SCOTT®

2004 Specialized Catalogue of United States Stamps & Covers

EIGHTY-SECOND EDITION

CONFEDERATE STATES • CANAL ZONE • DANISH WEST INDIES
GUAM • HAWAII • UNITED NATIONS

UNITED STATES ADMINISTRATION:
Cuba • Puerto Rico • Philippines • Ryukyu Islands

Released October 2003
Includes New Stamp Listings through the September 2003 *Scott Stamp Monthly* Catalogue Update

Scott Publishing Co.

911 Vandemark Road, Sidney, OH 45365-0828
A division of AMOS PRESS, INC., publishers of *Linn's Stamp News, Coin World* and *Cars & Parts* magazine.

Copyright Notice

Trademark Notice

Please Note

Effective as of 1978, designs of all United States stamps are copyrighted.

Scott Catalogue accepts all advertisements in good faith, but does not endorse or assume any responsibility for the contents of advertisements.

ISBN 0-89487-317-2

Library of Congress Card No. 2-3301

Scott Publishing Mission Statement

The Scott Publishing Team exists to serve the recreational, educational and commercial hobby needs of stamp collectors and dealers.

We strive to set the industry standard for philatelic information and products by developing and providing goods that help collectors identify, value, organize and present their collections.

Quality customer service is, and will continue to be, our highest priority. We aspire toward achieving total customer satisfaction.

Scott Publishing Co.

SCOTT 911 VANDEMARK ROAD, SIDNEY, OHIO 45365 937-498-0802

Dear Scott Catalogue User:

Earlier this year we received a letter from an elderly collector who informed us that his diminished eyesight and the huge amount of information on each page of the catalogue made it difficult for him to find the actual catalogue numbers of the stamps, which are in the same non-bold type as all the other information on the pages. The gentleman informed us that if we could not put the catalogue numbers in bold type, he feared that his catalogue-buying days were over. Well sir, I hope you are reading this, and get out your credit card, for the catalogue numbers ARE now in bold type and much easier to read. This feature will be incorporated into all the Scott catalogues beginning next year.

***What about value changes in the* 2004 Scott Specialized Catalogue of United States Stamps and Covers?**

More than 18,000 value changes highlight the 2004 U.S. Specialized Catalogue. Almost 3,500 of those changes are in the 19th century postage section, and another 2,800 value changes appear in 20th century postage. Nearly 5,000 changes were made in the section from Air Post through Postal Stationery, and more than 5,000 changes appear in the Revenue sections alone.

How about some specifics?

In the 19th century postage section, demand continues to be quite strong for very fine stamps, both unused and used. Value increases are not confined to rare and expensive items. Less expensive stamps also rise in value, such as the 1851 imperf 3¢ dull red type I, Scott 11, which moves unused to $275 from $250 in the 2004 Volume 1. In used condition, the value remains at $11.

There are new, higher values for many major rarities that made their way to the market in the last few months. For example, two 1869 inverted centers, unused with original gum, rise to new heights. Scott 119b, the 15¢ type I, jumps to $415,000 from "just" $275,000 last year, while Scott 121b, the 30¢ invert, moves to $275,000 from $210,000. Each of these stamps is the only example of its Scott number to possess original gum, so new categories for both stamps unused without gum have been added to the catalogue.

Selected 1870-93 Banknotes continue to climb, especially unused. Some value increases are large. The 1870 10¢ brown without grill, Scott 150, makes a big leap unused to $1,250 from $825 in the 2003 U.S. Specialized and $1,000 in the 2004 Volume 1. Another 10¢ brown, the American Bank Note Co. re-engraved printing of 1882, Scott 209, moves up slightly in unused condition, but its black brown minor, Scott 209b, jumps all the way to $1,400 from $1,000 last year and $1,200 in the 2004 Volume 1. In used condition, the black brown stamp climbs to $200 from $150 last year.

Values for some used early booklet panes increase sharply. An example is the very first booklet pane issued in 1900, Scott 279Be, which jumps to $1,250 used from $900 last year and $1,000 in the 2004 Volume 1.

In the Washington-Franklin section, used stamps were examined carefully, and values were raised where appropriate. This includes stamps with small values as well as those with higher values.

Some modern issues have become relatively scarce and show increases in value. Scott Nos. 2915B, 2915C and 2915D, three die cutting varieties of the 32¢ Flag over Porch design coils, show significant percentage moves, especially in used condition. Mint plate blocks of several recent lick-and-stick sheet stamps that were produced in panes of 100 with just one or two plate blocks per pane seem to be virtually unobtainable by dealers in any quantity. As just one example, the 1999 33¢ Flag and City plate block, Scott 3277, doubles in value to $25 from just $12.50 last year.

In modern booklet panes and complete booklets, the 1998 32¢ Christmas Wreaths panes, Scott 3248a-3248c, almost double in value, and the complete Wreath booklet, Scott BK270, moves to $90 from $50 last year. The 1999 Reindeer booklet, Scott BK276B, and the 2000 Submarine booklet, Scott BK276A, also show 50-100 percent gains in value.

Many stamps in the Postage Due section show increases, including many in the used column. In Officials, there is much upward movement evident in lower-valued as well as higher-valued stamps, both unused and used. Some especially large increases appear in the Official Special Printings of 1875, Scott O1S-O57xS, where virtually all stamps rise in value, often by large percentages.

In the Newspaper section, there are many increased values brought forward from the 2004 Volume 1, plus many additional increases. Some of the rarer stamps are now valued for the first time ever, such as the 1875 $36 brown rose reprint, Scott PR54, one of two sold by the Post Office and the only example currently recorded. This stamp sold for $250,000 unused this year, and that value is now reflected in the catalogue.

In Revenues, the 5,000+ value changes are almost all increases, with wholesale changes occurring in the dated red Documentaries, Scott R264-R732; Future Delivery, Scott RC1-RC28; Stock Transfer, Scott RD1-RD372; Beer, Scott REA1-REA199; and Silver Tax, Scott RG1-RG132.

What about editorial changes beyond those bold catalogue numbers?

Without doubt the new listings of United Nations die proofs, trial color proofs, progressive proofs and imperforate proofs on stamp paper are the most significant editorial change in the volume. In a Special Feature article on pages 834-835, New Issues Editor Martin Frankevicz relates the story of the listing of this new 23-page section of U.N. proofs, consisting of the items from the U.N. Postal Archives sold this year at auction, plus other archival proofs previously existing in the marketplace. Frankevicz not only constructed the listings, he spent more than two weeks examining these interesting proofs item by item, gaining an understanding of the range and detail of these proofs unequalled by anyone in philately. The new listings begin on page 833.

The Scott image-scanning project continues at a heated pace, with many additional images of actual stamps appearing this year. We still have a way to go, but much progress has been made this year.

New Earliest Documented Use covers continue to be found by collectors and dealers, and 50 new, earlier dates appear in the 2004 U.S. Specialized. They range from an earlier date for plate 4 of the 1¢ blue type III, Scott 8, to a first time EDU date for the 1923 1¢ green rotary sheet stamp, Scott 581.

Listings for additional varieties have been added for double transfers, color cancels, multiples, and tagging and gum varieties on modern definitives. For the first time, all modern precancels in mint condition have had values assigned, and varieties of these stamps, such as plate blocks and coil line pairs, have been added and valued.

Many new errors are added, such as the blue omitted on the 1993 29¢ Oregon Trail commemorative, now Scott 2747b, and many others. All new lettered minors will be found on the 2004 U.S. Specialized additions, deletions and number changes listings on page 860.

Collectors of Federal Duck stamps should be delighted to see all of the Duck stamps illustrated for the first time. Also in the Duck section, a new table has been created showing the designer of each stamp.

Happy Collecting,

James E Kloetzel

James E. Kloetzel/Catalogue Editor

Table of contents

Acknowledgments

Our appreciation and gratitude go to the following individuals and organizations who have assisted us in preparing information included in this year's edition of the Scott Specialized Catalogue of U.S. Stamps and Covers. Some helpers prefer anonymity. Those individuals have generously shared their stamp knowledge with others through the medium of the Scott Catalogue.

Those who follow provided information that is in addition to the hundreds of dealer price lists and advertisements and scores of auction catalogues and realizations which were used in producing the Catalogue Values provided herein. It is from those noted here that we have been able to obtain information on items not normally seen in published lists and advertisements. Support from these people of course goes beyond data leading to Catalogue Values, for they also are key to editorial changes.

Karl Agre, M.D., PhD
Michael E. Aldrich
(Michael E. Aldrich, Inc.)
Arthur L.-F. Askins
Steven R. Belasco
Alan Berkun
John Birkinbine II
Brian M. Bleckwenn
Victor Bove
John D. Bowman
(Carriers and Locals Society)
George W. Brett
Roger S. Brody
Randall Brooksbank
Lawrence A. Bustillo
(Suburban Stamp Inc.)
James R. Callis, Jr.
(Precancel Stamp Society)
A. Bryan Camarda
Alan C. Campbell
Gil Celli (Gold Mine Cover Co.)
Richard A. Champagne
Albert F. Chang
Harry Corrigan
William T. Crowe
Francis J. Crown, Jr.
Tony L. Crumbley (Carolina Coin & Stamp, Inc.)
Stephen R. Datz
John DeStefanis
Kenneth E. Diehl
Bob Dumaine (Sam Houston Duck Company)
William S. Dunn
Stephen G. Esrati
J. A. Farrington
Henry Fisher
Jeffrey M. Forster
Robert S. Freeman
Richard Friedberg
Melvin Getlan
Stan Goldfarb
Richard B. Graham
Fred F. Gregory
Harry Hagendorf
Calvet M. Hahn
Dr. Allan Hauck (International Society of Reply Coupon Collectors)
John B. Head
Robert R. Hegland
Dale Hendricks
(Dale Enterprises, Inc.)
Steven Hines
Wilson Hulme
Myron Hyman
Tom Jacks (Mountainside Stamps)
Eric Jackson
Michael Jaffe
(Michael Jaffe Stamps, Inc.)
Clyde Jennings
Allan Katz (Ventura Stamp Co.)
Lewis Kaufman
Patricia A. Kaufmann
Dr. Thomas C. Kingsley
Jim Kotanchik
Eliot Landau
Maurice J. Landry
Lester C. Lanphear III
Ken Lawrence
Richard L. Lazorow
(The Plate Block Stamp Co.)
James E. Lee
Ronald E. Lesher, Sr.
Steve Levine
John R. Lewis
(The William Henry Stamp Co.)
William A. Litle
W. C. Livingston
Larry Lyons
Robert L. Markovits
(Quality Investors, Ltd.)
Frank Marrelli
Peter Martin
(State Revenue Society)
William K. McDaniel
Robert Meyersburg
Allen Mintz
Harvey Mirsky
Jack E. Molesworth
William E. Mooz
Gary M. Morris
(Pacific Midwest Co.)
Bruce M. Moyer
(Moyer Stamps & Collectibles)
James Natale
Gerald Nylander
Michael O. Perry
Stanley M. Piller
(Stanley M. Piller & Associates)
Peter W. W. Powell
Louis E. Repeta
Peter A. Robertson
Peter Robin
Jon W. Rose
Christopher Rupp
Richard H. Salz
Byron Sandfield
(Park Cities Stamps)
Jacques C. Schiff, Jr.
(Jacques C. Schiff, Jr., Inc.)
Craig Selig
Merle Spencer
(The Stamp Gallery)
Richard Stambaugh
Frank J. Stanley, III
Philip & Henry Stevens
(postalstationery.com)
Jerry Summers
Alan Thomson (Plate Number Coil Collectors' Club)
Henry Tolman II
David R. Torre
Scott R. Trepel
(Robert A. Siegel Auction Galleries, Inc.)
George P. Wagner
Philip T. Wall
Daniel C. Warren
Dr. Gary B. Weiss
William R. Weiss, Jr.
(Weiss Philatelics)
Alan B. Whitman
Kirk Wolford
(Kirk's Stamp Company)
Robert Wurdeman
Robert F. Yacano
Dr. Clark Yarbrough
John P. Zuckerman
(Robert A. Siegel Auction Galleries, Inc.)

Expertizing Services

The following organizations will, for a fee, provide expert opinions about stamps submitted to them. Collectors should contact these organizations to find out about their fees and requirements before submitting philatelic material to them. The listing of these groups here is not intended as an endorsement by Scott Publishing Co.

General Expertizing Services

American Philatelic Expertizing Service (a service of the American Philatelic Society)
PO Box 8000
State College PA 16803
Ph: (814) 237-3803
Fax: (814) 237-6128
www.stamps.org
E-mail: ambristo@stamps.org

Philatelic Foundation
501 Fifth Ave., Rm. 1901
New York NY 10017
Ph: (212) 867-3699

Professional Stamp Experts
PO Box 6170
Newport Beach CA 92658
Ph: (877) STAMP-88
Fax: (949) 833-7955
www.collectors.com/pse
E-mail: pseinfo@collectors.com

Expertizing Services Covering Specific Fields Or Countries

American First Day Cover Society Expertizing Committee
P.O. Box 141379
Columbus, OH 43214

Confederate Stamp Alliance Authentication Service
c/o Patricia A. Kaufmann
10194 N. Old State Road
Lincoln, DE 19960-9797
Ph: (302) 422-2656
Fax: (302) 424-1990
www.webuystamps.com/csaauth.htm
E-mail: trish@ce.net

Errors, Freaks and Oddities Collectors Club Expertizing Service
138 East Lakemont Dr.
Kingsland GA 31548
Ph: (912) 729-1573

Hawaiian Philatelic Society Expertizing Service
PO Box 10115
Honolulu HI 96816-0115

Addresses, Telephone Numbers & E-Mail Addresses of General & Specialized Philatelic Societies

Collectors can contact the following groups for information about the philately of the areas within the scope of these societies, or inquire about membership in these groups. Many more specialized philatelic societies exist than those listed below. Aside from the general societies, we limit this list to groups which specialize in areas covered by the Scott U.S. Specialized Catalogue. These addresses were compiled two months prior to publication, and are, to the best of our knowledge, correct and current. Groups should inform the editors of address changes whenever they occur. The editors also want to hear from other such specialized groups not listed.

American Air Mail Society
Stephen Reinhard
P.O. Box 110
Mineola NY 11501
http://ourworld.compuserve.com/homepages/aams/
E-mail:sr1501@aol.com

American First Day Cover Society
Douglas Kelsey
P.O. Box 65960
Tucson AZ 85728-5960
Ph: (520) 321-0880
http://www.afdcs.org
E-mail:afdcs@aol.com

American Philatelic Society
P.O. Box 8000
State College PA 16803
Ph: (814) 237-3803
http://www.stamps.org
E-mail:relamb@stamps.org

American Plate Number Single Society
Norm J. Wood
777 W. State St., Apt 6H
Trenton NJ 08618
E-mail:stfia@pluto.njcc.com

American Revenue Association
Eric Jackson
P.O. Box 728
Leesport PA 19533-0728
Ph: (610) 926-6200
http://www.revenuer.org
E-mail:eric@revenuer.com

American Society for Philatelic Pages and Panels
Gerald N. Blankenship
539 North Gum Gully
Crosby TX 77532
Ph: (281) 324-2709
E-mail:gblank1941@aol.com

American Stamp Dealers Association
Joseph Savarese
3 School St.
Glen Cove NY 11542
Ph: (516) 759-7000
http://www.asdaonline.com
E-mail:asda@erols.com

American Topical Association
Paul E. Tyler
P.O. Box 50820
Albuquerque NM 87181-0820
Ph: (505) 323-8595
http://home/prcn.org/~pauld/ata/
E-mail:ATAStamps@aol.com

Canal Zone Study Group
Richard H. Salz
60 27th Ave.
San Francisco CA 94121

Carriers and Locals Society
John D. Bowman
P.O. Box 382436
Birmingham AL 35238-2436
Ph: (205) 967-6200
http://www.pennypost.org
E-mail:jdbowman@atlantabroadband.com

Christmas Seal & Charity Stamp Society
John Denune
234 East Broadway
Granville OH 43023
Ph: (614) 587-0276
http://members.aol.com/betsychuck/cscss.htm

Confederate Stamp Alliance
Ronald V. Teffs
19450 Yuma St.
Castro Valley CA 94546
http://www.flash.net/~rhbcsaps/

Errors, Freaks, and Oddities Collectors Club
Jim McDevitt
138 Lakemont Dr. East
Kingsland GA 31548
Ph: (912) 729-1573
E-mail:cwouscg@aol.com

Hawaiian Philatelic Society
Kay H. Hoke
P.O. Box 10115
Honolulu HI 96816-0115
Ph: (808) 521-5721
E-mail:bannan@pixi.com

International Philippine Philatelic Society
Robert F. Yacano
P.O. Box 100
Toast NC 27049
Ph: (336) 783-0768
E-mail:yacano@advi.net

International Society of Reply Coupon Collectors
Dr. Allan Hauck
P.O. Box 165
Somers WI 53171-0165
Ph: (262) 886-8535
E-mail:ashauck@pocketmail.com

Junior Philatelists of America
Jennifer Arnold
P.O. Box 2625
Albany OR 97321
http://www.jpastamps.org
E-mail:exec.sec@jpastamps.org

National Duck Stamp Collectors Society
Anthony J. Monico
P.O. Box 43
Harleysville PA 19438-0043
http://www.hwcn.org/links/ndscs
E-mail:ndscs@hwcn.org

Official Seal Study Group
Fred Scheuer
P.O. Box1518
Waldport OR 97394
Ph: (541) 563-4442

Perfins Club
Kurt Ottenheimer
462 West Walnut St.
Long Beach NY 11561
E-mail:oak462@juno.com

Plate Number Coil Collectors Club
Gene C. Trinks
3603 Bellows Court
Troy MI 48083
http://www.pnc3.org
E-mail:gctrinks@tir.com

Post Mark Collectors Club
Dave Proulx
7629 Homestead Dr.
Baldwinsville NY 13207
E-mail:stampdance@baldcom.net

Postal History Society
Kalman V. Illyefalvi
8207 Daren Court
Pikesville MD 21208-2211
Ph: (410) 653-0665

Precancel Stamp Society
Arthur Damm
176 Bent Pine Hill
North Wales PA 19454
Ph: (215) 368-6082

Ryukyu Philatelic Specialist Society
Carmine J. Di Vincenzo
P.O. Box 381
Clayton CA 94517-0381

Souvenir Card Collectors Society
Dana Marr
P.O. Box 4155
Tulsa OK 74159-0155
Ph: (918) 664-6724
E-mail:dmarr5569@aol.com

State Revenue Society
Scott Troutman
P.O. Box 270184
Oklahoma City OK 73137
http://hillcity-mail.com/SRS

United Nations Philatelists
Blanton Clement, Jr.
292 Springdale Terrace
Yardley PA 19067-3421
http://www.unpi.com
E-mail:bclement@prodigy.net

United Postal Stationery Society
Cora Collins
P.O. Box 1792
Norfolk VA 23501-1792
http://www.upss.org
E-mail:poststat@juno.com

U.S. Cancellation Club
Roger Rhoads
3 Ruthana Way
Hockessin DE 19707
http://www/geocities.com/athens/2088/uscchome.html
E-mail:rrrhoads@aol.com

U.S. Philatelic Classics Society
Mark D. Rogers
P.O. Box 80708
Austin TX 78708-0708
http://www.uspcs.org
E-mail:mdr3@swbell.net

U.S. Possessions Philatelic Society
David S. Durbin
1608 S. 22nd St.
Blue Springs MO 64015
Ph: (816) 224-3666

United States Stamp Society
Larry Ballantyne
P.O. Box 6634
Katy TX 77491-6634
http://www.usstamps.org

Information on Catalogue Values, Grade and Condition

Catalogue Value

The Scott Catalogue value is a retail value; that is, an amount you could expect to pay for a stamp in the grade of Very Fine with no faults. Any exceptions to the grade valued will be noted in the text. The general introduction on the following pages and the individual section introductions further explain the type of material that is valued. The value listed for any given stamp is a reference that reflects recent actual dealer selling prices for that item.

Dealer retail price lists, public auction results, published prices in advertising and individual solicitation of retail prices from dealers, collectors and specialty organizations have been used in establishing the values found in this catalogue. Scott Publishing Co. values stamps, but Scott is not a company engaged in the business of buying and selling stamps as a dealer.

Use this catalogue as a guide for buying and selling. The actual price you pay for a stamp may be higher or lower than the catalogue value because of many different factors, including the amount of personal service a dealer offers, or increased or decreased interest in the country or topic represented by a stamp or set. An item may occasionally be offered at a lower price as a "loss leader," or as part of a special sale. You also may obtain an item inexpensively at public auction because of little interest at that time or as part of a large lot.

Stamps that are of a lesser grade than Very Fine, or those with condition problems, generally trade at lower prices than those given in this catalogue. Stamps of exceptional quality in both grade and condition often command higher prices than those listed.

Values for pre-1900 unused issues are for stamps with approximately half or more of their original gum. Stamps with most or all of their original gum may be expected to sell for more, and stamps with less than half of their original gum may be expected to sell for somewhat less than the values listed. On rarer stamps, it may be expected that the original gum will be somewhat more disturbed than it will be on more common issues. Post-1900 unused issues are assumed to have full original gum. From breakpoints in most countries' listings, stamps are valued as never hinged, due to the wide availability of stamps in that condition. These notations are prominently placed in the listings and in the country information preceding the listings. Some countries also feature listings with dual values for hinged and never-hinged stamps.

Grade

A stamp's grade and condition are crucial to its value. The accompanying illustrations show examples of Very Fine stamps from different time periods, along with examples of stamps in Fine to Very Fine and Extremely Fine grades as points of reference.

FINE stamps (illustrations not shown) have designs that are noticeably off center on two sides. Imperforate stamps may have small margins, and earlier issues may show the design touching one edge of the stamp design. For perforated stamps, perfs may barely clear the design on one side, and very early issues normally will have the perforations slightly cutting into the design. Used stamps may have heavier than usual cancellations.

FINE-VERY FINE stamps may be somewhat off center on one side, or slightly off center on two sides. Imperforate stamps will have two margins of at least normal size, and the design will not touch any edge. For perforated stamps, the perfs are well clear of the design, but are still noticeably off center. *However, early issues of a country may be printed in such a way that the design naturally is very close to the edges. In these cases, the perforations may cut into the design very slightly.* Used stamps will not have a cancellation that detracts from the design.

VERY FINE stamps may be slightly off center on one side, but the design will be well clear of the edge. The stamp will present a nice, balanced appearance. Imperforate stamps will have three normal-sized margins. *However, early issues of many countries may be printed in such a way that the perforations may touch the design on one or more sides. Where this is the case, a boxed note will be found defining the centering and margins of the stamps being valued.* Used stamps will have light or otherwise neat cancellations. This is the grade used to establish Scott Catalogue values.

EXTREMELY FINE stamps are close to being perfectly centered. Imperforate stamps will have even margins that are larger than normal. Even the earliest perforated issues will have perforations clear of the design on all sides.

Scott Publishing Co. recognizes that there is no formally enforced grading scheme for postage stamps, and that the final price you pay or obtain for a stamp will be determined by individual agreement at the time of transaction.

Condition

Grade addresses only centering and (for used stamps) cancellation. *Condition* refers to factors other than grade that affect a stamp's desirability.

Factors that can increase the value of a stamp include exceptionally wide margins, particularly fresh color, the presence of selvage, and plate or die varieties. Unusual cancels on used stamps (particularly those of the 19th century) can greatly enhance their value as well.

Factors other than faults that decrease the value of a stamp include loss of original gum, regumming, a hinge remnant or foreign object adhering to the gum, natural inclusions, straight edges, and markings or notations applied by collectors or dealers.

Faults include missing pieces, tears, pin or other holes, surface scuffs, thin spots, creases, toning, short or pulled perforations, clipped perforations, oxidation or other forms of color changelings, soiling, stains, and such man-made changes as reperforations or the chemical removal or lightening of a cancellation.

Grading Illustrations

On the following two pages are illustrations of various stamps from countries appearing in this volume. These stamps are arranged by country, and they represent early or important issues that are often found in widely different grades in the marketplace. The editors believe the illustrations will prove useful in showing the margin size and centering that will be seen on the various issues.

In addition to the matters of margin size and centering, collectors are reminded that the very fine stamps valued in the Scott catalogues also will possess fresh color and intact perforations, and they will be free from defects.

Most examples shown are computer-manipulated images made from single digitized master illustrations.

Stamp Illustrations Used in the Catalogue

It is important to note that the stamp images used for identification purposes in this catlaogue may not be indicative of the grade of stamp being valued. Refer to the written discussion of grades on this page and to the grading illustrations on the following two pages for grading information.

	1847 ISSUES	1851-57 ISSUES	1857-61 ISSUES	1857-61 ISSUES	1861-67 ISSUES	1869 ISSUES
Fine-Very Fine →						
SCOTT CATALOGUES VALUE STAMPS IN THIS GRADE Very Fine →						
Extremely Fine →						

For purposes of helping to determine the gum condition and value of an unused stamp, Scott Publishing Co. presents the following chart which details different gum conditions and indicates how the conditions correlate with the Scott values for unused stamps. Used together, the Illustrated Grading Chart on the previous page and this Illustrated Gum Chart should allow catalogue users to better understand the grade and gum condition of stamps valued in the *Scott U.S. Specialized Catalogue.*

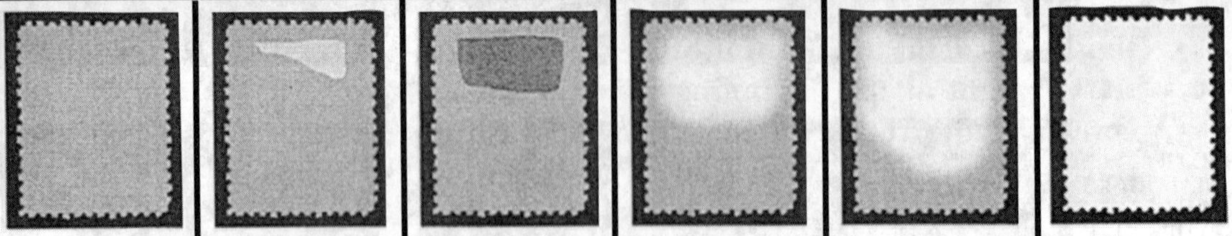

Gum Categories:	MINT N.H.	ORIGINAL GUM (O.G.)				NO GUM
	Mint Never Hinged *Free from any disturbance*	**Lightly Hinged** *Faint impression of a removed hinge over a small area*	**Hinge Mark or Remnant** *Prominent hinged spot with part or all of the hinge remaining*	**Large part o.g.** *Approximately half or more of the gum intact*	**Small part o.g.** *Approximately less than half of the gum intact*	**No gum** *Only if issued with gum*
Commonly Used Symbol:	★★	★	★	★	★	(★)
PRE-1890 ISSUES	*Very fine pre-1890 stamps in these categories trade at a premium over Scott value*			Scott Value for "Unused"		Scott "No Gum" Values thru No. 218
1890-1935 ISSUES	Scott "Never Hinged" Values for Nos. 219-771	Scott Value for "Unused" (Actual value will be affected by the degree of hinging of the full o.g.)				
1935 TO DATE	Scott Value for "Unused"					

Never Hinged (NH; ★★): A never-hinged stamp will have full original gum that will have no hinge mark or disturbance. The presence of an expertizer's mark does not disqualify a stamp from this designation.

Original Gum (OG; ★): Pre-1890 stamps should have approximately half or more of their original gum. On rarer stamps, it may be expected that the original gum will be somewhat more disturbed that it will be on more common issues. Stamps issued in 1890 or later should have full original gum. Original gum will show some disturbance caused by a previous hinge(s) which may be present or entirely removed. The actual value of an 1890 or later stamp will be affected by the degree of hinging of the full original gum.

Disturbed Original Gum: Gum showing noticeable effects of humidity, climate or hinging over more than half of the gum. The significance of gum disturbance in valuing a stamp in any of the Original Gum categories depends on the degree of disturbance, the rarity and normal gum condition of the issue and other variables affecting quality.

Regummed (RG; (★)): A regummed stamp is a stamp without gum that has had some type of gum privately applied at a time after it was issued. This normally is done to deceive collectors and/or dealers into thinking that the stamp has original gum and therefore has a higher value. A regummed stamp is considered the same as a stamp with none of its original gum for purposes of grading.

IMPORTANT INFORMATION REGARDING VALUES FOR NEVER-HINGED STAMPS

Collectors should be aware that the values given for never-hinged stamps from No. 219 on are for stamps in the grade of very fine. The never-hinged premium as a percentage of value will be larger for stamps in extremely fine or superb grades, and the premium will be smaller for fine-very-fine, fine or poor examples. This is particulary true of the issues of the late-19th and early 20th centuries. For example, in the grade of very fine, an unused stamp from this time period may be valued at $100 hinged and $180 never hinged. The never-hinged premium is thus 80%. But in a grade of extremely fine, this same stamp will not only sell for more hinged, but the never-hinged premium will increase, perhaps to 100%-300% or more over the higher extremely fine value. In a grade of superb, a hinged copy will sell for much more than a very fine copy, and additionally the never-hinged premium will be much larger, perhaps as large as 300%-400%. On the other hand, the same stamp in a grade of fine or fine-very fine not only will sell for less than a very fine stamp in hinged condition, but additionally the never-hinged premium will be smaller than the never-hinged premium on a very fine stamp, perhaps as small as 15%-30%.

Please note that the above statements and percentages are NOT a formula for arriving at the values of stamps in hinged or never-hinged condition in the grades of fine, fine to very fine, extremely fine or superb. The percentages given apply only to the size of the premium for never-hinged condition that might be added to the stamp value for hinged condition. The marketplace will determine what this value will be for grades other than very fine. Further, the percentages given are only generalized estimates. Some stamps or grades may have percentages for never-hinged condition that are higher or lower than the ranges given.

Never-Hinged Plate Blocks

Values given for never-hinged plate blocks are for blocks in which all stamps have original gum that has never been hinged and has no disturbances, and all selvage, whether gummed or ungummed, has never been hinged.

Catalogue Listing Policy

It is the intent of Scott Publishing Co. to list all postage stamps of the world in the *Scott Standard Postage Stamp Catalogue.* The only strict criteria for listing is that stamps be decreed legal for postage by the issuing country and that the issuing country actually have an operating postal system. Whether the primary intent of issuing a given stamp or set was for sale to postal patrons or to stamp collectors is not part of our listing criteria. Scott's role is to provide basic comprehensive postage stamp information. It is up to each stamp collector to choose which items to include in a collection.

It is Scott's objective to seek reasons why a stamp should be listed, rather than why it should not. Nevertheless, there are certain types of items that will not be listed. These include the following:

1. Unissued items that are not officially distributed or released by the issuing postal authority. If such items are officially issued at a later date by the country, they will be listed. Unissued items consist of those that have been printed and then held from sale for reasons such as change in government, errors found on stamps or something deemed objectionable about a stamp subject or design.

2. Stamps "issued" by non-existent postal entities or fantasy countries, such as Nagaland, Occusi-Ambeno, Staffa, Sedang, Torres Straits and others. Also, stamps "issued" in the names of legitimate, stamp-issuing countries that are not authorized by those countries.

3. Semi-official or unofficial items not required for postage. Examples include items issued by private agencies for their own express services. When such items are required for delivery, or are valid as prepayment of postage, they are listed.

4. Local stamps issued for local use only. Postage stamps issued by governments specifically for "domestic" use, such as Haiti Scott 219-228, or the United States non-denominated stamps, are not considered to be locals, since they are valid for postage throughout the country of origin.

5. Items not valid for postal use. For example, a few countries have issued souvenir sheets that are not valid for postage. This area also includes a number of worldwide charity labels (some denominated) that do not pay postage.

6. Intentional varieties, such as imperforate stamps that look like their perforated counterparts and are usually issued in very small quantities. Also, other egregiously exploitative issues such as stamps sold for far more than face value or stamps purposefully issued in artificially small quantities or only against advance orders. All of these kinds of items are usually controlled issues and/or are intended for speculation.

7. Items distributed by the issuing government only to a limited group, such as a stamp club, philatelic exhibition or a single stamp dealer, and later brought to market at inflated prices. These items normally will be included in a footnote.

The fact that a stamp has been used successfully as postage, even on international mail, is not in itself sufficient proof that it was legitimately issued. Numerous examples of so-called stamps from non-existent countries are known to have been used to post letters that have successfully passed through the international mail system.

There are certain items that are subject to interpretation. When a stamp falls outside our specifications, it may be listed along with a cautionary footnote.

A number of factors are considered in our approach to analyzing how a stamp is listed. The following list of factors is presented to share with you, the catalogue user, the complexity of the listing process.

Additional printings — "Additional printings" of a previously issued stamp may range from an item that is totally different to cases where it is impossible to differentiate from the original. At least a minor number (a small-letter suffix) is assigned if there is a distinct change in stamp shade, noticeably redrawn design, or a significantly different perforation measurement. A major number (numeral or numeral and capital-letter combination) is assigned if the editors feel the "additional printing" is sufficiently different from the original that it constitutes a different issue.

Commemoratives — Where practical, commemoratives with the same theme are placed in a set. For example, the U.S. Civil War Centennial set of 1961-65 and the Constitution Bicentennial series of 1989-90 appear as sets. Countries such as Japan and Korea issue such material on a regular basis, with an announced, or at least predictable, number of stamps known in advance. Occasionally, however, stamp sets that were released over a period of years have been separated. Appropriately placed footnotes will guide you to each set's continuation.

Definitive sets — Blocks of numbers generally have been reserved for definitive sets, based on previous experience with any given country. If a few more stamps were issued in a set than originally expected, they often have been inserted into the original set with a capital-letter suffix, such as U.S. Scott 1059A. If it appears that many more stamps than the originally allotted block will be released before the set is completed, a new block of numbers will be reserved, with the original one being closed off. In some cases, such as the U.S. Transportation and Great Americans series, several blocks of numbers exist. Appropriately placed footnotes will guide you to each set's continuation.

New country — Membership in the Universal Postal Union is not a consideration for listing status or order of placement within the catalogue. The index will tell you in what volume or page number the listings begin.

"No release date" items — The amount of information available for any given stamp issue varies greatly from country to country and even from time to time. Extremely comprehensive information about new stamps is available from some countries well before the stamps are released. By contrast some countries do not provide information about stamps or release dates. Most countries, however, fall between these extremes. A country may provide denominations or subjects of stamps from upcoming issues that are not issued as planned. Sometimes, philatelic agencies, those private firms hired to represent countries, add these later-issued items to sets well after the formal release date. This time period can range from weeks to years. If these items were officially released by the country, they will be added to the appropriate spot in the set. In many cases, the specific release date of a stamp or set of stamps may never be known.

Overprints — The color of an overprint is always noted if it is other than black. Where more than one color of ink has been used on overprints of a single set, the color used is noted. Early overprint and surcharge illustrations were altered to prevent their use by forgers.

Se-tenants — Connected stamps of differing features (se-tenants) will be listed in the format most commonly collected. This includes pairs, blocks or larger multiples. Se-tenant units are not always symmetrical. An example is Australia Scott 508, which is a block of seven stamps. If the stamps are primarily collected as a unit, the major number may be assigned to the multiple, with minors going to each component stamp. In cases where continuous-design or other unit se-tenants will receive significant postal use, each stamp is given a major Scott number listing. This includes issues from the United States, Canada, Germany and Great Britain, for example.

Understanding the Listings

On the opposite page is an enlarged "typical" listing from this catalogue. Following are detailed explanations of each of the highlighted parts of the listing.

1 Scott number — Stamp collectors use Scott numbers to identify specific stamps when buying, selling, or trading stamps, and for ease in organizing their collections. Each stamp issued by a country has a unique number. Therefore, U.S. Scott 219 can only refer to a single stamp. Although the Scott Catalogue usually lists stamps in chronological order by date of issue, when a country issues a set of stamps over a period of time the stamps within that set are kept together without regard to date of issue. This follows the normal collecting approach of keeping stamps in their natural sets.

When a country is known to be issuing a set of stamps over a period of time, a group of consecutive catalogue numbers is reserved for the stamps in that set, as issued. If that group of numbers proves to be too few, capital-letter suffixes are added to numbers to create enough catalogue numbers to cover all items in the set. Scott uses a suffix letter, e.g., "A," "b," etc., only once. If there is a Scott 296B in a set, there will not be a Scott 296b also.

There are times when the block of numbers is too large for the set, leaving some numbers unused. Such gaps in the sequence also occur when the editors move an item elsewhere in the catalogue or remove it from the listings entirely. Scott does not attempt to account for every possible number, but rather it does attempt to assure that each stamp is assigned its own number.

Scott numbers designating regular postage normally are only numerals. Scott numbers for other types of stamps, e.g., air post, special delivery, and so on, will have a prefix of either a capital letter or a combination of numerals and capital letters.

2 Illustration number — used to identify each illustration. Where more than one stamp in a set uses the same illustration number, that number needs to be used with the description line (noted below) to be certain of the exact variety of the stamp within the set. Illustrations normally are 75, 100, or 150 percent of the original size of the stamp. An effort has been made to note all illustrations not at those percentages. Overprints are shown at 100 percent of the original, unless otherwise noted. Letters *in parentheses* which follow an illustration number refer to illustrations of overprints or surcharges.

3 Listing styles — there are two principal types of catalogue listings: major and minor.

Majors may be distinguished by having as their catalogue number a numeral with or without a capital-letter suffix and with or without a prefix.

Minors have a small-letter suffix (or, only have the small letter itself shown if the listing is immediately beneath its major listing). These listings show a variety of the "normal," or major item. Examples include color variation or a different watermark used for that stamp only.

Examples of major numbers are 9X1, 16, 28A, 6LB1, C13, RW1, and TS1. Examples of minor numbers are 22b, 279Bc and C3a.

4 Denomination — normally value printed on the stamp (generally known as the *face value*), which is — unless otherwise stated — the cost of the stamp at the time of issue.

5 Basic information on stamp or set — introducing each stamp issue, this section normally includes the date of issue, method of printing, perforation, watermark, and sometimes additional information. New information on method of printing, watermark or perforation measurement may appear when that information changes. Dates of issue are as precise as Scott is able to confirm, either year only, month and year, or month, day and year.

In stamp sets issued over more than one date, the year or span of years will be in bold type above the first catalogue number. Individual stamps in the set will have a date-of-issue appearing in italics. Stamps without a year listed appeared during the first year of the span. Dates are not always given for minor varieties.

6 Color or other description — this line provides information to solidify identification of the stamp. Historically, when stamps normally were printed in a single color, only the color appeared here. With modern printing techniques, which include multicolor presses which mix inks on the paper, earlier methods of color identification are no longer applicable. When space permits, a description of the stamp design will replace the terms "multi" or "multicolored." The color of the paper is noted in italic type when the paper used is not white.

7 Date of issue — As precisely as Scott is able to confirm, either year only; month and year, or month, day and year. In some cases, the earliest known use (eku) is given. All dates, especially where no official date of issue has been given, are subject to change as new information is obtained. Many cases are known of inadvertent sale and use of stamps prior to dates of issue announced by postal officials. These are not listed here.

8 Value unused and **Value used** — the catalogue values are in U. S. dollars and are based on stamps that are in a grade of Very Fine. Unused values refer to items that have not seen postal or other duty for which they were intended. For pre-1890 issues, unused stamps must have at least most of their original gum; for later issues, complete gum is expected. Stamps issued without gum are noted. Unused values are for never-hinged stamps beginning at the point immediately following a prominent notice in the actual listing. The same information also appears at the beginning of the section's information. Scott values for used self-adhesive stamps are for examples either on piece or off piece.

Some sections in this book have more than two columns for values. Check section introductions and watch for value column headers. See the sections "Catalogue Values" and "Understanding Valuing Notations" for an explanation of the meaning of these values.

9 Changes in basic set information — bold or other type is used to show any change in the basic data between stamps within a set of stamps, e.g., perforation from one stamp to the next or a different paper or printing method or watermark.

10 Other varieties — these include additional shades, plate varieties, multiples, used on cover, plate number blocks. coil line pairs, coil plate number strips of three or five, ZIP blocks, etc.

On early issues, there may be a "Cancellation" section. Values in this section refer to single stamps off cover, unless otherwise noted. Values with a "+" are added to the basic used value. See "Basic Stamp Information" for more details on stamp and cancellation varieties.

11 Footnote — Where other important details about the stamps can be found.

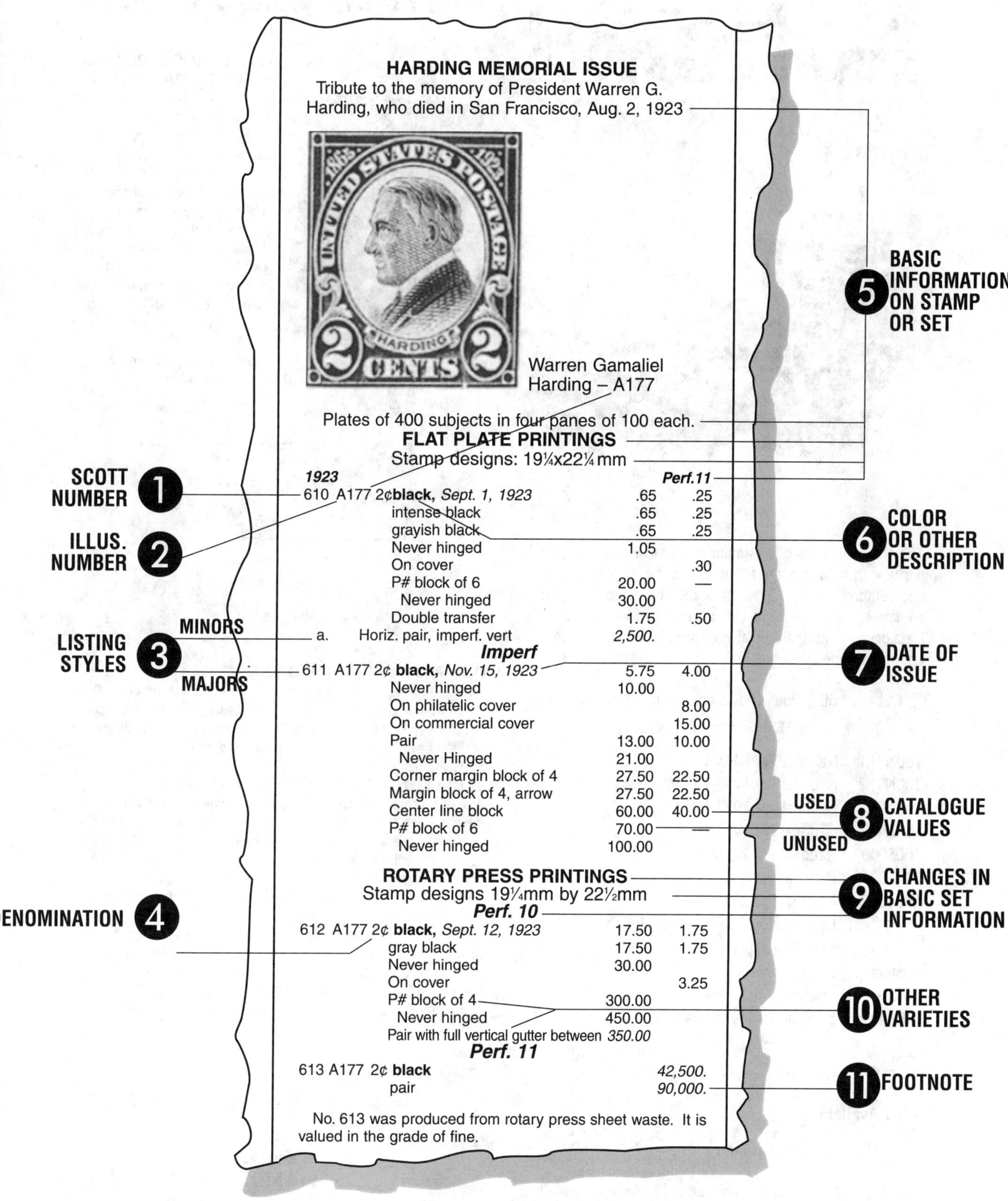
HARDING MEMORIAL ISSUE
Tribute to the memory of President Warren G. Harding, who died in San Francisco, Aug. 2, 1923
Warren Gamaliel Harding – A177
Plates of 400 subjects in four panes of 100 each.
FLAT PLATE PRINTINGS
Stamp designs: 19¼x22¼ mm
1923
Perf. 11
610 A177 2¢ black, Sept. 1, 1923 .65 .25
intense black .65 .25
grayish black .65 .25
Never hinged 1.05
On cover .30
P# block of 6 20.00 —
Never hinged 30.00
Double transfer 1.75 .50
a. Horiz. pair, imperf. vert 2,500.
Imperf
611 A177 2¢ black, Nov. 15, 1923 5.75 4.00
Never hinged 10.00
On philatelic cover 8.00
On commercial cover 15.00
Pair 13.00 10.00
Never Hinged 21.00
Corner margin block of 4 27.50 22.50
Margin block of 4, arrow 27.50 22.50
Center line block 60.00 40.00
P# block of 6 70.00 —
Never hinged 100.00
ROTARY PRESS PRINTINGS
Stamp designs 19¼mm by 22½mm
Perf. 10
612 A177 2¢ black, Sept. 12, 1923 17.50 1.75
gray black 17.50 1.75
Never hinged 30.00
On cover 3.25
P# block of 4 300.00
Never hinged 450.00
Pair with full vertical gutter between 350.00
Perf. 11
613 A177 2¢ black 42,500.
pair 90,000.
No. 613 was produced from rotary press sheet waste. It is valued in the grade of fine.
1 SCOTT NUMBER
2 ILLUS. NUMBER
3 LISTING STYLES
MINORS
MAJORS
4 DENOMINATION
5 BASIC INFORMATION ON STAMP OR SET
6 COLOR OR OTHER DESCRIPTION
7 DATE OF ISSUE
8 CATALOGUE VALUES
USED
UNUSED
9 CHANGES IN BASIC SET INFORMATION
10 OTHER VARIETIES
11 FOOTNOTE

Scott Numbering Practices and Special Notices

Classification of stamps

The *Scott Specialized Catalogue of United States Stamps* lists the stamps of the United States and its possessions and territories and the stamps of the United Nations. The next level is a listing by section on the basis of the function of the stamps or postal stationery. In each case, the items are listed in specialized detail. The principal sections cover regular postage stamps; air post stamps; postage due stamps, special delivery, and so on. Except for regular postage, catalogue numbers for most sections include a prefix letter (or number-letter combination) denoting the class to which the stamp belongs.

The Table of Contents, on page 4A, notes each section and, where pertinent, the prefix used. Some, such as souvenir cards and encased postage, do not have prefixes. Some sections, such as specimens and private perforations, have suffixes only.

New issue listings

Updates to this catalogue appear each month in the *Scott Stamp Monthly.* Included are corrections and updates to the current edition of this catalogue.

From time to time there will be changes in the listings from the *Scott Stamp Monthly* to the next edition of the catalogue, as additional information becomes available.

The catalogue update section of the *Scott Stamp Monthly* is the most timely presentation of this material available. For current subscription rates, see advertisements in this catalogue or write Scott Publishing Co., P.O. Box 828, Sidney, OH 45365-0828.

Additions, deletions & number changes

A list of catalogue additions, deletions, and number changes from the previous edition of the catalogue appears in each volume. See Catalogue Additions, Deletions & Number Changes in the Table of Contents for the location of this list..

Understanding valuing notations

The *absence of a value* does not necessarily suggest that a stamp is scarce or rare. In the U.S. listings, a dash in the value column means that the stamp is known in a stated form or variety, but information is lacking or insufficient for purposes of establishing a usable catalogue value. These could include rarities, such as Scott 3X4 on cover, or items that have a limited market, such as used plate blocks of Scott 1097.

Stamp values in *italics* generally refer to items which are difficult to value accurately. For expensive items, e.g., value at $1,000 or more, a value in italics represents an item which trades very seldom, such as a unique item. For inexpensive items, a value in italics represents a warning.

The Scott Catalogue values for used stamps reflect canceled-to-order material when such are found to predominate in the marketplace for the issue involved. Frequently notes appear in the stamp listings to specify items which are valued as canceled-to-order (Canal Zone Scott O1-O8) or if there is a premium for postally used examples.

Scott values for used stamps are not for precanceled examples, unless so stated. Precanceled copies must not have additional postal cancellations.

An example of a warning to collectors is a stamp that used has a value considerably higher than the unused version. Here, the collector is cautioned to be certain the used version has a readable, contemporaneous cancellation.

The *minimum catalogue value* of a stamp is 20 cents, to cover a dealer's costs of purchase and preparation for resale. The minimum catalogue value of a first day cover is one dollar. As noted, the sum of these values does not properly represent the "value" of a packet of unsorted or unmounted stamps sold in bulk. Such large collections, mixtures or packets generally consist of the lower-valued stamps. There are examples where the catalogue value of a block of stamps is less than the sum of the values of the individual stamps. This situation is caused by the overhead involved in handling single stamps, and should not be considered a suggestion that all blocks be separated into individual stamps to achieve a higher market value.

Values in the "unused" column are for stamps with original gum, if issued with gum. The stamp is valued as hinged if the listing appears *before* the point at which stamps are valued as never hinged. This point is marked by prominent notes in many sections. A similar note will appear at the beginning of the section's listing, noting exactly where the dividing point between hinged and never hinged is for each section of the listings. Where a value for a used stamp is considerably higher than for the unused stamp, the value applies to a stamp showing a distinct contemporaneous cancellation.

Covers

Prices paid for stamps on original covers vary greatly according to condition, appearance, cancellation or postmark and usage. Values given in this volume are for the commonest form with stamps in a grade of very fine "tied on" by the cancellation. A stamp is said to be "tied" to an envelope or card when the cancellation or postmark falls on both the stamp and envelope or card. Letters addressed to foreign countries showing unusual rates and transit markings normally are much in demand and often command large premiums.

Values are for covers bearing a single copy of the stamp referenced and used during the period when the stamp was on sale at post offices unless stated otherwise. If the postage rate was higher than the denomination of the stamp, then the stamp must represent the highest denomination possible to use in making up this rate. In this case, the value is the on-cover value of the stamp plus the used values of the additional stamps. As a general rule, the stamp must be tied to the cover.

Values for patriotic covers of the Civil War period (bearing pictorial designs of a patriotic nature) are for the commonest designs. Approximately 10,000 varieties of designs are known.

Cancellations

A complete treatment of this subject is impossible in a catalogue of this limited size. Only postal markings of meaning — those which were necessary to the proper function of the postal service — are recorded here, while those of value owing to their fanciness only are disregarded. The latter are the results of the whim of some postal official. Many of these odd designs, however, command high prices, based on their popularity, scarcity and clearness of impression.

Although there are many types of most of the cancellations listed, only one of each is illustrated. The values quoted are for the most common type of each.

Values for cancellation varieties are for stamp specimens off cover. Some cancellation varieties (e.g., pen, precancel, cut) are valued individually. Other varieties on pre-1900 stamps (e.g., less common colors, specific dates, foreign usages) are valued using premiums (denoted by "+") which are added to the stated value for the used stamp. When listed on cover, the distinctive cancellation must be on the stamp in order to merit catalogue valuation. Postal markings that denote origin or a service (as distinguished from canceling a stamp) merit catalogue valuation when on a cover apart from the stamp, provided the stamp is otherwise tied to the cover by a cancellation.

One type of "Paid" cancellation used in Boston, and shown in this introduction under "Postal Markings," is common and values given are for types other than this.

Examination

Scott Publishing Co. will not pass upon the genuineness, grade or condition of stamps, because of the time and responsibility involved. Rather, there are several expertizing groups which undertake this work for both collectors and dealers. Neither will Scott Publishing Co. appraise or identify philatelic material. The Company cannot take responsibility for unsolicited stamps or covers.

How to order from your dealer

It is not necessary to write the full description of a stamp as listed in this catalogue. All that you need is the name of the country or *U.S. Specialized* section, the Scott Catalogue number and whether the item is unused or used. For example, "U.S. Scott 833" is sufficient to identify the stamp of the United States listed as the 2-dollar value of a set of stamps issued between 1938-43. This stamp was issued September 29, 1938. It is yellow green and black in color, has a perforation of 11, and is printed on paper without a watermark by a flat plate press. Sections without a prefix or suffix must be mentioned by name.

Abbreviations

Scott Publishing Co. uses a consistent set of abbreviations throughout this catalogue and the *Standard Postage Stamp Catalogue* to conserve space while still providing necessary information. The first block shown here refers to color names only:

COLOR ABBREVIATIONS

amb.....amber
anil.....aniline
ap.....apple
aqua.....aquamarine
az.....azure
bis.....bister
bl.....blue
bld.....blood
blk.....black
bril.....brilliant
brn.....brown
brnsh.....brownish
brnz.....bronze
brt.....bright
brnt.....burnt
car.....carmine
cer.....cerise
chlky.....chalky
cham.....chamois
chnt.....chestnut
choc.....chocolate
chr.....chrome
cit.....citron
cl.....claret
cob.....cobalt
cop.....copper
crim.....crimson
cr.....cream
dk.....dark
dl.....dull
dp.....deep
db.....drab
emer.....emerald
gldn.....golden
grysh.....grayish
grn.....green
grnsh.....greenish
hel.....heliotrope
hn.....henna
ind.....indigo
int.....intense
lav.....lavender
lem.....lemon
lil.....lilac
lt.....light
mag.....magenta
man.....manila
mar.....maroon
mv.....mauve
multi.....multicolored
mlky.....milky
myr.....myrtle
ol.....olive
olvn.....olivine
org.....orange
pck.....peacock
pnksh.....pinkish
Prus.....Prussian
pur.....purple
redsh.....reddish
res.....reseda
ros.....rosine
ryl.....royal
sal.....salmon
saph.....sapphire
scar.....scarlet
sep.....sepia
sien.....sienna
sil.....silver
sl.....slate
stl.....steel
turq.....turquoise
ultra.....ultramarine
ven.....venetian
ver.....vermilion
vio.....violet
yel.....yellow
yelsh.....yellowish

When no color is given for an overprint or surcharge, black is the color used. Abbreviations for colors used for overprints and surcharges are: "(B)" or "(Blk)," black; "(Bl)," blue; "(R)," red; "(G)," green; etc.

Additional abbreviations used in this catalogue are shown below:

Adm. ....Administration
AFL..........American Federation of Labor
Anniv. ....Anniversary
APU..........Arab Postal Union
APS..........American Philatelic Society
ASEAN ....Association of South East Asian Nations
ASPCA..........American Society for the Prevention of Cruelty to Animals
Assoc. ....Association

b..........Born
BEP..........Bureau of Engraving and Printing
Bicent. ....Bicentennial
Bklt..........Booklet
Brit. ....British
btwn..........Between
Bur..........Bureau

c. or ca. ....Circa
CAR..........Central African Republic
Cat. ....Catalogue
Cent. ....Centennial, century, centenary
CEPT..........Conference Europeenne des Administrations des Postes et des Telecommunications
CIO ....Congress of Industrial Organizations
Conf. ....Conference
Cong..........Congress
Cpl. ....Corporal
CTO ....Canceled to order

d..........Died
Dbl. ....Double
DDR ....German Democratic Republic (East Germany)

EC ....European Community
ECU..........European currency unit
EEC ....European Economic Community
EKU..........Earliest known use
Engr. ....Engraved
Exhib. ....Exhibition
Expo. ....Exposition

FAO ....Food and Agricultural Organization of the United Nations
Fed. ....Federation
FIP..........Federation International de Philatelie

GB ....Great Britain
Gen. ....General
GPO ....General post office

Horiz. ....Horizontal

ICAO..........International Civil Aviation Organization
ICY..........International Cooperation Year
ILO..........International Labor Organization
Imperf..........Imperforate
Impt..........Imprint
Intl..........International
Invtd..........Inverted
IQSY..........International Quiet Sun Year
ITU..........International Telecommunications Union
ITY ....International Tourism Year
IWY..........International Women's Year
IYC ....International Year of the Child
IYD ....International Year of the Disabled
IYSH ....International Year of Shelter for the Homeless
IYY ....International Youth Year

L..........Left
Lieut. ....Lieutenant
Litho. ....Lithographed

LL..............Lower left
LR..............Lower right

mm............Millimeter
Ms.............Manuscript

NASA..........National Aeronautics and Space Administration
Natl. ....National
NATO ....North Atlantic Treaty Organization
No. ....Number
NY..............New York
NYC ....New York City

OAU ....Organization of African Unity
OPEC ....Organization of Petroleum Exporting Countries
Ovpt. ....Overprint
Ovptd. ....Overprinted

P#...............Plate number
Perf.............Perforated, perforation
Phil.............Philatelic
Photo..........Photogravure
PO..............Post office
Pr................Pair
P.R. ....Puerto Rico
PRC ....People's Republic of China (Mainland China)
Prec. ....Precancel, precanceled
Pres. ....President

R.................Right
Rio.............Rio de Janeiro
ROC ....Republic of China (Taiwan)

SEATO ....South East Asia Treaty Organization
Sgt. ....Sergeant
Soc. ....Society
Souv............Souvenir
SSR ....Soviet Socialist Republic
St................Saint, street
Surch. ....Surcharge

Typo. ....Typographed

UAE...........United Arab Emirate
UAMPT ......Union of African and Malagasy Posts and Telecommunications
UL ....Upper left
UN ....United Nations
UNESCO ....United Nations Educational, Scientific and Cultural Organization
UNICEF......United Nations Children's Fund
Univ ....University
UNPA ....United Nations Postal Administration
Unwmkd.....Unwatermarked
UPU............Universal Postal Union
UR ....Upper Right
US ....United States
USPO..........United States Post Office Department
USPS...........United States Postal Service (also "U.S. Postage Stamp" when referring to the watermark)
USSR ....Union of Soviet Socialist Republics

Vert.............Vertical
VP ....Vice president

WCY...........World Communications Year
WFUNA......World Federation of United Nations Associations
WHO..........World Health Organization
Wmk ....Watermark
Wmkd ....Watermarked
WMO ....World Meteorological Organization
WRY ....World Refugee Year
WWF..........World Wildlife Fund
WWI...........World War I
WWII ....World War II

YAR ....Yemen Arab Republic
Yemen PDR.Yemen People's Democratic Republic

Postmasters General of the United States

1775 Benjamin Franklin, July 26.
1776 Richard Bache, Nov. 7.
1782 Ebenezer Hazard, Jan. 28.
1789 Samuel Osgood, Sept. 26.
1791 Timothy Pickering, Aug. 12.
1795 Joseph Habersham, Feb. 25.
1801 Gideon Granger, Nov. 28.
1814 Return J. Meigs, Jr., Apr. 11.
1823 John McLean, July 1.
1829 William T. Barry, Apr. 6.
1835 Amos Kendall, May 1.
1840 John M. Niles, May 26.
1841 Francis Granger, Mar. 8.
1841 Charles A. Wickliffe, Oct. 13.
1845 Cave Johnson, Mar. 7.
1849 Jacob Collamer, Mar. 8.
1850 Nathan K. Hall, July 23.
1852 Samuel D. Hubbard, Sept. 14.
1853 James Campbell, Mar. 8.
1857 Aaron V. Brown, Mar. 7.
1859 Joseph Holt, Mar. 14.
1861 Horatio King, Feb. 12.
1861 Montgomery Blair, Mar. 9.
1864 William Dennison, Oct. 1.
1866 Alexander W. Randall, July 25.
1869 John A.J. Creswell, Mar. 6.
1874 Jas. W. Marshall, July 7.
1874 Marshall Jewell, Sept. 1.
1876 James N. Tyner, July 13.
1877 David McK. Key, Mar. 13.
1880 Horace Maynard, Aug. 25.
1881 Thomas L. James, Mar. 8.
1882 Timothy O. Howe, Jan. 5.
1883 Walter Q. Gresham, Apr. 11.
1884 Frank Hatton, Oct. 14.
1885 Wm. F. Vilas, Mar. 7.
1888 Don M. Dickinson, Jan. 17.
1889 John Wanamaker, Mar. 6.
1893 Wilson S. Bissell, Mar. 7.
1895 William L. Wilson, Apr. 4.
1897 James A. Gary, Mar. 6.
1898 Charles Emory Smith, Apr. 22.
1902 Henry C. Payne, Jan. 15.
1904 Robert J. Wynne, Oct. 10.
1905 Geo. B. Cortelyou, Mar. 7.
1907 Geo. von L. Meyer, Mar. 4.
1909 Frank H. Hitchcock, Mar. 6.
1913 Albert S. Burleson, Mar. 5.
1921 Will H. Hays, Mar. 5.
1922 Hubert Work, Mar. 4.
1923 Harry S. New, Mar. 4.
1929 Walter F. Brown, Mar. 6.
1933 James A. Farley, Mar. 4.
1940 Frank C. Walker, Sept. 11.
1945 Robert E. Hannegan, July 1.
1947 Jesse M. Donaldson, Dec. 16.
1953 Arthur E. Summerfield, Jan. 21.
1961 J. Edward Day, Jan. 21.
1963 John A. Gronouski, Sept. 30.
1965 Lawrence F. O'Brien, Nov. 3.
1968 W. Marvin Watson, Apr. 26.
1969 Winton M. Blount, Jan. 22.

U.S. POSTAL SERVICE

1971 Elmer T. Klassen, Dec. 7.
1975 Benjamin Bailar, Feb. 15.
1978 William F. Bolger, Mar. 1.
1985 Paul N. Carlin, Jan. 1.
1986 Albert V. Casey, Jan. 6.
1986 Preston R. Tisch, Aug. 17.
1988 Anthony M. Frank, Mar. 1.
1992 Marvin T. Runyon, Jr., July 6.
1998 William J. Henderson, May 16.
2001 John E. Potter, June 1

Basic Stamp Information

A stamp collector's knowledge of the combined elements that make a given issue of a stamp unique determines his or her ability to identify stamps. These elements include paper, watermark, method of separation, printing, design and gum. On the following pages these important areas are described in detail.

The guide below will direct you to those philatelic terms which are not major headings in the following introductory material. The major headings are:

Plate	Paper	Gum	Postal Markings
Printing	Perforations	Luminescence	General Glossary

Guide to Subjects

Arrows .... See Plate Markings
Bisect .... See General Glossary
Blocks .... See Plate
Booklet Panes .... See Plate
Booklets .... See Plate
Booklets A.E.F. .... See Plate
Bureau Issues .... See General Glossary
Bureau Prints .... See Postal Markings
Cancellations .... See Postal Markings
Carrier Postmark .... See Postal Markings
Center Line Block .... See Plate
Coarse Perforation .... See Perforations
Coils .... See Plate
Coil Waste .... See Plate
Color Registration Markings .... See Plate Markings
Color Trials .... See Printing
Commemorative Stamps .... See General Glossary
Compound Perforation .... See Perforations
Corner Blocks .... See Plate
Cracked Plate .... See Plate
Crystallization Cracks .... See Plate
Curvature Cracks .... See Plate
Cut Square .... See General Glossary
Diagonal Half .... See General Glossary (Bisect)
Die .... See Plate
Double Impression .... See Printing
Double Paper .... See Paper
Double Perforation .... See Perforations
Double Transfer .... See Plate
Dry Printings .... See note after Scott 1029
Electric Eye .... See Perforations
Embossed Printing .... See Printing
End Roller Grills .... See Paper
Engraving .... See Printing
Error .... See General Glossary
Essay .... See Printing
Fine Perforation .... See Perforations
First Day Covers .... See General Glossary
Flat Plate Printing .... See Printing
Flat Press Printing .... See Printing
Foreign Entry .... See Plate
Giori Press .... See Printing
Gridiron Cancellation .... See Postal Markings
Grills .... See Paper
Gripper Cracks .... See Plate
Guide Dots .... See Plate
Guide Lines .... See Plate Markings
Guide line Blocks .... See Plate
Gum Breaker Ridges .... See General Glossary
Gutter .... See Plate Markings
Hidden Plate Number .... See Plate
Horizontal Half .... See General Glossary (Bisect)
Imperforate .... See Perforations
Imprint .... See Plate Markings
Imprint Blocks .... See Plate
India Paper .... See Paper
Intaglio .... See Printing
Inverted Center .... See Printing
Joint Line Pair .... See Plate
Laid Paper .... See Paper
Line Engraved .... See Printing
Line Pair .... See Plate
Lithography .... See Printing
Luminescent Coating .... See Luminescence
Manila Paper .... See Paper
Margin .... See Plate Markings
Margin Blocks .... See Plate
Multicolored Stamps .... See Printing
New York City Foreign Mail Cancellations .... See Postal Markings
Offset Printing .... See Printing
Original Gum .... See General Glossary
Overprint .... See Printing
Pair Imperf. Between .... See Perforations
Pane .... See Plate
Part Perforate .... See Perforations
Paste-up .... See Plate
Paste-up Pair .... See Plate
Patent Cancellations .... See Postal Markings
Patriotic Covers .... See General Glossary
Pelure Paper .... See Paper
Phosphor Tagged .... See Luminescence
Plate Arrangement .... See Plate
Plate Flaws .... See Plate
Plate Markings .... See Plate
Postmarks .... See Postal Markings
Precancels .... See Postal Markings
Printed on Both Sides .... See Printing
Proofs .... See Printing
Propaganda Covers .... See General Glossary
Railroad Postmarks .... See Postal Markings
Receiving Mark .... See Postal Markings
Recut .... See Plate
Re-engraved .... See Plate
Re-entry .... See Plate
Re-issue .... See Printing
Relief .... See Plate
Reprints .... See Printing
Retouch .... See Plate
Rosette Crack .... See Printing
Rotary Press Printings .... See Printing
Rotary Press Double Paper .... See Paper
Rough Perforation .... See Perforations
Rouletting .... See Perforations
Se-Tenant .... See General Glossary
Service Indicators .... See Postal Markings
Sheet .... See Plate
Shifted Transfer .... See Plate
Ship Postmarks .... See Postal Markings
Short Transfer .... See Plate
Silk Paper .... See Paper
Specialization .... See General Glossary
Special Printings .... See Printing
Split Grill .... See Paper
Stampless Covers .... See Plate
Stitch Watermark .... See Paper
Strip .... See General Glossary
Surface Printing .... See Printing
Supplementary Mail Cancellations .... See Postal Markings
Surcharges .... See Printing

Plate

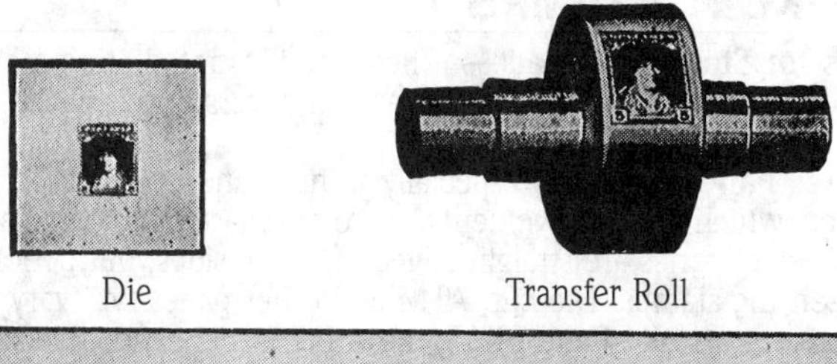

Die Transfer Roll

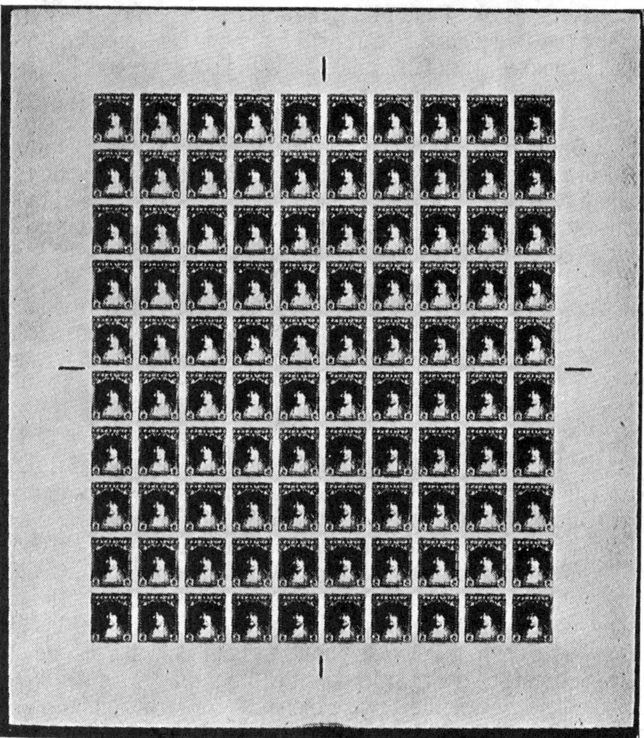

Plate

LINE ENGRAVING (INTAGLIO)

Die — Making the die is the initial operation in developing the intaglio plate. The die is a small flat piece of soft steel on which the subject (design) is recess-engraved in reverse. Dies are usually of a single-subject type, but dies exist with multiple subjects of the same design, or even different designs. After the engraving is completed, the die is hardened to withstand the stress of subsequent operations.

Transfer Roll — The next operation is making the transfer roll, which is the medium used to transfer the subject from the die to the plate. A blank roll of soft steel, mounted on a mandrel, is placed under the bearers of a transfer press. The hardened die is placed on the bed of the press and the face of the roll is brought to bear on the die. The bed is then rocked backed and forth under increasing pressure until the soft steel of the roll is forced into every line of the die. The resulting impression on the roll is known as a "relief" or "relief transfer." Several reliefs usually are rocked in on each roll. After the required reliefs are completed, the roll is hardened.

Relief — A relief is the normal reproduction of the design on the die, in reverse. A defective relief, caused by a minute piece of foreign material lodging on the die, may occur during the rocking-in process, or from other causes. Imperfections in the steel of the transfer roll may also result in a breaking away of parts of the design. If the damaged relief is continued in use, it will transfer a repeating defect to the plate. Also reliefs sometime are deliberately altered. "Broken relief" and "altered relief" are terms used to designate these changed conditions.

Plate — A flat piece of soft steel replaces the die on the bed of the transfer press and one of the reliefs on the transfer roll is brought to bear on this soft steel. The position of the plate is determined by position dots, which have been lightly marked on the plate in advance. After the position of the relief is determined, pressure is brought to bear and, by following the same method used in the making of the transfer roll, a transfer is entered. This transfer reproduces, in reverse, every detail of the design of the relief. As many transfers are entered on the plate as there are to be subjects printed at one time.

After the required transfers have been entered, the positions dots, layouts and lines, scratches, etc., are burnished out. Also, any required guide lines, plate numbers, or other marginal markings are added. A proof impression is then taken and if certified (approved), the plate is machined for fitting to the press, hardened and sent to the plate vault until used.

Rotary press plates, after being certified, require additional machining. They are curved to fit the press cylinder and gripper slots are cut into the back of each plate to receive the grippers, which hold the plate securely to the press. The rotary press plate is not hardened until these additional processes are completed.

Transfer — An impression entered on the plate by the transfer roll. A relief transfer is made when entering the design of the die onto the transfer roll.

Double Transfer — The condition of a transfer on a plate that shows evidences of a duplication of all or a portion of the design. A double transfer usually is the result of the changing of the registration between the relief and the plate during the rolling of the original entry.

Occasionally it is necessary to remove the original transfer from a plate and enter the relief a second time. When the finished re-transfer shows indications of the original transfer, because of incomplete erasure, the result is known as a double transfer.

Triple Transfer — Similar to a double transfer, this situation shows evidences of a third entry or two duplications.

Foreign Entry — When original transfers are erased incompletely from a plate, they can appear with new transfers of a different design which are entered subsequently on the plate.

Re-entry — When executing a re-entry, the transfer roll is reapplied to the plate at some time after the latter has been put to press. Thus, worn-out designs may be resharpened by carefully re-entering the transfer roll. If the transfer roll is not carefully entered, the registration will not be true and a double transfer will result. With the protective qualities of chromium plating, it is no longer necessary to resharpen the plate. In fact, after a plate has been curved for the rotary press, it is impossible to make a re-entry.

Shifted Transfer (Shift) — In transferring, the metal displaced on the plate by the entry of the ridges, constituting the design on the transfer roll, is forced ahead of the roll as well as pressed out at the sides. The amount of displaced metal increases with the depth of the entry. When the depth is increased evenly, the design will be uniformly entered. Most of the displaced metal is pressed ahead of the roll. If too much pressure is exerted on any pass (rocking), the impression on the previous partial entry may be floated (pushed) ahead of the roll and cause a duplication of the final design. The duplication appears as an increased width of frame lines or a doubling of the lines.

The ridges of the displaced metal are flattened out by the hammering or rolling back of the plate along the space occupied by the subject margins.

Short Transfer — Occasionally the transfer roll is not rocked its entire length in the entering of a transfer onto a plate, with the result that the finished transfer fails to show the complete design. This is known as a short transfer.

Short transfers are known to have been made deliberately, as in the Type III of the 1-cent issue of 1851-60 (Scott 8, 21), or accidentally, as in the 10-cent 1847 (Scott 2).

Re-engraved — Either the die that has been used to make a plate or the plate itself may have its temper drawn (softened) and be recut. The resulting impressions for such re-engraved die or plate may differ very slightly from the original issue and are given the label "re-engraved."

Re-cut — A re-cut is the strengthening or altering of a line by use of an engraving tool on unhardened plates.

Retouching — A retouch is the strengthening or altering of a line by means of etching.

PLATE ARRANGEMENT

Arrangement — The first engraved plates used to produce U.S. postage stamps in 1847 contained 200 subjects. The number of subjects to a plate varied between 100 and 300 until the issue of 1890, when the 400-subject plate was first laid down. Since that time, this size of plate has been used for a majority of the regular postal issues (those other than commemoratives). Exceptions to this practice exist, particularly among the more recent issues, and are listed under the headings of the appropriate issues in the catalogue.

Sheet — In single-color printings, the complete impression from a plate is termed a sheet. A sheet of multicolored stamps (two or more colors) may come from a single impression of a plate, i.e., many Giori-type press printings from 1957, or from as many impressions from separate plates as there are inks used for the particular stamp. Combination process printings may use both methods of multicolor production: Giori-type intaglio with offset lithography or with photogravure.

The Huck multicolor press used plates of different format (40, 72 or 80 subjects). The sheet it produced had 200 subjects for normal-sized commemoratives or 400 subjects for regular-issue stamps, similar to the regular products of other presses.

See the note on the Combination Press following the listing for Scott 1703.

In casual usage, a "pane" often is referred to as a "sheet."

Pane — A pane is the part of the original sheet that is issued for sale at post offices. A pane may be the same as an entire sheet, where the plate is small, or it may be a half, quarter, or some other fraction of a sheet where the plate is large.

The illustration shown later under the subtopic "Plate Markings" shows the layout of a 400-subject sheet from a flat plate, which for issuance would have been divided along the intersecting guide lines into four panes of 100.

Panes are classified into normal reading position according to their location on the printed sheet: U.L., upper left; U.R., upper right; L.L., lower left; and L.R., lower right. Where only two panes appear on a sheet, they are designed "R" (right) and "L" (left) or "T" (top) and "B" (bottom), on the basis of the division of the sheet vertically or horizontally.

To fix the location of a particular stamp on any pane, except for those printed on the Combination press, the pane is held with the subjects in the normal position, and a position number is given to each stamp starting with the first stamp in the upper left corner and proceeding horizontally to the right, then staring on the second row at the left and counting across to the right, and so on to the last stamp in the lower right corner.

In describing the location of a stamp on a sheet of stamps issued prior to 1894, the practice is to give the stamp position number first, then the pane position and finally the plate number, i.e., "1R22." Beginning with the 1894 issue and on all later issues the method used is to give the plate number first, then the position of the pane, and finally the position number of the stamp, i.e., "16807LL48" to identify an example of Scott 619 or "2138L2" to refer to an example of Scott 323.

BOOKLET STAMPS

Plates for Stamp Booklets — These are illustrated and described preceding the listing of booklet panes and covers in this catalogue.

Booklet Panes — Panes especially printed and cut to be sold in booklets which are a convenient way to purchase and store stamps. U.S. Booklet panes are straight-edged on three sides, but perforated between the stamps. Die cut, ATM and other panes will vary from this. Except for BK64 and BK65, the A.E.F. booklets, booklets were sold by the Post Office Department for a one-cent premium until 1962. Other sections of this catalogue with listings for booklet panes include Savings, Telegraphs and Canal Zone.

A.E.F. Booklets — These were special booklets prepared principally for use by the U.S. Army Post Office in France during World War I. They were issued in 1-cent and 2-cent denominations with 30 stamps to a pane (10 x 3), bound at right or left. As soon as Gen. John J. Pershing's organization reached France, soldiers' mail was sent free by means of franked envelopes.

Stamps were required during the war for the civilian personnel, as well as for registered mail, parcel post and other types of postal service. See the individual listings for Scott 498f and 499f and booklets BK64 and BK65.

COIL STAMPS

First issued in 1908-09, coils (rolls) originally were produced in two sizes, 500 and 1,000 stamps, with the individual stamps arranged endways or sideways and with and without perforations between.

Rolls of stamps for use in affixing or vending machines were first constructed by private companies and later by the Bureau of Engraving and Printing. Originally, it was customary for the Post Office Department to sell to the private vending companies and others imperforate sheets of stamps printed from the ordinary 400-subject flat plates. These sheets were then pasted together end-to-end or side-to-side by the purchaser and cut into rolls as desired, with the perforations being applied to suit the requirements of the individual machines. Such stamps with private perforations are listed in this catalogue under "Vending and Affixing Machine Perforations."

Later the Bureau produced coils by the same method, also in rolls of 500 and 1,000. These coils were arranged endways or sideways and were issued with or without perforation.

With the introduction of the Stickney rotary press, curved plates made for use on these presses were put into use at the Bureau of Engraving and Printing, and the sale of imperforate sheets was discontinued. This move marked the end of the private perforation. Rotary press coils have been printed on a number of presses over the years and have been made in sizes of 100, 500, 1,000, 3,000 and 10,000 stamps, etc.

Paste-up — the junction of two flat-plate printings joined by pasting the edge of one sheet onto the edge of another sheet to make coils. A two-stamp example of this joining is a "paste-up pair." See Splice.

Guide Line Pair — attached pair of flat-plate-printed coil stamps with printed line between. This line is identical with the guide line (See listing under "Plate Markings") found in sheets.

Joint Line — The edges of two curved plates do not meet exactly on the press and the small space between the plates takes ink and prints a line. A pair of rotary-press-printed stamps with such a line is called a "joint line pair."

Coil stamps printed on the Multicolor Huck Press do not consistently produce such lines. Occasionally accumulated ink will print partial lines in one or more colors, and very occasionally complete lines will be printed. Stamps resulting from such situations are not listed in this Catalogue. The "B" and "C" presses do not print joint lines at all.

Splice — the junction of two rotary-press printings by butting the ends of the web (roll) of paper together and pasting a strip of perforated translucent paper on the back of the junction. The two-stamp specimen to show this situation is a "spliced pair."

Splices occur when a web breaks and is repaired or when one web is finished and another begins.

Plate Number — for U.S. coil stamps prior to Scott 1891, Scott 1947, War Savings Coils and Canal Zone:

On a rotary-press horizontal coil the top or bottom part of a plate number may show. On a vertical coil, the left or right part of a plate number may show. The number was entered on the plate to be cut off when the web was sliced into coils and is found only when the web was sliced off center. Every rotary press coil plate number was adjacent to a joint line, so both features could occur together in one strip.

For U.S. stamps from Scott 1891 onward (excluding Scott 1947) and Official coils:

The plate number is placed in the design area of the stamp, so it will not be trimmed off. Such items are normally collected unused with the stamp containing the plate number in the center of a strip of three or five stamps. They normally are collected used as singles. The line, if any, will be at the right of the plate-number stamp. On the Cottrell press, the number occurs every 24th stamp, on the "B" press every 52nd stamp, on the "C" press every 48th stamp, etc.

Unused plate number strips of three and five are valued in this catalogue.

Hidden Plate Number — A plate number may be found entirely on a coil made from flat plates, but usually is hidden by a part of the next sheet which has been lapped over it.

Coil Waste — an occurrence brought about by stamps issued in perforated sheets from a printing intended for coils. These stamps came from short lengths of paper at the end of the coil run. Sometimes the salvaged sections were those which had been laid aside for mutilation because of some defect. Because the paper had been moistened during printing, it sometimes stretched slightly and provided added printing area. Sheets of 70, 100, and 170 are known. See Scott 538-541, 545-546, 578-579, and 594-595.

"T" — Letter which appears in the lower design area of Scott 2115b, which was printed on a experimental pre-phosphored paper. The stamp with the plate number is inscribed "T1."

SHEET STAMPS

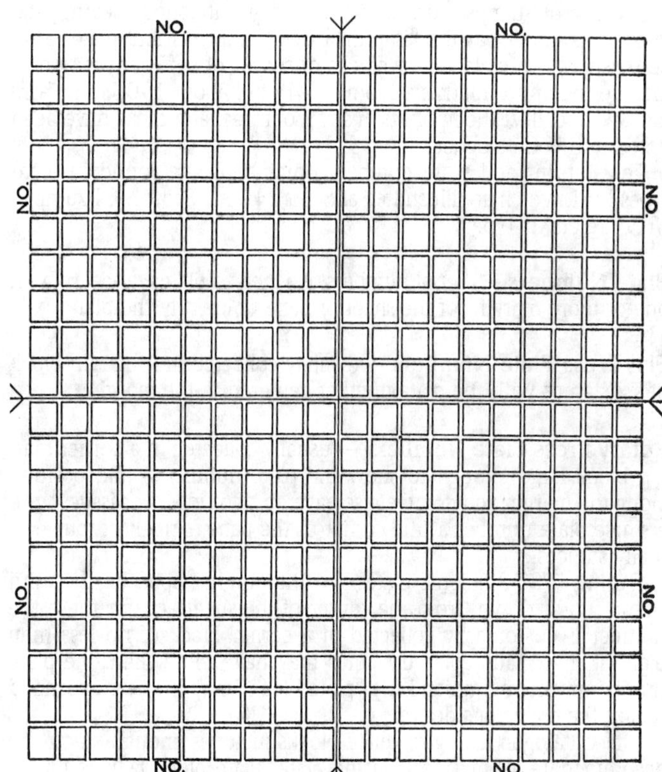

A typical 400-subject plate of 1922

Plate Markings — The illustration above shows a typical 400-subject plate of the 1922 issue with markings as found on this type of plate. Other layouts and markings are found further in the Catalogue text.

Guide Lines — Horizontal or vertical colored lines between the stamps, extending wholly or partially across the sheet. They serve as guides for the operators of perforating machines or to indicate the point of separation of the sheet into panes.

A block of stamps divided by any of the guide lines is known as a "line block" or "guide line block." The block of stamps from the exact center of the sheet, showing the crossed guide lines, is a "center line block."

Gutters — When guide lines are used to mark the division of the sheet into panes, the space between the stamps at the edge of the pane is no different than the space between any other stamps on the sheet. Some plates provide a wide space, or gutter, between the panes. These plates do not produce guide lines.

A pair of stamps with the wide space between is known as a "gutter pair", and blocks with that situation are "gutter blocks." A block of stamps from the exact center of the sheet, showing the two wide spaces crossing, is a "center gutter block" or "cross gutter block."

Gutter pairs or gutter blocks must contain complete stamps on both sides of the gutter, intact including perforation teeth unless imperforate. The stamps on either side of the gutter may or may not be creased; either way they qualify as the listed variety.

Arrows — arrow-shaped markings were used in the margins of stamp sheets, in place of guide lines, on the issues of 1870 through 1894. Since 1894, guide lines with arrows at both ends have been the standard practice on flat-plate printings.

A margin block of at least four stamps, showing the arrow centered at one edge, is known as a "margin block with arrow."

Color Registration Markings — marks of different sizes and shapes used as an aid in properly registering the colors in producing a bicolored or multicolored stamp.

Imprint — design containing the name of the producer of the stamps which appears on the sheet margin usually near the plate number.

A block of stamps with the sheet margin attached, bearing the imprint, is known as the "imprint block." Imprints and plate numbers usually are collected in blocks of six, or of sufficient length to include the entire marking. From 1894 until about 1907, one fashion was to collect the imprints in strips of three, and these have been noted in this Catalogue.

The imprint and plate number combination are found in eight types I-VII, which are illustrated at Scott 245 and Scott E3. Example: "T V" refers to Type V.

Plate Numbers — Serial numbers assigned to plates, appearing on one or more margins of the sheet or pane to identify the plate.

Flat Press Plate Numbers — usually collected in a margin block of six stamps with the plate number centered in the margin.

Rotary Press Plate Numbers — usually collected in a corner margin block large enough to show the plate number(s) and position along the margin and complete selvage on two sides. For issues with a single plate number at the corner of the pane a block of four normally suffices.

During 1933-39, some plates had the number opposite the third stamp (up or down) from the corner of the sheet and for these the number is customarily collected in a corner block of no less than eight stamps. Multicolored stamps may have more than one plate number in the margin and the "plate block" may then be expanded to suit the collector's desire.

The Catalogue listing for plate blocks includes enough stamps to accommodate all numbers on the plate. Plate block listings for se-tenant issues include all the designs as part of the block. When a continuous design is involved, such as Scott 1629-31, the complete design will be included in the plate number block. The entire pane constitutes the plate number block for issues such as the State Birds and Flowers (Scott 1953-2002).

Plate numbers take a further designation from the position on the sheet on which they appear, e.g. U.L. refers to upper left pane, etc.

See note following Scott 1703 for description of combination press markings.

Private Contractor Marks — On rotary plates from Scott 1789 onward: "A" denotes issues produced by private contractor American Bank Note Co., "U" by U.S. Bank Note Co., "K" by KCS Industries, Inc., "S" by Stamp Venturers, Inc., "P" by Ashton-Potter America, "B" by Banknote Corp. of America, "V" by Avery Dennison, "D" by Dittler Brothers, "M" by 3M Corp.

Stars — used on the flat plates to indicate a change from the previous spacing of the stamps. They also were used as a check on the assignment of the printed sheets to a perforating machine of the proper setting. Stars appear on certain rotary plates used for printing stamps for coils, appearing adjacent to the plate joint line and above stamp No. 1 on the 170-subject plates, and to the left of stamp No. 141 on the 150-subject plates.

"A" — On flat plates; used on plates having uniform vertical spacing between rows of subjects, but wider than those with the star marking.

"C.S." and "C" — plate has been chromium plated.

"E.I." — abbreviation for Electrolytic Iron. The designation is for plates made by the electrolytic process.

"F" — used to indicate the plate is ready for hardening. This appears only on flat plates and generally precedes the upper right plate number.

"Top" — marking on the top sheet margin of printings from both plates of some bicolored issues. This marking is used to check printings for "inverts." Beginning with the 6-cent bicolored airpost issue of 1938 (Scott C23), bicolored crosses also were used as an additional check.

"Coil Stamps" — appearing on the side sheet margins, designates plates used in the production of endwise coils.

"S 20," "S 30," "S 40" — marginal markings appearing on certain 150- and 170-subject rotary press plates to designate experimental variations in the depth and character of the frame line to over-come excess inking. "S 30" was adopted as the standard. Blocks showing these markings are listed as "Margin Block with S 20," etc., in this Catalogue.

Initials — used in sheet margins to identify individuals in the Bureau of Engraving and Printing who participated in the production or use of the plates.

Gutter Dashes — on the first 400-subject rotary plates, 3/16-inch horizontal dashes appear in the gutter between the 10th and 11th vertical rows of stamps. This arrangement was superseded by dashes 3/16-inch at the extreme ends of the vertical and horizontal gutters, and a 1/4-inch cross at the central gutter intersection. This latter arrangement continued until replaced by the scanning marks on the Electric Eye plates. See Electric Eye.

Margin — border outside the printed design or perforated area of a stamp, also known as selvage, or the similar border of a sheet of stamps. A block of stamps from the top, side or bottom of a sheet or pane to which is attached the selvage (margin) is known as a "margin block." A block of stamps from the corner of a sheet with full selvage attached to two adjoining sides is known as a "corner block."

NOTE — The descriptions and definitions above indicate that a certain number of stamps make up an arrow or plate number block. Any block of stamps, no matter how large or small, which had an arrow or plate number on its margin would be considered by that name. The usual practice is to collect flat-plate numbers in margin blocks of six and arrow blocks in margin blocks of four. Plate number blocks from rotary press printings generally are collected in blocks of 4 when the plate number appears beside the stamp at any of the four corners of the sheet. Particularly relative to bi-colored stamps, an arrow block is now separated from a plate number block. Thus, in those situations, the two individual types of blocks might form a block of eight or 10, as the situation dictates.

PRINTING

Methods Used — all four basic forms of printing have been used in producing U.S. stamps, engraved, photogravure, lithography, and typography. Holography has been used on some envelopes.

Engraved (Recess or Intaglio) — process where ink is received and held in lines depressed below the surface of the plate. Initially, in printing from such plate damp paper was forced into the depressed lines and therefore picked up ink. Consequently, ink lines on the stamp are slightly raised. This also is noted from the back of the stamp, where depressions mark where ink is placed on the front.

When the ornamental work for a stamp is engraved by a machine, the process is called "engine turned" or lathe-work engraving. An example of such lathe-work background is the 3-cent stamp of 1861 (Scott Illustration No. A25).

Engraved stamps were printed only with flat plates until 1914, when rotary press printing was introduced. "Wet" and "dry" printings are explained in the note in the text of the Catalogue following Scott 1029. The Giori press, used to print some U.S. stamps from 1957 (see Scott 1094, 4-cent Flag issue), applied two or three different colored inks simultaneously.

The Huck Multicolor press, put into service at the Bureau of

Engraving and Printing in 1968, was used first to produce the 1969 Christmas stamp (Scott 1363) and the 6-cent flag coil of 1969 (Scott 1338A). Developed by the Bureau's technical staff and the firm of graphic arts engineers whose name it bears, the Huck press printed, tagged with phosphor ink, gummed and perforated stamps in a continuous operation. Printing was accomplished in as many as nine colors. Fed by paper from a roll, the Huck Multicolor used many recess-engraved plates of smaller size than any used previously for U.S. stamp printing. Its product has certain characteristics which other U.S. stamps do not have. Post office panes of the 1969 Christmas stamp, for example, show seven or eight plate numbers in the margins. Joint lines appear after every two or four stamps. Other presses providing multiple plate numbers are the Andreotti, Champlain, Combination, Miller Offset, A Press, D Press and more.

Photogravure — the design of a stamp to be printed by photogravure usually is photographed through an extremely fine screen, lined in minute quadrille. The screen breaks up the reproduction into tiny dots, which are etched onto the plate and the depressions formed hold the ink. Somewhat similarly to engraved printing, the ink is lifted out of the lines by the paper, which is pressed against the plate. Unlike engraved printing, however, the ink does not appear to be raised relative to the surface of the paper.

Gravure is most often used for multicolored stamps, generally using the three primary colors (red, yellow and blue) and black. By varying the dot matrix pattern and density of these colors, virtually any color can be reproduced. A typical full-color gravure stamp will be created from four printing cylinders (one for each color). The original multicolored image will have been photographically separated into its component colors.

For U.S. stamps, photogravure first appeared in 1967 with the Thomas Eakins issue (Scott 1335). The early photogravure stamps were printed by outside contractors until the Bureau obtained the multicolor Andreotti press in 1971. The earliest stamp printed on that press was the 8-cent Missouri Statehood issue of 1971 (Scott 1426).

Color control bars, dashes or dots are printed in the margin of one pane in each "Andreotti" sheet of 200, 160 or 128 stamps. These markings generally are collected in blocks of 20 or 16 (two full rows of one pane), which include the full complement of plate numbers, Mr. Zip and the Zip and Mail Early slogans.

Details on the Combination Press follow the listing for Scott 1703.

Modern gravure printing may use computer-generated dot-matrix screens, and modern plates may be of various types including metal-coated plastic. The catalogue designation of Photogravure (or "Photo") covers any of these older and more modern gravure methods of printing.

Lithography — this is the most common and least expensive process for printing stamps. In this method, the design is drawn by hand or transferred in greasy ink from an original engraving to the surface of a lithographic stone or metal plate. The stone or plate is wet with an acid fluid, which causes it to repel the printing ink except at the greasy lines of the design. A fine lithographic print closely resembles an engraving, but the lines are not raised on the face or depressed on the back. Thus there usually is a more dull appearance to the lithograph than to the engraving.

Offset Printing or Offset Lithography — a modern development of the lithographic process. Anything that will print — type, woodcuts, photoengravings, plates engraved or etched in intaglio, halftone plates, linoleum blocks, lithographic stones or plates, photogravure plates, rubber stamps, etc. — may be used. Greasy ink is applied to the dampened plate or form and an impression made on a rubber blanket. Paper immediately is pressed against the blanket, which transfers the ink. Because of its greater flexibility, offset printing has largely displaced lithography.

Because the processes and results obtained are similar, stamps printed by either of these two methods normally are considered to be "lithographed."

The first application of lithographic printing for any U.S. items listed in this Catalogue was for Post Office seals, probably using stone printing bases. See also some Confederates States general issues. Offset lithography was used for the 1914 documentary revenues (Scott R195-R216). Postage stamps followed in 1918-20 (Scott 525-536) because of war-time shortages of ink, plates, and manpower relative to the regular intaglio production.

The next use of offset lithography for postage stamps was in 1964 with the Homemakers issue (Scott 1253), in combination with intaglio printing. Many similar issues followed, including the U.S. Bicentennial souvenir sheets of 1976 (Scott 1686-1689), all of which were produced by the combination of the two printing methods. The combination process serves best for soft backgrounds and tonal effects.

Typography — an exact reverse of engraved-plate printing, this process provides for the parts of the design which are to show in color to be left at the original level of the plate and the spaces between cut away. Ink is applied to the raised lines and the pressure of the printing forces these lines, more or less into the paper. The process impresses the lines on the face of the stamp and slightly raises them on the back. Normally, a large number of electrotypes of the original are made and assembled into a plate with the requisite number of designs for printing a sheet of stamps. Stamps printed by this process show greater uniformity, and the stamps are less expensive to print than with intaglio printing.

The first U.S. postal usage of an item printed by typography, or letterpress, under national authority was the 1846 "2" surcharge on the United States City Despatch Post 3-cent carrier stamp (Scott 6LB7). The next usage was the 1865 newspaper and periodical stamp issue, which for security reasons combined the techniques of machine engraving, colorless embossing and typography. This created an unusual first.

Most U.S. stamp typography consists of overprints, such as those for the Canal Zone, the Molly Pitcher and Hawaii Sesquicentennial stamps of 1928 (Scott 646-648), the Kansas-Nebraska control markings (Scott 658-679), Bureau-printed precancels, and "specimen" markings.

Embossed (relief) Printing — method in which the design is sunk in the metal of the die and the printing is done against a platen that is forced into the depression, thus forming the design on the paper in relief. Embossing may be done without ink (blind embossing), totally with ink, or a combination thereof. The U.S. stamped envelopes are an example of this form of printing.

Typeset — made from movable type.

Typeset Stamps — printed from ordinary printer's type. Sometimes electrotype or stereotype plates are made, but because such stamps usually are printed only in small quantities for temporary use, movable type often is used for the purpose. This method of printing is apt to show broken type and lack of uniformity. See Hawaii Scott 1-4 and 12-26.

Holograms — for objects to appear as holograms on stamps, a model exactly the same size as it is too appear on the hologram must be created. Rather than using photographic film to capture the image, holography records an image on a photoresist material. in processing, chemicals eat away at certain exposed areas, leaving a pattern of constructive and destructive interference. When the photoresist is developed, the result is a pattern of uneven ridges that acts as a mold. This mold is then coated with metal, and the resulting form is used to press copies in much the same way phonograph records are produced.

A typical reflective hologram used for stamps consists of a reproduction of the uneven patterns on a plastic film that is applied to a reflective background, ususally a silver or gold foil. Light is reflected off the background through the film, making the pattern present on the film visible. Because of the uneven pattern of the film, the viewer will perceive the objects in their proper three-dimensional relationships with appropriate brightness.

The first hologram on a stamp was produced by Austria in 1988 (Scott 1441).

Foil Application — A modern tecnique of applying color to stamps involves the application of metallic foil to the stamp paper. A pattern of foil is applied to the stamp paper by use of a stamping die. The foil usually is flat, but it may be textured. Canada Scott 1735 has three different foil applications in pearl, bronze, and gold. The gold foil was texured using a chemical-etch copper embossing die. The printing of this stamp also involved two-colored offset lithography plus embossing.

ADDITIONAL TERMS

Multicolored Stamps — until 1957 when the Giori press was introduced, bicolored stamps were printed on a flat-bed press in two runs, one for each color (example: Norse-American Issue of 1925, Scott 620-621). In the flat-press bicolors, if the sheet were fed to the press on the second run in reversed position, the part printed in the second color would be upside down, producing an "invert" such as the famed Scott C3a.

With the Giori press and subsequent presses, stamps could be printed in more than one color at the same time.

Many bicolored and multicolored stamps show varying degrees of poor color registration (alignment). Such varieties are not listed in this Catalogue.

Color Changeling — a stamp which, because of exposure to the environment, has naturally undergone a change of ink colors. Orange U.S. stamps of the early 1900's are notorious for turning brown as the ink reacts with oxygen. Exposure to light can cause some inks to fade. These are not considered color omitted errors. Exposure to other chemicals can cause ink colors to change. These stamps are merely altered stamps, and their value to collectors is greatly diminished.

Color Trials — printings in various colors, made to facilitate selection of color for the issued stamp.

Double Impression — a second impression of a stamp over the original impression.

This is not to be confused with a "double transfer," which is a plate imperfection and does not show a doubling of the entire design. A double impression shows every line clearly doubled. See also "Printed on Both Sides."

Essay — A proposed design, a designer's model or an incomplete engraving. Its design differs in some way — great or small — from the issued item.

Inverted Center — bicolored or multicolored stamp with the center printed upside down relative to the remainder of the design. A stamp may be described as having an inverted center even if the center is printed first. See "Multicolored Stamps."

Flat Plate Printing — stamp printed on a flat-bed press, rather than on a rotary press. See "Plate."

Overprint — any word, inscription or device printed across the face of a stamp to alter its use or locality or otherwise to serve a special purpose. An example is U.S. Scott 646, the "Molly Pitcher" overprint, which is Scott 634 with a black overprinted inscription as a memorial to the Revolutionary War heroine. See "Surcharge."

Printed on Both Sides — Occasionally a sheet of stamps already printed will, through error, be turned over and passed through the press a second time, creating the rare "printed on both sides" variety. On one side the impression is almost always poor or incomplete. This often is confused with an "offset," which occurs when sheets of stamps are stacked while the ink is still wet.

The "printed on both sides" variety will show the design as a positive (all inscriptions reading correctly) and the offset shows a reverse impression. See "Double Impression."

Progressive Proof — a type of essay that is an incomplete engraving of the finished accepted die.

Proofs — trial printings of a stamp made from the original die or the finished plate.

Reprints and Reissues — are impressions of stamps (usually obsolete) made from the original plates or stones. If they are valid for postage and reproduce obsolete issues (such as U.S. Scott 102-111), the stamps are *reissues.* If they are from current issues, they are designated as *second, third,* etc., *printing.* If designated for a particular purpose, they are called *special printings.*

When special printings are not valid for postage, but are made from original dies and plates by authorized persons, they are *official reprints. Private reprints* are made from the original plates and dies by private hands. An example of a private reprint is that of the 1871-1932 reprints made from the original die of the 1845 New Haven, Conn., postmaster's provisional. *Official reproductions* or imitations are made from new dies and plates by government authorization. Scott will list those reissues that are valid for postage if they differ significantly from the original printing.

The U.S. government made special printings of its first postage stamps in 1875. Produced were official imitations of the first two stamps (listed as Scott 3-4), reprints of the demonetized pre-1861 issues (Scott 40-47) and reissues of the 1861 stamps, the 1869 stamps and the then-current 1875 denominations. Even though the official imitations and the reprints were not valid for postage, Scott lists all of these U.S. special printings.

Most reprints or reissues differ slightly from the original stamp in some characteristic, such as gum, paper, perforation, color or watermark. Sometimes the details are followed so meticulously that only a student of that specific stamp is able to distinguish the reprint or reissue from the original.

Rotary Press Printings — stamps which have been printed on a rotary-type press from curved plates. Rotary press-printed stamps are longer or wider than stamps of the same design printed from flat plates. All rotary press printings through 1953, except coil waste (such as Scott 538), exist with horizontal "gum breaker ridges" varying from one to four per stamp. See: "Plate."

Surcharge — overprint which alters or restates the face value or denomination of the stamp to which it was applied. An example is Scott K1, where U.S. stamps were surcharged for use by U.S. Offices in China. Many surcharges are typeset. See: "Overprint" and "Typeset."

COMMON FLAWS

Cracked Plate — A term to describe stamps which show evidences that the plate from which they were printed was cracked.

Plate cracks have various causes, each which may result in a different formation and intensity of the crack. Cracks similar to the above illustration are quite common in older issues and are largely due to the plate being too-quickly immersed in the cooling bath when being tempered. These cracks are known as crystallization cracks. A jagged line running generally in one direction and most often in the gutter between stamps is due to the stress of the steel during the rolling in or transferring process.

In curved (rotary) plates, there are two types of cracks. Once is the bending or curving crack, which is quite marked and always runs in the direction in which the plate is curved.

The accompanying illustration shows the second type, the gripper crack. This type is caused by the cracking of the plate over the slots cut in the underside of the plate, which receive the "grippers" that fasten the plate to the press. These occur only on curved plates and are to be found in the row of stamps adjoining the plate joint. These appear on the printed impression as light irregularly colored lines, usually parallel to the plate joint line.

Rosette Crack — cluster of fine cracks radiating from a central point in irregular lines. These usually are caused by the plate receiving a blow.

Scratched Plate — caused by foreign matter scratching the plate, these usually are too minor to mention. See: "Gouge."

Gouge — exceptionally heavy and usually short scratches, these may be caused by a tool falling onto the plate.

Surface Stains — irregular surface marks resembling the outline of a point on a map. Experts differ on the cause. These are too minor to list.

PAPER

Paper falls broadly into two types: wove and laid. The difference in the appearance is caused by the wire cloth upon which the pulp is first formed.

Paper also is distinguished as thick or thin, hard or soft, and by its color (such as bluish, yellowish, greenish, etc.).

Wove — where the wire cloth is of even and closely woven nature, producing a sheet of uniform texture throughout. This type shows no light or dark figures when held to the light.

Laid — where the wire cloth is formed of closely spaced parallel wires crossed at much wider intervals by cross wires. The resultant paper shows alternate light and dark lines. The distances between the widely spaced lines and the thickness of these lines may vary, but on any one piece of paper they will be the same.

Pelure — type of paper which is very thin and semi-transparent. It may be either wove or laid.

Bluish — The 1909 so-called "bluish" paper was made with 35 percent rag stock instead of all wood pulp. The bluish (actually grayish-blue) color goes through the paper, showing clearly on back and face. See the note with Scott 331.

Manila — a coarse paper formerly made of Manila hemp fiber. Since about 1890, so-called "manila" paper has been manufactured entirely from wood fiber. It is used for cheaper grades of envelopes and newspaper wrappers and normally is a natural light brown. Sometimes color is added, such as in the U.S. "amber manila" envelopes. It may be either wove or laid.

Silk — refers to two kinds of paper found by stamp collectors.

One type has one or more threads of silk embedded in the substance of the paper, extending across the stamp. In the catalogues, this type of paper usually is designated as "with silk threads."

The other type, used to print many U.S. revenue stamps, has shortsilk fibers strewn over it and impressed into it during manufacture. This is simply called "silk paper."

Ribbed — paper which shows fine parallel ridges on one or both sides of a stamp.

India — a soft, silky appearing wove paper, usually used for proof impressions.

Double Paper — as patented by Charles F. Steel, this style of paper consists of two layers, a thin surface paper and a thicker backing paper. Double paper was supposed to be an absolute safeguard against cleaning cancellations off stamps to permit reuse, for any attempt to remove the cancellation would result in the destruction of the upper layer. The Continental Bank Note Co. experimented with this paper in the course of printing Scott 156-165. See "Rotary Press Double Paper."

China Clay Paper — See note preceding Scott 331.

Fluorescent or Bright Paper — See "Luminescence."

Rotary Press Double Paper — Rotary press printings occasionally are found on a double sheet of paper. The web (roll) of paper used on these press must be continuous. Therefore, any break in the web during the process of manufacture must be lapped and pasted. The overlapping portion, when printed upon, is known as a "double paper" variety. More recently, the lapped ends are joined with colored or transparent adhesive tape.

Such results of splicing normally are removed from the final printed material, although some slip through quality control efforts.

In one instance known, two splices have been made, thus leaving three thicknesses of paper. All rotary press stamps may exist on double paper.

Watermarks — Closely allied to the study of paper, watermarks normally are formed in the process of paper manufacture. Watermarks used on U.S. items consist of the letters "USPS" (found on postage stamps). "USPOD" (found on postal cards), the Seal of the United States (found on official seals), "USIR" (found on revenue items), and various monograms of letters, numbers, and so on, found on stamped envelopes.

The letters may be single- or double-lined and are formed from dies made of wire or cut from metal and soldered to the frame on which the pulp is caught or to a roll under which it is passed. The action of these dies is similar to the wires causing the prominent lines of laid paper, with the designs making thin places in the paper which show by more easily transmitting light.

The best method of detecting watermarks is to lay the stamp face down on a dark tray and immerse the stamp in a commercial brand of watermark fluid, which brings up the watermark in dark lines against a lighter background.

Note: This method of detecting watermarks may damage certain stamps printed with inks that run when immersed (such a U.S. Scott 1260 and 1832). It is advisable to first test a damaged stamp of the same type, if possible.

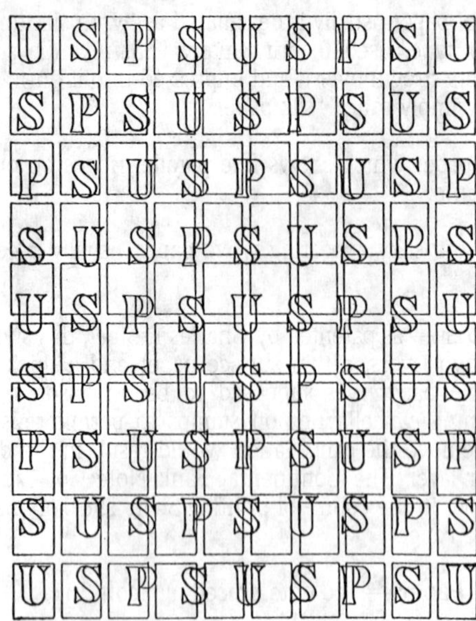

Wmk. 191
PERIOD OF USE
Postage: 1895-1910 Revenue: none

In the 1895-1903 U.S. issues, the paper was fed through the press so that the watermark letter read horizontally on 400 subject sheets and vertically on 200 subject sheets.

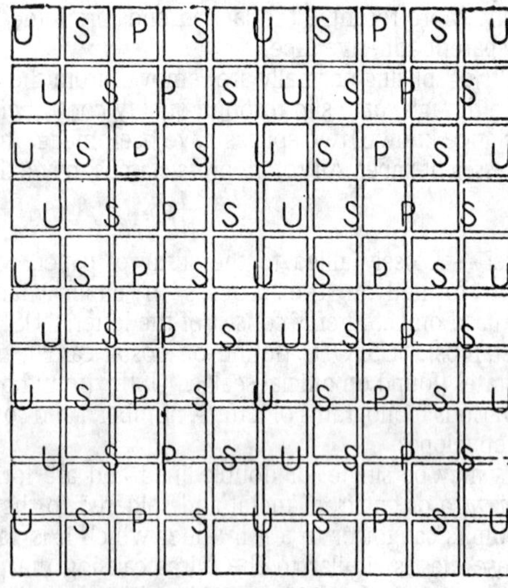

Wmk. 190
PERIOD OF USE
Postage: 1910-1916 Revenue: 1914

USIR
Wmk. 191R
PERIOD OF USE
Postage (unintentionally): 1895 (Scott 271a, 272a), 1951 (832b) Revenue: 1878-1958

Paper watermarked "USPOD" was used for postal cards from 1873 to 1875. For watermarks used on stamped envelopes, see Envelope Section in the text.

Watermarks may be found normal, reversed, inverted, inverted reversed and sideways, as seen from the back of the stamp.

Stitch Watermark — a type of watermark consisting of a row of short parallel lines. This is caused by the stitches which join the ends of the band on which the paper pulp is first formed. Stitch watermarks have been found on a great many issues, and may exist on all.

GRILLS

The grill consists of small square pyramids in parallel rows, impressed or embossed on the stamp. The object of the process is to break the fibers of the paper so that the ink from the cancellation would soak into the paper and make washing for reuse impossible. Grill impressions, when viewed from the face of the stamp, may be either "points up" or "points down." This process was used on U.S. Scott 79-101, 112-122 and 134-144 as well as some examples of 156-165 and 178-179.

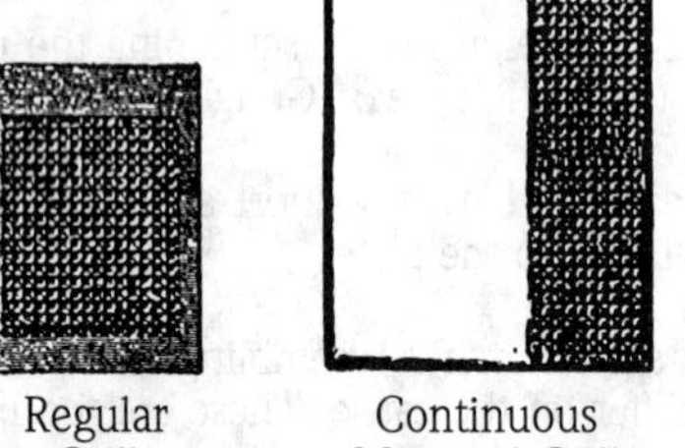

Regular Grill — Continuous Marginal Grill

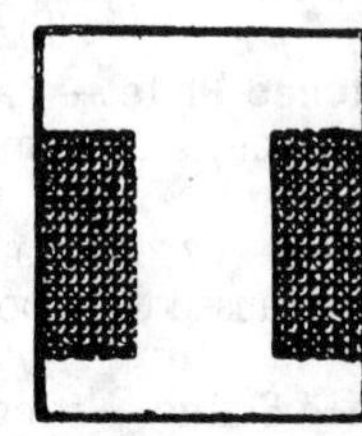

Split Grill

Continuous Marginal Grill — includes continuous rows of grill points impressed by the untrimmed parts of the ends of the grill rollers, noted as "end roller grill" on the 1870 and 1873 issues, and those grills which came from a continuous band lengthwise of the roller.

Split Grill — situation on a stamp showing portions of two or more grills, caused by a sheet being fed under the grill roller off center.

Double (or Triple) Grill — stamp showing two or more separate grill impressions. This is not to be confused with a split grill, which shows two or four partial impressions from a single grill impression.

Rotary Grills — grilled appearance occasionally found on rotary press printings that was produced unintentionally by a knurled roller during the perforating process.

Similarly, grill-like impressions can be left on stamps dispensed from vending machines.

SEPARATION

"Separation" is the general term used to describe methods used to separate stamps. The standard forms currently in use in the United States are perforating and die-cutting. These methods are done during the stamp production process, after printing. Sometimes these methods are done on-press or sometimes as a separate step. The earliest issues, such as the 1847 5¢ Franklin (Scott 1), did not have any means provided for separation. It was expected the stamps would be cut apart with scissors or folded and torn. These are examples of imperforate stamps. Many stamps were first issued in imperforate formats and were later issued with perforations. Therefore, care must be observed in buying single imperforate stamps to be certain they were issued imperforate and are not perforated copies that have been altered by having the perforations trimmed away. Stamps issued imperforate usually are valued as singles. However, imperforate varieties of normally perforated stamps should be collected in pairs or larger pieces as indisputable evidence of their imperforate character.

PERFORATIONS

The chief style of separation of U.S. stamps has been perforating. This is produced by cutting away the paper between the stamps in a line of holes (usually round) and leaving little bridges of paper between the stamps. These little bridges are the "teeth" of the perforation and, of course, project from the stamp when it is torn from the pane.

As the gauge of the perforation often is the distinguishing difference among stamps, it is necessary to measure and describe them by a gauge number. The standard for this measurement is the number of such teeth within two centimeters. Thus, we say that a stamp is perforated 12 or 10½ to note that there are either 12 or 10½ teeth counted within two centimeters.

Some later U.S. stamps are "stroke" perforated rather than "line" perforated. While it is difficult to tell the difference on a single stamp, with a block of four or more stamps the difference is more easily seen where the horizontal and vertical perforations cross. On the "stroke"-perforated items, the crossing point is clean and no holes are out of line. On the "line"-perforated stamps, the crossing point only rarely is perfect and generally there is a roughness.

Perforation Gauge — tool for measuring perforation, as described above.

Fine Perforation — perforation with small holes and teeth close together.

Coarse Perforation — perforation with large holes and teeth far apart, frequently irregularly spaced.

Rough Perforation — holes not clean cut, but jagged.

Compound Perforation — normally where perforations at the top and bottom differ from the perforations at the sides of the stamp. In describing compound perforations, the gauge of the top is given first, then the sides.

Some stamps are found where one side will differ from the other three, and in this case the reading will be the top first, then the right side, then the bottom, then the left side.

Double Perforations — often found on early U.S. revenue stamps and occasionally on postage issues, double perforations are applied in error. They do not generally command a premium over catalogue values of properly perforated stamps and are not to be confused with a variety found on occasional rotary press printings where stamps adjacent to the center gutters will show the entire width of the gutter and a line of perforations on the far end of the gutter. These are caused by the sheet having been cut off center and are called "gutter snipes." They command a small premium.

Many double perforations were privately made to increase the value of the stamp, and are to be considered damaged stamps.

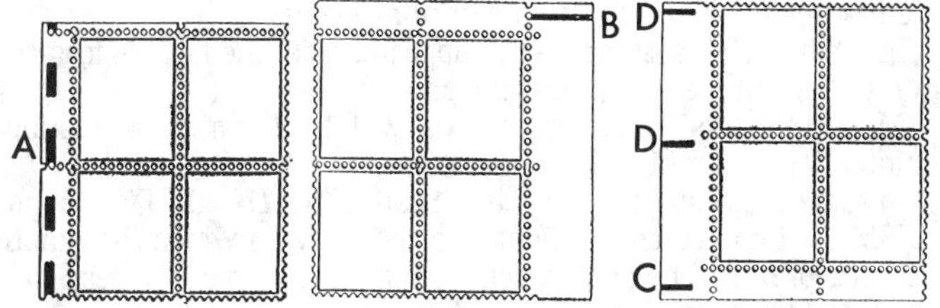

Electric Eye — an electronically controlled mechanical device acting as a guide in the operation of the perforating machine. Positive identification of stamps perforated by the electric eye process may be made by means of the distinctive marks in the gutters and margins of the full sheets on the printed web of paper. The original marks consisted of a series of heavy dashes dividing the vertical sheet gutter between the left and right panes (illustration A), together with a single line (margin line, illustration B), in the right sheet margin at the end of the horizontal sheet gutter between the upper and lower panes.

They first were used in 1933 on 400-subject plates for Scott 634, which was distributed to post offices in 1935 (used were plates 21149-50 and 21367-68). On these plates the plate numbers were placed opposite the ends of the third row of stamps from the top or bottom of the full sheet.

In later experiments, the margin line was broken into closely spaced thin vertical lines. Then it was again returned to its original form, but somewhat narrower.

In 1939, the Bureau of Engraving and Printing installed a new perforating machine which required a different layout to operate the centering mechanism. The vertical dashes remained the same, but the margin line was removed from the right sheet margin and a corresponding line ("gutter bar," illustration C) was placed in the left sheet margin at the end of the horizontal sheet gutter. Additional horizontal lines ("frame bars," illustration D) were added in the left sheet margin opposite the top frame line of the adjacent stamp design of all horizontal rows except the upper horizontal row of each left pane, where the frame bar is omitted. The plate numbers were moved back to their normal positions adjoining the corner stamps. Plates for the two types of machines could not be interchanged.

Later in 1939 a "convertible" plate was employed, consisting of a combination of the two previous layouts, the current one with the addition of a margin line (B) in its former position in the right sheet margin, thus making the perforation possible on either machine.

Originally laid out as 400-subject plates, electric eye plates were later used for 200-subject horizontal or vertical format (commemorative, special delivery and airpost issues), 280-subject (Famous Americans and those with similar formats) and 180- and 360-subject plates (booklet panes of definitives, airpost, postal savings and war savings issues).

In laying out the plates for the 400-subject and 200-subject horizontal format issues, the marks retained the same relative position to the stamp designs. This was changed, however, in entering the design for the stamps of the 200-subject vertical format and 280-subject issues because the stamp designs were turned 90 degrees. That is, the designs were entered on the plates with the longer dimension horizontal. Although the electric eye marks were entered on the plates in the usual positions, on the printed sheet they appear as though shifted 90 degrees when the stamps are held in the customary upright position.

Thus a "horizontal" mark on a 400-subject or 200-subject horizontal format sheet would become a "vertical" mark on a 200-subject vertical format or 280-subject sheet. This situation has caused confusion among collectors and dealers in determining a definite description of the various marks. The designation of the position of the plate numbers also has not been uniform for the "turned" designs.

To solve this confusion, the Bureau Issues Association adopted a standard terminology for all the marks appearing on the electric eye sheets. Dashes (A), Margin Line (B), Gutter Bar (C) and Frame Bars (D), whereby each type of mark may be identified readily without referring to its plate number position. The plate number designation of the panes will continue to be established by holding the pane of stamps with the designs in an upright position; the corner of the pane on which the plate number appears will determine the pane is upper left, upper right, lower left, or lower right.

DIE CUTTING

The other major form of U.S. stamp separation is die-cutting. This is a method where a die in the pattern of separation is created that later cuts the stamp paper in a stroke motion. This process is used for self-adhesive postage stamps. Die-cutting can appear in straight lines, such as U.S. Scott 2522; shapes, such as U.S. Scott 1552; or imitating the appearance of perforations, such as U.S. Scott 2920.

On stamps where the die cutting is unintentionally omitted, the terms "die cutting omitted" or "imperforate" may be used interchangeably.

GUM

The Illustrated Gum Chart in the first part of this introduction shows and defines various types of gum condition. Because gum condition has an important impact on the value of unused stamps, we recommend studying this chart and the accompanying text carefully.

The gum on the back of a stamp may be shiny, dull, smooth, rough, dark, white, colored or tinted. Most stamp gumming adhesives use gum arabic or dextrine as a base. Certain polymers such as polyvinyl alcohol (PVA) have been used extensively since World War II.

The *Scott Standard Postage Stamp Catalogue* does not list items by types of gum. The *Scott Specialized Catalogue of United States Stamps* does differentiate among some types of gum for certain issues.

As collectors generally prefer unused stamps with original gum, many unused stamps with no gum have been regummed to make them more desirable (and costly) to collectors who want stamps with full original gum. Some used stamps with faint cancels have had these cancels chemically removed and have been regummed. Skillful regumming can be difficult to detect, particularly on imperforate stamps. Certification of such stamps by competent authorities is suggested.

Reprints of stamps may have gum differing from the original issues. In addition, some countries have used different gum formulas for different seasons. These adhesives have different properties that may become more apparent over time.

Many stamps have been issued without gum, and the catalogue will note this fact. See United States Scott PR33-PR56.

LUMINESCENCE

Kinds of Luminescence — Fluorescence and phosphorescence, two different luminescent qualities, are found in U.S. postage stamps and postal stationery. While all luminescent stamps glow when exposed to short-wave ultraviolet (UV) light, only those with phosphorescent properties display brief afterglow when the UV light source is extinguished.

Fluorescent or "Hi-Bright" Papers — The Bureau of Engraving and Printing, at one point accepting paper for the printing of stamps without regard to fluorescent properties, unknowingly used a mix of paper with infinitely varying amounts of fluorescent optical brighteners added during the papermaking process. In March 1964, to preserve uniformity of product and as a safeguard for an emerging but still incomplete plan for nationwide use of luminescent stamps, BEP purchasing specifications were amended to limit the use of fluorescent paper brighteners. The amended specification permitted paper with some brightener content, but excluded brilliantly glowing papers known in the printing trade as "hi-bright."

Stamps printed on such papers emit a distinctive, intense whitish-violet glow when viewed with either long or short-wave UV. In following years, stamps were produced on papers with lower levels of fluorescence permitted by amended specifications.

Tagged Stamps — The Post Office Department (now the U.S. Postal Service) field-tested automated mail-handling equipment to face, cancel and sort mail at rates up to 30,000 pieces an hour, by sensing UV-light-activated afterglow from phosphorescent substances. For the first tests at Dayton, Ohio, started after August 1, 1963, the 8-cent carmine airpost stamp (Scott C64a) was over-printed (tagged) with a so-called "nearly-invisible" calcium silicate compound which phosphoresces orange-red when exposed to short-wave UV. A facer-canceler, with modifications that included a rapidly cycling on-off UV light, activated the phosphor-tagged airpost stamps and extracted envelopes bearing them from the regular flow of mail.

While the airpost extraction test was still in progress, the entire printing of the City Mail Delivery commemorative (Scott 1238) was ordered tagged with a yellow-green glowing zinc orthosilicate compound intended for use with the automated recognition circuits to be tested with surface transported letter mail.

After the first-day ceremonies October 26, 1963, at Washington, D.C., it was learned the stamps had been tagged to publicize the innovative test by coupling tagging with stamps memorializing "100 years of postal progress" and to provide the first national distribution of tagged stamps for collectors. Between October 28 and November 2, to broaden the scope of the test in the Dayton area, the 4-cent and 5-cent denominations of the regular issue then in use were issued with the same green glowing compound applied in an experimental tagging format (Scott 1036b, 1213b, 1213c, and 1229a).

By June 1964, testing had proven sufficiently effective for the Post Office Department to order all 8-cent airpost adhesive stamps phosphor-tagged for general distribution. By January 1966, all airpost stamps, regardless of denomination, were ordered tagged. Meanwhile, from 1963 through 1965, limited quantities of the Christmas issues were tagged for use in the continuing test in the Dayton area on the use of tagging to automatically position (face) and cancel mail. (Scott 1240a, 1254a-1257a, and 1276a).

On May 19, 1966, the use of phosphor-tagged stamps was expanded to the Cincinnati Postal Region, which then included offices in Ohio, Kentucky and Indiana. During the last half of 1966, primarily to meet postal needs of that region, phosphor-tagged issues were authorized to include additional denominations of regular issues, some postal stationery, and about 12 percent of each commemorative issue starting with the National Park Service 5-cent issue (Scott 1314a) and continuing through the Mary Cassatt 5-cent commemorative (Scott 1322a). After January 1, 1967, most regular values through the 16-cent, all commemoratives, and additional items of postal stationery were ordered tagged.

Adhesive stamps precanceled by the Bureau of Engraving and Printing (Bureau precancels), however, were not tagged, with the exception of Scott 1394, 1596, 1608, and 1610. Because there was no need to cancel mail with these stamps and since precancel permit holders post such mail already faced, postal officials by-passed facer-canceler operations and avoided the cost of tagging.

Overall phosphorescent overprints, when newly issued, are practically invisible in ordinary light. After aging three to five years, the tagging can discolor and become more easily visible. When viewed with UV light, there is little change in the hue of either orange-red or yellow-green emitted light. Even though observable discoloration exists, the presence or absence of tagging is best determined by examination with UV light.

Bar, or block, tagging, instead of the usual overall phosphorescent overprint, was used for some stamps beginning with the Andreotti-printed Mail Order Business commemorative (Scott 1468). These are much easier to identify than the overall overprint, often without need for a UV light.

Band tagging, a bar extending across two or more stamps, was first used with Scott 1489-1498.

Beginning in the 1990s, many stamps are printed on prephosphored paper. Unlike overall tagging, in which the tagging substance is applied to the entire stamp after it is printed, prephosphored paper has the tagging substance added to the surface of the paper during the paper-making process, before printing occurs.

In the late 1990s, some stamps appeared with the tagging formed in the shape of the stamp design elements.

Most of the luminescent issues exist with the luminescent coating unintentionally omitted.

In some postal stationery, such as Scott U551, UC40, UX48a, and UX55, the luminescent element is in the ink with which the stamp design is printed. The luminescent varieties of stamp envelopes Scott U550 and UC37 were made by adding a vertical phosphorescent bar or panel at left of the stamp. On Scott UC42, this "glow-bar" passes through the tri-globe design.

The *Scott Specialized Catalogue of U.S. Stamps and Covers* lists different tagging types when more than one type is known on a stamp. Currently, these types can be large or small block tagging, overall tagging and prephosphored paper. Prephosphored paper is further broken down into two types, each listed separately. It can have a "mottled tagging" appearance, which results from the application of the tagging substance to uncoated paper, or it can have a "solid tagging" appearance, either absolutely uniform or just slightly "grainy." The solid tagging appearance results from the application of the tagging substance to coated paper. Information in the catalogue reflects the most recent findings. Research on tagging is ongoing.

NOTE: Users of UV light should avoid prolonged exposure, which can burn the eyes. Sunglasses (particularly those that feature a "UV block") or prescription eyeglasses, tinted or plain, screen the rays and provide protection.

POSTAL MARKINGS

Postal markings are those marks placed by postal employees of this and other countries on the stamp or cover or both. These marks may indicate the mailing place of a letter, date, rate, route, accounting between post offices, and so on.

In addition to the basis town designations, there are many varieties of supplemental markings. Among these are rate marks, route marks, obliterators, special dating markings usually found on advertised or dead letter covers, transportation markings (rail, steam, ship, airpost, etc.), and service markings (advertised, forwarded, missent, second delivery, mail route, too late, charged, paid box, due, returned for postage, soldier's letter, held for postage, short paid, unpaid, not paid, paid, free, dead letter office, etc.).

These markings originated, for material mailed in what is now the United States, in the Colonial period when manuscript postal markings were first introduced under the Ordinance of December 10, 1672, of New York, which established an inland postal system between the colonies. A "Post Payd" is found on the first letter ever sent under the system, on January 22, 1673. Manuscript postal markings continued in use right through the pre-stamp period and even can be found on some letters today.

The earliest handstamp associated with the American service is a "NEW/YORK" blank handstamp found on letters conveyed via the Bristol Packet line in 1710-12 between New York and England. Following the demise of this operation, the first regular handstamp postal markings were introduced at New York in 1756, when a post office packet service was established between Falmouth, England, and New York. The marking merely was "NEW YORK" on two lines of type. The marking (see illustration), with each word of the city name on a separate line, is represented in presentations such as this as "NEW/YORK." Similar markings were later introduced at other towns, such as ANNA/POLIS, by 1766; CHARLES/TOWN, by 1770; PHILA/DELPHIA, by 1766; HART/FORD, by 1766; while other offices received a single line marking: BOSTON, by 1769; ALBANY, by 1773; PENSACOLA, by 1772; SAVANNA, by 1765, BALTIMORE, by 1772, and WMSBURG, by 1770.

Some of these early letters also bear a circular date stamp containing the month in abbreviated form, i.e., "IV" for June and "IY" for July, and the date in a 14-17mm circle. Known from at least nine towns, these are called "Franklin marks" after Benjamin Franklin, then deputy postmaster general for the English crown. The marks also are known as "American Bishopmarks" to distinguish them from the Bishopmark used in England, which has a center line.

First U.S. Handstamp

Franklin Mark

During 1774-1775, an American provisional postal system was established in opposition to that of the English crown. Both manuscript and handstamp markings have been attributed to it. This system was taken over by Congress on July 26, 1775, and the same markings were continued in use. The earliest reported Congressional marks are a manuscript "Camb Au 8" and a blue-green straightline "NEW*YORK*AU*24." Postal markings are known throughout the Congressional marks are a manuscript "Camb Au 8" and a blue-green straightline "NEW*YORK*AU*24." Postal markings are known throughout the Revolution, including English occupation markings. Most are manuscript.

In the post-war Confederation period, handstamped circular markings were introduced at Charleston, South Carolina, in 1778-1780, and later at New London, Connecticut. Straightlines and manuscripts continued to dominate until the use of oval markings became widespread about 1800, with circles becoming the predominant markings shortly thereafter.

Handstamp rate markings are known as early as the 1789 pennyweight markings of Albany. Such types of markings became more common in the 1830's and almost the standard by the "5" and "10"-cent rate period which began on July 1, 1845. This period also is when envelopes began to replace folded letter sheets. Before that date, envelopes were charged with an extra rate of postage. These "5," "10," and succeeding "3," "6," "5," and "10" rates of 1851-56 were common on domestic mail until prepayment became compulsory April 1, 1855, on all but drop or local letters domestically. The markings were common on foreign mail through about 1875.

Only 1.3 percent of all letters posted between 1847 and 1852 bore stamps. This proportion increased to 25 percent in 1852, 32 percent in 1853, 34 percent in 1854, 40 percent in 1855, and 64 percent in 1856. Stampless covers are commonplace, although there are some which are highly prized on the basis of their markings. Most are more common than stamped covers of the same period.

While the government began issuing handstamps as early as 1799 and obliterators in 1847, many postmasters were required, or at least permitted, to purchase their own canceling devices or to use pen strokes. Pen cancellations continued to be common in the smaller offices into the 1880's. Because of collector prejudice against pen-canceled stamps, many have ended up being "cleaned" (having the pen cancel removed). These are sold either as unused or with a different, faked cancellation to cover the evidence of cleaning. Ultraviolet light (long-wave) usually will reveal traces of the original pen markings.

From around 1850 until 1900, many postmasters used obliterators cut from wood or cork. Many bear fanciful designs, such as bees, bears, chickens, locks, eagles, Masonic symbols, flags, numerals and so on. Some of the designs symbolized the town of origin. These are not listed in this Catalogue, for they owe their origin to the whim of some individual rather than a requirement of the postal regulations. Many command high prices and are eagerly sought by collectors. This has led to extensive forgery of such markings so that collectors are advised to check them carefully.

Rapid machine cancellations were introduced at Boston in 1880-90 and later spread across the country. Each of the various canceling machine types had identifiable characteristics and collectors form collections based on type. One sub-specialty is that of flag cancellations. While handstamp flag designs are known earlier, the first machine flag cancellation was that of Boston in November-December 1894.

Specialists have noted that different canceling inks are used at different times, depending partly on the type of canceling device used. Rubber handstamps, prohibited in 1893 although used for parcel post and precanceling after that date, require a different type of ink from the boxwood or type-metal cancelers of the classic period, while a still different ink is used for the steel devices of the machine cancels.

Registry of letters was first authorized in this country in the Dutch colony of New Netherlands on overseas mail. Records of valuable letters were kept by postmasters throughout the stampless period while an "R" marking was introduced at Philadelphia in 1845 for registered mail. Cincinnati also had such a registry system. The first appearance of the word "registered" appears on mail in November 1847, in manuscript, and in handstamp in May 1850. The official registration for U.S. mail, however, did not begin until July 1, 1855.

In recent years, the handstamped and machine types of cancellations have been standardized by the Post Office Department and its successor and supplied to the various post offices.

Postmarks — markings to indicate the office of origin or manner of postal conveyance. In general terms, the postmark refers to the post office of origin, but sometimes there also are receiving postmarks of the post office of destination or of transit. Other post office markings include: advertised, forwarded, mail route, missent, paid, not paid, second delivery, too late, etc. Postmarks often serve to cancel postage stamps with or without additional obliterating cancels.

Cancellations — postal markings which make further use of the postage stamps impossible. As used in the listings in this Catalogue, cancellations include both postmarks used as cancellations and obliterations intended primarily to cancel (or "kill") the stamp.

Carrier Postmarks — usually show the words "Carrier" "City Delivery," or "U.S.P.O. Dispatch." They were applied to letters to indicate the delivery of mail by U.S. Government carriers. These markings should not be confused with those of local posts or other private mail services which used postmarks of their own. Free delivery of city mail by carriers was begun on July 1, 1863.

Free — handstamp generally used on free, franked mail. The marking occasionally is seen on early adhesives of the United States used as a canceling device.

Railroad Postmarks — usually handstamps, the markings were used to postmark unpouched mail received by route agents of the Post Office Department traveling on trains on railway mail route. The route name in an agent's postmark often was similar to the name of the railroad or included the terminals of the route. The earliest known use of the word "Railroad" as a postmark is 1838. Route agents gradually became R.P.O. clerks and some continued to use their handstamps after the route agent service ceased June 30, 1882. The railroad postmarks of the 1850 period and later usually carried the name of the railroad.

A sub-group of railroad postmarks is made up of those applied in the early days by railroad station agents, using the railroad's ticket dating handstamp as a postmark. Sometimes the station agent was also the postmaster.

In 1864, the Post Office Department equipped cars for the general distribution of mails between Chicago and Clinton, Iowa.

Modern railroad marks, such as "R.P.O." (Railway Mail Service) is a mark indicating transportation by railroad, and includes Railway Post Office, Terminal Railway Post Office, Transfer Office, Closed Mail Service, Air Mail Field, and Highway Post Office.

Effective November 1, 1949, the Railway Mail Service was merged with others of like nature under the consolidated title Postal Transportation Service (PTS). The service was discontinued June 30, 1977.

The modern "railway marks" are quite common and are not the types referred to under cancellations as listed in the Catalogue.

Way Markings — Way letters are those received by a mail carrier on his way between post offices and delivered at the first post office he reached. The postmaster ascertained where the carrier received them and charged, in his postbills, the postage from those places to destination. He wrote "Way" against those charges in his bills and also wrote or stamped "Way" on each letter. If the letter was exempt from postage, it should have been marked "Free."

The term "mail carrier" above refers to any carrier under contract to carry U.S. mail: a stage line, a horseback rider, or a steamboat or railroad that did not have a route agent on board. Only unpouched mail (not previously placed in a post office) was eligible for a Way fee of one cent. The postmaster paid this fee to the carrier, if demanded, for the carrier's extra work of bringing the letter individually to the post office. For a limited time at certain post offices, the Way fee was added to the regular postage. This explains the use of a numeral with the "Way" marking.

Packet Markings — Packet markings listed in this Catalogue are those applied on a boat traveling on inland or coastal waterways. This group does not include mail to foreign countries that contains the words "British Packet," "American Packet," etc, or their abbreviations. These are U.S. foreign-mail exchange-office markings.

Listed packet markings are in two groups: 1) waterways route agent markings which denote service exactly the same as that of the railroad route-agent markings, except that the route agent traveled on a boat instead of a train; 2) name-of-boat markings placed on the cover to advertise the boat or, as some believe, to expedite payment of Way and Steam fees at the post office where such letters entered the U.S. mails.

Occasionally waterways route-agent markings included the name of a boat, or "S.B.," "STEAMBOAT," or merely a route number. Such supplemental designations do not alter the character of the markings as those of a route-agent.

19th Century U.S. Express Mail Postmarks — In pre-stamp days these represented either an extra-fast mail service or mail under the care of an express-mail messenger who also carried out-of-mailexpress packages. The service was permitted as a practical means of competing with package express companies that also carried mail in competition with the U.S. Mail. Several of these early postmarks were later used by U.S. Mail route agents on the New York-Boston and New York-Albany runs, or by U.S. steamboat letter carriers on the coastal run between Boston and St. John, New Brunswick.

Steamboat or **Steam Markings** — Except for the circular markings "Maysville Ky. Steam" and "Terre Haute Stb." and the rectangular "Troy & New York Steam Boat," these markings contain only the word "STEAMBOAT" or "STEAM," with or without a rating numeral. They represent service the same as that of Way markings, except that the carrier was an inland or coastal steamer that had no contract to carry U.S. mails. Such boats, however, were required by law to carry to the nearest post office any mail given them at landings. The boat owner was paid a two-cent fee for each letter so delivered, except on Lake Erie where the fee was one-cent. At some post offices, the Steamboat fee was added to regular postage. In 1861, the two-cent fee was again added to the postage, and in 1863 double postage was charged.

Ship Postmarks — postal markings indicating arrival on a private ship (one not under contract to carry mail). This marking was applied to letters delivered by such ships to the post office at their port of entry as required by law, for which they received a fee and the letter were taxed with a specified fee for the service in place of the ordinary open postage.

The use of U.S. postage stamps on ship letters is unusual, except for letters from Hawaii, because the U.S. inland postage on ship letters from a foreign point did not need to be prepaid. "U.S. SHIP" is a special marking applied to mail posted on naval vessels, especially during the Civil War period.

Steamship Postmarks — akin to Ship postmarks, but they appear to have been used mostly on mail from Caribbean or Pacific ports to New Orleans or Atlantic ports carried on steamships having a U.S. mail contract. An associated numeral usually designates the through rate from where the letter was received by the ship to its inland destination.

Receiving Mark — impression placed on the back of envelopes by the receiving post office to indicate the name of the office and date of arrival. It also is known as a "backstamp." Generally discontinued about 1913, the marking was employed for a time on air mail service until it was found the practice slowed the service. The markings now are used on registry and special delivery mail.

Miscellaneous Route Markings — wordings associated with the previously described markings include Bay Route, River Mail, Steamer, Mail Route, etc. Classification of the marking ordinarily is evident from the usage, or it can be identified from publications on postal markings.

U.S. Foreign-Mail Exchange-Office Markings — These served to meet the accounting requirements of the various mail treaties before the Universal Postal Union was established. The markings usually designate the exchange office or the carrier (British Packet, Bremen Packet, American Packet, etc.). Sometimes these markings are a restatement of the through rate, or a numeral designating the amount credited or debited to the foreign country as a means of allocating the respective parts of the total postage, according to conditions of route, method of transit, weight, etc.

Gridiron Cancellation — commonest types of cancellations on early U.S. stamps. The markings consist of circles enclosing parallel lines. There are, however, many varieties of grid cancellations.

Paid Markings — generally consist of the word "PAID," sometimes within a frame, indicating regular postage prepaid by the sender of a letter. They are found as separate handstamps, within town or city postmarks, and as a part of obliterating cancels. In each case, the "paid" marking may be used with or without an accompany or combined rate numeral indication.

Precancels — stamps having the cancellation applied before the article is presented for mailing. The purpose is to reduce handling and speed up the mails. A permit is required for use by the public, except for special cases, such as the experiments using Scott 1384a, 1414a-1418a, or 1552 for Christmas mail. Normally the precanceling is done with devices not used for ordinary postal service. Most precancellations consist of the city and state names between two lines or bars.

Precancels are divided into two groups: locals and Bureaus. Locals are printed, usually from 100-subject plates, or handstamped, usually by means of a 10- or 25-subject device having a rubber, metal or vinyl surface, at the town using the stamps. Most locals are made with devices furnished by the Postal Service, but a number have been made with devices created in the city using them. Early locals include the printed "PAID" or "paid" on Scott 7 and 9, "CUMBERLAND, ME." on Scott 24-26 and the Glen Allen, Virginia stars.

Many styles of precancellation are known. More than 600,000 different precancels exist from more than 20,000 post offices in the United States.

The Bureaus, or Bureau Prints, are precancels furnished to the post offices by the Post Office Department in Washington. For 75 years these were printed by the Bureau of Engraving and Printing, hence the name "Bureaus." In late 1991, the American Bank Note Co. and J.W. Fergusson and Sons for Stamp Venturers also began producing precanceled stamps under contract with the Postal Service. Other companies have followed. Since the stamps go to the local post office from the same source, the Postal Service, and the method of production is essentially the same as used by the BEP, the term "Bureau precancel" has been retained in this catalogue. The cancellations consist of the name of the city and state where the stamps are to be used, lines or the class of mail. They originated in 1916 when postal officials were seeking ways to reduce costs as well as increase the legibility of the overprint. The BEP was low bidder in three cities, which resulted in the "experimentals." These 16 denominations, including two postage dues, were issued for Augusta, Maine (one value); Springfield, Massachusetts (14 values); and New Orleans (six values) in quanities ranging from 4,000,000 down to 10,000. Electrotype plates mounted on a flat bed press were used to print the precancellations.

Regular production of Bureau Prints began on May 2, 1923, with Scott 581 precanceled "New York, N.Y." All regular Bureaus until 1954 were produced by the Stickney rotary press, whereby the stamps, immediately after printing, pass under the precanceling plates. Then the roll is gummed, perforated and cut into sheets or coils. Since 1954, a variety of printing methods have been used.

Precancels are listed in the Catalogue only if the precanceled stamp is different from the nonprecanceled version (untagged stamps such as Scott 1582a); or, if the stamp only exists precanceled (Scott 2265). Classical locals and experimental bureaus are also included as cancellations. See Service Indicators.

Service Indicators — inscription included in the design of the stamp to indicate the category of postal service to be rendered. The first regular postage stamp to include a service indicator was the 7.9-cent Drum stamp of the Americana series, which was for bulk rate mailings. This stamp was issued with Bureau precancels for proper usage from 107 cities. Copies without the Bureau precancellation were for philatelic purposes.

A second category of service indicators came about when the USPS began to include the postal service between the lines of the Bureau precancellation. Examples of this group are "Bulk Rate" and "Nonprofit Organization."

Finally, with the 16.7-cent Transportation coil (Scott 2261), issued July 7, 1988, the USPS went back to including the service indicator in the design with the indicator serving as the cancellation. With the precancellation now part of the design, the USPS stopped offering tagged versions of the stamps for collectors.

In all cases, the "service indicator" stamp does not normally receive an additional cancellation when used for the indicated service. For examples see Postal Markings - Bureau Precancels.

Tied On — when the cancellation (or postmark) extends from the stamp to the envelope.

Postal Markings, Cancellations Examples

Numerals
Values are for rating marks such as those illustrated. Later types of numerals in grids targets, etc., are common.

The common Boston Paid cancellation
(Values are for types other than this)

PAID ALL

PAID

Steamship

STEAMBOAT

SHIP STEAM

FREE

Steamboat
(Route agent marking)

ST. LOUIS, CAIRO AND NEW ORLEANS
RAILROAD LINE STEAMER
CHAMPION
LEAVES NEW ORLEANS FOR
CAIRO AND ST LOUIS.
MAR 25

Packet Boat
(Name-of-boat marking)

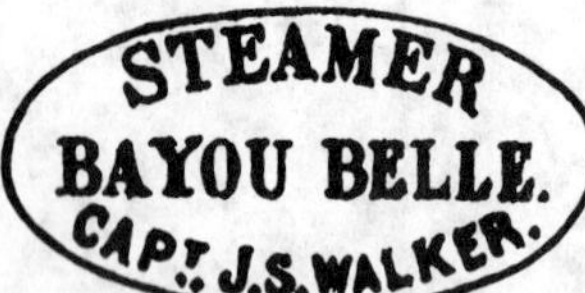

Packet Boat
(Name-of-boat marking)

Packet Boat
(Name-of-boat marking)

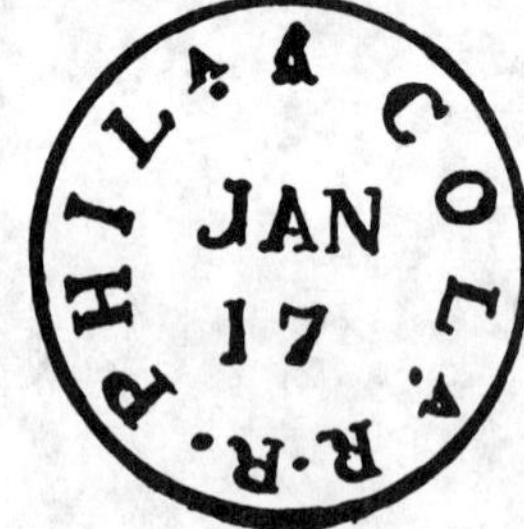

Railroad
(Route agent marking)

U.S. Express Mail
(Route agent marking)

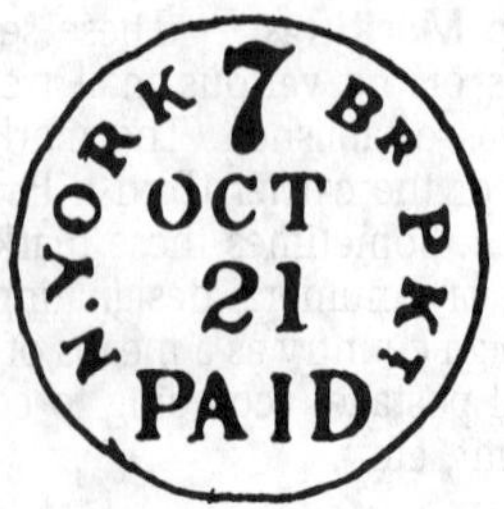

(In red on letter to Germany via Prussian Closed Mail, via British Packet. Credits 7 cent to Prussia.)

Express Company

Carrier

Army Field Post

Canadian

Town

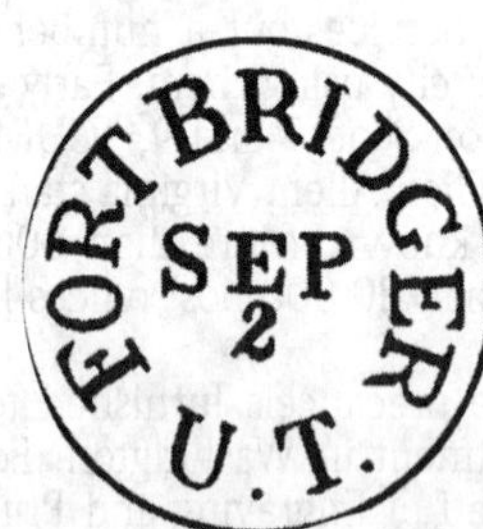

Fort

Year dated

Vera Cruz, Mexico 1914

U.S. Postmark used in Chin

Exposition Station
Used while exposition is open. Many styles.

U.S. Postmark used in Japan

Exposition advertising.
Used before exposition opens. Many styles.

New York City Foreign Mail — A group of design cancellations used between 1871 and 1877 in New York City on outgoing foreign mail only. This group of handstamps totals about 200 different fancy stars, geometric designs, wheels conventionalized flowers, etc., the majority within a circle 26-29 mm in diameter.

Patent Defacing Cancellations — When adhesive stamps came into general use, the Post Office Department made constant efforts to find a type of cancellation which would make the re-use of the stamp impossible. Many patents were granted to inventors and some of the cancellations (killers) came into more or less general use. Some of them appear in combination with the town postmarks.

About 125 different types are known on the stamps issues up to about 1887. Their principal use and greatest variety occur on Scott 65, 147, 158, 183 and 184.

Patent cancellations generally fall into three groups:

1) Small pins or punches which pierce the paper or depress it sufficiently to break the fiber.

2) Sharp blades or other devices for cutting the paper.

3) Rotation of a portion of the canceler so that part of the paper is scraped away.

1. Dot punches through paper

2. Blades cut the paper

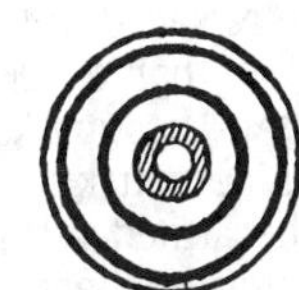

2. Small circle cuts the paper

3. Scraped in the shaded circle

Supplementary Mail — markings which designate the special post office service of dispatching mail after the regular mail closed. Two kinds of supplementary mail were available:

1. Foreign mail. For New York, the postmaster general established in 1853 a fee of double the regular rate. This paid to get the mail aboard ship after the regular mail closing and before sailing time. The service continued until 1939. Postmark Types A, D, E, F, and G were used.

2. Domestic mail. For Chicago, at no extra fee, supplementary mail entitled a letter to catch the last eastbound train. Postmark Types B and C were used. No foreign destination was implied.

Similar service with "Supplementary" in the postmark apparently available in Philadelphia and possibly elsewhere.

Type A

Type D

Type E

Type F
Combination Handstamp
(Also comes with numeral "1")
(Stamps with numeral cancel alone do not qualify for Supplementary Mail cancel premiums.)

Type G (also with other numerals)

Type B

Type C

World War I Soldiers' Letters — At the time the United States declared war against Germany on April 6, 1917, a postal regulation existed which permitted soldiers, sailors and Marines to send letters without prepayment of postage by endorsing them "Soldier letter" and having them countersigned by an officer. The single postage rate would then be collected from the recipient. Few of the enlisted men, however, took advantage of this privilege in sending letters while in the United States and practically all letters sent by soldiers from some 200 World War I military post offices in the United States bear regular postage stamps.

Fig. A

Soon after the arrival of the first units of the American Expeditionary Force in France, this regulation was modified to include letters which although not endorsed, bore the postmark of the United States Army Postal Service. The War Revenue Act of Congress of October 3, 1917, provided free postage for soldiers, sailors and marines assigned to duty overseas.

Therefore, letters from members of the A.E.F. sent before October 1917 without postage stamps were properly charged with postage due, while those sent after that time went through post free.

This provision for free postage did not ordinarily apply to civilians permitted to accompany the army, such as welfare workers, Post Office Department representatives, war correspondents and others. Neither did it apply to the registration fee on soldiers' letters nor to parcel post matter. It was necessary to pay such postage by means of postage stamps.

Fig. B Fig. C

The first U.S. Army post office, known as an A.P.O., was established at St. Nazaire, France, on July 10, 1917. The A.P.O.'s were at first operated by the Post Office Department, but in May 1918 the Military Express Service was established and the army took over the operation. Later the name was changed to Postal Express Service.

Fig. D Fig. E

Army post offices were given code numbers and were at first numbered from No. 1 (St. Nazaire) to No. 18 (Saumur). In December 1917, they were renumbered 701, 702, etc., and some 169 A.P.O.'s were established on the Western Front, including offices in Italy, Belgium, Netherlands, Luxembourg, and Germany after the Armistice. Most of the A.P.O.'s were located at fixed places, but "mobile" post offices were assigned to divisions, army corps and armies and were moved from place to place. Many A.P.O.'s had stations or branches, some of which used postmarks with different code numbers from those assigned to the main office.

Until July 1919, all A.E.F. mail was censored, and letters will be found with "company" censor marks (Fig. E) as well as "regimental" censor marks (Fig. F). Distinctive censor marks were used at the base censor's office in Paris (Fig. G).

Fig. F

Fig. G

An interesting variety of subsidiary markings may be found on soldiers' letters: "ADDRESSEE RETURNED TO U.S.A.," "CANNOT BE FOUND," "DECEASED - VERIFIED," "NO RECORD," "SOLDIER'S MAIL," and "UNIT RETURNED TO U.S."

Many styles of stationery were used, mainly those furnished by welfare organizations. Only a few pictorial envelopes were used, but a considerable variety of patriotic and pictorial postcards may be found in addition to officially printed-form postcards.

Fig. H Fig. I

A postal agency was in operation in Siberia from 1918 to 1920 and distinctive postmarks and censor marks were used there. A few American soldiers were sent to North Russia, and postmarks used there were those of the British Expeditionary Force's North Russia postal service (Fig. I).

World War I postmarks have been classified by collectors and the "American Classification System" prepared by the War Cover Club is in general use by collectors of these items.

World War II — Beginning in January 1941, U.S. post offices were established in Newfoundland, Bermuda and other naval bases acquired as a result of the exchange of destroyers with Great Britain. The names of the bases were at first included in the postmark. Later A.P.O. code numbers were adopted, in a similar manner to A.P.O. numbers were cut out of the postmark so that nothing appears to indicate the A.P.O. at which a letter was mailed, although the already established practice was continued of the writer giving the A.P.O. number in the return address. Early in 1943, A.P.O. numbers were replaced in the postmarks at many military post offices.

More than 1,000 different A.P.O. numbers were used. At least 90 types of postmarks exist, of which 45 are handstamped and 40 machine struck.

The armed services, both at home and abroad, were given the franking privilege early in April 1942, the frank consisting of the written word "Free" in the upper right corner of the envelope.

A wide variety of censor marks was used, differing radically in design from those used in World War I.

Bureau Precancels

AUGUSTA MAINE

NEW ORLEANS LA.

SPRINGFIELD MASS.

Experimentals

PERU IND.

LANSING MICH.

SAINT LOUIS MO.

New Orleans La.

San Francisco Calif.

PORTLAND ME.

LAKEWOOD N. J.

KANSAS CITY MO.

POUGHKEEPSIE N. Y.

LONG ISLAND CITY, N. Y.

CORPUS CHRISTI TEXAS

ATLANTA GEORGIA

ATLANTA GA.

PEORIA IL

CINCINNATI OH

Service Indicators

Blk. Rt. CAR-RT SORT

Bulk Rate

Nonprofit Org.

Nonprofit Org.

PRESORTED FIRST-CLASS

ZIP+4

Local Precancels

QUINCY ILLINOIS

FITCHBURG MASS.

LOS ANGELES CALIF.

Fergus Falls Minn.

COVINGTON KY.

REDWOOD CITY CALIF.

BELMONT CALIF.

ELGIN ILLINOIS

Electroplates

Ashland Wis.

PALMYRA N. Y.

Northhampton MASS.

DES PLAINES ILL.

RICHMOND VA.

BROOKFIELD ILLINOIS

PAONIA COLO.

GOSHEN IND

TOWER CITY N. DAK.

NEW BRUNSWICK N. J.

ORLANDO, FLA.

RICHTON PARK ILL.

M U L I N O, OREG.

PINE HILL N.Y.

FARRELL, PA

SACRAMENTO CA

Handstamps

General Glossary

Scott Publishing Co. uses the following terms in its Catalogues, as appropriate. Definitions follow each term.

Imperforate — stamps without perforations, rouletting, or other form of separation. Self-adhesive stamps are die cut, though they look imperforate.

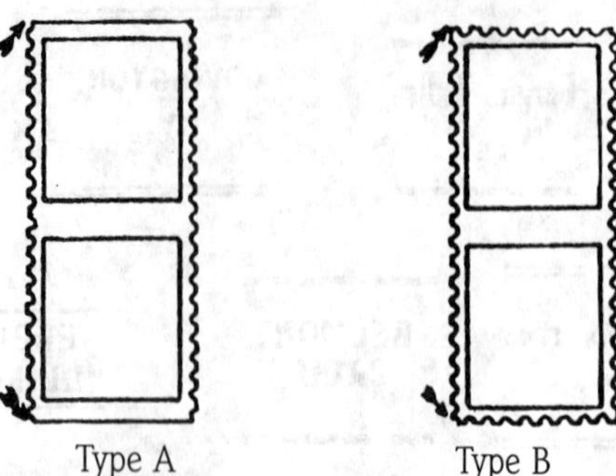

Type A Type B

Part-Perforate — Stamps with perforations on the two opposite sides, the other two sides remaining imperforate. See coils.

Vertical Pair, Imperforate Horizontally — (Type A illustrated) indicating that a pair of stamps is fully perforated vertically, but has no horizontal perforations.

Horizontal Pair, Imperforate Vertically — (Type A) indicating that a pair of stamps is fully perforated horizontally but has no vertical perforations.

Vertical Pair, Imperforate Between — (Type B illustrated) indicating that the vertical pair is fully perforated at the top, side and bottom, but has no perforations between the stamps.

Horizontal Pair, Imperforate Between — (Type B) indicating that the horizontal pair is fully perforated at the top, sides, and bottom, but has no perforations between the stamps.
Note: Of the above two types (A and B), Type A is the more common.

Blind Perforations — the slight impressions left by the perforating pins if they fail to puncture the paper. While multiples of stamps showing blind perforations may command a slight premium over normally perforated stamps, they are not imperforate errors. Fakers have removed gum from stamps to make blind perforations less evident.

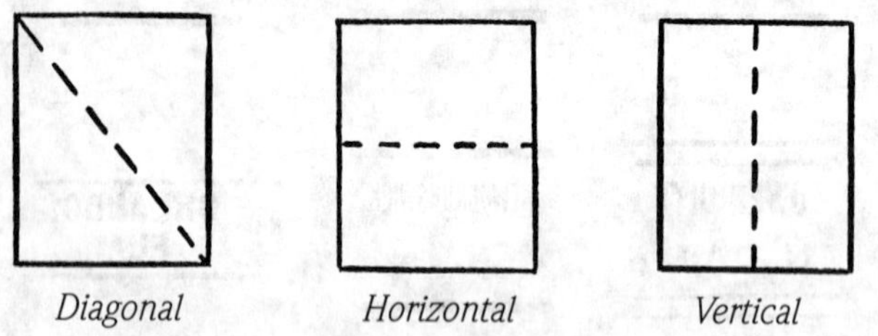

Diagonal *Horizontal* *Vertical*

Bisect — Stamps cut in half so that each portion prepaid postage. These items were used in emergencies where no stamps of the lower denomination were available. These may be diagonal, horizontal or vertical. Listings are for bisects on full covers with the bisected stamp tied to the cover on the cut side. Those on piece or part of a cover sell for considerably less. "Half-stamps" that receive a surcharge or overprint are not considered bisects.

This catalogue does not list unofficial bisects after the 1880's.

Block of Four, Imperforate Within — Examples exist of blocks of four stamps that are perforated on all four outside edges, but lack both horizontal and vertical perforations within the block. Scott 2096c, the Smokey the Bear commemorative, is an example of an accidental example of this phenomenon. Scott RS173j and RS174j are examples of a situation where internal perforations were omitted intentionally to create 4-cent "stamps" from four 1-cent stamps.

Rouletting — short consecutive cuts in the paper to facilitate separation of the stamps, made with a toothed wheel or disc.

Booklets — Many countries have issued stamps in booklets for the convenience of users. This idea is becoming increasingly popular today in many countries. Booklets have been issued in all sizes and forms, often with advertising on the covers, on the panes of stamps or on the interleaving.

The panes may be printed from special plates or made from regular sheets. All panes from booklets issued by the United States and many from those of other countries are imperforate on three sides, but perforated between the stamps. Any stamplike unit in the pane, either printed or blank, which is not a postage stamp, is considered a *label* in the Catalogue listings. The part of the pane through which stitches or staples bind the booklet together, or which affixes the pane to the booklet cover, is considered to be a *binding stub* or *tab.*

Scott lists and values booklets in this volume. Except for panes from Canal Zone, handmade booklet panes are not listed when they are fashioned from existing sheet stamps and, therefore, are not distinguishable from the sheet-stamp foreign counterparts.

Panes usually do not have a "used" value because there is little market activity in used panes, even though many exist used.

Cancellations — the marks or obliterations put on a stamp by the authorities to show that it has done service and is no longer valid for use. If made with a pen, it is a "pen cancellation." When the location of the post office appears in the cancellation, it is a "town cancellation." When calling attention to a cause or celebration, it is a "slogan cancellation." Many other types and styles of cancellations exist, such as duplex, numerals, targets, etc.

Coil Stamps — stamps issued in rolls for use in dispensers, affixing and vending machines. Those of the United States, and its territories are perforated horizontally or vertically only, with the outer edges imperforate. Coil stamps of some countries, such as Great Britain, are perforated on all four sides.

Commemorative Stamps — Special issues which commemorate some anniversary or event or person. Usually such stamps are used for a limited period concurrently with the regular issue of stamps. Examples of commemorative issues are Scott 230-245, 620-621, 946, 1266, C68, and U218-U221.

Covers — envelopes, with or without adhesive postage stamps, which have passed through the mail and bear postal or other markings of philatelic interest. Before the introduction of envelopes in about 1840, people folded letters and wrote the address on the outside. Many people covered their letters with an extra sheet of paper on the outside for the address, producing the term "cover." Used air letter sheets and stamped envelopes also are considered covers. Stamps on paper used to cover parcels are said to be "on wrapper." ("Wrapper" also is the term used for postal stationery items which were open at both sides and wrapped around newspapers or pamphlets.) Often stamps with high face values are rare on cover, but more common on wrapper. Some stamps and postal stationery items are difficult to find used in the manner for which they were intended, but quite common when used to make philatelic items such as flight or first day covers. High face-value stamps also may be more common on package address tags. See postal cards.

Earliest Documented Use (EDU) — For stamps that do not have a designated first day of issue, the earliest documented use is the date when a stamp was first used in the U.S. mails. These dates are listed in the U.S. Specialized catalog, and new dates must be documented with recognized certificates from leading expertizing committees.

rror — stamps having some unintentional major deviation from the ormal. Errors include, but are not limited to, mistakes in color, aper, or watermark, inverted centers or frames on multicolor printng, missing color or inverted or double surcharges or overprints, nperforates and part-perforates, and double impressions. A factually vrong or misspelled inscription, if it appears on all examples of a tamp, even if corrected later, is not classified as a philatelic error.

Color-Omitted Errors — This term refers to stamps where a missng color is caused by the complete failure of the printing plate to leliver ink to the stamp paper or any other paper. Generally, this is aused by the printing plate not being engaged on the press or the nk station running dry of ink during printing.

Color-Missing Errors — This term refers to stamps where a color or colors were printed somewhere but do not appear on the finished stamp. There are four different classes of color-missing errors, and the catalog indicates with a two-letter code appended to each such isting what caused the color to be missing:

FO = A *foldover* of the stamp sheet during printing may block ink from appearing on a stamp. Instead, the color will appear on the back of the foldover (where it might fall on the back of the selvage or perhaps on the back of another stamp).

EP = A piece of *extraneous paper* falling across the plate or stamp paper will receive the printed ink. When the extraneous paper is removed, an unprinted portion of stamp paper remains and shows partially or totally missing colors.

CM = A misregistration of the printing plates during printing will result in a *color misregistration*, and such a misregistration may result in a color not appearing on the finished stamp.

PS = A *perforation shift* after printing may remove a color from the finished stamp. Normally, this will occur on a row of stamps at the edge of the stamp pane.

First Day Cover — A philatelic term to designate the use of a certain stamp (on cover) or postal stationery item on the first day of sale at a place officially designated for such sale or so postmarked. Current U.S. stamps may have such a postal marking applied considerably after the actual issue date.

Gum Breaker Ridges — Colorless marks across the backs of some rotary press stamps, impressed during manufacture to prevent curling. Many varieties of "gum breaks" exist.

Original Gum — A stamp is described as "O.G." if it has the original gum as applied when printed. Some are issued without gum, such as Scott 730, 731, 735, 752, etc; government reproductions, such as Scott 3 and 4; and official reprints.

Overprinted and Surcharged Stamps — Overprinting is a wording or design placed on stamps to alter the place of use (e.g., "Canal Zone" on U.S. stamps), to adapt them for a special purpose ("I.R." on 1-cent and 2-cent U.S. stamps of the 1897-1903 regular issue for use as revenue stamps. Scott R153-R155A) or for a special occasion (U.S. Scott 646-648).

Surcharge is an overprint which changes or restates the face value of the item.

Surcharges and overprints may be handstamped, typeset or, occasionally, lithographed or engraved. A few hand-written overprints and surcharges are known. The world's first surcharge was a handstamped "2" on the United States City Despatch Post stamps of 1846.

Postal Cards — cards that have postage printed on them. Ones without printed stamps are referred to as "postcards."

Proofs and Essays — Proofs are impressions taken from an approved die, plate or stone in which the design and color are the same as the stamp issued to the public. Trial color proofs are impressions taken from approved dies, plates or stones in varying colors. An essay is the impression of a design that differs in some way from the stamp as issued.

Provisionals — stamps issued on short notice and intended for temporary use pending the arrival of regular (definitive) issues. They usually are issued to meet such contingencies as changes in government or currency, shortage of necessary values, or military occupation.

In the 1840's, postmasters in certain American cities issued stamps that were valid only at specific post offices. Postmasters of the Confederate States also issued stamps with limited validity. These are known as "postmaster's provisionals." See U.S. Scott 9X1-9X3 and Confederate States Scott 51X1.

Se-Tenant — joined, referring to an unsevered pair, strip or block of stamps differing in design, denomination or overprint. See U.S. Scott 2158a.

Tete Beche — A pair of stamps in which one is upside down in relation to the other. Some of these are the result of international sheet arrangements, i.e. Morocco Scott B10-B11. Others occurred when one or more electrotypes accidentally were placed upside down on the plate. See Hawaii Scott 21a and 22a. Separation of the stamps, of course, destroys the tete beche variety.

Specimens — One of the regulations of the Universal Postal Union requires member nations to send samples of all stamps they put into service to the International Bureau in Switzerland. Member nations, of the UPU receive these specimens as samples of what stamps are valid for postage. Many are overprinted, handstamped or initial-perforated "Specimen," "Canceled" or "Muestra."Stamps distributed to government officials or for publicity purposes, and stamps submitted by private security printers for official approval also may receive such defacements.

These markings prevent postal use, and all such items generally are known as "specimens." There is a section in this volume devoted to this type of material. U.S. officials with "specimen" overprints and printings are listed in the Special Printings section.

Territorial and Statehood Dates

	Territorial Date	Statehood Date	
Alabama	Sept. 25, 1817	Dec. 14, 1819	Territory by enabling act of March 3, 1817, effective Sept. 25, 1817. Created out c part of existing Mississippi Territory.
Alaska	Oct. 18, 1867	Jan. 3, 1959	A district from Oct. 18, 1867, until it became an organized territory Aug. 24, 1912.
Arizona	Feb. 24, 1863	Feb. 14, 1912	This region was sometimes called Arizona before 1863 though still in the Territory o New Mexico.
Arkansas	July 5, 1819*	June 15, 1836	The territory was larger than the state. After statehood, the left-over area to the wes had post offices that continued for some years to use an Arkansas abbreviation in the postmarks although really they were in the "Indian Country."
California		Sept. 9, 1850	Ceded by Mexico by the Treaty of Guadalupe-Hidalgo, concluded Feb. 2, 1848, and proclaimed July 4, 1848. From then until statehood, California had first a military government until Dec. 20, 1849, and then a local civil government. It never had a territorial form of government.
Colorado	Feb. 28, 1861	Aug. 1, 1876	
Connecticut		Jan. 9, 1788	The fifth of the original 13 colonies.
Delaware		Dec. 7, 1787	The first of the original 13 colonies.
Dakota	March 2, 1861	Nov. 2, 1889	Became two states: North and South Dakota.
Deseret	March 5, 1849		Brigham Young created the unofficial territory of Deseret. In spite of the fact that Utah Territory was created Sept. 9, 1850, Deseret continued to exist unofficially, in what is now Utah, at least as late as 1862.
Frankland or Franklin			This unofficial state was formed in Aug. 1784, in the northeast corner of what is now Tennessee, and the government existed until 1788. In reality it was part of North Carolina.
Florida	March 30, 1822	March 3, 1845	
Georgia		Jan. 2, 1788	The fourth of the original 13 colonies.
Hawaii	Aug. 12, 1898	Aug. 21, 1959	The territorial date given is that of the formal transfer to the United States, with Sanford B. Dole as first Governor.
Idaho	March 3, 1863	July 3, 1890	
Illinois	March 2, 1809*	Dec. 3, 1818	
Indiana	July 5, 1800*	Dec. 11, 1816	There was a residue of Indiana Territory which continued to exist under that name from Dec. 11, 1816 until Dec. 3, 1818, when it was attached to Michigan Territory.
Indian Territory		Nov. 16, 1907	In the region first called the "Indian Country," established June 30, 1834. It never had a territorial form of government. Finally, with Oklahoma Territory, it became the State of Oklahoma on Nov. 16, 1907.
Iowa	July 4, 1838	Dec. 28, 1846	
Jefferson	Oct. 24, 1859		An unofficial territory from Oct. 24, 1859, to Feb. 28, 1861. In reality it included parts of Kansas, Nebraska, Utah and New Mexico Territories, about 30% being in each of the first three and 10% in New Mexico. The settled portion was mostly in Kansas Territory until Jan. 29, 1861, when the State of Kansas was formed from the eastern part of Kansas Territory. From this date the heart of "Jefferson" was in unorganized territory until Feb. 28, 1861, when it became the Territory of Colorado.
Kansas	May 30, 1854	Jan. 29, 1861	
Kentucky		June 1, 1792	Never a territory, it was part of Virginia until statehood.
District of Louisiana	Oct. 1, 1804		An enormous region, it encompassed all of the Louisiana Purchase except the Territory of Orleans. Created by Act of March 26, 1804, effective Oct. 1, 1804, and attached for administrative purposes to the Territory of Indiana.
Territory of Louisiana	July 4, 1805		By Act of March 3, 1805, effective July 4, 1805, the District of Louisiana became the Territory of Louisiana.
Louisiana		April 30, 1812	With certain boundary changes, had been the Territory of Orleans.
District of Maine		March 16, 1820	Before statehood, what is now the State of Maine was called the District of Maine and belonged to Massachusetts.
Maryland		April 28, 1788	The seventh of the original 13 colonies.

	Territorial Date	Statehood Date	
Massachusetts		Feb. 6, 1788	The sixth of the original 13 colonies.
Michigan	July 1, 1805	Jan. 26, 1837	
Minnesota	March 3, 1849	May 11, 1858	
Mississippi	May 7, 1798	Dec. 10, 1817	Territory by Act of April 7, 1798, effective May 7, 1798.
Missouri	Dec. 7, 1812	Aug. 10, 1821	The state was much smaller than the territory. The area to the west and northwest of the state, which had been in the territory, was commonly known as the "Missouri Country" until May 30, 1854, and certain of the post offices in this area show a Missouri abbreviation in the postmark.
Montana	May 26, 1864	Nov. 8, 1889	
Nebraska	May 30, 1854	March 1, 1867	
Nevada	March 2, 1861	Oct. 31, 1864	
New Hampshire		June 21, 1788	The ninth of the original 13 colonies.
New Jersey		Dec. 18, 1787	The third of the original 13 colonies.
New Mexico	Dec. 13, 1850	Jan. 6, 1912	
New York		July 26, 1788	The 11th of the original 13 colonies.
North Carolina		Nov. 21, 1789	The 12th of the original 13 colonies.
North Dakota		Nov. 2, 1889	Had been part of the Territory of Dakota.
Northwest Territory	July 13, 1787		Ceased to exist March 1, 1803, when Ohio became a state. The date given is in dispute, Nov. 29, 1802 often being accepted.
Ohio		March 1, 1803	Had been part of Northwest Territory until statehood.
Oklahoma	May 2, 1890	Nov. 16, 1907	The state was formed from Oklahoma Territory and Indian Territory.
Oregon	Aug. 14, 1848	Feb. 14, 1859	
Orleans	Oct. 1, 1804		A territory by Act of March 26, 1804, effective Oct. 1, 1804. With certain boundary changes, it became the State of Louisiana, April 30, 1812.
Pennsylvania		Dec. 12, 1787	The second of the original 13 colonies.
Rhode Island		May 29, 1790	The 13th of the original 13 colonies.
South Carloina		May 23, 1788	The eighth of the original 13 colonies.
South Dakota		Nov. 2, 1889	Had been part of Dakota Territory.
Southwest Territory			Became the State of Tennessee, with minor boundary changes, June 1, 1796.
Tennessee		June 1, 1796	Had been Southwest Territory before statehood.
Texas		Dec. 29, 1845	Had been an independent Republic before statehood.
Utah	Sept. 9, 1850	Jan. 4, 1896	
Vermont		March 4, 1791	Until statehood, had been a region claimed by both New York and New Hampshire.
Virginia		June 25, 1788	The 10th of the original 13 colonies.
Washington	March 2, 1853	Nov. 11, 1889	
West Virginia		June 20, 1863	Had been part of Virginia until statehood.
Wisconsin	July 4, 1836	May 29, 1848	The state was smaller than the territory, and the left-over area continued to be called the Territory of Wisconsin until March 3, 1849.
Wyoming	July 29, 1868	July 10, 1890	

* The dates followed by an asterisk are one day later than those generally accepted. The reason is that the Act states, with Arkansas for example, "from and after July 4." While it was undoubtedly the intention of Congress to create Arkansas as a Territory on July 4, the U.S. Supreme Court decided that "from and after July 4," for instance, meant "July 5."

Territorial and statehood data compiled by Dr. Carroll Chase and Richard McP. Cabeen.

Domestic Letter Rates

Effective Date	Prepaid	Collect
1845, July 1		
Reduction from 6¢ to 25¢ range on single-sheet letters		
Under 300 miles, per ½ oz	5¢	5¢
Over 300 miles, per ½ oz	10¢	10¢
Drop letters	2¢	
1847-1848		
East, to or from Havana (Cuba) per ½ oz	12½¢	12½¢
East, to or from Chagres (Panama) per ½ oz	20¢	20¢
East, to or from Panama, across Isthmus, per ½ oz.	30¢	30¢
To or from Astoria (Ore.) or Pacific Coast, per ½ oz		40¢
40¢		
Along Pacific Coast, per ½ oz	12½¢	12½¢
1847, July 1		
Unsealed circulars		
1 oz. or less	3¢	
1851, July 1		
Elimination of rates of 1847-1848 listed above		
Up to 3,000 miles, per ½ oz.	3¢	5¢
Over 3,000 miles, per ½ oz	6¢	10¢
Drop letters	1¢	
Unsealed circular		
1 oz. or less up to 500 miles	1¢	
Over 500 miles to 1,500 miles	2¢	
Over 1,500 miles to 2,500 miles	3¢	
Over 2,500 miles to 3,500 miles	4¢	
Over 3,500 miles	5¢	
1852, September 30		
Unsealed circulars		
3 oz. or less anywhere in U.S.	1¢	
Each additional ounce	1¢	
(Double charge if collect)		
1855, April 1		
Prepayment made compulsory		
Not over 3,000 miles, per ½ oz.	3¢	
Over 3,000 miles, per ½ oz.	10¢	
Drop letters	1¢	
1863, July 1		
Distance differential eliminated		
All parts of United States, per ½ oz.	3¢	
1883, October 1		
Letter rate reduced one-third		
All parts of United States, per ½ oz.	2¢	
1885, July 1		
Weight increased to 1 oz.		

Effective Date	Prepaid
1896, October 1	
Rural Free Delivery started	
1917, November 2	
War emergency	
All parts of United States, per 1 oz.	3¢
1919, July 1	
Restoration of pre-war rate	
All parts of United States, per 1 oz.	2¢
1932, July 6	
Rise due to depression	
All parts of United States, per 1 oz.	3¢
1958, August 1	
All parts of United States, per 1 oz.	4¢
1963, January 7	
All parts of United States, per 1 oz.	5¢
1968, January 7	
All parts of United States, per 1 oz.	6¢
1971, May 16	
All parts of United States, per 1 oz.	8¢
1974, March 2	
All parts of United States, per 1 oz.	10¢
1975, December 31	
All parts of United States, 1st oz.	13¢
1978, May 29	
All parts of United States, 1st oz.	15¢
1981, March 22	
All parts of United States, 1st oz.	18¢
1981, November 1	
All parts of United States, 1st oz.	20¢
1985, February 17	
All parts of United States, 1st oz.	22¢
1988, April 3	
All parts of United States, 1st oz.	25¢
1991, February 3	
All parts of United States, 1st oz.	29¢
1995, January 1	
All parts of United States, 1st oz.	32¢
1999, January 10	
All parts of United States, 1st oz.	33¢
2001, January 7	
All parts of United States, 1st oz.	34¢
2002, June 30	
All parts of United States, 1st oz.	37¢

Domestic Air Mail Rates

Effective Date **Prepaid**

1911-1916 – The Pioneer Period

Special official Post Office Flights at Fairs, aviation meets, etc., per 1 oz. .... 2¢
Postal cards and postcards.......... 1¢
(Regulations prohibited an additional charge for air service on Post Office authorized flights.)

1918, May 15 - July 13, 1918

Service between Washington, DC, New York and Philadelphia (including 10¢ special delivery fee), per 1 oz. .... 24¢

1918, July 15-Dec. 14, 1918

Service between Washington, DC, New York and Philadelphia (including 10¢ special delivery fee), per 1 oz. .... 16¢
Additional ounces .... 6¢

1918, Dec. 15-July 17, 1919

Service between selected cities (other cities added later, special delivery no longer included), per 1 oz. .... 6¢

1919, July 18-June 29, 1924

No specific airmail rate: mail carried by airplane on space available basis but airmail service not guaranteed, per 1 oz. .... 2¢
Postal cards and postcards, per 1 oz.......... 1¢

1924, June 30-Jan. 31, 1927

Airmail service per zone (New York-Chicago; Chicago-Cheyenne, Wyo.; Cheyenne-San Francisco), per 1 oz. (each zone or portion thereof) .... 8¢

1925, July 1-Jan. 31, 1927

Special overnight service New York-Chicago (with three intermediate stops), per 1 oz. .... 10¢

1926, Feb. 15-Jan. 31, 1927

Contract routes not exceeding 1,000 miles (first flight Feb. 15) per 1 oz. (each route or portion thereof) .... 10¢
Contract routes between 1,000 and 1,500 miles (Seattle-Los Angeles, first flight Sept. 15) per 1 oz. .... 15¢
Mail traveling less than entire Seattle-Los Angeles route per 1 oz. .... 10¢
Contract routes exceeding 1,500 miles (none established during this rate period) per 1 oz. .... 20¢
Additional service on govt. route, per 1 oz. (each route or portion thereof) .... 5¢

1927, Feb. 1-July 31, 1928

All contract routes or govt. zones, or combinations thereof, per ½ oz. .... 10¢

1928, Aug. 1-July 5, 1932

All routes, 1st oz. .... 5¢
Each additional ounce or fraction thereof .... 10¢

Effective Date **Prepaid**

1932, July 6-June 30, 1934

All routes, 1st oz. .... 8¢
Each additional ounce or fraction thereof .... 13¢

1934, July 1-Mar. 25, 1934

All routes, per oz. .... 6¢

1944, Mar. 26-Sept. 30, 1946

All routes, per oz. .... 8¢

1946, Oct. 1-Dec. 31, 1948

All routes, per oz. .... 5¢

1949, Jan. 1-July 31, 1958

All routes, per oz. .... 6¢
Postal cards and postcards, per oz. .... 4¢

1958, Aug. 1-Jan. 6, 1963

All routes, per oz. .... 7¢
Postal cards and postcards, per oz. .... 5¢

1963, Jan. 7-Jan. 6, 1968

All routes, per oz. .... 8¢
Postal cards and postcards, per oz. .... 6¢

1968, Jan. 7-May 15, 1971

All routes, per oz. .... 10¢
Postal cards and postcards, per oz. .... 8¢

1971, May 16-Mar. 1, 1974

All routes, per oz. .... 11¢
Postal cards and postcards, per oz. .... 9¢

1974, Mar. 2-Oct. 10, 1975

All routes, per oz. .... 13¢
Postal cards and postcards, per oz. .... 11¢

As of Oct. 11, 1975, separate domestic airmail service was abolished, although at least one more airmail rate was published; effective Dec. 28, 1975, 17¢ per 1st oz., 15¢ each additional oz., 14¢ for postal cards and postcards. It lasted until May 1, 1977.

Many thanks to the American Air Mail Society for sharing information on airmail rates. For further study, we highly recommend the society's book, *Via Airmail, An Aerophilatelic Survey of Events, Routes, and Rates;* Simine Short, editor; James R. Adams, author (available from the American Airmail Society, P.O. Box 110, Mineola, NY 11501. Price: $20, plus $2.50 postage to U.S. addresses; $3.50 to addresses outside the U.S.).

Identifier of Definitive Issues — Arranged by Type Numbers

This section covers only listed postage stamps. See the Proofs section for imperforate items in the stamp colors mentioned which are not listed here and the Trial Color Proofs section for items in other colors.

ISSUES OF 1847-75

A1 Benjamin Franklin **A3 Reproduction**

5¢ On the originals the left side of the white shirt frill touches the oval on a level with the top of the "F" of "Five." On the reproductions it touches the oval about on a level with the top of the figure "5."

A2 George Washington **A4 Reproduction**

Original

Reproduction

10¢ On the originals line of coat (A) points to "T" of TEN and (B) it points between "T" and "S" of CENTS.

On the reproductions line of coat (A) points to right tip of "X" and line of coat (B) points to center of "S."

On the reproductions the eyes have a sleepy look, the line of the mouth is straighter, and in the curl of the hair near the left cheek is a strong black dot, while the originals have only a faint one.

Imperforate and Unwatermarked

Design Number			Scott Number
A1	5¢	red brown	1
A1	5¢	blue (reproduction)	948a
A3	5¢	red brown (reproduction, Special Printing)	3
A2	10¢	black	2
A2	10¢	brown orange (reproduction)	948b
A4	10¢	black (reproduction, Special Printing)	4

ISSUE OF 1851-75

A5 Franklin

A5

Type I Has a curved line outside the labels with "U.S. Postage" and "One Cent." The scrolls below the lower label are turned under, forming little balls. The scrolls and outer line at top are complete.

A6

Type Ia Same as I at bottom but top ornaments and outer line at top are partly cut away.

Type Ib Same as I but balls below the bottom label are not so clear. The plume-like scrolls at bottom are not complete.

Type Ic Same as type Ia, but bottom right plume and ball ornament is incomplete. The bottom left plume is complete or almost complete.

A7

Type II The little balls of the bottom scrolls and the bottoms of the lower plume ornaments are missing. The side ornaments are complete.

A8

Type III The top and bottom curved lines outside the labels are broken in the middle. The side ornaments are complete.

Type IIIa Similar to III with the outer line broken at top or bottom but not both. Type IIIa from Plate IV generally shows signs of plate erasure between the horizontal rows. Those from Plate IE show only a slight break in the line at top or bottom.

A9 Type IV

A20 Type V

Type IV Similar to II, but with the curved lines outside the labels recut at top or bottom or both.

The seven types listed account for most of the varieties of recutting.

Type V Similar to type III of 1851-56 but with side ornaments partly cut away.

A5	1¢	blue, type I, imperf.	5
A5	1¢	blue, type Ib, imperf.	5A
A5	1¢	blue, type I, perf. 15½	18
A5	1¢	bright blue, perf. 12 (Special Printing)	40
A6	1¢	blue, type Ia, imperf.	6
A6	1¢	blue, type Ic, imperf.	6b
A6	1¢	blue, type Ia, perf. 15½	19
A6	1¢	blue, type Ic, perf. 15½	19b
A7	1¢	blue, type II, imperf.	7
A7	1¢	blue, type II, perf. 15½	20

A8	1¢ blue, type III, imperf.	8
A8	1¢ blue, type IIIa, imperf.	8A
A8	1¢ blue, type III, perf. 15½	21
A8	1¢ blue, type IIIa, perf. 15½	22
A9	1¢ blue, type IV, imperf.	9
A9	1¢ blue, type IV, perf. 15½	23
A20	1¢ blue, type V, perf. 15½	24
A20	1¢ blue, type V, perf. 15½, laid paper	24b

A10 Washington, Type I

A10 Type I *There is an outer frame line on all four sides.*

A21 Type II *The outer line has been removed at top and bottom.*

Type IIa The side frame lines extend only to the top and bottom of the stamp design. All type IIa stamps are from plates 10 and 11 (each exists in 3 states), and these plates produced only type IIa. The side frame lines were recut individually for each stamp, thus being broken between the stamps vertically.

Beware of type II stamps with frame lines that stop at the top of the design (from top row of plate) or bottom of the design (from bottom row of plate). These are sometimes offered as No. 26a.

A11 Jefferson, Type I *There are projections on all four sides.*

A22 Type II *The projections at top and bottom are partly cut away. Several minor types could be made according to the extent of cutting of the projections.*

Nos. 40-47 are reprints produced by the Continental Bank Note Co. The stamps are on white paper without gum, perf. 12. They were not good for postal use. They also exist imperforate.

A10	3¢ orange brown, type I, imperf.	10
A10	3¢ dull red, type I, imperf.	11
A10	3¢ rose, type I, perf. 15½	25
A10	3¢ scarlet, perf. 12 (Special Printing)	41
A21	3¢ dull red, type II, perf. 15½	26
A21	3¢ dull red, type IIa, perf. 15½	26a
A11	5¢ red brown, type I, imperf.	12
A11	5¢ brick red, type I, perf. 15½	27
A11	5¢ red brown, type I, perf. 15½	28
A11	5¢ Indian red, type I, perf. 15½	28A
A11	5¢ brown, type I, perf. 15½	29
A22	5¢ orange brown, type II, perf. 15½	30
A22	5¢ brown, type II, perf. 15½	30A
A22	5¢ orange brown, type II, perf. 12 (Special Printing)	42

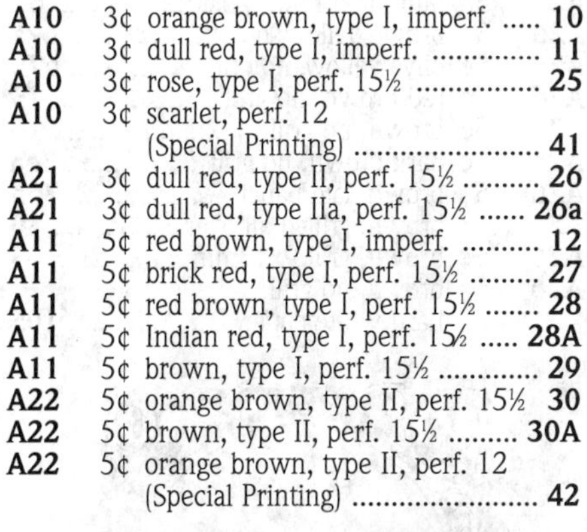

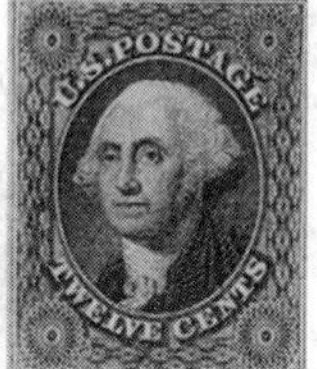

A12 Washington, Type I **A16** Washington

A12 Type I *The shells at the lower corners are practically complete. The outer line below the label is very nearly complete. The outer lines are broken above the middle of the top label and the "X" in each upper corner.*

A13 Type II *The design is complete at the top. The outer line at the bottom is broken in the middle. The shells are partly cut away.*

A14 Type III *The outer lines are broken above the top label and the "X" numerals. The outer line at the bottom and the shells are partly cut away as in Type II.*

A15 Type IV *The outer lines have been recut at top or bottom or both.*

A23 Type V *The side ornaments are slightly cut away. Usually only one pearl remains at each end of the lower label but some copies show two or three pearls at the right side. At the bottom, the outer line is complete and the shells nearly so. The outer lines at top are complete except over the right "X."*

A12	10¢ green, type I, imperf.	13
A12	10¢ green, type I, perf. 15½	31
A12	10¢ blue green, perf. 12 (Special Printing)	43
A13	10¢ green, type II, imperf.	14
A13	10¢ green, type II, perf. 15½	32
A14	10¢ green, type III, imperf.	15
A14	10¢ green, type III, perf. 15½	33
A15	10¢ green, type IV, imperf.	16
A15	10¢ green, type IV, perf. 15½	34
A23	10¢ green, type V, perf. 15½	35
A16	12¢ black, imperf.	17
A16	12¢ black, plate I, perf. 15½	36
A16	12¢ black, plate III	36b
A16	12¢ greenish black, perf. 12	44

A17 Washington

A18 Franklin **A19** Washington

A17	24¢ gray lilac, perf. 15½	37
A17	24¢ blackish violet, perf. 12 (Special Printing)	45
A18	30¢ orange, perf. 15½	38
A18	30¢ yellow orange, perf. 12 (Special Printing)	46
A19	90¢ blue, perf. 15½	39
A19	90¢ deep blue, perf. 12 (Special Printing)	47

ISSUES OF 1861-75

A24 Franklin

A24 *See the essay section for type A24 in indigo on perf. 12 thin, semi-transparent paper without the dash under the tip of the ornament at the right of the numeral in the upper left corner.*

A24 1¢ blue, perf. 12 ..... **63**
A24 1¢ blue, same, laid paper **63c**
A24 1¢ blue, grill 11x14mm **85A**
A24 1¢ blue, grill 11x13mm **86**
A24 1¢ blue, grill 9x13mm **92**
A24 1¢ blue, no grill, hard white paper (Special Printing) **102**

A25 Washington

A25 *See the essay section for type A25 in brown rose on perf. 12 thin, semi-transparent paper with smaller ornaments in the corners which do not end in a small ball.*

A25 3¢ pink, no grill, perf. 12 ..... **64**
A25 3¢ pigeon blood pink, same **64a**
A25 3¢ rose pink, same **64b**
A25 3¢ lake, same (Special Printing) **66**
A25 3¢ scarlet, same (Special Printing) ... **74**
A25 3¢ rose, same **65**
A25 3¢ rose, same, laid paper **65b**
A25 3¢ rose, grilled all over **79**
A25 3¢ rose, grill 18x15mm **82**
A25 3¢ rose, grill 13x16mm **83**
A25 3¢ rose, grill 12x14mm **85**
A25 3¢ rose, grill 11x14mm **85C**
A25 3¢ rose, grill 11x13mm **88**
A25 3¢ red, grill 9x13mm **94**
A25 3¢ brown red, no grill, hard white paper (Special Printing) .. **104**

A26 Jefferson

A26 *See the essay section for type A26 in brown on perf. 12 thin, semi-transparent paper without the leaflet in the foliated ornament at each corner.*

A26 5¢ buff, no grill **67**
A26 5¢ brown yellow, no grill **67a**
A26 5¢ olive yellow, no grill **67b**
A26 5¢ red brown, no grill **75**
A26 5¢ brown, no grill **76**
A26 5¢ dark brown, no grill **76a**
A26 5¢ brown, laid paper **76b**
A26 5¢ brown, grilled all over **80**
A26 5¢ brown, grill 9x13mm **95**
A26 5¢ brown, no grill, hard white paper **105**

A27a

A27 Washington

A27 *A heavy curved line has been cut below the stars and an outer line added to the ornaments above them.*

A27a 10¢ dark green, thin paper..... **62B**
A27 10¢ yellow green, see illustration A27 ..... **68**
A27 10¢ green, grill 11x14mm **85D**
A27 10¢ green, grill 11x13mm **89**
A27 10¢ yellow green, grill 9x13mm **96**
A27 10¢ green, no grill, hard white paper (Special Printing) **106**

A28 Washington

A28 *See the essay section for type A28 in black on perf. 12 thin, semi-transparent paper without corner ornaments.*

A28 12¢ black, no grill **69**
A28 12¢ black, grill 11x14mm **85E**
A28 12¢ black, grill 11x13mm **90**
A28 12¢ black, grill 9x13mm **97**
A28 12¢ black, no grill, hard white paper, (Special Printing) **107**

A29 Washington

A30 Franklin

See the Trial Color proof section for type A29 in dark violet on perf. 12 thin paper without grill and type A30 in red orange on perf. 12 thin paper without grill.

A29 24¢ red lilac, no grill **70**
A29 24¢ brown lilac, no grill **70a**
A29 24¢ steel blue, no grill **70b**
A29 24¢ violet, no grill, thin, transparent paper **70c**
A29 24¢ grayish lilac, no grill, thin, hard transparent paper **70d**
A29 24¢ lilac, no grill **78**
A29 24¢ grayish lilac, no grill **78a**
A29 24¢ gray, no grill **78b**
A29 24¢ blackish violet, no grill **78c**
A29 24¢ gray lilac, grill 9x13mm **99**
A29 24¢ deep violet, no grill, hard white paper, (Special Printing) **109**
A30 30¢ orange, no grill **71**
A30 30¢ orange, grilled all over **81**
A30 30¢ orange, grill 9x13mm **100**
A30 30¢ brownish orange, no grill, hard white paper, (Special Printing) .. **110**

A31 Washington

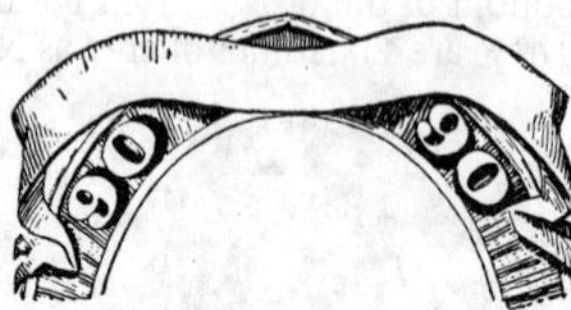

A31 *See the essay section for type A31 in dull blue on perf. 12 thin semi-transparent paper without dashes between the parallel lines which form the angle above the ribbon with "U.S. Postage," and without the point of color at the apex of the lower line.*

A31 90¢ blue, no grill **72**
A31 90¢ blue, grill 9x13mm **101**
A31 90¢ blue, no grill, hard white paper, (Special Printing) **111**

ISSUES OF 1861-75

A32 Jackson

A33 Lincoln

Perf. 12, Unwmkd.

A32 2¢ black, no grill 73

A32 2¢ black, laid paper 73d

A32 2¢ black, grill 12x14mm 84

A32 2¢ black, grill 11x14mm 85B

A32 2¢ black, grill 11x13mm 87

A32 2¢ black, grill 9x13mm 93

A32 2¢ black, no grill, hard white paper, (Special Printing) 103

A33 15¢ black, no grill 77

A33 15¢ black, grill 11x14mm 85F

A33 15¢ black, grill 11x13mm 91

A33 15¢ black, grill 9x13mm 98

A33 15¢ black, no grill, hard white paper, (Special Printing) 108

ISSUES OF 1869-80

A34 Franklin

A34 1¢ buff, grill 9½x9mm 112

A34 1¢ buff, no grill 112b

A34 1¢ buff, no grill, hard white paper (Special Printing) 123

A34 1¢ buff, no grill, soft porous paper (Special Printing) 133

A34 1¢ brown orange, same without gum (Special Printing) 133a

A35 Pony Express

A36 Baldwin 4-4-0 Locomotive, c. 1857

A35 2¢ brown, grill 9½x9mm 113

A35 2¢ brown, no grill 113b

A35 2¢ brown, no grill, hard white paper (Special Printing) 124

A36 3¢ ultramarine, grill 9½x9mm 114

A36 3¢ ultramarine, no grill 114a

A36 3¢ blue, no grill, hard white paper (Special Printing) 125

A37 Washington

A38 Shield and Eagle

A39 S.S. Adriatic

A37 6¢ ultramarine, grill 9½x9mm 115

A37 6¢ blue, no grill, hard white paper (Special Printing) 126

A38 10¢ yellow, grill 9½x9mm 116

A38 10¢ yellow, no grill, hard white paper (Special Printing) 127

A39 12¢ green, grill 9½x9mm 117

A39 12¢ green, no grill, hard white paper (Special Printing) 128

A40 Landing of Columbus

A40 Type I *Picture unframed*

A40a Type II *Picture framed*

Type III same as Type I but without the fringe of brown shading lines around central vignette.

A40 15¢ brown & blue, type I, grill 9½x9mm 118

A40 15¢ brown & blue, type I, no grill . 118a

A40 15¢ brown & blue, type III, no grill, hard white paper (Special Printing) 129

A40a 15¢ brown & blue, type II, grill 9½x9mm 119

A41 The Declaration of Independence

A42 Shield, Eagle and Flags

A43 Lincoln

A41 24¢ green & violet, grill 9½x9mm ... 120

A41 24¢ green & violet, no grill 120a

A41 24¢ green & violet, no grill, hard white paper (Special Printing) .. 130

A42 30¢ ultramarine & carmine, grill 9½x9mm 121

A42 30¢ ultramarine & carmine, no grill. 121a

A42 30¢ ultramarine & carmine, no grill, hard white paper (Special Printing) .. 131

A43 90¢ carmine & black, grill 9½x9mm 122

A43 90¢ carmine & black, no grill 122a

A43 90¢ carmine & black, no grill, hard white paper (Special Printing) .. 132

A43 90¢ carmine & black, 28x28mm, imperf., litho. & engraved 2433a

A43 90¢ blue & brown, 28x28mm, imperf., litho. & engraved 2433b

A43 90¢ green & blue, 28x28mm, imperf., litho. & engraved 2433c

A43 90¢ scarlet & blue, 28x28mm, imperf., litho. & engraved 2433d

ISSUES OF 1870-88

The secret mark shown in the detail of A45a is seldom found on the actual stamps. Stamps Nos. 146 and 157 are best identified by color which is red brown for No. 146 and brown for No. 157.

Note I: Special printings of 1880-83 — All denominations of this series were printed on special order from the Post Office Department during the period the stamps were current. The paper being the same as used on current issue, the special printings are extremely difficult to identify. The 2¢ brown, 7¢ scarlet vermilion, 12¢ blackish purple and 24¢ dark violet are easily distinguished by the soft porous paper as these denominations were never previously printed on soft paper. The other denominations can be distinguished by shades only, those of the special printings being slightly deeper and richer than the regular issue. The special printings except No. 211B were issued without gum. The only certain way to identify them is by comparison with stamps previously established as special printings.

A44 Franklin

A44

A44a With secret mark *In the pearl at the left of the numeral "1" there is a small dash.*

A44b Re-engraved *The vertical lines in the upper part of the stamp have been so deepened that the background often appears to be solid. Lines of shading have been added to the upper arabesques.*

A44 1¢ ultramarine, with grill 134

A44 1¢ ultramarine, no grill 145

A44a 1¢ ultramarine, white wove paper no grill 156

A44a 1¢ ultramarine, with grill 156e

A44a 1¢ ultramarine, hard white paper, without gum (Special Printing) . 167

A44a 1¢ dark ultra, soft porous paper 182

A44a 1¢ dark ultra, soft porous paper, without gum (Special Printing, see note I) 192

A44b 1¢ gray blue 206

A45 Jackson

A45

45a *Under the scroll at the left of "U.S." there is a small diagonal line.*

A45 2¢ red brown, with grill 135
A45 2¢ red brown, no grill 146
A45a 2¢ brown, white wove paper no grill 157
A45a 2¢ brown, with grill 157c
A45a 2¢ dark brown, hard white paper, without gum (Special Printing) . 168
A45a 2¢ black brown, soft porous paper, without gum (Special Printing) . 193
A45a 2¢ vermilion, yellowish paper 178
A45a 2¢ vermilion, same, with grill 178c
A45a 2¢ vermilion, soft porous paper 183
A45a 2¢ carmine vermilion, hard white paper, without gum (Special Printing) 180
A45a 2¢ scarlet vermilion, soft porous paper, without gum (Special Printing, see note I) 203

A46 Washington

A46

A46a With secret mark *The under part of the tail of the left ribbon is heavily shaded.*

A46b Re-engraved *The shading at the sides of the central oval appears only about one half the previous width. A short horizontal dash has been cut about 1mm. below the "TS" of "CENTS."*

A46 3¢ green, with grill 136
A46 3¢ green, no grill 147
A46a 3¢ green, white wove paper, no grill 158
A46a 3¢ green, same, with grill 158e
A46a 3¢ blue green, hard white paper, without gum (Special Printing) . 169
A46a 3¢ green, soft porous paper 184
A46a 3¢ blue green, soft porous paper, without gum (Special Printing see note I) 194
A46b 3¢ blue green, re-engraved 207
A46b 3¢ vermilion re-engraved 214

A47 Lincoln

A47

A47a With secret mark *The first four vertical lines of the shading in the lower part of the left ribbon have been strengthened.*

A47b Re-engraved. *6¢ on the original stamps four vertical lines can be counted from the edge of the panel to the outside of the stamp. On the re-engraved stamps there are but three lines in the same place.*

A47 6¢ carmine, with grill 137
A47 6¢ carmine, no grill 148
A47a 6¢ dull pink, no grill, white wove paper 159
A47a 6¢ dull pink, with grill 159b
A47a 6¢ dull rose, hard white paper, without gum (Special Printing) 170
A47a 6¢ pink, soft porous paper 186
A47a 6¢ dull rose, soft porous paper, without gum (Special Printing see note I) 195
A47b 6¢ rose, re-engraved 208

A48 Edwin McMasters Stanton

A49 Thomas Jefferson

A48

A48a With secret mark *Two small semi-circles are drawn around the ends of the lines which outline the ball in the lower right hand corner.*

A49

A49a With secret mark *A small semi-circle in the scroll at the right end of the upper label.*

A49b Re-engraved *On the original stamps there are five vertical lines between the left side of the oval and the edge of the shield. There are only four lines on the re-engraved stamps. In the lower part of the re-engraved stamps the horizontal lines of the background have been strengthened.*

A50 Henry Clay

A50

A50a With secret mark *The balls of the figure "2" are crescent shaped.*

A48 7¢ vermilion, with grill 138
A48 7¢ vermilion, no grill 149
A48a 7¢ orange verm., white wove paper no grill 160
A48a 7¢ orange verm., same, with grill 160a
A48a 7¢ reddish verm., hard white paper, without gum (Special Printing) 171
A48a 7¢ scarlet verm., soft porous paper, without gum (Special Printing) . 196
A49 10¢ brown, with grill 139
A49 10¢ brown, no grill 150
A49 10¢ brown, soft porous paper 187
A49a 10¢ brown, white wove paper no grill 161
A49a 10¢ brown, with grill 161c
A49a 10¢ pale brown, hard white paper, without gum (Special Printing) . 172
A49a 10¢ brown, soft porous paper 188
A49a 10¢ deep brown, soft porous paper, without gum (Special Printing, see note I) 197

A49b 10¢ brown, re-engraved **209**
A50 12¢ dull violet, with grill **140**
A50 12¢ dull violet, no grill **151**
A50a 12¢ blackish violet, white wove paper, no grill **162**
A50a 12¢ blackish violet, with grill **162a**
A50a 12¢ dark violet, hard white paper, without gum (Special Printing) . **173**
A50a 12¢ blackish purple, soft porous paper, without gum (Special Printing) **198**

A51 Webster   **A51**

A51a With secret mark *In the lower part of the triangle in the upper left corner two lines have been made heavier forming a "V." This mark can be found on some of the Continental and American (1879) printings, but not all stamps show it.*

A51 15¢ orange, with grill **141**
A51 15¢ bright orange, no grill **152**
A51a 15¢ yellow orange, white wove paper, no grill **163**
A51a 15¢ yellow orange, with grill **163a**
A51a 15¢ bright orange, hard white paper, without gum (Special Printing) . **174**
A51a 15¢ red orange, soft porous paper ... **189**
A51a 15¢ orange, soft porous paper, without gum (Special Printing, see note I) **199**

A52 General Winfield Scott

A53 Hamilton

A54 Perry

Secret marks were added to the dies of the 24¢, 30¢ and 90¢ but new plates were not made from them. The various printings of these stamps can be distinguished only by the shades and paper.

A52 24¢ purple, with grill **142**
A52 24¢ purple, no grill **153**
A52 24¢ purple, vertically ribbed white wove paper, no grill **164**
A52 24¢ dull purple, hard white paper, without gum (Special Printing) . **175**
A52 24¢ dark violet, soft porous paper, without gum (Special Printing) . **200**
A53 30¢ black, with grill **143**
A53 30¢ black, no grill **154**
A53 30¢ full black, soft porous paper **190**
A53 30¢ gray black, white wove paper, no grill **165**
A53 30¢ greenish black, with grill **165c**
A53 30¢ greenish black, hard white paper, without gum (Special Printing) . **176**
A53 30¢ greenish black, soft porous paper, without gum (Special Printing, see note I) **201**
A53 30¢ orange brown **217**
A54 90¢ carmine, with grill **144**
A54 90¢ carmine, no grill **155**
A54 90¢ carmine, soft porous paper **191**
A54 90¢ rose carmine, white wove paper **166**
A54 90¢ violet carmine, hard white paper, without gum (Special Printing) . **177**
A54 90¢ dull carmine, soft porous paper, without gum (Special Printing, see note I) **202**
A54 90¢ purple **218**

ISSUES OF 1875-88

A55 Taylor

A56 Garfield

Perf. 12, Unwmkd.

A55 5¢ blue, yellowish wove paper, no grill **179**
A55 5¢ blue, with grill **179c**
A55 5¢ bright blue, hard, white wove paper, without gum (Special Printing) **181**
A55 5¢ blue, soft porous paper **185**
A55 5¢ deep blue, soft porous paper, without gum (Special Printing, see note I) **204**
A56 5¢ yellow brown **205**
A56 5¢ gray brown, soft porous paper, without gum (Special Printing, see note I) **205C**
A56 5¢ indigo **216**

A57 Washington

A58 Jackson

A57 2¢ red brown **210**
A57 2¢ pale red brown, soft porous paper (Special Printing, see note I) .. **211B**
A57 2¢ green **213**
A58 4¢ blue green **211**
A58 4¢ deep blue green, soft porous paper, without gum (Special Printing, see note I) **211D**
A58 4¢ carmine **215**

A59 Franklin

A59 1¢ ultramarine **212**

ISSUES OF 1890-93

A60 Franklin   **A61** Washington

A62 Jackson   **A63** Lincoln

A64 Grant   **A65** Garfield

A66 William T. Sherman   **A67** Daniel Webster

A68 Henry Clay   **A69** Jefferson

A70 Perry

A60 1¢ dull blue **219**
A61 2¢ lake **219D**
A61 2¢ carmine **220**
A62 3¢ purple **221**
A63 4¢ dark brown **222**

A64	5¢ chocolate	**223**
A65	6¢ brown red	**224**
A66	8¢ lilac	**225**
A67	10¢ green	**226**
A68	15¢ indigo	**227**
A69	30¢ black	**228**
A70	90¢ orange	**229**

ISSUES OF 1894-1903

This series, the first to be printed by the Bureau of Engraving and Printing, closely resembles the 1890 series but is identified by the triangles which have been added to the upper corners of the designs.

The Catalogue divides this group into three separate series, the first of which was issued in 1894 and is unwatermarked. In 1895 the paper used was watermarked with the double line letters USPS (United States Postage Stamp). The stamps show one complete letter of the watermark or parts of two or more letters.

This watermark appears on all United States stamps issued from 1895 until 1910.

In 1898 the colors of some of the denominations were changed, which created the third series noted in the Catalogue.

Other than the watermark, or lack of it, there are three styles of the corner triangles used on the 2 cent stamps and two variations of designs are noted on the 10 cent and $1 denomination. In the following list all of these variations are illustrated and described immediately preceding the denominations on which they appear.

Wmkd. USPS **(191) Horizontally**

or USPS **Vertically**

(Actual size of letter)

A87 Franklin

A88 Washington

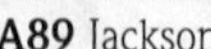

A89 Jackson

A90 Lincoln

A91 Grant

A92 Garfield

A93 Sherman

A94 Webster

A95 Clay

A96 Jefferson

A97 Perry

A98 James Madison

A99 John Marshall

A87	1¢ ultramarine, unwmkd.	**246**
A87	1¢ blue, unwmkd.	**247**
A87	1¢ blue, wmkd.	**264**
A87	1¢ deep green, wmkd.	**279**
A87	1¢ on 1¢ yellow green, "CUBA"	**Cuba 221**
A87	1¢ deep green, "GUAM"	**Guam 1**
A87	1¢ yellow green, "PHILIPPINES"	**Phil. 213**
A87	1¢ yellow green, "PORTO RICO"	**P.R. 210**
A87	1¢ yellow green, "PUERTO RICO"	**P.R. 215**

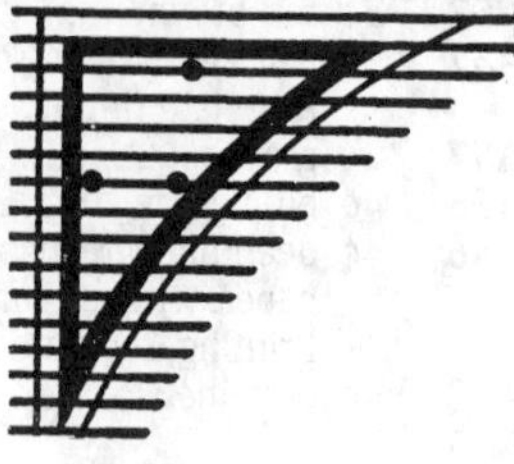

Triangle A (Type I) *The horizontal lines of the ground work run across the triangle and are of the same thickness within it as without.*

Triangle B (Type II) *The horizontal lines cross the triangle but are thinner within it than without. Other minor differences exist, but the change to Triangle B is a sufficient determinant.*

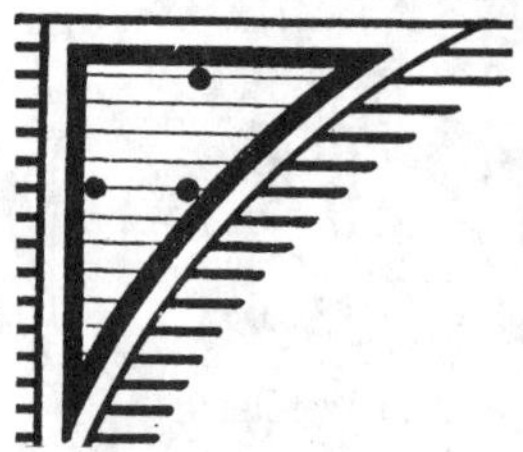

Triangle C (Types III & IV)
Type III: *The horizontal lines do not cross the double lines of the triangle. The lines within the triangle are thin, as in* Triangle *B.*

The rest of the design is the same as Type II, except that most of the designs had the dot in the "S" of "CENTS" removed. Stamps with this dot are listed; some specialists refer to them as "Type IIIa" varieties.

Type IV: *Same triangle C as type III, but other design differences including (1) recutting and lengthening of hairline, (2) shaded toga button, (3) strengthening of lines on sleeve, (4) additional dots on ear, (5) "T" of "TWO" straight at right, (6) background lines extend into white oval opposite "U" of "UNITED." Many other differences exist.*

A88	2¢ pink, type I, unwmkd.	**248**
A88	2¢ carmine lake, type I, unwmkd.	**249**
A88	2¢ carmine, type I, unwmkd.	**250**
A88	2¢ rose, type I, unwmkd.	**250a**
A88	2¢ scarlet, type I, unwmkd.	**250b**
A88	2¢ carmine, type I, wmkd.	**265**
A88	2¢ carmine, type II, unwmkd.	**251**
A88	2¢ carmine, type II, wmkd.	**266**
A88	2¢ carmine, type III, unwmkd.	**252**
A88	2¢ carmine, type III, wmkd.	**267**
A88	2¢ red, type IV, wmkd.	**279B**
A88	2¢ booklet pane of 6, wmkd., single stamps with 1 or 2 straight edges	**279Be**
A88	2c on 2¢ reddish carmine, type III "CUBA"	**Cuba 222**
A88	2c on 2¢ reddish carmine, type IV, "CUBA"	**Cuba 222A**
A88	2½c on 2¢ reddish carmine, type III, "CUBA"	**Cuba 223**
A88	2½c on 2¢ vermilion, type III, "CUBA"	**Cuba 223b**
A88	2½c on 2¢ reddish carmine, type IV, "CUBA"	**Cuba 223A**
A88	2¢ red, type IV, "GUAM"	**Guam 2**

A88 2¢ red, type IV, "PHILIPPINES" .... **Phil. 214**
A88 Same, booklet pane of 6 **Phil. 214b**
A88 2¢ reddish carmine, type IV, "PORTO RICO" .... **P.R. 211**
A88 Same, "PUERTO RICO" ... **P.R. 216**
A89 3¢ purple, unwmkd. **253**
A89 3¢ purple, wmkd. **268**
A89 3¢ on 3¢ purple, "CUBA" ... **Cuba 224**
A89 3¢ purple, "GUAM" .... **Guam 3**
A89 3¢ purple "PHILIPPINES" .... **Phil. 215**
A90 4¢ dark brown, unwmkd. **254**
A90 4¢ dark brown, wmkd. **269**
A90 4¢ rose brown, wmkd. **280**
A90 4¢ lilac brown, wmkd. **280a**
A90 4¢ orange brown, wmkd. **280b**
A90 4¢ lilac brown, "GUAM" .... **Guam 4**
A90 4¢ orange brown, "PHILIPPINES" .... **Phil. 220**
A91 5¢ chocolate, unwmkd. **255**
A91 5¢ chocolate, wmkd. **270**
A91 5¢ dark blue, wmkd. **281**
A91 5¢ on 5¢ blue, "CUBA" ...... **Cuba 225**
A91 5¢ blue, "GUAM" .... **Guam 5**
A91 5¢ blue, "PHILIPPINES" ...... **Phil. 216**
A91 5¢ blue, "PORTO RICO" .... **P.R. 212**
A92 6¢ dull brown, unwmkd. **256**
A92 6¢ dull brown, wmkd. USPS **271**
A92 6¢ dull brown, wmkd. USIR **271a**
A92 6¢ lake, wmkd. **282**
A92 6¢ lake, "GUAM" .... **Guam 6**
A92 6¢ lake, "PHILIPPINES" ...... **Phil. 221**
A93 8¢ violet brown, unwmkd. **257**
A93 8¢ violet brown, wmkd. USPS **272**
A93 8¢ violet brown, wmkd. USIR **272a**
A93 8¢ violet brown, "GUAM" ..... **Guam 7**
A93 8¢ violet brown, "PHILIPPINES" .... **Phil. 222**
A93 8¢ violet brown, "PORTO RICO" .... **P.R. 213**

Type I *The tips of the foliate ornaments do not impinge on the white curved line below "ten cents."*

Type II *The tips of the ornaments break the curved line below the "e" of "ten" and the "t" of "cents."*

A94 10¢ dark green, unwmkd. **258**
A94 10¢ dark green, wmkd. **273**
A94 10¢ brown, type I, wmkd. **282C**
A94 10¢ orange brown, type II, wmkd. .. **283**
A94 10¢ on 10¢ brown, type I, "CUBA" .... **Cuba 226**
A94 Same, type II, "CUBA" **Cuba 226A**
A94 10¢ brown, type I, "GUAM" ... **Guam 8**
A94 10¢ brown, type II, "GUAM" .. **Guam 9**
A94 10¢ brown, type I, "PHILIPPINES" .... **Phil. 217**
A94 10¢ orange brown, type II, "PHILIPPINES" .... **Phil. 217A**
A94 10¢ brown, type I, "PORTO RICO" .... **P.R. 214**
A95 15¢ dark blue, unwmkd. **259**
A95 15¢ dark blue, wmkd. **274**
A95 15¢ olive green, wmkd. **284**
A95 15¢ olive green, "GUAM" ..... **Guam 10**
A95 15¢ olive green, "PHILIPPINES" .... **Phil. 218**
A95 15¢ light olive green, "PHILIPPINES" .... **Phil. 218a**

A96 50¢ orange, unwmkd. **260**
A96 50¢ orange, wmkd. **275**
A96 50¢ orange, "GUAM" .... **Guam 11**
A96 50¢ red orange, "GUAM" .... **Guam 11a**
A96 50¢ orange, unwmkd., "PHILIPPINES" .... **Phil. 212**
A96 50¢ orange, wmkd., "PHILIPPINES" .... **Phil. 219**

A97 Type I *The circles enclosing "$1" are broken where they meet the curved line below "One Dollar."*

A97 Type II *The circles are complete.*

A97 $1 black, type I, unwmkd. **261**
A97 $1 black, type I, wmkd. **276**
A97 $1 black, type II, unwmkd. **261A**
A97 $1 black, type II, wmkd. **276A**
A97 $1 black, type I, "GUAM" ... **Guam 12**
A97 $1 black, type II, "GUAM" .. **Guam 13**
A97 $1 black, type I, "PHILIPPINES" .... **Phil. 223**
A97 $1 black, type II, "PHILIPPINES" .... **Phil. 223A**
A98 $2 bright blue, unwmkd. **262**
A98 $2 blue, perf. 11, tagged........... **2875a**
A98 $2 bright blue, wmkd. **277**
A98 $2 dark blue, "PHILIPPINES" .... **Phil. 224**
A99 $5 dark green, unwmkd. **263**
A99 $5 dark green, wmkd. **278**
A99 $5 dark green, "PHILIPPINES" .... **Phil. 225**

ISSUES OF 1902-17

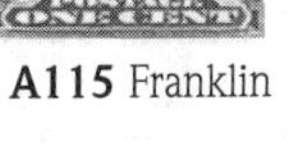

A115 Franklin **A116** Washington

A117 Jackson **A118** Grant

A119 Lincoln **A120** Garfield

A121 Martha Washington **A122** Daniel Webster

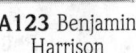

A123 Benjamin Harrison **A124** Henry Clay

A125 Jefferson **A126** David G. Farragut

A127 Madison **A128** Marshall

Unless otherwise noted all stamps are Perf. 12 and Wmkd. (191)

Single stamps from booklet panes show 1 or 2 straight edges.

A115 1¢ blue green **300**
A115 1¢ booklet pane of 6 .... **300b**
A115 1¢ blue green, imperf. **314**
A115 1¢ blue green, perf. 12 horiz., pair **316**
A115 1¢ blue green, perf. 12 vert., pair . **318**
A115 1¢ blue green, "CANAL ZONE PANAMA" .... **C.Z. 4**
A115 1¢ blue green, "PHILIPPINES" .... **Phil. 226**
A116 2¢ carmine **301**
A116 2¢ booklet pane of 6 .... **301c**
A116 2¢ carmine, "PHILIPPINES" **Phil. 227**
A117 3¢ bright violet **302**
A117 3¢ bright violet, "PHILIPPINES" .... **Phil. 228**
A118 4¢ brown **303**
A118 4¢ brown, imperf. **314A**
A118 4¢ brown, "PHILIPPINES" ... **Phil. 229**
A119 5¢ blue **304**
A119 5¢ blue, imperf. **315**
A119 5¢ blue, perf. 12 horiz. pair **317**
A119 5¢ blue, "CANAL ZONE PANAMA" .... **C.Z. 6**
A119 5¢ blue, "PHILIPPINES" ...... **Phil. 230**
A120 6¢ claret **305**
A120 6¢ brownish lake, "PHILIPPINES" .... **Phil. 231**
A121 8¢ violet black **306**
A121 8¢ violet black, "CANAL ZONE PANAMA" .... **C.Z. 7**
A121 8¢ violet black, "PHILIPPINES" .... **Phil. 232**
A122 10¢ pale red brown **307**
A122 10¢ pale red brown, "CANAL ZONE PANAMA" .... **C.Z. 8**

A122 10¢ pale red brown, "PHILIPPINES" .... **Phil. 233**
A123 13¢ purple black **308**
A123 13¢ purple black, "PHILIPPINES" .... **Phil. 234**
A124 15¢ olive green **309**
A124 15¢ olive green, "PHILIPPINES" .... **Phil. 235**
A125 50¢ orange **310**
A125 50¢ orange, "PHILIPPINES" .. **Phil. 236**
A126 $1 black **311**
A126 $1 black, "PHILIPPINES" ..... **Phil. 237**
A127 $2 dark blue **312**
A127 $2 dark blue, unwmkd., perf. 10 .. **479**
A127 $2 dark blue, "PHILIPPINES" .... **Phil. 238**
A128 $5 dark green **313**
A128 $5 light green, unwmkd., perf. 10 **480**
A128 $5 dark green, "PHILIPPINES" .... **Phil. 239**

ISSUES OF 1903

A129 Washington

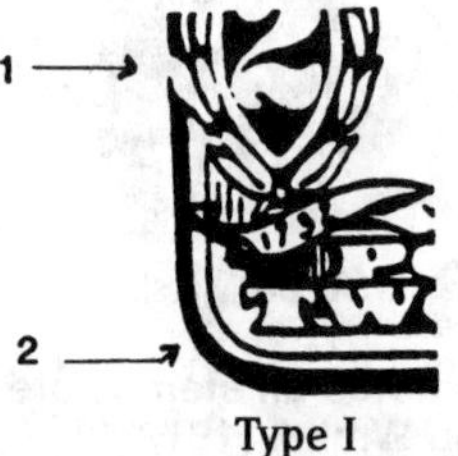

Type I

Type II

Specialists recognize over a hundred shades of this stamp in various hues of vermilion, red, carmine and lake. The Scott Catalogue lists only the most striking differences.

The Government coil stamp, No. 322 should not be confused with the scarlet vermilion coil of the International Vending Machine Co., which is perforated 12½ to 13.

A129 2¢ carmine, type I, wmkd. **319**
A129 2¢ lake, type I **319a**
A129 2¢ carmine rose, type I **319b**
A129 2¢ scarlet, type I **319c**
A129 2¢ lake, type II **319f**
A129 2¢ carmine, type I, booklet pane of 6 .... **319g**
A129 Same, type II **319h**
A129 2¢ carmine, type II **319i**
A129 2¢ carmine rose, type II **319j**
A129 2¢ scarlet, type II **319k**
A129 2¢ lake, type I, booklet pane of 6 .... **319m**
A129 2¢ carmine rose, type I, booklet pane of 6 .... **319n**
A129 2¢ scarlet, type I, booklet pane of 6 .... **319p**
A129 2¢ lake, type II, booklet pane of 6 .... **319q**
A129 2¢ carmine, type I, imperf. **320**
A129 2¢ lake, type II, imperf. **320a**
A129 2¢ scarlet, type I, imperf. **320b**
A129 2¢ carmine, perf. 12 horiz. pair **321**
A129 2¢ carmine, perf. 12 vert. pair **322**
A129 2¢ carmine, "CANAL ZONE PANAMA" .... **C.Z. 5**
A129 2¢ carmine, "PHILIPPINES" **Phil. 240**
A129 2¢ carmine, same, booklet pane of 6 .... **Phil. 240a**

ISSUES OF 1908-09

This series introduces for the first time the single line watermark USPS. Only a small portion of several letters is often all that can be seen on a single stamp.

A138 Franklin

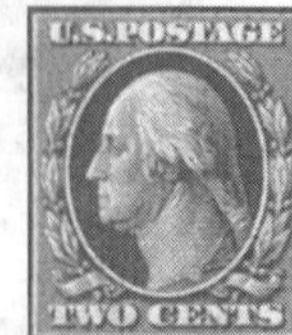

A139 Washington

Wmk. 190

A138 1¢ green, perf. 12, double line wmk. **331**
A138 1¢ green, same, China clay paper **331b**
A138 1¢ green, perf. 12, single line wmk. **374**
A138 1¢ green, perf. 12, bluish paper **357**
A138 1¢ green, imperf., double line wmk. **343**
A138 1¢ green, imperf., single line wmk. **383**
A138 1¢ green, perf. 12 horiz., double line wmk. **348**
A138 1¢ green, perf. 12 horiz., single line wmk. **385**
A138 1¢ green, perf. 12 vert., double line wmk. **352**
A138 1¢ green, perf. 12 vert., single line wmk. **387**
A138 1¢ green, perf. 8 ½ horiz., single line wmk. **390**
A138 1¢ green, perf. 8 ½ vert., single line wmk. **392**
A139 2¢ carmine, perf. 12, double line wmk. **332**
A139 2¢ carmine, same, China clay paper **332b**
A139 2¢ carmine, perf. 12, single line wmk. **375**
A139 2¢ carmine, perf. 12, bluish paper **358**
A139 2¢ carmine, perf. 11, double line wmk. **519**
A139 2¢ carmine, imperf., double line wmk. **344**
A139 2¢ carmine, imperf., single line wmk. **384**
A139 2¢ carmine, perf. 12 horiz., double line wmk. **349**
A139 2¢ carmine, perf. 12 horiz., single line wmk. **386**
A139 2¢ carmine, perf. 12 vert., double line wmk. **353**
A139 2¢ carmine, perf. 12 vert., single line wmk. **388**
A139 2¢ carmine, perf. 8½ horiz. single line wmk. **391**
A139 2¢ carmine, perf. 8½ vert., single line wmk. **393**

Single stamps from booklet panes show 1 or 2 straight edges.

A138 1¢ green, perf. 12, double line wmk., booklet pane of 6 .... **331a**
A138 1¢ green, perf.12, single line wmk., booklet pane of 6 .... **374a**
A139 2¢ carmine, perf. 12, double line wmk., booklet pane of 6 .... **332a**
A139 2¢ carmine, perf. 12, single line wmk., booklet pane of 6 .... **375a**

ISSUES OF 1908-21

FLAT BED AND ROTARY PRESS STAMPS

The Rotary Press Stamps are printed from plates that are curved to fit around a cylinder. This curvature produces stamps that are slightly larger, either horizontally or vertically, than those printed from flat plates. Designs of stamps from flat plates measure about 18½-19mm. wide by 22mm. high. When the impressions are placed sidewise on the curved plates the designs are 19½-20mm. wide; when they are placed vertically the designs are 22½ to 23mm. high. A line of color (not a guide line) shows where the curved plates meet or join on the press.

Rotary Press Coil Stamps were printed from plates of 170 subjects for stamps coiled sidewise, and from plates of 150 subjects for stamps coiled endwise.

A140 Washington

1¢ A138 Portrait of Franklin, value in words.
1¢ A140 Portrait of Washington, value in numerals.
2¢ A139 Portrait of Washington, value in words.
2¢ A140 Portrait of Washington, value in numerals.

A140 1¢ green, perf. 12, single line wmk. **405**
A140 1¢ green, same, booklet pane of 6 . **405b**
A140 1¢ green, perf. 11, flat plate, unwmkd. **498**
A140 1¢ green, same, booklet pane of 6 **498e**
A140 1¢ green, same, booklet pane of 30 **498f**
A140 1¢ green, perf. 11, rotary press measuring 19mmx22½mm, unwmkd. **544**
A140 1¢ green, same, measuring 19½ to 20mmx22mm **545**
A140 1¢ gray green, perf. 11, offset, unwmkd. **525**
A140 1¢ gray green, perf. 12½ **536**
A140 1¢ green, perf. 11x10 .... **538**
A140 1¢ green, perf. 10x11 .... **542**
A140 1¢ green, perf. 10, single line wmk. **424**
A140 1¢ green, same, perf. 12x10 ...... **423A**
A140 1¢ green, same, perf. 10x12 ...... **423D**
A140 1¢ green, perf.10, single line wmk., booklet pane of 6 .... **424d**
A140 1¢ green, perf. 10, flat plate, unwmkd. **462**
A140 1¢ green, same, booklet pane of 6 **462a**
A140 1¢ green, perf. 10, rotary press, unwmkd. **543**
A140 1¢ green, imperf., single line wmk. **408**
A140 1¢ green, imperf., unwmkd. **481**
A140 1¢ green, imperf., offset **531**
A140 1¢ green, perf. 10 horiz., flat plate, single line wmk. **441**
A140 1¢ green, same, rotary press **448**

A140 1¢ green, perf. 10 horiz., rotary press, unwmkd. **486**
A140 1¢ green, perf. 10 vert., flat plate, single line wmk. **443**
A140 1¢ green, same, rotary press **452**
A140 1¢ green, perf. 10 vert., rotary press, unwmkd. **490**
A140 1¢ green, perf. 8½ horiz. single line wmk. **410**
A140 1¢ green, perf. 8½ vert., same **412**

TYPES OF TWO CENTS

Type Ia *The design characteristics are similar to type I except that all of the lines of the design are stronger.*

The toga button, toga rope and rope shading lines are heavy.

The latter characteristics are those of type II, which, however, occur only on impressions from rotary plates.

Used only on flat plates 10208 and 10209.

Type II *Shading lines in ribbons as on type I.*

The toga button, rope and rope shading lines are heavy.

The shading lines of the face at the lock of hair end in a strong, vertical curved line.

Used on rotary press printings only.

Type III

Type III *Two lines of shading in the curves of the ribbons.*

Other characteristics similar to type II.

Used on rotary press printings only.

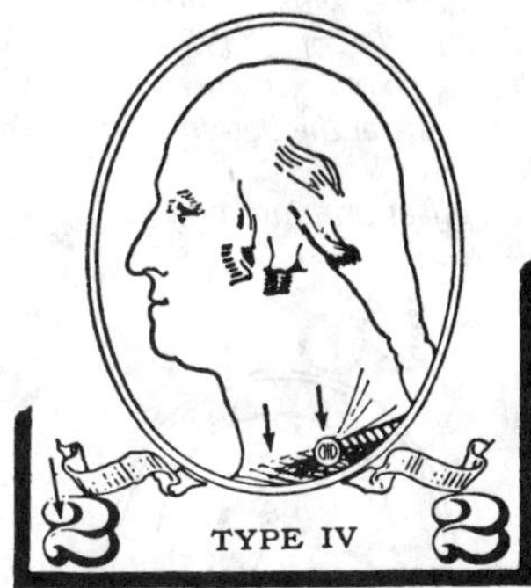

Type IV *Top line of the toga rope is broken.*

The shading lines in the toga button are so arranged that the curving of the first and last form "CID."

The line of color in the left "2" is very thin and usually broken. Used on offset printings only.

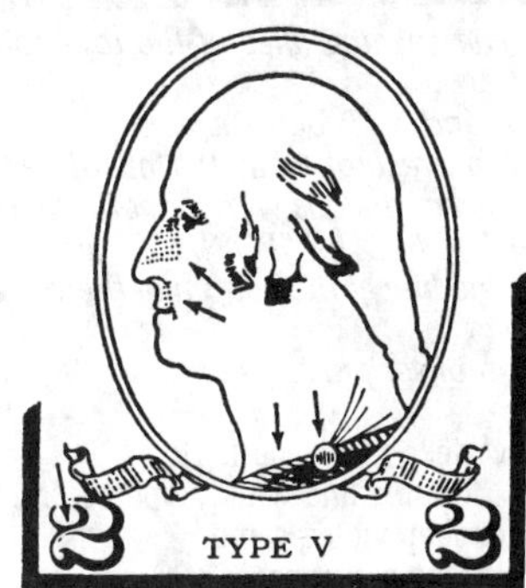

Type V *Top line of the toga is complete.*

There are five vertical shading lines in the toga button.

The line of color in the left "2" is very thin and usually broken.

The shading dots on the nose are as shown on the diagram.

Used on offset printings only.

Type Va *Characteristics are the same as type V except in the shading dots of the nose. The third row of dots from the bottom has four dots instead of six. The overall height is ⅓ mm shorter than type V.*

Used on offset printings only.

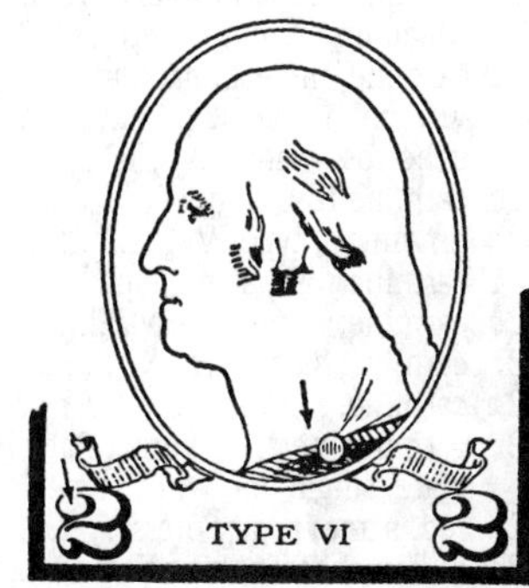

Type VI *General characteristics the same as type V except that the line of color in the left "2" is very heavy. Used on offset printings only.*

Type VII *The line of color in the left "2" is invariably continuous, clearly defined and heavier than in type V or Va but not as heavy as type VI.*

An additional vertical row of dots has been added to the upper lip.

Numerous additional dots have been added to the hair on top of the head.

Used on offset printings only.

A140 2¢ carmine, perf. 12, type I, single line wmk. **406**
A140 2¢ carmine, same, booklet pane of 6 .... **406a**
A140 2¢ pale car. red, perf. 11, single line wmk., type I **461**
A140 2¢ rose, perf. 11, flat plate, unwmkd., type I **499**
A140 2¢ rose, same, booklet pane of 6 . **499e**
A140 2¢ rose, same, booklet pane of 30 **499f**
A140 2¢ deep rose, perf. 11, unwmkd., type Ia **500**
A140 2¢ carmine rose, perf. 11, rotary press, unwmkd., type III **546**
A140 2¢ carmine, perf. 11, offset, unwmkd., type IV **526**
A140 2¢ carmine, same, type V **527**
A140 2¢ carmine, same, type Va **528**
A140 2¢ carmine, same, type VI **528A**
A140 2¢ carmine, same, type VII **528B**
A140 2¢ carmine rose, perf. 11x10, type II **539**
A140 2¢ carmine rose, same, type III **540**
A140 2¢ rose red, perf. 10x12, single line wmk., type I **423B**
A140 2¢ rose red, perf. 12x10, single line wmk., type I **423E**
A140 2¢ rose red, perf. 10, single line wmk., type I **425**
A140 2¢ rose red, same, perf. 10, booklet pane of 6 .... **425e**

A140 2¢ carmine, perf. 10, unwmkd., type I 463
A140 2¢ carmine, same, booklet pane of 6 .... 463a
A140 2¢ carmine, imperf., flat plate, single line wmk., type I 409
A140 2¢ carmine, imperf., rotary press, single line wmk., type I 459
A140 2¢ carmine, imperf., flat plate, unwmkd., type I 482
A140 2¢ deep rose, same, type Ia 482A
A140 2¢ carmine rose, imperf., offset, unwmkd., type IV 532
A140 2¢ carmine rose, same, type V 533
A140 2¢ carmine, same, type Va 534
A140 2¢ carmine, same, type VI 534A
A140 2¢ carmine, same, type VII 534B
A140 2¢ carmine, perf. 10 horiz., flat plate, single line wmk., type I .. 442
A140 2¢ red, same, rotary press 449
A140 2¢ carmine, same, type III 450
A140 2¢ carmine, perf. 10 horiz., rotary press unwmkd., type II .. 487
A140 2¢ carmine, same, type III 488
A140 2¢ carmine, perf. 10 vert., flat plate, single line wmk., type I .. 444
A140 2¢ carmine rose, same, rotary press 453
A140 2¢ red, same, type II 454
A140 2¢ carmine, same, type III 455
A140 2¢ carmine, perf. 10 vert., rotary press, unwmkd., type II . 491
A140 2¢ carmine, same, type III 492
A140 2¢ carmine, perf. 8½ horiz., type I 411
A140 2¢ carmine, perf. 8½ vert., type I .. 413

TYPES OF THREE CENTS

Type I *The top line of the toga rope is weak and the rope shading lines are thin. The 5th line from the left is missing. The line between the lips is thin.*

Type II *The top line of the toga rope is strong and the rope shading lines are heavy and complete.*

The line between the lips is heavy.

Used on both flat plate and rotary press printings.

Type III *The top line of the toga rope is strong but the 5th shading line is missing as in type I.*

Center shading line of the toga button consists of two dashes with a central dot.

The "P" and "O" of "POSTAGE" are separated by a line of color.

The frame line at the bottom of the vignette is complete.

Used on offset printings only.

Type IV *The shading lines of the toga rope are complete.*

The second and fourth shading lines in the toga button are broken in the middle and the third line is continuous with a dot in the center.

The "P" and "O" of "POSTAGE" are joined.

The frame line at the bottom of the vignette is broken.

Used on offset printings only.

A140 3¢ deep violet, perf. 12, double line wmk., type I 333
A140 3¢ deep violet, same, China clay paper 333a
A140 3¢ deep violet, perf. 12, single line wmk., type I 376
A140 3¢ deep violet, perf. 12, bluish paper, type I 359
A140 3¢ light violet, perf. 11, unwmkd., type I 501
A140 3¢ light violet, same, booklet pane of 6 .... 501b
A140 3¢ dark violet, perf. 11, unwmkd., type II 502
A140 3¢ dark violet, same, booklet pane of 6 .... 502b
A140 3¢ violet, perf. 11, offset, type III .. 529
A140 3¢ purple, same, type IV 530
A140 3¢ violet, perf. 11x10, type II 541
A140 3¢ deep violet, perf. 10, single line wmk., type I 426
A140 3¢ violet, perf. 10, unwmkd., type I 464
A140 3¢ deep violet, imperf., double line wmk., type I 345
A140 3¢ violet, imperf., unwmkd., type I 483
A140 3¢ violet, same, type II 484
A140 3¢ violet, imperf., offset, type IV ... 535
A140 3¢ deep violet, perf. 12 vert., single line wmk., type I 389
A140 3¢ violet, perf. 10 vert., flat plate, single line wmk., type I 445
A140 3¢ violet, perf. 10 vert., rotary press, single line wmk., type I 456
A140 3¢ violet, perf. 10 vert., rotary press, unwmkd., type I 493
A140 3¢ violet, same, type II 494
A140 3¢ violet, perf. 10 horiz., type I 489
A140 3¢ deep violet, perf. 8½ vert., type I 394
A140 4¢ orange brown, perf. 12, double line wmk. 334
A140 4¢ orange brown, same, China clay paper 334a
A140 4¢ orange brown, perf. 12, bluish paper 360
A140 4¢ brown, perf. 12, single line wmk. 377
A140 4¢ brown, perf. 11, unwmkd. 503
A140 4¢ brown, perf. 10, single line wmk. 427
A140 4¢ orange brown, perf. 10, unwmkd. 465
A140 4¢ orange brown, imperf. 346
A140 4¢ orange brown, perf. 12 horiz. .. 350
A140 4¢ orange brown, perf. 12 vert. 354
A140 4¢ brown, perf. 10 vert., flat plate, single line wmk. 446
A140 4¢ brown, same, rotary press 457
A140 4¢ orange brown, perf. 10 vert., rotary press, unwmkd. 495
A140 4¢ brown, perf. 8½ vert., single line wmk. 395
A140 5¢ blue, perf. 12, double line wmk. 335
A140 5¢ blue, same China clay paper ... 335a
A140 5¢ blue, perf. 12 bluish paper 361
A140 5¢ blue, perf. 12, single line wmk. 378
A140 5¢ blue, perf. 11, unwmkd. 504
A140 5¢ rose (error), same 505
A140 5¢ carmine (error), perf. 10, unwmkd. 467
A140 5¢ blue, perf. 10, single line wmk. 428
A140 5¢ blue, perf. 12x10 .... 423C
A140 5¢ blue, perf. 10, unwmkd. 466
A140 5¢ blue, imperf. 347
A140 5¢ carmine (error), imperf. 485
A140 5¢ blue, perf. 12 horiz. 351
A140 5¢ blue, perf. 12 vert. 355
A140 5¢ blue, perf. 10 vert., flat plate, single line wmk. 447
A140 5¢ blue, same, rotary press 458
A140 5¢ blue, perf. 10 vert., rotary press, unwmkd. 496
A140 5¢ blue, perf. 8½ vert. 396
A140 6¢ red orange, perf. 12, double line wmk. 336
A140 6¢ red orange, same, China clay paper 336a
A140 6¢ red orange, perf. 12, bluish paper 362
A140 6¢ red orange, perf. 12, single line wmk. 379
A140 6¢ red orange, perf. 11, unwmkd. 506
A140 6¢ red orange, perf. 10, single line wmk. 429
A140 6¢ red orange, perf. 10, unwmkd. 468
A140 7¢ black, perf. 12, single line wmk. 407
A140 7¢ black, perf. 11, unwmkd. 507
A140 7¢ black, perf. 10, single line wmk. 430
A140 7¢ black, perf. 10, unwmkd. 469
A140 8¢ olive green, perf. 12, double line wmk. 337
A140 8¢ olive green, same, China clay paper 337a

A140 8¢ olive green, perf. 12, bluish paper **363**
A140 8¢ olive green, perf. 12, single line wmk. **380**
A140 10¢ yellow, perf. 12, double line wmk. **338**
A140 10¢ yellow, same, China clay paper **338a**
A140 10¢ yellow, perf. 12, bluish paper ... **364**
A140 10¢ yellow, perf. 12, single line wmk. **381**
A140 10¢ yellow, perf. 12 vert. **356**
A140 13¢ blue green, perf. 12, double line wmk. **339**
A140 13¢ blue green, same, China clay paper **339a**
A140 13¢ blue green, perf. 12, bluish paper **365**
A140 15¢ pale ultra, perf. 12, double line wmk. **340**
A140 15¢ pale ultramarine, same, China clay paper **340a**
A140 15¢ pale ultra, perf. 12, bluish paper **366**
A140 15¢ pale ultra, perf. 12, single line wmk. **382**
A140 50¢ violet **341**
A140 $1 violet brown **342**

ISSUES OF 1912-19

A148

A149 Franklin

Designs of 8¢ to $1 denominations differ only in figures of value.

A148 8¢ pale olive green, perf. 12, single line wmk. **414**
A148 8¢ olive bister, perf. 11, unwmkd. **508**
A148 8¢ pale olive grn., perf. 10, single line wmk. **431**
A148 8¢ olive green, perf. 10, unwmkd. **470**
A148 9¢ salmon red, perf. 12, single line wmk. **415**
A148 9¢ salmon red, perf. 11, unwmkd. **509**
A148 9¢ salmon red, perf. 10, single line wmk. **432**
A148 9¢ salmon red, perf. 10, unwmkd. **471**
A148 10¢ orange yellow, perf. 12, single line wmk. **416**
A148 10¢ orange yellow, perf. 11, unwmkd. **510**
A148 10¢ orange yellow, perf. 10, single line wmk. **433**
A148 10¢ orange yellow, perf. 10, unwmkd. **472**
A148 10¢ orange yellow, perf. 10 vert., same **497**
A148 11¢ light green, perf. 11, unwmkd. **511**
A148 11¢ dark green, perf. 10, single line wmk. **434**
A148 11¢ dark green, perf. 10, unwmkd. **473**
A148 12¢ claret brown, perf. 12, single line wmk. **417**
A148 12¢ claret brown, perf. 11, unwmkd. **512**
A148 12¢ claret brown, perf. 10, single line wmk. **435**
A148 12¢ copper red, same **435a**
A148 12¢ claret brown, perf. 10, unwmkd. **474**
A148 13¢ apple green, perf. 11, unwmkd. **513**
A148 15¢ gray, perf. 12, single line wmk. **418**
A148 15¢ gray, perf. 11, unwmkd. **514**
A148 15¢ gray, perf. 10, single line wmk. **437**

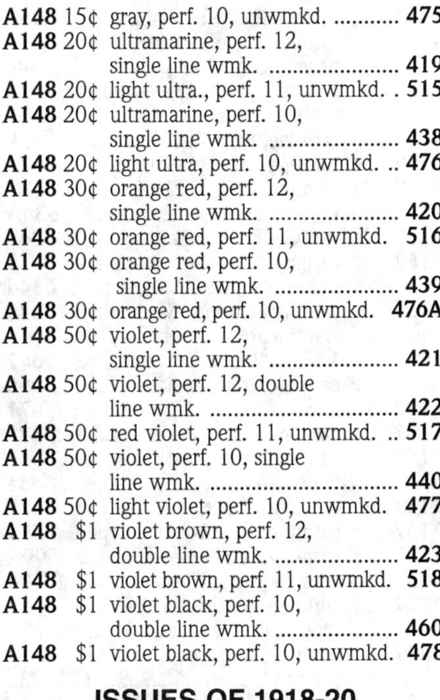

A148 15¢ gray, perf. 10, unwmkd. **475**
A148 20¢ ultramarine, perf. 12, single line wmk. **419**
A148 20¢ light ultra., perf. 11, unwmkd. . **515**
A148 20¢ ultramarine, perf. 10, single line wmk. **438**
A148 20¢ light ultra, perf. 10, unwmkd. .. **476**
A148 30¢ orange red, perf. 12, single line wmk. **420**
A148 30¢ orange red, perf. 11, unwmkd. **516**
A148 30¢ orange red, perf. 10, single line wmk. **439**
A148 30¢ orange red, perf. 10, unwmkd. **476A**
A148 50¢ violet, perf. 12, single line wmk. **421**
A148 50¢ violet, perf. 12, double line wmk. **422**
A148 50¢ red violet, perf. 11, unwmkd. .. **517**
A148 50¢ violet, perf. 10, single line wmk. **440**
A148 50¢ light violet, perf. 10, unwmkd. **477**
A148 $1 violet brown, perf. 12, double line wmk. **423**
A148 $1 violet brown, perf. 11, unwmkd. **518**
A148 $1 violet black, perf. 10, double line wmk. **460**
A148 $1 violet black, perf. 10, unwmkd. **478**

ISSUES OF 1918-20

Perf. 11 Unwmkd.

A149 $2 orange red & black **523**
A149 $2 carmine & black **547**
A149 $5 deep green & black **524**

ISSUES OF 1922-32

A154 Nathan Hale

A155 Franklin

A156 Warren G. Harding

A157 Washington

A158 Lincoln

A159 Martha Washington

A160 Theodore Roosevelt

A161 Garfield

A162 McKinley

A163 Grant

A164 Jefferson

A165 Monroe

A166 Hayes

A167 Cleveland

A168 American Indian

A169 Statue of Liberty

A170 Golden Gate

A171 Niagara Falls

A172 Buffalo

A173 Arlington Amphitheater and Tomb of the Unknown Soldier

A174 Lincoln Memorial

A175 United States Capitol

A176 "America"

Canal Zone Overprints:
Type A has flat-topped "A's" in "CANAL."
Type B has sharp-pointed "A's" in "CANAL."

Unwmkd.

A154 ½¢ olive brown, perf. 11 ... **551**
A154 ½¢ olive brown, perf. 11x10½ ... **653**
A154 ½¢ olive brown, "CANAL ZONE" ... **C.Z. 70**
A155 1¢ deep green, perf. 11, flat plate . **552**
A155 1¢ deep green, booklet pane of 6 **552a**
A155 1¢ green, perf. 11, rotary press 19¾x22¼mm ... **594**
A155 1¢ green, same, 19¼x22½mm (used) ... **596**
A155 1¢ green, perf. 11x10, rotary press ... **578**
A155 1¢ green, perf. 10 ... **581**
A155 1¢ green, perf. 11x10½ ... **632**
A155 1¢ green, same, booklet pane of 6 **632a**
A155 1¢ green, ovpt. Kans. ... **658**
A155 1¢ green, ovpt. Nebr. ... **669**
A155 1¢ green, imperf. ... **575**
A155 1¢ green, perf. 10 vert. ... **597**
A155 1¢ yellow green, perf. 10 horiz. ... **604**
A155 1¢ deep green, "CANAL ZONE" type A, perf. 11 ... **C.Z. 71**
A155 1¢ deep green, same, booklet pane of 6 ... **C.Z. 71e**
A155 1¢ green, "CANAL ZONE" type B, perf. 11x10½ ... **C.Z. 100**
A156 1½¢ yellow brown, perf. 11 ... **553**
A156 1½¢ yellow brown, perf. 11x10½ ... **633**
A156 1½¢ brown, ovpt. Kans. ... **659**
A156 1½¢ brown, ovpt. Nebr. ... **670**
A156 1½¢ brown, perf. 10 ... **582**
A156 1½¢ brown, perf. 10 vert. ... **598**
A156 1½¢ yellow brown, perf. 10 horiz. .. **605**
A156 1½¢ yellow brown, imperf., flat plate . **576**
A156 1½¢ yellow brown, imperf., rotary press, 19¼x22½mm ... **631**
A156 1½¢ yellow brown "CANAL ZONE" ... **C.Z. 72**

No heavy hair lines at top center of head. Outline of left acanthus scroll generally faint at top and toward base at left side.

Type I

Three heavy hair lines at top center of head; two being outstanding in the white area. Outline of left acanthus scroll very strong and clearly defined at top (under left edge of lettered panel) and at lower curve (above and to left of numeral oval).

Type II

A157 2¢ carmine, perf. 11, flat plate ... **554**
A157 2¢ carmine, same, booklet pane of 6 ... **554c**
A157 2¢ carmine, perf. 11, rotary press, 19¾x22¼mm ... **595**
A157 2¢ carmine, perf. 11x10 ... **579**
A157 2¢ carmine, perf. 11x10½, type I .. **634**
A157 2¢ carmine, perf. 11x10½, type II ... **634A**
A157 2¢ carmine lake, same, type I ... **634b**
A157 2¢ carmine lake, same, booklet pane of 6 ... **634d**
A157 2¢ carmine, overprt. Molly Pitcher **646**
A157 2¢ carmine, overprt. Hawaii 1778-1928 ... **647**
A157 2¢ carmine, overprt. Kans. ... **660**
A157 2¢ carmine, overprt. Nebr. ... **671**
A157 2¢ carmine, perf. 10 ... **583**
A157 2¢ carmine, same, booklet pane of 6 ... **583a**
A157 2¢ carmine, imperf. ... **577**
A157 2¢ carmine, perf. 10 vert., type I .. **599**
A157 2¢ carmine, same, type II ... **599A**
A157 2¢ carmine, perf. 10 horiz. ... **606**
A157 2¢ carmine, "CANAL ZONE" type A, perf. 11 ... **C.Z. 73**
A157 2¢ carmine, same, booklet pane of 6 ... **C.Z. 73a**
A157 2¢ carmine, "CANAL ZONE" type B, perf. 11 ... **C.Z. 84**
A157 2¢ carmine, same, booklet pane of 6 ... **C.Z. 84d**
A157 2¢ carmine, "CANAL ZONE" type B, perf. 10 ... **C.Z. 97**
A157 2¢ carmine, same, booklet pane of 6 ... **C.Z. 97b**
A157 2¢ carmine, "CANAL ZONE" type B, perf. 11x10½ ... **C.Z. 101**
A157 2¢ carmine, same, booklet pane of 6 ... **C.Z. 101a**
A158 3¢ violet, perf. 11 ... **555**
A158 3¢ violet, perf. 11x10½ ... **635**
A158 3¢ violet, overprt. Kans. ... **661**
A158 3¢ violet, overprt. Nebr. ... **672**
A158 3¢ violet, perf. 10 ... **584**
A158 3¢ violet, perf. 10 vert. ... **600**
A158 3¢ violet, "CANAL ZONE" perf. 11 ... **C.Z. 85**
A158 3¢ violet, "CANAL ZONE" perf. 10 ... **C.Z. 98**
A158 3¢ violet, "CANAL ZONE" perf. 11x10½ ... **C.Z. 102**
A159 4¢ yellow brown, perf. 11 ... **556**
A159 4¢ yellow brown, perf. 11x10½ ... **636**
A159 4¢ yellow brown, ovrpt. Kans. ... **662**
A159 4¢ yellow brown, ovrpt. Nebr. ... **673**
A159 4¢ yellow brown, perf. 10 ... **585**
A159 4¢ yellow brown, perf. 10 vert. ... **601**
A160 5¢ dark blue, perf. 11 ... **557**
A160 5¢ dark blue, perf. 11x10½ ... **637**
A160 5¢ dark blue, ovpt. Hawaii 1778-1928 ... **648**
A160 5¢ deep blue, ovpt. Kans. ... **663**
A160 5¢ deep blue, ovpt. Nebr. ... **674**
A160 5¢ blue, perf. 10 ... **586**
A160 5¢ dark blue, perf. 10 vert. ... **602**
A160 5¢ dark blue, "CANAL ZONE" type A, perf. 11 ... **C.Z. 74**
A160 5¢ dark blue, same, type B ... **C.Z. 86**
A160 5¢ dark blue, same, perf. 11x10½ ... **C.Z. 103**
A161 6¢ red orange, perf. 11 ... **558**
A161 6¢ red orange, perf. 11x10½ ... **638**
A161 6¢ red orange, ovrpt. Kans. ... **664**
A161 6¢ red orange, ovrpt. Nebr. ... **675**
A161 6¢ red orange, perf. 10 ... **587**
A161 6¢ deep orange, perf. 10 vert. ... **723**
A162 7¢ black, perf. 11 ... **559**
A162 7¢ black, perf. 11x10½ ... **639**
A162 7¢ black, ovrpt. Kans. ... **665**
A162 7¢ black, ovrpt. Nebr. ... **676**
A162 7¢ black, perf. 10 ... **588**
A163 8¢ olive green, perf. 11 ... **560**
A163 8¢ olive green, perf. 11x10½ ... **640**
A163 8¢ olive green, ovrpt. Kans. ... **666**
A163 8¢ olive green, ovrpt. Nebr. ... **677**
A163 8¢ olive green, perf. 10 ... **589**
A164 9¢ rose, perf. 11 ... **561**
A164 9¢ orange red, perf. 11x10½ ... **641**
A164 9¢ light rose, ovrpt. Kans. ... **667**
A164 9¢ light rose, ovrpt. Nebr. ... **678**
A164 9¢ rose, perf. 10 ... **590**
A165 10¢ orange, perf. 11 ... **562**
A165 10¢ orange, perf. 11x10½ ... **642**
A165 10¢ orange yellow, ovrpt. Kans. ... **668**
A165 10¢ orange yellow, ovrpt. Nebr. ... **679**
A165 10¢ orange, perf. 10 ... **591**
A165 10¢ orange, perf. 10 vert. ... **603**
A165 10¢ orange, "CANAL ZONE" type A, perf. 11 ... **C.Z. 75**
A165 10¢ orange, same, type B ... **C.Z. 87**
A165 10¢ orange, same, perf. 10 ... **C.Z. 99**
A165 10¢ orange, same, perf. 11x10½ ... **C.Z. 104**
A166 11¢ light blue, perf. 11 ... **563**
A166 11¢ light blue, perf. 11x10½ ... **692**
A167 12¢ brown violet, perf. 11 ... **564**
A167 12¢ brown violet, perf. 11x10½ ... **693**
A167 12¢ brown violet, "CANAL ZONE" type A ... **C.Z. 76**
A167 12¢ brown violet, same, type B . **C.Z. 88**
A168 14¢ blue, perf. 11 ... **565**
A168 14¢ dark blue, perf. 11x10½ ... **695**
A168 14¢ dark blue, "CANAL ZONE" type A, perf. 11 ... **C.Z. 77**
A168 14¢ dark blue, same, type B ... **C.Z. 89**
A168 14¢ dark blue, same, perf. 11x10½ ... **C.Z. 116**
A169 15¢ gray, perf. 11 ... **566**
A169 15¢ gray, perf. 11x10½ ... **696**
A169 15¢ gray, "CANAL ZONE" type A ... **C.Z. 78**
A169 15¢ gray, "CANAL ZONE" type B ... **C.Z. 90**
A170 20¢ carmine rose, perf. 11 ... **567**
A170 20¢ carmine rose, perf. 10½x11 ... **698**
A170 20¢ carmine rose, "CANAL ZONE" ... **C.Z. 92**
A171 25¢ yellow green, perf. 11 ... **568**
A171 25¢ blue green, perf. 10½x11 ... **699**
A172 30¢ olive brown, perf. 11 ... **569**
A172 30¢ brown, perf. 10½x11 ... **700**
A172 30¢ olive brown, "CANAL ZONE" type A ... **C.Z. 79**
A172 30¢ olive brown, "CANAL ZONE" type B ... **C.Z. 93**
A173 50¢ lilac, perf. 11 ... **570**
A173 50¢ lilac, perf. 10½x11 ... **701**
A173 50¢ lilac, "CANAL ZONE" type A ... **C.Z. 80**
A173 50¢ lilac, "CANAL ZONE" type B ... **C.Z. 94**
A174 $1 violet black, perf. 11 ... **571**
A174 $1 violet brown, "CANAL ZONE" type A ... **C.Z. 81**
A174 $1 violet brown, "CANAL ZONE" type B ... **C.Z. 95**
A175 $2 deep blue, perf. 11 ... **572**
A176 $5 carmine & blue, perf. 11 ... **573**

REGULAR ISSUES OF 1925-26, 1930 AND 1932

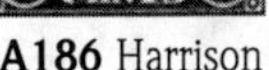
A186 Harrison

A187 Wilson

A186 13¢ green, perf. 11 .... **622**
A186 13¢ yellow green, perf. 11x10½ **694**
A187 17¢ black, perf. 11 .... **623**
A187 17¢ black, perf. 10½x11 .... **697**
A187 17¢ black, "CANAL ZONE" ..... **C.Z. 91**

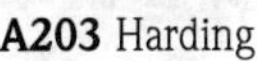
A203 Harding

A204 Taft

A203 1½¢ brown, perf. 11x10½ **684**
A203 1½¢ brown, perf. 10 vert. **686**
A204 4¢ brown, perf. 11x10½ **685**
A204 4¢ brown, perf. 10 vert. **687**

A226 Washington

A226 3¢ deep violet, perf. 11x10½ **720**
A226 3¢ deep violet, same, booklet pane of 6 .... **720b**
A226 3¢ deep violet, perf. 10 vert. **721**
A226 3¢ deep violet, perf. 10 horiz. **722**
A226 3¢ deep violet, "CANAL ZONE" .... **C.Z. 115**

PRESIDENTIAL ISSUE OF 1938

A275 Benjamin Franklin

A276 George Washington

A277 Martha Washington

A278 John Adams

A279 Thomas Jefferson

A280 James Madison

A281 The White House

A282 James Monroe

A283 John Quincy Adams

A284 Andrew Jackson

A285 Martin Van Buren

A286 William H. Harrison

A287 John Tyler

A288 James K. Polk

A289 Zachary Taylor

A290 Millard Fillmore

A291 Franklin Pierce

A292 James Buchanan

A293 Abraham Lincoln

A294 Andrew Johnson

A295 Ulysses S. Grant

A296 Rutherford B. Hayes

A297 James A. Garfield

A298 Chester A. Arthur

A299 Grover Cleveland

A300 Benjamin Harrison

A301 William McKinley

A302 Theodore Roosevelt

A303 William Howard Taft

A304 Woodrow Wilson

A305 Warren G. Harding

A306 Calvin Coolidge

Rotary Press Printing Unwmkd.

A275 ½¢ deep orange, perf. 11x10½ **803**
A275 ½¢ red orange, "CANAL ZONE" .... **C.Z. 118**

A276 1¢ green, perf. 11x10½ **804**
A276 1¢ green, booklet pane of 6 .... **804b**
A276 1¢ green, perf. 10 vert. **839**
A276 1¢ green, perf. 10 horiz. **848**
A277 1½¢ bister brown, perf. 11x10½ **805**
A277 1½¢ bister brown, perf. 10 vert. **840**
A277 1½¢ bister brown, perf. 10 horiz. ... **849**
A277 1½¢ bister brown, "CANAL ZONE" .... **C.Z. 119**
A278 2¢ rose carmine, perf. 11x10½ **806**
A278 2¢ booklet pane of 6 .... **806b**
A278 2¢ rose carmine, perf. 10 vert. **841**
A278 2¢ rose carmine, perf. 10 horiz. ... **850**
A279 3¢ deep violet, perf. 11x10½ **807**
A279 3¢ deep violet, booklet pane of 6 **807a**
A279 3¢ deep violet, perf. 10 vert. **842**
A279 3¢ deep violet, perf. 10 horiz. **851**
A280 4¢ red violet, perf. 11x10½ **808**
A280 4¢ red violet, perf. 10 vert. **843**
A281 4½¢ dark gray, perf. 11x10½ **809**
A281 4½¢ dark gray, perf. 10 vert. **844**
A282 5¢ bright blue, perf. 11x10½ **810**
A282 5¢ bright blue, perf. 10 vert. **845**
A283 6¢ red orange, perf. 11x10½ **811**
A283 6¢ red orange, perf. 10 vert. **846**
A284 7¢ sepia, perf. 11x10½ **812**
A285 8¢ olive green, perf. 11x10½ **813**
A286 9¢ rose pink, perf. 11x10½ **814**
A287 10¢ brown red, perf. 11x10½ **815**
A287 10¢ brown red, perf. 10 vert. **847**
A288 11¢ ultramarine, perf. 11x10½ **816**
A289 12¢ bright violet, perf. 11x10½ **817**
A290 13¢ blue green, perf. 11x10½ **818**
A291 14¢ blue, perf. 11x10½ **819**
A292 15¢ blue gray, perf. 11x10½ **820**
A293 16¢ black, perf. 11x10½ **821**
A294 17¢ rose red, perf. 11x10½ **822**
A295 18¢ brn. carmine, perf. 11x10½ **823**
A296 19¢ bright violet, perf. 11x10½ **824**
A297 20¢ bright blue green, perf. 11x10½ **825**
A298 21¢ dull blue, perf. 11x10½ **826**
A299 22¢ vermilion, perf. 11x10½ **827**
A300 24¢ gray black, perf. 11x10½ **828**
A301 25¢ dp. red lilac, perf. 11x10½ **829**
A302 30¢ deep ultra, perf. 11x10½ **830**
A303 50¢ lt. red violet, perf. 11x10½ **831**

Flat Plate Printing
Perf. 11

A304 $1 pur. & blk., unwmkd. **832**
A304 $1 pur. & blk., wmkd. USIR **832b**
A304 $1 red vio. & blk., thick white paper, smooth colorless gum **832c**
A305 $2 yellow green & black **833**
A306 $5 carmine & black **834**

LIBERTY ISSUE 1954-73

A477 Benjamin Franklin

A478 George Washington

A478a Palace of the Governors, Santa Fe

A479 Mount Vernon

A480 Thomas Jefferson

A481 Bunker Hill Monument and Massachusetts Flag 1776

A482 Statue of Liberty

A483 Abraham Lincoln

A484 The Hermitage

A485 James Monroe

A486 Theodore Roosevelt

A487 Woodrow Wilson

A488 Statue of Liberty (Rotary and flat plate printing)

A489 Design slightly altered; see position of torch (Giorgi press printing)

A489a John J. Pershing

A490 The Alamo

A491 Independence Hall

A491a Statue of Liberty

A492 Benjamin Harrison

A493 John Jay

A494 Monticello

A495 Paul Revere

A496 Robert E. Lee

A497 John Marshall

A498 Susan B. Anthony

A499 Patrick Henry

A500 Alexander Hamilton

Unwmkd.

A477 ½¢ red orange, perf. 11x10½ **1030**
A478 1¢ dark green, perf. 11x10½........ **1031**
A478 1¢ dark green, perf. 10 vert......... **1054**
A478a 1¼¢ turquoise, perf. 10½x11 ..... **1031A**
A478a 1¼¢ turquoise, perf. 10 horiz. ... **1054A**
A479 1½¢ brown carmine, perf. 10½x11 .... **1032**
A480 2¢ carmine rose, perf. 11x10 .... **1033**
A480 2¢ carmine rose, perf. 10 vert. **1055**
A481 2½¢ gray blue, perf. 11x10½ **1034**
A481 2½¢ gray blue, perf. 10 vert. **1056**
A482 3¢ deep violet, perf. 11x10½....... **1035**
A482 3¢ deep violet, perf. 10 vert., ... **1057**
A482 3¢ deep violet, imperf., size: 24x28mm **1075a**
A483 4¢ red violet, perf. 11x10½ **1036**
A483 4¢ red violet, perf. 10 vert. **1058**
A484 4½¢ blue green, perf. 10½x11 ...... **1037**
A484 4½¢ blue green, perf. 10 horiz. **1059**
A485 5¢ deep blue, perf. 11x10½ **1038**
A486 6¢ carmine, perf. 11x10½, ... **1039**
A487 7¢ rose carmine, same **1040**
A488 8¢ dark violet blue & carmine, flat plate printing, perf. 11, approx. 22.7mm high............. **1041**
A488 8¢ dark violet blue & carmine, rotary press printing, perf. 11, appprox. 22.9mm high......... **1041B**
A488 8¢ dark violet blue & carmine, imperf., size: 24x28mm **1075b**
A489 8¢ dark violet blue & carmine, perf. 11 .... **1042**

A489a 8¢ brown, perf. 11x10½ **1042A**
A490 9¢ rose lilac, perf. 10½x11 .... **1043**
A491 10¢ rose lake, same **1044**
A491a 11¢ carmine & dark violet blue, perf. 11 .... **1044A**
A492 12¢ red, perf. 11x10½ **1045**
A493 15¢ rose lake, perf. 11x10½ **1046**
A494 20¢ ultramarine, perf. 10½x11 .... **1047**
A495 25¢ green, perf. 11x10½ **1048**
A495 25¢ green, perf. 10 vert. **1059A**
A496 30¢ black, perf. 11x10½.................. **1049**
A497 40¢ brown red, perf. 11x10½........ **1050**
A498 50¢ bright purple, perf. 11x10½ ... **1051**
A499 $1 purple, perf. 11x10½ **1052**
A500 $5 black, perf. 11 .... **1053**

ISSUE OF 1962-66

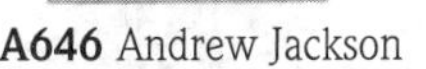
A646 Andrew Jackson

A650 George Washington

A646 1¢ green, perf. 11x10½ **1209**
A646 1¢ green, perf. 10 vert. **1225**
A650 5¢ dk. bl. gray, perf. 11x10½ **1213**
A650 5¢ dk. bl. gray, perf. 10 vert. **1229**

PROMINENT AMERICANS ISSUE 1965-81

A710 Thomas Jefferson

A711 Albert Gallatin

A712 Frank Lloyd Wright and Guggenheim Museum, New York

A713 Francis Parkman

A714 Abraham Lincoln

A715 George Washington

A715a Re-engraved

A716 Franklin D. Roosevelt

A727a Franklin D. Roosevelt (vertical coil)

A816 Benjamin Franklin and his signature

A717 Albert Einstein

A718 Andrew Jackson

A718a Henry Ford and 1909 Model T

A719 John F. Kennedy

A817a Fiorello H. LaGuardia and New York skyline

A720 Oliver Wendell Holmes

A818 Ernest (Ernie) Taylor Pyle

A818a Dr. Elizabeth Blackwell

A721 George C. Marshall

A818b Amadeo P. Giannini

A722 Frederick Douglass

A723 John Dewey

A724 Thomas Paine

A725 Lucy Stone

A726 Eugene O'Neill

A727 John Bassett Moore

Types of 15¢:

I - Necktie barely touches coat at bottom; cross-hatching of tie strong and complete. Flag of "5" is true horizontal. Crosshatching of "15" is colorless when visible.

II - Necktie does not touch coat at bottom; LL to UR crosshatching lines strong, UL to LR lines very faint. Flag of "5" slants down slightly at right. Crosshatching of "15" is colored and visible when magnified.

A third type, used only for No. 1288B, is smaller in overall size, and "15¢" is ¾mm closer to head.

Unwmkd.
Rotary Press Printing

A710 1¢ green, perf. 11x10½ **1278**
A710 1¢ green, perf. 10, vert., tagged . **1299**
A711 1¼¢ light green, perf. 11x10½ **1279**
A712 2¢ dk. bl. gray, perf. 11x10½ **1280**
A713 3¢ violet, perf. 10½x11 .... **1281**
A713 3¢ violet, perf. 10 horiz. **1297**
A714 4¢ black, perf. 11x10½ **1282**
A714 4¢ black, perf. 10, vert. **1303**
A715 5¢ blue, perf. 11x10½ **1283**
A715 5¢ blue, perf. 10 vert. **1304**
A715a 5¢ blue, perf. 11x10½ **1283B**
A715a 5¢ blue, perf. 10 vert. **1304C**
A716 6¢ gray brown, perf. 10½x11 ..... **1284**
A716 6¢ gray brown, perf. 10 horiz., tagged **1298**
A727a 6¢ gray brown, perf. 10 vert., tagged **1305**
A816 7¢ bright blue, perf. 10½x11 ... **1393D**
A717 8¢ violet, perf. 11x10½ **1285**
A718 10¢ lilac, perf. 11x10½ **1286**
A718a 12¢ black, perf. 10½x11 .... **1286A**
A719 13¢ brown, perf. 11x10½ **1287**
A817a 14¢ gray brown, perf. 11x10½ **1397**
A720 15¢ magenta, perf. 11x10½ **1288**
A720 15¢ magenta, perf. 10 (booklet panes only) **1288B**
A720 15¢ magenta, perf. 10 vert. **1305E**
A818 16¢ brown **1398**
A818a 18¢ violet, perf. 11x10½ **1399**
A721 20¢ deep olive, perf. 11x10½ **1289**
A818b 21¢ green, perf. 11x10½ **1400**
A722 25¢ rose lake, perf. 11x10½ **1290**
A723 30¢ red lilac, perf. 10½x11 .... **1291**
A724 40¢ blue black, perf. 11x10½ **1292**
A725 50¢ rose magenta, perf. 11x10½ .. **1293**

A726 $1 dull purple, perf. 11x10½ **1294**
A726 $1 dull purple, perf. 10 vert., tagged **1305C**
A727 $5 gray black, perf. 11x10½ **1295**

A815 Dwight D. Eisenhower

A815a

A815 6¢ dark blue gray, perf. 11x10½ .. **1393**
A815 6¢ dk. bl. gray, perf. 10, vert. **1401**
A815 8¢ deep claret, perf. 11x10½ (Booklet panes only) **1395**
A815 8¢ deep claret, perf. 10 vert. **1402**
A815a 8¢ blk., red & bl. gray, perf. 11 ... **1394**

FLAG ISSUE 1968-71

A760 Flag and White House

A760 6¢ dark blue, red & green, perf. 11, size: 19x22mm **1338**
A760 6¢ dark blue, red & green, perf. 11x10½, size: 18¼x21mm .. **1338D**
A760 6¢ dark blue, red & green, perf. 10 vert., size: 18¼x21mm **1338A**
A760 8¢ multicolored, perf. 11x10½ .. **1338F**
A760 8¢ multicolored, perf. 10 vert. . **1338G**

REGULAR ISSUE 1971-74

A817 U.S. Postal Service Emblem

A923 50-Star and 13-Star Flags

A924 Jefferson Memorial and quotation from Declaration of Independence

A925 Mail Transport and "Zip Code"

A926 Liberty Bell

A817 8¢ multicolored, perf. 11x10½ **1396**
A923 10¢ red & blue, perf. 11x10½ **1509**
A923 10¢ red & blue, perf. 10 vert. **1519**
A924 10¢ blue, perf. 11x10½ **1510**
A924 10¢ blue, perf. 10 vert. **1520**
A925 10¢ multicolored, perf. 11x10½ **1511**
A926 6.3¢ brick red, perf. 10 vert. **1518**

AMERICANA ISSUE 1975-81

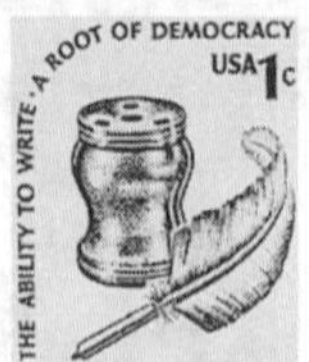

A984 Inkwell and Quill

A985 Speaker's Stand

A987 Early Ballot Box

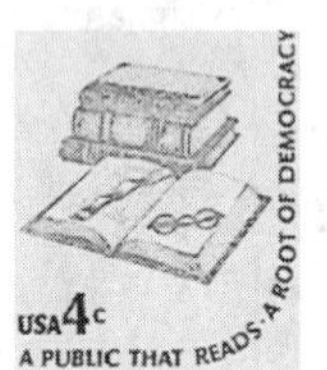

A988 Books, Bookmark, Eyeglasses

A994 Dome of Capitol

A995 Contemplation of Justice

A996 Early American Printing Press

A997 Torch Statue of Liberty

A998 Liberty Bell **A999** Eagle and Shield

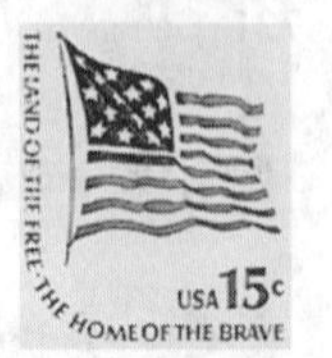

A1001 Ft. McHenry Flag

A1002 Head Statue of Liberty

A1003 Old North Church

A1004 Ft. Nisqually

A1005 Sandy Hook Lighthouse

A1006 Morris Township School No. 2, Devil's Lake

A1007 Iron "Betty" Lamp Plymouth Colony, 17th-18th Centuries

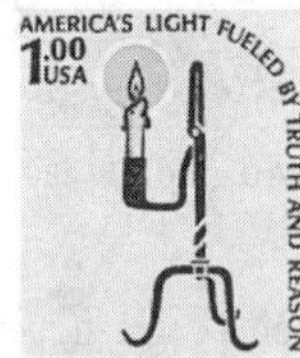

A1008 Rush Lamp and Candle Holder

A1009 Kerosene Table Lamp

A1010 Railroad Conductors Lantern, c. 1850

COIL STAMPS

A1011 Six-string guitar **A1199** Weaver violins

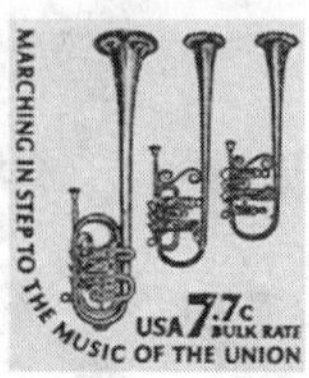

A1012 Saxhorns

A1013 Drum

A1014 Steinway Grand Piano, 1857

A984 1¢ dark blue, greenish, perf. 11x10½ **1581**
A984 1¢ dark blue, greenish, perf. 10 vert. **1811**
A985 2¢ red brown, greenish, perf. 11x10½ **1582**
A987 3¢ olive, greenish, perf. 11x10½ **1584**
A988 4¢ rose magenta, cream, perf. 11x10½ **1585**
A994 9¢ slate green, gray, perf. 11x10½ (booklet panes only) **1590**
A994 9¢ slate green, gray, perf. 11x9¾ (booklet panes only) **1590A**
A994 9¢ slate green, gray, perf. 11x10½ **1591**
A994 9¢ slate green, gray, perf. 10 vert. **1616**
A995 10¢ violet, gray, perf. 10 vert. **1617**
A995 10¢ violet, gray, perf. 11x10½ **1592**
A996 11¢ orange, gray, perf. 11x10½ .. **1593**
A997 12¢ red brown, beige, perf. 11x10½ **1594**
A997 12¢ red brown, beige, perf. 10 vert. **1816**
A998 13¢ brown, perf. 11x10½ **1595**
A998 13¢ brown, perf. 10 vert. **1618**
A999 13¢ multicolored **1596**
A1001 15¢ gray, dark blue & red, perf. 11 .... **1597**
A1001 15¢ gray, dark blue & red, perf. 11x 10½ (booklet panes only) **1598**
A1001 15¢ gray, dark blue & red, perf. 10 vert. **1618C**
A1002 16¢ blue, perf. 11x10½ **1599**
A1002 16¢ blue, perf. 10 vert. **1619**
A1003 24¢ red, blue, perf. 11x10½ **1603**
A1004 28¢ brown, blue, perf. 11x10½ .. **1604**
A1005 29¢ blue, blue, perf. 11x10½ **1605**
A1006 30¢ green, perf. 11x10½ **1606**
A1007 50¢ black & orange, perf. 11 ...... **1608**
A1008 $1 brown, orange & yellow, tan, perf. 11 .... **1610**
A1009 $2 dark green & red, tan, perf. 11 **1611**
A1010 $5 red brown, yellow & orange, tan, perf. 11 .... **1612**
A1011 3.1¢ brown, yellow, perf. 10 vert. **1613**
A1199 3.5¢ purple, yellow, perf. 10 vert. **1813**
A1012 7.7¢ brown, bright yellow, perf. 10 vert. **1614**
A1013 7.9¢ carmine, yellow, perf. 10 vert. **1615**
A1014 8.4¢ dark blue, yellow, perf. 10 vert. **1615C**

FLAG ISSUE 1975-77

A1015 13-star Flag over Independence Hall

A1016 Flag over Capitol

A1015 13¢ dark blue & red, perf. 11x10¾ **1622**
A1015 13¢ dark blue & red, perf. 11¼ **1622C**
A1015 13¢ dark blue & red, perf. 10 vert. **1625**
A1016 13¢ blue & red, perf. 11x10½ (booklet panes only) **1623**
A1016 13¢ blue & red, perf. 10x9¾ (booklet panes only) **1623B**

REGULAR ISSUE 1978

A1123 Indian Head Penny, 1877

A1209 Dolley Madison

A1126 Red Masterpiece and Medallion Roses

A1123 13¢ brown & blue, green, bister, perf. 11 .... **1734**
A1126 15¢ multicolored, perf. 10 (booklet panes only) **1737**
A1209 15¢ red brown & sepia, perf. 11 .. **1822**

REGULAR ISSUE 1978-85

A1124 "A" Eagle

A1207 "B" Eagle

A1332 "C" Eagle

A1333 "C" Eagle (Booklet)

A1496 "D" Eagle

A1497 "D" Eagle (Booklet)

A1124 (15¢) orange, Perf. 11 .... **1735**
A1124 (15¢) orange, perf. 11x10½ (booklet panes only) **1736**
A1124 (15¢) orange, perf. 10 vert. **1743**
A1207 (18¢) violet, perf. 11x10½ **1818**
A1207 (18¢) violet, perf. 10 (booklet panes only) **1819**
A1207 (18¢) violet, perf. 10 vert. **1820**
A1332 (20¢) brown, perf. 11x10½ **1946**
A1332 (20¢) brown, perf. 10 vert. **1947**
A1333 (20¢) brown, perf. 11x10½ (booklet panes only) **1948**
A1496 (22¢) green, perf. 11 .... **2111**
A1496 (22¢) green, perf. 10 vert. **2112**
A1497 (22¢) green, perf. 11 (booklet panes only) **2113**

GREAT AMERICANS ISSUE 1980-1999

A1231	A1551	A1232	A1552	A1233	A1553	A1234	A1554
A1235	A1555	A1556	A1236	A1237	A1238	A1239	A1240
A1557	A1241	A1242	A1243	A1558	A1559	A1244	A1560
A1245	A1246	A1247	A1248	A1249	A1561	A1562	A1250
A1563	A1564	A1565	A1566	A1567	A1251	A2248	A2249
A2250	A2251	A1252	A1568	A1253	A1254	A1255	A1569
A1570	A2253	A1256	A1571	A2255	A2256	A1572	A1573

A1574

A2257

A2258

A1575

A1576

A1577

A1578

GREAT AMERICANS ISSUE 1980-99

SEE ILLUSTRATIONS PAGE 62A

A1231 1¢ black, perf. 11 .... **1844**
A1551 1¢ brownish vermilion, perf. 11 **2168**
A1232 2¢ brown black, perf. 11x10½ .. **1845**
A1552 2¢ bright blue, perf. 11 .... **2169**
A1233 3¢ olive green, perf. 11x10½..... **1846**
A1553 3¢ bright blue, perf. 11 .... **2170**
A1234 4¢ violet, perf. 11x10½............ **1847**
A1554 4¢ blue violet, perf. 11 .... **2171**
A1235 5¢ henna brown, perf. 11x10½. **1848**
A1555 5¢ dark olive green, perf. 11..... **2172**
A1556 5¢ carmine, perf. 11 .... **2173**
A1236 6¢ orange vermilion, perf. 11.... **1849**
A1237 7¢ bright carmine, perf. 11 .... **1850**
A1238 8¢ olive black, perf. 11 .... **1851**
A1239 9¢ dark green, perf. 11 .... **1852**
A1240 10¢ Prussian blue, perf. 11 .... **1853**
A1557 10¢ lake, perf. 11 .... **2175**
A1241 11¢ dark blue, perf. 11 .... **1854**
A1242 13¢ light maroon, perf. 11x10½.. **1855**
A1243 14¢ slate green, perf. 11 .... **1856**
A1558 14¢ crimson, perf. 11 .... **2176**
A1559 15¢ claret, perf. 11 .... **2177**
A1244 17¢ green, perf. 11x10½............ **1857**
A1560 17¢ dull blue green, perf. 11....... **2178**
A1245 18¢ dark blue, perf. 11x10½....... **1858**
A1246 19¢ brown, perf. 11x10½ **1859**
A1247 20¢ claret, perf. 11x10½............ **1860**
A1248 20¢ green, perf. 11x10½............ **1861**
A1249 20¢ black, perf. 11 .... **1862**
A1561 20¢ red brown, perf. 11............. **2179**
A1562 21¢ blue violet, perf. 11 .... **2180**
A1250 22¢ dark chalky blue, perf. 11 .... **1863**
A1563 23¢ purple, perf. 11..................... **2181**
A1564 25¢ blue, perf. 11........................ **2182**
A1564 25¢ blue, perf. 10........................ **2197**
A1565 28¢ myrtle green, perf. 11 .... **2183**
A1566 29¢ blue, perf. 11........................ **2184**
A1567 29¢ indigo, perf. 11½x11 .... **2185**
A1251 30¢ olive gray, perf. 11 .... **1864**
A2248 32¢ brown, perf.11.1.................. **2933**
A2249 32¢ green, perf. 11.2................... **2934**
A2250 32¢ lake, perf. 11.2..................... **2935**
A2251 32¢ blue, perf. 11.2x11.1............ **2936**
A1252 35¢ gray, perf. 11x10½ **1865**
A1568 35¢ black, perf. 11 .... **2186**
A1253 37¢ blue, perf. 11x10½................ **1866**
A1254 39¢ rose lilac, perf. 11 .... **1867**
A1255 40¢ dark green, perf. 11 .... **1868**
A1569 40¢ dark blue, perf. 11 .... **2187**
A1570 45¢ bright blue, perf. 11 .... **2188**
A2253 46¢ carmine, perf. 11.1 .... **2938**
A1256 50¢ brown, perf. 11..................... **1869**
A1571 52¢ purple, perf. 11...................... **2189**
A2255 55¢ green, perf. 11 .... **2940**
A2256 55¢ black, serpentine die cut 11½, self-adhesive.........................**2941**
A1572 56¢ scarlet, perf. 11...................... **2190**
A1573 65¢ dark blue, perf. 11 .... **2191**
A1574 75¢ deep magenta, perf. 11 .... **2192**
A2257 77¢ blue, perf.11.8x11.6 .... **2942**
A2258 78¢ purple, perf. 11.2................. **2943**
A1575 $1 dark Prussian green, perf. 11 **2193**
A1576 $1 dark blue, perf. 11 .... **2194**
A1577 $2 bright violet, perf. 11 .... **2195**
A1578 $5 copper red, perf. 11 .... **2196**

WILDLIFE ISSUES 1981-82

A1267 Bighorn

A1268 Puma

A1269 Harbor Seal

A1270 Bison

A1271 Brown bear

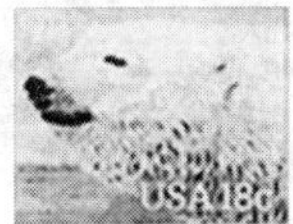

A1272 Polar bear

A1273 Elk (wapiti)

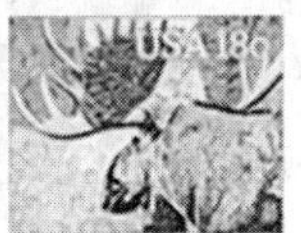

A1274 Moose

A1275 White-tailed deer

A1276 Pronghorn

A1334 Rocky Mountain Bighorn

From Booklet Panes

A1267 18¢ dark brown, perf. 11 .... **1880**
A1268 18¢ dark brown, perf. 11 .... **1881**
A1269 18¢ dark brown, perf. 11 .... **1882**
A1270 18¢ dark brown, perf. 11 .... **1883**
A1271 18¢ dark brown, perf. 11 .... **1884**
A1272 18¢ dark brown, perf. 11 .... **1885**
A1273 18¢ dark brown, perf. 11 .... **1886**
A1274 18¢ dark brown, perf. 11 .... **1887**
A1275 18¢ dark brown, perf. 11 .... **1888**
A1276 18¢ dark brown, perf. 11 .... **1889**
A1334 20¢ dark blue, perf. 11 .... **1949**

FLAG ISSUES 1981-85

A1277

A1278

A1279 Field of 1777 flag

A1280

A1281

A1498

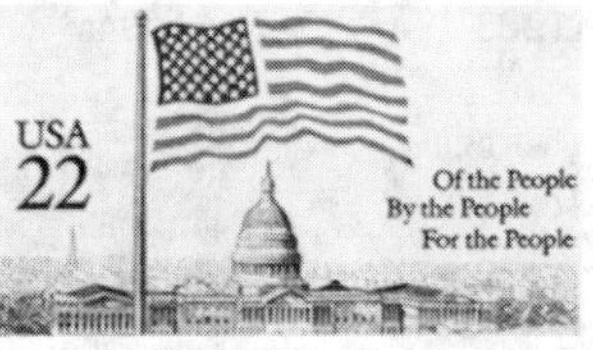

A1499 Of the People, By the People, For the People

A1277 18¢ multicolored, perf. 11 .... **1890**
A1278 18¢ multicolored, perf. 10 vert. ... **1891**
A1279 6¢ perf. 11 (booklet panes only) . **1892**
A1280 18¢ perf. 11 (booklet panes only) . **1893**
A1281 20¢ black, dark blue & red, perf. 11 .... **1894**
A1281 20¢ black, dark blue & red, perf. 10 vert. **1895**
A1281 20¢ black, dark blue & red, perf. 11x10½ (booklet panes only) **1896**
A1498 22¢ blue, red & black, perf. 11 ..... **2114**
A1498 22¢ blue, red & black, perf. 10 vert. **2115**
A1499 22¢ blue, red & black, perf. 10 horiz. (booklet panes only) **2116**

TRANSPORTATION ISSUE 1981-95

SEE ILLUSTRATIONS PAGE 64A

A1283 1¢ violet **1897**
A1604a 1¢ violet **2225**
A1284 2¢ black **1897A**
A1604b 2¢ black **2226**
A1284a 3¢ dark green **1898**
A1622 3¢ claret **2252**
A1506 3.4¢ dark bluish green **2123**
A1285 4¢ reddish brown, inscription 19½mm long **1898A**
A1285 4¢ reddish brown, inscription 17mm long **2228**
A1810 4¢ claret **2451**
A1507 4.9¢ brown black **2124**
A1286 5¢ gray green **1899**
A1623 5¢ black **2253**
A1811 5¢ carmine, engraved **2452**
A1811 5¢ carmine, photogravure **2452B**
A1811a 5¢ carmine........................... **2452D**
A1812 5¢ brown, engraved (Bureau precanceled) **2453**
A1812 5¢ red, photogravure (Bureau precanceled) **2454**
A1287 5.2¢ carmine **1900**
A1624 5.3¢ black (Bureau precanceled) **2254**
A1508 5.5¢ deep magenta **2125**
A1288 5.9¢ blue **1901**
A1509 6¢ red brown **2126**
A1510 7.1¢ lake **2127**
A1289 7.4¢ brown **1902**
A1625 7.6¢ brown (Bureau precanceled) **2255**
A1511 8.3¢ green, inscription 18½mm long **2128**
A1511 8.3¢ green, same, untagged (Bureau precanceled) **2128a**
A1511 8.3¢ green, inscription 18mm long, untagged (Bureau precanceled) **2231**
A1626 8.4¢ deep claret, (Bureau precanceled) **2256**
A1512 8.5¢ dark Prussian green **2129**

TRANSPORTATION ISSUE 1981-95

A1283 A1604a A1284 A1604b A1284a A1622 A1506

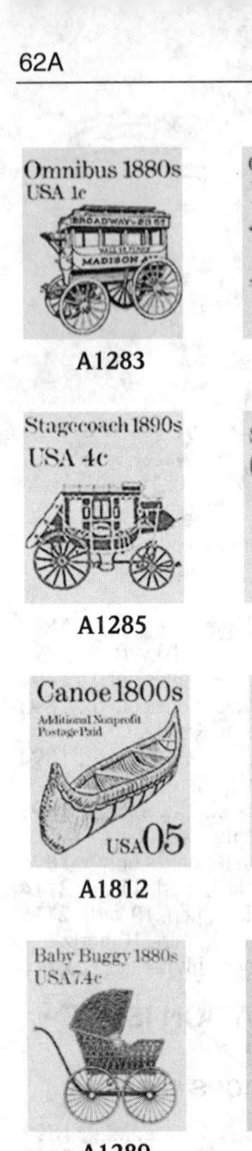

A1285 A1810 A1507 A1286 A1623 A1811 A1811a

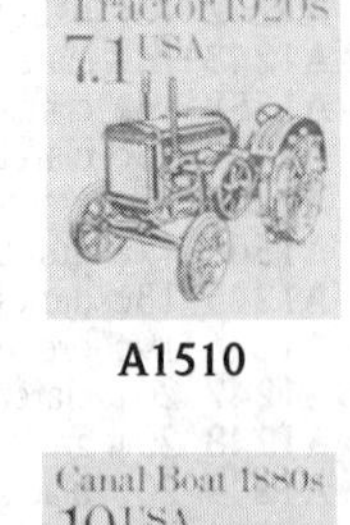

A1812 A1287 A1624 A1508 A1288 A1509 A1510

A1289 A1625 A1511 A1626 A1512 A1290 A1627

A1816 A1513 A1291 A1292 A1514 A1515 A1516

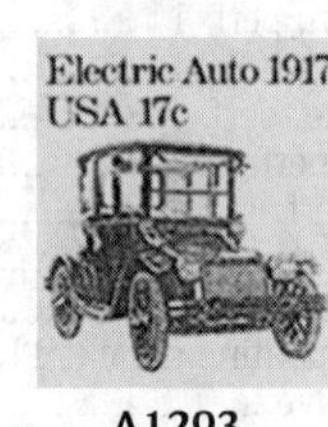

A1628 A1629 A1517 A1630 A1631 A1293 A1518

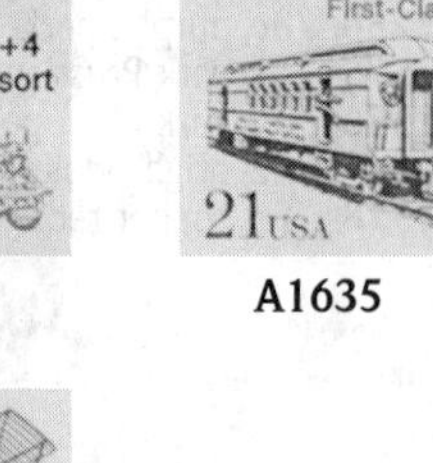

A1632 A1294 A1295 A1633 A1822 A1634 A1635

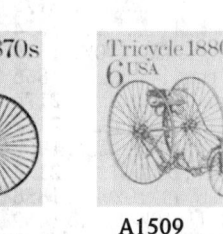

A1823 A1636 A1519 A1825 A1827

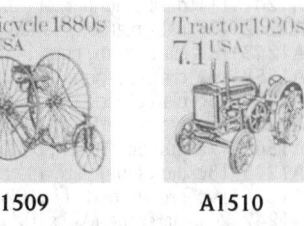

A1290 9.3¢ carmine rose **1903**
A1627 10¢ sky blue **2257**
A1816 10¢ green, engraved (Bureau precanceled) **2457**
A1816 10¢ green, photogravure (Bureau precanceled **2458**
A1513 10.1¢ slate blue **2130**
A1291 10.9¢ purple **1904**
A1292 11¢ red **1905**
A1514 11¢ dark green **2131**
A1515 12¢ dark blue **2132**
A1516 12.5¢ olive green **2133**
A1628 13¢ black, (Bureau precanceled) **2258**
A1629 13.2¢ slate green, (Bureau precanceled) **2259**
A1517 14¢ sky blue **2134**
A1630 15¢ violet **2260**
A1631 16.7¢ rose, (Bureau precanceled) **2261**
A1293 17¢ ultramarine **1906**
A1518 17¢ sky blue **2135**
A1632 17.5¢ dark violet **2262**
A1294 18¢ dark brown **1907**
A1295 20¢ vermilion **1908**
A1633 20¢ blue violet **2263**
A1822 20¢ green **2463**
A1634 20.5¢ rose, (Bureau precanceled) **2264**
A1635 21¢ olive green, (Bureau precanceled) **2265**
A1823 23¢ dark blue **2464**
A1636 24.1¢ deep ultramarine, (Bureau precanceled) **2266**
A1519 25¢ orange brown **2136**
A1825 32¢ blue **2466**
A1827 $1 dark blue & scarlet **2468**

REGULAR ISSUE 1983-99

A1894

A1897

A1898

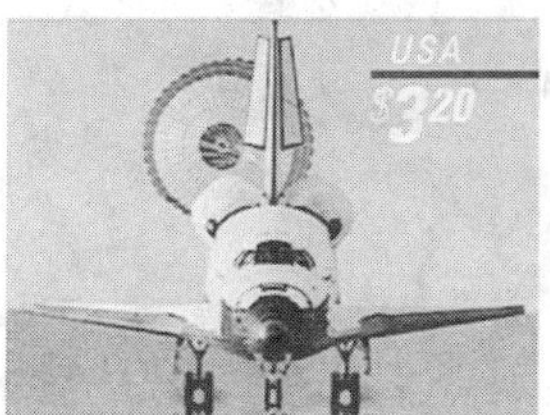

A2532

A1758

A1296 Eagle and Moon

A1895

A1505 Eagle and Half Moon

A1898a

A2533

A1896

A1894 $2.90 multicolored, perf. 11 ...... **2540**
A1897 $2.90 multicolored, perf. 11x 10½ **2543**
A1898 $3 multicolored, perf. 11....... **2544**
A2532 $3.20 multicolored, serpentine die cut 11.5......................**3261**
A1758 $8.75 multicolored, perf. 11 ...... **2394**
A1296 $9.35 multicolored, perf. 10 vert. (booklet panes only) **1909**
A1296 $9.35 multicolored, booklet pane of 3 .... **1909a**
A1895 $9.95 multicolored, perf. 11 ...... **2541**
A1505 $10.75 multicolored, perf. 10 vert. (booklet panes only) **2122**
A1898a $10.75 multicolored, perf 11 ... **2544A**
A2533 $11.75 multicolored, serpentine die cut 11.5........................... **3262**
A1896 $14 multicolored, perf 11 .... **2542**

REGULAR ISSUE 1982-85

A1532 George Washington Washington Monument

A1390 Consumer Education

A1533 Sealed Envelopes

A1532 18¢ multicolored, perf. 10 vert. **2149**
A1532 18¢ multicolored, same, untagged (Bureau precanceled) **2149a**
A1390 20¢ sky blue, perf. 10 vert. **2005**
A1533 21.1¢ multicolored, perf. 10 vert. **2150**
A1533 21.1¢ multicolored, same, untagged (Bureau precanceled) **2150a**

REGULAR ISSUE 1987-88

A1646

A1647

A1648

A1649

A1646 22¢ multicolored, perf. 11 .... **2276**
A1647 (25¢) multicolored, perf. 11 .... **2277**
A1647 (25¢) multicolored, perf. 10 .... **2282**
A1647 (25¢) multicolored, perf. 10 vert. **2279**
A1648 25¢ multicolored, perf. 11 .... **2278**
A1648 25¢ multicolored, perf. 10 ..... **2285A**
A1649 25¢ multicolored, perf. 10 vert. **2280**

FLORA & FAUNA ISSUE 1988-2001

A1840

A1841

A2335

A1842

A2336

A1843

A1847

A2350

A1649a

A1649b

A1649c

A1649d

A1848

A1849

A1852

A1853

A1854

A1875

A1879

A1844

A1850

A1851

A2351

A2550

A2551

A2552

A2553

A2634

A2635

A2636

A2637

A2694

A2695

A1845

A2339

A1846

A1840 1¢ multicolored, perf. 11 .... **2476**
A1841 1¢ multicolored, perf. 11 .... **2477**
A1841 1¢ multicolored, serpentine die cut 10½, self-adhesive **3031**
A1841 1¢ multicolored, blue inscriptions, serpentine die cut 11 1/4, self-adhesive **3031A**
A1841 1¢ multicolored, perf. 9.8 vert.... **3044**
A2335 2¢ multicolored, perf. 11.1 .... **3032**
A2335 2¢ multicolored, perf. 9¾ vert..... **3045**
A1842 3¢ multicolored, perf. 11 .... **2478**
A2336 3¢ multicolored, perf. 11.1 .... **3033**
A1843 19¢ multicolored, perf. 11½ x11... **2479**
A1847 20¢ multicolored, perf. 11x10 (booklet panes only) **2483**
A1847 20¢ multicolored, serpentine die cut 10½x11, self-adhesive **3048**
A1847 20¢ multicolored, serpentine die cut 11½ vert, self-adhesive **3053**
A2350 20¢ multicolored, serpentine die cut 11¼, self-adhesive **3050**
A2350 20¢ multicolored, serpentine die cut 10.6 on top and 10.6 on bottom or 10.6 on top and 10.4 on bottom, self-adhesive (booklet panes only)...................................... **3051**

A2350 20¢ multicolored, serpentine die cut 10.6x10.4 on 3 sides, self-adhesive (booklet panes only)....**3051A**
A2350 20¢ multicolored, serpentine die cut 9¾ vert., self-adhesive **3055**
A1649a 25¢ multicolored, perf. 11 (booklet panes only) **2283**
A1649b 25¢ multicolored, perf. 10 (booklet panes only) **2284**
A1649c 25¢ multicolored, perf. 10 .... **2285**
A1649d 25¢ multicolored, perf. 10 vert. . **2281**
A1848 29¢ black & multicolored, perf. 10 (booklet panes only) **2484**
A1848 29¢ red & multicolored, perf. 11 (booklet panes only) **2485**
A1849 29¢ multicolored, perf. 10x11 (booklet panes only) **2486**
A1852 29¢ multicolored, die cut, self-adhesive **2489**
A1853 29¢ red, green & black, die cut, self-adhesive **2490**
A1854 29¢ multicolored, die cut, self-adhesive **2491**
A1875 (29¢) yellow, black, red & yellow green, perf. 13 .... **2517**
A1875 (29¢) yellow, black, dull red & dark yellow green, perf. 10 vert. **2518**
A1875 (29¢) yellow, black, dull red & dark green, bullseye perf. 11.2 (booklet panes only) **2519**
A1875 (29¢) pale yellow, black, red & brightgreen, perf. 11 (booklet panes only) **2520**
A1879 29¢ dull yellow, black, red & yellow green, perf. 11 .... **2524**
A1879 29¢ dull yellow, black, red & yellow green, perf. 13x12¾ **2524A**
A1879 29¢ pale yellow, black, red & yellow green, roulette 10 vert. **2525**
A1879 29¢ pale yellow, black, red & yellow green, perf. 10 vert. **2526**
A1879 29¢ pale yellow, black, red & bright green, perf. 11 (booklet panes only) **2527**
A1844 30¢ multicolored, perf. 11½ x11. **2480**
A1850 32¢ multicolored, perf. 11x10 (booklet panes only) **2487**
A1850 32¢ multicolored, serpentine die cut, self-adhesive **2493**
A1850 32¢ multicolored, serpentine die cut vert., self-adhesive ... **2495**
A1851 32¢ multicolored, perf. 11x10 (booklet panes only) **2488**
A1851 32¢ multicolored, serpentine die cut, self-adhesive **2494**
A1851 32¢ multicolored, serpentine die cut vert., self-adhesive **2495A**
A1853 32¢ pink, green & black, serpentine die cut, self-adhesive............**2492**
A1853 32¢ yellow, orange, green & black, serpentine die cut 11.3x11.7, self-adhesive **3049**
A1853 32¢ yellow, orange, green & black, serpentine die cut 9.8 vert., self-adhesive **3054**
A2351 33¢ multicolored, serpentine die cut 11½x11¾ on 2, 3, or 4 sides, self-adhesive (booklet panes only) **3052**
A2351 33¢ multicolored, serpentine die cut 10¾x10½ on 2 or 3 sides, self-adhesive (booklet panes only) **3052E**
A2550 33¢ multicolored, serpentine die cut 11¼ x11½, self-adhesive (booklet panes only) **3294**
A2550 33¢ multicolored, serpentine die cut 9.5x10, self-adhesive (booklet panes only) **3298**
A2550 33¢ multicolored, serpentine die cut 8.5 vert., self-adhesive..........**3302**
A2551 33¢ multicolored, serpentine die cut 11¼ x11½, self-adhesive (booklet panes only) **3295**
A2551 33¢ multicolored, serpentine die cut 9.5x10, self-adhesive (booklet panes only) **3300**
A2551 33¢ multicolored, serpentine die cut 8.5 vert., self-adhesive..........**3303**
A2552 33¢ multicolored, serpentine die cut 11¼ x11½, self-adhesive (booklet panes only) **3296**
A2552 33¢ multicolored, serpentine die cut 9.5x10, self-adhesive (booklet panes only) **3299**
A2552 33¢ multicolored, serpentine die cut 8.5 vert., self-adhesive..........**3305**
A2553 33¢ multicolored, serpentine die cut 11¼ x11½, self-adhesive (booklet panes only) **3297**
A2553 33¢ multicolored, serpentine die cut 9.5x10, self-adhesive (booklet panes only) **3301**
A2553 33¢ multicolored, serpentine die cut 8.5 vert., self-adhesive..........**3304**
A2634 33¢ multicolored, serpentine die cut 8½ horiz., self-adhesive . **3404**
A2635 33¢ multicolored, serpentine die cut 8½ horiz., self-adhesive . **3405**
A2636 33¢ multicolored, serpentine die cut 8½ horiz., self-adhesive . **3406**
A2637 33¢ multicolored, serpentine die cut 8½ horiz., self-adhesive . **3407**
A2694 34¢ multicolored, serpentine die cut 11¼ on 2, 3 or 4 sides (booklet panes only), self-adhesive......**3491**
A2694 34¢ multicolored, serpentine die cut 11½x10¾ on 2 or 3 sides (booklet panes only), self-adhesive.........**3493**
A2695 34¢ multicolored, serpentine die cut 11¼ on 2, 3 or 4 sides (booklet panes only), self-adhesive......**3492**
A2695 34¢ multicolored, serpentine die cut 11½x10¾ on 2 or 3 sides (booklet panes only), self-adhesive.........**3494**
A1845 45¢ multicolored, perf. 11.......... **2481**
A2339 $1 multicolored, serpentine die cut 11½x11¼, self-adhesive.........**3036**
A1846 $2 multicolored, perf. 11.......... **2482**

REGULAR ISSUE 1989-98

A1793

A1834

A1877

A1884 A1947

A1950 A1951

A1793 25¢ multicolored, die cut, self-adhesive **2431**
A1834 25¢ dark red & dark blue, die cut, self-adhesive **2475**
A1877 (29¢) black, blue & dark red, die cut, self-adhesive **2522**
A1884 29¢ black, gold & green, die cut, self-adhesive **2531A**
A1947 29¢ brown & multicolored, die cut, self-adhesive **2595**
A1947 29¢ green & multicolored, die cut, self-adhesive **2596**
A1947 29¢ red & multicolored, die cut, self-adhesive **2597**
A1950 29¢ red, cream & blue, die cut, self-adhesive........................**2598**
A1951 29¢ multicolored, die cut, self-adhesive........................**2599**
A1951 32¢ red, light blue, dark blue & yellow, serpentine die cut 11, self-adhesive........................**3122**
A1951 32¢ red, light blue, dark blue & yellow, serpentine die cut 11.5x11.8, self-adhesive.....**3122E**

REGULAR ISSUE 1991-94

A1876 A1881

A1882 A1878

A1880 A1883

A1876 (4¢) bister & carmine, perf. 11 .... **2521**
A1881 19¢ multicolored, perf. 10 vert. .. **2529**
A1881 19¢ multicolored, perf. 10 vert., two rope loops on piling....... **2529**
A1881 19¢ multicolored, perf. 10 vert.,

one rope loop on piling...... **2529C**
A1882 19¢ multicolored, perf. 10 (booklet panes only) **2530**
A1878 29¢ multicolored, engraved, perf. 10 vert. **2523**
A1878 29¢ multicolored, photogravure, perf. 10 vert. **2523A**
A1880 29¢ multicolored, perf. 11 (booklet panes only) **2528**
A1883 29¢ multicolored, perf. 11 .... **2531**

REGULAR ISSUE 1991-98

A1956 A1957

A2534 A1959

A1960 A1946

A1961 A1939

A1942

A1944

A1956 (10¢) multicolored, perf. 10 vert. (Bureau precanceled).......... **2602**
A1957 (10¢) orange yellow & multicolored, perf. 10 vert. (Bureau precanceled)........................ **2603**
A1957 (10¢) gold & multicolored, perf. 10 vert. (Bureau precanceled) .. **2604**
A1957 (10¢) gold & multicolored, serpentine die cut 11.5 vert, self-adhesive **2907**
A2534 (10¢) multicolored, perf. 9.9 vert. (Bureau precanceled) **3270**
A2534 (10¢) multicolored, serpentine die cut 9.9 vert., self-adhesive (Bureau precanceled) **3271**
A1959 (23¢) multicolored, perf. 10 vert. (Bureau precanceled) **2605**
A1960 23¢ multicolored, perf. 10 vert. (Bureau precanceled) **2606**
A1960 23¢ multicolored, perf. 10 vert., "23" 7mm long (Bureau precanceled)........................ **2607**
A1960 23¢ violet blue, red & black, perf. 10 vert., "First Class" 8½ mm long (Bureau precanceled) **2608**
A1946 29¢ black & multicolored, perf. 10 (booklet panes only)............ **2593**
A1946 29¢ black & multicolored, perf. 11x10 (booklet panes only) **2593B**
A1946 29¢ red & multicolored, perf. 11x10 (booklet panes only)............ **2594**
A1961 29¢ blue & red, perf. 10 vert...... **2609**
A1939 32¢ red brown, perf. 11.2 .... **2587**
A1942 $1 blue, perf. 11½................... **2590**
A1944 $5 slate green, perf. 11½.......... **2592**

G RATE ISSUE 1994-95

A2206

A2210

A2207

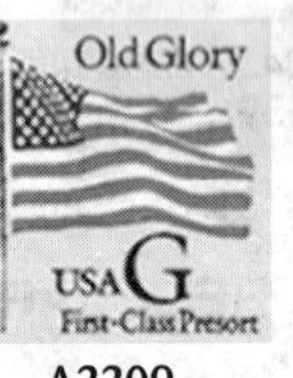

A2209

A2208

A2206 (3¢) tan, bright blue & red, perf. 11x10.8 .... **2877**
A2206 (3¢) tan, dark blue & red, perf. 10.8x10.9 .... **2878**
A2210 (5¢) green & multicolored, perf. 9.8 vert. (Bureau precanceled) .. **2893**
A2207 (20¢) black "G," yellow & multicolored, perf. 11.2x11.1 .... **2879**
A2207 (20¢) red "G," yellow & multicolored, perf. 11x10.9 .... **2880**
A2209 (25¢) black "G," blue & multicolored, perf. 9.8 vert.(Bureau precanceled) **2888**

A2208 (32¢) black "G" & multicolored, perf. 11.2x11.1 .... **2881**
A2208 (32¢) black "G" & multicolored, perf. 10x9.9 (booklet panes only) **2883**
A2208 (32¢) black "G" & multicolored, die cut, self-adhesive, small number of blue shading dots in white stripes below blue field.................. **2886**
A2208 (32¢) black "G" & multicolored, die cut, self-adhesive, thin translucent paper, more blue shading dots in white stripes below blue field.................. **2887**
A2208 (32¢) black "G" & multicolored, perf. 9.8 vert. **2889**
A2208 (32¢) red "G" & multicolored, perf. 11x10.9, distance from bottom of "G" to top of flag is 13¾ mm........................ **2882**
A2208 (32¢) red "G" & multicolored, perf. 11x10.9 on 2 or 3 sides (booklet panes only), distance from bottom of "G" to top of flag is 13½ mm......................... **2885**
A2208 (32¢) red "G" & multicolored, perf. 9.8 vert. **2891**
A2208 (32¢) red "G" & multicolored, rouletted. 9.8 vert.............. **2892**
A2208 (32¢) blue "G" & multicolored, perf. 10.9 (booklet panes only).... **2884**
A2208 (32¢) blue "G" & multicolored, perf. 9.8 vert. **2890**

REGULAR ISSUE 1995-2003

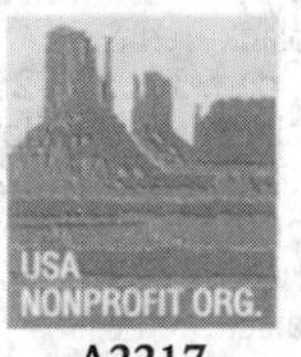

A2217

A2218

A2489

A2853

A2220

A2509

A2223

A2724

A2225

A2490

A2212

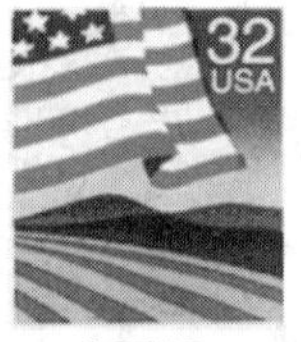
A2230

A2217 (5¢) yellow, red & blue, perf. 9.8 vert. 2902
A2217 (5¢) yellow, red & blue, serpentine die cut 11.5 vert, self-adhesive 2902B
A2218 (5¢) purple & multicolored, perf. 9.9 vert. 2903
A2218 (5¢) purple & multicolored, serpentine die cut 11.2 vert., self-adhesive 2904A
A2218 (5¢) purple & multicolored, serpentine die cut 9.8 vert., self-adhesive 2904B
A2218 (5¢) blue & multicolored, perf. 9.9 vert. 2904
A2489 (5¢) multicolored, perf. 10 vert. .. 3207
A2489 (5¢) multicolored, serpentine die cut 9.7 vert., self-adhesive (Bureau precanceled) 3207A
A2853 (5¢) multicolored, serpentine die cut 8½ vert. 3693
A2853 (5¢) multicolored, perf. 9¾ vert. 3775
A2853 (5¢) multicolored, serpentine die cut 9½x10 (coil stamp). 3785
A2220(10¢) black, red brown & brown, perf. 9.8 vert. 2905
A2220(10¢) black, red brown & brown, serpentine die cut 11.5 vert., self-adhesive 2906
A2509(10¢) multicolored, serpentine die cut 9.8 vert., self-adhesive (Bureau precanceled) 3228
A2509(10¢) multicolored, perf 9.9 vert. (Bureau precanceled) 3229
A2223(15¢) dark orange, yellow & multicolored (dark, bold colors, heavy shading lines, heavily shaded chrome), perf. 9.8 vert. 2908
A2223(15¢) buff & multicolored (more subdued colors, finer details, shinier chrome), perf. 9.8 vert. 2909
A2223(15¢) buff & multicolored, serpentine die cut 11.5 vert., self-adhesive 2910
A2724(15¢) multicolored, serpentine die cut 11½ vert., self-adhesive (Bureau precanceled 3522
A2225(25¢) dark red, dark yellow green & multicolored (dark, saturated colors, dark blue lines in music selection board), perf.9.8 vert. 2911
A2225(25¢) dark red, yellow green & multicolored, serpentine die cut 9.8 vert, self-adhesive 2912B
A2225(25¢) bright orange red, bright yellow green & multicolored (bright colors, less shading and light blue lines in music selection board), perf. 9.8 vert. 2912
A2225(25¢) bright orange red, bright yellow green & multicolored, serpentine die cut 11.5 vert., self-adhesive 2912A
A2225(25¢) bright orange red, bright yellow green & multicolored, imperf, with simulated perforations, self-adhesive 3132
A2490(25¢) multicolored, perf. 10 vert. .. 3208
A2490(25¢) multicolored, serpentine die cut 9.7 vert., self-adhesive (Bureau precanceled) 3208A
A2212 32¢ multicolored, perf. 10.4 2897
A2212 32¢ blue, tan, brown, red & light blue, perf. 10.8x9.8 (booklet panes only) 2916
A2212 32¢ blue, tan, brown, red & light blue (pronounced blue shading in flag and red "1995"), perf. 9.8 vert. 2913
A2212 32¢ blue, yellow brown, red & gray (gray shading in flag and blue "1995"), perf. 9.8 vert. 2914
A2212 32¢ multicolored, serpentine die cut 8.7 vert., self-adhesive 2915
A2212 32¢ dark blue, tan, brown, red & light blue, red "1996," serpentine die cut 9.7 vert., straight cut at bottom with 11 teeth above, self-adhesive 2915A
A2212 32¢ dark blue, tan, brown, red & light blue, red "1997," serpentine die cut 9.8 vert., straight cut at bottom and top with 9 teeth between, self-adhesive 2915D
A2212 32¢ dark blue, tan, brown, red & light blue (sky shows color graduation at lower right, blue "1996"), serpentine die cut 9.9 vert., self-adhesive 3133
A2212 32¢ dark blue, tan, brown, red & light blue, serpentine die cut 10.9 vert, self-adhesive 2915C
A2212 32¢ dark blue, tan, brown, red & light blue, serpentine die cut 11.5 vert, self-adhesive 2915B
A2212 32¢ multicolored, serpentine die cut 8.8 on 2, 3 or 4 adjacent sides, dated "1995" in blue, self-adhesive (booklet panes only) 2920
A2212 32¢ multicolored, serpentine die cut 11.3 on 2, 3 or 4 adjacent sides, dated "1996" in blue, self-adhesive (booklet panes only) 2920D
A2212 32¢ dark blue, tan, brown, red & light blue, serpentine die cut 9.8 on 2 or 3 adjacent sides, dated "1996" in red, self-adhesive (booklet panes only) 2921
A2212 32¢ dark blue, tan, brown, red & light blue, serpentine die cut 9.8 on 2 or 3 adjacent sides, dated "1997" in red, self-adhesive (booklet panes only) 2921b
A2230 32¢ multicolored, die cut, self-adhesive 2919

H RATE ISSUE 1999

A2529

A2530

A2531

A2529 (1¢) multicolored, white USA, black "1998," perf. 11.2 3257
A2529 (1¢) multicolored, pale blue USA, blue "1998," perf. 11.2 3258
A2530 22¢ multicolored, serpentine die cut 10.8, self-adhesive 3259
A2530 22¢ multicolored, serpentine die cut 9.9 vert, self-adhesive 3263
A2530 22¢ multicolored, perf. 9¾ vert. ... 3353
A2531(33¢) multicolored, perf. 11.2 3260
A2531(33¢) multicolored, perf. 9.8 vert... 3264
A2531(33¢) multicolored, serpentine die cut 9.9 vert., stamp corners at right angles, backing paper same size as stamp, self-adhesive 3265
A2531(33¢) multicolored, serpentine die cut 9.9 vert., stamp corners rounded, backing paper larger than stamp, self-adhesive 3266
A2531(33¢) multicolored, serpentine die cut 9.9, (booklet panes only), self-adhesive 3267
A2531(33¢) multicolored, serpentine die cut 11.2x11.1 (booklet panes only), self-adhesive 3268
A2531(33¢) multicolored, die cut 8 (booklet panes only), self-adhesive 3269

REGULAR ISSUE 1999

A2540

A2541

A2540 33¢ multicolored, perf. 11.2 3277
A2540 33¢ multicolored, serpentine die cut 11.1, self-adhesive 3278
A2540 33¢ multicolored, serpentine die cut 11½x11¾, self-adhesive 3278F
A2540 33¢ multicolored, serpentine die cut 9.8 (booklet panes only), self-adhesive 3279
A2540 33¢ multicolored, perf. 9.9 vert... 3280
A2540 33¢ multicolored, serpentine die cut 9.8 vert., stamp corners at right angles, backing paper same size as stamp, self-adhesive 3281
A2540 33¢ multicolored, serpentine die cut 9.8 vert., stamp corners rounded, backing paper same larger than stamp, self-adhesive 3282
A2541 33¢ multicolored, serpentine die cut 7.9 (booklet panes only), self-adhesive 3283

DISTINGUISED AMERICANS ISSUE 2000-02

A2650

A2656

A2661

A2662

A2650 10¢ red & black, perf 11 .... **3420**
A2656 33¢ red & black, perf 11 .... **3426**
A2661 76¢ red & black, serpentine die cut 11, self-adhesive **3431**
A2661 76¢ red & black, serpentine die cut 11½x11, self-adhesive. **3432**
A2662 83¢ red & black, serpentine die cut 11x11¾, self-adhesive. **3433**

AMERICAN CULTURE ISSUE 2000-03

A2677  A2722

A2875

A2677 (10¢) multicolored, serpentine die cut 11½ vert., self-adhesive (Bureau precanceled............ **3447**
A2677 (10¢) multicolored, perf. 10 vert. ..**3769**
A2722 (10¢) multicolored, serpentine die cut 8½ vert., self-adhesive (Bureau precanceled............ **3520**
A2875 $1 multicolored, serpentine die cut 11¼x11 vert., self-adhesive......................... **3766**

REGULAR ISSUE 2000-02

A2686  A2687

A2678  A2679

A2680  A2681

A2682  A2683

A2684  A2685

A2688  A2689

A2690  A2691

A2692  A2693

A2696

A2686 20¢ dark carmine, serpentine die cut 11¼ x11 on 3 sides (booklet panes only), self-adhesive...**3482**
A2686 20¢ dark carmine, serpentine die cut 10½ x11 on 3 sides (booklet panes only), self-adhesive...**3483**
A2687 21¢ multicolored, perf. 11¼x11 **3467**
A2687 21¢ multicolored, serpentine die cut 11¼ on 3 sides, self-adhesive (booklet panes only)...........**3484**
A2687 21¢ multicolored, serpentine die cut 101/2x111/4 on 3 sides, self-adhesive (booklet panes only **3484A**
A2687 21¢ multicolored, serpentine die cut 11, self-adhesive **3468**
A2687 21¢ multicolored, serpentine die cut 8½ vert., self-adhesive **3475**
A2686 23¢ green, perf. 11¼.................**3616**
A2686 23¢ green, serpentine die cut 11¼x11¾, self-adhesive ...**3468A**
A2686 23¢ green, serpentine die cut 8½ vert., self-adhesive (Banknote Corp. Printing).**3475A**
A2686 23¢ gray green, serpentine die cut 8½ vert., self-adhesive (Avery Printing) **3617**
A2686 23¢ green, serpentine die cut 11¼ on 3 sides, self-adhesive (booklet panes only............**3618**
A2686 23¢ green, serpentine die cut 101/2x111/4 on 3 sides, self-adhesive (booklet panes only).................................**3619**
A2678 (34¢) multicolored, perf. 11¼......**3448**
A2678 (34¢) multicolored, serpentine die cut 11¼, self-adhesive..............**3449**
A2678 (34¢) multicolored, serpentine die cut 8 on 2, 3 or 4 sides (booklet panes only), self-adhesive...**3450**
A2679 (34¢) multicolored, serpentine die cut 11 on 2, 3 or 4 sides (booklet panes only), self-adhesive...**3451**
A2680 (34¢) multicolored, perf. 9¾ vert.**3452**
A2680 (34¢) multicolored, serpentine die cut 10 vert., self-adhesive **3453**
A2681 (34¢) purple & multicolored, serpentine die cut 10¼x10¾ on 2 or 3 sides (booklet panes only), self-adhesive **3454**
A2681 (34¢) purple & multicolored, serpentine die cut 11¼x11¾ on 2 or 3 sides (booklet panes only), self-adhesive **3458**
A2681 (34¢) purple & multicolored, serpentine die cut 8½ vert., self-adhesive **3465**
A2682 (34¢) tan & multicolored, serpentine die cut 10¼x10¾ on 2 or 3 sides (booklet panes only), self-adhesive **3455**
A2682 (34¢) tan & multicolored, serpentine die cut 11½x11¾ on 2 or 3 sides (booklet panes only), self-adhesive **3459**
A2682 (34¢) tan & multicolored, serpentine die cut 8½ vert., self-adhesive ..**3463**
A2683 (34¢) green & multicolored, serpentine die cut 10¼x10¾ on 2 or 3 sides (booklet panes only), self-adhesive **3456**
A2683 (34¢) green & multicolored, serpentine die cut 11½x11¾ on 2 or 3 sides (booklet panes only), self-adhesive **3460**
A2683 (34¢) green & multicolored, serpentine die cut 8½ vert., self-adhesive **3462**
A2684 (34¢) red & multicolored, serpentine die cut 10¼x10¾ on 2 or 3 sides (booklet panes only), self-adhesive **3457**
A2684 (34¢) red & multicolored, serpentine die cut 11½x11¾ on 2 or 3 sides (booklet panes only), self-adhesive **3461**
A2684 (34¢) red & multicolored, serpentine die cut 8½ vert., self-adhesive ...**3463**
A2685 34¢ multicolored, serpentine die cut 9¾ vert., stamp corners rounded, backing paper larger than stamp, self-adhesive **3466**
A2685 34¢ multicolored, perf. 9¾ vert. **3476**
A2685 34¢ multicolored, serpentine die cut 9¾ vert., stamp corners at right angles, backing paper same size as stamp, self-adhesive **3477**
A2688 34¢ multicolored, perf. 11¼ ...**3469**
A2688 34¢ multicolored, serpentine die cut 11¼, self-adhesive.............**3470**
A2688 34¢ multicolored, serpentine die cut 8 on 2, 3 or 4 sides, self-adhesive (booklet panes only **3495**
A2689 34¢ multicolored, serpentine die cut 11 on 2, 3 or 4 sides (booklet panes only), self-adhesive...**3485**
A2690 34¢ green & multicolored, serpentine die cut 8½ vert., self-adhesive **3478**
A2690 34¢ green & multicolored, serpentine die cut 10¼x10¾ on 2 or 3 sides (booklet panes only), self-adhesive **3489**

A2691 34¢ red & multicolored, serpentine die cut 8½ vert., self-adhesive........................**3479**
A2692 34¢ tan & multicolored, serpentine die cut 8½ vert., self-adhesive...**3480**
A2692 34¢ tan & multicolored, serpentine die cut 10¼x10¾ on 2 or 3 sides (booklet panes only), self-adhesive.............................**3488**
A2693 34¢ purple & multicolored, serpentine die cut 8½ vert., self-adhesive...................................**3481**
A2693 34¢ & multicolored, serpentine die cut 10¼x10¾ on 2 or 3 sides (booklet panes only), self-adhesive...................................**3487**
A2696 55¢ multicolored, serpentine die cut 10¾, self-adhesive **3471**
A2696 57¢ multicolored, serpentine die cut 10¾, self-adhesive...........**3471A**

WASHINGTON VIEWS ISSUE 2001-02

A2697

A2818

A2698

A2819

A2697 $3.50 multicolored, serpentine die cut 11¼x11½, self-adhesive ...**3472**
A2818 $3.85 multicolored, serpentine die cut 11¼, self-adhesive.......**3647**
A2698 $12.25 multicolored, serpentine die cut 11¼x11½, self-adhesive.....................**3473**
A2819 $13.65 multicolored, serpentine die cut 11¼, self-adhesive.......**3648**

UNITED WE STAND ISSUE 2001-02

A2744

A2744 34¢ multicolored, serpentine die cut 11¼ on 2, 3 or 4 sides, self-adhesive (booklet panes only..................................**3549**
A2744 34¢ multicolored, serpentine die cut 10½x10¾ on 2 or 3 sides, self-adhesive (booklet panes only **3549B**
A2744 34¢ multicolored, serpentine die cut 9¾ vert., stamp corners at right angles, backing paper same size as stamp, self-adhesive...........................**3550**
A2744 34¢ multicolored, serpentine die cut 9¾ vert., stamp corners rounded, backing paper larger than stamp, self-adhesive **3550A**

AMERICAN DESIGN ISSUE 2002-03

A2866

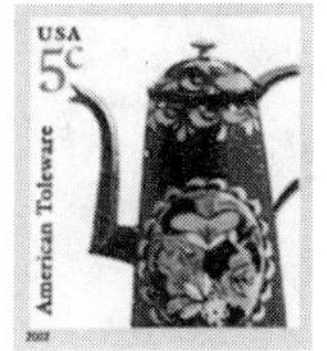

A2805

A2860

A2810 1¢ multicolored, perf. 10 vert....**3757**
A2805 5¢ multicolored, perf. 10 vert....**3612**
A2860 10¢ multicolored, serpentine die cut 11¼x11½, self-adhesive. **3751**

REGULAR ISSUE 2002-03

A2806

A2807

A2808 **A2809**

A2810 **A2811**

A2813 **A2814**

A2815 **A2816**

A2812 **A2817**

A2805 3¢ red, blue & black, serpentine die cut 11, self-adhesive, lithographed, year at lower left **3613**
A2806 3¢ red, blue & black, serpentine die cut 10, self-adhesive, photogravure, year at lower right......................................**3614**
A2806 (3¢) red, blue & black, perf. 10 vert., photogravure, year at lower left **3615**
A2807(37¢) multicolored, perf. 11¼x11....**3620**
A2807(37¢) multicolored, serpentine die cut 11¼x11, self-adhesive...............................**3621**
A2807(37¢) multicolored, serpentine die cut 10 vert., self-adhesive...............................**3622**
A2807(37¢) multicolored, serpentine die cut 11¼on 2, 3 or 4 sides, self-adhesive (booklet panes only) **3623**
A2807(37¢) multicolored, serpentine die cut 10½x10¾ on 2 or 3 sides, self-adhesive (booklet panes only)...........................**3624**
A2807(37¢) multicolored, serpentine die cut 8 on 2, 3 or 4 sides, self-adhesive (booklet panes only) **3625**

A2808 (37¢) multicolored, serpentine die cut 11 on 2, 3 or 4 sides, self-adhesive (booklet panes only) **3626**
A2809 (37¢) multicolored, serpentine die cut 11 on 2, 3 or 4 sides, self-adhesive (booklet panes only) **3627**
A2810 (37¢) multicolored, serpentine die cut 11 on 2, 3 or 4 sides, self-adhesive (booklet panes only) **3628**
A2811 (37¢) multicolored, serpentine die cut 11 on 2, 3 or 4 sides, self-adhesive (booklet panes only) **3629**
A2812 37¢ multicolored, serpentine die cut 11¼x11, self-adhesive.. **3630**
A2812 37¢ multicolored, perf. 10 vert. **3631**
A2812 37¢ multicolored, serpentine die cut 10 vert., self-adhesive .. **3632**
A2812 37¢ multicolored, serpentine die cut 8½ vert., stamp corners rounded, backing paper larger than stamp, self-adhesive **3633**
A2812 37¢ multicolored, serpentine die cut 11 on 3 sides, self-adhesive (booklet panes only) **3634**
A2812 37¢ multicolored, serpentine die cut 11¼ on 2 or 3 sides, self-adhesive (booklet panes only) **3635**
A2812 37¢ multicolored, serpentine die cut 10½x10¾ on 2 or 3 sides, self-adhesive (booklet panes only) **3636**
A2812 37¢ multicolored, serpentine die cut 8 on 2, 3 or 4 sides, self-adhesive (booklet panes only) **3637**
A2813 37¢ multicolored, serpentine die cut 8½ horz., self-adhesive . **3638**
A2813 37¢ multicolored, serpentine die cut 11 on 2, 3 or 4 sides, self-adhesive (booklet panes only) **3643**
A2814 37¢ multicolored, serpentine die cut 8½ horz., self-adhesive . **3639**
A2814 37¢ multicolored, serpentine die cut 11 on 2, 3 or 4 sides, self-adhesive (booklet panes only) **3642**
A2815 37¢ multicolored, serpentine die cut 8½ horz., self-adhesive . **3640**
A2815 37¢ multicolored, serpentine die cut 11 on 2, 3 or 4 sides, self-adhesive (booklet panes only) **3645**
A2816 37¢ multicolored, serpentine die cut 8½ horz., self-adhesive . **3641**
A2816 37¢ multicolored, serpentine die cut 11 on 2, 3 or 4 sides, self-adhesive (booklet panes only) **3644**
A2817 60¢ multicolored, serpentine die cut 11x11½ self-adhesive ... **3646**

EAGLE ISSUE 2003

A2898

A2899

A2898 (25¢) gray & gold, serpentine die 11¾ vert. **3792**
A2898 (25¢) dull blue & gold, serpentine die 11¾ vert. **3794**
A2898 (25¢) green & gold, serpentine die 11¾ vert. **3796**
A2898 (25¢) Prussian blue & gold, serpentine die 11¾ vert. **3798**
A2898 (25¢) red & gold, serpentine die 11¾ vert. **3800**
A2899 (25¢) gold & red, serpentine die 11¾ vert. **3793**
A2899 (25¢) gold & Prussian blue, serpentine die 11¾ vert. **3795**
A2899 (25¢) gold & gray, serpentine die 11¾ vert. **3797**
A2899 (25¢) gold & dull blue, serpentine die 11¾ vert. **3799**
A2899 (25¢) gold & green, serpentine die 11¾ vert. **3801**

SUBJECT INDEX OF REGULAR, COMMEMORATIVE & AIR POST ISSUES

POSTMASTERS' PROVISIONALS

The Act of Congress of March 3, 1845, effective July 1, 1845, established rates of postage as follows:

"For every single letter in manuscript or paper of any kind by or upon which information shall be asked or communicated in writing or by marks designs, conveyed in the mail, for any distance under 300 miles, five cents; and for any distance over 300 miles, ten cents; and for a double letter there shall be charged double these rates; and for a treble letter, treble these rates; and for a quadruple letter, quadruple these rates; and every letter or parcel not exceeding half an ounce in weight shall be deemed a single letter, and every additional weight of half an ounce, shall be charged with an additional single postage. All drop letters, or letters placed in any post office, not for transmission through the mail but for delivery only, shall be charged with postage at the rate of two cents each."

Circulars were charged 2 cents, magazines and pamphlets 2½ cents; newspapers according to size.

Between the time of the Act of 1845, effecting uniform postage rates, and the Act of Congress of March 3, 1847, authorizing the postmaster-general to issue stamps, postmasters in various cities issued provisional stamps.

Before adhesive stamps were introduced, prepaid mail was marked "Paid" either with pen and ink or handstamps of various designs. Unpaid mail occasionally was marked "Due." Most often, however, unpaid mail did not have a "Due" marking, only the amount of postage to be collected from the recipient, e.g. "5," "10," "18¾," etc. Thus, if a letter was not marked "Paid," it was assumed to be unpaid. These "stampless covers" are found in numerous types and usually carry the town postmark.

New York Postmaster Robert H. Morris issued the first postmaster provisional in July 1845. Other postmasters soon followed. The provisionals served until superseded by the federal government's 5c and 10c stamps issued July 1, 1847.

Postmasters recognized the provisionals as indicating postage prepaid. On several provisionals, the signature of initials of the postmaster vouched for their legitimate use.

On July 12, 1845, Postmaster Morris sent examples of his new stamp to the postmasters of Boston, Philadelphia, Albany and Washington, asking that they be treated as unpaid until they reached the New York office. Starting in that year, the New York stamps were distributed to other offices. Postmaster General Cave Johnson reportedly authorized this practice with the understanding that these stamps were to be sold for letters directed to or passing through New York. This was an experiment to test the practicality of the use of adhesive postage stamps.

ALEXANDRIA, VA

Daniel Bryan, Postmaster

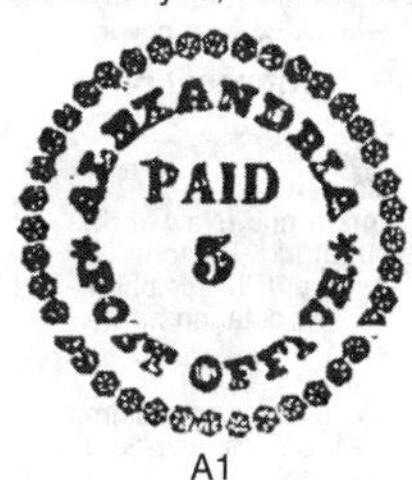

A1

All known copies cut to shape.
Type I - 40 asterisks in circle.
Type II - 39 asterisks in circle.

1846	Typeset		Imperf.
1X1 A1 5c **black,** *buff,* type I			—
a. 5c black, *buff,* type II		75,000.	
On cover (I or II)			150,000.
1X2 A1 5c **black,** *blue,* type I, on cover			—

Cancellations

Red circular town
Black "PAID"
Black ms. accounting number ("No. 45," "No. 70")

The approximately 6 copies of Nos. 1X1 and 1X1a known on cover or cover front are generally not tied by postmark and some are uncanceled. The value for "on cover" is for a stamp obviously belonging on a cover which bears the proper circular dated town, boxed "5" and straight line "PAID" markings.

No. 1X2 is unique. It is canceled with a black straight line "PAID" marking which is repeated on the cover. The cover also bears a black circular "Alexandria Nov. 25" postmark.

ANNAPOLIS, MD.

Martin F. Revell, Postmaster
ENVELOPE

E1

1846	Printed in upper right corner of envelope
2XU1 E1 5c **carmine red,** *white*	225,000.

No. 2XU1 exists in two sizes of envelope.

Envelopes and letter sheets are known showing the circular design and figure "2" handstamped in blue or red. They were used locally. Value, blue $3,000, red $5,000.

Letter sheets are known showing the circular design and figure "5" handstamped in blue or red. Value, blue $3,500, red $5,000.

Similar circular design in blue without numeral or "PAID" is known to have been used as a postmark.

BALTIMORE, MD.

James Madison Buchanan, Postmaster

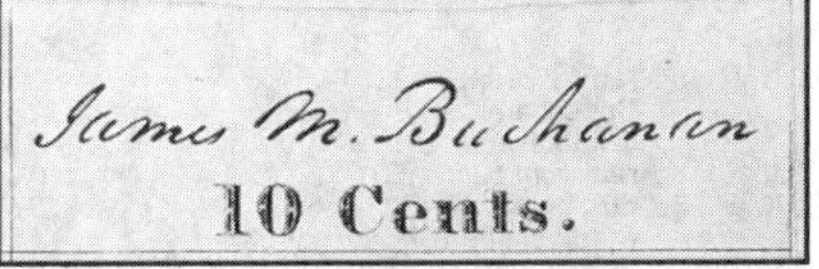

Signature of Postmaster—A1

Printed from a plate of 12 (2x6) containing nine 5c stamps (Pos. 1-6, 8, 10, 12) and three 10c (Pos. 7, 9, 11).

1845	Engr.		Imperf.
3X1 A1 5c **black**			5,250.
On cover			10,500.
Vertical pair on cover			30,000.
3X2 A1 10c **black,** on cover			50,000.
3X3 A1 5c **black,** *bluish*		65,000.	5,250.
On cover			10,500.
3X4 A1 10c **black,** *bluish*			60,000.
On cover			—

Nos. 3X3-3X4 preceded Nos. 3X1-3X2 in use.

No. 3X3 unused is unique. Value is based on 1997 auction sale.

Cancellations

Blue circular town
Blue straight line "PAID"
Blue "5" in oval
Blue "10" in oval
Black pen

Off cover values are for stamps canceled by either pen or handstamp. Stamps on cover tied by handstamps command premiums.

BALTIMORE, MD. Envelopes

E1

Three Separate Handstamps

The "PAID" and "5" in oval were handstamped in blue or red, always both in the same color on the same entire. "James M. Buchanan" was handstamped in black, blue or red. Blue town and rate with black signature was issued first and sells for more.

The paper is manila, buff, white, salmon or grayish. Manila is by far the most frequently found 5c envelope. All 10c envelopes are rare, with manila or buff the more frequent. Of the 10c on salmon, only one example is known.

The general attractiveness of the envelope and the clarity of the handstamps primarily determine the value.

The color listed is that of the "PAID" and "5" in oval.

1845	Various Papers	Handstamped
3XU1 E1 5c **blue**		6,500.
3XU2 E1 5c **red**		9,000.
3XU3 E1 10c **blue**		16,000.
3XU4 E1 10c **red**		19,000.

Earliest documented uses: Apr. 26, 1845 (No. 3XU2); June 12, 1845 (No. 3XU4).

Cancellations

Blue circular town
Blue "5" in oval

The second "5" in oval on the unlisted "5 + 5" envelopes is believed not to be part of the basic prepaid marking, but envelopes bearing this marking merit a premium over the values for Nos. 3XU1-3XU2.

BOSCAWEN, N. H.

Worcester Webster, Postmaster

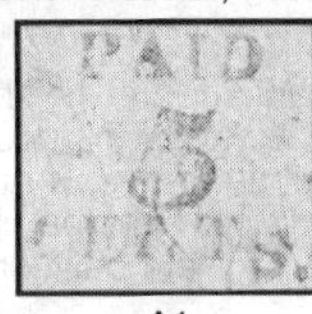

A1

1846 (?) **Typeset** ***Imperf.***

4X1 A1 5c **dull blue,** *yellowish,* on cover		*225,000.*

One copy known, uncanceled on cover with ms. postal markings.

BRATTLEBORO, VT.

Frederick N. Palmer, Postmaster

Initials of Postmaster (FNP)—A1

Printed from plate of 10 (5x2) separately engraved subjects with imprint "Eng'd by Thos. Chubbuck, Bratto." below the middle stamp of the lower row (Pos. 8).

1846 ***Imperf.***

Thick Softwove Paper Colored Through

5X1 A1 5c **black,** *buff*		*10,000.*
On cover		*35,000.*
Two singles on cover		*110,000.*

Earliest documented use: Aug. 28, 1846.

Cancellations

Red straight line "PAID"
Red pen
Blue "5"

The red pen-marks are small and lightly applied. They were used to invalidate a single sample sheet. One copy of each plate position is known so canceled.

LOCKPORT, N.Y.

Hezekiah W. Scovell, Postmaster

A1

"Lockport, N.Y." oval and "PAID" separately handstamped in red, "5" in black ms.

1846 ***Imperf.***

6X1 A1 5c **red,** *buff,* on cover		*225,000.*

Cancellation

Black ms. "X"

One copy of No. 6X1 is known. Small fragments of two other copies adhering to one cover have been found.

MILLBURY, MASS.

Asa H. Waters, Postmaster

George Washington—A1

Printed from a woodcut, singly, on a hand press.

1846 ***Imperf.***

7X1 A1 5c **black,** *bluish*	*130,000.*	*20,000.*
On cover		*90,000.*

Earliest documented use: Aug. 21, 1846.

Cancellations

Red straight line "PAID"
Red circular "MILBURY, MS.," date in center

NEW HAVEN, CONN.

Edward A. Mitchell, Postmaster
ENVELOPES

E1

Impressed from a brass handstamp at upper right of envelope.

Signed in blue, black or magenta ms., as indicated in parenthesis.

1845

8XU1 E1 5c **red** (Bl or M)	*80,000.*
Cut square	*22,500.*
Cut to shape	*9,000.*
8XU2 E1 5c **red,** *light bluish* (Bk)	*110,000.*
8XU3 E1 5c **dull blue,** *buff* (Bl)	*110,000.*
Cut to shape (Bk)	*11,000.*
8XU4 E1 5c **dull blue** (Bl)	*110,000.*

Values of Nos. 8XU1-8XU4 are a guide to value. They are based on auction realizations and take condition into consideration. All New Haven envelopes are of almost equal rarity. An entire of No. 8XU2 is the finest example known. The other envelopes and cut squares are valued according to condition as much as rarity.

REPRINTS

Twenty reprints in dull blue on white paper, signed by E. A. Mitchell in lilac rose ink, were made in 1871 for W. P. Brown and others, value $1,000. Thirty reprints in carmine on hard white paper, signed in dark blue or red, were made in 1874 for Cyrus B. Peets, Chief Clerk for Mitchell, value $750. Unsigned reprints were made for N. F. Seebeck and others about 1872, value $300.

Edward A. Mitchell, grandson of the Postmaster, in 1923 delivered reprints in lilac on soft white wove paper, dated "1923" in place of the signature, value $300.

In 1932, the New Haven Philatelic Society bought the original handstamp and gave it to the New Haven Colony Historical Society. To make the purchase possible (at the $1000 price) it was decided to print 260 stamps from the original handstamp. Of these, 130 were in red and 130 in dull blue, all on hard, white wove paper, value approximately $200 each.

According to Carroll Alton Means' booklet on the New Haven Provisional Envelope, after this last reprinting the brass handstamp was so treated that further reprints cannot be made. The reprints were sold originally at $5 each. A facsimile signature of the postmaster, "E. A. Mitchell," (blue on the red reprints, black on the blue) was applied with a rubber handstamp. These 260 reprints are all numbered to correspond with the number of the booklet issued then.

NEW YORK, N.Y.

Robert H. Morris, Postmaster

George Washington—A1

Printed by Rawdon, Wright & Hatch from a plate of 40 (5x8). The die for Washington's head on the contemporary bank notes was used for the vignette. It had a small flaw—a line extending from the corner of the mouth down the chin—which is quite visible on the paper money. This was corrected for the stamp.

The stamps were usually initialed "ACM" (Alonzo Castle Monson) in magenta ink as a control before being sold or passed through the mails. There are four or five styles of these initials. The most common is "ACM" without periods. The scarcest is "A.C.M.", believed written by Marcena Monson. The rare initials "RHM" (Robert H. Morris, the postmaster) and "MMJ (Marcena Monson) are listed separately.

The stamps were printed on a variety of wove papers varyin in thickness from pelure to thick, and in color from gray to bluis and blue. A thick brown gum was used first, succeeded by a th whitish transparent gum. Some stamps appear to have a slig ribbing or mesh effect. A few also show letters of a double-lin papermaker's watermark, a scarce variety. All used true blu copies carry "ACM" without periods; of the three unused copie two lack initials.

Nos. 9X1-9X3 and varieties unused are valued withou gum. Examples with original gum are extremely scarce an will command higher prices.

Earliest documented use: July 15, 1845 (Nos. 9X1, 9X1e).

1845-46 **Engr.** **Bluish Wove Paper** ***Imper***

9X1 A1 5c **black,** signed ACM, connected, *1846*	1,400.	500
On cover		650
On cover to France or England		*2,250*
On cover to other European countries		*5,500*
Pair	5,500.	1,300
Pair on cover		2,100
Pair on cover to England		*4,500*
Pair on cover to Canada		*5,500*
Strip of 3		*4,500*
Strip of 3 on cover		*9,000*
Strip of 4	*12,000.*	
Strip of 4 on cover		*20,000*
Block of 4		—
Double transfer at bottom (Pos. 2)	1,650.	575
Double transfer at top (Pos. 7)	1,650.	575
Bottom frame line double (Pos. 31)	1,650.	575
Top frame line double (Pos. 36)	1,650.	575

The only blocks currently known are a used block of 4 off cover (faulty) and a block of 9 on cover.

Cancellations

Blue pen	500.
Black pen	+25.
Magenta pen	+100.
Red square grid (New York)	+50.
Red round grid (Boston)	+350.
Blue numeral (Philadelphia)	+750.
Red "U.S" in octagon frame (carrier)	+1,200.
Red "PAID"	+50.
Red N.Y. circular date stamp	+75.
Large red N.Y. circular date stamp containing "5"	+125.

a. Signed ACM, AC connected	1,750.	550.
On cover		725.
On cover to France or England		*2,250.*
On cover to other European countries		*6,000.*
Pair	5,750.	1,550.
Pair, Nos. 9X1, 9X1a	—	3,500.
Pair on cover		*2,100.*
Double transfer at bottom (Pos. 2)	1,800.	675.
Double transfer at top (Pos. 7)	1,800.	675.
Bottom frame line double (Pos. 31)	1,800.	675.
Top frame line double (Pos. 36)	1,800.	675.

Cancellations

Blue pen	550.
Black pen	+25.
Magenta pen	+100.
Red N.Y. circular date stamp	+100.
Large red N.Y. circular date stamp	+150.
Red square grid	+100.
Red "PAID"	+50.

b. Signed A.C.M.	*3,750.*	*700.*
On cover		*850.*
On cover to France or England		*2,750.*
On cover to other European countries		*6,000.*
Pair		*2,400.*
Pair on cover		*3,250.*
Double transfer at bottom (Pos. 2)	—	*950.*
Double transfer at top (Pos. 7)	—	*950.*
Bottom frame line double (Pos. 31)		*950.*
Top frame line double (Pos. 36)		*950.*

Cancellations

Blue pen	*700.*
Black pen	+25.
Red square grid	+100.
Red N.Y. circular date stamp	+100.
Large red N.Y. circular date stamp containing "5"	+150.
Red "PAID"	+50.

c. Signed MMJr		*9,000.*
On cover		—
Pair on cover front		*26,500.*
d. Signed RHM	*13,000.*	*3,250.*
Pair		*12,000.*
On cover		*5,000.*
On cover from New Hamburgh, N.Y.		*10,000.*

Cancellations

Blue pen		*3,250.*
Black pen		+150.
Red square grid		+250.
Red N.Y. circular date stamp		+400.
Red "PAID"		+300.

Earliest documented use: July 17, 1845.

e. Without signature	3,250.	750.
On cover		1,250.
On cover to France or England		*2,250.*
On cover to other European countries		*6,000.*
On cover, July 15, 1845		*30,000.*
Pair		*2,400.*
Pair on cover		*2,600.*
Double transfer at bottom (Pos. 2)	3,500.	850.
Double transfer at top (Pos. 7)	3,500.	850.
Bottom frame line double (Pos. 31)	3,500.	850.
Top frame line double (Pos. 36)	3,500.	850.
Ribbed paper	—	—

Cancellations

Blue pen	750.
Black pen	+25.
Red square grid	+100.
Red N.Y. circular date stamp	+100.
Large red N.Y. circular date stamp containing "5"	+150.
Red "PAID"	+100.

Known used from Albany, Boston, Jersey City, N.J., New Hamburgh, N.Y., Philadelphia, Sing Sing, N.Y., Washington, D.C., and Hamilton, Canada, as well as by route agents on the Baltimore R.R. Covers originating in New Hamburgh are known only with No. 9X1d (one also bearing the U.S. City Despatch Post carrier); one also known used to Holland.

1847 Engr. Blue Wove Paper *Imperf.*

9X2 A1 5c **black,** signed ACM connected	*6,500.*	3,500.
On cover		*5,750.*
Pair		*13,000.*
Pair on cover		—
Double transfer at bottom (Pos. 2)		4,000.
Double transfer at top (Pos. 7)		4,000.
Bottom frame line double (Pos. 31)		4,000.
Top frame line double (Pos. 36)		4,000.
a. Signed RHM		—
d. Without signature	*11,000.*	*7,250.*

Earliest documented use: Mar. 4, 1847.

Cancellations

Red square grid	3,500.
Red "PAID"	+100.
Red N.Y. circular date stamp	+650.

On the only example known of No. 9X2a the 'R' is illegible and does not match those of the other 'RHM' signatures.

1847 Engr. Gray Wove Paper *Imperf.*

9X3 A1 5c **black,** signed ACM connected	5,250.	2,100.
On cover		*5,250.*
On cover to Europe		*8,500.*
Pair		*7,750.*
Pair on cover		*8,750.*
Double transfer at bottom (Pos. 2)		2,500.
Double transfer at top (Pos. 7)		2,500.
Bottom frame line double (Pos. 31)		2,500.
Top frame line double (Pos. 36)		2,500.
a. Signed RHM		*7,000.*
b. Without signature		*7,000.*

Earliest documented use: Feb. 8, 1847.

Cancellations

Red square grid	2,100.
Red N.Y. circular date stamp	2,100.
Red "PAID"	+100.

All used copies of No. 9X3a have red square grid or red "PAID" in arc cancel.

The first plate was of nine subjects (3x3). Each subject differs slightly from the others, with Position 8 showing the white stock shaded by crossed diagonal lines. At some point prints were struck from this plate in black on deep blue and white bond paper, as well as in blue, green, scarlet and brown on white bond paper. These are listed in the Proof and Trial Color Proof sections. Stamps from this plate were not issued.

ENVELOPES

Postmaster Morris, according to newspaper reports of July 2 and 7, 1845, issued envelopes. The design was not stated and no example has been seen.

PROVIDENCE, R. I.

Welcome B. Sayles, Postmaster

A1

A2

Engraved on copper plate containing 12 stamps (3x4). Upper right corner stamp (Pos. 3) "TEN"; all others "FIVE." The stamps were engraved directly on the plate, each differing from the other. The "TEN" and Pos. 4, 5, 6, 9, 11 and 12 have no period after "CENTS."

Yellowish White Handmade Paper

Earliest documented use: Aug. 25, 1846 (No. 10X1).

1846, Aug. 24 *Imperf.*

10X1 A1 5c **gray black**	350.	*1,750.*
On cover, tied by postmark		*20,000.*
On cover, pen canceled		*4,500.*
Two on cover		—
Pair	725.	
Block of four	1,450.	
10X2 A2 10c **gray black**	1,100.	*15,000.*
On cover, pen canceled		*35,000.*
a. Se-tenant with 5c	*1,650.*	
Complete sheet	*5,250.*	

Cancellations

Black pen check mark
Red circular town
Red straight line "PAID" (2 types)
Red "5"

All canceled copies of Nos. 10X1-10X2, whether or not bearing an additional handstamped cancellation, are obliterated with a black pen check mark. There is only one known certified used example off cover of No. 10X2, and it has a minor fault. Value represents a 1997 sale. All genuine covers must bear the red straight line "PAID," the red circular town postmark, and the red numeral "5" or "10" rating mark.

Reprints were made in 1898. In general, each stamp bears one of the following letters on the back: B. O. G. E. R. T. D. U. R. B. I. N. However, some reprint sheets received no such printing on the reverse. All reprints are without gum. Value for 5c, $50; for 10c, $125; for sheet, $725. Reprints without the printing on the reverse sell for more.

ST. LOUIS, MO.

John M. Wimer, Postmaster

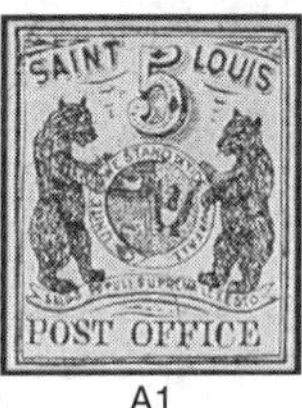

A1

A2

A3

Missouri Coat of Arms

Printed from a copper plate of 6 (2x3) subjects separately engraved by J. M. Kershaw.

The plate in its first state, referred to as Plate 1, comprised: three 5c stamps in the left vertical row and three 10c in the right vertical row. The stamps vary slightly in size, measuring from 17¾ to 18¼ by 22 to 22½mm.

Later a 20c denomination was believed necessary. So two of the 5c stamps, types I (pos. 1) and II (pos. 3) were changed to 20c by placing the plate face down on a hard surface and hammering on the back of the parts to be altered until the face was driven flush at those points. The new numerals were then engraved. Both 20c stamps show broken frame lines and the paw of the right bear on type II is missing. The 20c type II (pos. 3) also shows retouching in the dashes under "SAINT" and "LOUIS." The characteristics of types I and II of the 5c also serve to distinguish the two types of the 20c. This altered, second state of the plate is referred to as Plate 2. It is the only state to contain the 20c.

The demand for the 20c apparently proved inadequate, and the plate was altered again. The "20" was erased and "5" engraved in its place, resulting in noticeable differences from the 5c stamps from Plate 1. In type I (pos. 1) reengraved, the "5" is twice as far from the top frame line as in the original state, and the four dashes under "SAINT" and "LOUIS" have disappeared except for about half of the upper dash under each word. In type II (pos. 3) reengraved, the ornament in the flag of the "5" is a diamond instead of a triangle; the diamond in the bow is much longer than in the first state, and the ball of the "5," originally blank, contains a large dot. At right of the shading of the "5" is a short curved line which is evidently a remnant of the "0" of "20." Type III (pos. 5) of the 5c was slightly retouched. This second alteration of the plate is referred to as Plate 3.

Type characteristics common to Plates 1, 2 and 3:

5 Cent. Type I (pos. 1). Haunches of both bears almost touch frame lines.

Type II (pos. 3). Bear at right almost touches frame line, but left bear is about ¼mm from it.

Type III (pos. 5). Haunches of both bears about ½mm from frame lines. Small spur on "S" of "POST."

10 Cent. Type I (pos. 2). Three dashes below "POST OFFICE."

Type II (pos. 4). Three pairs of dashes.

Type III (pos. 6). Pairs of dashes (with rows of dots between) at left and right. Dash in center with row of dots above it.

20 Cent. Type I. See 5c Type I.

Type II. See 5c Type II.

Nos. 11X1-11X8 unused are valued without gum.

Wove Paper Colored Through

1845, Nov.-1846 *Imperf.*

11X1 A1 5c **black,** *greenish*	*7,000.*	*4,750.*
On cover		*10,500.*
Pair		*10,000.*
Two on cover		*11,500.*
Strip of 3 on cover		*17,000.*
11X2 A2 10c **black,** *greenish*	*7,000.*	*4,250.*
On cover		*8,000.*
Pair		*9,500.*
Pair on cover		*12,500.*
Strip of 3 on cover		*16,000.*
On cover, #11X2, 11X6		*50,000.*
11X3 A3 20c **black,** *greenish*		*30,000.*
On cover		—
On cover, #11X5, two #11X3		*150,000.*

Printed from Plate 1 (3 varieties each of the 5c and 10c) and Plate 2 (1 variety of the 5c, 3 of the 10c, 2 of the 20c).

1846

11X4 A1 5c **black,** *gray lilac*	—	*5,750.*
On cover		*8,250.*
11X5 A2 10c **black,** *gray lilac*	*5,500.*	*3,250.*
On cover		*6,000.*
Pair		*8,250.*
Pair, 10c (III), 5c		*22,000.*
Strip of 3		*14,500.*
Strip of 3 on cover		*32,500.*
Pair 10c (II), 10c (III) se-tenant with 5c		*25,000.*
Strip of 3 10c (I, II, III) se-tenant with 5c		*165,000.*
11X6 A3 20c **black,** *gray lilac*		*25,000.*
On cover		*35,000.*
Pair on cover		*60,000.*
On cover, #11X6 and #11X5		*42,500.*
Pair, #11X6 and #11X5		*42,500.*
Pair, #11X6 and #11X5, on cover		*100,000.*
Strip of 3, 2#11X6 and #11X5		*70,000.*

Printed from Plate 2 (1 variety of the 5c, 3 of the 10c, 2 of the 20c).

1846 Pelure Paper

11X7 A1 5c **black,** *bluish*	—	*6,500.*
On cover		*8,000.*
Two on cover		*22,500.*
11X8 A2 10c **black,** *bluish*		*6,500.*
On cover		*10,000.*
a. Impression of 5c on back		—

Printed from Plate 3 (3 varieties each of the 5c, 10c).
Earliest documented use: Nov. 25, 1846 (#11X8).

Cancellations, Nos. 11X1-11X8

Black pen
Ms. initials of postmaster (#11X2, type I)
Red circular town
Red straight line "PAID"
Red grid (#11X7)

Values of Nos. 11X7-11X8, on and off cover, reflect the usual poor condition of these stamps, which were printed on fragile pelure paper. Attractive copies with minor defects sell for considerably more.

Values for used off-cover stamps are for pen-canceled copies. Handstamp canceled copies sell for much more. Values for stamps on cover are pen cancels. Covers with the stamps tied by handstamp sell at considerable premiums depending upon the condition of the stamps and the general attractiveness of the cover. In general, covers with multiple frankings (unless separately valued) are valued at the "on cover" value of the highest item, plus the "off cover" value of the other stamps.

For Tuscumbia, Alabama, formerly listed as United States postmasters' provisional No. 12XU1, see the "3c 1861 Postmasters' Provisionals" section before the Confederate States of America Postmasters' Provisionals.

POSTAGE

GENERAL ISSUES

Please Note:
Stamps are valued in the grade of very fine unless otherwise indicated.
Values for early and valuable stamps are for examples with certificates of authenticity from acknowledged expert committees, or examples sold with the buyer having the right of certification. This applies to examples with original gum as well as examples without gum. Beware of stamps offered "as is," as the gum on some unused stamps offered with "original gum" may be fraudulent, and stamps offered as unused without gum may in some cases be altered or faintly canceled used stamps.

Issues from 1847 through 1894 are unwatermarked.

Benjamin Franklin — A1

Double transfer of top frame line — (A) position 80R1

Double transfer of top and bottom frame lines — (B) position 90R1

Double transfer of bottom frame line and lower part of left frame line — (C)

Double transfer of top, bottom and left frame lines, also numerals — (D)

Double transfer of "U," "POST OFFICE" and left numeral — (E)

Double transfer of top frame line, upper part of side frame lines, "U," and "POST OFFICE" — (F)

This issue was authorized by an Act of Congress, approved March 3, 1847, to take effect July 1, 1847, from which date the use of Postmasters' Stamps or any which were not authorized by the Postmaster General became illegal.
This issue was declared invalid as of July 1, 1851.

Produced by Rawdon, Wright, Hatch & Edson.
Plates of 200 subjects in two panes of 100 each.

1847, July 1 **Engr.** ***Imperf.***

Thin Bluish Wove Paper

No.	Design	Description	Unused	Used
1	A1	5c **red brown**	6,250.	550.
		pale brown	6,250.	550.
		brown	6,250.	550.
		No gum	2,500.	
		On cover		650.
		On cover to England or France		*2,750.*
		On cover to other European countries		3,250.
		Pair	15,000.	1,150.
		Pair on cover		1,300.
		Strip of 3	*24,000.*	2,350.
		Block of 4	*40,000.*	*27,500.*
		Block of 4 on cover		*80,000.*
		Dot in "S" in upper right corner	6,500.	600.
		Cracked plate (69R1)		—
a.		5c **dark brown**	7,250.	625.
		No gum	3,000.	
		grayish brown	7,500.	675.
		blackish brown	7,750.	725.
		No gum	3,250.	
		Pair	*18,500.*	1,400.
b.		5c **orange brown**	8,000.	850.
		No gum	3,500.	
		Block of 4 on cover		—
		brown orange	—	1,500.
		No gum	*4,500.*	
c.		5c **red orange**	*17,500.*	*5,500.*
		No gum	*7,500.*	
d.		Double impression		—
(A)		Double transfer of top frame line (80R1)		700.
(B)		Double transfer of top and bottom frame lines (90R1)	—	700.
(C)		Double transfer of bottom frame line and lower part of left frame line		3,000.
(D)		Double transfer of top, bottom and left frame lines, also numerals		3,000.
(E)		Double transfer of "U," "POST OFFICE" and left numeral		1,500.
(F)		Double transfer of top frame line, upper part of side frame lines, "U," and "POST OFFICE"		—

The only known double impression shows part of the design doubled.

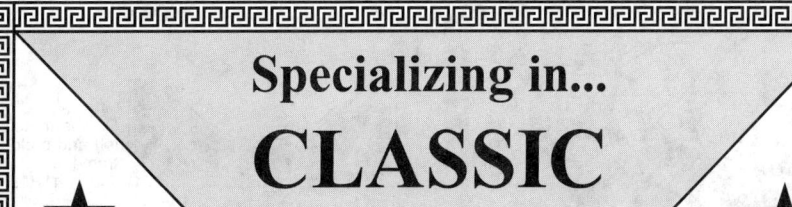

Some students believe that the "E double transfer" actually shows plate scratches instead.

Earliest documented use: July 7, 1847.

Cancellations

Red	550.
Red town	+200.
Orange red	+15.
Orange red town	+220.
Blue	+35.
Blue town	+125.
Black	+100.
Black town	+400.
Magenta	+250.
Orange	+750.
Ultramarine	+1,000.
Violet	+450.
Violet town	—
Green	+1,250.
"Paid"	+50.
"Paid" in grid (demonetized usage)	+300.
"Free"	+400.
Railroad	+200.
U. S. Express Mail (on the cover)	+100.
U. S. Express Mail (on stamp)	—
U. S. Express Mail in black (on stamp) (demonetized usage)	+12,500.
"Way"	+250.
"Way" with numeral	+500.
"Steamboat"	+350.
"Steam"	+200.
"Steamship"	+300.
Philadelphia RR	—
Hotel (on the cover)	*+2,000.*
Numeral	+100.
Canada	+3,000.
Wheeling, Va., grid	+6,000.
Pen	275.

George Washington — A2

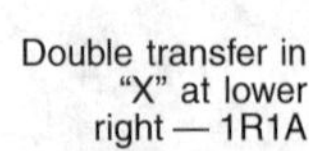

Double transfer in "X" at lower right — 1R1A

Double transfer in "Post Office" — 31R1B

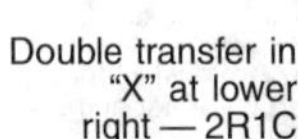

Double transfer in "X" at lower right — 2R1C

Double transfer of left and bottom frame line — 41R1D

2	A2	10c	**black**	*27,500.*	1,350.
			gray black	*27,500.*	1,350.
			No gum	*12,500.*	
			greenish black	—	1,700.
			On cover		1,750.
			On cover to Canada		2,000.
			On cover to Great Britain		3,250.
			On cover to France		*5,250.*
			On cover with 5c No. 1		*30,000.*
			Pair	*65,000.*	*3,250.*
			Pair on cover		*3,750.*
			Strip of 3	*95,000.*	*11,000.*
			Block of 4	*135,000.*	*75,000.*
			Short transfer at top	*29,000.*	1,450.
			Vertical line through second "F" of "OFFICE" (68R1)	—	1,900.
			With "Stick Pin" in tie (52L1)	—	1,900.
			With "harelip" (57L1)	—	1,900.
a.			Diagonal half used as 5c on cover		*13,000.*
b.			Vertical half used as 5c on cover		*35,000.*
c.			Horizontal half used as 5c on cover		—
(A)			Double transfer in "X" at lower right (1R1)	—	2,000.
(B)			Double transfer in "Post Office" (31R1)	—	2,500.
(C)			Double transfer in "X" at lower right (2R1)	—	2,000.
(D)			Double transfer of left and bottom frame line (41R1)	—	2,000.

Earliest documented use: July 2, 1847.

Two examples of the unused block are recorded. Value represents 1998 auction sale price of the only example available to collectors.

The value for the used block of 4 represents a block with manuscript cancel. One block is recorded with a handstamp cancellation and it is worth significantly more.

Cancellations

Red	1,400.
Orange red	+25.
Blue	+50.
Orange	+500.
Black	+350.
Magenta	+650
Violet	+850
Green	+2,000
Ultramarine	+900
"Paid"	+100
"Free"	+800
Railroad	+1,000
Philadelphia RR straightline	+500
U.S. Express Mail (on the cover)	+500
"Way"	+550
Numeral	+250
"Steam"	+350
"Steamship"	+400
"Steamboat"	+650
"Steamer 10"	+1,000
Canada	+3,000
Panama	—
Wheeling, Va., grid	+5,500.
Pen	750.

A3

A4

REPRODUCTIONS of 1847 ISSUE

Actually, official imitations made from new plates of 50 subjects made by the Bureau of Engraving and Printing by order of the Post Office Department. These were not valid for postal use.

Reproductions. The letters R. W. H. & E. at the bottom of each stamp are less distinct on the reproductions than on the originals.

5c. On the originals the left side of the white shirt frill touches the oval on a level with the top of the "F" of "Five." On the reproductions it touches the oval about on a level with the top of the figure "5." On the originals, the bottom of the right leg of the "N" in "CENTS" is blunt. On the reproductions, the "N" comes to a point at the bottom.

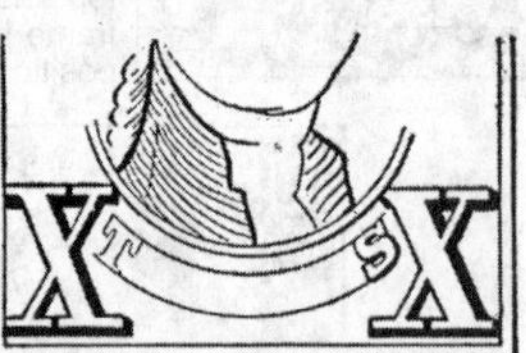

10c. On the originals line of coat (A) points to "T" of TEN and (B) it points between "T" and "S" of "CENTS."

On the reproductions line of coat (A) points to right tip of "X" and line of coat (B) points to center of "S."

The bottom of the right leg of the "N" of "CENTS" shows the same difference as on the 5c originals and reproductions.

On the reproductions the eyes have a sleepy look, the line of the mouth is straighter, and in the curl of the hair near the left cheek is a strong black dot, while the originals have only a faint one.

(See Nos. 948a and 948b for 1947 reproductions — 5c blue and 10c brown orange in larger size.)

1875 Bluish paper, without gum ***Imperf.***

3	A3	5c	**red brown** *(4779)*	725.
			brown	725.
			dark brown	725.
			Pair	1,600.
			Block of 4	*5,000.*
4	A4	10c	**black** *(3883)*	900.

gray black	900.
Pair	1,900.
Block of 4	*6,250.*

Numbers in parentheses are quantities sold.

Produced by Toppan, Carpenter, Casilear & Co.

Stamps of the 1847, 1851-57 series were printed from plates consisting of 200 subjects and the sheets were divided into panes of 100 each. In order that each stamp in the sheet could be identified easily in regard to its relative position it was devised that the stamps in each pane be numbered from one to one hundred, starting with the top horizontal row and numbering consecutively from left to right. Thus the first stamp at the upper left corner would be No. 1 and the last stamp at the bottom right corner, would be No. 100. The left and right panes are indicated by the letters "L" or "R." The number of the plate is last. As an example, the best-known of the scarce type III, 1c 1851 being the 99th stamp in the right pane of Plate No. 2 is listed as (99R2),*i.e.* 99th stamp, right pane, Plate No. 2.

One plate of the one cent and several plates of the three cents were reentered after they had been in use. The original state of the plate is called "Early" and the reentered state is termed "Late." If the plate was reentered twice, the inbetween state is called "Intermediate." Identification of "Early," "Intermediate" or "Late" state is explained by the addition of the letters "E," "I" or "L" after the plate numbers. The sixth stamp of the right pane of Plate No. 1 from the "Early" state would be 6R1E. The same plate position from the "Late" state would be 6R1L.

One plate of the three cents never had a plate number and is referred to by specialists as "Plate O."

The position of the stamp in the sheet is placed within parentheses, for example: (99R2).

The different values of this issue were intended primarily for the payment of specific rates, though any value might be used in making up a rate. The 1c stamp was to pay the postage on newspapers, drop letters and circulars, and the one cent carrier fee in some cities from 1856. The 3c stamp represented the rate on ordinary letters and two of them made up the rate for distances over 3000 miles prior to Apr. 1, 1855. The 5c stamp was originally for the registration fee but the fee was usually paid in cash. Occasionally two of them were used to pay the rate over 3000 miles, after it was changed in April, 1855. Singles paid the "Shore to ship" rate to certain foreign countries and, from 1857, triples paid the fifteen-cent rate to France. Ten cents was the rate to California and points distant more than 3000 miles. The 12c stamp was for quadruple the ordinary rate. Twenty-four cents represented the single letter rate to Great Britain. Thirty cents was the rate to Germany. The 90c stamp was apparently intended to facilitate the payment of large amounts of postage.

Act of Congress, March 3, 1851. "From and after June 30, 1851, there shall be charged the following rates: Every single letter not exceeding 3000 miles, prepaid postage, 3 cents; not prepaid, 5 cents; for any greater distance, double these rates. Every single letter or paper conveyed wholly or in part by sea, and to or from a foreign country over 2500 miles, 20 cents; under 2500 miles, 10 cents. Drop or local letters, 1 cent each. Letters uncalled for and advertised, to be charged 1 cent in addition to the regular postage."

Act of Congress, March 3, 1855. "For every single letter, in manuscript or paper of any kind, in writing, marks or signs, conveyed in the mail between places in the United States not exceeding 3000 miles, 3 cents; and for any greater distance, 10 cents. Drop or local letters, 1 cent."

The Act of March 3, 1855, made the prepayment of postage on domestic letters compulsory April 1, 1855, and prepayment of postage on domestic letters compulsory by stamps effective Jan. 1, 1856.

The Act authorized the Postmaster to establish a system for the registration of valuable letters, and to require prepayment of postage on such letters as well as registration fee of 5 cents. Stamps to prepay the registry fee were not required until June 1, 1867.

In Nos. 5-17 the 1c, 3c and 12c have very small margins between the stamps. The 5c and 10c have moderate size margins. The values of these stamps take the margin size into consideration.

Franklin — A5

ONE CENT. Issued July 1, 1851.

Type I. Has complete curved lines outside the labels with "U. S. Postage" and "One Cent." The scrolls below the lower label are turned under, forming little balls. The ornaments at top are substantially complete.

Type Ib. As I, but balls below bottom label are not so clear. Plume-like scrolls at bottom are incomplete.

1851-57 ***Imperf.***

No.	Type	Value	Description	Unused	Used
5	A5	1c	**blue,** type I (7R1E)	200,000.	*45,000.*
			Pair, types I, Ib		*70,000.*
			On cover		*55,000.*
			On cover, pair, one stamp type I		—
			On cover, strip of 3, one stamp type I		*80,000.*

Earliest documented use: July 5, 1851.

Cancellations

Blue	+500.
Blue town	—
Red grid	+2,000.
Red town	—
Red "Paid"	—

Values for No. 5 are for copies with margins touching or cutting slightly into the design, or for copies with four margins and minor faults. Very few sound copies with the design untouched exist, and these sell for much more than the values shown.

Value for No. 5 unused is for copy with no gum.

No.	Type	Value	Description	Unused	Used
5A	A5	1c	**blue,** type Ib, *July 1, 1851* (Less distinct examples 3-5, 9R1E)	*17,500.*	*7,000.*
			No gum	*8,500.*	
			Pair	*37,500.*	*15,000.*
			On cover		*7,500.*
			blue, type Ib (Best examples 6, 8R1E)	*22,500.*	*10,500.*
			No gum	*10,500.*	
			On cover		*11,500.*
			Pair, type Ib, II		*11,000*
			Block of 4, pair type Ib, pair type IIIa (8-9, 18-19R1E)		—

Earliest documented use: July 1, 1851 (FDC).

Cancellations

Blue town	+200.
Red town	—
Red Carrier	—
Red "Paid"	+450.
Pen (3, 4, 5 or 9R1E)	*3,500.*
Pen (6 or 8R1E)	*6,500.*

A6

Type Ia. Same as I at bottom but top ornaments and outer line at top are partly cut away. Type Ia comes only from the bottom row of both panes of Plate 4. All type Ia stamps have the flaw below "U" of "U.S.," but this flaw also appears on some stamps of types Ic, III and IIIa of Plate 4.

Type Ic. Same as Ia, but bottom right plume and ball ornament incomplete. Bottom left plume complete or nearly complete. Best examples are from bottom row, "F" relief, positions 91 and 96R4. Less distinct examples are "E" reliefs from 5th and 9th rows, positions 47L, 49L, 83L, 49R, 81R, 82R, and 89R, Plate 4, and early impressions of 41R4.

No.	Type	Value	Description	Unused	Used
6	A6	1c	**blue,** type Ia, *1857*	*37,500.*	*10,000.*
			No gum	*19,000.*	
			On cover		*14,000.*
			Pair	—	*22,500.*
			Strip of 3 on cover		*72,500.*
			Horizontal pair, types Ia, Ic		*22,500.*
			Horizontal strip of 3, types Ia, Ic, Ia		*30,000.*
			Vertical pair, types Ia, III	*55,000.*	*14,500.*
			Vertical pair, types Ia, IIIa	*44,000.*	*13,500.*
			Block of 4, types Ia, IIIa	*90,000.*	
			"Curl on shoulder" (97L4)	*40,000.*	*11,000.*
			"Curl in C" (97R4)	*40,000.*	*11,000.*

The horizontal strip of 3 represents positions 95-97R4, position 96R4 being type 1c.

Earliest documented use: Apr. 19, 1857.

Cancellations

Blue	+100.00
Black Carrier	+350.00
Red Carrier	+350.00
Pen	*5,000.*

No.	Type	Value	Description	Unused	Used
6b	A6	1c	**blue,** type Ic ("E" relief, less distinct examples)	*6,500.*	*2,000.*
			No gum	*2,800.*	
			On cover		*3,000.*
			Horizontal pair (81-82R4)		—
			Pair, types Ic, III		—
			Pair, types Ic, IIIa		—
			blue, type Ic ("F" relief, best examples, 91, 96R4)	*21,000.*	*7,000.*
			No gum	*12,500.*	
			On cover		*7,500.*
			Vertical pair (81-91R4)		—

Earliest documented use: May 20, 1857 (dated cancel on off-cover stamp); June 6, 1857 (on cover).

Cancellations

Blue ("E" relief)	—
Red ("E" relief)	—
Blue town ("F" relief)	—
Red("F" relief)	—
Pen ("E" relief)	*1,000.*
Pen ("F" relief)	*3,500.*

A7

Type II - Same as Type I at top, but the little balls of the bottom scrolls and the bottoms of the lower plume ornaments are missing. The side ornaments are substantially complete.

No.	Type	Value	Description	Unused	Used
7	A7	1c	**blue,** type II, (Plates 1E, 2); *July 1, 1851* (Plate 1E)	1,200.	160.00
			No gum	500.00	
			On cover		190.00
			Pair	2,750.	350.00
			Strip of 3	4,100.	550.00
			Block of 4 (Plate 1E)	—	—
			Block of 4 (Plate 2)	*5,500.*	1,100.
			P# block of 8, Impt. (Plate 2)	*36,000.*	
			Design complete at top (10R1E only)	—	*2,000.*
			Pair, types II, IIIa (Plate 1E)	6,150.	1,250.
			Block of 4, type II and types III, IIIa		—

Double transfer (Plate 1E or 2)	1,250.	170.00
Double transfer (89R2)	1,300.	210.00
Double transfer, one inverted (71L1E)	1,600.	375.00
Triple transfer, one inverted (91L1E)	1,600.	400.00
Cracked Plate (2L, 12L, 13L, 23L and 33L, Plate 2)	1,450.	375.00
Plate 1L (4R1L only, double transfer), *June 1852*	2,000.	360.00
Pair, types II (4R1L), IV	*3,900.*	*650.00*
Plate 3, *May, 1856*	—	400.00
On cover		625.00
Pair	—	900.00
Block of 4	—	—
Double transfer		450.00
Plate 4, *April, 1857*	*3,500.*	*1,100.*
On cover		*1,350.*
Pair	—	*2,300.*
Pair (vert.), types II, IIIa	—	—
"Curl in hair" (3R, 4R4)	—	*1,200.*
Double transfer (10R4)	—	—
Perf. 12½, unofficial	*20,000.*	*7,500.*
On cover		—

In addition to the cracked plates listed above (Plate 2) there exist a number of surface cracks coming from the rare Plate 3. These are valued at approximately $600 used.

See note concerning unofficial perfs following listings for No. 11.

Earliest documented uses: July 1, 1851 (Plate 1E) (FDC); Dec. 5, 1855 (Plate 2); May 6, 1856 (Plate 3).

Cancellations

Blue	+7.50
Red	+20.00
Magenta	+40.00
Ultramarine	+50.00
Green	+350.00
Orange	—
1855 year date	+10.00
1856 year date	+5.00
1857 year date	+2.50
1858 year date	—
"Paid"	+5.00
"Way"	+35.00
Red "Too Late"	+200.00
Numeral	+15.00
Railroad	+50.00
"Steam"	+50.00
"Steamboat"	+70.00
Red Carrier	+35.00
Black Carrier	+25.00
U. S. Express Mail	+25.00
Printed precancel "PAID"	+750.00
Pen	80.00

A8

Type III - The top and bottom curved lines outside the labels are broken in the middle. The side ornaments are substantially complete.

The most desirable examples of type III are those showing the widest breaks in the top and bottom framelines.

A special example is 99R2. All other stamps come from plate 4 and almost all show the breaks in the lines less clearly defined. Some of these breaks, especially of the bottom line, are very small.

Type IIIa - Similar to III with the outer line broken at top or, rarely, at bottom but not both. The side ornaments are substantially complete.

8 A8 1c **blue,** type III (Plate 4) see below for 99R2	*15,000.*	3,250.
No gum	*6,000.*	
On cover		3,500.
Pair	*32,500.*	6,250.
Pair, types III, IIIa	*22,500.*	*4,900.*
Strip of 3		*10,500.*
Block of 4, types III, IIIa	—	—

Earliest documented use: Sept. 21, 1857 (on off-cover stamp).

Cancellations

Blue	+60.00
Red	+150.00
Red Carrier	+200.00
Black Carrier	+250.00
Pen	1,625.

Values for type III are for at least a 2mm break in each outer line. Examples of type III with wider breaks in outer lines command higher prices; those with smaller breaks sell for much less.

(8) A8 1c **blue,** type III (99R2)	*18,000.*	*5,500.*
No gum	*8,500.*	
Pair, types III (99R2), II	—	*6,500.*
Pair, types III (99R2), IIIa	*26,000.*	—
Block of 4, type III (99R2), 3 type II	*33,500.*	
On cover (99R2)		*11,000.*

Cancellations

Blue	+100.00
Green	—
"Paid"	—
Red Carrier	+300.00

8A A8 1c **blue,** type IIIa (Plate 1E) *July 1, 1851*	4,750.	1,050.
No gum	2,100.	
On cover		1,150.
Pair	*10,000.*	2,600.
Double transfer, one inverted (81L1E)	*5,250.*	1,300.
Plate 1E (100R)	—	—
Plate 2 (100R)	—	—
Plate 4, *April, 1857*	*5,000.*	1,100.
No gum	2,250.	
On cover		1,250.
Pair	*11,000.*	2,250.
Block of 4	—	*9,000.*

Earliest documented uses: July 3, 1851 (Plate 1E); Apr. 4, 1857 (Plate 4).

Cancellations

Blue	+50.00
Red	+100.00
"Paid"	+90.00
Black Carrier	+160.00
Red Carrier	+150.00
Pen	500.00

Values are for stamps with at least a 2mm break in the top outer line. Examples with a wider break or a break in the lower line command higher prices, those with a smaller break sell for less.

"Paid" Cancellations

Values for "Paid" cancellations are for those OTHER than the common Boston type. See Postal Markings in the Introduction for illustrations.

A9

Type IV. Similar to II, but with the curved lines outside the labels recut at top or bottom or both.

9 A9 1c **blue,** type IV, *1852*	750.00	125.00
No gum	290.00	
On cover		150.00
Pair	1,600.	260.00
Strip of 3	2,500.	425.00
Block of 4	3,500.	*2,000.*
P# block of 8, Impt. (Plate 1)	—	
Double transfer	825.00	130.00
Triple transfer, one inverted (71L1L, 81L1L and 91L1L)	900.00	175.00
Cracked plate	900.00	175.00
Bottom frameline broken (89R1L)	—	275.00
Perf. 12½, unofficial		*12,500.*
Strip of 3		—
a. Printed on both sides, reverse inverted		—

See note concerning unofficial perfs following listings for No. 11.

VARIETIES OF RECUTTING

Stamps of this type were printed from Plate 1 after it had been reentered and recut in 1852. All but one stamp (4R, see No. 7 for listings) were recut and all varieties of recutting are listed below:

Recut once at top and once at bottom, (113 on plate)	750.00	125.00
Recut once at top, (40 on plate)	775.00	130.00
Recut once at top and twice at bottom, (21 on plate)	800.00	135.00
Recut twice at bottom, (11 on plate)	825.00	145.00
Recut once at bottom, (8 on plate)	850.00	155.00
Recut once at bottom and twice at top, (4 on plate)	875.00	165.00
Recut twice at bottom and twice at top, (2 on plate)	900.00	220.00

Earliest documented use: June 5, 1852.

Cancellations

Blue	+5.00
Red	+30.00
Ultramarine	+90.00
Brown	+150.00
Green	+350.00
Violet	+300.00
1853 year date	+250.00
1855 year date	+10.00
1856 year date	+7.50
1857 year date	+10.00
"Paid"	+10.00
"U. S. PAID"	+50.00
"Way"	+50.00
"Free"	+75.00
Railroad	+75.00
"Steam"	+60.0
Numeral	+10.0
"Steamboat"	+90.0
"Steamship"	+60.0
Red Carrier	+15.0
Black Carrier	+25.0
U. S. Express Mail	+60.0
Express Company	–
Packet boat	–
Printed precancel "PAID"	+2,50
Printed precancel "paid"	+2,50
Pen	62.5

These 1c stamps were often cut apart carelessly, destroying part or all of the top and bottom lines. This makes it difficult to determine whether a stamp is type II or IV without identifying the position. Such mutilated examples sell for much less.

PLEASE NOTE:

Stamps are valued in the grade of very fine unless otherwise indicated.

Values for early and valuable stamps are for examples with certificates of authenticity from acknowledged expert committees, or examples sold with the buyer having the right of certification. This applies to examples with original gum as well as examples without gum. Beware of stamps offered "as is," as the gum on some unused stamps offered with "original gum" may be fraudulent, and stamps offered as unused without gum may in some cases be altered or faintly canceled used stamps.

VALUES FOR NEVER-HINGED STAMPS PRIOR TO SCOTT No. 205

This catalogue does not value pre-1882 stamps in never-hinged condition. Premiums for never-hinged condition in the classic era invariably are even larger than those premiums listed for the post-1890 issues. Generally speaking, the earlier the stamp is listed in the catalogue, the larger will be the never-hinged premium. On some early classics, the premium will be several multiples of the unused, hinged values given in the catalogue.

Washington — A10

THREE CENTS. Issued July 1, 1851 (Plate 1E).

Type I - There is an outer frame line on all four sides.

10 A10 3c **orange brown,** type I	3,250.	110.00
No gum	1,400.	
deep orange brown	3,500.	150.00
No gum	1,500.	
copper brown	3,750.	260.00
No gum	1,600.	
On cover, orange brown		180.00
Pair	7,000.	425.00
Pair on cover		450.00
Strip of 3	*11,500.*	1,050.
Block of 4	*16,500.*	—
Double transfer		135.00
Triple transfer		375.00
Gash on shoulder		120.00
Dot in lower right diamond block (69L5E)		190.00
On part-India paper		*1,000.*
a. Printed on both sides		*12,000.*

Only one example of No. 10a is recorded.

VARIETIES OF RECUTTING

All of these stamps were recut at least to the extent of four outer frame lines and usually much more. Some of the most prominent varieties are listed below (others are described in "The 3c Stamp of U.S. 1851-57 Issue," by Carroll Chase). Basic values for No. 10 are for copies with recut inner frame lines:

No inner frame lines	3,500.	105.00.
Left inner line only recut		170.00
Right inner line only recut		115.00
1 line recut in upper left triangle	3,500.	105.00
2 lines recut in upper left triangle		115.00
3 lines recut in upper left triangle		140.00
5 lines recut in upper left triangle (47L0)		600.00
1 line recut in lower left triangle		130.00
1 line recut in lower right triangle		125.00

2 lines recut in lower right triangle (57L0)		600.00
2 lines recut in upper left triangle and 1 line recut in lower right triangle		180.00
1 line recut in upper right triangle		125.00
Upper part of top label and diamond block recut	3,500.	110.00
Top label and right diamond block joined		115.00
Top label and left diamond block joined		115.00
Lower label and right diamond block joined		115.00

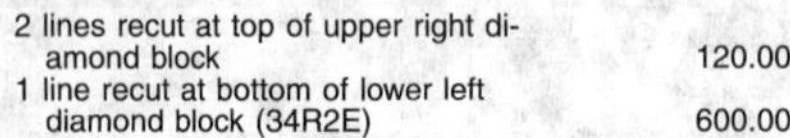

2 lines recut at top of upper right diamond block		120.00
1 line recut at bottom of lower left diamond block (34R2E)		600.00

Earliest documented uses: July 1, 1851 (Plate 1E) (FDC); July 12, 1851 (Plate 1i); July 23, 1851 (Plate 2E); July 19, 1851 (Plate 5E); Sept. 6, 1851 (Plate 0).

Cancellations

Blue	+3.00
Red	+5.00
Orange red	+10.00
Orange	—
Brown	+40.00
Ultramarine	+25.00
Green	+200.00
Violet	+150.00
1851 year date	*+350.00*
1852 year date	+350.00
"Paid"	+5.00
"Way"	+40.00
"Way" with numeral	+150.00
"Free"	+50.00
Numeral	+15.00
Railroad	+50.00
U. S. Express Mail	+20.00
"Steam"	+35.00
"Steamship"	+60.00
"Steamboat"	+70.00
Packet Boat	+300.00
Black Carrier (circular)	+400.00
Blue Carrier (circular)	+600.00
Blue Carrier (New Orleans "snowshovel")	+400.00
Green Carrier (New Orleans "snowshovel")	+500.00
Canadian	—
Territorial	+175.00
Pen	50.00

11 A10 3c **dull red** (1853-54-55), type I	275.00	11.00
orange red (1855)	275.00	11.00
rose red (1854-55)	275.00	11.00
No gum	100.00	
brownish carmine (1851-52 and 1856)	310.00	13.00
No gum	115.00	
claret (1852 and 1857)	330.00	16.00
No gum	130.00	
deep claret (1857)	360.00	19.00
No gum	150.00	
experimental orange brown	—	500.
On cover		600.00
plum (1857)	—	*2,000.*
No gum	—	
On cover, dull red		13.50
On cover, orange red		16.00
On cover, brownish carmine		19.00
On cover, claret		21.00
On cover, experimental orange brown	—	600.
On cover, plum		—
On propaganda cover, dull red		400.00
Pair	600.00	47.50
Pair on cover		50.00
Strip of 3	925.00	130.00
Block of 4	1,750.	900.00
P# block of 8, Impt.	*4,000.*	
Double transfer in "Three Cents"	310.00	13.00
Double transfer line through "Three Cents" and rosettes double (92L1L)	425.00	65.00
Triple transfer (92L2L)	410.00	50.00
Double transfer, "Gents" instead of "Cents" (66R2L)	410.00	50.00
Gash on shoulder	300.00	12.00
Dot in lower right diamond block (69L5L)	360.00	27.50
Major cracked plate (84L, 94L, 9R, Plate 5L)	*800.00*	160.00
Intermediate cracked plate (80L, 96L, 71R, Plate 5L)	*550.00*	80.00
Minor cracked plate (8L, 27L, 31L, 44L, 45L, 51L, 55L, 65L, 74L, 78L, 79L, 7R, 71R, and 72R, Plate 5L)	*425.00*	60.00
Worn plate	275.00	12.00
Perf. about 11, unofficial	*6,500.*	
Perf. 12½, unofficial		*6,000.*
On cover		*9,000.*
Pair on cover		—
c. Vertical half used as 1c on cover		*5,000.*
Strip of 4 No. 11c used as 6c on cover		*15,000.*
d. Diagonal half used as 1c on cover		*5,000.*
e. Double impression		*5,000.*

The unofficial perf varieties listed represent the first perforated stamps in the U. S. made using a true perforating machine. Known as the "Chicago perfs," both were made by Dr. Elijah W. Hadley, using a machine of his construction. None of the perf 11 stamps are believed to have been used.

The strip of 4 No. 11c on cover is the only recorded multiple of a bisected stamp in United States philately.

VARIETIES OF RECUTTING

All of these stamps were recut at least to the extent of three frame lines and usually much more. Some of the most prominent varieties are listed below (others are described in "The 3c Stamp of U.S. 1851-57 Issue," by Carroll Chase):

Recut inner frame lines	275.00	11.00
No inner frame lines	275.00	11.00
Right inner line only recut	300.00	16.00
1 line recut in upper left triangle	300.00	11.00
2 lines recut in upper left triangle	300.00	11.50
3 lines recut in upper left triangle	310.00	12.00
5 lines recut in upper left triangle (95L1L)	625.00	140.00
1 line recut in lower left triangle	310.00	12.00
1 line recut in lower right triangle	290.00	11.50
1 line recut in upper right triangle	410.00	16.00
Recut button on shoulder (10R2L)	450.00	70.00
Lines on bust and bottom of medallion circle recut (47R6)	*900.00*	300.00
Upper part of top label and diamond block recut	275.00	11.00
Top label and right diamond block joined	290.00	11.50
Top label and left diamond block joined	310.00	15.00
Lower label and right diamond block joined	310.00	15.00
1 extra vertical line outside of left frame line (29L, 39L, 49L, 59L, 69L, 79L, Plate 3)	300.00	15.00
2 extra vertical lines outside of left frame line (89L, 99L, Plate 3)	360.00	27.50
1 extra vertical line outside of right frame line (58L, 68L, 78L, 88L, 98L, Plate 3)	425.00	16.00
No inner line and frame line close to design at right (9L, 19L, Plate 3)	350.00	19.00
No inner line and frame line close to design at left (70, 80, 90, 100L, Plate 3)	310.00	16.00

Earliest documented uses: Oct. 6, 1851 (Plate 1L); Jan. 7, 1852 (Plate 2L); Jan. 15, 1852 (Plate 3); Mar. 28, 1855 (Plate 4); July 13, 1855 (Plate 5L); Feb. 18, 1856 (Plate 6); Feb. 9, 1856 (Plate 7); Apr. 14, 1856 (Plate 8).

Cancellations

Blue	+.50
Red	+1.00
Orange red	+5.00
Orange	+250.00
Brown	+30.00
Magenta	+40.00
Ultramarine	+40.00
Green	+175.00
Violet	+125.00
Purple	+125.00
Olive	+100.00
Yellow	*+5,000.*
Yellow, on cover	*10,000.*
1852 year date	*+300.00*
1853 year date	+100.00
1854 year date	—
1855 year date	+12.50
1858 year date	+.50
1859 year date	—
"Paid"	+1.25
"Way"	+10.00
"Way" with numeral	+60.00
"Free"	+25.00
Numeral	+7.50
Railroad	+20.00
U. S. Express Mail	+5.00
"Steam"	+15.00
"Ship"	+20.00
"New York Ship"	+35.00
"Steamboat"	+45.00
"Steamship"	+45.00
Packet boat	+120.00
Express Company	+120.00
Black Carrier	+60.00
Red Carrier (New York)	+50.00
Green Carrier (New Orleans)	+350.00
Blue Carrier (New Orleans)	+200.00
Canada	—
Territorial	+70.00
Pen	5.00

Thomas Jefferson — A11

FIVE CENTS.
Type I - Projections on all four sides.

12 A11 5c **red brown,** type I, *1856*	*20,000.*	950.
dark red brown	*20,000.*	950.
No gum	*8,500.*	
On domestic cover		1,400.
Single on cover to France		1,750.
Strip of 3 on cover to France		5,750.
Pair	*45,000.*	2,100.
Strip of 3	*67,500.*	4,750.
Block of 4	*160,000.*	*45,000.*
Double transfer (40R1)		*1,200.*
Defective transfer (23R1)		*1,400.*

Earliest documented use: Mar. 24, 1856.

Cancellations

Red	+150.
Magenta	+200.
Blue	+125.
Green	+900.
1856 year date	+25.
1857 year date	+25.
1858 year date	—
"Paid"	+125.
"Steamship"	+200.
U.S. Express Mail	+200.
Express Company	+400.
"Steamboat"	+350.
Railroad	+400.
Numeral	+1,000.
Pen	475.

Washington — A12

TEN CENTS

Type I - The "shells" at the lower corners are practically complete. The outer line below the label is very nearly complete. The outer lines are broken above the middle of the top label and the "X" in each upper corner. Beware of type V perforated (No. 35) trimmed to resemble type I imperforate (No. 13).

Types I, II, III and IV have complete ornaments at the sides of the stamps, and three pearls at each outer edge of the bottom panel.

Type I comes only from the bottom row of both panes of Plate 1.

13	A12 10c **green,** type I, *1855*	*16,000.*	800.
	dark green	*16,000.*	800.
	yellowish green	*16,000.*	800.
	No gum	*7,000.*	
	On domestic cover		900.
	Pair	*35,000.*	1,900.
	Strip of 3		2,700.
	Vert. pair, types III, I	*22,500.*	1,375.
	Vert. pair, types IV, I (86, 96L1)		*5,250.*
	Vertical strip of 3, types II, III, I		4,250.
	Block of 4, types III, I	*50,000.*	*10,500.*
	Block of 4, types III, IV, I		*16,000.*
	Double transfer (100R1)	*16,500.*	900.
	"Curl" in left "X" (99R1)	*16,500.*	900.

Earliest documented use: Aug. 27, 1855.

Cancellations

Blue	+40.
Red	+75.
Magenta	+200.
Orange	—
1855 year date	+25.
1856 year date	+25.
1857 year date	+25.
"Paid"	+50.
"Steamship"	+150.
Railroad	+175.
Territorial	+400.
Numeral	+50.
U.S. Express Mail	—
Pen	400.

A13

Type II - The design is complete at the top. The outer line at the bottom is broken in the middle. The shells are partly cut away.

14	A13 10c **green,** type II, *1855*	4,750.	200.
	dark green	4,750.	200.
	yellowish green	4,750.	200.
	No gum	2,000.	
	On domestic cover		260.
	Pair	10,000.	450.
	Strip of 3	16,000.	775.
	Block of 4	*22,500.*	*4,000.*
	Pair, types II, III	10,000.	450.
	Pair, types II, IV	*40,000.*	*2,100.*
	Vertical strip of 3, types II, III, IV		*2,500.*
	Block of 4, types II, III	—	*3,500.*
	Block of 4, types II, IV		—
	Block of 4, types II, III, IV		*10,000.*
	Double transfer (31L, 51L, and 20R, Plate 1)	5,250.	280.
	"Curl" opposite "X" (10R1)	5,250.	300.

Earliest documented use: May 12, 1855.

Cancellations

Blue	+10.
Red	+25.
Brown	+75.
Ultramarine	+100.
Magenta	+100.
Green	+200.
Violet	+150.
1855 year date	—
1856 year date	+50.
1857 year date	+10.
1858 year date	+10.
"Paid"	+25.
"Way"	+50.
"Free"	+75.
Railroad	+75.
Steamship	+75.
Steamboat	+100.
Numeral	+50.
Territorial	+150.
Express Company	+200.
U. S. Express Mail	+75.
Pen	90.

A14

Type III - The outer lines are broken above the top label and the "X" numerals. The outer line at the bottom and the shells are partly cut away similar to Type II.

15	A14 10c **green,** type III, *1855*	4,750.	200.
	dark green	4,750.	200.
	yellowish green	4,750.	200.
	No gum	2,000.	
	On domestic cover		260.
	Pair	10,000.	450.
	Strip of 3	16,000.	775.
	Pair, types III, IV	*40,000.*	*2,100.*
	Double transfer at top and at bottom		—
	"Curl" on forehead (85L1)	5,250.	300
	"Curl" to right of left "X" (87R1)	5,250.	300

Earliest documented use: May 19, 1855.

Cancellations

Blue	+10
Red	+25
Orange red	+35
Magenta	+100
Violet	+150
Brown	+75
Orange	—
Green	+200
1855 year date	—
1856 year date	+50
1857 year date	+10
1858 year date	+10
"Paid"	+25
Steamship	+75
U. S. Express Mail	+75.
Express Company	+200.
Packet boat	—
Canada (on cover)	+1000.
Territorial	+150.
Railroad	+75.
Numeral	+50.
Pen	90.

A15

Type IV - The outer lines have been recut at top or bottom or both.

16	A15 10c **green,** type IV, *1855*	*30,000.*	1,600.
	dark green	*30,000.*	1,600.
	yellowish green	*30,000.*	1,600.
	No gum	*14,000.*	
	On domestic cover		1,900.
	Pair	—	4,250.
	Block of 4 (54-55, 64-65L)		—

VARIETIES OF RECUTTING

Eight stamps on Plate 1 were recut. All are listed below.

Outer line recut at top (65L, 74L, 86L, and 3R, Plate 1)	*30,000.*	1,600.
Outer line recut at bottom (54L, 55L, 76L, Plate 1)	*31,500.*	1,700.
Outer line recut at top and bottom (64L1)	*35,000.*	2,000.

Positions 65L1 and 86L1 have both "X" ovals recut at top, as well as the outer line.

Earliest documented use: July 10, 1855.

Cancellations

Blue	+75.
Red	+150.
Brown	—
1857 year date	—
1859 year date	—
"Paid"	+150.
Steamship	+300.
Territorial	+500.
Express Company	+750.
Numeral	+150.
Pen	900.

Types I, II, III and IV occur on the same sheet, so it is possible to obtain pairs and blocks showing combinations of types. For listings of type combinations in pairs and blocks, see Nos. 13-15.

Washington — A16

17	A16 12c **black,** *July 1, 1851*	5,500.	325.
	gray black	5,500.	325.
	intense black	5,500.	325.
	No gum	2,200.	
	Single, on cover		1,500.
	Single on cover with No. 11 to France		1,150.
	Pair	*12,500.*	700.
	Pair, on cover to England		800.
	Block of 4	*27,500.*	*5,500.*
	Double transfer	5,750.	350.

Triple transfer (5R1 & 49R1) 6,000. 475.
Not recut in lower right corner 5,750. 350.
Recut in lower left corner (43L, 53L, 63L, 73L and 100L, Plate 1) 5,750. 400.
Cracked plate (32R1) —
On part-India paper — 850.
a. Diagonal half used as 6c on cover 2,500.
Diagonal half used as 6c on "Via Nicaragua" cover 5,750.
b. Vertical half used as 6c on cover 8,500.
c. Printed on both sides 10,000.

Earliest documented use: Aug. 4, 1851.

Cancellations

Red +20.
Orange red +45.
Blue +10.
Brown +60.
Magenta +75.
Orange —
Green +300.
"Paid" +25.
"Way" +75.
Steamship +100.
Steamboat +125.
Supplementary Mail Type A +125.
Railroad +100.
"Honolulu" in red (on cover) +400.
U. S. Express Mail +125.
Pen 160.

Please Note:

Stamps are valued in the grade of very fine unless otherwise indicated.

Values for early and valuable stamps are for examples with certificates of authenticity from acknowledged expert committees, or examples sold with the buyer having the right of certification. This applies to examples with original gum as well as examples without gum. Beware of stamps offered "as is," as the gum on some unused stamps offered with "original gum" may be fraudulent, and stamps offered as unused without gum may in some cases be altered or faintly canceled used stamps.

SAME DESIGNS AS 1851-57 ISSUES

Printed by Toppan, Carpenter & Co.

Nos. 18-39 have small or very small margins. The values take into account the margin size.

1857-61 ***Perf. 15½***

18 A5 1c **blue,** type I (Plate 12), *1861* 2,000. 600.
No gum 800.
On cover 750.
On patriotic cover 1,300.
Pair 4,400. 1,300.
Strip of 3 6,750. 2,200.
Block of 4 *12,000.*
Pair, types I, II 3,400. 900.
Pair, types I, IIIa 4,250. 1,150.
Block of 4, types I, II *8,000.* 4,850.
Block of 4, types I, II, IIIa *8,750.* 5,600.
Double transfer 2,150. 650.
Cracked plate (91R12) 850.

Plate 12 consists of types I & II. A few positions are type IIIa. Late printings of position 46L12 are type III.

Earliest documented use: Jan. 25, 1861.

Cancellations

Blue +10.
Red +35.
Violet +100.
Steamboat +100.
"Paid" +25.
"Free" +750.
Black Carrier +85.
Red Carrier +85.
Pen 300.

19 A6 1c **blue,** type Ia (Plate 4) *25,000.* *6,750.*
No gum *11,000.*
On cover *8,000.*
Pair *55,000.* *15,000.*
Strip of 3 *85,000.* *25,000.*
Vertical pair, types Ia, III *41,500.* *9,250.*
Vertical pair, types Ia, IIIa *31,000.* *7,750.*
Pair, types Ia, Ic — —
Strip of 3, types Ia, Ia, Ic —
Block of 4, types Ia, Ic, and IIIa *67,500.*
Block of 4, pair type Ia and types III or IIIa — —
"Curl on shoulder" (97L4) *26,500.* *7,000.*

Copies of this stamp exist with perforations not touching the design at any point. Such copies command very high prices.

Type Ia comes only from the bottom row of both panes of Plate 4.

Earliest documented use: Nov. 2, 1857 (dated postmark on off-cover stamp). No. 19 is known on a folded circular with Aug. 1 postmark, but the year of use has not been certified.

Cancellations

Red Carrier +200.
Green +1,750.
Pen 3,250.

19b A6 1c **blue,** type Ic ("E" relief, less distinct examples) *3,250.* *1,600.*
No gum *1,800.*
On cover *2,250.*
Horizontal pair (81-82R4) —
Pair, types Ic, III — —
Pair, types Ic, IIIa — —
blue, type Ic ("F" relief, best examples, 91, 96R4) *15,000.* *4,500.*
No gum *7,000.*
On cover *5,250.*

Type Ic - Same as Ia, but bottom right plume and ball ornament incomplete. Bottom left plume complete or nearly complete. Best examples are from bottom row, "F" relief, positions 91 and 96R4. Less distinct examples are "E" reliefs from 5th and 9th rows, positions 47L, 49L, 83L, 49R, 81R, 82R, and 89R, Plate 4, and early impressions of 41R4. Several combination type multiples can be found in the unused complete left pane of 100 from Plate 4.

Copies of the "F" relief type Ic stamps exist with perforations not touching the design at any point. Such copies command a substantial premium.

Cancellations

Pen ("E" relief) *650.*
Pen ("F" relief) *1,600.*

20 A7 1c **blue,** type II (Plate 2) 1,100. 250.
No gum 475.
On cover 290.
Pair 2,300. 550.
Strip of 3 3,500. 850.
Block of 4 *5,250.* 2,200.
Double transfer (Plate 2) 1,150. 290.
Double transfer (89R2) 1,200. 325.
Cracked plate (2L, 12L, 13L, 23L & 33L, Plate 2) 1,350. 750.
Plate 1L (4R1L only, double transfer), *July 1857* 750.
Pair, types II (4R1L), IV *1,900.*
Plate 4 3,150. *875.*
On cover *1,050.*
Pair 6,750. *1,850.*
Strip of 3 — —
Double transfer (10R4) 3,400. *1,450.*
"Curl in hair" (3R, 4R4) — *1,000.*
Plate 11 1,250. 325.
On cover 375.
On patriotic cover 750.
Pair 2,500. 700.
Strip of 3 —
Double transfer — —
Plate 12 1,050. 250.
On cover 290.
On patriotic cover 650.
Pair 2,200. 550.
Strip of 3 3,500. 850.
Block of 4 *5,250.* *2,200.*

Earliest documented uses: July 26, 1857 (Plate 2), July 26, 1857 (Plate 4), Jan. 12, 1861 (Plate 11), Jan. 21, 1861 (Plate 12).

No. 20, plate 2, is also known on two folded circulars dated July 24 and July 25, respectively, but no postal year date or docketing verifies the actual day of mailing.

Cancellations

Blue +5.
Red +20.
Green +200.
1857 year date +10.
1858 year date +5.
1861 year date +5.
"FREE" —
1863 year date +200.
"Paid" +15.
Railroad +60.
"Way" +75.
Steamboat +75.
Red Carrier +35.
Black Carrier +50.
Pen 125.

21 A8 1c **blue,** type III (Plate 4), see below for 99R2 *13,000.* 2,500.
No gum *6,000.*
On cover 3,000.
Pair *30,000.* 5,500.
Strip of 3 8,500.
Block of 4 —
Pair, types III, IIIa *16,000.* 3,250.
Vertical pair, types III, II — —
Block of 4, types III, IIIa —
Plate 12 (46L12) — —
a. Horiz. pair, imperf between *16,000.*

Earliest documented use: Sept. 18, 1857.

Cancellations

Blue +35.
Red +60.
Green +500.
1858 year date +35.
"Paid" +60.
Black Carrier +175.
Red Carrier +150.
Pen 1,250.

Values for type III are for at least a 2mm break in each outer line. Examples of type III with wider breaks in outer lines command higher prices; those with smaller breaks sell for less.

No. 21a is unique and is contained in a strip of three. Value reflects auction sale in 1999.

(21) A8 1c **blue,** type III (99R2) *20,000.*
On cover —
Pair, types III (99R2), II —
Pair, types III (99R2), IIIa —
Strip of 3, types III (99R2), II, IIIa —
Block of 9, one type III (99R2), others type II *110,000.*

The only recorded unused copy is the one in the block of 9. Only two covers are recorded bearing No. 21 (99R2).

Earliest documented use: Oct. 27, 1857.

22 A8 1c **blue,** type IIIa (Plate 4) 2,000. 500.
No gum 850.
On cover 550.
On patriotic cover 850.
Pair 4,400. 1,050.
Vertical pair, types IIIa, II — *1,800.*
Strip of 3 6,750. 1,750.
Block of 4 *9,750.* *5,000.*
Block of 4, types IIIa, II — —
Double transfer 2,100. 525.
Plate 2 (100R) — —
Plate 11 and Plate 12 2,100. 525.
On cover 575.
On patriotic cover 1,000.
Pair *4,600.* 1,150.
Vert. pair, types IIIa, II (Plate 11) *4,500.* 1000.
Strip of 3 *6,600.* 1,650.
Strip of 3, types IIIa, II, I (46-48L12) —
Block of 4 *9,750.*
Block of 4, types IIIa, II (Plate 11) *10,000.* *3,900.*
Double transfer 2,200. 550.
Triple transfer (Plate 11) — —
Bottom line broken (46L12) — —
b. Horizontal pair, imperf. between *5,000.*

One pair of No. 22b is reported. Beware of numerous pairs that have blind perforations. These are not to be confused with No. 22b.

Earliest documented uses: July 26, 1857 (Plate 4), Jan. 12, 1861 (Plate 11), Jan. 25, 1861 (Plate 12).

Cancellations

Blue +5.
Red +30.
Green +250.
1857 year date —
1858 year date —
1861 year date —
1863 year date —
"Paid" +25.
"Steamboat" —
Red Carrier +35.
Black Carrier +50.
Blue Carrier +100.
Pen 240.

23 A9 1c **blue,** type IV 8,500. 700.
No gum 3,750.
On cover 900.
Pair *18,500.* 1,600.
Strip of 3 *28,000.* 2,400.
Block of 4 *25,000.*
Double transfer *8,750.* 750.
Triple transfer, one inverted (71L1L, 81L1L and 91L1L) *9,250.* 900.
Cracked plate *8,750.* 825.
Bottom line broken (89R1L) — *1,450.*

Three or four used blocks of No. 23 are presently known. Value of used block of four is based on 1998 auction sale of the well-centered block of 5 sold at auction in 1998. Other blocks are poorly centered and will sell for much less.

VARIETIES OF RECUTTING

Recut once at top and once at bottom, (113 on plate) 8,500. 700.
Recut once at top, (40 on plate) 8,750. 725.
Recut once at top and twice at bottom, (21 on plate) 9,000. 725.
Recut twice at bottom, (11 on plate) 8,750. 750.
Recut once at bottom, (8 on plate) 9,000. 775.
Recut once at bottom and twice at top, (4 on plate) 9,250. 800.
Recut twice at bottom and once at top, (2 on plate) 9,500. 850.

Earliest documented use: July 25, 1857.

Cancellations

Blue +5.
Red +45.
1857 year date +50.
"Paid" +25.
Red Carrier +80.
Black Carrier +80.
Railroad +100.
"Way" +120.
"Steamboat" +135.
"Steam" +100.
Pen 325.

Franklin — A20

Type V - Similar to type III of 1851-57 but with side ornaments partly cut away. About one-half of all positions have side scratches. Wide breaks in top and bottom framelines.

Type Va - Stamps from Plate 5 with almost complete ornaments at right side and no side scratches. Many, but not all, stamps from Plate 5 are Type Va, the remainder being Type V.

24 A20 1c **blue,** type V (Plates 5, 7, 8, 9, 10) *1857*	175.00	40.00
No gum	75.00	
On cover		47.50
On patriotic cover		300.00
Pair	375.00	87.50
Strip of 3	550.00	140.00
Block of 4	775.00	425.00
P# strip of 4, Impt.	1,400.	
P# block of 8, Impt.	3,500.	—
Double transfer at top (8R and 10R, Plate 8)	240.00	85.00
Double transfer at bottom (52R9)	300.00	95.00
Curl on shoulder, (57R, 58R, 59R, 98R, 99R, Plate 7)	240.00	67.50
With "Earring" below ear (10L9)	600.00	95.00
"Curl" over "C" of "Cent"	250.00	67.50
"Curl" over "E" of "Cent" (41R and 81R8)	275.00	82.50
"Curl in hair," 23L7; 39, 69L8; 34, 74R9	240.00	57.50
"Curl" in "O" of "ONE" (62L5)	—	—
Horizontal dash in hair (24L7)	350.00	85.00
Horizontal dash in hair (36L8)	350.00	85.00
Long double "curl" in hair (52, 92R8)	300.00	80.00
Type Va	425.00	150.00
On cover (Type Va)		225.00
Pair (Type Va)	—	—
Strip of 3 (Type Va)	—	—
Block of 4 (Type Va)	—	—
"Curl" on shoulder (48L5)	—	—
b. Laid paper		*1,750.*

Earliest documented uses: Dec. 2, 1857 (Plate 5); Dec. 31, 1857 (Plate 7); Nov. 17, 1857 (Plate 8); Sept. 18, 1859 (Plate 9); June 14, 1860 (Plate 10).

Cancellations

Blue	+2.50
Red	+15.00
Green	+250.00
Brown	+150.00
Magenta	+150.00
Ultramarine	+100.00
1857 year date	+70.00
1858 year date	+2.50
1859 year date	+2.50
1860 year date	+2.50
1861 year date	+2.50
1863 year date	+250.00
Printed Precancel "CUMBERLAND, ME." (on cover)	—
"Paid"	+5.00
"Free"	+25.00
Railroad	+50.00
Numeral	+7.50
Express Company	+90.00
Steamboat	+55.00
"Steam"	+30.00
Steamship	+40.00
Packet boat	—
Supp. Mail Type A, B, or C	+55.00
"Way"	+30.00
Red Carrier	+20.00
Black Carrier	+12.50
Blue Carrier	+50.00
"Old Stamps-Not Recognized"	+1,500.
Territorial	+80.00
Pen	17.50

25 A10 3c **rose,** type I (no inner frame-lines), (Plates 4, 6, 7, 8)	2,750.	100.00
rose red	2,750.	100.00
dull red	2,750.	100.00
No gum	1,100.	
On cover		115.00
claret	3,000.	115.00
No gum	1,200.	
On patriotic cover		450.00
Pair	*6,000.*	225.00
Strip of 3	*9,000.*	375.00
Block of 4	*14,000.*	7,000.
Gash on shoulder	2,900.	105.00
Dot in lower right diamond block (69L5L)	—	*325.00*
Double transfer	3,000.	130.00
Double transfer "Gents" instead of "Cents" (66R2L)	—	625.00
Triple transfer (92L2L)	—	625.00
Worn plate	2,750.	100.00
Major cracked plate (84L, 94L, 9R, Plate 5L; 47R, 48R, Plate 7)	*4,250.*	550.00
Intermediate cracked plate (80L, 96L, 71R, Plate 5L)	*4,000.*	330.00
Minor cracked plate (8L, 27L, 31L, 44L, 45L, 51L, 55L, 65L, 74L, 78L, 79L, 7R, 71R, and 72R, Plate 5L)	*3,900.*	280.00
b. Vert. pair, imperf. horizontally		*10,000.*

All type I stamps were printed from 7 of the plates used for the imperfs., so many varieties exist both imperf. and perf.

VARIETIES OF RECUTTING

Recut inner lines (Plates 2L, 3, 5L)	4,000.	325.00
Recut inner line only at right (Plate 5L)		260.00
1 extra vertical line outside of left frame line (29L, 39L, 49L, 59L, 69L, 79L, Plate 3)	—	260.00
2 extra vertical lines outside of left frame line (89L, 99L, Plate 3)	—	290.00
1 extra vertical line outside of right frame line (58L, 68L, 78L, 88L, 98L, Plate 3)	—	235.00
No inner line and frame line close to design at right (9L, 19L, Plate 3)	—	290.00
No inner line and frame line close to design at left (70L, 80L, 90L, 100L, Plate 3)	—	260.00
Lines on bust and bottom of medallion circle recut (47R6)	—	1,250.
Recut button (10R2L)		950.00

Except for "5 lines recut in upper left triangle," all varieties of recutting listed under No. 11 are found on No. 25.

Earliest documented use: Feb. 28, 1857 (Plate 7).

Cancellations

Blue	+1.50
Red	+5.00
Orange red	+15.00
Orange	+150.00
Brown	+100.00
Ultramarine	+100.00
Green	+200.00
1857 year date	+1.00
1858 year date	+1.00
1859 year date	+1.00
"Paid"	+2.50
"Way"	+20.00
Railroad	+25.00
Numeral	+7.50
"Steam"	+20.00
Steamship	+35.00
Steamboat	+45.00
Packet Boat	+50.00
Supplementary Mail Type A	+40.00
U. S. Express Mail	+5.00
Express Company	+65.00
Black Carrier	+30.00
"Old Stamps-Not Recognized"	+1,000.
Territorial	+50.00
Printed precancel "Cumberland, Me." (on cover)	—
Pen	45.00

Washington—A21

Type II - There are no outer frame lines at top and bottom. The side frame lines were recut so as to be continuous from the top to the bottom of the plate. Stamps from the top or bottom rows show the ends of the side frame lines and may be mistaken for Type IIa.

Type IIa - The side frame lines extend only to the top and bottom of the stamp design. All Type IIa stamps are from plates 10 and 11 (each of which exists in three states), and these plates produced only Type IIa. The side frame lines were recut individually for each stamp, thus being broken between the stamps vertically.

Beware of type II stamps with frame lines that stop at the top of the design (from top row of plate) or bottom of the design (from bottom row of plate). These are often offered as No. 26a.

26 A21 3c **dull red,** type II	75.00	7.50
red	75.00	7.50
rose	75.00	7.50
No gum	27.50	
brownish carmine	150.00	18.00
No gum	57.50	
claret	170.00	23.00
No gum	70.00	
orange brown	—	—
plum		—
On cover, dull red		9.00
On cover, orange brown		*850.00*
On patriotic cover		100.00
On Confederate patriotic cover		2,000.
On Pony express cover		—
Pair	160.00	17.50
Strip of 3	240.00	37.50
Block of 4	400.00	150.0
P# block of 8, Impt.	3,000.	
Double transfer	110.00	17.5
Double transfer, rosettes double and line through "Postage" and "Three Cents" (87R15)	—	500.0
Left frame line double	110.00	17.5
Right frame line double	110.00	17.5
Cracked plate (62L, 71L, 72L, Plate 18)	*750.00*	*250.0*
Damaged transfer above lower left rosette	85.00	9.5
Same, retouched	105.00	10.5
Same, retouched with 2 vertical lines	120.00	11.5
Same, both damaged areas retouched	300.00	100.0
"Quadruple" plate flaw (18L28)	—	*600.0*
1 line recut in upper left triangle	—	30.0
5 lines recut in upper left triangle (52L25)		250.0
Inner line recut at right	—	200.0
Worn plate	85.00	8.0
b. Horiz. pair, imperf. vertically	*4,000.*	—
c. Vert. pair, imperf. horizontally		*10,000*
d. Horizontal pair, imperf. between		—
e. Double impression		*2,500*

Frame line double varieties are separate and distinct for virtually the entire length of the stamp. Copies with partly split lines are worth considerably less.

Earliest documented use: Sept. 14, 1857.

Cancellations

Blue	+.25
Red	+1.50
Orange red	+2.50
Orange	+150.00
Brown	+100.00
Ultramarine	+100.00
Violet	+100.00
Green	+150.00
1857 year date	+3.00
1858-1861 year date	+.25
Printed Circular Precancel "Cumberland, Me." (on cover)	—
"Paid"	+.50
"Paid All"	+15.00
"Free"	+20.00
"Collect"	+40.00
Numeral	+2.50
"Steam"	+12.50
Steamer	—
Steamboat	+22.50
Steamship	+22.50
"Way"	+12.50
Railroad	+15.00
U. S. Express Mail	+20.00
Express Company	+65.00
Packet boat	+65.00
Supp. Mail Type A, B or C	+75.00
Black Carrier	+30.00
Red Carrier	+25.00
"Southn. Letter Unpaid"	—
Territorial	+20.00
"Old Stamps-Not Recognized"	+500.00
Pen	3.00

26a A21 3c **dull red,** type IIa	225.00	65.00
brownish carmine	225.00	65.00
rose	225.00	65.00
No gum	95.00	
claret	250.00	75.00
No gum	105.00	
On cover		100.00
On patriotic cover		350.00
Pair	500.00	175.00
Strip of 3	1,000.	300.00
Block of 4	2,250.	1,000.
P# block of 8, Impt.	*10,000.*	
Double transfer	325.00	135.00
Double transfer, line through rosettes (61R10i, 61R10L, 98R10i, 98R10L)	—	300.00
Double transfer of rosettes and lower part of stamp (91R11L)	—	210.00
Triple transfer	—	425.00
Damaged transfer above lower left rosette	260.00	92.50
Same, retouched	250.00	85.00
Same, both damaged areas retouched (10R11)		135.00
Inner line recut at right	—	135.00
Inner line recut at left (79L10)	—	270.00
Left frame line double (70, 80, 90, 100R11)	—	160.00
Worn plate	225.00	65.00
f. Horiz. strip of 3, imperf. vert., on cover		*14,500.*

No. 26f is unique.

Earliest documented use: July 11, 1857.

Cancellations

Blue	+2.50
Red	+10.00
Orange red	+15.00
Orange	+150.00
Brown	+100.00
Ultramarine	+100.00
Violet	+150.00
Green	+175.00

1857 year date +2.50
1858 or 1859 year date +1.50
"Paid" +2.50
"Paid All" +15.00
"Free" +20.00
"Collect" +40.00
Numeral +2.50
"Steam" +15.00
Steamer —
Steamboat +25.00
Steamship +25.00
"Way" +15.00
Railroad +17.50
U. S. Express Mail +17.50
Express Company +65.00
Packet boat +65.00
Black Carrier +30.00
Red Carrier +20.00
Territorial +30.00
Pen 25.00

27 A11 5c **brick red,** type I, *1858* *30,000.* 1,400.
No gum *12,500.*
On cover 1,850.
On patriotic cover 4,750.
Pair *65,000.* 3,250.
Strip of 3 *5,400.*
Block of 4 *175,000.* *38,000.*
Defective transfer (23R1) — —

The unused block of 4 is unique.

Earliest documented use: Oct. 6, 1858.

Cancellations

Blue +150.
Red +175.
Ultramarine +450.
1859 year date +50.
1860 year date +50.
"Paid" +50.
Supplementary Mail Type A +150.
"Steamship" +150.
Pen 800.

28 A11 5c **red brown,** type I 5,500. 900.
pale red brown 5,500. 900.
No gum 2,350.
On cover 1,100.
Pair *12,000.* 2,000.
Strip of 3 3,100.
Block of 4 *42,500.* *6,500.*
Defective transfer (23R1) —

b. **Bright red brown** 6,000. 1,100.
No gum 2,500.

Earliest documented use: Aug. 23, 1857.

Cancellations

Blue +25.
Red +45.
1857 year date +20.

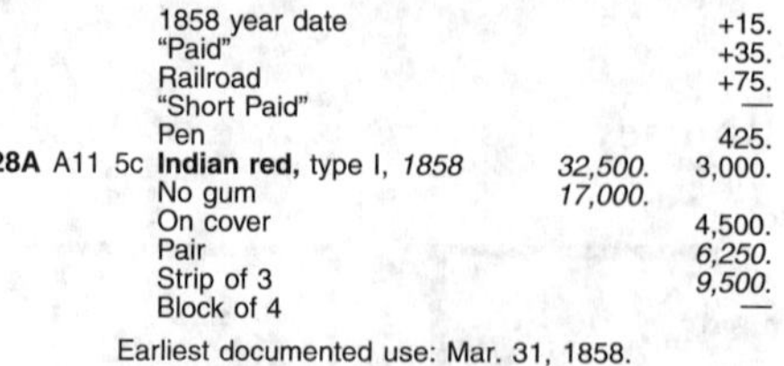

1858 year date +15.
"Paid" +35.
Railroad +75.
"Short Paid" —
Pen 425.

28A A11 5c **Indian red,** type I, *1858* *32,500.* 3,000.
No gum *17,000.*
On cover 4,500.
Pair *6,250.*
Strip of 3 *9,500.*
Block of 4 —

Earliest documented use: Mar. 31, 1858.

Cancellations

Red +75.
Blue +100.
1858 year date +50.
1859 year date +25.
Pen 1,750.

29 A11 5c **brown,** type I, *1859* 2,750. 375.
pale brown 2,750. 375.
deep brown 2,750. 375.
yellowish brown 2,750. 375.
No gum 1,150.
On cover 500.
Pair *6,000.* 800.
Strip of 3 *9,500.* 1,275.
Block of 4 *35,000.* *4,750.*
Defective transfer (23R1) — —

Earliest documented use: Mar. 21, 1859.

Cancellations

Blue +10.
Ultramarine —
Red +25.
Brown +75.
Magenta +125.
Green +350.
1859 year date +10.
1860 year date +10.
"Paid" +15.
"Steam" +75.
Steamship +100.
Numeral +80.
Pen 185.

Jefferson — A22

FIVE CENTS.
Type II - The projections at top and bottom are partly cut away. Several minor types could be made according to the extent of cutting of the projections.

30 A22 5c **orange brown,** Type II, *1861* 1,200. 1,150.
deep orange brown 1,200. 1,150.
No gum 525.
On cover *2,300.*
On patriotic cover —
Pair 2,500. *3,000.*
Strip of 3 3,900. —
Block of 4 *6,250.* —

Earliest documented use: May 8, 1861.

Cancellations

Blue +30.
Red +75.
Green —
"Paid" +75.
Steamship +110.
Supplementary Mail Type A +150.
Railroad —
Pen 575.

30A A22 5c **brown,** type II, *1860* 2,100. 300.
dark brown 2,100. 300.
yellowish brown 2,100. 300.
No gum 925.
On cover 350.
On patriotic cover —
Pair 4,500. 625.
Strip of 3 *7,000.* 950.
Block of 4 *10,500.* *3,000.*
Cracked plate —

b. Printed on both sides *4,500.* *4,750.*

Earliest documented use: May 4, 1860.

Cancellations

Blue +5.
Red +20.
Magenta +75.
Green +350.
"Paid" +20.
Supplementary Mail Type A +50.
"Steamship" +50.
"Steam" +40.

Express Company +25
Railroad —
Packet boat —
Pen 14

31 A12 10c **green,** type I *18,500.* 1,05
dark green *18,500.* 1,05
bluish green *18,500.* 1,05
yellowish green *18,500.* 1,05
No gum *8,250.*
On domestic cover 1,25
On patriotic cover 3,10
Pair *40,000.* 2,25
Vertical pair, types III, I *25,000.* 1,400
Vertical pair, types IV, I (86, 96 L 1) —
Strip of 3 —
Vertical strip of 3, types II, III, I —
Block of 4, types III, I *52,500.* —
Block of 4, types III, IV, I *8,750*
Vertical block of 6, 2 each types II, III, I *65,000.*
Double transfer (100R1) *20,000.* 1,150.
"Curl" in left "X" (99R1) *20,000.* 1,150.

Type I comes only from the bottom row of both panes of Plate 1.

Earliest documented use: Sept. 21, 1857.

Cancellations

Blue +15.
Red +50.
Green +500.
Supplementary Mail Type A —
"Steamship" +100.
Canadian —
Pen 525.

Act of February 27, 1861. Ten cent rate of postage to be prepaid on letters conveyed in the mail from any point in the United States east of the Rocky Mountains to any State or Territory on the Pacific Coast and vice versa, for each half-ounce.

32 A13 10c **green,** type II 5,250. 275.
dark green 5,250. 275.
bluish green 5,250. 275.
yellowish green 5,250. 275.
No gum 2,400.
On domestic cover 325.
On pony express cover 8,500.
Pair *11,000.* 575.
Strip of 3 — 875.
Block of 4 *25,000.* *4,500.*
Pair, types II, III *11,500.* 650.
Pair, types II, IV *41,000.* 2,650.
Vertical strip of 3, types II, III, IV —
Block of 4, types II, III *23,500.* *3,500.*
Block of 4, types II, IV —
Block of 4, types II, III, IV *80,000.* *18,000.*
Double transfer (31L, 51L and 20R, Plate 1) 5,500. 300.
"Curl opposite left X" (10R1) 350.

Earliest documented use: July 27, 1857 (dated cancel on off-cover stamp).

Cancellations

Blue +10.
Red +30.
Brown +125.
Green +300.
"Paid" +20.
1857 year date +10.
Supplementary Mail Type A —
Steamship +50.
Packet boat —
Railroad —
Express Company —
Pen 140.

33 A14 10c **green,** type III 5,250. 275.
dark green 5,250. 275.
bluish green 5,250. 275.
yellowish green 5,250. 275.
No gum 2,400.
On domestic cover 325.
Pair *11,000.* 575.
Strip of 3 — 875.
Pair, types III, IV 2,500.
"Curl" on forehead (85L1) — 350.
"Curl in left X" (87R1) 350.

Earliest documented use: Oct. 6, 1857.

Cancellations

Blue +10.
Red +30.
Brown +125.
Ultramarine +100.
1857 year date +10.
"Paid" +20.
"Steam" +45.
Steamboat —
Steamship +50.
Numeral +15.
Packet boat —
Pen 140.

34 A15 10c **green,** type IV *32,500.* 2,250.
dark green *32,500.* 2,250.
bluish green *32,500.* 2,250.
yellowish green *32,500.* 2,250.
No gum *17,000.*
On domestic cover 2,650.
Pair *5,750.*
Block of 4 (54-55, 64-65L) —

VARIETIES OF RECUTTING

Eight stamps on Plate I were recut. All are listed below.

Outer line recut at top (65L, 74L, 86L and 3R, Plate I)	*32,500.*	2,250.
Outer line recut at bottom (54L, 55L, 76L, Plate 1)	*33,500.*	2,300.
Outer line recut at top and bottom (64L1)	*35,000.*	2,350.

Earliest documented use: (?) 5, 1857 (Sept. or Dec.).

Cancellations

Blue	+40.
Red	+75.
Steamship	+200.
Packet boat	—
Pen	1,250.

Types I, II, III and IV occur on the same sheet, so it is possible to obtain pairs and blocks showing combinations of types. For listings of type combinations in pairs and blocks, see Nos. 31-33.

Washington (Two typical examples) — A23

Type V - The side ornaments are slightly cut away. Usually only one pearl remains at each end of the lower label, but some copies show two or three pearls at the right side. At the bottom the outer line is complete and the shells nearly so. The outer lines at top are complete except over the right "X."

35	A23 10c **green,** type V, (Plate 2), *1859*	275.00	65.00
	dark green	275.00	65.00
	yellowish green	275.00	65.00
	No gum	110.00	
	On domestic cover		77.50
	On patriotic cover		625.00
	On pony express cover		—
	On cover to Canada		125.00
	Pair	575.00	140.00
	Block of 4	1,200.	650.00
	P# block of 8, Impt.	*17,500.*	
	Double transfer at bottom (47R2)	350.00	90.00
	Small "Curl" on forehead (37, 78L2)	325.00	77.50
	Curl in "e" of "cents" (93L2)	350.00	90.00
	Curl in "t" of "cents" (73R2)	350.00	90.00
	Cracked plate		—

Earliest documented use: Apr. 29, 1859.

Cancellations

Red	+7.50
Orange red	+12.50
Brown	+100.00
Blue	+5.00
Orange	+150.00
Magenta	+100.00
Green	+250.00
1859 year date	+5.00
"Paid"	+5.00
Red carrier	—
Railroad	+40.00
Steamship	+35.00
"Steam"	+30.00
Numerals	+15.00
Supp. Mail Type A or C	+60.00
Express Company	+135.00
"Southn Letter Unpaid"	—
Territorial	—
Pen	30.00

TWELVE CENTS. Printed from two plates.

Plate I - Outer frame lines complete.

Plate III - Outer frame lines noticeably uneven or broken, sometimes partly missing.

36	A16 12c **black** (Plate 1)	1,500.	290.
	gray black	1,500.	290.
	No gum	650.	
	Single on cover		600.
	Single on cover with No. 26 to France		350.
	Pair on cover to England		675.
	Pair on patriotic cover		—
	Pair	3,500.	650.
	Block of 4	*8,500.*	2,250.
	Not recut in lower right corner	1,600.	325.
	Recut in lower left corner (43, 53, 63, 73, 100L)	1,650.	310.
	Double transfer	1,650.	325.
	Triple transfer	1,800.	—
a.	Diagonal half used as 6c on cover		*17,500.*
c.	Horizontal pair, imperf. between		*12,500.*

Earliest documented use: July 30, 1857.

Cancellations

Blue	+5.
Red	+10.
Brown	+75.
Magenta	+55.
Green	+250.
1857 year date	+20.
"Paid"	+10.
Supplementary Mail Type A	+60.
Express Company	—
Railroad	+60.
Numeral	+20.
"Southn Letter Unpaid"	—
Pen	140.

36b	A16 12c **black** (Plate 3)	800.	190.
	intense black	800.	190.
	No gum	350.	
	Single on cover		625.
	Single on cover with No. 26 to France		300.
	Pair on cover to England		450.
	Pair	1,650.	410.
	Block of 4	4,750.	2,350.
	Double frame line at right	850.	210.
	Double frame line at left	850.	210.
	Vertical line through rosette (95R3)	975.	270.

Earliest documented use: June 1, 1860. (The previously listed Dec. 3, 1859, cover requires expertization in order to be considered.)

Washington — A17

Franklin — A18

37	A17 24c **gray lilac,** *1860*	1,600.	350.
a.	24c **gray**	1,600.	350.
	No gum	650.	
	On cover to England		1,000.
	On patriotic cover		*4,000.*
	Pair	3,500.	775.
	Block of 4, gray lilac	*9,000.*	*6,250.*
	P# block of 12, Impt.	*31,500.*	

The technical configuration of a No. 37 plate block is eight stamps. The unique plate block currently is contained in the listed block of twelve stamps.

Earliest documented use: July 7, 1860.

Cancellations

Blue	+10.
Red	+40.
Magenta	+80.
Violet	+110.
Green	+450.
1860 year date	+15.
"Paid"	+25.
"Paid All"	+50.
"Free"	+100.
Supplementary Mail Type A	+150.
Railroad	+150.
Packet Boat	+200.
Red Carrier	—
Numeral	+40.
"Southn Letter Unpaid"	—
Pen	175.

See Trial Color Proofs for the 24c red lilac.

38	A18 30c **orange,** *1860*	1,900.	450.
	yellow orange	1,900.	425.
	reddish orange	1,900.	425.
	No gum	800.	
	On cover to Germany or France		*1,300.*
	On patriotic cover		*9,000.*
	Pair	*4,250.*	1,000.
	Block of 4	*11,000.*	*6,500.*
	Double transfer (89L1 and 99L1)	2,100.	525.
	Recut at bottom (52L1)	2,200.	575.
	Cracked plate	—	—

Earliest documented use: Aug. 8, 1860.

Cancellations

Blue	+20.
Red	+40.
Magenta	+90.
Violet	+90.
Green	+1000.
1860 year date	+30.
"Paid"	+35.
"Free"	—
Black town	+30.
Supplementary Mail Type A	+125.

Steamship		—
Express Company		—
Pen		225.

Washington — A19

39 A19 90c **blue,** *1860*	3,000.	*7,500.*
deep blue	3,000.	*7,500.*
No gum	1,250.	
On cover		*225,000.*
Pair	*6,250.*	—
Block of 4	*21,500.*	*45,000.*
Double transfer at bottom	3,250.	—
Double transfer at top	3,250.	—
Short transfer at bottom right and left (13L1 and 68R1)	3,250.	

The used block of 4 is believed to be unique and has perfs trimmed off at left and bottom clear of design. Value is based on 1993 auction sale.

Earliest documented use: Sept. 11, 1860.

Cancellations

Red	7,000.
Black	+200.
Blue	+300.
Black town	+1,000.
1861 year date	+1,000.
Boston "Paid"	+750.
Red Carrier	—
N.Y. Ocean Mail	+1,000.
Pen	2,500.

Genuine cancellations on the 90c are very scarce.
All used examples of No. 39 must be accompanied by certificates of authenticity issued by recognized expertizing committees.

See Die and Plate Proofs for imperfs. on stamp paper.

REPRINTS OF 1857-60 ISSUE

These were not valid for postal use, though one example each of Nos. 43 and 45 are known with contemporaneous cancels.

Produced by the Continental Bank Note Co.

White paper, without gum.

The 1, 3, 10 and 12c were printed from new plates of 100 subjects each differing from those used for the regular issue.

1875 ***Perf. 12***

40	A5	1c	**bright blue** *(3846)*	*625.*
			Pair	*1,350.*
			Block of 4	*3,500.*
			Cracked plate, pos. 91	*775.*
			Double transfer, pos. 94	*775.*
41	A10	3c	**scarlet** *(479)*	*3,250.*
42	A22	5c	**orange brown** *(878)*	*1,400.*
			Pair	*3,250.*
			Vertical margin strip of 4, Impt. & P#	*11,500.*
43	A12	10c	**blue green** *(516)*	*3,000.*
			Pair	*7,000.*
44	A16	12c	**greenish black** *(489)*	*3,250.*
			Pair	*7,500.*
45	A17	24c	**blackish violet** *(479)*	*3,250.*
46	A18	30c	**yellow orange** *(480)*	*3,250.*
47	A19	90c	**deep blue** *(454)*	*4,500.*

Nos. 41-46 are valued in the grade of fine.
Nos. 40-47 exist imperforate. Value, set of singles, $25,000. One set of imperforate pairs is recorded. A horizontal strip of 3 of No. 44 also is recorded.
Numbers in parentheses are quantities sold.

Produced by the National Bank Note Co.

Franklin — A24

Washington — A25

Jefferson — A26

Washington — A27

A27a

A27

Washington — A28

A29 Washington　A30 Franklin

Washington — A31

1c - There is a dash under the tip of the ornament at right the numeral in upper left corner.
3c - Ornaments at corners end in a small ball.
5c - There is a leaflet in the foliated ornaments at ea corner.
10c (A27) - A heavy curved line has been cut below the sta and an outer line added to the ornaments above them.
12c - There are corner ornaments consisting of ovals ar scrolls.
90c - Parallel lines form an angle above the ribbon with "U. S Postage"; between these lines there is a row of dashes and point of color at the apex of the lower line.

Patriotic Covers covering a wide range of historical interes were used during the Civil War period, in the North as well a the South, and are collected in State groups as well as gene ally, both used and unused. There are believed to be as mar as 12,000 varieties.
During the war, these stamps were used as small chang until Postage Currency was issued.
The Act of Congress of March 3, 1863, effective July 1, 1863 created a rate of three cents for each half ounce, first clas domestic mail. This Act was the first law which establishe uniform rate of postage regardless of the distance. This rat remained in effect until Oct. 1, 1883.

Plates of 200 subjects in two panes of 100 each.

The following items, formerly listed here as Nos. 55-62 are considered to be essays or trial color proofs. They wil be found in their respective sections as follows. Previous No. 58 has been combined with No. 62B.

Formerly	Currently	Formerly	Currently
55	63-E11e	59	69-E6e
56	65-E15h	60	70eTC
57	67-E9e	61	71bTC
58	62B	62	72-E7h

The paper of Nos. 62B-72 is thicker and more opaque than the essays and trial color proofs, except Nos. 62B, 70c, and 70d.

1861 ***Perf. 12***

62B A27a 10c **dark green**	*7,250.*	1,250.
dark yellow green	*7,250.*	1,250.
No gum	*3,250.*	
On cover		1,600.
On patriotic cover		2,750.
Pair	*16,000.*	2,750.
Block of 4	*34,000.*	*12,000.*
Foreign entry 94R4	*8,500.*	—
Block of 4, one stamp 94R4	—	

The foreign entry is of the 90c 1861.

Earliest documented use: Sept. 17, 1861.

Cancellations

Red	+80.
Blue	+50.
"Paid"	+60.
Steamship	+100.
Express Company	+200.
Supplementary Mail Type A	+125.

1861-62 ***Perf. 12***

63	A24	1c	**blue,** *Aug. 17, 1861*	325.00	35.00
			pale blue	325.00	35.00
			bright blue	325.00	35.00
			No gum	130.00	
			On cover (single)		42.50
			On prisoner's letter		—
			On patriotic cover		220.00
			Pair	700.00	75.00
			Block of 4	1,450.	425.00
			P# block of 8, Impt.	*6,000.*	
			Double transfer	—	47.50
			Dot in "U"	350.00	40.00
a.		1c	**ultramarine**	*2,000.*	*375.00*
			No gum	*900.00*	
b.		1c	**dark blue**	750.00	110.00
			No gum	275.00	
c.			Laid paper, horiz. or vert.	—	*4,000.*
d.			Vertical pair, imperf. horiz.		—
e.			Printed on both sides	—	*4,000.*

Earliest documented use: Aug. 17, 1861 (dated cancel on off-cover stamp); Aug. 21, 1861 (cover).

Cancellations

Blue	+2.00
Red	+7.50
Magenta	+50.00
Green	+250.00
Violet	+50.00
1861 year date	+7.50
1865 year date	+2.00
1866 year date	+2.00
"Free"	+40.00
"Paid"	+2.50
"Paid All"	+15.00
Supp. Mail Type A or B	+30.00
Steamship	+35.00
Steam	+30.00
Express Company	+175.00
Red Carrier	+10.00
Black Carrier	+10.00
Railroad	+30.00
Numeral	+10.00
"Steamboat"	+50.00
Printed Precancel "CUMBERLAND, ME." (on cover)	—

64	A25	3c	**pink,** *Aug. 17, 1861*	*9,500.*	850.00
			No gum	*3,750.*	
			On cover		950.00

			Unused	Used
		On patriotic cover		1,150.
		Pair	*20,000.*	*2,000.*
		Block of 4	*47,500.*	—

Earliest documented use: Aug. 17, 1861 (FDC).

Cancellations

Blue	+25.00
Red	+90.00
Green	+500.00
1861 date	—
"Paid"	+25.00
"Free"	+175.00
"Ship"	+85.00
Supplementary Mail Type B	+150.00
Railroad	+125.00
Steamboat	+175.00

a.		3c **pigeon blood pink**	*20,000.*	*3,500.*
		No gum	*9,000.*	
		On cover		*4,250.*
		On patriotic cover		*6,500.*

Earliest documented use: Aug. 21, 1861.

b.		3c **rose pink,** *Aug. 17, 1861*	600.00	150.00
		No gum	260.00	
		On cover		180.00
		On patriotic cover		240.00
		Pair	1,350.	325.00
		Block of 4	3,250.	850.00

Earliest documented use: Aug. 17, 1861 (FDC).

Cancellations

Blue	+10.00
Red	+20.00
Orange red	+25.00
Green	+150.00
Orange	—
"Paid"	+10.00
"Free"	+75.00
Supplementary Mail Type C	—
"Ship"	+30.00
Railroad	+60.00
Steamboat	+90.00

65	A25	3c **rose**	130.00	2.50
		bright rose	130.00	2.50
		dull red	130.00	2.50
		rose red	130.00	2.50
		No gum	50.00	
		On cover		3.00
		On patriotic cover		40.00
		On prisoner's letter		150.00
		On pony express cover		—
		Pair	300.00	5.75
		Block of 4	600.00	40.00
		P# block of 8, Impt.	4,250.	
		Double transfer	150.00	5.50
		Cracked plate		—
		brown red	*275.00*	5.00
		No gum	115.00	
		pale brown red	*210.00*	5.00
		No gum	85.00	
		dull brown red	*250.00*	5.00
		No gum	105.00	
		Block of 4	*1,250.*	
		deep pinkish rose	*275.00*	25.00
b.		Laid paper, horiz. or vert.	—	500.00
d.		Vertical pair, imperf. horiz.	*6,000.*	*750.00*
e.		Printed on both sides	*11,000.*	*3,750.*
f.		Double impression		*7,500.*

See Die and Plate Proofs for imperfs. on stamp paper.

Earliest documented use: Aug. 19, 1861.

Cancellations

Blue	+.25
Ultramarine	+2.75
Brown	+50.00
Red	+3.00
Orange red	+3.50
Violet	+35.00
Magenta	+8.00
Green	+90.00
Olive	+100.00
Orange	+150.00
Yellow	*+3,500.*
1861 year date	+.50
1867 or 1868 year date	+.50
"Paid"	+.35
"Paid All"	+7.50
"Mails Suspended"	—
Railroad	+12.50
"Way"	+20.00
"Free"	+20.00
"Collect"	+35.00
"Ship"	+15.00
"U. S. Ship"	+35.00
"Steam"	+12.00
Steamship	+15.00
Steamboat	+20.00
"Ship Letter"	+35.00
Red Carrier	+15.00
Blue Carrier	+25.00
Black Carrier	+20.00
Supplementary Mail Type A, B or C	+15.00
Numeral	+3.00
Express Company	+90.00
Army Field Post	+60.00
Packet Boat	+40.00
"Registered"	+30.00
"Postage Due"	+25.00
"Advertised"	+15.00
Territorial	+25.00
St. Thomas	—
China	—

The 3c lake can be found under No. 66 in the Trial Color Proofs section.

67	A26	5c **buff**	*21,000.*	875.
		No gum	*9,500.*	
		On cover		1,150.
		On patriotic cover		*4,000.*
		Pair	*45,000.*	2,000.
		Block of 4	*11,500.*	*12,000.*
a.		5c **brown yellow**	*21,000.*	900.
		No gum	*9,500.*	
b.		5c **olive yellow**	—	1,350.

The unused block of 4 is unique but very faulty. Value is based on actual 1993 sale.

Earliest documented uses: Aug. 19, 1861 (No. 67); Aug. 21, 1861 (No. 67a); Sept. 18, 1861 (No. 67b).

Cancellations

Red	+40.00
Blue	+20.00
Magenta	+125.00
Green	—
1861 year date	+10.00
"Paid"	+25.00
Supplementary Mail Type A	+100.00
Express Company	+250.00
Numeral	+50.00
"Steamship"	+100.00

Values of Nos. 67, 67a, 67b reflect the normal small margins.

68	A27	10c **yellow green**	850.00	50.00
		green	850.00	50.00
		No gum	375.00	
		On cover		67.50
		On patriotic cover		375.00
		On cover to Canada		90.00
		Pair	1,800.	110.00
		Block of 4	*4,000.*	600.00
		P# block of 8, Impt.	*9,000.*	
		Double transfer	925.00	55.00
		deep yellow green on thin paper	1,000.	60.00
a.		10c **dark green**	975.00	62.50
		blue green	975.00	65.00
		No gum	425.00	
b.		Vertical pair, imperf. horiz.		*3,500.*

Earliest documented use: Aug. 20, 1861.

Cancellations

Blue	+2.00
Red	+5.00
Purple	+50.00
Magenta	+50.00
Brown	+50.00
Green	+175.00
1865 year date	+3.50
"Paid"	+2.50
"Collect"	+32.50
"Short Paid"	+50.00
"P.D." in circle	+30.00
"Free"	+25.00
Numeral	+7.50
Red Carrier	+45.00
Railroad	+20.00
Steamship	+15.00
"Steamboat"	+35.00
Supplementary Mail Type A	+30.00
Red Supp. Mail Type D	—
Express Company	+70.00
China	—
Japan	+200.00
St. Thomas	—

Stamps are valued in the grade of very fine unless otherwise indicated.

Please Note:

Values for early and valuable stamps are for examples with certificates of authenticity from acknowledged expert committees, or examples sold with the buyer having the right of certification.

This applies to examples with original gum as well as examples without gum.

Beware of stamps offered "as is," as the gum on some unused stamps offered with "original gum" may be fraudulent, and stamps offered as unused without gum may in some cases be altered or faintly canceled used stamps.

69	A28	12c **black**	1,700.	100.00
		gray black	1,700.	110.00
		No gum	700.00	110.00
		intense black	1,750.	115.00
		No gum	725.00	
		On domestic cover		140.00
		On patriotic cover		900.00
		On cover to France or Germany with #65		160.00
		Pair	3,750.	240.00
		Block of 4	*8,250.*	1,050.
		Double transfer of top frame line	1,800.	130.00

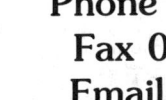

Double transfer of bottom frame line 1,800. 130.00
Double transfer of top and bottom frame lines 1,850. 135.00

Earliest documented use: Aug. 30, 1861.

Cancellations

Blue +2.50
Red +20.00
Purple +50.00
Magenta +100.00
Green +550.00
1861 year date +5.00
"Paid" +5.00
"Registered" +35.00
Supp. Mail Type A, B or C +45.00
Express Company +175.00
Railroad +50.00
Numeral +15.00

70 A29 24c **red lilac** 2,500. 200.00
No gum 1,000.
On cover 250.00
On patriotic cover *3,000.*
Pair 5,500. 425.00
Block of 4 *13,000.* *2,650.*
Scratch under "A" of "Postage" —
a. 24c **brown lilac** 2,250. 175.00
No gum 875.
Block of 4 *11,000.* *3,250.*
b. 24c **steel blue** ('61) *9,000.* 800.00
No gum *4,250.*
On cover 1,250.
Block of 4 *40,000.*
c. 24c **violet,** thin paper, *Aug. 20, 1861* *10,000.* 1,450.
No gum *5,000.*
d. 24c **pale gray violet,** thin paper 4,500. 1,450.
No gum 2,000.

There are numerous shades of the 24c stamp in this and the following issue.

Color changelings, especially of No. 78, are frequently offered as No. 70b. Obtaining a certificate from an acknowledged expert committee is strongly advised.

Nos. 70c and 70d are on a thinner, harder and more transparent paper than Nos. 70, 70a, 70b or the latter Nos. 78, 78a, 78b and 78c. No. 70eTC (formerly No. 60, see Trial Color Proofs section) is distinguished by its distinctive dark color.

Earliest documented uses: Jan. 7, 1862 (No. 70); Feb. 5, 1862 (No. 70a); Sept. 21, 1861 (No. 70b); Aug. 20, 1861 (No. 70c); Sept. 10, 1861 (No. 70d).

Cancellations, No. 70

Blue +5.00
Red +15.00
Magenta +200.00
Brown +125.00
Green +300.00
1865 year date +5.00
"Paid" +15.00
Supp. Mail Types A or B +75.00
Express Company +350.00

71 A30 30c **orange** 1,800. 160.
deep orange 1,800. 160.
No gum 800.
On cover to France or Germany 375.
On patriotic cover *3,500.*
Pair 3,800. 375.
Block of 4 *8,500.* *2,400.*
P# strip of 4, Impt. —
a. Printed on both sides —

Values for No. 71 are for copies with small margins, especially at sides. Large-margined examples sell for much more.

Earliest documented use: Aug. 20, 1861.

Cancellations

Blue +10.00
Magenta +100.00
Brown +100.00
Red +25.00
"Paid" +15.00
"Paid All" +35.00
Railroad —
Packet Boat —
"Steamship" +75.00
Supplementary Mail Type A +75.00
Red Supp. Mail Type D —
Express Company +350.00
Japan —

72 A31 90c **blue** 3,250. 425.
dull blue 3,250. 425.
No gum 1,400.
On cover *17,500.*
Pair *7,000.* 950.
Block of 4 *27,500.* *4,250.*
P# strip of 4, Impt. *24,000.*
a. 90c **pale blue** 3,000. 425.
No gum 1,350.
b. 90c **dark blue** 3,500. 650.
No gum 1,500.

The unique plate number and imprint strip of 4 of No. 72 has no gum and is valued thus.

Earliest documented use: Nov. 27, 1861.

Cancellations

Blue +15.
Red +40.
Green +750.
1865 year date +35.
"Paid" +25.
"Registered" +75.
Express Company +500.
Supplementary Mail Type A +100.

Nos. 68a, 69, 71 and 72 exist as imperforate sheet-margin singles with pen cancel. They were not regularly issued.

The 90c was distributed to several post offices in the last two weeks of August, 1861.

Owing to the Civil War, stamps and stamped envelopes in current use or available for postage in 1860, were demonetized by various post office orders, beginning in August, 1861, and extending to early January, 1862.

P. O. Department Bulletin.

"A reasonable time after hostilities began in 1861 was given for the return to the Department of all these (1851-56) stamps in the hands of postmasters, and as early as 1863 the Department issued an order declining to longer redeem them."

The Act of Congress, approved March 3, 1863, abolished carriers' fees and established a prepaid rate of two cents for drop letters, making necessary the 2-cent Jackson (No. 73).

Free City Delivery was authorized by the Act of Congress of March 3, 1863, effective in 49 cities with 449 carriers, beginning July 1, 1863.

Produced by the National Bank Note Co.
DESIGNS AS 1861 ISSUE

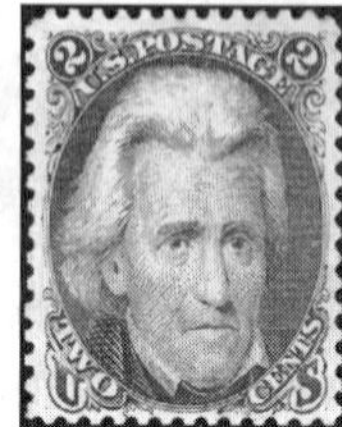

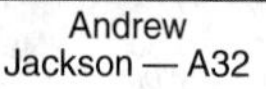
Andrew Jackson — A32

Abraham Lincoln — A33

1861-66 ***Perf. 12***

73 A32 2c **black**, *1863* 375.00 50.00
gray black 375.00 50.00
intense black 375.00 55.00
No gum 140.00
On cover 75.00
On prisoner's letter —
On patriotic cover *2,000.*
Pair 800.00 110.00
Block of 4 *3,750.* *1,250.*
P# strip of 4, Impt. *4,250.*
P# block of 8, Impt. *14,000.*
Double transfer 425.00 55.00
Major double transfer of top left corner and "Postage" ("Atherton shift") *12,500.*
Major double transfer of right side, pos. 81, right pane ("Preston shift") *5,000.* *4,500.*
Major double transfer of frame in all corners plus hair and chin ("Metzger shift") —
Triple transfer —
Short transfer 400.00 55.00
Cracked plate — —
a. Diagonal half used as 1c as part of 3c rate on cover 1,750.
b. Diagonal half used alone as 1c on cover *3,000.*
c. Horiz. half used as 1c as part of 3c rate on cover *3,500.*
d. Vert. half used as 1c as part of 3c rate on cover 1,800.
e. Vert. half used alone as 1c on cover —
f. Printed on both sides *10,000.*
g. Laid paper — *5,000.*

Earliest documented use: July 1, 1863 (dated cancel on off-cover stamp); July 6, 1863 (earliest known use on cover).

Cancellations

Blue +5.00
Brown +75.00
Red +50.00
Orange red +60.00
Magenta +200.00
Ultramarine +150.00
Orange +200.00
Green +750.00
1863 year date +5.00
Printed Precancel "Jefferson, Ohio" —
"PAID ALL" +40.00
"Paid" +10.00
Numeral +15.00
"Way" +150.00
Railroad +300.00
"Steam" +40.00
Steamship +100.00
"Steamboat" +65.00
"Ship Letter" +150.00
Black Carrier +20.00
Blue Carrier +35.00
Supp. Mail Type A or B +100.00
Express Company +300.00
"Short Paid" +250.00
Territorial +100.00
China —

The 3c scarlet, design A25, can be found under No. 74 in the Trial Color Proofs section.

75 A26 5c **red brown** 5,000. 475.
dark red brown 5,000. 475.
No gum 2,100.
On cover 700
On patriotic cover *2,500*
Pair *10,500.* 1,000
Block of 4 *29,000.* *7,250*
Double transfer *5,250.* 525

Values for No. 75 reflect the normal small margins.

Earliest documented use: Jan. 2, 1862.

Cancellations

Blue +10
Red +35
Magenta +65
"Paid" +25
Supplementary Mail Type A +50.
Express Company +300.

76 A26 5c **brown**, *1863* 1,400. 120.
pale brown 1,400. 120.
dark brown 1,400. 120.
No gum 550.
On cover 175.
On patriotic cover 850.
Pair 3,000. 250.
Block of 4 *6,750.* 1,050.
P# strip of 4, Impt. —
Double transfer of top frame line 1,500. 130.
Double transfer of bottom frame line 1,500. 130.
Double transfer of top and bottom frame lines 1,550. 145.
a. 5c **black brown** 1,750. 210.
No gum 675.
Block of 4 *7,750.* *1,500.*
b. Laid paper —

Values of Nos. 76, 76a reflect the normal small margins.

Earliest documented use: Feb. 3, 1863.

Cancellations

Blue +5.00
Magenta +75.00
Red +15.00
Brown +75.00
Green +300.00
1865 year date +10.00
"Paid" +15.00
"Short Paid" +75.00
Supp. Mail Type A or F +55.00
Express Company +175.00
"Steamship" +65.00
Packet boat —

77 A33 15c **black**, *1866* 2,750. 160.
full black 2,750. 160.
No gum 1,100.
On cover to France or Germany 240.
Pair 5,750. 340.
Block of 4 *23,500.* *1,000.*
P# block of 8, Impt. —
Double transfer 2,850. 170.
Cracked plate — —

Earliest documented use: Apr. 14, 1866.

Cancellations

Blue +5.
Indigo +10.
Purple +60.
Lavender +150.
Violet +75.
Magenta +100.
Red +35.
Brown +125.
Green +350.
Ultramarine +75.
"Paid" +15.
"Short Paid" +85.
"Insufficiently Paid" +150.
"Ship" +50.
Steamship +50.
Supplementary Mail Type A +70.

78 A29 24c **lilac,** *1862* 2,000. 175.
dark lilac 2,000. 175.
a. 24c **grayish lilac** 2,000. 150.
b. 24c **gray** 2,000. 150.
No gum 650.
On cover 250.
Pair 3,150. 375.
Block of 4 *12,500.* 1,500.
Scratch under "A" of "Postage" — —
c. 24c **blackish violet** *60,000.* *3,250.*
No gum *25,000.*
On cover *5,250.*
d. Printed on both sides —

Earliest documented uses: Oct. 23, 1862 (No. 78a); May 1, 1863 (No. 78c).

Cancellations

Blue +7.50
Red +15.00
Magenta +90.00
Green +400.00
"Paid" +15.00
Numeral +20.00
Supplementary Mail Type A +50.00
"Free" +100.00

Nos. 73, 76-78 exist as imperforate sheet-margin singles, all with pen cancel except No. 76 which is uncanceled. They were not regularly issued.

Only two examples are recorded of No. 78c unused with original gum. No. 78c unused with and without gum are valued in the grade of fine-very fine.

SAME DESIGNS AS 1861-66 ISSUES
Printed by the National Bank Note Co.

Grill

Embossed with grills of various sizes. Some authorities believe that more than one size of grill probably existed on one of the grill rolls.

A peculiarity of the United States issues from 1867 to 1870 is the grill or embossing. The object was to break the fiber of the paper so that the ink of the canceling stamp would soak in and make washing for a second using impossible. The exact date at which grilled stamps came into use is unsettled. Luff's "Postage Stamps of the United States" places the date as probably August 8, 1867.

Horizontal measurements are given first.

GRILL WITH POINTS UP

Grills A and C were made by a roller covered with ridges shaped like an inverted V. Pressing the ridges into the stamp paper forced the paper into the pyramidal pits between the ridges, causing irregular breaks in the paper. Grill B was made by a roller with raised bosses.

A. Grill Covering the Entire Stamp.

1867 ***Perf. 12***

79 A25 3c **rose** 7,500. 1,350.
No gum 2,500.
On cover 1,850.
Pair *16,000.* 3,250.
Block of 4 *50,000.*
b. Printed on both sides —

Earliest documented use: Aug. 13, 1867.

Cancellations

Blue +75.
Ultramarine +250.
Railroad —

Values for No. 79 are for fine-very fine copies with minor perf. faults.

An essay (#79-E15) which is often mistaken for No. 79 shows the points of the grill as small squares faintly impressed in the paper but not cutting through it. On the issued stamp the grill generally breaks through the paper. Copies without defects are rare.

See Die and Plate Proofs for imperf. on stamp paper.

80 A26 5c **brown** — *130,000.*
a. 5c **dark brown** *130,000.*
81 A30 30c **orange** *70,000.*

Eight copies of Nos. 80 and 80a (four unused and four used), and eight copies of No. 81 (one in a museum and not available to collectors) are known. All are more or less faulty and/or off center. Values are for off-center examples with small perforation faults.

B. Grill about 18x15mm
(22x18 points)

82 A25 3c **rose** *185,000.*

The four known copies of No. 82 are valued in the grade of fine.

Earliest documented use: Feb. 1?, 1869 (dated cancel on off-cover stamp).

C. Grill about 13x16mm
(16 to 17 by 18 to 21 points)

The grilled area on each of four C grills in the sheet may total about 18x15mm when a normal C grill adjoins a fainter grill extending to the right or left edge of the stamp. This is caused by a partial erasure on the grill roller when it was changed to produce C grills instead of the all-over A grill. Do not mistake these for the B grill. Unused exists and is very rare, value unused $7,500; value used $2,750; on cover $4,500.

83 A25 3c **rose** 5,250. 1,000.
No gum 2,250.
On cover 1,200.
Pair *11,500.* 3,000.
Block of 4 *23,500.* —
Double grill *6,500.* 2,300.
Grill with points down *6,000.* 1,250.

Earliest documented use: Nov. 16, 1867.

Cancellation

Blue +25.

See Die and Plate Proofs for imperf. on stamp paper.
The 1c, 3c, 5c, 10c, 12c, 30c of 1861 are known with experimental C grills. They are listed in the Essays section. The 3c differs slightly from No. 83.

GRILL WITH POINTS DOWN

The grills were produced by rollers with the surface covered, or partly covered, by pyramidal bosses. On the D, E and F grills the tips of the pyramids are vertical ridges. On the Z grill the ridges are horizontal.

D. Grill about 12x14mm
(15 by 17 to 18 points)

84 A32 2c **black** *15,000.* 3,500.
No gum *7,500.*
On cover 4,500.
Pair 33,500. 7,500.
Block of 4 *75,000.* —
Double transfer — —
Split grill 3,750.

No. 84 is valued in the grade of fine.

Earliest documented use: Feb. 15, 1868.

Cancellations

Red +100.
"Paid All" +100.

85 A25 3c **rose** 6,500. 1,000.
No gum 3,000.
On cover 1,150.
Pair *13,500.* 2,200.
Block of 4 *34,000.* —
Double grill —
Split grill 1,100.

Earliest documented use: Feb. 2, 1868.

Cancellations

Blue +20.
Green +400.
"Paid" +50.

Z. Grill about 11x14mm
(13 to 14 by 18 points)

85A A24 1c **blue** *935,000.*

Two copies of No. 85A are known. One is contained in the New York Public Library collection. Value represents 1998 auction sale price of the single example available to collectors.

85B A32 2c **black** 7,500. 1,200.
No gum 3,500.
On cover 1,350.
Pair *16,000.* 2,750.
Block of 4 *37,500.* —
Double transfer *8,000.* 1,250.
Double grill —
Split grill —

Earliest documented use: Jan. 17, 1868 (on piece); Feb. 11, 1868 (cover).

Cancellations

Blue +50.
Red +100.
Black Carrier +75.
"Paid All" +75.

85C A25 3c **rose** *13,500.* 3,500.
No gum *6,000.*
On cover 4,000.
Pair —
Block of 4 *62,500.*
Double grill *15,000.*

Earliest documented use: Feb. 12, 1868.

Cancellations

Green +250.
Blue +25.
Red +75.
"Paid" +50.

85D A27 10c **green** *95,000.*

Six copies of No. 85D are known. One is contained in the New York Public Library collection. Value is for a well-centered example with small faults.

85E A28 12c **black** *14,000.* 1,700.
No gum *5,750.*
On cover 2,200.
Strip of 3 —
Block of 4 — —
Double transfer of top frame line 1,800.

Earliest documented use: Feb. 15, 1868.

85F A33 15c **black** *240,000.*

Two copies of No. 85F are documented, one in the grade of very good, the other extremely fine. Value is for the extremely fine example.

E. Grill about 11x13mm
(14 by 15 to 17 points)

86 A24 1c **blue** 3,250. 475.
No gum 1,400.
a. 1c **dull blue** 3,250. 475.
No gum 1,400.
On cover 575.
Pair (blue) *6,750.* 1,000.
Block of 4 (blue) *15,000.* *2,900.*
Double grill — 600.
Split grill 3,400. 525.

Earliest documented use: Mar. 9, 1868.

Cancellations

Blue +10.
Red +60.
Green +300.
"Paid" +25.
Steamboat +90.
Red Carrier +80.

87 A32 2c **black** 1,600. 160.
gray black 1,600. 160.
No gum 675.
intense black 1,700. 200.
No gum 725.
On cover 270.
Pair 3,500. 350.
Block of 4 *8,000.* 6,250.
P# strip of 4, Impt. *9,000.*
Double grill — —
Double grill, one split —
Triple grill —
Split grill 1,750. 180.
Grill with points up —
Double transfer 1,750. 175.
a. Diagonal half used as 1c on cover *2,000.*
b. Vertical half used as 1c on cover *2,000.*

Earliest documented use: Mar. 7, 1868.

Cancellations

Blue +7.50
Purple +40.00
Brown +40.00
Red +50.00
Green +1,000.
"Paid" +10.00
Steamship +60.00
Black Carrier +35.00
"Paid All" +20.00
"Short Paid" +65.00
Japan —

88 A25 3c **rose** 900. 22.50
pale rose 900. 22.50
rose red 900. 22.50
No gum 375.
On cover 27.50
Pair 1,900. 47.50
Block of 4 *4,750.* 350.00
P# block of 8, Impt. *10,000.*
Double grill — —
Triple grill — —
Split grill 1,000. 27.50
Very thin paper 950. 25.00
a. 3c **lake red** 1,100. 40.00
No gum 450.

Earliest documented use: Feb. 12, 1868.

Cancellations

Blue +2.50
Red +5.00
Ultramarine +3.00
Green +80.00
"Paid" +3.00
"Way" +20.00
Numeral +2.00
Steamboat +35.00
Railroad +25.00
Express Company +80.00

89 A27 10c **green** 5,000. 300.
dark green 5,000. 300.
blue green 5,000. 300.
No gum 2,200.
On cover 400.
Pair *10,500.* 650.
Block of 4 *22,500.* *3,500.*
Double grill 6,400. 500.

Split grill 5,250. 325.
Double transfer — 325.
Very thin paper 5,250. 325.

Earliest documented use: Feb. 21, 1868.

Cancellations

Blue +20.
Red +60.
"Paid" +15.
Steamship +50.
Japan +225.

90 A28 12c **black** 5,000. 350.
gray black 5,000. 350.
intense black 5,000. 350.
No gum 2,200.
On cover 500.
Pair *10,500.* 750.
Block of 4 *31,500.* *2,500.*
Double transfer of top frame line 5,250. 375.
Double transfer of bottom frame line 5,250. 375.
Double transfer of top and bottom frame lines 5,500. 425.
Double grill 5,750. 700.
Split grill 5,250. 375.

Earliest documented use: Mar. 3, 1868.

Cancellations

Blue +20.
Red +65.
Purple —
Green +225.
Railroad +60.
"Paid" +20.

91 A33 15c **black** 10,000. 625.
gray black 10,000. 625.
No gum 4,500.
On cover 850.
Pair *21,500.* 1,300.
Block of 4 *55,000.* *12,500.*
Double grill — 950.
Split grill — 675.

Earliest documented use: May 2, 1868.

Cancellations

Blue +15.
Magenta +100.
Red +100.
"Paid" +30.
Supplementary Mail Type A +100.

F. Grill about 9x13mm
(11 to 12 by 15 to 17 points)

92 A24 1c **blue** 3,000. 450.
dark blue 3,000. 450.
No gum 900.
a. 1c **pale blue** 2,500. 375.
No gum 700.
On cover 490.
Pair 6,250. 950.
Block of 4 *14,500.* 2,750.
Double transfer 3,250. 500.
Double grill — 825.
Split grill 3,250. 500.
Very thin paper 3,250. 475.

Earliest documented use: Aug. 11 1868.

Cancellations

Blue +5.00
Red +20.00
Green +250.00
"Paid" +10.00
Red Carrier +25.00
"Paid All" +15.00

93 A32 2c **black** 500. 50.00
gray black 500. 50.00
No gum 200.
On cover 65.00
Pair 1,050. 105.00
Block of 4 2,500. 475.00
P# strip of 4, Impt. *6,250.*
P# block of 8, Impt. —
Double transfer 550. 57.50
Double grill — 180.00
Split grill 550. 57.50
Double grill, one split —
Double grill, one quadruple split *1,050.* —
Very thin paper 550. 57.50
a. Vertical half used as 1c as part of 3c rate on cover *1,250.*
b. Diagonal half used as 1c as part of 3c rate on cover *1,250.*
c. Horizontal half used alone as 1c on cover *2,500.*
d. Diagonal half used alone as 1c on cover *2,500.*

Earliest documented use: Mar. 27, 1868.

Cancellations

Blue +5.00
Red +15.00
Green +200.00
"Paid" +5.00
"Paid All" +15.00
Black Carrier +20.00
Red Carrier +30.00
Japan +350.00

94 A25 3c **red** 425. 7.50
rose red 425. 7.50
a. 3c **rose** 425. 7.50
No gum 150.
On cover 9.00
Pair 900. 15.50
Block of 4 *3,000.* 125.00
P# block of 8, Impt. *8,750.*
Double transfer 475. 10.00
Double grill —
Double grill, one normal, one partial with points up —
Triple grill — 160.00
End roller grill 350.00
Split grill 450. 8.00
Quadruple split grill 750. 130.00
Double grill, one quadruple split —
Grill with points up —
Very thin paper 425. 7.75
c. Vertical pair, imperf. horiz. *1,100.*
d. Printed on both sides *7,500.*

Seven examples of No. 94d are recorded. Six are in the top row of an unused top margin imprint block of 18 (6x3).

Earliest documented use: Mar. 21, 1868.

Cancellations

Blue +.25
Ultramarine +3.00
Red +3.50
Violet +5.50
Green +70.00
Numeral +3.00
"Paid" +2.25
"Paid All" +12.50
"Free" +20.00
Railroad +30.00
Steamboat +40.00
Packet boat +80.00
Express Company +50.00

See Die and Plate Proofs for imperf. on stamp paper.

95 A26 5c **brown** 3,500. 800.
No gum 1,300.
dark brown 3,650. 900.
No gum 1,350.
On cover 850.
Pair 7,250. 1,700.
Block of 4 *16,000.* *8,250.*
Double transfer of top frame line — —
Double transfer of bottom frame line —
Double grill — —
Split grill 4,000. 850.
Very thin paper 3,750. 825.
a. 5c **black brown** 4,000. 1,050.
No gum 1,600.

Earliest documented use: Aug. 19, 1868.

Cancellations

Blue +10.
Magenta +55.
Violet +60.
Red +50.
Green +200.
"Paid" +25.
"Free" +50.
"Steamship" +100.

Values of Nos. 95, 95a reflect the normal small margins.

96 A27 10c **yellow green** 3,250. 240.
green 3,250. 240.
a. 10c **dark green** 3,250. 240.
blue green 3,250. 240.
No gum 1,150.
On cover 290.
Pair 6,750. 500.
Block of 4 *25,000.* *3,500.*
P# strip of 4, Impt. *29,000.*
Double transfer — —
Double grill — 425.
Split grill 3,400. 275.
Quadruple split grill 700.
Very thin paper 3,400. 275.

Earliest documented use: May 28, 1868.

Cancellations

Blue +5.00
Red +25.00
Magenta +30.00
Green +200.00
"Paid" +10.00
"Free" +50.00
Supplementary Mail Type A —
Steamship +75.00
Japan +200.00
China —

97 A28 12c **black** 3,250. 250.
gray black 3,250. 250.
No gum 1,150.
On cover 300.
Pair 6,750. 525.
Block of 4 *23,500.* *2,300.*
P# strip of 4, Impt. *26,000.*
Double transfer of top frame line 3,600. 275.
Double transfer of bottom frame line 3,600. 275.
Double transfer of top and bottom frame lines — 300.
Double grill — 475.
Triple grill —
Split grill 3,600. 275.
End roller grill —
Very thin paper 3,600. 275.

Earliest documented use: May 27, 1868.

Cancellations

Blue +5.00
Red +50.00
Magenta +50.00
Brown +50.00
Green +250.0
Purple —
"Paid" +15.0
"Insufficiently Prepaid" +100.0
"Paid All" +25.0
Supplementary Mail Type A +50.0

98 A33 15c **black** 4,000. 300
gray black 4,000. 300
No gum 1,500.
On cover 350
Pair *8,500.* 625
Block of 4 *32,500.* *2,750*
P# block of 8, Impt. *45,000.*
Double transfer of upper right corner — —
Double grill — 450
Split grill 4,250. 325
Quadruple split grill 4,750. 625
Very thin paper 4,250. 300

Value for the plate block is for an example in fine condition.
Earliest documented use: May 4, 1868.

Cancellations

Blue +2.50
Magenta +75.00
Red +150.00
Orange red +40.00
Green +275.00
Orange +150.00
Purple —
"Paid" +20.00
"Insufficiently Prepaid" +135.00
"Insufficiently Paid" +135.00
Japan +300.00
Supplementary Mail Type A +60.00

99 A29 24c **gray lilac** 6,250. 950.
gray 6,250. 950.
No gum 2,750.
On cover 2,000.
Pair *13,000.* 2,000.
Block of 4 *31,500.* *7,500.*
P# block of 8, Impt. *65,000.*
Double grill 7,250. 1,900.
Split grill 6,500. 1,000.
Scratch under "A" of "Postage" —

Earliest documented use: Jan. 5, 1869.

Cancellations

Blue +15.
Red +100.
"Paid" +50.

100 A30 30c **orange** 7,000. 800.
deep orange 7,000. 800.
No gum 2,900.
On cover 2,000.
Pair *15,000.* 1,700.
Block of 4 *35,000.* *8,750.*
Double grill 9,250. 1,650.
Split grill 7,250. 850.
Double grill, one split —

Values for No. 100 are for copies with small margins, especially at sides. Large-margined examples sell for much more.

Earliest documented use: Nov. 10, 1868.

Cancellations

Blue +10.
Red +65.
Magenta +75.
"Paid" +50.
Supplementary Mail Type A +100.
Japan +400.

101 A31 90c **blue** 11,500. 1,600.
dark blue 11,500. 1,600.
No gum 5,250.
On cover *95,000.*
Pair *24,000.* 3,500.
Block of 4 *60,000.* *21,000.*
Double grill *15,500.*
Split grill 12,000. 1,650.

Two usages on cover are recorded (one being a cover front). Value is for use on full cover to Peru.

Earliest documented use: May 8, 1869.

Cancellations

Blue +40.
Red +100.
Japan +600.
"Paid" +50.

RE-ISSUE OF 1861-66 ISSUES

Produced by the National Bank Note Co.

Without grill, hard white paper, with white crackly gum.

The 1, 2, 5, 10 and 12c were printed from new plates of 100 subjects each.

1875 ***Perf. 12***

102 A24 1c **blue** *(3195)* *900.* *1,200.*
No gum *425.*
On cover —
Block of 4 *7,000.* —
103 A32 2c **black** *(979)* *4,000.* *5,500.*
No gum *2,000.*
Block of 4 *25,000.*
104 A25 3c **brown red** *(465)* *4,000.* *6,750.*
No gum *2,300.*
Block of 4 *30,000.*
105 A26 5c **brown** *(672)* *3,000.* *2,900.*
No gum *1,650.*
Block of 4 *22,500.*
106 A27 10c **green** *(451)* *3,250.* *12,500.*
No gum *1,800.*

No.	Type	Denom.	Description	Unused	Used
			Block of 4	*24,000.*	
107	A28	12c	**black** *(389)*	*4,500.*	*6,750.*
			No gum	*2,400.*	
			Block of 4	*27,500.*	
108	A33	15c	**black** *(397)*	*4,750.*	*9,000.*
			No gum	*2,500.*	
			Block of 4	*32,500.*	
109	A29	24c	**deep violet** *(346)*	*5,750.*	*10,000.*
			No gum	*3,250.*	
			Block of 4	*40,000.*	
110	A30	30c	**brownish orange** *(346)*	*5,750.*	*13,500.*
			No gum	*3,500.*	
			Pair	*15,500.*	
			Block of 4	*45,000.*	
111	A31	90c	**blue** *(317)*	*6,500.*	*55,000.*
			No gum	*3,900.*	

Earliest documented uses: No. 102, July 25, 1881; No. 104, July ?, 1883 (dated cancel on off-cover stamp); No. 111, Nov. 30, 1888 (dated cancel on off-cover stamp).

These stamps can be distinguished from the 1861-66 issue by the brighter colors, the sharper proof-like impressions and the paper which is very white instead of yellowish. The gum is almost always somewhat yellowed with age, and unused stamps with original gum are valued with such gum.

Numbers in parentheses are quantities sold.

Five examples are recorded of No. 111 used, one of which has a non-contemporaneous cancel. Value is for centered and sound example (two are known thus).

PLEASE NOTE:

Stamps are valued in the grade of very fine unless otherwise indicated.

Values for early and valuable stamps are for examples with certificates of authenticity from acknowledged expert committees, or examples sold with the buyer having the right of certification. This applies to examples with original gum as well as examples without gum. Beware of stamps offered "as is," as the gum on some unused stamps offered with "original gum" may be fraudulent, and unused stamps offered without may in some cases be altered or faintly canceled used stamps.

VALUES FOR NEVER-HINGED STAMPS PRIOR TO SCOTT No. 205

This catalogue does not value pre-1882 stamps in never-hinged condition. Premiums for never-hinged condition in the classic era invariably are even larger than those premiums listed for the post-1890 issues. Generally speaking, the earlier the stamp is listed in the catalogue, the larger will be the never-hinged premium. On some early classics, the premium will be several multiples of the unused, hinged values given in the catalogue.

Produced by the National Bank Note Co.

Plates for the 1c, 2c, 3c, 6c, 10c and 12c consisted of 300 subjects in two panes of 150 each. For the 15c, 24c, 30c and 90c plates of 100 subjects each.

NOTE: Stamps of the 1869 issue without grill cannot be guaranteed except when unused and with the original gum or traces of the original gum. This does not apply to No. 114 on gray paper.

Franklin — A34

Post Horse and Rider — A35

G. Grill measuring 9½x9mm (12 by 11 to 11½ points)

1869 Hard Wove Paper *Perf. 12*

No.	Type	Denom.	Description	Unused	Used
112	A34	1c	**buff**	825.	160.
			brown orange	825.	160.
			dark brown orange	825.	175.
			No gum	350.	
			On cover, single		300.
			Pair	1,700.	350.
			Block of 4	*6,000.*	*2,250.*
			Margin block of 4, arrow	*6,250.*	
			P# block of 10, Impt.	—	
			Double transfer	—	—
			Double grill	1,250.	340.
			Split grill	900.	200.
			Double grill, one split		—
			Double grill, one quadruple split		—
b.			Without grill, original gum	*6,000.*	

Earliest documented use: Apr. 1, 1869.

Cancellations

Cancel	Value
Blue	+15.
Ultramarine	+50.
Magenta	+55.
Purple	+75.
Red	+50.
Green	+800.
"Paid"	+50.
Numeral	+100.
Steamship	+75.
Black town	+30.
Blue town	+30.
Red town	+75.
Black Carrier	+80.
Blue Carrier	+100.
Japan	+400.

No.	Type	Denom.	Description	Unused	Used
113	A35	2c	**brown**	750.	85.
			pale brown	750.	85.
			dark brown	750.	85.
			yellow brown	750.	85.
			No gum	325.	
			On cover, single		130.
			Pair	1,600.	200.
			Block of 4	3,500.	1,300.
			Margin block of 4, arrow	3,750.	
			P# block of 10, Impt.	—	
			Double grill	—	325.
			Split grill	900.	110.
			Quadruple split grill	—	450.
			End roller grill	1,200.	
			Double transfer		105.
b.			Without grill, original gum	*2,750.*	
c.			Half used as 1c on cover, diagonal, vertical or horizontal		*4,000.*
d.			Printed on both sides		*9,000.*

Earliest documented use: Mar. 20, 1869.

Cancellations

Cancel	Value
Blue	+15.
Red	+30.
Orange red	+35.
Orange	+75.
Magenta	+35.
Purple	+40.
Ultramarine	+30.
Green	+450.
Brown	—
"Paid"	+15.
"Paid All"	+25.
Steamship	+60.
Black town	+10.
Blue town	+30.
Japan	+250.
Blue Carrier	+90.
Black Carrier	+80.
China	—
Printed Precancellation "Jefferson, Ohio"	—

Locomotive — A36

Washington — A37

No.	Type	Denom.	Description	Unused	Used
114	A36	3c	**ultramarine**	300.	18.
			pale ultramarine	300.	18.
			dark ultramarine	300.	18.
			No gum	125.	
			blue	575.	100.
			No gum	260.	
			violet blue		175.
			On cover		25.
			Pair	650.	40.
			Block of 4	1,500.	450.
			Margin block of 4, arrow	1,650.	
			P# block of 10, Impt.	*7,000.*	
			Double transfer	375.	35.00
			Double grill	600.	110.
			Triple grill	—	—
			Split grill	350.	37.50
			Quadruple split grill	650.	150.
			Sextuple grill	—	*3,250.*
			End roller grill	—	—
			Grill with points up		—
			Gray paper	—	95.
			On cover		250.
			Without grill		—
			Cracked plate	—	160.
a.			Without grill, original gum	*1,500.*	
b.			Vert. one-third used as 1c on cover		—
c.			Vert. two-thirds used as 2c on cover		*5,000.*
e.			Printed on both sides		—

The grill-with-points-up variety is found on a unique margin "pair" of stamps where the paper was folded over prior to perforating and grilling. The stamps have drastic freak perfs.

Earliest documented use: Mar. 27, 1869.

Cancellations

Cancel	Value
Blue	+5.
Ultramarine	+25.
Magenta	+35.
Purple	+75.
Violet	+65.
Red	+15.
Orange red	+20.
Brown	+200.
Green	+450.
Orange	—
Yellow	—
Black town	+3.
Blue town	+7.
Red town	+30.
Numeral	+10.
"Paid"	+20.
"Paid All"	+15.
"Steamboat"	—
"Steamship"	+50.
Ship	+35.
"U. S. Ship"	+450.
Railroad	+30.
Packet Boat	+100.
Black Carrier	+30.
Blue Carrier	+40.
Express Company	—
"Way"	—
"Free"	+150.
Alaska	—
Japan	+600.

The authenticity of the yellow cancel has been questioned by some specialists. The editors would like to see an expertizing certificate for this stamp and cancel.

No.	Type	Denom.	Description	Unused	Used
115	A37	6c	**ultramarine**	3,100.	210.
			pale ultramarine	3,100.	210.
			No gum	1,350.	
			On cover		425.
			Pair	6,500.	525.
			Block of 4	*15,500.*	*9,000.*
			Margin block of 4, arrow	*16,000.*	
			Double grill	—	650.
			Split grill	3,400.	300.
			Quadruple split grill	—	825.
			Double transfer		260.
b.			Vertical half used as 3c on cover		—

Earliest documented use: Apr. 26, 1869.

Cancellations

Cancel	Value
Blue	+5.
Brown	+80.
Magenta	+40.
Purple	+75.
Red	+50.
Green	+750
"Paid"	+15.
"Paid All"	+25.
Black town	+30.
"Short Paid"	+75.
"Insufficiently Paid"	+75.
Steamship	+40.
Railroad	+50.
Japan	+1,500.

Shield and Eagle — A38

S.S. "Adriatic" — A39

No.	Type	Denom.	Description	Unused	Used
116	A38	10c	**yellow**	2,500.	140.
			yellowish orange	2,500.	140.
			No gum	1,000.	
			On cover		375.
			Pair	5,250.	300.
			Block of 4	*13,000.*	*8,000.*
			Margin block of 4, arrow	*13,500.*	
			Double grill	—	425.
			Split grill	2,700.	150.
			End roller grill	—	—

Earliest documented use: Apr. 1, 1869.

Cancellations

Cancel	Value
Blue	+35.
Magenta	+30.
Purple	+100.
Red	+40.
Ultramarine	+60.
Green	+5,000.
Black town	+20.
Steamship	+35.
Railroad	+45.
"Paid"	+15.
"Paid All"	+30.
"Insufficiently Paid"	+50.
Supplementary Mail Type A	+150.
Express Company	—
St. Thomas	—
Hawaii	—
Japan	+125.
China	—

No.	Type	Denom.	Description	Unused	Used
117	A39	12c	**green**	2,600.	150.
			yellowish green	2,600.	150.
			bluish green	2,600.	175.
			No gum	1,100.	
			On cover		425.
			Pair	5,500.	325.
			Block of 4	*13,000.*	*1,750.*
			Margin block of 4, arrow	*13,500.*	
			Double grill	—	425.
			Split grill	3,100.	165.
			Double grill, one quadruple split		—
			End roller grill		600.

Earliest documented use: Apr. 1, 1869.

Cancellations

Cancel	Value
Blue	+150.
Magenta	+125.
Purple	+250.
Brown	+150.
Red	+150.

Cancellation	Value
Green	+4,000.
Numeral	+125.
"Paid"	+25.
"Paid All"	+40.
"Too Late"	+100.
"Insufficiently Paid"	+125.
Black town	+35.
Red town	+200.
Japan	+450.

Landing of Columbus — A40

No.	Type	Denom.	Description	Unused	Used
118	A40	15c	**brown & blue,** type I, Picture unframed	8,250.	650.
			dark brown & blue	8,250.	650.
			No gum	3,750.	
			On cover		1,850.
			Pair	*18,000.*	1,500.
			Block of 4	*52,500.*	*30,000.*
			Double grill	—	850.
			Split grill	8,750.	700.
a.			Without grill, original gum	*11,000.*	

Earliest documented use: Mar. 31, 1869 (dated cancel on off-cover stamp); Apr. 2, 1869 (on cover).

Cancellations

Cancellation	Value
Blue	+65.
Red	+90.
Brown	+150.
"Paid"	+50.
"Paid All"	+100.
"Insufficiently Paid"	+150.
Black town	+50.
Blue town	+120.
Steamship	+100.

A40a

No.	Type	Denom.	Description	Unused	Used
119	A40a	15c	**brown & blue,** type II, Picture framed	3,750.	250.
			dark brown & blue	3,750.	250.
			No gum	1,650.	
			On cover		875.
			Pair	8,000.	550.
			Block of 4	*18,500.*	*9,000.*
			P# block of 8, Impt.	*45,000.*	
			Double transfer	—	—
			Double grill	6,250.	500.
			Split grill	4,000.	325.
b.			Center inverted	*415,000.*	*15,000.*
			No gum	—	
c.			Center double, one inverted		*80,000.*

Earliest documented use: Apr. 5, 1869.

Cancellations

Cancellation	Value
Blue	+60.
Purple	+110.
Magenta	+110.
Red	+150.
Brown	+150.
Green	+1,500.
Numeral	+75.
"Paid"	+20.
"Paid All"	+35.
Black town	+30.
Blue town	+75.
Red town	+110.
"Steamship"	+75.
Supp. Mail Type A or F	+40.
Japan	+500.

Most copies of No. 119b are faulty. Values are for fine centered copies with only minimal faults. Three examples of No. 119b unused are recorded; only one has original gum.

Three examples of No. 119c are recorded. Value is for the finer of the two sound examples.

The Declaration of Independence — A41

No.	Type	Denom.	Description	Unused	Used
120	A41	24c	**green & violet**	8,000.	750
			bluish green & violet	8,000.	750
			No gum	3,600.	
			On cover		*20,000*
			Pair	*17,500.*	1,600
			Block of 4	*45,000.*	*20,000*
			Double grill	—	2,250
			Split grill	8,250.	875
a.			Without grill, original gum	*10,000.*	
b.			Center inverted	*285,000.*	*15,000*
			On cover		*105,000*
			Pair		*57,500*
			Block of 4		*600,000.*

Earliest documented use: Apr. 7, 1869.

Cancellations

Cancellation	Value
Blue	+250.
Red	+300.
Black town	+100.
Red town	+400.
"Paid All"	+150.
"Steamship"	+250.
Supp. Mail Type A	+200.
China	+750.

Most copies of No. 120b are faulty. Values are for fine centered copies with only minimal faults. No. 120b unused is valued without gum, as all of the three examples available to collectors are without gum.

Shield, Eagle and Flags — A42

Lincoln — A43

No.	Type	Denom.	Description	Unused	Used
121	A42	30c	**ultramarine & carmine**	7,500.	550.
			ultramarine & dark carmine	7,500.	550.
			No gum	3,500.	
			On cover		*27,500.*
			Pair	*16,000.*	1,150.
			Block of 4	*37,500.*	*3,250.*
			Double grill	—	1,100.
			Split grill	8,000.	600.
			Double paper (without grill), original gum	*8,250.*	
a.			Without grill, original gum	*11,000.*	
			Block of 4	*50,000.*	
			P# block of 8, Impt.	—	
b.			Flags inverted	*275,000.*	*67,500.*
			No gum	*210,000.*	

Seven examples of No. 121b unused are recorded. Only one has part of its original gum.

Earliest documented use: May 22, 1869. The previously listed May 15, 1869, date is questioned and requires certification.

Cancellations

Cancellation	Value
Blue	+200.
Red	+250.
Brown	+400.
Purple	+1,000.
Green	+7,500.
"Paid"	+50.
"Paid All"	+250.
Black town	+100.
Steamship	+75.
"Steam"	+60.
Supp. Mail Type A	+75.
Japan	+600.
China	—

No.	Type	Denom.	Description	Unused	Used
122	A43	90c	**carmine & black**	10,000.	2,300.
			carmine rose & black	10,000.	2,300.
			No gum	4,900.	
			Pair	*25,000.*	*5,750.*
			Block of 4	*105,000.*	*50,000.*
			Split grill	—	—
a.			Without grill, original gum	*16,000.*	

Cancellations

Cancellation	Value
Blue	+1,500.
Red	+400.
Orange red	+500.
Brown	+1,750.
Ultramarine	+1,000.
Black town	+1,500.
Red town	+1,750.
Magenta town	+2,000.
"Paid"	—
"Paid All"	—
N.Y. steamship	—

Students of the 1869 issue believe that No. 122 on cover no longer exists, though at one time one or two were known. The editors would appreciate receiving any information that might confirm the existence of No. 122 on cover.

Nos. 112, 114, 117, 118, 120b, 121, 122 exist as imperf. singles. They were not regularly issued.

CANCELLATIONS

The common type of cancellation on the 1869 issue is the block or cork similar to illustrations above. Japanese cancellations seen on this issue (not illustrated) resulted from the sale of U.S. stamps in Japanese cities where post offices were maintained for mail going from Japan to the United States.

RE-ISSUE OF 1869 ISSUE

Produced by the National Bank Note Co.

Without grill, hard white paper, with white crackly gum.

The gum is almost always somewhat yellowed with age, and unused stamps with original gum are valued with such gum.

A new plate of 150 subjects was made for the 1c and for the frame of the 15c. The frame on the 15c is the same as type I but without the fringe of brown shading lines around central vignette.

1875 ***Perf. 12***

123 A34	1c **buff** *(10,000)*	500.	325.
	No gum	250.	
	Block of 4	*2,750.*	
	On cover		*3,000.*
124 A35	2c **brown** *(4755)*	700.	500.
	No gum	350.	
	Block of 4	*4,000.*	
	On cover		*10,000.*
125 A36	3c **blue** *(1406)*	*5,500.*	*22,500.*
	No gum	3,150.	
	On cover		—

Cancellation

Supplementary Mail Type F —

Very few authenticated sound used copies of No. 125 are recorded. The used value is for an attractive fine to very fine example with minimal faults. Copies of No. 114 with faint or pressed-out grill are frequently offered as No. 125. Expertization by competent authorities is required.

126 A37	6c **blue** *(2226)*	1,900.	*2,100.*
	No gum	1,050.	
	Block of 4	*22,500.*	
	On cover		—
127 A38	10c **yellow** *(1947)*	2,000.	1,750.
	No gum	1,100.	
	Block of 4	*17,500.*	
	On cover		*22,500.*
128 A39	12c **green** *(1584)*	2,750.	2,750.
	No gum	1,550.	
	Block of 4	*29,000.*	
	On cover		—
129 A40	15c **brown & blue,** Type III, *(1981)*	1,900.	1,150.
	No gum	1,050.	
	Pair		*6,000.*
	Block of 4	*29,000.*	
	On cover		*22,500.*
a.	Imperf. horizontally, single	*6,000.*	*7,000.*
	No gum	4,000.	
130 A41	24c **green & violet** *(2091)*	2,250.	1,600.
	No gum	1,200.	
	Pair		*10,000.*
	On cover		*25,000.*
131 A42	30c **ultra & carmine** *(1535)*	3,000.	2,500.
	No gum	1,600.	
	Pair		*28,000.*
132 A43	90c **carmine & black** *(1356)*	5,000.	*5,500.*
	No gum	2,750.	
	Pair		*28,000.*
	Block of 4	*35,000.*	
	P# block of 10, Impt.	*325,000.*	

Numbers in parentheses are quantities sold.

Two used examples of No. 129a are recorded. Both are faulty and are valued thus.

Earliest documented uses:
No. 123, Dec. 9, 1877;
No. 124, Mar. 20, 1880;
No. 127, Nov. 11, 1880;
No. 128, Mar. 20, 1880.
No. 129, Mar. 20, 1880;
No. 130, Mar. 27, 1880.

RE-ISSUE OF 1869 ISSUE

Produced by the American Bank Note Co.

Without grill, soft porous paper.

1880-81

133 A34	1c **buff,** issued with gum (+23,252)	350.	225.
	No gum	160.	
	Block of 4, with gum	1,750.	
	Margin block of 10, Impt. & P#	*22,500.*	

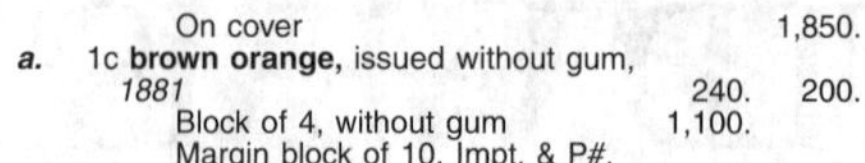

	On cover		1,850.
a.	1c **brown orange,** issued without gum, *1881*	240.	200.
	Block of 4, without gum	1,100.	
	Margin block of 10, Impt. & P#, without gum	*22,500.*	

+ This quantity includes No. 133a.

Earliest documented use: Oct. 5, 1880 (No. 133).

PRODUCED BY THE NATIONAL BANK NOTE COMPANY

Plates of 200 subjects in two panes of 100 each.

Franklin — A44

Jackson — A45

Washington — A46

Lincoln — A47

Edwin M. Stanton — A48

Jefferson — A49

Henry Clay — A50

Daniel Webster — A51

Two varieties of grill are known on this issue.

H. Grill about 10x12mm (11 to 13 by 14 to 16 points.) On all values 1c to 90c.

I. Grill about 8½x10mm (10 to 11 by 10 to 13 points.) On 1, 2, 3, 6, 7, 10 and 15c.

On the 1870-71 stamps the grill impressions are usually faint or incomplete. This is especially true of the H grill, which often shows only a few points.

Values for 1c-7c are for stamps showing well-defined grills.

Killer cancellation of the oval grid type with letters or numeral centers was first used in 1876 Bank Note issues. By order of the Postmaster-General (July 23, 1860) it was prohibited to use the town mark as a canceling instrument, and a joined town and killer cancellation was developed.

Numeral cancellations-see “Postal Markings-Examples.”

White Wove Paper, Thin to Medium Thick.

1870-71 ***Perf. 12***

134 A44	1c **ultramarine,** *Apr. 1870*	2,300.	150.00
	pale ultramarine	2,300.	150.00
	dark ultramarine	2,300.	150.00
	No gum	950.	
	On cover		185.00
	Pair	*4,850.*	310.00
	Block of 4	*10,500.*	850.00
	Double transfer	2,600.	165.00
	Double grill	—	290.00
	Split grill	2,700.	165.00
	Quadruple split grill	—	490.00
	End roller grill		675.00

Earliest documented use: Apr. 9, 1870.

Cancellations

Blue	+5.00
Red	+15.00
Green	+100.00
“Paid”	+10.00
“Paid All”	+20.00
“Steamship”	+45.00

135 A45	2c **red brown,** *Apr. 1870*	1,200.	70.00
	pale red brown	1,200.	70.00
	dark red brown	1,200.	70.00
	No gum	525.	
	On cover		95.00
	Pair	2,550.	150.00
	Block of 4	5,500.	425.00
	Double grill	1,575.	140.00
	Split grill	1,250	85.00
	Quadruple split grill	*2,400.*	225.00
	End roller grill	*1,900.*	*400.00*
	Grill with points up		*500.00*
a.	Diagonal half used as 1c on cover		—
b.	Vertical half used as 1c on cover		—

Earliest documented use: July 14, 1870.

Cancellations

Blue	+3.00
Red	+10.00
Brown	+8.00
Green	+100.00
“Paid”	+5.00
“Paid All”	+10.00
Numeral	+5.00
China	—

136 A46	3c **green,** *Mar. 1870*	725.	20.00
	pale green	725.	20.00
	yellow green	725.	20.00
	deep green	725.	20.00
	No gum	325.	
	On cover		27.50
	Pair	1,500.	42.50
	Block of 4	3,100.	180.00
	P# block of 10, Impt.	*7,750.*	
	P# block of 12, Impt.	*9,000.*	
	Printed on both sides	—	
	Double transfer	—	24.00
	Double grill	1,000.	77.50
	Split grill	775.	26.00
	Quadruple split grill	—	140.00
	End roller grill		275.00
	Cracked plate	—	90.00

Earliest documented use: Mar. 24, 1870.

Cancellations

Blue	+1.00
Purple	+2.50
Magenta	+5.00
Red	+5.00
Orange red	+6.00
Orange	+10.00
Brown	+2.50
Green	+45.00
"Paid"	+2.50
Railroad	+10.00
"Steamship"	+20.00
"Paid All"	+15.00
Numeral	+4.00
"Free"	+25.00

See Die and Plate Proofs for imperf. on stamp paper.

137 A47 6c	**carmine,** *Apr. 1870*	4,750.	525.00
	pale carmine	4,750.	525.00
	carmine rose	4,750.	525.00
	No gum	2,000.	
	On cover		750.00
	Pair	*10,000.*	1,100.
	Block of 4	*23,500.*	
	Double grill	—	900.00
	Split grill	*5,000.*	550.00
	Quadruple split grill	—	950.00
	End roller grill	*6,250.*	*1,100.*

Earliest documented use: Apr. 11, 1870.

Cancellations

Blue	+10.00
Red	+35.00
"Paid"	+35.00

138 A48 7c	**vermilion,** *1871*	3,750.	425.00
	deep vermilion	3,750.	425.00
	No gum	1,500.	
	On cover		600.00
	Pair	7,750.	900.00
	Block of 4	*16,500.*	
	Double grill		725.00
	Split grill	4,000.	450.00
	Quadruple split grill		775.00
	End roller grill		*900.00*

Earliest documented use: Feb. 12, 1871.

Cancellations

Blue	+10.00
Purple	+20.00
Red	+35.00
Green	+200.00
"Paid"	+25.00

The 7c stamps, Nos. 138 and 149, were issued for a 7c rate of July 1, 1870, to Prussia, German States and Austria, including Hungary, via Hamburg (on the Hamburg-American Line steamers), or Bremen (on North German Lloyd ships), but issue was delayed by the Franco-Prussian War.

The rate for this service was reduced to 6c in 1871.

For several months there was no 7c rate, but late in 1871 the Prussian closed mail rate via England was reduced to 7c which revived an important use for the 7c stamps.

The rate to Denmark direct via Baltic Lloyd ships, or via Bremen and Hamburg as above, was 7c from Jan. 1, 1872.

139 A49 10c	**brown,** *Apr. 1870*	5,000.	675.
	yellow brown	5,000.	675.
	dark brown	5,000.	675.
	No gum	2,250.	
	On cover		975.
	Pair	*10,500.*	1,400.
	Block of 4	*25,000.*	—
	Double grill		1,250.
	Split grill	5,250.	725.
	End roller grill		*1,600.*

Earliest documented use: June 2, 1870.

Cancellations

Blue	+15.
Red	+50.
"Steamship"	+50.
"Honolulu Paid All"	—

140 A50 12c	**dull violet,** *Apr. 1870*	*22,500.*	3,000.
	No gum	*11,000.*	
	On cover		*6,250.*
	Pair	*50,000.*	*7,000.*
	Strip of 3		*14,000.*
	Strip of 4		*17,500.*
	Block of 4	*110,000.*	
	Split grill	—	3,250.
	End roller grill		*6,500.*

Earliest documented use: June 17, 1870.

Cancellations

Blue	+50.
Red	+100.
"Paid all"	—

141 A51 15c	**orange,** *Apr. 1870*	7,500.	1,200.
	bright orange	7,500.	1,200.
	deep orange	7,500.	1,200.
	No gum	3,000.	
	On cover		1,900.
	Pair	16,000.	2,600.
	Block of 4	*37,500.*	—
	Double grill		—
	Split grill	7,750.	1,250.
	Quadruple split grill		—

Earliest documented use: June 2, 1870.

Cancellations

Blue	+20.
Purple	+50.
Red	+90.
Green	+300.

General Winfield Scott — A52

Alexander Hamilton — A53

142 A52 24c	**purple**	—	*6,500.*
	On cover		—
	Pair, double grill		—
	Split grill		—
	End roller grill		—

Earliest documented use: July 11, 1872.

Cancellations

Red	+500.
Blue	+500.
Purple	—

The pair of No. 142 is the unique multiple of this stamp.

143 A53 30c	**black,** *Apr. 1870*	17,000.	2,800.
	full black	17,000.	2,800.
	No gum	7,500.	
	On cover		3,750.
	Pair	*37,500.*	5,850.
	Block of 4	*85,000.*	—
	Double grill		—
	End roller grill		*4,250.*

Earliest documented use: Aug. 18, 1870.

Cancellations

Blue	+65.
Red	+125.

Commodore Oliver Hazard Perry — A54

144 A54 90c	**carmine,** *Apr. 12, 1870*	15,000.	1,800.
	dark carmine	15,000.	1,800.
	No gum	6,750.	
	On cover		—
	Pair	*31,500.*	4,000.
	Block of 4	*70,000.*	*9,000.*
	Double grill		—
	Split grill		1,900.

Cancellations

Blue	+75.
Red	+135.

PRODUCED BY THE NATIONAL BANK NOTE COMPANY.

White Wove Paper, Thin to Medium Thick.
Issued (except 3c and 7c) in April, 1870.
Without Grill.

1870-71 ***Perf. 12***

145 A44 1c	**ultramarine**	575.	15.00
	pale ultramarine	575.	15.00
	dark ultramarine	575.	15.00
	gray blue	575.	15.00
	No gum	210.	
	On cover		18.00
	Pair	1,200.	32.50
	Block of 4	2,600.	100.00
	P# block of 12, Impt.	*4,250.*	
	Double transfer	—	20.00
	Worn plate	575.	15.00

Only one plate block of No. 145 is known in private hands. It is of average condition and is without gum. Value is based on 1998 auction sale.

Earliest documented use: May 7, 1870.

Cancellations

Blue	+.1.00
Ultramarine	+2.50
Magenta	+2.00
Purple	+2.00
Brown	+2.00
Red	+5.00
Green	+55.00
"Paid"	+3.00
"Paid All"	+15.00
"Steamship"	+25.00
Railroad	+20.00
Numeral	+2.00

146 A45 2c	**red brown**	325.	12.00
	pale red brown	325.	12.00
	dark red brown	325.	12.00
	No gum	130.	
	orange brown	350.	13.00
	No gum	140.	
	On cover		14.00
	Pair	675.	25.00
	Block of 4	1,500.	90.00
	P# block of 10, Impt.	*6,250.*	
	Double transfer	—	15.00
a.	Diagonal half used as 1c on cover		*650.00*
b.	Vertical half used as 1c on cover		*750.00*
c.	Horiz. half used as 1c on cover		*750.00*
d.	Double impression		—

The No. 146 plate block is unique. Value is 1998 auction realization.

Earliest documented use: May 7, 1870.

Cancellations

Blue	+.50
Purple	+.75
Red	+3.00
Green	+55.00
Brown	+1.00
"Paid"	+2.00
"Paid All"	+10.00
Numeral	+2.00
"Steamship"	+22.50
Black Carrier	+12.50
Japan	—
China	—
Curacao	—

147 A46 3c	**green**	300.	1.50
	pale green	300.	1.50
	dark green	300.	1.50
	No gum	120.	
	yellow green	325.	1.60
	No gum	130.	
	On cover		2.10
	Pair	625.	3.10
	Block of 4	1,300.	22.50
	P# block of 10, Impt.	*3,500.*	
	Double transfer	—	12.00
	Short transfer at bottom	325.	20.00
	Cracked plate	—	55.00
	Worn plate	300.	1.50
a.	Printed on both sides		*1,750.*
b.	Double impression		*1,250.*

See Die and Plate Proofs for imperf. on stamp paper.

Earliest documented use: Mar. 1, 1870.

Cancellations

Blue	+.10
Purple	+.35
Magenta	+.35
Brown	+1.50
Red	+2.50
Ultramarine	+2.00
Green	+55.00
"Paid"	+2.00
"Paid All"	+10.00
"Free"	+15.00

				Unused	Used
			Numeral		+2.00
			Railroad		+10.00
			Express Company		—
			"Steamboat"		+20.00
			"Steamship"		+17.50
			Ship		+15.00
			Japan		+75.00
148	A47	6c	**carmine**	850.	25.00
			dark carmine	850.	25.00
			rose	850.	25.00
			No gum	325.	
			On cover		42.50
			Pair	1,800.	52.50
			Block of 4	3,750.	300.00
			Double transfer		35.00
			Double paper	—	—
			brown carmine	875.	50.00
			No gum	350.	
			violet carmine	1,000.	75.00
			No gum	450.	
a.			Vertical half used as 3c on cover		*3,500.*
b.			Double impression		*1,500.*

Earliest documented use: Mar. 28, 1870.

Cancellations

Blue	+.1.00
Purple	+1.50
Violet	+1.50
Ultramarine	+3.00
Brown	+1.50
Red	+5.00
Claret	+10.00
Orange red	+7.00
Orange	+10.00
Green	+90.00
"Paid"	+3.00
"Steamship"	+25.00
"Paid All"	+15.00
Numeral	—
Supp. Mail Type A or D	+25.00
China	+75.00
Japan	+150.00

				Unused	Used
149	A48	7c	**vermilion,** *Mar. 1871*	1,000.	90.00
			deep vermilion	1,000.	90.00
			No gum	425.	
			On cover		160.00
			Pair	2,100.	200.00
			Block of 4	4,750.	*725.00*
			Cracked plate		—

Earliest documented use: May 11, 1871.

Cancellations

Blue	+2.50
Purple	+7.50
Ultramarine	+12.50
Red	+10.00
Green	+450.00
Japan	+150.00

				Unused	Used
150	A49	10c	**brown**	1,250.	22.50
			dark brown	1,250.	22.50
			yellow brown	1,250.	22.50
			No gum	525.	
			On cover		40.00
			Pair	2,650.	47.50
			Block of 4	5,750.	*240.00*
			P# block of 10, Impt.	—	
			Double transfer	—	77.50

Earliest documented use: May 14, 1870 (stamp on piece); May 25, 1870 (on cover).

Cancellations

Blue	+.50
Purple	+2.00
Magenta	+2.00
Ultramarine	+4.00
Red	+4.00
Orange red	+5.00
Orange	+10.00
Green	+120.00
Brown	+3.00
"Paid All"	+20.00
"Steamship"	+20.00
Supp. Mail Type A or D	+25.00
Japan	+120.00
China	—
St. Thomas	—

				Unused	Used
151	A50	12c	**dull violet**	2,250.	160.00
			violet	2,250.	160.00
			dark violet	2,250.	160.00
			No gum	1,000.	
			On cover		425.00
			Pair	4,750.	350.00
			Block of 4	*10,500.*	*1,750.*

Earliest documented use: July 9, 1870.

Cancellations

Blue	+5.00
Magenta	+10.00
Red	+15.00
Green	+150.00
"Paid All"	+25.00
"Steamship"	+50.00
Supp. Mail Type A or D	+40.00
Japan	—

				Unused	Used
152	A51	15c	**bright orange**	2,400.	160.00
			deep orange	2,400.	160.00
			No gum	1,075.	
			On cover		310.00
			Pair	5,000.	350.00
			Block of 4	*11,000.*	*1,400.*
a.			Double impression		*1,650.*

Earliest documented use: June 24, 1870.

Cancellations

Blue	+2.50
Magenta	+7.50
Ultramarine	+10.00
Red	+15.00
"Paid"	+12.50
"Steamship"	+40.00
Supp. Mail Type A or F	+30.00
China	—

				Unused	Used
153	A52	24c	**purple**	1,750.	140.00
			bright purple	1,750.	140.00
			No gum	750.	
			On cover		*1,500.*
			Pair	3,750.	300.00
			Block of 4	*11,000.*	*3,400.*
			Double paper	—	—

Earliest documented use: Nov. 18, 1870.

Cancellations

Red	+15.00
Blue	+5.00
Purple	+7.50
China	—
"Paid"	+25.00
Town	+15.00
"Steamship"	—
Supp. Mail Type A, D or F	+30.00

				Unused	Used
154	A53	30c	**black**	6,000.	200.00
			full black	6,000.	200.00
			No gum	2,750.	
			On cover		775.00
			Pair	*13,000.*	425.00
			Block of 4	*31,500.*	

Earliest documented use: July 13, 1870.

Cancellations

Blue	+2.50
Brown	+50.00
Magenta	+15.00
Red	+50.00
"Steamship"	+55.00
Supplementary Mail Type A	+40.00

				Unused	Used
155	A54	90c	**carmine**	4,500.	300.00
			dark carmine	4,500.	300.00
			No gum	2,000.	
			On cover		—
			Pair	*9,250.*	625.00
			Block of 4	*21,000.*	2,000.
			P# strip of 5, Impt.	*28,500.*	

Earliest documented use: Sept. 1, 1872.

Cancellations

Blue	+10.00
Purple	+15.00
Magenta	+15.00
Green	+275.00
Red	+50.00
Town	+20.00
Supp. Mail Type A or F	+40.00
Japan	—

PLEASE NOTE:

Stamps are valued in the grade of very fine unless otherwise indicated.

Values for early and valuable stamps are for examples with certificates of authenticity from acknowledged expert committees, or examples sold with the buyer having the right of certification. This applies to examples with original gum as well as examples without gum. Beware of stamps offered "as is," as the gum on some unused stamps offered with "original gum" may be fraudulent, and stamps offered as unused without gum may in some cases be altered or faintly canceled used stamps.

VALUES FOR NEVER-HINGED STAMPS PRIOR TO SCOTT No. 205

This catalogue does not value pre-1882 stamps in never-hinged condition. Premiums for never-hinged conditions in the classic era invariably are even larger than those premiums listed for the post-1890 issues. Generally speaking, the earlier the stamp is listed in the catalogue, the larger will be the never-hinged premium. On some early classics, the premium will be several multiples of the unused, hinged values given in the catalogue.

PRINTED BY THE CONTINENTAL BANK NOTE COMPANY

Plates of 200 subjects in two panes of 100 each.

Designs of the 1870-71 Issue with secret marks on the values from 1c to 15c, as described and illustrated:

The object of secret marks was to provide a simple and positive proof that these stamps were produced by the Continental Bank Note Company and not by their predecessors.

Franklin — A44a

1c. In the pearl at the left of the numeral "1" there is a small crescent.

Jackson — A45a

2c. Under the scroll at the left of "U. S." there is a small diagonal line. This mark seldom shows clearly. The stamp, No. 157, can be distinguished by its color.

Washington — A46a

3c. The under part of the upper tail of the left ribbon is heavily shaded.

Lincoln — A47a

6c. The first four vertical lines of the shading in the lower part of the left ribbon have been strengthened.

Stanton — A48a

7c. Two small semi-circles are drawn around the ends of the lines that outline the ball in the lower right hand corner.

Jefferson — A49a

10c. There is a small semi-circle in the scroll at the right end of the upper label.

Clay — A50a

12c. The balls of the figure "2" are crescent shaped.

Webster — A51a

15c. In the lower part of the triangle in the upper left corner two lines have been made heavier forming a "V." This mark can be found on some of the Continental and American (1879) printings, but not all stamps show it.

Secret marks were added to the dies of the 24c, 30c and 90c but new plates were not made from them. The various printings of the 30c and 90c can be distinguished only by the shades and paper.

J. Grill about 7x9½mm exists on all values except 24c and 90c. Grill was composed of truncated pyramids and was so strongly impressed that some points often broke through the paper.

White Wove Paper, Thin to Thick

1873, July (?) *Perf. 12*

				Unused	Used
156	A44a	1c	**ultramarine**	275.	3.75
			pale ultramarine	275.	3.75
			gray blue	275.	3.75
			blue	275.	3.75
			No gum	110.	
			dark ultramarine	300.	3.75
			No gum	120.	
			On cover		5.00
			Pair	560.	7.75
			Block of 4	1,200.	40.00
			P# block of 12, Impt.	*6,000.*	
			Double transfer	350.	7.50
			Double paper	*1,000.*	200.00
			Ribbed paper	400.	15.00
			Paper with silk fibers	—	25.00
			Cracked plate		—
			Paper cut with "cogwheel" punch	*425.*	
e.			With grill	*2,000.*	
f.			Imperf., pair	—	*550.00*

The No. 156 plate block is unique. Value is 1998 auction sale.

No. 156f may not have been regularly issued.

Earliest documented use: Aug. 22, 1873.

Cancellations

Blue	+.25
Purple	+.35
Magenta	+.35
Ultramarine	+1.00
Red	+3.50
Orange red	+4.00
Orange	+5.00
Brown	+20.00
Green	+60.00
"Paid All"	+7.00
"Paid"	+1.00
Railroad	+12.00
"Free"	+12.00
Black carrier	+15.00
Numeral	+2.50
Alaska	—
Japan	—
Printed "G." Precancel (Glastonbury, Conn.)	+200.00
Printed Star Precancel (Glen Allen, Va.)	+100.00

No.	Type	Denom.	Description	Unused	Used
157	A45a	2c	**brown**	375.	17.50
			dark brown	375.	17.50
			dark reddish brown	375.	17.50
			yellowish brown	375.	17.50
			No gum	160.	
			With secret mark	410.	19.00
			No gum	180.	
			On cover		22.50
			Pair	775.	37.50
			Block of 4	1,600.	150.00
			P# block of 12, Impt.	*5,500.*	
			P# block of 14, Impt.	—	
			Double paper	1,000.	100.00
			Ribbed paper	500.	40.00
			Double transfer	—	22.50
			Cracked plate		—
c.			With grill	*1,850.*	*750.00*
d.			Double impression	—	*5,000.*
e.			Vertical half used as 1c on cover		—

Earliest documented use: July 12, 1873.

Cancellations

Blue	+.50
Magenta	+1.00
Purple	+1.00
Red	+5.00
Orange red	+5.50
Orange	+7.50
Green	+100.00
"Paid"	+2.50
"Insufficiently Paid"	—
"Paid All"	+13.50
"P. D." in circle	+15.00
Town	+2.00
Numeral	+1.50
Black Carrier	+8.50
"Steamship"	+15.00
Supplementary Mail Type F	+5.00
China	—
Japan	+100.00
Printed Star Precancellation (Glen Allen, Va.)	—

No.	Type	Denom.	Description	Unused	Used
158	A46a	3c	**green**	130.	.60
			bluish green	130.	.60
			yellow green	130.	.60
			dark yellow green	130.	.60
			dark green	130.	.60
			No gum	47.50	
			olive green, ribbed paper	*375.*	15.00
			No gum	160.	
			On cover		.75
			Pair	275.	1.25
			Block of 4	600.	13.00
			P# strip of 5, Impt.	775.	
			P# strip of 6, Impt.	900.	
			P# block of 10, Impt.	2,600.	
			P# block of 12, Impt.	*3,500.*	
			P# block of 14, Impt.	*4,400.*	
			Double paper	400.	50.00
			Paper cut with "cogwheel" punch	275.	225.
			Ribbed paper	300.	5.00
			Paper with silk fibers	—	5.00
			Cracked plate	—	32.50
			Major plate crack at bottom		*350.00*
			Double transfer	—	5.75
			Short transfer at bottom		15.00
e.			With grill	*500.*	
			End roller grill	*950.*	*425.*
h.			Horizontal pair, imperf. vert.		—
i.			Horizontal pair, imperf. between		*1,300.*
j.			Double impression		*3,750.*
k.			Printed on both sides		—

See Die and Plate Proofs for imperfs. on stamp paper, with and without grill.

Earliest documented use: July 17, 1873.

Cancellations

Blue	+.05
Magenta	+.20
Purple	+.20
Ultramarine	+1.25
Red	+2.50
Orange red	+2.75
Orange	+3.50
Green	+25.00
Town	+.05
"Paid"	+2.50
"Paid All"	+20.00
"Free"	+15.00
Numeral	+1.00
China	—
Railroad	+7.00
"R. P. O."	+1.50
"P. D." in circle	—
"Steamboat"	—
"Steamship"	—
Supplementary Mail Type D	+11.00
Supplementary Mail Type F	+8.50
Express Company	—
Black Carrier	+8.00
Red Carrier	+25.00
Japan	+65.00
Alaska	—

No.	Type	Denom.	Description	Unused	Used
159	A47a	6c	**dull pink**	425.	17.50
			brown rose	425.	17.50
			No gum	190.	
			On cover		45.00
			Pair	900.	37.50
			Block of 4	1,900.	*140.00*
			P# block of 12, Impt.	*16,000.*	
			Double paper	—	—
			Ribbed paper	—	40.00
			Paper with silk fibers	—	40.00
a.			Diagonal half used as 3c on cover		*3,750.*
b.			With grill	*1,800.*	
			End roller grill	*2,400.*	

Earliest documented use: June 8, 1873.

Cancellations

Blue	+.25
Indigo	+2.50
Magenta	+1.50
Purple	+1.50
Violet	+3.00
Ultramarine	+2.50
Red	+7.50
Orange red	+9.00
Green	+80.00
Numeral	+1.50
"Paid"	+7.00
"Paid All"	—
Supp. Mail Type D, E or F	+15.00
Japan	+100.00
China	—
Railroad	—
"R. P. O."	+2.00

No.	Type	Denom.	Description	Unused	Used
160	A48a	7c	**orange vermilion**	1,350.	80.00
			vermilion	1,350.	80.00
			No gum	575.	
			On cover		175.00
			Pair	2,600.	175.00
			Block of 4	5,500.	
			P# block of 12, Impt.	*14,000.*	
			Double transfer of "7 cents" (1R22)	—	200.00
			Double transfer in lower left corner	—	150.00
			Double paper		—
			Ribbed paper	—	95.00
			Paper with silk fibers	—	130.00
a.			With grill	*3,500.*	

The plate block of 12 is in fine condition. It is unique.

Earliest documented use: Sept. 10, 1873.

Cancellations

Blue	+4.00
Red	+10.00
Purple	+10.00
Brown	+5.00
"Paid"	+15.00

No.	Type	Denom.	Description	Unused	Used
161	A49a	10c	**brown**	950.	20.00
			dark brown	950.	20.00
			yellow brown	950.	20.00
			No gum	425.	
			On cover		35.00
			Pair	2,000.	42.50
			Block of 4	4,750.	*160.00*
			P# block of 10, Impt.	*14,000.*	
			P# block of 12, Impt.	*17,500.*	
			Double paper	—	
			Ribbed paper	—	50.00
			Paper with silk fibers	—	50.00
			Double transfer	—	50.00
c.			With grill	*3,500.*	
d.			Horizontal pair, imperf. between		*2,500.*

Earliest documented use: Aug. 2, 1873.

Cancellations

Blue	+1.50
Purple	+2.00
Red	+6.00
Orange red	+7.00
Orange	+10.00
Magenta	+2.00
Brown	+20.00
Green	+100.00
"Paid"	+4.00
"P. D." in circle	+20.00
"Steamship"	+15.00
Supplementary Mail Type E	+7.00
Supplementary Mail Type F	+2.50
Japan	+100.00
China	—
Alaska	—

No.	Type	Denom.	Description	Unused	Used
162	A50a	12c	**blackish violet**	2,500.	105.00
			No gum	1,100.	
			On cover		325.00
			Pair	5,250.	230.00
			Block of 4	*11,500.*	*850.00*
			Ribbed paper	—	200.00
a.			With grill	*5,500.*	

Earliest documented use: Jan. 3, 1874.

Cancellations

Blue	+2.50
Ultramarine	+15.00
Brown	+5.00
Red	+15.00
Supplementary Mail Type D	+15.00
Japan	+200.00

No.	Type	Denom.	Description	Unused	Used
163	A51a	15c	**yellow orange**	2,500.	125.00
			pale orange	2,500.	125.00
			reddish orange	2,500.	125.00
			No gum	1,100.	
			On cover		325.00
			Pair	5,250.	260.00
			Block of 4	*11,500.*	*1,050.*
			Double paper		—
			Paper with silk fibers	2,650.	175.00
			Vertical ribbed paper	2,600.	175.00
a.			With grill	*5,250.*	

Earliest documented use: July 22, 1873.

Cancellations

Blue	+5.00
Purple	+10.00
Red	+20.00
Green	+350.00
Brown	—
Supplementary Mail Type E	—
Supplementary Mail Type F	+10.00
"Steamship"	—
Numeral	+7.50
Puerto Rico	—
China	—

No.	Type	Denom.	Description	Unused	Used
164	A52	24c	**purple**		—

The Philatelic Foundation has certified as genuine a 24c on vertically ribbed paper, and that is the unique stamp listed as No. 164. Specialists believe that only Continental used ribbed paper. It is not known for sure whether or not Continental also printed the 24c value on regular paper; if it did, specialists currently are not able to distinguish these from No. 153.

No.	Type	Denom.	Description	Unused	Used
165	A53	30c	**gray black**	3,000.	110.00
			greenish black	3,000.	110.00
			No gum	1,350.	
			On cover		*725.00*
			Pair	6,500.	230.00
			Block of 4	*14,500.*	*1,150.*
			Double transfer	—	140.00
			Double paper	—	
			Ribbed paper	3,200.	125.00
			Paper with silk fibers	—	—
c.			With grill	*22,500.*	

Earliest documented use: Oct. 14, 1874.

Cancellations

Purple	+10.00
Blue	+5.00
Red	+25.00
Brown	+30.00
Magenta	+10.00
"Steamship"	—
Supplementary Mail Type E	+10.00
Supplementary Mail Type F	+5.00
Japan	+200.00

No.	Type	Denom.	Description	Unused	Used
166	A54	90c	**rose carmine**	2,750.	250.00
			pale rose carmine	2,750.	250.00
			No gum	1,250.	
			On cover		*7,500.*
			Pair	*5,750.*	525.00
			Block of 4	*12,000.*	*2,300.*
			P# strip of 5, Impt.	*15,000.*	

Earliest documented use: June 25, 1875.

Cancellations

Blue	+10.
Purple	+40.
Red	+40.
Supplementary Mail Type F	+30.

SPECIAL PRINTING OF 1873 ISSUE

Produced by the Continental Bank Note Co.

1875 ***Perf. 12***

Hard, white wove paper, without gum

No.	Type	Denom.	Description	Unused	Used
167	A44a	1c	**ultramarine**	*12,500.*	
168	A45a	2c	**dark brown**	*5,750.*	
169	A46a	3c	**blue green**	*15,000.*	—
			On cover		—
170	A47a	6c	**dull rose**	*14,500.*	
171	A48a	7c	**reddish vermilion**	*3,500.*	
172	A49a	10c	**pale brown**	*14,500.*	
173	A50a	12c	**dark violet**	*5,000.*	
			Horizontal pair	—	
174	A51a	15c	**bright orange**	*14,500.*	
175	A52	24c	**dull purple**	*3,500.*	*5,000.*
			Horizontal pair	—	
176	A53	30c	**greenish black**	*12,000.*	
177	A54	90c	**violet carmine**	*14,000.*	

Although perforated, these stamps were usually cut apart with scissors. As a result, the perforations are often much mutilated and the design is frequently damaged.

These can be distinguished from the 1873 issue by the shades; also by the paper, which is very white instead of yellowish.

These and the subsequent issues listed under the heading of "Special Printings" are special printings of stamps then in current use which, together with the reprints and re-issues, were made for sale to collectors. They were available for postage except for the Officials, Newspaper and Periodical, and demonetized issues.

Only No. 169 is documented on cover (unique; postmarked Mar. 5, 1876).

Only one example of No. 175 used has been certified. It is off-center and creased, and it is valued thus.

PRINTED BY THE CONTINENTAL BANK NOTE COMPANY

REGULAR ISSUE

Yellowish Wove Paper

1875 ***Perf. 12***

No.	Description	Unused	Used
178 A45a 2c	**vermilion,** *June 1875*	425.	10.00
	No gum	180.	
	On cover		12.50
	Pair	900.	21.00
	Block of 4	1,850.	115.00
	P# strip of 6, Impt.	*2,600.*	
	P# block of 12, Impt.	—	
	P# block of 14, Impt.	*6,500.*	
	Double transfer		—
	Double paper	—	—
	Ribbed paper	—	—
	Paper with silk fibers	475.	15.00
b.	Half used as 1c on cover		—
c.	With grill	775.	

See Die and Plate Proofs for imperf. on stamp paper.

Earliest documented use: July 15, 1875.

Cancellations

Blue	+.25
Purple	+.50
Magenta	+.50
Red	+6.00
"Paid"	+8.00
"Steamship"	—
Supplementary Mail Type F	+5.50
Black Carrier	+15.00
Railroad	+12.50

Zachary Taylor — A55

No.	Description	Unused	Used
179 A55 5c	**blue,** *June 1875*	600.	20.00
	dark blue	600.	20.00
	bright blue	600.	20.00
	light blue	600.	20.00
	No gum	260.	
	greenish blue	625.	25.00
	No gum	275.	
	On cover		32.50
	Pair	1,250.	42.50
	Block of 4	2,600.	350.00
	Cracked plate	—	*170.00*
	Double transfer	—	32.50
	Double paper	*675.*	—
	Ribbed paper	—	—
	Paper with silk fibers	—	32.50
c.	With grill	3,000.	
	End roller grill	—	

Earliest documented use: July 10, 1875.

Cancellations

Blue	+1.00
Ultramarine	+3.00
Purple	+2.00
Magenta	+2.00
Red	+10.00
Green	+70.00
Numeral	+5.00
Railroad	+17.50
"Steamship"	+12.50
Ship	+12.50
Supplementary Mail Type E	+5.00
Supplementary Mail Type F	+2.00
China	—
Japan	+100.00
Peru	—

The five cent rate to foreign countries in the Universal Postal Union began on July 1, 1875. No. 179 was issued for that purpose.

SPECIAL PRINTING OF 1875 ISSUE

Produced by the Continental Bank Note Co.

Hard, White Wove Paper, without gum

1875

No.	Description	Unused
180 A45a 2c	**carmine vermilion**	*40,000.*
181 A55 5c	**bright blue**	*95,000.*

Unlike Nos. 167-177, Nos. 180-181 were seldom cut apart with scissors.

PRINTED BY THE AMERICAN BANK NOTE COMPANY

The Continental Bank Note Co. was consolidated with the American Bank Note Co. on February 4, 1879. The American Bank Note Company used many plates of the Continental Bank Note Company to print the ordinary postage, Departmental and Newspaper stamps. Therefore, stamps bearing the Continental Company's imprint were not always its product.

The A. B. N. Co. also used the 30c and 90c plates of the N. B. N. Co. Some of No. 190 and all of No. 217 were from A. B. N. Co. plate 405.

Early printings of No. 188 were from Continental plates 302 and 303 which contained the normal secret mark of 1873. After those plates were re-entered by the A. B. N. Co. in 1880, pairs or multiple pieces contained combinations of normal, hairline or missing marks. The pairs or other multiples usually found contain at least one hairline mark which tended to disappear as the plate wore.

A. B. N. Co. plates 377 and 378 were made in 1881 from the National transfer roll of 1870. No. 187 from these plates has no secret mark.

Identification by Paper Type:

Collectors traditionally have identified American Bank Note Co. issues by the soft, porous paper on which they were printed. However, the Continental Bank Note Co. used a soft paper from August 1878 through early 1879, before the consolidation of the companies. When the consolidation occurred on Feb. 4, 1879, American Bank Note Co. took over the presses, plates, paper, ink, and the employees of Continental. Undoubtedly they also acquired panes of finished stamps and sheets of printed stamps that had not yet been gummed and/or perforated. Since the soft paper that was in use at the time of the consolidation and after is approximately the same texture and thickness as the soft paper that American Bank Note Co. began using regularly in June or July of 1879, all undated soft paper stamps have traditionally been classified as American Bank Note Co. printings.

However, if a stamp bears a dated cancellation or is on a dated cover from Feb. 3, 1879 or earlier, collectors (especially specialist collectors) must consider the stamp to be a Continental Bank Note printing. Undated stamps off cover, and stamps and covers dated Feb. 4 or later, traditionally have been considered to be American Bank Note Co. printings since that company held the contract to print U.S. postage stamps beginning on that date. The most dedicated and serious specialist students sometimes attempt to determine the stamp printer of the issues on soft, porous paper in an absolute manner (by scientifically testing the paper and/or comparing printing records).

Earliest documented uses for American Bank Note Co. issues are given for stamps on the soft, porous paper that has been traditionally associated with that company. But, for reasons given above, sometimes that date will precede the Feb. 4, 1879 consolidation date.

SAME AS 1870-75 ISSUES

Soft Porous Paper

1879 ***Perf. 12***

No.	Description	Unused	Used
182 A44a 1c	**dark ultramarine**	325.	3.50
	blue	325.	3.50
	gray blue	325.	3.50
	No gum	125.	
	On cover		4.00
	Pair	675.	7.50
	Block of 4	1,450.	55.00
	P# block of 10, Impt.	*4,750.*	
	Double transfer	—	9.50

Earliest documented use: Jan. 3, 1879.

Cancellations

Blue	+.05
Magenta	+.10
Purple	+.10
Red	+7.00
Printed Star Precancellation (Glen Allen, Va.)	+75.00
Green	+35.00
"Paid"	+4.00
Supplementary Mail Type F	+10.00
Railroad	+12.50
Printed "G." Precancellation (Glastonbury, Conn.)	+100.00

No.	Description	Unused	Used
183 A45a 2c	**vermilion**	140.	3.00
	orange vermilion	140.	3.00
	No gum	55.	
	On cover		3.50
	Pair	290.	6.50
	Block of 4	625.	50.00
	P# block of 10, Impt.	1,850.	
	P# block of 12, Impt.	*2,400.*	
	Double transfer	—	—
a.	Double impression	—	*5,500.*

Earliest documented use: Aug. 19, 1878.

Cancellations

Blue	+.25
Purple	+.40
Magenta	+.40
Red	+6.00
Green	+175.00
"Paid"	+5.00
"Paid All"	—
"Ship"	—
Numeral	+4.00
Railroad	+15.00
Supplementary Mail Type F	+8.00
China	—
Printed Star Precancellation in black (Glen Allen, Va.)	+350.00
Printed Star Precancellation in red (Glen Allen, Va.)	+1,750.

No.	Description	Unused	Used
184 A46a 3c	**green**	110.	.60
	light green	110.	.60
	dark green	110.	.60
	No gum	37.50	
	On cover		.70
	Pair	230.	1.25
	Block of 4	500.	11.00
	P# block of 10, Impt.	1,350.	
	P# block of 12, Impt.	1,600.	
	P# block of 14, Impt.	1,950.	
	Double transfer	—	—
	Short transfer	—	6.00
b.	Double impression		*5,500.*

See Die and Plate Proofs for imperf. on stamp paper.

Earliest documented use: Aug. 3, 1878.

Cancellations

Blue	+.10
Magenta	+.15
Purple	+.15
Violet	+.15
Brown	+1.00
Red	+7.50
Green	+25.00
"Paid"	+3.00
"Free"	+15.00
Numeral	+2.00
Railroad	+12.50
"Steamboat"	—
Supplementary Mail Type F	+8.00
Printed Star Precancel (Glen Allen, Va.)	—
China	+60.00
Alaska	—

No.	Description	Unused	Used
185 A55 5c	**blue**	525.	12.00
	light blue	525.	12.00
	bright blue	525.	12.00
	dark blue	525.	12.00
	No gum	225.	
	On cover		22.50
	Pair	1,100.	25.00
	Block of 4	2,300.	175.00
	P# block of 12, Impt.	*12,000.*	
	Double transfer	—	

Earliest documented use: Feb. 12, 1879.

Cancellations

Blue	+.25
Purple	+1.00
Magenta	+1.00
Ultramarine	+3.50
Red	+7.50
Railroad	+20.00
Numeral	+2.00
Supplementary Mail Type F	+1.50
"Steamship"	+35.00
China	+60.00
Peru	—
Panama	—

No.	Description	Unused	Used
186 A47a 6c	**pink**	1,100.	22.50
	dull pink	1,100.	22.50
	brown rose	1,100.	22.50
	No gum	450.	
	On cover		42.50
	Pair	2,300.	47.50
	Block of 4	5,000.	*600.00*

Earliest documented use: July 1, 1879.

Cancellations

Blue	+.50
Ultramarine	+3.00
Purple	+1.00
Magenta	+1.00
Red	+12.00
Supplementary Mail Type F	+4.00
Railroad	+22.50
Numeral	+4.00
China	+70.00

No.	Description	Unused	Used
187 A49 10c	**brown,** without secret mark	3,250.	25.00
	yellow brown	3,250.	25.00
	No gum	1,400.	
	On cover		47.50
	Pair	6,750.	52.50
	Block of 4	*15,000.*	—
	Double transfer	—	45.00
	Double paper	*6,000.*	

Earliest documented use: Sept. 5, 1879.

Cancellations

Blue	+.50
Magenta	+1.50
Red	+10.00
"Paid"	+3.50
Supplementary Mail Type F	+3.00
China	+70.00

No.	Description	Unused	Used
188 A49a 10c	**brown,** with secret mark	2,250.	25.00
	yellow brown	2,250.	25.00
	No gum	950.	
	black brown	2,450.	37.50
	No gum	1,000.	
	On cover		40.00
	Pair	4,750.	52.50
	Block of 4	*10,500.*	275.00
	Pair, one stamp No. 187	*7,000.*	700.00
	Double transfer		45.00
	Cracked plate	—	—

Earliest documented use: Oct. 5, 1878.

Cancellations

Blue	+.50
Ultramarine	+3.00
Purple	+2.00
Magenta	+2.00
Red	+10.00
Green	+70.00
"Paid"	+7.50
Supplementary Mail Type F	+5.00
Numeral	+3.00
Printed Star Precancel (Glen Allen, Va.)	—

No.	Description	Unused	Used
189 A51a 15c	**red orange**	350.	22.50
	orange	350.	22.50

		yellow orange	350.	22.50
		No gum	140.	
		On cover		85.00
		Pair	725.	47.50
		Block of 4	1,750.	225.00
		P# block of 12, Impt.	*7,250.*	
		Double transfer		—

Earliest documented use: Jan. 20, 1879.

Cancellations

Blue	+1.50
Purple	+3.00
Magenta	+3.00
Ultramarine	+5.00
Red	+12.00
"Steamship"	+22.50
Supplementary Mail Type E	—
Supplementary Mail Type F	+5.00
Japan	+120.00
China	—

190 A53	30c	**full black**	1,100.	65.00
		greenish black	1,100.	65.00
		No gum	450.	
		On cover		425.00
		Pair	2,300.	140.00
		Block of 4	5,000.	425.00
		P# block of 10, Impt.	*15,000.*	

Earliest documented use: Aug. 8, 1881.

Cancellations

Blue	+1.50
Purple	+3.00
Magenta	+3.00
Red	+20.00
Supplementary Mail Type F	+6.00
"Steamship"	+35.00
Tahiti	—
Samoa	—

191 A54	90c	**carmine**	2,250.	275.00
		rose	2,250.	275.00
		carmine rose	2,250.	275.00
		No gum	1,000.	
		On cover		*5,000.*
		Pair	4,750.	575.00
		Block of 4	*10,000.*	1,500.
		Double paper	—	

See Die and Plate Proofs for imperf. on stamp paper.

Earliest documented use: June 24, 1882.

Cancellations

Blue	+15.00
Purple	+20.00
Red	+45.00
Supplementary Mail Type F	+20.00

SPECIAL PRINTING OF 1879 ISSUE

Produced by the American Bank Note Co.

1880 ***Perf. 12***

Soft porous paper, without gum

192 A44a	1c	**dark ultramarine**	*27,500.*
193 A45a	2c	**black brown**	*16,000.*
194 A46a	3c	**blue green**	*50,000.*
195 A47a	6c	**dull rose**	*35,000.*
196 A48a	7c	**scarlet vermilion**	*5,500.*
197 A49a	10c	**deep brown**	*28,500.*
198 A50a	12c	**blackish purple**	*8,000.*
199 A51a	15c	**orange**	*27,500.*
200 A52	24c	**dark violet**	*7,750.*
201 A53	30c	**greenish black**	*18,000.*
202 A54	90c	**dull carmine**	*25,000.*
203 A45a	2c	**scarlet vermilion**	*55,000.*
204 A55	5c	**deep blue**	*85,000.*

Nos. 192 and 194 are valued in the grade of fine.

No. 197 was printed from Continental plate 302 (or 303) after plate was re-entered. Therefore, the stamp may show normal, hairline or missing secret mark.

The Post Office Department did not keep separate records of the 1875 and 1880 Special Printings of the 1873 and 1879 issues, but the total quantity sold of both is recorded.

Unlike the 1875 hard-paper Special Printings (Nos. 167-177), the 1880 soft-paper Special Printings were never cut apart with scissors.

Numbers Sold of 1875 and 1880 Special Printings.

1c ultramarine & dark ultramarine *(388)*
2c dark brown & black brown *(416)*
2c carmine vermilion & scarlet vermilion *(917)*
3c blue green *(267)*
5c bright blue & deep blue *(317)*
6c dull rose *(185)*
7c reddish vermilion & scarlet vermilion *(473)*
10c pale brown & deep brown *(180)*
12c dark violet & blackish purple *(282)*
15c bright orange & orange *(169)*
24c dull purple & dark violet *(286)*
30c greenish black *(179)*
90c violet carmine & dull carmine *(170)*

IMPORTANT INFORMATION REGARDING VALUES FOR NEVER-HINGED STAMPS

Collectors should be aware that the values given for never-hinged stamps from No. 205 on are for stamps in the grade of very fine, just as the values for all stamps in the catalogue are for very fine stamps unless indicated otherwise. The never-hinged premium as a percentage of value will be larger for stamps in extremely fine or superb grades, and the premium will be smaller for fine-very fine, fine or poor examples. This is particularly true of the issues of the late-19th and early-20th centuries. For example, in the grade of very fine, an unused stamp from this time period may be valued at $100 hinged and $180 never hinged. The never-hinged premium is thus 80%. But in a grade of extremely fine, this same stamp will not only sell for more hinged, but the never-hinged premium will increase, perhaps to 100%-300% or more over the higher extremely fine value. In a grade of superb, a hinged copy will sell for much more than a very fine copy, and additionally the never-hinged premium will be much larger, perhaps as large as 300%-400%. On the other hand, the same stamp in a grade of fine or fine-very fine not only will sell for less than a very fine stamp in hinged condition, but additionally the never-hinged premium will be smaller than the never-hinged premium on a very fine stamp, perhaps as small as 15%-30%.

Please note that the above statements and percentages are NOT a formula for arriving at the values of stamps in hinged or never-hinged condition in the grades of very good, fine, fine to very fine, extremely fine or superb. The percentages given apply only to the size of the premium for never-hinged condition that might be added to the stamp value for hinged condition. Further, the percentages given are only generalized estimates. Some stamps or grades may have percentages for never-hinged condition that are higher or lower than the ranges given. For values of the most popular U.S. stamps in the grades of very good, fine, fine to very fine, extremely fine and superb, see the *Scott Valuing Supplement*, updated and issued twice each year in April and October.

VALUES FOR NEVER-HINGED STAMPS PRIOR TO SCOTT 205

This catalogue does not value pre-1882 stamps in never-hinged condition. Premiums for never-hinged condition in the classic era invariably are even larger than those premiums listed for the post-1882 issues. Generally speaking, the earlier the stamp is listed in the catalogue, the larger will be the never-hinged premium. On some early classics, the premium will be several multiples of the unused, hinged values given in the catalogue.

NEVER-HINGED PLATE BLOCKS

Values given for never-hinged plate blocks are for blocks in which all stamps have original gum that has never been hinged and has no disturbances, and all selvage, whether gummed or ungummed, has never been hinged.

REGULAR ISSUE

Printed by the American Bank Note Co.

James A. Garfield — A56

1882, Apr. 10 ***Perf. 12***

205 A56	5c	**yellow brown**	300.	9.00
		brown	300.	9.00
		gray brown	300.	9.00
		Never hinged	675.	
		No gum	110.	
		On cover		17.50
		Pair	625.	20.00
		Block of 4	1,300.	115.00
		P# strip of 5, Impt.	1,800.	
		P# strip of 6, Impt.	2,100.	
		P# block of 10, Impt.	*5,500.*	
		P# block of 12, Impt.	*6,000.*	

Earliest documented use: Feb. 18, 1882.

Cancellations

Blue	+.50
Purple	+.75
Magenta	+.75
Red	+7.00
"Ship"	—
Numeral	+2.00
Supplementary Mail Type F	+2.50
Red Express Co.	—
China	+125.00
Japan	+125.00
Samoa	+150.00
Puerto Rico	—

SPECIAL PRINTING

Printed by the American Bank Note Co.

1882 ***Perf. 12***

Soft porous paper, without gum

205C A56 5c **gray brown** *40,000.*

Although Post Office records indicate that 2,463 copies of the 5c Garfield Special Printing were sold, almost all of these stamps appear to have been from supplies of the regular issue No. 205. The actual Special Printings, No. 205C, came from a small supply sent to the Third Assistant Post Master General before the regular issue was available. Only 22 examples have been certified as genuine Special Printings.

DESIGNS OF 1873 RE-ENGRAVED

Franklin — A44b

1c - The vertical lines in the upper part of the stamp have been so deepened that the background often appears to be solid. Lines of shading have been added to the upper arabesques.

1881-82

206 A44b	1c	**gray blue,** *Aug. 1881*	85.00	.90
		ultramarine	85.00	.90
		dull blue	85.00	.90
		slate blue	85.00	.90
		Never hinged	190.00	
		No gum	30.00	
		On cover		1.40
		Pair	180.00	1.90
		Block of 4	375.00	16.00
		P# strip of 5, Impt.	500.00	
		P# strip of 6, Impt.	600.00	
		P# block of 10, Impt.	*1,700.*	
		P# block of 12, Impt.	*1,900.*	
		Double transfer	110.00	6.00
		Punched with 8 small holes in a circle	*190.00*	
		P# block of 10, Impt. (8-hole punch)	*2,750.*	

Earliest documented use: Nov. 2, 1881.

Cancellations

Purple	+.10
Magenta	+.10
Blue	+.20
Red	+3.00
Orange red	+3.50
Orange	+5.00
Green	+50.00
"Paid"	+4.75
"Paid All"	+12.00
Numeral	+3.50
Supplementary Mail Type F	+5.00
Railroad	+10.00
Printed Star Precancel (Glen Allen, Va.)	+55.00
China	—

Washington — A46b

3c. The shading at the sides of the central oval appears only about one-half the previous width. A short horizontal dash has been cut about 1mm below the "TS" of "CENTS."

207 A46b	3c	**blue green,** *July 16, 1881*	85.00	.55
		green	85.00	.55
		yellow green	85.00	.55
		Never hinged	190.00	
		No gum	30.00	
		On cover		.70
		Pair	180.00	1.15
		Block of 4	375.00	30.00
		P# strip of 5, Impt.	525.00	
		P# block of 10, Impt.	*1,700.*	
		Double transfer	—	12.00
		Cracked plate	—	
		Punched with 8 small holes in a circle	*210.00*	
		P# block of 10, Impt. (8-hole punch)	*3,000.*	
c.		Double impression		—

Earliest documented use: Aug. 7, 1881.

Cancellations

Purple	+.10
Magenta	+.10
Blue	+.25
Brown	+1.50
Red	+2.50
"Paid"	+3.00
"Paid All"	—
Numeral	+2.50
"Ship"	—
Railroad	+5.00

Supplementary Mail Type F	+8.00
Printed Star Precancellation (Glen Allen, Va.)	—

Lincoln — A47b

6c. On the original stamps four vertical lines can be counted from the edge of the panel to the outside of the stamp. On the re-engraved stamps there are but three lines in the same place.

208 A47b 6c **rose**	625.	90.00
dull rose	625.	90.00
Never hinged	1,400.	
No gum	225.	
On cover (rose)		170.00
Pair (rose)	1,300.	190.00
Block of 4 (rose)	3,000.	775.00
P# block of 10, Impt.	*8,500.*	
Double transfer	750.	110.00
a. 6c **deep brown red**	550.	140.00
Never hinged	1,250.	
No gum	200.	
pale brown red	525.	95.00
Never hinged	1,175.	
No gum	190.	
On cover (deep brown red)		*425.00*
Pair (deep brown red)	1,150.	290.00
Block of 4 (deep brown red)	2,600.	1,100.
P# strip of 5, Impt.	3,100.	
P# strip of 6, Impt.	*3,900.*	
P# block of 10, Impt.	—	
P# block of 12, Impt.	—	

Earliest documented use: June 1, 1882.

Cancellations

Magenta	+3.00
Purple	+3.00
Blue	+5.00
Red	+15.00
Supplementary Mail Type F	+10.00

Jefferson — A49b

10c. On the original stamps there are five vertical lines between the left side of the oval and the edge of the shield. There are only four lines on the re-engraved stamps. In the lower part of the latter, also, the horizontal lines of the background have been strengthened.

209 A49b 10c **brown,** *Apr. 1882*	175.	6.00
yellow brown	175.	6.00
orange brown	175.	6.00
Never hinged	425.	
No gum	60.	
purple brown	190.	6.50
olive brown	190.	6.50
Never hinged	475.	
No gum	65.	
On cover		11.00
Pair	375.	12.50
Block of 4	850.	40.00
P# strip of 5, Impt.	1,200.	
P# strip of 6, Impt.	1,400.	
P# block of 10, Impt.	*3,500.*	
P# block of 12, Impt.	*4,250.*	
Never hinged	*8,000.*	
b. 10c **black brown**	1,400.	200.00
Never hinged	3,000.	
No gum	575.	
On cover		*450.00*
Pair	—	425.00
Block of 4	—	—
c. Double impression		—

Specimen stamps (usually overprinted "Sample") without overprint exist in a brown shade that differs from No. 209. The unoverprinted brown specimen is cheaper than No. 209. Expertization is recommended.

Earliest documented use: May 4, 1882.

Cancellations

Purple	+.50
Magenta	+.50
Blue	+1.00
Red	+4.00
Green	+35.00
Numeral	+2.00
"Paid"	+2.50
Supplementary Mail Type F	+3.00
Express Company	—
Japan	+75.00
China	—
Samoa	—

Printed by the American Bank Note Company.

Washington — A57

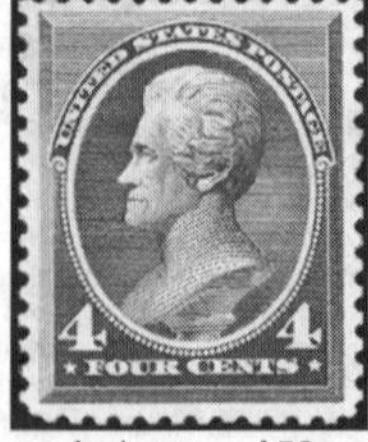

Jackson — A58

Nos. 210-211 were issued to meet the reduced first class rate of 2 cents for each half ounce, and the double rate, which Congress approved Mar. 3, 1883, effective Oct. 1, 1883.

1883, Oct. 1 ***Perf. 12***

210 A57 2c **red brown**	50.00	.60
dark red brown	50.00	.60
orange brown	50.00	.60
Never hinged	120.00	
No gum	17.50	
On cover		.70
Pair	105.00	1.25
Block of 4	225.00	12.00
P# strip of 5, Impt.	290.00	
P# strip of 6, Impt.	360.00	
P# block of 10, Impt.	*1,100.*	
P# block of 12, Impt.	*1,300.*	
Double transfer	55.00	2.25

See Die and Plate Proofs for imperf. on stamp paper.

Earliest documented use: Oct. 1, 1883 (FDC).

Cancellations

Purple	+.10
Margenta	+.10
Blue	+.20
Violet	+.30
Brown	+.30
Red	+3.50
Green	+25.00
Numeral	+2.50
"Paid"	+3.00
Railroad	+5.00
Express Company	—
Supplementary Mail Type F	+5.00
"Ship"	—
"Steamboat"	—
China	—

211 A58 4c **blue green**	300.	20.00
deep blue green	300.	20.00
Never hinged	675.	
No gum	125.	
On cover		47.50
Pair	625.	42.50
Block of 4	1,300.	110.00
P# strip of 5, Impt.	1,800.	
P# strip of 6, Impt.	2,150.	
P# block of 10, Impt.	*4,600.*	
P# block of 12, Impt.	*5,500.*	
Never hinged	*7,750.*	
Double transfer	—	—
Cracked plate	—	

See Die and Plate Proofs for imperf. on stamp paper.

Earliest documented use: Oct. 1, 1883 (FDC).

Cancellations

Purple	+1.00
Magenta	+1.00
Green	+50.00
Blue	+1.00
Numeral	+2.00
Supplementary Mail Type F	+5.00

SPECIAL PRINTING

Printed by the American Bank Note Company.

1883-85 **Soft porous paper** ***Perf. 12***

211B A57 2c **pale red brown,** with gum ('85)	450.	—
Never hinged	725.	
No gum	175.	
Block of 4	1,950.	
c. Horizontal pair, imperf. between	*1,900.*	
Never hinged	*2,750.*	
Top margin strip of 6, "Steamer - American Bank Note Co." imprint	*5,000.*	
Never hinged	*7,000.*	

Earliest documented use: May 23, 1885 (dated cancel on off-cover stamp).

211D A58 4c **deep blue green,** without gum *37,500.*

Postal records indicate that 26 copies of No. 211D were sold. Records also indicate an 1883 delivery and sales of 55 copies of the 2c red brown stamp, but there is no clear evidence that these can be differentiated from no gum examples of No. 210.

No. 211B is from a special trial printing by a new steam-powered American Bank Note Company press. Approximately 1,000 of these stamps (in sheets of 200 with an imperf gutter between the panes of 100) were delivered as samples to the Third Assistant Postmaster General and subsequently made their way to the public market.

REGULAR ISSUE

Printed by the American Bank Note Company.

Franklin — A59

1887 ***Perf. 12***

212 A59 1c **ultramarine,** *June*	120.00	2.00
bright ultramarine	120.00	2.00
Never hinged	280.00	
No gum	45.00	
On cover		2.75
Pair	250.00	4.10
Block of 4	550.00	35.00
P# strip of 5, Impt.	675.00	
P# strip of 6, Impt.	825.00	
P# block of 10, Impt.	*1,675.*	
P# block of 12, Impt.	*2,000.*	
Double transfer		—

See Die and Plate Proofs for imperf. on stamp paper.

Earliest documented use: July 15, 1887. The previously listed July 7, 1887, cover has not been adequately documented. The editors would like to see authenticated evidence of its existence.

Cancellations

Purple	+.10
Magenta	+.10
Blue	+.10
Red	+5.50
Numeral	+2.00
Railroad	+10.00
Supplementary Mail Type F	+5.00
China	—

213 A57 2c **green,** *Sept. 10*	50.00	.40
bright green	50.00	.40
dark green	50.00	.40
Never hinged	100.00	
No gum	17.50	
On cover		.55
Pair	105.00	.85
Block of 4	230.00	10.00
P# strip of 5, Impt.	300.00	
P# strip of 6, Impt.	375.00	
P# block of 10, Impt.	*1,250.*	
Never hinged	*2,250.*	
P# block of 12, Impt.	*1,500.*	
Double transfer	—	3.25
b. Printed on both sides		—

See Die and Plate Proofs for imperf. on stamp paper.

Earliest documented use: Sept. 20, 1887 (dated cancel on off-cover stamp); Sept. 21, 1887 (on cover).

Cancellations

Purple	+.10
Magenta	+.10
Blue	+.90
Red	+5.00
Green	+25.00
"Paid"	+5.00
Railroad	+12.00
Numeral	+2.00
"Steam"	—
"Steamboat"	—
Supplementary Mail Type F	+7.50
China	—
Japan	—

214 A46b 3c **vermilion,** *Sept.*	80.00	60.00
Never hinged	180.00	
No gum	27.50	
On cover (single)		105.00
Pair	170.00	125.00
Block of 4	375.00	350.00
P# strip of 5, Impt.	475.00	
P# strip of 6, Impt.	550.00	
P# block of 10, Impt.	*1,400.*	
P# block of 12, Impt.	*1,600.*	

Earliest documented use: Sept. 23, 1887.

Cancellations

Purple	+5.00
Magenta	+5.00
Green	+150.00
Blue	+10.00
Supplementary Mail Type F	+15.00
Railroad	+30.00

Printed by the American Bank Note Company.

SAME AS 1870-83 ISSUES

1888 ***Perf. 12***

215 A58 4c **carmine,** *Nov.*	250.	20.00
rose carmine	250.	20.00
pale rose	250.	20.00
Never hinged	650.	
No gum	90.	
On cover		45.00
Pair	525.	42.50
Block of 4	1,100.	140.00

			P# strip of 5, Impt.	1,550.	
			Never hinged	*3,250.*	
			P# strip of 6, Impt.	1,850.	
			P# block of 10, Impt.	*4,750.*	
			P# block of 12, Impt.	*5,500.*	

Earliest documented use: Jan. 18, 1889.

Cancellations

			Blue		+1.00
			Red		+5.00
			Purple		+2.00
			Magenta		+2.00
			Supplementary Mail Type F		+5.00
216	A56	5c	**indigo,** *Feb.*	275.	14.00
			deep blue	275.	14.00
			Never hinged	700.	
			No gum	100.	
			On cover		27.50
			Pair	575.	29.00
			Block of 4	1,200.	125.00
			P# strip of 5, Impt.	1,600.	
			P# strip of 6, Impt.	2,000.	
			P# block of 10, Impt.	*7,500.*	
			P# block of 12, Impt.	*9,000.*	

Earliest documented use: Mar. 15, 1888.

Cancellations

			Purple		+1.00
			Magenta		+1.00
			Blue		+1.00
			Supplementary Mail Type F		+3.00
			China		+85.00
			Japan		+85.00
			Puerto Rico		+75.00
			Samoa		—
217	A53	30c	**orange brown,** *Jan.*	450.	120.00
			deep orange brown	450.	120.00
			Never hinged	1,200.	
			No gum	170.	
			On cover		*1,400.*
			Pair	950.	250.00
			Block of 4	2,000.	625.00
			P# strip of 5, Impt.	*2,650.*	
			P# block of 10, Impt.	*7,000.*	
			P# block of 12, Impt.	—	

Earliest documented use: Aug. 8, 1888 (dated cancel on off-cover stamp); Sept. 7, 1888 (on cover).

Cancellations

			Blue		+5.00
			Magenta		+10.00
			Supplementary Mail Type F		+10.00
			"Paid All"		+25.00
			"Paid"		+15.00
218	A54	90c	**purple,** *Feb.*	1,200.	250.00
			bright purple	1,200.	250.00
			Never hinged	3,250.	
			No gum	500.	
			On cover		*10,000.*
			Pair	2,500.	525.00
			Block of 4	*5,750.*	1,400.
			P# strip of 5, Impt.	*7,000.*	
			P# block of 10, Impt.	*23,500.*	
			P# block of 12, Impt.	—	

Earliest documented use: Oct. 10, 1888 (on piece); Oct. 29, 1888 (cover).

Cancellations

			Blue		+10.00
			Purple		+15.00
			Supplementary Mail Type F		+25.00

See Die and Plate Proofs for imperfs. on stamp paper.

Printed by the American Bank Note Company. Plates for the 1c and 2c were of 400 subjects in 4 panes of 100 each. All other values were from plates of 200 subjects in two panes of 100 each.

Franklin — A60

Washington — A61

Jackson — A62

Lincoln — A63

Ulysses S. Grant — A64

Garfield — A65

William T. Sherman — A66

Daniel Webster — A67

Henry Clay — A68

Jefferson — A69

Perry — A70

1890-93 ***Perf. 12***

219	A60	1c	**dull blue,** *Feb. 22, 1890*	30.00	.60
			deep blue	30.00	.60
			ultramarine	30.00	.60
			Never hinged	70.00	
			On cover		.65
			Block of 4	130.00	4.75
			P# strip of 5, Impt. & letter	175.00	
			P# strip of 6, Impt. & letter	215.00	
			P# strip of 7, Impt. & letter	240.00	
			P# block of 10, Impt. & letter	800.00	
			P# block of 12, Impt. & letter	1,000.	
			P# block of 14, Impt. & letter	1,300.	
			Double transfer	—	—

Earliest documented use: Feb 27, 1890.

Cancellations

			Samoa		—
			China		—
219D	A61	2c	**lake,** *Feb. 22, 1890*	250.00	1.75
			Never hinged	575.00	
			On cover		2.40
			Block of 4	1,050.	17.50
			P# strip of 5, Impt.	1,350.	
			P# block of 10, Impt.	4,000.	
			Double transfer	—	—

Earliest documented use: Feb. 22, 1890 (FDC).

Cancellation

			Supplementary Mail Type F		+3.00
220	A61	2c	**carmine,** *1890*	25.00	.55
			dark carmine	25.00	.55
			carmine rose	25.00	.55
			rose	25.00	.75
			Never hinged	60.00	
			On cover		.60
			Block of 4	110.00	2.25
			P# strip of 5, Impt. & letter	165.00	
			P# strip of 6, Impt. & letter	200.00	
			Never hinged	360.00	
			P# strip of 7, Impt. & letter	230.00	
			P# block of 10, Impt. & letter	600.00	
			P# block of 12, Impt. & letter	750.00	
			P# block of 14, Impt. & letter	925.00	
			Double transfer	—	3.25
a.			Cap on left "2" (Plates 235-236, 246-247-248)	150.00	10.00
			Never hinged	350.00	
			Block of 4	700.00	*150.00*
			Pair, Nos. 220, 220a	—	—
			Never hinged	—	
c.			Cap on both "2's" (Plates 245, 246)	625.00	30.00
			Never hinged	1,400.	
			Pair, Nos. 220a, 220c	—	—
			Never hinged	—	

Earliest documented uses: Apr. 29, 1890 (No. 220); Sept. 9, 1892 (No. 220a); July 7, 1892 (No. 220c).

Cancellations

			Blue		+.05
			Purple		+.05
			Supp. Mail Types F or G		+3.00
			China		+20.00
221	A62	3c	**purple,** *Feb. 22, 1890*	85.00	7.50
			bright purple	85.00	7.50
			dark purple	85.00	7.50
			Never hinged	200.00	
			On cover		16.00
			Block of 4	360.00	50.00
			P# strip of 5, Impt.	525.00	
			P# block of 10, Impt.	2,850.	
			Never hinged	—	

Earliest documented use: Feb. 28, 1890.

Cancellation

			Samoa		—
222	A63	4c	**dark brown,** *June 2, 1890*	110.00	3.00
			blackish brown	110.00	3.00
			Never hinged	250.00	
			On cover		14.00
			Block of 4	460.00	25.00
			P# strip of 5, Impt.	675.00	
			P# block of 10, Impt.	3,500.	
			Never hinged	*5,500.*	
			Double transfer	125.00	—

Earliest documented use: July 16, 1890.

Cancellation

			China		+40.00
223	A64	5c	**chocolate,** *June 2, 1890*	90.00	3.00
			yellow brown	90.00	3.00
			Never hinged	210.00	
			On cover		13.00
			Block of 4	400.00	22.50
			P# strip of 5, Impt.	525.00	
			P# block of 10, Impt.	3,000.	
			Never hinged	—	
			Double transfer	110.00	3.75

Earliest documented use: June 14, 1890.

Cancellations

			China		+35.00
			Samoa		—
			Supp. Mail Types F or G		+3.00
224	A65	6c	**brown red,** *Feb. 22, 1890*	85.00	20.00
			dark brown red	85.00	20.00
			Never hinged	200.00	
			On cover		35.00
			Block of 4	350.00	110.00
			P# strip of 5, Impt.	500.00	
			P# block of 10, Impt.	2,900.	
			Never hinged	*4,500.*	

Earliest documented use: May 30, 1890.

Cancellation

			Supplementary Mail Type F		+3.00
225	A66	8c	**lilac,** *Mar. 21, 1893*	65.00	14.00
			grayish lilac	65.00	14.00
			magenta	65.00	14.00
			Never hinged	155.00	
			On cover		30.00
			Block of 4	270.00	90.00
			P# strip of 5, Impt.	370.00	
			P# block of 10, Impt.	1,950.	
			Never hinged	3,150.	

The 8c was issued because the registry fee was reduced from 10 to 8 cents effective Jan. 1, 1893.

Earliest documented use: May 21, 1893.

226	A67	10c	**green,** *Feb. 22, 1890*	200.00	3.75
			bluish green	200.00	3.75
			dark green	200.00	3.75
			Never hinged	475.00	
			On cover		10.00
			Block of 4	700.00	37.50
			P# strip of 5, Impt.	1,000.	
			P# block of 10, Impt.	4,200.	
			Never hinged	*6,750.*	
			Double transfer	—	—

Earliest documented use: Mar. 22, 1890.

Cancellations

			Samoa		—
			Supp. Mail Type F or G		+2.50
227	A68	15c	**indigo,** *Feb. 22, 1890*	275.00	22.50
			deep indigo	275.00	22.50
			Never hinged	650.00	
			On cover		65.00
			Block of 4	1,200.	125.00
			P# strip of 5, Impt.	1,650.	
			P# block of 10, Impt.	*9,250.*	
			Never hinged	—	
			Double transfer	—	—
			Triple transfer		—

Earliest documented use: May 27, 1890.

Cancellation

			Supplementary Mail Type F		+3.00
228	A69	30c	**black,** *Feb. 22, 1890*	425.00	32.50
			gray black	425.00	32.50
			full black	425.00	32.50
			Never hinged	1,000.	
			On cover		*600.00*
			Block of 4	1,800.	190.00
			P# strip of 5, Impt.	2,500.	
			P# block of 10, Impt.	*13,500.*	
			Never hinged	—	
			Double transfer	—	—

Earliest documented use: April 14, 1890.

Cancellation

		Supplementary Mail Type F		+5.00
229	A70 90c	**orange,** *Feb. 22, 1890*	650.00	130.00
		yellow orange	650.00	130.00
		red orange	650.00	130.00
		Never hinged	1,600.	
		On cover		—
		Block of 4	2,750.	675.00
		P# strip of 5, Impt.	3,800.	
		P# block of 10, Impt.	*27,500.*	
		Never hinged	*40,000.*	
		Short transfer at bottom	—	—

Earliest documented use: (?) 16, 1890 (dated cancel on off-cover stamp); Feb. 7, 1892 (on cover).

Cancellation

Supp. Mail Type F or G		+10.00
Nos. 219-229 (12)	2,290.	239.15

VALUES FOR VERY FINE STAMPS
Please note: Stamps are valued in the grade of Very Fine unless otherwise indicated.

COLUMBIAN EXPOSITION ISSUE

World's Columbian Exposition, Chicago, Ill., May 1 - Oct. 30, 1893, celebrating the 400th anniv. of the discovery of America by Christopher Columbus.

See Nos. 2624-2629 for souvenir sheets containing stamps of designs A71-A86 but with "1992" at upper right.

Columbus in Sight of Land — A71

Landing of Columbus — A72

"Santa Maria," Flagship of Columbus — A73

Fleet of Columbus — A74

Columbus Soliciting Aid from Queen Isabella — A75

Columbus Welcomed at Barcelona — A76

Columbus Restored to Favor — A77

Columbus Presenting Natives — A78

Columbus Announcing His Discovery — A79

Columbus at La Rábida — A80

Recall of Columbus — A81

Queen Isabella Pledging Her Jewels — A82

Columbus in Chains — A83

Columbus Describing His Third Voyage — A84

Queen Isabella and Columbus — A85

Columbus — A86

No. 57

Type of imprint and plate number

Exposition Station Handstamp Postmark

Printed by the American Bank Note Company.
Plates of 200 subjects in two panes of 100 each (1c, 2c).
Plates of 100 subjects in two panes of 50 each (2c-$5).
Issued (except 8c) Jan. 1 (a Sunday) and Jan. 2 (Monday), 1893. Jan. 1 and Jan. 2 first day covers are documented for the 1c, 2c, 3c, 4c, 5c and 10c. Jan. 2-only first day covers exist for the 6c and $2. See the First Day Cover section for values.

1893 *Perf. 12*

230	A71 1c	**deep blue**	22.50	.40
		blue	22.50	.40
		pale blue	22.50	.40
		Never hinged	45.00	
		On cover		.90
		Pair on cover, Expo. station machine canc.		85.00
		Pair on cover, Expo. station duplex handstamp canc.		150.00
		Block of 4	95.00	7.00
		P# strip of 3, Impt.	82.50	
		P# strip of 4, Impt. & letter	110.00	
		P# block of 6, Impt.	325.00	
		Never hinged	525.00	
		P# block of 8, Impt. & letter	525.00	
		Never hinged	850.00	
		Double transfer	27.50	.75
		Cracked plate	90.00	

Earliest documented use: Jan. 1, 1893 (FDC).

Cancellation

China	—
Philippines	—

"Broken hat" variety

231	A72 2c	**brown violet**	21.00	.30
		deep brown violet	21.00	.30
		gray violet	21.00	.30
		Never Hinged	42.50	

On cover		.35
On cover or card, Expo. station machine cancel		50.00
On cover or card, Expo. station duplex handstamp cancel		100.00
Block of 4	87.50	3.50
P# strip of 3, Impt.	75.00	
P# strip of 4, Impt. & letter	100.00	
Never Hinged	190.00	
P# block of 6, Impt.	275.00	
Never hinged	425.00	
P# block of 8, Impt. & letter	475.00	
Never hinged	775.00	
Double transfer	26.00	.35
Triple transfer	62.50	—
Quadruple transfer	95.00	
Broken hat on third figure to left of Columbus	65.00	.45
Never hinged	130.00	
Broken frame line	22.50	.35
Recut frame lines	22.50	—
Cracked plate	87.50	—

There are a number of different versions of the broken hat variety, some of which may be progressive.

Earliest documented use: Jan. 1, 1893 (FDC).

Cancellations

China		—
Supplementary Mail Type G		+3.50

See Die and Plate Proofs for the 2c, imperf. on stamp paper.

232 A73 3c **green**	60.00	15.00
dull green	60.00	15.00
dark green	60.00	15.00
Never hinged	120.00	
On cover		32.50
On cover, Expo. station machine canc.		200.00
On cover, Expo. station duplex handstamp cancel		300.00
Block of 4	260.00	100.00
P# strip of 3, Impt.	240.00	
Never Hinged	425.00	
P# strip of 4, Impt. & letter	310.00	
Never Hinged	550.00	
P# block of 6, Impt.	725.00	
Never hinged	1,250.	
P# block of 8, Impt. & letter	1,200.	
Never hinged	2,100.	
Double transfer	80.00	—

Earliest documented use: Jan. 1, 1893 (FDC).

Cancellations

China		—
Supp. Mail Type F or G		+7.50
233 A74 4c **ultramarine**	87.50	7.50
dull ultramarine	87.50	7.50
deep ultramarine	87.50	7.50
Never hinged	175.00	
On cover		22.50
On cover, Expo. station machine canc.		250.00
On cover, Expo. station duplex handstamp cancel		350.00
Block of 4	385.00	55.00
P# strip of 3, Impt.	340.00	
P# strip of 4, Impt. & letter	450.00	—
P# block of 6, Impt.	1,050.	
Never hinged	1,750.	
P# block of 8, Impt. & letter	2,200.	
Never hinged	3,750.	—
Double transfer	125.00	—
a. 4c **blue** (error)	*19,500.*	*15,000.*
Never hinged	*32,500.*	
Block of 4	*90,000.*	—
Never Hinged	*145,000.*	
P# strip of 4, Impt., letter	*145,000.*	

No. 233a exists in two shades.

Earliest documented use: Jan. 1, 1893 (FDC).

Cancellation

Supplementary Mail Type G		+3.00
234 A75 5c **chocolate**	95.00	8.00
pale brown	95.00	8.00
yellow brown	95.00	8.00
dark chocolate	95.00	8.00
Never hinged	190.00	
On cover		22.50
On cover, Expo. station machine canc.		250.00
On cover, Expo. station duplex handstamp cancel		375.00
Block of 4	400.00	60.00
P# strip of 3, Impt.	375.00	
P# strip of 4, Impt. & letter	525.00	
P# block of 6, Impt.	1,400.	
Never hinged	2,400.	
P# block of 8, Impt. & letter	2,750.	
Never hinged	4,600.	
Double transfer	145.00	—

Earliest documented use: Jan. 1, 1893 (FDC).

Cancellations

China		—
Philippines		—
Supplementary Mail Type F		+3.00
235 A76 6c **purple**	85.00	22.50
dull purple	85.00	22.50
Never hinged	170.00	
a. 6c **red violet**	85.00	22.50
Never hinged	170.00	
On cover		50.00
On cover, Expo. station machine canc.		275.00
On cover, Expo. station duplex handstamp cancel		400.00
Block of 4	375.00	115.00
P# strip of 3, Impt.	330.00	
P# strip of 4, Impt. & letter	425.00	
P# block of 6, Impt.	1,175.	
Never hinged	2,000.	
P# block of 8, Impt. & letter	2,150.	
Never hinged	3,600.	
Double transfer	110.00	30.00

Earliest documented use: Jan. 2, 1893 (FDC).

Cancellations

China		—
Supplementary Mail Type F		+5.00
236 A77 8c **magenta,** *Mar. 1893*	75.00	11.00
light magenta	75.00	11.00
dark magenta	75.00	11.00
Never hinged	150.00	
On cover		22.50
On cover, Expo. station machine canc.		275.00
On cover, Expo. station duplex handstamp cancel		450.00
Block of 4	325.00	65.00
P# strip of 3, Impt.	290.00	
P# strip of 4, Impt. & letter	400.00	
P# block of 6, Impt.	825.00	
Never hinged	1,400.	
P# block of 8, Impt. & letter	1,450.	
Never hinged	2,450.	
Double transfer	87.50	—

Earliest documented use: Mar. 18, 1893.

Cancellations

China		—
Supplementary Mail Type F		+4.50
237 A78 10c **black brown**	140.00	8.00
dark brown	140.00	8.00
gray black	140.00	8.00
Never hinged	280.00	
On cover		32.50
On cover, Expo. station machine canc.		350.00
On cover, Expo. station duplex handstamp cancel		500.00
Block of 4	600.00	60.00
P# strip of 3, Impt.	575.00	
P# strip of 4, Impt. & letter	700.00	
Never hinged	1,200.	
P# block of 6, Impt.	3,350.	
Never hinged	*5,750.*	
P# block of 8, Impt. & letter	5,000.	
Never hinged	*8,500.*	
Double transfer	180.00	12.50
Triple transfer	—	

Earliest documented use: Jan. 1, 1893 (FDC).

Cancellations

Philippines		—
Supp. Mail Types F or G		+4.00
238 A79 15c **dark green**	240.00	70.00
green	240.00	70.00
dull green	240.00	70.00
Never hinged	500.00	
On cover		225.00
On cover, Expo. station machine canc.		600.00
On cover, Expo. station duplex handstamp cancel		*900.00*
Block of 4	1,000.	450.00
P# strip of 3, Impt.	950.00	
P# strip of 4, Impt. & letter	1,200.	
P# block of 6, Impt.	*3,750.*	
Never hinged	*6,500.*	
P# block of 8, Impt. & letter	*6,500.*	
Never hinged	*11,500.*	
Double transfer	—	—

Earliest documented use: Jan. 26, 1893.

Cancellations

China		+75.00
Supp. Mail Type F or G		+10.00
239 A80 30c **orange brown**	300.00	90.00
bright orange brown	300.00	90.00
Never hinged	675.00	
On cover		400.00
On cover, Expo. station machine canc.		*1,000.*
On cover, Expo. station duplex handstamp cancel		*1,500.*
Block of 4	1,250.	600.00
P# strip of 3, Impt.	1,200.	
P# strip of 4, Impt. & letter	1,600.	
P# block of 6, Impt.	*8,500.*	
Never hinged	*14,500.*	
P# block of 8, Impt. & letter	*12,000.*	
Never hinged	*20,000.*	

Earliest documented use: Jan. 18, 1893 (dated cancel on off-cover stamp); Feb. 8, 1893 (cover).

Cancellations

Supp. Mail Types F or G		+25.00
240 A81 50c **slate blue**	600.00	180.00
dull state blue	600.00	180.00
Never hinged	1,400.	
On cover		625.00
On cover, Expo. station machine canc.		*1,500.*
On cover, Expo. station duplex handstamp cancel		2,000.
Block of 4	2,600.	1,100.
P# strip of 3, Impt.	2,500.	
P# strip of 4, Impt. & letter	*3,750.*	
Never hinged	6,250.	
P# block of 6, Impt.	*14,000.*	
Never hinged	*23,500.*	
P# block of 8, Impt. & letter	*22,500.*	
Never hinged	*37,500.*	
Double transfer	—	—
Triple transfer	—	—

Earliest documented use: Feb. 8, 1893.

Cancellation

Supp. Mail Types F or G		+30.00
241 A82 $1 **salmon**	1,250.	625.
dark salmon	1,250.	625.
Never hinged	3,250.	
No gum	650.	
On cover		*2,000.*
On cover, Expo. station machine canc.		*3,000.*
On cover, Expo. station duplex handstamp cancel		4,000.
Block of 4	5,250.	*4,500.*
P# strip of 3, Impt.	5,000.	
P# strip of 4, Impt. & letter	6,500.	
P# block of 6, Impt.	*47,500.*	
P# block of 8, Impt. & letter	*80,000.*	
Never hinged	*125,000.*	
Double transfer	—	—

Earliest documented use: Jan. 13, 1893 (dated cancel on off-cover stamp); Jan. 21, 1893 (on cover).

Cancellations

Supp. Mail Types F or G		+50.
242 A83 $2 **brown red**	1,300.	600.
deep brown red	1,300.	600.
Never hinged	3,500.	
No gum	675.	
On cover		*2,100.*
On cover, Expo. station machine canc.		*3,000.*
On cover, Expo. station duplex handstamp cancel		*4,000.*
Block of 4	5,500.	*3,250.*
P# strip of 3, Impt.	5,500.	
P# strip of 4, Impt. & letter	9,000.	
P# block of 6, Impt.	*67,500.*	
P# block of 8, Impt. & letter	*85,000.*	

Earliest documented use: Jan. 2, 1893 (FDC).

Cancellations

Supplementary Mail Type G		+50.

The No. 242 plate block of 8 is believed to be unique.

243 A84 $3 **yellow green**	2,000.	1,050.
pale yellow green	2,000.	1,050.
Never hinged	5,500.	
No gum	1,100.	
a. $3 **olive green**	2,000.	1,050.
Never hinged	5,500.	
No gum	1,100.	
On cover		*2,600.*
On cover, Expo. station machine canc.		*4,000.*
On cover, Expo. station duplex handstamp cancel		*6,000.*
Block of 4	*9,250.*	*9,000.*
P# strip of 3, Impt.	*8,250.*	
P# strip of 4, Impt. & letter	*11,000.*	
P# block of 6, Impt.	*85,000.*	

Earliest documented use: Mar. 24, 1893.

244 A85 $4 **crimson lake**	2,750.	1,300.
Never hinged	7,500.	
No gum	1,400.	
a. $4 **rose carmine**	2,750.	1,300.
pale aniline rose	2,750.	1,300.
Never hinged	7,500.	
No gum	1,400.	
On cover		*4,000.*
On cover, Expo. station machine canc.		*5,750.*
On cover, Expo. station duplex handstamp cancel		*8,000.*
Block of 4	*12,000.*	*12,500.*
P# strip of 3, Impt.	*10,750.*	
P# strip of 4, Impt. & letter	*15,500.*	
P# block of 6, Impt.	*250,000.*	
P# block of 8, Impt. & letter	*310,000.*	

The No. 244 plate block of 8 is unique; it has full original gum with light hinge marks.

Earliest documented use: Mar. 24, 1893.

245 A86 $5 **black**	3,100.	1,600.
grayish black	3,100.	1,600.
Never hinged	8,500.	
No gum	1,650.	
On cover		*4,750.*
On cover, Expo. station machine canc.		*8,000.*
On cover, Expo. station duplex handstamp cancel		*12,000.*
Block of 4	*14,000.*	*12,500.*
P# strip of 3, Impt.	*13,500.*	
P# strip of 4, Impt. & letter	*22,500.*	
Never hinged	*45,000.*	

P# block of 6, Impt.	*190,000.*	
Never hinged	*260,000.*	
P# block of 8, Impt. & letter	*250,000.*	

Earliest documented use: Jan. 6, 1893.

The No. 245 plate block of 8 is unique; it has traces of original gum.

See Nos. 2624-2629 for souvenir sheets containing stamps of designs A71-A86 but with "1992" at upper right.

Nos. 230-245 exist imperforate; not issued. See Die and Plate proofs for the 2c.

Never-Hinged Stamps

See note before No. 205 regarding premiums for never-hinged stamps.

BUREAU ISSUES

In the following listings of postal issues mostly printed by the Bureau of Engraving and Printing at Washington, D.C., the editors acknowledge with thanks the use of material prepared by the Catalogue Listing Committee of the Bureau Issues Association.

The Bureau-printed stamps until 1965 were engraved except the Offset Issues of 1918-19 (Nos. 525-536). Engraving and lithography were combined for the first time for the Homemakers 5c (No. 1253). The Bureau used photogravure first in 1971 on the Missouri 8c (No. 1426).

Stamps in this section which were not printed by the Bureau begin with Nos. 909-921 and are so noted.

"*On cover*" listings carry through No. 701. Beyond this point a few covers of special significance are listed. Many Bureau Issue stamps are undoubtly scarce properly used on cover. Most higher denominations exist almost exclusively on pieces of package wrapping and usually in combination with other values. Collector interest in covers is generally limited to fancy cancellations, attractive corner cards, use abroad and other special usages.

Plate number blocks are valued unused. Although many exist used, and are scarcer in that condition, they command only a fraction of the value of the unused examples because they are less sought after.

IMPRINTS AND PLATE NUMBERS

In listing the Bureau of Engraving & Printing Imprints, the editors have followed the classification of types adopted by the Bureau Issues Association. Types I, II, IV, V and VIII occur on postage issues and are illustrated below. Types III, VI and VII occur only on Special Delivery plates, so are illustrated with the listings of those stamps; other types are illustrated with the listings of the issues on which they occur.

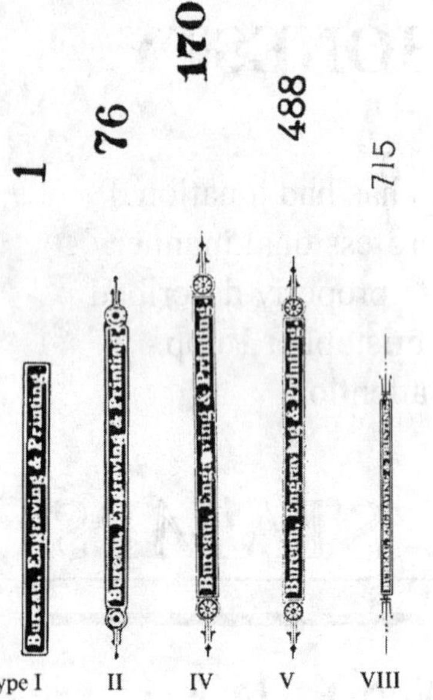

In listing Imprint blocks and strips, the editors have designated for each stamp the various types known to exist. If, however, the Catalogue listing sufficiently describes the Imprint, no type number is given. Thus a listing reading: "P# block of 6, Impt. (Imprint) & A" in the 1912-14 series would not be followed by a type number as the description is self-explanatory. Values are for the commonest types.

PLATE POSITIONS

At the suggestion of the Catalogue Listing Committee of the Bureau Issues Association, all plate positions of these issues are indicated by giving the plate number first, next the pane position, and finally the stamp position. For example: 20234 L.L. 58.

Franklin — A87

Washington — A88

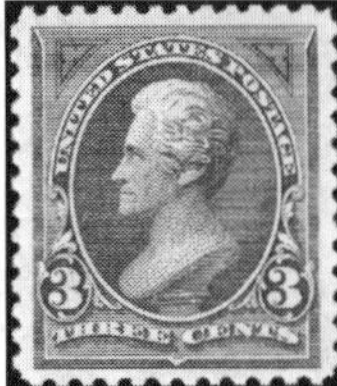

Jackson — A89

Lincoln — A90

Grant — A91

Garfield — A92

Sherman — A93

Webster — A94

Clay — A95

Jefferson — A96

Perry — A97

James Madison — A98

John Marshall — A99

REGULAR ISSUE

Plates for the issue of 1894 were of two sizes: 400 subjects for all 1c, 2c and 10c denominations; 200 subjects for all 6c, 8c, 15c, 50c, $1.00, $2.00 and $5.00, and both 400 and 200 subjects for the 3c, 4c and 5c denominations; all issued in panes of 100 each.

1894 Unwmk. *Perf. 12*

246	A87	1c **ultramarine,** *Oct. 1894*	32.50	4.50
		bright ultramarine	32.50	4.50
		dark ultramarine	32.50	4.50
		Never hinged	75.00	
		On cover		12.50
		Block of 4	140.00	32.50
		P# strip of 3, Impt., T I	145.00	
		Never hinged	300.00	
		P# block of 6, Impt., T I	450.00	
		Never hinged	800.00	
		Double transfer	40.00	5.50

Earliest documented use: Oct. 17, 1894.

Cancellation

		China		—
247	A87	1c **blue**	70.00	2.25
		bright blue	70.00	2.25
		dark blue	70.00	2.25
		Never hinged	160.00	
		On cover		20.00
		Block of 4	290.00	20.00
		P# strip of 3, Impt., T I or II	285.00	
		Never hinged	600.00	
		P# block of 6, Impt., T I or II	900.00	
		Never hinged	1,600.	
		Double transfer	—	3.75

Earliest documented use: Nov. 11, 1894.

TWO CENTS:

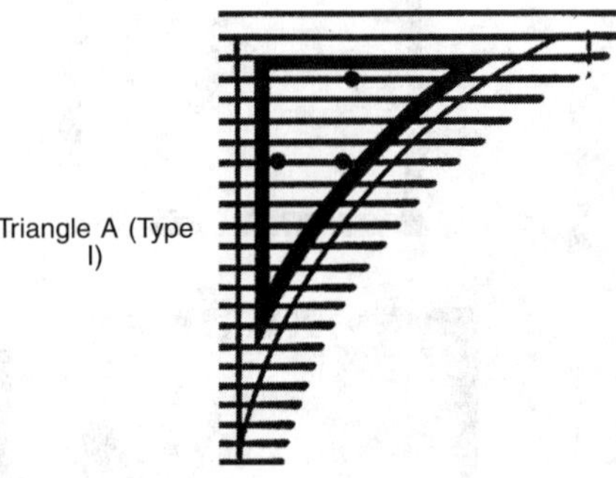

Triangle A (Type I)

Type I (Triangle A). The horizontal lines of the ground work run across the triangle and are of the same thickness within it as without.

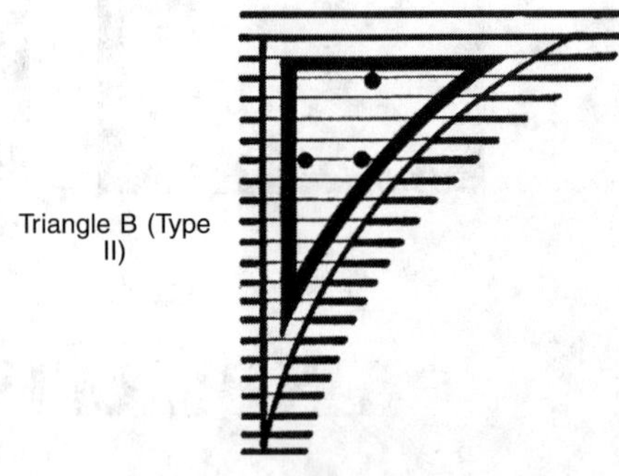

Triangle B (Type II)

Type II (Triangle B). The horizontal lines cross the triangle but are thinner within it than without. Other minor design differences exist, but the change to Triangle B is a sufficient determinant.

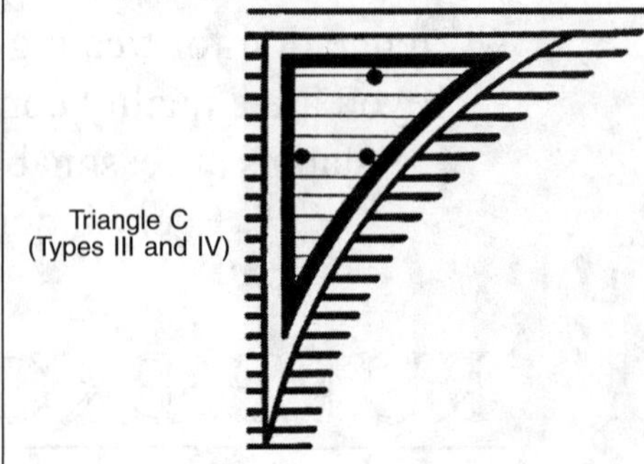

Triangle C (Types III and IV)

Type III (Triangle C). The horizontal lines do not cross the double lines of the triangle. The lines within the triangle are thin, as in Type II. The rest of the design is the same as Type II, except that most of the designs had the dot in the "S" of "CENTS" removed. Stamps with this dot present are listed; some specialists refer to them as "Type IIIa" varieties.

Type IV (Triangle C). See No. 279B and its varieties. Type IV is from a new die with many major and minor design variations including, (1) re-cutting and lengthening of hairline, (2) shaded toga button, (3) strengthening of lines on sleeve, (4) additional dots on ear, (5) "T" of "TWO" straight at right, (6) background lines extend into white oval opposite "U" of "UNITED." Many other differences exist.

For further information concerning type IV, see also George Brett's article in the Sept. 1993 issue of the "The United States Specialist" and the 23-part article by Kenneth Diehl in the Dec. 1994 through Aug. 1997 issues of the "The United States Specialist."

No.	Design	Description	Unused	Used
248	A88	2c **pink,** type I, *Oct. 1894*	27.50	6.00
		pale pink	27.50	6.00
		Never hinged	62.50	
		On cover		14.00
		Block of 4	120.00	35.00
		P# strip of 3, Impt., T I or II	110.00	
		Never hinged	235.00	
		P# block of 6, Impt., T I or II	275.00	
		Never hinged	550.00	
		Double transfer	—	—
a.		Vert. pair, imperf horiz.	*5,500.*	

Earliest documented use: Oct. 16, 1894.

No.	Design	Description	Unused	Used
249	A88	2c **carmine lake,** type I, *Oct. 1894*	160.00	5.50
		dark carmine lake	160.00	5.50
		Never hinged	375.00	
		On cover		11.50
		Block of 4	675.00	40.00
		P# strip of 3, Impt., T I or II	650.00	
		Never hinged	1,400.	
		P# block of 6, Impt., T I or II	2,250.	
		Never hinged	4,250.	
		Double transfer	—	6.50

Earliest documented use: Oct. 11, 1894.

No.	Design	Description	Unused	Used
250	A88	2c **carmine,** type I, *Oct. 1894*	30.00	2.50
		dark carmine	30.00	4.50
		Never hinged	65.00	
		On cover		3.50
		Block of 4	130.00	18.00
a.		2c **rose,** type I, *Oct. 1894*	30.00	4.50
		Never hinged	65.00	
		On cover		5.50
		Block of 4	130.00	20.00
b.		2c **scarlet,** type I, *Jan. 1895*	30.00	1.00
		Never hinged	65.00	
		On cover		1.50
		Block of 4	130.00	7.50
		P# strip of 3, Impt., T I or II	120.00	
		Never hinged	250.00	
		P# block of 6, Impt., T I or II	375.00	
		Never hinged	650.00	
		Double transfer	—	5.00
d.		Horizontal pair, imperf. between	*2,000.*	

Earliest documented uses: Oct. 17, 1894 (No. 250), Oct. 13, 1894 (No. 250a), Jan. 17, 1895 (No. 250b).

No.	Design	Description	Unused	Used
251	A88	2c **carmine,** type II, *Feb. 1895*	300.00	11.00
		dark carmine	300.00	11.00
		Never hinged	650.00	
		On cover		20.00
		Block of 4	1,250.	100.00
a.		2c **scarlet,** type II, *Feb. 1895*	300.00	7.50
		Never hinged	650.00	
		On cover		13.50
		Block of 4	1,250.	65.00
		P# strip of 3, Impt., T II	1,200.	
		Never hinged	2,500.	
		P# block of 6, Impt., T II	3,250.	
		Never hinged	5,500.	

Earliest documented uses: Feb. 16, 1895 (No. 251), Feb. 19, 1895 (No. 251a).

No.	Design	Description	Unused	Used
252	A88	2c **carmine,** type III, *Mar. 1895*	130.00	11.00
		pale carmine	130.00	11.00
		Never hinged	275.00	
a.		2c **scarlet,** type III, *Mar. 1895*	130.00	11.00
		Never hinged	275.00	
		On cover		15.00
		Block of 4	550.00	100.00
		P# strip of 3, Impt., T II or IV	525.00	
		Never hinged	1,100.	
		P# block of 6, Impt., T II or IV	1,900.	
		Never hinged	3,250.	
		Dot in "S" of "CENTS" (carmine)	150.00	5.75
		Never hinged	325.00	
b.		Horiz. pair, imperf. vert.	*1,500.*	
c.		Horiz. pair, imperf. between	*1,750.*	

Former Nos. 252a, 252b are now Nos. 252b, 252c.

Earliest documented uses: Apr. 2, 1895 (dated cancel tying No. 252 dot in "S" variety on piece); Apr. 5, 1895 (No. 252); Apr. 17, 1895 (No. 252a).

No.	Design	Description	Unused	Used
253	A89	3c **purple,** *Sept. 1894*	115.00	10.00
		dark purple	115.00	10.00
		Never hinged	250.00	
		On cover		25.00
		Block of 4	500.00	75.00
		Margin block of 4, arrow, R or L	525.00	
		P# strip of 3, Impt., T I or II	475.00	
		Never hinged	950.00	
		P# block of 6, Impt., T I or II	1,400.	
		Never hinged	2,500.	

Earliest documented use: Oct. 20, 1894 (dated cancel on off-cover stamp); Nov. 15, 1894 (on cover).

See Die and Plate Proofs for imperf. on stamp paper.

No.	Design	Description	Unused	Used
254	A90	4c **dark brown,** *Sept. 1894*	150.00	6.00
		brown	150.00	6.00
		Never hinged	350.00	
		On cover		20.00
		Block of 4	650.00	35.00
		Margin block of 4, arrow, R or L	675.00	
		P# strip of 3, Impt., T I or II	600.00	
		Never hinged	1,400.	
		P# block of 6, Impt., T I or II	1,900.	
		Never hinged	3,400.	

Earliest documented use: Oct. 16, 1894 (dated cancel on off-cover stamp); Dec. 5, 1894 (on cover).

See Die and Plate Proofs for imperf. on stamp paper.

Cancellations

		Supplementary Mail Type F		+2.00
255	A91	5c **chocolate,** *Sept. 1894*	110.00	7.00
		deep chocolate	110.00	7.00
		yellow brown	110.00	7.00
		Never hinged	240.00	
		On cover		20.00
		Block of 4	475.00	50.00
		Margin block of 4, arrow, R or L	500.00	
		P# strip of 3, Impt., T I, II or IV	475.00	
		Never hinged	950.00	
		P# block of 6, Impt., T I, II or IV	1,200.	
		Never hinged	2,100.	
		Double transfer	135.00	6.50
		Worn plate, diagonal lines missing in oval background	110.00	5.00
c.		Vert. pair, imperf. horiz.	*4,000.*	
		P# block of 6, Impt., T IV	—	

See Die and Plate Proofs for imperf. on stamp paper.

Earliest documented use: Oct. 23, 1894.

Cancellations

		Supplementary Mail Type G		+2.00
		China		—
256	A92	6c **dull brown,** *July 1894*	185.00	22.50
		Never hinged	400.00	
		On cover		45.00
		Block of 4	800.00	160.00
		Margin block of 4, arrow, R or L	825.00	
		P# strip of 3, Impt., T I	800.00	
		Never hinged	1,600.	
		P# block of 6, Impt., T I	2,900.	—
		Never hinged	*5,250.*	
a.		Vert. pair, imperf. horiz.	*1,600.*	
		P# block of 6, Impt., T I	*14,000.*	

Earliest documented use: Aug. 11, 1894.

257	A93	8c **violet brown,** *Mar. 1895*	140.00	17.50
		bright violet brown	140.00	17.50
		Never hinged	300.00	
		On cover		45.00
		Block of 4	600.00	125.00
		Margin block of 4, arrow, R or L	625.00	
		P# strip of 3, Impt., T I	575.00	
		Never hinged	1,150.	
		P# block of 6, Impt., T I	1,850.	
		Never hinged	*3,250.*	

Earliest documented use: May 8, 1895.

258	A94	10c **dark green,** *Sept. 1894*	300.00	12.50
		green	300.00	12.50
		dull green	300.00	12.50
		Never hinged	650.00	
		On cover		32.50
		Block of 4	1,250.	75.00
		P# strip of 3, Impt., T I	1,200.	
		Never hinged	2,500.	
		P# block of 6, Impt., T I	3,350.	
		Never hinged	*6,000.*	
		Double transfer	350.00	15.00

See Die and Plate Proofs for imperf. on stamp paper.

Earliest documented use: Nov. 19, 1894.

Cancellations

		China		—
		Supp. Mail Types F, G		+2.00
259	A95	15c **dark blue,** *Oct. 1894*	325.00	60.00
		indigo	325.00	60.00
		Never hinged	700.00	
		On cover		115.00
		Block of 4	1,350.	400.00
		Margin block of 4, arrow, R or L	1,400.	
		P# strip of 3, Impt., T I	1,500.	
		Never hinged	2,750.	
		P# block of 6, Impt., T I	5,000.	
		Never hinged	*9,000.*	

Earliest documented use: Dec. 6, 1894.

Cancellation

		China		—
260	A96	50c **orange,** *Nov. 1894*	575.	135.
		deep orange	575.	135.
		Never hinged	1,300.	
		On cover		1,000.
		Block of 4	2,500.	1,100.
		Margin block of 4, arrow, R or L	2,600.	
		P# strip of 3, Impt., T I	2,500.	
		Never hinged	*5,500.*	
		P# block of 6, Impt., T I	10,500.	
		Never hinged	*17,500.*	

Earliest documented use: Dec. 12, 1894 (dated cancel on off-cover stamp); Jan. 15, 1895 (cover).

Cancellations

Supp. Mail Type F or G	—
China	—

Type I

Type II

ONE DOLLAR

Type I. The circles enclosing "$1" are broken where they meet the curved line below "One Dollar."

Type II. The circles are complete.

The fifteen left vertical rows of impressions from plate 76 are Type I, the balance being Type II.

261	A97	$1 **black,** type I, *Nov. 1894*	1,000.	350.
		grayish black	1,000.	350.
		Never hinged	2,400.	
		No gum	350.	
		On cover		*2,750.*
		Block of 4	4,500.	*2,100.*
		Margin block of 4, arrow, L	4,750.	
		P# strip of 3, Impt., T V	4,250.	
		P# block of 6, Impt., T V	*17,500.*	

Earliest documented use: Jan. 18, 1895.

261A	A97	$1 **black,** type II, *Nov. 1894*	2,300.	750.
		Never hinged	5,500.	
		No gum	750.	
		On cover		*4,500.*
		Block of 4	*9,500.*	*4,750.*
		Margin block of 4, arrow, R	*9,750.*	
		Horizontal pair, types I and II	*4,000.*	*1,400.*
		Block of 4, two each of types I and II	*9,000.*	—
		P# strip of 3, Impt., T V, one stamp No. 261	6,250.	
		P# block of 6, Impt., T V, two stamps No. 261	*27,500.*	

Earliest documented use: Mar. 22, 1895. A Mar. 11, 1895, cover has been reported. The editors woyud like to see evidence of certification of this date.

262	A98	$2 **bright blue,** *Dec. 1894*	3,250.	1,200.
		Never hinged	7,750.	
		No gum	1,200.	
		dark blue	3,400.	1,250.
		Never hinged	8,000.	
		On cover		*5,000.*
		Block of 4	*14,500.*	*7,000.*
		Margin block of 4, arrow, R or L	*15,000.*	
		P# strip of 3, Impt., T V	*14,000.*	
		P# block of 6, Impt., T V	*42,500.*	

Earliest documented use: July 6, 1895 (dated cancel on off-cover stamp); July 15, 1895 (on cover).

263	A99	$5 **dark green,** *Dec. 1894*	5,000.	2,500.
		Never hinged	12,500.	
		No gum	2,600.	
		On cover		—
		Block of 4	*22,500.*	*14,000.*
		Margin block of 4, arrow, R or L	*23,500.*	
		P# strip of 3, Impt., T V	*23,500.*	

Earliest documented use: July 6, 1896 (dated cancel on off-cover stamp).

REGULAR ISSUE

(Actual size of letter)

repeated in rows, thus

Watermark 191

The letters stand for "United States Postage Stamp."

Plates for the 1895 issue were of two sizes:

400 subjects for all 1c, 2c and 10c denominations; 200 subjects for all 3c, 4c, 5c, 6c, 8c, 15c, 50c, $1, $2 and $5; all issued in panes of 100 each.

Printings from the 400 subject plates show the watermark reading horizontally, on the 200 subject printings the watermark reads vertically (with the tops and bottoms of the letters toward the vertical sides of the stamps).

Wmk. 191 Horizontally or Vertically

1895 ***Perf. 12***

264	A87	1c **blue,** *Apr. 1895*	6.50	.50
		dark blue	6.50	.50
		pale blue	6.50	.50
		Never hinged	14.00	
		On cover		1.25
		Block of 4	27.50	5.00
		P# strip of 3, Impt., T I, II, IV or V	26.00	
		Never hinged	55.00	
		P# block of 6, Impt., T I, II, IV or V	225.00	
		Never hinged	400.00	
		Double transfer	—	1.00

Earliest documented use: May 16, 1895.

Cancellations

		China		—
		Philippines		—
		Samoa		—
265	A88	2c **carmine,** type I, *May 1895*	30.00	2.80
		deep carmine	30.00	2.80
		Never hinged	65.00	
		On cover		4.75
		Block of 4	130.00	15.00
		P# strip of 3, Impt., T II	120.00	
		Never hinged	250.00	
		P# block of 6, Impt., T II	400.00	
		Never hinged	750.00	
		Double transfer	45.00	6.50

Earliest documented use: May 2, 1895.

266	A88	2c **carmine,** type II, *May 1895*	30.00	5.00
		Never hinged	65.00	
		On cover		8.50
		Block of 4	175.00	40.00
		Horizontal pair, types II and III	70.00	17.50
		Never hinged	145.00	
		P# strip of 3, Impt., T II or IV	120.00	
		Never hinged	250.00	
		P# block of 6, Impt., T II or IV	425.00	
		Never hinged	775.00	
		Never hinged	700.00	

Earliest documented use: May 27, 1895.

267	A88	2c **carmine,** type III *May 1895*	5.50	.40
		deep carmine	5.50	.40
		reddish carmine	5.50	.40
		Never hinged	12.00	
		On cover		.55
		Block of 4	24.00	3.25
		P# strip of 3, Impt., T II, IV or V	22.50	
		Never hinged	47.50	
		P# block of 6, Impt., T II, IV or V	190.00	
		Never hinged	300.00	
		Dot in "S" of "CENTS"	7.50	.50
		Never hinged	16.00	
		Double transfer	16.50	1.25
a.		2c **pink,** type III, *Nov. 1897*	7.50	1.00
		Never hinged	16.50	
		bright pink	12.50	4.50
		Never hinged	27.50	
		On cover		1.25
		Block of 4	32.50	7.50

P# strip of 3, Impt., T II, IV or V 27.50
Never hinged 60.00
P# block of 6, Impt., T II, IV or V 240.00
Never hinged 450.00
Dot in "S" of "CENTS" 15.00 .75
Never hinged 32.50
b. 2c **vermilion,** type III, *early 1899* *30.00* 4.50
c. 2c **rose carmine,** type III, *Mar. 1899* — 3.30

Earliest documented uses:
No. 267, May 31, 1895;
No. 267 with dot in "S", July 15, 1895;
No. 267a, Dec. 8, 1897;
No. 267a with dot in "S", Mar. 18, 1898.

Cancellations

Green —
China —
Hawaii —
Philippines —
Samoa —

The three left vertical rows of impressions from plate 170 are Type II, the balance being Type III.

268 A89 3c **purple,** *Oct. 1895* 37.50 2.00
dark purple 37.50 2.00
Never hinged 80.00
On cover 8.00
Block of 4 160.00 20.00
Margin block of 4, arrow, R or L 175.00
P# strip of 3, Impt., T II or V 150.00
Never hinged 300.00
P# block of 6, Impt., T II or IV 675.00
Never hinged 1,200.
Double transfer 45.00 4.50

Earliest documented use: Feb. 18, 1896.

Cancellations

Guam —
China —
Philippines —

269 A90 4c **dark brown,** *June, 1895* 40.00 3.00
dark yellow brown 40.00 3.00
Never hinged 87.50
On cover 11.00
Block of 4 170.00 27.50
Margin block of 4, arrow, R or L 180.00
P# strip of 3, Impt., T I, II, IV or V 160.00
Never hinged 325.00
P# block of 6, Impt., T I, II, IV or V 725.00
Never hinged 1,250.
Double transfer 45.00 5.00

Earliest documented use: July 22, 1895.

Cancellations

Philippines —
China —
Samoa —

270 A91 5c **chocolate,** *June, 1895* 37.50 3.00
deep brown 37.50 3.00
chestnut 37.50 3.00
Never hinged 80.00
On cover 7.50
Block of 4 160.00 27.50
Margin block of 4, arrow, R or L 170.00
P# strip of 3, Impt., T I, II, IV or V 150.00
Never hinged 300.00
P# block of 6, Impt., T I, II, IV or V 625.00
Never hinged 1,250.
Double transfer 45.00 4.50
Worn plate, diagonal lines missing in oval background 40.00 3.25

Earliest documented use: Sept. 12, 1895.

Cancellations

China —
Supplementary Mail G +2.50

271 A92 6c **dull brown,** *Aug. 1895* 110.00 7.50
claret brown 110.00 7.50
Never hinged 240.00
On cover 27.50
Block of 4 525.00 65.00
Margin block of 4, arrow, R or L 550.00
P# strip of 3, Impt., T I, IV or V 475.00
Never hinged 950.00
P# block of 6, Impt., T I, IV or V 2,750.
Never hinged 4,750.
Very thin paper 120.00 7.50
a. Wmkd. USIR *10,000.* *7,500.*
Pair —
P# strip of 3, Impt. —

Earliest documented use: Sept. 14, 1895.

Cancellation

Philippines —

Nos. 271a, 272a must have an identifiable portion of the letters "I" or "R." Single stamps from the same sheets, but showing the "U" or "S" are considered to be Nos. 271 and 272.

272 A93 8c **violet brown,** *July 1895* 70.00 2.50
dark violet brown 70.00 2.50
Never hinged 150.00
On cover 14.00
Block of 4 290.00 17.50
Margin block of 4, arrow, R or L 300.00
P# strip of 3, Impt., T I, IV or V 290.00
Never hinged 575.00
P# block of 6, Impt., T I, IV or V 975.00
Never hinged 1,600.
Double transfer 85.00 4.00
a. Wmkd. USIR *5,000.* 750.00
Block of 4 *5,000.*
P# strip of 3 Impt., T I *20,000.*

Earliest documented use: Dec. 24, 1895.

Cancellations

China —
Guam —
Philippines —
Puerto Rico, 1898 —
Samoa —
Supplementary Mail Type G +2.50

273 A94 10c **dark green,** *June 1895* 100.00 2.00
green 100.00 2.00
Never hinged 225.00
On cover 15.00
Block of 4 425.00 20.00
P# strip of 3, Impt., T I or IV 425.00
Never hinged 850.00
P# block of 6, Impt., T I or IV 1,750.
Never hinged 3,000.
Double transfer 125.00 4.50

Earliest documented use: July 25, 1895.

Cancellations

China —
Cuba —
Philippines —
Supp. Mail Types F, G +2.00

274 A95 15c **dark blue,** *Sept. 1895* 240.00 14.00
indigo 240.00 14.00
Never hinged 550.00
On cover 55.00
Block of 4 1,000. 90.00
Margin block of 4, arrow, R or L 1,025.
P# strip of 3, Impt., T I or IV 975.00
Never hinged 1,950.
P# block of 6, Impt., T I or IV 3,750.

Earliest documented use: May 6, 1896.

Cancellations

China —
Philippines —
Supplementary Mail Type G +3.00

275 A96 50c **orange,** *Nov. 1895* 300. 30.00
Never hinged 700.
On cover 400.00
Block of 4 1,300. 175.00
Margin block of 4, arrow, R or L 1,350.
P# strip of 3, Impt., T I 1,200.
P# block of 6, Impt., T I 6,000.
a. 50c **red orange** 325. 35.00
Never hinged 750.
On cover 400.00
Block of 4 1,400. 225.00
Margin block of 4, arrow, R or L 1,450.
P# strip of 3, Impt., T I 1,250.
P# block of 6, Impt., T I 6,000.

Earliest documented use: Feb. 27, 1897.

Cancellations

China —
Philippines —
Supp. Mail Types F, G +5.

276 A97 $1 **black,** type I, *Aug. 1895* 650. 90.00
greenish black 650. 90.00
Never hinged 1,850.
No gum 190.
On cover *2,250.*
Block of 4 2,750. 650.
Margin block of 4, arrow, L 2,900.
P# strip of 3, Impt., T V 2,750.
Never hinged *6,000.*
P# block of 6, Impt., T V *14,000.*

Earliest documented use: Mar. 1, 1898.

Cancellation

Philippines —

276A A97 $1 **black,** type II, *Aug. 1895* 1,400. 190.
greenish black 1,400. 190.
Never hinged 3,500.
No gum 450.
On cover *3,750.*
Block of 4 6,000. 1,500.
Margin block of 4, arrow, R 6,250.
Horizontal pair, types I and II *2,500.* *2,500.*
Block of 4, two each of types I and II *6,000.* *6,000.*
P# strip of 3, Impt., T V, one stamp No. 276 *4,750.*
P# block of 6, Impt., T V, two stamps No. 276 *25,000.*

Earliest documented use: Apr. 6, 1896.

Cancellation

China —
Philippines —

The fifteen left vertical rows of impressions from plate 76 are Type I, the balance being Type II.

277 A98 $2 **bright blue** 1,100. 350.
Never hinged 2,750.
No gum 400.
a. $2 **dark blue** 1,100. 350.
Never hinged 2,750.
No gum 400.
On cover *3,500.*
Block of 4 *4,750.* *2,500.*
Margin block of 4, arrow, R or L *5,000.*
P# strip of 3, Impt., T V *4,250.* —
P# block of 6, Impt., T V *21,000.*

Earliest documented use: July 18, 1895.

Cancellation

Supplementary Mail Type G		—
278 A99 $5 **dark green,** *Aug. 1895*	2,300.	550.
Never hinged	6,000.	
No gum	900.	
On cover		*12,500.*
Block of 4	*10,000.*	*3,500.*
Margin block of 4, arrow, R or L	*10,500.*	
P# strip of 3, Impt., T V	*9,500.*	
P# block of 6, Impt., T V	*75,000.*	

Earliest documented use: Nov. 3, 1896.

See Die and Plate Proofs for imperf. or horiz. pair, imperf. vert. (1c) on stamp paper.

REGULAR ISSUE

Wmk. 191 Horizontally or Vertically

1897-1903 ***Perf. 12***

Plates for the 1897-1903 issue were of two sizes:

400 subjects for the 1c and 2c denominations; 200 subjects for all 4c, 5c, 6c and 15c denominations; and both 400 and 200 for the 10c denomination; all issued in panes of 100 each.

Printings from the 400 subject plates show the watermark reading horizontally, on the 200 subject plate printings the watermark reads vertically.

In January, 1898, the color of the 1-cent stamp was changed to green and in March, 1898, that of the 5-cents to dark blue in order to conform to the colors assigned these values by the Universal Postal Union. These changes necessitated changing the colors of the 10c and 15c denominations in order to avoid confusion.

279 A87 1c **deep green,** *Jan. 1898*	9.00	.50
green	9.00	.50
yellow green	9.00	.50
dark yellow green	9.00	.50
Never hinged	20.00	
On cover		.60
Block of 4	37.50	5.00
P# strip of 3, Impt., T V	37.50	—
Never hinged	75.00	
P# block of 6, Impt., T V	185.00	
Never hinged	325.00	
Double transfer	12.00	1.10

Earliest documented use: Jan. 31, 1898

Cancellations

China		—
Guam		—
Puerto Rico, 1898		—
Philippines		—
279B A88 2c **red,** type IV *May 1899*	9.00	.40
light red, *May 1899*	9.00	.40
Never hinged	20.00	
deep red, *Sept. 1901*	13.50	1.25
Never hinged	30.00	
On cover		.50
Block of 4	37.50	3.00
P# strip of 3, Impt., T V	37.50	
Never hinged	75.00	
P# block of 6, Impt., T V	200.00	
Never hinged	350.00	
P# strip of 4, Impt., T V (plate 802, UR position)	*250.00*	
P# block of 8, Impt., T V (plate 802, UR position)	*750.00*	
Double transfer	18.00	.75
Triple transfer	—	
Triangle at upper right without shading	22.50	6.00
c. 2c **rose carmine,** type IV, *Mar. 1899*	250.00	75.00
bright carmine rose, *Mar. 1899*	250.00	75.00
Never hinged	575.00	
Block of 4	1,050.	—
P# strip of 3, Impt., T V	1,050.	
Never hinged	2,000.	
P# block of 6, Impt., T V	2,900.	
d. 2c **orange red,** type IV *June 1900*	11.50	.55
pale orange red	11.50	.55
dark orange red, *Sept. 1902*	11.50	.55
deep orange red, *Jan. 1903*	11.50	.55
Never hinged	25.00	
On cover		.70
Block of 4	50.00	4.00
P# strip of 3, Impt., T V	42.50	
Never hinged	85.00	
P# block of 6, Impt., T V	220.00	
Never hinged	385.00	
e. Booklet pane of 6, **red,** type IV, *Apr. 18, 1900*	425.00	*1,250.*
light red	425.00	*1,250.*
orange red, *1901*	425.00	*1,250.*
Never hinged	800.00	
f. 2c **carmine,** type IV, *Nov. 1897*	10.00	.50
reddish carmine, *Dec. 1898*	10.00	.50
Never hinged	22.00	
On cover		.65
Block of 4	42.50	3.00
P# strip of 3, Impt., T V	40.00	
Never hinged	85.00	
P# block of 6, Impt., T V	220.00	
Never hinged	385.00	
g. 2c **pink,** type IV, *Nov. 1897*	14.00	1.00
Never hinged	30.00	
bright pink	19.00	1.25
Never hinged	40.00	
On cover		1.25
Block of 4	60.00	7.50
P# strip of 3, Impt., T V	50.00	
Never hinged	115.00	
P# block of 6, Impt., T V	250.00	
Never hinged	450.00	
h. 2c **vermilion,** type IV, *Jan. 1899*	11.00	.55
pale vermilion	11.00	.55
Never hinged	24.00	
On cover		.75
Block of 4	47.50	4.00
P# strip of 3, Impt., T V	45.00	
Never hinged	100.00	
P# block of 6, Impt., T V	235.00	
Never hinged	400.00	
i. 2c **brown orange,** type IV, *Jan. 1899*	*100.00*	*10.00*
Never hinged	*220.00*	
P# strip of 3, Impt., T V	*450.00*	

Earliest documented uses:
No. 279B, July 6, 1899;
No. 279Bc, Mar 30, 1899;
No. 279Bc in bright rose carmine, July 16, 1899;
No. 279Bd, June 8, 1900;
No. 279Be booklet single (red), May 4, 1900;
No. 279Be booklet single (orange red), May 7, 1902;
No. 279Bf, Nov. 18, 1897;
No. 279Bg, Dec. 1, 1897;
No. 279Bh, Feb. 27, 1899.

Cancellations

Puerto Rico, 1898		—
Philippines, 1898		—
Guam, 1899 or 1900		—
Supplementary Mail Type G		+4.00
Cuba, 1898		—
China		—
Samoa		—
280 A90 4c **rose brown,** *Oct. 1898*	30.00	2.00
Never hinged	67.50	
a. 4c **lilac brown**	30.00	2.00
brownish claret	30.00	2.00
Never hinged	67.50	
b. 4c **orange brown**	30.00	2.00
Never hinged	67.50	
On cover		10.00
Block of 4	130.00	17.50
Margin block of 4, arrow, R or L	140.00	
P# strip of 3, Impt., T V	120.00	
Never hinged	230.00	
P# block of 6, Impt., T V	625.00	
Never hinged	1,050.	
Double transfer	35.00	3.00
Extra frame line at top (Plate 793 R 62)	50.00	7.50

Earliest documented use: Nov. 13, 1898.

Cancellations

Supplementary Mail Type G		+3.00
China		—
Philippines		—
281 A91 5c **dark blue,** *Mar. 1898*	35.00	1.80
blue	35.00	1.80
bright blue	35.00	1.80
Never hinged	80.00	
On cover		10.00
Block of 4	150.00	12.50
Margin block of 4, arrow, R or L	160.00	
P# strip of 3, Impt., T V	140.00	
Never hinged	275.00	
P# block of 6, Impt., T V	650.00	
Never hinged	1,200.	
Double transfer	45.00	3.75
Worn plate (diagonal lines missing in oval background)	40.00	2.00

Earliest documented use: Mar. 19, 1898.

Cancellations

Puerto Rico, 1898		—
Supplementary Mail Type G		+4.00
China		—
Cuba		—
Guam		—
Philippines		—
282 A92 6c **lake,** *Dec. 1898*	47.50	5.00
claret	47.50	5.00
Never hinged	110.00	
On cover		17.50
Block of 4	200.00	45.00
Margin block of 4, arrow, R or L	200.00	
P# strip of 3, Impt., T V	190.00	
Never hinged	375.00	
P# block of 6, Impt., T V	900.00	
Never hinged	1,500.	
Double transfer	60.00	7.50
a. 6c **purple lake**	65.00	10.00
Never hinged	150.00	
Block of 4	275.00	80.00
Margin block of 4, arrow	285.00	
P# strip of 3, Impt., T V	260.00	
Never hinged	550.00	
P# block of 6, Impt., T V	1,100.	
Never hinged	1,850.	

Earliest documented use: Mar. 13, 1899.

Cancellations

Supplementary Mail Type G		+4.00
China		—
Philippines		—

Type I. The tips of the foliate ornaments do not impinge on the white curved line below "ten cents."

282C A94 10c **brown,** type I, *Nov. 1898*	190.00	5.00
dark brown	190.00	5.00
Never hinged	450.00	
On cover		17.50
Block of 4	800.00	50.00
P# strip of 3, Impt., T IV or V	750.00	
Never hinged	1,500.	
P# block of 6, Impt., T IV or V	2,500.	
Never hinged	*4,000.*	
Double transfer	210.00	8.50

Earliest documented use: Dec. 10, 1898.

Cancellation

Supplementary Mail Type G		+2.50

Type II. The tips of the ornaments break the curved line below the "e" of "ten" and the "t" of "cents."

283 A94 10c **orange brown,** type II	135.00	4.50
brown	135.00	4.50
yellow brown	135.00	4.50
Never hinged	310.00	
On cover		17.50
Block of 4	575.00	45.00
Margin block of 4, arrow, R or L	600.00	—
P# strip of 3, Impt., T V	550.00	
Never hinged	1,000.	
P# block of 6, Impt., T V	1,750.	
Never hinged	2,850.	
Pair, type I and type II	*15,000.*	—

Earliest documented use: Mar. 13, 1899.

Cancellations

Supplementary Mail Type G		+2.50
China		—
Puerto Rico		—

On the 400 subject plate 932, all are Type I except the following: UL 20; UR 11, 12, 13; LL 61, 71, 86, these 7 being Type II.

284 A95 15c **olive green,** *Nov. 1898*	160.00	10.00
dark olive green	160.00	10.00
Never hinged	375.00	
On cover		32.50
Block of 4	700.00	85.00
Margin block of 4, arrow, R or L	750.00	
P# strip of 3, Impt., T IV	650.00	
Never hinged	1,400.	
P# block of 6, Impt., T IV	2,100.	
Never hinged	3,600.	

Earliest documented use: May 1, 1899.

Cancellations

Supp. Mail Type F or G		+2.50
China		—
Samoa		—
Nos. 279-284 (8)	615.50	29.20

VALUES FOR VERY FINE STAMPS

Please note: Stamps are valued in the grade of Very Fine unless otherwise indicated.

TRANS-MISSISSIPPI EXPOSITION ISSUE

Omaha, Nebr., June 1 - Nov. 1, 1898.

Jacques Marquette on the Mississippi A100

Farming in the West — A101

Indian Hunting Buffalo — A102

John Charles Frémont on the Rocky Mountains A103

Troops Guarding Wagon Train — A104

Hardships of Emigration A105

Western Mining Prospector A106

Western Cattle in Storm — A107

Mississippi River Bridge, St. Louis — A108

Exposition Station Handstamp Postmark

Plates of 100 (10x10) subjects, divided vertically into 2 panes of 50.

See Nos. 3209-3210 for bi-colored reproductions of Nos. 285-293.

1898, June 17 **Wmk. 191** ***Perf. 12***

No.	Type	Denom.	Description	Unused	Used
285	A100	1c	**dark yellow green**	30.00	6.50
			yellow green	30.00	6.50
			green	30.00	6.50
			Never hinged	65.00	
			On cover		9.75
			On card, Expo. station canc.		200.00
			Pair, on cover, Expo. station canc.		300.00
			Block of 4	120.00	45.00
			Margin block of 4, arrow, R or L	125.00	—
			P# pair, Impt., T VIII	67.50	
			Never hinged	140.00	
			P# strip of 3, Impt., T VIII	110.00	
			Never hinged	225.00	
			P# block of 4, Impt., T VIII	225.00	
			Never hinged	375.00	
			P# block of 6, Impt., T VIII	325.00	
			Never hinged	550.00	
			Double transfer	40.00	7.50

Earliest documented use: June 17, 1898 (FDC).

Cancellations

Cancellation	Value
Supp. Mail Type F or G	+1.50
China	—
Philippines	—
Puerto Rico, 1898	—

No.	Type	Denom.	Description	Unused	Used
286	A101	2c	**copper red**	27.50	2.50
			brown red	27.50	2.50
			light brown red	27.50	2.50
			Never hinged	60.00	
			On cover		3.50
			On cover, Expo. station canc.		175.00
			Block of 4	120.00	15.00
			Margin block of 4, arrow, R or L	125.00	—
			P# pair, Impt., T VIII	65.00	
			Never hinged	135.00	
			P# strip of 3, Impt., T VIII	110.00	
			Never hinged	220.00	
			P# block of 4, Impt., T VIII	190.00	
			Never hinged	325.00	
			P# block of 6, Impt., T VIII	300.00	
			Never hinged	500.00	
			Double transfer	42.50	3.75
			Worn plate	30.00	3.00

Earliest documented use: June 17, 1898 (FDC).

Cancellations

Cancellation	Value
China	—
Hawaii	—
Puerto Rico, 1898	—
Philippines	—

No.	Type	Denom.	Description	Unused	Used
287	A102	4c	**orange**	140.	24.00
			deep orange	140.	24.00
			Never hinged	325.	
			On cover		57.50
			On cover, Expo. station canc.		750.
			Block of 4	600.	185.
			Margin block of 4, arrow, R or L	625.	—
			P# pair, Impt., T VIII	350.	
			Never hinged	750.00	
			P# strip of 3, Impt., T VIII	600.	
			Never hinged	1,200.	
			P# block of 4, Impt., T VIII	900.	
			Never hinged	1,500.	
			P# block of 6, Impt., T VIII	1,500.	
			Never hinged	2,500.	

Earliest documented use: June 17, 1898 (FDC).

Cancellations

Cancellation	Value
Supp. Mail Type F or G	+5.
China	—
Philippines	—

No.	Type	Denom.	Description	Unused	Used
288	A103	5c	**dull blue**	140.	21.
			bright blue	140.	21.
			Never hinged	325.	
			On cover		50.
			On cover, Expo. station canc.		500.
			Block of 4	600.	150.
			Margin block of 4, arrow, R or L	625.	—
			P# pair, Impt., T VIII	325.	—
			Never hinged	750.	
			P# strip of 3, Impt., T VIII	500.	
			Never hinged	1,100.	
			P# block of 4, Impt., T VIII	825.	
			Never hinged	1,400.	
			P# block of 6, Impt., T VIII	1,400.	
			Never hinged	2,400.	

Earliest documented use: June 17, 1898 (FDC).

Cancellations

Cancellation	Value
Supp. Mail Type F or G	+5.
China	—
Philippines	—
Puerto Rico, 1898	—

No.	Type	Denom.	Description	Unused	Used
289	A104	8c	**violet brown**	180.	42.50
			dark violet brown	180.	42.50
			Never hinged	400.	
			On cover		115.
			On cover, Expo. station canc.		1,000.
			Block of 4	775.	275.
			Margin block of 4, arrow, R or L	800.	—
			P# pair, Impt., T VIII	390.	
			P# strip of 3, Impt., T VIII	725.	
			P# block of 4, Impt., T VIII	1,800.	
			Never hinged	3,000.	
			P# block of 6, Impt., T VIII	2,900.	
			Never hinged	4,750.	
a.			Vert. pair, imperf. horiz.	*22,500.*	
			P# block of 4, Impt., T VIII	*75,000.*	

Earliest documented use: June 17, 1898 (FDC).

Cancellations

Cancellation	Value
Philippines	—
Samoa	—

No.	Type	Denom.	Description	Unused	Used
290	A105	10c	**gray violet**	180.	30.00
			blackish violet	180.	30.00
			Never hinged	400.	
			On cover		87.50
			On cover, Expo. station canc.		750.
			Block of 4	775.	200.
			Margin block of 4, arrow, R or L	800.	—
			P# pair, Impt., T VIII	425.	
			Never hinged	950.	
			P# strip of 3, Impt., T VIII	650.	
			Never hinged	1,350.	
			P# block of 4, Impt., T VIII	1,900.	
			Never hinged	3,250.	
			P# block of 6, Impt., T VIII	3,250.	
			Never hinged	5,500.	

Earliest documented use: June 17, 1898 (FDC).

Cancellations

Cancellation	Value
Supplementary Mail Type G	+5.
China	—
Philippines	—

No.	Type	Denom.	Description	Unused	Used
291	A106	50c	**sage green**	700.	190.
			dark sage green	700.	190.
			Never hinged	1,600.	
			On cover		1,750.
			Block of 4	3,250.	1,250.
			Margin block of 4, arrow, R or L	3,400.	—
			P# pair, Impt., T VIII	1,950.	
			Never hinged	4,500.	
			P# strip of 3, Impt., T VIII	*2,800.*	
			Never hinged	*5,500.*	
			P# block of 4, Impt., T VIII	*14,000.*	
			Never hinged	*22,500.*	
			P# block of 6, Impt., T VIII	*26,000.*	

Earliest documented use: June 17, 1898 (FDC).

Cancellations

Cancellation	Value
Supp. Mail Type F or G	+25.
Cuba	—
Philippines	—

No.	Type	Denom.	Description	Unused	Used
292	A107	$1	**black**	1,250.	600.
			Never hinged	3,000.	
			No gum	650.	
			On cover		*4,000.*
			Block of 4	*5,750.*	*4,000.*
			Margin block of 4, arrow, R or L	*6,000.*	
			P# pair, Impt., T VIII	*3,000.*	
			Never hinged	*7,000.*	
			P# strip of 3, Impt., T VIII	*5,500.*	
			Never hinged	*10,500.*	
			P# block of 4, Impt., T VIII	*35,000.*	
			Never hinged	*50,000.*	
			P# block of 6, Impt., T VIII	*50,000.*	
			Never hinged	*67,500.*	

Earliest documented use: June 17, 1898 (FDC).

Cancellation

Cancellation	Value
Philippines	—

No.	Type	Denom.	Description	Unused	Used
293	A108	$2	**orange brown**	2,100.	1,000.
			dark orange brown	2,100.	1,000.
			Never hinged	5,000.	
			No gum	1,050.	
			On cover		*12,500.*
			Block of 4	*9,000.*	*6,000.*
			Margin block of 4, arrow, R or L	*9,500.*	
			P# pair, Impt., T VIII	*5,000.*	
			P# strip of 3, Impt., T VIII	*8,500.*	
			P# block of 4, Impt., T VIII	*80,000.*	
			Never hinged	—	
			P# block of 6, Impt., T VIII	*150,000.*	

Earliest documented use: June 24, 1898.

	Unused	Used
Nos. 285-293 (9)	4,747.	1,916.

Never-Hinged Stamps

See note before No. 205 regarding premiums for never-hinged stamps.

PAN-AMERICAN EXPOSITION ISSUE

Buffalo, N.Y., May 1 - Nov. 1, 1901.
On sale May 1-Oct. 31, 1901.

Fast Lake Navigation (Steamship "City of Alpena") — A109

Empire State Express — A110

Electric Automobile in Washington — A111

Bridge at Niagara Falls — A112

Canal Locks at Sault Ste. Marie — A113

Fast Ocean Navigation (Steamship "St. Paul") — A114

—PAN-AMERICAN STATION—
D

Exposition Station Machine Cancellation

Plates of 200 subjects in two panes of 100 each.

1901, May 1 Wmk. 191 ***Perf. 12***

No.	Description	Unused	Used
294 A109 1c	**green & black**	18.00	3.00
	dark blue green & black	18.00	3.00
	Never hinged	37.50	
	On cover		4.50
	On Expo. cover or card, Expo. station machine canc.		50.00
	On Expo. cover or card, Expo. station duplex handstamp canc.		150.00
	Block of 4	75.00	25.00
	Margin block of 4, top arrow & markers	72.50	
	Margin block of 4, bottom arrow & markers & black P#	80.00	
	P# strip of 3, Impt., T V	77.50	
	Never hinged	150.00	
	P# block of 6, Impt., T V	225.00	
	Never hinged	400.00	
	Margin strip of 5, bottom Impt. T V, two P#, arrow & markers	120.00	
	Never hinged	250.00	
	Margin block of 10, bottom Impt., T V, two P#, arrow & markers	475.00	
	Never hinged	800.00	
	Double transfer	25.00	5.25
a.	Center inverted	*9,500.*	*10,000.*
	Never hinged	*17,000.*	
	On cover		—
	Block of 4	*40,000.*	
	P# strip of 4, Impt.	*75,000.*	

Earliest documented uses: May 1, 1901 (No. 294 FDC); Aug. 2, 1901 (No. 294a). The No. 294a cover sold at auction in 1999 for $121,000. Two other uses on cover are recorded.

No.	Description	Unused	Used
295 A110 2c	**carmine & black**	17.50	1.00
	carmine & gray black	17.50	1.00
	dark carmine & black	17.50	1.00
	rose carmine & black	17.50	1.00
	scarlet & black	17.50	1.00
	Never hinged	35.00	
	On cover		1.50
	On Expo. cover or card, Expo. sta. machine cancel		60.00
	On Expo. cover or card, Expo. sta. duplex handstamp canc.		200.00
	Block of 4	72.50	8.00
	Margin block of 4, top arrow & markers	75.00	
	P# block of 4, bottom arrow & markers and black P#	77.50	
	P# strip of 3, Impt., T V	70.00	
	Never hinged	135.00	
	P# block of 6, Impt., T V	225.00	
	Never hinged	380.00	
	P# strip of 5, bottom Impt., T V, two P#, arrow & markers	130.00	
	Never hinged	240.00	
	P# block of 10, bottom Impt., T V, two P#, arrow & markers	450.00	
	Never hinged	825.00	
	Double transfer	25.00	2.25
a.	Center inverted	*42,500.*	*17,500.*
	Block of 4	*400,000.*	

Almost all unused copies of No. 295a have partial or disturbed gum. Values are for examples with full original gum that is slightly disturbed. Value for No. 295a used is for a well-centered example with faults, as there are no known fault-free examples.

Earliest documented use: May 1, 1901 (No. 295 FDC); Feb. 26, (1902?) (No. 295a, dated cancel on off-cover stamp). The dated No. 295a stamp is the only used example showing a date of any kind. Sold at auction in 2001 for $66,000.

No.	Description	Unused	Used
296 A111 4c	**deep red brown & black**	85.00	15.00
	chocolate & black	85.00	15.00
	Never hinged	170.00	
	On cover		37.50
	On cover, Expo. station machine cancel		350.00
	On cover, Expo. station duplex handstamp canc.		*750.00*
	Block of 4	340.00	125.00
	Margin block of 4, top arrow & markers	360.00	
	P# block of 4, bottom arrow & markers & black P#	375.00	
	P# strip of 3, Impt., T V	325.00	
	Never hinged	625.00	
	P# block of 6, Impt., T V	2,100.	
	Never hinged	*3,500.*	
	P# strip of 5, bottom Impt., T V, two P#, arrow & markers	600.00	
	Never hinged	1,150.	
	P# block of 10, bottom Impt., T V, two P#, arrow & markers	*4,250.*	
	Never hinged	*6,000.*	
a.	Center inverted	*35,000.*	—
	Block of 4	*150,000.*	
	P# strip of 4, Impt.	*175,000.*	

No. 296a was a Special Printing.

Almost all unused copies of No. 296a have partial or disturbed gum. Values are for examples with full orginal gum that is slightly disturbed.

See No. 296a-S, "Specimen" Stamps.

Earliest documented use: May 1, 1901 (FDC).

No.	Description	Unused	Used
297 A112 5c	**ultramarine & black**	95.00	14.00
	dark ultramarine & black	95.00	14.00
	Never hinged	190.00	
	On cover		40.00
	On cover, Expo. station machine cancel		350.00
	On cover, Expo. station duplex handstamp canc.		*750.00*
	Block of 4	400.00	110.00
	Margin block of 4, top arrow & markers	425.00	
	P# block of 4, bottom arrow & markers & black P#	450.00	
	P# strip of 3, Impt., T V	375.00	
	Never hinged	725.00	
	P# block of 6, Impt., T V	2,250.	
	Never hinged	*3,750.*	
	P# strip of 5, bottom Impt., T V, two P#, arrow & markers	700.00	
	Never hinged	1,350.	
	P# block of 10, bottom Impt., T V, two P#, arrow & markers	*4,250.*	
	Never hinged	*6,000.*	

Earliest documented use: May 1, 1901 (FDC).

No.	Description	Unused	Used
298 A113 8c	**brown violet & black**	120.00	50.00
	purplish brown & black	120.00	50.00
	Never hinged	240.00	
	On cover		110.00
	On cover, Expo. station machine cancel		*750.00*
	On cover, Expo. station duplex handstamp canc.		*1,250.*
	Block of 4	500.00	400.00
	Margin block of 4, top arrow & markers	525.00	
	P# block of 4, bottom arrow & markers & black P#	550.00	
	P# strip of 3, Impt., T V	475.00	
	Never hinged	900.00	
	P# block of 6, Impt., T V	*4,000.*	
	Never hinged	*5,500.*	
	P# strip of 5, bottom Impt., T V, two P#, arrow & markers	875.00	
	Never hinged	1,650.	
	P# block of 10, bottom Impt., T V, two P#, arrow & markers	*7,000.*	
	Never hinged	*9,500.*	

Earliest documented use: May 1, 1901 (FDC).

No.	Description	Unused	Used
299 A114 10c	**yellow brown & black**	160.00	25.00
	dark yellow brown & black	160.00	30.00
	Never hinged	325.00	
	On cover		125.00
	On cover, Expo. station machine cancel		*1,000.*
	On cover, Expo. station duplex handstamp canc.		*1,500.*
	Block of 4	675.00	250.00
	Margin block of 4, top arrow & markers	700.00	
	P# block of 4, bottom arrow & markers & black P#	750.00	
	P# strip of 3, Impt., T V	650.00	
	Never hinged	1,250.	
	P# block of 6, Impt., T V	6,750.	
	Never hinged	*9,000.*	
	P# strip of 5, bottom Impt., T V, two P#, arrow & markers	1,175.	
	Never hinged	2,250.	
	P# block of 10, bottom Impt., T V, two P#, arrow & markers	10,000.	
	Never hinged	*13,000.*	
	Nos. 294-299 (6)	495.50	108.00
	Nos. 294-299, never hinged	997.50	

Earliest documented use: May 1, 1901 (FDC).

VALUES FOR VERY FINE STAMPS
Please note: Stamps are valued in the grade of Very Fine unless otherwise indicated.

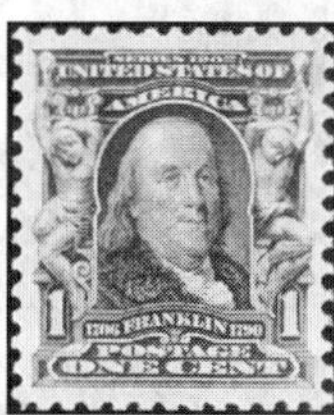

Franklin — A115

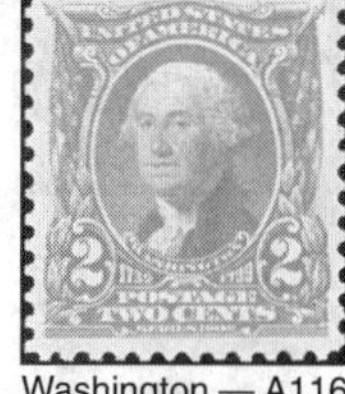

Washington — A116

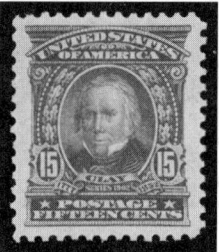

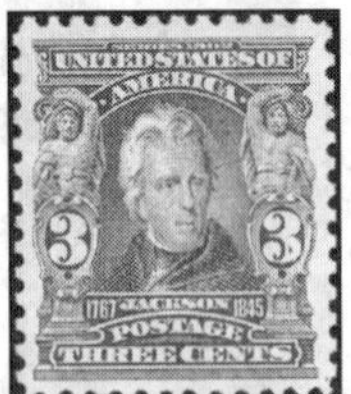

Jackson — A117

Grant — A118

Lincoln
A119

Garfield
A120

Martha
Washington — A121

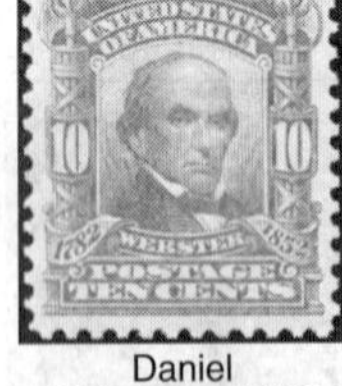

Daniel
Webster — A122

Benjamin
Harrison — A123

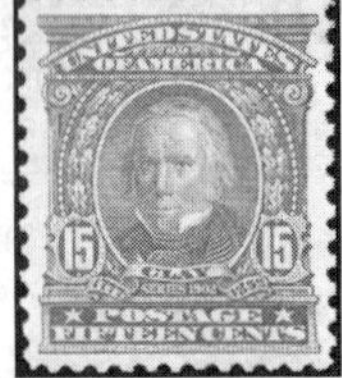

Henry Clay — A124

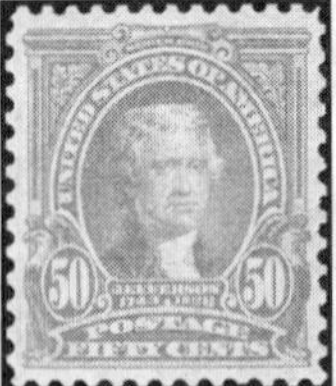

Jefferson — A125

David G.
Farragut — A126

Madison — A127

Marshall — A128

REGULAR ISSUE

Plates of 400 subjects in four panes of 100 each for all values from 1c to 15c inclusive. Certain plates of 1c, 2c type A129, 3c and 5c show a round marker in margin opposite the horizontal guide line at right or left.

Plates of 200 subjects in two panes of 100 each for 15c, 50c, $1, $2 and $5.

1902-03 Wmk. 191 *Perf. 12*

Many stamps of this issue are known with blurred printing due to having been printed on dry paper.

No.	Type	Denom.	Description	Unused	Used
300	A115	1c	**blue green,** *Feb. 1903*	12.00	.25
			green	12.00	.25
			deep green	12.00	.25
			gray green	12.00	.25
			yellow green	12.00	.25
			Never hinged	24.00	
			On cover		.30
			Block of 4	50.00	3.50
			P# strip of 3, Impt., T V	47.50	
			Never hinged	90.00	
			P# block of 6, Impt., T V	210.00	
			Never hinged	325.00	
			Double transfer	17.50	1.00
			Worn plate	13.00	.35
			Cracked plate	14.00	.30
b.			Booklet pane of 6, *Mar. 6, 1907*	600.00	*12,500.*
			Never hinged	1,100.	

Earliest documented uses: Feb. 3, 1903 (No. 300); Mar. 22, 1907 (No. 300b single).

No.	Type	Denom.	Description	Unused	Used
301	A116	2c	**carmine,** *Jan. 17, 1903*	16.00	.40
			bright carmine	16.00	.40
			deep carmine	16.00	.40
			carmine rose	16.00	.40
			Never hinged	32.50	
			On cover		.45
			Block of 4	67.50	5.00
			P# strip of 3, Impt., T V	65.00	
			Never hinged	120.00	
			P# block of 6, Impt., T V	250.00	
			Never hinged	400.00	
			Double transfer	27.50	1.25
			Cracked plate	—	1.25
c.			Booklet pane of 6, *Jan. 24, 1903*	500.00	*2,250.*
			Never hinged	900.00	

Earliest documented use: Mar. 28, 1903 (No. 301c single).

No.	Type	Denom.	Description	Unused	Used
302	A117	3c	**bright violet,** *Feb. 1903*	55.00	3.50
			violet	55.00	3.50
			deep violet	55.00	3.50
			Never hinged	110.00	
			On cover		11.00
			Block of 4	230.00	30.00
			P# strip of 3, Impt., T V	220.00	
			Never hinged	400.00	
			P# block of 6, Impt., T V	800.00	
			Never hinged	1,350.	
			Double transfer	77.50	4.75
			Cracked plate	—	—

Earliest documented use: Mar. 21, 1903.

No.	Type	Denom.	Description	Unused	Used
303	A118	4c	**brown,** *Feb. 1903*	60.00	2.30
			dark brown	60.00	2.30
			yellow brown	60.00	2.30
			orange brown	60.00	2.30
			red brown	60.00	2.30
			Never hinged	120.00	
			On cover		12.50
			Block of 4	250.00	25.00
			P# strip of 3, Impt., T V	240.00	
			Never hinged	450.00	
			P# block of 6, Impt., T V	825.00	
			Never hinged	1,375.	
			Double transfer	77.50	2.75

Earliest documented use: Mar. 13, 1903 (on cover front).

No.	Type	Denom.	Description	Unused	Used
304	A119	5c	**blue,** *Jan. 1903*	60.00	2.00
			pale blue	60.00	2.00
			bright blue	60.00	2.00
			dark blue	60.00	2.00
			Never hinged	120.00	
			On cover		7.50
			Block of 4	250.00	15.00
			P# strip of 3, Impt., T V	240.00	
			Never hinged	450.00	
			P# block of 6, Impt., T V	825.00	—
			Never hinged	1,375.	
			Double transfer	82.50	3.75
			Cracked plate	70.00	4.75

Earliest documented use: Feb. 9, 1903.

No.	Type	Denom.	Description	Unused	Used
305	A120	6c	**claret,** *Feb. 1903*	72.50	3.50
			deep claret	72.50	3.50
			brownish lake	72.50	3.50
			dull brownish lake	72.50	3.50
			Never hinged	150.00	
			On cover		12.50
			Block of 4	310.00	35.00
			P# strip of 3, Impt., T V	290.00	
			Never hinged	550.00	
			P# block of 6, Impt., T V	925.00	
			Never hinged	1,500.	
			Double transfer	77.50	4.50

Earliest documented use: May 8, 1903.

No.	Type	Denom.	Description	Unused	Used
306	A121	8c	**violet black,** *Dec. 1902*	45.00	3.00
			black	45.00	3.00
			slate black	45.00	3.00
			gray lilac	45.00	3.00
			Never hinged	90.00	
			lavender	55.00	3.75
			Never hinged	110.00	
			On cover		8.00
			Block of 4	190.00	27.50
			P# strip of 3, Impt., T V	180.00	
			Never hinged	335.00	
			P# block of 6, Impt., T V	750.00	
			Never hinged	1,250.	
			Double transfer	50.00	3.75

Earliest documented use: Dec. 27, 1902.

No.	Type	Denom.	Description	Unused	Used
307	A122	10c	**pale red brown,** *Feb. 1903*	70.00	2.80
			red brown	70.00	2.80
			dark red brown	70.00	2.80
			Never hinged	140.00	
			On cover		9.00
			Block of 4	280.00	17.50
			P# strip of 3, Impt., T V	275.00	
			Never hinged	525.00	
			P# block of 6, Impt., T V	1,100.	
			Never hinged	1,850.	
			Double transfer	80.00	10.00

Earliest documented use: Mar. 12, 1903.

No.	Type	Denom.	Description	Unused	Used
308	A123	13c	**purple black,** *Nov. 1902*	50.00	9.00
			brown violet	50.00	9.00
			Never hinged	100.00	
			On cover		37.50
			Block of 4	210.00	95.00
			P# strip of 3, Impt., T V	200.00	
			Never hinged	375.00	
			P# block of 6, Impt., T V	700.00	
			Never hinged	1,150.	

Earliest documented use: Nov. 18, 1902.

No.	Type	Denom.	Description	Unused	Used
309	A124	15c	**olive green,** *May 27, 1903*	170.00	7.50
			dark olive green	170.00	7.50
			Never hinged	375.00	
			On cover		75.00
			Block of 4	700.00	75.00
			Margin block of 4, arrow	725.00	
			P# strip of 3, Impt., T V	675.00	
			Never hinged	1,400.	
			P# block of 6, Impt., T V	3,250.	
			Never hinged	5,500.	
			Double transfer	210.00	9.00

Earliest documented use: July 1903 (on registry tag); Sept. 11, 1903 (on cover).

No.	Type	Denom.	Description	Unused	Used
310	A125	50c	**orange,** *Mar. 23, 1903*	475.	27.50
			deep orange	475.	27.50
			Never hinged	1,100.	
			On cover		700.00
			Block of 4	2,000.	225.00
			Margin block of 4, arrow	2,100.	
			P# strip of 3, Impt., T V	1,900.	
			Never hinged	4,000.	
			P# block of 6, Impt., T V	*7,500.*	

Earliest documented use: Oct. 6, 1903 (on cover front).

No.	Type	Denom.	Description	Unused	Used
311	A126	$1	**black,** *June 5, 1903*	750.00	75.00
			grayish black	750.00	75.00
			Never hinged	1,900.	
			No gum	180.00	
			On cover		1,500.
			Block of 4	3,150.	500.00
			Margin block of 4, arrow	3,300.	
			P# strip of 3, Impt., T V	3,000.	
			P# block of 6, Impt., T V	*18,000.*	

Earliest documented use: Sept. 30, 1903.

No.	Type	Denom.	Description	Unused	Used
312	A127	$2	**dark blue,** *June 5, 1903*	1,200.	200.00
			blue	1,200.	200.00
			Never hinged	2,900.	
			No gum	300.00	
			On cover		2,500.
			Block of 4	5,250.	1,750.
			Margin block of 4, arrow	5,500.	
			P# strip of 3, Impt., T V	5,000.	
			P# block of 6, Impt., T V	*32,500.*	

Earliest documented use: Feb. 17, 1904.

No.	Type	Denom.	Description	Unused	Used
313	A128	$5	**dark green,** *June 5, 1903*	2,900.	750.00
			Never hinged	*6,750.*	
			No gum	850.00	
			On cover		*5,000.*
			Block of 4	*13,500.*	*6,000.*
			Margin block of 4, arrow	*14,000.*	
			P# strip of 3, Impt., T V	*12,000.*	
			P# block of 6, Impt., T V	*110,000.*	

Earliest documented use: Feb. 17, 1904.

			Nos. 300-313 (14)	5,935.	1,086.

For listings of designs A127 and A128 with Perf. 10 see Nos. 479 and 480.

1906-08 *Imperf.*

No.	Type	Denom.	Description	Unused	Used
314	A115	1c	**blue green,** *Oct. 2, 1906*	18.00	15.00
			green	18.00	15.00
			deep green	18.00	15.00
			Never hinged	35.00	
			On cover		22.50
			Pair	37.50	31.00
			Never hinged	75.00	
			Block of 4	75.00	75.00
			Never hinged	150.00	
			Corner margin block of 4	77.50	72.50
			Margin block of 4, arrow	80.00	75.00
			Margin block of 4, arrow & round marker	150.00	125.00
			Center line block	135.00	100.00
			P# block of 6, Impt.	185.00	—
			Never hinged	275.00	
			Double transfer	32.50	17.50

Earliest documented use: Dec. 20, 1906.

No.	Type	Denom.	Description	Unused	Used
314A	A118	4c	**brown,** *Apr. 1908*	*70,000.*	*40,000.*
			Never hinged	*100,000.*	
			On cover		*130,000.*
			Pair	*150,000.*	
			Guide line pair	*240,000.*	

This stamp was issued imperforate but all copies were privately perforated with large oblong perforations at the sides (Schermack type III).

Beware of copies of No. 303 with trimmed perforations and fake private perfs. added.

Used and on-cover values are for contemporaneous usage.

Earliest documented use: May 27, 1908.

No.	Type	Denom.	Description	Unused	Used
315	A119	5c	**blue,** *May 12, 1908*	240.	*850.*
			Never hinged	425.	
			On cover, pair		*40,000.*
			Pair	500.	*2,750.*
			Never hinged	875.	
			Block of 4	1,000.	*6,500.*
			Never hinged	1,750.	
			Corner margin block of 4	1,100.	
			Margin block of 4, arrow	1,600.	
			Margin block of 4, arrow & round marker	2,150.	

Center line block 4,500.
P# block of 6, Impt. 2,600. —
Never hinged 3,750.

Earliest documented use: Sept. 15, 1908.

Beware of copies of No. 304 with perforations removed.
Used copies of No. 315 must have contemporaneous cancels. Single copies of No. 315 on cover are not known to exist.

COIL STAMPS

Warning! Imperforate stamps are known fraudulently perforated to resemble coil stamps and part-perforate varieties.

1908 ***Perf. 12 Horizontally***

316 A115 1c **blue green,** *Feb. 18* *50,000.*
Pair *120,000.*
Guide line pair *200,000.*
317 A119 5c **blue,** *Feb. 24* *6,000.* —
Never hinged *12,500.*
Pair *15,000.*
Never hinged *30,000.*
Guide line pair *35,000.*

Earliest documented use: Sept. 18, 1908.

Perf. 12 Vertically

318 A115 1c **blue green,** *July 31* *5,750.*
Never hinged *9,500.*
Pair *14,000.*
Guide line pair *22,500.*
Double transfer —

The No. 318 mint never hinged single is valued in the grade of fine.
Coil stamps for use in vending and affixing machines are perforated on two sides only, either horizontally or vertically. They were first issued in 1908, using perf. 12. This was changed to 8½ in 1910, and to 10 in 1914.
Imperforate sheets of certain denominations were sold to the vending machine companies which applied a variety of private perforations and separations (see Vending and Affixing Machine Perforations section of this catalogue).
Several values of the 1902 and later issues are found on an apparently coarse-ribbed paper. This is caused by worn blankets on the printing presses and is not a true paper variety.
All examples of Nos. 316-318 must be accompanied by certificates of authenticity issued by recognized expertizing committees.

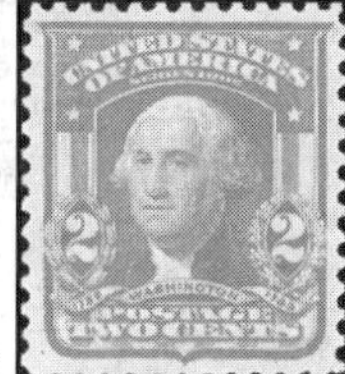

Washington — A129

Plate of 400 subjects in four panes of 100 each.

Type I

Type II

1903 **Wmk. 191** ***Perf. 12***

319 A129 2c **carmine,** type I, *Nov. 12, 1903* 6.00 .25
bright carmine 6.00 .25
red 6.00 .25
Never hinged 12.00
On cover .30
Block of 4 25.00 2.50
P# strip of 3, Impt., T V 24.00
Never hinged 45.00
P# block of 6, Impt., T V 110.00
Never hinged 175.00
Double transfer 12.50 2.00
a. 2c **lake,** type I — —
carmine lake —
b. 2c **carmine rose,** type I 7.50 .40
Never hinged 15.00
On cover .60
Block of 4 32.50 7.50
P# strip of 3, Impt., T V 32.50
Never hinged 60.00
P# block of 6, Impt., T V 150.00
Never hinged 240.00
c. 2c **scarlet,** type I 7.00 .30
Never hinged 14.00
On cover .35
Block of 4 30.00 4.50
P# strip of 3, Impt., T V 27.50
Never hinged 55.00
P# block of 6, Impt., T V 125.00
Never hinged 200.00
d. Vert. pair, imperf. horiz., No. 319 *7,500.*
Never hinged *15,000.*
e. Vertical pair, imperf. between, No. 319 1,750.
As "e," rouletted between *3,000.*

"Gash on Face" Variety

The gash may appear as double lines due to different plate wiping techniques.

f. 2c **lake,** type II 10.00 .30
carmine lake 10.00 .30
Never hinged 20.00
On cover .35
Block of 4 42.50 5.50
P# strip of 3, Impt., T V 45.00
Never hinged 85.00
P# block of 6, Impt., T V 300.00
Never hinged 450.00
"Gash on face" plate flaw (carmine lake, 4671 LL 16) —
g. Booklet pane of 6, **car.,** type I 125.00 *550.00*
Never hinged 240.00
h. Booklet pane of 6, **car.,** type II 500.00
Never hinged 800.00
i. 2c **carmine,** type II 75.00 *50.00*
red 75.00 *50.00*
Never hinged 150.00
On cover *150.00*
j. 2c **carmine rose,** type II 50.00 1.75
Never hinged 100.00
Block of 4 225.00 20.00
P# block of 6, Impt., T V *1,000.*
k. 2c **scarlet,** type II 50.00 .65
Never hinged 100.00
Block of 4 225.00 5.00
P# block of 6, Impt., T V *1,000.*
n. Booklet pane of 6, **car. rose** (I) 225.00 *650.00*
Never hinged 400.00
p. Booklet pane of 6, **scarlet** (I) 185.00 *575.00*
Never hinged 350.00
q. Booklet pane of 6, **lake** (II) 300.00 *750.00*
Never hinged 550.00

During the use of this stamp, the Postmaster at San Francisco discovered in his stock sheets of No. 319, each of which had the horizontal perforations missing between the two top rows of stamps. To facilitate their separation, the imperf. rows were rouletted, and the stamps sold over the counter. So vertical pairs are found with regular perforations all around and rouletted between.
Specialists have questioned the existence of No. 319m. The editors would like to receive authenticated evidence of its existence and would like to examine such a pane.
Earliest documented uses:
No. 319, Nov. 19, 1903;
No. 319a, Sept. 23, 1904;
No. 319b. Nov. 3, 1903;
No. 319c, Dec. 16, 1903;
No. 319f, Sept. 25, 1908;
No. 319g single, Jan. 22, 1904;
No. 319h single, Nov. 12, 1908;
No. 319i, June 5, 1908;
No. 319j, June 30, 1908;
No. 319k, June 11, 1908
No. 319p single, Apr. 12, 1904.

1906 ***Imperf.***

320 A129 2c **carmine,** type I *Oct. 2* 17.50 17.50
Never hinged 35.00
On cover 22.50
Pair 37.50 *37.50*
Never hinged 72.50
Block of 4 75.00 75.00
Corner margin block of 4 77.50 100.00
Margin block of 4, arrow 80.00 110.00
Margin block of 4, arrow & round marker —
Center line block 150.00 200.00
P# block of 6, Impt., T V, carmine 200.00 —
Never hinged 325.00
Double transfer 25.00 21.50

Earliest documented use: Oct. 26, 1906.

a. 2c **lake,** type II 45.00 40.00
carmine lake 45.00 40.00
Never hinged 95.00
On cover —
Pair 100.00 *95.00*
Never hinged 210.00
Block of 4 200.00 225.00
Corner margin block of 4 205.00
Margin block of 4, arrow 210.00
Center line block 425.00 —
P# block of 6, Impt., T V 725.00 —
Never hinged 1,100.
"Gash on face" plate flaw (see No. 319f) —
b. 2c **scarlet,** type I 18.50 12.50
Never hinged 40.00
On cover 20.00
Pair 39.00
Never hinged 85.00
Block of 4 77.50
Corner margin block of 4 80.00
Margin block of 4, arrow 82.50 —
Center line block 205.00 —
P# block of 6, Impt., T V 225.00
Never hinged 350.00
c. 2c **carmine rose,** type I 50.00 40.00
Never hinged 100.00
d. 2c **carmine,** type II *125.00* *275.00*
Never hinged 200.00
On cover *600.00*
Pair *260.00*
Never hinged 550.00
Guide line pair —

No. 320d was issued imperforate, but all copies were privately perforated with large oblong perforations at the sides (Schermack type III).

COIL STAMPS

1908 ***Perf. 12 Horizontally***

321 A129 2c **carmine,** type I, pair, *Feb. 18* *360,000.*
On cover, single *200,000.*
Guide line pair —

Four authenticated unused pairs of No. 321 are known. The value for an unused pair is for a fine-very fine example. Two fine pairs are recorded and one very fine pair. There are no authenticated unused single stamps recorded. There are 2 authenticated examples of the single used on cover, both used from Indianapolis in 1908. Numerous counterfeits exist.

Earliest documented use: Oct. 2, 1908.

Perf. 12 Vertically

322 A129 2c **carmine,** type II, *July 31* *5,500.* —
Never hinged *9,500.*
Pair *12,000.*
Guide line pair *15,500.*
Double transfer —

This Government Coil Stamp should not be confused with those of the International Vending Machine Co., which are perforated 12½.
All examples of Nos. 321-322 must be accompanied by certificates of authenticity issued by recognized expertizing committees.

VALUES FOR VERY FINE STAMPS
Please note: Stamps are valued in the grade of Very Fine unless otherwise indicated.

LOUISIANA PURCHASE EXPOSITION ISSUE

St. Louis, Mo., Apr. 30 - Dec. 1, 1904

Robert R. Livingston — A130

Thomas Jefferson — A131

James Monroe — A132

William McKinley — A133

Map of Louisiana Purchase — A134

Plates of 100 (10x10) subjects, divided vertically into 2 panes of 50.

—EXPOSITION STA.—
D

Exposition Station Machine Cancellation

1904, Apr. 30 **Wmk. 191** ***Perf. 12***

323 A130 1c **green**	30.00	5.00
dark green	30.00	5.00
Never hinged	60.00	
On cover		7.00
On Expo. card, Expo. station machine canc.		40.00
On Expo. card, Expo. station duplex handstamp canc.		100.00
Block of 4	125.00	35.00
Margin block of 4, arrow, R or L	130.00	—
P# pair, Impt., T V	82.50	
Never hinged	165.00	
P# strip of 3, Impt., T V	120.00	
Never hinged	225.00	
P# block of 4, Impt., T V	175.00	
Never hinged	280.00	
P# block of 6, Impt., T V	275.00	
Never hinged	440.00	
Diagonal line through left "1" (2138 L 2)	50.00	12.50
Double transfer		—

Earliest documented use: Apr. 30, 1904 (FDC).

324 A131 2c **carmine**	27.50	2.00
bright carmine	27.50	2.00
Never hinged	55.00	
On cover		3.00
On Expo. cover, Expo. station machine canc.		60.00
On Expo. cover, Expo. station duplex handstamp canc.		150.00
Block of 4	120.00	17.50
Margin block of 4, arrow, R or L	130.00	—
P# pair, Impt., T V	75.00	
Never hinged	150.00	
P# strip of 3, Impt., T V	110.00	
Never hinged	200.00	
P# block of 4, Impt., T V	175.00	
Never hinged	280.00	
P# block of 6, Impt., T V	275.00	
Never hinged	450.00	
a. Vertical pair, imperf. horiz.	*17,500.*	
Block of 4	*40,000.*	
P# block of 4, Impt., T V	*55,000.*	

Earliest documented use: Apr. 30, 1904 (FDC).

325 A132 3c **violet**	90.00	30.00
Never hinged	180.00	
On cover		65.00
On cover, Expo. station machine canc.		200.00
On cover, Expo. station duplex handstamp canc.		*400.00*
Block of 4	375.00	225.00
Margin block of 4, arrow, R or L	390.00	—
P# pair, Impt., T V	225.00	
Never hinged	450.00	
P# strip of 3, Impt., T V	350.00	
Never hinged	675.00	
P# block of 4, Impt., T V	625.00	
Never hinged	1,000.	
P# block of 6, Impt., T V	950.00	
Never hinged	1,650.	
Double transfer		—

Earliest documented use: Apr. 30, 1904 (FDC).

326 A133 5c **dark blue**	95.00	25.00
Never hinged	190.00	
On cover		50.00
On cover, Expo. station machine canc.		400.00
On cover, Expo. station duplex handstamp canc.		*500.00*
Block of 4	400.00	200.00
Margin block of 4, arrow, R or L	425.00	—
P# pair, Impt., T V	230.00	
Never hinged	475.00	
P# strip of 3, Impt., T V	375.00	
Never hinged	700.00	
P# block of 4, Impt., T V	675.00	
Never hinged	1,075.	
P# block of 6, Impt., T V	1,000.	
Never hinged	1,750.	

Earliest documented use: Apr. 30, 1904 (FDC).

327 A134 10c **red brown**	175.00	30.00
dark red brown	175.00	27.50
Never hinged	350.00	
On cover		125.00
On cover, Expo. station machine canc.		450.00
On cover, Expo. station duplex handstamp canc.		*750.00*
Block of 4	725.00	225.00
Margin block of 4, arrow, R or L	775.00	—
P# pair, Impt., T V	425.00	
Never hinged	800.00	
P# strip of 3, Impt., T V	725.00	
Never hinged	1,250.	
P# block of 4, Impt., T V	1,325.	
Never hinged	2,100.	
P# block of 6, Impt., T V	2,250.	
Never hinged	3,750.	

Earliest documented use: Apr. 30, 1904 (FDC).

Nos. 323-327 (5)	417.50	92.00
Nos. 323-327, never hinged	835.00	

JAMESTOWN EXPOSITION ISSUE

Hampton Roads, Va., Apr. 26 - Dec. 1, 1907

Captain John Smith — A135

Founding of Jamestown — A136

Pocahontas — A137

Plates of 200 subjects in two panes of 100 each.

—EXPOSITION STATION—
C

Exposition Station Machine Cancellation

1907 **Wmk. 191** ***Perf. 12***

328 A135 1c **green,** *Apr. 26*	30.00	5.00
dark green	30.00	5.00
Never hinged	60.00	
On cover		8.00
On Expo. card, Expo. station machine canc.		25.00
On Expo. card, Expo. station duplex handstamp canc.		125.00
Block of 4	125.00	50.00
Margin block of 4, arrow	130.00	—
P# strip of 3, Impt., T V	110.00	
Never hinged	210.00	
P# block of 6, Impt., T V	275.00	
Never hinged	450.00	
Double transfer	35.00	6.00

Earliest documented use: Apr. 26, 1907 (FDC).

329 A136 2c **carmine,** *Apr. 26*	35.00	4.50
bright carmine	35.00	4.50
Never hinged	70.00	
On cover		6.00
On Expo. cover, Expo. station machine canc.		100.00
On Expo. cover, Expo. station duplex handstamp canc.		150.00
Block of 4	150.00	35.00
Margin block of 4, arrow	160.00	—
P# strip of 3, Impt., T V	125.00	
Never hinged	250.00	
P# block of 6, Impt., T V	375.00	
Never hinged	575.00	
Double transfer	42.50	6.00

Earliest documented use: Apr. 26, 1907 (FDC).

330 A137 5c **blue**	150.00	30.00
deep blue	150.00	30.00
Never hinged	300.00	
On cover		82.50
On cover, Expo. station machine canc.		350.00
On cover, Expo. station duplex handstamp canc.		*500.00*
Block of 4	650.00	210.00
Margin block of 4, arrow	675.00	—
P# strip of 3, Impt., T V	525.00	
Never hinged	1,000.	
P# block of 6, Impt., T V	2,750.	
Never hinged	5,250.	
Double transfer	150.00	35.00

Earliest documented use: Apr. 26, 1907 (FDC).

Nos. 328-330 (3)	215.00	39.50
Nos. 328-330, never hinged	430.00	

Earliest documented use: May 8, 1907.

REGULAR ISSUE

Plates of 400 subjects in four panes of 100 each for all values 1c to 15c inclusive.

Plates of 200 subjects in two panes of 100 each for 50c and $1 denominations.

In 1909 the Bureau prepared certain plates with horizontal spacings of 3mm between the outer seven vertical stamp rows and 2mm between the others. This was done to try to counteract the effect of unequal shrinkage of the paper. *However, some unequal shrinkage still did occur and intermediate spacings are frequently found.* The listings of 2mm and 3mm spacings are for exact measurements. Intermediate spacings sell for approximately the same as the cheaper of the two listed spacings.

All such plates were marked with an open star added to the imprint and exist on the 1c, 2c, 3c, 4c, and 5c denominations only. A small solid star was added to the imprint and plate number for 1c plate No. 4980, 2c plate No. 4988 and for the 2c Lincoln. All other plates for this issue are spaced 2mm throughout.

There are several types of some of the 2c and 3c stamps of this and succeeding issues. These types are described under the dates at which they first appeared. Illustrations of Types I-VII of the 2c (A140) and Types I-IV of the 3c (A140) are reproduced by permission of H. L. Lindquist.

Bureau, Engraving & Printing ☆ 4968

Imprint, plate number and open star

Bureau, Engraving & Printing ★ 4976

Imprint, plate number and small solid star

Bureau, Engraving & Printing A 5557

Imprint, plate number and "A"

(Illustrations reduced in size)

"A" and number only **A 5805**

Number only **988**

The above illustrations are several of the styles used on plates of issues from 1908 to date.

China Clay Paper.

A small quantity of Nos. 331-340 was printed on paper containing a high mineral content (5-20%), instead of the specified 2%. The minerals, principally aluminum silicate, produced China clay paper. It is thick, hard and grayish, often darker than "bluish" paper.

Franklin — A138

Washington — A139

1908-09 **Wmk. 191** ***Perf. 12***

No.	Design	Description	Unused	Used
331	A138	1c **green,** *Dec. 1908*	7.25	.40
		bright green	7.25	.40
		dark green	7.25	.40
		yellow green	7.25	.40
		Never hinged	14.50	
		On cover		.55
		Block of 4 (2mm spacing)	32.50	2.50
		Block of 4 (3mm spacing)	35.00	3.00
		P# block of 6, Impt., T V	77.50	
		Never hinged	125.00	
		P# block of 6, Impt. & star	70.00	
		Never hinged	115.00	
		P# block of 6, Impt. & small solid star (plate 4980)	*1,500.*	
		Never hinged	*2,250.*	
		Double transfer	9.50	.75
		Cracked plate	—	—
a.		Booklet pane of 6, *Dec. 1908*	160.00	*450.00*
		Never hinged	250.00	
b.		"China Clay" paper	*1,000.*	

No. 331 exists in horizontal pair, imperforate between, a variety resulting from booklet experiments. Not regularly issued. Value, $2,500.

No. 331a used is valued with a contemporaneous cancel. A certificate of authenticity is advised.

Earliest documented uses: Dec. 1, 1908 (No. 331); Dec. 2, 1908 (No. 331a single).

No.	Design	Description	Unused	Used
332	A139	2c **carmine,** *Nov. 1908*	6.75	.35
		light carmine	6.75	.35
		dark carmine	6.75	.35
		Never hinged	13.50	
		On cover		.40
		Block of 4 (2mm spacing)	30.00	2.00
		Block of 4 (3mm spacing)	32.50	2.50
		P# block of 6, Impt., T V	70.00	
		Never hinged	110.00	
		P# block of 6, Impt. & star	67.50	
		Never hinged	105.00	
		P# block of 6, Impt. & small solid star (plate 4988)	*1,500.*	
		Never hinged	*2,500.*	
		Double transfer	12.50	—
		Foreign entry, design of 1c (plate 5299)	*1,750.*	*2,750.*
		On cover		—
		Rosette crack	—	
		Cracked plate	—	—
a.		Booklet pane of 6	135.00	*400.00*
		Never hinged	220.00	
b.		"China Clay" paper	*1,300.*	

No. 332a used is valued with a contemporaneous cancel. A certificate of authenticity is advised.

Earliest documented uses: Dec. 3, 1908 (No. 332), Nov. 16, 1908 (No. 332a single).

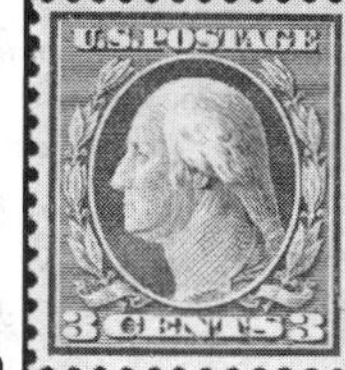

Washington — A140

TYPE I

THREE CENTS.

Type I. The top line of the toga rope is weak and the rope shading lines are thin. The 5th line from the left is missing. The line between the lips is thin. (For descriptions of 3c types II, III and IV, see notes and illustrations preceding Nos. 484, 529-530.)

Used on both flat plate and rotary press printings.

No.	Design	Description	Unused	Used
333	A140	3c **deep violet,** type I, *Dec. 1908*	35.00	3.00
		violet	35.00	3.00
		light violet	35.00	3.00
		Never hinged	70.00	
		On cover		8.50
		Block of 4 (2mm spacing)	145.00	26.50
		Block of 4 (3mm spacing)	150.00	29.00
		P# block of 6, Impt., T V	350.00	
		Never hinged	550.00	
		P# block of 6, Impt. & star	375.00	
		Never hinged	600.00	
		Double transfer	37.50	5.75
a.		"China Clay" paper	*1,000.*	
		P# block of 6, Impt., T V	*7,500.*	

Earliest documented use: Jan. 12, 1909.

No.	Design	Description	Unused	Used
334	A140	4c **orange brown,** *Dec. 1908*	42.50	1.50
		brown	42.50	1.50
		light brown	42.50	1.50
		dark brown	42.50	1.50
		Never hinged	85.00	
		On cover		7.00
		Block of 4 (2mm spacing)	180.00	12.50
		Block of 4 (3mm spacing)	190.00	14.00
		P# block of 6, Impt., T V	425.00	
		Never hinged	675.00	
		P# block of 6, Impt. & star	425.00	
		Never hinged	675.00	
		Double transfer	55.00	—
a.		"China Clay" paper	*1,300.*	

Earliest documented use: Jan. 12, 1909.

No.	Design	Description	Unused	Used
335	A140	5c **blue,** *Dec. 1908*	55.00	2.50
		bright blue	55.00	2.50
		dark blue	55.00	2.50
		Never hinged	110.00	
		On cover		8.50
		Block of 4 (2mm spacing)	230.00	20.00
		Block of 4 (3mm spacing)	240.00	17.50
		P# block of 6, Impt., T V	525.00	
		Never hinged	1,000.	
		P# block of 6, Impt. & star	550.00	
		Never hinged	1,050.	
		Double transfer	60.00	—
a.		"China Clay" paper	*1,000.*	

Earliest documented use: Jan. 12, 1909.

336 A140 6c **red orange,** *Jan. 1909* 65.00 6.50
pale red orange 65.00 6.50
orange 65.00 6.50
Never hinged 130.00
On cover 22.50
Block of 4 275.00 50.00
P# block of 6, Impt., T V 750.00
Never hinged 1,250.
a. "China Clay" paper *750.00*
Never hinged —

Earliest documented use: Jan. 6, 1909.

337 A140 8c **olive green,** *Dec. 1908* 50.00 3.00
deep olive green 50.00 3.00
Never hinged 100.00
On cover 18.00
Block of 4 210.00 25.00
P# block of 6, Impt., T V 525.00
Never hinged 850.00
Double transfer 57.50 —
a. "China Clay" paper *1,000.*

Earliest documented use: Jan. 8, 1909.

338 A140 10c **yellow,** *Jan. 1909* 70.00 2.00
Never hinged 140.00
On cover 10.00
Block of 4 300.00 15.00
P# block of 6, Impt., T V 800.00
Never hinged 1,350.
Double transfer — —
Very thin paper —
a. "China Clay" paper *1,000.*

Earliest documented use: Jan. 18, 1909.

339 A140 13c **blue green,** *Jan. 1909* 42.50 19.00
deep blue green 42.50 19.00
Never hinged 85.00
On cover 110.00
Block of 4 190.00 175.00
P# block of 6, Impt., T V 500.00
Never hinged 825.00
Line through "TAG" of "POSTAGE" (4948 LR 96) 70.00 —
a. "China Clay" paper *1,000.*
Never hinged —
P# block of 6, Impt., T V *7,500.*

Earliest documented use: Mar. 5, 1909.

340 A140 15c **pale ultramarine,** *Jan. 1909* 70.00 6.50
ultramarine 70.00 6.50
Never hinged 140.00
On cover 125.00
Block of 4 290.00 65.00
P# block of 6, Impt., T V 650.00
Never hinged 1,100.
a. "China Clay" paper *1,000.*
P# block of 6, Impt., T V *9,000.*

Earliest documented use: Mar. 12, 1909.

341 A140 50c **violet,** *Jan. 13, 1909* 350.00 20.00
dull violet 350.00 20.00
Never hinged 725.00
On cover *5,000.*
Block of 4 1,500. 150.00
Margin block of 4, arrow, right or left 1,550.
P# block of 6, Impt., T V *7,000.* —
Never hinged *11,000.*

Earliest documented use: Oct. 23, 1909 (on registry tag); June 2, 1916 (on cover).

342 A140 $1 **violet brown,** *Jan. 29, 1909* 525.00 100.00
light violet brown 525.00 100.00
Never hinged 1,100.
On cover *6,000.*
Block of 4 2,250. 700.00
Margin block of 4, arrow, right or left 2,350. 725.00
P# block of 6, Impt., T V *16,000.*
Double transfer — —

Earliest documented use: July 26, 1909.

Nos. 331-342 (12) 1,319. 164.75

For listings of other perforated sheet stamps of A138, A139 and A140 see:
Nos. 357-366 Bluish paper
Nos. 374-382, 405-407 Single line wmk. Perf. 12
Nos. 423A-423C Single line wmk. Perf 12x10
Nos. 423D-423E Single line wmk. Perf 10x12
Nos. 424-430 Single line wmk. Perf. 10
Nos. 461 Single line wmk. Perf. 11
Nos. 462-469 unwmk. Perf. 10
Nos. 498-507 unwmk. Perf. 11
Nos. 519 Double line wmk. Perf. 11
Nos. 525-530 and 536 Offset printing
Nos. 538-546 Rotary press printing

Plate Blocks

Scott values for plate blocks printed from flat plates are for very fine side and bottom positions. Top position plate blocks with full wide selvage sell for more.

Imperf

343 A138 1c **green,** *Dec. 1908* 5.00 4.50
dark green 5.00 4.50
yellowish green 5.00 4.50
Never hinged 9.50
On cover 10.00
Pair 10.50 10.00
Never hinged 19.00
Block of 4 (2mm or 3mm spacing) 21.50 20.00
Corner margin block of 4, 2mm or 3mm 22.50 21.00
Margin block of 4, arrow, 2mm or 3mm 23.50 21.00
Center line block 30.00 30.00
P# block of 6, Impt., T V 47.50 —
Never hinged 75.00
P# block of 6, Impt. & star 57.50 —
Never hinged 90.00
P# block of 6, Impt. & small solid star (plate 4980) *675.00*
Never hinged *1,050.*
Double transfer 11.00 7.00

Earliest documented use: Jan. 4, 1909.

344 A139 2c **carmine,** *Dec. 1908* 6.00 3.00
light carmine 6.00 3.00
dark carmine 6.00 3.00
Never hinged 11.50
On cover 7.50
Pair 12.50 7.50
Never hinged 22.50
Block of 4 (2mm or 3mm spacing) 27.50 15.00
Corner margin block of 4, 2mm or 3mm 30.00 21.00
Margin block of 4, arrow, 2mm or 3mm 32.50 21.00
Center line block 37.50 37.50
P# block of 6, Impt., T V 77.50 —
Never hinged 120.00
P# block of 6, Impt. & star 70.00 —
Never hinged 110.00
Double transfer 12.50 4.00
Foreign entry, design of 1c (plate 5299) *1,250.* —

Earliest documented use: Dec. 7, 1908.

The existence of the foreign entry on the imperforate sheet stamp No. 344 has been questioned by specialists. The editors would like to see evidence of the existence of the item, either unused or used.

345 A140 3c **deep violet,** type I, *1909* 11.50 *20.00*
violet 11.50 *20.00*
Never hinged 22.00
On cover 60.00
Pair 24.00 *50.00*
Never hinged 44.00
Block of 4 50.00 *100.00*
Corner margin block of 4 52.50 *105.00*
Margin block of 4, arrow 57.50 *105.00*
Center line block 75.00 *125.00*
P# block of 6, Impt., T V 155.00 —
Never hinged 240.00
Double transfer 22.50 —

Earliest documented use: Feb. 13, 1909.

346 A140 4c **orange brown,** *Feb. 25, 1909* 19.00 *22.50*
brown 19.00 *22.50*
Never hinged 37.50
On cover 90.00
Pair 40.00 *57.50*
Never hinged 72.50
Block of 4 (2 or 3mm spacing) 82.50 *115.00*
Corner margin block of 4 (2 or 3mm spacing) 87.50 *120.00*
Margin block of 4, arrow, (2 or 3mm spacing) 92.50 *120.00*
Center line block 120.00 *200.00*
P# block of 6, Impt., T V 175.00 —
Never hinged 275.00
P# block of 6, Impt. & star 210.00 —
Never hinged 325.00
Double transfer 37.50 —

Earliest documented use: Mar. 13, 1909.

347 A140 5c **blue,** *Feb. 25, 1909* 36.00 35.00
dark blue 36.00 35.00
Never hinged 70.00
On cover 125.00
Pair 75.00 *100.00*
Never hinged 145.00
Block of 4 160.00 *200.00*
Corner margin block of 4 170.00 *225.00*
Margin block of 4, arrow 180.00 *235.00*
Center line block 220.00 *300.00*
P# block of 6, Impt., T V 275.00 —
Never hinged 500.00
Cracked plate —

Earliest documented use: Mar. 4, 1909.

Nos. 343-347 (5) 77.50 85.00
Nos. 343-347, never hinged 150.50

For listings of other imperforate stamps of designs A138, A139 and A140 see Nos. 383, 384, 408, 409 and 459 Single line wmk.
Nos. 481-485 unwmk.
Nos. 531-535 Offset printing

COIL STAMPS

1908-10 ***Perf. 12 Horizontally***

348 A138 1c **green,** *Dec. 29, 1908* 37.50 25.00
dark green 37.50 25.00
Never hinged 75.00
On cover 50.00
Pair 100.00 *105.00*
Never hinged 200.00
Guide line pair 290.00 *550.00*
Never hinged 575.00

Earliest documented use: Jan. 25, 1909.

349 A139 2c **carmine,** *Jan. 1909* 80.00 17.50
dark carmine 80.00 17.50
Never hinged 160.00
On cover 37.50
Pair 200.00 75.00
Never hinged 400.00
Guide line pair 550.00 400.00
Never hinged 1,150.
Foreign entry, design of 1c (plate 5299) — *1,750.*

Earliest documented use: May 14, 1909.

350 A140 4c **orange brown,** *Aug. 15, 1910* 160.00 140.00
Never hinged 325.00
On cover 250.00
Pair 370.00 *500.00*
Never hinged 750.00
Guide line pair 1,250. *2,000.*
Never hinged 2,600.

Earliest documented use: Aug. 21, 1912.

351 A140 5c **blue,** *Jan. 1909* 175.00 175.00
dark blue 175.00 175.00
Never hinged 350.00
On cover 625.00
Pair 475.00 *600.00*
Never hinged 950.00
Guide line pair 1,250. *2,500.*
Never hinged 2,600.

Earliest documented use: Sept. 21, 1909.

1909 ***Perf. 12 Vertically***

352 A138 1c **green,** *Jan. 1909* 95.00 55.00
dark green 95.00 55.00
Never hinged 190.00
On cover 85.00
Pair (2mm spacing) 250.00 200.00
Never hinged 500.00
Pair (3mm spacing) 235.00 185.00
Never hinged 475.00
Guide line pair 750.00 *625.00*
Never hinged 1,500.
Double transfer — —

353 A139 2c **carmine,** *Jan. 12, 1909* 95.00 15.00
dark carmine 95.00 15.00
Never hinged 190.00
On cover 30.00
Pair (2mm spacing) 250.00 60.00
Never hinged 500.00
Pair (3mm spacing) 235.00 55.00
Never hinged 475.00
Guide line pair 750.00 *325.00*
Never hinged 1,500.

Earliest documented use: June 14, 1909.

354 A140 4c **orange brown,** *Feb. 23, 1909* 220.00 120.00
Never hinged 450.00
On cover 160.00
Pair (2mm spacing) 525.00 450.00
Never hinged 1,100.
Pair (3mm spacing) 500.00 450.00
Never hinged 1,050.
Guide line pair 1,500. *1,100.*
Never hinged 3,100.

Earliest documented use: June 9, 1909.

355 A140 5c **blue,** *Feb. 23, 1909* 230.00 130.00
Never hinged 475.00
On cover 260.00
Pair 575.00 *550.00*
Never hinged 1,200.
Guide line pair 1,500. *1,300.*
Never hinged 3,100.

Earliest documented use: Oct. 25, 1909.

These Government Coil Stamps, Nos. 352-355, should not be confused with those of the International Vending Machine Co., which are perf. 12½-13.

356 A140 10c **yellow,** *Jan. 7, 1909* 2,750. *2,750.*

Never hinged	6,000.	
On cover		*10,000.*
Pair	*6,750.*	*7,500.*
Never hinged	*12,500.*	
Guide line pair	*13,000.*	*29,000.*
Never hinged	*22,000.*	

Earliest documented use: Mar. 9, 1909.

The used guide line pair of No. 356 is unique. Value reflects price realized at auction in 2002.

For listings of other coil stamps of designs A138 A139 and A140 see:
Nos. 385-396, 410-413, 441-459, single line watermark.
Nos. 486-496, unwatermarked.

Beware of stamps offered as No. 356 which may be examples of No. 338 with perfs. trimmed at top and/or bottom. Beware also of plentiful fakes in the marketplace of Nos. 348-355. Authentication of all these coils is advised.

BLUISH PAPER

This was made with 35 per cent rag stock instead of all wood pulp. The "bluish" color (actually grayish blue) goes through the paper showing clearly on the back as well as on the face.

1909 ***Perf. 12***

357 A138 1c **green,** *Feb. 16, 1909*	90.00	*100.00*
Never hinged	180.00	
On postcard		120.00
On cover		220.00
Block of 4 (2mm spacing)	380.00	*600.00*
Block of 4 (3mm spacing)	*775.00*	
P# block of 6, Impt., T V	1,000.	
Never hinged	1,650.	
P# block of 6, Impt. & star	*3,000.*	
Never hinged	*4,750.*	

Earliest documented use: Feb. 22, 1909.

358 A139 2c **carmine,** *Feb. 16, 1909*	85.00	*100.00*
Never hinged	175.00	
On cover		190.00
Block of 4 (2mm spacing)	360.00	*650.00*
Block of 4 (3mm spacing)	425.00	
P# block of 6, Impt., T V	975.00	
Never hinged	1,750.	
P# block of 6, Impt. & star	1,500.	
Never hinged	2,500.	
Double transfer	—	

Earliest documented use: Feb. 23, 1909.

359 A140 3c **deep violet,** type I	2,000.	*2,600.*
Never hinged	4,000.	
On cover		—
Block of 4	*8,500.*	
P# block of 6, Impt., T V	*22,500.*	
Never hinged	*31,000.*	

Earliest documented use: Dec. 27, 1910.

360 A140 4c **orange brown**	*24,000.*	
Never hinged	*37,500.*	
Block of 4	*110,000.*	
P# strip of 3, Impt., T V	*125,000.*	
361 A140 5c **blue**	5,000.	*12,500.*
Never hinged	*10,000.*	
On cover		—
Block of 4	*22,000.*	—
P# block of 6, Impt., T V	*75,000.*	

The No. 361 plate block is unique.

Earliest documented use: June 20, 1910.

362 A140 6c **red orange**	1,500.	*5,000.*
Never hinged	3,000.	
On cover		*15,000.*
Block of 4	*6,250.*	
P# block of 6, Impt., T V	*16,000.*	
Never hinged	*28,500.*	

Earliest documented use: Sept. 14, 1911.

363 A140 8c **olive green**	*27,500.*	
Never hinged	*40,000.*	
Block of 4	*125,000.*	
P# strip of 3, Impt., T V	*125,000.*	
364 A140 10c **yellow**	1,850.	*5,500.*
Never hinged	3,750.	
On cover		—
Block of 4	7,750.	
P# block of 6, Impt., T V	*32,500.*	

Earliest documented use: Feb. 3, 1910.

365 A140 13c **blue green**	3,000.	*2,250.*
Never hinged	6,000.	
On cover		—
Block of 4	*13,000*	*10,000.*
P# block of 6, Impt., T V	*30,000.*	
366 A140 15c **pale ultramarine**	1,450.	*11,000.*
Never hinged	2,900.	
On cover		—
Block of 4	*6,000.*	
P# block of 6, Impt., T V	*11,000.*	
Never hinged	*17,500.*	

Earliest documented use: Jan. 15, 1911.

Nos. 360 and 363 were not regularly issued.

Used examples of Nos. 357-366 must bear contemporaneous cancels, and Nos. 359-366 used must be accompanied by certificates of authenticity issued by recognized expertizing committees.

IMPORTANT INFORMATION REGARDING VALUES FOR NEVER-HINGED STAMPS

Collectors should be aware that the values given for never-hinged stamps from No. 205 on are for stamps in the grade of very fine, just as the values for all stamps in the catalogue are for very fine stamps unless indicated otherwise. The never-hinged premium as a percentage of value will be larger for stamps in extremely fine or superb grades, and the premium will be smaller for fine-very fine, fine or poor examples. This is particularly true of the issues of the late-19th and early-20th centuries. For example, in the grade of very fine, an unused stamp from this time period may be valued at $100 hinged and $180 never hinged. The never-hinged premium is thus 80%. But in a grade of extremely fine, this same stamp will not only sell for more hinged, but the never-hinged premium will increase, perhaps to 100%-300% or more over the higher extremely fine value. In a grade of superb, a hinged copy will sell for much more than a very fine copy, and additionally the never-hinged premium will be much larger, perhaps as large as 300%-400%. On the other hand, the same stamp in a grade of fine or fine-very fine not only will sell for less than a very fine stamp in hinged condition, but additionally the never-hinged premium will be smaller than the never-hinged premium on a very fine stamp, perhaps as small as 15%-30%.

Please note that the above statements and percentages are NOT a formula for arriving at the values of stamps in hinged or never-hinged condition in the grades of very good, fine, fine to very fine, extremely fine or superb. The percentages given apply only to the size of the premium for never-hinged condition that might be added to the stamp value for hinged condition. Further, the percentages given are only generalized estimates. Some stamps or grades may have percentages for never-hinged condition that are higher or lower than the ranges given. For values of the most popular U.S. stamps in the grades of very good, fine, fine to very fine, extremely fine and superb, see the *Scott Valuing Supplement*, updated and issued twice each year in April and October.

VALUES FOR NEVER-HINGED STAMPS PRIOR TO SCOTT 205

This catalogue does not value pre-1882 stamps in never-hinged condition. Premiums for never-hinged condition in the classic era invariably are even larger than those premiums listed for the post-1882 issues. Generally speaking, the earlier the stamp is listed in the catalogue, the larger will be the never-hinged premium. On some early classics, the premium will be several multiples of the unused, hinged values given in the catalogue.

NEVER-HINGED PLATE BLOCKS

Values given for never-hinged plate blocks are for blocks in which all stamps have original gum that has never been hinged and has no disturbances, and all selvage, whether gummed or ungummed, has never been hinged.

Lincoln — A141

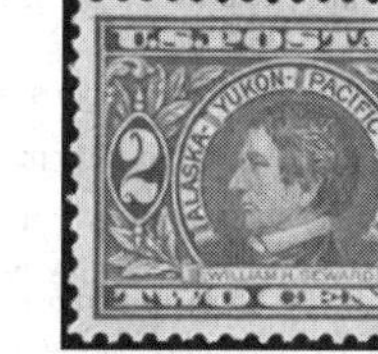

William H. Seward — A142

LINCOLN CENTENARY OF BIRTH ISSUE

Plates of 400 subjects in four panes of 100 each

1909 **Wmk. 191** ***Perf. 12***

367 A141 2c **carmine,** *Feb. 12*	5.50	1.75
bright carmine	5.50	1.75
Never hinged	9.50	
On cover		3.75
Block of 4 (2mm spacing)	22.50	15.00
Block of 4 (3mm spacing)	22.50	14.00
P# block of 6, Impt. & small solid star	150.00	
Never hinged	225.00	
Double transfer	7.50	2.50

Earliest documented use: Feb. 12, 1909 (FDC).

Imperf

368 A141 2c **carmine,** *Feb. 12*	19.00	20.00
Never hinged	35.00	
On cover		32.50
Pair	40.00	45.00
Never hinged	75.00	
Block of 4 (2mm or 3mm spacing)	82.50	95.00
Corner margin block of 4	87.50	95.00
Margin block of 4, arrow	92.50	100.00
Center line block	130.00	125.00
P# block of 6, Impt. & small solid star	180.00	—
Never hinged	275.00	
Double transfer	42.50	27.50

Earliest documented use: Feb. 12, 1909 (FDC).

BLUISH PAPER

Perf. 12

369 A141 2c **carmine,** *Feb.*	210.00	*275.00*
Never hinged	380.00	
On cover		425.00
Block of 4 (2mm or 3mm spacing)	950.00	*1,250.*
P# block of 6, Impt. & small solid star	*2,900.*	
Never hinged	*4,400.*	

Earliest documented use: Feb. 27, 1909 (dated cancel on off-cover stamp); Mar. 27, 1909 (on cover).

ALASKA-YUKON-PACIFIC EXPOSITION ISSUE

Seattle, Wash., June 1 - Oct. 16, 1909

Plates of 280 subjects in four panes of 70 each

1909 **Wmk. 191** ***Perf. 12***

370 A142 2c **carmine,** *June 1*	8.75	2.00
bright carmine	8.75	2.00
Never hinged	15.00	
On cover		4.75
On Expo. card or cover, Expo. station machine canc.		65.00
On Expo. card or cover, Expo. station duplex handstamp canc.		250.00
Block of 4	36.00	17.50
P# block of 6, Impt., T V	200.00	
Never hinged	310.00	
Double transfer (5249 UL 8)	10.50	4.50

Earliest documented use: June 1, 1909 (FDC).

Imperf

371 A142 2c **carmine,** *June*	22.50	22.50
Never hinged	40.00	
On cover		40.00
On cover, Expo. station machine canc.		*450.00*
Pair	47.50	50.00
Never hinged	85.00	
Block of 4	95.00	120.00
Corner margin block of 4	100.00	—
Margin block of 4, arrow	105.00	130.00
Center line block	165.00	160.00
P# block of 6, Impt., T V	220.00	—
Never hinged	340.00	
Double transfer	37.50	27.50

Earliest documented use: June 7, 1909.

HUDSON-FULTON CELEBRATION ISSUE

Tercentenary of the discovery of the Hudson River and the centenary of Robert Fulton's steamship, the "Clermont."

Henry Hudson's "Half Moon" and Fulton's Steamship "Clermont" A143

Plates of 240 subjects in four panes of 60 each

1909, Sept. 25 **Wmk. 191** ***Perf. 12***

372 A143 2c **carmine**	12.50	4.75
Never hinged	22.00	
On cover		8.50
Block of 4	52.50	30.00
P# block of 6, Impt., T V	280.00	
Never hinged	425.00	
Double transfer (5393 and 5394)	15.00	5.00

Earliest documented use: Sept. 25, 1909 (FDC).

Imperf

373 A143 2c **carmine**	25.00	25.00
Never hinged	47.50	
On cover		37.50
Pair	52.50	55.00
Never hinged	100.00	
Block of 4	105.00	120.00
Corner margin block of 4	110.00	—
Margin block of 4, arrow	115.00	125.00
Center line block	200.00	140.00
P# block of 6, Impt., T V	240.00	—
Never hinged	375.00	
Double transfer (5393 and 5394)	42.50	30.00

Earliest documented use: Sept. 25, 1909 (FDC).

REGULAR ISSUE

DESIGNS OF 1908-09 ISSUES

In this issue the Bureau used three groups of plates:

(1) The old standard plates with uniform 2mm spacing throughout (6c, 8c, 10c and 15c values);

(2) Those having an open star in the margin and showing spacings of 2mm and 3mm between stamps (for all values 1c to 10c); and

(3) A third set of plates with uniform spacing of approximately 2¾mm between all stamps. These plates have imprints showing

a. "Bureau of Engraving & Printing," "A" and number.
b. "A" and number only.
c. Number only.
(See above No. 331)

These were used for the 1c, 2c, 3c, 4c and 5c values.

On or about Oct. 1, 1910 the Bureau began using paper watermarked with single-lined letters:

(Actual size of letter)

repeated in rows, this way:

Watermark 190

Plates of 400 subjects in four panes of 100 each

1910-11 **Wmk. 190** ***Perf. 12***

374 A138 1c **green,** *Nov. 23, 1910*	7.00	.25
light green	7.00	.25
dark green	7.00	.25
Never hinged	14.00	
On cover		.30
Block of 4 (2mm spacing)	30.00	3.25
Block of 4 (3mm spacing)	32.50	3.00
P# block of 6, Impt., & star	77.50	
Never hinged	125.00	
P# block of 6, Impt. & "A"	90.00	—
Never hinged	150.00	
Double transfer	14.00	—
Cracked plate		—
Pane of 60	*1,750.*	—
a. Booklet pane of 6, *Oct. 7, 1910*	175.00	*200.00*
Never hinged	300.00	

Earliest documented uses: Feb. 13, 1911 (No. 374); Apr. 19, 1911 (No. 374a single).

Panes of 60 of No. 374 were regularly issued in Washington, D.C. during Sept. and Oct., 1912. They were made from the six outer vertical rows of imperforate "Star Plate" sheets that had been rejected for use in vending machines on account of the 3mm spacing.

These panes have sheet margins on two adjoining sides and are imperforate along the other two sides. Upper and lower right panes show plate number, star and imprint on both margins; upper and lower left panes show plate number, star and imprint on side margins, but only the imprint on top or bottom margins.

375 A139 2c **carmine,** *Nov. 23, 1910*	7.00	.25
bright carmine	7.00	.25
dark carmine	7.00	.25
Never hinged	14.00	
On cover		.30
Block of 4 (2mm spacing)	30.00	2.00
Block of 4 (3mm spacing)	29.00	1.75
P# block of 6, Impt. & star	85.00	
Never hinged	150.00	
P# block of 6, Impt. & "A"	95.00	
Never hinged	160.00	
Cracked plate	—	—
Double transfer	12.00	—
Foreign entry, design of 1c (plate 5299)	—	*1,450.*
a. Booklet pane of 6, *Nov. 30, 1910*	100.00	*175.00*
Never hinged	175.00	
b. 2c **lake**	*525.00*	
Never hinged	*1,050.*	
c. Double impression	*500.00*	
Never hinged	*1,000.*	

Earliest documented use: Dec. 29, 1910 (No. 375).

376 A140 3c **deep violet,** type I, *Jan. 16, 1911*	21.50	2.00
violet	21.50	2.00
Never hinged	42.50	
lilac	26.00	2.25
Never hinged	52.50	
On cover		8.00
Block of 4 (2mm spacing)	90.00	15.00
Block of 4 (3mm spacing)	92.50	14.00
P# block of 6, Impt. & star	200.00	
Never hinged	340.00	
P# block of 6	220.00	
Never hinged	360.00	

Earliest documented use: June 19, 1911.

377 A140 4c **brown,** *Jan. 20, 1911*	32.50	1.00
dark brown	32.50	1.00
orange brown	32.50	1.00
Never hinged	65.00	
On cover		7.50
Block of 4 (2mm spacing)	140.00	6.50
Block of 4 (3mm spacing)	135.00	6.00
P# block of 6, Impt. & star	240.00	
Never hinged	400.00	
P# block of 6	280.00	
Never hinged	450.00	
Double transfer	—	—

Earliest documented use: Mar. 7, 1911.

378 A140 5c **blue,** *Jan. 25, 1911*	32.50	.75
light blue	32.50	.75
dark blue	32.50	.75
bright blue	32.50	.75
Never hinged	67.50	
On cover		5.25
Block of 4 (2mm spacing)	140.00	6.00
Block of 4 (3mm spacing)	135.00	5.00
P# block of 6, Impt., T V	290.00	
Never hinged	475.00	
P# block of 6, Impt. & star	280.00	
Never hinged	450.00	
P# block of 6, "A"	325.00	
Never hinged	525.00	
P# block of 6	325.00	
Never hinged	525.00	
Double transfer	—	—

Earliest documented use: Feb. 14, 1911.

379 A140 6c **red orange,** *Jan. 1911*	37.50	1.00
light red orange	37.50	1.00
Never hinged	80.00	
On cover		13.00
Block of 4 (2mm spacing)	160.00	12.50
Block of 4 (3mm spacing)	155.00	11.00
P# block of 6, Impt., T V	500.00	
Never hinged	800.00	
P# block of 6, Impt. & star	440.00	
Never hinged	700.00	

Earliest documented use: Jan. 13, 1911.

380 A140 8c **olive green,** *Feb. 8, 1911*	115.00	15.00
dark olive green	115.00	15.00
Never hinged	240.00	
On cover		45.00
Block of 4 (2mm spacing)	475.00	100.00
Block of 4 (3mm spacing)	475.00	95.00
P# block of 6, Impt., T V	1,100.	
Never hinged	1,800.	
P# block of 6, Impt., & star	*1,300.*	
Never hinged	*2,100.*	

Earliest documented use: Aug. 2, 1911.

381 A140 10c **yellow,** *Jan. 24, 1911*	105.00	6.00
Never hinged	210.00	
On cover		22.50
Block of 4 (2mm spacing)	440.00	50.00
Block of 4 (3mm spacing)	440.00	47.50
P# block of 6, Impt., T V	1,125.	
Never hinged	1,850.	
P# block of 6, Impt. & star	1,250.	
Never hinged	2,250.	

Earliest documented use: Feb. 17, 1911.

382 A140 15c **pale ultramarine,** *Mar. 1, 1911*	275.00	17.50
Never hinged	575.00	
On cover		100.00
Block of 4	1,150.	125.00
P# block of 6, Impt., T V	2,400.	
Never hinged	3,750.	

Earliest documented use: May 16, 1912. A July 31, 1911, cover is reported. The editors request information on its certification.

Nos. 374-382 (9)	633.00	43.75

1910, Dec. ***Imperf.***

383 A138 1c **green**	2.25	2.00
dark green	2.25	2.00
yellowish green	2.25	2.00
bright green	2.25	2.00
Never hinged	4.25	
On cover		5.00
Pair	5.25	4.50
Never hinged	9.00	
Block of 4 (2mm or 3mm spacing)	10.50	14.00
Corner margin block of 4	11.50	
Margin block of 4, arrow	12.00	13.50
Center line block	24.00	16.00
P# block of 6, Impt., & star	45.00	—
Never hinged	67.50	
P# block of 6, Impt. & "A"	82.50	—
Never hinged	125.00	
Double transfer	6.50	—

Earliest documented use: Mar. 1, 1911.

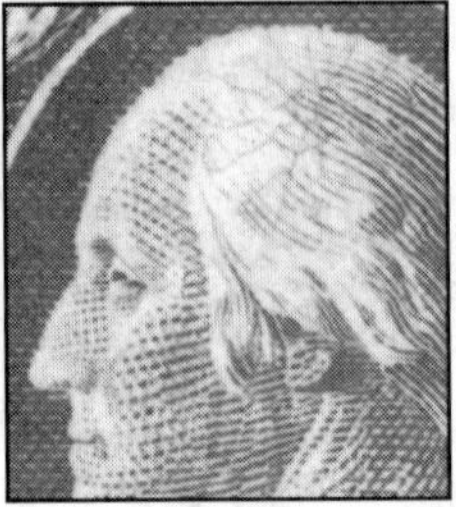

Rosette plate crack on head

384 A139 2c **carmine**	3.75	2.50
light carmine	3.75	2.50
Never hinged	7.00	
dark carmine	55.00	12.50
On cover		3.50
Horizontal pair	11.50	7.50
Never hinged	20.00	
Vertical pair	8.50	6.00
Never hinged	15.00	
Block of 4 (2mm or 3mm spacing)	25.00	16.00
Corner margin block of 4	27.50	20.00
Margin block of 4, arrow	27.50	21.00
Center line block	50.00	50.00
P# block of 6, Impt. & star	130.00	—
Never hinged	200.00	
P# block of 6, Impt. & "A"	170.00	—
Never hinged	260.00	
Double transfer	7.50	—
Rosette plate crack on head	*150.00*	—

Earliest documented use: Dec. 8, 1910.

COIL STAMPS

1910, Nov. 1 ***Perf. 12 Horizontally***

385 A138 1c **green**	40.00	20.00
dark green	40.00	20.00
Never hinged	80.00	
On cover		40.00
Pair	110.00	75.00
Never hinged	220.00	
Guide line pair	450.00	*500.00*
Never hinged	950.00	
386 A139 2c **carmine**	75.00	27.50
light carmine	75.00	27.50
Never hinged	150.00	
On cover		57.50
Pair	275.00	150.00
Never hinged	550.00	
Guide line pair	1,000.	*600.00*
Never hinged	2,000.	

Earliest documented use: Dec. 9, 1910.

1910-11 ***Perf. 12 Vertically***

387 A138 1c **green,** *Nov. 1, 1910*	200.00	75.00
Never hinged	400.00	
On cover		90.00
Pair (2mm spacing)	450.00	200.00
Never hinged	900.00	
Pair (3mm spacing)	475.00	190.00
Never hinged	950.00	
Guide line pair	900.00	*750.00*
Never hinged	1,800.	

Earliest documented use: Nov. 5, 1910.

388 A139 2c **carmine,** *Nov. 1, 1910*	1,050.	*525.00*
Never hinged	2,000.	
On cover		*1,300.*
Pair (2mm spacing)	3,250.	*6,500.*
Never hinged	6,750.	
Pair (3mm spacing)	3,500.	*6,750.*
Never hinged	7,000.	
Guide line pair	*8,500.*	*23,000.*
Never hinged	*15,000.*	

The used guide line pair of No. 388 is unique. It is fine-very fine and valued thus.

Stamps offered as No. 388 frequently are privately perforated examples of No. 384, or copies of No. 375 with top and/or bottom perfs trimmed.

Earliest documented use: Jan. 4, 1911.

389 A140 3c **deep vio.,** type I, *Jan. 24, 1911*	*65,000.*	*10,000.*
Never hinged	*150,000.*	
On cover		*27,500.*
Pair	*140,000.*	*37,500.*

No. 389 is valued in the grade of fine.

This is the rarest coil. Only a small supply of this coil was used at Orangeburg, N.Y. The used pair listed is part of a strip of 3 (two such strips exist). Each strip is in average condition, and the pairs are valued thus. No other used multiples are recorded. There is only one mint, never-hinged example recorded.

Stamps offered as No. 389 sometimes are examples of No. 376 with top and/or bottom perfs trimmed. Expertization by competent authorities is recommended.

Earliest documented use: Mar. 8, 1911.

1910 ***Perf. 8½ Horizontally***

No.	Type	Denom.	Description	Unused	Used
390	A138	1c	**green,** *Dec. 12, 1910*	5.00	*6.50*
			dark green	5.00	*6.50*
			Never hinged	9.50	
			On cover		10.50
			Pair	11.50	*30.00*
			Never hinged	23.00	
			Guide line pair	37.50	*85.00*
			Never hinged	75.00	
			Double transfer	—	—

Earliest documented use: Oct. 5, 1911.

No.	Type	Denom.	Description	Unused	Used
391	A139	2c	**carmine,** *Dec. 23, 1910*	40.00	15.00
			light carmine	40.00	15.00
			Never hinged	75.00	
			On cover		30.00
			Pair	110.00	80.00
			Never hinged	220.00	
			Guide line pair	260.00	*1,000.*
			Never hinged	525.00	

Earliest documented use: May 3, 1911.

1910-13 ***Perf. 8½ Vertically***

No.	Type	Denom.	Description	Unused	Used
392	A138	1c	**green,** *Dec. 12, 1910*	25.00	25.00
			dark green	25.00	25.00
			Never hinged	50.00	
			On cover		55.00
			Pair	67.50	*100.00*
			Never hinged	135.00	
			Guide line pair	200.00	*400.00*
			Never hinged	400.00	
			Double transfer	—	—

Earliest documented use: Dec. 16, 1910.

No.	Type	Denom.	Description	Unused	Used
393	A139	2c	**carmine,** *Dec. 16, 1910*	47.50	10.00
			dark carmine	47.50	10.00
			Never hinged	95.00	
			On cover		24.00
			Pair	125.00	65.00
			Never hinged	250.00	
			Guide line pair	300.00	225.00
			Never hinged	600.00	

Earliest documented use: Dec. 27, 1910.

No.	Type	Denom.	Description	Unused	Used
394	A140	3c	**deep violet,** type I, *Sept. 1911*	57.50	55.00
			violet	57.50	55.00
			red violet	57.50	55.00
			Never hinged	115.00	
			On cover		110.00
			Pair (2mm spacing)	145.00	160.00
			Never hinged	290.00	
			Pair (3mm spacing)	140.00	150.00
			Never hinged	280.00	
			Guide line pair	400.00	*500.00*
			Never hinged	800.00	

Earliest documented use: Sept. 18, 1911.

No.	Type	Denom.	Description	Unused	Used
395	A140	4c	**brown,** *Apr. 15, 1912*	60.00	52.50
			dark brown	60.00	52.50
			Never hinged	120.00	
			On cover		105.00
			Pair (2mm spacing)	150.00	140.00
			Never hinged	300.00	
			Pair (3mm spacing)	145.00	140.00
			Never hinged	290.00	
			Guide line pair	425.00	*550.00*
			Never hinged	850.00	

Earliest documented use: June 21, 1912.

No.	Type	Denom.	Description	Unused	Used
396	A140	5c	**blue,** *Mar. 1913*	57.50	50.00
			dark blue	57.50	50.00
			Never hinged	115.00	
			On cover		105.00
			Pair	150.00	150.00
			Never hinged	300.00	
			Guide line pair	400.00	*700.00*
			Never hinged	800.00	

Earliest documented use: May 14, 1913.

PANAMA-PACIFIC EXPOSITION ISSUE

San Francisco, Cal., Feb. 20 - Dec. 4, 1915

Vasco Nunez de Balboa — A144

Pedro Miguel Locks, Panama Canal — A145

Golden Gate — A146

Discovery of San Francisco Bay — A147

Exposition Station Cancellation.

Plates of 280 subjects in four panes of 70 each.

1913 **Wmk. 190** ***Perf. 12***

No.	Type	Denom.	Description	Unused	Used
397	A144	1c	**green,** *Jan. 1, 1913*	17.50	1.80
			deep green	17.50	1.80
			yellowish green	17.50	1.80
			Never hinged	35.00	
			On cover		3.25
			On Expo. card, Expo. station 1915 machine cancel		*30.00*
			Pair on cover, Expo. station 1915 duplex handstamp cancel		*150.00*
			Block of 4	70.00	12.50
			P# block of 6	175.00	
			Never hinged	290.00	
			Double transfer	21.00	2.75

Earliest documented use: Jan. 1, 1913 (FDC).

No.	Type	Denom.	Description	Unused	Used
398	A145	2c	**carmine,** *Jan. 1913*	20.00	.75
			deep carmine	20.00	.75
			Never hinged	40.00	
			brown lake	—	
			On cover		1.40
			On cover, Expo. station 1915 machine cancel		75.00
			On cover, Expo. station 1915 duplex handstamp cancel		*250.00*
			Block of 4	82.50	7.50
			P# block of 6	275.00	
			Never hinged	450.00	
			Double transfer	40.00	2.50
a.			2c **carmine lake**	*1,250.*	
			Never hinged	*1,900.*	

Earliest documented use: Jan. 17, 1913.

No.	Type	Denom.	Description	Unused	Used
399	A146	5c	**blue,** *Jan. 1, 1913*	80.00	9.50
			dark blue	80.00	9.50
			Never hinged	160.00	
			On cover		27.50
			On cover, Expo. station 1915 machine cancel		300.00
			Block of 4	325.00	67.50
			P# block of 6	1,900.	
			Never hinged	3,100.	

Earliest documented use: Jan. 1, 1913 (FDC).

No.	Type	Denom.	Description	Unused	Used
400	A147	10c	**orange yellow,** *Jan. 1, 1913*	135.00	20.00
			Never hinged	275.00	
			On cover		55.00
			On cover, Expo. station 1915 machine cancel		500.00
			Block of 4	575.00	140.00
			P# block of 6	2,350.	
			Never hinged	3,750.	

Earliest documented use: Jan. 1, 1913 (FDC).

No.	Type	Denom.	Description	Unused	Used
400A	A147	10c	**orange,** *Aug. 1913*	210.00	16.00
			Never hinged	425.00	
			On cover		75.00
			On cover, Expo. station 1915 machine cancel		550.00
			Block of 4	875.00	100.00
			P# block of 6	*11,500.*	
			Never hinged	*18,000.*	

Earliest documented use: Nov. 12, 1913.

	Unused	Used
Nos. 397-400A (5)	462.50	48.05
Nos. 397-400A, never hinged	935.00	

1914-15 ***Perf. 10***

No.	Type	Denom.	Description	Unused	Used
401	A144	1c	**green,** *Dec. 1914*	27.50	6.50
			dark green	27.50	6.50
			Never hinged	55.00	
			On cover		16.00
			On Expo. card, Expo. station 1915 machine cancel		75.00
			Block of 4	120.00	45.00
			P# block of 6	340.00	
			Never hinged	550.00	

Earliest documented use: Dec. 21, 1914.

No.	Type	Denom.	Description	Unused	Used
402	A145	2c	**carmine,** *Jan. 1915*	75.00	2.50
			deep carmine	75.00	2.50
			red	75.00	2.50
			Never hinged	150.00	
			On cover		6.50
			On cover, Expo. station 1915 machine cancel		150.00
			On cover, Expo. station 1915 duplex handstamp cancel		450.00
			Block of 4	325.00	17.50
			P# block of 6	1,950.	
			Never hinged	3,100.	

Earliest documented use: Jan. 13, 1915.

No.	Type	Denom.	Description	Unused	Used
403	A146	5c	**blue,** *Feb. 1915*	175.00	17.50
			dark blue	175.00	17.50
			Never hinged	350.00	
			On cover		55.00
			On cover, Expo. station 1915 machine cancel		450.00
			Block of 4	750.00	125.00
			P# block of 6	4,000.	
			Never hinged	6,500.	

Earliest documented use: Feb. 6, 1915.

No.	Type	Denom.	Description	Unused	Used
404	A147	10c	**orange,** *July 1915*	875.00	65.00
			Never hinged	1,750.	
			On cover		175.00
			On cover, Expo. station 1915 machine cancel		600.00
			Block of 4	*3,800.*	450.00
			P# block of 6	*12,500.*	
			Never hinged	20,000.	

Earliest documented use: Aug. 27, 1915.

	Unused	Used
Nos. 401-404 (4)	1,152.	91.50
Nos. 401-404, never hinged	2,305.	

VALUES FOR VERY FINE STAMPS
Please note: Stamps are valued in the grade of Very Fine unless otherwise indicated.

REGULAR ISSUE

Washington—A140

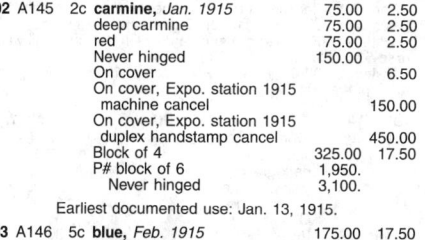

The plates for this and later issues were the so-called "A" plates with uniform spacing of 2¾mm between stamps.

Plates of 400 subjects in four panes of 100 each for all values 1c to 50c inclusive.

Plates of 200 subjects in two panes of 100 each for $1 and some of the 50c (No. 422) denomination.

1912-14 Wmk. 190 *Perf. 12*

405 A140 1c **green,** *Feb. 1912*	7.00	.25
light green	7.00	.25
dark green	7.00	.25
yellowish green	7.00	.25
Never hinged	14.00	
On cover		.30
Block of 4	30.00	2.50
P# block of 6, Impt. & "A"	110.00	
Never hinged	175.00	
P# block of 6, "A"	100.00	
Never hinged	160.00	
P# block of 6	95.00	
Never hinged	155.00	
Cracked plate	14.50	—
Double transfer	8.50	—
a. Vert. pair, imperf. horiz.	*1,500.*	—
b. Booklet pane of 6, *1912*	60.00	*75.00*
Never hinged	100.00	

Earliest documented uses: Feb. 12, 1912 (No. 405); Jan. 16, 1912 (No. 405b single).

TYPE I

TWO CENTS

Type I. There is one shading line in the first curve of the ribbon above the left "2" and one in the second curve of the ribbon above the right "2."

The button of the toga has only a faint outline.

The top line of the toga rope, from the button to the front of the throat, is also very faint.

The shading lines of the face terminate in front of the ear with little or no joining, to form a lock of hair.

Used on both flat plate and rotary press printings.

406 A140 2c **carmine,** type I, *Feb. 1912*	7.00	.25
bright carmine	7.00	.25
Never hinged	14.00	
dark carmine	7.50	.25
Never hinged	15.00	
On cover		.30
Block of 4	30.00	2.50
P# block of 6, Impt. & "A"	130.00	
Never hinged	210.00	
P# block of 6, "A"	125.00	
Never hinged	200.00	
P# block of 6	105.00	
Never hinged	170.00	
Margin block of 6, Electrolytic, (Pl. 6023)	*950.00*	
Never hinged	*1,500.*	
Double transfer	9.00	—
a. Booklet pane of 6, *Feb. 8, 1912*	60.00	*90.00*
Never hinged	100.00	
b. Double impression	—	
c. 2c **lake,** type I	*1,750.*	*2,750.*
Never hinged	*3,500.*	

Earliest documented uses: Feb. 15, 1912 (No. 406); May 2, 1912 (No. 406a single).

407 A140 7c **black,** *Apr. 1914*	80.00	12.50
grayish black	80.00	12.50
intense black	80.00	12.50
Never hinged	160.00	
On cover		75.00
Block of 4	350.00	95.00
P# block of 6	1,200.	
Never hinged	1,900.	

Earliest documented use: May 1, 1914.

1912 *Imperf.*

408 A140 1c **green,** *Mar. 1912*	1.10	.65
yellowish green	1.10	.65
dark green	1.10	.65
Never hinged	2.00	
On cover		1.20
Pair	2.25	1.50
Never hinged	4.00	
Block of 4	4.50	3.00
Corner margin block of 4	4.60	3.10
Margin block of 4, arrow	4.75	3.25
Center line block	10.00	10.00
P# block of 6, Impt. & "A," T, B or L	45.00	—
Never hinged	75.00	
P# block of 6, Impt. & "A," at right	*550.00*	—
Never hinged	*850.00*	
P# block of 6, "A"	26.00	—
Never hinged	42.50	
P# block of 6	18.00	—
Never hinged	29.00	
Double transfer	2.40	1.00
Cracked plate	—	—

Earliest documented use: Mar. 27, 1912.

409 A140 2c **carmine,** type I, *Feb. 1912*	1.30	.65
deep carmine	1.30	.65
scarlet	1.30	.65
Never hinged	2.30	
On cover		1.20
Pair	2.75	1.50
Never hinged	5.00	
Block of 4	5.50	3.00
Corner margin block of 4	5.75	
Margin block of 4, arrow	6.00	3.25
Center line block	11.00	10.00
P# block of 6, Impt. & "A"	47.50	—
Never hinged	77.50	
P# block of 6, "A"	45.00	—
Never hinged	72.50	
P# block of 6	35.00	—
Never hinged	57.50	
Cracked plate (Plates 7580, 7582)	14.00	—

Earliest documented use: Apr. 15, 1912.

In late 1914, the Post Office at Kansas City, Missouri, had on hand a stock of imperforate sheets of 400 of stamps Nos. 408 and 409, formerly sold for use in vending machines, but not then in demand. In order to make them salable, they were rouletted with ordinary tracing wheels and were sold over the counter with official approval of the Post Office Department given January 5, 1915.

These stamps were sold until the supply was exhausted. Except for one full sheet of 400 of each value, all were cut into panes of 100 before being rouletted and sold. They are known as "Kansas City Roulettes". Value, authenticated blocks of 4, 1c *$100*, 2c *$200*.

Earliest documented uses of "Kansas City Roulettes": Oct. 22, 1914 (No. 408); Nov. 25, 1914 (No. 409).

COIL STAMPS

1912 *Perf. 8½ Horizontally*

410 A140 1c **green,** *Mar. 1912*	6.00	4.25
dark green	6.00	4.25
Never hinged	11.50	
On cover		8.00
Pair	15.00	11.00
Never hinged	30.00	
Guide line pair	30.00	30.00
Never hinged	60.00	
Double transfer	—	—

Earliest documented use: Apr. 17, 1912.

411 A140 2c **carmine,** type I, *Mar. 1912*	10.00	4.00
deep carmine	10.00	4.00
Never hinged	19.00	
On cover		11.50
Pair	25.00	14.00
Never hinged	50.00	
Guide line pair	55.00	45.00
Never hinged	110.00	
Double transfer	12.50	—

Perf. 8½ Vertically

412 A140 1c **green,** *Mar. 18, 1912*	25.00	5.50
deep green	25.00	5.50
Never hinged	47.50	
On cover		14.50
Pair	60.00	22.50
Never hinged	120.00	
Guide line pair	120.00	72.50
Never hinged	240.00	

Earliest documented use: May 31, 1912.

413 A140 2c **carmine,** type I, *Mar. 1912*	50.00	2.00
dark carmine	50.00	2.00
Never hinged	95.00	
On cover		8.50
Pair	105.00	15.00
Never hinged	210.00	
Guide line pair	280.00	50.00
Never hinged	550.00	
Double transfer	52.50	—

Earliest documented use: April 16, 1912.

Plate Blocks

Scott values for plate blocks printed from flat plates are for very fine side and bottom positions. Top position plate blocks with full wide selvage sell for more.

Franklin — A148

1912-14 Wmk. 190 *Perf. 12*

414 A148 8c **pale olive green,** *Feb. 1912*	45.00	2.00
olive green	45.00	2.00
Never hinged	95.00	
On cover		15.00
Block of 4	200.00	15.00
P# block of 6, Impt. & "A"	475.00	
Never hinged	750.00	

415 A148 9c **salmon red,** *Apr. 1914*	55.00	13.50
rose red	55.00	13.50
Never hinged	110.00	
On cover		50.00
Block of 4	240.00	125.00
P# block of 6	650.00	
Never hinged	1,050.	

Earliest documented use: May 1, 1914.

416 A148 10c **orange yellow,** *Jan. 1912*	45.00	.75
yellow	45.00	.75
Never hinged	95.00	
On cover		2.70
Block of 4	200.00	5.00
P# block of 6, Impt. & "A"	500.00	
Never hinged	800.00	
P# block of 6, "A"	550.00	
Never hinged	875.00	
Double transfer	—	—
a. 10c **brown yellow**	*1,150.*	
Never hinged	*2,150.*	

Earliest documented use: Feb. 12, 1912.

417 A148 12c **claret brown,** *Apr. 1914*	50.00	5.00
deep claret brown	50.00	5.00
Never hinged	100.00	
On cover		25.00
Block of 4	225.00	37.50
P# block of 6	625.00	
Never hinged	1,000.	
Double transfer	55.00	—
Triple transfer	72.50	—

Earliest documented use: May 5, 1914.

418 A148 15c **gray,** *Feb. 1912*	85.00	4.50
dark gray	85.00	4.50
Never hinged	175.00	
On cover		17.50
Block of 4	350.00	35.00
P# block of 6, Impt. & "A"	675.00	
Never hinged	1,100.	
P# block of 6, "A"	775.00	
Never hinged	1,250.	
P# block of 6	850.00	
Never hinged	1,350.	
Double transfer	—	—

Earliest documented use: Apr. 26, 1912.

419 A148 20c **ultramarine,** *Apr. 1914*	200.00	18.50
dark ultramarine	200.00	18.50
Never hinged	400.00	
On cover		*150.00*
Block of 4	825.00	135.00
P# block of 6	2,000.	
Never hinged	3,250.	

Earliest documented use: May 1, 1914.

420 A148 30c **orange red,** *Apr. 1914*	125.00	17.50
dark orange red	125.00	17.50
Never hinged	250.00	
On cover		*250.00*
Block of 4	525.00	130.00
P# block of 6	1,450.	
Never hinged	2,300.	

Earliest documented use: May 1, 1914.

421 A148 50c **violet,** *1914*	425.00	22.50
bright violet	425.00	22.50
Never hinged	900.00	
On cover		*2,000.*
Block of 4	1,800.	175.00
P# block of 6	*10,000.*	
Never hinged	*16,000.*	

Earliest documented use: May 1, 1914.

No. 421 almost always has an offset of the frame lines on the back under the gum. Nos. 422 does not have this offset.

1912, Feb. 12 Wmk. 191

422 A148 50c **violet**	250.00	18.50
Never hinged	525.00	
On cover		*2,000.*
Block of 4	1,050.	140.00
Margin block of 4, arrow, R or L	1,100.	
P# block of 6, Impt. & "A"	*4,750.*	
Never hinged	*7,500.*	

Earliest documented use: Oct. 31, 1914.

423 A148 $1 **violet brown**	525.00	75.00
Never hinged	1,100.	
On cover		*7,000.*
Block of 4	2,200.	800.00
Margin block of 4, arrow, R or L	2,250.	
P# block of 6, Impt. & "A"	*12,000.*	
Never hinged	*19,000.*	
Double transfer (5782 L 66)	550.00	—

Earliest documented use: July 15, 1915.

During the United States occupation of Vera Cruz, Mexico, from April to November, 1914, letters sent from there show Provisional Postmarks.

For other listings of perforated sheet stamps of design A148, see:

Nos. 431-440 - Single line wmk. Perf. 10
Nos. 460 - Double line wmk. Perf. 10
Nos. 470-478 - Unwmkd. Perf. 10
Nos. 508-518 - Unwmkd. Perf. 11

1914 Compound Perforations

As the Bureau of Engraving and Printing made the changeover to perf 10 from perf 12, in the normal course of their stamp production they perforated limited quantities of 1c, 2c and 5c stamps with the old 12-gauge perforations in one direction and the new 10-gauge perforations in the other direction. These were not production errors. These compound-perforation stamps previously were listed as Nos. 424a, 424b, 425c, 425d and 428a.

All examples of Nos. 423A-423E must be accompanied by certificates of authenticity issued by a recognized expertizing committee. Fakes made from perf 12, perf 10 and imperfs exist.

1914 Wmk. 190 *Perf. 12x10*

423A A140 1c **green** *7,500. 5,000.*
Pair *10,500.*
Block of 4 *22,500.*
On postcard *8,000.*
On cover, pair *8,500.*

Formerly No. 424a. Eight unused and 53 used examples are recorded. Value for unused is for a sound stamp with perfs touching or just cutting the design. Value for used is for a sound stamp in the grade of fine-very fine. Of the used examples, 20 are precanceled Quincy IL (very scarce) or Chicago (sometimes inverted). The block of four, single on postcard and pair on cover are each unique (top stamp of pair on cover with small piece missing).

423B A140 2c **rose red,** type I *30,000. 10,000.*

Formerly No. 425d. One unused (a plate #7082 single) and 27 used examples are recorded. Value for used is for a sound stamp in the grade of fine-very fine. There are no precancels known on this issue.

423C A140 5c **blue** *12,500.*
Pair —

Formerly No. 428a. 24 used examples are recorded. No unused examples are recorded. Three examples are precanceled: Tampa FL (2) and Rahway NJ (1). Value is for a sound stamp in the grade of fine-very fine. The pair is unique (one stamp creased, the other with a small tear).

Earliest documented use: April 14, 1915 (dated cancel on off-cover stamp).

1914 Wmk. 190 *Perf. 10x12*

423D A140 1c **green** *7,500.*

Formerly No. 424b. 34 used examples are recorded. No unused examples are recorded. 32 examples are precanceled: Dayton OH (29), Buffalo NY (2) and Elkhart IN (1). Value is for a sound stamp in the grade of fine-very fine.

423E A140 2c **rose red,** type I —

Formerly No. 425c. Only one used example has been certified (by the Philatelic Foundation). It is well centered, has a machine cancel, and has small thinning and a crease.

Plates of 400 subjects in four panes of 100 each.

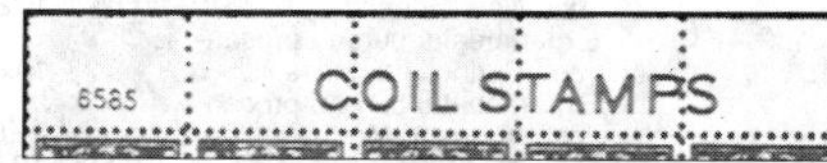

Type of plate number and imprint used for the 12 special 1c and 2c plates designed for the production of coil stamps.

1913-15 Wmk. 190 *Perf. 10*

424 A140 1c **green,** *Sept. 5, 1914* 2.50 .20
bright green 2.50 .20
deep green 2.50 .20
yellowish green 2.50 .20
Never hinged 5.00
On cover .25
Block of 4 10.50 1.50
P# block of 6 42.50
Never hinged 67.50
Block of ten with imprint "COIL STAMPS" and number (6581-82, 85, 89) 135.00
Never hinged 220.00
Cracked plate — —
Double transfer 4.75 —
c. Vert. pair, imperf. horiz. *2,000. 1,750.*
Never hinged *3,000.*
d. Booklet pane of 6 5.25 *7.50*
Never hinged 8.50
e. As "d," imperf. *1,600.*
f. Vert. pair, imperf. between and with straight edge at top *9,000.*

For former Nos. 424a and 424b, see Nos. 423A and 423D.
All known examples of No. 424e are without gum.
The unique example of No. 424f is never hinged, and it is valued thus.

Earliest documented uses: Oct. 21, 1914 (No. 424); Dec. 20, 1913 (No. 424d single).

425 A140 2c **rose red,** type I, *Sept. 5, 1914* 2.30 .20
dark rose red 2.30 .20
carmine rose 2.30 .20
carmine 2.30 .20
dark carmine 2.30 .20
scarlet 2.30 .20
red 2.30 .20
Never hinged 4.60
On cover .25
Block of 4 9.50 1.50
P# block of 6 27.50
Never hinged 45.00
Block of 10 with imprint "COIL STAMPS" and number (6568, 70-72) 145.00
Never hinged 230.00
Cracked plate 9.50 —
Double transfer — —
e. Booklet pane of 6, *Jan. 1914* 17.50 *25.00*
Never hinged 28.00

For former Nos. 425c and 425d, see Nos. 423E and 423B.
The aniline inks used on some printings of Nos. 425, 426 and 435a caused a pink tinge to permeate the paper and appear on the back. These are called "pink backs."

Earliest documented uses: Nov. 6, 1914 (No. 425); Jan. 6, 1914 (No. 425e single).

426 A140 3c **deep violet,** type I, *Sept. 18, 1914* 15.00 1.50
violet 16.00 1.50
bright violet 16.00 1.50
reddish violet 16.00 1.50
Never hinged 30.00
On cover 3.50
Block of 4 62.50 12.50
P# block of 6 200.00
Never hinged 325.00

See "pink backs" note after No. 425.

Earliest documented use: Oct. 11, 1914.

427 A140 4c **brown,** *Sept. 7, 1914* 35.00 1.00
dark brown 35.00 1.00
orange brown 35.00 1.00
yellowish brown 35.00 1.00
Never hinged 70.00
On cover 5.25
Block of 4 145.00 9.00
P# block of 6 475.00
Never hinged 775.00
Double transfer 45.00 —

Earliest documented use: Jan. 2, 1915.

428 A140 5c **blue,** *Sept. 14, 1914* 35.00 1.00
bright blue 35.00 1.00
dark blue 35.00 1.00
indigo blue 35.00 1.00
Never hinged 70.00
On cover 3.00
Block of 4 145.00 8.00
P# block of 6 390.00
Never hinged 625.00

For former No. 428a, see No. 423C.

Earliest documented use: Dec. 2, 1914.

429 A140 6c **red orange,** *Sept. 28, 1914* 50.00 2.00
deep red orange 50.00 2.00
pale red orange 50.00 2.00
Never hinged 100.00
On cover 9.00
Block of 4 (2mm spacing) 215.00 16.00
Block of 4 (3mm spacing) 210.00 15.00
P# block of 6, Impt. & star 425.00
Never hinged 700.00
P# block of 6 525.00
Never hinged 850.00

430 A140 7c **black,** *Sept. 10, 1914* 90.00 5.00
gray black 90.00 5.00
intense black 90.00 5.00
Never hinged 180.00
On cover 37.50
Block of 4 375.00 40.00
P# block of 6 950.00
Never hinged 1,500.

Earliest documented use: June 19, 1915.

431 A148 8c **pale olive green,** *Sept. 26, 1914* 37.50 3.00
olive green 37.50 3.00
Never hinged 75.00
On cover 8.00
Block of 4 160.00 25.00
P# block of 6, Impt. & "A" 450.00
Never hinged 725.00
P# block of 6, "A" 550.00
Never hinged 850.00
Double impression —
Double transfer — —

Earliest documented use: Jan. 20, 1915.

432 A148 9c **salmon red,** *Oct. 6, 1914* 50.00 9.00
dark salmon red 50.00 9.00
Never hinged 100.00
On cover 27.50
Block of 4 210.00 70.00
P# block of 6 700.00
Never hinged 1,100.

Earliest documented use: Feb. 25, 1916.

433 A148 10c **orange yellow,** *Sept. 9, 1914* 47.50 1.00
golden yellow 47.50 1.00
Never hinged 95.00
On cover 7.75
Block of 4 200.00 6.50
P# block of 6, Impt. & "A" 650.00
Never hinged 1,050.
P# block of 6, "A" 950.00
Never hinged 1,500.
P# block of 6 825.00
Never hinged 1,300.

Earliest documented use: Nov. 13, 1914.

434 A148 11c **dark green,** *Aug. 11, 1915* 25.00 8.50
bluish green 25.00 8.50
Never hinged 50.00
On cover 25.00
Block of 4 105.00 65.00
P# block of 6 240.00
Never hinged 390.00

435 A148 12c **claret brown,** *Sept. 10, 1914* 27.50 6.00
deep claret brown 27.50 6.00
Never hinged 60.00
On cover 17.50
Block of 4 115.00 45.00
P# block of 6 290.00
Never hinged 475.00
Double transfer 35.00 —
Triple transfer 40.00 —
a. 12c **copper red** 30.00 7.00
Never hinged 70.00
On cover 20.00
Block of 4 125.00 50.00
P# block of 6 325.00
Never hinged 525.00

All so-called vertical pairs, imperf. between, have at least one perf. hole or "blind perfs" between the stamps.
See "pink backs" note after No. 425.

Earliest documented use: Feb. 24, 1915.

437 A148 15c **gray,** *Sept. 16, 1914* 135.00 7.25
dark gray 135.00 7.25
Never hinged 280.00
On cover 52.50
Block of 4 575.00 70.00
P# block of 6, Impt. & "A" 1,050.
Never hinged 1,700.
P# block of 6, "A" 1,225.
Never hinged 1,950.
P# block of 6 1,125.
Never hinged 1,800.

Earliest documented use: Sept. 21, 1915.

438 A148 20c **ultramarine,** *Sept. 19, 1914* 220.00 6.00
dark ultramarine 220.00 6.00
Never hinged 450.00
On cover *150.00*
Block of 4 900.00 45.00
P# block of 6 3,250.
Never hinged *5,250.*

Earliest documented use: Nov. 28, 1914.

439 A148 30c **orange red,** *Sept. 19, 1914* 260.00 16.00
dark orange red 260.00 16.00
Never hinged 550.00
On cover *250.00*
Block of 4 1,050. 135.00
P# block of 6 *4,100.*
Never hinged *6,500.*

Earliest documented use: Feb. 13, 1915.

440 A148 50c **violet,** *Dec. 10, 1915* 575.00 16.00
Never hinged 1,250.
On cover *1,750.*
Block of 4 2,250. 120.00
P# block of 6 *15,000.*
Never hinged —
Nos. 424-440 (16) 1,607. 83.65

COIL STAMPS

1914 *Perf. 10 Horizontally*

441 A140 1c **green,** *Nov. 14, 1914* 1.00 1.00
deep green 1.00 1.00
Never hinged 1.90
On cover 2.25
Pair 2.75 4.00
Never hinged 5.50
Guide line pair 8.00 *11.00*
Never hinged 16.00

442 A140 2c **carmine,** type I, *July 22, 1914* 10.00 6.00
deep carmine 10.00 6.00
Never hinged 19.00
On cover 15.00
Pair 25.00 25.00
Never hinged 50.00
Guide line pair 60.00 *100.00*
Never hinged 125.00

1914 *Perf. 10 Vertically*

443 A140 1c **green,** *May 29, 1914* 25.00 7.50
deep green 25.00 7.50
Never hinged 47.50
On cover 15.00
Pair 75.00 20.00
Never hinged 150.00
Guide line pair 155.00 90.00
Never hinged 310.00

Earliest documented use: June. 19, 1914.

444 A140 2c **carmine,** type I, *Apr. 25, 1914* 40.00 3.00
deep carmine 40.00 3.00
red 40.00 3.00
Never hinged 80.00
On cover 12.50
Pair 120.00 6.50
Never hinged 240.00
Guide line pair 300.00 50.00
Never hinged 650.00
a. 2c **lake** *1,250.*

Earliest documented use: May 20, 1914.

445 A140 3c **violet,** type I, *Dec. 18, 1914* 225.00 125.00
deep violet 225.00 125.00
Never hinged 450.00
On cover *225.00*
Pair 575.00 *650.00*
Never hinged 1,150.
Guide line pair 1,300. *2,500.*
Never hinged 2,700.

Earliest documented use: August 13, 1915.

446 A140 4c **brown,** *Oct. 2, 1914* 125.00 50.00
Never hinged 250.00

On cover 115.00
Pair 325.00 325.00
Never hinged 650.00
Guide line pair 750.00 *900.00*
Never hinged 1,550.

Earliest documented use: Aug. 4, 1915.

447 A140 5c **blue,** *July 30, 1914* 47.50 27.50
Never hinged 85.00
On cover 57.50
Pair 115.00 *300.00*
Never hinged 230.00
Guide line pair 260.00 *800.00*
Never hinged 525.00

Earliest documented use: May 9, 1916.

ROTARY PRESS STAMPS

The Rotary Press Stamps are printed from plates that are curved to fit around a cylinder. This curvature produces stamps that are slightly larger, either horizontally or vertically, than those printed from flat plates. Designs of stamps from flat plates measure about 18½-19mm wide by 22mm high.

When the impressions are placed sidewise on the curved plates the designs are 19½-20mm wide; when they are placed vertically the designs are 22½ to 23mm high. A line of color (not a guide line) shows where the curved plates meet or join on the press.

Rotary Press Coil Stamps were printed from plates of 170 subjects for stamps coiled sidewise, and from plates of 150 subjects for stamps coiled endwise.

Double paper varieties of Rotary Press stamps are not listed in this catalogue. Collectors are referred to the note on "Rotary Press Double Paper" in the "Information for Collectors" in the front of the catalogue.

ROTARY PRESS COIL STAMPS

Stamp designs: 18½-19x22½mm

1915 ***Perf. 10 Horizontally***

448 A140 1c **green,** *Dec. 12, 1915* 6.00 4.00
light green 6.00 4.00
Never hinged 11.50
On cover 8.50
Pair 15.00 12.50
Never hinged 30.00
Joint line pair 45.00 35.00
Never hinged 90.00

Earliest documented use: Mar. 29, 1916.

TYPE II

TWO CENTS.
Type II. Shading lines in ribbons as on type I.
The toga button, rope and rope shading lines are heavy.
The shading lines of the face at the lock of hair end in a strong vertical curved line.
Used on rotary press printings only.

TYPE III

Type III. Two lines of shading in the curves of the ribbons.
Other characteristics similar to type II.
Used on rotary press printings only.

449 A140 2c **red,** type I, *1915* 2,600. 600.00
Never hinged 5,250.
carmine rose, type I —
On cover, type I 1,350.
Pair, type I 6,500. *5,000.*
Never hinged *13,500.*
Joint line pair, type I *15,000.* *11,000.*
Never hinged *30,000.*

Earliest documented uses: Oct. 29, 1915 (on cover front or dated cancel on off-cover stamp); Nov. 4, 1915 (on cover).

450 A140 2c **carmine,** type III, *1915* 10.00 5.00
carmine rose, type III 10.00 5.00
red, type III 10.00 5.00
Never hinged 19.00
On cover, type III 10.00
Pair, type III 25.00 17.50
Never hinged 50.00
Joint line pair, type III 100.00 85.00
Never hinged 200.00

Earliest documented use: Dec. 21, 1915.

1914-16 ***Perf. 10 Vertically***

Stamp designs: 19½-20x22mm

452 A140 1c **green,** *Nov. 11, 1914* 10.00 3.00
Never hinged 19.00
On cover 4.00
Pair 25.00 9.00
Never hinged 50.00
Joint line pair 75.00 22.50
Never hinged 150.00

Earliest documented use: Nov. 25, 1914.

453 A140 2c **carmine rose,** type I, *July 3, 1914* 150.00 6.00
Never hinged 290.00
On cover, type I 11.00
Pair, type I 325.00 20.00
Never hinged 675.00
Joint line pair, type I 725.00 250.00
Never hinged 1,550.
Cracked plate, type I — —

Earliest documented use: Sept. 26, 1914.

454 A140 2c **red,** type II, *June, 1915* 82.50 10.00
carmine, type II 82.50 10.00
Never hinged 160.00
On cover, type II 37.50
Pair, type II 175.00 45.00
Never hinged 350.00
Joint line pair, type II 425.00 260.00
Never hinged 850.00

Earliest documented use: July 7, 1915.

455 A140 2c **carmine,** type III, *Dec. 1915* 8.50 1.00
carmine rose, type III 8.50 1.00
Never hinged 16.00
On cover, type III 2.25
Pair, type III 21.00 3.50
Never hinged 42.50
Joint line pair, type III 50.00 12.50
Never hinged 100.00

Earliest documented use: Dec. 15, 1915.

Fraudulently altered copies of Type III (Nos. 455, 488, 492 and 540) have had one line of shading scraped off to make them resemble Type II (Nos. 454, 487, 491 and 539).

456 A140 3c **violet,** type I, *Feb. 2, 1916* 240.00 95.00
deep violet 240.00 95.00
red violet 240.00 95.00
Never hinged 475.00
On cover 200.00
Pair 600.00 450.00
Never hinged 1,200.
Joint line pair 1,250. *1,400.*
Never hinged 2,500.

Earliest documented use: Apr. 13, 1916.

457 A140 4c **brown,** *1915* 25.00 17.50
light brown 25.00 17.50
Never hinged 47.50
On cover 42.50
Pair 60.00 60.00
Never hinged 120.00
Joint line pair 150.00 *175.00*
Never hinged 300.00
Cracked plate 35.00 —

Earliest documented use: Nov. 5, 1915.

458 A140 5c **blue,** *Mar. 9, 1916* 30.00 17.50
Never hinged 57.50
On cover 42.50
Pair 72.50 60.00
Never hinged 145.00
Joint line pair 180.00 175.00
Never hinged 360.00
Double transfer — —

Earliest documented use: Apr. 6, 1916.

Horizontal Coil

1914, June 30 ***Imperf.***

459 A140 2c **carmine,** type I 240. *1,100.*
Never hinged 350.
Pair 475. *3,500.*
Never hinged 750.
Joint line pair, with crease 1,000. *15,000.*
Never hinged 1,600.
Joint line pair, without crease 1,500. —
Never hinged 2,500.

Most line pairs of No. 459 are creased. The value for joint line pair with crease is for a pair creased vertically between the stamps, but not touching the design.

When the value for a used stamp is higher than the unused value, the stamp must have a contemporaneous cancel. Valuable stamps of this type should be accompanied by certificates of authenticity issued by recognized expertizing committees. The used value for No. 459 is for an example with such a certificate.

Earliest documented use: Dec. 1914 (dated cancel on a used joint line pair, off cover).

FLAT PLATE PRINTINGS

1915 **Wmk. 191** ***Perf. 10***

460 A148 $1 **violet black,** *Feb. 8* 850. 100.
Never hinged 1,850.
On cover *12,000.*
Block of 4 3,750. 550.
Margin block of 4, arrow, R or L 3,850.
P# block of 6, Impt. & "A" *12,000.*
Never hinged *19,000.*
Double transfer (5782 L. 66) 900. —

Earliest documented uses: May 25, 1916 (dated cancel on stamp on mailing tag); June 2, 1916 (unique usage on cover is from Shanghai, China).

Wmk. 190 ***Perf. 11***

461 A140 2c **pale car. red,** type I, *June 17* 150. *300.*
Never hinged 300.
On cover *1,200.*
Block of 4 625. *1,250.*
P# block of 6 *1,500.*
Never hinged *2,500.*

Beware of fraudulently perforated copies of #409 being offered as #461.

See note on used stamps following No. 459.

Earliest documented use: July 14, 1915.

VALUES FOR VERY FINE STAMPS

Please note: Stamps are valued in the grade of Very Fine unless otherwise indicated.

FLAT PLATE PRINTINGS

Plates of 400 subjects in four panes of 100 each for all values 1c to 50c inclusive.

Plates of 200 subjects in two panes of 100 each for $1, $2 and $5 denominations.

The Act of Oct. 3, 1917, effective Nov. 2, 1917, created a 3 cent rate. Local rate, 2 cents.

1916-17 **Unwmk.** ***Perf. 10***

462 A140 1c **green,** *Sept. 27, 1916* 7.00 .35
light green 7.00 .35
dark green 7.00 .35
bluish green 7.00 .35
Never hinged 13.00
On cover .50
Block of 4 30.00 3.25
P# block of 6 160.00
Never hinged 260.00
Experimental bureau precancel, New Orleans 10.00
Experimental bureau precancel, Springfield, Mass. 10.00
Experimental bureau precancel, Augusta, Me. 25.00
a. Booklet pane of 6, *Oct. 15, 1916* 9.50 *12.50*
Never hinged 15.00

463 A140 2c **carmine,** type I, *Sept. 1916* 4.50 .40
dark carmine 4.50 .40
rose red 4.50 .40
Never hinged 8.50
On cover .45
Block of 4 20.00 3.50
P# block of 6 130.00
Never hinged 210.00
Double transfer 6.50 —
Experimental bureau precancel, New Orleans *500.00*
Experimental bureau precancel, Springfield, Mass. 22.50
a. Booklet pane of 6, *Oct. 8, 1916* 95.00 *110.00*
Never hinged 165.00

See No. 467 for P# block of 6 from plate 7942.

Earliest documented uses: Sept. 12, 1916 (No. 463).

464 A140 3c **violet,** type I, *Nov. 11, 1916* 75.00 17.50
deep violet 75.00 17.50
Never hinged 160.00
On cover 42.50
Block of 4 325.00 150.00
P# block of 6 1,350.
Never hinged 2,200.
Double transfer in "CENTS" *90.00* —
Experimental bureau precancel, New Orleans *1,000.*
Experimental bureau precancel, Springfield, Mass. 200.00

Earliest documented use: Mar. 9, 1917.

465 A140 4c **orange brown,** *Oct. 7, 1916* 45.00 2.50
deep brown 45.00 2.50
brown 45.00 2.50
Never hinged 90.00
On cover 11.00
Block of 4 190.00 25.00
P# block of 6 650.00
Never hinged 1,075.
Double transfer — —
Experimental bureau precancel, Springfield, Mass. 175.00

466 A140 5c **blue,** *Oct. 17, 1916* 75.00 2.50
dark blue 75.00 2.50
Never hinged 150.00

On cover 13.00
Block of 4 310.00 22.50
P# block of 6 950.00
Never hinged 1,550.
Experimental bureau precancel, Springfield, Mass. 175.00

467 A140 5c **carmine** (error in plate of 2c) 550.00 *750.00*
Never hinged 1,100.
On cover *5,000.*
Block of 9, #467 in middle 950.00 *1,450.*
Never hinged 1,650.
Block of 12, two middle stamps #467 1,800. *3,000.*
Never hinged 3,250.
P# block of 6 2c stamps (#463), P#7942 140.00
Never hinged 250.00

No. 467 is an error caused by using a 5c transfer roll in re-entering three subjects: 7942 UL 74, 7942 UL 84, 7942 LR 18; the balance of the subjects on the plate being normal 2c entries. No. 467 imperf. is listed as No. 485. The error perf 11 on unwatermarked paper is No. 505.

The first value given for the error in blocks of 9 and 12 is for blocks with the error stamp(s) never hinged. The second value given is for blocks in which all stamps are never hinged. See note on used stamps following No. 459.

Earliest documented use: May 22, 1917.

468 A140 6c **red orange,** *Oct. 10, 1916* 95.00 9.00
Never hinged 200.00
On cover 37.50
Block of 4 400.00 70.00
P# block of 6 1,350.
Never hinged 2,250.
Double transfer — —
Experimental bureau precancel, New Orleans *2,500.*
Experimental bureau precancel, Springfield, Mass. 175.00

469 A140 7c **black,** *Oct. 10, 1916* 130.00 15.00
gray black 130.00 15.00
Never hinged 275.00
On cover 45.00
Block of 4 550.00 125.00
P# block of 6 1,350.
Never hinged 2,250.
Experimental bureau precancel, Springfield, Mass. 175.00

Earliest documented use: Feb. 19, 1917.

470 A148 8c **olive green,** *Nov. 13, 1916* 60.00 8.00
dark olive green 60.00 8.00
Never hinged 120.00
On cover 27.50
Block of 4 250.00 65.00
P# block of 6, Impt. & "A" 550.00
Never hinged 900.00
P# block of 6, "A" 600.00
Never hinged 1,000.
Experimental bureau precancel, Springfield, Mass. 165.00

Earliest documented use: Oct. 17, 1917.

471 A148 9c **salmon red,** *Nov. 16, 1916* 60.00 18.50
Never hinged 125.00
On cover 42.50
Block of 4 250.00 135.00
P# block of 6 750.00
Never hinged 1,250.
Experimental bureau precancel, Springfield, Mass. 150.00

472 A148 10c **orange yellow,** *Oct. 17, 1916* 110.00 2.50
Never hinged 225.00
On cover 8.50
Block of 4 460.00 16.50
P# block of 6 1,350.
Never hinged 2,200.
Experimental bureau precancel, Springfield, Mass. 160.00

Earliest documented use: Oct. 24, 1916.

473 A148 11c **dark green,** *Nov. 16, 1916* 40.00 18.50
Never hinged 80.00
On cover 47.50
Block of 4 175.00 140.00
P# block of 6 360.00
Never hinged 600.00
Experimental bureau precancel, Springfield, Mass. *575.00*

Earliest documented use: Apr. 13, 1917.

474 A148 12c **claret brown,** *Oct. 1916* 55.00 7.50
Never hinged 105.00
On cover 22.50
Block of 4 230.00 55.00
P# block of 6 625.00
Never hinged 1,025.
Double transfer 65.00 8.50
Triple transfer 77.50 11.00
Experimental bureau precancel, Springfield, Mass. 200.00

Earliest documented uses: Oct. 6, 1916 (dated cancel on off-cover pair); Oct. 13, 1916 (on cover).

475 A148 15c **gray,** *Nov. 16, 1916* 200.00 16.00
dark gray 200.00 16.00
Never hinged 400.00
On cover 87.50
Block of 4 850.00 125.00
P# block of 6 3,000.
Never hinged 5,000.
P# block of 6, Impt. & "A" —
Experimental bureau precancel, Springfield, Mass. 150.00

Earliest documented use: Mar. 2, 1917.

476 A148 20c **light ultramarine,** *Dec. 5, 1916* 250.00 17.50
ultramarine 250.00 17.50
Never hinged 500.00
On cover *725.00*
Block of 4 1,050. 135.00
P# block of 6 3,600.
Never hinged *5,900.*
Experimental bureau precancel, Springfield, Mass. 125.00

476A A148 30c **orange red** *3,450.*
Never hinged *5,750.*
Block of 4 *15,500.*
P# block of 6, never hinged *40,000.*

No. 476A is valued in the grade of fine.

477 A148 50c **light violet,** *Mar. 2, 1917* 1,100. 80.00
Never hinged 2,350.
On cover *2,250.*
Block of 4 4,750. 575.00
P# block of 6 *57,500.*

Earliest documented use: Aug. 31, 1917.

478 A148 $1 **violet black,** *Dec. 22, 1916* 800.00 25.00
Never hinged 1,700.
On cover *3,000.*
Block of 4 3,500. 175.00
Margin block of 4, arrow, R or L 3,650.
P# block of 6, Impt. & "A" *13,000.*
Never hinged *21,000.*
Double transfer (5782 L 66) 825.00 32.50

Earliest documented use: June 26, 1917 (dated cancel on off-cover stamp); Aug. 31, 1917 (on piece).

TYPES OF 1902-03 ISSUE

1917, Mar. 22 Unwmk. *Perf. 10*

479 A127 $2 **dark blue** 275.00 42.50
Never hinged 550.00
On cover (other than first flight or Zeppelin) *1,250.*
On first flight cover *350.00*
On Zeppelin flight cover *750.00*
Block of 4 1,150. 325.00
Margin block of 4, arrow, R or L 1,300.
P# block of 6 *4,000.*
Never hinged *6,500.*
Double transfer —

Earliest documented use (on large piece of reg'd parcel wrapper): Apr. 6, 1917.

480 A128 $5 **light green** 225.00 40.00
Never hinged 450.00
On cover *1,250.*
Block of 4 950.00 300.00
Margin block of 4, arrow, R or L 1,050.
P# block of 6 3,100. —
Never hinged *5,000.*

Earliest documented use: Apr. 6, 1917 (on large piece of reg'd parcel wrapper).

1916-17 *Imperf.*

481 A140 1c **green,** *Nov. 1916* 1.00 .65
bluish green 1.00 .65
deep green 1.00 .65
Never hinged 1.90
On cover 1.50
Pair 2.10 1.60
Never hinged 3.90
Block of 4 4.20 3.50
Corner margin block of 4 4.40 5.50
Margin block of 4, arrow 4.50 3.75
Center line block 8.50 6.75
P# block of 6 13.00 —
Never hinged 22.00
Margin block of 6, Electrolytic (Pl. 13376) 375.00
Never hinged 650.00
Margin block of 6, Electrolytic (Pl. 13377) 525.00
Never hinged 800.00
Double transfer 2.50 1.50

Earliest documented use: Nov. 17, 1916.

During September, 1921, the Bureau of Engraving and Printing issued a 1c stamp printed from experimental electrolytic plates made in accordance with patent granted to George U. Rose. Tests at that time did not prove satisfactory and the method was discontinued. Four plates were made, viz., 13376, 13377, 13389 and 13390 from which stamps were issued. They are difficult to distinguish from the normal varieties. (See No. 498).

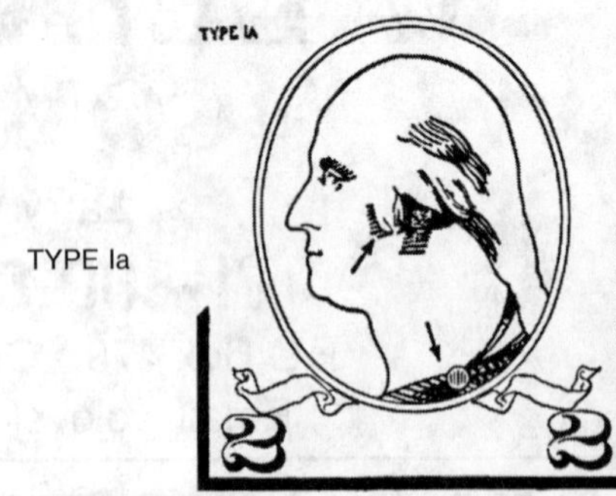

TYPE Ia

TWO CENTS

Type Ia. The design characteristics are similar to type I except that all of the lines of the design are stronger.

The toga button, toga rope and rope and rope shading lines are heavy.

The latter characteristics are those of type II, which, however, occur only on impressions from rotary plates.

Used only on flat plates 10208 and 10209.

482 A140 2c **carmine,** type I, *Dec. 8, 1916* 1.40 1.25
deep carmine 1.40 1.25
carmine rose 1.40 1.25
deep rose 1.40 1.25
Never hinged 2.60
On cover 2.50
Pair 2.90 2.75
Never hinged 5.50
Block of 4 5.80 6.50
Corner margin block of 4 6.00 5.75
Margin block of 4, arrow 6.25 6.00
Center line block 8.50 8.00
P# block of 6 22.50 —
Never hinged 37.50
Cracked plate — —

Earliest documented use: Dec. 16, 1916.

See No. 485 for P# block of 6 from plate 7942.

482A A140 2c **deep rose,** type Ia *50,000.*
On cover *55,000.*
Pair *105,000.*

Earliest documented use: Feb. 17, 1920.

The imperforate, type Ia, was issued but all known copies were privately perforated with large oblong perforations at the sides (Schermack type III).

The No. 482A pair is unique. Value reflects 1998 auction sale price.

No. 500 exists with imperforate top sheet margin. Copies have been altered by trimming perforations. Some also have faked Schermack perfs.

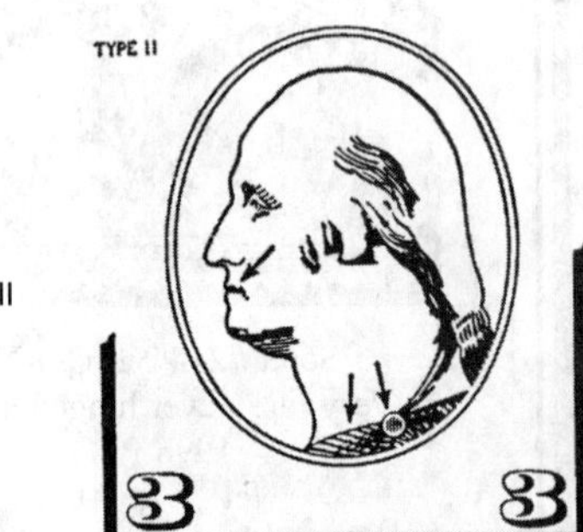

TYPE II

THREE CENTS

Type II. The top line of the toga rope is strong and the rope shading lines are heavy and complete.

The line between the lips is heavy.

Used on both flat plate and rotary press printings.

483 A140 3c **violet,** type I, *Oct. 13, 1917* 13.00 7.50
light violet 13.00 7.50
Never hinged 24.00
On cover 20.00
Pair 27.50 17.50
Never hinged 52.50
Block of 4 55.00 40.00
Corner margin block of 4 57.50 *42.50*
Margin block of 4, arrow 60.00 *42.50*
Center line block 75.00 *70.00*
P# block of 6 115.00 —
Never hinged 190.00
Double transfer 17.50 —
Triple transfer —

Earliest documented use: Nov. 2, 1917.

484 A140 3c **violet,** type II 10.00 5.00
deep violet 10.00 5.00
Never hinged 19.00
On cover 11.50
Pair 21.00 13.50
Never hinged 40.00
Block of 4 42.50 32.50
Corner margin block of 4 45.00 *35.00*
Margin block of 4, arrow 47.50 *35.00*
Center line block 67.50 *60.00*
P# block of 6 87.50 —
Never hinged 145.00
Double transfer 12.50 —

Earliest documented use: Apr. 5, 1918.

485 A140 5c **carmine** (error), *Mar. 1917* *12,000.*
Never hinged *20,000.*
Block of 9, #485 in middle *22,500.*
Never hinged *32,500.*
Block of 12, two middle stamps #485 *42,500.*
Never hinged *52,500.*
P# block of six 2c stamps (#482), P#7942 130.00
Never hinged 210.00

No. 485 is usually seen either as the center stamp in a block of 9 with 8 No. 482 (the first value given being with No. 485 never hinged) or as two center stamps in a block of 12 (the first value given being with both examples of No. 485 never hinged). A second value is given for each block with all stamps in the block never hinged.

See note under No. 467.

JOIN THE PRECANCEL STAMP SOCIETY

Jim Hirstein, Secretary, P.O. Box 4072, Missoula, MT 59806

TRY SOMETHING DIFFERENT •••••••••••••••• COLLECT PRECANCELS

Precancel Catalogs Now Available:

Town and Type Catalog	$25.00
Bureau Catalog	$10.00
Double Line Electros	$15.00
Style Chart Album	$3.00
City Type Coils	$7.00
Silent Precancels	$20.00
Precancelled Envelopes of the U.S.	$20.00
13 cent Apple Greens	$4.00
Style Chart	$4.50

The Town and Type computer program for Windows PC's, an online companion to the printed catalog. Track your inventory with all 20,000 towns and 42,000 types with this CD for only $39.00.

The new Bureau computer program for Windows PC's is now available for only $19.00. Track your buro inventory and value via this new tool.

All prices include postage via media mail rate. Sorry, no credit card orders. Send orders to:

PRECANCEL STAMP SOCIETY CATALOGS
3 SHADY CREEK LANE
SCARBOROUGH, ME. 04074
Ph. 207-883-2505

VISIT OUR SITE: WWW.PRECANCELS.COM

AND FIND OUT MORE ABOUT THE PRECANCEL STAMP SOCIETY AND THESE

Local Precancel Clubs:

Arizona Precancel Club
Eastern Pennsylvania Precancel Society
Florida Precancel Club
Golden Gate Precancel Society
Illini Precancel Stamp Club
Kentucky Precancel Society
Missouri Precancel Club
New England Precancel Club
Ohio Precancel Club
Southern California Precancel Club
Texas Precancel Club

Canceled equals Precanceled?...

Catalogue Value ~~15¢~~ $150

Catalogue Value ~~15¢~~ $300

Catalogue Value ~~$16.00~~ $500

Catalogue Value ~~15¢~~ $1500

...Obviously Not!!!

Are you missing out on gems like these? Bureau precancels were introduced late in 1916 to reduce the costs of local precanceling. These "experimentals" were used in three cities. In 1923 bureau precancels became part of the printing process done at the Bureau of Engraving and Printing in Washington, DC. There are now over 9,500 bureaus, including those pictured above, listed and priced in the Bureau Precancel Catalog and in the companion computer program. But if 9,500 varieties aren't enough, you can also collect the 42,000 locally printed types! These are listed in the Town and Type catalog and in its companion computer program.

ROTARY PRESS COIL STAMPS
(See note over No. 448)

1916-19 ***Perf. 10 Horizontally***

Stamp designs: 18½-19x22½mm

486 A140 1c **green,** *Jan. 1918* .90 .40
yellowish green .90 .40
Never hinged 1.70
On cover .65
Pair 2.10 1.00
Never hinged 4.25 1.00
Joint line pair 4.75 2.00
Never hinged 9.50
Cracked plate — —
Double transfer 2.25 —

Earliest documented use: June 30, 1918.

487 A140 2c **carmine,** type II, *Nov. 15, 1916* 13.50 5.00
Never hinged 26.00
On cover 10.00
Pair 30.00 12.50
Never hinged 60.00
Joint line pair 105.00 32.50
Never hinged 210.00
Cracked plate —

Earliest documented use: Sept. 21, 1917.

(See note after No. 455)

488 A140 2c **carmine,** type III, *1916* 2.50 1.75
carmine rose 2.50 1.75
Never hinged 4.75
On cover 3.50
Pair 5.75 5.00
Never hinged 11.50
Joint line pair 20.00 20.00
Never hinged 40.00
Cracked plate 12.00 7.50

Earliest documented use: Apr. 25, 1917.

489 A140 3c **violet,** type I, *Oct. 10, 1917* 5.00 1.50
dull violet 5.00 1.50
bluish violet 5.00 1.50
Never hinged 9.50
On cover 2.50
Pair 11.00 5.00
Never hinged 22.00
Joint line pair 32.50 16.00
Never hinged 65.00

Rosette plate crack on head

1916-22 ***Perf. 10 Vertically***

Stamp designs: 19½-20x22mm

490 A140 1c **green,** *Nov. 17, 1916* .55 .25
yellowish green .55 .25
Never hinged 1.05
On cover .40
Pair 1.30 1.00
Never hinged 2.60
Joint line pair 3.50 1.75
Never hinged 7.00
Double transfer — —
Cracked plate (horizontal) 7.50 —
Cracked plate (vertical) retouched 9.00 —
Rosette plate crack on head *60.00* —

Earliest documented use: Jan. 3, 1917 (dated cancel on off-cover pair).

491 A140 2c **carmine,** type II, *Nov. 17, 1916* 2,200. 750.00
Never hinged 4,250.
On cover, type II 725.00
Pair, type II 5,250. 3,750.
Never hinged *10,500.*
Joint line pair, type II *12,000.* *12,000.*
Never hinged *22,500.*

Earliest documented use: Jan. 2, 1917.

See note after No. 455.

492 A140 2c **carmine,** type III 9.50 .40
carmine rose, type III 9.50 .40
Never hinged 18.00
On cover, type III .55
Pair, type III 22.50 1.40
Never hinged 45.00
Joint line pair, type III 55.00 20.00
Never hinged 110.00
Double transfer, type III — —
Cracked plate — —

493 A140 3c **violet,** type I, *July 23, 1917* 16.00 3.50
reddish violet, type I 16.00 3.50
Never hinged 30.00
On cover, type I 7.50
Pair, type I 35.00 10.00
Never hinged 70.00
Joint line pair, type I 110.00 60.00
Never hinged 220.00

Earliest documented use: Nov. 2 1917.

494 A140 3c **violet,** type II, *Feb. 4, 1918* 10.00 1.10
dull violet, type II 10.00 1.10
gray violet, type II 10.00 1.10
Never hinged 19.00
On cover, type II 1.25
Pair, type II 24.00 3.50
Never hinged 48.00
Joint line pair, type II 75.00 9.00
Never hinged 150.00

Earliest documented use: Apr. 16, 1918.

495 A140 4c **orange brown,** *Apr. 15, 1917* 10.00 4.00
Never hinged 19.00
On cover 8.50
Pair 24.00 15.00
Never hinged 48.00
Joint line pair 75.00 27.50
Never hinged 150.00
Cracked plate 25.00 —

Earliest documented use: June 20, 1917.

496 A140 5c **blue,** *Jan. 15, 1919* 3.50 1.25
Never hinged 6.75
On cover 1.75
Pair 8.25 4.00
Never hinged 16.50
Joint line pair 30.00 12.50
Never hinged 60.00

Earliest documented use: Sept. 11, 1919.

497 A148 10c **orange yellow,** *Jan. 31, 1922* 20.00 11.00
Never hinged 38.00
On cover 17.00
Pair 47.50 *50.00*
Never hinged 95.00
Joint line pair 140.00 140.00
Never hinged 280.00

Earliest documented use: Jan. 31, 1922 (FDC).

Blind Perfs

Listings of imperforate-between varieties are for examples which show no trace of "blind perfs," traces of impressions from the perforating pins which do not cut into the paper.

Some unused stamps have had the gum removed to eliminate the impressions from the perforating pins. These copies do not qualify as the listed varieties.

FLAT PLATE PRINTINGS
Plates of 400 subjects in four panes of 100.
TYPES OF 1913-15 ISSUE

1917-19 **Unwmk.** ***Perf. 11***

498 A140 1c **green,** *Mar. 1917* .35 .25
light green .35 .25
dark green .35 .25
yellowish green .35 .25
Never hinged .60
On cover .30
Block of 4 1.40 1.50
P# block of 6 16.50
Never hinged 26.00
Margin block of 6, Electrolytic (Pl, 13376-7, 13389-90) *See note after No. 481* *550.00*
Cracked plate (10656 UL and 10645 LR) 7.50 —
Double transfer 5.50 2.00
a. Vertical pair, imperf. horiz. 600.00
Never hinged *1,200.*
b. Horizontal pair, imperf. between 325.00
Never hinged *650.00*
c. Vertical pair, imperf. between *450.00* —
d. Double impression 250.00 *2,500.*
e. Booklet pane of 6, *Apr. 6, 1917* 2.50 2.00
Never hinged 4.00
f. Booklet pane of 30, *Aug. 1917* *1,000.*
Never hinged *1,600.*
g. Perf. 10 at top or bottom *5,000* —
Never hinged *7,500.*

Earliest documented use: Aug. 8, 1917 (No. 498f single).
See No. 505 for P# block of 6 from plate 7942.

499 A140 2c **rose,** type I, *Mar. 1917* .35 .25
dark rose, type I .35 .25
carmine rose, type I .35 .25
deep rose, type I .35 .25
Never hinged .60
On cover, type I .30
Block of 4, type I 1.40 1.50
P# block of 6, type I 16.50
Never hinged 26.00
Double impression, type I, 15mm wide —
Cracked plate, type I — —
Recut in hair, type I *1,500.* *2,300.*
Double transfer, type I 6.00 —
a. Vertical pair, imperf. horiz., type I 175.00
Never hinged 350.00
b. Horiz. pair, imperf. vert., type I *300.00* *225.00*
Never hinged *600.00*
c. Vert. pair, imperf. btwn., type I *850.00* *225.00*
e. Booklet pane of 6, type I, *Mar. 31, 1917* 4.00 *2.50*
Never hinged 6.50
f. Booklet pane of 30, type I, *Aug. 1917* *28,000.* —
Never hinged *38,000.*
g. Double impression, type I 175.00 —
On cover *750.00*
h. 2c **lake,** type I 400.00 250.00
Never hinged *800.00*
On cover —

No. 499b is valued in the grade of fine.
Earliest documented uses: Mar. 27, 1917 (No. 499); July 19, 1917 (No. 499e single); Aug. 7, 1917 (No. 499f single).

500 A140 2c **deep rose,** type Ia 275.00 240.00
Never hinged 575.00
On cover, type Ia *650.00*
Block of 4, type Ia 1,150. *1,500.*
P# block of 6, type Ia 2,100.
Never hinged 3,750.
P# block of 6, two stamps type I (P# 10208 LL) *12,500.*
Never hinged *17,500.*
Pair, types I and Ia (10208 LL 95 or 96) *1,275.*

Earliest documented use: Dec. 15, 1919.

501 A140 3c **light violet,** type I, *Mar. 1917* 11.00 .40
violet, type I 11.00 .40
dark violet, type I 11.00 .40
reddish violet, type I 11.00 .40
Never hinged 22.50
On cover, type I .50
Block of 4, type I 45.00 4.00
P# block of 6, type I 125.00
Never hinged 210.00
Double transfer, type I 12.00
b. Bklt. pane of 6, type I, *Oct. 17, 1917* 75.00 *60.00*
Never hinged 120.00
c. Vert. pair, imper. horiz., type I *1,250.*
d. Double impression *2,750.* *2,750.*
Never hinged *5,000.*

Earliest documented uses: June 5, 1917 (No. 501); Feb. 18, 1918 (No. 501b single).

502 A140 3c **dark violet,** type II 14.00 .75
violet, type II 14.00 .75
Never hinged 30.00
On cover, type II 1.00
Block of 4, type II 57.50 5.50
P# block of 6, type II 140.00
Never hinged 240.00
b. Bklt. pane of 6, type II, *Feb. 25, 1918* 60.00 *55.00*
Never hinged 95.00
c. Vert. pair, imperf. horiz., type II *500.00* —
Never hinged *900.00*
On cover *1,500.*
d. Double impression 625.00 300.00
Never hinged 1,250.
e. Perf. 10 at top or bottom *9,500.* *6,000.*
Never hinged *13,500.*

Earliest documented uses: Jan. 30, 1918 (No. 502); June 12, 1918 (No. 502b single).

503 A140 4c **brown,** *Mar. 1917* 10.00 .40
dark brown 10.00 .40
orange brown 10.00 .40
yellow brown 10.00 .40
Never hinged 20.00
On cover 2.10
Block of 4 40.00 3.50
P# block of 6 130.00
Never hinged 220.00
Double transfer 15.00 —
b. Double impression —

504 A140 5c **blue,** *Mar. 1917* 9.00 .35
light blue 9.00 .35
dark blue 9.00 .35
Never hinged 18.00
On cover .45
Block of 4 37.50 3.00
P# block of 6 125.00
Never hinged 210.00
Double transfer 11.00 —
a. Horizontal pair, imperf. between *2,750.* —
b. Double impression *900.00*

Earliest documented use: June 9, 1917.

505 A140 5c **rose** (error) 350.00 *550.00*
Never hinged 625.00
On cover 2,250.
Block of 9, middle stamp #505 675.00 *1,000.*
Never hinged 1,100.
Block of 12, two middle stamps #505 1,300. *1,750.*
Never hinged 2,200.
Margin block of six 2c stamps (#499), P# 7942 25.00
Never hinged 40.00

Earliest documented use: Mar. 27, 1917.

Value notes under No. 467 also apply to No. 505.

506 A140 6c **red orange,** *Mar. 1917* 12.50 .40
orange 12.50 .40
Never hinged 25.00
On cover 2.50
Block of 4 52.50 4.00
P# block of 6 170.00
Never hinged 285.00
Double transfer — —
a. Perf. 10 at top or bottom *3,500.* *3,250.*

507 A140 7c **black,** *Mar. 1917* 27.50 1.25
gray black 27.50 1.25
intense black 27.50 1.25
Never hinged 55.00
On cover 7.75
Block of 4 115.00 12.50
P# block of 6 250.00
Never hinged 420.00
Double transfer —
a. Perf. 10 at top *7,500.*

508 A148 8c **olive bister,** *Mar. 1917* 12.00 .65
dark olive green 12.00 .65
olive green 12.00 .65
Never hinged 24.00
On cover 2.75
Block of 4 50.00 6.50
P# block of 6, Impt. & "A" 170.00
Never hinged 285.00

	P# block of 6, "A"	220.00	
	Never hinged	370.00	
	P# block of 6	140.00	
	Never hinged	235.00	
b.	Vertical pair, imperf. between	—	—
c.	Perf. 10 at top or bottom		*4,500.*
509 A148 9c	**salmon red,** *Mar. 1917*	14.00	1.75
	salmon	14.00	1.75
	Never hinged	28.00	
	On cover		13.00
	Block of 4	57.50	19.00
	P# block of 6	140.00	
	Never hinged	230.00	
	Double transfer	20.00	4.50
a.	Perf. 10 at top or bottom	*4,000.*	*6,000.*
	Never hinged	*6,500.*	

No. 509a also exists as a transitional stamp gauging partly perf 10 and partly perf 11 at top or bottom. Value thus the same as normal 509a.

510 A148 10c	**orange yellow,** *Mar. 1917*	17.50	.25
	golden yellow	17.50	.25
	Never hinged	35.00	
	On cover		2.00
	Block of 4	70.00	2.00
	P# block of 6, "A"	290.00	
	Never hinged	475.00	
	P# block of 6	180.00	
	Never hinged	300.00	
a.	10c **brown yellow**	*900.00*	
	Never hinged	*1,600.*	

Earliest documented use: Mar. 27, 1917.

511 A148 11c	**light green,** *May 1917*	9.00	2.50
	green	9.00	2.50
	Never hinged	18.00	
	dark green	10.00	2.50
	Never hinged	20.00	
	On cover		8.50
	Block of 4	37.50	22.50
	P# block of 6	125.00	
	Never hinged	210.00	
	Double transfer	12.50	3.25
a.	Perf. 10 at top or bottom	*4,000.*	*2,750.*
	Never hinged	*6,000.*	

No. 511a also exists as a transitional stamp gauging partly perf 10 and partly perf 11 at top or bottom. Value thus the same as normal 511a.

512 A148 12c	**claret brown,** *May 1917*	9.00	.40
	Never hinged	18.00	
	On cover		4.00
	Block of 4	37.50	3.75
	P# block of 6	125.00	
	Never hinged	210.00	
	Double transfer	12.50	—
	Triple transfer	20.00	—
a.	12c **brown carmine**	10.00	.50
	Never hinged	20.00	
	On cover		4.50
	Block of 4	40.00	4.50
	P# block of 6	130.00	
	Never hinged	215.00	
b.	Perf. 10 at top or bottom	—	*3,250.*

Earliest documented use: Oct. 13, 1917.

513 A148 13c	**apple green,** *Jan. 10, 1919*	11.00	6.00
	pale apple green	11.00	6.00
	Never hinged	22.00	
	deep apple green	12.50	6.50
	Never hinged	25.00	
	On cover		19.00
	Block of 4	45.00	45.00
	P# block of 6	125.00	
	Never hinged	200.00	

Earliest documented use: Feb. 4, 1919.

514 A148 15c	**gray,** *May 1917*	37.50	1.50
	dark gray	37.50	1.50
	Never hinged	75.00	
	On cover		25.00
	Block of 4	160.00	12.50
	P# block of 6	550.00	—
	Never hinged	900.00	
	Double transfer	—	—
a.	Perf. 10 at bottom		*7,500.*

Earliest documented use: Nov. 15, 1917.

515 A148 20c	**light ultramarine,** *May 1917*	45.00	.45
	gray blue	45.00	.45
	Never hinged	90.00	
	deep ultramarine	50.00	.55
	Never hinged	100.00	
	On cover		75.00
	Block of 4	200.00	3.50
	P# block of 6	600.00	
	Never hinged	975.00	
	Double transfer	—	—
b.	Vertical pair, imperf. between	*1,500.*	*1,750.*
c.	Double impression	*1,250.*	
d.	Perf. 10 at top or bottom	—	*10,000.*

No. 515b is valued in the grade of fine.

Beware of pairs with blind perforations inside the design of the top stamp that are offered as No. 515b.

Earliest documented use: May 4, 1918.

516 A148 30c	**orange red,** *May 1917*	37.50	1.50
	dark orange red	37.50	1.50
	Never hinged	75.00	
	On cover		150.00
	Block of 4	160.00	12.50
	P# block of 6	600.00	
	Never hinged	925.00	
	Double transfer	—	
a.	Perf. 10 at top or bottom	*5,000.*	*5,500.*
	Never hinged	*7,000.*	
b.	Double impression		—

Earliest documented use: Jan. 12, 1918.

517 A148 50c	**red violet,** *May 1917*	65.00	.75
	Never hinged	130.00	
	violet	75.00	.75
	Never hinged	150.00	
	light violet	80.00	.75
	Never hinged	160.00	
	On cover		*400.00*
	Block of 4	290.00	5.00
	P# block of 6	1,600.	
	Never hinged	2,550.	
	Double transfer	100.00	1.75
b.	Vertical pair, imperf. between & at bottom	—	*6,000.*
c.	Perf. 10 at top or bottom		*10,000.*

No. 517b is valued in average condition and may be a unique used pair. The editors would like to see authenticated evidence of an unused pair.

Earliest documented use: Dec. 28, 1917 (on registry tag).

518 A148 $1	**violet brown,** *May 1917*	50.00	1.50
	violet black	50.00	1.50
	Never hinged	100.00	
	On cover		*550.00*
	Block of 4	210.00	12.50
	Margin block of 4, arrow right or left	230.00	
	P# block of 6, Impt. & "A"	1,300.	—
	Never hinged	2,100.	
	Double transfer (5782 L. 66)	70.00	2.00
b.	$1 **deep brown**	*1,800.*	*1,050.*
	Never hinged	*3,000.*	
	Block of 4		*4,750.*

Earliest documented use: May 19, 1917.

No. 518b is valued in the grade of fine to very fine.

	Nos. 498-504,506-518 (20)	667.20	261.30

TYPE OF 1908-09 ISSUE

1917, Oct. 10 **Wmk. 191** ***Perf. 11***

This is the result of an old stock of No. 344 which was returned to the Bureau in 1917 and perforated with the then current gauge 11.

519 A139 2c	**carmine**	450.00	*1,200.*
	Never hinged	800.00	
	On cover		*2,400.*
	Block of 4	1,650.	—
	P# block of 6, T V, Impt.	2,700.	—
	Never hinged	*4,000.*	

Beware of copies of No. 344 fraudulently perforated and offered as No. 519. Obtaining a certificate from a recognized expertizing committee is strongly recommended.

Warning: See note following No. 459 regarding used stamps.

Earliest documented use: Oct. 10, 1917.

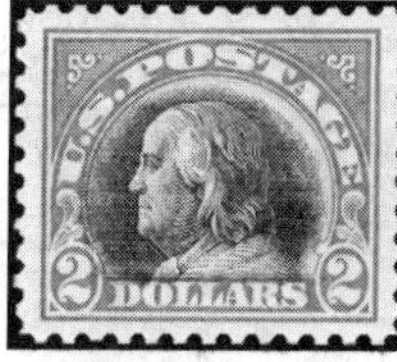

Franklin — A149

Plates of 100 subjects.

1918, Aug. **Unwmk.** ***Perf. 11***

523 A149 $2	**orange red & black**	600.	240.
	red orange & black	600.	240.
	Never hinged	1,250.	
	On cover		*2,000.*
	Block of 4	2,500.	1,300.
	Margin block of 4, arrow	2,600.	
	Center line block	2,850.	1,400.
	P# block of 8, 2# & arrow	*12,000.*	—
	Never hinged	*18,000.*	

Earliest documented use: Dec. 17, 1918.

524 A149 $5	**deep green & black**	200.	35.
	Never hinged	400.	
	On cover		*2,500.*
	Block of 4	875.	200.
	Margin block of 4, arrow	925.	210.
	Center line block	1,050.	225.
	P# block of 8, 2# & arrow	4,000.	
	Never hinged	*6,400.*	

Earliest documented use: Mar. 17, 1926 (on parcel tag). An Aug. 21, 1923, cover has been reported. The editors request information on its certification.

For other listing of design A149 see No. 547.

OFFSET PRINTING

Plates of 400, 800 or 1600 subjects in panes of 100 each, as follows:

No. 525- 400 and 1600 subjects
No. 526- 400, 800 and 1600 subjects
No. 529- 400 subjects
No. 531- 400 subjects
No. 532- 400, 800 and 1600 subjects
No. 535- 400 subjects
No. 536- 400 and 1600 subjects

TYPES OF 1917-19 ISSUE

1918-20 **Unwmk.** ***Perf. 11***

525 A140 1c	**gray green,** *Dec. 1918*	2.50	.90
	Never hinged	4.50	
	emerald	3.50	1.25
	Never hinged	6.25	
	On cover		1.75
	Block of 4	10.50	6.00
	P# block of 6	22.50	
	Never hinged	37.50	
	"Flat nose"	—	
a.	1c **dark green**	6.00	1.75
	Never hinged	11.00	
c.	Horizontal pair, imperf. between	100.00	
d.	Double impression	40.00	—
	Never hinged	80.00	

Earliest documented use: Dec. 24, 1918.

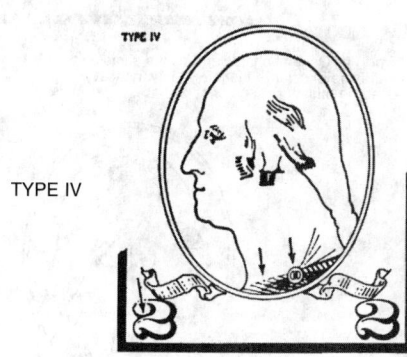

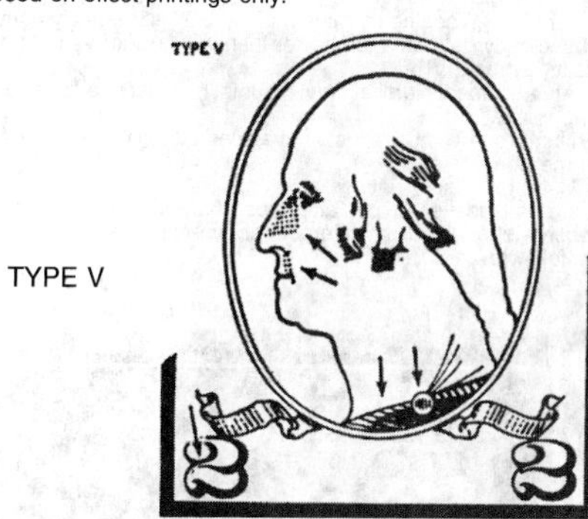

TYPE IV

TWO CENTS

Type IV - Top line of the toga rope is broken.

The shading lines in the toga button are so arranged that the curving of the first and last form "D (reversed) ID."

The line of color in the left "2" is very thin and usually broken.

Used on offset printings only.

TYPE V

Type V - Top line of the toga is complete.

There are five vertical shading lines in the toga button.

The line of color in the left "2" is very thin and usually broken.

The shading dots on the nose are as shown on the diagram.

Used on offset printings only.

TYPE Va

Type Va - Characteristics are the same as type V except in the shading dots of the nose. The third row of dots from the bottom has four dots instead of six. The overall height is ⅓mm shorter than type V.

Used on offset printings only.

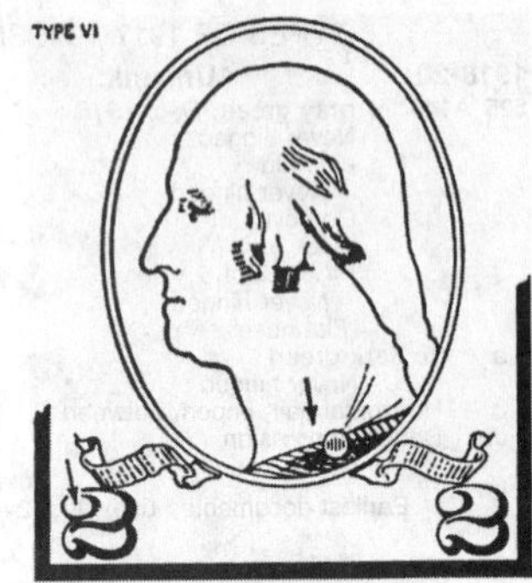

TYPE VI

Type VI - General characteristics the same as type V except that the line of color in the left "2" is very heavy.
Used on offset printings only.

TYPE VII

Type VII - The line of color in the left "2" is invariably continuous, clearly defined and heavier than in type V or Va but not as heavy as type VI.
An additional vertical row of dots has been added to the upper lip.
Numerous additional dots have been added to the hair on top of the head.
Used on offset printings only.
Dates of issue of types after type IV are not known but official records show the first plate of each type to have been certified as follows:

Type IV, Mar. 6, 1920
Type V, Mar. 20, 1920
Type Va, May 4, 1920
Type VI, June 24, 1920
Type VII, Nov. 3, 1920

526	A140 2c **carmine,** type IV, *1920*	27.50	4.00
	rose carmine, type IV	27.50	4.00
	Never hinged	50.00	
	On cover, type IV		11.00
	Block of 4, type IV	120.00	30.00
	P# block of 6, type IV	240.00	
	Never hinged	400.00	
	Gash on forehead, type IV	40.00	—
	Malformed "2" at left, type IV (10823 LR 93)	37.50	6.00

Earliest documented use: Mar. 15, 1920 (FDC).

527	A140 2c **carmine,** type V, *1920*	20.00	1.25
	bright carmine, type V	20.00	1.25
	rose carmine, type V	20.00	1.25
	Never hinged	36.00	
	On cover		2.75
	Block of 4, type V	85.00	10.00
	Block of 6, P# only, type V	165.00	
	Never hinged	275.00	
	Line through "2" & "EN," type V	30.00	—
a.	Double impression, type V	65.00	—
	Never hinged	130.00	
b.	Vert. pair, imperf. horiz., type V	*600.00*	
c.	Horiz. pair, imperf. vert., type V	*1,000.*	—

Earliest documented use: Apr. 20, 1920.

528	A140 2c **carmine,** type Va, *1920*	9.50	.40
	Never hinged	17.00	
	On cover, type Va		.75
	Block of 4, type Va	40.00	3.50
	Block of 6, P# only, type Va	82.50	
	Never hinged	130.00	
	Block of 6, monogram over P#	100.00	
	Never hinged	160.00	
	Retouches in "P" of Postage type Va	*52.50*	—
	Retouched on toga, type Va	—	—
	Variety C"R"NTS, type Va	*32.50*	
c.	Double impression, type Va	27.50	
g.	Vert. pair, imperf. between	*3,500.*	

Earliest documented use: June 18, 1920.

528A	A140 2c **carmine,** type VI, *1920*	52.50	2.00
	bright carmine, type VI	52.50	2.00
	Never hinged	110.00	
	On cover, type VI		3.75
	Block of 4, type VI	225.00	15.00
	P# block of 6, type VI	425.00	
	Never hinged	700.00	
	Block of 6, monogram over P#	525.00	
	Never hinged	850.00	
d.	Double impression, type VI	160.00	—
	Never hinged	290.00	
f.	Vert. pair, imperf. horiz., type VI	—	
h.	Vert. pair, imperf. between	*1,000.*	

Earliest documented use: July 30, 1920.

528B	A140 2c **carmine,** type VII, *1920*	22.50	.75
	Never hinged	40.00	
	On cover, type VII		1.00
	Block of 4, type VII	95.00	6.00
	P# block of 6, type VII	175.00	
	Never hinged	300.00	
	Retouched on cheek, type VII	400.00	—
e.	Double impression, type VII	70.00	

Earliest documented use: Nov. 10, 1920.

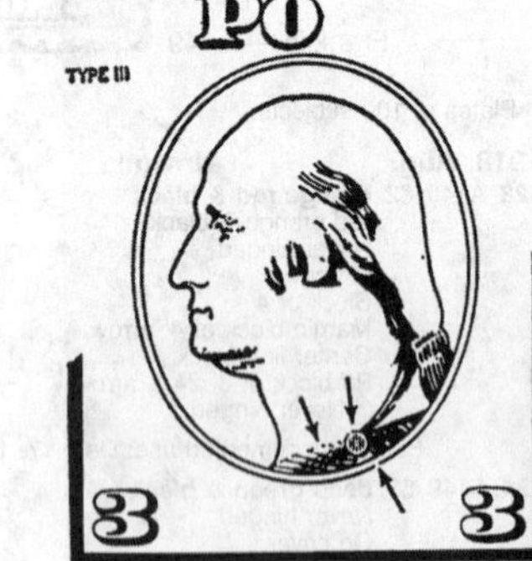

TYPE III

THREE CENTS
Type III - The top line of the toga rope is strong but the 5th shading line is missing as in type I.
Center shading line of the toga button consists of two dashes with a central dot.
The "P" and "O" of "POSTAGE" are separated by a line of color.
The frame line at the bottom of the vignette is complete.
Used on offset printings only.

TYPE IV

Type IV - The shading lines of the toga rope are complete.
The second and fourth shading lines in the toga button are broken in the middle and the third line is continuous with a dot in the center.
The "P" and "O" of "POSTAGE" are joined.
The frame line at the bottom of the vignette is broken.
Used on offset printings only.

529	A140 3c **violet,** type III, *Mar. 1918*	3.80	.50
	light violet, type III	3.80	.50
	dark violet, type III	3.80	.50
	Never hinged	7.50	
	On cover, type III		.60
	Block of 4, type III	16.00	4.00
	P# block of 6, type III	60.00	
	Never hinged	100.00	
a.	Double impression, type III	40.00	—
b.	Printed on both sides, type III	*1,500.*	

Earliest documented use: Apr. 8, 1918.

530	A140 3c **purple,** *June 1918* type IV	1.80	.30
	light purple, type IV	1.80	.30
	deep purple, type IV	1.80	.30
	violet, type IV	1.80	.30
	Never hinged	3.25	
	On cover, type IV		.35
	Block of 4, type IV	7.50	2.00
	P# block of 6, type IV	18.00	
	Never hinged	30.00	
	"Blister" under "U.S.," type IV	4.75	—
	Recut under "U.S.," type IV	4.75	—
a.	Double impression, type IV	30.00	—
b.	Printed on both sides, type IV	*350.00*	
	Nos. 525-530 (8)	140.10	10.10

Earliest documented use: June 30, 1918.

1918-20 ***Imperf.***

Dates of issue of 2c types are not known, but official records show that the first plate of each type known to have been issued imperforate was certified as follows:
Type IV, Mar. 1920
Type V, May 4, 1920
Type Va, May 25, 1920
Type VI, July 26, 1920
Type VII, Dec. 2, 1920

531	A140 1c **green,** *Jan. 1919*	9.50	8.00
	gray green	9.50	8.00
	Never hinged	17.00	
	On cover		15.00
	Pair	20.00	22.50
	Never hinged	35.00	
	Block of 4	37.50	50.00
	Corner margin block of 4	40.00	—
	Margin block of 4, arrow	40.00	52.50
	Center line block	55.00	*60.00*
	P# block of 6	85.00	—
	Never hinged	135.00	

Earliest documented use: Mar. 17, 1919 (dated cancel on off-cover plate block).

532	A140 2c **carmine rose,** type IV, *1920*	40.00	27.50
	Never hinged	72.50	
	On cover		65.00
	Pair	85.00	*100.00*
	Never hinged	150.00	
	Block of 4	160.00	200.00
	Corner margin block of 4	165.00	
	Margin block of 4, arrow	165.00	
	Center line block	190.00	
	P# block of 6	325.00	—
	Never hinged	550.00	
533	A140 2c **carmine,** type V, *1920*	110.00	80.00
	Never hinged	210.00	
	On cover		200.00
	Pair	240.00	225.00
	Never hinged	450.00	
	Block of 4	475.00	*525.00*
	Corner margin block of 4	500.00	*650.00*
	Margin block of 4, arrow	500.00	*650.00*
	Center line block	725.00	*650.00*
	P# block of 6	1,050.	—
	Never hinged	1,750.	

Earliest documented use: Sept. 29, 1920 (dated cancel on off-cover center line block of 4).

534	A140 2c **carmine,** type Va, *1920*	11.00	7.00
	carmine rose	11.00	7.00
	Never hinged	20.00	
	On cover		14.00
	Pair	24.00	19.00
	Never hinged	42.50	
	Block of 4	48.00	47.50
	Corner margin block of 4	50.00	
	Margin block of 4, arrow	50.00	50.00

Center line block 55.00 *75.00*
P# block of 6 105.00 —
Never hinged 165.00
Block of 6, monogram over P# 180.00
Never hinged 300.00

Earliest documented use: July 3, 1920 (dated cancel on off-cover block of 4).

534A A140 2c **carmine,** type VI, *1920* 45.00 25.00
Never hinged 90.00
On cover 37.50
Pair 95.00 70.00
Never hinged 190.00
Block of 4 190.00 200.00
Corner block of 4 210.00 225.00
Block of 4, arrow 210.00 —
Center line block 240.00 275.00
Block of 6, P# only 375.00 —
Never hinged 600.00

Earliest documented use: Sept. 7, 1920.

534B A140 2c **carmine,** type VII, *1920* 2,100. 1,250.
Never hinged 3,600.
On cover *3,500.*
Pair 4,400. *3,250.*
Never hinged 7,500.
Block of 4 9,000. *7,000.*
Corner margin block of 4 9,250.
Margin block of 4, arrow 9,500.
Center line block *10,500.*
P# block of 6 *17,000.*
Never hinged *25,000.*

Earliest documented use: Oct. 20, 1920.

Copies of the 2c type VII with Schermack type III vending machine perforations have been cut down at sides to simulate the rarer No. 534B imperforate. The No. 534B with Schermack type III perforations is much less expensive than the fully imperforate No. 534B listed here.

535 A140 3c **violet,** type IV, *1918* 9.00 5.00
Never hinged 16.00
On cover 11.00
Pair 20.00 15.00
Never hinged 36.00
Block of 4 40.00 32.50
Corner margin block of 4 42.50 35.00
Margin block of 4, arrow 42.50 35.00
Center line block 47.50 *50.00*
P# block of 6 75.00 —
Never hinged 120.00
a. Double impression 90.00 —
Never hinged 175.00

Earliest documented use: Sept. 30, 1918.

Cancellation

Haiti —

1919, Aug. 15 ***Perf. 12½***

536 A140 1c **gray green** 22.50 20.00
Never hinged 42.50
On cover 57.50
Block of 4 95.00 110.00
P# block of 6 200.00
Never hinged 350.00
a. Horiz. pair, imperf. vert. *900.00*

Earliest documented use: Aug. 21, 1919.

VICTORY ISSUE

Victory of the Allies in World War I

"Victory" and Flags of Allies — A150

Designed by Clair A. Huston

FLAT PLATE PRINTING

Plates of 400 subjects in four panes of 100 each

1919, Mar. 3 **Unwmk.** ***Perf. 11***

537 A150 3c **violet** 10.00 3.25
Never hinged 17.50
On cover 5.50
Block of 4 42.50 17.50
P# block of 6 115.00
Never hinged 190.00
Double transfer — —
a. 3c **deep red violet** *1,400.* *2,000.*
Never hinged *2,250.*
On cover —
Block of 4 *5,750.* *8,750.*
P# block of 6 *10,000.*
Never hinged *15,000.*
b. 3c **light reddish violet** 12.50 4.00
Never hinged 22.50
On cover 7.50
Block of 4 52.50 20.00
P# block of 6 140.00
Never hinged 225.00
c. 3c **red violet** 75.00 15.00
Never hinged 140.00
On cover 50.00
Block of 4 325.00
P# block of 6 625.00
Never hinged 1,000.

No. 537a is valued in the grade of fine.
Earliest documented date: Mar. 3, 1919 (FDC).

REGULAR ISSUE

ROTARY PRESS PRINTINGS

(See note over No. 448)

1919 **Unwmk.** ***Perf. 11x10***

Issued in panes of 170 stamps (coil waste), later in panes of 70 and 100 (#538, 540)

Stamp designs: 19½-20x22-22¼mm

538 A140 1c **green,** *June* 11.00 8.50
yellowish green 11.00 8.50
bluish green 11.00 8.50
Never hinged 20.00
On cover 22.50
Block of 4 47.50 *52.50*
P# block of 4 & "S 30" 95.00
Never hinged 150.00
P# block of 4 110.00
Never hinged 175.00
P# block of 4, star 140.00
Never hinged 225.00
Double transfer 17.50 —
a. Vert. pair, imperf. horiz. 50.00 *100.00*
Never hinged 87.50
Block of 4 110.00 *250.00*
Never hinged 190.00
P# block of 4 900.00
Never hinged 1,375.

No. 538a used is valued with a contemporaneous cancel. A certificate of authenticity is advised.
Earliest documented use: June 28, 1919.

539 A140 2c **carmine rose,** type II 2,750. *5,250.*
Never hinged 4,000.
On cover, type II *30,000.*
Block of 4, type II *11,000.* *27,500.*
P# block of 4, type II, & "S 20" *17,500.*
Never hinged *24,000.*

No. 539 is valued in the grade of fine.
(See note after No. 455.)
Earliest documented use: June 30, 1919. This is the unique usage on cover.

540 A140 2c **carmine rose,** type III, *June 14* 13.00 9.50
carmine 13.00 9.50
Never hinged 23.50
On cover, type III 25.00
Block of 4, type III 55.00 *60.00*
Never hinged 100.00
P# block of 4, type III, & "S 30" 105.00
Never hinged 170.00
P# block of 4, type III, & "S 30" inverted 450.00
Never hinged 725.00
P# block of 4, type III 105.00
Never hinged 170.00
P# block of 4, type III, star 150.00
Never hinged 250.00
Double transfer, type III 22.50 —

Earliest documented use: June 27, 1919.

a. Vert. pair, imperf. horiz., type III 50.00 *100.00*
Never hinged 87.50
Block of 4 110.00 *250.00*
Never hinged 190.00
P# block of 4, type III 1,000.
Never hinged 1,500.
P# block of 4, type III, Star 1,050.
Never hinged 1,600.
b. Horiz. pair, imperf. vert., type III *1,250.*

No. 540a used is valued with a contemporaneous cancel. A certificate of authenticity is advised.

541 A140 3c **violet,** type II, *June 14, 1919* 45.00 30.00
gray violet, type II 45.00 30.00
Never hinged 85.00
On cover 100.00
Block of 4 190.00 *250.00*
P# block of 4 360.00
Never hinged 600.00

Earliest documented use: June 14, 1919 (FDC).

1920, May 26 ***Perf. 10x11***

Plates of 400 subjects in four panes of 100.

Stamp design: 19x22½-22¾mm

542 A140 1c **green** 14.00 1.50
bluish green 14.00 1.50
Never hinged 27.50
On cover 5.50
Block of 4 60.00 12.50
Vertical margin block of 6, P# opposite center horizontal row 165.00
Never hinged 300.00

Earliest documented use: May 26, 1920 (FDC).

1921, May ***Perf. 10***

Plates of 400 subjects in four panes of 100 each

Stamp design: 19x22½mm

543 A140 1c **green** .50 .30
deep green .50 .30
Never hinged .90
On cover .35
Block of 4 2.00 2.00
Vertical margin block of 6, P# opposite center horizontal row 32.50
Never hinged 57.50
Corner margin block of 4, P# only 14.00
Never hinged 25.00
Double transfer —
Triple transfer — —
a. Horizontal pair, imperf. between *1,750.*

Earliest documented use: May 21, 1921.

1922 ***Perf. 11***

Rotary press sheet waste

Stamp design: 19x22½mm

544 A140 1c **green** *20,000.* *3,250.*
Never hinged *32,500.*
On cover *4,500.*

No. 544 is valued in the grade of fine.
Earliest documented use: Dec. 21, 1922.

1921, May

Issued in panes of 170 stamps (coil waste), later in panes of 70 and 100

Stamp designs: 19½-20x22mm

545 A140 1c **green** 200.00 175.00
yellowish green 200.00 175.00
Never hinged 400.00
On cover *1,800.*
Block of 4 825.00 *900.00*
P# block of 4, "S 30" 1,100.
Never hinged 1,725.
P# block of 4 1,150.
Never hinged 1,800.
P# block of 4, star 1,200.
Never hinged 1,900.

Earliest documented use: June 25, 1921.

546 A140 2c **carmine rose,** type III 125.00 *160.00*
deep carmine rose 125.00 *160.00*
Never hinged 240.00
On cover *775.00*
Block of 4 525.00 *850.00*
P# block of 4, "S 30" 750.00
Never hinged 1,200.
P# block of 4 775.00
Never hinged 1,250.
P# block of 4, star 800.00
Never hinged 1,275.
Recut in hair 140.00 *185.00*
a. Perf. 10 on left side *7,500.* *10,000.*

Earliest documented use: May 5, 1921.

FLAT PLATE PRINTING
Plates of 100 subjects

1920, Nov. 1				***Perf. 11***	
547	A149	$2	**carmine & black**	175.	40.
			Never hinged	325.	
			On cover (commercial)		1,000.
			On flown cover (philatelic)		250.
			Block of 4	725.	200.
			Margin block of 4, arrow	750.	
			Center line block	850.	—
			Margin block of 8, two P#, & arrow	4,000.	
			Never hinged	6,400.	
a.		$2	**lake & black**	220.	40.
			Never hinged	400.	

Earliest documented use: Dec. 6, 1920.

From No. 548 forward, almost all U.S. stamps have had officially designated first days of sale and use. Therefore, from this point, earliest documented uses are given only for those stamps for which there were not designated first days of sale. For first day covers, see the First Day Cover section later in the catalogue.

PILGRIM TERCENTENARY ISSUE

Landing of the Pilgrims at Plymouth, Mass.

The "Mayflower" — A151

Landing of the Pilgrims — A152

Signing of the Compact — A153

Designed by Clair A. Huston

Plates of 280 subjects in four panes of 70 each

1920, Dec. 21			**Unwmk.**	***Perf. 11***	
548	A151	1c	**green**	4.50	2.25
			dark green	4.50	2.25
			Never hinged	9.00	
			On cover		3.50
			Block of 4	19.00	14.00
			P# block of 6	47.50	
			Never hinged	72.50	
			Double transfer	—	—
549	A152	2c	**carmine rose**	6.50	1.60
			carmine	6.50	1.60
			rose	6.50	1.60
			Never hinged	13.00	
			On cover		2.50
			Block of 4	27.50	9.00
			P# block of 6	65.00	
			Never hinged	100.00	
			Cancellation		
			China		—
550	A153	5c	**deep blue**	40.00	14.00
			dark blue	40.00	14.00
			Never hinged	80.00	
			On cover		22.50
			Block of 4	175.00	75.00
			P# block of 6	450.00	
			Never hinged	650.00	
			Nos. 548-550 (3)	51.00	17.85
			Nos. 548-550, never hinged	92.75	

IMPORTANT INFORMATION
REGARDING VALUES FOR
NEVER-HINGED STAMPS

Collectors should be aware that the values given for never-hinged stamps from No. 205 on are for stamps in the grade of very fine, just as the values for all stamps in the catalogue are for very fine stamps unless indicated otherwise. The never-hinged premium as a percentage of value will be larger for stamps in extremely fine or superb grades, and the premium will be smaller for fine-very fine, fine or poor examples. This is particularly true of the issues of the late-19th and early-20th centuries. For example, in the grade of very fine, an unused stamp from this time period may be valued at $100 hinged and $180 never hinged. The never-hinged premium is thus 80%. But in a grade of extremely fine, this same stamp will not only sell for more hinged, but the never-hinged premium will increase, perhaps to 100%-300% or more over the higher extremely fine value. In a grade of superb, a hinged copy will sell for much more than a very fine copy, and additionally the never-hinged premium will be much larger, perhaps as large as 300%-400%. On the other hand, the same stamp in a grade of fine or fine-very fine not only will sell for less than a very fine stamp in hinged condition, but additionally the never-hinged premium will be smaller than the never-hinged premium on a very fine stamp, perhaps as small as 15%-30%.

Please note that the above statements and percentages are NOT a formula for arriving at the values of stamps in hinged or never-hinged condition in the grades of very good, fine, fine to very fine, extremely fine or superb. The percentages given apply only to the size of the premium for never-hinged condition that might be added to the stamp value for hinged condition. Further, the percentages given are only generalized estimates. Some stamps or grades may have percentages for never-hinged condition that are higher or lower than the ranges given. For values of the most popular U.S. stamps in the grades of very good, fine, fine to very fine, extremely fine and superb, see the *Scott Valuing Supplement*, updated and issued twice each year in April and October.

VALUES FOR NEVER-HINGED STAMPS
PRIOR TO SCOTT 205

This catalogue does not value pre-1882 stamps in never-hinged condition. Premiums for never-hinged condition in the classic era invariably are even larger than those premiums listed for the post-1882 issues. Generally speaking, the earlier the stamp is listed in the catalogue, the larger will be the never-hinged premium. On some early classics, the premium will be several multiples of the unused, hinged values given in the catalogue.

NEVER-HINGED PLATE BLOCKS

Values given for never-hinged plate blocks are for blocks in which all stamps have original gum that has never been hinged and has no disturbances, and all selvage, whether gummed or ungummed, has never been hinged.

REGULAR ISSUE

Nathan Hale — A154

Franklin — A155

Warren G. Harding — A156

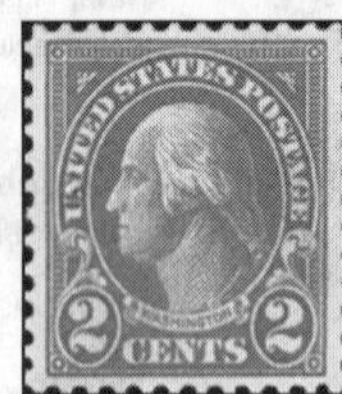

Washington — A157

Lincoln — A158

Martha Washington — A159

Theodore Roosevelt — A160

Garfield — A161

McKinley — A162

Grant — A163

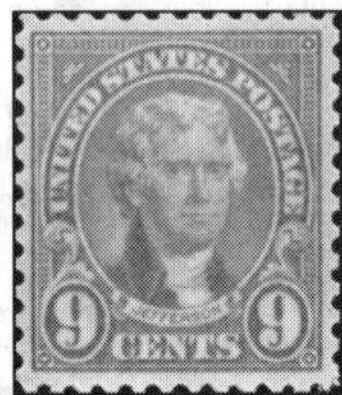

Jefferson — A164

Monroe — A165

Rutherford B. Hayes — A166

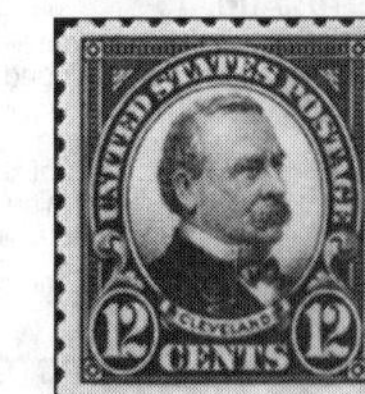

Grover Cleveland — A167

American Indian — A168

Statue of Liberty — A169

Golden Gate — A170

Niagara Falls — A171

American Buffalo — A172

Arlington Amphitheater — A173

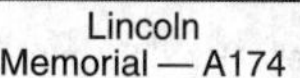

Lincoln Memorial — A174

United States Capitol — A175

Head of Freedom Statue, Capitol Dome — A176

Plates of 400 subjects in four panes of 100 each for all values ½c to 50c inclusive.

Plates of 200 subjects for $1 and $2. The sheets were cut along the horizontal guide line into two panes, upper and lower, of 100 subjects each.

Plates of 100 subjects for the $5 denomination, and sheets of 100 subjects were issued intact.

The Bureau of Engraving and Printing in 1925 in experimenting to overcome the loss due to uneven perforations, produced what is known as the "Star Plate." The vertical rows of designs on these plates are spaced 3mm apart in place of 2¾mm as on the regular plates. Most of these plates were identified with a star added to the plate number.

Designed by Clair Aubrey Huston.

FLAT PLATE PRINTINGS

1922-25 Unwmk. *Perf. 11*

551 A154 ½c **olive brown,** *Apr. 4, 1925* .30 .20
pale olive brown .30 .20
deep olive brown .30 .20
Never hinged .50
On 1c stamped envelope (3rd class) 2.50
Block of 4 1.20 .50
P# block of 6 5.75
Never hinged 9.00
"Cap" on fraction bar (Pl. 17041) .75 .20

552 A155 1c **deep green,** *Jan. 17, 1923* 1.50 .20
green 1.50 .20
pale green 1.50 .20
Never hinged 2.75
On postcard .25
Block of 4 6.25 .40
P# block of 6 22.50
Never hinged 37.50
Double transfer 3.50 —
a. Booklet pane of 6, *Aug. 11, 1923* 7.50 *4.00*
Never hinged 12.50

Earliest documented use: Dec. 26, 1923 (No. 552a single).

553 A156 1½c **yellow brown,** *Mar. 19, 1925* 2.50 .20
pale yellow brown 2.50 .20
brown 2.50 .20
Never hinged 4.50
On 3rd class cover 2.25
Block of 4 10.25 1.10
P# block of 6 30.00 —
Never hinged 45.00
Double transfer — —

554 A157 2c **carmine,** *Jan. 15, 1923* 1.30 .20
light carmine 1.30 .20
Never hinged 2.40
On cover .25
Block of 4 5.50 .30
P# block of 6 20.00
Never hinged 30.00
P# block of 6 & small 5 point star, top only 550.00
Never hinged 775.00
P# block of 6 & large 5 point star, side only 65.00
Never hinged 97.50
Same, large 5-pt. star, top 600.00
Never hinged 900.00
Same, large 6-pt. star, top 750.00
Never hinged 1,100.
Same, large 6-pt. star, side only (Pl. 17196) 875.00
Never hinged 1,300.
Double transfer 2.50 .80
a. Horiz. pair, imperf. vert. *300.00*
b. Vert. pair, imperf. horiz. *4,000.*
Never hinged —
c. Booklet pane of 6, *Feb. 10, 1923* 6.75 *3.00*
Never hinged 11.00
d. Perf. 10 at top or bottom *7,000.* *5,000.*
On cover *8,000.*

No. 554d unused is unique. It is never hinged and has a natural straight edge at left. Value represents the sale price at 2001 auction.

Earliest documented use: Feb. 10, 1923 (No. 554c single).

555 A158 3c **violet,** *Feb. 12, 1923* 17.50 1.25
deep violet 17.50 1.25
dark violet 17.50 1.25
red violet 17.50 1.25
bright violet 17.50 1.25
Never hinged 35.00
On 2c stamped envelope (single UPU rate) 8.00
Block of 4 72.50 9.00
P# block of 6 170.00
Never hinged 275.00

556 A159 4c **yellow brown,** *Jan. 15, 1923* 19.00 .50
brown 19.00 .50
Never hinged 37.50
On cover 9.00
Block of 4 77.50 3.00
P# block of 6 170.00
Never hinged 275.00
Double transfer — —
a. Vert. pair, imperf. horiz. *10,500.*
b. Perf. 10 at top or bottom *3,000.* *10,000.*

No. 556a is unique. It resulted from a sheet that was damaged and patched during production.

No. 556b also exists as a transitional stamp gauging 10 at left top and 11 at right top. Value the same.

557 A160 5c **dark blue,** *Oct. 27, 1922* 19.00 .30
deep blue 19.00 .30
Never hinged 37.50
On UPU-rate cover 6.00
Block of 4 77.50 2.00
P# block of 6 190.00
Never hinged 300.00
Double transfer (15571 UL 86) — *350.00*
a. Imperf., pair *1,500.*
Never hinged *2,500.*
b. Horiz. pair, imperf. vert. —
c. Perf. 10 at top or bottom — *7,500.*
On cover *15,000.*

Earliest documented use: Nov. 12, 1923 (No. 557c).

558 A161 6c **red orange,** *Nov. 20, 1922* 35.00 1.00
pale red orange 35.00 1.00
Never hinged 75.00
Pair on special delivery cover 17.50
Block of 4 145.00 7.50
P# block of 6 400.00
Never hinged 650.00
Double transfer (Plate 14169 LR 60 and 70) 55.00 2.00
Same, recut 55.00 2.00

559 A162 7c **black,** *May 1, 1923* 9.00 .75
gray black 9.00 .75
Never hinged 16.00
On registered cover with other values 27.50
Block of 4 40.00 6.00
P# block of 6 80.00
Never hinged 125.00
Double transfer — —

560 A163 8c **olive green,** *May 1, 1923* 50.00 1.00
pale olive green 50.00 1.00
Never hinged 100.00
Pair on airmail cover 12.50
Block of 4 210.00 7.50
P# block of 6 575.00
Never hinged 875.00
Double transfer — —

561 A164 9c **rose,** *Jan. 15, 1923* 14.00 1.25
pale rose 14.00 1.25
Never hinged 27.50
On registered cover with other values 22.50
Block of 4 57.50 9.00
P# block of 6 170.00
Never hinged 275.00
Double transfer — —

562 A165 10c **orange,** *Jan. 15, 1923* 17.50 .35
pale orange 17.50 .35
Never hinged 35.00
On special delivery cover with 2c 6.00
Block of 4 72.50 2.00
P# block of 6 200.00
Never hinged 325.00
a. Vert. pair, imperf. horiz. *2,250.*
Never hinged *3,250.*
b. Imperf., pair *1,500.*
P# block of 6 —
c. Perf. 10 at top or bottom *5,500.*
Pair *11,500.*

563 A166 11c **light blue,** *Oct. 4, 1922* 1.40 .60
greenish blue 1.40 .60
Never hinged 2.50
On registered cover with other values 12.50
Block of 4 5.75 3.50
P# block of 6 27.50
Never hinged 45.00
a. 11c **light bluish green** 1.40 .60
Never hinged 2.50
On registered cover with other values 14.00
Block of 4 5.75 4.00
P# block of 6 27.50
Never hinged 45.00
light yellow green 1.40 .60
Never hinged 2.50
d. Imperf., pair *17,500.*

Many other intermediate shades exist for Nos. 563 and 563a, all falling within the blue or green color families.

564 A167 12c **brown violet,** *Mar. 20, 1923* 6.00 .35
deep brown violet 6.00 .35
Never hinged 12.00
On special delivery cover 12.50
Block of 4 25.00 3.00
P# block of 6 80.00
Never hinged 125.00
P# block of 6 & large 5 point star, side only 115.00
Never hinged 185.00
P# block of 6 & large 6 point star, side only 240.00
Never hinged 375.00
Double transfer, (14404 UL 73 & 74) 12.50 1.10
a. Horiz. pair, imperf. vert. *1,750.*

565 A168 14c **blue,** *May 1, 1923* 4.00 .90
deep blue 4.00 .90
Never hinged 8.00
On registered cover with other values 15.00
Block of 4 16.50 7.50
P# block of 6 50.00
Never hinged 80.00
Double transfer — —

Horizontal pairs of No. 565 are known with spacings up to 3mm instead of 2mm between. These are from the 5th and 6th vertical rows of the right panes of Plate 14515 and also between stamps Nos. 3 and 4 of the same pane. A plate block of Pl. 14512 is known with 3mm spacing.

566 A169 15c **gray,** *Nov. 11, 1922* 20.00 .30
light gray 20.00 .30
Never hinged 40.00
On registered cover with 2c 3.50
Block of 4 85.00 2.00
P# block of 6 275.00
Never hinged 425.00
P# block of 6 & large 5 point star, side only 525.00
Never hinged 775.00

567 A170 20c **carmine rose,** *May 1, 1923* 20.00 .30
deep carmine rose 20.00 .30
Never hinged 40.00
On registered UPU-rate cover 12.50
Block of 4 85.00 2.00
P# block of 6 250.00
Never hinged 400.00
P# block of 6 & large 5 point star, side only 550.00
Never hinged 800.00
a. Horiz. pair, imperf. vert. *1,500.*
Never hinged *2,500.*

"Bridge over Falls" plate scratches

568 A171 25c **yellow green,** *Nov. 11, 1922* 18.00 .75
green 18.00 .75
deep green 18.00 .75
Never hinged 36.00
On contract airmail cover 27.50
Block of 4 75.00 6.00
P# block of 6 240.00
Never hinged 375.00
Double transfer — —
Plate scratches ("Bridge over Falls") — —
b. Vert. pair, imperf. horiz. *2,000.*
c. Perf. 10 at one side *5,000.* *11,000.*
Never hinged *7,500.*

No. 568b is valued in the grade of fine.

Double Transfer

569 A172 30c **olive brown,** *Mar. 20, 1923* 30.00 .60
Never hinged 60.00
On registered cover with other values 20.00
Block of 4 140.00 5.00
P# block of 6 240.00
Never hinged 375.00
Double transfer (16065 UR 52) 55.00 —

570 A173 50c **lilac,** *Nov. 11, 1922* 47.50 .40
dull lilac 47.50 .40
Never hinged 95.00
On Federal airmail cover 27.50
Block of 4 200.00 2.00
P# block of 6 575.00
Never hinged 900.00

571 A174 $1 **violet black,** *Feb. 12, 1923* 40.00 .65
violet brown 40.00 .65
Never hinged 80.00
On post-1932 registered cover with other values 22.50
Block of 4 170.00 4.50
Margin block of 4, arrow, top or bottom 180.00
P# block of 6 300.00
Never hinged 475.00

	Double transfers, Pl. 18642 L 30 and Pl. 18682	90.00	1.60
572 A175	$2 **deep blue,** *Mar. 20, 1923*	77.50	9.00
	Never hinged	155.00	
	On post-1932 registered cover with other values		55.00
	Block of 4	325.00	65.00
	Margin block of 4, arrow, top or bottom	335.00	
	P# block of 6	650.00	
	Never hinged	1,000.	
573 A176	$5 **carmine & blue,** *Mar. 20, 1923*	120.00	15.00
	Never hinged	225.00	
	On post-1932 registered cover with other values		175.00
	Block of 4	500.00	95.00
	Margin block of 4, arrow	525.00	
	Center line block	600.00	*105.00*
	Never hinged	1,025.	
	P# block of 8, two P# & arrow	1,800.	—
	Never hinged	2,500.	
a.	$5 **carmine lake & dark blue**	200.00	20.00
	Never hinged	375.00	
	On post-1932 registered cover with other values		190.00
	Block of 4	850.00	140.00
	Margin block of 4, arrow	875.00	
	Center line block	950.00	*175.00*
	Never hinged	1,600.	
	P# block of 8, two P# & arrow	2,400.	
	Never hinged	3,500.	
	Nos. 551-573 (23)	571.00	36.05
	Nos. 551-573, never hinged	1,127.	

For other listings of perforated stamps of designs A154 to A176 see:
Nos. 578 & 579, Perf. 11x10
Nos. 581-591, Perf. 10
Nos. 594-596, Perf. 11
Nos. 632-642, 653, 692-696, Perf. 11x10½
Nos. 697-701, Perf. 10½x11
This series also includes #622-623 (perf. 11), 684-687 & 720-723.

Plate Blocks

Scott values for plate blocks printed from flat plates are for very fine side and bottom positions. Top position plate blocks with full wide selvage sell for more.

1923-25 ***Imperf.***

Stamp design 19¼x22¼mm

575 A155	1c **green,** *Mar. 1923*	7.00	5.00
	deep green	7.00	5.00
	Never hinged	12.50	
	On commercial cover		*100.00*
	On philatelic cover		8.50
	Pair	15.00	12.50
	Never hinged	27.50	
	Block of 4	30.00	27.50
	Corner margin block of 4	32.50	*27.50*
	Margin block of 4, arrow	35.00	*30.00*
	Center line block	40.00	*40.00*
	P# block of 6	70.00	—
	Never hinged	100.00	

Earliest documented use: Mar. 16, 1923.

576 A156	1½c **yellow brown,** *Apr. 4, 1925*	1.40	1.50
	pale yellow brown	1.40	1.50
	brown	1.40	1.50
	Never hinged	2.50	
	On commercial cover		*25.00*
	On philatelic cover		6.00
	Pair	3.25	*3.75*
	Never hinged	5.00	
	Block of 4	6.50	*8.50*
	Corner margin block of 4	6.75	*8.00*
	Margin block of 4, arrow	7.00	*10.00*
	Center line block	11.00	*20.00*
	P# block of 6	20.00	—
	Never hinged	30.00	
	Double transfer	—	—

The 1½c A156 Rotary press imperforate is listed as No. 631.

577 A157	2c **carmine**	1.50	1.25
	light carmine	1.50	1.25
	Never hinged	2.70	
	On commercial cover		*20.00*
	On philatelic cover		6.00
	Pair	3.50	3.00
	Never hinged	5.50	
	Block of 4	7.25	7.00
	Corner margin block of 4	7.50	*8.00*
	Margin block of 4, arrow	8.00	*10.00*
	Center line block	13.00	*15.00*
	P# block of 6	25.00	—
	Never hinged	37.50	
	P# block of 6, large 5 point star	67.50	—
	Never hinged	95.00	
	Nos. 575-577 (3)	9.90	7.75
	Nos. 575-577, never hinged\17.70—		

ROTARY PRESS PRINTINGS
(See note over No. 448)
Issued in sheets of 70, 100 or 170 stamps, coil waste of Nos. 597, 599
Stamp designs: 19¾x22¼mm

1923 ***Perf. 11x10***

578 A155	1c **green**	95.00	*160.00*
	Never hinged	175.00	
	On cover		*700.00*
	Block of 4	400.00	*1,000.*
	P# block of 4, star	800.00	
	Never hinged	1,250.	

Earliest documented use: Nov. 7, 1923.

579 A157	2c **carmine**	85.00	*140.00*
	deep carmine	85.00	*140.00*
	Never hinged	160.00	
	Block of 4	360.00	*1,750.*
	On cover		*400.00*
	P# block of 4, star	600.00	
	Never hinged	900.00	
	Recut in eye, plate 14731	*110.00*	*150.00*

Earliest documented use: Feb. 20, 1923.

Plates of 400 subjects in four panes of 100 each
Stamp designs: 19¼x22½mm

1923-26 ***Perf. 10***

581 A155	1c **green,** *Apr. 21, 1923*	11.00	.75
	yellow green	11.00	.75
	pale green	11.00	.75
	Never hinged	18.00	
	On postcard		.85
	On 3rd class cover		1.35
	Block of 4	40.00	4.50
	P# block of 4	125.00	
	Never hinged	175.00	

Earliest documented use: May 18, 1923.

582 A156	1½c **brown,** *Mar. 19, 1925*	5.50	.65
	dark brown	5.50	.65
	Never hinged	9.00	
	On 3rd class cover		6.00
	Block of 4	24.00	4.00
	P# block of 4	45.00	
	Never hinged	65.00	
	Pair with full horiz. gutter btwn.	*160.00*	
	Pair with full vert. gutter btwn.	*210.00*	

No. 582 was available in full sheets of 400 subjects but was not regularly issued in that form.

583 A157	2c **carmine,** *Apr. 14, 1924*	3.00	.30
	deep carmine	3.00	.30
	Never hinged	5.00	
	On cover		2.50
	Block of 4	13.00	2.00
	P# block of 4	37.50	
	Never hinged	55.00	
a.	Booklet pane of 6, *Aug. 27, 1926*	95.00	*85.00*
	Never hinged	175.00	

Earliest documented use (unprecanceled): May 15, 1924.

584 A158	3c **violet,** *Aug. 1, 1925*	32.50	3.00
	Never hinged	55.00	
	On postcard (UPU rate)		12.50
	Block of 4	140.00	17.50
	P# block of 4	275.00	
	Never hinged	400.00	
585 A159	4c **yellow brown,** *Mar. 1925*	19.00	.65
	deep yellow brown	19.00	.65
	Never hinged	32.50	
	On cover		15.00
	Block of 4	80.00	4.00
	P# block of 4	230.00	
	Never hinged	350.00	
586 A160	5c **blue,** *Dec. 1924*	19.00	.40
	deep blue	19.00	.40
	Never hinged	32.50	
	On UPU-rate cover		6.00
	Block of 4	80.00	3.00
	P# block of 4	240.00	
	Never hinged	350.00	
	Double transfer	—	—
a.	Horizontal pair, imperf. vertically		*10,000.*

No. 586a is unique, precanceled, with average centering and small faults, and it is valued as such.

587 A161	6c **red orange,** *Mar. 1925*	9.25	.60
	pale red orange	9.25	.60
	Never hinged	16.00	
	On registered cover with other values		15.00
	Block of 4	40.00	4.00
	P# block of 4	110.00	
	Never hinged	160.00	
588 A162	7c **black,** *May 29, 1926*	13.50	6.25
	Never hinged	22.50	
	On registered cover with other values		30.00
	Block of 4	57.50	45.00
	P# block of 4	125.00	
	Never hinged	200.00	
589 A163	8c **olive green,** *May 29, 1926*	30.00	4.50
	pale olive green	30.00	4.50
	Never hinged	50.00	
	On airmail cover		22.50
	Block of 4	125.00	25.00
	P# block of 4	250.00	
	Never hinged	390.00	
590 A164	9c **rose,** *May 29, 1926*	6.00	2.50
	Never hinged	10.00	
	On registered cover with other values		22.50
	Block of 4	26.00	17.50
	P# block of 4	60.00	
	Never hinged	95.00	
591 A165	10c **orange,** *June 8, 1925*	70.00	.50
	Never hinged	120.00	
	On airmail cover		17.50
	Block of 4	310.00	3.00
	P# block of 4	475.00	
	Never hinged	750.00	
	Nos. 581-591 (11)	218.75	20.10
	Nos. 581-591, never hinged	370.50	

Bureau Precancels: 1c, 64 diff., 1½c, 76 diff., 2c, 58 diff., 3c, 41 diff., 4c, 36 diff., 5c, 38 diff., 6c, 36 diff., 7c, 18 diff., 8c, 18 diff., 9c, 13 diff., 10c, 39 diff.

Issued in sheets of 70 or 100 stamps, coil waste of Nos. 597, 599
Stamp designs approximately 19¾x22¼mm

1923 ***Perf. 11***

594 A155	1c **green**	*16,000.*	6,750.
	On cover		*11,000.*
	Pair		*14,500.*

No. 594 unused is valued without gum; both unused and used are valued with perforations just touching frameline on one side.

Earliest documented use: Mar. 25, 1924.

595 A157	2c **carmine**	300.00	*350.00*
	deep carmine	300.00	*350.00*
	Never hinged	500.00	
	On cover		550.00
	Block of 4	1,300.	*1,750.*
	P# block of 4, star	2,100.	
	Never hinged	3,000.	
	Recut in eye, plate 14731	—	

Earliest documented uses: Mar. 31, 1923 (dated cancel on off-cover pair of stamps); June 29, 1923 (on cover).

Rotary press sheet waste

Stamp design approximately 19¼x22½mm

596 A155	1c **green,** machine cancel		*120,000.*
	With Bureau precancel		*100,000.*

A majority of copies of No. 596 carry the Bureau precancel "Kansas City, Mo."
No. 596 is valued in the grade of fine.

COIL STAMPS
ROTARY PRESS

1923-29 ***Perf. 10 Vertically***

Stamp designs aproximately 19¾x22¼mm

597 A155	1c **green,** *July 18, 1923*	.30	.20
	yellow green	.30	.20
	Never hinged	.50	
	Three on cover		2.25
	Pair	.65	.25
	Never hinged	1.05	
	Joint line pair	2.25	.75
	Never hinged	3.60	
	Gripper cracks	2.60	1.00
	Double transfer	2.60	1.00
598 A156	1½c **brown,** *Mar. 19, 1925*	1.00	.20
	deep brown	1.00	.20
	Never hinged	1.60	
	On 3rd class cover		6.00
	Pair	2.20	.25
	Never hinged	3.50	
	Joint line pair	4.75	.75
	Never hinged	7.50	

TYPE I

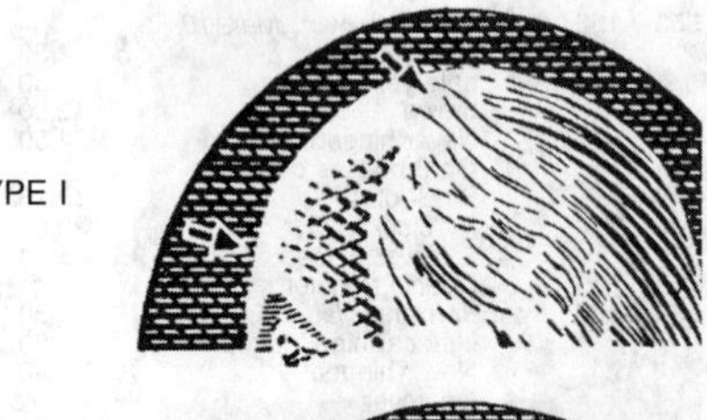

TYPE II

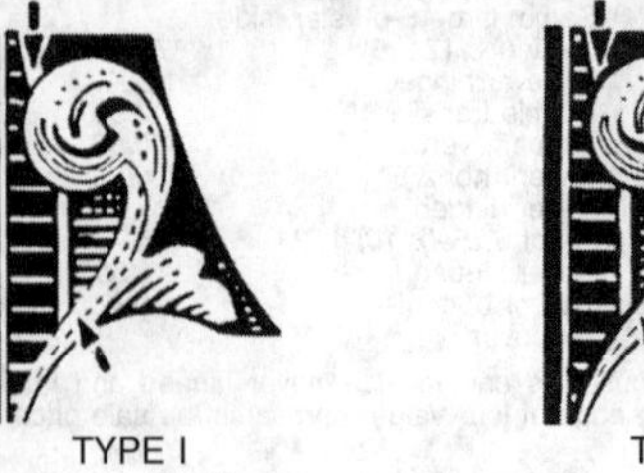

TYPE I TYPE II

TYPE I. No heavy hair lines at top center of head. Outline of left acanthus scroll generally faint at top and toward base at left side.

TYPE II. Three heavy hair lines at top center of head; two being outstanding in the white area. Outline of left acanthus scroll very strong and clearly defined at top (under left edge of lettered panel) and at lower curve (above and to left of numeral oval). This type appears only on Nos. 599A and 634A.

No.	Design	Denom.	Description	Unused	Used
599	A157	2c	**carmine,** type I, *Jan. 1923*	.40	.20
			deep carmine, type I	.40	.20
			Never hinged	.65	
			On cover		1.10
			Pair, type I	.85	.20
			Never hinged	1.35	
			Joint line pair, type I	2.30	.50
			Never hinged	3.75	
			Double transfer, type I	1.90	1.00
			Gripper cracks, type I	2.30	2.00

Earliest documented use: Jan. 10, 1923 (precanceled version).

No.	Design	Denom.	Description	Unused	Used
599A	A157	2c	**carmine,** type II, *Mar. 1929*	125.00	11.00
			Never hinged	200.00	
			On cover		30.00
			Pair, type II	260.00	30.00
			Never hinged	410.00	
			Joint line pair, type II	675.00	225.00
			Never hinged	1,125.	
			Joint line pair, types I & II	775.00	*850.00*
			Never hinged	1,350.	

Earliest documented use: Mar. 29, 1929.

No.	Design	Denom.	Description	Unused	Used
600	A158	3c	**violet,** *May 10, 1924*	7.25	.20
			deep violet	7.25	.20
			Never hinged	11.50	
			On cover		6.00
			Pair	15.50	.35
			Never hinged	25.00	
			Joint line pair	25.00	2.50
			Never hinged	40.00	
			Cracked plate	—	
601	A159	4c	**yellow brown,** *Aug. 5, 1923*	4.50	.35
			brown	4.50	.35
			Never hinged	7.25	
			On cover		14.00
			Pair	9.50	.95
			Never hinged	15.00	
			Joint line pair	30.00	6.00
			Never hinged	47.50	

Earliest documented use: Sept. 14, 1923.

No.	Design	Denom.	Description	Unused	Used
602	A160	5c	**dark blue,** *Mar. 5, 1924*	1.75	.20
			Never hinged	2.80	
			On UPU-rate cover		6.00
			Pair	3.75	.35
			Never hinged	6.00	
			Joint line pair	10.00	1.50
			Never hinged	16.00	
603	A165	10c	**orange,** *Dec. 1, 1924*	4.00	.20
			Never hinged	6.50	
			On special delivery cover with 2c		22.50
			Pair	9.00	.25
			Never hinged	14.50	
			Joint line pair	26.50	2.00
			Never hinged	42.50	

The 6c design A161 coil stamp is listed as No. 723.

Bureau Precancels: 1c, 296 diff., 1½c, 188 diff., 2c, type I, 113 diff., 2c, type II, Boston, Detroit, 3c, 62 diff., 4c, 34 diff., 5c, 36 diff., 10c, 32 diff.

1923-25 *Perf. 10 Horizontally*

Stamp designs: 19¼x22½mm

No.	Design	Denom.	Description	Unused	Used
604	A155	1c	**green,** *July 19, 1924*	.35	.20
			yellow green	.35	.20
			Never hinged	.55	
			Three on cover		6.00
			Pair	.80	.20
			Never hinged	1.30	
			Joint line pair	3.75	.55
			Never hinged	6.00	
605	A156	1½c	**yellow brown,** *May 9, 1925*	.35	.20
			brown	.35	.20
			Never hinged	.55	
			On 3rd class cover		17.50
			Pair	.80	.35
			Never hinged	1.30	
			Joint line pair	3.50	.75
			Never hinged	5.50	
606	A157	2c	**carmine,** *Dec. 31, 1923*	.35	.20
			Never hinged	.55	
			On cover		3.50
			Pair	.80	.45
			Never hinged	1.30	
			Joint line pair	2.60	1.00
			Never hinged	4.25	
			Cracked plate	5.25	2.00
			Nos. 597-599,600-606 (10)	20.25	2.15
			Nos. 597-599, 600-606, never hinged	32.45	

HARDING MEMORIAL ISSUE

Tribute to the memory of President Warren G. Harding, who died in San Francisco, Aug. 2, 1923.

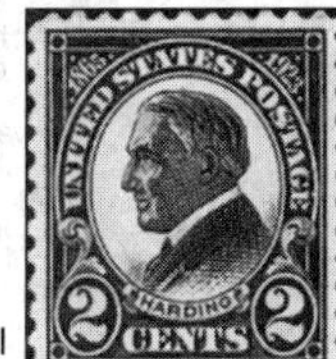

Warren Gamaliel Harding — A177

Plates of 400 subjects in four panes of 100 each
FLAT PLATE PRINTINGS
Stamp designs: 19¼x22¼mm

1923 *Perf. 11*

No.	Design	Denom.	Description	Unused	Used
610	A177	2c	**black,** *Sept. 1, 1923*	.65	.25
			intense black	.65	.25
			grayish black	.65	.25
			Never hinged	1.05	
			On cover		.30
			P# block of 6	20.00	—
			Never hinged	30.00	
			Double transfer	1.75	.50
a.			Horiz. pair, imperf. vert.	*2,500.*	

Imperf

No.	Design	Denom.	Description	Unused	Used
611	A177	2c	**black,** *Nov. 15, 1923*	5.75	4.00
			Never hinged	10.00	
			On philatelic cover		8.00
			On commercial cover		15.00
			Pair	13.00	10.00
			Never hinged	21.00	
			Corner margin block of 4	27.50	22.50
			Margin block of 4, arrow	27.50	22.50
			Center line block	60.00	40.00
			P# block of 6	70.00	—
			Never hinged	100.00	

ROTARY PRESS PRINTINGS
Stamp designs: 19¼x22½mm
Perf. 10

No.	Design	Denom.	Description	Unused	Used
612	A177	2c	**black,** *Sept. 12, 1923*	17.50	1.75
			gray black	17.50	1.75
			Never hinged	30.00	
			On cover		3.25
			P# block of 4	300.00	
			Never hinged	450.00	
			Pair with full vertical gutter between	*350.00*	

Perf. 11

No.	Design	Denom.	Description	Unused	Used
613	A177	2c	**black**		*42,500.*
			Pair		*90,000.*

No. 613 was produced from rotary press sheet waste. It is valued in the grade of fine.

HUGUENOT-WALLOON TERCENTENARY ISSUE

300th anniversary of the settling of the Walloons, and in honor of the Huguenots.

Ship "Nieu Nederland" A178

Walloons Landing at Fort Orange (Albany) — A179

Jan Ribault Monument at Duval County, Fla. — A180

"Broken Circle" flaw

Designed by Clair Aubrey Huston

FLAT PLATE PRINTINGS
Plates of 200 subjects in four panes of 50 each

1924, May 1 *Perf. 11*

No.	Design	Denom.	Description	Unused	Used
614	A178	1c	**dark green**	2.75	3.25
			green	2.75	3.25
			Never hinged	4.25	
			On cover		4.50
			P# block of 6	40.00	—
			Never hinged	65.00	
			Double transfer	6.50	6.50
615	A179	2c	**carmine rose**	5.00	2.25
			dark carmine rose	5.00	2.25
			Never hinged	8.75	
			On cover		3.50
			P# block of 6	55.00	—
			Never hinged	80.00	
			Double transfer	12.00	3.50
616	A180	5c	**dark blue**	22.50	13.00
			deep blue	22.50	13.00
			Never hinged	35.00	
			On UPU-rate cover		20.00
			P# block of 6	225.00	—
			Never hinged	350.00	
			Added line at bottom of white circle around right numeral, so-called "broken circle" (15754 UR 2, 3, 4, 5)	45.00	15.00
			Nos. 614-616 (3)	30.25	18.50
			Nos. 614-616, never hinged	48.00	

LEXINGTON-CONCORD ISSUE

150th anniv. of the Battle of Lexington-Concord.

Washington at Cambridge A181

"Birth of Liberty," by Henry Sandham A182

The Minute Man, by Daniel Chester French — A183

Plates of 200 subjects in four panes of 50 each

1925, Apr. 4 ***Perf. 11***

No.	Type	Denom.	Description	Unused	Used
617	A181	1c	**deep green**	2.50	2.50
			green	2.50	2.50
			Never hinged	4.00	
			On cover		3.75
			P# block of 6	40.00	—
			Never hinged	60.00	
618	A182	2c	**carmine rose**	5.00	4.00
			pale carmine rose	5.00	4.00
			Never hinged	8.00	
			On cover		5.50
			P# block of 6	55.00	—
			Never hinged	85.00	
619	A183	5c	**dark blue**	20.00	13.00
			blue	20.00	13.00
			Never hinged	32.50	
			On UPU-rate cover		20.00
			P# block of 6	200.00	—
			Never hinged	300.00	
			Line over head (16807 LL 48)	42.50	19.00
			Nos. 617-619 (3)	27.50	19.50
			Nos. 617-619, never hinged	44.50	

NORSE-AMERICAN ISSUE

Arrival in New York, on Oct. 9, 1825, of the sloop "Restaurationen" with the first group of immigrants from Norway.

Sloop "Restaurationen"
A184

Viking Ship
A185

Designed by Clair Aubrey Huston.

Plates of 100 subjects.

1925, May 18 ***Perf. 11***

No.	Type	Denom.	Description	Unused	Used
620	A184	2c	**carmine & black**	4.00	3.00
			deep carmine & black	4.00	3.00
			Never hinged	6.50	
			On cover		4.50
			Margin block of 4, arrow	17.50	
			Center line block	24.00	
			P# block of 8, two P# & arrow	180.00	—
			Never hinged	275.00	
			P# block of 8, carmine & arrow; black P# omitted	*3,250.*	—
621	A185	5c	**dark blue & black**	12.50	11.00
			Never hinged	24.00	
			On UPU-rate cover		17.50
			Margin block of 4, arrow	62.50	
			Center line block	75.00	
			P# block of 8, two P# & arrow	525.00	—
			Never hinged	725.00	

REGULAR ISSUE

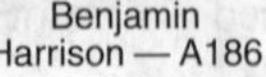
Benjamin
Harrison — A186

Woodrow
Wilson — A187

Plates of 400 subjects in four panes of 100.

1925-26 ***Perf. 11***

No.	Type	Denom.	Description	Unused	Used
622	A186	13c	**green,** *Jan. 11, 1926*	12.50	.75
			light green	12.50	.75
			Never hinged	21.00	
			On registered cover with other values		17.50
			P# block of 6	145.00	—
			Never hinged	225.00	
			P# block of 6, large 5 point star, right side only	*2,100.*	—
			Never hinged	*2,750.*	
623	A187	17c	**black,** *Dec. 28, 1925*	14.00	.30
			gray black	14.00	.30
			Never hinged	24.00	
			On registered cover		6.00
			P# block of 6	160.00	—
			Never hinged	240.00	

Plate Blocks

Scott values for plate blocks printed from flat plates are for very fine side and bottom positions. Top position plate blocks with full wide selvage sell for more.

SESQUICENTENNIAL EXPOSITION ISSUE

Sesquicentennial Exposition, Philadelphia, Pa., June 1 - Dec. 1, 1926, and 150th anniv. of the Declaration of Independence.

Liberty
Bell — A188

Designed by Clair Aubrey Huston.

Plates of 200 subjects in four panes of 50.

1926, May 10 ***Perf. 11***

No.	Type	Denom.	Description	Unused	Used
627	A188	2c	**carmine rose**	3.00	.50
			Never hinged	4.50	
			On cover		1.00
			On cover, Expo. station machine canc.		7.50
			On cover, Expo. station duplex handstamp canc.		35.00
			P# block of 6	37.50	—
			Never hinged	50.00	
			Double transfer	—	—

ERICSSON MEMORIAL ISSUE

Unveiling of the statue of John Ericsson, builder of the "Monitor," by the Crown Prince of Sweden, Washington, D.C., May 29, 1926.

Statue of John
Ericsson — A189

Designed by Clair Aubrey Huston.

Plates of 200 subjects in four panes of 50.

1926, May 29 ***Perf. 11***

No.	Type	Denom.	Description	Unused	Used
628	A189	5c	**gray lilac**	6.50	3.25
			Never hinged	9.50	
			On UPU-rate cover		8.00
			P# block of 6	75.00	—
			Never hinged	100.00	

BATTLE OF WHITE PLAINS ISSUE

150th anniv. of the Battle of White Plains, N. Y.

Alexander Hamilton's
Battery — A190

Designed by Clair Aubrey Huston.

Plates of 400 subjects in four panes of 100.

1926, Oct. 18 ***Perf. 11***

No.	Type	Denom.	Description	Unused	Used
629	A190	2c	**carmine rose**	2.25	1.70
			Never hinged	3.25	
			On cover		2.25
			P# block of 6	35.00	—
			Never hinged	50.00	
a.			Vertical pair, imperf. between		—

The existence of a genuine, non-spliced No. 629a has been questioned by specialists. The editors would like to see evidence of a non-spliced pair, imperf between.

INTERNATIONAL PHILATELIC EXHIBITION ISSUE

Souvenir Sheet

A190a

Illustration reduced.

Plates of 100 subjects in four panes of 25 each, separated by one inch wide gutters with central guide lines.

Condition valued:

Centering: Overall centering will average very fine, but individual stamps may be better or worse.

Perforations: No folds along rows of perforations.

Gum: There may be some light gum bends but no gum creases.

Hinging: There may be hinge marks in the selvage and on up to two or three stamps, but no heavy hinging or hinge remnants (except in the ungummed portion of the wide selvage.

Margins: Top panes should have about ½ inch bottom margin and 1 inch top margin.

Bottom panes should have about ½ inch top margin and just under ¾ inch bottom margin. Both will have one wide side (usually 1 inch plus) and one narrow (½ inch) side margin. The wide margin corner will have a small diagonal notch on top panes.

1926, Oct. 18 ***Perf. 11***

No.	Type	Denom.	Description	Unused	Used
630	A190a	2c	**carmine rose,** sheet of 25	375.00	450.00
			Never hinged	575.00	
			On cover		—
			Dot over first "S" of "States" 18774 LL 9 or 18773 LL 11, sheet	400.00	475.00

Issued in sheets measuring 158-160¼x136-146½mm containing 25 stamps with inscription "International Philatelic Exhibition, Oct. 16th to 23rd, 1926" in top margin.

VALUES FOR VERY FINE STAMPS
Please note: Stamps are valued in the grade of Very Fine unless otherwise indicated.

REGULAR ISSUE
ROTARY PRESS PRINTINGS
(See note over No. 448.)

Plates of 400 subjects in four panes of 100 each
Stamp designs 19¼x22½mm

1926, Aug. 27 ***Imperf.***

No.	Type	Denom.	Description	Unused	Used
631	A156	1½c	**yellow brown**	1.90	1.70
			light brown	1.90	1.70
			Never hinged	2.75	
			On philatelic cover		12.50
			Pair	4.00	4.00
			Never hinged	5.75	
			Pair, vert. gutter between	4.50	5.00
			Pair, horiz. gutter between	4.50	5.00
			Margin block with dash (left, right, top or bottom)	10.00	*14.00*
			Center block with crossed gutters and dashes	25.00	*27.50*
			P# block of 4	62.50	—
			Never hinged	85.00	
			Without gum breaker ridges	80.00	
			Pair, vert. gutter between	*200.00*	
			Pair, horiz. gutter btwn.	*200.00*	
			Margin block with dash (left, right, top or bottom)	*550.00*	
			Center block with crossed gutters and dashes	*1,250.*	
			Never hinged	*1,750.*	
			P# block of 4	1,250.	
			Never hinged	1,600.	

1926-34 ***Perf. 11x10½***

No.	Type	Denom.	Description	Unused	Used
632	A155	1c	**green,** *June 10, 1927*	.20	.20
			yellow green	.20	.20
			Never hinged	.20	
			Three on cover		1.25
			P# block of 4	2.00	—
			Never hinged	2.75	
			Pair with full vertical gutter btwn.	150.00	—
			Cracked plate	—	—
a.			Booklet pane of 6, *Nov. 2, 1927*	5.50	*4.00*
			Never hinged	8.00	
b.			Vertical pair, imperf. between	*3,500.*	*125.00*
			Never hinged	*5,500.*	
c.			Horiz. pair, imperf. between	*7,500.*	

No. 632c is valued in the grade of fine and never hinged. It is possibly unique.

No.	Type	Denom.	Description	Unused	Used
633	A156	1½c	**yellow brown,** *May 17, 1927*	1.90	.20

deep brown 1.90 .20
Never hinged 2.60
On 3rd class cover 2.50
P# block of 4 62.50 —
Never hinged 85.00

Normal

Recut ("long ear")

634 A157 2c **carmine,** type I, *Dec. 10, 1926* .20 .20
Never hinged .20
On cover .20
P# block of 4, type I, # opposite corner stamp 2.60 —
Never hinged 3.75
Vertical P# block of 10, # opposite 3rd horizontal row from top or bottom (Experimental Electric Eye plates) 5.00 —
Never hinged 7.50
Margin block of 4, Electric Eye marking .45 .25
Pair with full vertical gutter between 200.00
Recut ("long ear"), type I, 20342 UR 34 *400.00* —
Recut face, type I, 20234 LL 58 —
b. 2c **carmine lake,** type I — —
P# block of 4 —
c. Horizontal pair, type I, imperf. between *7,000.*
d. Booklet pane of 6, type I, *Feb. 25, 1927* 1.50 *1.50*
Never hinged 2.50

Shades of the carmine exist.
No. 634, Type I, exists on a thin, tough experimental paper.
No. 634c is valued in the grade of fine.

Earliest documented use: FDC (No. 634); Dec. 20, 1929 (No. 634b).

634A A157 2c **carmine,** type II, *Dec. 1928* 350.00 13.50
Never hinged 575.00
On cover 21.00
P# block of 4, type II 2,000. —
Never hinged 2,750.
Pair with full horiz. gutter btwn. 1,000. —
Pair with full vert. gutter btwn. 1,000. —
Center block with crossed gutters 4,000.

Earliest documented use: Dec. 15, 1928.

No. 634A, Type II, was available in full sheet of 400 subjects but was not regularly issued in that form.

635 A158 3c **violet,** *Feb. 3, 1927* .40 .20
Never hinged .55
On cover 2.00
P# block of 4 13.50 —
Never hinged 21.50
a. 3c **bright violet,** *Feb. 7, 1934* re-issue, Plates 21185 & 21186 .20 .20
Never hinged .30
On cover .25
P# block of 4 6.00 —
Never hinged 11.00
Gripper cracks 3.25 2.00
636 A159 4c **yellow brown,** *May 17, 1927* 2.10 .20
Never hinged 3.00
On cover 8.00
P# block of 4 75.00 —
Never hinged 110.00
Pair with full vert. gutter btwn. *200.00*
637 A160 5c **dark blue,** *Mar. 24, 1927* 2.10 .20
Never hinged 3.00
On UPU-rate cover 4.50
P# block of 4 14.00 —
Never hinged 20.00
Pair with full vert. gutter btwn. *275.00*
Double transfer — —
638 A161 6c **red orange,** *July 27, 1927* 2.10 .20
Never hinged 3.00
On airmail cover 6.00
P# block of 4 14.00 —
Never hinged 20.00
Pair with full horiz. gutter btwn. —
Pair with full vert. gutter btwn. *200.00*
639 A162 7c **black,** *Mar. 24, 1927* 2.10 .20
Never hinged 3.00
On registered cover with other values 15.00
P# block of 4 14.00 —
Never hinged 20.00
a. Vertical pair, imperf. between *325.00* 100.00
Never hinged *500.00*
640 A163 8c **olive green,** *June 10, 1927* 2.10 .20
olive bister 2.10 .20
Never hinged 3.00
On airmail cover 8.00
P# block of 4 14.00 —
Never hinged 20.00
641 A164 9c **rose,** *May 17, 1927* 2.10 .20
salmon rose 2.10 .20
orange red, *1931* 2.10 .20
Never hinged 3.00
On registered cover with other values 8.00
P# block of 4 13.00 —
Never hinged 19.00
Pair with full vert. gutter btwn. —
642 A165 10c **orange,** *Feb. 3, 1927* 3.50 .20
Never hinged 5.00
On special delivery cover with 2c 6.00
P# block of 4 20.00 —
Never hinged 30.00
Double transfer — —
Nos. 632-634,635-642 (11) 18.80 2.20
Nos. 632-634, never hinged 26.45

The 1½c, 2c, 4c, 5c, 6c, 8c imperf. (dry print) are printer's waste.
See No. 653.
Bureau Precancels: 1c, 292 diff., 1½c, 147 diff., 2c, type I, 99 diff., 2c, type II, 4 diff., 3c, 101 diff., 4c, 60 diff., 5c, 91 diff., 6c, 78 diff., 7c, 66 diff., 8c, 78 diff., 9c, 60 diff., 10c, 97 diff.

VERMONT SESQUICENTENNIAL ISSUE

Battle of Bennington, 150th anniv. and State independence.

Green Mountain Boy — A191

FLAT PLATE PRINTING

Plates of 400 subjects in four panes of 100.

1927, Aug. 3 ***Perf. 11***
643 A191 2c **carmine rose** 1.40 .80
Never hinged 2.00
On cover 1.50
P# block of 6 37.50 —
Never hinged 50.00

BURGOYNE CAMPAIGN ISSUE

Battles of Bennington, Oriskany, Fort Stanwix and Saratoga.

"The Surrender of General Burgoyne at Saratoga," by John Trumbull A192

Plates of 200 subjects in four panes of 50.

1927, Aug. 3 ***Perf. 11***
644 A192 2c **carmine rose** 3.75 2.10
Never hinged 5.50
On cover 3.00
P# block of 6 32.50 —
Never hinged 45.00

VALLEY FORGE ISSUE

150th anniversary of Washington's encampment at Valley Forge, Pa.

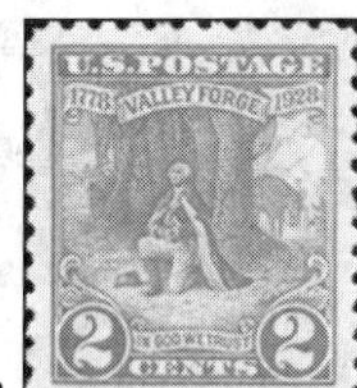

Washington at Prayer — A193

Plates of 400 subjects in four panes of 100.

1928, May 26 ***Perf. 11***
645 A193 2c **carmine rose** 1.05 .50
Never hinged 1.45
On cover .75
P# block of 6 25.00 —
Never hinged 32.50
a. 2c **lake** —
Never hinged —

BATTLE OF MONMOUTH ISSUE

150th anniv. of the Battle of Monmouth, N.J., and "Molly Pitcher" (Mary Ludwig Hayes), the heroine of the battle.

No. 634 Overprinted

ROTARY PRESS PRINTING

1928, Oct. 20 ***Perf. 11x10½***
646 A157 2c **carmine** 1.10 1.10
Never hinged 1.50
On cover 1.60
P# block of 4 35.00 —
Never hinged 50.00
Wide spacing, vert. pair 50.00 —
a. "Pitcher" only *500.00*

No. 646a is valued in the grade of fine.
The normal space between a vertical pair of the overprints is 18mm, but pairs are known with the space measuring 28mm.

HAWAII SESQUICENTENNIAL ISSUE

Sesquicentennial Celebration of the discovery of the Hawaiian Islands.

Nos. 634 and 637 Overprinted

ROTARY PRESS PRINTING

1928, Aug. 13 ***Perf. 11x10½***
647 A157 2c **carmine** 4.50 4.50
Never hinged 7.00
On cover 5.75
P# block of 4 135.00 —
Never hinged 200.00
Wide spacing, vert. pair 125.00
648 A160 5c **dark blue** 12.50 13.50
Never hinged 20.00
On cover 20.00
P# block of 4 275.00 —
Never hinged 400.00

Nos. 647-648 were sold at post offices in Hawaii and at the Postal Agency in Washington, D.C. They were valid throughout the nation.
Normally the overprints were placed 18mm apart vertically, but pairs exist with a space of 28mm between the overprints.

AERONAUTICS CONFERENCE ISSUE

Intl. Civil Aeronautics Conf., Washington, D.C., Dec. 12 - 14, 1928, and 25th anniv. of the 1st airplane flight by the Wright Brothers, Dec. 17, 1903.

Wright Airplane A194

Globe and Airplane A195

"Prairie Dog" plate flaw

FLAT PLATE PRINTING

Plates of 200 subjects in four panes of 50.

1928, Dec. 12 *Perf. 11*

649	A194	2c	**carmine rose**	1.25	.80
			Never hinged	1.75	
			On cover		1.50
			P# block of 6	10.00	—
			Never hinged	14.00	
650	A195	5c	**blue**	5.00	3.25
			Never hinged	7.25	
			On UPU-rate cover		5.00
			P# block of 6	47.50	—
			Never hinged	65.00	
			Plate flaw "prairie dog" (19658 LL 50)	27.50	12.50

GEORGE ROGERS CLARK ISSUE

150th anniv. of the surrender of Fort Sackville, the present site of Vincennes, Ind., to Clark.

Surrender of Fort Sackville A196

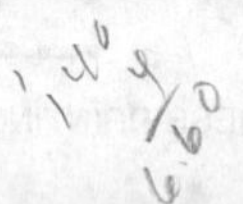

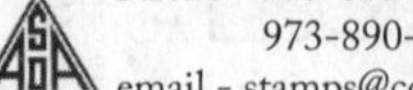

Plates of 100 subjects in two panes of 50.

1929, Feb. 25 *Perf. 11*

651	A196	2c	**carmine & black**	.65	.50
			Never hinged	.90	
			On cover		1.00
			Margin block of 4, arrow (line only) right or left	2.75	
			P# block of 6, two P# & "Top"	9.50	—
			Never hinged	12.50	
			P# block of 10, red P# only	—	—
			Double transfer (19721 R 14, 29 & 44)	4.25	2.25

REGULAR ISSUE

Type of 1922-26 Issue

ROTARY PRESS PRINTING

Plates of 400 subjects in four panes of 100.

1929, May 25 *Perf. 11x10½*

653	A154	½c	**olive brown**	.20	.20
			Never hinged	.20	
			On 1c stamped envelope (3rd class)		1.00
			P# block of 4	1.60	—
			Never hinged	2.50	
			Damaged plate, (19652 LL 72)	1.50	.75
			Retouched plate, (19652 LL 72)	1.50	.75
			Pair with full horiz. gutter btwn.	*150.00*	

Bureau Precancels: 99 diff.

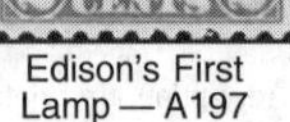

Edison's First Lamp — A197

Major General John Sullivan — A198

ELECTRIC LIGHT'S GOLDEN JUBILEE ISSUE

Invention of the 1st incandescent electric lamp by Thomas Alva Edison, Oct. 21, 1879, 50th anniv.

Designed by Alvin R. Meissner.

FLAT PLATE PRINTING

Plates of 400 subjects in four panes of 100.

1929 *Perf. 11*

654	A197	2c	**carmine rose,** *June 5*	.70	.70
			Never hinged	1.00	
			On cover		1.10
			P# block of 6	22.50	—
			Never hinged	32.50	

ROTARY PRESS PRINTING

Perf. 11x10½

655	A197	2c	**carmine rose,** *June 11*	.65	.20
			Never hinged	.90	
			On cover		.25
			P# block of 4	35.00	—
			Never hinged	47.50	

ROTARY PRESS COIL STAMP

Perf. 10 Vertically

656	A197	2c	**carmine rose,** *June 11*	14.00	1.75
			Never hinged	21.00	
			On cover		2.75
			Pair	27.50	4.00
			Never hinged	45.00	
			Joint line pair	65.00	27.50
			Never hinged	110.00	

SULLIVAN EXPEDITION ISSUE

150th anniversary of the Sullivan Expedition in New York State during the Revolutionary War.

PLAT PLATE PRINTING

Plates of 400 subjects in four panes of 100.

1929, June 17 *Perf. 11*

657	A198	2c	**carmine rose**	.70	.60
			Never hinged	1.00	
			On cover		1.00
			P# block of 6	22.50	—
			Never hinged	30.00	
a.		2c	**lake**	350.00	
			Never hinged	550.00	
			P# block of 6	*2,750.*	
			Never hinged	*3,750.*	

REGULAR ISSUE

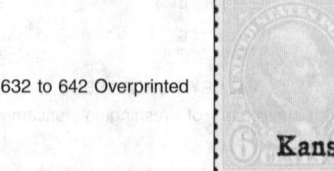

Nos. 632 to 642 Overprinted

Officially issued May 1, 1929.

Some values known canceled as early as Apr. 15.

This special issue was authorized as a measure of preventing losses from post office burglaries. Approximately a year's supply was printed and issued to postmasters. The P.O. Dept found it desirable to discontinue the State overprinted stamps after the initial supply was used.

ROTARY PRESS PRINTING

1929, May 1 *Perf. 11x10½*

658	A155	1c	**green**	2.50	2.00
			Never hinged	4.00	
			P# block of 4	35.00	—
			Never hinged	50.00	
			Wide spacing, pair	32.50	
a.			Vertical pair, one without ovpt.	*375.00*	
659	A156	1½c	**brown**	4.00	2.90
			Never hinged	6.25	
			P# block of 4	50.00	—
			Never hinged	70.00	
			Wide spacing, pair	70.00	
a.			Vertical pair, one without ovpt.	*425.00*	
660	A157	2c	**carmine**	4.50	1.00
			Never hinged	7.00	
			P# block of 4	47.50	—
			Never hinged	67.50	
			Wide spacing, pair	55.00	
661	A158	3c	**violet**	22.50	15.00
			Never hinged	35.00	
			P# block of 4	210.00	—
			Never hinged	300.00	
a.			Vertical pair, one without ovpt.	*525.00*	
			Never hinged	*675.00*	
662	A159	4c	**yellow brown**	22.50	9.00
			Never hinged	35.00	
			P# block of 4	210.00	—
			Never hinged	300.00	
a.			Vertical pair, one without ovpt.	*500.00*	
663	A160	5c	**deep blue**	14.00	9.75
			Never hinged	22.00	
			P# block of 4	150.00	—
			Never hinged	210.00	
664	A161	6c	**red orange**	32.50	18.00
			Never hinged	52.50	
			P# block of 4	450.00	—
			Never hinged	650.00	
665	A162	7c	**black**	30.00	27.50
			Never hinged	47.50	
			P# block of 4	500.00	—
			Never hinged	700.00	
a.			Vertical pair, one without ovpt.	—	

The existence of No. 665a has been questioned by specialists. The editors would like to see authenticated evidence of such a pair.

666	A163	8c	**olive green**	105.00	70.00
			Never hinged	170.00	
			P# block of 4	775.00	—
			Never hinged	1,150.	
667	A164	9c	**light rose**	16.00	11.25
			Never hinged	25.00	
			P# block of 4	225.00	—
			Never hinged	325.00	
668	A165	10c	**orange yellow**	25.00	12.00
			Never hinged	39.00	
			P# block of 4	350.00	—
			Never hinged	500.00	
			Pair with full horizontal gutter between	—	
			Nos. 658-668 (11)	278.50	178.40
			Nos. 658-668, never hinged	443.25	

See notes following No. 679.

Overprinted

1929, May 1

669	A155	1c	**green**	4.00	2.25
			Never hinged	6.25	
			P# block of 4	50.00	—
			Never hinged	70.00	
			Wide spacing, pair	40.00	45.00
a.			Vertical pair, one without ovpt.	—	
b.			No period after "Nebr." (19338, 19339 UR 26, 36)	50.00	

The existence of No. 669a has been questioned by specialists. The editors would like to see authenticated evidence of such a pair.

670	A156	1½c	**brown**	3.75	2.50
			Never hinged	5.75	
			P# block of 4	52.50	—
			Never hinged	75.00	
			Wide spacing, pair	37.50	
671	A157	2c	**carmine**	3.75	1.30
			Never hinged	5.75	
			P# block of 4	42.50	—
			Never hinged	60.00	
			Wide spacing, pair	57.50	
672	A158	3c	**violet**	15.00	12.00
			Never hinged	24.00	
			P# block of 4	165.00	—
			Never hinged	240.00	
			Wide spacing, pair	80.00	
a.			Vertical pair, one without ovpt.	*500.00*	

673 A159 4c **yellow brown** 21.00 15.00
Never hinged 35.00
P# block of 4 250.00 —
Never hinged 350.00
Wide spacing, pair 120.00
674 A160 5c **deep blue** 20.00 15.00
Never hinged 32.50
P# block of 4 275.00 —
Never hinged 400.00
675 A161 6c **red orange** 47.50 24.00
Never hinged 75.00
P# block of 4 525.00 —
Never hinged 750.00
676 A162 7c **black** 25.00 18.00
Never hinged 42.50
P# block of 4 300.00 —
Never hinged 425.00
677 A163 8c **olive green** 35.00 25.00
Never hinged 60.00
P# block of 4 400.00 —
Never hinged 575.00
Wide spacing, pair 175.00
678 A164 9c **light rose** 42.50 27.50
Never hinged 67.50
P# block of 4 525.00 —
Never hinged 750.00
Wide spacing, pair 160.00
a. Vertical pair, one without ovpt. *750.00*
679 A165 10c **orange yellow** 125.00 22.50
Never hinged 210.00
P# block of 4 950. —
Never hinged 1,350.
Nos. 669-679 (11) 342.50 165.05
Nos. 669-679, never hinged 562.75

Nos. 658-661, 669-673, 677-678 are known with the overprints on vertical pairs spaced 32mm apart instead of the normal 22mm.

Important: Nos. 658-679 with original gum have either one horizontal gum breaker ridge per stamp or portions of two at the extreme top and bottom of the stamps, 21mm apart. Multiple complete gum breaker ridges indicate a fake overprint. Absence of the gum breaker ridge indicates either regumming or regumming and a fake overprint.

General Wayne Memorial — A199

Lock No. 5, Monongahela River — A200

BATTLE OF FALLEN TIMBERS ISSUE

Memorial to Gen. Anthony Wayne and for 135th anniv. of the Battle of Fallen Timbers, Ohio.

FLAT PLATE PRINTING

Plates of 400 subjects in four panes of 100.

1929, Sept. 14 ***Perf. 11***
680 A199 2c **carmine rose** .80 .80
deep carmine rose .80 .80
Never hinged 1.10
On cover 1.10
P# block of 6 22.50 —
Never hinged 30.00

OHIO RIVER CANALIZATION ISSUE

Completion of the Ohio River Canalization Project, between Cairo, Ill. and Pittsburgh, Pa.

Plates of 400 subjects in four panes of 100.

1929, Oct. 19 ***Perf. 11***
681 A200 2c **carmine rose** .70 .65
Never hinged .95
On cover 1.10
P# block of 6 15.00 —
Never hinged 20.00

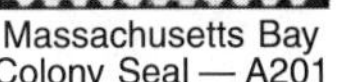
Massachusetts Bay Colony Seal — A201

Gov. Joseph West and Chief Shadoo, a Kiowa — A202

MASSACHUSETTS BAY COLONY ISSUE

300th anniversary of the founding of the Massachusetts Bay Colony.

Plates of 400 subjects in four panes of 100.

1930, Apr. 8 ***Perf. 11***
682 A201 2c **carmine rose** .60 .50
Never hinged .85
On cover 1.00
P# block of 6 22.50 —
Never hinged 30.00

CAROLINA-CHARLESTON ISSUE

260th anniv. of the founding of the Province of Carolina and the 250th anniv. of the city of Charleston, S.C.

Plates of 400 subjects in four panes of 100.

1930, Apr. 10 ***Perf. 11***
683 A202 2c **carmine rose** 1.20 1.20
Never hinged 1.65
On cover 1.40
P# block of 6 40.00 —
Never hinged 55.00

REGULAR ISSUE

Harding — A203

Taft — A204

Type of 1922-26 Issue
ROTARY PRESS PRINTING

1930 ***Perf. 11x10½***
684 A203 1½c **brown,** *Dec. 1* .35 .20
yellow brown .35 .20
Never hinged .50
On 3rd class cover 2.00
P# block of 4 1.75 —
Never hinged 2.50
Pair with full horiz. gutter btwn. *175.00*
Pair with full vert. gutter btwn. —
685 A204 4c **brown,** *June 4* .90 .25
deep brown .90 .25
Never hinged 1.25
On cover 5.00
P# block of 4 13.50 —
Never hinged 20.00
Gouge on right "4" (20141 UL 24) 2.10 .60
Recut right "4" (20141 UL 24) 2.10 .65
Pair with full horiz. gutter btwn. —

Bureau Precancels: 1½c, 96 diff., 4c, 46 diff.

ROTARY PRESS COIL STAMPS
Perf. 10 Vertically

686 A203 1½c **brown,** *Dec. 1* 1.80 .20
Never hinged 2.50
On 3rd class cover 5.00
Pair 3.75 .20
Never hinged 5.25
Joint line pair 6.50 .75
Never hinged 9.00
687 A204 4c **brown,** *Sept. 18* 3.25 .45
Never hinged 4.50
On cover 10.00
Pair 6.75 1.00
Never hinged 9.50
Joint line pair 13.00 2.50
Never hinged 18.00

Bureau Precancels: 1½c, 107 diff., 4c, 23 diff.

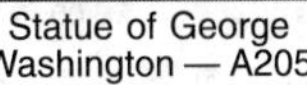
Statue of George Washington — A205

General von Steuben — A206

BRADDOCK'S FIELD ISSUE

175th anniversary of the Battle of Braddock's Field, otherwise the Battle of Monongahela.

Designed by Alvin R. Meissner.

FLAT PLATE PRINTING

Plates of 400 subjects in four panes of 100.

1930, July 9 ***Perf. 11***
688 A205 2c **carmine rose** 1.00 .85
Never hinged 1.40
On cover 1.00
P# block of 6 30.00 —
Never hinged 40.00

VON STEUBEN ISSUE

Baron Friedrich Wilhelm von Steuben (1730-1794), participant in the American Revolution.

FLAT PLATE PRINTING

Plates of 400 subjects in four panes of 100.

1930, Sept. 17 ***Perf. 11***
689 A206 2c **carmine rose** .55 .55
Never hinged .75
On cover 1.05
P# block of 6 20.00 —
Never hinged 26.50
a. Imperf., pair *2,750.*
Never hinged *3,500.*
P# block of 6 *12,500.*

The No. 689a plate block is unique but damaged. The value is for the item in its damaged condition.

General Casimir Pulaski — A207

"The Greatest Mother" — A208

PULASKI ISSUE

150th anniversary (in 1929) of the death of Gen. Casimir Pulaski, Polish patriot and hero of the American Revolutionary War.

Plates of 400 subjects in four panes of 100.

1931, Jan. 16 ***Perf. 11***
690 A207 2c **carmine rose** .30 .25
deep carmine rose .30 .25
Never hinged .40
On cover .50
P# block of 6 10.00 —
Never hinged 13.50

REGULAR ISSUE

TYPE OF 1922-26 ISSUES
ROTARY PRESS PRINTING

1931 ***Perf. 11x10½***
692 A166 11c **light blue,** *Sept. 4* 2.60 .25
Never hinged 3.70
On registered cover with other values 10.00
P# block of 4 14.00 —
Never hinged 20.00
Retouched forehead (20617 LL 2, 3) 20.00 1.00
693 A167 12c **brown violet,** *Aug. 25* 5.50 .20
violet brown 5.50 .20
Never hinged 7.75
Pair on registered cover 8.00
P# block of 4 25.00 —
Never hinged 33.50
694 A186 13c **yellow green,** *Sept. 4* 2.00 .25
light yellow green 2.00 .25
blue green 2.00 .25
Never hinged 2.80
On special delivery cover 25.00
P# block of 4 14.00 —
Never hinged 20.00
Pair with full vert. gutter btwn. 150.00
695 A168 14c **dark blue,** *Sept. 8* 3.75 .30
Never hinged 5.25
On registered cover with other values 20.00
P# block of 4 26.00 —
Never hinged 37.50
696 A169 15c **gray,** *Aug. 27* 8.00 .25
dark gray 8.00 .25
Never hinged 11.25
On registered cover with 3c 5.00
P# block of 4 37.50 —
Never hinged 50.00

Perf. 10½x11

697 A187 17c **black,** *July 25* 4.50 .25
Never hinged 6.25
On registered cover 5.00
P# block of 4 37.50 —
Never hinged 50.00
698 A170 20c **carmine rose,** *Sept. 8* 8.25 .25
Never hinged 11.50
On registered UPU-rate cover 12.50
P# block of 4 37.50 —
Never hinged 50.00
Double transfer (20538 LR 26) 20.00 —
699 A171 25c **blue green,** *July 25* 8.50 .25
Never hinged 12.00
On Federal airmail cover 20.00
P# block of 4 45.00 —
Never hinged 65.00
700 A172 30c **brown,** *Sept. 8* 15.00 .25
Never hinged 22.50
On Federal airmail cover 17.50
P# block of 4 67.50 —
Never hinged 95.00
Retouched in head (20552 UL 83) 27.50 .85
Cracked plate (20552 UR 30) 26.00 .85

701 A173 50c **lilac,** *Sept. 4* 37.50 .25
red lilac 37.50 .25
Never hinged 52.50
On Federal airmail cover 25.00
P# block of 4 180.00 —
Never hinged 250.00
Nos. 692-701 (10) 95.60 2.50
Nos. 692-701, never hinged 135.50

Bureau Precancels: 11c, 33 diff., 12c, 33 diff., 13c, 28 diff., 14c, 27 diff., 15c, 33 diff., 17c, 29 diff., 20c, 37 diff., 25c, 29 diff., 30c, 31 diff., 50c, 28 diff.

RED CROSS ISSUE

50th anniversary of the founding of the American Red Cross Society.

FLAT PLATE PRINTING

Plates of 200 subjects in two panes of 100.

1931, May 21 ***Perf. 11***

702 A208 2c **black & red** .25 .20
Never hinged .30
Margin block of 4, arrow right or left 1.05
P# block of 4, two P# 1.90 —
Never hinged 2.40
Double transfer 1.50 .50
a. Red cross missing (FO) *40,000.*

The cross tends to shift, appearing in many slightly varied positions. Two examples are recorded of No. 702a. Value reflects most recent sale price at auction in 1994.

YORKTOWN ISSUE

Surrender of Cornwallis at Yorktown, 1781.

Rochambeau, Washington, de Grasse — A209

First Plate Layout - Border and vignette plates of 100 subjects in two panes of 50 subjects each. Plate numbers between 20461 and 20602.

Second Plate Layout - Border plates of 100 subjects in two panes of 50 each, separated by a 1 inch wide vertical gutter with central guide line and vignette plates of 50 subjects. Plate numbers between 20646 and 20671.

Issued in panes of 50 subjects.

1931, Oct. 19 ***Perf. 11***

703 A209 2c **carmine rose & black** .40 .25
Never hinged .50
Margin block of 4, arrow marker, right or left 1.70
Center line block 1.80
P# block of 4, 2# 2.30 —
Never hinged 2.90
P# block of 4, 2# & arrow & marker block 2.25 —
Never hinged 2.75
P# block of 6, 2# & "TOP," arrow & marker 3.00 —
Never hinged 3.50
P# block of 8, 2# & "TOP" 3.75 —
Never hinged 4.50
Double transfer 1.75 .75
a. 2c **lake & black** 4.50 .75
Never hinged 6.25
b. 2c **dark lake & black** *450.00*
Never hinged *700.00*
P# block of 4, 2# *2,250.*
Never hinged *3,000.*
c. Horiz. pair, imperf. vertically *5,000.*
Never hinged *6,250.*
P# block of 6, 2# & arrow & marker block, hinged —

WASHINGTON BICENTENNIAL ISSUE

200th anniversary of the birth of George Washington. Various Portraits of George Washington.

By Charles Willson Peale, 1777 — A210

From Houdon Bust, 1785 — A211

By Charles Willson Peale, 1772 — A212

By Gilbert Stuart, 1796 — A213

By Charles Willson Peale, 1777 — A214

By Charles Peale Polk — A215

By Charles Willson Peale, 1795 — A216

By John Trumbull, 1792 — A217

By John Trumbull, 1780 — A218

By Charles B. J. F. Saint Memin, 1798 — A219

By W. Williams, 1794 — A220

By Gilbert Stuart, 1795 — A221

Broken Circle

ROTARY PRESS PRINTINGS

Plates of 400 subjects in four panes of 100 each

1932, Jan. 1 ***Perf. 11x10½***

704 A210 ½c **olive brown** .20 .20
Never hinged .20
P# block of 4 6.00 —
Never hinged 8.50
Broken circle (20560 U.R. 8) .75 .20
705 A211 1c **green** .20 .20
Never hinged .20
P# block of 4 4.50 —
Never hinged 6.00
Gripper cracks (20742 UL and UR) 2.75 1.75
706 A212 1½c **brown** .40 .20
Never hinged .55
P# block of 4 15.00 —
Never hinged 22.50
707 A213 2c **carmine rose** .20 .20
Never hinged .20
P# block of 4 1.50 —
Never hinged 2.00
Pair with full vert. gutter between —
Gripper cracks (20752 LR, 20755 LL & LR, 20756 LL, 20774 LR, 20792 LL & LR, 20796 LL & LR) 1.75 .65

Double Transfer

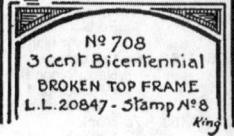

708 A214 3c **deep violet** .55 .20
Never hinged .80
P# block of 4 17.50 —
Never hinged 25.00
Double transfer 1.75 .65
Broken top frame line (20847 LL 8) 4.00 .90

Retouch in Eyes — 4c

Cracked Plate — 5c

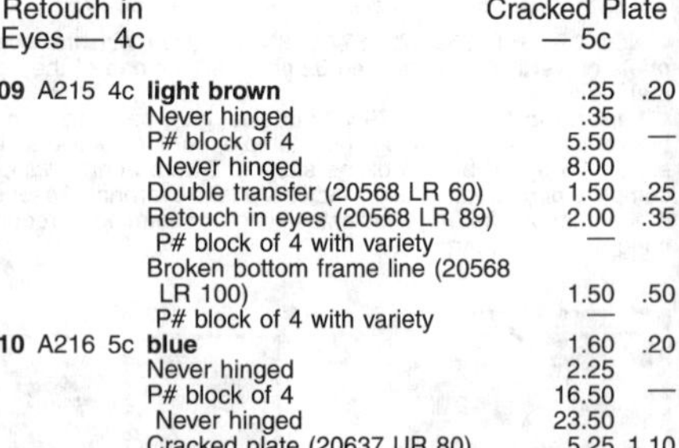

709 A215 4c **light brown** .25 .20
Never hinged .35
P# block of 4 5.50 —
Never hinged 8.00
Double transfer (20568 LR 60) 1.50 .25
Retouch in eyes (20568 LR 89) 2.00 .35
P# block of 4 with variety —
Broken bottom frame line (20568 LR 100) 1.50 .50
P# block of 4 with variety —
710 A216 5c **blue** 1.60 .20
Never hinged 2.25
P# block of 4 16.50 —
Never hinged 23.50
Cracked plate (20637 UR 80) 5.25 1.10
711 A217 6c **red orange** 3.25 .20
Never hinged 4.50
P# block of 4 52.50 —
Never hinged 70.00

Double Transfer

712 A218 7c **black** .25 .20
Never hinged .35
P# block of 4 9.00 —
Never hinged 12.50
Double transfer (20563 UL 1 or 20564 LL 91) 1.25 .25
P# block of 4 with variety —
713 A219 8c **olive bister** 2.75 .50
Never hinged 3.75
P# block of 4 50.00 —
Never hinged 70.00
Pair with full vert. gutter between —
714 A220 9c **pale red** 2.40 .20
orange red 2.40 .20
Never hinged 3.25
P# block of 4 35.00 —
Never hinged 47.50
715 A221 10c **orange yellow** 10.00 .20
Never hinged 14.00
P# block of 4 90.00 —
Never hinged 130.00
Nos. 704-715 (12) 22.05 2.70
Nos. 704-715, never hinged 30.25

Skier — A222

Boy and Girl Planting Tree — A223

OLYMPIC WINTER GAMES ISSUE

3rd Olympic Winter Games, held at Lake Placid, N.Y., Feb. 4-13, 1932.

FLAT PLATE PRINTING
Plates of 400 subjects in four panes of 100.

1932, Jan. 25 ***Perf. 11***
716 A222 2c **carmine rose** .40 .20
carmine .40 .20
Never hinged .50
P# block of 6 10.00 —
Never hinged 12.50
Cracked plate (20823 UR 41, 42; UL 48, 49, 50) 5.00 1.65
Recut (20823 UR 61) 3.50 1.50
Colored "snowball" (20815 UR 64) 25.00 5.00
a. 2c **lake** —
Never hinged —
carmine lake —
Never hinged —

ARBOR DAY ISSUE

1st observance of Arbor Day in the state of Nebraska, Apr. 1872, 60th anniv., and cent. of the birth of Julius Sterling Morton, who conceived the plan and the name "Arbor Day," while he was a member of the Nebraska State Board of Agriculture.

ROTARY PRESS PRINTING
Plates of 400 subjects in four panes of 100.

1932, Apr. 22 ***Perf. 11x10½***
717 A223 2c **carmine rose** .20 .20
Never hinged .20
P# block of 4 6.00 —
Never hinged 7.50

OLYMPIC GAMES ISSUE

Issued in honor of the 10th Olympic Games, held at Los Angeles, Calif., July 30 to Aug. 14, 1932.

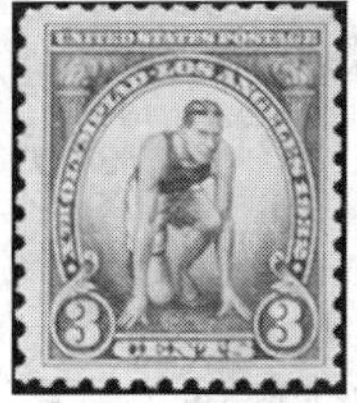
Runner at Starting Mark — A224

Myron's Discobolus — A225

Designed by Victor S. McCloskey, Jr.

ROTARY PRESS PRINTING
Plates of 400 subjects in four panes of 100.

1932, June 15 ***Perf. 11x10½***
718 A224 3c **violet** 1.40 .20
deep violet 1.40 .20
Never hinged 1.75
P# block of 4 11.50 —
Never hinged 17.50
Gripper cracks (20906 UL 1) 4.25 .75
P# block of 4 with variety —
719 A225 5c **blue** 2.20 .20
deep blue 2.20 .20
Never hinged 2.75
P# block of 4 20.00 —
Never hinged 25.00
Gripper cracks (20868 UL & UR) 4.25 1.00

Washington, by Gilbert Stuart — A226

REGULAR ISSUE
ROTARY PRESS PRINTING
Plates of 400 subjects in four panes of 100.

1932 ***Perf. 11x10½***
720 A226 3c **deep violet,** *June 16* .20 .20
light violet .20 .20
Never hinged .20
P# block of 4 1.30 —
Never hinged 1.60
Double transfer 1.00 .30
Recut face (20986 UR 15) 2.00 .75
Gripper cracks 1.25 .30
Pair with full vert. gutter btwn. *200.00*
Pair with full horiz. gutter btwn. *200.00*
b. Booklet pane of 6, *July 25* 35.00 *12.50*
Never hinged 60.00
c. Vertical pair, imperf. between *1,250.* *1,250.*
Never hinged *1,650.*

Bureau Precancels: 64 diff.

ROTARY PRESS COIL STAMPS

1932 ***Perf. 10 Vertically***
721 A226 3c **deep violet,** *June 24* 2.75 .20
light violet 2.75 .20
Never hinged 3.50
Pair 5.75 .25
Never hinged 7.00
Joint line pair 10.00 1.50
Never hinged 12.50
Gripper cracks — —
Recut face (20995, pos. 29) — —
Recut lines around eyes — —

Perf. 10 Horizontally
722 A226 3c **deep violet,** *Oct. 12* 1.50 .35
light violet 1.50 .35
Never hinged 2.00
Pair 3.25 .80
Never hinged 4.25
Joint line pair 6.25 2.75
Never hinged 8.00

Bureau Precancels: No. 721, 46 diff.

TYPE OF 1922-26 ISSUES

1932, Aug. 18 ***Perf. 10 Vertically***
723 A161 6c **deep orange** 11.00 .30
Never hinged 15.00
Pair 24.00 .70
Never hinged 32.50
Joint line pair 60.00 5.00
Never hinged 82.50

Bureau Precancels: 5 diff.

William Penn — A227

Daniel Webster (1782-1852), Statesman — A228

WILLIAM PENN ISSUE

250th anniv. of the arrival in America of Penn (1644-1718), English Quaker and founder of Pennsylvania.

FLAT PLATE PRINTING
Plates of 400 subjects in four panes of 100 each

1932, Oct. 24 ***Perf. 11***
724 A227 3c **violet** .35 .20
Never hinged .45
P# block of 6 8.00 —
Never hinged 10.00
a. Vert. pair, imperf. horiz. —

DANIEL WEBSTER ISSUE
FLAT PLATE PRINTING
Plates of 400 subjects in four panes of 100.

1932, Oct. 24 ***Perf. 11***
725 A228 3c **violet** .40 .25
light violet .40 .25
Never hinged .50
P# block of 6 16.50 —
Never hinged 20.00

Gen. James Edward Oglethorpe — A229

Washington's Headquarters at Newburgh, N.Y. — A230

GEORGIA BICENTENNIAL ISSUE

200th anniv. of the founding of the Colony of Georgia, and honoring Oglethorpe, who landed from England, Feb. 12, 1733, and personally supervised the establishing of the colony.

FLAT PLATE PRINTING
Plates of 400 subjects in four panes of 100.

1933, Feb. 12 ***Perf. 11***
726 A229 3c **violet** .35 .20
Never hinged .45
P# block of 6 10.00 —
Never hinged 12.50
P# block of 10, "CS" 14.00
Never hinged 17.50
Bottom margin block of 20, no P# —

PEACE OF 1783 ISSUE

150th anniv. of the issuance by George Washington of the official order containing the Proclamation of Peace marking officially the ending of hostilities in the War for Independence.

ROTARY PRESS PRINTING
Plates of 400 subjects in four panes of 100 each

1933, Apr. 19 ***Perf. 10½x11***
727 A230 3c **violet** .20 .20
Never hinged .20
P# block of 4 3.75 —
Never hinged 5.00
Pair with horiz. gutter between 100.00 —
Pair with vert. gutter between 100.00 —
Center block with crossed gutters and dashes —

No. 727 was available in full sheets of 400 subjects with gum, but was not regularly issued in that form. All examples of No. 727 must have original gum, including the gutter pairs and blocks, which are from the full sheets of 400. These should not be confused with similar blocks without gum, which are from the No. 752 Special Printing.

See No. 752 in the Special Printings following No. 751.

CENTURY OF PROGRESS ISSUES

"Century of Progress" Intl. Exhibition, Chicago, which opened June 1, 1933, and centenary of the incorporation of Chicago as a city.

Restoration of Fort Dearborn — A231

Federal Building — A232

ROTARY PRESS PRINTING
Plates of 400 subjects in four panes of 100.

1933, May 25 ***Perf. 10½x11***
728 A231 1c **yellow green** .20 .20
Never hinged .20
On card, Expo. station machine canc. 1.00
On card, Expo. station duplex handstamp canc. 3.00
P# block of 4 1.90 —
Never hinged 2.50
Pair with horizontal gutter between 200.00
Pair with vertical gutter between 200.00
Center block with crossed gutters and dashes *2,500.*
Gripper cracks (21133 UR & LR) 2.00 —
729 A232 3c **violet** .20 .20
Never hinged .20
On cover, Expo. station machine canc. 2.00
On cover, Expo. station duplex handstamp canc. 6.00
P# block of 4 2.40 —

Never hinged	4.00
Pair with horiz. gutter between	200.00
Pair with vert. gutter between	200.00
Center block with crossed gutters and dashes	*2,500.*

Nos. 728 and 729 were not regularly issued in full sheets of 400 with gum. The gutter pairs and blocks come from a very few non-issued sheets that were retained by Postmaster James A. Farley.

AMERICAN PHILATELIC SOCIETY ISSUE

SOUVENIR SHEETS

A231a

A232a

Illustrations reduced.

FLAT PLATE PRINTING

Plates of 225 subjects in nine panes of 25 each.

1933, Aug. 25 ***Imperf.***

Without Gum

730 A231a 1c **deep yellow green,** sheet of 25	27.50	27.50
a. Single stamp	.75	.50
Single on card, Expo. station machine canc.		1.50
Single on card, Expo. station duplex handstamp canc.		5.00
731 A232a 3c **deep violet,** sheet of 25	25.00	25.00
a. Single stamp	.65	.50
Single on cover, Expo. station machine canc.		3.00
Single on cover, Expo. station duplex handstamp canc.		7.50

Issued in sheets measuring 134x120mm containing twenty-five stamps, inscribed in the margins:

PRINTED BY THE TREASURY DEPARTMENT, BUREAU OF ENGRAVING AND PRINTING, - UNDER AUTHORITY OF JAMES A. FARLEY, POSTMASTER-GENERAL, AT CENTURY OF PROGRESS, - IN COMPLIMENT TO THE AMERICAN PHILATELIC SOCIETY FOR ITS CONVENTION AND EXHIBITION - CHICAGO, ILLINOIS, AUGUST, 1933. PLATE NO. 21145.

Also used were plates 21159 (1c), 21146 and 21160 (3c).

See Nos. 766-767 in the Special Printings following No. 751.

NATIONAL RECOVERY ACT ISSUE

Issued to direct attention to and arouse the support of the nation for the National Recovery Act.

Group of Workers — A233

ROTARY PRESS PRINTING

Plates of 400 subjects in four panes of 100.

1933, Aug. 15 ***Perf. 10½x11***

732 A233 3c **violet**	.20	.20
Never hinged	.20	
P# block of 4	1.50	—
Never hinged	1.80	
Gripper cracks (21151 UL & UR, 21153 UR & LR)	1.50	—
Recut at right (21151 UR 47)	2.00	

BYRD ANTARCTIC ISSUE

Issued in connection with the Byrd Antarctic Expedition of 1933 and for use on letters mailed through the Little America Post Office established at the Base Camp of the Expedition in the territory of the South Pole.

A Map of the World (on van der Grinten's Projection) — A234

Designed by Victor S. McCloskey, Jr.

FLAT PLATE PRINTING

Plates of 200 subjects in four panes of 50 each

1933, Oct. 9 ***Perf. 11***

733 A234 3c **dark blue**	.50	.50
Never hinged	.60	
P# block of 6	12.00	—
Never hinged	15.00	
Double transfer (21167 LR 2)	2.75	1.00

In addition to the postage charge of 3 cents, letters sent by the ships of the expedition to be canceled in Little America were subject to a service charge of 50 cents each.

See No. 753 in the Special Printings following No. 751.

KOSCIUSZKO ISSUE

Kosciuszko (1746-1807), Polish soldier and statesman served in the American Revolution, on the 150th anniv. of the granting to him of American citizenship.

Statue of General Tadeusz Kosciuszko — A235

Designed by Victor S. McCloskey, Jr.

FLAT PLATE PRINTING

Plates of 400 subjects in four panes of 100 each

1933, Oct. 13 ***Perf. 11***

734 A235 5c **blue**	.55	.25
Never hinged	.65	
P# block of 6	27.50	—
Never hinged	32.50	
Cracked plate	—	
a. Horizontal pair, imperf. vertically	*2,250.*	
Never hinged	*2,800.*	
P# block of 8	*25,000.*	

The No. 734a plate block is unique but damaged. Value reflects 1997 sale.

NATIONAL STAMP EXHIBITION ISSUE

SOUVENIR SHEET

A235a

Illustration reduced.

TYPE OF BYRD ISSUE

Plates of 150 subjects in 25 panes of six each.

1934, Feb. 10 ***Imperf.***

Without Gum

735 A235a 3c **dark blue,** sheet of 6	12.50	10.00
a. Single stamp	2.00	1.65

Issued in sheets measuring 87x93mm containing six stamps, inscribed in the margins: "Printed by the Treasury Department, Bureau of Engraving and Printing, under authority of James A. Farley, Postmaster General, in the National Stamp Exhibition of 1934. New York, N. Y., February 10-18, 1934. Plate No. 21184." Plate No. 21187 was used for sheets printed at the Exhibition, but all these were destroyed.

See No. 768 in the Special Printings following No. 751.

MARYLAND TERCENTENARY ISSUE

300th anniversary of the founding of Maryland.

"The Ark" and "The Dove" — A236

Designed by Alvin R. Meissner.

FLAT PLATE PRINTING

Plates of 400 subjects in four panes of 100.

1934, Mar. 23 ***Perf. 11***

736 A236 3c **carmine rose**	.20	.20
Never hinged	.20	
P# block of 6	6.00	—
Never hinged	8.00	
Double transfer (21190 UL 1)	—	—

MOTHERS OF AMERICA ISSUE

Issued to commemorate Mother's Day.

Adaptation of Whistler's Portrait of his Mother A237

Designed by Victor S. McCloskey, Jr.

Plates of 200 subjects in four panes of 50.

ROTARY PRESS PRINTING

1934, May 2 ***Perf. 11x10½***

737 A237 3c **deep violet**	.20	.20
Never hinged	.20	
P# block of 4	1.00	—
Never hinged	1.50	

FLAT PLATE PRINTING

Perf. 11

738 A237 3c **deep violet**	.20	.20
Never hinged	.20	
P# block of 6	4.25	—
Never hinged	5.00	

See No. 754 in the Special Printings following No. 751.

WISCONSIN TERCENTENARY ISSUE

Arrival of Jean Nicolet, French explorer, on the shores of Green Bay, 300th anniv. According to historical records, Nicolet was the 1st white man to reach the territory now comprising the State of Wisconsin.

Nicolet's Landing A238

Designed by Victor S. McCloskey, Jr.

FLAT PLATE PRINTING

Plates of 200 subjects in four panes of 50.

1934. July 7 ***Perf. 11***

No.	Type	Denom.	Description	Unused	Used
739	A238	3c	**deep violet**	.20	.20
			violet	.20	.20
			Never hinged	.20	
			P# block of 6	2.90	—
			Never hinged	3.40	
a.			Vert. pair, imperf. horiz.	*350.00*	
			Never hinged	*600.00*	
b.			Horiz. pair, imperf. vert.	*525.00*	
			Never hinged	*900.00*	
			P# block of 6	*2,000.*	

See No. 755 in the Special Printings following No. 751.

NATIONAL PARKS YEAR ISSUE

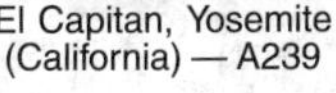

El Capitan, Yosemite (California) — A239

Old Faithful, Yellowstone (Wyoming) — A243

View of Grand Canyon (Arizona) A240

Mt. Rainier and Mirror Lake (Washington) A241

Cliff Palace, Mesa Verde Park (Colorado) A242

Crater Lake (Oregon) A244

Great Head, Acadia Park (Maine) — A245

Great White Throne, Zion Park (Utah) — A246

Great Smoky Mountains (North Carolina) — A248

Mt. Rockwell (Mt. Sinopah) and Two Medicine Lake, Glacier National Park (Montana) A247

FLAT PLATE PRINTING

Plates of 200 subjects in four panes of 50.

1934 **Unwmk.** ***Perf. 11***

No.	Type	Denom.	Description	Unused	Used
740	A239	1c	**green,** *July 16*	.20	.20
			light green	.20	.20
			Never hinged	.20	
			P# block of 6	1.00	—
			Never hinged	1.25	
			Recut	1.50	.50
a.			Vert. pair, imperf. horiz., with gum	*1,300.*	
			Never hinged	*1,800.*	
741	A240	2c	**red,** *July 24*	.20	.20
			orange red	.20	.20
			Never hinged	.20	
			P# block of 6	1.25	—
			Never hinged	1.50	
			Double transfer	1.25	—
a.			Vert. pair, imperf. horiz., with gum	*475.00*	
			Never hinged	*800.00*	
b.			Horiz. pair, imperf. vert., with gum	*600.00*	
			Never hinged	*1,000.*	
			P# block of 6	*2,750.*	
			Never hinged	*3,750.*	
742	A241	3c	**deep violet,** *Aug. 3*	.20	.20
			Never hinged	.20	
			P# block of 6	1.75	—
			Never hinged	2.10	
			Recut	1.50	—
a.			Vert. pair, imperf. horiz., with gum	*700.00*	
			Never hinged	*1,200.*	
743	A242	4c	**brown,** *Sept. 25*	.35	.40
			light brown	.35	.40
			Never hinged	.45	
			P# block of 6	7.00	—
			Never hinged	8.50	
a.			Vert. pair, imperf. horiz., with gum	*1,000.*	
			Never hinged	*1,700.*	
744	A243	5c	**blue,** *July 30*	.70	.65
			light blue	.70	.65
			Never hinged	.95	
			P# block of 6	8.75	—
			Never hinged	10.50	
a.			Horiz. pair, imperf. vert., with gum	*600.00*	
			Never hinged	*1,000.*	
745	A244	6c	**dark blue,** *Sept. 5*	1.10	.85
			Never hinged	1.50	
			P# block of 6	15.00	—
			Never hinged	18.00	
746	A245	7c	**black,** *Oct. 2*	.60	.75
			Never hinged	.85	
			P# block of 6	10.00	—
			Never hinged	12.00	
			Double transfer	3.00	1.25
a.			Horiz. pair, imperf. vert., with gum	*725.00*	
			Never hinged	*1,250.*	
			P# block of 6, never hinged	*6,000.*	
747	A246	8c	**sage green,** *Sept. 18*	1.60	1.50
			Never hinged	2.20	
			P# block of 6	15.00	—
			Never hinged	18.00	
748	A247	9c	**red orange,** *Aug. 27*	1.50	.65
			orange	1.50	.65
			Never hinged	2.10	
			P# block of 6	14.00	—
			Never hinged	19.00	
749	A248	10c	**gray black,** *Oct. 8*	3.00	1.25
			gray	3.00	1.25
			Never hinged	4.25	
			P# block of 6	22.50	—
			Never hinged	30.00	
			Nos. 740-749 (10)	9.45	6.65
			Nos. 740-749, never hinged	12.75	

Imperforate varieties of the 2c and 5c exist as errors of the perforated Parks set, but are virtually impossible to distinguish from gummed copies from the imperforate sheets of 200. (See note above No. 752 in the Special Printings following No. 751.

AMERICAN PHILATELIC SOCIETY ISSUE
SOUVENIR SHEET

A248a

Illustration reduced.

Plates of 120 subjects in 20 panes of 6 stamps each.

1934, Aug. 28 ***Imperf.***

No.	Type	Denom.	Description	Unused	Used
750	A248a	3c	**deep violet,** sheet of 6	30.00	27.50
			Never hinged	37.50	
a.			Single stamp	3.50	3.25
			Never hinged	4.50	

Issued in sheets measuring approximately 98x93mm containing six stamps, inscribed in the margins: PRINTED BY THE TREASURY DEPARTMENT, BUREAU OF ENGRAVING AND PRINTING, - UNDER AUTHORITY OF JAMES A. FARLEY, POSTMASTER GENERAL, - IN COMPLIMENT TO THE AMERICAN PHILATELIC SOCIETY FOR ITS CONVENTION AND EXHIBITION, - ATLANTIC CITY, NEW JERSEY, AUGUST, 1934. PLATE NO. 21303.

See No. 770 in the Special Printings following No. 751.

TRANS-MISSISSIPPI PHILATELIC EXPOSITION ISSUE
SOUVENIR SHEET

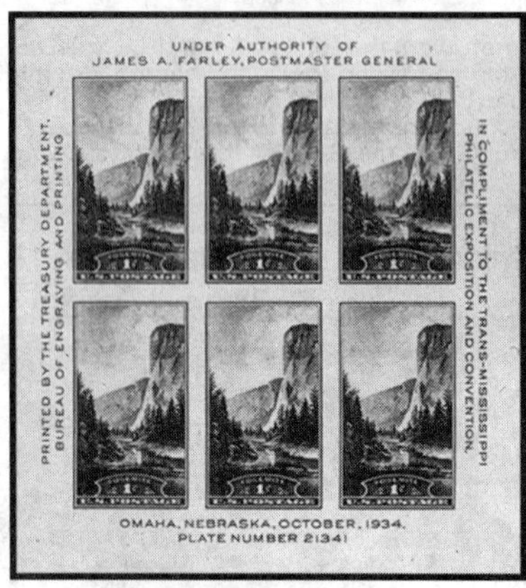

A248b

Illustration reduced.

Plates of 120 subjects in 20 panes of 6 stamps each.

1934, Oct. 10 *Imperf.*

751	A248b 1c	**green,** sheet of 6	12.50	12.50
		Never hinged	16.00	
a.		Single stamp	1.40	1.60
		Never hinged	1.85	

Issued in sheets measuring approximately 92x99mm containing six stamps, inscribed in the margins: PRINTED BY THE TREASURY DEPARTMENT, BUREAU OF ENGRAVING AND PRINTING, - UNDER AUTHORITY OF JAMES A. FARLEY, POSTMASTER GENERAL, - IN COMPLIMENT TO THE TRANS-MISSISSIPPI PHILATELIC EXPOSITION AND CONVENTION, OMAHA, NEBRASKA, - OCTOBER, 1934. PLATE NO. 21341.

See No. 769 in the Special Printings that follow.

SPECIAL PRINTING
(Nos. 752-771 inclusive)

"Issued for a limited time in full sheets as printed, and in blocks thereof, to meet the requirements of collectors and others who may be interested." -From Postal Bulletin No. 16614.

Issuance of the following 20 stamps in complete sheets resulted from the protest of collectors and others at the practice of presenting, to certain government officials, complete sheets of unsevered panes, imperforate (except Nos. 752 and 753) and generally ungummed.

Designs of Commemorative Issues
Without Gum

NOTE: In 1940 the P.O. Department offered to and did gum full sheets of Nos. 756-765 and 769-770 sent in by owners. No other Special Printings were accepted for gumming.

TYPE OF PEACE ISSUE

Issued in sheets of 400, consisting of four panes of 100 each, with vertical and horizontal gutters between and plate numbers at outside corners at sides.

ROTARY PRESS PRINTING

1935, Mar. 15 **Unwmk.** *Perf. 10½x11*

752	A230 3c	**violet**	.20	.20
		Pair with horiz. gutter between	5.75	—
		Pair with vert. gutter between	9.50	—
		Gutter block of 4 with dash (left or right)	12.50	—
		Gutter block of 4 with dash (top or bottom)	20.00	—
		Center block with crossed gutters and dashes	50.00	—
		P# block of 4	22.50	—

TYPE OF BYRD ISSUE

Issued in sheets of 200, consisting of four panes of 50 each, with vertical and horizontal guide lines in gutters between panes, and plate numbers centered at top and bottom of each pane. This applies to Nos. 753-765 and 771.

FLAT PLATE PRINTING
Perf. 11

753	A234 3c	**dark blue**	.50	.45
		Pair with horiz. line between	2.25	—
		Pair with vert. line between	25.00	—
		Margin block of 4, arrow & guide line (left or right)	4.75	—
		Margin block of 4, arrow & guide-line (top or bottom)	52.50	—
		Center line block	67.50	15.00
		P# block of 6, number at top or bottom	17.50	—

No. 753 is similar to No. 733. Positive identification is by blocks or pairs showing guide line between stamps. These lines between stamps are found only on No. 753.

TYPE OF MOTHERS OF AMERICA ISSUE
Issued in sheets of 200
FLAT PLATE PRINTING
Imperf

754	A237 3c	**deep violet**	.60	.60
		Pair with horiz. line between	1.75	—
		Pair with vert. line between	1.40	—
		Margin block of 4, arrow & guide-line (left or right)	3.75	—
		Margin block of 4, arrow & guide-line (top or bottom)	3.00	—
		Center line block	7.25	—
		P# block of 6, number at top or bottom	15.00	—

TYPE OF WISCONSIN ISSUE
Issued in sheets of 200
FLAT PLATE PRINTING
Imperf

755	A238 3c	**deep violet**	.60	.60
		Pair with horiz. line between	1.75	—
		Pair with vert. line between	1.40	—
		Margin block of 4, arrow & guide-line (left or right)	3.75	—
		Margin block of 4, arrow & guide-line (top or bottom)	3.00	—
		Center line block	7.25	—
		P# block of 6, number at top or bottom	15.00	—

TYPES OF NATIONAL PARKS ISSUE
Issued in sheets of 200
FLAT PLATE PRINTING
Imperf

756	A239 1c	**green**	.20	.20
		Pair with horiz. line between	.45	—
		Pair with vert. line between	.55	—
		Margin block of 4, arrow & guide-line (left or right)	1.00	—
		Margin block of 4, arrow & guide-line (top or bottom)	1.25	—
		Center line block	3.00	—
		P# block of 6, number at top or bottom	4.00	—
		See note above No. 766.		
757	A240 2c	**red**	.25	.25
		Pair with horiz. line between	.70	—
		Pair with vert. line between	.55	—
		Margin block of 4, arrow & guide-line (left or right)	1.60	—
		Margin block of 4, arrow & guide-line (top or bottom)	1.25	—
		Center line block	3.50	—
		P# block of 6, number at top or bottom	5.75	—
		Double transfer	—	
758	A241 3c	**deep violet**	.50	.45
		Pair with horiz. line between	1.40	—
		Pair with vert. line between	1.25	—
		Margin block of 4, arrow & guide-line (left or right)	3.10	—
		Margin block of 4, arrow & guide-line (top or bottom)	2.75	—
		Center line block	5.25	—
		P# block of 6, number at top or bottom	14.00	—
759	A242 4c	**brown**	.95	.95
		Pair with horiz. line between	2.75	—
		Pair with vert. line between	2.25	—
		Margin block of 4, arrow & guide-line (left or right)	5.75	—
		Margin block of 4, arrow & guide-line (top or bottom)	4.75	—
		Center line block	8.50	—
		P# block of 6, number at top or bottom	20.00	—
760	A243 5c	**blue**	1.50	1.40
		Pair with horiz. line between	3.50	—
		Pair with vert. line between	4.25	—
		Margin block of 4, arrow & guide-line (left or right)	7.50	—
		Margin block of 4, arrow & guide-line (top or bottom)	9.00	—
		Center line block	15.00	—
		P# block of 6, number at top or bottom	25.00	—
		Double transfer	—	
761	A244 6c	**dark blue**	2.40	2.25
		Pair with horiz. line between	6.50	—
		Pair with vert. line between	5.50	—
		Margin block of 4, arrow & guide-line (left or right)	14.00	—
		Margin block of 4, arrow & guide-line (top or bottom)	12.50	—
		Center line block	20.00	—
		P# block of 6, number at top or bottom)	37.50	—
762	A245 7c	**black**	1.50	1.40
		Pair with horiz. line between	4.25	—
		Pair with vert. line between	3.75	—
		Margin block of 4, arrow & guide-line (left or right)	9.25	—
		Margin block of 4, arrow & guide-line (top or bottom)	8.25	—
		Center line block	14.00	—
		P# block of 6, number at top or bottom	30.00	—
		Double transfer	—	
763	A246 8c	**sage green**	1.60	1.50
		Pair with horiz. line between	3.75	—
		Pair with vert. line between	4.75	—
		Margin block of 4, arrow & guide-line (left or right)	8.75	—
		Margin block of 4, arrow & guide-line (top or bottom)	11.00	—
		Center line block	17.50	—
		P# block of 6, number at top or bottom	37.50	—
764	A247 9c	**red orange**	1.90	1.75
		Pair with horiz. line between	5.00	—
		Pair with vert. line between	4.50	—
		Margin block of 4, arrow & guide-line (left or right)	11.50	—
		Margin block of 4, arrow & guide-line (top or bottom)	10.50	—
		Center line block	22.50	—
		P# block of 6, number at top or bottom	42.50	—
765	A248 10c	**gray black**	3.75	3.50
		Pair with horiz. line between	9.00	—
		Pair with vert. line between	10.50	—
		Margin block of 4, arrow & guide-line (left or right)	20.00	—
		Margin block of 4, arrow & guide-line (top or bottom)	24.00	—
		Center line block	30.00	—
		P# block of 6, number at top or bottom	50.00	—
		Nos. 756-765 (10)	14.55	13.65

SOUVENIR SHEETS

Note: Single items from these sheets are identical with other varieties, 766 and 730, 766a and 730a, 767 and 731, 767a and 731a, 768 and 735, 768a and 735a, 769 and 756, 770 and 758.

Positive identification is by blocks or pairs showing wide gutters between stamps. These wide gutters occur only on Nos. 766-770 and measure, horizontally, 13mm on Nos. 766-767; 16mm on No. 768, and 23mm on Nos. 769-770.

TYPE OF CENTURY OF PROGRESS ISSUE

Issued in sheets of 9 panes of 25 stamps each, with vertical and horizontal gutters between panes.

FLAT PLATE PRINTING
Imperf

766	A231a 1c	**yellow green,** pane of 25	25.00	25.00
a.		Single stamp	.70	.50
		Block of 4	2.80	1.70
		Pair with horiz. gutter between	5.50	—
		Pair with vert. gutter between	7.00	—
		Block with crossed gutters	15.00	—
		Block of 50 stamps (two panes)	70.00	
767	A232a 3c	**violet,** pane of 25	23.50	23.50
a.		Single stamp	.60	.50
		Pair with horiz. gutter between	5.25	—
		Pair with vert. gutter between	6.75	—
		Block with crossed gutters	15.00	—
		Block of 50 stamps (two panes)	65.00	

NATIONAL EXHIBITION ISSUE
TYPE OF BYRD ISSUE

Issued in sheets of 25 panes of 6 stamps each, with vertical and horizontal gutters between panes.

FLAT PLATE PRINTING
Imperf

768	A235a 3c	**dark blue,** pane of six	20.00	15.00
a.		Single stamp	2.80	2.40
		Pair with horiz. gutter between	7.50	—
		Pair with vert. gutter between	9.00	—
		Block of 4 with crossed gutters	20.00	—
		Block of 12 stamps (two panes)	47.50	

TYPES OF NATIONAL PARKS ISSUE

Issued in sheets of 20 panes of 6 stamps each, with vertical and horizontal gutters between panes.

FLAT PLATE PRINTING
Imperf

769	A248b 1c	**green,** pane of six	12.50	11.00
a.		Single stamp	1.85	1.80
		Pair with horiz. gutter between	6.00	—
		Pair with vert. gutter between	9.00	—
		Block of 4 with crossed gutters	15.00	—
		Block of 12 stamps (two panes)	30.00	
770	A248a 3c	**deep violet,** pane of six	30.00	24.00
a.		Single stamp	3.25	3.10
		Pair with horiz. gutter between	12.50	—
		Pair with vert. gutter between	11.00	—
		Block of 4 with crossed gutters	30.00	—
		Block of 12 stamps (two panes)	70.00	

TYPE OF AIR POST SPECIAL DELIVERY

Issued in sheets of 200, with vertical and horizontal guide lines between panes.

FLAT PLATE PRINTING
Imperf

771	APSD1 16c	**dark blue**	2.40	2.40
		Pair with horiz. line between	6.50	—
		Pair with vert. line between	5.50	—
		Margin block of 4, arrow & guideline (left or right)	15.00	—
		Margin block of 4, arrow & guideline (top or bottom)	12.50	—

Center line block	60.00	—
P# block of 6, number at top or bottom	50.00	—

Catalogue values for unused stamps in this section, from this point to the end, are for Never Hinged items.

VALUES FOR HINGED STAMPS AFTER NO. 771

This catalogue does not value unused stamps after No. 771 in hinged condition. Hinged unused stamps from No. 772 to the present are worth considerably less than the values given for unused stamps, which are for never-hinged examples.

CONNECTICUT TERCENTENARY ISSUE

300th anniv. of the settlement of Connecticut.

The Charter Oak — A249

ROTARY PRESS PRINTING

Plates of 200 subjects in four panes of 50.

1935, Apr. 26 **Unwmk.** ***Perf. 11x10½***

772	A249 3c **violet**	.20	.20
	rose violet	.20	.20
	P# block of 4	1.75	—
	Defect in cent sign (21395 UR 4)	1.00	.25

CALIFORNIA PACIFIC EXPOSITION ISSUE

California Pacific Exposition at San Diego.

View of San Diego Exposition A250

ROTARY PRESS PRINTING

Plates of 200 subjects in four panes of 50.

1935, May 29 **Unwmk.** ***Perf. 11x10½***

773	A250 3c **purple**	.20	.20
	On cover, Expo. station machine canc. (non-first day)		*2.50*
	On cover, Expo. station duplex handstamp canc. (non-first day)		*20.00*
	P# block of 4	1.10	—
	Pair with full vertical gutter between	—	

BOULDER DAM ISSUE

Dedication of Boulder Dam.

Boulder Dam (Hoover Dam) — A251

FLAT PLATE PRINTING

Plates of 200 subjects in four panes of 50.

1935, Sept. 30 **Unwmk.** ***Perf. 11***

774	A251 3c **purple**	.20	.20
	deep purple	.20	.20
	P# block of 6	1.65	—

MICHIGAN CENTENARY ISSUE

Advance celebration of Michigan Statehood centenary.

Michigan State Seal — A252

Designed by Alvin R. Meissner.

ROTARY PRESS PRINTING

Plates of 200 subjects in 4 panes of 50.

1935, Nov. 1 **Unwmk.** ***Perf. 11x10½***

775	A252 3c **purple**	.20	.20
	P# block of 4	1.25	—

TEXAS CENTENNIAL ISSUE

Centennial of Texas independence.

Sam Houston, Stephen F. Austin and the Alamo — A253

Designed by Alvin R. Meissner.

ROTARY PRESS PRINTING

Plates of 200 subjects in four panes of 50.

1936, Mar. 2 **Unwmk.** ***Perf. 11x10½***

776	A253 3c **purple**	.20	.20
	On cover, Expo. station machine canc.		2.00
	On cover, Expo. station duplex handstamp canc.		*40.00*
	P# block of 4	1.10	—

RHODE ISLAND TERCENTENARY ISSUE

300th anniv. of the settlement of Rhode Island.

Statue of Roger Williams — A254

ROTARY PRESS PRINTING

Plates of 200 subjects in four panes of 50.

1936, May 4 **Unwmk.** ***Perf. 10½x11***

777	A254 3c **purple**	.20	.20
	rose violet	.20	.20
	P# block of 4	1.10	—
	Pair with full gutter between	*200.00*	

THIRD INTERNATIONAL PHILATELIC EXHIBITION ISSUE

SOUVENIR SHEET

A254a

Illustration reduced.

Plates of 120 subjects in thirty panes of 4 each.

FLAT PLATE PRINTING

1936, May 9 **Unwmk.** ***Imperf.***

778	A254a **violet,** sheet of 4	1.75	1.75
a.	3c Type A249	.40	.35
b.	3c Type A250	.40	.35
c.	3c Type A252	.40	.35
d.	3c Type A253	.40	.35

Issued in sheets measuring 98x66mm containing four stamps, inscribed in the margins: "Printed by the Treasury Department, Bureau of Engraving and Printing, under authority of James A. Farley, Postmaster General, in compliment to the third International Philatelic Exhibition of 1936. New York, N. Y., May 9-17, 1936. Plate No. 21557 (or 21558)."

ARKANSAS CENTENNIAL ISSUE

100th anniv. of the State of Arkansas.

Arkansas Post, Old and New State Houses A255

ROTARY PRESS PRINTING

Plates of 200 subjects in four panes of 50.

1936, June 15 **Unwmk.** ***Perf. 11x10½***

782	A255 3c **purple**	.25	.20
	P# block of 4	1.25	—

OREGON TERRITORY ISSUE

Opening of the Oregon Territory, 1836, 100th anniv.

Map of Oregon Territory A256

ROTARY PRESS PRINTING

Plates of 200 subjects in four panes of 50.

1936, July 14 **Unwmk.** ***Perf. 11x10½***

783	A256 3c **purple**	.20	.20
	P# block of 4	1.10	—
	Double transfer (21579 UL 3)	1.00	.50

SUSAN B. ANTHONY ISSUE

Susan Brownell Anthony (1820-1906), woman-suffrage advocate, and 16th anniv. of the ratification of the 19th Amendment which grants American women the right to vote.

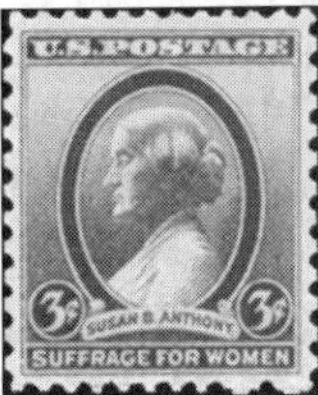

Susan B. Anthony — A257

ROTARY PRESS PRINTING

Plates of 400 subjects in four panes of 100.

1936, Aug. 26 **Unwmk.** ***Perf. 11x10½***

784	A257 3c **dark violet**	.20	.20
	P# block of 4	.75	—
	Period missing after "B" (21590 LR 100)	.75	.25

ARMY ISSUE

Issued in honor of the United States Army.

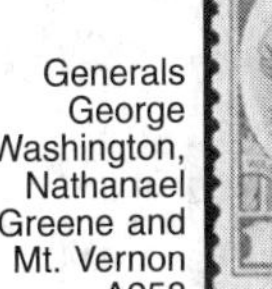

Generals George Washington, Nathanael Greene and Mt. Vernon A258

Maj. Gen. Andrew Jackson, Gen. Winfield Scott and the Hermitage A259

Generals William T. Sherman, Ulysses S. Grant and Philip H. Sheridan A260

Generals Robert E. Lee, "Stonewall" Jackson and Stratford Hall — A261

U. S. Military Academy, West Point — A262

ROTARY PRESS PRINTING

Plates of 200 subjects in four panes of 50.

1936-37			Unwmk.	Perf. 11x10½	
785	A258	1c	**green,** *Dec. 15, 1936*	.20	.20
			yellow green	.20	.20
			P# block of 4	.85	—
			Pair with full vertical gutter between	—	
786	A259	2c	**carmine,** *Jan. 15, 1937*	.20	.20
			P# block of 4	.85	—
787	A260	3c	**purple,** *Feb. 18, 1937*	.20	.20
			P# block of 4	1.25	—
788	A261	4c	**gray,** *Mar. 23, 1937*	.30	.20
			P# block of 4	8.00	—
789	A262	5c	**ultramarine,** *May 26, 1937*	.60	.25
			P# block of 4	8.50	—
			Nos. 785-789 (5)	1.50	1.05

NAVY ISSUE

Issued in honor of the United States Navy.

John Paul Jones and John Barry — A263

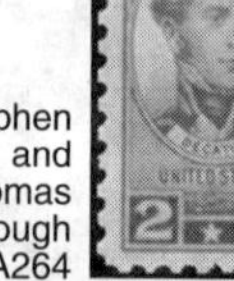

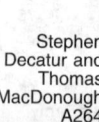

Stephen Decatur and Thomas MacDonough A264

Admirals David G. Farragut and David D. Porter — A265

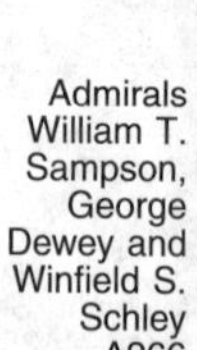

Admirals William T. Sampson, George Dewey and Winfield S. Schley A266

Seal of US Naval Academy and Naval Midshipmen A267

ROTARY PRESS PRINTING

Plates of 200 subjects in four panes of 50.

1936-37			Unwmk.	Perf. 11x10½	
790	A263	1c	**green,** *Dec. 15, 1936*	.20	.20
			yellow green	.20	.20
			P# block of 4	.85	—
791	A264	2c	**carmine,** *Jan. 15, 1937*	.20	.20
			P# block of 4	.75	—
792	A265	3c	**purple,** *Feb. 18, 1937*	.20	.20
			P# block of 4	1.00	—
793	A266	4c	**gray,** *Mar. 23, 1937*	.30	.20
			P# block of 4	9.00	—
794	A267	5c	**ultramarine,** *May 26, 1937*	.60	.25
			P# block of 4	9.00	—
			Pair with full vert. gutter btwn.	—	
			Nos. 790-794 (5)	1.50	1.05

ORDINANCE OF 1787 SESQUICENTENNIAL ISSUE

150th anniv. of the adoption of the Ordinance of 1787 and the creation of the Northwest Territory.

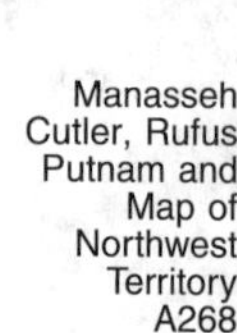

Manasseh Cutler, Rufus Putnam and Map of Northwest Territory A268

ROTARY PRESS PRINTING

Plates of 200 subjects in four panes of 50.

1937, July 13			Unwmk.	Perf. 11x10½	
795	A268	3c	**red violet**	.20	.20
			P# block of 4	1.10	—

VIRGINIA DARE ISSUE

350th anniv. of the birth of Virginia Dare, 1st child born in America of English parents (Aug. 18, 1587), and the settlement at Roanoke Island.

Virginia Dare and Parents — A269

FLAT PLATE PRINTING

Plates of 192 subjects in four panes of 48 each, separated by 1¼ inch wide gutters with central guide lines.

1937, Aug. 18			Unwmk.	Perf. 11	
796	A269	5c	**gray blue**	.20	.20
			P# block of 6	6.50	—

SOCIETY OF PHILATELIC AMERICANS ISSUE

SOUVENIR SHEET

A269a

Illustration reduced.

TYPE OF NATIONAL PARKS ISSUE

Plates of 36 subjects

FLAT PLATE PRINTING

1937, Aug. 26			Unwmk.	Imperf.	
797	A269a	10c	**blue green**	.60	.40

Issued in sheets measuring 67x78mm, inscribed in margins: "Printed by the Treasury Department, Bureau of Engraving and Printing - Under the Authority of James A. Farley, Postmasster General - In Compliment to the 43rd Annual Convention of the Society of Philatelic Americans - Asheville, N.C., August 26-28, 1937. Plate Number 21695 (6)."

CONSTITUTION SESQUICENTENNIAL ISSUE

150th anniversary of the signing of the Constitution on September 17, 1787.

"Adoption of the Constitution" A270

ROTARY PRESS PRINTING

Plates of 200 subjects in four panes of 50.

1937, Sept. 17			Unwmk.	Perf. 11x10½	
798	A270	3c	**bright red violet**	.20	.20
			P# block of 4	1.40	—

TERRITORIAL ISSUES

Hawaii

Statue of Kamehameha I, Honolulu — A271

Alaska

Mt. McKinley A272

Puerto Rico

La Fortaleza, San Juan — A273

Virgin Islands

Charlotte Amalie Harbor, St. Thomas A274

ROTARY PRESS PRINTING

Plates of 200 subjects in panes of 50.

1937			**Unwmk.**	***Perf. 10½x11***	
799	A271	3c	**violet,** *Oct. 18*	.20	.20
			P# block of 4	1.25	—
			Perf. 11x10½		
800	A272	3c	**violet,** *Nov. 12*	.20	.20
			P# block of 4	1.25	—
			Pair with full gutter between	—	
801	A273	3c	**bright violet,** *Nov. 25*	.20	.20
			P# block of 4	1.25	—
802	A274	3c	**light violet,** *Dec. 15*	.20	.20
			P# block of 4	1.25	—
			Pair with full vertical gutter between	*275.00*	
			Nos. 799-802 (4)	.80	.80

PRESIDENTIAL ISSUE

Benjamin Franklin — A275

George Washington — A276

Martha Washington A277

John Adams A278

Thomas Jefferson — A279

James Madison — A280

The White House — A281

James Monroe — A282

John Quincy Adams — A283

Andrew Jackson — A284

Martin Van Buren — A285

William H. Harrison — A286

John Tyler — A287

James K. Polk — A288

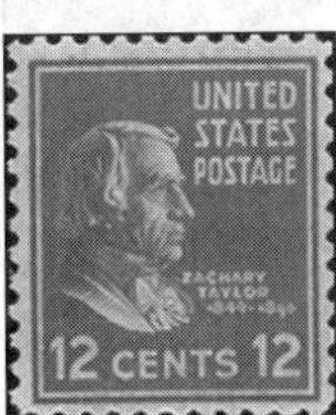

Zachary Taylor — A289

Millard Fillmore — A290

Franklin Pierce — A291

James Buchanan — A292

Abraham Lincoln — A293

Andrew Johnson — A294

Ulysses S. Grant — A295

Rutherford B. Hayes — A296

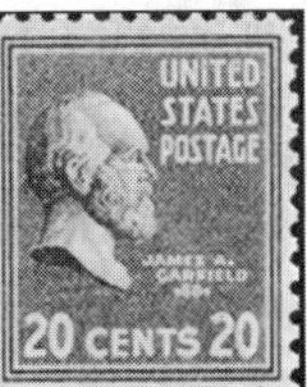

James A. Garfield — A297

Chester A. Arthur — A298

Grover Cleveland — A299

Benjamin Harrison — A300

William McKinley — A301

Theodore Roosevelt — A302

William Howard Taft — A303

Woodrow Wilson — A304

Warren G. Harding — A305

Calvin Coolidge — A306

ROTARY PRESS PRINTING

Ordinary and Electric Eye (EE) Plates of 400 subjects in four panes of 100. (For details of EE Markings, see Information for Collectors in first part of this Catalogue.)

1938			**Unwmk.**	***Perf. 11x10½***	
803	A275	½c	**deep orange,** *May 19*	.20	.20
			P# block of 4	.40	—
804	A276	1c	**green,** *Apr. 25*	.20	.20
			light green	.20	.20
			P# block of 4	.25	—
			Pair with full vert. gutter btwn.	*160.00*	—
b.			Booklet pane of 6	2.00	*.50*
805	A277	1½c	**bister brown,** *May 5*	.20	.20
			buff ('43)	.20	.20
			P# block of 4	.20	—
			Pair with full horiz. gutter btwn.	*175.00*	
			Pair with full vert. gutter btwn.	—	
b.			Horiz. pair, imperf. between	160.00	25.00

No. 805b used is always Bureau precanceled St. Louis, Mo., and is generally with gum. Value is for gummed pair.

806	A278	2c	**rose carmine,** *June 3*	.20	.20
			rose pink ('43)	.20	.20
			P# block of 4, # opposite corner stamp	.30	—
			Vertical margin block of 10, P# opposite 3rd horizontal row (Experimental EE plates)	4.00	
			Recut at top of head, Pl. 22156 U.L. 3	3.00	1.50
			Pair with full horiz. gutter btwn.	—	
			Pair with full vert. gutter btwn.	—	
b.			Booklet pane of 6	4.75	*.85*
807	A279	3c	**deep violet,** *June 16*	.20	.20
			P# block of 4, # opposite corner stamp	.25	.25

Vertical margin block of 10, P# opposite 3rd horizontal row (Experimental EE plates) 30.00
Pair with full vert. gutter btwn. *150.00*
Pair with full horiz. gutter btwn. *225.00*
a. Booklet pane of 6 8.50 *2.00*
Horiz. booklet pair with full vert. gutter between —
b. Horiz. pair, imperf. between *1,500.* —
c. Imperf., pair *2,500.*
808 A280 4c **red violet,** *July 1* .75 .20
rose violet ('43) .75 .20
P# block of 4 3.50 —
809 A281 4½c **dark gray,** *July 11* .20 .20
gray ('43) .20 .20
P# block of 4 1.50 —
810 A282 5c **bright blue,** *July 21* .20 .20
light blue .20 .20
P# block of 4 1.00 —
Pair with full vert. gutter btwn. —
811 A283 6c **red orange,** *July 28* .20 .20
P# block of 4 1.00 —
812 A284 7c **sepia,** *Aug. 4* .25 .20
violet brown .25 .20
P# block of 4 1.25 —
813 A285 8c **olive green,** *Aug. 11* .30 .20
light olive green ('43) .30 .20
olive ('42) .30 .20
P# block of 4 1.40 —
814 A286 9c **rose pink,** *Aug. 18* .30 .20
pink ('43) .30 .20
P# block of 4 1.40 —
Pair with full vert. gutter btwn. —
815 A287 10c **brown red,** *Sept. 2* .25 .20
pale brown red ('43) .25 .20
P# block of 4 1.25 —
816 A288 11c **ultramarine,** *Sept. 8* .65 .20
bright ultramarine .65 .20
P# block of 4 3.00 —
817 A289 12c **bright violet,** *Sept. 14* .90 .20
P# block of 4 4.00 —
818 A290 13c **blue green,** *Sept. 22* 1.25 .20
deep blue green 1.25 .20
P# block of 4 7.00 —
819 A291 14c **blue,** *Oct. 6* .90 .20
P# block of 4 4.50 —
820 A292 15c **blue gray,** *Oct. 13* .40 .20
P# block of 4 1.90 —
821 A293 16c **black,** *Oct. 20* .90 .25
P# block of 4 5.00 —
822 A294 17c **rose red,** *Oct. 27* .85 .20
deep rose red .85 .20
Block of 4 3.40 .75
P# block of 4 4.50 —
823 A295 18c **brown carmine,** *Nov. 3* 1.75 .20
rose brown ('43) 1.75 .20
Block of 4 7.00 .75
P# block of 4 8.75 —
824 A296 19c **bright violet,** *Nov. 10* 1.25 .35
P# block of 4 6.25 —
825 A297 20c **bright blue green,** *Nov. 10* .70 .20
deep blue green ('43) .70 .20
P# block of 4 3.50 —
826 A298 21c **dull blue,** *Nov. 22* 1.25 .20
Block of 4 5.00 1.25
P# block of 4 7.50 —
827 A299 22c **vermilion,** *Nov. 22* 1.00 .40
P# block of 4 9.50 —
828 A300 24c **gray black,** *Dec. 2* 3.50 .20
Block of 4 14.00 1.25
P# block of 4 15.00 —
829 A301 25c **deep red lilac,** *Dec. 2* .60 .20
rose lilac ('43) .60 .20
P# block of 4 3.00 —
Pair with full vert. gutter btwn. —
830 A302 30c **deep ultramarine,** *Dec. 8* 3.50 .20
blue 15.00 —
deep blue *125.00* —
Block of 4 14.00 .50
P# block of 4 15.00 —
831 A303 50c **light red violet,** *Dec. 8* 5.00 .20
P# block of 4 22.50 —

Bureau Precancels: ½c, 199 diff., 1c, 701 diff., 1½c, 404 diff., 2c, 161 diff., 3c, 87 diff., 4c, 30 diff., 4½c, 27 diff., 5c, 44 diff., 6c, 45 diff., 7c, 44 diff., 8c, 44 diff., 9c, 38 diff., 10c, 43 diff.

Also, 11c, 41 diff., 12c, 33 diff., 13c, 28 diff., 14c, 23 diff., 15c, 38 diff., 16c, 6 diff., 17c, 27 diff., 18c, 5 diff., 19c, 8 diff., 20c, 39 diff., 21c, 5 diff., 22c, 4 diff., 24c, 8 diff., 25c, 23 diff., 30c, 27 diff., 50c, 24 diff.

FLAT PLATE PRINTING

Plates of 100 subjects

1938 ***Perf. 11***
832 A304 $1 **purple & black,** *Aug. 29* 6.50 .20
Margin block of 4, bottom or side arrow 27.50 —
Center line block 31.50 *4.00*
Top P# block of 4, 2# 31.50 —
Top P# block of 20, 2#, arrow, 2 TOP, 2 registration markers and denomination 145.00 —
a. Vert. pair, imperf. horiz. *1,600.*
b. Watermarked USIR ('51) 210.00 65.00
Center line block —
P# block of 4, 2# —
c. $1 **red violet & black,** *Aug. 31, 1954* 6.00 .20
Top or bottom P# block of 4, 2# 30.00 —
d. As "c," vert. pair, imperf. horiz. *1,500.*
e. Vertical pair, imperf. between *2,750.*
f. As "c," vert. pair, imperf. btwn. *8,500.*

No. 832c is dry printed from 400-subject flat plates on thick white paper with smooth, colorless gum.

833 A305 $2 **yellow green & black,** *Sept. 29* 18.00 3.75
green & black ('43) 18.00 3.75
Margin block of 4, bottom or side arrow 77.50 —
Center line block 82.50 35.00
Top P# block of 4, 2# 90.00 —
Top P# block of 20, 2#, arrow, 2 TOP, 2 registration markers and denominations 450.00 —
Top P# block of 20, 2#, black # and marginal markings only (yellow green # and markings omitted) *3,000.*
834 A306 $5 **carmine & black,** *Nov. 17* 90.00 3.00
Margin block of 4, bottom or side arrow 380.00 —
Center line block 400.00 *25.00*
Top P# block of 4, 2# 400.00 —
Top P# block of 20, 2#, arrow, 2 TOP, 2 registration markers and denominations 2,200.
a. $5 **red brown & black** *3,000.* *7,000.*
Hinged *2,000.*
Top P# block of 4, 2# *13,000.*
Nos. 803-834 (32) 142.35 13.15
Nos. 803-834, P# blocks of 4 690.60

Top plate number blocks of Nos. 832, 833 and 834 are found both with and without top arrow or registration markers.

No. 834 can be chemically altered to resemble Scott 834a. No. 834a should be purchased only with competent expert certification.

Watermarks

All stamps from No. 835 on are unwatermarked.

CONSTITUTION RATIFICATION ISSUE

150th anniversary of the ratification of the United States Constitution.

Old Courthouse, Williamsburg, Va. — A307

ROTARY PRESS PRINTING

Plates of 200 subjects in four panes of 50.

1938, June 21 ***Perf. 11x10½***
835 A307 3c **deep violet** .25 .20
P# block of 4 3.50 —

SWEDISH-FINNISH TERCENTENARY ISSUE

Tercentenary of the founding of the Swedish and Finnish Settlement at Wilmington, Delaware.

"Landing of the First Swedish and Finnish Settlers in America," by Stanley M. Arthurs — A308

FLAT PLATE PRINTING

Plates of 192 subjects in four panes of 48 each, separated by 1¼ inch wide gutters with central guide lines.

1938, June 27 ***Perf. 11***
836 A308 3c **red violet** .20 .20
P# block of 6 2.50 —

NORTHWEST TERRITORY SESQUICENTENNIAL

"Colonization of the West," by Gutzon Borglum — A309

ROTARY PRESS PRINTING

Plates of 400 subjects in four panes of 100.

1938, July 15 ***Perf. 11x10½***
837 A309 3c **bright violet** .20 .20
rose violet .20 .20
P# block of 4 6.50 —

IOWA TERRITORY CENTENNIAL ISSUE

Old Capitol, Iowa City — A310

ROTARY PRESS PRINTING

Plates of 200 subjects in four panes of 50.

1938, Aug. 24 ***Perf. 11x10½***
838 A310 3c **violet** .20 .20
P# block of 4 6.00 —
Pair with full vertical gutter between —

REGULAR ISSUE

ROTARY PRESS COIL STAMPS

Types of 1938

1939, Jan. 20 ***Perf. 10 Vertically***
839 A276 1c **green** .30 .20
light green .30 .20
Pair .60 .20
Joint line pair 1.40 .35
840 A277 1½c **bister brown** .30 .20
buff .30 .20
Pair .60 .20
Joint line pair 1.50 .75
841 A278 2c **rose carmine** .40 .20
Pair .80 .20
Joint line pair 1.75 .35
842 A279 3c **deep violet** .50 .20
violet .50 .20
Pair 1.00 .20
Joint line pair 2.00 .35
Gripper cracks —
Thin translucent paper 2.50 —
843 A280 4c **red violet** 7.50 .40
Pair 16.50 .80
Joint line pair 27.50 5.00
844 A281 4½c **dark gray** .70 .40
Pair 1.50 .80
Joint line pair 5.00 2.25
845 A282 5c **bright blue** 5.00 .35
Pair 10.50 .70
Joint line pair 27.50 5.00
846 A283 6c **red orange** 1.10 .20
Pair 2.25 .40
Joint line pair 7.50 1.50
847 A287 10c **brown red** 11.00 .50
Pair 24.00 1.25
Joint line pair 42.50 3.00

Bureau Precancels: 1c, 269 diff., 1½c, 179 diff., 2c, 101 diff., 3c, 46 diff., 4c, 13 diff., 4½c, 3 diff., 5c, 6 diff., 6c, 8 diff., 10c, 4 diff.

1939, Jan. 27 ***Perf. 10 Horizontally***
848 A276 1c **green** .85 .20
Pair 1.75 .25
Joint line pair 2.75 .75
849 A277 1½c **bister brown** 1.25 .30
Pair 2.50 .60
Joint line pair 4.50 2.00
850 A278 2c **rose carmine** 2.50 .40
Pair 5.00 .80
Joint line pair 6.50 3.50
851 A279 3c **deep violet** 2.25 .35
Pair 4.50 .70
Joint line pair 6.25 3.00
Nos. 839-851 (13) 33.65 3.90

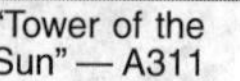

"Tower of the Sun" — A311

Trylon and Perisphere — A312

GOLDEN GATE INTL. EXPOSITION, SAN FRANCISCO

ROTARY PRESS PRINTING

Plates of 200 subjects in four panes of 50.

1939, Feb. 18 ***Perf. 10½x11***
852 A311 3c **bright purple** .20 .20
On cover, Expo. station machine canc. (non-first day) 3.00
On cover, Expo. station duplex handstamp canc. (non-first day) 15.00
P# block of 4 1.25 —

NEW YORK WORLD'S FAIR ISSUE

ROTARY PRESS PRINTING

Plates of 200 subjects in four panes of 50.

939, Apr. 1 *Perf. 10½x11*

53 A312 3c **deep purple** .20 .20
On cover, Expo. station machine canc. (non-first day) 3.00
On cover, Expo. station duplex handstamp canc. 10.00 —
P# block of 4 1.75

WASHINGTON INAUGURATION ISSUE

Sesquicentennial of the inauguration of George Washington as First President.

Washington Taking Oath of Office, Federal Building, New York City — A313

FLAT PLATE PRINTING

Plates of 200 subjects in four panes of 50.

1939, Apr. 30 *Perf. 11*

854 A313 3c **bright red violet** .40 .20
P# block of 6 3.50 —

BASEBALL CENTENNIAL ISSUE

Sandlot Baseball Game — A314

Designed by William A. Roach.

ROTARY PRESS PRINTING

Plates of 200 subjects in four panes of 50.

1939, June 12 *Perf. 11x10½*

855 A314 3c **violet** 1.75 .20
P# block of 4 7.50 —

PANAMA CANAL ISSUE

25th anniv. of the opening of the Panama Canal.

Theodore Roosevelt, Gen. George W. Goethals and Ship in Gaillard Cut — A315

Designed by William A. Roach.

FLAT PLATE PRINTING

Plates of 200 subjects in four panes of 50.

1939, Aug. 15 *Perf. 11*

856 A315 3c **deep red violet** .25 .20
P# block of 6 3.25 —

PRINTING TERCENTENARY ISSUE

Issued in commemoration of the 300th anniversary of printing in Colonial America. The Stephen Daye press is in the Harvard University Museum.

Stephen Daye Press — A316

Designed by William K. Schrage.

ROTARY PRESS PRINTING

E.E. Plates of 200 subjects in four panes of 50.

1939, Sept. 25 *Perf. 10½x11*

857 A316 3c **violet** .20 .20
P# block of 4 1.00 —

50th ANNIVERSARY OF STATEHOOD ISSUE

Map of North and South Dakota, Montana and Washington A317

ROTARY PRESS PRINTING

E.E. Plates of 200 subjects in four panes of 50.

1939, Nov. 2 *Perf. 11x10½*

858 A317 3c **rose violet** .20 .20
P# block of 4 1.10 —

FAMOUS AMERICANS ISSUES

ROTARY PRESS PRINTING

E.E. Plates of 280 subjects in four panes of 70.

AMERICAN AUTHORS

Washington Irving — A318

James Fenimore Cooper — A319

Ralph Waldo Emerson — A320

Louisa May Alcott — A321

Samuel L. Clemens (Mark Twain) — A322

1940 *Perf. 10½x11*

859 A318 1c **bright blue green,** *Jan. 29* .20 .20
P# block of 4 .95 —

860 A319 2c **rose carmine,** *Jan. 29* .20 .20
P# block of 4 .95 —

861 A320 3c **bright red violet,** *Feb. 5* .20 .20
P# block of 4 1.25 —

862 A321 5c **ultramarine,** *Feb. 5* .30 .20
P# block of 4 8.25 —

863 A322 10c **dark brown,** *Feb. 13* 1.65 1.20
P# block of 4 32.50 —
Nos. 859-863 (5) 2.55 2.00

AMERICAN POETS

Henry Wadsworth Longfellow — A323

John Greenleaf Whittier — A324

James Russell Lowell — A325

Walt Whitman — A326

James Whitcomb Riley — A327

864 A323 1c **bright blue green,** *Feb. 16* .20 .20
P# block of 4 1.75 —

865 A324 2c **rose carmine,** *Feb. 16* .20 .20
P# block of 4 1.75 —

866 A325 3c **bright red violet,** *Feb. 20* .20 .20
P# block of 4 2.25 —

867 A326 5c **ultramarine,** *Feb. 20* .35 .20
P# block of 4 9.00 —

868 A327 10c **dark brown,** *Feb. 24* 1.75 1.25
P# block of 4 30.00 —
Nos. 864-868 (5) 2.70 2.05

AMERICAN EDUCATORS

Horace Mann — A328

Mark Hopkins — A329

Charles W. Eliot — A330

Frances E. Willard — A331

Booker T. Washington — A332

869	A328	1c	**bright blue green,** *Mar. 14*	.20	.20
			P# block of 4	1.90	—
870	A329	2c	**rose carmine,** *Mar. 14*	.20	.20
			P# block of 4	1.25	—
871	A330	3c	**bright red violet,** *Mar. 28*	.20	.20
			P# block of 4	2.25	—
872	A331	5c	**ultramarine,** *Mar. 28*	.40	.20
			P# block of 4	9.00	—
873	A332	10c	**dark brown,** *Apr. 7*	1.25	1.10
			P# block of 4	27.50	—
			Nos. 869-873 (5)	2.25	1.90

AMERICAN SCIENTISTS

John James Audubon — A333

Dr. Crawford W. Long — A334

Luther Burbank — A335

Dr. Walter Reed — A336

Jane Addams — A337

874	A333	1c	**bright blue green,** *Apr. 8*	.20	.20
			P# block of 4	.95	—
875	A334	2c	**rose carmine,** *Apr. 8*	.20	.20
			P# block of 4	.95	—
876	A335	3c	**bright red violet,** *Apr. 17*	.20	.20
			P# block of 4	1.10	—
877	A336	5c	**ultramarine,** *Apr. 17*	.25	.20
			P# block of 4	5.00	—
878	A337	10c	**dark brown,** *Apr. 26*	1.10	.85
			P# block of 4	16.00	—
			Nos. 874-878 (5)	1.95	1.65

AMERICAN COMPOSERS

Stephen Collins Foster — A338

John Philip Sousa — A339

Victor Herbert — A340

Edward A. MacDowell — A341

Ethelbert Nevin — A342

879	A338	1c	**bright blue green,** *May 3*	.20	.20
			P# block of 4	1.00	—
880	A339	2c	**rose carmine,** *May 3*	.20	.20
			P# block of 4	1.00	—
881	A340	3c	**bright red violet,** *May 13*	.20	.20
			P# block of 4	1.10	—
882	A341	5c	**ultramarine,** *May 13*	.40	.20
			P# block of 4	9.25	—
883	A342	10c	**dark brown,** *June 10*	3.75	1.35
			P# block of 4	32.50	—
			Nos. 879-883 (5)	4.75	2.15

AMERICAN ARTISTS

Gilbert Charles Stuart — A343

James A. McNeill Whistler — A344

Augustus Saint-Gaudens — A345

Daniel Chester French — A346

Frederic Remington — A347

884	A343	1c	**bright blue green,** *Sept. 5*	.20	.20
			P# block of 4	1.00	—
885	A344	2c	**rose carmine,** *Sept. 5*	.20	.20
			P# block of 4	.95	—
886	A345	3c	**bright red violet,** *Sept. 16*	.20	.20
			P# block of 4	1.00	—
887	A346	5c	**ultramarine,** *Sept. 16*	.50	.20
			P# block of 4	8.00	—
888	A347	10c	**dark brown,** *Sept. 30*	1.75	1.25
			P# block of 4	20.00	—
			Nos. 884-888 (5)	2.85	2.05

AMERICAN INVENTORS

Eli Whitney — A348

Samuel F. B. Morse — A349

Cyrus Hall McCormick — A350

Elias Howe — A351

Alexander Graham Bell — A352

889	A348	1c	**bright blue green,** *Oct. 7*	.20	.20
			P# block of 4	1.90	—
890	A349	2c	**rose carmine,** *Oct. 7*	.20	.20
			P# block of 4	1.10	—
891	A350	3c	**bright red violet,** *Oct. 14*	.25	.20
			P# block of 4	1.75	—
892	A351	5c	**ultramarine,** *Oct. 14*	1.10	.30
			P# block of 4	12.50	—
893	A352	10c	**dark brown,** *Oct. 28*	11.00	2.00
			P# block of 4	65.00	—
			Nos. 889-893 (5)	12.75	2.90
			Nos. 859-893 (35)	29.80	14.70
			Nos. 859-894, P# blocks of 4	310.10	

PONY EXPRESS, 80th ANNIV. ISSUE

Pony Express Rider — A353

ROTARY PRESS PRINTING

E.E. Plates of 200 subjects in four panes of 50.

1940, Apr. 3 ***Perf. 11x10½***

894	A353	3c	**henna brown**	.25	.20
			P# block of 4	2.75	—

PAN AMERICAN UNION ISSUE

Founding of the Pan American Union, 50th anniv.

The Three Graces (Botticelli) — A354

ROTARY PRESS PRINTING

E.E. Plates of 200 subjects in four panes of 50.

1940, Apr. 14 ***Perf. 10½x11***

895	A354	3c	**light violet**	.20	.20
			P# block of 4	2.75	—

IDAHO STATEHOOD, 50th ANNIV.

Idaho State Capitol
A355

ROTARY PRESS PRINTING

E.E. Plates of 200 subjects in four panes of 50.

1940, July 3 *Perf. 11x10½*

896 A355 3c **bright violet**	.20	.20
P# block of 4	1.75	—

WYOMING STATEHOOD, 50th ANNIV.

Wyoming State Seal — A356

ROTARY PRESS PRINTING

E.E. Plates of 200 subjects in four panes of 50.

1940, July 10 *Perf. 10½x11*

897 A356 3c **brown violet**	.20	.20
P# block of 4	1.50	—

CORONADO EXPEDITION, 400th ANNIV.

"Coronado and His Captains" Painted by Gerald Cassidy
A357

ROTARY PRESS PRINTING

E.E. Plates of 200 subjects in four panes of 50.

1940, Sept. 7 *Perf. 11x10½*

898 A357 3c **violet**	.20	.20
P# block of 4	1.50	—

NATIONAL DEFENSE ISSUE

Statue of Liberty — A358

90-millimeter Anti-aircraft Gun — A359

Torch of Enlightenment — A360

ROTARY PRESS PRINTING

E.E. Plates of 400 subjects in four panes of 100

1940, Oct. 16 *Perf. 11x10½*

899 A358 1c **bright blue green**	.20	.20
P# block of 4	.45	—
Cracked plate (22684 UR 10)	3.00	
Gripper cracks	3.00	
Pair with full vert. gutter between	*200.00*	
a. Vertical pair, imperf. between	*650.00*	—
b. Horizontal pair, imperf. between	35.00	—

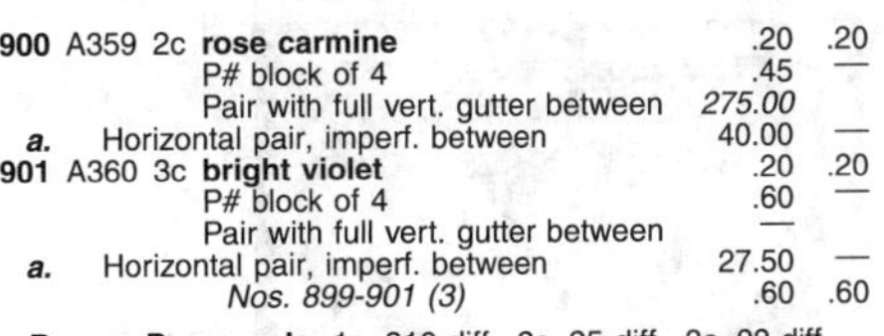

900 A359 2c **rose carmine**	.20	.20
P# block of 4	.45	—
Pair with full vert. gutter between	*275.00*	
a. Horizontal pair, imperf. between	40.00	—
901 A360 3c **bright violet**	.20	.20
P# block of 4	.60	—
Pair with full vert. gutter between	—	
a. Horizontal pair, imperf. between	27.50	—
Nos. 899-901 (3)	.60	.60

Bureau Precancels: 1c, 316 diff., 2c, 25 diff., 3c, 22 diff.

THIRTEENTH AMENDMENT ISSUE

75th anniv. of the 13th Amendment to the Constitution abolishing slavery.

Emancipation Monument; Lincoln and Kneeling Slave, by Thomas Ball — A361

Designed by William A. Roach.

ROTARY PRESS PRINTING

E.E. Plates of 200 subjects in four panes of 50.

1940, Oct. 20 *Perf. 10½x11*

902 A361 3c **deep violet**	.20	.20
dark violet	.20	.20
P# block of 4	3.00	—

VERMONT STATEHOOD, 150th ANNIV.

State Capitol, Montpelier
A362

Designed by Alvin R. Meissner.

ROTARY PRESS PRINTING

E.E. Plates of 200 subjects in four panes of 50.

1941, Mar. 4 *Perf. 11x10½*

903 A362 3c **light violet**	.20	.20
P# block of 4	1.75	—

KENTUCKY STATEHOOD, 150th ANNIV.

Daniel Boone and Three Frontiersmen, from Mural by Gilbert White — A363

Designed by William A. Roach.

ROTARY PRESS PRINTING

E.E. Plates of 200 subjects in four panes of 50.

1942, June 1 *Perf. 11x10½*

904 A363 3c **violet**	.20	.20
P# block of 4	1.10	—

WIN THE WAR ISSUE

American Eagle — A364

ROTARY PRESS PRINTING

E.E. Plates of 400 subjects in four panes of 100.

1942, July 4 *Perf. 11x10½*

905 A364 3c **violet**	.20	.20
light violet	.20	.20
P# block of 4	.40	—
Pair with full vert. or horiz. gutter between	*175.00*	
b. 3c **purple**	—	*500.00*

Bureau Precancels: 26 diff.

CHINESE RESISTANCE ISSUE

Issued to commemorate the Chinese people's five years of resistance to Japanese aggression.

Map of China, Abraham Lincoln and Sun Yat-sen, Founder of the Chinese Republic
A365

ROTARY PRESS PRINTING

E.E. Plates of 200 subjects in four panes of 50.

1942, July 7 *Perf. 11x10½*

906 A365 5c **bright blue**	.85	.20
P# block of 4	9.00	—

ALLIED NATIONS ISSUE

Allegory of Victory — A366

Designed by Leon Helguera.

ROTARY PRESS PRINTING

E.E. Plates of 400 subjects in four panes of 100.

1943, Jan. 14 *Perf. 11x10½*

907 A366 2c **rose carmine**	.20	.20
P# block of 4	.30	—
Pair with full vert. or horiz. gutter between	*225.00*	

Bureau Precancels: Denver, Baltimore.

FOUR FREEDOMS ISSUE

Liberty Holding the Torch of Freedom and Enlightenment — A367

Designed by Paul Manship.

ROTARY PRESS PRINTING

E.E. Plates of 400 subjects in four panes of 100.

1943, Feb. 12 *Perf. 11x10½*

908 A367 1c **bright blue green**	.20	.20
P# block of 4	.60	—

Bureau Precancels: 20 diff.

OVERRUN COUNTRIES ISSUE

Printed by the American Bank Note Co.

FRAMES ENGRAVED, CENTERS OFFSET LETTERPRESS

ROTARY PRESS PRINTING

Plates of 200 subjects in four panes of 50.

Due to the failure of the printers to divulge detailed information as to printing processes used, the editors omit listings of irregularities, flaws and blemishes which are numerous in this issue. An exception is made for certified double impressions and the widely recognized "KORPA" variety.

Flag of Poland
A368

1943-44 ***Perf. 12***

909 A368 5c **blue violet, bright red & black,** *June 22, 1943* .20 .20
Margin block of 4, Inscribed "Poland" 3.50 —
Top margin block of 6, with red & blue violet guide markings and "Poland" 4.75 —
Bottom margin block of 6, with red & black guide markings 1.20 —
a. Double impression of "Poland" —

Flag of Czechoslovakia — A368a

910 A368a 5c **blue violet, blue, bright red & black,** *July 12, 1943* .20 .20
Margin block of 4, inscribed "Czechoslovakia" 2.75 —
Top margin block of 6, with red & blue violet guide markings and "Czechoslovakia" 3.25 —
a. Double impression of "Czechoslovakia" —

Flag of Norway
A368b

911 A368b 5c **blue violet, dark rose, deep blue & black,** *July 27, 1943* .20 .20
Margin block of 4, inscribed "Norway" 1.30 —
Bottom margin block of 6 with dark rose & blue violet guide markings .90 —
a. Double impression of "Norway" —

Flag of Luxembourg
A368c

912 A368c 5c **blue violet, dark rose, light blue & black,** *Aug. 10, 1943* .20 .20
Margin block of 4, inscribed "Luxembourg" 1.20 —
Top margin block of 6 with light blue & blue violet guide markings & "Luxembourg" 1.60 —
a. Double impression of "Luxembourg" —

Flag of Netherlands
A368d

913 A368d 5c **blue violet, dark rose, blue & black,** *Aug. 24, 1943* .20 .20
Margin block of 4, inscribed "Netherlands" 1.20 —
Bottom margin block of 6 with blue & blue violet guide markings .90 —

Flag of Belgium
A368e

914 A368e 5c **blue violet, dark rose, yellow & black,** *Sept. 14, 1943* .20 .20
Margin block of 4, inscribed "Belgium" 1.10 —
Top margin block of 6, with yellow & blue violet guide markings and "Belgium" 1.50 —
a. Double impression of "Belgium" —

Flag of France
A368f

915 A368f 5c **blue violet, deep blue, dark rose & black,** *Sept. 28, 1943* .20 .20
Margin block of 4, inscribed "France" 1.25 —
Bottom margin block of 6 with dark rose & blue violet guide markings .90 —

Flag of Greece
A368g

916 A368g 5c **blue violet, pale blue & black,** *Oct. 12, 1943* .35 .25
Margin block of 4, inscribed "Greece" 9.00 —
Top margin block of 6 with pale blue & blue violet guide markings & "Greece" 10.00 —

Flag of Yugoslavia
A368h

Normal

Reverse Printing of Flag Colors

917 A368h 5c **blue violet, blue, dark rose & black,** *Oct. 26, 1943* .25 .20
Margin block of 4, inscribed "Yugoslavia" 4.25 —
Bottom margin block of 6 with dark rose & blue violet guide markings 1.50 —
a. Reverse printing of flag colors (blue and dark rose over black) —

On the normal printing, the black of the flag is printed over the red and blue. On No. 917a, the red and blue are printed over the black.

Flag of Albania
A368i

918 A368i 5c **blue violet, dark red & black,** *Nov. 9, 1943* .20 .20
Margin block of 4, inscribed "Albania" 4.25 —
Top margin block of 6, with dark red & blue violet guide markings & "Albania" 6.50 —
a. Double impression of "Albania" —

Flag of Austria
A368j

919 A368j 5c **blue violet, red & black,** *Nov. 23, 1943* .20 .20
Margin block of 4, inscribed "Austria" 3.50 —
Bottom margin block of 6, with red & blue violet guide markings 1.30 —
a. Double impression of "Austria" —

Flag of Denmark
A368k

920 A368k 5c **blue violet, red & black,** *Dec. 7, 1943* .20 .20
Margin block of 4, inscribed "Denmark" 5.25 —
Top margin block of 6, with red & blue violet guide markings & "Denmark" 6.00 —

Flag of Korea
A368m

"KORPA" plate flaw — 921var

921 A368m 5c **blue violet, red, black & light blue,** *Nov. 2, 1944* .20 .20
Margin block of 4, inscribed "Korea" 4.50 —
Top margin block of 6 with blue & black guide markings and "Korea" 5.25 —
"KORPA" plate flaw 17.50 12.50
a. Double impression of "Korea" —

The "P" of "KORPA" is actually a mangled "E." Occurs only on some panes, position 26.

Nos. 909-921 (13) 2.80 2.65
Nos. 909-921, Name blocks of 4 44.80

TRANSCONTINENTAL RAILROAD ISSUE

Completion of the 1st transcontinental railroad, 75th anniv.

"Golden Spike Ceremony" Painted by John McQuarrie A369

ENGRAVED
ROTARY PRESS PRINTING
E.E. Plates of 200 subjects in four panes of 50.

1944, May 10 *Perf. 11x10½*

922 A369 3c **violet** .20 .20
P# block of 4 1.40 —

STEAMSHIP ISSUE

1st steamship to cross the Atlantic, 125th anniv.

"Savannah" A370

ROTARY PRESS PRINTING
E.E. Plates of 200 subjects in four panes of 50.

1944, May 22 *Perf. 11x10½*

923 A370 3c **violet** .20 .20
P# block of 4 1.25 —

TELEGRAPH ISSUE

1st message transmitted by telegraph, cent.

Telegraph Wires and Morse's First Transmitted Words "What Hath God Wrought" A371

ROTARY PRESS PRINTING
E.E. Plates of 200 subjects in four panes of 50.

1944, May 24 *Perf. 11x10½*

924 A371 3c **bright red violet** .20 .20
P# block of 4 .90 —

PHILIPPINE ISSUE

Final resistance of the US and Philippine defenders on Corregidor to the Japanese invaders in 1942.

Aerial View of Corregidor, Manila Bay — A372

ROTARY PRESS PRINTING
E.E. Plates of 200 subjects in four panes of 50.

1944, Sept. 27 *Perf. 11x10½*

925 A372 3c **deep violet** .20 .20
P# block of 4 1.10 —

MOTION PICTURE, 50th ANNIV.

Motion Picture Showing for Armed Forces in South Pacific — A373

ROTARY PRESS PRINTING
E.E. Plates of 200 subjects in four panes of 50.

1944, Oct. 31 *Perf. 11x10½*

926 A373 3c **deep violet** .20 .20
P# block of 4 .90 —

FLORIDA STATEHOOD, CENTENARY

State Seal, Gates of St. Augustine and Capitol at Tallahassee A374

ROTARY PRESS PRINTING
E.E. Plates of 200 subjects in four panes of 50.

1945, Mar. 3 *Perf. 11x10½*

927 A374 3c **bright red violet** .20 .20
P# block of 4 .50 —

UNITED NATIONS CONFERENCE ISSUE

United Nations Conference, San Francisco, Calif.

"Toward United Nations, April 25, 1945" — A375

ROTARY PRESS PRINTING
E.E. Plates of 200 subjects in four panes of 50.

1945, Apr. 25 *Perf. 11x10½*

928 A375 5c **ultramarine** .20 .20
P# block of 4 .45 —

IWO JIMA (MARINES) ISSUE

Battle of Iwo Jima and honoring the achievements of the US Marines.

Marines Raising American Flag on Mount Suribachi, Iwo Jima — A376

ROTARY PRESS PRINTING
E.E. Plates of 200 subjects in four panes of 50.

1945, July 11 *Perf. 10½x11*

929 A376 3c **yellow green** .20 .20
P# block of 4 .55 —

FRANKLIN D. ROOSEVELT ISSUE

Franklin Delano Roosevelt (1882-1945).

Roosevelt and Hyde Park Residence A377

Roosevelt and the "Little White House" at Warm Springs, Ga. — A378

Roosevelt and White House A379

Roosevelt, Map of Western Hemisphere and Four Freedoms A380

ROTARY PRESS PRINTING
E.E. Plates of 200 subjects in four panes of 50.

1945-46 *Perf. 11x10½*

930 A377 1c **blue green,** *July 26, 1945* .20 .20
P# block of 4 .25 —
931 A378 2c **carmine rose,** *Aug. 24, 1945* .20 .20
P# block of 4 .45 —
932 A379 3c **purple,** *June 27, 1945* .20 .20
P# block of 4 .45 —
933 A380 5c **bright blue,** *Jan. 30, 1946* .20 .20
P# block of 4 .45 —
Nos. 930-933 (4) .80 .80

ARMY ISSUE

Achievements of the US Army in World War II.

United States Troops Passing Arch of Triumph, Paris — A381

ROTARY PRESS PRINTING
E.E. Plates of 200 subjects in four panes of 50.

1945, Sept. 28 *Perf. 11x10½*

934 A381 3c **olive** .20 .20
P# block of 4 .45 —

NAVY ISSUE

Achievements of the U.S. Navy in World War II.

United States Sailors A382

ROTARY PRESS PRINTING
E.E. Plates of 200 subjects in four panes of 50.

1945, Oct. 27 *Perf. 11x10½*

935 A382 3c **blue** .20 .20
P# block of 4 .55 —

COAST GUARD ISSUE

Achievements of the US Coast Guard in World War II.

Coast Guard Landing Craft and Supply Ship — A383

ROTARY PRESS PRINTING
E.E. Plates of 200 subjects in four panes of 50.

1945, Nov. 10 *Perf. 11x10½*

936 A383 3c **bright blue green** .20 .20
P# block of 4 .45 —

ALFRED E. SMITH ISSUE

Alfred E. Smith, Governor of New York — A384

ROTARY PRESS PRINTING
E.E. Plates of 400 subjects in four panes of 100.

1945, Nov. 26 *Perf. 11x10½*
937 A384 3c **purple** .20 .20
P# block of 4 .40
Pair with full vert. gutter btwn. —

TEXAS STATEHOOD, 100th ANNIV.

Flags of the United States and the State of Texas — A385

ROTARY PRESS PRINTING
E.E. Plates of 200 subjects in four panes of 50.

1945, Dec. 29 *Perf. 11x10½*
938 A385 3c **dark blue** .20 .20
P# block of 4 .40 —

MERCHANT MARINE ISSUE

Achievements of the US Merchant Marine in World War II.

Liberty Ship Unloading Cargo — A386

ROTARY PRESS PRINTING
E.E. Plates of 200 subjects in four panes of 50.

1946, Feb. 26 *Perf. 11x10½*
939 A386 3c **blue green** .20 .20
P# block of 4 .45 —

VETERANS OF WORLD WAR II ISSUE

Issued to honor all veterans of World War II.

Honorable Discharge Emblem — A387

ROTARY PRESS PRINTING
E.E. Plates of 400 subjects in four panes of 100.

1946, May 9 *Perf. 11x10½*
940 A387 3c **dark violet** .20 .20
P# block of 4 .40 —

TENNESSEE STATEHOOD, 150th ANNIV.

Andrew Jackson, John Sevier and State Capitol, Nashville A388

ROTARY PRESS PRINTING
E.E. Plates of 200 subjects in four panes of 50.

1946, June 1 *Perf. 11x10½*
941 A388 3c **dark violet** .20 .20
P# block of 4 .45 —

IOWA STATEHOOD, 100th ANNIV.

Iowa State Flag and Map — A389

ROTARY PRESS PRINTING
E.E. Plates of 200 subjects in four panes of 50.

1946, Aug. 3 *Perf. 11x10½*
942 A389 3c **deep blue** .20 .20
P# block of 4 .40 —

SMITHSONIAN INSTITUTION ISSUE

100th anniversary of the establishment of the Smithsonian Institution, Washington, D.C.

Smithsonian Institution A390

ROTARY PRESS PRINTING
E.E. Plates of 200 subjects in four panes of 50.

1946, Aug. 10 *Perf. 11x10½*
943 A390 3c **violet brown** .20 .20
P# block of 4 .35 —

KEARNY EXPEDITION ISSUE

100th anniversary of the entry of General Stephen Watts Kearny into Santa Fe.

"Capture of Santa Fe" by Kenneth M. Chapman A391

ROTARY PRESS PRINTING
E.E. Plates of 200 subjects in four panes of 50.

1946, Oct. 16 *Perf. 11x10½*
944 A391 3c **brown violet** .20 .20
P# block of 4 .30 —

THOMAS A. EDISON ISSUE

Thomas A. Edison (1847-1931), Inventor — A392

ROTARY PRESS PRINTING
E.E. Plates of 280 subjects in four panes of 70.

1947, Feb. 11 *Perf. 10½x11*
945 A392 3c **bright red violet** .20 .20
P# block of 4 .35 —

JOSEPH PULITZER ISSUE

Joseph Pulitzer (1847-1911), Journalist, and Statue of Liberty A393

Designed by Victor S. McCloskey, Jr.

ROTARY PRESS PRINTING
E.E. Plates of 200 subjects in four panes of 50.

1947, Apr. 10 *Perf. 11x10½*
946 A393 3c **purple** .20 .20
P# block of 4 .35 —

POSTAGE STAMP CENTENARY ISSUE

Centenary of the first postage stamps issued by the United States Government

Washington and Franklin, Early and Modern Mail-carrying Vehicles A394

Designed by Leon Helguera.

ROTARY PRESS PRINTING
E.E. Plates of 200 subjects in four panes of 50.

1947, May 17 *Perf. 11x10½*
947 A394 3c **deep blue** .20 .20
P# block of 4 .30 —

CENTENARY INTERNATIONAL PHILATELIC EXHIBITION ISSUE

SOUVENIR SHEET

A395

Illustration reduced.

FLAT PLATE PRINTING
Plates of 30 subjects

1947, May 19 ***Imperf.***
948 A395 Sheet of 2 .55 .45
a. 5c **blue**, type A1 .20 .20
b. 10c **brown orange**, type A2 .25 .25

Sheet inscribed below stamps: "100th Anniversary United States Postage Stamps" and in the margins:
"PRINTED BY THE TREASURY DEPARTMENT, BUREAU OF ENGRAVING AND PRINTING. - UNDER AUTHORITY OF ROBERT E. HANNEGAN, POSTMASTER GENERAL. - IN COMPLIMENT TO THE CENTENARY INTERNATIONAL PHILATELIC EXHIBITION. - NEW YORK, N.Y., MAY 17-25, 1947."
Sheet size varies: 96-98x66-68mm.

DOCTORS ISSUE

Issued to honor the physicians of America.

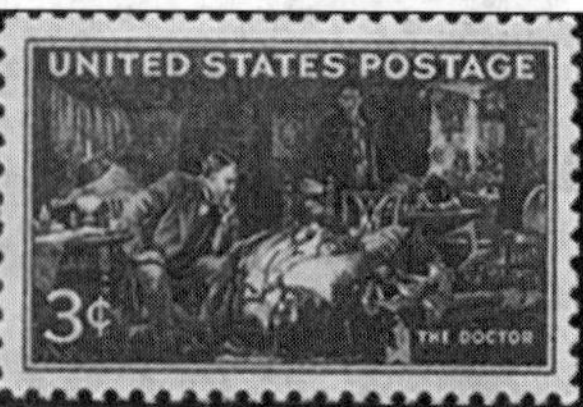

"The Doctor" by Sir Luke Fildes — A396

Designed by Charles R. Chickering.

ROTARY PRESS PRINTING
E.E. Plates of 200 subjects in four panes of 50.

1947, June 9 *Perf. 11x10½*
949 A396 3c **brown violet** .20 .20
P# block of 4 .30 —

UTAH ISSUE

Centenary of the settlement of Utah.

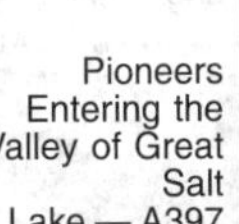
Pioneers Entering the Valley of Great Salt Lake — A397

Designed by Charles R. Chickering.

ROTARY PRESS PRINTING

E.E. Plates of 200 subjects in four panes of 50.

1947, July 24 *Perf. 11x10½*

950 A397 3c **dark violet** .20 .20
P# block of 4 .30 —

U.S. FRIGATE CONSTITUTION ISSUE

150th anniversary of the launching of the U.S. frigate Constitution ("Old Ironsides").

Naval Architect's Drawing of Frigate Constitution A398

Designed by Andrew H. Hepburn.

ROTARY PRESS PRINTING

E.E. Plates of 200 subjects in four panes of 50.

1947, Oct. 21 *Perf. 11x10½*

951 A398 3c **blue green** .20 .20
P# block of 4 .35 —

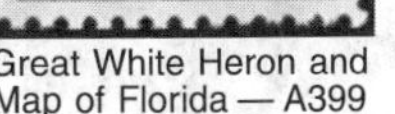
Great White Heron and Map of Florida — A399

Dr. George Washington Carver — A400

EVERGLADES NATIONAL PARK ISSUE

Dedication of the Everglades National Park, Florida, Dec. 6, 1947.

Designed by Robert I. Miller, Jr.

ROTARY PRESS PRINTING

E.E. Plates of 200 subjects in four panes of 50.

1947, Dec. 5 *Perf. 10½x11*

952 A399 3c **bright green** .20 .20
P# block of 4 .35 —

GEORGE WASHINGTON CARVER ISSUE

5th anniversary of the death of Dr. George Washington Carver, (1864-1943), botanist.

ROTARY PRESS PRINTING

E.E. Plates of 280 subjects in four panes of 70.

1948, Jan. 5 *Perf. 10½x11*

953 A400 3c **bright red violet** .20 .20
P# block of 4 .45 —

CALIFORNIA GOLD CENTENNIAL ISSUE

Sutter's Mill, Coloma, California A401

Designed by Charles R. Chickering.

ROTARY PRESS PRINTING

E.E. Plates of 200 subjects in four panes of 50.

1948, Jan. 24 *Perf. 11x10½*

954 A401 3c **dark violet** .20 .20
P# block of 4 .30 —

MISSISSIPPI TERRITORY ISSUE

Mississippi Territory establishment, 150th anniv.

Map, Seal of Mississippi Territory and Gov. Winthrop Sargent A402

Designed by William K. Schrage.

ROTARY PRESS PRINTING

E.E. Plates of 200 subjects in four panes of 50.

1948, Apr. 7 *Perf. 11x10½*

955 A402 3c **brown violet** .20 .20
P# block of 4 .50 —

FOUR CHAPLAINS ISSUE

George L. Fox, Clark V. Poling, John P. Washington and Alexander D. Goode, the 4 chaplains who sacrificed their lives in the sinking of the S.S. Dorchester, Feb. 3, 1943.

Four Chaplains and Sinking S.S. Dorchester A403

Designed by Charles R. Chickering.

ROTARY PRESS PRINTING

E.E. Plates of 200 subjects in four panes of 50.

1948, May 28 *Perf. 11x10½*

956 A403 3c **gray black** .20 .20
P# block of 4 .50 —

WISCONSIN STATEHOOD, 100th ANNIV.

Map on Scroll and State Capitol A404

Designed by Victor S. McCloskey, Jr.

ROTARY PRESS PRINTING

E.E. Plates of 200 subjects in four panes of 50.

1948, May 29 *Perf. 11x10½*

957 A404 3c **dark violet** .20 .20
P# block of 4 .35 —

SWEDISH PIONEER ISSUE

Centenary of the coming of the Swedish pioneers to the Middle West.

Swedish Pioneer with Covered Wagon Moving Westward A405

Designed by Charles R. Chickering.

ROTARY PRESS PRINTING

E.E. Plates of 200 subjects in four panes of 50.

1948, June 4 *Perf. 11x10½*

958 A405 5c **deep blue** .20 .20
P# block of 4 .45 —

PROGRESS OF WOMEN ISSUE

Century of progress of American Women.

Elizabeth Stanton, Carrie Chapman Catt and Lucretia Mott — A406

Designed by Victor S. McCloskey, Jr.

ROTARY PRESS PRINTING

E.E. Plates of 200 subjects in four panes of 50.

1948, July 19 *Perf. 11x10½*

959 A406 3c **dark violet** .20 .20
P# block of 4 .30 —

WILLIAM ALLEN WHITE ISSUE

William Allen White (1868-1944), Writer and Journalist — A407

ROTARY PRESS PRINTING

E.E. Plates of 280 subjects in four panes of 70.

1948, July 31 *Perf. 10½x11*

960 A407 3c **bright red violet** .20 .20
P# block of 4 .40 —

UNITED STATES-CANADA FRIENDSHIP ISSUE

Century of friendship between the US and Canada.

Niagara Railway Suspension Bridge — A408

Designed by Leon Helguera, modeled by V. S. McCloskey, Jr.

ROTARY PRESS PRINTING

E.E. Plates of 200 subjects in four panes of 50.

1948, Aug. 2 *Perf. 11x10½*

961 A408 3c **blue** .20 .20
P# block of 4 .30 —

FRANCIS SCOTT KEY ISSUE

Francis Scott Key (1779-1843), Maryland lawyer and author of "The Star-Spangled Banner" (1813).

Francis Scott Key and American Flags of 1814 and 1948 — A409

Designed by Victor S. McCloskey, Jr.

ROTARY PRESS PRINTING

E.E. Plates of 200 subjects in four panes of 50.

1948, Aug. 9 *Perf. 11x10½*

962 A409 3c **rose pink** .20 .20
P# block of 4 .40 —

SALUTE TO YOUTH ISSUE

Issued to honor the Youth of America and to publicize "Youth Month," September, 1948.

Girl and Boy Carrying Books — A410

ROTARY PRESS PRINTING
E.E. Plates of 200 subjects in four panes of 50.

1948, Aug. 11 ***Perf. 11x10½***
963 A410 3c **deep blue** .20 .20
P# block of 4 .30 —

OREGON TERRITORY ISSUE

Centenary of the establishment of Oregon Territory.

John McLoughlin, Jason Lee and Wagon on Oregon Trail — A411

ROTARY PRESS PRINTING
E.E. Plates of 200 subjects in four panes of 50.

1948, Aug. 14 ***Perf. 11x10½***
964 A411 3c **brown red** .20 .20
P# block of 4 .35 —

HARLAN F. STONE ISSUE

Harlan Fiske Stone (1872-1946) of New York, associate justice of the Supreme Court, 1925-1941, and chief justice, 1941-1946.

Chief Justice Harlan F. Stone — A412

ROTARY PRESS PRINTING
E.E. Plates of 280 subjects in four panes of 70.

1948, Aug. 25 ***Perf. 10½x11***
965 A412 3c **bright violet** .20 .20
P# block of 4 .60 —

PALOMAR MOUNTAIN OBSERVATORY ISSUE

Dedication, August 30, 1948.

Observatory, Palomar Mountain, California — A413

Designed by Victor S. McCloskey, Jr.

ROTARY PRESS PRINTING
E.E. Plates of 280 subjects in four panes of 70.

1948, Aug. 30 ***Perf. 10½x11***
966 A413 3c **blue** .20 .20
P# block of 4 .95 —
a. Vert. pair, imperf. between *525.00*

CLARA BARTON ISSUE

Clara Barton (1821-1912), Founder of the American Red Cross in 1882 — A414

Designed by Charles R. Chickering.

ROTARY PRESS PRINTING
E.E. Plates of 200 subjects in four panes of 50.

1948, Sept. 7 ***Perf. 11x10½***
967 A414 3c **rose pink** .20 .20
P# block of 4 .30 —

POULTRY INDUSTRY CENTENNIAL ISSUE

Light Brahma Rooster A415

Designed by Charles R. Chickering.

ROTARY PRESS PRINTING
E.E. Plates of 200 subjects in four panes of 50.

1948, Sept. 9 ***Perf. 11x10½***
968 A415 3c **sepia** .20 .20
P# block of 4 .40 —

GOLD STAR MOTHERS ISSUE

Issued to honor the mothers of deceased members of the United States armed forces.

Star and Palm Frond — A416

Designed by Charles R. Chickering.

ROTARY PRESS PRINTING
E.E. Plates of 200 subjects in four panes of 50.

1948, Sept. 21 ***Perf. 10½x11***
969 A416 3c **orange yellow** .20 .20
P# block of 4 .40 —

FORT KEARNY ISSUE

Establishment of Fort Kearny, Neb., centenary.

Fort Kearny and Pioneer Group — A417

ROTARY PRESS PRINTING
E.E. Plates of 200 subjects in four panes of 50.

1948, Sept. 22 ***Perf. 11x10½***
970 A417 3c **violet** .20 .20
P# block of 4 .40 —

VOLUNTEER FIREMEN ISSUE

300th anniv. of the organization of the 1st volunteer firemen in America by Peter Stuyvesant.

Peter Stuyvesant, Early and Modern Fire Engines A418

ROTARY PRESS PRINTING
E.E. Plates of 200 subjects in four panes of 50.

1948, Oct. 4 ***Perf. 11x10½***
971 A418 3c **bright rose carmine** .20 .20
P# block of 4 .50 —

INDIAN CENTENNIAL ISSUE

Centenary of the arrival in Indian Territory, later Oklahoma, of the Five Civilized Indian Tribes: Cherokee, Chickasaw, Choctaw, Muscogee and Seminole.

Map of Indian Territory and Seals of Five Tribes — A419

ROTARY PRESS PRINTING
E.E. Plates of 200 subjects in four panes of 50.

1948, Oct. 15 ***Perf. 11x10½***
972 A419 3c **dark brown** .20 .20
P# block of 4 .45 —

ROUGH RIDERS ISSUE

50th anniversary of the organization of the Rough Riders of the Spanish-American War.

Statue of Capt. William O. (Bucky) O'Neill by Solon H. Borglum A420

Designed by Victor S. McCloskey, Jr.

ROTARY PRESS PRINTING
E.E. Plates of 200 subjects in four panes of 50.

1948, Oct. 27 ***Perf. 11x10½***
973 A420 3c **violet brown** .20 .20
P# block of 4 .45 —

JULIETTE LOW ISSUE

Low (1860-1927), founded of the Girl Scouts of America. Mrs. Low organized the 1st Girl Guides troop in 1912 at Savannah. The name was changed to Girl Scouts in 1913 and headquarters moved to New York.

Juliette Gordon Low and Girl Scout Emblem A421

Designed by William K. Schrage.

ROTARY PRESS PRINTING
E.E. Plates of 200 subjects in four panes of 50.

1948, Oct. 29 ***Perf. 11x10½***
974 A421 3c **blue green** .20 .20
P# block of 4 .40 —

Will Rogers — A422

Fort Bliss, El Paso, Texas, and Rocket Firing — A423

WILL ROGERS ISSUE

Will Rogers, (1879-1935), humorist and political commentator.

ROTARY PRESS PRINTING
E.E. Plates of 280 subjects in four panes of 70.

1948, Nov. 4 ***Perf. 10½x11***
975 A422 3c **bright red violet** .20 .20
P# block of 4 .45 —

FORT BLISS CENTENNIAL ISSUE

Designed by Charles R. Chickering.

ROTARY PRESS PRINTING
E.E. Plates of 280 subjects in four panes of 70.

1948, Nov. 5 *Perf. 10½x11*
976 A423 3c **henna brown** .20 .20
P# block of 4 1.00 —

MOINA MICHAEL ISSUE

Moina Michael (1870-1944), educator who originated (1918) the Flanders Field Poppy Day idea as a memorial to the war dead.

Moina Michael and Poppy Plant — A424

ROTARY PRESS PRINTING
E.E. Plates of 200 subjects in four panes of 50.

1948, Nov. 9 *Perf. 11x10½*
977 A424 3c **rose pink** .20 .20
P# block of 4 .45 —

GETTYSBURG ADDRESS ISSUE

85th anniversary of Abraham Lincoln's address at Gettysburg, Pennsylvania.

Abraham Lincoln and Quotation from Gettysburg Address A425

Designed by Charles R. Chickering.

ROTARY PRESS PRINTING
E.E. Plates of 200 subjects in four panes of 50.

1948, Nov. 19 *Perf. 11x10½*
978 A425 3c **bright blue** .20 .20
P# block of 4 .50 —

Torch and Emblem of American Turners — A426

Joel Chandler Harris — A427

AMERICAN TURNERS ISSUE

Formation of the American Turners Soc., cent.

Designed by Alvin R. Meissner.

ROTARY PRESS PRINTING
E.E. Plates of 200 subjects in four panes of 50.

1948, Nov. 20 *Perf. 10½x11*
979 A426 3c **carmine** .20 .20
P# block of 4 .30 —

JOEL CHANDLER HARRIS ISSUE

Joel Chandler Harris (1848-1908), Georgia writer, creator of "Uncle Remus" and newspaperman.

ROTARY PRESS PRINTING
E.E. Plates of 280 subjects in four panes of 70.

1948, Dec. 9 *Perf. 10½x11*
980 A427 3c **bright red violet** .20 .20
P# block of 4 .55 —

MINNESOTA TERRITORY ISSUE

Establishment of Minnesota Territory, cent.

Pioneer and Red River Oxcart — A428

ROTARY PRESS PRINTING
E.E. Plates of 200 subjects in four panes of 50.

1949, Mar. 3 *Perf. 11x10½*
981 A428 3c **blue green** .20 .20
P# block of 4 .30 —

WASHINGTON AND LEE UNIVERSITY ISSUE

Bicentenary of Washington and Lee University.

George Washington, Robert E. Lee and University Building, Lexington, Va. — A429

ROTARY PRESS PRINTING
E.E. Plates of 200 subjects in four panes of 50.

1949, Apr. 12 *Perf. 11x10½*
982 A429 3c **ultramarine** .20 .20
P# block of 4 .30 —

PUERTO RICO ELECTION ISSUE

First gubernatorial election in the Territory of Puerto Rico, Nov. 2, 1948.

Puerto Rican Farmer Holding Cogwheel and Ballot Box — A430

ROTARY PRESS PRINTING
E.E. Plates of 200 subjects in four panes of 50.

1949, Apr. 27 *Perf. 11x10½*
983 A430 3c **green** .20 .20
P# block of 4 .30 —

ANNAPOLIS TERCENTENARY ISSUE

Founding of Annapolis, Maryland, 300th anniv.

James Stoddert's 1718 Map of Regions about Annapolis, Redrawn A431

ROTARY PRESS PRINTING
E.E. Plates of 200 subjects in four panes of 50.

1949, May 23 *Perf. 11x10½*
984 A431 3c **aquamarine** .20 .20
P# block of 4 .30 —

G.A.R. ISSUE

Final encampment of the Grand Army of the Republic, Indianapolis, Aug. 28 - Sept. 1, 1949.

Union Soldier and G.A.R. Veteran of 1949 — A432

Designed by Charles R. Chickering.

ROTARY PRESS PRINTING
E.E. Plates of 200 subjects in four panes of 50.

1949, Aug. 29 *Perf. 11x10½*
985 A432 3c **bright rose carmine** .20 .20
P# block of 4 .40 —

EDGAR ALLAN POE ISSUE

Edgar Allan Poe (1809-1849), Boston-born poet, story writer and editor.

Edgar Allan Poe — A433

ROTARY PRESS PRINTING
E.E. Plates of 280 subjects in four panes of 70.

1949, Oct. 7 *Perf. 10½x11*
986 A433 3c **bright red violet** .20 .20
P# block of 4 .45 —
Thin outer frame line at top, inner line missing (24143 LL 42) 6.00

AMERICAN BANKERS ASSOCIATION ISSUE

75th anniv. of the formation of the Association.

Coin, Symbolizing Fields of Banking Service A434

Designed by Charles R. Chickering.

ROTARY PRESS PRINTING
E.E. Plates of 200 subjects in four panes of 50.

1950, Jan. 3 *Perf. 11x10½*
987 A434 3c **yellow green** .20 .20
P# block of 4 .40 —

SAMUEL GOMPERS ISSUE

Samuel Gompers (1850-1924), British-born American labor leader.

Samuel Gompers — A435

ROTARY PRESS PRINTING
E.E. Plates of 280 subjects in four panes of 70.

1950, Jan. 27 *Perf. 10½x11*
988 A435 3c **bright red violet** .20 .20
P# block of 4 .30 —

NATIONAL CAPITAL SESQUICENTENNIAL ISSUE

150th anniversary of the establishment of the National Capital, Washington, D.C.

Statue of Freedom on Capitol Dome — A436

Executive Mansion A437

Supreme Court Building A438

United States Capitol — A439

ROTARY PRESS PRINTING

E.E. Plates of 200 subjects in four panes of 50.

1950 ***Perf. 10½x11, 11x10½***

989 A436 3c **bright blue,** *Apr. 20* .20 .20
P# block of 4 .30 —
990 A437 3c **deep green,** *June 12* .20 .20
P# block of 4 .40 —
991 A438 3c **light violet,** *Aug. 2* .20 .20
P# block of 4 .30 —
992 A439 3c **bright red violet,** *Nov. 22* .20 .20
P# block of 4 .40 —
Gripper cracks (24285 UL 11) 1.00 .50
Nos. 989-992 (4) .80 .80

RAILROAD ENGINEERS ISSUE

Issued to honor the Railroad Engineers of America. Stamp portrays John Luther (Casey) Jones (1864-1900), locomotive engineer killed in train wreck near Vaughn, Miss.

"Casey" Jones and Locomotives of 1900 and 1950 — A440

ROTARY PRESS PRINTING

E.E. Plates of 200 subjects in four panes of 50.

1950, Apr. 29 ***Perf. 11x10½***

993 A440 3c **violet brown** .20 .20
P# block of 4 .40 —

KANSAS CITY, MISSOURI, CENTENARY ISSUE

Kansas City, Missouri, incorporation.

Kansas City Skyline, 1950 and Westport Landing, 1850 — A441

ROTARY PRESS PRINTING

E.E. Plates of 200 subjects in four panes of 50.

1950, June 3 ***Perf. 11x10½***

994 A441 3c **violet** .20 .20
P# block of 4 .40 —

BOY SCOUTS ISSUE

Honoring the Boy Scouts of America on the occasion of the 2nd National Jamboree, Valley Forge, Pa.

Three Boys, Statue of Liberty and Scout Badge — A442

ROTARY PRESS PRINTING

E.E. Plates of 200 subjects in four panes of 50.

1950, June 30 ***Perf. 11x10½***

995 A442 3c **sepia** .20 .20
P# block of 4 .50 —

INDIANA TERRITORY ISSUE

Establishment of Indiana Territory, 150th anniv.

Gov. William Henry Harrison and First Indiana Capitol, Vincennes A443

ROTARY PRESS PRINTING

E.E. Plates of 200 subjects in four panes of 50.

1950, July 4 ***Perf. 11x10½***

996 A443 3c **bright blue** .20 .20
P# block of 4 .50 —

CALIFORNIA STATEHOOD ISSUE

Gold Miner, Pioneers and S.S. Oregon A444

ROTARY PRESS PRINTING

E.E. Plates of 200 subjects in four panes of 50.

1950, Sept. 9 ***Perf. 11x10½***

997 A444 3c **yellow orange** .20 .20
P# block of 4 .30 —

UNITED CONFEDERATE VETERANS FINAL REUNION ISSUE

Final reunion of the United Confederate Veterans, Norfolk, Virginia, May 30, 1951.

Confederate Soldier and United Confederate Veteran A445

ROTARY PRESS PRINTING

E.E. Plates of 200 subjects in four panes of 50.

1951, May 30 ***Perf. 11x10½***

998 A445 3c **gray** .20 .20
P# block of 4 .35 —

NEVADA CENTENNIAL ISSUE

Centenary of the settlement of Nevada.

Carson Valley, c. 1851 — A446

Designed by Charles R. Chickering.

ROTARY PRESS PRINTING

E.E. Plates of 200 subjects in four panes of 50.

1951, July 14 ***Perf. 11x10½***

999 A446 3c **light olive green** .20 .20
P# block of 4 .30 —

LANDING OF CADILLAC ISSUE

250th anniversary of the landing of Antoine de la Mothe Cadillac at Detroit.

Detroit Skyline and Cadillac Landing A447

ROTARY PRESS PRINTING

E.E. Plates of 200 subjects in four panes of 50.

1951, July 24 ***Perf. 11x10½***

1000 A447 3c **blue** .20 .20
P# block of 4 .30 —

COLORADO STATEHOOD, 75th ANNIV.

Colorado Capitol, Mount of the Holy Cross, Columbine and Bronco Buster by Proctor A448

ROTARY PRESS PRINTING

E.E. Plates of 200 subjects in four panes of 50.

1951, Aug. 1 ***Perf. 11x10½***

1001 A448 3c **blue violet** .20 .20
P# block of 4 .30 —

AMERICAN CHEMICAL SOCIETY ISSUE

75th anniv. of the formation of the Society.

A.C.S. Emblem and Symbols of Chemistry A449

ROTARY PRESS PRINTING

E.E. Plates of 200 subjects in four panes of 50.

1951, Sept. 4 ***Perf. 11x10½***

1002 A449 3c **violet brown** .20 .20
P# block of 4 .40 —

BATTLE OF BROOKLYN, 175th ANNIV.

Gen. George Washington Evacuating Army; Fulton Ferry House at Right — A450

ROTARY PRESS PRINTING

E.E. Plates of 200 subjects in four panes of 50.

1951, Dec. 10 ***Perf. 11x10½***

1003 A450 3c **violet** .20 .20
P# block of 4 .30 —

BETSY ROSS ISSUE

200th anniv. of the birth of Betsy Ross, maker of the first American flag.

"Birth of Our Nation's Flag," by Charles H. Weisgerber - Betsy Ross Showing Flag to Gen. George Washington, Robert Morris and George Ross — A451

ROTARY PRESS PRINTING

E.E. Plates of 200 subjects in four panes of 50.

1952, Jan. 2 ***Perf. 11x10½***

1004 A451 3c **carmine rose** .20 .20
P# block of 4 .35 —

4-H CLUB ISSUE

Farm, Club Emblem, Boy and Girl — A452

ROTARY PRESS PRINTING

E.E. Plates of 200 subjects in four panes of 50.

1952, Jan. 15 ***Perf. 11x10½***

1005 A452 3c **blue green** .20 .20
P# block of 4 .50 —

B. & O. RAILROAD ISSUE

125th anniv. of the granting of a charter to the Baltimore and Ohio Railroad Company by the Maryland Legislature.

Charter and Three Stages of Rail Transportation A453

ROTARY PRESS PRINTING

E.E. Plates of 200 subjects in four panes of 50.

1952, Feb. 28 ***Perf. 11x10½***

1006 A453 3c **bright blue** .20 .20
P# block of 4 .45 —

A. A. A. ISSUE

50th anniversary of the formation of the American Automobile Association.

School Girls and Safety Patrolman Automobiles of 1902 and 1952 — A454

ROTARY PRESS PRINTING

E.E. Plates of 200 subjects in four panes of 50.

1952, Mar. 4 ***Perf. 11x10½***

1007 A454 3c **deep blue** .20 .20
P# block of 4 .40 —

NATO ISSUE

Signing of the North Atlantic Treaty, 3rd anniv.

Torch of Liberty and Globe — A455

ROTARY PRESS PRINTING

E.E. Plates of 400 subjects in four panes of 100.

1952, Apr. 4 ***Perf. 11x10½***

1008 A455 3c **deep violet** .20 .20
P# block of 4 .30 —

GRAND COULEE DAM ISSUE

50 years of Federal cooperation in developing the resources of rivers and streams in the West.

Spillway, Grand Coulee Dam — A456

ROTARY PRESS PRINTING

E.E. Plates of 200 subjects in four panes of 50.

1952, May 15 ***Perf. 11x10½***

1009 A456 3c **blue green** .20 .20
P# block of 4 .30 —

LAFAYETTE ISSUE

175th anniversary of the arrival of Marquis de Lafayette in America.

Marquis de Lafayette, Flags, Cannon and Landing Party — A457

Designed by Victor S. McCloskey, Jr.

ROTARY PRESS PRINTING

E.E. Plates of 200 subjects in four panes of 50.

1952, June 13 ***Perf. 11x10½***

1010 A457 3c **bright blue** .20 .20
P# block of 4 .45 —

MT. RUSHMORE MEMORIAL ISSUE

Dedication of the Mt. Rushmore National Memorial in the Black Hills of South Dakota, 25th anniv.

Sculptured Heads on Mt. Rushmore — A458

Designed by William K. Schrage.

ROTARY PRESS PRINTING

E.E. Plates of 200 subjects in four panes of 50.

1952, Aug. 11 ***Perf. 10½x11***

1011 A458 3c **blue green** .20 .20
P# block of 4 .35 —

ENGINEERING CENTENNIAL ISSUE

American Society of Civil Engineers founding.

George Washington Bridge and Covered Bridge of 1850's A459

ROTARY PRESS PRINTING

E.E. Plates of 200 subjects in four panes of 50.

1952, Sept. 6 ***Perf. 11x10½***

1012 A459 3c **violet blue** .20 .20
P# block of 4 .45 —

SERVICE WOMEN ISSUE

Women in the United States Armed Services.

Women of the Marine Corps, Army, Navy and Air Force — A460

ROTARY PRESS PRINTING

E.E. Plates of 200 subjects in four panes of 50.

1952, Sept. 11 ***Perf. 11x10½***

1013 A460 3c **deep blue** .20 .20
P# block of 4 .30 —

GUTENBERG BIBLE ISSUE

Printing of the 1st book, the Holy Bible, from movable type, by Johann Gutenberg, 500th anniv.

Gutenberg Showing Proof to the Elector of Mainz — A461

ROTARY PRESS PRINTING

E.E. Plates of 200 subjects in four panes of 50.

1952, Sept. 30 ***Perf. 11x10½***

1014 A461 3c **violet** .20 .20
P# block of 4 .30 —

NEWSPAPER BOYS ISSUE

Newspaper Boy, Torch and Group of Homes A462

ROTARY PRESS PRINTING

E.E. Plates of 200 subjects in four panes of 50.

1952, Oct. 4 ***Perf. 11x10½***

1015 A462 3c **violet** .20 .20
P# block of 4 .30 —

RED CROSS ISSUE

Globe, Sun and Cross — A463

ROTARY PRESS PRINTING
Cross Typographed
E.E. Plates of 200 subjects in four panes of 50.

1952, Nov. 21 *Perf. 11x10½*
1016 A463 3c **deep blue & carmine** .20 .20
P# block of 4 .30 —

NATIONAL GUARD ISSUE

National Guardsman, Amphibious Landing and Disaster Service A464

ROTARY PRESS PRINTING
E.E. Plates of 200 subjects in four panes of 50.

1953, Feb. 23 *Perf. 11x10½*
1017 A464 3c **bright blue** .20 .20
P# block of 4 .30 —

OHIO STATEHOOD, 150th ANNIV.

Ohio Map, State Seal, Buckeye Leaf — A465

ROTARY PRESS PRINTING
E.E. Plates of 280 subjects in four panes of 70.

1953, Mar. 2 *Perf. 11x10½*
1018 A465 3c **chocolate** .20 .20
P# block of 4 .45 —

WASHINGTON TERRITORY ISSUE

Organization of Washington Territory, cent.

Medallion, Pioneers and Washington Scene — A466

ROTARY PRESS PRINTING
E.E. Plates of 200 subjects in four panes of 50.

1953, Mar. 2 *Perf. 11x10½*
1019 A466 3c **green** .20 .20
P# block of 4 .30 —

LOUISIANA PURCHASE, 150th ANNIV.

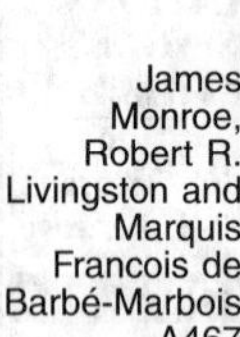

James Monroe, Robert R. Livingston and Marquis Francois de Barbé-Marbois A467

ROTARY PRESS PRINTING
E.E. Plates of 200 subjects in four panes of 50.

1953, Apr. 30 *Perf. 11x10½*
1020 A467 3c **violet brown** .20 .20
P# block of 4 .50 —

OPENING OF JAPAN CENTENNIAL ISSUE

Centenary of Commodore Matthew Calbraith Perry's negotiations with Japan, which opened her doors to foreign trade.

Commodore Matthew C. Perry and First Anchorage off Tokyo Bay — A468

ROTARY PRESS PRINTING
E.E. Plates of 200 subjects in four panes of 50.

1953, July 14 *Perf. 11x10½*
1021 A468 5c **green** .20 .20
P# block of 4 .65 —

AMERICAN BAR ASSOCIATION, 75th ANNIV.

Section of Frieze, Supreme Court Room — A469

ROTARY PRESS PRINTING
E.E. Plates of 200 subjects in four panes of 50.

1953, Aug. 24 *Perf. 11x10½*
1022 A469 3c **rose violet** .20 .20
P# block of 4 .30 —

SAGAMORE HILL ISSUE

Opening of Sagamore Hill, Theodore Roosevelt's home, as a national shrine.

Home of Theodore Roosevelt A470

ROTARY PRESS PRINTING
E.E. Plates of 200 subjects in four panes of 50.

1953, Sept. 14 *Perf. 11x10½*
1023 A470 3c **yellow green** .20 .20
P# block of 4 .35 —

FUTURE FARMERS ISSUE

25th anniversary of the organization of Future Farmers of America.

Agricultural Scene and Future Farmer A471

ROTARY PRESS PRINTING
E.E. Plates of 200 subjects in four panes of 50.

1953, Oct. 13 *Perf. 11x10½*
1024 A471 3c **deep blue** .20 .20
P# block of 4 .30 —

TRUCKING INDUSTRY ISSUE

50th anniv. of the Trucking Industry in the US.

Truck, Farm and Distant City — A472

ROTARY PRESS PRINTING
E.E. Plates of 200 subjects in four panes of 50.

1953, Oct. 27 *Perf. 11x10½*
1025 A472 3c **violet** .20 .2
P# block of 4 .30 —

GENERAL PATTON ISSUE

Honoring Gen. George S. Patton, Jr. (1885-1945) and the armored forces of the US Army.

Gen. George S. Patton, Jr., and Tanks in Action — A473

ROTARY PRESS PRINTING
E.E. Plates of 200 subjects in four panes of 50.

1953, Nov. 11 *Perf. 11x10½*
1026 A473 3c **blue violet** .20 .20
P# block of 4 .40 —

NEW YORK CITY, 300th ANNIV.

Dutch Ship in New Amsterdam Harbor A474

ROTARY PRESS PRINTING
E.E. Plates of 200 subjects in four panes of 50.

1953, Nov. 20 *Perf. 11x10½*
1027 A474 3c **bright red violet** .20 .20
P# block of 4 .35 —

GADSDEN PURCHASE ISSUE

Centenary of James Gadsden's purchase of territory from Mexico to adjust the US-Mexico boundary.

Map and Pioneer Group — A475

ROTARY PRESS PRINTING
E.E. Plates of 200 subjects in four panes of 50.

1953, Dec. 30 *Perf. 11x10½*
1028 A475 3c **copper brown** .20 .20
P# block of 4 .30 —

COLUMBIA UNIVERSITY, 200th ANNIV.

Low Memorial Library A476

ROTARY PRESS PRINTING
E.E. Plates of 200 subjects in four panes of 50.

1954, Jan. 4 *Perf. 11x10½*
1029 A476 3c **blue** .20 .20
P# block of 4 .30 —

Wet and Dry Printings

In 1953 the Bureau of Engraving and Printing began experiments in printing on "dry" paper (moisture content 5-10 per cent). In previous "wet" printings the paper had a moisture content of 15-35 per cent.

The new process required a thicker, stiffer paper, special types of inks and greater pressure to force the paper into the recessed plates. The "dry" printings show whiter paper, a higher sheen on the surface, feel thicker and stiffer, and the designs stand out more clearly than on the "wet" printings.

Nos. 832c and 1041 (flat plate) were the first "dry" printings to be issued of flat-plate, regular-issue stamps. No. 1063 was the first rotary press stamp to be produced entirely by "dry" printing.

Stamps printed by both the "wet" and "dry" process are Nos. 1030, 1031, 1035, 1035a, 1036, 1039, 1049, 1050-1052, 1054, 1055, 1057, 1058, C34-C36, C39, C39a, J78, J80-J84, QE1-QE3, RF26-RF28, S1, S1a, S2, S2a, S3. The "wet" printed 4c coil, No. 1058, exists only Bureau precanceled.

In the Liberty Issue listings that follow, wet printings are listed first, followed by dry printings. Where only one type of printing of a stamp is indicated, it is "dry."

All postage stamps have been printed by the "dry" process since the late 1950s.

LIBERTY ISSUE

Benjamin Franklin A477

George Washington A478

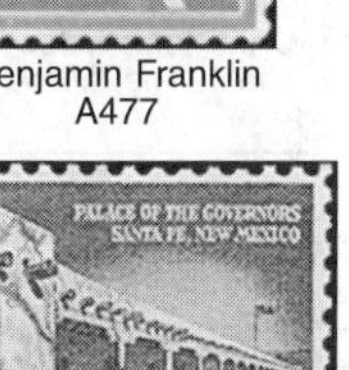

Palace of the Governors, Santa Fe — A478a

Mount Vernon — A479

Thomas Jefferson — A480

Bunker Hill Monument and Massachusetts Flag, 1776 — A481

Statue of Liberty — A482

Abraham Lincoln — A483

The Hermitage, Home of Andrew Jackson, near Nashville — A484

James Monroe — A485

Theodore Roosevelt — A486

Woodrow Wilson — A487

Statue of Liberty — A488

Statue of Liberty — A489

John J. Pershing — A489a

The Alamo, San Antonio — A490

Independence Hall — A491

Statue of Liberty — A491a

Benjamin Harrison — A492

John Jay — A493

Monticello, Home of Thomas Jefferson, near Charlottesville, Va. — A494

Paul Revere — A495

Robert E. Lee — A496

John Marshall — A497

Susan B. Anthony — A498

Patrick Henry — A499

Alexander Hamilton — A500

ROTARY PRESS PRINTING

E.E. Plates of 400 subjects in four panes of 100

1954-68 ***Perf. 11x10½***

No.	Design	Description	Unused	Used
1030a	A477	½c **red orange,** wet printing, *Oct. 20, 1955*	.20	.20
		P# block of 4	.35	—
1030	A477	½c **red orange,** dry printing, *May 1958*	.20	.20
		P# block of 4 (#25980 and up)	.25	—
1031b	A478	1c **dark green,** wet printing, *Aug. 26, 1954*	.20	.20
		P# block of 4	.25	—
1031	A478	1c **dark green,** dry printing, *Mar. 1956*	.20	.20
		P# block of 4 (#25326 and up)	.25	—
		Pair with full vert. gutter between	*150.00*	
		Pair with full horiz. gutter between	*150.00*	
		Perf. 10½x11		
1031A	A478a	1¼c **turquoise,** *June 17, 1960*	.20	.20
		P# block of 4	.45	—
1032	A479	1½c **brown carmine,** *Feb. 22, 1956*	.20	.20
		P# block of 4	1.75	—
		Perf. 11x10½		
1033	A480	2c **carmine rose,** *Sept. 15, 1954*	.20	.20
		P# block of 4	.25	—
		Pair with full vert. gutter between	—	
		Pair with full horiz. gutter between	—	
a.		Silkote paper	*750.00*	
		P# block of 4	*3,750.*	

Silkote paper was used in 1954 for an experimental printing of 50,000 stamps. The stamps were put on sale at the Westbrook, Maine post office in Dec. 1954. Only plates 25061 and 25062 were used to print No. 1033a. Competent expertization is required.

No.	Design	Description	Unused	Used
1034	A481	2½c **gray blue,** *June 17, 1959*	.20	.20
		P# block of 4	.50	—
1035e	A482	3c **deep violet,** wet printing, *June 24, 1954*	.20	.20
		P# block of 4	.35	—
a.		Booklet pane of 6, *June 30, 1954*	4.00	*1.25*
g.		As "a," vert. imperf. between	*5,000.*	
1035	A482	3c **deep violet,** dry printing	.20	.20
		P# block of 4 (#25235 and up)	.25	—
		Pair with full vert. gutter between	*150.00*	
		Pair with full horiz. gutter between	*150.00*	
b.		Tagged, *July 6, 1966*	.30	.25
		P# block of 4	5.50	—
c.		Imperf., pair	*2,000.*	
d.		Horiz. pair, imperf. between	—	
f.		Booklet pane of 6, untagged	5.00	*1.50*

No. 1057a measures about 19½x22mm; No. 1035c, about 18¾x22½mm.

No.	Design	Description	Unused	Used
1036c	A483	4c **red violet,** wet printing, *Nov. 19, 1954*	.20	.20
		P# block of 4	.50	—
1036	A483	4c **red violet,** dry printing	.20	.20
		P# block of 4 (#25445 and up)	.35	—
		Pair with full vert. gutter between	*650.00*	
		Pair with full horiz. gutter between	—	
a.		Booklet pane of 6, *July 31, 1958*	2.75	*1.25*
b.		Tagged, *Nov. 2, 1963*	.60	.40

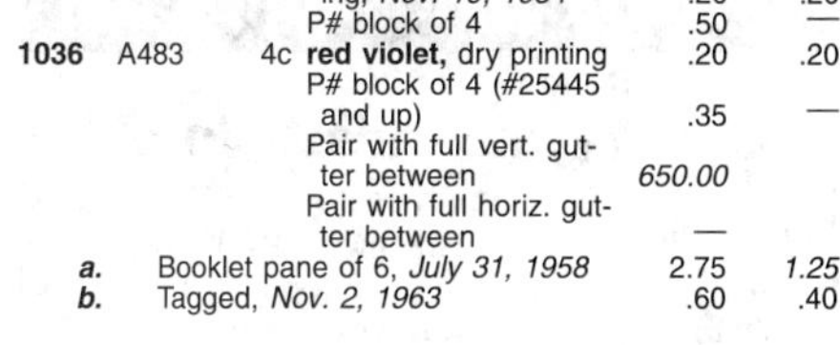

P# block of 4 8.50 —
d. As "a," imperf. horiz. —

Perf. 10½x11

1037 A484 4½c **blue green,** *Mar. 16, 1959* .20 .20
P# block of 4 .65 —

Perf. 11x10½

1038 A485 5c **deep blue,** *Dec. 2, 1954* .20 .20
P# block of 4 .45 —
Pair with full vert. gutter btwn. *200.00*

1039a A486 6c **carmine,** wet printing, *Nov. 18, 1955* .40 .20
P# block of 4 2.00 —
1039 A486 6c **carmine,** dry printing .25 .20
P# block of 4 (#25427 and up) 1.25 —
b. Imperf, pair *11,000.*

1040 A487 7c **rose carmine,** *Jan. 10, 1956* .20 .20
P# block of 4 1.00 —
a. 7c **dark rose carmine** .20 .20
P# block of 4 1.00 —

FLAT PLATE PRINTING

Plates of 400 subjects in four panes of 100 each

Size: 22.7mm high

Perf. 11

1041 A488 8c **dark violet blue & carmine,** *Apr. 9, 1954* .25 .20
P# block of 4, 2# 2.00 —
Corner P# block of 4, blue # only —
Corner P# block of 4, red # only —
a. Double impression of carmine *575.00*

FLAT PRINTING PLATES
Frame: 24912-13-14-15, 24926, 24929-30, 24932-33.
Vignette: 24916-17-18-19-20, 24935-36-37, 24939.
See note following No. 1041B.

ROTARY PRESS PRINTING

Plates of 400 subjects in four panes of 100 each

Size: 22.9mm high

Perf. 11

1041B A488 8c **dark violet blue & carmine,** *Apr. 9, 1954* .40 .20
P# block of 4, 2# 3.50 —

ROTARY PRINTING PLATES
Frame: 24923-24, 24928, 24940, 24942.
Vignette: 24927, 24938.

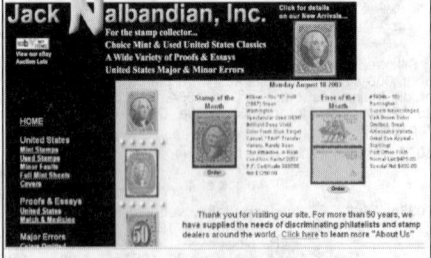

No. 1041B is slightly taller than No. 1041, about the thickness of one line of engraving.

GIORI PRESS PRINTING

Plates of 400 subjects in four panes of 100 each

Redrawn design

Perf. 11

1042 A489 8c **dark violet blue & carmine rose,** *Mar. 22, 1958* .20 .20
P# block of 4 .90 —

ROTARY PRESS PRINTING

E.E. Plates of 400 subjects in four panes of 100 each

Perf. 11x10½

1042A A489a 8c **brown,** *Nov. 17, 1961* .20 .20
P# block of 4 .90 —

Perf. 10½x11

1043 A490 9c **rose lilac,** *June 14, 1956* .30 .20
P# block of 4 1.30 —
a. 9c **dark rose lilac** .30 .20
P# block of 4 1.30 —

1044 A491 10c **rose lake,** *July 4, 1956* .30 .20
P# block of 4 1.40 —
b. 10c **dark rose lake** .25 .20
P# block of 4 1.10 —
d. Tagged, *July 6, 1966* 2.00 1.00
P# block of 4 *35.00* —

No. 1044b is from later printings and is on a harder, whiter paper than No. 1044.

GIORI PRESS PRINTING

Plates of 400 subjects in four panes of 100.

Perf. 11

1044A A491a 11c **carmine & dark violet blue,** *June 15, 1961* .30 .20
P# block of 4 1.50 —
c. Tagged, *Jan. 11, 1967* 2.00 1.60
P# block of 4 *35.00* —

ROTARY PRESS PRINTING

E.E. Plates of 400 subjects in four panes of 100 each

Perf. 11x10½

1045 A492 12c **red,** *June 6, 1959* .35 .20
P# block of 4 1.50 —
a. Tagged, *1968* .35 .20
P# block of 4 4.00 —

1046 A493 15c **rose lake,** *Dec. 12, 1958* .60 .20
P# block of 4 3.00 —
a. Tagged, *July 6, 1966* 1.10 .50
P# block of 4 13.00 —

Perf. 10½x11

1047 A494 20c **ultramarine,** *Apr. 13, 1956* .40 .20
P# block of 4 1.75 —
a. 20c **deep bright ultramarine** .40 .20
P# block of 4 1.75 —

No. 1047a is from later printings and is on a harder, whiter paper than No. 1047.

Perf. 11x10½

1048 A495 25c **green,** *Apr. 18, 1958* 1.10 .75
P# block of 4 4.75 —

1049a A496 30c **black,** wet printing, *Sept. 21, 1955* 1.10 .75
P# block of 4 5.00 —
1049 A496 30c **black,** dry printing, *June 1957* .70 .20
P# block of 4 (#25487 and up) 4.00 —
b. 30c **intense black** .70 .20
P# block of 4 3.50 —

No. 1049b is from later printings and is on a harder, whiter paper than No. 1049.

1050a A497 40c **brown red,** wet printing, *Sept. 24, 1955* 2.25 .25
P# block of 4 12.50 —
1050 A497 40c **brown red,** dry printing, *Apr. 1958* 1.50 .20
P# block of 4 (#25571 and up) 7.50 —

1051a A498 50c **bright purple,** wet printing, *Aug. 25, 1955* 1.75 .20
P# block of 4 11.00 —
Cracked plate (25231 UL 1) — —
1051 A498 50c **bright purple,** dry printing, *Apr. 1958* 1.50 .20
P# block of 4 (#25897 and up) 7.00 —

1052a A499 $1 **purple,** wet printing, *Oct. 7, 1955* 5.25 1.00
P# block of 4 22.50 —
1052 A499 $1 **purple,** dry printing, *Oct. 1958* 4.50 .20
P# block of 4 (#25541 and up) 19.00 —

FLAT PLATE PRINTING

Plates of 400 subjects in four panes of 100.

Perf. 11

1053 A500 $5 **black,** *Mar. 19, 1956* 60.00 6.75
P# block of 4 260.00 —

Bureau Precancels: ½c, 37 diff., 1c, 113 diff., 1¼c, 142 diff., 1½c, 45 diff.
2c, 86 diff., 2½c, 123 diff., 3c, 106 diff., 4c, 95 diff., 4½c, 23 diff., 5c, 20 diff., 6c, 23 diff., 7c, 16 diff.
Also, No. 1041, 12 diff., No. 1042, 12 diff., No. 1042A, 16 diff., 9c, 15 diff., 10c, 16 diff., 11c, New York, 12c, 6 diff.
15c, 12 diff., 20c, 20 diff., 25c, 11 diff., 30c, 17 diff., 40c, 10 diff., 50c, 19 diff., $1, 5 diff.

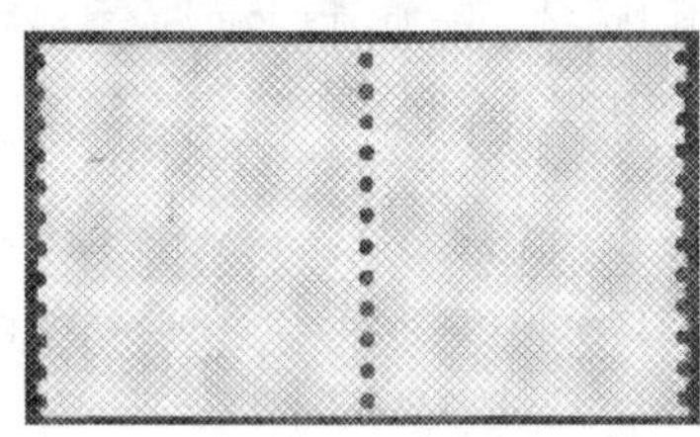

Large Holes

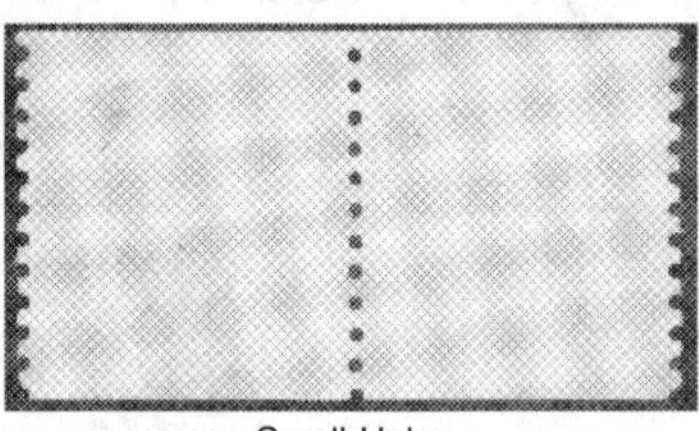

Small Holes

With the change from 384-subject plates to 432-subject plates the size of the perforation holes was reduced. While both are perf. 10 the later holes are smaller than the paper between them. The difference is most noticible on pairs.

ROTARY PRESS COIL STAMPS

1954-80 ***Perf. 10 Vertically***

1054c A478 1c **dark green,** large holes, wet printing, *Oct. 8, 1954* .35 .20
Pair .70 .40
Joint line pair 1.75 .90
1054 A478 1c **dark green,** small holes, *Feb. 1960* .20 .20
Pair .40 .25
Joint line pair 1.00 .65
Large holes, dry printing, *Aug. 1957* 1.00 .20
Pair 2.00 .25
Joint line pair 4.00 .65
b. Imperf., pair *2,500.* —

Perf. 10 Horizontally

1054A A478a 1¼c **turquoise,** *June 17, 1960,* small holes .20 .20
Pair .25 .25
Joint line pair 2.25 1.00
Large holes *8.00* .20
Pair *20.00* .25
Joint line pair *150.00* 1.25

Perf. 10 Vertically

1055d A480 2c **carmine rose,** large holes, wet printing, *Oct. 22, 1954* .40 .20
Pair .80 .20
Joint line pair 3.50 .40
1055 A480 2c **carmine rose,** large holes, dry printing, *May 1957* .35 .20
Pair .80 .20
Joint line pair 1.50 .25
Small holes, *Aug. 1961* 2.00 .20
Pair 5.00 .25
Joint line pair 25.00 .40
a. Tagged, small holes, shiny gum, *May 6, 1968* .20 .20
Pair .20 .20
Joint line pair .75 .20
Dull gum, tagged, small holes .35
Pair .80
Joint line pair 2.25
b. Imperf., pair, untagged, shiny gum (Bureau precanceled, Riverdale, MD) *550.00*
Joint line pair *1,400.*
c. Imperf. pair, tagged, shiny gum *600.00*
Joint line pair *1,250.*

1056 A481 2½c **gray blue,** large holes *Sept. 9, 1959* .35 .25
Pair .70 .50
Joint line pair 3.50 1.75
Small holes, *Jan. 1961* *400.00* *100.00*
Pair *850.00* *200.00*
Joint line pair *3,000.* *400.00*

No. 1056 with small holes only known with Bureau precancels. It was against postal regulations to make mint precanceled stamps available other than to permit holders for their use. Resale was prohibited. Since some mint examples do exist in the marketplace, values are furnished here.

1057c	A482	3c **deep violet,** large holes, wet printing, *July 20, 1954*	.35	.20
		Pair	.80	.25
		Joint line pair	2.75	.60
		Small holes, *Jan. 1961*	—	
		Pair	—	
		Joint line pair	—	
1057	A482	3c **deep violet,** large holes, dry printing, *Oct. 1956*	.35	.20
		Pair	.80	.20
		Joint line pair	2.75	.25
		Gripper cracks	—	—
		Small holes, *Mar. 1958*	.20	.20
		Pair	.20	.20
		Joint line pair	.55	.20
a.		Imperf., pair	*1,750.*	—
		Joint line pair	*2,750.*	—
b.		Tagged, small holes, philatelic printing, *June 26, 1967*	1.00	.50
		Pair	3.00	1.00
		Joint line pair	25.00	—
d.		Tagged, small holes, Look magazine printing, *Oct. 1966*	4.00	4.00
		Pair	11.00	8.00
		Joint line pair	*250.00*	

Earliest known use No. 1057d: Dec. 29, 1966.

No. 1057a measures about 19½x22mm; No. 1035c, about 18¾x22½mm.

The second tagged printing (No. 1057b) was a "philatelic reprint" made when the original stock of tagged stamps was exhausted. The original tagged printing (No. 1057d, specially printed for "Look" magazine) has a less intense color, the impression is less sharp and the tagging is brighter.

The reprint was printed on a slightly fluorescent paper, while the original paper is dead under longwave UV light.

1058b	A483	4c **red violet,** large holes, wet printing (Bureau precanceled)	*27.50*	.50
		Pair	*60.00*	—
		Joint line pair	*375.00*	

It was against postal regulations to make mint precanceled copies of No. 1058b available other than to permit holders for their use. Resale was prohibited. Since some mint examples do exist in the marketplace, values are furnished here.

1058	A483	4c **red violet,** large holes, dry printing, *July 31, 1958*	.50	.20
		Pair	1.50	.30
		Joint line pair	2.50	.40
		Small holes	.20	.20
		Pair	.35	.20
		Joint line pair	.70	.25
a.		Imperf., pair	120.00	120.00
		Joint line pair	200.00	

Perf. 10 Horizontally

1059	A484	4½c **blue green,** large holes, *May 1, 1959*	1.50	1.20
		Pair	3.00	2.40
		Joint line pair	14.00	3.00
		Small holes	12.00	—
		Pair	35.00	—
		Joint line pair	*450.00*	—

Perf. 10 Vertically

1059A	A495	25c **green,** *Feb. 25, 1965*	.50	.30
		Pair	1.00	.60
		Joint line pair	2.00	1.20
b.		Tagged, shiny gum, *Apr. 3, 1973*	.80	.20
		Pair	1.60	.40
		Joint line pair	3.25	1.25
		Tagged, dull gum, *1980*	1.25	
		Pair	2.50	
		Joint line pair	5.00	
c.		Imperf., pair	55.00	
		Joint line pair	100.00	

Value for No. 1059Ac is for fine centering.

Bureau Precancels: 1c, 118 diff., 1¼c, 105 diff., 2c, 191 diff., 2½c, 94 diff., 3c, 142 diff., 4c, 83 diff., 4½c, 23 diff.

NEBRASKA TERRITORY ISSUE

Establishment of the Nebraska Territory, centenary.

"The Sower," Mitchell Pass and Scotts Bluff — A507

ROTARY PRESS PRINTING

E.E. Plates of 200 subjects in four panes of 50.

1954, May 7 ***Perf. 11x10½***

1060	A507	3c **violet**	.20	.20
		P# block of 4	.30	—

KANSAS TERRITORY ISSUE

Establishment of the Kansas Territory, centenary

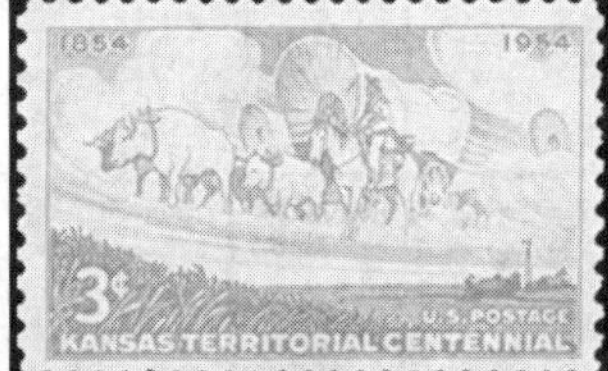

Wheat Field and Pioneer Wagon Train — A508

ROTARY PRESS PRINTING

E.E. Plates of 200 subjects in four panes of 50.

1954, May 31 ***Perf. 11x10½***

1061	A508	3c **brown orange**	.20	.20
		P# block of 4	.30	—

GEORGE EASTMAN ISSUE

Eastman (1854-1932), inventor of photographic dry plates, flexible film and the Kodak camera; Rochester, N.Y., industrialist.

George Eastman — A509

ROTARY PRESS PRINTING

E.E. Plates of 280 subjects in four panes of 70.

1954, July 12 ***Perf. 10½x11***

1062	A509	3c **violet brown**	.20	.20
		P# block of 4	.30	—

LEWIS AND CLARK EXPEDITION

150th anniv. of the Lewis and Clark expedition.

Meriwether Lewis, William Clark and Sacagawea Landing on Missouri Riverbank A510

ROTARY PRESS PRINTING

E.E. Plates of 200 subjects in four panes of 50.

1954, July 28 ***Perf. 11x10½***

1063	A510	3c **violet brown**	.20	.20
		P# block of 4	.35	—

PENNSYLVANIA ACADEMY OF THE FINE ARTS ISSUE

150th anniversary of the founding of the Pennsylvania Academy of the Fine Arts, Philadelphia.

Charles Willson Peale in his Museum, Self-portrait — A511

ROTARY PRESS PRINTING

E.E. Plates of 200 subjects in four panes of 50.

1955, Jan. 15 ***Perf. 10½x11***

1064	A511	3c **rose brown**	.20	.20
		P# block of 4	.45	—

LAND GRANT COLLEGES ISSUE

Centenary of the founding of Michigan State College and Pennsylvania State University, first of the land grant institutions.

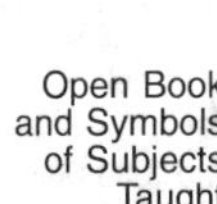

Open Book and Symbols of Subjects Taught A512

ROTARY PRESS PRINTING

E.E. Plates of 200 subjects in four panes of 50.

1955, Feb. 12 ***Perf. 11x10½***

1065	A512	3c **green**	.20	.20
		P# block of 4	.30	—

ROTARY INTERNATIONAL, 50th ANNIV.

Torch, Globe and Rotary Emblem A513

ROTARY PRESS PRINTING

E.E. Plates of 200 subjects in four panes of 50.

1955, Feb. 23 ***Perf. 11x10½***

1066	A513	8c **deep blue**	.20	.20
		P# block of 4	.95	—

ARMED FORCES RESERVE ISSUE

Marine, Coast Guard, Army, Navy and Air Force Personnel A514

ROTARY PRESS PRINTING

E.E. Plates of 200 subjects in four panes of 50.

1955, May 21 ***Perf. 11x10½***

1067 A514 3c **purple** .20 .20
P# block of 4 .30 —

NEW HAMPSHIRE ISSUE

Sesquicentennial of the discovery of the "Old Man of the Mountains."

Great Stone Face — A515

ROTARY PRESS PRINTING

E.E. Plates of 200 subjects in four panes of 50.

1955, June 21 ***Perf. 10½x11***

1068 A515 3c **green** .20 .20
P# block of 4 .50 —

SOO LOCKS ISSUE

Centenary of the opening of the Soo Locks.

Map of Great Lakes and Two Steamers A516

ROTARY PRESS PRINTING

E.E. Plates of 200 subjects in four panes of 50.

1955, June 28 ***Perf. 11x10½***

1069 A516 3c **blue** .20 .20
P# block of 4 .30 —

ATOMS FOR PEACE ISSUE

Issued to promote an Atoms for Peace policy.

Atomic Energy Encircling the Hemispheres A517

Designed by George R. Cox.

ROTARY PRESS PRINTING

E.E. Plates of 200 subjects in four panes of 50.

1955, July 28 ***Perf. 11x10½***

1070 A517 3c **deep blue** .20 .20
P# block of 4 .35 —

FORT TICONDEROGA ISSUE

Bicentenary of Fort Ticonderoga, New York.

Map of the Fort, Ethan Allen and Artillery A518

Designed by Enrico Arno.

ROTARY PRESS PRINTING

E.E. Plates of 200 subjects in four panes of 50.

1955, Sept. 18 ***Perf. 11x10½***

1071 A518 3c **light brown** .20 .20
P# block of 4 .30 —

Andrew W. Mellon — A519

"Franklin Taking Electricity from the Sky," by Benjamin West — A520

ANDREW W. MELLON ISSUE

Andrew W. Mellon (1855-1937), US Secretary of the Treasury (1921-32), financier and art collector.

Designed by Victor S. McCloskey, Jr.

ROTARY PRESS PRINTING

E.E. Plates of 280 subjects in four panes of 70.

1955, Dec. 20 ***Perf. 10½x11***

1072 A519 3c **rose carmine** .20 .20
P# block of 4 .35 —

BENJAMIN FRANKLIN ISSUE

250th anniv. of the birth of Benjamin Franklin.

Designed by Charles R. Chickering.

ROTARY PRESS PRINTING

E.E. Plates of 200 subjects in four panes of 50.

1956, Jan. 17 ***Perf. 10½x11***

1073 A520 3c **bright carmine** .20 .20
P# block of 4 .40 —

BOOKER T. WASHINGTON ISSUE

Washington (1856-1915), black educator, founder and head of Tuskegee Institute in Alabama.

Log Cabin — A521

Designed by Charles R. Chickering.

ROTARY PRESS PRINTING

E.E. Plates of 200 subjects in four panes of 50.

1956, Apr. 5 ***Perf. 11x10½***

1074 A521 3c **deep blue** .20 .20
P# block of 4 .40 —

FIFTH INTERNATIONAL PHILATELIC EXHIBITION ISSUES

FIPEX, New York City, Apr. 28 - May 6, 1956.

SOUVENIR SHEET

A522

Illustration reduced.

FLAT PLATE PRINTING

Plates of 24 subjects

1956, Apr. 28 ***Imperf.***

1075 A522 Sheet of 2 2.00 2.00
a. A482 3c deep violet .80 .80
b. A488 8c dark violet blue & carmine 1.00 1.00

No. 1075 measures 108x73mm. Nos. 1075a and 1075b measure 24x28mm.

Inscriptions printed in dark violet blue; scrolls and stars in carmine.

New York Coliseum and Columbus Monument A523

Designed by William K. Schrage.

ROTARY PRESS PRINTING

E.E. Plates of 200 subjects in four panes of 50.

1956, Apr. 30 ***Perf. 11x10½***

1076 A523 3c **deep violet** .20 .20
P# block of 4 .30 —

WILDLIFE CONSERVATION ISSUE

Issued to emphasize the importance of Wildlife Conservation in America.

Wild Turkey — A524

Pronghorn Antelope A525

King Salmon A526

Designed by Robert W. (Bob) Hines.

ROTARY PRESS PRINTING

E.E. Plates of 200 subjects in four panes of 50.

1956 ***Perf. 11x10½***

1077 A524 3c **rose lake,** *May 5* .20 .20
P# block of 4 .35 —
1078 A525 3c **brown,** *June 22* .20 .20
P# block of 4 .35 —
1079 A526 3c **blue green,** *Nov. 9* .20 .20
P# block of 4 .35 —
Nos. 1077-1079 (3) .60 .60

PURE FOOD AND DRUG LAWS, 50th ANNIV.

Harvey Washington Wiley — A527

Designed by Robert L. Miller

ROTARY PRESS PRINTING

E.E. Plates of 200 subjects in four panes of 50.

1956, June 27 ***Perf. 10½x11***

1080 A527 3c **dark blue green** .20 .20
P# block of 4 .50 —

WHEATLAND ISSUE

Pres. Buchanan's Home, Lancaster, Pa. — A528

ROTARY PRESS PRINTING
E.E. Plates of 200 subjects in four panes of 50.

1956, Aug. 5 *Perf. 11x10½*

1081 A528 3c **black brown**	.20	.20
P# block of 4	.30	—

LABOR DAY ISSUE

Mosaic, AFL-CIO Headquarters — A529

Designed by Victor S. McCloskey, Jr.

ROTARY PRESS PRINTING
E.E. Plates of 200 subjects in four panes of 50.

1956, Sept. 3 *Perf. 10½x11*

1082 A529 3c **deep blue**	.20	.20
P# block of 4	.30	—

NASSAU HALL ISSUE

200th anniv. of Nassau Hall, Princeton University.

Nassau Hall, Princeton, N.J. — A530

ROTARY PRESS PRINTING
E.E. Plates of 200 subjects in four panes of 50.

1956, Sept. 22 *Perf. 11x10½*

1083 A530 3c **black,** *orange*	.20	.20
P# block of 4	.50	—

DEVILS TOWER ISSUE

Issued to commemorate the 50th anniversary of the Federal law providing for protection of American natural antiquities. Devils Tower National Monument, Wyoming, is an outstanding example.

Devils Tower — A531

Designed by Charles R. Chickering.

ROTARY PRESS PRINTING
E.E. Plates of 200 subjects in four panes of 50.

1956, Sept. 24 *Perf. 10½x11*

1084 A531 3c **violet**	.20	.20
P# block of 4	.30	—
Pair with full horiz. gutter btwn.	—	

CHILDREN'S ISSUE

Issued to promote friendship among the children of the world.

Children of the World — A532

Designed by Ronald Dias.

ROTARY PRESS PRINTING
E.E. Plates of 200 subjects in four panes of 50.

1956, Dec. 15 *Perf. 11x10½*

1085 A532 3c **dark blue**	.20	.20
P# block of 4	.30	—

ALEXANDER HAMILTON (1755-1804)

Alexander Hamilton and Federal Hall — A533

Designed by William K. Schrage.

ROTARY PRESS PRINTING
E.E. Plates of 200 subjects in four panes of 50.

1957, Jan. 11 *Perf. 11x10½*

1086 A533 3c **rose red**	.20	.20
P# block of 4	.30	—

POLIO ISSUE

Honoring "those who helped fight polio," and on for 20th anniv. of the Natl. Foundation for Infantile Paralysis and the March of Dimes.

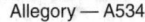

Allegory — A534

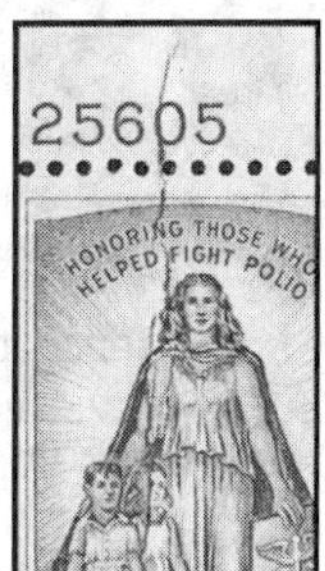

Major Plate Crack

Designed by Charles R. Chickering.

ROTARY PRESS PRINTING
E.E. Plates of 200 subjects in four panes of 50.

1957, Jan. 15 *Perf. 10½x11*

1087 A534 3c **red lilac**	.20	.20
P# block of 4	.30	—
Major plate crack (25605 UL 1)	—	

COAST AND GEODETIC SURVEY ISSUE

150th anniversary of the establishment of the Coast and Geodetic Survey.

Flag of Coast and Geodetic Survey and Ships at Sea — A535

Designed by Harold E. MacEwen.

ROTARY PRESS PRINTING
E.E. Plates of 200 subjects in four panes of 50.

1957, Feb. 11 *Perf. 11x10½*

1088 A535 3c **dark blue**	.20	.20
P# block of 4	.30	—

ARCHITECTS ISSUE

American Institute of Architects, centenary.

Corinthian Capital and Mushroom Type Head and Shaft — A536

Designed by Robert J. Schultz.

ROTARY PRESS PRINTING
E.E. Plates of 200 subjects in four panes of 50.

1957, Feb. 23 *Perf. 11x10½*

1089 A536 3c **red lilac**	.20	.20
P# block of 4	.30	—

STEEL INDUSTRY ISSUE

Centenary of the steel industry in America.

American Eagle and Pouring Ladle — A537

Designed by Anthonio Petruccelli.

ROTARY PRESS PRINTING
E.E. Plates of 200 subjects in four panes of 50.

1957, May 22 *Perf. 10½x11*

1090 A537 3c **bright ultramarine**	.20	.20
P# block of 4	.30	—

INTERNATIONAL NAVAL REVIEW ISSUE

Issued to commemorate the International Naval Review and the Jamestown Festival.

Aircraft Carrier and Jamestown Festival Emblem A538

Designed by Richard A. Genders.

ROTARY PRESS PRINTING
E.E. Plates of 200 subjects in four panes of 50.

1957, June 10 *Perf. 11x10½*

1091 A538 3c **blue green**	.20	.20
P# block of 4	.30	—

OKLAHOMA STATEHOOD, 50th ANNIV.

Map of Oklahoma, Arrow and Atom Diagram A539

Designed by William K. Schrage.

ROTARY PRESS PRINTING
E.E. Plates of 200 subjects in four panes of 50.

1957, June 14 *Perf. 11x10½*

1092 A539 3c **dark blue**	.20	.20
P# block of 4	.35	—

SCHOOL TEACHERS ISSUE

Teacher and Pupils — A540

ROTARY PRESS PRINTING
E.E. Plates of 200 subjects in four panes of 50.

1957, July 1 *Perf. 11x10½*
1093 A540 3c **rose lake** .20 .20
P# block of 4 .35 —

FLAG ISSUE

"Old Glory" (48 Stars) — A541

Designed by Victor S. McCloskey, Jr.

GIORI PRESS PRINTING
Plates of 200 subjects in four panes of 50.

1957, July 4 *Perf. 11*
1094 A541 4c **dark blue & deep carmine** .20 .20
P# block of 4 .35 —

"Virginia of Sagadahock" and Seal of Maine — A542

Ramon Magsaysay — A543

SHIPBUILDING ISSUE

350th anniversary of shipbuilding in America.

Designed by Ervine Metzel, Mrs. William Zorach, A. M. Main, Jr., and George F. Cary II.

ROTARY PRESS PRINTING
E.E. Plates of 280 subjects in four panes of 70.

1957, Aug. 15 *Perf. 10½x11*
1095 A542 3c **deep violet** .20 .20
P# block of 4 .45 —

CHAMPION OF LIBERTY ISSUE

Magsaysay (1907-57), Pres. of the Philippines.

Designed by Arnold Copeland, Ervine Metzl and William H. Buckley.

GIORI PRESS PRINTING
Plates of 192 subjects in four panes of 48 each.

1957, Aug. 31 *Perf. 11*
1096 A543 8c **carmine, ultramarine & ocher** .20 .20
P# block of 4, 2# .85 —
P# block of 4, ultra. # omitted —

Marquis de Lafayette (1757-1834) — A544

Whooping Cranes — A545

LAFAYETTE BICENTENARY ISSUE

Designed by Ervine Metzl.

ROTARY PRESS PRINTING
E.E. Plates of 200 subjects in four panes of 50.

1957. Sept. 6 *Perf. 10½x11*
1097 A544 3c **rose lake** .20 .20
P# block of 4 .30 —

WILDLIFE CONSERVATION ISSUE

Issued to emphasize the importance of Wildlife Conservation in America.

Designed by Bob Hines and C.R. Chickering.

GIORI PRESS PRINTING
Plates of 200 subjects in four panes of 50.

1957, Nov. 22 *Perf. 11*
1098 A545 3c **blue, ocher & green** .20 .20
P# block of 4 .35 —

Bible, Hat and Quill Pen — A546

"Bountiful Earth" — A547

RELIGIOUS FREEDOM ISSUE

300th anniv. of the Flushing Remonstrance.

Designed by Robert Geissmann.

ROTARY PRESS PRINTING
E.E. Plates of 200 subjects in four panes of 50.

1957, Dec. 27 *Perf. 10½x11*
1099 A546 3c **black** .20 .20
P# block of 4 .30 —

GARDENING HORTICULTURE ISSUE

Issued to honor the garden clubs of America and in connection with the centenary of the birth of Liberty Hyde Bailey, horticulturist.

Designed by Denver Gillen.

ROTARY PRESS PRINTING
E.E. Plates of 200 subjects in four panes of 50.

1958, Mar. 15 *Perf. 10½x11*
1100 A547 3c **green** .20 .20
P# block of 4 .30 —

BRUSSELS EXHIBITION ISSUE

Issued in honor of the opening of the Universal and International Exhibition at Brussels, April 17.

US Pavilion at Brussels A551

Designed by Bradbury Thompson.

ROTARY PRESS PRINTING
E.E. Plates of 200 subjects in four panes of 50.

1958, Apr. 17 *Perf. 11x10½*
1104 A551 3c **deep claret** .20 .20
On cover, Expo. station ("U.S. Pavilion") canc. 3.00
P# block of 4 .30 —

JAMES MONROE ISSUE

Monroe (1758-1831), 5th President of the US.

James Monroe — A552

Designed by Frank P. Conley.

ROTARY PRESS PRINTING
E.E. Plates of 280 subjects in four panes of 70.

1958, Apr. 28 *Perf. 11x10½*
1105 A552 3c **purple** .20 .20
P# block of 4 .30 —

MINNESOTA STATEHOOD, 100th ANNIV.

Minnesota Lakes and Pines — A553

Designed by Homer Hill.

ROTARY PRESS PRINTING
E.E. Plates of 200 subjects in four panes of 50.

1958, May 11 *Perf. 11x10½*
1106 A553 3c **green** .20 .20
P# block of 4 .30 —

GEOPHYSICAL YEAR ISSUE

International Geophysical Year, 1957-58.

Solar Disc and Hands from Michelangelo's "Creation of Adam" — A554

Designed by Ervine Metzl.

GIORI PRESS PRINTING
Plates of 200 subjects in four panes of 50.

1958, May 31 *Perf. 11*
1107 A554 3c **black & red orange** .20 .20
P# block of 4 .35 —

GUNSTON HALL ISSUE

Issued for the bicentenary of Gunston Hall and to honor George Mason, author of the Constitution of Virginia and the Virginia Bill of Rights.

Gunston Hall, Virginia A555

Designed by Rene Clarke.

ROTARY PRESS PRINTING
E.E. Plates of 200 subjects in four panes of 50.

1958, June 12 *Perf. 11x10½*
1108 A555 3c **light green** .20 .20
P# block of 4 .30 —

Mackinac Bridge — A556

Simon Bolívar — A557

MACKINAC BRIDGE ISSUE

Dedication of Mackinac Bridge, Michigan.

Designed by Arnold J. Copeland.

ROTARY PRESS PRINTING
E.E. Plates of 200 subjects in four panes of 50.

1958, June 25 ***Perf. 10½x11***
1109 A556 3c **bright greenish blue** .20 .20
P# block of 4 .30 —

CHAMPION OF LIBERTY ISSUE

Simon Bolívar, South American freedom fighter.

ROTARY PRESS PRINTING
E.E. Plates of 280 subjects in four panes of 70.

1958, July 24 ***Perf. 10½x11***
1110 A557 4c **olive bister** .20 .20
P# block of 4 .35 —

GIORI PRESS PRINTING
Plates of 288 subjects in four panes of 72 each.
Perf. 11

1111 A557 8c **carmine, ultramarine & ocher** .20 .20
P# block of 4, 2# 1.25 —
P# block of 4, ocher # only —

ATLANTIC CABLE CENTENNIAL ISSUE

Centenary of the Atlantic Cable, linking the Eastern and Western hemispheres.

Neptune, Globe and Mermaid A558

Designed by George Giusti.

ROTARY PRESS PRINTING
E.E. Plates of 200 subjects in four panes of 50.

1958, Aug. 15 ***Perf. 11x10½***
1112 A558 4c **reddish purple** .20 .20
P# block of 4 .35 —

LINCOLN SESQUICENTENNIAL ISSUE

Sesquicentennial of the birth of Abraham Lincoln. No. 1114 also for the centenary of the founding of Cooper Union, New York City. No. 1115 marks the centenary of the Lincoln-Douglas Debates.

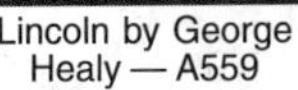

Lincoln by George Healy — A559

Lincoln by Gutzon Borglum — A560

Lincoln and Stephen A. Douglas Debating, from Painting by Joseph Boggs Beale — A561

Daniel Chester French Statue of Lincoln as Drawn by Fritz Busse — A562

Designed by Ervine Metzl.

ROTARY PRESS PRINTING
E.E. Plates of 200 subjects in four panes of 50.

1958-59 ***Perf. 10½x11***
1113 A559 1c **green,** *Feb. 12, 1959* .20 .20
P# block of 4 .25 —
1114 A560 3c **purple,** *Feb. 27, 1959* .20 .20
P# block of 4 .40 —

Perf. 11x10½

1115 A561 4c **sepia,** *Aug. 27, 1958* .20 .20
P# block of 4 .60 —
1116 A562 4c **dark blue,** *May 30, 1959* .20 .20
P# block of 4 .40 —
Nos. 1113-1116 (4) .80 .80

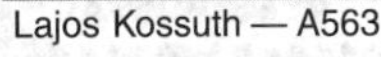

Lajos Kossuth — A563

Early Press and Hand Holding Quill — A564

CHAMPION OF LIBERTY ISSUE

Lajos Kossuth, Hungarian freedom fighter.

ROTARY PRESS PRINTING
E.E. Plates of 280 subjects in four panes of 70.

1958, Sept. 19 ***Perf. 10½x11***
1117 A563 4c **green** .20 .20
P# block of 4 .30 —

GIORI PRESS PRINTING
Plates of 288 subjects in four panes of 72 each.
Perf. 11

1118 A563 8c **carmine, ultramarine & ocher** .20 .20
P# block of 4, 2# 1.10 —

FREEDOM OF PRESS ISSUE

Honoring Journalism and freedom of the press in connection with the 50th anniv. of the 1st School of Journalism at the University of Missouri.

Designed by Lester Beall and Charles Goslin.

ROTARY PRESS PRINTING
E.E. Plates of 200 subjects in four panes of 50.

1958, Sept. 22 ***Perf. 10½x11***
1119 A564 4c **black** .20 .20
P# block of 4 .30 —

OVERLAND MAIL ISSUE

Centenary of Overland Mail Service.

Mail Coach and Map of Southwest US — A565

Designed by William H. Buckley.

ROTARY PRESS PRINTING
E.E. Plates of 200 subjects in four panes of 50.

1958, Oct. 10 ***Perf. 11x10½***
1120 A565 4c **crimson rose** .20 .20
P# block of 4 .30 —

Noah Webster — A566

Forest Scene — A567

NOAH WEBSTER ISSUE

Webster (1758-1843), lexicographer and author.

Designed by Charles R. Chickering.

ROTARY PRESS PRINTING
E.E. Plates of 280 subjects in four panes of 70.

1958, Oct. 16 ***Perf. 10½x11***
1121 A566 4c **dark carmine rose** .20 .20
P# block of 4 .40 —

FOREST CONSERVATION ISSUE

Issued to publicize forest conservation and the protection of natural resources and to honor Theodore Roosevelt, a leading forest conservationist, on the centenary of his birth.

Designed by Rudolph Wendelin.

GIORI PRESS PRINTING
Plates of 200 subjects in four panes of 50.

1958, Oct. 27 ***Perf. 11***
1122 A567 4c **green, yellow & brown** .20 .20
P# block of 4 .30 —

FORT DUQUESNE ISSUE

Bicentennial of Fort Duquesne (Fort Pitt) at future site of Pittsburgh.

British Capture of Fort Duquesne, 1758; Brig. Gen. John Forbes on Litter, Colonel Washington Mounted A568

Designed by William H. Buckley and Douglas Gorsline.

ROTARY PRESS PRINTING
E.E. Plates of 200 subjects in four panes of 50.

1958, Nov. 25 ***Perf. 11x10½***
1123 A568 4c **blue** .20 .20
P# block of 4 .35 —

OREGON STATEHOOD, 100th ANNIV.

Covered Wagon and Mt. Hood — A569

Designed by Robert Hallock.

ROTARY PRESS PRINTING
E.E. Plates of 200 subjects in four panes of 50.

1959, Feb. 14 ***Perf. 11x10½***
1124 A569 4c **blue green** .20 .20
P# block of 4 .30 —

José de San Martin — A570

NATO Emblem — A571

CHAMPION OF LIBERTY ISSUE

San Martin, So. American soldier and statesman.

ROTARY PRESS PRINTING

E.E. Plates of 280 subjects in four panes of 70.

1959, Feb. 25 ***Perf. 10½x11***

1125 A570 4c **blue** .20 .20
P# block of 4 .30 —
a. Horiz. pair, imperf. between *1,500.*

GIORI PRESS PRINTING

Plates of 288 subjects in four panes of 72 each.

Perf. 11

1126 A570 8c **carmine, ultramarine & ocher** .20 .20
P# block of 4 .90 —

NATO ISSUE

North Atlantic Treaty Organization, 10th anniv.

Designed by Stevan Dohanos.

ROTARY PRESS PRINTING

E.E. Plates of 280 subjects in four panes of 70.

1959, Apr. 1 ***Perf. 10½x11***

1127 A571 4c **blue** .20 .20
P# block of 4 .30 —

ARCTIC EXPLORATIONS ISSUE

Conquest of the Arctic by land by Rear Admiral Robert Edwin Peary in 1909 and by sea by the submarine "Nautilus" in 1958.

North Pole, Dog Sled and "Nautilus" A572

Designed by George Samerjan.

ROTARY PRESS PRINTING

E.E. Plates of 200 subjects in four panes of 50.

1959, Apr. 6 ***Perf. 11x10½***

1128 A572 4c **bright greenish blue** .20 .20
P# block of 4 .40 —

WORLD PEACE THROUGH WORLD TRADE ISSUE

Issued in conjunction with the 17th Congress of the International Chamber of Commerce, Washington, D.C., April 19-25.

Globe and Laurel — A573

Designed by Robert Baker.

ROTARY PRESS PRINTING

E.E. Plates of 200 subjects in four panes of 50.

1959, Apr. 20 ***Perf. 11x10½***

1129 A573 8c **rose lake** .20 .20
P# block of 4 .85 —

SILVER CENTENNIAL ISSUE

Discovery of silver at the Comstock Lode, Nevada.

Henry Comstock at Mount Davidson Site — A574

Designed by Robert L. Miller and W.K. Schrage.

ROTARY PRESS PRINTING

E.E. Plates of 200 subjects in four panes of 50.

1959, June 8 ***Perf. 11x10½***

1130 A574 4c **black** .20 .20
P# block of 4 .30 —

ST. LAWRENCE SEAWAY ISSUE

Opening of the St. Lawrence Seaway.

Great Lakes, Maple Leaf and Eagle Emblems A575

Designed by Arnold Copeland, Ervine Metzl, William H. Buckley and Gerald Trottier.

GIORI PRESS PRINTING

Plates of 200 subjects in four panes of 50.

1959, June 26 ***Perf. 11***

1131 A575 4c **red & dark blue** .20 .20
P# block of 4 .35 —
Pair with full horiz. gutter btwn. —

See Canada No. 387.

49-STAR FLAG ISSUE

U.S. Flag, 1959 — A576

Designed by Stevan Dohanos.

GIORI PRESS PRINTING

Plates of 200 subjects in four panes of 50.

1959, July 4 ***Perf. 11***

1132 A576 4c **ocher, dark blue & deep carmine** .20 .20
P# block of 4 .40 —

SOIL CONSERVATION ISSUE

Issued as a tribute to farmers and ranchers who use soil and water conservation measures.

Modern Farm — A577

Designed by Walter Hortens.

GIORI PRESS PRINTING

Plates of 200 subjects in four panes of 50.

1959, Aug. 26 ***Perf. 11***

1133 A577 4c **blue, green & ocher** .20 .20
P# block of 4 .35 —

PETROLEUM INDUSTRY ISSUE

Centenary of the completion of the nation's first oil well at Titusville, Pa.

Oil Derrick — A578

Designed by Robert Foster.

ROTARY PRESS PRINTING

E.E. Plates of 200 subjects in four panes of 50.

1959, Aug. 27 ***Perf. 10½x11***

1134 A578 4c **brown** .20 .20
P# block of 4 .40 —

DENTAL HEALTH ISSUE

Issued to publicize Dental Health and for the centenary of the American Dental Association.

Children A579

Designed by Charles Henry Carter.

ROTARY PRESS PRINTING

E.E. Plates of 200 subjects in four panes of 50.

1959, Sept. 14 ***Perf. 11x10½***

1135 A579 4c **green** .20 .20
P# block of 4 .40 —

Ernst Reuter — A580

Dr. Ephraim McDowell — A581

CHAMPION OF LIBERTY ISSUE

Ernst Reuter, Mayor of Berlin, 1948-53.

ROTARY PRESS PRINTING

E.E. Plates of 280 subjects in four panes of 70.

1959, Sept. 29 ***Perf. 10½x11***

1136 A580 4c **gray** .20 .20
P# block of 4 .30 —

GIORI PRESS PRINTING

Plates of 288 subjects in four panes of 72 each.

Perf. 11

1137 A580 8c **carmine, ultramarine & ocher** .20 .20
P# block of 4 .90 —
a. Ocher missing (EP) *3,750.*
b. Ultramarine missing (EP) *3,750.*
c. Ocher & ultramarine missing (EP) *4,000.*
d. All colors missing (EP) *2,500.*

DR. EPHRAIM McDOWELL ISSUE

Honoring McDowell (1771-1830) on the 150th anniv. of the 1st successful ovarian operation in the US, performed at Danville, Ky., 1809.

Designed by Charles R. Chickering.

ROTARY PRESS PRINTING

E.E. Plates of 280 subjects in four panes of 70.

1959, Dec. 3 ***Perf. 10½x11***

1138 A581 4c **rose lake** .20 .20
P# block of 4 .40 —
a. Vert. pair, imperf. btwn. *450.00*
b. Vert. pair, imperf. horiz. *350.00*

VALUES FOR HINGED STAMPS AFTER NO. 771
This catalogue does not value unused stamps after No. 771 in hinged condition. Hinged unused stamps from No. 772 to the present are worth considerably less than the values given for unused stamps, which are for never-hinged examples.

AMERICAN CREDO ISSUE

Issued to re-emphasize the ideals upon which America was founded and to honor those great Americans who wrote or uttered the credos.

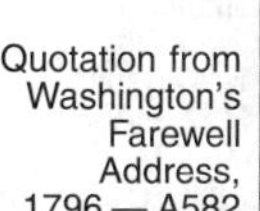

Quotation from Washington's Farewell Address, 1796 — A582

Benjamin Franklin Quotation A583

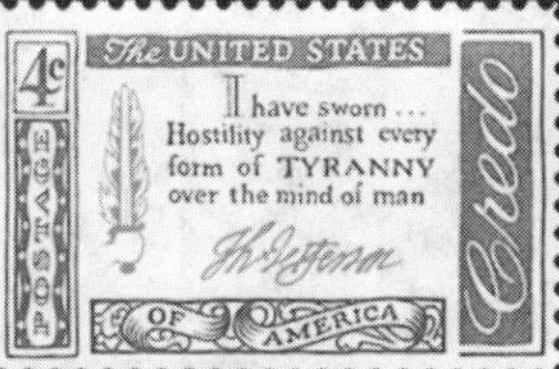

Thomas Jefferson Quotation A584

Francis Scott Key Quotation A585

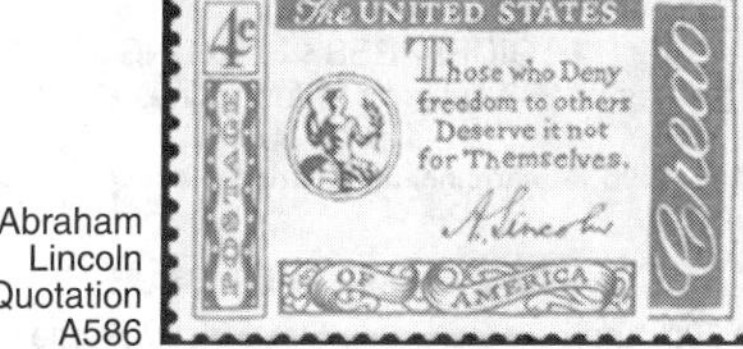

Abraham Lincoln Quotation A586

Patrick Henry Quotation A587

Designed by Frank Conley.

GIORI PRESS PRINTING
Plates of 200 subjects in four panes of 50.

1960-61 ***Perf. 11***

1139 A582 4c **dark violet blue, & carmine,** *Jan. 20, 1960* .20 .20
P# block of 4 .40 —
1140 A583 4c **olive bister & green,** *Mar. 31, 1960* .20 .20
P# block of 4 .40 —
1141 A584 4c **gray & vermilion,** *May 18, 1960* .20 .20
P# block of 4 .45 —
1142 A585 4c **carmine & dark blue,** *Sept. 14, 1960* .20 .20
P# block of 4 .50 —
1143 A586 4c **magenta & green,** *Nov. 19, 1960* .20 .20
P# block of 4 .50 —
Pair with full horiz. gutter between —
1144 A587 4c **green & brown,** *Jan. 11, 1961* .20 .20
P# block of 4 .50 —
Nos. 1139-1144 (6) 1.20 1.20

BOY SCOUT JUBILEE ISSUE

50th anniv. of the Boy Scouts of America.

Boy Scout Giving Scout Sign — A588

Designed by Norman Rockwell.

GIORI PRESS PRINTING
Plates of 200 subjects in four panes of 50.

1960, Feb. 8 ***Perf. 11***

1145 A588 4c **red, dark blue & dark bister** .20 .20
P# block of 4 .45 —

Olympic Rings and Snowflake — A589

Thomas G. Masaryk — A590

OLYMPIC WINTER GAMES ISSUE

Opening of the 8th Olympic Winter Games, Squaw Valley, Feb. 18-29, 1960.

Designed by Ervine Metzl.

ROTARY PRESS PRINTING
E.E. Plates of 200 subjects in four panes of 50.

1960, Feb. 18 ***Perf. 10½x11***

1146 A589 4c **dull blue** .20 .20
P# block of 4 .40 —

CHAMPION OF LIBERTY ISSUE

Issued to honor Thomas G. Masaryk, founder and president of Czechoslovakia (1918-35), on the 110th anniversary of his birth.

ROTARY PRESS PRINTING
E.E. Plates of 280 subjects in four panes of 70.

1960, Mar. 7 ***Perf. 10½x11***

1147 A590 4c **blue** .20 .20
P# block of 4 .30 —
a. Vert. pair, imperf. between *3,250.*

GIORI PRESS PRINTING
Plates of 288 subjects in four panes of 72 each.
Perf. 11

1148 A590 8c **carmine, ultramarine & ocher** .20 .20
P# block of 4 .95 —
a. Horiz. pair, imperf. between —

WORLD REFUGEE YEAR ISSUE

World Refugee Year, July 1, 1959-June 30, 1960.

Family Walking Toward New Life — A591

Designed by Ervine Metzl.

ROTARY PRESS PRINTING
E.E. Plates of 200 subjects in four panes of 50.

1960, Apr. 7 ***Perf. 11x10½***

1149 A591 4c **gray black** .20 .20
P# block of 4 .30 —

WATER CONSERVATION ISSUE

Issued to stress the importance of water conservation and to commemorate the 7th Watershed Congress, Washington, D.C.

Water: From Watershed to Consumer A592

Designed by Elmo White.

GIORI PRESS PRINTING
Plates of 200 subjects in four panes of 50.

1960, Apr. 18 ***Perf. 11***

1150 A592 4c **dark blue, brown orange & green** .20 .20
P# block of 4 .35 —
a. Brown orange missing (EP) *4,000.*

SEATO ISSUE

South-East Asia Treaty Organization and for the SEATO Conf., Washington, D.C., May 31-June 3.

SEATO Emblem — A593

Designed by John Maass.

ROTARY PRESS PRINTING
E.E. plates of 280 subjects in four panes of 70.

1960, May 31 ***Perf. 10½x11***

1151 A593 4c **blue** .20 .20
P# block of 4 .35 —
a. Vertical pair, imperf. between *140.00*

AMERICAN WOMAN ISSUE

Issued to pay tribute to American women and their accomplishments in civic affairs, education, arts and industry.

Mother and Daughter A594

Designed by Robert Sivard.

ROTARY PRESS PRINTING
E.E. Plates of 200 subjects in four panes of 50.

1960, June 2 ***Perf. 11x10½***

1152 A594 4c **deep violet** .20 .20
P# block of 4 .30 —

50-STAR FLAG ISSUE

US Flag, 1960 — A595

Designed by Stevan Dohanos.

GIORI PRESS PRINTING
Plates of 200 subjects in four panes of 50.

1960, July 4 ***Perf. 11***

1153 A595 4c **dark blue & red** .20 .20
P# block of 4 .30 —

PONY EXPRESS CENTENNIAL ISSUE

Pony Express Rider — A596

Designed by Harold von Schmidt.

ROTARY PRESS PRINTING

E.E. Plates of 200 subjects in four panes of 50.

1960, July 19 ***Perf. 11x10½***

1154 A596 4c **sepia** .20 .20
P# block of 4 .55 —

Man in Wheelchair Operating Drill Press — A597

World Forestry Congress Seal — A598

EMPLOY THE HANDICAPPED ISSUE

Promoting the employment of the physically handicapped and publicizing the 8th World Congress of the Intl. Soc. for the Welfare of Cripples, New York City.

Designed by Carl Bobertz.

ROTARY PRESS PRINTING

E.E. Plates of 200 subjects in four panes of 50.

1960, Aug. 28 ***Perf. 10½x11***

1155 A597 4c **dark blue** .20 .20
P# block of 4 .30 —

WORLD FORESTRY CONGRESS ISSUE

5th World Forestry Cong., Seattle, Wash., Aug. 29-Sept. 10.

ROTARY PRESS PRINTING

E.E. Plates of 200 subjects in four panes of 50.

1960, Aug. 29 ***Perf. 10½x11***

1156 A598 4c **green** .20 .20
P# block of 4 .30 —

Independence Bell — A599

Washington Monument and Cherry Blossoms — A600

MEXICAN INDEPENDENCE, 150th ANNIV.

Designed by Leon Helguera and Charles R. Chickering.

GIORI PRESS PRINTING

Plates of 200 subjects in four panes of 50.

1960, Sept. 16 ***Perf. 11***

1157 A599 4c **green & rose red** .20 .20
P# block of 4 .30 —

See Mexico No. 910.

US-JAPAN TREATY ISSUE

Centenary of the United States-Japan Treaty of Amity and Commerce.

Designed by Gyo Fujikawa.

GIORI PRESS PRINTING

Plates of 200 subjects in four panes of 50.

1960, Sept. 28 ***Perf. 11***

1158 A600 4c **blue & pink** .20 .20
P# block of 4 .35 —

Ignacy Jan Paderewski — A601

Robert A. Taft — A602

CHAMPION OF LIBERTY ISSUE

Jan Paderewski, Polish statesman and musician.

ROTARY PRESS PRINTING

E.E. Plates of 280 subjects in four panes of 70.

1960, Oct. 8 ***Perf. 10½x11***

1159 A601 4c **blue** .20 .20
P# block of 4 .30 —

GIORI PRESS PRINTING

Plates of 288 subjects in four panes of 72 each.

Perf. 11

1160 A601 8c **carmine, ultramarine & ocher** .20 .20
P# block of 4 .90 —

SENATOR TAFT MEMORIAL ISSUE

Senator Robert A. Taft (1889-1953) of Ohio.

Designed by William K. Schrage.

ROTARY PRESS PRINTING

E.E. Plates of 280 subjects in four panes of 70.

1960, Oct. 10 ***Perf. 10½x11***

1161 A602 4c **dull violet** .20 .20
P# block of 4 .45 —

WHEELS OF FREEDOM ISSUE

Issued to honor the automotive industry and in connection with the National Automobile Show, Detroit, Oct. 15-23.

Globe and Steering Wheel with Tractor, Car and Truck — A603

Designed by Arnold J. Copeland.

ROTARY PRESS PRINTING

E.E. Plates of 200 subjects in four panes of 50.

1960, Oct. 15 ***Perf. 11x10½***

1162 A603 4c **dark blue** .20 .20
P# block of 4 .30 —

BOYS' CLUBS OF AMERICA ISSUE

Boys' Clubs of America movement, centenary.

Profile of Boy — A604

Designed by Charles T. Coiner.

GIORI PRESS PRINTING

Plates of 200 subjects in four panes of 50.

1960, Oct. 18 ***Perf. 11***

1163 A604 4c **indigo, slate & rose red** .20 .20
P# block of 4 .30 —

FIRST AUTOMATED POST OFFICE IN THE US ISSUE

Publicizing the opening of the 1st automated post office in the US at Providence, R.I.

Architect's Sketch of New Post Office, Providence, R.I. — A605

Designed by Arnold J. Copeland and Victor S. McCloskey, Jr.

GIORI PRESS PRINTING

Plates of 200 subjects in four panes of 50.

1960, Oct. 20 ***Perf. 11***

1164 A605 4c **dark blue & carmine** .20 .20
P# block of 4 .30 —

Baron Gustaf Mannerheim — A606

Camp Fire Girls Emblem — A607

CHAMPION OF LIBERTY ISSUE

Baron Karl Gustaf Emil Mannerheim (1867-1951), Marshal and President of Finland.

ROTARY PRESS PRINTING

E.E. Plates of 280 subjects in four panes of 70.

1960, Oct. 26 ***Perf. 10½x11***

1165 A606 4c **blue** .20 .20
P# block of 4 .30 —

GIORI PRESS PRINTING

Plates of 288 subjects in four panes of 72 each.

Perf. 11

1166 A606 8c **carmine, ultramarine & ocher** .20 .20
P# block of 4 .80 —

CAMP FIRE GIRLS ISSUE

50th anniv. of the Camp Fire Girls' movement and in connection with the Golden Jubilee Convention celebration of the Camp Fire Girls.

Designed by H. Edward Oliver.

GIORI PRESS PRINTING

Plates of 200 subjects in four panes of 50.

1960, Nov. 1 ***Perf. 11***

1167 A607 4c **dark blue & bright red** .20 .20
P# block of 4 .55 —

Giuseppe Garibaldi — A608

Walter F. George — A609

CHAMPION OF LIBERTY ISSUE

Giuseppe Garibaldi (1807-1882), Italian patriot and freedom fighter.

ROTARY PRESS PRINTING
E.E. Plates of 280 subjects in four panes of 70.

1960, Nov. 2 ***Perf. 10½x11***
1168 A608 4c **green** .20 .20
P# block of 4 .30 —

GIORI PRESS PRINTING
Plates of 288 subjects in four panes of 72 each.
Perf. 11

1169 A608 8c **carmine, ultramarine & ocher** .20 .20
P# block of 4 .85 —

SENATOR GEORGE MEMORIAL ISSUE

Walter F. George (1878-1957) of Georgia.

Designed by William K. Schrage.

ROTARY PRESS PRINTING
E.E. Plates of 280 subjects in four panes of 70.

1960, Nov. 5 ***Perf. 10½x11***
1170 A609 4c **dull violet** .20 .20
P# block of 4 .45 —

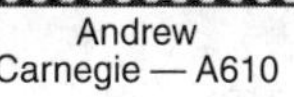
Andrew Carnegie — A610

John Foster Dulles — A611

ANDREW CARNEGIE ISSUE

Carnegie (1835-1919), industrialist & philanthropist.

Designed by Charles R. Chickering.

ROTARY PRESS PRINTING
E.E. Plates of 280 subjects in four panes of 70.

1960, Nov. 25 ***Perf. 10½x11***
1171 A610 4c **deep claret** .20 .20
P# block of 4 .35 —

JOHN FOSTER DULLES MEMORIAL ISSUE

Dulles (1888-1959), Secretary of State (1953-59).

Designed by William K. Schrage.

ROTARY PRESS PRINTING
E.E. Plates of 280 subjects in four panes of 70.

1960, Dec. 6 ***Perf. 10½x11***
1172 A611 4c **dull violet** .20 .20
P# block of 4 .35 —

ECHO I - COMMUNICATIONS FOR PEACE ISSUE

World's 1st communications satellite, Echo I, placed in orbit by the Natl. Aeronautics and Space Admin., Aug. 12, 1960.

Radio Waves Connecting Echo I and Earth — A612

Designed by Ervine Metzl.

ROTARY PRESS PRINTING
E.E. Plates of 200 subjects in four panes of 50.

1960, Dec. 15 ***Perf. 11x10½***
1173 A612 4c **deep violet** .20 .20
P# block of 4 .65 —

CHAMPION OF LIBERTY ISSUE

Mohandas K. Gandhi, leader in India's struggle for independence.

Mahatma Gandhi — A613

ROTARY PRESS PRINTING
E.E. Plates of 280 subjects in four panes of 70.

1961, Jan. 26 ***Perf. 10½x11***
1174 A613 4c **red orange** .20 .20
P# block of 4 .30 —

GIORI PRESS PRINTING
Plates of 288 subjects in four panes of 72 each.
Perf. 11

1175 A613 8c **carmine, ultramarine & ocher** .20 .20
P# block of 4 1.00 —

RANGE CONSERVATION ISSUE

Issued to stress the importance of range conservation and to commemorate the meeting of the American Society of Range Management, Washington, D.C. "The Trail Boss" from a drawing by Charles M. Russell is the Society's emblem.

The Trail Boss and Modern Range — A614

Designed by Rudolph Wendelin.

GIORI PRESS PRINTING
Plates of 200 subjects in four panes of 50.

1961, Feb. 2 ***Perf. 11***
1176 A614 4c **blue, slate & brown orange** .20 .20
P# block of 4 .40 —

HORACE GREELEY ISSUE

Greeley (1811-1872), publisher and editor.

Horace Greeley — A615

Designed by Charles R. Chickering.

ROTARY PRESS PRINTING
E.E. Plates of 280 subjects in four panes of 70.

1961, Feb. 3 ***Perf. 10½x11***
1177 A615 4c **dull violet** .20 .20
P# block of 4 .45 —

CIVIL WAR CENTENNIAL ISSUE

Centenaries of the firing on Fort Sumter (No. 1178), the Battle of Shiloh (No. 1179), the Battle of Gettysburg (No. 1180), the Battle of the Wilderness (No. 1181) and the surrender at Appomattox (No. 1182).

Sea Coast Gun of 1861 — A616

Rifleman at Battle of Shiloh, 1862 — A617

Blue and Gray at Gettysburg, 1863 — A618

Battle of the Wilderness, 1864 — A619

Appomattox, 1865 — A620

Designed by Charles R. Chickering (Sumter), Noel Sickles (Shiloh), Roy Gjertson (Gettysburg), B. Harold Christenson (Wilderness), Leonard Fellman (Appomattox).

ROTARY PRESS PRINTING
E.E. Plates of 200 subjects in four panes of 50.

1961-65 ***Perf. 11x10½***
1178 A616 4c **light green,** *Apr. 12, 1961* .25 .20
P# block of 4 1.10 —
1179 A617 4c **black,** *peach blossom, Apr. 7, 1962* .20 .20
P# block of 4 .75 —

GIORI PRESS PRINTING
Plates of 200 subjects in four panes of 50.
Perf. 11

1180 A618 5c **gray & blue,** *July 1, 1963* .20 .20
P# block of 4 .85 —
1181 A619 5c **dark red & black,** *May 5, 1964* .20 .20
P# block of 4 .60 —
Margin block of 4, Mr. Zip and "Use Zip Code" .55 —
1182 A620 5c **Prus. blue & black,** *Apr. 9, 1965* .30 .20
P# block of 4 1.40 —
Margin block of 4, Mr. Zip and "Use Zip Code" 1.30 —
a. Horiz. pair, imperf. vert. *4,500.*
Nos. 1178-1182 (5) 1.15 1.00

KANSAS STATEHOOD, 100th ANNIV.

Sunflower, Pioneer Couple and Stockade A621

GIORI PRESS PRINTING
Plates of 200 subjects in four panes of 50.

1961, May 10 ***Perf. 11***
1183 A621 4c **brown, dark red & green,** *yellow* .20 .20
P# block of 4 .35 —

SENATOR NORRIS ISSUE

Senator George W. Norris of Nebraska, and Norris Dam — A622

Designed by Charles R. Chickering.

ROTARY PRESS PRINTING
E.E. Plates of 200 subjects in four panes of 50.

1961, July 11 *Perf. 11x10½*
1184 A622 4c **blue green** .20 .20
P# block of 4 .40 —

NAVAL AVIATION, 50th ANNIV.

Navy's First Plane (Curtiss A-1 of 1911) and Naval Air Wings — A623

Designed by John Maass.

ROTARY PRESS PRINTING
E.E. Plates of 200 subjects in four panes of 50.

1961, Aug. 20 *Perf. 11x10½*
1185 A623 4c **blue** .20 .20
P# block of 4 .35 —
Pair with full vert. gutter btwn. *150.00*

WORKMEN'S COMPENSATION ISSUE

50th anniv. of the 1st successful Workmen's Compensation Law, enacted by the Wisconsin legislature.

Scales of Justice, Factory, Worker and Family — A624

Designed by Norman Todhunter.

ROTARY PRESS PRINTING
E.E. Plates of 200 subjects in four panes of 50.

1961, Sept. 4 *Perf. 10½x11*
1186 A624 4c **ultramarine,** *grayish* .20 .20
P# block of 4 .35 —
P# block of 4 inverted .60 —

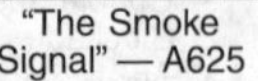

"The Smoke Signal" — A625

Sun Yat-sen — A626

FREDERIC REMINGTON ISSUE

Remington (1861-1909), artist of the West. The design is from an oil painting, Amon Carter Museum of Western Art, Fort Worth, Texas.

Designed by Charles R. Chickering.

GIORI PRESS PRINTING
Panes of 200 subjects in four panes of 50.

1961, Oct. 4 *Perf. 11*
1187 A625 4c **multicolored** .20 .20
P# block of 4 .40 —

REPUBLIC OF CHINA ISSUE

50th anniversary of the Republic of China.

ROTARY PRESS PRINTING
E.E. Plates of 200 subjects in four panes of 50.

1961, Oct. 10 *Perf. 10½x11*
1188 A626 4c **blue** .20 .20
P# block of 4 .45 —

Basketball — A627

Student Nurse Lighting Candle — A628

NAISMITH - BASKETBALL ISSUE

Honoring basketball and James Naismith (1861-1939), Canada-born director of physical education, who invented the game in 1891 at Y.M.C.A. College, Springfield, Mass.

Designed by Charles R. Chickering.

ROTARY PRESS PRINTING
E.E. Plates of 200 subjects in four panes of 50.

1961, Nov. 6 *Perf. 10½x11*
1189 A627 4c **brown** .20 .20
P# block of 4 .50 —

NURSING ISSUE

Issued to honor the nursing profession.

Designed by Alfred Charles Parker.

GIORI PRESS PRINTING
Plates of 200 subjects in four panes of 50.

1961, Dec. 28 *Perf. 11*
1190 A628 4c **blue, green, orange & black** .20 .20
P# block of 4, 2# .50 —

NEW MEXICO STATEHOOD, 50th ANNIV.

Shiprock A629

Designed by Robert J. Jones.

GIORI PRESS PRINTING
Plates of 200 subjects in four panes of 50.

1962, Jan. 6 *Perf. 11*
1191 A629 4c **lt. blue, maroon & bister** .20 .20
P# block of 4 .30 —

ARIZONA STATEHOOD, 50th ANNIV.

Giant Saguaro Cactus — A630

Designed by Jimmie E. Ihms and James M. Chemi.

GIORI PRESS PRINTING
Plates of 200 subjects in four panes of 50.

1962, Feb. 14 *Perf. 11*
1192 A630 4c **carmine, violet blue & green** .20 .20
P# block of 4 .30 —

PROJECT MERCURY ISSUE

1st orbital flight of a US astronaut, Lt. Col. John H. Glenn, Jr., Feb. 20, 1962.

"Friendship 7" Capsule and Globe — A631

GIORI PRESS PRINTING
Plates of 200 subjects in four panes of 50.

1962, Feb. 20 *Perf. 11*
1193 A631 4c **dark blue & yellow** .20 .20
P# block of 4 .35 —

Imperfs. are printers waste.

MALARIA ERADICATION ISSUE

World Health Organization's drive to eradicate malaria.

Great Seal of US and WHO Symbol A632

Designed by Charles R. Chickering.

GIORI PRESS PRINTING
Plates of 200 subjects in four panes of 50.

1962, Mar. 30 *Perf. 11*
1194 A632 4c **blue & bister** .20 .20
P# block of 4 .30 —

Charles Evans Hughes — A633

"Space Needle" and Monorail — A634

CHARLES EVANS HUGHES ISSUE

Hughes (1862-1948), Governor of New York, Chief Justice of the US.

Designed by Charles R. Chickering.

ROTARY PRESS PRINTING
E.E. Plates of 200 subjects in four panes of 50.

1962, Apr. 11 *Perf. 10½x11*
1195 A633 4c **black,** *buff* .20 .20
P# block of 4 .30 —

SEATTLE WORLD'S FAIR ISSUE

"Century 21" International Exposition, Seattle, Wash., Apr. 21-Oct. 21.

Designed by John Maass.

GIORI PRESS PRINTING
Plates of 200 subjects in four panes of 50.

1962, Apr. 25 *Perf. 11*
1196 A634 4c **red & dark blue** .20 .20
On cover, "Century 21" Expo. cancel 5.00
On cover, "Space Needle" Expo. cancel 2.00
P# block of 4 .30 —

LOUISIANA STATEHOOD, 150th ANNIV.

Riverboat on the Mississippi A635

Designed by Norman Todhunter.

GIORI PRESS PRINTING
Plates of 200 subjects in four panes of 50.

1962, Apr. 30 *Perf. 11*
1197 A635 4c **blue, dark slate green & red** .20 .20
P# block of 4 .50 —

HOMESTEAD ACT, CENTENARY

Sod Hut and Settlers A636

Designed by Charles R. Chickering.

ROTARY PRESS PRINTING
E.E. Plates of 200 subjects in four panes of 50.

1962, May 20 *Perf. 11x10½*
1198 A636 4c **slate** .20 .20
P# block of 4 .30 —

GIRL SCOUTS ISSUE

50th anniversary of the Girl Scouts of America.

Senior Girl Scout and Flag — A637

Designed by Ward Brackett.

ROTARY PRESS PRINTING
E.E. Plates of 200 subjects in four panes of 50.

1962, July 24 *Perf. 11x10½*
1199 A637 4c **rose red** .20 .20
P# block of 4 .30 —
Pair with full vertical gutter between *250.00*

SENATOR BRIEN McMAHON ISSUE

McMahon (1903-52) of Connecticut had a role in opening the way to peaceful uses of atomic energy through the Atomic Energy Act establishing the Atomic Energy Commission.

Brien McMahon and Atomic Symbol A638

Designed by V. S. McCloskey, Jr.

ROTARY PRESS PRINTING
E.E. Plates of 200 subjects in four panes of 50.

1962, July 28 *Perf. 11x10½*
1200 A638 4c **purple** .20 .20
P# block of 4 .40 —

APPRENTICESHIP ISSUE

National Apprenticeship Program and 25th anniv. of the National Apprenticeship Act.

Machinist Handing Micrometer to Apprentice A639

Designed by Robert Geissmann.

ROTARY PRESS PRINTING
E.E. Plates of 200 subjects in four panes of 50.

1962, Aug. 31 *Perf. 11x10½*
1201 A639 4c **black,** *yellow bister* .20 .20
P# block of 4 .30 —

SAM RAYBURN ISSUE

Rayburn (1882-1961), Speaker of the House of Representatives.

Sam Rayburn and Capitol — A640

Designed by Robert L. Miller.

GIORI PRESS PRINTING
Plates of 200 subjects in four panes of 50.

1962, Sept. 16 *Perf. 11*
1202 A640 4c **dark blue & red brown** .20 .20
P# block of 4 .30 —

DAG HAMMARSKJOLD ISSUE

Hammarskjold, UN Sec. General, 1953-61.

UN Headquarters and Dag Hammarskjold A641

Designed by Herbert M. Sanborn.

GIORI PRESS PRINTING
Plates of 200 subjects in four panes of 50.

1962, Oct. 23 *Perf. 11*
1203 A641 4c **black, brown & yellow** .20 .20
P# block of 4, 2# .30 —

Hammarskjold Special Printing

No. 1204 was issued following discovery of No. 1203 with yellow background inverted.

GIORI PRESS PRINTING
Plates of 200 subjects in four panes of 50.

1962, Nov. 16 *Perf. 11*
1204 A641 4c **black, brown & yel** (yellow inverted) .20 .20
P# block of 4, 2#, yellow # inverted 1.10 —

The inverted yellow impression is shifted to the right in relation to the black and brown impression. Stamps of first vertical row of UL and LL panes show no yellow at left side for a space of 11-11½mm in from the perforations.

Stamps of first vertical row of UR and LR panes show vertical no-yellow strip 9¾mm wide, covering UN Building. On all others, the vertical no-yellow strip is 3½mm wide, and touches UN Building.

CHRISTMAS ISSUE

Wreath and Candles — A642

Designed by Jim Crawford.

GIORI PRESS PRINTING
Plates of 400 subjects in four panes of 100.
Panes of 90 and 100 exist without plate numbers due to provisional use of smaller paper.

1962, Nov. 1 *Perf. 11*
1205 A642 4c **green & red** .20 .20
P# block of 4 .30 —

HIGHER EDUCATION ISSUE

Higher education's role in American cultural and industrial development and the centenary celebrations of the signing of the law creating land-grant colleges and universities.

Map of U.S. and Lamp — A643

Designed by Henry K. Bencsath.

GIORI PRESS PRINTING
Plates of 200 subjects in panes of 50.

1962, Nov. 14 *Perf. 11*
1206 A643 4c **blue green & black** .20 .20
P# block of 4, 2# .35 —

WINSLOW HOMER ISSUE

Homer (1836-1910), painter, showing his oil, "Breezing Up," which hangs in the National Gallery, Washington, D.C.

"Breezing Up" — A644

Designed by Victor S. McCloskey, Jr.

GIORI PRESS PRINTING
Plates of 200 subjects in four panes of 50.

1962, Dec. 15 *Perf. 11*
1207 A644 4c **multicolored** .20 .20
P# block of 4 .45 —
a. Horiz. pair, imperf. btwn. and at right *6,750.*

FLAG ISSUE

Flag over White House — A645

Designed by Robert J. Jones.

GIORI PRESS PRINTING
Plates of 400 subjects in four panes of 100.

1963-66 *Perf. 11*
1208 A645 5c **blue & red,** *Jan. 9, 1963* .20 .20
P# block of 4 .40 —
Pair with full horiz. gutter between —
a. Tagged, *Aug. 25, 1966* .20 .20
P# block of 4 2.00 —
b. Horiz. pair, imperf. between, tagged *1,500.*

Beware of pairs with faint blind perfs between offered as No. 1208b.

REGULAR ISSUE

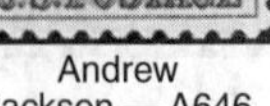

Andrew Jackson — A646

George Washington — A650

Designed by William K. Schrage.

ROTARY PRESS PRINTING

E.E. Plates of 400 subjects in four panes of 100.

1962-66 ***Perf. 11x10½***

No.	Type	Denom.	Description	Unused	Used
1209	A646	1c	**green,** *Mar. 22, 1963*	.20	.20
			P# block of 4	.20	—
			Pair with full vert. gutter btwn.	—	
a.			Tagged, *July 6, 1966*	.20	.20
			P# block of 4	.40	—
1213	A650	5c	**dark blue gray,** *Nov. 23, 1962*	.20	.20
			P# block of 4	.40	—
			Pair with full vert. gutter btwn.	—	
			Pair with full horiz. gutter btwn.	*450.00*	
a.			Booklet pane of 5 + label	3.00	*2.00*
b.			Tagged, *Oct. 28, 1963*	.50	.20
			P# block of 4	4.50	—
c.			As "a," tagged, *Oct. 28, 1963*	2.00	*1.50*
d.			Horiz. pair, imperf between	*2,750.*	

Bureau Precancels: 1c, 10 diff., 5c, 18 diff.

No. 1213d resulted from a paper foldover after perforating and before cutting into panes.

COIL STAMPS
(Rotary Press)

1962-66 ***Perf. 10 Vertically***

No.	Type	Denom.	Description	Unused	Used
1225	A646	1c	**green,** *May 31, 1963*	.20	.20
			Pair	.30	.20
			Joint line pair	2.00	.20
a.			Tagged, *July 6, 1966*	.20	.20
			Joint line pair	.75	.20
1229	A650	5c	**dark blue gray,** *Nov. 23, 1962*	1.10	.20
			Pair	2.25	.20
			Joint line pair	3.50	.35
a.			Tagged, *Oct. 28, 1963*	1.40	.20
			Joint line pair	6.50	.20
b.			Imperf., pair	*450.00*	
			Joint line pair	*1,250.*	

Bureau Precancels: 1c, 5 diff., 5c, 14 diff.

See Luminescence note in "Information for Collectors" at front of book.

CAROLINA CHARTER ISSUE

Tercentenary of the Carolina Charter granting to 8 Englishmen lands extending coast-to-coast roughly along the present border of Virginia to the north and Florida to the south. Original charter on display at Raleigh.

First Page of Carolina Charter A662

Designed by Robert L. Miller.

GIORI PRESS PRINTING

Plates of 200 subjects in four panes of 50.

1963, Apr. 6 ***Perf. 11***

No.	Type	Denom.	Description	Unused	Used
1230	A662	5c	**dark carmine & brown**	.20	.20
			P# block of 4	.40	—

FOOD FOR PEACE-FREEDOM FROM HUNGER ISSUE

American "Food for Peace" program and the "Freedom from Hunger" campaign of the FAO.

Wheat — A663

Designed by Stevan Dohanos.

GIORI PRESS PRINTING

Plates of 200 subjects in four panes of 50.

1963, June 4 ***Perf. 11***

No.	Type	Denom.	Description	Unused	Used
1231	A663	5c	**green, buff & red**	.20	.20
			P# block of 4	.40	—

WEST VIRGINIA STATEHOOD, 100th ANNIV.

Map of West Virginia and State Capitol A664

Designed by Dr. Dwight Mutchler.

GIORI PRESS PRINTING

Plates of 200 subjects in four panes of 50.

1963, June 20 ***Perf. 11***

No.	Type	Denom.	Description	Unused	Used
1232	A664	5c	**green, red & black**	.20	.20
			P# block of 4	.40	—

EMANCIPATION PROCLAMATION ISSUE

Centenary of Lincoln's Emancipation Proclamation freeing about 3,000,000 slaves in 10 southern states.

Severed Chain — A665

Designed by Georg Olden.

GIORI PRESS PRINTING

Plates of 200 subjects in four panes of 50.

1963, Aug. 16 ***Perf. 11***

No.	Type	Denom.	Description	Unused	Used
1233	A665	5c	**dark blue, black & red**	.20	.20
			P# block of 4	.50	—

ALLIANCE FOR PROGRESS ISSUE

2nd anniv. of the Alliance for Progress, which aims to stimulate economic growth and raise living standards in Latin America.

Alliance Emblem A666

Designed by William K. Schrage.

GIORI PRESS PRINTING

Plates of 200 subjects in four panes of 50.

1963, Aug. 17 ***Perf. 11***

No.	Type	Denom.	Description	Unused	Used
1234	A666	5c	**ultramarine & green**	.20	.20
			P# block of 4	.40	—

CORDELL HULL ISSUE

Hull (1871-1955), Secretary of State (1933-44).

Cordell Hull — A667

Designed by Robert J. Jones.

ROTARY PRESS PRINTING

E.E. Plates of 200 subjects in four panes of 50.

1963, Oct. 5 ***Perf. 10½x11***

No.	Type	Denom.	Description	Unused	Used
1235	A667	5c	**blue green**	.20	.20
			P# block of 4	.50	—

ELEANOR ROOSEVELT ISSUE

Mrs. Franklin D. Roosevelt (1884-1962).

Eleanor Roosevelt A668

Designed by Robert L. Miller.

ROTARY PRESS PRINTING

E.E. Plates of 200 subjects in four panes of 50.

1963, Oct. 11 ***Perf. 11x10½***

No.	Type	Denom.	Description	Unused	Used
1236	A668	5c	**bright purple**	.20	.20
			P# block of 4	.45	—

SCIENCE ISSUE

Honoring the sciences and in connection with the centenary of the Natl. Academy of Science.

"The Universe" A669

Designed by Antonio Frasconi.

GIORI PRESS PRINTING

Plates of 200 subjects in four panes of 50.

1963, Oct. 14 ***Perf. 11***

No.	Type	Denom.	Description	Unused	Used
1237	A669	5c	**Prussian blue & black**	.20	.20
			P# block of 4	.40	—

CITY MAIL DELIVERY ISSUE

Centenary of free city mail delivery.

Letter Carrier, 1863 — A670

Designed by Norman Rockwell.

GIORI PRESS PRINTING

Plates of 200 subjects in four panes of 50.

1963, Oct. 26 **Tagged** ***Perf. 11***

No.	Type	Denom.	Description	Unused	Used
1238	A670	5c	**gray, dark blue & red**	.20	.20
			P# block of 4	.50	—
a.			Tagging omitted	7.50	

RED CROSS CENTENARY ISSUE

Cuban Refugees on S.S. Morning Light and Red Cross Flag — A671

Designed by Victor S. McCloskey, Jr.

GIORI PRESS PRINTING

Plates of 200 subjects in four panes of 50.

1963, Oct. 29 *Perf. 11*

1239 A671 5c **bluish black & red** .20 .20
P# block of 4 .50 —

CHRISTMAS ISSUE

National Christmas Tree and White House — A672

Designed by Lily Spandorf; modified by Norman Todhunter.

GIORI PRESS PRINTING

Plates of 400 subjects in four panes of 100.

1963, Nov. 1 *Perf. 11*

1240 A672 5c **dark blue, bluish black & red** .20 .20
P# block of 4 .50 —
a. Tagged, *Nov. 2, 1963* .65 .50
P# block of 4 5.00 —
Pair with full horiz. gutter between —

"Columbia Jays" by Audubon — A673

Sam Houston — A674

JOHN JAMES AUDUBON ISSUE

Audubon (1785-1851), ornithologist and artist. The birds pictured are actually Collie's magpie jays. See No. C71.

Designed by Robert L. Miller.

GIORI PRESS PRINTING

Plates of 200 subjects in four panes of 50.

1963, Dec. 7 *Perf. 11*

1241 A673 5c **dark blue & multicolored** .20 .20
P# block of 4 .45 —

SAM HOUSTON ISSUE

Houston (1793-1863), soldier, president of Texas, US senator.

Designed by Tom Lea.

ROTARY PRESS PRINTING

E.E. Plates of 200 subjects in four panes of 50.

1964, Jan. 10 *Perf. 10½x11*

1242 A674 5c **black** .20 .20
P# block of 4 .45 —
Margin block of 4, Mr. Zip and "Use Zip Code" .40 —

CHARLES M. RUSSELL ISSUE

Russell (1864-1926), painter. The design is from a painting, Thomas Gilcrease Institute of American History and Art, Tulsa, Okla.

"Jerked Down" A675

Designed by William K. Schrage.

GIORI PRESS PRINTING

Plates of 200 subjects in four panes of 50.

1964, Mar. 19 *Perf. 11*

1243 A675 5c **multicolored** .20 .20
P# block of 4 .40 —
Margin block of 4, Mr. Zip and "Use Zip Code" .35 —

NEW YORK WORLD'S FAIR ISSUE

New York World's Fair, 1964-65.

Mall with Unisphere and "Rocket Thrower" by Donald De Lue — A676

Designed by Robert J. Jones.

ROTARY PRESS PRINTING

E.E. Plates of 200 subjects in four panes of 50.

1964, Apr. 22 *Perf. 11x10½*

1244 A676 5c **blue green** .20 .20
On cover, Expo. station machine cancel (non-first day) 2.00
On cover, Expo. station hand-stamp cancel (non-first day) 10.00
P# block of 4 .45 —
Margin block of 4, Mr. Zip and "Use Zip Code" .35 —

JOHN MUIR ISSUE

Muir (1838-1914), naturalist and conservationist.

John Muir and Redwood Forest — A677

Designed by Rudolph Wendelin.

GIORI PRESS PRINTING

Plates of 200 subjects in four panes of 50.

1964, Apr. 29 *Perf. 11*

1245 A677 5c **brown, green, yellow green & olive** .20 .20
P# block of 4 .45 —

KENNEDY MEMORIAL ISSUE

President John Fitzgerald Kennedy, (1917-1963).

John F. Kennedy and Eternal Flame — A678

Designed by Raymond Loewy/William Snaith, Inc.

Photograph by William S. Murphy.

ROTARY PRESS PRINTING

E.E. Plates of 200 subjects in four panes of 50.

1964, May 29 *Perf. 11x10½*

1246 A678 5c **blue gray** .20 .20
P# block of 4 .60 —

NEW JERSEY TERCENTENARY ISSUE

300th anniv. of English colonization of New Jersey. The design is from a mural by Howard Pyle in the Essex County Courthouse, Newark, N.J.

Philip Carteret Landing at Elizabethtown, and Map of New Jersey — A679

Designed by Douglas Allen.

ROTARY PRESS PRINTING

E.E. Plates of 200 subjects in four panes of 50.

1964, June 15 *Perf. 10½x11*

1247 A679 5c **brt. ultramarine** .20 .20
P# block of 4 .50 —
Margin block of 4, Mr. Zip and "Use Zip Code" .40 —

NEVADA STATEHOOD, 100th ANNIV.

Virginia City and Map of Nevada A680

Designed by William K. Schrage.

GIORI PRESS PRINTING

Plates of 200 subjects in four panes of 50.

1964, July 22 *Perf. 11*

1248 A680 5c **red, yellow & blue** .20 .20
P# block of 4 .40 —
Margin block of 4, Mr. Zip and "Use Zip Code" .35 —

Flag — A681

William Shakespeare — A682

REGISTER AND VOTE ISSUE

Campaign to draw more voters to the polls.

Designed by Victor S. McCloskey, Jr.

GIORI PRESS PRINTING

Plates of 200 subjects in four panes of 50.

1964, Aug. 1 *Perf. 11*

1249 A681 5c **dark blue & red** .20 .20
P# block of 4 .45 —
Margin block of 4, Mr. Zip and "Use Zip Code" .35 —

SHAKESPEARE ISSUE

William Shakespeare (1564-1616).

Designed by Douglas Gorsline.

ROTARY PRESS PRINTING

E.E. Plates of 200 subjects in four panes of 50.

1964, Aug. 14 ***Perf. 10½x11***

1250 A682 5c **black brown,** *tan* .20 .20
P# block of 4 .40 —
Margin block of 4, Mr. Zip and "Use Zip Code" .35 —

DOCTORS MAYO ISSUE

Dr. William James Mayo (1861-1939) and his brother, Dr. Charles Horace Mayo (1865-1939), surgeons who founded the Mayo Foundation for Medical Education and Research in affiliation with the Univ. of Minnesota at Rochester. Heads on stamp are from a sculpture by James Earle Fraser.

Drs. William and Charles Mayo — A683

ROTARY PRESS PRINTING

E.E. Plates of 200 subjects in four panes of 50.

1964, Sept. 11 ***Perf. 10½x11***

1251 A683 5c **green** .20 .20
P# block of 4 .60 —
Margin block of 4, Mr. Zip and "Use Zip Code" .40 —

AMERICAN MUSIC ISSUE

50th anniv. of the founding of the American Society of Composers, Authors and Publishers (ASCAP).

Lute, Horn, Laurel, Oak and Music Score — A684

Designed by Bradbury Thompson.

GIORI PRESS PRINTING

Plates of 200 subjects in four panes of 50.

1964, Oct. 15 ***Perf. 11***

Gray Paper with Blue Threads

1252 A684 5c **red, black & blue** .20 .20
P# block of 4 .40 —
Margin block of 4, Mr. Zip and "Use Zip Code" .35 —
a. Blue omitted *1,000.*
b. Blue missing (PS) —

Beware of copies offered as No. 1252a which have traces of blue.

HOMEMAKERS ISSUE

Honoring American women as homemakers and for the 50th anniv. of the passage of the Smith-Lever Act. By providing economic experts under an extension service of the U.S. Dept. of Agriculture, this legislation helped to improve homelife.

Farm Scene Sampler A685

Designed by Norman Todhunter.

Plates of 200 subjects in four panes of 50.

Engraved (Giori Press); Background Lithographed

1964, Oct. 26 ***Perf. 11***

1253 A685 5c **multicolored** .20 .20
P# block of 4 .40 —
Margin block of 4, Mr. Zip and "Use Zip Code" .35 —

CHRISTMAS ISSUE

Holly — A686

Mistletoe — A687

Poinsettia — A688

Sprig of Conifer — A689

Designed by Thomas F. Naegele.

GIORI PRESS PRINTING

Plates of 400 subjects in four panes of 100.
Panes contain 25 subjects each of Nos. 1254-1257

1964, Nov. 9 ***Perf. 11***

1254 A686 5c **green, carmine & black** .25 .20
a. Tagged, *Nov. 10* .60 .50
b. Printed on gummed side —
1255 A687 5c **carmine, green & black** .25 .20
a. Tagged, *Nov. 10* .60 .50
1256 A688 5c **carmine, green & black** .25 .20
a. Tagged, *Nov. 10* .60 .50
1257 A689 5c **black, green & carmine** .25 .20
a. Tagged, *Nov. 10* .60 .50
b. Block of 4, #1254-1257 1.00 1.00
P# block of 4 1.10 —
Margin block of 4, Zip and "Use Zip Code" 1.00 —
c. Block of 4, tagged 2.50 2.25
P# block of 4 5.50 —
Zip block of 4 3.00 —

No. 1254b resulted from a paper foldover before printing and perforating.

VERRAZANO-NARROWS BRIDGE ISSUE

Opening of the Verrazano-Narrows Bridge connecting Staten Island and Brooklyn.

Verrazano-Narrows Bridge and Map of New York Bay — A690

ROTARY PRESS PRINTING

E.E. Plates of 200 subjects in four panes of 50.

1964, Nov. 21 ***Perf. 10½x11***

1258 A690 5c **blue green** .20 .20
P# block of 4 .45 —
Margin block of 4, Mr. Zip and "Use Zip Code" .35 —

FINE ARTS ISSUE

Abstract Design by Stuart Davis — A691

GIORI PRESS PRINTING

Plates of 200 subjects in four panes of 50.

1964, Dec. 2 ***Perf. 11***

1259 A691 5c **ultra., black & dull red** .20 .20
P# block of 4, 2# .40 —
Margin block of 4, Mr. Zip and "Use Zip Code" .35 —

AMATEUR RADIO ISSUE

Issued to honor the radio amateurs on the 50th anniversary of the American Radio Relay League.

Radio Waves and Dial — A692

Designed by Emil J. Willett.

ROTARY PRESS PRINTING

E.E. Plates of 200 subjects in four panes of 50.

1964, Dec. 15 ***Perf. 10½x11***

1260 A692 5c **red lilac** .20 .20
P# block of 4 .60 —
Margin block of 4, Mr. Zip and "Use Zip Code" .35 —

BATTLE OF NEW ORLEANS ISSUE

Battle of New Orleans, Chalmette Plantation, Jan. 8-18, 1815, established 150 years of peace and friendship between the US and Great Britain.

General Andrew Jackson and Sesquicentennial Medal — A693

Designed by Robert J. Jones.

GIORI PRESS PRINTING

Plates of 200 subjects in four panes of 50.

1965, Jan. 8 ***Perf. 11***

1261 A693 5c **deep carmine, violet blue & gray** .20 .20
P# block of 4 .60 —
Margin block of 4, Mr. Zip and "Use Zip Code" .35 —

Discus Thrower — A694

Microscope and Stethoscope — A695

PHYSICAL FITNESS-SOKOL ISSUE

Publicizing the importance of physical fitness and for the centenary of the founding of the Sokol (athletic) organization in America.

Designed by Norman Todhunter.

GIORI PRESS PRINTING

Plates of 200 subjects in four panes of 50.

1965, Feb. 15 ***Perf. 11***

1262 A694 5c **maroon & black** .20 .20
P# block of 4 .50 —
Margin block of 4, Mr. Zip and "Use Zip Code" .40 —

CRUSADE AGAINST CANCER ISSUE

Issued to publicize the "Crusade Against Cancer" and to stress the importance of early diagnosis.

Designed by Stevan Dohanos.

GIORI PRESS PRINTING

Plates of 200 subjects in four panes of 50.

1965, Apr. 1 ***Perf. 11***

1263 A695 5c **black, purple & red orange** .20 .20
P# block of 4, 2# .40 —
Margin block of 4, Mr. Zip and "Use Zip Code" .35 —

CHURCHILL MEMORIAL ISSUE

Sir Winston Spencer Churchill (1874-1965), British statesman and World War II leader.

Winston Churchill — A696

Designed by Richard Hurd.

ROTARY PRESS PRINTING

E.E. Plates of 200 subjects in four panes of 50.

1965, May 13 ***Perf. 10½x11***

1264 A696 5c **black** .20 .20
P# block of 4 .40 —
Margin block of 4, Mr. Zip and "Use Zip Code" .35 —

MAGNA CARTA ISSUE

750th anniversary of the Magna Carta, the basis of English and American common law.

Procession of Barons and King John's Crown — A697

Designed by Brook Temple.

GIORI PRESS PRINTING

Plates of 200 subjects in four panes of 50.

1965, June 15 ***Perf. 11***

1265 A697 5c **black, yellow ocher & red lilac** .20 .20
P# block of 4, 2# .40 —
Margin block of 4, Mr. Zip and "Use Zip Code" .35 —
Corner block of 4, black # omitted —

INTERNATIONAL COOPERATION YEAR

ICY, 1965, and 20th anniv. of the UN.

International Cooperation Year Emblem A698

Designed by Herbert M. Sanborn and Olav S. Mathiesen.

GIORI PRESS PRINTING

Plates of 200 subjects in four panes of 50.

1965, June 26 ***Perf. 11***

1266 A698 5c **dull blue & black** .20 .20
P# block of 4 .40 —
Margin block of 4, Mr. Zip and "Use Zip Code" .35 —

SALVATION ARMY ISSUE

Centenary of the founding of the Salvation Army by William Booth in London.

A699

Designed by Sam Marsh.

GIORI PRESS PRINTING

Plates of 200 subjects in four panes of 50.

1965, July 2 ***Perf. 11***

1267 A699 5c **red, black & dark blue** .20 .20
P# block of 4 .40 —
Margin block of 4, Mr. Zip and "Use Zip Code" .35 —

Dante after a 16th Century Painting — A700

Herbert Hoover — A701

DANTE ISSUE

Dante Alighieri (1265-1321), Italian poet.

Designed by Douglas Gorsline.

ROTARY PRESS PRINTING

E.E. Plates of 200 subjects in four panes of 50.

1965, July 17 ***Perf. 10½x11***

1268 A700 5c **maroon,** *tan* .20 .20
P# block of 4 .40 —
Margin block of 4, Mr. Zip and "Use Zip Code" .35 —

HERBERT HOOVER ISSUE

President Herbert Clark Hoover, (1874-1964).

Designed by Norman Todhunter; photograph by Fabian Bachrach, Sr.

ROTARY PRESS PRINTING

E.E. Plates of 200 subjects in four panes of 50.

1965, Aug. 10 ***Perf. 10½x11***

1269 A701 5c **rose red** .20 .20
P# block of 4 .45 —
Margin block of 4, Mr. Zip and "Use Zip Code" .35 —

ROBERT FULTON ISSUE

Fulton (1765-1815), inventor of the 1st commercial steamship.

Robert Fulton and the Clermont A702

Designed by John Maass; bust by Jean Antoine Houdon.

GIORI PRESS PRINTING

Plates of 200 subjects in four panes of 50.

1965, Aug. 19 ***Perf. 11***

1270 A702 5c **black & blue** .20 .20
P# block of 4 .40 —
Margin block of 4, Mr. Zip and "Use Zip Code" .35 —

FLORIDA SETTLEMENT ISSUE

400th anniv. of the settlement of Florida, and the 1st permanent European settlement in the continental US, St. Augustine, Fla.

Spanish Explorer, Royal Flag of Spain and Ships — A703

Designed by Brook Temple.

GIORI PRESS PRINTING

Plates of 200 subjects with four panes of 50.

1965, Aug. 28 ***Perf. 11***

1271 A703 5c **red, yellow & black** .20 .20
P# block of 4, 3# .45 —
Margin block of 4, Mr. Zip and "Use Zip Code" .35 —
a. Yellow omitted *350.00*

See Spain No. 1312.

TRAFFIC SAFETY ISSUE

Issued to publicize traffic safety and the prevention of traffic accidents.

Traffic Signal — A704

Designed by Richard F. Hurd.

GIORI PRESS PRINTING

Plates of 200 subjects in four panes of 50.

1965, Sept. 3 ***Perf. 11***

1272 A704 5c **emerald, black & red** .20 .20
P# block of 4, 2# .45 —
Margin block of 4, Mr. Zip and "Use Zip Code" .35 —

JOHN SINGLETON COPLEY ISSUE

Copley (1738-1815), painter. The portrait of the artist's daughter is from the oil painting "The Copley Family," which hangs in the National Gallery of Art, Washington, D.C.

Elizabeth Clarke Copley — A705

Designed by John Carter Brown.

GIORI PRESS PRINTING

Plates of 200 subjects in four panes of 50.

1965, Sept. 17 ***Perf. 11***

1273 A705 5c **black, brown & olive** .20 .20
P# block of 4 .50 —
Margin block of 4, Mr. Zip and "Use Zip Code" .40 —

INTERNATIONAL TELECOMMUNICATION UNION, 100th ANNIV.

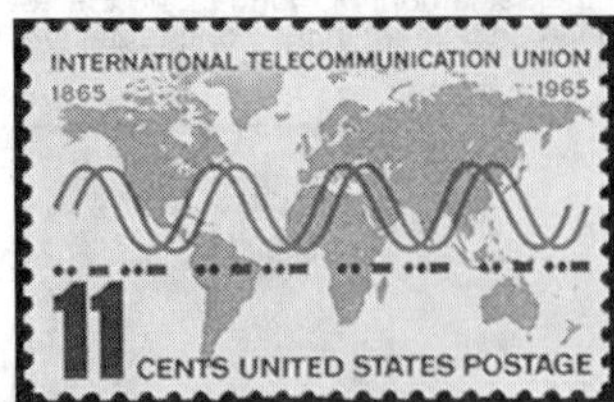

Galt Projection World Map and Radio Sine Wave — A706

Designed by Thomas F. Naegele.

GIORI PRESS PRINTING

Plates of 200 subjects with four panes of 50.

1965, Oct. 6 ***Perf. 11***

1274 A706 11c **black, carmine & bister** .35 .20
P# block of 4, 2# 2.25 —
Margin block of 4, Mr. Zip and "Use Zip Code" 1.50 —

ADLAI STEVENSON ISSUE

Adlai Ewing Stevenson (1900-65), governor of Illinois, US ambassador to the UN.

Adlai E. Stevenson — A707

Designed by George Samerjan; photograph by Philippe Halsman.

LITHOGRAPHED, ENGRAVED (Giori)

Plates of 200 subjects in four panes of 50.

1965, Oct. 23 ***Perf. 11***

1275 A707 5c **pale blue, black, carmine & violet blue** .20 .20
P# block of 4 .40 —

CHRISTMAS ISSUE

Angel with Trumpet, 1840 Weather Vane — A708

Designed by Robert Jones.

After a watercolor by Lucille Gloria Chabot of the 1840 weather vane from the People's Methodist Church, Newburyport, Mass.

GIORI PRESS PRINTING

Plates of 400 subjects in four panes of 100.

1965, Nov. 2 ***Perf. 11***

1276 A708 5c **carmine, dark olive green & bister** .20 .20
P# block of 4 .40 —
Margin block of 4, Mr. Zip and "Use Zip Code" .35 —
Pair with full vert. gutter btwn. —
a. Tagged, *Nov. 15* .75 .25
P# block of 4 5.50 —
Zip block of 4 3.50 —

PROMINENT AMERICANS ISSUE

Thomas Jefferson — A710

Albert Gallatin — A711

Frank Lloyd Wright and Guggenheim Museum, New York — A712

Abraham Lincoln A714

George Washington (redrawn) — A715a

Albert Einstein — A717

Henry Ford and 1909 Model T — A718a

Oliver Wendell Holmes — A720

Frederick Douglass — A722

Francis Parkman — A713

George Washington A715

Franklin D. Roosevelt — A716

Andrew Jackson — A718

John F. Kennedy — A719

George Catlett Marshall — A721

John Dewey — A723

Thomas Paine — A724

Lucy Stone — A725

Eugene O'Neill — A726

John Bassett Moore — A727

Designers: 1c, Robert Geissmann, after portrait by Rembrandt Peale. 1¼c, Robert Gallatin. 2c, Patricia Amarantides; photograph by Blackstone-Shelburne. 3c, Bill Hyde. 4c, Bill Hyde; photograph by Mathew Brady. 5c, Bill Hyde, after portrait by Rembrandt Peale. 5c, No. 1283B, Redrawn by Stevan Dohanos. 6c, 30c, Richard L. Clark. 8c, Frank Sebastiano; photograph by Philippe Halsman. 10c, Lester Beall. 12c, Norman Todhunter. 13c, Stevan Dohanos; photograph by Jacques Lowe. 15c, Richard F. Hurd. 20c, Robert Geissmann. 25c, Walter DuBois Richards. 40c, Robert Geissmann, after portrait by John Wesley Jarvis. 50c, Mark English. $1, Norman Todhunter. $5, Tom Laufer.

ROTARY PRESS PRINTING

E.E. Plates of 400 subjects in four panes of 100

1965-78 ***Perf. 11x10½, 10½x11***

Types of 15c:

I. Necktie barely touches coat at bottom; crosshatching of tie strong and complete. Flag of "5" is true horizontal. Crosshatching of "15" is colorless when visible.

II. Necktie does not touch coat at bottom; LL to UR crosshatching lines strong, UL to LR lines very faint. Flag of "5" slants down slightly at right. Crosshatching of "15" is colored and visible when magnified.

A third type, used only for No. 1288B, is smaller in overall size and "15¢" is ¾mm closer to head.

1278 A710 1c **green,** tagged, shiny gum, *Jan. 12, 1968* .20 .20
P# block of 4 .20 —
Margin block of 4, "Use Zip Codes" .20 —
Dull gum (from bklt. pane) .20
a. Booklet pane of 8, shiny gum, *Jan. 12, 1968* 1.00 *.75*
Dull gum 2.00
b. Bklt. pane of 4+2 labels, *May 10, 1971* .80 *.60*
c. Untagged (Bureau precanceled) 6.25 1.25
P# block of 4 175.00
Margin block of 4, "Use Zip Codes" 30.00
d. Tagging omitted (not Bureau precanceled) 3.50 —

1279 A711 1¼c **light green,** *Jan. 30, 1967* .20 .20
P# block of 4 6.00 —

1280 A712 2c **dark blue gray,** tagged, shiny gum, *June 8, 1966* .20 .20
P# block of 4 .25 —
Margin block of 4, "Use Zip Codes" .20 —
Pair with full vert. gutter btwn. —
Dull gum (from bklt. pane) .20
a. Bklt. pane of 5 + label, *Jan. 8, 1968* 1.25 *.80*
b. Untagged (Bureau precanceled) 1.35 .40
P# block of 4 27.50
Margin block of 4, "Use Zip Codes" 7.50
c. Bklt. pane of 6, shiny gum, *May 7, 1971* 1.00 *.75*
Dull gum 1.10
d. Tagging omitted (not Bureau precanceled) 3.50 —

1281 A713 3c **violet,** tagged, *Sept. 16, 1967* .20 .20
P# block of 4 .25 —
Margin block of 4, "Use Zip Codes" .20 —
a. Untagged (Bureau precanceled) 3.00 .75
P# block of 4 —
Margin block of 4, "Use Zip Codes" 30.00
b. Tagging omitted (not Bureau precanceled) 4.50 —

1282 A714 4c **black,** *Nov. 19, 1965* .20 .20
P# block of 4 .40 —
a. Tagged, *Dec. 1, 1965* .20 .20
P# block of 4 .55 —
Pair with full horiz. gutter between —

1283 A715 5c **blue,** *Feb. 22, 1966* .20 .20
P# block of 4 .50 —
Pair with full vert. gutter btwn. —
a. Tagged, *Feb. 23, 1966* .20 .20

P# block of 4 .60 —
1283B A715a 5c **blue,** tagged, shiny gum, *Nov. 17, 1967* .20 .20
P# block of 4 .50 —
Pair with full horiz. gutter btwn. —
Dull gum .20
P# block of 4 1.40
d. Untagged (Bureau precanceled) 13.25 1.00
P# block of 4 —
e. Tagging omitted (not Bureau precanceled) 4.50

No. 1283B is redrawn; highlights, shadows softened.

1284 A716 6c **gray brown,** *Jan. 29, 1966* .20 .20
P# block of 4 .60 —
Margin block of 4, "Use Zip Codes" (Bureau precanceled) 3.00
Pair with full horiz. gutter btwn. *150.00*
Pair with full vert. gutter btwn. *150.00*
a. Tagged, *Dec. 29, 1966* .20 .20
P# block of 4 .80 —
Margin block of 4, "Use Zip Codes" .65 —
b. Booklet pane of 8, *Dec. 28, 1967* 1.50 *1.00*
c. Bklt. pane of 5+ label, *Jan. 9, 1968* 1.50 *1.00*
d. Horiz. pair, imperf. between —
e. As "b," tagging omitted — —

For untagged sheet stamps, "Use Zip Codes" and "Mail Early in the Day" marginal markings are found only on panes with Bureau precancels.

1285 A717 8c **violet,** *Mar. 14, 1966* .20 .20
P# block of 4 .85 —
a. Tagged, *July 6, 1966* .20 .20
P# block of 4 .85 —
Margin block of 4, "Use Zip Codes" .85 —
1286 A718 10c **lilac,** tagged, *Mar. 15, 1967* .20 .20
P# block of 4 1.00 —
Margin block of 4, "Use Zip Codes" .85 —
b. Untagged (Bureau precanceled) 57.50 1.75
P# block of 4 —
Margin block of 4, "Use Zip Codes" 275.00
1286A 718a 12c **black,** tagged, *July 30, 1968* .25 .20
P# block of 4 1.00
Margin block of 4, "Use Zip Codes" 1.00 —
c. Untagged (Bureau precanceled) 4.75 1.00
P# block of 4 145.00
Margin block of 4, "Use Zip Codes" 27.50
d. Tagging omitted (not Bureau precanceled) 7.50
1287 A719 13c **brown,** tagged, *May 29, 1967* .30 .20
P# block of 4 1.50 —
a. Untagged (Bureau precanceled) 5.95 1.00
P# block of 4 100.00
b. Tagging omitted (not Bureau precanceled) *12.50* —
1288 A720 15c **magenta,** type I, tagged, *Mar. 8, 1968* .30 .20
P# block of 4 1.25 —
Margin block of 4, "Use Zip Codes" 1.25 —
a. Untagged (Bureau precanceled) .75 .75
P# block of 4 29.50
Margin block of 4, "Use Zip Codes" 7.50
d. Type II .55 .20
P# block of 4 8.00 —
Zip block of 4 3.50 —
Pair with full vert. gutter between *300.00*
f. As "d," tagging omitted (not Bureau precanceled) 5.00 —
Imperforates exist from printer's waste.

Values for No. 1288a are for the bars-only precancel. Also exists with city precancels, and worth more thus.

1288B A720 15c **magenta,** tagged, perf. 10 (from bklt. pane) .35 .20
c. Booklet pane of 8, *June 14, 1978* 2.80 *1.75*
e. As "c," vert. imperf. between —
g. Tagging omitted *5.00* —

No. 1288B issued in booklets only. All stamps have one or two straight edges. Plates made from redrawn die.

1289 A721 20c **deep olive,** *Oct. 24, 1967* .40 .20
P# block of 4 1.75 —
Margin block of 4, "Use Zip Codes" 1.65 —
a. Tagged, shiny gum, *Apr. 3, 1973* .40 .20
P# block of 4 1.75 —
Zip block of 4 1.65 —
Dull gum .40
P# block of 4 3.50
Zip block of 4 1.65
1290 A722 25c **rose lake,** *Feb. 14, 1967* .55 .20
P# block of 4 2.25 —
Margin block of 4, "Use Zip Codes" 2.20 —
a. Tagged, shiny gum, *Apr. 3, 1973* .45 .20
P# block of 4 2.00 —
Zip block of 4 1.90 —
Dull gum .45
P# block of 4 2.00
Zip block of 4 1.90
b. 25c **magenta** *25.00* —

On cover —
P# block of 4 *150.00*
1291 A723 30c **red lilac,** *Oct. 21, 1968* .65 .20
P# block of 4 2.90 —
Margin block of 4, "Use Zip Codes" 2.70 —
a. Tagged, *Apr. 3, 1973* .50 .20
P# block of 4 2.25 —
Zip block of 4 2.10 —
1292 A724 40c **blue black,** *Jan. 29, 1968* .80 .20
P# block of 4 3.25 —
Margin block of 4, "Use Zip Codes" 3.25 —
a. Tagged, shiny gum, *Apr. 3, 1973* .65 .20
P# block of 4 2.75 —
Zip block of 4 2.65 —
Dull gum .70
P# block of 4 3.00
Zip block of 4 2.90
1293 A725 50c **rose magenta,** *Aug. 13, 1968* 1.00 .20
P# block of 4 4.25 —
Margin block of 4, "Use Zip Codes" 4.00 —
Pair with full vert. gutter btwn. —
a. Tagged, *Apr. 3, 1973* .80 .20
P# block of 4 3.50 —
Zip block of 4 3.25 —
1294 A726 $1 **dull purple,** *Oct. 16, 1967* 2.25 .20
P# block of 4 10.00 —
Margin block of 4, "Use Zip Codes" 9.25 —
a. Tagged, *Apr. 3, 1973* 1.65 .20
P# block of 4 6.75 —
Zip block of 4 6.65 —
1295 A727 $5 **gray black,** *Dec. 3, 1966* 10.00 2.25
P# block of 4 42.50 —
a. Tagged, *Apr. 3, 1973* 8.50 2.00
P# block of 4 35.00 —
Nos. 1278-1295 (21) 18.85 6.25
Nos. 1278-1288, 1289-1295, P# blocks of 4 (20) 78.65

Bureau Precancels: 1c, 19 diff., 1¼c, 14 diff., 2c, 41 diff., 3c, 11 diff., 4c, 49 diff., No. 1283, 7 diff., No. 1283B, 29 diff., 6c, 35 diff., 8c, 18 diff., 10c, 12 diff., 12c, 3 diff., 13c, 3 diff., No. 1288a, 9 diff., 20c, 14 diff., 25c, 9 diff., 30c, 14 diff., 40c, 7 diff., 50c, 14 diff., $1, 8 diff.

See Luminescence note in "Information for Collectors" at front of book.

COIL STAMPS

1967-75 Tagged *Perf. 10 Horizontally*

1297 A713 3c **violet,** shiny gum, *Nov. 4, 1975* .20 .20
Pair .20 .20
Joint line pair .45 .20
Dull gum .75
Joint line pair 2.00
a. Imperf., pair *30.00*
Imperf., joint line pair *55.00*
b. Untagged (Bureau precanceled), shiny gum 1.05 .25
Pair 2.10 .50
Joint line pair 62.50 3.75
Dull gum .25
Pair .50
Joint line pair 3.75
c. As "b," imperf. pair *295.00* —
Joint line pair 25.00

No. 1297c is precanceled "Nonprofit Org. / CAR RT SORT."

1298 A716 6c **gray brown,** *Dec. 28, 1967* .20 .20
Pair .30 .20
Joint line pair 1.10 .25
a. Imperf., pair *2,000.*
Imperf., joint line pair *6,500.*
b. Tagging omitted 3.00

Bureau Precancels: 3c, 9 diff.

Franklin D. Roosevelt — A727a

Revised design by Robert J. Jones and Howard C. Mildner.

COIL STAMPS

1966-81 Tagged *Perf. 10 Vertically*

1299 A710 1c **green,** *Jan. 12, 1968* .20 .20
Pair .20 .20
Joint line pair .25 .20
a. Untagged (Bureau precanceled) 8.00 1.75
Pair 17.50 4.00
Joint line pair *295.00* —
b. Imperf., pair *30.00* —
Imperf., joint line pair *60.00*
1303 A714 4c **black,** *May 28, 1966* .20 .20
Pair .30 .20
Joint line pair .75 .20
a. Untagged (Bureau precanceled) 8.75 .75
Pair 19.00 1.75
Joint line pair *250.00* —
b. Imperf., pair *750.00*
Imperf., joint line pair *1,900.*
c. Tagging omitted (not Bureau precanceled) *12.50* —

1304 A715 5c **blue,** shiny gum, *Sept. 8, 1966* .20 .20
Pair .25 .20
Joint line pair .40 .20
Dull gum .75
Joint line pair 5.00
a. Untagged (Bureau precanceled) 6.50 .65
Pair 14.00 1.40
Joint line pair *195.00* —
b. Imperf., pair *175.00*
Joint line pair *400.00*
e. As "a," imperf., pair *375.00*
Joint line pair *850.00*
f. Tagging omitted (not Bureau precanceled) — —

No. 1304b is valued in the grade of fine.

No. 1304e is precanceled Mount Pleasant, IA. Also exists from Chicago, IL.

1304C A715a 5c **blue,** *1981* .20 .20
Pair .30 .20
Joint line pair 1.25 —
d. Imperf., pair *750.00*
1305 A727a 6c **gray brown,** *Feb. 28, 1968* .20 .20
Pair .30 .20
Joint line pair .55 .20
a. Imperf., pair *75.00*
Joint line pair *130.00*
b. Untagged (Bureau precanceled) 20.00 1.00
Pair 42.50 2.25
Joint line pair *675.00* —
k. Tagging omitted (not Bureau precanceled) 3.50 —
1305E A720 15c **magenta,** type I, shiny gum, *June 14, 1978* .25 .20
Pair .50 .20
Joint line pair 1.10 .30
Dull gum .60
Joint line pair 3.50
f. Untagged (Bureau precanceled, Chicago, IL) 37.50 37.50
Pair 80.00 80.00
Joint line pair *1,350.* —
g. Imperf., pair, shiny gum *30.00*
Joint line pair *75.00*
Imperf., pair, dull gum *50.00*
Joint line pair *125.00*
h. Pair, imperf. between *200.00*
Joint line pair *550.00*
i Type II, dull gum .60 .20
Joint line pair 2.75 —
j. Type II, dull gum, Imperf., pair *85.00*
Joint line pair *290.00*
l Tagging omitted —
1305C A726 $1 **dull purple,** shiny gum, *Jan. 12, 1973* 2.00 .40
Pair 4.00 .80
Joint line pair 5.50 1.50
Dull gum 2.25
Joint line pair 6.50
d. Imperf., pair *2,250.*
Joint line pair *4,000.*
Nos. 1297-1305C (9) 3.65 2.00

Bureau Precancels: 1c, 5 diff., 4c, 35 diff., No. 1304a, 45 diff., 6c, 30 diff.

MIGRATORY BIRD TREATY ISSUE

Migratory Birds over Canada-US Border A728

Designed by Burt E. Pringle.

GIORI PRESS PRINTING

Plates of 200 subjects in four panes of 50.

1966, Mar. 16 ***Perf. 11***

1306 A728 5c **black, crimson & dark blue** .20 .20
P# block of 4, 2# .40 —
Margin block of 4, Mr. Zip and "Use Zip Code" .35 —

HUMANE TREATMENT OF ANIMALS ISSUE

Issued to promote humane treatment of all animals and for the centenary of the American Society for the Prevention of Cruelty to Animals.

Mongrel A729

Designed by Norman Todhunter.

LITHOGRAPHED, ENGRAVED (Giori)
Plates of 200 subjects in four panes of 50.

1966, Apr. 9 *Perf. 11*

1307 A729 5c **orange brown & black** .20 .20
P# block of 4 .40 —
Margin block of 4, Mr. Zip and "Use Zip Code" .35 —

Sesquicentennial Seal; Map of Indiana with 19 Stars and old Capitol at Corydon — A730

Clown — A731

INDIANA STATEHOOD, 150th ANNIV.

Designed by Paul A. Wehr.

GIORI PRESS PRINTING
Plates of 200 subjects in four panes of 50.

1966, Apr. 16 *Perf. 11*

1308 A730 5c **ocher, brown & violet blue** .20 .20
P# block of 4, 2# .50 —
Margin block of 4, Mr. Zip and "Use Zip Code" .35 —

AMERICAN CIRCUS ISSUE

Issued to honor the American Circus on the centenary of the birth of John Ringling.

Designed by Edward Klauck.

GIORI PRESS PRINTING
Plates of 200 subjects in four panes of 50.

1966, May 2 *Perf. 11*

1309 A731 5c **multicolored** .20 .20
P# block of 4, 2# .50 —
Margin block of 4, Mr. Zip and "Use Zip Code" .40 —

SIXTH INTERNATIONAL PHILATELIC EXHIBITION ISSUES

Sixth International Philatelic Exhibition (SIPEX), Washington, D.C., May 21-30.

Stamped Cover — A732

Designed by Thomas F. Naegele.

LITHOGRAPHED, ENGRAVED (Giori)
Plates of 200 subjects in four panes of 50.

1966 *Perf. 11*

1310 A732 5c **multicolored**, *May 21* .20 .20
P# block of 4 .40 —
Margin block of 4, Mr. Zip and "Use Zip Code" .35 —

SOUVENIR SHEET

Designed by Brook Temple.

Plates of 24 subjects
Imperf

1311 A732 5c **multicolored**, *May 23* .20 .20

No. 1311 measures 108x74mm. Below the stamp appears a line drawing of the Capitol and Washington Monument. Marginal inscriptions and drawing are green.

"Freedom" Checking "Tyranny" — A734

Polish Eagle and Cross — A735

BILL OF RIGHTS, 175th ANNIV.

Designed by Herbert L. Block (Herblock).

GIORI PRESS PRINTING
Plates of 200 subjects in four panes of 50.

1966, July 1 *Perf. 11*

1312 A734 5c **carmine, dark & light blue** .20 .20
P# block of 4, 2# .45 —
Margin block of 4, Mr. Zip and "Use Zip Code" .40 —

POLISH MILLENNIUM ISSUE

Adoption of Christianity in Poland, 1000th anniv.

Designed by Edmund D. Lewandowski.

ROTARY PRESS PRINTING
E.E. Plates of 200 subjects in four panes of 50.

1966, July 30 *Perf. 10½x11*

1313 A735 5c **red** .20 .20
P# block of 4 .45 —
Margin block of 4, Mr. Zip and "Use Zip Code" .40 —

NATIONAL PARK SERVICE ISSUE

50th anniv. of the Natl. Park Service of the Interior Dept. The design "Parkscape U.S.A." identifies Natl. Park Service facilities.

National Park Service Emblem A736

Designed by Thomas H. Geismar.

LITHOGRAPHED, ENGRAVED (Giori)
Plates of 200 subjects in four panes of 50.

1966, Aug. 25 *Perf. 11*

1314 A736 5c **yellow, black & green** .20 .20
P# block of 4 .45 —
Margin block of 4, Mr. Zip and "Use Zip Code" .40 —
a. Tagged, *Aug. 26* .30 .25
P# block of 4 2.00 —
Zip block of 4 1.40 —

MARINE CORPS RESERVE ISSUE

US Marine Corps Reserve founding, 50th anniv.

Combat Marine, 1966; Frogman; World War II Flier; World War I "Devil Dog" and Marine, 1775 — A737

Designed by Stella Grafakos.

LITHOGRAPHED, ENGRAVED (Giori)
Plates of 200 subjects in four panes of 50.

1966, Aug. 29 *Perf. 11*

1315 A737 5c **black, bister, red & ultra.** .20 .20
P# block of 4 .45 —
Margin block of 4, Mr. Zip and "Use Zip Code" .40 —
a. Tagged .30 .20
P# block of 4 2.00 —
Zip block of 4 1.40 —
b. Black & bister (engraved) missing (EP) *16,000.*

GENERAL FEDERATION OF WOMEN'S CLUBS ISSUE

75 years of service by the General Federation of Women's Clubs.

Women of 1890 and 1966 — A738

Designed by Charles Henry Carter.

GIORI PRESS PRINTING
Plates of 200 subjects in four panes of 50.

1966, Sept. 12 *Perf. 11*

1316 A738 5c **black, pink & blue** .20 .20
P# block of 4, 2# .45 —
Margin block of 4, Mr. Zip and "Use Zip Code" .40 —
a. Tagged, *Sept. 13* .30 .20
P# block of 4, 2# 2.00 —
Zip block of 4 1.40 —

AMERICAN FOLKLORE ISSUE
Johnny Appleseed

Issued to honor Johnny Appleseed (John Chapman 1774-1845), who wandered over 100,000 square miles planting apple trees, and who gave away and sold seedlings to Midwest pioneers.

Johnny Appleseed — A739

Designed by Robert Bode.

GIORI PRESS PRINTING
Plates of 200 subjects in four panes of 50.

1966, Sept. 24 *Perf. 11*

1317 A739 5c **green, red & black** .20 .20
P# block of 4, 2# .45 —
Margin block of 4, Mr. Zip and "Use Zip Code" .40 —
a. Tagged, *Sept. 26* .30 .20
P# block of 4, 2# 2.00 —
Zip block of 4 1.40 —

BEAUTIFICATION OF AMERICA ISSUE

Issued to publicize President Johnson's "Plant for a more beautiful America" campaign.

Jefferson Memorial, Tidal Basin and Cherry Blossoms A740

Designed by Miss Gyo Fujikawa.

GIORI PRESS PRINTING

Plates of 200 subjects in four panes of 50.

1966, Oct. 5 *Perf. 11*

1318 A740 5c **emerald, pink & black**	.20	.20
P# block of 4, 2#	.45	—
Margin block of 4, Mr. Zip and "Use Zip Code"	.40	—
a. Tagged	.30	.20
P# block of 4, 2#	2.00	—
Zip block of 4	1.25	—

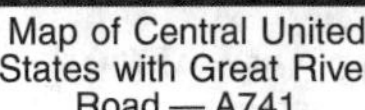
Map of Central United States with Great River Road — A741

Statue of Liberty and "Old Glory" — A742

GREAT RIVER ROAD ISSUE

Issued to publicize the 5,600-mile Great River Road connecting New Orleans with Kenora, Ontario, and following the Mississippi most of the way.

Designed by Herbert Bayer.

LITHOGRAPHED, ENGRAVED (Giori)

Plates of 200 subjects in four panes of 50.

1966, Oct. 21

1319 A741 5c **vermilion, yellow, blue & green**	.20	.20
P# block of 4	.60	—
Margin block of 4, Mr. Zip and "Use Zip Code"	.40	—
a. Tagged, *Oct. 22*	.30	.20
P# block of 4	2.00	—
Zip block of 4	1.40	—

SAVINGS BOND-SERVICEMEN ISSUE

25th anniv. of US Savings Bonds, and honoring American servicemen.

Designed by Stevan Dohanos, photo by Bob Noble.

LITHOGRAPHED, ENGRAVED (Giori)

Plates of 200 subjects in four panes of 50.

1966, Oct. 26 *Perf. 11*

1320 A742 5c **red, dark blue, light blue & black**	.20	.20
P# block of 4	.45	—
Margin block of 4, Mr. Zip and "Use Zip Code"	.40	—
a. Tagged, *Oct. 27*	.30	.20
P# block of 4	1.75	—
Zip block of 4	1.30	—
b. Red, dark blue & black missing (EP)	*4,250.*	
c. Dark blue (engr.) missing (EP)	*8,500.*	

No. 1320c is unique. Value represents price realized at 2001 auction sale.

CHRISTMAS ISSUE

Madonna and Child, by Hans Memling — A743

Designed by Howard C. Mildner.

Modeled after "Madonna and Child with Angels," by the Flemish artist Hans Memling (c.1430-1494), Mellon Collection, National Gallery of Art, Washington, D.C.

LITHOGRAPHED, ENGRAVED (Giori)

Plates of 400 subjects in four panes of 100.

1966, Nov. 1 *Perf. 11*

1321 A743 5c **multicolored**	.20	.20
P# block of 4	.40	—
Margin block of 4, Mr. Zip and "Use Zip Code"	.35	—
a. Tagged, *Nov. 2*	.30	.20
P# block of 4	1.50	—
Zip block of 4	1.25	—

MARY CASSATT ISSUE

Cassatt (1844-1926), painter. The painting "The Boating Party" is in the Natl. Gallery of Art, Washington, D.C.

"The Boating Party" — A744

Designed by Robert J. Jones.

GIORI PRESS PRINTING

Plates of 200 subjects in four panes of 50.

1966, Nov. 17 *Perf. 11*

1322 A744 5c **multicolored**	.20	.20
P# block of 4, 2#	.60	—
Margin block of 4, Mr. Zip and "Use Zip Code"	.50	—
a. Tagged	.30	.25
P# block of 4, 2#	1.75	—
Zip block of 4	1.25	—

NATIONAL GRANGE ISSUE

Centenary of the founding of the National Grange, American farmers' organization.

Grange Poster, 1870 — A745

Designed by Lee Pavao.

GIORI PRESS PRINTING

Plates of 200 subjects in four panes of 50.

1967, Apr. 17 **Tagged** *Perf. 11*

1323 A745 5c **orange, yellow, brown, green & black**	.20	.20
P# block of 4, 2#	.40	—
Margin block of 4, Mr. Zip and "Use Zip Code"	.35	—
a. Tagging omitted	*6.00*	—

CANADA CENTENARY ISSUE

Centenary of Canada's emergence as a nation.

Canadian Landscape A746

Designed by Ivan Chermayeff.

GIORI PRESS PRINTING

Plates of 200 subjects in four panes of 50.

1967, May 25 **Tagged** *Perf. 11*

1324 A746 5c **lt. blue, dp. green, ultra., olive & black**	.20	.20
On cover, Expo. station ("U.S. Pavilion") machine canc.		1.00
On cover, Expo. station handstamp canc.		2.50
P# block of 4, 2#	.40	—
Margin block of 4, Mr. Zip and "Use Zip Code"	.35	—
a. Tagging omitted	*6.00*	—

ERIE CANAL ISSUE

150th anniversary of the Erie Canal ground-breaking ceremony at Rome, N.Y. The canal links Lake Erie and New York City.

Stern of Early Canal Boat — A747

Designed by George Samerjan.

LITHOGRAPHED, ENGRAVED (Giori)

Plates of 200 subjects in four panes of 50.

1967, July 4 **Tagged** *Perf. 11*

1325 A747 5c **ultra., greenish blue, black & crimson**	.20	.20
P# block of 4	.40	—
Margin block of 4, Mr. Zip and "Use Zip Code"	.35	—
a. Tagging omitted	*11.00*	—

"SEARCH FOR PEACE" - LIONS ISSUE

Issued to publicize the search for peace. "Search for Peace" was the theme of an essay contest for young men and women sponsored by Lions International on its 50th anniversary.

Peace Dove — A748

Designed by Bradbury Thompson.

GIORI PRESS PRINTING

Plates of 200 subjects in four panes of 50.

1967, July 5 **Tagged** *Perf. 11*

Gray Paper with Blue Threads

1326 A748 5c **blue, red & black**	.20	.20
P# block of 4	.40	—
Margin block of 4, Mr. Zip and "Use Zip Code"	.35	—
a. Tagging omitted	*5.00*	—

HENRY DAVID THOREAU ISSUE

Henry David Thoreau (1817-1862), writer.

Henry David Thoreau — A749

Designed by Leonard Baskin.

GIORI PRESS PRINTING

Plates of 200 subjects in four panes of 50.

1967, July 12 **Tagged** *Perf. 11*

1327 A749 5c **carmine, black & blue green**	.20	.20
P# block of 4	.50	—
Margin block of 4, Mr. Zip and "Use Zip Code"	.35	—
a. Tagging omitted	—	

NEBRASKA STATEHOOD, 100th ANNIV.

Hereford Steer and Ear of Corn — A750

Designed by Julian K. Billings.

LITHOGRAPHED, ENGRAVED (Giori)
Plates of 200 subjects in four panes of 50.

1967, July 29 **Tagged** ***Perf. 11***

1328 A750 5c **dark red brown, lemon & yellow** .20 .20
P# block of 4 .40 —
Margin block of 4, Mr. Zip and "Use Zip Code" .35 —
a. Tagging omitted *7.50* —

VOICE OF AMERICA ISSUE

25th anniv. of the radio branch of the United States Information Agency (USIA).

Radio Transmission Tower and Waves — A751

Designed by Georg Olden.

LITHOGRAPHED, ENGRAVED (Giori)
Plates of 200 subjects in four panes of 50.

1967, Aug. 1 **Tagged** ***Perf. 11***

1329 A751 5c **red, blue, black & carmine** .20 .20
P# block of 4 .40 —
Margin block of 4, Mr. Zip and "Use Zip Code" .35 —
a. Tagging omitted *15.00* —

AMERICAN FOLKLORE ISSUE

Davy Crockett (1786-1836), frontiersman, hunter, and congressman from Tennessee who died at the Alamo.

Davy Crockett and Scrub Pine — A752

Designed by Robert Bode.

LITHOGRAPHED, ENGRAVED (Giori)
Plates of 200 subjects in four panes of 50.

1967, Aug. 17 **Tagged** ***Perf. 11***

1330 A752 5c **green, black, & yellow** .20 .20
P# block of 4 .60 —
Margin block of 4, Mr. Zip and "Use Zip Code" .40 —
a. Vertical pair, imperf. between *6,000.*
b. Green (engr.) missing (FO) —
c. Black & green (engr.) missing (FO) —
e. Tagging omitted *6.00* —

A foldover on a pane of No. 1330 resulted in one example each of Nos. 1330b-1330c. Part of the colors appear on the back of the selvage and one freak stamp. An engraved black-and-green-only impression appears on the gummed side of one almost-complete "stamp."

ACCOMPLISHMENTS IN SPACE ISSUE

US accomplishments in space. Printed with continuous design in horizontal rows of 5. In the left panes the astronaut stamp is 1st, 3rd and 5th, the spaceship 2nd and 4th. This arrangement is reversed in the right panes.

Space-Walking Astronaut A753

Gemini 4 Capsule A754

Designed by Paul Calle.

LITHOGRAPHED, ENGRAVED (Giori)
Plates of 200 subjects in four panes of 50.

1967, Sept. 29 **Tagged** ***Perf. 11***

1331 A753 5c **multicolored** .50 .20
b. Tagging omitted *15.00* —
1332 A754 5c **multicolored** .50 .20
P# block of 4 2.50 —
Margin block of 4, Mr. Zip and "Use Zip Code" 2.25 —
Plate flaw (red stripes of flag on capsule omitted; 29322, 29325 UL 19) 210.00
a. Tagging omitted *15.00* —
b. Pair, #1331-1332 1.10 *1.25*
c. As "b," tagging omitted *40.00* —

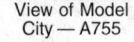

View of Model City — A755

Finnish Coat of Arms — A756

URBAN PLANNING ISSUE

Publicizing the importance of Urban Planning in connection with the Intl. Conf. of the American Institute of Planners, Washington, D.C., Oct. 1-6.

Designed by Francis Ferguson.

LITHOGRAPHED, ENGRAVED (Giori)
Plates of 200 subjects in four panes of 50.

1967, Oct. 2 **Tagged** ***Perf. 11***

1333 A755 5c **dark blue, light blue & black** .20 .20
P# block of 4 .50 —
Margin block of 4, Mr. Zip and "Use Zip Code" .40 —
a. Tagging omitted *20.00*

FINNISH INDEPENDENCE, 50th ANNIV.

Designed by Bradbury Thompson.

ENGRAVED (Giori)
Plates of 200 subjects in four panes of 50.

1967, Oct. 6 **Tagged** ***Perf. 11***

1334 A756 5c **blue** .20 .20
P# block of 4 .50 —
Margin block of 4, Mr. Zip and "Use Zip Code" .40 —
a. Tagging omitted —

THOMAS EAKINS ISSUE

Eakins (1844-1916), painter and sculptor. The painting is in the Natl. Gallery of Art, Washington, D.C.

"The Biglin Brothers Racing" (Sculling on Schuylkill River, Philadelphia) A757

Printed by Photogravure & Color Co., Moonachie, N.J.

PHOTOGRAVURE
Plates of 200 subjects in four panes of 50.

1967, Nov. 2 **Tagged** ***Perf. 12***

1335 A757 5c **gold & multicolored** .20 .20
P# block of 4, 6# .50 —
a. Tagging omitted *20.00* —

Plate number blocks from upper left or lower left panes show clipped corner of margin.

CHRISTMAS ISSUE

Madonna and Child, by Hans Memling — A758

LITHOGRAPHED, ENGRAVED (Giori)
Plates of 200 subjects in four panes of 50.

1967, Nov. 6 **Tagged** ***Perf. 11***

1336 A758 5c **multicolored** .20 .20
P# block of 4 .40 —
Margin block of 4, Mr. Zip and "Use Zip Code" .35 —
a. Tagging omitted *5.00* —

See note on painting above No. 1321.

MISSISSIPPI STATEHOOD, 150th ANNIV.

Magnolia A759

Designed by Andrew Bucci.

GIORI PRESS PRINTING
Plates of 200 subjects in four panes of 50.

1967, Dec. 11 **Tagged** ***Perf. 11***

1337 A759 5c **brt. greenish blue, green & red brown** .20 .20
P# block of 4, 2# .60 —
Margin block of 4, Mr. Zip and "Use Zip Code" .40 —
a. Tagging omitted *6.00* —

FLAG ISSUE

Flag and White House — A760

Designed by Stevan Dohanos.

GIORI PRESS PRINTING
Plates of 400 subjects in four panes of 100.

1968, Jan. 24 **Tagged** ***Perf. 11***
Size: 19x22mm

1338 A760 6c **dark blue, red & green** .20 .20
P# block of 4 .45 —
Margin block of 4, "Use Zip Code" .40 —
Pair with full vert. gutter btwn. —
k. Vert. pair, imperf. btwn. *500.00* —
m. Tagging omitted *4.00* —
s. Red missing (FO) —

Vertical pairs have been offered as imperf. horizontally. Some have had the gum washed off to make it difficult or impossible to detect blind perfs.
No. 1338s is unique.

COIL STAMP

MULTICOLOR HUCK PRESS

1969, May 30 **Tagged** ***Perf. 10 Vertically***
Size: 18¼x21mm

1338A A760 6c **dark blue, red & green** .20 .20
Pair .30 .20
b. Imperf., pair *500.00*
q. Tagging omitted *8.50* —

MULTICOLOR HUCK PRESS
Panes of 100 (10x10) each

1970-71 Tagged *Perf. 11x10½*
Size: 18¼x21mm

1338D A760 6c **dark blue, red & green,** *Aug. 7, 1970* .20 .20
Margin block of 20+ 2.60 —
e. Horiz. pair, imperf. between *175.00*
n. Tagging omitted *5.00* —
1338F A760 8c **dark blue, red & slate green,** *May 10, 1971* .20 .20
Margin block of 20+ 3.00 —
i. Imperf., vert. pair 45.00
j. Horiz. pair, imperf. between 55.00
o. Tagging omitted *6.50* —
p. Slate green omitted *400.00*
t. Horiz. pair, imperf. vertically —

+ Margin blocks of 20 come in four versions: (1) 2 P#, 3 ME, 3 zip; (2) 3 P#, 2 ME, 2 zip; (3) 2 P#, 3 ME, 2 zip; (4) 3 P#, 2 ME, 3 zip.

COIL STAMP
MULTICOLOR HUCK PRESS

1971, May 10 Tagged *Perf. 10 Vertically*
Size: 18¼x21mm

1338G A760 8c **dk blue, red & slate green** .20 .20
Pair .40 .20
h. Imperf., pair *55.00*
r. Tagging omitted *6.00* —

Farm Buildings and Fields of Ripening Grain — A761

Map of North and South America and Lines Converging on San Antonio — A762

ILLINOIS STATEHOOD, 150th ANNIV.

Designed by George Barford.

LITHOGRAPHED, ENGRAVED (Giori)
Plates of 200 subjects in four panes of 50.

1968, Feb. 12 Tagged *Perf. 11*

1339 A761 6c **dk blue, blue, red & ocher** .20 .20
P# block of 4 .60 —
Margin block of 4, Mr. Zip and "Use Zip Code" .45 —
a. Tagging omitted —

HEMISFAIR '68 ISSUE

HemisFair '68 exhibition, San Antonio, Texas, Apr. 6-Oct. 6, for the 250th anniv. of San Antonio.

Designed by Louis Macouillard.

LITHOGRAPHED, ENGRAVED (Giori)
Plates of 200 subjects in four panes of 50.

1968, Mar. 30 Tagged *Perf. 11*

1340 A762 6c **blue, rose red & white** .20 .20
On cover, Expo. station machine canc. 10.00
On cover, Expo. roller canc. 25.00
P# block of 4 .50 —
Margin block of 4, Mr. Zip and "Use Zip Code" .45 —
a. White omitted *1,250.*

AIRLIFT ISSUE

Issued to pay for airlift of parcels from and to US ports to servicemen overseas and in Alaska, Hawaii and Puerto Rico. Valid for all regular postage. On Apr. 26, 1969, the Post Office Department ruled that henceforth No. 1341 "may be used toward paying the postage or fees for special services on *airmail* articles."

Eagle Holding Pennant A763

Designed by Stevan Dohanos.

After a late 19th century wood carving, part of the Index of American Design, National Gallery of Art.

LITHOGRAPHED, ENGRAVED (Giori)
Plates of 200 subjects in four panes of 50.

1968, Apr. 4 Untagged *Perf. 11*

1341 A763 $1 **sepia, dk. blue, ocher & brown red** 2.00 1.25
P# block of 4 8.50 —
Margin block of 4, Mr. Zip and "Use Zip Code" 8.25 —
Pair with full horiz. gutter btwn. —

"SUPPORT OUR YOUTH" - ELKS ISSUE

Support Our Youth program, and honoring the Benevolent and Protective Order of Elks, which extended its youth service program in observance of its centennial year.

Girls and Boys — A764

Designed by Edward Vebell.

LITHOGRAPHED, ENGRAVED (Giori)
Plates of 200 subjects in four panes of 50.

1968, May 1 Tagged *Perf. 11*

1342 A764 6c **ultramarine & orange red** .20 .20
P# block of 4 .50 —
Margin block of 4, Mr. Zip and "Use Zip Code" .45 —
a. Tagging omitted *7.50* —

Policeman and Boy — A765

Eagle Weather Vane — A766

LAW AND ORDER ISSUE

Publicizing the policeman as protector and friend and to encourage respect for law and order.

Designed by Ward Brackett.

GIORI PRESS PRINTING
Plates of 200 subjects in four panes of 50 each

1968, May 17 Tagged *Perf. 11*

1343 A765 6c **chalky blue, black & red** .20 .20
P# block of 4 .50 —
Margin block of 4, Mr. Zip and "Use Zip Code" .45 —
a. Tagging omitted —

REGISTER AND VOTE ISSUE

Campaign to draw more voters to the polls. The weather vane is from an old house in the Russian Hill section of San Francisco, Cal.

Designed by Norman Todhunter and Bill Hyde; photograph by M. Halberstadt.

LITHOGRAPHED, ENGRAVED (Giori)
Plates of 200 subjects in four panes of 50.

1968, June 27 Tagged *Perf. 11*

1344 A766 6c **black, yellow & orange** .20 .20
P# block of 4 .50 —
Margin block of 4, Mr. Zip and "Use Zip Code" .45 —
a. Tagging omitted —

HISTORIC FLAG SERIES

Flags carried by American colonists and by citizens of the new United States. Printed se-tenant in vertical rows of 10. The flag sequence on the 2 upper panes is as listed. On the 2 lower panes the sequence is reversed with the Navy Jack in the 1st row and the Fort Moultrie flag in the 10th.

Ft. Moultrie, 1776 — A767

Ft. McHenry, 1795-1818 A768

Washington's Cruisers, 1775 — A769

Bennington, 1777 — A770

Rhode Island, 1775 — A771

First Stars and Stripes, 1777 — A772

Bunker Hill, 1775 — A773

Grand Union, 1776 — A774

Philadelphia Light Horse, 1775 — A775

First Navy Jack, 1775 — A776

ENGR. (Giori) (#1345-1348, 1350);
ENGR. & LITHO. (#1349, 1351-1354)
Plates of 200 subjects in four panes of 50.

1968, July 4	**Tagged**	***Perf. 11***	
1345 A767 6c	**dark blue**	.40	.25
1346 A768 6c	**dark blue & red**	.30	.25
1347 A769 6c	**dark blue & olive green**	.25	.25
1348 A770 6c	**dark blue & red**	.25	.25
1349 A771 6c	**dark blue, yellow & red**	.25	.25
1350 A772 6c	**dark blue & red**	.25	.25
1351 A773 6c	**dark blue, olive green & red**	.25	.25
1352 A774 6c	**dark blue & red**	.25	.25
1353 A775 6c	**dark blue, yellow & red**	.25	.25
1354 A776 6c	**dark blue, red & yellow**	.25	.25
a.	Strip of ten, #1345-1354	2.75	*3.25*
	P# block of 20, inscriptions, #1345-1354	6.00	—
b.	#1345b-1354b, any single, tagging omitted	—	

WALT DISNEY ISSUE

Walt Disney (1901-1966), cartoonist, film producer and creator of Mickey Mouse.

Walt Disney and Children of the World — A777

Designed by C. Robert Moore.

Designed after portrait by Paul E. Wenzel.
Printed by Achrovure Division of Union-Camp Corp., Englewood, N.J.

PHOTOGRAVURE
Plates of 400 subjects in eight panes of 50.

1968, Sept. 11	**Tagged**	***Perf. 12***	
1355 A777 6c	**multicolored**	.30	.20
	P# block of 4, 5#	1.40	—
	P# block of 4, 5#, 5 dashes	1.40	—
	Margin block of 4, Mr. Zip and "Use Zip Code"	1.25	—
a.	Ocher omitted ("Walt Disney," "6c," etc.)	*600.00*	—
b.	Vert. pair, imperf. horiz.	*700.00*	
c.	Imperf., pair	*600.00*	
d.	Black omitted	*1,500.*	
e.	Horiz. pair, imperf. between	*4,750.*	
f.	Blue omitted	*1,750.*	
g.	Tagging omitted	*15.00*	—

FATHER MARQUETTE ISSUE

Father Jacques Marquette (1637-1675), French Jesuit missionary, who together with Louis Jolliet explored the Mississippi River and its tributaries.

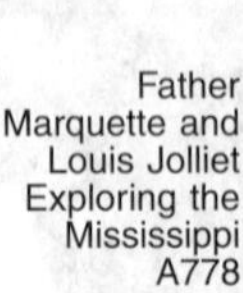

Father Marquette and Louis Jolliet Exploring the Mississippi A778

Designed by Stanley W. Galli.

GIORI PRESS PRINTING
Plates of 200 subjects in four panes of 50.

1968, Sept. 20	**Tagged**	***Perf. 11***	
1356 A778 6c	**black, apple green & orange brown**	.20	.20
	P# block of 4	.60	—
	Margin block of 4, Mr. Zip and "Use Zip Code"	.45	—
a.	Tagging omitted	—	—

AMERICAN FOLKLORE ISSUE

Daniel Boone (1734-1820), frontiersman and trapper.

Pennsylvania Rifle, Powder Horn, Tomahawk Pipe and Knife — A779

Designed by Louis Macouillard.

LITHOGRAPHED, ENGRAVED (Giori)
Plates of 200 subjects in four panes of 50.

1968, Sept. 26	**Tagged**	***Perf. 11***	
1357 A779 6c	**yellow, deep yellow, maroon & black**	.20	.20
	P# block of 4	.50	—
	Margin block of 4, Mr. Zip and "Use Zip Code"	.45	—
a.	Tagging omitted	—	

ARKANSAS RIVER NAVIGATION ISSUE

Opening of the Arkansas River to commercial navigation.

Ship's Wheel, Power Transmission Tower and Barge — A780

Designed by Dean Ellis.

LITHOGRAPHED, ENGRAVED (Giori)
Plates of 200 subjects in four panes of 50.

1968, Oct. 1	**Tagged**	***Perf. 11***	
1358 A780 6c	**bright blue, dark blue & black**	.20	.20
	P# block of 4	.50	—
	Margin block of 4, Mr. Zip and "Use Zip Code"	.45	—
a.	Tagging omitted	—	

LEIF ERIKSON ISSUE

Leif Erikson, 11th century Norse explorer, called the 1st European to set foot on the American continent, at a place he called Vinland. The statue by the American sculptor A. Stirling Calder is in Reykjavik, Iceland.

Leif Erikson by A. Stirling Calder — A781

Designed by Kurt Weiner.

LITHOGRAPHED & ENGRAVED
Plates of 200 subjects in four panes of 50.

1968, Oct. 9	**Tagged**	***Perf. 11***	
1359 A781 6c	**light gray brown & black brown**	.20	.20
	P# block of 4	.50	—
	Margin block of 4, Mr. Zip and "Use Zip Code"	.45	—

The luminescent element is in the light gray brown ink of the background. The engraved parts were printed on a rotary currency press.

CHEROKEE STRIP ISSUE

75th anniversary of the opening of the Cherokee Strip to settlers, Sept. 16, 1893.

Racing for Homesteads in Cherokee Strip, 1893 — A782

Designed by Norman Todhunter.

ROTARY PRESS PRINTING
E.E. Plates of 200 subjects in four panes of 50.

1968, Oct. 15	**Tagged**	***Perf. 11x10½***	
1360 A782 6c	**brown**	.20	.20
	P# block of 4	.60	—
	Margin block of 4, Mr. Zip and "Use Zip Code"	.50	—
a.	Tagging omitted	*6.00*	—

JOHN TRUMBULL ISSUE

Trumbull (1756-1843), painter. The stamp shows Lt. Thomas Grosvenor and his attendant Peter Salem. The painting hangs at Yale University.

Detail from "The Battle of Bunker's Hill" — A783

Modeled by Robert J. Jones.

LITHOGRAPHED, ENGRAVED (Giori)
Plates of 200 subjects in four panes of 50.

1968, Oct. 18	**Tagged**	***Perf. 11***	
1361 A783 6c	**multicolored**	.20	.20
	P# block of 4	.60	—
	Margin block of 4, Mr. Zip and "Use Zip Code"	.50	—
a.	Tagging omitted	—	—
b.	Black (engr.) missing (FO)	*11,000.*	—

WATERFOWL CONSERVATION ISSUE

Wood Ducks — A784

Designed by Stanley W. Galli.

LITHOGRAPHED, ENGRAVED (Giori)
Plates of 200 subjects in four panes of 50.

1968, Oct. 24	**Tagged**	***Perf. 11***		
1362 A784 6c	**black & multicolored**	.20	.20	
	P# block of 4	.65	—	
	Margin block of 4, Mr. Zip and "Use Zip Code"	.60	—	
a.	Vertical pair, imperf. between	*525.00*	—	
b.	Red & dark blue omitted	*900.00*		
c.	Red omitted			*1,750.*

Angel Gabriel, from "The Annunciation" by Jan van Eyck — A785

Chief Joseph, by Cyrenius Hall — A786

CHRISTMAS ISSUE

"The Annunciation" by the 15th century Flemish painter Jan van Eyck is in the National Gallery of Art, Washington, D.C.

Designed by Robert J. Jones.

ENGRAVED (Multicolor Huck press)
Panes of 50 (10x5)

1968, Nov. 1	**Tagged**	***Perf. 11***	
1363 A785 6c **multicolored**		.20	.20
	P# block of 10 +	2.00	—
a.	Untagged, *Nov. 2*	.20	.20
	P# block of 10 +	2.00	—
b.	Imperf., pair, tagged	*225.00*	
c.	Light yellow omitted	*65.00*	—
d.	Imperf., pair, untagged	*290.00*	

+ P# blocks come in two versions: (1) 7 P#, 3 ME; (2) 8 P#, 2 ME.

AMERICAN INDIAN ISSUE

Honoring the American Indian and to celebrate the opening of the Natl. Portrait Gallery, Washington, D.C. Chief Joseph (Indian name, Thunder Traveling over the Mountains), a leader of the Nez Percé, was born in eastern Oregon about 1840 and died at the Colesville Reservation in Washington State in 1904.

Designed by Robert J. Jones; lettering by Crimilda Pontes.

LITHOGRAPHED, ENGRAVED (Giori)
Plates of 200 subjects in four panes of 50.

1968, Nov. 4	**Tagged**	***Perf. 11***	
1364 A786 6c **black & multicolored**		.20	.20
	P# block of 4	.70	—
	Margin block of 4, Mr. Zip and "Use Zip Code"	.60	—
a.	Tagging omitted		—

BEAUTIFICATION OF AMERICA ISSUE

Publicizing the Natural Beauty Campaign for more beautiful cities, parks, highways and streets. In the left panes Nos. 1365 and 1367 appear in 1st, 3rd and 5th place, Nos. 1366 and 1368 in 2nd and 4th place. This arrangement is reversed in the right panes.

Capitol, Azaleas and Tulips — A787

Washington Monument, Potomac River and Daffodils A788

Poppies and Lupines along Highway A789

Blooming Crabapples Lining Avenue A790

Designed by Walter DuBois Richards.

LITHOGRAPHED, ENGRAVED (Giori)
Plates of 200 subjects in four panes of 50.

1969, Jan. 16	**Tagged**	***Perf. 11***	
1365 A787 6c **multicolored**		.25	.20
1366 A788 6c **multicolored**		.25	.20
1367 A789 6c **multicolored**		.25	.20
1368 A790 6c **multicolored**		.25	.20
a.	Block of 4, #1365-1368	1.00	*1.75*
	P# block of 4	1.25	—
	Margin block of 4, Mr. Zip and "Use Zip Code"	1.10	—
b.	#1365b-1368b, tagging omitted		—

Eagle from Great Seal — A791

July Fourth, by Grandma Moses — A792

AMERICAN LEGION, 50th ANNIV.

Designed by Robert Hallock.

LITHOGRAPHED, ENGRAVED (Giori)
Plates of 200 subjects in four panes of 50.

1969, Mar. 15	**Tagged**	***Perf. 11***	
1369 A791 6c **red, blue & black**		.20	.20
	P# block of 4	.45	—
	Margin block of 4, Mr. Zip and "Use Zip Code"	.40	—
a.	Tagging omitted		—

AMERICAN FOLKLORE ISSUE

Grandma Moses (Anna Mary Robertson Moses, 1860-1961), primitive painter of American life.

Designed by Robert J. Jones.

LITHOGRAPHED, ENGRAVED (Giori)
Plates of 200 subjects in four panes of 50.

1969, May 1	**Tagged**	***Perf. 11***	
1370 A792 6c **multicolored**		.20	.20
	P# block of 4	.50	—
	Margin block of 4, Mr. Zip and "Use Zip Code"	.45	—
a.	Horizontal pair, imperf. between	*225.00*	—
b.	Black ("6c U.S. Postage") & Prus. blue ("Grandma Moses") omitted (engraved)	*800.00*	
c.	Tagging omitted	7.50	—

Beware of pairs with blind perfs. being offered as No. 1370a.

No. 1370b often comes with mottled or disturbed gum. Such stamps sell for about two-thirds as much as copies with perfect gum.

APOLLO 8 ISSUE

Apollo 8 mission, which 1st put men into orbit around the moon, Dec. 21-27, 1968. The astronauts were: Col. Frank Borman, Capt. James Lovell and Maj. William Anders.

Moon Surface and Earth — A793

Designed by Leonard E. Buckley after a photograph by the Apollo 8 astronauts.

GIORI PRESS PRINTING
Plates of 200 subjects in four panes of 50.

1969, May 5	**Tagged**	***Perf. 11***	
1371 A793 6c **black, blue & ocher**		.20	.20
	P# block of 4	.65	—
	Margin block of 4, Mr. Zip and "Use Zip Code"	.60	—

Imperfs. exist from printer's waste.

W.C. HANDY ISSUE

Handy (1873-1958), jazz musician and composer.

William Christopher Handy — A794

Designed by Bernice Kochan.

LITHOGRAPHED, ENGRAVED (Giori)
Plates of 200 subjects in four panes of 50.

1969, May 17	**Tagged**	***Perf. 11***	
1372 A794 6c **violet, deep lilac & blue**		.20	.20
	P# block of 4	.65	—
	Margin block of 4, Mr. Zip and "Use Zip Code"	.40	—
a.	Tagging omitted	7.50	—

CALIFORNIA SETTLEMENT, 200th ANNIV.

Carmel Mission Belfry — A795

Designed by Leonard Buckley and Howard C. Mildner.

LITHOGRAPHED, ENGRAVED (Giori)
Plates of 200 subjects in four panes of 50.

1969, July 16	**Tagged**	***Perf. 11***	
1373 A795 6c **orange, red, black & light blue**		.20	.20
	P# block of 4	.45	—
	Margin block of 4, Mr. Zip and "Use Zip Code"	.40	—
a.	Tagging omitted	7.50	—
b.	Red (engr.) missing (CM)		—

JOHN WESLEY POWELL ISSUE

Powell (1834-1902), geologist who explored the Green and Colorado Rivers 1869-75, and ethnologist.

Major Powell Exploring Colorado River, 1869 — A796

Designed by Rudolph Wendelin.

LITHOGRAPHED, ENGRAVED (Giori)
Plates of 200 subjects in four panes of 50.

1969, Aug. 1 Tagged *Perf. 11*
1374 A796 6c **black, ocher & light blue** .20 .20
P# block of 4 .60 —
Margin block of 4, Mr. Zip and "Use Zip Code" .40 —
a. Tagging omitted 7.50 —

ALABAMA STATEHOOD, 150th ANNIV.

Camellia and Yellow-shafted Flicker — A797

Designed by Bernice Kochan

LITHOGRAPHED, ENGRAVED (Giori)
Plates of 200 subjects in four panes of 50.

1969, Aug. 2 Tagged *Perf. 11*
1375 A797 6c **magenta, rose red, yellow, dark green & brown** .20 .20
P# block of 4 .60 —
Margin block of 4, Mr. Zip and "Use Zip Code" .40 —
a. Tagging omitted —

BOTANICAL CONGRESS ISSUE

11th Intl. Botanical Cong., Seattle, Wash., Aug. 24-Sept. 2. In left panes Nos. 1376 and 1378 appear in 1st, 3rd and 5th place; Nos. 1377 and 1379 in 2nd and 4th place. This arrangement is reversed in right panes.

Douglas Fir (Northwest) A798

Lady's-slipper (Northeast) A799

Ocotillo (Southwest) A800

Franklinia (Southeast) A801

Designed by Stanley Galli.

LITHOGRAPHED, ENGRAVED (Giori)
Plates of 200 subjects in four panes of 50.

1969, Aug. 23 Tagged *Perf. 11*
1376 A798 6c **multicolored** .35 .20
1377 A799 6c **multicolored** .35 .20
1378 A800 6c **multicolored** .35 .20
1379 A801 6c **multicolored** .35 .20
a. Block of 4, #1376-1379 1.50 *2.50*
P# block of 4 1.75 —
Margin block of 4, Mr. Zip and "Use Zip Code" 1.60 —

DARTMOUTH COLLEGE CASE ISSUE

150th anniv. of the Dartmouth College Case, which Daniel Webster argued before the Supreme Court, reasserting the sanctity of contracts.

Daniel Webster and Dartmouth Hall — A802

Designed by John R. Scotford, Jr.

ROTARY PRESS PRINTING
E.E. Plates of 200 subjects in four panes of 50.

1969, Sept. 22 Tagged *Perf. 10½x11*
1380 A802 6c **green** .20 .20
P# block of 4 .50 —
Margin block of 4, Mr. Zip and "Use Zip Code" .45 —

PROFESSIONAL BASEBALL, 100th ANNIV.

Batter — A803

Designed by Alex Ross.

LITHOGRAPHED, ENGRAVED (Giori)
Plates of 200 subjects in four panes of 50.

1969, Sept. 24 Tagged *Perf. 11*
1381 A803 6c **yellow, red, black & green** .65 .20
P# block of 4 2.90 —
Margin block of 4, Mr. Zip and "Use Zip Code" 2.75 —
a. Black omitted ("1869-1969, United States, 6c, Professional Baseball") *1,100.*

INTERCOLLEGIATE FOOTBALL, 100th ANNIV.

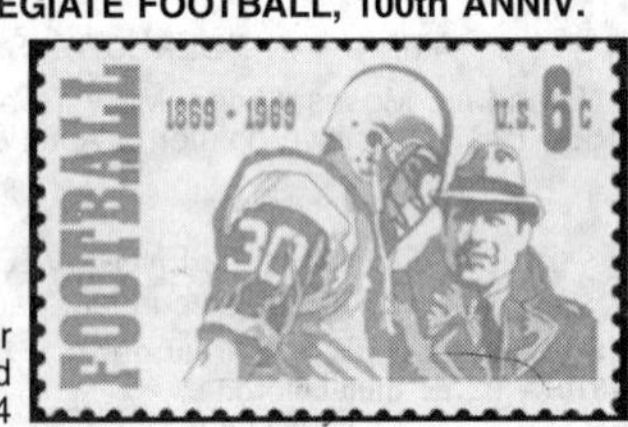

Football Player and Coach — A804

Designed by Robert Peak.

LITHOGRAPHED, ENGRAVED (Giori)
Plates of 200 subjects in four panes of 50.

1969, Sept. 26 Tagged *Perf. 11*
1382 A804 6c **red & green** .20 .20
P# block of 4 1.00 —
Margin block of 4, Mr. Zip and "Use Zip Code" .60 —
a. Tagging omitted —

The engraved parts were printed on a rotary currency press.

DWIGHT D. EISENHOWER ISSUE

Dwight D. Eisenhower, 34th President (1890-1969) — A805

Designed by Robert J. Jones; photograph by Bernie Noble.

GIORI PRESS PRINTING
Plates of 128 subjects in 4 panes of 32 each.

1969, Oct. 14 Tagged *Perf. 11*
1383 A805 6c **blue, black & red** .20 .20
P# block of 4 .50 —
Margin block of 4, Mr. Zip and "Use Zip Code" .45 —
a. Tagging omitted —
b. Blue ("U.S. 6c Postage") missing (PS) —

CHRISTMAS ISSUE

The painting, painted about 1870 by an unknown primitive artist, is the property of the N.Y. State Historical Association, Cooperstown, N.Y.

Winter Sunday in Norway, Maine A806

Designed by Stevan Dohanos.

ENGRAVED (Multicolor Huck)
Panes of 50 (5x10)

1969, Nov. 3 Tagged *Perf. 11x10½*
1384 A806 6c **dark green & multicolored** .20 .20
P# block of 10, 5#, 2-3 zip, 2-3 Mail Early 1.40 —
Precancel .50 .20
b. Imperf., pair *1,000.*
c. Light green omitted 22.50
d. Light green, red & yellow omitted *950.00* —
e. Yellow omitted *2,250.*
f. Tagging omitted 5.00 —
g. Red & yellow omitted *3,000.*
h. Light green and yellow omitted —

The precancel value applies to the least expensive of experimental precancels printed locally in four cities, on tagged stamps, with the names between lines 4½mm apart: in black or green, "ATLANTA, GA" and in green only "BALTIMORE, MD," "MEMPHIS, TN" and "NEW HAVEN, CT." They were sold freely to the public and could be used on any class of mail at all post offices during the experimental program and thereafter.

Most copies of No. 1384c show orange where the offset green was. Value is for this variety. Copies without orange sell for more.

Cured Child — A807

HOPE FOR CRIPPLED ISSUE

Issued to encourage the rehabilitation of crippled children and adults and to honor the National Society for Crippled Children and Adults (Easter Seal Society) on its 50th anniversary.

Designed by Mark English.

LITHOGRAPHED, ENGRAVED (Giori)
Plates of 200 subjects in four panes of 50.

1969, Nov. 20 **Tagged** ***Perf. 11***
1385 A807 6c **multicolored** .20 .20
P# block of 4 .50 —
Margin block of 4, Mr. Zip and "Use Zip Code" .45 —

WILLIAM M. HARNETT ISSUE

"Old Models" — A808

Harnett (1848-1892), painter. The painting hangs in the Museum of Fine Arts, Boston.

Designed by Robert J. Jones.

LITHOGRAPHED, ENGRAVED (Giori)
Plates of 128 subjects in 4 panes of 32 each.

1969, Dec. 3 **Tagged** ***Perf. 11***
1386 A808 6c **multicolored** .20 .20
P# block of 4 .55 —
Margin block of 4, Mr. Zip and "Use Zip Code" .45 —

NATURAL HISTORY ISSUE

Centenary of the American Museum of Natural History, New York City. Nos. 1387-1388 alternate in 1st row, Nos. 1389-1390 in 2nd row. This arrangement is repeated throughout the pane.

American Bald Eagle — A809

African Elephant Herd — A810

Tlingit Chief in Haida Ceremonial Canoe — A811

Brontosaurus, Stegosaurus and Allosaurus from Jurassic Period — A812

Designers: No. 1387, Walter Richards; No. 1388, Dean Ellis; No. 1389, Paul Rabut; No. 1390, detail from mural by Rudolph Zallinger in Yal Peabody Museum, adapted by Robert J. Jones.

LITHOGRAPHED, ENGRAVED (Giori)
Plates of 128 subjects in 4 panes of 32 each (4x8).

1970, May 6 **Tagged** ***Perf. 11***
1387 A809 6c **multicolored** .20 .20
1388 A810 6c **multicolored** .20 .20
1389 A811 6c **multicolored** .20 .20
1390 A812 6c **multicolored** .20 .20
a. Block of 4, #1387-1390 .55 *.80*
P# block of 4 .70 —
Margin block of 4, Mr. Zip and "Use Zip Code" .60 —
b. As "a," tagging omitted —

MAINE STATEHOOD, 150th ANNIV.

The painting hangs in the Metropolitan Museum of Art, New York City.

The Lighthouse at Two Lights, Maine, by Edward Hopper A813

Designed by Stevan Dohanos.

LITHOGRAPHED, ENGRAVED (Giori)
Plates of 200 subjects in four panes of 50.

1970, July 9 **Tagged** ***Perf. 11***
1391 A813 6c **black & multicolored** .20 .20
P# block of 4 .60 —
Margin block of 4, Mr. Zip and "Use Zip Code" .45 —
a. Tagging omitted —

WILDLIFE CONSERVATION ISSUE

American Buffalo A814

Designed by Robert Lougheed.

ROTARY PRESS PRINTING
E.E. Plates of 200 subjects in four panes of 50.

1970, July 20 **Tagged** ***Perf. 11x10½***
1392 A814 6c **black,** *light brown* .20 .20
P# block of 4 .50 —
Margin block of 4, Mr. Zip and "Use Zip Code" .45 —

REGULAR ISSUE
Dwight David Eisenhower

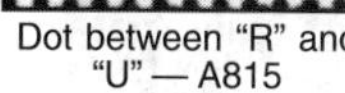

Dot between "R" and "U" — A815

No Dot between "R" and "U" — A815a

Benjamin Franklin — A816

U.S. Postal Service Emblem — A817

Fiorello H. LaGuardia — A817a

Ernest Taylor Pyle — A818

Dr. Elizabeth Blackwell — A818a

Amadeo P. Giannini — A818b

Designers: Nos. 1393-1395, 1401-1402, Robert Geissman; photograph by George Tames. 7c, Bill Hyde. No. 1396, Raymond Loewy/William Smith, Inc. 14c, Robert Geissman; photograph by George Fayer. 16c, Robert Geissman; photograph by Alfred Eisenstadt. 18c, Robert Geissman; painting by Joseph Kozlowski. 21c, Robert Geissman.

ROTARY PRESS PRINTING
E.E. Plates of 400 subjects in four panes of 100.

1970-74 **Tagged** ***Perf. 11x10½***
1393 A815 6c **dark blue gray,** shiny gum, *Aug. 6, 1970* .20 20
P# block of 4
Margin block of 4, "Use Zip Codes" .45 —
Dull gum .20
P# block of 4 1.00
Zip block of 4 .55
a. Booklet pane of 8, shiny gum 1.50 *.75*
Dull gum 1.90
b. Booklet pane of 5 + label 1.50 *.75*
c. Untagged (Bureau precanceled) 12.75 3.00
P# block of 4 *175.00*
Margin block of 4, "Use Zip Codes" 75.00
g. Tagging omitted (not Bureau precanceled) — —
h. As "a," tagging omitted *75.00* —

Perf. 10½x11
1393D A816 7c **bright blue,** shiny gum, *Oct. 20, 1972* .20 .20
P# block of 4 .60 —
Margin block of 4, "Use Zip Codes" .55 —
Dull gum .20
P# block of 4 1.25
Zip block of 4 .90
e. Untagged (Bureau precanceled) 4.25 1.00
P# block of 4 52.50
Margin block of 4, "Use Zip Codes" 22.50
f. Tagging omitted (not Bureau precanceled) 4.00 —

GIORI PRESS PRINTING
Plates of 400 subjects in four panes of 100.
Perf. 11

1394 A815a 8c **black, red & blue gray,** *May 10, 1971* .20 .20
P# block of 4 .60 —
Margin block of 4, "Use Zip Codes" .55 —
Pair with full vert. gutter btwn.
a. Tagging omitted 4.00 —
b. Red missing (PS) —
c. Red and blue missing (PS) —

ROTARY PRESS PRINTING
Perf. 11x10½ on 2 or 3 sides

1395 A815 8c **deep claret,** shiny gum (from blkt. pane) .20 .20
Dull gum .20
a. Booklet pane of 8, shiny gum, *May 10, 1971* 1.80 *1.25*

b. Booklet pane of 6, shiny gum, *May 10, 1971* 1.25 *1.10*
c. Booklet pane of 4 + 2 labels, dull gum, *Jan. 28, 1972* 1.65 *1.00*
d. Booklet pane of 7 + label, dull gum, *Jan. 28, 1972* 1.90 *1.10*
e. Vert. pair, imperf between *850.00*
f. As "a," tagging omitted *20.00* —
g. As "b," tagging omitted *35.00* —
h. As "c," tagging omitted *35.00* —

No. 1395 was issued only in booklets.

No. 1395e exists from two types of production errors. Apparently more common is the error from miscut panes separated at the perforations instead of being cut apart in the normal places. A rarer error resulted from a paper foldover after perforating and before cutting into panes. At least 4 pairs are recorded of this second type of error from 3 panes (one No. 1395a and two 1395d) with different foldover patterns. The value given for No. 1395e is for the more common error, while the errors from foldovers sell for more.

PHOTOGRAVURE (Andreotti)
Plates of 400 subjects in four panes of 100.
Perf. 11x10½

1396 A817 8c **multicolored,** *July 1, 1971* .20 .20
P# block of 12, 6# 2.00
P# block of 20, 6#, "Mail Early in the Day," "Use Zip Codes" and rectangular color contents (UL pane) 3.25
Margin block of 4, "Use Zip Codes" .65 —

ROTARY PRESS PRINTING
E.E. Plates of 400 subjects in four panes of 100.

1397 A817a 14c **gray brown,** *Apr. 24, 1972* .25 .20
P# block of 4 1.15 —
Margin block of 4, "Use Zip Codes" —
a. Untagged (Bureau precanceled) *145.00* 17.50
P# block of 4 —
Margin block of 4, "Use Zip Codes" —
1398 A818 16c **brown,** *May 7, 1971* .30 .20
P# block of 4 1.25 —
Margin block of 4, "Use Zip Codes" 1.20 —
a. Untagged (Bureau precanceled) 22.50 5.00
P# block of 4 —
Margin block of 4, "Use Zip Codes" 95.00
b. Tagging omitted (not Bureau precanceled) — —
1399 A818a 18c **violet,** *Jan. 23, 1974* .35 .20
P# block of 4 1.50 —
Margin block of 4, "Use Zip Codes" 1.40 —
1400 A818b 21c **green,** *June 27, 1973* .40 .20
P# block of 4 1.65 —
Margin block of 4, "Use Zip Codes" 1.60 —
Nos. 1393-1400 (9) 2.30 1.80

Bureau Precancels: 6c, 6 diff., 7c, 13 diff., No. 1394, 24 diff., 14c, 3 diff., 16c, NYC, 3 diff. Greensboro, NC.

COIL STAMPS
ROTARY PRESS PRINTING

1970-71 Tagged *Perf. 10 Vert.*

1401 A815 6c **dark blue gray,** shiny gum, *Aug. 6, 1970* .20 20
Pair
Joint line pair .50 .20
Dull gum .30
Joint line pair 1.40
a. Untagged (Bureau precanceled) 19.50 3.00
Pair 42.50 6.50
Joint line pair *525.00* —
b. Imperf., pair *2,000.*
Joint line pair —
1402 A815 8c **deep claret,** *May 10, 1971* .20 .20
Pair .30 .20
Joint line pair .60 .20
a. Imperf., pair 45.00
Joint line pair 70.00
b. Untagged (Bureau precanceled) 6.75 .75
Pair 15.00 1.60
Joint line pair *185.00* —
c. Pair, imperf. between *6,250.*

Bureau Precancels: 6c, 4 diff., 8c, 34 diff.

EDGAR LEE MASTERS ISSUE

Edgar Lee Masters (1869-1950), Poet — A819

Designed by Fred Otnes.

LITHOGRAPHED, ENGRAVED (Giori)
E.E. Plates of 200 subjects in four panes of 50.

1970, Aug. 22 Tagged *Perf. 11*

1405 A819 6c **black & olive bister** .20 .20
P# block of 4 .50 —
Margin block of 4, Mr. Zip and "Use Zip Code" .45 —
a. Tagging omitted 30.00 —

WOMAN SUFFRAGE ISSUE

50th anniversary of the 19th Amendment, which gave the vote to women.

Suffragettes, 1920, and Woman Voter, 1970 — A820

Designed by Ward Brackett.

GIORI PRESS PRINTING
Plates of 200 subjects in four panes of 50.

1970, Aug. 26 Tagged *Perf. 11*

1406 A820 6c **blue** .20 .20
P# block of 4 .50 —
Margin block of 4, Mr. Zip and "Use Zip Code" .45 —

SOUTH CAROLINA ISSUE

300th anniv. of the founding of Charles Town (Charleston), the 1st permanent settlement of South Carolina. Against a background of pine wood the line drawings of the design represent the economic and historic development of South Carolina: the spire of St. Phillip's Church, Capitol, state flag, a ship, 17th century man and woman, a Fort Sumter cannon, barrels, cotton, tobacco and yellow jasmine.

Symbols of South Carolina A821

Designed by George Samerjan.

LITHOGRAPHED, ENGRAVED (Giori)
Plates of 200 subjects in four panes of 50.

1970, Sept. 12 Tagged *Perf. 11*

1407 A821 6c **bister, black & red** .20 .20
P# block of 4 .55 —
Margin block of 4, Mr. Zip and "Use Zip Code" .45 —

STONE MOUNTAIN MEMORIAL ISSUE

Dedication of the Stone Mountain Confederate Memorial, Georgia, May 9, 1970.

Robert E. Lee, Jefferson Davis and "Stonewall" Jackson A822

Designed by Robert Hallock.

GIORI PRESS PRINTING
Plates of 200 subjects in four panes of 50.

1970, Sept. 19 Tagged *Perf. 11*

1408 A822 6c **gray** .20 .20
P# block of 4 .50 —
Margin block of 4, Mr. Zip and "Use Zip Code" .45 —

FORT SNELLING ISSUE

150th anniv. of Fort Snelling, Minnesota, an important outpost for the opening of the Northwest.

Fort Snelling, Keelboat and Tepees A823

Designed by David K. Stone.

LITHOGRAPHED, ENGRAVED (Giori)
Plates of 200 in four panes of 50.

1970, Oct. 17 Tagged *Perf. 11*

1409 A823 6c **yellow & multicolored** .20 .20
P# block of 4 .50 —
Margin block of 4, Mr. Zip and "Use Zip Code" .45 —
a. Tagging omitted —

ANTI-POLLUTION ISSUE

Issued to focus attention on the problems of pollution.

In left panes Nos. 1410 and 1412 appear in 1st, 3rd and 5th place; Nos. 1411 and 1413 in 2nd and 4th place. This arrangement is reversed in right panes.

Globe and Wheat — A824

Globe and City — A825

Globe and Bluegill A826

Globe and Seagull A827

Designed by Arnold Copeland and Walter DuBois Richards. Printed by Bureau of Engraving and Printing at Guilford Gravure, Inc., Guilford, Conn.

PHOTOGRAVURE
Plates of 200 subjects in four panes of 50.

1970, Oct. 28 Tagged *Perf. 11x10½*

1410 A824 6c **multicolored** .25 .20
1411 A825 6c **multicolored** .25 .20
1412 A826 6c **multicolored** .25 .20
1413 A827 6c **multicolored** .25 .20
a. Block of 4, #1410-1413 1.10 *1.50*
P# block of 10, 5# 2.25 —
Margin block of 4, Mr. Zip and "Use Zip Code" 1.25 —

CHRISTMAS ISSUE

In left panes Nos. 1415 and 1417 appear in 1st, 3rd and 5th place; Nos. 1416 and 1418 in 2nd and 4th place. This arrangement is reversed in right panes.

Nativity, by Lorenzo Lotto — A828

Tin and Cast-iron Locomotive A829

Toy Horse on Wheels A830

Mechanical Tricycle A831

Doll Carriage A832

Designers: No. 1414, Howard C. Mildner, from a painting by Lorenzo Lotto (1480-1556) in the National Gallery of Art, Washington, D.C. Nos. 1415-1418, Stevan Dohanos, from a drawing (locomotive) by Charles Hemming and from "Golden Age of Toys" by Fondin and Remise.

Printed by Guilford Gravure, Inc., Guilford, Conn.

PHOTOGRAVURE

Plates of 200 subjects in four panes of 50.

1970, Nov. 5 — **Tagged** — ***Perf. 10½x11***

No.		Description	Unused	Used
1414	A828	6c **multicolored**	.20	.20
		P# block of 8, 4#	1.10	—
		Margin block of 4, Mr. Zip and "Use Zip Code"	.50	—
a.		Precanceled	.20	.20
		P# block of 8, 4#	1.90	—
		Margin block of 4, Mr. Zip and "Use Zip Code"	.70	—
b.		Black omitted	*525.00*	
c.		As "a," blue omitted	*1,500.*	
d.		Type II	.20	.20
		P# block of 8, 4#	2.75	—
		Zip block of 4	.85	—
e.		Type II, precanceled	.25	.20
		P# block of 8, 4#	4.00	—
		Zip block of 4	1.25	—

No. 1414 has pregummed paper, a slightly blurry impression, snowflaking in the sky and no gum breaker ridges. No. 1414d has shiny surfaced paper, sharper impression, no snowflaking and vertical and horizontal gum breaker ridges.

No. 1414a has a slightly blurry impression, snowflaking in the sky, no gum breaker ridges and the precancel is grayish black. No. 1414e has sharper impression, no snowflaking, gum breaker ridges and the precancel is intense black.

Perf. 11x10½

No.		Description	Unused	Used
1415	A829	6c **multicolored**	.30	.20
a.		Precanceled	.75	.20
b.		Black omitted	*2,500.*	
c.		Tagging omitted		—
1416	A830	6c **multicolored**	.30	.20
a.		Precanceled	.75	.20
b.		Black omitted	*2,500.*	
c.		Imperf., pair (#1416, 1418)		*4,000.*
1417	A831	6c **multicolored**	.30	.20
a.		Precanceled	.75	.20
b.		Black omitted	*2,500.*	
c.		Tagging omitted		—
1418	A832	6c **multicolored**	.30	.20
a.		Precanceled	.75	.20
b.		Block of 4, #1415-1418	1.25	*1.75*
		P# block of 8, 4#	3.00	—
		Margin block of 4, Mr. Zip and "Use Zip Code"	1.25	—
c.		As "b," precanceled	3.25	*3.75*
		P# block of 8, 4P#	6.25	—
		Margin block of 4, Mr. Zip and "Use Zip Code"	3.50	—
d.		Black omitted	*2,500.*	
e.		As "b," black omitted	*10,000.*	
f.		As "b," black omitted on #1417 & 1418	*6,500.*	

The precanceled stamps, Nos. 1414a-1418a, were furnished to 68 cities. The plates include two straight (No. 1414a) or two wavy (Nos. 1415a-1418a) black lines that make up the precancellation. Unused values are for copies with gum and used values are for copies with an additional cancellation or without gum.

UNITED NATIONS, 25th ANNIV.

"UN" and UN Emblem A833

Designed by Arnold Copeland.

LITHOGRAPHED, ENGRAVED (Giori)

Plates of 200 subjects in four panes of 50.

1970, Nov. 20 — **Tagged** — ***Perf. 11***

No.		Description	Unused	Used
1419	A833	6c **black, verm. & ultra.**	.20	.20
		P# block of 4	.50	—
		Margin block of 4, Mr. Zip and "Use Zip Code"	.45	—
		Pair with full horiz. gutter btwn.	—	
a.		Tagging omitted	*25.00*	—

LANDING OF THE PILGRIMS ISSUE

350th anniv. of the landing of the Mayflower.

Mayflower and Pilgrims — A834

Designed by Mark English.

LITHOGRAPHED, ENGRAVED (Giori)

Plates of 200 subjects in four panes of 50.

1970, Nov. 21 — **Tagged** — ***Perf. 11***

No.		Description	Unused	Used
1420	A834	6c **blk., org., yel., magenta, bl. & brn.**	.20	.20
		P# block of 4	.50	—
		Margin block of 4, Mr. Zip and "Use Zip Code"	.45	—
a.		Orange & yellow omitted	*900.00*	
b.		Tagging omitted		—

DISABLED AMERICAN VETERANS AND SERVICEMEN ISSUE

No. 1421 for the 50th anniv. of the Disabled Veterans of America Organization; No. 1422 honors the contribution of servicemen, particularly those who were prisoners of war, missing or killed in action. Nos. 1421-1422 are printed se-tenant in horizontal rows of 10.

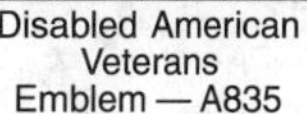
Disabled American Veterans Emblem — A835

A836

Designed by Stevan Dohanos.

LITHOGRAPHED, ENGRAVED (Giori)

Plates of 200 subjects in four panes of 50.

1970, Nov. 24 — **Tagged** — ***Perf. 11***

No.		Description	Unused	Used
1421	A835	6c **dark blue, red & multicolored**	.20	.20

ENGRAVED

No.		Description	Unused	Used
1422	A836	6c **dark blue, black & red**	.20	.20
a.		Pair, #1421-1422	.30	.40
		P# block of 4	1.00	—
		Margin block of 4, Mr. Zip and "Use Zip Code"	.65	—
b.		As "a," tagging omitted		—

Ewe and Lamb — A837

Gen. Douglas MacArthur — A838

AMERICAN WOOL INDUSTRY ISSUE

450th anniv. of the introduction of sheep to the North American continent and the beginning of the American wool industry.

Designed by Dean Ellis.

LITHOGRAPHED, ENGRAVED (Giori)

Plates of 200 subjects in four panes of 50.

1971, Jan. 19 — **Tagged** — ***Perf. 11***

No.		Description	Unused	Used
1423	A837	6c **multicolored**	.20	.20
		P# block of 4	.50	—
		Margin block of 4, Mr. Zip and "Use Zip Code"	.45	—
a.		Tagging omitted	11.00	—
b.		Teal blue ("United States") missing (CM)	—	

GEN. DOUGLAS MacARTHUR ISSUE

MacArthur (1880-1964), Chief of Staff, Supreme Commander for the Allied Powers in the Pacific Area during World War II and Supreme Commander in Japan after the war.

Designed by Paul Calle; Wide World photograph.

GIORI PRESS PRINTING

Plates of 200 subjects in four panes of 50.

1971, Jan. 26 — **Tagged** — ***Perf. 11***

No.		Description	Unused	Used
1424	A838	6c **black, red & dark blue**	.20	.20
		P# block of 4	.60	—
		Margin block of 4, Mr. Zip and "Use Zip Code"	.45	—
a.		Red missing (PS)	—	
b.		Tagging omitted		—
c.		Blue missing (PS)	—	

BLOOD DONOR ISSUE

Salute to blood donors and spur to increased participation in the blood donor program.

"Giving Blood Saves Lives" — A839

Designed by Howard Munce.

LITHOGRAPHED, ENGRAVED (Giori)
Plates of 200 subjects in four panes of 50.

1971, Mar. 12 **Tagged** ***Perf. 11***

1425 A839 6c **blue, scarlet & indigo** .20 .20
P# block of 4 .50 —
Margin block of 4, Mr. Zip and "Use Zip Code" .45 —
a. Tagging omitted 11.00 —

MISSOURI STATEHOOD, 150th ANNIV.

The stamp design shows a Pawnee facing a hunter-trapper and a group of settlers. It is from a mural by Thomas Hart Benton in the Harry S Truman Library, Independence, Mo.

"Independence and the Opening of the West," Detail, by Thomas Hart Benton A840

Designed by Bradbury Thompson.

PHOTOGRAVURE (Andreotti)
Plates of 200 subjects in four panes of 50.

1971, May 8 **Tagged** ***Perf. 11x10½***

1426 A840 8c **multicolored** .20 .20
P# block of 12, 6# 2.00 —
Margin block of 4, Mr. Zip and "Use Zip Code" .65 —
a. Tagging omitted —

See note on Andreotti printings and their color control markings in Information for Collectors under Printing, Photogravure.

WILDLIFE CONSERVATION ISSUE

Nos. 1427-1428 alternate in first row, Nos. 1429-1430 in second row. This arrangement repeated throughout pane.

Trout A841

Alligator — A842

Polar Bear and Cubs A843

California Condor — A844

Designed by Stanley W. Galli.

LITHOGRAPHED, ENGRAVED (Giori)
Plates of 128 subjects in 4 panes of 32 each (4x8).

1971, June 12 **Tagged** ***Perf. 11***

1427 A841 8c **multicolored** .20 .20
a. Red omitted 1,250.
b. Green (engr.) omitted —
1428 A842 8c **multicolored** .20 .20
1429 A843 8c **multicolored** .20 .20
1430 A844 8c **multicolored** .20 .20
a. Block of 4, #1427-1430 .80 1.00
P# block of 4 .90 —
Margin block of 4, Mr. Zip and "Use Zip Code" .85 —
b. As "a," light green & dark green omitted from #1427-1428 4,500.
c. As "a," red omitted from #1427, 1429-1430 7,500.

ANTARCTIC TREATY ISSUE

Map of Antarctica A845

Designed by Howard Koslow.

Adapted from emblem on official documents of Consultative Meetings.

GIORI PRESS PRINTING
Plates of 200 subjects in four panes of 50.

1971, June 23 **Tagged** ***Perf. 11***

1431 A845 8c **red & dark blue** .20 .20
P# block of 4 .65 —
Margin block of 4, Mr. Zip and "Use Zip Code" .60 —
a. Tagging omitted 9.00
b. Both colors missing (EP) 500.00

No. 1431b should be collected se-tenant with a normal stamp and/or a partially printed stamp.

AMERICAN REVOLUTION BICENTENNIAL

Bicentennial Commission Emblem — A846

Designed by Chermayeff & Geismar.

LITHOGRAPHED, ENGRAVED (Giori)
Plates of 200 subjects in four panes of 50.

1971, July 4 **Tagged** ***Perf. 11***

1432 A846 8c **gray, red, blue & black** .20 .20
P# block of 4 .85 —
Margin block of 4, Mr. Zip and "Use Zip Code" .80 —
a. Gray & black missing (EP) 500.00
b. Gray ("U.S. Postage 8c") missing (EP) 900.00

JOHN SLOAN ISSUE

John Sloan (1871-1951), painter. The painting hangs in the Phillips Gallery, Washington, D.C.

The Wake of the Ferry — A847

Designed by Bradbury Thompson.

LITHOGRAPHED, ENGRAVED (Giori)
Plates of 200 subjects in four panes of 50.

1971, Aug. 2 **Tagged** ***Perf. 11***

1433 A847 8c **multicolored** .20 .20
P# block of 4 .70 —
Margin block of 4, Mr. Zip and "Use Zip Code" .65 —
a. Tagging omitted —
b. Red engr. ("John Sloan" and "8") missing (CM) —

SPACE ACHIEVEMENT DECADE ISSUE

Decade of space achievements and the Apollo 15 moon exploration mission, July 26-Aug. 7. In the left panes the earth and sun stamp is 1st, 3rd and 5th, the rover 2nd and 4th. This arrangement is reversed in the right panes.

Earth, Sun and Landing Craft on Moon — A848

Lunar Rover and Astronauts A849

Designed by Robert McCall.

LITHOGRAPHED, ENGRAVED (Giori)
Plates of 200 subjects in four panes of 50.

1971, Aug. 2 **Tagged** ***Perf. 11***

1434 A848 8c **black, blue, gray, yellow & red** .20 .20
a. Tagging omitted 30.00
1435 A849 8c **black, blue, gray, yellow & red** .20 .20
a. Tagging omitted 30.00
b. Pair, #1434-1435 .40 .45
P# block of 4 .65 —
Margin block of 4, Mr. Zip and "Use Zip Code" .60 —
c. As "b," tagging omitted —
d. As "b," blue & red (litho.) omitted 1,500.

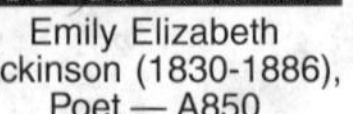

Emily Elizabeth Dickinson (1830-1886), Poet — A850

Sentry Box, Morro Castle, San Juan — A851

EMILY DICKINSON ISSUE

Designed by Bernard Fuchs after a photograph.

LITHOGRAPHED, ENGRAVED (Giori)
Plates of 200 subjects in four panes of 50.

1971, Aug. 28 Tagged *Perf. 11*

1436 A850 8c **multicolored,** *greenish* .20 .20
P# block of 4 .65 —
Margin block of 4, Mr. Zip and "Use Zip Code" .60 —
a. Black & olive (engr.) omitted *700.00*
b. Pale rose omitted *7,500.*
c. Red omitted —
d. Tagging omitted —

SAN JUAN ISSUE

450th anniversary of San Juan, Puerto Rico.

Designed as a woodcut by Walter Brooks.

LITHOGRAPHED, ENGRAVED (Giori)
Plates of 200 subjects in four panes of 50.

1971, Sept. 12 Tagged *Perf. 11*

1437 A851 8c **pale brown, black, yellow & dark brown** .20 .20
P# block of 4 .65 —
Margin block of 4, Mr. Zip and "Use Zip Code" .60 —
a. Tagging omitted *9.00*

VALUES FOR HINGED STAMPS AFTER NO. 771
This catalogue does not value unused stamps after No. 771 in hinged condition. Hinged unused stamps from No. 772 to the present are worth considerably less than the values given for unused stamps, which are for never-hinged examples.

Young Woman Drug Addict — A852

Hands Reaching for CARE — A853

PREVENT DRUG ABUSE ISSUE

Drug Abuse Prevention Week, Oct. 3-9.

Designed by Miggs Burroughs.

PHOTOGRAVURE (Andreotti)
Plates of 200 subjects in four panes of 50.

1971, Oct. 4 Tagged *Perf. 10½x11*

1438 A852 8c **blue, deep blue & black** .20 .20
P# block of 6, 3# 1.00 —
Margin block of 4, "Use Zip Code" .65 —

CARE ISSUE

25th anniversary of CARE, a US-Canadian Cooperative for American Relief Everywhere.

Designed by Soren Noring

PHOTOGRAVURE (Andreotti)
Plates of 200 subjects in four panes of 50.

1971, Oct. 27 Tagged *Perf. 10½x11*

1439 A853 8c **blue, blk., vio. & red lilac** .20 .20
P# block of 8, 4# 1.25 —
Margin block of 4, Mr. Zip and "Use Zip Code" .65 —
a. Black omitted *4,750.*
b. Tagging omitted 5.00

HISTORIC PRESERVATION ISSUE

Nos. 1440-1441 alternate in 1st row, Nos. 1442-1443 in 2nd row. This arrangement is repeated throughout the pane.

Decatur House, Washington, D.C. — A854

Whaling Ship Charles W. Morgan, Mystic, Conn. — A855

Cable Car, San Francisco — A856

San Xavier del Bac Mission, Tucson, Ariz. — A857

Designed by Melbourne Brindle.

LITHOGRAPHED, ENGRAVED (Giori)

1971, Oct. 29 Tagged *Perf. 11*

1440 A854 8c **black brown & ocher,** *buff* .20 .20
1441 A855 8c **black brown & ocher,** *buff* .20 .20
1442 A856 8c **black brown & ocher,** *buff* .20 .20
1443 A857 8c **black brown & ocher,** *buff* .20 .20
a. Block of 4, #1440-1443 .75 *1.00*
P# block of 4 .90 —
Margin block of 4, Mr. Zip and "Use Zip Code" .80 —
b. As "a," black brown omitted *2,100.*
c. As "a," ocher omitted —
d. As "a," tagging omitted *65.00*

CHRISTMAS ISSUE

Adoration of the Shepherds, by Giorgione — A858

"Partridge in a Pear Tree" — A859

Designers: No. 1444, Bradbury Thompson, using a painting by Giorgione in the National Gallery of Art, Washington, D.C. No. 1445, Jamie Wyeth.

PHOTOGRAVURE (Andreotti)
Plates of 200 subjects in four panes of 50.

1971, Nov. 10 Tagged *Perf. 10½x11*

1444 A858 8c **gold & multicolored** .20 .20
P# block of 12, 6# 1.80 —
Margin block of 4, Mr. Zip and "Use Zip Code" .60 —
a. Gold omitted *500.00*
1445 A859 8c **dark green, red & multicolored** .20 .20
P# block of 12, 6# 1.80
Margin block of 4, Mr. Zip and "Use Zip Code" .60 —

Sidney Lanier — A860

Peace Corps Poster, by David Battle — A861

SIDNEY LANIER ISSUE

Lanier (1842-81), poet, musician, lawyer, educator.

Designed by William A. Smith.

GIORI PRESS PRINTING
Plates of 200 subjects in four panes of 50.

1972, Feb. 3 Tagged *Perf. 11*

1446 A860 8c **black, brown & light blue** .20 .20
P# block of 4 .65 —
Margin block of 4, Mr. Zip and "Use Zip Code" .60 —
a. Tagging omitted 15.00

PEACE CORPS ISSUE

Designed by Bradbury Thompson.

PHOTOGRAVURE (Andreotti)
Plates of 200 subjects in four panes of 50.

1972, Feb. 11 Tagged *Perf. 10½x11*

1447 A861 8c **dark blue, light blue & red** .20 .20
P# block of 6, 3# 1.00 —
Margin block of 4, Mr. Zip and "Use Zip Code" .65 —
a. Tagging omitted 5.00

NATIONAL PARKS CENTENNIAL ISSUE

Centenary of Yellowstone National Park, the 1st National Park, and of the entire National Park System. See No. C84.

A862 A863

A864 A865
Cape Hatteras National Seashore

Wolf Trap Farm, Va. — A866

Old Faithful, Yellowstone — A867

Mt. McKinley, Alaska A868

Designers: 2c, Walter D. Richards; 6c, Howard Koslow; 8c, Robert Handville; 15c, James Barkley.

LITHOGRAPHED, ENGRAVED (Giori)

1972 Tagged *Perf. 11*

Plates of 400 subjects in 4 panes of 100 each

1448	A862	2c	**black & multi.,** *Apr. 5*	.20	.20
1449	A863	2c	**black & multi.,** *Apr. 5*	.20	.20
1450	A864	2c	**black & multi.,** *Apr. 5*	.20	.20
1451	A865	2c	**black & multi.,** *Apr. 5*	.20	.20
a.			Block of 4, #1448-1451	.25	*.45*
			P# block of 4	.50	—
			Margin block of 4, "Use Zip Codes"	.30	—
b.			As "a," black (litho.) omitted	*2,250.*	
c.			As "a," tagging omitted	—	

Plates of 200 subjects in four panes of 50 each

1452	A866	6c	**black & multicolored,** *June 26*	.20	.20
			P# block of 4	.55	—
			Margin block of 4, Mr. Zip and "Use Zip Code"	.50	—
a.			Tagging omitted	*11.00*	

Plates of 128 subjects in four panes of 32 (8x4)

1453	A867	8c	**blk., blue, brn. & multi.,** *Mar. 1*	.20	.20
			P# block of 4	.70	—
			Margin block of 4, Mr. Zip and "Use Zip Code"	.65	—
a.			Tagging omitted	15.00	

Plates of 200 subjects in four panes of 50 each

1454	A868	15c	**black & multi.,** *July 28*	.30	.20
			P# block of 4	1.30	—
			Margin block of 4, Mr. Zip	1.25	—
a.			Tagging omitted	—	
b.			Yellow omitted	—	

FAMILY PLANNING ISSUE

Family — A869

LITHOGRAPHED, ENGRAVED (Giori)

Plates of 200 subjects in four panes of 50.

1972, Mar. 18 Tagged *Perf. 11*

1455	A869	8c	**black & multicolored**	.20	.20
			P# block of 4	.65	—
			Margin block of 4, Mr. Zip and "Use Zip Code"	.60	—
a.			Yellow omitted	*1,000.*	
c.			Dark brown missing (FO)	*9,500.*	
d.			Tagging omitted	—	

AMERICAN BICENTENNIAL ISSUE
Colonial American Craftsmen

In left panes Nos. 1456 and 1458 appear in 1st, 3rd and 5th place; Nos. 1457 and 1459 in 2nd and 4th place. This arrangement is reversed in right panes.

Glass Blower A870

Silversmith A871

Wigmaker A872

Hatter — A873

Designed by Leonard Everett Fisher.

ENGRAVED

E.E. Plates of 200 subjects in four panes of 50.

1972, July 4 Tagged *Perf. 11x10½*

1456	A870	8c	**deep brown,** *dull yellow*	.20	.20
1457	A871	8c	**deep brown,** *dull yellow*	.20	.20
1458	A872	8c	**deep brown,** *dull yellow*	.20	.20
1459	A873	8c	**deep brown,** *dull yellow*	.20	.20
a.			Block of 4, #1456-1459	.65	*.90*
			P# block of 4	.80	—
			Margin block of 4, Mr. Zip and "Use Zip Code"	.70	—
b.			As "a," tagging omitted	—	

Margin includes Bicentennial Commission emblem and inscription: USA BICENTENNIAL / HONORS COLONIAL / AMERICAN CRAFTSMEN.

OLYMPIC GAMES ISSUE

11th Winter Olympic Games, Sapporo, Japan, Feb. 3-13 and 20th Summer Olympic Games, Munich, Germany, Aug. 26-Sept. 11. See No. C85.

Bicycling and Olympic Rings — A874

Bobsledding and Olympic Rings — A875

Running and Olympic Rings — A876

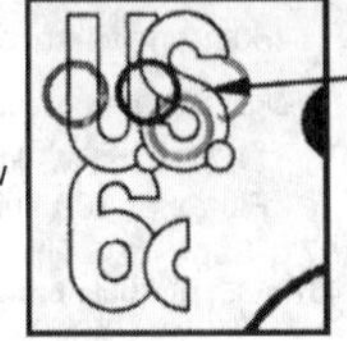

"Broken red ring" Cylinder Flaw

Designed by Lance Wyman.

PHOTOGRAVURE (Andreotti)

Plates of 200 subjects in four panes of 50.

1972, Aug. 17 Tagged *Perf. 11x10½*

1460	A874	6c	**black, blue, red, emerald & yellow**	.20	.20
			P# block of 10, 5#	1.25	—
			Margin block of 4, Mr. Zip and "Use Zip Code"	.60	—
			Cylinder flaw (broken red ring) (33313 UL 43)	10.00	
1461	A875	8c	**black, blue, red, emerald & yellow**	.20	.20
			P# block of 10, 5#	1.60	—
			Margin block of 4, Mr. Zip and "Use Zip Code"	.65	—
a.			Tagging omitted	7.50	
1462	A876	15c	**black, blue, red, emerald & yel**	.30	.20
			P# block of 10, 5#	3.00	—
			Margin block of 4, Mr. Zip and "Use Zip Code"	1.15	—
			Nos. 1460-1462 (3)	.70	.60

PARENT TEACHER ASSN., 75th ANNIV.

Blackboard A877

Designed by Arthur S. Congdon III.

PHOTOGRAVURE (Andreotti)

Plates of 200 subjects in four panes of 50.

1972, Sept. 15 Tagged *Perf. 11x10½*

1463	A877	8c	**yellow & black**	.20	.20
			P# block of 4, 2#	.65	—
			P# block of 4, yellow # reversed	.75	—
			Margin block of 4, Mr. Zip and "Use Zip Code"	.60	—

WILDLIFE CONSERVATION ISSUE

Nos. 1464-1465 alternate in 1st row, Nos. 1468-1469 in 2nd row. This arrangement repeated throughout pane.

Fur Seals A878

Cardinal — A879

Brown Pelican — A880

Bighorn Sheep — A881

Designed by Stanley W. Galli.

LITHOGRAPHED, ENGRAVED (Giori)
Plates of 128 subjects in 4 panes of 32 (4x8).

1972, Sept. 20 **Tagged** ***Perf. 11***

1464 A878 8c **multicolored** .20 .20
1465 A879 8c **multicolored** .20 .20
1466 A880 8c **multicolored** .20 .20
1467 A881 8c **multicolored** .20 .20
a. Block of 4, #1464-1467 .65 *.90*
P# block of 4 .75 —
Margin block of 4, Mr. Zip and "Use Zip Code" .70 —
b. As "a," brown omitted *4,000.*
c. As "a," green & blue omitted *4,500.*
d. As "a," red & brown omitted *4,000.*

MAIL ORDER BUSINESS ISSUE

Centenary of mail order business, originated by Aaron Montgomery Ward, Chicago. Design based on Headsville, W.Va., post office in Smithsonian Institution, Washington, D.C.

Rural Post Office Store — A882

Designed by Robert Lambdin.

PHOTOGRAVURE (Andreotti)
Plates of 200 subjects in four panes of 50.

1972, Sept, 27 **Tagged** ***Perf. 11x10½***

1468 A882 8c **multicolored** .20 .20
P# block of 12, 6# 1.75 —
Margin block of 4, Mr. Zip and "Use Zip Code" .60 —

The tagging on No. 1468 consists of a vertical bar of phosphor 10mm wide.

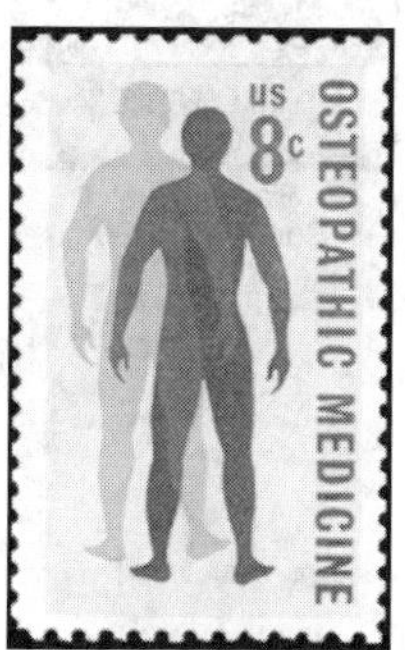

Man's Quest for Health — A883

Tom Sawyer, by Norman Rockwell — A884

OSTEOPATHIC MEDICINE ISSUE

75th anniv. of the American Osteopathic Assoc., founded by Dr. Andrew T. Still (1828-1917), who developed the principles of osteopathy in 1874.

Designed by V. Jack Ruther.

PHOTOGRAVURE (Andreotti)
Plates of 200 subjects in four panes of 50.

1972, Oct. 9 **Tagged** ***Perf. 10½x11***

1469 A883 8c **multicolored** .20 .20
P# block of 6, 3# 1.00 —
Margin block of 4, Mr. Zip and "Use Zip Code" .65 —

AMERICAN FOLKLORE ISSUE
Tom Sawyer

Designed by Bradbury Thompson.

LITHOGRAPHED, ENGRAVED (Giori)
Plates of 200 subjects in four panes of 50.

1972, Oct. 13 **Tagged** ***Perf. 11***

1470 A884 8c **black, red, yellow, tan, blue & rose red** .20 .20
P# block of 4 .65 —
Margin block of 4, Mr. Zip and "Use Zip Code" .60 —
a. Horiz. pair, imperf. between *4,500.*
b. Red & black (engr.) omitted *1,700.*
c. Yellow & tan (litho.) omitted *2,400.*
d. Tagging omitted —

CHRISTMAS ISSUE

Angels from "Mary, Queen of Heaven" — A885

Santa Claus — A886

Designers: No. 1471, Bradbury Thompson, using detail from a painting by the Master of the St. Lucy legend, in the National Gallery of Art, Washington, D.C. No. 1472, Stevan Dohanos.

PHOTOGRAVURE (Andreotti)
Plates of 200 subjects in four panes of 50.

1972, Nov. 9 **Tagged** ***Perf. 10½x11***

1471 A885 8c **multicolored** .20 .20
P# block of 12, 6# 1.75 —
Margin block of 4, Mr. Zip and "Use Zip Code" .60 —
a. Pink omitted *140.00*
b. Black omitted *4,000.*
1472 A886 8c **multicolored** .20 .20
P# block of 12, 6# 1.75 —
Margin block of 4, Mr. Zip and "Use Zip Code" .60 —

PHARMACY ISSUE

Honoring American druggists in connection with the 120th anniversary of the American Pharmaceutical Association.

Mortar and Pestle, Bowl of Hygeia, 19th Century Medicine Bottles A887

Designed by Ken Davies.

LITHOGRAPHED, ENGRAVED (Giori)
Plates of 200 subjects in four panes of 50.

1972, Nov. 10 **Tagged** ***Perf. 11***

1473 A887 8c **black & multicolored** .20 .20
P# block of 4 .65 —
Margin block of 4, Mr. Zip and "Use Zip Code" .60 —
a. Blue & orange omitted *750.00*
b. Blue omitted *2,100.*
c. Orange omitted *2,100.*
d. Tagging omitted —

STAMP COLLECTING ISSUE

Issued to publicize stamp collecting.

U.S. No. 1 under Magnifying Glass — A888

Designed by Frank E. Livia.

LITHOGRAPHED, ENGRAVED (Giori)
Plates of 160 subjects in four panes of 40.

1972, Nov. 17 **Tagged** ***Perf. 11***

1474 A888 8c **multicolored** .20 .20
P# block of 4 .65 —
Margin block of 4, Mr. Zip and "Use Zip Code" .60 —
a. Black (litho.) omitted *575.00*

LOVE ISSUE

"Love," by Robert Indiana A889

Designed by Robert Indiana.

PHOTOGRAVURE (Andreotti)
Plates of 200 subjects in four panes of 50.

1973, Jan. 26 **Tagged** ***Perf. 11x10½***

1475 A889 8c **red, emerald & violet blue** .20 .20
P# block of 6, 3# 1.00 —
Margin block of 4, Mr. Zip and "Use Zip Code" .65 —

AMERICAN BICENTENNIAL ISSUE
Communications in Colonial Times

Printer and Patriots Examining Pamphlet A890

Posting a Broadside A891

Postrider A892

Drummer A893

Designed by William A. Smith.

GIORI PRESS PRINTING

Plates of 200 subjects in four panes of 50.

1973 **Tagged** ***Perf. 11***

1476 A890 8c **ultra., greenish blk. & red,** *Feb. 16* .20 .20
P# block of 4 .65 —
Margin block of 4, Mr. Zip and "Use Zip Code" .60 —
a. Tagging omitted —
1477 A891 8c **black, vermilion & ultra.,** *Apr. 13* .20 .20
P# block of 4 .65 —
Margin block of 4, Mr. Zip and "Use Zip Code" .60 —
Pair with full horiz. gutter btwn. —

LITHOGRAPHED, ENGRAVED (Giori)

1478 A892 8c **blue, black, red & green,** *June 22* .20 .20
P# block of 4 .65 —
Margin block of 4, Mr. Zip and "Use Zip Code" .60 —
a. Red missing (CM) —
1479 A893 8c **blue, black, yellow & red,** *Sept. 28* .20 .20
P# block of 4 .65 —
Margin block of 4, Mr. Zip and "Use Zip Code" .60 —
Nos. 1476-1479 (4) .80 .80

Margin of Nos. 1477-1479 includes Bicentennial Commission emblem and inscription.

AMERICAN BICENTENNIAL ISSUE
Boston Tea Party

In left panes Nos. 1480 and 1482 appear in 1st, 3rd and 5th place, Nos. 1481 and 1483 appear in 2nd and 4th place. This arrangement is reversed in right panes.

British Merchantman A894

British Three-master A895

Boats and Ship's Hull — A896

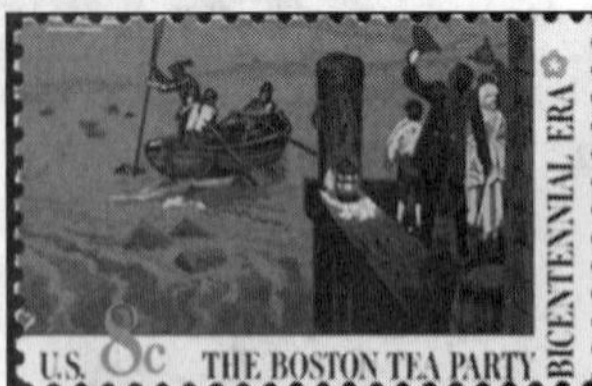

Boat and Dock — A897

Designed by William A. Smith.

LITHOGRAPHED, ENGRAVED (Giori)

Plates of 200 subjects in four panes of 50.

1973, July 4 **Tagged** ***Perf. 11***

1480 A894 8c **black & multicolored** .20 .20
1481 A895 8c **black & multicolored** .20 .20
1482 A896 8c **black & multicolored** .20 .20
1483 A897 8c **black & multicolored** .20 .20
a. Block of 4, #1480-1483 .65 *.90*
P# block of 4 .75 —
Margin block of 4, Mr. Zip and "Use Zip Code" .70 —
b. As "a," black (engraved) omitted *1,400.*
c. As "a," black (litho.) omitted *1,200.*
d. As "a," tagging omitted —

Margin includes Bicentennial Commission emblem and inscription.

AMERICAN ARTS ISSUE

George Gershwin (1898-1937), composer (No. 1484); Robinson Jeffers (1887-1962), poet (No. 1485); Henry Ossawa Tanner (1859-1937), black painter (No. 1486); Willa Cather (1873-1947), novelist (No. 1487).

Gershwin, Sportin' Life, Porgy and Bess — A898

Robinson Jeffers, Man and Children of Carmel with Burro — A899

Henry Ossawa Tanner, Palette and Rainbow A900

Willa Cather, Pioneer Family and Covered Wagon A901

Designed by Mark English.

PHOTOGRAVURE (Andreotti)

Plates of 160 subjects in four panes of 40.

1973 **Tagged** ***Perf. 11***

1484 A898 8c **dp. green & multi.,** *Feb. 28* .20 .20
P# block of 12, 6# 1.75 —
Margin block of 4, Mr. Zip, "Use Zip Code" and "Mail Early in the Day" .60 —
P# block of 16, 6#, Mr. Zip and slogans 2.50 —
a. Vertical pair, imperf. horiz. *225.00*
1485 A899 8c **Prussian blue & multi.,** *Aug. 13* .20 .20
P# block of 12, 6# 1.75 —
Margin block of 4, Mr. Zip, "Use Zip Code" "Mail Early in the Day" .60 —
P# block of 16, 6#, Mr. Zip and slogans 2.50 —
a. Vertical pair, imperf. horiz. *250.00*
1486 A900 8c **yellow brown & multi.,** *Sept. 10* .20 .20
P# block of 12, 6# 1.75 —
Margin block of 4, Mr. Zip, "Use Zip Code" "Mail Early in the Day" .60 —
P# block of 16, 6#, Mr. Zip and slogans 2.50 —
1487 A901 8c **deep brown & multi.,** *Sept. 20* .20 .20
P# block of 12, 6# 1.75 —
Margin block of 4, Mr. Zip, "Use Zip Code" "Mail Early in the Day" .60 —
P# block of 16, 6#, Mr. Zip and slogans 2.50 —
a. Vertical pair, imperf. horiz. *275.00*
Nos. 1484-1487 (4) .80 .80

COPERNICUS ISSUE

Nicolaus Copernicus (1473-1543), Polish Astronomer — A902

Designed by Alvin Eisenman after 18th century engraving.

LITHOGRAPHED, ENGRAVED (Giori)

Plates of 200 subjects in four panes of 50.

1973, Apr. 23 **Tagged** ***Perf. 11***

1488 A902 8c **black & orange** .20 .20
P# block of 4 .65 —
Margin block of 4, Mr. Zip and "Use Zip Code" .60 —
a. Orange omitted *1,000.*
b. Black (engraved) omitted *900.00*
c. Tagging omitted —

The orange can be chemically removed. Expertization of No. 1488a is required.

POSTAL SERVICE EMPLOYEES ISSUE

A tribute to US Postal Service employees. Nos. 1489-1498 are printed se-tenant in horizontal rows of 10. Emerald inscription on back, printed beneath gum in water-soluble ink, includes Postal Service emblem, "People Serving You" and a statement, differing for each of the 10 stamps, about some aspect of postal service.

Each stamp in top or bottom row has a tab with blue inscription enumerating various jobs in postal service.

Stamp Counter — A903

Mail Collection — A904

Letter Facing on Conveyor Belt — A905

Parcel Post Sorting — A906

Mail Canceling — A907

Manual Letter Routing — A908

Electronic Letter Routing — A909

Loading Mail on Truck — A910

Mailman — A911

Rural Mail Delivery — A912

Designed by Edward Vebell.

PHOTOGRAVURE (Andreotti)

Plates of 200 subjects in four panes of 50.

1973, Apr. 30 **Tagged** ***Perf. 10½x11***

1489 A903 8c **multicolored** .20 .20
1490 A904 8c **multicolored** .20 .20
1491 A905 8c **multicolored** .20 .20
1492 A906 8c **multicolored** .20 .20
1493 A907 8c **multicolored** .20 .20
1494 A908 8c **multicolored** .20 .20
1495 A909 8c **multicolored** .20 .20
1496 A910 8c **multicolored** .20 .20
1497 A911 8c **multicolored** .20 .20
1498 A912 8c **multicolored** .20 .20
a. Strip of 10, #1489-1498 1.75 *2.00*
P# block of 20, 5# and 10 tabs 3.25 —
b. As "a," tagging omitted —

The tagging on Nos. 1489-1498 consists of a ½-inch horizontal band of phosphor.

HARRY S TRUMAN ISSUE

Harry S Truman, 33rd President, (1884-1972) — A913

Designed by Bradbury [illegible]

GIORI [illegible]

Plates of 128 su[illegible]

1973, May 8

1499 A913 8c **carm**[illegible]
P# b[illegible]
a. Tagging o[illegible]

ELECT[illegible]

Microphone, Speaker, Vacuum Tube and TV Camera Tube — A916

Designed by Walter and Naiad Einsel.

LITHOGRAPHED, ENGRAVED (Giori)

Plates of 200 subjects in four panes of 50.

1973, July 10 **Tagged** ***Perf. 11***

1500 A914 6c **lilac & multicolored** .20 .20
P# block of 4 .55 —
Margin block of 4, Mr. Zip and "Use Zip Code" .50 —
a. Tagging omitted —
1501 A915 8c **tan & multicolored** .20 .20
P# block of 4 .70 —
Margin block of 4, Mr. Zip and "Use Zip Code" .65 —
a. Black (inscriptions & "U.S. 8c") omitted *450.00*
b. Tan (background) & lilac omitted *1,100.*

Many examples of No. 1501b are hinged. Value about one-half never hinged value.

1502 A916 15c **gray green & multicolored** .30 .20
P# block of 4 1.30 —
Margin block of 4, Mr. Zip and "Use Zip Code" 1.20 —
a. Black (inscriptions & "U.S. 15c") omitted *1,350.*
Nos. 1500-1502 (3) .70 .60

LYNDON B. JOHNSON ISSUE

Lyndon B. Johnson, 36th President (1908-1973) — A917

Designed by Bradbury Thompson, portrait by Elizabeth Shoumatoff.

PHOTOGRAVURE (Andreotti)

Plates of 128 subjects in four panes of 32 each.

1973, Aug. 27 **Tagged** ***Perf. 11***

1503 A917 8c **black & multicolored,** *Aug. 27* .20 .20
P# block of 12, 6# 1.90 —
a. Horiz. pair, imperf. vert. *350.00*

RURAL AMERICA ISSUE

[illegible]enary of the introduction of Aberdeen Angus [illegible] into the US (#1504); of the Chautauqua Institu[illegible] (#1505); and of the introduction of hard winter [illegible]t into Kansas by Mennonite immigrants (#1506).

Angus and Longhorn Cattle — A918

Chautauqua Tent and Buggies A919

Wheat Fields and Train — A920

No. 1504 modeled by Frank Waslick after painting by F. C. "Frank" Murphy. Nos. 1505-1506 designed by John Falter.

LITHOGRAPHED, ENGRAVED (Giori)

Plates of 200 subjects in four panes of 50.

1973-74 **Tagged** ***Perf. 11***

1504 A918 8c **multicolored,** *Oct. 5, 1973* .20 .20
P# block of 4 .65 —
Margin block of 4, Mr. Zip and "Use Zip Code" .60 —
a. Green & red brown omitted *950.00*
b. Vert. pair, imperf. between —
c. Tagging omitted —
1505 A919 10c **multicolored,** *Aug. 6, 1974* .20 .20
P# block of 4 .85 —
Margin block of 4, Mr. Zip and "Use Zip Code" .80 —
a. Black (litho.) omitted *2,000.*
b. Tagging omitted —
1506 A920 10c **multicolored,** *Aug. 16, 1974* .20 .20
P# block of 4 .85 —
Margin block of 4, Mr. Zip and "Use Zip Code" .80 —
a. Black and blue (engr.) omitted *700.00*
b. Tagging omitted —
Nos. 1504-1506 (3) .60 .60

CHRISTMAS ISSUE

Small Cowper Madonna, by Raphael — A921

Christmas Tree in Needlepoint — A922

Designers: No. 1507, Bradbury Thompson, using a painting in the National Gallery of Art, Washington, D.C. No. 1508, Dolli Tingle.

PHOTOGRAVURE (Andreotti)

Plates of 200 subjects in four panes of 50.

1973, Nov. 7 **Tagged** ***Perf. 10½x11***

1507 A921 8c **multicolored** .20 .20
P# block of 12, 6# 1.75 —
Margin block of 4, Mr. Zip and "Use Zip Code" .60 —
Pair with full vert. gutter btwn. —
1508 A922 8c **multicolored** .20 .20
P# block of 12, 6# 1.75 —

Margin block of 4, Mr. Zip and "Use Zip Code" .60 —
Pair with full horiz. gutter btwn. —
a. Vertical pair, imperf. between *300.00*

The tagging on Nos. 1507-1508 consists of a 20x12mm horizontal bar of phosphor.

50-Star and 13-Star Flags — A923

Jefferson Memorial and Signature — A924

Mail Transport — A925

Liberty Bell — A926

Designers: No. 1509, Ren Wicks. No. 1510, Dean Ellis. No. 1511, Randall McDougall. 6.3c, Frank Lionetti.

MULTICOLOR HUCK PRESS

Panes of 100 (10x10)

1973-74 Tagged *Perf. 11x10½*

1509 A923 10c **red & blue,** *Dec. 8, 1973* .20 .20
P# block of 20, 4-6#, 2-3 "Mail Early" and 2-3 "Use Zip Code" 4.25 —
a. Horizontal pair, imperf. between *50.00* —
b. Blue omitted *175.00* —
c. Imperf., vert. pair *900.00*
d. Horiz. pair, imperf., vert. *1,000.*
e. Tagging omitted *9.00*

ROTARY PRESS PRINTING

E.E. Plates of 400 subjects in four panes of 100.

1510 A924 10c **blue,** *Dec. 14, 1973* .20 .20
P# block of 4 .85 —
Margin block of 4, "Use Zip Codes" .80 —
a. Untagged (Bureau precanceled) 4.00 1.00
P# block of 4 50.00
Margin block of 4, "Use Zip Codes" 25.00
b. Booklet pane of 5 + label 1.65 *.90*
c. Booklet pane of 8 1.65 *1.00*
d. Booklet pane of 6, *Aug. 5, 1974* 5.25 *1.75*
e. Vert. pair, imperf. horiz. *525.00*
f. Vert. pair, imperf. between *700.00*
g. As No. 1510, tagging omitted (not Bureau precanceled) 5.00
h. As "c," tagging omitted —

Bureau Precancels: 10 different.

No. 1510f resulted from a paper foldover after perforating and before cutting into booklet panes.

PHOTOGRAVURE (Andreotti)

Plates of 400 subjects in four panes of 100.

1511 A925 10c **multicolored,** *Jan. 4, 1974* .20 .20
P# block of 8, 4# 1.75 —
Margin block of 4, "Use Zip Codes" .80 —
Pair with full horiz. gutter btwn. —
a. Yellow omitted *65.00*

Beware of copies with yellow chemically removed offered as No. 1511a.

COIL STAMPS

ROTARY PRESS PRINTING

1973-74 Tagged *Perf. 10 Vert.*

1518 A926 6.3c **brick red,** *Oct. 1, 1974* .20 .20
Pair .25 .20
Joint line pair .80 —
a. Untagged (Bureau precanceled) .35 .20
Pair .70 .30
Joint line pair 1.65 1.65
b. Imperf., pair *210.00*
Joint line pair *550.00*
c. As "a," imperf., pair *100.00*
Joint line pair *250.00*

A total of 129 different Bureau precancels were used by 117 cities.

No. 1518c is precanceled Washington, DC. Columbus, Ohio and Garden City, N.Y. values are higher.

MULTICOLOR HUCK PRESS

1519 A923 10c **red & blue,** *Dec. 8, 1973* .20 .20
Pair .40 .20
a. Imperf., pair 37.50

b. Tagging omitted *9.00*

ROTARY PRESS PRINTING

1520 A924 10c **blue,** *Dec. 14, 1973* .25 .20
Pair .50 .20
Joint line pair .75 —
a. Untagged (Bureau precanceled) 5.50 1.25
Pair 12.00 2.75
Joint line pair *185.00* —
b. Imperf., pair 40.00
Joint line pair 70.00

Bureau Precancels: No. 1520a, 14 diff.

VETERANS OF FOREIGN WARS ISSUE

75th anniversary of Veterans of Spanish-American and Other Foreign Wars.

Emblem and Initials of Veterans of Foreign Wars — A928

Designed by Robert Hallock.

GIORI PRESS PRINTING

Plates of 200 subjects in 4 plates of 50.

1974, Mar. 11 Tagged *Perf. 11*

1525 A928 10c **red & dark blue** .20 .20
P# block of 4 .85 —
Margin block of 4, Mr. Zip and "Use Zip Code" .80 —
a. Tagging omitted *15.00*
b. Blue missing (PS) —

ROBERT FROST ISSUE

Robert Frost (1873-1963), Poet — A929

Designed by Paul Calle; photograph by David Rhinelander.

ROTARY PRESS PRINTING

E.E. Plates of 200 subjects in four panes of 50.

1974, Mar. 26 Tagged *Perf. 10½x11*

1526 A929 10c **black** .20 .20
P# block of 4 .85 —
Margin block of 4, Mr. Zip and "Use Zip Code" .80 —

EXPO '74 WORLD'S FAIR ISSUE

EXPO '74 World's Fair "Preserve the Environment," Spokane, Wash., May 4-Nov. 4.

"Cosmic Jumper" and "Smiling Sage" — A930

Designed by Peter Max.

PHOTOGRAVURE (Andreotti)

Plates of 160 subjects in four panes of 40.

1974, Apr. 18 Tagged *Perf. 11*

1527 A930 10c **multicolored** .20 .20
On cover, Expo. station handstamp canc. 12.50
P# block of 12, 6# 2.50 —
Margin block of 4, Mr. Zip, "Use Zip Code" and "Mail Early in the Day" .80 —
P# block of 16, 6#, Mr. Zip and slogans 3.40 —

HORSE RACING ISSUE

Kentucky Derby, Churchill Downs, centenary.

Horses Rounding Turn — A931

Designed by Henry Koehler.

PHOTOGRAVURE (Andreotti)

Plates of 200 subjects in four panes of 50.

1974, May 4 Tagged *Perf. 11x10½*

1528 A931 10c **yellow & multicolored** .25 .20
P# block of 12, 6# 3.50 —
Margin block of 4, Mr. Zip and "Use Zip Code" 1.10 —
a. Blue ("Horse Racing") omitted *875.00*
b. Red ("U.S. postage 10 cents") omitted —
c. Tagging omitted —

Beware of stamps offered as No. 1528b that have traces of red.

SKYLAB ISSUE

First anniversary of the launching of Skylab I, honoring all who participated in the Skylab project.

Skylab — A932

Designed by Robert T. McCall.

LITHOGRAPHED, ENGRAVED (Giori)

Plates of 200 subjects in four panes of 50.

1974, May 14 Tagged *Perf. 11*

1529 A932 10c **multicolored** .20 .20
P# block of 4 .85 —
Margin block of 4, Mr. Zip and "Use Zip Code" .80 —
a. Vert. pair, imperf. between —
b. Tagging omitted *10.00*

UNIVERSAL POSTAL UNION ISSUE

UPU cent. In the 1st row Nos. 1530-1537 are in sequence as listed. In the 2nd row Nos. 1534-1537 are followed by Nos. 1530-1533. Every row of 8 and every horizontal block of 8 contains all 8 designs. The letter writing designs are from famous works of art; some are details. The quotation on every second stamp, "Letters mingle souls," is from a letter by poet John Donne.

Michelangelo, from "School of Athens," by Raphael, 1509 — A933

"Five Feminine Virtues," by Hokusai, c. 1811 — A934

Inkwell and Quill, from "Boy with a Top," by Jean-Baptiste Simeon Chardin, 1738 — A938

"Old Scraps," by John Fredrick Peto, 1894 — A935

Mrs. John Douglas, by Thomas Gainsborough, 1784 — A939

"The Lovely Reader," by Jean Etienne Liotard, 1746 — A936

Don Antonio Noriega, by Francisco de Goya, 1801 — A940

"Lady Writing Letter," by Gerard Terborch, 1654 — A937

Designed by Bradbury Thompson.

PHOTOGRAVURE (Andreotti)

Plates of 128 subjects in four panes of 32 each.

1974, June 6		**Tagged**		***Perf. 11***	
1530	A933	10c	**multicolored**	.20	.20
1531	A934	10c	**multicolored**	.20	.20
1532	A935	10c	**multicolored**	.20	.20
1533	A936	10c	**multicolored**	.20	.20
1534	A937	10c	**multicolored**	.20	.20
1535	A938	10c	**multicolored**	.20	.20
1536	A939	10c	**multicolored**	.20	.20
1537	A940	10c	**multicolored**	.20	.20
a.	Block or strip of 8 (#1530-1537)			1.75	1.60
	P# block of 16, 5#, "Mail Early in the Day," Mr. Zip and "Use Zip Code"			3.50	—
	P# block of 10, 5#; no slogans			2.25	—
b.	As "a," (block), imperf. vert.			*7,000.*	

MINERAL HERITAGE ISSUE

The sequence of stamps in 1st horizontal row is Nos. 1538-1541, 1538-1539. In 2nd row Nos. 1540-1541 are followed by Nos. 1538-1541.

Petrified Wood A941

Tourmaline A942

Amethyst A943

Rhodochrosite — A944

Designed by Leonard F. Buckley.

LITHOGRAPHED, ENGRAVED (Giori)

Plates of 192 subjects in four panes of 48 (6x8).

1974, June 13		**Tagged**		***Perf. 11***	
1538	A941	10c	**blue & multicolored**	.20	.20
a.	Light blue & yellow omitted			—	
1539	A942	10c	**blue & multicolored**	.20	.20
a.	Light blue omitted			—	
b.	Black & purple omitted			—	
1540	A943	10c	**blue & multicolored**	.20	.20
a.	Light blue & yellow omitted			—	
1541	A944	10c	**blue & multicolored**	.20	.20
a.	Block or strip of 4, #1538-1541			.80	.90
	P# block of 4			.90	—
	Margin block of 4, Mr. Zip and "Use Zip Code"			.85	—
b.	As "a," light blue & yellow omitted			*1,900.*	—
c.	Light blue omitted			—	
d.	Black & red omitted			—	
e.	As "a," tagging omitted			—	

KENTUCKY SETTLEMENT, 150th ANNIV.
Fort Harrod, first settlement in Kentucky.

Covered Wagons at Fort Harrod — A945

Designed by David K. Stone.

LITHOGRAPHED, ENGRAVED (Giori)
Plates of 200 subjects in four panes of 50.

1974, June 15 **Tagged** ***Perf. 11***

1542 A945 10c **green & multicolored** .20 .20
P# block of 4 .85 —
Margin block of 4, Mr. Zip and "Use Zip Code" .80 —
a. Dull black (litho.) omitted *750.00*
b. Green (engr. & litho.), black (engr. & litho.) & blue missing (EP) *3,000.*
c. Green (engr.) missing (EP) —
d. Green (engr.) & black (litho.) missing (EP) —
e. Tagging omitted —
f. Blue (litho.) omitted —

No. 1542f was caused by an occurrence that seems to be unique for U.S. total color omitted/missing errors. According to the BEP, oil on the printing blanket made a small area unreceptive to the blue ink. No blue at all was printed on one unique error stamp.

AMERICAN REVOLUTION BICENTENNIAL ISSUE
First Continental Congress

Nos. 1543-1544 alternate in 1st row, Nos. 1545-1546 in 2nd row. This arrangement is repeated throughout the pane.

Carpenters' Hall, Philadelphia A946

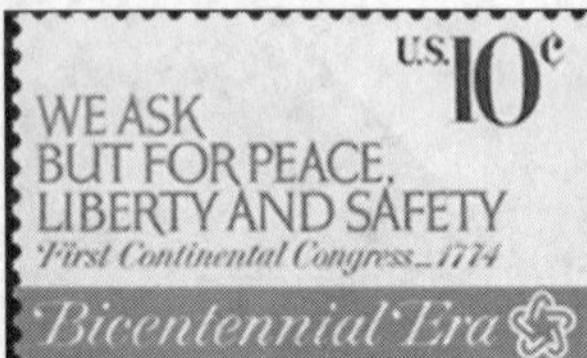

"We ask but for peace . . ." A947

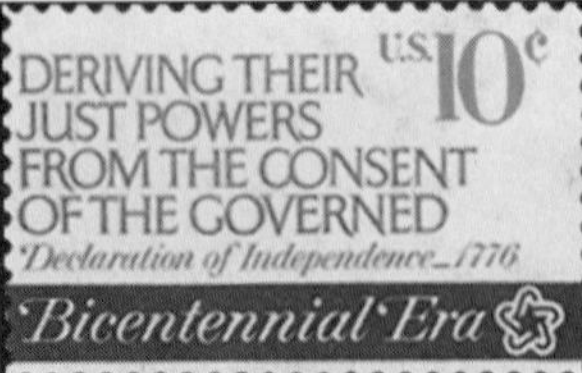

"Deriving their just powers . . ." A948

Independence Hall — A949

Designed by Frank P. Conley

GIORI PRESS PRINTING
Plates of 200 subjects in four panes of 50.

1974, July 4 **Tagged** ***Perf. 11***

1543 A946 10c **dark blue & red** .20 .20
1544 A947 10c **gray, dark blue & red** .20 .20
1545 A948 10c **gray, dark blue & red** .20 .20
1546 A949 10c **red & dark blue** .20 .20
a. Block of 4, #1543-1546 .80 .90
P# block of 4 .90 —
Margin block of 4, Mr. Zip and "Use Zip Code" .85 —
b. As "a," tagging omitted *60.00*

Margin includes Bicentennial Commission emblem and inscription.

ENERGY CONSERVATION ISSUE

Publicizing the importance of conserving all forms of energy.

Molecules and Drops of Gasoline and Oil — A950

Designed by Robert W. Bode.

LITHOGRAPHED, ENGRAVED (Giori)
Plates of 200 subjects in four panes of 50.

1974, Sept. 23 **Tagged** ***Perf. 11***

1547 A950 10c **multicolored** .20 .20
P# block of 4 .85 —
Margin block of 4, Mr. Zip and "Use Zip Code" .80 —
a. Blue & orange omitted *850.00*
b. Orange & green omitted *600.00*
c. Green omitted *825.00*
d. Tagging omitted 7.50

AMERICAN FOLKLORE ISSUE
Legend of Sleepy Hollow

The Headless Horseman in pursuit of Ichabod Crane from "Legend of Sleepy Hollow," by Washington Irving.

Headless Horseman and Ichabod A951

Designed by Leonard Everett Fisher.

LITHOGRAPHED, ENGRAVED (Giori)
Plates of 200 subjects in four panes of 50.

1974, Oct. 12 **Tagged** ***Perf. 11***

1548 A951 10c **dk. bl., blk., org. & yel.** .20 .20
P# block of 4 .85 —
Margin block of 4, Mr. Zip and "Use Zip Code" .80 —
a. Tagging omitted —

RETARDED CHILDREN ISSUE

Retarded Children Can Be Helped, theme of annual convention of the National Association of Retarded Citizens.

Retarded Child — A952

Designed by Paul Calle.

GIORI PRESS PRINTING
Plates of 200 subjects in four panes of 50.

1974, Oct. 12 **Tagged** ***Perf. 11***

1549 A952 10c **brown red & dark brown** .20 .20
P# block of 4 .85 —
Margin block of 4, Mr. Zip and "Use Zip Code" .80 —
a. Tagging omitted 7.50

CHRISTMAS ISSUE

Angel — A953

"The Road-Winter," by Currier and Ives — A954

Dove Weather Vane atop Mount Vernon — A955

Designers: No. 1550, Bradbury Thompson, using detail from the Pérussis altarpiece painted by anonymous French artist, 1480, in Metropolitan Museum of Art, New York City. No. 1551, Stevan Dohanos, using Currier and Ives print from drawing by Otto Knirsch. No. 1552, Don Hedin and Robert Geissman.

PHOTOGRAVURE (Andreotti)
Plates of 200 subjects in four panes of 50.

1974, Oct. 23 **Tagged** ***Perf. 10½x11***

1550 A953 10c **multicolored** .20 .20
P# block of 10, 5# 2.10 —
Margin block of 4, Mr. Zip and "Use Zip Code" .80 —

Perf. 11x10½

1551 A954 10c **multicolored** .20 .20
P# block of 12, 6# 2.50 —
Margin block of 4, Mr. Zip and "Use Zip Code" .80 —
a. Buff omitted 35.00

No. 1551a is difficult to identify. Competent expertization is necessary.

Die Cut, Paper Backing Rouletted

1974, Nov. 15 **Untagged**

Self-adhesive; Inscribed "Precanceled"

1552 A955 10c **multicolored** .20 .20
P# block of 20, 6#, 5 slogans 4.25
P# block of 12, 6#, 5 different slogans 2.60
Nos. 1550-1552 (3) .60 .60

Unused value of No. 1552 is for copy on rouletted paper backing as issued. Used value is for copy on piece, with or without postmark. **Most copies are becoming discolored, probably from the adhesive. The Catalogue value is for discolored copies.**

Die cutting includes crossed slashes through dove, applied to prevent removal and re-use of the stamp. The stamp will separate into layers if soaked.

Two different machines were used to roulette the sheet.

AMERICAN ARTS ISSUE

Benjamin West (1738-1820), painter (No. 1553); Paul Laurence Dunbar (1872-1906), poet (No. 1554); David (Lewelyn) Wark Griffith (1875-1948), motion picture producer (No. 1555).

Self-portrait — A956

A957

A958

Designers: No. 1553, Bradbury Thompson; No. 1554, Walter D. Richards; No. 1555, Fred Otnes.

PHOTOGRAVURE (Andreotti)
Plates of 200 subjects in four panes of 50.

1975 **Tagged** ***Perf. 10½x11***

1553 A956 10c **multicolored,** *Feb. 10* .20 .20
P# block of 10, 5# 2.10 —
Margin block of 4, Mr. Zip and "Use Zip Code" .80 —

Perf. 11

1554 A957 10c **multicolored,** *May 1* .20 .20
P# block of 10, 5# 2.10 —
Margin block of 4, Mr. Zip and "Use Zip Code" .80 —
a. Imperf., pair *1,300.*

LITHOGRAPHED, ENGRAVED (Giori)

Perf. 11

1555 A958 10c **brown & multicolored,** *May 27* .20 .20
P# block of 4 .85 —
Margin block of 4, Mr. Zip and "Use Zip Code" .80 —
a. Brown (engr.) omitted *625.00*
Nos. 1553-1555 (3) .60 .60

SPACE ISSUES

US space accomplishments with unmanned craft. Pioneer 10 passed within 81,000 miles of Jupiter, Dec. 10, 1973. Mariner 10 explored Venus and Mercury in 1974 and Mercury again in 1975.

Pioneer 10 Passing Jupiter A959

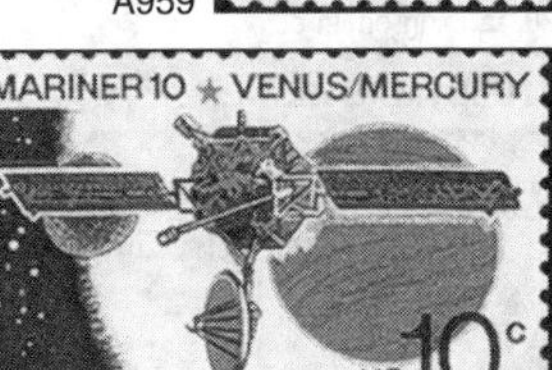

Mariner 10, Venus and Mercury A960

Designed by Robert McCall (No. 1556); Roy Gjertson (No. 1557).

LITHOGRAPHED, ENGRAVED (Giori)
Plates of 200 subjects in four panes of 50.

1975 **Tagged** ***Perf. 11***

1556 A959 10c **light yellow, dark yellow, red, blue & 2 dark blues** *Feb. 28* .20 .20
P# block of 4 .85 —
Margin block of 4, Mr. Zip and "Use Zip Code" .80 —
a. Red & dark yellow omitted *1,400.*
b. Dark blues (engr.) omitted *950.00*
c. Tagging omitted *9.00*
d. Dark yellow omitted —

Imperfs. exist from printer's waste.

1557 A960 10c **black, red, ultra. & bister,** *Apr. 4* .20 .20
P# block of 4 .85 —
Margin block of 4, Mr. Zip and "Use Zip Code" .80 —
a. Red omitted *450.00* —
b. Ultramarine & bister omitted *2,000.*
c. Tagging omitted *9.00*
d. Red missing (PS) —

COLLECTIVE BARGAINING ISSUE

Collective Bargaining law, enacted 1935, in Wagner Act.

"Labor and Management" A961

Designed by Robert Hallock.

PHOTOGRAVURE (Andreotti)
Plates of 200 subjects in four panes of 50.

1975, Mar. 13 **Tagged** ***Perf. 11***

1558 A961 10c **multicolored** .20 .20
P# block of 8, 4# 1.75 —
Margin block of 4, Mr. Zip and "Use Zip Code" .80 —

Imperforates exist from printer's waste.

AMERICAN BICENTENNIAL ISSUE

Contributors to the Cause

Sybil Ludington, age 16, rallied militia, Apr. 26, 1777; Salem Poor, black freeman, fought in Battle of Bunker Hill; Haym Salomon, Jewish immigrant, raised money to finance Revolutionary War; Peter Francisco, Portuguese-French immigrant, joined Continental Army at 15. Emerald inscription on back, printed beneath gum in water-soluble ink, gives thumbnail sketch of portrayed contributor.

Sybil Ludington A962

Salem Poor — A963

Haym Salomon A964

Peter Francisco A965

Designed by Neil Boyle.

PHOTOGRAVURE (Andreotti)
Plates of 200 subjects in four panes of 50.

1975, Mar. 25 **Tagged** ***Perf. 11x10½***

1559 A962 8c **multicolored** .20 .20
P# block of 10, 5# 1.50 —
Margin block of 4, Mr. Zip and "Use Zip Code" .65 —
a. Back inscriptions omitted *210.00*

1560 A963 10c **multicolored** .20 .20
P# block of 10, 5# 2.10 —
Margin block of 4, Mr. Zip and "Use Zip Code" .80 —
a. Back inscription omitted *210.00*

1561 A964 10c **multicolored** .20 .20
P# block of 10, 5# 2.10 —
Margin block of 4, Mr. Zip and "Use Zip Code" .80 —
a. Back inscription omitted *210.00*
b. Red omitted *250.00*

1562 A965 18c **multicolored** .35 .20
P# block of 10, 5# 3.60 —
Margin block of 4, Mr. Zip and "Use Zip Code" 1.45 —
Nos. 1559-1562 (4) .95 .80

Lexington-Concord Battle, 200th Anniv.

"Birth of Liberty," by Henry Sandham A966

Designed by Bradbury Thompson.

PHOTOGRAVURE (Andreotti)
Plates of 160 subjects in four panes of 40.

1975, Apr. 19 **Tagged** ***Perf. 11***

1563 A966 10c **multicolored** .20 .20
P# block of 12, 6# 2.50 —
Margin block of 4, Mr. Zip, "Use Zip Code" and "Mail Early in the Day" .80 —
P# block of 16, 6 P#, Mr. Zip and slogans 3.40 —
a. Vert. pair, imperf. horiz. *425.00*

Bunker Hill Battle, 200th Anniv.

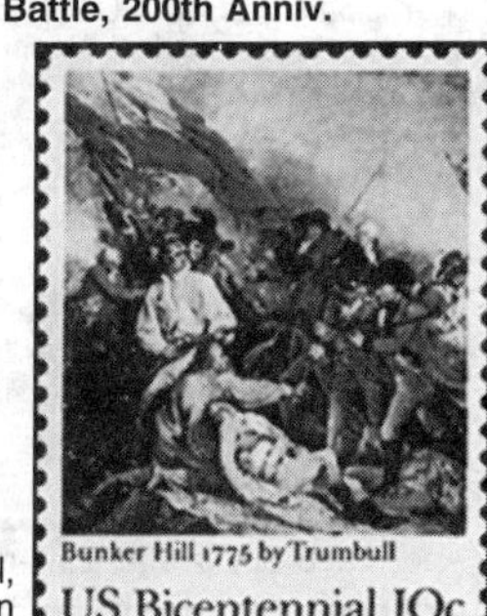

Battle of Bunker Hill, by John Trumbull — A967

Designed by Bradbury Thompson.

PHOTOGRAVURE (Andreotti)
Plates of 160 subjects in four panes of 40.

1975, June 17 **Tagged** ***Perf. 11***

1564 A967 10c **multicolored** .20 .20
P# block of 12, 6# 2.50 —
Margin block of 4, Mr. Zip, "Use Zip Code" and "Mail Early in the Day" .80 —
P# block of 16, 6#, Mr. Zip and slogans 3.40 —

Military Uniforms

Bicentenary of US Military Services. Nos. 1565-1566 alternate in one row, Nos. 1567-1568 in next row.

Soldier with Flintlock Musket, Uniform Button — A968

Sailor with Grappling Hook, First Navy Jack, 1775 — A969

Marine with Musket, Fullrigged Ship — A970

Militiaman with Musket and Powder Horn — A971

Designed by Edward Vebell.

PHOTOGRAVURE (Andreotti)
Plates of 200 subjects in four panes of 50.

1975, July 4 Tagged *Perf. 11*

1565	A968	10c	**multicolored**	.20	.20
1566	A969	10c	**multicolored**	.20	.20
1567	A970	10c	**multicolored**	.20	.20
1568	A971	10c	**multicolored**	.20	.20
a.			Block of 4, #1565-1568	.85	.90
			P# block of 12, 6#	2.50	—
			P# block of 20, 6#, Mr. Zip and slogans	4.50	—
			Margin block of 4, Mr. Zip and "Use Zip Code"	1.00	—

APOLLO SOYUZ SPACE ISSUE

Apollo Soyuz space test project, Russo-American cooperation, launched July 15; link-up, July 17. Nos. In the 1st row, No. 1569 is in 1st and 3rd space, No. 1570 is 2nd space; in the 2nd row No. 1570 is in 1st and 3rd space, No. 1569 in 2nd space, etc.

Participating US and USSR crews: Thomas P. Stafford, Donald K. Slayton, Vance D. Brand, Aleksei A. Leonov, Valery N. Kubasov.

Apollo and Soyuz after Link-up, and Earth — A972

Spacecraft before Link-up, Earth and Project Emblem — A973

Illustrations reduced.

Designed by Robert McCall (No. 1569) and Anatoly M. Aksamit of USSR (No. 1570).

PHOTOGRAVURE (Andreotti)
Plates of 96 subjects in four panes of 24 each.

1975, July 15 Tagged *Perf. 11*

1569	A972	10c	**multicolored**	.20	.20
			Pair with full horiz. gutter btwn.	—	
1570	A973	10c	**multicolored**	.20	.20
a.			Pair, #1569-1570	.45	.40
			P# block of 12, 6#	2.50	—
			Margin block of 4, Mr. Zip, "Use Zip Code"	.85	—
			P# block of 16, 6#, Mr. Zip, "Use Zip Code"	3.40	—
			Pair with full horiz. gutter btwn.	—	
b.			As "a," tagging omitted	*30.00*	—
c.			As "a," vert. pair imperf. horiz.	*2,150.*	
d.			As "a," yellow omitted	—	

Nos. 1569-1570 totally imperforate are printer's waste.
See Russia Nos. 4339-4340.

INTERNATIONAL WOMEN'S YEAR ISSUE

International Women's Year 1975.

Worldwide Equality for Women A974

Designed by Miriam Schottland.

PHOTOGRAVURE (Andreotti)
Plates of 200 subjects in four panes of 50.

1975, Aug. 26 Tagged *Perf. 11x10½*

1571	A974	10c	**blue, orange & dark blue**	.20	.20
			P# block of 6, 3#	1.30	—
			Margin block of 4, Mr. Zip and "Use Zip Code"	.80	—
a.			Tagging omitted		—

US POSTAL SERVICE BICENTENNIAL ISSUE

Nos. 1572-1573 alternate in 1st row, Nos. 1574-1575 in 2nd row. This arrangement is repeated throughout the pane.

Stagecoach and Trailer Truck — A975

Old and New Locomotives A976

Early Mail Plane and Jet — A977

Satellite for Transmission of Mailgrams A978

Designed by James L. Womer.

PHOTOGRAVURE (Andreotti)
Plates of 200 subjects in four panes of 50.

1975, Sept. 3 Tagged *Perf. 11x10½*

1572	A975	10c	**multicolored**	.20	.20
1573	A976	10c	**multicolored**	.20	.20
1574	A977	10c	**multicolored**	.20	.20
1575	A978	10c	**multicolored**	.20	.20
a.			Block of 4, #1572-1575	.85	.90
			P# block of 12, 6#	2.50	—
			P# block of 20, 6#, Mr. Zip and slogans	4.50	—
			Margin block of 4, Mr. Zip and "Use Zip Code"	1.00	—
b.			As "a," red "10c" omitted	*9,500.*	

WORLD PEACE THROUGH LAW ISSUE

A prelude to 7th World Law Conference of the World Peace Through Law Center at Washington, D.C., Oct. 12-17.

Law Book, Gavel, Olive Branch and Globe — A979

Designed by Melbourne Brindle.

GIORI PRESS PRINTING
Plates of 200 subjects in four panes of 50.

1975, Sept. 29 Tagged *Perf. 11*

1576	A979	10c	**green, Prussian blue & rose brown**	.20	.20
			P# block of 4	.85	—
			Margin block of 4, Mr. Zip and "Use Zip Code"	.80	—
a.			Tagging omitted	8.00	
b.			Horiz. pair, imperf vert.	—	

BANKING AND COMMERCE ISSUE

Banking and commerce in the U.S., and for the Centennial Convention of the American Bankers Association.

Designed by V. Jack Ruther.

Engine Turning, Indian Head Penny, Morgan-type Silver Dollar — A980

Seated Liberty Quarter, $20 Gold Double Eagle and Engine Turning A981

LITHOGRAPHED, ENGRAVED (Giori)
Plates of 160 subjects in four panes of 40.

1975, Oct. 6 Tagged *Perf. 11*

1577	A980	10c	**multicolored**	.25	.20
1578	A981	10c	**multicolored**	.25	.20
a.			Pair, #1577-1578	.50	.40
			P# block of 4	1.20	—
			Margin block of 4, Mr. Zip and "Use Zip Code"	1.00	—
b.			As "a," brown & blue (litho) omitted	*2,000.*	
c.			As "a," brown, blue & yellow (litho) omitted	*2,500.*	
d.			As No. 1578, tagging omitted		—

CHRISTMAS ISSUE

Madonna and Child, by Domenico Ghirlandaio — A982

Christmas Card, by Louis Prang, 1878 — A983

Designed by Stevan Dohanos.

PHOTOGRAVURE (Andreotti)
Plates of 200 subjects in four panes of 50.

1975, Oct. 14 **Tagged** ***Perf. 11***

1579 A982 (10c) **multicolored** .20 .20
P# block of 12, 6# 2.50 —
Margin block of 4, Mr. Zip and "Use Zip Code" .80 —
a. Imperf., pair *90.00*
Plate flaw ("d" damaged) (36741-36746 LL 47) 5.00 —

Perf. 11.2

1580 A983 (10c) **multicolored** .20 .20
P# block of 12, 6# 2.50 —
Margin block of 4, Mr. Zip and "Use Zip Code" .80 —
a. Imperf., pair *90.00*
c. Perf. 10.9 .25 .20
P# block of 12, 6# 3.50 —
Margin block of 4, Mr. Zip and "Use Zip Code" 1.00 —

Perf. 10.5x11.3

1580B A983 (10c) **multicolored,** .65 .20
P# block of 12, 6# 15.00 —
Margin block of 4, Mr. Zip and "Use Zip Code" 2.75 —

AMERICANA ISSUE

Inkwell and Quill — A984

Speaker's Stand — A985

Early Ballot Box — A987

Books, Bookmark, Eyeglasses — A988

Dome of Capitol — A994

Contemplation of Justice, by J. E. Fraser — A995

Early American Printing Press — A996

Torch, Statue of Liberty — A997

Liberty Bell — A998

Eagle and Shield — A999

Fort McHenry Flag (15 Stars) — A1001

Head, Statue of Liberty — A1002

Old North Church, Boston — A1003

Fort Nisqually, Wash. — A1004

Sandy Hook Lighthouse, NJ — A1005

Morris Township School No. 2, Devils Lake, ND — A1006

Iron "Betty" Lamp, Plymouth Colony, 17th-18th Centuries — A1007

Rush Lamp and Candle Holder — A1008

Kerosene Table Lamp — A1009

Railroad Conductor's Lantern, c. 1850 — A1010

Designed by: 2c, 4c, 15c, V. Jack Ruther Robert Hallock. 3c, Clarence Holbert. 9c, 10c, 11c, Walter Brooks. 12c, George Mercer. No. 1595, Bernard Glassman. No. 1596, James L. Womer.

ROTARY PRESS PRINTING
E.E. Plates of 400 subjects in four panes of 100.

1975-81 **Tagged** ***Perf. 11x10½***

Size: 18½x22½mm

1581 A984 1c **dark blue,** *greenish,* shiny gum, *Dec. 8, 1977* .20 .20
P# block of 4 .25 —
Margin block of 4, "Use Zip Code" .20 —
Dull gum .20
P# block of 4 .50
Zip block of 4 .20
Pair with full vert. gutter btwn. —
a. Untagged (Bureau precanceled) 4.50 1.50
P# block of 4 22.50
Margin block of 4, "Use Zip Codes" 18.50
c. White paper, dull gum — —
d. Tagging omitted (not Bureau precanceled) 4.50

1582 A985 2c **red brown,** *greenish,* shiny gum, *Dec. 8, 1977* .20 .20
P# block of 4 .25 —
Margin block of 4, "Use Zip Code" .20 —
Dull gum .20
P# block of 4 2.50
Zip block of 4 .50
a. Untagged (Bureau precanceled) 4.50 1.50
P# block of 4 22.50
Zip block of 4 18.50
b. Cream paper, dull gum, *1981* .20 .20
P# block of 4 .25
Zip block of 4 .20
c. Tagging omitted (not Bureau precanceled) 4.50

1584 A987 3c **olive,** *greenish,* shiny gum, *Dec. 8, 1977* .20 .20
P# block of 4 .30 —
Margin block of 4, "Use Zip Code" .25 —
Dull gum .20
P# block of 4 .50
Zip block of 4 .30
Pair with full horiz. gutter btwn. —
a. Untagged (Bureau precanceled) .75 .50
P# block of 4 9.50
Zip block of 4 5.00
b. Tagging omitted (not Bureau precanceled) 7.50

Values for No. 1584a are for the bars-only precancel. Also known with city precancels, and worth more thus.

1585 A988 4c **rose magenta,** *cream,* shiny gum, *Dec. 8, 1977* .20 .20
P# block of 4 .40 —
Margin block of 4, "Use Zip Code" .35 —
Dull gum .20
P# block of 4 1.10
Zip block of 4 .65
a. Untagged (Bureau precanceled) 1.05 .75
P# block of 4 13.50
Zip block of 4 6.00
b. Tagging omitted (not Bureau precanceled), dull gum *25.00*
Shiny gum *25.00*

Values for No. 1585a are for the bars-only precancel. Also known with city precancels, and worth more thus.

Size: 17½x20½mm

1590 A994 9c **slate green** (from bklt. pane #1623a), *Mar. 11, 1977* .45 .20

Perf. 10x9¾

1590A A994 9c **slate green** (from bklt. pane #1623Bc), *Mar. 11, 1977* 20.00 15.00

Size: 18½x22½mm

Perf. 11x10½

1591 A994 9c **slate green,** *gray,* shiny gum, *Nov. 24, 1975* .20 .20
P# block of 4 .85 —
Margin block of 4, "Use Zip Code" .80 —
Dull gum 1.00
P# block of 4 5.00
Zip block of 4 4.25
a. Untagged (Bureau precanceled) 1.75 1.00
P# block of 4 50.00
Zip block of 4 11.50
b. Tagging omitted (not Bureau precanceled) 5.00

Values for No. 1591a are for the bars-only precancel. Also known with city precancels, and worth more thus.

1592 A995 10c **violet,** *gray,* shiny gum, *Nov. 17, 1977* .20 .20
P# block of 4 .90 —
Margin block of 4, "Use Zip Code" .80 —
Dull gum .20
P# block of 4 .90
Zip block of 4 .80
a. Untagged (Bureau precanceled, Chicago) 9.50 5.00
P# block of 4 95.00
Zip block of 4 42.50
b. Tagging omitted (not Bureau precanceled) 7.50

1593 A996 11c **orange,** *gray, Nov. 13, 1975* .20 .20
P# block of 4 .90 —
Margin block of 4, "Use Zip Code" .85 —
Pair with full horiz. gutter btwn. —
a. Tagging omitted 4.00

1594 A997 12c **red brown,** *beige, Apr. 8, 1981* .25 .20
P# block of 4 1.60 —
Zip block of 4 1.10 —
a. Tagging omitted 5.00

1595 A998 13c **brown** (from bklt. pane), *Oct. 31, 1975* .30 .20
a. Booklet pane of 6 2.25 *1.00*
b. Booklet pane of 7 + label 2.25 *1.00*
c. Booklet pane of 8 2.25 *1.00*
d. Booklet pane of 5 + label, *Apr. 2, 1976* 1.75 *1.00*
e. Vert. pair, imperf. btwn. *800.00*
f. Tagging omitted —

No. 1595e resulted from a paper foldover after perforating and before cutting into panes. Beware of printer's waste consisting of complete panes with perfs around all outside edges.

PHOTOGRAVURE (Andreotti)
Plates of 400 subjects in four panes of 100.
Perf. 11.2

1596 A999 13c **multicolored,** *Dec. 1, 1975* .25 .20
P# block of 12, 6# 3.25 —
P# block of 20, 6# and slogans 5.50 —
Margin block of 4, "Use Zip Code" 1.00 —
Pair with full horiz. gutter btwn. *150.00*
a. Imperf., pair *50.00* —
b. Yellow omitted *160.00*
d. Line perforated *27.50* —
P# block of 12, 6# *375.00* —

On No. 1596 the entire sheet is perforated at one time so the perforations meet perfectly at the corners of the stamp. On No. 1596d the perforations do not line up perfectly and are perf. 11.

ENGRAVED (Combination Press)
Plates of 460 subjects (20x23) in panes of 100 (10x10)

1597 A1001 15c **gray, dark blue & red,** *June 30, 1978* .30 .20
P# block of 6 1.90 —
P# block of 20, 1-2# 6.50 —
a. Imperf., vert. pair *20.00*
b. Gray omitted *600.00*
c. Vert. strip of 3, imperf. btwn. and at top or bottom —
d. Tagging omitted 3.00

Plate number appears 3 times on each plate of 23 rows. With no separating gutters, each pane has only left or right sheet margin. Plate numbers appear on both margins; there are no slogans.

ENGRAVED
Perf. 11x10½

1598 A1001 15c **gray, dark blue & red** (from bklt. pane), *June 30, 1978* .40 .20
a. Booklet pane of 8 4.25 *.80*
1599 A1002 16c **blue,** *Mar. 31, 1978* .35 .20
P# block of 4 1.90 —
Margin block of 4, "Use Correct Zip Code" 1.40 —
1603 A1003 24c **red,** *blue, Nov. 14, 1975* .50 .20
P# block of 4 2.25 —
Margin block of 4, "Use Zip Code" 2.00 —
a. Tagging omitted 7.50
1604 A1004 28c **brown,** *blue,* shiny gum, *Aug. 11, 1978* .55 .20
P# block of 4 2.40 —
Margin block of 4, "Use Correct Zip Code" 2.25 —
Dull gum 1.10
P# block of 4 10.00
Zip block of 4 5.00
1605 A1005 29c **blue,** *light blue,* shiny gum, *Apr. 14, 1978* .60 .20
P# block of 4 3.00 —
Margin block of 4, "Use Correct Zip Code" 2.40 —
Dull gum 2.00
P# block of 4 15.00
Zip block of 4 9.00
1606 A1006 30c **green,** *blue, Aug. 27, 1979* .55 .20
P# block of 4 2.40 —
Margin block of 4, "Use Correct Zip Code" 2.25 —
a. Tagging omitted 15.00

LITHOGRAPHED AND ENGRAVED
Perf. 11

1608 A1007 50c **tan, black & orange,** *Sept. 11, 1979* .85 .20
P# block of 4 3.75 —
Margin block of 4, "Use Correct Zip Code" 3.50 —
a. Black omitted *300.00*
b. Vert. pair, imperf. horiz. *1,750.*
c. Tagging omitted 11.00

Beware of examples offered as No. 1608b that have blind perfs.

1610 A1008 $1 **tan, brown, orange & yellow,** *July 2, 1979* 2.00 .20
P# block of 4 8.50 —
Margin block of 4, "Use Correct Zip Code" 8.00 —
Pair with full vert. gutter btwn. —
a. Brown (engraved) omitted *225.00*
b. Tan, orange & yellow omitted *275.00*
c. Brown inverted *20,000.*
d. Tagging omitted *15.00*
1611 A1009 $2 **tan, dark green, orange & yellow,** *Nov. 16, 1978* 3.75 .75
P# block of 4 16.00 —
Margin block of 4, "Use Correct Zip Code" 15.00 —
a. Tagging omitted —
1612 A1010 $5 **tan, red brown, yellow & orange,** *Aug. 23, 1979* 8.50 1.75
P# block of 4 36.00 —
Margin block of 4, "Use Correct Zip Code" 34.00 —
Nos. 1581-1612 (23) 41.00 21.50

Nos. 1590, 1590A, 1595, 1598, 1623 and 1623b were issued only in booklets. All stamps have one or two straight edges.

Bureau Precancels: 1c, 3 diff., 2c, Chicago, Greensboro, NC, 3c, 6 diff., 4c, Chicago, lines only, No. 1591a, 4 diff., No. 1596, 5 diff., 30c, lines only, 50c, 2 spacings, lines only, $1, 2 spacings, lines only. The 30c, 50c, $1 and No. 1596 are precanceled on tagged stamps.

Six-string Guitar — A1011

Saxhorns — A1012

Drum — A1013

Steinway Grand Piano, 1857 — A1014

Designers: 3.1c, George Mercer. 7.7c, Susan Robb. 7.9c, Bernard Glassman. 10c, Walter Brooks. 15c, V. Jack Ruther.

COIL STAMPS
ENGRAVED

1975-79 ***Perf. 10 Vertically***

1613 A1011 3.1c **brown,** *yellow, Oct. 25, 1979* .20 .20
Pair .25 .20
Joint line pair 1.25 —
a. Untagged (Bureau precanceled, lines only) .35 .35
Pair .70 .70
Joint line pair 5.25 —
b. Imperf., pair *1,400.*
Joint line pair *3,600.*
1614 A1012 7.7c **brown,** *bright yellow, Nov. 20, 1976* .20 .20
Pair .40 .20
Joint line pair .90 —
a. Untagged (Bureau precanceled) .40 .30
Pair .80 .60
Joint line pair 3.25 —
b. As "a," imperf., pair *1,600.*
Joint line pair *4,250.*

A total of 160 different Bureau precancels were used by 153 cities.

No. 1614b is precanceled Washington, DC. Also exists from Marion, OH.

1615 A1013 7.9c **carmine,** *yellow,* shiny gum, *Apr. 23, 1976* .20 .20
Pair .40 .20
Joint line pair .75 —
Dull gum .35
Pair .70
Joint line pair 1.50
a. Untagged (Bureau precanceled), shiny gum .40 .40
Pair .80 .80
Joint line pair 2.75 —
Dull gum .45
Pair .90
Joint line pair 4.50
b. Imperf., pair *600.00*

A total of 109 different Bureau precancels were used by 107 cities plus CAR. RT./SORT.

1615C A1014 8.4c **dark blue,** *yellow,* shiny gum, *July 13, 1978* .20 .20
Pair .40 .20
Joint line pair 3.25 .30
d. Untagged (Bureau precanceled), shiny gum .50 .40
Pair 1.00 .80
Joint line pair 4.25 —
Dull gum .40
Pair .80
Joint line pair 3.25
e. As "d," pair, imperf. between 60.00
Joint line pair 125.00
f. As "d," imperf., pair 17.50
Joint line pair 35.00

A total of 145 different Bureau precancels were used by 144 cities.

No. 1615Ce is precanceled with lines only. No. 1615Cf is precanceled Newark, NJ. Also exists from Brownstown, Ind., Oklahoma City, Okla. and with lines only.

1616 A994 9c **slate green,** *gray, Mar. 5, 1976* .20 .20
Pair .40 .20
Joint line pair .90 —
a. Imperf., pair *160.00*
Joint line pair *375.00*
b. Untagged (Bureau precanceled), shiny gum 1.15 .75
Pair 2.30 1.50
Joint line pair 42.50 —
Dull gum .75
Pair 1.50
Joint line pair 19.50
c. As "b," imperf., pair *700.00*
Joint line pair —

Values for No. 1616b with shiny gum are for the bars-only precancel. Also known with city precancels, and worth more thus.

No. 1616c is precanceled Pleasantville, NY.

1617 A995 10c **violet,** *gray,* shiny gum, *Nov. 4, 1977* .20 .20
Pair .40
Joint line pair 1.00 —
Dull gum .30
Pair .60 .20
Joint line pair 2.50
a. Untagged (Bureau precanceled, shiny gum) 42.50 1.35
Pair 90.00 2.75
Joint line pair *1,150.* —
Dull gum 1.35
Pair 2.75
Joint line pair 47.50
b. Imperf., pair *60.00*
Joint line pair, shiny gum *125.00*
Imperf., pair, dull gum *70.00*
1618 A998 13c **brown,** shiny gum, *Nov. 25, 1975* .25 .20
Pair .50 .20
Joint line pair .75 —
Dull gum .75
Pair 1.50
Joint line pair 4.50
a. Untagged (Bureau precanceled), shiny gum 5.75 .75
Pair 12.00 1.50
Joint line pair 90.00 —
Dull gum .75
Pair 1.50
Joint line pair 35.00
b. Imperf., pair 25.00
Joint line pair *65.00*
g. Vertical pair, imperf. between —
h. As "a," imperf., pair —

Values for No. 1618a with shiny gum are for the bars-only precancel. Also known with city precancels, and worth more thus.

1618C A1001 15c **gray, dark blue & red,** *June 30, 1978* .50 .20
Pair 1.00 .20
d. Imperf., pair 25.00
e. Pair, imperf. between *150.00*
f. Gray omitted *40.00*
i. Tagging omitted 20.00
1619 A1002 16c **ultramarine,** overall tagging, *Mar. 31, 1978* .35 .20
Pair .70 .20
Joint line pair 1.50 —
a. Block tagging .50 .20
Pair 1.00 .25
Nos. 1613-1619 (9) 2.30 1.80

No. 1619a has a white background without bluish tinge, is a fraction of a millimeter smaller than No. 1619 and has no joint lines.

Nos. 1615a, 1615d, 1616b, 1617a, 1618a, issued also with dull gum.

Bureau Precancels: 9c, 7 diff., 10c, 3 diff., 13c, 12 diff.

See Nos. 1811, 1813, 1816.

13-Star Flag over Independence Hall — A1015

Flag over Capitol — A1016

Designers: No. 1622, Melbourne Brindle. No. 1623, Esther Porter.

Panes of 100 (10x10) each.

1975-81 *Perf. 11x10¾*

1622 A1015 13c **dk blue, red & brown red,** *Nov. 15, 1975* .25 .20
P# block of 20, 2-3#, 2-3 Zip, 2-3 Mail Early 5.75 —
a. Horiz. pair, imperf. between *50.00*
b. Vertical pair, imperf. *600.*
e. Horiz. pair, imperf. vert. —
f. Tagging omitted 4.00

No. 1622 was printed on the Multicolored Huck Press. Plate markings are at top or bottom of pane. It has large block tagging and nearly vertical multiple gum ridges.
See note after No. 1338F for marginal markings.

Perf. 11¼

1622C A1015 13c **dk blue, red & brown red,** *1981* 1.00 .25
P# block of 20, 1-2#, 1-2 Zip 40.00 —
P# block of 6 20.00 —
d. Vertical pair, imperf *150.00*

No. 1622C was printed on the Combination Press. Plate markings are at sides of pane. It has small block tagging and shiny flat gum.
See note after No. 1703.

BOOKLET STAMPS

1977, Mar. 11 **Engr.** *Perf. 11x10½*

1623 A1016 13c **blue & red** .25 .20
a. Booklet pane, 1 #1590 + 7 #1623 2.25 *1.25*
d. Pair, #1590 & #1623 .70 *1.00*
f. Tagging omitted —

Perf. 10x9¾

1623B A1016 13c **blue & red** .80 .80
c. Booklet pane, 1 #1590A + 7 #1623B 26.50 —
e. Pair, #1590A & #1623B 21.50 21.50

COIL STAMP

1975, Nov. 15 *Perf. 10 Vertically*

1625 A1015 13c **dk blue, red & brown red** .25 .20
Pair .50 .20
a. Imperf., pair 25.00
b. Tagging omitted —

AMERICAN BICENTENNIAL ISSUE
The Spirit of '76

Designed after painting by Archibald M. Willard in Abbot Hall, Marblehead, Massachusetts. Nos. 1629-1631 printed in continuous design.

Left panes contain 3 No. 1631a and one No. 1629; right panes contain one No. 1631 and 3 No. 1631a.

Drummer Boy — A1019

Old Drummer — A1020

Fifer — A1021

Designed by Vincent E. Hoffman.

PHOTOGRAVURE (Andreotti)
Plates of 200 subjects in four panes of 50.

1976, Jan. 1 **Tagged** *Perf. 11*

1629 A1019 13c **blue violet & multi** .25 .20
a. Imperf., vert. pair —
1630 A1020 13c **blue violet & multi** .25 .20
1631 A1021 13c **blue violet & multi** .25 .20
a. Strip of 3, #1629-1631 .75 .75
P# block of 12, 5# 3.50 —
P# block of 20, 5#, slogans 5.75 —
b. As "a," imperf. *1,050.*
c. Imperf., vert. pair, #1631 *800.00*

INTERPHIL ISSUE

Interphil 76 International Philatelic Exhibition, Philadelphia, Pa., May 29-June 6.

"Interphil 76" A1022

Designed by Terrence W. McCaffrey.

LITHOGRAPHED, ENGRAVED (Giori)
Plates of 200 subjects of four panes of 50.

1976, Jan. 17 **Tagged** *Perf. 11*

1632 A1022 13c **dark blue & red (engr.), ultra. & red (litho.)** .20 .20
P# block of 4 1.00 —
Margin block of 4, Mr. Zip and "Use Zip Code" 1.00 —
a. Dark blue & red (engr.) missing (CM) — —
b. Tagging omitted —
c. Red (engr,) missing (CM) —

AMERICAN BICENTENNIAL ISSUE

Illustration reduced.

Designed by Walt Reed.

PHOTOGRAVURE (Andreotti)
Plates of 200 subjects in four panes of 50.

1976, Feb. 23 **Tagged** *Perf. 11*

1633 A1023 13c Delaware .25 .20
1634 A1024 13c Pennsylvania .25 .20
1635 A1025 13c New Jersey .25 .20
1636 A1026 13c Georgia .25 .20
1637 A1027 13c Connecticut .25 .20
1638 A1028 13c Massachusetts .25 .20
1639 A1029 13c Maryland .25 .20
1640 A1030 13c South Carolina .25 .20
1641 A1031 13c New Hampshire .25 .20
1642 A1032 13c Virginia .25 .20
1643 A1033 13c New York .25 .20
1644 A1034 13c North Carolina .25 .20
1645 A1035 13c Rhode Island .25 .20
1646 A1036 13c Vermont .25 .20
1647 A1037 13c Kentucky .25 .20
1648 A1038 13c Tennessee .25 .20
1649 A1039 13c Ohio .25 .20
1650 A1040 13c Louisiana .25 .20
1651 A1041 13c Indiana .25 .20
1652 A1042 13c Mississippi .25 .20
1653 A1043 13c Illinois .25 .20
1654 A1044 13c Alabama .25 .20
1655 A1045 13c Maine .25 .20
1656 A1046 13c Missouri .25 .20
1657 A1047 13c Arkansas .25 .20
1658 A1048 13c Michigan .25 .20
1659 A1049 13c Florida .25 .20
1660 A1050 13c Texas .25 .20
1661 A1051 13c Iowa .25 .20
1662 A1052 13c Wisconsin .25 .20
1663 A1053 13c California .25 .20
1664 A1054 13c Minnesota .25 .20
1665 A1055 13c Oregon .25 .20
1666 A1056 13c Kansas .25 .20
1667 A1057 13c West Virginia .25 .20
a. Tagging omitted —
1668 A1058 13c Nevada .25 .20
1669 A1059 13c Nebraska .25 .20
1670 A1060 13c Colorado .25 .20
1671 A1061 13c North Dakota .25 .20
1672 A1062 13c South Dakota .25 .20
1673 A1063 13c Montana .25 .20
1674 A1064 13c Washington .25 .20
1675 A1065 13c Idaho .25 .20
1676 A1066 13c Wyoming .25 .20
1677 A1067 13c Utah .25 .20
1678 A1068 13c Oklahoma .25 .20
1679 A1069 13c New Mexico .25 .20
1680 A1070 13c Arizona .25 .20
1681 A1071 13c Alaska .25 .20
1682 A1072 13c Hawaii .25 .20
a. Pane of 50 15.00 —

TELEPHONE CENTENNIAL ISSUE

Centenary of first telephone call by Alexander Graham Bell, March 10, 1876.

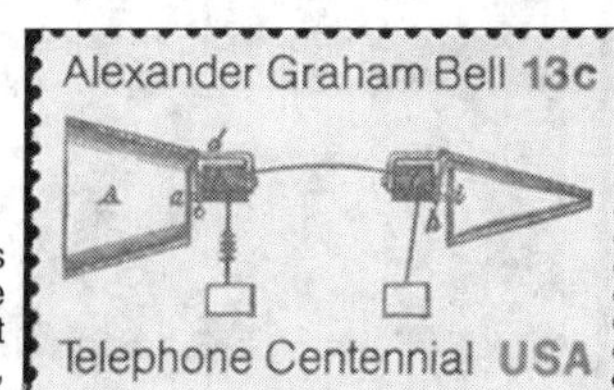

Bell's Telephone Patent Application, 1876 — A1073

Designed by George Tscherny.

ENGRAVED (Giori)
Plates of 200 subjects in four panes of 50.

1976, Mar. 10 **Tagged** *Perf. 11*

1683 A1073 13c **black, purple & red,** *tan* .25 .20
P# block of 4 1.10 —
Margin block of 4, Mr. Zip and "Use Zip Code" 1.00 —
a. Black & purple missing (EP) *500.00*
b. Red missing (EP) —
c. All colors missing (EP) —

On No. 1683a, the errors have only tiny traces of red present, so are best collected as a horiz. strip of 5 with 2 or 3 error stamps. No. 1683c also must be collected as a transitional strip.

COMMERCIAL AVIATION ISSUE

50th anniversary of first contract airmail flights: Dearborn, Mich. to Cleveland, Ohio, Feb. 15, 1926; and Pasco, Wash. to Elko, Nev., Apr. 6, 1926.

Ford-Pullman Monoplane and Laird Swallow Biplane A1074

Designed by Robert E. Cunningham.

PHOTOGRAVURE (Andreotti)
Plates of 200 subjects in four panes of 50 each

1976, Mar. 19 **Tagged** *Perf. 11*

1684 A1074 13c **blue & multicolored** .25 .20
P# block of 10, 5# 2.75 —
Margin block of 4, Mr. Zip and "Use Zip Code" 1.00 —

CHEMISTRY ISSUE

Honoring American chemists, in conjunction with the centenary of the American Chemical Society.

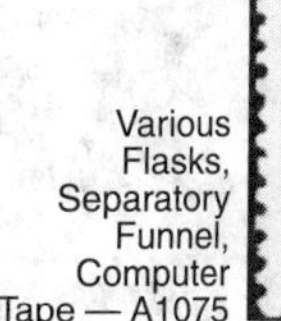

Various Flasks, Separatory Funnel, Computer Tape — A1075

Designed by Ken Davies.

PHOTOGRAVURE (Andreotti)
Plates of 200 subjects in four panes of 50.

1976, Apr. 6 **Tagged** *Perf. 11*

1685 A1075 13c **multicolored** .25 .20
P# block of 12, 6# 3.25 —
Margin block of 4, Mr. Zip and "Use Zip Code" 1.00 —
Pair with full vert. gutter btwn. —

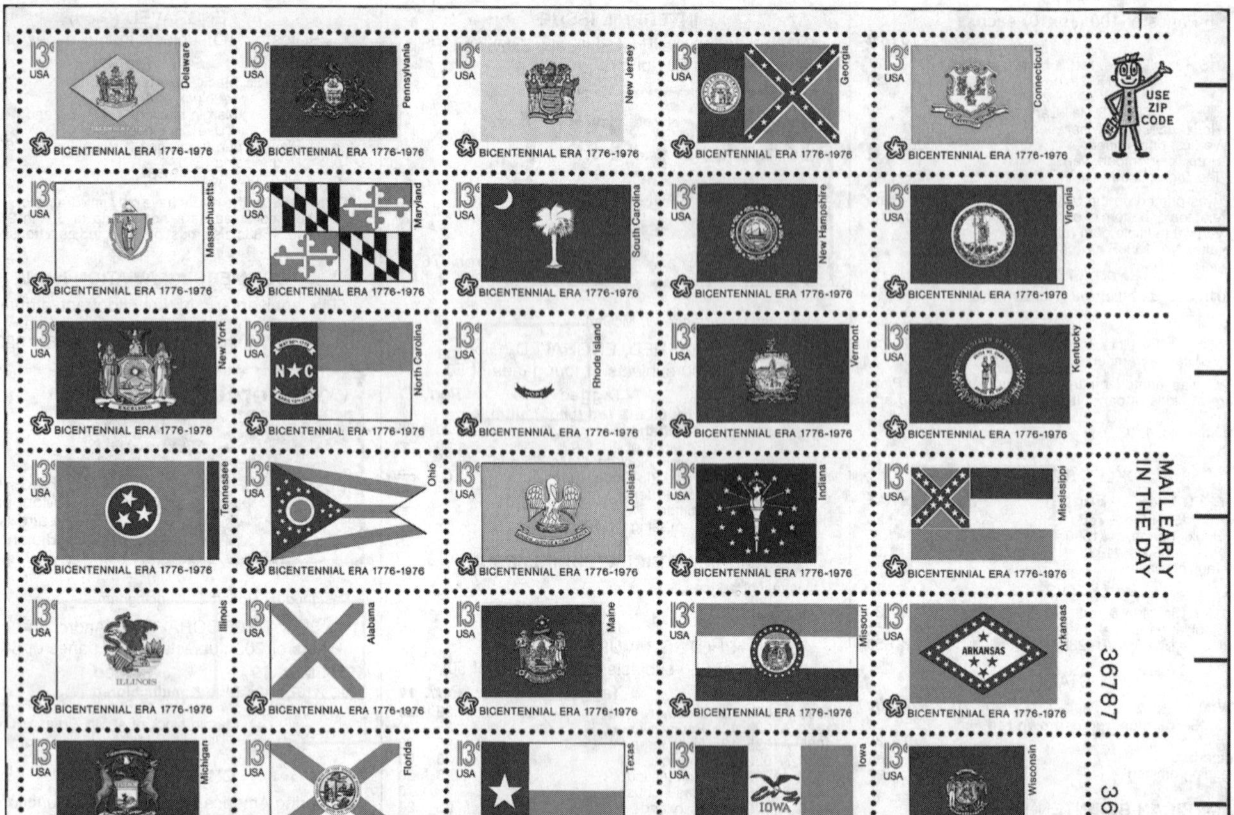

State Flags
A1023-A1072

AMERICAN BICENTENNIAL ISSUES
SOUVENIR SHEETS

Designs, from Left to Right, No. 1686: a, Two British officers. b, Gen. Benjamin Lincoln. c, George Washington. d, John Trumbull, Col. Cobb, von Steuben, Lafayette, Thomas Nelson. e, Alexander Hamilton, John Laurens, Walter Stewart (all vert.).

No. 1687: a, John Adams, Roger Sherman, Robert R. Livingston. b, Jefferson, Franklin. c, Thomas Nelson, Jr., Francis Lewis, John Witherspoon, Samuel Huntington. d, John Hancock, Charles Thomson. e, George Read, John Dickinson, Edward Rutledge (a, d, vert., b, c, e, horiz.).

No. 1688: a, Boatsman. b, Washington. c, Flag bearer. d, Men in boat. e, Men on shore (a, d, horiz., b, c, e, vert.).

No. 1689: a, Two officers. b, Washington. c, Officer, black horse. d, Officer, white horse. e, Three soldiers (a, c, e, horiz., b, d, vert.).

Surrender of Cornwallis at Yorktown, by John Trumbull — A1076

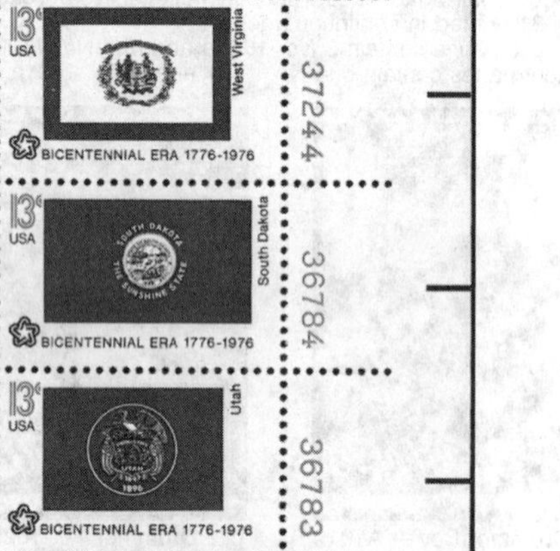

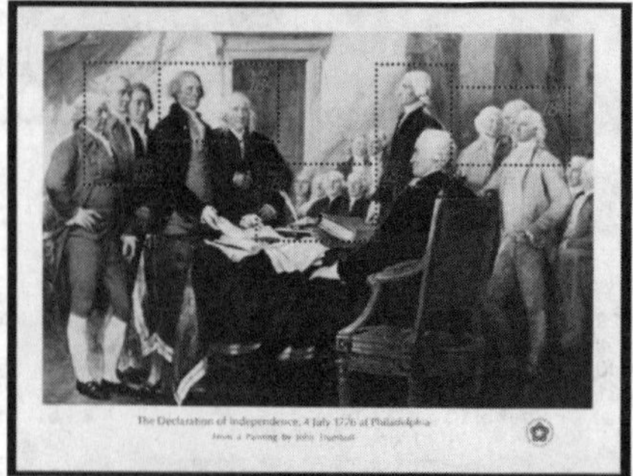
Declaration of Independence, by John Trumbull — A1077

Washington Crossing the Delaware, by Emmanuel Leutze / Eastman Johnson — A1078

Washington Reviewing Army at Valley Forge, by William T. Trego — A1079

Illustrations reduced.

Designed by Vincent E. Hoffman.

LITHOGRAPHED

Plates of 30 subjects in six panes of 5 each.

1976, May 29 **Tagged** ***Perf. 11***

1686 A1076 Sheet of 5 3.25 —
a.-e. 13c **multicolored** .45 .40
f. "USA/13c" omitted on "b," "c" & "d," imperf, tagging omitted — *2,250.*
g. "USA/13c" omitted on "a" & "e" *450.00* —
h. Imperf., tagging omitted *2,250.*
i. "USA/13c" omitted on "b," "c" & "d" *450.00*
j. "USA/13c" double on "b" —
k. "USA/13c" omitted on "c" & "d" *750.00*
l. "USA/13c" omitted on "e" *500.00*
m. "USA/13c" omitted, imperf., tagging omitted —
n. As "g," imperf., tagging omitted —

1687 A1077 Sheet of 5 4.25 —
a.-e. 18c **multicolored** .55 .55
f. Design & marginal inscriptions omitted *3,000.*
g. "USA/18c" omitted on "a" & "c" *750.00*
h. "USA/18c" omitted on "b," "d" & "e" *450.00*
i. "USA/18c" omitted on "d" *500.00* *500.00*
j. Black omitted in design *2,000.*
k. "USA/18c" omitted, imperf., tagging omitted *2,750.*
m. "USA/18c" omitted on "b" & "e" *500.00*
n. "USA/18c" omitted on "b" & "d" —
p. Imperf. (tagged) —
q. "USA/18c" omitted on "c" —

1688 A1078 Sheet of 5 5.25 —
a.-e. 24c **multicolored** .70 .70
f. "USA/24c" omitted, imperf., tagging omitted *3,500.*
g. "USA/24c" omitted on "d" & "e" *450.00* *450.00*
h. Design & marginal inscriptions omitted *3,250.*
i. "USA/24c" omitted on "a," "b" & "c" *500.00* —
j. Imperf., tagging omitted *3,000.*
k. "USA/24c" of "d" & "e" inverted —
l. As "i," imperf, tagging omitted *3,500.* —
m. Tagging omitted on "e" and "f" —
n. As No. 1688, perfs inverted —

1689 A1079 Sheet of 5 6.25 —
a.-e. 31c **multicolored** .85 .85
f. "USA/31c" omitted, imperf. *2,750.*
g. "USA/31c" omitted on "a" & "c" *400.00*
h. "USA/31c" omitted on "b," "d" & "e" *450.00* —
i. "USA/31c" omitted on "e" *450.00*
j. Black omitted in design *2,000.*
k. Imperf., tagging omitted *2,250.*
l. "USA/31c" omitted on "b" & "d" —
m. "USA/31c" omitted on "a," "b" & "e" —
n. As "m," imperf., tagging omitted —
p. As "h," imperf., tagging omitted *2,500.*
q. As "g," imperf., tagging omitted *2,750.*
r. "USA/31c" omitted on "d" & "e" —
s. As "f," tagging omitted *2,250.*
t. "USA/31c" omitted on "d" —
u. As No. 1689, tagging omitted —
v. As No. 1689, perfs inverted —
Nos. 1686-1689 (4) 19.00

Issued in connection with Interphil 76 International Philatelic Exhibition, Philadelphia, Pa., May 29-June 6. Size of sheets: 153x204mm; size of stamps: 25x39½mm, 39½x25mm.

Nos. 1688-1689 exist with inverted perforations.

Benjamin Franklin

American Bicentennial: Benjamin Franklin (1706-1790), deputy postmaster general for the colonies (1753-1774) and statesman. Design based on marble bust by anonymous Italian sculptor after terra cotta bust by Jean Jacques Caffieri, 1777. Map published by R. Sayer and J. Bennett in London.

Franklin and Map of North America, 1776 — A1080

Designed by Bernard Reilander (Canada).

LITHOGRAPHED, ENGRAVED (Giori)

Plates of 200 subjects in four panes of 50.

1976, June 1 **Tagged** ***Perf. 11***

1690 A1080 13c **ultramarine & multicolored** .25 .20
P# block of 4 1.10 —
Margin block of 4, Mr. Zip and "Use Zip Code" 1.00 —
a. Light blue omitted *225.00*
b. Tagging omitted 7.50

See Canada No. 691.

Declaration of Independence

Designed after painting of Declaration of Independence, by John Trumbull, in the Rotunda of the Capitol, Washington, D.C. Nos. 1691-1694 printed in continuous design. Left panes contain 10 No. 1694a and 5 each of Nos. 1691-1692; right panes contain 5 each of Nos. 1693-1694 and 10 No. 1694a.

A1081

A1082

A1083

A1084

Designed by Vincent E. Hoffman.

PHOTOGRAVURE (Andreotti)

Plates of 200 subjects in four panes of 50.

1976, July 4 **Tagged** ***Perf. 11***

1691 A1081 13c **blue & multicolored** .30 .20
1692 A1082 13c **blue & multicolored** .30 .20
1693 A1083 13c **blue & multicolored** .30 .20
1694 A1084 13c **blue & multicolored** .30 .20
a. Strip of 4, #1691-1694 1.20 1.10
P# block of 20, 5#, "Mail Early in the Day," Mr. Zip and "Use Zip Code" 7.75 —
P# block of 16, 5#, "Mail Early in the Day" 6.50 —
Margin block of 4, Mr. Zip and "Use Zip Code" 1.25 —

OLYMPIC GAMES ISSUE

12th Winter Olympic Games, Innsbruck, Austria, Feb. 4-15, and 21st Summer Olympic Games, Montreal, Canada, July 17-Aug. 1. Nos. 1695-1696 alternate in one row, Nos. 1697-1698 in other row.

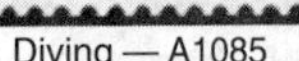
Diving — A1085

Skiing — A1086

Running — A1087

Skating — A1088

Designed by Donald Moss.

PHOTOGRAVURE (Andreotti)

Plates of 200 subjects in four panes of 50.

1976, July 16 **Tagged** ***Perf. 11***

1695 A1085 13c **multicolored** .25 .20
1696 A1086 13c **multicolored** .25 .20
1697 A1087 13c **multicolored** .25 .20
1698 A1088 13c **multicolored** .25 .20
a. Block of 4, #1695-1698 1.10 *1.40*
P# block of 12, 6# 3.25 —
P# block of 20, 6#, Mr. Zip and slogans 5.75 —
Margin block of 4, Mr. Zip and "Use Zip Code" 1.25 —
b. As "a," imperf. *650.00*

CLARA MAASS ISSUE

Clara Louise Maass (1876-1901), volunteer in fight against yellow fever, birth centenary.

Clara Maass and Newark German Hospital Pin — A1089

Designed by Paul Calle.

PHOTOGRAVURE (Andreotti)

Plates of 160 subjects in four panes of 40.

1976, Aug. 18 **Tagged** ***Perf. 11***

1699 A1089 13c **multicolored** .25 .20
P# block of 12, 6# 3.25 —
Margin block of 4, Mr. Zip, "Use Zip Code" and "Mail Early in the Day" 1.00 —
a. Horiz. pair, imperf. vert. *450.00*

ADOLPH S. OCHS ISSUE

Adolph S. Ochs (1858-1935), publisher of the New York Times, 1896-1935.

Adolph S. Ochs — A1090

Designed by Bradbury Thompson; photograph by S. J. Woolf.

GIORI PRESS PRINTING

Plates of 128 subjects in four panes of 32 (8x4).

1976, Sept. 18			**Tagged**	***Perf. 11***	
1700	A1090	13c	**black & gray**	.25	.20
			P# block of 4	1.10	—
			Margin block of 4, Mr. Zip and "Use Zip Code"	.90	—
a.			Tagging omitted		—

CHRISTMAS ISSUE

Nativity, by John Singleton Copley A1091

"Winter Pastime," by Nathaniel Currier A1092

Designers: No. 1701, Bradbury Thompson after 1776 painting in Museum of Fine Arts, Boston. No. 1702, Stevan Dohanos after 1855 lithograph in Museum of the City of New York.

PHOTOGRAVURE (Andreotti)

Plates of 200 subjects in four panes of 50.

1976, Oct. 27			**Tagged**	***Perf. 11***	
1701	A1091	13c	**multicolored**	.25	.20
			P# block of 12, 6#	3.25	—
			Margin block of 4, Mr. Zip and "Use Zip Code"	1.00	—
a.			Imperf., pair	*100.00*	
1702	A1092	13c	**multi,** overall tagging	.25	.20
			P# block of 10, 5#	2.75	—
			Margin block of 4, Mr. Zip and "Use Zip Code"	1.00	—
a.			Imperf., pair	*100.00*	

Plates of 230 (10x23) subjects in panes of 50 (5x10)

Tagged, Block

1703	A1092	13c	**multicolored**	.25	.20
			P# block of 20, 5-8#	6.00	—
a.			Imperf., pair	*100.00*	
b.			Vert. pair, imperf. between	*400.00*	
c.			Tagging omitted	12.50	
d.			Red omitted	—	
e.			Yellow omitted	—	

No. 1702 has overall tagging. Lettering at base is black and usually ½mm below design. As a rule, no "snowflaking" in sky or pond. Pane of 50 has margins on 4 sides with slogans. Plate Nos. 37465-37478.

No. 1703 has block tagging the size of printed area. Lettering at base is gray black and usually ¾mm below design. "Snowflaking" generally in sky and pond. Plate Nos. 37617-37621 or 37634-37638.

Copies of No. 1703 are known with various amounts of red or yellow missing. Nos. 1703d-1703e are stamps with the colors totally omitted. Expertization is recommended.

COMBINATION PRESS

Cylindrical plates consist of 23 rows of subjects, 10 across for commemoratives (230 subjects), 20 across for definitives (460 subjects), with selvage on the two outer edges only. Guillotining through the perforations creates individual panes of 50 or 100 with selvage on one side only.

Failure of the guillotine to separate through the perforations resulted in straight edges on some stamps. Perforating teeth along the center column and the tenth rows were removed for issues released on or after May 31, 1984 (the 10c Richard Russell, for definitives; the 20c Horace Moses, for commemoratives), creating panes with straight edged stamps on three sides.

Three sets of plate numbers, copyright notices (starting with No. 1787), and zip insignia (starting with No. 1927) are arranged identically on the left and right sides of the plate so that each pane has at least one of each marking. The markings adjacent to any particular row are repeated either seven or eight rows away on the cylinder.

Fifteen combinations of the three marginal markings and blank rows are possible on panes.

AMERICAN BICENTENNIAL ISSUE
Washington at Princeton

Washington's Victory over Lord Cornwallis at Princeton, N.J., bicentenary.

Washington, Nassau Hall, Hessian Prisoners and 13-star Flag, by Charles Willson Peale — A1093

Designed by Bradbury Thompson.

PHOTOGRAVURE (Andreotti)

Plates of 160 subjects in four panes of 40.

1977, Jan. 3			**Tagged**	***Perf. 11***	
1704	A1093	13c	**multicolored**	.25	.20
			P# block of 10, 5#	2.75	—
			Margin block of 4, Mr. Zip and "Use Zip Code", "Mail Early in the Day"	1.00	—
a.			Horiz. pair, imperf. vert.	*550.00*	

SOUND RECORDING ISSUE

Centenary of the invention of the phonograph by Thomas Alva Edison and development of sophisticated recording industry.

Tin Foil Phonograph A1094

Designed by Walter and Naiad Einsel.

LITHOGRAPHED, ENGRAVED (Giori)

Plates of 200 subjects in four panes of 50.

1977, Mar. 23			**Tagged**	***Perf. 11***	
1705	A1094	13c	**black & multicolored**	.25	.20
			P# block of 4	1.10	—
			Margin block of 4, Mr. Zip and "Use Zip Code"	1.00	—

AMERICAN FOLK ART SERIES
Pueblo Pottery

Pueblo art, 1880-1920, from Museums in New Mexico, Arizona and Colorado.

Nos. 1706-1709 are printed in blocks and strips of 4 in panes of 40. In the 1st row Nos. 1706-1709 are in sequence as listed. In the 2nd row Nos. 1708-1709 are followed by Nos. 1706-1709, 1708-1709.

Zia Pot — A1095

San Ildefonso Pot — A1096

Hopi Pot — A1097

Acoma Pot — A1098

Designed by Ford Ruthling.

PHOTOGRAVURE (Andreotti)

Plates of 160 subjects in four panes of 40.

1977, Apr. 13			**Tagged**	***Perf. 11***	
1706	A1095	13c	**multicolored**	.25	.20
1707	A1096	13c	**multicolored**	.25	.20
1708	A1097	13c	**multicolored**	.25	.20
1709	A1098	13c	**multicolored**	.25	.20
a.			Block or strip of 4, #1706-1709	1.00	1.00
			P# block of 10, 5#	2.75	—
			P# block of 16, 5#; Mr. Zip and slogans	4.25	—
			Margin block of 6, Mr. Zip and "Use Zip Code" "Mail Early in the Day"	1.50	—
b.			As "a," imperf. vert.	*2,250.*	

LINDBERGH FLIGHT ISSUE

Charles A. Lindbergh's solo transatlantic flight from New York to Paris, 50th anniversary.

Spirit of St. Louis
A1099

Designed by Robert E. Cunningham.

PHOTOGRAVURE (Andreotti)

Plates of 200 subjects in four panes of 50.

1977, May 20	**Tagged**	***Perf. 11***	
1710 A1099 13c **multicolored**		.25	.20
P# block of 12, 6#		3.25	—
Margin block of 4, Mr. Zip and "Use Zip Code"		1.00	—
a. Imperf., pair		*1,000.*	

Beware of private overprints on No. 1710.

COLORADO STATEHOOD ISSUE

Issued to honor Colorado as the "Centennial State." It achieved statehood in 1876.

Columbine and Rocky Mountains — A1100

Designed by V. Jack Ruther.

PHOTOGRAVURE (Andreotti)

Plates of 200 subjects in four panes of 50.

1977, May 21	**Tagged**	***Perf. 11***	
1711 A1100 13c **multicolored**		.25	.20
P# block of 12, 6#		3.25	—
Margin block of 4, Mr. Zip and "Use Zip Code"		1.00	—
a. Horiz. pair, imperf. between		*600.00*	
b. Horiz. pair, imperf. vertically		*900.00*	
c. Perf. 11.2		.35	.25
P# block of 12, 6#		20.00	

Perforations do not run through the sheet margin on about 10 percent of the sheets of No. 1711.

BUTTERFLY ISSUE

Nos. 1712-1713 alternate in 1st row, Nos. 1714-1715 in 2nd row. This arrangement is repeated throughout the pane. Butterflies represent different geographic US areas.

Swallowtail
A1101

Checkerspot
A1102

Dogface
A1103

Orange-Tip
A1104

Designed by Stanley Galli.

PHOTOGRAVURE (Andreotti)

Plates of 200 subjects in four panes of 50.

1977, June 6	**Tagged**	***Perf. 11***	
1712 A1101 13c **tan & multicolored**		.25	.20
1713 A1102 13c **tan & multicolored**		.25	.20
1714 A1103 13c **tan & multicolored**		.25	.20
1715 A1104 13c **tan & multicolored**		.25	.20
a. Block of 4, #1712-1715		1.00	1.00
P# block of 12, 6#		3.25	—
P# block of 20, 6#, Mr. Zip and slogans		5.50	—
Margin block of 4, Mr. Zip and "Use Zip Code"		1.05	—
b. As "a," imperf. horiz.		*15,000.*	

AMERICAN BICENTENNIAL ISSUES
Marquis de Lafayette

200th anniversary of Lafayette's Landing on the coast of South Carolina, north of Charleston.

Marquis de Lafayette — A1105

Designed by Bradbury Thompson.

GIORI PRESS PRINTING

Plates of 160 subjects in four panes of 40.

1977, June 13	**Tagged**	***Perf. 11***	
1716 A1105 13c **blue, black & red**		.25	.20
P# block of 4		1.10	—
Margin block of 4, Mr. Zip and "Use Zip Code"		1.00	—
a. Red missing (PS)		—	

Skilled Hands for Independence

Nos. 1717-1718 alternate in 1st row, Nos. 1719-1720 in 2nd row. This arrangement is repeated throughout the pane.

Seamstress
A1106

Blacksmith
A1107

Wheelwright
A1108

Leatherworker
A1109

Designed by Leonard Everett Fisher.

PHOTOGRAVURE (Andreotti)

Plates of 200 subjects in four panes of 50.

1977, July 4	**Tagged**	***Perf. 11***	
1717 A1106 13c **multicolored**		.25	.20
1718 A1107 13c **multicolored**		.25	.20
1719 A1108 13c **multicolored**		.25	.20
1720 A1109 13c **multicolored**		.25	.20
a. Block of 4, #1717-1720		1.00	1.00
P# block of 12, 6#		3.25	
P# block of 20, 6#, Mr. Zip and slogans		5.50	—
Margin block of 4, Mr. Zip and "Use Zip Code"		1.05	—

PEACE BRIDGE ISSUE

50th anniversary of the Peace Bridge, connecting Buffalo (Fort Porter), N.Y. and Fort Erie, Ontario.

Peace Bridge and Dove — A1110

Designed by Bernard Brussel-Smith (wood-cut).

ENGRAVED

Plates of 200 subjects in four panes of 50.

1977, Aug. 4	**Tagged**	***Perf. 11x10½***	
1721 A1110 13c **blue**		.25	.20
P# block of 4		1.10	—
Margin block of 4, Mr. Zip and "Use Zip Code"		1.00	—

AMERICAN BICENTENNIAL ISSUE
Battle of Oriskany

200th anniv. of the Battle of Oriskany, American Militia led by Brig. Gen. Nicholas Herkimer (1728-77).

Herkimer at Oriskany, by Frederick Yohn
A1111

Designed by Bradbury Thompson after painting in Utica, N.Y. Public Library.

PHOTOGRAVURE (Andreotti)

Plates of 160 subjects in four panes of 40.

1977, Aug. 6	**Tagged**	***Perf. 11***	
1722 A1111 13c **multicolored**		.25	.20
P# block of 10, 5#		2.75	—
Margin block of 6, Mr. Zip and "Use Zip Code" and "Mail Early in the Day"		1.50	—

ENERGY ISSUE

Conservation and development of nation}s energy resources. Nos. 1723-1724 se-tenant vertically.

"Conservation" A1112

"Development" A1113

Designed by Terrance W. McCaffrey.

PHOTOGRAVURE (Andreotti)
Plates of 160 subjects in four panes of 40.

1977, Oct. 20 **Tagged** ***Perf. 11***

1723 A1112 13c **multicolored**	.25	.20
1724 A1113 13c **multicolored**	.25	.20
a. Pair, #1723-1724	.50	.50
P# block of 12, 6#	3.25	—
Margin block of 4, Mr. Zip, "Use Zip Code" and "Mail Early in the Day"	1.00	—

ALTA CALIFORNIA ISSUE

Founding of El Pueblo de San José de Guadalupe, first civil settlement in Alta California, 200th anniversary.

Farm Houses A1114

Designed by Earl Thollander.

LITHOGRAPHED, ENGRAVED (Giori)
Plates of 200 subjects in four panes of 50.

1977, Sept. 9 **Tagged** ***Perf. 11***

1725 A1114 13c **black & multicolored**	.25	.20
P# block of 4	1.10	—
Margin block of 4, Mr. Zip and "Use Zip Code"	1.00	—
a. Tagging omitted		—

AMERICAN BICENTENNIAL ISSUE
Articles of Confederation

200th anniversary of drafting the Articles of Confederation, York Town, Pa.

Members of Continental Congress in Conference A1115

Designed by David Blossom.

ENGRAVED (Giori)
Plates of 200 subjects in four panes of 50.

1977, Sept. 30 **Tagged** ***Perf. 11***

1726 A1115 13c **red & brown,** *cream*	.25	.20
P# block of 4	1.10	—
Margin block of 4, Mr. Zip and "Use Zip Code"	1.00	—
a. Tagging omitted	—	
b. Red omitted	*600.00*	
c. Red & brown omitted	*400.00*	

No. 1726b also has most of the brown omitted. No. 1726c must be collected as a transition multiple, certainly with No. 1726b and preferably also with No. 1726.

TALKING PICTURES, 50th ANNIV.

Movie Projector and Phonograph A1116

Designed by Walter Einsel.

LITHOGRAPHED, ENGRAVED (Giori)
Plates of 200 subjects in four panes of 50.

1977, Oct. 6 **Tagged** ***Perf. 11***

1727 A1116 13c **multicolored**	.25	.20
P# block of 4	1.10	—
Margin block of 4, Mr. Zip and "Use Zip Code"	1.00	—

AMERICAN BICENTENNIAL ISSUE
Surrender at Saratoga

200th anniversary of Gen. John Burgoyne's surrender at Saratoga.

Surrender of Burgoyne, by John Trumbull A1117

Designed by Bradbury Thompson.

PHOTOGRAVURE (Andreotti)
Plates of 160 subjects in four panes of 40.

1977, Oct. 7 **Tagged** ***Perf. 11***

1728 A1117 13c **multicolored**	.25	.20
P# block of 10, 5#	2.75	—
Margin block of 6, Mr. Zip, "Use Zip Code" and "Mail Early in the Day"	1.50	—

CHRISTMAS ISSUE

Washington at Valley Forge — A1118

Rural Mailbox — A1119

Designers: No. 1729, Stevan Dohanos, after painting by J. C. Leyendecker. No. 1730, Dolli Tingle.

PHOTOGRAVURE (Combination Press)
Plates of 460 subjects (20x23) in panes of 100 (10x10).

1977, Oct. 21 **Tagged** ***Perf. 11***

1729 A1118 13c **multicolored**	.25	.20
P# block of 20, 5-8#	5.75	—
a. Imperf., pair	*75.00*	

See Combination Press note after No. 1703.

PHOTOGRAVURE (Andreotti)
Plates of 400 subjects in 4 panes of 100.

1730 A1119 13c **multicolored**	.25	.20
P# block of 10, 5#	2.75	—
Margin block of 4, Mr. Zip and "Use Zip Code"	1.00	—
Pair with full vert. gutter btwn.	—	
a. Imperf., pair	*300.00*	

CARL SANDBURG ISSUE

Carl Sandburg (1878-1967), poet, biographer and collector of American folk songs, birth centenary.

Carl Sandburg, by William A. Smith, 1952 — A1120

Designed by William A. Smith.

GIORI PRESS PRINTING
Plates of 200 subjects in four panes of 50.

1978, Jan. 6 **Tagged** ***Perf. 11***

1731 A1120 13c **black & brown**	.25	.20
P# block of 4	1.25	—
Margin block of 4, Mr. Zip	1.05	—
a. Brown omitted	—	

CAPTAIN COOK ISSUE

Capt. James Cook, 200th anniversary of his arrival in Hawaii, at Waimea, Kauai, Jan. 20, 1778, and of his anchorage in Cook Inlet, near Anchorage, Alaska, June 1, 1778. Nos. 1732-1733 printed in panes of 50, containing 25 each of Nos. 1732-1733 including 5 No. 1732a.

Capt. Cook, by Nathaniel Dance — A1121

"Resolution" and "Discovery," by John Webber A1122

Designed by Robert F. Szabo (No. 1732; Jak Katalan (No. 1733.

GIORI PRESS PRINTING
Plates of 200 subjects in four panes of 50.

1978, Jan. 20 **Tagged** ***Perf. 11***

1732 A1121 13c **dark blue**	.25	.20
1733 A1122 13c **green**	.25	.20
a. Vert. pair, imperf. horiz.	—	
b. Pair, #1732-1733	.50	.50
P# block of 4, #1732 or 1733	1.10	—
Margin block of 4, Mr. Zip, #1732 or 1733	1.05	—
P# block of 20, 10 each #1732-1733, P# and slogans	5.25	—
c. As "b," imperf. between	*4,500.*	

Indian Head Penny, 1877 — A1123

Eagle — A1124

Red Masterpiece and Medallion Roses — A1126

ENGRAVED (Giori)

Plates of 600 subjects in four panes of 150.

1978 **Tagged** ***Perf. 11***

1734 A1123 13c **brown & blue green,** *bister, Jan. 11, 1978*	.25	.20
P# block of 4	1.25	—
Margin block of 4, "Use Correct Zip Code"	1.00	—
Vert. pair with full horiz. gutter between	—	
a. Horiz. pair, imperf. vert.	*300.00*	

PHOTOGRAVURE (Andreotti)

Plates of 400 subjects in four panes of 100.

1735 A1124 (15c) **orange,** *May 22, 1978*	.25	.20
P# block of 4	1.25	—
Margin block of 4, "Use Zip Code"	1.00	—
Vert. pair with full horiz. gutter between	—	
a. Imperf., pair	*90.00*	
b. Vert. pair, imperf. horiz.	*700.00*	
c. Perf. 11.2	.25	.20
P# block of 4	1.75	—
Zip block of 4	1.10	—

BOOKLET STAMPS

ENGRAVED

Perf. 11x10½ on 2 or 3 sides

1736 A1124 (15c) **orange**	.25	.20
a. Booklet pane of 8, *May 22, 1978*	2.25	*1.25*
b. As "a," tagging omitted	—	
c. Vert. pair, imperf between	—	

Perf. 10

1737 A1126 15c **multicolored**	.25	.20
a. Booklet pane of 8, *July 11, 1978*	2.25	*1.25*
b. As "a," imperf.	—	
c. As "a," tagging omitted	*40.00*	—

A1127 A1128 A1129

A1130

A1131

Designed by Ronald Sharpe.

BOOKLET STAMPS

ENGRAVED

1980, Feb. 7 **Tagged** ***Perf. 11 on 2 or 3 sides***

1738 A1127 15c **sepia,** *yellow*	.30	.20
1739 A1128 15c **sepia,** *yellow*	.30	.20
1740 A1129 15c **sepia,** *yellow*	.30	.20
1741 A1130 15c **sepia,** *yellow*	.30	.20
1742 A1131 15c **sepia,** *yellow*	.30	.20
a. Booklet pane of 10, 2 each #1738-1742	3.50	*3.00*
b. Strip of 5, #1738-1742	1.50	1.40

COIL STAMP

1978, May 22 ***Perf. 10 Vert.***

1743 A1124 (15c) **orange**	.25	.20
Pair	.50	.20
Joint line pair	.65	—
a. Imperf., pair	90.00	
Joint line pair	—	

No. 1743a is valued in the grade of fine.

BLACK HERITAGE SERIES

Harriet Tubman (1820-1913), born a slave, helped more than 300 slaves escape to freedom.

Harriet Tubman and Cart Carrying Slaves — A1133

Designed by Jerry Pinkney after photograph.

PHOTOGRAVURE (Andreotti)

Plates of 200 subjects in four panes of 50.

1978, Feb. 1 **Tagged** ***Perf. 10½x11***

1744 A1133 13c **multicolored**	.25	.20
P# block of 12, 6#	3.25	—
Margin block of 4, Mr. Zip	1.00	—

AMERICAN FOLK ART SERIES
Quilts

Nos. 1745-1746 alternate in 1st row, Nos. 1747-1748 in 2nd.

Basket Design

A1134 A1135

A1136 A1137

Designed by Christopher Pullman after 1875 quilt made in New York City. Illustration reduced.

PHOTOGRAVURE (Andreotti)

Plates of 192 subjects in four panes of 48 (6x8).

1978, Mar. 8 ***Perf. 11***

1745 A1134 13c **multicolored**	.25	.20
1746 A1135 13c **multicolored**	.25	.20
1747 A1136 13c **multicolored**	.25	.20
1748 A1137 13c **multicolored**	.25	.20
a. Block of 4, #1745-1748	1.00	1.00
P# block of 12, 6#	3.25	—
P# block of 16, 6#, Mr. Zip and copyright	4.50	—
Margin block of 4, Mr. Zip, copyright	1.05	—

AMERICAN DANCE ISSUE

Nos. 1749-1750 alternate in 1st row, Nos. 1751-1752 in 2nd.

Ballet
A1138

Theater
A1139

Folk Dance
A1140

Modern Dance
A1141

Designed by John Hill.

PHOTOGRAVURE (Andreotti)

Plates of 192 subjects in four panes of 48 (6x8).

1978, Apr. 26 **Tagged** ***Perf. 11***

1749 A1138 13c **multicolored**	.25	.20
1750 A1139 13c **multicolored**	.25	.20
1751 A1140 13c **multicolored**	.25	.20
1752 A1141 13c **multicolored**	.25	.20
a. Block of 4, #1749-1752	1.00	1.00
P# block of 12, 6#	3.25	—
P# block of 16, 6#, Mr. Zip and copyright	4.50	—
Margin block of 4, Mr. Zip, copyright	1.05	—

AMERICAN BICENTENNIAL ISSUE

French Alliance, signed in Paris, Feb. 6, 1778 and ratified by Continental Congress, May 4, 1778.

King Louis XVI and Benjamin Franklin, by Charles Gabriel Sauvage — A1142

Designed by Bradbury Thompson after 1785 porcelain sculpture in Du Pont Winterthur Museum, Delaware.

GIORI PRESS PRINTING

Plates of 160 subjects in four panes of 40.

1978, May 4	**Tagged**	***Perf. 11***	
1753 A1142 13c	**blue, black & red**	.25	.20
	P# block of 4	1.10	—
	Margin block of 4, Mr. Zip	1.00	—

EARLY CANCER DETECTION ISSUE

George Papanicolaou, M.D. (1883-1962), cytologist and developer of Pap Test, early cancer detection in women.

Dr. Papanicolaou and Microscope — A1143

Designed by Paul Calle.

ENGRAVED

Plates of 200 subjects in four panes of 50.

1978, May 18	**Tagged**	***Perf. 10½x11***	
1754 A1143 13c	**brown**	.25	.20
	P# block of 4	1.10	—
	Margin block of 4, Mr. Zip	1.00	—

PERFORMING ARTS SERIES

Jimmie Rodgers (1897-1933), the "Singing Brakeman, Father of Country Music" (No. 1755); George M. Cohan (1878-1942), actor and playwright (No. 1756).

Jimmie Rodgers with Guitar and Brakeman's Cap, Locomotive — A1144

George M. Cohan, "Yankee Doodle Dandy" and Stars — A1145

Designed by Jim Sharpe.

PHOTOGRAVURE (Andreotti)

Plates of 200 subjects in four panes of 50.

1978	**Tagged**	***Perf. 11***	
1755 A1144 13c	**multicolored,** *May 24*	.25	.20
	P# block of 12, 6#	3.25	—
	Margin block of 4, Mr. Zip	1.00	—
1756 A1145 15c	**multicolored,** *July 3*	.30	.20
	P# block of 12, 6#	4.00	—
	Margin block of 4, Mr. Zip	1.25	—

CAPEX ISSUE

CAPEX '78, Canadian International Philatelic Exhibition, Toronto, Ont., June 9-18.

Wildlife from Canadian-United States Border — A1146

Illustration reduced.

Designed by Stanley Galli.

LITHOGRAPHED, ENGRAVED (Giori)

Plates of 24 subjects in four panes of 6 each.

1978, June 10	**Tagged**	***Perf. 11***	
1757 A1146	Block of 8, **multicolored**	2.00	2.00
a.	13c Cardinal	.25	.20
b.	13c Mallard	.25	.20
c.	13c Canada goose	.25	.20
d.	13c Blue jay	.25	.20
e.	13c Moose	.25	.20
f.	13c Chipmunk	.25	.20
g.	13c Red fox	.25	.20
h.	13c Raccoon	.25	.20
	P# block of 8	2.25	—
	Margin block of 8, Mr. Zip and copyright	2.10	—
	Pane of 6 No. 1757, P#, Mr. Zip and copyright	13.00	—
i.	As No. 1757, yellow, green, red, brown, blue, black (litho) omitted	*7,000.*	
j.	Strip of 4 (a-d), imperf. vert.	*7,000.*	
k.	Strip of 4 (e-h), imperf. vert.	*4,750.*	
l.	As No. 1757, "d" and "h" with black (engr.) omitted	—	

PHOTOGRAPHY ISSUE

Photography's contribution to communications and understanding.

Camera, Lens, Color Filters, Adapter Ring, Studio Light Bulb and Album — A1147

Designed by Ben Somoroff.

PHOTOGRAVURE (Andreotti)

Plates of 160 subjects in four panes of 40.

1978, June 26	**Tagged**	***Perf. 11***	
1758 A1147 15c	**multicolored**	.30	.20
	P# block of 12, 6#	4.00	—
	Margin block of 4, Mr. Zip and copyright	1.25	—
	P# block of 16, 6#, Mr. Zip and copyright	5.00	—

VIKING MISSIONS TO MARS ISSUE

Second anniv. of landing of Viking 1 on Mars.

Viking 1 Lander Scooping up Soil on Mars — A1148

Designed by Robert McCall.

LITHOGRAPHED, ENGRAVED (Giori)

Plates of 200 subjects in four panes of 50.

1978, July 20	**Tagged**	***Perf. 11***	
1759 A1148 15c	**multicolored**	.30	.20
	P# block of 4	1.35	—
	Margin block of 4, Mr. Zip	1.25	—

AMERICAN OWLS ISSUE

Nos. 1760-1761 alternate in one horizontal row. Nos. 1762-1763 in the next.

Great Gray Owl — A1149

Saw-whet Owl — A1150

Barred Owl — A1151

Great Horned Owl — A1152

Designed by Frank J. Waslick.

LITHOGRAPHED, ENGRAVED (Giori)

Plates of 200 subjects in four panes of 50.

1978, Aug. 26	**Tagged**	***Perf. 11***	
1760 A1149 15c	**multicolored**	.30	.20
1761 A1150 15c	**multicolored**	.30	.20
1762 A1151 15c	**multicolored**	.30	.20
1763 A1152 15c	**multicolored**	.30	.20
a.	Block of 4, #1760-1763	1.25	1.25
	P# block of 4	1.40	—
	Margin block of 4, Mr. Zip	1.25	—
b.	As "a," tagging omitted		—

AMERICAN TREES ISSUE

Nos. 1764-1765 alternate in 1st row, Nos. 1766-1767 in 2nd.

Giant Sequoia A1153

White Pine — A1154

White Oak — A1155

Gray Birch — A1156

Designed by Walter D. Richards.

PHOTOGRAVURE (Andreotti)
Plates of 160 subjects in four panes of 40.

1978, Oct. 9 **Tagged** ***Perf. 11***
1764 A1153 15c **multicolored** .30 .20
1765 A1154 15c **multicolored** .30 .20
1766 A1155 15c **multicolored** .30 .20
1767 A1156 15c **multicolored** .30 .20
a. Block of 4, #1764-1767 1.25 1.25
P# block of 12, 6# 4.00 —
P# block of 16, 6#, Mr. Zip and copyright 5.25 —
Margin block of 4, Mr. Zip, copyright 1.30 —
b. As "a," imperf. horiz. *15,000.*

No. 1767b is unique.

CHRISTMAS ISSUE

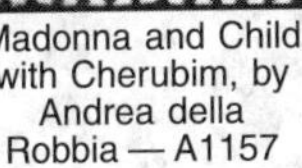

Madonna and Child with Cherubim, by Andrea della Robbia — A1157

Child on Hobby Horse and Christmas Trees — A1158

Designed by Bradbury Thompson (No. 1768) after terra cotta sculpture in National Gallery, Washington, D.C. by Dolli Tingle (No. 1769).

PHOTOGRAVURE (Andreotti)
Plates of 400 subjects in four panes of 100.

1978, Oct. 18 ***Perf. 11***
1768 A1157 15c **blue & multicolored** .30 .20
P# block of 12, 6# 4.00 —
Margin block of 4, "Use Correct Zip Code" 1.25 —
a. Imperf., pair *90.00*

Value for No. 1768a is for an uncreased pair.

1769 A1158 15c **red & multicolored** .30 .20
P# block of 12, 6# 4.00 —
Margin block of 4, "Use Correct Zip Code" 1.25 —
Pair with full horiz. gutter btwn. —
a. Imperf., pair *100.00*
b. Vert. pair, imperf. horiz. *2,000.*

Robert F. Kennedy — A1159

Martin Luther King, Jr. and Civil Rights Marchers — A1160

ROBERT F. KENNEDY ISSUE

Designed by Bradbury Thompson after photograph by Stanley Tretick.

ENGRAVED
Plates of 192 subjects in four panes of 48 (8x6).

1979, Jan. 12 **Tagged** ***Perf. 11***
1770 A1159 15c **blue** .35 .20
P# block of 4 1.75 —
Margin block of 4, Mr. Zip 1.50 —
a. Tagging omitted —

BLACK HERITAGE SERIES

Dr. Martin Luther King, Jr. (1929-1968), Civil Rights leader.

Designed by Jerry Pinkney.

PHOTOGRAVURE (Andreotti)
Plates of 200 subjects in four panes of 50.

1979, Jan. 13 **Tagged** ***Perf. 11***
1771 A1160 15c **multicolored** .30 .20
P# block of 12, 6# 4.00 —
Margin block of 4, Mr. Zip 1.25 —
a. Imperf., pair —

INTERNATIONAL YEAR OF THE CHILD ISSUE

Children of Different Races A1161

Designed by Paul Calle.

ENGRAVED
Plates of 200 subjects in four panes of 50.

1979, Feb. 15 **Tagged** ***Perf. 11***
1772 A1161 15c **orange red** .30 .20
P# block of 4 1.40 —
Margin block of 4, Mr. Zip 1.25 —

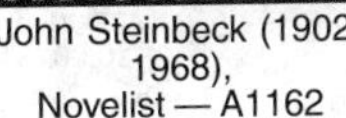

John Steinbeck (1902-1968), Novelist — A1162

Albert Einstein (1879-1955), Theoretical Physicist — A1163

LITERARY ARTS SERIES

Designed by Bradbury Thompson after photograph by Philippe Halsman.

ENGRAVED
Plates of 200 subjects in four panes of 50.

1979, Feb. 27 **Tagged** ***Perf. 10½x11***
1773 A1162 15c **dark blue** .30 .20
P# block of 4 1.40 —
Margin block of 4, Mr. Zip 1.25 —

ALBERT EINSTEIN ISSUE

Designed by Bradbury Thompson after photograph by Hermann Landshoff.

ENGRAVED
Plates of 200 subjects in four panes of 50.

1979, Mar. 4 **Tagged** ***Perf. 10½x11***
1774 A1163 15c **chocolate** .35 .20
P# block of 4 1.75 —
Margin block of 4, Mr. Zip 1.50 —
Pair, horiz. gutter btwn. —

AMERICAN FOLK ART SERIES
Pennsylvania Toleware, c. 1800

Coffeepot — A1164

Tea Caddy — A1165

Sugar Bowl — A1166

Coffeepot — A1167

Designed by Bradbury Thompson.

PHOTOGRAVURE (Andreotti)
Plates of 160 subjects in four panes of 40.

1979, Apr. 19 **Tagged** ***Perf. 11***
1775 A1164 15c **multicolored** .30 .20
1776 A1165 15c **multicolored** .30 .20
1777 A1166 15c **multicolored** .30 .20
1778 A1167 15c **multicolored** .30 .20
a. Block of 4, #1775-1778 1.25 1.25
P# block of 10, 5# 3.25 —
P# block of 16, 5#; Mr. Zip and copyright 5.25 —
Margin block of 6, Mr. Zip and copyright 2.00 —
b. As "a," imperf. horiz. *4,250.*

AMERICAN ARCHITECTURE SERIES

Nos. 1779-1780 alternate in 1st row, Nos. 1781-1782 in 2nd.

Virginia Rotunda, by Thomas Jefferson — A1168

Baltimore Cathedral, by Benjamin Latrobe — A1169

Boston State House, by Charles Bulfinch — A1170

Philadelphia Exchange, by William Strickland — A1171

Designed by Walter D. Richards.

ENGRAVED (Giori)

Plates of 192 subjects in four panes of 48 (6x8).

1979, June 4			**Tagged**	***Perf. 11***	
1779	A1168	15c	**black & brick red**	.30	.20
1780	A1169	15c	**black & brick red**	.30	.20
1781	A1170	15c	**black & brick red**	.30	.20
1782	A1171	15c	**black & brick red**	.30	.20
a.			Block of 4, #1779-1782	1.25	*1.50*
			P# block of 4	1.45	—
			Margin block of 4, Mr. Zip	1.30	—

ENDANGERED FLORA ISSUE

Nos. 1783-1784 alternate in one horizontal row. Nos. 1785-1786 in the next.

Persistent Trillium — A1172

Hawaiian Wild Broadbean — A1173

Contra Costa Wallflower — A1174

Antioch Dunes Evening Primrose — A1175

Designed by Frank J. Waslick.

PHOTOGRAVURE (Andreotti)

Plates of 200 subjects in four panes of 50.

1979, June 7			**Tagged**	***Perf. 11***	
1783	A1172	15c	**multicolored**	.30	.20
1784	A1173	15c	**multicolored**	.30	.20
1785	A1174	15c	**multicolored**	.30	.20
1786	A1175	15c	**multicolored**	.30	.20
a.			Block of 4, #1783-1786	1.25	1.25
			P# block of 12, 6#	4.00	—
			P# block of 20, 6#, Mr. Zip and copyright	6.50	—
			Margin block of 4, Mr. Zip	1.30	—
			As "a," full vert. gutter btwn.	—	
b.			As "a," imperf.	*600.00*	

SEEING EYE DOGS ISSUE

1st guide dog program in the US, 50th anniv.

German Shepherd Leading Man — A1176

Designed by Joseph Csatari.

PHOTOGRAVURE (Combination Press)

Plates of 230 (10x23) subjects in panes of 50 (10x5).

1979, June 15			**Tagged**	***Perf. 11***	
1787	A1176	15c	**multicolored**	.30	.20
			P# block of 20, 5-8#, 1-2 copyright	6.50	—
a.			Imperf., pair	*425.00*	
b.			Tagging omitted	10.00	

See Combination Press note after No. 1703.

Child Holding Winner's Medal — A1177

John Paul Jones, by Charles Willson Peale — A1178

SPECIAL OLYMPICS ISSUE

Special Olympics for special children, Brockport, N.Y., Aug. 8-13.

Designed by Jeff Cornell.

PHOTOGRAVURE (Andreotti)

Plates of 200 subjects in four panes of 50.

1979, Aug. 9			**Tagged**	***Perf. 11***	
1788	A1177	15c	**multicolored**	.30	.20
			P# block of 10, 5#	3.25	—
			Zip block of 4	1.25	—

JOHN PAUL JONES ISSUE

John Paul Jones (1747-1792), Naval Commander American Revolution.

Designed after painting in Independence National Historical Park, Philadelphia.

Printed by American Bank Note Co. and J. W. Fergusson and Sons.

Designed by Bradbury Thompson.

PHOTOGRAVURE (Champlain)

Plates of 200 subjects in four panes of 50.

1979, Sept. 23			**Tagged**	***Perf. 11x12***	
1789	A1178	15c	**multicolored**	.30	.20
			P# block of 10, 5#	3.25	—
			Zip block of 4	1.25	—
c.			Vert. pair, imperf. horiz.	*175.00*	

Numerous varieties of printer's waste exist. These include imperforates, perforated or imperforate gutter pairs or blocks and shifted or missing colors.

Perf. 11

1789A	A1178	15c	**multicolored**	.55	.20
			P# block of 10, 5#	4.00	—
			Zip block of 4	3.25	—
d.			Vertical pair, imperf. horiz.	*150.00*	

Perf. 12

1789B	A1178	15c	**multicolored**	*3,500.*	*3,500.*
			P# block of 10, 5#	*40,000.*	
			Zip block of 4	*15,000.*	—

OLYMPIC GAMES ISSUE

22nd Summer Olympic Games, Moscow, July 19-Aug. 3, 1980. Nos. 1791-1792 alternate in one horizontal row, Nos. 1793-1794 in next.

Javelin — A1179

Running A1180

Swimming A1181

Rowing A1182

Equestrian A1183

Designed by Robert M. Cunningham.

PHOTOGRAVURE
Plates of 200 subjects in four panes of 50.

1979, Sept. 5 **Tagged** ***Perf. 11***
1790 A1179 10c **multicolored** .20 .20
P# block of 12, 6# 3.00 —
Zip block of 4 .85 —

1979, Sept. 28
1791 A1180 15c **multicolored** .30 .20
1792 A1181 15c **multicolored** .30 .20
1793 A1182 15c **multicolored** .30 .20
1794 A1183 15c **multicolored** .30 .20
a. Block of 4, #1791-1794 1.25 *1.50*
P# block of 12, 6# 4.00 —
Zip block of 4 1.30 —
P# block of 20, 6#, zip, copyright 6.50 —
b. As "a," imperf. *1,500.*

OLYMPIC GAMES ISSUE

13th Winter Olympic Games, Lake Placid, N.Y., Feb. 12-24. Nos. 1795-1796 alternate in one horizontal row, Nos. 1797-1798 in next.

Speed Skating A1184

Downhill Skiing A1185

Ski Jump — A1186

Ice Hockey A1187

Designed by Robert M. Cunningham

PHOTOGRAVURE
Plates of 200 subject in four panes of 50.

1980, Feb. 1 **Tagged** ***Perf. 11¼x10½***
1795 A1184 15c **multicolored** .35 .20
1796 A1185 15c **multicolored** .35 .20
1797 A1186 15c **multicolored** .35 .20
1798 A1187 15c **multicolored** .35 .20
b. Block of 4, #1795-1798 1.50 1.40
P# block of 12, 6# 4.50 —
Zip block of 4 1.55 —
P# block of 20, 6#, zip and copyright 7.50 —

Perf. 11
1795A A1184 15c **multicolored** 1.05 .60
1796A A1185 15c **multicolored** 1.05 .60
1797A A1186 15c **multicolored** 1.05 .60
1798A A1187 15c **multicolored** 1.05 .60
c. Block of 4, #1795A-1798A 4.25 3.50
P# block of 12, 6# 14.00 —
Zip block of 4 4.50 —
P# block of 20, 6#, zip and copyright 25.00 —

CHRISTMAS ISSUE

Virgin and Child by Gerard David — A1188

Santa Claus, Christmas Tree Ornament — A1189

Designed by Bradbury Thompson (No. 1799) and by Eskil Ohlsson (No. 1800).

No. 1799 is designed after a painting in National Gallery of Art, Washington, D.C.

PHOTOGRAVURE (Andreotti)
Plates of 400 subjects in four panes of 100.

1979, Oct. 18 **Tagged** ***Perf. 11***
1799 A1188 15c **multicolored** .30 .20
P# block of 12, 6# 4.00 —
Zip block of 4 1.25 —
P# block of 20, 6#, zip, copyright 6.50 —
a. Imperf., pair *90.00*
b. Vert. pair, imperf. horiz. *700.00*
c. Vert. pair, imperf. between *2,250.*
d. Tagging omitted —
1800 A1189 15c **multicolored** .30 .20
P# block of 12, 6# 4.00 —
Zip block of 4 1.25 —
P# block of 20, 6#, zip, copyright 6.50 —
a. Green & yellow omitted *625.00*
b. Green, yellow & tan omitted *700.00*

Nos. 1800a and 1800b always have the remaining colors misaligned.
No. 1800b is valued in the grade of fine.

VALUES FOR HINGED STAMPS AFTER NO. 771
This catalogue does not value unused stamps after No. 771 in hinged condition. Hinged unused stamps from No. 772 to the present are worth considerably less than the values given for unused stamps, which are for never-hinged examples.

PERFORMING ARTS SERIES

Will Rogers (1879-1935), actor and humorist.

Will Rogers — A1190

Designed by Jim Sharpe.

PHOTOGRAVURE (Andreotti)
Plates of 200 subjects in four panes of 50.

1979, Nov. 4 **Tagged** ***Perf. 11***
1801 A1190 15c **multicolored** .30 .20
P# block of 12, 6# 4.00 —
Zip block of 4 1.25 —
P# block of 20, 6#, zip, copyright 6.50 —
a. Imperf., pair *225.00*

VIETNAM VETERANS ISSUE

A tribute to veterans of the Vietnam War.

Ribbon for Vietnam Service Medal A1191

Designed by Stevan Dohanos.

PHOTOGRAVURE (Andreotti)
Plates of 200 subjects in four panes of 50.

1979, Nov. 11 **Tagged** ***Perf. 11***
1802 A1191 15c **multicolored** .30 .20
P# block of 10, 5# 3.25 —
Zip block of 4 1.25 —

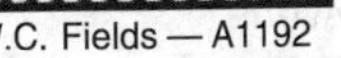
W.C. Fields — A1192

Benjamin Banneker — A1193

PERFORMING ARTS SERIES

W.C. Fields (1880-1946), actor and comedian.

Designed by Jim Sharpe.

PHOTOGRAVURE
Plates of 200 subjects in four panes of 50.

1980, Jan. 29 **Tagged** ***Perf. 11***
1803 A1192 15c **multicolored** .30 .20
P# block of 12, 6# 4.00 —
Zip block of 4 1.25 —
P# block of 20, 6#, zip, copyright 6.50 —
a. Imperf., pair —

BLACK HERITAGE SERIES

Benjamin Banneker (1731-1806), astronomer and mathematician.

Designed by Jerry Pinkney.

Printed by American Bank Note Co. and J. W. Fergusson and Sons.

PHOTOGRAVURE
Plates of 200 subjects in four panes of 50.

1980, Feb. 15 **Tagged** ***Perf. 11***
1804 A1193 15c **multicolored** .35 .20
P# block of 12, 6# 4.50 —
Zip block of 4 1.50 —
Plate block of 20, 6#, zip, copyright 6.50 —
a. Horiz. pair, imperf. vert. *800.00*

Imperfs, including gutter pairs and blocks, exist from printer's waste. These have been fraudulently perforated to simulate No. 1804a. Genuine examples of No. 1804a do not have colors misregistered.

NATIONAL LETTER WRITING WEEK ISSUE

National Letter Writing Week, Feb. 24-Mar. 1. Nos. 1805-1810 are printed vertically se-tenant.

Letters Preserve Memories — A1194

P.S. Write Soon — A1195

Letters Lift Spirits — A1196

Letters Shape Opinions — A1197

Designed by Randall McDougall.

Plates of 240 subjects in four panes of 60 (10x6) each.

PHOTOGRAVURE

1980, Feb. 25 **Tagged** ***Perf. 11***

1805 A1194 15c **multicolored** .30 .20
1806 A1195 15c **purple & multi** .30 .20
1807 A1196 15c **multicolored** .30 .20
1808 A1195 15c **green & multi** .30 .20
1809 A1197 15c **multicolored** .30 .20
1810 A1195 15c **red & multi** .30 .20
a. Vertical strip of 6, #1805-1810 1.85 *2.25*
P# block of 36, 6# 12.00 —
Zip block of 12 3.75 —
Nos. 1805-1810 (6) 1.80 1.20

AMERICANA TYPE

Weaver Violins — A1199

Designer: 3.5c, George Mercer.

COIL STAMPS

1980-81 **Engr.** ***Perf. 10 Vertically***

1811 A984 1c **dark blue,** *greenish,* shiny gum, *Mar. 6, 1980* .20 .20
Pair .20 .20
Joint line pair .40 —
Dull gum .20
Joint line pair .50
a. Imperf., pair *175.00*
Joint line pair *275.00*
b. Tagging omitted —
1813 A1199 3.5c **purple,** *yellow, June 23, 1980* .20 .20
Pair .20 .20
Joint line pair 1.00 —
a. Untagged (Bureau precanceled, lines only) .20 .20
Pair .35 .35
Joint line pair 1.95 —
b. Imperf., pair *225.00*
Joint line pair *450.00*
1816 A997 12c **red brown,** *beige, Apr. 8, 1981* .25 .20
Pair .50 .20
Joint line pair 1.50 —
a. Untagged (Bureau precanceled), **red brown,** *beige* 1.15 1.15
Pair 2.40 2.40
Joint line pair 47.50 —
b. Imperf., pair *175.00*
Joint line pair *350.00*
c. As "a," **brownish red,** *reddish beige* 1.65 1.65
Pair 2.50 2.50
Joint line pair 67.50 —
Nos. 1811-1816 (3) .65 .60

Bureau Precancels: 12c, lines only, PRESORTED/FIRST CLASS.

Eagle — A1207

PHOTOGRAVURE

Plates of 400 subjects in four panes of 100.

1981, Mar. 15 **Tagged** ***Perf. 11x10½***

1818 A1207 (18c) **violet** .35 .20
P# block of 4 1.60 —
Zip block of 4 1.50 —
Pair with full vert. gutter between —

BOOKLET STAMP

ENGRAVED

Perf. 10

1819 A1207 (18c) **violet** .40 .20
a. Booklet pane of 8 3.75 *2.25*

COIL STAMP

Perf. 10 Vert.

1820 A1207 (18c) **violet** .40 .20
Pair .80 .20
Joint line pair 1.60 —
a. Imperf., pair *100.00*
Joint line pair *250.00*

Frances Perkins A1208

Dolley Madison A1209

FRANCES PERKINS ISSUE

Frances Perkins (1882-1965), Secretary of Labor, 1933-1945 (first woman cabinet member).

Designed by F.R. Petrie.

ENGRAVED

Plates of 200 subjects in four panes of 50.

1980, Apr. 10 **Tagged** ***Perf. 10½x11***

1821 A1208 15c **Prussian blue** .30 .20
P# block of 4 1.30 —
Zip block of 4 1.25 —

DOLLEY MADISON ISSUE

Dolley Madison (1768-1849), First Lady, 1809-1817.

Designed by Esther Porter.

ENGRAVED

Plates of 600 subjects in four panes of 150.

1980, May 20 **Tagged** ***Perf. 11***

1822 A1209 15c **red brown & sepia** .30 .20
P# block of 4 1.40 —
Zip block of 4 1.25 —
a. Red brown missing (PS) —

Emily Bissell — A1210

Helen Keller and Anne Sullivan — A1211

EMILY BISSELL ISSUE

Emily Bissell (1861-1948), social worker; introduced Christmas seals in United States.

Designed by Stevan Dohanos.

ENGRAVED

Plates of 200 subjects in four panes of 50.

1980, May 31 **Tagged** ***Perf. 11***

1823 A1210 15c **black & red** .35 .20
P# block of 4 1.75 —
Zip block of 4 1.50 —
a. Vert. pair, imperf. horiz. *400.00*
b. All colors missing (EP) —

HELEN KELLER ISSUE

Helen Keller (1880-1968), blind and deaf writer an lecturer taught by Anne Sullivan (1867-1936).

Designed by Paul Calle.

LITHOGRAPHED AND ENGRAVED

Plates of 200 subjects in four panes of 50.

1980, June 27 **Tagged** ***Perf. 1***

1824 A1211 15c **multicolored** .30 .2
P# block of 4 1.30 —
Zip block of 4 1.25 —

Veterans Administration Emblem — A1212

Gen. Bernardo de Galvez — A1213

VETERANS ADMINISTRATION, 50th ANNIV.

Designed by Malcolm Grear.

Printed by American Bank Note Co. and J. W. Fergusson and Sons.

PHOTOGRAVURE

Plates of 200 subjects in four panes of 50.

1980, July 21 **Tagged** ***Perf. 11***

1825 A1212 15c **carmine & violet blue** .30 .20
P# block of 4, 2# 1.30 —
Zip block of 4 1.25 —
a. Horiz. pair, imperf. vert. *450.00*

BERNARDO DE GALVEZ ISSUE

Gen. Bernardo de Galvez (1746-1786), helped defeat British in Battle of Mobile, 1780.

Designed by Roy H. Andersen.

LITHOGRAPHED & ENGRAVED

Plates of 200 subjects in four panes of 50.

1980, July 23 **Tagged** ***Perf. 11***

1826 A1213 15c **multicolored** .30 .20
P# block of 4 1.30 —
Zip block of 4 1.25 —
a. Red, brown & blue (engr.) omitted *800.00*
b. Blue, brown, red (engr.) & yellow (litho.) omitted *1,400.*

CORAL REEFS ISSUE

Nos. 1827-1828 alternate in one horizontal row, Nos. 1829-1830 in the next.

Brain Coral, Beaugregory Fish — A1214

Elkhorn Coral, Porkfish — A1215

Chalice Coral, Moorish Idol — A1216

Finger Coral, Sabertooth Blenny — A1217

Designed by Chuck Ripper.

PHOTOGRAVURE

Plates of 200 subjects in four panes of 50.

1980, Aug. 26	Tagged	*Perf. 11*	
1827 A1214 15c **multi**		.30	.20
1828 A1215 15c **multi**		.30	.20
1829 A1216 15c **multi**		.30	.20
1830 A1217 15c **multi**		.30	.20
a. Block of 4, #1827-1830		1.25	1.10
P# block of 12, 6#		4.00	—
Zip block of 4		1.30	—
b. As "a," imperf.		*900.00*	
c. As "a," vert. imperf. between		—	
d. As "a," imperf. vert.		*3,000.*	

American Bald Eagle — A1218

Edith Wharton — A1219

ORGANIZED LABOR ISSUE

Designed by Peter Cocci.

PHOTOGRAVURE

Plates of 200 subjects in four panes of 50.

1980, Sept. 1	Tagged	*Perf. 11*	
1831 A1218 15c **multi**		.30	.20
P# block of 12, 6#		3.50	—
Zip block of 4		1.25	—
a. Imperf., pair		*375.00*	

LITERARY ARTS SERIES

Edith Wharton (1862-1937), novelist.

Designed by Bradbury Thompson after 1905 photograph.

ENGRAVED

Plates of 200 subjects in four panes of 50.

1980, Sept. 5	Tagged	*Perf. 10½x11*	
1832 A1219 15c **purple**		.30	.20
P# block of 4		1.30	—
Zip block of 4		1.25	—

EDUCATION ISSUE

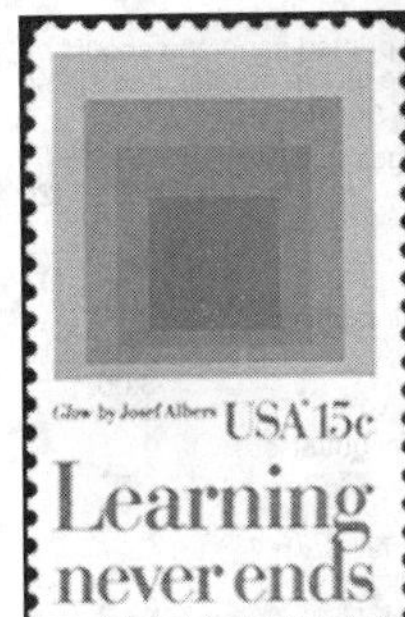

"Homage to the Square: Glow" by Josef Albers — A1220

Designed by Bradbury Thompson

Printed by American Bank Note Co. and J. W. Fergusson and Sons.

PHOTOGRAVURE

Plates of 200 subjects in four panes of 50.

1980, Sept. 12	Tagged	*Perf. 11*	
1833 A1220 15c **multi**		.30	.20
P# block of 6, 3#		1.90	—
Zip block of 4		1.25	—
a. Horiz. pair, imperf. vert.		*240.00*	

AMERICAN FOLK ART SERIES

Pacific Northwest Indian Masks

Heiltsuk, Bella Bella Tribe — A1221

Chilkat Tlingit Tribe — A1222

Tlingit Tribe — A1223

Bella Coola Tribe — A1224

Designed by Bradury Thompson after photographs.

PHOTOGRAVURE

Plates of 160 subjects in four panes of 40.

1980, Sept. 25	Tagged	*Perf. 11*	
1834 A1221 15c **multi**		.30	.20
1835 A1222 15c **multi**		.30	.20
1836 A1223 15c **multi**		.30	.20
1837 A1224 15c **multi**		.30	.20
a. Block of 4, #1834-1837		1.25	1.25
P# block of 10, 5#		4.50	—
Zip, copyright block of 6		1.90	—

AMERICAN ARCHITECTURE SERIES

Smithsonian A1225

Trinity Church A1226

Penn Academy A1227

Lyndhurst A1228

Designed by Walter D. Richards.

ENGRAVED (Giori)

Plates of 160 subjects in four panes of 40.

1980, Oct. 9	Tagged	*Perf. 11*	
1838 A1225 15c **black & red**		.30	.20
1839 A1226 15c **black & red**		.30	.20
1840 A1227 15c **black & red**		.30	.20
1841 A1228 15c **black & red**		.30	.20
a. Block of 4, #1838-1841		1.25	*1.50*
P# block of 4		1.50	—
Zip block of 4		1.30	—
b. As "a," red missing on Nos. 1838, 1839 (PS)		*400.00*	

CHRISTMAS ISSUE

Madonna and Child — A1229

Wreath and Toys — A1230

Designed by Esther Porter (No. 1842) after Epiphany Window, Washington Cathedral, and by Bob Timberlake (No. 1843).

PHOTOGRAVURE
Plate of 200 subjects in four panes of 50.

1980, Oct. 31 **Tagged** ***Perf. 11***

1842 A1229 15c **multi** .30 .20
P# block of 12, 6# 4.00 —
Zip block of 4 1.25 —
a. Imperf., pair *70.00*
Pair with full vert. gutter btwn. —

PHOTOGRAVURE (Combination Press)
Plates of 230 subjects (10x23) in panes of 50 (10x5).

1843 A1230 15c **multi** .30 .20
P# block of 20, 5-8 #, 1-2 copyright 6.50 —
a. Imperf., pair *70.00*
b. Buff omitted *25.00*
c. Vert. pair, imperf. horiz. —
d. Horiz. pair, imperf. between *4,000.*
e. Tagging omitted —

No. 1843b is difficult to identify and should have a competent certificate.

See Combination Press note after No. 1703.

GREAT AMERICANS ISSUE

A1231

A1232

A1233

A1234

A1235

A1236

A1237

A1238

A1239

A1240

A1241

A1242

A1243

A1244

A1245

A1246

A1247

A1248

A1249

A1250

A1251

A1252

A1253

A1254

A1255

A1256

Designers: 1c, Bernie Fuchs. 2c, Burt Silverman, 3c, 17c, 40c, Ward Brackett. 4c, 7c, 10c, 18c, 30c, Richard Sparks. 5c, Paul Calle. 6c, No. 1861, Dennis Lyall. 8c, Arthur Lidov. 9c, 11c, Robert Alexander Anderson. 13c, Brad Holland. 14c, Bradbury Thompson. 19c, 39c, Roy H. Andersen. No. 1860, Jim Sharpe. No. 1862, 22c, 50c, 37c, Christopher Calle. 35c, Nathan Jones.

ENGRAVED

1980-85 **Tagged** ***Perf. 11x10½***
Perf. 11 (1c, 6c-11c, 14c, No. 1862, 22c, 30c, 39c, 40c, 50c)

1844 A1231 1c **black,** perf. 11.2, small block tagging, *Sept. 23, 1983* .20 .20
P# block of 6 .35 —
P# block of 20, 1-2 #, 1-2 copyright 2.00 —
a. Imperf., pair *300.00*
b. Vert. pair, imperf. between and at bottom *3,000.*
c. Perf. 10.9, small block tagging .20 .20
P# block of 6 .35 —
P# block of 20, 1-2 #, 1-2 copyright 2.00 —
d. Perf. 10.9, large block tagging, *1985* .20 .20
P# block of 6 .35 —
P# block of 20, 1-2 #, 1-2 copyright 2.00 —
e. Vert. pair, imperf. horiz. —

1845 A1232 2c **brn blk,** overall tagging, *Nov. 18, 1982* .20 .20
P# block of 4 .35 —
Zip block of 4 .25 —
Vert. pair, full gutter between —
a. Tagging omitted —

1846 A1233 3c **olive green,** overall tagging, *July 13, 1983* .20 .20
P# block of 4 .55 —
Zip block of 4 .30 —
a. Tagging omitted 4.00

1847 A1234 4c **violet,** overall tagging, *June 3, 1983* .20 .20
P# block of 4 .65 —
Zip block of 4 .35 —
a. Tagging omitted 4.00

1848 A1235 5c **henna brown,** overall tagging, *June 25, 1983* .20 .20
P# block of 4 .70 —
Zip block of 4 .45 —

1849 A1236 6c **orange vermilion,** large block tagging, *Sept. 19, 1985* .20 .20
P# block of 6 .85 —
P# block of 20, 1-2 #, 1-2 zip, 1-2 copyright 3.50 —
a. Vert. pair, imperf. between and at bottom *2,000.*

1850 A1237 7c **bright carmine,** small block tagging, *Jan. 25, 1985* .20 .20
P# block of 6 .95 —
P# block of 20, 1-2 #, 1-2 zip, 1-2 copyright 4.00 —

1851 A1238 8c **olive black,** overall tagging, *July 25, 1985* .20 .20
P# block of 4 .85 —
Zip block of 4 .60 —
a. Tagging omitted —

1852 A1239 9c **dark green,** small block tagging, *June 7, 1985* .20 .20
P# block of 6 1.30 —
P# block of 20, 1-2 #. 1-2 zip, 1-2 copyright 5.00 —

1853 A1240 10c **Prus. blue,** small block tagging, *May 31, 1984* .25 .20
P# block of 6 2.00 —
P# block of 20, 1-2 #, 1-2 copyright, 1-2 zip 9.00 —
a. Large block tagging .30 .20
P# block of 6 2.25 —
P# block of 20, 1-2 #, 1-2 copyright, 1-2 zip 9.00 —
b. Vert. pair, imperf. between *850.00*
c. Horiz. pair, imperf. between *2,000.*

Completely imperforate tagged or untagged stamps are from printer's waste.

1854 A1241 11c **dark blue,** overall tagging, *Feb. 12, 1985* .30 .20
P# block of 4 1.60 —
Zip block of 4 1.20 —
a. Tagging omitted 9.00

1855 A1242 13c **light maroon,** overall tagging, *Jan. 15, 1982* .30 .20
P# block of 4 2.00 —
Zip block of 4 1.20 —
a. Tagging omitted 7.50

1856 A1243 14c **slate green,** small block tagging, *Mar. 21, 1985* .30 .20
P# block of 6 2.25 —
P# block of 20, 1-2 #, 1-2 zip, 1-2 copyright 9.00 —
a. Large block tagging .30 .20
P# block of 6 2.25 —
P# block of 20, 1-2 #, 1-2 zip, 1-2 copyright 9.00 —
b. Vert. pair, imperf. horiz. *120.00*
c. Horiz. pair, imperf. btwn. 9.00
d. Vert. pair, imperf. btwn. *1,500.*
e. All color omitted —

No. 1856e comes from a partially printed pane and should be collected as a vertical strip of 10, one stamp normal, one stamp transitional and 8 stamps with color omitted.

1857 A1244 17c **green,** overall tagging, *May 28, 1981* .35 .20
P# block of 4 2.00 —
Zip block of 4 1.40 —
a. Tagging omitted 10.00

1858 A1245 18c **dark blue,** overall tagging, *May 7, 1981* .35 .20
P# block of 4 3.00 —
Zip block of 4 1.40 —
Pair with full horiz. gutter between —
a. Tagging omitted 7.50

1859 A1246 19c **brown,** overall tagging, *Dec. 27, 1980* .40 .20
P# block of 4 2.75 —
Zip block of 4 1.75 —

1860 A1247 20c **claret,** overall tagging, *Jan. 12, 1982* .40 .20
P# block of 4 3.75 —
Zip block of 4 1.65 —
a. Tagging omitted 7.50

1861 A1248 20c **green,** overall tagging, *June 10, 1983* .50 .20
P# block of 4 4.00 —
Zip block of 4 2.00 —
1862 A1249 20c **black,** perf 10.9, small block tagging, dull gum, *Jan. 26, 1984* .40 .20
P# block of 6 4.50 —
P# block of 20, 1-2 #, 1-2 copyright, 1-2 zip 12.00 —
a. Perf. 11.2, large block tagging, dull gum .40 .20
Corner P# block of 4 3.00 —
Zip block of 4 1.60 —
b. Perf. 11.2, overall tagging, dull gum, *1990* .40 —
Corner P# block of 4 3.75 —
Zip block of 4 1.60 —
c. Tagging omitted, perf. 11.2 8.50
d. Prephosphored uncoated paper (mottled tagging), shiny gum, perf. 11.2, *1993* .40 .20
Corner P# block of 4 2.50 —
Zip block of 4 1.60
1863 A1250 22c **dark chalky blue,** small block tagging, *Apr. 23, 1985* .75 .20
P# block of 6 6.00 —
P# block of 20, 1-2 #, 1-2 zip, 1-2 copyright 17.50 —
a. Large block tagging 1.00 .20
P# block of 6 8.00 —
P# block of 20, 1-2 #, 1-2 zip, 1-2 copyright 22.50 —
b. Perf. 11.2, large block tagging, *1987* .55 .20
Corner P# block of 4 7.00 —
Zip block of 4 2.25 —
c. Tagging omitted 7.50
d. Vert. pair, imperf. horiz. *2,500.*
e. Vert. pair, imperf. between —
f. Horiz. pair, imperf. between *2,000.*
1864 A1251 30c **olive gray,** small block tagging, *Sept. 2, 1984* .60 .20
P# block of 6 3.50 —
P# block of 20, 1-2 #, 1-2 copyright, 1-2 zip 17.50 —
a. Perf. 11.2, large block tagging .55 .20
Corner P# block of 4 3.25 —
Zip block of 4 2.50 —
b. Perf. 11.2, overall tagging 1.75 .20
Corner P# block of 4 22.50 —
Zip block of 4 7.25 —
c. Tagging omitted —
1865 A1252 35c **gray,** overall tagging, *June 3, 1981* .75 .20
P# block of 4 4.25 —
Zip block of 4 3.25 —
a. Tagging omitted —
1866 A1253 37c **blue,** overall tagging, *Jan. 26, 1982* .80 .20
P# block of 4 3.75 —
Zip block of 4 3.25 —
a. Tagging omitted 10.00
1867 A1254 39c **rose lilac,** perf 10.9, small block tagging, *Mar. 20, 1985* .90 .20
P# block of 6 5.75 —
P# block of 20, 1-2 #, 1-2 zip, 1-2 copyright 22.50 —
a. Vert. pair, imperf. horiz. *500.00*
b. Vert. pair, imperf. between *2,000.*
c. Large block tagging, perf 10.9 .90 .20
P# block of 6 5.75 —
P# block of 20, 1-2 #, 1-2 zip, 1-2 copyright 20.00 —
d. Perf. 11.2, large block tagging .90 .20
Corner P# block of 4 5.75 —
Zip block of 4 3.75 —
1868 A1255 40c **dark green,** perf 10.9, small block tagging, *Feb. 24, 1984* .90 .20
P# block of 6 6.50 —
P# block of 20, 1-2 #, 1-2 copyright, 1-2 zip 20.00 —
a. Perf. 11.2, large block tagging .90 .20
Corner P# block of 4 6.50 —
Zip block of 4 3.75 —
1869 A1256 50c **brown,** perf 10.9, overall tagging, shiny gum, *Feb. 22, 1985* .95 .20
P# block of 4 7.50 —
Zip block of 4 4.00 —
a. Perf. 11.2, large block tagging, dull gum .95 .20
P# block of 4 6.25 —
Zip block of 4 4.00 —
b. Tagging omitted 11.00
c. Tagging omitted, perf. 11.2, dull gum 8.00
d. Perf. 11.2, overall tagging, dull gum 1.50 .20
P# block of 4 8.50 —
Zip block of 4 6.75 —
e. Perf. 11.2, prephosphored uncoated paper (mottled tagging), shiny gum, *1992* .90 .20
P# block of 4 5.00 —
Zip block of 4 4.00 —
Nos. 1844-1869 (26) 11.00 5.20

A1261

A1262

EVERETT DIRKSEN (1896-1969)

Senate minority leader, 1960-1969.

Designed by Ron Adair.

ENGRAVED

Plates of 200 subjects in four panes of 50.

1981, Jan. 4 **Tagged** ***Perf. 11***
1874 A1261 15c **gray** .30 .20
P# block of 4 1.40 —
Zip block of 4 1.25 —
a. All color omitted *500.00*

No. 1874a comes from a partially printed pane and may be collected as a vertical strip of 3 or 5 (1 or 3 stamps normal, one stamp transitional and one stamp with color omitted) or as a pair with one partially printed stamp.

BLACK HERITAGE SERIES

Whitney Moore Young, Jr. (1921-1971), civil rights leader.

Designed by Jerry Pinkney.

PHOTOGRAVURE

Plates of 200 subjects in four panes of 50.

1981, Jan. 30 **Tagged** ***Perf. 11***
1875 A1262 15c **multi** .35 .20
P# block of 4, 6# 1.75 —
Zip block of 4 1.50 —

FLOWER ISSUE

A1263 A1264

A1265 A1266

Illustration reduced.

Designed by Lowell Nesbitt. Illustration reduced.

PHOTOGRAVURE

Plates of 192 subjects in four panes of 48 (8x6).

1981, Apr. 23 **Tagged** ***Perf. 11***
1876 A1263 18c **multicolored** .35 .20
1877 A1264 18c **multicolored** .35 .20
1878 A1265 18c **multicolored** .35 .20
1879 A1266 18c **multicolored** .35 .20
a. Block of 4, #1876-1879 1.40 1.25
P# block of 4, 6# 1.75 —
Zip block of 4 1.45 —

American Wildlife

A1267

A1268

A1269

A1270

A1271

A1272

A1273

A1274

A1275

A1276

Designs from photographs by Jim Brandenburg.

ENGRAVED

1981, May 14 **Tagged** ***Perf. 11***

Dark brown

1880 A1267 18c Bighorn .55 .20
a. Tagging omitted —
1881 A1268 18c Puma .55 .20
1882 A1269 18c Harbor seal .55 .20
1883 A1270 18c American Buffalo .55 .20
1884 A1271 18c Brown bear .55 .20
1885 A1272 18c Polar bear .55 .20
1886 A1273 18c Elk (wapiti) .55 .20
1887 A1274 18c Moose .55 .20
a. Tagging omitted —
1888 A1275 18c White-tailed deer .55 .20
1889 A1276 18c Pronghorn .55 .20
a. Booklet pane of 10, #1880-1889 8.50 *7.00*
b. Tagging omitted —

Nos. 1880-1889 issued in booklet only. All stamps have one or two straight edges.

FLAG AND ANTHEM ISSUE

A1277

A1278

A1279

A1280

Designed by Peter Cocci.

ENGRAVED

Plates of 460 subjects (20x23) in panes of 100 (10x10).

1981, Apr. 24 **Tagged** ***Perf. 11***
1890 A1277 18c **multicolored** .35 .20
P# block of 6 2.25 —
P# block of 20, 1-2 # 10.00 —
a. Imperf., pair *100.00*
b. Vert. pair, imperf. horiz. *850.00*

See Combination Press note after No. 1703.

Coil Stamp

Perf. 10 Vert.

No.	Description	Unused	Used
1891 A1278 18c	**multicolored**	.35	.20
	Pair	.70	.20
	P# strip of 3, #1	85.00	
	P# strip of 3, #2	16.00	
	P# strip of 3, #3	225.00	
	P# strip of 3, #4	6.00	
	P# strip of 3, #5	4.00	
	P# strip of 3, #6	*1,450.*	
	P# strip of 3, #7	26.00	
	P# strip of 5, #1	350.00	
	P# strip of 5, #2	50.00	
	P# strip of 5, #3	875.00	
	P# strip of 5, #4	7.00	
	P# strip of 5, #5	4.75	
	P# strip of 5, #6	*3,600.*	
	P# strip of 5, #7	30.00	
	P# single, #1	—	2.50
	P# single, #2	—	1.00
	P# single, #3	—	10.00
	P# single, #4	—	1.00
	P# single, #5	—	1.00
	P# single, #6	—	*575.00*
	P# single, #7	—	25.00
a.	Imperf., pair	30.00	—
	P#2-5		
b.	Pair, imperf. between	*1,250.*	
a.	Tagging omitted		—
	P#2		—

Beware of pairs offered as No. 1891b that have faint blind perfs.

Vertical pairs and blocks exist from printer's waste.

Booklet Stamps

Perf. 11

No.	Description	Unused	Used
1892 A1279 6c	**multicolored**	.50	.20
1893 A1280 18c	**multicolored**	.30	.20
a.	Booklet pane of 8 (2 #1892, 6 #1893)	3.00	*2.50*
b.	As "a," vert. imperf. between	*75.00*	
c.	Se-tenant pair, #1892 & #1893	.90	*1.00*
d.	As "a," tagging omitted	—	

Bureau Precanceled Coils

Starting with No. 1895b, Bureau precanceled coil stamps are valued unused as well as used. The coils issued with dull gum may be difficult to distinguish.

When used normally these stamps do not receive any postal markings so that used stamps with an additional postal cancellation of any kind are worth considerably less than the values shown here.

FLAG OVER SUPREME COURT ISSUE

A1281

Designed by Dean Ellis

ENGRAVED

Plates of 460 subjects (20x23) in panes of 100 (10x10)

1981, Dec. 17 — Tagged — *Perf. 11*

No.	Description	Unused	Used
1894 A1281 20c	**black, dark blue & red,** dull gum	.40	.20
	P# block of 6	2.75	—
	P# block of 20, 1-2 #	9.00	—
a.	Vert. pair, imperf.	35.00	
b.	Vert. pair, imperf. horiz.	*525.00*	
c.	Dark blue omitted	*85.00*	
d.	Black omitted	*325.00*	
e.	Perf. 11.2, shiny gum	.35	.20
	P# block of 6	2.50	—
	P# block of 20, 1-2 #	8.50	—
f.	Tagging omitted	—	

Coil Stamp

Perf. 10 Vert.

No.	Description	Unused	Used
1895 A1281 20c	**black, dark blue & red,** wide block tagging	.40	.20
	Pair	.80	.20
	P# strip of 3, #1	5.00	
	P# strip of 3, #2	7.75	
	P# strip of 3, #3	3.50	
	P# strip of 3, #5	3.50	
	P# strip of 3, #11	8.00	
	P# strip of 3, #13, 14	3.25	
	P# strip of 5, #1	72.50	
	P# strip of 5, #2	8.00	
	P# strip of 5, #3	5.00	
	P# strip of 5, #5	4.25	
	P# strip of 5, #11	9.00	
	P# strip of 5, #13, 14	4.25	
	P# single, #1	—	.75
	P# single, #2-3	—	.50
	P# single, #5	—	.50
	P# single, #11	—	3.00
	P# single, #13, 14	—	1.00
a.	Narrow block tagging	.40	.20
	Pair	.80	.20
	P# strip of 3, #4	35.00	
	P# strip of 3, #6	85.00	
	P# strip of 3, #8	3.50	
	P# strip of 3, #9-10	3.25	
	P# strip of 3, #12	6.50	
	P# strip of 5, #4	*575.00*	
	P# strip of 5, #6	160.00	
	P# strip of 5, #8	12.50	
	P# strip of 5, #9	4.25	
	P# strip of 5, #10	5.00	
	P# strip of 5, #12	8.25	
	P# single, #4	—	1.00
	P# single, #6	—	2.50
	P# single, #8	—	.70
	P# single, #9	—	.50
	P# single, #10	—	.70
	P# single, #12	—	1.00
b.	Untagged (Bureau precanceled, lines only)	.50	.50
	P# strip of 3, #14	57.50	
	P# strip of 5, #14	60.00	
	P# single, #14		50.00
c.	Tagging omitted (not Bureau precanceled	—	
	P# strip of 3, #4		—
	P# strip of 3, #5, 8, 10, 11, 14	—	
	P# strip of 5, #5, 10, 11, 14	—	
	P# single, #5, 8-11, 14	—	—
d.	Imperf., pair	10.00	
	P#1-6, 8-14		
e.	Pair, imperf. between	*1,250.*	
f.	Black omitted	*50.00*	
g.	Dark blue omitted	*1,500.*	

The wide block tagging on No. 1895 and narrow block tagging on No. 1895a differentiate stamps printed on two different presses. The wide blocks are approximately 20-21mm high by 18mm wide with a 4mm untagged gutter between tagging blocks.

The narrow blocks are approximately 21-22mm high and approximately 16-16½mm wide with a 5½-6½ untagged gutter between tagging blocks.

BOOKLET STAMP

Perf. 11x10½

No.	Description	Unused	Used
1896 A1281 20c	**black, dark blue & red,** small block tagging	.40	.20
a.	Booklet pane of 6	3.00	*2.25*
	Scored perforations	3.00	*2.25*
b.	Booklet pane of 10, *June 1, 1982*	5.25	*3.25*
c.	As "b," tagging omitted	—	
d.	Large block tagging ('83)	.40	.20
e.	As "d," booklet pane of 10	5.25	*3.25*
	Scored perforations	5.25	*3.25*

Booklets containing two panes of ten of No. 1896e were issued Nov. 17, 1983.

The small block tagging is 16x18mm (Nos. 1896-1896b). The large block tagging is 18x21mm (Nos. 1896d-1896e).

TRANSPORTATION ISSUE

A1283

A1284

Designer: 1c, 2c, David Stone.

COIL STAMPS
ENGRAVED

1981-84 — Tagged — *Perf. 10 Vert.*

No.	Description	Unused	Used
1897 A1283 1c	**violet,** *Aug. 19, 1983*	.20	.20
	Pair	.20	.20
	P# strip of 3, line, #1, 2	.30	
	P# strip of 3, line, #3, 4	.50	
	P# strip of 3, line, #5, 6	.30	
	P# strip of 5, line, #1, 2	.45	
	P# strip of 5, line, #3, 4	.75	
	P# strip of 5, line, #5, 6	.50	
	P# single, #1, 2	—	.25
	P# single, #3, 4	—	.65
	P# single, #5, 6	—	.30
b.	Imperf., pair	*675.00*	
	P#5-6		
	Joint line pair	—	
1897A A1284 2c	**black,** *May 20, 1982*	.20	.20
	Pair	.20	.20
	P# strip of 3, line, #2	.50	
	P# strip of 3, line, #3, 4	.45	
	P# strip of 3, line, #6	.50	
	P# strip of 3, line, #8, 10	.45	
	P# strip of 5, line, #2	.55	
	P# strip of 5, line, #3, 4	.50	
	P# strip of 5, line, #6	.55	
	P# strip of 5, line, #8, 10	.50	
	P# single, #2	—	.45
	P# single, #3, 4	—	.40
	P# single, #6	—	.45
	P# single, #8, 10	—	.35
c.	Imperf., pair	52.50	
	P#3-4, 8, 10		
	Joint line pair	—	
d.	Tagging omitted	—	
	P#8		

A1284a

A1285

Designers: 3c, Walter Brooks. 4c, Jim Schleyer.

No.	Description	Unused	Used
1898 A1284a 3c	**dark green,** *Mar. 25, 1983*	.20	.20
	Pair	.20	.20
	P# strip of 3, line, #1-4	.65	
	P# strip of 5, line, #1-4	.70	
	P# single, #1-4	—	.55
1898A A1285 4c	**reddish brown,** *Aug. 19, 1982*	.20	.20
	Pair	.20	.20
	P# strip of 3, line, #1-4	.95	
	P# strip of 3, line, #5-6	2.10	
	P# strip of 5, line, #1-4	1.00	
	P# strip of 5, line, #5-6	2.25	
	P# single, #1-4	—	.75
	P# single, #5-6	—	2.00
b.	Untagged (Bureau precanceled, Nonprofit Org.)	.20	.20
	P# strip of 3, line, #3-6	4.75	
	P# strip of 5, line, #3-6	5.00	
	P# single, #3, 4	—	4.00
	P# single, #5, 6	—	4.25
c.	As "b," imperf., pair	*750.00*	
	P#5-6		
d.	Imperf. pair	*850.00*	—
	P#1-2		
e.	Tagging omitted (not Bureau precanceled)	—	
	P#3-4		

A1286

A1287

Designers: 5c, 5.2c, Walter Brooks.

1899 A1286 5c **gray green,** *Oct. 10, 1983* .20 .20
Pair .25 .20
P# strip of 3, line, #1-4 .85
P# strip of 5, line, #1-4 .90
P# single, #1-4 — .75
a. Imperf., pair *2,750.*
P#1-2
b. Tagging omitted 7.50 —
P# strip of 5, line, #1, 2 *250.00*

1900 A1287 5.2c **carmine,** *Mar. 21, 1983* .20 .20
Pair .25 .20
P# strip of 3, line, #1-2 6.00
P# strip of 3, line, #3 170.00
P# strip of 3, line, #5 140.00
P# strip of 5, line, #1-2 8.25
P# strip of 5, line, #3 260.00
P# strip of 5, line, #5 190.00
P# single, #1-2 — 5.50
P# single, #3 — *160.00*
P# single, #5 — *140.00*
a. Untagged (Bureau precanceled, lines only) .20 .20
P# strip of 3, line, #1-3 9.25
P# strip of 3, line, #4 12.00
P# strip of 3, line, #5 9.25
P# strip of 3, line, #6 12.00
P# strip of 5, line, #1-3 10.00
P# strip of 5, line, #4 13.00
P# strip of 5, line, #5 10.00
P# strip of 5, line, #6 13.00
P# single, #1, 2 — 3.00
P# single, #3 — 2.00
P# single, #4 — 9.00
P# single, #5 — 2.00
P# single, #6 — 9.00
b. Tagging omitted —

A1288

A1289

Designers: 5.9c, David Stone. 7.4c, Jim Schleyer.

1901 A1288 5.9c **blue,** *Feb. 17, 1982* .25 .20
Pair .50 .20
P# strip of 3, line, #3-4 6.75
P# strip of 5, line, #3-4 13.00
P# single, #3-4 — 5.75
a. Untagged (Bureau Precanceled, lines only) .20 .20
P# strip of 3, line, #3-4 24.00
P# strip of 3, line, #5-6 80.00
P# strip of 5, line, #3-4 30.00
P# strip of 5, line, #5-6 100.00
P# single, #3-4 — 5.50
P# single, #5-6 — 75.00
b. As "a," imperf., pair *200.00*
P#3-4
Joint line pair —

1902 A1289 7.4c **brown,** *Apr. 7, 1984* .20 .20
Pair .40 .20
P# strip of 3, #2 8.00
P# strip of 5, #2 8.25
P# single, #2 — 6.00
a. Untagged (Bureau precanceled, Blk. Rt. CAR-RT SORT) .20 .20
P# strip of 3, #2 5.00
P# strip of 5, #2 5.50
P# single, #2 — 4.00

A1290

A1291

Designers: 9.3c, Jim Schleyer. 10.9c, David Stone.

1903 A1290 9.3c **carmine rose,** *Dec. 15* .30 .20
Pair .60 .20
P# strip of 3, line, #1-2 7.50
P# strip of 3, line, #3-4 20.00
P# strip of 3, line, #5-6 250.00
P# strip of 5, line, #1-2 12.00
P# strip of 5, line, #3-4 32.50
P# strip of 5, line, #5-6 290.00
P# single, #1-2 — 7.00
P# single, #3-4 — 17.50
P# single, #5-6 — 190.00
a. Untagged (Bureau precanceled, lines only) .25 .25
P# strip of 3, line, #1 11.50
P# strip of 3, line, #2 10.50
P# strip of 3, line, #3 21.00
P# strip of 3, line, #4 16.00
P# strip of 3, line, #5-6 2.50
P# strip of 3, line, #8 240.00
P# strip of 5, line, #1 12.00
P# strip of 5, line, #2 11.00
P# strip of 5, line, #3 26.00
P# strip of 5, line, #4 18.00
P# strip of 5, line, #5-6 2.75
P# strip of 5, line, #8 260.00
P# single, #1-2 — 10.00
P# single, #3 — 12.50
P# single, #4 — 10.00
P# single, #5-6 — 1.75
P# single, #8 — 240.00
b. As "a," imperf., pair *120.00*
P#1-2
Joint line pair *200.00*

1904 A1291 10.9c **purple,** *Mar. 26, 1982* .30 .20
Pair .60 .20
P# strip of 3, line, #1-2 15.00
P# strip of 5, line, #1-2 29.00
P# single, #1-2 — 12.00
a. Untagged (Bureau precanceled, lines only) .30 .25
P# strip of 3, line, #1-2 20.00
P# strip of 3, line, #3-4 300.00
P# strip of 5, line, #1-2 29.00
P# strip of 5, line, #3-4 350.00
P# single, #1-2 — 8.75
P# single, #3-4 — 70.00
b. As "a," imperf., pair *150.00*
P#1-2
Joint line pair —

A1292

A1293

Designers: 11c, Jim Schleyer. 17c Chuck Jaquays.

1905 A1292 11c **red,** *Feb. 3, 1984* .30 .20
Pair .60 .20
P# strip of 3, #1 3.50
P# strip of 5, #1 3.75
P# single, #1 — 3.00
a. Untagged *Sept. 1991* .25 .20
Pair .50 .20
P# strip of 3, #1 3.00
P# strip of 3, #2 2.25
P# strip of 5, #1 3.75
P# strip of 5, #2 2.75
P# single, #1 — 2.75
P# single, #2 — 2.00

Untagged stamps from plate 1 come only Bureau precanceled with lines.

1906 A1293 17c **ultramarine,** *June 25* .35 .20
Pair .70 .20
P# strip of 3, line, #1-5 2.00
P# strip of 3, line, #6 13.00
P# strip of 3, line, #7 5.00
P# strip of 5, line, #1-5 2.25
P# strip of 5, line, #6 13.50
P# strip of 5, line, #7 5.25
P# single, #1-5 — 1.50
P# single, #6 — 12.00
P# single, #7 — 4.75
a. Untagged (Bureau precanceled, Presorted First Class) .35 .35
P# strip of 3, line, #1, 2 9.00
P# strip of 3, line, #3-5 3.50
P# strip of 3, line, #6, 7 11.00
P# strip of 5, line, #1, 2 9.25
P# strip of 5, line, #3-5 3.75
P# strip of 5, line, #6-7 11.50
P# single, #1, 2 — 7.25
P# single, #3-5 — 3.00
P# single, #6, 7 — 9.00

Three different precancel styles exist: "PRESORTED" measuring 11.3mm, 12.8mm and 13.4mm. The most common is the 11.3mm. Combination pairs exist.

b. Imperf., pair *165.00*
P#1-4
Joint line pair —
c. As "a," imperf., pair *650.00*
P#3-4
Joint line pair —

A1294

A1295

Designers: 18c, David Stone. 20c, Jim Schleyer.

No.	Type	Denom.	Description	Unused	Used
1907	A1294	18c	**dark brown,** *May 18*	.35	.20
			Pair	.70	.20
			P# strip of 3, line, #1	65.00	
			P# strip of 3, line, #2	2.75	
			P# strip of 3, line, #3, 4	62.50	
			P# strip of 3, line, #5, 6	2.75	
			P# strip of 3, line, #7	30.00	
			P# strip of 3, line, #8	2.75	
			P# strip of 3, line, #9-12	12.00	
			P# strip of 3, line, #13, 14	2.75	
			P# strip of 3, line, #15, 16	19.00	
			P# strip of 3, line, #17, 18	3.50	
			P# strip of 5, line, #1	95.00	
			P# strip of 5, line, #2	3.00	
			P# strip of 5, line, #3-4	82.50	
			P# strip of 5, line, #5, 6	3.00	
			P# strip of 5, line, #7	30.00	
			P# strip of 5, line, #8	3.00	
			P# strip of 5, line, #9-12	13.00	
			P# strip of 5, line, #13, 14	3.00	
			P# strip of 5, line, #15, 16	22.50	
			P# strip of 5, line, #17, 18	4.00	
			P# single, #1	—	9.50
			P# single, #2	—	1.00
			P# single, #3, 4	—	9.25
			P# single, #5, 6	—	1.00
			P# single, #7	—	9.50
			P# single, #8	—	1.00
			P# single, #9-14	—	4.00
			P# single, #15, 16	—	20.00
			P# single, #17, 18	—	3.75
a.			Imperf., pair	*140.00*	
			P#2, 8-10, 13 Joint line pair	—	
1908	A1295	20c	**vermilion,** *Dec. 10*	.35	.20
			Pair	.70	.20
			P# strip of 3, line, #1	30.00	
			P# strip of 3, line, #2	160.00	
			P# strip of 3, line, #3, 4	3.75	
			P# strip of 3, line, #5	2.00	
			P# strip of 3, line, #6	32.50	
			P# strip of 3, line, #7, 8	85.00	
			P# strip of 3, line, #9, 10	2.00	
			P# strip of 3, line, #11	29.00	
			P# strip of 3, line, #12	7.00	
			P# strip of 3, line, #13	3.75	
			P# strip of 3, line, #14	7.00	
			P# strip of 3, line, #15, 16	4.00	
			P# strip of 5, line, #1	140.00	
			P# strip of 5, line, #2	750.00	
			P# strip of 5, line, #3, 4	4.25	
			P# strip of 5, line, #5	2.75	
			P# strip of 5, line, #6	37.50	
			P# strip of 5, line, #7-8	200.00	
			P# strip of 5, line, #9-10	2.75	
			P# strip of 5, line, #11	80.00	
			P# strip of 5, line, #12	8.50	
			P# strip of 5, line, #13	4.25	
			P# strip of 5, line, #14	8.50	
			P# strip of 5, line, #15-16	4.25	
			P# single, #1	—	1.00
			P# single, #2	—	8.00
			P# single, #3, 4	—	.65
			P# single, #5	—	.75
			P# single, #6	—	1.25
			P# single, #7, 8	—	1.00
			P# single, #9, 10	—	.75
			P# single, #11	—	1.00
			P# single, #12	—	6.25
			P# single, #13	—	.65
			P# single, #14	—	6.25
			P# single, #15, 16	—	2.00
a.			Imperf., pair	*110.00*	
			P#1-5, 9-10, 15-16 Joint line pair	*300.00*	
b.			Tagging omitted		—
			Nos. 1897-1908 (14)	3.60	2.80

See Nos. 2225-2228.

Eagle and Moon — A1296

Booklet Stamp
PHOTOGRAVURE

1983, Aug. 12 **Tagged** ***Perf. 10 Vert.***

No.	Type	Denom.	Description	Unused	Used
1909	A1296	$9.35	**multicolored**	22.50	15.00
a.			Booklet pane of 3	70.00	—

A1297

A1298

AMERICAN RED CROSS CENTENNIAL

Designed by Joseph Csatari.

PHOTOGRAVURE
Plates of 200 subjects in four panes of 50.

1981, May 1 **Tagged** ***Perf. 10½x11***

No.	Type	Denom.	Description	Unused	Used
1910	A1297	18c	**multicolored**	.35	.20
			P# block of 4, 6#	1.50	—
			Zip block of 4	1.40	—

SAVINGS & LOAN SESQUICENTENNIAL

Designed by Don Hedin.

PHOTOGRAVURE
Plates of 200 subjects in four panes of 50.

1981, May 8 **Tagged** ***Perf. 11***

No.	Type	Denom.	Description	Unused	Used
1911	A1298	18c	**multicolored**	.35	.20
			P# block of 4, 6#	1.50	—
			Zip block of 4	1.40	—

SPACE ACHIEVEMENT ISSUE

A1299

A1302

A1300

A1301

A1303

A1306

A1304

A1305

Designed by Robert McCall.

Designs: A1299, Moon walk. A1300-A1301, A1304-A1305, Columbia space shuttle. A1302, Skylab. A1303, Pioneer 11. A1306, Telescope. Se-tenant in blocks of 8.

PHOTOGRAVURE
Plates of 192 subjects in four panes of 48 each.

1981, May 21 **Tagged** ***Perf. 11***

No.	Type	Denom.	Description	Unused	Used
1912	A1299	18c	**multicolored**	.40	.20
1913	A1300	18c	**multicolored**	.40	.20
1914	A1301	18c	**multicolored**	.40	.20
1915	A1302	18c	**multicolored**	.40	.20
1916	A1303	18c	**multicolored**	.40	.20
1917	A1304	18c	**multicolored**	.40	.20
1918	A1305	18c	**multicolored**	.40	.20
1919	A1306	18c	**multicolored**	.40	.20
a.			Block of 8, #1912-1919	3.25	3.00
			P# block of 8, 6#	3.75	—
			Zip, copyright block of 8	3.25	—
b.			As "a," imperf.	*8,000.*	
c.			As "a," tagging omitted	—	

PROFESSIONAL MANAGEMENT EDUCATION CENTENARY

Joseph Wharton (Founder of Wharton School of Business) A1307

Designed by Rudolph de Harak.

PHOTOGRAVURE
Plates of 200 subject in four panes of 50.

1981, June 18 **Tagged** ***Perf. 11***
1920 A1307 18c **blue & black** .35 .20
P# block of 4, 2# 1.50 —
Zip block of 4 1.40 —

PRESERVATION OF WILDLIFE HABITATS

Great Blue Heron — A1308

Badger — A1309

Grizzly Bear — A1310

Ruffed Grouse — A1311

Designed by Chuck Ripper

PHOTOGRAVURE
Plates of 200 subjects in four panes of 50.

1981, June 26 **Tagged** ***Perf. 11***
1921 A1308 18c **multicolored** .35 .20
1922 A1309 18c **multicolored** .35 .20
1923 A1310 18c **multicolored** .35 .20
1924 A1311 18c **multicolored** .35 .20
a. Block of 4, #1921-1924 1.50 1.25
P# block of 4, 5# 2.00 —
Zip block of 4 1.55 —

INTERNATIONAL YEAR OF THE DISABLED

Man Using Microscope A1312

Designed by Martha Perske

PHOTOGRAVURE
Plates of 200 subjects in four panes of 50.

1981, June 29 **Tagged** ***Perf. 11***
1925 A1312 18c **multicolored** .35 .20
P# block of 4, 6# 1.50 —
Zip block of 4 1.40 —
a. Vert. pair, imperf. horiz. *2,600.*

EDNA ST. VINCENT MILLAY ISSUE

A1313

Designed by Glenora Case Richards

LITHOGRAPHED AND ENGRAVED
Plates of 200 subjects in four panes of 50.

1981, July 10 **Tagged** ***Perf. 11***
1926 A1313 18c **multicolored** .35 .20
P# block of 4, 7# 1.50 —
Zip block of 4 1.40 —
a. Black (engr., inscriptions) omitted *300.00* —

ALCOHOLISM

A1314

Designed by John Boyd

ENGRAVED
Plates of 230 (10x23) subjects in panes of 50 (5x10)

1981, Aug. 19 **Tagged** ***Perf. 11***
1927 A1314 18c **blue & black** .40 .20
P# block of 6 10.00 —
P# block of 20, 1-2 #, 1-2 copyright, 1-2 Zip 20.00 —
a. Imperf., pair *400.00*
b. Vert. pair, imperf. horiz. *2,500.*

See Combination Press note after No. 1703.

AMERICAN ARCHITECTURE SERIES

New York University Library by Stanford White A1315

Biltmore House By Richard Morris Hunt — A1316

Palace of the Arts by Bernard Maybeck A1317

National Farmer's Bank by Louis Sullivan A1318

Designed by Walter D. Richards

ENGRAVED
Plates of 160 subjects in four panes of 40.

1981, Aug. 28 **Tagged** ***Perf. 11***
1928 A1315 18c **black & red** .40 .20
a. Tagging omitted —
1929 A1316 18c **black & red** .40 .20
1930 A1317 18c **black & red** .40 .20
a. Tagging omitted —
1931 A1318 18c **black & red** .40 .20
a. Block of 4, #1928-1931 1.65 1.75
P# block of 4 2.10 —
Zip block of 4 1.80 —

SPORTS PERSONALITIES

Mildred Didrikson Zaharias — A1319

Robert Tyre Jones — A1320

Designed by Richard Gangel

ENGRAVED
Plates of 200 subjects in four panes of 50.

1981, Sept. 22 **Tagged** ***Perf. 10½x11***
1932 A1319 18c **purple** .40 .20
P# block of 4 3.00 —
Zip block of 4 1.75 —
1933 A1320 18c **green** .40 .20
P# block of 4 3.00 —
Zip block of 4 1.75 —

FREDERIC REMINGTON

Coming Through the Rye — A1321

Designed by Paul Calle

LITHOGRAPHED AND ENGRAVED
Plates of 200 in four panes of 50.

1981, Oct. 9 **Tagged** ***Perf. 11***
1934 A1321 18c **gray, olive green & brown** .35 .20
P# block of 4, 3# 1.60 —
Zip block of 4 1.50 —
a. Vert. pair, imperf. between *275.00*
b. Brown omitted *425.00*

JAMES HOBAN

Irish-American Architect of the White House A1322

Designed by Ron Mercer and Walter D. Richards.

PHOTOGRAVURE
Plates of 200 in four panes of 50.

1981, Oct. 13 **Tagged** ***Perf. 11***
1935 A1322 18c **multicolored** .35 .20
P# block of 4, 6# 1.60 —
Zip block of 4 1.50 —
1936 A1322 20c **multicolored** .35 .20
P# block of 4, 6# 1.65 —
Zip block of 4 1.50 —

See Ireland No. 504.

AMERICAN BICENTENNIAL

Battle of Yorktown A1323

Battle of the Virginia Capes A1324

Designed by Cal Sacks.

LITHOGRAPHED AND ENGRAVED
Plates of 200 in four panes of 50.

1981, Oct. 16 Tagged *Perf. 11*

1937 A1323 18c **multicolored** .35 .20
1938 A1324 18c **multicolored** .35 .20
a. Pair, #1937-1938 .90 .75
P# block of 4, 7# 2.00 —
Zip block of 4 1.65 —
b. As "a," black (engr., inscriptions) omitted *400.00*
c. As "a," tagging omitted —

CHRISTMAS

Madonna and Child, Botticelli — A1325

Felt Bear on Sleigh A1326

Designed by Bradbury Thompson (No. 1939) and by Naiad Einsel (No. 1940).

PHOTOGRAVURE
Plates of 400 in four panes of 100 (No. 1939)
Plates of 200 in four panes of 50 (No. 1940)

1981, Oct. 28 Tagged *Perf. 11*

1939 A1325 (20c) **multicolored** .40 .20
P# block of 4, 6# 1.75 —
Zip block of 4 1.65 —
a. Imperf., pair *125.00*
b. Vert. pair, imperf. horiz. *1,650.*
c. Tagging omitted *15.00*
1940 A1326 (20c) **multicolored** .40 .20
P# block of 4, 5# 1.75 —
Zip block of 4 1.65 —
a. Imperf., pair *260.00*
b. Vert. pair, imperf. horiz. *2,500.*

JOHN HANSON

First President of the Continental Congress — A1327

Designed by Ron Adair.

PHOTOGRAVURE
Plates of 200 in panes of 50

1981, Nov. 5 Tagged *Perf. 11*

1941 A1327 20c **multicolored** .40 .20
P# block of 4, 5# 1.75 —
Zip block of 4 1.65 —

DESERT PLANTS

Barrel Cactus — A1328

Saguaro — A1331

Agave — A1329

Beavertail Cactus — A1330

Designed by Frank J. Waslick.

LITHOGRAPHED AND ENGRAVED
Plates of 160 in four panes of 40

1981 Dec. 11 Tagged *Perf. 11*

1942 A1328 20c **multicolored** .35 .20
1943 A1329 20c **multicolored** .35 .20
1944 A1330 20c **multicolored** .35 .20
1945 A1331 20c **multicolored** .35 .20
a. Block of 4, #1942-1945 1.50 1.25
P# block of 4, 7# 1.90 —
Zip block of 4 1.55 —
b. As "a," deep brown (litho.) omitted *3,500.*
c. No. 1945 imperf., vert. pair *5,250.*
d. As "a," tagging omitted —

A1332

A1333

Designed by Bradbury Thompson.

PHOTOGRAVURE
Plates of 400 in panes of 100.

1981, Oct. 11 Tagged *Perf. 11x10½*

1946 A1332 (20c) **brown** .40 .20
P# block of 4 2.00 —
Zip block of 4 1.65 —
a. Tagging omitted 9.00
b. All color omitted —

No. 1946b comes from a partially printed pane with most stamps normal. It must be collected as a vertical pair or strip with normal or partially printed stamps attached.

COIL STAMP
Perf. 10 Vert.

1947 A1332 (20c) **brown** .60 .20
Pair 1.20 .20
Joint line pair 1.50 —
a. Imperf. pair *1,400.*
Joint line pair —

BOOKLET STAMPS
Perf. 11

1948 A1333 (20c) **brown** .40 .20
a. Booklet pane of 10 4.50 *3.25*

Rocky Mountain Bighorn — A1334

BOOKLET STAMP
ENGRAVED

1982, Jan. 8 Tagged *Perf. 11*

1949 A1334 20c **dark blue** .55 .20
a. Booklet pane of 10 5.50 *2.50*
b. As "a," imperf. between *110.00*
c. Type II .55 .20
d. Type II, booklet pane of 10 11.00 —
e. As #1949, tagging omitted 5.00 —
f. As "e," booklet pane of 10 *50.00* —

No. 1949 is 18¾mm wide and has overall tagging. No. 1949c is 18½mm wide and has block tagging.

FRANKLIN DELANO ROOSEVELT

A1335

Designed by Clarence Holbert.

ENGRAVED
Plates of 192 in four panes of 48

1982, Jan. 30 Tagged *Perf. 11*

1950 A1335 20c **blue** .40 .20
P# block of 4 1.75 —
Zip block of 4 1.65 —

LOVE ISSUE

A1336

Designed by Mary Faulconer.

PHOTOGRAVURE

Plates of 200 in four panes of 50.

1982, Feb. 1		**Tagged**	*Perf. 11¼*	
1951	A1336 20c	**multicolored**	.40	.20
		P# block of 4, 5#	1.75	—
		Zip block of 4	1.65	—
b.		Imperf., pair	*260.00*	
c.		Blue omitted	*225.00*	
d.		Yellow omitted	*1,000.*	
e.		Purple omitted	—	
f.		Tagging omitted		—

No. 1951c is valued in the grade of fine.

Perf. 11¼x10½

1951A	A1336 20c	**multicolored**	.75	.25
		P# block of 4, 5#	3.50	—
		Zip block of 4	3.00	—

GEORGE WASHINGTON

A1337

Designed by Mark English.

PHOTOGRAVURE

Plates of 200 in four panes of 50.

1982, Feb. 22		**Tagged**	*Perf. 11*	
1952	A1337 20c	**multicolored**	.40	.20
		P# block of 4, 6#	1.75	—
		Zip block of 4	1.65	—

STATE BIRDS AND FLOWERS ISSUE

Illustration reduced.

Designed by Arthur and Alan Singer.

PHOTOGRAVURE (Andreotti)

Plates of 200 subjects in four panes of 50.

1982, Apr. 14		**Tagged**	*Perf. 10½x11¼*	
1953	A1338 20c	Alabama	.50	.25
1954	A1339 20c	Alaska	.50	.25
1955	A1340 20c	Arizona	.50	.25
1956	A1341 20c	Arkansas	.50	.25
1957	A1342 20c	California	.50	.25
1958	A1343 20c	Colorado	.50	.25
1959	A1344 20c	Connecticut	.50	.25
1960	A1345 20c	Delaware	.50	.25
1961	A1346 20c	Florida	.50	.25
1962	A1347 20c	Georgia	.50	.25
1963	A1348 20c	Hawaii	.50	.25
1964	A1349 20c	Idaho	.50	.25
1965	A1350 20c	Illinois	.50	.25
1966	A1351 20c	Indiana	.50	.25
1967	A1352 20c	Iowa	.50	.25
1968	A1353 20c	Kansas	.50	.25
1969	A1354 20c	Kentucky	.50	.25
1970	A1355 20c	Louisiana	.50	.25
1971	A1356 20c	Maine	.50	.25
1972	A1357 20c	Maryland	.50	.25
1973	A1358 20c	Massachusetts	.50	.25
1974	A1359 20c	Michigan	.50	.25
1975	A1360 20c	Minnesota	.50	.25
1976	A1361 20c	Mississippi	.50	.25
1977	A1362 20c	Missouri	.50	.25
1978	A1363 20c	Montana	.50	.25
1979	A1364 20c	Nebraska	.50	.25
1980	A1365 20c	Nevada	.50	.25
1981	A1366 20c	New Hampshire	.50	.25
b.		Black (engr.) missing (EP)	*6,000.*	
1982	A1367 20c	New Jersey	.50	.25
1983	A1368 20c	New Mexico	.50	.25
1984	A1369 20c	New York	.50	.25
1985	A1370 20c	North Carolina	.50	.25
1986	A1371 20c	North Dakota	.50	.25
1987	A1372 20c	Ohio	.50	.25
1988	A1373 20c	Oklahoma	.50	.25

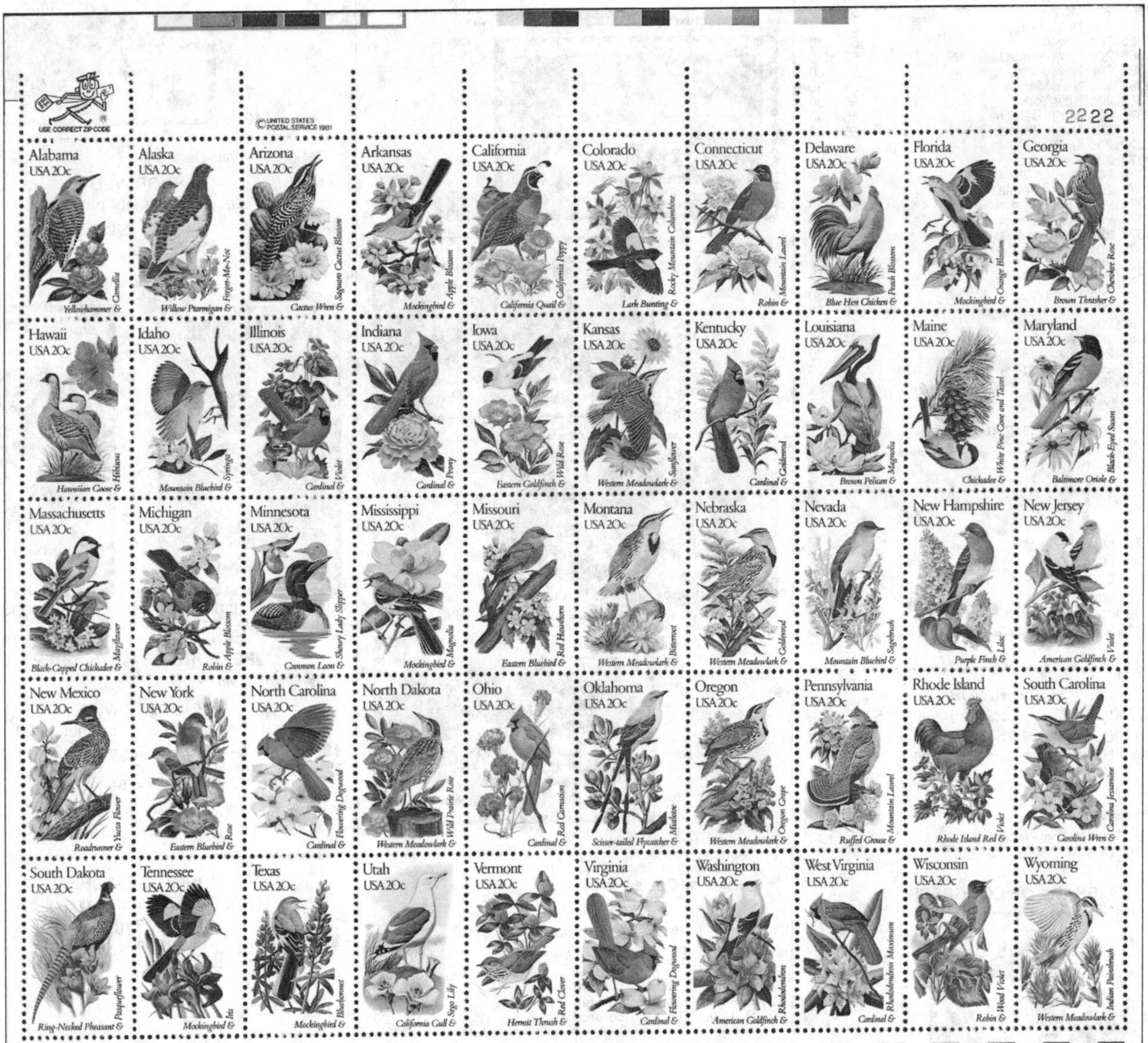

State Birds and Flowers
A1338-A1387

1989	A1374 20c Oregon	.50	.25
1990	A1375 20c Pennsylvania	.50	.25
1991	A1376 20c Rhode Island	.50	.25
b.	Black (engr.) missing (EP)	*6,000.*	
1992	A1377 20c South Carolina	.50	.25
1993	A1378 20c South Dakota	.50	.25
1994	A1379 20c Tennessee	.50	.25
1995	A1380 20c Texas	.50	.25
1996	A1381 20c Utah	.50	.25
1997	A1382 20c Vermont	.50	.25
1998	A1383 20c Virginia	.50	.25
1999	A1384 20c Washington	.50	.25
2000	A1385 20c West Virginia	.50	.25
2001	A1386 20c Wisconsin	.50	.25
b.	Black (engr.) missing (EP)	—	
2002	A1387 20c Wyoming	.50	.25
b.	A1338-A1387 Pane of 50, Nos. 1953-2002	25.00	—
d.	Pane of 50, imperf.	*27,500.*	

Perf. 11¼x11

1953A	A1338 20c Alabama	.55	.30
1954A	A1339 20c Alaska	.55	.30
1955A	A1340 20c Arizona	.55	.30
1956A	A1341 20c Arkansas	.55	.30
1957A	A1342 20c California	.55	.30
1958A	A1343 20c Colorado	.55	.30
1959A	A1344 20c Connecticut	.55	.30
1960A	A1345 20c Delaware	.55	.30
1961A	A1346 20c Florida	.55	.30
1962A	A1347 20c Georgia	.55	.30
1963A	A1348 20c Hawaii	.55	.30
1964A	A1349 20c Idaho	.55	.30
1965A	A1350 20c Illinois	.55	.30
1966A	A1351 20c Indiana	.55	.30
1967A	A1352 20c Iowa	.55	.30
1968A	A1353 20c Kansas	.55	.30
1969A	A1354 20c Kentucky	.55	.30
1970A	A1355 20c Louisiana	.55	.30
1971A	A1356 20c Maine	.55	.30
1972A	A1357 20c Maryland	.55	.30
1973A	A1358 20c Massachusetts	.55	.30
1974A	A1359 20c Michigan	.55	.30
1975A	A1360 20c Minnesota	.55	.30
1976A	A1361 20c Mississippi	.55	.30
1977A	A1362 20c Missouri	.55	.30
1978A	A1363 20c Montana	.55	.30
1979A	A1364 20c Nebraska	.55	.30
1980A	A1365 20c Nevada	.55	.30
1981A	A1366 20c New Hampshire	.55	.30
1982A	A1367 20c New Jersey	.55	.30
1983A	A1368 20c New Mexico	.55	.30
1984A	A1369 20c New York	.55	.30
1985A	A1370 20c North Carolina	.55	.30
1986A	A1371 20c North Dakota	.55	.30
1987A	A1372 20c Ohio	.55	.30
1988A	A1373 20c Oklahoma	.55	.30
1989A	A1374 20c Oregon	.55	.30
1990A	A1375 20c Pennsylvania	.55	.30
1991A	A1376 20c Rhode Island	.55	.30
1992A	A1377 20c South Carolina	.55	.30
1993A	A1378 20c South Dakota	.55	.30
1994A	A1379 20c Tennessee	.55	.30
1995A	A1380 20c Texas	.55	.30
1996A	A1381 20c Utah	.55	.30
1997A	A1382 20c Vermont	.55	.30
1998A	A1383 20c Virginia	.55	.30
1999A	A1384 20c Washington	.55	.30
2000A	A1385 20c West Virginia	.55	.30
2001A	A1386 20c Wisconsin	.55	.30
2002A	A1387 20c Wyoming	.55	.30
c.	A1338-A1387 Pane of 50, Nos. 1953A-2002A	27.50	—

US-NETHERLANDS

200th Anniv. of Diplomatic Recognition by The Netherlands
A1388

Designed by Heleen Tigler Wybrandi-Raue.

PHOTOGRAVURE

Plates of 230 (10x23) subjects in panes of 50 (5x10).

1982, Apr. 20 **Tagged** ***Perf. 11***

2003	A1388 20c **verm., brt. blue & gray blk.**	.40	.20
	P# block of 6	3.50	—
	P# block of 20, 1-2 #, 1-2 copyright, 1-2 zip	10.00	—
a.	Imperf., pair	*325.00*	

See Combination Press note after No. 1703.
See Netherlands Nos. 640-641.

LIBRARY OF CONGRESS

A1389

Designed by Bradbury Thompson.

ENGRAVED

Plates of 200 subjects in four panes of 50.

1982, Apr. 21 **Tagged** ***Perf. 11***

2004	A1389 20c **red & black**	.40	.20
	P# block of 4	1.75	—
	Zip block of 4	1.65	—
a.	All color missing	—	

No. 2004a must be collected as a right margin horiz. strip of 5 or 3 with 3 (or 1) normal, one transitional and one with color omitted.

A1390

Designed by John Boyd.

ENGRAVED

Coil Stamp

1982, Apr. 27 **Tagged** ***Perf. 10 Vert.***

2005	A1390 20c **sky blue**	.55	.20
	Pair	1.10	.20
	P# strip of 3, line, #1-4	22.50	
	P# strip of 5, line, #1-2	160.00	
	P# strip of 5, line, #3-4	100.00	
	P# single, #1-4	—	1.50
a.	Imperf., pair	*100.00*	
	P#1-4		
	Joint line pair	*400.00*	
b.	Tagging omitted	*7.50*	

KNOXVILLE WORLD'S FAIR

A1391

A1392

A1393

A1394

Illustration reduced.

Designed by Charles Harper.

PHOTOGRAVURE

Plates of 200 in four panes of 50.

1982, Apr. 29 **Tagged** ***Perf. 11***

2006	A1391 20c **multicolored**	.40	.20
2007	A1392 20c **multicolored**	.40	.20
2008	A1393 20c **multicolored**	.40	.20
2009	A1394 20c **multicolored**	.40	.20
	Any single on cover, Expo. station handstamp cancel		10.00
a.	Block of 4, #2006-2009	1.65	1.50
	P# block of 4, 6#	2.25	—
	Zip block of 4	1.75	—

HORATIO ALGER

A1395

Designed by Robert Hallock.

ENGRAVED

Plates of 200 in four panes of 50.

1982, Apr. 30 **Tagged** ***Perf. 11***

2010	A1395 20c **red & black,** *tan*	.40	.20
	P# block of 4	1.75	—
	Zip block of 4	1.65	—
a.	Red and black omitted	—	
b.	Tagging omitted		—

The Philatelic Foundation has issued a certificate for a pane of 50 with red and black colors omitted. Recognition of this error is by the paper and by a tiny residue of red ink from the tagging roller. The engraved plates did not strike the paper.

AGING TOGETHER

A1396

Designed by Paul Calle.

ENGRAVED

Plates of 200 in four panes of 50.

1982, May 21 **Tagged** ***Perf. 11***

2011	A1396 20c **brown**	.40	.20
	P# block of 4	1.75	—
	Zip block of 4	1.65	—

John, Ethel and Lionel Barrymore — A1397

A1398

PERFORMING ARTS SERIES

Designed by Jim Sharpe.

PHOTOGRAVURE

Plates of 200 in four panes of 50.

1982, June 8 **Tagged** ***Perf. 11***

2012	A1397 20c **multicolored**	.40	.20
	P# block of 4, 6#	1.75	—
	Zip block of 4	1.65	—

DR. MARY WALKER

Designed by Glenora Richards.

PHOTOGRAVURE

Plate of 200 in four panes of 50.

1982, June 10 **Tagged** ***Perf. 11***

2013	A1398 20c **multicolored**	.40	.20
	P# block of 4, 6#	1.75	—
	Zip block of 4	1.65	—

INTERNATIONAL PEACE GARDEN

Dunseith, ND-Boissevain, Manitoba — A1399

Designed by Gyo Fujikawa.

LITHOGRAPHED AND ENGRAVED
Plate of 200 in four panes of 50.

1982, June 30	Tagged		*Perf. 11*	
2014	A1399 20c **multicolored**		.40	.20
	P# block of 4, 5#		1.75	—
	Zip block of 4		1.65	—
a.	Black (engr.) omitted		*260.00*	

A1400

A1401

AMERICA'S LIBRARIES

Designed by Bradbury Thompson.

ENGRAVED
Plate of 200 subjects in four panes of 50.

1982, July 13	Tagged	*Perf. 11*	
2015	A1400 20c **red & black**	.40	.20
	P# block of 4	1.75	—
	Zip block of 4	1.65	—
a.	Vert. pair, imperf. horiz.	*300.00*	
b.	Tagging omitted	*7.50*	
c.	All colors missing (EP)	—	

BLACK HERITAGE SERIES

Jackie Robinson (1919-72), baseball player.

Designed by Jerry Pinkney.

PHOTOGRAVURE
Plate of 200 subjects in four panes of 50.

1982, Aug. 2	Tagged	*Perf. 10½x11*	
2016	A1401 20c **multicolored**	1.10	.20
	P# block of 4, 5#	5.50	—
	Zip block of 4	4.75	—

TOURO SYNAGOGUE

Oldest Existing Synagogue Building in the U.S. — A1402

Designed by Donald Moss and Bradbury Thompson.

PHOTOGRAVURE AND ENGRAVED
Plates of 230 (10x23) subjects in panes of 50 (5x10).

1982, Aug. 22	Tagged	*Perf. 11*	
2017	A1402 20c **multicolored**	.40	.20
	P# block of 20, 6-12 #, 1-2 copyright, 1-2 zip	12.50	—
a.	Imperf., pair	*2,500.*	

See Combination Press note after No. 1703.

WOLF TRAP FARM PARK

A1403

Designed by Richard Schlecht.

PHOTOGRAVURE
Plates of 200 in four panes of 50.

1982, Sept. 1	Tagged	*Perf. 11*	
2018	A1403 20c **multicolored**	.40	.20
	P# block of 4, 5#	1.75	—
	Zip block of 4	1.65	—

AMERICAN ARCHITECTURE SERIES

A1404

A1405

A1406

A1407

Designed by Walter D. Richards.

ENGRAVED
Plates of 160 subjects in four panes of 40.

1982, Sept. 30	Tagged	*Perf. 11*	
2019	A1404 20c **black & brown**	.45	.20
a.	Tagging omitted		—
b.	Red missing (PS)	—	
2020	A1405 20c **black & brown**	.45	.20
a.	Red missing (PS)	—	
2021	A1406 20c **black & brown**	.45	.20
2022	A1407 20c **black & brown**	.45	.20
a.	Block of 4, #2019-2022	2.00	1.75
	P# block of 4	2.50	—
	Zip block of 4	2.10	—

FRANCIS OF ASSISI

A1408

Designed by Ned Seidler.

Printed by American Bank Note Co. and J.W. Fergusson and Sons.

PHOTOGRAVURE
Plates of 200 subjects in four panes of 50.

1982, Oct. 7	Tagged	*Perf. 11*	
2023	A1408 20c **multicolored**	.40	.20
	P# block of 4, 6#	1.75	—
	Zip block of 4	1.65	—

PONCE DE LEON

A1409

Designed by Richard Schlecht.

PHOTOGRAVURE (Combination press)
Plates of 230 subjects (10x23) in panes of 50 (5x10).

1982, Oct. 12	Tagged	*Perf. 11*	
2024	A1409 20c **multicolored**	.40	.20
	P# block of 6, 5#	3.25	—
	P# block of 20, 5 or 10 #, 1-2 zip, 1-2 copyright	10.00	—
a.	Imperf., pair	*500.00*	
b.	Vert. pair, imperf. between and at top	—	

See Combination Press note after No. 1703.

CHRISTMAS ISSUES

A1410

A1411

A1412

A1413

A1414

A1415

PHOTOGRAVURE
Plates of 200 subjects in four panes of 50

Designed by Chuck Ripper.

1982, Nov. 3 **Tagged**
2025 A1410 13c **multicolored** .25 .20
P# block of 4 1.40 —
Zip block of 4 1.10 —
a. Imperf., pair *650.00*

PHOTOGRAVURE (Combination Press)
Plates of 230 subjects (10x23) in panes of 50 (5x10).

Designed by Bradbury Thompson.

1982, Oct. 28 **Tagged**
2026 A1411 20c **multicolored** .40 .20
P# block of 20, 5 or 10 #, 1-2 copyright, 1-2 zip 11.00 —
a. Imperf. pair *150.00*
b. Horiz. pair, imperf. vert. —
c. Vert. pair, imperf. horiz. —

See Combination Press note after No. 1703.

PHOTOGRAVURE
Plates of 200 in four panes of 50.

Designed by Dolli Tingle.

2027 A1412 20c **multicolored** .50 .20
2028 A1413 20c **multicolored** .50 .20
2029 A1414 20c **multicolored** .50 .20
2030 A1415 20c **multicolored** .50 .20
a. Block of 4, #2027-2030 2.10 1.50
P# block of 4, 4# 2.50 —
Zip block of 4 2.10 —
b. As "a," imperf. *2,750.*
c. As "a," imperf. horiz. *750.00*

SCIENCE & INDUSTRY

A1416

Designed by Saul Bass.

LITHOGRAPHED AND ENGRAVED
Plates of 200 in four panes of 50.

1983, Jan. 19 **Tagged** ***Perf. 11***
2031 A1416 20c **multicolored** .40 .20
P# block of 4, 4# 1.75 —
Zip block of 4 1.65 —
a. Black (engr.) omitted *1,400.*
b. Tagging omitted —

BALLOONS

Intrepid — A1417

Explorer II — A1420

A1418

A1419

Designed by David Meltzer.

PHOTOGRAVURE
Plates of 160 in four panes of 40.

1983, Mar. 31 **Tagged** ***Perf. 11***
2032 A1417 20c **multicolored** .40 .20
2033 A1418 20c **multicolored** .40 .20
2034 A1419 20c **multicolored** .40 .20
2035 A1420 20c **multicolored** .40 .20
a. Block of 4, #2032-2035 1.65 1.50
P# block of 4, 5# 1.75 —
Zip block of 4 1.70 —
b. As "a," imperf. *4,250.*
c. As "a," right stamp perf., otherwise imperf. *4,500.*

US-SWEDEN

Benjamin Franklin A1421

Designed by Czeslaw Slania, court engraver of Sweden.

ENGRAVED
Plates of 200 in four panes of 50.

1983, Mar. 24 **Tagged** ***Perf. 11***
2036 A1421 20c **blue, blk & red brn** .40 .20
P# block of 4 1.75 —
Zip block of 4 1.65 —

See Sweden No. 1453.

CCC, 50th ANNIV.

A1422

Designed by David K. Stone.

PHOTOGRAVURE
Plates of 200 in four panes of 50.

1983, Apr. 5 **Tagged** ***Perf. 11***
2037 A1422 20c **multicolored** .40 .20
P# block of 4, 6# 1.75 —
Zip block of 4 1.65 —
a. Imperf., pair *2,900.*
b. Vert. pair, imperf. horiz. —

JOSEPH PRIESTLEY

Discoverer of Oxygen — A1423

Designed by Dennis Lyall.

Printed by American Bank Note Company and J.W. Ferguson and Sons.

PHOTOGRAVURE
Plates of 200 in four panes of 50.

1983, Apr. 13 **Tagged** ***Perf. 11***
2038 A1423 20c **multicolored** .40 .20
P# block of 4, 6# 1.75 —
Zip block of 4 1.65 —

VOLUNTARISM

A1424

Designed by Paul Calle.

ENGRAVED (Combination Press)
Plates of 230 subjects (10x23) in panes of 50 (5x10).

1983, Apr. 20 **Tagged** ***Perf. 11***
2039 A1424 20c **red & black** .40 .20
P# block of 6 3.00 —
P# block of 20, 1-2 #, 1-2 copyright, 1-2 zip 10.00 —
a. Imperf., pair *750.00*

See Combination Press note after No. 1703.

US-GERMANY

A1425

Designed by Richard Schlecht.

ENGRAVED
Plates of 200 in four panes of 50.

1983, Apr. 29 **Tagged** ***Perf. 11***
2040 A1425 20c **brown** .40 .20
P# block of 4 1.75 —
Zip block of 4 1.65 —
a. Tagging omitted —

See Germany No. 1397.

BROOKLYN BRIDGE

A1426

Normal

"Unfinished Bridge" Short Transfer

Designed by Howard Koslow.

ENGRAVED

Plates of 200 in four panes of 50.

1983, May 17	Tagged		Perf. 11	
2041	A1426 20c **blue**		.40	.20
		P# block of 4	1.75	—
		Zip block of 4	1.65	—
		Short transfer (unfinished bridge) (UL 2)	8.00	.75
		P# block of 4	14.00	—
a.	Tagging omitted		*7.00*	
b.	All color missing (EP)		—	

On No. 2041b, an albino impression of the stamp is evident.

TVA

Norris Hydroelectric Dam — A1427

Designed by Howard Koslow.

PHOTOGRAVURE AND ENGRAVED (Combination Press)

Plates of 230 in panes of 50

1983, May 18	Tagged		Perf. 11	
2042	A1427 20c **multicolored**		.40	.20
		P# block of 20, 5-10 #, 1-2 copyright, 1-2 zip	10.00	—

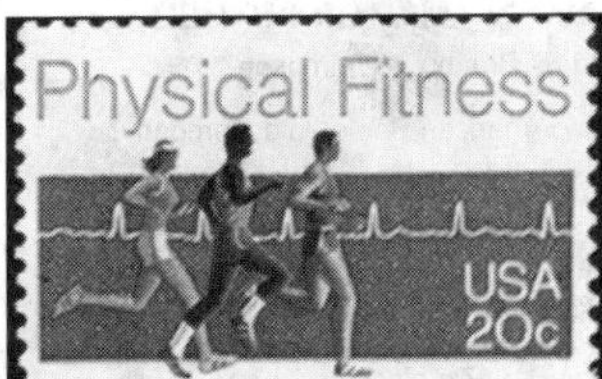

Runners, Electrocardiograph Tracing — A1428

Designed by Donald Moss.

PHOTOGRAVURE (Combination Press)

Plates of 230 in panes of 50.

1983, May 14	Tagged		Perf. 11	
2043	A1428 20c **multicolored**		.40	.20
		P# block of 6, 4#	3.00	—
		P# block of 20, 4-8 #, 1-2 copyright, 1-2 zip	10.00	—

BLACK HERITAGE SERIES

Scott Joplin (1868-1917), Ragtime composer.

A1429

Designed by Jerry Pinkney.

PHOTOGRAVURE

Plates of 200 in four panes of 50.

1983, June 9	Tagged		Perf. 11	
2044	A1429 20c **multicolored**		.40	.20
		P# block of 4, 6#	2.00	—
		Zip block of 4	1.65	—
a.	Imperf., pair		*475.00*	
b.	Tagging omitted			—

MEDAL OF HONOR

A1430

Designed by Dennis J. Hom.

LITHOGRAPHED AND ENGRAVED

Plates of 160 in four panes of 40.

1983, June 7	Tagged		Perf. 11	
2045	A1430 20c **multicolored**		.40	.20
		P# block of 4, 5#	1.75	—
		Zip block of 4	1.70	—
a.	Red omitted		*240.00*	

A1431

A1432

GEORGE HERMAN RUTH (1895-1948)

Designed by Richard Gangel.

ENGRAVED

Plates of 200 in four panes of 50.

1983, July 6	Tagged		Perf. 10½x11	
2046	A1431 20c **blue**		1.40	.20
		P# block of 4	6.50	—
		Zip block of 4	5.75	—

LITERARY ARTS SERIES

Nathaniel Hawthorne (1804-1864), novelist.

Designed by Bradbury Thompson after 1851 painting by Cephus Giovanni Thompson.

PHOTOGRAVURE

Plates of 200 in four panes of 50.

1983, July 8	Tagged		Perf. 11	
2047	A1432 20c **multicolored**		.45	.20
		P# block of 4, 4#	2.10	—
		Zip block of 4	1.90	—

1984 SUMMER OLYMPICS

Los Angeles, July 28-August 12

Discus A1433

High Jump — A1434

Archery A1435

Boxing A1436

Designed by Bob Peak.

PHOTOGRAVURE

Plates of 200 in four panes of 50.

1983, July 28	Tagged		Perf. 11	
2048	A1433 13c **multicolored**		.35	.20
2049	A1434 13c **multicolored**		.35	.20
2050	A1435 13c **multicolored**		.35	.20
2051	A1436 13c **multicolored**		.35	.20
a.	Block of 4, #2048-2051		1.50	1.25
		P# block of 4, 4#	1.75	—
		Zip block of 4	1.65	—

SIGNING OF TREATY OF PARIS

John Adams, B. Franklin, John Jay, David Hartley A1437

Designed by David Blossom based on unfinished painting by Benjamin West in Winterthur Museum.

PHOTOGRAVURE
Plates of 160 in four panes of 40.

1983, Sept. 2 Tagged *Perf. 11*

2052 A1437 20c **multicolored**		.40	.20
	P# block of 4, 4#	1.75	—
	Zip block of 4	1.65	—
a.	Tagging omitted		—

CIVIL SERVICE

A1438

Designed by MDB Communications, Inc.

PHOTOGRAVURE AND ENGRAVED
Plates of 230 in four panes of 50.

1983, Sept. 9 Tagged *Perf. 11*

2053 A1438 20c **buff, blue & red**		.40	.20
	P# block of 6	3.00	—
	P# block of 20, 1-2P#, 1-2 Zip, 1-2 Copyright	10.00	—
a.	Tagging omitted		—

METROPOLITAN OPERA

Original State Arch and Current 5-arch Entrance A1439

Designed by Ken Davies.

LITHOGRAPHED AND ENGRAVED
Plates of 200 in four panes of 50.

1983, Sept. 14 Tagged *Perf. 11*

2054 A1439 20c **yellow & maroon**		.40	.20
	P# block of 4, 2#	1.75	—
	Zip block of 4	1.65	—
a.	Tagging omitted	*8.50*	

AMERICAN INVENTORS

Charles Steinmetz and Curve on Graph A1440

Edwin Armstrong and Frequency Modulator A1441

Nikola Tesla and Induction Motor A1442

Philo T. Farnsworth and First Television Camera A1443

Designed by Dennis Lyall.

LITHOGRAPHED AND ENGRAVED
Plates of 200 in four panes of 50.

1983, Sept. 21 Tagged *Perf. 11*

2055 A1440 20c **multicolored**		.45	.20
2056 A1441 20c **multicolored**		.45	.20
2057 A1442 20c **multicolored**		.45	.20
2058 A1443 20c **multicolored**		.45	.20
a.	Block of 4, #2055-2058	1.80	1.25
	P# block of 4, 2#	2.50	—
	Zip block of 4	1.90	—
b.	As "a," black omitted	*375.00*	

STREETCARS

A1444

A1445

A1446

A1447

Designed by Richard Leech.

PHOTOGRAVURE AND ENGRAVED
Plates of 200 in four panes of 50.

1983, Oct. 8 Tagged *Perf. 11*

2059 A1444 20c **multicolored**		.45	.20
2060 A1445 20c **multicolored**		.45	.20
2061 A1446 20c **multicolored**		.45	.20
2062 A1447 20c **multicolored**		.45	.20
a.	Block of 4, #2059-2062	1.80	1.40
	P# block of 4, 5#	2.50	—
	Zip block of 4	1.90	—
b.	As "a," black omitted	*375.00*	
c.	As "a," black omitted on #2059, 2061		—

CHRISTMAS

Niccolini-Cowper Madonna, by Raphael — A1448

Santa Claus A1449

Designed by Bradbury Thompson (No. 2063), and John Berkey (No. 2064).

PHOTOGRAVURE
Plates of 200 in four panes of 50 (No. 2063),
Plates of 230 in panes of 50 (Combination Press, No. 2064)

1983, Oct. 28 Tagged *Perf. 11*

2063 A1448 20c **multicolored**		.40	.20
	P# block of 4, 5#	1.75	—
	Zip block of 4	1.65	—
2064 A1449 20c **multicolored**		.40	.20
	P# block of 6, 5#	3.00	—
	P# block of 20, 5-10 P#, 1-2 copyright, 1-2 zip	11.50	—
a.	Imperf., pair	*175.00*	

See Combination Press note after No. 1703.

German Religious Leader, Founder of Lutheran Church (1483-1546) — A1450

Caribou and Alaska Pipeline — A1451

MARTIN LUTHER

Designed by Bradbury Thompson.

Printed by American Bank Note Company.

PHOTOGRAVURE
Plates of 200 in four panes of 50.

1983, Nov. 11 Tagged *Perf. 11*

2065 A1450 20c **multicolored**		.40	.20
	P# block of 4, 5#	1.75	—
	Zip block of 4	1.65	—

ALASKA STATEHOOD, 25th ANNIV.

Designed by Bill Bond.

Printed by American Bank Note Company and J.W. Ferguson and Sons.

PHOTOGRAVURE
Plates of 200 in four panes of 50.

1984, Jan. 3 Tagged *Perf. 11*

2066 A1451 20c **multicolored**		.40	.20
	P# block of 4, 5#	1.75	—
	Zip block of 4	1.65	—

14th WINTER OLYMPIC GAMES, Sarajevo, Yugoslavia, Feb. 8-19

Ice Dancing — A1452

Downhill Skiing — A1453

Cross-country Skiing — A1454

Hockey — A1455

Designed by Bob Peak.

PHOTOGRAVURE

Plates of 200 in four panes of 50.

1984, Jan. 6 **Tagged** ***Perf. 10½x11***

2067 A1452 20c **multicolored** .50 .20
2068 A1453 20c **multicolored** .50 .20
2069 A1454 20c **multicolored** .50 .20
2070 A1455 20c **multicolored** .50 .20
a. Block of 4, #2067-2070 2.10 1.50
P# block of 4, 4# 3.00 —
Zip block of 4 2.25 —

Pillar, Dollar Sign — A1456

A1457

FEDERAL DEPOSIT INSURANCE CORPORATION, 50TH ANNIV.

Designed by Michael David Brown.

PHOTOGRAVURE

Plates of 200 in four panes of 50 (1 pane each #2071, 2074, 2075 and 2081)

1984, Jan. 12 **Tagged** ***Perf. 11***

2071 A1456 20c **multicolored** .40 .20
P# block of 4, 6#, UL only 1.75 —
Zip block of 4 1.65 —

LOVE

Designed by Bradbury Thompson.

PHOTOGRAVURE AND ENGRAVED (Combination Press)

Plates of 230 in four panes of 50.

1984, Jan. 31 **Tagged** ***Perf. 11x10½***

2072 A1457 20c **multicolored** .40 .20
P# block of 20, 6-12#, 1-2 copyright, 1-2 zip 11.50 —
a. Horiz. pair, imperf. vert. *175.00*
b. Tagging omitted *5.00*

See Combination Press note after No. 1703.

A1458

SOIL AND WATER CONSERVATION
USA 20c

A1459

BLACK HERITAGE SERIES

Carter G. Woodson (1875-1950), Black Historian.

Designed by Jerry Pinkney.

Printed by American Bank Note Company.

PHOTOGRAVURE

Plates of 200 in four panes of 50.

1984, Feb. 1 **Tagged** ***Perf. 11***

2073 A1458 20c **multicolored** .40 .20
P# block of 4, 6# 2.00 —
Zip block of 4 1.65 —
a. Horiz. pair, imperf. vert. *1,600.*

SOIL & WATER CONSERVATION

Designed by Michael David Brown.

See No. 2071 for printing information.

1984, Feb. 6 **Tagged** ***Perf. 11***

2074 A1459 20c **multicolored** .40 .20
P# block of 4, 6#, UR only 1.75 —
Zip block of 4 1.65 —

50TH ANNIV. OF CREDIT UNION ACT

Dollar Sign, Coin — A1460

Designed by Michael David Brown.

See No. 2071 for printing information.

1984, Feb. 10 **Tagged** ***Perf. 11***

2075 A1460 20c **multicolored** .40 .20
P# block of 4, 6#, LR only 1.75 —
Zip block of 4 1.65 —

ORCHIDS

Wild Pink — A1461

Yellow Lady's-slipper A1462

Spreading Pogonia — A1463

Pacific Calypso — A1464

Designed by Manabu Saito.

PHOTOGRAVURE

Plates of 192 in four panes of 48.

1984, Mar. 5 **Tagged** ***Perf. 11***

2076 A1461 20c **multicolored** .50 .20
2077 A1462 20c **multicolored** .50 .20
2078 A1463 20c **multicolored** .50 .20
2079 A1464 20c **multicolored** .50 .20
a. Block of 4, #2076-2079 2.00 1.50
P# block of 4, 5# 2.50 —
Zip block of 4 2.10 —

HAWAII STATEHOOD, 25th ANNIV.

Eastern Polynesian Canoe, Golden Plover, Mauna Loa Volcano A1465

Designed by Herb Kane.

Printed by American Bank Note Company.

PHOTOGRAVURE

Plates of 200 in four panes of 50.

1984, Mar. 12 **Tagged** ***Perf. 11***

2080 A1465 20c **multicolored** .40 .20
P# block of 4, 5# 1.70 —
Zip block of 4 1.65 —

50TH ANNIV., NATIONAL ARCHIVES

Abraham Lincoln, George Washington — A1466

Designed by Michael David Brown.

See No. 2071 for printing information.

1984, Apr. 16 **Tagged** ***Perf. 11***

2081 A1466 20c **multicolored** .40 .20
P# block of 4, 6#, LL only 1.70 —
Zip block of 4 1.65 —

LOS ANGELES SUMMER OLYMPICS
July 28-August 12

Diving — A1467

Long Jump — A1468

Wrestling — A1469

Kayak — A1470

Designed by Bob Peak.

PHOTOGRAVURE
Plates of 200 in four panes of 50.

1984, May 4	**Tagged**	***Perf. 11***	
2082 A1467 20c **multicolored**		.55	.20
2083 A1468 20c **multicolored**		.55	.20
2084 A1469 20c **multicolored**		.55	.20
2085 A1470 20c **multicolored**		.55	.20
a. Block of 4, #2082-2085		2.40	1.90
P# block of 4, 4#		3.50	—
Zip block of 4		2.50	—
b. As "a," imperf between vertically		—	

LOUISIANA WORLD EXPOSITION
New Orleans, May 12-Nov. 11

Bayou Wildlife
A1471

Designed by Chuck Ripper.

PHOTOGRAVURE
Plates of 160 in four panes of 40.

1984, May 11	**Tagged**	***Perf. 11***	
2086 A1471 20c **multicolored**		.40	.20
On cover, Expo. station pictorial handstamp cancel			2.50
P# block of 4, 5#		1.75	—
Zip block of 4		1.65	—

HEALTH RESEARCH

Lab Equipment
A1472

Designed by Tyler Smith.

Printed by American Bank Note Company.

PHOTOGRAVURE
Plates of 200 in four panes of 50.

1984, May 17	**Tagged**	***Perf. 11***	
2087 A1472 20c **multicolored**		.40	.20
P# block of 4, 5#		1.75	—
Zip block of 4		1.65	—

Actor Douglas Fairbanks (1883-1939) — A1473

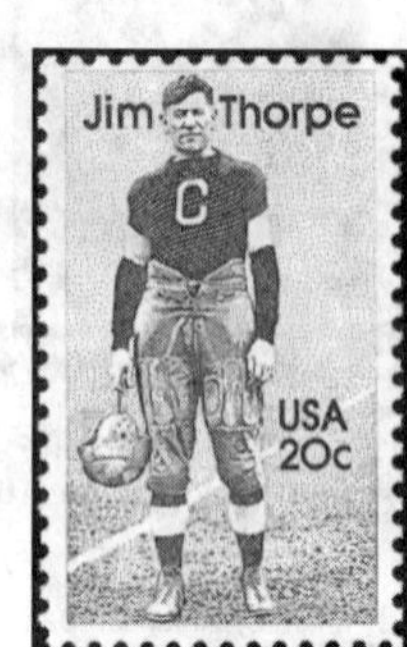

A1474

PERFORMING ARTS

Designed by Jim Sharpe.

PHOTOGRAVURE AND ENGRAVED (Combination Press)
Plates of 230 in panes of 50.

1984, May 23	**Tagged**	***Perf. 11***	
2088 A1473 20c **multicolored**		.40	.20
P# block of 20, 5-10#, 1-2 copyright, 1-2 zip		11.00	—
a. Tagging omitted		*15.00*	
b. Horiz. pair, imperf between		—	

See Combination Press note after No. 1703.

JIM THORPE, 1888-1953

Designed by Richard Gangel.

ENGRAVED
Plates of 200 in four panes of 50.

1984, May 24	**Tagged**	***Perf. 11***	
2089 A1474 20c **dark brown**		.40	.20
P# block of 4		2.00	—
Zip block of 4		1.65	—

PERFORMING ARTS

John McCormack (1884-1945), Operatic Tenor — A1475

Designed by Jim Sharpe (US) and Ron Mercer (Ireland).

PHOTOGRAVURE
Plates of 200 in four panes of 50.

1984, June 6	**Tagged**	***Perf. 11***	
2090 A1475 20c **multicolored**		.40	.20
P# block of 4, 5#		1.75	—
Zip block of 4		1.65	—

See Ireland No. 594.

ST. LAWRENCE SEAWAY, 25th ANNIV.

Aerial View of Seaway, Freighters
A1476

Designed by Ernst Barenscher (Canada).

Printed by American Bank Note Company.

PHOTOGRAVURE
Plates of 200 in four panes of 50.

1984, June 26	**Tagged**	***Perf. 11***	
2091 A1476 20c **multicolored**		.40	.20
P# block of 4, 4#		1.75	—
Zip block of 4		1.65	—

WATERFOWL PRESERVATION ACT, 50th ANNIV.

"Mallards Dropping In" by Jay N. Darling
A1477

Design adapted from Darling's work (No. RW1) by Donald M. McDowell.

ENGRAVED
Plates of 200 in four panes of 50.

1984, July 2	**Tagged**	***Perf. 11***	
2092 A1477 20c **blue**		.50	.20
P# block of 4		2.50	—
Zip block of 4		2.25	—
a. Horiz. pair, imperf. vert.		*400.00*	

The Elizabeth — A1478

A1479

ROANOKE VOYAGES

Designed by Charles Lundgren.

Printed by American Bank Note Company.

PHOTOGRAVURE
Plates of 200 in four panes of 50.

1984, July 13	**Tagged**	***Perf. 11***	
2093 A1478 20c **multicolored**		.40	.20
P# block of 4, 5#		1.75	—
Zip block of 4		1.65	—
Pair with full horiz. gutter btwn.		—	

LITERARY ARTS SERIES

Herman Melville (1819-1891), Author

Designed by Bradbury Thompson.

ENGRAVED
Plates of 200 in four panes of 50.

1984, Aug. 1	**Tagged**	***Perf. 11***	
2094 A1479 20c **sage green**		.40	.20
P# block of 4		1.75	—
Zip block of 4		1.65	—
a. Tagging omitted			—

Founder of Junior Achievement — A1480

Smokey Bear — A1481

HORACE MOSES (1862-1947)

Designed by Dennis Lyall.

ENGRAVED (Combination Press)
Plates of 200 in panes of 50.

1984, Aug. 6 **Tagged** ***Perf. 11***

2095 A1480 20c **orange & dark brown**	.45	.20
P# block of 6	3.50	—
P# block of 20, 1-2#, 1-2 copyright, 1-2 zip	12.50	—

See Combination Press note after No. 1703.

SMOKEY BEAR

Designed by Rudolph Wendelin.

LITHOGRAPHED AND ENGRAVED
Plates of 200 in panes of 50.

1984, Aug. 13 **Tagged** ***Perf. 11***

2096 A1481 20c **multicolored**	.40	.20
P# block of 4, 5#	2.00	—
Zip block of 4	1.65	—
a. Horiz. pair, imperf. btwn.	*300.00*	
b. Vert. pair, imperf. btwn.	*225.00*	
c. Block of 4, imperf. btwn. vert. and horiz.	*5,500.*	
d. Horiz. pair, imperf. vert.	*1,500.*	

ROBERTO CLEMENTE (1934-1972)

Clemente Wearing Pittsburgh Pirates Cap, Puerto Rican Flag — A1482

Designed by Juan Lopez-Bonilla.

PHOTOGRAVURE
Plates of 200 in panes of 50.

1984, Aug. 17 **Tagged** ***Perf. 11***

2097 A1482 20c **multicolored**	1.60	.20
P# block of 4, 6#	7.50	—
Zip block of 4	6.75	—
a. Horiz. pair, imperf. vert.	*2,000.*	

DOGS

Beagle and Boston Terrier A1483

Chesapeake Bay Retriever and Cocker Spaniel A1484

Alaskan Malamute and Collie A1485

Black and Tan Coonhound and American Foxhound A1486

Designed by Roy Andersen.

PHOTOGRAVURE
Plates of 160 in panes of 40.

1984, Sept. 7 **Tagged** ***Perf. 11***

2098 A1483 20c **multicolored**	.45	.20
2099 A1484 20c **multicolored**	.45	.20
2100 A1485 20c **multicolored**	.45	.20
2101 A1486 20c **multicolored**	.45	.20
a. Block of 4, #2098-2101	1.90	1.90
P# block of 4, 4#	3.00	—
Zip block of 4	2.00	—

CRIME PREVENTION

McGruff, the Crime Dog — A1487

Designed by Randall McDougall.

Printed by American Bank Note Company.

PHOTOGRAVURE
Plates of 200 in panes of 50.

1984, Sept. 26 **Tagged** ***Perf. 11***

2102 A1487 20c **multicolored**	.40	.20
P# block of 4, 4#	1.75	—
Zip block of 4	1.65	—

HISPANIC AMERICANS

A1488

Designed by Robert McCall.

PHOTOGRAVURE
Plates of 160 in four panes of 40.

1984, Oct. 31 **Tagged** ***Perf. 11***

2103 A1488 20c **multicolored**	.40	.20
P# block of 4, 6#	1.75	—
Zip block of 4	1.65	—
a. Vert. pair, imperf. horiz.	*2,250.*	

FAMILY UNITY

Stick Figures — A1489

Designed by Molly LaRue.

PHOTOGRAVURE AND ENGRAVED (Combination Press)
Plates of 230 in panes of 50.

1984, Oct. 1 **Tagged** ***Perf. 11***

2104 A1489 20c **multicolored**	.40	.20
P# block of 20, 3-6#, 1-2 copyright, 1-2 zip	12.50	—
a. Horiz. pair, imperf. vert.	*550.00*	
b. Tagging omitted	*7.50*	
c. Vert. pair, imperf. btwn. and at bottom	—	
d. Horiz. pair, imperf. between	—	

See Combination Press note after No. 1703.

A1490

Abraham Lincoln Reading to Son, Tad — A1491

ELEANOR ROOSEVELT (1884-1962)

Designed by Bradbury Thompson.

ENGRAVED
Plates of 192 in panes of 48.

1984, Oct. 11 **Tagged** ***Perf. 11***

2105 A1490 20c **deep blue**	.40	.20
P# block of 4	2.00	—
Zip block of 4	1.65	—

NATION OF READERS

Design adapted from Anthony Berger daguerrotype by Bradbury Thompson.

ENGRAVED
Plates of 200 in panes of 50.

1984, Oct. 16 **Tagged** ***Perf. 11***

2106 A1491 20c **brown & maroon**	.40	.20
P# block of 4	1.90	—
Zip block of 4	1.65	—

CHRISTMAS

Madonna and Child by Fra Filippo Lippi — A1492

Santa Claus — A1493

Designed by Bradbury Thompson (No. 2107) and Danny La Boccetta (No. 2108).

PHOTOGRAVURE
Plates of 200 in panes of 50.

1984, Oct. 30 **Tagged** ***Perf. 11***

2107 A1492 20c **multicolored**	.40	.20
P# block of 4, 5#	1.70	—
Zip block of 4	1.65	—
2108 A1493 20c **multicolored**	.40	.20
P# block of 4, 5#	1.70	—
Zip block of 4	1.65	—
a. Horiz. pair, imperf. vert.	*950.00*	

No. 2108a is valued in the grade of fine.

VIETNAM VETERANS MEMORIAL

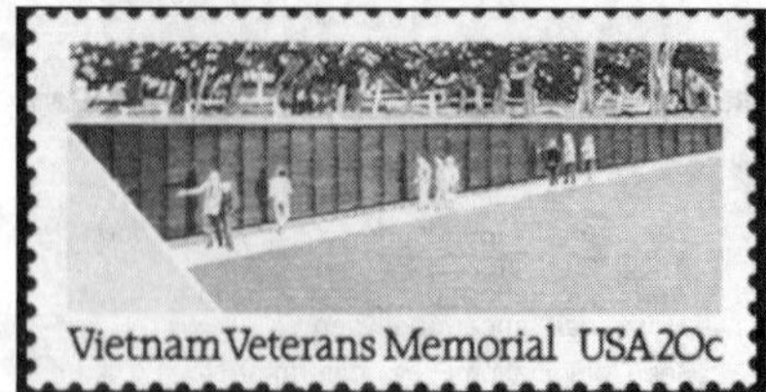

Memorial and Visitors — A1494

Designed by Paul Calle.

ENGRAVED

Plates of 160 in panes of 40.

1984, Nov. 10 **Tagged** ***Perf. 11***

No.	Description	Unused	Used
2109	A1494 20c **multicolored**	.40	.20
	P# block of 4	2.25	—
	Zip block of 4	1.65	—
a.	Tagging omitted	—	

PERFORMING ARTS

Jerome Kern (1885-1945), Composer — A1495

Designed by Jim Sharpe.

Printed by the American Bank Note Company.

PHOTOGRAVURE

Plates of 200 in four panes of 50.

1985, Jan. 23 **Tagged** ***Perf. 11***

No.	Description	Unused	Used
2110	A1495 22c **multicolored**	.40	.20
	P# block of 4, 5#	1.75	—
	Zip block of 4	1.65	—
a.	Tagging omitted	*7.50*	

A1496 A1497

Designed by Bradbury Thompson.

PHOTOGRAVURE

Plates of 460 (20x23) in panes of 100.

1985, Feb. 1 **Tagged** ***Perf. 11***

No.	Description	Unused	Used
2111	A1496 (22c) **green**	.55	.20
	P# block of 6	4.50	—
	P# block of 20, 1-2 #, 1-2 Zip, 1-2 Copyright	20.00	—
a.	Vert. pair, imperf.	*35.00*	
b.	Vert. pair, imperf. horiz.	*1,350.*	
c.	Tagging omitted		—

COIL STAMP

Perf. 10 Vert.

No.	Description	Unused	Used
2112	A1496 (22c) **green**	.60	.20
	Pair	1.20	.20
	P# strip of 3, #1, 2	5.00	
	P# strip of 5, #1, 2	6.50	
	P# single, #1, 2	—	.50
a.	Imperf., pair	*45.00*	
	P#1, 2		
b.	As "a," tagging omitted	*125.00*	
	P#1, 2		
c.	As No. 2112, tagging omitted	—	—
	P#1, 2		

BOOKLET STAMP

Perf. 11

No.	Description	Unused	Used
2113	A1497 (22c) **green**	.80	.20
a.	Booklet pane of 10	8.50	*3.00*
b.	As "a," imperf. btwn. horiz.	—	

A1498

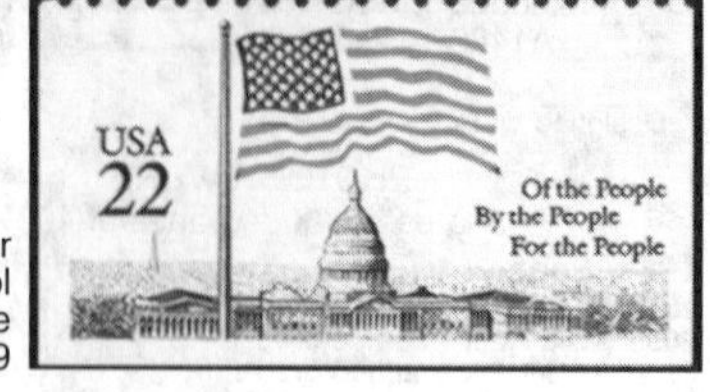

Flag Over Capitol Dome A1499

Designed by Frank Waslick.

ENGRAVED

Plates of 400 subjects in panes of 100.

1985, Mar. 29 **Tagged** ***Perf. 11***

No.	Description	Unused	Used
2114	A1498 22c **blue, red & black**	.40	.20
	P# block of 4	1.90	—
	Zip block of 4	1.65	—
	Pair with full horizontal gutter	—	

COIL STAMP

Perf. 10 Vert.

No.	Description	Unused	Used
2115	A1498 22c **blue, red & black,** wide block tagging	.40	.20
	Pair	.80	.20
	P# strip of 3, #2	3.00	
	P# strip of 3, #4	4.75	
	P# strip of 3, #6	6.00	
	P# strip of 3, #10	3.50	
	P# strip of 3, #13	10.50	
	P# strip of 3, #14	24.00	
	P# strip of 3, #15	3.00	
	P# strip of 3, #16	4.25	
	P# strip of 3, #21	5.00	
	P# strip of 5, #2	3.50	
	P# strip of 5, #4	5.50	
	P# strip of 5, #6	6.50	
	P# strip of 5, #10	3.75	
	P# strip of 5, #13	12.50	
	P# strip of 5, #14	29.00	
	P# strip of 5, #15	3.25	
	P# strip of 5, #16	5.50	
	P# strip of 5, #22	3.25	
	P# strip of 5, #21	6.00	
	P# single, #2	—	.50
	P# single, #4	—	.50
	P# single, #6	—	6.50
	P# single, #10	—	.65
	P# single, #13	—	9.00
	P# single, #14	—	27.50
	P# single, #15	—	1.50
	P# single, #16	—	2.25
	P# single, #21	—	2.25
a.	Narrow block tagging	.40	.20
	P# strip of 3, #1, 3	10.00	
	P# strip of 3, #5	4.50	
	P# strip of 3, #7	10.50	
	P# strip of 3, #8	3.00	
	P# strip of 3, #11	5.75	
	P# strip of 3, #12	3.00	
	P# strip of 3, #17, 18	5.00	
	P# strip of 3, #19	3.00	
	P# strip of 3, #20	5.00	
	P# strip of 3, #22	3.00	
	P# strip of 5, #1	12.00	
	P# strip of 5, #3	47.50	
	P# strip of 5, #5	5.75	
	P# strip of 5, #7	12.00	
	P# strip of 5, #8	3.25	
	P# strip of 5, #11	6.00	
	P# strip of 5, #12	3.25	
	P# strip of 5, #17-18	6.00	
	P# strip of 5, #19	3.25	
	P# strip of 5, #20	6.00	
	P# single, #1, 3, 5	—	.50
	P# single, #7-8	—	.65
	P# single, #11	—	1.00
	P# single, #12	—	.65
	P# single, #17-18	—	2.00
	P# single, #19	—	.65
	P# single, #20	—	2.25
	P# single, #22	—	.65
b.	Inscribed "T" at bottom, *May 23, 1987*	.50	.40
	P# strip of 3, #T1	3.00	
	P# strip of 5, #T1	3.50	
	P# single, #T1	—	3.00
c.	Black field of stars	—	—
d.	Tagging omitted	*4.50*	
e.	Imperf., pair	12.50	
	P#1-8, 10-12, 15, 17-20, 22		

No. 2115 is known with capitol in bluish black color, apparently from contaminated ink. Specialists often refer to this as "Erie blue."

BOOKLET STAMP

Perf. 10 Horiz.

No.	Description	Unused	Used
2116	A1499 22c **blue, red & black**	.50	.20
a.	Booklet pane of 5	2.50	*1.25*
	Scored perforations	2.50	

BOOKLET STAMPS

Frilled Dogwinkle — A1500

Reticulated Helmet — A1501

New England Neptune — A1502

Calico Scallop — A1503

Lightning Whelk — A1504

Designed by Pete Cocci.

ENGRAVED

1985, Apr. 4 **Tagged** ***Perf. 10***

No.	Description	Unused	Used
2117	A1500 22c **black & brown**	.40	.20
2118	A1501 22c **black & multi**	.40	.20
2119	A1502 22c **black & brown**	.40	.20
2120	A1503 22c **black & violet**	.40	.20
2121	A1504 22c **black & multi**	.40	.20
a.	Booklet pane of 10, 2 ea #2117-2121	4.00	*3.00*
b.	As "a," violet omitted on both Nos. 2120	*800.00*	
c.	As "a," vert. imperf. between	*600.00*	
d.	As "a," imperf.		—
e.	Strip of 5, Nos. 2117-2121	2.00	—

Eagle and Half Moon — A1505

Designed by Young & Rubicam.

TYPE I: washed out, dull appearance most evident in the black of the body of the eagle, and the red in the background between the eagle's shoulder and the moon. "$10.75" appears splotchy or grainy (P# 11111).

TYPE II: brighter, more intense colors most evident in the black on the eagle's body, and red in the background. "$10.75" appears smoother, brighter, and less grainy (P# 22222).

PHOTOGRAVURE

1985, Apr. 29 **Untagged** ***Perf. 10 Vert.***

No.	Description	Unused	Used
2122	A1505 $10.75 **multicolored,** type I	19.00	7.50
a.	Booklet pane of 3	60.00	—
b.	Type II, *June 19, 1989*	22.50	10.00
c.	As "b," booklet pane of 3	70.00	—

Coil Plate No. Strips of 3

Beginning with No. 2123, coil plate No. strips of 3 usually sell at the level of strips of 5 minus the face value of two stamps.

TRANSPORTATION ISSUE

A1506 A1507

A1508 A1509

A1510 A1511

A1512 A1513

A1514 A1515

A1516 A1517

A1518 A1519

Designers: 3.4c, 17c, Lou Nolan. 4.9c, 8.5c, 14c, 25c, William H. Bond. 5.5c, David K. Stone. 6c, 8.3c, 10.1c, 12.5c. James Schleyer. 7.1c, 11c, 12c, Ken Dallison.

COIL STAMPS
ENGRAVED

1985-87 Tagged *Perf. 10 Vert.*

2123	A1506	3.4c **dark bluish green,** *June 8*	.20	.20
		Pair	.20	.20
		P# strip of 5, line, #1-2	.90	
		P# single, #1-2	—	.80
a.		Untagged (Bureau precancel, Nonprofit Org. CAR-RT SORT)	.20	.20
		P# strip of 5, line, #1-2	4.25	
		P# single, #1-2	—	3.75
2124	A1507	4.9c **brown black,** *June 21*	.20	.20
		Pair	.20	.20
		P# strip of 5, line, #3-4	.85	
		P# single, #3-4	—	.80
a.		Untagged (Bureau precancel, Nonprofit Org.)	.20	.20
		P# strip of 5, line, #1-6	1.40	
		P# single, #1-6	—	1.25
2125	A1508	5.5c **deep magenta,** *Nov. 1, 1986*	.20	.20
		Pair	.20	.20
		P# strip of 5, #1	1.50	
		P# single, #1	—	1.25
a.		Untagged (Bureau precancel, Nonprofit Org. CAR-RT SORT)	.20	.20
		P# strip of 5, #1	1.75	
		P# strip of 5, #2	2.25	
		P# single, #1	—	1.00
		P# single, #2	—	1.75

On No. 2125a, both vignette and the precancel inscription were printed from a single printing sleeve.

2126	A1509	6c **red brown,** *May 6*	.20	.20
		Pair	.25	.20
		P# strip of 5, #1	1.50	
		P# single, #1	—	1.00
a.		Untagged (Bureau precancel, Nonprofit Org.)	.20	.20
		P# strip of 5, #1	1.75	
		P# strip of 5, #2	7.00	
		P# single, #1	—	1.00
		P# single, #2	—	2.75
b.		As "a," imperf., pair	*200.00*	
		P#2		
2127	A1510	7.1c **lake,** *Feb. 6, 1987*	.20	.20
		Pair	.30	.20
		P# strip of 5, #1	2.10	
		P# single, #1	—	1.50
a.		Untagged (Bureau precancel "Nonprofit Org." in black), *Feb. 6, 1987*	.20	.20
		P# strip of 5, #1	3.00	
		P# single, #1	—	1.75
b.		Untagged (Bureau precancel "Nonprofit 5-Digit Zip + 4" in black), *May 26, 1989*	.20	.20
		P# strip of 5, #1	1.75	
		P# single, #1	—	1.25

On Nos. 2127a and 2127b, both the vignette and the precancel inscription were printed from a single printing sleeve.

2128	A1511	8.3c **green,** *June 21*	.20	.20
		Pair	.40	.20
		P# strip of 5, line, #1-2	1.50	
		P# single, #1-2	—	1.00
a.		Untagged (Bureau precancel, Blk. Rt. CAR-RT SORT)	.20	.20
		P# strip of 5, line, #1-2	1.50	
		P# strip of 5, line, #3-4	4.50	
		P# single, #1-2	—	1.25
		P# single, #3-4	—	3.75

On No. 2231 "Ambulance 1860s" is 18mm long; on No. 2128, 18½mm long.

2129	A1512	8.5c **dark Prussian green,** *Jan. 24, 1987*	.20	.20
		Pair	.40	.20
		P# strip of 5, #1	3.00	
		P# single, #1	—	2.25
a.		Untagged (Bureau precancel, Nonprofit Org.)	.20	.20
		P# strip of 5, #1	2.75	
		P# strip of 5, #2	12.00	
		P# single, #1	—	2.00
		P# single, #2	—	8.00
2130	A1513	10.1c **slate blue,** *Apr. 18*	.25	.20
		Pair	.50	.20
		P# strip of 5, #1	2.50	
		P# single, #1	—	2.00
a.		Untagged (Bureau precancel "Bulk Rate Carrier Route Sort" in red)	.25	.25
		P# strip of 5, #2-3	2.25	
		P# single, #2-3	—	2.00
		Untagged (Bureau precancel "Bulk Rate" and lines in black)	.25	.25
		P# strip of 5, #1-2	2.50	
		P# single, #1-2	—	1.75
b.		As "a," red precancel, imperf, pair	15.00	
		P# strip of 6, #3	100.00	
		P# strip of 6, #2	—	
		As "a," black precancel, imperf, pair	*95.00*	
		P#1		
2131	A1514	11c **dark green,** *June 11*	.25	.20
		Pair	.50	.20
		P# strip of 5, line, #1-4	1.40	
		P# single, #1-4	—	1.00
a.		Tagging omitted	—	
2132	A1515	12c **dark blue,** type I, *Apr. 2*	.25	.20
		Pair	.50	.20
		P# strip of 5, line, #1-2	2.25	
		P# single, #1-2	—	1.50
a.		Untagged, type I (Bureau precancel, PRESORTED FIRST-CLASS), *Apr. 2*	.25	.25
		P# strip of 5, line, #1-2	2.40	
		P# single, #1-2	—	1.75
b.		Untagged, type II, (Bureau precancel, PRESORTED FIRST-CLASS) *1987*	.40	.30
		P# strip of 5, no line, #1	19.00	
		P# single, #1	—	17.00
c.		Tagging omitted, type I, (not Bureau precanceled), *1987*	6.00	
		P# strip of 5, #1, 2	—	

Type II has "Stanley Steamer 1909" ½mm shorter (17½mm) than No. 2132 (18mm).

2133	A1516	12.5c **olive green,** *Apr. 18*	.25	.20
		Pair	.50	.20
		P# strip of 5, #1	3.00	
		P# strip of 5, #2	4.75	
		P# single, #1	—	2.25
		P# single, #2	—	3.00
a.		Untagged (Bureau precancel, Bulk Rate)	.25	.25
		P# strip of 5, #1	3.00	
		P# strip of 5, #2	3.50	
		P# single, #1	—	1.75
		P# single, #2	—	3.00
b.		As "a," imperf., pair	50.00	
		P#1		

All No. 2133 from plate 1 and some No. 2133a from plate 1 were printed with luminescent ink that is orange under long wave UV light.

2134	A1517	14c **sky blue,** type I, *Mar. 23*	.30	.20
		Pair	.60	.20
		P# strip of 5, line, #1-4	2.25	
		P# single, #1-4	—	1.50
a.		Imperf., pair	100.00	
		P#1-2		
b.		Type II, *Sept. 30, 1986*	.30	.20
		P# strip of 5, no line, #2	3.25	
		P# single, #2	—	2.50
c.		Tagging omitted, type I	5.00	—

Type II design is ¼mm narrower (17¼mm) than the original stamp (17½mm) and has block tagging. No. 2134 has overall tagging.

2135	A1518	17c **sky blue,** *Aug. 20, 1986*	.35	.20
		Pair	.70	.20
		P# strip of 5, #2	3.25	
		P# single, #2	—	1.50
a.		Imperf., pair	*450.00*	
		P#2		
2136	A1519	25c **orange brown,** *Nov. 22, 1986*	.45	.20
		Pair	.90	.20
		P# strip of 5, #1-5	3.50	
		P# single, #1	—	2.50
		P# single, #2-4	—	.65
		P# single, #5	—	2.50
a.		Imperf., pair	10.00	
		P#2-5		
b.		Pair, imperf. between	*750.00*	
c.		Tagging omitted	*25.00*	
		P# strip of 5, #1	—	
		Nos. 2123-2136 (14)	3.50	2.80

Precancellations on Nos. 2125a, 2127a do not have lines. Precancellation on No. 2129a is in red. See No. 2231.

BLACK HERITAGE SERIES

Mary McLeod Bethune (1875-1955), educator.

A1520

Designed by Jerry Pinkney from a photograph.

Printed by American Bank Note Company.

PHOTOGRAVURE
Plates of 200 in four panes of 50.

1985, Mar. 5 Tagged *Perf. 11*

2137	A1520	22c **multicolored**	.40	.20
		P# block of 4, 6#	2.60	—
		Zip block of 4	1.70	—

AMERICAN FOLK ART SERIES
Duck Decoys

Broadbill
A1521

Mallard
A1522

Canvasback
A1523

Redhead
A1524

Designed by Stevan Dohanos.

Printed by American Bank Note Company.

PHOTOGRAVURE
Plates of 200 in four panes of 50.

1985, Mar. 22	**Tagged**	***Perf. 11***	
2138 A1521 22c **multicolored**		.65	.20
2139 A1522 22c **multicolored**		.65	.20
2140 A1523 22c **multicolored**		.65	.20
2141 A1524 22c **multicolored**		.65	.20
a. Block of 4, #2138-2141		4.00	2.75
P# block of 4, 5#		4.75	—
Zip block of 4		4.25	—

WINTER SPECIAL OLYMPICS

Ice Skater, Emblem, Skier — A1525

Designed by Jeff Carnell.

PHOTOGRAVURE
Plates of 160 in four panes of 40.

1985, Mar. 25	**Tagged**	***Perf. 11***	
2142 A1525 22c **multicolored**		.40	.20
P# block of 4, 6#		1.75	—
Zip block of 4		1.65	—
a. Vert. pair, imperf. horiz.		*525.00*	

LOVE

A1526

Designed by Corita Kent.

PHOTOGRAVURE
Plates of 200 in four panes of 50.

1985, Apr. 17	**Tagged**	***Perf. 11***	
2143 A1526 22c **multicolored**		.40	.20
P# block of 4, 6#		1.70	—
Zip block of 4		1.65	—
a. Imperf., pair		*1,500.*	

RURAL ELECTRIFICATION ADMINISTRATION

REA Power Lines, Farmland
A1527

Designed by Howard Koslow.

PHOTOGRAVURE & ENGRAVED (Combination Press)
Plates of 230 in panes of 50.

1985, May 11	**Tagged**	***Perf. 11***	
2144 A1527 22c **multicolored**		.45	.20
P# block of 20, 5-10 #, 1-2 Zip, 1-2 Copyright		17.50	—
a. Vert. pair, imperf between		—	

See Combination Press note after No. 1703.

AMERIPEX '86

US No. 134 — A1528

Designed by Richard Sheaff.

LITHOGRAPHED & ENGRAVED
Plates of 192 in four panes of 48

1985, May 25	**Tagged**	***Perf. 11***	
2145 A1528 22c **multicolored**		.40	.20
P# block of 4, 3#		1.75	—
Zip block of 4		1.65	—
a. Red, black & blue (engr.) omitted		*200.00*	
b. Red & black omitted		*1,250.*	
c. Red omitted		—	
d. Black missing (PS)		—	

ABIGAIL ADAMS (1744-1818)

A1529

Designed by Bart Forbes.

PHOTOGRAVURE
Plates of 200 in four panes of 50.

1985, June 14	**Tagged**	***Perf. 11***	
2146 A1529 22c **multicolored**		.40	.20
P# block of 4, 4#		2.00	—
Zip block of 4		1.65	—
a. Imperf., pair		*260.00*	

FREDERIC AUGUSTE BARTHOLDI (1834-1904)

Architect and Sculptor, Statue of Liberty
A1530

Designed by Howard Paine from paintings by Jose Frappa and James Dean.

LITHOGRAPHED & ENGRAVED
Plates of 200 in four panes of 50.

1985, July 18	**Tagged**	***Perf. 11***	
2147 A1530 22c **multicolored**		.40	.20
P# block of 4, 5#		1.90	—
Zip block of 4		1.65	—

Examples of No. 2147 exist with most, but not all, of the engraved black omitted.

George Washington, Washington Monument — A1532

Sealed Envelopes — A1533

Designed by Thomas Szumowski (#2149) based on a portrait by Gilbert Stuart, and Richard Sheaff (#2150).

COIL STAMPS
PHOTOGRAVURE

1985		***Perf. 10 Vertically***	
2149 A1532 18c **multicolored,** low gloss gum, *Nov. 6*		.35	.20
Pair		.70	.20
P# strip of 5, #1112		3.00	
P# strip of 5, #3333		4.25	
P# single, #1112		—	2.10
P# single, #3333		—	3.25
a. Untagged (Bureau Precanceled), low gloss gum		.35	.35
P# strip of 5, #11121		6.00	
P# strip of 5, #33333		3.00	
P# single, #11121		—	5.00
P# single, #33333		—	2.00
Dull gum		.35	
P# strip of 5, #33333		4.00	
P# strip of 5, #43444		6.50	
P# single, #43444		—	5.50
b. Imperf., pair		*950.00*	
P#1112			
c. As "a," imperf., pair		*800.00*	
P#33333			
d. Tagging omitted (not Bureau precanceled)		—	—
e. As "a," tagged (error), dull gum		2.00	1.75
Pair		4.00	3.75
P# strip of 5, #33333		*50.00*	
P# single, #33333		—	35.00
Low gloss gum		*2.00*	
P# strip of 5, #33333		50.00	
P# single, #33333		—	—
2150 A1533 21.1c **multicolored,** *Oct. 22*		.40	.20
Pair		.80	.20
P# strip of 5, #111111		3.25	
P# strip of 5, #111121		4.75	
P# single, #111111		—	2.50
P# single, #111121		—	3.75
a. Untagged (Bureau Precancel)		.40	.40
Pair		.80	.80
P# strip of 5, #111111		*40.00*	
P# single, #111111		—	2.75
b. As "a," tagged (error)		.40	.40
Pair		.80	.80
P# strip of 5, #111111		3.25	
P# strip of 5, #111121		4.75	
P# single, #111111		—	2.50
P# single, #111121		—	3.75

Precancellations on Nos. 2149a ("PRESORTED FIRST-CLASS"), 2150a and 2150b ("ZIP+4") do not have lines.

KOREAN WAR VETERANS

American Troops in Korea
A1535

Designed by Richard Sheaff from a photograph by David D. Duncan.

ENGRAVED
Plates of 200 in four panes of 50.

1985, July 26	**Tagged**	***Perf. 11***	
2152 A1535 22c **gray green & rose red**		.40	.20
P# block of 4		2.50	—
Zip block of 4		1.75	—

SOCIAL SECURITY ACT, 50th ANNIV.

Men, Women, Children, Corinthian Columns
A1536

Designed by Robert Brangwynne.

Printed by American Bank Note Company.

PHOTOGRAVURE
Plates of 200 in four panes of 50.

1985, Aug. 14	Tagged	Perf. 11	
2153 A1536 22c	**deep & light blue**	.40	.20
	P# block of 4, 2#	1.90	—
	Zip block of 4	1.70	—

WORLD WAR I VETERANS

The Battle of Marne, France
A1537

Designed by Richard Sheaff from Harvey Dunn's charcoal drawing.

ENGRAVED
Plates of 200 in four panes of 50.

1985, Aug. 26	Tagged	Perf. 11	
2154 A1537 22c	**gray green & rose red**	.40	.20
	P# block of 4	2.25	—
	Zip block of 4	1.85	—
a.	Red missing (PS)	—	
b.	Tagging omitted		—

HORSES

Quarter Horse
A1538

Morgan
A1539

Saddlebred
A1540

Appaloosa
A1541

Designed by Roy Andersen.

PHOTOGRAVURE
Plates of 160 in four panes of 40.

1985, Sept. 25	Tagged	Perf. 11	
2155 A1538 22c	**multicolored**	1.00	.20
2156 A1539 22c	**multicolored**	1.00	.20
2157 A1540 22c	**multicolored**	1.00	.20
2158 A1541 22c	**multicolored**	1.00	.20
a.	Block of 4, #2155-2158	6.00	5.00
	P# block of 4, 5#	7.50	—
	Zip block of 4	6.25	—

PUBLIC EDUCATION IN AMERICA

Quill Pen, Apple, Spectacles, Penmanship Quiz — A1542

Designed by Uldis Purins.

Printed by American Bank Note Company

PHOTOGRAVURE
Plates of 200 in four panes of 50.

1985, Oct. 1	Tagged	Perf. 11	
2159 A1542 22c	**multicolored**	.45	.20
	P# block of 4, 5#	2.75	—
	Zip block of 4	1.85	—

INTERNATIONAL YOUTH YEAR

YMCA Youth Camping, Cent. — A1543

Boy Scouts, 75th Anniv.
A1544

Big Brothers / Big Sisters Federation, 40th Anniv.
A1545

Camp Fire Inc., 75th Anniv.
A1546

Designed by Dennis Luzak.

Printed by American Bank Note Company.

PHOTOGRAVURE
Plates of 200 in four panes of 50.

1985, Oct. 7	Tagged	Perf. 11	
2160 A1543 22c	**multicolored**	.65	.20
2161 A1544 22c	**multicolored**	.65	.20
2162 A1545 22c	**multicolored**	.65	.20
2163 A1546 22c	**multicolored**	.65	.20
a.	Block of 4, #2160-2163	3.00	2.25
	P# block of 4, 5#	4.00	—
	Zip block of 4	3.25	—

HELP END HUNGER

Youths and Elderly Suffering from Malnutrition
A1547

Designed by Jerry Pinkney.

Printed by the American Bank Note Company.

PHOTOGRAVURE
Plates of 200 in four panes of 50.

1985, Oct. 15	Tagged	Perf. 11	
2164 A1547 22c	**multicolored**	.45	.20
	P# block of 4, 5#	2.00	—
	Zip block of 4	1.90	—

CHRISTMAS

Genoa Madonna, Enameled Terra-Cotta by Luca Della Robbia (1400-1482) — A1548

Poinsettia Plants
A1549

Designed by Bradbury Thompson (No. 2165) and James Dean (No. 2166).

PHOTOGRAVURE
Plates of 200 in panes of 50.

1985, Oct. 30	Tagged	Perf. 11	
2165 A1548 22c	**multicolored**	.40	.20
	P# block of 4, 4#	1.75	—
	Zip block of 4	1.65	—
a.	Imperf., pair	*100.00*	
2166 A1549 22c	**multicolored**	.40	.20
	P# block of 4, 5#	1.70	—
	Zip block of 4	1.65	—
a.	Imperf., pair	*130.00*	

ARKANSAS STATEHOOD, 150th ANNIV.

Old State House, Little Rock — A1550

Designed by Roger Carlisle.

Printed by the American Bank Note Company

PHOTOGRAVURE

Plates of 200 in four panes of 50.

1986, Jan. 3 **Tagged** ***Perf. 11***

2167 A1550 22c **multicolored** .50 .20
P# block of 4, 6# 2.50 —
Zip block of 4 2.10 —
a. Vert. pair, imperf. horiz. —

Marginal Inscriptions

Beginning with the Luis Munoz Marin issue a number of stamps include a descriptive inscription in the selvage.

GREAT AMERICANS ISSUE

A1551

A1552

Designed by Ron Adair.

Printed by the Bureau of Engraving & Printing.

ENGRAVED

Panes of 100 (#2168-2193, 2195), Panes of 20 (#2194, 2196)

Perf. 11, 11½x11 (#2185), 11x11.1 (20c)

1986-94 **Tagged**

2168 A1551 1c **brownish vermilion,** large block tagging, *June 30* .20 .20
P# block of 4 .25 —
Zip block of 4 .20 —
a. Tagging omitted *5.00*

2169 A1552 2c **bright blue,** large block tagging, *Feb. 28, 1987* .20 .20
P# block of 4 .30 —
Zip block of 4 .20 —
a. Untagged .20 .20
P# block of 4 .35 —
Zip block of 4 .20 —
b. Tagging omitted — —

The tagging omitted error No. 2169b appeared before No. 2169a was issued. Plate blocks from plate 1 are the error if untagged. No. 2169a is from plate 2. Other blocks and singles are indistiguishable, unless se-tenant with tagged stamps.

A1553

A1554

Designed by Christopher Calle.

Printed by the Bureau of Engraving & Printing.

2170 A1553 3c **bright blue,** large block tagging, dull gum, *Sept. 15* .20 .20
P# block of 4 .50 —
Zip block of 4 .25 —
a. Untagged, dull gum, *1994* .20 .20
P# block of 4 .50 —
Zip block of 4 .25 —
Shiny gum, *1994* .20
P# block of 4 .50 —
Zip block of 4 .25 —
b. Tagging omitted — —

The tagging omitted error No. 2170b appeared before No. 2170a was issued. Plate blocks from plates 2 and 3 are the error if untagged. No. 2170a is from plate 4. Other blocks and singles are indistiguishable, unless se-tenant with tagged stamps.

2171 A1554 4c **blue violet,** large block tagging, *July 14* .20 .20
P# block of 4 .60 —
Zip block of 4 .40 —
a. 4c **grayish violet,** untagged .20 .20
P# block of 4 .40 —
Zip block of 4 .35 —
b. 4c **deep grayish blue,** untagged, *1993* .20 .20
P# block of 4 .50 —
Zip block of 4 .40 —

A1555

A1556

Designers: No. 2172, Christopher Calle. No. 2173, Juan Maldonado.

Printed by the Bureau of Engraving & Printing.

2172 A1555 5c **dark olive green,** large block tagging, *Feb. 27* .20 .20
P# block of 4 .65 —
Zip block of 4 .35 —
a. Tagging omitted *10.00* —

2173 A1556 5c **carmine,** overall tagging, *Feb. 18, 1990* .20 .20
P# block of 4 .75 —
P# zip block of 4 .90 —
Zip block of 4 .45 —
a. Untagged, *1991* .20 .20
P# block of 4 .60 —
P# zip block of 4 .75 —
Zip block of 4 .45 —
b. Tagging omitted — —

The tagging omitted error No. 2173b appeared before No. 2173a was issued. Plate blocks from plate 1 are the error if untagged. No. 2173a is from plate 2. Other blocks and singles are indistiguishable, unless se-tenant with tagged stamps.

A1557

A1558

Designers: 10c, Robert Anderson. 14c, Ward Brackett.

Printed by the Bureau of Engraving & Printing.

2175 A1557 10c **lake,** large block tagging, dull gum, *Aug. 15, 1987* .20 .20
P# block of 4 .85 —
Zip block of 4 .80 —
a. Overall tagging, dull gum, *1990* .30 .20
P# block of 4 10.00 —
Zip block of 4 2.00 —
b. Tagging omitted *12.50*
c. Prephosphored coated paper (solid tagging), dull gum, *1991* .30 .20
P# block of 4 1.40 —
Zip block of 4 1.20 —
d. Prephosphored uncoated paper (mottled tagging), shiny gum, *1993* .20 .20
P# block of 4 1.25 —
Zip block of 4 .80 —
e. 10c **carmine,** prephosphored uncoated paper (mottled tagging), shiny gum, *1994* .25 .20
P# block of 4 1.25 —
Zip block of 4 1.00 —
f. As "c," all color omitted —

No. 2157f must be collected se-tenant with a partially printed stamp or longer vertical strip.

2176 A1558 14c **crimson,** large block tagging, *Feb. 12, 1987* .25 .20
P# block of 4 1.50 —
Zip block of 4 1.05 —

A1559

A1560

Designers: 15c, Jack Rosenthal. 17c, Christopher Calle.

Printed by the Bureau of Engraving & Printing.

2177 A1559 15c **claret,** large block tagging, *June 6, 1988* .35 .20
P# block of 4 10.00 —
Zip block of 4 1.50 —
a. Overall tagging, *1990* .30 —
P# block of 4 3.25 —
Zip block of 4 1.20 —
b. Prephosphored coated paper (solid tagging) .40 —
P# block of 4 3.25 —
Zip block of 4 1.60 —
c. Tagging omitted *15.00* —
d. All color omitted —

No. 2177d resulted from a partially printed pane. It must be collected se-tenant with a partially printed stamp or in a longer horizontal strip showing three error stamps plus partially/completely printed stamps.

2178 A1560 17c **dull blue green,** large block tagging, *June 18* .35 .20
P# block of 4 2.00 —
Zip block of 4 1.40 —
a. Tagging omitted *10.00*

A1561

A1562

Designers: 20c, Robert Anderson. 21c, Susan Sanford.

Printed by: 20c, Banknote Corporation of America. 21c, Bureau of Engraving & Printing.

2179 A1561 20c **red brown,** prephosphored coated paper (grainy solid tagging), *Oct. 24, 1994* .40 .20
P# block of 4, 1#+B 2.00 —
a. 20c **orange brown,** prephosphored coated paper (grainy solid tagging) .40 .20
P# block of 4, 1#+B 2.25 —

2180 A1562 21c **blue violet,** large block tagging, *Oct. 21, 1988* .40 .20
P# block of 4 2.50 —
Zip block of 4 1.65 —
a. Tagging omitted —

No. 2180 known with worn tagging mats on which horizontal untagged areas have taggant giving the appearance of vertical band tagging.

A1563

A1564

A1565

Designers: 23c, Dennis Lyall. 25c, Richard Sparks. 28c, Robert Anderson.

Printed by the Bureau of Engraving & Printing.

2181 A1563 23c **purple,** large block tagging, dull gum, *Nov. 4, 1988* .45 .20
P# block of 4 2.50 —
Zip block of 4 1.90 —
a. Overall tagging, dull gum .45 —
P# block of 4 5.00 —
Zip block of 4 1.80 —
b. Prephosphored coated paper (solid tagging), dull gum .60 —
P# block of 4 3.25 —
Zip block of 4 2.40 —
c. Prephosphored uncoated paper (mottled tagging), shiny gum .50 .20
P# block of 4 3.25 —
Zip block of 4 2.00 —
d. Tagging omitted *7.50*

2182 A1564 25c **blue,** large block tagging, *Jan. 11* .45 .20
P# block of 4 2.75 —

		Zip block of 4	1.85	—
a.		Booklet pane of 10, *May 3, 1988*	4.50	*3.75*
b.		As #2182, tagging omitted	—	—
c.		As "a," tagging omitted	—	
d.		Horiz. pair, imperf between	—	

See Nos. 2197, 2197a.

2183	A1565	28c **myrtle green,** large block tagging, *Sept. 14, 1989*	.50	.20
		P# block of 4	2.50	—
		Zip block of 4	2.25	—

A1566

A1567

Designed by Christopher Calle.

Printed by: No. 2184, Canadian Bank Note Co. for Stamp Venturers. No. 2185, Stamp Venturers.

2184	A1566	29c **blue,** prephosphored uncoated paper (mottled tagging), *Mar. 9, 1992*	.55	.20
		P# block of 4, #+S	2.50	—
		Zip block of 4	2.25	—
2185	A1567	29c **indigo,** prephosphored paper (solid tagging), *Apr. 13, 1993*	.50	.20
		P# block of 4, 1#+S	2.50	—
		Zip block of 4	2.25	—

A1568

A1569

A1575

(A1570: Harvey Cushing MD, USA 45)

Designers: 35c, 40c, Christopher Calle. 45c, Bradbury Thompson.

Printed by: 35c, Canadian Bank Note Co. for Stamp Venturers. 40c, 45c, Bureau of Engraving & Printing.

2186	A1568	35c **black,** prephosphored uncoated paper (mottled tagging), *Apr. 3, 1991*	.65	.20
		P# block of 4, #+S	3.25	—
		Zip block of 4	2.90	—
2187	A1569	40c **dark blue,** overall tagging, dull gum, *Sept. 6, 1990*	.70	.20
		P# block of 4	3.75	—
		Zip block of 4	3.00	—
a.		Prephosphored coated paper (solid tagging), dull gum	.75	.35
		P# block of 4	4.25	—
		Zip block of 4	3.00	—
b.		Prephosphored coated paper (grainy solid tagging), low gloss gum, *1998*	.75	.35
		P# block of 4	4.25	—
		Zip block of 4	4.00	—
c.		Prephosphored uncoated paper (mottled tagging), shiny gum, *1994*	.75	.20
		P# block of 4	7.50	—
		Zip block of 4	3.00	—
d.		Tagging omitted	—	
2188	A1570	45c **bright blue,** large block tagging, *June 17, 1988*	.85	.20
		P# block of 4	3.75	—
		Zip block of 4	3.50	—
a.		45c **blue,** overall tagging, *1990*	1.65	.20
		P# block of 4	11.00	—
		Zip block of 4	7.00	—
b.		Tagging omitted	*15.00*	

The blue on No. 2188a is noticeably lighter than on No. 2188. Color variety specialists, as well as tagging specialists, will want to consider it as a second variety of this stamp.

A1571

A1572

Designers: 52c, John Berkey. 56c, Robert Anderson.

Printed by the Bureau of Engraving & Printing.

2189	A1571	52c **purple,** prephosphored coated paper (solid tagging), dull gum, *June 3, 1991*	1.10	.20
		P# block of 4	7.50	—
		Zip block of 4	4.50	—
a.		Prephosphored uncoated paper (mottled tagging), shiny gum, *1993*	1.10	—
		P# block of 4	5.50	—
		Zip block of 4	4.50	—

Selvage inscriptions from the original printing of No. 2189 from plate 1 show the incorrect dates for Humphrey's vice-presidential term ("1964 to 1968"). Corrected plate 1 and plate 2 printings (No. 2189a) show the dates correctly as 1965 to 1969. Values for the two varieties of inscription blocks of 6 are approximately the same: $7.50.

2190	A1572	56c **scarlet,** large block tagging, *Sept. 3*	1.10	.20
		P# block of 4	6.00	—
		Zip block of 4	4.50	—

No. 2190 known with a "tagging spill" making stamp appear overall tagged.

A1573

A1574

Designed by Christopher Calle.

Printed by the Bureau of Engraving & Printing.

2191	A1573	65c **dark blue,** large block tagging, *Nov. 5, 1988*	1.20	.20
		P# block of 4	5.00	—
		Zip block of 4	4.90	—
a.		Tagging omitted	*20.00*	
2192	A1574	75c **deep magenta,** prephosphored coated paper (solid tagging), dull gum, *Feb. 16, 1992*	1.30	.20
		P# block of 4	5.50	—
		Zip block of 4	5.25	—
a.		Prephosphored uncoated paper (mottled tagging), shiny gum	1.30	—
		P# block of 4	5.50	—
		Zip block of 4	5.25	—

A1576

"Lipstick on Shirt Front" double gouge plate flaw

Designers: No. 2193, Tom Broad. No. 2194, Bradbury Thompson.

Printed by the Bureau of Engraving & Printing.

2193	A1575	$1 **dark Prussian green,** large block tagging, *Sept. 23*	2.50	.50
		P# block of 4	14.00	—
		Zip block of 4	10.50	—
2194	A1576	$1 **intense deep blue,** large block tagging, dull gum, *June 7, 1989*	1.75	.50
		P# block of 4	7.00	—
		Pane of 20	35.00	
		Double gouge plate flaw ("Lipstick on Shirt Front"), (pos. 6 on one plate #1 pane)	—	
b.		$1 **deep blue,** overall tagging, dull gum, *1990*	1.75	.50
		P# block of 4	7.00	—
		Pane of 20	35.00	
c.		Tagging omitted	*10.00*	
d.		$1 **dark blue,** prephosphored coated paper (solid tagging), dull gum, *1992*	1.75	.50
		P# block of 4	7.00	—
		Pane of 20	35.00	
e.		$1 **blue,** prephosphored uncoated paper (mottled tagging), shiny gum, *1993*	2.00	.60
		P# block of 4	8.00	—
		Pane of 20	40.00	
f.		$1 **blue,** prephosphored coated paper (grainy solid tagging), low gloss gum, *1998*	1.75	.50
		P# block of 4	7.00	—
		Pane of 20	35.00	

No. 2194 issued in pane of 20 (see No. 2196.)

The intense deep blue of No. 2194 is much deeper than the deep blue and dark blue of the other $1 varieties.

The "Lipstick on Shirt Front" flaw was discovered during production and the position was repaired. Very few have been found.

A1577

A1578

Designers: $2, Tom Broad. $5, Arthur Lidov.

Printed by the Bureau of Engraving & Printing.

2195	A1577	$2 **bright violet,** large block tagging, *Mar. 19*	4.00	.50
		P# block of 4	19.00	—
		Zip block of 4	17.00	—
a.		Tagging omitted	*45.00*	

No. 2195 is known with worn tagging mats on which horizontal untagged areas have taggant giving the appearance of vertical band tagging.

2196	A1578	$5 **copper red,** large block tagging, *Aug. 25, 1987*	8.50	1.00
		P# block of 4	35.00	—
		Pane of 20	170.00	
a.		Tagging omitted	—	
b.		Prephosphored coated paper (solid tagging), *1992*	8.50	—
		P# block of 4	35.00	—
		Pane of 20	170.00	
		Nos. 2168-2196 (28)	29.25	7.30

Booklet Stamp

Perf. 10 on 2 or 3 sides

2197	A1564	25c **blue,** large block tagging, *May 3, 1988*	.45	.20
a.		Booklet pane of 6	3.00	*2.25*
b.		Tagging omitted	*4.50*	
c.		As "b," booklet pane of 6	*60.00*	

UNITED STATES - SWEDEN STAMP COLLECTING

Handstamped Cover, Philatelic Memorabilia
A1581

Boy Examining Stamp Collection A1582

No. 836 Under Magnifying Glass, Sweden Nos. 268, 271 — A1583

1986 Presidents Miniature Sheet — A1584

Designed by Richard Sheaff and Eva Jern (No. 2200).

BOOKLET STAMPS
LITHOGRAPHED & ENGRAVED
Perf. 10 Vert. on 1 or 2 Sides

1986, Jan. 23 **Tagged**

2198 A1581 22c **multicolored** .45 .20
2199 A1582 22c **multicolored** .45 .20
2200 A1583 22c **multicolored** .45 .20
2201 A1584 22c **multicolored** .45 .20
a. Bklt. pane of 4, #2198-2201 2.00 *1.75*
b. As "a," black omitted on Nos. 2198, 2201 50.00 —
c. As "a," blue (litho.) omitted on Nos. 2198-2200 *2,500.*
d. As "a," buff (litho.) omitted —

See Sweden Nos. 1585-1588.

LOVE ISSUE

A1585

Designed by Saul Mandel.

Plates of 200 in four panes of 50.
PHOTOGRAVURE

1986, Jan. 30 **Tagged** ***Perf. 11***

2202 A1585 22c **multicolored** .40 .20
P# block of 4, 5# 1.75 —
Zip block of 4 1.65 —

Sojourner Truth (c. 1797-1883), Human Rights Activist — A1586

Texas State Flag and Silver Spur — A1587

BLACK HERITAGE SERIES

Designed by Jerry Pinkney.

Printed by American Bank Note Co.

Plates of 200 in four panes of 50
PHOTOGRAVURE

1986, Feb. 4 **Tagged** ***Perf. 11***

2203 A1586 22c **multicolored** .40 .20
P# block of 4, 6# 2.00 —
Zip block of 4 1.65 —

REPUBLIC OF TEXAS, 150th ANNIV.

Designed by Don Adair.

Printed by the American Bank Note Co.

Plates of 200 in four panes of 50.
PHOTOGRAVURE

1986, Mar. 2 **Tagged** ***Perf. 11***

2204 A1587 22c **dark blue, dark red & grayish black** .40 .20
P# block of 4, 3# 1.90 —
Zip block of 4 1.65 —
a. Horiz. pair, imperf. vert. *1,100.*
b. Dark red omitted *2,750.*
c. Dark blue omitted *8,500.*

FISH

Muskellunge — A1588

Atlantic Cod A1589

Largemouth Bass — A1590

Bluefin Tuna A1591

Catfish A1592

Designed by Chuck Ripper.

BOOKLET STAMPS
PHOTOGRAVURE

1986, Mar. 21 **Tagged** ***Perf. 10 Horiz.***

2205 A1588 22c **multicolored** .60 .20
2206 A1589 22c **multicolored** .60 .20
2207 A1590 22c **multicolored** .60 .20
2208 A1591 22c **multicolored** .60 .20
2209 A1592 22c **multicolored** .60 .20
a. Bklt. pane of 5, #2205-2209 5.50 *2.75*
b. As "a," red omitted —

PUBLIC HOSPITALS

A1593

Designed by Uldis Purins.

Printed by the American Bank Note Co.

PHOTOGRAVURE
Plates of 200 in four panes of 50.

1986, Apr. 11 **Tagged** ***Perf. 11***

2210 A1593 22c **multicolored** .40 .20
P# block of 4, 5# 1.75 —
Zip block of 4 1.65 —
a. Vert. pair, imperf. horiz. *325.00*
b. Horiz. pair, imperf. vert. *1,300.*

PERFORMING ARTS

Edward Kennedy "Duke" Ellington (1899-1974), Jazz Composer — A1594

Designed by Jim Sharpe.
Printed by the American Bank Note Co.

PHOTOGRAVURE
Plates of 200 in four panes of 50.

1986, Apr. 29 **Tagged** ***Perf. 11***

2211 A1594 22c **multicolored** .40 .20
P# block of 4, 6# 1.90 —
Zip block of 4 1.75 —
a. Vert. pair, imperf. horiz. *1,000.*

AMERIPEX '86 ISSUE

Miniature Sheets

Presidents of
the United States: I
AMERIPEX 86
International
Stamp Show
Chicago, Illinois
May 22-June 1, 1986

35 Presidents — A1599a

A1599b

A1599c

A1599d

Illustrations reduced.

Designs: No. 2216: a, George Washington. b, John Adams. c, Thomas Jefferson. d, James Madison. e, James Monroe. f, John Quincy Adams. g, Andrew Jackson. h, Martin Van Buren. i, William H. Harrison.

No. 2217: a, John Tyler. b, James Knox Polk. c, Zachary Taylor. d, Millard Fillmore. e, Franklin Pierce. f, James Buchanan. g, Abraham Lincoln. h, Andrew Johnson. i, Ulysses S. Grant.

No. 2218: a, Rutherford B. Hayes. b, James A. Garfield. c, Chester A. Arthur. d, Grover Cleveland. e, Benjamin Harrison. f, William McKinley. g, Theodore Roosevelt. h, William H. Taft. i, Woodrow Wilson.

No. 2219: a, Warren G. Harding. b, Calvin Coolidge. c, Herbert Hoover. d, Franklin Delano Roosevelt. e, White House. f, Harry S. Truman. g, Dwight D. Eisenhower. h, John F. Kennedy. i, Lyndon B. Johnson.

Designed by Jerry Dadds.

LITHOGRAPHED & ENGRAVED

1986, May 22 **Tagged** ***Perf. 11***

2216	A1599a Sheet of 9	4.25	—
a.-i.	22c, any single	.45	.25
j.	Blue (engr.) omitted	*3,250.*	
k.	Black inscription omitted	*2,000.*	
l.	Imperf.	*10,500.*	
m.	As "k," double impression of red	—	
2217	A1599b Sheet of 9	4.25	—
a-i.	22c, any single	.45	.25
j.	Black inscription omitted	*3,750.*	
2218	A1599c Sheet of 9	4.25	—
a.-i.	22c, any single	.45	.25
j.	Brown (engr.) omitted	—	
k.	Black inscription omitted	*2,900.*	
2219	A1599d Sheet of 9	4.25	—
a.-i.	22c, any single	.45	.25
j.	Blackish blue (engr.) inscription omitted on a-b, d-e, g-h	—	
k.	Tagging omitted on c, f, i	—	
l.	Blackish blue (engr.) omitted on all stamps	—	
	Nos. 2216-2219 (4)	17.00	

Issued in conjunction with AMERIPEX '86 Intl. Philatelic Exhibition, Chicago, IL May 22-June 1. Sheet size: 120x207mm (sheet size varied).

ARCTIC EXPLORERS

Elisha Kent Kane — A1600

Adolphus W. Greely A1601

Vilhjalmur Stefansson A1602

Robert E. Peary, Matthew Henson A1603

Designed by Dennis Lyall.
Printed by the American Bank Note Company

PHOTOGRAVURE

Plates of 200 in four panes of 50.

1986, May 28 **Tagged** ***Perf. 11***

2220	A1600 22c **multicolored**	.65	.20
2221	A1601 22c **multicolored**	.65	.20
2222	A1602 22c **multicolored**	.65	.20
2223	A1603 22c **multicolored**	.65	.20
a.	Block of 4, #2220-2223	2.75	2.25
	P# block of 4, 5#	4.50	—
	Zip block of 4	3.00	—
b.	As "a," black (engr.) omitted	*8,500.*	
c.	As "a," Nos. 2220, 2221 black (engr.) omitted	—	

STATUE OF LIBERTY, 100th ANNIV.

A1604

Designed by Howard Paine.

ENGRAVED

Plates of 200 in four panes of 50.

1986, July 4 **Tagged** ***Perf. 11***

No.	Type	Description	Unused	Used
2224	A1604	22c **scarlet & dark blue**	.40	.20
		P# block of 4	2.25	—
		Zip block of 4	1.65	—
a.		Scarlet omitted	—	

On No. 2224a, virtually all of the dark blue also is omitted, so the error stamp should be collected as part of a transition strip. See France No. 2014.

Coil Plate No. Strips of 3
Beginning with No. 2123, coil plate no. strips of 3 usually sell at the level of strips of 5 minus the face value of two stamps.

TRANSPORTATION ISSUE

A1604a

A1604b

Designers: 1c, 2c, David Stone.

COIL STAMPS
ENGRAVED

1986-87 **Tagged** ***Perf. 10 Vert.***

No.	Type	Description	Unused	Used
2225	A1604a	1c **violet,** large block tagging, dull gum, *Nov. 26*	.20	.20
		Pair	.20	.20
		P# strip of 5, #1	.60	
		P# strip of 5, #2	.65	
		P# single, #1	—	.40
		P# single, #2	—	.50
a.		Prephosphored uncoated paper (mottled tagging) (error), shiny gum	.20	.20
		Pair	.20	.20
		P# strip of 5, #3	15.00	
		P# single, #3	—	13.00
b.		Untagged, dull gum	.20	.20
		Pair	.20	.20
		P# strip of 5, #2-3	.65	
		P# single, #2-3	—	.45
		Shiny gum	.20	
		P# strip of 5, #3	.80	
		Low gloss gum	.20	
		P# strip of 5, #3	.80	
c.		Imperf., pair	*2,000.*	
2226	A1604b	2c **black,** dull gum, *Mar. 6, 1987*	.20	.20
		Pair	.20	.20
		P# strip of 5, #1	.70	
		P# single, #1	—	.45
a.		Untagged, dull gum	.20	.20
		Pair	.20	.20
		P# strip of 5, #2	.70	
		P# single, #2	—	.50
		Shiny gum	.20	
		P# strip of 5, #2	1.75	

REDUCED SIZE

No.	Type	Description	Unused	Used
2228	A1285	4c **reddish brown,** large block tagging, *Aug.*	.20	.20
		Pair	.20	.20
		P# strip of 5, #1	1.25	
		P# single, #1	—	.95
a.		Overall tagging, *1990*	.70	.20
		Pair	1.40	.20
		P# strip of 5, #1	11.00	
		P# single, #1	—	9.00
b.		Imperf., pair	300.00	
		P#1		

UNTAGGED

No.	Type	Description	Unused	Used
2231	A1511	8.3c **green** (Bureau precancel, Blk. Rt./CAR-RT/SORT), *Aug. 29*	.20	.20
		Pair	.40	.40
		P# strip of 5, #1	5.25	
		P# strip of 5, #2	5.75	
		P# single, #1	—	3.00
		P# single, #2	—	4.75

Earliest known usage of No. 2228: Aug. 15, 1986.

On No. 2228 "Stagecoach 1890s" is 17¾mm long; on No. 1898A, 19½mm long.

On No. 2231 "Ambulance 1860s" is 18mm long; on No. 2128, 18½mm long.

Joint lines do not appear on Nos. 2225-2231.

AMERICAN FOLK ART SERIES
Navajo Art

A1605

A1606

A1607

A1608

Designed by Derry Noyes.

LITHOGRAPHED & ENGRAVED

Plates of 200 in four panes of 50.

1986, Sept. 4 **Tagged** ***Perf. 11***

No.	Type	Description	Unused	Used
2235	A1605	22c **multicolored**	.50	.20
2236	A1606	22c **multicolored**	.50	.20
2237	A1607	22c **multicolored**	.50	.20
2238	A1608	22c **multicolored**	.50	.20
a.		Block of 4, #2235-2238	2.50	2.25
		P# block of 4, 5#	4.00	—
		Zip block of 4	2.75	—
b.		As "a," black (engr.) omitted	*350.00*	

LITERARY ARTS SERIES

T.S. Eliot (1888-1965), Poet — A1609

Designed by Bradbury Thompson.

ENGRAVED

Plates of 200 in four panes of 50.

1986, Sept. 26 **Tagged** ***Perf. 11***

No.	Type	Description	Unused	Used
2239	A1609	22c **copper red**	.40	.20
		P# block of 4	1.90	—
		Zip block of 4	1.65	—

AMERICAN FOLK ART SERIES
Woodcarved Figurines

A1610

A1611

A1612

A1613

Designed by Bradbury Thompson.
Printed by the American Bank Note Company

PHOTOGRAVURE

Plates of 200 in four panes of 50.

1986, Oct. 1 **Tagged** ***Perf. 11***

No.	Type	Description	Unused	Used
2240	A1610	22c **multicolored**	.40	.20
2241	A1611	22c **multicolored**	.40	.20
2242	A1612	22c **multicolored**	.40	.20
2243	A1613	22c **multicolored**	.40	.20
a.		Block of 4, #2240-2243	1.75	*2.00*
		P# block of 4, 5#	3.00	—
		Zip block of 4	1.90	—
b.		As "a," imperf. vert.	*1,250.*	

CHRISTMAS

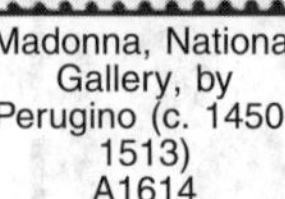
Madonna, National Gallery, by Perugino (c. 1450-1513) A1614

Village Scene A1615

Designed by Bradbury Thompson (#2244) & Dolli Tingle (#2245).

PHOTOGRAVURE

Plates of 200 in four panes of 50.

1986, Oct. 24 **Tagged** ***Perf. 11***

No.	Type	Description	Unused	Used
2244	A1614	22c **multicolored**	.40	.20
		P# block of 4, 6#	2.00	—
		Zip block of 4	1.65	—
a.		Imperf., pair	*800.00*	
2245	A1615	22c **multicolored**	.40	.20
		P# block of 4, 6#	1.90	—
		Zip block of 4	1.65	—

MICHIGAN STATEHOOD, 150th ANNIV.

White Pine — A1616

Designed by Robert Wilbert.

PHOTOGRAVURE

Plates of 200 in four panes of 50.

1987, Jan. 26 **Tagged** ***Perf. 11***

No.	Type	Description	Unused	Used
2246	A1616	22c **multicolored**	.40	.20
		P# block of 4, 5#	1.90	—
		Zip block of 4	1.65	—
		Pair with full vert. gutter between	—	

PAN AMERICAN GAMES
Indianapolis, Aug. 7-25

Runner in Full Stride
A1617

Designed by Lon Busch.

PHOTOGRAVURE
Plates of 200 in four panes of 50.

1987, Jan. 29 **Tagged** ***Perf. 11***

2247 A1617 22c **multicolored**	.40	.20
P# block of 4, 5#	1.90	—
Zip block of 4	1.65	—
a. Silver omitted	*1,500.*	

No. 2247a is valued in the grade of fine.

LOVE ISSUE

A1618

Designed by John Alcorn.

PHOTOGRAVURE
Panes of 100

1987, Jan. 30 **Tagged** ***Perf. 11½x11***

2248 A1618 22c **multicolored**	.40	.20
P# block of 4, 5#	1.90	—
Zip block of 4	1.65	—
Pair with full horiz. gutter between		—

BLACK HERITAGE SERIES

Jean Baptiste Pointe du Sable (c. 1750-1818), Pioneer Trader, Founder of Chicago — A1619

Designed by Thomas Blackshear.

PHOTOGRAVURE
Plates of 200 in four panes of 50.

1987, Feb. 20 **Tagged** ***Perf. 11***

2249 A1619 22c **multicolored**	.40	.20
P# block of 4, 5#	1.90	—
Zip block of 4	1.65	—
a. Tagging omitted	*10.00*	

Enrico Caruso (1873-1921), Opera Tenor — A1620

Fourteen Achievement Badges — A1621

PERFORMING ARTS SERIES

Designed by Jim Sharpe.

Printed by American Bank Note Co.

PHOTOGRAVURE & ENGRAVED
Plates of 200 in four panes of 50.

1987, Feb. 27 **Tagged** ***Perf. 11***

2250 A1620 22c **multicolored**	.40	.20
P# block of 4, 4#	1.90	—
Zip block of 4	1.65	—
a. Black (engr.) omitted	*5,000.*	

GIRL SCOUTS, 75TH ANNIVERSARY

Designed by Richard Sheaff.

LITHOGRAPHED & ENGRAVED
Plates of 200 in four panes of 50.

1987, Mar. 12 **Tagged** ***Perf. 11***

2251 A1621 22c **multicolored**	.40	.20
P# block of 4, 6#	1.90	—
Zip block of 4	1.65	—
a. All litho. colors omitted	*2,500.*	
b. Red & black (engr.) omitted	*2,000.*	

All known examples of No. 2251a have been expertized and certificate must accompany purchase. The unique pane of No. 2251b has been expertized and a certificate exists for the pane of 50.

Coil Plate No. Strips of 3
Beginning with No. 2123, coil plate no. strips of 3 usually sell at the level of strips of 5 minus the face value of two stamps.

TRANSPORTATION ISSUE

A1622

A1623

A1624

Carreta 1770s 7.6 USA Nonprofit

A1625

A1626

A1627

A1628

A1629

A1630

A1631

A1632

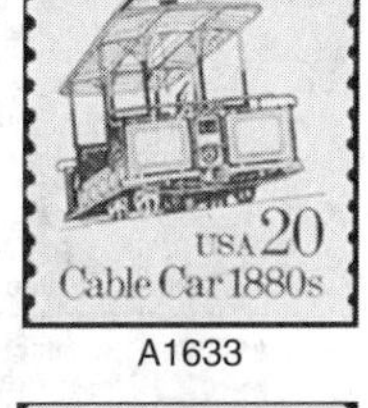

A1633

A1634

A1635

Tandem Bicycle 1890s 24.1 USA ZIP+4

A1636

Designers: 3c, 7.6c, 13.2c, 15c, Richard Schlecht. 5c, 5.3c, 16.7c, Lou Nolan. 8.4c, 20.5c, 24.1c, Christopher Calle. 10c, William H. Bond. 13c, Joe Brockert. 17.5c, Tom Broad. 20c, Dan Romano. 21c, David Stone.

COIL STAMPS
ENGRAVED

1987-88 ***Perf. 10 Vert.***

Tagged, Untagged (5.3c, 7.6c, 8.4c, 13c, 13.2c, 16.7c, 20.5c, 21c, 24.1c)

2252 A1622 3c **claret,** dull gum, *Feb. 29, 1988*	.20	.20
Pair	.20	.20
P# strip of 5, #1	.90	
P# single, #1	—	.60
a. Untagged, dull gum	.20	.20
P# strip of 5, #2-3	1.25	
P# single, #2	—	.95
P# single, #3	—	.80
Shiny gum, *1995*	.20	
P# strip of 5, #3	1.25	
P# strip of 5, #5	2.25	
P# strip of 5, #6	2.10	
P# single, #5	—	2.00
P# single, #6	—	2.00
Low gloss gum	.20	
P# strip of 5, #5	3.75	

The plate #5 on No. 2252a with low gloss gum is smaller than the #5 on No. 2252a with shiny gum. The smaller plate #5 represents a different printing sleeve (plate).

2253 A1623 5c **black,** *Sept. 25*	.20	.20
Pair	.20	.20
P# strip of 5, #1	.90	
P# single, #1	—	.75
2254 A1624 5.3c **black** (Bureau precancel "Nonprofit Carrier Route Sort" in red), *Sept. 16, 1988*	.20	.20
Pair	.20	.20
P# strip of 5, #1	1.10	
P# single, #1	—	.70
2255 A1625 7.6c **brown** (Bureau precancel "Nonprofit" in red), *Aug. 30, 1988*	.20	.20
Pair	.30	.30
P# strip of 5, #1-2	2.25	
P# strip of 5, #3	5.75	
P# single, #1-2	—	1.50
P# single, #3	—	4.00
2256 A1626 8.4c **deep claret** (Bureau precancel "Nonprofit" in red), *Aug. 12, 1988*	.20	.20
Pair	.30	.30
P# strip of 5, #1-2	1.90	
P# strip of 5, #3	13.50	
P# single, #1-2	—	1.00
P# single, #3	—	5.50
a. Imperf., pair	*700.00*	
P#1		
2257 A1627 10c **blue,** large block tagging, dull gum, *Apr. 11*	.20	.20
Pair	.40	.20
P# strip of 5, #1	2.50	
P# single, #1	—	1.00
a. Overall tagging, dull gum, *1993*	.20	.20
Pair	.40	.20
P# strip of 5, #1	4.00	
P# single, #1	—	3.25
Shiny gum, *1994*	.20	.20
Pair	.20	.20
P# strip of 5, #4	3.50	
P# single, #4	—	2.00
b. Prephosphored uncoated paper (mottled tagging), shiny gum	.20	.20

Pair .40 .20
P# strip of 5, #1, 2 3.25
P# strip of 5, #3, 4 3.75
P# single, #1, 2 — 2.50
P# single, #3, 4 — 2.75
c. Prephosphored coated paper (solid tagging), low gloss gum .20 .20
Pair .40 .20
P# strip of 5, #5 5.75
P# single, #5 — 4.00
d. Tagging omitted *20.00*
e. Imperf, pair, large block tagging —

2258 A1628 13c **black** (Bureau precancel "Presorted First-Class" in red), *Oct. 29, 1988* .30 .25
Pair .60 .50
P# strip of 5, #1 3.25
P# single, #1 — 2.00

2259 A1629 13.2c **slate green** (Bureau precancel "Bulk Rate" in red), *July 19, 1988* .25 .25
Pair .50 .50
P# strip of 5, #1-2 2.75
P# single, #1-2 — 1.50
a. Imperf., pair *100.00*
P#1-2

2260 A1630 15c **violet,** large block tagging, *July 12, 1988* .25 .20
Pair .50 .20
P# strip of 5, #1 2.00
P# strip of 5, #2 2.50
P# single, #1-2 — 1.50
a. Overall tagging, *1990* .25 .20
Pair .50 .20
P# strip of 5, #2 3.25
P# single, #2 — 2.75
b. Tagging omitted *3.75*
P# strip of 5, #2 *150.00*
c. Imperf., pair *800.00*
P#2

2261 A1631 16.7c **rose** (Bureau precancel "Bulk Rate " in black), *July 7, 1988* .30 .30
Pair .60 .60
P# strip of 5, #1 2.75
P# strip of 5, #2 3.75
P# single, #1 — 1.75
P# single, #2 — 2.75
a. Imperf., pair *225.00*
P#1

All known copies of No. 2261a are miscut top to bottom.

2262 A1632 17.5c **dark violet,** *Sept. 25* .30 .20
Pair .60 .20
P# strip of 5, #1 3.00
P# single, #1 — 2.50
a. Untagged (Bureau Precancel "ZIP + 4 Presort" in red) .35 .30
P# strip of 5, #1 3.50
P# single, #1 — 2.75
b. Imperf., pair *1,750.*
P#1

2263 A1633 20c **blue violet,** large block tagging, *Oct. 28, 1988* .35 .20
Pair .70 .20
P# strip of 5, #1-2 3.50
P# single, #1-2 — 1.50
a. Imperf., pair *65.00*
P#2
b. Overall tagging, *1990* .35 .20
Pair .70 .20
P# strip of 5, #2 8.00
P# single, #2 — 5.00

2264 A1634 20.5c **rose** (Bureau precancel "ZIP + 4 Presort" in black), *Sept. 28, 1988* .40 .40
Pair .80 .80
P# strip of 5, #1 4.75
P# single, #1 — 3.25

2265 A1635 21c **olive green** (Bureau precancel "Presorted First-Class" in red), *Aug. 16, 1988* .40 .40
Pair .80 .80
P# strip of 5, #1-2 3.50
P# single, #1-2 — 2.50
a. Imperf., pair *55.00*
P#1

2266 A1636 24.1c **deep ultra** (Bureau precancel ZIP + 4 in red), *Oct. 26, 1988* .45 .45
Pair .90 .90
P# strip of 5, #1 4.00
P# single, #1 — 2.50
Nos. 2252-2266 (15) 4.20 3.85

5.3c, 7.6c, 8.4c, 13.2c, 16.7c, 20.5c, 21c and 24.1c only available precanceled.

SPECIAL OCCASIONS

A1637

A1638

A1639

A1640

A1641

A1642

A1643

A1644

Designed by Oren Sherman.

BOOKLET STAMPS PHOTOGRAVURE

1987, Apr. 20 Tagged *Perf. 10 on 1, 2 or 3 Sides*

2267	A1637	22c	**multicolored**	.65	.20
2268	A1638	22c	**multicolored**	.80	.20
2269	A1639	22c	**multicolored**	.80	.20
2270	A1640	22c	**multicolored**	.80	.20
2271	A1641	22c	**multicolored**	.80	.20
2272	A1642	22c	**multicolored**	.65	.20
2273	A1643	22c	**multicolored**	1.25	.20
2274	A1644	22c	**multicolored**	.80	.20
a.	Bklt. pane of 10 (#2268-2271, 2273-2274, 2 each #2267, 2272)			10.00	*5.00*

UNITED WAY, 100th ANNIV.

Six Profiles
A1645

Designed by Jerry Pinkney.

LITHOGRAPHED & ENGRAVED
Plates of 200 in four panes of 50.

1987, Apr. 28 Tagged *Perf. 11*

2275 A1645 22c **multicolored** .40 .20
P# block of 4, 6# 1.90 —
Zip block of 4 1.65 —

A1646

A1647

A1648

A1649

Pheasant — A1649a

Grosbeak — A1649b

Owl
A1649c

Honeybee
A1649d

Designs: Nos. 2276, 2278, 2280, Peter Cocci. Nos. 2277, 2279, 2282, Robert McCall. Nos. 2281, 2283-2285, Chuck Ripper.

PHOTOGRAVURE (Nos. 2276-2279)
Panes of 100

1987-88 Tagged *Perf. 11*

2276 A1646 22c **multicolored,** *May 9* .40 .20
P# block of 4, 4# 1.90 —
Zip block of 4 1.65 —
a. Booklet pane of 20, *Nov. 30* 8.50 —
b. As "a," vert. pair, imperf. btwn. *1,750.*

2277 A1647 (25c) **multi,** *Mar. 22, 1988* .45 .20
P# block of 4, 4# 2.00 —
Zip block of 4 1.85 —

2278 A1648 25c **multi,** *May 6, 1988* .45 .20
P# block of 4, 4# 1.90 —
Zip block of 4 1.85 —
Pair with full vert. gutter between —

COIL STAMPS
Perf. 10 Vert.

2279 A1647 (25c) **multi,** *Mar. 22, 1988* .45 .20
Pair .90 .20
P# strip of 5, #1111 2.75
P# strip of 5, #1211 4.25
P# strip of 5, #1222 2.75
P# strip of 5, #2222 4.50
P# single, #1111 — .65
P# single, #1211 — 1.25
P# single, #1222 — .65
P# single, #2222 — 3.50
a. Imperf., pair *85.00* —
P#1111, 1211, 2222

ENGRAVED

2280 A1649 25c **multi,** large block tagging, *May 20, 1988* .45 .20
Pair .90 .20
P# strip of 5, #1 6.25
P# strip of 5, #2-5 3.50
P# strip of 5, #7 6.25
P# strip of 5, #8 3.50
P# strip of 5, #9 9.00
P# single, #1 — 2.50
P# single, #2-5 — .75
P# single, #7 — 2.50
P# single, #8 — .75
P# single, #9 — 2.00
a. Prephosphored uncoated paper (mottled tagging) .45 .20
P# strip of 5, #1 37.50
P# strip of 5, #2, 3 3.50
P# strip of 5, #5 6.50
P# strip of 5, #6 11.50
P# strip of 5, #7-14 3.50
P# strip of 5, #15 6.25
P# single, #1 — 30.00

	P# single, #2	—	.75
	P# single, #3	—	.55
	P# single, #5	—	1.25
	P# single, #6	—	5.75
	P# single, #7-14	—	.75
	P# single, #15	—	2.00
b.	Imperf., pair, large block tagging	32.50	
	P#2-9		
c.	Imperf., pair, prephosphored paper (mottled tagging)	14.00	
	P#2-3, 5-11, 13-15		
d.	Tagging omitted	*5.00*	
	P# strip of 5, #7, 8	—	
e.	Black trees	*100.00*	—
	P# strip of 5, #5, 15	*550.00*	
	P# strip of 5, #6	*650.00*	
f.	Pair, imperf. between	*750.00*	

LITHOGRAPHED AND ENGRAVED

2281	A1649d 25c **multi,** small block tagging *Sept. 2, 1988*	.45	.20
	Pair	.90	.20
	P# strip of 5, #1	3.75	
	P# single, #1	—	.65
a.	As No. 2281, imperf., pair	50.00	
	P#1-2		
b.	Black (engr.) omitted	*60.00*	—
c.	Black (litho.) omitted	*400.00*	
d.	Pair, imperf. between	*1,000.*	
e.	Yellow (litho.) omitted	*1,200.*	
f.	Large block tagging	.45	.20
	Pair	.90	
	P# strip of 5, #2	3.75	
	P# single, #2	—	.65
g.	As "f," imperf, pair	50.00	
h.	As "f," tagging omitted		—

No. 2281h can be distinguished as having come from the large block tagging stamp by its deeper colors and jet black "25," which is a characteristic of the plate 2 large block tagged printing.

No. 2281 from plate #1 is known with two types of "1" on the plate-numbered stamps. The original tall "1" was later shortened manually by removing the top of the "1," including the serif, so it would not penetrate the design. Value of plate # strip of 5 with tall "1," $24.

Beware of stamps with traces of the litho. black that are offered as No. 2281c.

Vertical pairs or blocks of No. 2281 and imperfs. with the engr. black missing are from printer's waste.

BOOKLET STAMPS

Printed by American Bank Note Co. (#2283)

PHOTOGRAVURE

Perf. 10, 11 (#2283)

2282	A1647 (25c) **multi,** *Mar. 22, 1988*	.50	.20
a.	Booklet pane of 10	6.50	*3.50*
2283	A1649a 25c **multi,** *Apr. 29, 1988*	.50	.20
a.	Booklet pane of 10	6.00	*3.50*
b.	25c multicolored, red removed from sky	6.25	.20
c.	As "b," bklt. pane of 10	*67.50*	—
d.	As "a," horiz. imperf. btwn.	*2,000.*	

Imperf. panes exist from printers waste, and a large number exist.

2284	A1649b 25c **multi,** *May 28, 1988*	.50	.20
2285	A1649c 25c **multi,** *May 28, 1988*	.50	.20
b.	Bklt. pane of 10, 5 each #2284-2285	5.00	*3.50*
d.	Pair, Nos. 2284-2285	1.10	.25
e.	As "d," tagging omitted	*12.50*	
2285A	A1648 25c **multi,** *July 5, 1988*	.50	.20
c.	Booklet pane of 6	3.00	*2.00*

Illustration reduced.

Designed by Chuck Ripper.

PHOTOGRAVURE

Plates of 200 in four panes of 50.

1987, June 13			**Tagged**	***Perf. 11***	
2286	A1650	22c	Barn swallow	*.85*	.20
2287	A1651	22c	Monarch butterfly	*.85*	.20
2288	A1652	22c	Bighorn sheep	*.85*	.20
2289	A1653	22c	Broad-tailed hummingbird	*.85*	.20
2290	A1654	22c	Cottontail	*.85*	.20
2291	A1655	22c	Osprey	*.85*	.20
2292	A1656	22c	Mountain lion	*.85*	.20
2293	A1657	22c	Luna moth	*.85*	.20
2294	A1658	22c	Mule deer	*.85*	.20
2295	A1659	22c	Gray squirrel	*.85*	.20
2296	A1660	22c	Armadillo	*.85*	.20
2297	A1661	22c	Eastern chipmunk	*.85*	.20
2298	A1662	22c	Moose	*.85*	.20
2299	A1663	22c	Black bear	*.85*	.20
2300	A1664	22c	Tiger swallowtail	*.85*	.20
2301	A1665	22c	Bobwhite	*.85*	.20
2302	A1666	22c	Ringtail	*.85*	.20
2303	A1667	22c	Red-winged blackbird	*.85*	.20
2304	A1668	22c	American lobster	*.85*	.20
2305	A1669	22c	Black-tailed jack rabbit	*.85*	.20
2306	A1670	22c	Scarlet tanager	*.85*	.20
2307	A1671	22c	Woodchuck	*.85*	.20
2308	A1672	22c	Roseate spoonbill	*.85*	.20
2309	A1673	22c	Bald eagle	*.85*	.20
2310	A1674	22c	Alaskan brown bear	*.85*	.20
2311	A1675	22c	Iiwi	*.85*	.20
2312	A1676	22c	Badger	*.85*	.20
2313	A1677	22c	Pronghorn	*.85*	.20
2314	A1678	22c	River otter	*.85*	.20
2315	A1679	22c	Ladybug	*.85*	.20
2316	A1680	22c	Beaver	*.85*	.20
2317	A1681	22c	White-tailed deer	*.85*	.20
2318	A1682	22c	Blue jay	*.85*	.20
2319	A1683	22c	Pika	*.85*	.20
2320	A1684	22c	American buffalo	*.85*	.20
2321	A1685	22c	Snowy egret	*.85*	.20
2322	A1686	22c	Gray wolf	*.85*	.20

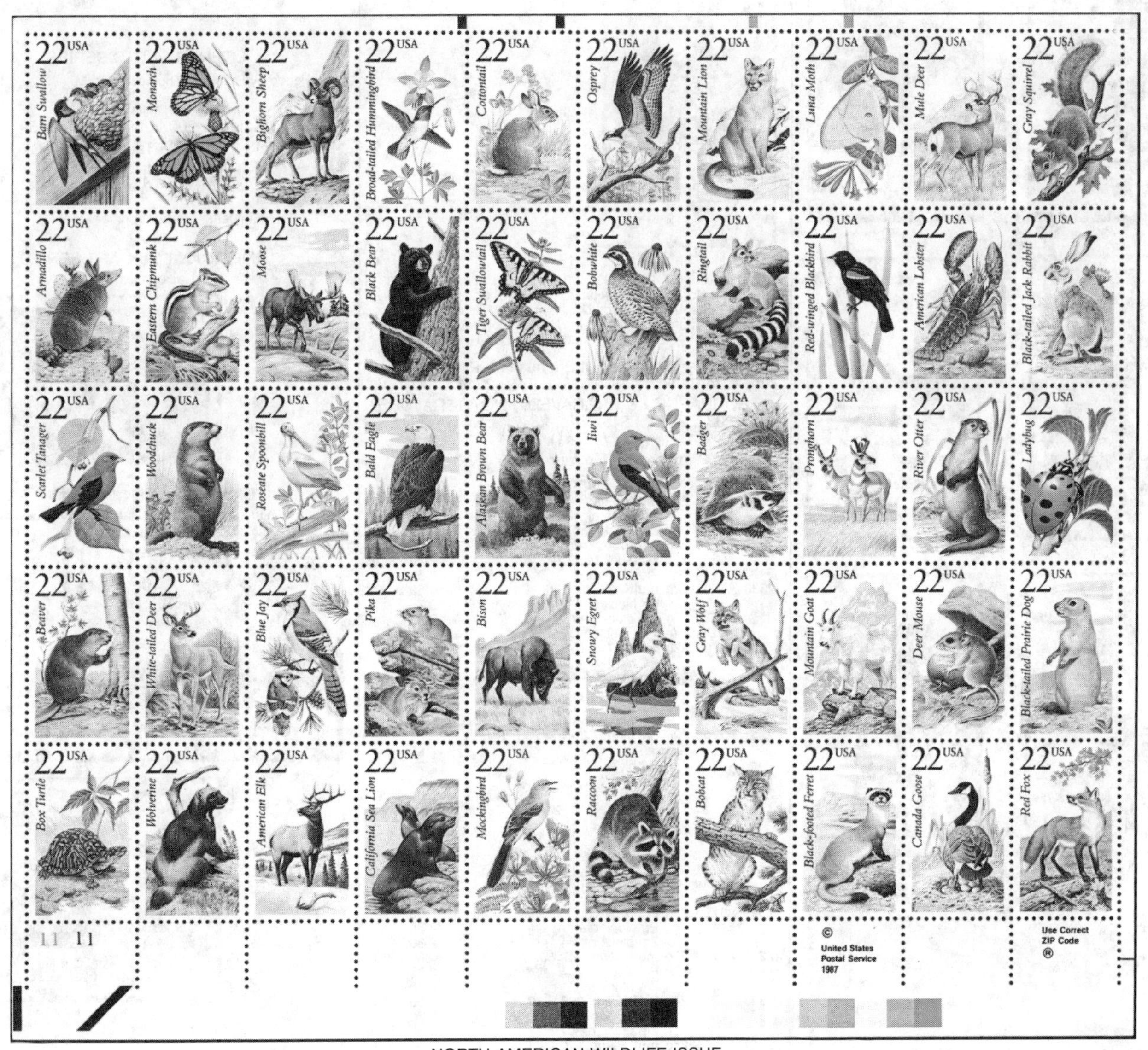

NORTH AMERICAN WILDLIFE ISSUE
A1650-A1699

No.	Design	Value	Description	Unused	Used
2323	A1687	22c	Mountain goat	*.85*	.20
2324	A1688	22c	Deer mouse	*.85*	.20
2325	A1689	22c	Black-tailed prairie dog	*.85*	.20
2326	A1690	22c	Box turtle	*.85*	.20
2327	A1691	22c	Wolverine	*.85*	.20
2328	A1692	22c	American elk	*.85*	.20
2329	A1693	22c	California sea lion	*.85*	.20
2330	A1694	22c	Mockingbird	*.85*	.20
2331	A1695	22c	Raccoon	*.85*	.20
2332	A1696	22c	Bobcat	*.85*	.20
2333	A1697	22c	Black-footed ferret	*.85*	.20
2334	A1698	22c	Canada goose	*.85*	.20
2335	A1699	22c	Red fox	*.85*	.20
a.	A1650-A1699		Pane of 50, #2286-2335	*47.50*	
2286b-2335b			Any single, red omitted		—

RATIFICATION OF THE CONSTITUTION BICENTENNIAL

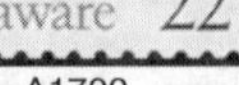
A1700

A1701

A1702

A1703

A1704

A1705

A1706

A1707

A1708

A1709

A1710

A1711

A1712

Designers: Nos. 2336-2337, 2341 Richard Sheaff. No. 2338, Jim Lamb. No. 2339, Greg Harlin. No. 2340, Christopher Calle. No. 2342, Stephen Hustvedt. Nos. 2343, 2347, Bob Timberlake. No. 2344, Thomas Szumowski. No. 2345, Pierre Mion. No. 2346, Bradbury Thompson. No. 2348, Robert Brangwynne.

Printed by the Bureau of Engraving & Printing or the American Bank Note Co. (Nos. 2343-2344, 2347).

LITHOGRAPHED & ENGRAVED, PHOTOGRAVURE (#2337, 2339, 2343-2344, 2347), ENGRAVED (#2341).

Plates of 200 in four panes of 50.

1987-90	**Tagged**		***Perf. 11***	
2336	A1700 22c **multi,** *July 4*		.60	.20
		P# block of 4, 5#	2.75	—
		Zip block of 4	2.50	—
2337	A1701 22c **multi,** *Aug. 26*		.60	.20
		P# block of 4, 5#	2.75	—
		Zip block of 4	2.50	—
2338	A1702 22c **multi,** *Sept. 11*		.60	.20
		P# block of 4, 5#	2.75	—
		Zip block of 4	2.50	—
a.	Black (engr.) omitted		*5,500.*	
2339	A1703 22c **multi,** *Jan. 6, 1988*		.60	.20
		P# block of 4, 5#	2.75	—
		Zip block of 4	2.50	—
2340	A1704 22c **multi,** *Jan. 9, 1988*		.60	.20
		P# block of 4, 5#	2.75	—
		Zip block of 4	2.50	—
2341	A1705 22c **dark blue & dark red,** *Feb. 6, 1988*		.60	.20
		P# block of 4, 1#	2.75	—
		Zip block of 4	2.50	—
2342	A1706 22c **multi,** *Feb. 15, 1988*		.60	.20
		P# block of 4, 6#	2.75	—
		Zip block of 4	2.50	—
2343	A1707 25c **multi,** *May 23, 1988*		.60	.20
		P# block of 4, 5#	2.75	—
		Zip block of 4	2.50	—
a.	Strip of 3, vert. imperf btwn.		—	
b.	Red missing (PS)		—	
2344	A1708 25c **multi,** *June 21, 1988*		.60	.20
		P# block of 4, 4#	2.75	—
		Zip block of 4	2.50	—
2345	A1709 25c **multi,** *June 25, 1988*		.60	.20
		P# block of 4, 5#	2.75	—
		Zip block of 4	2.50	—
2346	A1710 25c **multi,** *July 26, 1988*		.60	.20
		P# block of 4, 5#	2.75	—
		Zip block of 4	2.50	—
2347	A1711 25c **multi,** *Aug. 22, 1989*		.60	.20
		P# block of 4, 5#	2.75	—
		Zip block of 4	2.50	—
2348	A1712 25c **multi,** *May 29, 1990*		.60	.20
		P# block of 4, 7#	2.75	—
		Zip block of 4	2.50	—
		Nos. 2336-2348 (13)	7.80	2.60

No. 2343b resulted either from a shifting of all colors or from a shift of both the perforations and the cutting of the pane.

Arabesque, Dar Batha Palace Door, Fez — A1713

William Faulkner (1897-1962), Novelist — A1714

US-MOROCCO DIPLOMATIC RELATIONS, 200th ANNIV.

Designed by Howard Paine.

LITHOGRAPHED & ENGRAVED

Plates of 200 in four panes of 50.

1987, July 17	**Tagged**		***Perf. 11***	
2349	A1713 22c **scarlet & black**		.40	.20
		P# block of 4, 2#	1.75	—
		Zip block of 4	1.65	—
a.	Black (engr.) omitted		*275.00*	

See Morocco No. 642.

LITERARY ARTS SERIES

Designed by Bradbury Thompson.

ENGRAVED

Plates of 200 in four panes of 50

1987, Aug. 3	**Tagged**		***Perf. 11***	
2350	A1714 22c **bright green**		.40	.20
		P# block of 4	2.00	—
		Zip block of 4	1.65	—

Imperfs. are from printer's waste.

AMERICAN FOLK ART SERIES
Lacemaking

A1715

A1716

A1717

A1718

Designed by Libby Thiel.

LITHOGRAPHED & ENGRAVED
Plates of 160 in four panes of 40.

1987, Aug. 14 **Tagged** ***Perf. 11***
2351 A1715 22c **ultra & white** .45 .20
2352 A1716 22c **ultra & white** .45 .20
2353 A1717 22c **ultra & white** .45 .20
2354 A1718 22c **ultra & white** .45 .20
a. Block of 4, #2351-2354 1.90 1.90
P# block of 4, 4# 3.25 —
Zip block of 4 2.00 —
b. As "a," white omitted *950.00*

DRAFTING OF THE CONSTITUTION BICENTENNIAL

Excerpts from the Preamble

A1719

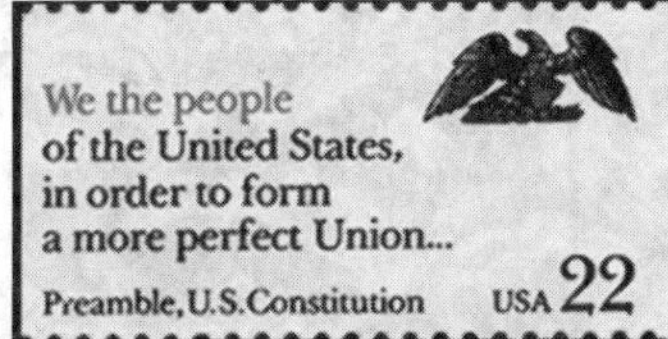

A1720

A1721

A1722

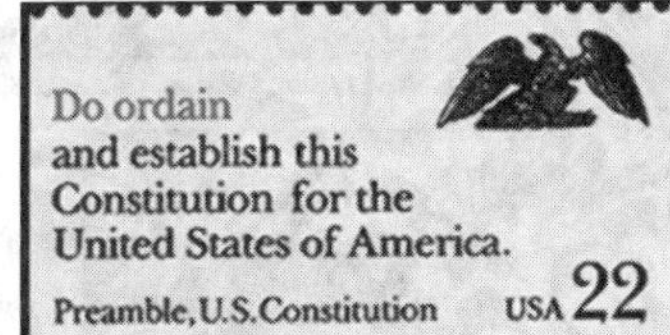

A1723

Designed by Bradbury Thompson.

BOOKLET STAMPS
PHOTOGRAVURE

1987, Aug. 28 **Tagged** ***Perf. 10 Horiz.***
2355 A1719 22c **multicolored** .55 .20
a. Grayish green (background) omitted —
2356 A1720 22c **multicolored** .55 .20
a. Grayish green (background) omitted —
2357 A1721 22c **multicolored** .55 .20
a. Grayish green (background) omitted —
2358 A1722 22c **multicolored** .55 .20
a. Grayish green (background) omitted —
2359 A1723 22c **multicolored** .55 .20
a. Bklt. pane of 5, #2355-2359 2.75 *2.25*
b. Grayish green (background) omitted —

A1724

A1725

SIGNING OF THE CONSTITUTION

Designed by Howard Koslow.

LITHOGRAPHED & ENGRAVED
Plates of 200 in four panes of 50.

1987, Sept. 17 **Tagged** ***Perf. 11***
2360 A1724 22c **multicolored** .45 .20
P# block of 4, 6# 2.25 —
Zip block of 4 1.90 —

CERTIFIED PUBLIC ACCOUNTING

Designed by Lou Nolan.

LITHOGRAPHED & ENGRAVED
Plates of 200 in four panes of 50.

1987, Sept. 21 **Tagged** ***Perf. 11***
2361 A1725 22c **multicolored** *1.50* .20
P# block of 4, 5# *7.00* —
Zip block of 4 *6.50* —
a. Black (engr.) omitted *725.00*

LOCOMOTIVES

Stourbridge Lion, 1829 — A1726

Best Friend of Charleston, 183 — A1727

John Bull, 1831 A1728

Brother Jonathan, 1832 A1729

Gowan & Marx, 1839 A1730

Designed by Richard Leech.

BOOKLET STAMPS
LITHOGRAPHED & ENGRAVED

1987, Oct. 1 **Tagged** ***Perf. 10 Horiz.***
2362 A1726 22c **multicolored** .55 .20
2363 A1727 22c **multicolored** .55 .20
2364 A1728 22c **multicolored** .55 .20
2365 A1729 22c **multicolored** .55 .20
a. Red omitted —
2366 A1730 22c **multicolored** .55 .20
a. Bklt. pane of 5, #2362-2366 2.75 *2.50*
b. As No. 2366, black (engr.) omitted (single) —
c. As No. 2366, blue omitted (single) —

CHRISTMAS

Moroni Madonna — A1731

Christmas Ornaments — A1732

Designed by Bradbury Thompson (No. 2367) and Jim Dean (No. 2368).

PHOTOGRAVURE
Plates of 800 in eight panes of 100.

1987, Oct. 23 **Tagged** ***Perf. 11***
2367 A1731 22c **multicolored** .40 .20
P# block of 4, 6# 2.00 —
Zip block of 4 1.65 —
2368 A1732 22c **multicolored** .40 .20
P# block of 4, 6# 1.75 —
Zip block of 4 1.65 —
Pair with full vert. gutter between —

1988 WINTER OLYMPICS, CALGARY

Skiing — A1733

Designed by Bart Forbes.

Printed by the American Bank Note Company

PHOTOGRAVURE
Plates of 200 in four panes of 50.

1988, Jan. 10 **Tagged** ***Perf. 11***
2369 A1733 22c **multicolored** .40 .20
P# block of 4, 4# 1.75 —
Zip block of 4 1.65 —

AUSTRALIA BICENTENNIAL

Caricature of an Australian Koala and an American Bald Eagle — A1734

Designed by Roland Harvey.

PHOTOGRAVURE
Plates of 160 in four panes of 40.

1988, Jan. 26 **Tagged** ***Perf. 11***
2370 A1734 22c **multicolored** .40 .20
P# block of 4, 5# 1.75 —
Zip block of 4 1.65 —

See Australia No. 1052.

BLACK HERITAGE SERIES

James Weldon Johnson (1871-1938), Author and Lyricist — A1735

Designed by Thomas Blackshear.

Printed by the American Bank Note Co.

PHOTOGRAVURE
Plates of 200 in four panes of 50.

1988, Feb. 2		**Tagged**	
2371 A1735 22c **multicolored**		.40	.20
	P# block of 4, 5#	2.00	—
	Zip block of 4	1.65	—

CATS

Siamese and Exotic Shorthair A1736

Abyssinian and Himalayan A1737

Maine Coon and Burmese A1738

American Shorthair and Persian A1739

Designed by John Dawson.

Printed by the American Bank Note Co.

PHOTOGRAVURE
Plates of 160 in four panes of 40.

1988, Feb. 5		**Tagged**	
2372 A1736 22c **multicolored**		.45	.20
2373 A1737 22c **multicolored**		.45	.20
2374 A1738 22c **multicolored**		.45	.20
2375 A1739 22c **multicolored**		.45	.20
a.	Block of 4, #2372-2375	1.90	1.90
	P# block of 4, 5#	4.00	—
	Zip block of 4	2.00	—

AMERICAN SPORTS

Knute Rockne (1883-1931), Notre Dame football coach.

Francis Ouimet (1893-1967), 1st amateur golfer to win the US Open championship.

A1740

A1741

Designed by Peter Cocci and Thomas Hipschen.

LITHOGRAPHED & ENGRAVED
Plates of 200 in four panes of 50.

1988, Mar. 9		**Tagged**	
2376 A1740 22c **multicolored**		.40	.20
	P# block of 4, 7#	2.50	—
	Zip block of 4	1.65	—

Designed by M. Gregory Rudd.
Printed by the American Bank Note Co.

PHOTOGRAVURE
Plates of 200 in four panes of 50.

1988, June 13		**Tagged**	
2377 A1741 25c **multicolored**		.45	.20
	P# block of 4, 5#	2.50	—
	Zip block of 4	1.85	—

LOVE ISSUE
Roses

A1742

A1743

Designed by Richard Sheaff.

PHOTOGRAVURE
Plates of 400 in four panes of 100 (25c).
Plates of 200 in four panes of 50 (45c).

1988		**Tagged**	
2378 A1742 25c **multicolored**, *July 4*		.45	.20
	P# block of 4, 5#	1.90	—
	Zip block of 4	1.85	—
	Pair with full horiz. gutter between	—	
a.	Imperf., pair	*3,250.*	
2379 A1743 45c **multicolored**, *Aug, 8*		.65	.20
	P# block of 4, 4#	3.25	—
	Zip block of 4	2.65	—

1988 SUMMER OLYMPICS, SEOUL

Gymnastic Rings A1744

Designed by Bart Forbes.

PHOTOGRAVURE
Plates of 200 in four panes of 50

1988, Aug. 19		**Tagged**	
2380 A1744 25c **multicolored**		.45	.20
	P# block of 4, 5#	1.90	—
	Zip block of 4	1.85	—

CLASSIC AUTOMOBILES

1928 Locomobile A1745

1929 Pierce-Arrow — A1746

1931 Cord A1747

1932 Packard A1748

1935 Duesenberg — A1749

Designed by Ken Dallison.

LITHOGRAPHED & ENGRAVED
BOOKLET STAMPS

1988, Aug. 25	**Tagged**	***Perf. 10 Horiz.***	
2381 A1745 25c **multicolored**		.60	.20
2382 A1746 25c **multicolored**		.60	.20
2383 A1747 25c **multicolored**		.60	.20
2384 A1748 25c **multicolored**		.60	.20
2385 A1749 25c **multicolored**		.60	.20
a. Bklt. pane of 5, #2381-2385		6.00	*2.25*

ANTARCTIC EXPLORERS

Nathaniel Palmer (1799-1877) A1750

Lt. Charles Wilkes (1798-1877) A1751

Richard E. Byrd (1888-1957) A1752

Lincoln Ellsworth (1880-1951) A1753

Designed by Dennis Lyall.

Printed by the American Bank Note Co.

PHOTOGRAVURE
Plates of 160 in four panes of 40.

1988, Sept. 14 **Tagged** ***Perf. 11***
2386 A1750 25c **multicolored** .65 .20
2387 A1751 25c **multicolored** .65 .20
2388 A1752 25c **multicolored** .65 .20
2389 A1753 25c **multicolored** .65 .20
a. Block of 4, #2386-2389 2.75 2.00
P# block of 4, 6# 4.50 —
Zip block of 4 3.00 —
b. As "a," black omitted *1,400.*
c. As "a," imperf. horiz. *3,000.*

AMERICAN FOLK ART SERIES
Carousel Animals

Deer — A1754

Horse — A1755

Camel — A1756

Goat — A1757

Designed by Paul Calle.

LITHOGRAPHED & ENGRAVED
Plates of 200 in four panes of 50.

1988, Oct. 1 **Tagged** ***Perf. 11***
2390 A1754 25c **multicolored** .65 .20
2391 A1755 25c **multicolored** .65 .20
2392 A1756 25c **multicolored** .65 .20
2393 A1757 25c **multicolored** .65 .20
a. Block of 4, #2390-2393 3.00 2.00
P# block of 4, 7# 4.00 —
Zip block of 4 3.25 —

EXPRESS MAIL RATE

Eagle and Moon — A1758

Designed by Ned Seidler.

LITHOGRAPHED & ENGRAVED
Panes of 20

1988, Oct. 4 **Tagged** ***Perf. 11***
2394 A1758 $8.75 **multicolored** 13.50 8.00
P# block of 4, 7# 54.00 —

SPECIAL OCCASIONS

Happy Birthday A1759

Best Wishes A1760

Thinking of You A1761

Love You A1762

Designed by Harry Zelenko

Printed by the American Bank Note Co.

BOOKLET STAMPS
PHOTOGRAVURE

1988, Oct. 22 **Tagged** ***Perf. 11***
2395 A1759 25c **multicolored** .50 .20
2396 A1760 25c **multicolored** .50 .20
a. Bklt. pane of 6, 3 #2395 + 3 #2396 with gutter between 3.50 *3.25*
2397 A1761 25c **multicolored** .50 .20
2398 A1762 25c **multicolored** .50 .20
a. Bklt. pane of 6, 3 #2397 + 3 #2398 with gutter between 3.50 *3.25*
b. As "a," imperf. horiz. —

CHRISTMAS

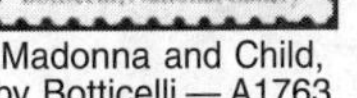

Madonna and Child, by Botticelli — A1763

One-horse Open Sleigh and Village Scene — A1764

"Missing Curlicue on Sleigh Runner" Cylinder Flaw

Designed by Bradbury Thompson (No. 2399) and Joan Landis (No. 2400).

LITHOGRAPHED & ENGRAVED (No. 2399), PHOTOGRAVURE (No. 2400)
Plates of 300 in 6 Panes of 50

1988, Oct 20 **Tagged** ***Perf. 11½***
2399 A1763 25c **multicolored** .45 .20
P# block of 4, 5+1# 1.90 —
Zip, copyright block of 4 1.85 —
Pair with full vert. gutter btwn. —
a. Gold omitted 30.00
2400 A1764 25c **multicolored** .45 .20
P# block of 4, 5# 1.90 —
Zip, copyright block of 4 1.85 —
Pair with full vert. gutter btwn. —
Cylinder flaw (missing curlicue on sleigh runner, 11111 UR19) 8.50

MONTANA STATEHOOD, 100th ANNIV.

C.M. Russell and Friends, by Charles M. Russell (1865-1926) A1765

Designed by Bradbury Thompson.

LITHOGRAPHED & ENGRAVED
Plates of 200 in four panes of 50.

1989, Jan. 15 **Tagged** ***Perf. 11***
2401 A1765 25c **multicolored** .45 .20
P# block of 4, 5# 2.00 —
Zip block of 4 1.85 —

Imperfs without gum exist from printer's waste.

BLACK HERITAGE SERIES

Asa Philip Randolph (1889-1979), Labor and Civil Rights Leader — A1766

Designed by Thomas Blackshear.

PHOTOGRAVURE
Plates of 200 in four panes of 50.

1989, Feb. 3 **Tagged** ***Perf. 11***
2402 A1766 25c **multicolored** .45 .20
P# block of 4, 5# 2.00 —
Zip block of 4 1.85 —

NORTH DAKOTA STATEHOOD, 100th ANNIV.

Grain Elevator on the Prairie
A1767

Designed by Wendell Minor.

Printed by the American Bank Note Co.

PHOTOGRAVURE
Plates of 200 in four panes of 50.

1989, Feb. 21 **Tagged** ***Perf. 11***

2403	A1767	25c	**multicolored**	.45	.20
			P# block of 4, 4#	2.00	—
			Zip block of 4	1.85	—

WASHINGTON STATEHOOD, 100th ANNIV.

Mt. Rainier — A1768

Designed by Howard Rogers.

Printed by the American Bank Note Co.

PHOTOGRAVURE
Plates of 200 in four panes of 50.

1989, Feb. 22 **Tagged** ***Perf. 11***

2404	A1768	25c	**multicolored**	.45	.20
			P# block of 4, 4#	2.00	—
			Zip block of 4	1.85	—

STEAMBOATS

Experiment, 1788-90 — A1769

Phoenix, 1809
A1770

New Orleans, 1812
A1771

Washington, 1816 — A1772

Walk in the Water, 1818
A1773

Designed by Richard Schlecht.

LITHOGRAPHED & ENGRAVED
BOOKLET STAMPS
Perf. 10 Horiz. on 1 or 2 Sides

1989, Mar. 3 **Tagged**

2405	A1769	25c	**multicolored**	.45	.20
2406	A1770	25c	**multicolored**	.45	.20
2407	A1771	25c	**multicolored**	.45	.20
2408	A1772	25c	**multicolored**	.45	.20
2409	A1773	25c	**multicolored**	.45	.20
a.			Booklet pane of 5, #2405-2409	2.25	*1.75*
b.			As "a," tagging omitted		—

No. 122 — A1774

Arturo Toscanini (1867-1957), Conductor — A1775

WORLD STAMP EXPO '89

Nov. 17-Dec. 3. Washington, D.C.

Designed by Richard Sheaff.

LITHOGRAPHED & ENGRAVED
Plates of 200 in four panes of 50.

1989, Mar. 16 **Tagged** ***Perf. 11***

2410	A1774	25c	**grayish brn, blk & car rose**	.45	.20
			P# block of 4, 4#	1.90	—
			Zip block of 4	1.85	—

PERFORMING ARTS

Designed by Jim Sharpe

Printed by the American Bank Note Co.

PHOTOGRAVURE
Plates of 200 in four panes of 50.

1989, Mar. 25 **Tagged** ***Perf. 11***

2411	A1775	25c	**multicolored**	.45	.20
			P# block of 4, 5#	2.00	—
			Zip block of 4	1.85	—

CONSTITUTION BICENTENNIAL SERIES

House of Representatives
A1776

Senate
A1777

Executive Branch — A1778

Supreme Court — A1779

Designed by Howard Koslow

LITHOGRAPHED & ENGRAVED
Plates of 200 in four panes of 50.

1989-90 **Tagged** ***Perf. 11***

2412	A1776	25c	**multi,** *Apr. 4, 1989*	.50	.20
			P# block of 4, 4#	2.25	—
			Zip block of 4	2.10	—
2413	A1777	25c	**multi,** *Apr. 6, 1989*	.50	.20
			P# block of 4, 4#	2.50	—
			Zip block of 4	2.10	—
2414	A1778	25c	**multi,** *Apr. 16, 1989*	.50	.20
			P# block of 4, 4#	2.25	—
			Zip block of 4	2.10	—
2415	A1779	25c	**multi,** *Feb. 2, 1990*	.50	.20
			P# block of 4, 4#	2.25	—
			Zip block of 4	2.10	—

SOUTH DAKOTA STATEHOOD, 100th ANNIV.

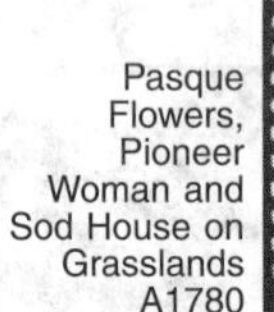

Pasque Flowers, Pioneer Woman and Sod House on Grasslands
A1780

Designed by Marian Henjum.

Printed by the American Bank Note Co.

PHOTOGRAVURE
Plates of 200 in four panes of 50.

1989, May 3 **Tagged** ***Perf. 11***

2416	A1780	25c	**multicolored**	.45	.20
			P# block of 4, 4#	1.90	—
			Zip block of 4	1.85	—

AMERICAN SPORTS

Henry Louis "Lou" Gehrig (1903-1941), New York Yankee Baseball Player — A1781

Designed by Bart Forbes.

Printed by the American Bank Note Co.

PHOTOGRAVURE
Plates of 200 in four panes of 50.

1989, June 10 **Tagged** ***Perf. 11***

2417	A1781	25c	**multicolored**	.50	.20
			P# block of 4, 6#	3.00	—
			Zip block of 4	2.25	—

LITERARY ARTS SERIES

Ernest Miller Hemingway (1899-1961), Nobel Prize winner for Literature in 1954 — A1782

Designed by M. Gregory Rudd.

Printed by the American Bank Note Co.

PHOTOGRAVURE
Plates of 200 in four panes of 50.

1989, July 17 **Tagged** ***Perf. 11***

2418 A1782 25c **multicolored**	.45	.20
P# block of 4, 5#	2.00	—
Zip block of 4	1.85	—
a. Vert. pair, imperf horiz.	—	

MOON LANDING, 20TH ANNIVERSARY

Raising of the Flag on the Lunar Surface, July 20, 1969 — A1783

Designed by Christopher Calle.

LITHOGRAPHED & ENGRAVED
Panes of 20

1989, July 20 **Tagged** ***Perf. 11x11½***

2419 A1783 $2.40 **multicolored**	4.00	2.00
P# block of 4, 6#	17.50	—
Pane of 20	82.50	—
a. Black (engr.) omitted	*2,500.*	
b. Imperf., pair	*750.00*	
c. Black (litho.) omitted	*3,250.*	

No. 2419 exists with a gray background instead of the normal dark blue. This was caused by a chemical wiping of the blue plate that contaminated the blue ink.

LETTER CARRIERS

A1784

Designed by Jack Davis.

Printed by the American Bank Note Co.

PHOTOGRAVURE
Plates of 160 in four panes of 40.

1989, Aug. 30 **Tagged** ***Perf. 11***

2420 A1784 25c **multicolored**	.45	.20
P# block of 4, 5#	1.90	—
Zip block of 4	1.85	—

CONSTITUTION BICENTENNIAL

Bill of Rights — A1785

Designed by Lou Nolan.

LITHOGRAPHED & ENGRAVED
Plates of 200 in four panes of 50.

1989, Sept. 25 **Tagged** ***Perf. 11***

2421 A1785 25c **multicolored**	.45	.20
P# block of 4	3.00	—
Zip block of 4	2.00	—
a. Black (engr.) omitted	*325.00*	

PREHISTORIC ANIMALS

Tyrannosaurus Rex — A1786

Pteranodon A1787

Stegosaurus A1788

Brontosaurus A1789

Designed by John Gurche.

LITHOGRAPHED & ENGRAVED
Plates of 160 in four panes of 40.

1989, Oct. 1 **Tagged** ***Perf. 11***

2422 A1786 25c **multicolored**	.65	.20
2423 A1787 25c **multicolored**	.65	.20
2424 A1788 25c **multicolored**	.65	.20
2425 A1789 25c **multicolored**	.65	.20
a. Block of 4, #2422-2425	3.00	2.00
P# block of 4, 6#	3.50	—
Zip block of 4	3.25	—
b. As "a," black (engr.) omitted	*750.00*	

The correct scientific name for Brontosaurus is Apatosaurus. Copyright block margin includes ad and Stamposaurus character trademark.

No. 2425b is valued in the grade of fine.

PRE-COLUMBIAN AMERICA ISSUE

Southwest Carved Figure, A.D. 1150-1350 — A1790

Designed by Lon Busch.

Printed by the American Bank Note Company.

PHOTOGRAVURE
Plate of 200 in four panes of 50.

1989, Oct. 12 **Tagged** ***Perf. 11***

2426 A1790 25c **multicolored**	.45	.20
P# block of 4, 6#	2.00	—
Zip block of 4	1.85	—

See No. C121.

CHRISTMAS

Madonna and Child, by Caracci — A1791

Sleigh Full of Presents — A1792

Designed by Bradbury Thompson (#2427) and Steven Dohanos (#2428-2429).

Printed by the Bureau of Engraving and Printing (#2427-2428) and American Bank Note Company (#2429).

LITHOGRAPHED & ENGRAVED,
PHOTOGRAVURE (#2428-2429)
Sheets of 300 in six panes of 50.

1989, Oct. 19 **Tagged** ***Perf. 11½***

2427 A1791 25c **multicolored**	.45	.20
P# block of 4, 5#	2.00	—
Zip, copyright block of 4	1.85	—
Pair with full horiz. gutter between	—	
a. Booklet pane of 10	4.75	*3.50*
b. As "a," red (litho.) omitted	*750.00*	
c. As "a," imperf.	—	

Perf. 11

2428 A1792 25c **multicolored**	.45	.20
P# block of 4, 5#	1.90	—
Zip, copyright block of 4	1.85	—
a. Vert. pair, imperf. horiz.	*2,000.*	

BOOKLET STAMP

Perf. 11½ on 2 or 3 sides

2429 A1792 25c **multicolored**	.45	.20
a. Booklet pane of 10	4.75	*3.50*
b. As "a," imperf. horiz.	—	
c. Vert. pair, imperf. horiz.	—	
d. As "a," red omitted	—	
e. Imperf., pair	—	

Marked differences exist between Nos. 2428 and 2429: No. 2429 was printed in four colors, No. 2428 in five colors. The runners on the sleigh in No. 2429 are twice as thick as those on No. 2428. On No. 2429 the package at the upper left in the sleigh has a red bow, whereas the same package in No. 2428 has a red and black bow; and the ribbon on the upper right package in No. 2429 is green, whereas the same ribbon in No. 2428 is black.

Eagle and Shield — A1793

Designed by Jay Haiden.

Printed by the American Bank Note Company.

PHOTOGRAVURE
BOOKLET STAMP

1989, Nov. 10 Tagged Self-Adhesive ***Die Cut***

2431 A1793 25c **multicolored** .50 .20
a. Booklet pane of 18 11.00
b. Vert. pair, no die cutting between *500.00*
c. Pair, no die cutting —

Panes sold for $5.

Also available in strips of 18 with stamps spaced for use in affixing machines to service first day covers. Sold for $5.

No. 2431c will include part of the margins around the stamps.

Sold only in 15 test cities (Atlanta, Chicago, Cleveland, Columbus, OH, Dallas, Denver, Houston, Indianapolis, Kansas City, MO, Los Angeles, Miami, Milwaukee, Minneapolis, Phoenix, St. Louis) and through the philatelic agency.

WORLD STAMP EXPO '89
Washington, DC, Nov. 17-Dec. 3

WORLD STAMP EXPO'89
The classic 1869 U.S. Abraham Lincoln stamp is reborn in these four larger versions commemorating World Stamp Expo'89, held in Washington, D.C. during the 20th Universal Postal Congress of the UPU. These stamps show the issued colors and three of the trial proof color combinations.

A1794

Illustration reduced.

Designed by Richard Sheaff.

LITHOGRAPHED & ENGRAVED

1989, Nov. 17 Tagged ***Imperf.***

2433 A1794 Sheet of 4 14.00 9.00
a. 90c like No. 122 2.00 1.75
b. 90c like 132TC (blue frame, brown center) 2.00 1.75
c. 90c like 132TC (green frame, blue center) 2.00 1.75
d. 90c like 132TC (scarlet frame, blue center) 2.00 1.75

20th UPU CONGRESS
Traditional Mail Delivery

Stagecoach, c. 1850 — A1795

Paddlewheel Steamer — A1796

Biplane — A1797

Depot-hack Type Automobile — A1798

Designed by Mark Hess.

LITHOGRAPHED & ENGRAVED
Plates of 160 in four panes of 40.

1989, Nov. 19 Tagged ***Perf. 11***

2434 A1795 25c **multicolored** .45 .20
2435 A1796 25c **multicolored** .45 .20
2436 A1797 25c **multicolored** .45 .20
2437 A1798 25c **multicolored** .45 .20
a. Block of 4, #2434-2437 2.00 1.75
P# block of 4, 5# 3.75 —
Zip block of 4 2.25 —
b. As "a," dark blue (engr.) omitted *600.00*

No. 2437b is valued in the grade of fine. Very fine blocks exist and sell for somewhat more.

Souvenir Sheet
LITHOGRAPHED & ENGRAVED

1989, Nov. 28 Tagged ***Imperf.***

2438 Sheet of 4 4.00 1.75
a. A1795 25c multicolored .65 .25
b. A1796 25c multicolored .65 .25
c. A1797 25c multicolored .65 .25
d. A1798 25c multicolored .65 .25
e. Dark blue & gray (engr.) omitted *5,500.*

20th Universal Postal Union Congress.

VALUES FOR HINGED STAMPS AFTER NO. 771

This catalogue does not value unused stamps after No. 771 in hinged condition. Hinged unused stamps from No. 772 to the present are worth considerably less than the values given for unused stamps, which are for never-hinged examples.

IDAHO STATEHOOD, 100th ANNIV.

Mountain Bluebird, Sawtooth Mountains — A1799

Designed by John Dawson.

Printed by the American Bank Note Company.

PHOTOGRAVURE
Plates of 200 in four panes of 50.

1990, Jan. 6 Tagged ***Perf. 11***

2439 A1799 25c **multicolored** .45 .20
P# block of 4, 5# 2.00 —
Zip block of 4 1.90 —

LOVE

A1800

Designed by Jayne Hertko.

Printed by the U.S. Banknote Company (#2440) and the Bureau of Engraving and Printing (#2441).

PHOTOGRAVURE
Plates of 200 in four panes of 50.

1990, Jan. 18 Tagged ***Perf. 12½x13***

2440 A1800 25c **black, bright blue, dark pink & emerald green** .45 .20
P# block of 4, 4# 2.00 —
Zip, copyright block of 4 1.90 —
a. Imperf., pair *800.00*

BOOKLET STAMP
Perf. 11½ on 2 or 3 sides

2441 A1800 25c **black, ultramarine, bright pink & dark green** .45 .20
a. Booklet pane of 10 4.75 *3.50*
b. As "a," bright pink omitted *1,700.*
c. As "b," single stamp *160.00*

No. 2441c may be obtained from booklet panes containing both normal and color-omitted stamps.

BLACK HERITAGE SERIES

Ida B. Wells (1862-1931), Journalist — A1801

Designed by Thomas Blackshear.

Printed by American Bank Note Company.

PHOTOGRAVURE
Plates of 200 in four panes of 50.

1990, Feb. 1 Tagged ***Perf. 11***

2442 A1801 25c **multicolored** .45 .20
P# block of 4, 5# 2.25 —
Zip block of 4 1.90 —

Beach Umbrella — A1802

Designed by Pierre Mion.

BOOKLET STAMP
PHOTOGRAVURE

1990, Feb. 3 Tagged ***Perf. 11***

2443 A1802 15c **multicolored** .30 .20
a. Booklet pane of 10 3.00 *2.00*
b. As "a," blue omitted *1,400.*
c. As No. 2443, blue omitted *140.00*

WYOMING STATEHOOD, 100th ANNIV.

High Mountain Meadows, by Conrad Schwiering A1803

Designed by Jack Rosenthal.

LITHOGRAPHED & ENGRAVED
Plates of 200 in four panes of 50.

1990, Feb. 23 Tagged ***Perf. 11***

2444 A1803 25c **multicolored** .45 .20
P# block of 4, 5# 2.00 —
Zip block of 4 1.90 —
a. Black (engr.) omitted *1,900.* —

CLASSIC FILMS

Judy Garland and Toto (The Wizard of Oz) — A1804

Clark Gable & Vivien Leigh (Gone With the Wind) — A1805

Gary Cooper (Beau Geste) — A1806

John Wayne (Stagecoach) A1807

Designed by Thomas Blackshear.

Printed by the American Bank Note Company.

PHOTOGRAVURE

Plates of 160 in four panes of 40.

1990, Mar. 23	**Tagged**		***Perf. 11***	
2445 A1804 25c	**multicolored**		1.00	.20
2446 A1805 25c	**multicolored**		1.00	.20
2447 A1806 25c	**multicolored**		1.00	.20
2448 A1807 25c	**multicolored**		1.00	.20
a.	Block of 4, #2445-2448		4.50	3.50
		P# block of 4, 5#	6.00	—
		Zip block of 4	4.75	—

LITERARY ARTS SERIES

Marianne Moore (1887-1972), Poet — A1808

Designed by M. Gregory Rudd.

Printed by the American Bank Note Company.

PHOTOGRAVURE

Plates of 200 in four panes of 50.

1990, Apr. 18	**Tagged**	***Perf. 11***	
2449 A1808 25c	**multicolored**	.45	.20
	P# block of 4, 3#	2.00	—
	Zip block of 4	1.90	—
a.	All colors missing (EP)	—	

No. 2449a must be collected se-tenant with a partially printed stamp or in longer horizontal strips with a partially printed stamp and normal stamps.

Coil Plate No. Strips of 3
Beginning with No. 2123, coil plate no. strips of 3 usually sell at the level of strips of 5 minus the face value of two stamps.

TRANSPORTATION ISSUE

A1810

A1811

A1811a

A1812

A1816

A1822

A1823

A1825

A1827

Designers: 4c, 32c, Richard Schlecht. Nos. 2452, 2452B, 2452D, Susan Sanford. No. 2453, Paul Calle. 10c, David K. Stone. 20c, 23c, Robert Brangwynne. $1, Chuck Hodgson.

Printed by: Guilford Gravure for American Bank Note Co. (No. 2452B), J.W. Fergusson & Sons for Stamp Venturers (No. 2454), Stamp Venturers (No, 2452D), others by BEP.

COIL STAMPS

ENGRAVED, PHOTOGRAVURE (#2452B, 2452D, 2454, 2458)

Tagged, Untagged (Nos. 2452B, 2452D, 2453, 2454, 2457-2458)

1990-95			***Perf. 9.8 Vert.***		
2451	A1810	4c	**claret,** *Jan. 25, 1991*	.20	.20
			Pair	.20	.20
			P# strip of 5, #1	1.10	
			P# single, #1	—	.95
a.			Imperf., pair	*700.00*	
			P#1		
b.			Untagged	.20	.20
			Pair	.20	.20
			P# strip of 5, #1	1.10	
			P# single, #1	—	.95
2452	A1811	5c	**carmine,** dull gum, *Aug. 31*	.20	.20
			Pair	.20	.20
			P# strip of 5, #1	1.25	
			P# single, #1	—	.90
a.			Untagged, dull gum	.20	.20
			Pair	.20	.20
			P# strip of 5, #1	1.25	
			P# single, #1	—	1.00
			Low gloss gum	.20	.20
			Pair	.20	.20
			P# strip of 5, #2	1.40	
			P# single, #2	—	1.20
c.			Imperf., pair	*700.00*	
2452B	A1811	5c	**carmine,** *Dec. 8, 1992*	.20	.20
			Pair	.25	.20
			P# strip of 5, #A1-A2	1.50	
			P# single, #A1-A2	—	1.00
f.			Printed with luminescent ink	.20	.20
			Pair	.20	.20
			P# strip of 5, #A3	2.10	
			P# single, #A3	—	2.00
2452D	A1811a	5c	**carmine,** low gloss gum, *Mar. 20, 1995*	.20	.20
			Pair	.20	.20
			P# strip of 5, #S1-S2	1.60	
			P# single, #S1-S2	—	1.10
e.			Imperf., pair	—	
g.			Printed with luminescent ink, shiny gum	.20	.20
			Pair	.20	.20
			P# strip of 5, #S2	1.90	
			P# single, #S2	—	1.75
			Low gloss gum	.20	
			P# strip of 5, #S3	1.90	
2453	A1812	5c	**brown** (Bureau precancel, Additional Nonprofit Postage Paid, in gray), *May 25, 1991*	.20	.20
			Pair	.20	.20
			P# strip of 5, #1-3	1.50	
			P# single, #1-3	—	1.00
a.			Imperf., pair	*300.00*	
			P#1		
b.			Gray omitted	—	
2454	A1812	5c	**red** (Bureau precancel, Additional Nonprofit Postage Paid, in gray), shiny gum, *Oct. 22, 1991*	.20	.20
			Pair	.20	.20
			P# strip of 5, #S11	1.40	
			P# single, #S11	—	1.25
			Low gloss gum	.50	
			Pair	1.00	
			P# strip of 5, #S11	10.00	
2457	A1816	10c	**green** (Bureau precancel, Additional Presort Postage Paid, in gray), *May 25, 1991*	.20	.20
			Pair	.40	.40
			P# strip of 5, #1	2.10	
			P# single, #1	—	1.50
a.			Imperf., pair	*250.00*	
			P#1		
b.			All color omitted	—	

No. 2457b must be collected as part of a transitional strip with normal stamps having freak perfs.

2458	A1816	10c	**green** (Bureau precancel, Additional Presort Postage Paid, in black), *May 25, 1994*	.30	.20
			Pair	.60	.40
			P# strip of 5, #11, 22	2.50	
			P# single, #11	—	2.25
			P# single, #22	—	2.00
2463	A1822	20c	**green,** *June 9, 1995*	.40	.20
			Pair	.80	.20
			P# strip of 5, #1-2	4.00	
			P# single, #1-2	—	2.25
a.			Imperf., pair	*125.00*	
2464	A1823	23c	**dark blue,** prephosphored coated paper (solid tagging), dull gum, *Apr. 12, 1991*	.45	.20
			Pair	.90	.20
			P# strip of 5, #2-3	3.75	
			P# single, #2-3	—	2.00
a.			Prephosphored uncoated paper (mottled tagging), dull gum, *1993*	.45	.20
			Pair	.90	.20
			P# strip of 5, #3	4.50	
			Shiny gum, *1993*	.45	

Pair .90
P# strip of 5, #3 4.50
P# strip of 5, #4 4.75
P# strip of 5, #5 11.50
P# single, #3-4 — 2.75
P# single, #5 — *5.00*

b. Imperf., pair *150.00*
P#2

2466 A1825 32c **blue,** prephosphored uncoated paper (mottled tagging), shiny gum, *June 2, 1995* .60 .20
Pair 1.25 .30
P# strip of 5, #2 5.50
P# strip of 5, #3 5.75
P# strip of 5, #4 5.50
P# strip of 5, #5 11.00
P# single, #2, 3 — 2.25
P# single, #4 — 2.50
P# single, #5 — 2.75
Low gloss gum .60
Pair 1.20
P# strip of 5, #3 9.00
P# strip of 5, #4 15.00
P# strip of 5, #5 8.00
P# single, #3 — 2.25
P# single, #4 — 2.50
P# single, #5 — 2.75

a. Imperf., pair *600.00*
b. 32c **bright blue,** prephosphored uncoated paper (mottled tagging), low gloss gum 6.00 4.50
Pair 12.00 11.00
P# strip of 5, #5 140.00
P# single, #5 — *110.00*

Some specialists refer to No. 2466b as "Bronx blue," and it is considered to be an error of color.

2468 A1827 $1 **blue & scarlet,** overall tagging, dull gum, *Apr. 20* 1.75 .50
Pair 3.50 1.00
P# strip of 5, #1 9.25
P# single, #1 — 3.00

a. Imperf., pair *2,750.* —
b. Prephosphored uncoated paper (mottled tagging), shiny gum, *1993* 1.75 .50
Pair 3.50 1.00
P# strip of 5, #3 9.25
P# single, #3 — 3.00
c. Prephosphored coated paper (grainy solid tagging), low gloss gum, *1998* 1.75 .50
Pair 3.50 1.00
P# strip of 5, #3 9.00
P# single, #3 — 3.00
Nos. 2451-2468 (12) 4.90 2.70

Some mint pairs of No. 2468 appear to be imperf. but have faint blind perforations on the gum.

LIGHTHOUSES

Admiralty Head, WA — A1829

Cape Hatteras, NC — A1830

West Quoddy Head, ME — A1831

American Shoals, FL — A1832

Sandy Hook, NJ — A1833

Designed by Howard Koslow.

BOOKLET STAMPS
LITHOGRAPHED & ENGRAVED
Perf. 10 Vert. on 1 or 2 sides

1990, Apr. 26 **Tagged**
2470 A1829 25c **multicolored** 1.00 .20
2471 A1830 25c **multicolored** 1.00 .20
2472 A1831 25c **multicolored** 1.00 .20
2473 A1832 25c **multicolored** 1.00 .20
2474 A1833 25c **multicolored** 1.00 .20
a. Bklt. pane of 5, #2470-2474 5.50 *2.00*
b. As "a," white ("USA 25") omitted 80.00 —

FLAG

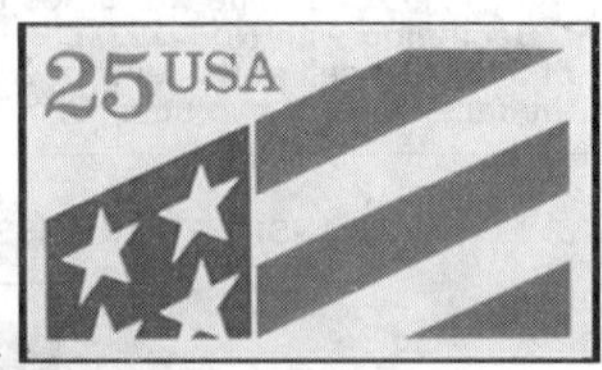

A1834

Designed by Harry Zelenko.

Printed by Avery International Corp.

PHOTOGRAVURE

1990, May 18 Untagged Self-adhesive *Die Cut*
Printed on Plastic
2475 A1834 25c **dark red & dark blue** .50 .25
a. Pane of 12 6.00

Sold only in panes of 12; peelable plastic backing inscribed in light ultramarine. Available for a test period of six months at 22 First National Bank automatic teller machines in Seattle.

FLORA and FAUNA

American Kestrel — A1840

A1841

Eastern Bluebird — A1842

Fawn — A1843

Cardinal — A1844

Pumpkinseed Sunfish — A1845

Bobcat A1846

Designers: 1c, 3c, 45c, Michael Matherly. 19c, Peter Cocci. 30c, Robert Giusti. $2, Chuck Ripper.

Printed by: No. 2476, 3c, American Bank Note Co. No. 2477, 19c, Bureau of Engraving & Printing. 30c, Stamp Venturers. 45c, Stamp Venturers (engraved) and The Press, Inc. (lithographed).

LITHOGRAPHED
Panes of 100

1990-95 Untagged *Perf. 11, 11.2 (#2477)*
2476 A1840 1c **multicolored,** *June 22, 1991* .20 .20
P# block of 4, 4#+A .20 —
Zip block of 4 .20 —
2477 A1841 1c **multicolored,** shiny gum, *May 10, 1995* .20 .20
P# block of 4, 4# .20 —
Low gloss gum .20
P# block of 4, 4# .20
a. Tagged (error), shiny gum —
2478 A1842 3c **multicolored,** *June 22, 1991* .20 .20
P# block of 4, 4#+A .30 —
Zip block of 4 .25 —
a. Vert. pair, imperf horiz. —
b. Double impression of all colors except yellow —

See Nos. 3032/3053. Compare design A1842 with design A2336.

PHOTOGRAVURE
Plates of 400 in four panes of 100.

Tagged ***Perf. 11½x11***
2479 A1843 19c **multicolored,** *Mar. 11, 1991* .35 .20
P# block of 4, 5# 1.75 —
Zip block of 4 1.50 —
a. Tagging omitted *10.00*
b. Red omitted *850.00*

On No. 2479b other colors are shifted.

2480 A1844 30c **multicolored,** *June 22, 1991* .50 .20
P# block of 4, 4#+S 2.25 —
Zip block of 4 2.10 —

LITHOGRAPHED & ENGRAVED
Panes of 100
Perf. 11
2481 A1845 45c **multicolored,** *Dec. 2, 1992* .80 .20
P# block of 4, 5#+S 3.90 —
Zip block of 4 3.50 —
a. Black (engr.) omitted *450.00* —

Panes of 20
2482 A1846 $2 **multicolored,** *June 1, 1990* 3.00 1.25
P# block of 4, 5# 12.00 —
Pane of 20 60.00
a. Black (engr.) omitted *300.00*
b. Tagging omitted 15.00

Blue Jay — A1847

Wood Duck — A1848

African Violets — A1849

Peach — A1850

Pear — A1851

Red Squirrel — A1852

Rose — A1853

Pine Cone — A1854

Designed by Robert Giusti (#2483-2485), Ned Seidler (#2486-2488, 2493-2495A), Michael R. Matherly (#2489), Gyo Fujikawa (#2490), Paul Breeden (#2491), Gyo Fujikawa (#2492).

Printed by Stamp Venturers (#2483, 2492), Bureau of Engraving and Printing (#2484, 2487-2488), J.W. Fergusson & Sons for KCS Industries, Inc. (#2485), KCS Industries (#2486), Dittler Brothers, Inc. (#2489), Stamp Venturers (#2490), Banknote Corporation of America (#2491), Avery-Dennison (#2493-2495, 2495A).

PHOTOGRAVURE
BOOKLET STAMPS

Perf. 10.9x9.8, 10 on 2 or 3 Sides (#2484)

1991-95

Tagged

2483 A1847 20c **multicolored,** *June 15, 1995* .50 .20
- *a.* Booklet pane of 10 5.25 *2.25*
- *b.* As "a," imperf —

2484 A1848 29c **black & multi,** overall tagging, *Apr. 12, 1991* .50 .20
- *a.* Booklet pane of 10 5.50 *3.75*
- *b.* Vert. pair, imperf. between *200.00*
- *c.* As "b," bklt. pane of 10 *1,000.*
- *d.* Prephosphored coated paper (solid tagging) .40 .20
- *e.* As "d," booklet pane of 10 5.50 *3.75*

Perf. 11 on 2 or 3 Sides

2485 A1848 29c **red & multi,** *Apr. 12, 1991* .50 .20
- *a.* Booklet pane of 10 5.50 *4.00*
- *b.* Vert. pair, imperf. between *3,000.*
- *c.* Imperf, pair —

Perf. 10x11 on 2 or 3 Sides

2486 A1849 29c **multicolored,** *Oct. 8, 1993* .50 .20
- *a.* Booklet pane of 10 5.50 *4.00*

Perf. 11x10 on 2 or 3 Sides

2487 A1850 32c **multicolored,** *July 8, 1995* .60 .20
2488 A1851 32c **multicolored,** *July 8, 1995* .60 .20
- *a.* Booklet pane, 5 each #2487-2488 6.00 *4.25*
- *b.* Pair, #2487-2488 1.25 .30

1993-95 **Tagged**

Die Cut

2489 A1852 29c **multicolored,** *June 25* .50 .20
- *a.* Booklet pane of 18 10.00
- *b.* As "a," die cutting omitted —

2490 A1853 29c **red, green & black,** *Aug. 19* .50 .20
- *a.* Booklet pane of 18 10.00

Nos. 2489-2490 also available in strips with stamps spaced for use in affixing machines to service first day covers. No plate numbers. Stamps removed from strips are indistinquishable from booklet stamps.

2491 A1854 29c **multicolored,** *Nov. 5* .50 .20
- *a.* Booklet pane of 18 11.00
- *b.* Horiz. pair, no die cutting between *250.00*
- *c.* Coil with plate # B1 — 5.00
  - P# strip of 5, #B1 6.75

Stamps without plate # from coil strips are indistinquishable from booklet stamps once they are removed from the backing paper.

Serpentine Die Cut 11.3x11.7 on 2, 3 or 4 Sides

2492 A1853 32c **pink, green & black,** *June 2, 1995* .60 .20
- *a.* Booklet pane of 20+label 12.00
- *b.* Booklet pane of 15+label 8.75
- *c.* Horiz. pair, no die cutting between —
- *d.* As "a," 2 stamps and parts of 7 others printed on backing liner —
- *e.* Booklet pane of 14 21.00
- *f.* Booklet pane of 16 21.00
- *g.* Coil with plate # S111 — 3.00
  - P# strip of 5, #S111 6.00
- *h.* Vert. pair, no die cutting between —

Stamps on plate # strips are separated on backing larger than the stamps. Stamps without plate # from coil strips are indistinquishable from interior position booklet stamps once they are removed from the backing paper.

For booklet panes containing No. 2492f with one stamp removed, see Nos. BK178B, BK178D-BK178E in Booklets section.

Serpentine Die Cut 8.8 on 2, 3 or 4 Sides

2493 A1850 32c **multicolored,** *July 8, 1995* .60 .20
2494 A1851 32c **multicolored,** *July 8, 1995* .60 .20
- *a.* Booklet pane, 10 each #2493-2494+label 12.50
- *b.* Pair, #2493-2494 1.20

COIL STAMPS

Serpentine Die Cut 8.8 Vert.

2495 A1850 32c **multicolored,** *July 8, 1995* .60 .20
2495A A1851 32c **multicolored,** *July 8, 1995* .60 .20
- *b.* Pair, #2495-2495A 1.20
  - P# strip of 5, 3 #2495A, 2 #2495, P#V11111 6.25
  - P# single, #V11111 — 3.50

See Nos. 3048, 3053-3054.

Scott values for used self-adhesive stamps are for examples either on piece or off piece.

OLYMPIANS

Jesse Owens, 1936 — A1855

Ray Ewry, 1900-08 A1856

Hazel Wightman, 1924 — A1857

Eddie Eagan, 1920, 1932 — A1858

Helene Madison, 1932 — A1859

Designed by Bart Forbes.

Printed by the American Bank Note Company.

PHOTOGRAVURE
Panes of 35.

1990, July 6 **Tagged** ***Perf. 11***

2496 A1855 25c **multicolored** .60 .20
2497 A1856 25c **multicolored** .60 .20
2498 A1857 25c **multicolored** .60 .20
2499 A1858 25c **multicolored** .60 .20
2500 A1859 25c **multicolored** .60 .20
- *a.* Strip of 5, #2496-2500 3.25 2.50
  - P# block of 10, 4# 8.00 —
  - Zip, inscription block of 10 6.50 —
- *b.* As "a," blue omitted —

INDIAN HEADDRESSES

Assiniboin A1860

Cheyenne A1861

Comanche A1862

Flathead A1863

Shoshone A1864

Designed by Lunda Hoyle Gill.

LITHOGRAPHED & ENGRAVED
BOOKLET STAMPS

1990, Aug. 17 **Tagged** ***Perf. 11 on 2 or 3 Sides***

2501 A1860 25c **multicolored** .80 .20
2502 A1861 25c **multicolored** .80 .20
2503 A1862 25c **multicolored** .80 .20
2504 A1863 25c **multicolored** .80 .20
2505 A1864 25c **multicolored** .80 .20
- *a.* Bklt. pane of 10, 2 each #2501-2505 8.50 *3.50*
- *b.* As "a," black (engr.) omitted *3,250.*
- *c.* Strip of 5, #2501-2505 2.75 1.00
- *d.* As "a," horiz. imperf. between —

MICRONESIA & MARSHALL ISLANDS

Canoe and Flag of the Federated States of Micronesia A1865

Stick Chart, Canoe and Flag of the Republic of the Marshall Islands
A1866

LITHOGRAPHED & ENGRAVED
Sheets of 200 in four panes of 50.

1990, Sept. 28 **Tagged** ***Perf. 11***

2506 A1865 25c **multicolored** .45 .20
2507 A1866 25c **multicolored** .45 .20
a. Pair, #2506-2507 .90 .60
P# block of 4, 6# 2.25 —
Zip block of 4 2.00 —
b. As "a," black (engr.) omitted *2,750.*

See Micronesia Nos. 124-126, Marshall Islands No. 381.

SEA CREATURES

Killer Whales
A1867

Northern Sea Lions — A1868

Sea Otter — A1869

Common Dolphin
A1870

Designed by Peter Cocci (Nos. 2508, 2511), Vladimir Beilin, USSR (Nos. 2509-2510).

LITHOGRAPHED & ENGRAVED
Sheets of 160 in four panes of 40.

1990, Oct. 3 **Tagged** ***Perf. 11***

2508 A1867 25c **multicolored** .45 .20
2509 A1868 25c **multicolored** .45 .20
2510 A1869 25c **multicolored** .45 .20
2511 A1870 25c **multicolored** .45 .20
a. Block of 4, #2508-2511 1.90 1.90
P# block of 4, 5# 2.50 —
Zip block of 4 2.00 —
b. As "a," black (engr.) omitted *700.00*

See Russia Nos. 5933-5936.

PRE-COLUMBIAN AMERICA ISSUE

Grand Canyon
A1871

Designed by Mark Hess.

Printed by the American Bank Note Company.

PHOTOGRAVURE
Plates of 200 in four panes of 50.
(3 panes of #2512, 1 pane of #C127)

1990, Oct. 12 **Tagged** ***Perf. 11***

2512 A1871 25c **multicolored** .45 .20
P# block of 4, 4#, UR, LL, LR 2.00 —
Zip block of 4 1.90 —

See No. C127.

DWIGHT D. EISENHOWER, BIRTH CENTENARY

A1872

Designed by Ken Hodges.

Printed by the American Bank Note Company.

PHOTOGRAVURE
Plates of 160 in four panes of 40.

1990, Oct. 13 **Tagged** ***Perf. 11***

2513 A1872 25c **multicolored** .60 .20
P# block of 4, 5# 3.00 —
P# block of 8, 5# and inscriptions 5.25 —
Zip block of 4 2.50 —
a. Imperf., pair *2,250.*

CHRISTMAS

Madonna & Child, by Antonello — A1873

Christmas Tree — A1874

Designed by Bradbury Thompson (#2514) and Libby Thiel (#2515-2516).

Printed by the Bureau of Engraving and Printing or the American Bank Note Company (#2515).

LITHOGRAPHED & ENGRAVED
Sheets of 300 in six panes of 50 (#2414-2415).

1990, Oct. 18 **Tagged** ***Perf. 11½***

2514 A1873 25c **multicolored**, large block tagging .45 .20
P# block of 4, 5# 2.00 —
Zip, copyright block of 4 1.90 —
a. Large block tagging over prephosphored coated paper (solid tagging) .45 .20
b. As "a," bklt. pane of 10 5.00 *3.25*

PHOTOGRAVURE
Perf. 11

2515 A1874 25c **multicolored** .45 .20
P# block of 4, 4# 2.00 —
Zip block of 4 1.90 —
a. Vert. pair, imperf. horiz. *1,100.*
b. All colors missing (EP) —

BOOKLET STAMP
Perf. 11½x11 on 2 or 3 sides

2516 A1874 25c **multicolored** .45 .20
a. Booklet pane of 10 5.00 *3.25*

No. 2515b must be collected se-tenant with normal and/or partially printed stamp(s).

Marked differences exist between Nos. 2515 and 2516. The background red on No. 2515 is even while that on No. 2516 is splotchy. The bands across the tree and "Greetings" are blue green on No. 2515 and yellow green on No. 2516.

A1875

A1876

Designed by Wallace Marosek (Nos. 2517-2520), Richard Sheaff (No. 2521).

Printed by U.S. Bank Note Company (No. 2517), Bureau of Engraving and Printing (No. 2518-2519), KCS Industries (No. 2520), American Bank Note Company (No. 2521).

PHOTOGRAVURE
Sheets of 100

1991, Jan. 22 **Tagged** ***Perf. 13***

2517 A1875 (29c) **yel, blk, red & yel grn** .55 .20
P# block of 4, 4# 2.60 —
Zip block of 4 2.40 —
a. Imperf., pair *700.00*
b. Horiz. pair, imperf. vert. *1,250.*

Do not confuse No. 2517a with No. 2518a. See note after No. 2518.

COIL STAMP
Perf. 10 Vert.

2518 A1875 (29c) **yel, blk, dull red & dk yel grn** .55 .20
Pair 1.10 .20
P# strip of 5, #1111 3.50
P# strip of 5, #1211 18.00
P# strip of 5, #1222 3.50
P# strip of 5, #2211 4.75
P# strip of 5, #2222 3.50
P# single, #1111 — .75
P# single, #1211 — 14.00
P# single, #1222 — .75
P# single, #2211 — 3.00
P# single, #2222 — .75
a. Imperf., pair *37.50*
P#1111, 1222, 2211, 2222

"For U.S. addresses only" is 17½mm long on No. 2517, 16½mm long on No. 2518. Design of No. 2517 measures 21½x17½mm, No. 2518, 21x18mm.

BOOKLET STAMPS
Perf. 11 on 2 or 3 Sides

2519 A1875 (29c) **yel, blk, dull red & dk grn** .55 .20
a. Booklet pane of 10 6.50 *4.50*
2520 A1875 (29c) **pale yel, blk, red & brt grn** .55 .20
a. Booklet pane of 10 18.00 *4.50*
b. As "a," imperf. horiz. —

No. 2519 has bullseye perforations that measure approximately 11.2. No. 2520 has less pronounced black lines in the leaf, which is a much brighter green than on No. 2519.

LITHOGRAPHED
Panes of 100

1991, Jan. 22 **Untagged** ***Perf. 11***

2521 A1876 (4c) **bister & carmine** .20 .20
P# block of 4, 2# .40 —
Zip block of 4 .30 —
a. Vert. pair, imperf. horiz. *100.00*
b. Imperf., pair *75.00*

FLAG

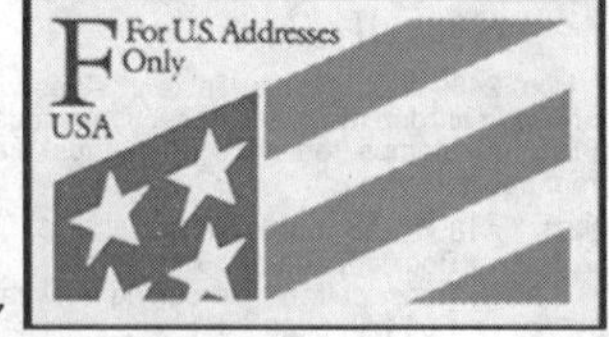

A1877

Designed by Harry Zelenko. Printed by Avery International Corp.

PHOTOGRAVURE

1991, Jan. 22 Untagged Self-Adhesive ***Die Cut***
Printed on Plastic

2522 A1877 (29c) **blk, blue & dk red** .55 .25
a. Pane of 12 7.00

Sold only in panes of 12; peelable plastic backing inscribed in light ultramarine. Available during a test period at First National Bank automatic teller machines in Seattle.

Flag Over Mt. Rushmore — A1878

Designed by Clarence Holbert.

COIL STAMP

ENGRAVED

1991, Mar. 29 **Tagged** ***Perf. 10 Vert.***

2523 A1878 29c **blue, red & claret,** prephosphored uncoated paper (mottled tagging) .55 .20
Pair 1.10 .20
P# strip of 5, #1-7 4.25
P# strip of 5, #8 6.00
P# strip of 5, #9 9.00
P# single, #1 — .60
P# single, #2-4 — .50
P# single, #5 — 2.25
P# single, #6, 7 — .60
P# single, #8 — 2.00
P# single, #9 — 2.00
b. Imperf., pair *25.00*
P#1, 3-4, 6-7, 9
c. 29c **blue, red & brown,** prephosphored uncoated paper (mottled tagging) 5.00 —
Pair 10.00
P# strip of 5, #1 *3,500.*
P# strip of 5, #7 *175.00*
P# single, #1, 7 — *160.00*
d. Prephosphored coated paper (solid tagging) 5.00 —
Pair 10.00 —
P# strip of 5, #2 *850.00*
P# strip of 5, #6 *200.00*
P# single, #2 — *175.00*
P# single, #6 — *150.00*

Specialists often call No. 2523c the "Toledo brown" variety, and No. 2523d "Lenz paper." It was from No. 2523d that it was discovered that "solid tagging" on prephosphored paper resulted from the application of taggant to coated paper.

COIL STAMP

PHOTOGRAVURE

Printed by American Bank Note Co.

1991, July 4 ***Perf. 10 Vert.***

2523A A1878 29c **blue, red & brown** .55 .20
Pair 1.10 .20
P# strip of 5, #A11111, A22211 4.00
P# single, #A11111, A22211 — 2.50

On No. 2523A, USA and 29 are not outlined in white and are farther from the bottom of the design.

A1879

Designed by Wallace Marosek.

Printed by U.S. Bank Note Co. (#2524), J.W. Fergusson & Sons for Stamp Venturers (#2525, 2526), J.W. Fergusson & Sons, Inc. for KCS Industries, Inc. (#2527).

PHOTOGRAVURE

Panes of 100

1991-92 **Tagged** ***Perf. 11***

2524 A1879 29c **dull yel, blk, red & yel grn,** *Apr. 5, 1991* .55 .20
P# block of 4, 4#+U 2.50 —
Zip block of 4 2.25 —

See note after No. 2527.

Perf. 13x12¾

2524A A1879 29c **dull yel, blk, red & yel grn,** *Apr. 5, 1991* .75 .20
P# block of 4, 4#+U 9.00 —
Zip block of 4 3.25 —

COIL STAMPS

Rouletted 10 Vert.

2525 A1879 29c **pale yel, blk, red & yel grn,** *Aug. 16, 1991* .55 .20
Pair 1.10 .30
P# strip of 5, P#S1111, S2222 4.50
P# single, #S1111, S2222 — .75

No. 2525 was issued in attached coils so that "blocks" and "vertical pairs" exist.

Perf. 10 Vert.

2526 A1879 29c **pale yel, blk, red & yel grn,** *Mar. 3, 1992* .55 .20
Pair 1.10 .30
P# strip of 5, P#S2222 4.50
P# single, #S2222 — 2.50

BOOKLET STAMP

Perf. 11 on 2 or 3 Sides

2527 A1879 29c **pale yel, blk, red & bright grn,** *Apr. 5* .55 .20
a. Booklet pane of 10 5.50 *3.50*
b. As "a," vert. imperf. between *1,500.*
c. Horiz. pair, imperf. vert. *225.00*
d. As "a," imperf. horiz. *2,500.*

Flower on Nos. 2524-2524A has grainy appearance, inscriptions look rougher.

Flag, Olympic Rings — A1880

Designed by John Boyd.

Printed by KCS Industries, Inc.

BOOKLET STAMP

PHOTOGRAVURE

1991, Apr. 21 **Tagged** ***Perf. 11 on 2 or 3 Sides***

2528 A1880 29c **multicolored** .55 .20
a. Booklet pane of 10 5.50 *3.50*
b. As "a," horiz. imperf. between, perfed at top and bottom —
c. Vert. pair, imperf between, perfed at top and bottom —
d. Vert. strip of 3, top or bottom pair imperf between —
e. Vert. pair, imperf horiz. *1,800.*

No. 2528c comes from the misperfed booklet pane of No. 2528b. No. 2528d resulted from paper foldovers after normal perforating and before cutting into panes. Two No. 2528d are known. No. 2528e is valued in the grade of fine.

Fishing Boat — A1881

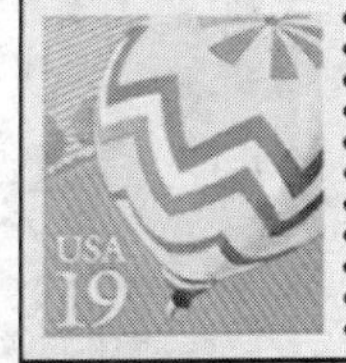

Balloon — A1882

Designed by Pierre Mion.

Printed by: Multi-Color Corp. for American Bank Note Co (type I); Guilford Gravure (type II); J. W. Fergusson & Sons for Stamp Venturers (No. 2529C).

COIL STAMPS

PHOTOGRAVURE

1991, Aug. 8 **Tagged** ***Perf. 9.8 Vert.***

2529 A1881 19c **multicolored** .35 .20
Pair .70 .30
P# strip of 5, #A1111, A1212, A2424 3.25
P# strip of 5, #A1112 6.25
P# single, #A1111, A1212, A2424 — 2.25
P# single, #A1112 — 5.00
a. Type II, *1993* .35 .20
Pair .70 .30
P# strip of 5, #A5555, A5556, A6667, A7667, A7679, A7766, A7779 3.75
P# single, same # — 2.50
b. As "a," untagged, *1993* 1.00 .40
Pair 2.00 .80
P# strip of 5, #A5555 7.50
P# single, #A5555 — 5.00

Design on Type II stamps is created by a finer dot pattern. Vertical sides of "1" are smooth on Type II and jagged on Type I stamps.

Imperforates are from printer's waste. Also, No. 2529a, Plate #A7767 is known only from printer's waste.

1994, June 25 **Tagged** ***Perf. 9.8 Vert.***

2529C A1881 19c **multicolored** .50 .20
Pair 1.00 .30
P# strip of 5, #S111 5.25
P# single, #S111 — 2.40

No. 2529C has one loop of rope tying boat to piling.

BOOKLET STAMP

1991, May 17 **Tagged** ***Perf. 10 on 2 or 3 Sides***

2530 A1882 19c **multicolored** .35 .20
a. Booklet pane of 10 3.50 *2.75*

Flags on Parade — A1883

Designed by Frank J. Waslick and Peter Cocci.

PHOTOGRAVURE

Panes of 100

1991, May 30 **Tagged** ***Perf. 11***

2531 A1883 29c **multicolored**, overall tagging .55 .20
P# block of 4, 4# 2.50 —
Zip block of 4 2.25 —
a. Prephosphored coated paper (solid tagging) .70 .25
P# block of 4, 4# 6.25 —
Zip block of 4 3.00 —

Liberty Torch — A1884

Designed by Harry Zelenko.

Printed by Avery Dennison Co.

PHOTOGRAVURE

1991, June 25 **Tagged** ***Die Cut***

Self-Adhesive

2531A A1884 29c **black, gold & green,** prephosphored coated paper (solid tagging) .55 .25
b. Booklet pane of 18 10.50
c. Pair, imperf. —
d. Overall tagging, *1992* .60 .25
e. As "d," booklet pane of 18 11.00

Sold only in panes of 18; peelable paper backing inscribed in light blue. Available for consumer testing at First National Bank automatic teller machines in Seattle, WA.

SWITZERLAND

Switzerland, 700th Anniv. A1887

Designed by Hans Hartman, Switzerland.

Printed by the American Bank Note Company.

PHOTOGRAVURE

Plates of 160 in four panes of 40

1991, Feb. 22 **Tagged** ***Perf. 11***

2532 A1887 50c **multicolored** 1.00 .25
P# block of 4, 5# 5.00 —
Zip block of 4 4.25 —
a. Vert. pair, imperf. horiz. *2,250.*

See Switzerland No. 888.

Imperfs exist from printer's waste.

A1888

A1889

VERMONT STATEHOOD, 200th ANNIV.

Designed by Sabra Field.

Printed by the American Bank Note Company.

PHOTOGRAVURE
Plates of 200 in four panes of 50

1991, Mar. 1 **Tagged** ***Perf. 11***

2533 A1888 29c **multicolored** .60 .20
P# block of 4, 4#+A 4.00 —
Zip block of 4 2.50 —

SAVINGS BONDS, 50TH ANNIVERSARY

Designed by Primo Angeli.

1991, Apr. 30 **Tagged** ***Perf. 11***

2534 A1889 29c **multicolored** .55 .20
P# block of 4, 6# 2.50 —
Zip block of 4 2.25 —

LOVE

A1890

A1891

Designed by Harry Zelenko (#2535-2536) and Nancy L. Krause (#2537).

Printed by U.S. Banknote Co. (#2535), the Bureau of Engraving and Printing (#2536) and American Bank Note Co. (#2537).

PHOTOGRAVURE
Panes of 50

1991, May 9 **Tagged** ***Perf. 12½x13***

2535 A1890 29c **multicolored** .55 .20
P# block of 4, 5#+U 2.50 —
Zip, copyright block of 4 2.25 —
b. Imperf., pair —

Perf. 11

2535A A1890 29c **multicolored** .75 .20
P# block of 4, 5#+U 4.00 —
Zip, copyright block of 4 3.00 —

BOOKLET STAMP

Perf. 11 on 2 or 3 Sides

2536 A1890 29c **multicolored** .55 .20
a. Booklet pane of 10 5.50 *3.50*

"29" is closer to edge of design on No. 2536 than on No. 2535.

Sheets of 200 in panes of 50

Perf. 11

2537 A1891 52c **multicolored** .90 .20
P# block of 4, 3#+A 4.50 —
Zip block of 4 4.00 —

LITERARY ARTS SERIES

William Saroyan
A1892

Designed by Ren Wicks.

Printed by J.W. Fergusson for American Bank Note Co.

PHOTOGRAVURE
Sheets of 200 in four panes of 50

1991, May 22 **Tagged** ***Perf. 11***

2538 A1892 29c **multicolored** .55 .20
P# block of 4, 5#+A 2.50 —
Zip block of 4 2.25 —

See Russia No. 6002.

Eagle, Olympic Rings — A1893

A1894

A1895

A1896

Futuristic Space Shuttle
A1897

Space Shuttle Challenger
A1898

Space Shuttle Endeavour
A1898a

Designed by: Terrence McCaffrey (Nos. 2539-2541), Timothy Knapp (No. 2542), Ken Hodges (No. 2543), Phil Jordan (Nos. 2544-2544A).

Printed by: J.W. Fergusson & Sons for Stamp Venturers (No. 2539); American Bank Note Co (Nos. 2540-2541); Jeffries Banknote Co. for the American Bank Note Co (No. 2542).

Nos. 2540, 2543-2544 for priority mail rate. Nos. 2541, 2544A for domestic express mail rate. No. 2542 for international express mail rate.

Nos. 2544-2544A printed by Ashton-Potter (USA) Ltd.

Sheet of 180 in nine panes of 20 (No. 2539)
Sheet of 120 in six panes of 20 (Nos. 2540-2542, 2544-2544A)
Pane of 40 (No. 2543)
PHOTOGRAVURE
Copyright information appears in the center of the top and bottom selvage.

1991, Sept. 29 **Tagged** ***Perf. 11***

2539 A1893 $1 **gold & multi** 1.75 .50
P# block of 4, 6#+S 8.00 —
Pane of 20 36.00
a. Black omitted —

LITHOGRAPHED & ENGRAVED

1991, July 7 **Tagged** ***Perf. 11***

2540 A1894 $2.90 **multicolored** 6.00 2.50
P# block of 4, 5#+A 24.00 —
Pane of 20 120.00
a. Vert. pair, imperf horiz. —
b. Black (engr.) omitted —

No. 2540 exists imperf and with color missing from printer's waste.

1991, June 16 **Untagged** ***Perf. 11***

2541 A1895 $9.95 **multicolored** 20.00 7.50
P# block of 4, 5#+A 80.00 —
Pane of 20 400.00
a. Imperf., pair —

No. 2541 exists imperf plus black (engr.) omitted from printer's waste.

1991, Aug. 31 **Untagged** ***Perf. 11***

2542 A1896 $14 **multicolored** 25.00 10.00
P# block of 4, 5#+A 100.00 —
Pane of 20 500.00
a. Red (engr. inscriptions) omitted *1,500.*

No. 2542 exists imperf plus red omitted from printer's waste.

1993, June 3 **Tagged** ***Perf. 11x10½***

2543 A1897 $2.90 **multicolored** 5.00 2.25
P# block of 4, 6# 22.50 —
Zip block of 4 21.00 —
a. Tagging omitted —

1995, June 22 **Tagged** ***Perf. 11.2***

2544 A1898 $3 **multicolored,** dated "1995" 5.25 2.25
b. Dated "1996" 5.25 2.25
P# block of 4, 5#+P 21.00 —
Pane of 20 105.00 —
c. As "b," horiz. pair, imperf between —
d. As "b," imperf pair *2,000.*

1995, Aug. 4 **Tagged** ***Perf. 11***

2544A A1898a $10.75 **multicolored** 19.00 7.50
P# block of 4, 5#+P 77.50 —
Pane of 20 380.00 —

FISHING FLIES

Royal Wulff — A1899

Jock Scott — A1900

Apte Tarpon Fly — A1901

Lefty's Deceiver A1902

Muddler Minnow A1903

Designed by Chuck Ripper.

Printed by American Bank Note Co.

PHOTOGRAVURE
BOOKLET STAMPS

1991, May 31 **Tagged** ***Perf. 11 Horiz.***

2545 A1899 29c **multicolored** 1.00 .20
a. Black omitted —
2546 A1900 29c **multicolored** 1.00 .20
a. Black omitted —
2547 A1901 29c **multicolored** 1.00 .20
a. Black omitted —
2548 A1902 29c **multicolored** 1.00 .20
2549 A1903 29c **multicolored** 1.00 .20
a. Bklt. pane of 5, #2545-2549 5.50 *2.50*

Horiz. pairs, imperf vert,. exist from printer's waste.

Cole Porter (1891-1964), Composer — A1904

S. W. Asia Service Medal — A1905

PERFORMING ARTS

Designed by Jim Sharpe.

Printed by American Bank Note Co.

PHOTOGRAVURE
Panes of 50

1991, June 8 **Tagged** ***Perf. 11***

2550 A1904 29c **multicolored** .55 .20
P# block of 4, 5#+A 2.50 —
Zip block of 4 2.25 —
a. Vert. pair, imperf. horiz. *650.00*

OPERATIONS DESERT SHIELD & DESERT STORM

Designed by Jack Williams.

Printed by J.W. Fergusson Co. for Stamp Venturers (No. 2551), Multi-Color Corp. for the American Bank Note Co. (No. 2552).

PHOTOGRAVURE
Panes of 50

1991, July 2 **Tagged** ***Perf. 11***

2551 A1905 29c **multicolored** .55 .20
P# block of 4, 7#+S 2.50 —
Zip block of 4 2.25 —
a. Vert. pair, imperf. horiz. *1,500.*

No. 2551 is 21mm wide.

BOOKLET STAMP
Perf. 11 Vert. on 1 or 2 Sides

2552 A1905 29c **multicolored** .55 .20
a. Booklet pane of 5 2.75 *2.25*

No. 2552 is 20½mm wide. Inscriptions are shorter than on No. 2551.

No. 2552 Vert. pairs, imperf horiz., are from printer's waste.

1992 SUMMER OLYMPICS, BARCELONA

Pole Vault — A1907

Discus A1908

Women's Sprints A1909

Javelin A1910

Women's Hurdles A1911

Designed by Joni Carter.

Printed by the American Bank Note Co.

PHOTOGRAVURE
Panes of 40

1991, July 12 **Tagged** ***Perf. 11***

2553 A1907 29c **multicolored** .55 .20
2554 A1908 29c **multicolored** .55 .20
2555 A1909 29c **multicolored** .55 .20
2556 A1910 29c **multicolored** .55 .20
2557 A1911 29c **multicolored** .55 .20
a. Strip of 5, #2553-2557 2.75 2.25
P# block of 10, 5#+A 7.50 —
Zip block of 10 5.50 —

NUMISMATICS

1858 Flying Eagle Cent, 1907 Standing Liberty Double Eagle, Series 1875 $1 Note, Series 1902 $10 National Currency Note — A1912

Designed by V. Jack Ruther.

LITHOGRAPHED & ENGRAVED
Sheets of 200 in four panes of 50

1991, Aug. 13 **Tagged** ***Perf. 11***

2558 A1912 29c **multicolored** .55 .20
P# block of 4, 7# 2.50 —
Zip block of 4 2.25 —

WORLD WAR II

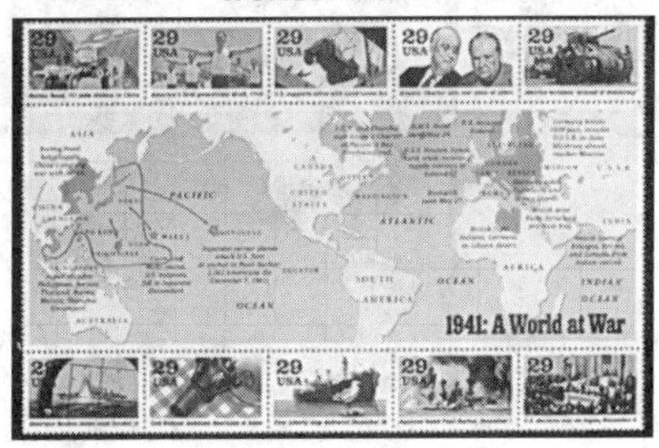

A1913

Illustration reduced.

Designed by William H. Bond.

Designs and events of 1941: a, Military vehicles (Burma Road, 717-mile lifeline to China). b, Recruits (America's first peacetime draft). c, Shipments for allies (U.S. supports allies with Lend-Lease Act). d, Franklin D. Roosevelt, Winston Churchill (Atlantic Charter sets war aims of allies). e, Tank (America becomes the "arsenal of democracy.") f, Sinking of Destoyer Reuben James, Oct. 31. g, Gas mask, helmet (Civil defense mobilizes Americans at home). h, Liberty Ship, sea gull (First Liberty ship delivered December 30). i, Sinking ships (Japanese bomb Pearl Harbor, December 7). j, Congress in session (U.S. declares war on Japan, December 8). Central label is the size of 15 stamps and shows world map, extent of axis control.

LITHOGRAPHED & ENGRAVED
Plates of eight subjects in four panes of 2 each

1991, Sept. 3 **Tagged** ***Perf. 11***

2559 A1913 Block of 10 5.50 5.00
Pane of 20 11.00 —
a.-j. 29c any single .55 .30
k. Black (engr.) omitted *10,000.*

No. 2559 has selvage at left and right and either top or bottom.

BASKETBALL, 100TH ANNIVERSARY

Basketball, Hoop, Players' Arms — A1914

Designed by Lon Busch.

PHOTOGRAVURE
Sheets of 200 in four panes of 50

1991, Aug. 28 **Tagged** ***Perf. 11***

2560	A1914 29c **multicolored**		.50	.20
	P# block of 4, 4#		2.50	—
	Zip block of 4		2.25	—

DISTRICT OF COLUMBIA BICENTENNIAL

Capitol Building from Pennsylvania Avenue, Circa 1903 — A1915

Designed by Pierre Mion.

LITHOGRAPHED & ENGRAVED
Plates of 200 in four panes of 50

1991, Sept. 7 **Tagged** ***Perf. 11***

2561	A1915 29c **multicolored**		.55	.20
	P# block of 4, 5#		2.50	—
	Zip block of 4		2.25	—
a.	Black (engr.) omitted		*110.00*	

COMEDIANS

Stan Laurel (1890-1965) and Oliver Hardy (1892-1957) A1916

Edgar Bergen (1903-1978) and Charlie McCarthy A1917

Jack Benny (1894-1974) A1918

Fanny Brice (1891-1951) A1919

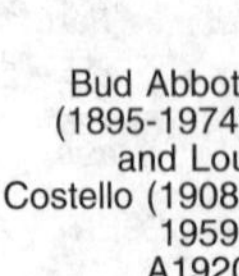

Bud Abbott (1895-1974) and Lou Costello (1908-1959) A1920

Designed by Al Hirschfeld.

LITHOGRAPHED & ENGRAVED
BOOKLET STAMPS

1991, Aug. 29 **Tagged** ***Perf. 11 on 2 or 3 Sides***

2562	A1916 29c **multicolored**		.65	.20
2563	A1917 29c **multicolored**		.65	.20
2564	A1918 29c **multicolored**		.65	.20
2565	A1919 29c **multicolored**		.65	.20
2566	A1920 29c **multicolored**		.65	.20
a.	Bklt. pane of 10, 2 each #2562-2566		9.00	*3.50*
b.	As "a," scar & brt violet (engr.) omitted		*700.00*	
c.	Strip of 5, #2562-2566		3.00	—

BLACK HERITAGE SERIES

Jan E. Matzeliger (1852-1889), Inventor — A1921

Designed by Higgins Bond.
Printed by J.W. Fergusson & Sons for the American Bank Note Co.

PHOTOGRAVURE
Plates of 200 in four panes of 50

1991, Sept. 15 **Tagged** ***Perf. 11***

2567	A1921 29c **multicolored**		.55	.20
	P# block of 4, 6#+A		2.50	—
	Zip block of 4		2.25	—
a.	Horiz. pair, imperf. vert.		*1,250.*	
b.	Vert. pair, imperf. horiz.		*1,250.*	
c.	Imperf., pair		*750.00*	

SPACE EXPLORATION

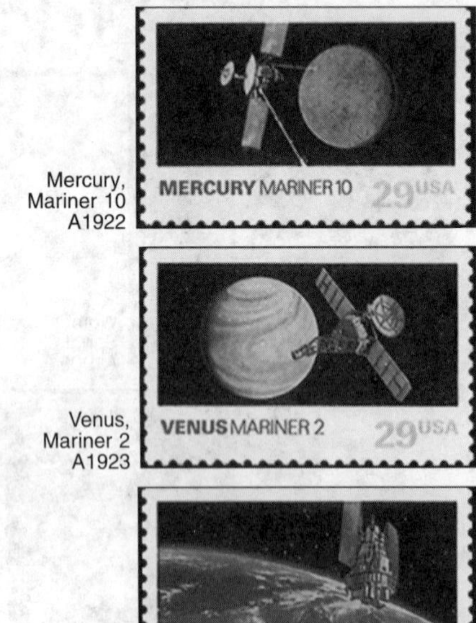

Mercury, Mariner 10 A1922

Venus, Mariner 2 A1923

Earth, Landsat A1924

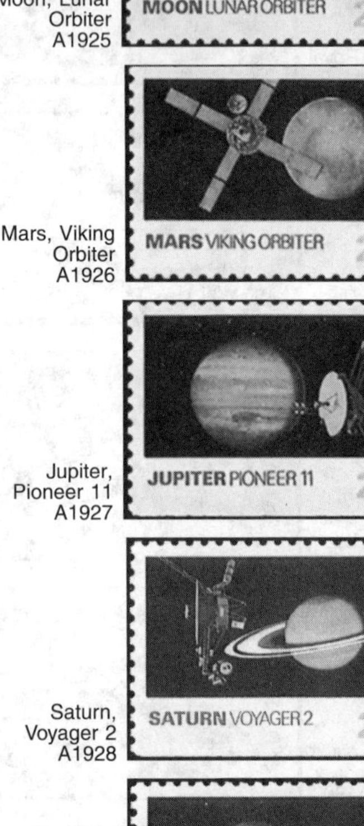

Moon, Lunar Orbiter A1925

Mars, Viking Orbiter A1926

Jupiter, Pioneer 11 A1927

Saturn, Voyager 2 A1928

Uranus, Voyager 2 A1929

Neptune, Voyager 2 A1930

Pluto — A1931

Designed by Ron Miller.

PHOTOGRAVURE
BOOKLET STAMPS

1991, Oct. 1 **Tagged** ***Perf. 11 on 2 or 3 Sides***

2568	A1922 29c **multicolored**		.85	.20
2569	A1923 29c **multicolored**		.85	.20
2570	A1924 29c **multicolored**		.85	.20
2571	A1925 29c **multicolored**		.85	.20
2572	A1926 29c **multicolored**		.85	.20
2573	A1927 29c **multicolored**		.85	.20
2574	A1928 29c **multicolored**		.85	.20
2575	A1929 29c **multicolored**		.85	.20
2576	A1930 29c **multicolored**		.85	.20
2577	A1931 29c **multicolored**		.85	.20
a.	Bklt. pane of 10, #2568-2577		9.00	*3.50*

CHRISTMAS

Madonna and Child by Antoniazzo Romano — A1933

Santa Claus in Chimney — A1934

Santa Checking List — A1935

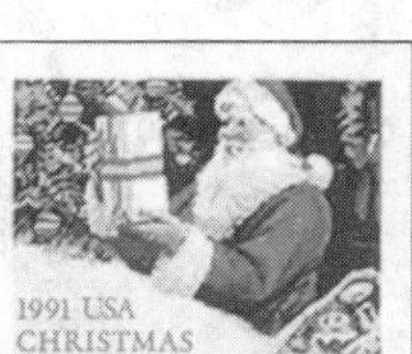

Santa with Present — A1936

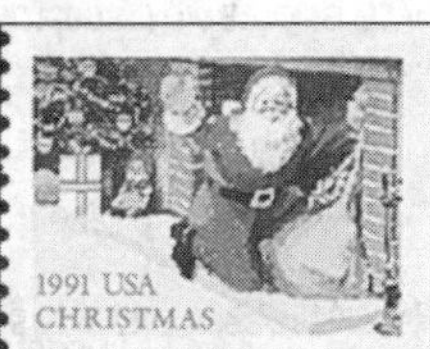

Santa at Fireplace — A1937

Santa and Sleigh — A1938

Designed by Bradbury Thompson (#2578) and John Berkey (#2579-2585).

Printed by the Bureau of Engraving and Printing (#2578); J.W. Fergusson & Sons (#2579) and Multi-Color Corp. (#2580-2585) for the American Bank Note Co.

LITHOGRAPHED & ENGRAVED

Sheets of 300 in six panes of 50

1991, Oct. 17 **Tagged** ***Perf. 11***

2578 A1933 (29c) **multicolored** .55 .20
P# block of 4, 5# 2.50 —
Zip, copyright block of 4 2.25 —
a. Booklet pane of 10 5.50 *3.25*
b. As "a," single, red & black (engr.) omitted *3,500.*

PHOTOGRAVURE

2579 A1934 (29c) **multicolored** .55 .20
P# block of 4, 3#+A 2.50 —
Zip block of 4 2.25 —
a. Horiz. pair, imperf. vert. *300.00*
b. Vert. pair, imperf. horiz. *500.00*

Booklet Stamps

Size: 25x18½mm

Perf. 11 on 2 or 3 Sides

2580 A1934 (29c) Type I 2.00 .20
2581 A1934 (29c) Type II 2.00 .20
a. Pair, #2580-2581 4.00 .50
b. Bklt. pane, 2 each, #2580, 2581 9.00 *1.25*
2582 A1935 (29c) **multicolored** .55 .20
a. Bklt. pane of 4 2.25 *1.25*
2583 A1936 (29c) **multicolored** .55 .20
a. Bklt. pane of 4 2.25 *1.25*
2584 A1937 (29c) **multicolored** .55 .20
a. Bklt. pane of 4 2.25 *1.25*
2585 A1938 (29c) **multicolored** .55 .20
a. Bklt. pane of 4 2.25 *1.25*
Nos. 2578-2585 (8) 7.30 1.60

The far left brick from the top row of the chimney is missing from Type II, No. 2581.

Imperfs of Nos. 2582-2585 are printer's waste.

James K. Polk (1795-1849) A1939

"The Surrender of General Burgoyne at Saratoga," by John Trumbull A1942

Washington and Jackson A1944

Designed by John Thompson (No. 2587), based on painting by John Trumbull (No. 2590), Richard D. Sheaff (No. 2592).

Printed by Banknote Corporation of America (No. 2587), Stamp Venturers (Nos. 2590, 2592).

ENGRAVED

Sheets of 400 in four panes of 100 (No. 2587)

Sheets of 120 in six panes of 20 (Nos. 2590, 2592)

1994-95 **Tagged** ***Perf. 11.2***

2587 A1939 32c **red brown,** *Nov. 2, 1995* .60 .20
P# block of 4, 1#+B 3.00 —

Perf. 11.5

2590 A1942 $1 **blue,** *May 5, 1994* 1.90 .50
P# block of 4, 1#+S 7.60 —
Pane of 20 38.00 —
2592 A1944 $5 **slate green,** *Aug. 19, 1994* 8.00 2.50
P# block of 4, 1#+S 40.00 —
Pane of 20 160.00 —

Some plate blocks contain either inscription or plate position diagram.

A1946

Eagle and Shield — A1947

A1950

Statue of Liberty — A1951

Designed by Lou Nolan (#2593-2594), Jay Haiden (#2595-2597), Richard Sheaff (#2598), Tom Engeman (#2599).

Printed by Banknote Corporation of America (#2595), Dittler Brothers, Inc. (#2596, 2599), Stamp Venturers (#2597), National Label Co. for 3M (#2598).

BOOKLET STAMPS

PHOTOGRAVURE

1992, Sept. 8 **Tagged** ***Perf. 10 on 2 or 3 sides***

2593 A1946 29c **black & multi** .55 .20
a. Booklet pane of 10 5.50 *4.25*

Perf. 11x10 on 2 or 3 sides

2593B A1946 29c **black & multi,** shiny gum 1.40 .50
Low gloss gum 2.00
c. Bklt. pane of 10, shiny gum 14.00 *7.50*
Low gloss gum *20.00*

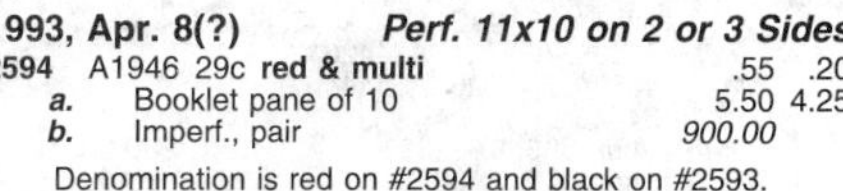

1993, Apr. 8(?) ***Perf. 11x10 on 2 or 3 Sides***

2594 A1946 29c **red & multi** .55 .20
a. Booklet pane of 10 5.50 4.25
b. Imperf., pair *900.00*

Denomination is red on #2594 and black on #2593.

LITHOGRAPHED & ENGRAVED

1992, Sept. 25 **Tagged** ***Die Cut***

Self-Adhesive

2595 A1947 29c **brown & multicolored** .55 .25
a. Bklt. pane of 17 + label 13.00
b. Pair, no die cutting *175.00*
c. Brown omitted *450.00*
d. As "a," no die cutting *1,500.*
2596 A1947 29c **green & multicolored** .55 .25
a. Bklt. pane of 17 + label 12.00

PHOTOGRAVURE

2597 A1947 29c **red & multicolored** .55 .25
a. Bklt. pane of 17 + label 10.00

Plate No. and inscription reads down on No. 2595a and up on Nos. 2596a-2597a. Design is sharper and more finely detailed on Nos. 2595, 2597.

Nos. 2595-2597 sold for $5.

Nos. 2595-2597 also available in strips with stamps spaced for use in affixing machines to service first day covers.

PHOTOGRAVURE

1994 **Tagged** ***Die Cut***

Self-Adhesive

2598 A1950 29c **red, cream & blue,** *Feb. 4* .55 .20
a. Booklet pane of 18 10.00
b. Coil with P#111 — 3.75
P# strip of 5, #111 6.75
2599 A1951 29c **multicolored,** *June 24* .55 .20
a. Booklet pane of 18 10.00
b. Coil with P#D1111 — 4.00
P# strip of 5, #D1111 6.75

Except for Nos. 2598b and 2599b with plate numbers, coil stamps of these issues are indistinguishable from booklet stamps once they are removed from the backing paper.

See Nos. 3122-3122E.

Scott values for used self-adhesvive stamps are for examples either on piece or off piece.

Eagle and Shield — A1956

Eagle and Shield — A1957

A1959

A1960

Flag Over White House — A1961

Designed by Chris Calle (#2602-2604), Terrence McCaffrey (#2605), Lon Busch (#2606-2608), V. Jack Ruther (29c).

Printed by Guildford Gravure, Inc. for the American Bank Note Co. (#2602, 2606), Bureau of Engraving and Printing (#2603, 2607), Stamp Venturers (#2604, 2608), American Bank Note Co. (#2605)

PHOTOGRAVURE

COIL STAMPS

1991-93 **Untagged** ***Perf. 10 Vert.***

2602 A1956 (10c) **multi** (Bureau precancel, Bulk Rate, in blue), *Dec. 13* .20 .20
Pair .40 .40
P# strip of 5, #A11111, A11112, A21112, A22112, A22113, A43325, A43334, A43335, A53335 2.50
P# strip of 5, #A12213 19.00

P# strip of 5, #A21113, A33333, A33335, A34424, A34426, A43324, A43326, A54444, A54445, 3.75
P# strip of 5, #A32333 *280.00*
P# strip of 5, #A33334 *80.00*
P# strip of 5, #A43426, A77777, A88888, A88889, A89999, A99998, A99999, A1010101010, A1011101010, A1011101011, A1011101012, A1110101010, A1110111010, A1111101010, A1111111010, A1211101010, A1411101010, A1411101011, A1412111110, A1412111111 3.00
P# strip of 5, #A1110101011 11.50
P# single, #A11111, A11112, A21112, A21113, A22112, A22113, A43324, A43325, A43326, A43334, A43426, A54444, A54445, A77777, A88888, A89999, A99998, A99999 — 2.25
P# single, #A12213 — 17.00
P# single, #A32333 — 275.00
P# single, #A33333, A33335, A34424, A34426 — 3.25
P# single, #A33334 — 80.00
P# single, #A53335, A88889, A1010101010, A1011101010, A1011101011, A1011101012, A1110101010, A1110111010, A1111101010, A1111111010, A1211101010, A1411101010, A1411101011, A1412111110, A1412111111 — 2.50
P# single, #A1110101011 — 9.00
a. Imperf., pair —

2603 A1957 (10c) **org yel & multi,** shiny gum (Bureau precancel, Bulk Rate, in red), *May 29, 1993* .20 .20
Pair .40 .40
P# strip of 5, #11111, 22221, 22222 3.00
P# single, same — 1.75
Low gloss gum .20
Pair .40
P# strip of 5, #22222, 33333, 44444 3.00
P# strip of 5, #11111 62.50
P# single, #33333, 44444 — 2.50
a. Imperf., pair *30.00*
b. Tagged (error), shiny gum 2.00 1.50
Pair 4.00 3.50
P# strip of 5, #11111, 22221 13.00
P# strip of 5, #22222 *310.00*
P# single, #11111, 22221 — 12.00
P# single, #22222 — *300.00*

All examples of Nos. 2603, 2603a and 2603b were printed with luminescent ink.

See No. 2907.

2604 A1957 (10c) **gold & multi,** shiny gum (Bureau precancel, Bulk Rate, in red), *May 29, 1993* .20 .20
Pair .40 .40
P# strip of 5, #S22222 3.25
P# single, same — 1.75
Low gloss gum .20
Pair .40
P# strip of 5, #S11111 3.00
P# strip of 5, #S22222 2.75
P# single, #S11111 — 2.00

2605 A1959 23c **multi** (Bureau precancel in blue), *Sept. 27* .40 .40
Pair .80 .80
P# strip of 5, #A111, A212, A222 3.50
P# strip of 5, #A112, A122, A333 4.50
P# single, #A111, A112, A122, A212, A222, A333 — 2.25

2606 A1960 23c **multi** (Bureau precanceled), *July 21, 1992* .40 .40
Pair .80 .80
P# strip of 5, #A1111, A2222, A2232, A2233, A3333, A4364, A4443, A4444, A4453 4.00
P# single, same # — 2.50

"First-Class" is 9½mm long and "23" is 6mm long on No. 2606.

2607 A1960 23c **multi,** shiny gum (Bureau precanceled), *Oct. 9, 1992* .40 .40
Pair .80 .80
P# strip of 5, #1111 4.00
P# single, #1111 — 2.50
Low gloss gum .40
Pair .80
P# strip of 5, #1111 4.00
a. Tagged (error), shiny gum 5.00 4.50
Pair 10.00 9.00
P# strip of 5, #1111 140.00
P# single, #1111 — 65.00
c. Imperf., pair *90.00*

"First-Class" is 9mm long and "23" is 6½mm long on No. 2607.

2608 A1960 23c **vio bl, red & blk** (Bureau precanceled), *May 14, 1993* .40 .40
Pair .80 .80
P# strip of 5, #S111 4.25
P# single, #S111 — 2.50
c. Imperf., pair —

"First-Class" is 8½mm long and "23" is 6½mm long on No. 2608.

ENGRAVED
Tagged

2609 A1961 29c **blue & red,** *Apr. 23, 1992* .55 .20
Pair 1.10 .20
P# strip of 5, #1-8 4.50
P# strip of 5, #9-16 5.50
P# strip of 5, #18 6.00
P# single, #1-4 — .75
P# single, #5 — 2.25
P# single, #6-8 — .75
P# single, #9 — 2.50
P# single, #10-16 — 1.00
P# single, #18 — 4.00
a. Imperf., pair *20.00*
P#3-7
b. Pair, imperf. between *90.00*

WINTER OLYMPICS

Hockey A1963

Figure Skating A1964

Speed Skating A1965

Skiing A1966

Bobsledding A1967

Designed by Lon Busch. Printed by J.W. Fergusson & Sons for Stamp Venturers.

PHOTOGRAVURE
Panes of 35

1992, Jan. 11 Tagged *Perf. 11*
2611 A1963 29c **multicolored** .55 .20
2612 A1964 29c **multicolored** .55 .20
2613 A1965 29c **multicolored** .55 .20
2614 A1966 29c **multicolored** .55 .20
2615 A1967 29c **multicolored** .55 .20
a. Strip of 5, #2611-2615 2.75 2.50
P# block of 10, 4#+S 6.50 —
Zip, copyright block of 15 8.50 —

Inscriptions on six marginal tabs.

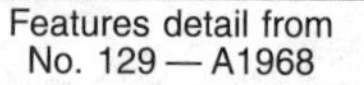

Features detail from No. 129 — A1968

W.E.B. Du Bois (1868-1963) — A1969

WORLD COLUMBIAN STAMP EXPO

Designed by Richard Sheaff.

LITHOGRAPHED & ENGRAVED
Plates of 200 in four panes of 50

1992, Jan. 24 Tagged *Perf. 11*
2616 A1968 29c **multicolored** .55 .20
P# block of 4, 4# 2.50 —
Zip block of 4 2.25 —
a. Tagging omitted 8.50

BLACK HERITAGE SERIES

W.E.B. Du Bois (1868-1963), Writer and Civil Rights Leader

Designed by Higgins Bond.

LITHOGRAPHED & ENGRAVED
Plates of 200 in four panes of 50

1992, Jan. 31 Tagged *Perf. 11*
2617 A1969 29c **multicolored** .55 .20
P# block of 4, 7# 2.50 —
Zip block of 4 2.25 —

A1970

A1971

LOVE

Designed by Uldis Purins. Printed by the U.S. Bank Note Co.

PHOTOGRAVURE
Panes of 50

1992, Feb. 6 Tagged *Perf. 11*
2618 A1970 29c **multicolored** .55 .20
P# block of 4, U+5# 2.50 —
Zip, copyright block of 4 2.25 —
a. Horiz. pair, imperf. vert. *700.00*
b. As "a," green omitted on right stamp —

OLYMPIC BASEBALL

Designed by Anthony DeLuz.

PHOTOGRAVURE
Plates of 200 in four panes of 50

1992, Apr. 3 Tagged *Perf. 11*
2619 A1971 29c **multicolored** .55 .20
P# block of 4, 5# 2.75 —
Zip block of 4 2.25 —

VOYAGES OF COLUMBUS

Seeking Queen Isabella's Support
A1972

Crossing the Atlantic
A1973

Approaching Land
A1974

Coming Ashore
A1975

Designed by Richard Schlecht.

LITHOGRAPHED & ENGRAVED
Plates of 160 in four panes of 40

1992, Apr. 24 **Tagged** *Perf. 11*

2620	A1972 29c **multicolored**	.55	.20
2621	A1973 29c **multicolored**	.55	.20
2622	A1974 29c **multicolored**	.55	.20
2623	A1975 29c **multicolored**	.55	.20
a.	Block of 4, #2620-2623	2.20	2.00
	P# block of 4, 5#	2.50	—
	Zip block of 4	2.25	—

See Italy Nos. 1877-1880.

Souvenir Sheets

A1976

A1977

A1978

A1979

A1980

A1981

Illustrations reduced.

Designed by Richard Sheaff.

Printed by the American Bank Note Co. Margins on Nos. 2624-2628 are lithographed. Nos. 2624a-2628c, 2629 are similar in design to Nos. 230-245 but are dated 1492-1992.

LITHOGRAPHED & ENGRAVED

1992, May 22 *Perf. 10½*

Tagged (15c-$5), Untagged

2624	A1976 Sheet of 3	1.90	—
a.	A71 1c **deep blue**	.20	.20
b.	A74 4c **ultramarine**	.20	.20
c.	A82 $1 **salmon**	1.75	1.00
d.	As No. 2624, tagging omitted on "c"	—	
2625	A1977 Sheet of 3	7.25	—
a.	A72 2c **brown violet**	.20	.20
b.	A73 3c **green**	.20	.20
c.	A85 $4 **crimson lake**	7.00	4.00
2626	A1978 Sheet of 3	1.50	—
a.	A75 5c **chocolate**	.20	.20
b.	A80 30c **orange brown**	.55	.30
c.	A81 50c **slate blue**	.85	.50
d.	As No. 2626, tagging omitted on "c"	—	—
2627	A1979 Sheet of 3	5.25	—
a.	A76 6c **purple**	.20	.20
b.	A77 8c **magenta**	.20	.20
c.	A84 $3 **yellow green**	5.00	3.00
2628	A1980 Sheet of 3	4.00	—
a.	A78 10c **black brown**	.20	.20
b.	A79 15c **dark green**	.30	.20
c.	A83 $2 **brown red**	3.50	2.00
2629	A1981 $5 Sheet of 1	8.75	—
a.	A86 $5 **black**, single stamp	8.50	5.00
	Nos. 2624-2629 (6)	28.65	

See Italy Nos. 1883-1888, Portugal Nos. 1918-1923 and Spain Nos. 2677-2682.

Imperforate examples are known of all the Columbus souvenir sheets, but these are not listed in this catalogue. Their appearance several years after the issue date, in substantial quantities of all six sheets at the same time and, evidently, from a single source, with many small faults such as wrinkles and light creases that are not normally seen on these sheets, raises serious concerns about the legitimacy of these imperforate sheets as issued errors.

These circumstances have led the Scott editors to adopt the position that these imperforate sheets are indeed almost certainly printer's waste rather than issued errors. While it is possible that actual imperforate errors of one or more of the sheets may exist that were legitimately sold by the USPS, it is not possible to separate these (should they exist) from the many more numerous examples that apparently are printer's waste.

NEW YORK STOCK EXCHANGE BICENTENNIAL

A1982

Designed by Richard Sheaff.

Printed by the Jeffries Bank Note Co. for the American Bank Note Co.

LITHOGRAPHED & ENGRAVED

1992, May 17 **Tagged** *Perf. 11*

2630	A1982 29c **green, red & black**	.55	.20
	P# block of 4, 3#+A	2.50	—
	Zip, Olympic block of 4	2.25	—
a.	Black missing (EP)	—	
b.	Black missing (CM)	—	
c.	Center (black engr.) inverted	—	

No. 2630a must be collected se-tenant with a normal stamp or with a stamp with half of black engraving missing, or se-tenant with a normal stamp and an additional 2630a.

No. 2630b may be collected alone or se-tenant with No. 2630c.

The unique pane containing 28 No. 2630c and 12 No. 2630b sold at a 2002 auction for $488,750. The unique pane containing 4 No. 2630a, one stamp with half of black center missing and 35 normal stamps sold at the same auction for $18,400.

SPACE ACCOMPLISHMENTS

Cosmonaut, US Space Shuttle — A1983

Astronaut, Russian Space Station, Russian Space Shuttle — A1984

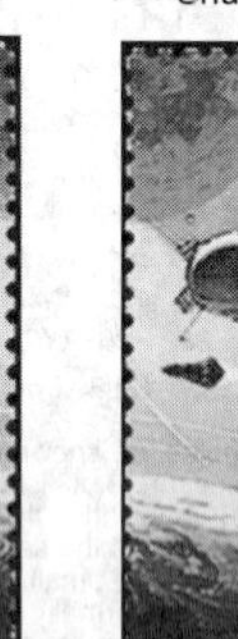

Sputnik, Vostok, Apollo Command & Lunar Modules — A1985

Soyuz, Mercury & Gemini Spacecraft — A1986

Designed by Vladimir Beilin (Russia) and Robert T. McCall.

PHOTOGRAVURE
Plates of 200 in four panes of 50

1992, May 29	**Tagged**	***Perf. 11***	
2631 A1983 29c **multicolored**		.55	.20
2632 A1984 29c **multicolored**		.55	.20
2633 A1985 29c **multicolored**		.55	.20
2634 A1986 29c **multicolored**		.55	.20
a. Block of 4, #2631-2634		2.20	1.90
P# block of 4, 4#		2.50	—
Zip block of 4		2.25	—

See Russia Nos. 6080-6083.

ALASKA HIGHWAY, 50th ANNIVERSARY

A1987

Designed by Byron Birdsall.

LITHOGRAPHED & ENGRAVED
Plates of 200 in four panes of 50

1992, May 30	**Tagged**	***Perf. 11***	
2635 A1987 29c **multicolored**		.55	.20
P# block of 4, 6#		2.50	—
Zip block of 4		2.25	—
a. Black (engr.) omitted		*500.00*	

Most known examples of No. 2635a have poor to fine centering. It is valued in the grade of fine. Very fine examples exist and sell for much more.

KENTUCKY STATEHOOD BICENTENNIAL

A1988

Designed by Joseph Petro.

Printed by J.W. Fergusson & Sons for Stamp Venturers.

PHOTOGRAVURE
Plates of 200 in four panes of 50

1992, June 1	**Tagged**	***Perf. 11***	
2636 A1988 29c **multicolored**		.55	.20
P# block of 4, 5#+S		2.50	—
Zip block of 4		2.25	—
a. Dark blue missing (EP)		—	
b. Dark blue and red missing (EP)		—	
c. All colors missing (EP)		—	

Nos. 2636a-2636c must be collected se-tenant with normal stamps.

SUMMER OLYMPICS

Soccer A1989

Gymnastics A1990

Volleyball A1991

Boxing A1992

Swimming A1993

Designed by Richard Waldrep.

Printed by J.W. Fergusson & Sons for Stamp Venturers.

PHOTOGRAVURE
Panes of 35

1992, June 11	**Tagged**	***Perf. 11***	
2637 A1989 29c **multicolored**		.55	.20
2638 A1990 29c **multicolored**		.55	.20
2639 A1991 29c **multicolored**		.55	.20
2640 A1992 29c **multicolored**		.55	.20
2641 A1993 29c **multicolored**		.55	.20
a. Strip of 5, #2637-2641		2.75	2.50
P# block of 10, 5#+S		6.00	—
Zip, copyright block of 15		8.50	—

Inscriptions on six marginal tabs.

HUMMINGBIRDS

Ruby-throated A1994

Broad-billed A1995

Costa's — A1996

Rufous — A1997

Calliope — A1998

Designed by Chuck Ripper.

Printed by Multi-Color Corp. for the American Bank Note Co.

PHOTOGRAVURE
BOOKLET STAMPS

Perf. 11 Vert. on 1 or 2 sides

1992, June 15		**Tagged**	
2642 A1994 29c **multicolored**		.55	.20
2643 A1995 29c **multicolored**		.55	.20
2644 A1996 29c **multicolored**		.55	.20
2645 A1997 29c **multicolored**		.55	.20
2646 A1998 29c **multicolored**		.55	.20
a. Bklt. pane of 5, #2642-2646		2.75	*2.50*

Imperfs of No. 2646a are printer's waste.

Illustration reduced.

Designed by Karen Mallary.

Printed by Ashton-Potter America, Inc.

LITHOGRAPHED
Plates of 300 in six panes of 50 and Plates of 200 in four panes of 50

1992, July 24	**Tagged**	***Perf. 11***	
2647 A1999 29c Indian paintbrush		.55	.20
2648 A2000 29c Fragrant water lily		.55	.20
2649 A2001 29c Meadow beauty		.55	.20
2650 A2002 29c Jack-in-the-pulpit		.55	.20
2651 A2003 29c California poppy		.55	.20

2652	A2004	29c	Large-flowered trillium	.55	.20
2653	A2005	29c	Tickseed	.55	.20
2654	A2006	29c	Shooting star	.55	.20
2655	A2007	29c	Stream violet	.55	.20
2656	A2008	29c	Bluets	.55	.20
2657	A2009	29c	Herb Robert	.55	.20
2658	A2010	29c	Marsh marigold	.55	.20
2659	A2011	29c	Sweet white violet	.55	.20
2660	A2012	29c	Claret cup cactus	.55	.20
2661	A2013	29c	White mountain avens	.55	.20
2662	A2014	29c	Sessile bellwort	.55	.20
2663	A2015	29c	Blue flag	.55	.20
2664	A2016	29c	Harlequin lupine	.55	.20
2665	A2017	29c	Twinflower	.55	.20
2666	A2018	29c	Common sunflower	.55	.20
2667	A2019	29c	Sego lily	.55	.20
2668	A2020	29c	Virginia bluebells	.55	.20
2669	A2021	29c	Ohi'a lehua	.55	.20
2670	A2022	29c	Rosebud orchid	.55	.20
2671	A2023	29c	Showy evening primrose	.55	.20
2672	A2024	29c	Fringed gentian	.55	.20
2673	A2025	29c	Yellow lady's slipper	.55	.20
2674	A2026	29c	Passionflower	.55	.20
2675	A2027	29c	Bunchberry	.55	.20
2676	A2028	29c	Pasqueflower	.55	.20
2677	A2029	29c	Round-lobed hepatica	.55	.20
2678	A2030	29c	Wild columbine	.55	.20
2679	A2031	29c	Fireweed	.55	.20
2680	A2032	29c	Indian pond lily	.55	.20
2681	A2033	29c	Turk's cap lily	.55	.20
2682	A2034	29c	Dutchman's breeches	.55	.20
2683	A2035	29c	Trumpet honeysuckle	.55	.20
2684	A2036	29c	Jacob's ladder	.55	.20
2685	A2037	29c	Plains prickly pear	.55	.20
2686	A2038	29c	Moss campion	.55	.20
2687	A2039	29c	Bearberry	.55	.20
2688	A2040	29c	Mexican hat	.55	.20
2689	A2041	29c	Harebell	.55	.20
2690	A2042	29c	Desert five spot	.55	.20
2691	A2043	29c	Smooth Solomon's seal	.55	.20
2692	A2044	29c	Red maids	.55	.20
2693	A2045	29c	Yellow skunk cabbage	.55	.20
2694	A2046	29c	Rue anemone	.55	.20
2695	A2047	29c	Standing cypress	.55	.20
2696	A2048	29c	Wild flax	.55	.20
a.	A1999-A2048		Pane of 50, #2647-2696	27.50	—

Sheet margin selvage contains a diagram of the plate layout with each pane's position shaded in gray.

WORLD WAR II

A2049

Illustration reduced.

Designed by William H. Bond.

Designs and events of 1942: a, B-25's take off to raid Tokyo, Apr. 18. b, Ration coupons (Food and other commodities rationed). c, Divebomber and deck crewman (US wins Battle of the Coral Sea, May). d, Prisoners of war (Corregidor falls to Japanese, May 6). e, Dutch Harbor buildings on fire (Japan invades Aleutian Islands, June). f, Headphones, coded message (Allies decipher secret enemy codes). g, Yorktown lost, U.S. wins at Midway. h, Woman with drill (Millions of women join war effort). i, Marines land on Guadalcanal, Aug. 7. j, Tank in desert (Allies land in North Africa, Nov.).

Central label is the size of 15 stamps and shows world map, extent of axis control.

LITHOGRAPHED & ENGRAVED

Plates of 80 in four panes of 20 each

1992, Aug. 17 **Tagged** ***Perf. 11***

2697	A2049	Block of 10	5.50	5.00
		Pane of 20	11.00	—
a.-j.		29c any single	.55	.30
k.		Red (litho.) omitted	*8,000.*	

No. 2697 has selvage at left and right and either top or bottom.

Dorothy Parker — A2050

Von Karman (1881-1963), Rocket Scientist — A2051

LITERARY ARTS SERIES

Designed by Greg Rudd.

Printed by J.W. Fergusson & Sons for Stamp Venturers.

PHOTOGRAVURE

Plates of 200 in four panes of 50

1992, Aug. 22 **Tagged** ***Perf. 11***

2698	A2050	29c	**multicolored**	.55	.20
			P# block of 4, 5# + S	2.50	—
			Zip block of 4	2.25	—

THEODORE VON KARMAN

Designed by Chris Calle.

Printed by J.W. Fergusson & Sons for Stamp Venturers.

PHOTOGRAVURE

Plates of 200 in four panes of 50

1992, Aug. 31 **Tagged** ***Perf. 11***

2699	A2051	29c	**multicolored**	.55	.20
			P# block of 4, 4# + S	2.50	—
			Zip block of 4	2.25	—

WILDFLOWERS

A1999-A2048

MINERALS

Azurite — A2052

Copper — A2053

Variscite — A2054

Wulfenite — A2055

Designed by Len Buckley.

LITHOGRAPHED & ENGRAVED
Sheets of 160 in four panes of 40.

1992, Sept. 17	**Tagged**	***Perf. 11***	
2700 A2052 29c **multicolored**		.55	.20
2701 A2053 29c **multicolored**		.55	.20
2702 A2054 29c **multicolored**		.55	.20
2703 A2055 29c **multicolored**		.55	.20
a. Block or strip of 4, #2700-2703		2.20	2.00
P# block of 4, 6#		2.50	—
Zip block of 4		2.25	—
b. As "a," silver (litho.) omitted		*8,500.*	
c. As "a," silver omitted on two stamps		—	

JUAN RODRIGUEZ CABRILLO

Cabrillo (d. 1543), Ship, Map of San Diego Bay Area — A2056

Designed by Ren Wicks.

Printed by The Press and J.W. Fergusson & Sons for Stamp Venturers.

LITHOGRAPHED & ENGRAVED
Plates of 200 in four panes of 50

1992, Sept. 28	**Tagged**	***Perf. 11***	
2704 A2056 29c **multicolored**		.55	.20
P# block of 4, 7# + 2 "S"s		2.50	—
Zip, Olympic block of 4		2.25	—
a. Black (engr.) omitted		*3,000.*	

WILD ANIMALS

Giraffe A2057

Giant Panda A2058

Flamingo A2059

King Penguins A2060

White Bengal Tiger — A2061

Designed by Robert Giusti.

Printed by J.W. Fergusson & Sons for Stamp Venturers.

PHOTOGRAVURE
BOOKLET STAMPS

1992, Oct. 1	**Tagged**	***Perf. 11 Horiz.***	
2705 A2057 29c **multicolored**		.55	.20
2706 A2058 29c **multicolored**		.55	.20
2707 A2059 29c **multicolored**		.55	.20
2708 A2060 29c **multicolored**		.55	.20
2709 A2061 29c **multicolored**		.55	.20
a. Booklet pane of 5, #2705-2709		2.75	*2.25*
b. As "a," imperf.		*3,000.*	

CHRISTMAS

Madonna and Child, by Giovanni Bellini — A2062

A2063 A2064

A2065 A2066

Designed by Bradbury Thompson (#2710) and Lou Nolan (#2711-2719). Illustration reduced.

Printed by the Bureau of Engraving and Printing, Ashton-Potter America, Inc. (#2711-2714), the Multi-Color Corporation for American Bank Note Company (#2715-2718), and Avery Dennison (#2719).

LITHOGRAPHED & ENGRAVED
Sheets of 300 in six panes of 50 (#2710, 2714a)

1992	**Tagged**	***Perf. 11½x11***	
2710 A2062 29c **multicolored,** *Oct. 22*		.55	.20
P# block of 4, 5#		2.50	—
Zip, copyright block of 4		2.25	—
a. Booklet pane of 10		5.50	*3.50*

LITHOGRAPHED

2711 A2063 29c **multicolored,** *Oct. 22*	.55	.20
2712 A2064 29c **multicolored,** *Oct. 22*	.55	.20
2713 A2065 29c **multicolored,** *Oct. 22*	.55	.20
2714 A2066 29c **multicolored,** *Oct. 22*	.55	.20
a. Block of 4, #2711-2714	2.20	1.10
P# block of 4, 5# + P	2.75	—
Zip, copyright block of 6	3.25	—

Booklet Stamps

PHOTOGRAVURE

Perf. 11 on 2 or 3 Sides

2715 A2063 29c **multicolored,** *Oct. 22*	.85	.20
2716 A2064 29c **multicolored,** *Oct. 22*	.85	.20
2717 A2065 29c **multicolored,** *Oct. 22*	.85	.20
2718 A2066 29c **multicolored,** *Oct. 22*	.85	.20
a. Booklet pane of 4, #2715-2718	3.50	*1.25*
b. As "a," imperf. horiz.	—	

No. 2718a completely imperf is printer's waste.

Self-Adhesive

Die Cut

2719 A2064 29c **multicolored,** *Oct. 28*	.60	.20
a. Booklet pane of 18	11.00	

"Greetings" is 27mm long on Nos. 2711-2714, 25mm long on Nos. 2715-2718 and 21½mm long on No. 2719. Nos. 2715-2719 differ in color from Nos. 2711-2714.

CHINESE NEW YEAR

Year of the Rooster A2067

Designed by Clarence Lee.

Printed by the American Bank Note Co.

LITHOGRAPHED & ENGRAVED
Panes of 20

1992, Dec. 30	Tagged	*Perf. 11*	
2720 A2067 29c **multicolored**		.55	.20
	P# block of 4, 5#+A	2.20	—
	Pane of 20	11.00	—

AMERICAN MUSIC SERIES

Elvis Presley
A2068

Oklahoma!
A2069

Hank Williams
A2070

Elvis Presley
A2071

Bill Haley
A2072

Clyde
McPhatter
A2073

Ritchie Valens
A2074

Otis Redding
A2075

Buddy
Holly — A2076

Dinah
Washington
A2077

Designed by Mark Stutzman (#2721, 2724-2725, 2727, 2729, 2731-2732, 2734, 2736), Wilson McLean (#2722), Richard Waldrep (#2723), John Berkey (#2726, 2728, 2730, 2733, 2735, 2737).

Printed by Stamp Venturers (#2723-2730), Multi-color Corp. (#2731-2737).

PHOTOGRAVURE
Panes of 40, Panes of 35 (#2724-2730)

1993	Tagged	*Perf. 11*	
2721	A2068 29c **multicolored,** *Jan. 8*	.55	.20
	P# block of 4, 5#	2.50	—
	Zip, copyright block of 4	2.25	—
a.	Imperf, pair		
	Perf. 10		
2722	A2069 29c **multicolored,** *Mar. 30*	.55	.20
	P# block of 4, 4#+S	4.00	—
	Zip block of 4	2.50	—
2723	A2070 29c **multicolored,** *June 9*	.55	.20
	P# block of 4, 6#+S	4.00	—
	Zip block of 4	2.50	—
	Perf. 11.2x11.5		
2723A	A2070 29c **multicolored,** *June 9*	22.50	10.00
	P# block of 4, 6#+S	140.00	—
	Zip block of 4	100.00	—

1993, June 16		*Perf. 10*	
2724	A2071 29c **multicolored**	.60	.20
2725	A2072 29c **multicolored**	.60	.20
2726	A2073 29c **multicolored**	.60	.20
2727	A2074 29c **multicolored**	.60	.20
2728	A2075 29c **multicolored**	.60	.20
2729	A2076 29c **multicolored**	.60	.20
2730	A2077 29c **multicolored**	.60	.20
a.	Vert. strip of 7, #2724-2730	4.25	
	Horiz. P# block of 10, 2 sets of 6P#+S, + top label	8.00	—
	Vert. P# block of 8, 6#+S	6.00	—
	Pane of 35	23.00	—

No. 2730a with Nos. 2724-2730 in numerical sequence cannot be obtained from the pane of 35.

Booklet Stamps
Perf. 11 Horiz.

2731	A2071 29c **multicolored**	.55	.20
2732	A2072 29c **multicolored**	.55	.20
2733	A2073 29c **multicolored**	.55	.20
2734	A2074 29c **multicolored**	.55	.20
2735	A2075 29c **multicolored**	.55	.20
2736	A2076 29c **multicolored**	.55	.20
2737	A2077 29c **multicolored**	.55	.20
a.	Booklet pane, 2 #2731, 1 each #2732-2737	5.00	*2.25*
b.	Booklet pane, #2731, 2735-2737 + tab	2.25	*1.50*

Nos. 2731-2737 have smaller design sizes, brighter colors and shorter inscriptions than Nos. 2724-2730, as well as framelines around the designs and other subtle design differences.

No. 2737b without tab is indistinguishable from broken No. 2737a.

See Nos. 2769, 2771, 2775 and designs A2112-A2117.

SPACE FANTASY

A2086

A2087

A2088

A2089

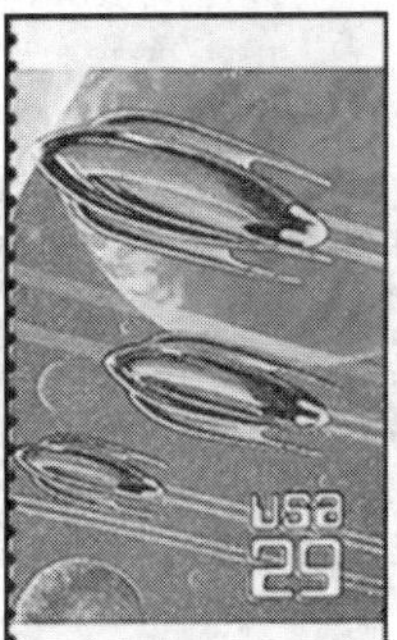

A2090

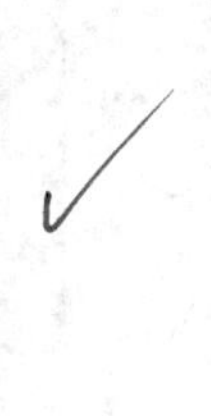

Designed by Stephen Hickman.

PHOTOGRAVURE
BOOKLET STAMPS

1993, Jan. 25	Tagged	*Perf. 11 Vert.*	
2741	A2086 29c **multicolored**	.55	.20
2742	A2087 29c **multicolored**	.55	.20
2743	A2088 29c **multicolored**	.55	.20
2744	A2089 29c **multicolored**	.55	.20
2745	A2090 29c **multicolored**	.55	.20
a.	Booklet pane of 5, #2741-2745	2.75	*2.25*

BLACK HERITAGE SERIES

Percy Lavon Julian (1899-1975), Chemist — A2091

Designed by Higgins Bond.

LITHOGRAPHED & ENGRAVED
Panes of 50

1993, Jan. 29 Tagged *Perf. 11*

2746 A2091 29c **multicolored**	.55	.20
P# block of 4, 7#	2.50	—
Zip block of 4	2.25	—

OREGON TRAIL

A2092

Designed by Jack Rosenthal.

LITHOGRAPHED & ENGRAVED
Panes of 50

1993, Feb. 12 Tagged *Perf. 11*

2747 A2092 29c **multicolored**	.55	.20
P# block of 4, 6#	2.50	—
Zip block of 4	2.25	—
a. Tagging omitted	20.00	
b. Blue omitted	—	

WORLD UNIVERSITY GAMES

A2093

Designed by David Buck.

PHOTOGRAVURE
Panes of 50

1993, Feb. 25 Tagged *Perf. 11*

2748 A2093 29c **multicolored**	.55	.20
P# block of 4, 5#	2.50	—
Zip block of 4	2.25	—

GRACE KELLY (1929-1982)

Actress, Princess of Monaco — A2094

Designed by Czeslaw Slania.

Printed by Stamp Venturers.

ENGRAVED
Panes of 50

1993, Mar. 24 Tagged *Perf. 11*

2749 A2094 29c **blue**	.55	.20
P# block of 4, 1# +S	2.50	—
Zip block of 4	2.25	—

See Monaco No. 1851.

CIRCUS

Clown — A2095

Ringmaster — A2096

Trapeze Artist — A2097

Elephant — A2098

Designed by Steve McCracken.

Printed by Ashton Potter America.

LITHOGRAPHED
Panes of 40

1993, Apr. 6 Tagged *Perf. 11*

2750 A2095 29c **multicolored**	.55	.20
2751 A2096 29c **multicolored**	.55	.20
2752 A2097 29c **multicolored**	.55	.20
2753 A2098 29c **multicolored**	.55	.20
a. Block of 4, #2750-2753	2.20	1.75
P# block of 6, 5#+P	5.00	—
Zip block of 6	3.50	—

Plate and zip blocks of 6 and copyright blocks of 9 contain one #2753a with continuous design (complete spotlight).

CHEROKEE STRIP LAND RUN, CENTENNIAL

A2099

Designed by Harold T. Holden.

Printed by American Bank Note. Co.

LITHOGRAPHED & ENGRAVED
Panes of 20

1993, Apr. 17 Tagged *Perf. 11*

2754 A2099 29c **multicolored**	.55	.20
P# block of 4, 5#+A	2.20	—
Pane of 20	11.00	—

DEAN ACHESON (1893-1971)

Secretary of State — A2100

Designed by Christopher Calle.

Printed by Stamp Venturers.

ENGRAVED
Sheets of 300 in six panes of 50

1993, Apr. 21 *Perf. 11*

2755 A2100 29c **greenish gray**	.55	.20
P# block of 4, 1#+S	2.50	—
Zip block of 4	2.25	—

SPORTING HORSES

Steeplechase A2101

Thoroughbred Racing A2102

Harness Racing A2103

Polo — A2104

Designed by Michael Dudash.

Printed by Stamp Venturers.

LITHOGRAPHED & ENGRAVED
Panes of 40

1993, May 1 **Tagged** ***Perf. 11x11½***

2756	A2101	29c **multicolored**		.55	.20
2757	A2102	29c **multicolored**		.55	.20
2758	A2103	29c **multicolored**		.55	.20
2759	A2104	29c **multicolored**		.55	.20
a.		Block of 4, #2756-2759		2.20	2.00
		P# block of 4, 5#+S		2.50	—
		Zip block of 4		2.25	—
b.		As "a," black (engr.) omitted		*1,000.*	

GARDEN FLOWERS

Hyacinth — A2105

Daffodil — A2106

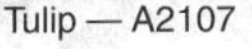

Tulip — A2107

Iris — A2108

Lilac — A2109

Designed by Ned Seidler.

LITHOGRAPHED & ENGRAVED
BOOKLET STAMPS

1993, May 15 **Tagged** ***Perf. 11 Vert.***

2760	A2105	29c **multicolored**	.55	.20
2761	A2106	29c **multicolored**	.55	.20
2762	A2107	29c **multicolored**	.55	.20
2763	A2108	29c **multicolored**	.55	.20
2764	A2109	29c **multicolored**	.55	.20
a.		Booklet pane of 5, #2760-2764	2.75	*2.25*
b.		As "a," black (engr.) omitted	*200.00*	
c.		As "a," imperf.	*2,250.*	

WORLD WAR II

A2110

Illustration reduced.

Designed by William H. Bond.

Designs and events of 1943: a, Destroyers (Allied forces battle German U-boats). b, Military medics treat the wounded. c, Amphibious landing craft on beach (Sicily attacked by Allied forces, July). d, B-24s hit Ploesti refineries, August. e, V-mail delivers letters from home. f, PT boat (Italy invaded by Allies, Sept.).

g, Nos. WS7, WS8, savings bonds, (Bonds and stamps help war effort). h, "Willie and Joe" keep spirits high. i, Banner in window (Gold Stars mark World War II losses). j, Marines assault Tarawa, Nov.

Central label is the size of 15 stamps and shows world map with extent of Axis control and Allied operations.

LITHOGRAPHED & ENGRAVED
Plates of 80 in four panes of 20 each

1993, May 31 **Tagged** ***Perf. 11***

2765	A2110	Block of 10	5.50	5.00
		Pane of 20	11.00	—
a.-j.		29c any single	.55	.30

No. 2765 has selvage at left and right and either top or bottom.

JOE LOUIS (1914-1981)

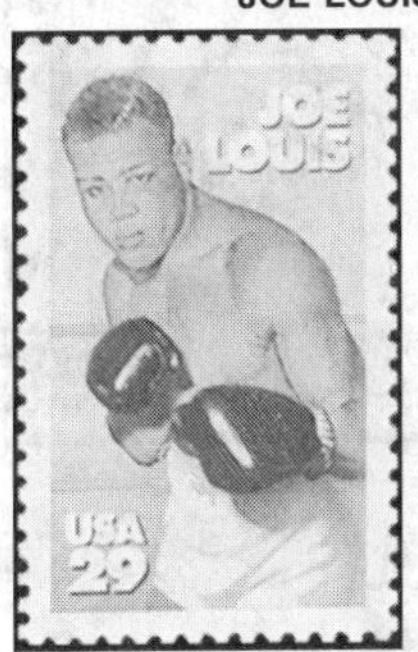

A2111

Designed by Thomas Blackshear.

LITHOGRAPHED & ENGRAVED
Plates of 200 in four panes of 50

1993, June 22 **Tagged** ***Perf. 11***

2766	A2111	29c **multicolored**	.55	.20
		P# block of 4, 5#	2.50	—
		Zip block of 4	2.25	—

AMERICAN MUSIC SERIES
Oklahoma! Type and

Show Boat — A2112

Porgy & Bess — A2113

My Fair Lady — A2114

Designed by Wilson McLean.

Printed by Multi-Color Corp.

BOOKLET STAMPS
PHOTOGRAVURE

Perf. 11 Horiz. on 1 or 2 Sides

1993, July 14 **Tagged**

2767	A2112	29c **multicolored**	.55	.20
2768	A2113	29c **multicolored**	.55	.20
2769	A2069	29c **multicolored**	.55	.20
2770	A2114	29c **multicolored**	.55	.20
a.		Booklet pane of 4, #2767-2770	2.75	*2.25*

No. 2769 has smaller design size, brighter colors and shorter inscription than No. 2722, as well as a frameline around the design and other subtle design differences.

AMERICAN MUSIC SERIES
Hank Williams Type and

Patsy Cline — A2115

The Carter Family A2116

Bob Wills — A2117

Designed by Richard Waldrep.

Printed by Stamp Venturers (#2771-2774) and American Bank Note Co. (#2775-2778).

PHOTOGRAVURE
Panes of 20

1993, Sept. 25 **Tagged** ***Perf. 10***

2771	A2070	29c **multicolored**	.55	.20
2772	A2115	29c **multicolored**	.55	.20
2773	A2116	29c **multicolored**	.55	.20
2774	A2117	29c **multicolored**	.55	.20
a.		Block or horiz. strip of 4, #2771-2774	2.20	1.75

	Horiz. P# block of 8, 2 sets of 6#+S + top label	6.00	—
	P# block of 4, 6#+S	3.00	—
	Pane of 20	13.00	—

Booklet Stamps

Perf. 11 Horiz. on one or two sides

With Black Frameline

2775	A2070 29c **multicolored**	.55	.20
2776	A2116 29c **multicolored**	.55	.20
2777	A2115 29c **multicolored**	.55	.20
2778	A2117 29c **multicolored**	.55	.20
a.	Booklet pane of 4, #2775-2778	2.50	*2.00*
b.	As "a," imperf	—	

Inscription at left measures 27½mm on No. 2723, 27mm on No. 2771 and 22mm on No. 2775. No. 2723 shows only two tuning keys on guitar, while No. 2771 shows those two and parts of two others.

NATIONAL POSTAL MUSEUM

Independence Hall, Benjamin Franklin, Printing Press, Colonial Post Rider — A2118

Pony Express Rider, Civil War Soldier, Concord Stagecoach A2119

JN-4H Biplane, Charles Lindbergh, Railway Mail Car, 1931 Model A Ford Mail Truck A2120

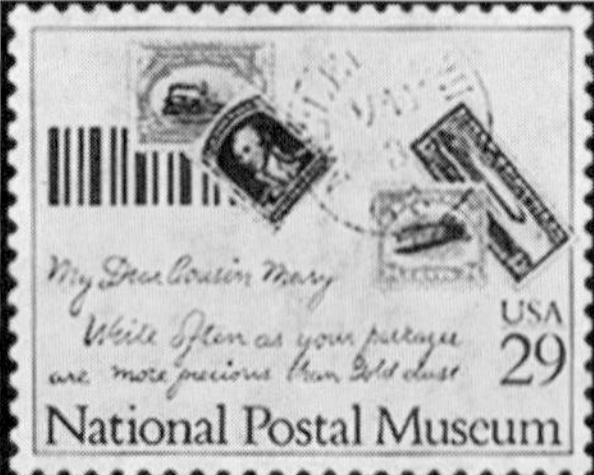

California Gold Rush Miner's Letter, Nos. 39, 295, C3a, C13, Barcode and Circular Date Stamp A2121

Designed by Richard Schlecht.

Printed by American Bank Note Co.

LITHOGRAPHED AND ENGRAVED

1993, July 30 **Tagged** ***Perf. 11***

2779	A2118 29c **multicolored**	.55	.20
2780	A2119 29c **multicolored**	.55	.20
2781	A2120 29c **multicolored**	.55	.20
2782	A2121 29c **multicolored**	.55	.20
a.	Block or strip of 4, #2779-2782	2.20	2.00
	P# block of 4, 7#+A	2.25	—
	Pane of 20	11.00	—
b.	As "a," engr. maroon (USA/29) and black ("My dear...") omitted	—	
c.	As "a," imperf	*3,500.*	

AMERICAN SIGN LANGUAGE

A2122

A2123

Designed by Chris Calle.

Printed by Stamp Venturers.

PHOTOGRAVURE

1993, Sept. 20 **Tagged** ***Perf. 11½***

2783	A2122 29c **multicolored**	.55	.20
2784	A2123 29c **multicolored**	.55	.20
a.	Pair, #2783-2784	1.10	.75
	P# block of 4, 4#+S	2.25	—
	Pane of 20	11.00	—

CLASSIC BOOKS

A2124

A2125

A2126

A2127

Designed by Jim Lamb.

Printed by American Bank Note Co.

Designs: No. 2785, Rebecca of Sunnybrook Farm, by Kate Douglas Wiggin. No. 2786, Little House on the Prairie, by Laura Ingalls Wilder. No. 2787, The Adventures of Huckleberry Finn, by Mark Twain. No. 2788, Little Women, by Louisa May Alcott.

LITHOGRAPHED & ENGRAVED

Panes of 40

1993, Oct. 23 **Tagged** ***Perf. 11***

2785	A2124 29c **multicolored**	.55	.20
2786	A2125 29c **multicolored**	.55	.20
2787	A2126 29c **multicolored**	.55	.20
2788	A2127 29c **multicolored**	.55	.20
a.	Block or horiz. strip of 4, #2785-2788	2.20	2.00
	P# block of 4, 5#+A	5.00	—
	Zip block of 4	2.25	—
b.	As "a," imperf	*3,000.*	

CHRISTMAS

Madonna and Child in a Landscape, by Giovanni Battista Cima — A2128

Jack-in-the-Box A2129

Red-Nosed Reindeer A2130

Snowman — A2131

Toy Soldier Blowing Horn — A2132

Designed by Bradbury Thompson (#2789-2790), Peter Good (#2791-2803).

Printed by Bureau of Engraving and Printing (#2789, 2791-2798), KCS Industries (#2790), Avery Dennison (#2799-2803).

LITHOGRAPHED & ENGRAVED

Panes of 50 (#2789, 2791-2794)

1993, Oct. 21 **Tagged** ***Perf. 11***

2789	A2128 29c **multicolored**	.55	.20
	P# block of 4, 4#	2.50	—
	Zip, copyright block of 4	2.25	—

Booklet Stamp
Size: 18x25mm
Perf. 11½x11 on 2 or 3 Sides

2790 A2128 29c **multicolored** .55 .20
a. Booklet pane of 4 2.25 *1.75*
b. Imperf., pair —
c. As "a," imperf. —

Nos. 2789-2790 have numerous design differences.

1993

PHOTOGRAVURE
Perf. 11½

2791 A2129 29c **multicolored,** *Oct. 21* .55 .20
2792 A2130 29c **multicolored,** *Oct. 21* .55 .20
2793 A2131 29c **multicolored,** *Oct. 21* .55 .20
2794 A2132 29c **multicolored,** *Oct. 21* .55 .20
a. Block or strip of 4, #2791-2794 2.20 2.00
P# block of 4, 6# 3.75 —
Zip, copyright block of 4 2.25 —

Snowman on Nos. 2793, 2799 has three buttons and seven snowflakes beneath nose (placement differs on both stamps). No. 2796 has two buttons and five snowflakes beneath nose. No. 2803 has two orange buttons and four snowflakes beneath nose.

Booklet Stamps
Size: 18x21mm
Perf. 11x10 on 2 or 3 Sides

2795 A2132 29c **multicolored,** *Oct. 21* .85 .20
2796 A2131 29c **multicolored,** *Oct. 21* .85 .20
2797 A2130 29c **multicolored,** *Oct. 21* .85 .20
2798 A2129 29c **multicolored,** *Oct. 21* .85 .20
a. Booklet pane, 3 each #2795-2796, 2 each #2797-2798 8.50 *4.00*
b. Booklet pane, 3 each #2797-2798, 2 each #2795-2796 8.50 *4.00*
c. Block of 4, #2795-2798 3.40 1.75

Self-Adhesive
Size: 19½x26½mm
Die Cut

2799 A2131 29c **multicolored,** *Oct. 28* .55 .20
a. Coil with plate # V1111111 — 3.50
P# strip of 5, 1 each #2799-2801, 2 #2802, P#V1111111 6.00
P# strip of 8, 2 each #2799-2802, P#V1111111 9.75
2800 A2132 29c **multicolored,** *Oct. 28* .55 .20
2801 A2129 29c **multicolored,** *Oct. 28* .55 .20
2802 A2130 29c **multicolored,** *Oct. 28* .55 .20
a. Booklet pane, 3 each #2799-2802 7.00
b. Block of 4, #2799-2802 2.20

Except for No. 2799a with plate number, coil stamps are indistinguishable from booklet stamps once they are removed from the backing paper.

Size: 17x20mm

2803 A2131 29c **multicolored,** *Oct. 28* .55 .20
a. Booklet pane of 18 10.00

Snowman on Nos. 2793, 2799 has three buttons and seven snowflakes beneath nose (placement differs on both stamps). No. 2796 has two buttons and five snowflakes beneath nose. No. 2803 has two orange buttons and four snowflakes beneath nose.

MARIANA ISLANDS

A2133

Designed by Herb Kane.

LITHOGRAPHED AND ENGRAVED

1993, Nov. 4 **Tagged** ***Perf. 11***

2804 A2133 29c **multicolored** .55 .20
P# block of 4, 6# 2.25 —
Pane of 20 11.00 —

COLUMBUS' LANDING IN PUERTO RICO, 500th ANNIVERSARY

A2134

Designed by Richard Schlecht.

Printed by Stamp Venturers.

PHOTOGRAVURE
Panes of 50

1993, Nov. 19 **Tagged** ***Perf. 11.2***

2805 A2134 29c **multicolored** .55 .20
P# block of 4, 5#+S 2.50 —
Zip block of 4 2.25 —

AIDS AWARENESS

A2135

Designed by Tom Mann.
Printed by Stamp Venturers.

PHOTOGRAVURE
Panes of 50

1993, Dec. 1 **Tagged** ***Perf. 11.2***

2806 A2135 29c **black & red** .55 .20
P# block of 4, 3#+S 2.50 —
Zip, copyright block of 6 3.50 —
a. Perf. 11 vert. on 1 or 2 sides, from bklt. pane .55 .20
b. As "a," booklet pane of 5 2.75 *2.00*

WINTER OLYMPICS

Slalom — A2136

Luge — A2137

Ice Dancing — A2138

Cross-Country Skiing — A2139

Ice Hockey — A2140

Designed by Lon Busch.
Printed by Ashton-Potter.

LITHOGRAPHED
Sheets of 120 in six panes of 20

1994, Jan. 6 **Tagged** ***Perf. 11.2***

2807 A2136 29c **multicolored** .55 .20
2808 A2137 29c **multicolored** .55 .20
2809 A2138 29c **multicolored** .55 .20
2810 A2139 29c **multicolored** .55 .20
2811 A2140 29c **multicolored** .55 .20
a. Strip of 5, #2807-2811 2.75 2.50
Horiz. P# block of 10, 2 sets of 4#+P and inscriptions 5.50 —
Horiz. P# block of 10, 2 sets of 4#+P 5.50 —
Pane of 20 11.00 —

EDWARD R. MURROW, JOURNALIST (1908-65)

A2141

Designed by Chris Calle.

ENGRAVED
Panes of 50

1994, Jan. 21 **Tagged** ***Perf. 11.2***

2812 A2141 29c **brown** .55 .20
P# block of 4, 1# 2.50 —

LOVE

A2142

A2143

A2144

Designed by Peter Goode (#2813), Lon Busch (#2814-2815).

Printed by Banknote Corp. of America (#2813), American Banknote Co. (#2814) and Bureau of Engraving and Printing (#2814C, 2815).

Booklet Stamps
LITHOGRAPHED & ENGRAVED

1994 **Tagged** ***Die Cut***
Self-adhesive

2813 A2142 29c **multicolored,** *Jan. 27* .55 .20
a. Booklet pane of 18 11.00
b. Coil with plate # B1 — 3.75
P# strip of 5, #B1 6.75

Except for No. 2813b with plate number, coil stamps are indistinguishable from booklet stamps once they are removed from the backing paper.

PHOTOGRAVURE
Perf. 10.9x11.1 on 2 or 3 sides

2814 A2143 29c **multicolored,** *Feb. 14* .55 .20
a. Booklet pane of 10 5.50 *3.50*
b. As "a," imperf —
e. Horiz. pair, imperf between —

LITHOGRAPHED & ENGRAVED
Sheets of 300 in six panes of 50
Tagged
Perf. 11.1

2814C A2143 29c **multicolored,** *June 11* .55 .20
P# block of 4, 5# 2.50 —

Size of No. 2814C is 20x28mm. No. 2814 is 18x24½mm.

PHOTOGRAVURE & ENGRAVED
Sheet of 300 in six panes of 50
Perf. 11.2

2815 A2144 52c **multicolored,** *Feb. 14*	1.00	.20
P# block of 4, 5#	5.00	—
P# block of 10, 2 sets of 5#, plate diagram, copyright and pane price inscriptions	11.00	—

BLACK HERITAGE SERIES

Dr. Allison Davis (1902-83), Social Anthropologist, Educator — A2145

Designed by Chris Calle.

Printed by Stamp Venturers.

ENGRAVED

1994, Feb. 1 **Tagged** ***Perf. 11.2***

2816 A2145 29c **red brown & brown**	.55	.20
P# block of 4, 1#+S	2.25	—
Pane of 20	11.00	—

CHINESE NEW YEAR

Year of the Dog — A2146

Designed by Clarence Lee.

Printed by J.W. Fergusson & Sons for Stamp Venturers.

PHOTOGRAVURE
Sheets of 180 in nine panes of 20

1994, Feb. 5 **Tagged** ***Perf. 11.2***

2817 A2146 29c **multicolored**	.55	.20
P# block of 4, 4#+S	2.25	—
Pane of 20	11.00	—

BUFFALO SOLDIERS

A2147

Designed by Mort Kuntsler.

Printed by Stamp Venturers.

LITHOGRAPHED & ENGRAVED
Plates of 180 in nine panes of 20

1994, Apr. 22 **Tagged** ***Perf. 11.5x11.2***

2818 A2147 29c **multicolored**	.55	.20
P# block of 4, 5#+S	2.25	—
Pane of 20	11.00	—
a. Double impression (second impression light) of red brown (engr. inscriptions)	—	

SILENT SCREEN STARS

Rudolph Valentino (1895-1926) — A2148

Clara Bow (1905-65) — A2149

Charlie Chaplin (1889-1977) — A2150

Lon Chaney (1883-1930) — A2151

John Gilbert (1895-1936) — A2152

Zasu Pitts (1898-1963) — A2153

Harold Lloyd (1894-1971) — A2154

Keystone Cops — A2155

Theda Bara (1885-1955) — A2156

Buster Keaton (1895-1966) — A2157

Designed by Al Hirschfeld.

LITHOGRAPHED & ENGRAVED
Plates of 160 in four panes of 40

1994, Apr. 27 **Tagged** ***Perf. 11.2***

2819 A2148 29c **red, black & bright violet**	.55	.20
2820 A2149 29c **red, black & bright violet**	.55	.20
2821 A2150 29c **red, black & bright violet**	.55	.20
2822 A2151 29c **red, black & bright violet**	.55	.20
2823 A2152 29c **red, black & bright violet**	.55	.20
2824 A2153 29c **red, black & bright violet**	.55	.20
2825 A2154 29c **red, black & bright violet**	.55	.20
2826 A2155 29c **red, black & bright violet**	.55	.20
2827 A2156 29c **red, black & bright violet**	.55	.20
2828 A2157 29c **red, black & bright violet**	.55	.20
a. Block of 10, #2819-2828	5.50	4.00
P# block of 10, 4#, plate diagram and copyright inscription	6.50	—
Half pane of 20	12.50	—
b. As "a," black (litho.) omitted	—	
c. As "a," blk, red & brt vio (litho.) omitted	—	

GARDEN FLOWERS

Lily — A2158

Zinnia — A2159

Gladiola — A2160

Marigold — A2161

Rose — A2162

Designed by Ned Seidler.

LITHOGRAPHED & ENGRAVED

1994, Apr. 28 **Tagged** ***Perf. 10.9 Vert.***

Booklet Stamps

2829 A2158 29c **multicolored**	.55	.20
2830 A2159 29c **multicolored**	.55	.20
2831 A2160 29c **multicolored**	.55	.20
2832 A2161 29c **multicolored**	.55	.20
2833 A2162 29c **multicolored**	.55	.20
a. Booklet pane of 5, #2829-2833	2.75	—
b. As "a," imperf	*2,000.*	
c. As "a," black (engr.) omitted	*200.00*	

1994 WORLD CUP SOCCER CHAMPIONSHIPS

A2163

USA 50 WorldCupUSA94

A2164

A2165

Illustration reduced.

Designed by Michael Dudash.

Printed by J.W. Fergusson & Sons for Stamp Venturers.
Design: 40c, Soccer player, diff.

PHOTOGRAVURE

Plates of 180 in nine panes of 20

1994, May 26	**Tagged**		***Perf. 11.1***
2834 A2163 29c	**multicolored**	.55	.20
	P# block of 4, 4#+S	2.25	—
	Pane of 20	11.00	—
2835 A2163 40c	**multicolored**	.80	.20
	P# block of 4, 4#+S	3.20	—
	Pane of 20	16.00	—
2836 A2164 50c	**multicolored**	1.00	.20
	P# block of 4, 4#+S	4.00	—
	Pane of 20	20.00	—

Souvenir Sheet

2837 A2165	Sheet of 3, #a.-c.	2.50	2.00

Nos. 2834-2836 are printed on phosphor-coated paper while Nos. 2837a (29c), 2837b (40c), 2837c (50c) are block tagged. No. 2837c has a portion of the yellow map in the LR corner.

WORLD WAR II

A2166

Illustration reduced.

Designed by William H. Bond.

Designs and events of 1944: a, Allied forces retake New Guinea. b, P-51s escort B-17s on bombing raids. c, Troops running from landing craft (Allies in Normandy, D-Day, June 6). d, Airborne units spearhead attacks. e, Officer at periscope (Submarines shorten war in Pacific). f, Parade (Allies free Rome, June 4; Paris, Aug. 25).

g, Soldier firing flamethrower (US troops clear Saipan bunkers). h, Red Ball Express speeds vital supplies. i, Battleship firing main battery (Battle for Leyte Gulf, Oct. 23-26). j, Soldiers in snow (Bastogne and Battle of the Bulge, Dec.).

Central label is size of 15 stamps and shows world map with extent of Axis control and Allied operations.

LITHOGRAPHED & ENGRAVED

Plates of eight subjects in four panes of 2 each

1994, June 6	**Tagged**		***Perf. 10.9***
2838 A2166	Block of 10	6.00	5.50
	Pane of 20	12.00	—
a.-j.	29c any single	.60	.30

No. 2838 has selvage at left and right and either top or bottom.

NORMAN ROCKWELL

A2167

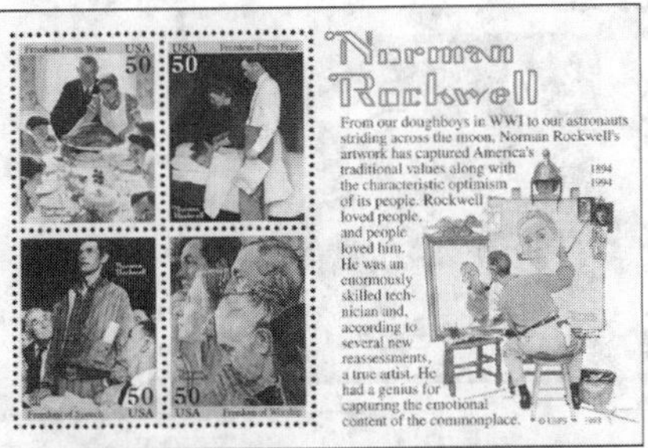

A2168

Illustration reduced.

Designed by Richard Sheaff based on Rockwell's works.

LITHOGRAPHED & ENGRAVED

Sheets of 200 in four panes of 50

1994, July 1	**Tagged**		***Perf. 10.9x11.1***
2839 A2167 29c	**multicolored**	.55	.20
	P# block of 4, 5#	2.50	—

Souvenir Sheet

LITHOGRAPHED

2840 A2168	Sheet of 4	4.00	2.75
a.	50c Freedom From Want	1.00	.65
b.	50c Freedom From Fear	1.00	.65
c.	50c Freedom of Speech	1.00	.65
d.	50c Freedom of Worship	1.00	.65

Panes of No. 2839 contain two plate blocks, one containing a plate position diagram.

Moon Landing, 25th Anniv.

A2169

A2170

Designed by Paul and Chris Calle.

Printed by Stamp Venturers (#2841) and Banknote Corp. of America (#2842).

Miniature Sheet

LITHOGRAPHED

1994, July 20	**Tagged**		***Perf. 11.2x11.1***
2841 A2169 29c	Sheet of 12	7.50	—
a.	Single stamp	.60	.60

LITHOGRAPHED & ENGRAVED

Sheets of 120 in six panes of 20

Perf. 10.7x11.1

2842 A2170 $9.95	**multicolored**	17.50	7.50
	P# block of 4, 5#+B	70.00	—

LOCOMOTIVES

Hudson's General A2171

McQueen's Jupiter A2172

Eddy's No. 242 — A2173

Ely's No. 10 — A2174

Buchanan's No. 999 — A2175

Designed by Richard Leech.

Printed by J.W. Ferguson & Sons for Stamp Venturers.

PHOTOGRAVURE

1994, July 28	**Tagged**		***Perf. 11 Horiz.***
	Booklet Stamps		
2843 A2171 29c	**multicolored**	.55	.20
2844 A2172 29c	**multicolored**	.55	.20
2845 A2173 29c	**multicolored**	.55	.20
2846 A2174 29c	**multicolored**	.55	.20
2847 A2175 29c	**multicolored**	.55	.20
a.	Booklet pane of 5, #2843-2847	2.75	*2.00*
b.	As "a," imperf.	—	

GEORGE MEANY, LABOR LEADER (1894-1980)

A2176

Designed by Chris Calle.

ENGRAVED
Sheets of 200 in four panes of 50

1994, Aug. 16	**Tagged**	***Perf. 11.1x11***	
2848 A2176 29c **blue**		.55	.20
P# block of 4, 1#		2.50	—

Panes of No. 2848 contain two plate blocks, one containing a plate position diagram.

AMERICAN MUSIC SERIES
Popular Singers

Al Jolson (1886-1950) A2177

Bing Crosby (1904-77) A2178

Ethel Waters (1896-1977) A2179

Nat "King" Cole (1919-65) A2180

Ethel Merman (1908-84) A2181

Jazz Singers

Bessie Smith (1894-1937) A2182

Muddy Waters (1915-83) A2183

Billie Holiday (1915-59) A2184

Robert Johnson (1911-38) A2185

Jimmy Rushing (1902-72) A2186

"Ma" Rainey (1886-1939) A2187

Mildred Bailey (1907-51) A2188

Howlin' Wolf (1910-76) A2189

Designed by Chris Payne (#2849-2853), Howard Koslow (#2854, 2856, 2858, 2860), Julian Allen (#2855, 2857, 2859, 2861).

Printed by J.W. Fergusson & Sons for Stamp Venturers (#2849-2853), Manhardt-Alexander for Ashton-Potter (USA) Ltd. (#2854-2861).

PHOTOGRAVURE
Plates of 180 in nine panes of 20, Plates of 210 in six panes of 35 (#2854-2861)

1994, Sept. 1	**Tagged**	***Perf. 10.1x10.2***	
2849 A2177 29c **multicolored**		.60	.20
2850 A2178 29c **multicolored**		.60	.20
2851 A2179 29c **multicolored**		.60	.20
2852 A2180 29c **multicolored**		.60	.20
2853 A2181 29c **multicolored**		.60	.20
a. Vert. strip of 5, #2849-2853		3.00	2.00
Vert. P# block of 6, 6#+S		6.50	—
Horiz. P# block of 12, 2 sets of 6#+S, + top label		13.50	—
Pane of 20		18.00	—

Some plate blocks of 6 will contain plate position diagram and copyright inscription, others will contain pane price inscription.

1994, Sept. 17	***Perf. 11x10.8***		
LITHOGRAPHED			
2854 A2182 29c **multicolored**		.60	.20
2855 A2183 29c **multicolored**		.60	.20
2856 A2184 29c **multicolored**		.60	.20
2857 A2185 29c **multicolored**		.60	.20
2858 A2186 29c **multicolored**		.60	.20
2859 A2187 29c **multicolored**		.60	.20
2860 A2188 29c **multicolored**		.60	.20
2861 A2189 29c **multicolored**		.60	.20
a. Block of 9, #2854-2861 +1 additional stamp		5.50	4.50
Vert. P# block of 10, 5#+P		8.50	—
P# block of 10, 2 sets of 5#+P, + top label		8.50	—
Pane of 35		23.00	—

Vertical plate blocks contain either pane price inscription or copyright inscription.

Nos. 2854-2861 were available on the first day in 9 other cities.

LITERARY ARTS SERIES

James Thurber (1894-1961) — A2190

Designed by Richard Sheaff based on drawing by James Thurber.

LITHOGRAPHED & ENGRAVED
Plates of 200 in four panes of 50

1994, Sept. 10	**Tagged**	***Perf. 11***	
2862 A2190 29c **multicolored**		.55	.20
P# block of 4, 2#		2.50	—

Panes of No. 2862 contain two plate blocks, one containing a plate position diagram.

WONDERS OF THE SEA

Diver, Motorboat A2191

Diver, Ship — A2192

Diver, Ship's Wheel A2193

Diver, Coral — A2194

Designed by Charles Lynn Bragg.

Printed by Barton Press for Banknote Corporation of America.

LITHOGRAPHED
Plates of 216 in nine panes of 24

1994, Oct. 3 Tagged *Perf. 11x10.9*

2863	A2191 29c **multicolored**		.55	.20
2864	A2192 29c **multicolored**		.55	.20
2865	A2193 29c **multicolored**		.55	.20
2866	A2194 29c **multicolored**		.55	.20
a.	Block of 4, #2863-2866		2.20	1.50
		P# block of 4, 4#+B	2.25	—
		Pane of 24	13.50	—
b.	As "a," imperf		*1,750.*	

CRANES

Black-Necked A2195

Whooping — A2196

Designed by Clarence Lee based on illustrations by Zhan Gengxi.

Printed by Barton Press for Banknote Corporation of America.

LITHOGRAPHED & ENGRAVED
Sheets of 120 in six panes of 20

1994, Oct. 9 Tagged *Perf. 10.8x11*

2867	A2195 29c **multicolored**	.55	.20
2868	A2196 29c **multicolored**	.55	.20
a.	Pair, #2867-2868	1.10	.75
	P# block of 4, 5#+B	2.25	—
	Pane of 20	11.00	
b.	As "a," black & magenta (engr.) omitted	*2,000.*	
c.	As "a," double impression of engr. black (Birds' names and "USA") & magenta ("29")	*5,000.*	
d.	As "a," double impression of engr. black ("USA") & magenta ("29")	—	

LEGENDS OF THE WEST

A2197

Illustration reduced.

g. Bill Pickett (1870-1932) (Revised)

Vertical Pair with Horizontal Gutter

Horizontal Pair with Vertical Gutter

Illustration reduced.

Designed by Mark Hess.

Printed by J.W. Fergusson & Sons for Stamp Venturers.

Designs: a, Home on the Range. b, Buffalo Bill Cody (1846-1917). c, Jim Bridger (1804-81). d, Annie Oakley (1860-1926). e, Native American Culture. f, Chief Joseph (c. 1840-1904). h, Bat Masterson (1853-1921). i, John C. Fremont (1813-90). j, Wyatt Earp (1848-1929). k, Nellie Cashman (c. 1849-1925). l, Charles Goodnight (1826-1929). m, Geronimo (1823-1909). n, Kit Carson (1809-68). o, Wild Bill Hickok (1837-76). p, Western Wildlife. q, Jim Beckwourth (c. 1798-1866). r, Bill Tilghman (1854-1924). s, Sacagawea (c. 1787-1812). t, Overland Mail.

PHOTOGRAVURE
Sheets of 120 in six panes of 20

1994, Oct. 18 Tagged *Perf. 10.1x10*

2869	A2197 Pane of 20	12.00	—
a.-t.	29c any single	.60	.20
	Sheet of 120 (6 panes)	72.50	
	Cross gutter block of 20	25.00	—
	Vert. pairs with horiz. gutter (each)	2.50	—
	Horiz. pairs with vert. gutter (each)	2.50	—
u.	As No. 2869, a.-e. imperf. f.-j. part perf.	—	

Cross gutter block of 20 consists of six stamps from each of two panes and four stamps from each of two other panes with the cross gutter between.

LEGENDS OF THE WEST (Recalled)

g. Bill Pickett (Recalled)

Nos. 2870b-2870d, 2870f-2870o, 2870q-2870s have a frameline around the vignette that is half the width of the frameline on similar stamps in No. 2869. Other design differences may exist.

PHOTOGRAVURE
Sheets of 120 in six panes of 20

1994 Tagged *Perf. 10.1x10*

2870	A2197 29c Pane of 20	*200.00*	—

150,000 panes of No. 2870 were made available through a drawing. Panes were delivered in an envelope. Value is for pane without envelope.

CHRISTMAS

Madonna and Child, by Elisabetta Sira — A2200

Stocking — A2201

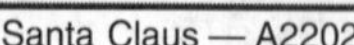

Santa Claus — A2202

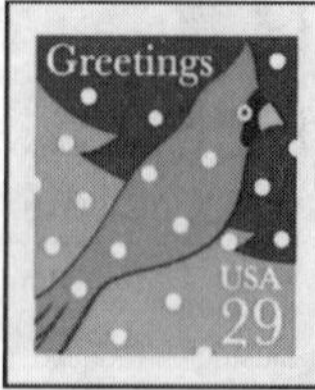

Cardinal in Snow — A2203

Designed by Bradbury Thompson (#2871), Lou Nolan (#2872), Harry Zelenko (#2873), Peter Good (#2874).

Printed by Bureau of Engraving and Printing (#2871), Ashton-Potter USA, Ltd. (#2872), Avery Dennison (#2873-2874).

LITHOGRAPHED & ENGRAVED
Sheets of 300 in six panes of 50

1994, Oct. 20 Tagged *Perf. 11¼*

2871 A2200 29c	**multicolored,** shiny gum	.55	.20
	P# block of 4, 5#	2.50	—
	Low gloss gum	.55	
	P# block of 4, 5#	2.50	

BOOKLET STAMP

Perf. 9¾x11

2871A A2200 29c	**multicolored**	.60	.20
b.	Booklet pane of 10	6.25	*3.50*
c.	As "b," imperf.	*2,250.*	

LITHOGRAPHED
Sheets of 400 in eight panes of 50

Perf. 11¼

2872 A2201 29c	**multicolored**	.55	.20
	P# block of 4, 5#+P	2.50	—
a.	Booklet pane of 20	11.00	*3.00*
b.	Imperf., pair	—	
c.	As "a," imperf. horiz.	—	
d.	Quadruple impression of black, triple impression of blue, double impressions of red and yellow, green normal	—	
e.	Vert. pair, imperf between	—	

Panes of Nos. 2871-2872 contain four plate blocks, one containing pane position diagram.

PHOTOGRAVURE
BOOKLET STAMPS
Self-Adhesive
Die Cut

2873 A2202 29c	**multicolored**	.55	.20
a.	Booklet pane of 12	6.75	
b.	Coil with plate # V1111	—	3.75
	P# strip of 5, P#V1111	6.75	

Except for No. 2873b with plate number, coil stamps are indistinguishable from booklet stamps once they are removed from the backing paper.

2874 A2203 29c	**multicolored**	.55	.20
a.	Booklet pane of 18	10.00	

BUREAU OF ENGRAVING & PRINTING
Souvenir Sheet

A2204

Illustration reduced.

Major Double Transfer

Minor Double Transfer

Designed by Peter Cocci, using original die for Type A98.

LITHOGRAPHED & ENGRAVED

1994, Nov. 3 Tagged *Perf. 11*

2875 A2204 $2	Sheet of 4	15.00	—
a.	Single stamp	3.00	1.25
	Sheet of 4 with major double transfer on right stamp	*90.00*	—
	Major double transfer, single stamp	—	—
	Sheet of 4 with minor double transfer on right stamp	*35.00*	—
	Minor double transfer, single stamp	—	—

CHINESE NEW YEAR

Year of the Boar — A2205

Designed by Clarence Lee.

Printed by Stamp Venturers.

PHOTOGRAVURE
Panes of 20

1994, Dec. 30 Tagged *Perf. 11.2x11.1*

2876 A2205 29c	**multicolored**	.55	.20
	P# block of 4, 5#+S	2.25	—
	Pane of 20	11.00	—

The first class rate was increased to 32c on Jan. 1, 1995.

A2206

A2207

A2208

A2208a

A2209

Designed by Richard D. Sheaff (#2877-2878), Lou Nolan (#2879-2892).

Printed by American Bank Note Co. (#2877, 2884, 2890), Bureau of Engraving and Printing (#2879, 2881, 2883, 2889), Stamp Venturers (#2878, 2880, 2882, 2888, 2891-2892), KCS Industries (#2885), Avery-Dennison (#2886-2887).

Coil Plate No. Strips of 3
Beginning with No. 2123, coil plate no. strips of 3 usually sell at the level of strips of 5 minus twice the face value of two stamps.

LITHOGRAPHED
Sheets of 100

1994, Dec. 13 Untagged *Perf. 11x10.8*

2877 A2206 (3c)	**tan, bright blue & red**	.20	.20
	P# block of 4, 3#+A	.30	—
	Zip block of 4	.25	—
a.	Imperf., pair	*200.00*	
b.	Double impression of red	—	

No. 2877 imperf and with blue omitted is known from printer's waste.

Perf. 10.8x10.9

2878 A2206 (3c)	**tan, dark blue & red**	.20	.20
	P# block of 4, 3#+S	.30	—
	Zip block of 4	.25	—

Inscriptions on #2877 are in a thin typeface. Those on #2878 are in heavy, bold type.

PHOTOGRAVURE
Tagged
Perf. 11.2x11.1

2879 A2207 (20c)	**black "G," yellow & multi**	.40	.20
	P# block of 4, 5#	5.00	—
	Zip block of 4	1.75	—
a.	Imperf., pair	—	

Perf. 11x10.9

2880 A2207 (20c)	**red "G," yellow & multi**	.50	.20
	P# block of 4, 5#+S	*9.00*	—
	Zip block of 4	2.25	—

Perf. 11.2x11.1

2881 A2208 (32c)	**black "G" & multi**	.75	.20
	P# block of 4, 4#	*70.00*	—
	Zip block of 4	*5.50*	—
a.	Booklet pane of 10	6.00	*3.75*

Perf. 11x10.9

2882 A2208a (32c)	**red "G" & multi**	.60	.20
	P# block of 4, 4#+S	3.00	—
	Zip block of 4	2.75	—

Distance on #2882 from bottom of red G to top of flag immediately above is 13¾mm. Illustration A2208a shows #2885 superimposed over #2882.

BOOKLET STAMPS

Perf. 10x9.9 on 2 or 3 Sides

2883 A2208 (32c)	**black "G" & multi**	.60	.20
a.	Booklet pane of 10	6.25	*3.75*

Perf. 10.9 on 2 or 3 Sides

2884 A2208 (32c)	**blue "G" & multi**	.60	.20
a.	Booklet pane of 10	6.00	*3.75*
b.	As "a," imperf	—	

Perf. 11x10.9 on 2 or 3 Sides

2885 A2208a (32c)	**red "G" & multi**	.85	.20
a.	Booklet pane of 10	8.50	*4.50*
b.	Pair, imperf vert.	—	
c.	Pair, imperf between	—	

Distance on #2885 from bottom of red G to top of flag immediately above is 13½mm. See note below #2882.

No. 2885c resulted from a paper foldover after perforating and before cutting into panes.

A2208b

A2208c

Self-Adhesive ***Die Cut***

2886 A2208b (32c)	**gray, blue, light blue, red & black**	.75	.20
a.	Booklet pane of 18	14.00	
b.	Coil with plate # V11111	—	3.25
	P# strip of 5, same #	5.50	

No. 2886 is printed on surface-tagged paper which is opaque, thicker and brighter than that of No. 2887 and has only a small number of blue shading dots in the white stripes immediately below the flag's blue field.

Except for No. 2886b with plate number, coil stamps are indistinguishable from booklet stamps once they are removed from the backing paper.

2887 A2208c (32c)	**black, blue & red**	.75	.20
a.	Booklet pane of 18	14.00	

No. 2887 has noticeable blue shading in the white stripes immediately below the blue field and has overall tagging. The paper is translucent, thinner and duller than No. 2886.

COIL STAMPS

Perf. 9.8 Vert.

2888 A2209 (25c)	**black "G," blue & multi**	.50	.50
	Pair	1.00	1.00
	P# strip of 5, #S11111	4.50	
	P# single, #S11111		2.50

2889 A2208 (32c) **black "G" & multi** .90 .20
Pair 1.80 .30
P# strip of 5, #1111, 2222 11.50
P# single, #1111, 2222 — 6.00
a. Imperf., pair *325.00*

2890 A2208 (32c) **blue "G" & multi** .60 .20
Pair 1.25 .30
P# strip of 5, #A1111, A1112, A1113, A1211, A1212, A1311, A1313, A1324, A2211, A2212, A2213, A2214, A2313, A3113, A3314, A3323, A3324, A3433, A3435, A3436, A4427, A5327, A5417, A5427 5.00
P# strip of 5, #A1222, A1314, A1417, A2223, A4426, A5437 6.25
P# strip of 5, #A1433 9.75
P# strip of 5, #A3114, A3315, A3423 7.25
P# strip of 5, #A3426 6.75
P# strip of 5, #A4435 *225.00*
P# single, #A1111, A1313, A2214, A3113, A3314, A3324, A4427, A5427 — 1.00
P# single, #A1212 — 3.00
P# single, #A2212, A3435 — 3.50
P# single, #A1112, A1311, A1324, A2213, A3323, A5327 — 2.50
P# single, #A1113, A5437 — 3.75
P# single, #A3315, A3423, A3426 4.75
P# single, #A1222, A2211, A2223, A3114 — 4.25
P# single, #A2313 — 6.00
P# single, #A1211, A1314, A4426 4.00
P# single, #A1417, A1433 — 6.75
P# single, #A3433, A3436 — 2.00
P# single, #A4435 — *225.00*
P# single, #A5417 3.00

2891 A2208 (32c) **red "G" & multi** .75 .20
Pair 1.50 .30
P# strip of 5, #S1111 6.00
P# single, #S1111 — 1.25

Rouletted 9.8 Vert.

2892 A2208 (32c) **red "G" & multi** .60 .20
Pair 1.25 .30
P# strip of 5, #S1111, S2222 6.00
P# single, #S1111, S2222 — 1.00

See note under No. 2525.

A2210

Flag Over Porch — A2212

Designed by Lou Nolan (#2893), Dave LaFleur (#2897).

Printed by American Bank Note Co. (#2893), Stamp Venturers (#2897).

PHOTOGRAVURE
COIL STAMP

1995 Untagged *Perf. 9.8 Vert.*

2893 A2210 (5c) **green & multi** .30 .20
Pair .60 .20
P# strip of 5, #A11111, A21111 2.50
P# single, #A11111, A21111 — 1.50

No. 2893 was only available through the Philatelic Fullfillment Center after its announcement 1/12/95. Covers submitted for first day cancels received a 12/13/94 cancel, even though the stamps were not available on that date.

Sheets of 400 in four panes of 100

1995 Tagged *Perf. 10.4*

2897 A2212 32c **multicolored,** shiny gum .60 .20
P# block of 4, 5#+S 3.00 —
Low gloss gum .60
P# block of 4, 5#+S 3.00
a. Imperf., vert. pair *80.00*

See Nos. 2913-2916D, 2920-2921, 3133. For booklet see No. BK243.

Butte — A2217

Mountain — A2218

Auto — A2220

Auto Tail Fin — A2223

Juke Box — A2225

Flag Over Field — A2230

Designed by Tom Engeman (#2902-2904B), Robert Brangwynne (#2905-2906), Chris Calle (#2907), Bill Nelson (#2908-2912B), Dave LaFleur (#2913-2916, 2921), Sabra Field (#2919).

Printed by J.W. Fergusson & Sons for Stamp Venturers (#2902, 2905, 2909, 2912, 2914), Bureau of Engraving and Printing (#2903, 2904B, 2908, 2911, 2912B, 2913, 2915A, 2915C-2915D, 2916, 2921), Stamp Venturers (#2902B, 2904, 2906-2907, 2910, 2912A, 2915B), Avery Dennison (#2904A, 2915, 2919, 2920).

Coil Plate No. Strips of 3
Beginning with No. 2123, coil plate No. strips of 3 usually sell at the level of strips of 5 minus the face value of two stamps.

COIL STAMPS
PHOTOGRAVURE

1995-97 Untagged *Perf. 9.8 Vert.*

Self-Adhesive (#2902B, 2904A-2904B, 2906-2907, 2910, 2912A, 2912B, 2915-2915D, 2919-2921)

2902 A2217 (5c) **yellow, red & blue,** *Mar. 10* .20 .20
Pair .20 .20
P# strip of 5, #S111, S222, S333 1.50
P# single, #S111, S222, S333 — 1.00
a. Imperf., pair 750.00

Serpentine Die Cut 11.5 Vert.

2902B A2217 (5c) **yellow, red & blue,** *June 15, 1996* .20 .20
Pair .20
P# strip of 5, #S111 1.50
P# single, #S111 — 1.10

Perf. 9.8 Vert.

2903 A2218 (5c) **purple & multi,** *Mar. 16, 1996* .20 .20
Pair .40 .20
P# strip of 5, #11111 1.50
P# single, #11111 — 1.00
a. Tagged (error) *4.00* 3.50
P# strip of 5, #11111 *85.00*
P# single, #11111 — 72.50

Letters of inscription "USA NONPROFIT ORG." outlined in purple on #2903.

2904 A2218 (5c) **blue & multi,** *Mar. 16, 1996* .20 .20
Pair .40 .20
P# strip of 5, #S111 1.50
P# single, #S111 — 1.00
c. Imperf., pair 500.00

Letters of inscription have no outline on #2904.

Serpentine Die Cut 11.2 Vert.

2904A A2218 (5c) **purple & multi,** *June 15, 1996* .20 .20
Pair .40
P# strip of 5, #V222222, V333323, V333342 1.75
P# strip of 5, #V333333 1.60
P# strip of 5, #V333343 2.50
P# single, #V222222, V333323, V333333, V333342 — 1.25
P# single, #V333343 2.10

Serpentine Die Cut 9.8 Vert.

2904B A2218 (5c) **purple & multi,** *Jan. 24, 1997* .20 .20
pair .40
P# strip of 5, #1111 1.50
P# single, #1111 — 1.25

Letters of inscription outlined in purple on #2904B, not outlined on No. 2904A.

Perf. 9.8 Vert.

2905 A2220 (10c) **black, red brown & brown,** *Mar. 10* .20 .20
Pair .40 .40
P# strip of 5, #S111, S222, S333 2.40
P# single, #S111, S222, S333 — 1.75

Serpentine Die Cut 11.5 Vert.

2906 A2220 (10c) **black, brown & red brown,** *June 15, 1996* .20 .20
Pair .40
P# strip of 5, #S111 2.50
P# single, #S111 — 1.75

2907 A1957 (10c) **gold & multi,** *May 21, 1996* .20 .20
Pair .40
P# strip of 5, #S11111 2.75
P# single, #S11111 — 2.00

Perf. 9.8 Vert.

2908 A2223 (15c) **dark orange yellow & multi,** tagged, *Mar. 17* .30 .30
Pair .60 .60
P# strip of 5, #11111 3.00
P# single, #11111 — 2.00

No. 2908 has dark, bold colors, heavy shading lines and heavily shaded chrome.

2909 A2223 (15c) **buff & multi,** *Mar. 17* .30 .30
Pair .60 .60
P# strip of 5, #S11111 2.75
P# single, #S11111 — 1.75

No. 2909 has shinier chrome, more subdued colors and finer details than No. 2908.

Serpentine Die Cut 11.5 Vert.

2910 A2223 (15c) **buff & multi,** *June 15, 1996* .30 .30
Pair .60
P# strip of 5, #S11111 2.90
P# single, #S11111 — 1.75

Perf. 9.8 Vert.

2911 A2225 (25c) **dark red, dark yellow green & multi,** tagged, *Mar. 17* .50 .50
Pair 1.00 1.00
P# strip of 5, #111111, 212222, 222222 4.25
P# strip of 5, #332222 4.75
P# single, #111111, 212222, 222222 — 12.50
P# single, #332222 — 3.00
a. Imperf, pair —

No. 2911 has dark, saturated colors and dark blue lines in the music selection board.

2912 A2225 (25c) **bright orange red, bright yellow green & multi,** *Mar. 17* .50 .50
Pair 1.00 1.00
P# strip of 5, #S11111, S22222 3.75
P# single, same # — 2.25

No. 2912 has bright colors, less shading and light blue lines in the music selection board.

Serpentine Die Cut 11.5 Vert.

2912A A2225 (25c) **bright orange red, bright yellow green & multi,** *June 15, 1996* .50 .50
Pair 1.00
P# strip of 5, #S11111, S22222 5.00
P# single, same # — 2.25

Serpentine Die Cut 9.8 Vert.

2912B A2225 (25c) **dark red, dark yellow green & multi,** *Jan. 24, 1997* .50 .50
pair 1.00
P# strip of 5, #111111 3.75
P# strip of 5, #222222 5.00
P# single, #111111, 222222 — 2.00

See No. 3132.

Tagged

Perf. 9.8 Vert.

2913 A2212 32c **blue, tan, brown, red & light blue,** shiny gum, *May 19* .60 .20
Pair 1.25 .30
P# strip of 5, #11111, 22221 5.25
P# strip of 5, #22222 6.25
P# single, #11111, 22222 — 1.00
P# single, #22221 — 3.50
Low gloss gum .60
Pair 1.25
P# strip of 5, #11111, 22222, 33333, 34333, 44444, 45444, 66646, 77767, 78767, 91161, 99969 5.00
P# strip of 5, #22322 12.00
P# strip of 5, #66666 11.00
P# single, #11111, 22222 — 1.00
P# single, #22322 — 6.50

P# single, #33333, 34333, 44444, 45444, 66646, 77767 — 1.75
P# single, #66666 — 8.00
P# single, #78767, 91161, 99969 — 2.50
a. Imperf., pair *45.00*

No. 2913 has pronounced light blue shading in the flag and red "1995" at left bottom. See No. 3133.

2914 A2212 32c **blue, yellow brown, red & gray,** *May 19* .60 .20
Pair 1.25 .30
P# strip of 5, #S11111 4.50
P# single, #S11111 — 2.50

No. 2914 has pale gray shading in the flag and blue "1995" at left bottom.

Serpentine Die Cut 8.7 Vert.

2915 A2212 32c **multicolored,** *Apr. 18* .75 .30
Pair 1.50
P# strip of 5, #V11111 7.50
P# single, #V11111 — 3.00

Serpentine Die Cut 9.8 Vert.

2915A A2212 32c **dk blue, tan, brown, red & light blue,** *May 21, 1996* .60 .20
Pair 1.25
P# strip of 5, #11111, 22222, 23222, 33333, 44444, 45444, 55555, 66666, 78777, 88888, 11111A, 13231A, 13311A, 22222A, 33333A, 44444A, 55555A, 66666A, 77777A, 78777A, 88888A, 99999 5.00
P# strip of 5, #87888 60.00
P# strip of 5, #87898 15.00
P# strip of 5, #88898 *300.00*
P# strip of 5, #89878, 97898 7.75
P# strip of 5, #89888 20.00
P# strip of 5, #89898 8.00
P# strip of 5, #89899 *575.00*
P# strip of 5, #99899 35.00
P# strip of 5, #13211A 100.00
P# single, #11111, 22222, 23222, 33333, 44444, 45444, 55555, 66666, 78777, 88888, 99999, 11111A, 13231A,13311A, 22222A, 33333A, 44444A, 55555A, 66666A, 77777A, 78777A, 88888A — 1.25
single, #13211A *75.00*
P# single, #87888 — *25.00*
P# single, #87898, 89878, 97898 — 4.50
P# single, #88898 — *225.00*
P# single, #89888 8.00
P# single, #89898 — 2.75
P# single, #89899 225.00
P# single, #99899 32.50
h. Imperf., pair *40.00*
i. Tan omitted *2,000.*
j. Double die cutting 30.00 —

Die cutting on No. 2915A shows either 10 serpentine "peaks" on each side, 11 "peaks" on the left side and 10 "peaks" on the right side, or 10 "peaks" on the left side and 11 "peaks" on the right side. The last configuration is considered by specialists to be an error, and it is rare.

Sky on No. 3133 shows color gradation at LR not on No. 2915A.

On No. 2915Ai all other colors except brown are severely shifted.

Serpentine Die Cut 11.5 Vert.

2915B A2212 32c **dk blue, tan, brown, red & light blue,** *June 15, 1996* .75 *.90*
Pair 1.50
P# strip of 5, #S11111 7.00
P# single, #S11111 — 2.75

Serpentine Die Cut 10.9 Vert.

2915C A2212 32c **dk blue, tan, brown, red & light blue,** *May 21, 1996* 1.00 .40
Pair 2.00
P# strip of 5, #55555, 66666 17.50
P# single, #55555, 66666 — 3.75
P# single, #88888 —

Serpentine Die Cut 9.8 Vert.

2915D A2212 32c **dark blue, tan, brown, red & light blue,** *Jan. 24, 1997* .75 *.90*
pair 1.50
P# strip of 5, #11111 7.50
P# single, #11111 — 3.25

No. 2915D shows 9 "peaks" at left and 10 at right or 10 "peaks" at left and 10 at right.

Stamps on multiples of No. 2915A touch, and are on a peelable backing the same size as the stamps, while those of No. 2915D are separated on the peelable backing, which is larger than the stamps.

No. 2915D has red "1997" at left bottom; No. 2915A has red "1996" at left bottom.

Sky on No. 3133 shows color gradation at LR not on No. 2915D, and it has blue "1996" at left bottom.

BOOKLET STAMPS

Perf. 10.8x9.8 on 2 or 3 Adjacent Sides

2916 A2212 32c **blue, tan, brown, red & light blue,** *May 19* .65 .20
a. Booklet pane of 10 6.50 *3.25*
b. As "a," imperf. —

Die Cut

2919 A2230 32c **multicolored,** *Mar. 17* .60 .20
a. Booklet pane of 18 11.00
b. Vert. pair, no die cutting btwn. —

Serpentine Die Cut 8.7 on 2, 3 or 4 Adjacent Sides

2920 A2212 32c **multicolored,** dated blue "1995," *Apr. 18* .60 .20
a. Booklet pane of 20+label 12.00
b. Small date 4.50 .35
c. As "b," booklet pane of 20+label *110.00*
f. As No. 2920, pane of 15+label *9.00*
g. As "a," partial pane of 10, 3 stamps and parts of 7 stamps printed on backing liner —
h. As No. 2920, booklet pane of 15 *35.00*
i. As No. 2920, imperf pair —
j. Dark blue omitted (from No. 2920a) —

Date on No. 2920 is nearly twice as large as date on No. 2920b. No. 2920f comes in various configurations.

No. 2920h is a pane of 16 with one stamp removed. The missing stamp is the lower right stamp in the pane or (more rarely) the upper left stamp. No. 2920h cannot be made from No. 2920f, a pane of 15 + label. The label is located in the sixth or seventh row of the pane and is die cut. If the label is removed, an impression of the die cutting appears on the backing paper.

Serpentine Die Cut 11.3 on 3 sides

2920D A2212 32c **multicolored,** dated blue "1996," *Jan. 20, 1996* .70 .25
e. Booklet pane of 10 7.50

Serpentine Die Cut 9.8 on 2 or 3 Adjacent Sides

2921 A2212 32c **dk bl, tan, brn, red & lt bl,** dated red 1996, *May 21, 1996* .75 .20
a. Booklet pane of 10, dated red "1996" 7.50
b. As No. 2921, dated red "1997" .75 .20
c. As "a," dated red "1997" 7.50
d. Booklet pane of 5 + label, dated red "1997," *Jan. 24, 1997* 3.75
e. As "a," imperf. *300.00*

Scott values for used self-adhesive stamps are for examples either on piece or off piece.

GREAT AMERICANS ISSUE

A2248 A2249

A2250 A2251

A2253 A2255

A2256 A2257

A2258

Designed by Dennis Lyall (#2933-2934), Richard Sheaff (#2935), Howard Paine (#2936, 2941-2942), Roy Andersen (#2938), Chris Calle (#2940, 2943).

Printed by Banknote Corporation of America (#2933-2935, 2940-2943), Ashton-Potter (USA) Ltd. (#2936), Bureau of Engraving & Printing (#2938).

ENGRAVED
Sheets of 400 in four panes of 100
Sheets of 160 in eight panes of 20 (#2935)
Sheets of 120 in six panes of 20 (#2936, 2941-2942)

1995-99 **Tagged**

Self-Adhesive (#2941-2942)

Perf. 11.2, Serpentine Die Cut 11.7x11.5 (#2941-2942)

2933 A2248 32c **brown,** prephosphored paper (solid tagging), *Sept. 13, 1995* .60 .20
P# block of 4, 1#+B 3.00 —
2934 A2249 32c **green,** prephosphored paper (solid tagging), *Apr. 26, 1996* .60 .20
P# block of 4, 1#+B 3.00 —
2935 A2250 32c **lake,** prephosphored paper (grainy solid tagging), *Apr. 3, 1998* .60 .20
P# block of 4, 1#+B 2.60 —
Pane of 20 12.75
2936 A2251 32c **blue,** prephosphored paper (solid tagging), *July 16, 1998* .60 .20
P# block of 4, 1#+P 2.60 —
Pane of 20 12.75 —
2938 A2253 46c **carmine,** prephosphored uncoated paper (mottled tagging), *Oct. 20, 1995* .90 .20
P# block of 4, 1# 4.50 —
2940 A2255 55c **green,** prephosphored paper (grainy solid tagging), *July 11, 1995* 1.10 .20
P# block of 4, 1#+B 5.50 —
a. Imperf., pair —
2941 A2256 55c **black,** prephosphored coated paper (solid tagging), *July 17, 1999* 1.10 .20
P# block of 4, 1#+B 4.40
Pane of 20 22.00
2942 A2257 77c **blue,** prephosphored paper (solid tagging), *Nov. 9, 1998* 1.50 .20
P# block of 4, 1#+B 6.00
Pane of 20 30.00
2943 A2258 78c **bright violet,** prephosphored paper (solid tagging), *Aug. 18, 1995* 1.60 .20
P# block of 4, 1#+B 7.50 —
a. 78c **dull violet,** prephosphored paper (grainy solid tagging) 1.60 .20
P# block of 4, 1#+B 7.50 —
b. 78c **pale violet,** prephosphored paper (grainy solid tagging) 1.75 .30
P# block of 4, 1#+B 12.00 —

The pale violet ink on No. 2943b luminesces bright pink under long-wave ultraviolet light.

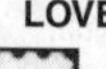

LOVE

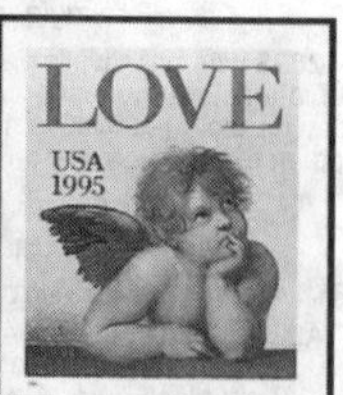

Cherub from Sistine Madonna, by Raphael
A2263 A2264

Designed by Terry McCaffrey.

Printed by the Bureau of Engraving and Printing (#2948) and Banknote Corp. of America (#2949).

LITHOGRAPHED & ENGRAVED
Sheets of 300 in six panes of 50

1995, Feb. 1 **Tagged** ***Perf. 11.2***

2948 A2263 (32c) **multicolored** .60 .20
P# block of 4, 5# 3.00 —

Self-Adhesive

Die Cut

2949 A2264 (32c) **multicolored** .60 .20
a. Booklet pane of 20 + label 12.00
b. Red (engr.) omitted *450.00*
c. As "a," red (engr.) omitted *9,000.*
d. Red (engr.) missing (CM) —

No. 2949d must be collected se-tenant with a normal stamp. See Nos. 2957-2960, 3030.

Florida Statehood, 150th Anniv. A2265

Designed by Laura Smith.
Printed by Ashton-Potter (USA) Ltd.

LITHOGRAPHED

Sheets of 160 in eight panes of 20

1995, Mar. 3 **Tagged** ***Perf. 11.1***
2950 A2265 32c **multicolored** .60 .20
P# block of 4, 5#+P 2.40 —
Pane of 20 12.00 —

EARTH DAY

Earth Clean-Up A2266

Solar Energy A2267

Tree Planting A2268

Beach Clean-Up A2269

Designed by Christy Millard (#2951), Jennifer Michalove (#2952), Brian Hailes (#2953) and Melody Kiper (#2954).
Printed by Ashton-Potter (USA) Ltd.

LITHOGRAPHED

Sheets of 96 in six panes of 16

1995, Apr. 20 **Tagged** ***Perf. 11.1x11***
2951 A2266 32c **multicolored** .60 .20
2952 A2267 32c **multicolored** .60 .20
2953 A2268 32c **multicolored** .60 .20
2954 A2269 32c **multicolored** .60 .20
a. Block of 4, #2951-2954 2.40 1.75

P# block of 4, 5#+P 2.40 —
Horiz. P# block of 8, 2 sets of 5#+P, + top or bottom label 4.80 —
Pane of 16 9.60 —

A2270

A2271

RICHARD M. NIXON

37th President (1913-94)

Designed by Daniel Schwartz.
Printed by Barton Press and Bank Note Corp. of America.

LITHOGRAPHED & ENGRAVED

Sheets of 200 in four panes of 50

1995, Apr. 26 **Tagged** ***Perf. 11.2***
2955 A2270 32c **multicolored** .60 .20
P# block of 4, 5#+B 3.00 —
a. Red (engr.) missing (CM) *1,250.*

No. 2955 is known with red (engr. "Richard Nixon") inverted, and with red engr. omitted but only half the Nixon portrait present, both from printer's waste. No. 2955a shows a complete Nixon portrait.

BLACK HERITAGE SERIES

Bessie Coleman (d. 1926), Aviator

Designed by Chris Calle.

ENGRAVED

Sheets of 200 in four panes of 50

1995, Apr. 27 **Tagged** ***Perf. 11.2***
2956 A2271 32c **red & black** .60 .20
P# block of 4, 1# 3.00 —

LOVE

A2272

A2273

Cherubs from Sistine Madonna, by Raphael — A2274

Designed by Terry McCaffrey.
Printed by Bureau of Engraving and Printing (#2957-2959), Bank Note Corp. of America (#2960).

LITHOGRAPHED & ENGRAVED

Sheets of 300 in six panes of 50

1995, May 12 **Tagged** ***Perf. 11.2***
2957 A2272 32c **multicolored** .60 .20
P# block of 4, 5# 3.00 —
Copyright block of 6 4.25 —

Compare with No. 3030. For booklet see No. BK244.

2958 A2273 55c **multicolored** 1.10 .20
P# block of 4, 5# 5.50 —

BOOKLET STAMPS

Perf. 9.8x10.8

2959 A2272 32c **multicolored** .60 .20
a. Booklet pane of 10 6.00 *3.25*
b. As "a," imperf —

Self-Adhesive

Die Cut

2960 A2274 55c **multicolored** 1.10 .20
a. Booklet pane of 20 + label 22.50

RECREATIONAL SPORTS

Volleyball A2275

Softball A2276

Bowling A2277

Tennis A2278

Golf — A2279

Designed by Don Weller.
Printed by Bank Note Corp. of America.

LITHOGRAPHED

Sheets of 120 in six panes of 20

1995, May 20 **Tagged** ***Perf. 11.2***
2961 A2275 32c **multicolored** .60 .20
2962 A2276 32c **multicolored** .60 .20
2963 A2277 32c **multicolored** .60 .20
2964 A2278 32c **multicolored** .60 .20
2965 A2279 32c **multicolored** .60 .20
a. Vert. strip of 5, #2961-2965 3.00 2.00
P# block of 10, 2 sets of 4#+B 6.00 —
Pane of 20 12.00 —
b. As "a," imperf *2,250.*
c. As "a," yellow omitted *2,250.*
d. As "a," yellow, blue & magenta omitted *2,250.*

PRISONERS OF WAR & MISSING IN ACTION

A2280

Designed by Carl Herrman.
Printed by Ashton-Potter (USA) Ltd.

LITHOGRAPHED

Sheets of 160 in eight panes of 20

1995, May 29 **Tagged** ***Perf. 11.2***
2966 A2280 32c **multicolored** .60 .20
P# block of 4, 6#+P 2.40 —
Pane of 20 12.00 —

LEGENDS OF HOLLYWOOD

Marilyn Monroe (1926-62) — A2281

Cross Gutter Block of 8

Illustration reduced.

Designed by Michael Deas.
Printed by Stamp Venturers.

PHOTOGRAVURE
Sheets of 120 in six panes of 20

1995, June 1 **Tagged** ***Perf. 11.1***

2967	A2281 32c **multicolored**		.60	.20
		P# block of 4, 6#+S	5.00	—
		Pane of 20	22.50	
		Sheet of 120 (six panes)	150.00	
		Cross gutter block of 8	55.00	—
		Block of 8 with vertical gutter	45.00	—
		Horiz. pair with vert. gutter	7.50	—
		Vert. pair with horiz. gutter	4.00	—
a.	Imperf., pair		*500.00*	
		Pane of 20, imperf.	*5,250.*	

Perforations in corner of each stamp are star-shaped.

TEXAS STATEHOOD

A2282

Designed by Laura Smith.
Printed by Sterling Sommer for Ashton-Potter (USA) Ltd.

LITHOGRAPHED
Sheets of 120 in six panes of 20

1995, June 16 **Tagged** ***Perf. 11.2***

2968	A2282 32c **multicolored**		.60	.20
		P# block of 4, 6#+P	2.40	—
		Pane of 20	12.00	—

GREAT LAKES LIGHTHOUSES

Split Rock, Lake Superior — A2283

St. Joseph, Lake Michigan — A2284

Spectacle Reef, Lake Huron — A2285

Marblehead, Lake Erie — A2286

Thirty Mile Point, Lake Ontario — A2287

Designed by Howard Koslow.
Printed by Stamp Venturers.

PHOTOGRAVURE
BOOKLET STAMPS

1995, June 17 **Tagged** ***Perf. 11.2 Vert.***

2969	A2283 32c **multicolored**	.60	.20
2970	A2284 32c **multicolored**	.60	.20
2971	A2285 32c **multicolored**	.60	.20
2972	A2286 32c **multicolored**	.60	.20
2973	A2287 32c **multicolored**	.60	.20
a.	Booklet pane of 5, #2969-2973	3.00	*2.75*

U.N., 50th ANNIV.

A2288

Designed by Howard Paine.
Printed by Banknote Corp. of America.

ENGRAVED
Sheets of 180 in nine panes of 20

1995, June 26 **Tagged** ***Perf. 11.2***

2974	A2288 32c **blue**		.60	.20
		P# block of 4, 1#+B	2.40	—
		Pane of 20	12.00	—

CIVIL WAR

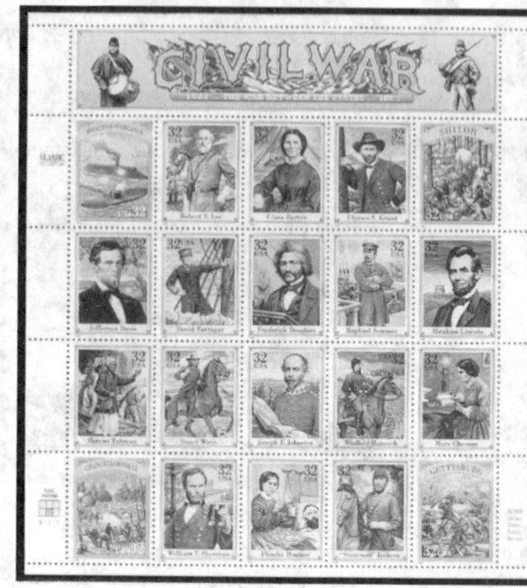

A2289

Illustration reduced.

Designed by Mark Hess.

Printed by Stamp Venturers.

Designs: a, Monitor and Virginia. b, Robert E. Lee. c, Clara Barton. d, Ulysses S. Grant. e, Battle of Shiloh. f, Jefferson Davis. g, David Farragut. h, Frederick Douglass. i, Raphael Semmes. j, Abraham Lincoln. k, Harriet Tubman. l, Stand Watie. m, Joseph E. Johnston. n, Winfield Hancock. o, Mary Chesnut. p, Battle of Chancellorsville. q, William T. Sherman. r, Phoebe Pember. s, "Stonewall" Jackson. t, Battle of Gettysburg.

PHOTOGRAVURE
Sheets of 120 in six panes of 20

1995, June 29 **Tagged** ***Perf. 10.1***

2975	A2289 Pane of 20		17.50	—
a.-t.	32c any single		.80	.20
		Sheet of 120 (6 panes)	105.00	
		Cross gutter block of 20	35.00	—
		Vert. pairs with horiz. gutter (each)	3.75	—
		Horiz. pairs with vert. gutter (each)	3.75	—
u.	As No. 2975, a.-e. imperf, f.-j. part perf			—
v.	As No. 2975, k.-t. imperf, f.-j. part perf			—
w.	As No. 2975, imperf		*1,500.*	
x.	Block of 9 (f.-h., k.-m., p.-r.) k.-l. & p.-q. imperf. vert.			—

Cross gutter block of 20 consists of six stamps from each of two panes and four stamps from each of two other panes with the cross gutter between.

AMERICAN FOLK ART SERIES
Carousel Horses

A2290

A2291

A2292

A2293

Designed by Paul Calle.

Printed at Sterling Sommer for Ashton-Potter (USA) Ltd.

LITHOGRAPHED

Sheets of 160 in eight panes of 20

1995, July 21	**Tagged**		***Perf. 11***	
2976	A2290 32c	**multicolored**	.60	.20
2977	A2291 32c	**multicolored**	.60	.20
2978	A2292 32c	**multicolored**	.60	.20
2979	A2293 32c	**multicolored**	.60	.20
a.		Block of 4, #2976-2979	2.40	2.00
		P# block of 4, 5#+P	2.40	—
		Pane of 20	12.00	—

WOMAN SUFFRAGE

A2294

Designed by April Greiman.
Printed by Ashton-Potter (USA) Ltd.

LITHOGRAPHED & ENGRAVED

Sheets of 160 in four panes of 40

1995, Aug. 26	**Tagged**	***Perf. 11.1x11***	
2980	A2294 32c **multicolored**	.60	.20
	P# block of 4, 5#+P	3.00	—
a.	Black (engr.) omitted	*425.00*	
b.	Imperf., pair	*1,500.*	

No. 2980a is valued in the grade of fine. Very fine examples exist and sell for much more.

WORLD WAR II

A2295

Illustration reduced.

Designed by Bill Bond.

Designs and events of 1945: a, Marines raise flag on Iwo Jima. b, Fierce fighting frees Manila by March 3, 1945. c, Soldiers advancing (Okinawa, the last big battle). d, Destroyed bridge (US and Soviets link up at Elbe River). e, Allies liberate Holocaust survivors. f, Germany surrenders at Reims. g, Refugees (By 1945, World War II has uprooted millions). h, Truman announces Japan's surrender. i, Sailor kissing nurse (News of victory hits home). j, Hometowns honor their returning veterans.

Central label is size of 15 stamps and shows world map with extent of Axis control and Allied operations.

LITHOGRAPHED & ENGRAVED

Plates of eight subjects in four panes of 2 each

1995, Sept. 2	**Tagged**	***Perf. 11.1***	
2981	A2295 Block of 10	6.00	5.50
	Pane of 20	12.00	—
a.-j.	32c any single	.60	.30

No. 2981 has selvage at left and right and either top or bottom.

AMERICAN MUSIC SERIES

Louis Armstrong (1901-71) A2296

Coleman Hawkins (1904-69) A2297

James P. Johnson (1894-1955) A2298

Jelly Roll Morton (1890-1941) A2299

Charlie Parker (1920-55) A2300

Eubie Blake (1883-1983) A2301

Charles Mingus (1922-79) A2302

Thelonious Monk (1917-82) A2303

John Coltrane (1926-67) A2304

Erroll Garner (1921-77) A2305

Designed by Dean Mitchell (#2982-2984, 2987, 2989, 2991-2992) and Thomas Blackshear (others).

Printed by Ashton-Potter (USA) Ltd. (#2982), Sterling Sommer for Ashton-Potter (USA) Ltd. (#2983-2992).

LITHOGRAPHED

Plates of 120 in six panes of 20

1995	**Tagged**		***Perf. 11.1x11***	
2982	A2296 32c	**white denomination,** *Sept. 1*	.80	.20
		P# block of 4, 4#+P	3.20	—
		Pane of 20	16.00	—
2983	A2297 32c	**multicolored,** *Sept. 16*	1.00	.20
2984	A2296 32c	**black denomination,** *Sept. 16*	1.00	.20
2985	A2298 32c	**multicolored,** *Sept. 16*	1.00	.20
2986	A2299 32c	**multicolored,** *Sept. 16*	1.00	.20
2987	A2300 32c	**multicolored,** *Sept. 16*	1.00	.20
2988	A2301 32c	**multicolored,** *Sept. 16*	1.00	.20
2989	A2302 32c	**multicolored,** *Sept. 16*	1.00	.20
2990	A2303 32c	**multicolored,** *Sept. 16*	1.00	.20
2991	A2304 32c	**multicolored,** *Sept. 16*	1.00	.20
2992	A2305 32c	**multicolored,** *Sept. 16*	1.00	.20
a.		Vert. block of 10, #2983-2992	10.00	—
		P# block of 10	10.00	—
		Pane of 20	20.00	—
b.		Pane of 20, dark blue (inscriptions) omitted		—

GARDEN FLOWERS

Aster A2306

Chrysanthemum A2307

Dahlia — A2308

Hydrangea — A2309

Rudbeckia — A2310

Designed by Ned Seidler.

LITHOGRAPHED & ENGRAVED
BOOKLET STAMPS

1995, Sept. 19 **Tagged** ***Perf. 10.9 Vert.***

2993 A2306 32c **multicolored** .60 .20
2994 A2307 32c **multicolored** .60 .20
2995 A2308 32c **multicolored** .60 .20
2996 A2309 32c **multicolored** .60 .20
2997 A2310 32c **multicolored** .60 .20
a. Booklet pane of 5, #2993-2997 3.00 *2.25*
b. As "a," imperf —

EDDIE RICKENBACKER (1890-1973), AVIATOR

A2311

Designed by Davis Meltzer.

PHOTOGRAVURE
Panes of 50

1995, Sept. 25 **Tagged** ***Perf. 11¼***

2998 A2311 60c **multicolored,** small "1995" year date 1.40 .30
P# block of 4, 5# 9.00 —
a. Large "1995" date, *Oct., 1999* 1.40 .30
P# block of 4, 5# 9.00 —

Date on No. 2998 is 1mm long, on No. 2998a 1½mm long.

REPUBLIC OF PALAU

A2312

Designed by Herb Kane.
Printed by Sterling Sommer for Ashton-Potter (USA) Ltd.

LITHOGRAPHED
Sheets of 200 in four panes of 50

1995, Sept. 29 **Tagged** ***Perf. 11.1***

2999 A2312 32c **multicolored** .60 .20
P# block of 4, 5#+P 3.00 —

See Palau Nos. 377-378.

COMIC STRIPS

A2313

Illustration reduced.

Designed by Carl Herrman.

Printed by Stamp Venturers.

Designs: a, The Yellow Kid. b, Katzenjammer Kids. c, Little Nemo in Slumberland. d, Bringing Up Father. e, Krazy Kat. f, Rube Goldberg's Inventions. g, Toonerville Folks. h, Gasoline Alley. i, Barney Google. j, Little Orphan Annie. k, Popeye. l, Blondie. m, Dick Tracy. n, Alley Oop. o, Nancy. p, Flash Gordon. q, Li'l Abner. r, Terry and the Pirates. s, Prince Valiant. t, Brenda Starr, Reporter.

PHOTOGRAVURE
Sheets of 120 in six panes of 20

1995, Oct. 1 **Tagged** ***Perf. 10.1***

3000 A2313 Pane of 20 12.00 —
a.-t. 32c any single .60 .20
Sheet of 120 (6 panes) 105.00
Cross gutter block of 20 35.00 —
Vert. pairs with horiz. gutter (each) 3.75 —
Horiz. pairs with vert. gutter (each) 3.75 —
u. As No. 3000, a.-h. imperf., i.-l. part perf —
v. As No. 3000, m.-t. imperf., i.-l. part perf —
w. As No. 3000, a.-l. imperf.,m.-t. imperf vert. —

Inscriptions on back of each stamp describe the comic strip.
Cross gutter block of 20 consists of six stamps from each of two panes and four stamps from each of two other panes with the cross gutter between.

U.S. NAVAL ACADEMY, 150th ANNIVERSARY

A2314

Designed by Dean Ellis. Printed by Sterling-Sommer for Aston-Potter (USA) Ltd.

LITHOGRAPHED
Sheets of 160 in eight panes of 20

1995, Oct. 10 **Tagged** ***Perf. 10.9***

3001 A2314 32c **multicolored** .60 .20
P# block of 4, 5#+P 2.40 —
Pane of 20 12.00 —

LITERARY ARTS SERIES

Tennessee Williams (1911-83) A2315

Designed by Michael Deas. Printed by Sterling-Sommer for Ashton-Potter (USA) Ltd.

LITHOGRAPHED
Sheets of 160 in eight panes of 20

1995, Oct. 13 **Tagged** ***Perf. 11.1***

3002 A2315 32c **multicolored** .60 .20
P# block of 4, 5#+P 2.40 —
Pane of 20 12.00 —

CHRISTMAS

Madonna and Child, by Giotto di Bondone — A2316

Santa Claus Entering Chimney — A2317

Child Holding Jumping Jack — A2318

Child Holding Tree — A2319

Santa Claus Working on Sled — A2320

Midnight Angel — A2321

Children Sledding — A2322

Designed by Richard Sheaff (#3003), John Grossman & Laura Alders (#3004-3018).

Printed by Bureau of Engraving and Printing (#3003), Sterling-Sommer for Ashton-Potter (USA) Ltd. (#3004-3007), Avery Dennison (#3008-3011, 3013-3017), Banknote Corporation of America (#3012, 3018).

LITHOGRAPHED & ENGRAVED
Sheets of 300 in six panes of 50

1995 **Tagged** ***Perf. 11.2***

3003 A2316 32c **multicolored,** *Oct. 19* .60 .20
P# block of 4, 5# 3.00 —
c. Black (engr., denomination) omitted *250.00*

BOOKLET STAMP
Perf. 9.8x10.9

3003A A2316 32c **multicolored,** *Oct. 19* .65 .20
b. Booklet pane of 10 6.50 *4.00*

LITHOGRAPHED
Sheets of 200 in four panes of 50
Perf. 11.25

3004 A2317 32c **multicolored,** *Sept. 30* .60 .20
3005 A2318 32c **multicolored,** *Sept. 30* .60 .20
3006 A2319 32c **multicolored,** *Sept. 30* .60 .20
3007 A2320 32c **multicolored,** *Sept. 30* .60 .20
a. Block or strip of 4, #3004-3007 2.40 1.25
P# block of 4, 4#+P 3.00 —
b. Booklet pane of 10, 3 each #3004-3005, 2 each #3006-3007 6.00 *4.00*
c. Booklet pane of 10, 2 each #3004-3005, 3 each #3006-3007 6.00 *4.00*
d. As "a," imperf *600.00*

PHOTOGRAVURE
Self-Adhesive Stamps
Serpentine Die Cut 11.25 on 2, 3 or 4 sides

No.	Type	Description	Unused	Used
3008	A2320	32c **multicolored,** *Sept. 30*	.75	.20
3009	A2318	32c **multicolored,** *Sept. 30*	.75	.20
3010	A2317	32c **multicolored,** *Sept. 30*	.75	.20
3011	A2319	32c **multicolored,** *Sept. 30*	.75	.20
a.		Booklet pane of 20, 5 each #3008-3011 + label	15.00	

LITHOGRAPHED
Serpentine Die Cut 11.3x11.6 on 2, 3 or 4 sides

No.	Type	Description	Unused	Used
3012	A2321	32c **multicolored,** *Oct. 19*	.60	.20
a.		Booklet pane of 20 + label	12.00	
b.		Vert. pair, no die cutting between	—	
c.		Booklet pane of 15 + label, *1996*	9.00	
d.		Booklet pane of 15	—	

No. 3012a comes either with no die cutting in the label (1995 printing) or with the die cutting (and deeper colors) from the 1996 printing.

No. 3012d is a pane of 16 with one stamp removed. The missing stamp can be from either row 1, 2, 3, 7 or 8 of the pane. No. 3012d cannot be made from No. 3012c, a pane of 15 + label. The label is die cut. If the label is removed, an impression of the die cutting appears on the backing paper.

PHOTOGRAVURE
Die Cut

No.	Type	Description	Unused	Used
3013	A2322	32c **multicolored,** *Oct. 19*	.60	.20
a.		Booklet pane of 18	11.00	

Self-Adhesive Coil Stamps
Serpentine Die Cut 11.2 Vert.

No.	Type	Description	Unused	Used
3014	A2320	32c **multicolored,** *Sept. 30*	.60	.30
3015	A2318	32c **multicolored,** *Sept. 30*	.60	.30
3016	A2317	32c **multicolored,** *Sept. 30*	.60	.30
3017	A2319	32c **multicolored,** *Sept. 30*	.60	.30
a.		Strip of 4, #3014-3017	2.40	
		P# strip of 5, 1 each #3014-3017 + 1 stamp, P#V1111	8.00	
		P# strip of 8, 2 each #3014-3017, P#V1111	11.00	
		P# single (#3017), #V1111	—	3.00

LITHOGRAPHED
Serpentine Die Cut 11.6 Vert.

No.	Type	Description	Unused	Used
3018	A2321	32c **multicolored,** *Oct. 19*	.60	.30
		P# strip of 5, #B1111	6.25	
		P# single, #B1111	—	3.00

Nos. 3014-3018 were only available through the Philatelic Fullfillment Center in Kansas City.

Nos. 3005-3006 have "USA" printed in green. It is red on the self-adhesive stamps.

ANTIQUE AUTOMOBILES

1893 Duryea
A2323

1894 Haynes
A2324

1898 Columbia
A2325

1899 Winton
A2326

1901 White
A2327

Designed by Ken Dallison.
Printed by Stamp Venturers.

PHOTOGRAVURE
Sheets of 200 in eight panes of 25

1995, Nov. 3 **Tagged** ***Perf. 10.1x11.1***

No.	Type	Description	Unused	Used
3019	A2323	32c **multicolored**	.90	.20
3020	A2324	32c **multicolored**	.90	.20
3021	A2325	32c **multicolored**	.90	.20
3022	A2326	32c **multicolored**	.90	.20
3023	A2327	32c **multicolored**	.90	.20
a.		Vert. or horiz. strip of 5, #3019-3023	4.50	2.00
		Vert. or Horiz. P# block of 10, 2 sets of 4#+S	9.00	—
		Pane of 25	22.50	—

Vert. and horiz. strips are all in different order.

UTAH STATEHOOD CENTENARY

Delicate Arch, Arches Natl. Park — A2328

Designed by McRay Magleby.
Printed by Sterling Sommer for Ashton-Potter (USA) Ltd.

LITHOGRAPHED
Sheets of 200 in four panes of 50

1996, Jan. 4 **Tagged** ***Perf. 11.1***

No.	Type	Description	Unused	Used
3024	A2328	32c **multicolored**	.60	.20
		P# block of 4, 5#+P	3.00	—

For booklet see No. BK245.

GARDEN FLOWERS

Crocus — A2329

Winter Aconite — A2330

Pansy — A2331

Snowdrop — A2332

Anemone — A2333

Designed by Ned Seidler.

LITHOGRAPHED & ENGRAVED
BOOKLET STAMPS

1996, Jan. 19 **Tagged** ***Perf. 10.9 Vert.***

No.	Type	Description	Unused	Used
3025	A2329	32c **multicolored**	.60	.20
3026	A2330	32c **multicolored**	.60	.20
3027	A2331	32c **multicolored**	.60	.20
3028	A2332	32c **multicolored**	.60	.20
3029	A2333	32c **multicolored**	.60	.20
a.		Booklet pane of 5, #3025-3029	3.00	*2.50*
b.		As "a," imperf.	—	

LOVE

Cherub from Sistine Madonna, by Raphael — A2334

Designed by Terry McCaffrey.
Printed by Banknote Corporation of America.

LITHOGRAPHED & ENGRAVED
BOOKLET STAMP
Serpentine Die Cut 11.3x11.7

1996, Jan. 20 **Tagged**

Self-Adhesive

No.	Type	Description	Unused	Used
3030	A2334	32c **multicolored**	.60	.20
a.		Booklet pane of 20 + label	12.00	
b.		Booklet pane of 15 + label	9.00	
c.		Red (engr.) omitted	*325.00*	
d.		Red (engr.) missing (CM)	—	

No. 3030d must be collected se-tenant with a stamp bearing the red engraving.

FLORA AND FAUNA SERIES
Kestrel, Blue Jay and Rose Types of 1993-95 and

Red-headed Woodpecker A2335

Eastern Bluebird A2336

Red Fox — A2339

Ring-necked Pheasant — A2350

Coral Pink Rose — A2351

Designed by Michael Matherly (#3031-3033, 3044-3045); Terry McCaffrey (#3050-3051, 3055); Derry Noyes (#3036, 3052, 3052E).

Printed by Banknote Corporation of America (#3031A, 3036); Bureau of Engraving & Printing (#3031-3033, 3044-3045); Stamp Venturers (#3048-3049, 3053); Avery Dennison (#3050-3051A). American Packaging Corp. for Sennett Security Products (#3052); Sennett Security Products (#3052E).

LITHOGRAPHED
Sheets of 300 in six panes of 50 (#3031).
Sheets of 400 in eight panes of 50 (#3031A).
Sheets of 400 in four panes of 100 (#3032-3033).
Sheets of 120 in six panes of 20 (#3036).
Sheets of 200 in ten panes of 20 (#3036a)

1996-2002 Untagged *Serpentine Die Cut 10¾*
Self-Adhesive (#3031, 3031A)

3031 A1841 1c **multicolored,** *Nov. 19, 1999* .20 .20
P# block of 4, 4# or 4# + A .25

Serpentine Die Cut 11¼

3031A A1841 1c **multicolored,** *Oct. 2000* .20 .20
P# block of 4, 6# + B .20

No. 3031A has blue inscription and year.

Perf. 11

3032 A2335 2c **multicolored,** *Feb. 2* .20 .20
P# block of 4, 5# .25 —
3033 A2336 3c **multicolored,** *Apr. 3* .20 .20
P# block of 4, 5# .25 —

Some plate blocks contain plate position diagram.

Tagged
Serpentine Die Cut 11½x11¼
Self-Adhesive

3036 A2339 $1 **multicolored,** *Aug. 14, 1998* 2.00 .50
P# block of 4, 4#+B 8.00
Pane of 20 40.00
3036a Serpentine die cut 11¾x11, *2002* 2.00 .50
P# block of 4, 4#+B 8.00
Pane of 20 40.00

The tagging of No. 3036 has a bright yellow-green appearance under shortwave ultraviolet light while that of No. 3036a appears light blue green.

COIL STAMPS
Untagged
Perf. 9¾ Vert.

3044 A1841 1c **multicolored,** small date, *Jan. 20* .20 .20
Pair .20 .20
P# strip of 5, #1111 in black, yellow, blue, magenta order .60
P# single, same — .40
P# strip of 5, #1111 in black, blue, yellow, magenta order .95
P# single, same — .65
a. Large date .20 .20
Pair .20 .20
P# strip of 5, #1111, 2222, 3333, 4444 in yellow, magenta, blue, black order .85
P# single, same — .55

Date on No. 3044 is 1mm long, on No. 3044a 1.5mm long.

Tagged

3045 A2335 2c **multicolored,** *June 22, 1999* .20 .20
Pair .20 .20
P# strip of 5, #11111 .80 —
P# strip of 5, #22222 1.90
P# single, #11111 — .65
P# single, #22222 — .75

BOOKLET STAMPS
PHOTOGRAVURE
Serpentine Die Cut 10.4x10.8 on 3 Sides
1996-2000 Tagged
Self-Adhesive

3048 A1847 20c **multicolored,** *Aug. 2, 1996* .40 .20
a. Booklet pane of 10 4.00
b. Booklet pane of 4 1.60
c. Booklet pane of 6 2.40

Nos. 3048b-3048c are from the vending machine booklet No. BK237 that has a glue strip at the top edge of the top pane, the peelable strip removed and the rouletting line 2mm lower than on No. 3048a, when the panes are compared with bottoms aligned.

Serpentine Die Cut 11.3x11.7 on 2, 3 or 4 Sides

3049 A1853 32c **yellow, orange, green & black,** *Oct. 24, 1996* .60 .20
a. Booklet pane of 20 + label 12.00
b. Booklet pane of 4, *Dec. 1996* 2.75
c. Booklet pane of 5 + label, *Dec. 1996* 3.20
P# single, #S1111 .80 *1.00*
d. Booklet pane of 6, *Dec. 1996* 3.60
Booklet pane of 6 containing P# single 4.00
P# single, #S1111 .80 *1.00*

The plate # single in No. 3049c is on the lower left stamp. In No. 3049d it is the lower right stamp on the bottom pane of the booklet.

Serpentine Die Cut 11.2 on 3 Sides

3050 A2350 20c **multicolored,** *July 31, 1999* .40 .20
a. Booklet pane of 10, all stamps upright 4.00
b. Serpentine die cut 11 .40 .20
c. As "b," booklet pane of 10, all stamps upright 4.00

Serpentine Die Cut 10½x11 on 3 Sides

3051 A2350 20c **multicolored,** *July 1999* .60 .20

No. 3051 represents the eight upright stamps on the booklet panes Nos. 3051Ab and 3051Ac. The two stamps turned sideways on those panes are No. 3051A.

Specialists should note that 3051 can be either die cut 10.4 at top and 10.6 at bottom or 10.6 at top and 10.4 at bottom. These two varieties exist in equal numbers.

Serpentine Die Cut 10.6x10.4 on 3 Sides

3051A A2350 20c **multicolored,** 3.75 .50
b. Booklet pane of 5, 4 #3051, 1 #3051A turned sideways at top 6.00
c. Booklet pane of 5, 4 #3051, 1 #3051A turned sideways at bottom 6.00

Serpentine Die Cut 11½x11¼ on 2, 3 or 4 Sides

3052 A2351 33c **multicolored,** *Aug. 13, 1999* .80 .20
a. Booklet pane of 4 3.20
b. Booklet pane of 5 + label 4.00
c. Booklet pane of 6 4.80
d. Booklet pane of 20 + label 13.00
i. Imperf, pair —

Serpentine Die Cut 10¾x10½ on 2 or 3 sides

3052E A2351 33c **multicolored,** *Apr. 7, 2000* .65 .20
f. Booklet pane of 20 13.00
g. As "f," all 12 stamps on one side with black ("33 USA," etc.) omitted —
h. Horiz. pair, imperf between —

No. 3052Ef is a double-sided booklet pane with 12 stamps on one side and 8 stamps plus label on the other side.

COIL STAMPS
Serpentine Die Cut 11½ Vert.

3053 A1847 20c **multicolored,** *Aug. 2, 1996* .40 .20
Pair .80
P# strip of 5, #S1111 3.25
P# single, #S1111 — 2.00

Yellow Rose, Ring-necked Pheasant Types of 1996-98

Printed by Bureau of Engraving and Printing (#3054-3055).

COIL STAMPS
LITHOGRAPHED

1997-98 Tagged *Serpentine Die Cut 9¾ Vert.*
Self-Adhesive

3054 A1853 32c **yellow, magenta, black & green,** *Aug. 1, 1997* .60 .20
Pair 1.25
P# strip of 5, #2222, 2223, 2333, 3344, 4455, 5455, 5555, 5556, 5566, 5666, 6666 5.25
P# strip of 5, #2233, 3444, 6677, 6777 6.75
P# strip of 5, #7777, 8888 5.75
P# single, #1111, 1112, 1122, 4445, 5555, 5556, 5566, 5666, 6666, 7777 — 2.00
P# single, #2222, 2333 — 2.50
P# single, #2223, 8888 — 2.75
P# single, #2233, 3444 — 3.75
P# single, #3344, 5455, 6677 — 3.50
P# single, #6777 — 5.50
a. Imperf., pair *90.00*
b. Black, yellow & green omitted —
c. Black, yellow & green omitted, imperf. pair —
d. Black omitted —
e. Black omitted, imperf. pair —
f. All colors omitted, imperf. —

Nos. 3054b and 3054d also are miscut and with shifted die cuttings.

No. 3054f must be collected se-tenant with a partially printed stamp(s).

3055 A2350 20c **multicolored,** *July, 31, 1998* .40 .20
Pair .80
P# strip of 5, P#1111, 2222 3.50
P# single, same — 2.25
a. Imperf., pair *200.00*

BLACK HERITAGE SERIES

Ernest E. Just (1883-1941), Marine Biologist — A2358

Designed by Richard Sheaff.
Printed by Banknote Corporation of America.

LITHOGRAPHED
Sheets of 160 in eight panes of 20

1996, Feb. 1 Tagged *Perf. 11.1*

3058 A2358 32c **gray & black** .60 .20
P# block of 4, 4#+B 2.40 —
Pane of 20 12.00 —

SMITHSONIAN INSTITUTION, 150TH ANNIVERSARY

A2359

Designed by Tom Engeman.
Printed by Ashton-Potter (USA) Ltd.

LITHOGRAPHED
Sheets of 160 in eight panes of 20

1996, Feb. 7 Tagged *Perf. 11.1*

3059 A2359 32c **multicolored** .60 .20
P# block of 4, 4#+P 2.40 —
Pane of 20 12.00 —

CHINESE NEW YEAR

Year of the Rat — A2360

Designed by Clarence Lee.
Printed by Stamp Venturers.

PHOTOGRAVURE
Sheets of 180 in nine panes of 20

1996, Feb. 8 Tagged *Perf. 11.1*

3060 A2360 32c **multicolored** .60 .20
P# block of 4, 4#+S 3.00 —
Pane of 20 12.75 —
a. Imperf., pair —

PIONEERS OF COMMUNICATION

Eadweard Muybridge (1830-1904), Photographer A2361

Ottmar Mergenthaler (1854-99), Inventor of Linotype A2362

Frederic E. Ives (1856-1937), Developer of Halftone Process A2363

William Dickson (1860-1935), Co-developer of Kinetoscope A2364

Designed by Fred Otnes.
Printed by Ashton-Potter USA.

LITHOGRAPHED
Sheets of 120 in six panes of 20

1996, Feb. 22	**Tagged**	***Perf. 11.1x11***	
3061 A2361 32c **multicolored**		.60	.20
3062 A2362 32c **multicolored**		.60	.20
3063 A2363 32c **multicolored**		.60	.20
3064 A2364 32c **multicolored**		.60	.20
a. Block or strip of 4, #3061-3064		2.40	2.00
P# block of 4, 5#+P		2.40	—
Pane of 20		12.00	—

FULBRIGHT SCHOLARSHIPS, 50th ANNIVERSARY

A2365

Designed by Richard D. Sheaff.

LITHOGRAPHED & ENGRAVED
Sheets of 200 in four panes of 50

1996, Feb. 28	**Tagged**	***Perf. 11.1***	
3065 A2365 32c **multicolored**		.60	.20
P# block of 4, 5#		3.00	—

For booklet see No. BK246.

JACQUELINE COCHRAN (1910-80), PILOT

A2366

Designed by Davis Meltzer.

LITHOGRAPHED & ENGRAVED
Sheets of 300 in six panes of 50

1996, Mar. 9	**Tagged**	***Perf. 11.1***	
3066 A2366 50c **multicolored**		1.00	.20
P# block of 4, 5#		5.00	—
a. Black (engr.) omitted		*60.00*	

MARATHON

A2367

Designed by Michael Bartalos.

Printed by Banknote Corporation of America.

LITHOGRAPHED
Sheets of 160 in eight panes of 20

1996, Apr. 11	**Tagged**	***Perf. 11.1***	
3067 A2367 32c **multicolored**		.60	.20
P# block of 4, 4#+B		2.40	—
Pane of 20		12.00	—

1996 SUMMER OLYMPIC GAMES

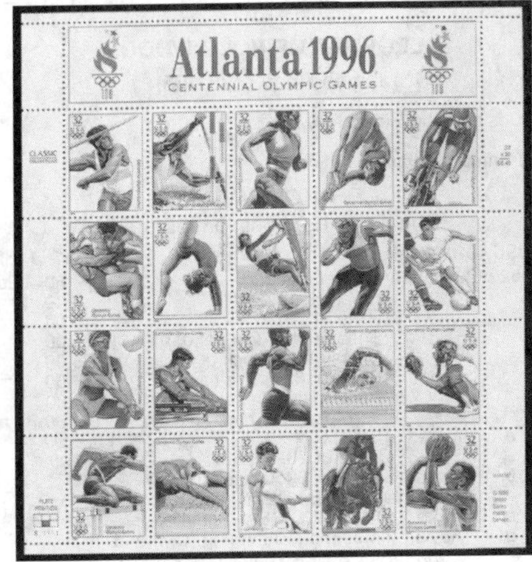

A2368

Illustration reduced.

Designed by Richard Waldrep. Printed by Stamp Venturers.

Designs: a, Decathlon (javelin). b, Men's canoeing. c, Women's running. d, Women's diving. e, Men's cycling. f, Freestyle wrestling. g, Women's gymnastics. h, Women's sailboarding. i, Men's shot put. j, Women's soccer. k, Beach volleyball. l, Men's rowing. m, Men's sprints. n, Women's swimming. o, Women's softball. p, Men's hurdles. q, Men's swimming. r, Men's gymnastics (pommel horse). s, Equestrian. t, Men's basketball.

PHOTOGRAVURE
Sheets of 120 in six panes of 20

1996, May 2	**Tagged**	***Perf. 10.1***	
3068 A2368 Pane of 20		12.00	—
a.-t. 32c any single		.60	.20
Sheet of 120 (6 panes)		120.00	
Cross gutter block of 20		45.00	—
Vert. pairs with horiz. gutter (each)		4.00	—
Horiz. pairs with vert. gutter (each)		4.00	—
u. As No. 3068, imperf		*1,250.*	
v. As No. 3068, back inscriptions omitted on a., f., k. & p., incorrect back inscriptions on others		—	

Inscription on back of each stamp describes the sport shown.
Cross gutter block of 20 consists of six stamps from each of two panes and four stamps from each of two other panes with the cross gutter between.

GEORGIA O'KEEFFE (1887-1986)

A2369

Designed by Margaret Bauer. Printed by Stamp Venturers.

PHOTOGRAVURE
Sheets of 90 in six panes of 15

1996, May 23	**Tagged**	***Perf. 11.6x11.4***	
3069 A2369 32c **multicolored**		.65	.20
P# block of 4, 5#+S		3.00	—
Pane of 15		10.50	—
a. Imperf., pair		*175.00*	
Pane of 15, imperf.		*1,250.*	—

For booklet see No. BK247.

TENNESSEE STATEHOOD BICENTENNIAL

A2370

Designed by Phil Jordan. Printed by Stamp Venturers.

PHOTOGRAVURE
Sheets of 200 in four panes of 50.

1996, May 31	**Tagged**	***Perf. 11.1***	
3070 A2370 32c **multicolored**		.60	.20
P# block of 4, 5#+S		3.00	—

For booklet see No. BK248.

Booklet Stamp
Self-Adhesive
Serpentine Die Cut 9.9x10.8

3071 A2370 32c **multicolored**		.70	.30
a. Booklet pane of 20, #S11111		14.00	
b. Horiz. pair, no die cutting btwn.		—	
c. Imperf., pair		—	
d. Horiz. pair, imperf vert.		—	

AMERICAN INDIAN DANCES

Fancy — A2371

Butterfly — A2372

Traditional — A2373

Raven — A2374

Hoop — A2375

Designed by Keith Birdsong. Printed by Ashton-Potter (USA) Ltd.

LITHOGRAPHED
Sheets of 120 in six panes of 20.

1996, June 7 Tagged *Perf. 11.1*

3072	A2371	32c	**multicolored**	.60	.20
3073	A2372	32c	**multicolored**	.60	.20
3074	A2373	32c	**multicolored**	.60	.20
3075	A2374	32c	**multicolored**	.60	.20
3076	A2375	32c	**multicolored**	.60	.20
a.			Strip of 5, #3072-3076	3.00	2.00
			P# block of 10, 4#+P	6.00	—
			Pane of 20	12.00	—

For booklet see No. BK249.

PREHISTORIC ANIMALS

Eohippus A2376

Woolly Mammoth A2377

Mastodon A2378

Saber-tooth Cat — A2379

Designed by Davis Meltzer. Printed by Ashton-Potter (USA) Ltd.

LITHOGRAPHED
Sheets of 120 in six panes of 20

1996, June 8 Tagged *Perf. 11.1x11*

3077	A2376	32c	**multicolored**	.60	.20
3078	A2377	32c	**multicolored**	.60	.20
3079	A2378	32c	**multicolored**	.60	.20
3080	A2379	32c	**multicolored**	.60	.20
a.			Block or strip of 4, #3077-3080	2.40	1.50
			P# block of 4, 4#+P	2.40	—
			Pane of 20	12.00	—

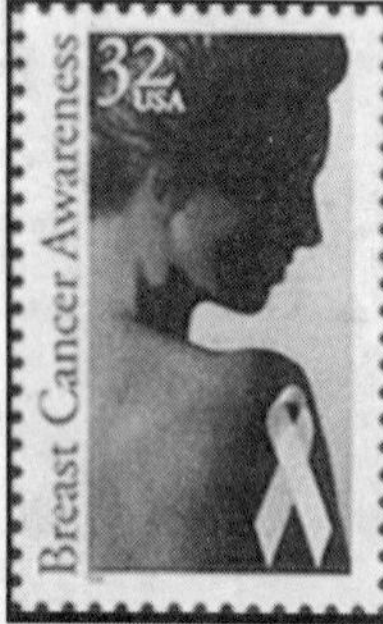

A2380

A2381

BREAST CANCER AWARENESS

Designed by Tom Mann. Printed by Ashton-Potter (USA) Ltd.

LITHOGRAPHED
Sheets of 120 in six panes of 20

1996, June 15 Tagged *Perf. 11.1*

3081	A2380	32c	**multicolored**	.60	.20
			P# block of 4, 5#+P	2.40	—
			Pane of 20	12.00	—

LEGENDS OF HOLLYWOOD

James Dean (1931-55)

Designed by Michael Deas.

Printed by Stamp Venturers.

PHOTOGRAVURE
Sheets of 120 in six panes of 20.

1996, June 24 Tagged *Perf. 11.1*

3082	A2381	32c	**multicolored**	.60	.20
			P# block of 4, 7#+S	3.00	—
			Pane of 20	15.00	—
			Sheet of 120 (six panes)	75.00	
			Cross gutter block of 8	25.00	—
			Block of 8 with vertical gutter	17.50	—
			Horiz. pair with vert. gutter	4.00	—
			Vert. pair with horiz. gutter	2.50	—
a.			Imperf., pair	*325.00*	
			Pane of 20, imperf.	*3,500.*	—
b.			As "a," red (USA 32c) missing (CM) and tan (JAMES DEAN) omitted		—
c.			As "a," tan (JAMES DEAN) omitted		—
d.			As "a," top stamp red missing (CM) and tan (JAMES DEAN) omitted, bottom stamp tan omitted		—

Perforations in corner of each stamp are star-shaped. No. 3082 was also available on the first day of issue in at least 127 Warner Bros. Studio stores.

Cross-gutter block consists of 3 stamps vertically from 2 upper panes and 1 stamp each from 2 lower panes.

For booklet see No. BK250.

Nos. 3082b-3082d come from the same error pane. The top row is No. 3082b; rows 2-4 are No. 3082c. No. 3082d is a vertical pair with one stamp from No. 3082b at top and one stamp from No. 3082c at bottom.

FOLK HEROES

A2382

A2383

A2384

A2385

Designed by David LaFleur.

Printed by Ashton-Potter (USA) Ltd.

LITHOGRAPHED
Sheets of 120 in six panes of 20

1996, July 11 Tagged *Perf. 11.1x11*

3083	A2382	32c	**multicolored**	.60	.20
3084	A2383	32c	**multicolored**	.60	.20
3085	A2384	32c	**multicolored**	.60	.20
3086	A2385	32c	**multicolored**	.60	.20
a.			Block or strip of 4, #3083-3086	2.40	2.00
			P# block of 4, 4#+P	2.40	—
			Pane of 20	12.00	—

For booklet see No. BK251.

Myron's Discobolus — A2386

Young Corn, by Grant Wood — A2387

CENTENNIAL OLYMPIC GAMES

Designed by Carl Herrman.

Printed by Ashton-Potter (USA) Ltd.

ENGRAVED
Sheets of 80 in four panes of 20

1996, July 19 Tagged *Perf. 11.1*

3087	A2386	32c	**brown**	.65	.20
			P# block of 4, 1#+P	4.00	—
			Pane of 20	18.50	—

Sheet margin of the pane of 20 is lithographed.

For booklet see No. BK252.

IOWA STATEHOOD, 150TH ANNIVERSARY

Designed by Carl Herrman.

Printed by Ashton-Potter (USA) Ltd. (#3088), Banknote Corporation of America (#3089)

LITHOGRAPHED
Sheets of 200 in four panes of 50

1996, Aug. 1 Tagged *Perf. 11.1*

3088	A2387	32c	**multicolored**	.60	.20
			P# block of 4, 4#+P	3.00	—

For booklet see No. BK253.

BOOKLET STAMP
Self-Adhesive
Serpentine Die Cut 11.6x11.4

3089	A2387	32c	**multicolored**	.70	.30
a.			Booklet pane of 20	14.00	

RURAL FREE DELIVERY, CENT.

A2388

Designed by Richard Sheaff.

LITHOGRAPHED & ENGRAVED
Sheets of 120 in six panes of 20

1996, Aug. 7 Tagged *Perf. 11.2x11*

3090	A2388	32c	**multicolored**	.60	.20
			P# block of 4, 5#	2.40	—
			Pane of 20	12.00	—

For booklet see No. BK254.

RIVERBOATS

Robt. E. Lee — A2389

Sylvan Dell — A2390

Far West
A2391

Rebecca Everingham
A2392

Bailey Gatzert
A2393

Designed by Dean Ellis.

Printed by Avery Dennison.

PHOTOGRAVURE
Sheets of 200 in 10 panes of 20
Serpentine Die Cut 11x11.1

1996, Aug. 22 Tagged

Self-Adhesive

3091 A2389 32c **multicolored**	.60	.20
3092 A2390 32c **multicolored**	.60	.20
3093 A2391 32c **multicolored**	.60	.20
3094 A2392 32c **multicolored**	.60	.20
3095 A2393 32c **multicolored**	.60	.20
a. Vert. strip of 5, #3091-3095	3.00	
P# block of 10, 5#+V	6.00	
Pane of 20	12.00	
b. Strip of 5, #3091-3095, with special die cutting	*75.00*	*50.00*
P# block of 10, 5#+V	*140.00*	
Pane of 20	*280.00*	

The serpentine die cutting runs through the peelable backing to which Nos. 3091-3095 are affixed. No. 3095a exists with stamps in different sequences.

On the long side of each stamp in No. 3095b, the die cutting is missing 3 "perforations" between the stamps, one near each end and one in the middle. This allows a complete strip to be removed from the backing paper for use on a first day cover. No. 3095b was also used to make Souvenir Page No. 1215.

For booklet see No. BK255.

AMERICAN MUSIC SERIES
Big Band Leaders

Count Basie
A2394

Tommy & Jimmy Dorsey
A2395

Glenn Miller
A2396

Benny Goodman
A2397

Songwriters

Harold Arlen
A2398

Johnny Mercer
A2399

Dorothy Fields
A2400

Hoagy Carmichael
A2401

Designed by Bill Nelson (#3096-3099), Gregg Rudd (#3100-3103).

Printed by Ashton-Potter (USA) Ltd.

LITHOGRAPHED
Sheets of 120 in six panes of 20

1996, Sept. 11 Tagged *Perf. 11.1x11*

3096 A2394 32c **multicolored**	.60	.20
3097 A2395 32c **multicolored**	.60	.20
3098 A2396 32c **multicolored**	.60	.20
3099 A2397 32c **multicolored**	.60	.20
a. Block or strip of 4, #3096-3099	2.40	1.75
P# block of 4, 6#+P	3.00	—
P# block of 8, 2 sets of P# + top label	6.00	—
Pane of 20	13.50	—
3100 A2398 32c **multicolored**	.70	.20
3101 A2399 32c **multicolored**	.70	.20
3102 A2400 32c **multicolored**	.70	.20
3103 A2401 32c **multicolored**	.70	.20
a. Block or strip of 4, #3100-3103	2.80	1.75
P# block of 4, 6#+P	3.00	—
P# block of 8, 2 sets of P# + top label	5.75	—
Pane of 20	14.50	—

LITERARY ARTS SERIES

F. Scott Fitzgerald (1896-1940)
A2402

Designed by Michael Deas.

PHOTOGRAVURE
Sheets of 200 in four panes of 50

1996, Sept. 27 Tagged *Perf. 11.1*

3104 A2402 23c **multicolored**	.45	.20
P# block of 4, 4#	2.25	—

ENDANGERED SPECIES

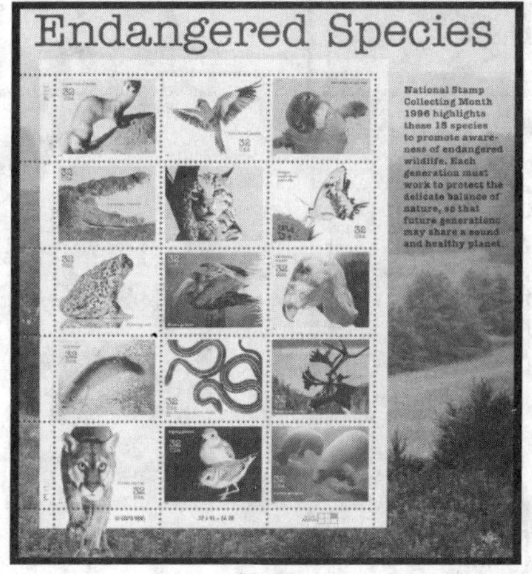

A2403

Illustration reduced.

Designed by James Balog. Printed by Ashton-Potter (USA) Ltd.

Designs: a, Black-footed ferret. b, Thick-billed parrot. c, Hawaiian monk seal. d, American crocodile. e, Ocelot. f, Schaus swallowtail butterfly. g, Wyoming toad. h, Brown pelican. i, California condor. j, Gila trout. k, San Francisco garter snake. l, Woodland caribou. m, Florida panther. n, Piping plover. o, Florida manatee.

LITHOGRAPHED
Sheets of 90 in six panes of 15

1996, Oct. 2 Tagged *Perf. 11.1x11*

3105 A2403 Pane of 15	9.00	—
a.-o. 32c any single	.60	.20

See Mexico No. 1995. For booklet see No. BK256.

COMPUTER TECHNOLOGY

A2404

Designed by Nancy Skolos & Tom Wedell.

Printed by Ashton-Potter (USA) Ltd.

LITHOGRAPHED & ENGRAVED
Sheets of 160 in four panes of 40

1996, Oct. 8 **Tagged** ***Perf. 10.9x11.1***

3106 A2404 32c **multicolored** .60 .20
P# block of 4, 6#+P 3.00 —

CHRISTMAS

Madonna and Child from Adoration of the Shepherds, by Paolo de Matteis — A2405

Family at Fireplace — A2406

Decorating Tree — A2407

Dreaming of Santa Claus — A2408

Holiday Shopping — A2409

Skaters — A2410

Designed by Richard D. Sheaff (#3107, 3112), Julia Talcott (#3108-3111, 3113-3117).

Printed by Bureau of Engraving and Printing (#3107, 3112), Ashton-Potter (USA) Ltd. (#3108-3111), Banknote Corporation of America (#3113-3116), Avery-Dennison (#3117).

LITHOGRAPHED & ENGRAVED
Sheets of 300 in six panes of 50

1996 **Tagged** ***Perf. 11.1x11.2***

3107 A2405 32c **multicolored,** *Nov. 1* .60 .20
P# block of 4, 5# 3.00 —

For booklet see No. BK257.

LITHOGRAPHED
Perf. 11.3

3108 A2406 32c **multicolored,** *Oct. 8* .60 .20
3109 A2407 32c **multicolored,** *Oct. 8* .60 .20
3110 A2408 32c **multicolored,** *Oct. 8* .60 .20
3111 A2409 32c **multicolored,** *Oct. 8* .60 .20
a. Block or strip of 4, #3108-3111 2.40 1.75
P# block of 4, 4#+P 3.00 —
b. Strip of 4, #3110-3111, 3108-3109, with #3109 imperf., #3108 imperf. at right —

BOOKLET STAMPS
Self-Adhesive

LITHOGRAPHED & ENGRAVED
Serpentine Die Cut 10 on 2, 3 or 4 Sides

3112 A2405 32c **multicolored,** *Nov. 1* .60 .20
a. Booklet pane of 20 + label 12.00
b. No die cutting, pair *70.00*
c. As "a," no die cutting —

LITHOGRAPHED
Serpentine Die Cut 11.8x11.5 on 2, 3 or 4 Sides

3113 A2406 32c **multicolored,** *Oct. 8* .60 .20
3114 A2407 32c **multicolored,** *Oct. 8* .60 .20
3115 A2408 32c **multicolored,** *Oct. 8* .60 .20
3116 A2409 32c **multicolored,** *Oct. 8* .60 .20
a. Booklet pane of 20, 5 ea #3113-3116 12.00
b. As "a," no die cutting *3,000.*

PHOTOGRAVURE
Die Cut

3117 A2410 32c **multicolored,** *Oct. 8* .60 .20
a. Booklet pane of 18 11.00

HANUKKAH

A2411

Designed by Hannah Smotrich.

Printed by Avery Dennison.

PHOTOGRAVURE
Sheets of 200 in 10 panes of 20

1996, Oct. 22 **Tagged** ***Serpentine Die Cut 11.1***
Self-Adhesive

3118 A2411 32c **multicolored** .60 .20
P# block of 4, 5#+V 2.40
Pane of 20 12.00

Backing on No. 3118 is die cut with a continuous horizontal wavy line. The 1997 reprint is die cut with two short horizontal lines on each side of a semi-circle on the backing of each stamp.

See No. 3352, Israel No. 1289. For booklet see No. BK258.

CYCLING
Souvenir Sheet

A2412

Illustration reduced.

Designed by McRay Magleby.

Printed by Stamp Venturers.

PHOTOGRAVURE

1996, Nov. 1 **Tagged** ***Perf. 11x11.1***

3119 A2412 Sheet of 2 2.00 2.00
a. 50c orange & multi 1.00 1.00
b. 50c blue green & multi 1.00 1.00

CHINESE NEW YEAR

Year of the Ox — A2413

Designed by Clarence Lee.

Printed by Stamp Venturers.

PHOTOGRAVURE
Sheets of 180 in 9 panes of 20

1997, Jan. 5 **Tagged** ***Perf. 11.2***

3120 A2413 32c **multicolored** .60 .20
P# block of 4, 4#+S 2.40 —
Pane of 20 12.00 —

BLACK HERITAGE SERIES

Brig. Gen. Benjamin O. Davis, Sr. (1880-1970) — A2414

Designed by Richard Sheaff.

Printed by Banknote Corp. of America.

LITHOGRAPHED
Sheets of 120 in six panes of 20

1997, Jan. 28 **Tagged** ***Serpentine Die Cut 11.4***
Self-Adhesive

3121 A2414 32c **multicolored** .60 .20
P# block of 4, 4#+B 2.40
Pane of 20 12.00

Statue of Liberty Type of 1994

Printed by Avery-Dennison.

PHOTOGRAVURE
Serpentine Die Cut 11 on 2, 3 or 4 Sides

1997, Feb. 1 **Tagged**
Self-Adhesive

3122 A1951 32c **red, light blue, dark blue & yellow** .60 .20
a. Booklet pane of 20 + label 12.00
b. Booklet pane of 4 2.50
c. Booklet pane of 5 + label 3.20
P# single, #V1111 .80 *1.00*
d. Booklet pane of 6 3.60
Booklet pane of 6 containing P# single 4.00
P# single, #V1111 .80 *1.00*
h. As "a," no die cutting —

The plate # single in No. 3122c is the lower left stamp and should be collected unused with the reorder label to its right to differentiate it from the plate # single in No. 3122d which is the lower left stamp in the bottom pane of the booklet and should be collected with a normal stamp adjoining it at right. In used condition, these plate # singles are indistinguishable.

Serpentine Die Cut 11.5x11.8 on 2, 3 or 4 Sides

1997 **Tagged**
Self-Adhesive

3122E A1951 32c **red, light blue, dark blue & yellow** 1.10 .20
f. Booklet pane of 20 + label 35.00
g. Booklet pane of 6 7.00
Booklet pane of 6 containing P# single 8.00
P# single, #V1111 2.00 2.00

The plate # single in No. 3122Eg is the lower left stamp in the bottom pane of the booklet.

LOVE

Swans
A2415 A2416

Designed by Marvin Mattelson.

Printed by Banknote Corp. of America.

LITHOGRAPHED
Serpentine Die Cut 11.8x11.6 on 2, 3 or 4 Sides

1997, Feb. 4 **Tagged**
Self-Adhesive

3123 A2415 32c **multicolored** .60 .20
a. Booklet pane of 20 + label 12.00
b. No die cutting, pair *175.00*
c. As "a," no die cutting *1,750.*
d. As "a," black omitted —

Serpentine Die Cut 11.6x11.8 on 2, 3 or 4 Sides

3124 A2416 55c **multicolored** 1.00 .20
a. Booklet pane of 20 + label 21.00

HELPING CHILDREN LEARN

A2417

Designed by Chris Van Allsburg.

Printed by Avery-Dennison.

PHOTOGRAVURE
Sheets of 160 in eight panes of 20
Serpentine Die Cut 11.6x11.7

1997, Feb. 18 **Tagged**

Self-Adhesive

3125 A2417 32c **multicolored**	.60	.20
P# block of 4, 4#+V	2.40	
Pane of 20	12.00	

The die cut perforations of #3125 are fragile and separate easily.

MERIAN BOTANICAL PRINTS

Citron, Moth, Larvae, Pupa, Beetle
A2418

Flowering Pineapple, Cockroaches
A2419

No. 3128 (r), No. 3129 (l), No. 3128a below

Designed by Phil Jordan based on works by Maria Sibylla Merian (1647-1717).

Printed by Stamp Venturers.

PHOTOGRAVURE
Serpentine Die Cut 10.9x10.2 on 2, 3 or 4 Sides

1997, Mar. 3 **Tagged**

Self-Adhesive

3126 A2418 32c **multicolored**	.60	.20
3127 A2419 32c **multicolored**	.60	.20
a. Booklet pane, 10 ea #3126-3127 + label	12.00	
b. Pair, #3126-3127	1.20	
c. Vert. pair, imperf between	*475.00*	

Size: 18.5x24mm

Serpentine Die Cut 11.2x10.8 on 2 or 3 Sides

3128 A2418 32c **multicolored**	1.25	.20
a. See footnote	2.50	.75
b. Booklet pane, 2 ea #3128-3129, 1 #3128a	7.50	
3129 A2419 32c **multicolored**	1.00	.20
a. See footnote	2.00	.65
b. Booklet pane, 2 ea #3128-3129, 1 #3129a	6.00	
c. Pair, #3128-3129	2.25	

Nos. 3128a-3129a are placed sideways on the pane and are serpentine die cut 11.2 on top and bottom, 10.8 on left side. The right side is 11.2 broken by a large perf where the stamp meets the vertical perforations of the two stamps above it. See illustration above.

PACIFIC 97

Sailing Ship — A2420

Stagecoach — A2421

Designed by Richard Sheaff.

Printed by Banknote Corporation of America.

ENGRAVED
Sheets of 96 in six panes of 16

1997, Mar. 13 **Tagged** ***Perf. 11.2***

3130 A2420 32c **blue**	.60	.20
3131 A2421 32c **red**	.60	.20
a. Pair, #3130-3131	1.25	.60
P# block of 4, 1#+B	2.50	—
Pane of 16	10.00	—
Sheet of 96 (6 panes)	80.00	
Cross gutter block of 16 (8 #3131a)	30.00	—
Vert. pairs with horiz. gutter (each)	10.00	—
Horiz. pairs with vert. gutter (each)	5.00	—

Juke Box and Flag Over Porch Types of 1995

Designed by Bill Nelson (#3132), Dave LaFleur (#3133).

Printed by Stamp Venturers.

PHOTOGRAVURE
COIL STAMPS

1997, Mar. 14 **Untagged** ***Imperf.***

Self-Adhesive

3132 A2225 (25c) **bright orange red, bright yellow green & multi**	.60	.50
Pair	1.20	
P# strip of 5, #M11111	5.00	
P#, single, #M11111		2.50

Tagged

Serpentine Die Cut 9.9 Vert.

3133 A2212 32c **dark blue, tan, brown, red & light blue**	.60	.20
Pair	1.25	
P# strip of 5, #M11111	6.50	
P#, single, #M11111		3.25

Nos. 3132-3133 were issued without backing paper. No. 3132 has simulated perforations ending in black bars at the top and bottom edges of the stamp. Sky on No. 3133 shows color gradation at LR not on Nos. 2915A or 2915D, and it has blue "1996" at left bottom.

LITERARY ARTS SERIES

Thornton Wilder (1897-1975)
A2422

Designed by Phil Jordan.

Printed by Ashton-Potter (USA) Ltd.

LITHOGRAPHED
Sheets of 180 in nine panes of 20

1997, Apr. 17 **Tagged** ***Perf. 11.1***

3134 A2422 32c **multicolored**	.60	.20
P# block of 4, 4#+P	2.40	—
Pane of 20	12.00	—

RAOUL WALLENBERG (1912-47)

Wallenberg and Jewish Refugees
A2423

Designed by Howard Paine.

Printed by Sterling Sommer for Ashton-Potter (USA) Ltd.

LITHOGRAPHED
Sheets of 180 in nine panes of 20

1997, Apr. 24 **Tagged** ***Perf. 11.1***

3135 A2423 32c **multicolored**	.60	.20
P# block of 4, 4#+P	2.40	—
Pane of 20	12.00	—

DINOSAURS

A2424

Illustration reduced.

Designed by James Gurney.
Printed by Sterling Sommer for Ashton-Potter (USA) Ltd.

Designs: a, Ceratosaurus. b, Camptosaurus. c, Camarasaurus. d, Brachiosaurus. e, Goniopholis. f, Stegosaurus. g, Allosaurus. h, Opisthias. i, Edmontonia. j, Einiosaurus. k, Daspletosaurus. l, Palaeosaniwa. m, Corythosaurus. n, Ornithominus. o, Parasaurolophus.

LITHOGRAPHED

1997, May 1 **Tagged** ***Perf. 11x11.1***

3136 A2424 Sheet of 15	9.00	—
a.-o. 32c any single	.60	.20
p. As No. 3136, bottom 7 stamps imperf.	*6,500.*	
q. As No. 3136, top 8 stamps imperf	—	
r. As No. 3136, all colors and tagging missing (EP)	—	

No. 3136r resulted from double sheeting in the sheet-fed press. It is properly gummed and perforated.

BUGS BUNNY

A2425

Cross Gutter Block of 12

Illustration reduced.

Designed by Warner Bros.

Printed by Avery Dennison.

PHOTOGRAVURE

1997, May 22 Tagged *Serpentine Die Cut 11*
Self-Adhesive

3137	Pane of 10	6.00	
a.	A2425 32c single	.60	.20
b.	Booklet pane of 9 #3137a	5.40	
c.	Booklet pane of 1 #3137a	.60	
	Sheet of 60 (six panes) top	*350.00*	
	Sheet of 60 (six panes) bottom, with plate #	*625.00*	
	Pane of 10 from uncut press sheet	*60.00*	
	Pane of 10 with plate #	*350.00*	
	Cross gutter block of 9 or 10	*200.00*	
	Cross gutter block of 12	*250.00*	
	Vert. pair with horiz. gutter	*25.00*	
	Horiz. pair with vert. gutter	*50.00*	

Die cutting on #3137 does not extend through the backing paper.

Booklet pane of 10 with P# comes from bottom uncut sheet of 60.

Nos. 3137b-3137c and 3138b-3138c are separated by a vertical line of microperforations that are absent on the uncut sheet of 60.

The horiz. pair with vert. gutter consists of a stamp at the left, from No. 3137b, part of the illustration of Bugs Bunny, the small gutter between the panes, and a stamp at the right from the left row of 3137b. Some pairs may include the single stamp from No. 3137c in addition to the two stamps at the right and left.

3138	Pane of 10	*125.00*	
a.	A2425 32c single	*2.00*	
b.	Booklet pane of 9 #3138a	—	
c.	Booklet pane of 1, imperf.	—	

Die cutting on #3138b extends through the backing paper. Used examples of No. 3138a are identical to those of No. 3137a.

An untagged promotional piece similar to No. 3137c exists on the same backing paper as the booklet pane, with the same design image, but without Bugs' signature and the single stamp. Replacing the stamp is an enlarged "32 / USA" in the same style as used on the stamp. This promotional piece was not valid for postage.

PACIFIC 97

Franklin — A2426

Washington — A2427

Designed by Richard Sheaff. Selvage on Nos. 3139-3140 is lithographed.

LITHOGRAPHED & ENGRAVED

1997 Tagged *Perf. 10.5x10.4*

3139	Pane of 12, *May 29*	12.00	—
a.	A2426 50c single	1.00	.50
3140	Pane of 12, *May 30*	14.50	—
a.	A2427 60c single	1.20	.60

Nos. 3139-3140 were sold through June 8.

MARSHALL PLAN, 50TH ANNIV.

Gen. George C. Marshall, Map of Europe
A2428

Designed by Richard Sheaff.

Printed by Stevens Security Press for Ashton-Potter (USA) Ltd.

LITHOGRAPHED & ENGRAVED
Sheets of 120 in six panes of 20

1997, June 4 Tagged *Perf. 11.1*

3141	A2428 32c **multicolored**	.60	.20
	P# block of 4, 5#+P	2.40	—
	Pane of 20	12.00	—

CLASSIC AMERICAN AIRCRAFT

A2429

Illustration reduced.

Designed by Phil Jordan.

Printed by Stamp Venturers.

Designs: a, Mustang. b, Model B. c, Cub. d, Vega. e, Alpha. f, B-10. g, Corsair. h, Stratojet. i, GeeBee. j, Staggerwing. k, Flying Fortress. l, Stearman. m, Constellation. n, Lightning. o, Peashooter. p, Tri-Motor. q, DC-3. r, 314 Clipper. s, Jenny. t, Wildcat.

PHOTOGRAVURE
Sheets of 120 in six panes of 20

1997, July 19 Tagged *Perf. 10.1*

3142	A2429 Pane of 20	12.00	—
a.-t.	32c any single	.60	.20
	Sheet of 120 (6 panes)	72.50	
	Cross gutter block of 20	22.50	
	Vert. pairs with horiz. gutter (each)	2.25	—
	Horiz. pairs with vert. gutter (each)	2.25	—

Inscriptions on back of each stamp describe the airplane.

Cross gutter block of 20 consists of six stamps from each of two panes and four stamps from each of two other panes with the cross gutter between.

FOOTBALL COACHES

Bear Bryant
A2430

Pop Warner
A2431

Vince Lombardi
A2432

George Halas
A2433

Designed by Carl Herrman.

Printed by Sterling Sommer for Ashton-Potter (USA) Ltd.

LITHOGRAPHED
Sheets of 120 in six panes of 20

1997 Tagged *Perf. 11.2*

3143	A2430 32c **multicolored,** *July 25*	.60	.20
3144	A2431 32c **multicolored,** *July 25*	.60	.20
3145	A2432 32c **multicolored,** *July 25*	.60	.20
3146	A2433 32c **multicolored,** *July 25*	.60	.20
a.	Block or strip of 4, #3143-3146	2.40	—
	P# block of 4, 5#+P	2.40	1.75
	P# block of 8, 2 sets of P# + top label	4.80	—
	Pane of 20	12.00	

With Red Bar Above Coach's Name
Perf. 11

3147	A2432 32c **multicolored,** *Aug. 5*	.60	.30
	P# block of 4, 4#+P	3.00	—
	Pane of 20	14.50	—
3148	A2430 32c **multicolored,** *Aug. 7*	.60	.30
	P# block of 4, 4#+P	3.00	—
	Pane of 20	14.50	—
3149	A2431 32c **multicolored,** *Aug. 8*	.60	.30
	P# block of 4, 4#+P	3.00	—
	Pane of 20	14.50	—
3150	A2433 32c **multicolored,** *Aug. 16*	.60	.30
	P# block of 4, 4#+P	3.00	—
	Pane of 20	14.50	—

AMERICAN DOLLS

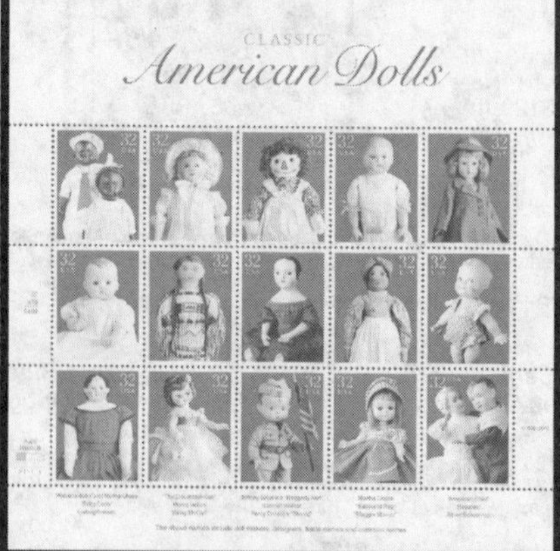

A2434

Illustration reduced.

Designed by Derry Noyes.

Printed by Sterling Sommer for Ashton-Potter (USA) Ltd.

Designs: a, "Alabama Baby," and doll by Martha Chase. b, "Columbian Doll." c, Johnny Gruelle's "Raggedy Ann." d, Doll by Martha Chase. e, "American Child." f, "Baby Coos." g, Plains Indian. h, Doll by Izannah Walker. i, "Babyland Rag." j, "Scootles." k, Doll by Ludwig Greiner. l, "Betsy McCall." m, Percy Crosby's "Skippy." n, "Maggie Mix-up." o, Dolls by Albert Schoenhut.

LITHOGRAPHED

Sheets of 90 in six panes of 15

1997, July 28	**Tagged**	***Perf. 10.9x11.1***	
3151 A2434	Pane of 15	12.50	—
a.-o.	32c any single	.80	.20

For booklet see No. BK266.

A2435

A2436

LEGENDS OF HOLLYWOOD

Humphrey Bogart (1899-1957).

Designed by Carl Herrman.

Printed by Stamp Venturers.

PHOTOGRAVURE

Sheets of 120 in six panes of 20

1997, July 31	**Tagged**	***Perf. 11.1***	
3152 A2435 32c	**multicolored**	.60	.20
	P# block of 4, 5#+S	2.50	—
	Pane of 20	12.50	—
	Sheet of 120 (6 panes)	75.00	—
	Cross gutter block of 8	17.50	—
	Block of 8 with vertical gutter	13.50	—
	Horiz. pair with vert. gutter	3.00	—
	Vert. pair with horiz. gutter	2.00	—

Perforations in corner of each stamp are star-shaped. Cross-gutter block consists of 6 stamps from upper panes and 2 stamps from panes below.

For booklet see No. BK267.

"THE STARS AND STRIPES FOREVER!"

Designed by Richard Sheaff.

Sheets of 300 in six panes of 50

PHOTOGRAVURE

1997, Aug. 21	**Tagged**	***Perf. 11.1***	
3153 A2436 32c	**multicolored**	.60	.20
	P# block of 4, 4#	3.00	—

For booklet see No. BK268.

AMERICAN MUSIC SERIES
Opera Singers

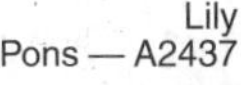

Lily Pons — A2437

Richard Tucker A2438

Lawrence Tibbett A2439

Rosa Ponselle A2440

Classical Composers & Conductors

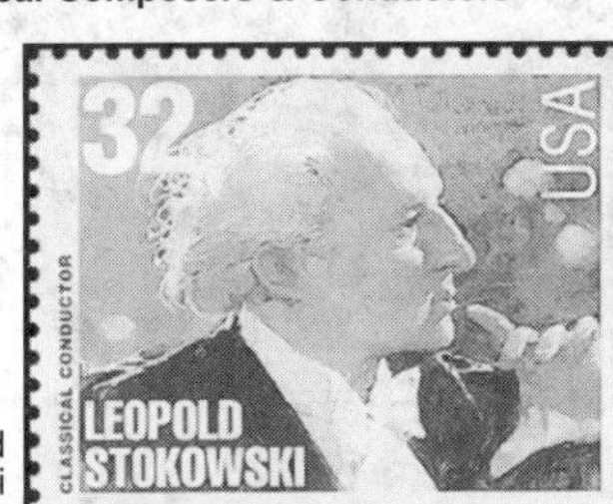

Leopold Stokowski A2441

Arthur Fiedler A2442

George Szell — A2443

Eugene Ormandy A2444

Samuel Barber A2445

Ferde Grofé A2446

Charles Ives — A2447

32 USA CLASSICAL COMPOSER LOUIS MOREAU GOTTSCHALK

Louis Moreau Gottschalk A2448

Designed by Howard Paine.

Printed by Ashton-Potter (USA) Ltd.

LITHOGRAPHED

Sheets of 120 in six panes of 20

1997	**Tagged**	***Perf. 11***	
3154 A2437 32c	**multicolored,** *Sept. 10*	.65	.20
3155 A2438 32c	**multicolored,** *Sept. 10*	.65	.20
3156 A2439 32c	**multicolored,** *Sept. 10*	.65	.20
3157 A2440 32c	**multicolored,** *Sept. 10*	.65	.20
a.	Block or strip of 4, #3154-3157	2.60	1.75
	P# block of 4, 5#+P	2.60	—
	P# block of 8, 2 sets of P# + top label	5.00	—
	Pane of 20	12.50	—
3158 A2441 32c	**multicolored,** *Sept. 12*	.65	.20
3159 A2442 32c	**multicolored,** *Sept. 12*	.65	.20
3160 A2443 32c	**multicolored,** *Sept. 12*	.65	.20
3161 A2444 32c	**multicolored,** *Sept. 12*	.65	.20
3162 A2445 32c	**multicolored,** *Sept. 12*	.65	.20
3163 A2446 32c	**multicolored,** *Sept. 12*	.65	.20
3164 A2447 32c	**multicolored,** *Sept. 12*	.65	.20
3165 A2448 32c	**multicolored,** *Sept. 12*	.65	.20
a.	Block of 8, #3158-3165	5.25	4.00
	P# block of 8, 2 sets of 5P#+P + top label	8.00	—
	Pane of 20	16.00	

PADRE FÉLIX VARELA (1788-1853)

A2449

Designed by Carl Herrman.

Printed by Sterling Sommer for Ashton-Potter (USA) Ltd.

LITHOGRAPHED

Sheets of 120 in six panes of 20

1997, Sept. 15	**Tagged**	***Perf. 11.2***	
3166 A2449 32c	**purple**	.60	.20
	P# block of 4, 1#+P	2.40	—
	Pane of 20	12.00	—

DEPARTMENT OF THE AIR FORCE, 50TH ANNIV.

Thunderbirds Aerial Demonstration Squadron
A2450

Designed by Phil Jordan.

Printed by Sterling Sommer for Ashton-Potter (USA) Ltd.

LITHOGRAPHED
Sheets of 180 in nine panes of 20

1997, Sept. 18 Tagged *Perf. 11.2x11.1*

3167 A2450 32c	**multicolored**	.60	.20
	P# block of 4, 4#+P	2.40	—
	Pane of 20	12.00	—

A hidden 3-D design can be seen on the stamp when it is viewed with a special viewer sold by the post office.

CLASSIC MOVIE MONSTERS

Lon Chaney as The Phantom of the Opera — A2451

Bela Lugosi as Dracula — A2452

Boris Karloff as Frankenstein's Monster — A2453

Boris Karloff as The Mummy — A2454

Lon Chaney, Jr. as The Wolf Man — A2455

Cross Gutter Block of 8

Designed by Derry Noyes.

Printed by Stamp Venturers.

PHOTOGRAVURE
Sheets of 180 in nine panes of 20

1997, Sept. 30 Tagged *Perf. 10.2*

3168 A2451 32c	**multicolored**	.60	.20
3169 A2452 32c	**multicolored**	.60	.20
3170 A2453 32c	**multicolored**	.60	.20
3171 A2454 32c	**multicolored**	.60	.20
3172 A2455 32c	**multicolored**	.60	.20
a.	Strip of 5, #3168-3172	3.00	2.25
	P# block of 10, 5#+S	6.00	—
	Pane of 20	12.00	—
	Sheet of 180 (9 panes)	100.00	
	Cross-gutter block of 8	15.00	
	Block of 10 with horiz. gutter	11.50	
	Vert. pairs with horiz. gutter (each)	2.25	—
	Horiz. pairs with vert. gutter (each)	2.25	—

Plate blocks may contain top label. See note after No. 3167.
For booklet see No. BK269.

FIRST SUPERSONIC FLIGHT, 50TH ANNIV.

A2456

Designed by Phil Jordan.

Printed by Banknote Corporation of America.

LITHOGRAPHED
Sheets of 180 in nine panes of 20

1997, Oct. 14 Tagged *Serpentine Die Cut 11.4*
Self-Adhesive

3173 A2456 32c	**multicolored**	.60	.20
	P# block of 4, 4#+B	2.40	
	Pane of 20	12.00	

WOMEN IN MILITARY SERVICE

A2457

Designed by Derry Noyes.

Printed by Banknote Corporation of America.

LITHOGRAPHED
Sheets of 120 in six panes of 20

1997, Oct. 18 Tagged *Perf. 11.1*

3174 A2457 32c	**multicolored**	.60	.20
	P# block of 4, 6#+B	2.40	—
	Pane of 20	12.00	

KWANZAA

A2458

Designed by Synthia Saint James. Printed by Avery Dennison.

PHOTOGRAVURE
Sheets of 250 in five panes of 50

1997, Oct. 22 Tagged *Serpentine Die Cut 11*
Self-Adhesive

3175 A2458 32c	**multicolored**	.60	.20
	P# block of 4, 4#+V	3.00	
	Sheet of 250 (5 panes)	*550.00*	
	P# block of 4, 4#+V and 4 sets of #+VO	*225.00*	
	Horiz. pair with vert. gutter	*11.00*	

See No. 3368.

CHRISTMAS

Madonna and Child, by Sano di Pietro — A2459

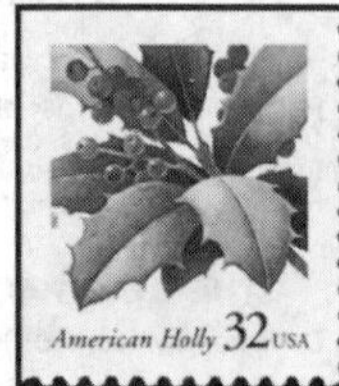

Holly — A2460

Designed by Richard D. Sheaff (#3176), Howard Paine (#3177).

Printed by Bureau of Engraving and Printing (#3176), Banknote Corporation of America (#3177).

LITHOGRAPHED
Serpentine Die Cut 9.9 on 2, 3 or 4 Sides
1997 Tagged
Booklet Stamps
Self-Adhesive

3176 A2459 32c	**multicolored,** *Oct. 27*	.60	.20
a.	Booklet pane of 20 + label	12.00	

Serpentine Die Cut 11.2x11.8 on 2, 3 or 4 Sides

3177 A2460 32c	**multicolored,** *Oct. 30*	.60	.20
a.	Booklet pane of 20 + label	12.00	
b.	Booklet pane of 4	2.50	
c.	Booklet pane of 5 + label	3.00	
d.	Booklet pane of 6	3.75	

MARS PATHFINDER
Souvenir Sheet

Mars Rover Sojourner — A2461

Illustration reduced.

Designed by Terry McCaffrey. Printed by Stamp Venturers.

PHOTOGRAVURE

1997, Dec. 10 Tagged ***Perf. 11x11.1***

3178 A2461 $3 **multicolored**	6.00	3.00
a. $3, single stamp	5.50	2.75
Sheet of 18	125.00	
Vert. pair with horiz. gutter	15.00	—
Single souvenir sheet from sheet of 18	7.00	—

The perforations at the bottom of the stamp contain the letters "USA." Vertical rouletting extends from the vertical perforations of the stamp to the bottom of the souvenir sheet.

Sheet of 18 has vertical perforations separating the three rows of souvenir sheets. These were cut away when No. 3178 was produced.

Souvenir sheet from sheet of 18 is wider and has vertical perforations on one or two sides.

See note after No. 3167.

CHINESE NEW YEAR

Year of the Tiger A2462

Designed by Clarence Lee. Printed by Stamp Venturers.

PHOTOGRAVURE

Sheets of 180 in nine panes of 20

1998, Jan. 5 Tagged ***Perf. 11.2***

3179 A2462 32c **multicolored**	.60	.20
P# block of 4, 4#+S	3.00	—
Pane of 20	14.25	

A2463

A2464

ALPINE SKIING

Designed by Michael Schwab.

Printed by Banknote Corporation of America.

LITHOGRAPHED

Sheets of 180 in nine panes of 20

1998, Jan. 22 Tagged ***Perf. 11.2***

3180 A2463 32c **multicolored**	.60	.20
P# block of 4, 6#+B	2.40	—
Pane of 20	12.00	

BLACK HERITAGE SERIES

Madam C.J. Walker (1867-1919), Entrepreneur

Designed by Richard Sheaff. Printed by Banknote Corp. of America.

LITHOGRAPHED

Sheets of 180 in nine panes of 20

Serpentine Die Cut 11.6x11.3

1998, Jan. 28 Tagged

Self-Adhesive

3181 A2464 32c **sepia & black**	.60	.20
P# block of 4, 3#+B	2.40	
Pane of 20	12.00	

CELEBRATE THE CENTURY

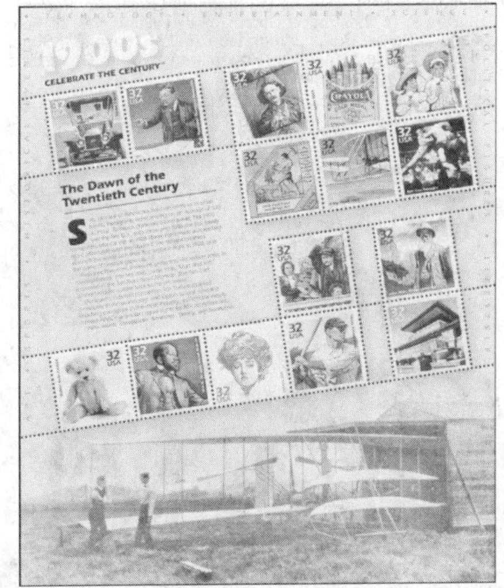

1900s — A2465

No. 3182: a, Model T Ford. b, Theodore Roosevelt. c, Motion picture "The Great Train Robbery," 1903. d, Crayola Crayons introduced, 1903. e, St. Louis World's Fair, 1904. f, Design used on Hunt's Remedy stamp (#RS56), Pure Food & Drug Act, 1906. g, Wright Brothers first flight, Kitty Hawk, 1903. h, Boxing match shown in painting "Stag at Sharkey's," by George Bellows of the Ash Can School. i, Immigrants arrive. j, John Muir, preservationist. k, "Teddy" Bear created. l, W.E.B. Du Bois, social activist. m, Gibson Girl. n, First baseball World Series, 1903. o, Robie House, Chicago, designed by Frank Lloyd Wright.

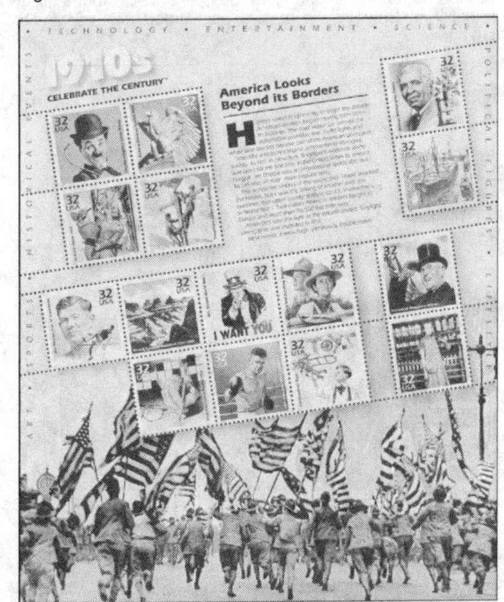

1910s — A2466

No. 3183: a, Charlie Chaplin as the Little Tramp. b, Federal Reserve System created, 1913. c, George Washington Carver. d, Avant-garde art introduced at Armory Show, 1913. e, First transcontinental telephone line, 1914. f, Panama Canal opens, 1914. g, Jim Thorpe wins decathlon at Stockholm Olympics, 1912. h, Grand Canyon National Park, 1919. i, U.S. enters World War I. j, Boy Scouts started in 1910, Girl Scouts formed in 1912. k, Woodrow Wilson. l, First crossword puzzle published, 1913. m, Jack Dempsey wins heavyweight title, 1919. n, Construction toys. o, Child labor reform.

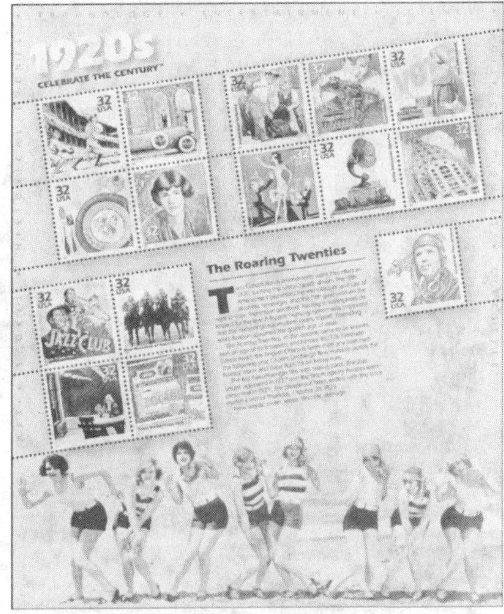

1920s — A2467

No. 3184: a, Babe Ruth. b, The Gatsby style. c, Prohibition enforced. d, Electric toy trains. e, 19th Amendment (woman voting). f, Emily Post's Etiquette. g, Margaret Mead, anthropologist. h, Flappers do the Charleston. i, Radio entertains America. j, Art Deco style (Chrysler Building). k, Jazz flourishes. l, Four Horsemen of Notre Dame. m, Lindbergh flies the Atlantic. n, American realism (The Automat, by Edward Hopper). o, Stock Market crash, 1929.

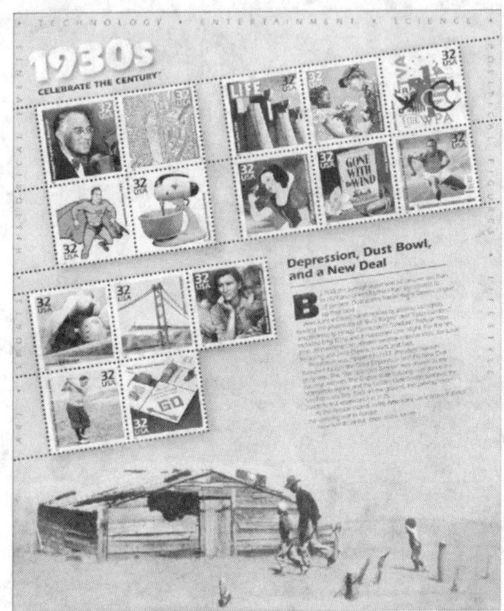

1930s — A2468

No. 3185: a, Franklin D. Roosevelt. b, The Empire State Building. c, 1st Issue of Life Magazine, 1936. d, Eleanor Roosevelt. e, FDR's New Deal. f, Superman arrives, 1938. g, Household conveniences. h, "Snow White and the Seven Dwarfs," 1937. i, "Gone with the Wind," 1936. j, Jesse Owens. k, Streamline design. l, Golden Gate Bridge. m, America survives the Depression. n, Bobby Jones wins golf Grand Slam, 1938. o, The Monopoly Game.

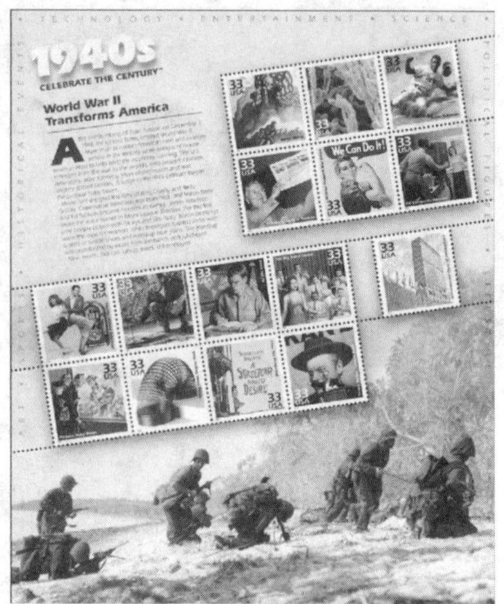

1940s — A2469

No. 3186: a, World War II. b, Antibiotics save lives. c, Jackie Robinson. d, Harry S Truman. e, Women support war effort. f, TV entertains America. g, Jitterbug sweeps nation. h, Jackson Pollock, Abstract Expressionism. i, GI Bill, 1944. j, Big Band Sound. k, Intl. style of architecture (UN Headquarters). l, Post-war baby boom. m, Slinky, 1945. n, "A Streecar Named Desire," 1947. o, Orson Welles' "Citizen Kane."

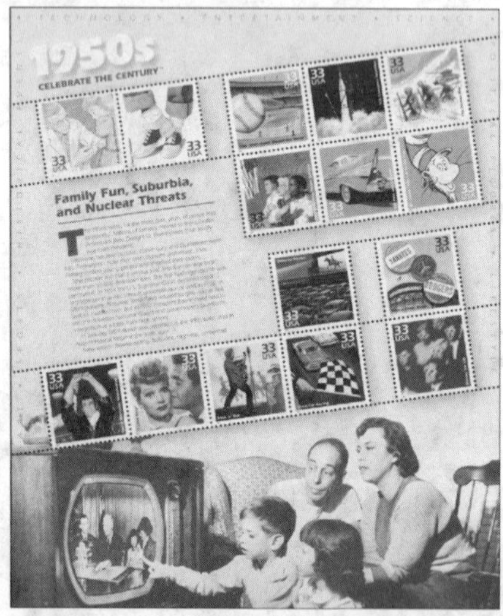

1950s — A2470

No. 3187: a, Polio vaccine developed. b, Teen fashions. c, The "Shot Heard 'Round the World." d, US launches satellites. e, Korean War. f, Desegregating public schools. g, Tail fins, chrome. h, Dr. Seuss' "The Cat in the Hat." i, Drive-in movies. j, World Series rivals. k, Rocky Marciano, undefeated boxer. l, "I Love Lucy." m, Rock 'n Roll. n, Stock car racing. o, Movies go 3-D.

1960s — A2471

No. 3188: a, Martin Luther King, Jr., "I Have a Dream." b, Woodstock. c, Man walks on the moon. d, Green Bay Packers. e, Star Trek. f, The Peace Corps. g, Viet Nam War. h, Ford Mustang. i, Barbie Doll. j, Integrated circuit. k, Lasers. l, Super Bowl I. m, Peace symbol. n, Roger Maris, 61 in '61. o, The Beatles "Yellow Submarine."

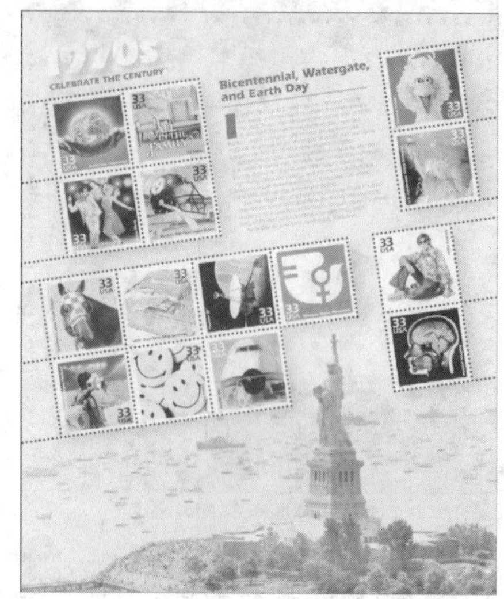

1970s — A2472

No. 3189: a, Earth Day celebrated. b, "All in the Family" television series. c, "Sesame Street" television series character, Big Bird. d, Disco music. e, Pittsburgh Steelers win four Super Bowls. f, US Celebrates 200th birthday. g, Secretariat wins Triple Crown. h, VCRs transform entertainment. i, Pioneer 10. j, Women's rights movement. k, 1970s fashions. l, "Monday Night Football." m, Smiley face buttons. n, Jumbo jets. o, Medical imaging.

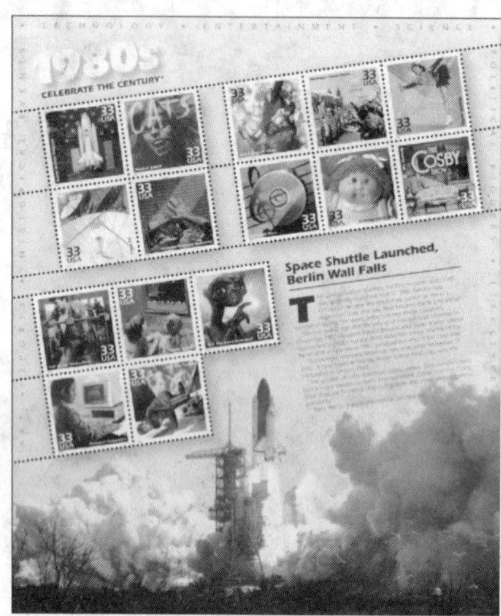

1980s — A2473

No. 3190: a, Space shuttle program. b, "Cats" Broadway show. c, San Francisco 49ers. d, Hostages in Iran come home. e, Figure skating. f, Cable TV. g, Vietnam Veterans Memorial. h, Compact discs. i, Cabbage Patch Kids. j, "The Cosby Show" television series. k, Fall of the Berlin Wall. l, Video games. m, "E. T. The Extra-Terrestrial" movie. n, Personal computers. o, Hip-hop culture.

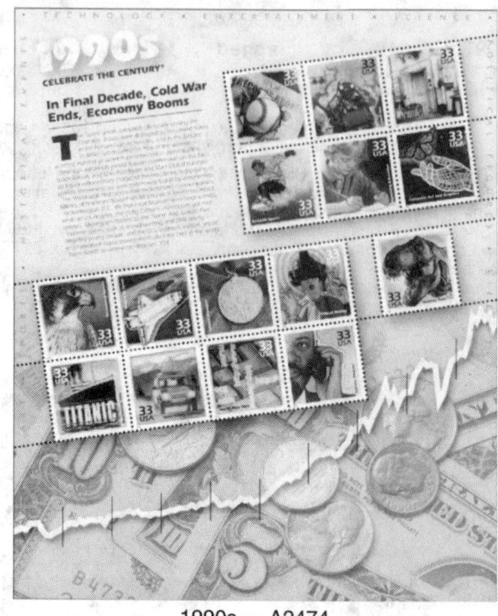

1990s — A2474

No. 3191: a, New baseball records. b, Gulf War. c, "Seinfeld" television series. d, Extreme sports. e, Improving education. f, Computer art and graphics. g, Recovering species. h, Return to space. i, Special Olympics. j, Virtual reality. k, Movie "Jurassic Park." l, Movie "Titanic." m, Sport utility vehicles. n, World Wide Web. o, Cellular phones.

Designed by Richard Waldrep (#3182), Dennis Lyall (#3183), Carl Herrman (#3184, 3188, 3190), Howard Paine (#3185-3187, 3189, 3191).

All illustrations reduced.

Printed by Ashton-Potter (USA) Ltd.

LITHOGRAPHED, ENGRAVED (#3182m, 3183f, 3184m, 3185b, 3186k, 3187a, 3188c, 3189h)

1998-2000		**Tagged**	***Perf. 11½***	
3182	A2465	Pane of 15, *Feb. 3, 1998*	9.00	—
a.-o.		32c any single	.60	.30
		Sheet of 4 panes	36.00	
p.		Engr. red (No. 3182m, Gibson girl) omitted, in pane of 15	—	
3183	A2466	Pane of 15, *Feb. 3, 1998*	9.00	—
a.-o.		32c any single	.60	.30
		Sheet of 4 panes	36.00	
p.		Nos. 3183g, 3183 l-3183o imperf, in pane of 15	—	
3184	A2467	Pane of 15, *May 28, 1998*	9.00	—
a.-o.		32c any single	.60	.30
		Sheet of 4 panes	36.00	
3185	A2468	Pane of 15, *Sept. 10, 1998*	9.00	—
a.-o.		32c any single	.60	.30
		Sheet of 4 panes	36.00	
3186	A2469	Pane of 15, *Feb. 18, 1999*	9.75	—
a.-o.		33c any single	.65	.30
		Sheet of 4 panes	40.00	
p.		Tagging omitted on b-j and m-o	—	
3187	A2470	Pane of 15, *May 26, 1999*	9.75	—
a.-o.		33c any single	.65	.30
		Sheet of 4 panes	40.00	
3188	A2471	Pane of 15, *Sept. 17, 1999*	9.75	—
a.-o.		33c any single	.65	.30
		Sheet of 4 panes	40.00	
3189	A2472	Pane of 15, *Nov. 18, 1999*	9.75	—
a.-o.		33c any single	.65	.30
		Sheet of 4 panes	40.00	
3190	A2473	Pane of 15, *Jan. 12, 2000*	9.75	—
a.-o.		33c any single	.65	.30
		Sheet of 4 panes	40.00	
3191	A2474	Pane of 15, *May 2, 2000*	9.75	—
a.-o.		33c any single	.65	.30
		Sheet of 4 panes	40.00	

"REMEMBER THE MAINE"

A2475

Designed by Richard Sheaff.

LITHOGRAPHED & ENGRAVED
Sheets of 120 in six panes of 20

1998, Feb. 15	**Tagged**	***Perf. 11.2x11***	
3192 A2475 32c **red & black**		.60	.20
P# block of 4, 2#		2.40	—
Pane of 20		12.00	

FLOWERING TREES

Southern Magnolia — A2476

Blue Paloverde — A2477

Yellow Poplar — A2478

Prairie Crab Apple — A2479

Pacific Dogwood — A2480

Designed by Howard Paine.

Printed by Banknote Corporation of America.

LITHOGRAPHED
Sheets of 120 in six panes of 20

1998, Mar. 19 **Tagged** ***Die Cut Perf 11.3***

Self-Adhesive

3193 A2476 32c **multicolored**	.60	.20
3194 A2477 32c **multicolored**	.60	.20
3195 A2478 32c **multicolored**	.60	.20
3196 A2479 32c **multicolored**	.60	.20
3197 A2480 32c **multicolored**	.60	.20
a. Strip of 5, #3193-3197	3.00	
P# block of 10, 2 sets of B+6#	6.00	
Pane of 20	12.00	
b. As "a," imperf	—	

ALEXANDER CALDER (1898-1976), SCULPTOR

Black Cascade, 13 Verticals, 1959 — A2481

Untitled, 1965 — A2482

Rearing Stallion, 1928 — A2483

Portrait of a Young Man, c. 1945 — A2484

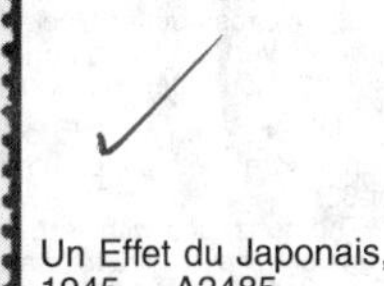

Un Effet du Japonais, 1945 — A2485

Designed by Derry Noyes. Printed by Stamp Venturers.

PHOTOGRAVURE
Sheets of 120 in six panes of 20

1998, Mar. 25 **Tagged** ***Perf. 10.2***

3198 A2481 32c **multicolored**	.60	.20
3199 A2482 32c **multicolored**	.60	.20
3200 A2483 32c **multicolored**	.60	.20
3201 A2484 32c **multicolored**	.60	.20
3202 A2485 32c **multicolored**	.60	.20
a. Strip of 5, #3198-3202	3.00	2.25
P# block of 10, 2 sets of S+6#	6.00	—
Pane of 20	12.00	—
Sheet of 120 (6 panes)	*110.00*	
Cross gutter block of 20	*37.50*	—
Block of 10 with horiz. gutter	*22.50*	—
Vert. pairs with horiz. gutter (each)	*4.00*	—
Horiz. pairs with vert. gutter (each)	*5.50*	—

Cross gutter block of 20 consists of six stamps from each of two panes and four stamps from each of two other panes with the cross gutter between. The sheet of 120 was quickly sold out.

A2486

CINCO DE MAYO

Designed by Carl Herrman.

Printed by Stamp Venturers.

PHOTOGRAVURE
Sheets of 180 in nine panes of 20
Serpentine Die Cut 11.7x10.9

1998, Apr. 16 **Tagged**

Self-Adhesive

3203 A2486 32c **multicolored**	.60	.20
P# block of 4, 5#+S	2.40	
Pane of 20	12.00	
Sheet of 180 (9 panes)	*110.00*	
Cross gutter block of 4	*12.50*	
Vert. pair with horiz. gutter	*2.00*	
Horiz. pair with vert. gutter	*2.00*	

See Mexico #2066. For 33c version, see #3309.

A2487

A2488

SYLVESTER & TWEETY

Designed by Brenda Guttman.

Printed by Avery Dennison.

PHOTOGRAVURE

1998, Apr. 27 Tagged *Serpentine Die Cut 11.1*

Self-Adhesive

3204	Pane of 10	6.00	
a.	A2487 32c single	.60	.20
b.	Booklet pane of 9 #3204a	5.40	
c.	Booklet pane of 1 #3204a	.60	
	Sheet of 60 (six panes) top	*65.00*	
	Sheet of 60 (six panes) bottom, with plate #	*100.00*	
	Pane of 10 from sheet of 60	*11.00*	
	Pane of 10 with plate #	*45.00*	
	Cross gutter block of 9 or 10	*40.00*	
	Cross gutter block of 12	*45.00*	
	Vert. pair with horiz. gutter	*6.00*	
	Horiz. pair with vert. gutter	*12.50*	

Die cutting on #3204b does not extend through the backing paper. Pane with plate number comes from bottom uncut sheet of 60.

The horiz. pair with vert. gutter consists of a stamp at the left from either No. 3204b, part of the illustration of Sylvester & Tweety, the small gutter between the panes, and a stamp at the right from the left row of No. 3204b. Some pairs may include the single stamp from No. 3204c in addition to the two stamps at the right and left.

3205	Pane of 10	*10.00*	
a.	A2487 32c single	*.60*	
b.	Booklet pane of 9 #3205a	—	
c.	Booklet pane of 1, imperf.	—	

Die cutting on #3205a extends through the backing paper. Used examples of No. 3205a are identical to those of No. 3204a.

Nos. 3204b-3204c and 3205b-3205c are separated by a vertical line of microperforations, which is absent on the uncut sheets of 60.

WISCONSIN STATEHOOD

Designed by Phil Jordan.

Printed by Sennett Security Products.

PHOTOGRAVURE

Sheets of 120 in six panes of 20

Serpentine Die Cut 10.8x10.9

1998, May 29 Tagged

Self-Adhesive

3206	A2488 32c	**multicolored**	.60	.30
		P# block of 4, 4#+S	2.40	
		Pane of 20	12.00	

See note after No. 3167.

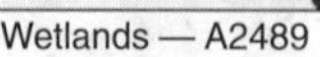

Wetlands — A2489 Diner — A2490

Designer by Phil Jordan (#3207-3207A), Carl Herrman (#3208, 308A).

Printed by Sennett Security Printers (#3207, 3208), Bureau of Engraving and Printing (#3207A, 3208A).

PHOTOGRAVURE

COIL STAMPS

1998 Untagged *Perf. 10 Vert.*

3207	A2489	(5c)	**multicolored,** *June 5*	.20	.20
			Pair	.20	.20
			P# strip of 5, #S1111	1.50	
			P#, single, #S1111		1.00

Serpentine Die Cut 9.8 Vert.

Self-adhesive

3207A	A2489	(5c)	**multicolored,** *Dec.14*	.20	.20
			Pair	.20	
			P# strip of 5, #1111, 2222, 3333, 4444, 5555, 6666	1.50	
			P# single, same		1.00

Perf. 10 Vert.

3208	A2490	(25c)	**multicolored,** *June 5*	.50	.50
			Pair	1.00	1.00
			P# strip of 5, #S11111	3.75	
			P#, single, #S11111		2.00

Serpentine Die Cut 9.8 Vert.

Self-Adhesive

3208A	A2490	(25c)	**multicolored,** *Sept. 30*	.50	.50
			Pair	1.00	
			P# strip of 5, #11111, 22211, 22222, 33333, 44444, 55555	4.00	
			P# single, same		2.00

1898 TRANS-MISSISSIPPI STAMPS, CENT.

A2491

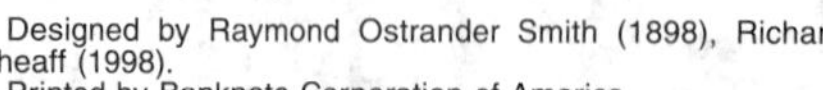

Illustration reduced.

Designed by Raymond Ostrander Smith (1898), Richard Sheaff (1998).

Printed by Banknote Corporation of America.

LITHOGRAPHED & ENGRAVED

Sheets of 54 in six panes of 9

1998, June 18 Tagged *Perf. 12x12.4*

3209	A2491	Pane of 9	7.75	5.00
a.	A100	1c green & black	.20	.20
b.	A108	2c red brown & black	.20	.20
c.	A102	4c orange & black	.20	.20
d.	A103	5c blue & black	.20	.20
e.	A104	8c dark lilac & black	.20	.20
f.	A105	10c purple & black	.20	.20
g.	A106	50c green & black	1.00	.60
h.	A107	$1 red & black	2.00	1.25
i.	A101	$2 red brown & black	4.00	2.50
		Block of 9 with horiz. gutter	35.00	
		Vert. pairs with horiz. gutter (each)	10.00	

Vignettes on Nos. 3209b and 3209i are reversed in comparison to the original issue.

Vert. pairs consist of #3209g-3209a, 3209h-3209b, 3209i-3209c.

3210	A107	$1	Pane of 9 #3209h	18.00	—
			Sheet of 6 panes, 3 each #3209-3210	*125.00*	
			Cross gutter block of 12	55.00	—
			Block of 18 (2 panes) with vert. gutter between & selvage on 4 sides	*47.50*	—
			Block of 12 with vert. gutter	*32.50*	—
			Vert. pair #3209h with horiz. gutter	10.00	
			Horiz. pairs with vert. gutter (each)	10.00	

Block of 12 contains #3209 and one column of 3 #3209h from #3210 separated by vert. gutter.

BERLIN AIRLIFT, 50th ANNIV.

A2492

Designed by Bill Bond.

Printed by Banknote Corporation of America.

PHOTOGRAVURE

Sheets of 120 in six panes of 20

1998, June 26 Tagged *Perf. 11.2*

3211	A2492 32c	**multicolored**	.60	.20
		P# block of 4, 4#+B	2.40	—
		Pane of 20	12.00	—

AMERICAN MUSIC SERIES
Folk Singers

Huddie "Leadbelly" Ledbetter (1888-1949) A2493

Woody Guthrie (1912-67) A2494

Sonny Terry (1911-86) A2495

Josh White (1908-69) A2496

Designed by Howard Paine.

Printed by American Packaging Corp. for Sennett Security Products.

PHOTOGRAVURE

Sheets of 180 in nine panes of 20

1998, June 26 Tagged *Perf. 10.1x10.2*

3212	A2493 32c	**multicolored**	.60	.20
3213	A2494 32c	**multicolored**	.60	.20
3214	A2495 32c	**multicolored**	.60	.20
3215	A2496 32c	**multicolored**	.60	.20
a.		Block or strip of 4, #3212-3215	2.50	2.00
		P# block of 4, 5#+S	2.50	—
		P# block of 8, 2 sets of P# + top label	5.00	—
		Pane of 20	12.50	—

AMERICAN MUSIC SERIES
Gospel Singers

Mahalia Jackson (1911-72) A2497

Roberta Martin (1917-69) A2498

Clara Ward (1924-73) A2499

Sister Rosetta Tharpe (1921-73) A2500

Designed by Howard Paine.
Printed by American Packaging Corp. for Sennett Security Products.

PHOTOGRAVURE
Sheets of 120 in six panes of 20

1998, July 15 — Tagged — *Perf. 10.1x10.3*

3216	A2497	32c	**multicolored**	.60	.20
3217	A2498	32c	**multicolored**	.60	.20
3218	A2499	32c	**multicolored**	.60	.20
3219	A2500	32c	**multicolored**	.60	.20
a.			Block or strip of 4, #3216-3219	2.40	2.00
			P# block of 4, 6#+S	3.00	—
			P# block of 8, 2 sets of P# + top label	6.00	—
			Pane of 20	14.50	—

SPANISH SETTLEMENT OF THE SOUTHWEST

La Mision de San Miguel de San Gabriel, Espanola, NM — A2501

Designed by Richard Sheaff.
Printed by Banknote Corporation of America.

LITHOGRAPHED
Sheets of 180 in nine panes of 20

1998, July 11 — Tagged — *Perf. 11.2*

3220	A2501	32c	**multicolored**	.60	.20
			P# block of 4, 4#+B	2.40	—
			Pane of 20	12.00	—

LITERARY ARTS SERIES

Stephen Vincent Benét (1898-43) A2502

Designed by Carl Herrman.
Printed by Ashton-Potter (USA) Ltd.

LITHOGRAPHED
Sheets of 180 in nine panes of 20

1998, July 22 — Tagged — *Perf. 11.2*

3221	A2502	32c	**multicolored**	.60	.20
			P# block of 4, 4#+P	2.40	—
			Pane of 20	12.00	—

TROPICAL BIRDS

Antillean Euphonia A2503

Green-throated Carib — A2504

Crested Honeycreeper A2505

Cardinal Honeyeater A2506

Designed by Phil Jordan.
Printed by Banknote Corporation of America.

LITHOGRAPHED
Sheets of 180 in nine panes of 20

1998, July 29 — Tagged — *Perf. 11.2*

3222	A2503	32c	**multicolored**	.60	.20
3223	A2504	32c	**multicolored**	.60	.20
3224	A2505	32c	**multicolored**	.60	.20
3225	A2506	32c	**multicolored**	.60	.20
a.			Block or strip of 4, #3222-3225	2.40	2.00
			P# block of 4, 4#+P	2.40	—
			Pane of 20	12.00	—

For booklet see No. BK272.

LEGENDS OF HOLLYWOOD

Alfred Hitchcock (1899-1980) — A2507

Designed by Rihard Sheaff.
Printed at American Packaging Corp. for Sennett Security Products.

PHOTOGRAVURE
Sheets of 120 in six panes of 20

1998, Aug. 3 — Tagged — *Perf. 11.1*

3226	A2507	32c	**multicolored**	.60	.20
			P# block of 4, 4#+S	3.00	—
			Pane of 20	14.50	—
			Sheet of 120 (6 panes)	72.50	
			Cross gutter block of 8	17.50	—
			Block of 8 with vert. gutter	13.50	—
			Horiz. pair with vert. gutter	3.00	—
			Vert. pair with horiz. gutter	2.00	—

Perforations in corner of each stamp are star-shaped. Cross-gutter block consists of 6 stamps from upper panes and 2 stamps from panes below. Hitchcock's profile in the UL corner of each stamp is laser cut.

ORGAN & TISSUE DONATION

A2508

Designed by Richard Sheaff. Printed by Avery Dennison.

PHOTOGRAVURE
Sheets of 160 in eight panes of 20

1998, Aug. 5 — Tagged — *Serpentine Die Cut 11.7*
Self-Adhesive

3227	A2508	32c	**multicolored**	.60	.20
			P# block of 4 5#+V	2.40	
			Pane of 20	12.00	

MODERN BICYCLE

A2509

Designed by Richard Sheaff. Printed by Bureau of Engraving and Printing (#3228), Sennett Security Printers (#3229).

PHOTOGRAVURE
COIL STAMP
Serpentine Die Cut 9.8 Vert.

1998, Aug. 14 — Untagged
Self-Adhesive (#3228)

3228	A2509	(10c)	**multicolored,** small "1998" year date	.20	.20
			Pair	.40	
			P# strip of 5, P#111, 221, 222, 333, 344, 444, 555	2.75	
			P# single, same #		1.75
a.			Large date	.20	.20
			Pair	.40	
			P# strip of 5, #666, 777, 888, 999	2.50	
			P# single, #666, 888	—	2.50
			P# single, #777, 999	—	1.75

Date on No. 3228a is approximately 1½mm; on No. 3228 approximately 1mm.

Untagged
Perf. 9.9 Vert.

3229	A2509	(10c)	**multicolored**	.20	.20
			Pair	.40	.25
			P# strip of 5, P#S111	2.50	
			P# single, same #		1.75

BRIGHT EYES

Dog — A2510

Fish — A2511

Cat — A2512

Parakeet
A2513

Hamster
A2514

Designed by Carl Herrman. Printed at Guilford Gravure for Banknote Corp. of America.

PHOTOGRAVURE

Sheets of 180 in nine panes of 20

1998, Aug. 20 Tagged *Serpentine Die Cut 9.9*

Self-Adhesive

3230	A2510 32c **multicolored**		.60	.20
3231	A2511 32c **multicolored**		.60	.20
3232	A2512 32c **multicolored**		.60	.20
3233	A2513 32c **multicolored**		.60	.20
3234	A2514 32c **multicolored**		.60	.20
a.	Strip of 5, #3230-3234		3.00	
		P# block of 8, 2 sets of 6#+B	6.00	
		Pane of 20	12.00	

Hidden 3-D designs can be seen on each stamp when viewed with a special viewer sold by the post office.

Plate blocks may contain top label.

KLONDIKE GOLD RUSH, CENTENNIAL

A2515

Designed by Howard Paine. Printed at Sterling Sommer for Ashton Potter (USA) Ltd.

LITHOGRAPHED

Sheets of 180 in nine panes of 20

1998, Aug. 21 Tagged *Perf. 11.1*

3235	A2515 32c **multicolored**		.60	.20
		P# block of 4, 5#+P	2.40	—
		Pane of 20	12.00	—

AMERICAN ART

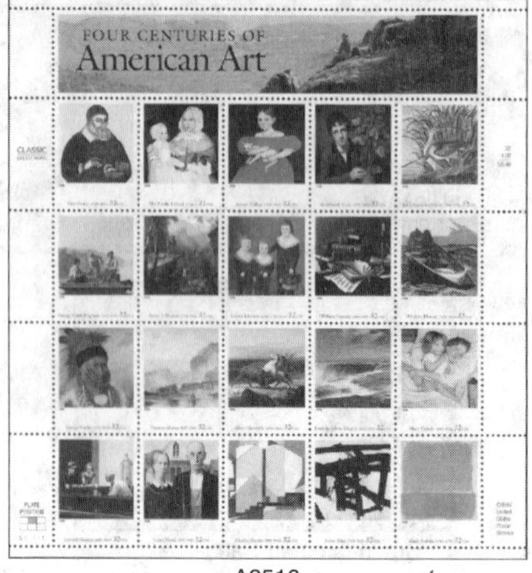

A2516

Illustration reduced.

Designed by Howard Paine. Printed by Sennett Security Products.

Paintings: a, "Portrait of Richard Mather," by John Foster. b, "Mrs. Elizabeth Freake and Baby Mary," by The Freake Limner. c, "Girl in Red Dress with Cat and Dog," by Ammi Phillips. d, "Rubens Peale with a Geranium," by Rembrandt Peale. e, "Long-billed Curlew, Numenius Longrostris," by John James Audubon. f, "Boatmen on the Missouri," by George Caleb Bingham. g, "Kindred Sprits," by Asher B. Durand. h, "The Westwood Children," by Joshua Johnson. i, "Music and Literature," by William Harnett. j, "The Fog Warning," by Winslow Homer. k, "The White Cloud, Head Chief of the Iowas," by George Catlin. l, "Cliffs of Green River," by Thomas Moran. m, "The Last of the Buffalo," by Alfred Bierstadt. n, "Niagara," by Frederic Edwin Church. o, "Breakfast in Bed," by Mary Cassatt. p, "Nighthawks," by Edward Hopper. q, "American Gothic," by Grant Wood. r, "Two Against the White," by Charles Sheeler. s, "Mahoning," by Franz Kline. t, "No. 12," by Mark Rothko.

PHOTOGRAVURE

Sheets of 120 stamps in six panes of 20

1998, Aug. 27 Tagged *Perf. 10.2*

3236	A2516	Pane of 20	12.00	—
a.-t.		32c any single	.60	.20
		Sheet of 120 (six panes)	72.50	
		Cross gutter block of 20	22.50	—
		Vert. pairs with horiz. gutter (each)	2.25	—
		Horiz. pairs with vert. gutter (each)	2.25	—

Inscriptions on the back of each stamp describe the painting and the artist.

Cross gutter block of 20 consists of six stamps from each of two panes and four stamps from each of two other panes with the cross gutter between.

AMERICAN BALLET

A2517

Designed by Derry Noyes. Printed by Sterling Sommer for Ashton-Potter (USA) Ltd.

LITHOGRAPHED

Sheets of 120 in six panes of 20

1998, Sept. 16 Tagged *Perf. 10.9x11.1*

3237	A2517 32c **multicolored**		.60	.20
		P# block of 4, 4#+P	2.40	—
		Pane of 20	12.00	
		Sheet of 120 (six panes)	72.50	
		Cross gutter block of 4	12.50	—
		Vert. pair with horiz. gutter	2.00	—
		Horiz. pair with vert. gutter	2.00	—

For booklet see No. BK273.

SPACE DISCOVERY

A2518

A2519

A2520

A2521

A2522

Designed by Phil Jordan. Printed at American Packaging Corp. for Sennett Security Products.

PHOTOGRAVURE

Sheets of 180 in nine panes of 20

1998, Oct. 1 Tagged *Perf. 11.1*

3238	A2518 32c **multicolored**		.60	.20
3239	A2519 32c **multicolored**		.60	.20
3240	A2520 32c **multicolored**		.60	.20
3241	A2521 32c **multicolored**		.60	.20
3242	A2522 32c **multicolored**		.60	.20
a.	Strip of 5, #3238-3242		3.00	2.25
		P# block of 10, 2 sets of 5#+S	6.00	—
		Pane of 20	12.00	
		Sheet of 180 (9 panes)	100.00	
		Cross gutter block of 10	17.50	—
		Vert. block of 10 with horiz. gutter	10.00	—
		Horiz. pair (#3238, 3242) with vert. gutter	2.00	—
		Vert. pairs with horiz. gutter (each)	2.00	
		Pane of 20 from sheet of 180	12.00	—

Hidden 3-D designs can be seen on each stamp when viewed with a special viewer sold by the post office.

Plate blocks may contain top label.

Cross gutter block of 10 consists of two stamps from each of two panes and three stamps from each of two other panes with the cross gutter between. Pane of 20 from sheet of 180 has vertical perforations on one or both sides and is wider than pane sold in local post offices.

For booklet see No. BK274.

GIVING AND SHARING

A2523

Designed by Bob Dinetz.

Printed by Avery Dennison.

PHOTOGRAVURE
Sheets of 200 in ten panes of 20

1998, Oct. 7 Tagged *Serpentine Die Cut 11.1*
Self-Adhesive

3243 A2523 32c **multicolored**		.60	.20
	P# block of 4, 4#+V	2.40	—
	Pane of 20	12.00	—

CHRISTMAS

Madonna and Child, Florence, 15th Cent. — A2524

Evergreen Wreath — A2525

Victorian Wreath — A2526

Chili Pepper Wreath — A2527

Tropical Wreath — A2528

Designed by Richard D. Sheaff (#3244), Lilian Dinihanian (A2525), George de Bruin (A2526), Chris Crinklaw (A2527), Micheale Thunin (A2528).

Printed by Bureau of Engraving and Printing (#3244), Banknote Corporation of America (#3245-3252).

LITHOGRAPHED
Sheets of 160 in 8 panes of 20 (#3249-3252)
Serpentine Die Cut 10.1x9.9 on 2, 3 or 4 Sides
1998, Oct. 15 Tagged
Self-Adhesive
Booklet Stamps

3244 A2524 32c **multicolored**		.60	.20
a.	Booklet pane of 20 + label	12.00	
b.	Imperf, pair	—	

Serpentine Die Cut 11.3x11.6 on 2 or 3 Sides

3245 A2525 32c **multicolored**		2.25	.20
3246 A2526 32c **multicolored**		2.25	.20
3247 A2527 32c **multicolored**		2.25	.20
3248 A2528 32c **multicolored**		2.25	.20
a.	Booklet pane of 4, #3245-3248	22.50	
b.	Booklet pane of 5, #3245-3246, 3248, 2 #3247 + label	27.50	
c.	Booklet pane of 6, #3247-3248, 2 each #3245-3246	32.50	

Size: 23x30mm
Serpentine Die Cut 11.4x11.6 on 2, 3, or 4 Sides

3249 A2525 32c **multicolored**		.60	.20
3250 A2526 32c **multicolored**		.60	.20
3251 A2527 32c **multicolored**		.60	.20
3252 A2528 32c **multicolored + label**		.60	.20
a.	Block of 4, #3249-3252	2.40	
	P#block of 4, 6#+B	3.00	
	Pane of 20	14.50	
b.	Booklet pane, 5 each #3249-3252 + label	12.00	
c.	Block or strip of 4, red ("Greetings 32 USA" and "1998") omitted on #3249, 3252	—	

Weather Vane — A2529

Uncle Sam — A2530

Uncle Sam's Hat — A2531

Space Shuttle Landing A2532

Piggyback Space Shuttle A2533

Designed by Terry McCaffrey (#3257-3258, 3260, 3264-3269), Richard Sheaff (#3259, 3263), Phil Jordan (#3261-3262).

Printed by Ashton Potter (USA) Ltd. (#3257), American Packaging Corp. for Sennett Security Products (#3259), Stamp Venturers (#3260), Banknote Corporation of America (#3258, 3261-3262), Bureau of Engraving and Printing (#3263-3267), Avery Dennison (#3268-3269).

LITHOGRAPHED
Sheets of 400 in eight panes of 50 (#3257, 3260), Sheets of 300 in six panes of 50 (#3258), Sheets of 160 in eight panes of 20 (#3259), Sheets of 120 in six panes of 20 (#3261-3262)

1998 Untagged *Perf. 11.2*

3257 A2529 (1c) **multicolored** *Nov. 9*		.20	.20
	P# block of 4, 5# + P	.25	—
a.	Black omitted	—	
3258 A2529 (1c) **multicolored,** *Nov. 9*		.20	.20
	P# block of 4, 5# + B	.25	—

No. 3257 is 18mm high, has thin letters, white USA, and black 1998. No. 3258 is 17mm high, has thick letters, pale blue USA and blue 1998.

PHOTOGRAVURE
Tagged
Serpentine Die Cut 10.8
Self-Adhesive (#3259, 3261-3263, 3265-3269)

3259 A2530 22c **multicolored,** *Nov. 9*		.45	.20
a.	Die cut 10.8x10.5	1.00	.25
	P# block of 4, 4# + S, all No. 3259	2.50	
	P# block of 4, top stamps No. 3259, bottom stamps No. 3259a	—	
	P# block of 4, top stamps No. 3259a, bottom stamps No. 3259	7.50	
	Pane of 20, all No. 3259	9.00	
	Pane of 20, row 1 No. 3259a, rows 2-4 No. 3259	—	
	Pane of 20, row 2 No. 3259a, rows 1, 3-4 No. 3259	—	
	Pane of 20, row 3 No. 3259a, rows 1-2, 4 No. 3259	12.50	
	Pane of 20, row 4 No. 3259a, rows 1-3 No. 3259	—	

See No. 3353.

Perf. 11.2

3260 A2531 (33c) **multicolored,** shiny gum, *Nov. 9*		.65	.20
	P# block of 4 4#+S	2.60	—
	Low-gloss gum	.65	.20
	P# block of 4 5#+S	2.60	—

LITHOGRAPHED
Serpentine Die Cut 11.5

3261 A2532 $3.20 **multicolored,** *Nov. 9*		6.00	3.00
	P# block of 4, 4#+B	24.00	
	Pane of 20	120.00	
3262 A2533 $11.75 **multicolored,** *Nov. 19*		22.50	11.50
	P# block of 4, 4#+B	90.00	
	Pane of 20	450.00	

COIL STAMPS
PHOTOGRAVURE
Serpentine Die Cut 9.9 Vert.

3263 A2530 22c **multicolored,** *Nov. 9*		.45	.20
	Pair	.90	
	P# strip of 5, #1111	3.50	
	P# single, same #		2.50
a.	Imperf, pair	—	

See No. 3353.

Perf. 9.8 Vert.

3264 A2531 (33c) **multicolored,** shiny gum, *Nov. 9*		.65	.20
	Pair	1.30	.30
	P# strip of 5, #1111, 3333, 3343, 3344, 3444	5.00	
	P# single, same #		2.50
	Low-gloss gum	.70	
	Pair	1.40	
	Plate strip of 5, #1111	6.00	

Serpentine Die Cut 9.9 Vert.

3265 A2531 (33c) **multicolored,** *Nov. 9*		.65	.20
	Pair	1.30	
	P# strip of 5, #1111, 1131, 2222, 3333	5.50	
	P# single, same #		2.25
a.	Imperf., pair	—	
b.	Red omitted	—	
c.	Black omitted	—	
d.	Black omitted, Imperf., pair	—	

Unused examples of No. 3265 are on backing paper the same size as the stamps. Corners of the stamp are 90 degree angles.

On No. 3265b, the blue and gray colors are shifted down and to the right.

Serpentine Die Cut 9.9 Vert.

3266 A2531 (33c) **multicolored,** *Nov. 9*		.65	.20
	Pair	1.30	
	P# strip of 5, #1111	5.00	
	P# single, same #		3.50

Unused examples of No. 3266 are on backing paper larger than the stamps, and the stamps are spaced approximately 2mm. apart. Corners of stamps are rounded.

BOOKLET STAMPS
Serpentine Die Cut 9.9 on 2 or 3 Sides

3267 A2531 (33c) **multicolored,** *Nov. 9*		.65	.20
a.	Booklet pane of 10	6.50	

Serpentine Die Cut 11¼ on 3 Sides (#3268, 3268a)
or 11 on 2, 3 or 4 sides (#3268b, 3268c)

3268 A2531 (33c) **multicolored,** *Nov. 9*		.65	.20
a.	Booklet pane of 10	6.50	
b.	Serpentine die cut 11	.65	.20
c.	As "b," booklet pane of 20 + label	13.00	

Die Cut 8 on 2, 3 or 4 Sides

3269 A2531 (33c) **multicolored,** *Nov. 9*		.65	.20
a.	Booklet pane of 18	12.00	

> Used examples of an "H" non-denominated stamp inscribed "Postcard Rate" exist in the marketplace. There is no evidence that these "stamps" were ever issued.

A2534

Designed by Chris Calle.

PHOTOGRAVURE
COIL STAMPS

1998, Dec. 14 Untagged *Perf. 9.8 Vert.*

3270 A2534 (10c) **multicolored,** small date		.20	.20
	Pair	.40	.40
	P# strip of 5, #11111	2.75	
	P# single, #11111		1.75
a.	Large date	.20	.20
	Pair	.40	.40
	P# strip of 5, #22222	7.00	—
	P# single, same #	—	2.25

Self-Adhesive

Serpentine Die Cut 9.9 Vert.

3271 A2534 (10c) **multicolored,** small date .20 .20
Pair .40
P# strip of 5, #11111, 22222 2.75
P# single, #11111, 22222 1.75
a. Large date .20 .20
Pair .40
P# strip of 5, #33333 3.25
P# single, #33333 — 1.75
b. Tagged (error) 1.25 1.10
Pair 2.50
P# strip of 5, #11111 10.50
P# single, #11111 — 9.50

No. 3271 is known with eagle in red brown rather than the normal golden brown, apparently from contaminated ink. Values slightly higher than normal No. 3271.

No. 3271a is known in plate #11111 strips with blue "1" of plate numbers omitted.

Dates on Nos. 3270a and 3271a are approximately 1 ¾mm; on Nos. 3270-3271 approximately 1 ¼mm.

Compare to Nos. 2602-2604, 2907.

Scott values for used self-adhesvive stamps are for examples either on piece or off piece.

CHINESE NEW YEAR

Year of the Rabbit A2535

Designed by Clarence Lee.

Printed at American Packaging Corp. for Sennett Security Printers.

PHOTOGRAVURE

Sheets of 180 in nine panes of 20

1999, Jan. 5 Tagged *Perf. 11.2*

3272 A2535 33c **multicolored** .65 .20
P# block of 4, 4#+S 2.60 —
Pane of 20 13.00 —

BLACK HERITAGE SERIES

Malcolm X (1925-65), Civil Rights Activist — A2536

Designed by Richard Sheaff. Printed by Banknote Corp. of America.

LITHOGRAPHED

Sheets of 180 in nine panes of 20

1999, Jan. 20 Tagged *Serpentine Die Cut 11.4*

Self-Adhesive

3273 A2536 33c **multicolored** .65 .20
P# block of 4, 3#+B 2.60
Pane of 20 13.00

LOVE

A2537

A2538

Designed by John Grossman, Holly Sudduth.

Printed by Avery Dennison.

PHOTOGRAVURE

1999, Jan. 28 Tagged *Die Cut*

Booklet Stamp

Self-Adhesive

3274 A2537 33c **multicolored** .65 .20
a. Booklet pane of 20 13.00
b. Imperf, pair —

Sheets of 160 in eight panes of 20

3275 A2538 55c **multicolored** 1.10 .20
P# block of 4, 7#+B 4.40
Pane of 20 22.00

HOSPICE CARE

A2539

Designed by Phil Jordan.

Printed by Banknote Corp. of America.

LITHOGRAPHED

Sheets of 120 in six panes of 20

1999, Feb. 9 Tagged *Serpentine Die Cut 11.4*

3276 A2539 33c **multicolored** .65 .20
P# block of 4, 4#+B 2.80
Pane of 20 13.50

Flag and City — A2540

Flag and Chalkboard — A2541

Designed by Richard Sheaff. Printed by Bureau of Engraving and Printing (#3277, 3279-3282), Avery Dennison (#3278, 3278F, 3283).

PHOTOGRAVURE

Sheets of 400 in four panes of 100 (#3277), Sheets of 200 in ten panes of 20 (#3278)

1999, Feb. 25 Tagged *Perf. 11.2*

Self-Adhesive (#3278, 3278F, 3279, 3281-3282)

3277 A2540 33c **multicolored** .65 .20
P# block of 4, 4# 25.00 —

No. 3277 has red date.

Serpentine Die Cut 11 on 2, 3 or 4 Sides

3278 A2540 33c **multicolored** .65 .20
P# block of 4, 4#+V 4.00
Pane of 20 19.00
a. Booklet pane of 4 2.60
b. Booklet pane of 5 + label 3.25
P# single, #V1111, V1112, V1121, V1122, V1212, V2212 .80 *1.00*
c. Booklet pane of 6 3.90
d. Booklet pane of 10 6.50
e. Booklet pane of 20 + label 13.00
h. As "e," imperf —
i. Serpentine die cut 11 ¼ .65 .20
j. As "i," booklet pane of 10 6.50

No. 3278 has black date.

The plate # single in No. 3278b is the lower left single.

BOOKLET STAMPS

Serpentine Die Cut 11½x11¾ on 2, 3 or 4 Sides

3278F A2540 33c **multicolored** .65 .20
g. Booklet pane of 20 + label 13.00

No. 3278F has black date.

Serpentine Die Cut 9.8 on 2 or 3 Sides

3279 A2540 33c **multicolored** .65 .20
a. Booklet pane of 10 6.50

No. 3279 has red date.

COIL STAMPS

Perf. 9.9 Vert.

3280 A2540 33c **multicolored,** small "1999" year date .65 .20
Pair 1.30 .30
P# strip of 5, #1111, 2222 5.00 —
P# single, same # 2.50
a. Large date .65 .20
Pair 1.30 .30
P# strip of 5, #3333 5.00 —
P# single, same # — 3.50
b. As No. 3280, imperf pair —
P#2222 —

Serpentine Die Cut 9.8 Vert.

3281 A2540 33c **multicolored,** large "1999" year date .65 .20
Pair 1.30
P# strip of 5, #6666, 7777, 8888, 9999, 1111A, 2222A, 3333A, 4444A, 5555A, 6666A, 7777A, 8888A, 1111B,2222B 5.00
P# single, same # 2.00
a. Imperf., pair 27.50
b. Light blue and yellow omitted *600.00*
c. Small date .65 .20
Pair 1.30
P# strip of 5, #1111, 2222, 3333, 3433, 4443, 4444, 5555, 9999A 5.00
P# single, same # — 2.00

Corners are square on #3281. Unused examples are on backing paper the same size as the stamps, and the stamps are adjoining.

Date on Nos. 3280a and 3281 is approximately 1 ¾mm; on Nos. 3280 and 3281c approximately 1 ¼mm.

3282 A2540 33c **multicolored** .65 .20
Pair 1.30
P# strip of 5, #1111, 2222 5.00
P# single, same # 3.25

Corners are rounded on #3282. Unused examples are on backing paper larger than the stamps, and the stamps are spaced approximately 2mm. apart.

PHOTOGRAVURE

Serpentine Die Cut 7.9 on 2, 3 or 4 Sides

1999, Mar. 13 Tagged

Self-Adhesive

BOOKLET STAMP

3283 A2541 33c **multicolored** .65 .20
a. Booklet pane of 18 12.00

IRISH IMMIGRATION

A2542

Designed by Howard Paine. Printed by Ashton-Potter (USA) Ltd.

LITHOGRAPHED

Sheets of 180 in nine panes of 20

1999, Feb. 26 Tagged *Perf. 11.2*

3286 A2542 33c **multicolored** .65 .20
P# block of 4, 4#+P 2.60 —
Pane of 20 13.00 —

See Ireland No. 1168.

PERFORMING ARTS SERIES

Alfred Lunt (1892-1977), Lynn Fontanne (1887-1983), Actors

A2543

Designed by Carl Herrman. Printed by Sterling Sommer for Ashton-Potter (USA) Ltd.

LITHOGRAPHED

Sheets of 180 in nine panes of 20

1999, Mar. 2 Tagged *Perf. 11.2*

3287 A2543 33c **multicolored** .65 .20
P# block of 4, 4#+P 2.60 —
Pane of 20 13.00 —

ARCTIC ANIMALS

Arctic Hare — A2544

Arctic Fox — A2545

Snowy Owl — A2546

Polar Bear — A2547

Gray Wolf — A2548

Designed by Derry Noyes. Printed by Banknote Corp. of America.

LITHOGRAPHED

Sheets of 90 in six panes of 15

1999, Mar. 12 **Tagged** *Perf. 11*

3288 A2544 33c **multicolored**	.65	.20
3289 A2545 33c **multicolored**	.65	.20
3290 A2546 33c **multicolored**	.65	.20
3291 A2547 33c **multicolored**	.65	.20
3292 A2548 33c **multicolored**	.65	.20
a. Strip of 5, #3288-3292	3.25	—
Pane of 15, 6#+B	12.00	

While the normal definition of a plate block dictates a block of 10, this would require collectors to discard the decorative label and top row of stamps from the pane of 15. To avoid destroying the more collectible entire, Scott is listing the entire pane as the plate block, and will provide space for this item in the Commemorative Plate Block supplement.

SONORAN DESERT

A2549

Illustration reduced.

Designed by Ethel Kessler. Printed by Banknote Corporation of America.

Designs: a, Cactus wren, brittlebush, teddy bear cholla. b, Desert tortoise. c, White-winged dove, prickly pear. d, Gambel quail. e, Saguaro cactus. f, Desert mule deer. g, Desert cottontail, hedgehog cactus. h, Gila monster. i, Western diamondback rattlesnake, cactus mouse. j, Gila woodpecker.

LITHOGRAPHED

Sheets of 60 in six panes of 10

Serpentine Die Cut Perf 11.2

1999, Apr. 6 **Tagged**

Self-Adhesive

3293 A2549 Pane of 10	6.50	
a.-j. 33c any single	.65	.20
Sheet of 6 panes	40.00	

BERRIES

Blueberries
A2550

Raspberries
A2551

Strawberries
A2552

Blackberries
A2553

Designed by Howard Paine. Printed by Guilford Gravure for Banknote Corporation of America.

PHOTOGRAVURE

Serpentine Die Cut 11¼x11½ on 2, 3 or 4 Sides (Nos. 3294-3297), or 2 or 3 sides (Nos. 3294a-3297a)

1999, Apr. 10 **Tagged**

Self-Adhesive

3294 A2550 33c **multicolored**	.65	.20
a. Dated "2000," *Mar. 15, 2000*	.65	.20
3295 A2551 33c **multicolored**	.65	.20
a. Dated "2000," *Mar. 15, 2000*	.65	.20
3296 A2552 33c **multicolored**	.65	.20
a. Dated "2000," *Mar. 15, 2000*	.65	.20
3297 A2553 33c **multicolored**	.65	.20
a. Dated "2000," *Mar. 15, 2000*	.65	.20
b. Booklet pane of 20, 5 each #3294-3297 + label	13.00	
c. Block of 4, #3294-3297	2.60	
d. Booklet pane of 20, 5 #3297e + label	13.00	
e. Block of 4, #3294a-3297a	2.60	

No. 3297d is a double-sided booklet pane, with 12 stamps on one side and eight stamps plus label on the other side.

Serpentine Die Cut 9½x10 on 2 or 3 Sides

3298 A2550 33c **multicolored**	.65	.20
3299 A2552 33c **multicolored**	.65	.20
3300 A2551 33c **multicolored**	.65	.20
3301 A2553 33c **multicolored**	.65	.20
a. Booklet pane of 4, #3298-3301	2.60	
b. Booklet pane of 5, #3298, 3299, 3301, 2 #3300 + label	3.25	
c. Booklet pane of 6, #3300, 3301, 2 #3298, 3299	4.00	
d. Block of 4, #3298-3301	2.60	

COIL STAMPS

Serpentine Die Cut 8.5 Vert.

3302 A2550 33c **multicolored**	.75	.20
3303 A2551 33c **multicolored**	.75	.20
3304 A2553 33c **multicolored**	.75	.20
3305 A2552 33c **multicolored**	.75	.20
a. Strip of 4, #3302-3305	3.00	
P# strip of 5, 2 #3302, 1 ea #3303-3305, P#B1111, B1112, B2211, B2221, B2222	6.00	
P# strip of 9, 2 ea #3302-3303, 3305, 3 #3304, same P#	8.50	
P# single (#3304), same P#	—	1.50

A2554

A2555

DAFFY DUCK

Designed by Ed Wieczyk.
Printed by Avery Dennison.

PHOTOGRAVURE

1999, Apr. 16 **Tagged** ***Serpentine Die Cut 11.1***

Self-Adhesive

3306 Pane of 10	6.50	
a. A2554 33c single	.65	.20
b. Booklet pane of 9 #3306a	5.85	
c. Booklet pane of 1 #3306a	.65	
Sheet of 60 (six panes) top	40.00	
Sheet of 60 (six panes) bottom, with plate # in selvage	47.50	
Pane of 10 from sheet of 60	8.00	
Pane of 10 with plate # in selvage	15.00	
Cross gutter block of 9 or 10	15.00	
Cross gutter block of 12	18.00	
Vert. pair with horiz. gutter	2.00	
Horiz. pair with vert. gutter	4.00	

Nos. 3306b-3306c and 3307b-3307c are separated by a vertical line of microperforations, which is absent on the uncut sheet of 60.

Die cutting on #3306b does not extend through the backing paper.

3307 Pane of 10	*6.50*	
a. A2554 33c single	*.65*	
b. Booklet pane of 9 #3307a	—	
c. Booklet pane of 1, imperf.	—	

Die cutting on #3307a extends through the backing paper. Used examples of No. 3307a are identical to those of No. 3306a.

Nos. 3306b-3306c and 3307b-3307c are separated by a vertical line of microperforations.

LITERARY ARTS SERIES

Ayn Rand (1905-82).

Designed by Phil Jordan.

Printed by Sterling Sommer for Ashton-Potter (USA) Ltd.

LITHOGRAPHED

Sheets of 180 in nine panes of 20

1999, Apr. 22 **Tagged** ***Perf. 11.2***

3308 A2555 33c **multicolored**	.65	.20
P# block of 4, 4#+P	2.60	—
Pane of 20	13.00	—

Cinco De Mayo Type of 1998

Designed by Carl Herrman.

Printed by Banknote Corporation of America.

LITHOGRAPHED
Sheets of 160 in eight panes of 20
Serpentine Die Cut 11.6x11.3

1999, Apr. 27 **Tagged**

Self-Adhesive

3309 A2486 33c **multicolored** .65 .20
P# block of 4, 6#+B 2.60
Pane of 20 13.00

TROPICAL FLOWERS

Bird of Paradise A2556

Royal Poinciana A2557

Gloriosa Lily — A2558

Chinese Hibiscus A2559

Designed by Carl Herrman.

Printed by Sennett Security Products.

PHOTOGRAVURE
BOOKLET STAMPS
Serpentine Die Cut 10.9 on 2 or 3 Sides

1999, May 1 **Tagged**

Self-Adhesive

3310 A2556 33c **multicolored** .65 .20
3311 A2557 33c **multicolored** .65 .20
3312 A2558 33c **multicolored** .65 .20
3313 A2559 33c **multicolored** .65 .20
a. Block of 4, #3310-3313 2.60
b. Booklet pane, 5 each #3313a 13.00

No. 3313b is a double-sided booklet pane with 12 stamps on one side and 8 stamps plus label on the other side.

A2560

A2561

JOHN (1699-1777) & WILLIAM (1739-1823) BARTRAM, BOTANISTS

Designed by Phil Jordan. Printed by Banknote Corporation of America.

LITHOGRAPHED
Sheets of 180 in nine panes of 20

1999, May 18 **Tagged** ***Serpentine Die Cut 11½***

Self-Adhesive

3314 A2560 33c Franklinia Alatamaha, by William Bartram .65 .20
P# block of 4, 4#+B 2.60
Pane of 20 13.00

PROSTATE CANCER AWARENESS

Designed by Michael Cronan. Printed by Avery Dennison.

PHOTOGRAVURE
Sheets of 200 in ten panes of 20

1999, May 28 **Tagged** ***Serpentine Die Cut 11***

Self-Adhesive

3315 A2561 33c **multicolored** .65 .20
P# block of 4, 5#+V 2.60
Pane of 20 13.00

CALIFORNIA GOLD RUSH, 150TH ANNIV.

A2562

Designed by Howard Paine. Printed by Ashton-Potter (USA) Ltd.

LITHOGRAPHED
Sheets of 180 in nine panes of 20

1999, June 18 **Tagged** ***Perf. 11¼***

3316 A2562 33c **multicolored** .65 .20
P# block of 4, 5#+P 2.60 —
Pane of 20 13.00 —

AQUARIUM FISH

Reef Fish

A2563

A2564

A2565

A2566

Designed by Richard Sheaff. Printed by Banknote Corporation of America.

Designs: No. 3317, Yellow fish, red fish, cleaner shrimp. No. 3318, Fish, thermometer. No. 3319, Red fish, blue & yellow fish. No. 3320, Fish, heater/aerator.

LITHOGRAPHED
Sheets of 120 in six panes of 20

1999, June 24 **Tagged** ***Serpentine Die Cut 11½***

Self-Adhesive

3317 A2563 33c **multicolored,** block tagging .65 .20
a. Overall tagging 10.00 *10.00*
3318 A2564 33c **multicolored,** block tagging .65 .20
a. Overall tagging 10.00 *10.00*
3319 A2565 33c **multicolored,** block tagging .65 .20
a. Overall tagging 10.00 *10.00*
3320 A2566 33c **multicolored,** block tagging .65 .20
a. Overall tagging 10.00 *10.00*
b. Strip of 4, #3317-3320 2.60
P# block of 8, 2 sets of 4#+B 5.20
Pane of 20 13.00
Sheet of 6 panes 80.00
Cross gutter block of 8 20.00
Block of 8 with horiz. gutter 9.00
Horiz. pair with vert. gutter 2.00
Vert. pairs with horiz. gutter (each) 2.25
c. Strip of 4, #3317a-3320a 45.00
P# block of 8, 2 sets of 4#+B 95.00
Pane of 20 190.00

Plate blocks will have either top label or list of fish shown on bottom selvage. Cross gutter block of 8 consists of 4 horiz. pairs separated by vert. gutter with horiz. gutter between.

Press sheets were printed with large block tagging.

EXTREME SPORTS

Skateboarding — A2567

BMX Biking — A2568

Snowboarding — A2569

Inline Skating — A2570

Designed by Carl Herrman. Printed by Avery Dennison.

PHOTOGRAVURE
Sheets of 160 in eight panes of 20

1999, June 25 **Tagged** ***Serpentine Die Cut 11***

Self-Adhesive

3321 A2567 33c **multicolored** .65 .20
3322 A2568 33c **multicolored** .65 .20
3323 A2569 33c **multicolored** .65 .20
3324 A2570 33c **multicolored** .65 .20
a. Block or strip of 4, #3321-3324 2.60
P# block of 4, 4#+V 2.60
Pane of 20 13.00
Sheet of 80 (four panes) top 60.00
Sheet of 80 (four panes) bottom, with plate # in sheet margin 60.00
Pane of 20 with extra selvage from sheet of 80 13.00
Pane of 20 with plate # in sheet margin 20.00
Cross gutter block of 8 5.25
Vert. pairs with horiz. gutter (each) 1.60
Horiz. pairs with vert. gutter (each) 1.60
Block of 4 with horiz. gutter 5.25
Block of 8 with vert. gutter 10.50

Cross gutter block of 8 consists of 4 horiz. pairs separated by vert. gutter with horiz. gutter between

AMERICAN GLASS

Free-Blown Glass — A2571

Mold-Blown Glass — A2572

Pressed Glass — A2573

Art Glass — A2574

Designed by Richard Sheaff. Printed by Sterling Sommer for Ashton-Potter (USA) Ltd.

LITHOGRAPHED
Sheets of 90 in six panes of 15

1999, June 29 **Tagged** ***Perf. 11***

3325	A2571 33c **multicolored**		.65	.20
3326	A2572 33c **multicolored**		.65	.20
3327	A2573 33c **multicolored**		.65	.20
3328	A2574 33c **multicolored**		.65	.20
a.	Strip or block of 4, #3325-3328		2.60	—
		Pane of 15, 4 each #3325, 3327-3328, 3 #3326	9.75	—

A2575

A2576

LEGENDS OF HOLLYWOOD
James Cagney (1899-1986)

Designed by Howard Paine.

Printed by Sennett Security Products.

PHOTOGRAVURE
Sheets of 120 in six panes of 20

1999, July 22 **Tagged** ***Perf. 11***

3329	A2575 33c **multicolored**	.65	.20
	P# block of 4, 5#+S	2.60	—
	Pane of 20	13.00	—
	Sheet of 120 (6 panes)	80.00	—
	Cross gutter block of 8	17.50	—
	Block of 8 with vertical gutter	10.00	—
	Horiz. pair with vert. gutter	3.00	—
	Vert. pair with horiz. gutter	2.00	—

Perforations in corner of each stamp are star-shaped. Cross-gutter block consists of 2 stamps from upper panes and 6 stamps from panes below.

GEN. WILLIAM "BILLY" L. MITCHELL (1879-1936), AVIATION PIONEER

Designed by Phil Jordan.

Printed by Guilford Gravure for Banknote Corporation of America.

PHOTOGRAVURE
Sheets of 180 in nine panes of 20

1999, July 30 **Tagged** ***Serpentine Die Cut 9¾x10***
Self-Adhesive

3330	A2576 55c **multicolored**	1.10	.20
	P# block of 4, 5#+B	4.40	
	Pane of 20	22.00	

HONORING THOSE WHO SERVED

A2577

Designed by Richard Sheaff and Uldis Purins.
Printed by Avery Dennison.

PHOTOGRAVURE
Sheets of 200 in 10 panes of 20

1999, Aug. 16 **Tagged** ***Serpentine Die Cut 11***
Self-Adhesive

3331	A2577 33c **black, blue & red**	.65	.20
	P# block of 4, 3#+V	2.60	
	Pane of 20	13.00	

UNIVERSAL POSTAL UNION

A2578

Designed by Gerald Gallo.
Printed by Sterling Sommer for Ashton-Potter (USA) Ltd.

LITHOGRAPHED
Sheets of 180 in nine panes of 20

1999, Aug. 25 **Tagged** ***Perf. 11***

3332	A2578 45c **multicolored**	.90	.20
	P# block of 4, 3#+P	3.60	—
	Pane of 20	18.00	—

FAMOUS TRAINS

Daylight A2579

Congressional A2580

20th Century Limited A2581

Hiawatha A2582

Super Chief A2583

Designed by Howard Paine.
Printed by Ashton-Potter (USA) Ltd.

LITHOGRAPHED
Sheets of 120 in six panes of 20

1999, Aug. 26 **Tagged** ***Perf. 11***

3333	A2579 33c **multicolored**	.65	.20
3334	A2580 33c **multicolored**	.65	.20
3335	A2581 33c **multicolored**	.65	.20
3336	A2582 33c **multicolored**	.65	.20
3337	A2583 33c **multicolored**	.65	.20
a.	Strip of 5, #3333-3337	3.25	—
	Pane of 20, 4 #3337a	13.00	—
	P# block of 8, 2 sets of 4#+P	5.25	—
	Sheet of 120 (6 panes)	82.50	—
	Block of 10 with vert. gutter	11.00	—
	Cross gutter block of 8	17.50	—
	Horiz. pairs with vert. gutter (each)	2.00	—
	Vert. pairs with horiz. gutter (each)	2.00	—

Stamps in No. 3337a are arranged in four different orders. Plate block may contain top label.

FREDERICK LAW OLMSTED (1822-1903), LANDSCAPE ARCHITECT

A2584

Designed by Ethel Kessler.
Printed by Ashton-Potter (USA) Ltd.

LITHOGRAPHED
Sheets of 120 in six panes of 20

1999, Sept. 12 **Tagged** ***Perf. 11***

3338	A2584 33c **multicolored**	.65	.20
	P# block of 4, 4#+P	2.60	—
	Pane of 20	13.00	—

AMERICAN MUSIC SERIES
Hollywood Composers

Max Steiner (1888-1971) A2585

Dimitri Tiomkin (1894-1975)
A2586

Bernard Herrmann (1911-75)
A2587

Franz Waxman (1906-67)
A2588

Alfred Newman (1907-70)
A2589

Erich Wolfgang Korngold (1897-1957)
A2590

Designed by Howard Paine.
Printed by Sterling Sommer for Ashton-Potter (USA) Ltd.

LITHOGRAPHED
Sheets of 120 in six panes of 20

1999, Sept. 16 Tagged *Perf. 11*

3339	A2585 33c **multicolored**			.65	.20
3340	A2586 33c **multicolored**			.65	.20
3341	A2587 33c **multicolored**			.65	.20
3342	A2588 33c **multicolored**			.65	.20
3343	A2589 33c **multicolored**			.65	.20
3344	A2590 33c **multicolored**			.65	.20
a.	Block of 6, #3339-3344			3.90	—
	P# block of 6, 5#+P			3.90	—
	P# block of 8, 2 sets of 5#+P + top label			5.25	—
	Pane of 20			13.00	—

AMERICAN MUSIC SERIES
Broadway Songwriters

Ira (1896-1983) & George (1898-1937) Gershwin
A2591

Alan Jay Lerner (1918-86) & Frederick Loewe (1901-88)
A2592

Lorenz Hart (1895-1943)
A2593

Richard Rodgers (1902-79) & Oscar Hammerstein II (1895-1960)
A2594

Meredith Willson (1902-84)
A2595

Frank Loesser (1910-69)
A2596

Designed by Howard Paine.
Printed by Sterling Sommer for Ashton-Potter (USA) Ltd.

LITHOGRAPHED
Sheets of 120 in six panes of 20

1999, Sept. 21 Tagged *Perf. 11*

3345	A2591 33c **multicolored**	.65	.20
3346	A2592 33c **multicolored**	.65	.20
3347	A2593 33c **multicolored**	.65	.20
3348	A2594 33c **multicolored**	.65	.20
3349	A2595 33c **multicolored**	.65	.20
3350	A2596 33c **multicolored**	.65	.20
a.	Block of 6, #3345-3350	3.90	—
	P# block of 6, 5#+P	3.90	—
	P# block of 8, 2 sets of 5#+P + top label	5.25	—
	Pane of 20	13.00	—

INSECTS & SPIDERS

A2597

Illustration reduced.

Designed by Carl Herrman.
Printed by Ashton-Potter (USA) Ltd.

Designs: a, Black widow. b, Elderberry longhorn. c, Lady beetle. d, Yellow garden spider. e, Dogbane beetle. f, Flower fly. g, Assassin bug. h, Ebony jewelwing. i, Velvet ant. j, Monarch caterpillar. k, Monarch butterfly. l, Eastern Hercules beetle. m, Bombardier beetle. n, Dung beetle. o, Spotted water beetle. p, True katydid. q, Spinybacked spider. r, Periodical cicada. s, Scorpionfly. t, Jumping spider.

LITHOGRAPHED
Sheets of 80 in four panes of 20

1999, Oct. 1 Tagged *Perf. 11*

3351	A2597 Pane of 20	13.00	—
a.-t.	33c any single	.65	.20
	Sheet of 4 panes	52.50	
	Cross gutter block of 20	20.00	
	Vert. pair with horiz. gutter (each)	1.60	
	Horiz. pair with vert. gutter (each)	1.60	

Cross gutter block of 20 consists of six stamps from each of two panes and four stamps from each of the two other panes with the cross gutter between.

Hanukkah Type of 1996

Designed by Hannah Smotrich.
Printed by Avery Dennison.

PHOTOGRAVURE
Sheets of 200 in 10 panes of 20

1999, Oct. 8 Tagged *Serpentine Die Cut 11*
Self-Adhesive

3352	A2411 33c **multicolored**	.65	.20
	P# block of 4, 5#+V	2.60	
	Pane of 20	13.00	

Uncle Sam Type of 1998

Designed by Richard Sheaff.
Printed by Bureau of Engraving and Printing.

COIL STAMP
PHOTOGRAVURE

1999, Oct. 8 Tagged *Perf. 9¾ Vert.*

3353	A2530 22c **multicolored**	.45	.20
	Pair	.90	.30
	P# strip of 5, #1111	3.50	—
	P# single, same #	—	2.50

NATO, 50TH ANNIV.

A2598

Designed by Michael Cronan.
Printed by Ashton-Potter (USA) Ltd.

LITHOGRAPHED
Sheets of 180 in nine panes of 20

1999, Oct. 13 Tagged *Perf. 11¼*

3354	A2598 33c **multicolored**	.65	.20
	P# block of 4, 4#+P	2.60	—
	Pane of 20	13.00	—

CHRISTMAS

Madonna and Child, by Bartolomeo Vivarini — A2599

Deer — A2600

Designed by Richard Sheaff (#3355), Tom Nikosey (#3356-3367).
Printed by Banknote Corp. of America.

LITHOGRAPHED

Serpentine Die Cut 11¼ on 2 or 3 sides

1999, Oct. 20 **Tagged**

Booklet Stamp

Self-Adhesive

3355	A2599 33c **multicolored**		.65	.15
a.	Booklet pane of 20		13.00	

Sheets of 120 in six panes of 20

Serpentine Die Cut 11¼

3356	A2600 33c **gold & red**	.65	.20
3357	A2600 33c **gold & blue**	.65	.20
3358	A2600 33c **gold & purple**	.65	.20
3359	A2600 33c **gold & green**	.65	.20
a.	Block or strip of 4, #3356-3359	2.60	
	P# block of 4, 6#+B	2.60	
	Pane of 20	13.00	

Booklet Stamps

Serpentine Die Cut 11¼ on 2, 3 or 4 sides

3360	A2600 33c **gold & red**	.65	.20
3361	A2600 33c **gold & blue**	.65	.20
3362	A2600 33c **gold & purple**	.65	.20
3363	A2600 33c **gold & green**	.65	.20
a.	Booklet pane of 20, 5 each #3360-3363	13.00	
b.	Block of 4, #3360-3363	4.00	
c.	As "b," imperf	—	
d.	As "a," imperf	—	

Size: 21x19mm

Serpentine Die Cut 11½x11¼ on 2 or 3 sides

3364	A2600 33c **gold & red**	1.00	.20
3365	A2600 33c **gold & blue**	1.00	.20
3366	A2600 33c **gold & purple**	1.00	.20
3367	A2600 33c **gold & green**	1.00	.20
a.	Booklet pane of 4, #3364-3367	4.25	
b.	Booklet pane of 5, #3364, 3366, 3367, 2 #3365 + label	5.25	
c.	Booklet pane of 6, #3365, 3367, 2 each #3364 & 3366	6.50	
d.	Block of 4, #3364-3367	4.00	

The frame on Nos. 3356-3359 is narrow and the space between it and the hoof is a hairline. The frame on Nos. 3360-3363 is much thicker, and the space between it and the hoof is wider.

Kwanzaa Type of 1997

Designed by Synthia Saint James
Printed by Avery Dennison.

PHOTOGRAVURE

Sheets of 240 in twelve pane of 20

1999, Oct. 29 **Tagged** ***Serpentine Die Cut 11***

Self-Adhesive

3368	A2458 33c **multicolored**	.65	.20
	P# block of 4, 4#+V	2.60	
	Pane of 20	13.00	

YEAR 2000

Baby New Year — A2601

Designed by Carl Herrman.
Printed by Banknote Corporation of America.

LITHOGRAPHED

Sheets of 120 in six panes of 20

1999, Dec. 27 **Tagged** ***Serpentine Die Cut 11¼***

Self-Adhesive

3369	A2601 33c **multicolored**	.65	.20
	P# block of 4, 5#+B	3.00	
	Pane of 20	14.50	

CHINESE NEW YEAR

Year of the Dragon A2602

Designed by Clarence Lee.
Printed by Sterling Sommer.

LITHOGRAPHED

Sheets of 180 in nine panes of 20

2000, Jan. 6 **Tagged** ***Perf. 11¼***

3370	A2602 33c **multicolored**	.65	.20
	P# block of 4, 4#+P	2.60	—
	Pane of 20	13.00	—

BLACK HERITAGE SERIES

Patricia Roberts Harris (1924-85), First Black Woman Cabinet Secretary — A2603

Designed by Richard Sheaff.
Printed by Ashton-Potter (USA) Ltd.

LITHOGRAPHED

Sheets of 180 in nine panes of 20

Serpentine Die Cut 11½x11¼

2000, Jan. 27 **Tagged**

Self-Adhesive

3371	A2603 33c **indigo**	.65	.20
	P# block of 4, 4#+P	2.60	
	Pane of 20	13.00	

SUBMARINES

S Class A2604

Los Angeles Class A2605

Ohio Class A2606

USS Holland A2607

Gato Class — A2608

Illustration of No. 3377 reduced.

Designed by Carl Herrman.
Printed by Banknote Corporation of America.

LITHOGRAPHED

Sheets of 180 in nine panes of 20

2000, Mar. 27 **Tagged** ***Perf. 11***

3372	A2605 33c **multicolored,** with microprinted "USPS" at base of sail	.75	.20
	P# block of 4, 4#+B	3.00	—
	Pane of 20	15.00	—

BOOKLET STAMPS

3373	A2604 22c **multicolored**	.75	.20
3374	A2605 33c **multicolored,** no microprinting	1.00	.30
3375	A2606 55c **multicolored**	1.60	.50
3376	A2607 60c **multicolored**	2.00	.55
3377	A2608 $3.20 **multicolored**	10.00	3.00
a.	Booklet pane of 5, #3373-3377	17.50	—

No. 3377a was issued with two types of text in the selvage.

PACIFIC COAST RAIN FOREST

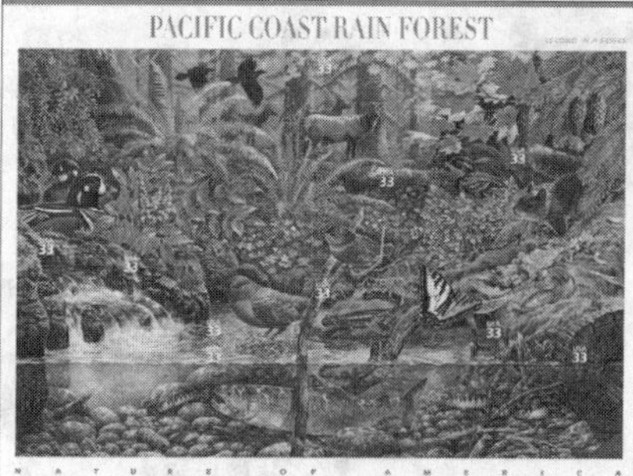

A2609

Illustration reduced.

Designed by Ethel Kessler.
Printed by Banknote Corporation of America.

Designs: a, Harlequin duck. b, Dwarf oregongrape, snail-eating ground beetle. c, American dipper, horiz. d, Cutthroat trout, horiz. e, Roosevelt elk. f, Winter wren. g, Pacific giant salamander, Rough-skinned newt. h, Western tiger swallowtail, horiz. i, Douglas squirrel, foliose lichen. j, Foliose lichen, banana slug.

LITHOGRAPHED

Sheets of 60 in six panes of 10

Serpentine Die Cut 11¼x11½, 11½ (horiz. stamps)

2000, Mar. 29 **Tagged**

Self-Adhesive

3378 A2609 Pane of 10 6.50
a.-j. 33c any single .65 .20
Sheet of 6 panes 39.00

LOUISE NEVELSON (1899-1988), SCULPTOR

Silent Music I — A2610

Royal Tide I — A2611

Black Chord — A2612

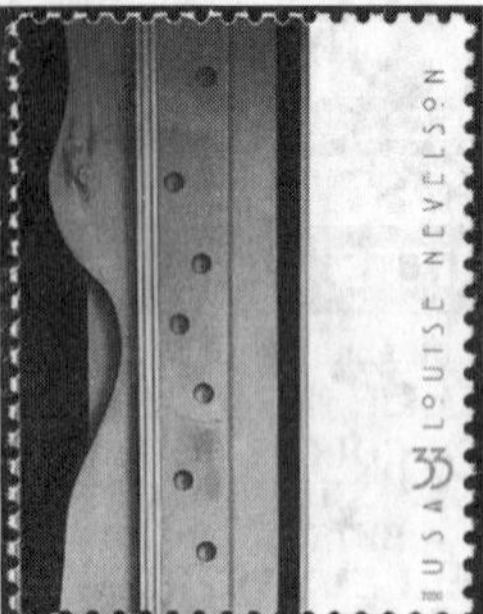

Nightsphere-Light A2613

Dawn's Wedding Chapel I — A2614

Designed by Ethel Kessler.
Printed by Ashton-Potter (USA) Ltd.

LITHOGRAPHED

Sheets of 80 in four panes of 20.

2000, Apr. 6 **Tagged** ***Perf. 11x11¼***

3379 A2610 33c **multicolored** .65 .20
3380 A2611 33c **multicolored** .65 .20
3381 A2612 33c **multicolored** .65 .20
3382 A2613 33c **multicolored** .65 .20
3383 A2614 33c **multicolored** .65 .20
a. Strip of 5, #3379-3383 3.25 —
P# block of 10, 4#+P 6.50 —
Pane of 20 13.00 —

HUBBLE SPACE TELESCOPE IMAGES

Eagle Nebula — A2615

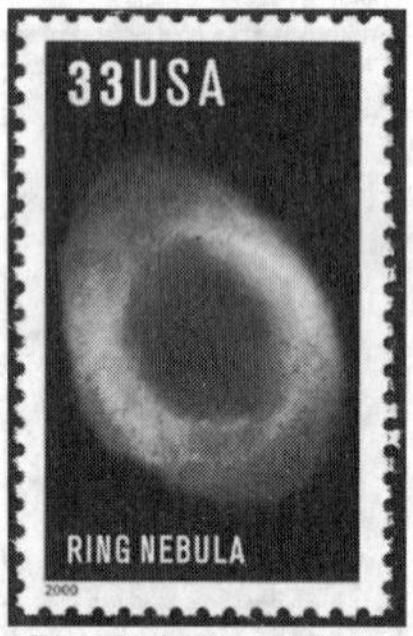

Ring Nebula — A2616

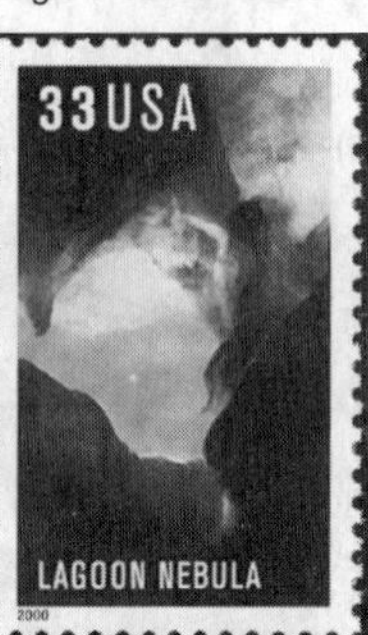

Lagoon Nebula — A2617

Egg Nebula — A2618

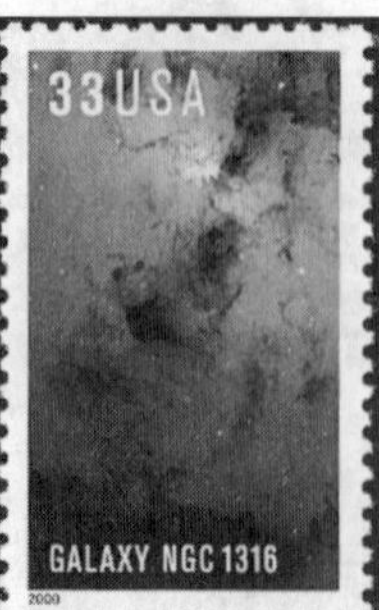

Galaxy NGC 1316 — A2619

Designed by Phil Jordan. Printed at American Packaging Corp. for Sennett Security Products.

PHOTOGRAVURE

Sheets of 120 in six panes of 20.

2000, Apr. 10 **Tagged** ***Perf. 11***

3384 A2615 33c **multicolored** .65 .20
3385 A2616 33c **multicolored** .65 .20
3386 A2617 33c **multicolored** .65 .20
3387 A2618 33c **multicolored** .65 .20
3388 A2619 33c **multicolored** .65 .20
a. Strip of 5, #3384-3388 3.25 —
P# block of 10, 6#+S 6.50 —
Pane of 20 13.00 —
b. As "a," imperf *1,200.*
As "b," pane of 20 *5,000.*

AMERICAN SAMOA

Samoan Double Canoe A2620

Designed by Howard Paine.
Printed by Ashton-Potter (USA) Ltd.

LITHOGRAPHED

Sheets of 120 in six panes of 20

2000, Apr. 17 **Tagged** ***Perf. 11***

3389 A2620 33c **multicolored** .65 .20
P# block of 4, 4#+P 2.60 —
Pane of 20 13.00 —

LIBRARY OF CONGRESS

Interior Dome and Arched Windows in Main Reading Room, Thomas Jefferson Building — A2621

Designed by Ethel Kessler.
Printed by Ashton-Potter (USA) Ltd.

LITHOGRAPHED

Sheets of 120 in six panes of 20

2000, Apr. 24 **Tagged** ***Perf. 11***

3390 A2621 33c **multicolored** .65 .20
P# block of 4, 5#+P 2.60 —
Pane of 20 13.00 —

ROAD RUNNER & WILE E. COYOTE

A2622

Cross Gutter Block of 9

Illustration reduced.

Designed by Ed Wleczyk, Warner Bros.
Printed by Banknote Corp. of America, Inc.

LITHOGRAPHED

2000, Apr. 26 Tagged ***Serpentine Die Cut 11***
Self-Adhesive

3391	Pane of 10	6.50	
a.	A2622 33c single	.65	.20
b.	Booklet pane of 9 #3391a	5.85	
c.	Booklet pane of 1 #3391a	.65	
	Sheet of 60 (six panes) top, with plate # in selvage on reverse	47.50	
	Sheet of 60 (six panes) bottom, with plate # in selvage	50.00	
	Pane of 10 from sheet of 60	8.00	
	Two panes of 10 with plate numbers on front	18.00	
	Cross gutter block of 9 or 10	16.00	
	Vert. pair with horiz. gutter	2.00	
	Horiz. pair with vert. gutter	4.00	
d.	All die cutting omitted, pane of 10	*8,500.*	

Die cutting on #3391b does not extend through the backing paper.

3392	Pane of 10	*6.50*	
a.	A2622 33c single	*.65*	
b.	Booklet pane of 9 #3392a	—	
c.	Booklet pane of 1, imperf.	—	

Die cutting on #3392a extends through the backing paper. Used examples of No. 3392a are identical to those of No. 3391a.

Nos. 3391b-3391c and 3392b-3392c are separated by a vertical line of microperforations.

DISTINGUISHED SOLDIERS

Maj. Gen. John L. Hines (1868-1968) A2623

Gen. Omar N. Bradley (1893-1981) A2624

Sgt. Alvin C. York (1887-1964) A2625

Second Lt. Audie L. Murphy (1924-71) A2626

Designed by Phil Jordan.
Printed by Sterling Sommer for Ashton-Potter (USA) Ltd.

LITHOGRAPHED
Sheets of 120 in six panes of 20

2000, May 3 Tagged ***Perf. 11***

3393	A2623 33c	**multicolored**	.65	.20
3394	A2624 33c	**multicolored**	.65	.20
3395	A2625 33c	**multicolored**	.65	.20
3396	A2626 33c	**multicolored**	.65	.20
a.		Block or strip of 4, #3393-3396	2.60	—
		P# block of 4, 4#+P	2.60	—
		Pane of 20	13.00	—

SUMMER SPORTS

Runners A2627

Designed by Richard Sheaff.
Printed by Ashton-Potter (USA) Ltd.

LITHOGRAPHED
Sheets of 120 in six panes of 20

2000, May 5 Tagged ***Perf. 11***

3397	A2627 33c	**multicolored**	.65	.20
		P# block of 4, 4#+P	2.60	—
		Pane of 20	13.00	—

ADOPTION

Stick Figures — A2628

Designed by Greg Berger.
Printed by Banknote Corporation of America.

LITHOGRAPHED
Sheets of 120 in six panes of 20

2000, May 10 Tagged ***Serpentine Die Cut 11½***
Self-Adhesive

3398	A2628 33c	**multicolored**	.65	.20
		P# block of 4, 5#+B	2.60	
		Pane of 20	13.00	

YOUTH TEAM SPORTS

Basketball — A2629

Football — A2630

Soccer — A2631

Baseball — A2632

Designed by Derry Noyes.
Printed by Sterling Sommer for Ashton-Potter (USA) Ltd.

LITHOGRAPHED
Sheets of 120 in six panes of 20

2000, May 27 Tagged ***Perf. 11***

3399	A2629 33c	**multicolored**	.65	.20
3400	A2630 33c	**multicolored**	.65	.20
3401	A2631 33c	**multicolored**	.65	.20
3402	A2632 33c	**multicolored**	.65	.20
a.		Block or strip of 4, #3399-3402	2.60	—
		P# block of 4, 4#+P	2.60	—
		Pane of 20	13.00	—

THE STARS AND STRIPES

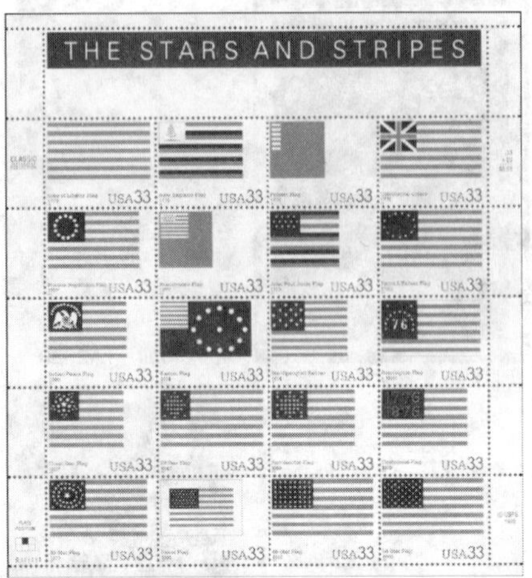

A2633

Illustration reduced.

Designed by Richard Sheaff.
Printed by Banknote Corp. of America.

Designs: a, Sons of Liberty Flag, 1775. b, New England Flag, 1775. c, Forster Flag, 1775. d, Continental Colors, 1776. e, Francis Hopkinson Flag, 1777. f, Brandywine Flag, 1777. g, John Paul Jones Flag, 1779. h, Pierre L'Enfant Flag, 1783. i, Indian Peace Flag, 1803. j, Easton Flag, 1814. k, Star-Spangled Banner, 1814. l, Bennington Flag, c. 1820. m, Great Star Flag, 1837. n, 29-Star Flag, 1847. o, Fort Sumter Flag, 1861. p, Centennial Flag, 1876. q, 38-Star Flag, 1877. r, Peace Flag, 1891. s, 48-Star Flag, 1912. t, 50-Star Flag, 1960.

LITHOGRAPHED

2000, June 14 **Tagged** ***Perf. 10½x11***

3403	A2633 Pane of 20	13.00	—
a.-t.	33c any single	.65	.30
	Sheet of 120 (6 panes)	80.00	
	Cross gutter block of 20	22.50	—
	Vert. pairs with horiz. gutter (each)	2.25	—
	Horiz. pairs with vert. gutter (each)	2.25	—

Inscriptions on the back of each stamp describe the flag.

Cross gutter block of 20 consists of six stamps from each of two panes and four stamps from each of two other panes with the cross gutter between.

BERRIES

Blueberries — A2634

Strawberries — A2635

Blackberries — A2636

Raspberries — A2637

Designed by Howard Paine. Printed by Guilford Gravure.

See designs A2550-A2553.

PHOTOGRAVURE
COIL STAMPS
Serpentine Die Cut 8½ Horiz.

2000, June 16 **Tagged**

Self-Adhesive

3404	A2634 33c **multicolored**	.75	.20
3405	A2635 33c **multicolored**	.75	.20
3406	A2636 33c **multicolored**	.75	.20
3407	A2637 33c **multicolored**	.75	.20
a.	Strip of 4, #3404-3407	3.00	
	P# strip of 5, 2 #3404, 1 each #3405-3407, #G1111	6.00	
	P# strip of 9, 2 each #3404-3405, 3407, 3 #3406, #G1111	8.50	
	P# single (#3406), #G1111	—	1.50

The adhesive on Nos. 3404-3407 is strong and can remove the ink from stamps in the roll.

LEGENDS OF BASEBALL

A2638

Illustration reduced.

Designed by Phil Jordan. Printed by Ashton-Potter (USA) Ltd.

Designs: a, Jackie Robinson. b, Eddie Collins. c, Christy Mathewson. d, Ty Cobb. e, George Sisler. f, Rogers Hornsby. g, Mickey Cochrane. h, Babe Ruth. i, Walter Johnson. j, Roberto Clemente. k, Lefty Grove. l, Tris Speaker. m, Cy Young. n, Jimmie Foxx. o, Pie Traynor. p, Satchel Paige. q, Honus Wagner. r, Josh Gibson. s, Dizzy Dean. t, Lou Gehrig.

LITHOGRAPHED
Sheets of 120 in six panes of 20

2000, July 6 **Tagged** ***Serpentine Die Cut 11¼***

Self-Adhesive

3408	A2638 Pane of 20	13.00	
a.-t.	33c any single	.65	.20
	Sheet of 120 (6 panes)	80.00	
	Cross gutter block of 20	22.50	—
	Vert. pairs with horiz. gutter (each)	2.25	—
	Horiz. pairs with vert. gutter (each)	2.25	—

Cross gutter block of 20 consists of six stamps from each of two panes and four stamps from each of two other panes with the cross gutter between.

SPACE
Souvenir Sheets

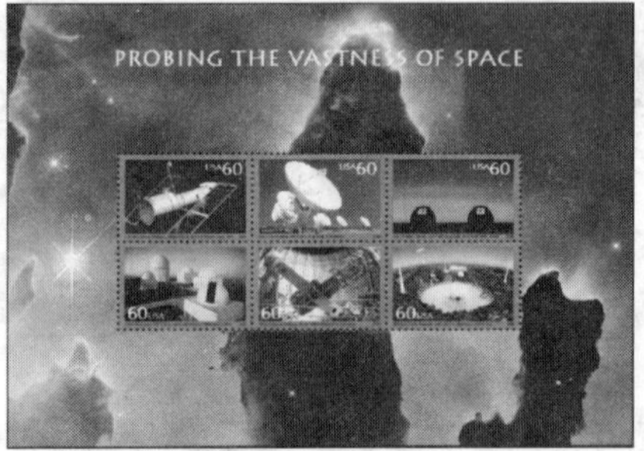

Probing the Vastness of Space — A2639

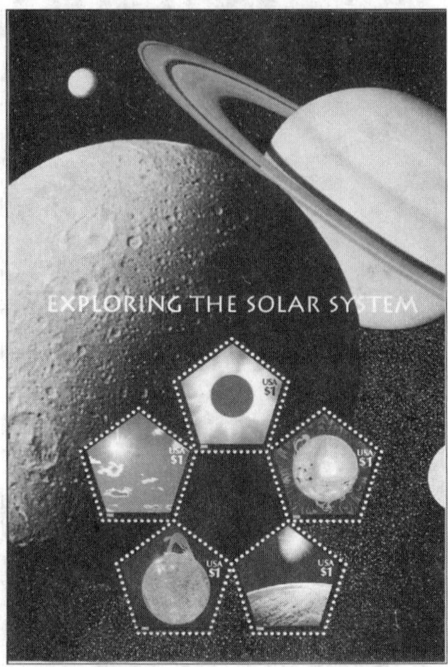

Exploring the Solar System — A2640

Escaping the Gravity of Earth — A2641

Space Achievement and Exploration — A2642

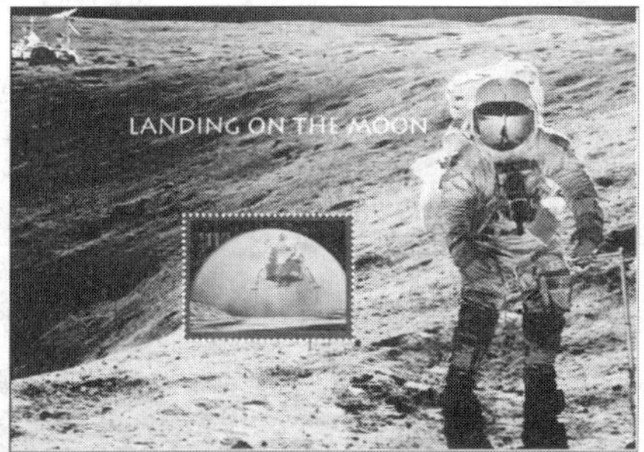

Landing on the Moon — A2643

Designed by Richard Sheaff. Printed by American Packaging Corporation for Sennett Security Products.

Designs: No. 3409: a, Hubble Space Telescope. b, Radio interferometer very large array, New Mexico. c, Optical and infrared telescopes, Keck Observatory, Hawaii. d, Optical telescopes, Cerro Tololo Observatory, Chile. e, Optical telescope, Mount Wilson Observatory, California. f, Radio telescope, Arecibo Observatory, Puerto Rico.

No. 3410: a, Sun and corona. b, Cross-section of sun. c, Sun and earth. d, Sun and solar flare. e, Sun and clouds.

No. 3411: a, Space Shuttle and Space Station. b, Astronauts working in space.

Illustrations reduced.

PHOTOGRAVURE

2000 Tagged ***Perf. 10½x11***

3409	A2639	Sheet of 6, *July 10*	7.50	—
a.-f.		60c any single	1.25	.60

Perf. 10¾

3410	A2640	Sheet of 5 + label, *July 11*	10.00	—
a.-e.		$1 any single	2.00	1.00
f.		As No. 3410, imperf	—	
g		As No. 3410, with hologram from No. 3411b applied	—	

Untagged

Photogravure with Hologram Affixed

Perf. 10½, 10¾ (#3412)

3411	A2641	Sheet of 2, *July 9*	12.50	—
a.-b.		$3.20 any single	6.25	3.00
c.		Hologram omitted on right stamp	—	
3412	A2642	**multicolored,** *July 7*	22.50	11.50
a.		$11.75 single	20.00	10.00
b.		Hologram omitted	—	
c.		Hologram omitted on No. 3412 in uncut sheet of 5 panes	—	
3413	A2643	**multicolored,** *July 8*	22.50	11.50
		Uncut sheet of 5 panes, #3409-3412	75.00	
a.		$11.75 single	20.00	10.00
b.		Double hologram	—	
c.		Double hologram on No. 3413 in uncut sheet of 5 panes	—	
d.		Hologram omitted on No. 3413 in uncut sheet of 5 panes	—	
		Nos. 3409-3413 (5)	75.00	

Warning: Soaking in water may affect holographic images.

STAMPIN' THE FUTURE CHILDREN'S STAMP DESIGN CONTEST WINNERS

By Zachary Canter A2644

By Sarah Lipsey A2645

By Morgan Hill — A2646

By Ashley Young A2647

Designed by Richard Sheaff. Printed by Ashton-Potter (USA) Ltd.

LITHOGRAPHED

Sheets of 120 in six panes of 20

2000, July 13 Tagged ***Serpentine Die Cut 11¼***

Self-Adhesive

3414	A2644	33c	**multicolored**	.65	.20
3415	A2645	33c	**multicolored**	.65	.20
3416	A2646	33c	**multicolored**	.65	.20
3417	A2647	33c	**multicolored**	.65	.20
a.			Horiz. strip of 4, #3414-3417	2.60	
			P# block of 8, 2 sets of 5#+P	5.25	
			Pane of 20	13.00	

Plate block may contain top label.

DISTINGUISHED AMERICANS

Gen. Joseph W. Stilwell (1883-1946) A2650

Sen. Claude Pepper (1900-89) A2656

Sen. Hattie Caraway (1878-1950) A2661

Edna Ferber (1887-1968), Writer A2662

Designed by: 10c, 33c, 76c, 83c Richard Sheaff.
Printed by Banknote Corporation of America.

LITHOGRAPHED & ENGRAVED

Sheets of 120 in six panes of 20

Perf. 11 (#3420, 3426), Serpentine Die Cut 11 (#3431), 11½x11 (#3432), 11x11¾ (#3433)

2000-02 Tagged

3420	A2650	10c	**red & black,** *Aug. 24*	.20	.20
			P# block of 4, 3#+B	.80	—
			Pane of 20	4.00	—
a.			Imperf, pair	*450.00*	
3426	A2656	33c	**red & black,** *Sept. 7*	.65	.20
			P# block of 4, 3#+B	2.60	—
			Pane of 20	13.00	—
3431	A2661	76c	**red & black,** *Feb. 21, 2001*	1.50	.20
			P# block of 4, 3#+B	6.00	
			Pane of 20	30.00	
3432	A2661	76c	**red & black,**	*3.25*	*3.00*
			P# block of 4, 3#+B	*14.00*	
			Pane of 20	*70.00*	
3433	A2662	83c	**red & black,** *July 29, 2002*	1.60	.30
			P# block of 4, 3#+B1	6.50	
			Pane of 20	32.50	

This is an ongoing set. Numbers may change.

CALIFORNIA STATEHOOD, 150TH ANNIV.

Big Sur and Iceplant — A2668

Designed by Carl Herrman.
Printed by Avery Dennison.

PHOTOGRAVURE

Sheets of 200 in ten panes of 20

2000, Sept. 8 Tagged ***Serpentine Die Cut 11***

Self-Adhesive

3438	A2668	33c	**multicolored**	.65	.20
			P# block of 4, 5#+V	2.60	
			Pane of 20	13.00	

DEEP SEA CREATURES

Fanfin Anglerfish A2669

Sea Cucumber A2670

Fangtooth A2671

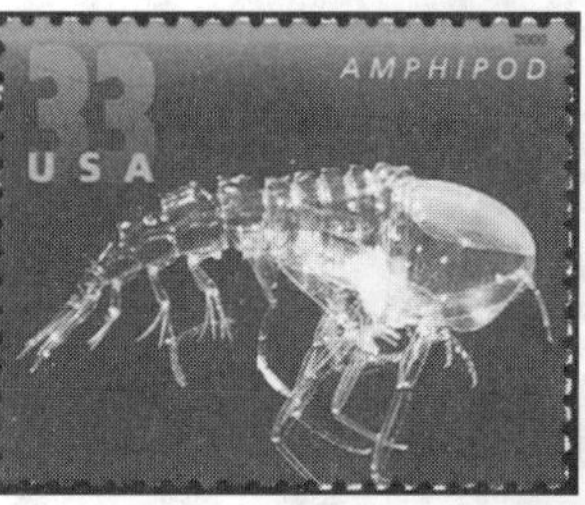

Amphipod A2672

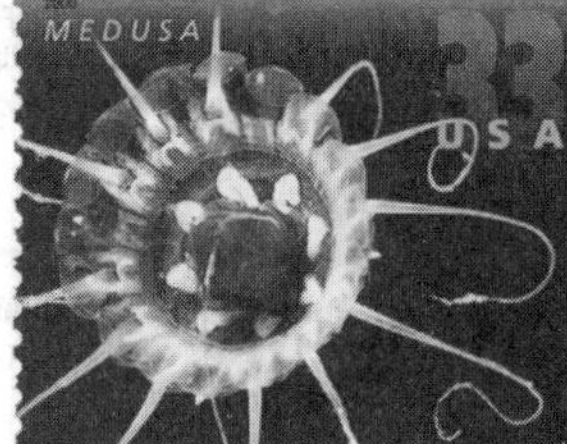

Medusa A2673

Designed by Ethel Kessler.

Printed by American Packaging Corp. for Sennett Security Products.

PHOTOGRAVURE

Sheets of 135 in nine panes of 15

2000, Oct. 2 **Tagged** ***Perf. 10x10¼***

3439 A2669 33c **multicolored** .65 .20
3440 A2670 33c **multicolored** .65 .20
3441 A2671 33c **multicolored** .65 .20
3442 A2672 33c **multicolored** .65 .20
3443 A2673 33c **multicolored** .65 .20
a. Vert. strip of 5, #3439-3443 3.25 —
Pane of 15, 4#+S 9.75 —
Sheet of 135 (nine panes) 90.00 —
Cross gutter block of 10 15.00 —
Horiz. block of 10 with vert. gutter 10.00 —
Horiz. pairs with vert. gutter (each) 2.00 —
Vert. pair with horiz. gutter 1.75 —

See note under No. 3292 regarding lack of plate block listing.

Cross gutter block of 10 consists of three stamps from each of two panes and two stamps from each of the other two panes with the cross gutter between.

LITERARY ARTS SERIES

Thomas Wolfe (1900-38), Novelist A2674

Designed by Phil Jordan.
Printed by Ashton-Potter (USA) Ltd.

LITHOGRAPHED

Sheets of 120 in six panes of 20

2000, Oct. 3 **Tagged** ***Perf. 11***

3444 A2674 33c **multicolored** .65 .20
P# block of 4, 5#+P 2.60 —
Pane of 20 13.00 —

WHITE HOUSE, 200TH ANNIV.

A2675

Designed by Derry Noyes.
Printed by Ashton-Potter (USA) Ltd.

LITHOGRAPHED

Sheets of 180 in nine panes of 20

2000, Oct. 18 **Tagged** ***Serpentine Die Cut 11¼***

Self-Adhesive

3445 A2675 33c **multicolored** .65 .20
P# block of 4, 4#+P 2.60
Pane of 20 13.00

LEGENDS OF HOLLYWOOD

Edward G. Robinson (1893-1973) — A2676

Designed by Howard Paine.
Printed by American Packaging Corporation for Sennett Security Products.

PHOTOGRAVURE

Sheets of 120 in six panes of 20

2000, Oct. 24 **Tagged** ***Perf. 11***

3446 A2676 33c **multicolored** .65 .20
P# block of 4, 7#+S 2.60 —
Pane of 20 13.00 —
Sheet of 120 80.00
Cross gutter block of 8 17.50
Block of 8 with vertical gutter 10.00
Horiz. pair with vert. gutter 3.00
Vert. pair with horiz. gutter 2.00

Perforations in corner of each stamp are star-shaped. Cross gutter block consists of 6 stamps from upper panes and 2 stamps from panes below.

New York Public Library Lion — A2677

Designed by Carl Herrman.
Printed by American Packaging Corporation for Sennett Security Products.

PHOTOGRAVURE
COIL STAMP

Serpentine Die Cut 11½ Vert.

2000, Nov. 9 **Untagged**

Self-Adhesive

3447 A2677 (10c) **multicolored** .20 .20
Pair .40
P# strip of 5, #S11111, S22222, S33333 3.00
P# single, #S11111, S22222, S33333 — 1.75

Flag Over Farm — A2678

Designed by Richard Sheaff.
Printed by Sterling Sommer for Ashton-Potter (USA) Ltd. (#3448), Ashton-Potter (USA) Ltd. (#3449), Avery Dennison (#3450).

LITHOGRAPHED (#3448-3449), PHOTOGRAVURE (#3450)

Sheets of 120 in six panes of 20

2000, Dec. 15 **Tagged** ***Perf. 11¼***

3448 A2678 (34c) **multicolored** .65 .20
P# block of 4, 4# + P 2.60 —
Pane of 20 13.00 —

Self-Adhesive

Serpentine Die Cut 11¼

3449 A2678 (34c) **multicolored** .65 .20
P# block of 4, 4# + P 2.60
Pane of 20 13.00

Booklet Stamp

Self-Adhesive

Serpentine Die Cut 8 on 2, 3 or 4 sides

3450 A2678 (34c) **multicolored** .75 .20
a. Booklet pane of 18 14.00

A2679

Statue of Liberty — A2680

Designed by Derry Noyes.
Printed by Avery Dennison (#3451), Bureau of Engraving and Printing (#3452-3453).

PHOTOGRAVURE

Serpentine Die Cut 11 on 2, 3 or 4 sides

2000, Dec. 15 **Tagged**

Self-Adhesive (#3451, 3453)

Booklet Stamp

3451 A2679 (34c) **multicolored** .65 .20
a. Booklet pane of 20 13.00
b. Booklet pane of 4 2.60
Booklet pane of 4 containing P# single 2.60
P# single, #V1111 .65 .50
c. Booklet pane of 6 3.90
d. As "a," imperf —

Coil Stamps

Perf. 9¾ Vert.

3452 A2680 (34c) **multicolored** .65 .20
Pair 1.30 .30
P# strip of 5, #1111 5.00 —
P# single, same # — 2.50

Serpentine Die Cut 10 Vert.

3453 A2680 (34c) **multicolored** .65 .20
Pair 1.30
P# strip of 5, #1111 5.00
P# single, same # — 3.00
a. Imperf, pair —

A2681

A2682

A2683

Flowers — A2684

Designed by Derry Noyes.
Printed by American Packaging Corporation for Sennett Security Products (#3454-3461), Guilford Gravure for Banknote Corporation of America, Inc. (#3462-3465).

PHOTOGRAVURE

Serpentine Die Cut 10½x10¾ on 2 or 3 sides

2000, Dec. 15 **Tagged**

Booklet Stamps

Self-Adhesive

3454 A2681 (34c) **purple & multi** .65 .20
3455 A2682 (34c) **tan & multi** .65 .20
3456 A2683 (34c) **green & multi** .65 .20
3457 A2684 (34c) **red & multi** .65 .20
a. Block of 4, #3454-3457 2.60
b. Booklet pane of 4, #3454-3457 2.60
c. Booklet pane of 6, #3456, 3457, 2 each #3454-3455 3.90
d. Booklet pane of 6, #3454, 3455, 2 each #3456-3457 3.90
e. Booklet pane of 20, 5 each #3454-3457 + label 13.00

No. 3457e is a double-sided booklet pane, with 12 stamps on one side and eight stamps plus label on the other side.

Serpentine Die Cut 11½x11¾ on 2 or 3 sides

3458 A2681 (34c) **purple & multi** .65 .20
3459 A2682 (34c) **tan & multi** .65 .20
3460 A2683 (34c) **green & multi** .65 .20
3461 A2684 (34c) **red & multi** .65 .20
a. Block of 4, #3458-3461 2.60
b. Booklet pane of 20, 2 each #3461a, 3 each #3457a *25.00*
c. Booklet pane of 20, 2 each #3457a, 3 each #3461a *30.00*

Nos. 3461b and 3461c are double-sided booklet panes, with 12 stamps on one side and eight stamps plus label on the other side.

Coil Stamps

Serpentine Die Cut 8½ Vert.

3462 A2683 (34c) **green & multi** .75 .20
3463 A2684 (34c) **red & multi** .75 .20
3464 A2682 (34c) **tan & multi** .75 .20
3465 A2681 (34c) **purple & multi** .75 .20
a. Strip of 4, #3462-3465 3.00
P# strip of 5, 2 #3462, 1 each #3463-3465, P#B1111 6.00
P# strip of 9, 2 each #3462-3463, 3465, 3 #3464, same P# 8.50
P# single (#3464) — 2.50

Lettering on No. 3462 has black outline not found on No. 3456. Zeroes of "2000" are rounder on Nos. 3454-3457 than on Nos. 3462-3465.

Statue of Liberty
A2685

George Washington
A2686

American
Buffalo — A2687

Flag Over
Farm — A2688

Statue of
Liberty — A2689

A2690

A2691

A2692

Flowers — A2693

Apple — A2694

Orange — A2695

Eagle — A2696

Capitol
Dome — A2697

Washington
Monument — A2698

Designed by Sterling Sommer for Ashton-Potter (USA) Ltd. (#3467), Carl Herrman (#3467, 3468, 3471, 3471A, 3475, 3484, 3484A), Richard Sheaff (#3468A, 3469, 3470, 3475A, 3482-3483, 3495), Derry Noyes (#3466, 3472-3473, 3476, 3477-3481, 3485, 3487-3490), Ned Seidler (#3491-3494).

Printed by Avery Dennison (#3468, 3475, 3485, 3495) Ashton-Potter (USA) Ltd. (#3469-3470, 3482-3484A), American Packaging Corporation for Sennett Security Printers (#3471, 3471A, 3487-3490), Bureau of Engraving and Printing (#3466, 3476-3477), Guilford Gravure, Inc. for Banknote Corporation of America (#3475A, 3478-3481), Banknote Corporation of America (#3468A, 3472-3473, 3491-3494).

PHOTOGRAVURE

Serpentine Die Cut 9¾ Vert.

2001, Jan. 7 **Tagged**

Coil Stamp

Self-Adhesive

3466 A2685 34c **multicolored** .65 .20
Pair 1.30
P# strip of 5, #1111, 2222 5.00
P# single, same # — 2.50

Sheets of 400 in four panes of 100 (#3467), Sheets of 200 in ten panes of 20 (#3468), Sheets of 200 in two panes of 100 (#3469), Sheets of 120 in six panes of 20 (#3468A, 3470-3473), Sheets of 160 in eight panes of 20 (#3471A)

Self-Adhesive (#3468-3468A, 3470-3473)

2001 **Photo.** **Tagged** ***Perf. 11¼x11***

3467 A2687 21c **multicolored,** *Sept. 20* .40 .20
P# block of 4, 6#+P 5.00 —

Serpentine Die Cut 11

3468 A2687 21c **multicolored,** *Feb. 22* .40 .20
P# block of 4, 4#+V 1.60
Pane of 20 8.00

Litho.

Serpentine Die Cut 11¼x11¾

3468A A2686 23c **green,** *Sept. 20* .45 .20
P# block of 4, 3#+B 1.80
Pane of 20 9.00

Photo.

Perf. 11¼

3469 A2688 34c **multicolored,** *Feb. 7* .65 .20
P# block of 4, 4#+P 9.00 —

Serpentine Die Cut 11¼

3470 A2688 34c **multicolored,** *Mar. 6* .65 .20
P# block of 4, 4#+P 2.60
Pane of 20 13.00

Photo.

Serpentine Die Cut 10¾

3471 A2696 55c **multicolored,** *Feb. 22* 1.10 .20
P# block of 4, 5#+S 4.40
Pane of 20 22.00

Serpentine Die Cut 10¾

3471A A2696 57c **multicolored,** *Sept. 20* 1.10 .20
P# block of 4, 5#+S 4.40
Pane of 20 22.00

LITHOGRAPHED

Serpentine Die Cut 11¼x11½

3472 A2697 $3.50 **multicolored,** *Jan. 29* 7.00 3.50
P# block of 4, 4#+B 28.00
Pane of 20 140.00
a. Imperf, pair —

3473 A2698 $12.25 **multicolored,** *Jan. 29* 22.50 10.00
P# block of 4, 4#+B 90.00
Pane of 20 450.00

COIL STAMPS

Self-Adhesive (#3475-3475A, 3477-3481)

Photo.

Serpentine Die Cut 8½ Vert.

3475 A2687 21c **multicolored,** *Feb. 22* .40 .20
Pair .80 .30
P# strip of 5, #V1111, V2222 3.50 —
P# single, same # — 1.25

3475A A2686 23c **green,** *Sept. 20* .45 .20
Pair .90
P# strip of 5, #B11 2.50
P# single, same # — .60

Compare No. 3475A ("2001" date at lower left) with No. 3617 ("2002" date at lower left).

Perf. 9¾ Vert.

3476 A2685 34c **multicolored,** prephosphored coated paper (grainy solid tagging), *Feb. 7* .65 .20
Pair 1.30 .30
P# strip of 5, #1111 5.00 —
P# single, same # — 2.50
a. Prephosphored coated paper (solid tagging) .65 .20
Pair 1.30 .30
P# strip of 5, #1111 5.00 —
P# single, same # — 2.00

Serpentine Die Cut 9¾ Vert.

3477 A2685 34c **multicolored,** *Feb. 7* .65 .20
Pair 1.30 .30
P# strip of 5, #1111, 2222, 3333, 4444, 5555, 6666, 7777 5.00 —
P# single, same # — 2.00

No. 3477 has right angle corners and backing paper as high as the stamp. No. 3466 has rounded corners and is on backing paper larger than the stamp.

Serpentine Die Cut 8½ Vert.

3478 A2690 34c **green & multi,** *Feb. 7* .65 .20
3479 A2691 34c **red & multi,** *Feb. 7* .65 .20
3480 A2692 34c **tan & multi,** *Feb. 7* .65 .20
3481 A2693 34c **purple & multi,** *Feb. 7* .65 .20
a. Strip of 4, #3478-3481 2.60
P# strip of 5, 2 #3478, 1 each #3479-3481, P#B1111, B2111, B2122, B2211, B2222 4.50
P# strip of 9, 3 #3480, 2 each #3478-3479, 3481, P# B1111, B2111, B2122, B2211, B2222 6.50 —
P# single, (#3480), same # — 2.00

BOOKLET STAMPS

Litho.

Self-Adhesive, Tagged

Serpentine Die Cut 11¼ on 3 Sides

3482 A2686 20c **dark carmine,** *Feb. 22* .40 .20
a. Booklet pane of 10 4.00
b. Booklet pane of 4 1.60
c. Booklet pane of 6 2.40

Serpentine Die Cut 10½x11¼ on 3 Sides

3483 A2686 20c **dark carmine,** *Feb. 22* 1.75 1.50
a. Booklet pane of 4, 2 #3482 at L, 2 #3483 at R *9.00*
b. Booklet pane of 6, 3 #3482 at L, 3 #3483 at R *15.00*
c. Booklet pane of 10, 5 #3482 at L, 5 #3483 at R *16.00*
d. Booklet pane of 4, 2 #3483 at L, 2 #3482 at R *9.00*
e. Booklet pane of 6, 3 #3483 at L, 3 #3482 at R *15.00*
f. Booklet pane of 10, 5 #3483 at L, 5 #3482 at R *16.00*
g. Pair, #3482 at L, #3483 at R *4.00*
h. Pair, #3483 at L, #3482 at R *4.00*

Serpentine Die Cut 11¼ on 3 Sides

3484 A2687 21c **multicolored,** *Sept. 20* .40 .20
b. Booklet pane of 4 1.60
c. Booklet pane of 6 2.40
d. Booklet pane of 10 4.00

Serpentine Die Cut 10½x11¼

3484A A2687 21c **multicolored,** *Sept. 20* *1.75* 1.50
e. Booklet pane of 4, 2 #3484 at L, 2 #3484A at R *9.00*
f. Booklet pane of 6, 3 #3484 at L, 3 #3484A at R *15.00*
g. Booklet pane of 10, 5 #3484 at L, 5 #3484A at R *16.00*
h. Booklet pane of 4, 2 #3484A at L, 2 #3484 at R *9.00*
i. Booklet pane of 6, 3 #3484A at L, 3 #3484 at R *15.00*
j. Booklet pane of 10, 5 #3484A at L, 5 #3484 at R *16.00*
k. Pair, #3484 at L, #3484A at R *4.00*
l. Pair, #3484A at L, #3484 at R *4.00*

Photo.

Serpentine Die Cut 11 on 2, 3 or 4 Sides

3485 A2689 34c **multicolored,** *Feb. 7* .65 .20
a. Booklet pane of 10 6.50
b. Booklet pane of 20 13.00
c. Booklet pane of 4 2.60
Booklet pane of 4 containing P# single 2.60
P# single, #V1111, V1122, V2212, V2222 .65 .65
P# single, #V1112, V1121 — —
d. Booklet pane of 6 3.90
e. Imperf, pair (from No. 3485b) —
f. As "e," booklet pane of 20 —

Photo.

Serpentine Die Cut 10½x10¾ on 2 or 3 Sides

3487 A2693 34c **purple & multi,** *Feb. 7* .65 .20
3488 A2692 34c **tan & multi,** *Feb. 7* .65 .20
3489 A2690 34c **green & multi,** *Feb. 7* .65 .20
3490 A2691 34c **red & multi,** *Feb. 7* .65 .20
a. Block of 4, #3487-3490 2.60
b. Booklet pane of 4, #3487-3490 2.60

c. Booklet pane of 6, #3489-3490, 2 each #3487-3488 3.90
d. Booklet pane of 6, #3487-3488, 2 each #3489-3490 3.90
e. Booklet pane of 20, 5 each #3490a + label 13.00

No. 3490e is a double-sided booklet pane, with 12 stamps on one side and eight stamps plus label on the others side.

Litho.

Serpentine Die Cut 11¼ on 2, 3 or 4 Sides

3491 A2694 34c **multicolored,** *Mar. 6* .65 .20
3492 A2695 34c **multicolored,** *Mar. 6* .65 .20
a. Pair, #3491-3492 1.30
b. Booklet pane, 10 each #3491-3492 13.00
c. As "a," black ("34 USA") omitted —
d. As "a," imperf —
e. As "b," imperf —

Serpentine Die Cut 11½x10¾ on 2 or 3 Sides

3493 A2694 34c **multicolored,** *May* .65 .20
3494 A2695 34c **multicolored,** *May* .65 .20
a. Pair, #3493-3494 1.30
b. Booklet pane, 2 each #3493-3494 2.60
Booklet pane, 2 each #3493-3494, containing P# single 2.60
P# single, #B1111 .65 .65
c. Booklet pane, 3 each #3493-3494, #3493 at UL 3.90
d. Booklet pane, 3 each #3493-3494, #3494 at UL 3.90

Serpentine Die Cut 8 on 2, 3 or 4 sides

3495 A2688 34c **multicolored,** *Dec. 17* .65 .20
a. Booklet pane of 18 12.00

LOVE

Rose, Apr. 20, 1763 Love Letter by John Adams — A2699

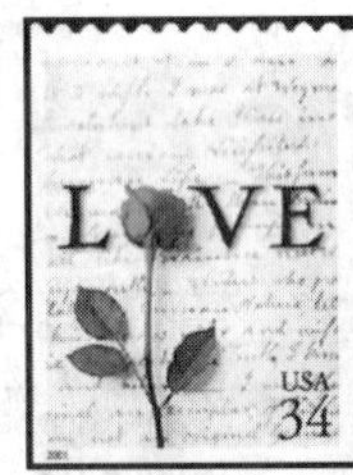

Rose, Apr. 20, 1763 Love Letter by John Adams — A2700

Rose, Aug. 11, 1763 Love Letter by Abigail Smith (Abigail Adams in 1764) — A2701

Designed by Lisa Catalone. Printed by Banknote Corporation of America, Inc.

LITHOGRAPHED
Sheets of 180 in nine panes of 20 (#3499)

Serpentine Die Cut 11¼ on 2, 3 or 4 Sides

2001 **Tagged**

Self-Adhesive

Booklet Stamps (Nos. 3496-3498)

3496 A2699 (34c) **multicolored,** *Jan. 19* .65 .20
a. Booklet pane of 20 13.00
b. Vert. pair, imperf horiz. —

Serpentine Die Cut 11¼ on 2, 3 or 4 Sides

3497 A2700 34c **multicolored,** *Feb. 14* .65 .20
a. Booklet pane of 20 13.00

Size: 18x21mm

Serpentine Die Cut 11½x10¾ om 2 or 3 Sides

3498 A2700 34c **multicolored,** *Feb. 14* .65 .20
a. Booklet pane of 4 2.60
Booklet pane of 4 containing P# single 2.60
P# single, #B1111 .65 .65
b. Booklet pane of 6 3.90

Plate number single on No. 3498 is on the lower left stamp of the bottom pane of 4 of the booklet.

Serpentine Die Cut 11¼

3499 A2701 55c **multicolored,** *Feb. 14* 1.10 .20
P# block of 4, 4#+B 4.50
Pane of 20 22.50

See No. 3551.

CHINESE NEW YEAR

Year of the Snake — A2702

Designed by Clarence Lee. Printed by Sterling Sommer for Ashton-Potter (USA) Ltd.

LITHOGRAPHED
Sheets of 180 in nine panes of 20

2001, Jan. 20 **Tagged** ***Perf. 11¼***

3500 A2702 34c **multicolored** .65 .20
P# block of 4, 5#+P 2.60 —
Pane of 20 13.00 —

BLACK HERITAGE SERIES

Roy Wilkins (1901-81), Civil Rights Leader — A2703

Designed by Richard Sheaff. Printed by Ashton-Potter (USA) Ltd.

LITHOGRAPHED
Sheets of 180 in nine panes of 20

Serpentine Die Cut 11½x11¼

2001, Jan. 24 **Tagged**

Self-Adhesive

3501 A2703 34c **blue** .65 .20
P# block of 4, 2#+P 2.60
Pane of 20 13.00

AMERICAN ILLUSTRATORS

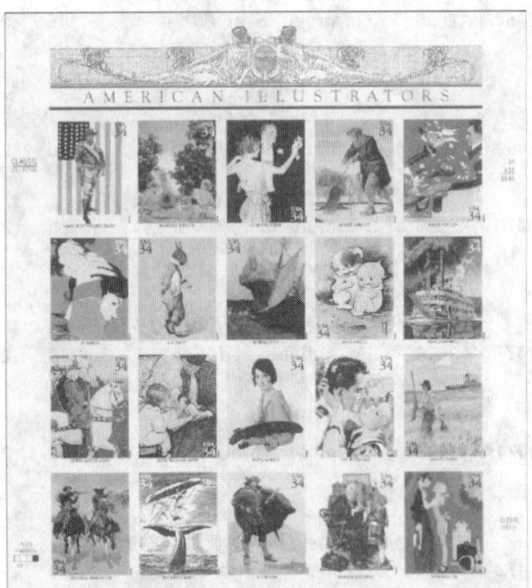

A2704

Illustration reduced.

Designed by Carl Herrman.
Printed by Avery Dennison.

Designs: a, Marine Corps poster "First in the Fight, Always Faithful," by James Montgomery Flagg. b, "Interlude (The Lute Players)," by Maxfield Parrish. c, Advertisement for Arrow Collars and Shirts, by J. C. Leyendecker. d, Advertisement for Carrier Corp. Refrigeration, by Robert Fawcett. e, Advertisement for Luxite Hosiery, by Coles Phillips. f, Illustration for correspondence school lesson, by Al Parker. g, "Br'er Rabbit," by A. B. Frost. h, "An Attack on a Galleon," by Howard Pyle. i, Kewpie and Kewpie Doodle Dog, by Rose O'Neill. j, Illustration for cover of True Magazine, by Dean Cornwell. k, "Galahad's Departure," by Edwin Austin Abbey. l, "The First Lesson," by Jessie Willcox Smith. m, Illustration for cover of McCall's Magazine, by Neysa McMein. n, "Back Home For Keeps," by Jon Whitcomb. o, "Something for Supper," by Harvey Dunn. p, "A Dash for the Timber," by Frederic Remington. q, Illustration for "Moby Dick," by Rockwell Kent. r, "Captain Bill Bones," by N. C. Wyeth. s, Illustration for cover of The Saturday Evening Post, by Norman Rockwell. t, "The Girl He Left Behind," by John Held, Jr.

PHOTOGRAVURE
Sheets of 80 in four panes of 20

2001, Feb. 1 **Tagged** ***Serpentine Die Cut 11¼***

Self-Adhesive

3502 A2704 Pane of 20 16.00
a.-t. 34c any single 1.00 .35
Sheet of 80 (4 panes) 52.50
Block of 20 different stamps with vert. gutter between any 2 columns 27.50
Pairs with vert. gutter between (each) 2.00

DIABETES AWARENESS

A2705

Designed by Richard Sheaff. Printed by Ashton-Potter (USA) Ltd.

LITHOGRAPHED
Sheets of 180 in nine panes of 20

Serpentine Die Cut 11¼x11½

2001, Mar. 16 **Tagged**

Self-Adhesive

3503 A2705 34c **multicolored** .65 .20
P# block of 4, 4#+P 2.60
Pane of 20 13.00

NOBEL PRIZE CENTENARY

Alfred Nobel and Obverse of Medals A2706

Designed by Olof Baldursdottir of Sweden. Printed by De La Rue Security Printing.

LITHOGRAPHED & ENGRAVED
Sheets of 120 in six panes of 20

2001, Mar. 22 **Tagged** ***Perf. 11***

3504 A2706 34c **multicolored** .65 .20
P# block of 4, 3#+S 2.60 —
Pane of 20 13.00 —

See Sweden No. 2415.

PAN-AMERICAN EXPOSITION INVERT STAMPS, CENT.

A2707

Illustration reduced.

Reproductions (dated 2001) of: a, #294a. b, #295a. c, #296a. d, Commemorative "cinderella" stamp depicting a buffalo.

Designed by Richard Sheaff. Printed by Banknote Corporation of America.

LITHOGRAPHED (#3505d), ENGRAVED (others)
Sheets of 28 in four panes of 7

2001, Mar. 29 ***Perf. 12 (#3505d), 12½x12 (others)***
Tagged (#3505d), Untagged (others)

3505	A2707 Pane of 7, #3505a-3505c, 4 #3505d	6.75	—
a.	A109 1c **green & black**	.20	.20
b.	A110 2c **carmine & black**	.20	.20
c.	A111 4c **deep red brown & black**	.20	.20
d.	80c **red & blue**	1.60	.35
	Sheet of 4 panes	45.00	

GREAT PLAINS PRAIRIE

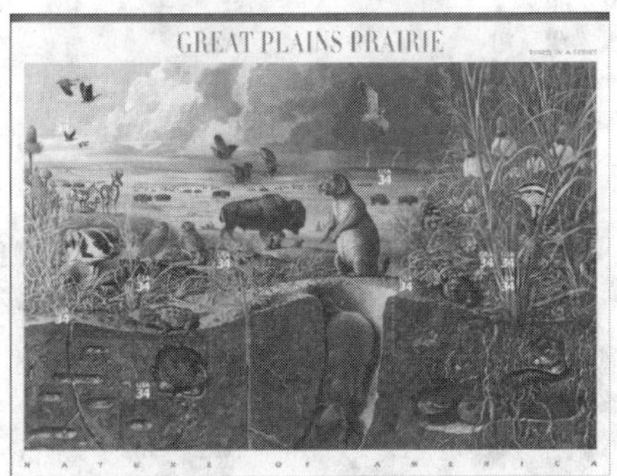

A2708

Illustration reduced.

Designed by Ethel Kessler. Printed by Ashton-Potter (USA) Ltd.

Wildlife and flowers: a, Pronghorns, Canada geese. b, Burrowing owls, American buffalos. c, American buffalo, Black-tailed prairie dogs, wild alfalfa, horiz. d, Black-tailed prairie dog, American buffalos,. e, Painted lady butterfly, American buffalo, prairie coneflowers, prairie wild roses, horiz. f, Western meadowlark, camel cricket, prairie coneflowers, prairie wild roses. g, Badger, harvester ants. h, Eastern short-horned lizard, plains pocket gopher. i, Plains spadefoot, dung beetle, prairie wild roses, horiz. j, Two-striped grasshopper, Ord's kangaroo rat.

LITHOGRAPHED
Sheets of 60 in six panes of 10

2001, Apr. 19 **Tagged** ***Serpentine Die Cut 10***
Self-Adhesive

3506	A2708 Pane of 10	7.00	
a.-j.	34c Any single	.65	.20
	Sheet of 6 panes	42.50	

PEANUTS COMIC STRIP

Snoopy A2709

Designed by Paige Braddock. Printed by Ashton-Potter (USA) Ltd.

LITHOGRAPHED
Sheets of 180 in nine panes of 20
Serpentine Die Cut 11¼x11½

2001, May 17 **Tagged**
Self-Adhesive

3507	A2709 34c **multicolored**	.65	.20
	P# block of 4, 5#+P	2.60	
	Pane of 20	13.00	

HONORING VETERANS

A2710

Designed by Carl Herrman. Printed by Ashton-Potter (USA) Ltd.

LITHOGRAPHED
Sheets of 180 in nine panes of 20
Serpentine Die Cut 11¼x11½

2001, May 23 **Tagged**
Self-Adhesive

3508	A2710 34c **multicolored**	.65	.20
	P# block of 4, 4#+P	2.60	
	Pane of 20	13.00	

FRIDA KAHLO (1907-54), PAINTER

Self-portrait — A2711

Designed by Richard Sheaff. Printed by Sterling Sommer for Ashton-Potter (USA) Ltd..

LITHOGRAPHED
Sheets of 80 in four panes of 20

2001, June 21 **Tagged** ***Perf. 11¼***

3509	A2711 34c **multicolored**	.65	.20
	P# block of 4, 4#+P	2.60	—
	Pane of 20	13.00	—

LEGENDARY PLAYING FIELDS

Ebbets Field — A2712

Tiger Stadium A2713

Crosley Field — A2714

Yankee Stadium A2715

Polo Grounds A2716

Forbes Field — A2717

Fenway Park — A2718

Comiskey Park — A2719

Shibe Park — A2720

Wrigley Field — A2721

Designed by Phil Jordan. Printed by Avery Dennison.

PHOTOGRAVURE
Sheets of 160 in eight panes of 20
Serpentine Die Cut 11¼x11½

2001, June 27 **Tagged**
Self-Adhesive

3510	A2712 34c **multicolored**	.65	.20
3511	A2713 34c **multicolored**	.65	.20
3512	A2714 34c **multicolored**	.65	.20
3513	A2715 34c **multicolored**	.65	.20
3514	A2716 34c **multicolored**	.65	.20
3515	A2717 34c **multicolored**	.65	.20
3516	A2718 34c **multicolored**	.65	.20
3517	A2719 34c **multicolored**	.65	.20
3518	A2720 34c **multicolored**	.65	.20
3519	A2721 34c **multicolored**	.65	.20
a.	Block of 10, #3510-3519	6.50	
	P# block of 10, 4#+V	6.50	
	Pane of 20	13.00	
	Sheet of 160	105.00	
	Cross-gutter block of 12	14.00	
	Horiz. block of 10 with vert. gutter	9.50	
	Block of 4 with horiz. gutter	4.00	
	Vert. pairs with horiz. gutter (each)	1.75	
	Horiz. pairs with vert. gutter (each)	1.75	

Cross gutter block contains one each Nos. 3510-3517, two each of Nos. 3518-3519, and vertical and horizontal gutters.

ATLAS STATUE, NEW YORK CITY

A2722

Designed by Kevin Newman. Printed by Banknote Corporation of America.

PHOTOGRAVURE
COIL STAMP

Serpentine Die Cut 8½ Vert.

2001, June 29 **Untagged**

Self-Adhesive

3520 A2722 (10c) **multicolored**	.20	.20
Pair	.40	
P# strip of 5, #B1111	2.75	
P# single, same #	—	1.75

LEONARD BERNSTEIN (1918-90), CONDUCTOR

A2723

Designed by Howard Paine. Printed by Sterling Sommer for Ashton-Potter (USA) Ltd.

LITHOGRAPHED
Sheets of 180 in nine panes of 20

2001, July 10 **Tagged** ***Perf. 11¼***

3521 A2723 34c **multicolored**	.65	.20
P# block of 4, 4#+P	2.60	—
Pane of 20	13.00	—

WOODY WAGON

A2724

Designed by Kevin Newman. Printed by American Packaging Corporation for Sennett Security Products.

PHOTOGRAVURE
COIL STAMP

Serpentine Die Cut 11½ Vert.

2001, Aug. 3 **Untagged**

Self-Adhesive

3522 A2724 (15c) **multicolored**	.30	.20
Pair	.60	
P# strip of 5, #S11111	3.00	
P# single, same #	—	1.75

LEGENDS OF HOLLYWOOD

Lucille Ball (1911-89) — A2725

Designed by Derry Noyes. Printed by Banknote Corporation of America.

LITHOGRAPHED
Sheets of 180 in nine panes of 20

2001, Aug. 6 **Tagged** ***Serpentine Die Cut 11***

Self-Adhesive

3523 A2725 34c **multicolored**	.65	.20
P# block of 4, 4#+B	2.60	
Pane of 20	13.00	
Sheet of 180	120.00	
Cross-gutter block of 8	17.50	
Block of 8 with vert. gutter	10.00	
Horiz. pair with vert. gutter	3.00	
Vert. pairs with horiz. gutter	2.00	
a. As No. 3523, die cutting omitted	—	

Cross gutter block consists of 6 stamps from upper panes and 2 stamps from lower panes.

AMERICAN TREASURES SERIES
Amish Quilts

Diamond in the Square, c. 1920 — A2726

Lone Star, c. 1920 — A2727

Sunshine and Shadow, c. 1910 — A2728

Double Ninepatch Variation — A2729

Designed by Derry Noyes. Printed by Ashton-Potter (USA) Ltd.

LITHOGRAPHED
Sheets of 120 in six panes of 20

Serpentine Die Cut 11¼x11½

2001, Aug. 9 **Tagged**

Self-Adhesive

3524 A2726 34c **multicolored**	.65	.20
3525 A2727 34c **multicolored**	.65	.20
3526 A2728 34c **multicolored**	.65	.20
3527 A2729 34c **multicolored**	.65	.20
a. Block or strip of 4, #3524-3527	2.60	
P# block of 4, 5#+P	2.60	
Pane of 20	13.00	

CARNIVOROUS PLANTS

Venus Flytrap — A2730

Yellow Trumpet — A2731

Cobra Lily — A2732

English Sundew — A2733

Designed by Steve Buchanan.
Printed by Avery Dennison.

PHOTOGRAVURE
Sheets of 160 in eight panes of 20

2001, Aug. 23 **Tagged** ***Serpentine Die Cut 11½***

Self-Adhesive

3528 A2730 34c **multicolored**	.65	.20
3529 A2731 34c **multicolored**	.65	.20
3530 A2732 34c **multicolored**	.65	.20
3531 A2733 34c **multicolored**	.65	.20
a. Block or strip of 4, #3528-3531	2.60	
P# block of 4, 4#+V	2.60	
Pane of 20	13.00	

EID

"Eid Mubarak" — A2734

Designed by Mohamed Zakariya.
Printed by Avery Dennison.

PHOTOGRAVURE
Sheets of 240 in twelve panes of 20

2001, Sept. 1 **Tagged** ***Serpentine Die Cut 11¼***

Self-Adhesive

3532 A2734 34c **multicolored**	.65	.20
P# block of 4, 3#+V	2.60	
Pane of 20	13.00	

ENRICO FERMI (1901-54), PHYSICIST

A2735

Designed by Richard Sheaff. Printed by Sterling Sommer for Ashton-Potter (USA) Ltd.

LITHOGRAPHED
Sheets of 180 in nine panes of 20

2001, Sept. 29 **Tagged** ***Perf. 11***

3533 A2735 34c **multicolored** .65 .20
P# block of 4, 4#+P 2.60 —
Pane of 20 13.00 —

THAT'S ALL FOLKS!

Porky Pig at Mailbox — A2736

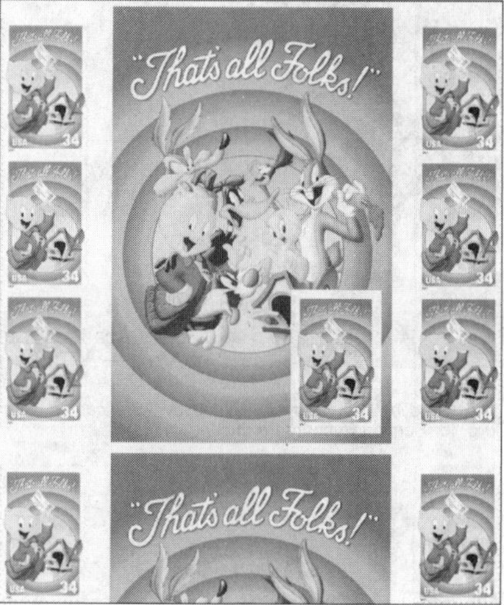

Cross Gutter Block of 9

Illustration reduced.
Designed by Ed Wleczyk, Warner Bros.
Printed by Avery Dennison.

PHOTOGRAVURE

2001, Oct. 1 **Tagged** ***Serpentine Die Cut 11***
Self-Adhesive

3534 Pane of 10 6.50
a. A2736 34c single .65 .20
b. Booklet pane of 9 or 10 #3534a 5.85
c. Booklet pane of 1 #3534a .65
Sheet of 60 (six panes) no plate numbers 47.50
Sheet of 60 (six panes) with plate # in selvage on front and reverse 50.00
Pane of 10 from sheet of 60 8.00
Pane of 10 with plate numbers on front 12.50
Cross gutter block of 9 or 10 16.00
Cross gutter block of 12 18.00
Vert. pair with horiz. gutter 2.00
Horiz. pair with vert. gutter 4.00

Die cutting on No. 3534b does not extend through the backing paper.

3535 Pane of 10 6.50
a. A2736 34c single .65
b. Booklet pane of 9 #3535a —
c. Booklet pane of 1, imperf. —

Die cutting on No. 3535a extends through backing paper. Used examples of No. 3535a are identical to those of No. 3534a.

Nos. 3534b-3534c and 3535b-3535c are separated by a vertical line of microperforations.

CHRISTMAS

Virgin and Child, by Lorenzo Costa — A2737

A2738 A2739

A2740 A2741

19th Century Chromolithographs of Santa Claus

Designed by Richard Sheaff.

Printed by Guilford Gravure, Inc., for Banknote Corporation of America (#3536), American Packaging Corporation for Sennett Security Products (#3537-3540), Avery Dennison (#3541-3544).

PHOTOGRAVURE
Sheets of 160 in eight panes of 20 (#3537-3540)

Serpentine Die Cut 11½ on 2, 3 or 4 Sides
2001, Oct. 10 **Tagged**
Self-Adhesive
Booklet Stamps (#3536, 3537a-3540a, 3541-3544)

3536 A2737 34c **multicolored** .65 .20
a. Booklet pane of 20 13.00

Serpentine Die Cut 10¾x11
Black Inscriptions

3537 A2738 34c **multicolored,** large date .65 .20
a. Small date (from booklet pane) .65 .20
b. Large date (from booklet pane) .65 .20
3538 A2739 34c **multicolored,** large date .65 .20
a. Small date (from booklet pane) .65 .20
b. Large date (from booklet pane) .65 .20
3539 A2740 34c **multicolored,** large date .65 .20
a. Small date (from booklet pane) .65 .20
b. Large date (from booklet pane) .65 .20
3540 A2741 34c **multicolored,** large date .65 .20
a. Small date (from booklet pane) .65 .20
b. Block of 4, #3537-3540 2.60
P# block of 4, 4#+S 2.60
Pane of 20 13.00
c. Block of 4, small date, #3537a-3540a 2.60
d. Booklet pane of 20, 5 #3540c + label 13.00
e. Large date (from booklet pane) .65 .20
f. Block of 4, large date, #3537b-3539b, 3540e 2.60
g. Booklet pane, 5 #3540f + label 13.00

Nos. 3540d and 3540g are double-sided booklet panes, with 12 stamps on one side and eight stamps plus label on the other side.

Numerals "3" and "4" are distinctly separate on Nos. 3537-3540, and touching or separated by a slight hairline on the booklet pane stamps.

Designs of Nos. 3537a-3540a are slightly taller than Nos. 3537-3540.

Serpentine Die Cut 11 on 2 or 3 Sides
Size: 21x18½mm
Green and Red Inscriptions

3541 A2738 34c **multicolored** .65 .20
3542 A2739 34c **multicolored** .65 .20
3543 A2740 34c **multicolored** .65 .20
3544 A2741 34c **multicolored** .65 .20
a. Block of 4, #3541-3544 2.60
b. Booklet pane of 4, #3541-3544 2.60
c. Booklet pane of 6, #3543-3544, 2 #3541-3542 3.90
d. Booklet pane of 6, #3541-3542, 2 #3543-3544 3.90
Nos. 3536-3544 (9) 5.85 1.80

JAMES MADISON (1751-1836)

Madison and His Home, Montpelier
A2742

Designed by John Thompson.

Printed by Banknote Corporation of America.

LITHOGRAPHED & ENGRAVED
Sheets of 120 in six panes of 20

2001, Oct. 18 **Tagged** ***Perf. 11x11¼***

3545 A2742 34c **green & black** .65 .20
P# block of 4, 2#+B 2.60 —
Pane of 20 13.00 —
Sheet of 120 80.00
Cross gutter block of 4 8.25 —
Horiz. pair with vert. gutter 3.00 —
Vert. pair with horiz. gutter 2.00 —

THANKSGIVING

Cornucopia — A2743

Designed by Richard Sheaff.

Printed by Ashton-Potter (USA) Ltd.

LITHOGRAPHED
Sheets of 180 in nine panes of 20

2001, Oct. 19 **Tagged** ***Serpentine Die Cut 11¼***
Self-Adhesive

3546 A2743 34c **multicolored** .65 .20
P# block of 4, 4#+P 2.60
Pane of 20 13.00

Hanukkah Type of 1996

Designed by Hannah Smotrich.

Printed by Avery Dennison.

PHOTOGRAVURE
Sheets of 200 in ten panes of 20

2001, Oct. 21 **Tagged** ***Serpentine Die Cut 11***
Self-Adhesive

3547 A2411 34c **multicolored** .65 .20
P# block of 4, 5#+V 2.60
Pane of 20 13.00

Kwanzaa Type of 1997

Designed by Synthia Saint James.

Printed by Avery Dennison.

PHOTOGRAVURE
Sheets of 240 in twelve panes of 20

2001, Oct. 21 **Tagged** ***Serpentine Die Cut 11***
Self-Adhesive

3548 A2458 34c **multicolored** .65 .20
P# block of 4, 4#+V 2.60
Pane of 20 13.00

UNITED WE STAND

A2744

Designed by Terry McCaffrey.

Printed by Banknote Corporation of America (#3549), Bureau of Engraving and Printing (#3550).

LITHOGRAPHED
BOOKLET STAMPS

Serpentine Die Cut 11¼ on 2, 3, or 4 Sides
2001, Oct. 24 **Tagged**
Self-Adhesive

3549 A2744 34c **multicolored** .65 .20
a. Booklet pane of 20 13.00

PHOTOGRAVURE

Serpentine Die Cut 10½x10¾ on 2 or 3 Sides
2002, Jan. **Tagged**
Self-Adhesive

3549B A2744 34c **multicolored,** *Jan. 2002* .65 .20
c. Booklet pane of 4 2.60
d. Booklet pane of 6 3.90
e. Booklet pane of 20 13.00

No. 3549Be is a double-sided booklet pane, with 12 stamps on one side and eight stamps plus label on the other side.

COIL STAMP

Serpentine Die Cut 9¾ Vert.

2001, Oct. 24 **Tagged**

Self-Adhesive

3550 A2744 34c **multicolored, perpendicular corners** .65 .20
Pair 1.30
P# strip of 5, #1111, 2222, 3333 5.00
P# single, same # — 2.00

3550A A2744 34c **multicolored** .65 .20
Pair 1.30
P# strip of 5, #1111 5.00
P# single, same # — 2.00

No. 3550 has right angle corners and backing paper as high as the stamp. No. 3550A has rounded corners, the backing paper larger than the stamp, and the stamps are spaced approximately 2mm apart.

Love Letters Type of 2001

Designed by Lisa Catalone.
Printed by Banknote Corporation of America.

LITHOGRAPHED

Sheets of 160 in eight panes of 20

2001, Nov. 19 **Tagged** ***Serpentine Die Cut 11¼***

Self-Adhesive

3551 A2701 57c **multicolored** 1.10 .20
P# block of 4, 4# + B 4.40
Pane of 20 22.00

WINTER OLYMPICS

Ski Jumping
A2745

Snowboarding
A2746

Ice Hockey
A2747

Figure Skating
A2748

Designed by Jager Di Paola Kemp. Printed by American Packaging Corporation for Sennett Security Products.

PHOTOGRAVURE

Sheets of 180 in nine panes of 20

Serpentine Die Cut 11½x10¾

2002, Jan. 8 **Tagged**

Self-Adhesive

3552 A2745 34c **multicolored** .65 .20
3553 A2746 34c **multicolored** .65 .20
3554 A2747 34c **multicolored** .65 .20
3555 A2748 34c **multicolored** .65 .20
a. Block or strip of 4, #3552-3555 2.60
P# block of 4, 6#+S (UL and UR only) 2.60
Pane of 20 13.00
Sheet of 180 120.00
Cross gutter block of 8 15.00
Block of 4 with vert. gutter 4.00
Block of 8 with horiz. gutter 8.00
Vert. pair with horiz. gutter, each 1.75
Horiz. pair with vert. gutter, each 1.75
b. Die cutting inverted, pane of 20 —
c. Imperf, block of 4 —
As "c," pane of 20 —

Cross gutter blocks of 8 may be either 2x4 or 4x2 in configuration. The former will not show equal numbers of each stamp; the latter will.

Blocks of 4 with vertical gutter must show one of each of the stamps.

MENTORING A CHILD

Child and Adult — A2749

Designed by Lance Hidy. Printed by American Packaging Corporation for Sennett Security Products.

PHOTOGRAVURE

Sheets of 120 in six panes of 20

Serpentine Die Cut 11x10¾

2002, Jan. 10 **Tagged**

Self-Adhesive

3556 A2749 34c **multicolored** .65 .20
P# block of 4, 5#+S 2.60
Pane of 20 13.00

BLACK HERITAGE SERIES

Langston Hughes (1902-67), Writer — A2750

Designed by Richard Sheaff. Printed by Banknote Corporation of America.

LITHOGRAPHED

Sheets of 120 in six panes of 20

Serpentine Die Cut 10¼x10½

2002, Feb. 1 **Tagged**

Self-Adhesive

3557 A2750 34c **multicolored** .65 .20
P# block of 4, 5#+B 2.60
Pane of 20 13.00
a. Imperf, pair —
As "a," pane of 20 —

Beware of pairs/panes with extremely faint die cutting offered as imperf errors.

HAPPY BIRTHDAY

A2751

Designed by Harry Zelenko. Printed by Avery Dennison.

PHOTOGRAVURE

Sheets of 200 in ten panes of 20

2002, Feb. 8 **Tagged** ***Serpentine Die Cut 11***

Self-Adhesive

3558 A2751 34c **multicolored** .65 .20
P# block of 4, 4#+V 2.60
Pane of 20 13.00

CHINESE NEW YEAR

Year of the Horse
A2752

Designed by Clarence Lee. Printed by Banknote Corporation of America.

LITHOGRAPHED

Sheets of 120 in six panes of 20

Serpentine Die Cut 10½x10¼

2002, Feb. 11 **Tagged**

Self-Adhesive

3559 A2752 34c **multicolored** .65 .20
P# block of 4, 5#+B 2.60
Pane of 20 13.00

U.S. MILITARY ACADEMY, BICENT.

Military Academy Coat of Arms — A2753

Designed by Derry Noyes. Printed by American Packaging Corp. for Sennett Security Products.

PHOTOGRAVURE

Sheets of 180 in nine panes of 20

Serpentine Die Cut 10½x11

2002, Mar. 16 **Tagged**

Self-Adhesive

3560 A2753 34c **multicolored** .65 .20
P# block of 4, 6#+S 2.60
Pane of 20 13.00

GREETINGS FROM AMERICA

A2754-A2803

Illustration reduced.

Designed by Richard Sheaff. Printed by American Packaging Corp. for Sennett Security Products.

PHOTOGRAVURE

Sheets of 100 in two panes of 50

2002, Apr. 4 **Tagged** ***Serpentine Die Cut 10¾***

Self-Adhesive

3561 A2754 34c Alabama .65 .20
3562 A2755 34c Alaska .65 .20
3563 A2756 34c Arizona .65 .20
3564 A2757 34c Arkansas .65 .20
3565 A2758 34c California .65 .20
3566 A2759 34c Colorado .65 .20

No.	Type	Denom.	Description	Unused	Used
3567	A2760	34c	Connecticut	.65	.20
3568	A2761	34c	Delaware	.65	.20
3569	A2762	34c	Florida	.65	.20
3570	A2763	34c	Georgia	.65	.20
3571	A2764	34c	Hawaii	.65	.20
3572	A2765	34c	Idaho	.65	.20
3573	A2766	34c	Illinois	.65	.20
3574	A2767	34c	Indiana	.65	.20
3575	A2768	34c	Iowa	.65	.20
3576	A2769	34c	Kansas	.65	.20
3577	A2770	34c	Kentucky	.65	.20
3578	A2771	34c	Louisiana	.65	.20
3579	A2772	34c	Maine	.65	.20
3580	A2773	34c	Maryland	.65	.20
3581	A2774	34c	Massachusetts	.65	.20
3582	A2775	34c	Michigan	.65	.20
3583	A2776	34c	Minnesota	.65	.20
3584	A2777	34c	Mississippi	.65	.20
3585	A2778	34c	Missouri	.65	.20
3586	A2779	34c	Montana	.65	.20
3587	A2780	34c	Nebraska	.65	.20
3588	A2781	34c	Nevada	.65	.20
3589	A2782	34c	New Hampshire	.65	.20
3590	A2783	34c	New Jersey	.65	.20
3591	A2784	34c	New Mexico	.65	.20
3592	A2785	34c	New York	.65	.20
3593	A2786	34c	North Carolina	.65	.20
3594	A2787	34c	North Dakota	.65	.20
3595	A2788	34c	Ohio	.65	.20
3596	A2789	34c	Oklahoma	.65	.20
3597	A2790	34c	Oregon	.65	.20
3598	A2791	34c	Pennsylvania	.65	.20
3599	A2792	34c	Rhode Island	.65	.20
3600	A2793	34c	South Carolina	.65	.20
3601	A2794	34c	South Dakota	.65	.20
3602	A2795	34c	Tennessee	.65	.20
3603	A2796	34c	Texas	.65	.20
3604	A2797	34c	Utah	.65	.20
3605	A2798	34c	Vermont	.65	.20
3606	A2799	34c	Virginia	.65	.20
3607	A2800	34c	Washington	.65	.20
3608	A2801	34c	West Virginia	.65	.20
3609	A2802	34c	Wisconsin	.65	.20
3610	A2803	34c	Wyoming	.65	.20
a.			Pane of 50, #3561-3610	32.50	
			Sheet of 100 (two panes)	65.00	
			Block of 50 different stamps with vert. gutter between any 2 columns	32.50	
			Pair with vert. gutter between (each)	2.00	

LONGLEAF PINE FOREST

A2804

Illustration reduced.

Designed by Ethel Kessler. Printed by American Packaging Corp. for Sennett Security Products.

Wildlife and flowers: a, Bachman's sparrow. b, Northern bobwhite, yellow pitcher plants. c, Fox squirrel, red-bellied woodpecker. d, Brown-headed nuthatch. e, Broadhead skink, yellow pitcher plants, pipeworts. f, Eastern towhee, yellow pitcher plants, Savannah meadow beauties, toothache grass. g, Gray fox, gopher tortoise, horiz. h, Blind click beetle, sweetbay, pine woods treefrog. i, Rosebud orchid, pipeworts, southern toad, yellow pitcher plants. j, Grass-pink orchid, yellow-sided skimmer, pipeworts, yellow pitcher plants, horiz.

PHOTOGRAVURE

Sheets of 90 in nine panes of 10

Serpentine Die Cut 10½x10¾, 10¾x10½

2002, Apr. 26 **Tagged**

Self-Adhesive

3611	A2804	Pane of 10	7.00	
a.-j.		34c Any single	.65	.20
		Sheet of 9 panes	65.00	
k.		As No. 3611, imperf	—	

AMERICAN DESIGN SERIES

Toleware Coffeepot — A2805

Designed by Derry Noyes.

Printed by American Packaging Corp. for Sennett Security Products.

PHOTOGRAVURE

COIL STAMP

2002, May 31 **Untagged** ***Perf. 10 Vert.***

3612	A2805 5c	**multicolored**	.20	.20
		Pair	.20	.20
		P# strip of 5, #S1111111	1.60	—
		P# single, #S1111111	—	1.25

Star — A2806

Designed by Phil Jordan. Printed by Banknote Corporation of America.

LITHOGRAPHED, PHOTOGRAVURE (No. 3614, 3615)

Sheets of 400 in eight panes of 50

2002, June 7 **Untagged** ***Serpentine Die Cut 11***

Self-Adhesive (#3613-3614)

Year at Lower Left

3613	A2806 3c	**red, blue & black**	.20	.20
		P# block of 4, 3#+B	.25	
a.		Imperf, pair	—	

Serpentine Die Cut 10

Year at Lower Right

3614	A2806 3c	**red, blue & black**	.20	.20
		P# block of 4, 3#+B	.25	

Year at Lower Left

3615	A2806 3c	**red, blue & black**	.20	.20
		Pair	.20	.20
		P# strip of 5, #S111	1.00	—
		P# single, same #	—	.65

Washington Type of 2001

Designed by Richard Sheaff. Printed by Ashton-Potter (USA) Ltd. (#3616, 3618, 3619), Avery Dennison (#3617).

LITHOGRAPHED, PHOTOGRAVURE (#3617)

Sheets of 400 in four panes of 100 (#3616)

2002, June 7 **Tagged** ***Perf. 11¼***

3616	A2686 23c	**green**	.45	.20
		P# block of 4, 1#+P	1.80	—

Self-Adhesive

Coil Stamp

Serpentine Die Cut 8½ Vert.

3617	A2686 23c	**gray green**	.45	.20
		Pair	.90	
		P# strip of 5, #V11, V13, V21, V22, V24	3.00	
		P# single, same #	—	.60

Compare No. 3617 ("2002" date at lower left) with No. 3475A ("2001" date at lower left).

Booklet Stamps

Serpentine Die Cut 11¼ on 3 Sides

3618	A2686 23c	**green**	.45	.20
a.		Booklet pane of 4	1.80	
b.		Booklet pane of 6	2.70	
c.		Booklet pane of 10	4.50	

Serpentine Die Cut 10½x11¼ on 3 Sides

3619	A2686 23c	**green**	1.75	1.25
a.		Booklet pane of 4, 2 #3619 at L, 2 #3618 at R	*6.00*	
b.		Booklet pane of 6, 3 #3619 at L, 3 #3618 at R	*9.50*	
c.		Booklet pane of 4, 2 #3618 at L, 2 #3619 at R	*6.50*	
d.		Booklet pane of 6, 3 #3618 at L, 3 #3619 at R	*9.50*	
e.		Booklet pane of 10, 5 #3619 at L, 5#3618 at R	*10.00*	
f.		Booklet pane of 10, 5 #3618 at L, 5 #3619 at R	*10.00*	
g.		Pair, #3619 at L, #3618 at R	*2.50*	
h.		Pair, #3618 at L, #3619 at R	*2.50*	

Flag — A2807

Designed by Terrence W. McCaffrey. Printed by Sterling Sommer for Ashton-Potter (USA) Ltd. (#3620), Ashton-Potter (USA) Ltd. (#3621), Bureau of Engraving and Printing (#3622), Banknote Corporation of America (#3623), American Packaging Corporation for Sennett Security Products (#3624), Avery Dennison (#3625).

LITHOGRAPHED, PHOTOGRAVURE (#3622, 3624, 3625)

Sheets of 400 in four panes of 100 (#3620), Sheets of 120 in six panes of 20 (#3621)

2002, June 7 **Tagged** ***Perf. 11¼x11***

3620	A2807 (37c)	**multicolored**	.70	.20
		P# block of 4, 4#+P	2.80	—

Self-Adhesive

Serpentine Die Cut 11¼x11

3621	A2807 (37c)	**multicolored**	.70	.20
		P# block of 4, 4#+P	2.80	
		Pane of 20	14.00	

Coil Stamp

Serpentine Die Cut 10 Vert.

3622	A2807 (37c)	**multicolored**	.70	.20
		Pair	1.40	
		P# strip of 5, #1111, 2222	5.25	
		P# single, same #	—	2.00
a.		Imperf, pair	—	

Booklet Stamps

Serpentine Die Cut 11¼ on 2, 3 or 4 Sides

3623	A2807 (37c)	**multicolored**	.70	.20
a.		Booklet pane of 20	14.00	

Serpentine Die Cut 10½x10¾ on 2 or 3 Sides

3624	A2807 (37c)	**multicolored**	.70	.20
a.		Booklet pane of 4	2.80	
b.		Booklet pane of 6	4.20	
c.		Booklet pane of 20	14.00	

Serpentine Die Cut 8 on 2, 3 or 4 sides

3625	A2807 (37c)	**multicolored**	.70	.20
a.		Booklet pane of 18	13.00	

Toy Mail Wagon — A2808

Toy Locomotive — A2809

Toy Taxicab — A2810

Toy Fire Pumper — A2811

Designed by Derry Noyes. Printed by Avery Dennison

PHOTOGRAVURE

Serpentine Die Cut 11 on 2, 3 or 4 Sides

2002, June 7 **Tagged**

Booklet Stamps

Self-Adhesive

3626	A2808 (37c)	**multicolored**	.70	.20
3627	A2809 (37c)	**multicolored**	.70	.20
3628	A2810 (37c)	**multicolored**	.70	.20
3629	A2811 (37c)	**multicolored**	.70	.20
a.		Block of 4, #3626-3629	2.80	
b.		Booklet pane of 4, #3626-3629	2.80	
c.		Booklet pane of 6, #3627, 3629, 2 each #3626, 3628	4.20	
d.		Booklet pane of 6, #3626, 3628, 2 each #3627, 3629	4.20	
e.		Booklet pane of 20, 5 each #3626-3629	14.00	

Flag — A2812

Designed by Terrence W. McCaffrey. Printed by Ashton-Potter (USA) Ltd. (#3630), American Packaging Corporation for Sennett Security Products (#3631, 3636), Bureau of Engraving and Printing (#3632), Banknote Corporation of America (#3633, 3635), Guilford Gravure for Banknote Corporation of America (#3633A), Avery Dennison (#3637).

LITHOGRAPHED, PHOTOGRAVURE (#3631-3633, 3634, 3636)

Sheets of 120 in six panes of 20

2002-03 Tagged *Serpentine Die Cut 11¼x11*

Self-Adhesive

3630 A2812 37c **multicolored** .70 .20
P# block of 4, 4#+P 2.80
Pane of 20 14.00

COIL STAMPS

Water-Activated Gum

Perf. 10 Vert.

3631 A2812 37c **multicolored,** *June 7* .70 .20
Pair 1.40 —
P# strip of 5, #S1111 5.25 —
P# single, same # — 2.00

Self-Adhesive

Serpentine Die Cut 9¾ Vert.

3632 A2812 37c **multicolored,** *June 7* .70 .20
Pair 1.40
P# strip of 5, #1111, 2222, 3333, 4444, 5555, 6666 4.75
P# single, same # — 2.00
a. Imperf, pair —

Serpentine Die Cut 8½ Vert.

3633 A2812 37c **multicolored,** *June 7* .70 .20
Pair 1.40
P# strip of 5, #B1111 5.25
P# single, same # — 2.00

Backing paper of No. 3633 is larger than the stamp.

3633A A2812 37c **multicolored** .70 .20
Pair 1.40
P# strip of 5 #B1111 5.25
P# single, same # — 2.00

No. 3633A has right angle corners and backing paper as high as the stamp, and is dated "2003." No. 3633 is dated "2002," has rounded corners, the backing paper larger than the stamp, and the stamps are spaced approximately 2mm apart.

Booklet Stamps

Serpentine Die Cut 11 3 Sides

3634 A2812 37c **multicolored,** *June 7* .70 .20
a. Booklet pane of 10 7.00

Serpentine Die Cut 11¼ on 2, 3 or 4 Sides

3635 A2812 37c **multicolored**
3637 A2812 37c **multicolored**
a. Booklet pane of 18 13.00
a. Booklet pane of 20 14.00

Serpentine Die Cut 10½x10¾ on 2 or 3 Sides

3636 A2812 37c **multicolored,** *June 7* .70 .20
a. Booklet pane of 4 2.80
b. Booklet pane of 6 4.20
c. Booklet pane of 20 14.00

No. 3636c is a double-sided booklet pane, with 12 stamps on one side and eight stamps plus label on the other side.

Serpentine Die Cut 8 on 2, 3 or 4 Sides

3637 A2812 37c **multicolored,** *Feb. 4, 2003* .70 .20
a. Booklet pane of 18 13.00

Toy Locomotive — A2813

Toy Mail Wagon — A2814

Toy Fire Pumper — A2815

Toy Taxicab — A2816

Designed by Derry Noyes. Printed by Banknote Corporation of America, Avery Dennison (#3642-3645)

PHOTOGRAVURE

Serpentine Die Cut 8½ Horiz.

2002, July 26 Tagged

Self-Adhesive

Coil Stamps

3638 A2813 37c **multicolored** .70 .20
3639 A2814 37c **multicolored** .70 .20
3640 A2815 37c **multicolored** .70 .20
3641 A2816 37c **multicolored** .70 .20
a. Strip of 4, #3638-3641 2.80
P# strip of 5, 2 #3638, 1 each #3639-3641, #B11111, B12222 5.50
P# strip of 9, 2 each #3638-3639, 3641, 3 #3640, #B11111, B12222 8.75
P# single (#3640), #B11111, B12222 — 2.00

Serpentine Die Cut 11 on 2, 3 or 4 Sides

Booklet Stamps

3642 A2814 37c **multicolored** .70 .20
3643 A2813 37c **multicolored** .70 .20
3644 A2816 37c **multicolored** .70 .20
3645 A2815 37c **multicolored** .70 .20
a. Block of 4, #3642-3645 2.80
b. Booklet pane of 4, #3642-3645 2.80
c. Booklet pane of 6, #3643, 3645, 2 each #3642, 3644 4.20
d. Booklet pane of 6, #3642, 3644, 2 each #3643, 3645 4.20
e. Booklet pane of 20, 5 each #3642-3645 14.00

Coverlet Eagle — A2817

Designed by Richard Sheaff. Printed by Ashton-Potter (USA) Ltd.

LITHOGRAPHED

Sheets of 120 in six panes of 20

Serpentine Die Cut 11x11¼

2002, July 12 Tagged

Self-Adhesive

3646 A2817 60c **multicolored** 1.25 .25
P# block of 4, 4#+P 5.00
Pane of 20 25.00

Jefferson Memorial A2818

Capitol Dome — A2819

Designed by Derry Noyes. Printed by Banknote Corporation of America.

LITHOGRAPHED

Sheets of 180 in nine panes of 20

2002, July 30 Tagged *Serpentine Die Cut 11¼*

Self-Adhesive

3647 A2818 $3.85 **multicolored** 7.50 3.75
P# block of 4, 4#+B 30.00
Pane of 20 150.00
3648 A2819 $13.65 **multicolored** 27.50 12.50
P# block of 4, 4#+B 110.00
Pane of 20 550.00

MASTERS OF AMERICAN PHOTOGRAPHY

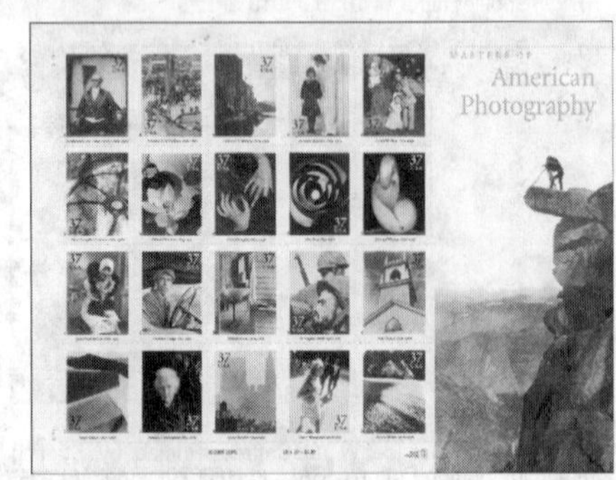

A2820

Illustration reduced.

Designed by Derry Noyes. Printed by American Packaging Corporation for Sennett Security Products.

Designs: a, Portrait of Daniel Webster, by Albert Sands Southworth and Josiah Johnson Hawes. b, Gen. Ulysses S. Grant and Officers, by Timothy H. O'Sullivan. c, "Cape Horn, Columbia River," by Carleton E. Watkins. d, "Blessed Art Thou Among Women," by Gertrude Käsebier. e, "Looking for Lost Luggage, Ellis Island," by Lewis W. Hine. f, "The Octopus," by Alvin Langdon Coburn. g, "Lotus, Mount Kisco, New York," by Edward Steichen. h, "Hands and Thimble," by Alfred Stieglitz. i, "Rayograph," by Man Ray. j, "Two Shells," by Edward Weston. k, "My Corsage," by James VanDerZee. l, "Ditched, Stalled, and Stranded, San Joaquin Valley, California," by Dorothea Lange. m, "Washroom and Dining Area of Floyd Burroughs' Home, Hale County, Alabama," by Walker Evans. n, "Frontline Soldier with Canteen, Saipan," by W. Eugene Smith. o, "Steeple," by Paul Strand. p, "Sand Dunes, Sunrise," by Ansel Adams. q, "Age and Its Symbols," by Imogen Cunningham. r, New York cityscape, by André Kertész. s, Photograph of pedestrians, by Garry Winogrand. t, "Bristol, Vermont," by Minor White.

PHOTOGRAVURE

Sheets of 120 in six panes of 20

Serpentine Die Cut 10½x10¾

2002, June 13 Tagged

Self-Adhesive

3649 A2820 Pane of 20 14.00
a.-t. 37c Any single .70 .30
Sheet of 120 85.00
Cross-gutter block of 20 27.50
Horiz. block of 8 with vert. gutter 10.00
Vert. block of 10 with horiz. gutter 12.50
Vert. pairs with horiz. gutter (each) 2.25
Horiz. pairs with vert. gutter (each) 2.25

Cross gutter block of 20 consists of six stamps from each of two panes and four stamps from each of two other panes with the cross gutter between.

AMERICAN TREASURES SERIES

Scarlet and Louisiana Tanagers, by John James Audubon — A2821

Designed by Derry Noyes. Printed by American Pacakaging Corporation for Sennett Security Products.

PHOTOGRAVURE

Sheets of 120 in six panes of 20

2002, June 27 Tagged *Serpentine Die Cut 10¾*

Self-Adhesive

3650 A2821 37c **multicolored** .70 .20
P# block of 4, 7#+S 2.80
Pane of 20 14.00

HARRY HOUDINI (1874-1926), MAGICIAN

A2822

Designed by Richard Sheaff. Printed by Ashton-Potter (USA) Ltd.

LITHOGRAPHED

Sheets of 180 in nine panes of 20

2002, July 3 Tagged *Serpentine Die Cut 11¼*

Self-Adhesive

3651 A2822 37c **multicolored** .70 .20
P# block of 4, 4#+P 2.80 —
Pane of 20 14.00 —

ANDY WARHOL (1928-87), ARTIST

Self-Portrait — A2823

Designed by Richard Sheaff.
Printed by American Packaging Corporation for Sennett Security Products.

PHOTOGRAVURE
Sheets of 80 in four panes of 20
Serpentine Die Cut 10½x10¾

2002, Aug. 9 **Tagged**

Self-Adhesive

3652	A2823 37c **multicolored**	.70	.20
	P# block of 4, 6#+S	2.80	
	Pane of 20	14.00	

TEDDY BEARS, CENTENNIAL

Bruin Bear, c. 1907 — A2824

"Stick" Bear, 1920s — A2825

Gund Bear, c. 1948 — A2826

Ideal Bear, c. 1905 — A2827

Designed by Margaret Bauer.
Printed by American Packaging Corporation for Sennett Security Products.

PHOTOGRAVURE
Sheets of 120 in six panes of 20

2002, Aug. 15 **Tagged** ***Serpentine Die Cut 10½***

Self-Adhesive

3653	A2824 37c **multicolored**	.70	.20
3654	A2825 37c **multicolored**	.70	.20
3655	A2826 37c **multicolored**	.70	.20
3656	A2827 37c **multicolored**	.70	.20
a.	Block or vert. strip of 4, #3653-3656	2.80	
	P# block of 4, 7#+S	2.80	
	P# block of 10, 2 sets of P# + top label	7.00	
	Pane of 20	14.00	
	Sheet of 120 (six panes)	85.00	
	Cross gutter block of 8	15.00	
	Block of 8 with vert. gutter	9.00	
	Block of 4 with horiz. gutter	5.00	
	Vert. pair with horiz. gutter (each)	2.00	
	Horiz. pair with vert. gutter (each)	2.00	

Cross gutter block can be either a vertical or horizontal block showing all designs.

LOVE

A2828

A2829

Designed by Michael Osborne.
Printed by Banknote Corporation of America (#3657), Avery Dennison.

LITHOGRAPHED (#3657), PHOTOGRAVURE
Sheets of 200 in ten panes of 20 (#3658)
Serpentine Die Cut 11 on 2, 3 or 4 Sides

2002, Aug. 16 **Tagged**

Booklet Stamp (#3657)

Self-Adhesive

3657	A2828 37c **multicolored**	.70	.20
a.	Booklet pane of 20	14.00	

Serpentine Die Cut 11

3658	A2829 60c **multicolored**	1.25	.25
	P# block of 4, 5#+V	5.00	
	Pane of 20	25.00	

OGDEN NASH (1902-7187), POET

Nash and Poems A2830

Designed by Carl T. Herrman.
Printed by Avery Dennison.

PHOTOGRAVURE
Sheets of 200 in ten panes of 20

2002, Aug. 19 **Tagged** ***Serpentine Die Cut 11***

Self-Adhesive

3659	A2830 37c **multicolored**	.70	.20
	P# block of 4, 8#+V	2.80	
	Pane of 20	14.00	

DUKE KAHANAMOKU (1890-1968), "FATHER OF SURFING" AND OLYMPIC SWIMMER

Kahanamoku and Surfers at Waikiki Beach — A2831

Designed by Carl T. Herrman.
Printed by Avery Dennison.

PHOTOGRAVURE
Sheets of 200 in ten panes of 20
Serpentine Die Cut 11½x11¾

2002, Aug. 24 **Tagged**

Self-Adhesive

3660	A2831 37c **multicolored**	.70	.20
	P# block of 4, 4#+V	2.80	
	Pane of 20	14.00	

AMERICAN BATS

Red Bat — A2832

Leaf-nosed Bat — A2833

Pallid Bat — A2834

Spotted Bat — A2835

Designed by Phil Jordan.
Printed by American Packaging Corporation for Sennett Security Products.

PHOTOGRAVURE
Sheets of 120 in six panes of 20

2002, Sept. 13 **Tagged** ***Serpentine Die Cut 10¾***

Self-Adhesive

3661	A2832 37c **multicolored**	.70	.20
3662	A2833 37c **multicolored**	.70	.20
3663	A2834 37c **multicolored**	.70	.20
3664	A2835 37c **multicolored**	.70	.20
a.	Block or horiz. strip of 4, #3661-3664	2.80	
	P# block of 4, 7#+S	2.80	
	P# block of 8, 2 sets of P# + top label	5.60	
	Pane of 20	14.00	

WOMEN IN JOURNALISM

Nellie Bly (1864-1922) A2836

Ida M. Tarbell (1857-1944) A2837

Ethel L. Payne (1911-91) A2838

Marguerite Higgins (1920-66) A2839

Designed by Fred Otnes.
Printed by American Packaging Corporation for Sennett Security Products.

PHOTOGRAVURE
Sheets of 120 in six panes of 20
Serpentine Die Cut 11x10½

2002, Sept. 14 **Tagged**

Self-Adhesive

3665 A2836 37c **multicolored** .70 .20
3666 A2837 37c **multicolored** .70 .20
3667 A2838 37c **multicolored** .70 .20
3668 A2839 37c **multicolored** .70 .20
a. Block or horiz. strip of 4, #3665-3668 2.80
P# block of 4, 5#+S 2.80
P# block of 8, 2 sets of P# + top label 5.60
Pane of 20 14.00

IRVING BERLIN (1888-1989), COMPOSER

Berlin and Score of "God Bless America" — A2840

Designed by Greg Berger.
Printed by Avery Dennison.

PHOTOGRAVURE
Sheets of 200 in ten panes of 20

2002, Sept. 15 **Tagged** ***Serpentine Die Cut 11***

Self-Adhesive

3669 A2840 37c **multicolored** .70 .20
P# block of 4, 4#+V 2.80
Pane of 20 14.00

NEUTER AND SPAY

Kitten — A2841

Puppy A2842

Designed by Derry Noyes. Printed by American Packaging Corporation for Sennett Security Products.

PHOTOGRAVURE
Sheets of 120 in six panes of 20
Serpentine Die Cut 10¾x10½

2002, Sept. 20 **Tagged**

Self-Adhesive

3670 A2841 37c **multicolored** .70 .20
3671 A2842 37c **multicolored** .70 .20
a. Horiz. or vert. pair, #3670-3671 1.40
P# block of 4, 5#+S 2.80
P# block of 8, 2 sets of P# + top label 5.60
Pane of 20 14.00

Hanukkah Type of 1996

Designed by Hannah Smotrich.
Printed by Avery Dennison.

PHOTOGRAVURE
Sheets of 200 in ten panes of 20

2002, Oct. 10 **Tagged** ***Serpentine Die Cut 11***

Self-Adhesive

3672 A2411 37c **multicolored** .70 .20
P# block of 4, 5#+V 2.80
Pane of 20 14.00

Kwanzaa Type of 1997

Designed by Synthia Saint James.
Printed by Avery Dennison.

PHOTOGRAVURE
Sheets of 200 in ten panes of 20

2002, Oct. 10 **Tagged** ***Serpentine Die Cut 11***

Self-Adhesive

3673 A2458 37c **multicolored** .70 .20
P# block of 4, 4#+V 2.80
Pane of 20 14.00

Eid Type of 2001

Designed by Mohamed Zakariya.
Printed by Avery Dennison.

PHOTOGRAVURE
Sheets of 240 in twelve panes of 20

2002, Oct. 10 **Tagged** ***Serpentine Die Cut 11***

Self-Adhesive

3674 A2734 37c **multicolored** .70 .20
P# block of 4, 3#+V 2.80
Pane of 20 14.00

CHRISTMAS

Madonna and Child, by Jan Gossaert — A2843

Designed by Richard Sheaff.
Printed by Banknote Corporation of America.

LITHOGRAPHED
Serpentine Die Cut 11x11¼ on 2, 3 or 4 Sides

2002, Oct. 10 **Tagged**

Self-Adhesive

Booklet Stamp

3675 A2843 37c **multicolored** .70 .20
a. Booklet pane of 20 14.00

CHRISTMAS

Snowman with Red and Green Plaid Scarf — A2844

Snowman with Blue Plaid Scarf — A2845

Snowman with Pipe — A2846

Snowman with Top Hat — A2847

Snowman with Blue Plaid Scarf — A2848

Snowman with Pipe — A2849

Snowman with Top Hat — A2850

Snowman with Red and Green Plaid Scarf — A2851

Designed by Derry Noyes.

Printed by Avery Dennison (#3676-3679, 3688-3691), Guilford Gravure (#3680-3683), and American Packaging Corp. for Sennett Security Products (#3684-3687).

PHOTOGRAVURE
Sheets of 200 in ten panes of 20

2002, Oct. 28 **Tagged** ***Serpentine Die Cut 11***

Self-Adhesive

3676 A2844 37c **multicolored** .70 .20
3677 A2845 37c **multicolored** .70 .20
3678 A2846 37c **multicolored** .70 .20
3679 A2847 37c **multicolored** .70 .20
a. Block or vert. strip of 4, #3676-3679 2.80
P# block of 4, 4#+V 2.80
Pane of 20 14.00

COIL STAMPS

Serpentine Die Cut 8½ Vert.

3680 A2848 37c **multicolored** .70 .20
3681 A2849 37c **multicolored** .70 .20
3682 A2850 37c **multicolored** .70 .20
3683 A2851 37c **multicolored** .70 .20
a. Strip of 4, #3680-3683 2.80
P# strip of 5, 2 #3680, 1 each #3681-3683, #G1111 5.50
P# strip of 9, 2 each #3680, 3681, 3683, 3 #3682 8.75
P# single (#3682) — 2.00
P# single #G1112 —

BOOKLET STAMPS

Serpentine Die Cut 10¾x11 on 2 or 3 Sides

3684 A2844 37c **multicolored** .70 .20
3685 A2845 37c **multicolored** .70 .20
3686 A2846 37c **multicolored** .70 .20
3687 A2847 37c **multicolored** .70 .20
a. Block of 4, #3684-3687 2.80
b. Booklet pane of 20, 5 #3687a + label 14.00

No. 3687b is a double-sided booklet pane with 12 stamps on one side and eight stamps plus label on the other side.

Serpentine Die Cut 11 on 2 or 3 Sides

No.	Design		Description	Unused	Used
3688	A2851	37c	**multicolored**	.70	.20
3689	A2848	37c	**multicolored**	.70	.20
3690	A2849	37c	**multicolored**	.70	.20
3691	A2850	37c	**multicolored**	.70	.20
a.			Block of 4, #3688-3691	2.80	
b.			Booklet pane of 4, #3688-3691	2.80	
c.			Booklet pane of 6, #3690-3691, 2 each #3688-3689	4.20	
d.			Booklet pane of 6, #3688-3689, 2 each #3690-3691	4.20	
			Nos. 3676-3691 (16)	11.20	3.20

Colors of Nos. 3684-3687 are deeper and designs are slightly smaller than those found on Nos. 3676-3679.

LEGENDS OF HOLLYWOOD

Cary Grant (1904-86), Actor — A2852

Designed by Carl Herrman.

Printed by American Packaging Corporation for Sennett Security Products.

PHOTOGRAVURE

Sheets of 120 in six panes of 20

2002, Oct. 15 Tagged *Serpentine Die Cut 10¾*

Self-Adhesive

No.	Design		Description	Unused	Used
3692	A2852	37c	**multicolored**	.70	.20
			P# block of 4, 6#+S	2.80	
			Pane of 20	14.00	
			Sheet of 120	85.00	
			Cross gutter block of 8	17.50	
			Block of 8 with vertical gutter	10.00	
			Horiz. pair with vert. gutter	3.00	
			Vert. pair with horiz. gutter	2.00	

Cross gutter block consists of 6 stamps from upper panes and 2 stamps from panes below.

Sea Coast — A2853

Designed by Tom Engelman.

Printed by Banknote Corporation Of America.

PHOTOGRAVURE

COIL STAMP

Serpentine Die Cut 8½ Vert.

2002, Oct. 21 Tagged

Self-Adhesive

No.	Design		Description	Unused	Used
3693	A2853	(5c)	**multicolored**	.20	.20
			Pair	.20	
			P# strip of 5, #B111	1.50	
			P# single, #B111	—	1.00

See Nos. 3775, 3785.

HAWAIIAN MISSIONARY STAMPS

A2854

Designed by Richard Sheaff.

Printed by Banknote Corporation of America.

Designs: a, 2c stamp of 1851 (Hawaii Scott 1). b, 5c stamp of 1851 (Hawaii Scott 2) c, 13c stamp of 1851 (Hawaii Scott 3). d, 13c stamp of 1852 (Hawaii Scott 4).

LITHOGRAPHED

Sheets of 24 in six panes of 4

2002, Oct. 24 Tagged *Perf. 11*

No.	Design		Description	Unused	Used
3694	A2854		Pane of 4	2.80	.80
a.-d.		37c	Any single	.70	.20
			Sheet of 6 panes	17.00	

Happy Birthday Type of 2002

Designed by Harry Zelenko.

Printed by Avery Dennison.

PHOTOGRAVURE

Sheets of 200 in ten panes of 20

2002, Oct. 25 Tagged *Serpentine Die Cut 11*

Self-Adhesive

No.	Design		Description	Unused	Used
3695	A2751	37c	**multicolored**	.70	.20
			P# block of 4, 4#+V	2.80	
			Pane of 20	14.00	

Greetings From America Type of 2002

Designed by Richard Sheaff. Printed by American Packaging Corp. for Sennett Security Products.

PHOTOGRAVURE

Sheets of 100 in two panes of 50

2002, Oct. 25 Tagged *Serpentine Die Cut 10¾*

Self-Adhesive

No.	Design		Description	Unused	Used
3696	A2754	37c	Alabama	.70	.20
3697	A2755	37c	Alaska	.70	.20
3698	A2756	37c	Arizona	.70	.20
3699	A2757	37c	Arkansas	.70	.20
3700	A2758	37c	California	.70	.20
3701	A2759	37c	Colorado	.70	.20
3702	A2760	37c	Connecticut	.70	.20
3703	A2761	37c	Delaware	.70	.20
3704	A2762	37c	Florida	.70	.20
3705	A2763	37c	Georgia	.70	.20
3706	A2764	37c	Hawaii	.70	.20
3707	A2765	37c	Idaho	.70	.20
3708	A2766	37c	Illinois	.70	.20
3709	A2767	37c	Indiana	.70	.20
3710	A2768	37c	Iowa	.70	.20
3711	A2769	37c	Kansas	.70	.20
3712	A2770	37c	Kentucky	.70	.20
3713	A2771	37c	Louisiana	.70	.20
3714	A2772	37c	Maine	.70	.20
3715	A2773	37c	Maryland	.70	.20
3716	A2774	37c	Massachusetts	.70	.20
3717	A2775	37c	Michigan	.70	.20
3718	A2776	37c	Minnesota	.70	.20
3719	A2777	37c	Mississippi	.70	.20
3720	A2778	37c	Missouri	.70	.20
3721	A2779	37c	Montana	.70	.20
3722	A2780	37c	Nebraska	.70	.20
3723	A2781	37c	Nevada	.70	.20
3724	A2782	37c	New Hampshire	.70	.20
3725	A2783	37c	New Jersey	.70	.20
3726	A2784	37c	New Mexico	.70	.20
3727	A2785	37c	New York	.70	.20
3728	A2786	37c	North Carolina	.70	.20
3729	A2787	37c	North Dakota	.70	.20
3730	A2788	37c	Ohio	.70	.20
3731	A2789	37c	Oklahoma	.70	.20
3732	A2790	37c	Oregon	.70	.20
3733	A2791	37c	Pennsylvania	.70	.20
3734	A2792	37c	Rhode Island	.70	.20
3735	A2793	37c	South Carolina	.70	.20
3736	A2794	37c	South Dakota	.70	.20
3737	A2795	37c	Tennessee	.70	.20
3738	A2796	37c	Texas	.70	.20
3739	A2797	37c	Utah	.70	.20
3740	A2798	37c	Vermont	.70	.20
3741	A2799	37c	Virginia	.70	.20
3742	A2800	37c	Washington	.70	.20
3743	A2801	37c	West Virginia	.70	.20
3744	A2802	37c	Wisconsin	.70	.20
3745	A2803	37c	Wyoming	.70	.20
a.			Pane of 50, #3696-3745	35.00	

BLACK HERITAGE SERIES

Thurgood Marshall (1908-93), Supreme Court Justice — A2855

Designed by Richard Sheaff. Printed by Ashton-Potter (USA) Ltd.

LITHOGRAPHED

Sheets of 180 in nine panes of 20

2003, Jan. 7 Tagged *Serpentine Die Cut 11½*

Self-Adhesive

No.	Design		Description	Unused	Used
3746	A2855	37c	**black & gray**	.70	.20
			P# block of 4, 3#+P	2.80	
			Pane of 20	14.00	

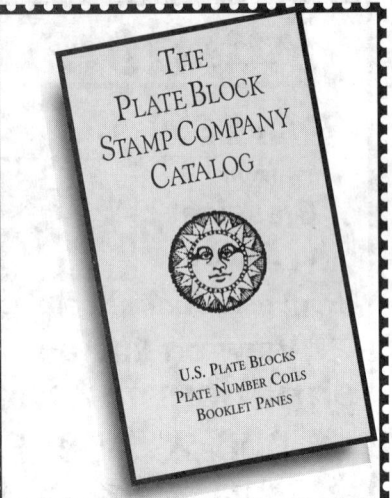

CHINESE NEW YEAR

Year of the Ram — A2856

Designed by Clarence Lee. Printed by Banknote Corporation of America.

LITHOGRAPHED
Sheets of 120 in six panes of 20

2003, Jan. 15 Tagged ***Serpentine Die Cut 11½***
Self-Adhesive

3747 A2856 37c **multicolored** .70 .20
P# block of 4, 4#+B 2.80
Pane of 20 14.00

LITERARY ARTS

Zora Neale Hurston (1891-1960), Writer A2857

Designed by Howard E. Paine. Printed by American Packaging Corporation for Sennett Security Products.

PHOTOGRAVURE
Sheets of 120 in six panes of 20

2003, Jan. 24 Tagged ***Serpentine Die Cut 10¾***
Self-Adhesive

3748 A2857 37c **multicolored** .70 .20
P# block of 4, 5#+S 2.80
Pane of 20 14.00

AMERICAN DESIGN SERIES

American Clock — A2860

Tiffany Lamp — A2866

Designed by Derry Noyes. Printed by Ashton-Potter (USA) Ltd. (#3751), American Packaging Corp. for Sennett Security Products (#3757).

LITHOGRAPHED
Sheets of 120 in six panes of 20

2003 Tagged ***Serpentine Die Cut 11¼x11***
Self-Adhesive

3751 A2860 10c **multicolored**, *Jan. 24* .20 .20
P# block of 4, 4#+P .80
Pane of 20 4.00

PHOTOGRAVURE
COIL STAMP

Untagged ***Perf. 10 Vert.***

3757 A2866 1c **multicolored,** *Mar. 1* .20 .20
Pair .20 .20
P# strip of 5, #S11111 .60 —
P# single, #S11111 — .30

This is an ongoing set. Numbers may change.

AMERICAN CULTURE SERIES

Wisdom, Rockefeller Center, New York City — A2875

Designed by Carl Herrman. Printed by Ashton-Potter (USA) Ltd.

LITHOGRAPHED
Sheets of 120 in six panes of 20
Serpentine Die Cut 11¼x11

2003, Feb. 28 Tagged
Self-Adhesive

3766 A2875 $1 **multicolored** 2.00 .50
P# block of 4, 5# + P 8.00
Pane of 20 40.00

New York Public Library Lion Type of 2000

Designed by Carl Herrman. Printed by American Packaging Corporation for Sennett Security Products.

PHOTOGRAVURE
COIL STAMP

2003, Feb. 4 Untagged ***Perf. 10 Vert.***

3769 A2677 (10c) **multicolored** .20 .20
Pair .40 .20
P# strip of 5, #S11111 3.00 —
P# single, #S11111 — 1.75

SPECIAL OLYMPICS

Athlete with Medal — A2879

Designed by Derry Noyes. Printed by Avery Dennison.

PHOTOGRAVURE
Sheets of 200 in ten panes of 20

2003, Feb. 13 Tagged ***Serpentine Die Cut 11***
Self-Adhesive

3771 A2879 80c **multicolored** 1.60 .35
P# block of 4, 6# + V 6.40
Pane of 20 32.00

AMERICAN FILMMAKING: BEHIND THE SCENES

A2880

Block of 10 With Vertical Gutter Between

Designed by Imaginary Forces. Printed by American Packaging Corporation for Sennett Security Products.

Designs: a, Screenwriting (segment of script from *Gone With the Wind*). b, Directing (John Cassavetes). c, Costume design (Edith Head). d, Music (Max Steiner working on score). e, Makeup (Jack Pierce working on Boris Karloff's makeup for *Frankenstein*). f, Art direction (Perry Ferguson working on sketch for *Citizen Kane*). g, Cinematography (Paul Hill, assistant cameraman for *Nagana*). h, Film editing (J. Watson Webb editing *The Razor's Edge*). i, Special effects (Mark Siegel working on model for *E.T. The Extra-Terrestrial*). j, Sound (Gary Summers works on control panel).

PHOTOGRAVURE
Sheets of 60 in six panes of 10
Serpentine Die Cut 11 Horiz.

2003, Feb. 25 **Tagged**

Self-Adhesive

3772 A2880	Pane of 10	7.00	
a.-j.	37c Any single	.70	.20
	Sheet of 6 panes	42.00	
	Block of 10 with vertical gutter between	9.00	

OHIO STATEHOOD BICENTENNIAL

Aerial View of Farm Near Marietta — A2881

Designed by Phil Jordan. Printed by Banknote Corporation of America.

LITHOGRAPHED
Sheets of 120 in six panes of 20
Serpentine Die Cut 11¾x11½

2003, Mar. 1 **Tagged**

Self-Adhesive

3773 A2881 37c **multicolored**		.70	.20
	P# block of 4, 4# + B	2.80	
	Pane of 20	14.00	

PELICAN ISLAND NATIONAL WILDLIFE REFUGE, CENT.

Brown Pelican — A2882

Designed by Carl T. Herrman. Printed by Banknote Corporation of America.

LITHOGRAPHED
Sheets of 120 in six panes of 20
Serpentine Die Cut 12x11½

2003, Mar. 14 **Tagged**

Self-Adhesive

3774 A2882 37c **multicolored**		.70	.20
	P# block of 4, 4#+B	2.80	
	Pane of 20	14.00	

Sea Coast Type of 2002

Designed by Tom Engeman. Printed by Banknote Corporation of America.

PHOTOGRAVURE
COIL STAMP

2003, Mar. 19 **Untagged** ***Perf. 9¾ Vert.***

3775 A2853 (5c) **multicolored**		.20	.20
	Pair	.20	—
	P# strip of 5, #B111	1.50	
	P# single, #B111		1.00

OLD GLORY

Uncle Sam on Bicycle with Liberty Flag, 20th Cent. — A2883

1888 Presidential Campaign Badge — A2884

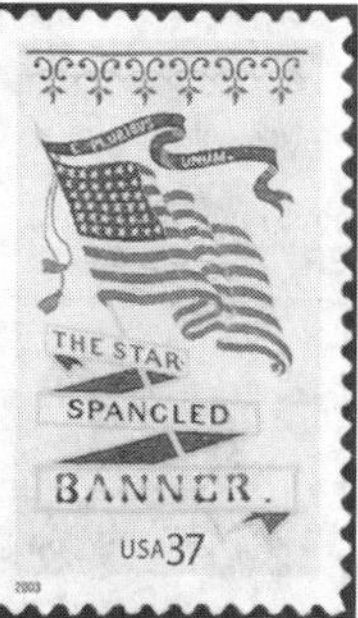

1893 Silk Bookmark — A2885

Modern Hand Fan — A2886

Carving of Woman with Flag and Sword, 19th Cent. — A2887

Designed by Richard Sheaff. Printed by Ashton-Potter (USA) Ltd.

LITHOGRAPHED
BOOKLET STAMPS

2003, Apr. 3 **Tagged** ***Serpentine Die Cut 10x9¾***

Self-Adhesive

3776 A2883 37c **multicolored**	.70	.20
3777 A2884 37c **multicolored**	.70	.20
3778 A2885 37c **multicolored**	.70	.20
3779 A2886 37c **multicolored**	.70	.20

3780	A2887 37c **multicolored**	.70	.20
a.	Horiz. strip of 5, #3776-3780	3.50	
b.	Booklet pane, 2 #3780a	7.00	

No. 3780b was issued with two types of backing.

CESAR E. CHAVEZ (1927-93), LABOR ORGANIZER

A2888

Designed by Carl Herrman. Printed by Banknote Corporation of America.

LITHOGRAPHED

Sheets of 120 in six panes of 20

Serpentine Die Cut 11¾x11½

2003, Apr. 23 **Tagged**

Self-Adhesive

3781	A2888 37c **multicolored**	.70	.20
	P# block of 4, 4# + B	2.80	
	Pane of 20	14.00	

LOUISIANA PURCHASE, BICENT.

English Translation of Treaty, Map of US, Treaty Signers — A2889

Designed by Richard Sheaff. Printed by American Packaging Corporation for Sennett Security Products

PHOTOGRAVURE

Sheets of 120 in six panes of 20

2003, Apr. 30 **Tagged** ***Serpentine Die Cut 10¾***

Self-Adhesive

3782	A2889 37c **multicolored**	.70	.20
	P# block of 4, 6# + S	2.80	
	Pane of 20	14.00	

FIRST FLIGHT OF WRIGHT BROTHERS, CENT.

Orville Wright Piloting 1903 Wright Flyer — A2890

Designed by McRay Magleby. Printed by Avery Dennison.

PHOTOGRAVURE

BOOKLET STAMP

2003, May 22 **Tagged** ***Serpentine Die Cut 11***

Self-Adhesive

3783	A2890 37c **multicolored**	.70	.20
a.	Booklet pane of 9	6.30	
b.	Booklet pane of 1	.70	

PURPLE HEART

A2891

Designed by Carl Herrman. Printed by Banknote Corporation of America.

LITHOGRAPHED

Sheets of 200 in ten panes of 20

Serpentine Die Cut 11¼x10¾

2003, May 30 **Tagged**

Self-Adhesive

3784	A2891 37c **multicolored**	.70	.20
	P# block of 4, 4#+B	2.80	
	Pane of 20	14.00	

Sea Coast Type of 2002

Designed by Tom Engeman. Printed by Ashton-Potter (USA) Ltd.

LITHOGRAPHED

COIL STAMP

2003, June **Untagged** ***Serpentine Die Cut 9½x10***

Self-Adhesive

3785	A2853 (5c) **multicolored**	.20	.20
	Pair	.20	
	P# strip of 5, #P1111	1.50	
	P# single, same #	—	1.00

LEGENDS OF HOLLYWOOD

Audrey Hepburn (1929-93), Actress — A2892

Designed by Michael J. Deas. Printed by American Packaging Corporation for Sennett Security Products.

PHOTOGRAVURE

Sheets of 120 in six panes of 20

2003, June 11 **Tagged** ***Serpentine Die Cut 10¾***

Self-Adhesive

3786	A2892 37c **multicolored**	.70	.20
	P# block of 4, 6#+S	2.80	
	Pane of 20	14.00	
	Sheet of 120	85.00	
	Cross gutter block of 8	17.50	
	Block of 8 with vertical gutter	10.00	
	Horiz. pair with vert. gutter	3.00	
	Vert. pair with horiz. gutter	2.00	

Cross gutter block consists of 6 stamps from upper panes and 2 stamps from panes below.

SOUTHEASTERN LIGHTHOUSES

Old Cape Henry, Virginia — A2893

Cape Lookout, North Carolina — A2894

Morris Island, South Carolina — A2895

Tybee Island, Georgia — A2896

Hillsboro Inlet, Florida — A2897

Designed by Howard E. Paine. Printed by American Packaging Corporation for Sennett Security Products.

PHOTOGRAVURE

Sheets of 120 in six panes of 20

2003, June 13 **Tagged** ***Serpentine Die Cut 10¾***

Self-Adhesive

3787	A2893 37c **multicolored**	.70	.20
3788	A2894 37c **multicolored**	.70	.20
a.	Bottom of "USA" even with top of upper half-diamond of lighthouse (pos. 2)	.70	.20
3789	A2895 37c **multicolored**	.70	.20
3790	A2896 37c **multicolored**	.70	.20
3791	A2897 37c **multicolored**	.70	.20
a.	Strip of 5, #3587-3791	3.50	
b.	Strip of 5, #3787, 3788a, 3789-3791	3.50	
	P# block of 10, 2 sets of 6#+S	7.00	
	Pane of 20	14.00	

Eagle in Gold on Colored Background A2898

Colored Eagle on Gold Background A2899

Designed by Tom Engeman. Printed by American Packaging Corporation for Sennett Security Products.

PHOTOGRAVURE

COIL STAMPS

Serpentine Die Cut 11¾ Vert.

2003, June 26 **Untagged**

Self-Adhesive

3792	A2898 (25c) **gray & gold**	.50	.20
3793	A2899 (25c) **gold & red**	.50	.20
3794	A2898 (25c) **dull blue & gold**	.50	.20
3795	A2899 (25c) **gold & Prussian blue**	.50	.20
3796	A2898 (25c) **green & gold**	.50	.20
3797	A2899 (25c) **gold & gray**	.50	.20
3798	A2898 (25c) **Prussian blue & gold**	.50	.20
3799	A2899 (25c) **gold & dull blue**	.50	.20
3800	A2898 (25c) **red & gold**	.50	.20
3801	A2899 (25c) **gold & green**	.50	.20
a.	Strip of 10, #3792-3801	5.00	
	P# strip of 11, 2 # 3801, 1 each #3792-3800, #S1111111, S2222222	7.50	
	P# strip of 21, 3 # 3796, 2 each #3792-3795, 3797-3801, #S1111111, S2222222	15.00	
	P# single (#3796), same #	—	2.00

ARCTIC TUNDRA

A2900

Illustration reduced.

Designed by Ethel Kessler. Printed by Banknote Corporation of America.

Wildlife and vegetation: a, Gyrfalcon. b, Gray wolf, vert. c, Common raven, vert. d, Musk oxen and caribou, vert. e, Grizzly bears, caribou. f, Caribou, willow ptarmigans. g, Arctic ground squirrel, vert. h, Willow ptarmigan, bearberry. i, Arctic grayling. j, Singing vole, thin-legged wolf spider, lingonberry, Labrador tea.

LITHOGRAPHED

Sheets of 80 in eight panes of 10

Serpentine Die Cut 10¾x10½, 10½x10¾

2003, July 2 **Tagged**

Self-Adhesive

3802	A2900 Pane of 10	7.00	
a.-j.	37c Any single	.70	.20
	Sheet of 8 panes	65.00	
	Pair of tete-beche panes	14.00	

2003 END-OF-YEAR ISSUES

The USPS has announced that the following items will be released in late 2003. Dates, denominations and cities are tentative.

Korean War Veterans Memorial, 37c self-adhesive, *July 27,* Washington DC

Mary Cassatt, 4x37c self-adhesives, *Aug. 7,* Columbus OH

Early Football Heroes, 4x37c self-adhesives, *Aug. 8,* South Bend, IN

Roy Acuff, 37c self-adhesive, *Sept. 13,* Nashville TN

Reptiles and Amphibians, 5x37c self-adhesives, *Oct. 7,*

Christmas, 4x37c self-adhesive sheet stamps, *Oct. 15,* New York NY

Christmas, 4x37c self-adhesives in convertible booklet of 20, *Oct. 15,* New York NY

Christmas, 4x37c self-adhesives in vending machine booklet of 20, *Oct. 15,* New York NY

Christmas, 4x37c postal cards, *Oct. 24,* New York NY

Snowy Egret, 37c self-adhesive, *Nov.,* Denver CO

Domestic Violence, 37c stamped envelope, *Aug. 2,* Washington DC & nationwide

Listings as of 10:00PM, July 23, 2003.

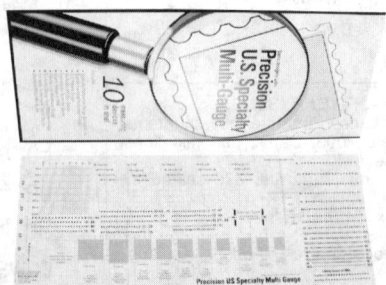

SEMI-POSTAL STAMP

The genesis of the U.S. semi-postal stamp program was a July 1997 bill passed by both houses of Congress that directed the USPS to issue a stamp to benefit breast-cancer research. On August 13, the President signed it into law. The surcharge was to be up to 25% of the current first-class rate.

BREAST CANCER AWARENESS

SP1

Designed by Ethel Kessler. Printed by Avery Dennison.

PHOTOGRAVURE

Sheets of 160 in eight panes of 20

1998, July 29 Tagged ***Serpentine Die Cut 11***

Self-Adhesive

B1	SP1	(32c+8c) **multicolored**	.80	.25
		P# block of 4, 6#+V	3.25	
		Pane of 20	16.00	

The 8c surtax was for cancer research. After the Jan. 10, 1999, first class postage rate changes, No. B1 became a 33c stamp with a 7c surtax; after Jan. 7, 2001, it became a 34c stamp with a 6c surtax. Effective Mar. 23, 2002, the stamp was sold for 45c, but the face value remained at 34c until June 30, 2002, at which time the face value rose to 37c.

HEROES OF 2001

Firemen Atop World Trade Center Rubble — SP2

Designed by Derry Noyes. Printed by Ashton-Potter (USA) Ltd..

LITHOGRAPHED

Sheets of 120 in six panes of 20

2002, June 7 Tagged ***Serpentine Die Cut 11¼***

Self-Adhesive

B2	SP2	(34c+11c) **multicolored**	.90	.65
		P# block of 4, 4#+P	3.60	
		Pane of 20	18.00	

The 11c surtax was for assistance to families of emergency relief personnel killed or permanently disabled in the line of duty in connection with the terrorist attacks of Sept. 11, 2001. No. B2 became a 37c stamp with an 8c surtax June 30, 2002.

AIR POST STAMPS

Air mail in the U. S. postal system developed in three stages: pioneer period (with many unofficial or semi-official flights before 1918), government flights and contract air mail (C.A.M.). Contract air mail began on February 15, 1926.

All C.A.M. contracts were canceled on February 19, 1934, and air mail was carried by Army planes for six months. After that the contract plan was resumed. Separate domestic airmail service was abolished Oct. 11, 1975.

See Domestic Air Mail Rates chart in introduction.

Curtiss Jenny — AP1

No. C3 first used on airplane mail service between Washington, Philadelphia and New York, on May 15, 1918, but was valid for ordinary postage. The rate of postage was 24 cents per ounce, which included immediate individual delivery.

Rate of postage was reduced to 16 cents for the first ounce and 6 cents for each additional ounce, which included 10 cents for immediate individual delivery, on July 15, 1918, by Postmaster General's order of June 26, 1918. No. C2 was first used for air mail in the tri-city service on July 15.

Rate of postage was reduced on December 15, 1918, by Postmaster General's order of November 30, 1918, to 6 cents per ounce. No. C1 was first used for air mail (same three-way service) on Dec. 16.

FLAT PLATE PRINTINGS

Plates of 100 subjects.

1918 Unwmk. Engr. ***Perf. 11***

C1	AP1	6c **orange,** *Dec. 10*	65.	30.
		pale orange	65.	30.
		Never hinged	110.	
		On cover		50.
		First flight cover, *Dec. 16*		2,000.
		Margin block of 4, arrow top or left	275.	140.
		Center line block	290.	150.
		P# block of 6, arrow	725.	—
		Never hinged	1,050.	
		Double transfer (#9155-14)	90.	45.
C2	AP1	16c **green,** *July 11*	80.	35.
		dark green	80.	35.
		Never hinged	140.	
		On cover		55.
		First flight cover, *July 15*		800.
		Margin block of 4, arrow top or left	330.	175.
		Center line block	360.	190.
		P# block of 6, arrow	1,000.	—
		Never hinged	1,500.	
C3	AP1	24c **carmine rose & blue,** *May 13*	80.	35.
		dark carmine rose & blue	80.	35.
		Never hinged	140.	
		On cover		75.
		First flight cover, *May 15*		750.
		Margin block of 4, arrow top or left	330.	150.
		Margin block of 4, arrow bottom	375.	160.
		Margin block of 4, arrow right	425.	200.
		Center line block	375.	175.
		P# block of 4, red P# only	400.	—
		P# block of 12, two P#, arrow & two "TOP"	1,225.	—
		Never hinged	2,000.	
		P# block of 12, two P#, arrow & blue "TOP" only	*12,500.*	
	a.	Center inverted	*170,000.*	
		Never hinged	*200,000.*	
		Block of 4	*750,000.*	
		Block of 4 with horiz. guide line	*850,000.*	
		Corner margin block of 4 with siderographer's initials	*1,100,000.*	
		Center line block	*825,000.*	
		P# block of 4, blue P#	*1,200,000.*	
		Nos. C1-C3 (3)	225.00	100.00
		Nos. C1-C3, never hinged	390.00	

Plate Blocks

Scott values for plate blocks printed from flat plates are for very fine side and bottom positions. Top position plate blocks with full wide selvage sell for more.

Airplane Radiator and Wooden Propeller — AP2

Air Service Emblem — AP3

DeHavilland Biplane — AP4

Nos. C4-C6 were issued primarily for use in the new night-flying air mail service between New York and San Francisco, but valid for all purposes. Three zones were established; New York-Chicago, Chicago-Cheyenne, Cheyenne-San Francisco, and the rate of postage was 8 cents an ounce for each zone. Service was inaugurated on July 1, 1924.

These stamps were placed on sale at the Philatelic Agency at Washington on the dates indicated in the listings but were not issued to postmasters at that time.

Plates of 400 subjects in four panes of 100 each.

1923 Unwmk. ***Perf. 11***

C4	AP2	8c **dark green,** *Aug. 15*	22.50	14.00
		deep green	22.50	14.00
		Never hinged	40.00	
		On cover		22.50
		P# block of 6	225.00	—
		Never hinged	325.00	
		Double transfer	40.00	22.50
C5	AP3	16c **dark blue,** *Aug. 17*	80.00	30.00
		Never hinged	140.00	
		On cover		47.50
		P# block of 6	1,550.	—
		Never hinged	2,350.	
		Double transfer	120.00	50.00
C6	AP4	24c **carmine,** *Aug. 21*	90.00	30.00
		Never hinged	150.00	
		On cover		42.50
		P# block of 6	2,050.	—
		Never hinged	3,100.	
		Double transfer (Pl. 14841)	160.00	42.50
		Nos. C4-C6 (3)	192.50	74.00
		Nos. C4-C6, never hinged	330.00	

Map of United States and Two Mail Planes — AP5

Double Transfer

The Act of Congress of February 2, 1925, created a rate of 10 cents per ounce for distances to 1000 miles, 15 cents per ounce for 1500 miles and 20 cents for more than 1500 miles on contract air mail routes.

Plates of 200 subjects in four panes of 50 each.

1926-27 **Unwmk.** ***Perf. 11***

C7	AP5	10c	**dark blue,** *Feb. 13, 1926*	2.60	.35
			light blue	2.60	.35
			Never hinged	4.50	
			P# block of 6	35.00	—
			Never hinged	47.50	
			Double transfer (18246 UL 11)	5.75	1.10
C8	AP5	15c	**olive brown,** *Sept. 18, 1926*	3.00	2.50
			light brown	3.00	2.50
			Never hinged	5.25	
			P# block of 6	35.00	—
			Never hinged	50.00	
C9	AP5	20c	**yellow green,** *Jan. 25, 1927*	7.50	2.00
			green	7.50	2.00
			Never hinged	13.50	
			P# block of 6	75.00	—
			Never hinged	105.00	
			Nos. C7-C9 (3)	13.10	4.85
			Nos. C7-C9, never hinged	23.25	

Lindbergh's Plane "Spirit of St. Louis" and Flight Route — AP6

A tribute to Col. Charles A. Lindbergh, who made the first non-stop (and solo) flight from New York to Paris, May 20-21, 1927.

Plates of 200 subjects in four panes of 50 each.

1927, June 18 **Unwmk.** ***Perf. 11***

C10	AP6	10c	**dark blue**	7.25	2.50
			Never hinged	12.50	
			P# block of 6	90.00	—
			Never hinged	130.00	
			Double transfer	11.50	3.25
a.			Booklet pane of 3, *May 26, 1928*	80.00	*65.00*
			Never hinged	120.00	

Beacon on Rocky Mountains AP7

Issued to meet the new rate, effective August 1, of 5 cents per ounce.

Plates of 100 subjects in two panes of 50

1928, July 25 **Unwmk.** ***Perf. 11***

C11	AP7	5c	**carmine and blue**	5.00	.75
			Never hinged	8.50	
			On cover, first day of 5c airmail rate, Aug. 1		3.00
			Margin block of 4, arrow, (line) right or left	22.50	4.50
			P# block of 8, two P# only (no "TOP")	175.00	—
			Never hinged	240.00	
			P# block of 6, two P# & red "TOP"	40.00	—
			Never hinged	55.00	
			P# block of 6, two P# & blue "TOP"	40.00	—
			Never hinged	55.00	
			P# block of 6, two P# & double "TOP"	110.00	—
			Never hinged	150.00	
			Recut frame line at left	6.50	1.25
			Double transfer	—	—
a.			Vert. pair, imperf. between	*5,500.*	

Winged Globe — AP8

Plates of 200 subjects in four panes of 50 each.

1930, Feb. 10 **Unwmk.** ***Perf. 11***

Stamp design: 46½x19mm

C12	AP8	5c	**violet**	10.00	.50
			Never hinged	17.50	
			P# block of 6	135.00	—
			Never hinged	190.00	
			Double transfer (Pl. 20189)	19.00	1.25
a.			Horiz. pair, imperf. between	*4,500.*	

See Nos. C16-C17, C19.

GRAF ZEPPELIN ISSUE

Zeppelin Over Atlantic Ocean — AP9

Zeppelin Between Continents — AP10

Zeppelin Passing Globe — AP11

Issued for use on mail carried on the first Europe-Pan-America round trip flight of the Graf Zeppelin in May, 1930. They were withdrawn from sale June 30, 1930.

Plates of 200 subjects in four panes of 50 each.

1930, Apr. 19 **Unwmk.** ***Perf. 11***

C13	AP9	65c	**green**	240.	160.
			Never hinged	350.	
			On cover or card		175.
			Block of 4	1,000.	700.
			P# block of 6	2,250.	—
			Never hinged	3,100.	
C14	AP10	$1.30	**brown**	450.	375.
			Never hinged	700.	
			On cover		400.
			Block of 4	2,150.	1,500.
			P# block of 6	5,600.	—
			Never hinged	7,750.	
C15	AP11	$2.60	**blue**	700.	575.
			Never hinged	1,050.	
			On cover		600.
			Block of 4	3,250.	2,500.
			P# block of 6	8,000.	—
			Never hinged	11,250.	
			Nos. C13-C15 (3)	1,390.	1,110.
			Nos. C13-C15, never hinged	2,110.	

ROTARY PRESS PRINTING

Plates of 200 subjects in four panes of 50 each.

1931-32 **Unwmk.** ***Perf. 10½x11***

Stamp design: 47½x19mm

C16	AP8	5c	**violet,** *Aug. 19, 1931*	5.25	.60
			Never hinged	8.75	
			Block of 4	22.00	2.00
			P# block of 4	75.00	—
			Never hinged	100.00	

Issued to conform with new air mail rate of 8 cents per ounce which became effective July 6, 1932.

C17	AP8	8c	**olive bister,** *Sept. 26, 1932*	2.25	.40
			Never hinged	3.75	
			Block of 4	9.50	2.00
			P# block of 4	27.50	—
			Never hinged	37.50	

CENTURY OF PROGRESS ISSUE

"Graf Zeppelin," Federal Building at Chicago Exposition and Hangar at Friedrichshafen — AP12

Issued in connection with the flight of the airship "Graf Zeppelin" in October, 1933, to Miami, Akron and Chicago and from the last city to Europe.

FLAT PLATE PRINTING

Plates of 200 subjects in four panes of 50 each.

1933, Oct. 2 **Unwmk.** ***Perf. 11***

C18 AP12 50c **green** 65.00 65.00
Never hinged 100.00
On cover 80.00
Block of 4 275.00 290.00
P# block of 6 525.00 —
Never hinged 725.00

Catalogue values for unused stamps in this section, from this point to the end, are for Never Hinged items.

Type of 1930 Issue

ROTARY PRESS PRINTING

Issued to conform with new air mail rate of 6 cents per ounce which became effective July 1, 1934.

Plates of 200 subjects in four panes of 50 each.

1934, June 30 **Unwmk.** ***Perf. 10½x11***

C19 AP8 6c **dull orange** 3.50 .25
On cover, first day of 6c airmail rate, July 1 10.00
Block of 4 14.00 1.10
P# block of 4 21.00 —
Horiz. pair with full vert. gutter btwn. *425.00*
Vert. pair with full horiz. gutter btwn. —

TRANSPACIFIC ISSUES

"China Clipper" over Pacific AP13

Issued to pay postage on mail transported by the Transpacific air mail service, inaugurated Nov. 22, 1935.

FLAT PLATE PRINTING

Plates of 200 subjects in four panes of 50 each.

1935, Nov. 22 **Unwmk.** ***Perf. 11***

C20 AP13 25c **blue** 1.40 1.00
P# block of 6 20.00 —

"China Clipper" over Pacific AP14

Issued primarily for use on the Transpacific service to China, but valid for all air mail purposes.

FLAT PLATE PRINTING

Plates of 200 subjects in four panes of 50 each.

1937, Feb. 15 **Unwmk.** ***Perf. 11***

C21 AP14 20c **green** 11.00 1.75
dark green 11.00 1.75
Block of 4 47.50 8.50
P# block of 6 100.00 —
C22 AP14 50c **carmine** 10.00 5.00
Block of 4 42.50 21.00
P# block of 6 100.00 —

Wide full selvage top margin plate blocks of No. C22 are extremely scarce and sell for six to seven times the value listed.

Eagle Holding Shield, Olive Branch and Arrows — AP15

FLAT PLATE PRINTING

Frame plates of 100 subjects in two panes of 50 each separated by a 1½-inch wide vertical gutter with central guide line, and vignette plates of 50 subjects. Some plates were made of iron, then chromed; several of these carry an additional imprint, "E.I." (Electrolytic Iron).

1938, May 14 **Unwmk.** ***Perf. 11***

C23 AP15 6c **dark blue & carmine** .50 .20
Margin block of 4, bottom or side arrow 2.25 .55
P# block of 4, 2 P# 7.00 —
Center line block 2.75 .95
Top P# block of 10, with two P#, arrow, two "TOP" and two registration markers 13.50
Ultramarine & carmine *150.00* *1,500.*
P# block of 4, 2 P# *1,500.*
a. Vert. pair, imperf. horiz. *325.00*
P# block of 4, 2 P# *1,250.* —
b. Horiz. pair, imperf. vert. *12,500.*
P# block of 4, 2 P# *37,500.* —

Top plate number blocks of No. C23 are found both with and without top arrow.

The plate block of No. C23b is unique and never hinged; value is based on 1994 auction sale.

TRANSATLANTIC ISSUE

Winged Globe — AP16

Inauguration of Transatlantic air mail service.

FLAT PLATE PRINTING

Plates of 200 subjects in four panes of 50 each.

1939, May 16 **Unwmk.** ***Perf. 11***

C24 AP16 30c **dull blue** 10.50 1.50
P# block of 6 130.00 —

Twin-Motored Transport Plane — AP17

ROTARY PRESS PRINTING

E. E. Plates of 200 subjects in four panes of 50 each.

1941-44 **Unwmk.** ***Perf. 11x10½***

C25 AP17 6c **carmine,** *June 25, 1941* .20 .20
P# block of 4 .60 —
Pair with full vert. gutter btwn. *225.00*
Pair with full horiz. gutter btwn. —
a. Booklet pane of 3, *Mar. 18, 1943* 5.00 *1.50*
b. Horiz. pair, imperf. between *2,250.*

Singles from No. C25a are imperf. at sides or at sides and bottom.

Value of No. C25b is for pair without blue crayon P. O. rejection mark on front. Very fine pairs with crayon mark sell for about $1,750.

C26 AP17 8c **olive green,** *Mar. 21, 1944* .20 .20
P# block of 4 1.10 —
Pair with full horiz. gutter btwn. *325.00*
C27 AP17 10c **violet,** *Aug. 15, 1941* 1.25 .20
P# block of 4 5.75 —
C28 AP17 15c **brown carmine,** *Aug. 19, 1941* 2.25 .35
P# block of 4 10.50 —
C29 AP17 20c **bright green,** *Aug. 27, 1941* 2.25 .30
P# block of 4 10.00 —
C30 AP17 30c **blue,** *Sept. 25, 1941* 2.25 .35
P# block of 4 10.50 —
C31 AP17 50c **orange,** *Oct. 29, 1941* 11.00 3.25
P# block of 4 52.50 —
Nos. C25-C31 (7) 19.40 4.85

DC-4 Skymaster AP18

ROTARY PRESS PRINTING

E. E. Plates of 200 subjects in four panes of 50 each.

1946, Sept. 25 **Unwmk.** ***Perf. 11x10½***

C32 AP18 5c **carmine** .20 .20
P# block of 4 .45 —

DC-4 Skymaster — AP19

ROTARY PRESS PRINTING

E. E. Plates of 400 subjects in four panes of 100 each.

1947, Mar. 26 **Unwmk.** ***Perf. 10½x11***

C33 AP19 5c **carmine** .20 .20
P# block of 4 .55 —

Pan American Union Building, Washington, D.C., and Martin 2-0-2 — AP20

Statue of Liberty, New York Skyline and Lockheed Constellation AP21

San Francisco-Oakland Bay Bridge and Boeing B377 Stratocruiser — AP22

Designed by Victor S. McCloskey, Jr., Leon Helguera and William K. Schrage.

ROTARY PRESS PRINTING

E. E. Plates of 200 subjects in four panes of 50 each.

1947 **Unwmk.** ***Perf. 11x10½***

C34 AP20 10c **black,** *Aug. 30* .25 .20
P# block of 4 1.10 —
a. Dry printing .40 .20
P# block of 4 (#25613, 25614) 1.75 —
C35 AP21 15c **bright blue green,** *Aug. 20* .35 .20
blue green .35 .20
P# block of 4 1.50 —

Pair with full horiz. gutter btwn. *650.00*
a. Horiz. pair, imperf. between *2,400.*
b. Dry printing .55 .20
P# block of 4 (#25492 and up) 2.50 —
C36 AP22 25c **blue,** *July 30* .90 .20
P# block of 4 3.75 —
a. Dry printing 1.10 .20
P# block of 4 (#25615 and up) 4.75 —
Nos. C34-C36 (3) 1.50 .60

See note on wet and dry printings following No. 1029. No. C35a is valued in the grade of fine.

ROTARY PRESS COIL STAMP
Type of 1947

1948, Jan. 15 Unwmk. *Perf. 10 Horizontally*
C37 AP19 5c **carmine** 1.00 .80
Pair 2.10 1.75
Joint line pair 10.00 3.00

NEW YORK CITY ISSUE

Map of Five Boroughs, Circular Band and Planes — AP23

50th anniv. of the consolidation of the five boroughs of New York City.

ROTARY PRESS PRINTING
E. E. Plates of 400 subjects in four panes of 100 each.

1948, July 31 Unwmk. *Perf. 11x10½*
C38 AP23 5c **bright carmine** .20 .20
P# block of 4 3.50 —

Type of 1947
ROTARY PRESS PRINTING
E. E. Plates of 400 subjects in four panes of 100 each.

1949 Unwmk. *Perf. 10½x11*
C39 AP19 6c **carmine,** *Jan. 18* .20 .20
P# block of 4 .50 —
Pair with full horiz. gutter btwn. —
a. Booklet pane of 6, *Nov. 18* 10.00 *5.00*
b. Dry printing .50 .20
P# block of 4 (#25340 and up) 2.25 —
c. As "a," dry printing 20.00 —

See note on wet and dry printings following No. 1029.

ALEXANDRIA BICENTENNIAL ISSUE

Home of John Carlyle, Alexandria Seal and Gadsby's Tavern AP24

200th anniv. of the founding of Alexandria, Va.

ROTARY PRESS PRINTING
E. E. Plates of 200 subjects in four panes of 50 each.

1949, May 11 Unwmk. *Perf. 11x10½*
C40 AP24 6c **carmine** .20 .20
P# block of 4 .50 —

ROTARY PRESS COIL STAMP
Type of 1947

1949, Aug. 25 Unwmk. *Perf. 10 Horizontally*
C41 AP19 6c **carmine** 3.00 .20
Pair 6.25 .20
Joint line pair 14.00 1.35

UNIVERSAL POSTAL UNION ISSUE

Post Office Department Building AP25

Globe and Doves Carrying Messages AP26

Boeing Stratocruiser and Globe — AP27

Universal Postal Union, 75th Anniv.

ROTARY PRESS PRINTING
E. E. Plates of 200 subjects in four panes of 50 each.

1949 Unwmk. *Perf. 11x10½*
C42 AP25 10c **violet,** *Nov. 18* .20 .20
P# block of 4 1.40 —
C43 AP26 15c **ultramarine,** *Oct. 7* .30 .25
P# block of 4 1.25 —
C44 AP27 25c **rose carmine,** *Nov. 30* .60 .40
P# block of 4 5.25 —
Nos. C42-C44 (3) 1.10 .85

WRIGHT BROTHERS ISSUE

Wilbur and Orville Wright and their Plane, 1903 — AP28

46th anniv. of the 1st successful flight in a motor-powered airplane, Dec. 17, 1903, at Kill Devil Hill near Kitty Hawk, NC, by Wilbur (1867-1912) and Orville Wright (1871-1948) of Dayton, OH. The plane flew 852 feet in 59 seconds.

ROTARY PRESS PRINTING
E. E. Plates of 200 subjects in four panes of 50 each.

1949, Dec. 17 Unwmk. *Perf. 11x10½*
C45 AP28 6c **magenta** .20 .20
P# block of 4 .65 —

Diamond Head, Honolulu, Hawaii AP29

ROTARY PRESS PRINTING
E. E. Plates of 200 subjects in four panes of 50 each.

1952, Mar. 26 Unwmk. *Perf. 11x10½*
C46 AP29 80c **bright red violet** 5.00 1.25
P# block of 4 22.50 —

POWERED FLIGHT, 50th ANNIV.

First Plane and Modern Plane — AP30

ROTARY PRESS PRINTING
E. E. Plates of 200 subjects in four panes of 50 each.

1953, May 29 Unwmk. *Perf. 11x10½*
C47 AP30 6c **carmine** .20 .20
P# block of 4 .55 —

Eagle in Flight — AP31

Issued primarily for use on domestic post cards.

ROTARY PRESS PRINTING
E. E. Plates of 400 subjects in four panes of 100 each.

1954, Sept. 3 Unwmk. *Perf. 11x10½*
C48 AP31 4c **bright blue** .20 .20
P# block of 4 1.25 —

AIR FORCE, 50th ANNIV.

B-52 Stratofortress and F-104 Starfighters AP32

Designed by Alexander Nagy, Jr.

ROTARY PRESS PRINTING
E. E. Plates of 200 subjects in four panes of 50 each.

1957, Aug. 1 Unwmk. *Perf. 11x10½*
C49 AP32 6c **blue** .20 .20
P# block of 4 .65 —

Type of 1954

Issued primarily for use on domestic post cards.

1958, July 31 Unwmk. *Perf. 11x10½*
C50 AP31 5c **red** .20 .20
P# block of 4 1.25 —

Silhouette of Jet Airliner — AP33

Designed by William H. Buckley and Sam Marsh.

ROTARY PRESS PRINTING
E. E. Plates of 400 subjects in four panes of 100 each.

1958, July 31 Unwmk. *Perf. 10½x11*
C51 AP33 7c **blue** .20 .20
P# block of 4 .60 —
a. Booklet pane of 6 12.50 *7.00*
b. Vert. pair, imperf. between (from booklet pane) —

No. C51b resulted from a paper foldover after perforating and before cutting into panes. Two pairs are known.

ROTARY PRESS COIL STAMP
Perf. 10 Horizontally

C52 AP33 7c **blue** 2.00 .20
Pair 4.25 .40
Joint line pair 14.00 1.25
Small holes 10.00 —
Pair 20.00
Joint line pair 200.00

ALASKA STATEHOOD ISSUE

Big Dipper, North Star and Map of Alaska AP34

Designed by Richard C. Lockwood.

ROTARY PRESS PRINTING

E. E. Plates of 200 subjects in four panes of 50 each.

1959, Jan. 3 Unwmk. *Perf. 11x10½*

C53 AP34 7c **dark blue** .20 .20
P# block of 4 .60 —

BALLOON JUPITER ISSUE

Balloon and Crowd — AP35

Designed by Austin Briggs.

Centenary of the carrying of mail by the balloon Jupiter from Lafayette to Crawfordsville, Ind.

GIORI PRESS PRINTING

Plates of 200 subjects in four panes of 50 each.

1959, Aug. 17 Unwmk. *Perf. 11*

C54 AP35 7c **dark blue & red** .20 .20
P# block of 4 .60 —

HAWAII STATEHOOD ISSUE

Alii Warrior, Map of Hawaii and Star of Statehood AP36

Designed by Joseph Feher.

ROTARY PRESS PRINTING

E. E. Plates of 200 subjects in four panes of 50 each.

1959, Aug. 21 Unwmk. *Perf. 11x10½*

C55 AP36 7c **rose red** .20 .20
P# block of 4 .60 —

PAN AMERICAN GAMES ISSUE

Runner Holding Torch — AP37

Designed by Suren Ermoyan.

3rd Pan American Games, Chicago, Aug. 27-Sept. 7, 1959.

GIORI PRESS PRINTING

Plates of 200 subjects in four panes of 50 each.

1959, Aug. 27 Unwmk. *Perf. 11*

C56 AP37 10c **violet blue & bright red** .25 .25
P# block of 4 1.25 —

Liberty Bell — AP38

Statue of Liberty AP39

Abraham Lincoln AP40

GIORI PRESS PRINTING

Plates of 200 subjects in four panes of 50 each.

1959-66 Unwmk. *Perf. 11*

C57 AP38 10c **black & green,** *June 10, 1960* 1.10 .70
P# block of 4 4.75 —
C58 AP39 15c **black & orange,** *Nov. 20, 1959* .35 .20
P# block of 4 1.50 —
C59 AP40 25c **black & maroon,** *Apr. 22, 1960* .50 .20
P# block of 4 2.00 —
a. Tagged, *Dec. 29, 1966* .60 .30
P# block of 4 2.50 —
Nos. C57-C59 (3) 1.95 1.10

See Luminescence data in Information for Collectors section.

Type of 1958

ROTARY PRESS PRINTING

E. E. Plates of 400 subjects in four panes of 100 each.

1960, Aug. 12 Unwmk. *Perf. 10½x11*

C60 AP33 7c **carmine** .20 .20
P# block of 4 .60 —
Pair with full horiz. gutter btwn. 125.00
a. Booklet pane of 6, *Aug. 19* 14.00 *8.00*
b. Vert. pair, imperf between (from booklet pane) *5,500.*

No. C60b resulted from a paper foldover after perforating and before cutting into panes. Two pairs are known.

Type of 1958

ROTARY PRESS COIL STAMP

1960, Oct. 22 Unwmk. *Perf. 10 Horizontally*

C61 AP33 7c **carmine** 4.00 .25
Pair 8.25 .55
Joint line pair 35.00 3.75

Type of 1959-60 and

Statue of Liberty AP41

GIORI PRESS PRINTING

Plates of 200 subjects in four panes of 50 each.

1961-67 Unwmk. *Perf. 11*

C62 AP38 13c **black & red,** *June 28, 1961* .40 .20
P# block of 4 1.65 —
a. Tagged, *Feb. 15, 1967* .75 .50
P# block of 4 5.00 —
C63 AP41 15c **black & orange,** *Jan. 13, 1961* .30 .20
P# block of 4 1.25 —
a. Tagged, *Jan. 11, 1967* .35 .20
P# block of 4 1.50 —
b. As "a," horiz. pair, imperf. vert. *15,000.*

Jet Airliner over Capitol — AP42

Designed by Henry K. Bencsath.

ROTARY PRESS PRINTING

E.E. Plates of 400 subjects in four panes of 100 each.

1962, Dec. 5 Unwmk. *Perf. 10½x11*

C64 AP42 8c **carmine** .20 .20
P# block of 4 .65 —
a. Tagged, *Aug. 1, 1963* .20 .20
P# block of 4 .65 —
As "a," pair with full horiz. gutter between —
b. Booklet pane of 5 + label 7.00 *3.00*
c. As "b," tagged, *1964* 2.00 *.75*

Nos. C64a and C64c were made by overprinting Nos. C64 and C64b with phosphorescent ink. No. C64a was first issued at Dayton, O., for experiments in high speed mail sorting. The tagging is visible in ultraviolet light.

COIL STAMP; ROTARY PRESS

Perf. 10 Horizontally

C65 AP42 8c **carmine** .40 .20
Pair .80 .20
Joint line pair 3.75 .35
a. Tagged, *Jan. 14, 1965* .35 .20
Pair .70 .20
Joint line pair 1.50 .30

MONTGOMERY BLAIR ISSUE

Montgomery Blair — AP43

Designed by Robert J. Jones

Montgomery Blair (1813-83), Postmaster General (1861-64), who called the 1st Intl. Postal Conf., Paris, 1863, forerunner of the UPU.

GIORI PRESS PRINTING

Plates of 200 subjects in four panes of 50 each.

1963, May 3 Unwmk. *Perf. 11*

C66 AP43 15c **dull red, dark brown & blue** .60 .55
P# block of 4 2.60 —

Bald Eagle — AP44

Designed by V. S. McCloskey, Jr.

Issued primarily for use on domestic post cards.

ROTARY PRESS PRINTING

E.E. Plates of 400 subjects in four panes of 100 each.

1963, July 12 Unwmk. *Perf. 11x10½*

C67 AP44 6c **red** .20 .20
P# block of 4 1.60 —
a. Tagged, *Feb. 15, 1967* 4.00 3.00
P# block of 4 55.00 —

AMELIA EARHART ISSUE

Amelia Earhart and Lockheed Electra — AP45

Designed by Robert J. Jones.

Amelia Earhart (1898-1937), 1st woman to fly across the Atlantic.

GIORI PRESS PRINTING

Plates of 200 subjects in four panes of 50 each.

1963, July 24 **Unwmk.** ***Perf. 11***

C68 AP45 8c **carmine & maroon** .20 .20
P# block of 4 1.00 —

ROBERT H. GODDARD ISSUE

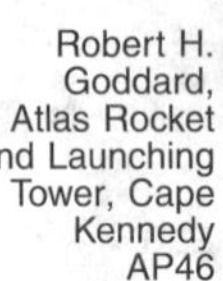

Robert H. Goddard, Atlas Rocket and Launching Tower, Cape Kennedy AP46

Designed by Robert J. Jones.

Dr. Robert H. Goddard (1882-1945), physicist and pioneer rocket researcher.

GIORI PRESS PRINTING

Plates of 200 subjects in four panes of 50 each.

1964, Oct. 5 **Tagged** ***Perf. 11***

C69 AP46 8c **blue, red & bister** .40 .20
P# block of 4 1.75 —
Margin block of 4, Mr. Zip and "Use Zip Code" 1.65 —

Luminescence

Air Post stamps issued after mid-1964 are tagged.

ALASKA PURCHASE ISSUE

Tlingit Totem, Southern Alaska — AP47

Designed by Willard R. Cox

Centenary of the Alaska Purchase. The totem pole shown is in the Alaska State Museum, Juneau.

GIORI PRESS PRINTING

Plates of 200 subjects in four panes of 50 each.

1967, Mar. 30 **Unwmk.** ***Perf. 11***

C70 AP47 8c **brown** .25 .20
P# block of 4 1.25 —
Margin block of 4, Mr. Zip and "Use Zip Code" 1.05 —

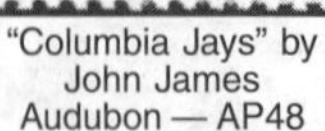

"Columbia Jays" by John James Audubon — AP48

Fifty-Star Runway — AP49

GIORI PRESS PRINTING

Designed by Robert J. Jones.

Plates of 200 subjects in four panes of 50 each.

1967, Apr. 26 ***Perf. 11***

C71 AP48 20c **multicolored** .80 .20
P# block of 4 3.50 —
Margin block of 4, Mr. Zip and "Use Zip Code" 3.25 —
a. Tagging omitted *10.00*

See note over No. 1241.

ROTARY PRESS PRINTING

Designed by Jaan Born.

E. E. Plates of 400 subjects in four panes of 100 each.

1968, Jan. 5 **Unwmk.** ***Perf. 11x10½***

C72 AP49 10c **carmine** .20 .20
P# block of 4 .90 —
Margin block of 4, "Use Zip Codes" .85 —
Vert. pair with full horiz. gutter between —
b. Booklet pane of 8 2.00 *.75*
c. Booklet pane of 5 + label, *Jan. 6* 3.75 *.75*
d. Vert. pair, imperf. between (from bklt. pane) *8,000.*
e. Tagging omitted *10.00* —
f. As "b," tagging omitted —

Red is the normal color of the tagging. Copies of No. C72b exist that have a mixture of the two tagging compounds.

No. C72d resulted from a paper foldover after perforating and before cutting into panes. Only one pair is known.

ROTARY PRESS COIL STAMP

Perf. 10 Vertically

C73 AP49 10c **carmine** .30 .20
Pair .65 .20
Joint line pair 1.75 .20
a. Imperf., pair *600.00*
Joint line pair *900.00*

$1 Air Lift

This stamp, listed as No. 1341, was issued Apr. 4, 1968, to pay for airlift of parcels to and from U.S. ports to servicemen overseas and in Alaska, Hawaii and Puerto Rico.

It was "also valid for paying regular rates for other types of mail," the Post Office Department announced to the public in a philatelic release dated Mar. 10, 1968. The stamp is inscribed "U.S. Postage" and is untagged.

On Apr. 26, 1969, the P.O.D. stated in its Postal Manual (for postal employees) that this stamp "may be used toward paying the postage or fees for special services on *airmail* articles." On Jan. 1, 1970, the Department told postal employees through its Postal Bulletin that this $1 stamp "can only be used to pay the airlift fee or toward payment of postage or fees on *airmail* articles."

Some collectors prefer to consider No. 1341 an airmail stamp.

50th ANNIVERSARY OF AIR MAIL ISSUE

Curtiss Jenny — AP50

Designed by Hordur Karlsson.

50th anniv. of regularly scheduled air mail service.

LITHOGRAPHED, ENGRAVED (GIORI)

Plates of 200 subjects in four panes of 50 each.

1968, May 15 ***Perf. 11***

C74 AP50 10c **blue, black & red** .25 .20
P# block of 4 2.00 —
Margin block of 4, Mr. Zip and "Use Zip Code" 1.05 —
b. Tagging omitted *7.50*

"USA" and Jet — AP51

Designed by John Larrecq.

LITHOGRAPHED, ENGRAVED (GIORI)

Plates of 200 subjects in four panes of 50 each.

1968, Nov. 22 ***Perf. 11***

C75 AP51 20c **red, blue & black** .35 .20
P# block of 4 1.75 —
Margin block of 4, Mr. Zip and "Use Zip Code" 1.50 —
a. Tagging omitted *10.00*

MOON LANDING ISSUE

First Man on the Moon AP52

Designed by Paul Calle.

Man's first landing on the moon July 20, 1969, by U.S. astronauts Neil A. Armstrong and Col. Edwin E. Aldrin, Jr., with Lieut. Col. Michael Collins piloting Apollo 11.

LITHOGRAPHED, ENGRAVED (GIORI)

Plates of 128 subjects in four panes of 32 each.

1969, Sept. 9 ***Perf. 11***

C76 AP52 10c **yellow, black, lt. blue, ultra., rose red & carmine** .25 .20
P# block of 4 1.10 —
Margin block of 4, Mr. Zip and "Use Zip Code" 1.05 —
a. Rose red (litho.) omitted *500.00* —
b. Tagging omitted —

On No. C76a, the lithographed rose red is missing from the entire vignette-the dots on top of the yellow areas as well as the flag shoulder patch.

Silhouette of Delta Wing Plane — AP53

Silhouette of Jet Airliner — AP54

Winged Airmail Envelope — AP55

Statue of Liberty AP56

Designed by George Vander Sluis (9c, 11c), Nelson Gruppo (13c) and Robert J. Jones (17c).

ROTARY PRESS PRINTING

E. E. Plates of 400 subjects in four panes of 100 each.

1971-73 ***Perf. 10½x11***

C77 AP53 9c **red,** *May 15, 1971* .20 .20
P# block of 4 .90 —
Margin block of 4, "Use Zip Codes" .85 —

No. C77 issued primarily for use on domestic post cards.

Perf. 11x10½

C78 AP54 11c **carmine,** *May 7, 1971* .20 .20
P# block of 4 .90 —
Margin block of 4, "Use Zip Codes" .85 —
Pair with full vert. gutter btwn. —
a. Booklet pane of 4 + 2 labels 1.25 *.75*
b. Untagged (Bureau precanceled) .85 .85
P# block of 4 28.50 —
Margin block of 4, "Use Zip Codes" 13.75 —
c. Tagging omitted (not Bureau precanceled) 7.50
C79 AP55 13c **carmine,** *Nov. 16, 1973* .25 .20
P# block of 4 1.10 —
Margin block of 4, "Use Zip Codes" 1.05 —
a. Booklet pane of 5 + label, *Dec. 27, 1973* 1.50 *.75*
b. Untagged (Bureau precanceled) .85 .85

P# block of 4 11.50 —
Margin block of 4, "Use Zip Codes" 9.50 —
c. Green instead of red tagging (single from booklet pane) —
d. Tagging omitted (not precanceled) 7.50 —

No. C78b Bureau precanceled "WASHINGTON D.C." (or "DC"), No. C79b "WASHINGTON DC" only; both for use of Congressmen, but available to any permit holder.

Red is the normal color of the tagging. Copies also exist that have a mixture of the two tagging compounds.

GIORI PRESS PRINTING

Panes of 200 subjects in four panes of 50 each.

Perf. 11

C80 AP56 17c **bluish black, red, & dark green,** *July 13, 1971* .35 .20
P# block of 4 1.60 —
Margin block of 4, Mr. Zip and "Use Zip Code" 1.50 —
a. Tagging omitted 10.00 —

"USA" & Jet Type of 1968

LITHOGRAPHED, ENGRAVED (GIORI)

Plates of 200 subjects in four panes of 50 each.

Perf. 11

C81 AP51 21c **red, blue & black,** *May 21, 1971* .40 .20
P# block of 4 2.00 —
Margin block of 4, Mr. Zip and "Use Zip Code" 1.75 —
a. Tagging omitted *10.00*
b. Black (engr.) missing (FO) —

COIL STAMPS

ROTARY PRESS PRINTING

1971-73 *Perf. 10 Vertically*

C82 AP54 11c **carmine,** *May 7, 1971* .25 .20
Pair .50 .25
Joint line pair .80 .35
a. Imperf., pair *275.00*
Joint line pair *425.00*
b. Tagging omitted 4.00
C83 AP55 13c **carmine,** *Dec. 27, 1973* .30 .20
Pair .60 .25
Joint line pair 1.10 —
a. Imperf., pair *75.00*
Joint line pair *150.00*

NATIONAL PARKS CENTENNIAL ISSUE

City of Refuge, Hawaii

Kii Statue and Temple — AP57

Designed by Paul Rabut.

Centenary of national parks. This 11c honors the City of Refuge National Historical Park, established in 1961 at Honaunau, island of Hawaii.

LITHOGRAPHED, ENGRAVED (GIORI)

Plates of 200 subjects in four panes of 50 each.

1972, May 3 *Perf. 11*

C84 AP57 11c **orange & multicolored** .20 .20
P# block of 4 .90 —
Margin block of 4, Mr. Zip and "Use Zip Code" .85 —
a. Blue & green (litho.) omitted *800.00*
b. Tagging omitted —

OLYMPIC GAMES ISSUE

Skiing and Olympic Rings — AP58

Designed by Lance Wyman.

11th Winter Olympic Games, Sapporo, Japan, Feb. 3-13, and 20th Summer Olympic Games, Munich, Germany, Aug. 26-Sept. 11.

PHOTOGRAVURE (Andreotti)

Plates of 200 subjects in four panes of 50 each.

1972, Aug. 17 *Perf. 11x10½*

C85 AP58 11c **black, blue, red, emerald & yellow** .20 .20
P# block of 10, 5 P# 2.50 —
Margin block of 4, "Use Zip Code" .85 —

ELECTRONICS PROGRESS ISSUE

De Forest Audions AP59

Designed by Walter and Naiad Einsel.

LITHOGRAPHED, ENGRAVED (GIORI)

Plates of 200 subjects in four panes of 50 each.

1973, July 10 *Perf. 11*

C86 AP59 11c **vermilion, lilac, pale lilac, olive, brown, deep carmine & black** .20 .20
P# block of 4 .95 —
Margin block of 4, Mr. Zip and "Use Zip Code" .90 —
a. Vermilion & olive (litho.) omitted *1,100.*
b. Tagging omitted *20.00*
c. Olive omitted —

Statue of Liberty AP60

Mt. Rushmore National Memorial AP61

Designed by Robert (Gene) Shehorn.

GIORI PRESS PRINTING

Panes of 200 subjects in four panes of 50 each.

1974 *Perf. 11*

C87 AP60 18c **carmine, black & ultramarine,** *Jan. 11* .35 .30
P# block of 4, 2# 1.50 —
Margin block of 4, Mr. Zip and "Use Zip Code" 1.45 —
a. Tagging omitted *17.50*
C88 AP61 26c **ultramarine, black & carmine,** *Jan. 2* .50 .20
P# block of 4 2.25 —
Margin block of 4, Mr. Zip and "Use Zip Code" 2.10 —
Pair with full vert. gutter btwn. —
a. Tagging omitted *17.50*
b. Yellow-green instead of orange-red tagging — —

Plane and Globes AP62

Plane, Globes and Flags — AP63

Designed by David G. Foote.

GIORI PRESS PRINTING

Panes of 200 subjects in four panes of 50 each.

1976, Jan. 2 *Perf. 11*

C89 AP62 25c **red, blue & black** .50 .20
P# block of 4 2.25 —
Margin block of 4, Mr. Zip and "Use Zip Code" 2.10 —
a. Tagging omitted —
C90 AP63 31c **red, blue & black** .60 .20
P# block of 4 2.60 —
Margin block of 4, Mr. Zip and "Use Zip Code" 2.50 —
a. Tagging omitted *10.00*

WRIGHT BROTHERS ISSUE

Orville and Wilbur Wright, and Flyer A — AP64

Wright Brothers, Flyer A and Shed — AP65

Designed by Ken Dallison.

75th anniv. of 1st powered flight, Kill Devil Hill, NC, Dec. 17, 1903.

LITHOGRAPHED, ENGRAVED (GIORI)

Plates of 400 subjects in four panes of 100 each.

1978, Sept. 23 *Perf. 11*

C91 AP64 31c **ultramarine & multicolored** .65 .30
C92 AP65 31c **ultramarine & multicolored** .65 .30
a. Vert. pair, #C91-C92 1.30 1.20
P# block of 4 3.00 —
Margin block of 4, "Use Correct Zip Code" 2.75 —
b. As "a," ultra. & black (engr.) omitted *750.00*
c. As "a," black (engr.) omitted —
d. As "a," black, yellow, magenta, blue & brown (litho.) omitted *2,250.*

OCTAVE CHANUTE ISSUE

Chanute and Biplane Hang-glider — AP66

Biplane Hang-glider and Chanute — AP67

Designed by Ken Dallison.

Octave Chanute (1832-1910), civil engineer and aviation pioneer.

LITHOGRAPHED, ENGRAVED (GIORI)

Plates of 400 subjects in four panes of 100 each.

1979, Mar. 29 **Tagged** *Perf. 11*

C93 AP66 21c **blue & multicolored** .70 .35
C94 AP67 21c **blue & multicolored** .70 .35
a. Vert. pair, #C93-C94 1.40 1.20
P# block of 4 3.25 —
Margin block of 4, Mr. Zip 2.85 —
b. As "a," ultra & black (engr.) omitted *4,500.*

WILEY POST ISSUE

Wiley Post and "Winnie Mae" — AP68

NR-105-W, Post in Pressurized Suit, Portrait — AP69

Designed by Ken Dallison.

Wiley Post (1899-1935), first man to fly around the world alone and high-altitude flying pioneer.

LITHOGRAPHED, ENGRAVED (GIORI)
Plates of 400 subjects in four panes of 100 each.

1979, Nov. 20 **Tagged** ***Perf. 11***

C95	AP68 25c **blue & multicolored**	1.10	.45
C96	AP69 25c **blue & multicolored**	1.10	.45
a.	Vert. pair, #C95-C96	2.25	1.50
	P# block of 4	5.00	—
	Margin block of 4, Mr. Zip	4.50	—

OLYMPIC GAMES ISSUE

High Jump — AP70

Designed by Robert M. Cunningham.

22nd Olympic Games, Moscow, July 19-Aug. 3, 1980.

PHOTOGRAVURE
Plates of 200 subjects in four panes of 50 each.

1979, Nov. 1 **Tagged** ***Perf. 11***

C97	AP70 31c **multicolored**	.70	.30
	P# block of 12, 6#	9.50	—
	Zip block of 4	3.00	—

PHILIP MAZZEI (1730-1816)

Italian-born Political Writer — AP71

Designed by Sante Graziani

PHOTOGRAVURE
Plates of 200 subjects in four panes of 50 each.

1980, Oct. 13 **Tagged** ***Perf. 11***

C98	AP71 40c **multicolored**	.80	.20
	P# block of 12, 6#	10.00	—
	Zip block of 4	3.50	—
b.	Imperf., pair	*2,750.*	
d.	Tagging omitted	*10.00*	

1982 **Tagged** ***Perf. 10½x11¼***

C98A	AP71 40c **multicolored**	7.50	1.50
	P# block of 12, 6#	125.00	—
c.	Horiz. pair, imperf. vert.	—	

BLANCHE STUART SCOTT (1886-1970)

First Woman Pilot — AP72

Designed by Paul Calle.

PHOTOGRAVURE
Plates of 200 subjects in four panes of 50.

1980, Dec. 30 **Tagged** ***Perf. 11***

C99	AP72 28c **multicolored**	.60	.20
	P# block of 12, 6#	8.50	—
	Zip block of 4	2.50	—
a.	Imperf., pair	*3,250.*	

GLENN CURTISS (1878-1930)

Aviation Pioneer and Aircraft Designer AP73

Designed by Ken Dallison.

PHOTOGRAVURE
Plates of 200 subjects in four panes of 50.

1980, Dec. 30 **Tagged** ***Perf. 11***

C100	AP73 35c **multicolored**	.65	.20
	P# block of 12, 6#	9.00	—
	Zip block of 4	2.75	—

SUMMER OLYMPICS 1984

Women's Gymnastics — AP74

Hurdles — AP75

Women's Basketball — AP76

Soccer — AP77

Shot Put — AP78

Men's Gymnastics AP79

Women's Swimming AP80

Weight Lifting AP81

Women's Fencing AP82

Cycling AP83

Women's Volleyball AP84

Pole Vaulting AP85

Designed by Robert Peak.

23rd Olympic Games, Los Angeles, July 28-Aug. 12, 1984.

PHOTOGRAVURE
Plates of 200 subjects in four panes of 50.

1983, June 17 **Tagged** ***Perf. 11***

C101	AP74 28c **multicolored**	1.00	.30
C102	AP75 28c **multicolored**	1.00	.30
C103	AP76 28c **multicolored**	1.00	.30
C104	AP77 28c **multicolored**	1.00	.30
a.	Block of 4, #C101-C104	4.25	2.50
	P# block of 4, 4#	5.50	—
	Zip block of 4	4.25	—
b.	As "a," imperf. vert.	*7,500.*	

1983, Apr. 8 **Tagged** ***Perf. 11.2 Bullseye***

C105	AP78 40c **multicolored**	.90	.40
a.	Perf. 11 line	1.00	.45
C106	AP79 40c **multicolored**	.90	.40
a.	Perf. 11 line	1.00	.45
C107	AP80 40c **multicolored**	.90	.40
a.	Perf. 11 line	1.00	.45
C108	AP81 40c **multicolored**	.90	.40
a.	Perf. 11 line	1.00	.45
b.	Block of 4, #C105-C108	4.25	3.00
	P# block of 4, 4#	5.00	—
	Zip block of 4	4.50	—
c.	Block of 4, #C105a-C108a	5.00	4.00
	P# block of 4, 4#	7.50	—
d.	Block of 4, imperf.	*1,250.*	

1983, Nov. 4 **Tagged** ***Perf. 11***

C109	AP82 35c **multicolored**	.90	.55
C110	AP83 35c **multicolored**	.90	.55
C111	AP84 35c **multicolored**	.90	.55
C112	AP85 35c **multicolored**	.90	.55
a.	Block of 4, #C109-C112	4.00	3.25
	P# block of 4, 4#	7.00	—
	Zip block of 4	4.25	—

AVIATION PIONEERS

Alfred V. Verville (1890-1970), Inventor, Verville-Sperry R-3 Army Racer — AP86

Lawrence Sperry (1892-1931), Aircraft Designer, and Father Elmer (1860-1930), Designer and Pilot, 1st Seaplane AP87

Designed by Ken Dallison (No. C113) and Howard Koslow (No. C114)

PHOTOGRAVURE
Plates of 200 in four panes of 50
(2 panes each, No. C113 and No. C114)
Plates of 200 in four panes of 50 (No. C114)

1985, Feb. 13 **Tagged** ***Perf. 11***

C113 AP86 33c	**multicolored**	.65	.20
	P# block of 4, 5#, UL, LR	3.25	—
	Zip block of 4	2.90	—
a.	Imperf., pair	*850.00*	
C114 AP87 39c	**multicolored**	.80	.25
	P# block of 4, 5#, UR, LL	3.75	—
	Zip block of 4	3.50	—
a.	Imperf., pair	*1,500.*	

Philatelic Foundation certificates issued prior to August 1994 for No. C114 with magenta missing have been rescinded. At this time no true magenta missing copies are known.

TRANSPACIFIC AIRMAIL
50th Anniversary

Martin M-130 China Clipper AP88

Designed by Chuck Hodgson.

PHOTOGRAVURE
Plates of 200 in four panes of 50

1985, Feb. 15 **Tagged** ***Perf. 11***

C115 AP88 44c	**multicolored**	.85	.25
	P# block of 4, 5#	4.00	—
	Zip block of 4	3.50	—
a.	Imperf., pair	*850.00*	

FR. JUNIPERO SERRA (1713-1784)
California Missionary

Outline Map of Southern California, Portrait, San Gabriel Mission AP89

Designed by Richard Schlecht from a Spanish stamp.

PHOTOGRAVURE
Plates of 200 in four panes of 50

1985, Aug. 22 **Tagged** ***Perf. 11***

C116 AP89 44c	**multicolored**	1.00	.35
	P# block of 4	8.50	—
	Zip block of 4	4.25	—
a.	Imperf., pair	*1,500.*	

SETTLING OF NEW SWEDEN, 350th ANNIV.

Settler, Two Indians, Map of New Sweden, Swedish Ships "Kalmar Nyckel" and "Fogel Grip" — AP90

Designed by Goran Osterland based on an 18th century illustration from a Swedish book about the Colonies.

LITHOGRAPHED AND ENGRAVED
Plates of 200 in four panes of 50

1988, Mar. 29 **Tagged** ***Perf. 11***

C117 AP90 44c	**multicolored**	1.00	.25
	P# block of 4, 5#	6.75	—
	Zip block of 4	5.00	—

See Sweden No. 1672 and Finland No. 768.

SAMUEL P. LANGLEY (1834-1906)

Langley and Unmanned Aerodrome No. 5 — AP91

Designed by Ken Dallison.

LITHOGRAPHED AND ENGRAVED
Plates of 200 in four panes of 50

1988, May 14 **Tagged** ***Perf. 11***

C118 AP91 45c	**multicolored,** large block tagging	.90	.20
	P# block of 4, 7#	4.25	—
	Zip block of 4	4.00	—
a.	Overall tagging	3.00	.50
	P# block of 4, 7#	30.00	—
	Zip block of 4	14.00	—

IGOR SIKORSKY (1889-1972)

Sikorsky and 1939 VS300 Helicopter AP92

Designed by Ren Wicks.

PHOTOGRAVURE AND ENGRAVED
Plates of 200 in four panes of 50

1988, June 23 **Tagged** ***Perf. 11***

C119 AP92 36c	**multicolored**	.70	.25
	P# block of 4, 6#	3.25	—
	Zip block of 4	3.10	—

Beware of copies with traces of red offered as "red omitted" varieties.

FRENCH REVOLUTION BICENTENNIAL

Liberty, Equality and Fraternity — AP93

Designed by Richard Sheaff.

LITHOGRAPHED AND ENGRAVED
Plates of 120 in four panes of 30.

1989, July 14 **Tagged** ***Perf. 11½x11***

C120 AP93 45c	**multicolored**	.95	.20
	P# block of 4, 4#	4.75	—
	Zip block of 4	4.00	—

See France Nos. 2143-2145a.

PRE-COLUMBIAN AMERICA ISSUE

Southeast Carved Figure, 700-1430 A.D. — AP94

Designed by Lon Busch.
Printed by American Bank Note Co.

PHOTOGRAVURE
Plates of 200 in four panes of 50

1989, Oct. 12 ***Perf. 11***

C121 AP94 45c	**multicolored**	.90	.20
	P# block of 4, 4#	5.25	—
	Zip block of 4	3.75	—

20th UPU CONGRESS
Futuristic Mail Delivery

Spacecraft — AP95

Air-suspended Hover Car — AP96

Moon Rover — AP97

Space Shuttle — AP98

Designed by Ken Hodges.

LITHOGRAPHED & ENGRAVED
Plates of 160 in four panes of 40.

1989, Nov. 27 **Tagged** ***Perf. 11***

C122	AP95 45c **multicolored**		1.00	.50
C123	AP96 45c **multicolored**		1.00	.50
C124	AP97 45c **multicolored**		1.00	.50
C125	AP98 45c **multicolored**		1.00	.50
a.	Block of 4, #C122-C125		4.25	3.25
	P# block of 4, 5#		5.50	—
	Zip block of 4		4.50	—
b.	As "a," light blue (engr.) omitted		*800.00*	

Souvenir Sheet
LITHOGRAPHED & ENGRAVED

1989, Nov. 24 **Tagged** ***Imperf.***

C126	Sheet of 4	4.75	3.75
a.	AP95 45c multicolored	1.00	.50
b.	AP96 45c multicolored	1.00	.50
c.	AP97 45c multicolored	1.00	.50
d.	AP98 45c multicolored	1.00	.50

PRE-COLUMBIAN AMERICA ISSUE

Tropical Coast — AP99

Designed by Mark Hess.
Printed by the American Bank Note Company.

PHOTOGRAVURE
Plates of 200 in four panes of 50
(3 panes of #2512, 1 pane of #C127)

1990, Oct. 12 **Tagged** ***Perf. 11***

C127	AP99 45c **multicolored**	.90	.20
	P# block of 4, 4#, UL only	6.75	—
	Zip block of 4	3.75	—

HARRIET QUIMBY, 1ST AMERICAN WOMAN PILOT

Quimby (1884-1912), Bleriot Airplane AP100

Designed by Howard Koslow. Printed by Stamp Venturers.

PHOTOGRAVURE
Panes of 200 in four panes of 50

1991, Apr. 27 **Tagged** ***Perf. 11***

C128	AP100 50c **multicolored**	1.00	.25
	P# block of 4, 4#+S	5.50	—
	Zip block of 4	4.25	—
a.	Vert. pair, imperf. horiz.	1,900.	
b.	Perf. 11.2	1.10	.25
	P# block of 4, 4#+S	6.00	—
	Zip block of 6	4.50	—

WILLIAM T. PIPER, AIRCRAFT MANUFACTURER

Piper and Piper Cub — AP101

Designed by Ren Wicks.
Printed by J. W. Fergusson and Sons for American Bank Note Co.

PHOTOGRAVURE
Panes of 200 in four panes of 50

1991, May 17 **Tagged** ***Perf. 11***

C129	AP101 40c **multicolored**	.80	.20
	P# block of 4, 4#+A	4.00	—
	Zip block of 4	3.60	—

Blue sky is plainly visible all the way across stamp above Piper's head.
See No. C132.

ANTARCTIC TREATY, 30TH ANNIVERSARY

AP102

Designed by Howard Koslow. Printed by Stamp Venturers.

PHOTOGRAVURE
Panes of 50

1991, June 21 **Tagged** ***Perf. 11***

C130	AP102 50c **multicolored**	1.00	.35
	P# block of 4, 4#+S	5.00	—
	Zip block of 4	4.25	—

PRE-COLUMBIAN AMERICA ISSUE

Bering Land Bridge AP103

Designed by Richard Schlect.

PHOTOGRAVURE
Plates of 200 in 4 panes of 50

1991, Oct. 12 **Tagged** ***Perf. 11***

C131	AP103 50c **multicolored**	1.00	.35
	P# block of 4, 6#	5.25	—
	Zip block of 4	4.75	—

Piper Type of 1991

Printed by Stamp Venturers.

PHOTOGRAVURE
Panes of 200 in four panes of 50

1993 **Tagged** ***Perf. 11.2***

C132	AP101 40c **multicolored**	1.40	.35
	P# block of 4, 4#+S	35.00	—
	Zip block of 4	6.50	—

Piper's hair touches top edge of design. No inscriptions. Bullseye perf.

"All LC (Letters and Cards) mail receives First-Class Mail service in the United States, is dispatched by the fastest transportation available, and travels by airmail or priority service in the destination country. All LC mail should be marked 'AIRMAIL' or 'PAR AVION.'" (U.S. Postal Service, Pub. 51).

No. C133 listed below was issued to meet the LC rate to Canada and Mexico and is inscribed with the silhouette of a jet plane next to the denomination indicating the need for airmail service. This is unlike No. 2998, which met the LC rate to other countries, but contained no indication that it was intended for that use.

Future issues that meet a specific international airmail rate and contain the airplane silhouette will be treated by Scott as Air Post stamps. Stamps similar to No. 2998 will be listed in the Postage section.

NIAGARA FALLS

AP104

Designed by Ethel Kessler. Printed by Avery Dennison.

PHOTOGRAVURE
Sheets of 200 in ten panes of 20

1999, May 12 **Tagged** ***Perf. 11***
Self-Adhesive

C133	AP104 48c **multicolored**	.95	.20
	P# block of 4, 5#+V	4.00	
	Pane of 20	20.00	

RIO GRANDE

AP105

Designed by Ethel Kessler. Printed by Avery Dennison.

PHOTOGRAVURE
Sheets of 200 in ten panes of 20

1999, July 30 **Tagged** ***Serpentine Die Cut 11***
Self-Adhesive

C134	AP105 40c **multicolored**	.80	.60
	P# block of 4, 5#+V	3.20	
	Pane of 20	16.00	

GRAND CANYON

AP106

Designed by Ethel Kessler.
Printed by Banknote Corp. of America.

LITHOGRAPHED
Sheets of 180 in nine panes of 20
Serpentine Die Cut 11¼x11½

2000, Jan. 20 **Tagged**
Self-Adhesive

C135	AP106 60c **multicolored**	1.25	.25
	P# block of 4, 4#+B	5.00	
	Pane of 20	25.00	
a.	Imperf, pair	—	

NINE-MILE PRAIRIE, NEBRASKA

AP107

Designed by Ethel Kessler. Printed by Ashton-Potter (USA) Ltd.

LITHOGRAPHED
Sheets of 180 in nine panes of 20
Serpentine Die Cut 11¼x11½

2001, Mar. 6 **Tagged**
Self-Adhesive

C136	AP107 70c **multicolored**	1.40	.30
	P# block of 4, 5#+P	5.60	
	Pane of 20	28.00	

MT. MCKINLEY

AP108

Designed by Ethel Kessler. Printed by Avery Dennison.

PHOTOGRAVURE
Sheets of 200 in ten panes of 20.

2001, Apr. 17 **Tagged** ***Serpentine Die Cut 11***
Self-Adhesive

C137	AP108 80c **multicolored**	1.60	.35
	P# block of 4, 5 #+V	6.40	
	Pane of 20	32.00	

ACADIA NATIONAL PARK

AP109

Designed by Ethel Kessler. Printed by Banknote Corporation of America.

LITHOGRAPHED
Sheets of 180 in nine panes of 20
Serpentine Die Cut 11¼x11½

2001, May 30 **Tagged**

Self-Adhesive

C138 AP109 60c **multicolored**	1.25	.25
P# block of 4, 4#+B	5.00	
Pane of 20	25.00	

AIR POST SPECIAL DELIVERY STAMPS

Great Seal of United States
APSD1

No. CE1 was issued for the prepayment of the air postage and the special delivery fee in one stamp. First day sale was at the American Air Mail Society Convention.

FLAT PLATE PRINTING
Plates of 200 subjects in four panes of 50 each.

1934, Aug. 30 **Unwmk.** ***Perf. 11***

CE1 APSD1 16c **dark blue**	.60	.70
blue	.60	.70
Never hinged	.80	
P# block of 6	15.00	—
Never hinged	20.00	
First day cover, Chicago *(40,171)*		25.00
First day cover, Washington, D.C., *Aug. 31*		15.00

For imperforate variety see No. 771.

Type of 1934

Frame plates of 100 subjects in two panes of 50 each separated by a 1½ inch wide vertical gutter with central guide line, and vignette plates of 50 subjects.

The "seal" design for No. CE2 was from a new engraving, slightly smaller than that used for No. CE1.

Top plate number blocks of No. CE2 are found both with and without top arrow.

Issued in panes of 50 each.

1936, Feb. 10

CE2 APSD1 16c **red & blue**	.40	.25
Never hinged	.50	
Margin block of 4, bottom or side arrow	2.00	1.50
Center line block	2.50	2.25
P# block of 4, 2#	6.50	—
Never hinged	8.00	
P# block of 4, 2#, blue dotted registration marker	75.00	
Never hinged	95.00	
Same, arrow, thick red registration marker	70.00	
Never hinged	90.00	
P# block of 10, 2#, two "TOP" and two registration markers	17.50	6.00
Never hinged	22.50	
First day cover Washington, D.C. *(72,981)*		17.50
a. Horiz. pair, imperf. vert.	*4,250.*	
P# block of 6, 2#, two "TOP" and registration markers	*40,000.*	

The No. CE2a plate block is unique. Value represents sale in 1997.

Quantities issued: #CE1, 9,215,750; #CE2, 72,517,850.

AIR POST SEMI-OFFICIAL STAMPS

Buffalo Balloon

This stamp was privately issued by John F. B. Lillard, a Nashville reporter. It was used on covers carried on a balloon ascension of June 18, 1877, which began at Nashville and landed at Gallatin, Tenn., and possibly on other flights. The balloon was owned and piloted by Samuel Archer King. The stamp was reported to have been engraved by (Mrs.?) J. H. Snively and printed in tete beche pairs from a single die. Lillard wrote that 300 were printed and 23 used.

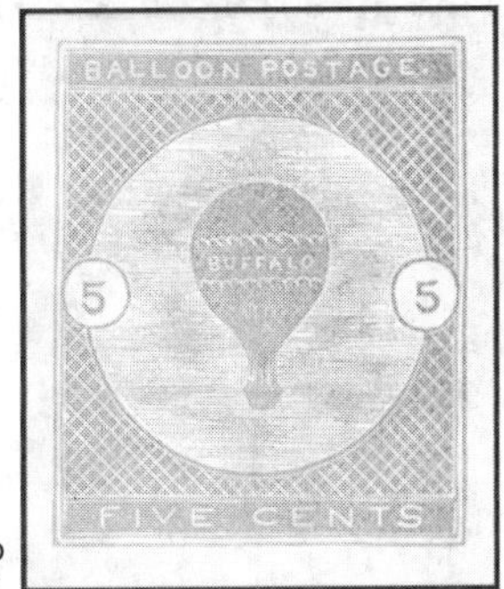

Buffalo Balloon—APSO1

1877, June 18 **Typo.** ***Imperf.***

CL1 APSO1 5c **deep blue**	*7,500.*	
Never hinged	*10,000.*	
On cover with 3c #158		—
On cover with 1c #156 & 2c #178		—
a. Tête bêche pair, vertical	*21,500.*	
Never hinged	—	

A black proof exists of No. CL1, value *$7,500.*

Rodgers Aerial Post

This stamp was privately issued by Calbraith Perry Rodgers' wife who acted as unofficial postmaster during her husband's cross-country airplane flight in 1911. Rodgers was competing for the $50,000 prize offered by William Randolph Hearst to whomever completed the trip within a 30-day period. Rodgers' flight was sponsored by the Armour meat-packing company, makers of the soft drink, Vin Fiz.

The stamp probably was first available in Texas about October 19. Recorded dated examples exist from Oct. 19 to Nov. 8.

Each of the thirteen known copies is trimmed close to the design on one or more sides.

APSO2

1911, Oct. ***Imperf.***

CL2 APSO2 25c **black**	*35,000.*	
Tied on postcard with 1c #374		*50,000.*

No. CL2 is the first stamp in the world to picture an airplane.

R.F. OVERPRINTS

Authorized as a control mark by the United States Fleet Post Office during 1944-45 for the accommodation of and exclusive use by French naval personnel on airmail correspondence to the United States and Canada. All "R.F." (Republique Francaise) mail had to be posted on board ship or at one of the Mediterranean naval bases and had to bear the return address, rank and/or serial number of a French officer or seaman. It also had to be reviewed by a censor.

All "R.F." overprints were handstamped by the French naval authorities after the stamps were affixed for mailing. The stamps had to be canceled by a special French naval cancellation. The status of unused copies seems questionable; they are alleged to have been handstamped at a later date.

Several types of "R.F." overprints other than those illustrated are known, but their validity is doubtful.

United States No. C25 Handstamped in Black

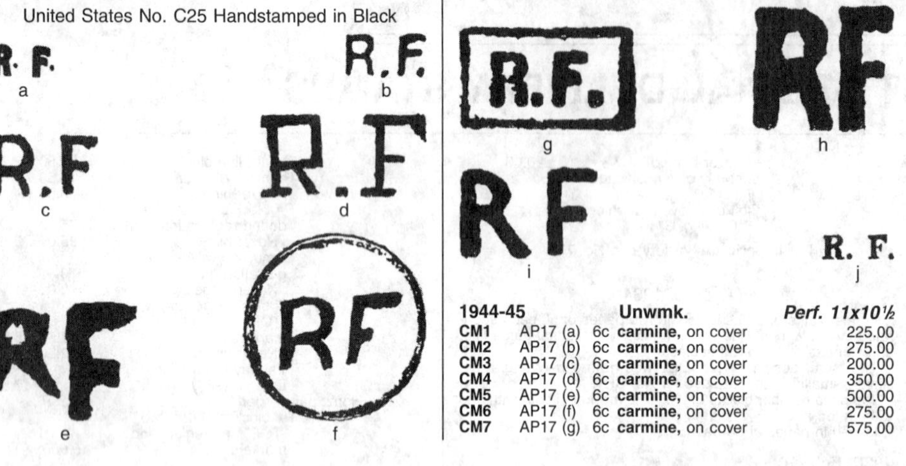

1944-45 **Unwmk.** ***Perf. 11x10½***

CM1	AP17 (a)	6c **carmine,** on cover	225.00
CM2	AP17 (b)	6c **carmine,** on cover	275.00
CM3	AP17 (c)	6c **carmine,** on cover	200.00
CM4	AP17 (d)	6c **carmine,** on cover	350.00
CM5	AP17 (e)	6c **carmine,** on cover	500.00
CM6	AP17 (f)	6c **carmine,** on cover	275.00
CM7	AP17 (g)	6c **carmine,** on cover	575.00
CM8	AP17 (h)	6c **carmine,** on cover	600.00
CM9	AP17 (i)	6c **carmine,** on cover	750.00
CM10	AP17 (j)	6c **carmine,** on cover	—

Counterfeits of several types exist.

No. 907 is known with type "c" overprint; No. C19 with type "e" or "h"; No. C25a (single) with type "c", and No. C26 with type "b" or "f." Type "i" exists in several variations.

STAMPED ENVELOPES

Nos. UC3, UC4 or UC6 Handstamped in Black

1944-45

UCM1	UC2 (a)	6c **orange,** entire	300.00
UCM2	UC2 (b)	6c **orange,** entire	400.00
UCM3	UC2 (d)	6c **orange,** entire	450.00
UCM4	UC2 (f)	6c **orange,** entire	450.00
UCM5	UC2 (h)	6c **orange,** entire	—
UCM6	UC2 (i)	6c **orange,** entire	—
UCM7	UC2 (j)	6c **orange,** entire	—

Values for Nos. UCM1-UCM7 reflect the scarcity of the actual overprint types. Use of No. UC6 envelopes was by far the most common. Overprints on Nos. UC3 or UC4 merit a very slight premium.

SPECIAL DELIVERY STAMPS

Special Delivery service was instituted by the Act of Congress of March 3, 1885, and put into operation on October 1, 1885. The Act limited the service to free delivery offices and such others as served places with a population of 4,000 or more, and its privileges were thus operative in but 555 post offices. The Act of August 4, 1886, made the stamps and service available at all post offices and upon any article of mailable matter. To consume the supply of stamps of the first issue, Scott No. E2 was withheld until September 6, 1888.

A Special Delivery stamp, when affixed to any stamped letter or article of mailable matter, secures later delivery during daytime and evening at most post offices, so that the item will not have to wait until the next day for delivery.

Messenger Running SD1

ENGRAVED

Printed by the American Bank Note Co.

Plates of 100 subjects in two panes of 50 each

1885 **Unwmk.** ***Perf. 12***

E1 SD1 10c **blue**	400.00	50.00
deep blue	400.00	50.00
Never hinged	900.00	
On cover		85.00
First day of service cover (Oct. 1)		*8,500.*
P# block of 8, Impt. 495 or 496	*15,000.*	
Margin strip of 4, same	3,500.	
Double transfer at top	500.00	75.00

Earliest documented use: Sept. 29, 1885, on a cover delivered Oct. 1. There is also a Sept. 30 cover recorded, received for delivery at 7:00 a.m. Oct. 1.

Messenger Running SD2

1888, Sept. 6

E2 SD2 10c **blue**	375.00	20.00
deep blue	375.00	20.00
Never hinged	800.00	
On cover		55.00
P# block of 8, Impt. 73 or 552	*11,500.*	
Never hinged	*15,500.*	
Margin strip of 4, same	3,500.	

Earliest known use: Dec. 18, 1888.

See note above No. E3.

COLUMBIAN EXPOSITION ISSUE

Though not issued expressly for the Exposition, No. E3 is considered to be part of that issue. It was released in orange because No. E2 was easily confused with the 1c Columbian, No. 230.

From Jan. 24, 1893, until Jan. 5, 1894, the special delivery stamp was printed in orange; the issue in that color continued until May 19, 1894, when the stock on hand was exhausted. The stamp in blue was not issued from Jan. 24, 1893 to May 19, 1894. However, on Jan. 5, 1894, printing of the stamp in blue was resumed. Presumably it was reissued from May 19, 1894 until the appearance of No. E4 on Oct. 10, 1894. The emissions of the blue stamp of this design before Jan. 24, 1893 and after Jan. 5, 1894 are indistinguishable.

1893, Jan. 24

E3 SD2 10c **orange**	225.00	27.50
deep orange	225.00	27.50
Never hinged	475.00	
On cover		75.00
On cover, Columbian Expo. station machine canc.		450.00
On cover, Columbian Expo. station duplex handstamp cancel		675.00
P# block of 8, Impt. 73 or 552	*7,500.*	
Never hinged	*10,500.*	
Margin strip of 4, same	1,750.	

Earliest known use: Feb. 11, 1893.

Messenger Running — SD3

77 257 381

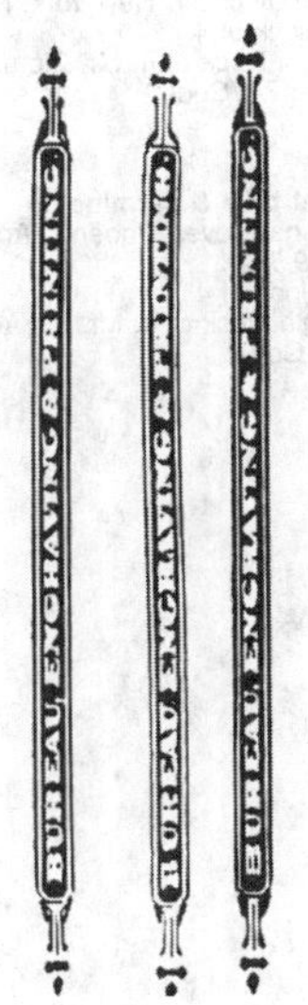

Type III Type VI Type VII

Printed by the Bureau of Engraving and Printing.

1894, Oct. 10

Line under "TEN CENTS"

E4 SD3 10c **blue** 800.00 35.00
dark blue 800.00 35.00
bright blue 800.00 35.00
Never hinged 1,750.
On cover 160.00
Block of four 3,350.
Margin block of 4, arrow 3,500.
P#77 block of 6, T III Impt. *15,000.*
Never hinged *20,000.*
Margin strip of 3, same 4,000.
Double transfer — —

Earliest known use: Oct. 25, 1894.

Imperfs of No. E4 on stamp paper, currently listed as No. E4aP, may not be proofs, but it is also unlikely that they were regularly issued. They most likely are from printer's waste.

1895, Aug. 16 **Wmk. 191**

E5 SD3 10c **blue** 175.00 5.00
dark blue 175.00 5.00
deep blue 175.00 5.00
Never hinged 350.00
On cover 17.50
Margin block of 4, arrow 775.00
P# block of 6, T III, VI or VII Impt. *4,000.*
Never hinged *5,750.*
Margin strip of 3, same 825.00
Never hinged 1,400.
Double transfer — 22.50
Line of color through "POSTAL DELIVERY," from bottom row of Plates 1257-1260 275.00 25.00
Dots in curved frame above messenger (Pl. 882) 210.00 10.00
b. Printed on both sides —

Earliest known use: Oct. 3, 1895.

See Die and Plate Proofs for imperf. on stamp paper.

Messenger on Bicycle — SD4

1902, Dec. 9

E6 SD4 10c **ultramarine** 150.00 4.50
dark ultramarine 150.00 4.50
pale ultramarine 150.00 4.50
Never hinged 350.00
a. 10c **blue** 150.00 4.50
Never hinged 350.00
On cover 10.00
Margin block of 4, arrow 650.00
P# block of 6, T VII Impt. *2,500.*
Never hinged *3,500.*
Margin strip of 3, same 550.00
Never hinged 1,000.
P# block of 6, "09" *2,100.*
Never hinged *3,000.*
Margin strip of 3, same 525.00
Never hinged 950.00
Double transfer — —
Damaged transfer under "N" of "CENTS" 175.00 5.00

Earliest known use: Jan. 22, 1903.

No. E6 was re-issued in 1909 from new plates 5240, 5243-5245. After a few months use the Bureau added "09" to these plate numbers. The stamp can be identified only by plate number.

Helmet of Mercury — SD5

Designed by Whitney Warren.

Plates of 280 subjects in four panes of 70 each

1908, Dec. 12

E7 SD5 10c **green** 60.00 40.00
dark green 60.00 40.00
yellowish green 60.00 40.00
Never hinged 120.00
On cover 100.00
P# block of 6, T V Impt. *925.00* —
Never hinged *1,300.*
Margin strip of 3, same 275.00
Never hinged 500.00
Double transfer 140.00 75.00

Earliest known use: Dec. 14, 1908.

Plates of 200 subjects in four panes of 50 each

1911, Jan. **Wmk. 190** ***Perf. 12***

E8 SD4 10c **ultramarine** 100.00 7.50
pale ultramarine 100.00 7.50
dark ultramarine 100.00 7.50
Never hinged 200.00
b. 10c **violet blue** 100.00 7.50
Never hinged 200.00
On cover 15.00
P# block of 6, T VII Impt. *1,850.*
Never hinged *2,750.*
P# block of 6 *1,700.*
Never hinged *2,500.*
Top frame line missing (Pl. 5514) 140.00 15.00

Earliest known use: Jan. 14, 1911.

1914, Sept. ***Perf. 10***

E9 SD4 10c **ultramarine** 180.00 7.50
pale ultramarine 180.00 7.50
Never hinged 375.00
On cover 32.50
P# block of 6, T VII Impt. *3,750.* —
Never hinged *5,500.*
P# block of 6 *3,000.* —
Never hinged *4,500.*
Margin block of 8, T VII Impt. & P# (side) —
a. 10c **blue** 210.00 8.50
Never hinged 425.00
On cover 37.50
P# block of 6, T VII Impt. *4,000.* —
Never hinged *5,750.*
P# block of 6 *3,500.* —
Never hinged *5,250.*
Margin block of 8, T VII Impt. & P# (side) —

Earliest known use: Oct. 26, 1914.

1916, Oct. 19 **Unwmk.** ***Perf. 10***

E10 SD4 10c **pale ultramarine** 290.00 30.00
ultramarine 290.00 30.00
Never hinged 575.00
On cover 67.50
P# block of 6, T VII Impt. 5520 *5,250.* —
Never hinged *6,850.*
P# block of 6 *4,750.* —
Never hinged *6,250.*
a. 10c **blue** 325.00 27.50
Never hinged 650.00
On cover 75.00
P# block of 6, T VII Impt. 5520 *5,500.* —
P# block of 6 *4,750.* —

Earliest known use: Nov. 4, 1916.

1917, May 2 **Unwmk.** ***Perf. 11***

E11 SD4 10c **ultramarine** 22.50 .50
pale ultramarine 22.50 .50
dark ultramarine 22.50 .50
Never hinged 40.00
On cover 3.25
P# block of 6, T VII Impt. 725.00 —
P# block of 6 225.00 —
Never hinged 325.00
Margin block of 8, T VII Impt. & P# (side) —
b. 10c **gray violet** 22.50 .50
Never hinged 40.00
c. 10c **blue** 60.00 2.50
Never hinged 110.00
On cover 15.00
P# block of 6, T VII Impt. 2,000.
P# block of 6 600.00
Margin block of 8, T VII Impt. & P# (side) —
d. Perf. 10 at left —

Earliest known use: June 12, 1917.

The aniline ink used on some printings of No. E11 permeated the paper causing a pink tinge to appear on the back. Such stamps are called "pink backs." They are scarce and valued slightly higher than the normal stamp.

Motorcycle Delivery SD6

Post Office Truck — SD7

1922, July 12 **Unwmk.** ***Perf. 11***

E12 SD6 10c **gray violet** 35.00 .50
Never hinged 70.00
On cover 2.00
First day cover 475.00
P# block of 6 400.00 —
Never hinged 600.00
Double transfer — —
a. 10c **deep ultramarine** 42.50 .60
Never hinged 85.00
On cover 2.00
P# block of 6 425.00 —
Never hinged 650.00
Double transfer — —

FLAT PLATE PRINTING

1925 **Unwmk.** ***Perf. 11***

Issued to facilitate special delivery service for parcel post.

E13 SD6 15c **deep orange,** *Apr. 11, 1925* 24.00 1.50
Never hinged 45.00
On cover 12.50
First day cover 300.00
P# block of 6 300.00 —
Never hinged 450.00
Double transfer 35.00 2.25
E14 SD7 20c **black,** *Apr. 25, 1925* 1.75 1.00
Never hinged 3.00
On cover 1.50
First day cover 100.00
P# block of 6 30.00
Never hinged 45.00

Motorcycle Type of 1922

ROTARY PRESS PRINTING

1927-31 **Unwmk.** ***Perf. 11x10½***

E15 SD6 10c **gray violet,** *Nov. 29, 1927* .60 .20
violet .60 .20
Never hinged 1.00
a. 10c **red lilac** .60 .20
Never hinged 1.00
b. 10c **gray lilac** .60 .20
Never hinged 1.00
On cover .25
First day cover 110.00
First day cover, electric eye plate, *Sept. 8, 1941* 30.00
P# block of 4 3.75 —
Never hinged 6.00
Gouged plate —
Cracked plate 19280 LR 35.00
c. Horizontal pair, imperf. between 300.00
Never hinged *500.00*
E16 SD6 15c **orange,** *Aug. 1931* .70 .20
Never hinged 1.05
On cover .25
First day cover, Washington, D.C., *Aug. 13, 1931* 125.00
P# block of 4 2.75 —
Never hinged 4.50

The Washington, D.C. Aug. 13, 1931 first day cover reflects the first day of sale at the philatelic agency. The actual earliest documented use of No. E16 is Aug. 6, 1931, at Easton, PA; value, $2,500.

Catalogue values for unused stamps in this section, from this point to the end, are for Never Hinged items.

Motorcycle Type of 1922
ROTARY PRESS PRINTING
E. E. Plates of 200 subjects in four panes of 50 each.

1944-51 **Unwmk.** ***Perf. 11x10½***

E17 SD6 13c	**blue**, *Oct. 30, 1944*	.60	.20
	First day cover		12.00
	P# block of 4	2.75	—
E18 SD6 17c	**orange yellow**, *Oct. 30, 1944*	2.75	1.75
	First day cover		12.00
	First day cover, Nos. E17 & E18		30.00
	P# block of 4	17.50	—
E19 SD7 20c	**black**, *Nov. 30, 1951*	1.25	.20
	First day cover		5.00
	P# block of 4	5.50	—

Special Delivery Letter, Hand to Hand — SD8

ROTARY PRESS PRINTING
E.E. Plates of 200 subjects in four panes of 50 each

1954, Oct. 13 **Unwmk.** ***Perf. 11x10½***

E20 SD8 20c	**deep blue**	.40	.20
	light blue	—	—
	First day cover, Boston *(194,043)*		3.00
	P# block of 4	2.00	—

1957, Sept. 3

E21 SD8 30c	**lake**	.50	.20
	First day cover, Indianapolis, Ind. *(111,451)*		2.25
	P# block of 4	2.25	—

Arrows SD9

Designed by Norman Ives.

GIORI PRESS PRINTING
Plates of 200 subjects in four panes of 50 each

1969, Nov. 21 **Unwmk.** ***Perf. 11***

E22 SD9 45c	**carmine & violet blue**	1.25	.25
	First day cover, New York, N.Y.		4.00
	P# block of 4	5.50	—
	Margin block of 4, Mr. Zip and "Use Zip Code"	5.10	—

1971, May 10 ***Perf. 11***

E23 SD9 60c	**violet blue & carmine**	1.25	.20
	First day cover, Phoenix, Ariz. *(129,562)*		3.50
	P# block of 4	5.50	—
	Margin block of 4, Mr. Zip and "Use Zip Code"	5.25	—

REGISTRATION STAMP

The Registry System for U.S. mail went into effect July 1, 1855, the fee being 5 cents. On June 30, 1863, the fee was increased to 20 cents.

On January 1, 1869, the fee was reduced to 15 cents and on January 1, 1874, to 8 cents. On July 1, 1875, the fee was increased to 10 cents. On January 1, 1893 the fee was again reduced to 8 cents and again it was increased to 10 cents on November 1, 1909.

Early registered covers with various stamps, rates and postal markings are of particular interest to collectors.

Registry stamps (10c ultramarine) were issued on December 1, 1911, to prepay registry fees (not postage), but ordinary stamps were valid for registry fees then as now. These special stamps were abolished May 28, 1913, by order of the Postmaster General, who permitted their use until supplies on hand were exhausted.

Eagle — RS1

ENGRAVED

1911, Dec. 1 **Wmk. 190** ***Perf. 12***

F1 RS1 10c	**ultramarine**	75.00	7.50
	pale ultramarine	75.00	7.50
	Never hinged	140.00	
	On cover		40.00
	Block of 4	325.00	*75.00*
	P# block of 6, Impt. & "A"	*1,600.*	—
	Never hinged	*2,500.*	
	First day cover		*15,000.*

CERTIFIED MAIL STAMP

Certified Mail service was started on June 6, 1955, for use on first class mail for which no indemnity value is claimed, but for which proof of mailing and proof of delivery are available at less cost than registered mail. The mailer receives one receipt and the addressee signs another when the postman delivers the letter. The second receipt is kept on file at the post office for six months. The Certified Mail charge, originally 15 cents, is in addition to regular postage, whether surface mail, air mail, or special delivery.

Catalogue value for the unused stamp in this section is for a Never Hinged item.

Letter Carrier — CM1

ROTARY PRESS PRINTING
E. E. Plates of 200 subjects in four panes of 50

1955, June 6 **Unwmk.** ***Perf. 10½x11***

FA1 CM1 15c	**red**	.45	.30
	P# block of 4	4.25	—
	First day cover		5.00

POSTAGE DUE STAMPS

For affixing, by a postal clerk, to any piece of mailable matter, to denote the amount to be collected from the addressee because of insufficient prepayment of postage.

Prior to July 1879, whenever a letter was unpaid, or insufficiently prepaid, the amount of postage due was written by hand or handstamped on the envelope, and the deficiency collected by the carrier. No vouchers were given for money thus collected.

Postage Due Stamps were authorized by the Act of Congress, approved March 3, 1879, effective July 1, 1879.

Printed by the American Bank Note Co.
Plates of 200 subjects in two panes of 100 each.

D1

D2

1879 Unwmk. Engr. *Perf. 12*

J1 D1 1c	**brown**	70.00	10.00
	pale brown	70.00	10.00
	deep brown	70.00	10.00
	Block of 4	300.00	65.00
	P# block of 10, Impt.	*1,250.*	
J2 D1 2c	**brown**	400.00	10.00
	pale brown	400.00	10.00
	Block of 4	1,650.	—
J3 D1 3c	**brown**	62.50	5.00
	pale brown	62.50	5.00
	deep brown	62.50	5.00
	yellowish brown	65.00	6.00
	Block of 4	275.00	30.00
	P# block of 10, Impt.	*1,150.*	
J4 D1 5c	**brown**	700.00	50.00
	pale brown	700.00	50.00
	deep brown	700.00	50.00
	Block of 4	3,000.	—
J5 D1 10c	**brown,** *Sept. 19*	800.00	55.00
	pale brown	800.00	55.00
	deep brown	800.00	55.00
	Block of 4	3,500.	—
a.	Imperf., pair	*2,000.*	
J6 D1 30c	**brown,** *Sept. 19*	350.00	55.00
	pale brown	350.00	55.00
	Block of 4	1,500.	—
	P# block of 10, Impt.	*4,500.*	
J7 D1 50c	**brown,** *Sept. 19*	575.00	75.00
	pale brown	575.00	75.00
	Block of 4	2,500.	—
	P# block of 10, Impt.	*12,000.*	

SPECIAL PRINTING

1879 Unwmk. *Perf. 12*
Soft porous paper
Printed by the American Bank Note Co.

J8 D1 1c	deep brown *(9,420)*	*19,000.*
J9 D1 2c	deep brown *(1,361)*	*9,500.*
J10 D1 3c	deep brown *(436)*	*19,000.*
J11 D1 5c	deep brown *(249)*	*9,500.*
J12 D1 10c	deep brown *(174)*	*4,500.*
J13 D1 30c	deep brown *(179)*	*4,500.*
J14 D1 50c	deep brown *(179)*	*4,500.*

Identifying characteristics for the final 8,920 copies of No. J8 delivered to the Post Office are unknown, and it is likely that these were regular issue stamps (No. J1) that were then sold as special printings.

1884 Unwmk. *Perf. 12*

J15 D1 1c	**red brown**	65.00	6.00
	pale red brown	65.00	6.00
	deep red brown	65.00	6.00
	Block of 4	300.00	40.00
	P# block of 10, Impt.	*1,400.*	
J16 D1 2c	**red brown**	75.00	5.00
	pale red brown	75.00	5.00
	deep red brown	75.00	5.00
	Block of 4	325.00	32.50
	P# block of 10, Impt.	*1,500.*	
J17 D1 3c	**red brown**	1,100.	225.00
	deep red brown	1,100.	225.00
	Block of 4	4,750.	—
J18 D1 5c	**red brown**	575.00	35.00
	pale red brown	575.00	35.00
	deep red brown	575.00	35.00
	Block of 4	2,600.	—
J19 D1 10c	**red brown**	575.00	30.00
	deep red brown	575.00	30.00
	Block of 4	2,600.	—
	P# block of 10, Impt.	*13,500.*	
J20 D1 30c	**red brown**	185.00	55.00
	deep red brown	185.00	55.00
	Block of 4	850.00	325.00
	P# block of 10, Impt.	*3,150.*	
J21 D1 50c	**red brown**	1,750.	200.00
	Block of 4	7,750.	—

1891 Unwmk. *Perf. 12*

J22 D1 1c	**bright claret**	35.00	1.50
	light claret	35.00	1.50
	dark claret	35.00	1.50
	Block of 4	160.00	8.50
	P# block of 10, Impt.	*625.00*	
J23 D1 2c	**bright claret**	37.50	1.50
	light claret	37.50	1.50
	dark claret	37.50	1.50
	Block of 4	170.00	8.50
	P# block of 10, Impt.	*700.00*	
J24 D1 3c	**bright claret**	70.00	15.00
	dark claret	70.00	15.00
	Block of 4	325.00	75.00
	P# block of 10, Impt.	*1,050.*	
J25 D1 5c	**bright claret**	90.00	15.00
	light claret	90.00	15.00
	dark claret	90.00	15.00
	Block of 4	400.00	75.00
	P# block of 10, Impt.	*1,300.*	
J26 D1 10c	**bright claret**	150.00	25.00
	light claret	150.00	25.00
	Block of 4	700.00	165.00
	P# block of 10, Impt.	*2,250.*	
J27 D1 30c	**bright claret**	575.00	185.00
	Block of 4	2,600.	—
	P# block of 10, Impt.	*8,500.*	
J28 D1 50c	**bright claret**	575.00	175.00
	dark claret	575.00	175.00
	Block of 4	2,600.	—
	P# block of 10, Impt.	*9,500.*	
	Nos. J22-J28 (7)	1,532.	418.00

See Die and Plate Proofs for imperfs. on stamp paper.

Printed by the Bureau of Engraving and Printing.

1894 Unwmk. *Perf. 12*

J29 D2 1c	**vermilion**	2,000.	550.
	pale vermilion	2,000.	550.
	Never hinged	4,250.	
	Block of 4	*8,750.*	*2,500.*
	P# block of 6, Impt.	—	
J30 D2 2c	**vermilion**	800.	225.
	deep vermilion	800.	225.
	Never hinged	1,700.	
	Block of 4	3,500.	
	P# block of 6, Impt.	*6,750.*	

1894-95

J31 D2 1c	**deep claret,** *Aug. 14, 1894*	60.00	8.00
	claret	60.00	8.00
	lake	60.00	8.00
	Never hinged	125.00	
	Block of 4	275.00	50.00
	P# block of 6, Impt.	525.00	
	Never hinged	750.00	
b.	Vertical pair, imperf. horiz.	—	

See Die and Plate Proofs for imperf. on stamp paper.

J32 D2 2c	**deep claret,** *July 20, 1894*	50.00	6.00
	claret	50.00	6.00
	lake	50.00	6.00
	Never hinged	100.00	
	Block of 4	220.00	37.50
	P# block of 6, Impt.	475.00	
	Never hinged	675.00	
J33 D2 3c	**deep claret,** *Apr. 27, 1895*	200.00	40.00
	lake	200.00	40.00
	Never hinged	425.00	
	Block of 4	875.00	—
	P# block of 6, Impt.	2,150.	
	Never hinged	*3,150.*	
J34 D2 5c	**deep claret,** *Apr. 27, 1895*	325.00	45.00
	claret	325.00	45.00
	Never hinged	675.00	
	Block of 4	1,400.	—
	P# block of 6, Impt.	2,600.	
	Never hinged	*3,750.*	
J35 D2 10c	**deep claret,** *Sept. 24, 1894*	325.00	30.00
	Never hinged	675.00	
	Block of 4	1,400.	—
	P# block of 6, Impt.	2,600.	
J36 D2 30c	**deep claret,** *Apr. 27, 1895*	525.00	175.00
	claret	525.00	175.00
	Never hinged	1,100.	
	Block of 4	2,300.	—
	P# block of 6, Impt.	4,250.	
	Never hinged	6,000.	
a. 30c	**carmine**	600.00	200.00
	Never hinged	1,250.	
	Block of 4	2,750.	—
	P# block of 6, Impt.	4,750.	
	Never hinged	*7,000.*	
b. 30c	**pale rose**	425.00	140.00
	Never hinged	900.00	
	Block of 4	1,850.	—
	P# block of 6, Impt.	3,600.	
	Never hinged	*5,000.*	
J37 D2 50c	**deep claret,** *Apr. 27, 1895*	1,700.	600.00
	Never hinged	3,500.	
	Block of 4	7,250.	—
a. 50c	**pale rose**	1,550.	500.00
	Never hinged	3,250.	
	Block of 4	6,750.	—
	P# block of 6, Impt.	*11,750.*	

Shades are numerous in the 1894 and later issues.

Wmk. 191 Horizontally or Vertically

1895-97 *Perf. 12*

J38 D2 1c	**deep claret,** *Aug. 29, 1895*	11.50	.75
	claret	11.50	.75
	carmine	11.50	.75
	lake	11.50	.75
	Never hinged	23.50	
	Block of 4	50.00	7.50
	P# block of 6, Impt.	250.00	
J39 D2 2c	**deep claret,** *Sept. 14, 1895*	11.50	.70
	claret	11.50	.70
	carmine	11.50	.70
	lake	11.50	.70
	Never hinged	23.50	
	Block of 4	50.00	7.50
	P# block of 6, Impt.	250.00	
	Double transfer	—	—

In October, 1895, the Postmaster at Jefferson, Iowa, surcharged a few 2 cent stamps with the words "Due I cent" in black on each side, subsequently dividing the stamps vertically and using each half as a 1 cent stamp. Twenty of these were used.

J40 D2 3c	**deep claret,** *Oct. 30, 1895*	70.00	3.00
	claret	70.00	3.00
	rose red	70.00	3.00
	carmine	70.00	3.00
	Never hinged	145.00	
	Block of 4	300.00	18.50
	P# block of 6, Impt.	700.00	
	Never hinged	1,000.	
J41 D2 5c	**deep claret,** *Oct. 15, 1895*	75.00	3.00
	claret	75.00	3.00
	carmine rose	75.00	3.00
	Never hinged	160.00	
	Block of 4	325.00	18.50
	P# block of 6, Impt.	750.00	

Never hinged 1,050.
J42 D2 10c **deep claret,** *Sept. 14, 1895* 75.00 5.00
claret 75.00 5.00
carmine 75.00 5.00
lake 75.00 5.00
Never hinged 160.00
Block of 4 325.00 32.50
P# block of 6, Impt. 750.00
Never hinged 1,050.
J43 D2 30c **deep claret,** *Aug. 21, 1897* 600.00 55.00
claret 600.00 55.00
Never hinged 1,300.
Block of 4 2,600. 350.00
P# block of 6, Impt. *5,750.*
J44 D2 50c **deep claret,** *Mar. 17, 1896* 425.00 40.00
claret 425.00 40.00
Never hinged 900.00
Block of 4 1,850. 200.00
P# block of 6, Impt. *4,500.* —
Nos. J38-J44 (7) 1,268. 107.45

Plates of 400 subjects in four panes of 100.

1910-12 Wmk. 190 *Perf. 12*

J45 D2 1c **deep claret,** *Aug. 30, 1910* 35.00 3.50
Never hinged 75.00
a. 1c **rose carmine** 32.50 3.50
Never hinged 67.50
Block of 4 (2 or 3mm spacing) 150.00 20.00
P# block of 6, Impt. & star 490.00
J46 D2 2c **deep claret,** *Nov. 25, 1910* 40.00 1.50
lake 40.00 1.50
Never hinged 85.00
a. 2c **rose carmine** 35.00 1.50
Never hinged 75.00
Block of 4 (2 or 3mm spacing) 170.00 7.50
P# block of 6, Impt. & star 450.00 —
P# block of 6 475.00
Double transfer — —
J47 D2 3c **deep claret,** *Aug. 31, 1910* 600.00 40.00
lake 600.00 40.00
Never hinged 1,300.
Block of 4 (2 or 3mm spacing) 2,600. 225.00
P# block of 6, Impt. & star 5,500.
Never hinged *8,000.*
J48 D2 5c **deep claret,** *Aug. 31, 1910* 115.00 9.00
Never hinged 230.00
a. 5c **rose carmine** 110.00 9.00
Never hinged 220.00
Block of 4 (2 or 3mm spacing) 500.00 50.00
P# block of 6, Impt. & star 1,075.
Never hinged *1,550.*
J49 D2 10c **deep claret,** *Aug. 31, 1910* 130.00 15.00
Never hinged 275.00
Block of 4 (2 or 3mm spacing) 575.00 90.00
P# block of 6, Impt. & star 1,450.
a. 10c **rose carmine** 125.00 15.00
Never hinged 260.00
J50 D2 50c **deep claret,** *Sept. 23, 1912* 1,100. 140.00
Never hinged 2,350.
Block of 4 (2 or 3mm spacing) 4,750.
P# block of 6, Impt. & star *10,000.*

1914 *Perf. 10*

J52 D2 1c **carmine lake** 65.00 12.50
deep carmine lake 65.00 12.50
Never hinged 140.00
Block of 4 (2 or 3mm spacing) 275.00 67.50
P# block of 6, Impt. & star 600.00 —
Never hinged 900.00
a. 1c **dull rose** 75.00 12.50
Never hinged 160.00
Block of 4 (2 or 3mm spacing) 325.00 75.00
P# block of 6, Impt. & star 675.00 —
J53 D2 2c **carmine lake** 47.50 .50
Never hinged 105.00
Block of 4 200.00 4.00
P# block of 6 450.00 —
a. 2c **dull rose** 52.50 1.00
Block of 4 10.00
Never hinged 115.00
b. 2c **vermilion** 55.00 .75
Never hinged 120.00
Block of 4 240.00 7.50
P# block of 6 500.00 —
Never hinged 750.00
J54 D2 3c **carmine lake** 950.00 57.50
Never hinged 2,250.
a. 3c **dull rose** 950.00 57.50
Never hinged 2,250.
Block of 4 (2 or 3mm spacing) 4,250. —
P# block of 6, Impt. & star *8,000.* —
J55 D2 5c **carmine lake** 37.50 3.50
Never hinged 80.00
a. 5c **dull rose** 37.50 2.50
carmine rose 37.50 2.50
Never hinged 80.00
deep claret — —
Block of 4 (2 or 3mm spacing) 160.00 20.00
P# block of 6, Impt. & star 350.00 —
Never hinged 525.00
J56 D2 10c **carmine lake** 60.00 2.50
Never hinged 125.00
Block of 4 (2 or 3mm spacing) 260.00 14.00
P# block of 6, Impt. & star 675.00 —
a. 10c **dull rose** 70.00 4.00
carmine rose 70.00 4.00
Never hinged 150.00
Block of 4 (2 or 3mm spacing) 300.00 20.00
P# block of 6, Impt. & star 800.00 —
Never hinged 1,200.
J57 D2 30c **carmine lake** 240.00 20.00
Never hinged 480.00
Block of 4 (2 or 3mm spacing) 1,050. 125.00
P# block of 6, Impt. & star 2,750. —
J58 D2 50c **carmine lake** *12,500.* 1,200.
Never hinged *22,500.*
Precanceled 650.00
Block of 4 (2 or 3mm spacing) *55,000.* *5,750.*
P# block of 6, Impt. & star *85,000.*

No. J58, precanceled, was used at Buffalo (normal, inverted) and Chicago (normal, inverted, double, double inverted).

1916 Unwmk. *Perf. 10*

J59 D2 1c **rose** 4,000. 550.00
Never hinged 8,000.
Block of 4 (2 or 3mm spacing) 17,500. *3,250.*
P# block of 6, Impt. & star *27,500.*
Experimental bureau precancel, New Orleans *250.00*
J60 D2 2c **rose** 230.00 60.00
Never hinged 500.00
Block of 4 1,000. 300.00
P# block of 6 2,000. —
Experimental bureau precancel, New Orleans 25.00

1917 Unwmk. *Perf. 11*

J61 D2 1c **carmine rose** 3.00 .25
dull rose 3.00 .25
Never hinged 6.00
a. 1c **rose red** 3.00 .25
Never hinged 6.00
b. 1c **deep claret** 3.00 .25
claret brown 3.00 .25
Never hinged 6.00
Block of 4 (2 or 3mm spacing) 13.00 2.00
P# block of 6, Impt. & star 125.00 —
Never hinged 250.00
P# block of 6 45.00 —
Never hinged 80.00
J62 D2 2c **carmine rose** 3.00 .25
Never hinged 6.00
a. 2c **rose red** 3.00 .25
Never hinged 6.00
b. 2c **deep claret** 3.00 .25
claret brown 3.00 1.10
Never hinged 6.00
Block of 4 13.00 2.00
Never hinged 26.00
P# block of 6 45.00 —
Never hinged 75.00
Double transfer — —
J63 D2 3c **carmine rose** 12.50 .35
Never hinged 25.00
a. 3c **rose red** 12.50 .35
Never hinged 25.00
b. 3c **deep claret** 12.50 .50
claret brown 12.50 .50
Never hinged 25.00
Block of 4 (2 or 3mm spacing) 52.50 3.00
P# block of 6, Impt. & star 125.00 —
Never hinged 190.00
P# block of 6 105.00 —
Never hinged 155.00
J64 D2 5c **carmine** 12.50 .35
carmine rose 12.50 .35
Never hinged 25.00
a. 5c **rose red** 12.50 .35
Never hinged 25.00
b. 5c **deep claret** 12.50 .35
claret brown 12.50 .35
Never hinged 25.00
Block of 4 (2 or 3mm spacing) 52.50 3.00
P# block of 6, Impt. & star 125.00 —
Never hinged 190.00
P# block of 6 105.00 —
Never hinged 155.00
J65 D2 10c **carmine rose** 17.00 .40
Never hinged 35.00
a. 10c **rose red** 17.00 .40
Never hinged 35.00
b. 10c **deep claret** 17.00 .40
claret brown 17.00 .40
Never hinged 35.00
Block of 4 (2 or 3mm spacing) 72.50 3.50
P# block of 6, Impt. & star 150.00 —
Never hinged 225.00
P# block of 6 160.00 —
Never hinged 250.00
Double transfer — —
J66 D2 30c **carmine rose** 87.50 1.00
Never hinged 175.00
a. 30c **deep claret** 87.50 1.00
claret brown 87.50 1.00
Never hinged 175.00
Block of 4 (2 or 3mm spacing) 375.00 7.50
P# block of 6, Impt. & star 700.00 —
P# block of 6 725.00 —
J67 D2 50c **carmine rose** 125.00 .50
Never hinged 250.00
a. 50c **rose red** 125.00 .50
Never hinged 250.00
b. 50c **deep claret** 125.00 .30
claret brown 125.00 .30
Never hinged 250.00
Block of 4 (2 or 3mm spacing) 525.00 4.00
P# block of 6, Impt. & star 900.00 —
Never hinged 1,375.
P# block of 6 950.00 —

1925, Apr. 13

J68 D2 ½c **dull red** 1.00 .25
Never hinged 1.60
Block of 4 4.00 1.50
P# block of 6 12.50 —
Never hinged 17.50

D3

D4

1930 Unwmk. *Perf. 11*

Design measures 19x22mm

J69 D3 ½c **carmine** 4.50 1.40
Never hinged 8.00
P# block of 6 42.50 —
Never hinged 62.50
J70 D3 1c **carmine** 3.00 .25
Never hinged 5.00
P# block of 6 30.00 —
Never hinged 45.00
J71 D3 2c **carmine** 4.00 .25
Never hinged 7.00
P# block of 6 45.00 —
Never hinged 67.50
J72 D3 3c **carmine** 21.00 2.00
Never hinged 37.50
P# block of 6 275.00 —
Never hinged 400.00
J73 D3 5c **carmine** 19.00 3.00
Never hinged 35.00
P# block of 6 250.00 —
Never hinged 375.00
J74 D3 10c **carmine** 40.00 1.50
Never hinged 75.00
P# block of 6 450.00 —
Never hinged 675.00
J75 D3 30c **carmine** 140.00 3.00
Never hinged 225.00
P# block of 6 1,100. —
Never hinged *1,650.*
J76 D3 50c **carmine** 190.00 1.50
Never hinged 325.00
P# block of 6 1,700. —
Never hinged *2,500.*

Design measures 22x19mm

J77 D4 $1 **carmine** 30.00 .25
Never hinged 50.00
P# block of 6 225.00 —
Never hinged 325.00
a. $1 **scarlet** 25.00 .25
Never hinged 42.50
P# block of 6 275.00 —
Never hinged 400.00
J78 D4 $5 **carmine** 37.50 .25
Never hinged 60.00
P# block of 6 300.00 —
Never hinged 450.00
a. $5 **scarlet** 32.50 .25
Never hinged 52.50
P# block of 6 250.00 —
Never hinged 375.00
b. As "a," wet printing 35.00 .25
Never hinged 55.00
P# block of 6 275.00 —
Never hinged 400.00

See note on Wet and Dry Printings following No. 1029.

Type of 1930-31 Issue
Rotary Press Printing
Ordinary and Electric Eye Plates
Design measures 19x22½mm

1931 Unwmk. *Perf. 11x10½*

J79 D3 ½c **dull carmine** .90 .20
Never hinged 1.30
a. ½c **scarlet** .90 .20
Never hinged 1.30
P# block of 4 20.00 —
Never hinged 30.00
J80 D3 1c **dull carmine** .20 .20
Never hinged .30
a. 1c **scarlet** .20 .20
Never hinged .30
P# block of 4 (#25635, 25636) 1.50 —
Never hinged 2.25
b. As "a," wet printing .20 .20
Never hinged .20
P# block of 4 1.75 —
Never hinged 2.50
Pair with full vertical gutter between —
J81 D3 2c **dull carmine** .20 .20
Never hinged .30
a. 2c **scarlet** .20 .20
Never hinged .30
P# block of 4 (#25637, 25638) 1.50 —
Never hinged 2.25
b. As "a," wet printing .20 .20
Never hinged .30
P# block of 4 2.00 —
Never hinged 2.75
J82 D3 3c **dull carmine** .25 .20
Never hinged .40
a. 3c **scarlet** .25 .20
Never hinged .40
P# block of 4 (#25641, 25642) 2.25 —
Never hinged 3.25
b. As "a," wet printing .30 .20
Never hinged .45
P# block of 4 2.50 —
Never hinged 3.50

J83 D3 5c **dull carmine** .40 .20
Never hinged .60
a. 5c **scarlet** .40 .20
Never hinged .60
P# block of 4 (#25643, 25644) 3.00 —
Never hinged 4.25
b. As "a," wet printing .50 .20
Never hinged .75
P# block of 4 3.50 —
Never hinged 4.75
J84 D3 10c **dull carmine** 1.10 .20
Never hinged 1.80
a. 10c **scarlet** 1.10 .20
Never hinged 1.80
P# block of 4 (#25645, 25646) 6.50 —
Never hinged 8.75
b. As "a," wet printing 1.25 .20
Never hinged 1.90
P# block of 4 7.00 —
Never hinged 9.25
J85 D3 30c **dull carmine** 7.50 .25
Never hinged 11.50
a. 30c **scarlet** 7.50 .25
Never hinged 11.50
P# block of 4 35.00 —
Never hinged 50.00
J86 D3 50c **dull carmine** 9.00 .25
Never hinged 15.00
a. 50c **scarlet** 9.00 .25
Never hinged 15.00
P# block of 4 52.50 —
Never hinged 75.00

Design measures 22½x19mm

1956 ***Perf. 10½x11***
J87 D4 $1 **scarlet** 30.00 .25
Never hinged 47.50
P# block of 4 190.00 —
Never hinged 275.00
Nos. J79-J87 (9) 49.55 1.95

Catalogue values for unused stamps in this section, from this point to the end, are for Never Hinged items.

D5

Rotary Press Printing

Denominations added in black by rubber plates in an operation similar to precanceling.

1959, June 19 **Unwmk.** ***Perf. 11x10½***

Denomination in Black

J88 D5 ½c **carmine rose** 1.50 1.10
P# block of 4 175.00 —
J89 D5 1c **carmine rose**, shiny gum .20 .20
P# block of 4 .35 —
Dull gum .25
P# block of 4 4.50
a. Denomination omitted 300.00
P# block of 4 — —
b. Pair, one without "1 CENT" *500.00*
J90 D5 2c **carmine rose**, shiny gum .20 .20
P# block of 4 .45 —
Wide spacing, pair *120.00*
Dull gum .25
P# block of 4 4.50
J91 D5 3c **carmine rose**, shiny gum .20 .20
P# block of 4 .50 —
Dull gum .25
P# block of 4 3.25
a. Pair, one without "3 CENTS" *725.00*
J92 D5 4c **carmine rose** .20 .20
P# block of 4 .60 —
Wide spacing, pair *120.00*
J93 D5 5c **carmine rose**, shiny gum .20 .20
P# block of 4 .65 —
Dull gum .25
P# block of 4 5.00
a. Pair, one without "5 CENTS" *1,250.*
J94 D5 6c **carmine rose**, shiny gum .20 .20
P# block of 4 .70 —
Pair with full vertical gutter between —
Dull gum *100.00*
P# block of 4 *1,250.*
a. Pair, one without "6 CENTS" *850.00*
J95 D5 7c **carmine rose**, shiny gum .20 .20
P# block of 4 .80 —
Wide spacing, pair *120.00*
Dull gum *750.00*
P# block of 4 —
J96 D5 8c **carmine rose** .20 .20
P# block of 4 .90 —
Wide spacing, pair *120.00*
a. Pair, one without "8 CENTS" *850.00*
J97 D5 10c **carmine rose**, shiny gum .20 .20
P# block of 4 1.00 —
Dull gum .35
P# block of 4 5.00
J98 D5 30c **carmine rose**, shiny gum .75 .20
P# block of 4 3.50 —
Dull gum .90
P# block of 4 11.00
J99 D5 50c **carmine rose**, shiny gum 1.10 .20
P# block of 4 5.00 —
Dull gum 1.50
P# block of 4 17.50

Straight Numeral Outlined in Black

J100 D5 $1 **carmine rose, shiny gum** 2.00 .20
P# block of 4 8.50 —
Dull gum 2.50
P# block of 4 15.00
J101 D5 $5 **carmine rose**, shiny gum 9.00 .20
P# block of 4 40.00 —
Dull gum 10.00
P# block of 4 —
Nos. J88-J101 (14) 16.15 3.70

All single copies with denomination omitted are catalogued as No. J89a.

Rotary Press Printing

1978-85 ***Perf. 11x10½***

Denomination in Black

J102 D5 11c **carmine rose,** *Jan. 2, 1978* .25 .20
P# block of 4 2.00 —
J103 D5 13c **carmine rose,** *Jan. 2, 1978* .25 .20
P# block of 4 2.00 —
J104 D5 17c **carmine rose,** *June 10, 1985* .40 .35
P# block of 4 22.50 —

U.S. POSTAL AGENCY IN CHINA

Postage stamps of the 1917-19 U.S. series (then current) were issued to the U.S. Postal Agency, Shanghai, China, surcharged at double the original value of the stamps.

These stamps were intended for sale at Shanghai at their surcharged value in local currency, valid for prepayment on mail despatched from the U.S. Postal Agency at Shanghai to addresses in the U.S.

Stamps were first issued May 24, 1919, and were placed on sale at Shanghai on July 1, 1919. These stamps were not issued to postmasters in the U.S. The Shanghai post office, according to the U.S.P.O. Bulletin, was closed in December 1922. The stamps were on sale at the Philatelic Agency in Washington, D.C. for a short time after that.

The cancellations of the China office included "U.S. Postal Agency Shanghai China", "U.S. Pos. Service Shanghai China" duplexes, and the Shanghai parcel post roller cancel.

United States Stamps #498-499, 502-504, 506-510, 512, 514-518 Surcharged in Black or Red (Nos. K7, K16)

1919 **Unwmk.** ***Perf. 11***

K1 A140 2c on 1c **green** 25.00 *32.50*
Never hinged 50.00
Block of 4 110.00 *210.00*
P# block of 6 300.00 —
Never hinged 475.00
Double transfer 42.50
Never hinged 85.00
K2 A140 4c on 2c **rose,** type I 25.00 *32.50*
Never hinged 50.00
Block of 4 110.00 *210.00*
P# block of 6 300.00 —
Never hinged 475.00
K3 A140 6c on 3c **violet,** type II 52.50 *75.00*
Never hinged 115.00
Block of 4 225.00 *450.00*
P# block of 6 600.00 —
Never hinged 950.00
K4 A140 8c on 4c **brown** 57.50 *75.00*
Never hinged 120.00
Block of 4 250.00 *450.00*
P# block of 6 650.00 —
Never hinged 1,025.
K5 A140 10c on 5c **blue** 65.00 *75.00*
Never hinged 140.00
Block of 4 280.00 *450.00*
P# block of 6 600.00
Never hinged 950.00
K6 A140 12c on 6c **red orange** 85.00 *110.00*
Never hinged 180.00
Block of 4 375.00 *650.00*
P# block of 6 800.00
Never hinged *1,250.*
K7 A140 14c on 7c **black** 87.50 *125.00*
Never hinged 190.00
Block of 4 400.00 *800.00*
P# block of 6 1,050.
Never hinged *1,650.*
K8 A148 16c on 8c **olive bister** 65.00 *80.00*
Never hinged 140.00
Block of 4 280.00 *550.00*
P# block of 6 600.00
Never hinged 950.00
a. 16c on 8c **olive green** 60.00 *60.00*
Never hinged 130.00
Block of 4 260.00 *475.00*
P# block of 6 575.00
Never hinged 875.00
K9 A148 18c on 9c **salmon red** 65.00 *85.00*
Never hinged 140.00
Block of 4 280.00 *550.00*
P# block of 6 700.00
Never hinged *1,100.*
K10 A148 20c on 10c **orange yellow** 60.00 *70.00*
Never hinged 130.00
Block of 4 260.00 *425.00*
P# block of 6 725.00
Never hinged 1,150.
K11 A148 24c on 12c **brown carmine** 80.00 *80.00*
Never hinged 175.00
Block of 4 350.00 *425.00*
P# block of 6 1,000.
a. 24c on 12c **claret brown** 105.00 *125.00*
Never hinged 230.00
Block of 4 450.00 *675.00*
P# block of 6 1,100.
Never hinged *1,700.*
K12 A148 30c on 15c **gray** 87.50 *140.00*
Never hinged 190.00
Block of 4 375.00 —
P# block of 6 1,100.
Never hinged *1,700.*
K13 A148 40c on 20c **deep ultramarine** 130.00 *225.00*
Never hinged 275.00
Block of 4 550.00 *1,350.*
P# block of 6 1,300.
Never hinged *2,050.*
K14 A148 60c on 30c **orange red** 120.00 *175.00*
Never hinged 260.00
Block of 4 525.00 *1,150.*
P# block of 6 1,050.
Never hinged *1,600.*
K15 A148 $1 on 50c **light violet** 575.00 *650.00*
Never hinged 1,200.
Block of 4 2,500. *4,750.*
P# block of 6 *17,500.*
K16 A148 $2 on $1 **violet brown** 450.00 *550.00*
Never hinged 950.00
Block of 4 2,000. *4,500.*
Margin block of 4, arrow, right or left 2,100.
P# block of 6 *7,000.*
Never hinged *11,000.*
a. Double surcharge *7,000.* *7,500.*
Never hinged *11,500.*
Block of 4 —
Nos. K1-K16 (16) 2,030. *2,580.*

A fake of No. K1 has recently been discovered. Other values may exist.

OFFICIAL STAMPS

The original official stamps were authorized by Act of Congress, approved March 3, 1873, abolishing the franking privilege. Stamps for each government department were issued July 1, 1873. These stamps were supplanted on May 1, 1879, by penalty envelopes and on July 5, 1884, were declared obsolete.

DESIGNS. Stamps for departments other than the Post Office picture the same busts used in the regular postage issue: 1c Franklin, 2c Jackson, 3c Washington, 6c Lincoln, 7c Stanton, 10c Jefferson, 12c Clay, 15c Webster, 24c Scott, 30c Hamilton, and 90c Perry. William H. Seward appears on the $2, $5, $10 and $20.

Designs of the various denominations are not identical, but resemble those illustrated.

PLATES. Plates of 200 subjects in two panes of 100 were used for Post Office Department 1c, 3c, 6c; Treasury Department 1c, 2c, 3c, and War Department 2c, 3c. Plates of 10 subjects were used for State Department $2, $5, $10 and $20. Plates of 100 subjects were used for all other Official stamps up to No. O120.

CANCELLATIONS. Odd or Town cancellations on Departmental stamps are relatively much scarcer than those appearing on the general issues of the same period. Town cancellations, especially on the 1873 issue, are scarce. The "Kicking Mule" cancellation is found used on stamps of the War Department and has also been seen on some stamps of the other Departments. Black is usual.

Grade, condition and presence of original gum are very important in valuing Nos. O1-O120.

As is done elsewhere in this catalogue, all Officials are valued in the grade of very fine. If unused, they will have original gum. Unused examples without original gum are often encountered and sell for less.

Printed by the Continental Bank Note Co.
Thin Hard Paper

Franklin
O1 O2

AGRICULTURE

1873 Engr. Unwmk. *Perf. 12*

No.	Design	Denom.	Variety	Unused	Used
O1	O1	1c	**yellow**	175.00	160.00
			golden yellow	180.00	170.00
			olive yellow	185.00	175.00
			On cover		—
			Block of 4	800.00	
			Ribbed paper	185.00	160.00
			Cancellations		
			Magenta		+7.50
			Violet		+7.50
			Blue		+5.00
			Red		+50.00
			Town		+7.50
			Fort		+150.00
O2	O1	2c	**yellow**	140.00	70.00
			golden yellow	145.00	72.50
			olive yellow	150.00	75.00
			On cover		*1,750.*
			Block of 4	625.00	
			P# block of 12	—	
			Ribbed paper	150.00	85.00
			Cancellations		
			Blue		+3.00
			Violet		+3.00
			Red		+15.00
			Magenta		+5.00
			Town		+5.00
O3	O1	3c	**yellow**	125.00	13.00
			golden yellow	130.00	14.00
			olive yellow	135.00	15.00
			On cover		*900.00*
			Block of 4	550.00	—
			P# block of 12, Impt., never hinged	*2,600.*	
			Ribbed paper	135.00	13.00
			Double transfer	—	—

The never hinged, bottom left plate block of No. O3 is the only plate block of this number recorded.

No.	Design	Denom.	Variety	Unused	Used
			Cancellations		
			Blue		+.50
			Purple		+1.00
			Magenta		+1.00
			Violet		+1.00
			Red		+17.50
			Indigo		+10.00
			Green		+200.00
			Town		+4.00
			"Paid"		+27.50
			Numeral		+35.00
			Railroad		+75.00
			Express Company		+900.00
O4	O1	6c	**yellow**	140.00	52.50
			golden yellow	145.00	55.00
			olive yellow	150.00	57.50
			On cover		—
			Block of 4	625.00	
			Cancellations		
			Blue		+3.00
			Magenta		+4.00
			Violet		+5.00
			Red		+50.00
			Town		+7.00
			"Paid"		+27.50
			Numeral		+35.00
			Express Company		—
			Revenue		—
O5	O1	10c	**yellow**	290.00	180.00
			golden yellow	300.00	185.00
			olive yellow	310.00	190.00
			On cover (parcel label)		—
			Block of 4	1,300.	
			Cancellations		
			Violet		+5.00
			Blue		+5.00
			Red		+50.00
			Town		+25.00
O6	O1	12c	**yellow**	380.00	240.00
			golden yellow	400.00	250.00
			olive yellow	420.00	255.00
			On cover		—
			Block of 4	1,500.	
			Cancellations		
			Violet		+10.00
			Blue		+10.00
			Red		+50.00
			Town		+30.00
O7	O1	15c	**yellow**	325.00	210.00
			golden yellow	350.00	220.00
			olive yellow	375.00	230.00
			Block of 4	1,400.	—
			Cancellations		
			Purple		+10.00
			Blue		+10.00
O8	O1	24c	**yellow**	325.00	200.00
			golden yellow	350.00	210.00
			On parcel label		—
			Block of 4	1,400.	
			Cancellation		
			Violet		+10.00
O9	O1	30c	**yellow**	400.00	250.00
			golden yellow	425.00	260.00
			olive yellow	450.00	275.00
			Block of 4	1,800.	
			Cancellations		
			Blue		+10.00
			Red		+65.00

EXECUTIVE

1873

No.	Design	Denom.	Variety	Unused	Used
O10	O2	1c	**carmine**	675.00	425.00
			deep carmine	675.00	425.00
			On cover with No. O11		—
			On cover, single franking		—
			Block of 6	*5,750.*	

The only known block is off-center and has original gum.

No.	Design	Denom.	Variety	Unused	Used
			Cancellations		
			Violet		+10.00
			Blue favor		+10.00
			Red		+50.00
			Town		+30.00
O11	O2	2c	**carmine**	450.00	210.00
			deep carmine	450.00	210.00
			On cover, single franking		*1,500.*
			Block of 4	*2,750.*	
			Foreign entry of 6c Agriculture	—	
			Cancellations		
			Violet		+10.00
			Blue favor		+10.00
			Red		+50.00
O12	O2	3c	**carmine**	500.00	175.00
a.		3c	**violet rose**	500.00	175.00
			On cover		*700.00*
			On cover from Long Branch, N.J.		*3,500.*
			Block of 4	*2,400.*	
			Cancellations		
			Blue favor		+10.00
			Violet		+10.00
			Indigo		+20.00
			Red		+50.00
			Town		+35.00
O13	O2	6c	**carmine**	750.00	500.00
			pale carmine	750.00	500.00
			deep carmine	750.00	500.00
			On cover		*3,500.*
			Strip of 4	*4,500.*	
			Cancellations		
			Violet		+15.00
			Blue favor		+15.00
			Town		+50.00
O14	O2	10c	**carmine**	725.00	575.00
			pale carmine	725.00	575.00
			deep carmine	725.00	575.00
			On cover		—
			Block of 4	*4,250.*	
			Cancellations		
			Violet		+15.00
			Blue favor		+15.00

O3

O4

INTERIOR

1873

No.	Design	Denom.	Variety	Unused	Used
O15	O3	1c	**vermilion**	42.50	8.50
			dull vermilion	42.50	8.50
			bright vermilion	42.50	8.50
			On cover		160.00
			Block of 4	175.00	—
			P# block of 10, Impt.	*600.00*	
			Never hinged	*850.00*	
			Ribbed paper	47.50	9.50
			Cancellations		
			Violet		+1.00
			Blue		+1.00
			Red		+12.50
			Ultramarine		+8.00
			Town		+3.00
O16	O3	2c	**vermilion**	35.00	10.00
			dull vermilion	35.00	10.00
			bright vermilion	35.00	10.00
			On cover		65.00
			Block of 4	150.00	—
			P# block of 10, Impt.	*500.00*	
			P# block of 12, Impt.	*575.00*	

Cancellations
Purple +.75
Violet +75
Blue +.75
Red +6.00
Town +7.50
Numeral +20.00
"Paid" +20.00

O17 O3 3c **vermilion** 55.00 5.25
dull vermilion 55.00 5.25
bright vermilion 55.00 5.25
On cover 40.00
First day cover, Nos. O17, O18, *July 1, 1873* —
Block of 4 210.00 —
P# block of 10, Impt. *625.00*
Ribbed paper 62.50 6.75

Cancellations
Violet +1.00
Blue +1.00
Indigo +3.00
Magenta +5.00
Red +15.00
Green +65.00
Town +7.50
Numeral +20.00
Express Company +75.00
"Paid" +20.00
Fort —

O18 O3 6c **vermilion** 42.50 7.50
dull vermilion 42.50 7.50
bright vermilion 42.50 7.50
scarlet vermilion 42.50 8.50
On cover 95.00
Block of 4 190.00 —
P# block of 10, Impt. *575.00*

Cancellations
Violet +1.00
Blue +1.00
Red +15.00
Town +7.50
Express Company —
Railroad —
Fort —

See No. O17 first day cover listing.

O19 O3 10c **vermilion** 42.50 16.00
dull vermilion 42.50 16.00
bright vermilion 42.50 16.00
On cover *450.00*
Block of 4 190.00 —
P# block of 12, Impt. *675.00*

Cancellations
Violet +1.00
Blue +1.00
Red +25.00
Town +10.00
Fort —

O20 O3 12c **vermilion** 55.00 9.00
bright vermilion 55.00 9.00
On cover *450.00*
Block of 4 230.00 —
P# block of 10, Impt. *775.00*

Cancellations
Violet +1.00
Magenta +1.00
Blue +1.00
Red +15.00
Brown +20.00
Town +7.50
Fort —

O21 O3 15c **vermilion** 100.00 18.00
bright vermilion 100.00 18.00
On cover *650.00*
Block of 4 450.00 —
P# block of 12, Impt. —
Double transfer of left side 160.00 26.00

Cancellations
Blue +1.50
Violet +1.50
Town +5.00

O22 O3 24c **vermilion** 75.00 15.00
dull vermilion 75.00 15.00
bright vermilion 75.00 15.00
On cover —
Block of 4 300.00 —
P# block of 12, Impt. *1,050.*
a. Double impression —

Cancellations
Violet +1.50
Blue +1.50
Red +15.00
Town +5.00

O23 O3 30c **vermilion** 100.00 15.00
bright vermilion 100.00 15.00
On parcel label —
Block of 4 450.00 —
P# block of 12, Impt. *1,400.*

Cancellations
Violet +2.00
Blue +2.00
Red +15.00
Town +7.50

O24 O3 90c **vermilion** 210.00 40.00
bright vermilion 210.00 40.00
On cover *4,500.*
Block of 4 950.00 —
P# block of 12, Impt. *3,150.*
Double transfer *270.00*
Major double transfer (Pos. 17) *450.00* *70.00*
Silk paper —

Cancellations
Violet +4.00
Blue +4.00
Magenta +10.00
Red +50.00
Brown +60.00
Town +17.50

JUSTICE

1873

O25 O4 1c **purple** 130.00 90.00
dark purple 130.00 90.00
On cover *1,100.*
Block of 4 575.00 —

Cancellations
Violet +3.00
Blue +3.00
Indigo +5.00
Magenta +5.00
Red +20.00
Town +7.50

O26 O4 2c **purple** 220.00 90.00
light purple 220.00 90.00
On cover —
Block of 4 975.00

Cancellations
Violet +4.00
Blue +4.00
Ultramarine +10.00
Indigo +5.00
Magenta +5.00
Red +20.00
Town +20.00

O27 O4 3c **purple** 220.00 25.00
dark purple 220.00 25.00
bluish purple 220.00 25.00
On cover *575.00*
Block of 4 1,000. —
Double transfer —

Cancellations
Violet +2.00
Magenta +2.00
Blue +2.00
Ultramarine +10.00
Indigo +5.00
Red +12.00
Green +100.00
Town +15.00

O28 O4 6c **purple** 200.00 35.00
light purple 200.00 35.00
bluish purple 200.00 35.00
On cover *800.00*
Block of 4 900.00 —

Cancellations
Violet +2.00
Blue +2.00
Indigo +5.00
Magenta +5.00
Red +15.00
Town +17.50

O29 O4 10c **purple** 225.00 75.00
bluish purple 225.00 75.00
On cover *2,000.*
Block of 4 1,100. —
P# block of 12, Impt. —
Double transfer — —

Cancellations
Violet +4.00
Blue +4.00
Magenta +5.00
Town +17.50

O30 O4 12c **purple** 180.00 60.00
dark purple 180.00 60.00
On cover *1,100.*
Block of 4 825.00

Cancellations
Purple +2.00
Violet +2.00
Blue +2.00
Magenta +5.00
Red +35.00
Town +17.50

O31 O4 15c **purple** 350.00 160.00
On cover *1,250.*
Block of 4 —
Double transfer — —

Cancellations
Violet +5.00
Blue +5.00
Indigo +5.00
Magenta +10.00
Red +35.00
Town +10.00

O32 O4 24c **purple** 900.00 350.00
On cover *2,750.*
Block of 4 —
Short transfer (pos. 98) —

The existence of the block of 4 of No. O32 has been questioned by specialists. The editors would like to see evidence of the current existence of this item.

Cancellations
Violet +10.00
Blue +10.00
Magenta +10.00
Red +35.00
Town +40.00

O33 O4 30c **purple** 900.00 275.00
On cover 7,500.
Block of 4 —
Double transfer at top 975.00 300.00

Cancellations
Purple +10.00
Violet +10.00
Blue +10.00
Magenta +10.00
Red +35.00
Town +40.00

O34 O4 90c **purple** 1,350. 525.00
dark purple 1,350. 525.00
On cover *16,500*
Block of 4 —

Cancellations
Purple +25.00
Violet +25.00
Blue +25.00
Magenta +25.00

No. O34 on cover is unique. The cover bears three No. O34 and four No. O33. Value represents auction sale price in 1998.

The existence of the block of 4 of No. O34 has been questioned by specialists. The editors would like to see evidence of the current existence of this item.

O5 O6

NAVY

1873

O35 O5 1c **ultramarine** 85.00 42.50
dark ultramarine 85.00 42.50
On cover *600.00*
Block of 4 400.00 —
P# block of 12, Impt. *1,250.*
a. 1c **dull blue** 90.00 45.00

Cancellations
Violet +2.00
Blue +2.00
Indigo +5.00
Red +20.00
Town +7.50
Steamship +100.00

O36 O5 2c **ultramarine** 70.00 20.00
dark ultramarine 70.00 20.00
On cover *350.00*
Block of 4 325.00 —
P# block of 12, Impt. *1,500.*
Double transfer — —
a. 2c **dull blue** 75.00 18.00
gray blue 75.00 18.00

The 2c deep green and the 2c black, both perforated and imperforate, are trial color proofs.

Cancellations
Violet +1.50
Blue +1.50
Indigo +5.00
Red +15.00
Green +75.00
Town +10.00
Steamship +100.00

O37 O5 3c **ultramarine** 125.00 11.50
pale ultramarine 125.00 11.50
dark ultramarine 125.00 11.50
On cover *160.00*
Block of 4 600.00 —
P# block of 12, Impt. *1,800.*
Double transfer — —
a. 3c **dull blue** 120.00 12.50

Cancellations
Violet +1.50
Blue +1.50
Indigo +5.00
Ultramarine +10.00
Magenta +5.00
Red +15.00
Town +5.00
Blue town +15.00
Steamship +75.00

O38 O5 6c **ultramarine** 65.00 17.50
bright ultramarine 65.00 17.50
On cover *600.00*
Block of 4 325.00 —
P# block of 12, Impt. *925.00*
Vertical line through "N" of "Navy" 130.00 25.00
Double transfer —
a. 6c **dull blue** 70.00 17.50

Cancellations
Violet +1.50
Purple +1.50
Blue +1.50
Magenta +10.00
Red +17.50
Green +100.00
Town +5.00
Steamship +100.00

O39 O5 7c **ultramarine** 450.00 200.00
dark ultramarine 450.00 200.00
On cover *2,000.*
Block of 4 *2,250.*
Double transfer — —
a. 7c **dull blue** 450.00 200.00

Cancellations
Blue +10.00
Violet +10.00
Magenta +10.00
Red +45.00
Town +25.00

O40 O5 10c **ultramarine** 90.00 35.00
dark ultramarine 90.00 35.00
On cover 4,000.
Block of 4 450.00
P# block of 12, Impt. 1,300.
Plate scratch, pos. 3 180.00 —
Ribbed paper 105.00 40.00
a. 10c **dull blue** 90.00 35.00

Cancellations
Violet +2.00
Blue +2.00
Brown +20.00
Red +25.00
Town +10.00
Steamship +100.00

O41 O5 12c **ultramarine** 110.00 35.00
pale ultramarine 110.00 35.00
dark ultramarine 110.00 35.00
On cover 3,000.
Block of 4 525.00
P# block of 12, Impt. —
Double transfer of left side, pos. 50 270.00 180.00

Cancellations
Violet +2.50
Magenta +2.50
Blue +2.50
Red +25.00
Town +10.00
Supplementary Mail +80.00
Steamship +100.00

O42 O5 15c **ultramarine** 190.00 60.00
dark ultramarine 190.00 60.00
Block of 4 900.00
P# block of 12, Impt. —

Cancellations
Violet +2.50
Blue +2.50
Red +35.00
Yellow —
Town +20.00

O43 O5 24c **ultramarine** 220.00 70.00
dark ultramarine 220.00 70.00
On cover —
Block of 4 1,000.
a. 24c **dull blue** 210.00 —

Cancellations
Violet +5.00
Magenta +5.00
Red +50.00
Blue +5.00
Green +150.00
Town +40.00
Steamship +125.00

O44 O5 30c **ultramarine** 160.00 40.00
dark ultramarine 160.00 40.00
Block of 4 750.00 —
Double transfer 190.00 45.00

Cancellations
Blue +4.00
Red +30.00
Violet +4.00
Town +20.00
Supplementary Mail +125.00

O45 O5 90c **ultramarine** 750.00 250.00
Block of 4 4,000.
P# block of 12, Impt. —
Short transfer at upper left (pos. 1, 5) — —
a. Double impression 4,000.

Cancellations
Purple +15.00
Violet +15.00
Red +75.00
Town +40.00

POST OFFICE

Stamps of the Post Office Department are often on paper with a gray surface. This is due to insufficient wiping of the excess ink off plates during printing.

1873

O47 O6 1c **black** 15.00 10.00
gray black 15.00 10.00
On cover 60.00
Block of 4 65.00 —
P# block of 12, Impt. 260.00
Never hinged 375.00

Cancellations
Purple +1.00
Violet +1.00
Magenta +1.00
Blue +1.00
Red +12.50
Town +3.50

O48 O6 2c **black** 20.00 7.50
gray black 20.00 7.50
On cover 160.00
Block of 4 85.00 —
P# block of 12, Impt. 325.00
a. Double impression 500.00 400.00

Cancellations
Purple +1.00
Violet +1.00
Blue +1.00
Indigo +5.00
Magenta +1.00
Red +12.50
Town +3.50
Blue town +7.50

O49 O6 3c **black** 6.50 1.25
gray black 6.50 1.25
On cover 20.00
Block of 4 30.00 —
P# block of 14, Impt. 150.00
Never hinged 220.00 —
Cracked plate — —
Double transfer at bottom — —
Double paper — —
Vertical ribbed paper — —
a. Printed on both sides 3,250.

Cancellations
Purple +.75
Violet +.75
Blue +.75
Indigo +5.00
Ultramarine +1.50
Magenta +.75
Red +10.00
Brown +20.00
Green +60.00
Numeral +20.00
Town +1.50
Railroad +25.00
"Paid" +12.00

O50 O6 6c **black** 20.00 6.50
gray black 20.00 6.50
On cover 75.00
Block of 4 85.00 —
P# block of 14, Impt. 375.00
Vertical ribbed paper — 11.00
a. Diagonal half used as 3c on cover 3,250.

Cancellations
Purple +.75
Violet +.75
Magenta +.75
Blue +.75
Indigo +5.00
Red +12.00
Brown +20.00
Numeral +20.00
Town +2.50
"Paid" +15.00

O51 O6 10c **black** 80.00 45.00
gray black 80.00 45.00
On cover 400.00
Block of 4 400.00 —
P# block of 12, Impt. 1,100.

Cancellations
Violet +3.50
Red +15.00
Magenta +3.50
Blue +3.50
Town +10.00

O52 O6 12c **black** 40.00 9.00
gray black 40.00 9.00
On cover 1,000.
Block of 4 175.00 —
P# block of 12, Impt. 625.00

Cancellations
Purple +1.00
Magenta +1.00
Blue +1.00
Indigo +5.00
Red +12.50
Town +4.00

O53 O6 15c **black** 55.00 15.00
gray black 55.00 15.00
On cover 1,500.
Block of 4 250.00 —
P# block of 14, Impt. 825.00
Double transfer — —

Cancellations
Violet +1.50
Magenta +1.50
Red +20.00
Blue +1.50
Town +7.50

O54 O6 24c **black** 70.00 18.50
gray black 70.00 18.50
Block of 4 300.00 —
P# block of 12, Impt. —
Double paper — —

Cancellations
Violet +1.50
Blue +1.50
Red +20.00
Town +7.50

O55 O6 30c **black** 75.00 18.50
gray black 75.00 18.50
On cover —
Block of 4 325.00 —
P# block of 12, Impt. 1,050.

Cancellations
Purple +1.50
Blue +1.50
Red +20.00
Magenta +1.50
Town +12.50

O56 O6 90c **black** 100.00 17.50
gray black 100.00 17.50
Block of 4 450.00 —
P# block of 12, Impt. 1,450.
Double transfer — —
Double paper — —
Silk paper —

Cancellations
Purple +1.50
Magenta +1.50
Blue +1.50
Town +6.50

STATE

Franklin — O7

William H. Seward — O8

1873

O57 O7 1c **dark green** 140.00 60.00
dark yellow green 140.00 60.00
light green 140.00 60.00
On cover —
Block of 4 700.00

Cancellations
Violet +2.00
Blue favor +2.00
Red +17.50
Town +7.50

O58 O7 2c **dark green** 225.00 85.00
dark yellow green 225.00 85.00
yellow green — —
On cover 1,000.
Block of 4 —
Double transfer — —

Cancellations
Violet +5.00
Blue favor +5.00
Indigo +5.00
Red +50.00
Town +25.00

The existence of any multiple of No. O58 larger than a strip of 3 used on cover has been questioned by specialists. The editors would like to see evidence that any blocks of 4 or larger are still in existence, either unused or used.

O59 O7 3c **bright green** 110.00 20.00
yellow green 110.00 20.00
dark green 110.00 20.00
On cover 450.00
First day cover, *July 1, 1873* —
Block of 4 550.00 —
Double paper — —

Cancellations
Violet +1.50
Blue favor +1.50
Indigo +1.50
Red +10.00
Town +6.50

O60 O7 6c **bright green** 100.00 25.00
dark green 100.00 25.00
yellow green 100.00 25.00
On cover 650.00
Block of 4 500.00 —
P# block of 12, Impt. —
Double transfer — —
Foreign entry of 6c Executive, pos. 41 & 91 — —
Double transfer plus foreign entry of 6c Executive, pos. 61 —

Cancellations
Violet +2.00
Blue favor +10.00
Indigo +2.00
Red +20.00
Town +17.50

O61 O7 7c **dark green** 180.00 55.00
dark yellow green 180.00 55.00
On cover 1,000.
Block of 4 1,000.
Ribbed paper 200.00 60.00

Cancellations
Violet +2.00
Blue favor +2.00
Indigo +2.00
Red +25.00
Town +10.00

O62 O7 10c **dark green** 140.00 45.00
bright green 140.00 45.00
yellow green — —
On cover 1,200.
Block of 4 700.00
P# block of 12, Impt. —
Short transfer, pos. 34 180.00 57.50

Cancellations
Violet +2.50
Blue favor +2.50
Indigo +2.50
Red +35.00
Town +25.00
Blue town +10.00
Numeral +50.00

O63 O7 12c **dark green** 220.00 110.00
dark yellow green — —
On cover 1,500.
Block of 4 1,250.

Cancellations
Violet +5.00
Blue favor +5.00
Red +30.00

Town +15.00
O64 O7 15c **dark green** 230.00 75.00
dark yellow green 230.00 75.00
On cover —
Block of 4 1,250.

Cancellations
Violet +2.50
Blue favor +2.50
Red +30.00
Town +30.00

O65 O7 24c **dark green** 450.00 200.00
dark yellow green 450.00 200.00
On cover *1,750.*
Block of 4 *2,750.* —

Cancellations
Violet +15.00
Blue favor +15.00
Indigo +15.00
Red +85.00
Town +55.00

O66 O7 30c **dark green** 425.00 150.00
dark yellow green 425.00 150.00
On cover —
Block of 4 — —

Cancellations
Violet +5.00
Blue favor +5.00
Indigo +5.00
Red +50.00
Town +50.00
Blue town +75.00

O67 O7 90c **dark green** 850.00 300.00
dark yellow green —
On cover —
Block of 4 —

The existence of the block of 4 No. O67 has been questioned by specialists. The editors would like to see evidence of the current existence of this item.

Cancellations
Violet +15.00
Blue favor +15.00
Red +85.00
Town +90.00

O68 O8 $2 **green & black** 1,250. 800.00
yellow green & black 1,250. 800.00
On parcel label —
Block of 4 *14,000.*
Ribbed paper —

Cancellations
Violet +25.00
Blue favor +25.00
Red +175.00
Town +125.00
Blue town +200.00
Pen *175.00*

O69 O8 $5 **green & black** 6,000. 4,250.
dark green & black 6,000. 4,250.
yellow green & black 6,000. 4,250.
Block of 4 *30,000.*

Cancellations
Blue favor +250.00
Red favor +250.00
Pen *1,600.*

The block of 4 is contained in the only known multiple: an irregular block of 6.

O70 O8 $10 **green & black** 4,500. 3,500.
dark green & black 4,500. 3,500.
yellow green & black 4,500. 3,500.
Block of 4 *22,500.*
P# sheet of 10, Impt. *55,000.*

Cancellations
Blue favor +200.00
Pen *1,150.*

O71 O8 $20 **green & black** 3,500. 2,500.
dark green & black 3,500. 2,500.
yellow green & black 3,500. 2,500.
Block of 4 *18,500.*
Block of 4, pen cancel *6,500.*
P# sheet of 10, Impt. *45,000.*

Cancellations
Blue favor +200.00
Red favor +200.00
Pen *1,100.*

The design of Nos. O68 to O71 measures 25½x39½mm.

O9

O10

TREASURY

1873

O72 O9 1c **brown** 40.00 5.50
dark brown 40.00 5.50
yellow brown 40.00 5.50
On cover 100.00
Block of 4 170.00 —
P# block of 14, Impt. *800.00*
Never hinged *1,150.*
Double transfer 47.50 6.75

Cancellations
Purple +1.00
Violet +1.00
Magenta +1.00
Blue +1.00
Red +10.00
Brown +20.00
Green +50.00
Town +2.00
Blue town +4.00

O73 O9 2c **brown** 50.00 5.50
dark brown 50.00 5.50
yellow brown 50.00 5.50
On cover 75.00
Block of 4 210.00 —
P# block of 14, Impt. *850.00*
Double transfer — 9.00
Cracked plate 67.50 —

Cancellations
Purple +1.00
Violet +1.00
Magenta +1.00
Blue +1.00
Indigo +3.00
Red +10.00
Town +2.00
Blue town +4.00

O74 O9 3c **brown** 50.00 1.50
dark brown 50.00 1.50
yellow brown 50.00 1.50
On cover 30.00
First day cover, *July 1, 1873* *3,250.*
Block of 4 225.00 —
P# block of 14, Impt. *850.00*
Double paper —
Shaded circle outside of right frame line — —
a. Double impression —

Cancellations
Purple +.50
Violet +.50
Blue +.50
Indigo +3.00
Ultramarine +2.00
Magenta +.50
Red +3.50
Brown +20.00
Green +50.00
Town +1.00
Railroad +20.00
"Paid" +10.00

O75 O9 6c **brown** 50.00 3.00
dark brown 50.00 3.00
yellow brown 50.00 3.00
On cover 75.00
Block of 4 225.00 *500.00*
P# block of 12, Impt. *875.00*
Never hinged *1,250.*
Dirty plate 50.00 4.50
Double transfer — —

Cancellations
Purple +.50
Violet +.50
Magenta +.50
Blue +.50
Indigo +3.00
Ultramarine +1.50
Red +5.00
Green +50.00
"Paid" +20.00
Town +1.50

O76 O9 7c **brown** 100.00 27.50
dark brown 100.00 27.50
yellow brown 100.00 27.50
On cover 750.00
Block of 4 475.00 —
P# block of 12, Impt. —

Cancellations
Purple +2.00
Violet +2.00
Blue +2.00
Indigo +3.00
Red +30.00
Green +60.00
Town +7.50
Blue town +12.50

O77 O9 10c **brown** 100.00 9.00
dark brown 100.00 9.00
yellow brown 100.00 9.00
On cover *450.00*
Block of 4 450.00 —
P# block of 12, Impt. —
Double paper — —
Double transfer —

Cancellations
Purple +1.00
Violet +1.00
Blue +1.00
Indigo +3.00
Ultramarine +4.00
Magenta +1.00
Red +12.00
Brown +20.00
Green +50.00
Town +4.00
Blue town +8.50

O78 O9 12c **brown** 100.00 6.50
dark brown 100.00 6.50
yellow brown 100.00 6.50
On cover 600.00
Block of 4 450.00 —

Cancellations
Purple +.50
Blue +.50
Ultramarine +10.00
Red +10.00
Green +50.00
Town +2.50
Railroad +20.00

O79 O9 15c **brown** 95.00 9.00
yellow brown 95.00 9.00
On cover *850.00*
Block of 4 425.00 —
P# block of 12, Impt. *1,650.*
Never hinged *2,400.*

Cancellations
Blue +1.00
Purple +1.00
Red +10.00
Green +50.00
Town +2.50
Blue town +7.50
Numeral +15.00

O80 O9 24c **brown** 500.00 75.00
dark brown 500.00 75.00
yellow brown 500.00 75.00
Block of 4 2,250.
Double transfer at top — —

Cancellations
Violet +10.00
Blue +5.00
Ultramarine +10.00
Magenta +5.00
Red +30.00
Town +15.00
Blue town +25.00

O81 O9 30c **brown** 200.00 10.00
dark brown 200.00 10.00
yellow brown 200.00 10.00
On cover *3,000.*
Block of 4 900.00 —
Short transfer at left top (pos. 95) 250.00 20.00
Short transfer at right top (pos. 45) 250.00 20.00
Block of 4, one pos. 45 —
Short transfer across entire top (pos. 41) 250.00 20.00

Cancellations
Purple +1.00
Blue +1.00
Magenta +1.00
Red +12.00
Green +50.00
Town +3.50
Blue town +7.50

O82 O9 90c **brown** 200.00 11.00
dark brown 200.00 11.00
yellow brown 200.00 11.00
Block of 4 900.00 300.00
Double paper — —

Cancellations
Purple +1.00
Magenta +1.00
Blue +1.00
Red +30.00
Brown +7.50
Green +50.00
Town +3.50
Blue town +7.50

WAR

1873

O83 O10 1c **rose** 150.00 12.00
rose red 150.00 12.00
On cover 140.00
Block of 4 650.00
P# block of 12, Impt. *2,000.*

Cancellations
Purple +1.00
Blue +1.00
Magenta +5.00
Red +15.00
Town +3.50
Fort +80.00
Numeral +12.50
"Paid" —

O84 O10 2c **rose** 135.00 12.00
rose red 135.00 12.00
On cover 70.00
Block of 4 575.00 —
P# block of 14, Impt. *2,250*
Ribbed paper 145.00 14.00

Cancellations
Purple +1.50
Magenta +1.50
Blue +1.50
Red +15.00
Town +4.00
Fort +75.00

O85 O10 3c **rose** 140.00 4.00
rose red 140.00 4.00
On cover 40.00
Block of 4 600.00 —
P# block of 14, Impt. *2,150.*

Cancellations
Purple +1.00
Blue +1.00
Ultramarine +10.00
Magenta +1.00
Red +20.00
Green +35.00
Town +1.50
Fort +65.00
"Paid" +12.00

O86 O10 6c **rose** 475.00 7.50
pale rose 475.00 7.50
On cover 60.00
Block of 4 *2,250.* —
P# block of 12, Impt. —

No.	Type	Denom.	Description	Unused	Used
			Cancellations		
			Purple		+1.50
			Blue		+1.50
			Indigo		+3.00
			Magenta		+3.00
			Red		+15.00
			Town		+3.50
			Blue town		+6.50
			Fort		+65.00
O87	O10	7c	**rose**	130.00	77.50
			pale rose	130.00	77.50
			rose red	130.00	77.50
			On cover		—
			Block of 4	550.00	—
			P# block of 10, Impt.	*1,850.*	
			Cancellations		
			Purple		+2.50
			Blue		+3.50
			Magenta		+10.00
			Red		+25.00
			Town		+7.50
O88	O10	10c	**rose**	50.00	17.50
			rose red	50.00	17.50
			On cover		—
			Block of 4	200.00	*900.00*
			P# block of 12, Impt.	*850.00*	

All copies of No. O88 show a crack at lower left. It was on the original die.

No.	Type	Denom.	Description	Unused	Used
			Cancellations		
			Purple		+1.00
			Blue		+1.00
			Town		+3.50
			Fort		+65.00
O89	O10	12c	**rose**	180.00	10.00
			On cover		300.00
			Block of 4	750.00	—
			P# block of 12, Impt.	*2,200.*	
			Never hinged	*3,150.*	
			Ribbed paper	200.00	11.00
			Cancellations		
			Purple		+1.00
			Magenta		+1.00
			Blue		+1.00
			Indigo		+5.00
			Red		+10.00
			Town		+3.00
			Fort		+70.00
O90	O10	15c	**rose**	45.00	12.00
			pale rose	45.00	12.00
			rose red	45.00	12.00
			On cover		—
			Block of 4	200.00	—
			P# block of 10, Impt.	*575.00*	
			Ribbed paper	50.00	15.00
			Cancellations		
			Purple		+1.00
			Blue		+1.00
			Ultramarine		+10.00
			Magenta		+3.00
			Red		+10.00
			Town		+2.50
			Fort		+100.00
			Express Company		—
O91	O10	24c	**rose**	45.00	10.00
			pale rose	45.00	10.00
			rose red	45.00	10.00
			On cover		—
			Block of 4	200.00	*900.00*
			P# block of 10, Impt.	*825.00*	
			Cancellations		
			Purple		+1.00
			Blue		+1.00
			Magenta		+5.00
			Town		+2.50
			Fort		+100.00
O92	O10	30c	**rose**	47.50	9.00
			rose red	47.50	9.00
			On cover		—
			Block of 4	210.00	—
			P# block of 12, Impt.	*750.00*	
			Ribbed paper	52.50	11.50
			Cancellations		
			Purple		+1.00
			Magenta		+1.00
			Blue		+1.00
			Red		+20.00
			Town		+2.50
			Fort		+100.00
O93	O10	90c	**rose**	100.00	42.50
			rose red	100.00	42.50
			On cover		—
			Block of 4	450.00	*900.00*
			P# block of 12, Impt.	*2,200.*	
			Cancellations		
			Purple		+2.00
			Magenta		+2.00
			Blue		+2.00
			Red		+20.00
			Numeral		+40.00
			Town		+7.50
			Fort		+125.00

Printed by the American Bank Note Co.

The Continental Bank Note Co. was consolidated with the American Bank Note Co. on February 4, 1879. The American Bank Note Company used many plates of the Continental Bank Note Company to print the ordinary postage, Departmental and Newspaper stamps. Therefore, stamps bearing the Continental Company's imprint were not always its product.

1879 — Soft Porous Paper

AGRICULTURE

No.	Type	Denom.	Description	Unused	Used
O94	O1	1c	**yellow** (issued without gum)	*4,250.*	
			Block of 4	*20,000.*	
O95	O1	3c	**yellow**	400.00	75.00
			On cover		—
			Block of 4	2,000.	*1,300.*
			P# block of 12, Impt.	*5,250.*	
			Cancellations		
			Purple		+5.00
			Blue		+5.00
			Town		+30.00

INTERIOR

No.	Type	Denom.	Description	Unused	Used
O96	O3	1c	**vermilion**	250.00	230.00
			pale vermilion	250.00	230.00
			Block of 4	1,200.	—
			P# block of 12, Impt.	*3,750.*	
			Cancellations		
			Purple		+5.00
			Blue		+5.00
			Town		+15.00
O97	O3	2c	**vermilion**	6.00	2.50
			pale vermilion	6.00	2.50
			scarlet vermilion	6.00	2.50
			On cover		35.00
			Block of 4	27.50	—
			P# block of 12, Impt.	*160.00*	
			Cancellations		
			Purple		+.50
			Violet		+.50
			Blue		+.50
			Red		+5.00
			Town		+1.50
			Blue town		+3.00
			Railroad		+40.00
			Fort		+75.00
O98	O3	3c	**vermilion**	5.50	1.50
			pale vermilion	5.50	1.50
			On cover		30.00
			Block of 4	25.00	—
			P# block of 10, Impt.	*165.00*	
			Cancellations		
			Purple		+.50
			Violet		+.50
			Blue		+.50
			Red		+5.00
			Town		+1.50
			Blue town		+3.00
			Railroad		+40.00
			Numeral		+5.00
O99	O3	6c	**vermilion**	10.00	6.50
			pale vermilion	10.00	6.50
			scarlet vermilion	10.00	6.50
			On cover		200.00
			Block of 4	45.00	—
			P# block of 10, Impt.	*225.00*	
			Cancellations		
			Purple		+.50
			Blue		+.50
			Red		+5.00
			Town		+1.50
O100	O3	10c	**vermilion**	90.00	65.00
			pale vermilion	90.00	65.00
			On cover		*800.00*
			Block of 4	400.00	—
			P# block of 12, Impt.	*1,350.*	
			Cancellations		
			Purple		+5.00
			Blue		+5.00
			Town		+10.00
O101	O3	12c	**vermilion**	180.00	100.00
			pale vermilion	180.00	100.00
			On cover		—
			Block of 4	750.00	*500.00*
			Block of 6		*1,500.*
			P# block of 12, Impt.	*2,400.*	
			Cancellation		
			Violet		+5.00
O102	O3	15c	**vermilion**	350.00	240.00
			Block of 4	1,500.	
			P# block of 12, Impt.	—	
			On cover		—
			Double transfer	400.00	—
			Cancellations		
			Purple		+5.00
			Blue		+5.00
O103	O3	24c	**vermilion**	*4,000.*	—
			Block of 4	*20,000.*	
			P# block of 12, Impt.	—	
			Cancellation		
			Blue		—

JUSTICE

No.	Type	Denom.	Description	Unused	Used
O106	O4	3c	**bluish purple**	110.00	75.00
			deep bluish purple	110.00	75.00
			On cover		700.00
			Block of 4	500.00	
			Cancellations		
			Violet		+5.00
			Blue		+5.00
			Indigo		+5.00
			Ultramarine		+10.00
O107	O4	6c	**bluish purple**	275.00	190.00
			On cover		—
			Block of 4	1,200.	
			Cancellations		
			Blue		+10.00
			Indigo		+5.00
			Town		+20.00

POST OFFICE

No.	Type	Denom.	Description	Unused	Used
O108	O6	3c	**black**	20.00	6.50
			gray black	20.00	6.50
			On cover		—
			Block of 4	87.50	—
			P# block of 14, Impt.	*325.00*	
			Cancellations		
			Purple		+1.00
			Violet		+1.00
			Blue		+1.00
			Indigo		+10.00
			Magenta		+1.00
			Red		+20.00
			Green		+40.00
			Town		+2.00
			"Paid"		+12.00

TREASURY

No.	Type	Denom.	Description	Unused	Used
O109	O9	3c	**brown**	65.00	7.50
			yellow brown	65.00	7.50
			On cover		110.00
			Block of 4	300.00	—
			P# block of 14, Impt.	*1,050.*	
			Cancellations		
			Purple		+1.50
			Blue		+1.50
			Indigo		+3.00
			Town		+2.00
			Numeral		+7.50
O110	O9	6c	**brown**	100.00	40.00
			yellow brown	100.00	40.00
			dark brown	100.00	40.00
			On cover		300.00
			Block of 4	450.00	—
			P# block of 12, Impt.	*1,500.*	
			Cancellations		
			Purple		+6.00
			Magenta		+6.00
			Blue		+6.00
O111	O9	10c	**brown**	180.00	65.00
			yellow brown	180.00	65.00
			dark brown	180.00	65.00
			On cover		*750.00*
			Block of 4	900.00	—
			P# block of 12, Impt.	*3,150.*	
			Cancellations		
			Purple		+2.50
			Blue		+2.50
			Magenta		+5.00
			Town		+7.50
O112	O9	30c	**brown**	1,600.	325.00
			Block of 4	*8,000.*	
			Cancellations		
			Blue		+25.00
			Indigo		+25.00
			Town		+50.00
O113	O9	90c	**brown**	2,500.	325.00
			dark brown	2,500.	325.00
			Block of 4	*12,500.*	
			Cancellations		
			Purple		+25.00
			Blue		+25.00
			Town		+75.00

WAR

No.	Type	Denom.	Description	Unused	Used
O114	O10	1c	**rose red**	4.50	4.00
			rose	4.50	4.00
			dull rose red	4.50	4.00
			brown rose	4.50	4.00
			On cover		55.00
			Block of 4	20.00	—
			P# block of 12, Impt.	*140.00*	
			Never hinged	*200.00*	
			Cancellations		
			Purple		+.50
			Blue		+.50
			Town		+1.00
			Fort		+50.00
O115	O10	2c	**rose red**	7.00	3.50
			dark rose red	7.00	3.50
			dull vermilion	7.00	3.50
			On cover		40.00
			Block of 4	30.00	—
			P# block of 12, Impt.	*180.00*	
			Never hinged	*260.00*	
			Cancellations		
			Purple		+.50
			Blue		+.50
			Magenta		+.50
			Green		+35.00
			Town		+2.00
			Fort		+45.00
O116	O10	3c	**rose red**	7.00	1.50
			dull rose red	7.00	1.50
			On cover		35.00
			Block of 4	30.00	—
			P# block of 12, Impt.	*180.00*	
			Never hinged	*260.00*	
			Double transfer	11.00	5.00
			Plate flaw at upper left (32 R 20)	—	—
		a.	Imperf., pair	*1,000.*	
		b.	Double impression	*900.00*	
			Cancellations		
			Purple		+.50
			Violet		+.50
			Blue		+.50
			Ultramarine		+5.00
			Magenta		+1.00
			Red		+5.00
			Town		+1.00
			Fort		+45.00
O117	O10	6c	**rose red**	7.00	2.50
			dull rose red	7.00	2.50
			dull vermilion	—	—
			On cover		50.00
			Block of 4	30.00	—
			P# block of 12, Impt.	*180.00*	

Cancellations
Purple +.50
Blue +.50
Magenta +1.00
Brown +20.00
Town +1.00
Fort +45.00
Numeral +7.50

O118 O10 10c **rose red** 45.00 40.00
dull rose red 45.00 40.00
On cover —
Block of 4 200.00
P# block of 10, Impt. *650.00*

Cancellations
Violet +3.00
Town +5.00
Fort +75.00

O119 O10 12c **rose red** 35.00 11.00
dull rose red 35.00 11.00
brown rose 35.00 11.00
On cover —
Block of 4 150.00 —
P# block of 10, Impt. *450.00*

Cancellations
Purple +1.00
Violet +1.00
Red +10.00
Town +2.50
Fort +75.00

O120 O10 30c **rose red** 120.00 75.00
dull rose red 120.00 75.00
Block of 4 525.00 —
P# block of 10, Impt. *2,100.*

Cancellations
Violet +5.00
Town +10.00
Fort +125.00

SPECIAL PRINTINGS

Special printings of Official stamps were made in 1875 at the time the other Reprints, Re-issues and Special Printings were printed. They are ungummed. Though overprinted "SPECIMEN," these stamps are Special Printings, and they are not considered to be in the same category as the stamps listed in the Specimen section of this catalogue.

Although perforated, these stamps were sometimes (but not always) cut apart with scissors. As a result the perforations may be mutilated and the design damaged.

Number sold indicated in brackets.

All values exist imperforate.

Blocks of 4 are now listed. All are scarce, a few are rare. They will be valued when sufficient information has been received. Imprint and plate number strips or blocks are very scarce.

The "SEPCIMEN" error appears once on some panes of 100. The error was discovered and corrected part way through the printing. Blocks of 4 or larger with the "SEPCIMEN" error are rare and worth much more than the value of the individual stamps.

Printing flaws which resemble broken type (but are not) are commonly found on the SPECIMEN overprint on these and other overprinted stamps. The variety listed as a "small dotted i" is actually an "i"; it is not one of the printing flaws noted in the preceding sentence.

Printed by the Continental Bank Note Co.

Overprinted in Block Letters

1875 **Thin, hard white paper** ***Perf. 12***

Type D

AGRICULTURE

Carmine Overprint

O1S D 1c **yellow** (10,234) 16.00
Block of 4 *200.00*
a. "Sepcimen" error 1,250.
b. Small dotted "i" in "Specimen" 450.00
c. Horiz. ribbed paper (10,000) 21.00
Block of 4 *200.00*
O2S D 2c **yellow** (4,192) 30.00
Block of 4 *350.00*
a. "Sepcimen" error 1,500.
O3S D 3c **yellow** (389) 100.00
a. "Sepcimen" error *5,000.*
O4S D 6c **yellow** (373) 175.00
a. "Sepcimen" error *7,500.*
O5S D 10c **yellow** (390) 175.00
a. "Sepcimen" error *5,000.*
O6S D 12c **yellow** (379) 170.00
a. "Sepcimen" error *5,000.*
O7S D 15c **yellow** (370) 170.00
a. "Sepcimen" error *5,000.*
O8S D 24c **yellow** (352) 170.00
a. "Sepcimen" error *5,000.*
O9S D 30c **yellow** (354) 170.00
a. "Sepcimen" error *5,000.*

EXECUTIVE

Blue Overprint

O10S D 1c **carmine** (10,000) 16.00
Block of 4 *175.00*
a. Small dotted "i" in "Specimen" 350.00
b. Horiz. ribbed paper (10,000) 21.00
Block of 4 *190.00*
O11S D 2c **carmine** (7,430) 32.50
Block of 4 —
Foreign entry of 6c Agriculture —
O12S D 3c **carmine** (3,735) 37.50
Block of 4 —
O13S D 6c **carmine** (3,485) 37.50
Block of 4 —
O14S D 10c **carmine** (3,461) 37.50
Block of 4 —

INTERIOR

Blue Overprint

O15S D 1c **vermilion** (7,194) 32.50
Block of 4 —
P# block of 12, impt. —
O16S D 2c **vermilion** (1,263) 40.00
Block of 4 —
P# Block of 12, Impt. —
a. "Sepcimen" error *4,500.*
O17S D 3c **vermilion** (88) 700.00
O18S D 6c **vermilion** (83) 700.00
O19S D 10c **vermilion** (82) 700.00
O20S D 12c **vermilion** (75) 700.00
O21S D 15c **vermilion** (78) 700.00
O22S D 24c **vermilion** (77) 700.00
O23S D 30c **vermilion** (75) 700.00
O24S D 90c **vermilion** (77) 700.00

JUSTICE

Blue Overprint

O25S D 1c **purple** (10,000) 16.00
Block of 4 *150.00*
a. "Sepcimen" error 750.00
b. Small dotted "i" in "Specimen" 300.00
c. Horiz. ribbed paper (9,729) 21.00
Block of 4 *190.00*
O26S D 2c **purple** (3,395) 32.50
Block of 4 —
a. "Sepcimen" error 1,500.
O27S D 3c **purple** (178) 425.00
Plate scratches —
a. "Sepcimen" error *4,500.*
O28S D 6c **purple** (163) 425.00
O29S D 10c **purple** (163) 425.00
O30S D 12c **purple** (154) 425.00
a. "Sepcimen" error *5,000.*
O31S D 15c **purple** (157) 425.00
a. "Sepcimen" error *5,000.*
O32S D 24c **purple** (150) 450.00
a. "Sepcimen" error *5,000.*
O33S D 30c **purple** (150) 450.00
a. "Sepcimen" error *5,000.*
O34S D 90c **purple** (152) 450.00

NAVY

Carmine Overprint

O35S D 1c **ultramarine** (10,000) 21.00
Block of 4 *190.00*
a. "Sepcimen" error 900.00
O36S D 2c **ultramarine** (1,748) 37.50
Block of 4 *375.00*
a. "Sepcimen" error 1,500.
O37S D 3c **ultramarine** (126) 425.00
O38S D 6c **ultramarine** (116) 475.00
O39S D 7c **ultramarine** (501) 200.00
Block of 4 —
a. "Sepcimen" error 3,750.
O40S D 10c **ultramarine** (112) 475.00
a. "Sepcimen" error *5,500.*
O41S D 12c **ultramarine** (107) 425.00
Double transfer at left side, pos. 50 —
a. "Sepcimen" error *5,000.*
O42S D 15c **ultramarine** (107) 425.00
a. "Sepcimen" error *7,500.*
O43S D 24c **ultramarine** (106) 425.00
a. "Sepcimen" error *5,000.*
O44S D 30c **ultramarine** (104) 425.00
Double transfer —
a. "Sepcimen" error *5,500.*
O45S D 90c **ultramarine** (102) 425.00

POST OFFICE

Carmine Overprint

O47S D 1c **black** (6,015) 27.50
Block of 4 *300.00*
a. "Sepcimen" error 1,100.
b. Inverted overprint *1,100.*
O48S D 2c **black** (590) 75.00
Block of 4 —
a. "Sepcimen" error 2,100.
O49S D 3c **black** (91) 625.00
a. "Sepcimen" error —
O50S D 6c **black** (87) 600.00
O51S D 10c **black** (177) 375.00
a. "Sepcimen" error *5,250.*
O52S D 12c **black** (93) 550.00
O53S D 15c **black** (82) 650.00
a. "Sepcimen" error *5,250.*
O54S D 24c **black** (84) 575.00
a. "Sepcimen" error *5,250.*
O55S D 30c **black** (81) 575.00
O56S D 90c **black** (82) 575.00
a. "Sepcimen" error *12,500.*

STATE

Carmine Overprint

O57S D 1c **bluish green** (10,000) 16.00
Block of 4 *160.00*
a. "Sepcimen" error 500.00
b. Small dotted "i" in "Specimen" 425.00
c. Horiz. ribbed paper (10,000) 21.00
d. Double overprint —
Block of 4 —
O58S D 2c **bluish green** (5,145) 32.50
Block of 4 *350.00*
a. "Sepcimen" error 900.00
O59S D 3c **bluish green** (793) 60.00
Block of 4 —
a. "Sepcimen" error 3,500.
O60S D 6c **bluish green** (467) 130.00
a. "Sepcimen" error 4,250.
O61S D 7c **bluish green** (791) 65.00
Block of 4 —
a. "Sepcimen" error 3,500.
O62S D 10c **bluish green** (346) 250.00
Short transfer, pos. 34 —
a. "Sepcimen" error *7,500.*
O63S D 12c **bluish green** (280) 250.00
a. "Sepcimen" error *4,500.*
O64S D 15c **bluish green** (257) 250.00
O65S D 24c **bluish green** (253) 250.00
a. "Sepcimen" error *4,500.*
O66S D 30c **bluish green** (249) 250.00
a. "Sepcimen" error *6,000.*
O67S D 90c **bluish green** (245) 250.00
a. "Sepcimen" error *6,000.*
O68S D $2 **green & black** (32) *7,500.*
O69S D $5 **green & black** (12) *15,000.*
O70S D $10 **green & black** (8) *25,000.*
O71S D $20 **green & black** (7) *35,000.*

TREASURY

Blue Overprint

O72S D 1c **dark brown** (2,185) 30.00
Block of 4 *300.00*
Double transfer —
O73S D 2c **dark brown** (309) 145.00
Block of 4 —
O74S D 3c **dark brown** (84) 650.00
O75S D 6c **dark brown** (85) 575.00
O76S D 7c **dark brown** (198) 375.00
Block of 4 1,600.
P# block of 12, impt. 8,500.
O77S D 10c **dark brown** (82) 625.00
O78S D 12c **dark brown** (75) 650.00
O79S D 15c **dark brown** (75) 650.00
O80S D 24c **dark brown** (99) 525.00
O81S D 30c **dark brown** (74) 700.00
Short transfer at left top (pos. 95) (1) —
Short transfer at right top (pos. 45) (1) —
O82S D 90c **dark brown** (72) 700.00

WAR

Blue Overprint

O83S D 1c **deep rose** (9,610) 18.50
Block of 4 *185.00*
a. "Sepcimen" error 900.00
O84S D 2c **deep rose** (1,618) 37.50
Block of 4 *375.00*
a. "Sepcimen" error 1,600.
O85S D 3c **deep rose** (118) 450.00
a. "Sepcimen" error *5,000.*
O86S D 6c **deep rose** (111) 450.00
a. "Sepcimen" error *5,250.*
O87S D 7c **deep rose** (539) 100.00
Block of 4 *900.00*
a. "Sepcimen" error 3,000.
O88S D 10c **deep rose** (119) 425.00
a. "Sepcimen" error *5,250.*
O89S D 12c **deep rose** (105) 525.00
a. "Sepcimen" error *5,250.*
O90S D 15c **deep rose** (105) 525.00
a. "Sepcimen" error *5,250.*
O91S D 24c **deep rose** (106) 525.00
a. "Sepcimen" error *5,250.*
O92S D 30c **deep rose** (104) 525.00
a. "Sepcimen" error *5,250.*
O93S D 90c **deep rose** (106) 525.00
a. "Sepcimen" error *5,500.*

SOFT POROUS PAPER

EXECUTIVE

1881

Blue Overprint

O10xS D 1c **violet rose** (4,652) 60.00
Block of 4 *500.00*

NAVY

Carmine Overprint

O35xS D 1c **gray blue** (4,182) 70.00
deep blue 70.00
Block of 4 *500.00*
a. Double overprint 900.00

STATE

O57xS D 1c **yellow green** (1,672) 275.00
Block of 4 —

POSTAL SAVINGS MAIL

The Act of Congress, approved June 25, 1910, establishing postal savings depositories, provided:

"Sec. 2. That the Postmaster General is hereby directed to prepare and issue special stamps of the necessary denominations for use, in lieu of penalty or franked envelopes, in the transmittal of free mail resulting from the administration of this act."

The use of postal savings official stamps was discontinued by the Act of Congress, approved September 23, 1914. The unused stamps in the hands of postmasters were returned and destroyed.

O11

1910-11 Engr. Wmk. 191

O121 O11 2c **black,** *Dec. 22, 1910* 15.00 1.75
Never hinged 30.00
On cover 12.50
Block of 4 (2mm spacing) 67.50 10.00
Block of 4 (3mm spacing) 65.00 9.00
P# block of 6, Impt. & Star 325.00
Double transfer 20.00 3.50
O122 O11 50c **dark green,** *Feb. 1, 1911* 145.00 50.00
Never hinged 275.00
On cover 225.00
Block of 4 (2mm spacing) 625.00 250.00
Block of 4 (3mm spacing) 600.00 250.00
Margin block of 4, arrow 625.00
P# block of 6, Impt. & Star 2,400.
Never hinged *3,500.*
O123 O11 $1 **ultramarine,** *Feb. 1, 1911* 135.00 12.50
Never hinged 250.00
On cover 110.00
Block of 4 (2mm spacing) 600.00 65.00
Block of 4 (3mm spacing) 575.00 65.00
Margin block of 4, arrow 600.00
P# block of 6, Impt. & Star 2,200. —

Wmk. 190

O124 O11 1c **dark violet,** *Mar. 27, 1911* 8.00 1.50
Never hinged 15.00
On cover 15.00
Block of 4 (2mm spacing) 35.00 6.50
Block of 4 (3mm spacing) 32.50 6.25
P# block of 6, Impt. & Star 185.00
O125 O11 2c **black** 47.50 5.50
Never hinged 90.00
On cover 25.00
Block of 4 (2mm spacing) 210.00 25.00
Block of 4 (3mm spacing) 200.00 25.00
P# block of 6, Impt. & Star 675.00
Double transfer 52.50 6.50
O126 O11 10c **carmine,** *Feb. 1, 1911* 18.00 6.50
Never hinged 32.50
On cover 20.00
Block of 4 (2mm spacing) 75.00 30.00
Block of 4 (3mm spacing) 72.50 7.50
P# block of 6, Impt. & Star 370.00
Double transfer 24.00 3.00

Catalogue values for unused stamps in this section, from this point to the end, are for Never Hinged items.

From No. O127 onward, all official stamps are tagged unless noted.

OFFICIAL MAIL

O12

Designed by Bradbury Thompson

ENGRAVED

1983, Jan. 12-1985 Unwmk. *Perf. 11*

O127 O12 1c **red, blue & black** .20 .20
FDC, Washington, DC 1.00
P# block of 4, UL or UR .25
O128 O12 4c **red, blue & black** .20 .25
FDC, Washington, DC 1.00
P# block of 4, LR only .40
O129 O12 13c **red, blue & black** .45 .75
FDC, Washington, DC 1.00
P# block of 4, UR only 2.00
O129A O12 14c **red, blue & black,** *May 15, 1985* .45 .50
FDC, Washington, DC 1.00
Zip-copyright block of 6 2.90
O130 O12 17c **red, blue & black** .60 .40
FDC, Washington, DC 1.00
P# block of 4, LL only 3.00
O132 O12 $1 **red, blue & black** 2.00 1.00
FDC, Washington, DC 2.25
P# block of 4, UL only 9.50
O133 O12 $5 **red, blue & black** 9.00 9.00
FDC, Washington, DC 12.50
P# block of 4, LL only 42.50
Nos. O127-O133 (7) 12.90 12.10

No. O129A does not have a "c" after the "14."

COIL STAMPS

Perf. 10 Vert.

O135 O12 20c **red, blue & black** 1.75 2.00
FDC, Washington, DC 1.00
Pair 3.50 4.00
P# strip of 3, P# 1 12.50
P# strip of 5, P# 1 57.50
P# single, #1 — 16.00
a. Imperf., pair *2,000.*
O136 O12 22c **red, blue & blk,** *May 15, 1985* .80 *2.00*
FDC, Washington, DC 1.00
Pair 1.60 *4.00*
Dull finish gum *75.00*

Used Values of Nos. O135-O138, O140, etc., do not apply to copies removed from first day covers.

Inscribed: Postal Card Rate D

1985, Feb. 4 *Perf. 11*

O138 O12 (14c) **red, blue & black** 5.25 *5.00*
FDC, Washington, DC 1.00
P# block of 4, LR only 42.50 —

Frame line completely around the design — O13

Inscribed: No. O139, Domestic Letter Rate D; No. O140, Domestic Mail E.

COIL STAMPS

1985-88 Litho., Engr. (#O139) *Perf. 10 Vert.*

O138A O13 15c **red, blue & blk,** *June 11, 1988* .45 .50
FDC, Corpus Christi, TX 1.25
Pair .90 1.00
O138B O13 20c **red, blue & blk,** *May 19, 1988* .45 .30
FDC, Washington 1.25
Pair .90 .60
O139 O12 (22c) **red, blue & blk,** *Feb. 4* 5.25 3.00
FDC, Washington, DC 1.00
Pair 10.50 —
P# strip of 3, P# 1 32.50
P# strip of 5, P# 1 65.00
P# single, #1 — 32.50
O140 O13 (25c) **red, blue & black,** *Mar. 22, 1988* .75 *2.00*
FDC, Washington 1.25
Pair 1.50 —
O141 O13 25c **red, blue & blk,** *June 11, 1988* .65 .50
FDC, Corpus Christi, TX 1.25
Pair 1.30 1.00
a. Imperf., pair *1,750.* —
Nos. O138A-O141 (5) 7.55 *6.30*

First day cancellation was applied to 137,721 covers bearing Nos. O138A and O141.

Plates of 400 in four panes of 100.

1989, July 5 Litho. *Perf. 11*

O143 O13 1c **red, blue & black** .20 .20
FDC, Washington, DC 1.25

Type of 1985 and

O14

COIL STAMPS

1991 Litho. *Perf. 10 Vert.*

O144 O14 (29c) **red, blue & blk,** *Jan. 22* .75 .50
FDC, Washington, DC 1.25
Pair 1.50 —
O145 O13 29c **red, blue & blk,** *May 24* .65 .30
FDC, Seattle, WA 1.25
Pair 1.30 .60

Plates of 400 in four panes of 100.

1991-93 Litho. *Perf. 11*

O146 O13 4c **red, blue & blk,** *Apr. 6* .20 *.30*
FDC, Oklahoma City, OK 1.25
O146A O13 10c **red, blue & black,** *Oct. 19, 1993* .25 *.30*
FDC, Washington, DC 1.25
O147 O13 19c **red, blue & blk,** *May 24* .40 *.50*
FDC, Seattle, WA 1.25
O148 O13 23c **red, blue & blk,** *May 24* .45 .30
FDC, Seattle, WA 1.25
Horiz. pair with full vert. gutter between —
Vert. pair with full horiz. gutter between —
a. Imperf., pair *100.00*
O151 O13 $1 **red, blue & black,** *Sept. 1993* 2.00 .75
Nos. O146-O151 (5) 3.30 2.15

COIL STAMPS

Inscribed: No. O152, For U.S. addresses only G.

Perf. 9.8 Vert.

O152 O14 (32c) **red, blue & black,** *Dec. 13, 1994* .65 —
FDC, Washington, DC 1.25
Pair 1.30 —
O153 O13 32c **red, blue & black,** *May 9, 1995* .65 .30
FDC, Washington, DC 1.25
Pair 1.30 —

Nos. O146A, O151, O153 have a line of microscopic text below the eagle.

1995, May 9 Litho. *Perf. 11.2*

O154 O13 1c **red, blue & black,** untagged .20 .20
FDC, Washington, DC 1.25
Pair .20 —
O155 O13 20c **red, blue & black** .45 .30
FDC, Washington, DC 1.25
Pair .90 —
O156 O13 23c **red, blue & black** .50 .30
FDC, Washington, DC 1.25
Pair 1.00 —

Nos. O154-O156 have a line of microscopic text below the eagle.

COIL STAMP

1999, Oct. 8 Litho. *Perf. 9¾ Vert.*

O157 O13 33c **red, blue & black** .65 —
FDC, Washington, DC 1.25
Pair 1.30 —

No. O157 has a line of microscopic text below the eagle.

Type of 1985
COIL STAMP

2001, Feb. 27 Litho. Tagged *Perf. 9¾ Vert.*

O158 O13 34c **red, blue & black** .65 .30
FDC, Washington, DC 1.25
Pair 1.30 —

Type of 1985
COIL STAMP

2002, Aug. 2 Photo. Tagged *Perf. 10 Vert.*

O159 O13 37c **red, blue & black** .70 .35
First day cover, Washington, DC 1.25
First day cover, any other city 1.25
Pair 1.40 —
P# strip of 5, P#S111 5.25 —
P# single, same # — .70

NEWSPAPER AND PERIODICAL STAMPS

First issued in September 1865 for prepayment of postage on bulk shipments of newspapers and periodicals. From 1875 on, the stamps were affixed to pages of receipt books, sometimes canceled, and retained by the post office.

Virtually all used stamps of Nos. PR1-PR4 are canceled by blue brush strokes. All are rare. Most used stamps of Nos. PR9-PR32, PR57-PR79 and PR81-PR89 are pen canceled (or uncanceled). Handstamp cancellations on any of these issues are rare and sell for much more than catalogue values which are for pen-canceled examples. Used values for Nos. PR102-PR125 are for stamps with handstamp cancellations.

Discontinued on July 1, 1898.

Washington — N1

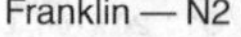

Franklin — N2

Lincoln — N3

(Illustrations N1, N2 and N3 are half the size of the stamps.)

Printed by the National Bank Note Co.
Plates of 20 subjects in two panes of 10 each.

Typographed and Embossed

1865 **Unwmk.** ***Perf. 12***

Thin hard paper, without gum

Size of design: 51x95mm

Colored Border

No.	Design	Description	Unused	Used
PR1	N1	5c **dark blue**	525.00	—
		blue	525.00	—
		Block of 4	2,500.	—
a.		5c **light blue**	550.00	—
PR2	N2	10c **blue green**	220.00	—
a.		10c **green**	220.00	—
		Block of 4	950.00	—
b.		Pelure paper	250.00	—
PR3	N3	25c **orange red**	280.00	—
		Block of 4	1,275.	—
a.		25c **carmine red**	300.00	—
		Block of 4	1,350.	—
b.		Pelure paper	280.00	

White Border

Yellowish paper

No.	Design	Description	Unused	Used
PR4	N1	5c **light blue**	150.00	—
		blue	150.00	—
a.		5c **dark blue**	150.00	—
		Block of 4	775.00	
b.		Pelure paper	150.00	—

REPRINTS of 1865 ISSUE

Printed by the National Bank Note Co.

1875 ***Perf. 12***

Hard white paper, without gum

5c White Border, 10c and 25c Colored Border

No.	Design	Description	Unused
PR5	N1	5c **dull blue** *(10,000)*	135.00
		dark blue	135.00
		Block of 4	600.00
a.		Printed on both sides	*5,750.*
PR6	N2	10c **dark bluish green** *(7765)*	150.00
		deep green	150.00
		Block of 4	650.00
a.		Printed on both sides	*3,000.*
PR7	N3	25c **dark carmine** *(6684)*	185.00
		dark carmine red	185.00
		Block of 4	850.00

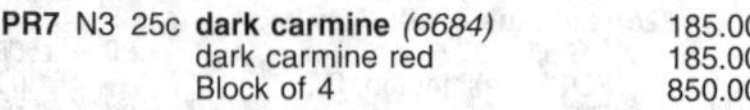

750 examples of each value, which were remainders from the regular issue, were sold as reprints because of delays in obtaining Nos. PR5-PR7. These remainders cannot be distinguished from Nos. PR2-PR4, and are not included in the reprint quantities.

On No. PR5, there is no thin line of color in the second white area on each side of the stamp. On No. PR8, there is a thin line of color in this area.

#PR5

#PR8

Printed by the American Bank Note Co.
Soft porous paper, without gum
White Border

1881

No.	Design	Description	Unused
PR8	N1	5c **dark blue** (5645)	400.00
		Block of 4	2,000.

The Continental Bank Note Co. made another special printing from new plates, which did not have the colored border. These exist imperforate and perforated, but they were not regularly issued.

Statue of Freedom on Capitol Dome, by Thomas Crawford — N4

"Justice" — N5

Ceres — N6

"Victory" — N7

Clio — N8

Minerva — N9

Vesta — N10

"Peace" — N11

"Commerce" — N12

Hebe — N13

Indian Maiden — N14

Printed by the Continental Bank Note Co.
Plates of 100 subjects in two panes of 50 each
Size of design: 24x35mm

1875, Jan. 1 **Engr.** ***Perf. 12***

Thin hard paper

No.	Design	Description	Unused	Used
PR9	N4	2c **black**	75.00	25.00
		gray black	75.00	25.00
		greenish black	75.00	25.00
		Block of 4	350.00	160.00
PR10	N4	3c **black**	80.00	27.50
		gray black	80.00	27.50
		Block of 4	375.00	140.00
PR11	N4	4c **black**	80.00	25.00
		gray black	80.00	25.00
		greenish black	80.00	25.00
		Block of 4	360.00	
PR12	N4	6c **black**	100.00	27.50
		gray black	100.00	27.50
		greenish black	100.00	27.50
		Block of 4	450.00	
PR13	N4	8c **black**	125.00	40.00
		gray black	125.00	40.00
		greenish black	125.00	40.00
PR14	N4	9c **black**	240.00	87.50
		gray black	240.00	87.50
		Double transfer at top	275.00	100.00
PR15	N4	10c **black**	140.00	32.50
		gray black	140.00	32.50
		greenish black	140.00	32.50
		Block of 4	675.00	
PR16	N5	12c **rose**	325.00	82.50
		pale rose	325.00	82.50
PR17	N5	24c **rose**	375.00	100.00
		pale rose	375.00	100.00
PR18	N5	36c **rose**	450.00	110.00
		pale rose	450.00	110.00
PR19	N5	48c **rose**	750.00	175.00
		pale rose	750.00	175.00
PR20	N5	60c **rose**	550.00	100.00
		pale rose	550.00	100.00
PR21	N5	72c **rose**	900.00	230.00
		pale rose	900.00	230.00
PR22	N5	84c **rose**	1,200.	330.00
		pale rose	1,200.	330.00
PR23	N5	96c **rose**	950.00	225.00
		pale rose	950.00	225.00

No.	Type	Denom.	Color	Unused	Used
PR24	N6	$1.92	**dark brown**	1,100.	300.00
PR25	N7	$3	**vermilion**	1,400.	325.00
PR26	N8	$6	**ultramarine**	2,100.	475.00
			dull ultramarine	2,100.	475.00
PR27	N9	$9	**yellow orange**	2,750.	525.00
PR28	N10	$12	**blue green**	3,500.	675.00
PR29	N11	$24	**dark gray violet**	3,750.	700.00
PR30	N12	$36	**brown rose**	3,850.	850.00
PR31	N13	$48	**red brown**	4,500.	1,000.
PR32	N14	$60	**violet**	5,250.	1,100.

SPECIAL PRINTING of 1875 ISSUE

Printed by the Continental Bank Note Co.
Hard white paper, without gum

1875 *Perf. 12*

No.	Type	Denom.	Color	Unused	Used
PR33	N4	2c	**gray black** *(5,000)*	475.00	
a.			Horizontally ribbed paper (10,000)	475.00	
			Block of 4	2,400.	
PR34	N4	3c	**gray black** *(5,000)*	525.00	
			Block of 4	2,750.	
a.			Horizontally ribbed paper (1,952)	550.00	
PR35	N4	4c	**gray black** *(4451)*	600.00	
			Block of 4	3,150.	
a.			Horizontally ribbed paper	650.00	
PR36	N4	6c	**gray black** *(2348)*	675.00	
PR37	N4	8c	**gray black** *(1930)*	750.00	
PR38	N4	9c	**gray black** *(1795)*	850.00	
PR39	N4	10c	**gray black** *(1499)*	1,050.	
a.			Horizontally ribbed paper	—	
PR40	N5	12c	**pale rose** *(1313)*	1,250.	
PR41	N5	24c	**pale rose** *(411)*	1,800.	
PR42	N5	36c	**pale rose** *(330)*	2,400.	
PR43	N5	48c	**pale rose** *(268)*	2,800.	
PR44	N5	60c	**pale rose** *(222)*	3,250.	
PR45	N5	72c	**pale rose** *(174)*	3,750.	
PR46	N5	84c	**pale rose** *(164)*	*4,000.*	
PR47	N5	96c	**pale rose** *(141)*	*6,250.*	
PR48	N6	$1.92	**dark brown** *(41)*	*17,500.*	
PR49	N7	$3	**vermilion** *(20)*	*45,000.*	
PR50	N8	$6	**ultramarine** *(14)*	*80,000.*	
PR51	N9	$9	**yellow orange** *(4)*	*115,000.*	
PR52	N10	$12	**blue green** *(5)*	*115,000.*	
PR53	N11	$24	**dark gray violet** *(2)*	—	
PR54	N12	$36	**brown rose** *(2)*	*250,000.*	
PR55	N13	$48	**red brown** *(1)*	—	
PR56	N14	$60	**violet** *(1)*	—	

No. PR54 is valued in the grade of fine. Although two stamps were sold, only one is currently recorded.

All values of this issue, Nos. PR33 to PR56, exist imperforate but were not regularly issued. Value, set $50,000.

Numbers in parenthesis are quantities sold.

The existence of No. PR39a has been questioned by specialists. The editors would like to see evidence of its existence.

Printed by the American Bank Note Co.
Soft porous paper

1879 **Unwmk.** *Perf. 12*

No.	Type	Denom.	Color	Unused	Used
PR57	N4	2c	**black**	35.00	6.50
			gray black	35.00	6.50
			greenish black	35.00	6.50
			Block of 4	150.00	
			Double transfer at top	40.00	12.00
			Cracked plate	—	—
PR58	N4	3c	**black**	40.00	8.00
			gray black	40.00	8.00
			intense black	40.00	8.00
			Block of 4	185.00	
			Double transfer at top	45.00	12.50
PR59	N4	4c	**black**	40.00	8.00
			gray black	40.00	8.00
			intense black	40.00	8.00
			greenish black	40.00	8.00
			Block of 4	185.00	
			Double transfer at top	40.00	12.50
PR60	N4	6c	**black**	75.00	16.50
			gray black	75.00	16.50
			intense black	75.00	16.50
			greenish black	75.00	16.50
			Block of 4	350.00	
			Double transfer at top	80.00	22.50
PR61	N4	8c	**black**	75.00	16.50
			gray black	75.00	16.50
			greenish black	75.00	16.50
			Block of 4	350.00	
			Double transfer at top	80.00	22.50
PR62	N4	10c	**black**	75.00	16.50
			gray black	75.00	16.50
			greenish black	75.00	16.50
			Block of 4	350.00	
			Double transfer at top	80.00	
PR63	N5	12c	**red**	375.00	65.00
			Block of 4	1,750.	
PR64	N5	24c	**red**	375.00	65.00
			Block of 4	1,750.	
PR65	N5	36c	**red**	750.00	185.00
			Block of 4	3,500.	
PR66	N5	48c	**red**	700.00	140.00
PR67	N5	60c	**red**	575.00	120.00
			Block of 4	2,600.	
a.			Imperf., pair	*3,500.*	
PR68	N5	72c	**red**	1,150.	230.00
PR69	N5	84c	**red**	1,150.	175.00
			Block of 4	—	
PR70	N5	96c	**red**	850.00	125.00
			Block of 4	3,900.	
PR71	N6	$1.92	**pale brown**	450.00	105.00
			brown	450.00	105.00
			Block of 4	2,000.	
			Cracked plate	500.00	
PR72	N7	$3	**red vermilion**	500.00	115.00
			Block of 4	2,250.	
PR73	N8	$6	**blue**	950.00	175.00
			ultramarine	950.00	175.00
PR74	N9	$9	**orange**	650.00	125.00
PR75	N10	$12	**yellow green**	750.00	160.00
PR76	N11	$24	**dark violet**	800.00	200.00
PR77	N12	$36	**Indian red**	850.00	220.00
PR78	N13	$48	**yellow brown**	900.00	300.00
PR79	N14	$60	**purple**	850.00	280.00
			bright purple	850.00	280.00

See Die and Plate Proofs for other imperfs. on stamp paper.

SPECIAL PRINTING of 1879 ISSUE

Printed by the American Bank Note Co.

1883

No.	Type	Denom.	Color	Unused	Used
PR80	N4	2c	**intense black** (4,514)	1,050.	
			Block of 4	4,750.	

Printed by the American Bank Note Co.

1885, July 1 **Unwmk.** *Perf. 12*

No.	Type	Denom.	Color	Unused	Used
PR81	N4	1c	**black**	45.00	7.50
			gray black	45.00	7.50
			intense black	45.00	7.50
			Block of 4	200.00	
			Double transfer at top	47.50	11.00
PR82	N5	12c	**carmine**	130.00	18.00
			deep carmine	130.00	18.00
			rose carmine	130.00	18.00
			Block of 4	625.00	
PR83	N5	24c	**carmine**	130.00	20.00
			deep carmine	130.00	20.00
			rose carmine	130.00	20.00
			Block of 4	625.00	
PR84	N5	36c	**carmine**	175.00	32.50
			deep carmine	175.00	32.50
			rose carmine	175.00	32.50
			Block of 4	800.00	
PR85	N5	48c	**carmine**	250.00	47.50
			deep carmine	250.00	47.50
			Block of 4	1,100.	
PR86	N5	60c	**carmine**	330.00	70.00
			deep carmine	330.00	70.00
			Block of 4	1,500.	
PR87	N5	72c	**carmine**	330.00	75.00
			deep carmine	330.00	75.00
			rose carmine	330.00	75.00
			Block of 4	1,500.	
PR88	N5	84c	**carmine**	650.00	175.00
			rose carmine	650.00	175.00
			Block of 4	3,000.	
PR89	N5	96c	**carmine**	550.00	135.00
			rose carmine	550.00	135.00
			Block of 4	2,500.	

See Die and Plate Proofs for imperfs. on stamp paper.

Printed by the Bureau of Engraving and Printing

1894 **Unwmk.** *Perf. 12*

Soft wove paper

No.	Type	Denom.	Color	Unused	Used
PR90	N4	1c	**intense black**	275.00	*600.00*
			Block of 4	1,200.	
			Double transfer at top	300.00	
PR91	N4	2c	**intense black**	300.00	
			Block of 4	1,300.	
			Double transfer at top	325.00	
PR92	N4	4c	**intense black**	350.00	
			Block of 4	1,600.	
PR93	N4	6c	**intense black**	4,250.	
			Block of 4	—	
PR94	N4	10c	**intense black**	800.00	
			Block of 4	3,750.	
PR95	N5	12c	**pink**	2,000.	*1,500.*
			Block of 4	9,250.	
PR96	N5	24c	**pink**	2,500.	*1,750.*
			Block of 4	11,000.	
PR97	N5	36c	**pink**	*50,000.*	
			Block of 4	—	
PR98	N5	60c	**pink**	*60,000.*	*7,500.*
			Block of 4	—	
PR99	N5	96c	**pink**	*50,000.*	
PR100	N7	$3	**scarlet**	*60,000.*	
			Block of 4	—	
PR101	N8	$6	**pale blue**	*60,000.*	—

Nos. PR97-PR100 unused are valued in the grade of fine-very fine.

Nos. PR95-PR96, PR98 used are valued with fine centering and small faults.

Statue of Freedom — N15

N16

N17

N18

N19

N20

N21

N22

1895, Feb. 1 **Unwmk.** *Perf. 12*

Size of designs: 1c-50c, 21x34mm
$2-$100, 24x35mm

No.	Type	Denom.	Color	Unused	Used
PR102	N15	1c	**black**	135.00	20.00
			Never hinged	270.00	
			Block of 4	625.00	90.00
PR103	N15	2c	**black**	135.00	20.00
			gray black	135.00	20.00
			Never hinged	270.00	
			Block of 4	625.00	—
			Double transfer at top	150.00	—
PR104	N15	5c	**black**	200.00	35.00
			gray black	200.00	35.00
			Never hinged	400.00	
			Block of 4	900.00	
PR105	N15	10c	**black**	400.00	80.00
			Never hinged	800.00	
			Block of 4	1,700.	
PR106	N16	25c	**carmine**	550.00	90.00
			Never hinged	1,100.	
			Block of 4	2,500.	
PR107	N16	50c	**carmine**	1,250.	200.00
			Never hinged	2,250.	
			Block of 4	5,700.	
PR108	N17	$2	**scarlet**	1,500.	200.00
			Never hinged	2,750.	
PR109	N18	$5	**ultramarine**	1,750.	300.00
			Never hinged	3,250.	
PR110	N19	$10	**green**	2,250.	350.00
			Never hinged	4,000.	
PR111	N20	$20	**slate**	2,500.	600.00
			Never hinged	4,500.	
PR112	N21	$50	**dull rose**	2,500.	500.00
			Never hinged	4,500.	
PR113	N22	$100	**purple**	3,000.	750.00
			Never hinged	5,500.	

Nos. PR102-PR113 were printed from plates with arrows in the top, bottom and side margins, but no guidelines between the stamps.

1895-97 **Wmk. 191** *Perf. 12*

No.	Type	Denom.	Color	Unused	Used
PR114	N15	1c	**black,** *Jan. 11, 1896*	6.50	7.50
			gray black	6.50	7.50
			Never hinged	12.50	
			Block of 4	27.50	—
PR115	N15	2c	**black,** *Nov. 21, 1895*	6.50	7.50
			gray black	12.50	7.50
			Never hinged	11.25	
			Block of 4	27.50	—
PR116	N15	5c	**black,** *Feb. 12, 1896*	10.00	10.00
			gray black	10.00	10.00
			Never hinged	18.50	
			Block of 4	45.00	—
PR117	N15	10c	**black,** *Sept. 13, 1895*	7.50	7.50
			gray black	7.50	7.50
			Never hinged	15.00	
			Block of 4	32.50	—
PR118	N16	25c	**carmine,** *Oct. 11, 1895*	12.50	18.00
			lilac rose	12.50	18.00

			Never hinged	25.00	
			Block of 4	55.00	—
PR119	N16	50c	**carmine,** *Sept. 19, 1895*	15.00	20.00
			rose carmine	15.00	20.00
			lilac rose	15.00	20.00
			Never hinged	30.00	
			Block of 4	65.00	—
PR120	N17	$2	**scarlet,** *Jan. 23, 1897*	20.00	32.50
			scarlet vermilion	20.00	32.50
			Never hinged	40.00	
			Block of 4	87.50	—
PR121	N18	$5	**dark blue,** *Jan. 16, 1896*	35.00	45.00
			Never hinged	70.00	
			Block of 4	160.00	
a.			$5 light blue	190.00	110.00
			Never hinged	380.00	
			Block of 4	*800.00*	*700.00*
			Never hinged	*1,550.*	
PR122	N19	$10	**green,** *Mar. 5, 1896*	35.00	45.00
			Never hinged	70.00	
			Block of 4	160.00	—
PR123	N20	$20	**slate,** *Jan. 27, 1896*	37.50	50.00
			Never hinged	75.00	
			Block of 4	170.00	—
PR124	N21	$50	**dull rose,** *July 31, 1897*	50.00	60.00
			Never hinged	100.00	
			Block of 4	220.00	
PR125	N22	$100	**purple,** *Jan. 23, 1896*	55.00	75.00
			Never hinged	110.00	
			Block of 4	240.00	
			Nos. PR114-PR125 (12)	290.50	378.00
			Nos. PR114-PR125, never hinged	578.50	

Nos. PR114-PR125 were printed from the original plates with guide lines added in November 1895. Top and bottom plate strips and blocks of Nos. PR114-PR119 exist both with and without vertical guidelines.

In 1899 the Government sold 26,989 sets of these stamps but, as the stock of high values was not sufficient to make up the required number, an additional printing was made of the $5, $10, $20, $50 and $100. These are virtually indistinguishable from earlier printings.

POSTAL NOTE STAMPS

Postal note stamps were issued to supplement the regular money order service. They were a means of sending amounts under $1. One or two Postal note stamps, totaling 1c to 99c, were affixed to United States Postal Notes and canceled by the clerk. The stamps were on the second of three parts, the one retained by the post office redeeming the Postal Note. They were discontinued March 31, 1951.

MO1

ROTARY PRESS PRINTING

1945, Feb. 1 **Unwmk.** ***Perf. 11x10½***

PN1	MO1	1c	**black** (155950-155951)	.20	.20
PN2	MO1	2c	**black** (156003-156004)	.20	.20
PN3	MO1	3c	**black** (156062-156063)	.20	.20
PN4	MO1	4c	**black** (156942-156943)	.25	.20
PN5	MO1	5c	**black** (156261-156262)	.35	.20
PN6	MO1	6c	**black** (156064-156065)	.40	.20
PN7	MO1	7c	**black** (156075-156076)	.55	.20
PN8	MO1	8c	**black** (156077-156078)	.65	.20
PN9	MO1	9c	**black** (156251-156252)	.75	.20
PN10	MO1	10c	**black** (156274-156275)	.85	.20
PN11	MO1	20c	**black** (156276-156277)	1.75	.20
PN12	MO1	30c	**black** (156303-156304)	2.25	.20
PN13	MO1	40c	**black** (156283-156284)	2.75	.20
PN14	MO1	50c	**black** (156322-156323)	3.25	.20
PN15	MO1	60c	**black** (156324-156325)	4.25	.20
PN16	MO1	70c	**black** (156344-156345)	5.25	.20
PN17	MO1	80c	**black** (156326-156327)	6.00	.20
PN18	MO1	90c	**black** (156352-156353)	6.75	.20
			Nos. PN1-PN18 (18)	36.65	3.60

Blocks of four and plate number blocks of four are valued at 4 and 15 times the unused single value.

Postal note stamps exist on postal note cards with first day cancellation.

Numbers in parentheses are plate Nos.

PARCEL POST STAMPS

The Act of Congress approved Aug. 24, 1912, created postage rates on 4th class mail weighing 4 ounces or less at 1 cent per ounce or fraction. On mail over 4 ounces, the rate was by the pound. These rates were to be prepaid by distinctive postage stamps. Under this provision, the Post Office Department prepared 12 parcel post and 5 parcel post due stamps, usable only on parcel post packages starting Jan. 1, 1913. Other stamps were not usable on parcel post starting on that date.

Beginning on Nov. 27, 1912, the stamps were shipped to post offices offering parcel post service. Approximate shipping dates were: 1c, 2c, 5c, 25c, 1c due, 5c due, Nov. 27; 10c, 2c due, Dec. 9; 4c, 10c due, Dec. 12; 15c, 20c, 25c due, Dec. 16; 75c, Dec. 18. There was no prohibition on sale of the stamps prior to Jan. 1, 1913. Undoubtedly many were used on 4th class mail in Dec. 1912. Fourth class mail was expanded by adding former 2nd and 3rd class categories and was renamed "parcel post" effective Jan. 1, 1913. Normally 4th class (parcel post) mail did not receive a dated cancel unless a special service was involved. Small pieces, such as samples, are known with 1st class cancels.

With the approval of the Interstate Commerce Commission, the Postmaster General directed, in Order No. 7241 dated June 26, 1913, and effective July 1, 1913, that regular postage stamps should be valid on parcels. Parcel post stamps then became usable as regular stamps.

Parcel post and parcel post due stamps remained on sale, but no further printings were made. Remainders, consisting of 3,510,345 of the 75c, were destroyed in Sept. 1921.

The 20c was the first government-issued postage stamp of any country to show an airplane.

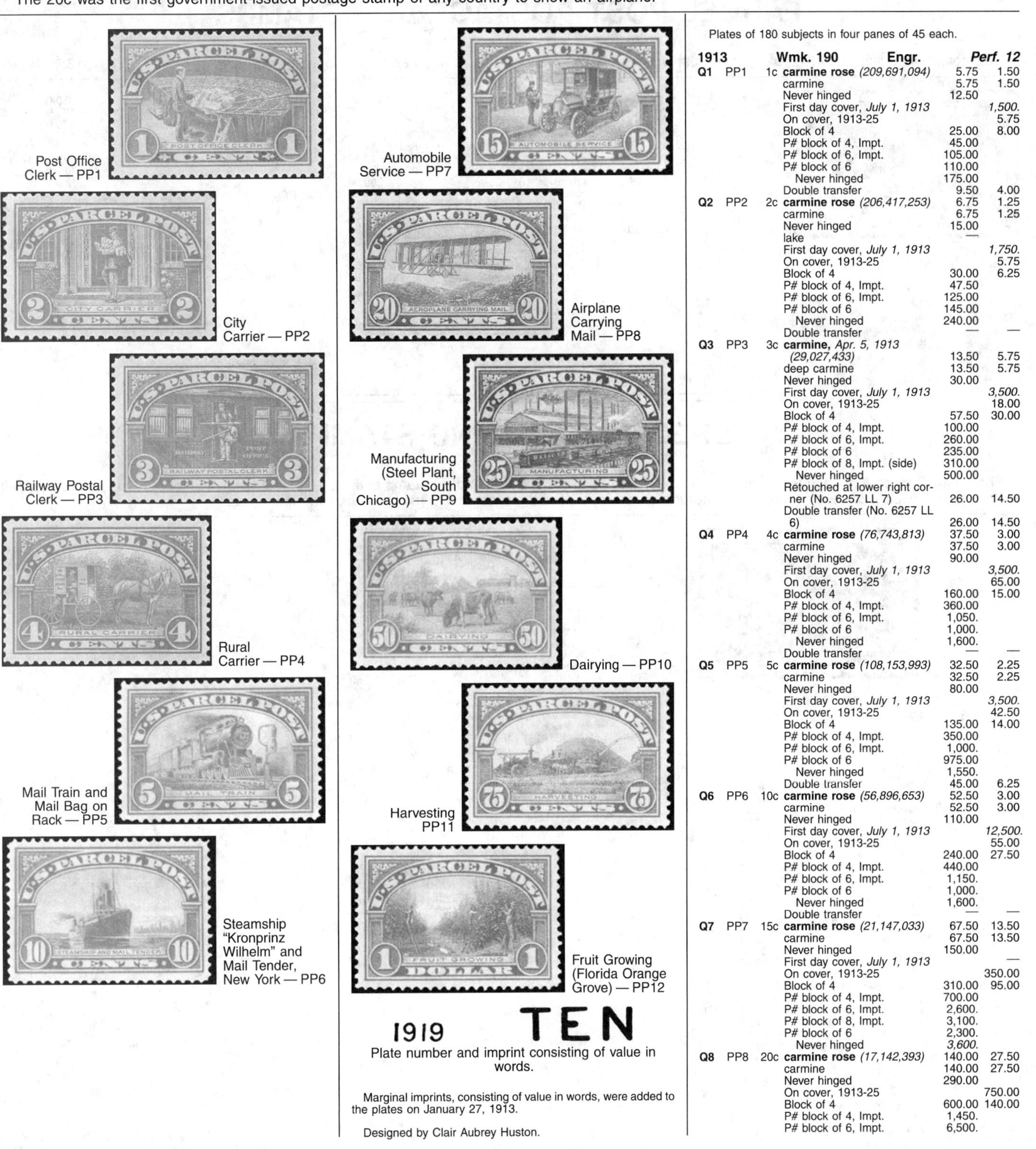

Post Office Clerk — PP1

City Carrier — PP2

Railway Postal Clerk — PP3

Rural Carrier — PP4

Mail Train and Mail Bag on Rack — PP5

Steamship "Kronprinz Wilhelm" and Mail Tender, New York — PP6

Automobile Service — PP7

Airplane Carrying Mail — PP8

Manufacturing (Steel Plant, South Chicago) — PP9

Dairying — PP10

Harvesting PP11

Fruit Growing (Florida Orange Grove) — PP12

Plate number and imprint consisting of value in words.

Marginal imprints, consisting of value in words, were added to the plates on January 27, 1913.

Designed by Clair Aubrey Huston.

Plates of 180 subjects in four panes of 45 each.

1913			Wmk. 190 Engr.		*Perf. 12*
Q1	PP1	1c	**carmine rose** *(209,691,094)*	5.75	1.50
			carmine	5.75	1.50
			Never hinged	12.50	
			First day cover, *July 1, 1913*		*1,500.*
			On cover, 1913-25		5.75
			Block of 4	25.00	8.00
			P# block of 4, Impt.	45.00	
			P# block of 6, Impt.	105.00	
			P# block of 6	110.00	
			Never hinged	175.00	
			Double transfer	9.50	4.00
Q2	PP2	2c	**carmine rose** *(206,417,253)*	6.75	1.25
			carmine	6.75	1.25
			Never hinged	15.00	
			lake	—	
			First day cover, *July 1, 1913*		*1,750.*
			On cover, 1913-25		5.75
			Block of 4	30.00	6.25
			P# block of 4, Impt.	47.50	
			P# block of 6, Impt.	125.00	
			P# block of 6	145.00	
			Never hinged	240.00	
			Double transfer	—	—
Q3	PP3	3c	**carmine,** *Apr. 5, 1913 (29,027,433)*	13.50	5.75
			deep carmine	13.50	5.75
			Never hinged	30.00	
			First day cover, *July 1, 1913*		*3,500.*
			On cover, 1913-25		18.00
			Block of 4	57.50	30.00
			P# block of 4, Impt.	100.00	
			P# block of 6, Impt.	260.00	
			P# block of 6	235.00	
			P# block of 8, Impt. (side)	310.00	
			Never hinged	500.00	
			Retouched at lower right corner (No. 6257 LL 7)	26.00	14.50
			Double transfer (No. 6257 LL 6)	26.00	14.50
Q4	PP4	4c	**carmine rose** *(76,743,813)*	37.50	3.00
			carmine	37.50	3.00
			Never hinged	90.00	
			First day cover, *July 1, 1913*		*3,500.*
			On cover, 1913-25		65.00
			Block of 4	160.00	15.00
			P# block of 4, Impt.	360.00	
			P# block of 6, Impt.	1,050.	
			P# block of 6	1,000.	
			Never hinged	1,600.	
			Double transfer	—	—
Q5	PP5	5c	**carmine rose** *(108,153,993)*	32.50	2.25
			carmine	32.50	2.25
			Never hinged	80.00	
			First day cover, *July 1, 1913*		*3,500.*
			On cover, 1913-25		42.50
			Block of 4	135.00	14.00
			P# block of 4, Impt.	350.00	
			P# block of 6, Impt.	1,000.	
			P# block of 6	975.00	
			Never hinged	1,550.	
			Double transfer	45.00	6.25
Q6	PP6	10c	**carmine rose** *(56,896,653)*	52.50	3.00
			carmine	52.50	3.00
			Never hinged	110.00	
			First day cover, *July 1, 1913*		*12,500.*
			On cover, 1913-25		55.00
			Block of 4	240.00	27.50
			P# block of 4, Impt.	440.00	
			P# block of 6, Impt.	1,150.	
			P# block of 6	1,000.	
			Never hinged	1,600.	
			Double transfer	—	—
Q7	PP7	15c	**carmine rose** *(21,147,033)*	67.50	13.50
			carmine	67.50	13.50
			Never hinged	150.00	
			First day cover, *July 1, 1913*		—
			On cover, 1913-25		350.00
			Block of 4	310.00	95.00
			P# block of 4, Impt.	700.00	
			P# block of 6, Impt.	2,600.	
			P# block of 8, Impt.	3,100.	
			P# block of 6	2,300.	
			Never hinged	*3,600.*	
Q8	PP8	20c	**carmine rose** *(17,142,393)*	140.00	27.50
			carmine	140.00	27.50
			Never hinged	290.00	
			On cover, 1913-25		750.00
			Block of 4	600.00	140.00
			P# block of 4, Impt.	1,450.	
			P# block of 6, Impt.	6,500.	

P# block of 8, Impt. (side) 7,000.
P# block of 6 6,500.
Never hinged *10,000.*
Q9 PP9 25c **carmine rose** *(21,940,653)* 67.50 7.50
carmine 67.50 7.50
Never hinged 150.00
On cover, 1913-25 300.00
Block of 4 310.00 55.00
P# block of 6, Impt. 2,700.
P# block of 8, Impt. (side) 3,500.
P# block of 6 2,400.
Never hinged *3,850.*
Q10 PP10 50c **carmine rose,** *Mar. 15, 1913 (2,117,793)* 280.00 45.00
carmine 280.00 45.00
Never hinged 600.00
On cover, 1913-25 —
Block of 4 1,275. 300.00
P# block of 4, Impt. 1,950.
Never hinged 3,000.
P# block of 6, Impt. *22,500.*
Never hinged *30,000.*
Q11 PP11 75c **carmine rose** *(2,772,615)* 95.00 35.00
carmine 95.00 35.00
Never hinged 200.00
On cover, 1913-25 —
Block of 4 425.00 200.00
P# block of 6, Impt. 4,000.
P# block of 8, Impt. (side) 3,600.
P# block of 6 3,000.
Never hinged *4,500.*
Q12 PP12 $1 **carmine rose,** *Jan. 3, 1913 (1,053,273)* 350.00 40.00
carmine 350.00 40.00
Never hinged 750.00
On cover, 1913-25 1,250.
Block of 4 1,550. 200.00
P# block of 6, Impt. *20,000.*
Never hinged *29,000.*
P# block of 8, Impt. (side) *21,000.*
P# block of 6 *18,000.*
Nos. Q1-Q12 (12) 1,148. 185.25
Nos. Q1-Q12, never hinged 2,478.

The 1c, 2c, 4c and 5c are known in parcel post usage postmarked Jan. 1, 1913.

PARCEL POST POSTAGE DUE STAMPS

See notes preceding Scott No. Q1. Parcel Post Due stamps were allowed to be used as regular postage due stamps from July 1, 1913.

PPD1

Designed by Clair Aubrey Huston

Plates of 180 subjects in four panes of 45

1913 Wmk. 190 Engr. *Perf. 12*
JQ1 PPD1 1c **dark green** (7,322,400) 11.00 4.50
yellowish green 11.00 4.50
Never hinged 25.00
On cover, 1913-25 150.00
Block of 4 50.00 35.00
P# block of 6 550.00
Never hinged 875.00
JQ2 PPD1 2c **dark green** (3,132,000) 85.00 17.50
yellowish green 85.00 17.50
Never hinged 200.00
On cover, 1913-25 200.00
Block of 4 375.00 125.00
P# block of 6 *3,750.*
Never hinged *6,000.*
JQ3 PPD1 5c **dark green** (5,840,100) 15.00 5.50
yellowish green 15.00 5.50
Never hinged 32.50
On cover, 1913-25 185.00
Block of 4 65.00 37.50
P# block of 6 600.00
Never hinged 950.00
JQ4 PPD1 10c **dark green** (2,124,540) 175.00 45.00
yellowish green 175.00 45.00
Never hinged 375.00
On cover, 1913-25 650.00
Block of 4 775.00 375.00
P# block of 6 *9,750.*
Never hinged *14,000.*
JQ5 PPD1 25c **dark green** (2,117,700) 105.00 5.00
yellowish green 105.00 5.00
Never hinged 225.00
On cover, 1913-25 —
Block of 4 475.00 35.00
P# block of 6 *5,000.*
Nos. JQ1-JQ5 (5) 391.00 77.50
Nos. JQ1-JQ5, never hinged 857.50

SPECIAL HANDLING STAMPS

The Postal Service Act, approved February 28, 1925, provided for a special handling stamp of the 25-cent denomination for use on fourth-class mail matter, which would secure for such mail matter the expeditious handling accorded to mail matter of the first class.

PP13

FLAT PLATE PRINTING

Plates of 200 subjects in four panes of 50

1925-55 Unwmk. *Perf. 11*
QE1 PP13 10c **yellow green,** *1955* 1.60 1.00
Never hinged 2.60
Block of 4 6.75 5.75
P# block of 6 32.50
Never hinged 47.50
a. Wet printing, *June 25, 1928* 3.25 1.00
Never hinged 5.25
P# block of 6 22.50
Never hinged 32.50
First day cover 45.00
QE2 PP13 15c **yellow green,** *1955* 1.75 .90
Never hinged 2.75
Block of 4 7.50 5.75
P# block of 6 42.50
Never hinged 62.50
a. Wet printing, *June 25, 1928* 3.50 .90
Never hinged 5.50
P# block of 6 30.00
Never hinged 40.00
First day cover 45.00
QE3 PP13 20c **yellow green,** *1955* 2.75 1.50
Never hinged 4.40
Block of 4 12.50 11.00
P# block of 6 47.50
Never hinged 70.00
a. Wet printing, *June 25, 1928* 4.25 1.50
Never hinged 6.75
P# block of 6 37.50
Never hinged 55.00
First day cover 45.00
First day cover, Nos. QE1a-QE3a 350.00
QE4 PP13 25c **yellow green,** *1929* 20.00 7.50
Never hinged 36.00
Block of 4 95.00 32.50
P# block of 6 260.00
Never hinged 375.00
a. 25c **deep green,** *Apr. 11, 1925* 32.50 5.50
Never hinged 52.50
First day cover 225.00
Block of 4 140.00 30.00
P# block of 6 330.00
Never hinged 475.00
"A" and second "T" of "States" joined at top (Pl. 17103) 50.00 22.50
"A" and second "T" of "States" and "T" and "A" of "Postage" joined at top (Pl. 17103) 50.00 45.00
Nos. QE1-QE4 (4) 26.10 10.90
Nos. QE1-QE4, never hinged 45.75

See note on Wet and Dry Printings following No. 1029.

POSTAL INSURANCE STAMPS

Postal insurance stamps were issued to pay insurance on parcels for loss or damage. The stamps come in a booklet of one which also carries instructions for use and a receipt form for use if there is a claim. The booklets were sold by vending machine. Values in unused column are for complete booklets. Values in used column are for used stamps.

PPI1

1965, Aug. **Typo.** ***Rouletted 9 at Top***

QI1 PPI1 (10c) **dark red** 135.00 —

No. QI1 paid insurance up to $10. It was sold at the Canoga Park, Calif., automatic post office which opened Aug. 19, 1965. The "V" stands for "Vended."

PPI2

1966, Mar. 26 **Litho.** ***Perf. 11 at Top***

QI2 PPI2 (20c) **red** 4.00 —

No. QI2 paid insurance up to $15. The rate increased from 20c to 25c on Apr. 18, 1976, and to 40c on July 18, 1976.

The QI2 booklet comes with two types of front covers, the first beginning "Vended..." and the second "Domestic Vended...." There also are two types of back covers, the first with some white on black lettering, the second with all black on white lettering.

No 25c postal insurance stamps were printed. Existing copies of No. QI2 had 5c postage stamps added and the value on the cover was changed to 25c, usually by hand, but sometimes by handstamp or label. Twenty-cent stamps were added to make the 40c rate since new postal insurance stamps were not issued until 1977. Some 25c provisional booklets were further revalued to 40c by the addition of a 15c stamp. Each provisional booklet comes with both cover types.

Type PPI2 with "FEE PAID THROUGH VENDING MACHINE" Added Below

1977-81 **Litho.** ***Perf. 11 at Top***

QI3 PPI2 (40c) **black** 8.50 —

Available for use by Nov. 28, 1977 or earlier.

QI4 PPI2 (50c) **green** 7.50 —

The rate increased to 50c on May 29, 1978. Examples of QI2 and QI3 exist revalued to 50c by the addition of stamps.

QI5 PPI2 (45c) **red,** *1981* 8.50 —

No. QI3 booklets exist revalued to 45c by the addition of a 5c stamp, and the QI4 booklet is known revalued to 45c on its cover.

FIRST DAY COVERS

All envelopes or cards are postmarked Washington, D.C., unless otherwise stated. Minors and sublistings without dates have the same date and city (if none is otherwise mentioned) as the previous listing. Minors and sublistings with dates differing from the previous listing are postmarked in Washington, D.C. unless otherwise stated.

Values are for first day covers in very fine condition, without tears, stains or smeared postmarks, and with sound stamps that have fresh color and are not badly off center.

Printed cachets on covers before Scott Nos. 772 and C20 sell at a substantial premium. Values for covers of Nos. 772-986 and C20-C45 are for those with the most common cachets and addressed. Unaddressed covers sell at a substantial premium and covers without cachet sell at a substantial discount. Values for covers from Scott 987 and C46 onward are for those with the most common cachets and unaddressed.

Values for 1st class rate stamps are for covers bearing single stamps. Blocks of 4 on first day covers usually sell for about 1½ times as much as singles; Plate number blocks of 4 at about 3 times; Plate number blocks of 6 at about 4 times; coil line pairs at about 3 times. Stamps with denominations less than the first class rate will have the proper multiple to make the rate if practical or additional postage. (See Nos. 899, 907-908, 930-931, etc.)

Dates given are those on which the stamps were first *officially* placed on sale. Many instances are known of stamps being sold in advance, contrary to regulations.

Numbers in parentheses are quantities stated to have received the first day cancel.

Listings from Scott Nos. 551 and C4 are for covers canceled at cities officially designated by the Post Office Department or Postal Service. Some tagged varieties and cities of special interest are exceptions.

Air post first day covers are listed following the Postage first day covers. Envelope, postal card and other first day covers are with the regular listings. Quantities given for se-tenant issues include the multiple and any single or combination of singles (see No. 2375a).

1851-57

5A 1c **blue, type Ib,** *July 1, 1851,* Boston, Mass. *120,000.*
7 1c **blue, type II,** *July 1, 1851,* any city *17,500.*
Same on printed circular *4,000.*
10 3c **orange brown,** *July 1, 1851,* any city *12,500.*

The No. 5A cover is unique. Value is based on 1996 auction sale.

1861

64 3c **pink,** *Aug. 17, 1861,* Baltimore, Md. *17,500.*
64b 3c **rose pink,** *Aug. 17, 1861,* Baltimore, Md. *23,000.*

The Nos. 64 and 64b covers are each unique. Values based on 1999 and 1996 auction sales, respectively.

1883

210 2c **red brown,** *Oct. 1,* any city *2,000.*
210, 211 2c, 4c **blue green,** *Oct. 1,* New York, N.Y. *36,000.*

The Nos. 210, 211 cover is unique. Value is based on 1996 auction sale.

1890

219D 2c **lake,** *Feb. 22,* any city *12,500.*

1893

COLUMBIAN EXPOSITION ISSUE

230 1c **deep blue,** *Jan. 1,* any city *6,000.*
Jan. 2, any city *3,500.*
231 2c **brown violet,** *Jan. 1,* any city *11,000.*
Jan. 2, any city *3,500.*
232 3c **green,** *Jan. 1,* any city *10,000.*
Jan. 2, any city *6,500.*
230, 232 on one cover, *Jan. 2,* Boston, Mass. *7,500.*
233 4c **ultramarine,** *Jan. 1,* any city *15,000.*
Jan. 2, any city *9,500.*
234 5c **chocolate,** *Jan. 1,* any city *25,000.*
Jan. 2, any city *16,000.*
235 6c **purple,** *Jan. 2,* any city *20,000.*
237 10c **black brown,** *Jan. 1,* any city *30,000.*
Jan. 2, any city *25,000.*
242 $2 **brown red,** *Jan. 2,* any city *60,000.*

As Jan. 1, 1893, was a Sunday, specialists recognize both Jan. 1 and 2 as "first day."

1898

TRANS-MISSISSIPPI EXPOSITION ISSUE

285 1c **green,** *June 17,* any city *12,500.*
286 2c **copper red,** *June 17,* any city *12,500.*
Pittsburgh, Pa, *9,500.*
287 4c **orange,** *June 17* *27,500.*
288 5c **dull blue,** *June 17,* any city *17,500.*
285-288 on one cover *75,000.*
289 8c **violet brown,** *June 17,* any city *20,000.*
290 10c **gray violet,** *June 17* *27,500.*
285-290, all 6 on one cover, *June 17* *100,000.*
291 50c **sage green,** *June 17,* any city *50,000.*
292 $1 **black,** *June 17,* any city —

1901

PAN AMERICAN EXPOSITION ISSUE

294 1c **green & black,** *May 1,* any city *4,500.*
295 2c **carmine & black,** *May 1,* any city *2,750.*
297 5c **ultra. & blk.,** *May 1,* any city *15,000.*
294, 295, 297 on one cover, *May 1,* Boston, Mass. *9,500.*
294, 296, 297 on one cover, *May 1,* Boston, Mass. *24,000.*
295, 298 on one cover, *May 1,* Washington, D.C. *9,500.*
296, 298 on one cover, *May 1,* Boston, Mass. *15,000.*
297, 298 on one cover, *May 1,* Philadelphia, Pa. *15,000.*
294-299, complete set of 6 on one cover *May 1,* any city *35,000.*

1904

LOUISIANA PURCHASE EXPOSITION ISSUE

323 1c **green,** *Apr. 30,* any city *6,000.*
324 2c **carmine,** *Apr. 30,* any city *4,750.*
325 3c **violet,** *Apr. 30,* any city *5,000.*
326 5c **dark blue,** *Apr. 30,* any city *22,500.*
327 10c **red brown,** *Apr. 30,* any city *24,000.*
323-327, all 5 on one cover, *Apr. 30,* New York *80,000.*

The Nos. 323-327 combination cover is unique. Value is based on 1996 auction sale.

1907

328 1c **Jamestown,** *Apr. 26,* any city *6,000.*
329 2c **Jamestown,** *Apr. 26,* any city *9,000.*

1909

367 2c **Lincoln,** *Feb. 12,* any city *500.*

Imperf

368 2c **Lincoln,** *Feb. 12,* any city *12,500.*

1909

ALASKA-YUKON ISSUE

370 2c **carmine,** *June 1,* any city *3,000.*
On Expo-related picture postcard, *June 1* *4,000.*

1909

HUDSON-FULTON ISSUE

372 2c **carmine,** *Sept. 25,* any city *750.*
On Expo-related picture postcard, *Sept. 25* *1,250.*

Imperf

373 2c **carmine,** *Sept. 25,* any city *7,000.*

1913

PANAMA-PACIFIC ISSUE

397 1c **green,** *Jan. 1,* any city *5,000.*
399 5c **blue,** *Jan. 1* *21,000.*
400 10c **orange yellow,** *Jan. 1* 10,000.
397, 399 & 400, all 3 on one cover, San Francisco, Cal. *10,000.*

1916-22

COIL STAMP

497 10c **orange yellow,** *Jan. 31, 1922,* any city *4,500.*

1918-20

OFFSET PRINTING

526 2c **carmine,** type IV, *Mar. 15, 1920* *800.*

1919

537 3c **Victory,** *Mar. 3,* any city *800.*

1919 ***Perf. 11x10***

541 3c **violet,** type II, *June 14, 1919,* any city —

1920 ***Perf. 10x11***

REGULAR ISSUE

542 1c **green,** *May 26* *1,750.*

1920

548 1c **Pilgrim,** *Dec. 21, any city,* pair *900.*
549 2c **Pilgrim,** *Dec. 21,* any city *700.*
Plymouth, Mass. *950.*
550 5c **Pilgrim,** *Dec. 21* —
548-550, complete set of 3 on one cover, *Dec. 21,* any city *2,500.*
Washington, D.C. *3,000.*

1922-26 ***Perf. 11***

551 ½c **Hale,** *Apr. 4, 1925,* block of 4 17.50
New Haven, Conn. *22.50*
551 & 576 on one cover, *Apr. 4, 1925,* New Haven, Conn. *150.00*
552 1c **Franklin,** *Jan. 17, 1923,* pair 25.00
Philadelphia, Pa. *42.50*
553 1½c **Harding,** *Mar. 19, 1925,* pair 30.00
553, 582, 598 on one cover, *Mar. 19, 1925* *175.00*
554 2c **Washington,** *Jan. 15, 1923* 37.50
555 3c **Lincoln,** *Feb. 12, 1923* 35.00
Hodgenville, Ky. *300.00*
556 4c **Martha Washington,** *Jan. 15, 1923* 60.00
557 5c **Roosevelt,** *Oct. 27, 1922* *125.00*
New York, N.Y. *175.00*
Oyster Bay, N.Y. *1,000.*
558 6c **Garfield,** *Nov. 20, 1922* 225.00
559 7c **McKinley,** *May 1, 1923* 175.00
Niles, O. *250.00*
560 8c **Grant,** *May 1, 1923* 175.00
561 9c **Jefferson,** *Jan. 15, 1923* 175.00
562 10c **Monroe,** *Jan. 15, 1923* 175.00
554, 556, 561 & 562, all 4 stamps issued *Jan. 15* on one cover *3,500.*
563 11c **Hayes,** *Oct. 4, 1922* 600.00
Fremont, O. *4,000.*
564 12c **Cleveland,** *Mar. 20, 1923* 175.00
Boston, Mass. (Philatelic Exhibition) *175.00*
Caldwell, N.J. *210.00*
565 14c **American Indian,** *May 1, 1923* 400.00
Muskogee, Okla. *1,250.*
566 15c **Statue of Liberty,** *Nov. 11, 1922* 550.00
567 20c **Golden Gate,** *May 1, 1923* *500.00*
San Francisco, Cal. *2,000.*
559, 560, 565 & 567, all 4 stamps issued *May 1* on one cover *10,000.*
568 25c **Niagara Falls,** *Nov. 11, 1922* *650.00*
569 30c **American Buffalo,** *Mar. 20, 1923* *850.00*
570 50c **Arlington,** *Nov. 11, 1922* *1,250.*
571 $1 **Lincoln Memorial,** *Feb. 12, 1923* *7,000.*
Springfield, Ill. *6,500.*
572 $2 **U.S. Capitol,** *Mar. 20, 1923* *20,000.*
573 $5 **America,** *Mar. 20, 1923* *32,500.*

Imperf

576 1½c **Harding,** *Apr. 4, 1925* 45.00

Perf. 10

581 1c **Franklin,** *Oct. 17, 1923,* not precanceled *6,000.*
582 1½c **Harding,** *Mar. 19, 1925* 40.00
583a 2c **Washington booklet pane of 6,** *Aug. 27, 1926* *1,800.*
584 3c **Lincoln,** *Aug. 1, 1925* 55.00
585 4c **Martha Washington,** *Apr. 4, 1925* 55.00
586 5c **Roosevelt,** *Apr. 4, 1925* 57.50
587 6c **Garfield,** *Apr. 4, 1925* 60.00
585-587, all 3 stamps issued *April 4* on one cover *1,000.*
588 7c **McKinley,** *May 29, 1926* 70.00
589 8c **Grant,** *May 29, 1926* 72.50
590 9c **Jefferson,** *May 29, 1926* 72.50
591 10c **Monroe,** *June 8, 1925* 95.00

Perf. 10 Vertically

597 1c **Franklin,** *July 18, 1923* *600.00*
598 1½c **Harding,** *Mar. 19, 1925* 60.00
599 2c **Washington,** *Jan. 15, 1923* *1,500.*
600 3c **Lincoln,** *May 10, 1924* 80.00
602 5c **Roosevelt,** *Mar. 5, 1924* 85.00
603 10c **Monroe,** *Dec. 1, 1924* 100.00

No. 599 is known used on Jan. 10, 11 and 13, 1923 (one each day). Jan. 15 was the first day of sale in Washington, D. C.

Perf. 10 Horizontally

604 1c **Franklin,** *July 19, 1924* 90.00
605 1½c **Harding,** *May 9, 1925* 70.00
606 2c **Washington,** *Dec. 31, 1923* 125.00

1923

610 2c **Harding,** perf. 11, *Sept. 1* 30.00
Marion, O. 20.00
611 2c **Harding,** imperf., *Nov. 15* 90.00
612 2c **Harding,** perf. 10, *Sept. 12* 100.00

1924

614 1c **Huguenot-Walloon,** *May 1,* pair 40.00
Albany, N.Y 40.00
Allentown, Pa. 40.00
Charleston, S.C. 40.00
Jacksonville, Fla. 40.00
Lancaster, Pa. 40.00
Mayport, Fla. 40.00
New Rochelle, N.Y. 40.00
New York, N.Y. 40.00
Philadelphia, Pa. 40.00
Reading, Pa. 40.00
615 2c **Huguenot-Walloon,** *May 1* 55.00
Albany, N.Y. 55.00
Allentown, Pa. 55.00
Charleston, S.C. 55.00
Jacksonville, Fla. 55.00
Lancaster, Pa. 55.00
Mayport, Fla. 55.00
New Rochelle, N.Y. 55.00
New York, N.Y. 55.00
Philadelphia, Pa. 55.00
Reading, Pa. 55.00
616 5c **Huguenot-Walloon,** *May 1* 80.00
Albany, N.Y. 80.00
Allentown, Pa. 80.00
Charleston, S.C. 80.00
Jacksonville, Fla. 80.00
Lancaster, Pa. 80.00
Mayport, Fla. 80.00
New Rochelle, N.Y. 80.00
New York, N.Y. 80.00
Philadelphia, Pa. 80.00
Reading, Pa. 80.00
614-616 on one cover, any city 175.00

1925

617 1c **Lexington-Concord,** *Apr. 4,* pair 35.00
Boston, Mass. 35.00
Cambridge, Mass. 32.50
Concord, Mass. 35.00
Concord Junction, Mass. 37.50
Lexington, Mass. 37.50
618 2c **Lexington-Concord,** *Apr. 4* 37.50
Boston, Mass. 37.50
Cambridge, Mass. 37.50
Concord, Mass 37.50
Concord Junction, Mass. 37.50
Lexington, Mass. 37.50
619 5c **Lexington-Concord,** *Apr. 4* 85.00
Boston, Mass. 85.00
Cambridge, Mass. 85.00
Concord, Mass. 85.00
Concord Junction, Mass. 85.00
Lexington, Mass. 85.00
617-619 on one cover, Concord Junction or Lexington 210.00
Set of 3 on one cover, any other city 160.00

1925

620 2c **Norse-American,** *May 18* 25.00
Algona, Iowa 25.00
Benson, Minn. 25.00
Decorah, Iowa 25.00
Minneapolis, Minn. 25.00
Northfield, Minn. 25.00
St. Paul, Minn. 25.00
621 5c **Norse-American,** *May 18* 40.00
Algona, Iowa 40.00
Benson, Minn. 40.00
Decorah, Iowa 40.00
Minneapolis, Minn. 40.00
Northfield, Minn. 40.00
St. Paul, Minn. 40.00
620-621 on one cover, any city 55.00

1925-26

622 13c **Harrison,** *Jan. 11, 1926* 22.50
Indianapolis, Ind. 32.50
North Bend, Ohio *(500)* 160.00
623 17c **Wilson,** *Dec. 28, 1925* 27.50
New York, N.Y. 27.50
Princeton, N.J. 27.50
Staunton, Va. 27.50

1926

627 2c **Sesquicentennial,** *May 10* 10.00
Boston, Mass. 10.00
Philadelphia, Pa. 10.00
628 5c **Ericsson,** *May 29* 30.00
Chicago, Ill. 30.00
Minneapolis, Minn. 30.00
New York, N.Y. 30.00
629 2c **White Plains,** New York, N.Y., *Oct. 18* 6.25
New York, N.Y., Inter-Philatelic Exhibition Agency cancellation 6.25
White Plains, N.Y. 6.25
Washington, D.C., *Oct. 28* 3.50
630 Sheet of 25, *Oct. 18* 1,500.
Sheet of 25, *Oct. 28* 1,000.

1926-34 ***Imperf.***

631 1½c **Harding,** *Aug. 27, 1926,* pair 35.00

Perf. 11x10½

632 1c **Franklin,** *June 10, 1927,* pair 45.00
632a Booklet pane of 6, *Nov. 2, 1927* *3,250.*
633 1½c **Harding,** *May 17, 1927,* pair 45.00
634 2c **Washington,** *Dec. 10, 1926* 47.50
635 3c **Lincoln,** *Feb. 3, 1927* 47.50
635a 3c **bright violet,** *Feb. 7, 1934* 25.00
636 4c **Martha Washington,** *May 17, 1927* 50.00
637 5c **Roosevelt,** *Mar. 24, 1927* 50.00
638 6c **Garfield,** *July 27, 1927* 57.50
639 7c **McKinley,** *Mar. 24, 1927* 57.50
637, 639, both stamps issued *Mar. 24* 500.00
640 8c **Grant,** *June 10, 1927* 67.50
632, 640, both stamps issued *June 10* 350.00
641 9c **Jefferson,** *May 17, 1927* 72.50
633, 636, 641 all three stamps issued *May 17* 550.00
642 10c **Monroe,** *Feb. 3, 1927* 90.00

1927

643 2c **Vermont,** *Aug. 3* 6.00
Bennington, Vt. 6.00
644 2c **Burgoyne,** *Aug. 3* 12.50
Albany, N.Y. 12.50
Rome, N.Y. 12.50
Syracuse, N.Y. 12.50
Utica, N.Y. 12.50

1928

645 2c **Valley Forge,** *May 26* 4.00
Cleveland, O. 67.50
Lancaster, Pa. 4.00
Norristown, Pa. 4.00
Philadelphia, Pa. 4.00
Valley Forge, Pa. 4.00
West Chester, Pa. 4.00
Cleveland, Midwestern Philatelic Sta. cancellation 4.00
646 2c **Molly Pitcher,** *Oct. 20* 15.00
Freehold, N.J. 15.00
Red Bank, N.J. 15.00

1928

647 2c **Hawaii,** *Aug. 13* 15.00
Honolulu, Hawaii 17.50
648 5c **Hawaii,** *Aug. 13* 22.50
Honolulu, Hawaii 25.00
647-648 on one cover 40.00
649 2c **Aero Conf.,** *Dec. 12* 7.00
650 5c **Aero Conf.,** *Dec. 12* 10.00
649-650 on one cover 15.00

1929

651 2c **Clark,** Vincennes, Indiana, *Feb. 25* 6.00
Washington, *Feb. 26,* first day of sale by Philatelic Agency 3.00

Perf. 11x10½

653 ½c **olive brown,** *May 25,* block of four 27.50
654 2c **Electric Light,** perf. 11, Menlo Park, N.J., *June 5* 10.00
Washington, D.C., *June 6,* first day of sale by Philatelic Agency 4.00
655 2c **Electric Light,** perf. 11x10½, *June 11* 80.00
656 2c **Electric Light,** perf. 10 vert., *June 11* 90.00
657 2c **Sullivan,** Auburn, N.Y., *June 17* 4.00
Binghamton, N.Y. 4.00
Canajoharie, N.Y. 4.00
Canandaigua, N.Y. 4.00
Elmira, N.Y. 4.00
Geneseo, N.Y. 4.00
Geneva, N.Y. 4.00
Horseheads, N.Y. 4.00
Owego, N.Y. 4.00
Penn Yan, N.Y 4.00
Perry, N.Y. 4.00
Seneca Falls, N.Y. 4.00
Waterloo, N.Y. 4.00
Watkins Glen, N.Y. 4.00
Waverly, N.Y. 4.00
Washington, D.C., *June 18* 2.00

1929

658 1c **Kansas,** *May 1,* pair 50.00
Newton, Kan., *Apr. 15* 325.00
659 1½c **Kansas,** *May 1,* pair 52.50
Colby, Kan., *Apr. 16* —
660 2c **Kansas,** *May 1* 52.50
Colby, Kan., *Apr. 16* —
661 3c **Kansas,** *May 1* 60.00
Colby, Kan., *Apr. 16* —
662 4c **Kansas,** *May 1* 62.50
Colby, Kan., *Apr. 16* —
663 5c **Kansas,** *May 1* 80.00
Colby, Kan., *Apr. 16* —
664 6c **Kansas,** *May 1* 90.00
Newton, Kan., *Apr. 15* 600.00
665 7c **Kansas,** *May 1* 100.00
Colby, Kan., *Apr. 16* —
666 8c **Kansas,** *May 1* 125.00
Newton, Kan., *Apr. 15* 575.00

667 9c **Kansas,** *May 1* 140.00
Colby, Kan., *Apr. 16* —
668 10c **Kansas,** *May 1* 175.00
Colby, Kan., *Apr. 16* —
658-668 on 1 cover, Washington, D.C., *May 1* 1,300.
669 1c **Nebraska,** *May 1,* pair 50.00
Beatrice, Neb., *Apr. 15* 125.00
670 1½c **Nebraska,** *May 1,* pair 50.00
Hartington, Neb., *Apr. 15* 275.00
671 2c **Nebraska,** *May 1* 55.00
Auburn, Neb., *Apr. 15* 1,200.
Beatrice, Neb., *Apr. 15* —
Hartington, Neb., *Apr. 15* 225.00
672 3c **Nebraska,** *May 1* 65.00
Beatrice, Neb., *Apr. 15* 190.00
Hartington, Neb., *Apr. 15* 190.00
673 4c **Nebraska,** *May 1* 75.00
Beatrice, Neb., *Apr. 15* 240.00
Hartington, Neb., *Apr. 15* 240.00
674 5c **Nebraska,** *May 1* 75.00
Beatrice, Neb., *Apr. 15* 225.00
Hartington, Neb., *Apr. 15* 225.00
675 6c **Nebraska,** *May 1* 100.00
Ravenna, Neb., *Apr. 17* —
Wahoo, Neb., *Apr. 17* —
676 7c **Nebraska,** *May 1* 100.00
Auburn, Neb., *Apr. 17* 250.00
677 8c **Nebraska,** *May 1* 125.00
Humbolt, Neb., *Apr. 17* 250.00
Pawnee City, Neb., *Apr. 17* 250.00
678 9c **Nebraska,** *May 1* 140.00
Cambridge, Neb., *Apr. 17* 250.00
679 10c **Nebraska,** *May 1* 175.00
Tecumseh, Neb., *Apr. 18* —
669-679 on 1 cover, Washington, D.C., *May 1* 1,300.
658-679 on 1 cover, Washington, D.C., *May 1* *4,000.*
680 2c **Fallen Timbers,** Erie, Pa., *Sept. 14* 3.50
Maumee, O. 3.50
Perrysburg, O. 3.50
Toledo, O. 3.50
Waterville, O. 3.50
Washington, D.C., *Sept. 16* 2.00
681 2c **Ohio River,** Cairo, Ill., *Oct. 19* 3.50
Cincinnati, O. 3.50
Evansville, Ind. 3.50
Homestead, Pa. 3.50
Louisville, Ky. 3.50
Pittsburgh, Pa. 3.50
Wheeling, W. Va. 3.50
Washington, D.C., *Oct. 21* 2.00

1930

682 2c **Massachusetts Bay Colony,** Boston, Mass. *Apr. 8 (60,000)* 3.50
Salem, Mass. 3.50
Washington, D.C., *Apr. 11* 2.00
683 2c **Carolina-Charleston,** Charleston, S.C. *Apr. 10* 3.50
Washington, D.C., *Apr. 11* 2.00

Perf. 11x10½

684 1½c **Harding,** Marion, O., *Dec. 1,* pair 4.50
Washington, D.C., *Dec. 2* 2.50
685 4c **Taft,** Cincinnati, O., *June 4* 6.00
Washington, D.C., *June 5* 3.00

Perf. 10 Vertically

686 1½c **Harding,** Marion, Ohio, *Dec. 1* 5.00
Washington, D.C., *Dec. 2* 3.00
687 4c **Taft,** *Sept. 18* 20.00

Perf. 11

688 2c **Braddock,** Braddock, Pa., *July 9* 4.00
Washington, D.C., *July 10* 2.00
689 2c **Von Steuben,** New York, N.Y., *Sept. 17* 4.00
Washington, D.C., *Sept. 18* 2.00

1931

690 2c **Pulaski,** Brooklyn, N.Y., *Jan. 16* 4.00
Buffalo, N.Y. 4.00
Chicago, Ill. 4.00
Cleveland, O. 4.00
Detroit, Mich. 4.00
Gary, Ind. 4.00
Milwaukee, Wis. 4.00
New York, N.Y. 4.00
Pittsburgh, Pa. 4.00
Savannah, Ga. 4.00
South Bend, Ind. 4.00
Toledo, O. 4.00
Washington, D.C., *Jan. 17* 2.00

1931 ***Perf. 11x10½, 10½x11***

692 11c **Hayes,** *Sept. 4* 100.
693 12c **Cleveland,** *Aug. 25* 100.
694 13c **Harrison,** *Sept. 4* 100.
695 14c **American Indian,** *Sept. 8* 100.
696 15c **Liberty,** *Aug. 27* 125.
697 17c **Wilson,** *July 25,* Brooklyn, N.Y. *2,750.*
Washington, D.C., *July 27* 400.
698 20c **Golden Gate,** *Sept. 8* 325.
699 25c **Niagara Falls,** *July 25,* Brooklyn, N.Y. *2,000.*
Washington, D.C., *July 27* 400.
697, 699 on one cover, Brooklyn, *July 25* *5,750.*
697, 699 on one cover, Washington, *July 27* *2,500.*
700 30c **American Buffalo,** *Sept. 8* 300.
701 50c **Arlington,** *Sept. 4* 425.
Woolrich, Pa., *Sept. 4* 625.

1931

702 2c **Red Cross,** *May 21* 3.00
Dansville, N.Y. 3.00
703 2c **Yorktown,** *Oct. 19,* Wethersfield, Conn. 3.50
Yorktown, Va. 3.50
Washington, D.C., *Oct. 20* 2.00

1932

WASHINGTON BICENTENNIAL ISSUE

704 ½c *Jan. 1,* block of 4 5.00
705 1c *Jan. 1,* pair 4.00
706 1½c *Jan. 1,* pair 4.00
707 2c *Jan. 1* 4.00
708 3c *Jan. 1* 4.00
709 4c *Jan. 1* 4.00
710 5c *Jan. 1* 4.00
711 6c *Jan. 1* 4.00
712 7c *Jan. 1* 4.00
713 8c *Jan. 1* 4.50
714 9c *Jan. 1* 4.50
715 10c *Jan. 1* 4.50
704-715, set of 12 on one cover, *Jan. 1* 70.00

1932

716 2c **Olympic Winter Games,** *Jan. 25,* Lake Placid, N.Y. 6.00
Washington, D.C., *Jan. 26* 1.50
717 2c **Arbor Day,** *Apr. 22,* Nebraska City, Neb. 4.00
Washington, D.C., *Apr. 23* 1.50
Adams, N.Y., *Apr. 23* 6.50
718 3c **Olympic Summer Games,** *June 15,* Los Angeles, Cal. 6.00
Washington, D.C., *June 16* 2.75
719 5c **Olympic Summer Games,** *June 15,* Los Angeles, Cal. 8.00
Washington, D.C., *June 16* 2.75
718, 719 on one cover, Los Angeles, Cal. 10.00
718, 719 on one cover, Washington, D.C. 4.50
720 3c **Washington,** *June 16* 7.50
720b Booklet pane of 6, *July 25* 100.00
721 3c **Washington Coil,** Sideways, *June 24* 15.00
722 3c **Washington Coil,** Endways, *Oct. 12* 15.00
723 6c **Garfield Coil,** Sideways, *Aug. 18,* Los Angeles, Cal. 15.00
Washington, D.C., *Aug. 19* 4.00
724 3c **William Penn,** *Oct. 24,* New Castle, Del. 3.25
Chester, Pa. 3.25
Philadelphia, Pa. 3.25
Washington, D.C., *Oct. 25* 1.25
725 3c **Daniel Webster,** *Oct. 24,* Franklin, N.H. 3.25
Exeter, N.H. 3.25
Hanover, N.H. 3.25
Washington, D.C., *Oct. 25* 1.25

1933

726 3c **Gen. Oglethorpe,** *Feb. 12,* Savannah, Ga., *(200,000)* 3.25
Washington, D.C., *Feb. 13* 1.50
727 3c **Peace Proclamation,** *Apr. 19,* Newburgh, N.Y. *(349,571)* 3.50
Washington, D.C., *Apr. 20* 1.25
728 1c **Century of Progress,** *May 25,* Chicago, Ill., strip of 3 3.00
Washington, D.C., *May 26* 1.00
729 3c **Century of Progress,** *May 25,* Chicago, Ill. 3.00
Washington, D.C., *May 26* 1.00
728, 729 on one cover 5.00

Covers mailed May 25, bearing Nos. 728 and 729 total 232,251.

730 1c **American Philatelic Society,** sheet of 25, *Aug. 25,* Chicago, Ill. 100.00
730a 1c **A.P.S.,** imperf., *Aug. 25,* Chicago, Ill., strip of 3 3.25
Washington, D.C., *Aug. 28* 1.25
731 3c **American Philatelic Society,** sheet of 25, *Aug. 25,* Chicago, Ill. 100.00
731a 3c **A.P.S.,** single, imperf., *Aug. 25,* Chicago, Ill. 3.25
Washington, D.C., *Aug. 28* 1.25
730a, 731a on one cover 5.50

Covers mailed Aug. 25 bearing Nos. 730, 730a, 731, 731a total 65,218.

732 3c **National Recovery Administration,** *Aug. 15,(65,000)* 3.25
Nira, Iowa, *Aug. 17* 2.50
733 3c **Byrd Antarctic,** *Oct. 9* 10.00
734 5c **Kosciuszko,** *Oct. 13,* Boston, Mass. *(23,025)* 4.50
Buffalo, N.Y. *(14,981)* 5.50
Chicago, Ill, *(26,306)* 4.50
Detroit, Mich. *(17,792)* 5.25
Pittsburgh, Pa. *(6,282)* 32.50
Kosciuszko, Miss. *(27,093)* 5.25
St. Louis, Mo. *(17,872)* 5.25
Washington, D.C., *Oct. 14* 1.60

1934

735 3c **National Exhibition,** sheet of 6, Byrd imperf., *Feb. 10,* New York, N.Y. 40.00
Washington, D.C., *Feb. 19* 27.50
735a 3c **National Exhibition,** single, imperf., New York, N.Y., *Feb. 10 (450,715)* 5.00
Washington, D.C., *Feb. 19* 2.75
736 3c **Maryland Tercentenary,** *Mar. 23* St. Mary's City, Md. *(148,785)* 1.60
Washington, D.C., *Mar. 24* 1.00
737 3c **Mothers of America,** perf. 11x10½, *May 2, any city* 1.60
738 3c **Mothers of America,** perf. 11, *May 2, any city* 1.60
737, 738 on one cover 4.00

Covers mailed at Washington, May 2 bearing Nos. 737 and 738 total 183,359.

739 3c **Wisconsin,** *July 7,* Green Bay, Wisc. *(130,000)* 1.10
Washington, D.C., *July 9* 1.00
740 1c **Parks, Yosemite,** *July 16* 2.25
Yosemite, Cal., *(60,000),* strip of 3 2.75
741 2c **Parks, Grand Canyon,** *July 24* 2.25
Grand Canyon, Ariz., *(75,000),* pair 2.75
742 3c **Parks, Mt. Rainier,** *Aug. 3* 2.50
Longmire, Wash., *(64,500)* 3.00
743 4c **Parks, Mesa Verde,** *Sept. 25* 2.25
Mesa Verde, Colo., *(51,882)* 2.75
744 5c **Parks, Yellowstone,** *July 30* 2.25
Yellowstone, Wyo., *(87,000)* 2.50
745 6c **Parks, Crater Lake,** *Sept. 5* 3.00
Crater Lake, Ore., *(45,282)* 3.25
746 7c **Parks, Arcadia,** *Oct. 2* 3.00
Bar Harbor, Maine *(51,312)* 3.25
747 8c **Parks, Zion,** *Sept. 18* 3.25
Zion, Utah, *(43,650)* 3.75
748 9c **Parks, Glacier Park,** *Aug. 27* 3.50
Glacier Park, Mont., *(52,626)* 3.75
749 10c **Parks, Smoky Mountains,** *Oct. 8* 6.00
Sevierville, Tenn., *(39,000)* 7.50

Imperf

750 3c **American Philatelic Society,** sheet of 6, *Aug. 28,* Atlantic City, N.J. 40.00
750a 3c **A.P.S.,** single, *Aug. 28,* Atlantic City, N.J. *(40,000)* 3.25
Washington, D.C., *Sept. 4* 2.00
751 1c **Trans-Mississippi Philatelic Expo.,** sheet of 6, *Oct. 10,* Omaha, Neb. 35.00
751a 1c **Trans-Miss. Phil. Expo.,** Omaha. Neb., *Oct. 10 (125,000),* strip of 3 3.25
Washington, D.C., Oct. 15 2.00

1935

SPECIAL PRINTING

Nos. 752-771 issued Mar. 15

752 3c **Peace Commemoration** 5.00
753 3c **Byrd** 6.00
754 3c **Mothers of America** 6.00
755 3c **Wisconsin Tercentenary** 6.00
756 1c **Parks, Yosemite,** strip of 3 6.00
757 2c **Parks, Grand Canyon,** pair 6.00
758 3c **Parks, Mount Rainier** 6.00
759 4c **Parks, Mesa Verde** 6.50
760 5c **Parks, Yellowstone** 6.50
761 6c **Parks, Crater Lake** 6.50
762 7c **Parks, Acadia** 6.50
763 8c **Parks, Zion** 7.50
764 9c **Parks, Glacier Park** 7.50
765 10c **Parks, Smoky Mountains** 7.50
766a 1c **Century of Progress,** strip of 3 5.50
Pane of 25 *250.00*
767a 3c **Century of Progress** 5.50
Pane of 25 *250.00*
768a 3c **Byrd** 6.50
Pane of 6 *250.00*
769a 1c **Parks, Yosemite,** strip of 3 4.00
Pane of 6 *250.00*
770a 3c **Parks, Mount Rainier** 5.00
Pane of 6 *250.00*
771 16c **Airmail Special Delivery** 12.50

Catalogue values from this point to No. 986 are for addressed covers with the most common cachets.

772 3c **Connecticut Tercentenary,** *Apr. 26,* Hartford, Conn. *(217,800)* 10.00
Washington, D.C., *Apr. 27* 2.25
773 3c **California Exposition,** *May 29,* San Diego, Cal. *(214,042)* 10.00
Washington, D.C., *May 31* 1.50
774 3c **Boulder Dam,** *Sept. 30,* Boulder City, Nev. *(166,180)* 10.00
Washington, D.C., *Oct. 1* 2.00
775 3c **Michigan Centenary,** *Nov. 1,* Lansing, Mich. *(176,962)* 10.00
Washington, D.C., *Nov. 2* 1.50

1936

776 3c **Texas Centennial,** *Mar. 2,* Gonzales, Texas *(319,150)* 17.50
Washington, D.C., *Mar. 3* 2.00
777 3c **Rhode Island Tercentenary,** *May 4,* Providence, R.I. *(245,400)* 9.00
Washington, D.C., *May 5* 2.25
778 **TIPEX** souvenir sheet, *May 9 (297,194) New York, N.Y.* (TIPEX cancellation) 13.00
Washington, D.C., *May 11* 3.50
782 3c **Arkansas Centennial,** *June 15,* Little Rock, Ark. *(376,693)* 12.00
Washington, D.C, *June 16* 1.25
783 3c **Oregon Territory Centennial,** *July 14,* Astoria, Ore. *(91,110)* 8.50
Daniel, Wyo., *(67,013)* 8.50
Lewiston, Ida., *(86,100)* 8.00
Missoula, Mont., *(59,883)* 8.50
Walla Walla, Wash., *(106,150)* 8.00
Washington, D.C., *July 15* 1.25
784 3c **Susan B. Anthony,** *Aug. 26 (178,500)* 12.00

1936-37

785 1c **Army,** *Dec. 15, 1936,* strip of 3 6.00
786 2c **Army,** *Jan. 15, 1937,* pair 6.00
787 3c **Army,** *Feb. 18, 1937* 6.00
788 4c **Army,** *Mar. 23, 1937* 6.00

No.	Denom.	Description	Price
789	5c	**Army,** *May 26, 1937,* West Point, N.Y., *(160,000)*	6.00
		Washington, D.C., *May 27*	1.50
790	1c	**Navy,** *Dec. 15, 1936,* strip of 3	6.00
791	2c	**Navy,** *Jan. 15, 1937,* pair	6.00
792	3c	**Navy,** *Feb. 18, 1937*	6.00
793	4c	**Navy,** *Mar. 23, 1937*	6.00
794	5c	**Navy,** *May 26, 1937,* Annapolis, Md., *(202,806)*	6.00
		Washington, D.C., *May 27*	1.50

Covers for #785 & 790 total 390, 749; #786 & 791 total 292,570; #787 & 792 total 320,888; #788 & 793 total 331,000.

1937

No.	Denom.	Description	Price
795	3c	**Ordinance of 1787,** *July 13* Marietta, Ohio *(130,531)*	9.00
		New York, N.Y. *(125,134)*	9.00
		Washington, D.C., *July 14*	1.25
796	5c	**Virginia Dare,** *Aug. 18,* Manteo, N.C. *(226,730)*	11.00
797	10c	**Souvenir Sheet,** *Aug. 26,* Asheville, N.C. *(164,215)*	10.00
798	3c	**Constitution,** *Sept. 17,* Philadelphia, Pa. *(281,478)*	9.00
799	3c	**Hawaii,** *Oct. 18,* Honolulu, Hawaii *(320,334)*	10.00
800	3c	**Alaska,** *Nov. 12,* Juneau, Alaska *(230,370)*	10.00
801	3c	**Puerto Rico,** *Nov. 25,* San Juan, P.R. *(244,054)*	10.00
802	3c	**Virgin Islands,** *Dec. 15,* Charlotte Amalie, V.I. *(225,469)*	10.00

1938

PRESIDENTIAL ISSUE

No.	Denom.	Description	Price
803	½c	**Franklin,** *May 19,* Philadelphia, Pa. *(224,901),* block of 6	3.00
804	1c	**G. Washington,** *Apr. 25 (124,037),* strip of 3	3.00
804b		Booklet pane of 6, *Jan. 27, 1939*	
805	1½c	**M. Washington,** *May 5 (128,339),* pair	3.00
806	2c	**J. Adams,** *June 3 (127,806),* pair	3.00
806b		Booklet pane of 6, *Jan. 27, 1939*	15.00
807	3c	**Jefferson,** *June 16 (118,097)*	3.00
807a		Booklet pane of 6, *Jan. 27, 1939*	17.50
808	4c	**Madison,** *July 1 (118,765)*	3.00
809	4½c	**White House,** *July 11 (115,820)*	3.00
810	5c	**Monroe,** *July 21 (98,282)*	3.00
811	6c	**J.Q. Adams,** *July 28 (97,428)*	3.00
812	7c	**Jackson,** *Aug. 4 (98,414)*	3.00
813	8c	**Van Buren,** *Aug. 11 (94,857)*	3.00
814	9c	**W.H. Harrison,** *Aug. 18 (91,229)*	3.00
815	10c	**Tyler,** *Sept. 2 (83,707)*	3.00
816	11c	**Polk,** *Sept. 8 (63,966)*	5.00
817	12c	**Taylor,** *Sept. 14 (62,935)*	5.00
818	13c	**Fillmore,** *Sept. 22 (58,965)*	5.00
819	14c	**Pierce,** *Oct. 6 (49,819)*	5.00
820	15c	**Buchanan,** *Oct. 13 (52,209)*	5.00
821	16c	**Lincoln,** *Oct. 20 (59,566)*	6.00
822	17c	**A. Johnson,** *Oct. 27 (55,024)*	6.00
823	18c	**Grant,** *Nov. 3 (53,124)*	6.00
824	19c	**Hayes,** *Nov. 10 (54,124)*	6.00
825	20c	**Garfield,** *Nov. 10 (51,971)*	7.00
826	21c	**Arthur,** *Nov. 22 (44,367)*	7.00
827	22c	**Cleveland,** *Nov. 22 (44,358)*	8.00
828	24c	**B. Harrison,** *Dec. 2 (46,592)*	8.00
829	25c	**McKinley,** *Dec. 2 (45,691)*	8.00
830	30c	**T. Roosevelt,** *Dec. 8 (43,528)*	9.00
831	50c	**Taft,** *Dec. 8 (41,984)*	12.50
832	$1	**Wilson, purple & black,** *Aug. 29 (24,618)*	50.00
832c		**red violet & black,** *Aug. 31, 1954 (20,202)*	25.00
833	$2	**Harding,** *Sept. 29 (19,895)*	100.00
834	$5	**Coolidge,** *Nov. 17 (15,615)*	160.00

1938

No.	Denom.	Description	Price
835	3c	**Constitution,** *June 21,* Philadelphia, Pa. *(232,873)*	15.00
836	3c	**Swedes and Finns,** *June 27,* Wilmington, Del. *(225,617)*	15.00
837	3c	**Northwest Sesqui.,** *July 15,* Marietta, Ohio *(180,170)*	15.00
838	3c	**Iowa,** *Aug. 24,* Des Moines, Iowa *(209,860)*	15.00

1939

COIL STAMPS

Perf. 10 Vertically

No.	Denom.	Description	Price
839	1c	**G. Washington,** *Jan. 20,* strip of 3	4.75
840	1½c	**M. Washington,** *Jan. 20,* pair	4.75
841	2c	**J. Adams,** *Jan. 20,* pair	4.75
842	3c	**Jefferson,** *Jan. 20*	4.75
843	4c	**Madison,** *Jan. 20*	5.00
844	4½c	**White House,** *Jan. 20*	5.00
845	5c	**Monroe,** *Jan. 20*	5.00
846	6c	**J.Q. Adams,** *Jan. 20*	6.50
847	10c	**Tyler,** *Jan. 20*	9.00
		839-847 on one cover, *Jan. 20*	45.00

Perf. 10 Horizontally

No.	Denom.	Description	Price
848	1c	Strip of 3, *Jan. 27*	5.00
849	1½c	Pair, *Jan. 27*	5.00
850	2c	Pair, *Jan. 27*	5.00
851	3c	*Jan. 27*	5.50
		848-851 on one cover, *Jan. 27*	25.00

1939

No.	Denom.	Description	Price
852	3c	**Golden Gate Expo,** *Feb. 18,* San Francisco, Cal. *(352,165)*	15.00
853	3c	**N.Y. World's Fair,** *Apr. 1,* New York, N.Y. *(585,565)*	15.00
854	3c	**Washington Inauguration,** *Apr. 30,* New York, N.Y. *(395,644)*	15.00
855	3c	**Baseball Centennial,** *June 12,* Cooperstown, N.Y. *(398,199)*	35.00
856	3c	**Panama Canal,** *Aug. 15,* U.S.S. Charleston, Canal Zone *(230,974)*	17.50
857	3c	**Printing Tercentenary,** *Sept. 25,* New York, N.Y. *(295,270)*	14.00
858	3c	**50th Statehood Anniversary,** Bismarck, N.D. *Nov. 2 (142,106)*	12.50
		Pierre, S.D., *Nov. 2 (150,429)*	12.50
		Helena, Mont., *Nov. 8 (130,273)*	12.50
		Olympia, Wash., *Nov. 11 (150,429)*	12.50

1940

FAMOUS AMERICANS

No.	Denom.	Description	Price
859	1c	**Washington Irving,** *Jan. 29,* Tarrytown, N.Y. *(170,969),* strip of 3	3.00
860	2c	**James Fenimore Cooper,** *Jan. 29,* Cooperstown, N.Y. *(154,836),* pair	3.00
861	3c	**Ralph Waldo Emerson,** *Feb. 5,* Boston, Mass. *(185,148)*	3.00
862	5c	**Louisa May Alcott,** *Feb. 5,* Concord, Mass. *(134,325)*	4.00
863	10c	**Samuel L. Clemens,** *Feb. 13,* Hannibal, Mo. *(150,492)*	8.00
864	1c	**Henry W. Longfellow,** *Feb. 16,* Portland, Me. *(160,508),* strip of 3	3.00
865	2c	**John Greenleaf Whittier,** *Feb. 16,* Haverhill, Mass. *(148,423),* pair	3.00
866	3c	**James Russell Lowell,** *Feb. 20,* Cambridge, Mass. *(148,735)*	3.00
867	5c	**Walt Whitman,** *Feb. 20,* Camden, N.J. *(134,185)*	4.00
868	10c	**James Whitcomb Riley,** *Feb. 24,* Greenfield, Ind. *(131,760)*	6.00
869	1c	**Horace Mann,** *Mar. 14,* Boston, Mass. *(186,854),* strip of 3	3.00
870	2c	**Mark Hopkins,** *Mar. 14,* Williamstown, Mass. *(140,286),* pair	3.00
871	3c	**Charles W. Eliot,** *Mar. 28,* Cambridge, Mass. *(155,708)*	3.00
872	5c	**Frances E. Willard,** *Mar. 28,* Evanston, Ill. *(140,483)*	4.00
873	10c	**Booker T. Washington,** *Apr. 7,* Tuskegee Institute, Ala. *(163,507)*	10.00
874	1c	**John James Audubon,** *Apr. 8,* St. Francisville, La. *(144,123),* strip of 3	3.00
875	2c	**Dr. Crawford W. Long,** *Apr. 8,* Jefferson, Ga. *(158,128),* pair	3.00
876	3c	**Luther Burbank,** *Apr. 17,* Santa Rosa, Cal. *(147,033)*	3.00
877	5c	**Dr. Walter Reed,** *Apr. 17 (154,464)*	4.00
878	10c	**Jane Addams,** *Apr. 26,* Chicago, Ill. *(132,375)*	6.00
879	1c	**Stephen Collins Foster,** *May 3,* Bardstown, Ky. *(183,461),* strip of 3	3.00
880	2c	**John Philip Sousa,** *May 3 (131,422),* pair	3.00
881	3c	**Victor Herbert,** *May 13,* New York, N.Y. *(168,200)*	3.00
882	5c	**Edward A. MacDowell,** *May 13,* Peterborough, N.H. *(135,155)*	4.00
883	10c	**Ethelbert Nevin,** *June 10,* Pittsburgh, Pa. *(121,951)*	6.00
884	1c	**Gilbert Stuart,** *Sept. 5,* Narragansett, R.I. *(131,965),* strip of 3	3.00
885	2c	**James A. McNeill Whistler,** *Sept. 5,* Lowell, Mass. *(130,962),* pair	3.00
886	3c	**Augustus Saint-Gaudens,** *Sept. 16,* New York, N.Y. *(138,200)*	3.00
887	5c	**Daniel Chester French,** *Sept. 16,* Stockbridge, Mass. *(124,608)*	4.00
888	10c	**Frederic Remington,** *Sept. 30,* Canton, N.Y. *(116,219)*	6.00
889	1c	**Eli Whitney,** *Oct. 7,* Savannah, Ga. *(140,868),* strip of 3	3.00
890	2c	**Samuel F.B. Morse,** *Oct. 7,* New York, N.Y. *(135,388),* pair	3.00
891	3c	**Cyrus Hall McCormick,** *Oct. 14,* Lexington, Va. *(137,415)*	3.00
892	5c	**Elias Howe,** *Oct. 14,* Spencer, Mass. *(126,334)*	4.00
893	10c	**Alexander Graham Bell,** *Oct. 28,* Boston, Mass. *(125,372)*	8.00

1940

No.	Denom.	Description	Price
894	3c	**Pony Express,** *Apr. 3,* St. Joseph, Mo. *(194,589)*	10.00
		Sacramento, Cal. *(160,849)*	10.00
895	3c	**Pan American Union,** *Apr. 14 (182,401)*	7.00
896	3c	**Idaho Statehood,** *July 3,* Boise, Idaho *(156,429)*	7.00
897	3c	**Wyoming Statehood,** *July 10* Cheyenne, Wyo. *(156,709)*	7.00
898	3c	**Coronado Expedition,** *Sept. 7,* Albuquerque, N.M. *(161,012)*	7.00
899	1c	**Defense,** *Oct. 16,* strip of 3	4.25
900	2c	**Defense,** *Oct. 16,* pair	4.25
901	3c	**Defense,** *Oct. 16*	4.25
		899-901 on one cover	10.00

First day cancel was applied to 450,083 covers bearing one or more of Nos. 899-901.

No.	Denom.	Description	Price
902	3c	**Thirteenth Amendment,** *Oct. 20,* World's Fair, N.Y. *(156,146)*	10.00

1941

No.	Denom.	Description	Price
903	3c	**Vermont Statehood,** *Mar. 4,* Montpelier, Vt. *(182,423)*	10.00

MacArthur, W. Va.

Apr 15, 1942

First Day Cover

Covers exist with this cancellation. "First Day" refers to the first day of the new name of the town, previously known as Hollywood, W. Va.

1942

No.	Denom.	Description	Price
904	3c	**Kentucky Statehood,** *June 1,* Frankfort, Ky. *(155,730)*	5.50
905	3c	**"Win the War",** *July 4 (191,168)*	5.50
906	5c	**Chinese Resistance,** *July 7,* Denver, Colo. *(168,746)*	12.00

1943-44

No.	Denom.	Description	Price
907	2c	**Allied Nations,** *Jan. 14, 1943 (178,865),* pair	5.50
908	1c	**Four Freedoms,** *Feb. 12, 1943 (193,800),* strip of 3	5.50
909	5c	**Poland,** *June 22, 1943,* Chicago, Ill. *(88,170)*	5.00
		Washington, D.C. *(136,002)*	4.00
910	5c	**Czechoslovakia,** *July 12, 1943 (145,112)*	4.00
911	5c	**Norway,** *July 27, 1943 (130,054)*	4.00
912	5c	**Luxemborg,** *Aug. 10, 1943 (166,367)*	4.00
913	5c	**Netherlands,** *Aug. 24, 1943 (148,763)*	4.00
914	5c	**Belgium,** *Sept. 14, 1943 (154,220)*	4.00
915	5c	**France,** *Sept. 28, 1943 (163,478)*	4.00
916	5c	**Greece,** *Oct. 12, 1943 (166,553)*	4.00
917	5c	**Yugoslavia,** *Oct. 26, 1943 (161,835)*	4.00
918	5c	**Albania,** *Nov. 9, 1943 (162,275)*	4.00
919	5c	**Austria,** *Nov. 23, 1943 (172,285)*	4.00
920	5c	**Denmark,** *Dec. 7, 1943 (173,784)*	4.00
921	5c	**Korea,** *Nov. 2, 1944 (192,860)*	5.00

1944

No.	Denom.	Description	Price
922	3c	**Railroad,** *May 10,* Ogden, Utah *(151,324)*	9.00
		Omaha, Neb. *(171,000)*	9.00
		San Francisco, Cal. *(125,000)*	9.00
923	3c	**Steamship,** *May 22,* Kings Point, N.Y. *(152,324)*	7.50
		Savannah, Ga. *(181,472)*	7.50
924	3c	**Telegraph,** *May 24 (141,907)*	7.50
		Baltimore, Md. *(136,480)*	7.50
925	3c	**Philippines,** *Sept. 27 (214,865)*	7.50
926	3c	**Motion Picture,** *Oct. 31,* Hollywood, Cal. *(190,660)*	7.50
		New York, N.Y. *(176,473)*	7.50

1945

No.	Denom.	Description	Price
927	3c	**Florida,** *Mar. 3,* Tallahassee, Fla. *(228,435)*	7.50
928	5c	**United Nations Conference,** *Apr. 25,* San Francisco, Cal. *(417,450)*	7.50
929	3c	**Iwo Jima,** *July 11 (391,650)*	14.00

1945-46

No.	Denom.	Description	Price
930	1c	**Roosevelt,** *July 26, 1945,* Hyde Park, N.Y. *(390,219),* strip of 3	3.50
931	2c	**Roosevelt,** *Aug. 24, 1945,* Warm Springs, Ga. *(426,142),* pair	3.50
932	3c	**Roosevelt,** *June 27, 1945 (391,650)*	3.50
933	5c	**Roosevelt,** *Jan. 30, 1946 (466,766)*	3.50

1945

No.	Denom.	Description	Price
934	3c	**Army,** *Sept. 28 (392,300)*	8.00
935	3c	**Navy,** *Oct. 27,* Annapolis, Md. *(460,352)*	8.00
936	3c	**Coast Guard,** *Nov. 10* New York, N.Y. *(405,280)*	8.00
937	3c	**Alfred E. Smith,** *Nov. 26* New York, N.Y. *(424,950)*	2.50
938	3c	**Texas,** *Dec. 29,* Austin, Tex. *(397,860)*	7.50

1946

No.	Denom.	Description	Price
939	3c	**Merchant Marine,** *Feb. 26 (432,141)*	8.00
940	3c	**Veterans of WWII,** *May 9 (492,786)*	8.00
941	3c	**Tennessee,** *June 1, 1946,* Nashville, Tenn. *(463,512)*	3.00
942	3c	**Iowa,** *Aug. 3,* Iowa City, Iowa *(517,505)*	3.00
943	3c	**Smithsonian,** *Aug. 10 (402,448)*	3.00
944	3c	**Kearny Expedition,** *Oct. 16,* Santa Fe, N.M. *(384,300)*	3.00

1947

No.	Denom.	Description	Price
945	3c	**Thomas A. Edison,** *Feb. 11,* Milan, Ohio *(632,473)*	3.25
946	3c	**Joseph Pulitzer,** *Apr. 10,* New York, N.Y. *(580,870)*	3.00
947	3c	**Stamp Centenary,** *May 17,* New York, N.Y. *(712,873)*	3.00
948	5c	and 10c **Centenary Exhibition Sheet,** *May 19,* New York, N.Y. *(502,175)*	3.50
949	3c	**Doctors,** *June 9,* Atlantic City, N.J. *(508,016)*	6.50
950	3c	**Utah,** *July 24,* Salt Lake City, Utah *(456,416)*	1.00
951	3c	**"Constitution,"** *Oct. 21,* Boston, Mass. *(683,416)*	6.00
952	3c	**Everglades Park,** *Dec. 5,* Florida City, Fla. *(466,647)*	3.00

1948

No.	Denom.	Description	Price
953	3c	**Carver,** *Jan. 5,* Tuskegee Institute, Ala. *(402,179)*	2.50
954	3c	**California Gold,** *Jan. 24,* Coloma, Calif. *(526,154)*	1.50
955	3c	**Mississippi Territory,** *Apr. 7,* Natchez, Miss. *(434,804)*	1.50
956	3c	**Four Chaplains,** *May 28 (459,070)*	5.00
957	3c	**Wisconsin Centennial,** *May 29,* Madison, Wis. *(470,280)*	1.00
958	5c	**Swedish Pioneers,** *June 4* Chicago, Ill. *(364,318)*	1.00
959	3c	**Women's Progress,** *July 19,* Seneca Falls, N.Y. *(401,923)*	1.00
960	3c	**William Allen White,** *July 31,* Emporia, Kans. *(385,648)*	1.00
961	3c	**U.S.-Canada Friendship,** *Aug. 2,* Niagara Falls, N.Y. *(406,467)*	1.00
962	3c	**Francis Scott Key,** *Aug. 9,* Frederick, Md. *(505,930)*	1.00
963	3c	**Salute to Youth,** *Aug. 11 (347,070)*	1.00
964	3c	**Oregon Territory Establishment,** *Aug. 14,* Oregon City, Ore. *(365,898)*	1.00

965 3c **Harlan Fiske Stone,** *Aug. 25,* Chesterfield, N.H. *(362,170)* 1.00
966 3c **Palomar Observatory,** *Aug. 30,* Palomar Mountain, Calif. *(401,365)* 3.00
967 3c **Clara Barton,** *Sept. 7,* Oxford, Mass. *(362,000)* 2.75
968 3c **Poultry Industry,** *Sept. 9,* New Haven, Conn. *(475,000)* 1.50
969 3c **Gold Star Mothers,** *Sept. 21 (386,064)* 1.50
970 3c **Fort Kearny,** *Sept. 22,* Minden, Neb. *(429,633)* 1.50
971 3c **Volunteer Firemen,** *Oct. 4,* Dover, Del. *(399,630)* 7.00
972 3c **Indian Centennial,** *Oct. 15,* Muskogee, Okla. *(459,528)* 1.00
973 3c **Rough Riders,** *Oct. 27,* Prescott, Ariz. *(399,198)* 1.00
974 3c **Juliette Low,** *Oct. 29,* Savannah, Ga. *(476,573)* 6.00
975 3c **Will Rogers,** *Nov. 4,* Claremore, Okla. *(450,350)* 1.50
976 3c **Fort Bliss,** *Nov. 5,* El Paso, Tex. *(421,000)* 2.50
977 3c **Moina Michael,** *Nov. 9,* Athens, Ga. *(374,090)* 1.00
978 3c **Gettysburg Address,** *Nov. 19,* Gettysburg, Pa. *(511,990)* 1.75
979 3c **American Turners Society,** *Nov. 20,* Cincinnati, Ohio *(434,090)* 1.25
980 3c **Joel Chandler Harris,** *Dec. 9,* Eatonton, Ga. *(426,199)* 1.25

1949
981 3c **Minnesota Territory,** *Mar. 3,* St. Paul, Minn. *(458,750)* 2.00
982 3c **Washington and Lee University,** *Apr. 12,* Lexington, Va. *(447,910)* 2.00
983 3c **Puerto Rico Election,** *Apr. 27,* San Juan, P.R. *(390,416)* 2.00
984 3c **Annapolis, Md.,** *May 23,* Annapolis, Md. *(441,802)* 2.00
985 3c **G.A.R.,** *Aug. 29,* Indianapolis, Ind. *(471,696)* 2.00
986 3c **Edgar Allan Poe,** *Oct. 7,* Richmond, Va. *(371,020)* 2.50

Catalogue values from this point to the end of the section are for unaddressed covers with the most common cachets.

1950
987 3c **American Bankers Assoc.,** *Jan. 3,* Saratoga Springs, N.Y. *(388,622)* 2.00
988 3c **Samuel Gompers,** *Jan. 27 (332,023)* 1.00

National Capital Sesquicentennial

989 3c **Freedom,** *Apr. 20 (371,743)* 1.00
990 3c **Executive,** *June 12 (376,789)* 1.00
991 3c **Judicial,** *Aug. 2 (324,007)* 1.00
992 3c **Legislative,** *Nov. 22 (352,215)* 1.00
993 3c **Railroad Engineers,** *Apr. 29,* Jackson, Tenn. *(420,830)* 3.00
994 3c **Kansas City Centenary,** *June 3,* Kansas City, Mo. *(405,390)* 1.00
995 3c **Boy Scouts,** *June 30,* Valley Forge, Pa. *(622,972)* 6.00
996 3c **Indiana Territory Sesquicentennial,** *July 4,* Vincennes, Ind. *(359,643)* 1.00
997 3c **California Statehood,** *Sept. 9,* Sacramento, Cal. *(391,919)* 2.00

1951
998 3c **United Confederate Veterans,** *May 30,* Norfolk, Va. *(374,235)* 1.50
999 3c **Nevada Centennial,** *July 14,* Genoa, Nev. *(336,890)* 1.00
1000 3c **Landing of Cadillac,** *July 24,* Detroit, Mich. *(323,094)* 1.00
1001 3c **Colorado Statehood,** *Aug. 1,* Minturn, Colo. *(311,568)* 1.00
1002 3c **American Chemical Society,** *Sept. 4,* New York, N.Y. *(436,419)* 1.50
1003 3c **Battle of Brooklyn,** *Dec. 10,* Brooklyn, N.Y. *(420,000)* 1.00

1952
1004 3c **Betsy Ross,** *Jan. 2,* Philadelphia, Pa. *(314,312)* 1.00
1005 3c **4-H Club,** *Jan. 15,* Springfield, Ohio *(383,290)* 3.00
1006 3c **B. & O. Railroad,** *Feb. 28,* Baltimore, Md. *(441,600)* 2.00
1007 3c **American Automobile Association,** *Mar. 4,* Chicago, Ill. *(520,123)* 1.50
1008 3c **NATO,** *Apr. 4 (313,518)* 1.00
1009 3c **Grand Coulee Dam,** *May 15,* Grand Coulee, Wash. *(341,680)* 1.00
1010 3c **Lafayette,** *June 13,* Georgetown, S.C. *(349,102)* 1.00
1011 3c **Mt. Rushmore Memorial,** *Aug. 11,* Keystone, S.D. *(337,027)* 1.00
1012 3c **Civil Engineers,** *Sept. 6,* Chicago, Ill. *(318,483)* 1.00
1013 3c **Service Women,** *Sept. 11 (308,062)* 1.50
1014 3c **Gutenberg Bible,** *Sept. 30 (387,078)* 1.00
1015 3c **Newspaper Boys,** *Oct. 4,* Philadelphia, Pa. *(626,000)* 1.00
1016 3c **Red Cross,** *Nov. 21,* New York, N.Y. *(439,252)* 1.50

1953
1017 3c **National Guard,** *Feb. 23 (387,618)* 1.00
1018 3c **Ohio Sesquicentennial,** *Mar. 2,* Chillicothe, Ohio *(407,983)* 1.00
1019 3c **Washington Territory,** *Mar. 2,* Olympia, Wash. *(344,047)* 1.00
1020 3c **Louisiana Purchase,** *Apr. 30,* St. Louis, Mo. *(425,600)* 1.00
1021 5c **Opening of Japan,** *July 14 (320,541)* 1.25
1022 3c **American Bar Association,** *Aug. 24,* Boston, Mass. *(410,036)* 4.50
1023 3c **Sagamore Hill,** *Sept. 14,* Oyster Bay, N.Y. *(379,750)* 1.00
1024 3c **Future Farmers,** *Oct. 13,* Kansas City, Mo. *(424,193)* 1.00
1025 3c **Trucking Industry,** *Oct. 27,* Los Angeles, Calif. *(875,021)* 1.25
1026 3c **Gen. G.S. Patton, Jr.,** *Nov. 11,* Fort Knox, Ky. *(342,600)* 2.00
1027 3c **New York City,** *Nov. 20,* New York, N.Y. *(387,914)* 1.00
1028 3c **Gadsden Purchase,** *Dec. 30,* Tucson, Ariz. *(363,250)* 1.00

1954
1029 3c **Columbia University,** *Jan. 4,* New York, N.Y. *(550,745)* 1.00

1954-67

LIBERTY ISSUE

1030a ½c **Franklin,** *Oct. 20, 1955 (223,122),* block of 6 1.00
1031b 1c **Washington,** *Aug. 26, 1954,* Chicago, Ill. *(272,581),* strip of 3 1.00
1031A 1¼c **Palace of Governors,** *June 17, 1960,* Santa Fe, N.M., strip of 3 1.00
1031A and 1054A on one cover 1.50

First day cancel was applied to 501,848 covers bearing one or more of Nos. 1031A, 1054A.

1032 1½c **Mt. Vernon,** *Feb. 22, 1956,* Mount Vernon, Va. *(270,109),* pair 1.00
1033 2c **Jefferson,** *Sept. 15, 1954,* San Francisco, Cal. *(307,300),* pair 1.00
1034 2½c **Bunker Hill,** *June 17, 1959,* Boston, Mass. *(315,060),* pair 1.00
1035e 3c **Statue of Liberty,** *June 24, 1954,* Albany, N.Y. *(340,001)* 1.00
1035a Booklet pane of 6, *June 30, 1954* 3.50
1035b 3c Tagged, *July 6, 1966* 40.00
1036c 4c **Lincoln,** *Nov. 19, 1954,* New York, N.Y. *(374,064)* 1.00
1036a Booklet pane of 6, *July 31, 1958,* Wheeling, W. Va. *(135,825)* 4.00
1036b 4c Tagged, *Nov. 2, 1963* 50.00

No. 1036b was supposed to have been issued at Dayton Nov. 2, but a mix-up delayed its issuance there until Nov. 4. About 510 Covers received the Nov. 2 cancellation.

1037 4½c **Hermitage,** *Mar. 16, 1959,* Hermitage, Tenn. *(320,000)* 1.00
1038 5c **Monroe,** *Dec. 2, 1954,* Fredericksburg, Va. *(255,650)* 1.00
1039a 6c **T. Roosevelt,** *Nov. 18, 1955,* New York, N.Y. *(257,551)* 1.00
1040 7c **Wilson,** *Jan. 10, 1956,* Staunton, Va. *(200,111)* 1.00
1041 8c **Statue of Liberty** (flat plate), *Apr. 9, 1954* 1.00
1041B 8c **Statue of Liberty** (rotary press), *Apr. 9, 1954* 1.00

First day cancellation was applied to 340,077 covers bearing one or more of Nos. 1041-1041B.

1042 8c **Statue of Liberty** (Giori press), *Mar. 22, 1958,* Cleveland, O. *(223,899)* 1.00
1042A 8c **Pershing,** *Nov. 17, 1961,* New York, N.Y. *(321,031)* 1.25
1043 9c **Alamo,** *June 14, 1956,* San Antonio, Texas *(207,086)* 1.25
1044 10c **Independence Hall,** *July 4, 1956,* Philadelphia, Pa., *(220,930)* 1.00
1044b 10c Tagged, *July 6, 1966* 40.00
1044A 11c **Statue of Liberty,** *June 15, 1961* *(238,905)* 1.25
1044Ac 11c Tagged, *Jan. 11, 1967* 40.00
1045 12c **B. Harrison,** *June 6, 1959,* Oxford, O. *(225,869)* 1.25
1045a 12c Tagged, *May 6, 1968* 40.00
1046 15c **Jay,** *Dec. 12, 1958 (205,680)* 1.25
1046a 15c Tagged, *July 6, 1966* 40.00
1047 20c **Monticello,** *Apr. 13, 1956,* Charlottesville, Va. *(147,860)* 1.25
1048 25c **Revere,** *Apr. 18, 1958,* Boston, Mass. *(196,530)* 1.25
1049a 30c **Lee,** *Sept. 21, 1955,* Norfolk, Va. *(120,166)* 2.00
1050a 40c **Marshall,** *Sept. 24, 1955,* Richmond, Va. *(113,972)* 2.00
1051a 50c **Anthony,** *Aug. 25, 1955,* Louisville, Ky. *(110,220)* 6.00
1052a $1 **Henry,** *Oct. 7, 1955,* Joplin, Mo. *(80,191)* 10.00
1053 $5 **Hamilton,** *Mar. 19, 1956,* Paterson, N.J. *(34,272)* 50.00

1954-73

COIL STAMPS

1054c 1c **Washington,** *Oct. 8, 1954,* Baltimore, Md. *(196,318),* strip of 3 1.00
1054A 1¼c **Palace of Governors,** *June 17, 1960,* Santa Fe, N.M., strip of 3 1.00
1055d 2c **Jefferson,** *Oct. 22, 1954,* St. Louis, Mo. *(162,050),* pair 1.00
1055a 2c Tagged, *May 6, 1968,* pair 32.50
1056 2½c **Bunker Hill,** *Sept. 9, 1959,* Los Angeles, Calif. *(198,680),* pair 2.00
1057c 3c **Statue of Liberty,** *July 20, 1954* *(137,139)* 1.00
1058 4c **Lincoln,** *July 31, 1958,* Mandan, N.D. *(184,079)* 1.00
1059 4½c **Hermitage,** *May 1, 1959,* Denver, Colo. *(202,454)* 1.75
1059A 25c **Revere,** *Feb. 25, 1965,* Wheaton, Md. *(184,954)* 1.25
1059Ab 25c Tagged, *Apr. 3, 1973,* New York, N.Y. 40.00

1954
1060 3c **Nebraska Territory,** *May 7,* Nebraska City, Neb. *(401,015)* 1.00
1061 3c **Kansas Territory,** *May 31,* Fort Leavenworth, Kans. *(349,145)* 1.00
1062 3c **George Eastman,** *July 12,* Rochester, N.Y. *(630,448)* 1.00
1063 3c **Lewis & Clark Expedition,** *July 28,* Sioux City, Iowa *(371,557)* 1.00

1955
1064 3c **Pennsylvania Academy of the Fine Arts,** *Jan. 15,* Philadelphia, Pa. *(307,040)* 1.00
1065 3c **Land Grant Colleges,** *Feb. 12,* East Lansing, Mich. *(419,241)* 1.25
1066 8c **Rotary International,** *Feb. 23,* Chicago, Ill. *(350,625)* 2.25
1067 3c **Armed Forces Reserve,** *May 21 (300,436)* 1.00
1068 3c **New Hampshire,** *June 21,* Franconia, N.H. *(330,630)* 1.50
1069 3c **Soo Locks,** *June 28,* Sault Sainte Marie, Mich. *(316,616)* 1.00
1070 3c **Atoms for Peace,** *July 28 (351,940)* 1.00
1071 3c **Fort Ticonderoga,** *Sept. 18,* Fort Ticonderoga, N.Y. *(342,946)* 1.00
1072 3c **Andrew W. Mellon,** *Dec. 20 (278,897)* 1.00

1956
1073 3c **Benjamin Franklin,** *Jan. 17,* Philadelphia, Pa. *(351,260)* 1.00
1074 3c **Booker T. Washington,** *Apr. 5,* Booker T. Washington Birthplace, Va. *(272,659)* 1.50
1075 11c **FIPEX Souvenir Sheet,** *Apr. 28,* New York, N.Y. *(429,327)* 5.00
1076 3c **FIPEX,** *Apr. 30,* New York, N.Y. *(526,090)* 1.00
1077 3c **Wildlife (Turkey),** *May 5,* Fond du Lac, Wis. *(292,121)* 1.50
1078 3c **Wildlife (Antelope),** *June 22,* Gunnison, Colo. *(294,731)* 1.50
1079 3c **Wildlife (Salmon),** *Nov. 9,* Seattle, Wash. *(346,800)* 1.50
1080 3c **Pure Food and Drug Laws,** *June 27,* Washington, D.C. *(411,761)* 1.00
1081 3c **Wheatland,** *Aug. 5,* Lancaster, Pa. *(340,142)* 1.00
1082 3c **Labor Day,** *Sept. 3,* Camden, N.J. *(338,450)* 1.00
1083 3c **Nassau Hall,** *Sept. 22,* Princeton, N.J. *(350,756)* 1.00
1084 3c **Devils Tower,** *Sept. 24,* Devils Tower, Wyo. *(285,090)* 1.00
1085 3c **Children,** *Dec. 15 (305,125)* 1.00

1957
1086 3c **Alexander Hamilton,** *Jan. 11,* New York, N.Y. *(305,117)* 1.00
1087 3c **Polio,** *Jan. 15 (307,630)* 1.50
1088 3c **Coast & Geodetic Survey,** *Feb. 11,* Seattle, Wash. *(309,931)* 1.00
1089 3c **Architects,** *Feb. 23,* New York, N.Y. *(368,840)* 1.25
1090 3c **Steel Industry,** *May 22,* New York, N.Y. *(473,284)* 1.00
1091 3c **Naval Review,** *June 10,* U.S.S. Saratoga, Norfolk, Va. *(365,933)* 1.00
1092 3c **Oklahoma Statehood,** *June 14,* Oklahoma City, Okla. *(327,172)* 1.00
1093 3c **School Teachers,** *July 1,* Philadelphia, Pa. *(357,986)* 2.00
(Spelling error) Philadelpia 5.00
1094 4c **Flag,** *July 4 (523,879)* 1.00
1095 3c **Shipbuilding,** *Aug. 15,* Bath, Maine *(347,432)* 1.00
1096 8c **Ramon Magsaysay,** *Aug. 31 (334,558)* 1.25
1097 3c **Lafayette Bicentenary,** *Sept. 6,* Easton, Pa. *(260,421)* 1.00
Fayetteville, N.C. *(230,000)* 1.00
Louisville, Ky. *(207,856)* 1.00
1098 3c **Wildlife** (Whooping Cranes), *Nov. 22,* New York, N.Y. *(342,970)* 1.25
New Orleans, La. *(154,327)* 1.25
Corpus Christi, Tex. *(280,990)* 1.25
1099 3c **Religious Freedom,** *Dec. 27,* Flushing, N.Y. *(357,770)* 1.00

1958
1100 3c **Gardening-Horticulture,** *Mar. 15,* Ithaca, N.Y. *(451,292)* 1.00
1104 3c **Brussels Exhibition,** *Apr. 17,* Detroit, Mich. *(428,073)* 1.00
1105 3c **James Monroe,** *Apr. 28,* Montross, Va. *(326,988)* 1.00
1106 3c **Minnesota Statehood,** *May 11,* Saint Paul, Minn. *(475,552)* 1.00
1107 3c **International Geophysical Year,** *May 31,* Chicago, Ill. *(397,000)* 1.00
1108 3c **Gunston Hall,** *June 12,* Lorton, Va. *(349,801)* 1.00
1109 3c **Mackinac Bridge,** *June 25,* Mackinac Bridge, Mich. *(445,605)* 1.00

1110 4c **Simon Bolivar,** *July 24* 1.25
1111 8c **Simon Bolivar,** *July 24* 1.25
1110-1111 on one cover 2.00

First day cancellation was applied to 708, 777 covers bearing one or more of Nos. 1110-1111.

1112 4c **Atlantic Cable,** *Aug. 15,* New York, N.Y. *(365,072)* 1.00

1958-59

1113 1c **Lincoln Sesquicentennial,** *Feb. 12, 1959,* Hodgenville, Ky. *(379,862)* block of four 1.00
1114 3c **Lincoln Sesquicentennial,** *Feb. 12, 1959,* New York, N.Y. *(437,737)* 1.00
1115 4c **Lincoln-Douglas Debates,** *Aug. 27, 1958,* Freeport, Ill. *(373,063)* 1.00
1116 4c **Lincoln Sesquicentennial,** *May, 30, 1959 (894,887)* 1.00

1958

1117 4c **Lajos Kossuth,** *Sept. 19* 1.25
1118 8c **Lajos Kossuth,** *Sept. 19* 1.25
1117-1118 on one cover 2.00

First day cancellation was applied to 722,188 covers bearing one or more of Nos. 1117-1118.

1119 4c **Freedom of Press,** *Sept. 22,* Columbia, Mo. *(411,752)* 1.00
1120 4c **Overland Mail,** *Oct. 10,* San Francisco, Cal. *(352,760)* 1.00
1121 4c **Noah Webster,** *Oct. 16,* West Hartford, Conn. *(364,608)* 1.00
1122 4c **Forest Conservation,** *Oct. 27,* Tucson, Ariz. *(405,959)* 1.00
1123 4c **Fort Duquesne,** *Nov. 25,* Pittsburgh, Pa. *(421,764)* 1.00

1959

1124 4c **Oregon Statehood,** *Feb. 14,* Astoria, Ore. *(452,764)* 1.00
1125 4c **San Martin,** *Feb. 25* 1.25
1126 8c **San Martin,** *Feb. 25* 1.25
1125-1126 on one cover 2.00

First day cancellation was applied to 910,208 covers bearing one or more of No. 1125-1126.

1127 4c **NATO,** *Apr. 1 (361,040)* 1.00
1128 4c **Arctic Exploration,** *Apr. 6,* Cresson, Pa. *(397,770)* 1.00
1129 8c **World Trade,** *Apr. 20 (503,618)* 1.00
1130 4c **Silver Centennial,** *June 8,* Virginia City, Nev. *(337,233)* 1.00
1131 4c **St. Lawrence Seaway,** *June 26,* Massena, N.Y. *(543,211)* 1.25
1132 4c **Flag** (49 stars), *July 4,* Auburn, N.Y. *(523,773)* 1.00
1133 4c **Soil Conservation,** *Aug. 26,* Rapid City, S.D. *(400,613)* 1.00
1134 4c **Petroleum Industry,** *Aug. 27,* Titusville, Pa. *(801,859)* 1.50
1135 4c **Dental Health,** *Sept. 14,* New York, N.Y. *(649,813)* 3.50
1136 4c **Reuter,** *Sept. 29* 1.25
1137 8c **Reuter,** *Sept. 29* 1.25
1136-1137 on one cover 2.00

First day cancellation was applied to 1,207,933 covers bearing one or more of Nos. 1136-1137.

1138 4c **Dr. Ephraim McDowell,** *Dec. 3,* Danville, Ky. *(344,603)* 1.25

1960-61

1139 4c **Washington "Credo,"** *Jan. 20, 1960,* Mount Vernon, Va. *(438,335)* 1.00
1140 4c **Franklin "Credo,"** *Mar. 31, 1960,* Philadelphia, Pa. *(497,913)* 1.00
1141 4c **Jefferson "Credo,"** *May 18, 1960,* Charlottesville, Va. *(454,903)* 1.00
1142 4c **Francis Scott Key "Credo,"** *Sept. 14, 1960,* Baltimore, Md. *(501,129)* 1.00
1143 4c **Lincoln "Credo,"** *Nov. 19, 1960,* New York, N.Y. *(467,780)* 1.00
1144 4c **Patrick Henry "Credo,"** *Jan. 11, 1961,* Richmond, Va. *(415,252)* 1.00

1960

1145 4c **Boy Scouts,** *Feb. 8 (1,419,955)* 4.00
1146 4c **Olympic Winter Games,** *Feb. 18,* Olympic Valley, Calif, *(516,456)* 1.00
1147 4c **Masaryk,** *Mar. 7* 1.25
1148 8c **Masaryk,** *Mar. 7* 1.25
1147-1148 on one cover 2.00

First day cancellation was applied to 1,710,726 covers bearing one or more of Nos. 1147-1148.

1149 4c **World Refugee Year,** *Apr. 7 (413,298)* 1.00
1150 4c **Water Conservation,** *Apr. 18 (648,988)* 1.00
1151 4c **SEATO,** *May 31 (514,926)* 1.00
1152 4c **American Woman,** *June 2 (830,385)* 1.25
1153 4c **50-Star Flag,** *July 4,* Honolulu, Hawaii *(820,900)* 1.00
1154 4c **Pony Express Centennial,** *July 19,* Sacramento, Calif, *(520,223)* 1.50
1155 4c **Employ the Handicapped,** *Aug. 28,* New York, N.Y. *(439,638)* 1.50
1156 4c **World Forestry Congress,** *Aug. 29,* Seattle, Wash. *(350,848)* 1.00
1157 4c **Mexican Independence,** *Sept. 16,* Los Angeles, Calif, *(360,297)* 1.00
1158 4c **U.S.-Japan Treaty,** *Sept. 28 (545,150)* 1.00
1159 4c **Paderewski,** *Oct. 8* 1.25
1160 8c **Paderewski,** *Oct. 8* 1.25
1159-1160 on one cover 2.00

First day cancellation was applied to 1,057,438 covers bearing one or more of Nos. 1159-1160.

1161 4c **Robert A. Taft,** *Oct. 10,* Cincinnati, Ohio *(312,116)* 1.00
1162 4c **Wheels of Freedom,** *Oct. 15,* Detroit, Mich. *(380,551)* 1.00
1163 4c **Boys' Clubs,** *Oct. 18,* New York, N.Y. *(435,009)* 1.00
1164 4c **Automated P.O.,** *Oct. 20,* Providence, R.I. *(458,237)* 1.00
1165 4c **Mannerheim,** *Oct. 26* 1.25
1166 8c **Mannerheim,** *Oct. 26* 1.25
1165-1166 on one cover 2.00

First day cancellation was applied to 1,168,770 covers bearing one or more of Nos. 1165-1166.

1167 4c **Camp Fire Girls,** *Nov. 1,* New York, N.Y. *(324,944)* 2.50
1168 4c **Garibaldi,** *Nov. 2* 1.25
1169 8c **Garibaldi,** *Nov. 2* 1.25
1168-1169 on one cover 2.00

First day cancellation was applied to 1,001,490 covers bearing one or more of Nos. 1168-1169.

1170 4c **Senator George,** *Nov. 5,* Vienna, Ga. *(278,890)* 1.00
1171 4c **Andrew Carnegie,** *Nov. 25,* New York, N.Y. *(318,180)* 1.00
1172 4c **John Foster Dulles,** *Dec. 6 (400,055)* 1.00
1173 4c **Echo I,** *Dec. 15 (583,747)* 2.50

1961-65

1174 4c **Gandhi,** *Jan. 26, 1961* 1.25
1175 8c **Gandhi,** *Jan. 26, 1961* 1.25
1174-1175 on one cover 2.00

First day cancellation was applied to 1,013,515 covers bearing one or more of Nos. 1174-1175.

1176 4c **Range Conservation,** *Feb. 2, 1961,* Salt Lake City, Utah *(357,101)* 1.00
1177 4c **Horace Greeley,** *Feb. 3, 1961,* Chappaqua, N.Y. *(359,205)* 1.00
1178 4c **Fort Sumter,** *Apr. 12, 1961,* Charleston, S.C. *(602,599)* 4.00
1179 4c **Battle of Shiloh,** *Apr. 7, 1962,* Shiloh, Tenn. *(526,062)* 4.00
1180 5c **Battle of Gettysburg,** *July 1, 1963,* Gettysburg, Pa. *(600,205)* 4.00
1181 5c **Battle of Wilderness,** *May 5, 1964,* Fredericksburg, Va. *(450,904)* 4.00
1182 5c **Appomattox,** *Apr. 9, 1965,* Appomattox, Va. *(653,121)* 4.00

1961

1183 4c **Kansas Statehood,** *May 10,* Council Grove, Kansas *(480,561)* 1.00
1184 4c **Senator Norris,** *July 11 (482,875)* 1.00
1185 4c **Naval Aviation,** *Aug. 20,* San Diego, Calif. *(416,391)* 1.00
1186 4c **Workmen's Compensation,** *Sept. 4,* Milwaukee, Wis, *(410,236)* 1.00
1187 4c **Frederic Remington,** *Oct. 4 (723,443)* 1.25
1188 4c **China Republic,** *Oct. 10 (463,900)* 5.50
1189 4c **Naismith-Basketball,** *Nov. 6,* Springfield, Mass. *(479,917)* 6.50
1190 4c **Nursing,** *Dec. 28 (964,005)* 10.00

1962

1191 4c **New Mexico Statehood,** *Jan. 6,* Sante Fe, N.M. *(365,330)* 1.50
1192 4c **Arizona Statehood,** *Feb. 14,* Phoenix, Ariz. *(508,216)* 1.50
1193 4c **Project Mercury,** *Feb. 20,* Cape Canaveral, Fla. *(3,000,000)* 3.00
Any other city 5.00
1194 4c **Malaria Eradication,** *Mar. 30 (554,175)* 1.00
1195 4c **Charles Evans Hughes,** *Apr. 11* *(544,424)* 1.00
1196 4c **Seattle World's Fair,** *Apr. 25,* Seattle, Wash. *(771,856)* 1.00
1197 4c **Louisiana Statehood,** *Apr. 30,* New Orleans, La. *(436,681)* 1.00
1198 4c **Homestead Act,** *May 20,* Beatrice, Nebr. *(487,450)* 1.00
1199 4c **Girl Scouts,** *July 24,* Burlington, Vt. *(634,347)* 5.00
1200 4c **Brien McMahon,** *July 28,* Norwalk, Conn. *(384,419)* 1.00
1201 4c **Apprenticeship,** *Aug. 31 (1,003,548)* 1.00
1202 4c **Sam Rayburn,** *Sept. 16,* Bonham, Texas *(401,042)* 1.50
1203 4c **Dag Hammarskjold,** *Oct. 23,* New York, N.Y. *(500,683)* 1.00
1203 4c **Dag Hammarskjold,** original yellow inverted, *Oct. 23,* New York, N.Y. *2,500.*
1204 4c **Hammarskjold,** yellow inverted, *Nov. 16,* (about *75,000*) 5.00
1205 4c **Christmas,** *Nov. 1,* Pittsburgh, Pa. *(491,312)* 1.10
1206 4c **Higher Education,** *Nov. 14 (627,347)* 1.25
1207 4c **Winslow Homer,** *Dec. 15,* Gloucester, Mass. *(498,866)* 1.25

1963-66

1208 5c **Flag,** *Jan. 9, 1963 (696,185)* 1.00
1208a 5c Tagged, *Aug. 25, 1966* 30.00

1962-66

REGULAR ISSUE

1209 1c **Jackson,** *Mar. 22, 1963,* New York, N.Y. *(392,363),* block of 5 or 6 1.00
1209a 1c Tagged, *July 6, 1966,* block of 5 or 6 30.00
1213 5c **Washington,** *Nov. 23, 1962,* New York, N.Y. *(360,531)* 1.00
1213a Booklet pane of 5 + label, *Nov. 23, 1962,* New York, N.Y. *(111,452)* 4.00
1213b 5c Tagged, *Oct. 28, 1963,* Dayton, Ohio (about *15,000*) 30.00
1213c Booklet pane of 5 + label, tagged, *Oct. 28, 1963,* Dayton, Ohio 100.00
Washington, D.C. *(750)* 110.00
1225 1c **Jackson,** Coil, *May 31, 1963,* Chicago, Ill. *(238,952),* pair and strip of 3 1.00
1225a 1c Coil, tagged, *July 6, 1966,* pair and strip of 3 30.00
1229 5c **Washington,** Coil, *Nov. 23, 1962,* New York, N.Y. *(184,627)* 1.00
1229a 5c Coil, tagged, *Oct. 28, 1963,* Dayton, Ohio (about *2,000*) 30.00

1963

1230 5c **Carolina Charter,** *Apr. 6,* Edenton, N.C. *(426,200)* 1.00
1231 5c **Food for Peace,** *June 4 (624,342)* 1.00
1232 5c **West Virginia Statehood,** *June 20,* Wheeling, W. Va. *(413,389)* 1.00
1233 5c **Emancipation Proclamation,** *Aug. 16,* Chicago, Ill, *(494,886)* 1.75
1234 5c **Alliance for Progress,** *Aug. 17 (528,095)* 1.00
1235 5c **Cordell Hull,** *Oct. 5* Carthage, Tenn. *(391,631)* 1.00
1236 5c **Eleanor Roosevelt,** *Oct. 11 (860,155)* 1.00
1237 5c **Science,** *Oct. 14 (504,503)* 1.25
1238 5c **City Mail Delivery,** *Oct. 26 (544,806)* 1.25
1239 5c **Red Cross,** *Oct. 29 (557,678)* 1.50
1240 5c **Christmas,** *Nov. 1,* Santa Claus, Ind. *(458,619)* 1.25
1240a 5c **Christmas,** tagged, *Nov. 2,* (about *500*) 60.00

Note below No. 1036b also applies to No. 1240a.

1241 5c **Audubon,** *Dec. 7,* Henderson, Ky. *(518,855)* 1.25

1964

1242 5c **Sam Houston,** *Jan. 10,* Houston, Tex. *(487,986)* 1.75
1243 5c **Charles Russell,** *Mar. 19,* Great Falls, Mont. *(658,745)* 1.25
1244 5c **N.Y. World's Fair,** *Apr. 22,* World's Fair, N.Y. *(1,656,346)* 1.25
1245 5c **John Muir,** *Apr. 29,* Martinez, Calif. *(446,925)* 1.50
1246 5c **John F. Kennedy,** *May 29,* Boston, Mass. *(2,003,096)* 2.25
Any other city 4.00
1247 5c **New Jersey Tercentenary,** *June 15,* Elizabeth, N.J. *(526,879)* 1.00
1248 5c **Nevada Statehood,** *July 22,* Carson City, Nev. *(584,973)* 1.00
1249 5c **Register & Vote,** *Aug. 1 (533,439)* 1.25
1250 5c **Shakespeare,** *Aug. 14,* Stratford, Conn. *(524,053)* 1.50
1251 5c **Drs. Mayo,** *Sept. 11,* Rochester, Minn. *(674,846)* 2.75
1252 5c **American Music,** *Oct. 15,* New York, N.Y. *(466,107)* 1.50
1253 5c **Homemakers,** *Oct. 26,* Honolulu, Hawaii *(435,392)* 1.00
1257b 5c **Christmas,** *Nov. 9,* Bethlehem, Pa. 3.00
1254-1257, any single 1.00
1257c 5c Tagged, *Nov. 10,* Dayton, O. 57.50
1254a-1257a, any single 30.00

First day cancellation was applied to 794,900 covers bearing Nos. 1254-1257 in singles or multiples and at Dayton to about 2,700 covers bearing Nos. 1254a-1257a in singles or multiples.

1258 5c **Verrazano-Narrows Bridge,** *Nov. 21,* Staten Island, N.Y. *(619,780)* 1.00
1259 5c **Fine Arts,** *Dec. 2 (558,046)* 1.00
1260 5c **Amateur Radio,** *Dec. 15,* Anchorage, Alaska *(452,255)* 5.00

1965

1261 5c **Battle of New Orleans,** *Jan. 8,* New Orleans, La. *(466,029)* 1.00
1262 5c **Physical Fitness-Sokol,** *Feb. 15* *(864,848)* 1.25
1263 5c **Cancer Crusade,** *Apr. 1 (744,485)* 2.50
1264 5c **Churchill,** *May 13,* Fulton, Mo. *(773,580)* 1.25
1265 5c **Magna Carta,** *June 15,* Jamestown, Va. *(479,065)* 1.00
1266 5c **Intl. Cooperation Year,** *June 26,* San Francisco, Cal. *(402,925)* 1.00
1267 5c **Salvation Army,** *July 2,* New York, N.Y. *(634,228)* 2.00
1268 5c **Dante,** *July 17,* San Francisco, Cal. *(424,893)* 1.00
1269 5c **Herbert Hoover,** *Aug. 10,* West Branch, Iowa *(698,182)* 1.00
1270 5c **Robert Fulton,** *Aug. 19,* Clermont, N.Y. *(550,330)* 1.00
1271 5c **Florida Settlement,** *Aug. 28,* St. Augustine, Fla. *(465,000)* 1.00
1272 5c **Traffic Safety,** *Sept. 3,* Baltimore, Md. *(527,075)* 1.00
1273 5c **Copley,** *Sept. 17 (613,484)* 1.00
1274 11c **Intl. Telecommunication Union,** *Oct. 6* *(332,818)* 1.10
1275 5c **Adlai Stevenson,** *Oct. 23,* Bloomington, Ill. *(755,656)* 1.00
1276 5c **Christmas,** *Nov. 2,* Silver Bell, Ariz. *(705,039)* 1.00
1276a 5c Tagged, *Nov. 15,* (about *300*) 42.50

1965-78

PROMINENT AMERICANS ISSUE

1278 1c **Jefferson**, *Jan. 12, 1968,* Jeffersonville, Ind., block of 5 or 6 1.00
1278a Booklet pane of 8, *Jan. 12, 1968,* Jeffersonville, Ind. 2.50
1278b Booklet pane of 4 + 2 labels, *May 10, 1971* 11.50

First day cancellation was applied to 655,680 covers bearing one or more of Nos. 1278, 1278a and 1299.

1279 1¼c **Gallatin**, *Jan. 30, 1967,* Gallatin, Mo. *(439,010)* 1.00
1280 2c **Wright**, *June 8, 1966,* Spring Green, Wis. *(460,427)* 1.00
1280a Booklet pane of 5 + label, *Jan. 8, 1968,* Buffalo, N.Y. *(147,244)* 3.50
1280c Booklet pane of 6, *May 7, 1971,* Spokane, Wash. 15.00
1281 3c **Parkman**, *Sept. 16, 1967,* Boston, Mass. *(518,355)* 1.00
1282 4c **Lincoln**, *Nov. 19, 1965,* New York, N.Y. *(445,629)* 1.00
1282a 4c Tagged, *Dec. 1, 1965,* Dayton, O. *(about 2,000)* 30.00
Washington, D.C. *(1,200)* 32.50
1283 5c **Washington**, *Feb. 22, 1966 (525,372)* 1.00
1283a 5c Tagged, *Feb. 23, 1966,* (about *900*) 30.00
Dayton, Ohio (about *200*) 75.00
1283B 5c **Washington**, Redrawn, *Nov. 17, 1967,* New York, N.Y. *(328,983)* 1.00
1284 6c **Roosevelt**, *Jan. 29, 1966,* Hyde Park, N.Y. *(448,631)* 1.00
1284a 6c Tagged, *Dec. 29, 1966* 30.00
1284b Booklet pane of 8, *Dec. 28, 1967* 2.75
1284c Booklet pane of 5 + label, *Jan. 9, 1968* 100.00
1285 8c **Einstein**, *Mar. 14, 1966,* Princeton, N.J. *(366,803)* 2.50
1285a 8c Tagged, *July 6, 1966* 30.00
1286 10c **Jackson**, *Mar. 15, 1967,* Hermitage, Tenn. *(255,945)* 1.00
1286A 12c **Ford**, *July 30, 1968,* Greenfield Village, Mich. *(342,850)* 1.50
1287 13c **Kennedy**, *May 29, 1967,* Brookline, Mass. *(391,195)* 1.75
1288 15c **Holmes**, type I, *Mar. 8, 1968 (322,970)* 1.00
1288B 15c **Holmes**, from bklt., *June 14, 1978,* Boston, Mass. 1.00
1288Bc Booklet pane of 8 3.00

First day cancellation was applied to 387,119 covers bearing one or more of Nos. 1288B and 1305E.

1289 20c **Marshall**, *Oct. 24, 1967,* Lexington, Va. *(221,206)* 1.10
1289a 20c Tagged, *Apr. 3, 1973,* New York, N.Y. 30.00
1290 25c **Douglass**, *Feb. 14, 1967 (213,730)* 2.50
1290a 25c Tagged, *Apr. 3, 1973,* New York, N.Y. 30.00
1291 30c **Dewey**, *Oct. 21, 1968,* Burlington, Vt. *(162,790)* 1.75
1291a 30c Tagged, *Apr. 3, 1973,* New York, N.Y. 30.00
1292 40c **Paine**, *Jan. 29, 1968,* Philadelphia, Pa. *(157,947)* 1.75
1292a 40c Tagged, *Apr. 3, 1973,* New York, N.Y. 30.00
1293 50c **Stone**, *Aug. 13, 1968,* Dorchester, Mass. *(140,410)* 2.50
1293a 50c Tagged, *Apr. 3, 1973,* New York, N.Y. 30.00
1294 $1 **O'Neill**, *Oct. 16, 1967,* New London, Conn. *(103,102)* 6.00
1294a $1 Tagged, *Apr. 3, 1973,* New York, N.Y. 50.00
1295 $5 **Moore**, *Dec. 3, 1966,* Smyrna, Del. *(41,130)* 40.00
1295a $5 Tagged, *Apr. 3, 1973,* New York, N.Y. 90.00

First day cancellation was applied to 17,533 covers bearing one or more of Nos. 1059b, 1289a, 1290a, 1291a, 1292a, 1293a, 1294a and 1295a.

COIL STAMPS

1297 3c **Parkman**, *Nov. 4, 1975,* Pendleton, Ore. *(166,798)* 1.00
1298 6c **Roosevelt**, Perf. 10 Horiz., *Dec. 28, 1967* 1.00

First day cancellation was applied to 312,330 covers bearing one or more of Nos. 1298 and 1284b.

1299 1c **Jefferson**, *Jan. 12, 1968,* Jeffersonville, Ind., pair and strip of 3 1.00
1303 4c **Lincoln**, *May 28, 1966,* Springfield, Ill. *(322,563)* 1.00
1304 5c **Washington**, *Sept. 8, 1966,* Cincinnati, O. *(245,400)* 1.00
1305 6c **Roosevelt**, Perf. 10 vert., *Feb. 28, 1968 (317,199)* 1.00
1305E 15c **Holmes**, type I, *June 14, 1978,* Boston, Mass. 1.00
1305C $1 **O'Neill**, *Jan. 12, 1973,* Hempstead, N.Y. *(121,217)* 4.00

1966

1306 5c **Migratory Bird Treaty**, *Mar. 16,* Pittsburgh, Pa. *(555,485)* 1.75
1307 5c **Humane Treatment of Animals**, *Apr. 9,* New York, N.Y. *(524,420)* 1.25
1308 5c **Indiana Statehood**, *Apr. 16,* Corydon, Ind. *(575,557)* 1.00
1309 5c **Circus**, *May 2,* Delavan, Wis. *(754,076)* 2.00
1310 5c **SIPEX**, *May 21 (637,802)* 1.00
1311 5c **SIPEX, souvenir sheet**, *May 23 (700,882)* 1.10
1312 5c **Bill of Rights**, *July 1,* Miami Beach, Fla. *(562,920)* 1.75
1313 5c **Polish Millennium**, *July 30 (715,603)* 1.25
1314 5c **Natl. Park Service**, *Aug. 25,* Yellowstone National Park, Wyo. *(528,170)* 1.00
1314a 5c Tagged, *Aug. 26* 35.00
1315 5c **Marine Corps Reserve**, *Aug. 29 (585,923)* 1.50
1315a 5c Tagged, *Aug. 29* 35.00
1316 5c **Gen. Fed. of Women's Clubs**, *Sept. 12,* New York, N.Y. *(383,334)* 1.25
1316a 5c Tagged, *Sept. 13* 35.00
1317 5c **Johnny Appleseed**, *Sept. 24,* Leominster, Mass. *(794,610)* 1.00
1317a 5c Tagged, *Sept. 26* 35.00
1318 5c **Beautification of America**, *Oct. 5 (564,440)* 1.00
1318a 5c Tagged, *Oct. 5* 35.00
1319 5c **Great River Road**, *Oct. 21,* Baton Rouge, La. *(330,933)* 1.00
1319a 5c Tagged, *Oct. 22* 35.00
1320 5c **Savings Bond-Servicemen**, *Oct. 26,* Sioux City, Iowa *(444,421)* 1.00
1320a 5c Tagged, *Oct. 27* 35.00
1321 5c **Christmas**, *Nov. 1,* Christmas, Mich. *(537,650)* 1.00
1321a 5c Tagged, *Nov. 2* 35.00
1322 5c **Mary Cassatt**, *Nov. 17 (593,389)* 1.00
1322a 5c Tagged, *Nov. 17* 35.00

1967

1323 5c **National Grange**, *Apr. 17 (603,460)* 1.00
1324 5c **Canada Centenary**, *May 25,* Montreal, Canada *(711,795)* 1.00
1325 5c **Erie Canal**, *July 4,* Rome, N.Y. *(784,611)* 1.00
1326 5c **Search for Peace-Lions**, *July 5,* Chicago, Ill. *(393,197)* 1.00
1327 5c **Thoreau**, *July 12,* Concord, Mass. *(696,789)* 1.00
1328 5c **Nebraska Statehood**, *July 29,* Lincoln, Nebr. *(1,146,957)* 1.00
1329 5c **Voice of America**, *Aug. 1 (455,190)* 2.00
1330 5c **Davy Crockett**, *Aug. 17,* San Antonio, Tex. *(462,291)* 1.25
1331a 5c **Space Accomplishments**, *Sept. 29,* Kennedy Space Center, Fla. *(667,267)* 7.50
1331-1332, any single 3.00
1333 5c **Urban Planning**, *Oct. 2 (389,009)* 1.00
1334 5c **Finland Independence**, *Oct. 6,* Finland, Minn. *(408,532)* 1.00
1335 5c **Thomas Eakins**, *Nov. 2 (648,054)* 1.40
1336 5c **Christmas**, *Nov. 6,* Bethlehem, Ga. *(462,118)* 1.25
1337 5c **Mississippi Statehood**, *Dec. 11,* Natchez, Miss. *(379,612)* 1.00

1968-71

1338 6c **Flag** (Giori), *Jan. 24, 1968 (412,120)* 1.00
1338A 6c **Flag coil**, *May 30, 1969,* Chicago, Ill. *(248,434)* 1.00
1338D 6c **Flag** (Huck) *Aug. 7, 1970 (365,280)* 1.00
1338F 8c **Flag**, *May 10, 1971* 1.00
1338G 8c **Flag coil**, *May 10, 1971* 1.00

First day cancellation (May 10) was applied to 235,543 covers bearing one or more of Nos. 1338F-1338G.

1968

1339 6c **Illinois Statehood**, *Feb. 12,* Shawneetown, Ill. *(761,640)* 1.00
1340 6c **HemisFair'68**, *Mar. 30,* San Antonio, Tex. *(469,909)* 1.00
1341 $1 **Airlift**, *Apr. 4,* Seattle, Wash. *(105,088)* 7.00
1342 6c **Youth-Elks**, *May 1,* Chicago, Ill. *(354,711)* 1.00
1343 6c **Law and Order**, *May 17 (407,081)* 2.00
1344 6c **Register and Vote**, *June 27 (355,685)* 1.00
1354a 6c **Historic Flag series of 10**, *July 4,* Pittsburgh, Pa. *(2,924,962)* 12.50
1345-1354, any single 3.00
1355 6c **Disney**, *Sept. 11,* Marceline, Mo. *(499,505)* 25.00
1356 6c **Marquette**, *Sept. 20,* Sault Ste. Marie, Mich. *(379,710)* 1.00
1357 6c **Daniel Boone**, *Sept. 26,* Frankfort, Ky. *(333,440)* 1.25
1358 6c **Arkansas River**, *Oct. 1,* Little Rock, Ark. *(358,025)* 1.00
1359 6c **Leif Erikson**, *Oct. 9,* Seattle, Wash. *(376,565)* 1.00
1360 6c **Cherokee Strip**, *Oct. 15,* Ponca, Okla. *(339,330)* 1.00
1361 6c **John Trumbull**, *Oct. 18,* New Haven, Conn. *(378,285)* 2.00
1362 6c **Waterfowl Conservation**, *Oct. 24,* Cleveland, Ohio, *(349,719)* 1.25
1363 6c **Christmas**, tagged, *Nov. 1 (739,055)* 1.25
1363a 6c Untagged, *Nov. 2* 10.00
1364 6c **American Indian**, *Nov. 4 (415,964)* 1.25

1969

1368a 6c **Beautification of America**, *Jan. 16 (1,094,184)* 4.00
1365-1368, any single 1.00
1369 6c **American Legion**, *Mar. 15 (632,035)* 1.00
1370 6c **Grandma Moses**, *May 1 (367,880)* 1.10
1371 6c **Apollo 8**, *May 5,* Houston, Texas *(908,634)* 2.25
1372 6c **W.C. Handy**, *May 17,* Memphis, Tenn. *(398,216)* 2.25
1373 6c **California Bicentenary**, *July 16,* San Diego, Calif. *(530,210)* 1.00
1374 6c **J.W. Powell**, *Aug. 1,* Page, Ariz. *(434,433)* 1.00
1375 6c **Alabama Statehood**, *Aug. 2,* Huntsville, Ala. *(485,801)* 1.00
1379a 6c **Botanical Congress**, *Aug. 23,* Seattle, Wash. *(737,935)* 5.00
1376-1379, any single 1.50
1380 6c **Dartmouth Case**, *Sept. 22,* Hanover, N.H. *(416,327)* 1.00
1381 6c **Professional Baseball**, *Sept. 24,* Cincinnati, Ohio *(414,942)* 12.00
1382 6c **Intercollegiate Football**, *Sept. 26,* New Brunswick, N.J. *(414,860)* 6.50
1383 6c **Dwight D. Eisenhower**, *Oct. 14,*Abilene, Kans. *(1,009,560)* 1.00
1384 6c **Christmas**, *Nov. 3,* Christmas, Fla. *(555,500)* 1.25
1385 6c **Hope for Crippled**, *Nov. 20,* Columbus, Ohio *(342,676)* 1.25
1386 6c **William M. Harnett**, *Dec. 3,* Boston, Mass. *(408,860)* 1.00

1970-74

1390a 6c **National History**, *May 6, 1970,* New York, N.Y. *(834,260)* 4.00
1387-1390, any single 1.50
1391 6c **Maine Statehood**, *July 9, 1970,* Portland, Maine, *(472,165)* 2.00
1392 6c **Wildlife Conservation**, *July 20, 1970,* Custer, S.D. *(309,418)* 1.00
1393 6c **Eisenhower**, *Aug. 6, 1970* 1.00
1393a Booklet pane of 8 3.00
1393b Booklet pane of 5 + label 1.50

First day cancellations were applied to 823,540 covers bearing one or more of Nos. 1393 and 1401.

1393D 7c **Franklin**, *Oct. 20, 1972,* Philadelphia, Pa. *(309,276)* 1.00
1394 8c **Eisenhower** (multi), *May 10, 1971* 1.00
1395 8c **Eisenhower** (claret), *May 10, 1971* 1.00
1395a Booklet pane of 8 2.50
1395b Booklet pane of 6 2.50
1395c Booklet pane of 4 + 2 labels, *Jan. 28, 1972,* Casa Grande, Ariz. 2.25
1395d Booklet pane of 7 + label, *Jan. 28, 1972,* Casa Grande, Ariz. 2.25

First day cancellations were applied to 813,947 covers bearing one or more of Nos. 1394, 1395 and 1402. First day cancellations were applied to 181,601 covers bearing one or more of Nos. 1395c or 1395d.

1396 8c **Postal Service Emblem**, *July 1, 1971, any city (est. 16,300,000)* 1.00

First day cancels from over 16,000 different cities are known. Some are rare.

1397 14c **Fiorello H. LaGuardia**, *Apr. 24, 1972,* New York, N.Y. *(180,114)* 1.00
1398 16c **Ernie Pyle**, *May 7, 1971 (444,410)* 1.50
1399 18c **Elizabeth Blackwell**, *Jan. 23, 1974,* Geneva, N.Y. *(217,938)* 1.25
1400 21c **Amadeo Giannini**, *June 27, 1973,* San Mateo, Calif. *(282,520)* 1.50
1401 6c **Eisenhower coil**, *Aug. 6, 1970* 1.00
1402 8c **Eisenhower coil**, *May 10, 1971* 1.00

1970

1405 6c **Edgar Lee Masters**, *Aug. 22,* Petersburg Ill. *(372,804)* 1.00
1406 6c **Woman Suffrage**, *Aug. 26,* Adams, Mass. *(508,142)* 1.00
1407 6c **South Carolina Anniv.** *Sept. 12,* Charleston, S.C. *(533,000)* 1.00
1408 6c **Stone Mt. Memorial**, *Sept. 19,* Stone Mountain, Ga. *(558,546)* 1.00
1409 6c **Fort Snelling**, *Oct. 17,* Fort Snelling, Minn. *(497,611)* 1.00
1413a 6c **Anti-Pollution**, *Oct. 28,* San Clemente, Calif. *(1,033,147)* 4.00
1410-1413, any single 1.25
1414 6c **Christmas (Nativity)**, *Nov. 5* 1.25
1414a 6c Precanceled, *Nov. 5* 7.50
1418b 6c **Christmas**, *Nov. 5* 5.50
1415-1418, any single 1.50
1414-1418 on one cover 8.50
1418c 6c Precanceled, *Nov. 5* 15.00
1415a-1418a, any single 5.00
1414a-1418a on one cover 30.00

First day cancellation was applied to 2,014,450 covers bearing one or more of Nos. 1414-1418 or 1414a-1418a.

1419 6c **United Nations**, *Nov. 20,* New York, N.Y. *(474,070)* 1.00
1420 6c **Pilgrims' Landing**, *Nov. 21,* Plymouth, Mass. *(629,850)* 1.00
1421 6c **Disabled Veterans**, *Nov. 24,* Cincinnati, Ohio, or Montgomery, Ala. 2.00
1422 6c **U.S. Servicemen**, *Nov. 24,* Cincinnati, Ohio, or Montgomery, Ala. 2.00
1421a 3.00

First day cancellation was applied to 476,610 covers at Cincinnati and 336,417 at Montgomery, each cover bearing one or more of Nos. 1421-1422.

1971

1423 6c **Wool Industry**, *Jan. 19,* Las Vegas, Nev. *(379,911)* 1.00
1424 6c **MacArthur**, *Jan. 26,* Norfolk, Va. *(720,035)* 1.50
1425 6c **Blood Donor**, *Mar. 12,* New York, N.Y. *(644,497)* 1.00
1426 8c **Missouri Sesquicentennial**, *May 8,* Independence, Mo. *(551,000)* 1.00
1430a 8c **Wildlife Conservation**, *June 12,* Avery Island, La. *(679,483)* 3.00
1427-1430, any single 1.25
1431 8c **Antarctic Treaty**, *June 23 (419,200)* 1.00
1432 8c **American Revolution Bicentennial**, *July 4 (434,930)* 1.00
1433 8c **John Sloan**, *Aug. 2,* Lock Haven, Pa. *(482,265)* 1.00
1434a 8c **Space Achievement Decade**, *Aug. 2,* Kennedy Space Center, Fla. *(1,403,644)* 2.00
Houston, Texas *(811,560)* 2.00
Huntsville, Ala. *(524,000)* 2.00
1436 8c **Emily Dickinson**, *Aug. 28,* Amherst, Mass. *(498,180)* 1.00

1437 8c **San Juan,** *Sept. 12,* San Juan, P.R. *(501,668)* 1.00
1438 8c **Drug Abuse,** *Oct. 4,* Dallas, Texas *(425,330)* 1.00
1439 8c **CARE,** *Oct. 27,* New York, N.Y. *(402,121)* 1.00
1443a 8c **Historic Preservation,** *Oct. 29,* San Diego, Calif. *(783,242)* 3.00
1440-1443, any single 1.25
1444 8c **Christmas (religious),** *Nov. 10* 1.25
1445 8c **Christmas (secular),** *Nov. 10* 1.25
1444-1445 on one cover 1.50

First day cancellation was applied to 348,038 covers with No. 1444 and 580,062 with No. 1445.

1972

1446 8c **Sidney Lanier,** *Feb. 3,* Macon Ga. *(394,800)* 1.00
1447 8c **Peace Corps,** *Feb. 11 (453,660)* 1.00
1451a 2c **National Parks Centennial,** *Apr. 5,* Hatteras, N.C., block of 4 *(505,697)* 2.00
1452 6c **National Parks,** *June 26,* Vienna, Va. *(403,396)* 1.00
1453 8c **National Parks,** *Mar. 1,* Yellowstone National Park, Wyo. 1.00
Washington, D.C. *(847,500)* 1.00
1454 15c **National Parks,** *July 28,* Mt. McKinley National Park, Alaska *(491,456)* 1.00
1455 8c **Family Planning,** *Mar. 18,* New York, N.Y. *(691,385)* 1.00
1459a 8c **Colonial Craftsmen** (Rev. Bicentennial), *July 4,* Williamsburg, Va. *(1,914,976)* 2.50
1456-1459, any single 1.00
1460 6c **Olympics,** *Aug. 17* 1.00
1461 8c **Winter Olympics,** *Aug. 17* 1.00
1462 15c **Olympics,** *Aug. 17* 1.00
1460-1462 and C85 on one cover 2.00

First day cancellation was applied to 971,536 covers bearing one or more of Nos. 1460-1462 and C85.

1463 8c **P.T.A.,** *Sept. 15,* San Francisco, Cal. *(523,454)* 1.00
1467a 8c **Wildlife,** *Sept. 20,* Warm Springs, Ore. *(733,778)* 3.00
1464-1467, any single 1.50
1468 8c **Mail Order,** *Sept. 27,* Chicago, Ill. *(759,666)* 1.00
1469 8c **Osteopathy,** *Oct. 9,* Miami, Fla. *(607,160)* 1.50
1470 8c **Tom Sawyer,** *Oct. 13,* Hannibal, Mo. *(459,013)* 1.50
1471 8c **Christmas (religious),** *Nov. 9* 1.00
1472 8c **Christmas (secular),** *Nov. 9* 1.00
1471-1472 on one cover 2.00

First day cancellation was applied to 713,821 covers bearing one or more of Nos. 1471-1472.

1473 8c **Pharmacy,** *Nov. 10,* Cincinnati, Ohio *(804,320)* 8.00
1474 8c **Stamp Collecting,** *Nov. 17,* New York, N.Y. *(434,680)* 1.25

1973

1475 8c **Love,** *Jan. 26,* Philadelphia, Pa. *(422,492)* 2.00
1476 8c **Pamphleteer** (Rev. Bicentennial), *Feb. 16,* Portland, Ore. *(431,784)* 1.00
1477 8c **Broadside** (Rev. Bicentennial), *Apr. 13,* Atlantic City, N.J. *(423,437)* 1.00
1478 8c **Post Rider** (Rev. Bicentennial), *June 22,* Rochester, N.Y. *(586,850)* 1.00
1479 8c **Drummer** (Rev. Bicentennial), *Sept. 28,* New Orleans, La. *(522,427)* 1.00
1483a 8c **Boston Tea Party** (Rev. Bicentennial), *July 4,* Boston, Mass. *(897,870)* 3.00
1480-1483, any single 1.00
1484 8c **George Gershwin,** *Feb. 28,* Beverly Hills, Calif. *(448,814)* 1.00
1485 8c **Robinson Jeffers,** *Aug. 13,* Carmel, Calif. *(394,261)* 1.00
1486 8c **Henry O. Tanner,** *Sept. 10,* Pittsburgh, Pa. *(424,065)* 2.50
1487 8c **Willa Cather,** *Sept. 20,* Red Cloud, Nebr. *(435,784)* 1.00
1488 8c **Nicolaus Copernicus,** *Apr. 23 (734,190)* 1.25
1498a 8c **Postal People,** *Apr. 30, any city* 5.00
1489-1498, any single 1.00

First day cancellation was applied at Boston to 1,205,212 covers bearing one or more of Nos. 1489-1498. Cancellations at other cities unrecorded.

1499 8c **Harry S Truman,** *May 8,* Independence, Mo. *(938,636)* 1.25
1500 6c **Electronics,** *July 10,* New York, N.Y. 1.00
1501 8c **Electronics,** *July 10,* New York, N.Y. 1.00
1502 15c **Electronics,** *July 10,* New York, N.Y. 1.00
1500-1502 and C86 on one cover 4.00

First day cancellation was applied to 1,197,700 covers bearing one or more of Nos. 1500-1502 and C86.

1503 8c **Lyndon B. Johnson,** *Aug. 27,* Austin, Texas *(701,490)* 1.00

1973-74

1504 8c **Angus Cattle,** *Oct. 5, 1973,* St. Joseph, Mo. *(521,427)* 1.00
1505 10c **Chautauqua,** *Aug. 6, 1974,* Chautauqua, N.Y. *(411,105)* 1.00
1506 10c **Wheat,** *Aug. 16, 1974,* Hillsboro, Kans. *(468,280)* 1.00
1507 8c **Christmas (religious),** *Nov. 7, 1973* 1.00
1508 8c **Christmas (secular),** *Nov. 7, 1973* 1.00
1507-1508 on one cover 1.10

First day cancellation was applied to 807,468 covers bearing one or both of Nos. 1507-1508.

1509 10c **Crossed Flags,** *Dec. 8, 1973,* San Francisco, Calif. 1.00

First day cancellation was applied to 341,528 covers bearing one or more of Nos. 1509 and 1519.

1510 10c **Jefferson Memorial,** *Dec. 14, 1973* 1.00
1510b Booklet pane of 5 + label 2.25
1510c Booklet pane of 8 2.50
1510d Booklet pane of 6, *Aug. 5, 1974,* Oakland, Calif. 3.00

First day cancellation was applied to 686,300 covers bearing one or more of Nos. 1510, 1510b, 1510c, 1520.

1511 10c **Zip Code,** *Jan. 4, 1974 (335,220)* 1.00
1518 6.3c **Bell Coil,** *Oct. 1, 1974 (221,141)* 1.00
1519 10c **Crossed Flags coil,** *Dec. 8, 1973,* San Francisco, Calif. 1.00
1520 10c **Jefferson Memorial coil,** *Dec. 14, 1973* 1.00

1974

1525 10c **Veterans of Foreign Wars,** *Mar. 11 (543,598)* 1.25
1526 10c **Robert Frost,** *Mar. 26,* Derry, N.H. *(500,425)* 1.00
1527 10c **EXPO '74,** *Apr. 18,* Spokane, Wash. *(565,548)* 1.00
1528 10c **Horse Racing,** *May 4,* Louisville, Ky. *(623,983)* 3.00
1529 10c **Skylab,** *May 14,* Houston, Tex. *(972,326)* 1.50
1537a 10c **UPU Centenary,** *June 6 (1,374,765)* 4.00
1530-1537, any single 1.00
1541a 10c **Mineral Heritage,** *June 13,* Lincoln, Neb. *(865,368)* 2.75
1538-1541, any single 1.00
1542 10c **Kentucky Settlement,** *June 15,* Harrodsburg, Ky. *(478,239)* 1.00
1546a 10c **Continental Congress** (Rev. Bicentennial), *July 4,* Philadelphia, Pa. *(2,124,957)* 2.75
1543-1546, any single 1.00
1547 10c **Energy Conservation,** *Sept. 23,* Detroit, Mich. *(587,210)* 1.00
1548 10c **Sleepy Hollow,** *Oct. 10,* North Tarrytown, N.Y. *(514,836)* 1.50
1549 10c **Retarded Children,** *Oct. 12,* Arlington Tex. *(412,882)* 1.00
1550 10c **Christmas (Religious),** *Oct. 23,* New York, N.Y. *(634,990)* 1.00
1551 10c **Christmas (Currier & Ives),** *Oct. 23,* New York, N.Y. *(634,990)* 1.00
1550-1551 on one cover 1.10
1552 10c **Christmas (Dove),** *Nov. 15,* New York, N.Y. *(477,410)* 1.50

1975

1553 10c **Benjamin West,** *Feb. 10,* Swarthmore, Pa. *(465,017)* 1.00
1554 10c **Paul L. Dunbar,** *May 1,* Dayton, Ohio *(397,347)* 1.50
1555 10c **D.W. Griffith,** *May 27,* Beverly Hills, Calif. *(424,167)* 1.00
1556 10c **Pioneer-Jupiter,** *Feb. 28,* Mountain View, Calif. *(594,896)* 1.25
1557 10c **Mariner 10,** *Apr. 4,* Pasadena, Calif. *(563,636)* 1.25
1558 10c **Collective Bargaining,** *Mar. 13 (412,329)* 1.00
1559 8c **Sybil Ludington** (Rev. Bicentennial), *Mar. 25,* Carmel, N.Y. *(394,550)* 1.00
1560 10c **Salem Poor** (Rev. Bicentennial), *Mar. 25,* Cambridge, Mass. *(415,565)* 1.50
1561 10c **Haym Salomon** (Rev. Bicentennial), *Mar. 25,* Chicago, Ill. *(442,630)* 1.00
1562 18c **Peter Francisco** (Rev. Bicentennial), *Mar. 25,* Greensboro, N.C. *(415,000)* 1.00
1563 10c **Lexington-Concord** (Rev. Bicentennial), *Apr. 19,* Lexington, Mass., or Concord, Mass. *(975,020)* 1.00
1564 10c **Bunker Hill** (Rev. Bicentennial), *June 17,* Charlestown, Mass. *(557,130)* 1.00
1568a 10c **Military Services** (Rev. Bicentennial), *July 4 (1,134,831)* 2.50
1565-1568, any single 1.00
1569a 10c **Apollo-Soyuz,** *July 15,* Kennedy Space Center, Fla. *(1,427,046)* 5.00
1569-1570, any single 3.00
1571 10c **International Women's Year,** *Aug. 26,* Seneca Falls, N.Y. *(476,769)* 1.00
1575a 10c **Postal Service Bicentenary,** *Sept. 3,* Philadelphia, Pa. *(969,999)* 2.50
1572-1575, any single 1.00
1576 10c **World Peace through Law,** *Sept. 29 (386,736)* 1.25
1577a 10c **Banking-Commerce,** *Oct. 6,* New York, N.Y. *(555,580)* 1.75
1577-1578, any single 1.00
1579 (10c) **Christmas (religious),** *Oct. 14* 1.00
1580 (10c) **Christmas (secular),** *Oct. 14* 1.00
1579-1580 on one cover 2.00

First day cancellation was applied to 730,079 covers bearing one or more of Nos. 1579-1580.

1975-79

AMERICANA ISSUE

1581 1c **Inkwell,** *Dec. 8, 1977,* St. Louis, Mo., multiple for 1st class rate 1.00
1582 2c **Speaker's Stand,** *Dec. 8, 1977,* St. Louis, Mo., multiple for 1st class rate 1.00
1584 3c **Ballot Box,** *Dec. 8, 1977,* St. Louis, Mo., multiple for 1st class rate 1.00
1585 4c **Books and Eyeglasses,** *Dec. 8, 1977,* St. Louis, Mo., multiple for 1st class rate 1.00

First day cancellation was applied to 530,033 covers bearing one or more of Nos. 1581-1582, 1584-1585.

1590 9c **Capitol Dome,** from bklt.,*Mar. 11, 1977,* New York, N.Y., plus postage for 1st class rate 1.00
1591 9c **Capitol Dome,** *Nov. 24, 1975 (190,117),* multiple for 1st class rate 1.00
1592 10c **Justice,** *Nov. 17, 1977,* New York, N.Y. *(359,050),* multiple for 1st class rate 1.00
1593 11c **Printing Press,** *Nov. 13, 1975,* Philadelphia, Pa. *(217,755),* multiple for 1st class rate 1.00
1594 12c **Torch,** *Apr. 8, 1981,* Dallas, TX, multiple for 1st class rate 1.00

First day cancellation was applied to 280,930 covers bearing one or more of Nos. 1594 and 1816.

1595 13c **Liberty Bell,** *Oct. 31, 1975,* Cleveland, Ohio *(256,734)* 1.00
1595a Booklet pane of 6 2.00
1595b Booklet pane of 7 + label 2.75
1595c Booklet pane of 8 2.50
1595d Booklet pane of 5 + label, *Apr. 2, 1976,* Liberty, Mo. 2.25
1596 13c **Eagle and Shield,** *Dec. 1, 1975,* Juneau, Alaska *(418,272)* 1.00
1597 15c **Flag,** *June 30, 1978,* Baltimore, Md. 1.00
1598 15c **Flag,** from bklt., *June 30, 1978,* Baltimore, Md. 1.00
1598a Booklet pane of 8 2.50

First day cancellation was applied to 315,359 covers bearing one or more of Nos. 1597, 1598, and 1618C.

1599 16c **Statue of Liberty,** *Mar. 31, 1978,* New York, N.Y. 1.00
1603 24c **Old North Church,** *Nov. 14, 1975,* Boston, Mass. *(208,973)* 1.00
1604 28c **Fort Nisqually,** *Aug. 11, 1978,* Tacoma, Wash. *(159,639)* 1.00
1605 29c **Sandy Hook Lighthouse,** *Apr. 14, 1978,* Atlantic City, N.J. *(193,476)* 1.50
1606 30c **Schoolhouse,** *Aug. 27, 1979,* Devils Lake, N.D. *(186,882)* 1.25
1608 50c **Betty Lamp,** *Sept. 11, 1979,* San Juan, P.R. *(159,540)* 1.50
1610 $1 **Rush Lamp,** *July 2, 1979,* San Francisco, Calif. *(255,575)* 3.00
1611 $2 **Kerosene Lamp,** *Nov. 16, 1978,* New York, N.Y. *(173,596)* 5.00
1612 $5 **Railroad Lantern,** *Aug. 23, 1979,* Boston, Mass. *(129,192)* 12.50

COIL STAMPS

1613 3.1c **Guitar,** *Oct. 25, 1979,* Shreveport, La. *(230,403)* 1.00
1614 7.7c **Saxhorns,** *Nov. 20, 1976,* New York, N.Y. *(285,290)* 1.00
1615 7.9c **Drum,** *Apr. 23, 1976,* Miami, Fla. *(193,270)* 1.00
1615C 8.4c **Piano,** *July 13, 1978,* Interlochen, Mich. *(200,392)* 1.00
1616 9c **Capitol Dome,** *Mar. 5, 1976,* Milwaukee, Wis. *(128,171)* 1.00
1617 10c **Justice,** *Nov. 4, 1977,* Tampa, Fla. *(184,954)* 1.00
1618 13c **Liberty Bell,** *Nov. 25, 1975,* Allentown, Pa. *(320,387)* 1.00
1618C 15c **Flag,** *June 30, 1978,* Baltimore, Md. 1.00
1619 16c **Statue of Liberty,** *Mar. 31, 1978,* New York, N.Y. 1.00

First day cancellation was applied to 376,338 covers bearing one or more of Nos. 1599 and 1619.

1975

1622 13c **13-Star Flag,** *Nov. 15,* Philadelphia, Pa. 1.00
1623 13c **Flag over Capitol,** *Mar. 11,* New York, N.Y. 1.50
1623a Booklet pane of 8, perf 11 (1 #1590 +7 #1623) 25.00
1623Bc Booklet pane of 8, perf. 10x9¾ (1 #1590A + 7 #1623B) 12.50

First day cancellation was applied to 242,208 covers bearing Nos. 1623, 1623a, 1623B or 1623Bc.

1625 13c **13-Star Flag coil,** *Nov. 15,* Philadelphia, PA 1.00

First day cancellation was applied to 362,959 covers bearing one or more of Nos. 1622 and 1625.

1976

1631a 13c **Spirit of '76,** *Jan. 1,* Pasadena, CA *(1,013,067)* 2.00
1629-1631, any single 1.25
1632 13c **Interphil '76,** *Jan. 17,* Philadelphia, Pa. *(519,902)* 1.00
1682a 13c **State Flags,** *Feb. 23* 27.50
1633-1682, any single 1.50
1683 13c **Telephone,** *Mar. 10,* Boston, Mass. *(662,515)* 1.00
1684 13c **Commercial Aviation,** *Mar. 19,* Chicago Ill. *(631,555)* 1.25
1685 13c **Chemistry,** *Apr. 6,* New York, N.Y. *(557,600)* 1.50

Bicentennial Souvenir Sheets of 5

1686 13c **Surrender of Cornwallis,** *May 29,* Philadelphia, Pa. 7.50
1687 18c **Declaration of Independence,** *May 29,* Philadelphia, Pa. 7.50

1688 24c **Declaration of Independence,** *May 29,* Philadelphia, Pa. 7.50
1689 31c **Washington at Valley Forge,** *May 29,* Philadelphia, Pa. 7.50

First day cancellation was applied to 879,890 covers bearing singles, multiples or complete sheets of Nos. 1686-1689.

1690 13c **Franklin,** *June 1,* Philadelphia, Pa. *(588,740)* 1.00
1694a 13c **Declaration of Independence,** *July 4,* Philadelphia, Pa. *(2,093,880)* 2.00
1691-1694, any single 1.00
1698a 13c **Olympic Games,** *July 16,* Lake Placid, N.Y. *(1,140,189)* 2.00
1695-1698, any single 1.00
1699 13c **Clara Maass,** *Aug. 18,* Belleville, N.J. *(646,506)* 1.25
1700 13c **Adolph S. Ochs,** *Sept. 18,* New York, N.Y. *(582,580)* 1.00
1701 13c **Christmas (religious),** *Oct. 27,* Boston, Mass. (540,050) 1.00
1702 13c **Christmas (secular),** *Oct. 27,* Boston, Mass. (181,410) 1.00
1703 13c **Christmas (secular),** block tagged, *Oct. 27,* Boston, Mass. (330,450) 1.00
1701 and 1702 or 1703 on one cover 1.25

1977

1704 13c **Washington at Princeton,** *Jan. 3,* Princeton, N.J. *(695,335)* 1.00
1705 13c **Sound Recording,** *Mar. 23 (632,216)* 1.25
1709a 13c **Pueblo Art,** *Apr. 13,* Santa Fe, N.M. *(1,194,554)* 2.00
1706-1709, any single 1.00
1710 13c **Lindbergh Flight,** *May 20,* Roosevelt Sta., N.Y. *(3,985,989)* 2.00
1711 13c **Colorado Statehood,** *May 21,* Denver, Colo. *(510,880)* 1.00
1715a 13c **Butterflies,** *June 6,* Indianapolis, Ind. *(1,218,278)* 2.00
1712-1715, any single 2.00
1716 13c **Lafayette's Landing,** *June 13,* Charleston, S.C. *(514,506)* 1.00
1720a 13c **Skilled Hands,** *July 4,* Cincinnati, Ohio *(1,263,568)* 2.00
1717-1720, any single 1.00
1721 13c **Peace Bridge,** *Aug. 4,* Buffalo, N.Y. *(512,995)* 1.00
1722 13c **Battle of Oriskany,** *Aug. 6,* Utica, N.Y. *(605,906)* 1.00
1723a 13c **Energy Conservation,** *Oct. 20 (410,299)* 1.50
1723-1724, any single 1.25
1725 13c **Alta California,** *Sept. 9,* San Jose, Calif. *(709,457)* 1.00
1726 13c **Articles of Confederation,** *Sept. 30,* York, Pa. *(605,455)* 1.00
1727 13c **Talking Pictures,** *Oct. 6,* Hollywood, Calif. *(570,195)* 1.50
1728 13c **Surrender at Saratoga** *Oct. 7,* Schuylerville, N.Y. *(557,529)* 1.00
1729 13c **Christmas (Valley Forge),** *Oct. 21,* Valley Forge, Pa. *(583,139)* 1.00
1730 13c **Christmas (mailbox),** *Oct. 21,* Omaha, Nebr. *(675,786)* 1.00

1978

1731 13c **Carl Sandburg,** *Jan. 6,* Galesburg, Ill. *(493,826)* 1.00
1732a 13c **Captain Cook,** *Jan. 20,* Honolulu, Hawaii, or Anchorage, Alaska 1.75
1732-1733, any single 1.25

First day cancellation was applied to 823,855 covers at Honolulu, and 672,804 at Anchorage, each cover bearing one or both of Nos. 1732-1733.

1734 13c **Indian Head Penny,** *Jan. 11,* Kansas City, Mo. *(512,426)* 1.00

1978-80

REGULAR ISSUE

1735 (15c) **"A" Eagle,** *May 22,* Memphis, Tenn. 1.00
1736 (15c) **"A" Eagle,** bklt. single *May 22,* Memphis, Tenn. 1.00
1736a Booklet pane of 8 2.50
1737 15c **Roses,** *July 11,* Shreveport, La. *(445,003)* 1.00
1737a Booklet pane of 8 2.50
1742a 15c **Windmills Booklet pane of 10,** *Feb. 7, 1980,* Lubbock, TX 3.50
1738-1742, any single 1.00
1743 15c **"A" Eagle coil,** *May 22,* Memphis, Tenn. 1.00

First day cancellation was applied to 689,049 covers bearing one or more of Nos. 1735, 1736 and 1743. First day cancellation was applied to 708,411 covers bearing one or more of Nos. 1738-1742a.

1978

1744 13c **Harriet Tubman,** *Feb. 1 (493,495)* 1.75
1748a 13c **American Quilts,** *Mar. 8,* Charleston, W.Va. 2.00
1745-1748, any single 1.00

First day cancellation was applied to 1,081,827 covers bearing one or more of Nos. 1745-1748.

1752a 13c **American Dance,** *Apr. 26,* New York, N.Y. *(1,626,493)* 2.00
1749-1752, any single 1.00
1753 13c **French Alliance,** *May 4,* York, Pa. *(705,240)* 1.00
1754 13c **Papanicolaou,** *May 18 (535,584)* 1.00
1755 13c **Jimmie Rodgers,** *May 24,* Meridian, Miss. *(599,287)* 1.00
1756 15c **George M. Cohan,** *July 3,* Providence, R.I. *(740,750)* 1.25
1757 **CAPEX** souv. sheet, *June 10,* Toronto, Canada *(1,994,067)* 2.75
1758 15c **Photography,** *June 26,* Las Vegas, Nev. *(684,987)* 1.00
1759 15c **Viking Missions,** *July 20,* Hampton, Va. *(805,051)* 1.00
1763a 15c **American Owls,** *Aug. 26,* Fairbanks, Alas. *(1,690,474)* 2.00
1760-1763, any single 1.25
1767a 15c **American Trees,** *Oct. 9,* Hot Springs National Park, Ark. *(1,139,100)* 2.00
1764-1767, any single 1.25
1768 15c **Christmas (Madonna),** *Oct. 18 (553,064)* 1.00
1769 15c **Christmas (Hobby Horse),** *Oct. 18,* Holly, Mich. *(603,008)* 1.00

1979-80

1770 15c **Robert Kennedy,** *Jan. 12 (624,582)* 1.50
1771 15c **Martin L. King,** *Jan. 13,* Atlanta, Ga. *(726,149)* 2.00
1772 15c **Year of Child,** *Feb. 15,* Philadelphia, Pa. *(716,782)* 1.00
1773 15c **John Steinbeck,** *Feb. 27,* Salinas, Calif. *(709,073)* 1.00
1774 15c **Albert Einstein,** *Mar. 4,* Princeton, N.J. *(641,423)* 3.00
1778a 15c **Toleware,** *Apr. 19,* Lancaster, Pa. *(1,581,962)* 2.00
1775-1778, any single 1.00
1782a 15c **American Architecture,** *June 4,* Kansas City, Mo. *(1,219,258)* 2.00
1779-1782, any single 1.00
1786a 15c **Endangered Flora,** *June 7,* Milwaukee, Wis. *(1,436,268)* 2.00
1783-1786, any single 1.00
1787 15c **Guide Dogs,** *June 15,* Morristown, N.J. *(588,826)* 1.25
1788 15c **Special Olympics,** *Aug. 9,* Brockport, N.Y. *(651,344)* 1.25
1789 15c **John Paul Jones,** *Sept. 23,* Annapolis, Md. 1.50
1789A 15c **John Paul Jones,** *Sept. 23,* Annapolis, Md. 1.50

Total for 1789 and 1789A is 587,018.

1790 10c **Olympic Javelin,** *Sept. 5,* Olympia, Wash. *(305,122)* 1.00
1794a 15c **Olympics 1980,** *Sept. 28,* Los Angeles, Calif. *(1,561,366)* 2.00
1791-1794, any single 1.25
1798b 15c **Winter Olympics,** *Feb. 1, 1980,* Lake Placid, N.Y. *(1,166,302)* 2.00
1795-1798, any single 1.25

1979

1799 15c **Christmas (Madonna),** *Oct. 18 (686,990)* 1.25
1800 15c **Christmas (Santa Claus),** *Oct. 18,* North Pole, Alaska *(511,829)* 1.25
1799-1800, both stamps issued *Oct. 18* 2.00
1801 15c **Will Rogers,** *Nov. 4,* Claremore, Okla. *(1,643,151)* 1.50
1802 15c **Viet Nam Veterans,** *Nov. 11,* Arlington, VA *(445,934)* 2.75

1980

1803 15c **W.C. Fields,** *Jan. 29,* Beverly Hills, CA *(633,303)* 1.75
1804 15c **Benjamin Banneker,** *Feb. 15,* Annapolis, MD *(647,126)* 2.00
1810a 15c **Letter Writing,** *Feb. 25 (1,083,360)* 2.50
1805-1810, any single 1.00

1980-81

DEFINITIVES

1811 1c **Quill Pen,** coil, *Mar. 6, 1980,* New York, NY *(262,921)* 1.00
1813 3.5c **Violins,** coil, *June 23, 1980,* Williamsburg, PA 1.00

FD cancel was applied to 716,988 covers bearing Nos. 1813 or U590.

1816 12c **Torch,** coil, *Apr. 8, 1981,* Dallas, TX 1.00
1818 (18c) **"B" Eagle,** *Mar. 15, 1981,* San Francisco, CA 1.25

FD cancel was applied to 511,688 covers bearing one or more of Nos. 1818-1820, U592 or UX88.

1819 (18c) **"B" Eagle,** bklt. single, *Mar. 15, 1981,* San Francisco, CA 1.00
1819a Booklet pane of 8 3.00
1820 (18c) **"B" Eagle,** coil, *Mar. 15, 1981,* San Francisco, CA 1.00

1980

1821 15c **Frances Perkins,** *Apr. 10 (678,966)* 1.00
1822 15c **Dolley Madison,** *May 20 (331,048)* 1.00
1823 15c **Emily Bissell,** *May 31,* Wilmington, DE *(649,509)* 1.00
1824 15c **Helen Keller, Anne Sullivan,** *June 27,* Tuscumbia, AL *(713,061)* 1.00
1825 15c **Veterans Administration,** *July 21 (634,101)* 1.50
1826 15c **Bernardo de Galvez,** *July 23,* New Orleans, LA *(658,061)* 1.00
1830a 15c **Coral Reefs,** *Aug. 26,* Charlotte Amalie, VI *(1,195,126)* 2.00
1827-1830, any single 1.00
1831 15c **Organized Labor,** *Sept. 1 (759,973)* 1.00
1832 15c **Edith Wharton,** *Sept. 5,* New Haven, CT *(633,917)* 1.00
1833 15c **Education,** *Sept. 12,*Franklin, MA *(672,592)* 1.50
1837a 15c **Indian Masks,** *Sept. 25,* Spokane, WA *(2,195,136)* 2.00
1834-1837, any single 1.00
1841a 15c **Architecture,** *Oct. 9,* New York, NY *(2,164,721)* 1.75
1838-1841, any single 1.00
1842 15c **Christmas (Madonna),** *Oct. 31 (718,614)* 1.25
1843 15c **Christmas (Toys),** *Oct. 31,* Christmas, MI *(755,108)* 1.25

1980-85

GREAT AMERICANS ISSUE

1844 1c **Dorothea Dix,** *Sept. 23, 1983,* Hampden, ME *(164,140)* 1.00
1845 2c **Igor Stravinsky,** *Nov. 18, 1982,* New York, NY *(501,719)* 1.00
1846 3c **Henry Clay,** *July 13, 1983 (204,320)* 1.00
1847 4c **Carl Schurz,** *June 3, 1983,* Watertown, WI *(165,010)* 1.00
1848 5c **Pearl Buck,** *June 25, 1983,* Hillsboro, WV *(231,852)* 1.00
1849 6c **Walter Lippman,** *Sept. 19, 1985,* Minneapolis, MN *(371,990)* 1.00
1850 7c **Abraham Baldwin,** *Jan. 25, 1985,* Athens, GA *(402,285)* 1.00
1851 8c **Henry Knox,** *July 25, 1985,* Thomaston, ME *(315,937)* 1.00
1852 9c **Sylvanus Thayer,** *June 7, 1985,* Braintree, MA *(345,649)* 1.25
1853 10c **Richard Russell,** *May 31, 1984,* Winder, GA *(183,581)* 1.00
1854 11c **Alden Partridge,** *Feb. 12, 1985,* Northfield, VT *(442,311)* 1.25
1855 13c **Crazy Horse,** *Jan. 15, 1982,* Crazy Horse, SD 1.25
1856 14c **Sinclair Lewis,** *Mar. 21, 1985,* Sauk Centre, MN *(308,612)* 1.00
1857 17c **Rachel Carson,** *May 28, 1981,* Springdale, PA *(273,686)* 1.00
1858 18c **George Mason,** *May 7, 1981,* Gunston Hall, VA *(461,937)* 1.00
1859 19c **Sequoyah,** *Dec. 27, 1980,* Tahlequah, OK *(241,325)* 1.25
1860 20c **Ralph Bunche,** *Jan. 12, 1982,* New York, NY 1.75
1861 20c **Thomas Gallaudet,** *June 10, 1983,* West Hartford, CT *(261,336)* 1.25
1862 20c **Harry S Truman,** *Jan. 26, 1984 (267,631)* 1.25
1863 22c **John J. Audubon,** *Apr. 23, 1985,* New York, NY *(516,249)* 1.25
1864 30c **Frank Laubach,** *Sept. 2, 1984,* Benton, PA *(118,974)* 1.25
1865 35c **Charles Drew,** *June 3, 1981 (383,882)* 1.75
1866 37c **Robert Millikan,** *Jan. 26, 1982,* Pasadena, CA 1.25
1867 39c **Grenville Clark,** *Mar. 20, 1985,* Hanover, NH *(297,797)* 1.25
1868 40c **Lillian Gilbreth,** *Feb. 24, 1984,* Montclair, NJ *(110,588)* 1.50
1869 50c **Chester W. Nimitz,** *Feb. 22, 1985,* Fredericksburg, TX *(376,166)* 2.00

1981

1874 15c **Everett Dirksen,** *Jan. 4,* Pekin, IL *(665,755)* 1.00
1875 15c **Whitney M. Young,** *Jan. 30,* New York, NY *(963,870)* 1.75
1879a 18c **Flowers,** *Apr. 23,* Fort Valley, GA *(1,966,599)* 2.50
1876-1879, any single 1.00

DEFINITIVES

1889a 18c **Animals Booklet pane of 10,** *May 14,* Boise, ID 5.00
1880-1889, any single 1.00
1890 18c **Flag-Anthem (grain),** *Apr. 24,* Portland, ME 1.00
1891 18c **Flag-Anthem (sea),** *Apr. 24,* Portland, ME 1.50
1892 6c **Star Circle,** *Apr. 24,* Portland, ME 1.00
1893 18c **Flag-Anthem (mountain),** *Apr. 24,* Portland, ME 1.00
1893a Booklet pane of 8 (2 #1892, 6 #1893) 2.50

FDC cancel was applied to 691,526 covers bearing one or more of Nos. 1890-1893 & 1893a.

1894 20c **Flag-Court,** *Dec. 17* 1.00
1895 20c **Flag-Court,** coil, *Dec. 17* 1.00
1896 20c **Flag-Court,** perf. 11x10½, *Dec. 17 (185,543)* 1.00
1896a Booklet pane of 6 6.00
1896b Booklet pane of 10, *June 1, 1982* *10.00*

First day cancellations were applied to 598,169 covers bearing one or more of Nos. 1894-1896.

1981-84

TRANSPORTATION ISSUE

1897 1c **Omnibus,** *Aug. 19, 1983,* Arlington, VA *(109,463)* 1.00
1897A 2c **Locomotive,** *May 20, 1982,* Chicago, IL *(290,020)* 1.50
1898 3c **Handcar,** *Mar. 25, 1983,* Rochester, NY *(77,900)* 1.00
1898A 4c **Stagecoach,** *Aug. 19, 1982,* Milwaukee, WI *(152,940)* 1.00
1899 5c **Motorcycle,** *Oct. 10, 1983,* San Francisco, CA *(188,240)* 1.50
1900 5.2c **Sleigh,** *Mar. 21, 1983,* Memphis, TN *(141,979)* 1.00
1901 5.9c **Bicycle,** *Feb. 17, 1982,* Wheeling, WV *(814,419)* 1.25
1902 7.4c **Baby Buggy,** *Apr. 7, 1984,* San Diego, CA 1.00
1903 9.3c **Mail Wagon,** *Dec. 15, 1981,* Shreveport, LA *(199,645)* 1.00

1904 10.9c **Hansom,** *Mar. 26, 1982,* Chattanooga, TN 1.00
1905 11c **Railroad Caboose,** *Feb. 3, 1984,* Chicago, IL *(172,753)* 1.50
1906 17c **Electric Auto,** *June 25, 1982,* Greenfield Village, MI *(239,458)* 1.00
1907 18c **Surrey,** *May 18, 1981,* Notch, MO *(207,801)* 1.00
1908 20c **Fire Pumper,** *Dec. 10, 1981,* Alexandria, VA *(304,668)* 2.00
1909 $9.35 **Eagle,** *Aug. 12, 1983,* Kennedy Space Center, FL *(77,858)* 47.50
1909a Booklet pane of 3 *125.00*

1981

1910 18c **Red Cross,** *May 1 (874,972)* 1.25
1911 18c **Savings & Loan,** *May 8,* Chicago, IL *(740,910)* 1.00
1919a 18c **Space Achievement,** *May 21,* Kennedy Space Center, FL *(7,027,549)* 3.00
1912-1919, any single 1.00
1920 18c **Professional Management,** *June 18,* Philadelphia, PA *(713,096)* 1.00
1924a 18c **Wildlife Habitats,** *June 26,* Reno, NV *(2,327,609)* 2.50
1921-1924, any single 1.00
1925 18c **Year of Disabled,** *June 29,* Milford, MI *(714,244)* 1.00
1926 18c **Edna St. V. Millay,** *July 10,* Austerlitz, NY *(725,978)* 1.00
1927 18c **Alcoholism,** *Aug. 19 (874,972)* 2.00
1931a 18c **Architecture,** *Aug. 28,* New York, NY *(1,998,208)* 2.50
1928-1931, any single 1.00
1932 18c **Babe Zaharias,** *Sept. 22,* Pinehurst, NC 6.50
1933 18c **Bobby Jones,** *Sept. 22,* Pinehurst, NC 10.00
1932-1933, both stamps issued *Sept. 22,* Pinehurst, NC 12.50

First day cancel was applied to 1,231,543 covers bearing one or more of Nos. 1932-1933.

1934 18c **Frederic Remington,** *Oct. 9,* Oklahoma City, OK *(1,367,099)* 1.25
1935 18c **James Hoban,** *Oct. 13* 1.00
1936 20c **James Hoban,** *Oct. 13* 1.00
1935-1936, both stamps issued *Oct. 13* 2.50

FD cancel was applied to 635,012 covers bearing Nos. 1935-1936.

1938a 18c **Yorktown-Va. Capes Battle,** *Oct. 16,* Yorktown, VA *(1,098,278)* 1.50
1937-1938, any single 1.00
1939 (20c) **Christmas (Madonna),** *Oct. 28,* Chicago, IL *(481,395)* 1.00
1940 (20c) **Christmas (Teddy Bear),** *Oct. 28,* Christmas Valley, OR *(517,898)* 1.00
1941 20c **John Hanson,** *Nov. 5,* Frederick, MD *(605,616)* 1.00
1945a 20c **Desert Plants,** *Dec. 11,* Tucson, AZ *(1,770,187)* 2.50
1942-1945, any single 1.00

REGULAR ISSUE

1946 (20c) **"C" Eagle,** *Oct. 11,* Memphis, TN 1.00
1947 (20c) **"C" Eagle,** coil, *Oct. 11,* Memphis, TN 1.00
1948 (20c) **"C" Eagle,** bklt. single, *Oct. 11,* Memphis, TN 1.00
1948a Booklet pane of 10 *3.50*

First day cancellations were applied to 304,404 covers bearing one or more of Nos. 1946-1948.

1982

1949 20c **Bighorn,** *Jan. 8,* Bighorn, MT 1.25
1949a Booklet pane of 10 *6.00*
1950 20c **F.D. Roosevelt,** *Jan. 30,* Hyde Park, NY 1.00
1951 20c **Love,** *Feb. 1,* Boston, MA *(325,727)* 1.00
1952 20c **Washington,** *Feb. 22,* Mt. Vernon, VA 1.25
2002b 20c **Birds-Flowers,** *Apr. 14,* Washington, DC, or State Capital 30.00
1953-2002, any single 1.25
2003 20c **U.S.-Netherlands,** *Apr. 20* 1.00
2004 20c **Library of Congress,** *Apr. 21* 1.00
2005 20c **Consumer Education,** *Apr. 27* 1.00
2009a 20c **Knoxville Fair,** *Apr. 29,* Knoxville, TN 2.50
2006-2009, any single 1.00
2010 20c **Horatio Alger,** *Apr. 30,* Willow Grove, PA 1.00
2011 20c **Aging,** *May 21,* Sun City, AZ *(510,677)* 1.00
2012 20c **Barrymores,** *June 8,* New York, NY 1.00
2013 20c **Dr. Mary Walker,** *June 10,* Oswego, NY 1.00
2014 20c **Peace Garden,** *June 30,* Dunseith, ND 1.00
2015 20c **America's Libraries,** *July 13,* Philadelphia, PA 1.00
2016 20c **Jackie Robinson,** *Aug. 2,* Cooperstown, NY 6.00
2017 20c **Touro Synagogue,** *Aug. 22,* Newport, RI *(517,264)* 1.50
2018 20c **Wolf Trap Farm Park,** *Sept. 1,* Vienna, VA *(704,361)* 1.00
2022a 20c **Architecture,** *Sept. 30 (1,552,567)* 2.50
2019-2022, any single 1.00
2023 20c **St. Francis,** *Oct. 7,* San Francisco, CA *(530,275)* 1.00
2024 20c **Ponce de Leon,** *Oct. 12,* San Juan, PR *(530,275)* 1.00
2025 13c **Puppy, Kitten,** *Nov. 3,* Danvers, MA *(239,219)* 1.25
2026 20c **Christmas (Madonna),** *Oct. 28 (462,982)* 1.00
2030a 20c **Christmas (Children),** *Oct. 28,* Snow, OK *(676,950)* 2.50
2027-2030, any single 1.00

1983

2031 20c **Science & Industry,** *Jan. 19,* Chicago, IL *(526,693)* 1.00
2035a 20c **Balloons,** *Mar. 31,* Albuquerque, NM or Washington, DC *(989,305)* 2.50
2032-2035, any single 1.00
2036 20c **U.S.-Sweden,** *Mar. 24,* Philadelphia, PA *(526,373)* 1.00
2037 20c **Civilian Conservation Corps.,** *Apr. 5,* Luray, VA *(483,824)* 1.00
2038 20c **Joseph Priestley,** *Apr. 13,* Northumberland, PA *(673,266)* 1.00
2039 20c **Voluntarism,** *Apr. 20 (574,708)* 1.00
2040 20c **U.S.-Germany,** *Apr. 29,* Germantown, PA *(611,109)* 1.00
2041 20c **Brooklyn Bridge,** *May 17,* Brooklyn, NY *(815,085)* 1.75
2042 20c **TVA,** *May 18,* Knoxville, TN *(837,588)* 1.00
2043 20c **Physical Fitness,** *May 14,* Houston, TX *(501,336)* 1.25
2044 20c **Scott Joplin,** *June 9,* Sedalia, MO *(472,667)* 1.75
2045 20c **Medal of Honor,** *June 7 (1,623,995)* 4.50
2046 20c **Babe Ruth,** *July 6,* Chicago, IL *(1,277,907)* 5.00
2047 20c **Nathaniel Hawthorne,** *July 8,* Salem, MA *(442,793)* 1.00
2051a 13c **Summer Olympics,** *July 28,* South Bend, IN *(909,332)* 2.50
2048-2051, any single 1.25
2052 20c **Treaty of Paris,** *Sept. 2 (651,208)* 1.00
2053 20c **Civil Service,** *Sept. 9 (422,206)* 1.00
2054 20c **Metropolitan Opera,** *Sept. 14,* New York, NY *(807,609)* 1.50
2058a 20c **American Inventors,** *Sept. 21 (1,006,516)* 2.50
2055-2058, any single 1.00
2062a 20c **Streetcars,** *Oct. 8,* Kennebunkport, ME *(1,116,909)* 2.50
2059-2062, any single 1.00
2063 20c **Christmas (Madonna),** *Oct. 28 (361,874)* 1.00
2064 20c **Christmas (Santa),** *Oct. 28,* Santa Claus, IN *(388,749)* 1.00
2065 20c **Martin Luther,** *Nov. 11 (463,777)* 1.50

1984

2066 20c **Alaska Statehood,** *Jan. 3,* Fairbanks, AK *(816,591)* 1.00
2070a 20c **Winter Olympics,** *Jan. 6,* Lake Placid, NY *(1,245,807)* 2.50
2067-2070, any single 1.00
2071 20c **Federal Deposit Ins. Corp.,** *Jan. 12 (536,329)* 1.00
2072 20c **Love,** *Jan. 31 (327,727)* 1.00
2073 20c **Carter Woodson,** *Feb. 1 (387,583)* 1.75
2074 20c **Soil & Water Conservation,** *Feb. 6,* Denver, CO *(426,101)* 1.00
2075 20c **Credit Union Act,** *Feb. 10,* Salem, MA *(523,583)* 1.00
2079a 20c **Orchids,** *Mar. 5,* Miami, FL *(1,063,237)* 2.50
2076-2079, any single 1.00
2080 20c **Hawaii Statehood,** *Mar. 12,* Honolulu, HI *(546,930)* 1.00
2081 20c **National Archives,** *Apr. 16 (414,415)* 1.00
2085a 20c **Olympics 1984,** *May 4,* Los Angeles, CA *(1,172,313)* 2.50
2082-2085, any single 1.25
2086 20c **Louisiana Exposition,** *May 11,* New Orleans, LA *(467,408)* 1.00
2087 20c **Health Research,** *May 17,* New York, NY *(845,007)* 1.00
2088 20c **Douglas Fairbanks,** *May 23,* Denver CO *(547,134)* 1.00
2089 20c **Jim Thorpe,** *May 24,* Shawnee, OK *(568,544)* 3.00
2090 20c **John McCormack,** *June 6,* Boston, MA *(464,117)* 1.00
2091 20c **St. Lawrence Seaway,** *June 26,* Massena, NY *(550,173)* 1.00
2092 20c **Waterfowl Preservation Act,** *July 2,* Des Moines, IA *(549,388)* 1.00
2093 20c **Roanoke Voyages,** *July 13,* Manteo, NC *(443,725)* 1.00
2094 20c **Herman Melville,** *Aug. 1,* New Bedford, MA *(378,293)* 1.50
2095 20c **Horace A. Moses,** *Aug. 6,* Bloomington, IN *(459,386)* 1.00
2096 20c **Smokey Bear,** *Aug. 13,* Capitan, NM *(506,833)* 3.00
2097 20c **Roberto Clemente,** *Aug. 17,* Carolina, PR *(547,387)* 9.00
2101a 20c **Dogs,** *Sept. 7,* New York, NY *(1,157,373)* 3.00
2098-2101, any single 1.50
2102 20c **Crime Prevention,** *Sept. 26 (427,564)* 1.25
2103 20c **Hispanic Americans,** *Oct. 31 (416,796)* 1.75
2104 20c **Family Unity,** *Oct. 1,* Shaker Heights, OH *(400,659)* 1.00
2105 20c **Eleanor Roosevelt,** *Oct. 11,* Hyde Park, NY *(479,919)* 1.00
2106 20c **Nation of Readers,** *Oct. 16 (437,559)* 1.00
2107 20c **Christmas (Madonna),** *Oct. 30 (386,385)* 1.00
2108 20c **Christmas (Santa),** *Oct. 30,* Jamaica, NY *(430,843)* 1.00
2109 20c **Vietnam Veterans' Memorial,** *Nov. 10 (434,489)* 3.50

1985

2110 22c **Jerome Kern,** *Jan. 23,* New York, NY (503,855) 1.00

REGULAR ISSUE

2111 (22c) **"D" Eagle,** *Feb. 1,* Los Angeles, CA 1.00
2112 (22c) **"D" Eagle, coil,** *Feb. 1,* Los Angeles, CA 1.00
2113 (22c) **"D" Eagle, bklt. single,** *Feb. 1,* Los Angeles, CA 1.00
2113a Booklet pane of 10 *7.50*

First Day cancel was applied to 513,027 covers bearing one or more of Nos. 2111-2113.

2114 22c **Flag over Capitol Dome,** *Mar. 29* 1.00
2115 22c **Flag over Capitol Dome,** coil, *Mar. 29* 1.00
2115b Inscribed "T" at bottom, *May 23, 1987,* Secaucus, NJ *1.00*

First Day Cancel was applied to 268,161 covers bearing one or more of Nos. 2114-2115.

2116 22c **Flag Over Capitol Dome,** bklt. single, *Mar. 29,* Waubeka, WI *(234,318)* 1.00
2116a Booklet pane of 5 3.50
2121a 22c **Seashells Booklet pane of 10,** *Apr. 4,* Boston, MA *(426,290)* *7.50*
2117-2121, any single 1.00
2122 $10.75 **Eagle and Half Moon,** *Apr. 29,* San Francisco, CA *(93,154)* 40.00
2122a Booklet pane of 3 *95.00*
2122c Booklet pane of 3, type II, *June 19, 1989* —

1985-87

TRANSPORTATION ISSUE

2123 3.4c **School Bus,** *June 8, 1985,* Arlington, VA *(131,480)* 1.00
2124 4.9c **Buckboard,** *June 21, 1985,* Reno, NV 1.00
2125 5.5c **Star Route Truck,** *Nov. 1, 1986,* Fort Worth, TX *(136,021)* 1.00
2126 6c **Tricycle,** *May 6, 1985,* Childs, MD *(151,494)* 1.00
2127 7.1c **Tractor,** *Feb. 6, 1987,* Sarasota, FL *(167,555)* 1.00
2127a 7.1c **Tractor,** Zip+4 precancel, untagged, *May 26, 1989,* Rosemont, IL *(202,804)* 5.00
2128 8.3c **Ambulance,** *June 21, 1986,* Reno, NV 1.00

First day cancel was applied to 338,765 covers bearing one or more of Nos. 2124 and 2128.

2129 8.5c **Tow Truck,** *Jan. 24, 1987,* Tucson, AZ *(224,285)* 1.25
2130 10.1c **Oil Wagon,** *Apr. 18, 1985,* Oil Center, NM 1.25
2130a 10.1c "Bulk Rate Carrier Route Sort" precancel, *June 27, 1988 (136,428)* 1.25
2131 11c **Stutz Bearcat,** *June 11, 1985,* Baton Rouge, LA *(135,037)* 1.25
2132 12c **Stanley Steamer,** *Apr. 2, 1985,* Kingfield, ME *(173,998)* 1.25
2133 12.5c **Pushcart,** *Apr. 18, 1985,* Oil Center, NM 1.25

First day cancel was applied to 319,953 covers bearing one or more of Nos. 2130 and 2133.

2134 14c **Ice Boat,** *Mar. 23, 1985,* Rochester, NY *(324,710)* 1.25
2135 17c **Dog Sled,** *Aug. 20, 1986,* Anchorage, AK 1.25
2136 25c **Bread Wagon,** *Nov. 22, 1986,* Virginia Beach, VA *(151,950)* 1.25

1985

2137 22c **Mary McLeod Bethune,** *Mar. 5 (413,244)* 1.50
2141a 22c **Duck Decoys,** *Mar. 22,* Shelburne, VT *(932,249)* 2.50
2138-2141, any single 1.00
2142 22c **Winter Special Olympics,** *Mar. 25,* Park City, UT *(253,074)* 1.00
2143 22c **Love,** *Apr. 17,* Hollywood, CA *(283,072)* 1.00
2144 22c **Rural Electrification Administration,** *May 11,* Madison, SD *(472,895)* 1.00
2145 22c **AMERIPEX '86,** *May 25,* Rosemont, IL *(457,038)* 1.00
2146 22c **Abigail Adams,** *June 14,* Quincy, MA *(491,026)* 1.00
2147 22c **Frederic Auguste Bartholdi,** *July 18,* New York, NY *(594,896)* 1.00
2149 18c **George Washington, Washington Monument,** *Nov. 6 (376,238)* 1.00
2150 21.1c **Envelopes,** *Oct. 22 (119,941)* 1.00
2152 22c **Korean War Veterans,** *July 26 (391,754)* 2.00
2153 22c **Social Security Act,** *Aug. 14,* Baltimore, MD *(265,143)* 1.00
2154 22c **World War I Veterans,** *Aug. 26,* Milwaukee, WI 1.50
2158a 22c **Horses,** *Sept. 25,* Lexington, KY *(1,135,368)* 2.50
2155-2158, any single 1.50
2159 22c **Public Education in America,** *Oct. 1,* Boston, MA *(356,030)* 1.00
2163a 22c **International Youth Year,** *Oct. 7,* Chicago, IL *(1,202,541)* 2.50
2160, 2162-2163, any single 1.00
2161 2.00
2164 22c **Help End Hunger,** *Oct. 15 (299,485)* 1.00
2165 22c **Christmas (Madonna & Child),** *Oct. 30,* Detroit, MI 1.00
2166 22c **Christmas (Poinsettia),** *Oct. 30,* Nazareth, MI *(524,929)* 1.00

1986

2167 22c **Arkansas Statehood,** *Jan. 3,* Little Rock, AR *(364,729)* 1.00

1986-94

GREAT AMERICANS ISSUE

2168 1c **Margaret Mitchell,** *June 30, 1986,* Atlanta, GA *(316,764)* 2.00
2169 2c **Mary Lyon,** *Feb. 28, 1987,* South Hadley, MA *(349,831)* 1.00

2170 3c **Dr. Paul Dudley White,** *Sept. 15, 1986* 1.00
2171 4c **Father Flanagan,** *July 14, 1986,* Boys Town, NE *(367,883)* 1.00
2172 5c **Hugo Black,** *Feb. 27, 1986 (303,012)* 1.00
2173 5c **Luis Munoz Marin,** *Feb. 18, 1990,* San Juan, PR *(269,618)* 1.00
2175 10c **Red Cloud,** *Aug. 15, 1987,* Red Cloud, NE *(300,472)* 1.50
2176 14c **Julia Ward Howe,** *Feb. 12, 1987,* Boston, MA *(454,829)* 1.00
2177 15c **Buffalo Bill Cody,** *June 6, 1988* Cody, WY *(356,395)* 1.25
2178 17c **Belva Ann Lockwood,** *June 18, 1986,* Middleport, NY *(249,215)* 1.00
2179 20c **Virginia Apgar,** *Oct. 24, 1994,* Dallas, TX *(28,461)* 1.00
2180 21c **Chester Carlson,** *Oct. 21, 1988,* Rochester, NY *(288,073)* 1.00
2181 23c **Mary Cassatt,** *Nov. 4, 1988,* Philadelphia, PA *(322,537)* 1.00
2182 25c **Jack London,** *Jan. 11, 1986,* Glen Ellen, CA *(358,686)* 1.25
2182a Booklet pane of 10, *May 3, 1988,* San Francisco, CA 6.00
2183 28c **Sitting Bull,** *Sept. 14, 1989,* Rapid City, SD *(126,777)* 1.50
2184 29c **Earl Warren,** *Mar. 9, 1992 (175,517)* 1.25
2185 29c **Thomas Jefferson,** *Apr. 13, 1993,* Charlottesville, VA *(202,962)* 1.25
2186 35c **Dennis Chavez,** *Apr. 3, 1991,* Albuquerque, NM *(285,570)* 1.25
2187 40c **Claire Chennault,** *Sept. 6, 1990,* Monroe, LA *(186,761)* 2.00
2188 45c **Harvey Cushing,** *June 17, 1988,* Cleveland, OH *(135,140)* 1.25
2189 52c **Hubert Humphrey,** *June 3, 1991,* Minneapolis, MN *(93,391)* 1.40
2190 56c **John Harvard,** *Sept. 3, 1986,* Cambridge, MA 2.50
2191 65c **Hap Arnold,** *Nov. 5, 1988,* Gladwyne, PA *(129,829)* 2.50
2192 75c **Wendell Willkie,** *Feb. 18, 1992,* Bloomington, IN *(47,086)* 2.50
2193 $1 **Dr. Bernard Revel,** *Sept. 23, 1986,* New York, NY 3.50
2194 $1 **Johns Hopkins,** *June 7, 1989,* Baltimore, MD *(159,049)* 3.00
2195 $2 **William Jennings Bryan,** *Mar. 19, 1986,* Salem, IL *(123,430)* 5.50
2196 $5 **Bret Harte,** *Aug. 25, 1987,* Twain Harte, CA *(111,431)* 15.00
2197 25c **Jack London,** bklt. single, *May 3, 1988,* San Francisco, CA 1.00
2197a Booklet pane of 6 4.00

First day cancel was applied to 94,655 covers bearing one or more of Nos. 2183a, 2197, and 2197a.

1986

2201a 22c **Stamp Collecting Booklet pane of 4,** *Jan. 23,* State College, PA 4.00
2198-2201, any single 1.00

First day cancellation was applied to 675,924 covers bearing one or more of Nos. 2198-2201a.

2202 22c **Love,** *Jan. 30,* New York, NY 1.00
2203 22c **Sojourner Truth,** *Feb. 4,* New Paltz, NY *(342,985)* 1.75
2204 22c **Republic of Texas,** *Mar. 2,* San Antonio, TX *(380,450)* 1.75
2209a 22c **Fish Booklet pane of 5,** *Mar. 21,* Seattle, WA 3.50
2205-2209, any single 1.25

First day cancellation was applied to 988,184 covers bearing one or more of Nos. 2205-2209a.

2210 22c **Public Hospitals,** *Apr. 11,* New York, NY *(403,665)* 1.00
2211 22c **Duke Ellington,** *Apr. 29,* New York, NY *(397,894)* 2.25
2216 22c **Presidents Souvenir Sheet of 9 (Washington-Harrison),** *May 22,* Chicago, IL 4.00
2217 22c **Presidents Souvenir Sheet of 9 (Tyler-Grant),** *May 22,* Chicago, IL 4.00
2218 22c **Presidents Souvenir Sheet of 9 (Hayes-Wilson),** *May 22,* Chicago, IL 4.00
2219 22c **Presidents Souvenir Sheet of 9 (Harding-Johnson),** *May 22,* Chicago, IL 4.00
2216a-2219g, 2219i, any single 1.50
2219h 2.50

First day cancellation was applied to 9,009,599 covers bearing one or more of Nos. 2216-2219, 2216a-2219i.

2223a 22c **Polar Explorers,** *May 28,* North Pole, AK *(760,999)* 3.75
2220-2223, any single 1.25
2224 22c **Statue of Liberty,** *July 4,* New York, NY *(1,540,308)* 1.25

1986-87

TRANSPORTATION ISSUE

2225 1c **Omnibus,** *Nov. 26, 1986 (57,845)* 1.00
2226 2c **Locomotive,** *Mar. 6, 1987,* Milwaukee, WI *(169,484)* 1.50

1986

2238a 22c **Navajo Art,** *Sept. 4,* Window Rock, AZ *(1,102,520)* 2.00
2235-2238, any single 1.00
2239 22c **T.S. Eliot,** *Sept. 26,* St. Louis, MO *(304,764)* 1.00
2243a 22c **Woodcarved Figurines,** *Oct. 1 (629,399)* 2.00
2240-2243, any single 1.00
2244 22c **Christmas (Madonna),** *Oct. 24 (467,999)* 1.00
2245 22c **Christmas (Winter Village),** *Oct. 24,* Snow Hill, MD *(504,851)* 1.00

1987

2246 22c **Michigan Statehood Sesquicent.,** *Jan. 26,* Lansing, MI *(379,117)* 1.00
2247 22c **Pan American Games,** *Jan. 29,* Indianapolis, IN *(344,731)* 1.00
2248 22c **Love,** *Jan. 30,* San Francisco, CA *(333,329)* 1.00
2249 22c **Pointe du Sable,** *Feb. 20,* Chicago, IL *(313,054)* 1.50
2250 22c **Enrico Caruso,** *Feb. 27,* New York, NY *(389,834)* 1.00
2251 22c **Girl Scouts of America,** *Mar. 12 (556,391)* 2.50

1987-88

TRANSPORTATION ISSUE

2252 3c **Conestoga Wagon,** *Feb. 29, 1988,* Conestoga, PA *(155,203)* 1.00
2253 5c **Milk Wagon,** *Sept. 25, 1987,* Indianapolis, IN 1.00

First day cancel was applied to 162,571 covers bearing one or more of Nos. 2253 and 2262.

2254 5.3c **Elevator,** *Sept. 16, 1988,* New York, NY *(142,705)* 1.00
2255 7.6c **Carretta,** *Aug. 30, 1988,* San Jose, CA *(140,024)* 1.00
2256 8.4c **Wheelchair,** *Aug. 12, 1988,* Tucson, AZ *(136,337)* 1.00
2257 10c **Canal Boat,** *Apr. 11, 1987,* Buffalo, NY *(171,952)* 1.00
2258 13c **Police Patrol Wagon,** *Oct. 29, 1988,* Anaheim, CA *(132,928)* 1.50
2259 13.2c **Railway Coal Car,** *July 19, 1988,* Pittsburgh, PA *(123,965)* 1.00
2260 15c **Tugboat,** *July 12, 1988,* Long Beach, CA *(134,926)* 1.00
2261 16.7c **Popcorn Wagon,** *July 7, 1988,* Chicago, IL *(117,908)* 1.00
2262 17.5c **Racing Car,** *Sept. 25, 1987,* Indianapolis, IN 1.00
2263 20c **Cable Car,** *Oct. 28, 1988,* San Francisco, CA *(150,068)* 1.00
2264 20.5c **Fire Engine,** *Sept. 28, 1988,* San Angelo, TX *(123,043)* 1.50
2265 21c **Railway Mail Car,** *Aug. 16, 1988,* Santa Fe, NM *(124,430)* 1.00
2266 24.1c **Tandem Bicycle,** *Oct. 26, 1988,* Redmond, WA *(138,593)* 1.25

1987

2274a 22c **Special Occasions Booklet pane of 10,** *Apr. 20,* Atlanta, GA 5.00
2267-2274, any single 1.00

First day cancellation was applied to 1,588,129 covers bearing one or more of Nos. 2267-2274a.

2275 22c **United Way,** *Apr. 28 (556,391)* 1.00

1987-89

2276 22c **Flag and Fireworks,** *May 9, 1987* Denver, CO *(398,855)* 1.00
2276a Booklet pane of 20, *Nov. 30, 1987* 8.00
2277 (25c) **"E" Earth,** *Mar. 22, 1988* 1.25
2278 25c **Flag and Clouds,** *May 6, 1988,* Boxborough, MA *(131,265)* 1.25
2279 (25c) **"E" Earth,** coil, *Mar. 22, 1988* 1.25
2280 25c **Flag over Yosemite,** *May 20, 1988,* Yosemite, CA *(144,339)* 1.25
Prephosphored paper, *Feb. 14, 1989,* Yosemite, CA *(118,874)* 1.25
2281 25c **Honey Bee,** *Sept. 2, 1988,* Omaha, NE *(122,853)* 1.25
2282 (25c) **"E" Earth,** bklt. single, *Mar. 22, 1988* 1.25
2282a Booklet pane of 10 6.00

First day cancel was applied to 363,639 covers bearing one or more of Nos. 2277, 2279 and 2282.

2283 25c **Pheasant,** *Apr. 29, 1988,* Rapid City, SD *(167,053)* 1.25
2283a Booklet pane of 10 6.00
2285b 25c **Grosbeak & Owl, booklet pane of 10** *May 28, 1988,* Arlington, VA 6.00
2284-2285, any single 1.25

First day cancel was applied to 272,359 covers bearing one or more of Nos. 2284 and 2285.

2285A 25c **Flag and Clouds,** bklt. single, *July 5, 1988 (117,303)* 1.00
2285Ac Booklet pane of 6 4.00
2335a 22c **American Wildlife,** *June 13, 1987,* Toronto, Canada 50.00
2286-2335, any single 1.50

1987-90 RATIFICATION OF THE CONSTITUTION

2336 22c **Delaware,** *July 4, 1987,* Dover, DE *(505,770)* 1.50
2337 22c **Pennsylvania,** *Aug. 26, 1987,* Harrisburg, PA *(367,184)* 1.50
2338 22c **New Jersey,** *Sept. 11, 1987,* Trenton, NJ *(432,899)* 1.50
2339 22c **Georgia,** *Jan. 6, 1988,* Atlanta, GA *(467,804)* 1.50
2340 22c **Connecticut,** *Jan. 9, 1988,* Hartford, CT *(379,706)* 1.50
2341 22c **Massachusetts,** *Feb. 6, 1988,* Boston, MA *(412,616)* 1.50
2342 22c **Maryland,** *Feb. 15, 1988,* Annapolis, MD *(376,403)* 1.50
2343 25c **South Carolina,** *May 23, 1988,* Columbia, SC *(322,938)* 1.50
2344 25c **New Hampshire,** *June 21, 1988,* Concord, NH *(374,402)* 1.50
2345 25c **Virginia,** *June 25, 1988,* Williamsburg, VA *(474,079)* 1.50
2346 25c **New York,** *July 26, 1988,* Albany, NY *(385,793)* 1.50
2347 25c **North Carolina,** *Aug. 22, 1989,* Fayetteville, NC *(392,953)* 1.50
2348 25c **Rhode Island,** *May 29, 1990,* Pawtucket, RI *(305,566)* 1.50

1987

2349 22c **U.S.-Morocco Diplomatic Relations Bicent.,** *July 17 (372,814)* 1.00
2350 22c **William Faulkner,** *Aug. 3,* Oxford, MS *(480,024)* 1.00
2354a 22c **Lacemaking,** *Aug. 14,* Ypsilanti, MI 2.50
2351-2354, any single 1.00
2359a 22c **Drafting of Constitution Bicent. Booklet pane of 5,** *Aug. 28* 4.00
2355-2359, any single 1.25

First day cancellation was applied to 1,008,799 covers bearing one or more of Nos. 2355-2359a.

2360 22c **Signing of Constitution Bicent.,** *Sept. 17,* Philadelphia, PA *(719,975)* 1.25
2361 22c **Certified Public Accounting,** *Sept. 21,* New York, NY *(362,099)* 7.50
2366a 22c **Locomotives booklet pane of 5,** *Oct. 1,* Baltimore, MD 3.00
2362-2366, any single 1.25

First day cancellation was applied to 976,694 covers bearing one or more of Nos. 2362-2366a.

2367 22c **Christmas (Madonna),** *Oct. 23 (320,406)* 1.25
2368 22c **Christmas (Ornaments),** *Oct. 23,* Holiday-Anaheim, CA *(375,858)* 1.25

1988

2369 22c **Winter Olympics, Calgary,** *Jan. 10,* Anchorage, AK *(395,198)* 1.00
2370 22c **Australia Bicentennial,** *Jan. 26 (523,465)* 1.75
2371 22c **James Weldon Johnson,** *Feb. 2,* Nashville, TN *(465,282)* 1.75
2375a 22c **Cats,** *Feb. 5,* New York, NY *(872,734)* 4.50
2372-2375, any single 2.00
2376 22c **Knute Rockne,** *Mar. 9,* Notre Dame, IN *(404,311)* 3.50
2377 25c **Francis Ouimet,** *June 13,* Brookline, MA *(383,168)* 4.50
2378 25c **Love,** *July 4,* Pasadena, CA *(399,038)* 1.00
2379 45c **Love,** *Aug. 8,* Shreveport, LA *(121,808)* 1.25
2380 25c **Summer Olympics, Seoul,** *Aug. 19,* Colorado Springs, CO *(402,616)* 1.25
2385a 25c **Automobiles booklet pane of 5,** *Aug. 25,* Detroit, MI 3.00
2381-2385, any single 1.25

First day cancel was applied to 875,801 covers bearing one or more of Nos. 2381-2385a.

2389a 25c **Antarctic Explorers,** *Sept. 14 (720,537)* 3.00
2386-2389, any single 1.25
2393a 25c **Carousel Animals,** *Oct. 1,* Sandusky, OH *(856,380)* 3.00
2390-2393, any single 1.25
2394 $8.75 **Express Mail,** *Oct. 4,* Terre Haute, IN *(66,558)* 27.50
2396a 25c **Special Occasions (Happy Birthday, Best Wishes),** *Oct. 22,* King of Prussia, PA 4.00
2395-2396, any single 1.25
2398a 25c **Special Occasions (Thinking of You, Love You),** *Oct. 22,* King of Prussia, PA 4.00
2397-2398, any single 1.25

First day cancel was applied to 126,767 covers bearing one or more of Nos. 2395-2398, 2396a, 2398a.

2399 25c **Christmas (Madonna),** *Oct. 20 (247,291)* 1.25
2400 25c **Christmas (Contemporary),** *Oct. 20,* Berlin, NH *(412,213)* 1.25

1989

2401 25c **Montana,** *Jan. 15,* Helena, MT *(353,319)* 1.25
2402 25c **A. Philip Randolph,** *Feb. 3,* New York, NY *(363,174)* 1.75
2403 25c **North Dakota,** *Feb. 21,* Bismarck, ND *(306,003)* 1.00
2404 25c **Washington Statehood,** *Feb. 22,* Olympia, WA *(445,174)* 1.00
2409a 25c **Steamboats Booklet pane of 5,** *Mar. 3,* New Orleans, LA 3.00
2405-2409, any single 1.25

First day cancel was applied to 981,674 covers bearing one or more of Nos. 2405-2409a.

2410 25c **World Stamp Expo,** *Mar. 16,* New York, NY *(296,310)* 1.00
2411 25c **Arturo Toscanini,** *Mar. 25,* New York, NY *(309,441)* 1.00

1989-90

BRANCHES OF GOVERNMENT

2412 25c **House of Representatives,** *Apr. 4, 1989 (327,755)* 1.25
2413 25c **Senate,** *Apr. 6, 1989 (341,288)* 1.25
2414 25c **Executive Branch,** *Apr. 16, 1989* Mount Vernon, VA *(387,644)* 1.25
2415 25c **Supreme Court,** *Feb. 2, 1990 (233,056)* 1.25

1989

2416 25c **South Dakota,** *May 3,* Pierre, SD *(348,370)* 1.00
2417 25c **Lou Gehrig,** *June 10,* Cooperstown, NY *(694,227)* 4.00

2418 25c **Ernest Hemingway,** *July 17,* Key West, FL *(345,436)* 1.25
2419 $2.40 **Moon Landing,** *July 20 (208,982)* 7.50
2420 25c **Letter Carriers,** *Aug. 30,* Milwaukee, WI *(372,241)* 1.25
2421 25c **Bill of Rights,** *Sept. 25,* Philadelphia, PA *(900,384)* 1.00
2425a 25c **Dinosaurs,** *Oct. 1,* Orlando, FL *(871,634)* 3.00
2422-2425, any single 1.50
2426 25c **Southwest Carved Figure,** *Oct. 12,* San Juan, PR *(215,285)* 1.00
2427 25c **Christmas (Madonna),** *Oct. 19 (395,321)* 1.00
2427a Booklet pane of 10 6.00
2428 25c **Christmas (Sleigh with Presents),** *Oct. 19,* Westport, CT 1.00
2429 25c **Christmas (Sleigh with Presents) from bklt.,** *Oct. 19,* Westport, CT 1.00
2429a Booklet pane of 10 6.00

First day cancel was applied to 345,931 covers bearing one or more of Nos. 2428-2429a.

2431 25c **Eagle and Shield,** *Nov. 10,* Virginia Beach, VA 1.25
2433 90c **World Stamp Expo '89 Souvenir Sheet,** *Nov. 17 (281,725)* 7.00
2437a 25c **Classic Mail Transportation,** *Nov. 19 (916,389)* 2.50
2434-2437, any single 1.25
2438 25c **Classic Mail Transportation Souvenir Sheet,** *Nov. 28 (241,634)* 3.00

1990

2439 25c **Idaho Statehood,** *Jan. 6,* Boise, ID *(252,493)* 1.25
2440 25c **Love,** *Jan. 18,* Romance, AR 1.25
2441 25c **Love, from bklt.,** *Jan. 18,* Romance, AR 1.00
2441a Booklet pane of 10 6.00

First day cancel was applied to 257,788 covers bearing one or more of Nos. 2440-2441a.

2442 25c **Ida B. Wells,** *Feb. 1,* Chicago, IL *(229,226)* 2.00
2443 15c **Beach Umbrella,** *Feb. 3,* Sarasota, FL 1.25
2443a Booklet pane of 10 4.25

First day cancel was applied to 72,286 covers bearing one or more of Nos. 2443-2443a.

2444 25c **Wyoming Statehood,** *Feb. 23,* Cheyenne, WY *(317,654)* 1.00
2448a 25c **Classic Films,** *Mar. 23,* Hollywood, CA *(863,079)* 5.00
2445-2448, any single 2.50
2449 25c **Marianne Moore,** *Apr. 18,* Brooklyn, NY *(390,535)* 1.25

1990-95

TRANSPORTATION COILS

2451 4c **Steam Carriage,** *Jan. 25, 1991,* Tucson, AZ *(100,393)* 1.25
2452 5c **Circus Wagon,** engraved, *Aug. 31, 1990,* Syracuse, NY *(71,806)* 1.50
2452B 5c **Circus Wagon,** photogravure, *Dec. 8, 1992,* Cincinnati, OH 1.50
2452D 5c **Circus Wagon,** with cent sign, photogravure, *Mar. 20, 1995,* Kansas City MO *(20,835)* 2.00
2453 5c **Canoe,** engraved, *May 25, 1991,* Secaucus, NJ *(108,634)* 1.25
2454 5c **Canoe,** photogravure, *Oct. 22, 1991,* Secaucus, NJ 1.25
2457 10c **Tractor Trailer,** engr., *May 25, 1991,* Secaucus, NJ *(84,717)* 1.25
2458 10c **Tractor Trailer,** photo., *May 25, 1994,* Secaucus, NJ *(15,431)* 1.25
2463 20c **Cog Railway,** *June 9, 1995,* Dallas, TX *(28,883)* 1.25
2464 23c **Lunch Wagon,** *Apr. 12, 1991,* Columbus, OH *(115,830)* 1.25
2466 32c **Ferry Boat,** *June 2, 1995,* McLean VA 1.25

First day cancellation was applied to 59,100 covers bearing one or more of Nos. 2466, 2492.

2468 $1 **Seaplane,** *Apr. 20, 1990* Phoenix, AZ *(244,775)* 2.50

1990

2474a 25c **Lighthouses booklet pane of 5,** *Apr. 26* 3.00
2470-2474, any single 1.50

First day cancel was applied to 805,133 covers bearing one or more of Nos. 2470-2474a.

2475 25c **Flag,** *May 18,* Seattle, WA *(97,567)* 1.00

1990-95

FLORA AND FAUNA ISSUE

2476 1c **Kestrel,** *June 22,* Aurora, CO *(77,781)* 1.00
2477 1c **Kestrel, with cent sign,** *May 10, 1995* Aurora, CO *(21,767)* 1.00
2478 3c **Eastern Bluebird,** *June 22,* Aurora, CO *(76,149)* 1.00
2479 19c **Fawn,** *Mar. 11 (100,212)* 1.00
2480 30c **Cardinal,** *June 22,* Aurora, CO *(101,290)* 1.25
2481 45c **Pumpkinseed Sunfish,** *Dec. 2, 1992 (38,696)* 1.75
2482 $2 **Bobcat,** *June 1,* Arlington, VA *(49,660)* 5.00
2483 20c **Blue Jay,** booklet single, *June 15, 1995,* Kansas City MO 1.25

First day cancellation was applied to 16,847 covers bearing one or more of Nos. 2483, 2483a.

2484 29c **Wood Duck,** black denomination bklt. single, *Apr. 12,* Columbus, OH 1.00
2484a Booklet pane of 10 4.00
2485 29c **Wood Duck,** red denomination bklt. single, *Apr. 12,* Columbus, OH 1.00
2485a Booklet pane of 10 4.00

First day cancel was applied to 205,305 covers bearing one or more of Nos. 2484-2485, 2484a-2485a.

2486 29c **African Violet,** *Oct. 8, 1993,* Beaumont, TX 1.00
2486a Booklet pane of 10 4.00

First day cancellation was applied to 40,167 covers bearing one or more of Nos. 2486-2486a.

2487 32c **Peach,** booklet single, *July 8, 1995,* Reno NV 1.50
2488 32c **Pear,** booklet single, *July 8, 1995,* Reno NV 1.50

First day cancellation was applied to 71,086 covers bearing one or more of Nos. 2487-2488, 2488a, 2493-2495A.

2488a Booklet pane, 5 each #2488-2489 7.50
2489 29c **Red Squirrel,** self-adhesive, *June 25, 1993* Milwaukee, WI *(48,564)* 1.25
2490 29c **Red Rose,** self-adhesive, *Aug. 19, 1993* Houston, TX *(37,916)* 1.25
2491 29c **Pine Cone,** self-adhesive, *Nov. 5, 1993* Kansas City, MO *(110,924)* 1.25
2492 32c **Pink Rose,** self-adhesive, *June 2, 1995,* McLean VA 1.25

First day cancellation was applied to 59,100 covers bearing one or more of Nos. 2466, 2492.

2493 32c **Peach,** self-adhesive, *July 8, 1995,* Reno NV 1.25
2494 32c **Pear,** self-adhesive, *July 8, 1995,* Reno NV 1.25
2495 32c **Peach,** self-adhesive, serpentine die cut vert., *July 8, 1995,* Reno NV 1.25
2495A 32c **Pear,** self-adhesive, serpentine die cut vert., *July 8, 1995,* Reno NV 1.25

First day cancellation was applied to 71,086 covers bearing one or more of Nos. 2487-2488, 2488a, 2493-2495A.

1990

2500a 25c **Olympians,** *July 6,* Minneapolis, MN *(1,143,404)* 4.00
2496-2500, any single 1.25
2505a 25c **Indian Headdresses, booklet pane of 10** *Aug. 17,* Cody, WY 6.00
2501-2505, any single 1.25

First day cancel was applied to 979,580 covers bearing one or more of Nos. 2501-2505a.

2507a 25c **Micronesia, Marshall Islands,** *Sept. 28 (343,816)* 2.00
2506-2507, any single 1.25
2511a 25c **Sea Creatures,** *Oct. 3,* Baltimore, MD *(706,047)* 3.00
2508-2511, any single 1.25
2512 25c **Grand Canyon,** *Oct. 12,* Grand Canyon, AZ *(164,190)* 1.25
2513 25c **Dwight D. Eisenhower,** *Oct. 13,* Abilene, KS *(487,988)* 1.25
2514 25c **Christmas (traditional),** *Oct. 18* 1.25
2514a Booklet pane of 10 6.00

First day cancel was applied to 378,383 covers bearing one or more of Nos. 2514-2514a.

2515 25c **Christmas (secular),** *Oct. 18,* Evergreen, CO 1.25
2516 25c **Christmas (secular),** *Oct. 18,* Evergreen, CO 1.00
2516a Booklet pane of 10 6.00

First day cancel was applied to 230,586 covers bearing one or more of Nos. 2515-2516a.

1991-94

2517 (29c) **"F" Flower,** *Jan. 22, 1991 (106,698)* 1.25
2518 (29c) **"F" Flower,** coil, *Jan. 22, 1991 (39,311)* 1.25
2519 (29c) **"F" Flower,** bklt. single (bullseye perf. 11.2), *Jan. 22, 1991* 1.00
2519a Booklet pane of 10 7.25
2520 (29c) **"F" Flower,** bklt. single (perf. 11), *Jan. 22, 1991* 1.25
2520a Booklet pane of 10 8.00

First day cancel was applied to 32,971 covers bearing one or more of Nos. 2519-2520, 2519a-2520a.

2521 (4c) **Makeup Stamp,** *Jan. 22, 1991 (51,987)* 1.25
2522 (29c) **"F" Flag,** *Jan. 22, 1991 (48,821)* 1.25
2523 29c **Flag over Mt. Rushmore,** engraved, *Mar. 29, 1991* Mt. Rushmore, SD *(233,793)* 1.25
2523A 29c **Flag over Mt. Rushmore,** photogravure, *July 4, 1991* Mt. Rushmore, SD *(80,662)* 1.25
2524 29c **Flower,** *Apr. 5, 1991,* Rochester, NY *(132,233)* 1.00
2525 29c **Flower,** roulette 10 coil, *Aug. 16, 1991,* Rochester, NY *(144,750)* 1.00
2526 29c **Flower,** perf. 10 coil, *Mar. 3, 1992,* Rochester, NY *(35,877)* 1.00
2527 29c **Flower,** bklt. single, *Apr. 5, 1991,* Rochester, NY 1.00
2527a Booklet pane of 10 4.00

First day cancel was applied to 16,975 covers bearing one or more of Nos. 2527-2527a.

2528 29c **Flag and Olympic Rings,** bklt. single, *Apr. 21, 1991,* Atlanta, GA 1.25
2528a Booklet pane of 10 5.00

First day cancel was applied to 319,488 covers bearing one or more of Nos. 2528-2528a.

2529 19c **Fishing Boat,** two loops, *Aug. 8, 1991 (82,698)* 1.50
2529C 19c **Fishing Boat,** one loop, *June 25, 1994,* Arlington, VA *(14,538)* 1.50
2530 19c **Balloon,** *May 17, 1991,* Denver, CO 1.25
2530a Booklet pane of 10 5.00

First day cancel was applied to 96,351 covers bearing one or more of Nos. 2530-2530a.

2531 29c **Flags on Parade,** *May 30, 1991,* Waterloo, NY *(104,046)* 1.00
2531A 29c **Liberty Torch,** *June 25, 1991,* New York, NY *(68,456)* 1.25

1991-95

2532 50c **Switzerland,** *Feb. 22,* Washington, DC *(316,047)* 1.40
2533 29c **Vermont,** *Mar. 1,* Bennington, VT *(308,105)* 1.50
2534 29c **Savings Bonds,** *Apr. 30,* Washington, DC *(341,955)* 1.25
2535 29c **Love,** *May 9,* Honolulu, HI *(336,132)* 1.25
2536 29c **Love,** bklt. single, *May 9,* Honolulu, HI 1.25
2536a Booklet pane of 10 5.00

First day cancel was applied to 43,336 covers bearing one or more of Nos. 2536-2536a.

2537 52c **Love,** *May 9,* Honolulu, HI *(90,438)* 1.25
2538 29c **William Saroyan,** *May 22,* Fresno, CA *(334,373)* 1.50
2539 $1 **Eagle & Olympic Rings,** *Sept. 29,* Orlando, FL *(69,241)* 2.25
2540 $2.90 **Eagle & Olympic Rings,** *July 7,* San Diego, CA *(79,555)* 5.50
2541 $9.95 **Eagle & Olympic Rings,** *June 16,* Sacramento, CA *(68,657)* 15.00
2542 $14 **Eagle,** *Aug. 31,* Hunt Valley, MD *(54,727)* 19.00
2543 $2.90 **Futuristic Space Shuttle,** *June 3, 1993,* Kennedy Space Center, FL *(36,359)* 6.00
2544 $3 **Space Shuttle Challenger,** *June 22, 1995* Anaheim CA *(16,502)* 6.00
2544A $10.75 **Space Shuttle Endeavour,** *Aug. 4, 1995* Irvine CA *(10,534)* 15.00

1991

2549a 29c **Fishing Flies booklet pane of 5,** *May 31,* Cuddebackville, NY *(1,045,726)* 3.00
2545-2549, any single 1.25
2550 29c **Cole Porter,** *June 8,* Peru, IN *(304,363)* 1.25
2551 29c **Desert Storm/ Desert Shield,** *July 2* 2.50
2552 29c **Desert Storm/ Desert Shield,** bklt. single, *July 2* 2.50
2552a Booklet pane of 5 4.75

First day cancel was applied to 860,455 covers bearing one or more of Nos. 2551-2552, 2552a.

2557a 29c **Summer Olympics,** *July 12,* Los Angeles, CA *(886,984)* 3.00
2553-2557, any single 1.25
2558 29c **Numismatics,** *Aug. 13,* Chicago, IL *(288,519)* 1.25
2559 29c **World War II block of 10,** *Sept. 3,* Phoenix, AZ *(1,832,967)* 7.00
2559a-2559j, any single 1.50
2560 29c **Basketball,** *Aug. 28,* Springfield, MA *(295,471)* 2.25
2561 29c **District of Columbia,** *Sept. 7 (299,989)* 1.25
2566a 29c **Comedians booklet pane of 10,** *Aug. 29,* Hollywood, CA 3.00
2562-2566, any single 1.25

First day cancel was applied to 954,293 covers bearing one or more of Nos. 2562-2566a.

2567 29c **Jan Matzeliger,** *Sept. 15,* Lynn, MA *(289,034)* 1.75
2577a 29c **Space Exploration booklet pane of 10,** *Oct. 1,* Pasadena, CA 5.00
2568-2577, any single 1.25

First day cancel was applied to 1,465,111 covers bearing one or more of Nos. 2568-2577a.

2578 (29c) **Christmas (religious),** *Oct. 17,* Houston, TX 1.25
2579 (29c) **Christmas (secular),** *Oct. 17,* Santa, ID *(169,750)* 1.25
2581b (29c) **Christmas booklet pane of 4,** *Oct. 17,* Santa, ID 2.50
2580-2581, any single 1.25
2582 (29c) **Christmas,** bklt. single, *Oct. 17,* Santa, ID 1.25
2582a Booklet pane of 4 2.50
2583 (29c) **Christmas,** bklt. single, *Oct. 17,* Santa, ID 1.25
2583a Booklet pane of 4 2.50
2584 (29c) **Christmas,** bklt. single, *Oct. 17,* Santa, ID 1.25
2584a Booklet pane of 4 2.50
2585 (29c) **Christmas,** bklt. single, *Oct. 17,* Santa, ID 1.25
2585a Booklet pane of 4 2.50

First day cancel was applied to 168,794 covers bearing one or more of Nos. 2580-2585, 2581b, 2582a, 2583a, 2584a and 2585a.

1991-95

2587 32c **James K. Polk,** *Nov. 2, 1995,* Columbia TN *(189,429)* 1.25
2590 $1 **Surrender of Gen. John Burgoyne,** *May 5, 1994,* New York, NY *(379,629)* 2.50
2592 $5 **Washington & Jackson,** *Aug. 19, 1994,* Pittsburgh, PA *(16,303)* 12.50

2593 29c **Pledge of Allegiance,** black denomination, *Sept. 8, 1992,* Rome, NY 1.25
2593a Booklet pane of 10 5.00

First day cancel was applied to 61,464 covers bearing one or more of Nos. 2593-2593a.

2595 29c **Eagle & Shield,** brown denomination, *Sept. 25, 1992,* Dayton, OH 1.50
2596 29c **Eagle & Shield,** green denomination, *Sept. 25, 1992,* Dayton, OH 1.50
2597 29c **Eagle & Shield,** red denomination, *Sept. 25, 1992,* Dayton, OH 1.50

First day cancel was applied to 65,822 covers bearing one or more of Nos. 2595-2597.

2598 29c **Eagle,** *Feb. 4, 1994,* Sarasota, FL *(67,300)* 1.25
2599 29c **Statue of Liberty,** *June 24, 1994,* Haines City, FL *(39,810)* 1.25
2602 (10c) **Eagle & Shield,** Bulk Rate USA, *Dec. 13, 1991,* Kansas City, MO *(21,176)* 1.25
2603 (10c) **Eagle & Shield,** USA Bulk Rate, *May 29, 1993,* Secaucus, NJ 1.25
2604 (10c) **Eagle & Shield,** gold eagle, *May 29, 1993,* Secaucus, NJ 1.25

First day cancellation was applied to 36,444 covers bearing one or more of Nos. 2603-2604.

2605 23c **Flag,** *Sept. 27, 1991* 1.25
2606 23c **Reflected Flag,** *July 21, 1992,* Kansas City, MO *(35,673)* 1.25
2607 23c **Reflected Flag,** 7mm "23," *Oct. 9, 1992,* Kansas City, MO 1.25
2608 23c **Reflected Flag,** 8 ½mm "First Class" *May 14, 1993,* Denver, CO *(15,548)* 1.25
2609 29c **Flag over White House,** *Apr. 23, 1992 (56,505)* 1.25

1992

2615a 29c **Winter Olympics,** *Jan. 11,* Orlando, FL *(1,062,048)* 3.50
2611-2615, any single 1.25
2616 29c **World Columbian Stamp Expo,** *Jan. 24,* Rosemont, IL *(309,729)* 1.25
2617 29c **W.E.B. Du Bois,** *Jan. 31,* Atlanta, GA *(196,219)* 1.75
2618 29c **Love,** *Feb. 6,* Loveland, CO *(218,043)* 1.25
2619 29c **Olympic Baseball,** *Apr. 3,* Atlanta, GA *(105,996)* 2.00
2623a 29c **Voyages of Columbus,** *Apr. 24,* Christiansted, VI 2.75
2620-2623, any single 1.25

First day cancellation was applied to 509,270 covers bearing one or more of Nos. 2620-2623a.

2624 **First Sighting of Land Souvenir Sheet of 3,** *May 22,* Chicago, IL 2.10
2624a 1c 1.50
2624b 4c 1.50
2624c $1 2.00
2625 **Claiming a New World Souvenir Sheet of 3,** *May 22,* Chicago, IL 8.00
2625a 2c 1.50
2625b 3c 1.50
2625c $4 8.00
2626 **Seeking Royal Support Souvenir Sheet of 3,** *May 22,* Chicago, IL 1.75
2626a 5c 1.50
2626b 30c 1.50
2626c 50c 1.50
2627 **Royal Favor Restored Souvenir Sheet of 3,** *May 22,* Chicago, IL 6.25
2627a 6c 1.50
2627b 8c 1.50
2627c $3 6.00
2628 **Reporting Discoveries Souvenir Sheet of 3,** *May 22,* Chicago, IL 4.50
2628a 10c 1.50
2628b 15c 1.50
2628c $2 4.00
2629 $5 **Christopher Columbus Souvenir Sheet,** *May 22,* Chicago, IL 10.00

First day cancel was applied to 211,142 covers bearing one or more of Nos. 2624-2629.

2630 29c **New York Stock Exchange,** *May 17,* New York, NY *(261,897)* 2.50
2634a 29c **Space Accomplishments,** *May 29,* Chicago, IL 2.75
2631-2634, any single 1.50

First day cancel was applied to 277,853 covers bearing one or more of Nos. 2631-2634a.

2635 29c **Alaska Highway,** *May 30,* Fairbanks, AK *(186,791)* 1.25
2636 29c **Kentucky,** *June 1,* Danville, KY *(251,153)* 1.25
2641a 29c **Summer Olympics,** *June 11,* Baltimore, MD *(713,942)* 3.00
2637-2641, any single 1.25
2646a 29c **Hummingbirds booklet pane of 5,** *June 15* 3.00
2642-2646, any single 1.25

First day cancel was applied to 995,278 covers bearing one or more of Nos. 2642-2646a.

2696a 29c **Wildflowers,** *July 24,* Columbus, OH 30.00
2647-2696, any single 1.25

First day cancellation was applied to 3,693,972 covers bearing one or more of Nos. 2647-2696a.

2697 29c **World War II block of 10,** *Aug. 17,* Indianapolis, IN *(1,734,880)* 7.00
2697a-2697j, any single 1.50

First day cancellation was applied to 1,734,880 covers bearing one or more of Nos. 2697, 2697a-2697j.

2698 29c **Dorothy Parker,** *Aug. 22,* West End, NJ *(266,323)* 1.50
2699 29c **Theodore von Karman,** *Aug. 31 (256,986)* 1.50
2703a 29c **Minerals,** *Sept. 17* 2.75
2700-2703, any single 1.25

First day cancellation was applied to 681,416 covers bearing one or more of Nos. 2700-2703.

2704 29c **Juan Rodriguez Cabrillo,** *Sept. 28,* San Diego, CA *(290,720)* 1.25
2709a 29c **Wild Animals booklet pane of 5,** *Oct. 1,* New Orleans, LA 3.25
Any other city 4.00
2705-2709, any single 1.25

First day cancel was applied to 604,205 New Orleans covers bearing one or more of Nos. 2705-2709a.

2710 29c **Christmas (religious),** *Oct. 22* 1.25
2710a Booklet pane of 10 7.25

First day cancel was applied to 201,576 covers bearing one or more of Nos. 2710-2710a.

2714a 29c **Christmas (secular),** *Oct. 22,* Kansas City, MO 2.75
2711-2714, any single 1.25
2718a 29c **Christmas (secular) booklet pane of 4,** *Oct. 22,* Kansas City, MO 2.75
2715-2718, any single 1.25

First day cancel was applied to 461,937 covers bearing one or more of Nos. 2711-2714, 2715-2718 and 2718a.

2719 29c **Christmas (secular),** self-adhesive, *Oct. 28,* New York, NY *(48,873)* 1.25
2720 29c **Chinese New Year,** *Dec. 30,* San Francisco, CA *(138,238)* 2.25

1993

2721 29c **Elvis (Presley),** *Jan. 8,* Memphis, TN, AM cancellation, *(4,452,815)* 1.75
Any city, PM cancellation 2.00
2722 29c **Oklahoma!,** *Mar. 30,* Oklahoma City, OK *(283,837)* 1.25
2723 29c **Hank Williams,** perf 10, *June 9,* Nashville, TN 1.25
2723A 29c **Hank Williams,** perf 11.2x11.5, *June 9,* Nashville, TN —

First day cancel was applied to 311,106 covers bearing one or more of Nos. 2723-2723A.

2730a 29c **Rock & Roll/Rhythm & Blues Musicians,** *June 16,* Cleveland OH or Santa Monica CA 5.00
Any other city 5.00
2724-2730, any single 1.25
Any single, any other city 1.25

Value for No. 2730a is also for any se-tenant configuration of seven different stamps.

First day cancel was applied to 540,809 covers bearing one or more of Nos. 2724-2730a, 2731-2737b.

2737a 29c **Rock & Roll/Rhythm & Blues Musicians booklet pane of 8,** *June 16,* Cleveland, OH or Santa Monica CA 5.25
Any other city 5.25
2731-2737, any single 1.25
Any single, any other city 1.25
2737b 29c **Rock & Roll/Rhythm & Blues Musicians booklet pane of 4,** *June 16,* Cleveland, OH or Santa Monica CA 2.75
Any other city 2.75

For first day cancellation quantities, see No. 2730a.

2745a 29c **Space Fantasy booklet pane of 5,** *Jan. 25,* Huntsville, AL 3.25
2741-2745, any single 1.25

First day cancel was applied to 631,203 covers bearing one or more of Nos. 2741-2745a.

2746 29c **Percy Lavon Julian,** *Jan. 29,* Chicago, IL *(120,877)* 1.75
2747 29c **Oregon Trail,** *Feb. 12,* Salem, OR *(436,550)* 1.25

No. 2747 was also available on the first day of issue in 36 cities along the route of the Oregon Trail.

2748 29c **World University Games,** *Feb. 25,* Buffalo, NY *(157,563)* 1.50
2749 29c **Grace Kelly,** *Mar. 24,* Beverly Hills, CA *(263,913)* 2.50
2753a 29c **Circus,** *Apr. 6* 3.00
2750-2753, any single 1.50

First day cancel was applied to 676,927 covers bearing one or more of Nos. 2750-2753a.

2754 29c **Cherokee Strip Land Run,** *Apr. 17,* Enid, OK *(260,118)* 1.25
2755 29c **Dean Acheson,** *Apr. 21, (158,783)* 1.25
2759a 29c **Sporting Horses,** *May 1,* Louisville, KY 3.50
2756-2759, any single 1.75

First day cancel was applied to 448,059 covers bearing one or more of Nos. 2756-2759a.

2764a 29c **Garden Flowers booklet pane of 5,** *May 15,* Spokane, WA 3.00
2760-2764, any single 1.50

First day cancel was applied to 492,578 covers bearing one or more of Nos. 2760-2764a.

2765 29c **World War II block of 10,** *May 31,* 7.00
2765a-2765j, any single 1.50

First day cancel was applied to 543,511 covers bearing one or more of Nos. 2765, 2765a-2765j.

2766 29c **Joe Louis,** *June 22,* Detroit, MI *(229,272)* 2.50

2770a 29c **Broadway Musicals booklet pane of 4,** *July 14,* New York, NY 3.50
2767-2770, any single 1.25

First day cancel was applied to 308,231 covers bearing one or more of Nos. 2767-2770a.

2774a 29c **Country Music,** *Sept. 25,* Nashville, TN 3.00
2771-2774, any single 1.25
2778a 29c **Country Music booklet pane of 4,** *Sept. 25,* Nashville, TN 3.00
2775-2778, any single 1.25

First day cancel was applied to 362,904 covers bearing one or more of Nos. 2771-2774a, 2775-2778a.

2782a 29c **National Postal Museum,** *July 30* 2.75
2779-2782, any single 1.25

First day cancel was applied to 371,115 covers bearing one or more of Nos. 2779-2782a.

2784a 29c **Deafness/Sign Language,** *Sept. 20,* Burbank, CA 2.25
2783-2784, any single 1.25

First day cancel was applied to 112,350 covers bearing one or more of Nos. 2783-2784a.

2788a 29c **Classic Books,** *Oct. 23,* Louisville, KY 2.75
2785-2788, any single 1.25

First day cancel was applied to 269,457 covers bearing one or more of Nos. 2785-2788a.

2789 29c **Christmas (religious),** *Oct. 21,* Raleigh, NC 1.25
2790 29c **Christmas (religious),** booklet single, *Oct. 21,* Raleigh, NC 1.25
2790a Booklet pane of 4 2.50

First day cancellation was applied to 155,192 covers bearing one or more of Nos. 2789-2790a.

2794a 29c **Christmas (secular),** sheet stamps, *Oct. 21,* New York, NY 2.75
2791-2794, any single 1.25
2798a 29c **Christmas (secular) booklet pane of 10,** *Oct. 21,* New York, NY 6.50
2798b 29c **Christmas (secular) booklet pane of 10,** *Oct. 21,* New York, NY 6.50
2795-2798, any single 1.25
2799 29c **Christmas (snowman),** large self-adhesive, *Oct. 28,* New York, NY 1.25
2800 29c **Christmas (soldier),** self-adhesive, *Oct. 28,* New York, NY 1.25
2801 29c **Christmas (jack-in-the-box),** self-adhesive, *Oct. 28,* New York, NY 1.25
2802 29c **Christmas (reindeer),** self-adhesive, *Oct. 28,* New York, NY 1.25
2799-2802 on one cover 2.50
2803 29c **Christmas (snowman),** small self-adhesive, *Oct. 28,* New York, NY 1.25

First day cancel was applied to 384,262 covers bearing one or more of Nos. 2791-2794a, 2795-2798b, 2799-2803.

2804 29c **Mariana Islands,** *Nov. 4,* Saipan, MP *(157,410)* 1.25
2805 29c **Columbus' Landing in Puerto Rico,** *Nov. 19,* San Juan, PR *(222,845)* 1.25
2806 29c **AIDS Awareness,** *Dec. 1,* New York, NY 1.75
2806a Booklet single, perf. 11 vert. 1.75
2806b Booklet pane of 5 3.75

First day cancellation was applied to 209,200 covers bearing one or more of Nos. 2806-2806b.

1994

2811a 29c **Winter Olympics,** *Jan. 6,* Salt Lake City, UT 3.00
2807-2811, any single 1.25

First day cancellation was applied to 645,636 covers bearing one or more of Nos. 2807-2811a.

2812 29c **Edward R. Murrow,** *Jan. 21,* Pullman, WA *(154,638)* 1.25
2813 29c **Love,** self-adhesive, *Jan. 27,* Loveland, OH *(125,146)* 1.25
2814 29c **Love,** booklet single, *Feb. 14,* Niagara Falls, NY 1.25
2814a Booklet pane of 10 6.50
2814C 29c **Love,** *June 11,* Niagara Falls, NY *(42,109)* 1.25
2815 52c **Love,** *Feb. 14,* Niagara Falls, NY 1.50
2816 29c **Dr. Allison Davis,** *Feb. 1,* Williamstown, MA *(162,404)* 2.00
2817 29c **Chinese New Year,** *Feb. 5,* Pomona, CA *(148,492)* 1.75
2818 29c **Buffalo Soldiers,** *Apr. 22,* Dallas, TX *(107,223)* 2.50

No. 2818 was also available on the first day of issue in forts in Kansas, Texas and Arizona.

2828a 29c **Silent Screen Stars,** *Apr. 27,* San Francisco, CA 6.50
2819-2828, any single 1.50

First day cancellation was applied to 591,251 covers bearing one or more of Nos. 2819-2828a.

2833a 29c **Garden Flowers booklet pane of 5,** *Apr. 28,* Cincinnati, OH 3.25
2829-2833, any single 1.25

First day cancellation was applied to 153,069 covers bearing one or more of Nos. 2829-2833a.

2834 29c **World Cup Soccer,** *May 26,* New York, NY 1.25
2835 40c **World Cup Soccer,** *May 26,* New York, NY 1.40
2836 50c **World Cup Soccer,** *May 26,* New York, NY 1.50

First day cancellation was applied to 443,768 covers bearing one or more of Nos. 2834-2836.

2837 **World Cup Soccer souvenir sheet of 3,** *May 26,* New York, NY *(59,503)* 3.00
2838 29c **World War II block of 10,** *June 6,* USS Normandy 7.00
2838a-2838j, any single 1.50

No. 2838 was also available on the first day of issue in 13 other locations.
First day cancellation was applied to 744,267 covers bearing one or more of Nos. 2838, 2838a-2838j.

2839 29c **Norman Rockwell,** *July 1,* Stockbridge, MA *(232,076)* 1.25
2840 50c **Norman Rockwell Souvenir Sheet of 4,** *July 1,* Stockbridge, MA 3.50
2840a-2840d, any single 1.50

First day cancellation was applied to 19,734 covers bearing one or more of Nos. 2840-2840d.

2841 29c **Moon Landing Sheet of 12,** *July 20,* 6.50
2841a, single stamp 1.50

First day cancellation was applied to 303,707 covers bearing one or more of Nos. 2841-2841a.

2842 $9.95 **Moon Landing,** *July 20 (11,463)* 17.50
2847a 29c **Locomotives booklet pane of 5,** *July 28,* Chama, NM 3.25
2843-2847, any single 1.50

First day cancellation was applied to 169,016 covers bearing one or more of Nos. 2843-2847a.

2848 29c **George Meany,** *Aug. 16 (172,418)* 1.25
2853a 29c **American Music Series,** *Sept. 1,* New York, NY 4.50
2849-2853, any single 1.50

First day cancellation was applied to 156,049 covers bearing one or more of Nos. 2849-2853a.

2861a 29c **American Music Series,** *Sept. 17,* Greenville MS 6.00
2854-2861, any single 1.25

First day cancellation was applied to 483,737 covers bearing one or more of Nos. 2854-2861a.

2862 29c **James Thurber,** *Sept. 10,* Columbus OH *(39,064)* 1.25
2866a 29c **Wonders of the Sea,** *Oct. 3,* Honolulu HI 2.75
2863-2866, any single 1.25

First day cancellation was applied to 284,678 covers bearing one or more of Nos. 2863-2866a.

2868a 29c **Cranes,** *Oct. 9* 2.50
2867-2868, any single 1.25

First day cancellation was applied to 202,955 covers bearing one or more of Nos. 2867-2868a, 24,942 with the People's Republic of China stamps.

2869 29c **Legends of the West Pane of 20,** *Oct. 18,* Laramie WY *(429,680)* 14.00
Tucson, AZ *(220,417)* 14.00
Lawton, OK *(191,393)* 14.00
2869a-2869t, any single, any city 1.75

First day cancellation was applied to covers bearing one or more of Nos. 2869-2869t.

2871 29c **Christmas (religious),** perf 11¼, *Oct. 20 (155,192)* 1.25
2871A 29c **Christmas (religious),** perf 9¾x11, *Oct. 20 (155,192)* 1.25
2872 29c **Christmas (stocking),** *Oct. 20,* Harmony MN 1.25
2873 29c **Christmas (Santa Claus),** self-adhesive, *Oct. 20,* Harmony MN 1.25
2874 29c **Christmas (cardinal),** small self-adhesive, *Oct. 20,* Harmony MN 1.25

First day cancellation was applied to 132,005 covers bearing one or more of Nos. 2872, 2872a, 2873, 2874.

2875 $2 **Bureau of Printing and Engraving Souvenir sheet,** *Nov. 3,* New York, NY *(13,126)* 17.50
2876 29c **Chinese New Year (Boar),** *Dec. 30,* Sacramento CA 1.50
2877 (3c) **Dove, bright blue,** *Dec. 13* 1.25
2878 (3c) **Dove, dark blue,** *Dec. 13* 1.25
2879 (20c) **G, black,** *Dec. 13* 1.25
2880 (20c) **G, red,** *Dec. 13* 1.25
2881 (32c) **G, black,** *Dec. 13* 1.25
2881a Booklet pane of 10 6.75
2882 (32c) **G, red,** *Dec. 13* 1.25
2883 (32c) **G, black,** *Dec. 13* 1.25
2883a Booklet pane of 10 6.75
2884 (32c) **G, black,** *Dec. 13* 1.25
2884a Booklet pane of 10 6.75
2885 (32c) **G, red,** *Dec. 13* 1.25
2885a Booklet pane of 10 6.75
2886 (32c) **G, gray, blue, light blue, red & black,** self-adhesive, *Dec. 13* 1.25
2887 (32c) **G, black, blue & red,** self-adhesive, *Dec. 13* 1.25
2888 (25c) **G, black,** coil, *Dec. 13* 1.25
2889 (32c) **G, black,** coil, *Dec. 13* 1.25
2890 (32c) **G, blue,** coil, *Dec. 13* 1.25
2891 (32c) **G, red,** coil, *Dec. 13* 1.25
2892 (32c) **G, red,** rouletted coil, *Dec. 13* 1.25

Originally, No. 2893 (the 5c green Non-profit Presort G rate stamp) was only available through the Philatelic Fullfillment Center after their announcement 1/12/95. Requests for first day cancels received a 12/13/94 cancel, even though they were not available on that date. Value, $1.25.

First day cancellation was applied to 338,107 covers bearing one or more of Nos. 2877-2893(?), and U633-U634.

2897 32c **Flag Over Porch,** *May 19,* Denver CO 1.25

First day cancellation was applied to 66,609 covers bearing one or more of Nos. 2897, 2913-2914, 2916 and possibly, 2920.

1995-98

2902 (5c) **Butte,** coil, *Mar. 10,* State College PA 1.25

First day cancellation was applied to 80,003 covers bearing one or more of Nos. 2902, 2905, and U635-U636.

2902B (5c) **Butte,** self-adhesive coil, *June 15, 1996,* San Antonio TX 1.25

First day cancellation was applied to 87,400 covers bearing one or more of Nos. 2902B, 2904A, 2906, 2910, 2912A, 2915B.

2903 (5c) **Mountain,** purple & multi coil, *Mar. 16, 1996* San Jose CA 1.25
2904 (5c) **Mountain,** blue & multi coil, *Mar. 16,1996* San Jose CA 1.25

First day cancellation was applied to 28,064 covers bearing one or more of Nos. 2903-2904.

2904A (5c) **Mountain,** purple & multi self-adhesive coil, *June 15, 1996,* San Antonio TX 1.25

First day cancellation was applied to 87,400 covers bearing one or more of Nos. 2902B, 2904A, 2906, 2910, 2912A, 2915B.

2904B (5c) **Mountain,** purple & multi self-adhesive coil, inscription outlined, *Jan. 24, 1997,* Tucson, AZ 1.25
2905 (10c) **Auto,** coil, *Mar. 10,* State College PA 1.25
2906 (10c) **Auto,** self-adhesive coil, *June 15, 1996* San Antonio TX 1.25

First day cancellation was applied to 87,400 covers bearing one or more of Nos. 2902B, 2904A, 2906, 2910, 2912A, 2915B.

2907 (10c) **Eagle & Shield,** USA Bulk Rate self-adhesive coil, *May 21, 1996* 1.25

First day cancellation was applied to 54,102 covers bearing one or more of Nos. 2907, 2915A, 2915C, 2921.

2908 (15c) **Auto tail fin (dark orange yellow),** coil, *Mar. 17,* New York NY 1.25
2909 (15c) **Auto tail fin (buff),** coil, *Mar. 17,* New York, NY 1.25

First day cancellation was applied to 93,770 covers bearing one or more of Nos. 2908-2909, 2911-2912, 2919.

2910 (15c) **Auto tail fin (buff),** self-adhesive coil, *June 15, 1996,* San Antonio TX 1.25

First day cancellation was applied to 87,400 covers bearing one or more of Nos. 2902B, 2904A, 2906, 2910, 2915B.

2911 (25c) **Juke box,** coil, *Mar. 17,* New York NY 1.25
2912 (25c) **Juke box,** coil, *Mar. 17,* New York NY 1.25

First day cancellation was applied to 93,770 covers bearing one or more of Nos. 2908-2909, 2911-2912, 2919.

2912A (25c) **Juke box,** self-adhesive coil, bright orange red & multi, microperfs, *June 15, 1996,* New York NY 1.25

First day cancellation was applied to 87,400 covers bearing one or more of Nos. 2902B, 2904A, 2906, 2910, 2912A, 2915B.

2912B (25c) **Juke box,** self-adhesive coil, dark red & multi, *Jan. 24, 1997,* Tucson, AZ 1.25
2913 32c **Flag Over Porch,** coil, *May 19,* Denver CO 1.25
2914 32c **Flag Over Porch,** coil, *May 19,* Denver CO 1.25
2915 32c **Flag Over Porch,** self-adhesive, die cut 8.7 vert., *Apr. 18* 1.25
2915A 32c **Flag Over Porch,** self-adhesive, die cut 9.8 vert., 11 teeth, *May 21, 1996* 1.25
2915B 32c **Flag Over Porch,** self-adhesive die cut 11.5 vert., *June 15, 1996,* San Antonio TX 1.25

First day cancellation was applied to 87,400 covers bearing one or more of Nos. 2902B, 2904A, 2906, 2910, 2912A, 2915B.

2915C 32c **Flag Over Porch,** self-adhesive, die cut 10.9, *May 21, 1996* 2.00
2915D 32c **Flag Over Porch,** self-adhesive coil, self-adhesive die cut 9.8 vert., 9 teeth, *Jan. 24, 1997,* Tucson, AZ 1.25

First day cancellation was applied to 56,774 covers bearing one or more of Nos. 2904B, 2912B, 2915D and 2921b.

2916 32c **Flag Over Porch,** booklet single, *May 19,* Denver CO 1.25
2916a Booklet pane of 10 7.50
2919 32c **Flag Over Field,** self-adhesive, *Mar. 17,* New York NY 1.25

First day cancellation was applied to 93,770 covers bearing one or more of Nos. 2908-2909, 2911-2912, 2919.

2920 32c **Flag Over Porch,** self-adhesive, *Apr. 18* 1.25

First day cancellation was applied to 66,609 covers bearing one or more of Nos. 2897, 2913-2914, 2916 and possibly, 2920.

First day cancellation was applied to 57,639 covers bearing one or more of Nos. 2920d, 3030, 3044.

2921 32c **Flag Over Porch,** self-adhesive, booklet stamp, die cut 9.8 on 2 or 3 sides, *May 21, 1996* 1.25

First day cancellation was applied to 54,102 covers bearing one or more of Nos. 2907, 2915A, 2915C, 2921.

GREAT AMERICANS ISSUE

2933 32c **Milton Hershey,** *July 11,* Hershey PA *(121,228)* 1.25
2934 32c **Cal Farley,** *Apr. 26, 1996,* Amarillo TX *(109,440)* 1.25
2935 32c **Henry Luce,** *Apr. 3, 1998,* New York NY *(76,982)* 1.25
2936 32c **Wallace,** *July 16, 1998,* Pleasantville NY *(72,183)* 1.25
2938 46c **Ruth Benedict,** *Oct. 20,* Virginia Beach VA *(24,793)* 1.40
2940 55c **Alice Hamilton,** *July 11,* Boston MA *(24,225)* 1.40
2941 55c **Justin Morrill,** *July 17, 1999* Strafford VT *(19,699)* 1.40
2942 77c **Mary Breckinridge,** *Nov. 9, 1998* Troy, NY 1.75

First day cancellation was applied to 121,662 covers bearing one or more of Nos. 2942, 3257-3261, 3263-3269.

2943 78c **Alice Paul,** *Aug. 18,* Mount Laurel NJ *(25,071)* 1.75

1995

2948 (32c) **Love,** *Feb. 1,* Valentines VA 1.50
2949 (32c) **Love,** self-adhesive, *Feb. 1,* Valentines VA 1.50

First day cancellation was applied to 70,778 covers bearing one or more of Nos. 2948, 2949.

2950 32c **Florida Statehood,** *Mar. 3,* Tallahassee FL *(167,499)* 1.25
2954a 32c **Earth Day,** *Apr. 20* 2.75
2951-2954, any single 1.25

First day cancellation was applied to 328,893 covers bearing one or more of Nos. 2951-2954, 2954a.

2955 32c **Richard Nixon,** *Apr. 26,* Yorba Linda CA *(377,605)* 1.25
2956 32c **Bessie Coleman,** *Apr. 27,* Chicago IL *(299,834)* 1.75
2957 32c **Love,** *May 12,* Lakeville PA 1.25
2958 55c **Love,** *May 12,* Lakeville PA 1.25
2959 32c **Love,** booklet single, *May 12,* Lakeville PA 1.25
2959a Booklet pane of 10 7.50
2960 55c **Love,** self-adhesive, *May 12,* Lakeville PA 1.40

First day cancellation was applied to 273,350 covers bearing one or more of Nos. 2957-2959, 2959a, and U637.

2965a 32c **Recreational Sports,** *May 20,* Jupiter FL 3.25
2961-2965, any single 1.50

First day cancellation was applied to 909,807 covers bearing one or more of Nos. 2961-2965, 2965a.

2966 32c **Prisoners of War & Missing in Action,** *May 29 (231,857)* 2.00
2967 32c **Marilyn Monroe,** *June 1,* Universal City CA *(703,219)* 2.50
Any other city 1.75
2968 32c **Texas Statehood,** *June 16,* Austin TX *(177,550)* 1.75
2973a 32c **Great Lakes Lighthouses booklet pane of 5,** *June 17,* Cheboygan MI 5.00
2969-2973, any single 2.00

First day cancellation was applied to 626,055 covers bearing one or more of Nos. 2969-2973, 2973a.

2974 32c **UN, 50th Anniv.,** *June 26,* San Francisco CA *(160,383)* 1.50
2975 32c **Civil War pane of 20,** *June 29,* Gettysburg PA 16.00
Any other city 16.00
2975a-2975t, any single, Gettysburg PA 1.50
Any other city 1.50

First day cancellation was applied to 1,950,134 covers bearing one or more of Nos. 2975, 2975a-2975t, and UX200-UX219.

2979a 32c **Carousel Horses,** *July 21,* Lahaska PA 3.25
2976-2979, any single 1.25

First day cancellation was applied to 479,038 covers bearing one or more of Nos. 2976-2979, 2979a.

2980 32c **Woman Suffrage,** *Aug. 26 (196,581)* 1.25
2981 32c **World War II block of 10,** *Sept. 2,* Honolulu HI 7.00
2981a-2981j, any single 1.50

First day cancellation was applied to 1,562,094 covers bearing one or more of Nos. 2981, 2981a-2981j.

2982 32c **American Music Series,** *Sept. 1,* New Orleans LA *(258,996)* 1.75
2992a 32c **American Music Series,** *Sept. 16,* Monterey CA 6.50
2983-2992, any single 1.50

First day cancellation was applied to 629,956 covers bearing one or more of Nos. 2983-2992, 2992a.

2997a 32c **Garden Flowers booklet pane of 5,** *Sept. 19,* Encinitas CA 4.00
2993-2997, any single 1.25

First day cancellation was applied to 564,905 covers bearing one or more of Nos. 2993-2997, 2997a.

2998 60c **Eddie Rickenbacker,** *Sept. 25,* Columbus OH *(24,283)* 1.75
2999 32c **Republic of Palau,** *Sept. 29,* Agana GU *(157,377)* 1.25
3000 32c **Comic Strips Pane of 20,** *Oct. 1,* Boca Raton FL 13.00
3000a-3000t, any single 2.00

First day cancellation was applied to 1,362,990 covers bearing one or more of Nos. 3000, 3000a-3000t.

3001 32c **US Naval Academy,** *Oct. 10,* Annapolis, MD *(222,183)* 1.75

3002 32c **Tennessee Williams,** *Oct. 13,* Clarksdale MS *(209,812)* 1.25
3003 32c **Christmas, Madonna,** perf 11.2, *Oct. 19* 1.25
3003A 32c **Christmas, Madonna,** perf 9.8x10.9. *Oct. 19* 1.25
3003Ab Booklet pane of 10 7.25

First day cancellation was applied to 223,301 covers bearing one or more of Nos. 3003, 3003A-3003Ab.

3007a 32c **Christmas (secular) sheet,** *Sept. 30,* North Pole NY 3.25
3004-3007, any single 1.25
3007b 32c Booklet pane of 10, 3 #3004, etc. 7.25
3007c 32c Booklet pane of 10, 2 #3004, etc. 7.25

First day cancellation was applied to 487,816 covers bearing one or more of Nos. 3004-3007, 3007a.

3008-3011 32c **Christmas (secular) self-adhesive booklet stamps,** *Sept. 30,* North Pole NY 3.25
3008-3011, any single 1.25
3012 32c **Angel,** *Oct. 19,* Christmas FL 1.25
3013 32c **Children sledding,** *Oct. 19,* Christmas FL 1.25

First day cancellation was applied to 77,675 covers bearing one or more of Nos. 3012, 3013, 3018.

3014-3017 32c **Self-adhesive coils,** *Sept. 30,* North Pole NY 2.50
3014-3017, any single 1.25
3018 32c **Self-adhesive coil,** *Oct. 19,* Christmas FL 1.25

First day cancellation was applied to 77,675 covers bearing one or more of Nos. 3012, 3013, 3018.

3023a 32c **Antique Automobiles,** *Nov. 3,* New York NY 3.00
3019-3023, any single 1.25

First day cancellation was applied to 757,003 covers bearing one or more of Nos. 3019-3023, 3023a.

1996

3024 32c **Utah Statehood Cent.,** *Jan. 4,* Salt Lake City UT *(207,089)* 1.25
3029a 32c **Garden Flowers booklet pane,** *Jan. 19,* Kennett Square PA 3.50
3025-3029, any single 1.25

First day cancellation was applied to 876,176 covers bearing one or more of Nos. 3025-3029, 3029a.

3030 32c **Love self-adhesive,** *Jan. 20,* New York NY 1.25

First day cancellation was applied to 57,639 covers bearing one or more of Nos. 2920d, 3030, 3044.

1996-2000

FLORA AND FAUNA

3031 1c **Kestrel,** *Nov. 19, 1999,* New York, NY *(14,431)* 1.50
3032 2c **Red-headed woodpecker,** *Feb. 2,* Sarasota FL *(37,319)* 1.25
3033 3c **Eastern Bluebird,** *Apr. 3 (23,405)* 1.25
3036 $1 **Red Fox,** *Aug. 14, 1998* 3.50

First day cancellation was applied to 46,557 covers bearing one or more of Nos. 3228-3229, 3036.

3044 1c **American Kestrel, coil,** *Jan. 20,* New York NY 1.25

First day cancellation was applied to 57,639 covers bearing one or more of Nos. 2920d, 3030, 3044.

3045 2c **Red-Headed Woodpecker,** *June 22, 1999 (14,377)* 1.25
3048 20c **Blue Jay, booklet stamp, self-adhesive,** *Aug. 2,* St. Louis MO 1.25

First day cancellation was applied to 32,633 covers bearing one or more of Nos. 3048, 3053.

3049 32c **Yellow Rose, booklet stamp, self-adhesive,** *Oct. 24,* Pasadena, CA *(7,849)* 1.25
3050 20c **Ring-necked Pheasant, booklet stamp, self-adhesive,** *July 31, 1998* Somerset NJ 1.25

First day cancellation was applied to 32,220 covers bearing one or more of Nos. 3050, 3055.

3052 33c **Coral Pink Rose,** serpentine die cut 11½x11¼, *Aug. 13, 1999,* Indianapolis, IN 1.25
3052E 33c **Coral Pink Rose,** serpentine die cut 10¾x10½, *Apr. 7, 2000,* New York, NY *(18,199)* 1.25
3053 20c **Blue Jay, coil, self-adhesive,** *Aug. 2,* St. Louis MO 1.25
3054 32c **Yellow Rose, self-adhesive,** *Aug. 1, 1997,* Falls Church VA *(20,029)* 1.25
3055 20c **Ring-necked Pheasant,coil, self-adhesive,** *July 31, 1998* Somerset NJ 1.25

First day cancellation was applied to 32,220 covers bearing one or more of Nos. 3050, 3055.

1996

3058 32c **Ernest E. Just,** *Feb. 1 (191,360)* 1.75
3059 32c **Smithsonian, 150th anniv.,** *Feb. 7, (221,399)* 1.25
3060 32c **Chinese New Year,** *Feb. 8,* San Francisco CA *(237,451)* 1.50
3064a 32c **Pioneers of Communication,** *Feb. 22,* New York NY 2.50
3061-3064, any single 1.25

First day cancellation was applied to 567,205 covers bearing one or more of Nos. 3061-3064, 3064a.

3065 32c **Fulbright Scholarships,** *Feb. 28,* Fayetteville AR *(227,330)* 1.25
3066 50c **Jacqueline Cochran,** *Mar. 9,* Indio CA *(30,628)* 1.40
3067 32c **Marathon,** *Apr. 11,* Boston MA *(177,050)* 1.75
3068 32c **Olympics, pane of 20,** *May 2* 13.00
3068a-3068t, any single 1.25
Atlanta, GA —

Washington DC first day cancellation was applied to 1,807,316 covers bearing one or more of Nos. 3068, 3068a-3068t. Atlanta was also an official first day city, and covers postmarked there are scarce.

3069 32c **Georgia O'Keeffe,** *May 23,* Santa Fe NM *(200,522)* 1.25
3070 32c **Tennessee Statehood, Bicen.,** *May 31,* Knoxville, Memphis or Nashville TN 1.25
3071 32c **Tennessee, self-adhesive,** *May 31,* Knoxville, Memphis or Nashville TN 1.25

First day cancellation was applied to 217,281 covers bearing one or more of Nos. 3070-3071.

3076a 32c **American Indian Dances, strip of 5,** *June 7,* Oklahoma City OK 2.75
3072-3076, any single 1.25

First day cancellation was applied to 653,057 covers bearing one or more of Nos. 3072-3076, 3076a.

3080a 32c **Prehistoric Animals,** *June 8,* Toronto, Canada 2.75
3077-3080, any single 1.50

First day cancellation was applied to 485,929 covers bearing one or more of Nos. 3077-3080, 3080a.

3081 32c **Breast Cancer Awareness,** *June 15 (183,896)* 1.25
Any other city 1.25
3082 32c **James Dean,** *June 24,* Burbank CA *(263,593)* 1.75
3086a 32c **Folk Heroes,** *July 11,* Anaheim CA 2.75
3083-3086, any single 1.25

First day cancellation was applied to 739,706 covers bearing one or more of Nos. 3083-3086, 3086a.

3087 32c **Centennial Olympic Games,** *July 19,* Atlanta GA *(269,056)* 1.25
3088 32c **Iowa Statehood, 150th Anniv.,** *Aug. 1,* Dubuque IA 1.25
3089 32c **Iowa Statehood, self-adhesive** *Aug. 1,* Dubuque IA 1.25
3088, 3089, both stamps issued *Aug. 1,* Dubuque, IA 1.75

First day cancellation was applied to 215,181 covers bearing one or more of Nos. 3088-3089.

3090 32c **Rural Free Delivery,** *Aug. 7,* Charleston WV *(192,070)* 1.25
3091-3095 32c **Riverboats,** *Aug. 22,* Orlando FL 3.50
3091-3095, any single 1.25
3095b 32c **Riverboats, special die cutting,** *Aug. 22,* Orlando FL 3.50

First day cancellation was applied to 770,384 covers bearing one or more of Nos. 3091-3095, 3095b.

3099a 32c **Big Band Leaders,** *Sept. 11,* New York NY 3.25
3096-3099, any single 1.25

First day cancellation was applied to 1,235,166 covers bearing one or more of Nos. 3096-3103, 3099a, 3103a.

3103a 32c **Songwriters,** *Sept. 11,* New York NY 3.25
3100-3103, any single 1.25

First day cancellation was applied to 1,235,166 covers bearing one or more of Nos. 3096-3103, 3099a, 3103a.

3104 23c **F. Scott Fitzgerald,** *Sept. 27,* St. Paul MN *(150,783)* 1.25
3105 32c **Endangered Species,** *Oct. 2,* San Diego CA 7.50
3105a-3105o, any single 1.25

First day cancellation was applied to 941,442 covers bearing one or more of Nos. 3105, 3105a-3105o.

3106 32c **Computer Technology,** *Oct. 8,* Aberdeen Proving Ground MD *(153,688)* 1.75
3107 32c **Christmas Madonna,** *Nov. 1,* Richmond VA 1.25

First day cancellation was applied to 164,447 covers bearing one or more of Nos. 3107, 3112.

3111a 32c **Christmas (secular),** *Oct. 8,* North Pole AK 2.75
3108-3111, any single 1.25

First day cancellation was applied to 884,339 covers bearing one or more of Nos. 3108-3111, 3111a, 3113-3117.

3112 32c **As No. 3107, self-adhesive,** *Nov. 1,* Richmond VA 1.25
3113-3116 32c **Christmas (secular), self-adhesive,** *Oct. 8,* North Pole AK 3.25
3113-3116, any single 1.25
3117 32c **Skaters, self-adhesive,** *Oct. 8,* North Pole AK 1.25

First day cancellation was applied to 884,339 covers bearing one or more of Nos. 3108-3111, 3111a, 3113-3117.

3118 32c **Hanukkah,** *Oct. 22 (179,355)* 1.75
3119 50c **Cycling,** *Nov. 1,* New York NY 3.25
3119a-3119b, any single 1.75

First day cancellation was applied to 290,091 covers bearing one or more of Nos. 3119, 3119a-3119b.

1997

3120 32c **Chinese New Year,** *Jan. 5,* Honolulu *(233,638)* 1.50
3121 32c **Benjamin O. Davis, Sr.,** *Jan. 28 (166,527)* 1.75
3122 32c **Statue of Liberty, self-adhesive,** *Feb. 1,* San Diego CA *(40,003)* 1.25
3123 32c **Love, Swans, self-adhesive,** *Feb. 4,* Los Angeles CA 1.25
3124 55c **Love, Swans, self-adhesive,** *Feb. 4,* Los Angeles CA 1.50

First day cancellation was applied to 257,380 covers bearing one or more of Nos. 3123-3124.

3125 32c **Helping Children Learn, self-adhesive** *Feb. 18 (175,410)* 1.25
3126 32c **Merian Botanical Prints, Citron, etc., self-adhesive, die cut 10.9x10.2,** *Mar. 3* 1.25
3127 32c **Merian Botanical Prints, Pineapple, etc., self-adhesive, die cut 10.9x10.2,** *Mar. 3* 1.25
3128 32c **Merian Botanical Prints, Citron, etc., self-adhesive, die cut 11.2x10.8,** *Mar. 3* 1.25
3128a 32c **Merian Botanical Prints, Citron, etc., self-adhesive, die cut mixed perf,** *Mar. 3* 1.25
3129 32c **Merian Botanical Prints, Pineapple, etc., self-adhesive, die cut 11.2x10.8,** *Mar. 3* 1.25
3129a 32c **Merian Botanical Prints, Pineapple, etc., self-adhesive, die cut mixed perf,** *Mar. 3* 1.25

First day cancellation was applied to 336,897 covers bearing one or more of Nos. 3126-3129, 3128a-3129a.

3131a 32c **Pacific 97,** *Mar. 13,* New York NY 1.75
3130-3131, any single 1.25

First day cancellation was applied to 371,908 covers bearing one or more of Nos. 3130-3131, 3131a.

3132 (25c) **Juke Box, self-adhesive** *Mar. 14,* New York NY 1.25
3133 32c **Flag over Porch, Self-adhesive** *Mar. 14,* New York NY 1.25

First day cancellation was applied to 26,0820 covers bearing one or more of Nos. 3132-3133.

3134 32c **Thornton Wilder,** *Apr. 17,* Hamden CT *(157,299)* 1.25
3135 32c **Raoul Wallenberg,** *Apr. 24 (168,668)* 2.00
3136 32c **Dinosaurs, pane of 15** *May 1,* Grand Junction CO 7.50
3136a-3136o, any single 1.25

First day cancellation was applied to 1,782,1221 covers bearing one or more of Nos. 3136, 3136a-3136o.

3137a 32c **Bugs Bunny,** *May 22,* Burbank CA *(378,142)* 1.75
3139 50c **Pacific 97, Franklin, pane of 12** *May 29,* San Francisco CA 12.00
3139a, single 2.00
3140 60c **Pacific 97,, pane of 12,** *May 30,* San Francisco CA 12.00
3140a, single 2.00

First day cancellation was applied to 328,401 covers bearing one or more of Nos. 3139-3140, 3139a-3140b.

3141 32c **Marshall Plan,** *June 4,* Cambridge MA *(157,622)* 1.25
3142 32c **Classic American Aircraft,** *July 19,* Dayton OH 10.00
3142a-3142t, any single 1.25

First day cancellation was applied to 1,413,833 covers bearing one or more of Nos. 3142, 3142a-3142t.

3146a 32c **Football Coaches** *July 25,* Canton OH 2.50
3143-3146, any single 1.50

First day cancellation was applied to 586,946 covers bearing one or more of Nos. 3143-3146.

3147 32c **Bear Bryant,** *Aug. 5,* Green Bay WI *(119,428)* 1.50
3148 32c **Pop Warner,** *Aug. 7,* Tuscaloosa AL *(23,858)* 1.50
3149 32c **Vince Lombardi,** *Aug. 8,* Philadelphia PA *(37,839)* 1.50
3150 32c **George Halas,** *Aug. 16,* Chicago IL *(26,760)* 1.50
3151 32c **American Dolls,** *July 28,* Anaheim CA 8.00
3151a-3151o, any single 1.25

First day cancellation was applied to 831,359 covers bearing one or more of Nos. 3151, 3151a-3151o.

3152 32c **Humphrey Bogart,** *July 31,* Los Angeles CA *(220,254)* 1.50
3153 32c **"The Star and Stripes Forever,"** *Aug. 21,* Milwaukee WI *(36,666)* 1.25
3157a 32c **Opera Singers,** *Sept. 10,* New York NY 2.75
3154-3157, any single 1.25

First day cancellation was applied to 386,689 covers bearing one or more of Nos. 3154-3157.

3165a 32c **Classical Composers and Conductors,** *Sept. 12,* Cincinnati OH 5.25
3158-3165, any single 1.25

First day cancellation was applied to 424,344 covers bearing one or more of Nos. 3158-3165.

3166 32c **Padre Felix Varela,** *Sept. 15,* Miami FL *(120,079)* 1.25
3167 32c **Department of the Air Force,** *Sept. 18 (178,519)* 1.50
3172a 32c **Classic Movie Monsters,** *Sept. 30,* Universal City CA 3.75
3168-3172, any single 1.50

First day cancellation was applied to 476,993 covers bearing one or more of Nos. 3168-3172.

3173 32c **First Supersonic Flight,** *Oct. 14,* Edwards AFB CA *(173,778)* 1.50
3174 32c **Women in Military Service,** *Oct. 18 (106,121)* 1.50
3175 32c **Kwanzaa,** *Oct. 22,* Los Angeles CA *(92,489)* 1.75
3176 32c **Christmas Madonna,** *Oct. 27 (35,809)* 1.25
3177 32c **Holly,** *Oct. 30,* New York NY *(87,332)* 1.25
3178 $3 **Mars Pathfinder,** *Dec. 10* Pasadena CA *(11,699)* 7.50

1998

3179 32c **Chinese New Year,** *Jan. 5,* Seattle WA *(234,269)* 1.50
3180 32c **Alpine Skiing,** *Jan. 22,* Salt Lake City UT *(196,504)* 1.25
3181 32c **Madam C. J. Walker,** *Jan. 28,* Indianapolis IN *(146,348)* 1.75

1998-2000

CELEBRATE THE CENTURY

3182 32c **1900s,** *Feb. 3 (11,699)* 8.50
3182a-3182o, any single 1.50
3183 32c **1910s,** *Feb. 3* 8.50
3183a-3183o, any single 1.50

First day cancellation was applied to 3,896,387 covers bearing one or more of Nos. 3182-3182o, 3183-3183o.

3184 32c **1920s,** *May 28* 8.50
3184a-3184o, any single 1.50

First day cancellation was applied to 1,057,909 covers bearing one or more of Nos. 3184-3184o.

3185 32c **1930s,** *Sept. 10,* Cleveland OH 8.50
3185a-3185o, any single 1.50

First day cancellation was applied to 999,017 covers bearing one or more of Nos. 3185-3185o.

3186 33c **1940s,** *Feb. 18, 1999,* Dobbins AFB GA 8.50
3186a-3186o, any single 1.50

First day cancellation was applied to 1,459,138 covers bearing one or more of Nos. 3186-3186o.

3187 33c **1950s,** *May 26, 1999,* Springfield MA 8.50
3187a-3187o, any single 1.50

First day cancellation was applied to 1,454,906 covers bearing one or more of Nos. 3187-3187o.

3188 33c **1960s,** *Sept. 17, 1999,* Green Bay, WI 8.50
3188a-3188a, any single 1.50

First day cancellation was applied to 1,252,243 covers bearing one or more of Nos. 3188-3188o.

3189 33c **1970s,** *Nov. 18, 1999,* New York, NY 8.50
3189a-3189o, any single 1.50

First day cancellation was applied to 894,084 covers bearing one or more of Nos. 3189-3189o.

3190 33c **1980s,** *Jan. 12, 2000,* Kennedy Space Center, FL 8.50
3190a-3190o, any single 1.50
3191 33c **1990s,** *May 2, 2000,* Escondido, CA 8.50
3191a-3191o, any single 1.50

First day cancellation was applied to 1,172,962 covers bearing one or more of Nos. 3191-3190o.

1998

3192 32c **"Remember the Maine,"** *Feb. 15,* Key West FL *(161,657)* 1.75
3193-3197 32c **Flowering Trees,** *Mar. 19,* New York NY 3.75
3193-3197, any single 1.50

First day cancellation was applied to 666,199 covers bearing one or more of Nos. 3193-3197.

3202a 32c **Alexander Calder,** *Mar. 25* 3.75
3198-3202, any single 1.50

First day cancellation was applied to 588,887 covers bearing one or more of Nos. 3198-3202, 3202a.

3203 32c **Cinco de Mayo,** *Apr. 16,* San Antonio TX *(144,443)* 1.25
3204a 32c **Sylvester & Tweety,** *Apr. 27,* New York NY *(213,839)* 1.25
3206 32c **Wisconsin Statehood,** *May 29,* Madison WI *(130,810)* 1.25

1998-99

3207 (5c) **Wetlands,** *June 5,* McLean VA 1.25
3207A (5c) **Wetlands, Serpentine die cut,** *Dec. 14* 1.25
3208 (25c) **Diner,** *June 5,* McLean VA 1.25

First day cancellation was applied to 35,333 covers bearing one or more of Nos. 3207, 3208; 13,378 covers bearing one of more of Nos. 3207A, 3270-3271.

3208A (25c) **Diner, Serpentine die cut,** *June 5 (13,984)* 1.25

1998

1898 TRANS-MISSISSIPPI STAMPS, CENT.

3209 **Sheet of 9,** *June 18,* Anaheim CA 6.50
3209a 1c 1.50
3209b 2c 1.50
3209c 4c 1.50
3209d 5c 1.50
3209e 8c 1.50
3209f 10c 1.50
3209g 50c 2.00
3209h $1 2.50
3209i $2 4.50
3210 $1 **Sheet of 9,** *June 18,* Anaheim CA 15.00

First day cancellation was applied to 203,649 covers bearing one or more of Nos. 3209-3210, 3209a-3209i.

1998

3211 32c **Berlin Airlift,** *June 26,* Berlin, Germany *(137,894)* 1.25
3215a 32c **Folk Musicians,** *June 26* 3.25
3212-3215, any single 1.25

First day cancellation was applied to 341,015 covers bearing one or more of Nos. 3212-3215, 3215a.

3219a 32c **Gospel Music,** *July 15,* New Orleans LA 3.25
3216-3219, any single 1.25

First day cancellation was applied to 330,533 covers bearing one or more of Nos. 3216-3219, 3219a.

3220 32c **Spanish Settlement of the Southwest,** *July 11,* Española NM *(122,182)* 1.25
3221 32c **Stephen Vincent Benét,** *July 22,* Harpers Ferry WV *(107,412)* 1.25
3225a 32c **Tropical Birds,** *July 29,* Ponce PR 3.00
3222-3225, any single 1.25

First day cancellation was applied to 371,354 covers bearing one or more of Nos. 3222-3225, 3225a.

3226 32c **Alfred Hitchcock,** *Aug. 3,* Los Angeles CA *(140,628)* 1.50
3227 32c **Organ & Tissue Donation,** *Aug. 5,* Columbus OH *(110,601)* 1.25
3228 (10c) **Modern Bicycle, Serpentine die cut,** *Aug. 14* 1.25
3229 (10c) **Modern Bicycle,** *Aug. 14* 1.25

First day cancellation was applied to 46,557 covers bearing one or more of Nos. 3228-3229, 3036.

3230-3234 32c **Bright Eyes,** *Aug. 20,* Boston MA 3.25
3230-3234, any single 1.50

First day cancellation was applied to 394,280 covers bearing one or more of Nos. 3230-3234.

3235 32c **Klondike Gold Rush Cent.,** *Aug. 21,* Nome or Skagway AK *(123,559)* 1.50
3236 32c **American Art, pane of 20,** *Aug. 27,* Santa Clara CA 9.00
3236a-3236t, any single 1.25

First day cancellation was applied to 924,031 covers bearing one or more of Nos. 3236, 3236a-3236t.

3237 32c **American Ballet,** *Sept. 16,* New York NY *(133,034)* 1.25
3242a 32c **Space Discovery,** *Oct. 1,* Kennedy Space Center FL 3.75
3238-3242, any single 1.25

First day cancellation was applied to 399,807 covers bearing one or more of Nos. 3238-3242, 3242a.

3243 32c **Giving & Sharing,** *Oct. 7,* Atlanta GA *(124,051)* 1.25
3244 32c **Christmas, Madonna,** *Oct. 15 (105,835)* 1.25
3245-3248 32c **Christmas, Secular,** *Oct. 15,* Christmas MI 3.25
3245-3248, any single 1.25
3249-3252 32c **Christmas, Secular, size: 23x30mm,** *Oct. 15,* Christmas MI 3.00
3249-3252, any single 1.25

First day cancellation was applied to 328,199 covers bearing one or more of Nos. 3245-3252.

3257 (1c) **Weather Vane, white USA,** *Nov. 9,* Troy NY 1.25
3258 (1c) **Weather Vane, pale blue USA,** *Nov. 9,* Troy NY 1.25
3259 22c **Uncle Sam,** *Nov. 9,* Troy NY 1.25
3260 (33c) **Uncle Sam's Hat,** *Nov. 9,* Troy NY 1.25
3261 $3.20 **Space Shuttle Landing,** *Nov. 9,* 5.00
3262 $11.75 **Piggyback Space Shuttle,** *Nov. 9,* New York NY *(3,703)* 25.00
3263 22c **Uncle Sam, coil,** *Nov. 9,* Troy NY 1.25
3264 (33c) **Uncle Sam's Hat, coil,** *Nov. 9,* Troy NY 1.25
3265 (33c) **Uncle Sam's Hat, self-adhesive coil, die cut 9.9, round corners,** *Nov. 9,* Troy NY 1.25
3266 (33c) **Uncle Sam's Hat, self-adhesive coil, die cut 9.9, square corners,** *Nov. 9,* Troy NY 1.50
3267 (33c) **Uncle Sam's Hat, self-adhesive booklet single, die cut 9.9** *Nov. 9,* Troy NY 1.25
3268 (33c) **Uncle Sam's Hat, self-adhesive booklet single, die cut 11.2x11.1** *Nov. 9,* Troy NY 1.25
3269 (33c) **Uncle Sam's Hat, self-adhesive booklet single, die cut 8** *Nov. 9,* Troy NY 1.25

First day cancellation was applied to 121,662 covers bearing one or more of Nos. 2942, 3257-3261, 3263-3269.

3270 (10c) **Eagle & Shield, Presorted Std.,** *Dec. 14* 1.25
3271 (10c) **Eagle & Shield, Presorted Std., self-adhesive, Serpentine die cut,** *Dec. 14* 1.25

First day cancellation was applied to 13,378 covers bearing one of more of Nos. 3207A, 3270-3271.

1999

3272 33c **Chinese New Year,** *Jan. 5,* Los Angeles CA *(151,436)* 1.50
3273 33c **Malcolm X,** *Jan. 20,* New York NY *(107,226)* 1.75
3274 33c **Love,** *Jan. 28,* Loveland CO 1.25
3275 55c **Love,** *Jan. 28,* Loveland CO 1.50

First day cancellation was applied to 189,331 covers bearing one of more of Nos. 3274, 3275, UX300.

3276 33c **Hospice Care,** *Feb. 9,* Largo FL *(136,976)* 1.25
3277 33c **Flag & City,** *Feb. 25,* Orlando FL 1.25
3278 33c **Flag & City, self-adhesive, die cut 11.1** *Feb. 25,* Orlando FL 1.25
3279 33c **Flag & City, self-adhesive, die cut 9.8** *Feb. 25,* Orlando FL 1.25
3280 33c **Flag & City, coil, perf. 9.9 vert.** *Feb. 25,* Orlando FL 1.25
3281 33c **Flag & City, self-adhesive coil, die cut 9.8 vert, square corners,** *Feb. 25,* Orlando FL 1.25
3282 33c **Flag & City, self-adhesive coil, die cut 9.8 vert., round corners,** *Feb. 25,* Orlando FL 1.25

First day cancellation was applied to 88,569 covers bearing one of more of Nos. 3277-3282.

3283 33c **Flag & Blackboard, self-adhesive, die cut 7.9,** *Mar. 13 (26,067)* 1.25
3286 33c **Irish Immigration,** *Feb. 26,* Boston MA *(127,213)* 1.50
3287 33c **Lunt & Fontanne,** *Mar. 2,* New York NY *(120,423)* 1.25
3292a 33c **Arctic Animals,** *Mar. 12,* Barrow AK 3.25
3288-3292, any single 1.25

First day cancellation was applied to 476,863 covers bearing one of more of Nos. 3288-3292, 3292a.

3293 33c **Sonoran Desert, Pane of 10,** *Apr. 6,* Tucson AZ 6.75
3293a-3293j, any single 1.25

First day cancellation was applied to 410,985 covers bearing one of more of Nos. 3293-3293j.

3294-3297 33c **Christmas Berries, die cut 11.2x11.7** *Apr. 10,* Ponchatoula LA 3.25
3294-3297, any single 1.25
3297e, dated 2000, *Mar. 15, 2000,* Ponchatoula LA 3.25
3294a-3296a, 3297c, any single 1.25
3298-3301 33c **Christmas Berries, die cut 9.5x10** *Apr. 10,* Ponchatoula LA 3.25
3298-3301, any single 1.25
3302-3305 33c **Christmas Berries, die cut 8.5 vert.** *Apr. 10,* Ponchatoula LA 3.25
3302-3305, any single 1.25

First day cancellation was applied to 101,344 covers bearing one of more of Nos. 3294-3305.

3306a 33c **Daffy Duck,** *Apr. 16,* Los Angeles CA 1.50

First day cancellation was applied to 177,988 covers bearing one of more of Nos. 3306-3307c, UX304.

3308 33c **Ayn Rand,** *Apr. 22,* New York NY *(123,660)* 1.25
3309 33c **Cinco de Mayo,** *Apr. 27,* San Antonio TX *(20,904)* 1.25
3310-3313 33c **Tropical Flowers,** *May 1,* Honolulu HI 3.25
3310-3313, any single 1.25

First day cancellation was applied to 311,495 covers bearing one of more of Nos. 3310-3313, 3313a, 3313b.

3314 33c **Bartram,** *May 18,* Philadelphia PA *(110,381)* 1.25
3315 33c **Prostate Cancer Awareness,** *July 22,* Austin TX *(113,299)* 1.25
3316 33c **California Gold Rush,** *June 18,* Sacramento CA *(123,648)* 1.25
3317-3320 33c **Aquarium Fish,** *June 24,* Anaheim CA 3.25
3317-3320, any single 1.25

First day cancellation was applied to 301,719 covers bearing one of more of Nos. 3317-3320, 3320a-3320c.

3321-3324 33c **Extreme Sports,** *June 25,* San Francisco CA 3.00
3321-3324, any single 1.25

First day cancellation was applied to 278,068 covers bearing one of more of Nos. 3321-3324, 3324a.

3328a 33c **American Glass,** *June 29,* Corning NY 3.00
3325-3328, any single 1.25

First day cancellation was applied to 272,792 covers bearing one of more of Nos. 3325-3328, 3328a.

3329 33c **James Cagney,** *July 22,* Burbank CA *(135,867)* 1.50
3330 55c **"Billy" Mitchell,** *July 30,* Milwaukee WI 1.50

First day cancellation was applied to 42,144 covers bearing one of more of Nos. 3330, C134.

3331 33c **Honoring Those Who Served,** *Aug. 16,* Kansas City MO *(130,306)* 1.50
3332 45c **Universal Postal Union,** *Aug. 25,* Beijing, China (20,371) 1.25
3337a 33c **Famous Trains,** *Aug. 26,* Cleveland, OH 3.75
any other city 3.75
#3333-3337, any single, Cleveland, OH 1.50
#3333-3337, any single, any other city 1.50

First day cancellation was applied to 518,446 covers bearing one of more of Nos. 3333-3337, 3337a, UX307-UX311a.

3338 33c **Frederick Law Olmsted,** *Sept. 12,* Boston, MA (109,735) 1.25
3344a 33c **Hollywood Composers,** *Sept. 16,* Los Angeles, CA 3.75
#3339-3344, any single, Los Angeles, CA 1.25

First day cancellation was applied to 287,407 covers bearing one of more of Nos. 3339-3344, 3344a.

3350a 33c **Broadway Songwriters,** *Sept. 21,* New York, NY 3.75
#3345-3350, any single, New York, NY 1.25

First day cancellation was applied to 284,840 covers bearing one of more of Nos. 3345-3350, 3350a.

3351 33c **Insects & Spiders,** *Oct. 1,* Indianapolis, IN 10.00
#3351a-3351t, any single 1.25

First day cancellation was applied to 773,590 covers bearing one of more of Nos. 3351-3351t.

3352 33c **Hanukkah,** *Oct. 8,* Washington, DC 1.50
3353 22c **Uncle Sam perforated coil,** *Oct. 8,* Washington, DC 1.25

First day cancellation was applied to 44,534 covers bearing one of more of Nos. 3352-3353, O157.

3354 33c **NATO,** *Oct. 13,* Brussels, Belgium *(110,415)* 1.25
3355 33c **Christmas Madonna,** *Oct. 20,* Washington, DC *(110,460)* 1.25
3356-3359 33c **Christmas Deer, narrow frame (sheet),** *Oct. 20,* Rudolph, WI 3.00
3356-3359, any single 1.25
3360-3363 33c **Christmas Deer, thick frame (booklet),** *Oct. 20,* Rudolph, WI 3.00
3360-3363, any single 1.25
3364-3367 33c **Christmas Deer, smaller size (booklet),** *Oct. 20,* Rudolph, WI 3.00
3364-3367, any single 1.25

First day cancellation was applied to 239,350 covers bearing one of more of Nos. 3356-3367, 3359a, 3363a, 3367a-3367c.

3368 33c **Kwanzaa,** *Oct. 29,* Los Angeles, CA *(20,493)* 1.75
3369 33c **Year 2000,** *Dec. 27,* Washington, DC *(145,928)* 1.25

2000

3370 33c **Chinese New Year,** *Jan. 6,* San Francisco, CA *(155,586)* 1.50
3371 33c **Patricia Roberts Harris,** *Jan. 27,* Washington, DC *(82,211)* 1.75
3372 33c **Los Angeles Class Submarine,** with microprinting, *Mar. 27,* Groton, CT 1.50
3373 22c **S Class Submarine,** *Mar. 27,* Groton, CT 1.50
3374 33c **Los Angeles Class Submarine,** no microprinting, *Mar. 27,* Groton, CT 1.50
3375 55c **Ohio Class Submarine,** *Mar. 27,* Groton, CT 1.75
3376 60c **USS Holland,** *Mar. 27,* Groton, CT 1.75
3377 $3.20 **Gato Class Submarine,** *Mar. 27,* Groton, CT 6.00
3377a, Booklet pane of 5, #3373-3377, either selvage 8.00

First day cancellation was applied to 265,226 covers bearing one of more of Nos. 3372-3377, 3377a.

3378 33c **Pacific Coast Rain Forest Pane of 10,** *Mar. 29,* Seattle, WA 6.75
3378a-3378j, any single 1.25

First day cancellation was applied to 435,549 covers bearing one of more of Nos. 3378-3378j.

3383a 33c **Louise Nevelson,** *Apr. 6,* New York, NY 3.25
3379-3383, any single 1.25

First day cancellation was applied to 389,200 covers bearing one of more of Nos. 3379-3383, 3383a.

3388a 33c **Hubble Space Telescope,** *Apr. 10,* Greenbelt, MD 3.25
3384-3388, any single 1.25

First day cancellation was applied to 411,449 covers bearing one of more of Nos. 3384-3388, 3388a.

3389 33c **American Samoa,** *Apr. 17,* Pago Pago, AS *(107,346_* 1.25
3390 33c **Library of Congress,** *Apr. 24,* Washington, DC *(115,679)* 1.25
3391a 33c **Road Runner & Wile E. Coyote,** *Apr. 26,* Phoenix, AZ 1.25

First day cancellation was applied to 154,903 covers bearing one of more of Nos. 3391-3392, 3391a-3391c, 3392a-3392c.

3396a 33c **Distinguished Soldiers,** *May 3,* Washington, DC 3.25
Any other city 3.25
3393-3396, any single, Washington, DC 1.50
Any other city 1.25

First day cancellation was applied to 322,278 covers bearing one of more of Nos. 3393-3396, 3396a.

3397 33c **Summer Sports,** *May 5,* Spokane, WA *(110,768)* 1.25
3398 33c **Adoption,** *May 10,* Beverly Hills, CA 1.25

First day cancellation was applied to 137,903 covers bearing one of more of Nos. 3398, UX315.

3402a 33c **Youth Team Sports,** *May 27,* Lake Buena Vista, FL 3.25
3399-3402, any single 1.25

First day cancellation was applied to 309,349 covers bearing one of more of Nos. 3399-3402, 3402a.

3403 33c **The Stars and Stripes, pane of 20,** *June 14,* Baltimore, MD 10.00
3403a-3403t, any single 1.25

First day cancellation was applied to 1,121,071 covers bearing one of more of Nos. 3403-3403t.

3404-3407 33c **Berries,** die cut 8½ horiz., *June 16,* Buffalo, NY 3.25
3404-3707, any single 1.25

First day cancellation was applied to 35,671 covers bearing one of more of Nos. 3404-3407, 3407a.

3408 33c **Legends of Baseball, pane of 20,** *July 6,* Atlanta, GA 10.00
3408a-3708t, any single 1.50

First day cancellation was applied to 1,214,413 covers bearing one of more of Nos. 3408-3408t.

3409 60c **Probing the Vastness of Space,** *July 10,* Anaheim, CA 6.00
3409a-3409f, any single 1.50

First day cancellation was applied to 296,252 covers bearing one of more of Nos. 3409-3409f.

3410 $1 **Exploring the Solar System,** *July 11,* Anaheim, CA 9.00
3410a-3410e, any single 2.00

First day cancellation was applied to 49,500 covers bearing one of more of Nos. 3410-3410e.

3411 $3.20 **Escaping the Gravity of Earth,** *July 9,* Anaheim, CA 9.50
3411a-3411b, any single 3.75

First day cancellation was applied to 22,321 covers bearing one of more of Nos. 3411-3411b.

3412 $11.75 **Space Achievement and Exploration,** *July 7,* Anaheim, CA *(12,070)* 17.50
3413 $11.75 **Landing on the Moon,** *July 8,* Anaheim, CA *(11,639)* 17.50
3414-3417 33c **Stampin' The Future,** *July 13,* Anaheim, CA 3.25
3414-3417, any single 1.25

First day cancellation was applied to 294,434 covers bearing one of more of Nos. 3414-3417, 3417a.

Distinguished Americans Issue 2000-2001

3420 10c **Joseph W. Stilwell,** *Aug. 24,* Providence, RI *(21,669)* 1.50
3426 33c **Claude Pepper,** *Sept. 7,* Washington, DC *(60,689)* 1.25
3431 76c **Hattie Caraway,** *Feb. 21, 2001,* Little Rock, AR 1.75
3432 83c **Edna Ferber,** *July 29, 2002,* Appleton, WI 1.75
3438 33c **California Statehood,** *Sept. 8,* Sacramento, CA *(119,729)* 1.25
3443a 33c **Deep Sea Creatures,** *Oct. 2,* Monterey, CA 3.75
#3439-3443, any single 1.25

First day cancellation was applied to 385,406 covers bearing one of more of Nos. 3439-3443, 3443a.

3444 33c **Thomas Wolfe,** *Oct. 3,* Asheville, NC *(112,293)* 1.25
3445 33c **White House,** *Oct. 18,* Washington, DC *(135,844)* 1.25
3446 33c **Edward G. Robinson,** *Oct. 24,* Los Angeles, CA *(120,125)* 1.50
3447 (10c) **New York Public Library Lion,** *Nov. 9,* New York, NY *(18,477)* 1.25
3448 (34c) **Flag Over Farm, perf,** *Dec. 15,* Washington, DC 1.25
3449 (34c) **Flag Over Farm, litho. self-adhesive,** *Dec. 15,* Washington, DC 1.25
3450 (34c) **Flag Over Farm, photo. self-adhesive,** *Dec. 15,* Washington, DC 1.25
3451 (34c) **Statue of Liberty, booklet stamp,** *Dec. 15,* Washington, DC 1.25
3452 (34c) **Statue of Liberty perforated coil,** *Dec. 15,* Washington, DC 1.25
3453 (34c) **Statue of Liberty self-adhesive coil,** *Dec. 15,* Washington, DC 1.25
3454-3457 (34c) **Flowers, booklet stamps die cut 10¼x10¾,** *Dec. 15,* Washington, DC 3.25
3454-3457, any single 1.25
3458-3461 (34c) **Flowers, booklet stamps die cut 11½x11¾,** *Dec. 15,* Washington, DC 3.25
3458-3461, any single 1.25
3462-3465 (34c) **Flowers, coil stamps,** *Dec. 15,* Washington, DC 3.25
3462-3465, any single 1.25

First day cancellation was applied to 178,635 covers bearing one of more of Nos. 3448-3465, 3450a, 3451a-3451d, 3457a-3457e, 3461a-3461c, 3465a.

2001

3466 34c **Statue of Liberty coil (rounded corners),** *Jan. 7,* Washington, DC 1.25
3467 21c **American Buffalo, perforated sheet stamp,** *Sept. 20,* Washington, DC 1.25
3468 21c **American Buffalo, perforated sheet stamp,** *Feb. 22,* Wall, SD 1.25
3468A 23c **George Washington, sheet stamp,** *Sept. 20,* Washington, DC 1.25
3469 34c **Flag Over Farm, perforated sheet stamp,** *Feb. 7,* New York, NY 1.25
3470 34c **Flag Over Farm, self-adhesive sheet stamp,** *Mar. 6,* Lincoln, NE 1.25
3471 55c **Eagle,** *Feb. 22,* Wall, SD 1.50
3471A 57c **Eagle,** *Sept. 20,* Washington, DC 1.50
3472 $3.50 **Capitol Dome,** *Jan. 29,* Washington, DC 6.25
3473 $12.25 **Washington Monument,** *Jan. 29,* Washington, DC 15.00
3475 21c **American Buffalo coil stamp,** *Feb. 22,* Wall, SD 1.25
3475A 23c **George Washington, coil stamp,** *Sept. 20,* Washington, DC 1.25
3476 34c **Statue of Liberty, perforated coil stamp,** *Feb. 7,* New York, NY 1.25
3477 34c **Statue of Liberty coil stamp (right angle corners),** *Feb. 7,* New York, NY 1.25
3478-3481 34c **Flower coil stamps,** *Feb. 7,* New York, NY 3.25
3478-3481, any single 1.25

Serpentine Die Cut 11¼

3482 20c **George Washington booklet stamp,** *Feb. 22,* Wall, SD 1.25

Serpentine Die Cut 10½x11¼

3483 21c **George Washington booklet stamp,** *Feb. 22,* Wall, SD 1.25
3484 21c **American Buffalo, booklet stamp, serp. die cut 11¼,** *Sept. 20,* Washington, DC 1.25
3484A 21c **American Buffalo, booklet stamp, serp. die cut 10½x11¼,** *Sept. 20,* Washington, DC *1.25*
3485 34c **Statue of Liberty booklet stamp,** *Feb. 7,* New York, NY 1.25
3487-3490 34c **Flower booklet stamps,** *Feb. 7,* New York, NY 3.25
3487-3490, any single 1.25
3491-3492 34c **Apple & Orange booklet stamps,** *Feb. 7,* Lincoln, NE 2.25
3491-3492, any single 1.25
3495 34c **Flag Over Farm, booklet stamp,** *Dec. 17,* Washington, DC 1.25
3496 (34c) **Love Letter,** *Jan. 19,* Tucson, AZ 1.25
3497 34c **Love Letters,** *Feb. 14,* Lovejoy, GA 1.25

Serpentine Die Cut 11½x10¾

3498 34c **Love Letters, die cut 11½x10¾,** *Feb. 14,* Lovejoy, GA 1.25
3499 55c **Love Letter,** *Feb. 14,* Lovejoy, GA 1.50
3500 34c **Chinese New Year,** *Jan. 20,* Oakland, CA 1.50
3501 34c **Roy Wilkins,** *Jan. 24,* Minneapolis, MN 1.25
3502 34c **American Illustrations pane of 20,** *Feb. 1,* New York, NY 9.50
3502a-3502t, any single 1.25
3503 34c **Diabetes Awareness,** *Mar. 16,* Boston, MA 1.25
3504 34c **Nobel Prize Centenary,** *Mar. 22,* Washington, DC 1.50
3505 **Pan-American Inverts Pane,** *Mar. 29,* New York, NY 6.00
3505a 1c 1.25
3505b 2c 1.25
3505c 4c 1.25
3505d 80c 1.75
3506 34c **Great Plains Prairie Pane of 10,** *Apr. 19,* Lincoln, NE 7.00
3507 34c **Peanuts,** *May 17,* Santa Rosa, CA 1.25
3508 34c **Honoring Veterans,** *May 23,* Washington, DC 1.50
Any other city 1.25
3509 34c **Frida Kahlo,** *June 21,* Phoenix, AZ 1.25
3519a 34c **Legendary Playing Fields,** *June 27,* New York, NY, Boston, MA, Chicago, IL or Detroit, MI 6.50

3510-3519, any single, New York, NY, Boston, MA, Chicago, IL or Detroit, MI 1.50
3520 (10c) **Atlas Statue,** *June 29,* New York, NY 1.25
3521 34c **Leonard Bernstein,** *July 10,* New York, NY 1.25
3522 (15c) **Woody Wagon,** *Aug. 3,* Denver, CO 1.25
3523 34c **Lucille Ball,** *Aug. 6,* Los Angeles, CA 1.50
3527a 34c **Amish Quilts,** *Aug. 9,* Nappanee, IN 3.25
3524-3527, any single 1.25

2001
3533 34c **Enrico Fermi,** *Sept. 29,* Chicago, IL 1.25
3534a 34c **That's All Folks!,** *Oct. 1,* Beverly Hills, CA 1.25
3536 34c **Christmas, Madonna,** *Oct. 10,* Philadelphia, PA 1.25
3537-3540 34c **Christmas, Santas, black inscriptions, large date** *Oct. 10,* Santa Claus, IN 3.25
3537-3540, any single 1.25
3537a-3540a, small date (from booklet) 3.25
3537a-3540a, any single 1.25
3541-3544 34c **Christmas, Santas, green and red inscriptions,** *Oct. 10,* Santa Claus, IN 3.25
3541-3544, any single 1.25

2001
3545 34c **James Madison,** *Oct. 18,* New York, NY 1.25
3546 34c **Thanksgiving,** *Oct. 19,* Dallas, TX 1.25
3547 34c **Hanukkah,** *Oct. 21,* New York, NY 1.25
3548 34c **Kwanzaa,** *Oct. 21,* New York, NY 1.25

2001-02
3549 34c **United We Stand,** *Oct. 24,* Washington, DC 1.50
3549B 34c **United We Stand,** serpentine die cut 10½x10¾ booklet stamp *Oct. 24, 2001,* Washington, DC 1.50

Though No. 3549B was issued in Jan. 2002, first day covers received the Oct. 24, 2001 cancel.

2001
Any other city in NY, NJ, CT, PA or DC metropolitan area 1.50
3550 34c **United We Stand coil, right angle corners,** *Oct. 24,* Washington, DC 1.50
Any other city in NY, NJ, CT, PA or DC metropolitan area 1.50
3550A 34c **United We Stand coil,** rounded corners, *Oct. 24,* Washington, DC 1.50
Any other city in NY, NJ, CT, PA or DC metropolitan area 1.25
3551 57c **Love Letters,** *Nov. 19,* Washington, DC 1.50

2002
3552-3555 34c **Winter Sports,** *Jan. 8,* Park City, UT 3.25
3552-3555, any single 1.25
3556 34c **Mentoring a Child,** *Jan. 10,* Annapolis, MD 1.25
3557 34c **Langston Hughes,** *Feb. 1,* New York, NY 1.25
3558 34c **Happy Birthday,** *Feb. 8,* Riverside, CA 1.25
3559 34c **Chinese New Year,** *Feb. 11,* New York, NY 1.25
3560 34c **U.S. Military Academy Bicent.,** *Mar. 16,* West Point, NY 1.25
3610a 34c **Greetings from America Pane,** *Apr. 4,* New York, NY 32.50
3561-3610, Any single, New York, NY 1.25
3610a, Any other city 32.50
3561-3610, Any single, any other city 1.25
3561-3610, any state capital 1.50
3611 34c **Longleaf Pine Forest Pane of 10,** *Apr. 26,* Tallahassee, FL 7.00
3611a-3611j, any single 1.25
3612 5c **Toleware Coffeepot,** *May 31,* McLean, VA 1.25
3613 3c **Litho. Star sheet stamp,** *June 7,* Washington, DC 1.25
Any other city 1.25
3614 3c **Photo. Star sheet stamp,** *June 7,* Washington, DC 1.25
Any other city 1.25
3615 3c **Star coil stamp,** *June 7,* Washington, DC 1.25
3616 23c **George Washington,** water-activated gum sheet stamp, *June 7,* Washington, DC 1.00
3617 23c **George Washington,** gray green coil stamp, *June 7,* Washington, DC 1.00
3618 23c **George Washington,** booklet stamp, serp. die cut 11¼ on 3 sides, *June 7,* Washington, DC 1.00
3620 (37c) **Flag,** water-activated gum sheet stamp, *June 7,* Washington, DC 1.25
Any other city 1.25
3621 (37c) **Flag,** self-adhesive sheet stamp, serp. die cut 11¼x11, *June 7,* Washington, DC 1.25
Any other city 1.25
3622 (37c) **Flag,** coil stamp, *June 7,* Washington, DC 1.25
Any other city 1.25
3623 (37c) **Flag,** booklet stamp, serp. die cut 11¼ on 2, 3 or 4 sides, *June 7,* Washington, DC 1.25
Any other city 1.25
3624 (37c) **Flag,** booklet stamp, serp. die cut 10½x10¾ on 2 or 3 sides, *June 7,* Washington, DC 1.25
Any other city 1.25
3625 (37c) **Flag,** booklet stamp, serp. die cut 8 on 2, 3 or 4 sides, *June 7,* Washington, DC 1.25
Any other city 1.25
3626-3629 (37c) **Antique Toys,** booklet stamps, *June 7,* Washington, DC 3.25
Any other city 3.25
3626-3629, any single 1.25
3626-3629, any single, any other city 1.25
3630 37c **Flag,** self-adhesive sheet stamp, serp. die cut 11¼x11, *June 7,* Washington, DC 1.25
Any other city 1.25
3631 37c **Flag,** water-activated gum coil stamp, *June 7,* Washington, DC 1.25
3632 37c **Flag,** self-adhesive coil stamp, serp. die cut 10 vert., *June 7,* Washington, DC 1.25
3633 37c **Flag,** self-adhesive coil stamp, serp. die cut 8½ vert., *June 7,* Washington, DC 1.25
3634 37c **Flag,** self-adhesive booklet stamps, serp. die cut 11 on 3 sides, *June 7,* Washington, DC 1.25
3635 37c **Flag,** booklet stamp, serp. die cut 11¼ on 2, 3 or 4 sides, *June 7,* Washington, DC 1.25
3636 37c **Flag,** booklet stamp, serp. die cut 10½x10¾ on 2 or 3 sides, *June 7,* Washington, DC 1.25
3637 37c **Flag,** booklet stamp, serp. die cut 8 on 2, 3 or 4 sides, *Feb. 4, 2003* Washington, DC 1.25

2002
3638-3641 37c **Antique Toys coil stamps,** *July 26,* Rochester, NY 3.25
3638-3641, any single 1.25
3642-3645 37c **Antique Toys booklet stamps,** *July 26,* Rochester, NY 3.25
3642-3645, any single 1.25
3646 60c **Coverlet Eagle,** *July 12,* Oak Brook, IL 1.50
3647 $3.85 **Jefferson Memorial,** *July 30,* Washington, DC 7.00
Any other city 7.00
3648 $13.65 **Capitol Dome,** *July 30,* Washington, DC 25.00
Any other city 25.00
3649 37c **Masters of American Photography,** *June 13,* San Diego, CA 10.00
3649a-3649t, any single 1.25
3650 37c **John James Audubon,** *June 27,* Santa Clara, CA 1.25
3651 37c **Harry Houdini,** *July 3,* New York, NY 1.25
3652 37c **Andy Warhol,** *Aug. 9,* Pittsburgh, PA 1.25
3653-3656 37c **Teddy Bears,** *Aug. 15,* Atlantic City, NJ 3.25
3653-3656, any single 1.25
3657 37c **Love,** *Aug. 16,* Atlantic City, NJ 1.25
3658 60c **Love,** *Aug. 16,* Atlantic City, NJ 1.50
3659 37c **Ogden Nash,** *Aug. 19,* Baltimore, MD 1.25
3660 37c **Duke Kahanamoku,** *Aug. 24,* Honolulu, HI 1.25
3661-3664 37c **American Bats,** *Sept. 13,* Austin, TX 3.25
3661-3664, any single 1.25
3665-3668 37c **Women in Journalism,** *Sept. 14,* Fort Worth, TX 3.25
3665-3668, any single 1.25
3669 37c **Irving Berlin,** *Sept. 15,* New York, NY 1.25
3670-3671 37c **Neuter and Spay,** *Sept. 20,* Washington, DC 2.25
Any other city 2.25
3670-3671, either single, Washington, DC 1.25
3670-3671, either single, any other city 1.25
3672 37c **Hanukkah,** *Oct. 10,* Washington, DC 1.25
3673 37c **Kwanzaa,** *Oct. 10,* Washington, DC 1.25
3674 37c **Eid,** *Oct. 10,* Washington, DC 1.25
3675 37c **Christmas Madonna,** *Oct. 10,* Chicago, IL 1.25
3676-3679 37c **Christmas Snowmen,** serp. die cut 11 (sheet stamps), *Oct. 28,* Houghton, MI 3.25
3676-3679, any single 1.25
3680-3683 37c **Christmas Snowmen,** serp. die cut 8½ vert. (coil stamps), *Oct. 28,* Houghton, MI 3.25
3680-3683, any single 1.25
3684-3687 37c **Christmas Snowmen,** serp. die cut 10¾x11 on 2 or 3 sides (large booklet stamps), *Oct. 28,* Houghton, MI 3.25
3684-3687, any single 1.25
3688-3691 37c **Christmas Snowmen,** serp. die cut 11 on 2 or 3 sides (small booklet stamps), *Oct. 28,* Houghton, MI 3.25
3688-3691, any single 1.25
3692 37c **Cary Grant,** *Oct. 15,* Los Angeles, CA 1.25
3693 (5c) **Sea Coast,** *Oct. 21,* Washington, DC 1.25
3694 37c **Hawaiian Missionary Stamps sheet,** *Oct. 24,* New York, NY 3.25
3694a-3694d, any single 1.25
3695 37c **Happy Birthday,** *Oct. 25,* New York, NY 1.25
3745a 37c **Greetings From America,** *Oct. 25,* New York, NY 35.00
3696-3745, any single 1.25
3696-3745, any state capital 1.50
3746 37c **Thurgood Marshall,** *Jan. 7,* Washington, DC 1.25
3747 37c **Chinese New Year,** *Jan. 15,* Chicago, IL 1.25
3748 37c **Zora Neale Hurston,** *Jan. 24,* Eatonville, FL 1.25
3751 10c **American Clock,** *Jan. 24,* Tucson, AZ 1.25

American Design Series

2003
3757 1c **Tiffany Lamp Coil,** *Mar. 1,* Biloxi, MS 1.25

American Culture Series

3766 $1 **Wisdom,** *Feb. 28,* Biloxi, MS 2.50
3769 (10c) **New York Public Library Lion,** perf. 10 vert., *Feb. 4,* Washington, DC 1.25

2003
3771 80c **Special Olympics,** *Feb. 13,* Chicago, IL 1.75
3772 37c **American Filmmaking: Behind the Scenes Pane of 10,** *Feb. 25,* Beverly Hills, CA 7.25
3772a-3772j, any single 1.25
3773 37c **Ohio Statehood Bicentennial,** *Mar. 1,* Chillicothe, OH 1.25
3774 37c **Pelican Island National Wildlife Refuge, Cent.,** *Mar. 14,* Sebastian, FL 1.25
3775 (5c) **Sea Coast,** perf. 9¾ vert. *Mar. 19,* Washington, DC 1.25
3776-3780 37c **Old Glory,** *Apr. 3,* New York, NY 4.00
3776-3780, any single 1.25
3781 37c **Cesar E. Chavez,** *Apr. 23,* Los Angeles, CA 1.25
3782 37c **Louisiana Purchase, Bicent.,** *Apr. 30,* New Orleans, LA 1.25
3783 37c **First Flight,** *May 22,* Dayton, OH or Kill Devil Hills, NC 1.25
3784 37c **Purple Heart,** *May 30,* Mount Vernon, VA 1.25
3786 37c **Audrey Hepburn,** *June 11,* Los Angeles, CA 1.25
3787-3791 37c **Southeastern Lighthouses,** *June 13,* Tybee Island, GA 4.00
3787, 3788a, 3789-3791, Tybee Island, GA 4.00
3787-3791, 3788a, any single 1.25
3792-3801 (25c) **Eagle coils,** *June 26,* Santa Clara, CA 6.00
3792-3801, any single 1.25
3802 37c **Arctic Tundra,** *July 2,* Fairbanks, AK 7.50
3802a-3802j, any single 1.25

SEMI-POSTAL FIRST DAY COVERS

1998
B1 32c +8c **Breast Cancer,** *July 29,* Washington, DC (51,775) 1.50

2002
B2 (34c+11c) **Heroes of 2001,** *June 7,* New York, NY 2.00
Any other city 2.00

AIR POST FIRST DAY COVERS

1918

C1 6c **orange,** *Dec. 10* *32,500.*
C2 16c **green,** *July 11* *32,500.*
C3 24c **carmine rose & blue,** *May 13* *27,500.*

1923

C4 8c **dark green,** *Aug. 15* 450.00
C5 16c **dark blue,** *Aug. 17* 650.00
C6 24c **carmine,** *Aug. 21* 850.00

1926-27

C7 10c **dark blue,** *Feb. 13, 1926* 60.00
Chicago, Ill. 75.00
Detroit, Mich. 75.00
Cleveland, Ohio 140.00
Dearborn, Mich. 140.00
C8 15c **olive brown,** *Sept. 18, 1926* 75.00
C9 20c **yellow green,** *Jan. 25, 1927* 100.00
New York, N.Y. 125.00
C10 10c **dark blue,** *June 18, 1927* 25.00
St. Louis, Mo. 25.00
Little Falls, Minn. 35.00
Detroit, Mich. 35.00
C10a Booklet pane of 3, *May 26, 1928* 875.00
Cleveland Midwestern Philatelic Sta. cancel 800.00
C10a & 645 on one cover, Washington, D.C. 1,000.

1928-30

C11 5c **carmine & blue,** *July 25, 1928,* pair 50.00
C12 5c **violet,** *Feb. 10, 1930* 12.00
C13 65c **green,** *Apr. 19, 1930* 1,250.
C14 $1.30 **brown,** *Apr. 19, 1930* 1,100.
C15 $2.60 **blue,** *Apr. 19, 1930* 1,250.
C13-C15 on one cover 15,000.

Values are for first day covers flown on Zeppelin flights with appropriate markings. Non-flown covers sell for less.

1931-33

C16 5c **violet,** *Aug. 19, 1931* 175.00
C17 8c **olive bister,** *Sept. 26, 1932* 15.00
C18 50c **green,** *Oct. 2, 1933,* New York, N.Y. *(3,500)* 200.00
Akron, Ohio, *Oct. 4* 300.00
Washington, D.C., *Oct. 5* 275.00
Miami, Fla., *Oct. 6* 150.00
Chicago, Ill., *Oct. 7* 250.00

1934-37

C19 6c **dull orange,** *June 30, 1934,* Baltimore, Md. *190.00*
New York, N.Y. *700.00*
Washington, D.C., *July 1* 10.00

Catalogue values for Nos. C20-C45 are for addressed covers with the most common cachets.

C20 25c **blue,** *Nov. 22, 1935 (10,910)* 40.00
San Francisco, Cal. *(15,000)* 35.00
C21 20c **green,** *Feb. 15, 1937* 45.00
C22 50c **carmine,** *Feb. 15, 1937* 50.00
C21-C22 on one cover 100.00

First day covers of Nos. C21 and C22 total 40,000.

1938-39

C23 6c **dark blue & carmine,** *May 14, 1938,* Dayton, Ohio *(116,443)* 15.00
St. Petersburg, Fla. *(95,121)* 15.00
Washington, D.C., *May 15* 3.50
C24 30c **dull blue,** *May 16, 1939,* New York, N.Y. *(68,634)* 47.50

1941-44

C25 6c **carmine,** *June 25, 1941 (99,986)* 3.75
C25a Booklet pane of 3, *Mar. 18, 1943* 25.00
C26 8c **olive green,** *Mar. 21, 1944 (147,484)* 3.75
C27 10c **violet,** *Aug. 15, 1941,* Atlantic City, N.J. *(87,712)* 8.00
C28 15c **brown carmine,** *Aug. 19, 1941,* Baltimore, Md. *(74,000)* 10.00
C29 20c **bright green,** *Aug. 27, 1941,* Philadelphia, Pa. *(66,225)* 12.50
C30 30c **blue,** *Sept. 25, 1941,* Kansas City, Mo. *(57,175)* 20.00
C31 50c **orange,** *Oct. 29, 1941,* St. Louis, Mo. *(54,580)* 40.00

1946-48

C32 5c **carmine,** *Sept. 25, 1946* 2.00

First day covers of Nos. C32 & UC14 total 396,669.

C33 5c **carmine,** *Mar. 26, 1947 (342,634)* 2.00
C34 10c **black,** *Aug. 30, 1947 (265,773)* 2.00
C35 15c **bright blue green,** *Aug. 20, 1947,* New York, N.Y. *(230,338)* 1.75
C36 25c **blue,** *July 30, 1947,* San Francisco, Cal. *(201,762)* 2.25
C37 5c **carmine, coil,** *Jan. 15, 1948 (192,084)* 1.75
C38 5c **New York City,** *July 31, 1948,* New York, N.Y. *(371,265)* 1.75

1949

C39 6c **carmine,** *Jan. 18 (266,790)* 1.50
C39a Booklet pane of 6, *Nov. 18, 1949,* New York, N.Y. 10.00
C40 6c **Alexandria Bicentennial,** *May 11,* Alexandria, Va. *(386,717)* 1.50
C41 6c **carmine coil,** *Aug. 25 (240,386)* 1.25
C42 10c **U.P.U.,** *Nov. 18,* New Orleans, La. *(270,000)* 1.75
C43 15c **U.P.U.,** *Oct. 7,* Chicago, Ill. *(246,833)* 2.75
C44 25c **U.P.U.,** *Nov. 30,* Seattle, Wash. *(220,215)* 3.75
C45 6c **Wright Brothers,** *Dec. 17,* Kitty Hawk, N.C. *(378,585)* 2.75

Catalogue values from this point to the end of the section are for unaddressed covers with the most common cachets.

1952-59

C46 80c **Hawaii,** *Mar. 26, 1952,* Honolulu, Hawaii, *(89,864)* 17.50
C47 6c **Powered Flight,** *May 29, 1953,* Dayton, Ohio *(359,050)* 1.50
C48 4c **bright blue,** *Sept. 3, 1954,* Philadelphia, Pa. *(295,720)* 1.00
C49 6c **Air Force,** *Aug. 1, 1957 (356,683)* 1.25
C50 5c **red,** *July 31, 1958,* Colorado Springs, Colo. *(207,954)* 1.00
C51 7c **blue,** *July 31, 1958,* Philadelphia, Pa. *(204,401)* 1.00
C51a Booklet pane of 6, San Antonio, Tex. *(119,769)* 9.00
C52 7c **blue coil,** *July 31, 1958,* Miami, Fla. *(181,603)* 1.00
C53 7c **Alaska Statehood,** *Jan. 3, 1959,* Juneau, Alaska *(489,752)* 1.25
C54 7c **Balloon Jupiter,** *Aug. 17, 1959,* Lafayette, Ind.*(383,556)* 1.75
C55 7c **Hawaii Statehood,** *Aug. 21, 1959,* Honolulu, Hawaii *(533,464)* 1.00
C56 10c **Pan American Games,** *Aug. 27, 1959,* Chicago, Ill. *(302,306)* 1.00

1959-66

C57 10c **Liberty Bell,** *June 10, 1960,* Miami, Fla. *(246,509)* 1.25
C58 15c **Statue of Liberty,** *Nov. 20, 1959,* New York, N.Y. *(259,412)* 1.25
C59 25c **Abraham Lincoln,** *Apr. 22, 1960,* San Francisco, Cal. *(211,235)* 1.25
C59a 25c Tagged, *Dec. 29, 1966 (about 3,000)* 50.00
C60 7c **carmine,** *Aug. 12, 1960,* Arlington, Va. *(247,190)* 1.00
C60a Booklet pane of 6, *Aug. 19, 1960,* St. Louis, Mo. *(143,363)* 8.00
C61 7c **carmine coil,** *Oct. 22, 1960,* Atlantic City, N.J. *(197,995)* 1.00

1961-67

C62 13c **Liberty Bell,** *June 28, 1961,* New York, N.Y. *(316,166)* 1.00
C62a 13c Tagged, *Feb. 15, 1967* 50.00
C63 15c **Redrawn Statue of Liberty,** *Jan. 13, 1961,* Buffalo, N.Y. *(192,976)* 1.00
C63a 15c Tagged, *Jan. 11, 1967* 50.00
C64 8c **carmine,** *Dec. 5, 1962 (288,355)* 1.00
C64b Booklet pane of 5 + label *(146,835)* 3.50
C64a 8c Tagged, *Aug. 1, 1963,* Dayton, Ohio *(262,720)* 1.25
C65 8c **carmine coil,** *Dec. 5, 1962 (220,173)* 1.00
C65a 8c Tagged, *Jan. 14, 1965,* New Orleans, La. 50.00

1963-69

C66 15c **Montgomery Blair,** *May 3, 1963,* Silver Spring, Md. *(260,031)* 1.10
C67 6c **Bald Eagle,** *July 12, 1963,* Boston, Mass. *(268,265)* 1.00
C67a 6c Tagged, *Feb. 15, 1967* 50.00
C68 8c **Amelia Earhart,** *July 24, 1963,* Atchison, Kan. *(437,996)* 3.00
C69 8c **Robert H. Goddard,** *Oct. 5, 1964,* Roswell, N.M. *(421,020)* 3.00
C70 8c **Alaska Purchase,** *Mar. 30, 1967,* Sitka, Alaska *(554,784)* 1.25
C71 20c **Audubon,** *Apr. 26, 1967,* Audubon (Station of N.Y.C.), N.Y. *(227,930)* 2.00
C72 10c **carmine,** *Jan. 5, 1968,* San Francisco, Cal. 1.00
C72b Booklet pane of 8 3.75
C72c Booklet pane of 5 + label, slogan 4 *Jan. 6, 1968* 125.00
With slogan 5 110.00
C73 10c **carmine coil,** *Jan. 5, 1968,* San Francisco, Cal. 1.00
C74 10c **Air Mail Service,** *May 15, 1968 (521,084)* 1.50
C75 20c **USA and Jet,** *Nov. 22, 1968,* New York, N.Y. *(276,244)* 1.25
C76 10c **Moon Landing,** *Sept. 9, 1969 (8,743,070)* 5.00

1971-73

C77 9c **red,** *May 15, 1971,* Kitty Hawk, N.C. 1.00

First day cancellation was applied to 379,442 covers of Nos. C77 and UXC10.

C78 11c **carmine,** *May 7, 1971,* Spokane, Wash. 1.00
C78a Booklet pane of 4 + 2 labels 2.25
C79 13c **carmine,** *Nov. 16, 1973,* New York, N.Y. *(282,550)* 1.00
C79a Booklet pane of 5 + label, *Dec. 27, 1973,* Chicago, Ill. 2.25

First day cancellation was applied to 464,750 covers of Nos. C78, C78a and C82, and to 204,756 covers of Nos. C79a and C83.

C80 17c **Statue of Liberty,** *July 13, 1971,* Lakehurst, N.J. *(172,269)* 1.25
C81 21c **USA and Jet,** *May 21, 1971 (293,140)* 1.00
C82 11c **carmine coil,** *May 7, 1971,* Spokane, Wash. 1.00
C83 13c **carmine coil,** *Dec. 27, 1973,* Chicago, Ill. 1.00
C84 11c **National Parks Centennial,** *May 3, 1972,* Honaunau, Hawaii *(364,816)* 1.00
C85 11c **Olympics,** *Aug. 17, 1972* 1.00

First day cancellation was applied to 971,536 covers of Nos. 1460-1462 and C85.

C86 11c **Electronics,** *July 10, 1973,* New York, N.Y. 1.00

First day cancellation was applied to 1,197,700 covers of Nos. 1500-1502 and C86.

1974-79

C87 18c **Statue of Liberty,** *Jan. 11, 1974,* Hempstead, N.Y. *(216,902)* 1.00
C88 26c **Mt. Rushmore,** *Jan. 2, 1974,* Rapid City, S.D. *(210,470)* 1.50
C89 25c **Plane and Globes,** *Jan. 2, 1976,* Honolulu, Hawaii 1.00
C90 31c **Plane, Globes and Flag,** *Jan. 2, 1976,* Honolulu, Hawaii 1.25
C92a 31c **Wright Brothers,** *Sept. 23, 1978,* Dayton, Ohio 4.00
C91-C92, any single 3.00
C94a 21c **Octave Chanute,** *Mar. 29, 1979,* Chanute, Kan. *(459,235)* 4.00
C93-C94, any single 3.00
C96a 25c **Wiley Post,** *Nov. 20, 1979,* Oklahoma City, Okla. 4.00
C95-C96, any single 3.00
C97 31c **Olympics,** *Nov. 1, 1979,* Colorado Springs, CO 1.50

1980

C98 40c **Philip Mazzei,** *Oct. 13* 1.50
C99 28c **Blanche Stuart Scott,** *Dec. 30,* Hammondsport, NY *(238,502)* 1.50
C100 35c **Glenn Curtiss,** *Dec. 30,* Hammondsport, NY *(208,502)* 1.50

1983

C104a 28c **Olympics,** *June 17,* San Antonio, TX *(901,028)* 3.75
C101-C104, any single 1.75
C108a 40c **Olympics,** *Apr. 8,* Los Angeles, CA *(1,001,657)* 5.00
C105-C108, any single 1.75
C112a 35c **Olympics,** *Nov. 4,* Colorado Springs, CO*(897,729)* 4.50
C109-C112, any single 1.75

1985

C113 33c **Alfred V. Verville,** *Feb. 13,* Garden City, NY 1.50
C114 39c **Lawrence & Elmer Sperry,** *Feb. 13,* Garden City, NY 1.50

First day cancel was applied to 429,290 covers bearing one more of Nos. C113-C114.

C115 44c **Transpacific Air Mail,** *Feb. 15,* San Francisco, CA *(269,229)* 1.75

A total of 269,229 first day cancels were applied for Nos. C115 and UXC22.

C116 44c **Junipero Serra,** *Aug. 22,* San Diego, CA *(254,977)* 2.00

1988

C117 44c **Settling of New Sweden,** *Mar. 29,* Wilmington, DE *(213,445)* 1.50
C118 45c **Samuel P. Langley,** *May 14,* San Diego, CA 1.50
C119 36c **Igor Sikorsky,** *June 23,* Stratford, CT *(162,986)* 1.75

1989

C120 45c **French Revolution,** *July 14 (309,975)* 1.50
C121 45c **Southeast Carved Figure,** *Oct. 12,* San Juan, PR *(93,569)* 1.50
C125a 45c **Future Mail Transportation,** *Nov. 27 (765,479)* 6.50
C122-C125, any single 1.75
C126 45c **Future Mail Transportation Souvenir Sheet,** *Nov. 24 (257,826)* 6.50

1990

C127 45c **Tropical Coast,** *Oct. 12,* Grand Canyon, AZ *(137,068)* 1.50

1991

C128 50c **Harriet Quimby,** *Apr. 27,* Plymouth, MI 1.50
C129 40c **William T. Piper,** *May 17,* Denver, CO 1.50
C130 50c **Antarctic Treaty,** *June 21* 1.50
C131 50c **Bering Land Bridge,** *Oct. 12,* Anchorage, AK 1.50

1999

C133 48c **Niagara Falls,** *May 12,* Niagara Falls, NY *(20,878)* 1.40

C134 40c **Rio Grande,** *July 30,* Milwaukee, WI 1.25
any other city 1.25

First day cancel was applied to 42,144 covers bearing one more of Nos. 3330, C134.

C135 60c **Grand Canyon,** *Jan. 20,* Grand Canyon, AZ *(64,282)* 1.50

2001

C136 70c **Nine-mile Prairie,** *Mar. 6,* Lincoln, NE 1.50

C137 80c **Mt. McKinley,** *Apr. 17,* Fairbanks, AK 1.75

C138 60c **Acadia National Park,** *May 30,* Bar Harbor, ME 1.50

BOOKLETS: PANES & COVERS

Most booklet panes issued before 1962 consist of a vertical block of 6 stamps perforated vertically through the center. The panes are perforated horizontally on all but the bottom edge and the top of the selvage tab. The selvage top, the two sides and the bottom are straight edged. Exceptions for panes issued before 1962 are the 1917 American Expeditionary Forces panes (30 stamps); Lindbergh and 6¢ 1943 air mails (3), and the Savings Stamps (10). Since 1962, panes have been issued with 3 to 20 stamps and various configurations. They have included one or more labels and two or more stamps se-tenant.

Flat plate booklet panes, with the exceptions noted above, were made from specially designed plates of 180 or 360 subjects. They are collected in plate positions. There are nine collectible positions on the 180-subject plate and 12 on the 360-subject plate.

Rotary booklet panes issued from 1926 to May 1978 (except for Nos. 1623a and 1623c) were made from specially designed plates of 180, 320, 360, and 400 subjects. They also are collected in plate positions. There are five collectible positions on the 360-subject plates which were printed before electric eye plates came into use, and 20 collectible positions on the Type II "new design" 360-subject rotary plates. There are 21 collectible positions in the rotary air mail 180-subject plate as well as the Type IV "modified design" 360-subject plate. There are 16 collectible positions on the 320-subject plates and 20 on the 400 subject plates. There are five collectible positions on Defense and War Savings 300-subject plates.

The generally accepted methods of designating pane positions as illustrated and explained hereafter are those suggested by George H. Beans in the May 1913 issue of "Everybody's Philatelist" and by B. H. Mosher in his monograph "Discovering U.S. Rotary Pane Varieties 1926-78." Some collectors seek all varieties possible, but the majority collect unused (A) panes and plate number (D) panes from flat plate issues, and plain panes and panes with electric eye bars and electric eye dashes, where available, from rotary plates.

Starting in 1977, BEP made two major changes in booklet production. Printing of panes was gradually moved from rotary plates to sleeves for modern high speed presses. Also, booklet production was transferred to Goebel booklet-forming machines. These changes virtually eliminated collectible pane positions for several years. However, beginning with No. BK156 (No. 2276a), BEP and other printers began placing printing process control marks in pane tabs. As a result, specialist booklet pane collectors actively resumed collecting pane positions. Collectible positions on these issues are not shown in this catalogue but can be found in the United States Stamp Society's Research Paper No. 2 "Folded Style Checklist," Michael O. Perry, editor. Also, because of the requirements of the Goebel machine, the subject size of printing plates or sleeves varied widely. For these reasons, plate layouts are not shown for each issue. The plate layout for No. 1288c and the sleeve layout for No. 1623a are shown as typical.

The following panes, issued after Mar. 11, 1977, were printed from pairs of rotary plates and assembled into booklets on the Goebel machine: Nos. 1288c, 1742a, 1819a, 1889a, and 1949a. One pane in 12 of those issues may have a join line along either long side of the pane, creating three collectible positions: no join line, join line top (or right) and join line bottom (or left). Except for Nos. 1736a and 2276a, all other booklet panes issued from Mar. 11, 1977 on were printed from intaglio sleeves, gravure cylinders, and/or offset plates.

At least one pane in every booklet produced on the BEP's Goebel machines contain two register marks in the tab: a cross register line (CRL) 1.5mm wide which runs across the width of the tab and a length register mark (LRM), typically 1.5x5mm, usually placed above the right hand (or top) stamp of the pane. Nos. 1623a and 1623Bc were regularly issued with the LRM over either stamp. Some copies of Nos. 1893a, 2121a and 3003Ab were issued with the LRM over the left stamp.

Starting with No. 1889a (except for No. 1948a), plate numbers (1 to 5 digits) were placed in the tab, normally over the left stamp. On booklets containing Nos. 1889a, 1949a and 2113a, the plate number is supposed to be on the top pane, the second pane not having a number. All subsequent multi-pane booklets have the plate number on each pane. Some multi-pane booklets contain panes with different plate numbers. The booklet value is determined by the top pane.

Some recent booklets have been printed by contractors other than the BEP so markings may differ or be absent.

Panes in all booklets assembled on the Goebel machine will be folded at least once. **Repeated handling of booklets with folded panes may cause the panes to fall apart.**

Booklet panes with tabs attached to the cover by adhesive instead of staples are valued on the basis of the tab intact. Minor damage on the back of the tab due to removal from the booklet does not affect the value. Some of these panes were furnished to first day cover processors unfolded and not pasted into covers. Around 1989, these panes were available to collectors through the Philatelic Agency.

All panes from 1967 to date are tagged, unless otherwise stated.

Dr. William R. Bush, Morton Dean Joyce, Robert E. Kitson, Richard F. Larkin, Dr. Robert Marks, Bruce H. Mosher, the United States Stamp Society (formerly the Bureau Issues Association), and the Booklet Collectors Club helped the editors extensively in compiling the listings and preparing the illustrations of booklets, covers and plate layouts.

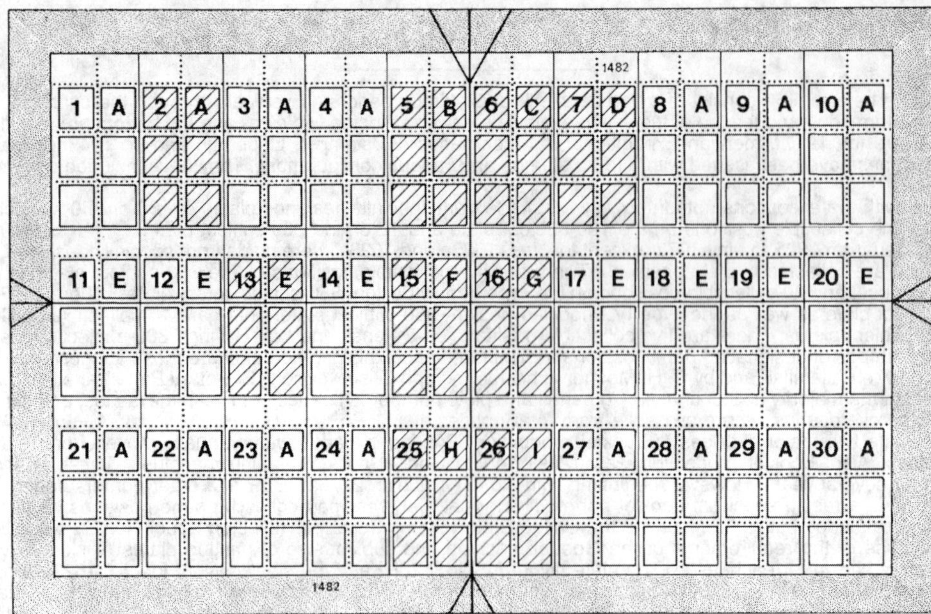

180-SUBJECT PLATE - 9 Collectible Positions

Beginning at upper left and reading from left to right, the panes are designated from 1 to 30. All positions not otherwise identifiable are designated by the letter A: Pane 1A, 2A, 3A, 4A, etc.

The identifiable positions are as follows:

A — The ordinary booklet pane without distinguishing features. Occurs in Position 1, 2, 3, 4, 8, 9, 10, 21, 22, 23, 24, 27, 28, 29, 30.
B — Split arrow and guide line at right. Occurs in Position 5 only.
C — Split arrow and guide line at left. Occurs in Position 6 only.
D — Plate number pane. Occurs in Position 7 only.
E — Guide line pane showing horizontal guide line between stamps 1-2 and 3-4 of the pane. Occurs in Positions 11, 12, 13, 14, 17, 18, 19, and 20.
F — Guide line through pane and at right. Occurs in Position 15 only.
G — Guide line through pane and at left. Occurs in Position 16 only.
H — Guide line at right. Occurs in Position 25 only.
I — Guide line at left. Occurs in Position 26 only.

Only positions B, F and H or C, G and I may be obtained from the same sheet, depending on whether the knife which separated the panes fell to right or left of the line.

Side arrows, bottom arrows, or bottom plate numbers are seldom found because the margin of the sheets is usually cut off, as are the sides and bottom of each pane.

In the illustrations, the dotted lines represent the rows of perforations, the unbroken lines represents the knife cut.

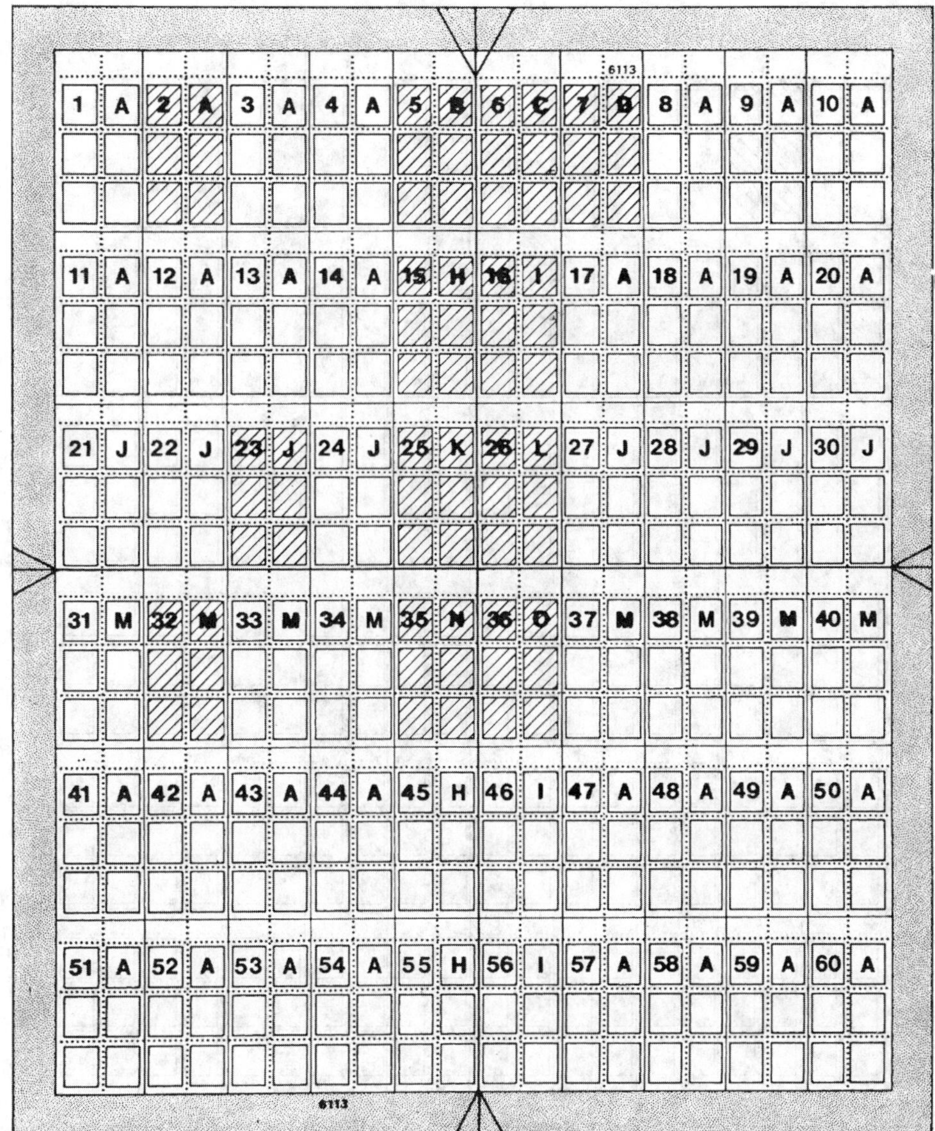

360-SUBJECT PLATE - 12 Collectible Positions

As with the 180-Subject Sheets, the position of the various panes is indicated by numbers beginning in the upper left corner with the No. 1 and reading from left to right to No. 60.

The identifiable positions are as follows:

A — The ordinary booklet pane without distinguishing features. Occurs in Positions 1, 2, 3, 4, 8, 9, 10, 11, 12, 13, 14, 17, 18, 19, 20, 41, 42, 43, 44, 47, 48, 49, 50, 51, 52, 53, 54, 57, 58, 59, and 60.

B — Split arrow and guide line at right. Occurs in Position 5 only.

C — Split arrow and guide line at left. Occurs in Position 6 only.

D — Plate number pane. Occurs in Position 7 only.

E, F, G — Do not occur in the 360-Subject Plate.

H — Guide line at right. Occurs in Positions 15, 45, and 55.

I — Guide line at left. Occurs in Positions 16, 46, and 56.

J — Guide line at bottom. Occurs in Positions 21, 22, 23, 24, 27, 28, 29 and 30.

K — Guide line at right and bottom. Occurs in Position 25 only.

L — Guide line at left and bottom. Occurs in Position 26 only.

M — Guide line at top. Occurs in Positions 31, 32, 33, 34, 37, 38, 39 and 40.

N — Guide line at top and right. Occurs in Position 35 only.

O — Guide line at top and left. Occurs in Position 36 only.

Only one each of Positions B or C, K, L, N or O; four positions of H or I, and eight or nine positions of J or M may be obtained from each 360 subject sheet, depending on whether the knife fell to the right or left, top or bottom of the guide lines.

Because the horizontal guide line appears so close to the bottom row of stamps on panes Nos. 21 to 30, Positions M, N, and O occur with great deal less frequency than Positions J, K and L.

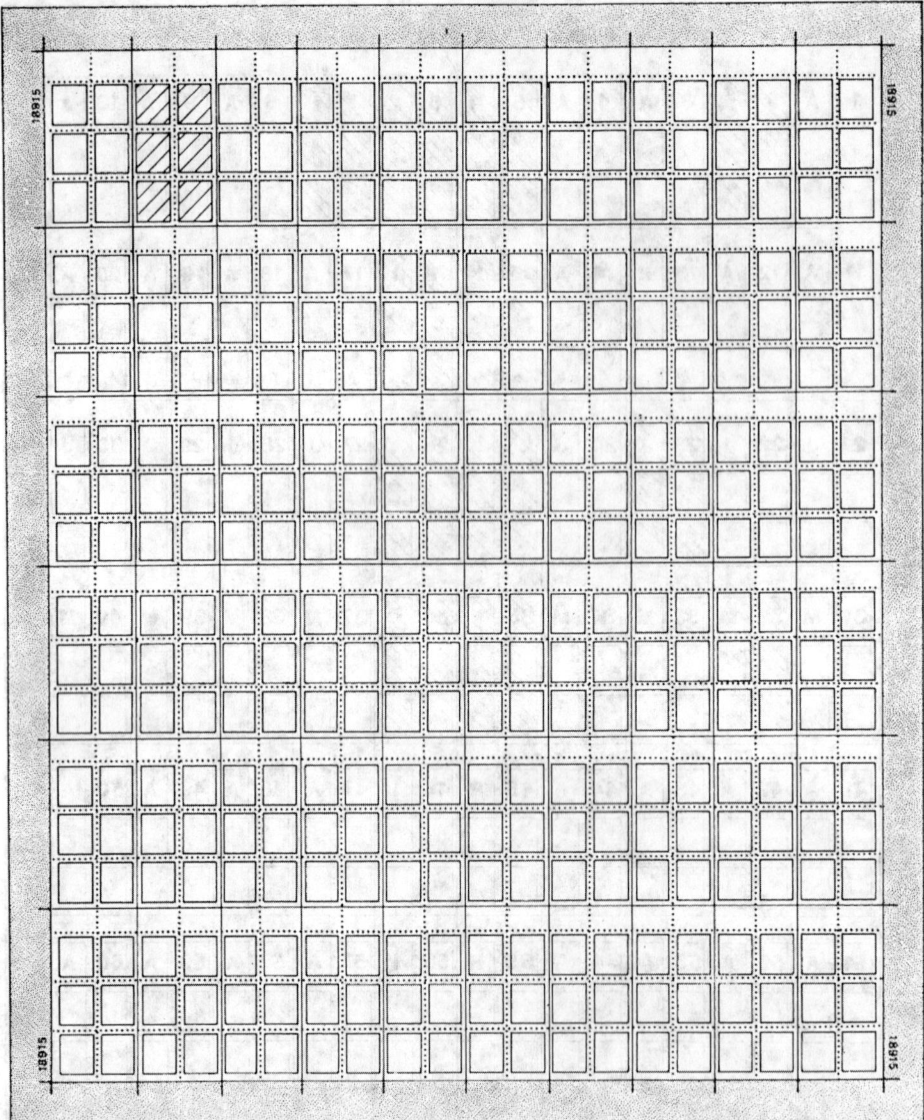

The 360-Subject Rotary Press Plate (before Electric Eye) Position A only

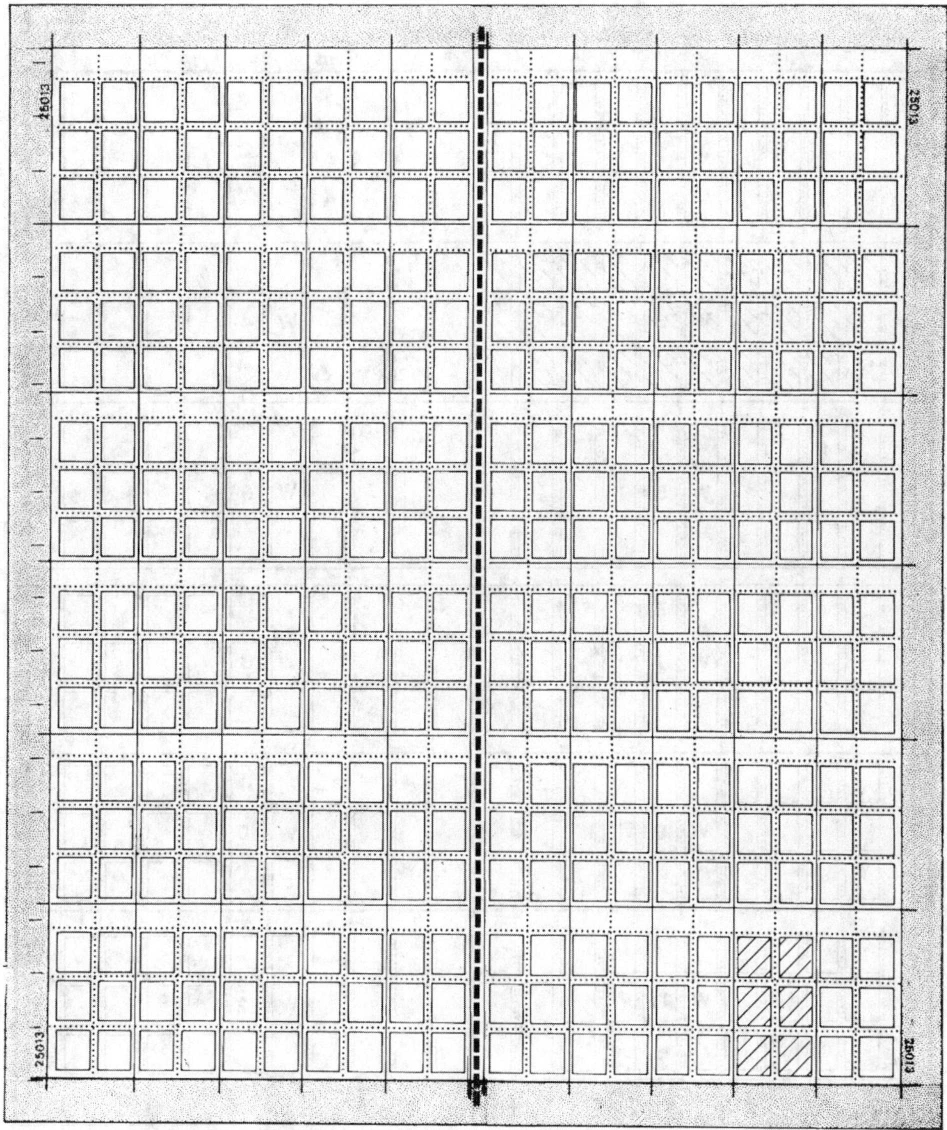

The 360-Subject Rotary Press Plate - Electric Eye

A modified design was put into use in 1956. The new plates have 20 frame bars instead of 17.

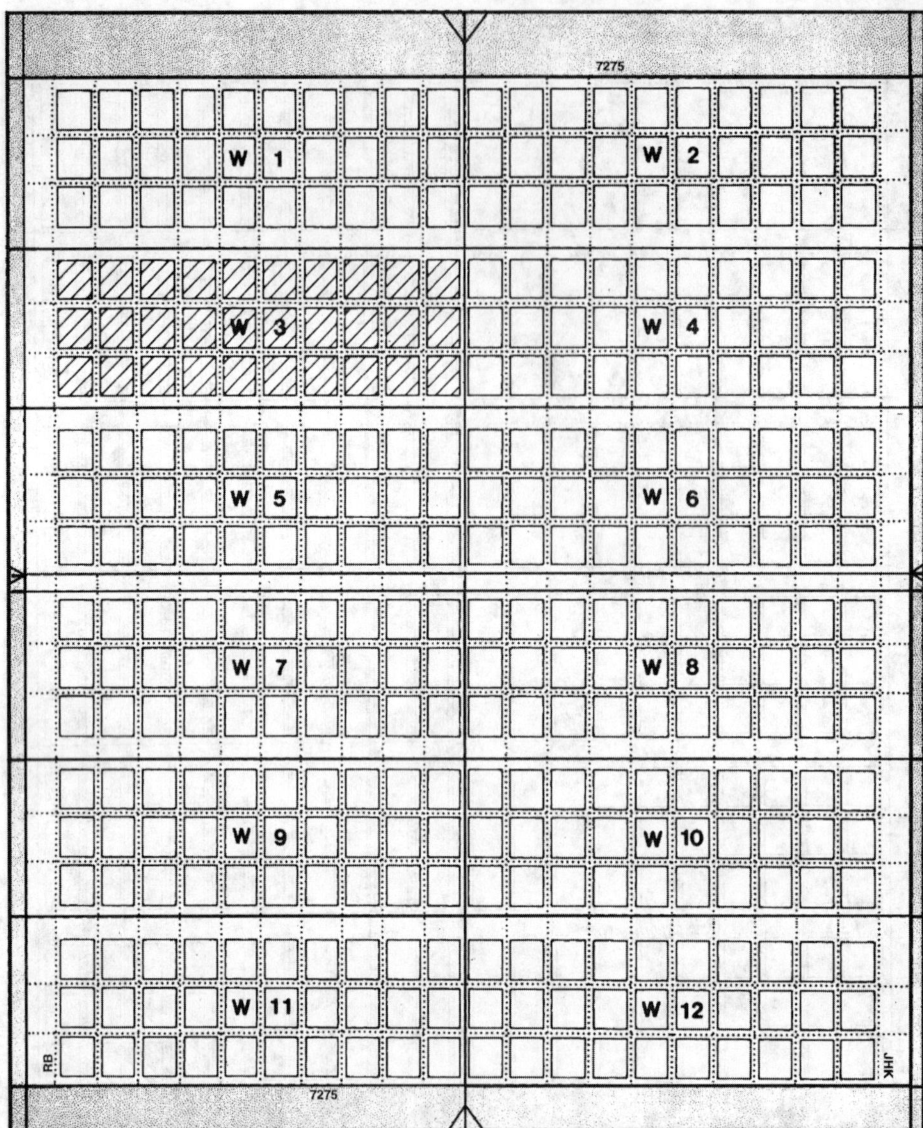

The A.E.F. Plate - 360-Subject Flat Plate - 8 Collectible Positions (See listings)

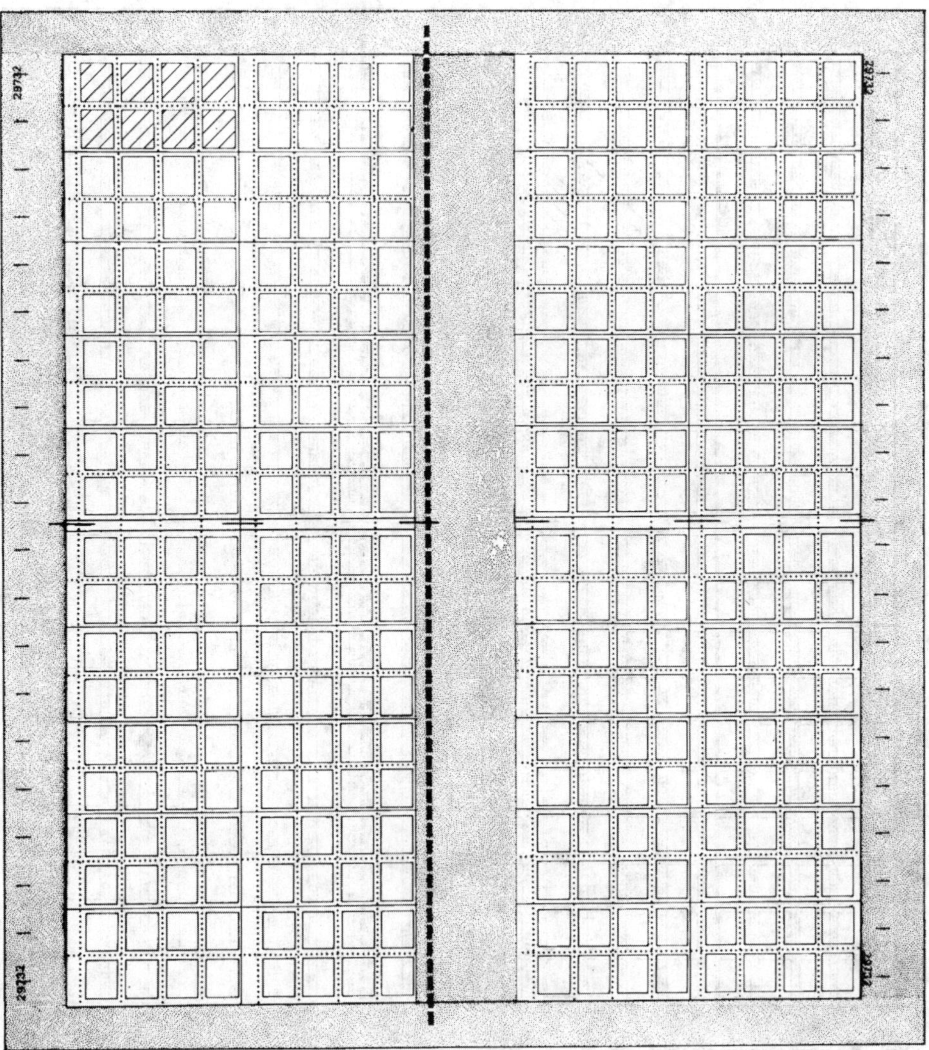

The 320-Subject plate

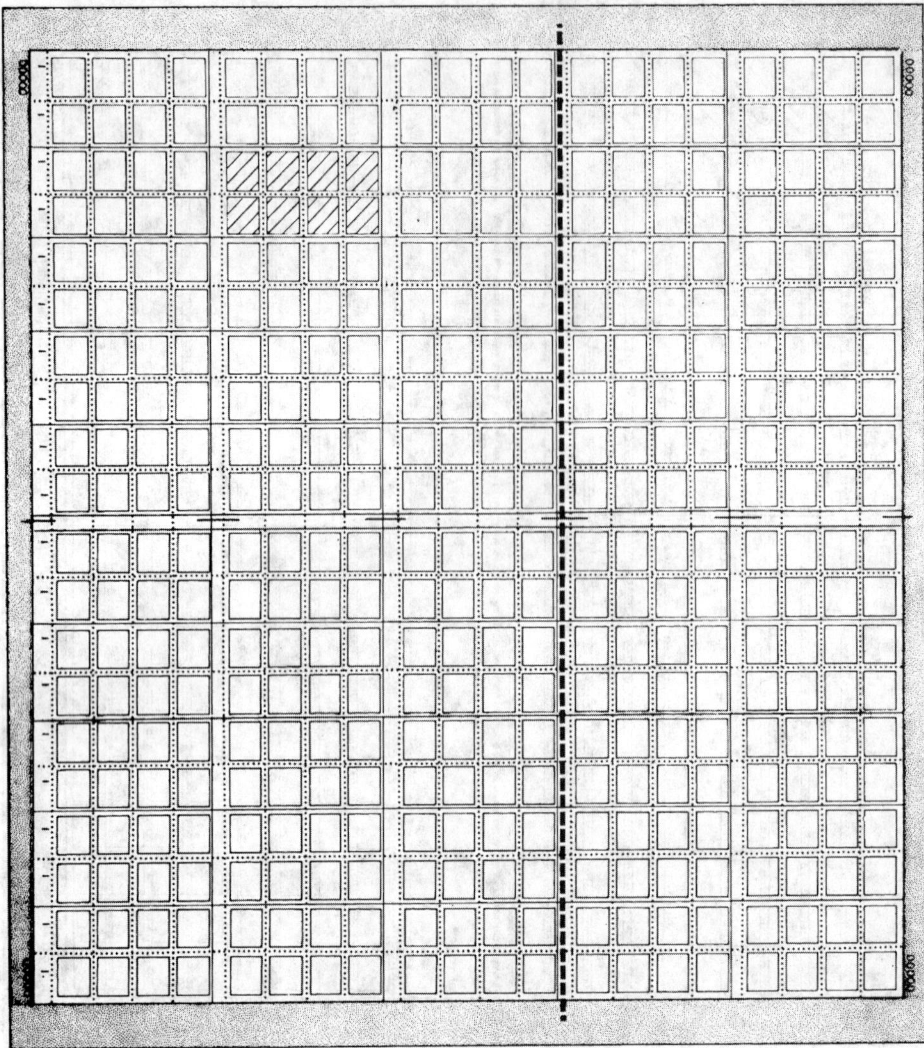

400-Subject Plate —The 300-Subject plate with double labels has the same layout.

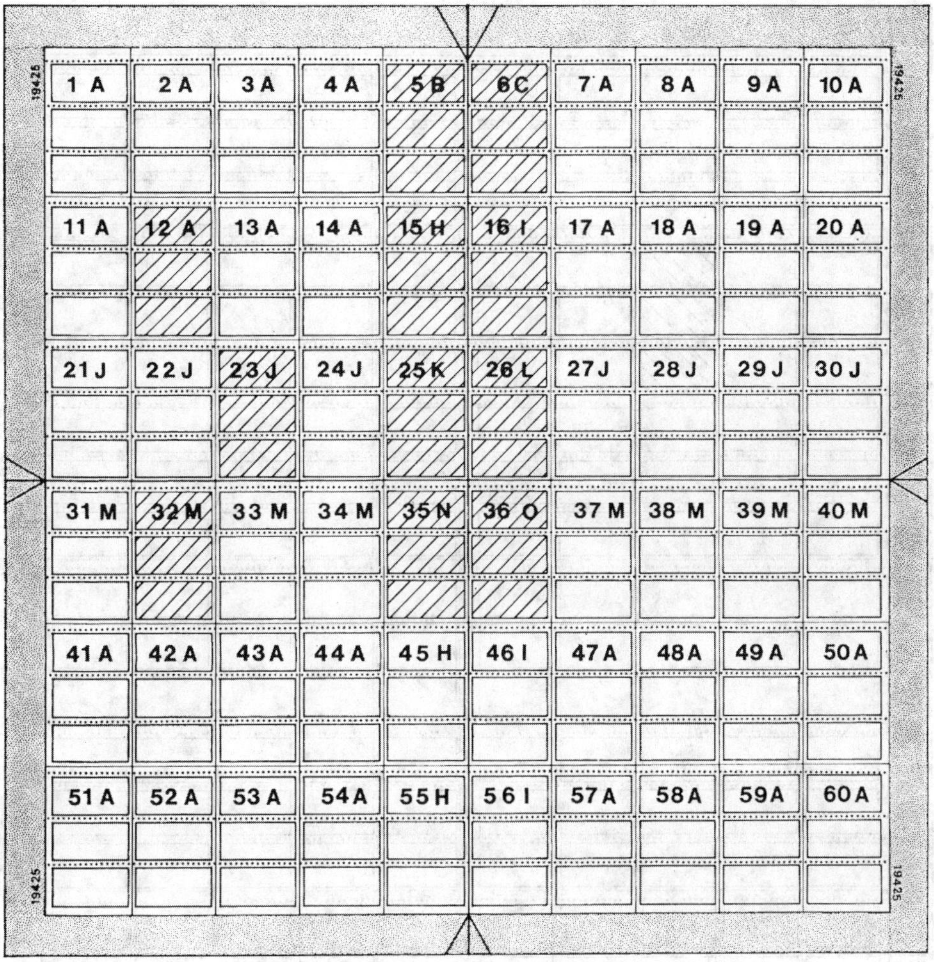

19425

1 A	2 A	3 A	4 A	5 B	6 C	7 A	8 A	9 A	10 A
11 A	12 A	13 A	14 A	15 H	16 I	17 A	18 A	19 A	20 A
21 J	22 J	23 J	24 J	25 K	26 L	27 J	28 J	29 J	30 J
31 M	32 M	33 M	34 M	35 N	36 O	37 M	38 M	39 M	40 M
41 A	42 A	43 A	44 A	45 H	46 I	47 A	48 A	49 A	50 A
51 A	52 A	53 A	54 A	55 H	56 I	57 A	58 A	59 A	60 A

19425

Lindbergh Booklet Plate-180 Subjects - 11 Collectible Positions

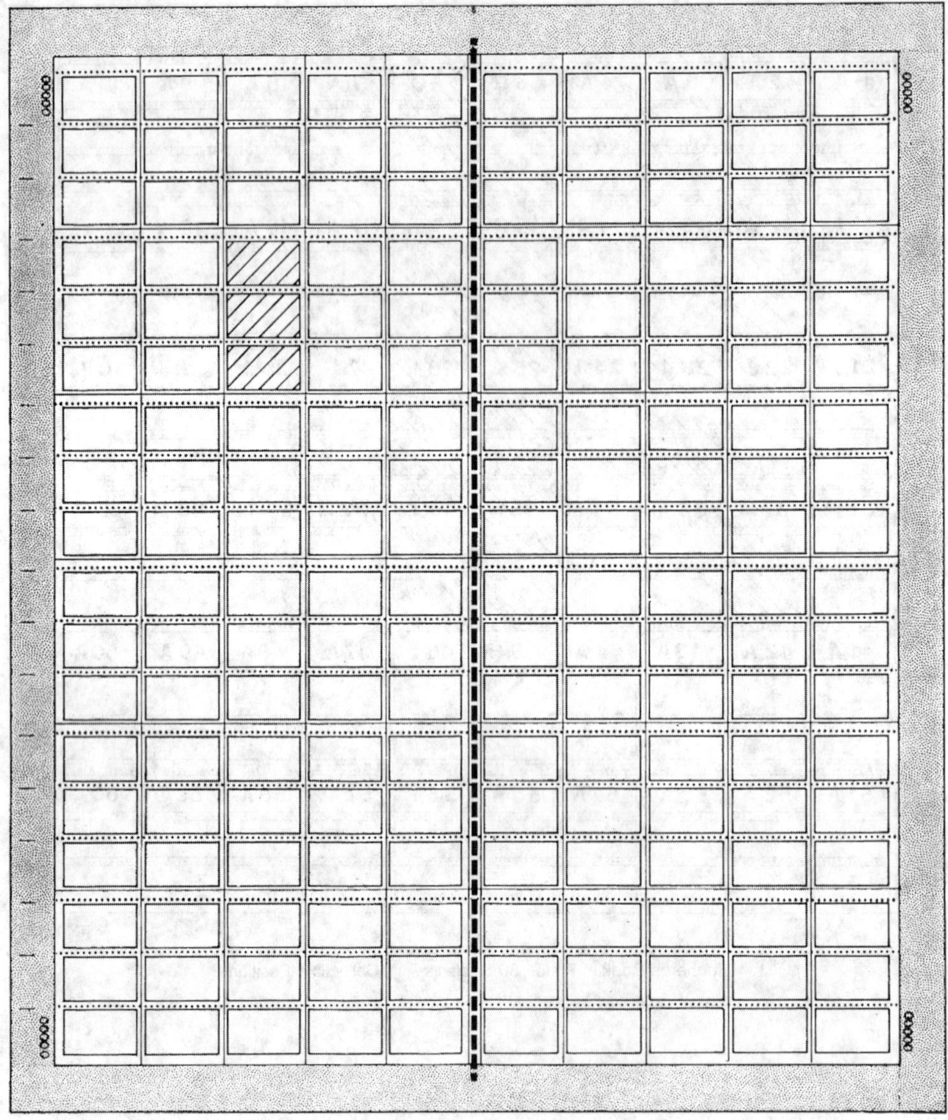

Airmail 180-Subject Rotary Press Plate - Electric Eye

Plate Sizes: No. 1288Bc to date.

Since 1978 numerous plate sizes from 78 to 1080 subjects have been used. Since plate size is not relevant to collecting these panes, we are not including this information in the catalogue.

BOOKLET COVERS

Front covers of booklets of postage and airmail issues are illustrated and numbered.

Included are the Booklet Cover number (BC2A); and the catalogue numbers of the Booklet Panes (300b, 331a). The text of the inside and or back covers changes. Some modern issues have minor changes on the front covers also. When more than one combination of covers exists, the number of possible booklets is noted in parenthesis after the booklet listing.

POST OFFICE DEPARTMENT.

THIS BOOK CONTAINS 12 TWO-CENT STAMPS.
Price, 25 cents.

DOMESTIC POSTAGE RATES.

(Apply to mail matter sent to Puerto Rico, Guam, Philippines, Canada, and Mexico.)

First-class. Letters and sealed matter: 2 cts. for each ounce or fraction.

Second-class. Newspapers and periodicals: 1 ct. for each four ounces or fraction.

Third-class. Miscellaneous printed matter: 1 ct. for each two ounces or fraction.

Fourth-class. All matter not included in first three classes: 1 ct. for each ounce or fraction.

279Be — BC1

1900-03

Text only cover

25c booklet contains 2 panes of six 2c stamps.
49c booklet contains 4 panes of six 2c stamps.
97c booklet contains 8 panes of six 2c stamps.

Booklets sold for 1c more than the face value of the stamps.

POST OFFICE DEPARTMENT, U. S. A.

25c. —THIS BOOK CONTAINS 24 ONE-CENT STAMPS— 25c.
PRICE, 25 CENTS.

DOMESTIC POSTAGE RATES.

(Apply to Guam, Hawaii, Philippines, Porto Rico, Tutuila, Canal Zone, and to Canada, Cuba, Mexico, and the Republic of Panama.)

First-class. Letters and sealed matter: 2 cts. for each ounce or fraction. Postal cards and post cards 1 ct. each.

Second-class. Newspapers and periodicals: 1 ct. for each four ounces or fraction.

Third-class. Miscellaneous printed matter: 1 ct. for each two ounces or fraction.

Fourth-class. All matter not included in first three classes: 1 ct. for each ounce or fraction.

Special-delivery. A special-delivery stamp, in addition to postage, secures immediate delivery within the carrier-delivery limit of city free delivery and within one mile of any other United States post office.

300b, 331a — BC2A

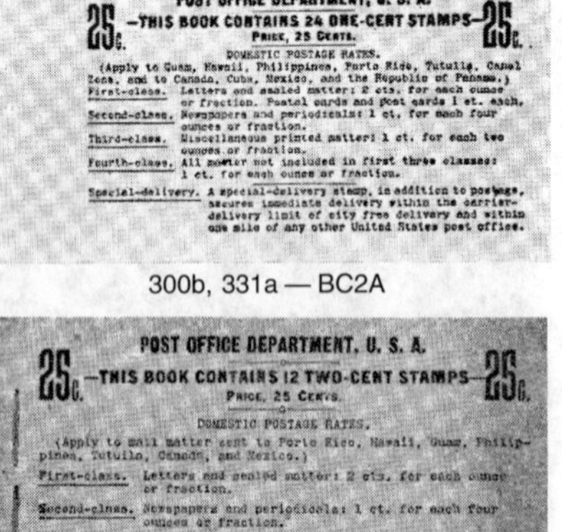

POST OFFICE DEPARTMENT, U. S. A.

25c. —THIS BOOK CONTAINS 12 TWO-CENT STAMPS— 25c.
PRICE, 25 CENTS.

DOMESTIC POSTAGE RATES.

(Apply to mail matter sent to Porto Rico, Hawaii, Guam, Philippines, Tutuila, Canada, and Mexico.)

First-class. Letters and sealed matter: 2 cts. for each ounce or fraction.

Second-class. Newspapers and periodicals: 1 ct. for each four ounces or fraction.

Third-class. Miscellaneous printed matter: 1 ct. for each two ounces or fraction.

Fourth-class. All matter not included in first three classes: 1 ct. for each ounce or fraction.

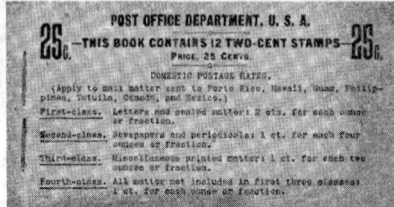

279Be, 301c, 319, 332a — BC2B

1900-08

Text cover with price added in upper corners

25c booklets contain 4 panes of six 1c stamps or 2 panes of six 2c stamps.
49c booklet contains 4 panes of six 2c stamps.
97c booklet contains 8 panes of six 2c stamps.

331a, 332a, 374a, 375a, 405b, 406a — BC3

1908-12 **Postrider**

25c booklet contains 4 panes of six 1c stamps.
25c booklet contains 2 panes of six 2c stamps.
49c booklet contains 4 panes of six 2c stamps.
97c booklet contains 8 panes of six 2c stamps.

405b, 424d, 462a, 498e, 804b — BC4A

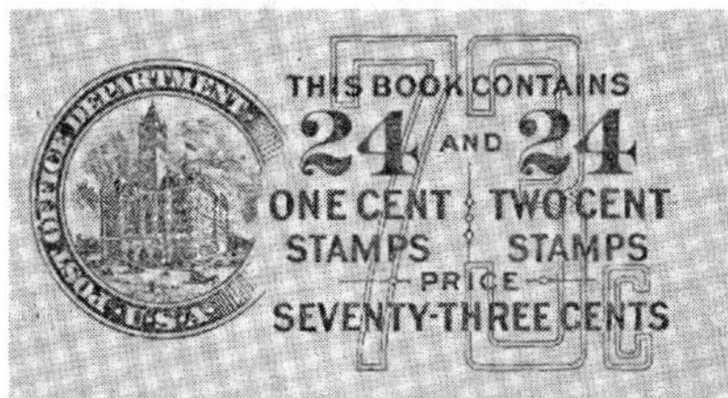

405b, 424d, 462a, 498e, 552a, 632a — BC4B

1912-39 **Washington P.O.**

Price of booklet in large numerals behind contents information

25c booklet contains 4 panes of six 1c stamps.
73c booklet contains 4 panes of six 1c stamps and 4 panes of six 2c stamps.
97c booklet contains 16 panes of six 1c stamps.

406a, 425e, 463a, 499e, 554c, 583a, 632a, 634d, 804b, 806b — BC5A

632a, 804b — BC5D

1912-39 **Small Postrider**

Large background numerals

25c booklets contain 4 panes of six 1c stamps or 2 panes of six 2c stamps.
49c booklet contains 4 panes of six 2c stamps.
73c booklet contains 4 panes of six 1c stamps and 4 panes of six 2c stamps.
97c booklets contain 16 panes of six 1c stamps or 8 panes of six 2c stamps.

498e, 552a — BC6A

501b, 502b — BC6B

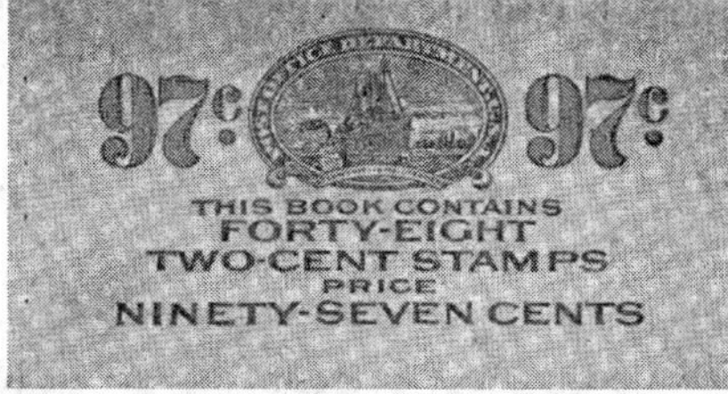

499e, 554c, 583a, 634d — BC6C

1917-27 **Oval designs**

25c booklet contains 4 panes of six 1c stamps.
37c booklet contains 2 panes of six 3c stamps.
97c booklet contains 8 panes of six 2c stamps.

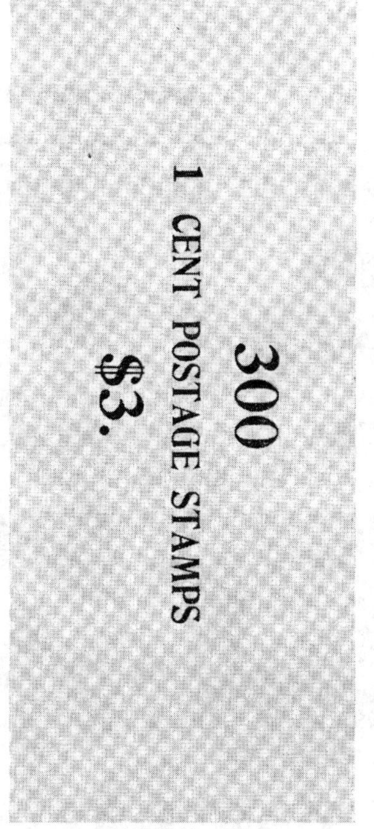

498f, 499f — BC7

Illustration reduced.

1917 **A.E.F.**

$3 booklet contains 10 panes of thirty 1c stamps.
$6 booklet contains 10 panes of thirty 2c stamps.

Booklets sold for face value.

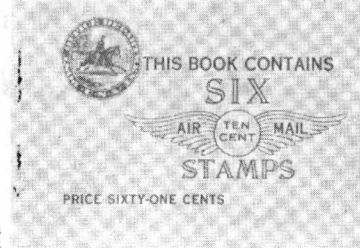

C10a
BC8

1928 **Postrider and Wings**

61c booklet contains 2 panes of three 10c stamps.

720b, 806b, 807a, 1035a — BC9A

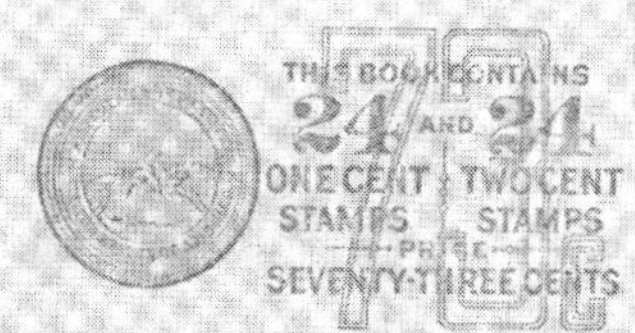

804b — BC9E

1932-54 **Post Office Seal**

Large background numerals

25c booklet contains 2 panes of six 2c stamps.
37c booklet contains 2 panes of six 3c stamps.
49c booklet contains 4 panes of six 2c stamps.
73c booklets contain 4 panes of six 3c stamps or 4 panes of six 1c stamps and 4 panes of six 2c stamps.

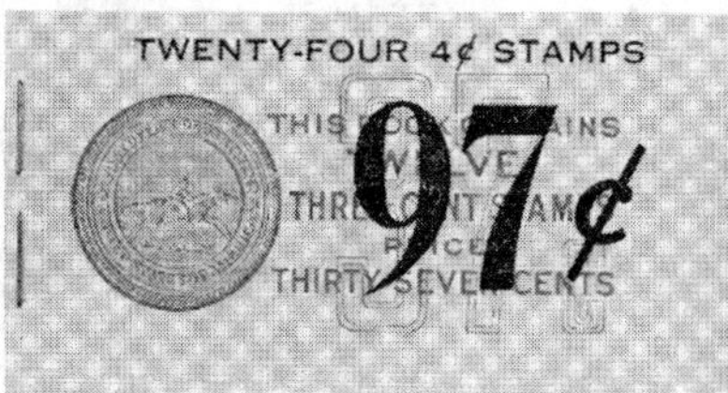

1036a — BC9F

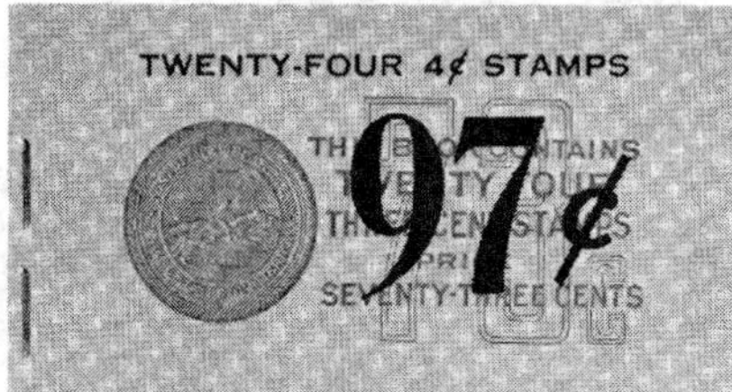

1036a — BC9G

1036a — BC9H

1958

97c booklet contains 4 panes of six 4c stamps.

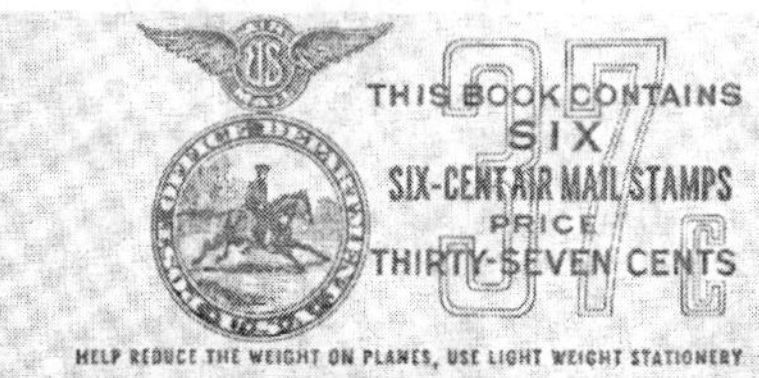

C25a — BC10

Large background numerals

1943 **Postrider and Wings**

37c booklet contains 2 panes of three 6c stamps.
73c booklet contains 4 panes of three 6c stamps.

C39a — BC11A

C51a — BC11B

C51a, C60a — BC11C

C64b, C64c — BC11D

1949-63 **U.S. Airmail Wings**

The 73c and 85c booklets were the last sold for 1c over face value.

73c booklet contains 2 panes of six 6c stamps.
85c booklet contains 2 panes of six 7c stamps.
80c booklet contains 2 panes of five 8c stamps.
$2 booklet contains 5 panes of five 8c stamps.

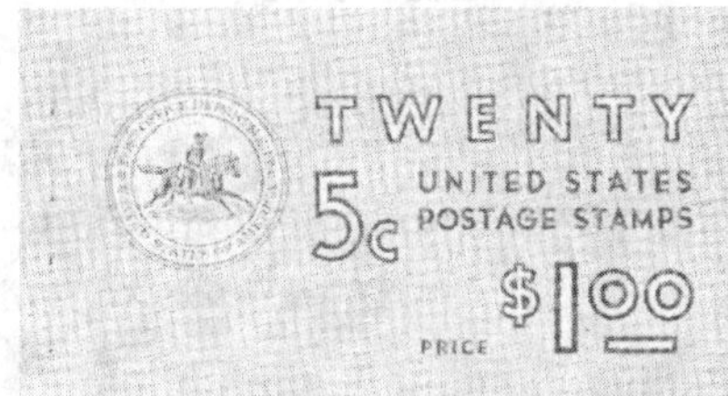

1213a — BC12A

1962-63 **Small Postrider**

$1 booklet contains 4 panes of five 5c stamps.

1213a, 1213c — BC13A

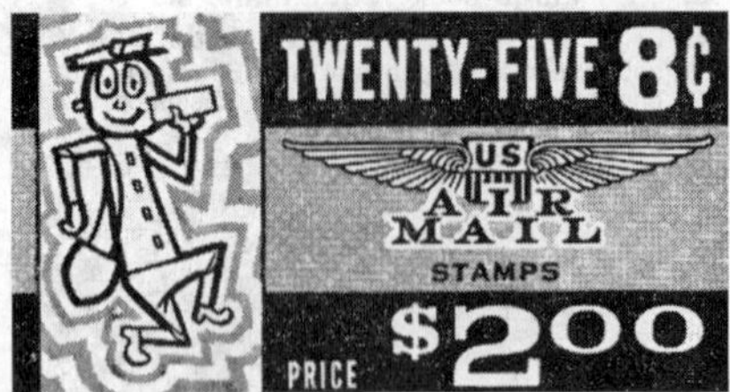

C64b, C64c — BC13B

1963-64 **Mr. Zip**

$1 booklet contains 4 panes of five 5c stamps.
$2 booklet contains 5 panes of five 8c stamps.

1278a, 1284b, 1393a — BC14A

C72b — BC14B

1967-68

$2 booklet contains 4 panes of eight 6c stamps and 1 pane of eight 1c stamps.
$4 booklet contains 5 panes of eight 10c stamps.

1284c, 1393b, 1395b, C72c, C78a — BC15

1968-71

$1 booklets contain 2 panes of five 10c stamps or 2 panes of six 8c stamps and 1 pane of four 1c stamps; 3 panes of five 6c stamps and 1 pane of five 2c stamps or 2 panes of four 11c stamps and 1 pane of six 2c stamps.

1278a, 1393a, 1395a — BC16

1970-71 **Eisenhower**

$2 booklet contains 4 panes of eight 6c stamps and 1 pane of eight 1c stamps.
$1.92 booklet contains 3 panes of eight 8c stamps.

1395d — BC17A

1510b — BC17B

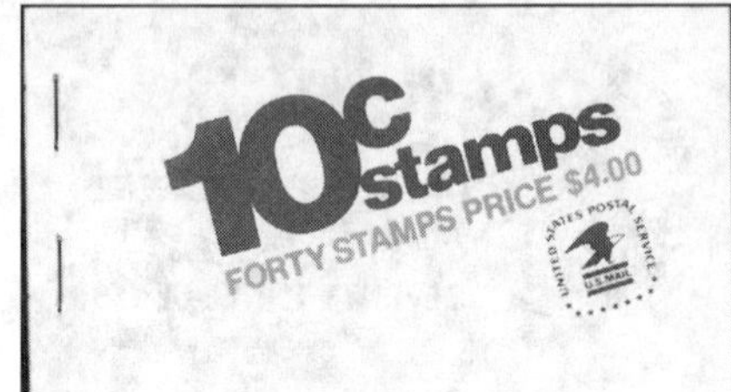

1510c — BC17C

1510d — BC17D

1972-74 **Postal Service Emblem**

$2 booklet contains 3 panes of seven 8c stamps and 1 pane of four 8c stamps.
$1 booklet contains 2 panes of five 10c stamps.
$4 booklet contains 5 panes of eight 10c stamps.
$1.25 booklet contains 1 pane of five 13c stamps and 1 pane of six 10c stamps.

C79a — BC18

1973

$1.30 booklet contains 2 panes of five 13c stamps.

13c Stamps

1595a, 1595d — BC19A

13c STAMPS

1595c — BC19B

1975-76

90c booklet contains 1 pane of six 13c stamps and 1 pane of six 2c stamps.
$1.30 booklet contains 2 panes of five 13c stamps.
$2.99 booklet contains 2 panes of eight 13c stamps and 1 pane of seven 13c stamps.

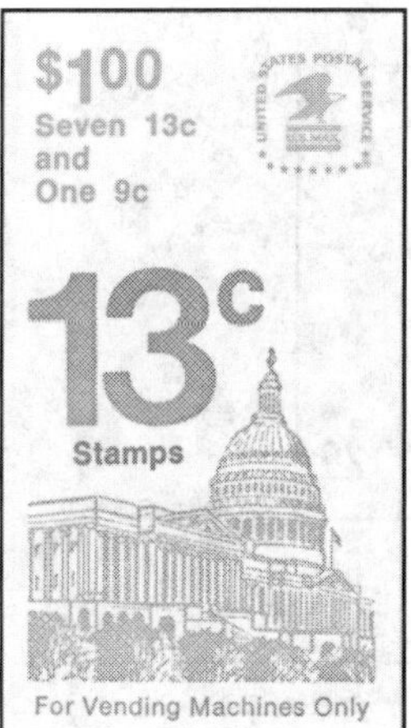

1623a — BC20

1598a — BC21

1737a — BC22

1288c — BC23

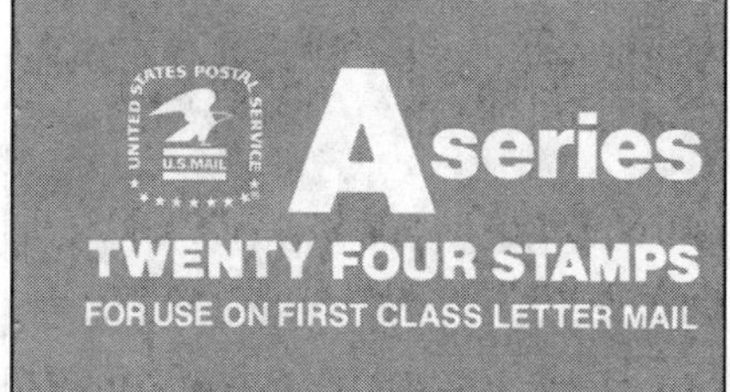

1736c — BC24

BC24 illustration reduced.

1977-78

$1 booklet contains 1 pane of one 9c stamp and seven 13c stamps.
$1.20 booklet contains 1 pane of eight 15c stamps.
$2.40 booklet contains 2 panes of eight 15c stamps.
$3.60 booklet contains 3 panes of eight 15c stamps.

1742a — BC25

1980

$3 booklet contains 2 panes of ten 15c stamps.

1819a, 1948a, 2113a — BC26

1981-82

$4.32 booklet contains 3 panes of eight B stamps.
$4 booklet contains 2 panes of ten C stamps.
$4.40 booklet contains 2 panes of ten D stamps.

1893a — BC27

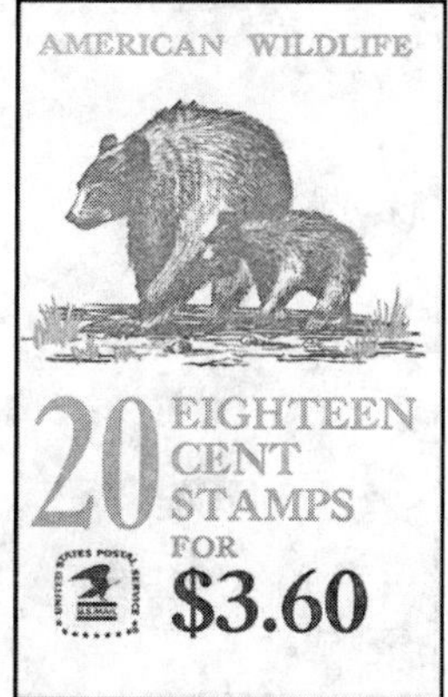

1889a — BC28

1981

$1.20 booklet contains 1 pane of two 6c and six 18c stamps.
$3.60 booklet contains 2 panes of ten 18c stamps.

1896a — BC29

1896b — BC29A

1896b — BC29B

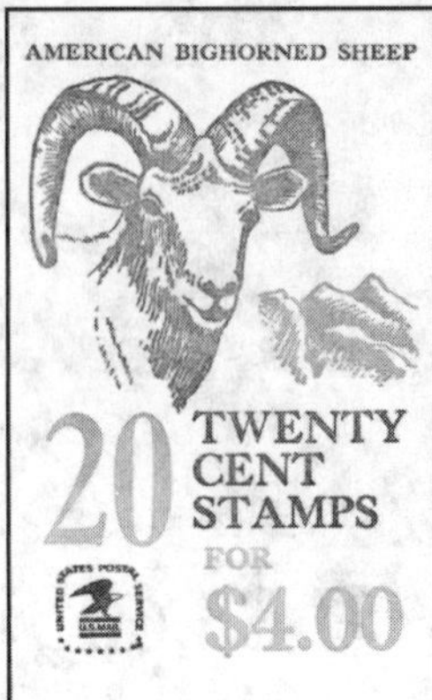

1949a — BC30

1982

$1.20 booklet contains 2 panes of six 20c stamps.
$2 booklet contains 1 pane of ten 20c stamps.
$4 booklet contains 2 panes of ten 20c stamps.

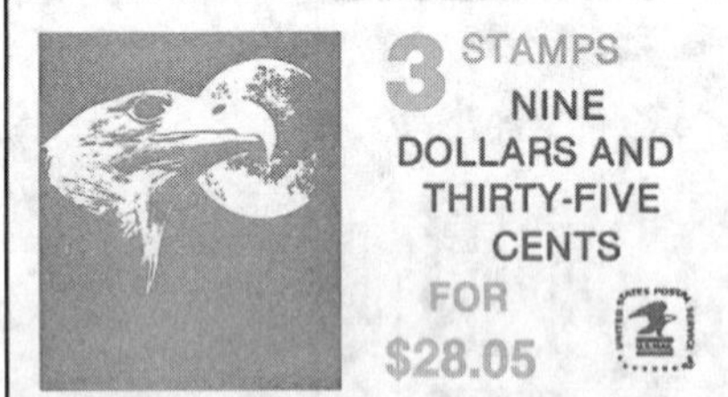

1909a — BC31

2122a — BC31A

2122c — BC31B

1983-89

$28.05 booklet contains 1 pane of three $9.35 stamps.
$32.25 booklet contains 1 pane of three $10.75 stamps.

2116a — BC32

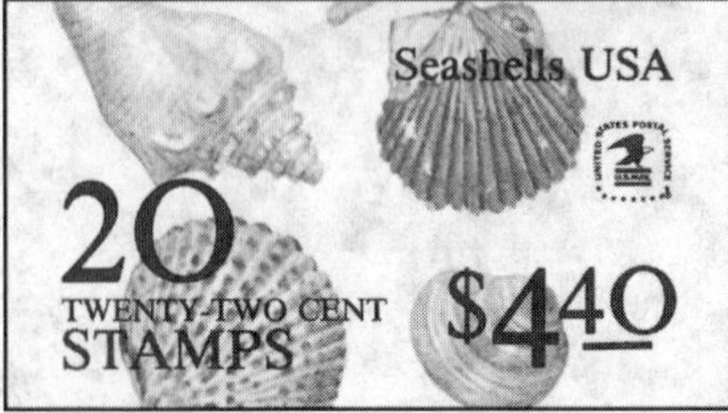

2121a — BC33A

Many different seashell configurations are possible on BC33A. Seven adjacent covers are necessary to show all 25 shells.

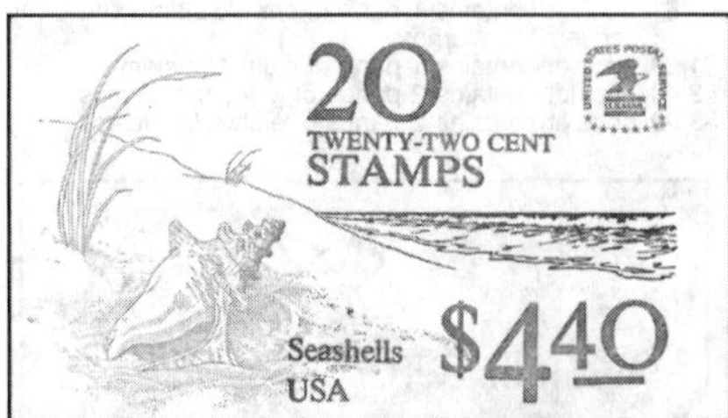

2121a — BC33B

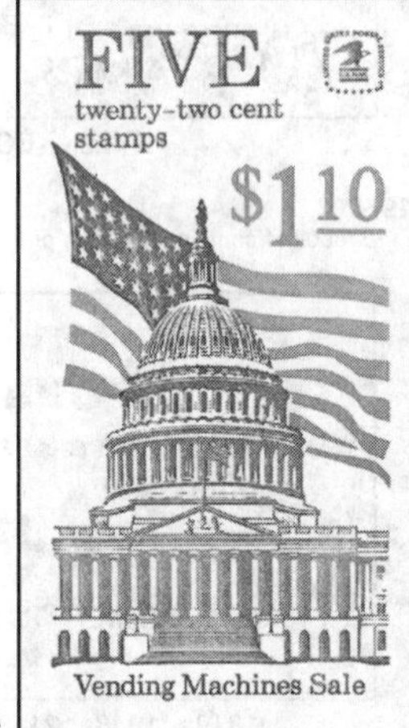

2116a — BC33C

1985

$1.10 booklet contains one pane of five 22c stamps.
$2.20 booklet contains two panes of five 22c stamps.
$4.40 booklet contains two panes of ten 22c stamps.

2201a — BC34

2209a — BC35

1986

$1.76 booklet contains 2 panes of four 22c stamps.
$2.20 booklet contains 2 panes of five 22c stamps.

FOR 22 CENTS, YOU CAN ADD ONE OF THESE GREETINGS TO A LETTER TO ANYONE IN THE UNITED STATES, CANADA OR MEXICO.
Get Well!
Thank You!
Best Wishes!
Keep in Touch!
Love You, Dad!
Happy Birthday!
Congratulations!
Love You, Mother!
10 TWENTY-TWO CENT U.S. POSTAGE STAMPS 2 20

2274a — BC36

1987

$2.20 booklet contains 1 pane of ten 22c stamps.

2359a — BC37

1987

$4.40 booklet contains four panes of five 22c stamps.

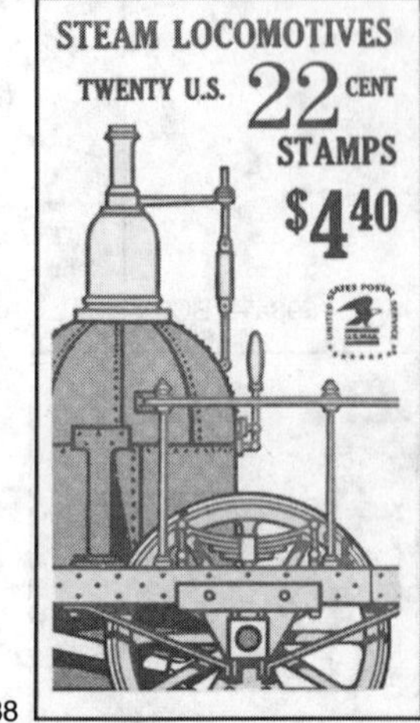

2366a — BC38

1987

$4.40 booklet contains four panes of five 22c stamps.

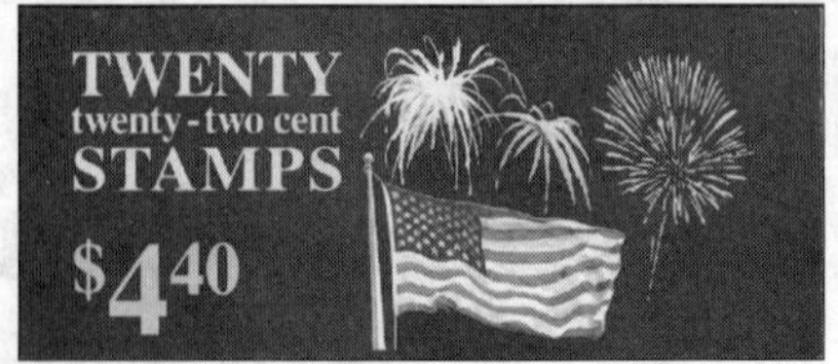

2276a — BC39

Illustration reduced.

1987

$4.40 booklet contains one pane of twenty 22c stamps.

2282a — BC40

1988
$5 booklet contains two panes of ten E stamps.

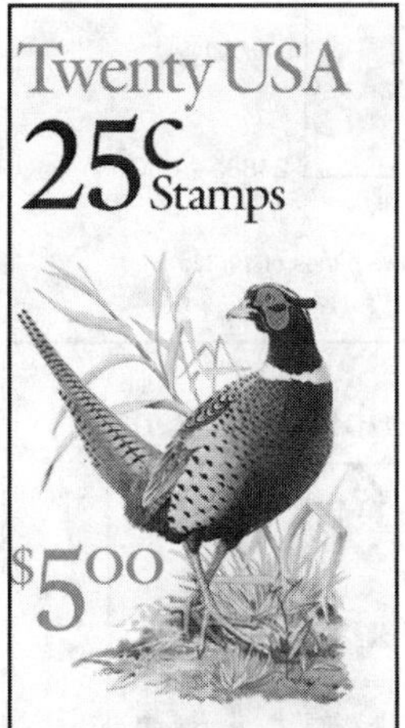

2283a, 2283c — BC41

1988
$5 booklet contains two panes of ten 25c stamps.

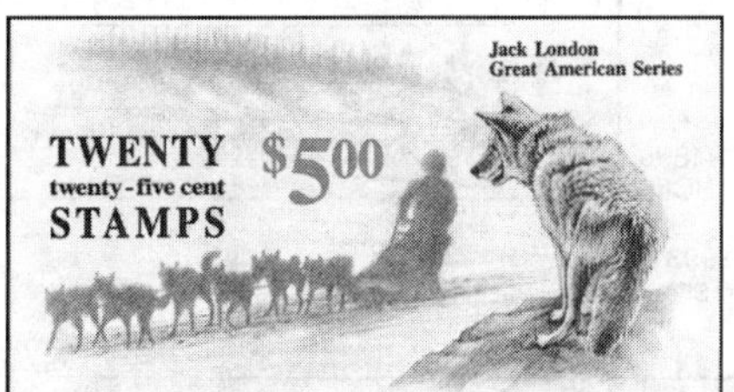

2182a, 2197a — BC43

1988
$1.50 booklet contains one pane of six 25c stamps.
$3 booklet contains two panes of six 25c stamps.
$5 booklet contains two panes of ten 25c stamps.

2285b — BC45

1988
$5 booklet contains two panes of ten 25c stamps.

2285c — BC46

1988
$3 booklet contains two panes of six 25c stamps.

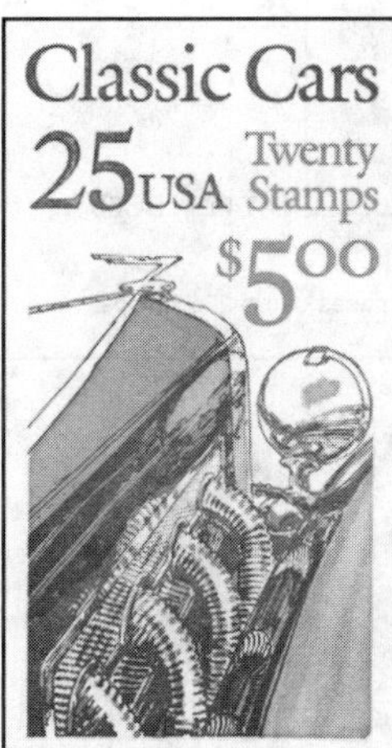

2385a — BC47

1988
$5 booklet contains four panes of five 25c stamps.

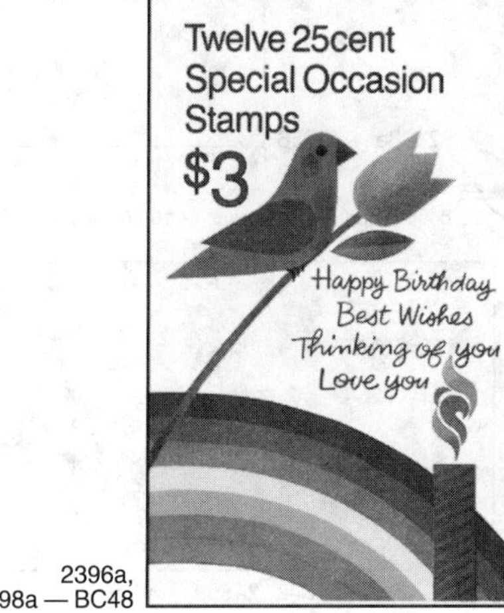

2396a, 2398a — BC48

1988
$3 booklet contains two panes of six 25c stamps.

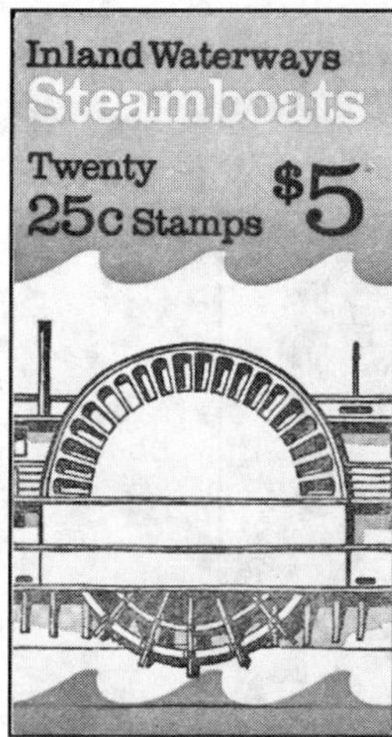

2409a — BC49

1989
$5 booklet contains four panes of five 25c stamps.

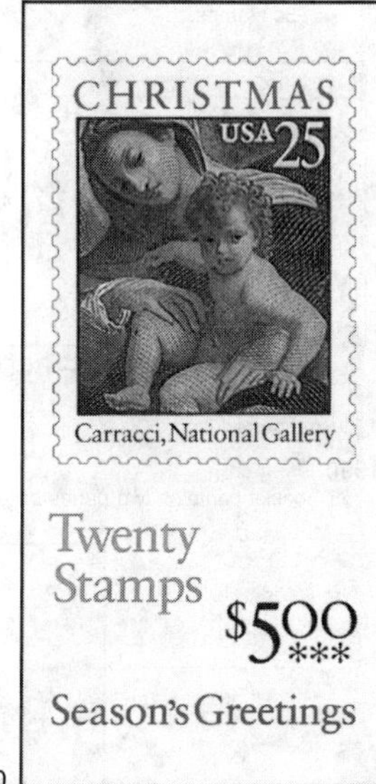

2427a — BC50

1989
$5 booklet contains two panes of ten 25c stamps.

2429a — BC51

Illustration reduced.

1989
$5 booklet contains two panes of ten 25c stamps.

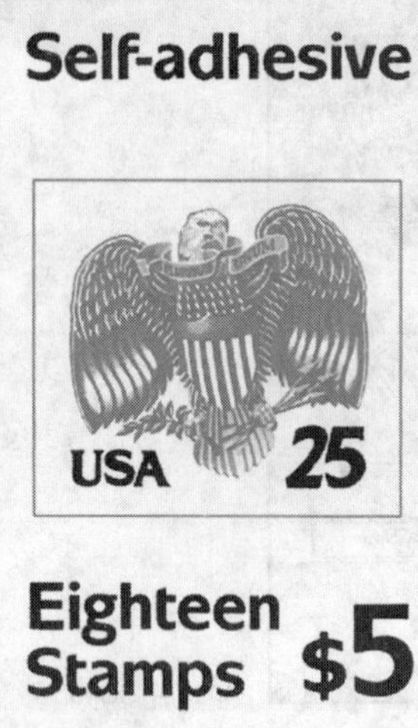

2431a — BC52

1989
$5 fold-it-yourself booklet contains eighteen self-adhesive 25c stamps.

2441a — BC53

Illustration reduced.

1990
$5 booklet contains two panes of ten 25c stamps.

2443a — BC54

1990
$3 booklet contains two panes of ten 15c stamps.

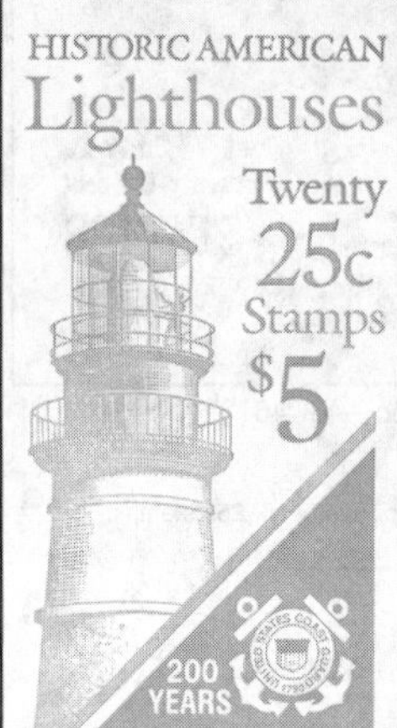

2474a — BC55

1990
$5 booklet contains four panes of five 25c stamps.

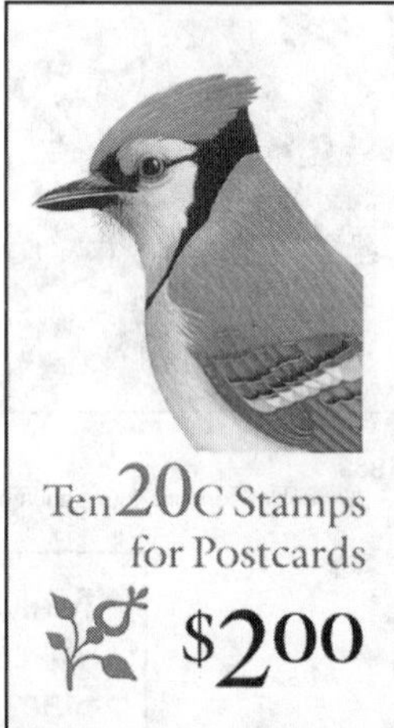

2483a — BC56

1995
$2 booklet contains one pane of 10 20c stamps.

2484a, 2485a — BC57

Illustration reduced.

1991-92
$2.90 booklet contains one pane of 10 29c stamps.
$5.80 booklet contains two panes of 10 29c stamps.

2486a — BC58

1993
$2.90 booklet contains one pane of 10 29c stamps.
$5.80 booklet contains two panes of 10 29c stamps.

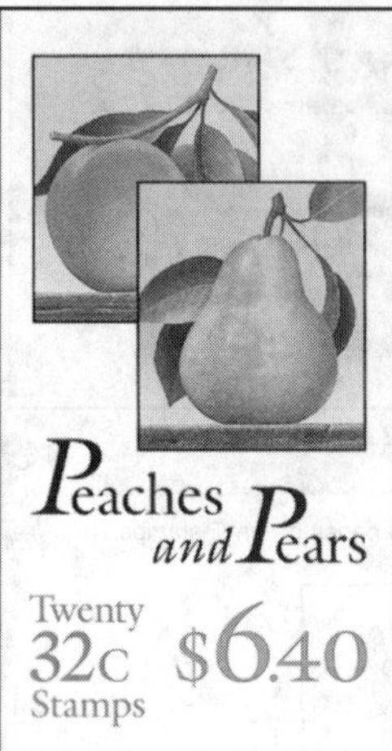

2488a — BC59

1995
$6.40 booklet contains two panes of 10 32c stamps.

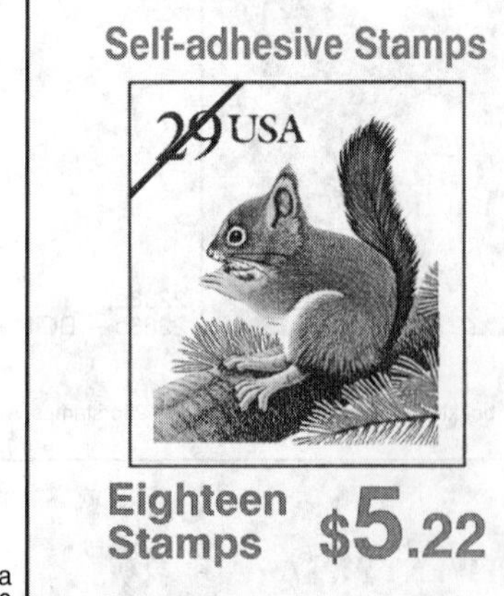

2489a
BC60

1993
$5.22 fold-it-yourself booklet contains 18 self-adhesive 29c stamps.

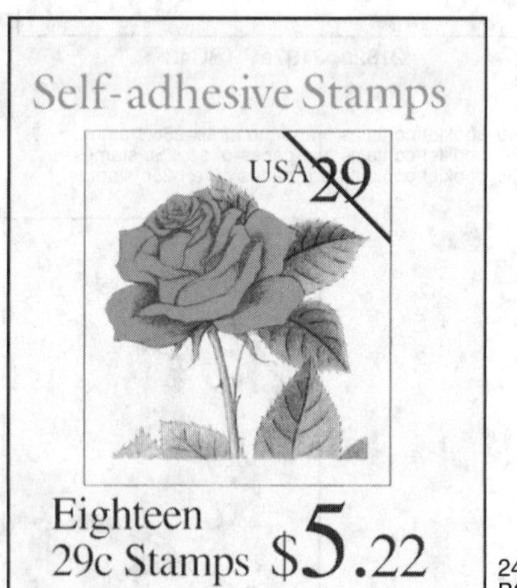

Self-adhesive Stamps
USA 29
Eighteen
29c Stamps $5.22

2490a
BC61

1993
$5.22 fold-it-yourself booklet contains 18 self-adhesive 29c stamps.

2491a — BC61A

1993

$5.22 fold-it-yourself booklet contains 18 self-adhesive stamps.

2492a — BC61B

1995

$6.40 fold-it-yourself booklet contains 20 self-adhesive 32c stamps.

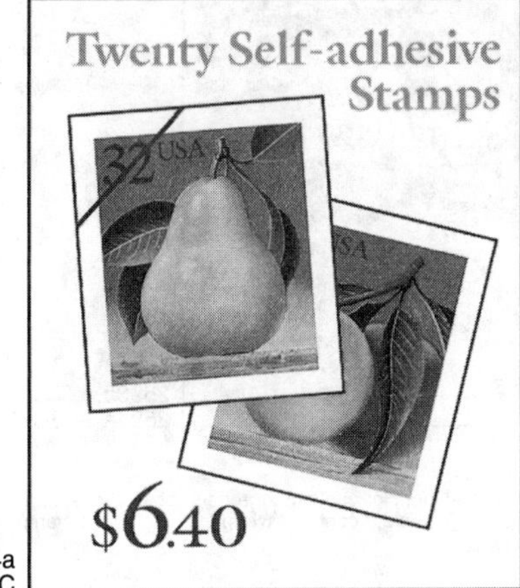

2494a BC61C

1995

$6.40 fold-it-yourself booklet contains 20 self-adhesive 32c stamps.

2505a — BC62

2514a — BC63

2516a — BC64

1990

$5 booklet contains two panes of 10 25c stamps.

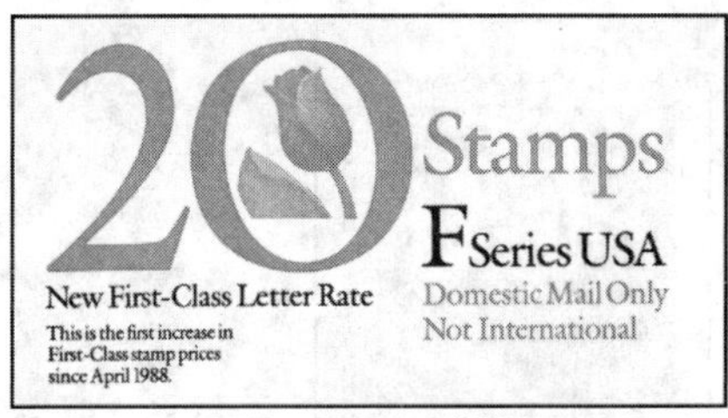

20 Stamps
F Series USA
New First-Class Letter Rate
This is the first increase in First-Class stamp prices since April 1988.
Domestic Mail Only
Not International

2519a, 2520a — BC65

1991

$2.90 booklet contains one pane of 10 F stamps.
$5.80 booklet contains two panes of 10 F stamps.

2527a — BC66

2528a — BC67

2528a — BC67A

1991

$2.90 booklet contains one pane of 10 29c stamps.

2530a — BC68

1991
$3.80 booklet contains two panes of 10 19c stamps.

Self-adhesive • DO NOT WET • © USPS 1991 • Patent Pending
The U.S. Postal Service offers prestamped First-Class envelopes with printed return addresses at reasonable prices including shipping & handling. Convenient quantities of 50 available; several styles & sizes offered.
Ask for an order form at your post office or write to: STAMPED ENVELOPE AGENCY PO BOX 500 WILLIAMSBURG PA 16693-0500

Self-adhesive • DO NOT WET • © USPS 1991 • Patent Pending
The U.S. Postal Service offers prestamped First-Class envelopes with printed return addresses at reasonable prices including shipping & handling. Convenient quantities of 50 available; several styles & sizes offered.
Ask for an order form at your post office or write to: STAMPED ENVELOPE AGENCY PO BOX 500 WILLIAMSBURG PA 16693-0500

2531Ab — BC68A

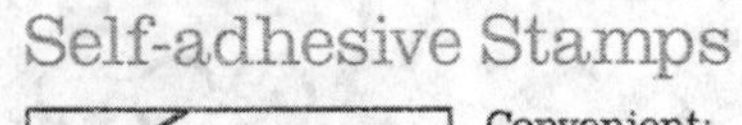

Convenient: No Licking!

Strong Adhesive: Stays on Envelopes!

Easy to Use: No Tearing!

Eighteen Stamps

2531Ab — BC68B

1991
$5.22 fold-it-yourself booklet contains 18 self-adhesive 29c stamps.

2536a — BC69

1991
$5.80 booklet contains two panes of 10 29c stamps.

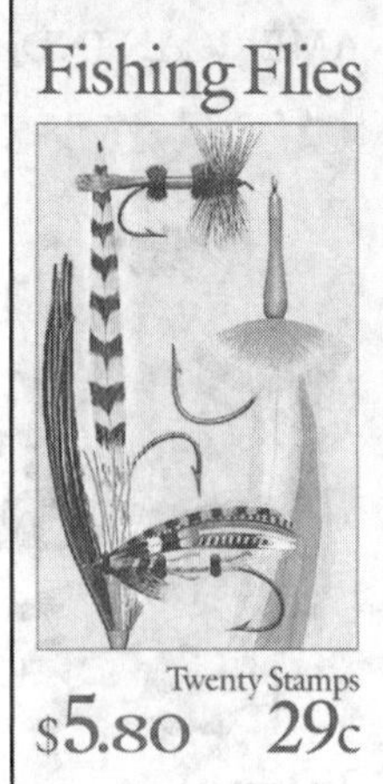

2549a — BC70

2552a — BC71

1991
$5.80 booklet contains four panes of 5 29c stamps.

2566a — BC72

1991
$5.80 booklet contains two panes of ten 29c stamps.

2577a — BC73

1991
$5.80 booklet contains two panes of 10 29c stamps.

2578a — BC74

1991
($5.80) booklet contains two panes of 10 (29c) stamps.

2581b, 2582a-2585a — BC75

1991
($5.80) booklet contains five panes of 4 (29c) stamps.

2593a,
2594a — BC76

1992
$2.90 booklet contains one pane of 10 29c stamps.
$5.80 booklet contains two panes of 10 29c stamps.

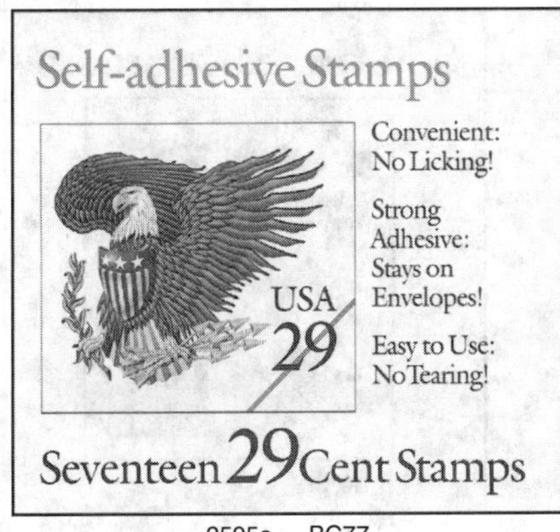

2595a — BC77

1992

$5 fold-it-yourself booklet contains 17 self-adhesive 29c stamps.

Nos. BC77 differs in size and style of type as well as location of UPC labels.

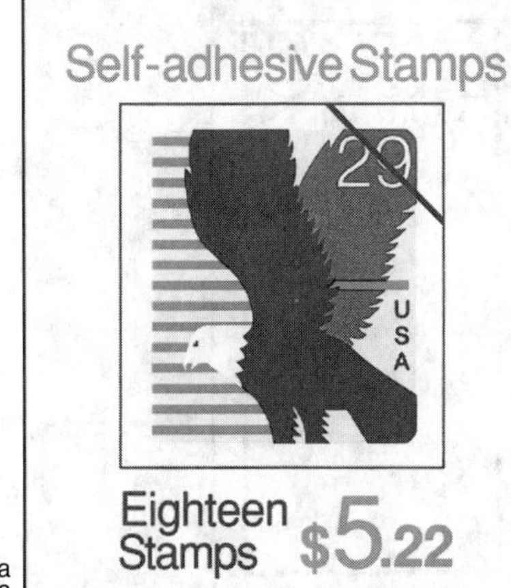

2598a BC78

1994

$5.22 fold-it-yourself booklet contains 18 self-adhesive 29c stamps.

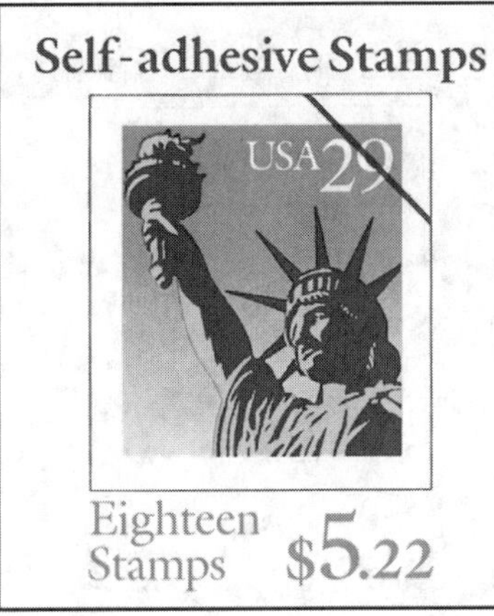

2599a BC79

1994

$5.22 fold-it-yourself booklet contains 18 self-adhesive 29c stamps.

2646a — BC80

2709a — BC83

1992

$5.80 booklet contains four panes of 5 29c stamps.

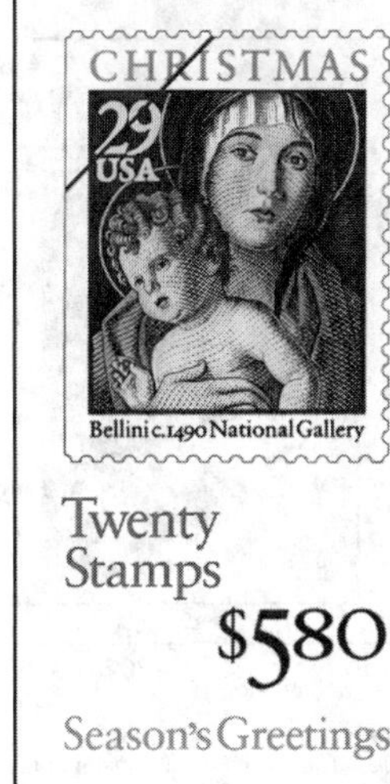

2710a — BC83A

1992

$5.80 booklet contains two panes of 10 29c stamps.

2718a — BC84

1992

$5.80 booklet contains five panes of 4 29c stamps.

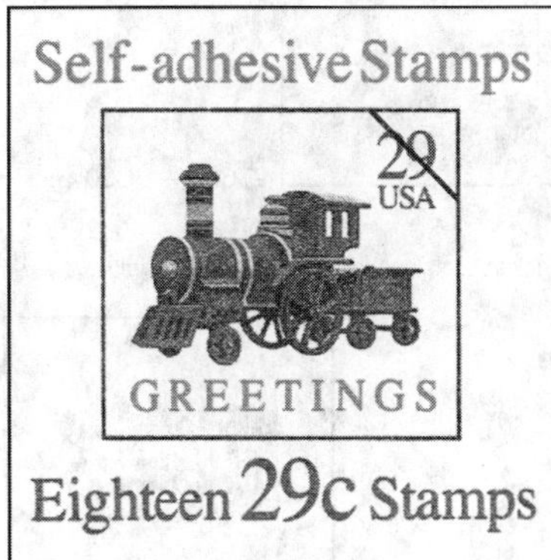

2719a BC85

1992

$5.22 fold-it-yourself booklet contains 18 self-adhesive 29c stamps.

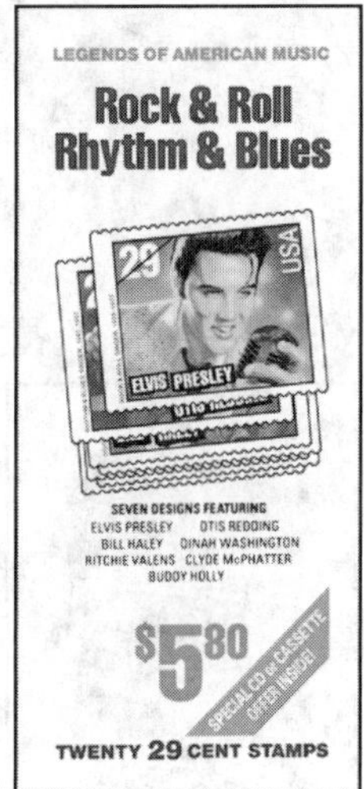

2737a — BC86

1993

$5.80 booklet contains one pane of four 29c stamps and two panes of eight 29c stamps.

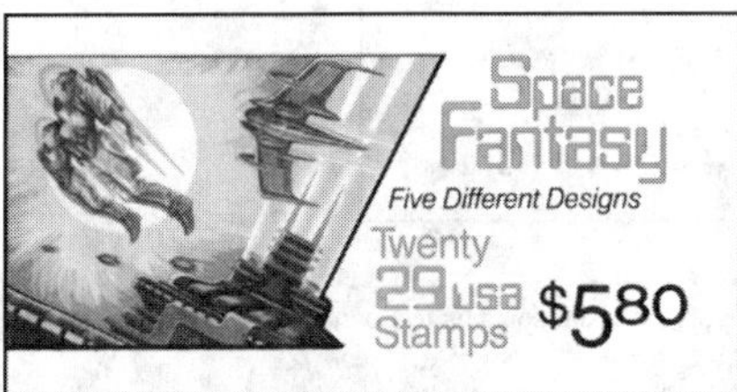

2745a — BC89

1993

$5.80 booklet contains four panes of 5 29c stamps.

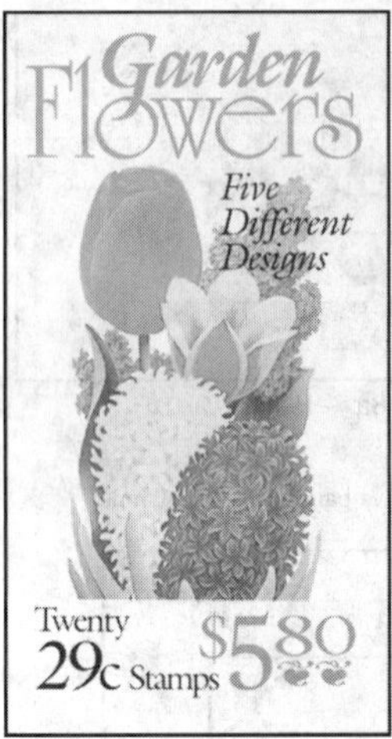

2764a — BC90

1993
$5.80 booklet contains four panes of 5 29c stamps.

2770a — BC91

2778a — BC92

1993
$5.80 booklet contains five panes of 4 29c stamps.

2790a — BC93

1993
$5.80 booklet contains five panes of 4 29c stamps.

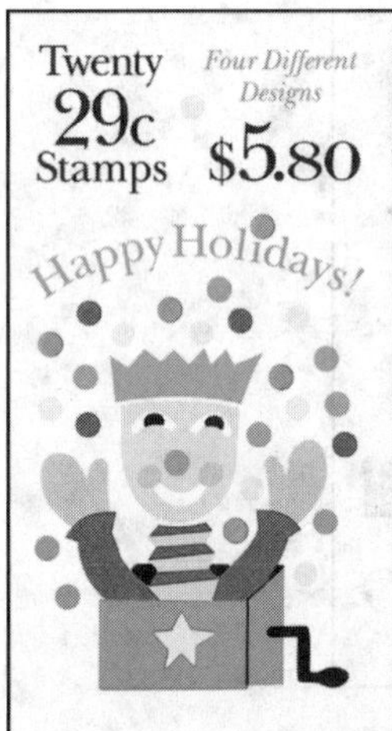

2798a — BC94

1993
$5.80 booklet contains two panes of 10 29c stamps.

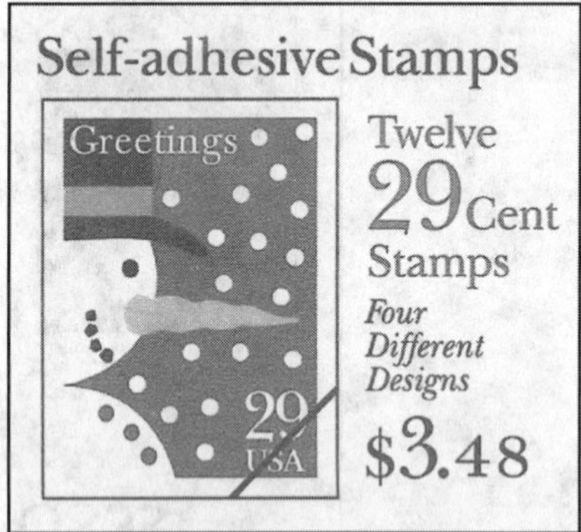

2802a — BC95

1993
$3.48 fold-it-yourself booklet contains 12 self-adhesive 29c stamps.

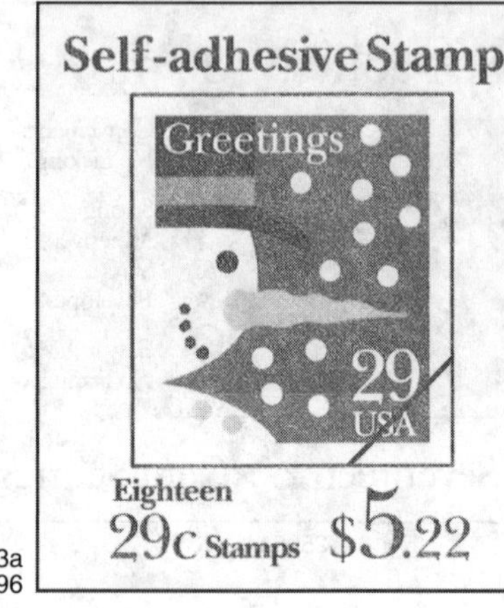

2803a
BC96

1993
$5.22 fold-it-yourself booklet contains 18 self-adhesive 29c stamps.

2806b — BC97

1993
$2.90 booklet contains two panes of 5 29c stamps.

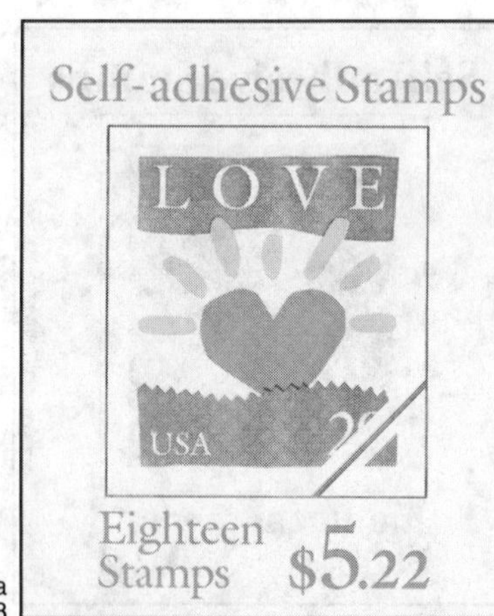

2813a
BC98

1994
$5.22 fold-it-yourself booklet contains 18 self-adhesive 29c stamps.

2814a — BC99

1994
$5.80 booklet contains two panes of 10 29c stamps.

2833a — BC100

1994
$5.80 booklet contains four panes of 5 29c stamps.

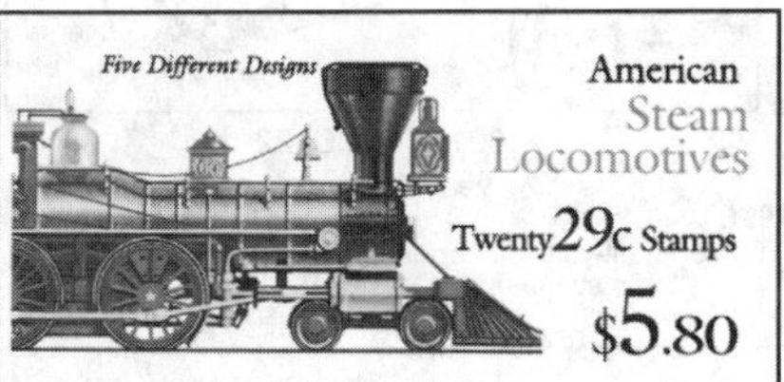

2847a — BC101

1994
$5.80 booklet contains four panes of 5 29c stamps.

2871Ab — BC102

1994
$5.80 booklet contains two panes of 10 29c stamps.

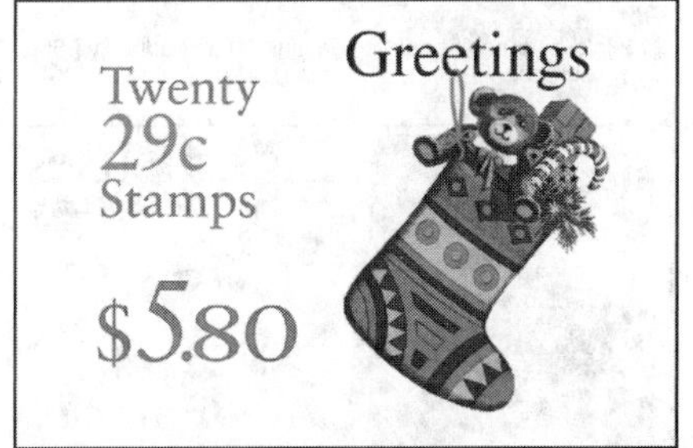

2872a — BC103

1994
$5.80 booklet contains one pane of 20 29c stamps.

2873a — BC104

1994
$3.48 fold-it-yourself booklet contains 12 self-adhesive 29c stamps.

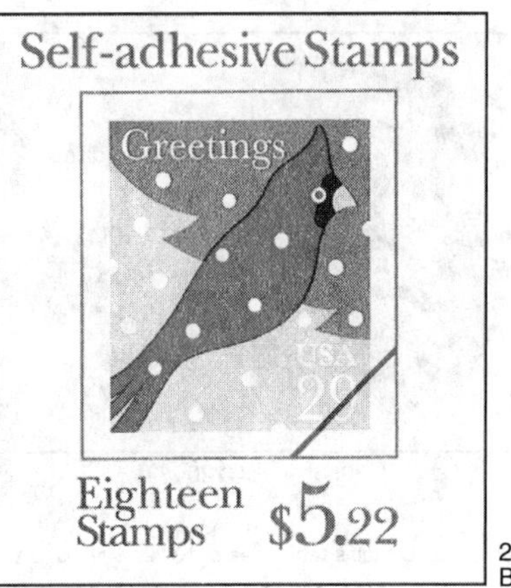

2874a
BC105

1994
$5.22 fold-it-yourself booklet contains 18 self-adhesive 29c stamps.

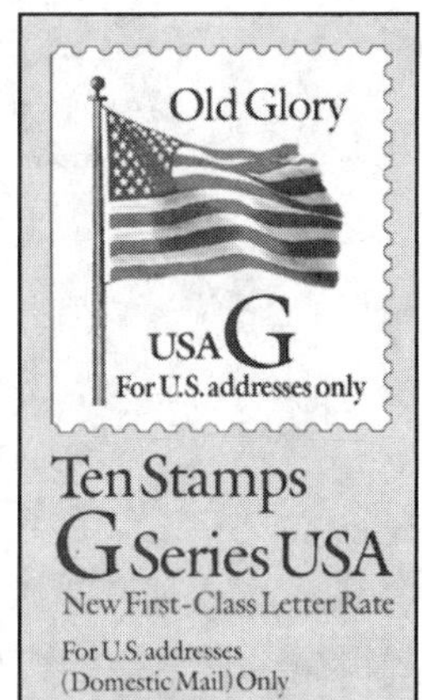

2881a, 2883a, 2884a,
2885a — BC106

1994
($3.20) booklet contains one pane of 10 G stamps.
($6.40) booklet contains two panes of 10 G stamps.

No. BC106 was printed by three different manufacturers in either two- or four-color formats, with G in different colors and with other minor design differences.

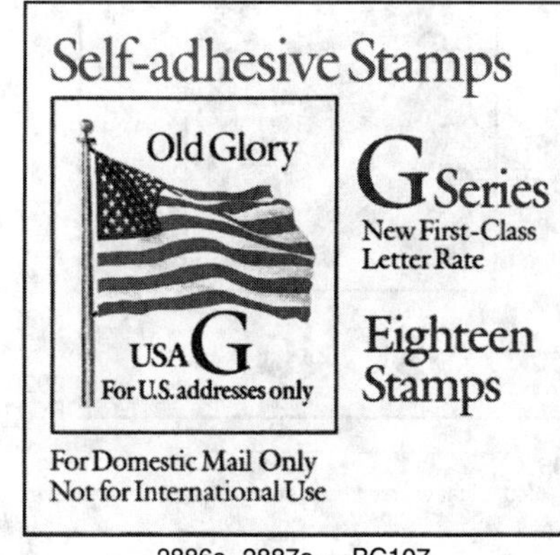

2886a, 2887a — BC107

1994
($5.76) fold-it-yourself booklet contains 18 self-adhesive G stamps.

2916a — BC108

1995
$3.20 booklet contains one pane of 10 32c stamps.
$6.40 booklet contains two panes of 10 32c stamps.

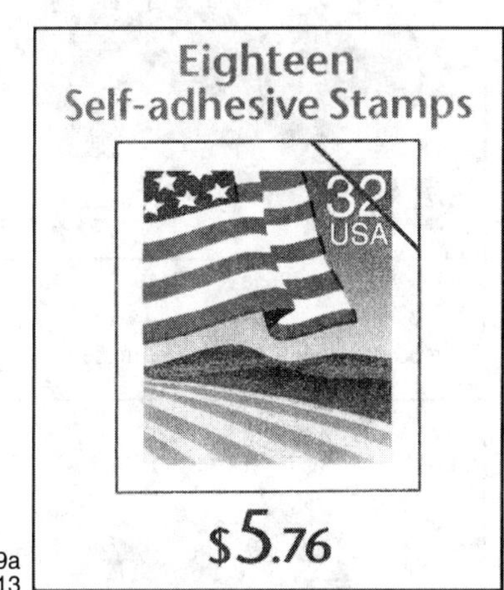

2919a
BC113

1995
$5.76 fold-it-yourself booklet contains 18 self-adhesive 32c stamps.

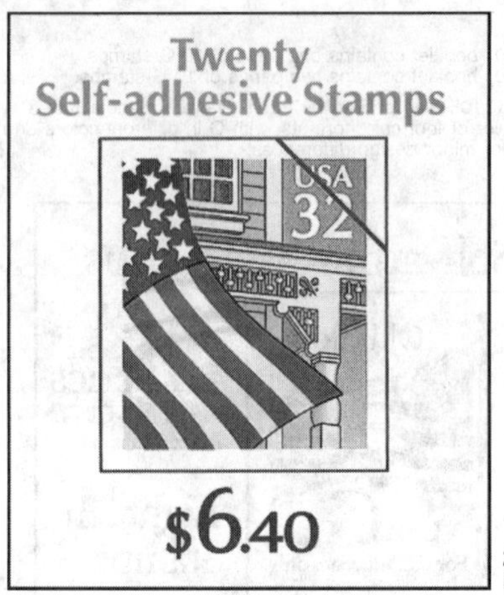

2920a
BC114

1995
$6.40 fold-it-yourself booklet contains 20 self-adhesive 32c stamps.

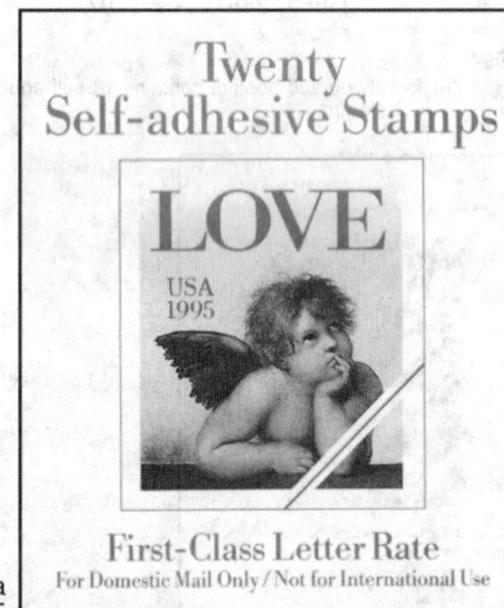

2949a
BC115

1995
($6.40) fold-it-yourself booklet contains 20 self-adhesive non-denominated 32c stamps.

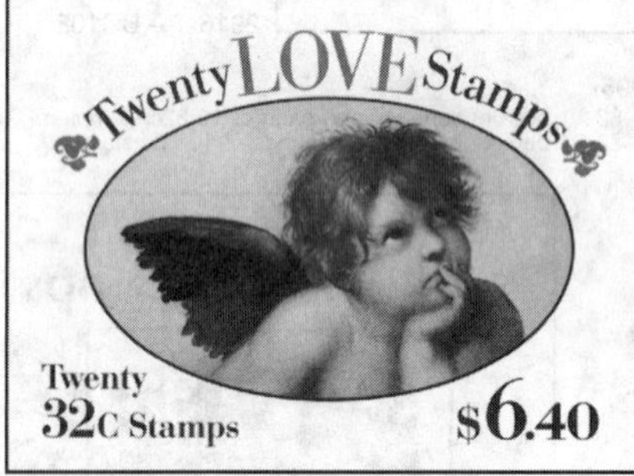

2959a — BC116

1995
$6.40 booklet contains two panes of 10 32c stamps.

2960a — BC117

1995
$11 fold-it-yourself booklet contains 20 self-adhesive 55c stamps.

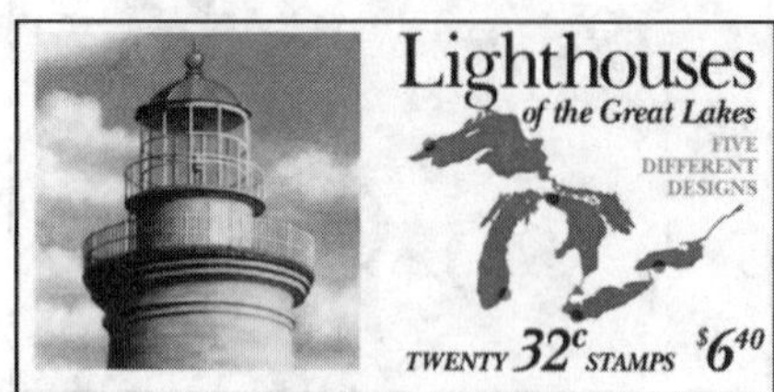

2973a — BC118

1995
$6.40 booklet contains four panes of 5 32c stamps.

2997a — BC119

1995
$6.40 booklet contains four panes of 5 32c stamps

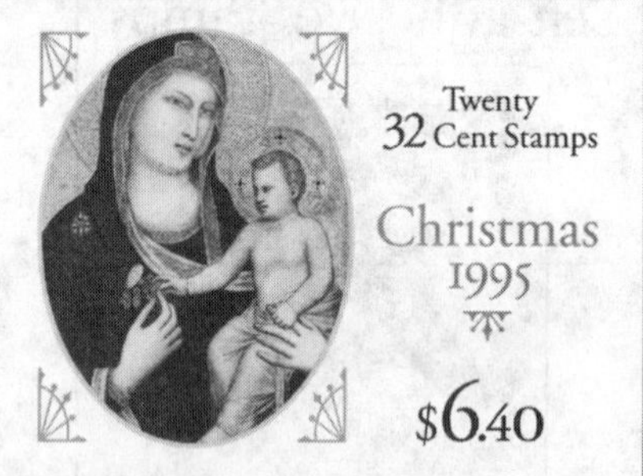

3003b — BC120

1995
$6.40 booklet contains two panes of 10 32c stamps

3007b-3007c
BC121

1995
$6.40 booklet contains two panes of 10 32c stamps

3011a — BC122

1995
$6.40 fold-it-yourself booklet contains 20 self-adhesive 32c stamps

3012a
BC123

1995
$6.40 fold-it-yourself booklet contains 20 self-adhesive 32c stamps

3013a
BC124

1995
$5.76 fold-it-yourself booklet contains 18 self-adhesive 32c stamps

3029a — BC125

1996
$6.40 booklet contains four panes of 5 32c stamps

Front

Now you can order stamps by phone:
1•800•STAMP•24
(1•800•782•6724)
Call toll free:
24 hours
per day,
7 days
per week

Fifteen Stamps (15)
15-32¢ Love Cherubs PSA
Item No. 3627
Value $4.80

Back — BC126

1996
$4.80 booklet contains 15 32c stamps
$9.60 booklet contains 30 2c stamps

A number of different stamps have been sold in BC126. The text on the front and back changes to describe the contents of the booklet. The enclosed stamps are affixed to the cover with a spot of glue.

3071a — BC127

1996
$6.40 fold-it-yourself booklet contains 20 self-adhesive 32c stamps

3048a-3048c
BC128

3049b — BC129

1996
$2.00 fold-it-yourself booklet contains 10 self-adhesive 20c stamps
$2.00 booklet contains 10 self-adhesive 20c stamps

1996
$4.80 booklet contains 15 self-adhesive 32c stamps

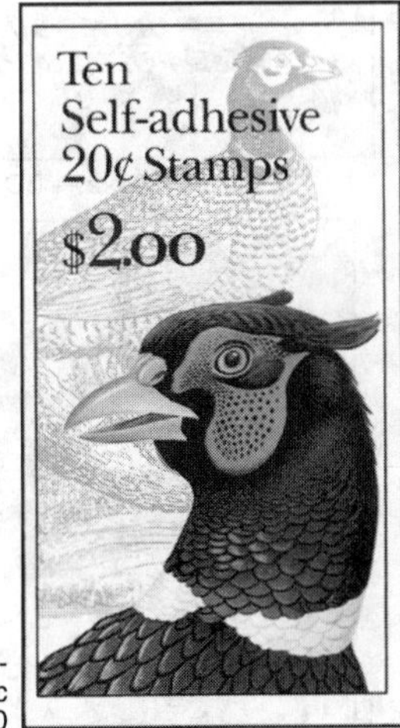

3050a, 3051Ab-
3051Ac
BC130

1998
$2.00 fold-it-yourself booklet contains 10 self-adhesive 20c stamps
$2.00 booklet contains 10 self-adhesive 20c stamps

Coral Pink Rose
Twenty Self-adhesive
33¢ Stamps
$6.60

3052a-3052E — BC131

1999
$4.95 booklet contains 15 self-adhesive 33c stamps + label
$6.60 fold-it-yourself booklet contains 20 self-adhesive 33c stamps + label

Twenty
Self-adhesive Stamps

USA 32
1846
IOWA

$6.40

UNITED STATES
POSTAL SERVICE™
We Deliver For You.

3089a — BC133

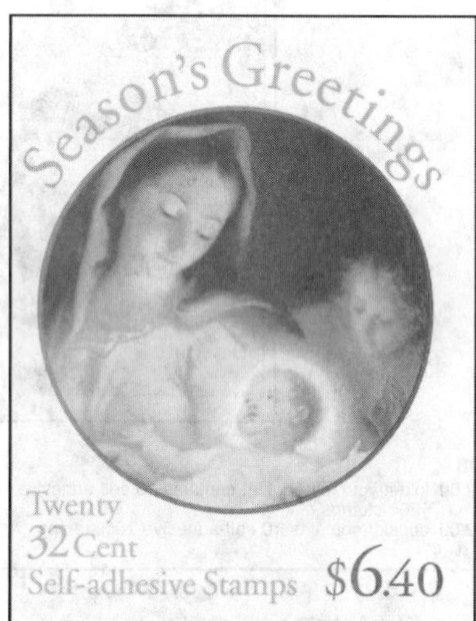

Season's Greetings
Twenty
32 Cent
Self-adhesive Stamps
$6.40

3112a — BC134

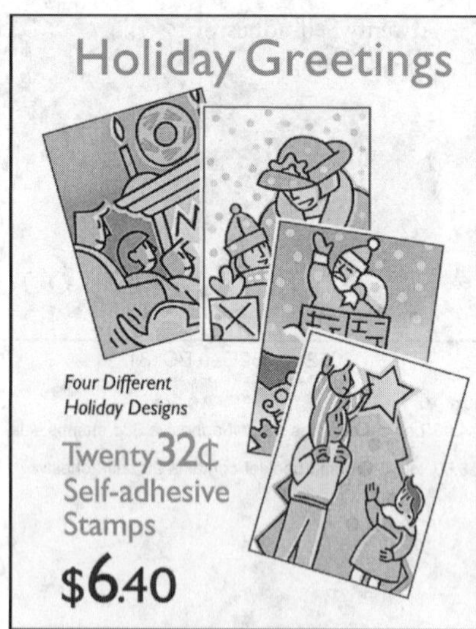

3116a — BC135

1996
$6.40 fold-it-yourself booklet contains 20 self-adhesive 32c stamps

3117a
BC136

1996
$5.76 fold-it-yourself booklet contains 18 self-adhesive 32c stamps

3123a — BC137

1997
$6.40 fold-it-yourself booklet contains 20 self-adhesive 32c stamps
$11 fold-it-yourself booklet contains 20 self-adhesive 55c stamps

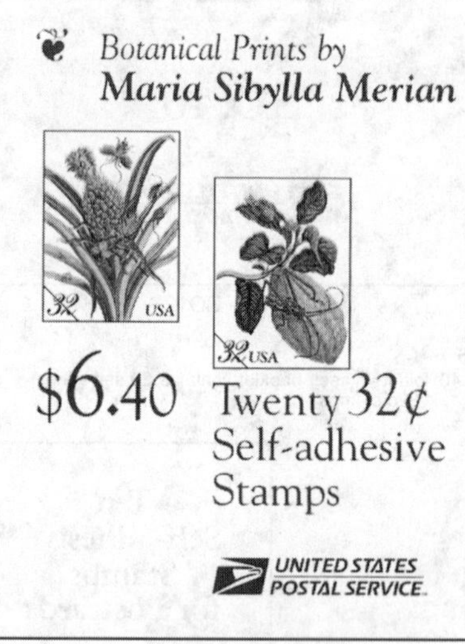

3127a, 3128b, 3129b — BC138

1997
$4.80 booklet contains 15 32c stamps
$6.40 fold-it-yourself booklet contains 20 32c stamps

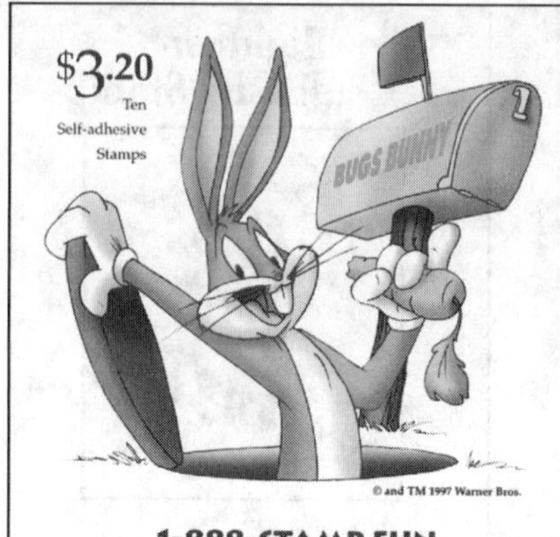

© and TM 1997 Warner Bros.

1-888-STAMP FUN

If you like *this* stamp, the Postal Service has about a million more of them. Call the number – get free stuff about other stamps you can save and trade. And guess what? The phone call is free!

3137-3138 — BC139

1997
$3.20 booklet contains 10 32c self-adhesive stamps

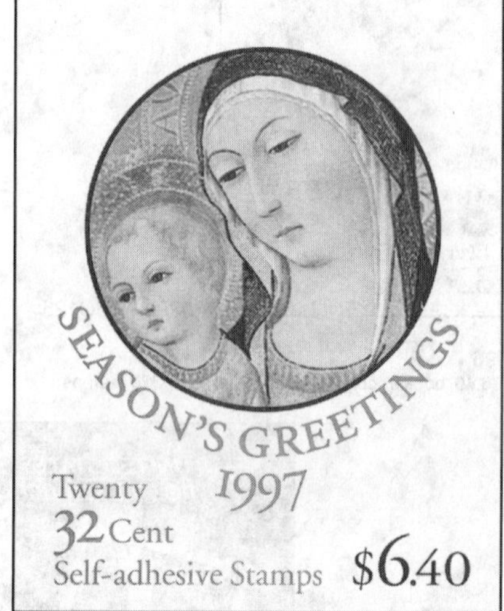

3176a — BC140

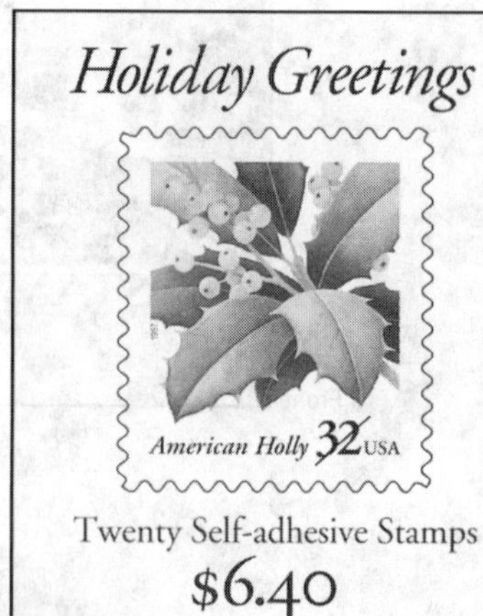

Holiday Greetings
American Holly 32 USA
Twenty Self-adhesive Stamps
$6.40

3177a
BC141

1997
$6.40 fold-it-yourself booklet contains 20 self-adhesive 32c stamps

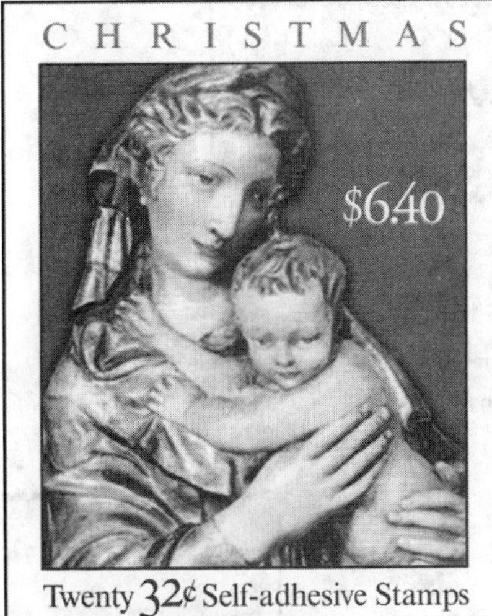

3244a — BC142

3248a-3248c, 3252b — BC143

1998
$4.80 booklet contains 15 self-adhesive 32c stamps
$6.40 fold-it-yourself booklet contains 20 self-adhesive 32c stamps

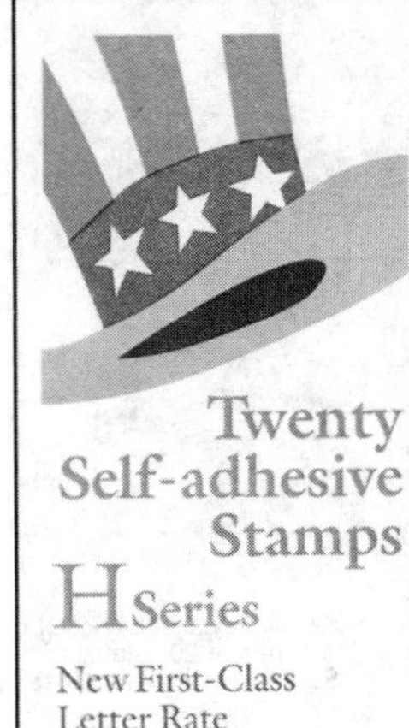

3267a, 3268a-3268b, 3269a — BC144

1998
($6.60) booklet contains 20 self-adhesive (33c) stamps
($3.30) fold-it-yourself booklet contains 10 self-adhesive (33c) stamps
($6.60) fold-it-yourself booklet contains 20 self-adhesive (33c) stamps
($5.94) fold-it-yourself booklet contains 18 self-adhesive (33c) stamps

3274a BC145

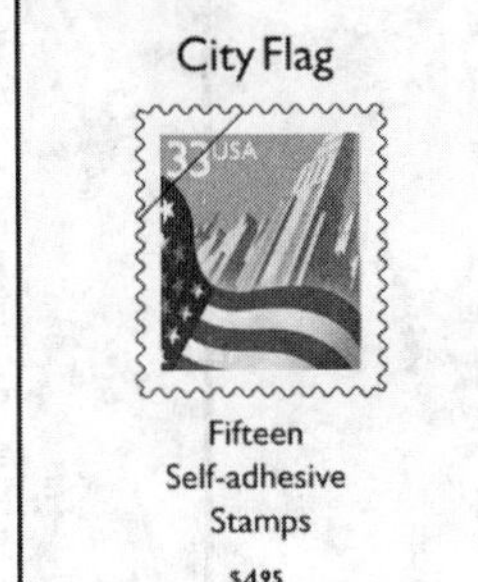

3278a-3278e, 3279a — BC146

1999
$3.30 Fold-it-yourself booklet contains 10 self-adhesive 33c stamps
$4.95 Booklet contains 15 self-adhesive 33c stamps
$6.60 Fold-it-yourself booklet contains 20 self-adhesive 33c stamps
$6.60 Booklet contains 20 self-adhesive 33c stamps

3283a — BC147

1999
$5.94 fold-it-yourself booklet contains 18 self-adhesive 33c stamps

3297a BC148

1999
$6.60 fold-it-yourself booklet contains 20 self-adhesive 33c stamps + label
$4.95 booklet contains 15 self-adhesive 33c stamps + label

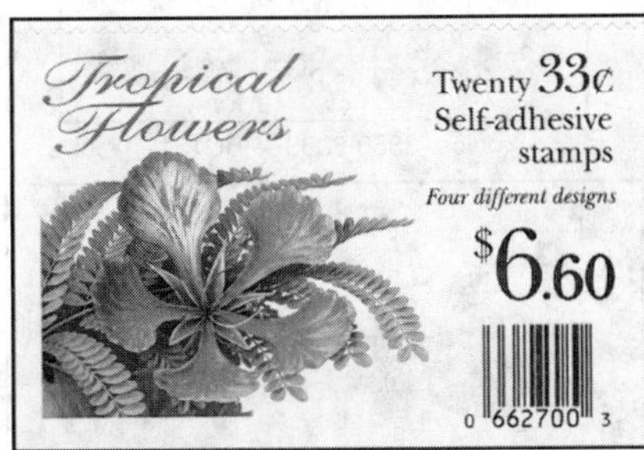

3313b — BC149

1999
$6.60 fold-it-yourself booklet contains 20 self-adhesive 33c stamps

No. 3355 — BC150

Nos. 3360-3363 — BC151

Nos. 3364-3367 — BC152

1999

$6.60 fold-it-yourself booklets contains 20 self-adhesive 33c stamps

$4.95 fold-it-yourself booklet contains 15 self-adhesive 33c stamps

3377a — BC153

2000

$9.80 booklet contains 2 panes of one 22c, 33c, 55c, 60c and $3.20 stamps and 6 leaves of text.

3450a — BC154

2000

$6.12 fold-it-yourself booklet contains 18 self-adhesive (34c) stamps

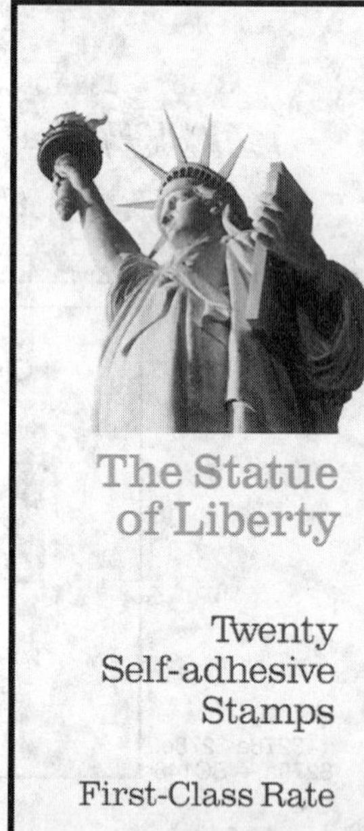

3451a — BC155

2000

$6.80 fold-it-yourself booklet contains 20 self-adhesive (34c) stamps

3451b, 3451c — BC156

2000

$6.80 booklet contains 20 self-adhesive (34c) stamps

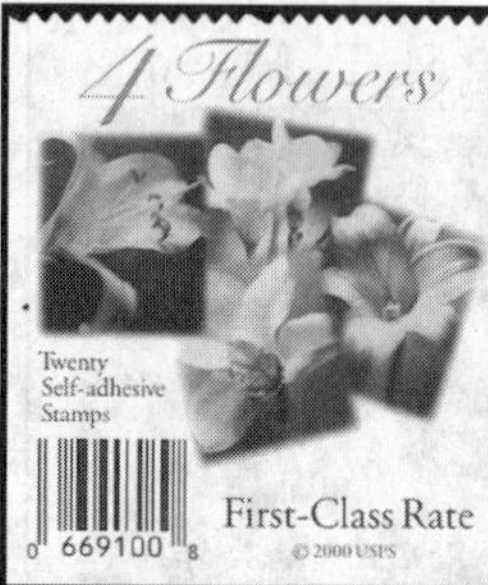

3457a — BC157

2000

$6.80 fold-it-yourself booklet contains 20 self-adhesive (34c) stamps

3457b, 3457c, 3457d — BC158

2000

$6.80 booklet contains 20 self-adhesive (34c) stamps

3482a, 3483a, 3483b — BC159

2001

$2 fold-it-yourself booklet contains 10 self-adhesive 20c stamps

$2 booklet contains 10 self-adhesive 20c stamps

3484b, 3484c, 3484d, 3484Ae, 3484Af, 3484Ag, 3484Ah, 3484Ai, 3484Aj — BC159A

2001

$2.10 fold-it-yourself booklet contains 10 self-adhesive 21c stamps

$2.10 booklet contains 10 self-adhesive 21c stamps

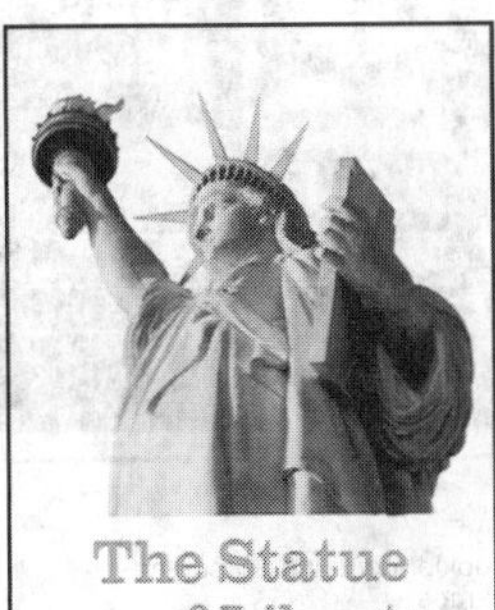

3485a, 3485b — BC160

2001

$3.40 fold-it-yourself booklet contains 10 self-adhesive 34c stamps

$6.80 fold-it-yourself booklet contains 20 self-adhesive 34c stamps

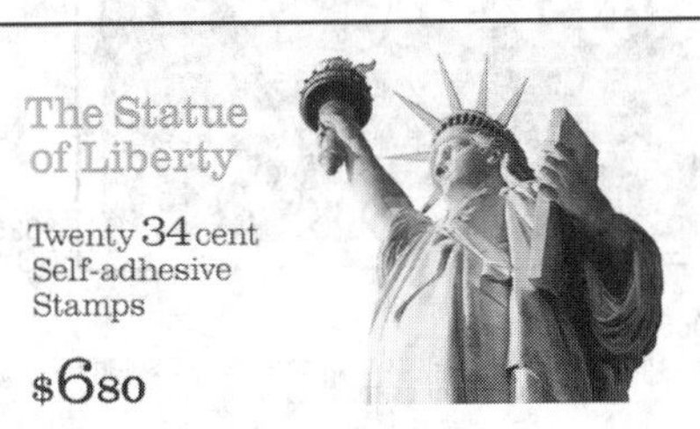

3485c, 3485d — BC160A

2001

$6.80 booklet contains 20 self-adhesive 34c stamps

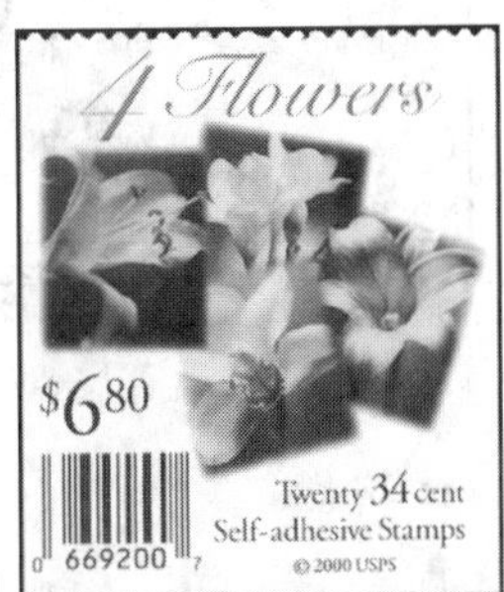

3490a — BC161

2001

$6.80 fold-it-yourself booklet contains 20 self-adhesive 34c stamps

3490b, 3490c, 3490d — BC162

2001

$6.80 booklet contains 20 self-adhesive 34c stamps

3492b — BC163

2001

$6.80 fold-it-yourself booklet contains 20 self-adhesive 34c stamps

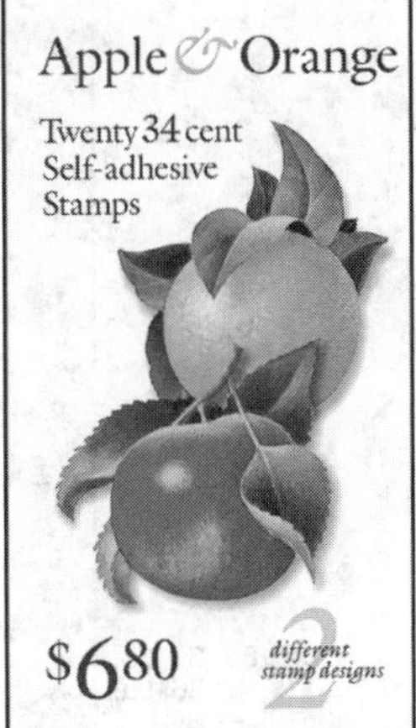

3494b, 3494c, 3494d — BC163A

2001

$6.80 booklet contains 20 self-adhesive 34c stamps

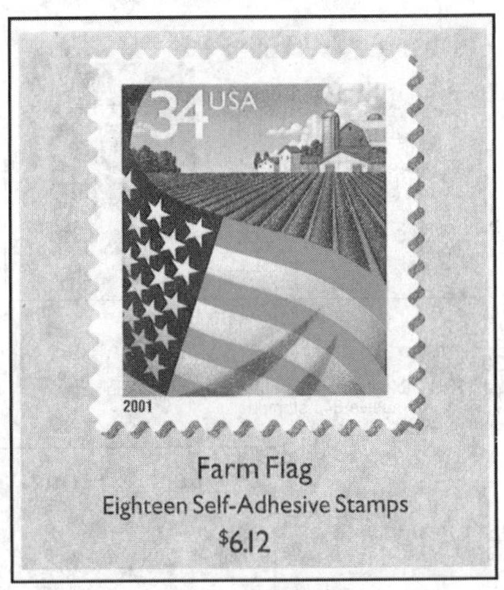

3495a — BC163B

2001

$6.12 booklet contains 18 self-adhesive 34c stamps

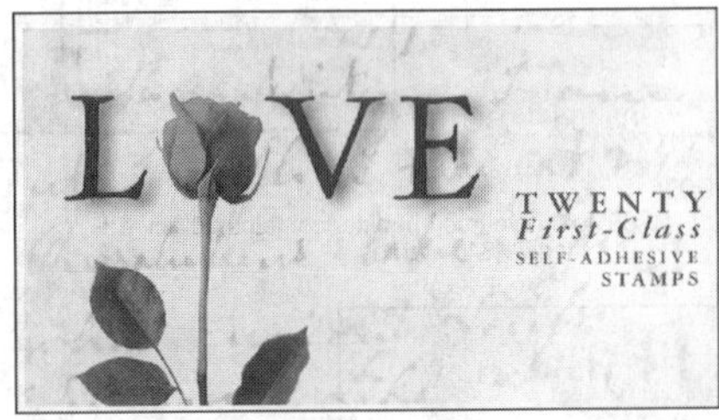

3496a — BC164

2001

$6.80 fold-it-yourself booklet contains 20 self-adhesive (34c) stamps

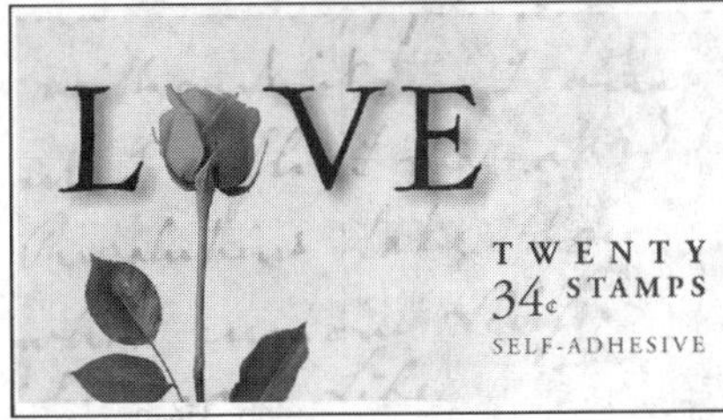

3497a — BC165

2001

$6.80 fold-it-yourself booklet contains 20 self-adhesive 34c stamps

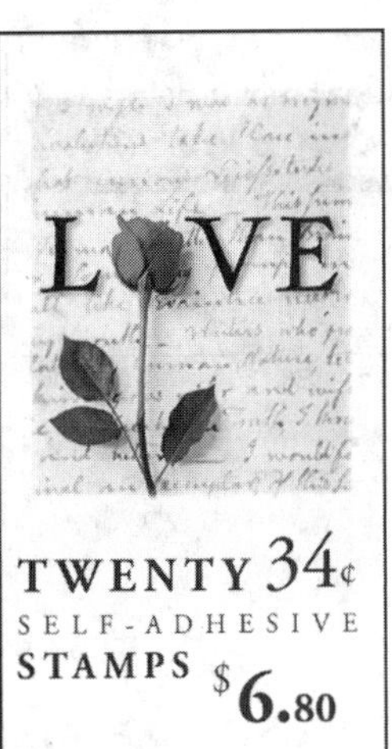

3498a, 3498b — BC166

2001

$6.80 booklet contains 20 self-adhesive 34c stamps

3536a — BC167

2001
$6.80 fold-it-yourself booklet contains 20 self-adhesive 34c stamps

3540d — BC168

2001
$6.80 fold-it-yourself booklet contains 20 self-adhesive 34c stamps

3544b, 3544c, 3544d — BC169

2001
$6.80 booklet contains 20 self-adhesive 34c stamps

3549a — BC170

2001
$6.80 booklet contains 20 self-adhesive 34c stamps

3549Bc, 3549Bd — BC171

2002
$6.80 booklet contains 20 self-adhesive 34c stamps

3549Be — BC172

2002
$6.80 fold-it-yourself booklet contains 20 self-adhesive 34c stamps

3618a, 3618b, 3619a, 3619b — BC173

2002
$2.30 booklet contains 10 self-adhesive 23c stamps

3623a — BC174

2002
$7.40 fold-it-yourself booklet contains 20 self-adhesive (37c) stamps

3624a, 3624b — BC175

2002
$7.40 booklet contains 20 self-adhesive (37c) stamps

3624c — BC176

2002
$7.40 fold-it-yourself booklet contains 20 self-adhesive (37c) stamps

3625a BC177

2002
$6.66 fold-it-yourself booklet contains 18 self-adhesive (37c) stamps

3629b, 3629c, 3629d — BC178

2002
$7.40 booklet contains 20 self-adhesive (37c) stamps

3629e — BC179

2002
$7.40 fold-it-yourself booklet contains 20 self-adhesive (37c) stamps

3634a — BC180

2002
$3.70 booklet contains 10 self-adhesive 37c stamps

3635a — BC181

2002
$7.40 fold-it-yourself booklet contains 20 self-adhesive 37c stamps

3636c — BC183

2002
$7.40 fold-it-yourself booklet contains 20 self-adhesive 37c stamps

3636a, 3636b — BC182

2002
$7.40 fold-it-yourself booklet contains 20 self-adhesive 37c stamps

3637a—BC184

2003
$6.66 fold-it-yourself booklet contains 18 self-adhesive 37c stamps

3645b, 3645c, 3645d — BC185

2002
$7.40 booklet contains 20 self-adhesive 37c stamps

3645e — BC186

2002
$7.40 fold-it-yourself booklet contains 20 self-adhesive 37c stamps

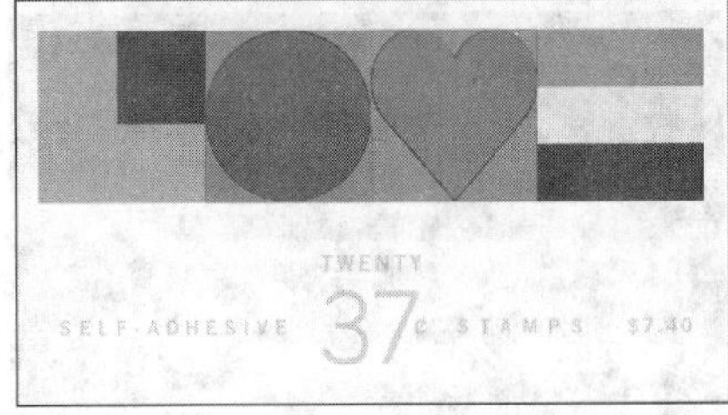

3657a — BC187

2002
$7.40 fold-it-yourself booklet contains 20 self-adhesive 37c stamps

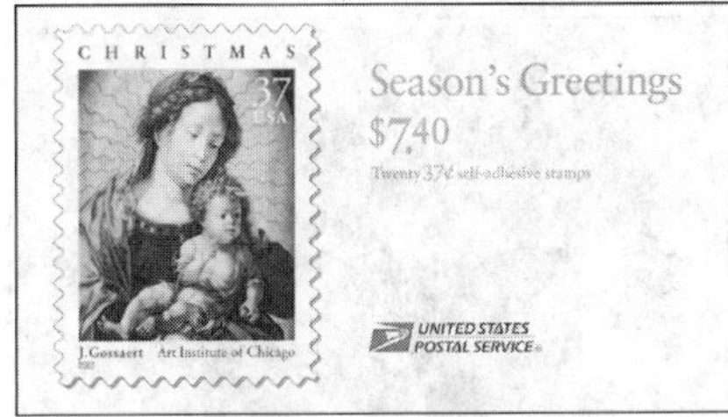

3675a — BC188

2002
$7.40 fold-it-yourself booklet contains 20 self-adhesive 37c stamps

3687b — BC189

2002
$7.40 booklet contains 20 self-adhesive 37c stamps

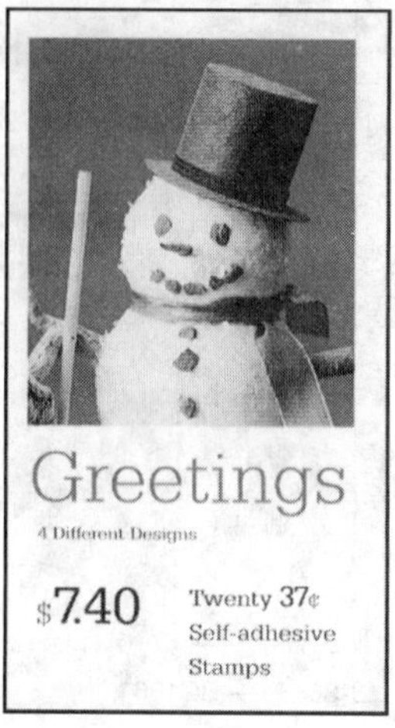

3691b, 3691c, 3691d — BC190

2002

$7.40 booklet contains 20 self-adhesive 37c stamps

3780b — BC191

2003

$7.40 booklet contains 20 self-adhesive stamps

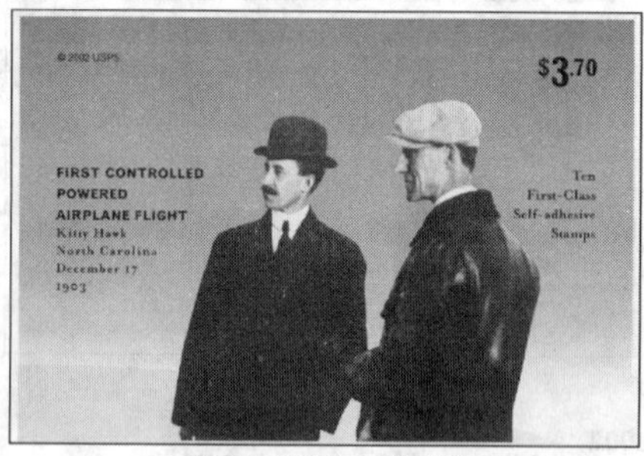

3783a, 3783b — BC192

2003

$3.70 fold-it-yourself booklet contains 10 self-adhesive 37c stamps

---

BOOKLET PANES

Values for both unused and used booklet panes are for complete panes with selvage, and for panes of six unless otherwise stated. Panes in booklets are Never Hinged. Values for stapled booklets are for those with creasing along the lines of the staples. Values for booklets which were glued shut are for opened booklets without significant damage to the cover.

See other notes in the introduction to this section.

Washington — A88

Wmk. 191 Horizontally or Vertically

1900-03 *Perf. 12*

279Be A88 2c **red**, *Apr. 18* 425. *1,250.*
light red 425.
orange red, *1902* 425.
Never hinged 800.
With plate number (D) 1,250. *3,000.*
Never hinged 1,900.

180- and 360-Subject Plates. All plate positions exist, except J, K, and L, due to the horizontal guide line being placed too far below stamps to appear on the upper panes.

Booklets

BK1 BC1 25c **black,** *cream* —
BK2 BC1 25c **black,** *buff* *6,000.*
BK3 BC1 49c **green,** *cream* —
BK4 BC1 49c **black,** *buff* —
BK5 BC1 97c **red,** *cream* —
BK6 BC1 97c **black,** *gray* —
BK7 BC2B 25c **black,** *cream* (3) *7,000.*
BK8 BC2B 49c **black,** *buff* (3) —
BK9 BC2B 97c **black,** *gray* (3) *15,000.*

Nos. BK1-BK6 and one type each of Nos. BK7-BK9 exist with specimen overprints handstamped on cover and individual stamps.

All covers of BK7-BK9 exist with "Philippines" overprint in 50mm or 48mm.

Franklin — A115

Washington — A116

1903-07 **Wmk. 191 Vertically**

300b A115 1c **blue green,** *Mar. 6, 1907* 600. *12,500.*
Never hinged 1,100.
With plate number (D) 1,300.
Never hinged *2,250.*
With plate number 3472 over left stamp (D) *4,000.*

180-Subject Plates only. All plate positions exist.

Booklet

BK10 BC2A 25c **black,** *green* (6) *6,500.*

301c A116 2c **carmine,** *Jan. 24, 1903* 500. *2,250.*
Never hinged 900.
With plate number (D) 1,500. *3,000.*

180-Subject Plates only. All plate positions exist.

Booklets

BK11 BC2B 25c **black,** *cream* *3,000.*
BK12 BC2B 49c **black,** *buff* *4,000.*
BK13 BC2B 97c **black,** *gray* —

Washington — A129

1903 **Wmk. 191 Vertically**

319g A129 2c **carmine,** type I, *Dec. 3, 1903* 125.00 *550.00*
Never hinged 240.00
With plate number (D) 275.00 *850.00*
Never hinged 475.00
Wmk. horizontal *700.00*
Never hinged *1,150.*
With Plate number (D) *1,250.*
319n A129 2c **carmine rose** (I) 225.00 *650.00*
Never hinged 400.00
With plate number (D) 400.00 *950.00*
Never hinged 650.00
319p A129 2c **scarlet** (I) 185.00 *575.00*
Never hinged 350.00
With plate number (D) 350.00 *900.00*
Never hinged 575.00
319h A129 2c **carmine,** type II, *1907* 500.00
Never hinged 800.00
With plate number (D) 850.00
Never hinged 1,350.
319q A129 2c **lake** (II) 300.00 *750.00*
Never hinged 550.00
With plate number (D) 550.00
Never hinged 850.00

180-Subject Plates only. All plate positions exist.

Booklet

BK14 BC2B 25c **black,** *cream* (11) 1,000.
BK15 BC2A 49c **black,** *buff* (11) *1,250.*
BK16 BC2A 49c **black,** *pink* *2,500.*
BK17 BC2B 97c **black,** *gray* (11) *2,750.*

Booklet Covers

When more than one combination of covers exists, the number of possible booklets is noted in parenthesis after the booklet listing.

Franklin — A138

Washington — A139

1908 **Wmk. 191 Vertically**

331a A138 1c **green,** *Dec. 1908* 160.00 *450.00*
Never hinged 250.00
With plate number (D) 240.00
Never hinged 375.00

180- and 360-Subject Plates. All plate positions exist.

No. 331 exists in horizontal pair, imperforate between, a variety resulting from booklet experiments. Not regularly issued. Value, unused $2,500.

Booklets

BK18 BC2A 25c **black,** *green* (3) *2,000.*
BK19 BC3 25c **black,** *green* *2,250.*

332a A139 2c **carmine,** *Nov. 16, 1908* 135.00 *400.00*
Never hinged 220.00
With plate number (D) 175.00
Never hinged 275.00

180- and 360-Subject Plates. All plate positions exist.

Booklets

BK20 BC2B 25c **black,** *cream* (2) *1,250.*
BK21 BC2A 49c **black,** *buff* (2) *2,750.*
BK22 BC2A 49c **black,** *pink* *2,750.*
BK23 BC2B 97c **black,** *gray* (3) *3,000.*
BK24 BC3 25c **black,** *cream* *1,250.*
BK25 BC3 49c **black,** *pink* —
BK26 BC3 97c **black,** *gray* *3,000.*

1910 **Wmk. 190 Vertically** *Perf. 12*

374a A138 1c **green,** *Oct. 7, 1910* 175.00 *200.00*
Never hinged 300.00
With plate number (D) 225.00
Never hinged 360.00

360-Subject Plates only. All plate positions exist.

Booklet

BK27 BC3 25c **black,** *green* (2) *2,000.*

375a A139 2c **carmine,** *Nov. 30, 1910* 100.00 *175.00*
Never hinged 175.00
With plate number (D) 135.00
Never hinged 225.00

360-Subject Plates only. All plate positions exist.

Booklets

BK28 BC3 25c **black,** *cream* (2) *850.00*
BK29 BC3 49c **black,** *pink* (2) *2,500.*
BK30 BC3 97c **black,** *gray* (2) *3,000.*

Washington — A140

1912 **Wmk. 190 Vertically**

405b A140 1c **green,** *Feb. 8, 1912* 60.00 *75.00*
Never hinged 100.00
With plate number (D) 75.00
Never hinged 125.00

360-Subject Plates only. All plate positions exist.

Ordinary Booklets

BK31 BC3 25c **black,** *green* (2) *1,000.*
BK32 BC4A 25c **green,** *green* (3) *1,250.*
BK33 BC4A 97c **green,** *lavender* *1,750.*

Combination Booklet

BK34 BC4B 73c **red,** 4 #405b + 4 #406a —

406a A140 2c **carmine,** *Feb. 8, 1912* 60.00 *90.00*
Never hinged 100.00
With plate number (D) 77.50
Never hinged 130.00

360-Subject Plates only. All plate positions exist.

Ordinary Booklets

BK35 BC3 25c **black,** *cream* (2) *825.00*
BK36 BC3 49c **black,** *pink* (2) *1,500.*
BK37 BC3 97c **black,** *gray* (2) 2,000.
BK38 BC5A 25c **red,** *buff* (3) *1,000.*
BK39 BC5A 49c **red,** *pink* (3) 1,750.
BK40 BC5A 97c **red,** *blue,* (3) 2,250.

Combination Booklet

See No. BK34.

1914 **Wmk. 190 Vertically** ***Perf. 10***

424d A140 1c **green** 5.25 *7.50*
Never hinged 8.50
Double transfer, Plate 6363 — —
With plate number (D) 14.00
Never hinged 22.50
Cracked plate —
e. As "d," imperf. *1,600.*
With plate number (D) —

360-Subject Plates only. All plate positions exist.
All known examples of No. 424e are without gum.

Ordinary Booklets

BK41 BC4A 25c **green,** *green* (3) 300.00
BK42 BC4A 97c **green,** *lavender* (2) 135.00

Combination Booklet

BK43 BC4B 73c **red,** 4 #424d + 4 #425e (3) 300.00

425e A140 2c **carmine,** *Jan. 6, 1914* 17.50 *25.00*
Never hinged 28.00
With plate number (D) 42.50
Never hinged 67.50

360-Subject Plates only. All plate positions exist.

Ordinary Booklets

BK44 BC5A 25c **red,** *buff* (3) 500.00
BK45 BC5A 49c **red,** *pink* (3) 1,000.
BK46 BC5A 97c **red,** *blue* (3) 1,250.

Combination Booklet

See No. BK43.

1916 **Unwmk.** ***Perf. 10***

462a A140 1c **green,** *Oct. 15, 1916* 9.50 *12.50*
Never hinged 15.00
Cracked plate at right 200.00 —
Never hinged 310.00
Cracked plate at left 200.00
Never hinged 310.00
With plate number (D) 25.00
Never hinged 37.50

360-Subject Plates only. All plate positions exist.

Ordinary Booklets

BK47 BC4A 25c **green,** *green* 650.00
BK48 BC4A 97c **green,** *lavender* 500.00

Combination Booklets

BK49 BC4B 73c **red,** 4 #462a + 4 #463a (2) 900.00

463a A140 2c **carmine,** *Oct. 8, 1916* 95.00 *110.00*
Never hinged 165.00
With plate number (D) 125.00
Never hinged 200.00

360-Subject Plates only. All plate positions exist.

Ordinary Booklets

BK50 BC5A 25c **red,** *buff* *650.00*
BK51 BC5A 49c **red,** *pink* *1,200.*
BK52 BC5A 97c **red,** *blue* *2,250.*

Combination Booklets

See No. BK49.

1917-18 **Unwmk.** ***Perf. 11***

498e A140 1c **green,** *Apr. 6, 1917* 2.50 *2.00*
Never hinged 4.00
Double transfer — —
With plate number (D) 6.00 *2.00*
Never hinged 9.00

360-Subject Plates only. All plate positions exist.

Ordinary Booklets

BK53 BC4A 25c **green,** *green* (2) 300.00
BK54 BC4A 97c **green,** *lavender* (4) 85.00
BK55 BC6A 25c **green,** *green* (5) 120.00

Combination Booklets

BK56 BC4B 73c **red,** 4 #498e + 4 #499e (4) 80.00
BK57 BC4B 73c **red,** 4 #498e + 4 #554c (3) 100.00

499e A140 2c **rose,** type I, *Mar. 31, 1917* 4.00 *2.50*
Never hinged 6.50
With plate number (D) 7.00 *2.25*
Never hinged 10.00

360-Subject Plates only. All plate positions exist.

Ordinary Booklets

BK58 BC5A 25c **red,** *buff* (5) 250.00
BK59 BC5A 49c **red,** *pink* (4) 400.00
BK60 BC5A 97c **red,** *blue* (3) 750.00
BK61 BC6C 97c **red,** *blue* (2) 1,250.

Combination Booklets

See No. BK56.

501b A140 3c **violet,** type I, *Oct. 17, 1917* 75.00 *60.00*
Never hinged 120.00
With plate number (D) 105.00
Never hinged 160.00

360-Subject Plates only. All plate positions exist.

Booklet

BK62 BC6B 37c **violet,** *sage* 550.00

502b A140 3c **violet,** type II, *Mar. 1918* 60.00 *55.00*
Never hinged 95.00
With plate number (D) 77.50
Never hinged 120.00

360-Subject Plates only. All plate positions exist.

Booklet

BK63 BC6B 37c **violet,** *sage* 235.00

Washington — A140

A.E.F. Panes of 30

1917, Aug.

498f A140 1c **green** (pane of 30) *1,000.*
Never hinged *1,600.*

Booklet

BK64 BC7 $3 **black,** *green* *25,000.*

499f A140 2c **rose,** (pane of 30) type I *28,000.* —
Never hinged *38,000.*

Booklet

BK65 BC7 $6 **black,** *pink*

No copies of No. BK65 are known. The number and description is provided only for specialist reference.

Nos. 498f and 499f were for use of the American Expeditionary Force in France.

They were printed from the ordinary 360-Subject Plates, the sheet being cut into 12 leaves of 30 stamps each in place of 60 leaves of 6 stamps each, and, of course, the lines of perforations changed accordingly.

The same system as used for designating plate positions on the ordinary booklet panes is used for designating the war booklet, only each war booklet pane is composed of 5 ordinary panes. Thus, No. W1 booklet pane would be composed of positions 1, 2, 3, 4, and 5 of an ordinary pane, etc.

The A. E. F. booklet panes were bound at side margins which accounts for side arrows sometimes being found on positions W5 and W6. As the top and bottom arrows were always removed when the sheets were cut, positions W1 and W2 cannot be distinguished from W7 and W8. Cutting may remove guidelines on these, but identification is possible by wide bottom margins. Positions W3 and W4 cannot be distinguished from W9 and W10.

There are thus just 8 collectible positions from the sheet as follows:

W1 or W7 Narrow top and wide bottom margins. Guide line at right.
W2 or W8 As W1, but guide line at left.
W3 or W9 Approximately equal top and bottom margins. Guide line at right.
W4 or W10 As W3, but guide line at left.
W5 Narrow bottom margin showing guideline very close to stamps. Wide top margin. Guide line at right. Pane with extra long tab may show part of split arrow at left.
W6 As W5, but guide line at left, split arrow at right. Guide line at left and at bottom. Arrow at lower right.
W11 Narrow bottom and wide top margins. Guide line at right. Siderographer initials on left tab.
W12 Narrow bottom and wide top margins. Guide line at left. Finisher initials on right tab.

Franklin — A155

Washington — A157

1923 **Unwmk.** ***Perf. 11***

552a A155 1c **deep green,** *Aug. 1923* 7.50 *4.00*
Never hinged 12.50
With plate number (D) 13.00
Never hinged 21.00

360-Subject Plates only. All plate positions exist.

Ordinary Booklets

BK66 BC6A 25c **green,** *green* (2) 75.00
BK67 BC4A 97c **green,** *lavender* (3) *650.00*

Combination Booklet

BK68 BC4B 73c **white,** *red,* 4 #552a + 4 #554c (3) 85.00

554c A157 2c **carmine** 6.75 *3.00*
Never hinged 11.00
With plate number (D) 12.00
Never hinged 20.00

360-Subject Plates only. All plate positions exist.

Ordinary Booklets

BK69 BC5A 25c **red,** *buff* (3) *400.00*
BK70 BC5A 49c **red,** *pink* (3) 950.00
BK71 BC6C 97c **red,** *blue* (3) 1,500.

Combination Booklets

See Nos. BK57 and BK68.

ROTARY PRESS PRINTINGS

Two experimental plates were used to print No. 583a. At least one guide line pane (H) is known from these plates. The rest of rotary press booklet panes were printed from specially prepared plates of 360-subjects in arrangement as before, but without the guide lines and the plate numbers are at the sides instead of at the top as on the flat plates.

The only varieties possible are the ordinary pane (A) and partial plate numbers appearing at the right or left of the upper or lower stamps of a booklet pane when the trimming of the sheets is off center. The note applies to Nos. 583a, 632a, 634d, 720b, 804b, 806b and 807a, before Electric Eyes.

1926 ***Perf. 10***

583a A157 2c **carmine,** *Aug. 1926* 95.00 *85.00*
Never hinged 175.00

Ordinary Booklets

BK72 BC5A 25c **red,** *buff* (3) *575.00*
BK73 BC5A 49c **red,** *pink* *800.00*
BK74 BC6C 97c **red,** *blue* *1,250.*

1927 ***Perf. 11x10½***

632a A155 1c **green,** *Nov. 2, 1927* 5.50 *4.00*
Never hinged 8.00

Ordinary Booklets

BK75 BC5A 25c **green,** *green* (3) 65.00
BK76 BC4A 97c **green,** *lavender* 600.00
BK77 BC5A 97c **green,** *lavender* 850.00

Combination Booklets

BK78 BC4B 73c **red,** 4 #632a + 4 #634d —
BK79 BC5D 73c **red,** 4 #632a + 4 #634d (2) 90.00

634d A157 2c **carmine,** type I, *Feb. 25, 1927* 1.50 *1.50*
Never hinged 2.50

Ordinary Booklets

BK80 BC5A 25c **red,** *buff* (2) 10.00
a. With experimental cellophane interleaving *1,500.*
BK81 BC5A 49c **red,** *pink* (2) 15.00
BK82 BC5A 97c **red,** *blue* (3) 50.00
BK83 BC6C 97c **red,** *blue* 900.00

Combination Booklets

See Nos. BK78 and BK79.

56,000 booklets of BK80a were produced in 1928 using .00125 inch thick cellophane interleaving. Scarce, as few were saved.

Washington — A226

1932

720b A226 3c **deep violet,** *July 25, 1932* 35.00 *12.50*
Never hinged 60.00

Ordinary Booklets

BK84 BC9A 37c **violet,** *buff* (2) 135.00
a. With experimental cellophane interleaving *1,750.*
BK85 BC9A 73c **violet,** *pink* (2) 375.00

30,000 booklets of No. BK84a were made with .001 inch thick cellophane interleaving, similar to but thinner than the experimental interleaving used for No. BK80a. Poor handling qualities during booklet assembly plus higher cost prevented wider use. Placed on sale in Wash. D.C. post office in Sept., 1936. Extremely scarce, as few were saved.

Catalogue values for unused panes in this section, from this point to the end, are for Never Hinged items.

Washington — A276

Adams — A278

Jefferson — A279

In 1942 plates were changed to the Type II "new design" and the E. E. marks may appear at the right or left margins of panes of Nos. 804b, 806b and 807a. Panes printed from E. E. plates have 2½mm vertical gutter; those from pre-E. E. plates have 3mm vertical gutter.

1939-42 ***Perf. 11x10½***

804b A276 1c 3mm vert. gutter, *Jan. 27, 1939* 4.00 *.85*

Ordinary Booklets

BK86 BC5A 25c **green,** *green* 75.00
BK87 BC5A 97c **green,** *lavender* *600.00*
BK88 BC4A 97c **green,** *lavender* —

Combination Booklet

BK89 BC5D 73c **red,** 4 #804b + 4 #806b 135.00

804b A276 1c 2½mm vert. gutter, *Apr. 14, 1942* 2.00 *.50*
Horiz. pair, perf. only at bottom —

Ordinary Booklets

BK90 BC5A 25c **green,** *green* 8.25
BK91 BC5A 97c **green,** *lavender* 600.00

Combination Booklets

BK92 BC5D 73c **red,** 4 #804b + 4 #806b 30.00
BK93 BC9E 73c **red,** 4 #804b + 4 #806b 37.50

806b A278 2c 3mm vert. gutter, *Jan. 27, 1939* 9.00 *1.00*

Ordinary Booklets

BK94 BC5A 97c **red,** *blue* *400.00*

Combination Booklets

See No. BK89.

806b A278 2c 2½mm vert. gutter, *Apr. 25, 1942* 4.75 *.85*

Ordinary Booklets

BK95 BC5A 97c **red,** *blue* 1,250.
BK96 BC5A 25c **red,** *buff* 19.00
BK97 BC9A 25c **red,** *buff* 100.00
BK98 BC5A 49c **red,** *pink* 45.00
BK99 BC9A 49c **red,** *pink* 75.00

Combination Booklets

See Nos. BK92 and BK93.

807a A279 3c 3mm vert. gutter, *Jan. 27, 1939* 12.50 *3.25*

Booklets

BK100 BC9A 37c **violet,** *buff* 65.00
BK101 BC9A 73c **violet,** *pink* *875.00*

807a A279 3c 2½mm vert. gutter, *Mar. 6, 1942* 10.00 *2.00*
Horiz. pair with full vert. pane gutter btwn. —

Booklets

BK102 BC9A 37c **violet,** *buff* (3) 20.00
BK103 BC9A 73c **violet,** *pink* (3) 45.00

Statue of Liberty — A482

Lincoln — A483

1954-58 ***Perf. 11x10½***

1035a A482 3c pane of 6, *June 30, 1954* 4.00 *1.25*
1035f Dry printing 5.00 *1.50*

Booklets

BK104 BC9A 37c **violet,** *buff,* with #1035a 17.50
a. With #1035f 22.50
BK105 BC9A 73c **violet,** *pink,* with #1035a 25.00
a. With #1035f 30.00

Varieties

1035g As "a," vert. imperf. betwn. *5,000.*

1036a A483 4c pane of 6, *July 31, 1958* 2.75 *1.25*

Booklets

BK106 BC9F 97c on 37c **violet,** *buff* 60.00
BK107 BC9G 97c on 73c **violet,** *pink* 30.00
BK108 BC9H 97c **blue,** *yellow* 150.00
BK109 BC9H 97c **blue,** *pink* (3) 18.00
a. With experimental silicone interleaving *150.00*

Varieties

1036d As "a," imperf. horiz. —

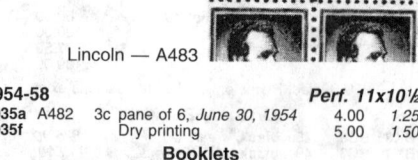

Washington (Slogan 1) — A650

Slogan 2

ADD ZIP TO YOUR MAIL ALWAYS USE ZIP CODE

Slogan 3

1962-64 ***Perf. 11x10½***

Plate of 300 stamps, 60 labels

1213a A650 5c pane of 5+label, slogan 1, *Nov. 23, 1962* 7.00 *4.00*
With slogan 2, *1963* 16.00 *7.00*

With slogan 3, *1964* 3.00 *2.00*

Booklets

BK110	BC12A	$1 **blue,** slogan 1	30.00
BK111	BC12A	$1 **blue,** slogan 2	135.00
BK112	BC13A	$1 **blue,** slogan 2	110.00
BK113	BC13A	$1 **blue,** slogan 3 (4)	15.00

1213c A650 As No. 1213a, tagged, slogan 2, *Oct. 28, 1963* 90.00 *10.00*
With slogan 3, *1964* 2.00 *1.50*

Booklets

BK114	BC13A	$1 **blue,** slogan 2	375.00
BK115	BC13A	$1 **blue,** slogan 3 (4)	10.50

Jefferson — A710

Wright — A712

Slogan 4

Slogan 5

1967-78 ***Perf. 11x10½***

1278a A710 1c pane of 8, shiny gum, *Jan. 12, 1968* 1.00 *.75*
Dull gum 2.00

Combination Booklets

See Nos. BK116, BK117B, BK118 and BK119.

1278b A710 1c pane of 4+2 labels, slogans 5 & 4, *May 10, 1971* .80 *.60*

Combination Booklet

See No. BK122.

1280a A712 2c pane of 5+label, slogan 4, *Jan. 8, 1968* 1.25 *.80*
With slogan 5 1.25 *.80*

Combination Booklets

See Nos. BK117 and BK120.

1280c A712 2c pane of 6, shiny gum, *May 7, 1971* 1.00 *.75*
Dull gum 1.10

Combination Booklets

See Nos. BK127 and BKC22.

The 1c and 6c panes of 8, Nos. 1278a and 1284b, were printed from 320-subject plates and from 400-subject plates, both with electric eye markings. The 2c and 6c panes of 5 stamps plus label, Nos. 1280a and 1284c, were printed from 360-subject plates.

An experimental moisture-resistant gum was used on 1,000,000 panes of No. 1278a and 4,000,000 of No. 1393a released in March, 1971. This dull finish gum shows no breaker ridges. The booklets lack interleaving. This gum was also used for Nos. 1395c, 1395d, 1288c and all engraved panes from No. 1510b on unless noted.

Roosevelt — A716

Oliver Wendell Holmes — A720

Perf. 10½x11

1284b A716 6c pane of 8, *Dec. 28, 1967* 1.50 *1.00*

Combination Booklet

BK116 BC14A $2 **brown,** 4 #1284b (6c)+1 #1278a(1c)(2) 7.75

1284c A716 6c pane of 5+label, slogan 4, *Jan. 9, 1968* 1.50 *1.00*
With slogan 5 1.50 *1.00*

Combination Booklet

BK117 BC15 $1 **brown,** 3 #1284c (6c) + 1 #1280a (2c) (2) 7.00

No. BK117 contains panes with slogan 4, slogan 5 or combinations of 4 and 5.

Perf. 10

1288Bc A720 15c pane of 8, *June 14, 1978* 2.80 *1.75*

Booklet

BK117A BC23 $3.60 **red & light blue,** no P# 8.75

Varieties

1288Be As "c," vert. imperf. btwn. —

1288Bg Tagging omitted, booklet single 5.00 —

Eisenhower — A815

Plate of 400 subjects for No. 1393a. Plate of 300 stamps and 60 labels for No. 1393b.

1970 Tagged ***Perf. 11x10½***

1393a A815 6c pane of 8, shiny gum, *Aug. 6* 1.50 *.75*
Dull gum 1.90

Combination Booklets

BK117B BC14A $2 **blue,** 4 #1393a (6c) + 1 #1278a (1c) 9.00

BK118 BC16 $2 **blue,** 4 #1393a (6c) + 1 #1278a (1c) (2) 7.25

BK119 BC16 $2 **blue,** dull gum, 4 #1393a (6c) + 1 #1278a (1c) (2) 8.75

1393b A815 6c pane of 5+label, slogan 4, *Aug. 6* 1.50 *.75*
With slogan 5 1.50 *.75*

Combination Booklet

BK120 BC15 $1 **blue,** 3 #1393b (6c) + 1 #1280a (2c) 6.00

No. BK120 contains panes with slogan 4, slogan 5 or combinations of 4 and 5.

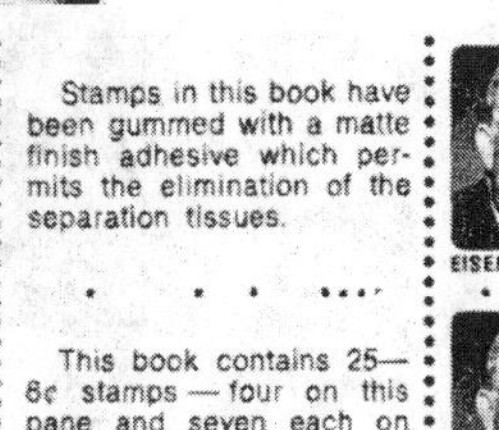

Stamps in this book have been gummed with a matte finish adhesive which permits the elimination of the separation tissues.
This book contains 25—8¢ stamps — four on this pane and seven each on three additional panes.
Selling price $2.00.

Slogans 6 and 7

Eisenhower — A815a

1971-72 **Shiny Gum** ***Perf. 11x10½***

1395a A815a 8c **deep claret,** pane of 8, *May 10, 1971* 1.80 *1.25*

Booklet

BK121 BC16 $1.92 **claret** (2) 6.50

1395b A815a 8c pane of 6, *May 10, 1971* 1.25 *1.10*

Combination Booklet

BK122 BC15 $1 **claret,** 2 #1395b (8c) + 1 #1278b (1c) (2) 4.00

Dull Gum

1395c A815a 8c pane of 4+2 labels, slogans 6 and 7, *Jan. 28, 1972* 1.65 *1.00*

1395d A815a 8c pane of 7+label, slogan 4, *Jan. 28, 1972* 1.90 *1.10*
With slogan 5 1.90 *1.10*

Combination Booklet

BK123 BC17A $2 **claret,** *yellow,* 3 #1395d + 1 #1395c 7.75

Varieties

1395e Vert. pair, imperf between *600.00*
1395f As "a," tagging omitted *20.00* —
1395g As "b," tagging omitted *35.00* —
1395h As "c," tagging omitted *35.00* —

Plate of 400 subjects for No. 1395a. Plate of 360 subjects for No. 1395b. Plate of 300 subjects (200 stamps and 100 double-size labels) for No. 1395c. Plate of 400 subjects (350 stamps and 50 labels) for No. 1395d.

No. 1395e resulted from a paper foldover after perforating and before cutting into panes. At least 4 pairs are recorded from 3 panes (one 1395a, two 1395d) with different foldover patterns.

No. BK123 exists with covers printed on both thin and thick card stock.

Booklet Covers

When more than one combination of covers exists, the number of possible booklets is noted in parenthesis after the booklet listing.

Slogan 8

Jefferson Memorial — A924

1973-74 ***Perf. 11x10½***

1510b A924 10c pane of 5+label, slogan 8, *Dec. 14, 1973* 1.65 *.90*

Booklet

BK124 BC17B $1 **red & blue** 3.75

1510c A924 10c pane of 8, *Dec. 14, 1973* 1.65 *1.00*

Booklet

BK125 BC17C $4 **red & blue** 8.50

1510d A924 10c pane of 6, *Aug. 5, 1974* 5.25 *1.75*

Combination Booklet

BK126 BC17D $1.25 **red & blue,** 1 #1510d (10c) + 1 #C79a (13c) 7.25

No. BK125 exists with covers printed on both thin and thick card stock.

Varieties

1510f Vert. pair, imperf between *700.00*
1510h As "c," tagging omitted —

No. 1510f resulted from a paper foldover after perforating and before cutting into panes.

Slogan 9

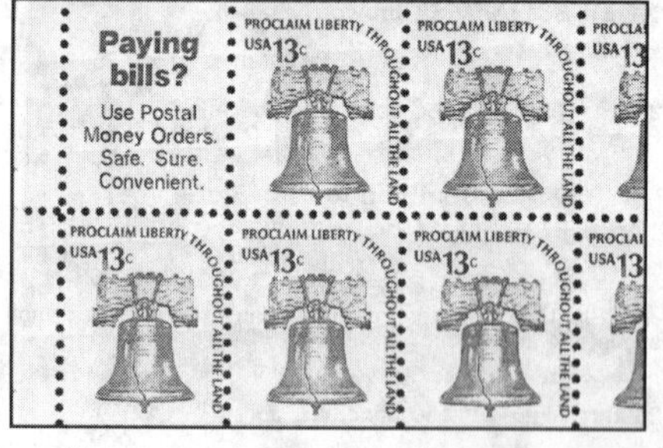

Liberty Bell — A998

1975-78 ***Perf. 11x10½***

1595a A998 13c pane of 6, *Oct. 31, 1975* 2.25 *1.00*

Combination Booklet

BK127 BC19A 90c **red & blue,** 1 #1595a (13c) + 1 #1280c (2c) (2) 3.25

1595b A998 13c pane of 7+label, slogan 8, *Oct. 31, 1975* 2.25 *1.00*

1595c A998 13c pane of 8, *Oct. 31, 1975* 2.25 *1.00*

Combination Booklet

BK128 BC19B $2.99 **red & blue,** 2 #1595c (13c) + 1 #1595b (13c) (2) 7.75

No. BK128 exists with covers printed on both thin and thick card stock.

1595d A998 13c pane of 5+label, slogan 9, *Apr. 2, 1976* 1.75 *1.00*

Booklet

BK129 BC19A $1.30 **red & blue** 4.00

Varieties

1595e Vert. pair, imperf. btwn. *800.00*

No. 1595e resulted from a paper foldover after perforating and before cutting into panes. Beware of printer's waste consisting of complete panes with perfs around all outside edges.

A994, A1018a

Fort McHenry Flag (15 Stars) — A1001

1977-78 ***Perf. 11x10½***

1598a A1001 15c pane of 8, *June 30, 1978* 4.25 *.80*

Booklet

BK130 BC21 $1.20 **red & light blue,** no P# 4.50

1623a A1018a Pane of 8 (1 #1590 + 7 #1623), *Mar. 11, 1977* 2.25 *1.25*

Booklet

BK131 BC20 $1 **red & light blue,** no P# (3) 2.50

Varieties

1623d Pair, Nos. 1590, 1623 .70 *1.00*
1623f Tagging omitted, single stamp —

Perf. 10

1623Bc A1018a Pane of 8 (1 #1590A + 7 #1623B), *Mar. 11, 1977* 26.50 —

Booklet

BK132 BC20 $1 **red & light blue,** no P# (2) 27.50

Varieties

1623Be Pair, Nos. 1590A, 1623B 21.50 21.50

BOOKLET PANES

Eagle — A1124

1978 **Tagged** ***Perf. 11x10½***

1736a	A1124	A pane of 8, *May 22*	2.25	*1.25*

Booklet

BK133	BC24	$3.60 **deep orange**	7.00

No. BK133 exists with covers printed on both thin and thick card stock.

Varieties

1736b	As "a," tagging omitted		—
1736c	Vert. pair, imperf between	—	

Red Masterpiece and Medallion — A1126 Roses

Perf. 10

1737a	A1126	15c pane of 8, *July 11*	2.25	*1.25*

Booklet

BK134	BC22	$2.40 **rose red & yel grn,** no P# (4)	5.25

Varieties

1737b	As "a," imperf.	—	
1737c	As "a," tagging omitted	*40.00*	—

Windmills — A1127-A1131

1980 ***Perf. 11***

1742a	A1131	15c pane of 10, *Feb. 7*	3.50	*3.00*

Booklet

BK135	BC25	$3 **light blue & dark blue,** *blue,* no P#	7.50

Varieties

1742b	Strip of 5, #1738-1742	1.50	1.40

A1207

A1267-A1276

A1279-A1280

1981

1819a	A1207	B pane of 8, *Mar. 15*	3.75	*2.25*

Booklet

BK136	BC26	$4.32 **dull violet,** no P#	11.75

1889a	A1267	18c pane of 10, *May 14*	8.50	*7.00*

Booklet

BK137	BC28	$3.60 **gray & olive,** P#1-10	17.00
		P#11-13	40.00
		P#14-16	35.00

Varieties

1880a	Tagging omitted		—
1887a	Tagging omitted		—
1889b	Tagging omitted		—

1893a	A1279	Pane of 8 (2 #1892, 6 #1893), *Apr. 24*	3.00	*2.50*

Booklet

BK138	BC27	$1.20 **blue & red,** P#1	3.25

Varieties

1893b	As "a," vert. imperf. btwn.	*75.00*	
1893c	Pair, Nos. 1892, 1893	.90	*1.00*
1893d	As "a," tagging omitted	—	

Booklet

BK138a	BC27	$1.20 With No. 1893b, P#1	75.00
BK138b	BC27	$1.20 With No. 1893d, P#1	—

A1281

1981-83

1896a	A1281	20c pane of 6, small block tagging, *Dec. 17, 1981*	3.00	*2.25*
		Scored perforations	3.00	—

Booklet

BK139	BC29	$1.20 **blue & red,** P#1 (2)	3.25

1896b	A1281	20c pane of 10, *June 1, 1982*	5.25	*3.25*
BK140	BC29A	$2 **blue & red,** P#1 (4)	5.50	
		P#4	47.50	
1896e	A1281	20c pane of 10, large block tagging, *Nov. 17, 1983*	5.25	*3.25*
		Scored perforations	5.25	—

Booklet

BK140A	BC29B	$4 **blue & red,** *Nov. 17, 1983,* P#2	11.00
		P#3	17.50
		P#4	—

Varieties

1896c	As "b," tagging omitted	—

The small block tagging is 16x18mm (Nos. 1896a-1896b). The large block tagging is 18x21mm (No. 1896e).

Booklet Covers

When more than one combination of covers exists, the number of possible booklets is noted in parenthesis after the booklet listing.

A1296

1983

1909a	A1296	$9.35 pane of 3, *Aug. 12*	70.00	—

Booklet

BK140B	BC31	28.05 **blue & red,** P#1111	72.50

A1333

1981

1948a	A1333	C pane of 10, *Oct. 11*	4.50	*3.25*

Booklet

BK141	BC26	$4 **brown,** *blue,* no P#	10.00

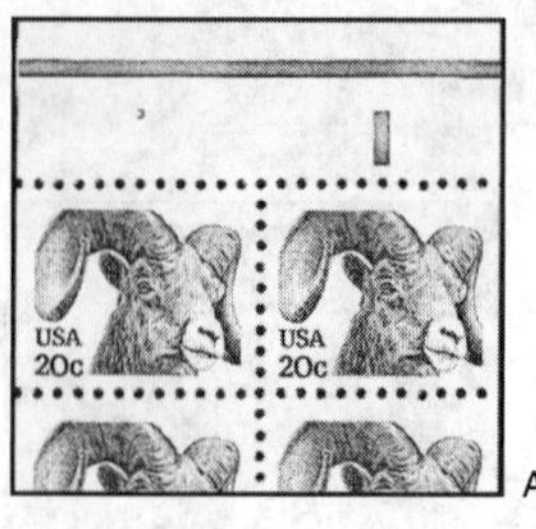

A1334

1982

1949a	A1334	20c	pane of 10, type I, *Jan. 8*	5.50	*2.50*
1949d			As "a," type II	11.00	—

Booklets

BK142	BC30	$4	**blue & yellow green,** P#1-6, 9-10	16.00
			P#11, 12, 15	40.00
			P#14	30.00
			P#16	75.00
			P#17-19	55.00
			P#20, 22-24	100.00
			P#21, 28, 29	*350.00*
			P#25-26	*150.00*
a.			Type II, P#34	22.00

Varieties

1949b	As "a," vert. imperf. btwn.	*110.00*	
1949f	As "a," tagging omitted	*50.00*	—

Booklets

BK142b	As BK142, with 2 #1949b	—
BK142c	As BK142, with 2 #1949f, P#5	*100.00*

Stamps in No. 1949a are 18¾mm wide and have overall tagging. Stamps in No. 1949d are 18½mm wide and have block tagging.

Plate number does not always appear on top pane in Nos. BK142, BK142a. These booklets sell for more.

A1497

1985 ***Perf. 11***

2113a	A1497	D	pane of 10 *Feb. 1*	8.50	*3.00*

Booklet

BK143	BC26	$4.40	**green,** P#1, 3, 4	17.00
			P#2	*700.00*

Varieties

2113b	As "a," imperf. between, horiz.	—

Plate number does not always appear on top pane in No. BK143. These booklets sell for more.

A1499

Perf. 10 Horiz.

2116a	A1499	22c	pane of 5, *Mar. 29*	2.50	*1.25*
			Scored perforations	2.50	—

Booklets

BK144	BC33C	$1.10	**blue & red,** P#1, 3 (2)	2.75
BK145	BC32	$2.20	**blue & red,** P#1, 3 (2)	5.25

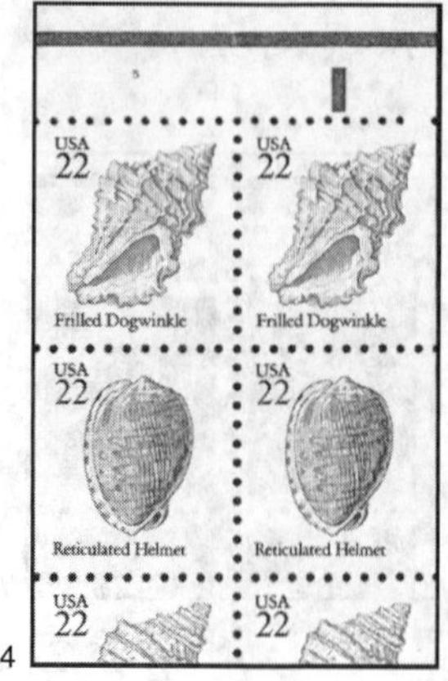

A1500-A1504

Perf. 10

2121a	A1500	22c	pane of 10, *Apr. 4*	4.00	*3.00*

Booklets

BK146	BC33A	$4.40	**multicolored,** P#1, 3	8.50
			P#2	10.00
BK147	BC33B	$4.40	**brown & blue,** P#1, 3, 5, 6, 7, 10	8.50
			P#8	10.00

Varieties

2121b	As "a," violet omitted on both Nos. 2120	*800.00*	
2121c	As "a," vert. imperf. btwn.	*600.00*	
2121d	As "a," imperf.		—
2121e	Strip of 5, Nos. 2117-2121	2.00	—

A1505

1985-89 ***Perf. 10 Vert.***

2122a	A1505	10.75	type I, pane of 3, *Apr. 29, 1985*	60.00	—

Booklet

BK148	BC31A	32.25	**multicolored,** P#11111	62.50

2122c	A1505	10.75	type II, pane of 3, *June 19, 1989*	70.00	—

Booklet

BK149	BC31B	32.25	**blue & red,** P#22222 (2)	72.50

No. 2182a — A1564

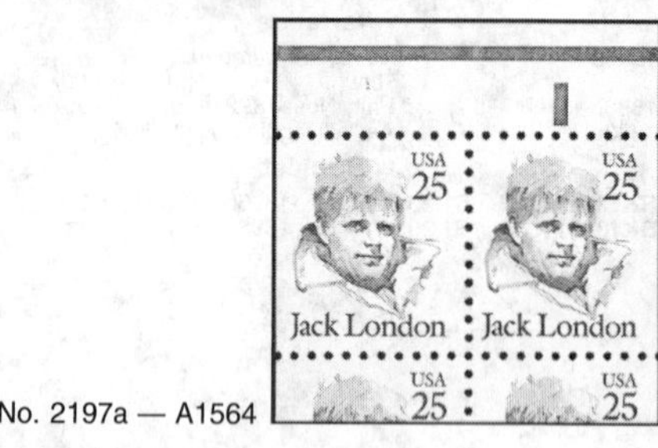

No. 2197a — A1564

1988 ***Perf. 11***

2182a	A1564	25c	pane of 10, *May 3*	4.50	*3.75*

Booklet

BK150	BC43	$5	**multicolored,** P#1-2	9.25

Varieties

2182c	As "a," tagging omitted	—
2182d	Horiz. pair, imperf between	—

Booklet

BK150a	BC43	$1.50	As BK150, with #2182c	—

Perf. 10 on 2 or 3 Sides

2197a	A1564	25c	pane of 6, *May 3*	3.00	*2.25*

Booklets

BK151	BC43	$1.50	**blue & brown,** P#1	3.00
BK152	BC43	$3	**brown & blue,** P#1	6.00

BK151 and BK152 exist with covers printed on both thin and thick card stock.

Varieties

2197c	A1564	25c	As "a," tagging omitted	*65.00*

Booklet

BK151a	BC43	$1.50	As BK151, with #2197c	*70.00*

A1581-A1584

1986

2201a	A1581	22c	pane of 4, *Jan. 23*	2.00	*1.75*

Booklet

BK153	BC34	$1.76	**purple & black,** P#1	4.00

Varieties

2201b	As "a," black omitted on Nos. 2198, 2201	50.00
2201c	As "a," blue (litho.) omitted on Nos. 2198-2200	*2,500.*
2201d	As "a," buff (litho.) omitted	—

Booklets

BK153a	BC34	$1.76	As No. BK153, with 2 #2201b	100.00
BK153b	BC34	$1.76	As No. BK153, with 2 #2201c	*5,000.*

A1588-A1592

2209a	A1588	22c	pane of 5, *Mar. 21*	5.50	*2.75*

Booklet

BK154	BC35	$2.20	**blue green and red,** P#11111, 22222	12.00

Varieties

2209b	As "a," red omitted	—

A1637-A1644

1987

2274a A1637 22c pane of 10, *Apr. 20* 10.00 *5.00*

Booklet

BK155 BC36 $2.20 **blue & red,** P#111111, 222222 12.50

A1646

Perf. 11

2276a A1646 22c pane of 20, *Nov. 30* 8.50 —

Booklet

BK156 BC39 $4.40 **multicolored,** no P# 9.00
P#1111, 2222 12.00
P#2122 19.00

Varieties

2276b As "a," vert. pair, imperf. between *1,750.*

No. 2276a was made from sheets of No. 2276 which had alternating rows of perforations removed and the right sheet margins trimmed off.

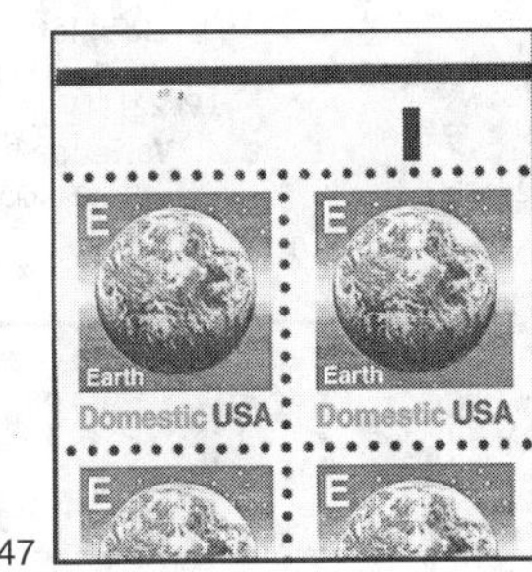

A1647

1988 ***Perf. 10***

2282a A1647 E pane of 10, *Mar. 22* 6.50 *3.50*
Scored perforations 6.50 —

Booklet

BK157 BC40 $5 **blue,** P#1111, 2222 13.00
P#2122 15.00

A1649a

Perf. 11

2283a A1649a 25c pane of 10, *Apr. 29* 6.00 *3.50*

Booklet

BK158 BC41 $5 **multicolored,** P#A1111 12.00

Varieties

2283d As "a," horiz. imperf. between *2,000.*

Imperf. panes exist from printers waste.

Color Change

2283c A1649a 25c red removed from sky, pane of 10 *67.50* —

Booklet

BK159 BC41 $5 **multicolored,** P#A3111, A3222 *135.00*

A1649b-A1649c

Perf. 10

2285b A1649b 25c pane of 10, *May 28* 5.00 *3.50*

Booklet

BK160 BC45 $5 **red & black,** P#1111, 1112, 1211, 1433, 1434, 1734, 2121, 2321, 3333, 5955 (2) 12.00
P#1133, 2111, 2122, 2221, 2222, 3133, 3233, 3412, 3413, 3422, 3521, 4642, 4644, 4911, 4941 20.00
P#1414 95.00
P#1634, 3512 50.00
P#3822 40.00
P#5453 165.00

Varieties

2285d Pair, Nos. 2284-2285 1.10 .25
2285e As "d," tagging omitted 12.50

A1648

2285Ac A1648 25c pane of 6, *July 5* 3.00 *2.00*

Booklet

BK161 BC46 $3 **blue & red,** P#1111 6.00

A1719-A1723

1987

2359a A1719 22c pane of 5, *Aug. 28* 2.75 *2.25*

Booklet

BK162 BC37 $4.40 **red & blue,** P#1111, 1112 11.00

Varieties

2355a Grayish green (background) omitted, single stamp —
2356a As No. 2355a —
2357a As No. 2355a —
2358a As No. 2355a —
2359b As No. 2355a —

A1726-A1730

2366a A1726 22c pane of 5, *Oct. 1* 2.75 *2.50*

Booklet

BK163 BC38 $4.40 **black & yellow,** P#1, 2 11.00

Varieties

2365a Red omitted, single stamp —
2366b Black omitted, single stamp —
2366c Blue omitted, single stamp —

A1745-A1749

1988

2385a A1745 25c pane of 5, *Aug. 25* 6.00 *2.25*

Booklet

BK164 BC47 $5 **black & red,** P#1 25.00

A1759-A1760

A1761-A1762

Perf. 11

2396a A1759 25c pane of 6, *Oct. 22* 3.50 *3.25*
2398a A1761 25c pane of 6, *Oct. 22* 3.50 *3.25*

Combination Booklet

BK165 BC48 $3 **multicolored,** 1 #2396a, 1 #2398a, P#A1111 (2) 7.00

Varieties

2398b As "a," imperf. horiz. —

Unused never folded panes of No. 2398a are known but were not regularly issued. The USPS used never folded panes on first day programs and souvenir pages for this issue. Value, unused $1,250.

A1769-A1773

1989 ***Perf. 10***

2409a A1769 25c pane of 5, *Mar. 3* 2.25 *1.75*
Never folded pane, P#1 8.00
P#2 20.00

Booklet

BK166 BC49 $5 **blue & black,** P#1, 2 10.00

Varieties

2409b As "a," tagging omitted —

A1791

Perf. 11½

2427a A1791 25c pane of 10, *Oct. 19* 4.75 *3.50*
Never folded pane, P#1 10.00

Booklet

BK167 BC50 $5 **multicolored,** P#1 9.50

Varieties

2427b As "a," red (litho.) omitted *750.00*
2427c As "a," imperf —

A1792

2429a A1792 25c pane of 10, *Oct. 19* 4.75 *3.50*
Never folded pane, P#1111 17.50

Booklet

BK168 BC51 $5 **multicolored,** P#1111, 2111 10.00

Varieties

2429b As "a," imperf. horiz. —
2429c Vert. pair, imperf. horiz. —
2429d As "a," red omitted —
2429e Imperf., pair —

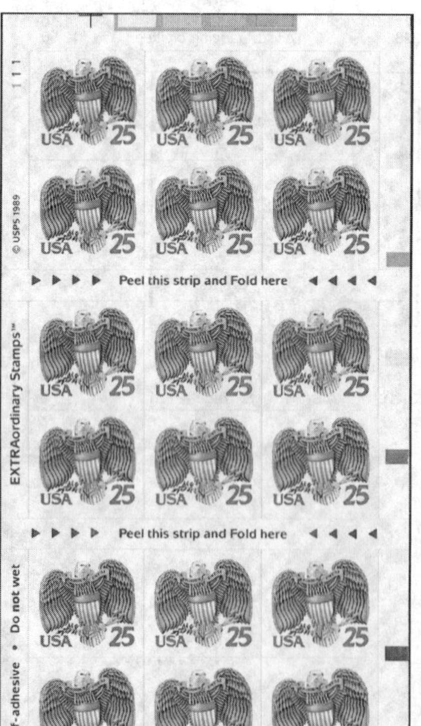

A1793

Illustration reduced.

Self-adhesive ***Die cut***

2431a A1793 25c pane of 18, *Nov. 10,* P#A1111 11.00

By its nature, No. 2431a constitutes a complete booklet. Blue & red peelable paper backing is booklet cover (BC52). Sold for $5.

Varieties

2431b Vert. pair, no die cutting between *500.00*
2431c Pair, no die cutting —

A1800

1990 ***Perf. 11½***

2441a A1800 25c pane of 10, *Jan. 18* 4.75 *3.50*
Never folded pane, P#1211 35.00

Varieties

2441b As "a," bright pink omitted *1,700.*
2441c As "b," single stamp *160.00*

Panes exist containing both normal and bright pink omitted stamps. Value is less than that of No. 2441b.

Booklet

BK169 BC53 $5 **multicolored,** P#1211 10.50
P#2111 20.00
P#2211 30.00
P#2222 17.50

A1802

Perf. 11

2443a A1802 15c pane of 10, *Feb. 3* 3.00 *2.00*
Never folded pane, P#111111 9.00

Booklet

BK170 BC54 $3 **multi,** P#111111 6.00
P#221111 10.00

Varieties

2443b As #2443a, blue omitted *1,400.*
2443c As "b," single stamp *140.00*

A1829-A1833

Perf. 10

2474a A1829 25c pane of 5, *Apr. 26* 5.50 *2.00*
Never folded pane, P#1, 3, 5 6.00
P#2 8.00
P#4 —

Booklet

BK171 BC55 $5 **blue & red,** P#1-5 (2) 22.50

Varieties

2474b As #2474a, white omitted 80.00 —

Booklet

BK171a As No. BK171, with 4 No. 2474b 300.00

A1847

1991-95

2483a A1847 20c **multicolored,** pane of 10, *June 15, 1995* 5.25 *2.25*
Never folded pane 6.25

Booklet

BK172 BC56 $2 **multicolored,** P#S1111 5.25

Varieties

2483b As "a," imperf —

A1848

Perf. 10

2484a A1848 29c **black & multi,** overall tagging, pane of 10, *Apr. 12, 1991* 5.50 *3.75*
Never folded pane, P#1111 9.00

Booklets

BK173 BC57 $2.90 **black & green,** *1992,* P#4444 5.75
BK174 BC57 $5.80 **black & red,** P#1111, 2222 11.00
P#1211, 3221 125.00
P#2122, 3222, 3333 20.00
P#3331 —
P#4444 15.00

Varieties

2484b Vert. pair, imperf. between *200.00*
As "b," pane of 10 1,000.
2484e Prephosphered paper (solid tagging), pane of 10 5.50 3.75

Booklet

BK173a As No. BK173, with No. 2484e 5.75
BK174a As No. BK174, with 2 #2484e 11.00

Perf. 11

2485a A1848 29c **red & multi,** pane of 10, *Apr. 12, 1991* 5.50 *4.00*
Never folded pane, P#K11111 12.00

Booklets

BK175 BC57 $5.80 **black & multi,** P#K11111 12.00

Varieties

2485b Vert. pair, imperf. between *3,000.*
2485c Imperf, pair —

A1849

2486a A1849 29c pane of 10, *Oct. 8, 1993* 5.50 *4.00*

Never folded pane, P#K1111 6.25

Booklet

BK176 BC58 $2.90 **multicolored,** P#K1111 6.00
BK177 BC58 $5.80 **multicolored,** P#K1111 11.50

A1850-A1851

2488a A1850 32c **multicolored,** pane of 10, *July 8, 1995* 6.00 *4.25*
Never folded pane 6.75

Booklet

BK178 BC59 $6.40 **multicolored,** P#11111 12.00

Varieties

2488b Pair, Nos. 2487-2488 *1.25* .30

A1852

Self-Adhesive ***Die Cut***

2489a A1852 29c pane of 18, *June 25, 1993* P#D11111, D22211 10.00
P#D22221, D22222, D23133 12.50

By its nature, No. 2489a constitutes a complete booklet (BC60). The peelable backing serves as a booklet cover.

Varieties

2489b As "a," die cutting omitted —

Red Rose — A1853

Self-Adhesive ***Die Cut***

2490a A1853 29c pane of 18, *Aug. 19, 1993,* P#S111 10.00

By its nature, No. 2490a constitutes a complete booklet (BC61). The peelable backing, of which two types are known, serves as a booklet cover.

A1854

Self-Adhesive ***Die Cut***

2491a A1854 29c pane of 18, *Nov. 5, 1993,* P#B3-11, 13-14, 16 11.00
P#B1 17.50
P#B2, 12, 15 15.00

By is nature, No. 2491a constitutes a complete booklet (BC61A). The peelable backing serves as a booklet cover.

Varieties

2491b Horiz. pair, no die cutting btwn. *250.00*

Pink Rose (No. 2492a) — A1853

Serpentine Die Cut 11.3x11.7 on 2, 3 or 4 Sides

Self-Adhesive

2492a A1853 32c pane of 20+label, *June 2, 1995,* P#S111, S112, S333, S444, S555 12.00
2492b A1853 32c pane of 15+label, *1996* 8.75
2492e A1853 32c pane of 14, *1996* 21.00
2492f A1853 32c pane of 16, *1996* 21.00

By its nature, No. 2492a is a complete booklet (BC61B). The peelable backing serves as a booklet cover.

No. 2492e contains blocks of 4, 6 and 4 stamps. No. 2492f contains blocks of 6,6, and 4 stamps. The blocks are on rouletted backing paper. The peel-a-way strips that were between the blocks have been removed to fold the pane.

Booklets

BK178A BC126 $4.80 **blue,** No. 2492b (5) 10.00
BK178B BC126 $4.80 **blue,** No. 2492f with bottom right stamp removed 40.00
BK178C BC126 $9.60 **blue,** 2 #2492b, No P# (3) 18.00
BK178D BC126 $9.60 **blue,** 2 panes of #2492f ea with a stamp removed from either the top or bottom row, No P# (3) 20.00

Combination Booklets

BK178E BC126 $9.60 **blue,** 1 ea #2492e, 2492f, no P# (3) 45.00
BK178F BC126 $9.60 **blue,** #2492b, 2492f with bottom right stamp removed, no P# *225.00*

No. BK178A was issued wrapped in cellophane and not wrapped in cellophane. The two cellophane-wrapped versions are scarcer.

No. BK178E was sold wrapped in cellophane with the contents of the booklet listed on a label. Three versions exist. No. 2492f is affixed to the booklet cover, and No. 2492e is loose.

The panes of #2492f with one stamp removed that are contained in Nos. BK178B, BK178D and BK178F cannot be made from No. 2492b, a pane of 15 + label. The label is located in the sixth or seventh row of the pane and is sometimes die cut. The panes with one stamp removed all have the stamp removed from the top or bottom row of the pane.

Varieties

2492c Horiz. pair, no die cutting btwn. —
2492d As "a," 2 stamps and parts of 7 others printed on backing liner —
2492h Vert. pair, no die cutting btwn. —

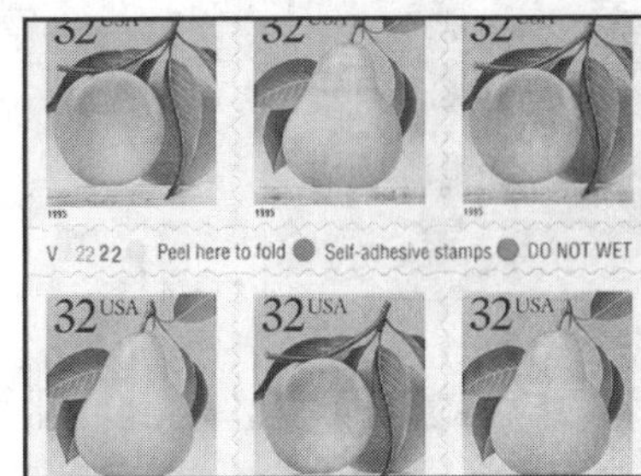
A1850-A1851

Serpentine Die Cut 8.8

2494a A1850 32c pane of 20+label, *July 8, 1995,*
P# list 1 12.50
P# list 2 18.00
P#V11132, V33353 15.00
P#V33323 25.00
P#V11232 —

By its nature, No. 2494a is a complete booklet (BC61C). The peelable backing serves as a booklet cover.

List 1 - P#V11111, V11122, V12132, V12211, V12221, V22212, V22222, V33142, V33243, V33333, V33343, V33363, V44424, V44434, V44454, V45434, V45464, V54365, V54565, V55365, V55565.

List 2 - P#V11131, V12131, V12232, V22221, V33143, V33453.

Varieties

2494b Pair, #2493-2494 1.20

A1860-A1864

1990 *Perf. 11*

2505a A1860 25c pane of 10, *Aug. 17* 8.50 *3.50*
Never folded pane, P#1-2 15.00

Booklet

BK179 BC62 $5 **multicolored,** P#1, 2 17.50

Varieties

2505b As "a," black (engr.) omitted *3,250.*
2505c Strip of 5, Nos. 2501-2505 2.75 1.00
2505d As "a," horiz. imperf. —

A1873

1990 *Perf. 11½*

2514b A1873 25c pane of 10, *Oct. 18* 5.00 *3.25*
Never folded pane 12.50

Booklet

BK180 BC63 $5 **multicolored,** P#1 10.00

A1874

1990 *Perf. 11½x11*

2516a A1874 25c pane of 10, *Oct. 18* 5.00 *3.25*
Never folded pane, P#1211 15.00

Booklet

BK181 BC64 $5 **multicolored,** P#1211 11.00

No. 2519a — A1875

No. 2520a — A1875

1991 ***Perf. 11.2 Bullseye***

2519a A1875 F pane of 10, *Jan. 22* 6.50 *4.50*

Booklets

BK182 BC65 ($2.90) **yellow & multi,** P#2222 6.50
BK183 BC65 ($5.80) **grn, red & blk,** P#1111, 2121, 2222 13.00
P#1222, 2111, 2212 25.00

Perf. 11

2520a A1875 F pane of 10, *Jan. 22* 18.00 *4.50*

Booklet

BK184 BC65 ($2.90) like #BK182, **grn, red & blk,** P#K1111 18.00

Varieties

2520b As "a," imperf. horiz. —

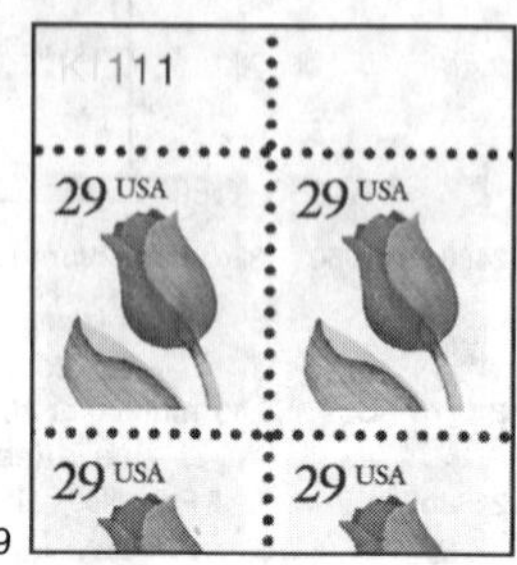

A1879

Perf. 11

2527a A1879 29c pane of 10, *Apr. 5* 5.50 *3.50*
Never folded pane, P#K1111 7.50

Booklet

BK185 BC66 $5.80 **multicolored,** P#K1111, K2222, K3333 11.00

Varieties

2527b As "a," vert. imperf. between *1,500.*
2527c Horiz. pair, imperf. vert. *225.00*
2527d As "a," imperf. horiz. *2,500.*

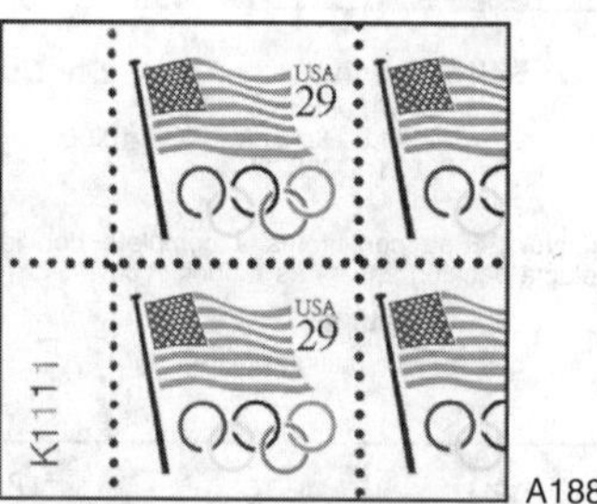

A1880

Perf. 11

2528a A1880 29c pane of 10, *Apr. 21* 5.50 *3.50*
Never folded pane 6.50

Booklets

BK186 BC67 $2.90 **black & multicolored,** P#K11111 5.75
BK186A BC67A $2.90 **red & multicolored,** P#K11111 (2) 6.75

Varieties

2528b As "a," horiz. imperf. between, perfed at top and bottom —
2528c Vert. pair, imperf between, perfed at top and bottom —
2528d Vert. strip of 3, top or bottom pair imperf between —
2528e Vert. pair, imperf horiz. *1,800.*

No. 2528c comes from the misperfed booklet pane of No. 2528b. No. 2528d resulted from paper foldovers after normal perforating and before cutting into panes. Two No. 2528d are known. No. 2528e is valued in the grade of fine.

Booklet Covers

When more than one combination of covers exists, the number of possible booklets is noted in parenthesis after the booklet listing.

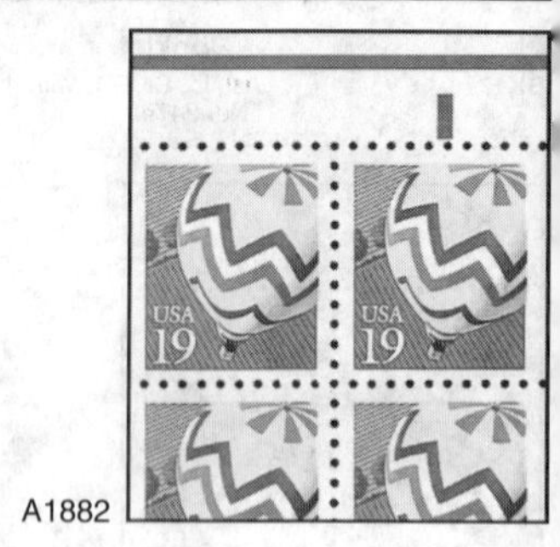

A1882

1991 ***Perf. 10***

2530a A1882 19c pane of 10, *May 17* 3.50 *2.75*
Never folded pane, P#1111 4.50

Booklet

BK187 BC68 $3.80 **black & blue,** P#1111, 2222 7.00
P#1222 30.00

A1884

Self-Adhesive

Die Cut

2531Ab A1884 29c pane of 18, prephosphored coated paper (solid tagging), *June 25,* no P# 10.50

By its nature, No. 2531Ab constitutes a complete booklet (BC68A). The peelable backing serves as a booklet cover.

Varieties

2531Ac As "b," no die cutting, pair —
2531Ae As "b," overall tagging (BC68B), *1992* 11.00

A1890

1991 ***Perf. 11***

2536a A1890 29c pane of 10, *May 9* 5.50 *3.50*
Never folded pane, P#1111, 1112 7.75

Booklet

BK188 BC69 $5.80 **multicolored,** P#1111, 1112 11.00
P#1113, 1123, 2223 15.00
P#1212 40.00

A1899-A1903

Perf. 11

2549a A1899 29c pane of 5, *May 31* 5.50 *2.50*
Never folded pane,
P#A23133, A23213 10.00
P#A11111, A22122,
A33213 —
P#A23124 42.50
P#A32225, A33233 27.50

Booklet

BK189 BC70 $5.80 **multicolored,**
P#A22122, A23123,
A23124, A33235,
A44446, A45546,
A45547 22.50
P#A11111, A22133, A23133,
A23213 47.50
P#A22132, A32224, A32225,
A33233 27.50
P#A31224 —

No. BK189 exists assembled from panes with different plate numbers.

P#33213 has yet to be found as top pane in booklets.

Varieties

2545a Black omitted, single stamp —
2546a Black omitted, single stamp —
2547a Black omitted, single stamp —

A1905

Perf. 11

2552a A1905 29c pane of 5, *July 2* 2.75 *2.25*
Never folded pane,
P#A11121111 4.50

Booklet

BK190 BC71 $5.80 **multicolored,**
P#A11111111,
A11121111 10.50

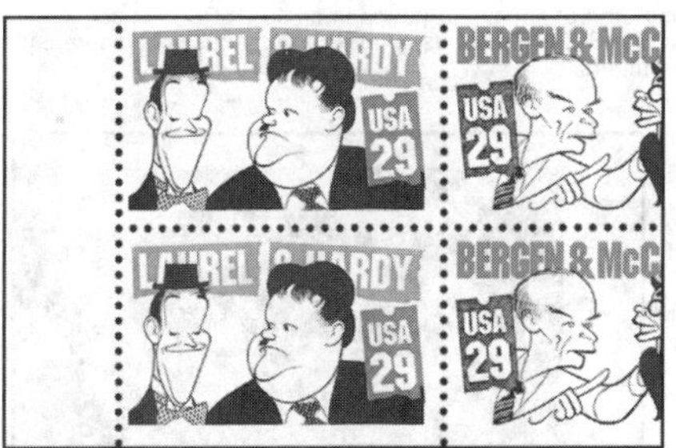

A1916-A1920

2566a A1916 29c pane of 10, *Aug. 29* 9.00 *3.50*
Never folded pane, P#1 10.50

Booklet

BK191 BC72 $5.80 **scar, blk & brt vio,**
P#1, 2 19.00

Varieties

2566b As "a," scar & brt violet (engr.) omitted *700.00*
2566c Strip of 5, Nos. 2562-2566 3.00 —

A1922-A1931

2577a A1922 29c pane of 10, *Oct. 1* 9.00 *3.50*
Never folded pane,
P#111111 12.50

Booklet

BK192 BC73 $5.80 **blue, black & red,**
P#111111 19.00
P#111112 24.00

A1933

2578a A1933 (29c) pane of 10, *Oct. 17* 5.50 *3.25*
Never folded pane 7.50

Booklet

BK193 BC74 ($5.80) **multicolored,** P#1 11.00

Varieties

2578b As "a," single, red & black (engr.) omitted *3,500.*

A1934

2581b A1934 (29c) pane, 2 each, #2580, 2581, *Oct. 17* 9.00 *1.25*
Never bound pane,
P#A11111 11.00
2582a A1935 (29c) pane of 4, *Oct. 17* 2.25 *1.25*
Never bound pane,
P#A11111 3.50
2583a A1936 (29c) pane of 4, *Oct. 17* 2.25 *1.25*
Never bound pane,
P#A11111 3.50
2584a A1937 (29c) pane of 4, *Oct. 17* 2.25 *1.25*
Never bound pane,
P#A11111 3.50
2585a A1938 (29c) pane of 4, *Oct. 17* 2.25 *1.25*
Never bound pane,
P#A11111 3.50

Combination Booklet

BK194 BC75 ($5.80) **multicolored,** 1 each #2581b, 2582a-2585a,
P#A11111, A12111 20.00

Varieties

2581a Pair, Nos. 2580-2581 4.00 .50

For illustrations A1935-A1938 see regular listings. Panes are similar to A1934.

Nos. 2581b-2585a are unfolded panes.

A1946

1992-94 ***Perf. 10***

2593a A1946 29c **black & multi,** pane of 10, *Sept. 8* 5.00 *4.25*
Never folded pane,
P#1111 7.00

Booklets

BK195 BC76 $2.90 **blue & red,** P#1111,
2222 5.50
BK196 BC76 $5.80 **blue & red,** P#1111,
2222 11.00
P#1211, 2122 —

Perf. 11x10

2593Bc A1946 29c **black & multi,** pane of 10, shiny gum, *1993* 14.00 *6.00*
Low gloss gum 20.00

Booklet

BK197 BC76 $5.80 **blue & red,** P#1111,
1211, 2122, 2222,
2232, 3333 28.00
P#2232, 4444, low
gloss gum 45.00
P#2333 —
P#3333, low gloss gum *125.00*
2594a A1946 29c **red & multi,** pane of 10, *1993* 5.50 *4.25*
Never folded pane 7.00

Booklet

BK198 BC76 $2.90 **black, red & blue,**
P#K1111 5.75
BK199 BC76 $5.80 **multicolored,** *1994,*
P#K1111 13.50

Varieties

2594b Imperf, pair *900.00*

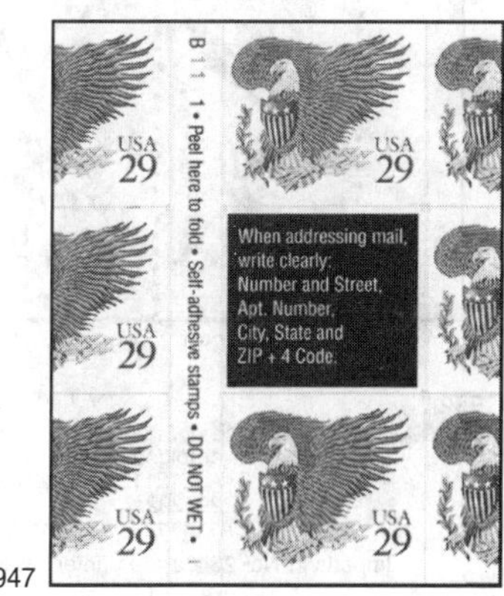

A1947

Self-adhesive

Die Cut

2595a A1947 29c **brown & multi,** pane of 17 + label, *Sept. 25,*
P#B1111-1, B1111-2,
B3434-1 12.50
P#B2222-1, B2222-2,
B3333-1, B3333-3,
B3434-3, B4344-1,
B4444-1, B4444-3 25.00
P#B4344-3 *300.00*

Varieties

2595b Pair, no die cutting *175.00*
2595c Brown omitted, single *450.00*
2595d As "a," no die cutting *1,500.*
2596a A1947 29c **green & multi,** pane of 17 + label, *Sept. 25, 1992,*
P#D11111, D21221,
D22322, D32322 12.00
P#D32332, D43352,
D43452, D43453,
D54563, D54571,
D54573, , D54673,
D61384, D65784 15.00
P#D32342, D42342 35.00
P#D54561 25.00
2597a A1947 29c **red & multi,** pane of 17 + label, *Sept. 25,* P#S1111 10.00

By their nature, Nos. 2595a-2597a constitute complete booklets (BC77). A peelable paper backing serves as a booklet cover for each. No. 2595a has a black and multicolored backing with serifed type. No. 2596a has a blue and multicolored backing, No. 2597a a black and multicolored backing with unserifed type.

A1950

Self-Adhesive ***Die Cut***

2598a A1950 29c pane of 18, *Feb. 4, 1994,* P#M111, M112 10.00

By its nature, No. 2598a constitutes a complete booklet (BC78). The peelable backing serves as a booklet cover.

A1951

Self-Adhesive ***Die Cut***

2599a A1951 29c pane of 18, *June 24, 1994,* P#D1111, D1212 10.00

By its nature, No. 2599a constitutes a complete booklet (BC79). The peelable backing serves as a booklet cover.

A1994-A1998

1992

2646a A1994 29c pane of 5, *June 15* 2.75 *2.50*
Never folded pane, P#A2212112, A2212122, A2222222 3.75
P#A1111111, A2212222 10.00

Imperfs of No. 2646a are printer's waste.

Booklet

BK201 BC80 $5.80 **multicolored,** P#A1111111, A2212112, A2212222, A2222222 11.00
P#A2212122 17.00

A2057-A2061

2709a A2057 29c pane of 5, *Oct. 1* 2.75 *2.25*
Never folded pane 3.75

Booklet

BK202 BC83 $5.80 **multicolored,** P#K1111 12.00

Varieties

2709b As "a," imperf. *3,000.*

A2062

2710a A2062 29c pane of 10, *Oct. 22* 5.50 *3.50*
Never folded pane 6.25

Booklet

BK202A BC83A $5.80 **multicolored,** P#1 11.50

A2063-A2066

2718a A2063 29c pane of 4, *Oct. 22* 3.50 *1.25*
Never bound pane, P#A111111, A222222 4.50
P#A112211 —

Booklet

BK203 BC84 $5.80 **multi,** P#A111111, A112211, A222222 17.50

Varieties

2718b As "a," imperf. horiz. —

No. 2718a completely imperf is printer's waste.

A2064

Self-Adhesive

Die Cut

2719a A2064 29c **multicolored,** pane of 18, *Oct. 29,* P#V11111 11.00

By its nature, No. 2719a constitutes a complete booklet (BC85). The peelable paper backing serves as a booklet cover.

A2071, A2075-A2077

Tab format on No. 2737a is similar to that shown for No. 2737b.

1993

2737a A2071 29c pane of 8, 2 #2731, 1 each #2732-2737, *June 16* 5.00 *2.25*
Never folded pane, P#A22222 6.25
P#A13113 —

2737b A2071 29c pane of 4, #2731, 2735-2737 + tab, *June 16* 2.25 *1.50*
Never folded pane, P#A22222 3.25
P#A13113 —

Combination Booklet

BK204 BC86 $5.80 **multicolored,** 2 #2737a, + 1 #2737b, P#A11111, A22222 11.00
P#A13113, A44444 14.00

No. 2737b without tab is indistinguishable from broken No. 2737a.

Never folded panes of No. 2737a with P#A11111 exist missing the bottom stamp (found in some USPS mint sets).

No. BK204 exists assembled from panes with different plate numbers.

A2086-A2090

2745a A2086 29c pane of 5, *Jan. 25* 2.75 *2.25*
Never folded pane, P#1111, 1211 3.75
P#2222 6.25

Booklet

BK207 BC89 $5.80 **multi,** P#1111, 1211, 2222 11.00

A2105-A2109

2764a A2105 29c pane of 5, *May 15* 2.75 *2.25*
Never folded pane, P#1 3.75

Booklet

BK208 BC90 $5.80 **multicolored,** P#1, 2 12.00

Varieties

2764b As "a," black (engr.) omitted *200.00*
2764c As "a," imperf. *2,250.*

Booklet

BK208a As #BK208, with 4 #2764b *1,000.*

A2069, A2112-A2114

2770a A2069 29c pane of 4, *July 14* 2.75 *2.25*
Never folded pane, P#A11111, A11121, A22222 3.75

Booklet

BK209 BC91 $5.80 **multicolored,** P#A11111, A11121, A22222, A23232, A23233 12.00

A2070, A2115-A2117

2778a A2070 29c pane of 4, *Sept. 25, 1993* 2.50 *2.00*
Never folded pane, P#A222222 3.50

Booklet

BK210 BC92 $5.80 **multicolored,** P#A111111, A222222, A333333, A422222 11.00
P#A333323 —

Varieties

2778b As "a," imperf. —

A2128

2790a A2128 29c pane of 4, *Oct. 21, 1993* 2.25 *1.75*
Never bound pane, P#K111111, K133333, K144444 3.25
P#K255555 *85.00*

Booklet

BK211 BC93 $5.80 **multicolored,** P#K111111, K133333, K144444, K255555, K266666 11.50
P#K222222 35.00

Varieties

2790b Imperf., pair —
2790c As "a," imperf. —

No. 2798a — A2129-A2132

2798a A2129 29c pane of 10, 3 each #2795-2796, 2 each #2797-2798, *Oct. 21, 1993* 8.50 *4.00*
Never folded pane, P#111111 10.00
2798b A2129 29c pane of 10, 3 each #2797-2798, 2 each #2795-2796, *Oct. 21, 1993* 8.50 *4.00*
Never folded pane, P#111111 10.00

Combination Booklet

BK212 BC94 $5.80 **multicolored,** 1 each #2798a, 2798b, P#111111, 222222 17.50

Varieties

2798c Block of 4, Nos. 2795-2798 3.40 1.75

On No. 2798b the plate number appears close to the top row of perfs. Different selvage markings can be found there.

A2129-A2132

A2131

Self-Adhesive *Die Cut*

2802a A2129 29c pane of 3 each #2799-2802, *Oct. 28, 1993,* P#V1111111, V2221222, V2222112, V2222122, V2222221, V2222222 7.00
P#V3333333 9.00
2803a A2131 29c pane of 18, *Oct. 28, 1993,* P#V1111 10.00
P# V2222 12.50

Varieties

2802c Block of 4, Nos. 2799-2802 2.20

By their nature, Nos. 2802a-2803a constitute complete booklets (BC95-BC96). The peelable backing serves as a booklet cover.

A2135

2806b A2135 29c pane of 5, *Dec. 1, 1993* 2.75 *2.00*
Never folded pane 3.75

Booklet

BK213 BC97 $2.90 **black & red,** P#K111 5.75

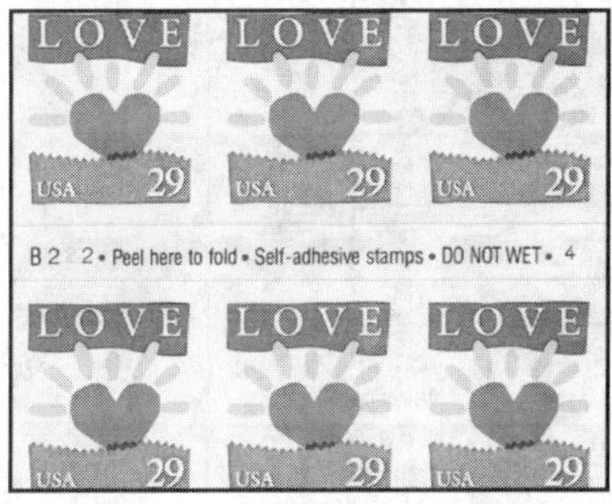

A2142

1994 Self-Adhesive *Die Cut*

2813a A2142 29c pane of 18, *Jan. 27,* P#, see list 11.00
P#B111-5, B333-14 *75.00*
P#B121-5, B444-7, B444-8, B444-9, B444-14 14.00
P#B333-5, B333-7, B333-8 22.50
P#B334-11 *750.00*
P#B344-11 50.00
P#B434-10 100.00

By its nature, No. 2813a constitutes a complete booklet (BC98). The peelable backing serves as a booklet cover.
List - #B111-1, B111-2, B111-3, B111-4, B221-5, B222-4, B222-5, B222-6, B333-9, B333-10, B333-11, B333-12, B333-17, B344-12, B344-13, B444-10, B444-13, B444-15, B444-16, B444-17, B444-18, B444-19, B555-20, B555-21

A2143

2814a A2143 29c pane of 10, *Feb. 14, 1994* 5.50 *3.50*
Never folded pane, P#A11111 6.00

Booklet

BK214 BC99 $5.80 **multicolored,** P#A11111, A11311, A12112, A21222, A22122, A22322 11.00
P#A12111, A12211, A12212, A21311 25.00
P#A22222 16.00

Varieties

2814b As #2814a, imperf —
2814e Horiz. pair, imperf between —

A2158-A2162

2833a A2158 29c pane of 5, *Apr. 28, 1994* 2.75 2.25
Never folded pane, P#2 3.25

Booklet

BK215 BC100 $5.80 **multicolored,** P#1, 2 12.00

Varieties

2833b As "a," imperf *2,000.*
2833c As "a," black (engr.) omitted *200.00*

Booklet

BK215a As #BK215, with 4 #2833c *800.00*

A2171-A2175

2847a A2171 29c pane of 5, *July 28, 1994* 2.75 *2.00*
Never folded pane 3.75

Booklet

BK216 BC101 $5.80 **multicolored,** P#S11111 12.00

Varieties

2847b As "a," imperf —

A2200

2871Ab A2200 29c pane of 10, *Oct. 20, 1994* 6.25 *3.50*
Never folded pane, P#1, 2 7.00

Booklet

BK217 BC102 $5.80 **multicolored,** P#1, 2 12.50

Varieties

2871Ac As "b," imperf. *2,250.*

A2201

2872a A2201 29c pane of 20, *Oct. 20, 1994* 11.00 *3.00*
Never folded pane, P#P11111, P22222, P44444 12.50
P#P33333 —

Booklet

BK218 BC103 $5.80 **multicolored,** P#P11111, P22222, P33333, P44444 11.50

Varieties

2872c As "a," imperf. horiz. —

A2202

2873a A2202 29c pane of 12, *Oct. 20, 1994,* P#V1111 6.75

By is nature, No. 2873a constitutes a complete booklet (BC104). The peelable backing serves as a booklet cover.

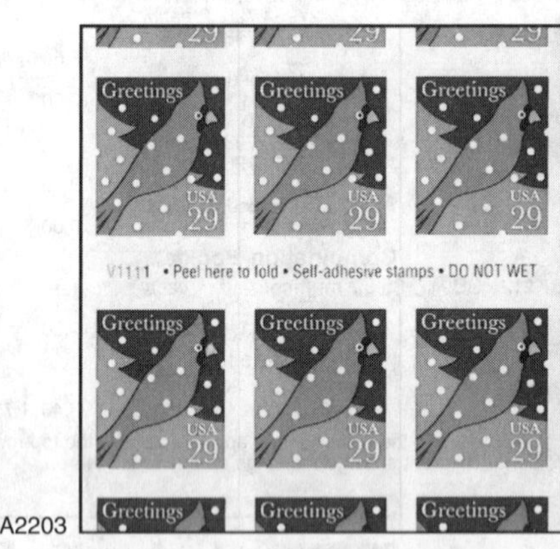

A2203

2874a A2203 29c pane of 18, *Oct. 20, 1994,* P#V1111, V2222 10.00

By its nature, No. 2874a constitutes a complete booklet (BC105). The peelable backing serves as a booklet cover.

A2208

1994 ***Perf. 11.2x11.1***

2881a A2208 (32c) **black "G" & multi,** pane of 10, *Dec. 13, 1994* 6.00 *3.75*

Booklet

BK219 BC106 ($3.20) **pale blue & red,** P#1111 6.00

Perf. 10x9.9

2883a A2208 (32c) **black "G" & multi,** pane of 10, *Dec. 13, 1994* 6.25 *3.75*

Booklets

BK220 BC106 ($3.20) **pale blue & red,** P#1111, 2222 6.25
BK221 BC106 ($6.40) **blue & red,** P#1111, 2222 12.50

Perf. 10.9

2884a A2208 (32c) **blue "G" & multi,** pane of 10, *Dec. 13, 1994* 6.00 *3.75*

Booklet

BK222 BC106 ($6.40) **blue "G" & multi,** P#A1111, A1211, A2222, A3333, A4444 12.00

No. BK222 exists with panes that have different plate numbers.

Varieties

2884b As "a," imperf. —

Perf. 11x10.9

2885a A2208 (32c) **red "G" & multi,** pane of 10, *Dec. 13, 1994* 8.50 *4.50*

Booklet

BK223 BC106 ($6.40) **red "G" & multi,** P#K1111 17.50

Varieties

2885b Pair, imperf vert. —
2885c Pair, imperf between —

No. 2885c resulted from a paper foldover after perforating and before cutting into panes.

No. 2886a — A2208b

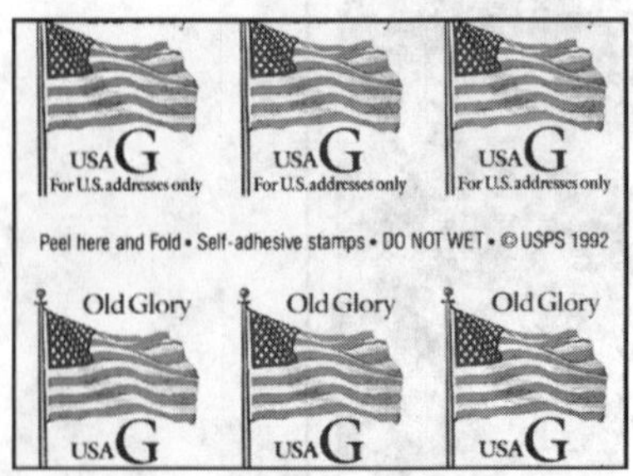

No. 2887a — A2208c

Self-Adhesive ***Die Cut***

2886a A2208b (32c) pane of 18, *Dec. 13, 1994,* P#V11111, V22222 14.00
2887a A2208c (32c) pane of 18, *Dec. 13, 1994,* no P# 14.00

By their nature, Nos. 2886a and 2887a constitute complete booklets (BC107). The peelable backing serves as a booklet cover. The backing on No. 2886a contains a UPC symbol, while the backing on No. 2887a does not.

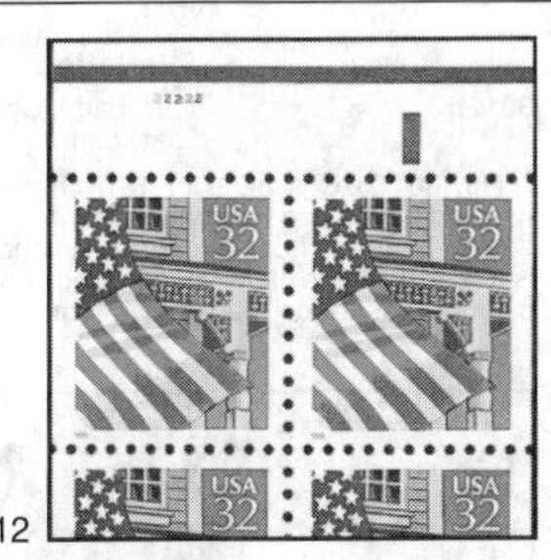
A2212

Perf. 10.8x9.8

2916a A2212 32c **blue, tan, brown, red & light blue,** pane of 10, *May 19, 1995* 6.50 *3.25*
Never folded pane, P#11111 7.25

Booklets

BK225 BC108 $3.20 **blue & red,** P#11111, 22222, 33332 6.50
P#23222, 44444 —
BK226 BC108 $6.40 **multicolored,** P#11111, 13111, 22222, 23222, 33332, 44444 13.00

Varieties

2916b As "a," imperf. —

A2230

Self-Adhesive ***Die Cut***

2919a A2230 32c pane of 18, *Mar. 17, 1995,* P#V1111, V1311, V1433, V2222, V2322 11.00
P#V2111 45.00

Varieties

2919b Vert. pair, no die cutting between —

By its nature No. 2919a is a complete booklet (BC113). The peelable backing serves as a booklet cover.

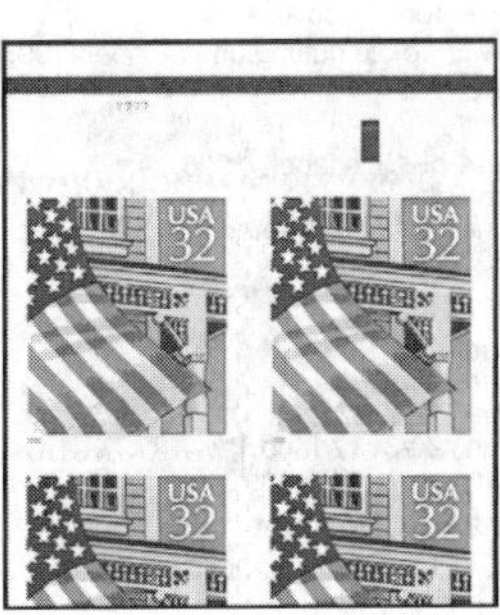

Nos. 2920a, 2920c — A2212

Serpentine Die Cut 8.7 on 2 or 3 Sides

Self-Adhesive

2920a A2212 32c pane of 20+label, large date, *Apr. 18, 1995* (see List 1) 12.00
P#V23422 25.00
P#V23522 40.00
P#V57663 —
2920c A2212 32c pane of 20+label, small date, *Apr. 18, 1995,* P#V11111 *110.00*

Varieties

2920g As "a," partial pane of 10, 3 stamps and parts of 7 stamps printed on backing liner —
2920i Imperf, pair —
2920j Dark blue omitted (from 2920a) —

By their nature Nos. 2920a, 2920c are complete booklets (BC114). The rouletted peelable backing, of which two types are known, serves as a booklet cover.

Date on No. 2920a is nearly twice as large as date on No. 2920c.

List 1 - P#V12211, V12212, V12312, V12321, V12322, V12331, V13322, V13831, V13834, V13836, V22211, V23322, V23432, V34743, V34745, V36743, V42556, V45554, V56663, V56665, V56763, V65976, V78989.

Nos. 2920f, 2920h — A2212

Serpentine Die Cut 8.7

Self-Adhesive

2920f A2212 32c pane of 15+label 9.00
2920h A2212 32c pane of 15, see note, *1996 35.00*

Booklets

BK226A BC126 $4.80 **blue,** 1 #2920f, no P# (4) 9.00
BK226B BC126 $4.80 **blue,** 1 #2920h, no P# (3) 65.00
BK227 BC126 $9.60 **blue,** 2 #2920f (3) 18.00

No. 2920h is a pane of 16 with one stamp removed. The missing stamp is the lower right stamp in the pane or (more rarely) the upper left stamp. No. 2920h cannot be made from No. 2920f, a pane of 15 + label. The label is located in the sixth or seventh row of the pane and is die cut. If the label is removed, an impression of the die cutting appears on the backing paper.

No. 2920De — A2212

Serpentine Die Cut 11.3

Self-Adhesive

2920De A2212 32c pane of 10, *Jan. 20, 1996* 7.50

By its nature No. 2920De is a complete booklet (BC114). The rouletted peelable backing serves as a booklet cover.

Below is a list of known plate numbers. Some numbers may be scarcer than the value indicated in the listing.

No. 2920De - P#V11111, V12111, V23222, V31121, V32111, V32121, V44322, V44333, V44444, V55555, V66666, V66886, V67886, V68886, V68896, V76989, V77666, V77668, V77766, V77776, V78698, V78886, V78896, V78898, V78986, V78989, V89999.

Nos. 2921a, 2921c, 2921d — A2212

Serpentine Die Cut 9.8

Self-Adhesive

2921a A2212 32c pane of 10, dated red "1996," *May 21, 1996* 7.50
Never folded pane, P#21221, 22221, 22222 9.00
2921c A2212 32c pane of 10, dated red "1997,"*May 21, 1996* 7.50
Never folded pane, P#11111 9.00
2921d A2212 32c pane of 5 + label, dated red "1997," *Jan. 24, 1997* 3.75
Never folded pane, P#11111 5.25

Combination Booklet

BK227A BC108 $4.80 **multicolored,** 1 ea #2921c-2921d P#11111 11.25

Booklets

BK228 BC108 $6.40 **blue, red & black,** 2 #2921a (5) 15.00

Known numbers for BK228: P#11111, 13111, 21221, 22221, 22222, 44434, 44444, 55555, 55556, 66666, 77777, 88788, 88888, 99999. Some numbers may be scarcer than the value indicated in the listing.

BK228A BC108 $9.60 **multicolored,** 3 #2921c, P#11111 20.00

Varieties

2921e As "a," imperf. *300.00*

Booklet

BK228b As #BK228, with 2 #2921e, P#11111 *600.00*

A2264

Self-Adhesive ***Die Cut***

2949a A2264 (32c) pane of 20 + label, *Feb. 1, 1995,* P#B1111-1, B2222-1, B2222-2, B3333-2 12.00

By its nature, No. 2949a is a complete booklet (BC115). The peelable backing serves as a booklet cover.

Varieties

2949b As "a," red (engr.) omitted, single stamp *450.00*
2949c As "a," red (engr.) omitted *9,000.*
2949d As "a," red (engr.) missing (CM) —

No. 2949d must be collected se-tenant with a normal stamp.

A2272

Perf. 9.8x10.8

2959a A2272 32c pane of 10, *May 12, 1995* 6.00 *3.25*
Never folded pane 6.25

Booklet

BK229 BC116 $6.40 **multicolored,** P#1 12.00

Varieties

2959b As "a," Imperf. —

A2274

Self-Adhesive *Die Cut*

2960a A2274 55c pane of 20 + label, *May 12, 1995,* P#B1111-1, B2222-1 22.50

By its nature, No. 2960a is a complete booklet (BC117). The peelable backing serves as a booklet cover.

A2283-A2287

2973a A2283 32c pane of 5, *June 17, 1995* 3.00 *2.75*
Never folded pane 3.50

Booklet

BK230 BC118 $6.40 **multicolored,** P#S11111 12.00

A2306-A2310

2997a A2306 32c pane of 5, *Sept. 19, 1995* 3.00 *2.25*
Never folded pane 4.00

Booklet

BK231 BC119 $6.40 **multicolored,** P#2 12.00

Varieties

2997b As "a," imperf. —

A2316

3003Ab A2316 32c pane of 10, *Oct. 19, 1995* 6.50 *4.00*
Never folded pane 7.50

Booklet

BK232 BC120 $6.40 **multicolored,** P#1 13.00

A2317-A2320

3007b A2317 32c pane of 10, 3 each #3004-3005, 2 each #3006-3007, *Sept. 30, 1995* 6.00 *4.00*
Never folded pane, P#P1111 7.00

3007c A2317 32c pane of 10, 2 each #3004-3005, 3 each #3006-3007, *Sept. 30, 1995* 6.00 *4.00*
Never folded pane, P#P1111 7.00

Combination Booklet

BK233 BC121 $6.40 **multicolored,** 1 each #3007b, 3007c, P#P1111, P2222 12.00

Varieties

3007d As "a," imperf. *600.00*

A2317-A2320

Serpentine Die Cut

3011a A2317 32c pane of 20 +label, *Sept. 30, 1995* P#V1111, V1211, V3233, V3333, V4444 15.00
P#V1212 25.00

By is nature, No. 3011a is a complete booklet (BC122). The peelable backing serves as a booklet cover.

P#V1111, V1211, V1212, V3233, V3333, V4444.

No. 3012a — A2321

Serpentine Die Cut

3012a A2321 32c pane of 20 + label, *Oct. 19, 1995,* P#B1111, B2222, B3333 12.00

By its nature, No. 3012a is a complete booklet (BC123). The peelable backing serves as a booklet cover.

No. 3012a comes either with no die cutting on the label (1995 printing) or with die cutting (and deeper colors) from the 1996 printing.

3012c A2321 32c pane of 15 + label, *1996,* no P# 9.00

3012d A2321 32c pane of 15, see note, *1996* —

Booklets

BK233A BC126 $4.80 **blue,** #3012c (2) 9.00
BK233B BC126 $4.80 **blue,** #3012d —
BK233C BC126 $9.60 **blue** 2 #3012c (3) 18.00
BK233D BC126 $9.60 **blue,** 2 #3012d, no P# (3) 25.00

Combination Booklet

BK233E BC126 $9.60 **blue,** 1 ea #3012c, 3012d (2) 40.00

Varieties

3012b Vert. pair, no die cutting between —

No. 3012d is a pane of 16 with one stamp removed. The missing stamp can be from either row 1, 2, 3, 7 or 8. No. 3012d cannot be made from No. 3012c, a pane of 15 + label. The label is die cut. If the label is removed, an impression of the die cutting appears on the backing paper.

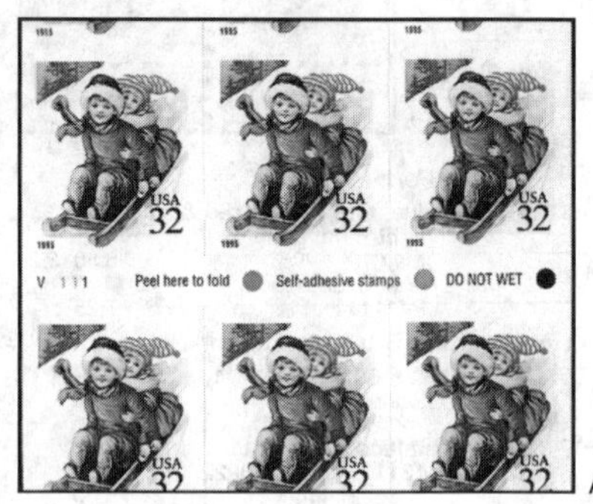

A2322

Die Cut

3013a A2322 32c Pane of 18, *Oct. 19, 1995,* P#V1111 11.00

By its nature, No. 3013a is a complete booklet (BC124). The peelable backing serves as a booklet cover.

A2329-A2333

3029a A2329 32c pane of 5, *Jan. 19, 1996* 3.00 *2.50*
Never folded pane 3.50

Booklet

BK234 BC125 $6.40 **multicolored,** P#1 12.00

Varieties

3029b As "a," imperf. —

No. 3030a — A2334

Serpentine Die Cut 11.3x11.7

3030a A2334 32c pane of 20+label, *Jan. 20, 1996* 12.00

By its nature, No. 3030a is a complete booklet (BC115). The peelable backing serves as a booklet cover.

P#B1111-1, B1111-2, B2222-1, B2222-2.

3030b A2334 32c pane of 15+label, *1996* 9.00

Booklet

BK235 BC126 $4.80 **blue** (4) 9.00
BK236 BC126 $9.60 **blue** (3) 18.00

Varieties

3030c Red (engr.) omitted, single stamp *325.00*

3030d Red (engr.) missing (CM), single stamp —

No. 3030d must be collected se-tenant with a stamp bearing the red engraving.

A1847

Serpentine Die Cut 10.4x10.8

3048a A1847 20c pane of 10, *Aug. 2, 1996,* P#S1111, S2222 4.00

By is nature, No. 3048a is a complete booklet (BC128). The peelable backing serves as a booklet cover.

3048b A1847 20c Booklet pane of 4 1.60
3048c A1847 20c Booklet pane of 6 2.40

Nos. 3048b-3048c are from the vending machine booklet No. BK237 that has a glue strip at the top edge of the top pane, the peelable strip removed and the rouletting line 2mm lower than on No. 3048a when the panes are compared with the bottoms aligned

Booklet

BK237 BC128 $2.00 **multicolored,** 1 ea #3048b, 3048c, P#S1111, S2222 4.00

A1853

Serpentine Die Cut 11.3x11.7

3049a A1853 32c pane of 20, *Oct. 24, 1996,* P#S1111, S2222, S3333 12.00

By its nature, No. 3049a is a complete booklet (BC61B). The peelable backing, of which three types are known, serves as a booklet cover.

3049b A1853 32c pane of 4, *Dec. 1996,* no P# 2.75
3049c A1853 32c pane of 5 + label, *Dec. 1996,* P#S1111 3.20
3049d A1853 32c pane of 6, *Dec. 1996,* without P# 3.60

Combination Booklet

BK241 BC129 $4.80 **multicolored,** 1 ea #3049b-3049d, P#S1111 10.00

Booklet

BK242 BC129 $9.60 **multicolored,** 5 #3049d, P#S1111 19.00

The backing on Nos. BK241-BK242 is rouletted between each pane.
P# on Nos. 3049c-3049d is on a stamp, not the removable strip.

Varieties

3049c P# single, #S1111 .80 *1.00*
3049d Pane of 6 containing P# single 4.00
P# single, #S1111 .80 1.00

The plate # single in No. 3049c is on the lower left stamp. In No. 3049d it is the lower right stamp on the bottom pane of the booklet.

A2350

1998 ***Serpentine Die Cut 11.2***

3050a A2350 20c pane of 10, *July 31, 1998,* P#V1111, V2222, V2232, V3233 4.00
P#V2342, V3232 —
3050c A2350 20c pane of 10, *July 31, 1998,* P#V2332, V2333, V2342, V2343, V3232, V3233, V3243, V3333 4.00
P#V2232, V2332 —

By their nature Nos. 3050a and 3050c are complete booklets (BC130). The peelable backing serves as a booklet cover. All stamps in Nos. 3050a and 3050c are upright.

3051Ac — A2350

1999 ***Serpentine Die Cut 10½x11 on 3 Sides***

Self-Adhesive

3051Ab A2350 20c pane, 4 #3051, 1 #3051A turned sideways at top, *July 1999* 6.00
3051Ac A2350 20c pane, 4 #3051, 1 #3051A turned sideways at bottom, *July 1999* 6.00

BOOKLET

BK242A BC130 $2.00 **multicolored,** #3051b, 3051c, P#V1111, *July 1999* 12.00

3052a-3052c — A2351

3052d — A2351

3052Ef — A2351

Serpentine Die Cut 11½x11¼

3052a A2351 33c pane of 4, no P# 3.20
3052b A2351 33c pane of 5 + label, no P# 4.00
3052c A2351 33c pane of 6 4.80
3052d A2351 33c pane of 20 + label, P#S222 13.00

COMBINATION BOOKLET

BK242B BC131 $4.95 **multicolored,** 1 each #3052a-3052c, P#S111, *Aug. 13, 1999* 12.00

Varieties

3052i Imperf, pair —

No. BK242B has a self-adhesive strip on #3052b that adhers to the plastic-coated peelable backing of #3052a when the booklet is closed. When the booklet is opened, this strip is sticky and my adhere firmly to mounts, album pages, etc. Removal of this strip will damage the backing paper of #3052b. Plate numbers for No. BK242B are on backing paper below bar code.
No. 3052d is a complete booklet (BC131). The peelable backing serves as a booklet cover.

Serpentine Die Cut 10¾x10½ on 2 or 3 Sides

2000

3052Ef A2351 33c pane of 20, *Apr. 7, 2000,* P#S111 13.00

By its nature, No. 3052Ef is a complete booklet. Eight #3052E and the booklet cover (similar to BC131) are printed on one side of the peelable backing and twelve #3052E appear on the other side of the backing.

Varieties

3052Eg As "f," all 12 stamps on one side with black ("33 USA," etc.) omitted —
3052Eh Horiz. pair, imperf between —

3071a — A2370

Serpentine Die Cut 9.9x10.8

3071a A2370 32c pane of 20, *May 31, 1996,* P#S11111 14.00

Varieties

3071b Horiz. pair, no die cutting between —
3071c Imperf, pair —
3071d Horiz. pair, inperf vert. —

By its nature, No. 3071a is a complete booklet (BC127). The peelable backing serves as a booklet cover.

A2387

Serpentine Die Cut 11.6x11.4

3089a A2387 32c pane of 20, *Aug. 1, 1996,* P#B1111 14.00

By its nature, No. 3089a is a complete booklet (BC133). The peelable backing serves as a booklet cover.

A2405

Serpentine Die Cut 10 on 2, 3 or 4 Sides

3112a A2405 32c pane of 20 + label, *Nov. 1, 1996* 12.00

Varieties

3112b	No die cutting, pair	*70.00*
3112c	As "a," no die cutting	—

By its nature No. 3112a is a complete booklet (BC134). The peelable backing serves as a booklet cover.

Below is a list of known plate numbers. Some numbers may be scarcer than the value indicated in the listing.

P#1111-1, 1211-1, 2212-1, 2222-1, 2323-1, 3323-1, 3333-1, 3334-1, 4444-1, 5544-1, 5555-1, 5556-1, 5556-2, 5656-2, 6656-2, 6666-1, 6666-2, 6766-1, 7887-1, 7887-2, 7888-2, 7988-2.

A2406-2409

Serpentine Die Cut 11.8x11.5 on 2, 3 or 4 Sides

3116a A2406 32c pane of 20 + label, *Oct. 8, 1996*, P#B1111, B2222, B3333 12.00

Varieties

3116b	As "a," no die cutting	*3,000.*

By its nature No. 3116a is a complete booklet (BC135). The peelable backing serves as a booklet cover.

A2410

Die Cut

3117a A2410 32c pane of 18, *Oct. 8, 1996*, P#V1111, V2111 11.00

By its nature No. 3117a is a complete booklet (BC136). The peelable backing serves as a booklet cover.

MAKESHIFT VENDING MACHINE BOOKLETS

The booklets listed below were released in 1996 to meet the need for $4.80 and $9.60 vending machine booklets. The booklets consist of blocks of sheet stamps folded and affixed to a standard cover (BC126) with a spot of glue.

The cover varies from issue to issue in the line of text on the front that indicates the number of stamps contained in the booklet and in the four lines of text on the back that describe the contents of the booklet and list the booklet's item number. Due to the folding required to make stamps fit within the covers, the stamp blocks may easily fall apart when booklets are opened. Stamps may also easily detach from booklet cover.

1996

Booklets

BK243	BC126	$4.80	**blue,** 15 #2897	11.00
BK244	BC126	$4.80	**blue,** 15 #2957	11.00
BK245	BC126	$4.80	**blue,** 15 #3024	12.50
BK246	BC126	$4.80	**blue,** 15 #3065	11.00
BK247	BC126	$4.80	**blue,** 15 #3069	11.00
BK248	BC126	$4.80	**blue,** 15 #3070	11.00
BK249	BC126	$4.80	**blue,** 3 #3076a	11.00
BK250	BC126	$4.80	**blue,** 15 #3082	13.50
BK251	BC126	$4.80	**blue,** 15(#3083-3086)	11.00
BK252	BC126	$4.80	**blue,** 15 #3087	15.00
BK253	BC126	$4.80	**blue,** 15 #3088	11.00
BK254	BC126	$9.60	**blue,** 30 #3090	22.50
BK255	BC126	$4.80	**blue,** 3 #3095a	12.50
BK256	BC126	$4.80	**blue,** #3105a-3105o	11.00
BK257	BC126	$4.80	**blue,** 15 #3107	11.00
BK258	BC126	$4.80	**blue,** 15 #3118	11.00

The contents of #BK251 may vary.

See Nos. BK266-BK269, BK272-BK274, BK277-BK278.

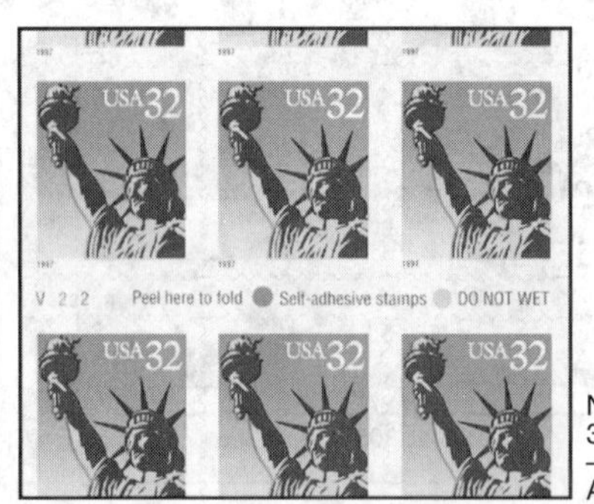

No. 3122a — A1951

1997

Serpentine Die Cut 11

3122a A1951 32c pane of 20 + label, *Feb. 1,* P#V1111, V1211, V1311, V2122, V2222, V2311, V2331, V3233, V3333, V3513, V4532 12.00

Varieties

3122h	As "a," no die cutting	—

By its nature, No. 3122a is a complete booklet (BC79). The peelable backing, of which two types are known, serves as a booklet cover.

3122b	A1951	32c pane of 4, *Feb. 1,* no P#	2.50
3122c	A1951	32c pane of 5 + label, *Feb. 1,* P#V1111	3.20
3122d	A1951	32c pane of 6, *Feb. 1,* without P#	3.60

Varieties

3122c	P# single, #V1111	.80	*1.00*
3122d	pane of 6 containing P# single	4.00	
	P#Single, #V1111	.80	*1.00*

The plate # single in No. 3122c is the lower left stamp and should be collected unused with the reorder label to its right to differentiate it from the plate # single in No. 3122d which is the lower left stamp in the bottom pane of the booklet and should be collected with a normal stamp adjoining it at right. In used condition, these plate # singles are indistinguishable.

Serpentine Die Cut 11.5x11.8 on 2, 3 or 4 Sides

3122Ef	A1951	32c pane of 20 + label, P#V1111, V1211, V2122, V2222	35.00
3122Eg	A1951	32c pane of 6, *1997,* without plate # single	7.00

By its nature, No. 3122Ef is a complete booklet (BC79). The peelable backing serves as a booklet cover.

Combination Booklet

BK259 BC79 $4.80 **multicolored,** 1 ea #3122b-3122d, P#V1111 10.00

Booklets

BK260	BC79	$9.60	**multicolored,** 5 #3122d, P#V1111	19.00
BK260A	BC79	$9.60	**multicolored,** 5 #3122Eg	37.50

The backing on Nos. BK259-BK260 is rouletted between each pane.

Varieties

3122Eg	pane of 6 containing P# single	8.00	
	P# single, #V1111	2.00	2.00

The plate # single in No. 3122Eg is the lower left stamp in the bottom pane of the booklet.

A2415

1997

Serpentine Die Cut 11.8x11.6 on 2, 3 or 4 Sides

3123a A2415 32c pane of 20 + label, *Feb. 4,* P#B1111, B2222, B3333, B4444, B5555, B6666, B7777 12.00

Serpentine Die Cut 11.6x11.8 on 2, 3 or 4 Sides

3124a A2416 55c pane of 20 + label, *Feb. 4,* P#B1111, B2222, B3333, B4444 21.00

By their nature, Nos. 3123a-3124a are complete booklets (BC137). The peelable backing serves as a booklet cover.

Varieties

3123b	No die cutting, pair	*175.00*
3123c	As "a," no die cutting	*1,750.*
3123d	As "a," black omitted	—

No. 3127a — A2418-A2419

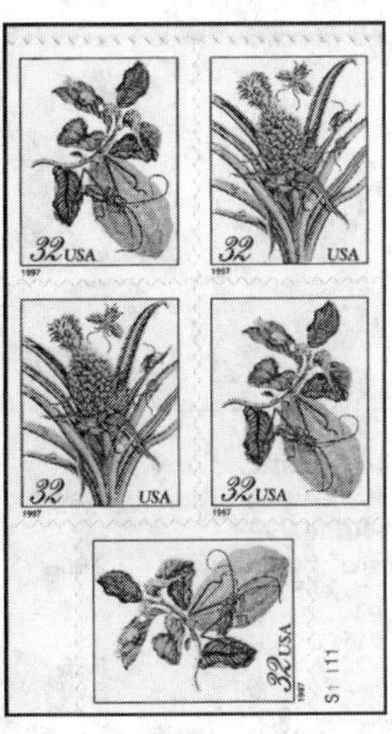
No. 3128b, 3129b — A2418-A2419

Serpentine Die Cut 10.9x10.2 on 2,3 or 4 Sides

1997

3127a A2418 32c pane of 20, 10 ea #3126-3127 + label, *Mar. 3,* P#S11111, S22222, S33333 12.00

By its nature, No. 3127a is a complete booklet (BC138). The peelable backing serves as a booklet cover.

See Footnote

3128b A2418 32c pane of 5, 2 ea #3128-3129, 1 #3128a, *Mar. 3,* P#S11111 7.50
3129b A2419 32c pane of 5, 2 ea #3128-3129, 1 #3129a, *Mar. 3,* no P# 6.00

Combination Booklet

BK261 BC138 $4.80 2 #3128b, 1 #3129b, P#S11111 20.00

Varieties

3127b Pair, Nos. 3126-3127 1.20
3127c Vert. pair, imperf between *475.00*
3129c Pair, Nos. 3128-3129 2.25

Nos. 3128-3129 are serpentine die cut 11.2x10.8 on 2 or 3 sides. Nos. 3128a-3129a are placed sideways on the pane and are serpentine die cut 11.2 on top and bottom, 10.8 on left side. The right side is 11.2 broken by a large perf where the stamp meets the vertical perforations of the two stamps above it.

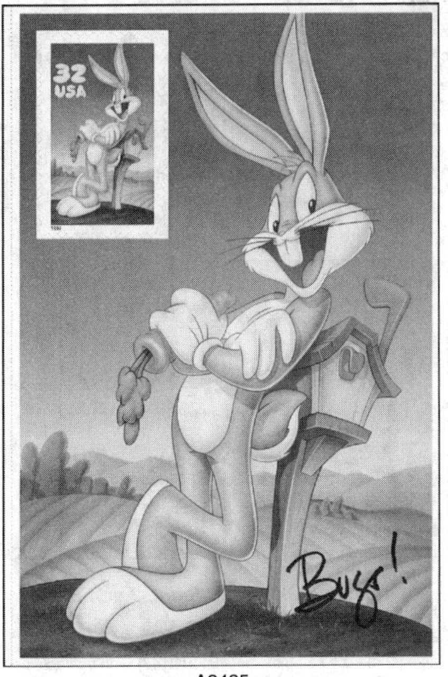

A2425

1997, May 22

Serpentine Die Cut 11

Self-Adhesive

3137 A2425 32c pane of 10, Nos. 3137b, 3137c, no P# 6.00
3137b A2425 32c pane of 9, no P# 5.40
3137c A2425 32c pane of 1, no P# .60

Varieties

Pane of 10 from uncut press sheet *60.00*
Pane of 10 with plate # *350.00*

Die cutting on #3137 does not extend through the backing paper.

3138 A2425 32c pane of 10, Nos. 3138b, 3138c, no P# *125.00*
3138b A2425 32c pane of 9, no P# —

Imperf

3138c A2425 32c pane of 1, no P# —

Die cutting on #3138b extends through the backing paper.
By their nature, Nos. 3137-3138 are complete booklets (BC139). The peelable backing serves as a booklet cover.

3176a — A2459

Serpentine Die Cut 9.9 on 2, 3 or 4 Sides

1997, Oct. 27 **Tagged**

3176a A2459 32c pane of 20+label, P#1111, 2222, 3333 12.00

By its nature, No. 3176a is a complete booklet (BC140). The peelable backing serves as a booklet cover.

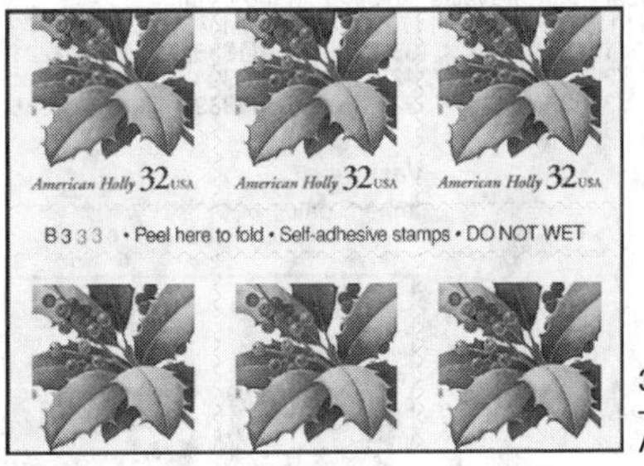

3177a — A2460

Serpentine Die Cut 11.2x11.8 on 2, 3 or 4 Sides

1997, Oct. 30 **Tagged**

Self-Adhesive

3177a A2460 32c pane of 20 + label, P#B1111, B2222, B3333 12.00

By its nature No. 3177a is a complete booklet (BC141). The peelable backing serves as a booklet cover.

3177b A2460 32c Booklet pane of 4, no P# 2.50
3177c A2460 32c Booklet pane of 5 + label, no P# 3.00
3177d A2460 32c Booklet pane of 6, no P# or P#B1111 3.75

Combination Booklet

BK264 BC141 $4.80 **black & green,** 1 ea #3177b-3177d, P#B1111 9.25

Booklet

BK265 BC141 $9.60 **black & green,** 5 #3177d, P#B1111 19.00

Panes in Nos. BK264-BK265 are separated by rouletting between each pane.

MAKESHIFT VENDING MACHINE BOOKLETS

See note before No. BK243.

1997

BK266 BC126 $4.80 #3151a-3151o 9.00
BK267 BC126 $4.80 15 #3152 9.00
BK268 BC126 $4.80 15 #3153 9.00
BK269 BC126 $4.80 3 ea #3168-3172 9.00

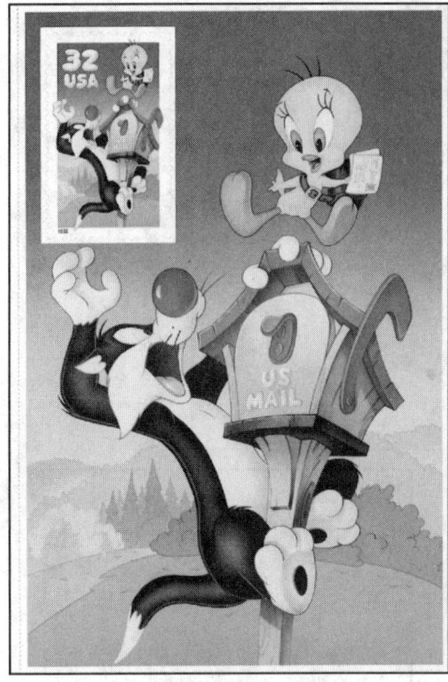

A2487

1998, Apr. 27 ***Serpentine Die Cut 11.1***

Self-Adhesive

3204 A2487 32c Pane of 10, 1 each #3204b, 3204c 6.00
3204b A2487 32c Pane of 9, no P# 5.40
3204c A2487 32c Pane of 1, no P# .60
3205 A2487 32c Pane of 10, 1 each #3205b, 3205c *10.00*
3205b A2487 32c Pane of 9, no P# —

Imperf

3205c A2487 32c Pane of 1, no P# —

Varieties

Pane of 10 from sheet of 60 *11.00*
Pane of 10 with plate # *45.00*

Die cutting on No. 3205b extends through the backing paper. By their nature, Nos. 3204 and 3205 are complete booklets. The peelable backing (BC139) serves as a booklet cover.

3244a — A2524

Serpentine Die Cut 10.1x9.9 on 2, 3 or 4 Sides

1998, Oct. 15 **Tagged**

3244a A2524 32c pane of 20+label, P#11111, 22222, 33333 12.00

No. 3244a is a complete booklet (BC142). The peelable backing serves as a booklet cover.

Varieties

3244b Imperf, pair —

3248a-3248c

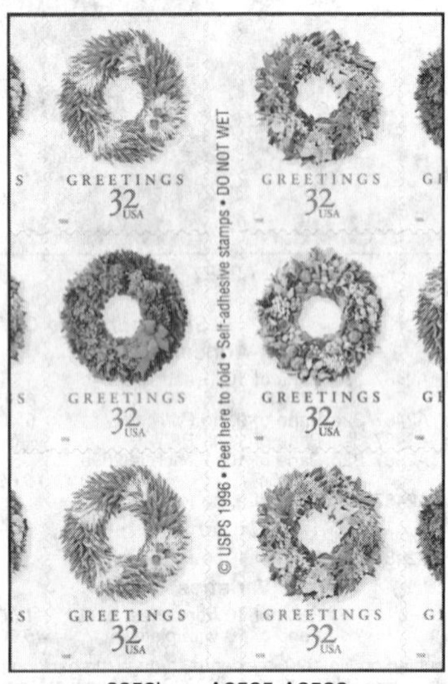

3252b — A2525-A2528

Serpentine Die Cut 11.3x11.6 on 2, or 3 Sides

1998, Oct. 15 **Tagged**

3248a	A2525	32c pane of 4, #3245-3248, no P#	22.50
3248b	A2525	32c pane of 5, #3245-3246, 3248, 2 #3247 + label, no P#	27.50
3248c	A2525	32c pane of 6, #3247-3248, 2 each #3245-3246, P#B111111	32.50

Combination Booklet

BK270	BC143 $4.80	**multi,** 1 each #3248a-3248c, P#B111111	*90.00*

Serpentine Die Cut 11.4x11.6 on 2, 3 or 4 Sides

3252b	A2525	32c pane of 5 each #3249-3252 + label, P#B111111, B222222, B333333, B444444, B555555	12.00

No. 3252b is a complete booklet (BC143). The peelable backing serves as a booklet cover.

Varieties

3252c	Block or strip of 4, red ("Greetings 32 USA" and "1998") omitted on #3249, 3252	—

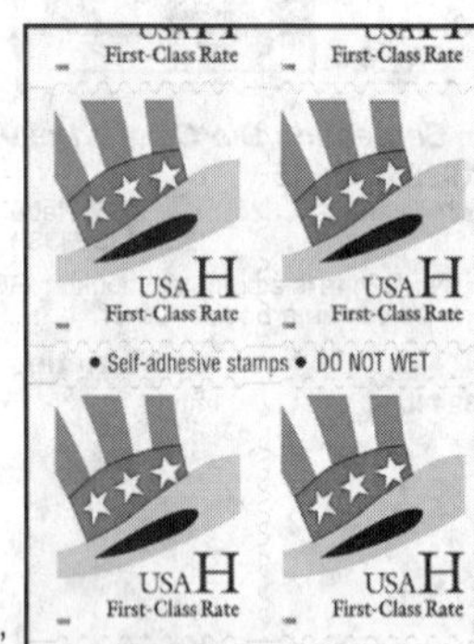

3267a, 3268a-3268b, 3269a — A2531

Serpentine Die Cut 9.9 on 2 or 3 Sides

1998, Nov. 9

3267a	A2531	(33c) pane of 10	6.50

Booklet

BK271	BC144 ($6.60)	**multi** P#1111, 2222, 3333	13.00

Die cut 11¼ on 3 sides (No. 3268a), 11 on 2, 3 or 4 Sides (No. 3268c)

3268a	A2531	(33c) pane of 10, P#V1111, V1211, V2211, V2222	6.50
3268c	A2531	(33c) pane of 20 + label, P#V1111, V1112, V1113, V1213, V1222, V2113, V2122, V2213, V2223	13.00
		P# V1122, V2222	20.00

Die Cut 8

3269a	A2531	(33c) pane of 18, P#V1111	12.00

Nos. 3268a, 3268c, 3269a are complete booklets (BC144). The peelable backing serves as a booket cover.

MAKESHIFT VENDING MACHINE BOOKLETS

See note before No. BK243.

1998

BK272	BC126 $4.80	15 (#3222-3225)	9.00
BK273	BC126 $4.80	15 #3237	9.00
BK274	BC126 $4.80	3 #3242a	9.00

Configuration of stamps in #BK272 may vary.

3274a — A2537

Tagged **Die Cut**

3274a	A2537	33c pane of 20, *Jan. 28, 1999*	13.00

No. 3274a is a complete booklet (BC145). The peelable backing serves as a booklet cover.

Below is a list of known plate numbers. Some numbers may be scarcer than the value indicated in the listing.

P#V1111, V1112, V1117, V1118, V1211, V1212, V1213, V1233, V1313, V1314, V1333, V1334, V1335, V2123, V2221, V2222, V2223, V2424, V2425, V2426, V2324, V3123, V3124, V3125, V3133, V3134, V3323, V3327, V3333, V3334, V3336, V4529, V5650.

Varieties

3274b	Imperf, pair	—

Nos. 3278a-3278c

No. 3278d

Nos. 3278e, 3278Fg

No. 3279a — A2540

Serpentine Die Cut 11 on 2, 3 or 4 Sides

1999 **Tagged**

Self-Adhesive

3278a	A2540	33c pane of 4, no P#	2.60
3278b	A2540	33c pane of 5 + label, P#V1111, V1112, V1121, V1122, V1212, V2212	3.25
3278c	A2540	33c pane of 6, no P#	3.90
3278d	A2540	33c pane of 10, P#V1111, V1112, V1113, V2222, V2322, V2324, V3433, V3434, V3545	6.50
3278e	A2540	33c pane of 20 + label, P#V1111, V1211, V2122, V2222, V2223, V3333, V4444	13.00

Serpentine Die Cut 11½x11¾ on 2, 3 or 4 Sides

3278Fg	A2540	33c pane of 20 + label	13.00

No. 3278Fg is a complete booklet. The peelable backing serves as a booklet cover and is similar to BC146.

Below is a list of known plate numbers. Some numbers may be scarcer than the value indicated in the listing.

P# V1111, V1131, V2222, V2223, V2323, V2423, V2443, V3333, V4444, V5428, V5445, V5576, V5578, V6423, V6456, V6546, V6556, V6575, V6576, V7567, V7667.

Serpentine Die Cut 11¼

3278j	A2540	33c pane of 10, P#V1111, V1112, V2222	6.50

By its nature No. 3278j is a complete booklet. The peelable backing serves as a booklet cover and is similar to BC146.

Serpentine Die Cut 9.8 on 2 or 3 Sides

3279a	A2540	33c pane of 10	6.50

COMBINATION BOOKLET

BK275	BC146 $4.95	**multi,** 1 each #3278a-3278c, P#V1111, V1112, V1121, V1212, V2212	10.00

BOOKLET

BK276	BC146 $6.60	**multi,** 2 #3279a, P#1111, 1121	13.00

Nos. 3278d-3278e are complete booklets. The peelable backing serves as a booklet cover and is similar to BC146.

Varieties

3278b	variety, P# single, #V1111, V1112, V1121, V1122, V1212, V2212	.80	*1.00*
3278h	As "e," imperf	—	

No. 3278 has black date.

The plate # single in No. 3278b is the lower left single.

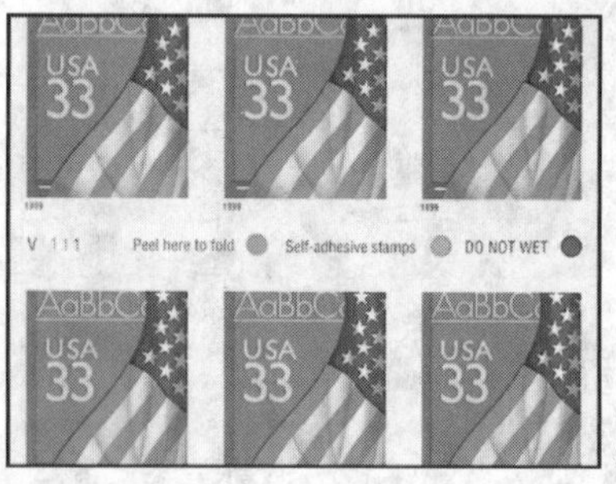

No. 3283a

Serpentine Die Cut 7.9 on 2, 3 or 4 Sides

Tagged

3283a	A2541	33c pane of 18, P#V1111	12.00

No. 3283a is a complete booklet (BC147). The peelable backing serves as a booklet cover.

Nos. 3297b, 3301a

No. 3297d

No. 3301c — A2550-A2553

Serpentine Die Cut 11¼x11½ on 2, 3 or 4 Sides

1999-2000 **Tagged**

Self-Adhesive

3297b 33c pane of 20, 5 ea #3294-3297 + label 13.00

No. 3297b is a complete booklet (BC148). The peelable backing serves as a booklet cover.

P#B1111, B1112, B2211, B2222, B3331, B3332, B3333, B4444, B5555.

Serpentine Die Cut 11¼x11½ on 2 or 3 Sides

3297d 33c pane of 20, 5 #3297e + label *Mar. 15, 2000,* P#B1111 13.00

By its nature, No. 3297d is a double-sided complete booklet. Two #3297e and the booklet cover (similar to BC148) are printed on one side of the peelable backing and three #3297e appear on the other side of the backing.

Varieties

3297c Block of 4, Nos. 3294-3297 2.60
3297e Block of 4, Nos. 3294a-3297a 2.60

Serpentine Die Cut 9½x10 on 2 or 3 sides

3301a A2550 33c pane of 4, no P# 2.60
3301b A2550 33c pane of 5 + label, no P# 3.25
3301c A2550 33c pane of 6, P#B1111, B1112, B2212, B2222 4.00
P#B2221 —

Only one example of No. 3301c with Plate #B2221 is recorded.

COMBINATION BOOKLET

BK276A BC148 $4.95 **multicolored,** 1 each #3301a-3301c, P# see 3301c 10.00

Varieties

3301d Block of 4, Nos. 3298-3301 2.60

A2554

1999, Apr. 16 ***Serpentine Die Cut 11.1***

Self-Adhesive

3306 33c Pane of 10, 1 each #3306b, 3306c 6.50
3306b 33c Pane of 9, no P# 5.85
3306c 33c Pane of 1, no P# .65
3307 33c Pane of 10, 1 each #3307b, 3307c *6.50*
3307b 33c Pane of 9, no P# *5.85*

Imperf

3307c 33c Pane of 1, no P# *.65*

Varieties

Pane of 10 from sheet of 60 *8.00*
Pane of 10 with plate # *15.00*

Die cutting on No. 3306b extends through the backing paper. By their nature, Nos. 3306 and 3307 are complete booklets. The peelable backing (BC139) serves as a booklet cover.

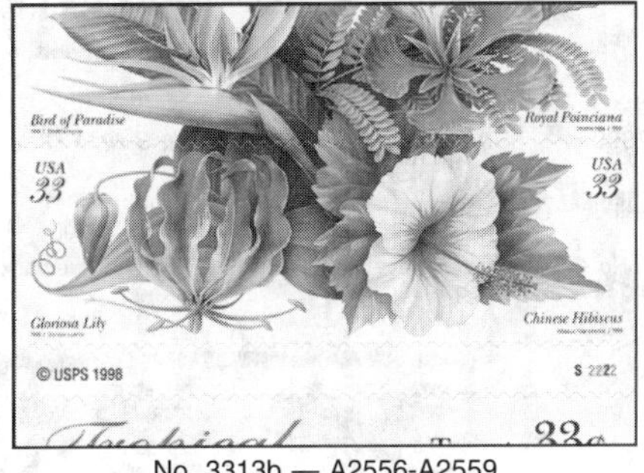
No. 3313b — A2556-A2559

Serpentine Die Cut 10.9 on 2 or 3 Sides

1999 **Tagged**

3313b 33c pane of 20, all P# (see below) except P#S22444 13.00
P#S22444 —

By its nature, No. 3313b is a complete booklet. Two #3313a and the booklet cover (BC149) are printed on one side of the peelable backing and 3 #3313a appear on the other side of the backing.

P#S11111, S22222, S22244, S22344, S22444, S22452, S22462, S23222, S24222, S24224, S24242, S24244, S24422, S24442, S24444, S26462, S32323, S32333, S32444, S33333, S44444, S45552, S46654, S55452, S55552, S56462, S62544, S62562, S64452, S64544, S65552, S66462, S66544, S66552, S66562, S66652.

Only one example of No. 3313b with Plate #S22444 is recorded.

Varieties

3313a Block of 4, Nos. 3310-3313 2.60

A2599

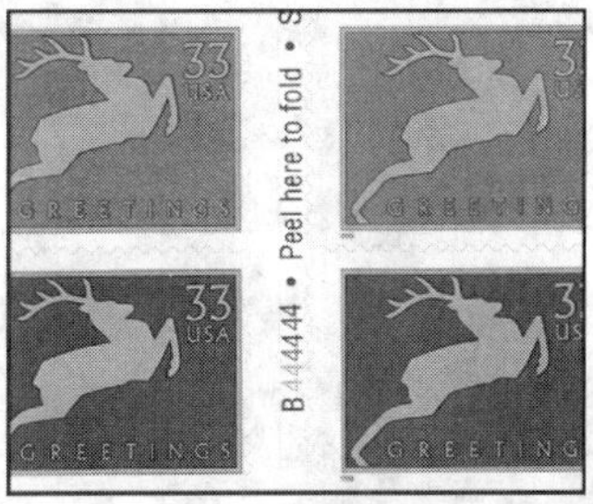

Nos. 3360-3363 — A2600

Nos. 3364-3367 — A2600

No. 3367c — A2600

1999, Oct. 20 ***Serpentine Die Cut 11¼***

Self-Adhesive

3355a A2599 33c pane of 20, P#B1111, B2222, B3333 13.00
3363a A2600 33c pane of 20, P#B111111, B222222, B333333, B444444, B555555, B666666, B777777, B888888, B999999, B000000, BAAAAAA, BBBBBBB 13.00

By their nature, Nos. 3355a and 3363a are complete booklets. Twelve #3355 are printed on one side of the peelable backing and 8 #3355 and BC150 appear on the other side of the backing. The peelable backing (BC151) serves as a booklet cover on No. 3363a.

Serpentine Die Cut 11½x11¼ on 2 or 3 sides

Stamp Size: 21x19mm

3367a A2600 33c pane of 4, no P# 4.25
3367b A2600 33c pane of 5 + label, no P# 5.25
3367c A2600 33c pane of 6, P#B111111, B222222 6.50

COMBINATION BOOKLET

BK276B BC152 $4.95 **green & gold,** 1 each #3367a-3367c, P#B see 3367c 16.00

Varieties

3367d A2600 33c Block of 4, Nos. 3364-3367 4.00

MAKESHIFT VENDING MACHINE BOOKLETS

See note before No. BK243.

1999

BK277 BC126 $4.95 4 each #3325, 3327-3328, 3 #3326 11.00
BK278 BC126 $4.95 3 each #3333-3337 11.00

No. 3377a — A2604-A2608

THE DOLPHIN PIN

The U.S. Navy Submarine Force insignia is a pin featuring a pair of dolphins flanking a sub with its bow planes rigged for diving. The pin is gold plated for officers, silver plated for enlisted personnel. Training prepares submariners not only for day-to-day responsibilities such as navigation and depth control, but also for the most extreme situations, from floods and fires to fighting the enemy. Only after the ability to handle these difficult scenarios has been confirmed can a candidate finally wear the coveted "dolphins."

Selvage 1

THE SUBMARINE STAMPS
U.S. Navy Submarines
A Century of Service to America

USS *Holland,* the U.S. Navy's first submarine, was purchased in 1900.

S-class submarines were designed during WWI.

***Gato* class** submarines played a key role in the destruction of Japanese maritime power in the Pacific during WWII.

***Los Angeles* class** attack submarines, armed with "smart" torpedoes and cruise missiles, are nuclear powered.

***Ohio* class** submarines—also nuclear powered—carry more than half of America's strategic weapons, making them a vital part of America's nuclear deterrence.

Selvage 2

2000, Mar. 27 ***Perf. 11***

3377a	pane of 5 with selvage 1	17.50	—
	With selvage 2	17.50	—

Booklet

BK279 BC153 $9.80 **multicolored,** no P# 40.00

No. BK279 contains one pane with selvage 1 and one pane with selvage 2.

A2622

2000, Apr. 26 ***Serpentine Die Cut 11***

Self-Adhesive

3391	A2622	33c	Pane of 10, 1 each # 3391b, 3391c	6.50
3391b	A2622	33c	Pane of 9, no P#	5.85
3391c	A2622	33c	Pane of 1, no P#	.65
3392	A2622	33c	Pane of 10, 1 each # 3392b, 3392c	6.50
3392b	A2622	33c	Pane of 9, no P#	5.85

Imperf

3392c	A2622	33c	Pane of 1, no P#	.65

Varieties

	Pane of 10 from sheet of 60	8.00
	Two panes of 10 with plate number on front	18.00
3391d	All die cutting omitted, pane of 10	*8,500.*

Die cutting on No. 3392a extends through backing paper. By their nature, Nos. 3391 and 3392 are complete booklets. The peelable backing (BC139) serves as a booklet cover.

3450a — A2678

2000 ***Serpentine Die Cut 8 on 2, 3 or 4 Sides***

Self-Adhesive

3450a A2678 (34c) pane of 18, P#V1111, *Dec. 15* 14.00

No. 3450a is a complete booklet (BC154). The peelable backing serves as a booklet cover.

3451a — A2679

3451b — A2679

3451c — A2679

Serpentine Die Cut 11 on 2, 3 or 4 Sides
2000, Dec. 15

Self-Adhesive

3451a A2679 (34c) pane of 20, P#V1111, V2222 13.00

No. 3451a is a complete booklet (BC155). The peelable backing serves as a booklet cover.

3451b	A2679	(34c)	pane of 4, without plate #	2.60
3451c	A2679	(34c)	pane of 6, no P#	3.90

COMBINATION BOOKLET

BK280 BC156 ($6.80) **multicolored,** 2 each #3451b, 3451c 13.00

P# on No. 3451b is on the lower right stamp of the right pane of 4 of the booklet.

Varieties

3451b	pane of 4, containing P# single	2.60	
	P# single, #V1111, V2222	.65	.50

3457a — A2681-A2684

3457b, 3457c, 3457d — A2681-A2684

Serpentine Die Cut 10½x10¾ on 2 or 3 Sides
2000

Self-Adhesive

3457e (34c) pane of 20, 5 each # 3454-3457, P#S1111, *Dec. 15* 13.00

No. 3457e is a complete booklet. Two #3457a and the booklet cover (BC157) are printed on one side of the peelable backing and three #3457a appear on the other side of the backing.

3457b	(34c)	pane of 4, #3454-3457, *Dec. 15*	2.60
3457c	(34c)	pane of 6, #3456, 3457, 2 each #3454-3455, no P#, *Dec. 15*	3.90
3457d	(34c)	pane of 6, #3454, 3455, 2 each #3456-3457, no P#, *Dec. 15*	3.90

COMBINATION BOOKLET

BK281 BC158 ($6.80) **multicolored,** #3457c, 3457d, 2 #3457b, P#S1111 13.00

P# on No. BK281 is on the backing paper of the top pane of No. 3457b.

Varieties

3457a Block of 4, #3454-3457 2.60
3461b pane of 20, 2 each #3461a, 3 each #3457a, #S1111, *Dec. 15* *25.00*
3461c pane of 20, 2 each #3457a, 3 each #3461a, #S1111, *Dec. 15* *30.00*
3461a Block of 4, #3458-3461 2.60

Nos. 3461b and 3461c are complete booklets. Two blocks of four with the same gauge die cutting and the booklet cover (BC157) are printed on one side of the peelable backing and three blocks of four with the other gauge die cutting appear on the other side of the backing.

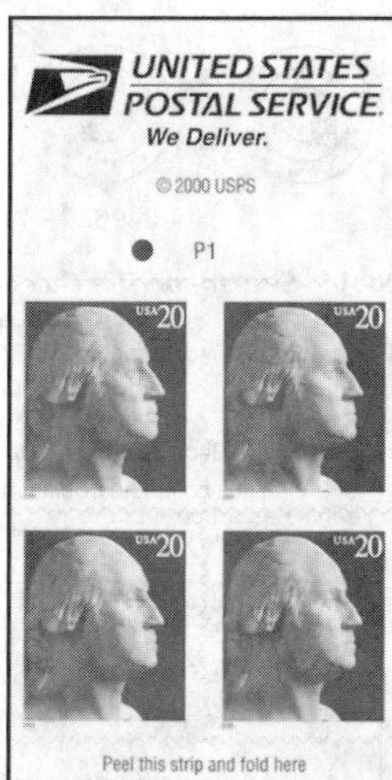

Nos. 3482a, 3483a, 3483b — A2686

2001, Feb. 22 ***Serpentine Die Cut 11¼ on 3 Sides***

Self-Adhesive

3482a A2686 20c pane of 10, P#P1, P2, P3 4.00
3482b A2686 20c pane of 4, P#P1, P2, P3 1.60
3482c A2686 20c pane of 6, no P# 2.40

COMBINATION BOOKLET

BK281A BC159 $2 **multicolored,** #3482b-3482c, P#P1, P2, P3 4.00

No. BK281A has slightly smaller cover than No. 3482a and lacks self-adhesive panel that covers the rouletting.

Serpentine Die Cut 10½x11¼ on 3 Sides

3483a A2686 20c pane of 4, 2 #3482 at L, 2 #3483 at R, P#P1, P2, P3 9.00
3483b A2686 20c pane of 6, 3 #3482 at L, 3 #3483 at R, no P# 15.00
3483c A2686 20c pane of 10, 5 #3482 at L, 5 #3483 at R, P#P1, P2, P3 16.00
3483d A2686 20c pane of 4, 2 #3483 at L, 2 #3282 at R, P#P1, P2, P3 9.00
3483e A2686 20c pane of 6, 3 #3483 at L, 3 #3282 at R, no P# 15.00
3483f A2686 20c pane of 10, 5 #3483 at L, 5 #3282 at R, P#P1, P2, P3 16.00

Nos. 3482a, 3483c and 3483f are complete booklets (BC159) and include a self-adhesive panel that covers the rouletting. The peelable backing, which is slightly longer than that on Nos. BK282 and BK282A, serves as a booklet cover.

COMBINATION BOOKLETS

BK282 BC159 $2 **multicolored,** #3483a-3483b, P#P1, P2, P3 24.00
BK282A BC159 $2 **multicolored,** #3483d-3483e, P#P1, P2, P3 24.00

Varieties

3483g Pair, #3482 at L, #3483 at R 4.00
3483h Pair, #3483 at L, #3482 at R 4.00

Nos. 3484b, 3484c, 3484d, 3484Ae, 3484Af, 3484Ag, 3484Ah, 3484Ai, 3484Aj—A2687

Serpentine Die Cut 11¼ on 3 Sides

2001, Sept. 20

Self-Adhesive

3484b A2687 21c pane of 4, P#P111111, P333333, P444444 1.60
3484c A2687 21c pane of 6, no P# 2.40
3484d A2687 21c pane of 10, P#P111111, P222222, P333333, P444444, P555555 4.00

Serpentine Die Cut 10½x11¼ on 3 Sides

3484Ae A2687 21c pane of 4, 2 #3484 at L, 2# 3484A at R, P#P111111, P333333, P444444 *9.00*
3484Af A2687 21c pane of 6, 3 #3484 at L, 3# 3484A at R, no P# *15.00*
3484Ag A2687 21c pane of 10, 5 #3484 at L, 5# 3484A at R, P#P111111, P222222, P333333, P444444, P555555 *16.00*
3484Ah A2687 21c pane of 4, 2 #3484A at L, 2# 3484 at R, P#P111111, P333333, P444444 *9.00*
3484Ai A2687 21c pane of 6, 3 #3484A at L, 3# 3484 at R, no P# *15.00*
3484Aj A2687 21c pane of 10, 5 #3484A at L, 5# 3484 at R, P#P111111, P222222, P333333, P444444, P555555 *16.00*

COMBINATION BOOKLETS

BK282B BC159A $2.10 **multi,** #3484b-3484c, P#P111111, P333333, P444444 4.00
BK282C BC159A $2.10 **multi,** #3484Ae-3484Af, P#P111111, P333333, P444444 *24.00*
BK282D BC159A $2.10 **multi,** #3484Ah-3484Ai, P#P111111, P333333, P444444 *24.00*

Nos. 3484d, 3484Ag and 3484Aj are complete booklets (BC159A). The peelable backing serves as a booklet cover. Nos. BK282-BK282D lack self-adhesive panel that covers the rouletting. Nos. BK282B-BK282D have a small 662900 UPC code on cover back, while Nos. 3484d, 3484Ag and 3484Aj have a large 662800 UPC code on cover back.

Varieties

3484Ak Pair, #3484 at L, #3484A at R *4.00*
3484Al Pair, #3484A at L, #3484 at R *4.00*

No. 3485a - A2689

No. 3485b - A2689

No. 3485c - A2689

2001, Feb. 7 ***Serpentine Die Cut 11 on 3 Sides***

Self-Adhesive

3485a A2689 34c pane of 10, P#V1111, V1221 6.50
3485b A2689 34c pane of 20, P#V1111, V1211, V1221, V2111, V2112, V2121, V2122, V2212, V2222 13.00
3485c A2689 34c pane of 4, without P# 2.60
3485d A2689 34c pane of 6, no P# 3.90

COMBINATION BOOKLET

BK283 BC160A $6.80 **multicolored,** 2 each #3485c-3485d, P#V1111, V1122, V2212, V2222 13.00
P#V1112, V1121 —

Varieties

3485c pane of 4, containing P# single 2.60
P# single, #V1111, V1122, V2212, V2222 .65 .65
Pane containing P#V1112, V1121 —
P# single, #V1112, V1121 — —
3485e Imperf pair (from No. 3485b) —
3485f Imperf, pane of 20 —

Nos. 3485a-3485b are complete booklets (BC160). The peelable backing serves as a booklet cover.

Nos. 3490b, 3490c, 3490d — A2690-A2693

No. 3490e — A2690-A2693

Serpentine Die Cut 10½x 10¾ on 2 or 3 Sides
2001, Feb. 7

Self-Adhesive

3490b	34c pane of 4	2.60
3490c	34c pane of 6, #3490-3491, 2 each #3487-3488	3.90
3490d	34c pane of 6, #3487-3488, 2 each #3490-3491	3.90
3490e	34c pane of 20, 5 #3490a, P#S1111, S2222	13.00

COMBINATION BOOKLET

BK284	BC162 $6.80 **multicolored,** #3490c-3490d, 2 #3490b, P#S1111	13.00

No. 3490e is a complete booklet (BC161) with 12 stamps on one side and eight stamps plus label on the other side. The peelable backing serves as a booklet cover.

P# on No. BK284 is on the backing paper of the bottom pane of No. 3490b.

Varieties

3490a	Block of 4, #3487-3490	2.60

Nos. 3492b — A2694-A2695

Serpentine Die Cut 11¼ on 2, 3 or 4 sides
2001, Mar. 6

Self-Adhesive

3492b	34c pane of 20, 10 each #3491-3492, P# B1111, B2222, B3333, B4444, B5555, B6666, B7777	13.00

No. 3492b is a complete booklet (BC163). The peelable backing serves as a booklet cover.

Varieties

3492a	Pair, #3491-3492	1.30
3492c	As "a," black ("34 USA") omitted	—
3492d	As "a," imperf	—
3492e	As "b," imperf	—

No. 3494b — A2694-A2695

No. 3494c — A2694-A2695

No. 3494d — A2694-A2695

2001, May ***Serpentine Die Cut 11½x10¾***

Self-Adhesive

3494b	34c pane of 4, 2 each #3493-3494, without P#	2.60
3494c	34c pane of 6, 3 each #3493-3494, #3493 at UL, no P#	3.90
3494d	34c pane of 6, 3 each #3493-3494, #3494 at UL, no P#	3.90

COMBINATION BOOKLET

BK284A	BC163A $6.80 **multi,** #3494c, 3494d, 2 #3494b, P#B1111	13.00

Varieties

3494a	Pair, #3493-3494	1.30	
3494b	Pane of 4 with P#	2.60	
	P# single #B1111	.65	.65

3495a—A2688

Serpentine Die Cut 8 on 2, 3 or 4 Sides
2001, Dec. 17

Self-Adhesive

3495a	34c pane of 18, #V1111	12.00

Nos. 3495a is a complete booklet (BC163B). The peelable backing serves as a booklet cover.

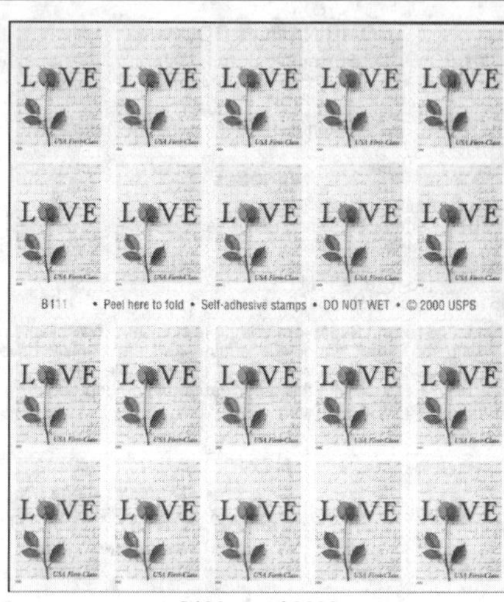

3496a — A2699

2001 ***Serpentine Die Cut 11¼ on 2, 3, or 4 Sides***

Self-Adhesive

3496a	A2699 (34c) pane of 20, P#B1111, B2222, *Jan. 19*	13.00

Varieties

3496b	A2699 (34c) Vert. pair, imperf horiz.	—

No. 3496a is a complete booklet (BC164). The peelable backing serves as a booklet cover.

3497a - A2700

3498a, 3498b - A2700

2001 ***Serpentine Die Cut 11¼ on 2, 3 or 4 Sides***

Self-Adhesive

3497a	A2700 34c pane of 20, P#B1111, B2222, B3333, B4444, B5555, *Feb. 14*	13.00

Size: 18x21mm

Serpentine Die Cut 11½x10¾

3498a	A2700 34c pane of 4, without P#, *Feb. 14*	2.60
3498b	A2700 34c pane of 6, no P#, *Feb. 14*	3.90

COMBINATION BOOKLET

BK285	BC166 $6.80 **multicolored,** 2 each #3498a-3498b, P#B1111	13.00

Varieties

3498a	pane of 4, containing plate # single	3.90	
	P# single, #B1111	.65	.65

No. 3497a is a complete booklet (BC165). The peelable backing serves as a booklet cover.

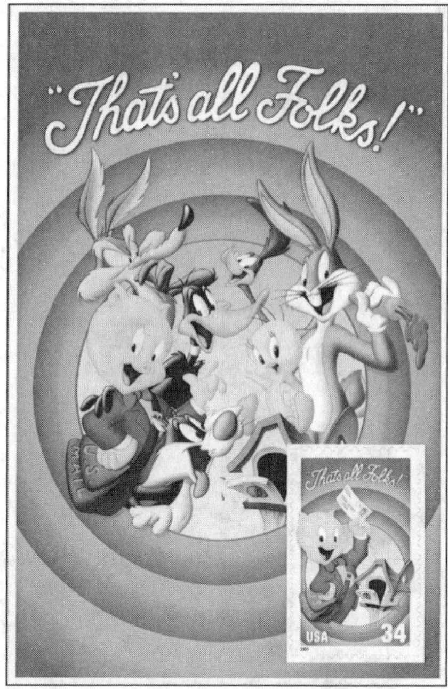

A2736

2001, Oct. 1 *Serpentine Die Cut 11*

Self-Adhesive

3534 A2736 34c pane of 10, 1 each #3534b, 3534c 6.50
3534b A2736 34c pane of 9, no P# 5.85
3534c A2736 34c pane of 1, no P# .65
3535 A2736 34c pane of 10, 1 each #3535b, 3535c 6.50
3535b A2736 34c pane of 9, no P# —

Imperf

3535c A2736 34c pane of 1, no P# —

Die cutting on No. 3535b extends through backing paper. By their nature, Nos. 3534 and 3535 are complete booklets. The peelable backing serves as a booklet cover (BC139).

A2737

No. 3540d— A2738-A2741

3544b

Serpentine Die Cut 11½ on 2, 3 or 4 Sides

2001, Oct. 10

Self-Adhesive

3536a A2737 34c pane of 20, P#B1111 13.00

Serpentine Die Cut 10¾x11 on 2 or 3 Sides

3540d 34c pane of 20, 5 each #3537a-3540a + label, P#S1111, S3333, S4444 13.00
3540g Booklet pane, 5 #3540f + label, P#S2222, S3333, S4444 13.00

No. 3540g is a complete booklet (BC168). The peelable backing serves as a booklet cover.

Green Inscriptions

Stamp Size: 21x18½mm

Serpentine Die Cut 11 on 2 or 3 sides

3544b 34c pane of 4, #3541-3544 2.60
3544c 34c pane of 6, #3543-3544, 2 #3541-3542 3.90
3544d 34c pane of 6, #3541-3542, 2 #3543-3544 3.90

COMBINATION BOOKLET

BK286 BC169 $6.80 **multi,** #3544c-3544d, 2 #3544b, P#V1111 13.00

No. 3536a is a complete booklet (BC167). No. 3540d is a complete booklet (BC168) with 12 stamps on one side and eight stamps plus label on the other side. The peelable backing serves as a booklet cover.

P# on No. BK286 is on the backing paper of the bottom pane of No. 3544b.

Varieties

3540c Block of 4, #3537a-3540a 2.60
3544a Block of 4, #3541-3544 2.60

Varieties

3540f Block of 4, large date, #3537b-3539b, 3540e —

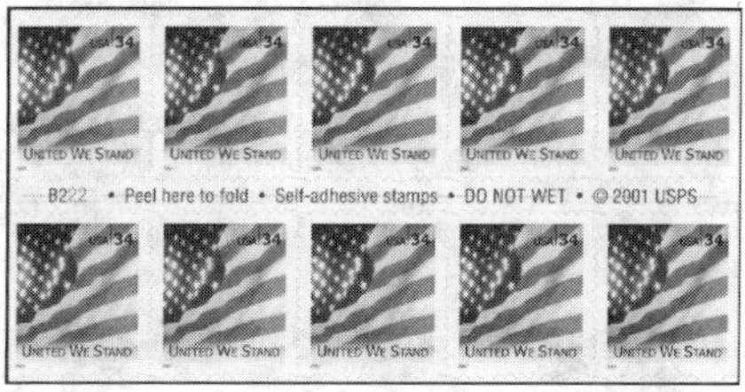

No. 3549a — A2744

Serpentine Die Cut 11¼ on 2, 3 or 4 Sides

2001, Oct. 24

Self-Adhesive

3549a A2744 34c Pane of 20, P#B1111, B2222, B3333, B4444 13.00

No. 3549a is a complete booklet (BC170). The peelable backing serves as a booklet cover.

3549Bc, 3549Bd—A2744

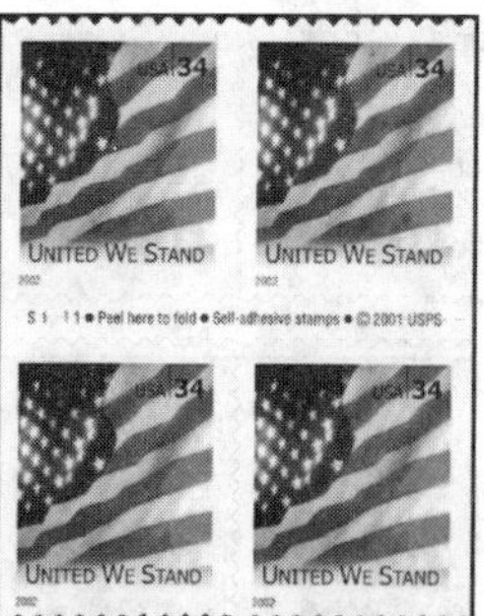

3549Be—A2744

Serpentine Die Cut 10½x10¾ on 2 or 3 Sides

2002, Jan.

Self-Adhesive

3549Bc A2744 34c pane of 4 2.60
3549Bd A2744 34c pane of 6 3.90
3549Be A2744 34c pane of 20, P#S1111 13.00

COMBINATION BOOKLET

BK287 BC171 $6.80 **multi,** 2 each #3549Bc, 3549Bd, P#S1111 13.00

P# on No. BK287 is on the backing paper of the lower example of No. 3549Bd. No. 3549Be is a complete booklet (BC172) with 12 stamps on one side and eight stamps plus label on the other side. The peelable backing serves as a booklet cover.

Washington Type of 2002

2002, June 7 *Serpentine Die Cut 11¼*

Self-Adhesive

3618a A2686 23c pane of 4, P#P1, P2, P4 1.80
3618b A2686 23c pane of 6, no P# 2.70

Serpentine Die Cut 11¼ on 3 Sides

3618c A2686 23c pane of 10, P#P1, P2, P3 4.50

COMBINATION BOOKLET

BK288 BC173 $2.30 **multi,** #3618a-3618b, P#P1, P2, P4 4.50

No. BK288 has a 671800 UPC code on cover back, while No. 3618c has a 671000 UPC code on cover back.

Serpentine Die Cut 10½x11¼ on 3 Sides

3619a A2686 23c pane of 4, 2 #3619 at L, 2 #3618 at R, P#P1, P2, P4 *6.00*
3619b A2686 23c pane of 6, 3 #3619 at L, 3 #3618 at R, no P# *9.50*
3619c A2686 23c pane of 4, 2 #3618 at L, 2 #3619 at R, P#P1, P2, P4 *5.00*
3619d A2686 23c pane of 6, 3 #3618 at L, 3 #3619 at R, no P# *8.00*

Washington Type of 2002

Serpentine Die Cut 10½x11¼ on 3 Sides

2002, June 7

Self-Adhesive

3619e A2686 23c pane of 10, 5 #3619 at L, 5 #3618 at R, P#P1, P2, P3 *10.00*

No. 3619e is a complete booklet (BC173) and includes a self-adhesive panel that covers the rouletting. The peelable backing, which is slightly longer than those on Nos. BK289 and BK289A, serves as a booklet cover.

3619f A2686 23c pane of 10, 5 #3618 at L, 5 #3619 at R, P#P1, P2, P3 *10.00*

No. 3619f is a complete booklet (BC173) and includes a self-adhesive panel that covers the rouletting. The peelable backing, which is slightly longer than those on Nos. BK289 and BK289A, serves as a booklet cover.

COMBINATION BOOKLET

BK289 BC173 $2.30 **multi,**#3619a-3619b, P#P1, P2, P4 15.50
BK289A BC173 $2.30 **multi,**#3619c-3619d, P#P1, P2, P4 15.50

Variety

3619g Pair, #3619 at L, #3618 at R *2.50*
3619h Pair, #3618 at L, #3619 at R —

No. 3618c is a complete booklet (BC173) and includes a self-adhesive panel that covers the rouletting. The peelable backing, which is slightly longer than those on Nos. BK289 and BK289A, serves as a booklet cover.

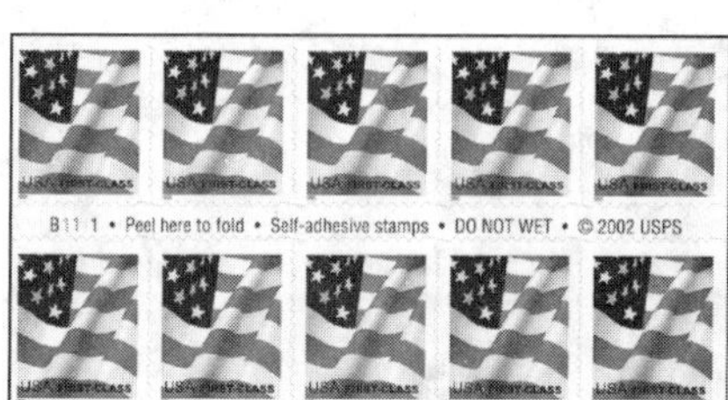

No. 3623a—A2807

Serpentine Die Cut 11¼ on 2, 3 or 4 Sides

2002, June 7 **Litho.**

Self-Adhesive

3623a A2807 (37c) pane of 20, P#B1111, B2222, B3333 14.00

No. 3623a is a complete booklet (BC174). The peelable backing serves as a booklet cover.

No. 3624a—A2807

No. 3624b—A2807

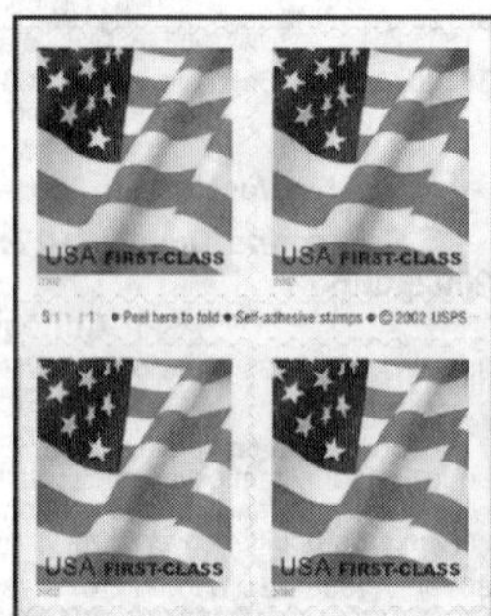

No. 3624c—A2807

Serpentine Die Cut 10½x10¾ on 2 or 3 Sides

2002, June 7 **Photo.**

Self-Adhesive

3624a A2807 (37c) pane of 4, no P# 2.80
3624b A2807 (37c) pane of 6, no P# 3.60
3624c A2807 (37c) pane of 20, P#S1111 14.00

COMBINATION BOOKLET

BK290 BC175 ($7.40) **multi,** 2 each #3624a, 3624b, P#S11111 14.00

Plate number appears on the backing of the lower example of No. 3624b in No. BK290.

No. 3624c is a complete booklet pane (BC176). The peelable backing serves as a booklet cover.

No. 3625a—A2807

Serpentine Die Cut 8 on 2, 3 or 4 Sides

2002, June 7 **Photo.**

Self-Adhesive

3625a A2807 (37c) pane of 18, P#V1111 13.00

No. 3625a is a complete booklet (BC177). The peelable backing serves as a booklet cover.

No. 3629b—A2808-A2811

No. 3629c—A2808-A2811

No. 3629d—A2808-A2811

No. 3629e—A2808-A2811

Serpentine Die Cut 11 on 2, 3 or 4 Sides

2002, June 7 **Photo.**

Self-Adhesive

3629b (37c) pane of 4, #3626-3629, no P# 2.80
3629c (37c) pane of 6, #3627, 3629, 2 each #3626, 3628, no P# 4.20
3629d (37c) pane of 6, #3626, 3628, 2 each #3627, 3629, no P# 4.20
3629e (37c) pane of 20, 5 each #3626-3629, P#V1111, V1112, V2222 14.00

COMBINATION BOOKLET

BK291 BC178 ($7.40) **multi,**#3629c-3629d, 2 #3629b, no P# 14.00

No. 3629e is a complete booklet (BC179). The peelable backing serves as a booklet cover.

Variety

3629a Block of 4, #3626-3629 2.80

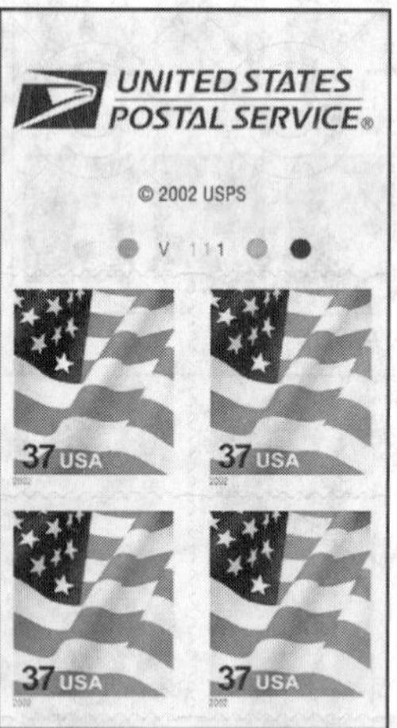

No. 3634a—A2812

Serpentine Die Cut 11 on 3 Sides

2002, June 7 **Photo.**

Self-Adhesive

3634a A2812 37c pane of 10, P#V1111 7.00

No. 3634a is a complete booklet (BC180). The peelable backing serves as a booklet cover.

No. 3635a—A2812

Serpentine Die Cut 11¼ on 2, 3 or 4 Sides

2002, June 7 **Litho.**

Self-Adhesive

3635a A2812 37c pane of 20, P#B1111, B2222, B3333, B4444, B5555, B6666, B7777 14.00

No. 3635a is a complete booklet (BC181). The peelable backing serves as a booklet cover.

No. 3636a—A2812

No. 3636b—A2812

Serpentine Die Cut 10½x10¾ on 2 or 3 Sides

2002, June 7 **Photo.**

Self-Adhesive

3636a A2812 37c pane of 4, no P# 2.80
3636b A2812 37c pane of 6, no P# 3.60

COMBINATION BOOKLET

BK291A BC182 $7.40 **multi,** 2 each #3636a, 3636b, P#S11111 14.00

Plate number appears on the backing of the lower example of No. 3636b in No. BK291A.

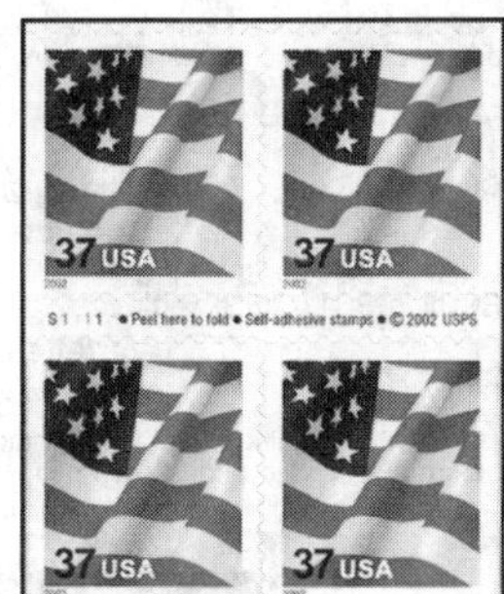

No. 3636c—A2812

Serpentine Die Cut 10½x10¾ on 2 or 3 Sides

2002, June 7 **Photo.**

Self-Adhesive

3636c A2812 37c pane of 20, P#S1111, S2222, S3333, S4444 14.00

No. 3636c is a complete booklet (BC183) with 12 stamps on one side and eight stamps plus label on the other side. The peelable backing serves as a booklet cover.

No. 3637a—A2812

Serpentine Die Cut 8 on 2, 3 or 4 Sides

2003, Feb. 4 **Photo.**

Self-Adhesive

3637a A2812 37c pane of 18, #V1111 13.00

No. 3637a is a complete booklet (BC184). The peelable backing serves as a booklet cover.

No. 3645b—A2813-A2816

No. 3645c—A2813-A2816

No. 3645d—A2813-A2816

No. 3645e—A2813-A2816

Serpentine Die Cut 11 on 2, 3 or 4 Sides

2002, July 26 **Photo.**

Self-Adhesive

3645b 37c pane of 4, #3642-3645, no P# 2.80
3645c 37c pane of 6, #3643, 3645, 2 each #3642, 3644, no P# 4.20
3645d 37c pane of 6, #3642, 3644, 2 each #3643, 3645, no P# 4.20
3645e 37c pane of 20, 5 each #3642-3645, P#V1111, V1112, V2221, V2222 14.00

COMBINATION BOOKLET

BK292 BC185 $7.40 **multi,**#3645c-3645d, 2 #3645b, P#V1111 14.00

No. 3645e is a complete booklet (BC186). The peelable backing serves as a booklet cover. Plate number on No. BK292 is on backing paper of No. 3645d.

Variety

3645a Block of 4, #3642-3645 2.80

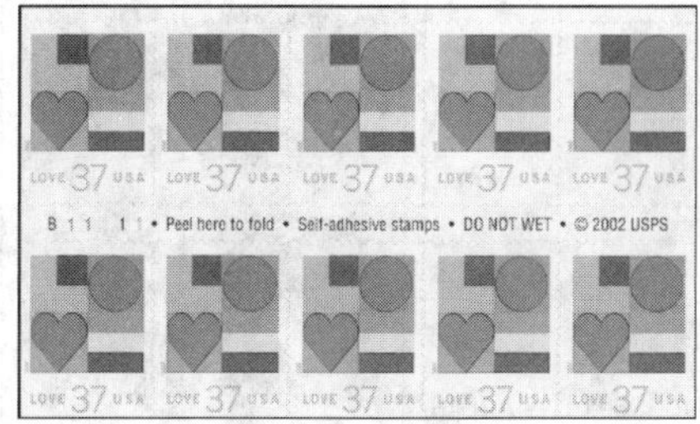

No. 3657a—A2828

Serpentine Die Cut 11 on 2, 3 or 4 Sides

2002, Aug. 16 **Litho.**

Self-Adhesive

3657a A2828 37c pane of 20, P#B11111, B22222, B33333, B44444, B55555, B66666, B77777 14.00

No. 3657a is a complete booklet (BC187). The peelable backing serves as a booklet cover.

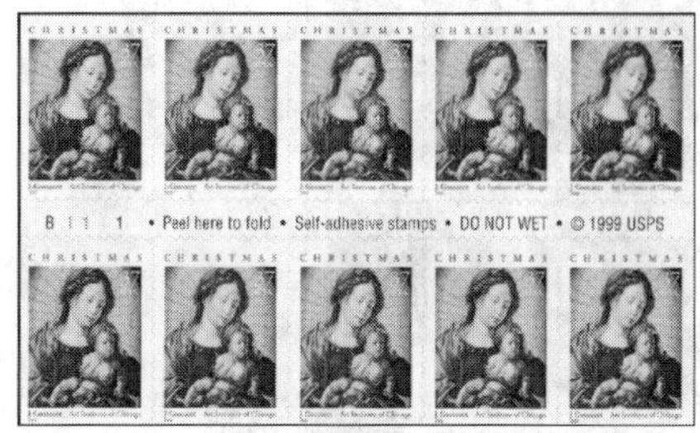

Nos. 3675a—A2843

Serpentine Die Cut 11x11¼ on 2, 3 or 4 Sides

2002, Oct. 10

Self-Adhesive

3675a A2843 37c pane of 20, P#B1111, B2222 14.00

No. 3675a is a complete booklet (BC188). The peelable backing serves as a booklet cover.

No. 3687b — A2844-A2847

No. 3691b — A2848-A2851

No. 3691c — A2848-A2851

No. 3691d — A2848-A2851

Serpentine Die Cut 10¾ on 2 or 3 Sides

2002, Oct. 28

Self-Adhesive

3687b 37c Pane of 20, P#S111, S1113, S2222, S4444 14.00

Serpentine Die Cut 11 on 2 or 3 Sides

3691b 37c Pane of 4, #3688-3691, no P# 2.80
3691c 37c Pane of 6, #3690-3691, 2 each #3688-3689, no P# 4.20
3691d 37c Pane of 6, #3688-3689, 2 each #3690-3691, no P# 4.20

COMBINATION BOOKLET

BK293 BC190 $7.40 **multi,** #3691c, 3691d 2 each #3691b, P#V1111 14.00

No. 3687b is a complete booklet (BC189) with 12 stamps on one side and eight stamps plus label on the other side. The peelable backing serves as a booklet cover. Plate number appears on the backing of the upper example of No. 3691b in BK293.

Varieties

3687a Block of 4, #3684-3687 2.80
3691a Block of 4, #3688-3691 2.80

No. 3780b—A2883-A2887

Backing 1

Backing 2

2003, Apr. 3 Litho. ***Serpentine Die Cut 10x9¾***

Self-Adhesive

3780b 37c Pane of 2 #3780a with backing 1 7.00
With backing 2 7.00

Booklet

BK294 BC191 $7.40 **multi,** no P# 14.00

No. BK294 contains one pane with backing 1 and one pane with backing 2.

Variety

3780a Horiz. strip of 5, #3776-3780 3.50

No. 3783a—A2890

No. 3783b—A2890

2003, May 22 Photo. ***Serpentine Die Cut 11***

Self-Adhesive

3783a A2890 37c Pane of 9, no P# 6.30
3783b A2890 37c Pane of 1, no P# .70

COMBINATION BOOKLET

BK295 BC192 $3.70 **multi,** #3783a-3783b, no P# 7.00

AIR POST BOOKLET PANES

Spirit of St. Louis — AP6

FLAT PLATE PRINTING

1928 ***Perf. 11***

C10a AP6 10c **dark blue,** *May 26* 80.00 *65.00*
Never hinged 120.00
Tab at bottom —

No. C10a was printed from specially designed 180-subject plates arranged exactly as a 360-subject plate-each pane of three occupying the relative position of a pane of six in a 360-subject plate. Plate numbers appear at the sides, therefore Position D does not exist except partially on panes which have been trimmed off center. All other plate positions common to a 360-subject plate are known.

Booklet

BKC1 BC8 61c **blue** 250.00
Tab at bottom, one pane in complete booklet *13,500.*

Catalogue values for unused panes in this section, from this point to the end, are for Never Hinged items.

AP17

ROTARY PRESS PRINTINGS

1943

C25a AP17 6c **carmine,** *Mar. 18* 5.00 *1.50*

180-Subject Plates Electric Eye Convertible.

Booklets

BKC2 BC10 37c **red** 11.00
BKC3 BC10 73c **red** 22.50

AP19

1949 ***Perf. 10½x11***

C39a AP19 6c **carmine,** *Nov. 18* 10.00 *5.00*
C39c Dry printing 20.00 —

Booklets

BKC4 BC11A 73c **red,** with #C39a (2) 25.00
BKC4a BC11A 73c **red,** with #C39c 50.00

AP33

1958

C51a AP33 7c **blue,** *July 31* 12.50 *7.00*

Booklets

BKC5 BC11B 85c on 73c **red** 26.50
BKC6 BC11C 85c **blue** 25.50

Varieties

C51b Vert. pair, imperf. between (from booklet pane) —

No. C51b resulted from a paper foldover after perforating and before cutting into panes. Two pairs are known.

1960

C60a AP33 7c **carmine,** *Aug. 19* 14.00 *8.00*

Booklets

BKC7 BC11C 85c **blue** 28.50
BKC8 BC11C 85c **red** 28.50

Varieties

C60b Vert. pair, imperf between *5,500.*

No. C60b resulted from a paper foldover after perforating and before cutting into panes. Twp pairs are known.

AP42

1962-64

C64b AP42 8c **carmine,** pane of 5+label, slogan 1, *Dec. 5, 1962* 7.00 *3.00*
With slogan 2, *1963* 50.00 *5.00*
With slogan 3, *1964* 13.00 *2.50*

Booklets (No. C64b)

BKC9 BC11D 80c **black,** *pink,* slogan 1 22.50
BKC10 BC11D $2 **red,** *pink,* slogan 1 35.00
BKC11 BC11D 80c **black,** *pink,* slogan 3 (2) 30.00
BKC12 BC11D $2 **red,** *pink,* slogan 2 300.00

BKC13 BC13B $2 **red,** *pink,* slogan 2 300.00
BKC14 BC13B $2 **red,** slogan 3 *3,500.*
BKC15 BC13B $2 **red,** *pink,* slogan 3 100.00

C64c AP42 As No. C64b, tagged, slogan 3, *1964* 2.00 *.75*

Plate of 360 subjects (300 stamps, 60 labels).

Booklets (No. C64c)

BKC16 BC11D 80c **black** (2) 35.00
BKC17 BC11D 80c **black,** *pink* *1,000.*
BKC18 BC13B $2 **red,** *pink* *325.00*
BKC19 BC13B $2 **red** (3) 13.00

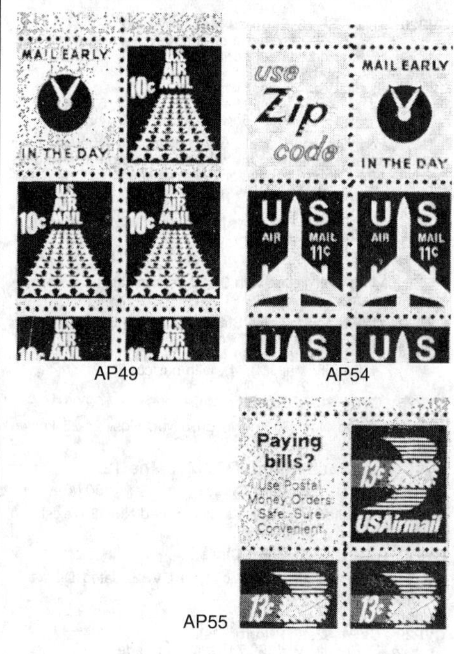

AP49 AP54

AP55

1968-73 *Perf. 11x10½*

C72b AP49 10c **carmine,** pane of 8, *Jan. 5, 1968* 2.00 *.75*

Booklet

BKC20 BC14B $4 **red** (2) 12.00

C72c AP49 10c **carmine,** pane of 5+label, slogan 4, *Jan. 6, 1968* 3.75 *.75*
With slogan 5 3.75 *.75*

Booklet

BKC21 BC15 $1 **red** (2) 8.00

Varieties

C72d Vert. pair, imperf. between *8,000.*
C72f As "b," tagging omitted —

No. C72d resulted from a paper foldover after perforating and before cutting into booklet panes. Two pairs are known.

C78a AP54 11c **carmine,** pane of 4+2 labels, slogans 5 & 4, *May 7, 1971* 1.25 *.75*

Combination Booklet

BKC22 BC15 $1 **red,** 2 #C78a + 1 #1280c (2) 3.75

C79a AP55 13c **carmine,** pane of 5+label, slogan 8, *Dec. 27, 1973* 1.50 *.75*

Booklet

BKC23 BC18 $1.30 **blue & red** 3.25

Combination Booklet

See No. BK126.

No. C72b, the 8-stamp pane, was printed from 320-subject plate and from 400-subject plate; No. C72c, C78a and C79a from 360-subject plates.

COMPUTER VENDED POSTAGE STAMPS

Unlike meters, except for the limits of the service requested, computer vended postage stamps are usable from any post office at any date.

Self-service user-interactive mailing system machines which vended computer-printed postage were in service and available to the general public at the Martin Luther King, Jr., Station of the Washington, DC, Post Office, and at the White Flint Mall in Kensington, MD, until May 7, 1990.

Machines were also available for use by delegates to the 20th Universal Postal Congress at the Washington Convention Center between Nov. 13 and Dec. 14, 1989. These machines, Washington Nos. 11 and 12, were not readily accessible by the general public.

A variety of services were available by using the machines, which could weigh items to be sent, determine postage rates through the connected computer, permit the customer to cancel the transaction or continue with it and generate a postage stamp, a label and a receipt. The stamps produced were valid only for domestic postage.

A tagged orange strip runs along the left side of the stamp. The requested mail service is in a double line box.

The denomination is in the upper box at right under "U.S. Postage." The date of the transaction is below the denomination. Next to the date is a number which indicates the item number within the transaction. The maximum number of items per transaction may be five.

Above the post office location is a box at right which gives the machine number, followed by the transaction or serial number. Stamps from the same transaction, which are generated and printed at the same time, will have the same transaction number, but different item numbers, even if different mail services are requested. Transaction numbers go back to 00001 every time the machine is reset. Below this is the weight of the item to be mailed.

Along with each stamp generated came an unattached label with one of three slogan types: "We Deliver. . .," used from September to November, "We Deliver. . . / United States Postal Service," used thereafter, and "Developed by / Technology Resource Department," used only on Machine 11 during its limited use.

Listings and values are for the basic denominations of the five postal services, though others are known or possible (45c, 65c, 85c for first class over 1 oz., $1.10 for certified first class, $3.25 for priority mail, $8.50 for express mail to post office boxes, parcel post weight and zone variations, etc.). Values for used copies are for those with a regular cancellation.

A total of 3,000 unused sets of five different service stamps and unused sets of two 25c (Nos. 02501-12500) first class stamps furnished to the Philatelic Agency have a first day date and serial numbers with the final three digits matching. First day dates Nos. 00101-02500 were sold over the counter at post offices.

Stamps were intended to be dispensed individually. The height of the stamps produced differs from machine to machine. Unsevered strips of stamps are known, as are unsevered strips of a slogan and one or more stamps. Printing varieties such as squeezes (more than one impression condensed on to one stamp) and stretches (impression stretched out so that a complete impression will not fit on the paper) also are known.

Issues starting with No. 31 will be explained with the listings.

CVP1

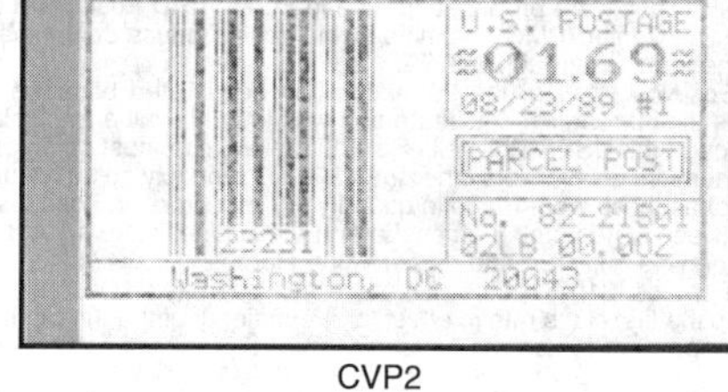

CVP2

1989, Aug. 23 **Tagged** *Guillotined*

Self-Adhesive

Washington, DC, Machine 82

CVP1 CVP1 25c **First Class,** any date other than first day 6.00 —
a. First day dated, serial Nos. 12501-15500 4.50 —
b. First day dated, serial Nos. 00001-12500 4.50 —
On cover with first day cancel *150.00*
c. First day dated, over No. 27500 — —
On cover with first day cancel *150.00*

CVP2 CVP1 $1 **Third Class,** any date other than first day — —
a. First day dated, serial Nos. 24501-27500 — —
b. First day dated, over No. 27500 — —

CVP3 CVP2 $1.69 **Parcel Post,** any date other than first day — —
a. First day dated, serial Nos. 21501-24500 — —
b. First day dated, over No. 27500 — —

CVP4 CVP1 $2.40 **Priority Mail,** any date other than first day — —
a. First day dated, serial Nos. 18501-21500 — —
b. Priority Mail ($2.74), with bar code (CVP2) *100.00*
c. First day dated, over No. 27500 — —
On cover with first day cancel or verifying receipt *500.00*

CVP5 CVP1 $8.75 **Express Mail,** any date other than first day — —
a. First day dated, serial Nos. 15501-18500 — —
b. First day dated, over No. 27500 — —
On cover with first day cancel or verifying receipt —
Nos. 1a-5a (5) 82.50

Washington, DC, Machine 83

CVP6 CVP1 25c **First Class,** any date other than first day 6.00 —
a. First day dated, serial Nos. 12501-15500 4.50 —
b. First day dated, serial Nos. 00001-12500 4.50 —
On cover with first day cancel *150.00*
c. First day dated, over No. 27500 — —
On cover with first day cancel *150.00*

Error dates 11/17/90 and 11/18/90 exist.

CVP7 CVP1 $1 **Third Class,** any date other than first day — —
a. First day dated, serial Nos. 24501-27500 — —
b. First day dated, over No. 27500 — —

CVP8 CVP2 $1.69 **Parcel Post,** any date other than first day — —
a. First day dated, serial Nos. 21501-24500 — —
b. First day dated, over No. 27500 — —

CVP9 CVP1 $2.40 **Priority Mail,** any date other than first day — —
a. First day dated, serial Nos. 18501-21500 — —
b. First day dated, over No. 27500 — —
On cover with first day cancel or verifying receipt *500.00*

Error date 11/17/90 exists.

c. Priority Mail ($2.74), with bar code (CVP2) *100.00*

Error date 11/18/90 exists.

CVP10 CVP1 $8.75 **Express Mail,** any date other than first day — —
a. First day dated, serial Nos. 15501-18500 — —
b. First day dated, over No. 27500 — —
On cover with first day cancel or verifying receipt —
Nos. 6a-10a (5) 57.50 —

Error date 11/17/90 exists.

1989, Sept. 1 Kensington, MD, Machine 82

CVP11 CVP1 25c **First Class,** any date other than first day 6.00 —
a. First day dated, serial Nos. 12501-15500 4.50 —
b. First day dated, serial Nos. 00001-12500 4.50 —
On cover with first day cancel *100.00*
c. First day dated, over No. 27500 — —
On cover with first day cancel *100.00*

CVP12 CVP1 $1 **Third Class,** any date other than first day — —
a. First day dated, serial Nos. 24501-27500 — —
b. First day dated, over No. 27500 — —

CVP13 CVP2 $1.69 **Parcel Post,** any date other than first day — —
a. First day dated, serial Nos. 21501-24500 — —
b. First day dated, over No. 27500 — —

CVP14 CVP1 $2.40 **Priority Mail,** any date other than first day — —
a. First day dated, serial Nos. 18501-21500 — —
b. First day dated, over No. 27500 — —
c. Priority Mail ($2.74), with bar code (CVP2) *100.00*

CVP15 CVP1 $8.75 **Express Mail,** any date other than first day — —
a. First day dated, serial Nos. 15501-18500 — —
b. First day dated, over No. 27500 — —
Nos. 11a-15a (5) 57.50 —
Nos. 1b, 11b (2) 9.00 —

Kensington, MD, Machine 83

CVP16 CVP1 25c **First Class,** any date other than first day 6.00 —
a. First day dated, serial Nos. 12501-15500 4.50 —
b. First day dated, serial Nos. 00001-12500 4.50 —
c. First day dated, over No. 27500 — —
On cover with first day cancel *100.00*

CVP17 CVP1 $1 **Third Class,** any date other than first day — —
a. First day dated, serial Nos. 24501-27500 — —
b. First day dated, over No. 27500 — —

CVP18 CVP2 $1.69 **Parcel Post,** any date other than first day — —
a. First day dated, serial Nos. 21501-24500 — —
b. First day dated, over No. 27500 — —

CVP19 CVP1 $2.40 **Priority Mail,** any date other than first day — —
a. First day dated, serial Nos. 18501-21500 — —
b. First day dated, over No. 27500 — —
c. Priority Mail ($2.74), with bar code (CVP2) 100.00

CVP20 CVP1 $8.75 **Express Mail,** any date other than first day — —
a. First day dated, serial Nos. 15501-18500 — —
b. First day dated, over No. 27500 — —
Nos. 16a-20a (5) 57.50 —
Nos. 6b, 16b (2) 9.00 —

Unsevered pairs and single with advertising label exist for most, if not all, of the machine vended items from Kensington machine #83. Other combinations also exist.

1989, Nov. Washington, DC, Machine 11

CVP21 CVP1 25c **First Class** *150.00*
a. First Class, with bar code (CVP2) —

Stamps in CVP1 design with $1.10 denominations exist (certified first class).

CVP22 CVP1 $1 **Third Class** *500.00*
CVP23 CVP2 $1.69 **Parcel Post** *500.00*
CVP24 CVP1 $2.40 **Priority Mail** *500.00*
a. Priority Mail ($2.74), with bar code (CVP2) —
CVP25 CVP1 $8.75 **Express Mail** *500.00*

No. 21 dated Nov. 30 known on cover, Nos. 24-25 known dated Dec. 2.

Washington, DC, Machine 12

CVP26 CVP1 25c **First Class** *150.00*

A $1.10 certified First Class stamp, dated Nov. 20, exists on cover.

CVP27 CVP1 $1 **Third Class** —

A $1.40 Third Class stamp of type CVP2, dated Dec. 1 is known on a Dec. 2 cover.

CVP28 CVP2 $1.69 **Parcel Post** —
CVP29 CVP1 $2.40 **Priority Mail** —
a. Priority Mail ($2.74), with bar code (CVP2) —
CVP30 CVP1 $8.75 **Express Mail** —

Nos. 29-30 known dated Dec. 1. An $8.50 Express Mail stamp, dated Dec. 2, exists on cover.

CVP3 - Type I

CVP3 - Type II

Denomination printed by ECA GARD Postage and Mailing Center machines.

COIL STAMPS

1992, Aug. 20 Engr. Tagged *Perf. 10 Horiz.*

CVP31 CVP3 29c **red & blue,** type I, prephosphered paper (solid tagging), dull gum .60 .25
Pair 1.20 —
P# strip of 5, P#1 8.50
P# single, #1 5.50
a. 29c Type I, prephosphered paper (mottled tagging), shiny gum .60 .25
Pair 1.20 —
P# strip of 5, P#1 8.50
P# single, #1 5.50
First day cover, Oklahoma City, OK 1.25
b. 32c Type II, prephosphered paper (solid tagging), dull gum, *Nov. 1994* .90 .40
Pair 1.80
P# strip of 5, P#1 10.00
P# single, #1 *5.50*
c. 32c Type II, prephosphered paper (mottled tagging), shiny gum .90 .40
Pair 1.80
P# strip of 5, P#1 8.75
P# single, #1 *6.00*

Types I and II differ in style of asterisk, period between dollar and cent figures and font used for figures, as shown in illustrations.

No. 31 was available at five test sites in the Southern Maryland, Miami, Oklahoma City, Detroit and Santa Ana, CA, divisions. They were produced for use in ECA GARD Postage and Mailing Center (PMC) machines which can produce denominations from 1c through $99.99.

For Nos. 31-31a, the 29c value has been listed because it was the current first class rate and was the only value available through the USPS Philatelic Sales Division. The most common denomination available other than 29c will probably be 1c (value 20c) as these were made in quantity, by collectors and dealers, between plate number strips. Later the machines were adjusted to provide only 19c and higher value stamps.

For Nos. 31b-31c, the 32c value has been listed because it was the first class rate in effect for the majority of the period the stamps were in use.

CVP4

Denominations printed by Unisys PMC machines.

1994, Feb. 19 Photo. Tagged *Perf. 9.9 Vert.*

CVP32 CVP4 29c **dark red & dark blue** .60 .35
Pair 1.20 —
P# strip of 5, #A11 8.00 —
P# single, #A11 5.50
First day cover, Merrifield, VA *(26,390)* 1.25

No. 32 was available at six test sites in northern Virginia. It was produced for use in machines which can produce values from 19c to $99.99. See note following No. 31.

For No. 32, the 29c value has been listed because it was the first class rate in effect at the time the stamp was issued.

1996, Jan. 26 Photo. Tagged *Perf. 9.9 Vert.*

CVP33 CVP4 32c **bright red & blue,** "1996" below design .60 .25
Pair 1.20 —
P# strip of 5, same, #11 7.25 —
P# single, #11 6.00

Letters in "USA" on No. 33 are thicker than on No. 32. Numerous other design differences exist in the moire pattern and in the bunting. No. 33 has "1996" in the lower left corner; No. 32 has no date.

For No. 33, the 32c value has been listed because it was the first class rate in effect at the time the stamp was issued.

CVP5

Illustration reduced.

1999 Tagged *Die Cut*
Self-Adhesive

CVP34 CVP5 33c **black** *22.50* —

No. CVP34 was available from 15 NCR Automated Postal Center machines located in central Florida. Machines could produce values as low as 1c as well as values higher than 33c. The backing paper is taller and wider than the stamp.

Sales of No. CVP34 were discontinued in 2000 or 2001.

CVP6

Illustration reduced.

1999 Tagged *Die Cut*
Self-Adhesive

CVP35 CVP6 33c **black & red orange** — —
a. With Priority Mail inscription instead of identification number at LL — —

No. CVP35 was available from 18 IBM machines located in central Florida. The backing paper is taller than the stamp. Machines could produce values as low as 1c as well as values higher than 33c.

Test Labels

TL1

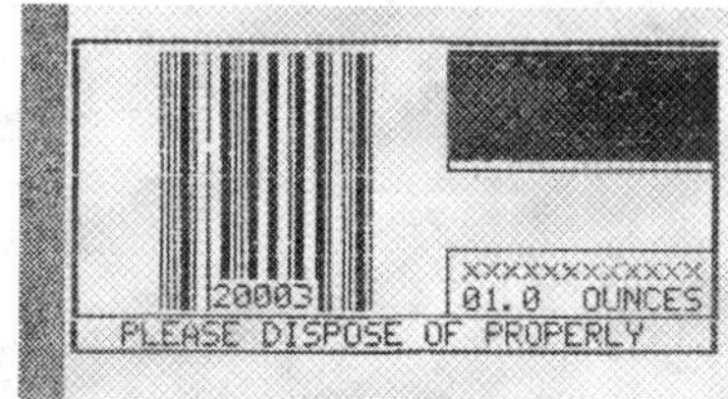

TL2

Test labels were generated when machines were activated. They were not intended for public distribution.

Other samples, advertizing labels, proofs, etc. exist.

POSTAL CARDS

On July 5, 1990 the first of a number of "Postal Buddy" machines was placed in service at the Merrifield, VA post office. The machine printed out numerous items such as address labels (including monogram if you wished), fax labels, "penalty" cards, denominated postal cards, etc. Certain services were free, such as the penalty card mailed to your post office for change of address. The 15-cent denominated card cost 33-cents each and could be used to notify others of address change, meeting notices, customized messages, etc. Borders, messages, backs are different. The cards also came in sheets of 4.

These machines were tested in at least 30 locations in Virginia, including 16 post offices.

Denominated Postal Cards

10005-90-198-022

Number under design includes machine number, year, date (1 through 366) and transaction number.

1990, July 5

CVUX1	15c	6.00	*10.00*
	First day cancel, Merrifield, VA *(6,500)*		5.00

1991, Feb. 3

CVUX2	19c	3.00	*8.00*
	First day cancel, any location		35.00

Number under design includes ZIP Code of the originating machine (22033 in illustration), machine number (101), last digit of year, numbers of month and day (21203 for Dec. 3, 1992) and transaction number (041).

1992, Nov. 13

CVUX3	19c	6.00	*15.00*
	First day dated, Reston or Chantilly, VA		25.00

A total of 171 machines were used in the greater Washington, DC area including locations in Virginia and Maryland (109), the greater San Diego area (59), and in Denver (3). The machine numbers (011, 012, 021, 101, 111, 121, 131) when combined with the zip code created unique identification numbers for each machine.

No. 3 is known also on fluorescent paper. Two different designs on back known for each paper type.

The contract for Postal Buddy machines was canceled Sept. 16, 1993. After the contract was canceled, the Postal Buddy Corporation sold remaining stocks of card stock to the public with both reverse designs imprinted. By using this stock and a high quality copier, very dangerous counterfeits can be created. The duplication of numbers in the transaction line will be one indicator.

VENDING & AFFIXING MACHINE PERFORATIONS

Imperforate sheets of 400 were first issued in 1906 on the request of several makers of vending and affixing machines. The machine manufacturers made coils from the imperforate sheets and applied various perforations to suit the particular needs of their machines. These privately applied perforations were used for many years and form a chapter of postal history.

Unused values are for pairs, used values for singles. "On cover" values are for single stamps used commercially in the proper period when known that way. Several, primarily the Alaska-Yukon and Hudson-Fulton commemoratives, are known almost exclusively on covers from contemporaneous stamp collectors and stamp dealers. Virtually all are rare and highly prized by specialists.

The 2mm and 3mm spacings refer only to the 1908-10 issues. (See note following No. 330 in the Postage section.) Values for intermediate spacings would roughly correspond to the lower-valued of the two listed spacings. Guide line pairs of 1906-10 issues have 2mm spacing except the Alaska-Yukon and Hudson-Fulton issues, which have 3mm spacing. Scott Nos. 408-611 have 3mm spacing, except the "A" plates which have 2¾mm spacing and Scott No. 577, which has both 2¾mm and 3mm spacing. (All spacing measurements are approximate.)

Spacing on paste-up pairs is not a factor in valuing them. Because they were joined together by hand, many different spacings can occur, from less than 2mm to more than 3mm.

Perfins listed here are punched into the stamp at the same time as the perforation. The most common pattern consisted of a 7mm square made up of nine holes. Pins would be removed to create unique perfins for each company using the machines. The catalogue value is for the most common perfin pattern on each stamp.

* — Many varieties are suspected or known to have been perforated for philatelic purposes and not actually used in machines. These are indicated by an asterisk before the number. Several of these privately applied perforation varieties exist in blocks, which were not produced in the regular course of business. They are generally valued at a premium over the multiple of the coil pairs contained, with an additional premium for plate numbers attached.

Counterfeits are prevalent, especially of items having a basic imperf. variety valued far lower than the vending machine coil.

The Vending and Affixing Machine Perforations Committee of the Bureau Issues Association and William R. Weiss, Jr., compiled these listings.

The Attleboro Stamp Co.

See following U.S. Automatic Vending Company.

THE BRINKERHOFF COMPANY

Sedalia, Mo., Clinton, Iowa

Manufacturers of Vending Machines

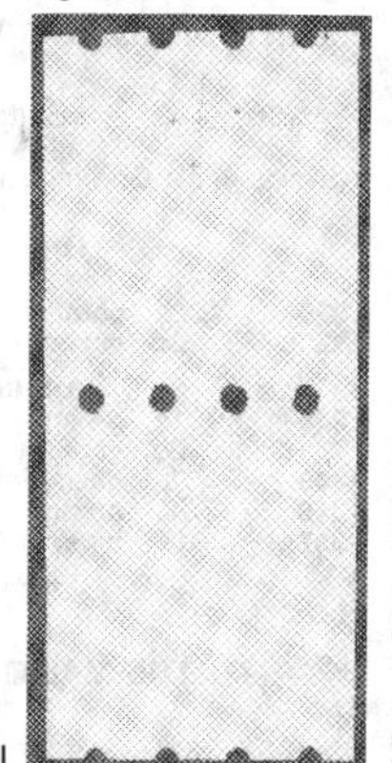
Perforations Type I

Stamps were cut into strips and joined before being perforated.

			Unused Pair	Used Single
		On Issue of 1906-08		
314	1c	**blue green**	190.00	25.00
		Guide line pair	300.00	
320	2c	**carmine**	210.00	25.00
		Guide line pair	375.00	
*320a	2c	**lake**	140.00	20.00
		Guide line pair	300.00	
		On Issue of 1908-09		
*343	1c	**green**	105.00	16.00
		Guide line pair	250.00	
		Pasteup pair	220.00	
*344	2c	**carmine**	90.00	16.00
		On cover		*1,500.*
		Guide line pair	175.00	—
*345	3c	**deep violet**	130.00	—
		Guide line pair	250.00	
*346	4c	**orange brown**	150.00	75.00
		Guide line pair	240.00	
*347	5c	**blue**	290.00	75.00
		On cover		**3,000.**
		Guide line pair	400.00	
		On Lincoln Issue of 1909		
*368	2c	**carmine,** coiled endwise	160.00	160.00
		Guide line pair	275.00	
		On Alaska-Yukon Issue of 1909		
*371	2c	**carmine,** coiled sideways	*550.00*	—
		Guide line pair	*750.00*	
		On Issue of 1910		
*383	1c	**green**	*190.00*	

			Unused Pair	Used Single
		On Issue of 1912		
*408	1c	**green**	27.50	12.00
		On cover		*750.00*
		Guide line pair	55.00	
		Pasteup pair	50.00	
*409	2c	**carmine**	27.50	12.00
		On cover		*1,000.*
		Guide line pair	55.00	
		Pasteup pair	50.00	

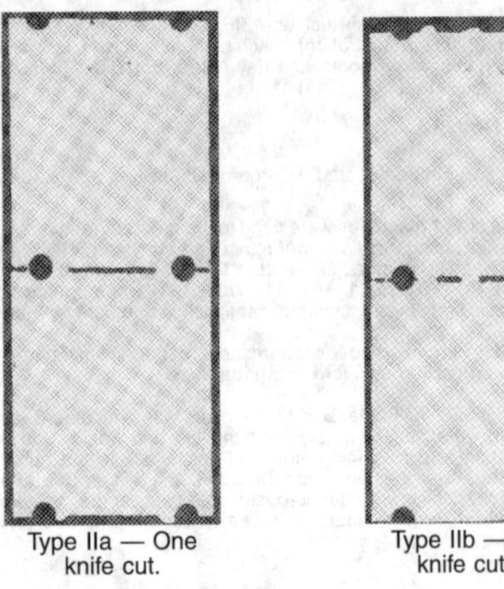

Type IIa — One knife cut.

Type IIb —Two knife cuts.

Perforations Type II, 2 Holes

The Type II items listed below are without knife cuts and did not pass through the vending machine. Types IIa and IIb (illustrated above) have knife cuts, applied by the vending machine, to help separate the stamps.

	Type			Unused Pair	Used Single
			On Issue of 1906-08		
314	*II	1c	**blue green**	90.00	10.00
			On cover		*750.00*
	IIa	1c	**blue green**	65.00	10.00
			Guide line pair	140.00	
	*IIb	1c	**blue green**	360.00	—
320	*II	2c	**carmine**	190.00	*60.00*
	IIa	2c	**carmine**	32.50	10.00
			On cover		*500.00*
			Guide line pair	110.00	
320a	*II	2c	**lake**	190.00	*60.00*
	IIa	2c	**lake**	50.00	10.00
			On cover		*500.00*
			Guide line pair	100.00	
			Pasteup pair	90.00	
	*IIb	2c	**lake**	310.00	*70.00*
			On Issue of 1908-09		
343	*II	1c	**green**	60.00	
			On cover		*600.00*
			Guide line pair	95.00	
	IIa	1c	**green**	16.00	3.00
			On cover		600.00
			Pasteup pair	27.50	
	IIb	1c	**green**	27.50	
			Pasteup pair	47.50	
344	*II	2c	**carmine**	70.00	
			On cover, pair		*600.00*
			Pasteup pair	120.00	
	IIa	2c	**carmine**	16.00	3.00
			Guide line pair	30.00	
			On cover		*700.00*
	IIb	2c	**carmine**	32.50	6.00
			Guide line pair	65.00	
			Pasteup pair	55.00	
345	*II	3c	**deep violet**	90.00	10.00
	*IIa	3c	**deep violet**	75.00	*10.00*
			On cover		*1,500.*
			Guide line pair	140.00	
	*IIb	3c	**deep violet**	250.00	
346	*II	4c	**orange brown**	140.00	
			Guide line pair	240.00	
	*IIa	4c	**orange brown**	120.00	**45.00**
			On cover		*1,200.*
			Guide line pair	210.00	
			Pasteup pair	190.00	
	*IIb	4c	**orange brown**	130.00	**45.00**
			On cover		*1,500.*
347	*II	5c	**blue**	225.00	
			Guide line pair	350.00	
	*IIa	5c	**blue**	130.00	*100.00*
			On cover		**3,000.**
	*IIb	5c	**blue**	160.00	
			On Lincoln Issue of 1909		
368	*II	2c	**carmine**	70.00	
			Guide line pair	120.00	
	IIa	2c	**carmine**	65.00	12.00
			On cover		*1,200.*
			Guide line pair	200.00	
	IIb	2c	**carmine**	190.00	20.00
			On cover		*1,500.*
			Guide line pair	400.00	
			On Alaska-Yukon Issue of 1909		
371	*II	2c	**carmine,** coiled sideways	130.00	*90.00*
			On cover		*1,000.*
			Guide line or pasteup pair	250.00	
	II	2c	**carmine,** coiled endwise	*525.00*	
			Guide line pair	*1,050.*	
	IIa	2c	**carmine,** coiled sideways	160.00	**40.00**
			On cover		*750.00*
			Guide line pair	260.00	
			Pasteup pair	240.00	
			On Hudson-Fulton Issue of 1909		
373	*II	2c	**carmine,** coiled sidewise	*250.00*	
			Guide line or pasteup pair	**400.00**	
			On Issue of 1910		
383	*II	1c	**green**	32.50	
			Guide line pair	65.00	
	IIa	1c	**green**	42.50	8.00
			On cover		*800.00*
	IIb	1c	**green**	80.00	**45.00**
			On cover		*1,000.*
			Guide line pair	130.00	
384	*II	2c	**carmine**	32.50	
			Guide line pair	60.00	
	IIa	2c	**carmine**	110.00	
			On cover		*1,000.*
	IIb	2c	**carmine**	55.00	8.00
			On cover		*1,500.*
			On Issue of 1912		
408	*II	1c	**green**	60.00	—
			On cover		*800.00*
			Guide line pair	110.00	
			Pasteup pair	100.00	
	*IIa	1c	**green**	100.00	
			Guide line pair	190.00	
	IIb	1c	**green**	22.50	5.00
			On cover		800.00
			Guide line pair	45.00	
409	*II	2c	**carmine**	65.00	
			On cover		*800.00*
			Guide line pair	130.00	
			Pasteup pair	120.00	
	*IIa	2c	**carmine**	240.00	—
			On cover		*800.00*
			Guide line pair	375.00	
	IIb	2c	**carmine**	27.50	5.00
			On cover		*625.00*
			Guide line pair	50.00	

THE FARWELL COMPANY

Chicago, Ill.

A wholesale dry goods firm using Schermack (Mailometer) affixing machines. In 1911 the Farwell Company began to make and perforate their own coils. These were sometimes wrongly called "Chambers" perforations.

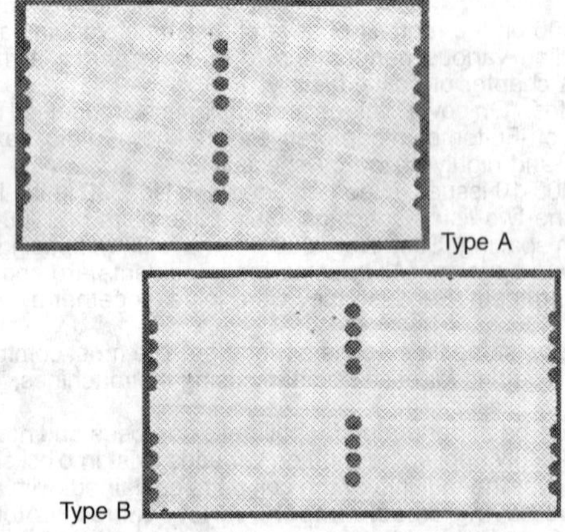

Type A

Type B

Stamps were perforated in sheets, then cut into strips and coiled. Blocks exist.

The following listings are grouped according to the number of holes, further divided into two types of spacing, narrow and wide.

The type symbols (3A2) indicate 3 holes over 2 holes with narrow, type A, spacing between groups.

Types A and B occurred in different rows on the same sheet. Left margin or pasteup stamps sometimes show different perforation type on the two sides.

Commercial usages of Farwell perforations are generally, but not always, on printed Farwell Co. corner card covers.

	Type			Unused Pair Spacing 2mm	3mm	Used Single
			Group I, no spacing			
			On Issue of 1910			
384		2c	**carmine**, 7 holes	*2,000.*	*2,000.*	*850.00*
			On cover			*5,000.*
384		2c	**carmine,** 6 holes	**3,500.**	**3,500.**	
			On cover			*5,000.*
			Group 2, two and three holes			
			On Issue of 1910			
383	2B3	1c	**green**	**350.00**	*600.00*	*200.00*
	3A2	1c	**green**	**350.00**	*600.00*	
			On cover			—
			Guide line pair	*525.00*		
384	2A3	2c	**carmine**	*250.00*	**450.00**	*200.00*
			On cover			*950.00*
			Guide line pair	1,050.	950.00	
			Pasteup pair		750.00	
	2B3	2c	**carmine**	*600.00*	*675.00*	*225.00*
			On cover			—
			Pasteup pair		*1,000.*	
	3A2	2c	**carmine**	**400.00**	**450.00**	*210.00*
			On cover			*1,100.*
			Guide line pair	*600.00*		
	3B2	2c	**carmine**	**350.00**	**350.00**	*235.00*
			Guide line pair	*750.00*		
			Group 3, three and four holes			
			On Issue of 1910			
383	3B4	1c	**green**	*240.00*	*240.00*	*200.00*
			Pasteup pair	*525.00*		
	4B3	1c	**green**	**350.00**	**350.00**	*200.00*
384	3B4	2c	**carmine**	**450.00**	**450.00**	*200.00*
			On cover			—
			Guide line pair	*650.00*		
	4B3	2c	**carmine**	*600.00*	*600.00*	*175.00*
			On cover			*700.00*
			Guide line pair	—		
	4A3	2c	Carmine			—
			Group 4, four and four holes			
			On Issue of 1908-09			
343	*A	1c	**green**	*225.00*		
	*B	1c	**green**	*225.00*		
344	*A	2c	**carmine**	*225.00*	**350.00**	
	*B	2c	**carmine**	*175.00*	*160.00*	*115.00*
			On Lincoln Issue of 1909			
368	*A	2c	**carmine**	*800.00*	*800.00*	
	*B	2c	**carmine**	*800.00*	*800.00*	
			On Issue of 1910			
383	A	1c	**green**	55.00	50.00	*55.00*
			Guide line pair	100.00		
	B	1c	**green**	55.00	50.00	—
			Guide line pair	100.00		
384	A	2c	**carmine**	60.00	55.00	15.00
			Guide line pair	110.00		
	B	2c	**carmine**	60.00	55.00	15.00
			On cover			**300.00**
			Guide line pair	110.00		
			On Issue of 1912			
408	A	1c	**green**		30.00	2.50
			On cover			275.00
			Guide line pair		52.50	
	B	1c	**green**		30.00	2.50
			On cover			200.00
			Guide line pair		52.50	
409	A	2c	**carmine**		24.00	2.50
			On cover			75.00
	B	2c	**carmine**		24.00	2.50
			On cover			75.00
			Guide line pair		45.00	
			On Issue of 1916-17			
482	A	2c	**carmine**		**375.00**	*55.00*
			On cover			*1,100.*
			Guide line pair		*525.00*	
			Pasteup pair		*550.00*	
	B	2c	**carmine**		**425.00**	*55.00*
			On cover			*1,100.*
			Guide line pair		*650.00*	
			Group 5, four and five holes			
			On Issue of 1910			
383	4A5	1c	**green**	*575.00*	475.00	—
			Guide line pair	*850.00*		
384	4A5	2c	**carmine**	*600.00*	475.00	—
			Guide line pair	*900.00*		
			On Issue of 1912			
408	4A5	1c	**green**		800.00	
			Guide line pair		*1,100.*	
	*5A4	1c	**green**		800.00	
			Guide line pair		*1,100.*	
409	*4A5	2c	**carmine**		925.00	—
			Guide line or pasteup pair		*1,300.*	
	*5A4	2c	**carmine**		800.00	
			Guide line pair		*1,100.*	

INTERNATIONAL VENDING MACHINE CO.

Baltimore, Md.

Similar to the Government Coil stamp #322, but perf. 12½.

		On Issue of 1906		
320	2c	**carmine**	**3,000.**	
320b	2c	**scarlet**	*1,000.*	*1,300.*
		On Issue of 1908-09		
343	1c	**green**	*2,750.*	
344	2c	**carmine**	*1,100.*	
345	3c	**deep violet**	*1,100.*	
346	4c	**orange brown**	—	
347	5c	**blue**	*5,750.*	

THE MAILOMETER COMPANY

Detroit, Mich.

Formerly the Schermack Mailing Machine Co., then Mail-om-eter Co., and later the Mail-O-Meter Co. Their round-hole perforations were developed in an attempt to get the Bureau of Engraving and Printing to adopt a larger perforation for coil stamps.

Perforations Type I

Used experimentally in Detroit and Chicago in August, 1909. Later used regularly in the St. Louis branch.

Two varieties exist: six holes 1.95mm in diameter spaced an average 1.2mm apart with an overall length of 17.7mm, and six holes 1.95mm in diameter spaced an average 1.15mm apart with an overall length of 17.45mm.

To date, only the 17.7mm length perfs. have been found on commercial covers.

			Unused Pair Spacing 2mm	3mm	Used Single
		On Issue of 1906-08			
*320	2c	**carmine**	450.00		
*320a	2c	**lake**	350.00		
		Guide line pair	800.00		
*320b	2c	**scarlet**	325.00		
		On Issue of 1908-09			
343	1c	**green**	40.00	45.00	22.50
		On cover			*500.00*
		Guide line pair	70.00		
344	2c	**carmine**	40.00	45.00	4.50
		On cover, St. Louis			*75.00*
		On cover, Detroit or Chicago			*1,250.*
		On cover, Washington, D.C.			*1,750.*
		Guide line pair	70.00		
		With perforated control mark, single			*75.00*
		Same, on cover			**325.00**
345	3c	**deep violet**	55.00		17.50
		Guide line pair	100.00		
346	4c	**orange brown**	105.00	75.00	35.00
		Guide line pair	160.00		
347	5c	**blue**	120.00		35.00
		Guide line pair	190.00		
		On Lincoln Issue of 1909			
*368	2c	**carmine**	150.00	100.00	*110.00*
		Guide line or pasteup pair	300.00		
		On Alaska-Yukon Issue of 1909			
*371	2c	**carmine**		200.00	*110.00*
		Guide line pair		325.00	
		On Hudson-Fulton Issue of 1909			
*373	2c	**carmine**		180.00	*100.00*
		Guide line pair		325.00	
		On Issue of 1910			
383	1c	**green**	37.50	32.50	3.25
		On cover			—
		Guide line pair	65.00		
384	2c	**carmine**	45.00	37.50	4.50
		On cover			75.00
		Guide line pair	75.00		
		On Issue of 1912			
*408	1c	**green**		24.00	4.00
		Guide line pair		45.00	
*409	2c	**carmine**		25.00	4.00
		Guide line pair		47.50	

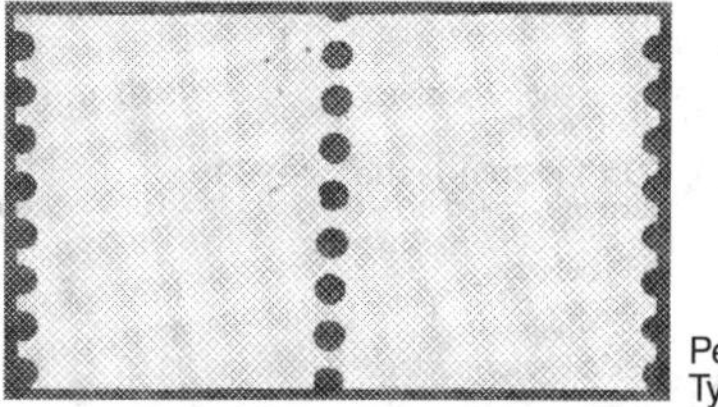

Perforations Type II

Used experimentally: Chicago, 1909; Detroit, 1911.

			2mm	3mm	Used
		On Issue of 1906-08			
*320	2c	**carmine**	600.00		
*320b	2c	**scarlet**	1,000.		
		On Issue of 1908-09			
343	1c	**green**	35.00	35.00	12.50
		Guide line pair	60.00		
344	2c	**carmine**	40.00	40.00	12.50
		On cover			*5,000.*
		Guide line pair	75.00		
*345	3c	**deep violet**	200.00		*65.00*
*346	4c	**orange brown**	290.00	290.00	
*347	5c	**blue**	525.00		
		On Lincoln Issue of 1909			
*368	2c	**carmine**	525.00	500.00	
		On Alaska-Yukon Issue of 1909			
*371	2c	**carmine**		575.00	
		On Hudson-Fulton Issue of 1909			
*373	2c	**carmine**		260.00	
		Guide line or pasteup pair		375.00	
		On Issue of 1910			
383	1c	**green**	90.00	90.00	25.00
		Guide line or pasteup pair	175.00		
384	2c	**carmine**	110.00	95.00	*50.00*
		On cover			**4,000.**

Perforations Type III

Used experimentally in Detroit in 1910.

			2mm	3mm	Used
		On Issue of 1906-08			
*320	2c	**carmine**	600.00		
*320b	2c	**scarlet**	800.00		
		On Issue of 1908-09			
343	1c	**green**	120.00	120.00	
		Guide line pair	240.00		
344	2c	**carmine**	175.00	175.00	
		Guide line pair	275.00		
		Pasteup pair		**350.00**	
*345	3c	**deep violet**	260.00		
*346	4c	**orange brown**	375.00	290.00	
*347	5c	**blue**	*625.00*		
		Pasteup pair		*1,050.*	
		On Lincoln Issue of 1909			
*368	2c	**carmine**	290.00	240.00	*90.00*
		Pasteup pair		375.00	
		On Alaska-Yukon Issue of 1909			
*371	2c	**carmine**		625.00	
		On Hudson-Fulton Issue of 1909			
*373	2c	**carmine**		575.00	
		Guide line pair		*1,300.*	

Perforations Type IV

Used in St. Louis branch office. Blocks exist but were not regularly produced or issued.

			2mm	3mm	Used
		On Issue of 1906-08			
*320	2c	**carmine**	200.00		*75.00*
*320b	2c	**scarlet**	120.00		*60.00*
		On Issue of 1908-09			
343	1c	**green**	45.00	40.00	8.00
		Guide line pair	85.00		
344	2c	**carmine**	55.00	45.00	8.00
		On cover			—
		Guide line or pasteup pair	100.00		
345	3c	**deep violet**	95.00		
		Guide line or pasteup pair	180.00		
346	4c	**orange brown**	150.00	120.00	
		Guide line pair	275.00		
347	5c	**blue**	175.00		*50.00*
		Guide line pair	300.00		
		On Lincoln Issue of 1909			
*368	2c	**carmine**	95.00	95.00	25.00
		Guide line or pasteup pair	180.00		
		On Alaska-Yukon Issue of 1909			
*371	2c	**carmine**		**325.00**	
		Guide line pair		*550.00*	
		On Hudson-Fulton Issue of 1909			
*373	2c	**carmine**		**325.00**	
		On cover		—	
		Guide line pair		*525.00*	
		On Issue of 1910			
383	1c	**green**	14.00	10.00	2.00
		On cover			*200.00*
		Guide line pair	22.50		
384	2c	**carmine**	25.00	22.50	1.00
		On cover			*110.00*
		Guide line pair	40.00		
		On Issue of 1912			
408	1c	**green**		7.00	1.00
		On cover			50.00
		Guide line or pasteup pair		11.00	
409	2c	**carmine**		8.00	.50
		On cover			50.00
		Guide line or pasteup pair		13.00	
		On Issue of 1916-17			
482	2c	**carmine**		*100.00*	*60.00*
		On cover			*275.00*
		Guide line pair		*175.00*	
		Pasteup pair		*210.00*	
483	3c	**violet,** type I		*130.00*	*60.00*
		On cover			*275.00*
		Guide line pair		*250.00*	
		Pasteup pair		*175.00*	

THE SCHERMACK COMPANY

Detroit, Mich.

These perforations were developed by the Schermack Mailing Machine Co. before it became the Mailometer Co. The Type III perforation was used in the company's affixing machines from 1908 through 1927 or 1928.

Perforations Type I. Eight Holes

Perforated in sheets, then cut into strips and coiled.

			Unused Pair Spacing 2mm	3mm	Used Single
		On Issue of 1906-08			
314	1c	**blue green**	140.00		*90.00*
		Guide line pair	250.00		
		*Seven holes	1,000.		
		*Pasteup pair	*1,350.*		
		*Six holes	900.00		
		Guide line pair	1,600.		
320	2c	**carmine**	110.00		*50.00*
		On cover			*2,000.*
		Guide line pair	190.00		
		Seven holes	1,000.		**300.00**
		On cover			*8,000.*
		Guide line pair	1,500.		
		Pasteup pair	1,100.		
		*Six holes	1,000.		
		Guide line pair	*2,250.*		
*320a	2c	**lake**	300.00		*100.00*
		*Seven holes	600.00		
		Guide line pair	*1,500.*		
		*Six holes	*1,250.*		
*320b	2c	**scarlet,** six holes			
		Guide line pair	*1,500.*		
*315	5c	**blue**	—		
		On Issue of 1908-09			
*343	1c	**green**	210.00	—	75.00
		Guide line pair	—		
*344	2c	**carmine**	1,000.	—	
		Guide line pair	*1,400.*		
*345	3c	**deep violet**	*1,400.*		
		Guide line pair	*1,750.*		
*346	4c	**orange brown**	600.00	—	
		Guide line pair	—		
*347	5c	**blue**	600.00		
		Guide line pair	—		
		On Lincoln Issue of 1909			
*368	2c	**carmine**	175.00	200.00	*75.00*
		Guide line pair	275.00		
		*Seven holes	875.00	—	
		*Six holes	1,000.	—	

Perforations Type II

Cut into strips and joined before being perforated.

			2mm	3mm	Used
		On Issue of 1906-08			
314	1c	**blue green**	260.00		*75.00*
		Guide line pair	375.00		
320	2c	**carmine**	130.00		*50.00*
		Guide line pair	225.00		
*320a	2c	**lake**	225.00		*90.00*

No.	Denom.	Description	Unused Pair 2mm	Unused Pair 3mm	Used Single
		Guide line pair	375.00		
*315	5c	**blue**	*11,000.*		*1,750.*
		Guide line pair	—		

On Issue of 1908-09

No.	Denom.	Description	Unused Pair 2mm	Unused Pair 3mm	Used Single
*343	1c	**green**	*600.00*	*625.00*	
		Guide line pair	*850.00*		
*344	2c	**carmine**	*600.00*	*575.00*	
		Guide line pair	*775.00*		
*345	3c	**deep violet**	*600.00*		
		Guide line pair	*800.00*		
*346	4c	**orange brown**	*800.00*	—	
		Guide line pair	*1,050.*		
*347	5c	**blue**	*750.00*		
		Guide line pair	*1,400.*		

On Lincoln Issue of 1909

No.	Denom.	Description	Unused Pair 2mm	Unused Pair 3mm	Used Single
*368	2c	**carmine**	140.00	125.00	*60.00*
		Guide line pair	225.00		

On Issue of 1910

No.	Denom.	Description	Unused Pair 2mm	Unused Pair 3mm	Used Single
*383	1c	**green**	—	—	
		Guide line or pasteup pair	—		
*384	2c	**carmine**	—	—	

Existance of genuine copies of Nos. 383-384 has been questioned.

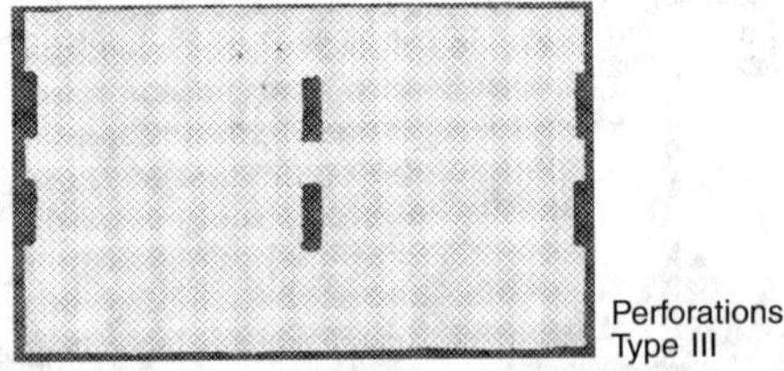

Perforations Type III

Blocks exist but were not regularly produced or issued.

On Issue of 1906-08

No.	Denom.	Description	Unused Pair Spacing 2mm	Unused Pair Spacing 3mm	Used Single
314	1c	**blue green**	11.00		2.00
		On cover			*125.00*
		Guide line pair	22.50		
		Pasteup pair	19.00		
320	2c	**carmine,** type I	16.00		5.00
		On cover			80.00
		Guide line pair	30.00		
320a	2c	**lake,** type II	22.50		2.50
		On cover			*80.00*
		Guide line pair	45.00		
		Pasteup pair	40.00		
		With perforated control mark, single			—
*320b	2c	**scarlet,** type I	22.50		5.00
		On cover			—
		Guide line pair	40.00		
320c	2c	**carmine rose,** type I	55.00		
320d	2c	**carmine,** type II, single	125.00		
		On cover			600.00
		Pair	260.00		
		Guide line pair	—		
314A	4c	**brown,** single	*70,000.*		**40,000.**
		Pair	*150,000.*		
		On cover			*130,000.*
		Guide line pair	*240,000.*		
*315	5c	**blue**	**4,000.**		

On Issue of 1908-09

No.	Denom.	Description	Unused Pair Spacing 2mm	Unused Pair Spacing 3mm	Used Single
343	1c	**green**	5.50	6.50	1.00
		On cover			25.00
		Guide line or pasteup pair	10.00		
		With perforated control mark, single			*50.00*
		Same, on cover			**450.00**
344	2c	**carmine**	5.50	6.50	1.00
		On cover			22.50
		Guide line or pasteup pair	10.00		
		With perforated control mark, single			*50.00*
		Same, on cover			**450.00**
345	3c	**deep violet**	22.50	*150.00*	10.00
		On cover			30.00
		Guide line pair	40.00		
		With perforated control mark, single			*750.00*
		Same, on cover			*7,500.*
346	4c	**orange brown**	32.50	22.50	15.00
		On cover			**3,000.**
		Guide line or pasteup pair	55.00		
		With perforated control mark, single			*1,250.*
		On cover			*9,000.*
347	5c	**blue**	55.00		15.00
		On cover			*2,250.*
		Guide line pair	100.00		

On Lincoln Issue of 1909

No.	Denom.	Description	Unused Pair Spacing 2mm	Unused Pair Spacing 3mm	Used Single
368	2c	**carmine**	65.00	50.00	10.00
		On cover			*175.00*
		Guide line or pasteup pair	110.00		

On Alaska-Yukon Issue of 1909

No.	Denom.	Description	Unused Pair Spacing 2mm	Unused Pair Spacing 3mm	Used Single
*371	2c	**carmine**		77.50	
		On cover			**4,000.**

No.	Denom.	Description	Unused Pair Spacing 2mm	Unused Pair Spacing 3mm	Used Single
		Guide line or pasteup pair		140.00	

On Hudson-Fulton Issue of 1909

No.	Denom.	Description	Unused Pair Spacing 2mm	Unused Pair Spacing 3mm	Used Single
*373	2c	**carmine**		95.00	
		Guide line or pasteup pair		175.00	

On Issue of 1910

No.	Denom.	Description	Unused Pair Spacing 2mm	Unused Pair Spacing 3mm	Used Single
383	1c	**green**	4.50	3.25	1.00
		On cover			27.50
		Guide line or pasteup pair	8.75		
		With perforated control mark, single			**30.00**
		Same, on cover			*250.00*
384	2c	**carmine**	10.00	7.75	1.00
		On cover			25.00
		Guide line pair	16.00		
		With perforated control mark, single			**30.00**
		Same, on cover			*200.00*

On Issue of 1912

No.	Denom.	Description	Unused Pair Spacing 2mm	Unused Pair Spacing 3mm	Used Single
408	1c	**green**		2.25	.50
		On cover			30.00
		Guide line or pasteup pair		4.50	
		With perforated control mark, single			**35.00**
		Same, on cover			*275.00*
409	2c	**carmine**		2.25	.40
		On cover			25.00
		Guide line or pasteup pair		4.50	
		Aniline ink ("pink back")		—	
		With perforated control mark, single			**35.00**
		Same, on cover			*275.00*

On Issue of 1916-17

No.	Denom.	Description	Unused Pair Spacing 2mm	Unused Pair Spacing 3mm	Used Single
481	1c	**green**		3.25	.30
		On cover			20.00
		Guide line or pasteup pair		6.50	
482	2c	**carmine,** type I		4.50	.50
		On cover			15.00
		Guide line or pasteup pair		8.50	
		Aniline ink ("pink back")		—	
482A	2c	**deep rose,** type Ia, single			*50,000.*
		Pair			*105,000.*
		On cover			*55,000.*
483	3c	**violet,** type I		11.00	2.50
		On cover			100.00
		Guide line or pasteup pair		19.00	
484	3c	**violet,** type II		16.00	4.00
		On cover			75.00
		Guide line or pasteup pair		27.50	

On Issue of 1918-20

No.	Denom.	Description	Unused Pair Spacing 2mm	Unused Pair Spacing 3mm	Used Single
531	1c	**green**		11.00	4.00
		On cover			100.00
		Guide line or pasteup pair		22.00	
532	2c	**carmine,** type IV		32.50	3.00
		On cover			75.00
		Guide line or pasteup pair		60.00	
		Pasteup strip of 4, left pair No. 532, right pair No. 482		*1,900.*	
533	2c	**carmine,** type V		*250.00*	**40.00**
		On cover			*250.00*
		Guide line or pasteup pair		*750.00*	
534	2c	**carmine,** type Va		16.00	2.00
		On cover			90.00
		Guide line or pasteup pair		50.00	
534A	2c	**carmine,** type VI		37.50	4.00
		On cover			75.00
		Guide line or pasteup pair		72.50	
534B	2c	**carmine,** type VII		*1,100.*	80.00
		On cover			**425.00**
		Guide line or pasteup pair		*1,550.*	
535	3c	**violet,** type IV		15.00	3.00
		On cover			75.00
		Guide line or pasteup pair		22.50	

On Issue of 1923-26

No.	Denom.	Description	Unused Pair Spacing 2mm	Unused Pair Spacing 3mm	Used Single
575	1c	**green**		*250.00*	6.00
		Unused single		22.50	
		On cover			*500.00*
		Guide line or pasteup pair		**400.00**	
		Precanceled		4.50	1.00
		On cover, precanceled			*100.00*
576	1½c	**yellow brown**		22.50	4.00
		On cover			*200.00*
		Guide line or pasteup pair		40.00	
		Precanceled		4.50	1.00
		On cover, precanceled			*75.00*
577	2c	**carmine**	27.50	22.50	1.00
		On cover			20.00
		Guide line or pasteup pair	50.00	40.00	

On Harding Issue of 1923

No.	Denom.	Description	Unused Pair Spacing 2mm	Unused Pair Spacing 3mm	Used Single
611	2c	**black**		95.00	15.00
		On cover			*7,500.*
		Guide line or pasteup pair		160.00	

U.S. AUTOMATIC VENDING COMPANY

New York, N.Y.

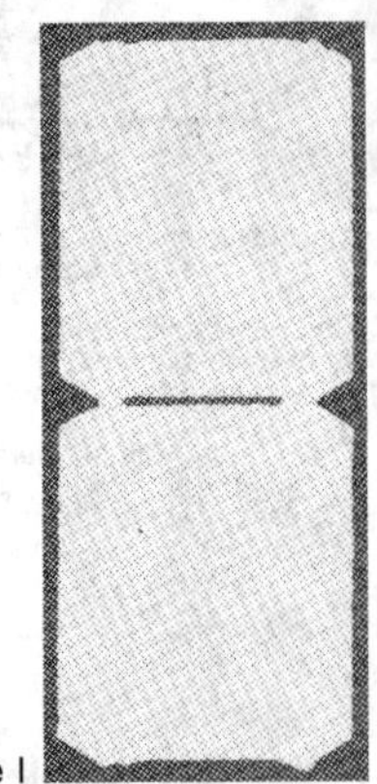

Separations Type I

Cut into strips and joined before being perforated.

Two varieties exist: 15½ and 16mm between notches of the perforations.

On Issue of 1906-08
Coiled Endwise

No.	Denom.	Description	Unused Pair	Used Single
314	1c	**blue green**	50.00	10.00
		On cover		*1,900.*
		Guide line or pasteup pair	85.00	
320	2c	**carmine**	45.00	8.00
		Guide line pair	80.00	
*320a	2c	**lake**	100.00	9.00
		Guide line or pasteup pair	200.00	
320b	2c	**scarlet**	55.00	7.00
		On cover		**3,500.**
		Guide line pair	110.00	
315	5c	**blue**	650.00	—
		On cover		*10,000.*
		Guide line pair	*2,500.*	
		Pasteup pair	*2,750.*	

On Issue of 1908-09
Coiled Endwise

No.	Denom.	Description	Unused Pair	Used Single
343	1c	**green**	11.00	1.50
		On cover		100.00
		On postcard		60.00
		Guide line or pasteup pair	22.00	
344	2c	**carmine**	9.00	1.50
		On cover		100.00
		Guide line or pasteup pair	17.50	
*345	3c	**deep violet**	32.50	8.00
		On cover		*500.00*
		Guide line or pasteup pair	65.00	
*346	4c	**orange brown**	50.00	9.00
		Guide line or pasteup pair	105.00	
347	5c	**blue**	90.00	40.00
		On cover		*2,250.*
		On cover (pair) with No. 373 USAV type II pair		*7,500.*
		Guide line or pasteup pair	175.00	

On Lincoln Issue of 1909

No.	Denom.	Description	Unused Pair	Used Single
368	2c	**carmine,** coiled endwise	40.00	7.00
		On cover		*500.00*
		First day cover, *Feb. 12, 1909*		*14,500.*
		Guide line or pasteup pair	80.00	

On Alaska-Yukon Issue of 1909

No.	Denom.	Description	Unused Pair	Used Single
*371	2c	**carmine,** coiled sideways	75.00	10.00
		On cover		*500.00*
		Guide line pair	140.00	

			Unused Pair	Used Single
		Type Ia, No T. and B. margins	140.00	15.00
		Type Ia, Guide line or pasteup pair	225.00	

Type Ia stamps are a deep shade and have a misplaced position dot in the "S" of "Postage." Beware of trimmed copies of No. 371 type I.

On Issue of 1910

383	1c	**green**	6.50	2.50
		On cover		100.00
		On postcard		40.00
		Guide line or pasteup pair	11.00	
*384	2c	**carmine**	22.50	4.50
		Guide line pair	40.00	

On Issue of 1912

*408	1c	**green**	11.00	2.00
		Guide line pair	19.00	
*409	2c	**carmine**	14.00	4.00
		Guide line pair	22.50	

Separations Type II

Similar to Type I but with notches farther apart and a longer slit. Cut into strips and joined before being perforated.

On Issue of 1906-08
Coiled Sideways

			Unused Pair Spacing 2mm	3mm	Used Single
*314	1c	**blue green**	50.00		8.00
		On cover			—
		Guide line or pasteup pair	82.50		
*320	2c	**carmine**	87.50		
*320b	2c	**scarlet**	60.00		5.00
		Guide line pair	100.00		
*315	5c	**blue**	1,400.		
		Guide line pair	*2,500.*		

On Issue of 1908-09

			2mm	3mm	Used Single
343	1c	**green**	14.00		3.00
		On cover			*1,000.*
		Guide line or pasteup pair	22.50		
344	2c	**carmine**	16.00		
		On cover			*2,500.*
		Guide line pair	25.00		
*345	3c	**deep violet**	65.00	—	
		Guide line pair	110.00		
*346	4c	**orange brown**	95.00	82.50	
		Guide line pair	160.00		
*347	5c	**blue**	190.00		
		Guide line pair	300.00		

On Lincoln Issue of 1909

			2mm	3mm	Used Single
368	2c	**carmine**	100.00	87.50	20.00
		Guide line pair	175.00		

On Alaska-Yukon Issue of 1909

			2mm	3mm	Used Single
*371	2c	**carmine**		65.00	35.00
		On cover			—
		Guide line or pasteup pair		110.00	

On Hudson-Fulton Issue of 1909

			2mm	3mm	Used Single
*373	2c	**carmine**		70.00	*15.00*
		On cover			*2,000.*
		Guide line or pasteup pair		120.00	

See No. 347 USAV type I for combination cover.

On Issue of 1910

			2mm	3mm	Used Single
383	1c	**green**	16.00	12.50	
		On cover			*1,000.*
		Guide line pair	27.50		
384	2c	**carmine**	22.50	16.00	
		On cover			*2,500.*
		Guide line pair	40.00		

On Issue of 1912

			2mm	3mm	Used Single
408	1c	**green**		11.00	2.00
		On cover			*1,500.*
		Guide line pair		19.00	
409	2c	**carmine**		16.00	4.00

			Unused Pair Spacing 2mm	3mm	Used Single
		Guide line pair		27.50	

Perforations Type III

Cut into strips and joined before being perforated.

On Issue of 1906-08

			2mm	3mm	Used Single
*314	1c	**blue green**	55.00		10.00
		Guide line pair	100.00		
*320	2c	**carmine**	100.00		
*320b	2c	**scarlet**	65.00		10.00
		Guide line pair	110.00		
*315	5c	**blue**	1,200.		
		Guide line or pasteup pair	*2,500.*		

On Issue of 1908-09

			2mm	3mm	Used Single
343	1c	**green**	27.50	25.00	5.00
		Guide line or pasteup pair	45.00		
344	2c	**carmine**	27.50		5.00
		Guide line pair	45.00		
*345	3c	**deep violet**	110.00		
		Guide line pair	190.00		
*346	4c	**orange brown**	110.00	100.00	12.00
		Guide line pair	190.00		
*347	5c	**blue**	140.00		
		Guide line pair	250.00		

On Lincoln Issue of 1909

			2mm	3mm	Used Single
*368	2c	**carmine**	70.00	60.00	16.00
		Guide line pair	120.00		
		Experimental perf. 12	*2,750.*		
		Guide line pair	**4,000.**		

On Alaska-Yukon Issue of 1909

			2mm	3mm	Used Single
*371	2c	**carmine**		90.00	16.00
		On cover			—
		Guide line or pasteup pair		140.00	

On Hudson-Fulton Issue of 1909

			2mm	3mm	Used Single
*373	2c	**carmine**		100.00	16.00
		On cover			—
		Guide line or pasteup pair		140.00	

On Issue of 1910

			2mm	3mm	Used Single
383	1c	**green**	15.00	13.00	2.50
		Guide line pair	25.00		
384	2c	**carmine**	17.50	15.00	2.50
		Guide line pair	27.50		

On Issue of 1912

			2mm	3mm	Used Single
408	1c	**green**		8.75	
		Guide line pair		14.00	
409	2c	**carmine**		13.00	
		Guide line pair		19.00	

On 1914 Rotary Press Coil

			2mm	3mm	Used Single
459	2c	**carmine**		*24,000.*	*11,500.*

This firm also produced coil strips of manila paper, folded so as to form small "pockets", each "pocket" containing one 1c stamp and two 2c stamps, usually imperforate but occasionally with either government or U.S.A.V. private perforations. The manila "pockets" were perforated type II, coiled sideways. They fit U.S.A.V. ticket vending machines. Multiples exist.

Values are for "pockets" with known combinations of stamps, listed by basic Scott Number. Other combinations exist, but are not listed due to the fact that the stamps may have been added at a later date.

Pocket Type 1 (1908)
("Patents Pending" on front and green advertising on reverse)

Type 1-1	314 + 320	*2,500.*
Type 1-2	314 + 320b	*2,500.*

Pocket Type 2 (1909)
("Patents Applied For" Handstamped in greenish blue)

Type 2-1	343 + 371	1,250.
Type 2-2	343 + 372	900.
Type 2-3	343 (USAV Type I) + 371	1,900.
Type 2-4	343 + 375	900.

Pocket Type 3 (1909)
("Patents Pending" printed in red)

Type 3-1	343 + 372	900.
Type 3-2	343 + 373	700.
Type 3-3	343 + 375	800.
Type 3-4	383 + 406	800.

Pocket Type 4 (1909)
(No printing on front, serial number on back)

Type 4-1	343 + 344	300.
Type 4-2	343 + 368	300.
Type 4-3	343 + 371	300.
Type 4-4	383 + 344	300.
Type 4-5	383 (USAV Type II) + 344	300.
Type 4-6	383 + 384	300.
Type 4-7	383 + 406	300.

THE ATTLEBORO STAMP COMPANY

Attleboro, Mass.

This Company used an affixing machine to stamp its newletters during the summer and fall of 1909.

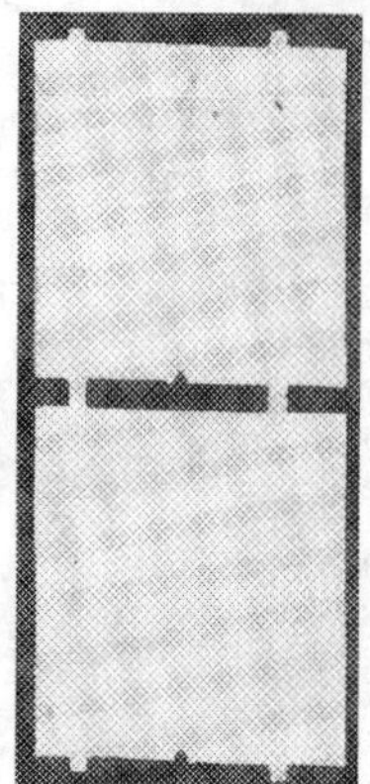

Nos. 343-344

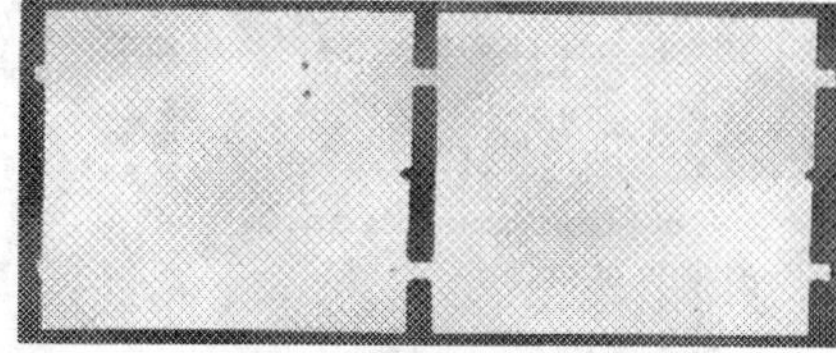

No. 371

On Issue of 1908-09

			Unused Pair	Used Single
343	1c	**green**	*1,300.*	850.
		On Attleboro Philatelist wrapper		*5,000.*
		On cover		*19,000.*
		Guide line or pasteup pair	*2,000.*	
344	2c	**carmine**	**45,000.**	

The No. 344 pair is unique.

On Alaska-Yukon Issue of 1909

			Unused Pair	Used Single
371	2c	**carmine**, coiled sidewise	**3,500.**	*1,100.*
		Guide line or pasteup pair	*5,500.*	—
		On wrapper or cover		*6,000.*

FLAT PLATE IMPERFORATE COIL STAMPS

These flat plate imperforate coil stamps were made from imperforate sheets of the regular issues, and were issued in coils of 500 or 1,000. The numbers assigned below are those of the regularly issued imperforate sheet stamps to which "H" or "V" has been added to indicate that the stamps are coiled horizontally (side by side), or vertically (top to bottom). These coil stamps are virtually indistinguishable from the corresponding imperforate sheet stamps, although they can be authenticated, particularly when in strips of four or longer. Many genuine imperforate coil stamps bear authenticating signatures of contemporaneous experts.

Values for stamps on cover are for single stamps.

FLAT PLATE PRINTING

1908 — Wmk. 191 — *Imperf.*

314V	A115	1c	**blue green,** pair	300.00	—
			Strip of 4	700.00	—
			Guide line pair	600.00	
			Guide line strip of 4	—	
314H	A115	1c	**blue green,** pair	*1,800.*	—
			On cover		*1,300.*
			Strip of 4	—	—

Earliest documented use: Oct. 11, 1908.

			Guide line pair	*4,500.*	
			Guide line strip of 4	—	
320V	A129	2c	**carmine,** pair	*1,000.*	—
			Strip of 4	—	—
			Guide line pair	—	
			Guide line strip of 4	—	

Earliest documented use: July 10, 1908.

320H	A129	2c	**carmine,** pair	350.00	—
			Strip of 4	—	—
			Guide line pair	—	
			Guide line strip of 4	—	

1908-10 — *Imperf.*

343V	A138	1c	**green,** pair	25.00	8.50
			On cover		10.00
			Strip of 4	55.00	—
			Guide line pair	50.00	—
			Guide line strip of 4	72.50	

Earliest documented use: May 24, 1910.

343H	A138	1c	**green,** pair	47.50	—
			Strip of 4	115.00	—
			Guide line pair	90.00	—
			Guide line strip of 4	—	
344V	A139	2c	**carmine,** pair	30.00	20.00
			On cover		15.00
			Strip of 4	70.00	—
			Guide line pair	60.00	—
			Guide line strip of 4	95.00	
			Foreign entry, design of 1c	*1,500.*	*2,500.*

Earliest documented use: Oct. 13, 1909.

344H	A139	2c	**carmine,** pair (2mm spacing)	30.00	20.00
			On cover		—
			Strip of 4	—	
			Guide line pair	60.00	
			Guide line strip of 4	—	
			Pair (3mm spacing)	32.50	—
			Strip of 4	—	
			Guide line pair	65.00	—
			Guide line strip of 4	—	

Earliest documented use: March 23, 1909.

345H	A140	3c	**deep violet,** type I, pair	—	
346V	A140	4c	**orange brown,** pair	125.00	
			Strip of 4	290.00	—
			Guide line pair	250.00	75.00
			Guide line strip of 4	—	

Earliest documented use: Mar. 13, 1909.

347V	A140	5c	**blue,** pair	175.00	—
			On cover		—
			Strip of 4	425.00	—
			Guide line pair	375.00	—
			Guide line strip of 4	575.00	

1909 — *Imperf.*

368V	A141	2c	**carmine,** *Lincoln,* pair	200.00	—
			On cover		—
			Strip of 4	500.00	—
			Guide line pair	400.00	—
			Guide line strip of 4	800.00	—

Earliest documented use: May 3, 1909.

368H	A141	2c	**carmine,** *Lincoln,* pair	275.00	—
			On cover		—
			Strip of 4	750.00	
			Guide line pair	525.00	
			Guide line strip of 4	900.00	

Earliest documented use: Dec. 9, 1909.

1910 — Wmk. 190 — *Imperf.*

383V	A138	1c	**green,** pair	12.00	—
			On cover		6.00
			Strip of 4	27.50	—
			Guide line pair	25.00	—
			Guide line strip of 4	55.00	—
			Double transfer	—	—

Earliest documented use: Apr. 22, 1911.

383H	A138	1c	**green,** pair (2mm spacing)	13.00	—
			Strip of 4	27.50	—
			Guide line pair	—	—
			Guide line strip of 4	—	—
			Pair (3mm spacing)	13.00	—
			Strip of 4	27.50	—
			Guide line pair	26.00	—
			Guide line strip of 4	—	—
384V	A139	2c	**carmine,** pair	14.00	—
			On cover		7.00
			Strip of 4	30.00	—
			Guide line pair	27.50	—
			Guide line strip of 4	45.00	—
			Foreign entry, design of 1c	*1,500.*	—

Earliest documented use: Dec. 10, 1910.

384H	A139	2c	**carmine,** pair (2mm spacing)	27.50	—
			Strip of 4	65.00	
			Guide line pair	—	—
			Guide line strip of 4	—	—
			Pair (3mm spacing)	25.00	—
			Strip of 4	60.00	—
			Guide line pair	50.00	—
			Guide line strip of 4	—	—

1912 — Wmk. 190 — *Imperf.*

408V	A140	1c	**green,** pair	3.75	
			On cover		—
			Strip of 4	8.50	
			Guide line pair	7.75	
			Guide line strip of 4	14.00	

Earliest documented use: Jan. 6, 1922.

408H	A140	1c	**green,** pair	4.25	
			Strip of 4	—	
			Guide line pair	—	
			Guide line strip of 4	—	
409V	A140	2c	**carmine,** pair	4.25	
			Strip of 4	9.00	
			Guide line pair	8.25	
			Guide line strip of 4	14.00	

Earliest documented use: June 1, 1912.

409H	A140	2c	**carmine,** pair	5.50	
			Strip of 4	—	
			Guide line pair	—	
			Guide line strip of 4	—	
			Double transfer	—	

Earliest documented use: Dec. 17, 1914.

COMMEMORATIVE STAMPS, QUANTITIES ISSUED

Quantities issued fall into four categories. First are stamps where reasonably accurate counts are made of the number of copies sold.

Second are stamps where the counts are approximations of the number sold.

Third are stamps where the count is of quantities shipped to post offices and philatelic sales units, but no adjustments are made for returned or destroyed copies.

Fourth are stamps for which the quantity printed is furnished but no other adjustments are made.

Occasionally more accurate figures are determined. In these cases the quantities here will be adjusted. For example, it is now known that while 2,000,000 sets of the Voyages of Columbus souvenir sheets were printed, the number sold was 1,185,170 sets.

Scott No.		Quantity
230		449,195,550
231		1,464,588,750
232		11,501,250
233		19,181,550
234		35,248,250
235		4,707,550
236		10,656,550
237		16,516,950
238		1,576,950
239		617,250
240		243,750
241		55,050
242		45,550
243		27,650
244		26,350
245		27,350
285		70,993,400
286		159,720,800
287		4,924,500
288		7,694,180
289		2,927,200
290		4,629,760
291		530,400
292		56,900
293		56,200
294		91,401,500
295		209,759,700
296		5,737,100
297		7,201,300
298		4,921,700
299		5,043,700
323		79,779,200
324		192,732,400
325		4,542,600
326		6,926,700
327		4,011,200
328		77,728,794
329		149,497,994
330		7,980,594
367		148,387,191
368		1,273,900
369		637,000
370		152,887,311
371		525,400
372		72,634,631
373		216,480
397 & 401		334,796,926
398 & 402		503,713,086
399 & 403		29,088,726
400 & 404		16,968,365
537		99,585,200
548		137,978,207
549		196,037,327
550		11,321,607
610		1,459,487,085
611		770,000
612		99,950,300
614		51,378,023
615		77,753,423
616		5,659,023
617		15,615,000
618		26,596,600
619		5,348,800
620		9,104,983
621		1,900,983
627		307,731,900
628		20,280,500
629		40,639,485
630	(sheet of 25)	107,398
643		39,974,900
644		25,628,450
645		101,330,328
646		9,779,896
647		5,519,897
648		1,459,897
649		51,342,273
650		10,319,700
651		16,684,674
654		31,679,200
655		210,119,474
656		133,530,000
657		51,451,880
658		13,390,000
659		8,240,000
660		87,410,000
661		2,540,000
662		2,290,000
663		2,700,000
664		1,450,000

Scott No.		Quantity
665		1,320,000
666		1,530,000
667		1,130,000
668		2,860,000
669		8,220,000
670		8,990,000
671		73,220,000
672		2,110,000
673		1,600,000
674		1,860,000
675		980,000
676		850,000
677		1,480,000
678		530,000
679		1,890,000
680		29,338,274
681		32,680,900
682		74,000,774
683		25,215,574
688		25,609,470
689		66,487,000
690		96,559,400
702		99,074,600
703		25,006,400
704		87,969,700
705		1,265,555,100
706		304,926,800
707		4,222,198,300
708		456,198,500
709		151,201,300
710		170,565,100
711		111,739,400
712		83,257,400
713		96,506,100
714		75,709,200
715		147,216,000
716		51,102,800
717		100,869,300
718		168,885,300
719		52,376,100
724		49,949,000
725		49,538,500
726		61,719,200
727		73,382,400
728		348,266,800
729		480,239,300
730	(sheet of 25)	456,704
730a		11,417,600
731	(sheet of 25)	441,172
731a		11,029,300
732		1,978,707,300
733		5,735,944
734		45,137,700
735	(sheet of 6)	811,404
735a		4,868,424
736		46,258,300
737		193,239,100
738		15,432,200
739		64,525,400
740		84,896,350
741		74,400,200
742		95,089,000
743		19,178,650
744		30,980,100
745		16,923,350
746		15,988,250
747		15,288,700
748		17,472,600
749		18,874,300
750	(sheet of 6)	511,391
750a		3,068,346
751	(sheet of 6)	793,551
751a		4,761,306
752		3,274,556
753		2,040,760
754		2,389,288
755		2,294,948
756		3,217,636
757		2,746,640
758		2,168,088
759		1,822,684
760		1,724,576
761		1,647,696
762		1,682,948
763		1,638,644
764		1,625,224
765		1,644,900
766	(pane of 25)	98,712
766a		2,467,800
767	(pane of 25)	85,914
767a		2,147,850
768	(pane of 6)	267,200
768a		1,603,200
769	(pane of 6)	279,960
769a		1,679,760
770	(pane of 6)	215,920
770a		1,295,520
771		1,370,560
772		70,726,800
773		100,839,600
774		73,610,650
775		75,823,900
776		124,324,500
777		67,127,650
778	(sheet of 4)	2,809,039
778a		2,809,039
778b		2,809,039
778c		2,809,039
778d		2,809,039
782		72,992,650
783		74,407,450
784		269,522,200
785		105,196,150
786		93,848,500
787		87,741,150
788		35,794,150
789		36,839,250

Scott No.	Quantity
790	104,773,450
791	92,054,550
792	93,291,650
793	34,552,950
794	36,819,050
795	84,825,250
796	25,040,400
797	5,277,445
798	99,882,300
799	78,454,450
800	77,004,200
801	81,292,450
802	76,474,550
835	73,043,650
836	58,564,368
837	65,939,500
838	47,064,300
852	114,439,600
853	101,699,550
854	72,764,550
855	81,269,600
856	67,813,350
857	71,394,750
858	66,835,000
859	56,348,320
860	53,177,110
861	53,260,270
862	22,104,950
863	13,201,270
864	51,603,580
865	52,100,510
866	51,666,580
867	22,207,780
868	11,835,530
869	52,471,160
870	52,366,440
871	51,636,270
872	20,729,030
873	14,125,580
874	59,409,000
875	57,888,600
876	58,273,180
877	23,779,000
878	15,112,580
879	57,322,790
880	58,281,580
881	56,398,790
882	21,147,000
883	13,328,000
884	54,389,510
885	53,636,580
886	55,313,230
887	21,720,580
888	13,600,580
889	47,599,580
890	53,766,510
891	54,193,580
892	20,264,580
893	13,726,580
894	46,497,400
895	47,700,000
896	50,618,150
897	50,034,400
898	60,943,700
902	44,389,550
903	54,574,550
904	63,558,400
906	21,272,800
907	1,671,564,200
908	1,227,334,200
909	19,999,646
910	19,999,646
911	19,999,646
912	19,999,646
913	19,999,646
914	19,999,646
915	19,999,646
916	14,999,646
917	14,999,646
918	14,999,646
919	14,999,646
920	14,999,646
921	14,999,646
922	61,303,000
923	61,001,450
924	60,605,000
925	50,129,350
926	53,479,400
927	61,617,350
928	75,500,000
929	137,321,000
930	128,140,000
931	67,255,000
932	133,870,000
933	76,455,400
934	128,357,750
935	138,863,000
936	111,616,700
937	308,587,700
938	170,640,000
939	135,927,000
940	260,339,100
941	132,274,500
942	132,430,000
943	139,209,500
944	114,684,450
945	156,540,510
946	120,452,600
947	127,104,300
948	10,299,600
949	132,902,000
950	131,968,000
951	131,488,000
952	122,362,000
953	121,548,000
954	131,109,500
955	122,650,500

Scott No.	Quantity
956	121,953,500
957	115,250,000
958	64,198,500
959	117,642,500
960	77,649,600
961	113,474,500
962	120,868,500
963	77,800,500
964	52,214,000
965	53,958,100
966	61,120,010
967	57,823,000
968	52,975,000
969	77,149,000
970	58,332,000
971	56,228,000
972	57,832,000
973	53,875,000
974	63,834,000
975	67,162,200
976	64,561,000
977	64,079,500
978	63,388,000
979	62,285,000
980	57,492,610
981	99,190,000
982	104,790,000
983	108,805,000
984	107,340,000
985	117,020,000
986	122,633,000
987	130,960,000
988	128,478,000
989	132,090,000
990	130,050,000
991	131,350,000
992	129,980,000
993	122,315,000
994	122,170,000
995	131,635,000
996	121,860,000
997	121,120,000
998	119,120,000
999	112,125,000
1000	114,140,000
1001	114,490,000
1002	117,200,000
1003	116,130,000
1004	116,175,000
1005	115,945,000
1006	112,540,000
1007	117,415,000
1008	2,899,580,000
1009	114,540,000
1010	113,135,000
1011	116,255,000
1012	113,860,000
1013	124,260,000
1014	115,735,000
1015	115,430,000
1016	136,220,000
1017	114,894,600
1018	118,706,000
1019	114,190,000
1020	113,990,000
1021	89,289,600
1022	114,865,000
1023	115,780,000
1024	115,244,600
1025	123,709,600
1026	114,789,600
1027	115,759,600
1028	116,134,600
1029	118,540,000
1060	115,810,000
1061	113,603,700
1062	128,002,000
1063	116,078,150
1064	116,139,800
1065	120,484,800
1066	53,854,750
1067	176,075,000
1068	125,944,400
1069	122,284,600
1070	133,638,850
1071	118,664,600
1072	112,434,000
1073	129,384,550
1074	121,184,600
1075	2,900,731
1076	119,784,200
1077	123,159,400
1078	123,138,800
1079	109,275,000
1080	112,932,200
1081	125,475,000
1082	117,855,000
1083	122,100,000
1084	118,180,000
1085	100,975,000
1086	115,299,450
1087	186,949,627
1088	115,235,000
1089	106,647,500
1090	112,010,000
1091	118,470,000
1092	102,230,000
1093	102,410,000
1094	84,054,400
1095	126,266,000
1096	39,489,600
1097	122,990,000
1098	174,372,800
1099	114,365,000
1100	122,765,200
1104	113,660,200
1105	120,196,580

Scott No.	Quantity
1106	120,805,200
1107	125,815,200
1108	108,415,200
1109	107,195,200
1110	115,745,280
1111	39,743,640
1112	114,570,200
1113	120,400,200
1114	91,160,200
1115	114,860,200
1116	126,500,000
1117	120,561,280
1118	44,064,576
1119	118,390,200
1120	125,770,200
1121	114,114,280
1122	156,600,200
1123	124,200,200
1124	120,740,200
1125	133,623,280
1126	45,569,088
1127	122,493,280
1128	131,260,200
1129	47,125,200
1130	123,105,000
1131	126,105,050
1132	209,170,000
1133	120,835,000
1134	115,715,000
1135	118,445,000
1136	111,685,000
1137	43,099,200
1138	115,444,000
1139	126,470,000
1140	124,560,000
1141	115,455,000
1142	122,060,000
1143	120,540,000
1144	113,075,000
1145	139,325,000
1146	124,445,000
1147	113,792,000
1148	44,215,200
1149	113,195,000
1150	121,805,000
1151	115,353,000
1152	111,080,000
1153	153,025,000
1154	119,665,000
1155	117,855,000
1156	118,185,000
1157	112,260,000
1158	125,010,000
1159	119,798,000
1160	42,696,000
1161	106,610,000
1162	109,695,000
1163	123,690,000
1164	123,970,000
1165	124,796,000
1166	42,076,800
1167	116,210,000
1168	126,252,000
1169	42,746,400
1170	124,117,000
1171	119,840,000
1172	117,187,000
1173	124,390,000
1174	112,966,000
1175	41,644,200
1176	110,850,000
1177	98,616,000
1178	101,125,000
1179	124,865,000
1180	79,905,000
1181	125,410,000
1182	112,845,000
1183	106,210,000
1184	110,810,000
1185	116,995,000
1186	121,015,000
1187	111,600,000
1188	110,620,000
1189	109,110,000
1190	145,350,000
1191	112,870,000
1192	121,820,000
1193	289,240,000
1194	120,155,000
1195	124,595,000
1196	147,310,000
1197	118,690,000
1198	122,730,000
1199	126,515,000
1200	130,960,000
1201	120,055,000
1202	120,715,000
1203	121,440,000
1204	40,270,000
1205	861,970,000
1206	120,035,000
1207	117,870,000
1230	129,945,000
1231	135,620,000
1232	137,540,000
1233	132,435,000
1234	135,520,000
1235	131,420,000
1236	133,170,000
1237	130,195,000
1238	128,450,000
1239	118,665,000
1240	1,291,250,000
1241	175,175,000
1242	125,995,000
1243	128,025,000
1244	145,700,000

Scott No.	Quantity
1245	120,310,000
1246	511,750,000
1247	123,845,000
1248	122,825,000
1249	453,090,000
1250	123,245,000
1251	123,355,000
1252	126,970,000
1253	121,250,000
1254-1257	1,407,760,000
1258	120,005,000
1259	125,800,000
1260	122,230,000
1261	115,695,000
1262	115,095,000
1263	119,560,000
1264	125,180,000
1265	120,135,000
1266	115,405,000
1267	115,855,000
1268	115,340,000
1269	114,840,000
1270	116,140,000
1271	116,900,000
1272	114,085,000
1273	114,880,000
1274	26,995,000
1275	128,495,000
1276	1,139,930,000
1306	116,835,000
1307	117,470,000
1308	123,770,000
1309	131,270,000
1310	122,285,000
1311	14,680,000
1312	114,160,000
1313	128,475,000
1314	119,535,000
1315	125,110,000
1316	114,853,200
1317	124,290,000
1318	128,460,000
1319	127,585,000
1320	115,875,000
1321	1,173,547,420
1322	114,015,000
1323	121,105,000
1324	132,045,000
1325	118,780,000
1326	121,985,000
1327	111,850,000
1328	117,225,000
1329	111,515,000
1330	114,270,000
1331-1332	120,865,000
1333	110,675,000
1334	110,670,000
1335	113,825,000
1336	1,208,700,000
1337	113,330,000
1339	141,350,000
1340	144,345,000
1342	147,120,000
1343	130,125,000
1344	158,700,000
1345-1354	228,040,000
1355	153,015,000
1356	132,560,000
1357	130,385,000
1358	132,265,000
1359	128,710,000
1360	124,775,000
1361	128,295,000
1362	142,245,000
1363	1,410,580,000
1364	125,100,000
1365-1368	192,570,000
1369	148,770,000
1370	139,475,000
1371	187,165,000
1372	125,555,000
1373	144,425,000
1374	135,875,000
1375	151,110,000
1376-1379	159,195,000
1380	129,540,000
1381	130,925,000
1382	139,055,000
1383	150,611,200
1384	1,709,795,000
1385	127,545,000
1386	145,788,800
1387-1390	201,794,200
1391	171,850,000
1392	142,205,000
1405	137,660,000
1406	135,125,000
1407	135,895,000
1408	132,675,000
1409	134,795,000
1410-1413	161,600,000
1414-1414a	683,730,000
1415-1418, 1415a-1418a	489,255,000
1419	127,610,000
1420	129,785,000
1421-1422	134,380,000
1423	136,305,000
1424	134,840,000
1425	130,975,000
1426	161,235,000
1427-1430	175,679,600
1431	138,700,000
1432	138,165,000
1433	152,125,000
1434-1435	176,295,000
1436	142,845,000

Scott No.	Quantity
1437	148,755,000
1438	139,080,000
1439	130,755,000
1440-1443	170,208,000
1444	1,074,350,000
1445	979,540,000
1446	137,355,000
1447	150,400,000
1448-1451	172,730,000
1452	104,090,000
1453	164,096,000
1454	53,920,000
1455	153,025,000
1456-1459	201,890,000
1460	67,335,000
1461	179,675,000
1462	46,340,000
1463	180,155,000
1464-1467	198,364,800
1468	185,490,000
1469	162,335,000
1470	162,789,950
1471	1,003,475,000
1472	1,017,025,000
1473	165,895,000
1474	166,508,000
1475	320,055,000
1476	166,005,000
1477	163,050,000
1478	159,005,000
1479	147,295,000
1480-1483	196,275,000
1484	139,152,000
1485	128,048,000
1486	146,008,000
1487	139,608,000
1488	159,475,000
1489-1498	486,020,000
1499	157,052,800
1500	53,005,000
1501	159,775,000
1502	39,005,000
1503	152,624,000
1504	145,840,000
1505	151,335,000
1506	141,085,000
1507	885,160,000
1508	939,835,000
1525	143,930,000
1526	145,235,000
1527	135,052,000
1528	156,750,000
1529	164,670,000
1530-1537	190,156,800
1538-1541	167,212,800
1542	156,265,000
1543-1546	195,585,000
1547	148,850,000
1548	157,270,000
1549	150,245,000
1550	835,180,000
1551	882,520,000
1552	213,155,000
1553	156,995,000
1554	146,365,000
1555	148,805,000
1556	173,685,000
1557	158,600,000
1558	153,355,000
1559	63,205,000
1560	157,865,000
1561	166,810,000
1562	44,825,000
1563	144,028,000
1564	139,928,000
1565-1568	179,855,000
1569-1570	161,863,200
1571	145,640,000
1572-1575	168,655,000
1576	146,615,000
1577-1578	146,196,000
1579	739,430,000
1580	878,690,000
1629-1631	219,455,000
1632	157,825,000
1633-1682	436,005,000
1683	159,915,000
1684	156,960,000
1685	158,470,000
1686	1,990,000
1687	1,983,000
1688	1,953,000
1689	1,903,000
1690	164,890,000
1691-1694	208,035,000
1695-1698	185,715,000
1699	130,592,000
1700	158,332,800
1701	809,955,000
1702-1703	963,370,000
1704	150,328,000
1705	176,830,000
1706-1709	195,976,000
1710	208,820,000
1711	192,250,000
1712-1715	219,830,000
1716	159,852,000
1717-1720	188,310,000
1721	163,625,000
1722	156,296,000
1723-1724	158,676,000
1725	154,495,000
1726	168,050,000
1727	156,810,000
1728	153,736,000
1729	882,260,000
1730	921,530,000

Scott No.	Quantity
1731	156,560,000
1732-1733	202,155,000
1744	156,525,000
1745-1748	165,182,400
1749-1752	157,598,400
1753	102,856,000
1754	152,270,000
1755	94,600,000
1756	151,570,000
1757	15,170,400
1758	161,228,000
1759	158,880,000
1760-1763	186,550,000
1764-1767	168,136,000
1768	963,120,000
1769	916,800,000
1770	159,297,600
1771	166,435,000
1772	162,535,000
1773	155,000,000
1774	157,310,000
1775-1778	174,096,000
1779-1782	164,793,600
1783-1786	163,055,000
1787	161,860,000
1788	165,775,000
1789	160,000,000
1790	67,195,000
1791-1794	186,905,000
1795-1798	208,295,000
1799	873,710,000
1800	931,880,000
1801	161,290,000
1802	172,740,000
1803	168,995,000
1804	160,000,000
1805-1810	232,134,000
1821	163,510,000
1822	256,620,000
1823	95,695,000
1824	153,975,000
1825	160,000,000
1826	103,850,000
1827-1830	204,715,000
1831	166,545,000
1832	163,310,000
1833	160,000,000
1834-1837	152,404,000
1838-1841	152,420,000
1842	692,500,000
1843	718,715,000
1874	160,155,000
1875	159,505,000
1876-1879	210,633,000
1910	165,175,000
1911	107,240,000
1912-1919	337,819,000
1920	99,420,000
1921-1924	178,930,000
1925	100,265,000
1926	99,615,000
1927	97,535,000
1928-1931	167,308,000
1932	101,625,000
1922	99,170,000
1934	101,155,000
1935	101,200,000
1936	167,360,000
1937-1938	162,420,000
1939	597,720,000
1940	792,600,000
1941	167,130,000
1942-1945	191,560,000
1950	163,939,200
1952	180,700,000
1953-2002	666,950,000
2003	109,245,000
2004	112,535,000
2006-2009	124,640,000
2010	107,605,000
2011	173,160,000
2012	107,285,000
2013	109,040,000
2014	183,270,000
2015	169,495,000
2016	164,235,000
2017	110,130,000
2018	110,995,000
2019-2022	165,340,000
2023	174,180,000
2024	110,261,000
2026	703,295,000
2027-2030	788,880,000
2031	118,555,000
2032-2035	226,128,000
2036	118,225,000
2037	114,290,000
2038	165,000,000
2039	120,430,000
2040	117,025,000
2041	181,700,000
2042	114,250,000
2043	111,775,000
2044	115,200,000
2045	108,820,000
2046	184,950,000
2047	110,925,000
2048-2051	395,424,000
2052	104,340,000
2053	114,725,000
2054	112,525,000
2055-2058	193,055,000
2059-2062	207,725,000
2063	715,975,000
2064	848,525,000
2065	165,000,000
2066	120,000,000
2067-2070	319,675,000
2071	103,975,000
2072	554,675,000
2073	120,000,000
2074	106,975,000
2075	107,325,000
2076-2079	306,912,000
2080	120,000,000
2081	108,000,000
2082-2085	313,350,000
2086	130,320,000
2087	120,000,000
2088	117,050,000
2089	115,725,000
2090	116,600,000
2091	120,000,000
2092	123,575,000
2093	120,000,000
2094	117,125,000
2095	117,225,000
2096	95,525,000
2097	119,125,000
2098-2101	216,260,000
2102	120,000,000
2103	108,140,000
2104	117,625,000
2105	112,896,000
2106	116,500,000
2107	751,300,000
2108	786,225,000
2109	105,300,000
2110	124,500,000
2137	120,000,000
2138-2141	300,000,000
2142	120,580,000
2143	729,700,000
2144	124,750,000
2145	203,496,000
2146	126,325,000
2147	130,000,000
2152	119,975,000
2153	120,000,000
2154	119,975,000
2155-2158	147,940,000
2159	120,000,000
2160-2163	130,000,000
2164	120,000,000
2165	759,200,000
2166	757,600,000
2198-2201	67,996,800
2202	947,450,000
2203	130,000,000
2204	136,500,000
2205-2209	219,990,000
2210	130,000,000
2211	130,000,000
2216	5,825,050
2217	5,825,050
2218	5,825,050
2219	5,825,050
2220-2223	130,000,000
2224	220,725,000
2235-2238	240,525,000
2239	131,700,000
2240-2243	240,000,000
2244	690,100,000
2245	882,150,000
2246	167,430,000
2247	166,555,000
2248	811,560,000
2249	142,905,000
2250	130,000,000
2251	149,980,000
2267-2274	610,425,000
2275	156,995,000
2286-2335	645,975,000
2336	166,725,000
2337	186,575,000
2338	184,325,000
2339	165,845,000
2340	155,170,000
2341	102,100,000
2342	103,325,000
2343	162,045,000
2344	153,295,000
2345	160,245,000
2346	183,290,000
2347	179,800,000
2348	164,130,000
2349	157,475,000
2350	156,225,000
2351-2354	163,980,000
2355-2359	584,340,000
2360	168,995,000
2361	163,120,000
2362-2366	394,776,000
2367	528,790,000
2368	978,340,000
2369	158,870,000
2370	145,560,000
2371	97,300,000
2372-2375	158,556,000
2376	97,300,000
2377	153,045,000
2378	841,240,000
2379	169,765,000
2380	157,215,000
2381-2385	635,238,000
2386-2389	162,142,500
2390-2393	305,015,000
2395-2398	480,000,000
2399	821,285,000
2400	1,030,850,000
2401	165,495,000
2402	151,675,000
2403	163,000,000
2404	264,625,000
2405-2409	204,984,000
2410	103,835,000
2411	152,250,000
2412	138,760,000
2413	137,985,000
2414	138,580,000
2415	150,545,000
2416	164,680,000
2417	262,755,000
2418	191,755,000
2420	188,400,000
2421	191,860,000
2422-2425	406,988,000
2426	137,410,000
2427	913,335,000
2428	900,000,000
2429	399,243,000
2433	2,017,225
2434-2437	163,824,000
2438	2,047,200
2439	173,000,000
2440	886,220,000
2441	995,178,000
2442	153,125,000
2444	169,495,000
2445-2448	176,808,000
2449	150,000,000
2470-2474	733,608,000
2496-2500	178,587,500
2501-2505	619,128,000
2506-2507	151,430,000
2508-2511	278,264,000
2512	143,995,000
2513	142,692,000
2514	728,919,000
2515	599,400,000
2516	320,304,000
2532	103,648,000
2533	179,990,000
2534	150,560,000
2538	161,498,000
2545-2549	744,918,000
2550	149,848,000
2551	200,003,000
2552	200,000,000
2553-2557	170,025,600
2558	150,310,000
2560	149,810,000
2561	149,260,000
2562-2566	699,978,000
2567	148,973,000
2577a	33,394,800
2615a	32,000,000
2616	148,665,000
2617	149,990,000
2618	835,000,000
2619	160,000,000
2623a	40,005,000
2624	1,185,170
2625	1,185,170
2626	1,185,170
2627	1,185,170
2628	1,185,170
2629	1,185,170
2630	148,000,000
2634a	37,315,000
2635	146,610,000
2636	160,000,000
2641a	32,000,000
2646a	87,728,000
2696a	11,000,000
2697	12,000,000
2698	105,000,000
2699	142,500,000
2703a	36,831,000
2704	85,000,000
2709a	80,000,000
2721	517,000,000
2722	150,000,000
2723	152,000,000
2730a	14,285,715
2731	98,841,000
2732	32,947,000
2733	32,947,000
2734	32,947,000
2735	65,894,000
2736	65,894,000
2737	65,894,000
2745a	140,000,000
2746	105,000,000
2747	110,000,000
2748	110,000,000
2749	172,870,000
2753a	65,625,000
2754	110,000,000
2755	115,870,000
2759a	40,000,000
2764a	199,784,500
2765	120,000,000
2766	160,000,000
2770a	128,735,000
2774a	25,000,000
2778a	170,000,000
2782a	37,500,000
2784a	41,840,000
2788a	37,550,000
2804	88,300,000
2805	105,000,000
2806	100,000,000
2806a	250,000,000
2811a	35,800,000
2812	150,500,000
2813	357,949,584
2814	830,000,000
2814C	300,000,000
2815	274,800,000
2816	155,500,000

Scott No.	Quantity
2817	105,000,000
2818	185,500,000
2828a	18,600,000
2833a	166,000,000
2834	201,000,000
2835	300,000,000
2836	269,370,000
2837	60,000,000
2838	120,600,000
2839	209,000,000
2840	20,000,000
2841	12,958,000
2842	100,500,000
2847a	159,200,000
2848	150,500,000
2853a	35,436,000
2854	24,986,000
2855	24,986,000
2856	24,986,000
2857	19,988,800
2858	19,988,800
2859	19,988,800
2860	19,988,800
2861	19,988,800
2862	150,750,000
2866a	56,475,000
2868a	77,748,000
2869	20,000,000
2870	150,186
2871	518,500,000
2872	602,500,000
2873	236,997,600
2874	45,000,000
2875	5,000,000
2876	80,000,000
2948	214,700,000
2949	1,220,970,000
2950	94,500,000
2954a	50,000,000
2955	80,000,000
2956	97,000,000
2957	315,000,000
2958	300,000,000
2965a	30,000,000
2966	125,000,000
2967	400,000,000
2968	99,424,000
2973a	120,240,000
2974	60,000,000
2975	300,000,000
2979a	62,500,000
2980	105,000,000
2981	100,000,000
2982	150,000,000
2983-2992	15,000,000
2992	15,000,000
2997a	200,000,000
2998	300,000,000
2999	85,000,000
3000	300,000,000
3001	80,000,000
3002	80,000,000
3003	300,000,000
3007a	75,000,000
3008	350,495,000
3009	350,495,000
3010	350,495,000
3011	350,495,000
3013	90,000,000
3023a	30,000,000
3024	120,000,000
3029a	160,000,000
3030	2,550,000,000
3058	92,100,000
3059	115,600,000
3060	93,150,000
3064a	23,292,500
3065	111,000,000
3066	314,175,000
3067	209,450,000
3068	16,207,500
3069	156,300,000
3070	100,000,000
3071	60,120,000
3076a	27,850,000
3080a	22,218,000
3081	95,600,000
3082	300,000,000
3086a	23,681,250
3087	133,613,000
3088	103,400,000
3089	60,000,000
3090	134,000,000
3095a	32,000,000
3099a	23,025,000
3103a	23,025,000
3104	300,000,000
3105	14,910,000
3106	93,612,000
3107	243,575,000
3111a	56,479,000
3112	847,750,000
3116a	451,312,500
3117	495,504,000
3118	103,520,000
3120	106,000,000
3121	112,000,000
3123	1,660,000,000
3124	814,000,000
3125	122,000,000
3131a	65,000,000
3134	97,500,000
3135	96,000,000
3136	14,600,000
3137	37,800,000
3138	118,000
3139	593,775

Scott No.	Quantity
3140	592,849
3141	45,250,000
3142	8,050,000
3146a	22,500,000
3147	20,000,000
3148	20,000,000
3149	10,000,000
3150	10,000,000
3151	7,000,000
3152	195,000,000
3153	323,000,000
3157a	21,500,000
3158-3161	12,900,000
3162-3165	8,600,000
3166	25,250,000
3167	45,250,000
3172a	36,250,000
3173	173,000,000
3174	37,000,000
3175	133,000,000
3176	882,500,000
3177	1,621,465,000
3178	15,000,000
3179	51,000,000
3180	80,000,000
3181	45,000,000
3182	12,533,000
3183	12,533,000
3184	12,533,000
3185	12,533,000
3186	12,533,000
3187	12,533,000
3188	8,000,000
3189	6,000,000
3190	6,000,000
3191	8,250,000
3192	30,000,000
3193-3197	250,000,000
3198-3202	80,000,000
3203	85,000,000
3204	39,600,000
3205	650,000
3206	32,000,000
3209	2,200,000
3210	2,200,000
3211	30,000,000
3212-3215	45,000,000
3216-3219	45,000,000
3220	46,300,000
3221	30,000,000
3222-3225	70,000,000
3226	65,000,000
3227	50,000,000
3230-3234	180,000,000
3235	28,000,000
3236	4,000,000
3237	130,750,000
3238-3242	185,000,000
3243	50,000,000
3244	925,200,000
3245-3248	116,760,000
3249-3252	991,750,000
3272	51,000,000
3273	100,000,000
3274	1,000,000,000
3275	
3276	100,000,000
3286	40,400,000
3287	42,500,000
3288-3292	73,155,000
3293	10,000,000
3306	42,700,000
3307	500,000
3308	42,500,000
3309	105,000,000
3310-3313	1,500,000,000
3314	145,375,000
3315	78,100,000
3316	89,270,000
3317-3320	141,175,000
3321-3324	151,976,000
3325-3328	116,083,500
3329	75,500,000
3330	100,750,000
3331	101,800,000
3332	43,150,000
3333-3337	120,000,000
3338	42,500,000
3339-3344	42,500,000
3345-3350	42,500,000
3351	4,235,000
3352	65,000,000
3354	44,600,000
3355	1,555,560,000
3356-3359	116,500,000
3360-3363	1,785,060,000
3364-3367	118,125,000
3368	95,000,000
3369	120,000,000

Quantities for Nos. 3370-on, and for Nos. 3190, 3191 and 3236, are for Quantities ordered.

Scott No.	Quantity
3370	56,000,000
3371	150,000,000
3372	65,150,000
3373-3377	15,000,000
3378	10,000,000
3379-3383	55,000,000
3384-3388	105,350,000
3389	16,000,000
3390	55,000,000
3391	30,000,000
3392	236,000
3393-3396	55,000,000
3397	90,600,000
3398	200,000,000
3399-3402	88,000,000
3403	4,000,000
3408	11,250,000
3409	1,695,000
3410	1,695,000
3411	1,695,000
3412	1,695,000
3413	1,695,000
3414-3417	100,000,000
3438	53,000,000
3439-3443	85,000,000
3444	53,000,000
3445	125,000,000
3446	52,000,000

AIRPOST STAMPS

Cat. No.	Quantity
C1	3,395,854
C2	3,793,887
C3	2,134,888
C4	6,414,576
C5	5,309,275
C6	5,285,775
C7	42,092,800
C8	15,597,307
C9	17,616,350
C10	20,379,179
C11	106,887,675
C12	97,641,200
C13	93,536
C14	72,428
C15	61,296
C16	57,340,050
C17	76,648,803
C18	324,070
C19	302,205,100
C20	10,205,400
C21	12,794,600
C22	9,285,300
C23	349,946,500
C24	19,768,150
C25	4,746,527,700
C26	1,744,878,650
C27	67,117,400
C28	78,434,800
C29	42,359,850
C30	59,880,850
C31	11,160,600
C32	864,753,100
C33	971,903,700
C34	207,976,550
C35	756,186,350
C36	132,956,100
C37	33,244,500
C38	38,449,100
C39	5,070,095,200
C40	75,085,000
C41	260,307,500
C42	21,061,300
C43	36,613,100
C44	16,217,100
C45	80,405,000
C46	18,876,800
C47	78,415,000
C48	50,483,977
C49	63,185,000
C50	72,480,000
C51	1,326,960,000
C52	157,035,000
C53	90,055,200
C54	79,290,000
C55	84,815,000
C56	38,770,000
C57	39,960,000
C58	98,160,000
C59	
C60	1,289,460,000
C61	87,140,000
C62	
C63	
C64	
C65	
C66	42,245,000
C67	
C68	63,890,000
C69	62,255,000
C70	55,710,000
C71	+ 50,000,000
C72	
C73	
C74	+ 60,000,000
C75	
C76	152,364,800
C77	
C78	
C79	
C80	
C81	
C82	
C83	
C84	78,210,000
C85	96,240,000
C86	58,705,000
C87	
C88	
C89	
C90	
C91-C92	
C93-C94	
C95-C96	
C97	

Cat. No.	Quantity	Cat. No.	Quantity	Cat. No.	Quantity
C101-C104	+ 165,000,000	*C119*	111,550,000	*C131*	15,260,000
C105-C108	+ 165,000,000	*C120*	38,532,000	*C132*	100,000,000
C109-C112	+ 175,000,000	*C121*	39,325,000	*C133*	100,750,000
C113	98,600,000	*C122-C125*	106,360,000	*C134*	100,750,000
C114	110,475,000	*C126*	1,944,000	*C135*	+ 100,800,000
C115	167,625,000	*C127*	48,000,000		
C116	45,700,000	*C128*	250,000,000		
C117	22,975,000	*C129*	182,400,000		
C118	201,150,000	*C130*	113,000,000		

+ Quantity ordered printed.

CARRIERS' STAMPS

The term "Carriers' Stamps" is applied to certain stamps of the United States used to defray delivery to a post office on letters going to another post office, and for collection and delivery in the same city (local letters handled only by the carrier department). A less common usage was for a collection fee from the addressee at the post office ("drop letters"). During the period when these were in use, the ordinary postage fee defrayed the carriage of mail matter from post office to post office only.

In many of the larger cities the private ("Local") posts delivered mail to the post office or to an addressee in the city direct for a fee of 1 or 2 cents (seldom more), and adhesive stamps were often employed to indicate payment. (See introduction to "Local Stamps" section.)

Carrier service dates back at least to 1689 when the postmaster of Boston was instructed "to receive all letters and deliver them at 1d." In 1794, the law allowed a penny post to collect 2 cents for the delivery of a letter. As these early fees were paid in cash, little evidence survives.

In 1851 the Federal Government, under the acts of 1825 and 1836, began to deliver letters in many cities and so issued Carriers' stamps for local delivery service. This Act of Congress of March 3, 1851, effective July 1, 1851 (succeeding Act of 1836), provided for the collecting and delivering of letters to the post office by carriers, "for which not exceeding 1 or 2 cents shall be charged."

Carriers' stamps were issued under the authority of, or derived from, the postmaster general. The "Official Issues" (Nos. LO1-LO2) were general issues of which No. LO2 was valid for postage at face value, and No. LO1 at the value set upon sale, in any post office. They were issued under the direct authority of the postmaster general. The "Semi-official Issues" were valid in the city in which they were issued either directly by or sanctioned by the local postmaster under authority derived from the postmaster general.

These "Official" and "Semi-official" Carriers' stamps prepaid the fees of official letter carriers who were appointed by the postmaster general and were under heavy bond to the United States for the faithful performance of their duties. Some of the letter carriers received fixed salaries from the government. Others were paid from the fees received for the delivery and collection of letters carried by them. After discontinuance of carrier fees on June 30, 1863, all carriers of the United States Post Office were government employees, paid by salary at a yearly rate.

Some Carriers' stamps are often found on cover with the regular government stamps and have the official post office cancellation applied to them as well. Honour's City Express and the other Charleston, S.C., Carrier stamps almost always have the stamp uncanceled or canceled with pen, or less frequently pencil.

Unless indicated otherwise, values for Carriers' stamps on cover are for covers having the stamp tied by a handstamped cancellation. Carriers' stamps, either uncanceled or pen-canceled, **on covers to which they apparently belong**, also are valued where possible. For covers with stamps canceled by pen or pencil with initials or name of carrier, as sometimes seen on No. LO2 from Washington, and on Baltimore carrier stamps, the premium is 75% of the on-cover value.

All Carriers' stamps are imperforate and on wove paper, either white or colored through, unless otherwise stated.

Counterfeits exist of many Carriers' stamps.

OFFICIAL ISSUES

Franklin — OC1

Eagle — OC2

Engraved and printed by Toppan, Carpenter, Casilear & Co. Plate of 200 subjects divided into two panes of 100 each, one left, one right

1851, Sept. Unwmk. *Imperf.*

LO1	OC1	(1c)	**dull blue** (shades), *rose*	*5,000.*	*5,000.*
			On cover from Philadelphia		*15,000.*
			On cover from New York		*27,500.*
			On cover from New Orleans with 3c #10 (a 2nd #LO1 removed)		*10,500.*
			Pair	*12,500.*	*12,500.*
			Strip of 3	*20,000.*	*20,000.*
			Major plate crack	—	
			Major plate crack, on cover		*60,000.*
			Corner plate cracks (91L)	—	—
			Double transfer	—	—
			Double transfer, on cover		*25,000.*

Earliest known use: Oct. 28, 1851.

Cancellations

Red star (Philadelphia)	*5,000.*
Blue town (Philadelphia)	+1,000.
Red town (New York)	+1,000.
Black town (New York), unique	+3,000.
Blue grid (New York)	—
Black grid (New York)	—
Black grid (New Orleans)	—
Green grid (New Orleans)	—

Of the entire issue of 310,000 stamps, 250,000 were sent to New York, 50,000 to New Orleans, 10,000 to Philadelphia. However, the quantity sent to each city is not indicative of proportionate use. More appear to have been used in Philadelphia than in the other two cities. The use in all three cities was notably limited.

No. LO1, major plate crack on cover, is unique. The double transfer on cover also is unique.

U.S.P.O. Despatch

Engraved and printed by Toppan, Carpenter, Casilear & Co. Plate of 200 subjects divided into two panes of 100 each, one upper, one lower

1851, Nov. 17 Unwmk. *Imperf.*

LO2	OC2	1c	**blue** (shades)	25.	*50.*
			On cover, used alone		500.
			On cover, precanceled		600.
			On cover, pair or 2 singles		*1,500.*
			On cover with block of 3, 1c #9		*4,500.*
			On cover with 3c #11		400.
			On cover with 3c #25		—
			On cover with 3c #26		*600.*
			On cover with strip of 3, 3c #26		—
			On cover with 5c #30A and 10c #32		*33,000.*
			On cover with 3c #65 (Washington, D.C.)		*4,500.*
			On 3c envelope #U1, #LO2 pen canceled		—
			On 3c envelope #U2, tied by handstamp		—
			On 3c envelope #U2, #LO2 pen canceled		—
			Pair	60.	
			Pair on cover (Cincinnati)		*1,000.*
			Block of 4	250.00	
			Margin block of 8, imprint	*800.00*	
			Double transfer	—	—
			Double transfer on cover		—

Earliest known use: Jan. 3, 1852.

Cancellations

Red star	*50.*
Philadelphia	+50.
Cincinnati	+200.
Black grid	—
Blue grid	+300.
Red grid	+300.
Black town	+5.
Blue town	+100.
Red town	+300.
Kensington, Pa. (red)	—
Kensington, Pa. red "3c"	—
Washington, D.C.	+1,000.
Blue squared target	—
Red squared target	—
Railroad	—
Black carrier (Type C32)	—
Red carrier (Type C32)	—
Carrier's initial, manuscript	—

Earliest known use: Jan. 3, 1852. Used principally in Philadelphia, Cincinnati, Washington, D.C., and Kensington, Pa.

GOVERNMENT REPRINTS

Printed by the Continental Bank Note Co.
First reprinting-10,000 copies, on May 19, 1875.
Second reprinting-10,000 copies, on Dec. 22, 1875.

The first reprinting of the Franklin stamp was on the rose paper of the original, obtained from Toppan, Carpenter, Casilear & Co. Two batches of ink were used, both darker than the original. The second reprinting was on much thicker, paler paper in an indigo color. All of these differ under ultraviolet light. The design of the reprints is not as distinct as the original design and may appear a bit "muddy" in the lathework above the vignette.

Most of the reprints of the Eagle stamp are on the same hard white paper used for special printings of the postage issue, but a few have been found on both very thin and very thick soft porous white paper. A very small number are known to fluoresce green. Reprints may be differentiated from the originals under ultraviolet light by the whiteness of the paper. Nos. LO3-LO6 are ungummed, Nos. LO1-LO2 have brown gum.

1875

Franklin Reprints

Imperf

LO3	OC1	(1c)	**blue,** *rose*	50.
			indigo, *rose*	70.
			Block of 4	225.
			Margin block of 4, imprint	—
			Corner plate cracks (91L)	100.

Perf. 12

LO4	OC1	(1c)	**blue**	*16,000.*
			Pair	*35,000.*

No. LO4 is valued in the grade of average to fine.

Eagle Reprints

Imperf.

LO5	OC2	1c	**blue**	25.

Block of 4 125.

Perf. 12

LO6 OC2 1c **blue** 160.
Block of 4 900.
Margin block of 8, imprint & Pl.# *12,500.*

SEMI-OFFICIAL ISSUES

All are imperforate.

Baltimore, Md.

C1

1850-55 Typo. Settings of 10 (2x5) varieties

1LB1 C1 1c **red** (shades), *bluish* 180. 160.
On cover, tied by handstamp *1,000.*
On cover with 1c #9 —
On cover (tied) with 3c #11 *500.*
1LB2 C1 1c **blue** (shades), *bluish* 200. 150.
On cover, tied *1,000.*
a. Bluish laid paper — —
1LB3 C1 1c **blue** (shades) 160. 100.
On cover, tied by handstamp *1,000.*
On cover, tied by ms. *250.*
Block of 4 *1,000.*
a. Laid paper 200. 150.
On cover, tied by handstamp *1,000.*
b. Block of 14 containing three tete-beche gutter pairs (unique) *5,500.*
1LB4 C1 1c **green** — 850.
On cover, tied by handstamp *3,500.*
On cover, not tied *1,100.*
On cover with 1c #7, tied by handstamp *2,250.*
On cover with 3c #11, ms. tied —
On 3c envelope #U10 *3,500.*
Pair 5,500.
1LB5 C1 1c **red** 2,250. 1,750.
On cover, tied by handstamp *4,500.*
On cover (tied) with 3c #11 *5,000.*

The No. 1LB4 pair is the unique multiple of this stamp.

Cancellations on Nos. 1LB1-1LB5:

Black grid —
Blue grid —
Black cross —
Black town —
Blue town +100.
Black numeral —
Blue numeral —
Black pen —

C2

1856 Typo.

1LB6 C2 1c **blue** (shades) 130. 90.
On cover 400.
On cover with 3c #11 *1,000.*
On cover with 3c #26 *1,250.*
1LB7 C2 1c **red** (shades) 130. 90.
On cover *300.*
On cover (tied) with 3c #25 *350.*
On cover (tied) with 3c #26 *350.*
On 3c envelope #U9, tied *300.*
On 3c envelope #U10, tied *350.*
Block of 4 *850.*

C3

Plate of 10 (2x5); 10 Varieties

The sheet consisted of at least four panes of 10 placed horizontally, the two center panes tete beche. This makes possible five horizontal tete beche gutter pairs.

1857 Typo.

1LB8 C3 1c **black** (shades) 65. 50.
On cover, tied by handstamp *125.*
On cover, tied by handstamp, to Germany *3,750.*
On cover (tied) with 3c #26 175.
On 3c envelope #U9, tied *225.*
On 3c envelope #U10 *225.*
On 3c envelope #U27, tied *250.*
Strip of 3 (not tied), on cover *4,000.*
Block of 4 275.
Pane of 10 *1,000.*
Tete beche gutter pair *650.*
a. "SENT," Pos. 7 100. 75.
On cover, tied by handstamp *175.*
On cover with 3c #26 *250.*
On 3c envelope #U9, tied *250.*
On 3c envelope #U10, tied *250.*
b. Short rays, Pos. 2 100. 75.
On cover (tied) with 3c #26 *600.*

Cancellations

Black pen (or pencil) 20.00
Blue town +2.50
Black town +2.50
Black Steamship —

1LB9 C3 1c **red** (shades) 100. 90.
On cover *175.*
On cover with 3c #26 *300.*
On 3c envelope #U9 *325.*
On 3c envelope #U10 *325.*
Block of 6 *2,250.*
a. "SENT," Pos. 7 140. 110.
On cover (tied) with 3c #26 *500.*
b. Short rays, Pos. 2 140. 110.
c. As "b," double impression —

The block of 6 of No. 1LB9 is the only recorded multiple of this stamp.

Cancellations on Nos. 1LB6-1LB7, 1LB9:

Black town —
Blue town —
Blue numeral —
Black pen —
Carrier's initial, manuscript +25.

Boston, Mass.

C6

Several Varieties

1849-50 Pelure Paper Typeset

3LB1 C6 1c **blue** 375. 180.
On cover, tied by handstamp 275.
On cover with 5c #1 *4,000.*
On cover with two 5c #1 *6,750.*
On cover with 3c #10 *450.00*
a. Wrong ornament at left *400.00*
On cover, not tied —

Cancellations

Red town —
Red grid —
Black ornate double oval —
Black "Penny Post Paid" in 3-bar circle —
Black "Penny Post Paid" in 3-bar circle —
Red "Penny Post Paid" in 3-bar circle —

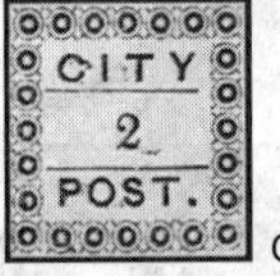

C7

1851 Typeset

Several Varieties

Wove Paper Colored Through

3LB2 C7 1c **blue** (shades), *slate* 190. 100.
On cover 220.
On cover with 5c #1 *12,500.*
On cover with 3c #10 500.
On cover with 3c #11 325.
On 3c envelope #U2, #U5 or #U9 350.
Tete beche gutter pair *600.*

Cancellations on Nos. 3LB2:

Black small fancy circle —
Black diamond grid +100.00
Red town —
Black grid —
Black PAID —
Black crayon —
Red small fancy circle +50.00
Red diamond grid +100.00
Black railroad —
Black hollow star —
Black pencil —
Red crayon —

Charleston, S. C.

John H. Honour was appointed a letter carrier at Charleston, in 1849, and engaged his brother-in-law, E. J. Kingman, to assist him. They separated in 1851, dividing the carrier business of the city between them. At the same time Kingman was appointed a letter carrier. In March, 1858, Kingman retired, being replaced by Joseph G. Martin. In the summer of 1858, John F. Steinmeyer, Jr., was added to the carrier force. When Honour retired in 1860, John C. Beckman was appointed in his place.

Each of these carriers had stamps prepared. These stamps were sold by the carriers. The Federal Government apparently encouraged their use.

Honour's City Express

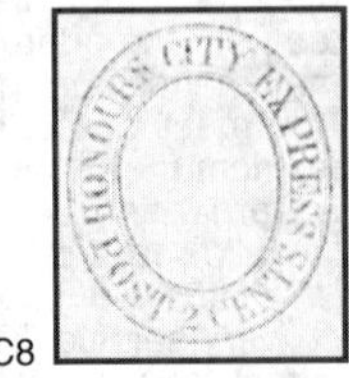

C8

1849 Typo. Wove Paper Colored Through

4LB1 C8 2c **black,** *brown rose* *10,000.*
Cut to shape *4,000.* *4,000.*
On cover, not canceled, with certificate *13,500.*
On cover, cut to shape, tied, with 10c #2 *40,000.*
4LB2 C8 2c **black,** *yellow,* cut to shape —
On cover, not tied, with certificate *12,500.*
On cover, cut to shape, uncanceled —
On cover , rectangular-cut, tied, with 10c #2 —

Cancellations on Nos. 4LB1-4LB2: Red grid, red town, red crayon.

No. 4LB1 unused is a unique uncanceled stamp on piece. The used cut-to-shape stamp is also unique. Additionally, each of the listed covers bearing No. 4LB1 is unique.

Four examples of No. 4LB2 are recorded, each listing above being unique.

C10

1854 Wove Paper Typeset

4LB3 C10 2c **black** *1,500.*
On cover, tied by pen cancel *3,000.*
On cover with 3c #11, tied *4,500.*
On cover with 3c #11, not tied *2,750.*

Cancellations

Black town —
Blue town —
Black pen —
Black pencil —
Brown "PAID" —
Initial "H" —

C11

Several Varieties

1849-50 Typeset

Wove Paper Colored Through

4LB5 C11 2c **black,** *bluish,* pelure *750.* *500.*
On cover with pair 5c #1b —
On cover with two 5c #1b —
On cover (tied) with 3c #11 *4,000.*
a. "Ceuts" *5,750.*
4LB7 C11 2c **black,** *yellow* *750.* *1,000.*
On cover, tied by handstamp *9,000.*
a. "Ccnts," ms. tied on cover *14,500.*

No. 4LB5a is unique. It is without gum and is valued thus. No. 4LB7a also is unique.

The varieties of type C11 on bluish wove (thicker) paper and pink, pelure paper are not believed genuine.

Cancellation Nos. 4LB5, 4LB7:

Red town —
Black pen —
Red pen —
Red crayon —

C13

C14

C15

Several varieties of each type

1851-58 **Typeset**

Wove Paper Colored Through

4LB8 C13 2c **black,** *bluish* 350. 175.
On cover, tied by handstamp *700.*
On cover, not tied *300.*
On cover, tied, with 3c #10 *1,500.*
On cover, tied, with 3c #11 *1,500.*
On cover, tied, with 3c #26 *1,500.*
Pair *1,500.*
a. Period after "PAID" 500. 250.
On cover *650.*
On cover, ms. tied, with 3c #11 *750.*
b. "Cens" 700. *900.*
On cover, ms. tied, with 3c #11 *3,250.*
c. "Conours" and "Bents" —
4LB9 C13 2c **black,** *bluish,* pelure *850.* *950.*
4LB11 C14 (2c) **black,** *bluish* — *375.*
On cover, tied by handstamp, with 3c #11 *12,500.*
On cover, ms. tied, with 3c #11 *3,000.*
4LB12 C14 (2c) **black,** *bluish,* pelure — —
4LB13 C15 (2c) **black,** *bluish* ('58) 750. 400.
On cover with 3c #11, Aiken, S.C. postmark, tied by handstamp (unique) *6,000.*
On cover with 3c #26, tied by pen cancel *4,000.*
Horiz. pair *3,500.*
a. Comma after "PAID" *1,100.*
b. No period after "Post" *1,400.*

The pair of No. 4LB13 is the unique multiple of this stamp.

A 2c of design C13 exists on pink pelure paper. It is believed not to have been issued by the post, but to have been created later and perhaps accidentally.

Cancellations on Nos. 4LB8-4LB13

Black town —
Blue town —
Red town —
Black pen —
Black pencil —
Red crayon —
Brown cork initial "H"

Kingman's City Post

C16

C17

Several varieties of each

1851(?)-58(?) **Typeset**

Wove Paper Colored Through

4LB14 C16 2c **black,** *bluish* *1,400.* *900.*
Vert. pair, ms. tied, on Valentine cover *6,750.*
On cover with 3c #11 *7,500.*
On cover with 3c #26 *6,000.*
a. "Kingman's" erased *5,000.*
4LB15 C17 2c **black,** *bluish* *800.* *800.*
On cover —
Vertical pair —
Horiz. pair, not tied, on Valentine cover *6,500.*
Vertical strip of 3 *22,500.*
a. "Kingman's" erased, on cover with 3c #11, tied by pen cancel (unique) *5,000.*

The No. 4LB14 pair on cover is the only recorded multiple of this stamp.

The 4LB15 pair and strip of 3 actually are uncanceled on covers and are valued thus. The horiz. pair on cover is ms. canceled.

Cancellations on Nos. 4LB14-4LB15: Black town, black pen.

Martin's City Post

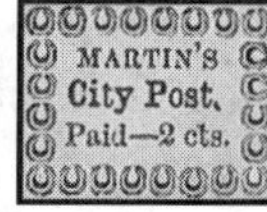

C18

Several varieties

1858 **Wove Paper Colored Through** **Typeset**

4LB16 C18 2c **black,** *bluish* *8,000.*

Beckman's City Post

Same as C19, but inscribed "Beckmann's City Post."

1860

4LB17 C19 2c **black,** on cover —

No. 4LB17 is unique. It is on cover with 3c No. 26, both tied by black circle townmark: "CHARLESTON, S.C. JUN 18, 1860".

Steinmeyer's City Post

C19

C20

Several varieties of Type C19

Type C20 printed from plate of 10 (2x5) varieties

1859 **Wove Paper Colored Through** **Typeset**

4LB18 C19 2c **black,** *bluish* *21,000.*
On cover, uncanceled —
4LB19 C20 2c **black,** *bluish* *4,500.* —
4LB20 C20 2c **black,** *pink* *200.* —
Block of 4 *850.*
Sheet of 10 *2,250.*
4LB21 C20 2c **black,** *yellow* 200.
Block of 4 850.
Sheet of 10 *2,250.*

Sheets of 10 of Nos. 4LB20-4LB21 exist signed by J.F. Steinmeyer Jr. These sell for about 50% more than the unsigned sheets.

Two examples of No. 4LB18 are known on cover, both uncanceled.

Cancellation on Nos. 4LB19-4LB21: Black pen.

Cincinnati, Ohio

Williams' City Post

Organized by C. C. Williams, who was appointed and commissioned by the Postmaster General.

C20a

1854 **Wove Paper** **Litho.**

9LB1 C20a 2c **brown** — *3,000.*
On cover, tied by handstamp —
On cover, tied by pen cancel *3,500.*
On cover with 1c #9 *9,500.*
Pair *7,500.*

Cancellations

Red squared target —
Black pen —
Blue company circle —

Fraser & Co.

Local stamps of designs L146-L147 were carrier stamps when used on cover between Feb. 3, 1848 and June 30, 1849.

Cleveland, Ohio

Bishop's City Post.

Organized by Henry S. Bishop, "Penny Postman" who was appointed and commissioned by the Postmaster General.

C20b

C20c

1854 **Wove Paper** **Litho.**

10LB1 C20b **blue** *5,000.* *2,000.*
On cover, tied by handstamp *15,000.*
Pair on cover, canceled by pencil, with 3c #11, with certificate *16,500.*

Vertically Laid Paper

10LB2 C20c 2c **black,** *bluish* *7,000.* *3,750.*
On cover —
Pair —

Cancellations on #10LB1-10LB2

Red town —
Red boxed numeral —
Black pencil —
Black pen —

Louisville, Ky.

Carrier Service was first established by the Louisville Post Office about 1854, with one carrier. David B. Wharton, appointed a carrier in 1856, issued an adhesive stamp in 1857, but as he was soon thereafter replaced in the service, it is believed that few, if any, of these stamps were used. Brown & McGill, carriers who succeeded Wharton, issued stamps in April, 1858.

Wharton's U.S.P.O. Despatch

C21

Sheet of 50 subjects in two panes of 25 (5x5) each, one upper, one lower

1857 **Lithographed by Robyn & Co.**

5LB1 C21 (2c) **bluish green** (shades) 125.
Block of 4 *650.*
Pane of 25 *3,250.*
Sheet of 50 *7,000.*

Brown & McGill's U. S. P. O. Despatch

C22

1858 **Litho. by Hart & Maypother**

5LB2 C22 (2c) **blue** (shades) 250. *750.*
On cover, not tied, with 3c #26 *750.00*
On cover with 3c #26, tied by handstamp *6,250.*
Block of 4 *1,250.*
5LB3 C22 (2c) **black** *4,500.* *15,000.*

The value for No. 5LB3 used refers to the finer of the two known used (canceled) examples; it is on a piece with a 3c #26.

Cancellations on Nos. 5LB2-5LB3: Blue town, black pencil.

New York, N. Y.

UNITED STATES CITY DESPATCH POST

By an order made on August 1, 1842, the Postmaster General established a carrier service in New York known as the "United States City Despatch Post." Local delivery service had been authorized by the Act of Congress of July 2, 1836.

Greig's City Despatch Post was sold to the U. S. P. O. Department and on August 16, 1842, began operation as the "United States City Despatch Post" under the superintendence of Alexander M. Greig who was appointed a U. S. letter carrier for that purpose.

The Greig circular introducing this service stated that letter boxes had been placed throughout the city, that letters might be sent prepaid or collect, and that registry service was available for an extra 3 cents.

The City Despatch Post stamps were accepted for the service of the United States City Despatch Post. The stamps thus used bear the cancellation of the New York Post Office, usually "U.S." in an octagon which served as a type of overprint indicating that the carrier service was now a government operation (no longer a private local post) as well as a cancellation.

Some examples are canceled by a circular date stamp reading "U.S. CITY DESPATCH POST" or, infrequently, a New York town postmark. When canceled "FREE" in frame they were used as local stamps. See No. 40L1 in Locals section.

No. 6LB3 was the first stamp issued by authority of the U.S.P.O. Department. The 3c denomination included 1 cent in lieu of drop letter postage until June 30, 1845, and the maximum legal carrier fee of 2 cents. Service was discontinued late in November, 1846.

C23

C24

Engraved and printed by Rawdon, Wright & Hatch.

Plate of 42 (6x7) subjects
Wove Paper Colored Through

1842

6LB1	C23	3c **black,** *grayish*		*1,750.*
		On cover, tied by handstamp		*10,000.*

Cancellations

Red "U.S" in octagon	*1,750.*
Red circle "U.S. City Despatch Post"	—
Red town	—

Used copies which do not bear the official cancellation of the New York Post Office and unused copies are classed as Local stamps. See No. 40L1.

Plate of 100 subjects

1842-45 Engraved by Rawdon, Wright & Hatch
Wove Paper (unsurfaced) Colored Through

6LB2	C24	3c **black,** *rosy buff*	*2,500.*	
6LB3	C24	3c **black,** *light blue*	*550.*	500.
		On cover, tied by handstamp		*1,750.*
		On cover, not tied		*750.00*
		Pair	*2,250.*	
6LB4	C24	3c **black,** *green*	*11,500.*	

Some authorities consider No. 6LB2 to be an essay, and No. 6LB4 a color changeling.

Glazed Paper, Surface Colored

6LB5	C24	3c **black,** *blue green* (shades)	200.	175.
		On cover, tied by handstamp		600.
		Five on cover		*20,000.*
		Pair	—	400.
		Strip of 3		*650.*
		Strip of 4		800.
		Strip of 5		—
		Ribbed paper	—	—
		Double transfer		—
a.		Double impression		*1,500.*
b.		3c **black,** *blue*	650.	*250.*
		On cover		*750.*
		Strip of 3 + single on cover		*14,000.*
		Strip of 3	*2,500.*	—
		Block of 12	*23,000.*	—
c.		As "b," double impression		*850.*
d.		3c **black,** *green*	1,000.	*900.*
		On cover		—
		Strip of 4 + single on cover		*36,000.*
e.		As "d," double impression	—	
		On cover		—

Cancellations

Red curved PAID	—
Red "U.S City Despatch Post"	—
Red "U.S" in octagon	—
Red New York	—
Red double line circle "U.S. City Despatch Post"	—

No. 6LB5 has been noted on cover with the 5c New York signed "R.H.M.," No. 9X1d.

6LB6	C24	3c **black,** *pink,* on cover front	*14,500.*

No. 6LB6 is unique.

C25

1846

No. 6LB5 Surcharged in Red

6LB7	C25	2c on 3c **black,** *bluish green,* on cover, not tied, with certificate	*55,000.*

The City Dispatch 2c red formerly listed as No. 6LB8 is now listed under Local Stamps as No. 160L1.

U.S. MAIL

C27

Issued by the Postmaster at New York, N.Y.

1849 Wove Paper, Colored Through Typo.

6LB9	C27	1c **black,** *rose*	90.	90.
		On cover, tied by handstamp		*250.*
		On cover with 5c #1		*2,000.*
		Pair	*250.*	
		Block of 4	*600.*	

1849-50

Glazed Surface Paper

6LB10	C27	1c **black,** *yellow*	90.	90.
		On cover, tied by handstamp		*250.*
		On cover with 5c #1		*1,500.*
		Pair	*250.*	
		Block of 4	*600.*	
6LB11	C27	1c **black,** *buff*	90.	90.
		On cover		*250.*
		On cover with 5c #1, not tied, with certificate		*3,000.*
a.		Pair, one stamp sideways	*2,250.*	

Cancellations on #6LB9-6LB11

Red town	—
Red grid	—
Red "PAID"	+50.
Black numeral in circle	—
Red "N.Y. U.S. CITY MAIL" in circle	+150.
Black pen	—
Black pencil	—

Philadelphia, Pa.

C28

Several Varieties
Thick Wove Paper Colored Through

1849-50 Typeset

7LB1	C28	1c **black,** *rose* (with "L P")	450.	
		On cover, tied by handstamp		*3,000.*
		On cover, not canceled		*2,000.*
		On cover with 5c #1		—
7LB2	C28	1c **black,** *rose* (with "S")	*3,000.*	
		On cover, not canceled		*4,500.*
7LB3	C28	1c **black,** *rose* (with "H")	275.	
		On cover, tied by handstamp		*3,750.*
		On cover, not canceled		*1,000.*
		On cover with 5c #1		—
7LB4	C28	1c **black,** *rose* (with "L S")	400.	*500.*
		On cover, not canceled		*2,500.*
7LB5	C28	1c **black,** *rose* (with "J J")		*7,500.*
		On cover with 5c #1, uncanceled		*70,000.*

The unique used No. 7LB5 in an uncanceled stamp on a cover front.

C29

Several Varieties

7LB6	C29	1c **black,** *rose*	300.	250.
		On cover, tied by handstamp		*2,500.*
		On cover, uncanceled		*500.00*
7LB7	C29	1c **black,** *blue,* glazed	*1,000.*	
		On cover, tied by handstamp		*6,500.*
		On cover, uncanceled		*1,500.*
		On cover with 5c #1		—
7LB8	C29	1c **black,** *vermilion,* glazed	*700.*	
		On cover, tied by handstamp		*1,500.*
		On cover with 5c dark brown #1a, uncanceled		*12,500.*
		On cover with 5c orange brown #1b, uncanceled		*21,000.*
7LB9	C29	1c **black,** *yellow,* glazed	*2,750.*	*2,250.*
		On cover, not canceled		*4,500.*
		On cover with 3c #10, uncanceled		*2,000.*

Cancellations on Nos. 7LB1-7LB9: Normally these stamps were left uncanceled on the letter, but occasionally were accidentally tied by the Philadelphia town postmark which was normally struck in blue ink.

A 1c black on buff (unglazed) of type C29 is believed to be a color changeling.

C30

Settings of 25 (5x5) varieties (Five basic types)

1850-52 Litho.

7LB11	C30	1c **gold,** *black,* glazed	175.	110.
		On cover, tied by handstamp		*600.*
		On cover (tied) with 5c #1		*3,500.*
		On cover (tied) with 3c #10		*800.*
		On cover (uncanceled) with 3c #10		*250.*
		Block of 19	*8,250.*	
7LB12	C30	1c **blue**	400.	275.
		On cover, tied by handstamp		*1,250.*
		On cover (tied) with 3c #10		*1,750.*
		On cover (tied) with 3c #11		*1,250.*
		Pair		1,600.
7LB13	C30	1c **black**	*750.*	550.
		On cover, tied by handstamp		2,500.
		On cover (tied) with 3c #10		—
		On cover (not tied) with 3c #11		*3,250.*

Cancellations on #7LB11-7LB13

Red star	—
Red town	—
Blue town	—

C31

Handstamped

7LB14	C31	1c **blue,** *buff*	3,000.

No. 7LB14 was handstamped on coarse dark buff paper on which rectangles in the approximate size of the type C31 handstamp had been ruled in pencil. The stamps so produced were later cut out and show traces of the adjoining handstamp markings as well as parts of the penciled rectangle. Some uncanceled examples exist on covers.

1855(?)

7LB16	C31	1c **black**	*5,000.*
		On cover with strip of 3, 1c #9	—
		On cover with 3c 1851 stamp removed, tied by handstamp	*7,000.*

C32

1856(?) Handstamped

7LB18	C32	1c **black**	*1,250.*	*2,000.*
		On cover (cut diamond-shaped) with pair 1c #7 and single 1c #9		—
		On cover with strip of 3, 1c #7		*17,000.*
		On cover with 3c #11		*9,500.*
		On 3c envelope #U5		—
		On 3c envelope #U10, not canceled		*9,000.*

Cancellations on #7LB16, 7LB18

Black circled grid —
Black town —

Nos. 7LB16 and 7LB18 were handstamped on the sheet margins of U.S. 1851 1c stamps, cut out and used as adhesives. The paper therefore has some surface bluing, and some stamps show parts of the plate imprint.

Values are for stamps cut square unless otherwise mentioned.

ENVELOPES

Handstamps of types C31 and C32 were also used to make stamped envelopes and letter sheets or circulars. These same types were also used as postmarks or cancellations in the same period.

A handstamp similar to C32, but with "U.S.P. DESPATCH" in serif capitals, is believed to have been used only as a postmark.

Type C31 exists struck in blue or red, type C32 in blue, black or red. When found on cover, on various papers, struck alone, they are probably postmarks and not prepaid stamped envelopes. As such, these entire covers, depending upon the clarity of the handstamp and the general attractiveness of the letter are valued between $400 and $800.

When found on envelopes with the Carrier stamp canceled by a handstamp (such as type C31 struck in blue on a buff envelope canceled by the red solid star cancellation) they can be regarded as probably having been sold as prepaid envelopes. Value approximately $3,000.

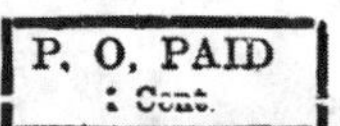

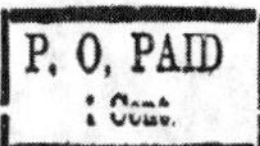

Labels of these designs are believed by most specialists not to be carrier stamps. Those seen are uncanceled, either off cover or affixed to stampless covers of the early 1850s. Some students believe they should be given carrier status.

St. Louis, Mo.

C36

C37

Illustrations enlarged to show details of the two types (note upper corners especially).

1849 **White Wove Paper** **Litho.**
Two Types

8LB1	C36	2c **black**	*7,000.*	—
8LB2	C37	2c **black**	*6,000.*	—

Cancellation on Nos. 8LB1-8LB2: Black town.

C38

1857 **Litho.**

8LB3	C38	2c **blue**	*22,500.*
		On cover, tied by handstamp	*55,000.*
		On Valentine cover, ms. cancel, not tied	*35,000.*

The used example off cover is unique. Four covers are recorded.

Cancellations on No. 8LB3: Black boxed "1ct," "Paid" in arc, black pen.

LOCAL STAMPS

This listing of Local stamps includes stamps issued by Local Posts (city delivery), Independent Mail Routes and Services, Express Companies and other private posts which competed with, or supplemented, official services.

The Independent Mail Routes began using stamps early in 1844 and were put out of business by an Act of March, 1845, which became effective July 1, 1845. By this Act, the Government reduced the zones to two, reduced the rates to 5c and 10c and applied them to weight instead of the number of sheets of paper which composed a letter.

Most of the Local Posts still in business were forced to discontinue service by an Act of 1861, except Boyd's and Hussey's which were able to continue about 20 years longer because of the particular nature of their business. Other posts appeared illegally and sporadically after 1861 and were quickly suppressed.

City posts generally charged 1c to deliver a letter to the Post Office (usually the letter bore a government stamp as well) and 2c for intracity delivery (such letters naturally bore only local stamps). These usages are not catalogued separately because the value of a cover is determined as much by its attractiveness as its franking, rarity being the basic criterion.

Only a few Local Posts used special handstamps for canceling. The stamps frequently were left uncanceled, were canceled by pen, or less often by pencil. **Unless indicated otherwise, values for stamps on cover are for covers having the stamp tied by a handstamped cancellation, either private or governmental.** Local stamps, either uncanceled or pen canceled, **on covers to which they apparently belong**, also are valued where possible.

The absence of any specific cancellation listed indicates that no company handstamp is known so used, and that the canceling, if any, was done by pen, pencil or government handstamp. Local stamps used on letters directed out of town (and consequently bearing government stamps) sometimes, because of their position, are tied together with the government stamp by the cancellation used to cancel the latter.

Values for envelopes are for entires unless specifically mentioned.

All Local stamps are imperforate and on wove paper, either white or colored through, unless otherwise stated.

Counterfeits exist of many Local stamps, but most of these are crude reproductions and would deceive only the novice.

Adams & Co.'s Express, California

This post started in September, 1849, operating only on the Pacific Coast.

D. H. Haskell, Manager
L1 L2

Nos. 1L2-1L5 Printed in Sheets of 40 (8x5).

1854 **Litho.**

1L1	L1	25c **black,** *blue*	*2,750.*	—
		On cover		—
1L2	L2	25c **black** (initials in black)	75.00	—
		Block of 4	375.00	
		Sheet of 40	—	
a.		Initials in red		—
b.		Without initials		—

Cancellation (1L1-1L2): Black Express Co.

Nos. 1L1-1L2 were the earliest adhesive franks issued west of the Mississippi River.

No. 1L2 usually bear manuscript control markings "LR" for Louis Reed or less commonly "IBW" for Isaiah B. Wood.

Glazed Surface Cardboard

1L3 L2 25c **black,** *pink* 30.00
Block of 4 160.00
Sheet of 40 2,000.
Retouched flaw above LR "25" 100.00

No. 1L3 was probably never placed in use as a postage stamp.

L3

Overprinted in red "Over our California lines only"

1L4 L3 25c **black** (with initials "LR") 750.00 —

L4

L5

1L5 L4 25c **black** (black surcharge) *2,750.* —
1L6 L5 25c **black** *2,000.*
Pair *6,500.*

The pair of No. 1L6 is unique.

NEWSPAPER STAMP

L6

1LP1 L6 **black,** *claret* — *2,000.*

Cancellation: Blue company oval.

ENVELOPES

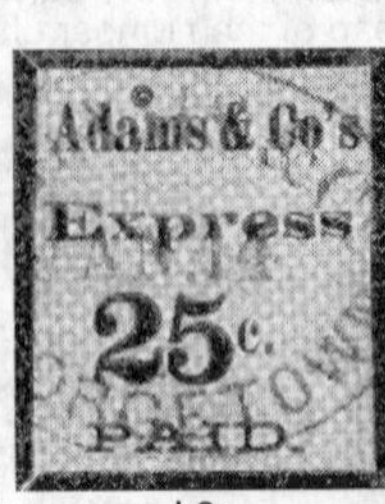

L6a

L6b

Typo.

1LU1 L6a 25c **blue** (cut square) *15,000.*
1LU2 L6b 25c **black,** on U.S. #U9 —
1LU3 L6b 50c **black,** on U.S. #U9 *2,500.* *2,500.*
1LU4 L6b 50c **black,** *buff* *15,000.*

Nos. 1LU2 and 1LU3 exist cut out and apparently used as adhesives.
Cancellation: Blue company oval.

Adams' City Express Post, New York, N.Y.

L7

L7a

L8

1850-51 **Typo.**

2L2 L7 2c **black,** *buff* *5,000.* *2,250.*
On cover, canceled, not tied, with certificate *10,000.*
2L3 L7a 1c **black,** *gray* — —
2L4 L8 2c **black,** *gray* *450.00* *450.00*
On cover, tied by handstamp *5,500.*

Nos. 2L3-2L4 were reprinted in black and in blue on white wove paper. Some students claim that the 1c and 2c in blue exist as originals.

Allen's City Dispatch, Chicago, Ill.

Established by Edwin Allen for intracity delivery of letters and circulars. The price of the stamps is believed to have been determined on a quantity basis. Uncanceled and canceled remainders were sold to collectors after suppression of the post in February, 1883.

L9

1882 **Typo.** ***Perf. 10***
Sheet of 100

3L1 L9 **pink** 7.50 *25.00*
On cover *900.00*
Block of 4 *40.00*
a. Horizontal pair, imperf. between —
3L2 L9 **black** 12.50 *100.00*
On cover —
Block of 4 55.00
a. Horizontal pair, imperf. between —
3L3 L9 **red,** *yellow* .75 *20.00*
On cover *800.00*
Block of 4 *3.25*
a. Imperf., pair *150.00*
b. Horizontal pair, imperf. between —
3L4 L9 **blackish purple** 120.00

Cancellations: Violet company oval, violet "eagle."

American Express Co., New York, N.Y.

Believed by some researchers to have been established by Smith & Dobson in 1856, and short-lived.

L10

Typeset
Glazed Surface Paper

4L1 L10 2c **black,** *green* *9,000.*

American Letter Mail Co.

Lysander Spooner established this independent mail line operating to and from New York, Philadelphia and Boston.

L12

L13

1844 **Engr.**
Sheet of 20 (5x4)

5L1 L12 5c **black,** thin paper (2nd printing) 7.50 *35.00*
Thick paper (1st printing) 35.00 *50.00*
On cover *850.00*
Pair on cover —
Block of 4, thin paper 40.00
Sheet of 20, thin paper 225.00

No. 5L1 has been extensively reprinted in several colors, distinguishable by the rust marks on the plate, which were mostly removed from the margins and gutters between stamps but remain within the stamp designs. Cancellations: Red dotted star (2 types). Red "PAID," black brush, red brush.

Engr.

5L2 L13 **black,** *gray* 150.00 *250.00*
On cover, tied by handstamp *1,000.*
On cover, ms. tied *500.00*
On cover, not tied *350.00*
Pair on cover —
Vertical strip of 4 *3,000.*
Block of 4 *4,000.*
5L3 L13 **blue,** *gray* *2,000.* *1,750.*
On cover, uncanceled, with certificate *12,500.*

Cancellations: Red "PAID," red company oval.

A. W. Auner's Despatch Post, Philadelphia, Pa.

L13a

1851 **Typeset**
Cut to shape

154L1 L13a **black,** *grayish* *9,000.*
On cover, not tied, with certificate *16,500.*

Nos. 154L1 unused and on cover are each unique.

Baker's City Express Post, Cincinnati, Ohio

L14

1849

6L1 L14 2c **black,** *pink* *2,250.*
On cover, uncanceled, with certificate *12,500.*

Bank & Insurance Delivery Office or City Post

See Hussey's Post.

Barnard's Cariboo Express, British Columbia

The adhesives were used on British Columbia mail and the post did not operate in the United States, so the formerly listed PAID and COLLECT types are omitted. This company had an arrangement with Wells, Fargo & Co. to exchange mail at San Francisco.

Barnard's City Letter Express, Boston, Mass.

Established by Moses Barnard

L19

1845

7L1 L19 **black,** *yellow,* glazed paper *1,250.* *1,000.*
7L2 L19 **red** *1,000.*
On cover, ms. cancel, not tied, with certificate *5,000.*

No. 7L2 unused and on cover are each unique.

Barr's Penny Dispatch, Lancaster, Pa.

Established by Elias Barr.

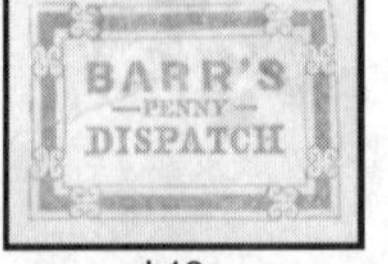

L19a

L20

1855 **Typeset**

Five varieties of each

8L1	L19a	**red**	1,000.	1,000.
		On cover, ms. cancel, not tied, with certificate		*2,000.*
8L2	L20	**black,** *green*	250.	200.00
		On cover with 3c #11		—
		Pair	*650.*	

Bayonne City Dispatch, Bayonne City, N.J.

Organized April 1, 1883, to carry mail, with three daily deliveries. Stamps sold at 80 cents per 100.

L21

1883 **Electrotyped**

Sheet of 10

9L1	L21	1c **black**	200.	200.
		On cover		*750.*
		On cover with 1c & 2c #183, 206		*2,750.*
		On cover with 3c #207		*1,600.*

Cancellation: Purple concentric circles.

ENVELOPE

1883, May 15 **Handstamped**

9LU1	L21	1c **purple,** *amber*	.175	*1,000.*

Bentley's Dispatch, New York, N.Y.

Established by H. W. Bentley, who acquired Cornwell's Madison Square Post Office, operating until 1856, when the business was sold to Lockwood. Bentley's postmark was double circle handstamp.

L22

L22a

1856(?) **Glazed Surface Paper**

10L1	L22	**gold**	*6,500.*	*9,000.*
10L2	L22a	**gold**		*8,000.*
		Pair	*15,000.*	

Two unused examples of No. 10L1 are known, while the used example is unique.

Cancellation: Black "PAID."

Berford & Co.'s Express, New York, N.Y.

Organized by Richard G. Berford and Loring L. Lombard. Carried letters, newspapers and packages by steamer to Panama and points on the West Coast, North and South America. Agencies in West Indies, West Coast of South America, Panama, Hawaii, etc.

L23

1851

11L1	L23	3c **black**	*5,000.*	*7,000.*
		On cover, not canceled		—
11L2	L23	6c **green**	—	—
		On cover, tied		—
11L3	L23	10c **violet**	*5,000.*	
		On cover, not canceled		—
		Four cut to shape on cover		*16,500.*
		Pair		—
a.		Horiz. tete beche pair		
		On cover with normal pair		*55,000.*
		Two tete beche pair on cover		*57,500.*
11L4	L23	25c **red**	*17,000.*	
		On cover with #11L1 & 2 #11L2		*55,000.*

Values of cut to shape copies are about half of those quoted.
No. 11L4 unused and on cover are each unique.
Cancellation: Red "B & Co. Paid" (sometimes impressed without ink). Dangerous counterfeits exist of Nos. 11L1-11L4.

Bicycle Mail Route, California

During the American Railway Union strike, Arthur C. Banta, Fresno agent for Victor bicycles, established this post to carry mail from Fresno to San Francisco and return, employing messengers on bicycles. The first trip was made from Fresno on July 6, 1894. Service was discontinued on July 18 when the strike ended. In all, 380 letters were carried. Stamps were used on covers with U.S. Government adhesive stamps and on stamped envelopes.

L24

Printed from single die. Sheet of six.
Error of spelling "SAN FRANSISCO"

1894 **Typo.** ***Rouletted 10***

12L1	L24	25c **green**	150.	*200.*
		On cover		1,500.
		Block of 4	700.	
		Pane of 6	*1,750.*	

(Illustration reduced size) — L25

Retouched die. Spelling error corrected.

12L2	L25	25c **green**	30.	75.
		On cover		1,250.
		Block of 4	125.	
		Pane of 6	250.	
a.		"Horiz." pair, imperf. "vert"	75.	
		As "a," pane of 6	—	

ENVELOPES

12LU1	L25	25c **brown,** on 2c No. U311	200.	*1,350.*
12LU2	L25	25c **brown,** on 2c No. U312	200.	*1,350.*

Cancellation: Two black parallel bars 2mm apart.
Stamps and envelopes were reprinted from the defaced die.

Bigelow's Express, Boston, Mass.

Authorities consider items of this design to be express company labels rather than stamps.

Bishop's City Post, Cleveland, Ohio

See Carriers' Stamps, Nos. 10LB1-10LB2.

Blizzard Mail

Organized March, 1888, to carry mail to New York City during the interruption of U.S. mail by the Blizzard of 1888. Used March 12-16.

L27

1888, Mar. 12 **Quadrille Paper** **Typo.**

163L1	L27	5c **black**	*2,000.*	

D.O. Blood & Co., Philadelphia, Pa.

I. Philadelphia Despatch Post

Operated by Robertson & Co., predecessor of D.O. Blood & Co.

L28

L29

Initialed "R & Co."

1842 **Handstamped**

Cut to Shape

15L1	L28	3c **red,** *bluish*		*1,500.*
		On cover		*12,500.*
15L2	L28	3c **black**		*1,500.*
		On cover, not tied, with certificate		*15,000.*

Cancellations on Nos. 15L1-15L2: Red "3," red pattern of segments.

With or without shading in background.
Initialed "R & Co"

1843 **Litho.**

15L3	L29	(3c) **black,** *grayish*		750.
		On cover, tied by handstamp		*10,000.*
		On cover, not tied, with certificate		*3,500.*
a.		Double impression		—

Cancellation on No. 15L3: Red "3"

The design shows a messenger stepping over the Merchants' Exchange Building, which then housed the Government Post Office, implying that the private post gave faster service.

See illustration L161 for similar design.

II. D.O. Blood & Co.

Formed by Daniel Otis Blood and Walter H. Blood in 1845. Successor to Philadelphia Despatch Post which issued Nos. 15L1-15L3.

L30

Initialed "Dob & Cos" or "D.O.B. & Co."

1845

Shading in background

15L4	L30	(3c) **black,** *grayish*		400.
		On cover, tied by handstamp		*6,000.*
		On cover, not tied		*1,500.*

L31

L32

1846

15L5 L31 (2c) **black** 125. *250.*
On cover —
On cover, not tied, with certificate *800.*
Block of 4 *475.*
Pane of 12 *5,500.*

1847

15L6 L32 (2c) **black** — 200.
On cover —
On cover, not tied, with certificate *1,250.*

Cancellations on Nos. 15L4-15L6: Black dot pattern, black cross, red "PAID."
Dangerous counterfeits exist of Nos. 15L3-15L6.

L33

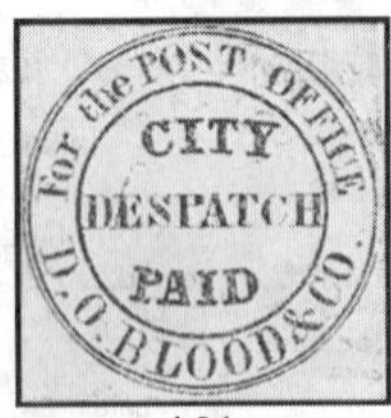

L34

L35

1846-47

15L7 L33 (2c) **black** 125.00 300.00
On cover, tied by handstamp *1,750.*
On cover, cut to shape, tied by handstamp *1,100.*
On cover, not tied *750.00*

15L8 L34 (2c) **black** 110.00 75.00
On cover, tied by handstamp *950.00*
On cover, uncanceled *500.00*

15L9 L35 (2c) **black** 100.00 60.00
On cover, tied by handstamp *1,500.*
On cover, with 5c #1 —
On cover, not tied *500.00*
Block of 4 —

Values for Nos. 15L7-15L9 cut to shape are half of those quoted.
"On cover" listings of Nos. 15L7-15L9 are for stamps tied by government town postmarks, either Philadelphia, or rarely Baltimore.

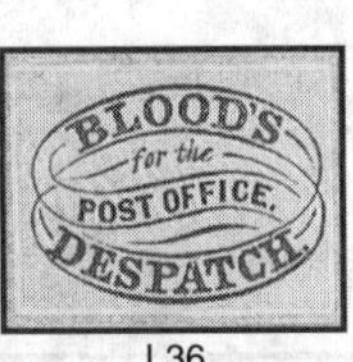

L36

L37

1848

15L10 L36 (2c) **black & blue** 350.00 *500.00*
On cover, tied by handstamp —
On cover, not canceled *1,250.*
On cover, with 5c #1 —
Pair *1,300.*

15L11 L37 (2c) **black,** *pale green* 300.00 300.00
On cover, tied by handstamp *1,250.*
On cover, not tied *800.00*

Cancellation: Black grid.

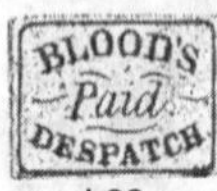

L38

L39

L40

L41

1848-54

15L12 L38 (2c) **gold,** *black,* glazed *110.00* 100.00
On cover, tied by handstamp *500.00*
On cover, acid tied 150.00
On cover with 5c #1 —

15L13 L39 1c **bronze,** *black,* glazed ('50) 25.00 12.50
On cover, tied by handstamp *225.00*
On cover, acid tied 75.00
On cover, acid tied, with 5c #1 *1,600.*
On cover with 10c #2 —
On cover, acid tied, with three 1c #7 *1,100.*
On cover with, tied by handstamp, 3c #10 *250.00*
Block of 4 150.00
Pane of 24 *1,250.*

15L14 L40 (1c) **bronze,** *lilac* ('54) 4.25 2.50
On cover, tied by handstamp *200.00*
On cover, acid tied 30.00
On cover, acid tied, with 1c #9 *300.00*
On cover with 3c #11 *375.00*
On cover, tied by handstamp, with 3c #26 *200.00*
On cover, acid tied, with 3c #64b *125.00*
Block of 4 50.00
Pane of 25 *750.00*
a. Laid paper — —

15L15 L40 (1c) **blue & pink,** *bluish* ('53) 22.50 12.50
On cover, tied by handstamp *200.00*
On cover, acid tied 50.00
Block of 4 80.00
Pane of 25 *1,250.*
a. Laid paper — —

15L16 L40 (1c) **bronze,** *black,* glazed ('54) 30.00 25.00
On cover, tied by handstamp *225.00*
On cover, acid tied 75.00
On cover, tied by handstamp, with 3c #11 *275.00*

15L17 L41 (2c) **bronze,** *black,* glazed 35.00 20.00
On cover, tied by handstamp *225.00*
On cover, acid tied 75.00
On cover, acid tied, with 5c #1 *1,250.*
On cover, handstamp tied, with pair of 5c #1a *11,000.*

D.O. Blood & Co. reduced the cost for mailing letters from 2c to 1c as of Jan. 8, 1849, in anticipation of the government carrier rate reduction. As a result, Nos. 15L12 and 15L17 could be purchased for 1c after this date.
Cancellations: Black grid (No. 15L12, 15L17). Nos. 15L13-15L16 were almost always canceled with an acid which discolored both stamp and cover.

III. Blood's Penny Post

Blood's Penny Post was acquired by the general manager, Charles Kochersperger, in 1855, when Daniel O. Blood died.

Henry Clay — L42

1855 **Engr. by Draper, Welsh & Co.**

15L18 L42 (1c) **black** 35.00 10.00
On cover 150.00
On cover, tied by handstamp, with 3c #11 *400.00*
On cover, tied by handstamp, with 3c #26 *350.00*
On 3c entire #U9 300.00
Block of 4 175.00

Cancellations: Black or red circular "Blood's Penny Post," black "1" in frame, red "1" in frame.

ENVELOPES

L42A

L43

L44

1848-60 **Embossed**

15LU1 L42A **albino embossing,** *white* —
15LU1A L42A **albino embossing,** *buff* — 4,500.
15LU1B L43 **red,** *white* 75.00 *100.00*
a. **Pink,** *white* *100.00*
b. Impressed on US Env. #U9 225.00
15LU2 L43 **red,** *buff* — 150.00
15LU3 L44 **red,** *white* 75.00 160.00
15LU4 L44 **red,** *buff* 75.00 125.00

One example of No. 15LU1 is recorded, uncanceled, with the embossed stamp cut out and reattached. Two examples of No. 15LU1A are recorded, canceled by the "Blood's Despatch/28 So. Sixth" handstamp.

L45

15LU5 L45 **red,** *white* 35.00 75.00
Used with 3c #11 350.00
Used with 3c #26 *350.00*
a. Impressed on US Env. #U7 *250.00*
b. Impressed on US Env. #U9 *250.00*
c. Impressed on US Env. #U1 *300.00*
d. Impressed on US Env. #U3 *500.00*
e. Impressed on US Env. #U2 *275.00*
15LU6 L45 **red,** *amber* 35.00 100.00
15LU6A L45 **red,** *buff* *350.00*
On cover with 10c #2 —
On cover with three 1c #9 —
b. **Red,** *brown* *500.00*

Laid Paper

15LU7 L45 **red,** *white* 35.00 125.00
Used with acid tied #15L14 *200.00*
a. Impressed on US env. #U9 350.00
15LU8 L45 **red,** *amber* 35.00 125.00
Used with 3c No. 25 200.00
15LU9 L45 **red,** *buff* 35.00 125.00
15LU10 L45 **red,** *blue* *6,500.*

Nos. 15LU1-15LU9 exist in several envelope sizes.
Cancellations: Black grid (Nos. 15LU1-15LU4), black company circle (2 sizes and types). When on government envelope, the Blood stamp was often left uncanceled.

Bouton's Post, New York, N.Y.
I. Franklin City Despatch Post

Organized by John R. Bouton

L46

1847 **Glazed Surface Paper** **Typo.**

16L1 L46 (2c) **black,** *green* *7,500.*
a. "Bouton" in blk. ms. vert. at side *7,000.*
On cover *14,000.*

II. Bouton's Manhattan Express

Acquired from William V. Barr

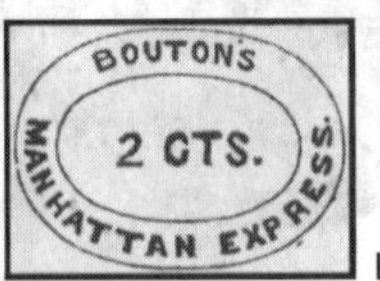

L47

1847 **Typo.**

17L1 L47 2c **black,** *pink* *4,000.*
Cut to shape *900.*
On cover, uncanceled *4,500.*

III. Bouton's City Dispatch Post

(Sold to Swarts' in 1849.)

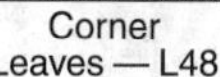
Corner Leaves — L48

Corner Dots — L49

Design: Zachary Taylor

1848 **Litho.**

18L1 L48 2c **black** — 600.
On cover *2,000.*
On cover with 5c #1 *27,500.*
On cover with 10c #2 *50,000.*

18L2 L49 2c **black,** *gray blue* 200. 250.
On cover, tied by handstamp 600.
On cover tied by Swarts' handstamp *1,000.*
On cover with 5c #1 *25,000.*
On cover with 10c #2 *7,500.*

Cancellations on Nos. 18L1-18L2: Red "PAID BOUTON."

Boyce's City Express Post, New York, N.Y.

L50

Center background has 17 parallel lines

1852 **Glazed Surface Paper** **Typo.**

19L1 L50 2c **black,** *green* *1,500.* *1,000.*
Cut to shape *600.00*
On cover, tied by manuscript cancel *4,000.*

Boyd's City Express, New York, N.Y.

Boyd's City Express, as a post, was established by John T. Boyd, on June 17, 1844. In 1860 the post was briefly operated by John T. Boyd, Jr., under whose management No. 20L15 was issued.

For about six months in 1860 the post was suspended. It was then sold to William and Mary Blackham who resumed operation on Dec. 24, 1860.

The Blackham issues began with No. 20L16. Boyd's had arrangements to handle local delivery mail for Pomeroy, Letter Express, Brooklyn City Express Post, Staten Island Express Post and possibly others.

L51

Designs L51-L56, L59-L60 have a rectangular frame of fine lines surrounding the design.

1844 **Glazed Surface Paper** **Litho.**

20L1 L51 2c **black,** *green* 600.
On cover *4,000.*
On cover, not tied, with #117L4 *7,000.*

Cancellation: Red "FREE."

L52

L53

L54

Plain background. Map on globe.

1844 **Litho.**

20L2 L52 2c **black,** *yellow green* 175.00
On cover *450.00*

Cancellation: Red "FREE."

Plain background. Only globe shaded.

1845 **Engr.**

20L3 L53 2c **black,** *bluish green* — 250.00
On cover *500.00*

Cancellation: Red "FREE."

Inner oval frame of two thin lines. Netted background, showing but faintly on late impressions.

1845 **Engr.**

20L4 L54 2c **black,** *green* — 15.00
On cover, tied by handstamp 250.00
On cover, tied, with 5c U.S. Postmaster Provisional #9X1, on cover front —
On cover, tied, with 5c #1 *5,000.*
Double transfer 35.00
a. Diagonal half used as 1c on cover *2,300.*

Cancellations: Red "FREE." Black grid.

The 20L4 and 9X1 on cover front is the only recorded usage of a local stamp and a Postmaster Provisional.

1847

20L5 L54 2c **gold,** *cream* *350.00* *600.00*
On cover *1,750.*

Designs L54-L59 (except No. 20L23) were also obtainable die cut. An extra charge was made for such stamps. In general, genuine Boyd die-cuts sell for 75% of rectangular cut copies. Stamps hand cut to shape are worth much less.

L55 L56 L57

No period after "CENTS." Inner oval frame has heavy inner line.

1848 **Engr.**

20L7 L55 2c **black,** *green* (glazed) 10.00 15.00
On cover, tied by handstamp 175.00
On cover, tied by handstamp, with 5c #1 *3,250.*
On cover, tied, with 3c #11 *275.00*
Block of 4 40.00
a. 2c **black,** *yellow green* 15.00
On cover 135.00

Cancellation: Black grid.

No. 20L7a is on unglazed surface-colored paper.

1852 **Litho.**

Period after "CENTS." Inner frame as in L55.

20L8 L56 2c **black,** *green* 25.00 35.00
On cover *150.00*
Vert. strip of 3 on cover *300.00*

20L9 L56 2c **gold,** 12.50 80.00
On cover, tied by handstamp *750.00*
On cover with 3c #11 *1,250.*
Block of 4 80.00

Cancellations on Nos. 20L8-20L9: Black cork. Black "PAID J.T.B."

No. 20L8 was reprinted in 1862 on unglazed paper, and about 1880 on glazed paper without rectangular frame.

1854

Period after "CENTS." Inner oval frame has heavy outer line. Eagle's tail pointed. Upper part of "2" open, with heavy downstroke at left shorter than one at right. "2C" closer than "T2."

20L10 L57 2c **black,** *green* 32.50 25.00
On cover, tied by handstamp 200.00

Cancellation: Black "PAID J.T.B."

L58

L59

1855 **Unglazed Paper Colored Through** **Typo.**

Outer oval frame of three lines, outermost heavy. Solid background.

20L11 L58 2c **black,** *olive green* *65.00* 90.00
On cover, tied by handstamp *350.00*

1857

20L12 L58 2c **brick red,** *white* 50.00 45.00
On cover, tied by handstamp *500.00*

20L13 L58 2c **dull orange,** *white* 50.00 45.00
On cover *400.00*
a. Printed on both sides —

Cancellation on Nos. 20L11-20L13: Black "PAID J.T.B."

Nos. 20L11-20L13 were reprinted in the 1880's for sale to collectors. They were printed from a new small plate of 25 on lighter weight paper and in colors of ink and paper lighter than the originals.

1857 **Glazed Surface Paper** **Litho.**

Similar to No. 20L10, but eagle's tail square. Upper part of "2" closed (in well printed specimens) forming a symmetrical "o" with downstrokes equal. "T2" closer than "2C."

20L14 L59 2c **black,** *green* 12.50 *25.00*
On cover 125.00
On cover, tied by handstamp, with 3c #26 —
Pair on cover —
Block of 4 65.00
a. Serrate perf. —

The serrate perf. is probably of private origin.

No. 20L15 was made by altering the stone of No. 20L14, and many traces of the "S" of "CENTS" remain.

1860

20L15 L59 1c **black,** *green* 1.00 *50.00*
On cover, tied by handstamp *400.00*
Block of 4 7.50
a. "CENTS" instead of "CENT" — —
On cover *450.00*

Cancellation on Nos. 20L14-20L15: Black "PAID J.T.B."

L60

L61

Center dots before "POST" and after "CENTS."

1861

20L16 L60 2c **black,** *red* 7.50 20.00
On cover, tied by handstamp 200.00
Block of 4 37.50
a. Tete beche pair 45.00

20L17 L60 1c **black,** *lilac* 12.50 17.50
On cover, tied by handstamp 250.00
On cover, tied by handstamp, with 3c #26 *200.00*
On cover, tied by handstamp, with 3c #65 *500.00*
Block of 4 50.00
a. "CENTS" instead of "CENT" 50.00 *75.00*
Two on cover (No. 20L17a) —
b. "1" inverted —

20L18 L60 1c **black,** *blue gray* 22.50 35.00
On cover, tied by handstamp *250.00*
On cover, tied by handstamp, with 3c #26 *225.00*
On cover, tied by handstamp, with 3c #65 *225.00*
Block of 4 90.00
a. "CENTS" instead of "CENT" 75.00 90.00
On cover 250.00
On cover, tied by handstamp, with 1c #24 and three 3c #26 *2,000.*
b. "1" inverted —

Cancellations on Nos. 20L16-20L18: Black or blue company oval, black company circle, black or blue "PAID" in circle.

1861

20L19 L60 2c **gold,** *250.00*
Block of 4 —
a. Tete beche pair —

20L20 L60 2c **gold,** *green* 20.00
Block of 4 —
a. Tete beche pair —

20L21 L60 2c **gold,** *dark blue* 12.50
On cover, tied by handstamp *150.00*
Block of 4 —
a. Tete beche pair —

20L22 L60 2c **gold,** *crimson* 25.00
Block of 4 —
a. Tete beche pair —

1866 **Typo.**

20L23 L58 2c **black,** *red* 7.50 25.00
On cover, tied by handstamp 250.00
Block of 4 37.50
a. Tete beche pair 55.00

Cancellations: Black company, black "PAID" in circle.

No. 20L23 was reprinted from a new stone on paper of normal color. See note after No. 20L13.

1866 **Typo.**

No period or center dots.

20L24 L61 1c **black,** *lilac* *30.00* *65.00*
On cover, tied by handstamp *500.00*
Block of 4 —

20L25 L61 1c **black,** *blue* 6.00 *50.00*
On cover, tied by handstamp *500.00*
Block of 4 30.00

Cancellation on Nos. 20L24-20L25: Black company.

Reprints exist of Nos. 20L24 and 20L25. Originals of No. 20L24 are grayish black on glazed paper, while the reprints are deep black on unglazed paper. Reprints of No. 20L25 are identical to the originals, and it is customary to regard stamps with original gum as originals and those without gum as reprints.

Boyd's City Dispatch

(Change in Name)

L62

1874 Glazed Surface Paper Litho.

20L26	L62	2c **light blue**	35.00	40.00
		On cover		—
		Block of 4	—	

A unique sheet of 100 exists. It demonstrates 10 transfer types (2x5) repeated ten times to produce the printing stone. The same stone was modified to produce Nos. 20L30-20L36.

The 2c black on wove paper, type L62, is a cut-out from the Bank Notices Nos. 20LU45, 20LU46 or 20LU47.

Surface Colored Paper

20L28	L62	2c **black,** *red*		—
20L29	L62	2c **blue,** *red*	*250.00*	

The adhesives of type L62 were made from the third state of the envelope die.

Nos. 20L28 and 20L29 are color trials, possibly used postally.

L63

L64

1877 Litho.

20L30	L63	2c **lilac,** *roseate*		—

Laid Paper

20L31	L63	2c **lilac,** *roseate*		—

Perf *12½*, Wove Paper

20L32	L63	2c **lilac,** *roseate*	27.50	25.00
		On cover		*200.00*
a.		2c **lilac,** *grayish*	27.50	25.00

Laid Paper

20L33	L63	2c **lilac,** *roseate*		25.00
a.		2c **lilac,** *grayish*		—

Glazed Surface Paper

20L34	L63	2c **brown,** *yellow*	35.00	35.00
		On cover, tied by handstamp		—
a.		Imperf. horizontally	—	

1877 Laid Paper *Perf. 11, 12, 12½*

20L35	L64	(1c) **violet,** *lilac*	15.00	17.50
		On cover, tied by handstamp		*350.00*
a.		(1c) **red lilac,** *lilac*	27.50	27.50
b.		(1c) **gray lilac,** *lilac*	17.50	17.50
c.		Vert. pair, imperf. horiz.	*400.00*	
20L36	L64	(1c) **gray,** *roseate*	15.00	15.00
		On cover, tied by handstamp		*250.00*
a.		(1c) **gray,** *grayish*		15.00

Cancellations on Nos. 20L30-20L36: Black "PAID" in circle. Purple company oval.

Boyd's Dispatch

(Change in Name)

Mercury Series-Type I — L65

Printed in sheets of 100.
Inner frame line at bottom broken below foot of Mercury.
Printed by C.O. Jones.

1878 Litho. Wove Paper *Imperf.*

20L37	L65	**black,** *pink*	*400.00*	*300.00*

Surface Colored Wove Paper

20L38	L65	**black,** *orange red*	*750.00*	*500.00*
20L39	L65	**black,** *crimson*	*450.00*	*300.00*

Laid Paper

20L40	L65	**black,** *salmon*	*450.00*	
20L41	L65	**black,** *lemon*	*450.00*	*400.00*
20L42	L65	**black,** *lilac pink*	*450.00*	

Nos. 20L37-20L42 are color trials, some of which may have been used postally.

Surface Colored Paper

Perf. 12

20L43	L65	**black,** *crimson*	60.00	50.00
		On cover, tied by handstamp		*300.00*
a.		**black,** *dull brown red*	40.00	40.00
		On cover, tied by handstamp		*300.00*
20L43A	L65	**black,** *orange red*	150.00	150.00
		On cover, tied by handstamp		*1,000.*

Cancellations on Nos. 20L37-20L43A: Black "PAID" in circle. Purple company oval.

Wove Paper

Perf. 11, 11½, 12, 12½ and Compound

20L44	L65	**black,** *pink*	1.50	2.50
		On cover		*200.00*
a.		Horizontal pair, imperf. between	—	—

1879 *Perf. 11, 11½, 12*

20L45	L65	**black,** *blue*	10.00	15.00
		On cover, tied by handstamp		200.00
20L46	L65	**blue,** *blue*	27.50	32.50
		On cover, tied by handstamp		*400.00*

1880 *Perf. 11, 12, 13½*

20L47	L65	**black,** *lavender*	8.00	20.00
		On cover, tied by handstamp		*300.00*
		Block of 4	50.00	
a.		Horizontal pair, imperf. between	*400.00*	
20L48	L65	**blue,** *lavender*	—	—

1881 Laid Paper *Perf. 12, 12½, 14*

20L49	L65	**black,** *pink*	*350.00*	
		On cover, tied by handstamp		*600.00*
20L50	L65	**black,** *lilac pink*	7.00	25.00
		On cover, tied by handstamp		*325.00*

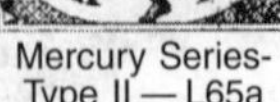

Mercury Series-Type II — L65a

Mercury Series-Type III — L65b

No break in frame, the great toe raised, other toes touching line.

Printed by J. Gibson

1881 Wove Paper *Perf. 12, 16 & Compound.*

20L51	L65a	**black,** *blue*	35.00	30.00
20L52	L65a	**black,** *pink*	75.00	75.00
		On cover, tied by handstamp		*400.00*

Laid Paper

20L53	L65a	**black,** *pink*	7.50	7.50
		On cover, tied by handstamp		125.00
20L54	L65a	**black,** *lilac pink*	12.50	10.00
		On cover		*200.00*

No break in frame, the great toe touching.
Printed by the "Evening Post"

Perf. 10, 11½, 12, 16 & Compound

1882 Wove Paper

20L55	L65b	**black,** *blue*	4.00	10.00
		On cover, tied by handstamp		*225.00*
		Pair on cover		225.00
20L56	L65b	**black,** *pink*	.40	*1.50*
		On cover, tied by handstamp		100.00
		Block of 4	2.00	

Cancellations on Nos. 20L44-20L56: black or purple company ovals of various types, purple company circle, purple "SPECIAL," purple Maltese cross.

ENVELOPES

Boyd's City Post

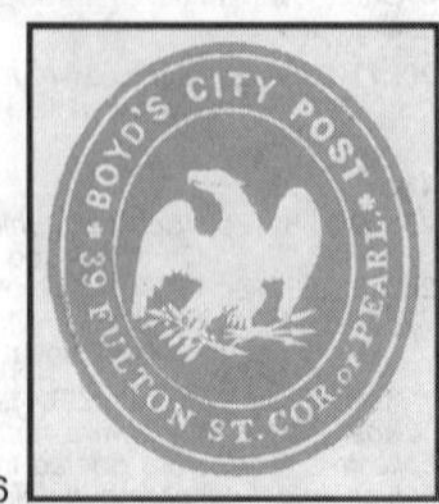

L66

Imprinted in upper right corner.
Used envelopes show Boyd's handstamps.

1864 Diagonally Laid Paper Embossed

20LU1	L66	**red**	*175.00*	
20LU2	L66	**red,** *amber*	*90.00*	
20LU3	L66	**red,** *yellow*	—	—
20LU4	L66	**blue**	*175.00*	—
20LU5	L66	**blue,** *amber*	*175.00*	
20LU6	L66	**blue,** *yellow*	—	—

Several shades of red and blue.

20LU7	L66	**deep blue,** *orange,* cut square	*600.00*	
		Entire		*5,500.*

Reprinted on pieces of white, fawn and oriental buff papers, vertically, horizontally or diagonally laid.

Wove Paper

20LU8	L66	**red,** *cream*	*175.00*	
20LU9	L66	**red,** *orange*	—	*2,500.*
20LU10	L66	**blue,** *cream*	—	—
20LU11	L66	**blue,** *orange*	—	
		Impression at upper left	—	*4,000.*
20LU11A	L66	**blue,** *amber*	—	—

Boyd's City Dispatch

L67a

L67b

L67a. Lines and letters sharp and clear. Trefoils at sides pointed and blotchy, middle leaf at right long and thick at end.

L67b. Lines and letters thick and rough. Lobes of trefoils rounded and definitely outlined. Stamp impressed normally in upper right corner of envelope; L67b rarely in upper left.

1867 Diagonally Laid Paper Typo.

20LU12	L67	2c **red** (a) (b)	—	*800.00*
20LU13	L67	2c **red,** *amber* (b)	—	*300.00*
20LU14	L67	2c **red,** *cream* (b)	—	*300.00*
a.		On horiz. laid paper		—
20LU15	L67	2c **red,** *yellow* (a) (b)	—	*300.00*
20LU16	L67	2c **red,** *orange* (b)	—	*300.00*
a.		Stamp impressed at upper left		—

Wove Paper

20LU17	L67	2c **red** (a) (b)	—	*300.00*
20LU18	L67	2c **red,** *cream* (a) (b)	—	*300.00*
20LU19	L67	2c **red,** *yellow* (a)	—	—
20LU20	L67	2c **red,** *orange* (a) (b)	—	—
20LU21	L67	2c **red,** *blue* (a) (b)	500.00	*400.00*

Design as Type L62

First state of die, showing traces of old address.

1874

Diagonally Laid Paper

20LU22	L62	2c **red,** *amber*		*200.00*
20LU23	L62	2c **red,** *cream*	—	*200.00*

Wove Paper

20LU24	L62	2c **red,** *amber*		*200.00*
20LU25	L62	2c **red,** *yellow*		*200.00*

Second state of die, no traces of address.

1875

Diagonally Laid Paper

20LU26	L62	2c **red,** *amber*		*1,250.*
20LU27	L62	2c **red,** *cream*	—	*375.00*

Wove Paper

20LU28	L62	2c **red,** *amber*		*450.00*

L68

L69

1877

Laid Paper

20LU29	L68	2c **red,** *amber*		*800.00*

Stamp usually impressed in upper left corner of envelope.

1878

Diagonally Laid Paper

20LU30	L69	(1c) **red,** *amber*	—	*650.00*

Wove Paper

20LU31	L69	(1c) **red,** *cream*	—	
20LU32	L69	(1c) **red,** *yellow*	—	

Boyd's Dispatch

L70

Mercury Series-Type IV — L71

Shading omitted in banner. No period after "Dispatch." Short line extends to left from great toe.

1878

Diagonally Laid Paper

20LU33	L70	**black**	40.00	*100.00*
20LU34	L70	**black,** *amber*		*80.00*
20LU35	L70	**black,** *cream*	50.00	*100.00*
20LU36	L70	**red**		*50.00*
20LU37	L70	**red,** *amber*	35.00	*45.00*
20LU38	L70	**red,** *cream*	35.00	*80.00*
20LU39	L70	**red,** *yellow green*		—
20LU40	L70	**red,** *orange*		*350.00*
20LU41	L70	**red,** *fawn*		—

Wove Paper

20LU42	L70	**red**	—	*800.00*

Mercury Series-Type V

Colorless crosshatching lines in frame work

1878

Diagonally Laid Paper

20LU43	L71	**red**	—	*450.00*
20LU44	L71	**red,** *cream*	25.00	*50.00*

Wove Paper

20LU44A	L71	**red**		*1,000.*

BANK NOTICES

IMPORTERS' AND TRADERS' NATIONAL BANK

1874

Thin to Thick White Wove Paper
Incomplete Year Date on Card

20LU45 L62 (2c) **black**		*200.00*

1875-83

Complete Year Date on Card

20LU46 L62 2c **black**		*200.00*
20LU47 L68 2c **black** ('76-'77)		*200.00*
20LU48 L69 (1c) **black** ('78)		*200.00*
20LU49 L70 (1c) **black** ('79)		*200.00*
20LU50 L70 (1c) **black** ('80)	75.00	*200.00*
20LU51 L70 (1c) **black** ('81)		—
20LU52 L71 (1c) **black** ('82)	—	
20LU53 L71 (1c) **black** ('83)	—	

NATIONAL PARK BANK

1880

20LU54 L71 (1c) **black,** 120x65mm —

The Bank Notices are in the class of postal cards. No postmarks or cancellations were used on Bank Notices.

Bradway's Despatch, Millville, N.J.

Operated by Isaac Bradway

L72

1857 **Typo.**

21L1 L72 **gold,** *lilac,* on cover, not tied, with certificate *9,250.*
On cover, not tied, with 3c #11, with certificate *12,000.*

Brady & Co., New York, N.Y.

Operated by Abner S. Brady at 97 Duane St. Successor to Clark & Co.

L73

1857 **Typo.**

22L1 L73 1c **red,** *yellow* *1,000.* *1,000.*
On cover, tied by company handstamp *22,000.*
On cover, tied by "PAID" handstamp *10,000.*

Cancellations: Blue boxed "PAID," blue company oval.
Reprints exist.
No. 22L1 tied on corner by company handstamp is unique. Three covers recorded with stamp tied by "PAID."

Brady & Co.}s Penny Post, Chicago, Ill.

L74

1860(?) **Litho.**

23L1 L74 1c **violet** *650.00* —

The authenticity of this stamp has not been fully established.

Brainard & Co.

Established by Charles H. Brainard in 1844, operating between New York, Albany and Troy, Exchanged mail with Hale & Co. by whom Brainard had been employed.

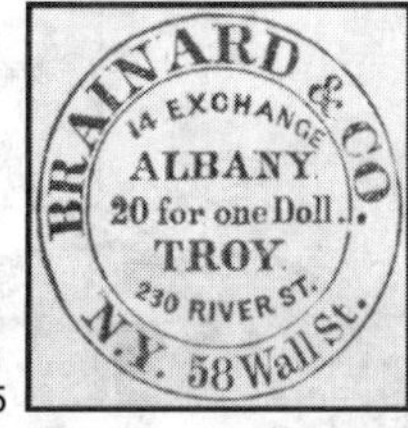

L75

1844 **Typo.**

24L1 L75 **black** *1,000.* *1,250.*
On cover, two stamps tied —
On cover, not tied *2,000.*
On cover, cut to shape, not tied *1,750.*
24L2 L75 **blue** *1,000.* *1,250.*
On cover, not tied *3,250.*

Nos. 21L1-24L2 cut to shape are one half of values quoted.

Brigg's Despatch, Philadelphia, Pa.

Established by George W. Briggs

L76

L77

1847

25L1 L76 (2c) **black,** *yellow buff* *1,000.*
On cover, not tied, with certificate *11,500.*
25L2 L76 (2c) **black,** *blue,* cut to shape *7,500.*

No. 25L2 is unique. It is on cover, manuscript "X" cancel, genuine, but Philatelic Foundation has declined to give an opinion as to whether the stamp originated on the cover.

1848

25L4 L77 (2c) **gold,** *yellow,* glazed *5,500.*
On cover, not tied —
25L5 L77 (2c) **gold,** *black,* glazed *4,000.*
On cover —
25L6 L77 (2c) **gold,** *pink* —

No. 25L4 used and on cover are each unique.

Handstamps formerly illustrated as types L78 and L79 are included in the section "Local Handstamped Covers" at the end of the Local Stamp listings. They were used as postmarks and there is no evidence that any prepaid handstamped envelopes or letter sheets were ever sold.

Broadway Post Office, New York, N.Y.

Started by James C. Harriott in 1848. Sold to Dunham & Lockwood in 1855.

L80

1849(?) **Typo.**

26L1 L80 (1c) **gold,** *black,* glazed *1,000.* *1,250.*
Cut to shape 250.
On cover —
Pair on cover —

1851(?)

26L2 L80 (1c) **black** 250. *400.*
On cover *1,500.*
On cover with 3c #11 *2,750.*
Pair *1,000.*
Pair on part of cover *1,500.*
Block of 4 1,750.

Cancellation: Black oval "Broadway City Express Post-Office 2 Cts."

Bronson & Forbes' City Express Post, Chicago, Ill.

Operated by W.H. Bronson and G.F. Forbes.

L81

1855 **Typo.**

27L1 L81 **black,** *green* *600.* *1,500.*
On cover —
On cover, tied by handstamp, with 3c #11 *10,000.*
27L2 L81 **black,** *lilac* *3,500.*

Cancellation: Black circle "Bronson & Forbes' City Express Post" (2 types).
No. 27L2 is unique.

Brooklyn City Express Post, Brooklyn, N.Y.

According to the foremost students of local stamps, when this concern was organized its main asset was the business of Kidder's City Express Post, of which Isaac C. Snedeker was the proprietor.

L82

L83

1855-64 **Glazed Surface Paper** **Typo.**

28L1 L82 1c **black,** *blue* (shades) 25.00 *80.00*
On cover, tied by handstamp *400.00*
Block of 4 125.00
a. Tete beche pair *80.00*
28L2 L82 1c **black,** *green* 20.00 50.00
On cover, tied by handstamp *350.00*
On cover, tied by handstamp, with 3c #65 *1,250.*
Block of 4 100.00
a. Tete beche pair *125.00*

28L3 L83 2c **black,** *crimson* 60.00 70.00
On cover, tied by handstamp *400.00*
Block of 4 *300.00*
28L4 L83 2c **black,** *pink* 17.50 *100.00*
On cover, tied by handstamp *550.00*
On cover, tied by handstamp, with 3c #65 *1,750.*
Block of 4 100.00
a. Tete beche pair 60.00
28L5 L83 2c **black,** *dark blue* 50.00 *90.00*
On cover, tied by handstamp *500.00*
On cover, tied by handstamp, with 3c #11 *500.00*
Block of 4 *250.00*

No. 28L5 has frame (dividing) lines around design.

28L6 L83 2c **black,** *orange* — —
On cover —
a. Tete beche pair —

Unsurfaced Paper Colored Through

28L7 L83 2c **black,** *pink* *300.00* *750.00*

Cancellations: Black ring, red "PAID."
Reprints exist of Nos. 28L1-28L4, 28L6.

Browne & Co.'s City Post Office, Cincinnati, Ohio

Operated by John W.S. Browne

L84

L85

1852-55 **Litho.**

29L1	L84	1c **black** (Brown & Co.)	175.00	150.00
		On cover		*1,000.*
		On cover with 3c #11		*2,750.*
		Pair	*450.00*	
29L2	L85	2c **black** (Browne & Co.)	175.00	175.00
		On cover, tied by handstamp		*3,500.*
		On cover with 3c #11		*3,000.*
		Pair	*575.*	

Cancellations: Black, blue or red circle "City Post*," red, bright blue or dull blue circle "Browne & Co. City Post Paid."

Browne's Easton Despatch, Easton, Pa.

Established by William J. Browne

L87

L88

1857 **Glazed Surface Paper** **Typeset**

30L1	L87	2c **black,** *red*	—	*5,000.*
30L2	L88	2c **black,** *red*	—	—

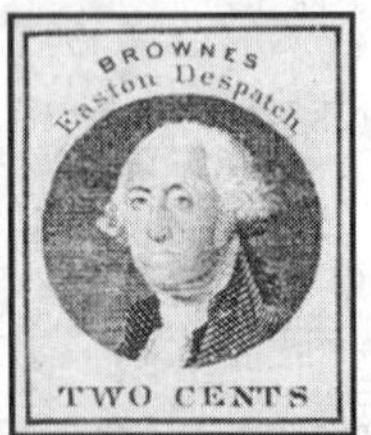

George Washington — L89

Wove Paper **Engr.**

30L3	L89	2c **black**	*700.*	*1,000.*
		Pair	*1,600.*	
		Block of 6	*5,750.*	

The No. 30L3 block of 6 is the only reported block of this stamp. Three pairs are reported.

Cancellation on No. 30L3: Black oval "Browne's Despatch Easton Pa."

Brown's City Post, New York, N.Y.

Established by stamp dealer William P. Brown for philatelic purposes.

L86

1876 **Glazed Surface Paper** **Typo.**

31L1	L86	1c **black,** *bright red*	200.00	*275.00*
		On cover		*800.00*
31L2	L86	1c **black,** *yellow*	200.00	*275.00*
		On cover		*800.00*
31L3	L86	1c **black,** *green*	200.00	*275.00*
		On cover		*800.00*
31L4	L86	1c **black,** *violet*	200.00	*275.00*
		On cover		*800.00*
31L5	L86	1c **black,** *vermilion*	200.00	*275.00*
		On cover		*800.00*

Cancellation: Black circle "Brown's Despatch Paid."

Bury's City Post, New York, N.Y.

L90

L91

1857 **Embossed without color**

32L1	L90	1c *blue*	*8,000.*	

Handstamped

32L2	L91	**black,** *blue*		—

Bush's Brooklyn City Express, Brooklyn, N.Y.

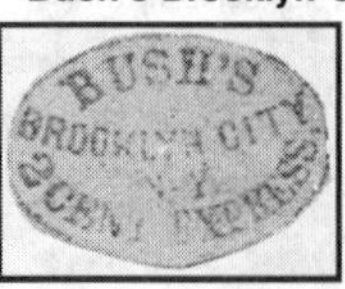

L91a

1848(?) **Cut to shape** **Handstamped**

157L1	L91a	2c **red,** *green,* glazed	*27,500.*	

No. 157L1 is unique. It is uncanceled on a large piece. See Bush handstamp in Local Handstamped Covers section.

California City Letter Express Co., San Francisco, Calif.

Organized by J.W. Hoag, proprietor of the Contra-Costa Express, for local delivery. Known also as the California Letter Express Co.

L92

L93

1862-66 **Typeset**

33L1	L92	10c **red**	—	—
		On cover, not tied, with 10c #68, with certificate		*23,000.*
33L2	L92	10c **blue**		—
		On cover, not tied, with certificate		*16,500.*
33L3	L92	10c **green**	5,500.	
		On cover, uncanceled, with certificate		*18,000.*
33L4	L93	10c **red**	—	—
33L5	L93	10c **blue**		*14,000.*
33L6	L93	10c **green**	*19,000.*	
		On cover, not tied, with certificate		*31,000.*

No side ornaments, "Hoogs & Madison's" in one line

33L7	L93	10c **red**		*1,200.*
		On cover, not tied, with certificate		*19,000.*
33L8	L93	10c **blue**		—
		On cover, not tied, with 10c #68, with certificate		*60,000.*

Nos. 33L1 unused, 33L1 on cover with #68, 33L3 used, 33L3 on cover, 33L6 unused, 33L6 on (patriotic) cover, 33L7 used, 33L7 on cover, 33L8 used and 33L8 on cover with #68 each are unique. The other varieties of Nos. 33L1-33L8 are all rare.

California Penny Post Co.

Established in 1855 by J. P. Goodwin and partners. At first confined its operations to San Francisco, Sacramento, Stockton and Marysville, but branches were soon established at Benicia, Coloma, Nevada, Grass Valley and Mokelumne Hill. Operation was principally that of a city delivery post, as it transported mail to the General Post Office and received mail for local delivery. Most of the business of this post was done by means of prepaid envelopes.

L94

L94a

L95

L95a

1855 **Litho.**

34L1	L94	2c **blue**	*700.*	*750.*
		On cover		*20,000.*
		Block of 4	*3,000.*	
34L1A	L94a	3c **blue**	*850.*	
34L2	L95	5c **blue**	*250.*	*425.*
		On cover		*1,250.*
		Block of 4	750.	
34L3	L95a	10c **blue**	475.	—
		On cover		*3,000.*

Cancellation: Blue circle "Penny Post Co."

Only one example of No. 34L1 on cover is recorded. The stamp is tied by manuscript cancel. Three examples of No. 34L1A are recorded, each uncanceled on cover.

L96

34L4	L96	5c **blue**	*600.*	*1,750.*
		On cover		*3,000.*
		Strip of 3	*3,500.*	

The strip of 3 of No. 34L4 has faults but is unique. Value is for strip in faulty condition.

ENVELOPES

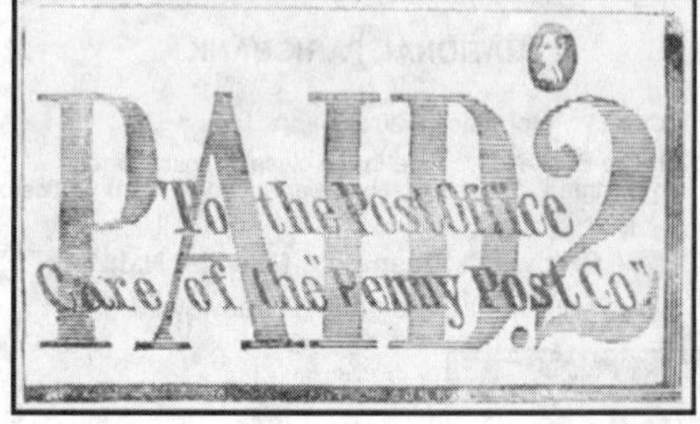

L97

1855-59

34LU1	L97	2c **black,** *white*	200.00	*900.00*
		With 3c #11		*9,000.*
a.		Impressed on 3c US env. #U10	250.00	*1,000.*
34LU2	L97	5c **blue,** *blue*	200.00	*900.00*
34LU3	L97	5c **black,** *buff*	200.00	*900.00*
a.		Impressed on 3c US env. #U10		*1,500.*
34LU4	L97	7c **black,** *buff*	200.00	—

L98

34LU6	L98	7c **vermilion** on 3c US env. #U9	200.00	*1,000.*
34LU7	L98	7c **vermilion** on 3c US env. #U10	225.00	*1,750.*

PENNY-POSTAGE PAID, 5.

L98A

34LU8 L98A 5c **black,** *white* 150. *1,200.*
34LU9 L98A 5c **black,** *buff* 150. *1,200.*
a. Impressed on 3c US env. #U10 *1,250.*
34LU10 L98A 7c **black,** *white* 150. *1,000.*
a. Impressed on 3c US env. #U9 *1,750.*
34LU11 L98A 7c **black,** *buff* 150.00 *1,100.*
a. Impressed on 3c US env. #U10 *1,500.*
34LU11C L98A **black,** *buff,* "Collect Penny Postage" (no denomination) 250. *1,500.*

L98B

34LU11B L98B 7c **black** on 3c US env. #U10 250. *1,400.*
34LU12 L98B 7c **black** on 3c US env. #U9 250. *4,500.*

OCEAN PENNY POSTAGE.
PAID 5.

L98C

34LU13 L98C 5c **black,** *buff* 250. *1,300.*

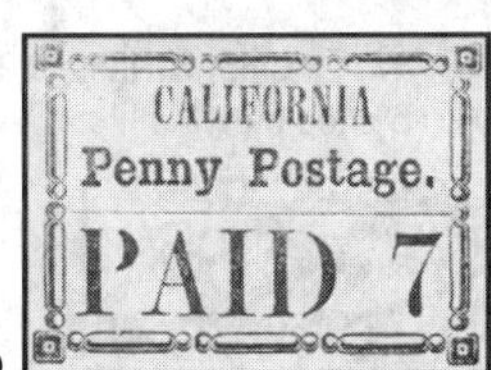

L98D

34LU13A L98D 5c **black,** *buff* —
34LU14 L98D 7c **black,** *buff* 300. *3,000.*
With 3c #11 *5,000.*
34LU15 L98D 7c **black** on 3c US env. #U9 350. *2,500.*

The non-government envelopes of types L97, L98A, L98C and L98D bear either 1c No. 9 or 3c No. 11 adhesives. These adhesives are normally canceled with the government postmark of the town of original mailing. Values are for covers of this kind. The U.S. adhesives are seldom canceled with the Penny Post cancellation. When they are, the cover sells for more.

Carnes' City Letter Express, San Francisco, Calif.

Established by George A. Carnes, former P.O. clerk.

L99

L100

1864 **Typo.**
35L1 L99 (5c) **rose** 175. 300.
On cover, tied *17,500.*
Block of 4 *750.*

Cancellations: Black dots. Blue dots. Blue "Paid." Blue oval "Wm. A. Frey."

Overprinted "X" in Blue

35L2 L99 10c **rose** 200.00

Litho.

35L3 L100 5c **bronze** 125.00
a. Tete beche pair 300.00
35L4 L100 5c **gold** 125.00
a. Tete beche pair 300.00
35L5 L100 5c **silver** 125.00
a. Tete beche pair 300.00
35L6 L100 5c **black** 125.00
a. Tete beche pair 300.00
35L7 L100 5c **blue** 125.00
a. Tete beche pair 300.00
35L8 L100 5c **red** 125.00
a. Tete beche pair 300.00

Printed in panes of 18 (3x6) from three settings of 6 (3x2), with the bottom setting inverted, creating three tete-beche pairs.

G. Carter's Despatch, Philadelphia, Pa.

Operated by George Carter

L101

1849-51
36L1 L101 2c **black** — 100.00
On cover, tied by pen cancel *225.00*
a. Ribbed paper — 140.00
On cover, tied by pen cancel *300.00*

No. 36L1 exists on paper with a blue, red or maroon wash. The origin and status are unclear.

Cancellation: Black circle "Carter's Despatch."

ENVELOPE

L102

36LU1 L102 **blue,** *buff* *1,000.*
Cut to shape *150.*
On cover with 3c No. 10 *3,250.*
On cover with 3c No. 11 *1,750.*

Cheever & Towle, Boston, Mass.

Sold to George H. Barker in 1851

L104

1849(?)
37L1 L104 2c **blue** *275.* *275.*
On cover, tied by handstamp *5,000.*
On cover, not tied *1,500.*
On cover, not tied, cut to shape *500.*

Cancellation: Red oval "Towle's City Despatch Post 7 State Street."

Chicago Penny Post, Chicago, Ill.

L105

1862 **Typo.**
38L1 L105 (1c) **orange brown** 800. 1,250.
On cover, serrated perforations *5,000.*

Reprints exist.

Cancellation: Black circle "Chicago Penny Post A. E. Cooke Sup't."

Cincinnati City Delivery, Cincinnati, Ohio

Operated by J. Staley, who also conducted the St. Louis City Delivery Co. He established the Cincinnati post in January, 1883. The government suppressed both posts after a few weeks. Of the 25,000 Cincinnati City Delivery stamps printed, about 5,000 were sold for postal use. The remainders, both canceled and uncanceled, were sold to collectors.

L106

1883 **Typo.** ***Perf. 11***
39L1 L106 (1c) **carmine** 2.50 *12.50*
a. Imperf., pair — —

Cancellation: Purple target.

City Despatch Post, New York, N.Y.

The City Despatch Post was started Feb. 1, 1842, by Alexander M. Greig and Henry T. Windsor. Greig's Post extended to 23rd St. Its operations were explained in a circular which throws light on the operations of all Local Posts:

New York City Despatch Post, Principal Office, 46 William Street.

"The necessity of a medium of communication by letter from one part of the city to another being universally admitted, and the Penny Post, lately existing having been relinquished, the opportunity has been embraced to reorganize it under an entirely new proprietory and management, and upon a much more comprehensive basis, by which Despatch, Punctuality and Security-those essential elements of success-may at once be attained, and the inconvenience now experienced be entirely removed."

"*** Branch Offices-Letter boxes are placed throughout every part of the city in conspicuous places; and all letters deposited therein not exceeding two ounces in weight, will be punctually delivered three times a day *** at three cents each."

"*** Post-Paid Letters.-Letters which the writers desire to send free, must have a free stamp affixed to them. An ornamental stamp has been prepared for this purpose *** 36 cents per dozen or 2 dolls. 50c per hundred. ***"

"No money must be put in boxes. All letters intended to be sent forward to the General Post Office for the inland mails must have a free stamp affixed to them."

"Unpaid Letters.-Letters not having a free stamp will be charged three cents, payable by the party to whom they are addressed, on delivery."

"Registry and Despatch.-A Registry will be kept for letters which it may be wished to place under special charge. Free stamps must be affixed for such letters for the ordinary postage, and three cents additional be paid (or an additional fee stamp be affixed), for the Registration."

NOTE: The word "Free," as used in this circular, should be read as "Prepaid." Likewise, the octagonal "FREE" cancellation should be taken to mean "Prepaid" (that is, "Free" of further charge).

The City Despatch Post was purchased by the United States Government and ceased to operate as a private carrier on August 15, 1842. It was replaced by the "United States City Despatch Post" which began operation on August 16, 1842, as a Government carrier.

No. 40L1 was issued by Alexander M. Greig; No. 40L2 and possibly No. 40L3 by Abraham Mead; Nos. 40L4-40L8 probably by Charles Cole.

L106a

Cancellation

Plate of 42 (6x7) subjects

This was the first adhesive stamp used in the United States. This stamp was also used as a carrier stamp. See No. 6LB1.

Engraved by Rawdon, Wright & Hatch

1842, Feb. 1
40L1 L106a 3c **black,** *grayish* 375. 275.
On cover, tied by handstamp *1,500.*
First day cover *25,000.*
Pair 850.
Block of 4 1,900.
Sheet of 42 *27,500.*

Cancellations: Red framed "FREE" (see illustration above), red circle "City Despatch Post" (2 types).

Die reprints of No. 40L1 were made in 1892 on grayish white, orange, red and green surface-colored papers. It is believed that only four sets were made. Value, each reprint $500.

1847

Glazed Surface Paper

40L2 L106a 2c **black,** *green* *200.00* 150.00
On cover, tied by handstamp *600.00*
On cover, not tied *400.00*
40L3 L106a 2c **black,** *pink* *2,250..*
On cover, not tied, with certificate *9,000.*

Cancellations: Red framed "FREE," black framed "FREE," red circle "City Despatch Post."

L107

Similar to L106a with "CC" at sides.

1847-50

40L4 L107 2c **black,** *green* 350.00 200.00
On cover, tied by handstamp 1,500.
a. "C" at right inverted —
b. "C" at left sideways —
On cover, tied by handstamp —
c. "C" at right only —

Some students think No. 40L4c may have just a badly worn sideways "C" at left.

40L5 L107 2c **black,** *grayish* 500.00
On cover, tied by handstamp 850.00
a. "C" at right inverted —
b. "C" at left sideways —
c. "C" in ms. between "Two" and "Cents" *1,000.*
d. "C" at left sideways plus "C" in ms. between "Two" and "Cents" *1,900.*
On cover, tied by handstamp *4,000.*

40L6 L107 2c **black,** *vermilion* 450.00 300.00
On cover, tied by handstamp *1,000.*
a. "C" at right inverted —
b. "C" at left sideways *4,500.*
On cover, tied by handstamp 4,000.
On cover, not tied 2,750.

40L8 L107 2c **black,** *yellowish buff* — —
a. "C" at right inverted —
b. "C" at left sideways *4,500.*

An uncanceled copy of No. 40L8 exists on cover.

Cancellations: Red framed "FREE," black framed "FREE," black "PAID," red "PAID," red circle company, black grid of 4 short parallel bars.

Each of the No. 40L6b covers are unique as listed.

City Dispatch, New York, N.Y.

L107a

1846 **Typo.**

160L1 L107a 2c **red** *3,000.* *2,750.*
On cover —
Vertical pair *16,500.*

The unique vertical pair is the only reported multiple of No. 160L1.

Cancellation: Red "PAID."

City Dispatch, Philadelphia, Pa.

Justice — L108

1860 **Thick to Thin Wove Paper** **Litho.**

41L1 L108 1c **black** 7.50 50.00
On cover, tied by handstamp *500.00*
Block of 4 55.00

Cancellations: Black circle "Penny Post Philada.," black circled grid of X's.

City Dispatch, St. Louis, Mo.

L109

Initials in black ms.

1851 **Litho.**

42L1 L109 2c **black,** *blue* *22,000.*

No. 42L1 used is unique. A second example, on cover, is recorded.

City Dispatch Post Office, New Orleans, La.

Stamps sold at 5c each, or 30 for $1.

L110

1847 **Glazed Surface Paper** **Typeset**

43L1 L110 (5c) **black,** *green* *6,000.*
On cover —
43L2 L110 (5c) **black,** *pink* *6,000.*
On cover, not canceled —

City Express Post, Philadelphia, Pa.

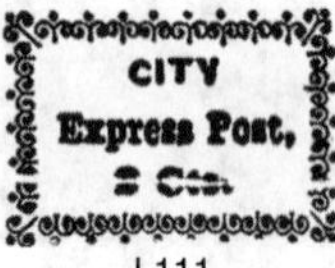

L111

L112

184-(?) **Typeset**

44L1 L111 2c **black,** on cover, uncanceled, with certificate *11,000.*
44L2 L112 (2c) **black,** *pink* *10,000.*
On cover, uncanceled, with certificate *20,000.*
44L3 L112 (2c) **red,** *yellow,* on cover, uncanceled *30,000.*

One example recorded of Nos. 44L1 and 44L3. Six No. 44L2 recorded, five of these uncanceled on covers.

See illustration L8.

City Letter Express Mail, Newark, N.J.

Began business under the management of Augustus Peck at a time when there was no free city delivery in Newark.

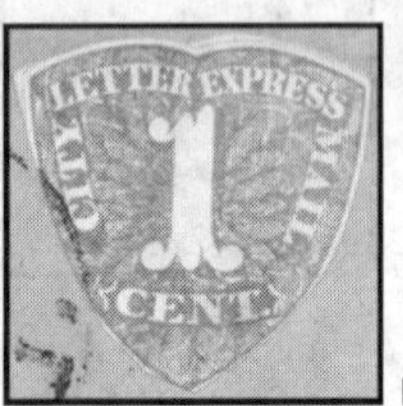

L113

1856 **Litho.**

45L1 L113 1c **red** *275.00* *450.00*
Cut to shape 75.00
On cover —
On cover, cut to shape, tied by handstamp, with 3c #11 *17,000.*
45L2 L113 2c **red,** on cover, cut to shape, uncanceled, with certificate *11,000.*

On No. 45L2, the inscription reads "City Letter/Express/City Delivery" in three lines across the top. The example on cover is unique.

See illustration L206.

City Mail Co., New York, N.Y.

There is evidence that Overton & Co. owned this post.

L114

1845

46L1 L114 (2c) **black,** *grayish* *1,500.* *1,500.*
On cover, not tied, with certificate *8,000.*

Cancellation: Red "PAID."

City One Cent Dispatch, Baltimore, Md.

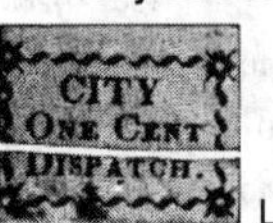

L115

1851

47L1 L115 1c **black,** *pink* (on cover) —

Clark & Co., New York, N.Y.

(See Brady & Co.)

L116

1857 **Typo.**

48L1 L116 1c **red,** *yellow* 600. *900.*
On cover *2,500.*

Cancellation: Blue boxed "PAID."

Clark & Hall, St. Louis, Mo.

Established by William J. Clark and Charles F. Hall.

L117

Several varieties

1851 **Typeset**

49L1 L117 1c **black,** *pink,* on cover, uncanceled, with certificate 19,000.

Clarke's Circular Express, New York, N.Y.

Established by Marion M. Clarke

George Washington — L118

Impression handstamped through inked ribbon. Cut squares from envelopes or wrappers.

1865-68(?)

50LU1 L118 **blue,** wove paper *5,750.*
a. Diagonally laid paper *4,500.*
50LU2 L118 **black,** diag. laid paper *5,750.*

No. 50LU1 unused is unique.

Cancellation: Blue dated company circle.

Clinton's Penny Post, Philadelphia, Pa.

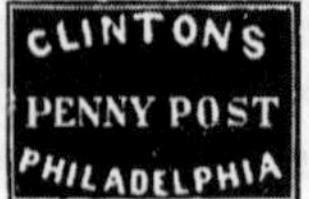

L118a

Typo.

161L1 L188a (1c) **black** *22,500.*

Cook's Dispatch, Baltimore, Md.

Established by Isaac Cook

L119

1853

51L1 L119 (1c) **green,** *white* *4,000.* *3,000.*
Cut to shape *1,500.*
On cover —

Cancellation: Red straight-line "I cook."

Cornwell's Madison Square Post Office, New York, N.Y.

Established by Daniel H. Cornwell. Sold to H.W. Bentley.

L120

1856 **Typo.**

52L1 L120 (1c) **red,** *blue* 600. —
52L2 L120 (1c) **red** 200. *500.*
On cover, tied by handstamp *10,000.*
Pair 325.

Cancellation: Black oval "Cornwall's Madison Square Post Office." Covers also bear black boxed "Paid Swarts."

Cressman & Co.'s Penny Post, Philadelphia, Pa.

L121

1856

Glazed Surface Paper

53L1 L121 (1c) **gold,** *black* 250. 250.
Pair *1,200.*
53L2 L121 (1c) **gold,** *lilac,* on cover, acid tied *25,000.*

The vertical pair of No. 53L1 is unique. No. 53L2 also is unique.

Cancellation: Acid. (See D.O. Blood & Co. Nos. 15L13-15L16.)

Crosby's City Post, New York, N.Y.

Established by Oliver H. Crosby. Stamps printed by J.W. Scott & Co.

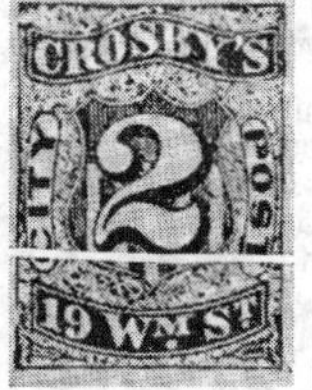

L123

1870 **Typo.**

Printed in sheets 25 (5x5), imprint at left.

54L1 L123 2c **carmine** (shades) 2.00 50.00
On cover *400.00*
Sheet of 25 75.00

Cancellation: Black oval "Crosby's City Post."

Cummings' City Post, New York, N.Y.

Established by A. H. Cummings.

L124

1844 **Glazed Surface Paper** **Typo.**

55L1 L124 2c **black,** *rose* *1,000.*
On cover, tied, with certificate *5,750.*
55L2 L124 2c **black,** *green* *650.*
On cover *2,500.*
55L3 L124 2c **black,** *yellow* *750.*
On cover, tied by handstamp *2,000.*
On cover, not tied, with certificate *1,250.*

Cancellations: Red boxed "FREE," red boxed "PAID AHC," black cork (3 types).

L125

55L4 L125 2c **black,** *green* *750.00* *750.00*
55L5 L125 2c **black,** *olive* *750.00* *750.00*

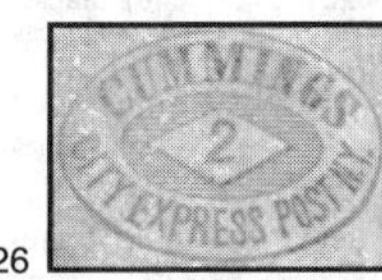

L126

55L7 L126 2c **black,** *vermilion* *8,250.*
On cover, uncanceled, with certificate *22,000.*

As L124, but "Cummings" erased on cliche

55L8 L124 2c **black,** *vermilion* —

Nos. 55L7 on cover and 55L8 each are unique.

Cutting's Despatch Post, Buffalo, N.Y.

Established by Thomas S. Cutting

L127

Cut to shape

1847

Glazed Surface Paper

56L1 L127 2c **black,** *vermilion,* on cover *22,000.*

No. 56L1 is unique. It is cut to shape, uncanceled, on cover, with certificate. There is a second possible example, not authenticated, uncanceled off cover.

Davis's Penny Post, Baltimore, Md.

Established by William D. Davis and brother.

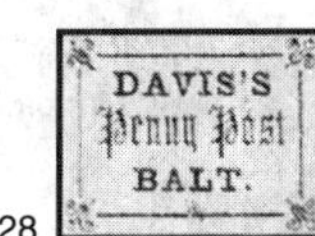

L128

1856 **Typeset**

Several varieties

57L1 L128 (1c) **black,** *lilac* *2,750.*
On cover, tied by handstamp *11,000.*
a. "Pennq," pos. 2 *8,250.* *8,250.*

Cancellation: Red company circle.

Deming's Penny Post, Frankford, Pa.

Established by Sidney Deming

L129

1854 **Litho.**

58L1 L129 (1c) **black,** *grayish* *5,750.*
On cover, with 3c #11 *18,000.*

Douglas' City Despatch, New York, N.Y.

Established by George H. Douglas

L130

L131

Printed in sheets of 25

1879 **Typo.** ***Perf. 11***

59L1 L130 (1c) **pink** 10.00 *15.00*
On cover *300.00*
a. Imperf. 30.00 —
59L2 L130 (2c) **blue** 10.00 *15.00*
On cover, tied by handstamp *500.00*
a. Imperf. 50.00 —
b. Printed on both sides —

Printed in sheets of 50 (10x5).

Perf. 11, 12 & Compound

59L3 L131 1c **vermilion** 15.00 *35.00*
On cover *325.00*
a. Imperf. 1.00 —
59L4 L131 1c **orange** 25.00 *50.00*
On cover, tied by handstamp *600.00*
59L5 L131 1c **blue** 30.00 *50.00*
On cover *300.00*
a. Imperf. 1.00 —
59L6 L131 1c **slate blue** 20.00 25.00
a. Imperf. 7.50 —

Cancellations on Nos. 59L1-59L6: Ornate purple design, purple circular design composed of bars and wedges.

Imperforates are believed to be remainders sold by the printer.

Dupuy & Schenck, New York, N.Y.

Established by Henry J. Dupuy and Jacob H. Schenck, formerly carriers for City Despatch Post and U. S. City Despatch Post.

Beehive — L132

1846-48 **Engr.**

60L1 L132 (1c) **black,** glazed paper 175. *300.*
On cover, tied by handstamp *1,750.*
On cover, tied by ms. *1,250.*
60L2 L132 (1c) **black,** *gray* 175. *300.*
On cover, tied by handstamp *1,600.*

Cancellation: Red "PAID."

Eagle City Post, Philadelphia, Pa.

Established by W. Stait, an employee of Adams' Express Co.

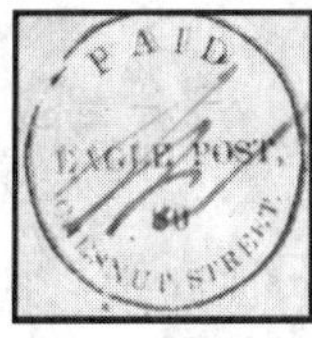

L133

Black manuscript "WS" on used examples

1847 **Pelure Paper** **Typeset**

61L1 L133 (2c) **black,** *grayish* *14,000.* *10,000.*
Cut to shape, on cover —

No. 61L1 unused is unique. Value reflects a 1997 auction sale.

L134

L135

Two types: 39 and 46 points around circle

1846 **Litho.**

61L2 L134 (2c) **black** 125.00 *250.00*
On cover, tied by handstamp *1,500.*
On cover, not tied *1,000.*
Block of 4 600.00
a. Tete beche pair 500.00
Block of 18, containing 4 tete beche pairs *3,300.*

Paper varies in thickness.
Five types identified of Nos. 61L3-61L4.

1850

61L3 L135 (1c) **red,** *bluish* 225.00 225.00
On cover, not tied, with certificate *2,250.*
61L4 L135 (1c) **blue,** *bluish* 175.00 250.00

On cover, tied by handstamp 6,500.
On cover, not tied 400.00
Block of 4 1,150.

Cancellations on Nos. 61L2-61L4: Red "PAID" in large box, red circular "Stait's at Adams Express."

East River Post Office, New York, N. Y.

Established by Jacob D. Clark and Henry Wilson in 1850, and sold to Sigmund Adler in 1852.

L136

1852 **Typo.**
62L1 L136 (1c) **black,** *rose* (on cover) —

L137 L138

1852-54 **Litho.**
62L3 L137 (1c) **black,** *green,* glazed *1,000.* —

1855
62L4 L138 (1c) **black,** *green,* glazed 250.00 250.00
On cover *800.00*
On cover, not tied *400.00*
Vertical pair *2,500.*

The unique No. 62L4 pair is the only recorded multiple of any of the East River Post Office stamps.

Eighth Avenue Post Office, New York, N.Y.

L139

1852 **Typo.**
63L1 L139 **red,** on cover *19,000.*

One example known, uncanceled on cover.

Empire City Dispatch, New York, N.Y.

Established by J. Bevan & Son and almost immediately suppressed by the Government.

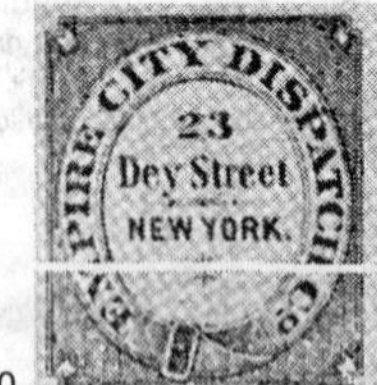

L140

1881 **Typo.** **Laid Paper** ***Perf. 12***
64L1 L140 **black,** *green* 1.50
Block of 4 7.50
a. Imperf. —
b. Horiz. pair, imperf. btwn. 85.00
c. Vert. pair, imperf. btwn. 85.00

Essex Letter Express, New York, N.Y.

L141

1856 **Glazed Surface Paper** **Typo.**
65L1 L141 2c **black,** *red* *1,250.*

Though uncanceled examples exist affixed to covers, some authorities doubt that No. 65L1 was placed in use.

Faunce's Penny Post, Atlantic City, N.J.

Established in 1884 by Ancil Faunce to provide local delivery of letters to and from the post office. Discontinued in 1887.

L141a

1885 **Die cut**
152L1 L141a (1c) **black,** *red* 225. 350.
On cover *1,500.*

Jabez Fearey & Co.'s Mustang Express, Newark, N.J.

Established by Jabez Fearey, Local Agent of the Pacific & Atlantic Telegraph Co.

L142

1870 **Glazed Surface Paper** **Typeset**
66L1 L142 **black,** *red* *225.00*

Some authorities consider this item to be an express company label rather than a stamp.

Fiske & Rice

Authorities consider items of this design to be express company labels rather than stamps.

Floyd's Penny Post, Chicago, Ill.

Established by John R. Floyd early in 1860, operated by him until June 20, 1861, then continued by Charles W. Mappa.

John R. Floyd — L144

1860 **Typo.**
68L1 L144 (1c) **blue** (shades) — 125.
On cover, tied by handstamp *1,000.*
On cover with 3c #26 —
On cover with 3c #65 *1,500.*
Pair 275.
Strip of 4 *1,250.*
68L2 L144 (1c) **brown** *500.* 850.
On cover *4,250.*
68L3 L144 (1c) **green** *4,500.* *2,750.*
On cover —
On 3c pink entire —

Cancellations: Black circle "Floyd's Penny Post Chicago," black circle "Floyd's Penny Post" and sunburst, black or blue oval "Floyd's Penny Post Chicago."

Franklin City Despatch Post, N.Y.

(See Bouton's Manhattan Express.)

Frazer & Co., Cincinnati, Ohio.

Established by Hiram Frazer. Stamps used while he was a Cincinnati letter carrier. Stamps of designs L146 and L147 were carrier stamps when used on cover betweeen Feb, 3, 1848 and June 30, 1849.

L145

Cut to shape

1845
Glazed Surface Paper
69L1 L145 2c **black,** *green* —
On cover —

L146

L147

1845-51 **Wove Paper** **Litho.**
69L2 L146 2c **black,** *pink* — *3,500.*
On cover, ms. tied *5,500.*
69L3 L146 2c **black,** *green* *2,500.* *2,750.*
On 1847 cover, tied by handstamp *11,000.*
On cover, not tied *3,000.*
69L4 L146 2c **black,** *yellow* *2,500.* *2,500.*
69L5 L146 2c **black,** *grayish* *2,500.* *2,500.*

Two stamps of type L146 show manual ms. erasure of "& Co."

1848-51
69L6 L147 2c **black,** *rose* *2,750.*
On 1848 cover, not tied, with certificate *6,500.*
69L7 L147 2c **black,** *blue* (shades) *3,500.* —
69L8 L147 2c **black,** *yellow* *2,750.*
On 1848 part-printed notice *7,500.*

Hiram Frazer was a government letter carrier until June 5, 1849. Therefore, any usage before that date is a government-carrier usage, not a local-post usage.

Freeman & Co.'s Express, New York, N.Y.

L147a

1855 (?) **Litho.**
164L1 L147a (25c) **blue** *3,500.*

Friend's Boarding School, Barnesville, Ohio.

(Barclay W. Stratton, Supt.)

On Nov. 6, 1877 the school committee decided to charge the students one cent for each letter carried to or from the post office, one and a half miles away. Adhesive labels were prepared and sold for one cent each. Their sale and use continued until 1884.

L147b — Type I

F. B. S.
L147b — Type II

L147b — Type III

Three main types and sizes of frame

1877 **Typo.**
151L1 L147b (1c) **black** *175.00* —
On cover, uncanceled, affixed to backflap *400.00*
On cover, tied by handstamp, with 3c #158 *2,400.*
On cover, tied by handstamp, with 2c #210 *2,750.*

No. 151L1 was usually affixed to the back of the envelope and left uncanceled.

Gahagan & Howe City Express, San Francisco, Calif.

Established by Dennis Gahagan and C. E. B. Howe, as successors to John C. Robinson, proprietor of the San Francisco Letter Express. Sold in 1865 to William E. Loomis, who later purchased the G. A. Carnes business. Loomis used the adhesive stamps and handstamps of these posts, changing the Carnes stamp by erasing his name.

L148

L149

1849-70 **Typeset**

70L1	L148	5c	**light blue**	400.	*800.*
70L2	L149	(5c)	**blue**	150.	400.
a.			Tete beche pair	*450.*	
			Sheet of 20, with 4 tete beche pairs	—	

Sheets of No. 70L2 contain five vertical rows of 4, the first two rows being reversed against the others, making horizontal tete beche pairs with wide margins between. The pairs were not evenly locked up in the form.

L150

70L3	L150	(5c)	**black**	40.00	45.00
			Pair		100.00
			Strip of 3		175.00

Overprinted "X" in Blue

70L4	L150	10c	**black**	*750.00*	

Cancellations: Blue or black oval "Gahagan & Howe," blue or black oval "San Francisco Letter Express" and horseman (Robinson), blue or black oval "PAID" (Loomis).

Glen Haven Daily Mail, Glen Haven, N.Y.

Glen Haven was located at the head of Skaneateles Lake, Cayuga County, N.Y., until 1910 when the City of Syracuse, having purchased the land for reservoir purposes, razed all the buildings.

Glen Haven, by 1848, had become a famous Water Cure resort, with many sanitariums conducted there. The hamlet had a large summer colony interested in dress reform under the leadership of Amelia Jenks Bloomer; also antislavery, and other reform movements.

A local post was established by the hotel and sanitarium managements for their guests' convenience to deliver mail to the U.S. post offices at Homer or Scott, N.Y. The local stamps were occasionally pen canceled. They are known tied to cover with the Homer or Scott town postmark when the local stamp was placed adjacent to the government stamp and received the cancellation accidentally. The local stamps are only known used in conjunction with government stamps.

L151

L152

1854-58 **Typeset**

Several varieties of each

71L1	L151	1c	**black,** *dark green*	1,000.	
a.			"Gien" instead of "Glen"	*3,500.*	
			On cover, uncanceled, with 3c #26, with certificate		*5,500.*

No. 71L1a unused (actually uncanceled on piece) and on cover with #26 each are unique.

Glazed Surface Paper

71L2	L152	1c	**black,** *green*	*500.*	*500.*
			On cover		*2,000.*

Links at corners — L153

Varying ornaments at corners — L153a

Several varieties of each

Glazed Surface Paper

71L3	L153	1c	**black,** *green*	200.	*225.*
			On cover		*2,000.*
			On cover, tied by handstamp, with 3c #11		*1,750.*
			On cover, not tied, with 3c #11		*500.00*
			Pair	700.	
71L4	L153a	1c	**black,** *green*	300.	350.
			On cover		*1,000.*
			On 3c entire #U9, tied by handstamp		*1,000.*
			"Block" of 3	*900.00*	

The strip of 3 of No. 71L4 is the only known multiple of any Glen Haven stamp. It has faults and is valued thus.

Gordon's City Express, New York, N. Y.

Established by Samuel B. Gordon

L154

1848-52 **Typo.** **Surface Colored Paper**

72L1	L154	2c	**black,** *vermilion*		*7,000.*
			On cover, uncanceled, with certificate		*15,000.*
72L2	L154	2c	**black,** *green*	150.	*175.*
			On cover		650.

Glazed Surface Paper

72L3	L154	2c	**black,** *green*	125.	*200.*
			On cover		650.

Cancellation: Small black or red "PAID."

Grafflin's Baltimore Despatch, Baltimore, Md.

Established by Joseph Grafflin; operated from Apr. 1, 1855, until June 30, 1863

L155

Printed in sheets of 49

1856 **Litho.**

73L1	L155	1c	**black**	200.	*350.*
			On cover, tied by handstamp		*4,000.*
			On cover, tied by handstamp, with 3c #11		*3,000.*
			Block of 4	*1,050.*	

Originals show traces of a fine horizontal line through tops of most of the letters in "BALTIMORE."

Guy's City Despatch, Philadelphia, Pa.

Established by F. A. Guy, who employed 8 carriers.

L156

Sheets of 25 (5x5)

1879 **Typo.** ***Perf. 11, 12, 12½***

74L1	L156	(1c)	**pink**	30.00	35.00
			On cover, tied by handstamp		800.00
			Block of 4	150.00	
a.			Imperf., pair	—	
74L2	L156	(1c)	**blue**	45.00	60.00
			On cover, tied by handstamp		1,500.
			Block of 4	225.00	
a.			Imperf., pair	—	
b.		(1c)	**Ultramarine**	*75.00*	*100.00*

Cancellation: Purple company oval.

Guy's City Despatch was in operation from April to June, 1879. When Guy's was suppressed, the remainders were sold to a New York stamp dealer.

Hackney & Bolte Penny Post, Atlantic City, N.J.

Established in 1886 by Evan Hackney and Charles Bolte to provide delivery of mail to and from the post office. Discontinued in 1887.

L156a

Die cut

153L1	L156a	(1c)	**black,** *red*	250.	375.
			On cover		*1,500.*
			On cover, tied by handstamp, with 2c #210		*5,000.*

Hale & Co.

Established by James W. Hale at New York, N.Y., to carry mail to points in New England, New York State, Philadelphia and Baltimore. Stamps sold at 6 cents each or "20 for $1.00."

L157

L158

Printed in sheets of 20 (5x4)

1844 **Wove Paper (several thicknesses)** **Typo.**

75L1	L157	(6c)	**light blue** (shades)	65.00	40.00
			Cut to shape		17.50
			On cover, tied by handstamp		500.00
			Cut to shape on cover, tied by handstamp		200.00
			Strip of 3 on cover, tied by handstamp		*7,000.*
			Strip of 3 on cover, not tied		*2,750.*
75L2	L157	(6c)	**red,** *bluish*	*300.00*	*300.00*
			Cut to shape		75.00
			On cover, tied by handstamp		*2,500.*
			On cover, not tied		*500.00*
			Cut to shape on cover, tied by handstamp		*1,000.*
			Pair on cover		—
			Ms. "23 State," cut to shape		*1,900.*
			On cover		*4,000.*

Two covers recorded showing the manuscript change of address.

Same Handstamped in Black or Red, "City Despatch Office, 23 State St."

75L3	L157	(6c)	**red,** *bluish* (Bk), cut to shape	*2,000.*	
			Pair, partly cut to shape	*44,000.*	
75L4	L157	(6c)	**blue** (R), cut to shape	*2,000.*	

No. 75L3 single and pair each are unique.

No. 75L3 and 75L4 represent the first handstamped overprints in philately.

Same as Type L157 but street address omitted

75L5	L158	(6c)	**blue** (shades)	40.00	20.00
			Cut to shape		5.00
			On cover, tied by handstamp		450.00
			Cut to shape on cover, tied by handstamp		200.00
			Pair on cover		700.00
			Strip of 3 on cover, not tied		—
			Pair	*500.00*	
			Block of 9	—	
			Block of 15	*9,500.*	
			Sheet of 20 (5x4)	*17,000.*	
			Ms. "23 State St.," on cover		*2,500.*

Cancellations on Nos. 75L1-75L5: Large red "PAID," red, black or blue oval "Hale & Co." (several types and cities), small red ornamental framed box (several types), red negative monogram "WE," magenta ms. "NB" (New Bedford).

The No. 75L5 sheet of 20 is unique.

Hall & Mills' Despatch Post, New York, N.Y.

Established by Gustavus A. Mills and A. C. Hall.

L159

Several Varieties

1847		Glazed Surface Paper		Typeset
76L1	L159 (2c)	**black,** *green*	300.	300.
		On cover		750.
		On cover with 5c #1		2,500.

T.A. Hampton City Despatch, Philadelphia, Pa.

L159a

L159b

Several Varieties of L159a

1847		Cut to shape		Typeset
77L1	L159a (2c)	**black**	1,500.	
		On cover, tied by handstamp		14,000.
		On cover, uncanceled, with certificate		5,000.
77L2	L159b	**black,** on cover		13,000.

Only one cover known with No. 77L1 tied by handstamp. Five or six covers are known with stamp uncanceled.

Two covers known with No. 77L2, each with stamp canceled, not tied. May 23 cover with certificate is valued above. Second cover is undated Valentine cover.

A handstamp similar to type L159b with denomination "2cts" or "3c" instead of "PAID." in center has been used as a postmark.

Hanford's Pony Express, New York, N.Y.

Established by John W. Hanford.

L160

1845		Glazed Surface Paper		Typo.
78L1	L160 2c	**black,** *orange yellow* (shades)	300.	400.
		Cut to shape		60.
		On cover, tied by handstamp		1,250.

Cancellation: Small red "PAID."

The handstamp in black or red formerly listed as Nos. 78LU1-78LU6 is illustrated in the Local Handstamped Covers section. It was used as a postmark and there is no evidence that any prepaid handstamped envelopes or lettersheets were ever sold.

George S. Harris City Despatch Post, Philadelphia, Pa.

L160a

L160b

1847 (?)				Typeset
79L1	L160a (2c)	**black,** on cover		—
79L2	L160b	**black,** on cover		30,000.

One example each known of Nos. 79L1-79L2, each uncanceled on cover, No. 79L2 with certificate.

Hartford, Conn. Mail Route

L161

Plate of 12 (6x2) varieties

1844		Glazed Surface Paper		Engr.
80L1	L161 (5c)	**black,** *yellow*	1,250.	2,000.
		On cover		—
		Pair		5,000.
		Pair on cover, not canceled		32,500.
80L3	L161	**black,** *pink*		3,500.

Chemically affected copies of No. 80L1 appear as buff, and of No. 80L3 as salmon.

Cancellations are usually initials or words ("S," "W," "South," etc.) in black ms. This may indicate destination or routing.

Hill's Post, Boston, Mass.

Established by Oliver B. Hill

L162

1849				Typo.
81L1	L162 1c	**black,** *rose,* on cover, tied by handstamp		7,500.
		On cover, canceled but not tied, with certificate		6,500.

Only one No. 81L1 tied to cover recorded. Six covers recorded bearing No. 80L1 not tied, all but one of those also uncanceled.

A. M. Hinkley's Express Co., New York, N.Y.

Organized by Abraham M. Hinkley, Hiram Dixon and Hiram M. Dixon, in 1855, and business transferred to the Metropolitan Errand & Carrier Express Co. in same year.

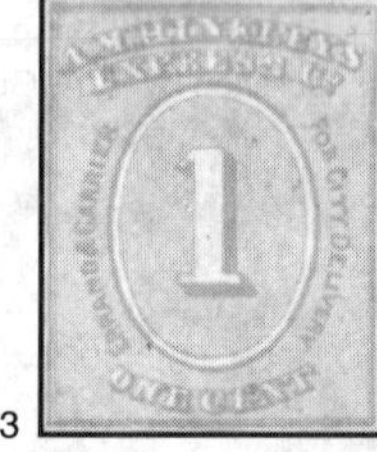

L163

Sheets of 64 (8x8)

1855				Litho.
82L1	L163 1c	**red,** *bluish*	500.00	
		Block of 4	—	
a.		Tete-beche pair	—	

It is doubtful that No. 82L1 was ever placed in use.

Only one example of No. 82L1a is recorded. It is contained in a block of 16 of No. 82L1.

Reprints exist on white paper somewhat thicker than the originals.

Homan's Empire Express, New York, N.Y.

Established by Richard S. Homan

L164

Several varieties

1852				Typeset
83L1	L164	**black,** *yellow*	—	—
a.		"1" for "I" in "PAID"		8,250.

No. 83L1a is unique. It is affixed to a cover front, uncanceled, with certificate.

Hopedale Penny Post, Milford, Mass.

Hopedale was a large farm community southwest of Milford, Mass. The community meeting of Feb. 2, 1849, voted to arrange for regular transportation of mail to the nearest post office, which was at Milford, a mile and a half distant, at a charge of 1c a letter. A complete history of this community may be found in "The Hopedale Community," published in 1897.

Rayed asterisks in corners
L165

Plain asterisks in corners
L166

Several varieties of Types L165-L166

1849		Glazed Surface Paper		Typeset
84L1	L165 (1c)	**black,** *pink*	800.00	800.00
		On cover with 3c #11, handstamp tied		3,750.
		On cover with 3c #11, not canceled		1,250.
84L2	L166 (1c)	**black,** *pink*	1,000.	1,000.

Types L165 and L166 probably were printed together in a single small plate.

L167

		Wove Paper		Typo.
84L3	L167 (1c)	**black,** *yellow*	—	2,400.
		Cut to shape	900.	
		On cover		—
84L4	L167 (1c)	**black,** *pink*	600.	600.
		Pair	4,500.	

The No. 84L4 pair is unique, defective at top. It is the only recorded multiple of any Hopedale Penny Post issue.

J. A. Howell's City Despatch, Philadelphia, Pa.

L167a

184?				Typo.
165L1	L167a	**black**		—

Hoyt's Letter Express, Rochester, N.Y.

David Hoyt, agent at Rochester for the express company of Livingston, Wells & Pomeroy, operated a letter and package express by boats on the Genesee Canal between Dansville, N.Y., and Rochester, where connection was also made with Pomeroy's Letter Express.

L168

Several varieties

1844		Glazed Surface Paper		Typeset
85L1	L168 (5c)	**black,** *vermilion*	4,000.	—
a.		"Lettcr" instead of "Letter"		—
		Pair, #85L1, 85L1a, on cover front		—

Humboldt Express, Nevada

A branch of Langton's Pioneer Express, connecting with the main line of Pioneer Express at Carson City, Nevada, and making tri-weekly trips to adjacent points.

L169

1863 **Litho.**

86L1	L169 25c **brown**		*1,750.*	*1,250.*
	Pair			*2,750.*
	On cover (U.S. Envelopes Nos. U34 or U35)			*40,000.*
	On cover with 3c #65			—

Cancellations: Blue oval "Langton's Pioneer Express Unionville." Red "Langton & Co."

Hussey's Post, New York, N.Y.

Established by George Hussey.
Reprints available for postage are so described.

L170

L171

1854 **Litho.**

87L1	L170 (1c) **blue**		*500.*
	On cover, tied by handstamp		*2,750.*
	On cover, with U.S. 3c (#11)		—

1856

87L2	L171 (1c) **black**	*300.*	*200.*
	On cover, tied by handstamp		*1,200.*
87L3	L171 (1c) **red**		*200.*
	On cover, tied by handstamp		*750.*

Cancellation on Nos. 87L1-87L3: Black "FREE."

L172

L173

1858

87L4	L172 1c **brown red**	45.	*125.*
	On cover, tied by handstamp		*450.*
	Pair on cover		*1,000.*
87L5	L172 1c **black**	*175.*	—
	On cover		—
	Block of 4	—	
	Strip of 7	—	

Cancellation on Nos. 87L4-87L5: Black circle "1ct PAID HUSSEY 50 Wm. ST," date in center.
The No. 87L5 block of 4 and strip of 7 are unique.

1858

87L6	L173 (1c) **black**	5.00	—
	On cover		—
87L7	L173 (1c) **rose red**	5.00	—
	On cover		—
	Sheet of 46	*275.00*	
87L8	L173 (1c) **red**	60.00	—
	On cover		—
	Sheet of 46	—	

Type L173 was printed in sheets of 46: 5 horizontal rows of 8, one row of 6 sideways at botton. Type L173 saw little, if any, commercial use and was probably issued mainly for collectors. Covers exist, many with apparently contemporaneous corner cards. On-cover stamps bear a black HUSSEY'S POST handstamp, but most if not all of Nos. 87L6-87L8 were canceled after the post ceased to operate.

L174

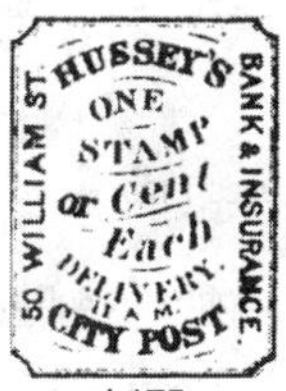

L175

1858 **Typo.**

87L9	L174 (1c) **blue**	5.00

1859 **Litho.**

87L10	L175 1c **rose red**	15.00	*40.00*
	On cover		*400.00*

No. 87L10 in orange red is not known to have been placed in use.

Cancellations: Black "FREE," black company circle "1 CT PAID HUSSEY 50 WM ST.," no date in center (smaller than cancel on Nos. 87L4-87L5).

87L11	L175 1c **lake**	—
87L12	L175 1c **black**	—

L176

L177

1862

87L13	L176 1c **black**	25.00	
87L14	L176 1c **blue**	15.00	*25.00*
	On cover		*450.00*
87L15	L176 1c **green**	20.00	
	On cover		*450.00*
87L16	L176 1c **red**	30.00	
87L17	L176 1c **red brown**	30.00	
87L18	L176 1c **brown**	30.00	
87L19	L176 1c **lake**	—	
87L20	L176 1c **purple**	30.00	
87L21	L176 1c **yellow**	30.00	

Similar to L174 but has condensed "50" and shows a short flourish line over the "I" of "DELIVERY."
Printed in sheets of 49

1862

87L22	L177 (1c) **blue**	3.00	*25.00*
	On cover		—

L178

Similar to L171, but no dots in corners — L179

Printed in sheets of 30

1863

87L23	L178 (1c) **blue**	7.50	
87L24	L179 (1c) **black**	5.00	
	Sheet of 30	225.00	
87L25	L179 (1c) **red**	6.50	
	Sheet of 30	250.00	
	On cover with 6c #115		*17,500.*

See No. 87L52.

L180

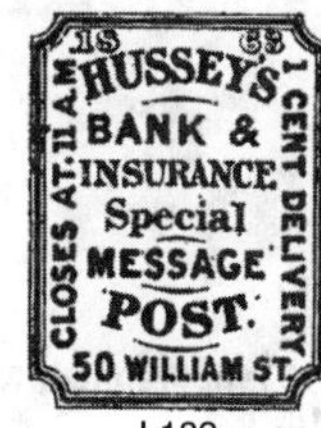

L182

87L26	L180 1c **brown red**	5.00	*25.00*
	Block of 4	25.00	
	On cover, tied by handstamp		*450.00*

A so-called "reprint" of No. 87L26, made for J. W. Scott, has a colored flaw extending diagonally upward from the "I" in "CITY."

Reprints of types L173, L174, L178, L179 and L180 were made in 1875-76 on thicker paper in approximately normal colors and were available for postage.

1863

Dated 1863

87L27	L182 1c **blue**	20.00	
	Cut to shape	12.50	
	On cover, tied by handstamp		*500.00*
87L28	L182 1c **green**	27.50	—
	Cut to shape	14.00	
	On cover, tied by handstamp		*550.00*
87L29	L182 1c **yellow**	25.00	—
	Cut to shape	12.50	
	On cover, tied by handstamp		*500.00*
87L30	L182 1c **brown**	27.50	
	Cut to shape	14.00	
87L31	L182 1c **red brown**	30.00	
	Cut to shape	15.00	
87L32	L182 1c **red**	27.50	
	Cut to shape	14.00	
87L33	L182 1c **black**	40.00	
	Cut to shape	20.00	
87L34	L182 1c **violet**	40.00	
	Cut to shape	20.00	
87L35	L182 2c **brown**	40.00	*75.00*
	Cut to shape	20.00	
	On cover, tied by handstamp		*650.00*

The 2c blue dated 1863 exists only as a counterfeit.

1865

Dated 1865

87L38	L182 2c **blue**	35.00	*45.00*
	On cover, tied by handstamp		*475.00*

1867

Dated 1867

87L39	L182 2c **blue**	45.00	40.00
	On cover, tied by handstamp		*450.00*

1868

Dated 1868

87L40	L182 2c **blue**	40.00	*65.00*
	On cover, tied by handstamp		*500.00*

1869

Dated 1870

87L41	L182 2c **blue**	45.00	*70.00*
	On cover, tied by handstamp		*500.00*

1871

Dated 1871

87L42	L182 2c **blue**	40.00	*65.00*
	On cover, tied by handstamp		*750.00*

L183

L184

1872

Wove Paper

87L43	L183 **black**	5.00	*20.00*
	On cover, tied by handstamp		*300.00*
	Pair on cover, tied by handstamp		*1,500.*
87L44	L183 **red lilac**	9.00	*40.00*
	On cover, tied by handstamp		*300.00*
87L45	L183 **blue**	6.00	*40.00*
	On cover, tied by handstamp		*300.00*
	Pair on cover, tied by handstamp		*750.00*
87L46	L183 **green**	10.00	*45.00*
	On cover, tied by handstamp		*300.00*

Sheets contain four panes of 28 each. Double periods after "A.M." on two stamps in two panes, and on four stamps in the other two panes.

Covers show postmark reading: "HUSSEY'S SPECIAL-MESSENGER EXPRESS-PAID-54 PINE ST."

1872

Thick Laid paper

87L47	L184 **black**	10.00	*35.00*
	On cover		—
	Block of 4	45.00	
87L48	L184 **yellow**	17.50	*65.00*
87L49	L184 **red brown**	17.50	*50.00*
	On cover		*200.00*
87L50	L184 **red**	17.50	*40.00*
	On cover		—

L185

L186

1873

Thin Wove Paper

87L51 L185 2c **black** 75.00 *150.00*
On cover *500.00*

A reprint of No. 87L51, believed to have been made for J. W. Scott, shows a 4mm break in the bottom frameline under "54."

Type of 1863

1875

Thick Wove Paper

87L52 L179 (1c) **blue** *750.00*

1875

L186 in imitation of L180, but no corner dots, "S" for "$," etc.

87L53 L186 1c **black** 2.00

Some authorities believe Nos. 87L52-87L53 are imitations made from new stones. Attributed to J. W. Scott.

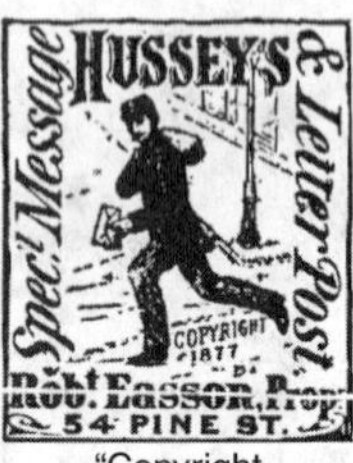

"Copyright 1877" — L188

L188a

1877

Thick Wove Paper

87L55 L188 **black** *175.00* —
On cover *600.00*

Error of design, used provisionally. Stamp was never copyrighted. Printed singly.

87L56 L188a **black** *350.00*

Thin Wove Paper

87L57 L188a **blue** *45.00*
87L58 L188a **rose** 30.00
On cover —

Perf. 12½

87L59 L188a **blue** 3.00 *10.00*
On cover *250.00*
a. Imperf. horizontally, pair —
87L60 L188a **rose** 3.00 *10.00*
On cover *250.00*

"TRADE MARK" small — L189

"TRADE MARK" medium — L190

"TRADE MARK" larger, touching "s" of "Easson." — L191

1878 **Wove Paper** ***Perf. 11, 11½, 11x12, 12***

87L61 L189 **blue** 15.00 *50.00*
On cover, tied by handstamp *150.00*
87L62 L189 **carmine** 12.50 *40.00*
On cover, tied by handstamp *200.00*
87L63 L189 **black** 100.00

Nos. 87L61-87L63 exist imperforate.

Perf. 11, 12, 12½, 14, 16 and Compound

87L64 L190 **blue** 5.00 *17.50*
On cover, tied by handstamp *200.00*
87L65 L190 **red** 5.00 *10.00*
On cover, tied by handstamp *150.00*
87L66 L190 **black** —

Nos. 87L64-87L66 imperf. are reprints.

1879 ***Perf. 11, 12, and Compound***

87L67 L191 **blue** 3.00 *10.00*
On cover, tied by handstamp *300.00*
87L69 L191 **black** —

1880 ***Imperf.***

87L70 L191 **blue** 4.00 *50.00*
On cover, tied by handstamp *450.00*
87L71 L191 **red** 5.00 *75.00*
87L72 L191 **black** 4.00

The authenticity of Nos. 87L69-87L72 has not been fully established.

L192

Two types of L192:
I. Imprint "N. F. Seebeck, 97 Wall St. N. Y." is in lower tablet below "R Easson, etc."
II. Imprint in margin below stamp.

1880 **Glazed Surface Wove Paper** ***Perf. 12***

87L73 L192 **brown,** type I 10.00 *20.00*
On cover, tied by handstamp *250.00*
Block of 4 —
a. Type II 3.00 *5.00*
On cover, tied by handstamp *250.00*
b. Horiz. pair, imperf. between 50.00
c. Imperf., pair 50.00
87L74 L192 **ultramarine,** type I 12.50 *25.00*
On cover, tied by handstamp *350.00*
a. Imperf., pair —
Imperf (single) on cover *135.00*
b. Deep blue, type II 40.00
87L75 L192 **red,** type II 1.50 *3.50*
On cover, tied by handstamp *175.00*
Block of 4 6.50
a. Imperf, single on cover *150.00*

1882 ***Perf. 16, 12x16***

87L76 L192 **brown,** type I 12.50 *30.00*
On cover, tied by handstamp *125.00*
87L77 L192 **ultramarine,** type I 10.00 *20.00*
On cover, tied by handstamp *125.00*

Cancellations: Violet 3-ring target, violet ornamental "T."
Imperf. impressions of Type I in various colors, on horizontally laid paper, ungummed, are color trials.

SPECIAL DELIVERY STAMPS

L181

Typographed; Numerals Inserted Separately

1863 **Glazed Surface Paper**

87LE1 L181 5c **black,** *red* 2.00 *17.50*
On cover *350.00*
87LE2 L181 10c **gold,** *green* 2.50 *20.00*
On cover *350.00*
87LE3 L181 15c **gold,** *black* 3.50 *27.50*
On cover *400.00*
On cover with 1c #87L10, tied by handstamps —
87LE4 L181 20c **black** 2.00 *17.50*
On cover *400.00*
87LE5 L181 25c **gold,** *blue* 4.00 *40.00*
On cover *400.00*
87LE6 L181 30c **gold,** *red* —
87LE7 L181 50c **black,** *green* —

Nos. 87LE1-87LE7 on cover show Hussey handstamp cancellations in various types.

Nos. 87LE4 and 87LE5 are on unglazed paper, the latter surface colored. Ten minor varieties of each value, except the 30c and 50c, which have the figures in manuscript. Printed in two panes of 10, certain values exist in horizontal cross-gutter tete beche pairs.

Originals of the 5c to 20c have large figures of value. The 25c has condensed figures with decimal point. Reprints exist with both large and condensed figures. Reprints of the 25c also exist with serifs on large figures.

Most of the Hussey adhesives are known on cover, tied with Hussey Express postmarks. Many of these were canceled after the post ceased to operate as a mail carrier. "On cover" values are for original stamps used while the post was operating.

WRAPPERS

L192a

1856 **Handstamped** **Inscribed: "82 Broadway"**

87LUP1 L192 **black** — *500.00*

1858 **Inscribed: "50 William St. Basement"**

87LUP2 L192a **black,** *manila* — *600.*
With 1c #87L3, tied by handstamp *1,250.*
87LUP3 L192a **black** — *650.*
With 1c #87L2, tied by handstamp *2,750.*
With 1c #87L3, tied by handstamp *850.*

Jefferson Market P. O., New York, N. Y.

Established by Godfrey Schmidt

L193

1850 **Glazed Surface Paper** **Litho.**

88L1 L193 (2c) **black,** *pink* *7,000.*
88L2 L193 (2c) **black,** *blue* —
On cover, tied by handstamp —

Four examples recorded of No. 88L1, all unused. Five No. 88L2 recorded, all on covers (two with stamp tied by handstamp).

Jenkins' Camden Dispatch, Camden, N. J.

Established by Samuel H. Jenkins and continued by William H. Jenkins.

George Washington—L194a
L194

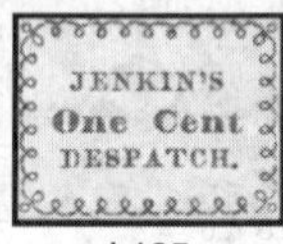

L195

There are two types of design L194.

1853 **Litho.**

89L1 L194 **black** (fine impression) *350.00* *450.00*
On cover, tied by ms., with certificate *3,500.*
Block of 4 *2,250.*

Type L194 printed on envelopes at upper left is considered a corner card.

Typo. from Woodcut

89L2 L194a **black,** *yellow* (coarse impression) *3,000.*
On cover, tied by ms., with certificate *6,500.*

Typeset

89L3 L195 1c **black,** *bluish* — —
On cover, tied by ms. *17,500.*

Johnson & Co.'s City Despatch Post, Baltimore, Md.

Operated by Ezekiel C. Johnson, letter carrier

L196

1848 **Typeset**

90L1 L196 2c **black,** *lavender* —

Two recorded examples of No. 90L1, each uncanceled on cover.

Jones' City Express, Brooklyn, N. Y.

George Washington — L197

1845 **Glazed Surface Paper** **Engr.**

91L1 L197 2c **black,** *pink* *1,000.* *1,500.*
On cover, not tied, with certificate *3,500.*

Cancellation: Red oval "Boyd's City Express Post."

Kellogg's Penny Post & City Despatch, Cleveland, Ohio

L198

1853 **Typo.**

92L1 L198 (1c) **vermilion** *1,500.*
On cover, tied by handstamp —
On cover, tied by handstamp, with 3c #11, with certificate *42,500.*
On cover, not tied, with 3c #11, with certificate *15,000.*
On 3c entire #U2, tied by handstamp *9,000.*

Cancellation: Black grid.

Kidder's City Express Post, Brooklyn, N.Y.

In 1847, Henry A. Kidder took over the post of Walton & Co., and with the brothers Isaac C. Snedeker and George H. Snedeker increased its scope. In 1851, the business was sold to the Snedekers. It was operated under the old name until 1853 when the Brooklyn City Express Post was founded.

L199

Stamps bear black manuscript "I S" control in two styles.

1847 **Glazed Surface Paper** **Typo.**

93L1 L199 2c **black,** *pale blue* *750.* 500.
On cover, tied by handstamp *6,000.*
Block of 4 3,500.

Cancellation: Red "PAID."

Reprinted on green paper.

Kurtz Union Despatch Post, New York, N.Y.

L200

Typeset; "T" in Black Ms.

1853

Glazed Surface Paper

94L1 L200 2c **black,** *green* *3,500.*

Langton & Co.

(See Humboldt Express.)

Ledger Dispatch, Brooklyn, N.Y.

Established by Edwin Pidgeon. Stamps reported to have been sold at 80 cents per 100. Suppressed after a few months.

L201

1882 **Typo.** ***Rouletted 12 in color***

95L1 L201 **rose** (shades) 250. *550.*
Block of 4 *1,250.*

Letter Express

Established by Henry Wells. Carried mail for points in Western New York, Chicago, Detroit and Duluth.

L202

L203

1844 **Glazed Surface Paper** **Typo.**

96L1 L202 5c **black,** *pink* 300.00 200.00
On cover, tied by ms. cancel *1,000.*
On cover, not tied *500.00*
Pair on cover, tied by ms. cancel *2,000.*
Pair on cover, not tied *1,000.*
Pair 700.00 450.00
Block of 10 *28,500.*

96L2 L202 5c **black,** *green* — 500.00
On cover, tied by ms. cancel *5,000.*
On cover, not tied *3,500.*
Pair *1,500.*

96L3 L203 10c **black,** *pink* — 500.00
On cover, tied by ms. cancel *1,500.*
On cover, not tied *750.00*
Pair *1,500.* *1,500.*
Strip of 3 *9,250.*

a. Bisect on cover, tied by ms. cancel —

No. 96L3a was sold as a horizontal or vertical bisect. It is known used singly for 5c (rare), or as two bisects for 10c (extremely rare). Stamps are known almost exclusively tied with black ms. "X" covering the cut, and can be authenticated by experts.

The block of 10 of No. 96L1 is the only block recorded of any Letter Express issue. Value represents actual auction sale price in 1999.

L204

96L4 L204 10c **black,** *scarlet* — *2,500.*
On cover, tied by ms. cancel, with certificate *9,250.*

a. Tete beche pair, one stamp a horiz. bisect, on piece *8,750.*

Cancellations: Red large partly boxed "PAID," red boxed "Boyd's City Express Post."

Locomotive Express Post

L205

1847 (?) **Handstamped**

97L1 L205 **black** —

Wm. E. Loomis Letter Express, San Francisco, Calif.

William E. Loomis established this post as the successor to the Gahagan & Howe City Express, which he bought in 1865. He continued to use the Gahagan & Howe stamps unchanged. Later Loomis bought Carnes' City Letter Express. He altered the Carnes stamp by erasing "CARNES}" from the plate and adding the address below the oval: "S.E. cor. Sans'e & Wash'n."

L206

1868 **Typo.**

98L1 L206 (5c) **rose** 275.00 *650.00*

Cancellation: Blue "PAID."

McGreely's Express, Alaska

Established in 1898 by S. C. Marcuse to carry letters and packages by motorboat between Dyea and Skagway, Alaska.

L208

1898 **Typo.** ***Perf. 14***

155L1 L208 25c **blue** 50.00 —
Block of 4 *250.00*

The status of No. 155L1 is questioned.

McIntire's City Express Post, New York, N.Y.

Established by William H. McIntire

Mercury — L207

1859 **Litho.**

99L1 L207 2c **pink** 10.00 *75.00*
Block of 4 75.00
On cover, tied by handstamp *3,250.*

a. Period after CENTS omitted —

Cancellation: Black oval "McIntire's City Express Post Paid."

McMillan's City Dispatch Post, Chicago, Ill.

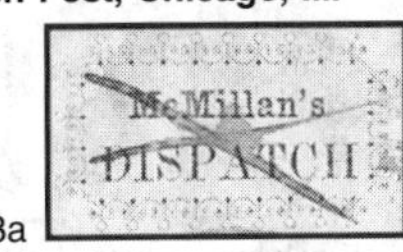

L208a

1855 **Typeset**

100L1 L208a **black,** *rose* *25,000.*

No. 100L1 is unique.

Mac & Co's Dispatch, Fallsington-Morrisville, Pa.

L208b

Typo.

166L1 L208b 1c **black,** on 3c entire #U1, uncanceled, with certificate *14,000.*

No. 166L1 is unique.

Magic Letter Express, Richmond, Va.

Established by Evans, Porter & Co.

L209

L209a

1865 **Typo.**

101L1 L209 1c **black,** on cover, not tied by cancel — 24,000.
101L2 L209a 2c **black,** *brown* — 11,000.
101L3 L209a 5c **black,** *brown* — —

Nos. 101L1-101L2 each are unique.

Mason's New Orleans City Express, New Orleans, La.

J. Mason, proprietor

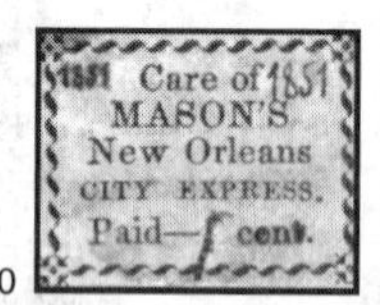

L210

1850-57 **Typeset**

102L1 L210 ½c **black,** *blue* (value changed to "1" in black ms.) 12,500.
On cover, tied —
102L2 L210 2c **black,** *yellow* — 3,000.
On cover, tied by handstamp 10,000.

Cancellations: Red grid, small red circle "Mason's City Express."

Mearis' City Despatch Post, Baltimore, Md.

Established by Malcom W. Mearis

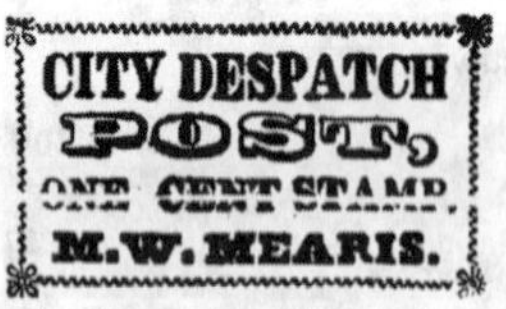

L211

L212

Black ms. initials "M W M" control on all stamps

1846 **Typeset**

103L1 L211 1c **black,** *gray* — —
On cover, tied by handstamp 22,000.
103L2 L212 1c **black,** *gray* —
103L3 L212 2c **black,** *gray* —
On cover, uncancelled, with certificate 16,500.
a. Horiz. pair, #103L2-103L3 —

Two types of No. 103L3.

L213

Two types of each.

103L4 L213 1c **black,** *gray* —
103L5 L213 2c **black,** *gray* —
a. Horiz. pair, #103L4-103L5 —

L214

103L6 L214 1c **black,** *gray* 11,000.

No. 103L6 is unique; tied on small piece by handstamp.

Corner ornaments of Nos. 103L1-103L6 differ on each stamp. All varieties of Nos. 103L1-103L6 contained in one plate.

Menant & Co.'s Express, New Orleans, La.

L215

1853 (?) **Typo.**

104L1 L215 2c **dark red** 15,000.

Only four examples are known. Two have Philatelic Foundation Certificates. All four have faults, and the stamp is valued thus.

Reprints are fairly common and are orange red, not dark red.

Mercantile Library Association, New York, N.Y.

Stamps paid for special delivery service of books ordered from the library, and of forms especially provided to subscribers. The forms bore a government stamp on the outside, a library stamp inside.

L216

1870-75 **Litho.**

105L1 L216 5c **black,** *maroon* 250. 350.
105L2 L216 5c **black,** *yellow* 350. 500.
105L3 L216 5c **blue** 350. 500.
Pair, on postal card 1,400.
105L5 L216 6c **black,** *maroon* 2,250.
105L6 L216 10c **black,** *yellow* 500. 750.

No. 105L5 is slightly larger than the 5c and 10c stamps.

The stamps "on cover" are affixed to cutouts from order blanks showing order number, title of book desired, and subscriber's name and address. When canceled, the stamps and order blanks show a dull blue double-lined oval inscribed "MERCANTILE LIBRARY ASSOCIATION" and date in center. The stamps are really more a form of receipt for a prepaid parcel delivery service than postage stamps.

POSTAL CARD

Printed on U. S. Postal Card, First Issue

105LU1 L216 10c **yellow** 3,500.

No. 105LU1 is unique.

Messenkope's Union Square Post Office, New York, N. Y.

Established by Charles F. Messenkope in 1849 and sold to Joseph E. Dunham in 1850.

L217

1849 **Glazed Surface Paper** **Litho.**

106L1 L217 (1c) **black,** *green* 90. 90.
On cover, tied by handstamp 500.
Pair on cover (2c rate), tied by handstamp 1,750.
On cover with 5c #1 2,750.
On cover, tied by handstamp, with 3c #10 1,250.
On cover, tied by handstamp, with 3c #11 2,000.
On cover with 3c #26 950.
Strip of 3 400.
106L2 L217 (2c) **black,** *pink* — —
On cover —

Some examples of No. 106L1 are found with "MESSENKOPES" crossed through in black ms. in an apparent attempt (by Dunham?) to obliterate it.

Cancellations: Red "PAID," red oval "DUNHAMS UNION SQUARE POST OFFICE," red grid of dots.

Metropolitan Errand and Carrier Express Co., New York, N.Y.

Organized Aug. 1, 1855, by Abraham M. Hinkley, Hiram Dixon, and others.

L218

L219

Printed in sheets of 100 (10x10), each stamp separated by thin ruled lines.

1855 **Thin to Medium Wove Paper** **Engr.**

107L1 L218 1c **red orange** (shades) 20.00 17.50
Cut to shape 5.00 4.00
On cover, tied by handstamp 325.00
On cover, cut to shape, tied by handstamp 150.00
On cover, cut to shape, tied by handstamp, with 3c #11 900.00
Pair 35.00
Pair on cover, uncanceled 1,000.
Block of 4 90.00
107L2 L218 5c **red orange** 225.00
Cut to shape 60.00
107L3 L218 10c **red orange** 300.00
Cut to shape 60.00
107L4 L218 20c **red orange** 325.00
Cut to shape 60.00

Cancellations: Black, blue or green boxed "PAID."

The imprint "Baldwin, Bald & Cousland New York" appears in the bottom margin of the two stamps at the bottom right of the sheets.

Nos. 107L1-107L4 have been extensively reprinted in brown and in blue on paper much thicker than the originals.

ENVELOPE

Embossed

Wide Diagonally Laid Paper

107LU1 L219 2c **red,** *amber,* entire 125.00 —

No. 107LU1 has been reprinted on amber wove, diagonally laid or horizontally laid paper with narrow lines. The embossing is sharper than on the original.

Metropolitan Post Office, New York, N. Y.

Established by Lemuel Williams who later took William H. Laws as a partner.

L220

L221

L222

L223

Nos. 108L1-108L5 were issued die cut.

1852-53 **Glazed Surface Paper** **Embossed**

108L1 L220 (2c) **red** (L. Williams) 550. 550.
On cover, tied by pencil, with certificate —
On cover, tied by blue ms., with two 3c #11 and strip of 3 12c #17 —
108L2 L221 (2c) **red** (address and name erased) 1,000. 1,000.
On cover, uncanceled, with certificate 5,500.
108L3 L222 (2c) **red** 275. 350.

On cover, tied by handstamp — 3,000.

108L3A L222 (2c) **blue** 600. 700.
On cover, tied by handstamp — 7,500.
On cover, tied by handstamp, with 3c #11 — 8,250.

Wove Paper

108L4 L223 1c **red** 75. 90.
On cover — 300.
On cover, tied by handstamp, with 3c #11 — 1,500.

108L5 L223 1c **blue** 85. 100.
On cover — 350.
On cover, tied by handstamp, with 3c #26 — 700.

Cancellations: Black circle "METROPOLITAN P. O.," black boxed "PAID W. H. LAWS," black smudge.

G. A. Mills' Despatch Post, New York, N.Y.

Established by Gustavus A. Mills at 6 Wall St., succeeding Hall & Mills.

L224

Several varieties

1847 Glazed Surface Paper Typeset

109L1 L224 (2c) **black,** *green* 500. 500.
On cover —

Moody's Penny Dispatch, Chicago, Ill.

Robert J. Moody, proprietor

"CHICAGO" 8mm — L225

Several varieties

1856 Glazed Surface Paper Typeset

110L1 L225 (1c) **black,** *red,* 1,750. 1,750.
On cover, tied by handstamp, with 3c #11 — 16,000.
On cover with three 1c #9 — 70,000.
Vert. strip of 3 showing 3 varieties: period, colon, comma after "Dispatch" 18,000. 6,000.
a. "CHICAGO" sans serif and 12½mm — 2,750.
b. "Henny" instead of "Penny," on cover, tied by handstamp, with 3c #11 — 40,000.

Cancellations: Blue circle "Moody's Despatch."
The vertical strip of 3, the cover with the three 1c stamps and No. 110L1b, are each unique.

Morton's Post, Philadelphia, Pa.

L225a

167L1 L225a 2c **black,** *grayish,* on cover, uncanceled, with certificate — 13,000.

No. 167L1 is unique.

New York City Express Post, New York, N.Y.

L226

Several varieties

1847 Glazed Surface Paper Engr.

111L1 L226 2c **black,** *green* 1,200. 1,500.
Cut to shape 400. 450.
On cover, tied by handstamp — 4,000.
On cover, cut to shape, tied by handstamp — 1,750.

Wove Paper

111L2 L226 2c **orange** — —
On cover — 8,000.

One Cent Despatch, Baltimore, Md., Washington, D.C.

Established by J.H. Wiley to deliver mail in Washington, Georgetown and Baltimore. Made as many as five deliveries daily at 1 cent if prepaid, or 2 cents payable on delivery.

L227

L228

Two types:
I. Courier's letter points to "O" of "ONE."
II. Letter points to "N" of "ONE."

1856 Washington, D.C. Litho.

Inscribed at bottom "Washington City"

112L1 L227 1c **violet** 225. 150.
On cover, tied by handstamp — 750.
On cover, tied by handstamp, with 3c #11 — 1,500.
On 3c entire #U1, tied by handstamp — 750.
Horiz. pair, types I & II — 1,250.

Baltimore, Maryland

No name at bottom

112L2 L228 1c **red** 450. 250.
On cover, tied by handstamp — 2,000.
On cover with 3c #11 — 2,250.

The No. 112L1 pair is the unique multiple of either One Cent Despatch stamp.

Cancellation on Nos. 112L1-112L2: Black circle "City Despatch."

Overton & Co.

Carried mail principally between New York and Boston; also to Albany. Stamps sold for 6c each, 20 for $1.

L229

1844

113L1 L229 (6c) **black,** *greenish* 400. 400.
On cover, tied by ms. — 5,000.
On cover, not tied — 2,250.
Pair — 850.
a. "FREE" printed below design — 1,750.
On cover — 4,000.
Pair on cover, not tied, with certificate — 18,500.

Cancellation: Black "PAID." Red "Cd."

Penny Express Co.

Little information is available on this post, but a sheet is known carrying the ms. initials of Henry Reed of the Holladay staff. The post was part of the Holladay Overland Mail and Express Co. system.

In 1866 in the West the "short-bit" or 10 cents was the smallest currency generally used. The word "penny" is believed to refer to the "half-bit" or 5 cents (nickel).

L230

Printed in sheets of 32 (8x4)

1866 Litho.

114L1 L230 5c **black** 300.00
Pair 650.
a. Sheet of 32 initialed "HR," black ms., original gum 7,000.

114L2 L230 5c **blue** 12.50
Block of 4 55.00
Sheet of 32, no gum 550.00

114L3 L230 5c **red** 12.50
Block of 4 55.00
Sheet of 32, no gum 550.00

Nos. 114L1-114L3 lack gum and probably were never placed in use.

Philadelphia Despatch Post, Philadelphia, Pa.

See D.O. Blood & Co.

Pinkney's Express Post, New York, N.Y.

L231

1851 Glazed Surface Paper Typo.

115L1 L231 2c **black,** *green* 1,400.
Cut to shape 800.
On cover, tied by ms., with certificate — 5,750.
On cover, not canceled, with certificate — 9,000.
On cover, cut to shape, with certificate — 3,500.

On the cover with No. 115L1 tied, the stamp is faulty. It is valued thus.

Pips Daily Mail, Brooklyn, N.Y.

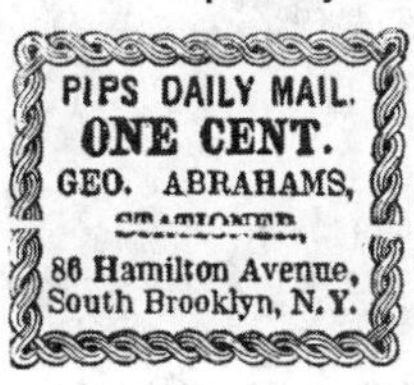

L232

1862 (?) Litho.

116L1 L232 1c **black** 300.
116L2 L232 1c **black,** *buff* 250. 2,250.
116L3 L232 1c **black,** *yellow* 250.
116L4 L232 1c **black,** *dark blue* 300.
116L5 L232 1c **black,** *rose* 300.
Block of 4 —

No. 116L2 used is unique.

Pomeroy's Letter Express.

Established in 1844 by George E. Pomeroy. Carried mail principally to points in New York State. Connected with Letter Express for Western points.

L233

Engraved by John E. Gavit, Albany, N.Y. (Seen as "GAVIT" in bottom part of stamp). Sheets of 40 (8x5).

1844

Surface Colored Wove Paper

117L1 L233 5c **black,** *yellow* 6.50 65.00
On cover, tied by ms. — 900.00
Pair — 250.00
Pair on cover — 3,500.
Block of 4 40.00

117L2 L233 **black,** *yellow* (value incomplete) 750. 1,250.
On cover, tied by ms. — 3,000.
On cover, ms. cancel, not tied

Thin Bond Paper

117L3 L233 5c **blue** 5.00 125.00
On cover, not tied — 2,000.
Pair on cover, not tied — 4,000.

117L4 L233 5c **black** 3.50 125.00
On cover — —
Strip of 4 on cover
Block of 4 30.00
Sheet of 40 —

117L5 L233 5c **red** 3.50 125.00
On cover, not tied — 3,500.
Strip of 3 on cover —
Block of 4 25.00

117L6 L233 5c **lake** 200.00 300.00
On cover, tied by ms. — 900.00
Pair on cover —

117L7 L233 5c **orange** 7.50 —

Cancellations: Large red partly boxed "PAID" (Nos. 117L1, 117L6), red "Cd" (Nos. 117L1-117L2, 117L4); stamps are considered "tied to cover" by this "Cd" when the impression shows through the letter paper.

All stamps except No. 117L2 have "20 for $1" in tablet at the bottom. On No. 117L2 the value is incomplete.

Remainders of Nos. 117L1, 117L3, 117L4 and 117L5 are plentiful in unused condition, including multiples and sheets. A 5c black on yellow paper colored through and a 5c brown were prepared for use but never issued. No. 117L2 was never remaindered.

P. O. Paid, Philadelphia, Pa.

See note in Carriers' Stamps Section.

Price's City Express, New York, N.Y.

L235

L236

1857-58 Glazed Surface Paper Litho.

119L1 L235 2c **black,** *vermilion* 275.
On cover, tied by handstamp *5,000.*
On cover, ms. tied *1,000.*
On cover, not tied, with certificate *750.00*
On cover, tied by handstamp, with 3c #26 —
119L2 L235 2c **black,** *green* 250.
Cut to shape 85.

1858

Sheets of 108 (12x9)

119L3 L236 2c **black,** *green* 5.00 *150.00*
On cover —
Block of 4 27.50

Cancellation on #119L3: Black oval "Price's City Express."

Price's Eighth Avenue Post Office, New York, N.Y.

Established by James Price at 350 Eighth Avenue, in 1854, and sold to Russell in the same year.

L237

1854 Litho.

120L1 L237 (2c) **red,** *bluish* *600.00*
On cover, uncanceled, with certificate *7,500.*

Priest's Despatch, Philadelphia, Pa.

Established by Solomon Priest

L238

L239

1851 Glazed Surface Paper Typo.

121L1 L238 (2c) **silver,** *vermilion* *2,250.* —
121L2 L238 (2c) **gold,** *dark blue* *500.*

Wove Paper

121L2A L238 (2c) **bronze,** *bluish* *500.* *1,000.*
121L3 L238 (2c) **black,** *yellow* *500.*
On cover, uncanceled, with 3c #11, with certificate *5,500.*
121L4 L238 (2c) **black,** *rose* *500.*
On cover, uncanceled, with certificate *2,500.*
121L5 L238 (2c) **black,** *blue* *1,000.*
121L6 L239 (2c) **black,** *yellow* *500.*
On cover, uncanceled, with 3c #11, with certificate *4,500.*
121L7 L239 (2c) **black,** *blue* *500.*
On cover, uncanceled, with certificate *3,250.*
121L8 L239 (2c) **black,** *rose* *500.00*
121L9 L239 (2c) **black,** *emerald,* uncanceled, on cover *6,500.*

No. 121L9 is believed to be unique.

Prince's Letter Dispatch, Portland, Maine

Established by J. H. Prince of Portland. Mail carried nightly by messenger travelling by steamer to Boston. Stamp engraved by Lowell of Lowell & Brett, Boston, his name appearing in the design below the steamship.

L240

Printed in sheets of 40 (5x8)

1861 Litho.

122L1 L240 **black** 7.50 *125.00*
On cover, tied by handstamp *5,000.*
On cover, tied by handstamp, with 3c #65 *8,000.*
On cover, tied by handstamp, with 3c #94 *4,750.*
Block of 4 40.00
Sheet of 40 550.00

Cancellations: Black, blue or red Boston datestamps, blue company serrated oval, black "Boston & Portland/Express/11 State Street, Boston/34 Exchange Street, Portland" framed ribbon-marker handstamp.

Private Post Office, San Francisco, Calif.
ENVELOPES

L241

(Illustration reduced size.)

Impressed on U. S. Envelopes, 1863-64 Issue

1864 Typo.

123LU1 L241 15c **blue,** *orange* (on US #U56) *600.00*
123LU2 L241 15c **blue,** *buff* (on US #U54) *600.00*
a. 15c **blue,** *buff* (on US #U58) *700.00*
b. 15c **blue,** *buff* (on US #U59) *600.00*
123LU3 L241 25c **blue,** *buff* (on US #U54) *600.00*

Providence Despatch, Providence, R.I.

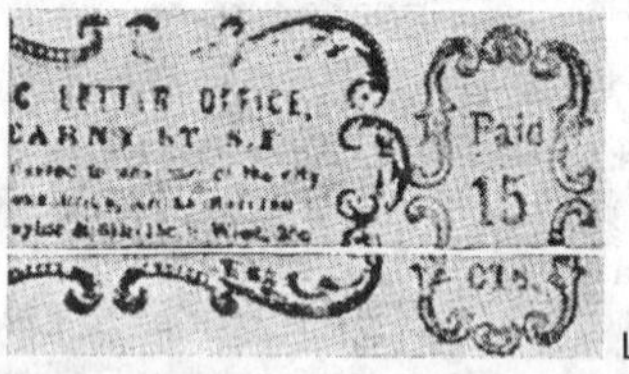

L242

1849 Typeset

124L1 L242 **black** *2,000.*

Public Letter Office, San Francisco, Calif.
ENVELOPES

L243

Illustration reduced.

Impressed on U. S. Envelopes, 1863-64 Issue

1864 Typeset

125LU1 L243 **black** *350.00*
125LU2 L243 **blue** *350.00*
125LU3 L243 15c **blue** *400.00* *5,000.*
125LU4 L243 25c **blue** *400.00*

Reed's City Despatch Post, San Francisco, Calif.

Pioneer San Francisco private post. Also serving Adams & Co. for city delivery.

L244

1853-54 Glazed Surface Paper Litho.

126L1 L244 **black,** *green,* on cover, tied by handstamp —
126L2 L244 **black,** *blue,* on cover, uncanceled *27,500.*

No. 126L1 is unique. Two No. 126L2 recorded, each uncanceled on cover.

Cancellation: Blue double-circle "Adams & Co. San Francisco."

Ricketts & Hall, Baltimore, Md.

Successors to Cook's Dispatch

L244a

1857 Cut to shape Typo.

127L1 L244a 1c **red,** *bluish* — *9,000.*

Robison & Co., Brooklyn, N. Y.

L245

1855-56 Typo.

128L1 L245 1c **black,** *blue* *4,500.* *4,500.*
On cover, tied *6,500.*

Cancellation: Blue "PAID."

Roche's City Dispatch, Wilmington, Del.

L246

1850 Glazed Surface Paper Typo.

129L1 L246 (2c) **black,** *green* *2,250.*
Cut to shape *1,500.*
On cover, uncanceled, with certificate *8,250.*
On cover, cut to shape, uncanceled, with certificate *3,500.*

A black negative handstamp similar to type L246 served solely as a postmark and no evidence exists that any prepaid handstamped envelopes or lettersheets were ever sold.

Rogers' Penny Post, Newark, N.J.

Established by Alfred H. Rogers, bookseller, at 194 Broad St., Newark, N.J.

L246a

Cut to shape

1856 Glazed Surface Paper Handstamped

162L1 L246a (1c) **black,** *green* *30,000.*

No. 162L1 is unique. It is on a tiny piece. Value represents 2000 auction sale price.

See Rogers' handstamp in Local Handstamp Covers section.

Russell 8th Ave. Post Office, New York, N.Y.

(See Price's Eighth Avenue Post Office.)

L247

1854-58 **Wood Engraving**

No.	Illus.	Denom.	Description	Unused	Used
130L1	L247	(2c)	**blue,** *rose*	*600.*	*500.*
			On cover, tied		—
130L2	L247	(2c)	**black,** *yellow*	*750.*	*650.*
			On cover, tied		*5,000.*
			On cover, uncanceled, with 3c #11, with certificate		*9,250.*
130L3	L247	(2c)	**red,** *bluish*	*900.*	*750.*
			On cover, tied by handstamp		*8,750.*
			On cover, not tied, with 3c #11, with certificate		*5,750.*
130L4	L247	(2c)	**blue green,** *green*		—

No. 130L4 used is unique.

St. Louis City Delivery Company, St. Louis, Mo.

(See Cincinnati City Delivery.)

L249

1883 **Typo.** ***Perf. 12***

No.	Illus.	Denom.	Description	Unused	Used
131L1	L249	(1c)	**red**	4.00	7.50
			Block of 4	17.50	
			On cover, tied by handstamp		*2,750.*
a.			Imperf., pair		—
b.			Horiz. pair, imperf between	*350.00*	

Cancellation: Purple target.

Smith & Stephens' City Delivery, St. Louis, Mo.

L284

Typeset

No.	Illus.	Denom.	Description	Unused	Used
158L1	L284	1c	**black,** *pale rose,* on cover, tied by ms. cancel		25,000.

No. 158L1 is unique.

Spaulding's Penny Post, Buffalo, N.Y.

L283

L283a

1848-49

No.	Illus.	Denom.	Description	Unused	Used
156L1	L283	2c	**vermilion**	*27,500.*	
156L2	L283a	2c	**carmine**	*27,500.*	
			On cover		—

Nos. 156L1 unused, 156L2 unused and 156L2 on cover each are unique.

A No. 156L1 on cover, uncanceled, was reported but has not been seen.

Spence & Brown Express Post, Philadelphia, Pa.

L285

L286

(Illustrations reduced size.)

Typeset

1847 (?)

No.	Illus.	Denom.	Description	Unused	Used
159L1	L285	2c	**black,** *bluish*	*10,000.*	*11,500.*

One each recorded of No. 159L1 unused and used.

1848 **Litho.**

No.	Illus.	Denom.	Description	Unused	Used
159L2	L286	(2c)	**black**	*1,500.*	—
			Block of 4	*6,500.*	

Squier & Co. City Letter Dispatch, St. Louis, Mo.

(Jordan & Co.)

This post began to operate as a local carrier on July 6, 1859 and was discontinued in the early part of 1860. Squier & Co. used imperforate stamps; their successors (Jordan & Co.) about Jan. 1 1860, used the roulettes.

L248

1859 **Litho.** ***Imperf.***

No.	Illus.	Denom.	Description	Unused	Used
132L1	L248	1c	**green**	*150.*	*175.*
			On cover		*1,500.*
			On cover, tied by handstamp, with 3c #26		—
			On cover, tied by ms., with 3c #26		*1,000.*
			On cover, uncanceled, with 3c #26		*600.*
			Block of 4	*750.*	

1860 ***Rouletted 19***

No.	Illus.	Denom.	Description	Unused	Used
132L2	L248	1c	**rose brown**	*250.*	*250.*
			On cover		*1,000.*
132L3	L248	1c	**brownish purple**	*250.*	*250.*
			On cover		*1,000.*
132L4	L248	1c	**green**	*250.*	*300.*
			On cover		*1,000.*
			On cover, tied by handstamp, with 3c #26		*5,000.*

Cancellation: Black circle "Jordan's Penny Post Saint Louis."

Staten Island Express Post, Staten Island, N. Y.

Established by Hagadorn & Co., with office at Stapleton, Staten Island. Connected with Boyd for delivery in New York City.

L250

1849 **Typo.**

No.	Illus.	Denom.	Description	Unused	Used
133L1	L250	3c	**vermilion**	*1,400.*	*1,100.*
			On cover, tied by ms.		*4,750.*
			On cover, uncanceled, with certificate		*3,250.*
133L2	L250	6c	**vermilion**	—	*3,000.*

Stringer & Morton's City Despatch, Baltimore, Md.

According to an advertisement in the Baltimore newspapers, dated October 19, 1850, this post aimed to emulate the successful posts of other cities, and divided the city into six districts, with a carrier in each district. Stamps were made available throughout the city.

L251

1850 **Glazed Surface Paper**

No.	Illus.	Denom.	Description	Unused	Used
134L1	L251	(1c)	**gold,** *black*	*500.*	—
			On cover, uncanceled		*700.*

Cancellation: Black circle "Baltimore City Despatch & Express Paid."

Sullivan's Dispatch Post, Cincinnati, Ohio

L252

1853 **Glazed Surface Paper** **Litho.**

No.	Illus.	Denom.	Description	Unused	Used
135L1	L252	(2c)	**black,** *green,* uncanceled, on cover		—

Wove Paper

No.	Illus.	Denom.	Description	Unused	Used
135L2	L252	(2c)	**bluish black,** uncanceled, on magazine, with certificate		*22,000.*
135L3	L252	(2c)	**green**	*60,000.*	
			On cover		—

Nos. 135L1-135L2 are either die cut octagonally or cut round. They do not exist cut square.

Each listed Sullivan Post item is unique. Additionally, a second No. 135L2 on magazine is in the Smithsonian Institution collection.

Swarts' City Dispatch Post, New York, N.Y.

Established by Aaron Swarts, at Chatham Square, in 1847, becoming one of the largest local posts in the city.

The postmarks of Swarts' Post Office are often found on stampless covers, as this post carried large quantities of mail without using adhesive stamps.

Zachary Taylor
L253

George Washington
L254

1849-53 **Glazed Surface Paper** **Litho.**

No.	Illus.	Denom.	Description	Unused	Used
136L1	L253	(2c)	**black,** *light green*	—	*175.00*
			On cover, tied by handstamp		*450.00*
			On cover, not tied		*300.00*
			On cover with 3c #10		*450.00*
136L2	L253	(2c)	**black,** *dark green*	—	135.00
			On cover, tied by handstamp		*375.00*

Wove Paper

No.	Illus.	Denom.	Description	Unused	Used
136L3	L253	(2c)	**pink**	—	35.00
			On cover, tied by handstamp		*350.00*
			On cover with 5c #1		—
136L4	L253	(2c)	**red** (shades)	20.00	20.00
			On cover, tied by handstamp		*275.00*
			On cover with 5c #1		—
			On cover, tied by handstamp, with 3c #11		*325.00*
			Block of 4	85.00	
			Sheet of 25	*600.00*	
136L5	L253	(2c)	**pink,** *blue*		60.00
			On cover, tied by handstamp		*375.00*
136L6	L253	(2c)	**red,** *blue*		60.00
			On cover, tied by handstamp		*400.00*
136L7	L253	(2c)	**black,** *blue gray*	200.00	150.00
			On cover, tied by handstamp		*400.00*
136L8	L253	(2c)	**blue**		200.00
			On cover, tied by handstamp		*650.00*
136L9	L254	(1c)	**red**	—	40.00
			On cover, tied by handstamp		*400.00*
			On cover with 3c #11		—
136L10	L254	(1c)	**pink**	—	30.00
			On cover, tied by handstamp		*250.00*
			On cover, tied by handstamp, with 3c #11		*800.00*
136L11	L254	(1c)	**red,** *bluish*	—	100.00
			On cover		*500.00*
136L12	L254	(1c)	**pink,** *bluish*	—	100.00
			On cover		*450.00*

Bouton's Stamp with Red ms. "Swarts" at Top

No.	Illus.	Denom.	Description	Unused	Used
136L13	L49	2c	**black,** *gray blue*	*500.*	*550.*
			On cover, tied by handstamp		*1,500.*
			On cover, not tied		*600.*

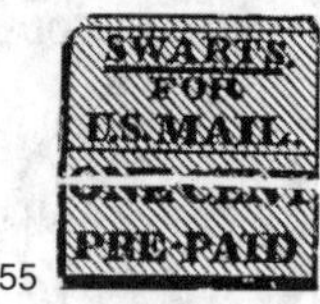

L255

Printed in sheets of 25 (5x5). Five minor varieties, the stamps in each vertical row being identical.

136L14 L255 1c **blue** 15. 60.
On cover, tied by handstamp 175.
On cover, tied by handstamp, with 3c #11 *225.*
Block of 4 *65.*
a. Thin paper 8.00
Block of 4 35.
Sheet of 25 *225.00*
136L15 L255 1c **red** — *125.*
On cover, tied by handstamp *1,000.*
On cover with 3c #10 *1,650.*
On cover, tied by handstamp, with 3c #11 *3,500.*
136L16 L255 1c **red,** *bluish* — 135.
On cover, tied by handstamp *1,000.*
136L17 L255 1c **black,** on cover *36,000.*

Nos. 136L3-136L4, 136L9-136L10, 136L14-136L15 have been reprinted.

Cancellations: Red boxed "PAID" (mostly on Nos. 136L1-136L8, 136L13), black boxed "PAID SWARTS" (mostly on Nos. 136L9-136L12), black oval "Swarts Post Office Chatham Square" (Nos. 136L9-136L12), black oval "Swarts B Post Chatham Square," black grids (5-bar rectangle, 6-bar circle, solid star, hollow star, star in circle, etc). Other handstamp postmarks of the post have been found as cancellations. Government town postmarks exist on almost all Swarts stamps.

Teese & Co. Penny Post, Philadelphia, Pa.

L256

Printed in sheet of 200 divided into two panes of 100. Each pane includes setting of 20, repeated 5 times. Vertical or horizontal tete beche pairs appear twice in each setting. Twenty varieties.

1852 **Wove Paper** **Litho.**
137L1 L256 (1c) **blue,** *bluish* 20.00 125.00
On cover, tied by handstamp *3,000.*
On cover, tied by handstamp, with 3c #11 —
Block of 4 90.00
a. Tete beche pair 100.00

Telegraph Despatch P. O., Philadelphia, Pa.

L257

1848
138L1 L257 1c **black,** *yellowish* *2,750.*
On cover, tied by ms., with certificate *15,000.*
On cover, not tied, with certificate *5,500.*
138L2 L257 2c **black,** *yellowish,* on cover with 5c #1 *10,500.*

The 2c differs in design, including the address, "Office No. 6 Sth 8 St" at bottom.

One example known of No. 138L2.

Third Avenue Post Office, New York, N.Y.

Established by S. Rothenheim, a former carrier for Boyd's City Express. All stamps were cut to shape by hand before being sold and exist only in that form.

L258

1855 **Glazed Surface Paper** **Handstamped**
139L1 L258 2c **black,** *green* *500.* *500.*
On cover, uncanceled *1,250.*
On cover, uncanceled, with 3c #11, with certificate *1,600.*
139L1A L258 2c **blue,** *green,* on cover, uncanceled, with certificate *2,250.*
139L2 L258 2c **black,** *maroon* *3,250.* *2,250.*

Unsurfaced Paper colored through
139L3 L258 2c **black,** *yellow* *2,250.*
On cover, uncanceled, with 3c #11, with certificate *3,000.*
139L4 L258 2c **black,** *blue* —
On cover, uncanceled, with 3c #11, with certificate *7,750.*
139L5 L258 2c **black,** *brown* *2,250.*
139L6 L258 2c **black,** *buff* *2,500.*
139L7 L258 2c **black,** *pink* *5,250.*
On cover, uncanceled, with 3c #11 *6,500.*
139L8 L258 2c **black,** *green* *4,150.* *2,200.*

Nos. 139L1A, 139L2, 139L4 on cover, 139L7-139L8 unused and 139L8 used are each unique.

Cancellation on No. 139L1: Black "PAID."

Union Post, New York, N.Y.

UNION
POST
HRS
L259

1846 **Handstamped**
Thick Glazed Surface Paper
140L3 L259 **blue,** *green* ("UNOIN") *3,000.*
140L4 L259 **red,** *blue* ("UNION") *2,000.*
On cover —

Type L259 was used also as a postmark, usually struck in blue.

Union Square Post Office, New York, N.Y.

Established by Joseph E. Dunham about 1850. In 1851 Dunham acquired Messenkope's Union Square Post Office, operating the combined posts until 1854 or 1855. The business was sold in 1855 to Phineas C. Godfrey.

L259a

L260

Printed in sheets of 120 (6x20)

1852 **Typo.**
141L1 L259a 1c **black,** *dark green* 9.00 *45.00*
On cover, tied by handstamp *900.00*
On cover, tied by handstamp, with 3c #11 *1,500.*
Block of 4 45.00
141L2 L259a 1c **black,** *light apple green* 40.00 *75.00*
On cover, tied by handstamp *700.00*
On cover, tied by handstamp, with 3c #11 *1,500.*
On cover, cut to shape, tied by handstamp, with 3c #11 *200.00*
141L3 L260 2c **black,** *rose* 3.50 *2,000.*
On cover *750.00*
Block of 4 17.50

Used stamps must bear handstamp cancels.

Walton & Co.'s City Express, Brooklyn, N.Y.

Operated by Wellington Walton.

L261

1846 **Glazed Surface Paper** **Litho.**
142L1 L261 2c **black,** *pink* *700.* *900.*
On cover, tied by ms. —
On cover, ms. cancel, not tied, with certificate *15,000.*
On cover, handstamp cancel, not tied —
On cover, cut to shape, tied by handstamp, with certificate *4,500.*
On cover, cut to shape, handstamp cancel, not tied, with certificate *6,000.*

Cancellations: Black "PAID / W. W." Black oblong quad (ties stamp "through" to cover).

Wells, Fargo and Co.

Wells, Fargo & Company entered the Western field about July 1, 1852, to engage in business on the Pacific Coast, and soon began to acquire other express businesses, eventually becoming the most important express company in its territory.

The Central Overland, California and Pikes Peak Express Company, inaugurated in 1860, was the pioneer Pony Express system and was developed to bring about quicker communication between the extreme portions of the United States. Via water the time was 28 to 30 days, with two monthly sailings, and by the overland route the time was 28 days. In 1860 the pioneer Pony Express carried letters only, reducing the time for the 2,100 miles (St. Joseph to San Francisco) to about 12 days. The postage rate was originally $5 the half-ounce.

About April 1, 1861, Wells, Fargo & Company became agents for the Central Overland, California and Pikes Peak Express Company and issued $2 red and $4 green stamps.

The rates were cut in half about July 1, 1861, and new stamps were issued: the $1 red, $2 green and $4 black, and the $1 garter design.

The revival of the Pony Express in 1862, known as the "Virginia City Pony" resulted in the appearance of the "cents" values, first rate.

Advertisement in the Placerville newspaper, Aug. 7, 1862: "Wells, Fargo & Co.'s Pony Express. On and after Monday, the 11th inst., we will run a Pony Express Daily between Sacramento and Virginia City, carrying letters and exchange papers, through from San Francisco in 24 hours, Sacramento in 15 hours and Placerville in 10 hours. Rates: All letters to be enclosed in our franks, and TEN CENTS PREPAID, in addition, for each letter weighing half an ounce or less, and ten cents for each additional half-ounce."

Wells, Fargo & Company used various handstamps to indicate mail transit. These are illustrated and described in the handbook, "Wells, Fargo & Co.'s Handstamps and Franks" by V. M. Berthold, published by Scott Stamp & Coin Co., Ltd. (out of print). The history of the Pony Express, a study of the stamps and reprints, and a survey of existing covers are covered in "The Pony Express," by M. C. Nathan and Winthrop S. Boggs, published by the Collectors Club, 22 E. 35th., New York, N.Y. 10016.

Wells Fargo stamps of types L262-L264 were lithographed by Britton & Rey, San Francisco.

L262

Front hoof missing

Printed in sheets of 40 (8x5), two panes of 20 (4x5) each.

1861 **(April to July 1)** **Litho.**
143L1 L262 $2 **red** 150. *800.*
On US envelope #U10 —
On US envelope #U16 *12,500.*
On US envelope #U17 *12,500.*
On US envelope #U18 *12,500.*
On US envelope #U32 (patriotic cover) *100,000.*
On US envelope #U33 *15,000.*
On US envelope #U65 —
143L2 L262 $4 **green** 300. *1,250.*
Block of 4 *9,000.*
On US envelope #U33 —

The No. 143L2 block is the only recorded $4 block.

1861
(July 1 to Nov.)
143L3 L262 $1 **red** 90. *750.*
Block of 4 750.
Sheet of 40 *7,000.*
On US envelope #U11 —
On US envelope #U15 *8,500.*
On US envelope #U17 *8,500.*
On US envelope #U32 *9,000.*
On US envelope #U33 *9,000.*
On US envelope #U35 *8,500.*
On US envelope #U40 *9,000.*
On US envelope #U41 *8,500.*
Front hoof missing (9R) *175.*
143L4 L262 $2 **green** 250. *1,750.*
Block of 4 1,200.
On US envelope #U41 *50,000.*
143L5 L262 $4 **black** 175. *1,100.*
Block of 4 —
On cover to Wash., D.C., tied by handstamp *350,000.*

Cancellations: Blue, black or magenta express company.

Nos. 143L1-143L5 and 143L7-143L9 were reprinted in 1897. The reprints are retouched. Shades vary from originals. Originals and reprints are fully described in "The Pony Express," by M. C. Nathan and W. S. Boggs (Collectors Club).

L263

Printed in sheets of 16 (4x4)

1861

Thin Wove Paper

143L6	L263	$1	**blue**	*750.*	*1,250.*
			Strip of 3	—	
			On 10c US env. #U40		*75,000.*

No. 143L6 apparently used only from east to west.

Most counterfeits have a horizontal line bisecting the shield. Some genuine stamps have a similar line drawn in with blue or red ink. Value for genuine, $300.

L264

Printed in sheets of 40 (8x5), four panes of 10, each pane 2x5.

1862-64

143L7	L264	10c	**brown** (shades)	50.	*150.*
			Pair	125.	*500.*
			Block of 4	500.	
			Block of 6	*750.*	
			On US envelope #U26		*5,000.*
			On US envelope #U32		*3,500.*
			On US envelope #U34		*4,500.*
			On US envelope #U35		*3,500.*
			On cover with 3c #65		—
143L8	L264	25c	**blue**	75.	*140.*
			Pair	175.	
			Block of 4	500.	
			Block of 8	*1,750.*	
			On plain cover		*2,250.*
			Strip of 3 on cover		—
			On US envelope #U10		—
			On US envelope #U26		*2,000.*
			On US envelope #U34		*3,500.*
			On US envelope #U35		*4,000.*
143L9	L264	25c	**red**	30.	*80.*
			Pair	80.	
			Block of 4	225.	
			Block of 6	*550.*	
			Sheet of 40	*4,500.*	
			On US envelope #U9		—
			On US envelope #U10		*4,000.*
			On US envelope #U34		*4,000.*
			On US envelope #U35		*4,000.*
			Pair on US envelope #U35		*9,000.*
			On US envelope #U59		*2,750.*

Cancellations on Nos. 143L7-143L9: Blue or black express company, black town.

NEWSPAPER STAMPS

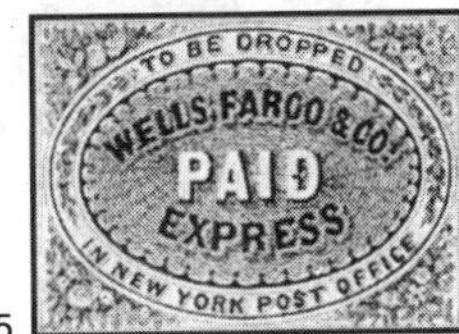

L265

L266

L267

L268

L269

L270

1861-70

143LP1	L265	**black**	*1,250.*	—
		On cover, uncanceled, with certificate		*11,000.*
143LP2	L266	**blue**	*1,250*	
143LP3	L267	**blue**	20.00	*75.00*
		Pair	100.00	
		Block of 4	—	
		Sheet of 50	—	
a.		Thin paper	40.00	*100.00*
143LP4	L268	**blue**	50.00	

Rouletted 10

143LP5	L267	**blue**	25.00	*125.00*
		On wrapper		*1,500.*
		Pair	55.00	
		Block of 4	125.00	
a.		Thin paper	—	
143LP6	L268	**blue**	22.50	
a.		Tete beche pair	350.00	

Design L267 was printed in sheets of 50 (5x10).

1883-88 ***Perf. 11, 12, 12½***

143LP7	L268	**blue**	12.50	*25.00*
143LP8	L269	**blue**	25.00	*35.00*
143LP9	L270	**blue**	3.50	*5.00*
		Double transfer	—	
		On wrapper		*1,500.*
		Strip of 3 on wrapper		—
a.		Vertical pair, imperf. between	125.00	
b.		Horiz. pair, imperf. vert.	*350.00*	

FOR PUBLISHERS' USE

PUBLISHERS'
PAID STAMP
W.F.& Co's Express.

L271

1876 **Typo.**

143LP10	L271	**blue**	8.50	*25.00*
		Pair	17.50	*60.00*
		Block of 4	45.00	
		Sheet of 50	—	
		On wrapper		*1,750.*
		On wrapper with #143LP9		—

Cancellation: Blue company.

ENVELOPES

1862

143LU1	L264	10c	**red**	—	*1,250.*
			On US envelope #U34	—	*1,500.*
143LU2	L264	10c	**blue**		—
			On US envelope #U34		*5,500.*
143LU3	L264	25c	**red**	700.	
			On "Gould & Curry" overall advertising env.	700.	

Westervelt's Post, Chester, N.Y.

Operated by Charles H. Westervelt. Rate was 1 cent for letters and 2 cents for packages carried to the post office. Local and government postage required prepayment.

Westervelt's
POST,
Chester, N. Y.

L273

Several varieties

1863 (?) **Typeset**

144L1	L273	(1c)	**black,** *buff*	35.00	—
			On cover		*650.00*
			On cover, tied by handstamp, with 3c #65		*1,000.*
			Sheet of 6	*675.00*	
144L2	L273		**black,** *lavender*	40.00	—
			On cover		—

Indian Chief — L274

General U. S. Grant — L275

Six varieties

1864 (?) **Typeset**

144L9	L274	(1c)	**red,** *pink*	75.00	—
			On cover		*650.00*
			On cover, tied by handstamp, with 3c #65		*2,000.*

Six varieties

1865 **Typo.**

144L29	L275	2c	**black,** *yellow*	35.00	—
144L30	L275	2c	**black,** *gray green*	40.00	—
144L40	L275	2c	**red,** *pink*	40.00	—

All of the Westervelt stamps are believed to have a philatelic flavor, although it is possible that Nos. 144L1-144L2 were originally issued primarily for postal purposes. It is possible that Nos. 144L9, 144L29-144L30 and 144L40 were used in the regular course of business, particularly No. 144L9.

However, the large number of varieties on various colors of paper, which exist both as originals as well as contemporaneous and near-contemporaneous reprints, are believed to have been produced solely for sale to collectors. Design L275 was certainly issued primarily for sale to collectors. Many of the unlisted colors in all three types exist only as reprints. Forgeries of all three designs also exist.

L276

ENVELOPES

Impressed at top left

1865				Typo.
144LU1	L276	**red,** *white*	—	
144LU2	L276	**red brown,** *orange*	—	250.00
144LU3	L276	**black,** *bluish*	—	
144LU4	L276	**black,** *buff*	—	
144LU5	L276	**black,** *white*	—	

It is possible that Nos. 114LU1-144LU5 were corner cards and had no franking value.

Westtown, Westtown, Pa.

The Westtown School at Westtown, Pa., is the oldest of the secondary schools in America, managed by the Society of Friends. It was established in 1799. In 1853 the school authorities decided that all outgoing letters carried by stage should pay a fee of 2 cents. Prepaid stamps were placed on sale at the school. Stamps were usually affixed to the reverse of the letter sheets or envelopes.

At first, letters were usually mailed at West Chester, Pa. After March 4, 1859, letters were sent from Street Road Post Office, located at the railroad station. Later this became the Westtown Post Office. The larger stamp was the first used. The smaller stamp came into use about 1867.

L277 — Type I

L277 — Type II

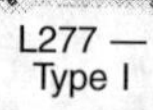

L277 — Type III

L277 — Type IV

L277a — Type V

L277a — Type VI

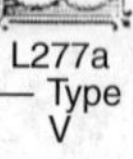

L277a — Type VII

1853-67(?)					Litho.
145L1	L277	(2c)	**gold**	45.	—
			On front of cover, tied with 3c #11		4,500.
			On front of cover, uncanceled, with 1c #9		1,000.
			On front of cover, uncanceled, with 3c #11		150.00
			On front of cover, uncanceled, with 3c #26a		200.00
145L2	L277a	(2c)	**gold**	30.	—
			On cover		400.
			On cover, tied by handstamp, with 3c #158		2,250.
			Block of 4	400.	
			Block of 6	1,000.	
a.			Tete beche pair	300.	

No. 145L1 in red brown is a fake.

Whittelsey's Express, Chicago, Ill.

Operated by Edmund A. and Samuel M. Whittelsey

George Washington — L278

1857					Typo.
146L1	L278	2c	**red**	2,000.	5,500.
			Block of 11	20,000.	

Cancellation: Blue oval "Whittelsey's Express."

Williams' City Post, Cincinnati, Ohio.

See Carriers' Stamps, No. 9LB1.

Wood & Co. City Despatch, Baltimore, Md.

Operated by W. Wood

L280

1856				Typeset
148L1	L280	(1c)	**black,** *yellow,* on cover, ms. cancel, not tied, with certificate	11,000.
			On printed matter, tied by ms.	7,500.
			On 3c red entire #U10, tied by ms., with certificate	14,500.

W. Wyman, Boston, Mass.

Established to carry mail between Boston and New York

L281

1844					Litho.
149L1	L281	5c	**black**	—	750.00
			On cover, tied by ms., Wyman handstamp		3,850.
			On cover, tied by ms., Overton handtsamp		10,000.
			On cover, not tied		2,000.

No. 149L1 may have been sold singly at 6 cents each.

Zieber's One Cent Dispatch, Pittsburgh, Pa.

L282

1851				Typeset
150L1	L282	1c	**black,** *gray blue*	20,000.
			On cover, acid cancel, with 3c #10	—

No. 150L1 used and on cover are each unique.

Cancellation: Acid

For Local #151L1 see **Friend's Boarding School.**
For Local #152L1 see **Faunce's Penny Post.**
For Local #153L1 see **Hackney & Bolte Penny Post.**
For Local #154L1 see **A. W. Auner's Despatch Post.**
For Local #155L1 see **McGreely's Express.**
For Local #156L1-156L2 see **Spaulding's Penny Post.**
For Local #157L1 see **Bush's Brooklyn City Express.**
For Local #158L1 see **Smith & Stephens City Delivery.**
For Local #159L1-159L2 see **Spence & Brown Express Post.**
For Local #160L1 see **City Dispatch, New York City.**
For Local #161L1 see **Clinton's Penny Post.**
For Local #162L1 see **Rogers' Penny Post.**
For Local #163L1 see **Blizzard Mail.**
For Local #164L1 see **Freeman & Co.'s Express, New York City.**
For Local #165L1 see **J. A. Howell's City Despatch.**
For Local #166L1 see **Mac & Co's Dispatch.**
For Local #167L1 see **Morton's Post.**

LOCAL HANDSTAMPED COVERS

In 1835-1860 when private companies carried mail, many of them used handstamps on the covers they carried. Examples of these handstamps are shown on this and following pages.

Accessory Transit Co. of Nicaragua

Blue or Black

VIA NICARAGUA
AHEAD OF THE MAILS.

Red, Black or Blue

A sub-variety shows "Leland" below "MAILS" in lower right corner.

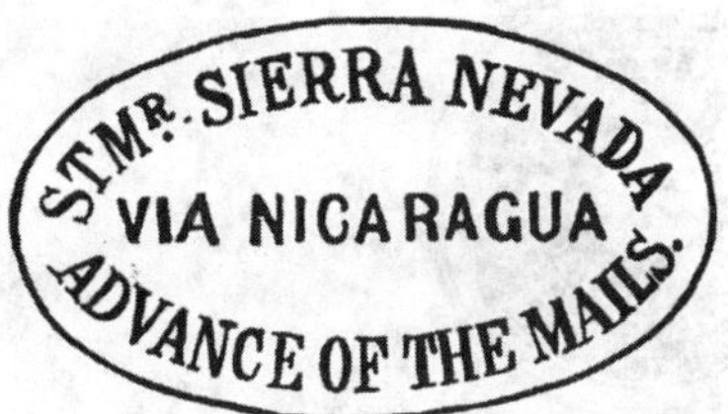

Red or Blue

1853

Barker's City Post, Boston, Mass.

Black

1855-59

Also known with "10" instead of "34" Court Square.

E. N. Barry's Despatch Post, New York, N.Y.

Black

1852

Bates & Co., New Bedford, Mass.
(Agent for Hale & Co. at New Bedford)

Red

1845

Branch Post Office, New York, N. Y.
(Swarts' Chatham Square Post Office)

Red

1847

Brigg's Despatch, Philadelphia, Pa.

Black

1848

Bush's Brooklyn City Express, Brooklyn, N. Y.

Red

1848

Cover shows red PAID.

Central Post Office, New York, N.Y.

Black

1856

Cover shows black PAID.

City Despatch Post, New York, N. Y.
(Used by Mead, successor to United States City Despatch Post.)

Black

1848

City Dispatch Post, Baltimore, Md.

Red

1846-47

City Despatch & Express, Baltimore, Md.

Black

1850

Cole's City Despatch P. O., New York, N. Y.
(Used by Cole with some of the City Despatch Post stamps.)

Black or Red

1848-50

Dunhams Post Office, New York, N. Y.
(See Union Square Post Office).

Red

1850-52

Gay, Kinsley & Co., Boston, Mass.
(A package express)

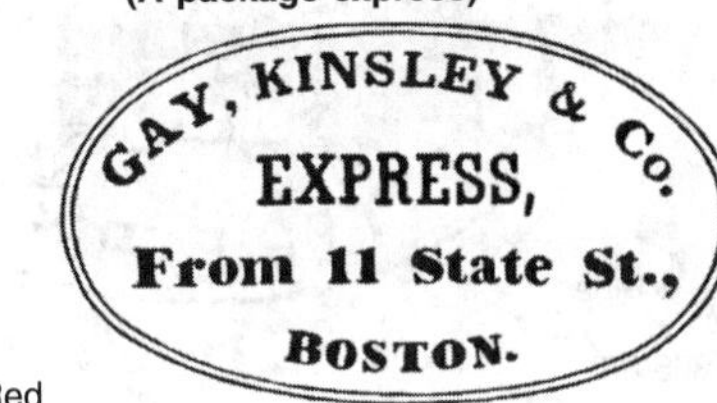

Red

Hanford's Pony Express Post, New York, N.Y.

Black or Red

1845-51

Hartford Penny Post, Hartford, Conn.

Black

1852-61

Hudson Street Post Office, New York, N. Y.

Red

1850

Cover shows red PAID.

Jones & Russell's Pikes Peak Express Co., Denver, Colo.

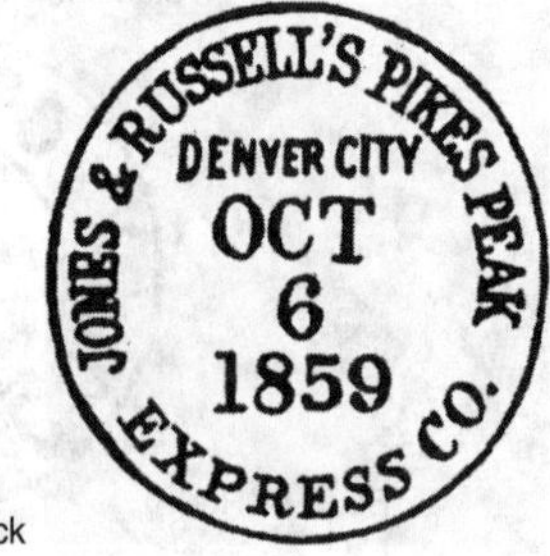

Black

1859-60

Kenyon's Letter Office, 91 Wall St., New York City

Red

1846-60

Letter Express, San Francisco, Cal.
(See Gahagan & Howe, San Francisco, Cal.)

Blue

1865-66

Libbey & Co.'s City Post, Boston, Mass.

LIBBEY & CO'S
CITY POST.
10 COURT SQUARE Black or Red

1852

Cover has 3c 1851 postmarked Boston, Mass.

Manhattan Express, New York, N. Y.
(W. V. Barr. See Bouton's Manhattan Express.)

Red

1847

New York Penny Post, New York, N. Y.

Black or Red

1840-41

Also known with hour indicated.

Noisy Carriers, San Francisco, Cal.

Blue or Green

Blue

By Mail Steamer FROM NOISY CARRIER'S

Black or Red

Black, Blue or Green

NOISY CARRIER'S MAIL. SAN FRANCISCO.

Black

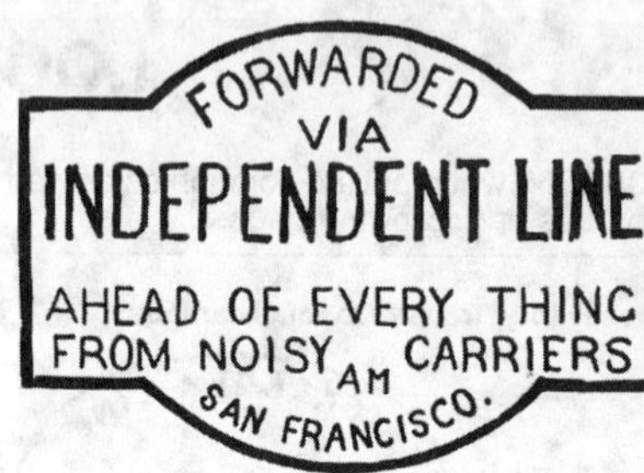

Black or Blue

1853-56

Northern Liberties News Rooms, Philadelphia, Pa.
(Actually a carrier marking mechanically applied.)

Black

Black

1835-36

Overton & Co.'s City Mail, New York, N. Y.

Red

1844-45

Pony Express

Blue or Red

1860

Blue (Enlarged)

1861

Black or Carmine

1860-61

Blue or Red

1853-56

from

St. Joseph, Mo.	Black or Green
Denver City, K. T.	Black
Leavenworth City, K. T.	Black
San Francisco, Cal.	Blue

Black or Green

1860-61

Red

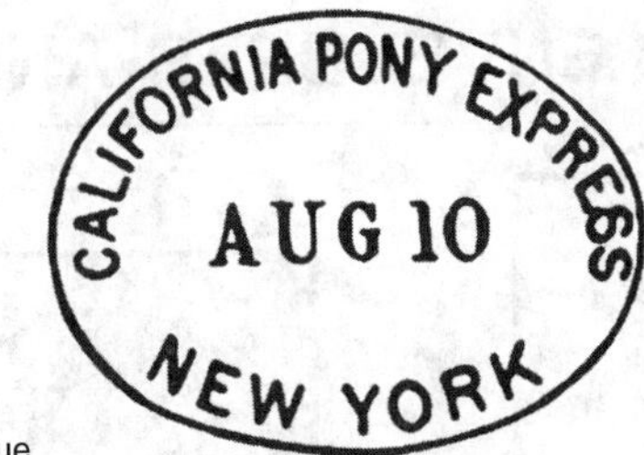

Blue

1860

Rogers' Penny Post, Newark, N. J.

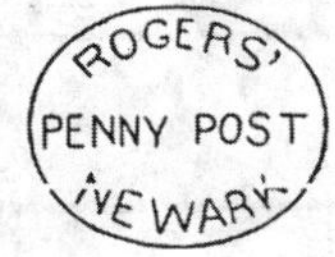

Black

1856

Spark's Post Office, New York, N. Y.

Red, Green, Blue or Black

1848

Spaulding's Penny Post, Buffalo, N. Y.

Black

1848

Spence & Brown Express Post, Philadelphia, Pa.

Black

1848

Stait's Despatch Post, Philadelphia, Pa.
(Eagle City Post)

Red or Black

1850-51

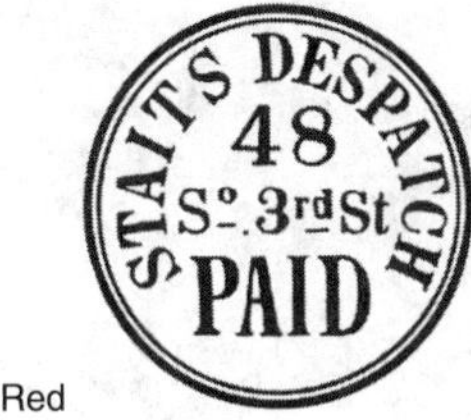

Red

1850-55

Stone's City Post, New York, N. Y.

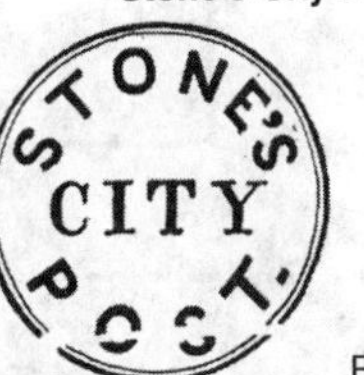

Red

1858-59

J. W. Sullivan's Newspaper Office,
San Francisco, Cal.

Black or Red

1854-55

Towle & Co. Letter Delivery, Boston, Mass.

Red

1847

Towle's City Dispatch Post, Boston, Mass.

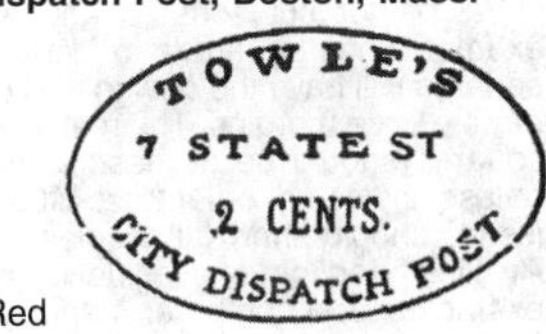

Red

1849

Towle's City Post, Boston, Mass.

(Also 10 Court Sq.) Red

1849-50

Cover shows PAID.

STAMPED ENVELOPES AND WRAPPERS

Fine-Very Fine

THE SCOTT CATALOGUE VALUES CUT SQUARES IN THIS GRADE

Very Fine

Extremely Fine

VALUES

Values for cut squares and most entires are for examples in the grade of very fine. Very fine cut squares will have the design well centered within moderately large margins. The margins on 20th century cut squares should be at least ¼ inch on the cut sides unless indicated otherwise. Cut squares of modern issues should show full tagging bars when they exist. An illustrated grading guide is shown above. These examples are computer-manipulated images made from single digitized master illustrations. Selected issues from both the 19th and 20th centuries are shown in the grades of fine-very fine, very fine and extremely fine. In addition to margin size, collectors are reminded that very fine cut squares (and entires) also will possess a fresh appearance and be free from defects.

Precanceled cut squares must include the entire precancellation. Values for unused entires are for those without printed or manuscript address, and for the most popular sizes. In a number of cases the larger envelopes are less expensive than the values shown here, for example, Nos. U348-U351. Values for letter sheets and wrappers are for folded entires. Unfolded copies sell for more.

"Full corner" cut squares include both back and side flaps. These items generally command a premium of 25% or more above the cut square values shown here, which are not for "full corners."

A plus sign (+) before a Catalogue number indicates that the item was not regularly issued and is not known used.

Envelopes are not available before the First day of issue so most cachets are applied after the envelope has been canceled. First day covers are valued uncacheted. First day covers prior to Nos. U532, UC18 and UO73 are addressed. Minimum values are $1 through 1986, and $1.25 after.

PRECANCELED CUT SQUARES

Precanceled envelopes do not normally receive another cancellation. Since the lack of a cancellation makes it impossible to distinguish between cut squares from used and unused envelopes, they are valued here as used only. Precanceled entires are valued mint and used since entires will show evidence of usage.

HISTORY

STAMPED ENVELOPES were first issued on July 1, 1853. They have always been made by private contractors, after public bidding, usually at four-year intervals. They have always been sold to the public at postage value plus cost of manufacture. They have appeared in many sizes and shapes, made of a variety of papers, with a number of modifications.

George F. Nesbitt & Co. made the government envelopes during the 1853-70 period. The Nesbitt seal or crest on the tip of the top flap was officially ordered discontinued July 7, 1853.

Watermarks in envelope paper, illustrated in this introduction, were mandatory from their first appearance in 1853. One important exception started in 1919 and lasted until the manila newspaper wrappers were discontinued in October 1934. The envelope contractor, due to inability to obtain watermarked Manila paper, was permitted to buy unwatermarked stock in the open market, a procedure that accounts for the wide range of shades and weights in this paper, including glazed and unglazed brown (kraft) paper. No. U615, and other unwatermarked envelopes that follow will be so noted in the listings. Diagonally laid paper has been used for some envelopes beginning with Scott U571.

A few stamped envelopes, in addition to the Manila items noted above, have been found without watermarks or with unauthorized watermarks. Such unusual watermarks or lack of watermarks are errors, bidders' samples or "specimen" envelopes, and most of them are quite rare.

Watermarks usually have been changed with every four-year contract, and thus serve to identify the envelope contractor, and since 1911, the manufacturer of the paper.

Envelope paper watermarks can be seen by spreading the envelope open and holding it against the light.

COLORS IN ENVELOPE PAPER

Stamped envelopes usually have been supplied in several colors and qualities of paper, some of which blend into each other and require study for identification. The following are the principal colors and their approximate years of use for stamped envelopes and wrappers:

Amber: 1870-1920 and 1929-1943; in two qualities; a pale yellow color; its intentional use in the Nesbitt series is doubtful.

Amber-Manila: 1886-98; same as Manila-amber.

Blue: 1874-1943; usually in two qualities; light and dark shades.

Buff: 1853-70; called cream, 1870-78; and oriental buff, 1886-1920; varies widely in shades.

Canary: 1873-78; another designation given to lemon.

Cream: 1870-78; see buff; second quality in 1c and 2c envelopes.

Fawn: 1874-86; very dark buff, almost light chocolate.

Lemon: 1873-78; Post Office official envelopes only, same as canary.

Manila: 1861-1934; second quality envelopes 1886-1928, and most wrappers; light and dark shades 1920-34; also kraft colored paper in later years.

Manila-Amber: 1886-98; amber shade of Manila quality.

Orange: 1861-83; second and third qualities only.

Oriental Buff: 1886-1920; see buff.

White: 1853-date; two qualities 1915-date; three qualities 1915-25; many shades including ivory, light gray, and bluish; far more common than any other color of paper. Envelopes that have no paper color given are white.

Laid paper was used almost exclusively from 1853 to 1915, but there were a few exceptions, mostly in the Manila papers. Wove paper has been the rule since 1915.

EMBOSSING AND PRINTING DIES

Until the modern era, stamped envelopes were always embossed, with the colorless areas slightly raised above the colored (or printed) flat background. While this process was not made mandatory in the original act, custom and tradition firmly established this policy. In 1977, No. U584 became the first envelope to have no embossing. Since 1977, most envelopes are not embossed. Embossing is an unusual procedure, seldom seen in other printed matter. Embossed impressions without color and those where lines are raised are not unusual. The method of making envelope embossings has few counterparts in the typographic industries, and hence is not well understood, even by stamp collectors.

Three types of dies are used, closely interrelated in their derivation, MASTER dies, HUB dies and WORKING (or PRINTING) dies. These types and the ways in which they are made, have undergone many changes with the years, and some of the earlier techniques are unrecorded and rather vague. No attempt will be made to describe other than the present day-methods. As an aid to clarity, the design illustrated herewith is the interlocked monogram "US," within a single circular border. Dies with curved faces for rotary printing are used extensively, as well as with straight faces for flat printing; only the latter will be described, since the basic principles are the same for both.

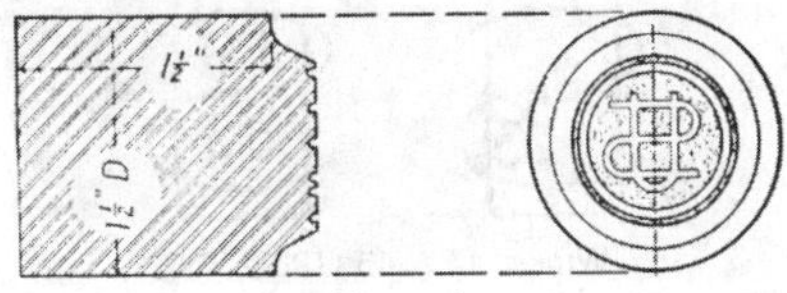

Figure 1

Master Die for Envelope Stamps

Colorless Lines are Recessed Below the Printing Surface.

It Reads Backward.

The MASTER die (Figure 1) is engraved on the squared end of a small soft steel cylinder, before hardening. The lines that are to remain colorless are cut or engraved into the face of this die, leaving the flat area of the face to carry the printing ink. The monogram is reversed, reading backward, as with any printing type or plate. Instead of engraving, a master die may be made by transfer under heavy pressure, usually for some modification in design, in which case it is called a sub-master or supplementary-master die. Sub-master dies are sometimes made without figures of value, when the balance of the design is as desired, and only the figures of value engraved by hand. Various other combinations of transfer and engraving are known, always resulting in a reversed design, with recessed lines and figures, from which proofs can be pulled, and which accurately represents the printing surface that is desired in the eventual working die. The soft steel of a master die, after engraving and transferring is completed, is hardened by heat treatments before it can be used for making hubs.

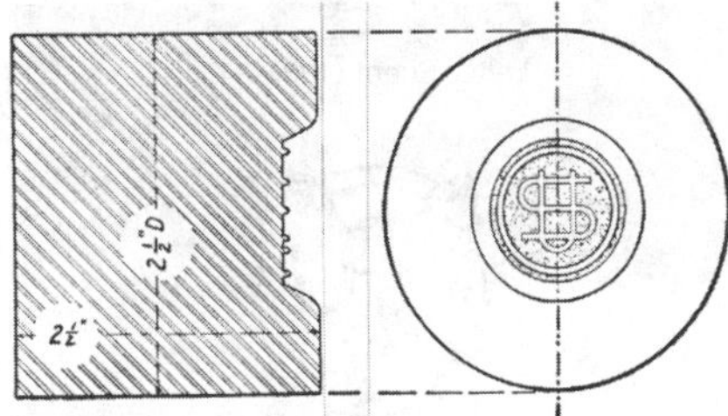

Figure 2

Hub Die for Envelope Stamps

Colorless Lines Protrude above the Surface.

The Monogram Reads Forward.

The HUB die (Figure 2), also called HOB die, is made from soft steel by transfer under pressure from the hardened master or sub-master die, which serves as a matrix or pattern. Since it is a transfer from the master die, the colorless lines protrude from the surface and it reads forward. This transfer impression of the hub die is made in a depression at the end of a sturdy cylinder, as it is subject to extremely hard service in making many working dies.

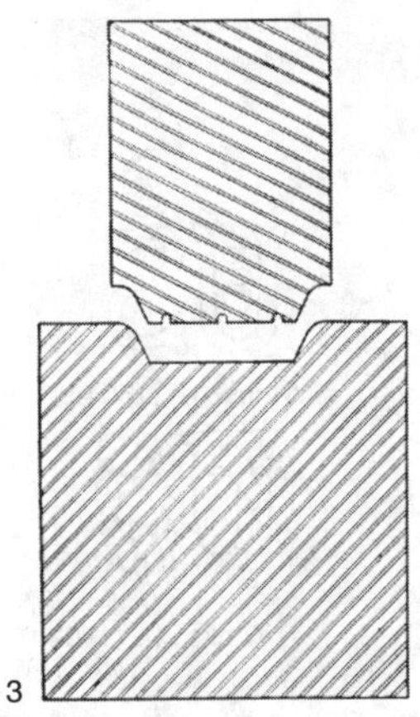

Figure 3

Pressure Transfer From Master Die to Hub Die

Above, Hardened Steel Master Die with Recessed Monogram.

Below, Soft Steel Hub Die Blank.

Figure 3 shows the relative position of the hardened steel master die as it enters the depression in the soft steel hub die blank. Some surplus metal may be squeezed out as the master die is forced into the hub blank, and require removal, leading to possible minor differences between the hub and master dies. At the completion of the pressure transfer the engraver may need to touch up the protruding surfaces to eliminate imperfections, to make letters and figures more symmetrical, and to improve the facial lines of the bust.

A hub die may be made by normal transfer, as above, the figures of value then ground off, and thus be ready for use in making a sub-master die without figures of value, and in which the figures of value may be engraved or punched. Since a hub die may be used to make a hundred or more working dies, it must be exceedingly sturdy and withstand terrific punishment without damage. Duplicate hub dies are frequently made from master dies, as stand-bys or reserves. After completion, hub dies are hardened. Hub dies cannot be engraved, nor can proof impressions be taken from them.

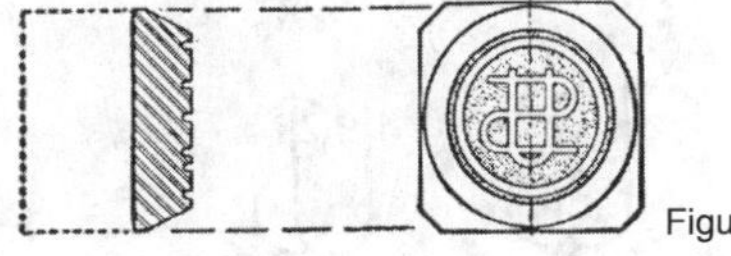

Figure 4

Working or Printing Die for Envelope Stamps

An exact Replica of the Master Die, except for size and shape of shank, which is designed for Printers} lock-up.

It Reads Backward.

The WORKING, or PRINTING, die (Figure 4) is like the type or plate that printers use, and may be thin to clamp to a base block, or type-high with square sides to lock in a printer's form. Its face reads backward, i.e., in reverse, and it is an exact replica of the master die as well as an exact matrix of the hub die.

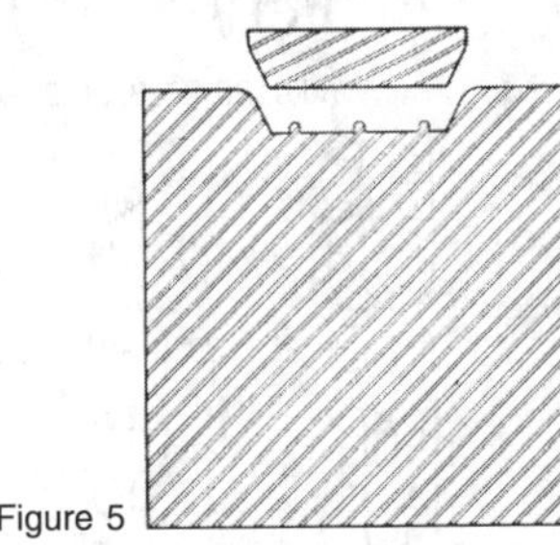

Figure 5

Pressure Transfer from Hub to Working Die

Above, Soft Steel Blank for Working Die.

Below, Hardened Steel Hub Die with Protruding Lines.

The process of pressure transfer is shown in Figure 5. where the soft steel blank of the working die is entering the depression on the top end of the hardened hub die, In fact the pressure transfer of working dies from hub dies closely resembles that of minting coins, and many of these envelope stamp dies are made at the United States Mint in Philadelphia.

In some cases even working dies may be made without figures of value, and the figures of value individually engraved thereon. This is known to be the case in Die B of the 6c orange airmail stamped envelope die, where the size and position of the "6" has eleven variations.

There are some known instances, as in the case of the 4c and 5c envelopes dies of 1903 and 1907, where the engraved master dies were used as printing dies, since the anticipated demand did not justify the expense of making hub dies.

While working envelope dies are heat treated to the hardest temper known, they do wear down eventually to a point where impressions deteriorate and are unsatisfactory, due to shallow recesses or to broken areas, and such dies are destroyed. In many cases these printing dies can be reworked, or deepened, by annealing the steel, touching up the lines or busts by hand engraving to restore the letters or renew the facial contour lines, and then rehardened for subsequent use. This recutting is the principal cause for minor die varieties in envelope stamps. When working dies are no longer useful, they are mutilated and eventually melted down into scrap metal.

The average "life" (in number of good impressions obtained) of a hardened steel working die, as used in envelope printing and embossing machines is around 30,000,000 on flat bed presses, and 43,000,000 on rotary presses. With a production of stamped envelopes of approximately 2 billion annually, 60 to 75 working dies are worn out each year, and require replacement with new dies or a reworking of old dies. Some 200 to 250 working dies can be in constant use, since most envelope printing presses are set up for a special size, type or value, and few can be operated continuously at maximum capacity.

Master and hub dies of obsolete envelope issues are kept in the vaults of the Bureau of Engraving and printing in Washington, as are the original dies of adhesive stamps, revenue paper, government securities and paper currency.

PRINTING ENVELOPE STAMPS

Embossed envelope stamps are not printed against a rigid flat platen, as is the normal printed page, but against a somewhat flexible or resilient platen or make-ready (Figure 6). This resilient platen is hard enough to produce a clear full impression from the ink on the face of the working die, and soft enough to push the paper into the uninked recesses that correspond to the engraved lines cut into the master die. The normal result is raised lines or embossments without ink or color, standing out in relief against an inked or colored background. The method differs from the usual embossing technique, where rigid dies are used on both sides of the paper, as in notarial seals. The use of the resilient platen in envelope embossing permits far higher operating speeds than can be obtained with rigid embossing dies, without the need of such accurate register between the printing surface and the platen.

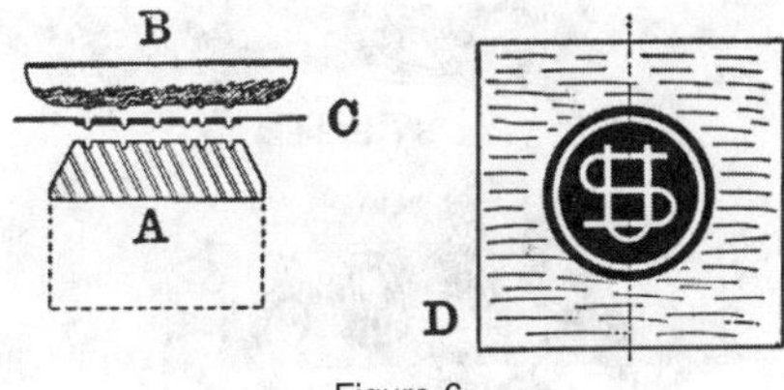

Figure 6

Printing Process for Embossed

A. Working Die, Carrying ink on its surface.

B. Resilient Platen, or Make-ready, Pushing Paper into uninked recesses, so that lines of Embossed Monogram receive no color.

C. Paper of Envelope Blank, after Printing and Embossing. Heavy line shows deposit of ink on surface of paper, but Embossed Lines are not inked.

D. Front view of Embossed impression.

When these recessed lines in a working die become filled with ink or other foreign material, the paper is not pushed in, the plugged area receives ink, and the corresponding colorless line does not appear on the stamp. This accounts for missing letters, lines or figures, and is a printing error, not a die variety.

An ALBINO impression is where two or more envelope blanks are fed into the printing press. The one adjacent to the printing die receives the color and the embossing, while the others are embossed only. Albinos are printing errors and are worth more than normal, inked impressions. Albinos of earlier issues, canceled while current, are scarce.

Before January 1, 1965, stamped envelopes were printed by two processes: (1.) The rotary, with curved dies, on Huckins and Harris presses. (2.) The flat process, with straight dies, as illustrated, on the O'Connell-type press, which is a redesigned Hartford press. The flat bed presses include a gumming and folding attachment, while the rotary presses, running at higher speeds, require separate folding machines.

Different master dies in every denomination are required for Huckins, Harris and flat bed presses. This difference gives rise to most of the major die varieties in envelope stamps.

Web-fed equipment which converts paper from a roll into finished envelopes in a continuous operation has produced envelopes starting with Nos. U547 and UC37. Albino impressions do not occur on envelopes produced by web-fed equipment.

Some authorities claim that Scott U37, U48, U49, U110, U124, U125, U130, U133A, U137A, U137B, U137C, W138, U140A, U145, U162, U178A, U185, U220, U285, U286, U298, U299, UO3, UO32, UO38, UO45 and UO45A (with plus sign + before number), were not regularly issued and are not known to have been used.

Wrappers are listed with envelopes of corresponding design, and are numbered with the prefix "W" instead of "U."

ENVELOPE WATERMARKS

Watermark Illustrations 5, 6, 17 and 18 are condensed. Watermark 4 was used only on Officials. Watermarks 9 and 10 are found on Specimens and Errors. Watermarks 17-18 were the last laid paper watermarks; watermarks 19-21 the first wove paper watermarks. Beginning with No. U615 unwatermarked papers were used for some issues.

Wmks. 1 (1853-70) & 2 (1870-78)

Wmk. 3 (1876)

Wmk. 4 (1877-82)

Wmk. 5 (1878-82)

Wmk. 6 (1882-86)

Wmks. 7 (1886-90) & 8 (1890-94)

Wmks. 9 (1886-87) & 10 (1886-99)

Wmk. 11 (1893)

Wmks. 12 (1894-98) & 13 (1899-1902)

Wmks. 14 (1903-07) & 15 (1907-11)

Wmks. 15A (1907-11) & 16 (1911-15)

USSE US-SE

1911 1911

Wmks. 17 & 18 (1911-15)

Wmk. 19, 20 & 21 (1915-19)

Wmks. 22 & 23 (1919-20)

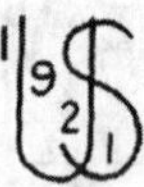

Wmks. 24 & 25 (1921-24)

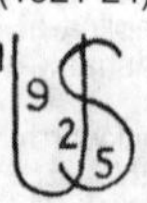

Wmks. 26 & 27 (1925-28)

Wmks. 28 & 28A (1929-32)

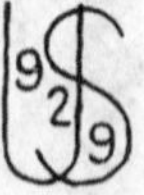

Wmks. 29, 30 & 30A (1929-32)

Wmks. 31, 32, 33 (1933-36)

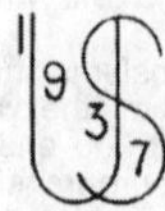

Wmks. 35 & 36 (1937-40)

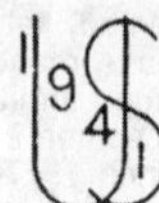
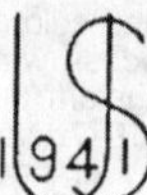

Wmks. 38 & 39 (1941-44)

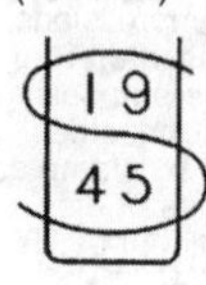

Wmks. 40 & 41 (1945-48)

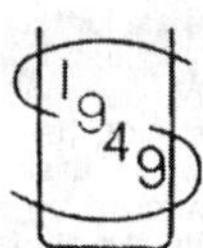
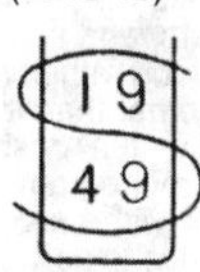

Wmks. 42 & 43 (1949-52)

Wmks. 44 & 45 (1953-56)

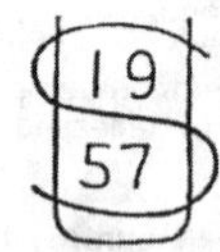

Wmk. 46 (1957-60)

Wmks. 47 & 48 (1961-64)

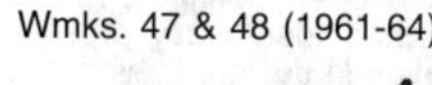

Wmks. 49 & 50 (1965-68)

Letter Sheet (1886-94)

Official Envelopes (1991)

Washington — U1

"THREE" in short label with curved ends; 13mm wide at top. Twelve varieties.

U2

"THREE" in short label with straight ends; 15½mm wide at top. Three varieties.

U3

"THREE" in short label with octagonal ends. Two varieties.

U4

"THREE" in wide label with straight ends; 20mm wide at top.

U5

"THREE" in medium wide label with curved ends; 14½mm wide at top. Ten varieties. A sub-variety shows curved lines at either end of label omitted; both T's have longer cross stroke; R is smaller (20 varieties).

U6

Four varieties.

U7

"TEN" in short label; 15½mm wide at top.

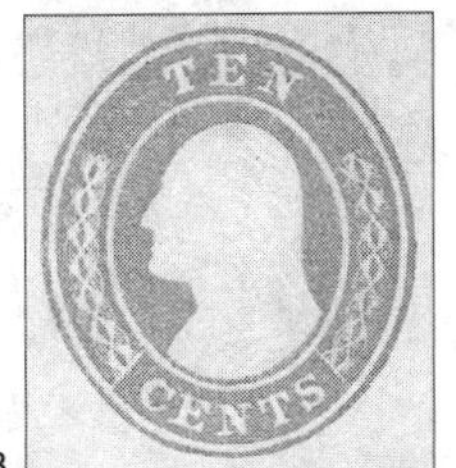
U8

"TEN" in wide label; 20mm wide at top.

Printed by George F. Nesbitt & Co., New York, N.Y.

1853-55

On Diagonally Laid Paper (Early printings of No. U1 on Horizontally Laid Paper)

U1	U1	3c **red**	350.00	35.00
		Entire	2,250.	45.00
U2	U1	3c **red,** *buff*	97.50	25.00
		Entire	975.00	30.00
U3	U2	3c **red**	1,250.	45.00
		Entire	6,000.	100.00
U4	U2	3c **red,** *buff*	350.00	40.00
		Entire	2,500.	75.00
U5	U3	3c **red** ('54)	6,250.	500.00
		Entire	*37,500.*	850.00
U6	U3	3c **red,** *buff* ('54)	5,000.	75.00
		Entire	—	150.00
U7	U4	3c **red**	5,000.	125.00
		Entire	—	300.00
U8	U4	3c **red,** *buff*	*8,500.*	150.00
		Entire	—	300.00
U9	U5	3c **red** ('54)	40.00	4.00
		Entire	150.00	8.00
U10	U5	3c **red,** *buff* ('54)	22.50	4.00
		Entire	72.50	6.00
U11	U6	6c **red**	300.00	80.00
		Entire	400.00	175.00
U12	U6	6c **red,** *buff*	160.00	80.00
		Entire	275.00	200.00
U13	U6	6c **green**	350.00	125.00
		Entire	675.00	225.00
U14	U6	6c **green,** *buff*	225.00	100.00
		Entire	450.00	225.00
U15	U7	10c **green** ('55)	525.00	100.00
		Entire	850.00	150.00
U16	U7	10c **green,** *buff* ('55)	160.00	75.00
		Entire	450.00	150.00
a.		10c **pale green,** *buff*	150.00	65.00
		Entire	425.00	125.00
U17	U8	10c **green** ('55)	400.00	140.00
		Entire	750.00	225.00
a.		10c **pale green**	400.00	125.00
		Entire	750.00	200.00
U18	U8	10c **green,** *buff* ('55)	400.00	90.00
		Entire	700.00	175.00
a.		10c **pale green,** *buff*	375.00	90.00
		Entire	750.00	175.00

Nos. U9, U10, U11, U12, U13, U14, U17, and U18 have been reprinted on white and buff papers, wove or vertically laid, and are not known entire. The originals are on diagonally laid paper. Value, set of 8 reprints on laid, $225. Reprints on wove sell for more.

Franklin — U9

Period after "POSTAGE." (Eleven varieties.)

Franklin — U10

Bust touches inner frame-line at front and back.

Franklin — U11

No period after "POSTAGE." (Two varieties.)

Washington — U12

Nine varieties of type U12.

Envelopes are on diagonally laid paper.
Wrappers on vertically or horizontally laid paper.

Wrappers of the 1 cent denomination were authorized by an Act of Congress, February 27, 1861, and were issued in October, 1861. These were suspended in 1863, and their use resumed in June, 1864.

1860-61

W18B	U9	1c **blue**	*4,500.*	
U19	U9	1c **blue,** *buff*	40.00	15.00
		Entire	90.00	32.50
W20	U9	1c **blue,** *buff* ('61)	70.00	50.00
		Entire	125.00	75.00
W21	U9	1c **blue,** *manila* ('61)	60.00	45.00
		Entire	125.00	100.00
U21A	U9	1c **blue,** *orange,* entire	*2,400.*	
W22	U9	1c **blue,** *orange* ('61)	*4,000.*	
		Entire	*7,750.*	
U23	U10	1c **blue,** *orange*	750.00	350.00
		Entire	1,000.	500.00
U24	U11	1c **blue,** *amber*	375.00	125.00
		Entire	725.00	225.00
W25	U11	1c **blue,** *manila* ('61)	*7,500.*	*2,000.*
		Entire	*20,000.*	*4,500.*
U26	U12	3c **red**	35.00	20.00
		Entire	60.00	32.50
U27	U12	3c **red,** *buff*	26.00	13.00
		Entire	45.00	22.50
U28	U12 + U9	3c + 1c **red & blue**	375.00	240.00
		Entire	825.00	500.00
U29	U12 + U9	3c + 1c **red & blue,** *buff*	375.00	240.00
		Entire	825.00	500.00
U30	U12	6c **red**	3,500.	1,500.
		Entire	*6,000.*	

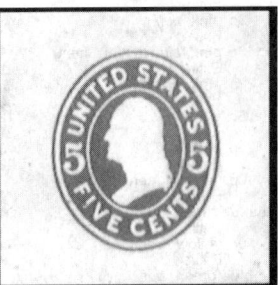

U31	U12	6c	**red,** *buff*	4,000.	1,500.
			Entire	*7,000.*	*15,000.*
U32	U12	10c	**green**	1,650.	450.00
			Entire	*14,000.*	650.00
U33	U12	10c	**green,** *buff*	1,650.	275.00
			Entire	*4,500.*	550.00

Nos. U26, U27, U30 to U33 have been reprinted on the same vertically laid paper as the reprints of the 1853-55 issue, and are not known entire. Value, Nos. U26-U27, $160; Nos. U30-U33, $100.

Washington — U13

17 varieties for Nos. U34-U35; 2 varieties for No. U36.

Washington — U14

Washington — U15

Washington — U16

Envelopes are on diagonally laid paper.

U36 and U45 come on vertically or horizontally laid paper. U36 appeared in August, 1861, and was withdrawn in 1864. Total issue 211,800.

1861

U34	U13	3c	**pink**	30.00	5.75
			Entire	60.00	12.50
U35	U13	3c	**pink,** *buff*	30.00	5.25
			Entire	60.00	12.50
U36	U13	3c	**pink,** *blue* (Letter Sheet)	80.00	50.00
			Entire	290.00	125.00
+U37	U13	3c	**pink,** *orange*	*5,500.*	
			Entire	*7,750.*	
U38	U14	6c	**pink**	125.00	80.00
			Entire	210.00	190.00
U39	U14	6c	**pink,** *buff*	80.00	62.50
			Entire	225.00	160.00
U40	U15	10c	**yellow green**	45.00	30.00
			Entire	80.00	60.00
a.		10c	**blue green**	45.00	27.50
			Entire	80.00	60.00
U41	U15	10c	**yellow green,** *buff*	45.00	30.00
			Entire	80.00	50.00
a.		10c	**blue green,** *buff*	45.00	30.00
			Entire	80.00	52.50
U42	U16	12c	**red & brown,** *buff*	250.00	160.00
			Entire	550.00	*650.00*
a.		12c	**lake & brown,** *buff*	*1,400.*	
U43	U16	20c	**red & blue,** *buff*	300.00	200.00
			Entire	575.00	*1,250.*
U44	U16	24c	**red & green,** *buff*	240.00	200.00
			Entire	750.00	*1,500.*
a.		24c	**lake & green,** *salmon*	325.00	225.00
			Entire	850.00	*1,750.*
U45	U16	40c	**black & red,** *buff*	375.00	350.00
			Entire	850.00	*4,500.*

Nos. U38 and U39 have been reprinted on the same papers as the reprints of the 1853-55 issue, and are not known entire. Value, set of 2 reprints, $60.

Jackson — U17

"U.S. POSTAGE" above. Downstroke and tail of "2" unite near the point (seven varieties).

Jackson — U18

"U.S. POSTAGE" above. The downstroke and tail of the "2" touch but do not merge.

Jackson — U19

"U.S. POST" above. Stamp 24-25mm wide (Sixteen varieties).

Jackson — U20

"U.S. POST" above. Stamp 25½-26¼mm wide. (Twenty-five varieties.)

Envelopes are on diagonally laid paper.
Wrappers on vertically or horizontally laid paper.

1863-64

U46	U17	2c	**black,** *buff*	50.00	20.00
			Entire	80.00	35.00
W47	U17	2c	**black,** *dark manila*	70.00	45.00
			Entire	92.50	77.50
+U48	U18	2c	**black,** *buff*	*3,250.*	
			Entire	*6,000.*	
+U49	U18	2c	**black,** *orange*	1,600.	
			Entire	4,250.	
U50	U19	2c	**black,** *buff* ('64)	17.00	9.00
			Entire	37.50	20.00
W51	U19	2c	**black,** *buff* ('64)	375.00	160.00
			Entire	550.00	325.00
U52	U19	2c	**black,** *orange* ('64)	17.50	9.00
			Entire	32.50	17.50
W53	U19	2c	**black,** *dark manila* ('64)	45.00	35.00
			Entire	175.00	125.00
U54	U20	2c	**black,** *buff* ('64)	17.50	9.00
			Entire	35.00	15.00
W55	U20	2c	**black,** *buff* ('64)	90.00	57.50
			Entire	140.00	110.00
U56	U20	2c	**black,** *orange* ('64)	20.00	8.25
			Entire	30.00	15.00
W57	U20	2c	**black,** *light manila* ('64)	19.00	11.50
			Entire	32.50	22.50

Washington — U21

79 varieties for Nos. U58-U61; 2 varieties for Nos. U63-U65.

Washington — U22

1864-65

U58	U21	3c	**pink**	10.00	1.60
			Entire	17.50	3.25
U59	U21	3c	**pink,** *buff*	9.00	1.25
			Entire	15.00	3.00
U60	U21	3c	**brown** ('65)	60.00	30.00
			Entire	110.00	100.00
U61	U21	3c	**brown,** *buff* ('65)	55.00	26.00
			Entire	110.00	72.50
U62	U21	6c	**pink**	87.50	29.00
			Entire	175.00	60.00
U63	U21	6c	**pink,** *buff*	45.00	27.50
			Entire	100.00	50.00
U64	U21	6c	**purple** ('65)	55.00	26.00
			Entire	77.50	55.00
U65	U21	6c	**purple,** *buff* ('65)	50.00	20.00
			Entire	80.00	55.00
U66	U22	9c	**lemon,** *buff* ('65)	450.00	250.00
			Entire	575.00	*1,000.*
U67	U22	9c	**orange,** *buff* ('65)	150.00	90.00
			Entire	200.00	275.00
a.		9c	**orange yellow,** *buff*	150.00	90.00
			Entire	225.00	275.00
U68	U22	12c	**brown,** *buff* ('65)	325.00	250.00
			Entire	575.00	*1,150.*
U69	U22	12c	**red brown,** *buff* ('65)	150.00	55.00
			Entire	200.00	360.00
U70	U22	18c	**red,** *buff* ('65)	95.00	95.00
			Entire	200.00	*800.00*
U71	U22	24c	**blue,** *buff* ('65)	100.00	95.00
			entire	200.00	*750.00*
U72	U22	30c	**green,** *buff* ('65)	125.00	80.00
			Entire	175.00	*1,500.*
a.		30c	**yellow green,** *buff*	125.00	*80.00*
			Entire	175.00	*1,500.*
U73	U22	40c	**rose,** *buff* ('65)	125.00	*250.00*
			Entire	350.00	*2,000.*

Printed by George H. Reay, Brooklyn, N. Y.
The engravings in this issue are finely executed.

Franklin — U23

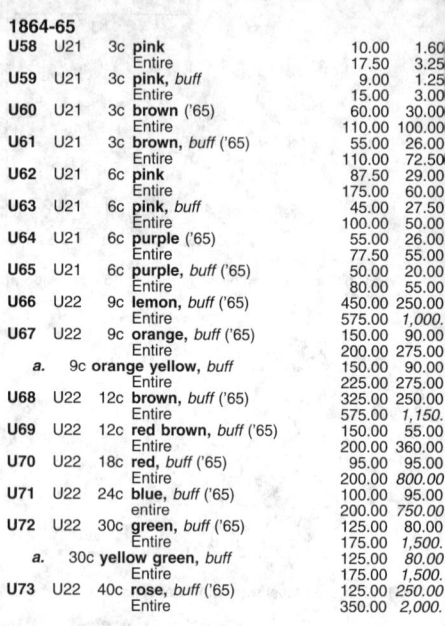

Bust points to the end of the "N" of "ONE."

Jackson — U24

Bust narrow at back. Small, thick figures of value.

Washington — U25

Queue projects below bust.

Lincoln — U26

Neck very long at the back.

Stanton — U27

Bust pointed at the back; figures "7" are normal.

Jefferson — U28

Queue forms straight line with the bust.

Clay — U29

Ear partly concealed by hair, mouth large, chin prominent.

Webster — U30

Has side whiskers.

Scott — U31

Straggling locks of hair at top of head; ornaments around the inner oval end in squares.

Hamilton — U32

Back of bust very narrow, chin almost straight; labels containing figures of value are exactly parallel.

Perry — U33

Front of bust very narrow and pointed; inner lines of shields project very slightly beyond the oval.

1870-71

U74	U23	1c	**blue**	45.00	30.00
			Entire	80.00	45.00
a.		1c	**ultramarine**	72.50	35.00
			Entire	140.00	60.00
U75	U23	1c	**blue,** *amber*	37.50	27.50
			Entire	60.00	40.00
a.		1c	**ultramarine,** *amber*	70.00	30.00
			Entire	100.00	55.00
U76	U23	1c	**blue,** *orange*	20.00	15.00
			Entire	35.00	22.50
W77	U23	1c	**blue,** *manila*	42.50	35.00
			Entire	80.00	67.50
U78	U24	2c	**brown**	40.00	16.00
			Entire	60.00	22.50
U79	U24	2c	**brown,** *amber*	20.00	9.00
			Entire	40.00	17.50
U80	U24	2c	**brown,** *orange*	12.00	6.50
			Entire	17.50	11.00
W81	U24	2c	**brown,** *manila*	27.50	21.00
			Entire	60.00	55.00
U82	U25	3c	**green**	8.00	1.00
			Entire	16.00	4.00
a.		3c	**brown** (error), entire	*13,000.*	
U83	U25	3c	**green,** *amber*	6.75	2.00
			Entire	17.50	5.00
U84	U25	3c	**green,** *cream*	10.00	4.25
			Entire	16.00	10.00
U85	U26	6c	**dark red**	30.00	16.00
			Entire	42.50	21.00
a.		6c	**vermilion**	30.00	16.00
			Entire	50.00	20.00
U86	U26	6c	**dark red,** *amber*	32.50	15.00
			Entire	50.00	30.00
a.		6c	**vermilion,** *amber*	32.50	15.00
			Entire	50.00	30.00
U87	U26	6c	**dark red,** *cream*	37.50	16.00
			Entire	60.00	30.00
a.		6c	**vermilion,** *cream*	37.50	16.00
			Entire	60.00	27.50
U88	U27	7c	**vermilion,** *amber* ('71)	50.00	*190.00*
			Entire	80.00	*800.00*
U89	U28	10c	**olive black**	925.00	850.00
			Entire	1,250.	1,200.
U90	U28	10c	**olive black,** *amber*	925.00	900.00
			Entire	1,350.	*1,200.*
U91	U28	10c	**brown**	90.00	70.00
			Entire	125.00	110.00
U92	U28	10c	**brown,** *amber*	100.00	50.00
			Entire	125.00	110.00
a.		10c	**dark brown,** *amber*	100.00	50.00
			Entire	125.00	110.00
U93	U29	12c	**plum**	110.00	82.50
			Entire	240.00	*450.00*
U94	U29	12c	**plum,** *amber*	125.00	110.00
			Entire	240.00	*650.00*
U95	U29	12c	**plum,** *cream*	275.00	250.00
			Entire	375.00	
U96	U30	15c	**red orange**	80.00	75.00
			Entire	175.00	
a.		15c	**orange**	80.00	
			Entire	175.00	
U97	U30	15c	**red orange,** *amber*	210.00	*300.00*
			Entire	400.00	
a.		15c	**orange,** *amber*	210.00	
			Entire	400.00	
U98	U30	15c	**red orange,** *cream*	325.00	350.00
			Entire	425.00	
a.		15c	**orange,** *cream*	325.00	
			Entire	425.00	
U99	U31	24c	**purple**	140.00	*140.00*
			Entire	200.00	
U100	U31	24c	**purple,** *amber*	200.00	*325.00*
			Entire	375.00	
U101	U31	24c	**purple,** *cream*	275.00	*500.00*
			Entire	475.00	
U102	U32	30c	**black**	80.00	*110.00*
			Entire	300.00	*750.00*
U103	U32	30c	**black,** *amber*	250.00	*500.00*
			Entire	650.00	
U104	U32	30c	**black,** *cream*	225.00	*500.00*
			Entire	400.00	
U105	U33	90c	**carmine**	175.00	*350.00*
			Entire	250.00	
U106	U33	90c	**carmine,** *amber*	300.00	*450.00*
			Entire	900.00	*4,500.*
U107	U33	90c	**carmine,** *cream*	225.00	*2,500.*
			Entire	950.00	*5,000.*

Printed by Plimpton Manufacturing Co.

U34

Bust forms an angle at the back near the frame. Lettering poorly executed. Distinct circle in "O" of "Postage."

U35

Lower part of bust points to the end of the "E" in "ONE." Head inclined downward.

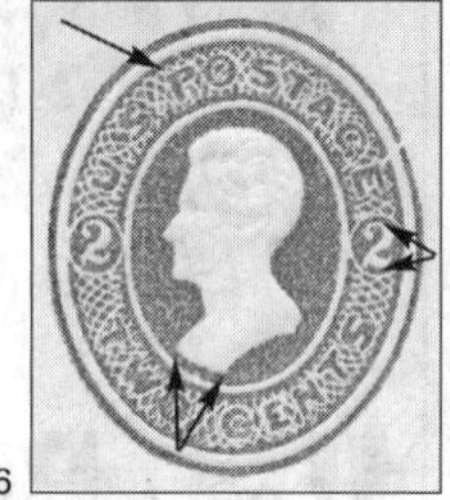
U36

Bust narrow at back. Thin numerals. Head of "P" narrow. Bust broad at front, ending in sharp corners.

U37

Bust broad. Figures of value in long ovals.

U38

Similar to U37 but the figure "2" at the left touches the oval.

U39

Similar to U37 but the "O" of "TWO" has the center netted instead of plain and the "G" of "POSTAGE" and the "C" of "CENTS" have diagonal crossline.

U40

Bust broad: numerals in ovals short and thick.

U41

Similar to U40 but the ovals containing the numerals are much heavier. A diagonal line runs from the upper part of the "U" to the white frame-line.

U42

Similar to U40 but the middle stroke of "N" in "CENTS" is as thin as the vertical strokes.

U43

Bottom of bust cut almost semi-circularly.

U44

Thin lettering, long thin figures of value.

U45

Thick lettering, well-formed figures of value, queue does not project below bust.

U46

Top of head egg-shaped; knot of queue well marked and projects triangularly.

Taylor — U47

Die 1 - Figures of value with thick, curved tops.

Die 2 - Figures of value with long, thin tops.

U48

Neck short at back.

U49

Figures of value turned up at the ends.

U50

Very large head.

U51

Knot of queue stands out prominently.

U52

Ear prominent, chin receding.

U53

No side whiskers, forelock projects above head.

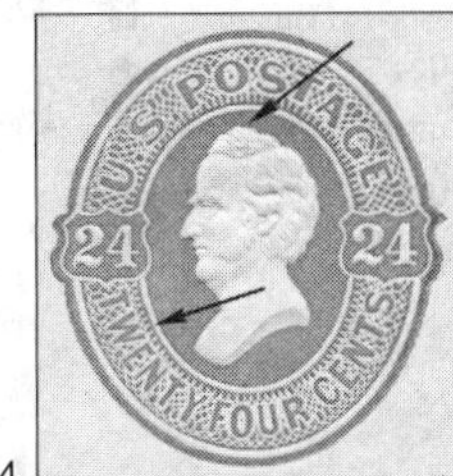
U54

Hair does not project; ornaments around the inner oval end in points.

U55

Back of bust rather broad, chin slopes considerably; labels containing figures of value are not exactly parallel.

U56

Front of bust sloping; inner lines of shields project considerably into the inner oval.

1874-86

No.	Design	Description	Unused	Used
U108	U34	1c **dark blue**	210.00	70.00
		Entire	275.00	110.00
a.		1c **light blue**	210.00	70.00
		Entire	275.00	125.00
U109	U34	1c **dark blue,** *amber*	180.00	75.00
		Entire	200.00	140.00
+U110	U34	1c **dark blue,** *cream*	1,600.	
U111	U34	1c **dark blue,** *orange*	25.00	17.50
		Entire	35.00	25.00
a.		1c **light blue,** *orange*	25.00	17.50
		Entire	35.00	25.00
W112	U34	1c **dark blue,** *manila*	70.00	40.00
		Entire	100.00	72.50
U113	U35	1c **light blue**	1.75	1.00
		Entire	2.75	1.10
a.		1c **dark blue**	8.50	7.50
		Entire	27.50	20.00
U114	U35	1c **light blue,** *amber*	4.25	4.00
		Entire	8.00	6.00
a.		1c **dark blue,** *amber*	19.00	10.00
		Entire	29.00	20.00
U115	U35	1c **blue,** *cream*	5.00	4.50
		Entire	10.00	6.50
a.		1c **dark blue,** *cream*	19.00	8.50
		Entire	30.00	20.00
U116	U35	1c **light blue,** *orange*	.80	.40
		Entire	1.00	.75
a.		1c **dark blue,** *orange*	4.00	2.50
		Entire	15.00	8.00
U117	U35	1c **light blue,** *blue* ('80)	8.00	5.25
		Entire	13.00	9.00
U118	U35	1c **light blue,** *fawn* ('79)	8.00	5.25
		Entire	15.00	10.00
U119	U35	1c **light blue,** *manila* ('86)	8.50	3.25
		Entire	16.00	5.00
W120	U35	1c **light blue,** *manila*	1.60	1.10
		Entire	2.75	1.75
a.		1c **dark blue,** *manila*	8.50	8.00
		Entire	15.00	15.00
U121	U35	1c **light blue,** *amber manila* ('86)	17.50	10.00
		Entire	27.50	20.00
U122	U36	2c **brown**	125.00	40.00
		Entire	160.00	85.00
U123	U36	2c **brown,** *amber*	70.00	40.00
		Entire	110.00	70.00
+U124	U36	2c **brown,** *cream*	1,250.	
+U125	U36	2c **brown,** *orange*	*25,000.*	
		Entire	*45,000.*	
W126	U36	2c **brown,** *manila*	160.00	80.00
		Entire	275.00	150.00
W127	U36	2c **vermilion,** *manila*	2,750.	250.00
		Entire	4,500.	2,500.
U128	U37	2c **brown**	55.00	32.50
		Entire	100.00	72.50
U129	U37	2c **brown,** *amber*	80.00	37.50
		Entire	110.00	75.00
+U130	U37	2c **brown,** *cream*	*50,000.*	
W131	U37	2c **brown,** *manila*	19.00	16.00
		Entire	27.50	25.00
U132	U38	2c **brown**	80.00	27.50
		Entire	110.00	77.50
U133	U38	2c **brown,** *amber*	350.00	65.00
		Entire	575.00	125.00
+U133A	U38	2c **brown,** *cream*	*75,000.*	
U134	U39	2c **brown**	1,400.	150.00
		Entire	2,000.	275.00
U135	U39	2c **brown,** *amber*	525.00	125.00
		Entire	700.00	160.00
U136	U39	2c **brown,** *orange*	55.00	29.00
		Entire	85.00	37.50
W137	U39	2c **brown,** *manila*	75.00	35.00
		Entire	110.00	50.00
+U137A	U39	2c **vermilion**	*35,000.*	
+U137B	U39	2c **vermilion,** *amber*	*35,000.*	
		Entire	—	
+U137C	U39	2c **vermilion,** *orange*	*35,000.*	
+W138	U39	2c **vermilion,** *manila*	*32,500.*	
U139	U40	2c **brown** ('75)	60.00	35.00
		Entire	80.00	45.00
U140	U40	2c **brown,** *amber* ('75)	95.00	60.00
		Entire	125.00	75.00
+U140A	U40	2c **reddish brown,** *orange* ('75)	*25,000.*	
		Entire	*40,000.*	
W141	U40	2c **brown,** *manila* ('75)	35.00	26.00
		Entire	42.50	30.00
U142	U40	2c **vermilion** ('75)	8.50	3.00
		Entire	10.00	5.00
a.		2c **pink**	8.50	5.00
		Entire	10.00	7.50
U143	U40	2c **vermilion,** *amber* ('75)	8.50	3.00
		Entire	10.00	4.00
U144	U40	2c **vermilion,** *cream* ('75)	17.50	6.25
		Entire	22.50	11.00
+U145	U40	2c **vermilion,** *orange* ('75)	*50,000.*	
U146	U40	2c **vermilion,** *blue* ('80)	140.00	40.00
		Entire	*200.00*	140.00
U147	U40	2c **vermilion,** *fawn* ('75)	9.00	4.50
		Entire	14.00	6.50
W148	U40	2c **vermilion,** *manila* ('75)	4.00	3.75
		Entire	8.00	6.00
U149	U41	2c **vermilion** ('78)	60.00	30.00
		Entire	90.00	40.00
a.		2c **pink**	60.00	30.00
		Entire	90.00	40.00
U150	U41	2c **vermilion,** *amber* ('78)	40.00	17.50
		Entire	60.00	22.50
U151	U41	2c **vermilion,** *blue* ('80)	13.00	9.25
		Entire	20.00	15.00
a.		2c **pink,** *blue*	10.00	9.00
		Entire	15.00	11.00
U152	U41	2c **vermilion,** *fawn* ('78)	12.50	4.75
		Entire	17.50	9.50
U153	U42	2c **vermilion** ('76)	75.00	26.00
		Entire	100.00	35.00
U154	U42	2c **vermilion,** *amber* ('76)	400.00	90.00
		Entire	450.00	175.00
W155	U42	2c **vermilion,** *manila* ('76)	22.50	9.50
		Entire	45.00	15.00
U156	U43	2c **vermilion** ('81)	1,600.	150.00
		Entire	2,100.	*400.00*
U157	U43	2c **vermilion,** *amber* ('81)	*57,500.*	*35,000.*
		Entire	*70,000.*	
W158	U43	2c **vermilion,** *manila* ('81)	100.00	60.00
		Entire	175.00	160.00
U159	U44	3c **green**	35.00	6.75
		Entire	60.00	17.50
U160	U44	3c **green,** *amber*	35.00	10.50
		Entire	65.00	20.00
U161	U44	3c **green,** *cream*	40.00	15.00
		Entire	65.00	30.00
+U162	U44	3c **green,** *blue*	—	
U163	U45	3c **green**	1.40	.30
		Entire	4.00	2.25
U164	U45	3c **green,** *amber*	1.50	.70
		Entire	4.00	2.00
U165	U45	3c **green,** *cream*	9.00	6.50
		Entire	17.50	9.00
U166	U45	3c **green,** *blue*	8.25	6.25
		Entire	16.00	11.00
U167	U45	3c **green,** *fawn* ('75)	5.00	3.50
		Entire	9.00	5.00
U168	U46	3c **green** ('81)	1,500.	75.00
		Entire	5,000.	275.00
U169	U46	3c **green,** *amber*	300.00	110.00
		Entire	600.00	300.00
U170	U46	3c **green,** *blue* ('81)	*12,500.*	*3,750.*
		Entire	*20,000.*	*4,750.*
U171	U46	3c **green,** *fawn* ('81)	*45,000.*	*3,250.*
		Entire		*14,000.*
U172	U47	5c **blue,** die 1 ('75)	14.00	8.00
		Entire	20.00	12.50
U173	U47	5c **blue,** die 1, *amber* ('75)	14.00	9.00
		Entire	20.00	12.00
U174	U47	5c **blue,** die 1, *cream* ('75)	110.00	40.00
		Entire	175.00	85.00
U175	U47	5c **blue,** die 1, *blue* ('75)	37.50	15.00
		Entire	55.00	19.00
U176	U47	5c **blue,** die 1, *fawn* ('75)	150.00	57.50
		Entire	275.00	
U177	U47	5c **blue,** die 2 ('75)	11.00	6.75
		Entire	17.50	15.00
U178	U47	5c **blue,** die 2, *amber* ('75)	10.00	7.50
		Entire	19.00	16.00
+U178A	U47	5c **blue,** die 2, *cream* ('76)	*14,000.*	
		Entire	*22,500.*	
U179	U47	5c **blue,** die 2, *blue* ('75)	30.00	9.00
		Entire	45.00	22.50
U180	U47	5c **blue,** die 2, *fawn* ('75)	125.00	45.00
		Entire	225.00	125.00
U181	U48	6c **red**	9.00	6.25
		Entire	14.00	11.00
a.		6c **vermilion**	9.00	6.25
		Entire	14.00	11.00
U182	U48	6c **red,** *amber*	14.00	6.25
		Entire	22.50	13.00
a.		6c **vermilion,** *amber*	14.00	6.25
		Entire	22.50	13.00
U183	U48	6c **red,** *cream*	50.00	13.00
		Entire	85.00	27.50
a.		6c **vermilion,** *cream*	50.00	13.00
		Entire	85.00	27.50
U184	U48	6c **red,** *fawn* ('75)	22.50	13.00
		Entire	32.50	27.50
+U185	U49	7c **vermilion**	*1,800.*	
U186	U49	7c **vermilion,** *amber*	140.00	62.50
		Entire	190.00	
U187	U50	10c **brown**	42.50	20.00
		Entire	62.50	
U188	U50	10c **brown,** *amber*	80.00	32.50
		Entire	150.00	
U189	U51	10c **chocolate** ('75)	7.50	4.00
		Entire	12.00	9.00
a.		10c **bister brown**	8.50	5.00
		Entire	12.50	10.00
b.		10c **yellow ocher**	*4,500.*	
		Entire	*8,500.*	
U190	U51	10c **chocolate,** *amber* ('75)	8.00	7.00
		Entire	13.50	11.00
a.		10c **bister brown,** *amber*	8.50	7.50
		Entire	13.50	11.00
b.		10c **yellow ocher** *amber*	*3,500.*	
		Entire	*6,500.*	
U191	U51	10c **brown,** *oriental buff* ('86)	14.00	8.25
		Entire	18.00	11.00
U192	U51	10c **brown,** *blue* ('86)	17.50	8.25
		Entire	20.00	15.00
a.		10c **gray black,** *blue*	17.50	8.25
		Entire	20.00	15.00
b.		10c **red brown,** *blue*	17.50	8.25
		Entire	20.00	15.00
U193	U51	10c **brown,** *manila* ('86)	18.00	10.00
		Entire	22.50	16.00
a.		10c **red brown,** *manila*	18.00	10.00
		Entire	22.50	16.00
U194	U51	10c **brown,** *amber manila* ('86)	21.00	9.00
		Entire	27.50	17.50
a.		10c **red brown,** *amber manila*	21.00	9.00
		Entire	27.50	17.50
U195	U52	12c **plum**	475.00	100.00
		Entire	700.00	
U196	U52	12c **plum,** *amber*	275.00	175.00
		Entire	350.00	
U197	U52	12c **plum,** *cream*	225.00	150.00
		Entire	950.00	
U198	U53	15c **orange**	52.50	37.50
		Entire	90.00	50.00
U199	U53	15c **orange,** *amber*	160.00	100.00
		Entire	300.00	
U200	U53	15c **orange,** *cream*	600.00	350.00
		Entire	1,100.	
U201	U54	24c **purple**	175.00	150.00
		Entire	250.00	
U202	U54	24c **purple,** *amber*	190.00	125.00
		Entire	260.00	
U203	U54	24c **purple,** *cream*	175.00	125.00
		Entire	750.00	
U204	U55	30c **black**	62.50	27.50
		Entire	80.00	65.00
U205	U55	30c **black,** *amber*	72.50	60.00
		Entire	140.00	*250.00*
U206	U55	30c **black,** *cream* ('75)	400.00	375.00
		Entire	800.00	
U207	U55	30c **black,** *oriental buff* ('81)	100.00	82.50
		Entire	160.00	
U208	U55	30c **black,** *blue* ('81)	110.00	82.50
		Entire	140.00	
U209	U55	30c **black,** *manila* ('81)	95.00	80.00
		Entire	160.00	
U210	U55	30c **black,** *amber manila* ('86)	175.00	85.00
		Entire	210.00	
U211	U56	90c **carmine** ('75)	110.00	85.00
		Entire	160.00	95.00
U212	U56	90c **carmine,** *amber* ('75)	225.00	300.00
		Entire	275.00	
U213	U56	90c **carmine,** *cream* ('75)	1,350.	
		Entire	3,000.	
U214	U56	90c **carmine,** *oriental buff* ('86)	200.00	275.00
		Entire	275.00	300.00
U215	U56	90c **carmine,** *blue* ('86)	190.00	250.00
		Entire	250.00	275.00
U216	U56	90c **carmine,** *manila* ('86)	175.00	250.00
		Entire	250.00	275.00
U217	U56	90c **carmine,** *amber manila* ('86)	150.00	200.00
		Entire	225.00	275.00

Note: No. U206 has watermark #2; No. U207 watermark #6 or #7. No U213 has watermark #2; No. U214 watermark #7. These envelopes cannot be positively identified except by the watermark.

U57

Single line under "POSTAGE."

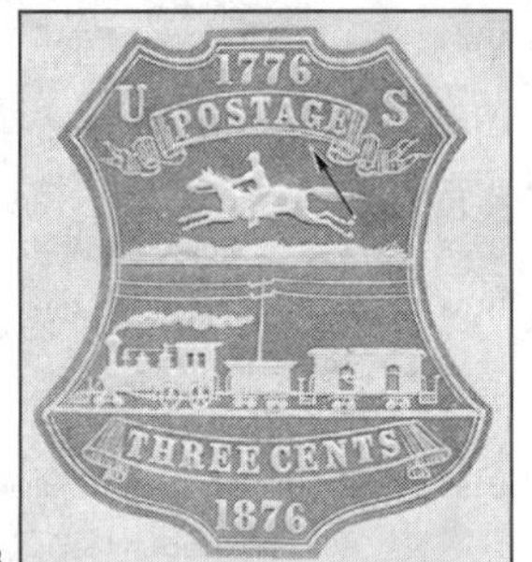

U58

Double line under "POSTAGE."

1876

Printed by Plimpton Manufacturing Co.

U218	U57	3c	**red**	50.00	25.00
			Entire	75.50	50.00
U219	U57	3c	**green**	45.00	17.50
			Entire	65.00	40.00
U220	U58	3c	**red**	*42,500.*	
			Entire	*60,000.*	
U221	U58	3c	**green**	52.50	21.00
			Entire	85.00	50.00

Garfield — U59

1882-86

Printed by Plimpton Manufacturing Co. and Morgan Envelope Co.

U222	U59	5c	**brown**	5.00	2.75
			Entire	10.00	7.00
U223	U59	5c	**brown,** *amber*	5.00	3.25
			Entire	10.50	8.50
U224	U59	5c	**brown,** *oriental buff* ('86)	125.00	72.50
			Entire	175.00	
U225	U59	5c	**brown,** *blue*	80.00	35.00
			Entire	110.00	75.00
U226	U59	5c	**brown,** *fawn*	350.00	
			Entire	500.00	

Washington — U60

1883, October

U227	U60	2c	**red**	4.25	2.25
			Entire	9.50	3.00
a.		2c	**brown** (error), entire	*10,000.*	
U228	U60	2c	**red,** *amber*	5.25	2.75
			Entire	10.00	6.00
U229	U60	2c	**red,** *blue*	8.00	5.00
			Entire	12.00	8.00
U230	U60	2c	**red,** *fawn*	9.00	5.25
			Entire	14.50	7.00

Washington — U61

Wavy lines fine and clear.

1883, November

Four Wavy Lines in Oval

U231	U61	2c	**red**	4.25	2.25
			Entire	8.50	4.00
U232	U61	2c	**red,** *amber*	5.25	3.75
			Entire	10.00	5.75
U233	U61	2c	**red,** *blue*	9.00	7.25
			Entire	16.00	10.00
U234	U61	2c	**red,** *fawn*	6.50	4.75
			Entire	10.50	6.00
W235	U61	2c	**red,** *manila*	19.00	6.25
			Entire	29.00	12.50

U62

Retouched die. Wavy lines thick and blurred.

1884, June

U236	U62	2c	**red**	12.50	4.00
			Entire	19.00	7.75
U237	U62	2c	**red,** *amber*	15.00	10.00
			Entire	24.00	11.00
U238	U62	2c	**red,** *blue*	27.50	10.00
			Entire	37.50	12.50
U239	U62	2c	**red,** *fawn*	16.00	10.00
			Entire	21.00	11.00

U63

3½ links over left "2."

U240	U63	2c	**red**	95.00	42.50
			Entire	150.00	67.50
U241	U63	2c	**red,** *amber*	1,000.	325.00
			Entire	2,750.	750.00
U242	U63	2c	**red,** *fawn*		*37,500.*
			Entire		*55,000.*

U64

2 links below right "2."

U243	U64	2c	**red**	110.00	57.50
			Entire	150.00	90.00
U244	U64	2c	**red,** *amber*	325.00	75.00
			Entire	475.00	110.00
U245	U64	2c	**red,** *blue*	475.00	200.00
			Entire	625.00	210.00
U246	U64	2c	**red,** *fawn*	425.00	140.00
			Entire	650.00	250.00

U65

Round "O" in "TWO." White lines above "WO" of "TWO" joined to form thick white dash.

U247	U65	2c	**red**	2,900.	500.00
			Entire	4,000.	*950.00*
U248	U65	2c	**red,** *amber*	4,750.	1,050.
			Entire	7,500.	*1,500.*
U249	U65	2c	**red,** *fawn*	1,150.	425.00
			Entire	1,700.	*600.00*

Jackson, Die 1 — U66

Die 1 - Numeral at left is 2¾mm wide.

Die 2 - Numeral at left is 3¼mm wide

1883-86

U250	U66	4c	**green,** die 1	3.75	3.50
			Entire	6.25	6.00
U251	U66	4c	**green,** die 1, *amber*	4.75	3.50
			Entire	7.00	5.25
U252	U66	4c	**green,** die 1, *oriental buff* ('86)	12.00	9.00
			Entire	17.50	12.50
U253	U66	4c	**green,** die 1, *blue* ('86)	12.00	6.50
			Entire	17.50	8.00
U254	U66	4c	**green,** die 1, *manila* ('86)	15.00	7.50
			Entire	20.00	15.00
U255	U66	4c	**green,** die 1, *amber manila* ('86)	22.50	10.00
			Entire	30.00	15.00
U256	U66	4c	**green,** die 2	10.00	5.00
			Entire	18.00	6.75
U257	U66	4c	**green,** die 2, *amber*	14.50	7.00
			Entire	24.00	10.00
U258	U66	4c	**green,** die 2, *manila* ('86)	14.50	7.50
			Entire	24.00	12.50
U259	U66	4c	**green,** die 2, *amber manila* ('86)	14.50	7.50
			Entire	24.00	12.50

1884, May

U260	U61	2c	**brown**	16.00	5.75
			Entire	20.00	9.00
U261	U61	2c	**brown,** *amber*	16.00	6.50
			Entire	20.00	7.50
U262	U61	2c	**brown,** *blue*	20.00	10.00
			Entire	27.50	14.00
U263	U61	2c	**brown,** *fawn*	16.00	9.25
			Entire	19.00	12.50
W264	U61	2c	**brown,** *manila*	17.50	10.50
			Entire	25.00	17.50

1884, June

Retouched Die

U265	U62	2c	**brown**	17.50	6.25
			Entire	25.00	11.00
U266	U62	2c	**brown,** *amber*	67.50	40.00
			Entire	75.00	50.00
U267	U62	2c	**brown,** *blue*	22.50	6.25
			Entire	30.00	10.00
U268	U62	2c	**brown,** *fawn*	17.50	11.00
			Entire	21.00	15.00
W269	U62	2c	**brown,** *manila*	27.50	15.00
			Entire	32.50	22.50

2 Links Below Right "2"

U270	U64	2c	**brown**	110.00	45.00
			Entire	150.00	100.00
U271	U64	2c	**brown,** *amber*	450.00	100.00
			Entire	525.00	300.00
U272	U64	2c	**brown,** *fawn*	*9,000.*	*2,500.*
			Entire	*12,000.*	*4,000.*

Round "O" in "Two"

U273	U65	2c	**brown**	300.00	100.00
			Entire	375.00	190.00
U274	U65	2c	**brown,** *amber*	300.00	85.00
			Entire	400.00	175.00
U275	U65	2c	**brown,** *blue*		*20,000.*
			Entire		*47,500.*
U276	U65	2c	**brown,** *fawn*	1,050.	700.00
			Entire	1,550.	*900.00*

Washington — U67

Extremity of bust below the queue forms a point.

U68

Extremity of bust is rounded. Similar to U61. Two wavy lines in oval.

1884-86

U277	U67	2c	**brown**	.50	.20
			Entire	.75	.40
	a.	2c	**brown lake,** die 1	22.50	21.00
			Entire	27.50	26.00
U278	U67	2c	**brown,** *amber*	.65	.50
			Entire	1.25	.75
	a.	2c	**brown lake,** *amber*	35.00	25.00
			Entire	42.50	32.50
U279	U67	2c	**brown,** *oriental buff* ('86)	5.00	2.10
			Entire	7.50	3.00
U280	U67	2c	**brown,** *blue*	3.00	2.10
			Entire	4.50	3.50
U281	U67	2c	**brown,** *fawn*	3.50	2.40
			Entire	5.50	4.00
U282	U67	2c	**brown,** *manila* ('86)	13.00	4.00
			Entire	17.50	6.50
W283	U67	2c	**brown,** *manila*	7.25	5.00
			Entire	10.50	6.50
U284	U67	2c	**brown,** *amber manila* ('86)	9.00	5.75
			Entire	15.00	7.00
+U285	U67	2c	**red**	775.00	
			Entire	1,650.	
+U286	U67	2c	**red,** *blue*	325.00	
			Entire	375.00	
W287	U67	2c	**red,** *manila*	140.00	
			Entire	200.00	
U288	U68	2c	**brown**	375.00	42.50
			Entire	800.00	125.00
U289	U68	2c	**brown,** *amber*	17.50	12.50
			Entire	22.50	16.00
U290	U68	2c	**brown,** *blue*	1,750.	250.00
			Entire	2,250.	400.00
U291	U68	2c	**brown,** *fawn*	30.00	19.00
			Entire	42.50	24.00
W292	U68	2c	**brown,** *manila*	24.00	17.50
			Entire	32.50	21.00

Gen. U.S. Grant — US1

1886

Printed by American Bank Note Co.

Issued August 18, 1886. Withdrawn June 30, 1894.

Letter Sheet, 160x271mm

Stamp in upper right corner

Creamy White Paper

U293	US1	2c	**green,** entire	27.50	17.00

Perforation varieties:

83 perforations at top	27.50	17.00
33 perforations at top	50.00	20.00

All with 41 perforations at top

Inscribed: Series 1	27.50	17.00
Inscribed: Series 2	27.50	17.00
Inscribed: Series 3	27.50	17.00
Inscribed: Series 4	27.50	17.00
Inscribed: Series 5	27.50	17.00
Inscribed: Series 6	27.50	17.00
Inscribed: Series 7	27.50	17.00

Franklin — U69

Washington — U70

Bust points between third and fourth notches of inner oval "G" of "POSTAGE" has no bar.

U71

Bust points between second and third notches of inner oval; "G" of "POSTAGE" has a bar; ear is indicated by one heavy line; one vertical line at corner of mouth.

U72

Frame same as U71; upper part of head more rounded; ear indicated by two curved lines with two locks of hair in front; two vertical lines at corner of mouth.

Jackson — U73

Grant — U74

There is a space between the beard and the collar of the coat. A button is on the collar.

U75

The collar touches the beard and there is no button.

1887-94

Printed by Plimpton Manufacturing Co. and Morgan Envelope Co., Hartford, Conn.; James Purcell, Holyoke, Mass.

U294	U69	1c	**blue**	.55	.20
			Entire	1.00	.50
U295	U69	1c	**dark blue** ('94)	7.50	2.50
			Entire	10.50	6.50
U296	U69	1c	**blue,** *amber*	3.50	1.25
			Entire	6.00	3.50
U297	U69	1c	**dark blue,** *amber* ('94)	47.50	22.50
			Entire	57.50	27.50
+U298	U69	1c	**blue,** *oriental buff*	*14,000.*	
			Entire	*20,000.*	
+U299	U69	1c	**blue,** *blue*	*20,000.*	
			Entire	*30,000.*	
U300	U69	1c	**blue,** *manila*	.65	.35
			Entire	1.25	.75
W301	U69	1c	**blue,** *manila*	.45	.30
			Entire	1.25	.60
U302	U69	1c	**dark blue,** *manila* ('94)	27.50	11.00
			Entire	35.00	20.00
W303	U69	1c	**dark blue,** *manila* ('94)	15.00	9.50
			Entire	22.50	13.00
U304	U69	1c	**blue,** *amber manila*	10.00	4.25
			Entire	15.00	6.00
U305	U70	2c	**green**	17.50	9.00
			Entire	32.50	13.00
U306	U70	2c	**green,** *amber*	40.00	14.00
			Entire	50.00	17.50
U307	U70	2c	**green,** *oriental buff*	90.00	30.00
			Entire	110.00	42.50
U308	U70	2c	**green,** *blue*	*9,000.*	1,250.
			Entire		*20,000.*
U309	U70	2c	**green,** *manila*	*17,500.*	750.00
			Entire	*25,000.*	1,050.
U310	U70	2c	**green,** *amber manila*	—	1,250.
			Entire	—	*3,500.*
U311	U71	2c	**green**	.35	.20
			Entire	.75	.25
	a.	2c	**dark green** ('94)	.50	.30
			Entire	1.10	.85
U312	U71	2c	**green,** *amber*	.45	.20
			Entire	.80	.30
	a.		Double impression	—	
	b.	2c	**dark green,** *amber* ('94)	.60	.35
			Entire	1.10	.85
U313	U71	2c	**green,** *oriental buff*	.60	.25
			Entire	1.20	.40
	a.	2c	**dark green,** *oriental buff* ('94)	2.00	1.00
			Entire	4.00	4.00
U314	U71	2c	**green,** *blue*	.65	.30
			Entire	1.25	.40
	a.	2c	**dark green** *blue* ('94)	.85	.40
			Entire	1.75	1.50
U315	U71	2c	**green,** *manila*	1.75	.50
			Entire	2.75	1.00
	a.	2c	**dark green** *manila* ('94)	2.75	.75
			Entire	4.00	1.50
W316	U71	2c	**green,** *manila*	4.00	2.50
			Entire	11.00	7.00
U317	U71	2c	**green,** *amber manila*	2.75	1.90
			Entire	6.00	3.00
	a.	2c	**dark green,** *amber manila* ('94)	4.00	3.00
			Entire	7.50	4.00
U318	U72	2c	**green**	150.00	12.50
			Entire	200.00	45.00
U319	U72	2c	**green,** *amber*	190.00	25.00
			Entire	275.00	50.00
U320	U72	2c	**green,** *oriental buff*	175.00	40.00
			Entire	240.00	70.00
U321	U72	2c	**green,** *blue*	190.00	65.00
			Entire	300.00	82.50
U322	U72	2c	**green,** *manila*	275.00	65.00
			Entire	325.00	110.00
U323	U72	2c	**green,** *amber manila*	575.00	80.00
			Entire	675.00	160.00
U324	U73	4c	**carmine**	3.00	2.00
			Entire	5.50	2.10
	a.	4c	**lake**	3.00	2.00
			Entire	6.00	3.75
	b.	4c	**scarlet** ('94)	3.00	2.00
			Entire	6.00	3.75
U325	U73	4c	**carmine,** *amber*	3.50	2.50
			Entire	7.00	3.25
	a.	4c	**lake,** *amber*	3.50	2.50
			Entire	7.25	3.75
	b.	4c	**scarlet,** *amber* ('94)	3.50	3.25
			Entire	7.25	4.25
U326	U73	4c	**carmine,** *oriental buff*	7.00	3.50
			Entire	13.00	4.75
	a.	4c	**lake,** *oriental buff*	7.50	3.50
			Entire	14.50	6.25
U327	U73	4c	**carmine,** *blue*	6.00	4.00
			Entire	12.00	7.00
	a.	4c	**lake,** *blue*	6.00	4.00
			Entire	12.00	6.00
U328	U73	4c	**carmine,** *manila*	8.00	6.00
			Entire	12.00	7.50
	a.	4c	**lake,** *manila*	8.50	6.00
			Entire	12.00	7.50
	b.	4c	**pink,** *manila*	14.00	4.50
			Entire	20.00	8.00
U329	U73	4c	**carmine,** *amber manila*	6.00	3.25
			Entire	11.50	5.00
	a.	4c	**lake,** *amber manila*	7.00	3.25
			Entire	12.50	5.00
	b.	4c	**pink,** *amber manila*	15.00	3.75
			Entire	21.00	6.50
U330	U74	5c	**blue**	3.75	4.00
			Entire	7.50	11.00
U331	U74	5c	**blue,** *amber*	5.25	2.25
			Entire	10.00	14.00
U332	U74	5c	**blue,** *oriental buff*	5.75	3.75
			Entire	16.00	17.50
U333	U74	5c	**blue,** *blue*	10.00	5.50

		Entire	16.00	14.00
U334	U75	5c **blue** ('94)	25.00	7.50
		Entire	40.00	20.00
U335	U75	5c **blue,** *amber* ('94)	14.00	7.50
		Entire	22.50	17.50
U336	U55	30c **red brown**	55.00	47.50
		Entire	70.00	*475.00*
a.		30c **yellow brown**	55.00	47.50
		Entire	70.00	*475.00*
b.		30c **chocolate**	55.00	47.50
		Entire	70.00	*475.00*
U337	U55	30c **red brown,** *amber*	55.00	47.50
		Entire	70.00	*475.00*
a.		30c **yellow brown,** *amber*	55.00	47.50
		Entire	70.00	*475.00*
b.		30c **chocolate,** *amber*	55.00	47.50
		Entire	70.00	*475.00*
U338	U55	30c **red brown,** *oriental buff*	55.00	47.50
		Entire	70.00	*475.00*
a.		30c **yellow brown,** *oriental buff*	55.00	47.50
		Entire	70.00	*475.00*
U339	U55	30c **red brown,** *blue*	55.00	47.50
		Entire	70.00	*475.00*
a.		30c **yellow brown,** *blue*	55.00	47.50
		Entire	70.00	*475.00*
U340	U55	30c **red brown,** *manila*	55.00	47.50
		Entire	70.00	*475.00*
a.		30c **brown,** *manila*	55.00	47.50
		Entire	70.00	*475.00*
U341	U55	30c **red brown,** *amber manila*	60.00	30.00
		Entire	70.00	*475.00*
a.		30c **yellow brown,** *amber manila*	60.00	30.00
		Entire	70.00	*475.00*
U342	U56	90c **purple**	77.50	*75.00*
		Entire	100.00	*1,050.*
U343	U56	90c **purple,** *amber*	92.50	80.00
		Entire	125.00	*1,050.*
U344	U56	90c **purple,** *oriental buff*	92.50	85.00
		Entire	140.00	*1,050.*
U345	U56	90c **purple,** *blue*	92.50	*90.00*
		Entire	140.00	*1,050.*
U346	U56	90c **purple,** *manila*	100.00	*92.50*
		Entire	150.00	*1,050.*
U347	U56	90c **purple,** *amber manila*	100.00	*92.50*
		Entire	150.00	*1,050.*

Columbus and Liberty — U76

Four dies were used for the 1c, 2c and 5c:
1 - Meridian behind Columbus' head. Period after "CENTS" and "AMERICA." Appears on 1c, 2c and 5c.
2 - No meridian. With periods. Appears on 1c, 2c and 5c.
3 - With meridian. No periods. Appears on 1c, 2c and 10c.
4 - No meridian. No periods. Appears on 2c.

1893

U348	U76	1c **deep blue**	2.25	1.25
		Entire	3.00	1.50
		Entire, Expo. station machine cancel		100.00
		Entire, Expo. station duplex handstamp cancel		250.00
U349	U76	2c **violet**	1.75	.50
		Entire	3.50	.60
		Entire, Expo. station machine cancel		40.00
		Entire, Expo. station duplex handstamp cancel		85.00
a.		2c **dark slate** (error)	*2,500.*	
		Entire	*3,500.*	
U350	U76	5c **chocolate**	8.50	7.50
		Entire	13.00	10.00
		Entire, Expo. station machine cancel		150.00
		Entire, Expo. station duplex handstamp cancel		250.00
a.		5c **slate brown** (error)	*800.00*	*950.00*
		Entire	*1,000.*	*1,400.*
U351	U76	10c **slate brown**	35.00	30.00
		Entire	70.00	60.00
		Entire, Expo. station machine cancel		250.00
		Entire, Expo. station duplex handstamp cancel		450.00

Franklin — U77

Washington — U78

Bust points to first notch of inner oval and is only slightly concave below.

U79

Bust points to middle of second notch of inner oval and is quite hollow below. Queue has ribbon around it.

U80

Same as die 2, but hair flowing. No ribbon on queue.

Lincoln — U81

Bust pointed but not draped.

U82

Bust broad and draped.

U83

Head larger, inner oval has no notches.

Grant — U84

Similar to design of 1887-95 but smaller.

1899

U352	U77	1c **green**	1.00	.20
		Entire	2.50	.50
U353	U77	1c **green,** *amber*	5.50	1.50
		Entire	8.75	2.75
U354	U77	1c **green,** *oriental buff*	14.00	2.75
		Entire	18.00	3.75
U355	U77	1c **green,** *blue*	14.00	7.50
		Entire	18.00	12.50
U356	U77	1c **green,** *manila*	2.25	.95
		Entire	6.50	2.00
W357	U77	1c **green,** *manila*	2.50	1.10
		Entire	9.00	4.00
U358	U78	2c **carmine**	3.00	1.75
		Entire	7.50	3.25
U359	U78	2c **carmine,** *amber*	22.50	14.00
		Entire	30.00	20.00
U360	U78	2c **carmine,** *oriental buff*	22.50	8.00
		Entire	32.50	9.50
U361	U78	2c **carmine,** *blue*	62.50	27.50
		Entire	75.00	35.00
U362	U79	2c **carmine**	.35	.20
		Entire	.65	.30
a.		2c **dark lake**	30.00	30.00
		Entire	37.50	35.00
U363	U79	2c **carmine,** *amber*	1.40	.20
		Entire	3.00	.60
U364	U79	2c **carmine,** *oriental buff*	1.20	.20
		Entire	3.00	.60
U365	U79	2c **carmine,** *blue*	1.50	.55
		Entire	3.50	2.00
W366	U79	2c **carmine,** *manila*	8.00	3.25
		Entire	12.00	6.50
U367	U80	2c **carmine**	6.00	2.75
		Entire	11.00	6.75
U368	U80	2c **carmine,** *amber*	9.00	6.75
		Entire	15.00	12.00
U369	U80	2c **carmine,** *oriental buff*	25.00	12.50
		Entire	32.50	20.00
U370	U80	2c **carmine,** *blue*	12.50	10.00
		Entire	25.00	15.00
U371	U81	4c **brown**	19.00	11.00
		Entire	29.00	14.00
U372	U81	4c **brown,** *amber*	19.00	12.50
		Entire	30.00	22.50
U373	U82	4c **brown**	*12,500.*	1,100.
		Entire	*17,500.*	
U374	U83	4c **brown**	14.00	8.00
		Entire	26.00	12.50
U375	U83	4c **brown,** *amber*	60.00	17.50
		Entire	75.00	24.00
W376	U83	4c **brown,** *manila*	17.50	8.25
		Entire	26.00	12.00
U377	U84	5c **blue**	12.50	9.50
		Entire	17.50	16.00
U378	U84	5c **blue,** *amber*	16.00	10.00
		Entire	24.00	17.50

Franklin — U85

Washington — U86

"D" of "UNITED" contains vertical line at right that parallels the left vertical line. One short and two long vertical lines at the right of "CENTS."

Grant — U87

Lincoln — U88

1903

Printed by Hartford Manufacturing Co., Hartford, Conn.

No.	Design	Description	Unused	Used
U379	U85	1c **green**	.70	.20
		Entire	1.20	.35
U380	U85	1c **green,** *amber*	15.00	2.00
		Entire	21.00	2.50
U381	U85	1c **green,** *oriental buff*	17.50	2.50
		Entire	22.50	3.00
U382	U85	1c **green,** *blue*	22.50	2.50
		Entire	30.00	3.00
U383	U85	1c **green,** *manila*	4.00	.90
		Entire	5.00	1.25
W384	U85	1c **green,** *manila*	2.50	.40
		Entire	4.00	.80
U385	U86	2c **carmine**	.40	.20
		Entire	.85	.35
		Pink	1.60	1.00
U386	U86	2c **carmine,** *amber*	1.90	.20
		Entire	3.50	.80
		Pink, *amber*	3.25	1.50
U387	U86	2c **carmine,** *oriental buff*	1.75	.30
		Entire	2.50	.35
		Pink, *oriental buff*	2.50	1.25
U388	U86	2c **carmine,** *blue*	1.30	.50
		Entire	2.75	.60
		Pink, *blue*	3.25	1.75
W389	U86	2c **carmine,** *manila*	17.50	9.50
		Entire	22.50	14.00
U390	U87	4c **chocolate**	22.50	11.00
		Entire	27.50	14.00
U391	U87	4c **chocolate,** *amber*	20.00	12.50
		Entire	25.00	15.00
W392	U87	4c **chocolate,** *manila*	20.00	12.50
		Entire	26.00	16.00
U393	U88	5c **blue**	20.00	12.50
		Entire	25.00	17.50
U394	U88	5c **blue,** *amber*	20.00	12.50
		Entire	27.50	20.00

U89

Re-cut die - "D" of "UNITED" is well rounded at right. The three lines at the right of "CENTS" and at the left of "TWO" are usually all short; the lettering is heavier and the ends of the ribbons slightly changed.

1904

Re-cut Die

No.	Design	Description	Unused	Used
U395	U89	2c **carmine**	.55	.20
		Entire	1.00	.45
		Pink	5.00	2.50
U396	U89	2c **carmine,** *amber*	8.00	1.00
		Entire	12.50	2.00
		Pink, *amber*	10.00	3.00
U397	U89	2c **carmine,** *oriental buff*	5.50	1.10
		Entire	7.50	1.50
		Pink, *oriental buff*	7.00	2.75
U398	U89	2c **carmine,** *blue*	3.50	.90
		Entire	5.00	1.40
		Pink, *blue*	5.75	2.50
W399	U89	2c **carmine,** *manila*	12.00	9.50
		Entire	20.00	14.00
		Pink, *manila*	17.50	12.50

Franklin — U90

U90 Die 1

U90 Die 2

U90 Die 3

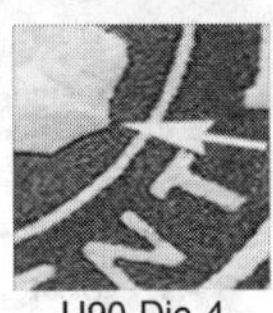
U90 Die 4

Die 1 - Wide "D" in "UNITED."
Die 2 - Narrow "D" in "UNITED."
Die 3 - Wide "S-S" in "STATES" (1910).
Die 4 - Sharp angle at back of bust, "N" and "E" of "ONE" are parallel (1912).

1907-16

Printed by Mercantile Corp. and Middle West Supply Co., Dayton, Ohio

No.	Design	Description	Unused	Used
U400	U90	1c **green,** die 1	.30	.20
		Entire	.50	.30
a.	Die 2		.80	.25
		Entire	1.10	.45
b.	Die 3		.80	.35
		Entire	1.20	.65
c.	Die 4		.75	.30
		Entire	1.00	.45
U401	U90	1c **green,** *amber,* die 1	1.75	.40
		Entire	2.10	.60
a.	Die 2		1.90	.70
		Entire	2.75	.80
b.	Die 3		2.40	.75
		Entire	3.50	.80
c.	Die 4		1.90	.65
		Entire	2.75	.75
U402	U90	1c **green,** *oriental buff,* die 1	8.50	1.00
		Entire	10.50	1.75
a.	Die 2		10.50	1.50
		Entire	16.00	1.75
b.	Die 3		12.00	1.50
		Entire	16.00	2.50
c.	Die 4		9.25	1.50
		Entire	11.50	2.25
U403	U90	1c **green,** *blue,* die 1	9.25	1.50
		Entire	11.50	2.25
a.	Die 2		9.25	1.50
		Entire	11.50	2.00
b.	Die 3		9.25	3.00
		Entire	11.50	3.25
c.	Die 4		8.00	1.25
		Entire	10.00	3.00
U404	U90	1c **green,** *manila,* die 1	3.00	1.90
		Entire	4.50	2.75
a.	Die 3		3.75	3.00
		Entire	5.75	4.50
W405	U90	1c **green,** *manila,* die 1	.80	.25
		Entire	1.00	.35
a.	Die 2		40.00	25.00
		Entire	45.00	30.00
b.	Die 3		7.50	4.00
		Entire	15.00	6.50
c.	Die 4		40.00	—

Washington— — U406

U91 Die 1

U91 Die 2

U91 Die 3

U91 Die 4

U91 Die 5

U91 Die 6

U91 Die 7

U91 Die 8

Die 1 - Oval "O" in "TWO" and "C" in "CENTS." Front of bust broad.
Die 2 - Similar to 1 but hair re-cut in two distinct locks at top of head.
Die 3 - Round "O" in "TWO" and "C" in "CENTS," coarse lettering.
Die 4 - Similar to 3 but lettering fine and clear, hair lines clearly embossed. Inner oval thin and clear.
Die 5 - All "S's" wide (1910).

Die 6 - Similar to 1 but front of bust narrow (1913).
Die 7 - Similar to 6 but upper corner of front of bust cut away (1916).
Die 8 - Similar to 7 but lower stroke of "S" in "CENTS" is a straight line. Hair as in Die 2 (1916).

No.	Design	Value	Description	Unused	Used
U406	U91	2c	**brown red,** die 1	.80	.20
			Entire	1.75	.30
a.			Die 2	40.00	6.25
			Entire	50.00	20.00
b.			Die 3	.60	.20
			Entire	1.00	.40
U407	U91	2c	**brown red,** *amber,* die 1	5.75	2.00
			Entire	7.75	5.00
a.			Die 2	250.00	45.00
			Entire	300.00	70.00
b.			Die 3	3.75	1.00
			Entire	6.25	1.65
U408	U91	2c	**brown red,** *oriental buff,* die 1	7.25	1.50
			Entire	10.50	3.75
a.			Die 2	175.00	55.00
			Entire	200.00	90.00
b.			Die 3	6.75	2.50
			Entire	10.00	5.00
U409	U91	2c	**brown red,** *blue,* die 1	4.75	1.75
			Entire	6.75	3.50
a.			Die 2	300.00	100.00
			Entire	400.00	125.00
b.			Die 3	4.50	1.50
			Entire	6.50	3.00
W410	U91	2c	**brown red,** *manila,* die 1	40.00	32.50
			Entire	50.00	42.50
U411	U91	2c	**carmine,** die 1	.25	.20
			Entire	.60	.35
a.			Die 2	.45	.20
			Entire	2.00	1.50
b.			Die 3	.75	.35
			Entire	1.20	.50
c.			Die 4	.40	.20
			Entire	.70	.35
d.			Die 5	.55	.30
			Entire	.95	.50
e.			Die 6	.40	.20
			Entire	.85	.30
f.			Die 7	35.00	25.00
			Entire	42.50	30.00
g.			Die 8	37.50	25.00
			Entire	47.50	30.00
h.			#U411 with added impression of #U400, entire	350.00	
i.			#U411 with added impression of #U416a, entire	350.00	
U412	U91	2c	**carmine,** *amber,* die 1	.25	.20
			Entire	.90	.20
a.			Die 2	.90	.25
			Entire	4.00	3.00
b.			Die 3	1.75	.45
			Entire	2.25	.75
c.			Die 4	.40	.25
			Entire	.75	.40
d.			Die 5	.70	.35
			Entire	1.25	.55
e.			Die 6	.55	.35
			Entire	1.00	.50
f.			Die 7	30.00	20.00
			Entire	35.00	27.50
U413	U91	2c	**carmine,** *oriental buff,* die 1	.45	.20
			Entire	.65	.25
a.			Die 2	1.25	.45
			Entire	4.00	3.75
b.			Die 3	7.00	3.00
			Entire	11.00	5.50
c.			Die 4	.40	.20
			Entire	.75	.40
d.			Die 5	3.25	1.25
			Entire	4.00	3.25
e.			Die 6	.55	.35
			Entire	1.00	.55
f.			Die 7	95.00	42.50
			Entire	125.00	62.50
g.			Die 8	30.00	21.00
			Entire	47.50	27.50
U414	U91	2c	**carmine,** *blue,* die 1	.50	.20
			Entire	1.00	.25
a.			Die 2	1.10	.35
			Entire	5.00	5.00
b.			Die 3	1.75	.60
			Entire	2.00	.70
c.			Die 4	.50	.25
			Entire	.70	.45
d.			Die 5	1.75	.30
			Entire	2.25	.40
e.			Die 6	.55	.30
			Entire	1.00	.40
f.			Die 7	32.50	19.00
			Entire	45.00	35.00
g.			Die 8	32.50	19.00
			Entire	42.50	35.00
W415	U91	2c	**carmine,** *manila,* die 1	4.50	2.00
			Entire	7.00	4.75
a.			Die 2	4.50	1.10
			Entire	5.25	4.50
b.			Die 5	4.50	2.25
			Entire	7.00	2.50
c.			Die 7	110.00	87.50
			Entire	150.00	125.00

U90 4c Die 1

U90 4c Die 2

Die 1 - "F" close to (1mm) left "4."
Die 2 - "F" far from (1¾mm) left "4."

No.	Design	Value	Description	Unused	Used
U416	U90	4c	**black,** die 2	4.75	3.00
			Entire	9.25	5.00
a.			Die 1	4.75	3.00
			Entire	9.25	5.00
U417	U90	4c	**black,** *amber,* die 2	6.50	2.50
			Entire	10.00	4.00
a.			Die 1	6.50	2.50
			Entire	10.00	4.00

Die 1 - Tall "F" in "FIVE"

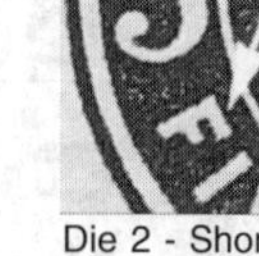

Die 2 - Short "F" in "FIVE"

Die 1 - Tall "F" in "FIVE."
Die 2 - Short "F" in "FIVE."

No.	Design	Value	Description	Unused	Used
U418	U91	5c	**blue,** die 2	6.50	2.25
			Entire	12.50	6.50
a.			Die 1	6.50	2.25
			Entire	12.50	6.50
b.			5c **blue,** *buff,* die 2 (error)	*3,000.*	
c.			5c **blue,** *blue,* die 2 (error)	*3,000.*	
d.			As "c," die 1 (error)	*3,000.*	
			Entire	*5,500.*	
U419	U91	5c	**blue,** *amber,* die 2	15.00	11.00
			Entire	21.00	13.00
a.			Die 1	15.00	11.00
			Entire	21.00	13.00

On July 1, 1915 the use of laid paper was discontinued and wove paper was substituted. Nos. U400 to W405 and U411 to U419 exist on both papers: U406 to W410 come on laid only. Nos. U429 and U430 exist on laid paper.

Franklin — U92

Die 1

Die 2

Die 3 Die 4 Die 5

(The 1c and 4c dies are the same except for figures of value.)
Die 1 - UNITED nearer inner circle than outer circle.
Die 2 - Large U; large NT closely spaced.
Die 3 - Knob of hair at back of neck. Large NT widely spaced.
Die 4 - UNITED nearer outer circle than inner circle.
Die 5 - Narrow oval C, (also O and G).

Printed by Middle West Supply Co. and International Envelope Corp., Dayton, Ohio.

1915-32

No.	Design	Value	Description	Unused	Used
U420	U92	1c	**green,** die 1 ('16)	.20	.20
			Entire	.35	.20
a.			Die 2	140.00	55.00
			Entire, size 8	200.00	70.00
b.			Die 3	.30	.20
			Entire	.45	.25
c.			Die 4	.40	.40
			Entire	.60	.50
d.			Die 5	.40	.35
			Entire	.60	.45
U421	U92	1c	**green,***amber,*die 1 ('16)	.50	.30
			Entire	.75	.45
a.			Die 2	475.00	175.00
			Entire, size 8	625.00	200.00
b.			Die 3	1.10	.65
			Entire	1.60	.95
c.			Die 4	1.50	.85
			Entire	2.00	1.25
d.			Die 5	1.00	.55
			Entire	1.40	.80
U422	U92	1c	**green,** *oriental buff,* die 1 ('16)	2.00	.90
			Entire	2.75	1.40
a.			Die 4	4.25	1.25
			Entire	6.00	2.75
U423	U92	1c	**green,** *blue,* die 1 ('16)	.45	.35
			Entire	.75	.50
a.			Die 3	.75	.45
			Entire	1.00	.70
b.			Die 4	1.25	.65
			Entire	1.95	.95
c.			Die 5	.80	.35
			Entire	1.50	.65
U424	U92	1c	**grn,** *manila* (unglazed), die 1 ('16)	6.50	4.00
			Entire	8.50	5.00
W425	U92	1c	**grn,** *manila* (unglazed), die 1 ('16)	.20	.20
			Entire	.35	.20
a.			Die 3	160.00	125.00
			Entire	200.00	140.00
U426	U92	1c	**green,** (glazed) *brown,* die 1 ('20)	45.00	15.00
			Entire	55.00	17.50
W427	U92	1c	**green,** (glazed) *brown,* die 1 ('20)	65.00	
			Entire	75.00	
U428	U92	1c	**green,** (unglazed) *brown,* die 1 ('20)	16.00	7.50
			Entire	22.50	9.00
W428A	U92	1c	**green,** (unglazed) *brown,* die 1 ('20), entire		*3,000.*

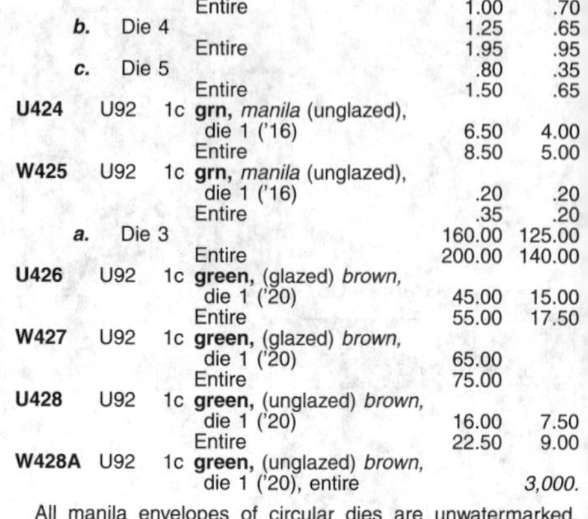

All manila envelopes of circular dies are unwatermarked. Manila paper, including that of Nos. U424 and W425, exists in many shades.

Washington — U93

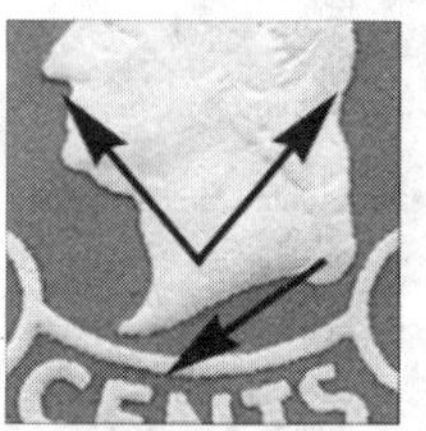

Die 1

Die 2

Die 3

Die 4

Die 5

Die 6

Die 7

Die 8

Die 9

(The 1½c, 2c, 3c, 5c, and 6c dies are the same except for figures of value.)

Die 1 - Letters broad. Numerals vertical. Large head (9¼mm). from tip of nose to back of neck. E closer to inner circle than N of cents.

Die 2 - Similar to 1; but U far from left circle.

Die 3 - Similar to 2; but all inner circles very thin (Rejected die).

Die 4 - Large head as in Die 1. C of CENTS close to circle. Baseline of right numeral "2" slants downward to right. Left numeral "2" is larger.

Die 5 - Small head (8¾mm) from tip of nose to back of neck. T and S of CENTS close at bottom.

Die 6 - Similar to 5; but T and S of CENTS far apart at bottom. Left numeral slopes to right.

Die 7 - Large head. Both numerals slope to right. Clean cut lettering. All letters T have short top strokes.

Die 8 - Similar to 7; but all letters T have long top strokes.

Die 9 - Narrow oval C (also O and G).

U429 U93 2c **carmine,** die 1, *Dec. 20, 1915* .20 .20
Entire .35 .20
a. Die 2 14.00 6.00
Entire 20.00 9.00
b. Die 3 45.00 25.00
Entire 55.00 40.00
c. Die 4 30.00 15.00
Entire 37.50 20.00
d. Die 5 .50 .35
Entire .80 .45
e. Die 6 .60 .30
Entire 1.10 .60
f. Die 7 .65 .25
Entire .95 .75
g. Die 8 .45 .20
Entire .75 .50
h. Die 9 .40 .20
Entire .75 .45
i. 2c **green,** die 1 (error), entire *14,000.*
j. #U429 with added impression of #U420 1,100.
Entire 1,500.
k. #U429 with added impression of #U416a, entire 1,000.
l. #U429 with added impression of #U400, entire 1,000.
m. #U429, double impression, entire 1,750.

U430 U93 2c **carmine,** *amber,* die 1 ('16) .25 .20
Entire .45 .20
a. Die 2 15.00 7.50
Entire 21.00 10.00
b. Die 4 50.00 20.00
Entire 62.50 25.00
c. Die 5 1.10 .35
Entire 1.75 .60
d. Die 6 .95 .40
Entire 1.75 .75
e. Die 7 .70 .35
Entire 1.50 .95
f. Die 8 .65 .30
Entire .95 .45
g. Die 9 .60 .20
Entire .80 .35

U431 U93 2c **carmine,** *oriental buff,* die 1 ('16) 2.25 .65
Entire 4.50 1.40
a. Die 2 160.00 40.00
Entire 210.00 *70.00*
b. Die 4 75.00 60.00
Entire 90.00 75.00
c. Die 5 2.75 1.75
Entire 5.00 2.50
d. Die 6 3.00 2.00
Entire 5.50 2.75
e. Die 7 2.75 1.75
Entire 4.50 3.00

U432 U93 2c **carmine,** *blue,* die 1 ('16) .25 .20
Entire .50 .20
b. Die 2 32.50 20.00
Entire 40.00 30.00
c. Die 3 150.00 90.00
Entire 190.00 *110.00*
d. Die 4 65.00 50.00
Entire 75.00 55.00
e. Die 5 .80 .30
Entire 1.90 .75
f. Die 6 .85 .40
Entire 1.50 .60
g. Die 7 .75 .35
Entire 1.45 .65
h. Die 8 .60 .25
Entire 1.25 .50
i. Die 9 .90 .30
Entire 2.50 .55

U432A U93 2c **car,** *manila,* die 7, unwatermarked, entire *35,000.*

W433 U93 2c **carmine,** *manila,* die 1 ('16) .25 .20
Entire .45 .30

W434 U93 2c **carmine,** (glazed) *brown* ('20), die 1 90.00 50.00
Entire 115.00 60.00

W435 U93 2c **carmine,** (unglazed) *brown,* die 1 ('20) 95.00 50.00
Entire 120.00 60.00

U436 U93 3c **purple,** die 1 ('32) .30 .20
Entire .55 .25
a. 3c **dark violet,** die 1 ('17) .55 .20
Entire .70 .25
b. 3c **dark violet,** die 5 1.65 .75
Entire 3.00 .90
c. 3c **dark violet,** die 6 2.00 1.40
Entire 3.25 1.50
d. 3c **dark violet,** die 7 1.40 .95
Entire 2.50 1.00
e. 3c **purple,** die 7 ('32) .65 .30
Entire 1.50 .75
f. 3c **purple,** die 9 ('32) .40 .20
Entire .50 .30
g. 3c **carmine** (error), die 1 32.50 30.00
Entire 55.00 45.00
h. 3c **carmine** (error), die 5 35.00 30.00
Entire 50.00 45.00
i. #U436 with added impression of #U420, entire 900.00
j. #U436 with added impression of #U429, entire 900.00 950.00

U437 U93 3c **purple,** *amber,* die 1 ('32) .35 .20
Entire .60 .35
a. 3c **dark violet,** die 1 ('17) 5.00 1.25
Entire 9.00 2.25
b. 3c **dark violet,** die 5 8.00 2.50
Entire 12.00 3.00
c. 3c **dark violet,** die 6 8.00 2.50
Entire 12.00 3.00
d. 3c **dark violet,** die 7 8.00 2.25
Entire 12.00 2.50
e. 3c **purple,** die 7 ('32) .75 .20
Entire 1.25 .50
f. 3c **purple,** die 9 ('32) .50 .20
Entire 1.00 .30
g. 3c **carmine** (error), die 5 475.00 275.00
Entire 525.00 *325.00*
h. 3c **black** (error), die 1 200.00 —
Entire 275.00 —

U438 U93 3c **dark violet,** *oriental buff,* die 1 ('17) 22.50 1.50
Entire 27.50 2.00
a. Die 5 22.50 1.00
Entire 27.50 1.10
b. Die 6 32.50 1.65
Entire 35.00 2.50
c. Die 7 32.50 3.50
Entire 37.50 7.75

U439 U93 3c **purple,** *blue,* die 1 ('32) .30 .20
Entire .75 .25
a. 3c **dark violet,** die 1 ('32) 8.00 2.00
Entire 14.00 6.00
b. 3c **dark violet,** die 5 9.00 4.00
Entire 14.00 4.50
c. 3c **dark violet,** die 6 9.00 4.25
Entire 14.00 4.50
d. 3c **dark violet,** die 7 12.00 5.50
Entire 17.50 7.50
e. 3c **purple,** die 7 ('32) .75 .25
Entire 1.50 .50
f. 3c **purple,** die 9 ('32) .50 .20
Entire 1.20 .45
g. 3c **carmine** (error), die 5 350.00 300.00
Entire 450.00 *725.00*

U440 U92 4c **black,** die 1 ('16) 1.50 .60
Entire 3.00 2.00
a. With added impression of 2c carmine (#U429), die 1, entire 400.00

U441 U92 4c **black,** *amber,* die 1 ('16) 3.00 .85
Entire 4.75 2.00

U442 U92 4c **black,** *blue,* die 1 ('21) 3.25 .85
Entire 5.50 1.75

U443 U93 5c **blue,** die 1 ('16) 3.25 2.75
Entire 5.75 3.25

U444 U93 5c **blue,** *amber,* die 1 ('16) 3.75 1.60
Entire 5.50 3.50

U445 U93 5c **blue,** *blue,* die 1 ('21) 4.00 3.25
Entire 8.00 4.25

For 1½c and 6c see Nos. U481-W485, U529-U531.

Surcharged Envelopes

The provisional 2c surcharges of 1920-21 were made at central post offices with canceling machines using slugs provided by the Post Office Department.

Double or triple surcharge listings of 1920-25 are for specimens with surcharge directly or partly upon the stamp.

Surcharged on 1874-1920 Envelopes indicated by Numbers in Parentheses

Surcharged

Type 1

1920-21

Surcharged in Black

U446 U93 2c on 3c **dark vio** (U436, die 1) 15.00 10.00
Entire 22.50 12.50
a. On No. U436b (die 5) 14.00 10.00
Entire 19.00 12.50

Surcharged

Type 2

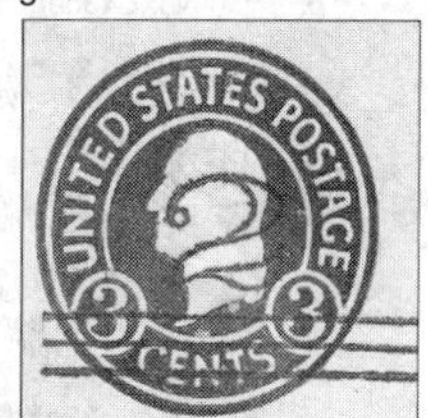

Rose Surcharge

U447 U93 2c on 3c **dark vio** (U436, die 1) 7.75 6.50
Entire 10.00 8.50
b. On No. U436c (die 6) 10.00 8.50
Entire 12.50 10.00

Black Surcharge

U447A U93 2c on 2c **carmine** (U429, die 1) *50,000.*

U447C U93 2c on 2c **carmine,** *amber* (U430, die 1) —

U448 U93 2c on 3c **dark vio** (U436, die 1) 2.50 2.00
Entire 3.50 2.50
a. On No. U436b (die 5) 2.50 2.00
Entire 3.50 2.50
b. On No. U436c (die 6) 3.25 2.00
Entire 4.50 2.50
c. On No. U436d (die 7) 2.50 2.00
Entire 3.50 2.50

U449 U93 2c on 3c **dark violet,** *amber* (U437, die 1) 6.50 6.00
Entire 8.50 7.50
a. On No. U437b (die 5) 10.00 7.50
Entire 13.50 10.00
b. On No. U437c (die 6) 7.50 6.00
Entire 10.00 7.50
c. On No. U437d (die 7) 7.00 6.50
Entire 9.50 8.00

U450 U93 2c on 3c **dark violet,** *oriental buff* (U438, die 1) 17.50 14.00
Entire 20.00 17.50
a. On No. U438a (die 5) 17.50 14.00
Entire 20.00 17.50
b. On No. U438b (die 6) 17.50 14.00
Entire 20.00 17.50
c. On No. U438c (die 7) 110.00 90.00
Entire 160.00 125.00

U451 U93 2c on 3c **dark violet,** *blue* (U439, die 1) 12.50 10.00
Entire 19.00 10.50
b. On No. U439b (die 5) 12.50 10.00
Entire 19.00 10.50
c. On No. U439c (die 6) 12.50 10.00
Entire 19.00 10.50
d. On No. U439d (die 7) 25.00 20.00
Entire 35.00 25.00

Type 2 exists in three city sub-types.

Surcharged

Type 3

Bars 2mm apart, 25 to 26mm in length

No.	Die	Description	Unused	Used
U451A	U90	2c on 1c **green** (U400, die 1)	*30,000.*	
		Entire	—	
U452	U92	2c on 1c **green** (U420, die 1)	3,500.	
		Entire	4,000.	
a.		On No. U420b (die 3)	3,500.	
		Entire	4,000.	
b.		As No. U452, double surcharge	4,000.	
		Entire	4,500.	
U453	U91	2c on 2c **car** (U411b, die 3)	4,250.	
		Entire	7,500.	
a.		On No. U411 (die 1)	4,750.	
		Entire	8,000.	
U453B	U91	2c on 2c **carmine,** *blue* (U414e, die 6)	2,750.	
		Entire	3,750.	
U453C	U91	2c on 2c **carmine,** *oriental buff* (U413e, die 6)	2,100.	*750.00*
		Entire	3,000.	
d.		On No. U413 (die 1)	2,100.	
		Entire	3,250.	
U454	U93	2c on 2c **car** (U429e, die 6)	125.00	
		Entire	175.00	
a.		On No. U429 (die 1)	350.00	
		Entire	400.00	
b.		On No. U429d (die 5)	500.00	
		Entire	650.00	
c.		On No. U429f (die 7)	125.00	
		Entire	175.00	
U455	U93	2c on 2c **carmine,** *amber* (U430, die 1)	2,000.	
		Entire	3,750.	
a.		On No. U430d (die 6)	2,250.	
		Entire	4,250.	
b.		On No. U430e (die 7)	2,250.	
		Entire	4,250.	
U456	U93	2c on 2c **carmine,** *oriental buff* (U431a, die 2)	300.00	
		Entire	350.00	
a.		On No. U431c (die 5)	325.00	
		Entire	400.00	
b.		On No. U431e (die 7)	800.00	
		Entire	850.00	
c.		As No. U456, double surcharge	500.00	
U457	U93	2c on 2c **carmine,** *blue* (U432f, die 6)	350.00	
		Entire	400.00	
a.		On No. U432e (die 5)	350.00	
		Entire	450.00	
b.		On No. U432g (die 7)	750.00	
		Entire	800.00	
U458	U93	2c on 3c **dark vio** (U436, die 1)	.50	.35
		Entire	.70	.45
a.		On No. U436b (die 5)	.50	.40
		Entire	.70	.50
b.		On No. U436c (die 6)	.50	.35
		Entire	.70	.45
c.		On No. U436d (die 7)	.50	.35
		Entire	.70	.45
d.		As #U458, double surcharge	25.00	7.50
		Entire	35.00	10.00
e.		As #U458, triple surcharge	110.00	
		Entire	150.00	
f.		As #U458, dbl. surch., 1 in **magenta**	110.00	
		Entire	150.00	
g.		As #U458, dbl. surch., types 2 & 3	140.00	
		Entire	190.00	
h.		As "a," double surcharge	27.50	15.00
		Entire	37.50	20.00
i.		As "a," triple surcharge	110.00	
		Entire	160.00	
j.		As "a," double surch., both **magenta**	110.00	
		Entire	150.00	
k.		As "b," double surcharge	25.00	8.00
		Entire	35.00	11.00
l.		As "c," double surcharge	25.00	8.00
		Entire	35.00	11.00
m.		As "c," triple surcharge	110.00	
		Entire	150.00	
U459	U93	2c on 3c **dark violet,** *amber* (U437c, die 6)	3.00	1.00
		Entire	4.50	1.75
a.		On No. U437 (die 1)	4.00	1.00
		Entire	5.50	1.75
b.		On No. U437b (die 5)	4.00	1.00
		Entire	5.50	1.75
c.		On No. U437d (die 7)	3.00	1.00
		Entire	4.50	1.75
d.		As #U459, double surcharge	35.00	
		Entire	50.00	
e.		As "a," double surcharge	35.00	
		Entire	50.00	
f.		As "b," double surcharge	35.00	
		Entire	50.00	
g.		As "b," double surcharge, types 2 & 3	125.00	
		Entire	175.00	
h.		As "c," double surcharge	35.00	
		Entire	50.00	
U460	U93	2c on 3c **dark violet,** *oriental buff* (U438a, die 5)	3.50	1.00
		Entire	4.50	1.40
a.		On No. U438 (die 1)	4.00	1.50
		Entire	5.00	2.00
b.		On No. U438b (die 6)	4.00	2.00
		Entire	5.00	2.50
c.		As #U460, double surcharge	20.00	
		Entire	30.00	
d.		As "a," double surcharge	20.00	
		Entire	30.00	
e.		As "b," double surcharge	20.00	
		Entire	30.00	
f.		As "b," triple surcharge	150.00	
		Entire	250.00	
U461	U93	2c on 3c **dark violet,** *blue* (U439, die 1)	6.00	1.00
		Entire	8.00	1.50
a.		On No. U439b (die 5)	6.00	1.00
		Entire	8.00	1.50
b.		On No. U439c (die 6)	6.00	1.00
		Entire	8.00	1.50
c.		On No. U439d (die 7)	12.50	2.00
		Entire	17.50	3.00
d.		As #U461, double surcharge	20.00	
		Entire	30.00	
e.		As "a," double surcharge	20.00	
		Entire	30.00	
f.		As "b," double surcharge	20.00	
		Entire	30.00	
g.		As "c," double surcharge	20.00	
		Entire	30.00	
U462	U87	2c on 4c **chocolate** (U390)	625.00	260.00
		Entire	1,000.	500.00
U463	U87	2c on 4c **chocolate,** *amber* (U391)	1,250.	250.00
		Entire	1,600.	500.00
U463A	U90	2c on 4c **black** (U416, die 2)	1,400.	400.00
		Entire	2,000.	
U464	U93	2c on 5c **blue** (U443)	1,250.	
		Entire	2,000.	

Type 3 exists in 11 city sub-types.

Surcharged

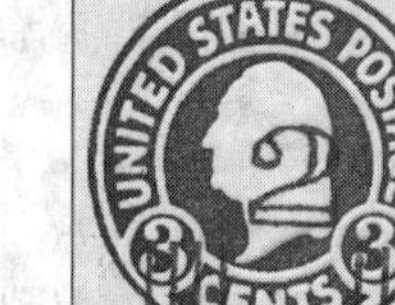

Type 4

Bars 1 mm apart, 21 to 23 mm in length

No.	Die	Description	Unused	Used
U465	U92	2c on 1c **green** (U420, die 1)	1,500.	
		Entire	2,900.	
a.		On No. U420b (die 3)	1,600.	
		Entire	3,000.	
U466	U91	2c on 2c **car** (U411e, die 6)	*14,000.*	
		Entire	*27,500.*	

The existence of U466 as a cut square has been questioned by specialists.

No.	Die	Description	Unused	Used
U466A	U93	2c on 2c **carmine** (U429, die 1)	750.00	
		Entire	1,600.	
c.		On No. U429d (die 5)	1,250.	
		Entire	1,750.	
d.		On No. U429e (die 6)	1,250.	
		Entire	1,750.	
e.		On No. U429f (die 7)	1,250.	
		Entire	1,750.	
U466B	U93	2c on 2c **carmine,** *amber* (U430)	*14,000.*	
		Entire	*30,000.*	
U466C	U93	2c on 2c **carmine,** *oriental buff* (U431), entire	—	
U466D	U25	2c on 3c **green,** die 2 (U82)	*7,500.*	
U467	U45	2c on 3c **green,** die 2 (U163)	350.00	
		Entire	500.00	
U468	U93	2c on 3c **dark vio** (U436, die 1)	.70	.45
		Entire	1.00	.75
a.		On No. U436b (die 5)	.70	.50
		Entire	1.00	.75
b.		On No. U436c (die 6)	.70	.50
		Entire	1.00	.75
c.		On No. U436d (die 7)	.70	.50
		Entire	1.00	.75
d.		As #U468, double surcharge	20.00	
		Entire	30.00	
e.		As #U468, triple surcharge	100.00	
		Entire	150.00	
f.		As #U468, dbl. surch., types 2 & 4	125.00	
		Entire	175.00	
g.		As "a," double surcharge	20.00	
		Entire	30.00	
h.		As "b," double surcharge	20.00	
		Entire	30.00	
i.		As "c," double surcharge	20.00	
		Entire	30.00	
j.		As "c," triple surcharge	100.00	
		Entire	150.00	
k.		As "c," inverted surcharge	75.00	
		Entire	125.00	
l.		2c on 3c **carmine** (error), (U436h)	650.00	
		Entire	800.00	
m.		As #U468, triple surcharge, one inverted, entire		—
U469	U93	2c on 3c **dark violet,** *amber* (U437, die 1)	3.50	2.25
		Entire	4.75	2.75
a.		On No. U437b (die 5)	3.50	2.25
		Entire	4.75	2.75
b.		On No. U437c (die 6)	3.50	2.25
		Entire	4.75	2.75
c.		On No. U437d (die 7)	3.50	2.25
		Entire	4.75	2.75
d.		As #U469, double surcharge	30.00	
		Entire	40.00	
e.		As "a," double surcharge	30.00	
		Entire	40.00	
f.		As "a," double surcharge, types 2 & 4	100.00	
		Entire	150.00	
g.		As "b," double surcharge	30.00	
		Entire	40.00	
h.		As "c," double surcharge	30.00	
		Entire	40.00	
U470	U93	2c on 3c **dark violet,** *oriental buff* (U438, die 1)	5.50	2.50
		Entire	9.00	4.00
a.		On No. U438a (die 5)	5.50	2.50
		Entire	9.00	4.00
b.		On No. U438b (die 6)	5.50	2.50
		Entire	9.00	4.00
c.		On No. U438c (die 7)	40.00	32.50
		Entire	60.00	45.00
d.		As #U470, double surcharge	25.00	
		Entire	35.00	
e.		As #U470, double surch., types 2 & 4	100.00	
		Entire	150.00	
f.		As "a," double surcharge	25.00	
		Entire	35.00	
g.		As "b," double surcharge	25.00	
		Entire	35.00	
U471	U93	2c on 3c **dark violet,** *blue* (U439, die 1)	7.00	1.75
		Entire	12.50	3.50
a.		On No. U439b (die 5)	7.00	1.75
		Entire	12.50	3.50
b.		On No. U439c (die 6)	7.00	1.75
		Entire	12.50	3.50
c.		On No. U439d (die 7)	10.00	6.00
		Entire	20.00	10.00
d.		As #U471, double surcharge	30.00	
		Entire	40.00	
e.		As #U471, double surch., types 2 & 4	175.00	
		Entire	250.00	
f.		As "a," double surcharge	30.00	
		Entire	40.00	
g.		As "b," double surcharge	30.00	
		Entire	40.00	
U472	U87	2c on 4c **chocolate** (U390)	12.00	8.00
		Entire	25.00	14.00
a.		Double surcharge	150.00	
U473	U87	2c on 4c **chocolate,** *amber* (U391)	16.00	10.00
		Entire	25.00	13.50

Type 4 exists in 30 city sub-types.

Surcharged

Double Surcharge, Type 4 and 1c as above

No.	Die	Description	Unused	Used
U474	U93	2c on 1c on 3c **dark violet** (U436, die 1)	275.	
		Entire	350.	
a.		On No. U436b (die 5)	325.	
		Entire	475.	
b.		On No. U436d (die 7)	750.	
		Entire	950.	
U475	U93	2c on 1c on 3c **dark violet,** *amber* (U437, die 1)	275.	
		Entire	400.	

Surcharged

U476	U93	2c on 3c **dark violet,** *amber* (U437, die 1)	275.	
		Entire	450.	
a.		On No. U437c (die 6)	750.	
		Entire	1,000.	
b.		As #U476, double surcharge	—	

Surcharged at Duncan, OK.

Surcharged

U477	U93	2c on 3c **dark vio** (U436, die 1)	125.	
		Entire	175.	
a.		On No. U436b (die 5)	200.	
		Entire	250.	
b.		On No. U436c (die 6)	200.	
		Entire	250.	
c.		On No. U436d (die 7)	200.	
		Entire	250.	
U478	U93	2c on 3c **dark violet,** *amber* (U437, die 1)	300.	
		Entire	400.	

Surcharged at Frederick, OK.

Handstamped Surcharged in Black or Violet

U479	U93	2c on 3c **dark violet** (Bk) (U436, die 1)	450.	
		Entire	550.	
a.		On No. U436b (die 5)	900.	
		Entire	1,100.	
b.		On No. U436d (die 7)	450.	
		Entire	550.	
U480	U93	2c on 3c **dark violet** (V) (U436d, die 7)	*5,500.*	
		Entire	*8,000.*	
a.		Double overprint	—	

Expertization by competent authorities is recommended for Nos. U476-U480.

Surcharged at Daytona, FL (#U479) and Orlando Beach, FL (#U480).

1925

Type of 1916-32 Issue

U481	U93	1½c **brown,** die 1, *Mar. 19*	.20	.20
		Entire	.55	.20
		Entire, 1st day cancel		60.00
a.		Die 8	.60	.25
		Entire	.80	.50
b.		1½c purple, die 1 (error) ('34)	90.00	
		Entire	110.00	—
U482	U93	1½c **brown,** die 1, *amber*	.90	.40
		Entire	1.50	.60
a.		Die 8	1.75	.75
		Entire	2.25	.80
U483	U93	1½c **brown,** die 1, *blue*	1.50	.95
		Entire	2.40	1.25
a.		Die 8	2.25	1.25
		Entire	3.00	1.40
U484	U93	1½c **brown,** die 1, *manila*	6.00	3.00
		Entire	11.00	6.00
W485	U93	1½c **brown,** die 1, *manila*	.80	.20
		Entire	1.25	.45
a.		With added impression of #W433	120.00	—

The manufacture of newspaper wrappers was discontinued in 1934.

New rates on printed matter effective Apr. 15, 1925, resulted in revaluing some of the current envelopes.

Under the caption "Revaluation of Surplus Stocks of the 1 cent envelopes," W. Irving Glover, Third Assistant Postmaster-General, distributed through the Postal Bulletin a notice to postmasters authorizing the surcharging of envelopes under stipulated conditions.

Surcharging was permitted "at certain offices where the excessive quantities of 1 cent stamped envelopes remained in stock on April 15, 1925."

Envelopes were revalued by means of post office canceling machines equipped with special dies designed to imprint "1 ½" in the center of the embossed stamp and four vertical bars over the original numerals "1" in the lower corners.

Postmasters were notified that the revaluing dies would be available for use only in the International and "Universal" Model G machines and that the overprinting of surplus envelopes would be restricted to post offices having such canceling equipment available.

Envelopes of Preceding Issues Surcharged

1925

On Envelopes of 1887

U486	U71	1½c on 2c **green** (U311)	725.	
		Entire	1,250.	
U487	U71	1½c on 2c **green,** *amber* (U312)	1,250.	
		Entire	1,750.	

On Envelopes of 1899

U488	U77	1½c on 1c **green** (U352)	625.	
		Entire	1,000.	
U489	U77	1½c on 1c **green,** *amber* (U353)	125.	60.
		Entire	200.	90.

On Envelopes of 1907-16

U490	U90	1½c on 1c **green** (U400, die 1)	6.00	3.50
		Entire	9.00	5.50
a.		On No. U400a (die 2)	17.50	9.00
		Entire	20.00	12.00
b.		On No. U400b (die 3)	30.00	17.50
		Entire	40.00	22.50
c.		On No. U400c (die 4)	9.00	2.50
		Entire	12.00	4.00
U491	U90	1½c on 1c **green,** *amber* (U401c, die 4)	7.00	2.25
		Entire	10.00	4.50
a.		On No. U401 (die 1)	11.00	2.50
		Entire	15.00	6.00
b.		On No. U401a (die 2)	90.00	65.00
		Entire	110.00	95.00
c.		On No. U401b (die 3)	42.50	30.00
		Entire	57.50	40.00
U492	U90	1½c on 1c **green,** *oriental buff* (U402a, die 2)	500.00	100.00
		Entire	600.00	125.00
a.		On No. U402c (die 4)	1,000.	100.00
		Entire	1,400.	125.00
U493	U90	1½c on 1c **grn,** *blue* (U403c, die 4)	100.00	55.00
		Entire	140.00	80.00
a.		On No. U403a (die 2)	100.00	55.00
		Entire	140.00	80.00
U494	U90	1½c on 1c **grn,** *manila* (U404, die 1)	350.00	80.00
		Entire	500.00	110.00
a.		On No. U404a (die 3)	1,000.	
		Entire	1,250.	

On Envelopes of 1916-20

U495	U92	1½c on 1c **green** (U420, die 1)	.75	.25
		Entire	1.00	.45
a.		On No. U420a (die 2)	70.00	52.50
		Entire	100.00	90.00
b.		On No. U420b (die 3)	1.60	.60
		Entire	2.25	.80
c.		On No. U420c (die 4)	1.75	.75
		Entire	2.40	1.00
d.		As #U495, double surcharge	10.00	3.00
		Entire	15.00	5.00
e.		As "b," double surcharge	10.00	3.00
		Entire	15.00	5.00
f.		As "c," double surcharge	10.00	3.00
		Entire	15.00	5.00
U496	U92	1½c on 1c **grn,** *amber* (U421, die 1)	20.00	12.50
		Entire	27.50	15.00
a.		On No. U421b (die 3)	600.00	
		Entire	700.00	
b.		On No. U421c (die 4)	20.00	12.50
		Entire	27.50	15.00
U497	U92	1½c on 1c **green,** *oriental buff* (U422, die 1)	4.00	1.90
		Entire	6.50	2.25
a.		On No. U422b (die 4)	52.50	
		Entire	80.00	
U498	U92	1½c on 1c **grn,** *blue* (U423c, die 4)	1.25	.75
		Entire	2.00	1.00
a.		On No. U423 (die 1)	2.25	1.50
		Entire	3.75	2.00
b.		On No. U423b (die 3)	1.75	1.50
		Entire	2.75	2.00
U499	U92	1½c on 1c **green,** *manila* (U424)	12.50	6.00
		Entire	19.00	7.00
U500	U92	1½c on 1c **green,** *brown* (unglazed) (U428)	82.50	30.00
		Entire	95.00	35.00
U501	U92	1½c on 1c **green,** *brown* (glazed) (U426)	82.50	30.00
		Entire	95.00	35.00
U502	U93	1½c on 2c **carmine** (U429, die 1)	275.00	—
		Entire	475.00	—
a.		On No. U429d (die 5)	375.00	
		Entire	550.00	
b.		On No. U429f (die 7)	375.00	
		Entire	550.00	
c.		On No. U429e (die 6)	—	
		Entire	—	
d.		On No. U429g (die 8)	—	
U503	U93	1½c on 2c **carmine,** *oriental buff* (U431c, die 5)	375.00	—
		Entire	500.00	—
a.		Double surcharge	—	
b.		Double surcharge, one inverted	*700.00*	
U504	U93	1½c on 2c **car,** *blue* (U432, die 1)	400.00	—
		Entire	525.00	—
a.		On No. U432g (die 7)	350.00	
		Entire	450.00	

On Envelopes of 1925

U505	U93	1½c on 1½c **brown** (U481, die 1)	450.00	
		Entire	625.00	
a.		On No. U481a (die 8)	450.00	
		Entire	625.00	
U506	U93	1½c on 1½c **brown,** *blue* (U483a, die 8)	450.00	
		Entire	625.00	

The paper of No. U500 is not glazed and appears to be the same as that used for the wrappers of 1920.

Type 8 exists in 20 city sub-types.

Surcharged

Black Surcharge
On Envelopes of 1887

U507	U69	1½c on 1c **blue** (U294)	3,250.	
		Entire	4,000.	
U507A	U69	1½c on 1c **blue,** *amber* (U296)	—	
U507B	U69	1½c on 1c **blue,** *manila* (U300), entire	—	

On Envelope of 1899

U508	U77	1½c on 1c **green,** *amber* (U353)	67.50	
		Entire	72.50	

On Envelopes of 1903

U508A	U85	1½c on 1c **green** (U379)	4,750.	
		Entire	6,750.	
U509	U85	1½c on 1c **green,** *amber* (U380)	15.00	10.00
		Entire	27.50	15.00
a.		Double surcharge	75.00	
		Entire	100.00	
U509B	U69	1½c on 1c **green,** *oriental buff* (U381)	60.00	40.00
		Entire	70.00	50.00

On Envelopes of 1907-16

U510	U90	1½c on 1c **green** (U400, die 1)	2.75	1.25
		Entire	4.50	1.50
b.		On No. U400a (die 2)	9.00	4.00
		Entire	12.50	6.00
c.		On No. U400b (die 3)	30.00	8.00
		Entire	40.00	11.00
d.		On No. U400c (die 4)	4.00	1.25
		Entire	7.25	2.00
e.		As No. U510, double surcharge	25.00	
		Entire	50.00	
U511	U90	1½c on 1c **green,** *amber* (U401, die 1)	250.00	72.50
		Entire	375.00	90.00
U512	U90	1½c on 1c **green,** *oriental buff* (U402, die 1)	8.50	4.00
		Entire	15.00	6.50
a.		On No. U402c (die 4)	20.00	14.00
		Entire	27.50	17.00
U513	U90	1½c on 1c **grn,** *blue* (U403, die 1)	6.00	4.00
		Entire	9.00	5.00
a.		On No. U403c (die 4)	6.00	4.00
		Entire	9.00	5.00
U514	U90	1½c on 1c **green,** *manila* (U404, die 1))	32.50	9.00

		Entire	42.50	22.50
a.		On No. U404a (die 3)	60.00	37.50
		Entire	70.00	45.00

On Envelopes of 1916-20

U515	U92	1½c on 1c **green** (U420, die 1)	.35	.20
		Entire	.65	.30
a.		On No. U420a (die 2)	20.00	15.00
		Entire	25.00	20.00
b.		On No. U420b (die 3)	.35	.20
		Entire	.65	.30
c.		On No. U420c (die 4)	.35	.20
		Entire	.65	.30
d.		As #U515, double surcharge	10.00	
		Entire	15.00	
e.		As #U515, inverted surcharge	20.00	
		Entire	30.00	
f.		As #U515, triple surcharge	20.00	
		Entire	30.00	
g.		As #U515, dbl. surch., one invtd., entire	—	
h.		As "b," double surcharge	10.00	
		Entire	15.00	
i.		As "b," inverted surcharge	20.00	
		Entire	30.00	
j.		As "b," triple surcharge	30.00	
		Entire	40.00	
k.		As "c," double surcharge	10.00	
		Entire	15.00	
l.		As "c," inverted surcharge	20.00	
		Entire	30.00	
U516	U92	1½c on 1c **green,** *amber* (U421c, die 4)	47.50	25.00
		Entire	57.50	35.00
a.		On No. U421 (die 1)	52.50	30.00
		Entire	62.50	40.00
U517	U92	1½c on 1c **green,** *oriental buff* (U422, die 1))	6.00	1.25
		Entire	8.00	1.50
a.		On No. U422a (die 4)	7.00	1.50
		Entire	9.00	2.00
U518	U92	1½c on 1c **green,** *blue* (U423b, die 4)	5.50	1.25
		Entire	7.50	1.50
a.		On No. U423 (die 1)	7.50	2.50
		Entire	10.00	3.00
b.		On No. U423a (die 3)	20.00	7.50
		Entire	27.50	9.00
c.		As "a," double surcharge	25.00	
		Entire	37.50	
U519	U92	1½c on 1c **green,** *manila* (U424, die 1)	25.00	10.00
		Entire	32.50	12.50
a.		Double surcharge	100.00	
U520	U93	1½c on 2c **car** (U429, die 1)	350.00	—
		Entire	500.00	—
a.		On No. U429d (die 5)	350.00	
		Entire	500.00	
b.		On No. U429e (die 6)	350.00	
		Entire	500.00	
c.		On No. U429f (die 7)	400.00	
		Entire	550.00	
U520D	U93	1½c on 2c **car,** *amber* (U430c, die 5), entire	—	

Magenta Surcharge

U521	U92	1½c on 1c **green** (U420b, die 3), *Oct. 22, 1925*	4.50	3.50
		Entire	5.25	5.50
		Entire, 1st day cancel, Washington, D.C.		100.00
a.		Double surcharge	75.00	
		Entire	125.00	

Sesquicentennial Exposition Issue

150th anniversary of the Declaration of Independence.

Liberty Bell — U94

Die 1. The center bar of "E" of "postage" is shorter than top bar.

Die 2. The center bar of "E" of "postage" is of same length as top bar.

1926, July 27

U522	U94	2c **carmine,** die 1	1.10	.50
		Entire	1.60	.95
a.		Die 2	7.00	3.75
		Entire	11.00	5.50
		Entire, die 2, 1st day cancel, Washington, D.C.		32.50
		Entire, die 2, 1st day cancel, Philadelphia		27.50

Washington Bicentennial Issue

200th anniversary of the birth of George Washington.

Mount Vernon — U95

2c Die 1 - "S" of "Postage" normal.
2c Die 2 - "S" of "Postage" raised.

1932

U523	U95	1c **olive green,** *Jan. 1*	1.00	.80
		Entire	1.50	1.75
		Entire, 1st day cancel		18.00
U524	U95	1½c **chocolate,** *Jan. 1*	2.00	1.50
		Entire	2.75	2.50
		Entire, 1st day cancel		18.00
U525	U95	2c **carmine,**die 1,*Jan. 1*	.40	.20
		Entire	.50	.25
		Entire, 1st day cancel		16.00
a.		2c **carmine,** die 2	70.00	16.00
		Entire	85.00	55.00
b.		2c **carmine,** *blue,* die 1 (error) entire	*27,500.*	
U526	U95	3c **violet,** *June 16*	2.00	.35
		Entire	2.50	.40
		Entire, 1st day cancel		18.00
U527	U95	4c **black,** *Jan. 1*	18.00	16.00
		Entire	22.50	21.00
		Entire, 1st day cancel		30.00
U528	U95	5c **dark blue,** *Jan. 1*	4.00	3.50
		Entire	4.75	4.75
		Entire, 1st day cancel		20.00
		Nos. U523-U528 (6)	27.40	22.35

1932, Aug. 18

Type of 1916-32 Issue

U529	U93	6c **orange,** die 7	5.50	4.00
		Entire	8.50	7.50
		Entire, 1st day cancel, Los Angeles		20.00
U530	U93	6c **orange,** *amber,* die 7	11.00	10.00
		Entire	15.00	12.00
		Entire, 1st day cancel, Los Angeles		20.00
U531	U93	6c **orange,** *blue,* die 7	11.00	10.00
		Entire	15.00	12.50
		Entire, 1st day cancel		20.00

Franklin — U96

Die 1

Die 2

Die 3

Die 1 - Short (3½mm) and thick "I" in thick circle.
Die 2 - Tall (4½mm) and thin "1" in thin circle; upper and lower bars of E in ONE long and 1mm from circle.
Die 3 - As in Die 2, but E normal and 1½mm from circle.

Printed by International Envelope Corp.

1950

U532	U96	1c **green,** die 1, *Nov. 16*	5.50	1.75
		Entire	8.75	2.25
		Entire, 1st day cancel, NY, NY		1.00
a.		Die 2	7.00	3.00
		Entire	10.00	3.75
b.		Die 3	7.00	3.00
		Entire	9.50	3.75
		Precanceled, die 3		1.25
		Entire, precanceled, die 3	2.50	1.50

Washington — U97

Die 1

Die 2

Die 3

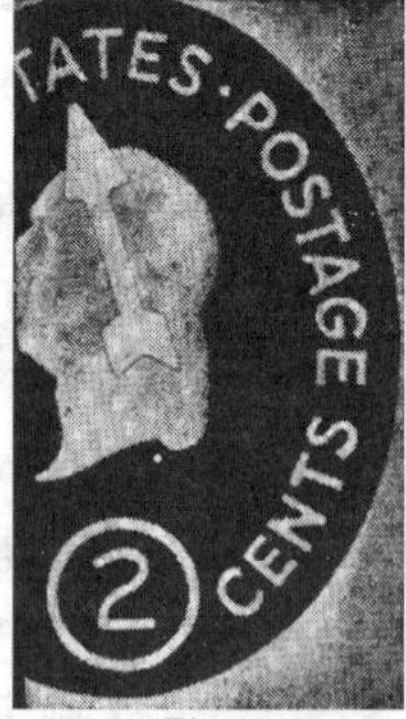
Die 4

Die 1 - Thick "2" in thick circle; toe of "2" is acute angle.

Die 2 - Thin "2" in thin circle; toe of "2" is almost right angle; line through left stand of "N" in UNITED and stand of "E" in POSTAGE goes considerably below tip of chin; "N" of UNITED is tall; "O" of TWO is high.

Die 3 - Figure "2" as in Die 2. Short UN in UNITED thin crossbar in A of STATES.

Die 4 - Tall UN in UNITED; thick crossbar in A of STATES; otherwise like Die 3.

U533	U97	2c **carmine,** die 3	.75	.25
		Entire	1.25	.35
a.		Die 1, *Nov. 17*	.85	.30
		Entire	1.50	.45
		Entire, 1st day cancel, NY, NY		1.00
b.		Die 2	1.50	.85
		Entire	2.00	.95
c.		Die 4	1.40	.60
		Entire	1.60	.65

Die 1

Die 2

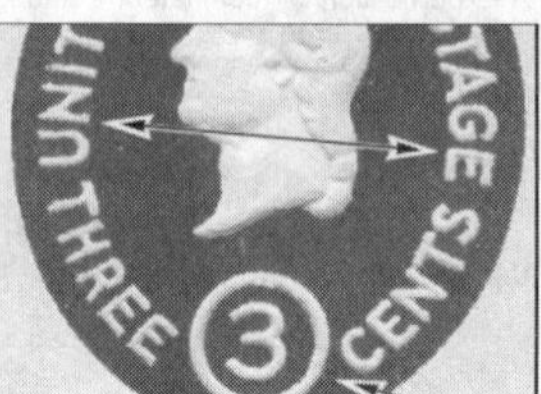
Die 3

Die 4

Die 5

Die 1 - Thick and tall (4½mm) "3" in thick circle; long top bars and short stems in T's of STATES.

Die 2 - Thin and tall (4½mm) "3" in medium circle; short top bars and long stems in T's of STATES.

Die 3 - Thin and short (4mm) "3" in thin circle; lettering wider than Dies 1 and 2; line from left stand of N to stand of E is distinctly below tip of chin.

Die 4 - Figure and letters as in Die 3. Line hits tip of chin; short N in UNITED and thin crossbar in A of STATES.

Die 5 - Figure, letter and chin line as in Die 4; but tall N in UNITED and thick crossbar in A of STATES.

U534 U97 3c	**dark violet,** die 4	.40	.20
	Entire	.50	.25
a.	Die 1, *Nov. 18*	2.00	.70
	Entire	2.50	1.20
	Entire, 1st day cancel, NY, NY		1.00
b.	Die 2, *Nov. 19*	.80	.50
	Entire	1.60	.55
	Entire, 1st day cancel, NY, NY		4.00
c.	Die 3	.60	.25
	Entire	1.10	.45
d.	Die 5	.80	.45
	Entire	1.25	.65

Washington — U98

1952

U535 U98 1½c	**brown**	5.50	3.50
	Entire	6.25	4.25
	Precanceled		1.25
	Entire, precanceled	2.50	1.50

Die 1

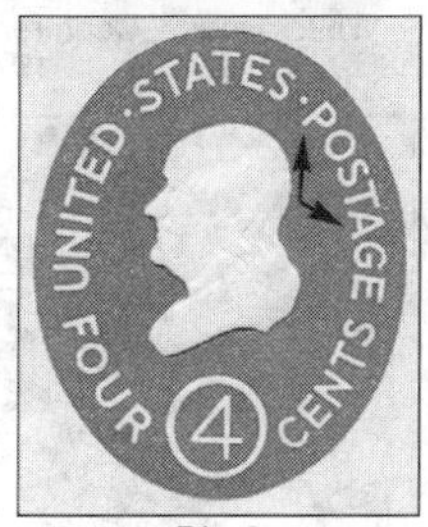

Die 2 Die 3

Die 1 - Head high in oval (2mm below T of STATES). Circle near (1mm) bottom of colored oval.

Die 2 - Head low in oval (3mm). Circle 1½mm from edge of oval. Right leg of A in POSTAGE shorter than left. Short leg on P.

Die 3 - Head centered in oval (2½mm). Circle as in Die 2. Legs of A of POSTAGE about equal. Long leg on P.

1958

U536 U96 4c	**red violet,** die 1, *July 31*	.80	.20
	Entire	.95	.25
	Entire, 1st day cancel, Montpelier, Vt. *(163,746)*		1.00
a.	Die 2	1.05	.20
	Entire	1.30	.25
b.	Die 3	1.05	.20
	Entire	1.30	.25

Nos. U429, U429f, U429h, U533, U533a-U533c Surcharged in Red at Left of Stamp

b

1958

U537 U93 2c	+ 2c **carmine,** die 1	3.50	1.50
	Entire	4.25	—
a.	Die 7	11.00	7.00
	Entire	13.50	—
b.	Die 9	5.50	5.00
	Entire	7.00	—
U538 U97 2c	+ 2c **carmine,** die 1	.75	*1.25*
	Entire	.90	*2.50*
a.	Die 2	1.00	*1.25*
	Entire	1.50	*2.50*
b.	Die 3	.80	*1.25*
	Entire	1.10	*2.50*
c.	Die 4	.80	*1.25*
	Entire	1.00	*2.50*

Nos. U436a, U436e-U436f, U534, U534b-U534d Surcharged in Green at Left of Stamp

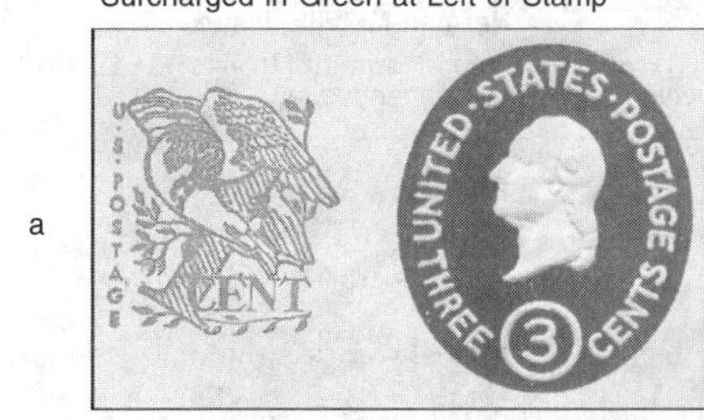

a

U539 U93 3c	+ 1c **purple,** die 1	15.00	11.00
	Entire	17.50	—
a.	Die 7	12.00	9.00
	Entire	15.00	—
b.	Die 9	30.00	15.00
	Entire	35.00	—
U540 U97 3c	+ 1c **dark violet,** die 3	.50	*1.00*
	Entire	.60	*2.00*
a.	Die 2	—	—
	Entire	*2,500.*	—
b.	Die 4	.75	*1.00*
	Entire	.90	*2.00*
c.	Die 5	.75	*1.00*
	Entire	1.00	*2.00*

Benjamin Franklin — U99

George Washington — U100

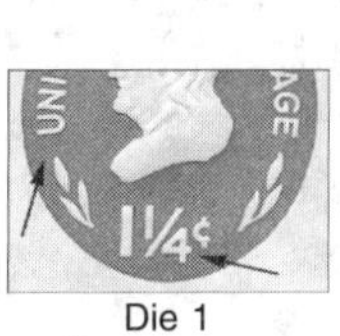

Die 1 Die 2

Dies of 1¼c

Die 1 - The "4" is 3mm high. Upper leaf in left cluster is 2mm from "U."

Die 2 - The "4" is 3½mm high. Leaf clusters are larger. Upper leaf at left is 1mm from "U."

1960

U541 U99 1¼c	**turquoise,** die 1, *June 25, 1960*	.75	.50
	Entire	.90	.55
	Entire, 1st day cancel, Birmingham, Ala. *(211,500)*		1.00
	Precanceled		.20
	Entire, precanceled	.45	.45
a.	Die 2, precanceled		1.50
	Entire, precanceled	2.00	2.00
U542 U100 2½c	**dull blue,** *May 28, 1960*	.85	.50
	Entire	1.00	.60
	Entire, 1st day cancel, Chicago, Ill. *(196,977)*		1.00
	Precanceled		.25
	Entire, precanceled	.55	.55

Pony Express Centennial Issue

Pony Express Rider — U101

White Outside, Blue Inside.

1960

U543 U101 4c	**brown,** *July 19, 1960*	.60	.30
	Entire	.75	.40
	Entire, 1st day cancel, St. Joseph, Mo. *(407,160)*		1.00

Abraham Lincoln — U102

Die 1

Die 2

Die 3

Die 1 - Center bar of E of POSTAGE is above the middle. Center bar of E of STATES slants slightly upward. Nose sharper, more pointed. No offset ink specks inside envelope on back of die impression.

Die 2 - Center bar of E of POSTAGE in middle. P of POSTAGE has short stem. Ink specks on back of die impression.

Die 3 - FI of FIVE closer than Die 1 or 2. Second T of STATES seems taller than ES. Ink specks on back of die impression.

1962

U544 U102 5c	**dark blue,** die 2, *Nov. 19, 1962*	.85	.20
	Entire	1.10	.30
	Entire, 1st day cancel, Springfield, Ill. *(163,258)*		1.00
a.	Die 1	.85	.25
	Entire	1.10	.30
b.	Die 3	.90	.35
	Entire	1.20	.40
c.	Die 2 with albino impression of 4c (#U536), entire	85.00	—
d.	Die 3 with albino impression of 4c (#U536), entire	85.00	—
e.	Die 3 on complete impression of 4c (#U536), cut square		—

No. U536 Surcharged in Green at left of Stamp

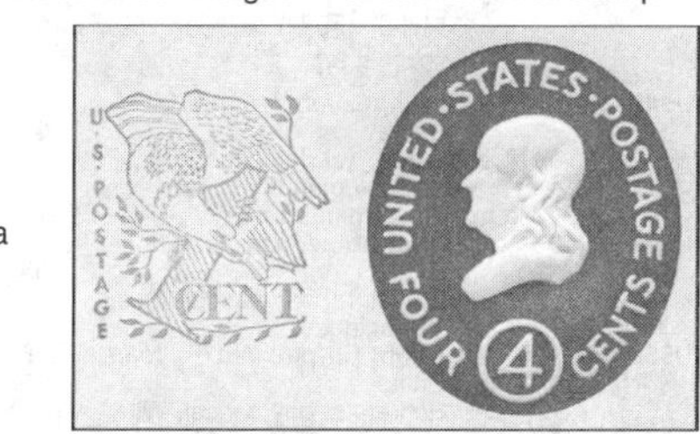

a

Two types of surcharge:

Type I - "U.S. POSTAGE" 18½mm high. Serifs on cross of T both diagonal. Two lines of shading in C of CENT.

Type II - "U.S. POSTAGE" 17½mm high. Right serif on cross of T is vertical. Three shading lines in C.

1962

U545 U96 4c + 1c **red vio.,** die 1, type I, *Nov. 1962* 1.40 *1.25*
Entire 1.60 *2.50*
a. Type II 1.40 *1.25*
Entire 1.60 *2.50*

New York World's Fair Issue

Issued to publicize the New York World's Fair, 1964-65.

Globe with Satellite Orbit — U103

1964

U546 U103 5c **maroon,** *Apr. 22, 1964* .60 .40
Entire .75 .50
Entire, 1st day cancel World's Fair, N.Y. *(466,422)* 1.00

Precanceled cut squares

Precanceled envelopes do not normally receive another cancellation. Since the lack of a cancellation makes it impossible to distinguish between cut squares from used and unused envelopes, they are valued here as used only.

Liberty Bell — U104

Old Ironsides — U105

Eagle — U106

Head of Statue of Liberty — U107

Printed by the United States Envelope Company, Williamsburg, Pa. Designed (6c) by Howard C. Mildner and (others) by Robert J. Jones.

1965-69

U547 U104 1¼c **brown,** *Jan. 6, 1965* .20
Entire .90 .75
Entire, 1st day cancel, Washington, D.C. 1.00
U548 U104 1 4/10c **brown,** *Mar. 26, 1968* .20
Entire 1.00 .75
Entire, 1st day cancel, Springfield, Mass. *(134,832)* 1.00
U548A U104 1 6/10c **orange,** *June 16, 1969* .20
Entire .85 .70
Entire, 1st day cancel, Washington, D.C. 1.00
b. 1 6/10c **brown (error), entire** —
U549 U105 4c **bright blue,** *Jan. 6, 1965* .75 .20
Entire .95 .20
Entire, 1st day cancel, Washington, D.C. 1.00
U550 U106 5c **bright purple,** *Jan. 5, 1965* .75 .20
Entire .85 .25
Entire, 1st day cancel, Williamsburg, Pa. *(246,496)* 1.00
a. Tagged, *Aug. 15, 1967* 2.00 .50
Entire 2.50 .75
Entire, tagged, 1st day cancel 3.50
b. orange-red (air post) instead of yellow-green tagging, entire —

Tagged

U551 U107 6c **light green,** *Jan. 4, 1968* .70 .20
Entire .80 .25
Entire, 1st day cancel, New York, N.Y. *(184,784)* 1.25

No. U550a has a 9x29mm panel at left of stamp that glows yellow green under ultraviolet light.
First day covers of the 1¼c and 4c total 451,960.

Nos. U549-U550 Surcharged Types "b" and "a" in Red or Green at Left of Stamp

1968, Feb. 5

U552 U105 4c + 2c **bright blue** (R) 3.75 2.00
Entire 4.00 2.50
Entire, 1st day cancel 6.00
U553 U106 5c + 1c **bright purple** (G) 3.50 2.75
Entire 4.00 3.25
Entire, 1st day cancel 6.00
a. Tagged 3.50 2.75
Entire 4.00 3.25
Entire, 1st day cancel 6.00

Tagged

Envelopes from No. U554 onward are tagged, with the tagging element in the ink unless otherwise noted.

Herman Melville Issue

Issued to honor Herman Melville (1819-1891), writer, and the whaling industry.

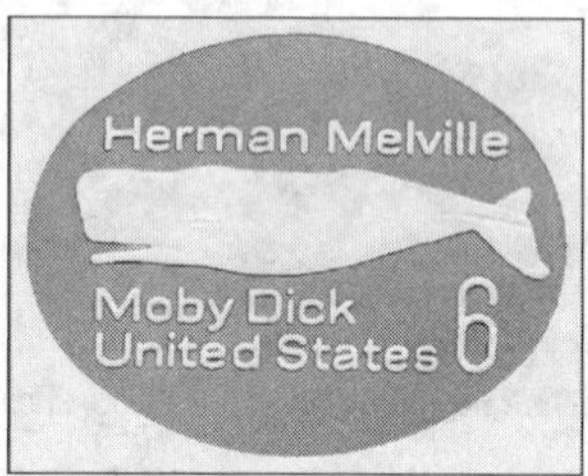

Moby Dick — U108

1970, Mar. 7

U554 U108 6c **blue** .50 .20
Entire .60 .25
Entire, 1st day cancel, New Bedford, Mass. *(433,777)* 1.00

Youth Conference Issue

Issued to publicize the White House Conference on Youth, Estes Park, Colo., Apr. 18-22.

Conference Emblem Symbolic of Man's Expectant Soul and of Universal Brotherhood U109

Printed by United States Envelope Company, Williamsburg, Pa. Designed by Chermayeff and Geismar Associates.

1971, Feb. 24

U555 U109 6c **light blue** .75 .20
Entire .85 .40
Entire, 1st day cancel, Washington, D.C. *(264,559)* 1.00

Liberty Bell Type of 1965 and U110

Eagle — U110

Printed by the United States Envelope Co., Williamsburg, Pa. Designed (8c) by Bradbury Thompson.

1971

U556 U104 1 7/10c **deep lilac,** untagged, *May 10* .20
Entire .30 .20
Entire, 1st day cancel, Baltimore, Md. *(150,767)* 1.00
U557 U110 8c **ultramarine,** *May 6* .40 .20
Entire .50 .25
Entire, 1st day cancel, Williamsburg, Pa. *(193,000)* 1.00

Nos. U551 and U555 Surcharged in Green at Left of Stamp

c

1971, May 16

U561 U107 6c + (2c) **light green** 1.00 1.25
Entire 1.10 2.50
Entire, 1st day cancel, Washington, D.C. 2.50
U562 U109 6c + (2c) **light blue** 2.00 2.50
Entire 2.50 3.00
Entire, 1st day cancel, Washington, D.C. 3.00

Bowling Issue

Issued as a salute to bowling and in connection with the 7th World Tournament of the International Bowling Federation, Milwaukee, Wis.

Bowling Ball and Pin — U111

Designed by George Giusti.

1971, Aug. 21

U563 U111 8c **rose red** .70 .20
Entire .80 .20
Entire, 1st day cancel, Milwaukee, Wis. *(281,242)* 1.00

Aging Conference Issue

White House Conference on Aging, Washington, D.C., Nov. 28-Dec. 2, 1971.

Conference Symbol — U112

Designed by Thomas H. Geismar.

1971, Nov. 15

U564 U112 8c **light blue** .50 .20
Entire .65 .20
Entire, 1st day cancel, Washington, D.C. *(125,000)* 1.00

International Transportation Exhibition Issue

U.S. International Transportation Exhibition, Dulles International Airport, Washington, D.C., May 27-June 4.

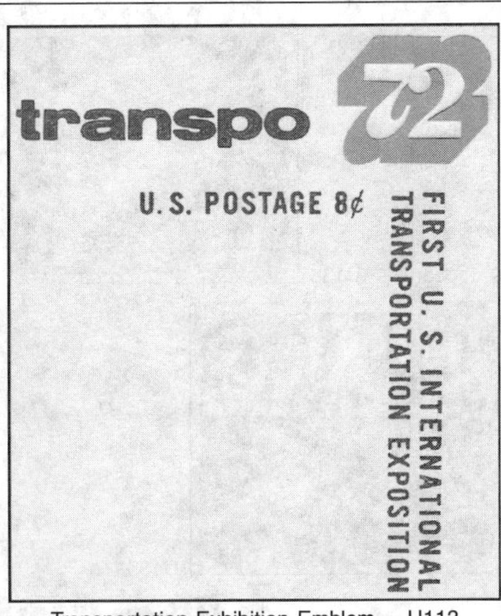

Transportation Exhibition Emblem — U113

Emblem designed by Toshihiki Sakow.

1972, May 2

U565 U113 8c **ultramarine & rose red** .50 .20
Entire .75 .25
Entire, 1st day cancel, Washington, D.C. 1.00

No. U557 Surcharged Type "b" in Ultramarine at Left of Stamp

1973, Dec. 1

U566 U110 8c + 2c **brt. ultramarine** .40 *1.25*
Entire .50 *2.50*
Entire, 1st day cancel, Washington, D.C. 1.50

Liberty Bell — U114

1973, Dec. 5

U567 U114 10c **emerald** .40 .20
Entire .50 .20
Entire, 1st day cancel, Philadelphia, Pa. *(142,141)* 1.00

"Volunteer Yourself" — U115

Designed by Norman Ives.

1974, Aug. 23

Untagged

U568 U115 1 8/10c **blue green** .20
Entire .30 *.75*
Entire, 1st day cancel, Cincinnati, Ohio 1.00

Tennis Centenary Issue

Centenary of tennis in the United States.

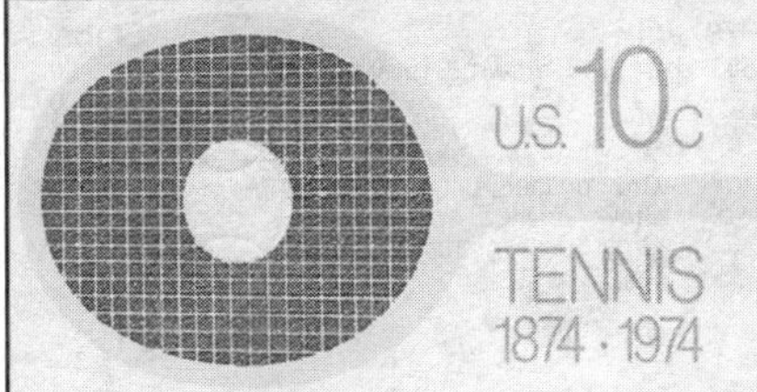

Tennis Racquet — U116

Designed by Donald Moss.

1974, Aug. 31

U569 U116 10c **yellow, brt. blue & light green** .65 .20
Entire .75 .25
Entire, 1st day cancel, Forest Hills, N.Y. *(245,000)* 1.00

Bicentennial Era Issue

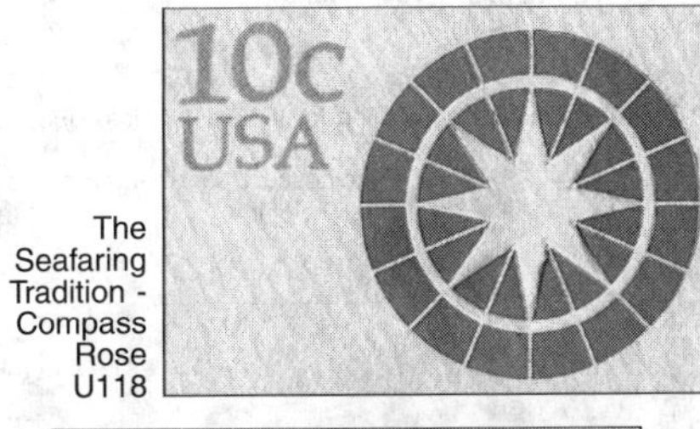

The Seafaring Tradition - Compass Rose U118

The American Homemaker - Quilt Pattern — U119

The American Farmer - Sheaf of Wheat U120

The American Doctor - Mortar U121

The American Craftsman - Tools, c. 1750 U122

Designs (in brown on left side of envelope): 10c, Norwegian sloop Restaurationen. No. U572, Spinning wheel. No. U573, Plow. No. U574, Colonial era medical instruments and bottle. No. U575, Shaker rocking chair.
Designed by Arthur Congdon.

1975-76 **Embossed**

Diagonally Laid Paper

U571 U118 10c **brown & blue,** *light brown, Oct. 13, 1975* .30 .20
Entire .45 .20
Entire, 1st day cancel, Minneapolis, Minn. *(255,304)* 1.00
a. Brown ("10c/USA," etc.) omitted, entire *150.00*

U572 U119 13c **brown & blue green,** *light brown, Feb. 2, 1976* .35 .20
Entire .50 .20
Entire, 1st day cancel, Biloxi, Miss. *(196,647)* 1.00
a. Brown ("13c/USA," etc.) omitted, entire *150.00*

U573 U120 13c **brown & bright green,** *light brown, Mar. 15, 1976* .35 .20
Entire .50 .20
Entire, 1st day cancel, New Orleans, La. *(214,563)* 1.00
a. Brown ("13c/USA," etc.) omitted, entire *150.00*

U574 U121 13c **brown & orange,** *light brown, June 30, 1976* .35 .20
Entire .50 .20
Entire, 1st day cancel, Dallas, Texas 1.00
a. Brown ("13c/USA," etc.) omitted, entire *150.00*

U575 U122 13c **brown & carmine,** *lt. brown, Aug. 6, 1976* .35 .20
Entire .50 .20
Entire, 1st day cancel, Hancock, Mass. 1.00
a. Brown ("13c/USA," etc.) omitted, entire *150.00*
Nos. U571-U575 (5) 1.70 1.00

Liberty Tree, Boston, 1646 — U123

Designed by Leonard Everett Fisher.

1975, Nov. 8 **Embossed**

U576 U123 13c **orange brown** .30 .20
Entire .40 .20
Entire, 1st day cancel, Memphis, Tenn. *(226,824)* 1.00

Star and Pinwheel — U124

U125

U126

Eagle — U127

Uncle Sam — U128

Designers: 2c, Rudolph de Harak. 2.1c, Norman Ives. 2.7c, Ann Sforza Clementino. 15c, George Mercer.

1976-78 **Embossed**

U577 U124 2c **red,** untagged, *Sept. 10, 1976* .20
Entire .30 *1.00*
Entire, 1st day cancel, Hempstead, N.Y. *(81,388)* 1.00

U578 U125 2.1c **green,** untagged, *June 3, 1977* .20
Entire .30 *.50*
Entire, 1st day cancel, Houston, Tex. *(120,280)* 1.00

U579 U126 2.7c **green,** untagged, *July 5, 1978* .20
Entire .35 *.50*
Entire, 1st day cancel, Raleigh, N.C. *(92,687)* 1.00

U580 U127 (15c) **orange,** *May 22, 1978* .40 .20
Entire .55 .20
Entire, 1st day cancel, Memphis, Tenn. 1.00

U581 U128 15c **red,** *June 3, 1978* .40 .20
Entire .55 .20
Entire, 1st day cancel, Williamsburg, Pa. *(176,000)* 1.00

Bicentennial Issue

Centennial Envelope, 1876 — U129

1976, Oct. 15 **Embossed**

U582 U129 13c **emerald** .35 .20
Entire .45 .20
Entire, 1st day cancel, Los Angeles, Cal. *(277,222)* 1.00

Golf Issue

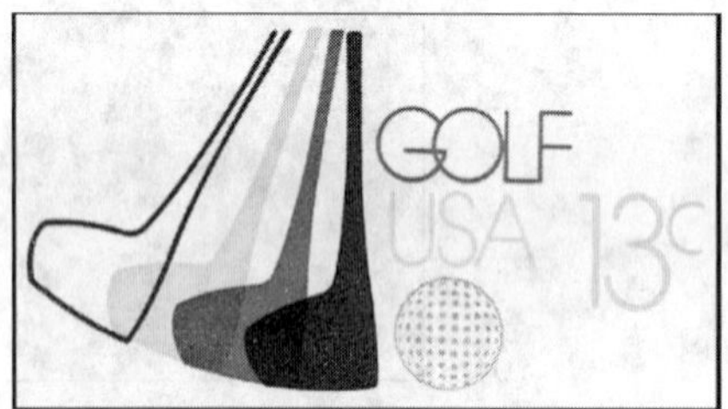

Golf Club in Motion and Golf Ball — U130

Designed by Guy Salvato.

1977, Apr. 7 **Photogravure and Embossed**

U583 U130 13c **black, blue & yellow green** .65 .20
Entire .75 *1.00*
Entire, 1st day cancel, Augusta, Ga. *(252,000)* 1.00
a. Black omitted, entire *650.00*
b. Black & blue omitted, entire *550.00*

Energy Issue

Conservation and development of national resources.

"Conservation" U131

"Development" U132

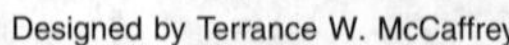
Designed by Terrance W. McCaffrey.

1977, Oct. 20 **Embossed**

U584 U131 13c **black, red & yellow** .40 .20
Entire .50 .20
Entire, 1st day cancel, Ridley Park, Pa. 1.00
a. Red & yellow omitted, entire *250.00*
b. Yellow omitted, entire *175.00*
c. Black omitted, entire *175.00*
d. Black & red omitted, entire *425.00*

U585 U132 13c **black, red & yellow** .40 .20
Entire .50 .20
Entire, 1st day cancel, Ridley Park, Pa. 1.00

First day cancellation applied to 353,515 of Nos. U584 and U585.

Nos. U584-U585 have a luminescent panel at left of stamp which glows green under ultraviolet light.

Olive Branch and Star — U133

Designed by George Mercer.

1978, July 28 **Embossed**

Black Surcharge

U586 U133 15c on 16c **blue** .35 .20
Entire .50 *1.00*
Entire, 1st day cancel, Williamsburg, Pa. *(193,153)* 1.00
a. Surcharge omitted, entire *375.00* —
b. Surcharge on No. U581, entire 100.00 —
c. As "a," with surcharge printed on envelope flap 175.00 —

Auto Racing Issue

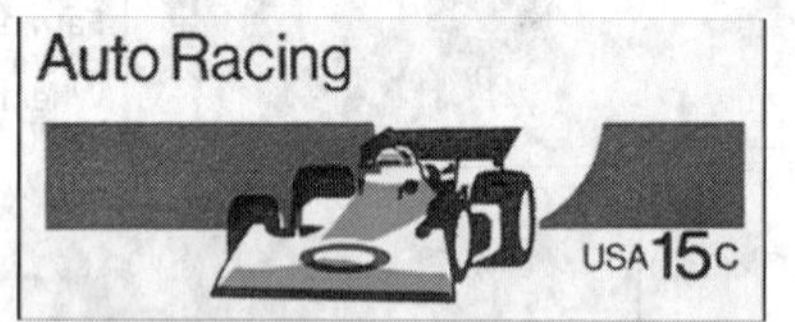

Indianapolis 500 Racing Car — U134

Designed by Robert Peak.

1978, Sept. 2 **Embossed**

U587 U134 15c **red, blue & black** .35 .20
Entire .50 *1.00*
Entire, 1st day cancel, Ontario, Cal. *(209,147)* 1.00
a. Black omitted, entire *120.00*
b. Black & blue omitted, entire —
c. Red omitted, entire *120.00*
d. Red & blue omitted, entire —

No. U576 Surcharged Like No. U586

1978, Nov. 28 **Embossed**

U588 U123 15c on 13c **orange brown** .35 .20
Entire .50 .20
Entire, 1st day cancel, Williamsburg, Pa. *(137,500)* 1.00

U135

Weaver Violins — U136

U137

Eagle — U138

U139

Eagle — U140

1979, May 18 **Untagged** **Embossed**

U589 U135 3.1c **ultramarine** .20
Entire .25 *.40*
Entire, 1st day cancel, Denver, Colo. *(117,575)* 1.00

1980, June 23 **Untagged** **Embossed**

U590 U136 3.5c **purple** .20
Entire .30 *.50*
Entire, 1st day cancel, Williamsburg, Pa. 1.00

1982, Feb. 17 **Untagged** **Embossed**

U591 U137 5.9c **brown** .20
Entire .30 *.40*
Entire, 1st day cancel, Wheeling, WV 1.00

1981, Mar. 15 **Embossed**

U592 U138 (18c) **violet** .45 .20
Entire .55 .25
Entire, 1st day cancel, Memphis, TN *(179,171)* 1.00

1981, Apr. 2 **Embossed**

U593 U139 18c **dark blue** .45 .20
Entire .55 .25
Entire, 1st day cancel, Star City, IN *(160,439)* 1.00

1981, Oct. 11 **Embossed**

U594 U140 (20c) **brown** .45 .20
Entire .55 .20
Entire, 1st day cancel, Memphis, TN *(304,404)* 2.00

Veterinary Medicine Issue

Seal of Veterinarians U141

Design at left side of envelope shows 5 animals and bird in brown, "Veterinary Medicine" in gray.
Designed by Guy Salvato.

1979, July 24 **Embossed**

U595 U141 15c **brown & gray** .50 .20
Entire .60 *1.00*
Entire, 1st day cancel, Seattle, WA *(209,658)* 1.00
a. Gray omitted, entire *750.00*
b. Brown omitted, entire *1,050.*
c. Gray & brown omitted, entire —

Olympic Games Issue

22nd Olympic Games, Moscow, July 19-Aug. 3, 1980.

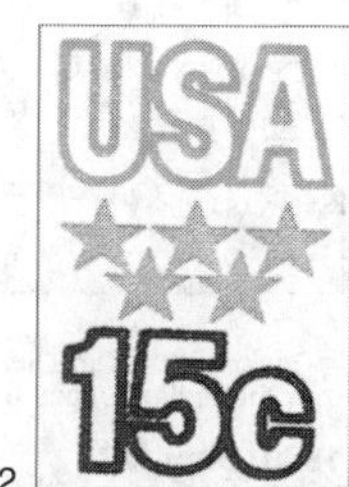

U142

Design (multicolored on left side of envelope) shows two soccer players with ball.

Designed by Robert M. Cunningham.

1979, Dec. 10 **Embossed**

U596 U142 15c **red, green & black** .60 .20
Entire .70 *1.00*
Entire, 1st day cancel, East Rutherford, NJ *(179,336)* 1.00
a. Red & green omitted, untagged, entire *225.00*
b. Black omitted, untagged, entire *225.00*
c. Black & green omitted, entire *225.00*
d. Red omitted, untagged, entire *400.00*

Highwheeler Bicycle — U143

Design (blue on left side of envelope) shows racing bicycle.

Designed by Robert Hallock.

1980, May 16 **Embossed**

U597 U143 15c **blue & rose claret** .40 .20
Entire .55 .20
Entire, 1st day cancel, Baltimore, MD *(173,978)* 1.00
a. Blue ("15c USA") omitted, entire *100.00*

Yacht — U144

Designed by Cal Sachs.

1980, Sept. 15 **Embossed**

U598 U144 15c **blue & red** .40 .20
Entire .55 .20
Entire, 1st day cancel, Newport, RI *(192,220)* 1.00

Italian Honeybee and Orange Blossoms U145

Bee and petals colorless embossed.

Designed by Jerry Pinkney.

1980, Oct. 10 **Photogravure and Embossed**

U599 U145 15c **brown, green & yellow** .35 .20
Entire .50 .20
Entire, 1st day cancel, Paris, IL *(202,050)* 1.00
a. Brown ("USA 15c") omitted, entire *125.00*
b. Green omitted, entire —

No. U599b also has almost all of the brown color missing.

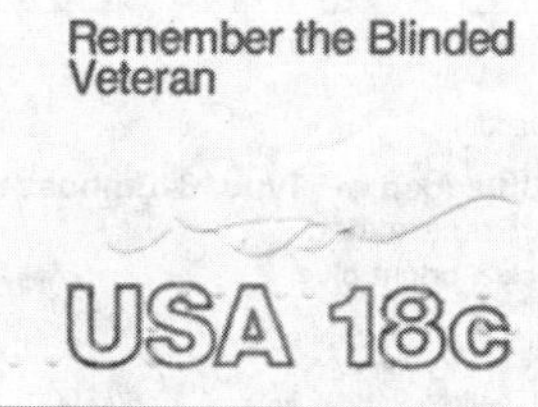

Hand and Braille — U146

Hand and braille colorless embossed.

Designed by John Boyd.

1981, Aug. 13 **Embossed**

U600 U146 18c **blue & red** .45 .20
Entire .55 .25
Entire, 1st day cancel, Arlington, VA *(175,966)* 1.00
a. Blue omitted, entire —
b. Red omitted, entire —

Capital Dome — U147

1981, Nov. 13 **Embossed**

U601 U147 20c **deep magenta** .45 .20
Entire .55 .20
Entire, 1st day cancel, Los Angeles, CA 1.00
a. Bar tagged 3.00 1.50

U148

Designed by Bradbury Thompson.

1982, June 15 **Embossed**

U602 U148 20c **dark blue, black & magenta** .45 .20
Entire .55 .20
Entire, 1st day cancel, Washington, DC *(163,905)* 1.00
a. Dark blue omitted, entire *150.00*
b. Dark blue & magenta omitted, entire —

U149

Designed by John Boyd.

1982, Aug. 6 **Embossed**

U603 U149 20c **purple & black** .65 .20
Entire .75 .20
Entire, 1st day cancel, Washington, DC *(110,679)* 1.00
a. Black omitted, entire —
b. Purple omitted, entire —

U150

1983, Mar. 21 **Untagged** **Embossed**

U604 U150 5.2c **orange** .20
Entire .40 *1.00*
Entire, 1st day cancel, Memphis, TN *(141,979)* 1.00

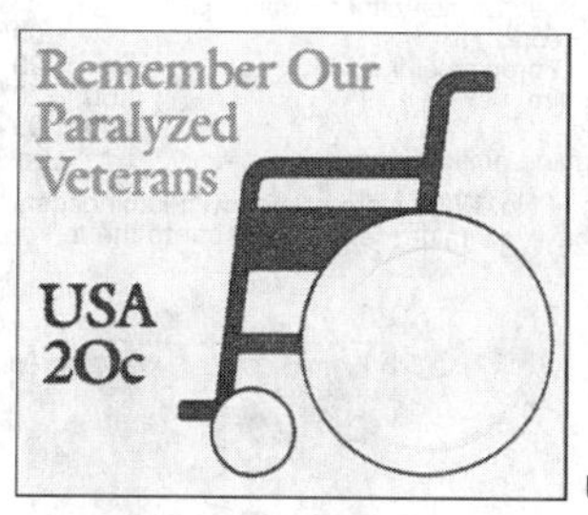

U151

1983, Aug. 3 **Embossed**

U605 U151 20c **red, blue & black** .45 .20
Entire .55 .20
Entire, 1st day cancel, Portland, OR *(21,500)* 1.00
a. Red omitted, entire —
b. Blue omitted, entire —
c. Red & black omitted, entire *140.00*
d. Blue & black omitted, entire *140.00*
e. Black omitted, entire *225.00*

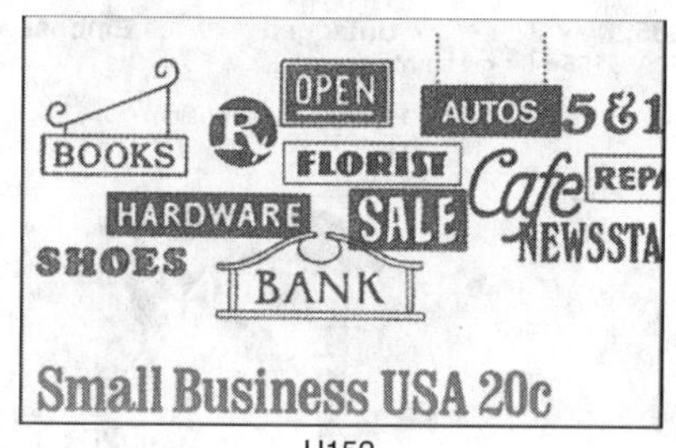

U152

Designed by Peter Spier and Pat Taylor.

Design shows storefronts at lower left. Stamp and design continue on back of envelope.

1984, May 7

U606 U152 20c **multi** .50 .20
Entire .60 .20
Entire, 1st day cancel, Washington, DC *(77,665)* 1.00

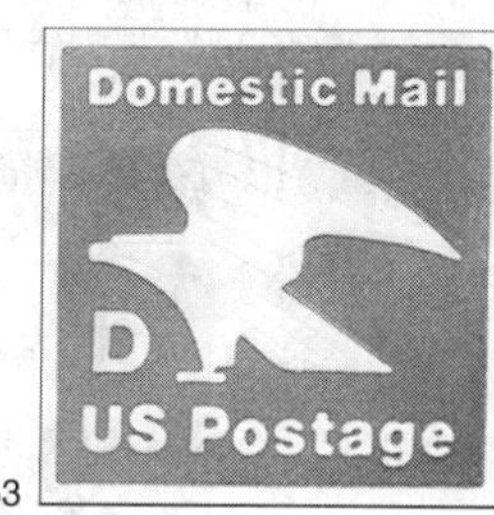

U153

Designed by Bradbury Thompson.

1985, Feb. 1 **Embossed**

U607 U153 (22c) **deep green** .55 .20
Entire .65 .20
Entire, 1st day cancel, Los Angeles, CA 1.00

American Buffalo — U154

Designed by George Mercer.

1985, Feb. 25 **Embossed**

U608 U154 22c **violet brown** .55 .20
Entire .65 .20
Entire, 1st day cancel, Bison, SD *(105,271)* 1.00
a. Untagged, 3 precancel lines .20
Entire .60 .20
b. Bar tagged 2.00 1.00
c. As "b," tagging omitted — —

Original printings of No. U608 were printed with luminescent ink. later printings have a luminescent vertical bar to the left of the stamp.

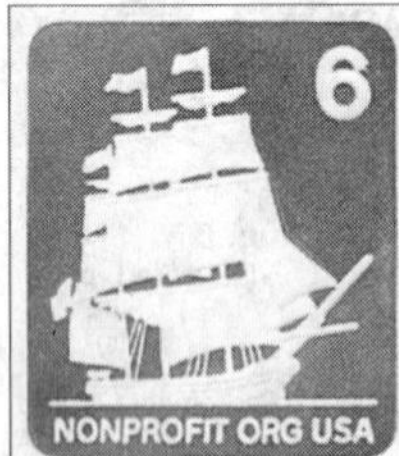

Frigate U.S.S. Constitution — U155

Designed by Cal Sacks.

1985, May 3 **Untagged** **Embossed**

U609 U155 6c **green blue** .20
Entire .25 *.35*
Entire, 1st day cancel, Boston, MA *(170,425)* 1.00

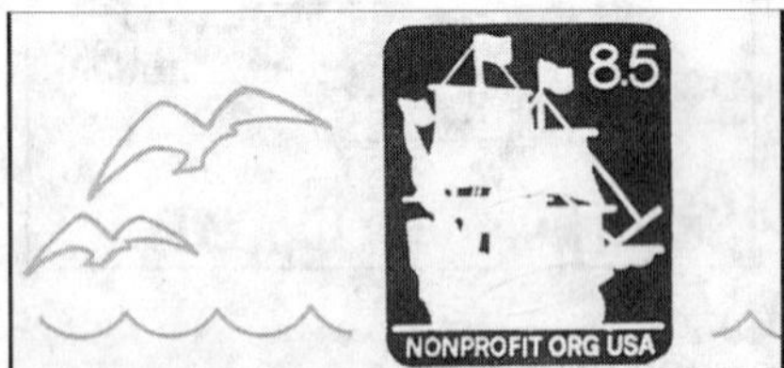

The Mayflower — U156

Designed by Robert Brangwynne.

1986, Dec. 4 **Untagged Precanceled** **Embossed**

U610 U156 8.5c **black & gray** .20
Entire .30 .30
Entire, 1st day cancel, Plymouth, MA *(105,164)* 1.00

Stars U157

Designed by Joe Brockert.

1988, Mar. 26 **Typo. & Embossed**

U611 U157 25c **dark red & deep blue** .60 .20
Entire .70 .25
Entire, 1st day cancel, Star, MS *(29,393)* 1.25
a. Dark red (25) omitted, entire *75.00* —

U.S. Frigate Constellation — U158

Designed by Jerry Dadds.

1988, Apr. 12 **Untagged Precanceled** **Typo. & Embossed**

U612 U158 8.4c **black & bright blue** .20
Entire .30 .30
Entire, 1st day cancel, Baltimore, MD *(41,420)* 1.25
a. Black omitted, entire *600.00*

Snowflake — U159

Designed by Randall McDougall. "Holiday Greetings!" inscribed in lower left.

1988, Sept. 8 **Typo.**

U613 U159 25c **dark red & green** 1.00 *5.00*
Entire 1.25 .30
Entire, 1st day cancel, Snowflake, AZ *(32,601)* 1.25

Stars U160

Designed by Joe Brockert. "Philatelic Mail" and asterisks in dark red below vignette; continuous across envelope face and partly on reverse.

1989, Mar. 10 **Typo.**

U614 U160 25c **dark red & deep blue** .50 .25
Entire .60 .30
Entire, 1st day cancel, Cleveland, OH 1.25

Stars — U161

Designed by Joe Brockert.

1989, July 10 **Typo.** **Unwmk.**

U615 U161 25c **dark red & deep blue** .50 .25
Entire .60 .30
Entire, 1st day cancel, Washington, DC *(33,461)* 1.25
a. Dark red omitted, entire —

Lined with a blue design to provide security for enclosures.

Love! U162

Designed by Tim Girvin. Light blue lines printed diagonally over the entire surface of the envelope.

1989, Sept. 22 **Litho. & Typo.** **Unwmk.**

U616 U162 25c **dark red & bright blue** .50 .25
Entire .60 .30
Entire, 1st day cancel, McLean, VA *(69,498)* 1.25
a. Dark red and bright blue omitted, entire 175.00

Shuttle Docking at Space Station — U163

Designed by Richard Sheaff.

1989, Dec. 3 **Typo. Die Cut** **Unwmk.**

U617 U163 25c **ultramarine** .90 .60
Entire 1.00 .70
Entire, 1st day cancel, Washington, DC 1.25
a. Ultramarine omitted, entire *600.00*

A hologram, visible through the die cut window to the right of "USA 25," is affixed to the inside of the envelope.
Available only in No. 9 size.
See Nos. U625, U639.

Vince Lombardi Trophy, Football Players — U164

Designed by Bruce Harman.

1990, Sept. 9 **Typo.** **Unwmk.** ***Die Cut***

U618 U164 25c **vermilion** .90 .60
Entire 1.00 .70
Entire, 1st day cancel, Green Bay, WI *(54,589)* 1.25

A hologram, visible through the die cut window to the right of "USA 25," is affixed to the inside of the envelope.
Available only in No. 10 size.

Star — U165

Designed by Richard Sheaff.

1991, Jan. 24 **Typo. & Embossed** **Wmk.**

U619 U165 29c **ultramarine & rose** .60 .30
Entire .70 .35
Entire, unwatermarked, *May 1, 1992* .70 .35

Entire, 1st day cancel, Washington, DC *(33,025)* 1.25
a. Ultramarine omitted, entire 600.00
b. Rose omitted, entire *400.00*

Unwatermarked envelopes are on recycled paper, and have an imprint under the flap.
See No. U623.

Birds — U166

Designed by Richard Sheaff
Stamp and design continue on back of envelope. Illustration reduced.

1991, May 3 Typo. Wmk.
Untagged Precanceled

U620 U166 11.1c **blue & red**			.20
Entire		.35	.25
Entire, 1st day cancel, Boxborough, MA *(20,720)*			1.25
Entire, unwatermarked, *May 1, 1992*		.35	.25

Unwatermarked envelopes are on recycled paper, and have an imprint under the flap.

Love — U167

Designed by Salahattin Kanidinc.

1991, May 9 Litho. Unwmk.

U621 U167 29c **light blue, maroon & bright rose**	.60	.30
Entire	.70	.35
Entire, 1st day cancel, Honolulu, HI *(40,110)*		1.25
a. Bright rose omitted, entire	*500.00*	

Examples on recycled paper were issued May 1, 1992 and have imprint under the flap.

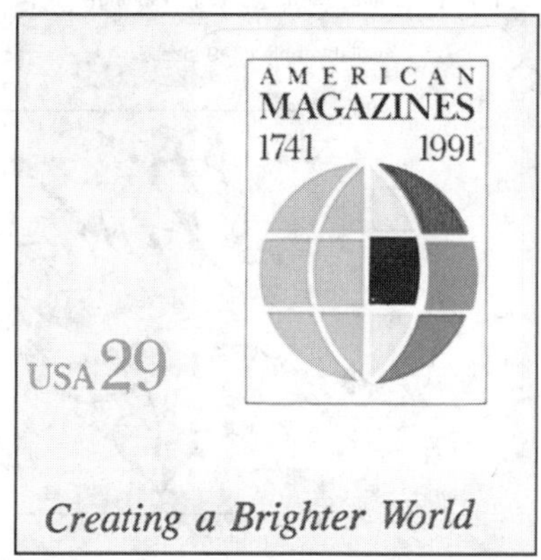

Magazine Industry, 250th Anniv. — U168

Designed by Bradbury Thompson.

1991, Oct. 7 Photo. & Typo. Unwmk.

U622 U168 29c **multicolored**	.60	.30
Entire	.70	*1.00*
Entire, 1st day cancel, Naples, FL *(26,020)*		1.25

The photogravure vignette, visible through the die cut window to the right of "USA 29", is affixed to the inside of the envelope. Available only in No. 10 size.

Star U169

Designed by Richard Sheaff.
Stamp and design continue on back of envelope.

1991, July 20 Typo.

U623 U169 29c **ultra & rose**	.60	.30
Entire	.70	.35
Entire, 1st day cancel, Washington, DC *(16,038)*		1.25
a. Ultra omitted, entire	—	
b. Rose omitted, entire	—	

Lined with a blue design to provide security for enclosures. Examples on recycled paper were issued May 1, 1992 and have imprint under the flap. Available only in No. 9 size.

Country Geese U170

Designed by Marc Zaref.

1991, Nov. 8 Litho. & Typo. Wmk.

U624 U170 29c **blue gray & yellow**	.60	.60
Entire	.70	.70
Entire, 1st day cancel, Virginia Beach, VA *(21,031)*		1.25
Entire, unwatermarked, *May 1, 1992*	.70	.70

Unwatermarked envelopes are on recycled paper, and have an imprint under the flap.

Space Shuttle Type of 1989

Designed by Richard Sheaff.

1992, Jan. 21 Typo. Unwmk. *Die Cut*

U625 U163 29c **yellow green**	.90	.50
Entire	1.00	.60
Entire, 1st day cancel, Virginia Beach, VA *(37,646)*		1.25

A hologram, visible through the die cut window to the right of "USA 29," is affixed to the inside of the envelope. Examples on recycled paper were issued May 1, 1992 and have imprint under the flap.

U171

Designed by Harry Zelenko.

1992, Apr. 10 Typo. & Litho. Unwmk. *Die Cut*

U626 U171 29c **multicolored**	.60	.30
Entire	.70	*1.00*
Entire, 1st day cancel, Dodge City, KS *(34,258)*		1.25

The lithographed vignette, visible through the die cut window to the right of "USA 29," is affixed to the inside of the envelope. Available only in the No. 10 size.

Hillebrandia — U172

Designed by Joseph Brockert. Illustration reduced.

1992, Apr. 22

U627 U172 29c **multicolored**	.60	.30
Entire	.70	*1.50*
Entire, 1st day cancel, Chicago, IL *(29,432)*		1.25

The lithographed vignette, visible through the die cut window to the right of "29 USA," is affixed to the inside of the envelope. Inscribed "Save the Rain Forests" in the lower left. Available only in the No. 10 size.

Star — U173

Designed by Joseph Brockert.

1992, May 19 Typo. & Embossed Precanceled
Untagged

U628 U173 19.8c **red & blue**			.40
Entire		.50	.45
Entire, 1st day cancel, Las Vegas, NV *(18,478)*			1.25

Available only in No. 10 size.

U174

Designed by Richard Sheaff. Illustration reduced.

1992, July 22 Typo. Unwmk.

U629 U174 29c **red & blue**	.60	.30
Entire	.70	.35
Entire, 1st day cancel, Washington, DC *(28,218)*		1.25

U175

Designed by Nancy Krause. Illustration reduced.

1993, Oct. 2 Typo. & Litho. Unwmk. *Die Cut*

U630 U175 29c **multicolored**	.90	.50
Entire	1.00	*1.50*
Entire, 1st day cancel, King of Prussia, PA *(6,511)*		1.25

The lithographed vignette, visible through the die cut window to the right of "USA 29," is affixed to the inside of the envelope. Available only in the No. 10 size.

U176

Designed by Richard Sheaff.

1994, Sept. 17 Typo. & Embossed Unwmk.

U631 U176 29c **brown & black** .60 .30
Entire .70 .35
Entire, 1st day cancel, Canton, OH *(28,977)* 1.25
a. Black ("29/USA") omitted, entire *400.00*

Available only in No. 10 size.

Liberty Bell — U177

Designed by Richard Sheaff.

1995, Jan. 3 Typo. & Embossed Unwmk.

U632 U177 32c **greenish blue & blue** .65 .30
Entire .75 .40
Entire, 1st day cancel, Williamsburg, PA 1.25
a. Greenish blue omitted, entire *500.00*
b. Blue ("USA 32") omitted, entire *150.00*

First day cancellation was applied to 54,102 of Nos. U632, UX198.
See No. U638.

U178

Design sizes: 49x38mm (#U633), 53x44mm (U634). Stamp and design continue on back of envelope.

1995 Typo. Unwmk.

U633 U178 (32c) **blue & red** .65 .30
Entire, #6¾ .75 .40
U634 U178 (32c) **blue & red** .65 .30
Entire, #10 .75 .40
a. Red & tagging omitted, entire *500.00*
b. Blue omitted, entire *500.00*

Originally, Nos. U633-U634 were only available through the Philatelic Fullfillment Center after their announcement 1/12/95. Envelopes submitted for first day cancels received a 12/13/94 cancel, even though they were not available on that date.
See No. U638.

U179

Design size: 58x25mm. Stamp and design continue on back of envelope.
Designed by Douglas Smith.

1995, Mar. 10 Typo. Unwmk.
Precanceled

U635 U179 (5c) **green & red brown** .20
Entire .25 .25
Entire, 1st day cancel, State College, PA 1.25

Graphic Eagle — U180

Designed by Uldis Purins.

1995, Mar. 10 Typo. Unwmk.
Precanceled

U636 U180 (10c) **dark carmine & blue** .20
Entire .30 .20
Entire, 1st day cancel, State College, PA 1.25

Available only in No. 10 size.

Spiral Heart — U181

Designed by Uldis Purins.

1995, May 12 Typo. Unwmk.

U637 U181 32c **red,** *light blue* .65 .30
Entire .75 .40
Entire, 1st day cancel, Lakeville, PA 1.25

Liberty Bell Type

1995, May 16 Typo. Unwmk.

U638 U177 32c **greenish blue & blue** .65 .30
Entire .70 .35
Entire, 1st day cancel, Washington, DC 1.25
a. Greenish blue omitted, entire —

No. U638 was printed on security paper and was available only in No. 9 size.

Space Shuttle Type of 1989

Designed by Richard Sheaff.

1995, Sept. 22 Typo. Unwmk. *Die Cut*

U639 U163 32c **carmine rose** .65 .35
Entire .70 .40
Entire, 1st day cancel, Milwaukee, WI 1.25

A hologram, visible through the die cut window to the right of "USA 32," is affixed to the inside of the envelope. No. U639 was available only in No. 10 size.

U182

Designed by Richard Sheaff.

1996, Apr. 20 Typo. & Litho. Unwmk. *Die Cut*

U640 U182 32c **multicolored** .60 .30
Entire .70 .35
Entire, 1st day cancel, Chicago, IL *(9,921)* 1.25

The lithographed vignette, visible through the die cut window to the right of "USA 32c," is affixed to the inside of the envelope. Available only in the No. 10 size.

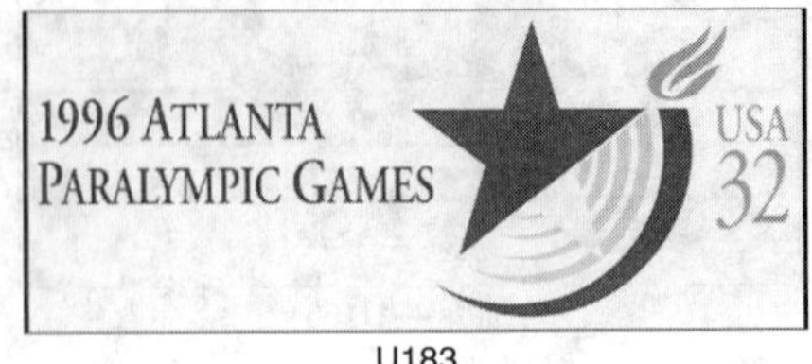

U183

Designed by Brad Copeland. Illustration reduced.

1996, May 2

U641 U183 32c **multicolored** .60 .30
Entire .70 .35
Entire, 1st day cancel, Washington, DC 1.25
a. Blue & red omitted, entire —
b. Blue & gold omitted, entire *500.00*
c. Red omitted, entire —
d. Black & red omitted, entire *500.00*

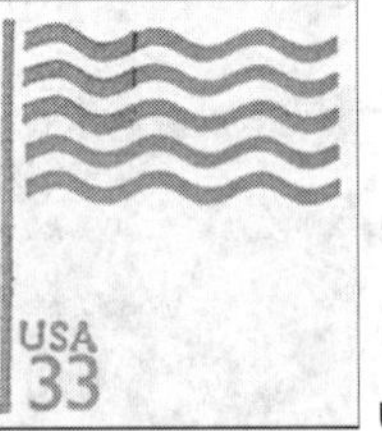

U184

Designer by Richard Sheaff.

1999, Jan. 11 Typo. & Embossed Unwmk.

U642 U184 33c **yellow, blue & red** .65 .30
Entire .80 .40
Entire, 1st day cancel, Washington, DC 1.25
a. Tagging bar to right of design .65 .30
Entire .80 .40
b. As "a," blue omitted, entire —
c. Yellow omitted, entire —

Earliest documented use of No. U642a, 10/12/99.

1999, Jan. 11 Typo. Unwmk.

U643 U184 33c **blue & red** .65 .30
Entire .80 .40
Entire, 1st day cancel, Washington, DC 1.25

Available only in #9 size.

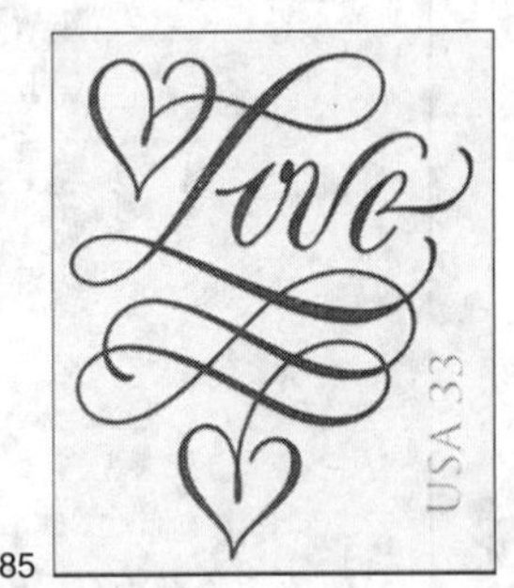

U185

Designed by Julian Waters.

1999, Jan. 28 Litho.

U644 U185 33c **violet** .65 .30
Entire .80 .40
Entire, 1st day cancel, Loveland, CO 1.25

Lincoln — U186

Designed by Richard Sheaff.

1999, June 5 Typo. & Litho. Unwmk.

U645	U186	33c	**blue & black**	.65	.30
			Entire	.80	.40
			Entire, 1st day cancel, Springfield, IL		1.25

Eagle — U187

Designed by Michael Doret.

2001, Jan. 7 Typo. Tagged Unwmk.

U646	U187	34c	**blue gray & gray**	.65	.30
			Entire	.85	.40
			Entire, 1st day cancel, Washington, DC		1.25
a.			Blue gray omitted, entire	—	

Many color shades known.

This envelope was also produced using recycled blue-gray paper starting in 2002.

Lovebirds U188

Designed by Robert Brangwynne.

2001, Feb. 14 Litho. Tagged Unwmk.

U647	U188	34c	**rose & dull violet**	.65	.30
			Entire	.85	.40
			Entire, 1st day cancel, Lovejoy, GA		1.25

Community Colleges, Cent. — U189

Designed by Howard Paine.

2001, Feb. 20 Typo. Tagged Unwmk.

U648	U189	34c	**dark blue & orange brown**	.65	.30
			Entire	.85	.40
			Entire, 1st day cancel, Joliet, IL		1.25

Ribbon Star — U190

Designed by Terrence W. McCaffrey.

2002, June 7 Typo. Unwmk.

U649	U190	37c	**red, blue & gray**	.75	.35
			Entire	.90	.45
			Entire, 1st day cancel, Washington, DC		1.25
			Entire, 1st day cancel, any other city		1.25
a.			Gray omitted, entire	—	
b.			Blue and gray omitted, entire	—	

This envelope was also produced using recycled blue-gray paper starting in 2002.

Type of 1995 Inscribed "USA / Presorted / Standard"

Designed by Uldis Purins.

2002, Aug. 8 Typo. Unwmk.

Untagged

Precanceled

U650	U180	(10c)	**dark carmine & blue**		.20
			Entire	.35	.20
			Entire, 1st day cancel, Washington, DC		1.25

Available only in No. 10 size.

Nurturing Love — U191

Designed by Craig Frazier.

2003, Jan. 25 Typo. Unwmk.

U651	U191	37c	**olive green & yellow orange**	.75	.35
			Entire	.90	.45
			Entire, 1st day cancel, Tucson, AZ		1.25

AIR POST STAMPED ENVELOPES AND AIR LETTER SHEETS

All envelopes have carmine and blue borders, unless noted. There are seven types of borders:

Carmine Diamond in Upper Right Corner.

a- Diamonds measure 9 to 10mm paralled to edge of envelope and 11 to 12mm along oblique side (with top flap open). Sizes 5 and 13 only.

b- Like "a" except diamonds measure 7 to 8mm along oblique side (with top flap open). Sizes 5 and 13 only.

c- Diamonds measure 11 to 12mm parallel to edge of envelope. Size 8 only.

Blue Diamond in Upper Right Corner.

d- Lower points of top row of diamonds point to left. Size 8 only.

e- Lower points of top row of diamonds point to right. Size 8 only.

Diamonds Omitted in Upper Right Corner (1965 Onward)

f- Blue diamond above at left of stamp.

g- Red diamond above at left of stamp.

UC1

5c - Vertical rudder is not semi-circular but slopes down to the left. The tail of the plane projects into the G of POSTAGE. Border types a, b, c, d and e.

UC2

Die 2 (5c and 8c): Vertical rudder is semi-circular. The tail of the plane touches but does not project into the G of POSTAGE. Border types b, d, and e for the 5c; b and d for the 8c.

Die 2 (6c)- Same as UC2 except three types of numeral.

2a- The numeral "6" is 6½mm wide.

2b- The numeral "6" is 6mm wide.

2c- The numeral "6" is 5½mm wide.

Eleven working dies were used in printing the 6c. On each, the numeral "6" was engraved by hand, producing several variations in position, size and thickness.

Nos. UC1 and UC2 occur with varying size blue blobs, caused by a shallow printing die. They are not constant.

Border types b and d for dies 2a and 2b; also without border (June 1944 to Sept. 1945) for dies 2a, 2b and 2c.

Die 3 (6c): Vertical rudder leans forward. S closer to O than to T of POSTAGE. E of POSTAGE has short center bar. Border types b and d, also without border.

No. UC1 with 1933 and 1937 watermarks and No. UC2 with 1929 and 1933 watermarks were issued in Puerto Rico.

No. UC1 in blue black, with 1925 watermark #26 and border type a, is a proof.

1929-44

UC1	UC1	5c	**blue,** *Jan. 12, 1929*	3.50	2.00
			Entire, border a or b	4.50	2.25
			Entire, border c, d or e	8.50	5.75
			First day cancel, border a, entire		40.00
			1933 wmk. #33, border d, entire	*750.00*	*750.00*
			1933 wmk. #33, border b, entire	—	—
			1937 wmk. #36, border d, entire	—	*2,500.*
			1937 wmk. #36, border b, entire	—	—
			Bicolored border omitted, entire	1,300.	
a.			Orange and blue border, type b	350.00	
UC2	UC2	5c	**blue,** die 2	11.00	5.00
			Entire, border b	13.50	6.50
			Entire, border e	19.50	12.50
			1929 wmk. #28, border d, entire	—	*1,500.*
			1933 wmk. #33, border b, entire	*650.00*	—
			1933 wmk. #33, border d, entire	325.00	—
UC3	UC2	6c	**orange,** die 2a, *July 1, 1934*	1.50	.40
			Entire, bicolored border	1.75	.60
			Entire, without border	2.50	1.25
			Entire, 1st day cancel		14.00
a.			With added impression of 3c purple (#U436a), entire without border	*4,000.*	
UC4	UC2	6c	**orange,** die 2b ('42)	2.75	2.00
			Entire, bicolored border, 1941 wmk. #39	60.00	20.00
			Entire, without border	4.50	2.00
UC5	UC2	6c	**orange,** die 2c ('44)	.75	.30
			Entire, without border	1.00	.45
UC6	UC2	6c	**orange,** die 3 ('42)	1.00	.35
			Entire, bicolored border	1.50	.75
			Entire, without border	2.50	.90
			Entire, carmine of border omitted	*4,000.*	
			Double impression, entire	400.00	
a.			6c orange, *blue,* die 3 (error) Entire, without border	*3,500.*	*2,400.*
UC7	UC2	8c	**olive green,** die 2, *Sept. 26, 1932*	13.00	3.50
			Entire, bicolored border	16.00	6.50
			Entire, 1st day cancel		11.00

Surcharged in black on envelopes indicated by number in parenthesis

1945

UC8	U93	6c on 2c	**carmine** (U429, die 1)	1.25	.65
			Entire	1.60	1.00
a.			On U429f, die 7	2.25	1.50
			Entire	3.00	2.00
b.			On U429g, die 8	1.75	1.10
			Entire	2.25	1.75
c.			On U429h, die 9	10.00	7.50

Entire 15.00 11.00
d. 6c on 1c green (error) (U420) *1,750.*
Entire *2,500.*
e. 6c on 3c purple (error) (U436a) *2,000.*
Entire *3,250.*
f. 6c on 3c purple (error), *amber* (U437a) *3,000.*
Entire *3,500.*
g. 6c on 3c violet (error) (U526) *3,000.*
Entire *3,500.*
UC9 U95 6c on 2c **carmine** (U525) 70.00 35.00
Entire 95.00 45.00

Ten surcharge varieties are found on Nos. UC8-UC9.

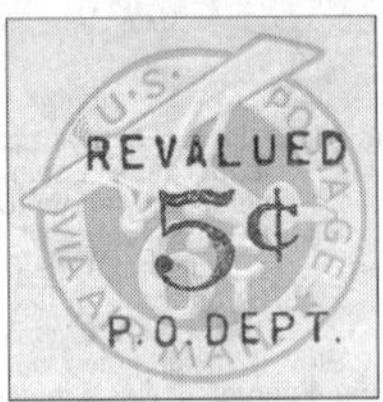

Surcharged in Black on 6c Air Post Envelopes without borders

1946
UC10 UC2 5c on 6c **orange,** die 2a 2.75 1.50
Entire 3.50 2.50
First day of rate, *Oct. 1, 1946,* entire 100.00
a. Double surcharge 60.00
UC11 UC2 5c on 6c **orange,** die 2b 9.00 5.50
Entire 10.00 7.00
First day of rate, *Oct. 1, 1946,* entire 150.00
UC12 UC2 5c on 6c **orange,** die 2c .75 .50
Entire 1.25 .60
First day of rate, *Oct. 1, 1946,* entire 75.00
a. Double surcharge 60.00 60.00
UC13 UC2 5c on 6c **orange,** die 3 .80 .60
Entire 1.00 .75
First day of rate, *Oct. 1, 1946,* entire 75.00
a. Double surcharge 60.00

The 6c borderless envelopes and the revalued envelopes were issued primarily for use to and from members of the armed forces. The 5c rate came into effect Oct. 1, 1946.

Ten surcharge varieties are found on Nos. UC10-UC13.

DC-4 Skymaster — UC3

Envelopes with borders types b and d.

Die 1 - The end of the wing at the right is a smooth curve. The juncture of the front end of the plane and the engine forms an acute angle. The first T of STATES and the E's of UNITED STATES lean to the left.

Die 2 - The end of the wing at the right is a straight line. The juncture of the front end of the plane and the engine is wide open. The first T of STATES and the E's of UNITED STATES lean to the right.

1946
UC14 UC3 5c **carmine,** die 1, *Sept. 25, 1946* .75 .20
Entire, bicolored border 1.10 .40
Entire, 1st day cancel 1.50
Entire, bicolored border omitted —
UC15 UC3 5c **carmine,** die 2 .85 .25
Entire, bicolored border 1.10 .40

No. UC14, printed on flat bed press, measures 21½mm high. No. UC15, printed on rotary press, measures 22mm high. See No. UC18.

DC-4 Skymaster — UC4

1947-55 Typographed, Without Embossing
Letter Sheets for Foreign Postage

UC16 UC4 10c **bright red,** *pale blue,* "Air Letter" on face, 2-line inscription on back, entire 8.50 6.00
Entire, 1st day cancel, *Apr. 29, 1947* 2.00
Die cutting reversed, entire 110.00
UC16a UC4 10c **bright red,** *pale blue, Sept. 1951,* "Air Letter" on face, 4-line inscription on back, entire 17.50 14.00
Die cutting reversed, entire 275.00
b. 10c **chocolate,** *pale blue,* entire 450.00
UC16c UC4 10c **bright red,** *pale blue, Nov. 1953,* "Air Letter" and "Aerogramme" on face, 4-line inscription on back, entire 45.00 12.50
Die cutting reversed, entire 150.00
UC16d UC4 10c **bright red,** *pale blue, 1955,* "Air Letter" and "Aerogramme" on face, 3-line inscription on back, entire 9.00 8.00
Die cutting reversed, entire 60.00
Dark blue (inscriptions & border diamonds) omitted —

Printed on protective tinted paper containing colorless inscription,

UNITED STATES FOREIGN AIR MAIL multiple, repeated in parallel vertical or horizontal lines.

Postage Stamp Centenary Issue

Centenary of the first postage stamps issued by the United States Government.

Washington and Franklin, Early and Modern Mail-carrying Methods — UC5

Two dies: Rotary, design measures 22¼mm high; and flat bed press, design 21¾mm high.

1947, May 21 Embossed
For Domestic Postage
UC17 UC5 5c **carmine** (rotary) .40 .25
Entire, bicolored border b .55 .35
Entire, 1st day cancel, NY, NY 1.25
a. Flat plate printing .50 .30
Entire .60 .40

Type of 1946

Type I: 6's lean to right.
Type II: 6's upright.

1950
UC18 UC3 6c **carmine,** type I, *Sept. 22, 1950* .35 .20
Entire, bicolored border .60 .30
Entire, 1st day cancel, Philadelphia 1.00
a. Type II .75 .25
Entire 1.00 .30

Several other types differ slightly from the two listed.

Nos. UC14, UC15, UC18 Surcharged in Red at Left of Stamp

1951
UC19 UC3 6c on 5c **carmine,** die 1 .85 .50
Entire 1.25 .80
UC20 UC3 6c on 5c **carmine,** die 2 .85 .50
Entire 1.25 .80
a. 6c on 6c **carmine** (error) entire *1,500.*
b. Double surcharge *500.00* —

Nos. UC14 and UC15 Surcharged in Red at Left of Stamp

1952
UC21 UC3 6c on 5c **carmine,** die 1 27.50 17.50
Entire 32.50 22.50
UC22 UC3 6c on 5c **carmine,** die 2, *Aug. 29, 1952* 4.00 2.50
Entire 5.75 4.25
a. Double surcharge 200.00

Same Surcharge in Red on No. UC17

UC23 UC5 6c on 5c **carmine** 1,250.
Entire 2,400.

The 6c on 4c black (No. U440) is believed to be a favor printing.

Fifth International Philatelic Exhibition Issue

FIPEX, the Fifth International Philatelic Exhibition, New York, N.Y., Apr. 28-May 6, 1956.

Eagle in Flight — UC6

1956, May 2
UC25 UC6 6c **red** .75 .50
Entire 1.00 .80
Entire, 1st day cancel, New York, N.Y. *(363,239)* 1.25

Two types exist, differing slightly in the clouds at top.

Skymaster Type of 1946

1958, July 31
UC26 UC3 7c **blue** .65 .50
Entire 1.00 .55
Entire, 1st day cancel, Dayton, O. *(143,428)* 1.00

Nos. UC3-UC5, UC18 and UC25 Surcharged in Green at Left of Stamp

1958
UC27 UC2 6c + 1c **orange,** die 2a 325.00 225.00
Entire, without border 350.00 275.00
Entire, with border 8,000.
UC28 UC2 6c + 1c **orange,** die 2b 75.00 75.00
Entire, without border 100.00 110.00
UC29 UC2 6c + 1c **orange,** die 2c 45.00 50.00
Entire 50.00 75.00
UC30 UC3 6c + 1c **carmine,** type I 1.00 .50
Entire 1.25 .65
a. Type II 1.00 .50
Entire 1.25 .65
UC31 UC6 6c + 1c **red** 1.00 .50
Entire 1.40 .85

Jet Airliner — UC7

Letter Sheet for Foreign Postage

Type I: Back inscription in 3 lines.
Type II: Back inscription in 2 lines.

1958-59 Typographed, Without Embossing
UC32 UC7 10c **blue & red,** *blue,* II, *May, 1959,* entire 6.00 5.00
b. Red omitted, II, entire —
c. Blue omitted, II, entire *1,000.*
d. Red omitted, I, entire *1,000.*
UC32a UC7 10c **blue & red,** *blue,* I, *Sept. 12, 1958,* entire 10.00 5.00
Entire, 1st day cancel, St. Louis, Mo. *(92,400)* 1.25
Die cutting reversed, entire 75.00

Silhouette of Jet Airliner — UC8

1958, Nov. 21 Embossed
UC33 UC8 7c **blue** .60 .25
Entire .70 .30
Entire, 1st day cancel, New York, N.Y. *(208,980)* 1.00

1960, Aug. 18
UC34 UC8 7c **carmine** .60 .25
Entire .70 .30
Entire, 1st day cancel, Portland, Ore. *(196,851)* 1.00

Jet Airliner and Globe — UC9

Letter Sheet for Foreign Postage
Typographed, Without Embossing

1961, June 16
UC35 UC9 11c **red & blue,** *blue,* entire 2.75 2.25
Entire, 1st day cancel, Johnstown, Pa. *(163,460)* 1.00
Die cutting reversed, entire 35.00
a. Red omitted, entire *1,000.*
b. Blue omitted, entire *1,000.*

Jet Airliner — UC10

1962, Nov. 17 **Embossed**
UC36 UC10 8c **red** .55 .20
Entire .75 .30
Entire, 1st day cancel, Chantilly, Va. *(194,810)* 1.00

Jet Airliner — UC11

1965-67
UC37 UC11 8c **red,** *Jan. 7* .35 .20
Entire, border "f" .45 .30
Entire, border "g" *20.00*
Entire, 1st day cancel, Chicago, Ill. *(226,178)* 1.00
a. Tagged, *Aug. 15, 1967* 3.50 .30
Entire 5.00 .75
Tagged, 1st day cancel 3.50

No. UC37a has a 8x24mm panel at left of stamp that glows orange red under ultraviolet light.

Pres. John F. Kennedy and Jet Plane UC12

Letter Sheets for Foreign Postage
Typographed, Without Embossing

1965, May 29
UC38 UC12 11c **red & dark blue,** *blue,* entire 3.25 2.75
Entire, 1st day cancel, Boston, Mass. *(337,422)* 1.00
Die cutting reversed, entire 40.00

1967, May 29
UC39 UC12 13c **red & dark blue,** *blue,* entire 3.00 2.75
Entire, 1st day cancel, Chicago, Ill. *(211,387)* 1.00
Die cutting reversed, entire —
a. Red omitted, entire *900.00*
b. Dark blue omitted, entire *500.00*

Jet Liner — UC13

Designed by Robert J. Jones.

1968, Jan. 8 **Tagged** **Embossed**
UC40 UC13 10c **red** .50 .20
Entire .80 .20
Entire, 1st day cancel, Chicago, Ill. *(157,553)* 1.00

No. UC37 Surcharged in Red at Left of Stamp

1968, Feb. 5
UC41 UC11 8c + 2c **red** .65 .20
Entire .90 .40
Entire, 1st day cancel, Washington, D.C. 8.00

Human Rights Year Issue

Issued for International Human Rights Year, and to commemorate the 20th anniversary of the United Nations' Declaration of Human Rights.

Globes and Flock of Birds — UC14

Printed by Acrovure Division of Union-Camp Corporation, Englewood, N.J. Designed by Antonio Frasconi.

Letter Sheet for Foreign Postage

1968, Dec. 3 **Tagged** **Photo.**
UC42 UC14 13c **gray, brown, orange & black,** *blue,* entire 8.00 4.00
Entire, 1st day cancel, Washington, D.C. *(145,898)* 1.25
Die cutting reversed, entire 75.00
a. Orange omitted, entire —
b. Brown omitted, entire *500.00*
c. Black omitted, entire —

No. UC42 has a luminescent panel ⅜x1 inch on the right globe. The panel glows orange red under ultraviolet light.

Jet Plane — UC15

Printed by United States Envelope Co., Williamsburg, Pa. Designed by Robert Geissmann.

1971, May 6 **Embossed (Plane)**
Center Circle Luminescent
UC43 UC15 11c **red & blue** .50 .20
Entire .60 .20
Entire, 1st day cancel, Williamsburg, Pa. *(187,000)* 1.00

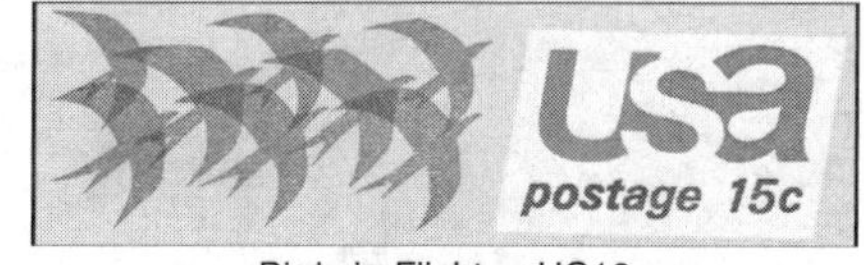

Birds in Flight — UC16

Printed by Bureau of Engraving and Printing. Designed by Soren Noring.

Letter Sheet for Foreign Postage

1971 **Tagged** **Photo.**
UC44 UC16 15c **gray, red, white & blue,** *blue,* entire, *May 28* 1.50 1.10
Entire, 1st day cancel, Chicago, Ill. *(130,669)* 1.25
Die cutting reversed, entire 30.00
a. "AEROGRAMME" added to inscription, entire, *Dec. 13* 1.50 1.10
Entire, 1st day cancel, Philadelphia, Pa. 1.25
Die cutting reversed, entire 30.00

Folding instructions (2 steps) in capitals on No. C44; (4 steps) in upper and lower case on No. UC44a.

On Nos. UC44-UC44a the white rhomboid background of "USA postage 15c" is luminescent. No. UC44 is inscribed: "VIA AIR MAIL-PAR AVION". "postage 15c" is in gray. See No. UC46.

No. UC40 Surcharged in Green at Left of Stamp

1971, June 28 **Embossed**
UC45 UC13 10c + (1c) **red** 1.50 .20
Entire 1.90 .50
Entire, 1st day cancel, Washington, D.C. 8.00

HOT AIR BALLOONING CHAMPIONSHIPS ISSUE

Hot Air Ballooning World Championships, Albuquerque, N.M., Feb. 10-17, 1973.

"usa" Type of 1971

Design: Three balloons and cloud at left in address section; no birds beside stamp. Inscribed "INTERNATIONAL HOT AIR BALLOONING." "postage 15c" in blue.

Printed by Bureau of Engraving and Printing. Designed by Soren Noring (vignette) and Esther Porter (balloons).

Letter Sheet for Foreign Postage

1973, Feb. 10 **Tagged** **Photo.**
UC46 UC16 15c **red, white & blue,** *blue,* entire .75 .40
Entire, 1st day cancel, Albuquerque, N.M. *(210,000)* 1.00

Folding instructions as on No. UC44a. See notes after No. UC44.

Bird in Flight — UC17

1973, Dec. 1 **Luminescent Ink**
UC47 UC17 13c **rose red** .30 .20
Entire .40 .20
Entire, 1st day cancel, Memphis, Tenn. *(132,658)* 1.00

UC18

Printed by the Bureau of Engraving and Printing. Designed by Bill Hyde.

Letter Sheet for Foreign Postage.

1974, Jan. 4 **Tagged** **Photo.**
UC48 UC18 18c **red & blue,** *blue,* entire .90 .30
Entire, 1st day cancel, Atlanta, Ga. *(119,615)* 1.00
Die cutting reversed, entire —
a. Red omitted, entire —

25TH ANNIVERSARY OF NATO ISSUE

UC19

Design: "NATO" and NATO emblem at left in address section.
Printed by Bureau of Engraving and Printing. Designed by Soren Noring.

Letter Sheet for Foreign Postage

1974, Apr. 4 **Tagged** **Photo.**
UC49 UC19 18c **red & blue,** *blue,* entire .90 .40
Entire, 1st day cancel, Washington, D.C. 1.00

UC20

Printed by Bureau of Engraving and Printing. Designed by Robert Geissmann.

Letter Sheet for Foreign Postage

1976, Jan. 16 **Tagged** **Photo.**
UC50 UC20 22c **red & blue,** *blue,* entire .90 .40
Entire, 1st day cancel, Tempe, Ariz. *(118,303)* 1.00
Die cutting reversed, entire 15.00

"USA" — UC21

Printed by Bureau of Engraving and Printing. Designed by Soren Noring.

Letter Sheet for Foreign Postage

1978, Nov. 3 **Tagged** **Photo.**
UC51 UC21 22c **blue,** *blue,* entire .70 .25
Entire, 1st day cancel, St. Petersburg, Fla. *(86,099)* 1.00
Die cutting reversed, entire 25.00

22nd OLYMPIC GAMES, MOSCOW, JULY 19-AUG. 3, 1980.

UC22

Design (multicolored in bottom left corner) shows discus thrower.
Printed by Bureau of Engraving and Printing. Designed by Robert M. Cunningham.

Letter Sheet for Foreign Postage

1979, Dec. 5 **Tagged** **Photo.**
UC52 UC22 22c **red, black & green,** *bluish,* entire 1.50 .25
Entire, 1st day cancel, Bay Shore, N.Y. 1.00

"USA" — UC23

Design (brown on No. UC53, green and brown on No. UC54): lower left, Statue of Liberty. Inscribed "Tour the United States." Folding area shows tourist attractions.
Printed by Bureau of Engraving and Printing.
Designed by Frank J. Waslick.

Letter Sheet for Foreign Postage

1980, Dec. 29 **Tagged** **Photo.**
UC53 UC23 30c **blue, red & brown,** *blue,* entire .65 *1.00*
Entire, 1st day cancel, San Francisco, CA 1.25
Die cutting reversed, entire 20.00
a. Red (30) omitted, entire *70.00*
Die cutting reversed, entire —

1981, Sept. 21 **Tagged** **Photo.**
UC54 UC23 30c **yellow, magenta, blue & black,** *blue,* entire .65 *1.00*
Entire, 1st day cancel, Honolulu, HI 1.25
Die cutting reversed, entire 20.00

UC24

Design: "Made in USA . . . world's best buys!" on flap, ship, tractor in lower left. Reverse folding area shows chemicals, jet silhouette, wheat, typewriter and computer tape disks. Printed by Bureau of Engraving and Printing.
Designed by Frank J. Waslick.

Letter Sheet for Foreign Postage

1982, Sept. 16 **Tagged** **Photo.**
UC55 UC24 30c **multi,** *blue,* entire .65 *1.00*
Entire, 1st day cancel, Seattle, WA 1.25
Die cutting reversed, entire —

WORLD COMMUNICATIONS YEAR

World Map Showing Locations of Satellite Tracking Stations — UC25

Design: Reverse folding area shows satellite, tracking station.
Printed by Bureau of Engraving and Printing.
Designed by Esther Porter.

Letter Sheet for Foreign Postage

1983, Jan. 7 **Tagged** **Photo.**
UC56 UC25 30c **multi,** *blue,* entire .65 *1.00*
Entire, 1st day cancel, Anaheim, CA 1.25
Die cutting reversed, entire 25.00

1984 OLYMPICS

UC26

Design: Woman equestrian at lower left with montage of competitive events on reverse folding area.
Printed by the Bureau of Engraving & Printing.
Designed by Bob Peak.

Letter Sheet for Foreign Postage

1983, Oct. 14 **Tagged** **Photo.**
UC57 UC26 30c **multi,** *blue,* entire .65 *1.50*
Entire, 1st day cancel, Los Angeles, CA 1.25
Die cutting reversed, entire —

WEATHER SATELLITES, 25TH ANNIV.

Landsat Infrared and Thermal Mapping Bands UC27

Design: Landsat orbiting the earth at lower left with three Landsat photographs on reverse folding area. Inscribed: "Landsat views the Earth."
Printed by the Bureau of Engraving & Printing.
Designed by Esther Porter.

Letter Sheet for Foreign Postage

1985, Feb. 14 **Tagged** **Photo.**
UC58 UC27 36c **multi,** *blue,* entire .70 *1.00*
Entire, 1st day cancel, Goddard Flight Center, MD 1.40
Die cutting reversed, entire 30.00

NATIONAL TOURISM WEEK

Urban Skyline — UC28

Design: Inscribed "Celebrate America" at lower left and "Travel. . . the perfect freedom" on folding area. Skier, Indian chief, cowboy, jazz trumpeter and pilgrims on reverse folding area.
Printed by the Bureau of Engraving & Printing.
Designed by Dennis Luzak.

Letter Sheet for Foreign Postage

1985, May 21 **Tagged** **Photo.**
UC59 UC28 36c **multi,** *blue,* entire .70 *1.00*
Entire, 1st day cancel, Washington, DC 1.40
Die cutting reversed, entire 25.00
a. Black omitted, entire —

MARK TWAIN AND HALLEY'S COMET

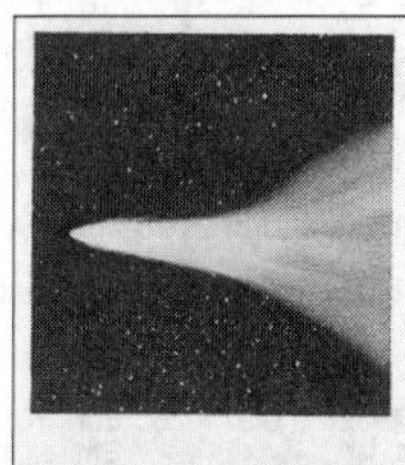

Comet Tail Viewed from Space — UC29

Design: Portrait of Twain at lower left and inscribed "I came in with Halley's Comet in 1835. It is coming again next year, and I expect to go out with it. It will be the greatest disappointment of my life if I don't go out with Halley's Comet." "1835 . Mark Twain . 1910 . Halley's Comet . 1985" and Twain, Huckleberry Finn, steamboat and comet on reverse folding areas.
Printed by the Bureau of Engraving & Printing.
Designed by Dennis Luzak.

Letter Sheet for Foreign Postage

1985, Dec. 4 **Tagged** **Photo.**

UC60 UC29 36c **multi,** entire 1.00 *1.50*
Entire, 1st day cancel, Hannibal, MO 1.50
Die cutting reversed, entire 25.00

UC30

Printed by the Bureau of Engraving & Printing.

Letter Sheet for Foreign Postage

1988, May 9 **Litho.** **Tagged**

UC61 UC30 39c **multi,** entire .80 *1.00*
Entire, 1st day cancel, Miami, FL *(27,446)* 1.60
a. Tagging bar to left of design ('89) .80 *1.00*

On No. UC61, the tagging bar is between "USA" and "39."

MONTGOMERY BLAIR, POSTMASTER GENERAL 1861-64

Blair and Pres. Abraham Lincoln — UC31

Design: Mail bags and "Free city delivery," "Railway mail service" and "Money order system" at lower left. Globe, locomotive, bust of Blair, UPU emblem and "The Paris conference of 1863, initiated by Postmaster General Blair, led, in 1874, to the founding of the Universal Postal Union" contained on reverse folding area.
Printed by the Bureau of Engraving & Printing.
Designed by Ned Seidler.

Letter Sheet for Foreign Postage

1989, Nov. 20 **Litho.** **Tagged**

UC62 UC31 39c **multicolored,** entire .80 *1.00*
Entire, 1st day cancel, Washington, DC 1.60

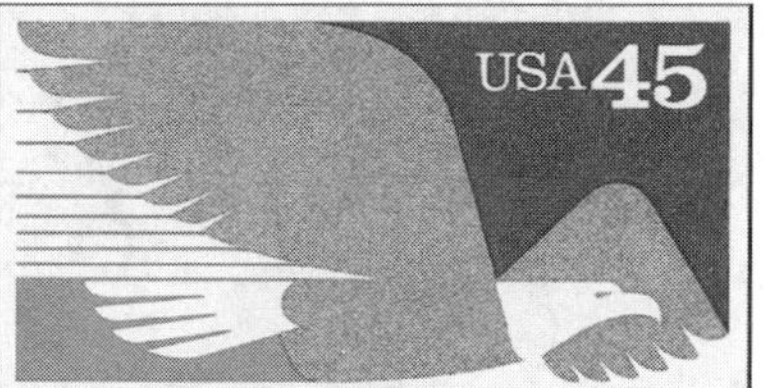

UC32

Designed by Bradbury Thompson.
Printed by the Bureau of Engraving and Printing.

Letter Sheet for Foreign Postage

1991, May 17 **Litho.** **Tagged**

UC63 UC32 45c **gray, red & blue,** *blue,* entire .90 *1.00*
a. White paper .90 *1.00*
Entire, 1st day cancel, Denver, CO *(19,941)* 1.40

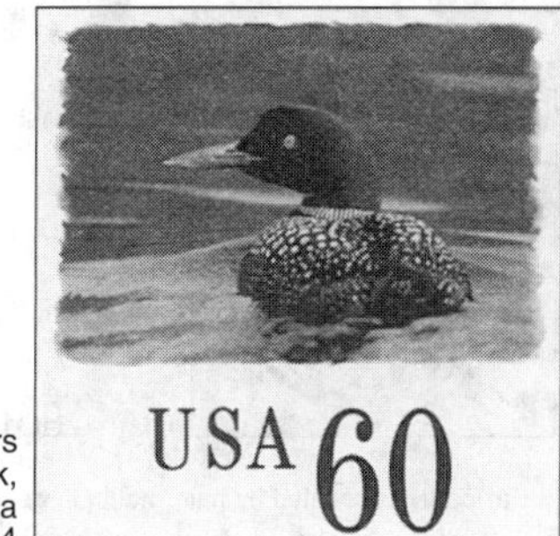

Thaddeus Lowe (1832-1913), Balloonist — UC33

Designed by Davis Meltzer.
Printed by the Bureau of Engraving & Printing.

Letter Sheet for Foreign Postage

1995, Sept. 23 **Litho.** **Tagged**

UC64 UC33 50c **multicolored,** *blue,* entire 1.00 1.00
Entire, 1st day cancel, Tampa, FL 1.25

Voyageurs Natl. Park, Minnesota UC34

Designed by Phil Jordan.

Printed by Burean of Engraving & Printing.

Letter Sheet for Foreign Postage

1999, May 15 **Litho.** **Tagged**

UC65 UC34 60c **multicolored,** *blue,* entire 1.25 1.00
Entire, 1st day cancel, Denver, CO 1.50

OFFICIAL ENVELOPES & WRAPPERS

By the Act of Congress, January 31, 1873, the franking privilege of officials was abolished as of July 1, 1873 and the Postmaster General was authorized to prepare official envelopes. At the same time official stamps were prepared for all Departments. Department envelopes became obsolete July 5, 1884. After that, government offices began to use franked envelopes of varied design. These indicate no denomination and lie beyond the scope of this Catalogue.

Post Office Department

UO1

Numeral 9mm high.

UO2

Numeral 9mm high.

UO3

Numeral 9½mm high.

Printed by George H. Reay, Brooklyn, N.Y.

1873

UO1	UO1	2c **black,** *lemon*		22.50	9.00
		Entire		32.50	12.50
UO2	UO2	3c **black,** *lemon*		15.00	6.00
		Entire		27.50	9.00
+UO3	UO2	3c **black**		*22,500.*	
		Entire		*30,000.*	
UO4	UO3	6c **black,** *lemon*		25.00	15.00
		Entire		32.50	20.00

The No. UO3 entire is unique. It has a tear through the stamp that has been professionally repaired. Value based on auction sale in 1999.

UO4

Numeral 9¼mm high.

UO5

Numeral 9¼mm high.

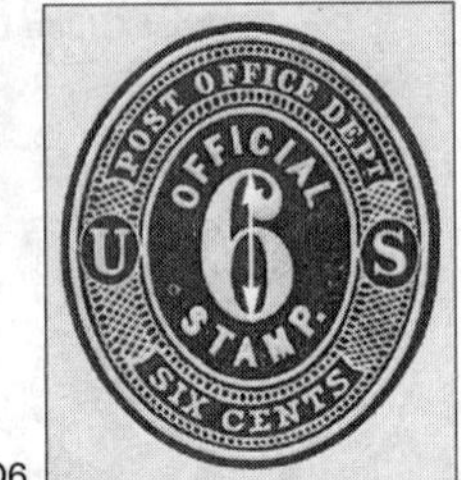

UO6

Numeral 10½mm high.

Printed by Plimpton Manufacturing Co., Hartford, Conn.

1874-79

No.	Type	Denom.	Description	Unused	Used
UO5	UO4	2c	**black,** *lemon*	10.00	4.00
			Entire	14.00	5.75
UO6	UO4	2c	**black**	125.00	32.50
			Entire	160.00	40.00
UO7	UO5	3c	**black,** *lemon*	3.25	.85
			Entire	4.25	1.50
UO8	UO5	3c	**black**	3,000.	2,250.
			Entire	5,750.	
UO9	UO5	3c	**black,** *amber*	110.00	35.00
			Entire	150.00	50.00
UO10	UO5	3c	**black,** *blue*	*45,000.*	
			Entire	*50,000.*	
UO11	UO5	3c	**blue,** *blue* ('75)	*45,000.*	
			Entire	*50,000.*	
UO12	UO6	6c	**black,** *lemon*	15.00	5.50
			Entire	25.00	10.00
UO13	UO6	6c	**black**	3,000.	1,500.
			Entire	5,750.	

Fakes exist of Nos. UO3, UO8 and UO13.

Postal Service

UO7

1877

No.	Type	Description	Unused	Used
UO14	UO7	**black**	6.50	3.75
		Entire	10.50	5.00
UO15	UO7	**black,** *amber*	210.00	27.50
		Entire	425.00	40.00
UO16	UO7	**blue,** *amber*	200.00	30.00
		Entire	425.00.	45.00
UO17	UO7	**blue,** *blue*	8.50	6.00
		Entire	12.50	9.00

War Department

Franklin — UO8

Bust points to the end of "N" of "ONE".

Jackson — UO9

Bust narrow at the back.

Washington — UO10

Queue projects below the bust.

Lincoln — UO11

Neck very long at the back.

Jefferson — UO12

Queue forms straight line with bust.

Clay — UO13

Ear partly concealed by hair, mouth large, chin prominent.

Webster — UO14

Has side whiskers.

Scott — UO15

Hamilton — UO16

Back of bust very narrow; chin almost straight; the labels containing the letters "U S" are exactly parallel.

Printed by George H. Reay.

1873

No.	Type	Denom.	Description	Unused	Used
UO18	UO8	1c	**dark red**	700.00	300.00
			Entire	1,200.	325.00
WO18A	UO8	1c	**dark red,** *manila*		—
UO19	UO9	2c	**dark red**	2,250.	400.00
			Entire	3,000.	
UO20	UO10	3c	**dark red**	70.00	40.00
			Entire	95.00	60.00
UO21	UO10	3c	**dark red,** *amber*	*40,000.*	
			Entire	*50,000.*	
UO22	UO10	3c	**dark red,** *cream*	900.00	250.00
			Entire	1,100.	300.00
UO23	UO11	6c	**dark red**	325.00	90.00
			Entire	425.00	150.00
UO24	UO11	6c	**dark red,** *cream*	8,250.	425.00
			Entire	10,000.	*2,000.*
UO25	UO12	10c	**dark red**	*17,500.*	2,250.
			Entire	*27,500.*	4,000.
UO26	UO13	12c	**dark red**	175.00	50.00
			Entire	250.00	—
UO27	UO14	15c	**dark red**	160.00	55.00
			Entire	210.00	*375.00*
UO28	UO15	24c	**dark red**	175.00	50.00
			Entire	225.00	*1,250.*
UO29	UO16	30c	**dark red**	550.00	150.00
			Entire	725.00	500.00

1873

No.	Type	Denom.	Description	Unused	Used
UO30	UO8	1c	**vermilion**	200.00	
			Entire	400.00	
WO31	UO8	1c	**vermilion,** *manila*	17.50	12.50
			Entire	32.50	20.00
+UO32	UO9	2c	**vermilion**	500.00	
			Entire	—	
WO33	UO9	2c	**vermilion,** *manila*	225.00	
			Entire	375.00	
UO34	UO10	3c	**vermilion**	100.00	40.00
			Entire	175.00	125.00
UO35	UO10	3c	**vermilion,** *amber*	125.00	
			Entire	375.00	
UO36	UO10	3c	**vermilion,** *cream*	17.00	12.50
			Entire	37.50	22.50
UO37	UO11	6c	**vermilion**	100.00	
			Entire	175.00	
+UO38	UO11	6c	**vermilion,** *cream*	575.00	
			Entire	*27,500.*	
UO39	UO12	10c	**vermilion**	350.00	
			Entire	450.00	
UO40	UO13	12c	**vermilion**	175.00	
			Entire	225.00	
UO41	UO14	15c	**vermilion**	250.00	
			Entire	3,000.	
UO42	UO15	24c	**vermilion**	450.00	
			Entire	650.00	
UO43	UO16	30c	**vermilion**	500.00	
			Entire	625.00	

UO17

Bottom serif on "S" is thick and short; bust at bottom below hair forms a sharp point.

UO18

Bottom serif on "S" is thick and short; front part of bust is rounded.

UO19

Bottom serif on "S" is short; queue does not project below bust.

UO20

Neck very short at the back.

UO21

Knot of queue stands out prominently.

UO22

Ear prominent, chin receding.

UO23

Has no side whiskers; forelock projects above head.

UO24

Back of bust rather broad; chin slopes considerably; the label containing letters "U S" are not exactly parallel.

Printed by Plimpton Manufacturing Co.

1875

UO44	UO17	1c	**red**	175.00	80.00
			Entire	225.00	150.00
+UO45	UO17	1c	**red,** *amber*	1,000.	
+UO45A	UO17	1c	**red,** *orange*	*37,500.*	
WO46	UO17	1c	**red,** *manila*	4.25	2.75
			Entire	9.50	6.50
UO47	UO18	2c	**red**	125.00	—
			Entire	175.00	
UO48	UO18	2c	**red,** *amber*	35.00	14.00
			Entire	42.50	25.00
UO49	UO18	2c	**red,** *orange*	60.00	13.50
			Entire	70.00	19.00
WO50	UO18	2c	**red,** *manila*	95.00	40.00
			Entire	210.00	—
UO51	UO19	3c	**red**	16.00	9.00
			Entire	20.00	15.00
UO52	UO19	3c	**red,** *amber*	20.00	9.00
			Entire	25.00	14.00
UO53	UO19	3c	**red,** *cream*	7.00	3.75
			Entire	9.75	6.50
UO54	UO19	3c	**red,** *blue*	3.75	2.75
			Entire	5.50	4.50
UO55	UO19	3c	**red,** *fawn*	6.00	2.75
			Entire	10.00	4.00
UO56	UO20	6c	**red**	60.00	30.00
			Entire	95.00	—
UO57	UO20	6c	**red,** *amber*	90.00	40.00
			Entire	110.00	—
UO58	UO20	6c	**red,** *cream*	225.00	85.00
			Entire	275.00	
UO59	UO21	10c	**red**	250.00	80.00
			Entire	300.00	—
UO60	UO21	10c	**red,** *amber*	1,250.	
			Entire	1,650.	
UO61	UO22	12c	**red**	60.00	40.00
			Entire	175.00	*250.00*
UO62	UO22	12c	**red,** *amber*	800.00	
			Entire	950.00	
UO63	UO22	12c	**red,** *cream*	700.00	
			Entire	950.00	
UO64	UO23	15c	**red**	250.00	140.00
			Entire	300.00	—
UO65	UO23	15c	**red,** *amber*	950.00	
			Entire	1,200.	
UO66	UO23	15c	**red,** *cream*	800.00	
			Entire	1,000.	
UO67	UO24	30c	**red**	190.00	140.00
			Entire	225.00	—
UO68	UO24	30c	**red,** *amber*	950.00	
			Entire	2,400.	
UO69	UO24	30c	**red,** *cream*	1,000.	
			Entire	1,350.	

POSTAL SAVINGS ENVELOPES

Issued under the Act of Congress, approved June 25, 1910, in lieu of penalty or franked envelopes. Unused remainders, after October 5, 1914, were overprinted with the Penalty Clause. Regular stamped envelopes, redeemed by the Government, were also overprinted for official use.

UO25

1911

UO70	UO25	1c	**green**	70.00	20.00
			Entire	82.50	40.00
UO71	UO25	1c	**green,** *oriental buff*	200.00	67.50
			Entire	250.00	85.00
UO72	UO25	2c	**carmine**	11.50	3.75
			Entire	20.00	11.00
a.		2c	**carmine,** *manila* (error)	*1,750.*	*1,000.*
			Entire	*2,500.*	*1,400.*

Tagged
Envelopes from No. UO73 onward are tagged unless otherwise noted.

OFFICIAL MAIL

Great Seal — UO26

1983, Jan. 12 **Embossed**

UO73 UO26 20c **blue,** entire 1.25 *30.00*
First day cancel, Washington, DC 1.00

UO27

1985, Feb. 26 **Embossed**

UO74 UO27 22c **blue,** entire .90 *15.00*
First day cancel, Washington, DC 1.00

UO28

1987, Mar. 2 **Typo.**

UO75 UO28 22c **blue,** entire 1.00 *20.00*
First day cancel, Washington, DC 1.00

Used exclusively to mail U.S. Savings Bonds.

UO29

1988, Mar. 22 **Typo.**

UO76 UO29 (25c) **black & blue,** entire 1.10 *20.00*
First day cancel, Washington, DC 1.25

Used exclusively to mail U.S. Savings Bonds.

UO30

Official Mail 25 USA

UO31

POSTAL CARDS

Values are for unused cards as sold by the Post Office, without printed or written address or message, and used cards with Post Office cancellation, when current. Used cards with postage added to meet higher rates sell for less. Used cards for international rates are for proper usage. Those used domestically sell for less.

The "Preprinted" values are for unused cards with printed or written address or message.

Starting with No. UX21, all postal cards have been printed by the Government Printing Office.

Nos. UX1-UX48 are typographed; others are lithographed (offset) unless otherwise stated.

Numerous printing varieties exist. Varieties of surcharged cards include (a) inverted surcharge at lower left, (b) double surcharge, one inverted at lower left, (c) surcharge in other abnormal positions, including back of card. Such surcharge varieties command a premium.

Colored cancellations sell for more than black in some instances. **All values are for entire cards.**

As of Jan. 1, 1999, postal cards were sold individually for 1c over face value.

See Computer Vended Postage section for "Postal Buddy" cards.

Since 1875 it has been possible to purchase some postal cards in sheets for multiple printing, hence pairs, strips and blocks are available. Some sheets have been cut up so that cards exist with stamp inverted, in center of card, two on one card, in another corner, etc. These are only curiosities and of minimal value.

Liberty — PC1

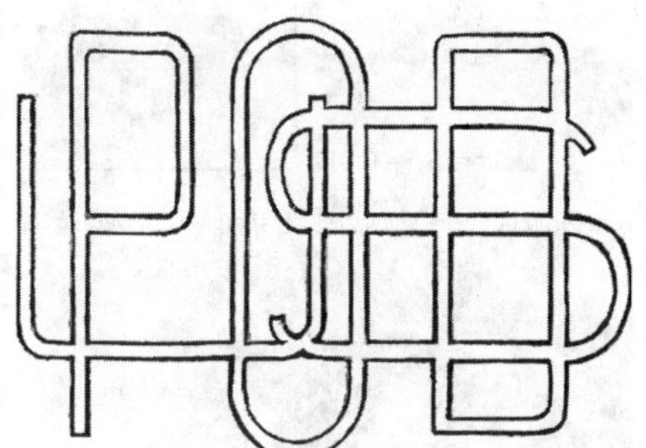

Wmk. Large "U S P O D" in Monogram, (90x60mm)

1873, May 13 **Size: 130x76mm**

UX1	PC1 1c **brown,**	350.00	20.00
	Preprinted	57.50	
	First day cancel, Boston, New York or Washington		*3,500.*

One card is documented canceled May 11 in Providence, R.I., another May 12 in Springfield, Mass.

Wmk. Small "U S P O D" in Monogram, (53x36mm)

1873, July 6

UX3	PC1 1c **brown,** *buff*	75.00	2.50
	Preprinted	20.00	
a.	Without watermark		800.00

The watermarks on Nos. UX1, UX3 and UX4 are found in normal position, inverted, reversed, and inverted and reversed. They are often dim, especially on No. UX4. Values listed are for clear watermarks.

No. UX3a is not known unused. Cards offered as such are either unwatermarked proofs, or have partial or vague watermarks. See No. UX65.

Liberty — PC2

Inscribed: "WRITE THE ADDRESS . . ."

1875 **Wmk. Small "U S P O D" in Monogram**

UX4	PC2 1c **black,** *buff, Sept. 28*	2,500.	350.
	Preprinted	600.	

Unwmk.

UX5	PC2 1c **black,** *buff, Sept. 30*	75.00	.45
	Preprinted	6.50	

For other postal card of type PC2 see No. UX7.

Liberty — PC3

For International Use

1879, Dec. 1

UX6	PC3 2c **blue,** *buff*	32.50	25.00
	Preprinted	11.00	
a.	2c **dark blue,** *buff*	30.00	25.00
	Preprinted	11.00	

See Nos. UX13 and UX16.

Design of PC2, Inscribed "NOTHING BUT THE ADDRESS."

1881, Oct. 17 (?)

UX7	PC2 1c **black,** *buff*	65.00	.40
	Preprinted	6.00	
a.	23 teeth below "ONE CENT"	1,250.	50.00
	Preprinted	210.00	
b.	Printed on both sides	*800.00*	*400.00*

Jefferson — PC4

1885, Aug. 24

UX8	PC4 1c **brown,** *buff*	50.00	1.25
	Preprinted	9.00	
c.	1c **dark chocolate,** *buff*	175.00	40.00
	Preprinted	75.00	
d.	Double impression		—
e.	Double impression, one inverted	—	
f.	Printed on both sides	—	

Card was printed in many shades of brown ink.

PC5

Head of Jefferson facing right, centered on card.

1886, Dec 1

UX9	PC5 1c **black,** *buff*	22.50	.55
	Preprinted	1.50	
a.	1c **black,** *dark buff*	45.00	5.00
	Preprinted	10.00	
b.	Double impression	—	
c.	Double impression, one inverted	*7,000.*	

Grant — PC6

1891 **Size: 155x95mm**

UX10	PC6 1c **black,** *buff*	40.00	1.50
	Preprinted	6.00	
a.	Double impression, one inverted	*3,000.*	
b.	Double impression	*1,250*	
c.	Triple impression, one inverted	3,250.	
d.	Quintuple impression, three inverted	3,250.	

Two types exist of No. UX10.

Earliest documented use; Dec. 21.

Size: 117x75mm

UX11	PC6 1c **blue,** *grayish white*	20.00	3.00
	Preprinted	4.50	
b.	Double impression, one inverted	*3,000.*	

Cards printed in black instead of blue are invariably proofs.

Earliest documented use; Dec. 26.

PC7

Head of Jefferson facing left.
Small wreath and name below.
Size: 140x89mm

1894, Jan. 2

UX12	PC7 1c **black,** *buff*	40.00	.65
	Preprinted	2.10	
a.	Double impression	—	

Two types exist of No. UX12: flat bed printing and rotary press printing.

For International Use

1897, Jan. 25 **Design of PC3**

Size: 140x89mm

UX13	PC3 2c **blue,** *cream*	190.00	85.00
	Preprinted	85.00	

PC8

Head same as PC7. Large wreath and name below.

1897, Dec. 1

Size: 139x82mm

UX14 PC8 1c **black,** *buff*	35.00	.45
Preprinted	2.50	
a. Double impression, one inverted	4,500.	—
Preprinted	—	
b. Printed both sides		—
Preprinted	—	
c. Double impression	—	—
Preprinted	—	
d. **Black,** *salmon pink,* preprinted	1,500.	

John Adams — PC9

1898

Size: 126x74mm

UX15 PC9 1c **black,** *buff, Mar. 31*	42.50	15.00
Preprinted	11.00	

Design same as PC3, without frame around card.

For International Use

Size: 140x82mm

UX16 PC3 2c **black,** *buff*	14.00	*17.00*
Preprinted	5.00	

McKinley — PC10

1902

UX17 PC10 1c **black,** *buff*	*7,000.*	
Preprinted	*3,250.*	*2,750.*

Earliest documented use; May 27, 1902.

McKinley — PC11

1902

UX18 PC11 1c **black,** *buff*	14.00	.35
Preprinted	1.60	

Earliest documented use; July 14, 1902.
Two types exist of Nos. UX18-UX20.

McKinley — PC12

1907

UX19 PC12 1c **black,** *buff*	40.00	.50
Preprinted	2.00	

Earliest documented use; June 28, 1907.

Same design, correspondence space at left

1908, Jan. 2

UX20 PC12 1c **black,** *buff*	52.50	4.25
Preprinted	7.50	

PC13

McKinley, background shaded.

1910

UX21 PC13 1c **blue,** *bluish*	95.00	13.00
Preprinted	16.00	
a. 1c **bronze blue,** *bluish*	200.00	30.00
Preprinted	25.00	
b. Double impression	*1,200.*	
Preprinted	—	
c. Triple impression	—	
d. Double impression, one inverted	—	
e. Four arcs above and below "IS" of inscription to left of stamp impression are pointed	*1,900.*	*600.00*
Preprinted	*900.00*	

A No. UX21 card exists with Philippines No. UX11 printed on the back.

PC14

Same design, white background.

1910, Apr. 13

UX22 PC14 1c **blue,** *bluish*	17.00	.35
Preprinted	1.50	
a. Double impression	*600.00*	
b. Triple impression	*3,250.*	*2,250.*
c. Triple impression, one inverted	—	
d. Quintuple impression	*5,500.*	

See No. UX24.

PC15

Head of Lincoln, solid background.

1911, Jan. 21

Size: 127x76mm

UX23 PC15 1c **red,** *cream*	10.00	5.50
Preprinted	3.00	
a. Triple impression	—	
b. Double impression	*7,250.*	

See No. UX26.

Design same as PC14

1911, Aug. 10 **Size: 140x82mm**

UX24 PC14 1c **red,** *cream*	10.00	.35
Preprinted	1.25	
a. Double impression	—	
b. Triple impression	—	

Copies with 1920 2-line surcharge are considered favor items.

Grant — PC16

1911, Oct. 27

For International Use

Size: 140x82mm

UX25 PC16 2c **red,** *cream*	1.50	16.00
Preprinted	.65	
a. Double impression	—	

For surcharge see No. UX36.

1913, July 29

Size: 127x76mm

UX26 PC15 1c **green,** *cream*	13.00	7.50
Preprinted	2.50	

Jefferson — PC17

Die I-End of queue small, sloping sharply downward to right.

Die II (re-cut)-End of queue large and rounded.

1914-16

Size: 140x82mm

UX27 PC17 1c **green,** *buff,* die I, *June 4*	.25	.25
Preprinted	.20	
a. 1c **green,** *cream*	3.50	.65
Preprinted	1.25	
b. Double impression	—	

On gray, rough surfaced card

UX27C PC17 1c **green,** die I, *1916*	*4,000.*	190.00
Preprinted	*275.00*	
UX27D PC17 1c **dark green,** die II, *Dec. 22, 1916*	*12,000.*	160.00
Preprinted	375.00	

For surcharges see Nos. UX39 and UX41.

Lincoln — PC19

1917, Mar. 14 **Size: 127x76mm**

UX28 PC19 1c **green,** *cream* .60 .30
Preprinted .30
a. 1c **green,** *dark buff* 1.50 .60
Preprinted .50
b. Double impression —
Preprinted *2,250.*

No. UX28 was printed also on light buff and canary.
See No. UX43. For surcharges see Nos. UX40 and UX42.

Jefferson — PC20

Die I - Rough, coarse impression. End of queue slopes sharply downward to right. Left basal ends of "2" form sharp points.

Size: 140x82mm

Die II - Clear fine lines in hair. Left basal ends of "2" form balls.

1917-18

UX29 PC20 2c **red,** *buff,* die I, *Oct. 22* 42.50 2.10
Preprinted 6.50
a. 2c **lake,** *cream,* die I 50.00 4.00
Preprinted 9.00
c. 2c **vermilion,** *buff,* die I 925.00 75.00
Preprinted 70.00
UX30 PC20 2c **red,** *cream,* die II, *Jan. 23, 1918* 30.00 1.60
Preprinted 4.50

2c Postal Cards of 1917-18 Revalued

Surcharged in one line by canceling machine at Washington, DC

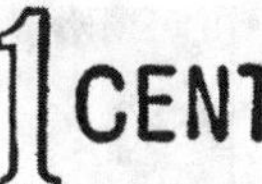

1920, Apr.

UX31 PC20 1c on 2c **red,** *cream,* die II *5,000.* *4,500.*
Preprinted *3,250.*

Surcharged in two lines by canceling machine (46 Types)

UX32 PC20 1c on 2c **red,** *buff,* die I 52.50 12.50
Preprinted 15.00
a. 1c on 2c **vermilion,** *buff* 150.00 60.00
Preprinted 60.00
b. Double surcharge 150.00 100.00
Preprinted 100.00 —
UX33 PC20 1c on 2c **red,** *cream,* die II 12.00 1.90
Preprinted 2.50
a. Inverted surcharge 100.00 100.00
Preprinted 40.00 —
b. Double surcharge 55.00 35.00
Preprinted 35.00
c. Double surcharge, one inverted, preprinted 325.00
d. Triple surcharge 350.00

Surcharge varieties with the values listed here for Nos. UX32 and UX33 **must have** the surcharges *on the stamp.* Copies having the surcharge inverted in the lower left corner, either alone or in combination with a normal surcharge, exist in many of the 46 types.

Surcharged in Two Lines by Press Printing

1920

UX34 PC20 1c on 2c **red,** *buff,* die I 550.00 52.50
Preprinted 125.00
a. Double surcharge 750.00
UX35 PC20 1c 2c **red,** *cream,* die II 225.00 37.50
Preprinted 55.00

Surcharges were prepared from (a) special dies fitting International and Universal post office canceling machines (Nos. UX31-UX33), and (b) printing press dies (Nos. UX34-UX35). There are 38 canceling machine types on Die I, and 44 on Die II. There are two printing press types of each die.

UX36 PC16 1c on 2c **red,** *cream* (#UX25) *50,000.*

Unused copies of No. UX36 (New York surcharge) were probably made by favor. Used copies of No. UX36 (Los Angeles surcharge, three to four examples used in Long Beach are recorded) are unquestionably authentic. Surcharges on other numbers exist, but their validity is doubtful.

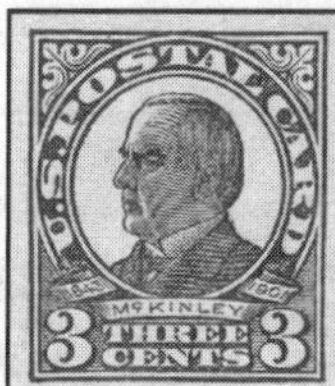

McKinley — PC21

1926, Feb. 1

For International Use

UX37 PC21 3c **red,** *buff* 4.50 *15.00*
Preprinted 1.75
First day cancel, Washington, DC 225.00
a. 3c **red,** *yellow* 4.50 *15.00*
Preprinted 1.75
b. Double impression *5,000.*

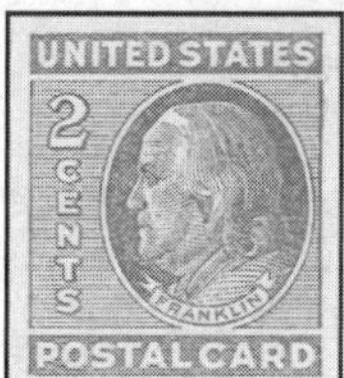

Franklin — PC22

1951, Nov. 16

UX38 PC22 2c **carmine rose,** *buff* .35 .25
Preprinted .25
First day cancel 1.00
a. Double impression 500.00
b. 2c **carmine rose,** *dark buff,* (error) 700.00

No. UX38b was printed on spacer paper used for counting.
For surcharge see No. UX47.

Nos. UX27 and UX28 Surcharged by Canceling Machine at Left of Stamp in Light Green

1952

UX39 PC17 2c on 1c **green,** *buff, Jan. 1* .50 .35
Preprinted .25
First day cancel, any city 12.00
a. Surcharged vertically, reading down 8.00 *10.00*
Preprinted 3.00
b. Double surcharge 20.00 *25.00*
UX40 PC19 2c on 1c **green,** *cream, Mar. 22* .65 .45
Preprinted .40
First day cancel, Washington, D.C. 15.00
a. Surcharged vertically, reading down 7.00 5.50
Preprinted 4.00

Nos. UX27 and UX28 with Similar Surcharge Typographed at Left of Stamp in Dark Green.

1952

UX41 PC17 2c on 1c **green,** *buff* 4.50 2.00
Preprinted 1.75
a. Inverted surcharge at lower left 77.50 125.00
Preprinted 50.00
UX42 PC19 2c on 1c **green,** *cream* 5.00 2.50
Preprinted 3.00
a. Surcharged by offset lithography 5.00 2.50
b. Surcharged on back 160.00

Type of 1917

1952, July 31 **Size: 127x76mm**

UX43 PC19 2c **carmine,** *buff* .30 *1.00*
Preprinted .20
First day cancel 1.00

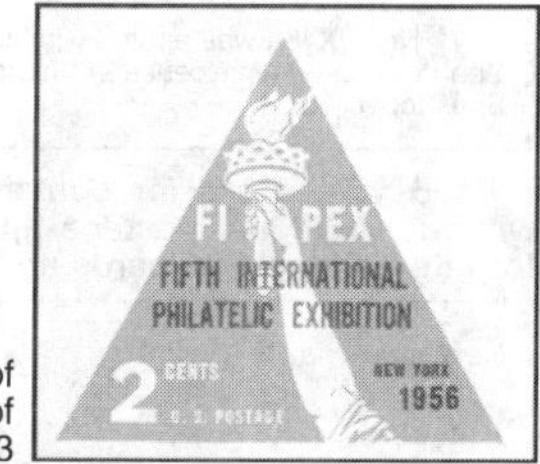

Torch and Arm of Statue of Liberty — PC23

Fifth International Philatelic Exhibition (FIPEX), New York City, Apr. 28-May 6, 1956.

1956, May 4

UX44 PC23 2c **deep carmine & dark violet blue,** *buff* .25 *1.00*
First day cancel, New York, NY *(537,474)* 1.00
a. 2c **rose pink & dark violet blue,** *buff* 100.00 75.00
b. Dark violet blue omitted 625.00 600.00
c. Double impression of dark violet blue 40.00 20.00
d. Double impression of deep carmine & dark violet blue *650.00*

Statue of Liberty
PC24 PC25

For International Use

1956, Nov. 16

UX45 PC24 4c **deep red & ultramarine,** *buff* 1.50 *75.00*
First day cancel, New York, NY *(129,841)* 1.00

See No. UY16.

1958, Aug. 1

UX46 PC25 3c **purple,** *buff* .50 .20
First day cancel, Philadelphia, Pa. *(180,610)* 1.00
a. "N GOD WE TRUST" 13.50 *25.00*
b. Double impression *250.00*
c. Double impression one inverted *4,500.*
d. Precanceled with 3 printed purple lines, *1961* 4.25 2.50
e. Indicia omitted (inscription normal) *325.00*
f. 3c **purple,** *dark buff* (error) 350.00

On No. UX46c, the precanceling lines are incorporated with the design. The earliest documented postmark on this experimental card is Oct. 31, 1961. UX46f was printed on spacer paper used for counting.
See No. UY17.

No. UX38 Surcharged by Canceling Machine at Left of Stamp in Black

ONE CENT
ADDITIONAL
PAID

1958

UX47 PC22 2c + 1c **carmine rose,** *buff* 225.00 600.00

The surcharge was applied to 750,000 cards for the use of the General Electric Co., Owensboro, Ky. A variety of the surcharge shows the D of PAID beneath the N of ADDITIONAL. All known examples of No. UX47 have a printed advertisement on the back and a small punch hole near lower left corner.
No. UX47 exists with inverted surcharge at lower left. Value, $500.
Used value is for commercially used card.

Lincoln
PC26

1962, Nov. 19

Precanceled with 3 printed red violet lines

UX48 PC26 4c **red violet** .50 .20
First day cancel, Springfield, IL *(162,939)* 1.00
a. Tagged, *June 25, 1966* .50 .20
First day cancel, Bellevue, OH 30.00

No. UX48a was printed with luminescent ink.
See note on Luminescence in "Information for Collectors."
See No. UY18.

Used values are for contemporaneous usage without additional postage applied. Used values for international-rate cards are for proper usage.

Map of Continental United States — PC27

Designed by Suren H. Ermoyan

For International Use

1963, Aug. 30

UX49 PC27 7c **blue & red** 4.00 *45.00*
First day cancel, New York, NY 1.00
a. Blue omitted *6,750.*

First day cancellation was applied to 270,464 of Nos. UX49 and UY19. See Nos. UX54, UX59, UY19-UY20.

Flags and Map of U.S. PC28

175th anniv. of the U.S. Customs Service.

Designed by Gerald N. Kurtz

1964, Feb. 22

Precanceled with 3 printed blue lines

UX50 PC28 4c **red & blue** .50 *1.00*
First day cancel, Washington, DC *(313,275)* 1.00
a. Blue omitted 625.00
b. Red omitted —
c. Double red impression *650.00*

Americans "Moving Forward" (Street Scene) — PC29

Issued to publicize the need to strengthen the US Social Security system. Released in connection with the 15th conf. of the Intl. Social Security Association at Washington, DC.

Designed by Gerald N. Kurtz

1964, Sept. 26

Precanceled with a blue and 2 red printed lines

UX51 PC29 4c **dull blue & red** .40 *1.00*
First day cancel, Washington, D.C. *(293,650)* 1.00
a. Red omitted —
b. Blue omitted *700.00* 650.00

Coast Guard Flag — PC30

175th anniv. of the U.S. Coast Guard.

Designed by Muriel R. Chamberlain

1965, Aug. 4

Precanceled with 3 printed red lines

UX52 PC30 4c **blue & red** .30 *1.00*
First day cancel, Newburyport, Mass. *(338,225)* 1.00
a. Blue omitted —

Crowd and Census Bureau Punch Card — PC31

Designed by Emilio Grossi

1965, Oct. 21

Precanceled with 3 bright blue printed lines

UX53 PC31 4c **bright blue & black** .30 *1.00*
First day cancel, Philadelphia, Pa. *(275,100)* 1.00

Map Type of 1963

For International Use

1967, Dec. 4

UX54 PC27 8c **blue & red** 4.00 *45.00*
First day cancel, Washington, DC 1.00

First day cancellation was applied to 268,077 of Nos. UX54 and UY20.

Lincoln PC33

Designed by Robert J. Jones

Luminescent Ink

1968, Jan. 4

Precanceled with 3 printed green lines

UX55 PC33 5c **emerald** .30 *.60*
First day cancel, Hodgenville, Ky. 1.00
a. Double impression —

First day cancellation was applied to 274,000 of Nos. UX55 and UY21.

Woman Marine, 1968, and Marines of Earlier Wars — PC34

25th anniv. of the Women Marines.

Designed by Muriel R. Chamberlain

1968, July 26

UX56 PC34 5c **rose red & green** .35 *1.00*
First day cancel, San Francisco, Cal. *(203,714)* 1.00

Tagged

Postal cards from No. UX57 onward are either tagged or printed with luminescent ink unless otherwise noted.

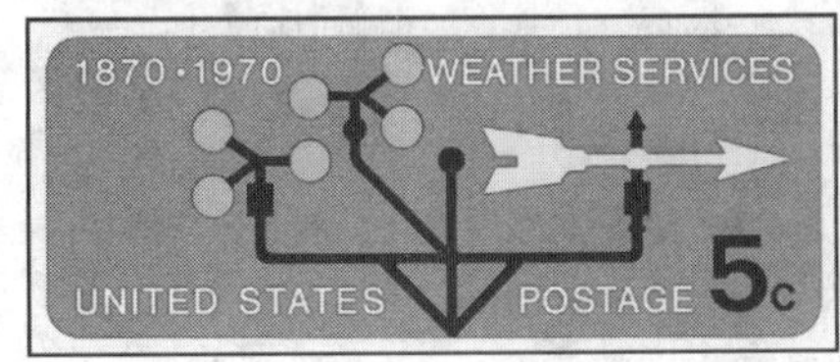

Weather Vane — PC35

Centenary of the Army's Signal Service, the Weather Services (Weather Bureau).

Designed by Robert Geissmann

1970, Sept. 1

UX57 PC35 5c **blue, yellow, red & black** .30 *1.00*
First day cancel, Fort Myer, Va. *(285,800)* 1.00
a. Yellow & black omitted *1,400. 850.00*
b. Blue omitted *1,400.* —
c. Black omitted *1,400. 850.00*

Paul Revere PC36

Issued to honor Paul Revere, Revolutionary War patriot.

Designed by Howard C. Mildner after statue near Old North Church, Boston

1971, May 15

Precanceled with 3 printed brown lines

UX58 PC36 6c **brown** .30 *1.00*
First day cancel, Boston, Mass. 1.00
a. Double impression *300.00*

First day cancellation was applied to 340,000 of Nos. UX58 and UY22.

Map Type of 1963

For International Use

1971, June 10

UX59 PC27 10c **blue & red** 4.50 *45.00*
First day cancel, New York, NY 1.00

First day cancellation was applied to 297,000 of Nos. UX59 and UXC11.

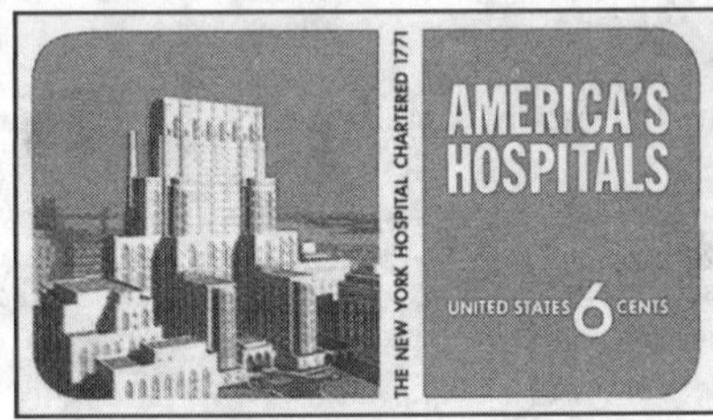

New York Hospital, New York City — PC37

Issued as a tribute to America's hospitals in connection with the 200th anniversary of New York Hospital.

Designed by Dean Ellis

1971, Sept. 16

UX60 PC37 6c **blue & multicolored** .30 *1.00*
First day cancel, New York, NY *(218,200)* 1.00
a. Blue & yellow omitted *1,150.*
b. Yellow omitted —
c. Red & black omitted —
d. Red omitted —
e. Tagging omitted 150.00

U.S.F. Constellation — PC38

Monument Valley — PC39

Gloucester, Mass. — PC40

Tourism Year of the Americas.

Designed by Melbourne Brindle

1972, June 29

Size: 152½x108½mm

UX61 PC38 6c **black,** *buff* (Yosemite, Mt. Rushmore, Niagara Falls, Williamsburg on back) .85 *10.00*
First day cancel, any city 1.00
a. Address side blank *300.00*
b. Reverse blank —
c. Tagging omitted 200.00

UX62 PC39 6c **black,** *buff* (Monterey, Redwoods, Gloucester, U.S.F. Constellation on back) .40 *10.00*
First day cancel, any city 10.00
a. Black omitted on back —
b. Orange omitted on back —
c. Reverse blank 350.00
d. Tagging omitted 200.00

UX63 PC40 6c **black,** *buff* (Rodeo, Mississippi Riverboat, Grand Canyon, Monument Valley on back) .40 *6.00*
First day cancel, any city 1.00
a. Black inverted —
b. Reverse blank 500.00
c. Tagging omitted 200.00
Nos. UX61-UX63,UXC12-UXC13 (5) 3.15 *101.00*

Nos. UX61-UX63, UXC12-UXC13 went on sale throughout the United States. They were sold as souvenirs without postal validity at Belgica Philatelic Exhibition in Brussels and were displayed at the American Embassies in Paris and Rome. This is reflected in the first day cancel.

Varieties of the pictorial back printing include: black omitted (UX62), black and pale salmon omitted (UX63), and back inverted in relation to address side (UX63).

John Hanson — PC41

Designed by Thomas Kronen after statue by Richard Edwin Brooks in Maryland Capitol

1972, Sept. 1

Precanceled with 3 printed blue lines.

UX64 PC41 6c **blue** .50 *1.00*
First day cancel, Baltimore, MD 1.00
a. Coarse paper .60 *1.25*

Liberty Type of 1873

Centenary of first U.S. postal card.

1973, Sept. 14

UX65 PC1 6c **magenta** .25 *1.00*
First day cancel, Washington, D.C. *(289,950)* 1.00
a. Tagging omitted —

Samuel Adams — PC42

Designed by Howard C. Mildner

1973, Dec. 16

Precanceled with 3 printed orange lines

UX66 PC42 8c **orange** .50 *1.00*
First day cancel, Boston, Mass. *(147,522)* 1.00
a. Coarse paper .75 *1.00*
b. Double impression *1,200.*

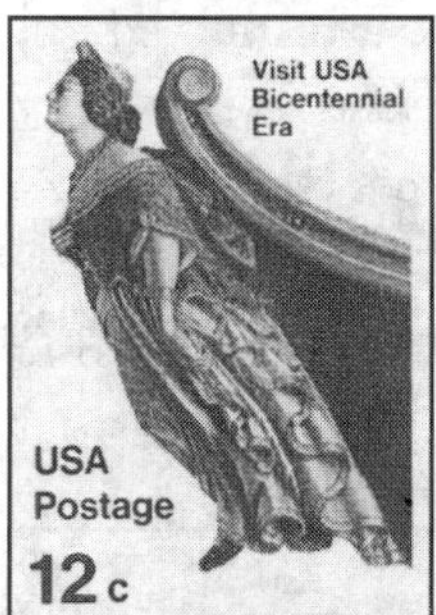

Ship's Figurehead, 1883 — PC43

Design is after a watercolor by Elizabeth Moutal of the oak figurehead by John Rogerson from the barque Edinburgh.

1974, Jan. 4

For International Use

UX67 PC43 12c **multicolored** .35 *45.00*
First day cancel, Miami, Fla. *(138,500)* 1.00
a. Yellow omitted *700.00*

Charles Thomson — PC44

John Witherspoon — PC45

Caesar Rodney — PC46

Designed by Howard C. Mildner

1975-76

Precanceled with 3 printed emerald lines

UX68 PC44 7c **emerald,** *Sept. 14, 1975* .30 *9.00*
First day cancel, Bryn Mawr, Pa. 1.00

Precanceled with 3 printed brown lines

UX69 PC45 9c **yellow brown,** *Nov. 10, 1975* .30 *1.00*
First day cancel, Princeton, N.J. 1.00

Precanceled with 3 printed blue lines

UX70 PC46 9c **blue,** *July 1, 1976* .30 *1.00*
First day cancel, Dover, Del. 1.00
a. Double impression *4,500.*

First day cancellation applied to 231,919 of Nos. UX68 and UY25; 254,239 of Nos. UX69 and UY26; 304,061 of Nos. UX70 and UY27.

Federal Court House, Galveston, Texas — PC47

The Court House, completed in 1861, is on the National Register of Historic Places.

Designed by Donald Moss

1977, July 20

UX71 PC47 9c **multicolored** .25 *1.00*
First day cancel, Galveston, Tex. *(245,535)* 1.00
a. Black Omitted *8,250.*
b. Tagging omitted 150.00

Nathan Hale PC48

Designed by Howard C. Mildner

1977, Oct. 14

Precanceled with 3 printed green lines

UX72 PC48 9c **green** .25 *1.00*
First day cancel, Coventry, Conn. 1.00
a. Cent sign missing after "9" 125.00
b. Double impression 275.00

First day cancellation applied to 304,592 of Nos. UX72 and UY28.

No. UX72a also exists on fluorescent stock. Value thus is 4 times the listed value.

Cincinnati Music Hall — PC49

Centenary of Cincinnati Music Hall, Cincinnati, Ohio.

Designed by Clinton Orlemann

1978, May 12

UX73 PC49 10c **multicolored** .30 *1.00*
First day cancel, Cincinnati, O. *(300,000)* 1.75

John Hancock — PC50

Designed by Howard Behrens

1978

Precanceled with 3 printed brown orange lines.

UX74 PC50 (10c) **brown orange,** *May 19* .30 *1.00*
First day cancel, Quincy, Mass. *(299,623)* 1.00

Inscribed "U.S. Postage 10¢"

UX75 PC50 10c **brown orange,** *June 20* .30 1.00
First day cancel, Quincy, Mass. *(187,120)* 1.00

Coast Guard Cutter Eagle — PC51

Designed by Carl G. Evers

For International Use

1978, Aug. 4

UX76 PC51 14c **multicolored** .40 *30.00*
First day cancel, Seattle, Wash. *(196,400)* 1.00

Molly Pitcher Firing Cannon at Monmouth — PC52

Bicentennial of Battle of Monmouth, June 28, 1778, and to honor Molly Pitcher (Mary Ludwig Hays).

Designed by David Blossom

1978, Sept. 8 **Litho.**

UX77 PC52 10c **multicolored** .30 *1.60*
First day cancel, Freehold, N.J. *(180,280)* 1.00

Clark and his Frontiersmen Approaching Fort Sackville — PC53

Bicentenary of capture of Fort Sackville from the British by George Rogers Clark.

Designed by David Blossom

1979, Feb. 23 **Litho.**

UX78 PC53 10c **multicolored** .30 *1.50*
First day cancel, Vincennes, Ind. 1.00
a. Yellow omitted —

Gen. Casimir Pulaski — PC54

Bicentenary of the death of Gen. Casimir Pulaski (1748-1779), Polish nobleman who served in American Revolutionary Army.

1979, Oct. 11 **Litho.**

UX79 PC54 10c **multicolored** .30 *1.50*
First day cancel, Savannah. GA *(210,000)* 1.00

Olympic Games Issue

Sprinter PC55

22nd Olympic Games, Moscow, July 19-Aug. 3, 1980.

Designed by Robert M. Cunningham

1979, Sept. 17 **Litho.**

UX80 PC55 10c **multicolored** .60 *1.50*
First day cancel, Eugene, Ore. 1.00
a. Tagging omitted 200.00

Iolani Palace, Honolulu — PC56

1979, Oct. 1 **Litho.**

UX81 PC56 10c **multicolored** .30 *1.50*
First day cancel, Honolulu, HI *(242,804)* 1.00
a. Tagging omitted —

Women's Figure Skating PC57

13th Winter Olympic Games, Lake Placid, N.Y., Feb. 12-24.

Designed by Robert M. Cunningham

For International Use

1980, Jan. 15 **Litho.**

UX82 PC57 14c **multicolored** .60 *20.00*
First day cancel, Atlanta, GA *(160,977)* 1.00

Salt Lake Temple, Salt Lake City — PC58

1980, Apr. 5 **Litho.**

UX83 PC58 10c **multicolored** .25 *1.50*
First day cancel, Salt Lake City, UT *(325,260)* 1.00
a. Tagging omitted 300.00

Rochambeau's Fleet — PC59

Count Jean-Baptiste de Rochambeau's landing at Newport, R.I. (American Revolution) bicentenary.

Designed by David Blossom

1980, July 11 **Litho.**

UX84 PC59 10c **multicolored** .25 *1.50*
First day cancel, Newport, R.I. *(180,567)* 1.00
a. Front normal, black & yellow on back *4,000.*
b. Magenta & blue omitted —

Whig Infantrymen — PC60

Bicentenary of the Battle of Kings Mountain (American Revolution).

Designed by David Blossom

1980, Oct. 7 **Litho.**

UX85 PC60 10c **multicolored** .25 *1.50*
First day cancel, Kings Mountain, NC *(136,130)* 1.00

Golden Hinde — PC61

300th anniv. of Sir Francis Drake's circumnavigation (1578-1580).

Designed by Charles J. Lundgren

For International Use

1980, Nov. 21

UX86 PC61 19c **multicolored** .70 *35.00*
First day cancel, San Rafael, CA *(290,547)* 1.00

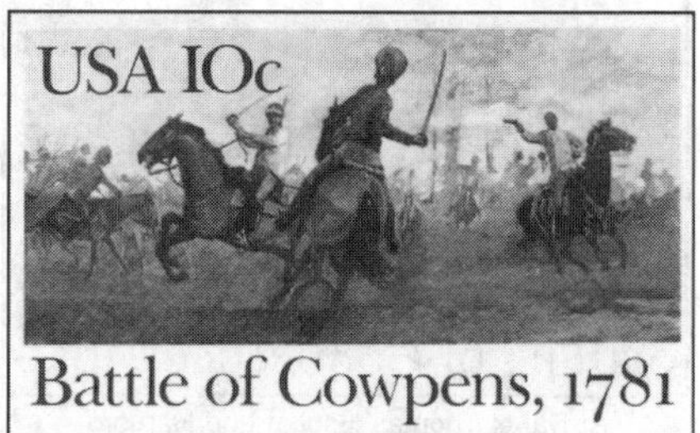

Cols. Washington and Tarleton — PC62

Bicentenary of the Battle of Cowpens (American Revolution).

Designed by David Blossom

1981, Jan. 17

UX87 PC62 10c **multicolored** .25 *16.00*
First day cancel, Cowpens, SC *(160,000)* 1.00

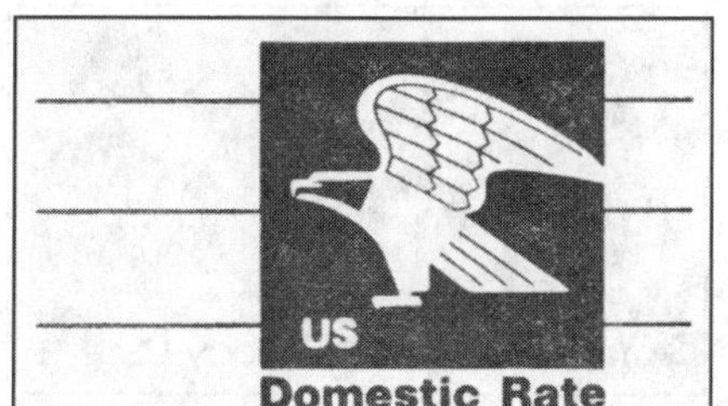

Eagle — PC63

1981, Mar. 15

Precanceled with 3 printed violet lines

UX88 PC63 (12c) **violet** .30 *.65*
First day cancel, Memphis, TN 1.00

See No. 1818, FDC section.

Isaiah Thomas — PC64

Designed by Chet Jezierski

1981, May 5 Precanceled with 3 printed lines

UX89 PC64 12c **light blue** .30 *.60*
First day cancel, Worcester, MA *(185,610)* 1.00

PC65

Bicentenary of the Battle at Eutaw Springs (American Revolution)

Designed by David Blossom

1981, Sept. 8 Litho.

UX90 PC65 12c **multicolored** .30 *10.00*
First day cancel, Eutaw Springs, SC *(115,755)* 1.00
a. Red & yellow omitted *2,500.*

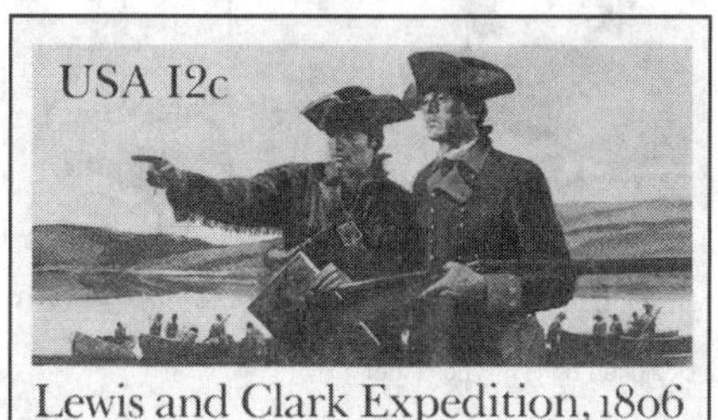

PC66

Designed by David Blossom

1981, Sept. 23

UX91 PC66 12c **multicolored** .30 *20.00*
First day cancel, Saint Louis, MO 1.00

Robert Morris — PC67

1981

Precanceled with 3 printed lines

UX92 PC67 (13c) **buff,** *Oct. 11* .30 *.60*
First day cancel, Memphis, TN 1.00

See No. 1946, FDC section.

Inscribed: U.S. Postage 13¢

UX93 PC67 13c **buff,** *Nov. 10* .30 *.60*
First day cancel, Philadelphia, PA 1.00
a. Buff omitted 500.00

On No. UX93a, the copyright symbol and "1981" in buff is present at the lower left corner of the card.

General Francis Marion (1732?-1795) — PC68

Designed by David Blossom

1982, Apr. 3 Litho.

UX94 PC68 13c **multicolored** .30 *1.00*
First day cancel, Marion, SC *(141,162)* 1.00

Rene Robert Cavelier, Sieur de la Salle (1643-1687) — PC69

Designed by David Blossom

1982, Apr. 7 Litho.

UX95 PC69 13c **multicolored** .30 *1.00*
First day cancel, New Orleans, LA 1.00

PC70

Designed by Melbourne Brindle

1982, June 18 Litho.

UX96 PC70 13c brown, red & cream, *buff* .30 *1.00*
First day cancel, Philadelphia, PA 1.00
a. Brown & cream omitted *775.00*

PC71

Designed by Clint Orlemann

1982, Oct. 14 Litho.

UX97 PC71 13c **multicolored** .30 *1.00*
First day cancel, St. Louis, MO 1.00

Gen. Oglethorpe Meeting Chief Tomo-Chi-Chi of the Yamacraw — PC72

Designed by David Blossom

1983, Feb. 12 Litho.

UX98 PC72 13c **multicolored** .30 *1.00*
First day cancel, Savannah, GA *(165,750)* 1.00

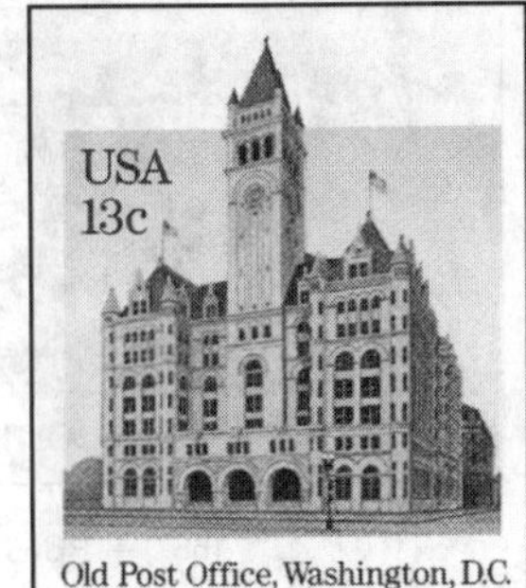

PC73

Designed by Walter Brooks

1983, Apr. 19 **Litho.**

UX99 PC73 13c **multicolored** .30 *1.00*
First day cancel, Washington, DC *(125,056)* 1.00

Olympics 84, Yachting — PC74

Designed by Bob Peak

1983, Aug. 5 **Litho.**

UX100 PC74 13c **multicolored** .30 *1.00*
First day cancel, Long Beach, CA *(132,232)* 1.00
a. Yellow & red omitted *4,000.*

The Ark and the Dove — PC75

Designed by David Blossom

1984, Mar. 25 **Litho.**

UX101 PC75 13c **multicolored** .30 *1.00*
First day cancel, St. Clement's Island, MD *(131,222)* 1.00

Runner Carrying Olympic Torch — PC76

Designed by Robert Peak

1984, Apr. 30 **Litho.**

UX102 PC76 13c **multicolored** .30 *1.00*
First day cancel, Los Angeles, CA *(110,627)* 1.00
a. Black & yellow inverted —
b. Tagging omitted 350.00

Father Baraga and Indian Guide in Canoe — PC77

Designed by David Blossom

1984, June 29 **Litho.**

UX103 PC77 13c **multicolored** .30 *1.00*
First day cancel, Marquette, MI *(100,156)* 1.00

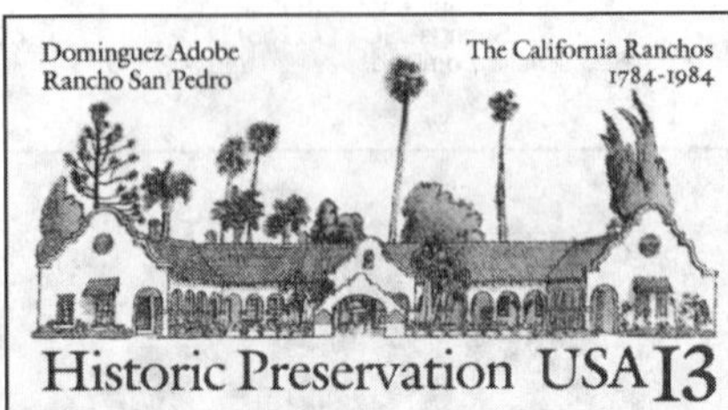

Dominguez Adobe at Rancho San Pedro — PC78

Designed by Earl Thollander

1984, Sept. 16 **Litho.**

UX104 PC78 13c **multicolored** .30 *1.00*
First day cancel, Compton, CA *(100,545)* 1.00
a. Black & blue omitted *1,600.*
b. Tagging omitted —

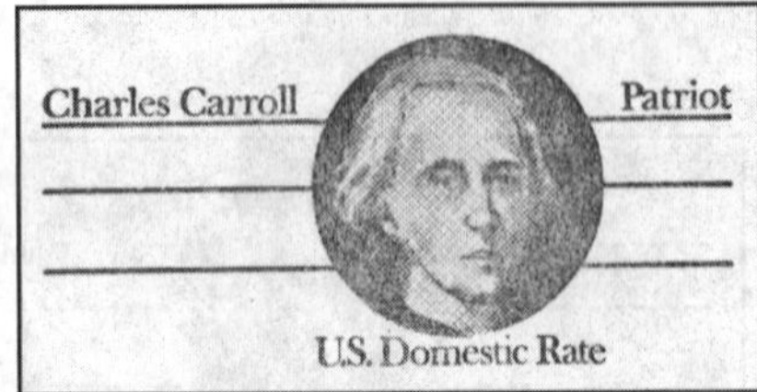

Charles Carroll (1737-1832) — PC79

Designed by Richard Sparks

1985

Precanceled with 3 printed lines

UX105 PC79 (14c) **pale green,** *Feb. 1* .45 *.50*
First day cancel, New Carrollton, MD *(135,642)* 1.00

Inscribed: USA 14

UX106 PC79 14c **pale green,** *Mar. 6* .45 .50
First day cancel, Annapolis, MD *(111,122)* 1.00

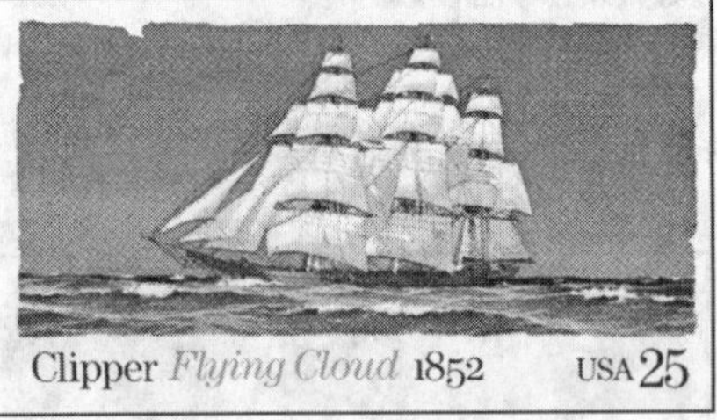

Clipper Flying Cloud — PC80

Designed by Richard Schlecht

For International Use

1985, Feb. 27 **Litho.**

UX107 PC80 25c **multicolored** .70 *20.00*
First day cancel, Salem, MA *(95,559)* 1.25

No. UX107 was sold by the USPS at CUP-PEX 87, Perth, Western Australia, with a cachet honoring CUP-PEX 87 and the America's Cup race.

George Wythe (1726-1806) — PC81

Designed by Chet Jezierski from a portrait by John Fergusson.

1985, June 20

Precanceled with 3 printed lines

UX108 PC81 14c **bright apple green** .30 *.75*
First day cancel, Williamsburg, VA *(133,334)* 1.00
a. Indicia missing —

On No. UX108a, the left precancel, "George Wythe" and the copyright symbol are normal.

Arrival of Thomas Hooker and Hartford Congregation — PC82

Settlement of Connecticut, 350th Anniv.

Designed by David Blossom

1986, Apr. 18 **Litho.**

UX109 PC82 14c **multicolored** .30 *1.25*
First day cancel, Hartford, CT *(76,875)* 1.00

Stamp Collecting — PC83

Designed by Ray Ameijide

1986, May 23 **Litho.**

UX110 PC83 14c **multicolored** .30 *1.25*
First day cancel, Chicago, IL *(75,548)* 1.00

No. UX110 was sold by the USPS at "najubria 86" with a show cachet.

Francis Vigo (1747-1836) — PC84

Designed by David Blossom

1986, May 24 **Litho.**

UX111 PC84 14c **multicolored** .30 *1.25*
First day cancel, Vincennes, IN *(100,141)* 1.00

Roger Williams (1603-1683), Clergyman, Landing at Providence — PC85

Settling of Rhode Island, 350th Anniv.

Designed by David Blossom

1986, June 26 **Litho.**
UX112 PC85 14c **multicolored** .30 *1.25*
First day cancel, Providence, RI *(54,559)* 1.00

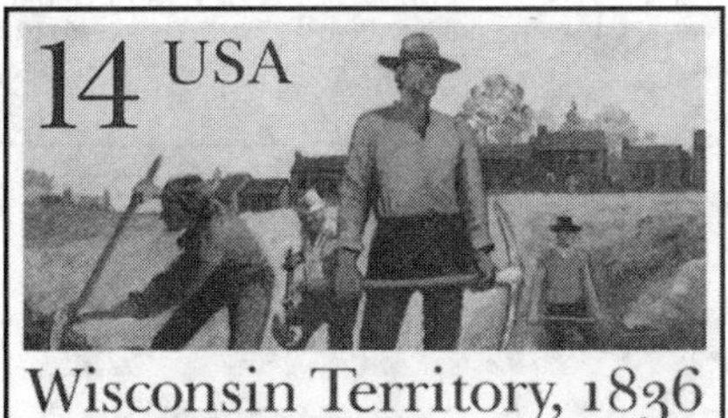

Miners, Shake Rag Street Housing — PC86

Wisconsin Territory Sesquicentennial.

Designed by David Blossom

1986, July 3 **Litho.**
UX113 PC86 14c **multicolored** .30 *.85*
First day cancel, Mineral Point, WI *(41,224)* 1.00
a. Tagging omitted 200.00

The First Muster, by Don Troiani — PC87

Designed by Bradbury Thompson

1986, Dec. 12 **Litho.**
UX114 PC87 14c **multicolored** .30 *1.25*
First day cancel, Boston, MA *(72,316)* 1.00

PC88

The self-scouring steel plow invented by blacksmith John Deere in 1837 pictured at lower left.

Designed by William H. Bond

1987, May 22 **Litho.**
UX115 PC88 14c **multicolored** .30 *1.25*
First day cancel, Moline, IL *(160,009)* 1.00

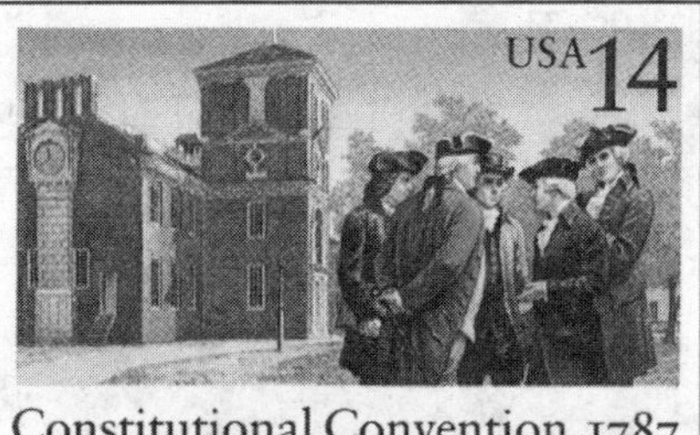

Convening of the Constitutional Convention, 1787 — PC89

George Mason, Gouverneur Morris, James Madison, Alexander Hamilton and Charles C. Pinckney are listed in the lower left corner of the card.

Designed by David K. Stone

1987, May 25 **Litho.**
UX116 PC89 14c **multicolored** .30 *.60*
First day cancel, Philadelphia, PA *(138,207)* 1.00
a. Double black and blue, with first day cancel *650.00*

Stars and Stripes — PC90

Designed by Steven Dohanos

1987, June 14 **Litho.**
UX117 PC90 14c **black, blue & red** .30 *.60*
First day cancel, Baltimore, MD 1.00

No. UX117 was sold by the USPS at Cologne, Germany, with a cachet for Philatelia'87.

Take Pride in America — PC91

Designed by Lou Nolan

1987, Sept. 22 **Litho.**
UX118 PC91 14c **multicolored** .30 *1.25*
First day cancel, Jackson, WY *(47,281)* 1.00

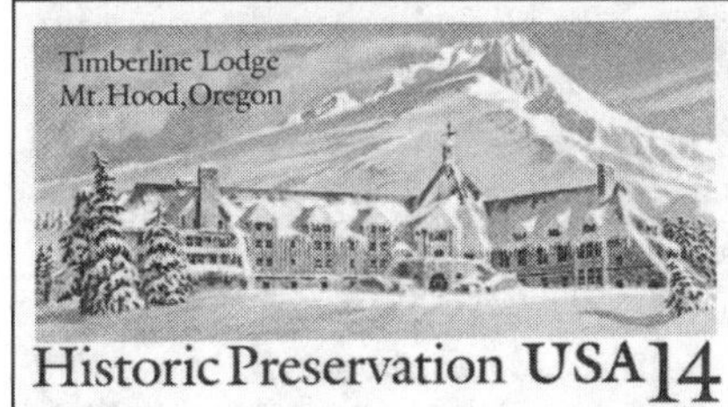

Timberline Lodge, 50th Anniversary — PC92

Designed by Walter DuBois Richards

1987, Sept. 28 **Litho.**
UX119 PC92 14c **multicolored** .30 *1.25*
First day cancel, Timberline, OR *(63,595)* 1.00

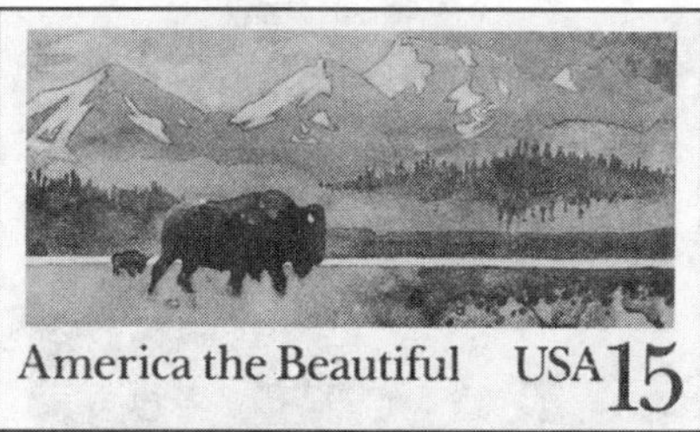

American Buffalo and Prairie — PC93

Designed by Bart Forbes

1988, Mar. 28 **Litho.**
UX120 PC93 15c **multicolored** .30 *.60*
First day cancel, Buffalo, WY *(52,075)* 1.00
a. Black omitted 1,750.
b. Printed on both sides *450.00*
c. Front normal, blue & black on back *650.00*
d. Black & magenta omitted *1,500.*
e. Black, yellow, blue & tagging omitted *1,000.*
f. Black, blue & tagging omitted *1,500.*
g. Black, magenta, yellow & tagging omitted *1,500.*
h. Double black impression —
i. Triple black impression —
j. Double black and blue impression —
k. Double magenta & blue, and triple black impression —

Tagged

Postal cards from No. UX57 onward are either tagged or printed with luminescent ink unless otherwise noted.

PC94

Designed by Pierre Mion

1988, May 4 **Litho.**
UX121 PC94 15c **multicolored** .30 *.75*
First day cancel, Washington, DC *(52,188)* 1.00

Yorkshire, Squarerigged Packet — PC95

Inscribed: Yorkshire, Black Ball Line, Packet Ship, circa 1850 at lower left.

Designed by Richard Schlect

For International Use

1988, June 29 **Litho.**
UX122 PC95 28c **multicolored** .60 *15.00*
First day cancel, Mystic, CT *(46,505)* 1.00
a. Black & blue omitted *850.00*
b. Black, blue, yellow & tagging omitted *1,200.*
c. Black, magenta & tagging omitted *1,000.*
d. Black, magenta, yellow & tagging omitted *1,000.*
e. Black & tagging omitted *2,000.*

Harvesting Corn Fields — PC96

Iowa Territory Sesquicentennial.

Designed by Greg Hargreaves

1988, July 2 **Litho.**
UX123 PC96 15c **multicolored** .30 *.75*
First day cancel, Burlington, IA *(45,565)* 1.00

Flatboat Ferry Transporting Settlers Down the Ohio River — PC97

Bicentenary of the settlement of Ohio, the Northwest Territory. Design at lower left shows map of the eastern United States with Northwest Territory highlighted.

Designed by James M. Gurney and Susan Sanford

1988, July 15 **Litho.**
UX124 PC97 15c **multicolored** .30 *.75*
First day cancel, Marietta, OH *(28,778)* 1.00
a. Black, blue, yellow & tagging omitted *1,000.*
b. Black, magenta & tagging omitted *750.00*
c. Blue, black & tagging omitted *1,000.*
d. Black & tagging omitted *2,000.*

PC98

Designed by Robert Reynolds

1988, Sept. 20 **Litho.**
UX125 PC98 15c **multicolored** .30 *.60*
First day cancel, San Simeon, CA *(84,786)* 1.00
a. Black, magenta & tagging omitted *750.00*
b. Black, blue, yellow & tagging omitted *2,000.*
c. Black, magenta, yellow & tagging omitted *1,000.*
d. Black & tagging omitted *2,000.*
e. Black, blue & tagging omitted —

Pressman, New Yorker Reading Newspaper, 1787 — PC99

Designed by Roy Andersen

1988, Oct. 27 **Litho.**
UX126 PC99 15c **multicolored** .30 *.75*
First day cancel, New York, NY *(37,661)* 1.00

Red-tailed Hawk and Sonora Desert at Sunset — PC100

Designed by Bart Forbes

1989, Jan. 13 **Litho.**
UX127 PC100 15c **multicolored** .30 *.75*
First day cancel, Tucson, AZ *(51,891)* 1.00

Healy Hall, Georgetown University — PC101

Designed by John Morrell. Inscription at lower left: "Healy Hall / Georgetown / Washington, DC / HISTORIC PRESERVATION."

1989, Jan. 23 **Litho.**
UX128 PC101 15c **multicolored** .40 *.75*
First day cancel, Washington, DC *(54,897)* 1.00

Great Blue Heron, Marsh — PC102

Designed by Bart Forbes

1989, Mar. 17 **Litho.**
UX129 PC102 15c **multicolored** .30 *.75*
First day cancel, Okefenokee, GA *(58,208)* 1.00

Settling of Oklahoma — PC103

Designed by Bradbury Thompson

1989, Apr. 22 **Litho.**
UX130 PC103 15c **multicolored** .30 *.75*
First day cancel, Guthrie, OK *(68,689)* 1.00

Used values are for contemporaneous usage without additional postage applied. Used values for international-rate cards are for proper usage.

Canada Geese and Mountains — PC104

Designed by Bart Forbes

1989, May 5 **Litho.** **For Use to Canada**
UX131 PC104 21c **multicolored** .40 *10.00*
First day cancel, Denver, CO *(59,303)* 1.25

Seashore — PC105

Designed by Bart Forbes

1989, June 17 **Litho.**
UX132 PC105 15c **multicolored** .30 *.75*
First day cancel, Cape Hatteras, NC *(67,073)* 1.00

PC106

Designed by Bart Forbes

1989, Aug. 26 **Litho.**
UX133 PC106 15c **multicolored** .30 *.75*
First day cancel, Cherokee, NC *(67,878)* 1.00

Jane Addams' Hull House Community Center 1889, Chicago — PC107

Designed by Michael Hagel

1989, Sept. 16 **Litho.**
UX134 PC107 15c **multicolored** .30 *.75*
First day cancel, Chicago, IL *(53,773)* 1.00

Aerial View of Independence Hall, Philadelphia — PC108

Designed by Bart Forbes

1989, Sept. 25 **Litho.**

UX135 PC108 15c **multicolored** .30 *.75*
First day cancel, Philadelphia, PA *(61,659)* 1.00

See No. UX139.

Inner Harbor, Baltimore — PC109

Designed by Bart Forbes

1989, Oct. 7 **Litho.**

UX136 PC109 15c **multicolored** .30 *.75*
First day cancel, Baltimore, MD *(58,746)* 1.00

See No. UX140.

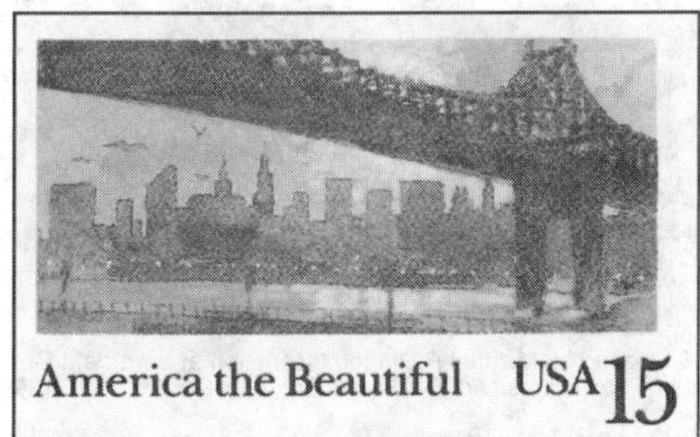

59th Street Bridge, New York City — PC110

Designed by Bart Forbes

1989, Nov. 8 **Litho.**

UX137 PC110 15c **multicolored** .30 *.75*
First day cancel, New York, NY *(48,044)* 1.00

See No. UX141.

West Face of the Capitol, Washington D.C. — PC111

Designed by Bart Forbes

1989, Nov. 26 **Litho.**

UX138 PC111 15c **multicolored** .30 *.75*
First day cancel, Washington, DC 1.00

See No. UX142.

1989, Dec. 1 **Litho.**

Designed by Bart Forbes. Issued in sheets of 4 + 2 inscribed labels picturing 20th UPU Congress or World Stamp Expo '89 emblems, and rouletted 9½ on 2 or 3 sides.

UX139 PC108 15c **multicolored** 3.25 *4.00*
First day cancel, Washington, DC 1.00
UX140 PC109 15c **multicolored** 3.25 *4.00*
First day cancel, Washington, DC 1.00
UX141 PC110 15c **multicolored** 3.25 *4.00*
First day cancel, Washington, DC 1.00
UX142 PC111 15c **multicolored** 3.25 *4.00*
First day cancel, Washington, DC 1.00
a. Sheet of 4, #UX139-UX142 13.00
Nos. UX135-UX142 (8) 14.20 *19.00*

Unlike Nos. UX135-UX138, Nos. UX139-UX142 do not contain inscription and copyright symbol at lower left. Order on sheet is Nos. UX140, UX139, UX142, UX141.

Many copies of No. UX142a and UX139 are bent at the upper right corner.

The White House — PC112

Jefferson Memorial — PC113

Designed by Pierre Mion. Space for message at left.

1989 **Litho.**

UX143 PC112 15c **multicolored**, *Nov. 30* 1.50 *2.50*
First day cancel, Washington, DC 2.00
UX144 PC113 15c **multicolored**, *Dec. 2* 1.50 *2.00*
First day cancel, Washington, DC 2.00

Nos. UX143-UX144 sold for 50c each. Illustrations of the buildings without denominations are shown on the back of the card

Rittenhouse Paper Mill, Germantown, PA — PC114

Designed by Harry Devlin.

1990, Mar. 13 **Litho.**

UX145 PC114 15c **multicolored** .30 .40
First day cancel, New York, NY *(9,866)* 1.00

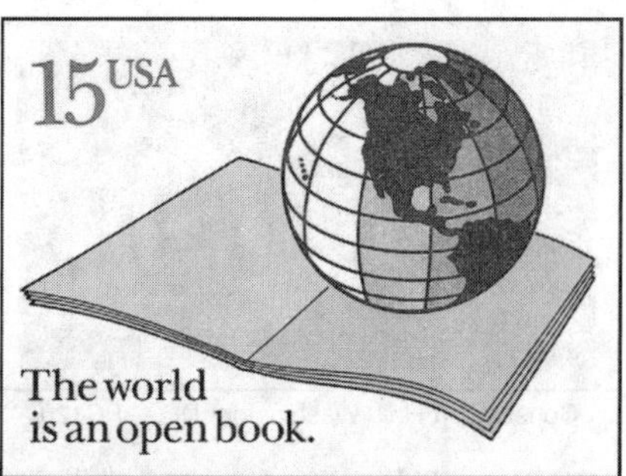

World Literacy Year — PC115

Designed by Joe Brockert.

1990, Mar. 22 **Litho.**

UX146 PC115 15c **multicolored** .30 *.75*
First day cancel, Washington, DC *(11,163)* 1.00

PC116

Designed by Bradbury Thompson. Inscription in upper left corner: "Fur Traders Descending the Missouri / George Caleb Bingham, 1845 / Metropolitan Museum of Art".

1990, May 4 **Litho.**

UX147 PC116 15c **multicolored** 1.50 *2.50*
First day cancel, St. Louis, MO *(13,632)* 2.00

No. UX147 sold for 50c and shows more of the painting without the denomination on the back.

PC117

Designed by Frank Constantino. Inscription at lower left: "HISTORIC PRESERVATION SERIES / Isaac Royall House, 1700s / Medford, Massachusetts / National Historic Landmark".

1990, June 16 **Litho.**

UX148 PC117 15c **multicolored** .30 *.75*
First day cancel, Medford, MA *(21,708)* 1.00

Quadrangle, Stanford University — PC119

Designed by Jim M'Guinness.

1990, Sept. 30 **Litho.**

UX150 PC119 15c **multicolored** .30 *.60*
First day cancel, Stanford, CA *(28,430)* 1.00

Constitution Hall, Washington, DC — PC120

Designed by Pierre Mion. Inscription at upper left: "Washington: Constitution Hall (at right)/ Memorial Continental Hall (reverse side) / Centennial, Daughters of the American Revolution".

1990, Oct. 11 **Litho.**

UX151 PC120 15c **multicolored** 1.50 2.00
First day cancel, Washington, DC *(33,254)* 2.00

No. UX151 sold for 50c.

Chicago Orchestra Hall — PC121

Designed by Michael Hagel. Inscription at lower left: "Chicago: Orchestra Hall / HISTORIC PRESERVATION / Chicago Symphony Orchestra / Centennial, 1891-1991".

1990, Oct. 19 **Litho.**

UX152 PC121 15c **multicolored** .30 *.75*
First day cancel, Chicago, IL *(28,546)* 1.00

PC122

Designed by Richard Sheaff.

1991, Jan. 24 **Litho.**

UX153 PC122 19c **rose, ultramarine & black** .40 *.60*
First day cancel, Washington, DC *(26,690)* 1.00

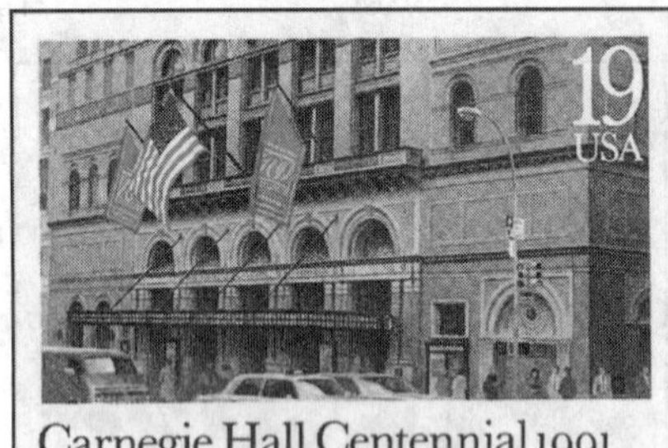

PC123

Designed by Howard Koslow.

1991, Apr. 1 **Litho.**

UX154 PC123 19c **multicolored** .40 *.60*
First day cancel, New York, NY *(27,063)* 1.00

Old Red, University of Texas Medical Branch, Galveston, Cent. — PC124

Designed by Don Adair.

1991, June 14 **Litho.**

UX155 PC124 19c **multicolored** .50 *.60*
First day cancel, Galveston, TX *(24,308)* 1.00

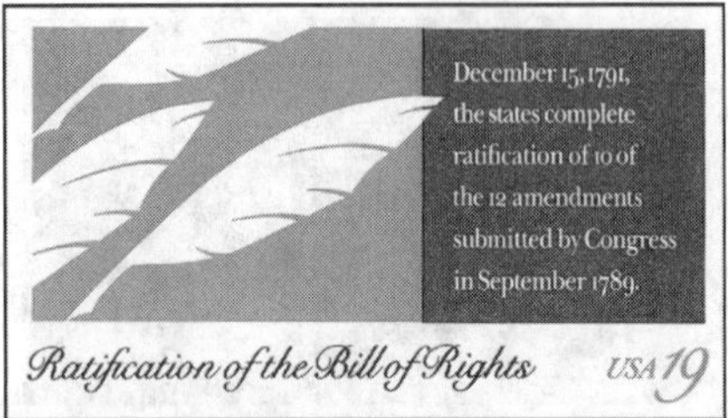

Ratification of the Bill of Rights, Bicent. — PC125

Designed by Mark Zaref.

1991, Sept. 25 **Litho.**

UX156 PC125 19c **red, blue & black** .40 *.60*
First day cancel, Richmond, VA *(27,457)* 1.00

Main Building, University of Notre Dame PC126

Designed by Frank Costantino. Inscription at lower left: Notre Dame / Sesquicentennial / 1842-1992.

1991, Oct. 15 **Litho.**

UX157 PC126 19c **multicolored** .50 *.60*
First day cancel, Notre Dame, IN *(34,325)* 1.00

Niagara Falls — PC127

Designed by Wendell Minor.

1991, Aug. 21 **Litho.**

For Use to Canada & Mexico

UX158 PC127 30c **multicolored** .75 *7.50*
First day cover, Niagara Falls, NY *(29,762)* 1.25

Tagged

Postal cards from No. UX57 onward are either tagged or printed with luminescent ink unless otherwise noted.

The Old Mill — PC128

Designed by Harry Devlin. Inscription at lower left: The Old Mill / University of Vermont / Bicentennial.

1991, Oct. 29 **Litho.**

UX159 PC128 19c **multicolored** .50 *.75*
First day cancel, Burlington, VT *(23,965)* 1.00

Wadsworth Atheneum, Hartford, CT — PC129

Designed by Frank Costantino. Inscription at lower left: Wadsworth Atheneum / Hartford, Connecticut / 150th Anniversary / 1842-1992.

1992, Jan. 16 **Litho.**

UX160 PC129 19c **multicolored** .40 *.75*
First day cancel, Hartford, CT *(41,499)* 1.00

Cobb Hall, University of Chicago — PC130

Designed by Michael P. Hagel. Inscription at lower left: Cobb Hall / The University of Chicago / Centennial Year, 1991-1992.

1992, Jan. 23 **Litho.**

UX161 PC130 19c **multicolored** .50 *.75*
First day cancel, Chicago, IL *(27,150)* 1.00

Waller Hall, Willamette University — PC131

Designed by Bradbury Thompson. Inscription at lower left: Waller Hall / Salem, Oregon / Willamette University / Sesquicentennial / 1842-1992.

1992, Feb. 1 **Litho.**

UX162 PC131 19c **multicolored** .50 *.75*
First day cancel, Salem, OR *(28,463)* 1.00

PC132

Designed by Dennis Simon. Space for message at left. Inscription at upper left: "At right: The Reliance, USA 1903 / Reverse: The Ranger, USA 1937."

1992, May 6 **Litho.**
UX163 PC132 19c **multicolored** 1.00 *3.00*
First day cancel, San Diego, CA *(19,944)* 2.00

No. UX163 sold for 50 cents.

PC133

Designed by Ken Hodges.

1992, May 9 **Litho.**
UX164 PC133 19c **multicolored** .40 *.75*
First day cancel, Stevenson, WA *(32,344)* 1.00

Ellis Island Immigration Museum — PC134

Designed by Howard Koslow. Inscription at lower left: "Ellis Island / Centennial 1992."

1992, May 11 **Litho.**
UX165 PC134 19c **multicolored** .40 *.75*
First day cancel, Ellis Island, NY *(38,482)* 1.00

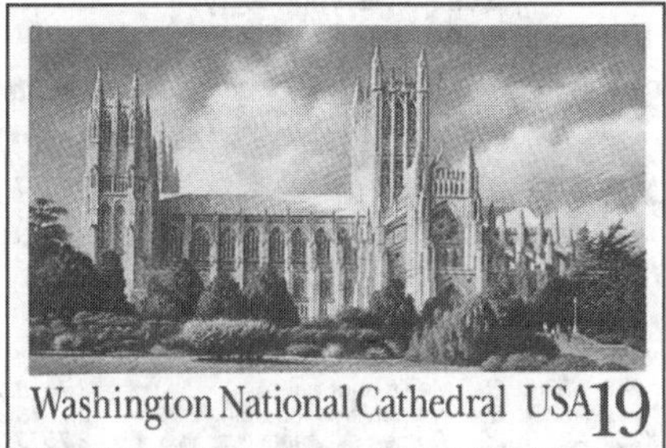

PC135

Designed by Howard Koslow.

1993, Jan. 6 **Litho.**
UX166 PC135 19c **multicolored** .40 *.75*
First day cancel, Washington, DC *(8,315)* 1.00

PC136

Designed by Pierre Mion.

1993, Feb. 8 **Litho.**
UX167 PC136 19c **multicolored** .50 *.75*
First day cancel, Williamsburg, VA *(9,758)* 1.00

Opening of Holocaust Memorial Museum — PC137

Designed by Tom Engeman. Space for message at left. Inscription at upper left: "Washington, DC: / United States / Holocaust Memorial Museum."

1993, Mar. 23 **Litho.**
UX168 PC137 19c **multicolored** 1.00 *3.00*
First day cancel, Washington, DC *(8,234)* 2.00

No. UX168 sold for 50c, and shows aerial view of museum on the back.

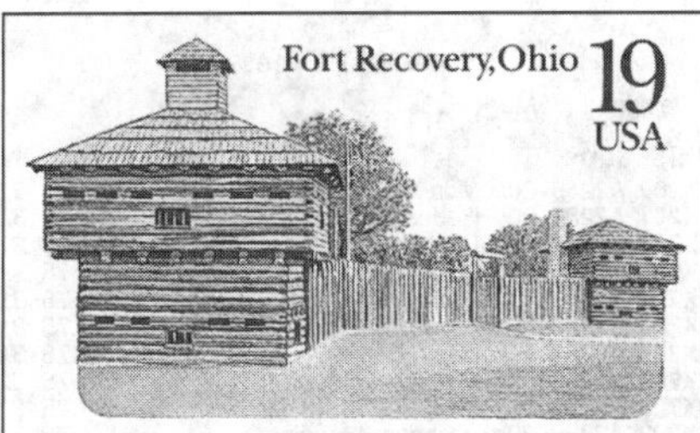

PC138

Designed by Michael Hagel.

1993, June 13 **Litho.**
UX169 PC138 19c **multicolored** .40 *.75*
First day cancel, Fort Recovery, OH *(8,254)* 1.00

PC139

Designed by Robert Timberlake.

1993, Sept. 14 **Litho.**
UX170 PC139 19c **multicolored** .50 *.75*
First day cancel, Chapel Hill, NC *(7,796)* 1.00

PC140

Designed by Frank Constantino.

1993, Sept. 17 **Litho.**
UX171 PC140 19c **multicolored** .50 *.75*
First day cancel, Worcester, MA *(4,680)* 1.00

PC141

Designed by Michael Hagel.

1993, Oct. 9 **Litho.**
UX172 PC141 19c **multicolored** .50 *.75*
First day cancel, Jacksonville, IL *(5,269)* 1.00

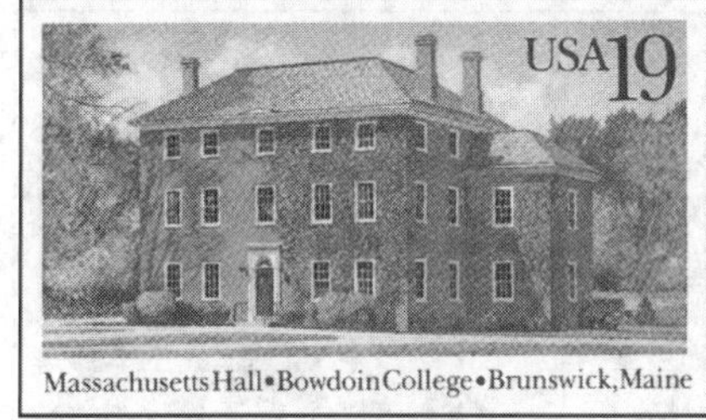

PC142

Designed by Harry Devlin.

1993, Oct. 14 **Litho.**
UX173 PC142 19c **multicolored** .50 *.75*
First day cancel, Brunswick, ME *(33,750 est.)* 1.00

PC143

Designed by Michael Hagel.

1994, Feb. 12 **Litho.**
UX174 PC143 19c **multicolored** .40 *.75*
First day cancel, Springfield, IL *(26,164)* 1.00

PC144

Designed by Michael Hagel.

1994, Mar. 11 **Litho.**
UX175 PC144 19c **multicolored** .50 *.75*
First day cancel, Springfield, OH *(20,230)* 1.00

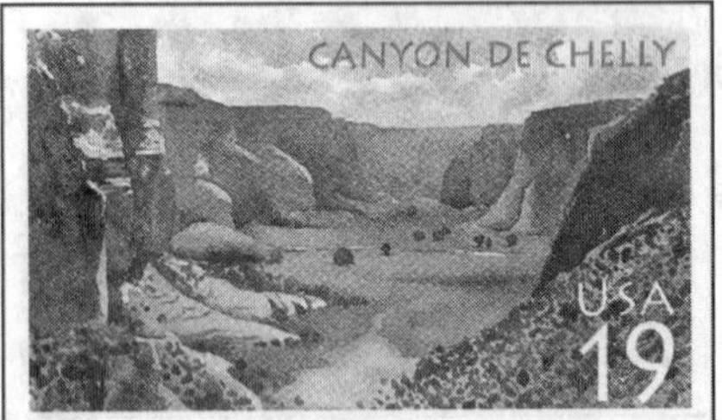

PC145

Designed by William Matthews.

1994, Aug. 11 **Litho.**
UX176 PC145 19c **multicolored** .40 *.75*
First day cancel, Chinle, AZ *(19,826)* 1.00

St. Louis Union Station — PC146

Designed by Harry Devlin.

1994, Sept. 3 **Litho.**
UX177 PC146 19c **multicolored** .40 *.75*
First day cancel, St. Louis, MO *(38,881)* 1.00

Legends of the West Type

Designed by Mark Hess.

1994, Oct. 18 **Litho.**

UX178 A2197 19c Home on the Range 1.10 *3.00*
UX179 A2197 19c Buffalo Bill 1.10 *3.00*
UX180 A2197 19c Jim Bridger 1.10 *3.00*
UX181 A2197 19c Annie Oakley 1.10 *3.00*
UX182 A2197 19c Native American Culture 1.10 *3.00*
UX183 A2197 19c Chief Joseph 1.10 *3.00*
UX184 A2197 19c Bill Pickett (revised) 1.10 *3.00*
UX185 A2197 19c Bat Masterson 1.10 *3.00*
UX186 A2197 19c John Fremont 1.10 *3.00*
UX187 A2197 19c Wyatt Earp 1.10 *3.00*
UX188 A2197 19c Nellie Cashman 1.10 *3.00*
UX189 A2197 19c Charles Goodnight 1.10 *3.00*
UX190 A2197 19c Geronimo 1.10 *3.00*
UX191 A2197 19c Kit Carson 1.10 *3.00*
UX192 A2197 19c Wild Bill Hickok 1.10 *3.00*
UX193 A2197 19c Western Wildlife 1.10 *3.00*
UX194 A2197 19c Jim Beckwourth 1.10 *3.00*
UX195 A2197 19c Bill Tilghman 1.10 *3.00*
UX196 A2197 19c Sacagawea 1.10 *3.00*
UX197 A2197 19c Overland Mail 1.10 *3.00*
Nos. UX178-UX197 (20) 22.00
First day cancel, #UX178-UX197, any card, Tucson, AZ, Lawton, OK or Laramie, WY *(10,000 USPS est.)* 1.50

Nos. UX178-UX197 sold in packages of 20 different for $7.95.

Red Barn — PC147

Designed by Wendell Minor.

1995, Jan. 3 **Litho.**
UX198 PC147 20c **multicolored** .40 .60
First day cancel, Williamsburg, PA 1.00

First day cancellation was applied to 54,102 of Nos. U632, UX198.

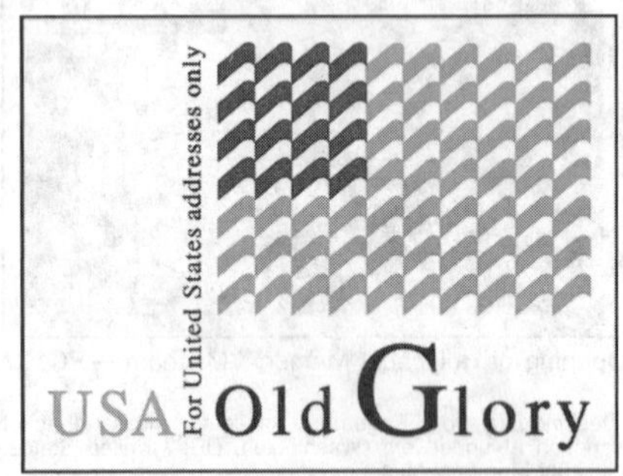

PC148

1995 **Litho.**
UX199 PC148 (20c) **black, blue & red** 3.00 2.50

No. UX199 was only available through the Philatelic Fullfillment Center after its announcement 1/12/95. Cards submitted for first day cancels received a 12/13/94 cancel, even though they were not available on that date.

Civil War Types

Designed by Mark Hess.

1995, June 29 **Litho.**

UX200 A2289 20c Monitor & Virginia 1.75 *3.00*
UX201 A2289 20c Robert E. Lee 1.75 *3.00*
UX202 A2289 20c Clara Barton 1.75 *3.00*
UX203 A2289 20c Ulysses S. Grant 1.75 *3.00*
UX204 A2289 20c Battle of Shiloh 1.75 *3.00*
UX205 A2289 20c Jefferson Davis 1.75 *3.00*
UX206 A2289 20c David Farragut 1.75 *3.00*
UX207 A2289 20c Frederick Douglass 1.75 *3.00*
UX208 A2289 20c Raphael Semmes 1.75 *3.00*
UX209 A2289 20c Abraham Lincoln 1.75 *3.00*
UX210 A2289 20c Harriet Tubman 1.75 *3.00*
UX211 A2289 20c Stand Watie 1.75 *3.00*
UX212 A2289 20c Joseph E. Johnston 1.75 *3.00*
UX213 A2289 20c Winfield Hancock 1.75 *3.00*
UX214 A2289 20c Mary Chesnut 1.75 *3.00*
UX215 A2289 20c Battle of Chancellorsville 1.75 *3.00*
UX216 A2289 20c William T. Sherman 1.75 *3.00*
UX217 A2289 20c Phoebe Pember 1.75 *3.00*
UX218 A2289 20c Stonewall Jackson 1.75 *3.00*
UX219 A2289 20c Battle of Gettysburg 1.75 *3.00*
Nos. UX200-UX219 (20) 35.00
First day cancel, any card, Gettysburg, PA 1.50
First day cancel, any card, any other city 1.50

Nos. UX200-UX219 sold in packages of 20 different for $7.95.

PC148a

For International Use

1995, Aug. 24 **Litho.**
UX219A PC148a 50c **multicolored** 1.00 *7.50*
First day cancel, St. Louis, MO *(6,008)* 1.25

PC149

Designed by Richard Sheaff.

1995, Sept. 3 **Litho.**
UX220 PC149 20c **multicolored** .40 .75
First day cancel, Hunt Valley, MD *(5,281)* 1.00

Comic Strip Types

Designed by Carl Herrman.

1995, Oct. 1 **Litho.**

UX221 A2313 20c The Yellow Kid 2.50 *3.00*
UX222 A2313 20c Katzenjammer Kids 2.50 *3.00*
UX223 A2313 20c Little Nemo in Slumberland 2.50 *3.00*
UX224 A2313 20c Bringing Up Father 2.50 *3.00*
UX225 A2313 20c Krazy Kat 2.50 *3.00*
UX226 A2313 20c Rube Goldberg's Inventions 2.50 *3.00*
UX227 A2313 20c Toonerville Folks 2.50 *3.00*
UX228 A2313 20c Gasoline Alley 2.50 *3.00*
UX229 A2313 20c Barney Google 2.50 *3.00*
UX230 A2313 20c Little Orphan Annie 2.50 *3.00*
UX231 A2313 20c Popeye 2.50 *3.00*
UX232 A2313 20c Blondie 2.50 *3.00*
UX233 A2313 20c Dick Tracy 2.50 *3.00*
UX234 A2313 20c Alley Oop 2.50 *3.00*
UX235 A2313 20c Nancy 2.50 *3.00*
UX236 A2313 20c Flash Gordon 2.50 *3.00*
UX237 A2313 20c Li'l Abner 2.50 *3.00*
UX238 A2313 20c Terry and the Pirates 2.50 *3.00*
UX239 A2313 20c Prince Valiant 2.50 *3.00*
UX240 A2313 20c Brenda Starr Reporter 2.50 *3.00*
Nos. UX221-UX240 (20) 50.00
First day cancel, any card, Boca Raton, FL 1.50

Nos. UX221-UX240 sold in packages of 20 different for $7.95.

Winter Scene — PC150

1996, Feb. 23 **Litho.**
UX241 PC150 20c **multicolored** .40 .40
First day cancel, Watertown, NY *(11,764)* 1.00

Summer Olympics Type

Designed by Richard Waldrep.

1996, May 2 **Litho.**

Size: 150x108mm

UX242 A2368 20c Men's cycling 2.75 *3.00*
UX243 A2368 20c Women's diving 2.75 *3.00*
UX244 A2368 20c Women's running 2.75 *3.00*
UX245 A2368 20c Men's canoeing 2.75 *3.00*
UX246 A2368 20c Decathlon (javelin) 2.75 *3.00*
a. Inverted impression of entire address side, men's cycling picture on reverse 2.75
UX247 A2368 20c Women's soccer 2.75 *3.00*
UX248 A2368 20c Men's shot put 2.75 *3.00*
UX249 A2368 20c Women's sailboarding 2.75 *3.00*
UX250 A2368 20c Women's gymnastics 2.75 *3.00*
UX251 A2368 20c Freestyle wrestling 2.75 *3.00*
UX252 A2368 20c Women's softball 2.75 *3.00*
UX253 A2368 20c Women's swimming 2.75 *3.00*
UX254 A2368 20c Men's sprints 2.75 *3.00*
UX255 A2368 20c Men's rowing 2.75 *3.00*
UX256 A2368 20c Beach volleyball 2.75 *3.00*
UX257 A2368 20c Men's basketball 2.75 *3.00*
UX258 A2368 20c Equestrian 2.75 *3.00*
UX259 A2368 20c Men's gymnastics 2.75 *3.00*
UX260 A2368 20c Men's swimming 2.75 *3.00*

UX261 A2368 20c Men's hurdles 2.75 *3.00*
a. Booklet of 20 postal cards, #UX242-UX261 55.00
First day cancel, any card, Washington, DC 1.50

First day cancels of Nos. UX242-UX261 were available as sets from the US Postal Service. Unused sets of Nos. UX242-UX261 were not available from the US Philatelic Fullfillment Center for several months after the "official" first day.

PC151

Designed by Harry Devlin.

1996, June 1 **Litho.**
UX262 PC151 20c **multicolored** .50 .75
First day cancel, Annapolis, MD *(8,793)* 1.00

PC152

Designed by Howard Koslow.

1996, Sept. 20 **Litho.**
UX263 PC152 20c **multicolored** .50 .75
First day cancel, Princeton, NJ *(11,621)* 1.00

Endangered Species Type

Designed by James Balog.

1996, Oct. 2 **Litho.**
UX264 A2403 20c Florida panther 3.50 1.75
UX265 A2403 20c Black-footed ferret 3.50 1.75
UX266 A2403 20c American crocodile 3.50 1.75
UX267 A2403 20c Piping plover 3.50 1.75
UX268 A2403 20c Gila trout 3.50 1.75
UX269 A2403 20c Florida manatee 3.50 1.75
UX270 A2403 20c Schaus swallowtail butterfly 3.50 1.75
UX271 A2403 20c Woodland caribou 3.50 1.75
UX272 A2403 20c Thick-billed parrot 3.50 1.75
UX273 A2403 20c San Francisco garter snake 3.50 1.75
UX274 A2403 20c Ocelot 3.50 1.75
UX275 A2403 20c Wyoming toad 3.50 1.75
UX276 A2403 20c California condor 3.50 1.75
UX277 A2403 20c Hawaiian monk seal 3.50 1.75
UX278 A2403 20c Brown pelican 3.50 1.75
a. Booklet of 15 cards, #UX264-UX278 50.00
First day cancel, #UX264-UX278, any card, San Diego, CA *(5,000)* 1.75

Nos. UX264-UX278 were issued bound three-to-a-page in a souvenir booklet that was sold for $11.95.

Love (Swans) Type

Designed by Supon Design.

1997, Feb. 4 **Litho.**
UX279 A2415 20c multicolored .80 1.10

Stamp Designs Depicted on Reverse of Card

Scott 2814 2.50 1.10
Scott 2815 2.50 1.10
Scott 3123 2.50 1.10
Scott 3124 2.50 1.10
Sheet of 4, #2814-2815, 3123-3124 10.00
Scott 2202 7.50 1.10
Scott 2248 7.50 1.10
Scott 2440 7.50 1.10
Scott 2813 7.50 1.10
Sheet of 4, #2202, 2248, 2440, 2813 30.00

No. UX279 was sold in sets of 3 sheets of 4 picture postal cards with 8 different designs for $6.95 (two sheets of #2814-2815, 3123-3124 and one sheet of #2202, 2248, 2440, 2813). The cards are separated by microperfs. The picture side of each card depicted a previously released Love stamp design without the inscriptions and value.

First day cancels were not available on Feb. 4. It was announced after Feb. 4 that collectors could purchase the cards and send them to the U.S.P.S. for First Day cancels.

PC153

Designed by Howard Koslow.

1997, May 7 **Litho.**
UX280 PC153 20c **multicolored** .50 .50
First day cancel, New York, NY *(9,576)* 1.00

Bugs Bunny Type

Designed by Warner Bros.

1997, May 22 **Litho.**
UX281 A2425 20c **multicolored** 1.25 *2.00*
First day cancel, Burbank, CA 1.75
a. Booklet of 10 cards 12.50

No. UX281a sold for $5.95.

First day cancellations applied to 378,142 of Nos. UX281 and 3138.

Golden Gate in Daylight — PC154

Golden Gate at Sunset — PC155

Designed by Carol Simowitz.

1997, June 2 **Litho.**
UX282 PC154 20c **multicolored,** *June 2* .40 *.65*
First day cancel, San Francisco, CA 1.00

For International Use

UX283 PC155 50c **multicolored,** *June 3* 1.00 2.50
First day cancel, San Francisco, CA 2.00

First day cancellation was applied to 21,189 of Nos. UX282-UX283.

PC156

Designed by Richard Sheaff.

1997, Sept. 7 **Litho.**
UX284 PC156 20c **multicolored** .40 .50
First day cancel, Baltimore, MD *(9,611)* 1.00

Similar to Types A2451-A2455 with 20c Denomination

Designed by Derry Noyes.

1997, Sept. 30 **Litho.**
UX285 A2451 20c Phantom of the Opera 1.50 .60
UX286 A2452 20c Dracula 1.50 .60
UX287 A2453 20c Frankenstein's Monster 1.50 .60
UX288 A2454 20c The Mummy 1.50 .60
UX289 A2455 20c The Wolf Man 1.50 .60
a. Booklet of 20 cards, 4 each #UX285-UX289 25.00
First day cancel, #UX285-UX289, any card, Universal City, CA 1.75

Nos. UX285-UX289 were issued bound in a booklet of 20 cards containing four of each card. Booklet was sold in package for $5.95.

PC157

Designed by Howard Paine.

1998, Apr. 20 **Litho.**
UX290 PC157 20c **multicolored** .50 .50
First day cancel, University, MS *(22,276)* 1.00

Similar to Sylvester & Tweety with 20c Denomination

Designed by Brenda Guttman.

1998, Apr. 27 **Litho.**
UX291 A2487 20c **multicolored** 1.25 *2.00*
First day cancel, New York, NY 1.75
a. Booklet of 10 cards 14.00

No. UX291a sold for $5.95.

First day cancellations applied to 231,839 of Nos. UX291, 3204 and 3205.

PC158

Designed by Phil Jordan.

1998, May 1 **Litho.**
UX292 PC158 20c **multicolored** .50 .50
First day cancel, Philadelphia, PA *(13,853)* 1.00

Similar to Tropical Birds with 20c Denomination and No Inscription

Designed by Phil Jordan.

1998, July 29 **Litho.**

UX293 A2503 20c Antillean euphonia 1.00 .75
UX294 A2504 20c Green-throated carib 1.00 .75
UX295 A2505 20c Crested honeycreeper 1.00 .75
UX296 A2506 20c Cardinal honeyeater 1.00 .75
a. Booklet of 20 cards, 5 ea #UX293-UX296 20.00
First day cancel, #UX293-UX296, any card, Ponce PR 1.75

Nos. UX293-UX296 were issued bound in a booklet of 20 cards containing five of each card. Illustration of the stamp without denomination is shown on the back of each card. Booklet was sold in packages for $6.95.

American Ballet Type

Designed by Derry Noyes.

1998, Sept. 16 **Litho.**

UX297 A2517 20c **multicolored** 1.25 *1.40*
a. Booklet of 10 cards 12.50
First day cancel, New York, NY 1.75

No. UX297a was sold for $5.95.

PC159

Designed by Richard Sheaff.

1998, Oct. 3 **Litho.**

UX298 PC159 20c **multicolored** .50 .50
First day cancel, Boston, MA *(14,812)* 1.00

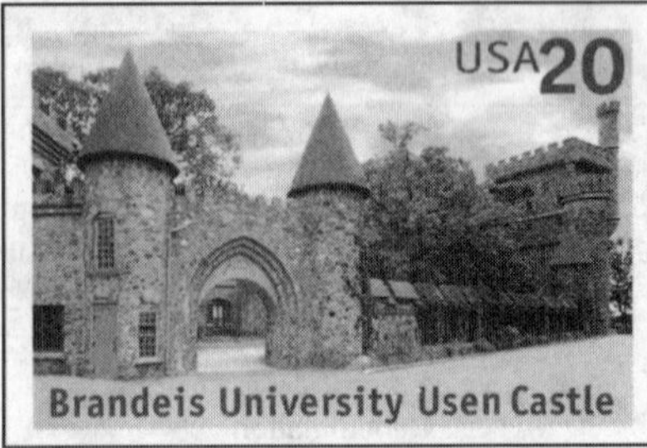

PC160

Designed by Richard Sheaff.

1998, Oct. 17 **Litho.**

UX299 PC160 20c **multicolored** .50 .50
First day cancel, Waltham, MA *(14,137)* 1.00

Love Type

Designed by John Grossman, Holly Sudduth

1999, Jan. 28 **Litho.**

UX300 A2537 20c **multicolored** .70 .70

No. UX300 was sold in packs containing 5 sheets of 4 cards for $6.95.

150 YEARS
USA20
University of Wisconsin-Madison • Bascom Hill

PC161

Designed by Carl Herrman.

1999, Feb. 5 **Litho.**

UX301 PC161 20c **multicolored** .50 .50
First day cancel, Madison, WI *(12,582)* 1.00

PC162

Designed by Derry Noyes.

1999, Feb. 11 **Litho.**

UX302 PC162 20c **multicolored** .50 .50
First day cancel, Lexington, VA *17,556* 1.00

PC163

Designed by Richard Sheaff.

1999, Mar. 11 **Litho.**

UX303 PC163 20c **red & black** .50 .50
First day cancel, Newport, RI *(13,649)* 1.00

Daffy Duck Type

Designed by Ed Wieczyk.

1999, Apr. 16 **Litho.**

UX304 A2554 20c **multicolored** 1.40 1.40
First day cancel, Los Angeles, CA 1.40
a. Booklet of 10 cards 14.00

No. UX304a sold for $6.95.

First day cancellation was applied to 177,988 of UX304, 3306 and 3307.

PC164

Designed by Richard Sheaff.

1999, May 14 **Litho.**

UX305 PC164 20c **multicolored** .40 .40
First day cancel, Mount Vernon, VA *(14,642)* 1.00

Block Island Lighthouse — PC165

Designed by Derry Noyes.

1999, July 24 **Litho.**

UX306 PC165 20c **multicolored** .40 .45
First day cancel, Block Island, RI *(12,694)* 1.00

Famous Trains Type

Designed by Howard Paine.

1999, Aug. 26 **Litho.**

UX307 A2583 20c Super Chief .85 1.00
UX308 A2582 20c Hiawatha .85 1.00
UX309 A2579 20c Daylight .85 1.00
UX310 A2580 20c Congressional .85 1.00
UX311 A2581 20c 20th Century Limited .85 1.00
a. Booklet of 20 cards, 4 ea #UX307-UX311 17.50
First day cancel, #UX307-UX311, any card, Cleveland, OH 1.75
First day cancel, #UX307-UX311, any card, any other city 1.75

Nos. UX307-UX311 were issued bound in a booklet of 20 cards containing four of each card. Booklet sold for $6.95.

PC166

Designed by Ethel Kessler.

2000, Feb. 28 **Litho.**

UX312 PC166 20c **multicolored** .40 .45
First day cancel, Salt Lake City, UT *(14,230)* 1.00

PC167

Designed by Richard Sheaff.

2000, Mar. 18 **Litho.**

UX313 PC167 20c **multicolored** .40 .45
First day cancel, Nashville, TN *(12,690)* 1.00

Road Runner & Wile E. Coyote Type

Designed by Ed Wleczyk, Warner Bros.

2000, Apr. 26 **Litho.**

UX314 A2622 20c **multicolored** 1.40 1.40
First day cancel, Phoenix, AZ 1.40
a. Booklet of 10 cards 14.00

No. UX314a sold for $6.95.

First day cancellation was applied to 154,903 of UX314 and 3391.

Adoption Type

Designed by Greg Berger.

2000, May 10 **Litho.**
UX315 A2628 20c **multicolored** 1.40 1.50
First day cancel, Beverly Hills, CA 1.40
a. Booklet of 10 cards 14.00

No. UX315a sold for $6.95. The design, without denominations, is shown on the back of the card.
First day cancellation was applied to 137,903 of UX315 and 3398.

PC168

Designed by Howard Paine.

2000, May 19 **Litho.**
UX316 PC168 20c **multicolored** .40 .45
First day cancel, Middlebury, VT *(13,586)* 1.00

Stars and Stripes Type

Designed by Richard Sheaff.

2000, June 14 **Litho.**
UX317 A2633 20c Sons of Liberty Flag, 1775 1.50 1.25
UX318 A2633 20c New England Flag, 1775 1.50 1.25
UX319 A2633 20c Forster Flag, 1775 1.50 1.25
UX320 A2633 20c Continental Colors, 1776 1.50 1.25
a. Sheet of 4 cards, #UX317-UX320 6.50
UX321 A2633 20c Francis Hopkinson Flag, 1777 1.50 1.25
UX322 A2633 20c Brandywine Flag, 1777 1.50 1.25
UX323 A2633 20c John Paul Jones Flag, 1779 1.50 1.25
UX324 A2633 20c Pierre L'Enfant Flag, 1783 1.50 1.25
a. Sheet of 4 cards, #UX321-UX324 6.50
UX325 A2633 20c Indian Peace Flag, 1803 1.50 1.25
UX326 A2633 20c Easton Flag, 1814 1.50 1.25
UX327 A2633 20c Star-Spangled Banner, 1814 1.50 1.25
UX328 A2633 20c Bennington Flag, c. 1820 1.50 1.25
a. Sheet of 4 cards, #UX325-UX328 6.50
UX329 A2633 20c Great Star Flag, 1837 1.50 1.25
UX330 A2633 20c 29-Star Flag, 1847 1.50 1.25
UX331 A2633 20c Fort Sumter Flag, 1861 1.50 1.25
UX332 A2633 20c Centennial Flag, 1876 1.50 1.25
a. Sheet of 4 cards, #UX329-UX332 6.50
UX333 A2633 20c 38-Star Flag, 1877 1.50 1.25
UX334 A2633 20c Peace Flag, 1891 1.50 1.25
UX335 A2633 20c 48-Star Flag, 1912 1.50 1.25
UX336 A2633 20c 50-Star Flag, 1960 1.50 1.25
a. Sheet of 4 cards, #UX333-UX336 6.50
First day cancel, any card, Baltimore, MD .90
Nos. UX317-UX336 (20) 30.00 25.00

Nos. UX320a, UX324a, UX328a, UX332a and UX336a were sold together in a package for $8.95. Microperforations are between individual cards on each sheet. Illustrations of the flags, without denominations, are shown on the back of the cards.

Legends of Baseball Type

Designed by Phil Jordan.

2000, July 6 **Litho.**
UX337 A2638 20c Jackie Robinson 1.10 *1.25*
UX338 A2638 20c Eddie Collins 1.10 *1.25*
UX339 A2638 20c Christy Mathewson 1.10 *1.25*
UX340 A2638 20c Ty Cobb 1.10 *1.25*
UX341 A2638 20c George Sisler 1.10 *1.25*
UX342 A2638 20c Rogers Hornsby 1.10 *1.25*
UX343 A2638 20c Mickey Cochrane 1.10 *1.25*
UX344 A2638 20c Babe Ruth 1.10 *1.25*
UX345 A2638 20c Walter Johnson 1.10 *1.25*
UX346 A2638 20c Roberto Clemente 1.10 *1.25*
UX347 A2638 20c Lefty Grove 1.10 *1.25*
UX348 A2638 20c Tris Speaker 1.10 *1.25*
UX349 A2638 20c Cy Young 1.10 *1.25*
UX350 A2638 20c Jimmie Foxx 1.10 *1.25*
UX351 A2638 20c Pie Traynor 1.10 *1.25*
UX352 A2638 20c Satchel Paige 1.10 *1.25*
UX353 A2638 20c Honus Wagner 1.10 *1.25*
UX354 A2638 20c Josh Gibson 1.10 *1.25*
UX355 A2638 20c Dizzy Dean 1.10 *1.25*
UX356 A2638 20c Lou Gehrig 1.10 *1.25*
a. Booklet of 20 cards, #UX337-UX356 25.00
First day cancel, any card, Atlanta, GA .90

No. UX356a sold for $8.95.

Christmas Deer Type of 1999

Designed by Tom Nikosey.

2000, Oct. 12 **Litho.** ***Rouletted on 2 sides***
UX357 A2600 20c **gold & blue** 1.25 1.25
UX358 A2600 20c **gold & red** 1.25 1.25
UX359 A2600 20c **gold & purple** 1.25 1.25
UX360 A2600 20c **gold & green** 1.25 1.25
a. Sheet of 4, #UX357-UX360 5.00
First day cancel, any card, Rudolph, WI 1.75

Nos. UX357-UX360 were sold in packs containing five No. UX360a for $8.95.

PC169

Designed by Derry Noyes.

2001, Mar. 30 **Litho.**
UX361 PC169 20c **multicolored** .40 .60
First day cancel, New Haven, CT 1.00

PC170

Designed by Ethel Kessler.

2001, Apr. 26 **Litho.**
UX362 PC170 20c **multicolored** .40 .60
First day cancel, Columbia, SC 1.00

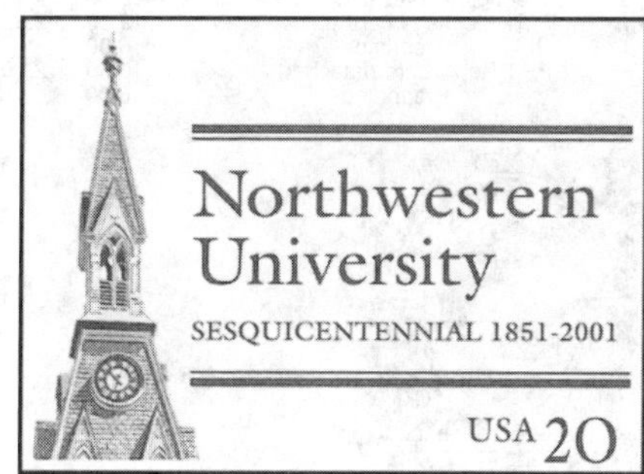

PC171

Designed by Howard Paine.

2001, Apr. 28 **Litho.**
UX363 PC171 20c **multicolored** .40 .60
First day cancel, Evanston, IL 1.00

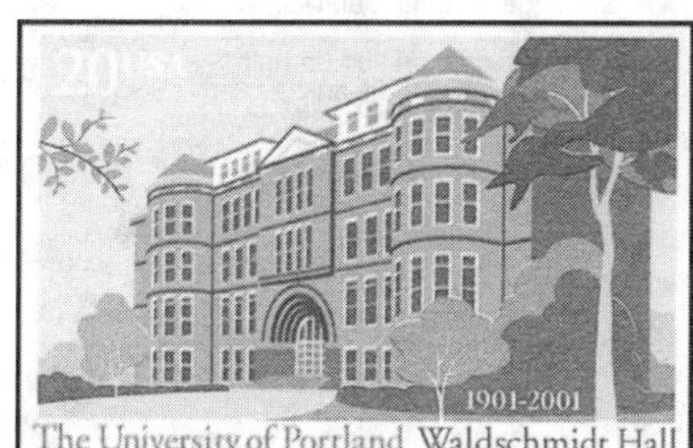

PC172

Designed by Richard Sheaff.

2001, May 1 **Litho.**
UX364 PC172 20c **multicolored** .40 .50
First day cancel, Portland, OR 1.00

Legendary Playing Fields Type with 21c Denomination

Designed by Phil Jordan.

2001, June 27 **Litho.**
UX365 A2712 21c Ebbets Field 1.40 1.40
UX366 A2713 21c Tiger Stadium 1.40 1.40
UX367 A2714 21c Crosley Field 1.40 1.40
UX368 A2715 21c Yankee Stadium 1.40 1.40
UX369 A2716 21c Polo Grounds 1.40 1.40
UX370 A2717 21c Forbes Field 1.40 1.40
UX371 A2718 21c Fenway Park 1.40 1.40
UX372 A2719 21c Comiskey Park 1.40 1.40
UX373 A2720 21c Shibe Park 1.40 1.40
UX374 A2721 21c Wrigley Field 1.40 1.40
a. Booklet of 10 cards, #UX365-UX374 14.00

No. UX374a sold for $6.95.

White Barn — PC173

Designed by Derry Noyes.

2001, Sept. 20 **Litho.**
UX375 PC173 21c **multicolored** .45 .45
First day cancel, Washington, DC 1.00

That's All Folks! Type

Designed by Ed Wleczyk, Warner Bros.

2001, Oct. 1 **Litho.**
UX376 A2736 21c **multicolored** 1.50 1.50
First day cancel, Beverly Hills, CA 1.50
a. Booklet of 10 cards 15.00

No. UX376a sold for $7.25.

Christmas Type

Designed by Richard Sheaff.

2001, Oct. 10 **Litho.** ***Rouletted on 2 Sides***
UX377 A2740 21c **multicolored** 1.25 .95
First day cancel, Santa Claus, IN 1.25
UX378 A2741 21c **multicolored** 1.25 .95
First day cancel, Santa Claus, IN 1.25
UX379 A2738 21c **multicolored** 1.25 .95
First day cancel, Santa Claus, IN 1.25
UX380 A2739 21c **multicolored** 1.25 .95
First day cancel, Santa Claus, IN 1.25
a. Sheet of 4, #UX377-UX380 5.00

Packages of 5 No. UX380a sold for $9.25.

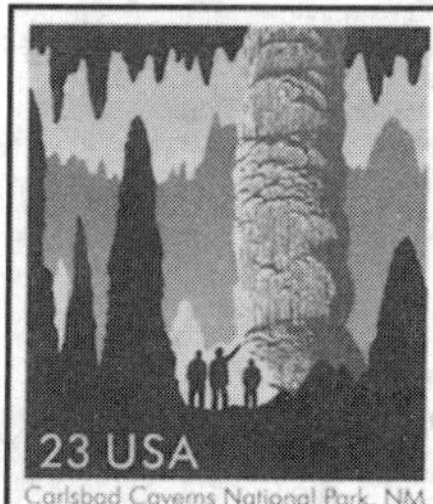

Carlsbad Caverns National Park — PC174

Designed by Carl Herrman.

2002, June 7 **Litho.**
UX381 PC174 23c **multicolored** .50 .50
First day cancel, Carlsbad, NM 1.00
First day cancel, any other city 1.00

Teddy Bears Type

Designed by Margaret Bauer.

2002, Aug. 15 **Litho.** ***Rouletted on 2 Sides***
UX382 A2827 23c Ideal Bear, c. 1905 .90 .90
First day cancel, Atlantic City, NJ .90
UX383 A2826 23c Gund Bear, c. 1948 .90 .90
First day cancel, Atlantic City, NJ .90
UX384 A2824 23c Bruin Bear, c. 1907 .90 .90
First day cancel, Atlantic City, NJ .90

UX385 A2825 23c "Stick" Bear, 1920s .90 .90
First day cancel, Atlantic City, NJ .90
a. Sheet of 4, #UX382-UX385 3.75

Packages of 5 No. UX385a sold for $9.25.

Christmas Snowmen Type

Designed by Derry Noyes.

2002, Oct. 28 Litho. *Rouletted on 2 Sides*
Design Size: 28x38mm

UX386 A2844 23c **multicolored** 1.00 1.00
First day cancel, Houghton, MI 1.00
UX387 A2845 23c **multicolored** 1.00 1.00
First day cancel, Houghton, MI 1.00
UX388 A2846 23c **multicolored** 1.00 1.00
First day cancel, Houghton, MI 1.00
UX389 A2847 23c **multicolored** 1.00 1.00
First day cancel, Houghton, MI 1.00
a. Sheet of 4, #UX386-UX389 4.00

Packages of 5 #UX389a sold for $9.75.

Old Glory Type

Designed by Richard Sheaff.

2003, Apr. 3 Litho. *Rouletted on 1 Side*

UX390 A2883 23c **multicolored** 1.00 1.00
First day cancel, New York, NY 1.00
UX391 A2884 23c **multicolored** 1.00 1.00
First day cancel, New York, NY 1.00
UX392 A2885 23c **multicolored** 1.00 1.00
First day cancel, New York, NY 1.00
UX393 A2886 23c **multicolored** 1.00 1.00
First day cancel, New York, NY 1.00
UX394 A2887 23c **multicolored** 1.00 1.00
First day cancel, New York, NY 1.00
a. Booklet of 20 cards, 4 each #UX390-UX394 20.00

No. UX394a sold for $9.75.

Southeastern Lighthouses Type

Designed by Howard E. Paine.

2003, June 13 Litho. *Rouletted on 1 Side*

UX395 A2893 23c **multicolored** 1.00 1.00
First day cancel, Tybee Island, GA 1.00
UX396 A2894 23c **multicolored** 1.00 1.00
First day cancel, Tybee Island, GA 1.00
UX397 A2895 23c **multicolored** 1.00 1.00
First day cancel, Tybee Island, GA 1.00
UX398 A2896 23c **multicolored** 1.00 1.00
First day cancel, Tybee Island, GA 1.00
UX399 A2897 23c **multicolored** 1.00 1.00
First day cancel, Tybee Island, GA 1.00
a. Booklet of 20 cards, 4 each #UX395-UX399 20.00

No. UX399a sold for $9.75.

PAID REPLY POSTAL CARDS

These are sold to the public as two unsevered cards, one for message and one for reply. These are listed first as unsevered cards and then as severed cards. Values are for:

Unused cards (both unsevered and severed) without printed or written address or message.

Unsevered cards sell for a premium if never folded.

Used unsevered cards, Message Card with Post Office cancellation and Reply Card uncanceled (from 1968 value is for a single used severed card); and used severed cards with cancellation when current.

Used values for International Paid Reply Cards are for proper usage. Those domestically used or with postage added sell for less than the unused value.

"Preprinted," unused cards (both unsevered and severed) with printed or written address or message. Used value applies after 1952.

First day cancel values are for cards without cachets.

PM1

Head of Grant, card framed.
PR1 inscribed "REPLY CARD."

1892, Oct. 25 Size: 140x89mm

UY1 PM1+PR1 1c +1c **black,** *buff,* unsevered 37.50 9.00
Preprinted 15.00
a. Message card printed on both sides, reply card blank 250.00
b. Message card blank, reply card printed on both sides 300.00
c. Cards joined at bottom 200.00 100.00
Preprinted 100.00
m. PM1 Message card detached 6.00 1.75
Preprinted 3.00
r. PR1 Reply card detached 6.00 1.75
Preprinted 3.00

For other postal cards of types PM1 and PR1 see No. UY3.

Liberty — PM2

PR2 inscribed "REPLY CARD."

1893, Mar. 1 For International Use

UY2 PM2+PR2 2c +2c **blue,** *grayish white,* unsevered 20.00 20.00
Preprinted 12.50
a. 2c+2c **dark blue,** *grayish white,* unsevered 20.00 20.00
Preprinted 12.50
b. Message card printed on both sides, reply card blank 500.00
c. Message card blank, reply card printed on both sides —
d. Message card normal, reply card blank 300.00
m. PM2 Message card detached 5.00 *6.00*
Preprinted 2.50
r. PR2 Reply card detached 5.00 *6.00*
Preprinted 2.50

For other postal cards of types PM2 and PR2 see No. UY11.

Design same as PM1 and PR1, without frame around card

1898, Sept.
Size: 140x82mm

UY3 PM1+PR1 1c +1c **black,** *buff,* unsevered 62.50 12.50
Preprinted 12.50
a. Message card normal, reply card blank 400.00
b. Message card printed on both sides, reply card blank 400.00
c. Message card blank, reply card printed on both sides 400.00
d. Message card without "Detach annexed card/for answer" 250.00 150.00
Preprinted —
e. Message card blank, reply card normal 250.00
f. Message card normal, reply card double impression, preprinted *825.00*
m. PM1 Message card detached 12.50 2.50
Preprinted 6.00
r. PR1 Reply card detached 12.50 2.50
Preprinted 6.00

PM3

PR3 pictures Sheridan.

1904, Mar, 31

UY4 PM3+PR3 1c +1c **black,** *buff,* unsevered 52.50 6.50
Preprinted 9.00
a. Message card normal, reply card blank 275.00
b. Message card printed on both sides, reply card blank *950.00*
c. Message card blank, reply card normal 275.00
d. Message card blank, reply card printed on both sides — 175.00
Preprinted 200.00
m. PM3 Message card detached 9.00 1.10
Preprinted 4.00
r. PR3 Reply card detached 9.00 1.10
Preprinted 4.00

PM4

PR4 pictures Martha Washington.

Double frame line around instructions

1910, Sept. 14

UY5 PM4+PR4 1c +1c **blue,** *bluish,* unsevered 160.00 25.00
Preprinted 40.00
a. Message card normal, reply card blank 325.00
m. PM4 Message card detached 15.00 3.75
Preprinted 9.00
r. PR4 Reply card detached 15.00 3.75
Preprinted 9.00

1911, Oct. 27

UY6 PM4+PR4 1c +1c **green,** *cream,* unsevered 160.00 25.00
Preprinted 60.00
a. Message card normal, reply card blank —
m. PM4 Message card detached 22.50 6.50
Preprinted 12.50
r. PR4 Reply card detached 22.50 6.50
Preprinted 12.50

Single frame line around instructions

1915, Sept. 18

UY7 PM4+PR4 1c +1c **green,** *cream,* unsevered 1.25 .50
Preprinted .60
a. 1c+1c **dark green,** *buff,* unsevered 1.25 .50
Preprinted .60
b. Message card normal, reply card blank —
m. PM4 Message card detached .30 .20
Preprinted .20
r. PR4 Reply card detached .30 .20
Preprinted .20
s. As "a," missing Reply indicia *1,850.*

See No. UY13.

PR5

PM5 pictures George Washington.

1918, Aug. 2

UY8 PM5+PR5 2c +2c **red,** *buff,* unsevered 82.50 40.00
Preprinted 30.00
m. PM5 Message card detached 20.00 7.50
Preprinted 10.00
r. PR5 Reply card detached 20.00 7.50
Preprinted 10.00

Same Surcharged

Fifteen canceling machine types

1920, Apr.

UY9 PM5+PR5 1c on 2c+1c on 2c **red,** *buff,* unsevered 20.00 11.00
Preprinted 10.00
a. Message card normal, reply card no surcharge 85.00 —
Preprinted —
b. Message card normal, reply card double surcharge 85.00 —
Preprinted —
c. Message card double surcharge, reply card normal 85.00 —
Preprinted —
d. Message card no surcharge, reply card normal 85.00 —
Preprinted —
e. Message card no surcharge, reply card double surcharge 85.00
m. PM5 Message card detached 5.00 4.00
Preprinted 3.00
r. PR5 Reply card detached 5.00 4.00
Preprinted 3.00

One press printed type

UY10 PM5+PR5 1c on 2c+1c on 2c **red,** *buff,* unsevered 325.00 200.00
Preprinted 150.00
a. Message card no surcharge, reply card normal — —
Preprinted —
b. Surcharge double on message card, reply card normal *950.00*
m. PM5 Message card detached 75.00 45.00
Preprinted 40.00
r. PR5 Reply card detached 75.00 45.00
Preprinted 40.00

Designs same as PM2 and PR2

1924, Mar. 18 **For International Use**

Size: 139x89mm

UY11 PM2+PR2 2c +2c **red,** *cream,* unsevered 2.00 *35.00*
Preprinted 1.50
m. PM2 Message card detached .50 *12.50*
Preprinted .40
r. PR2 Reply card detached .50 *12.50*
Preprinted .40

PM6

PR6 inscribed "REPLY CARD."

For International Use

1926, Feb. 1

UY12 PM6+PR6 3c +3c **red,** *buff,* unsevered 10.00 *25.00*
Preprinted 6.00
a. 3c +3c **red,** *yellow,* unsevered 10.00 *25.00*
Preprinted 6.00
First day cancel —
m. PM6 Message card detached 3.00 *6.00*
Preprinted 1.50
r. PR6 Reply card detached 3.00 *6.00*
Preprinted 1.50

Type of 1910

Single frame line around instructions

1951, Dec. 29

UY13 PM4+PR4 2c +2c **carmine,** *buff,* unsevered 1.25 *2.00*
Preprinted .65
First day cancel, Washington, D.C. 1.25
m. PM4 Message card detached .35 *1.00*
Preprinted .25
r. PR4 Reply card detached .35 *1.00*
Preprinted .25

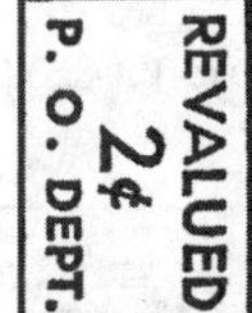

No. UY7a Surcharged Below Stamp in Green by Canceling Machine

1952, Jan. 1

UY14 PM4+PR4 2c on 1c+2c on 1c **green,** *buff,* unsevered 1.00 *2.00*
Preprinted .50
a. Surcharge vertical at left of stamps 12.50 7.50
Preprinted 7.50
b. Surcharge horizontal at left of stamps 15.00 12.50
Preprinted 8.50
c. Inverted surcharge horizontal at left of stamps 140.00 90.00
Preprinted 75.00
d. Message card normal, reply card no surcharge 40.00 40.00
Preprinted —
e. Message card normal, reply card double surcharge 40.00 40.00
Preprinted —
f. Message card no surcharge, reply card normal 40.00 40.00
Preprinted —
g. Message card double surcharge, reply card normal 40.00 40.00
Preprinted —
h. Both cards, dbl. surch. 50.00 50.00
Preprinted —
m. PM4 Message card detached .40 *1.00*
Preprinted .30
r. PR4 Reply card detached .40 *1.00*
Preprinted .30

No. UY7a with Similar Surcharge (horizontal) Typographed at Left of Stamp in Dark Green

1952

UY15 PM4+PR4 2c on 1c+2c on 1c **green,** *buff,* unsevered 110.00 45.00
Preprinted 35.00
a. Surcharge on message card only 150.00
m. PM4 Message card detached 17.50 10.00
Preprinted 9.00
r. PR4 Reply card detached 17.50 10.00
Preprinted 9.00

On No. UY15a, the surcharge also appears on blank side of card.

Liberty Type

For International Use

1956, Nov. 16

UY16 PC24 4c +4c **carmine & dark violet blue,** *buff,* unsevered 1.00 *75.00*
First day cancel, New York, N. Y. *(127,874)* 1.00
a. Message card printed on both halves 125.00 —
b. Reply card printed on both halves 125.00 —
c. Double scarlet on reply side 200.00
d. Double scarlet on message side 200.00
e. Double violet blue on message side —
f. Double violet blue on both sides —
g. Message side blank, reply side normal —
m. Message card detached .40 *45.00*
r. Reply card detached .40 *45.00*

Liberty Type of 1956

1958, July 31

UY17 PC25 3c +3c **purple,** *buff,* unsevered 3.00 *2.00*
First day cancel, Boise, Idaho *(136,768)* 1.00
a. One card blank 575.00

Both halves of No. UY17 are identical, inscribed as No. UX46, "This side of card is for address."

Lincoln Type

1962, Nov. 19

Precanceled with 3 printed red violet lines

UY18 PC26 4c +4c **red violet,** unsevered 3.00 *2.50*
First day cancel, Springfield, Ill. *(107,746)* 1.00
a. Tagged, *Mar. 7, 1967* 6.50 3.00
First day cancel, Dayton, OH 30.00

Both halves of No. UY18 are identical, inscribed as No. UX48, "This side of card is for address."

No. UY18a was printed with luminescent ink.

Map Type

1963, Aug. 30 **For International Use**

UY19 PC27 7c +7c **blue & red,** unsevered 2.50 *60.00*
First day cancel, New York 1.00
a. Message card normal, reply card blank 400.00 100.00
b. Message card blank, reply card normal 400.00 —
c. Additional message card on back of reply card 550.00
d. Double red on message side —
e. Double red & blue on message side —
m. Message card detached .85 *40.00*
r. Reply card detached .85 *40.00*

Message card inscribed "Postal Card With Paid Reply" in English and French. Reply card inscribed "Reply Postal Card Carte Postale Reponse".

Map Type of 1963

1967, Dec. 4 **For International Use**

UY20 PC27 8c +8c **blue & red,** unsevered 2.50 *60.00*
First day cancel, Washington, D.C. 1.00
m. Message card detached .85 *40.00*
r. Reply card detached .85 *40.00*
s. Reply imprint omitted —

Message card inscribed "Postal Card With Paid Reply" in English and French. Reply card inscribed "Reply Postal Card Carte Postale Résponse."

Tagged

Paid Reply Postal cards from No. UY21 onward are either tagged or printed with luminescent ink unless otherwise noted.

Lincoln Type

1968, Jan. 4

UY21 PC33 5c +5c **emerald,** unsevered 1.25 *2.00*
First day cancel, Hodgenville, Ky. 1.00
a. Printed on one side only —

Paul Revere Type

1971, May 15

Precanceled with 3 printed brown lines.

UY22 PC36 6c +6c **brown,** unsevered .85 *2.00*
First day cancel, Boston, Mass. 1.00

John Hanson Type

1972, Sept. 1

Precanceled with 3 printed blue lines.

UY23 PC41 6c +6c **blue,** unsevered 1.00 *2.00*
First day cancel, Baltimore, Md. 1.00

Samuel Adams Type

1973, Dec. 16

Precanceled with 3 printed orange lines

UY24 PC42 8c +8c **orange,** unsevered .75 *2.00*
First day cancel, Boston, Mass. *(105,369)* 1.00
a. Coarse paper 1.25 *2.00*
b. Printed on one side only, preprinted 750.00

Thomson, Witherspoon, Rodney, Hale & Hancock Types

1975-78

Precanceled with 3 printed emerald lines

UY25 PC44 7c +7c **emerald,** unsevered, *Sept. 14, 1975* .75 *5.00*
First day cancel, Bryn Mawr, Pa. 1.00

Precanceled with 3 printed yellow brown lines

UY26 PC45 9c +9c **yellow brown,** unsevered, *Nov. 10, 1975* .75 *2.00*
First day cancel, Princeton, N.J. 1.00

Precanceled with 3 printed blue lines

UY27 PC46 9c +9c **blue,** unsevered, *July 1, 1976* 1.00 *2.00*
First day cancel, Dover, Del. 1.00

Precanceled with 3 printed green lines

UY28 PC48 9c +9c **green,** unsevered, *Oct. 14, 1977* 1.00 *2.00*
First day cancel, Coventry, Conn. 1.00

Inscribed "U.S. Domestic Rate"

Precanceled with 3 printed brown orange lines

UY29 PC50 (10c +10c) **brown orange,** unsevered, *May 19, 1978* 9.00 *9.00*
First day cancel, Quincy, Mass. 1.75

Precanceled with 3 printed brown orange lines

UY30 PC50 10c +10c **brown orange,** unsevered, *June 20, 1978* 1.00 .25
First day cancel, Quincy, Mass. 1.00
a. One card "Domestic Rate," other "Postage 10¢" —
b. Printed on one side only *800.00*
Nos. UY25-UY30 (6) 13.50

Eagle Type

Inscribed "U. S. Domestic Rate"

1981, Mar. 15

Precanceled with 3 printed violet lines

UY31 PC63 (12c +12) **violet,** unsevered 1.00 *2.00*
First day cancel, Memphis, TN 1.00

Isaiah Thomas Type

1981, May 5

Precanceled with 3 printed lines

UY32 PC64 12c +12c **light blue,** unsevered 1.50 *2.00*
First day cancel, Worcester, MA 1.00
a. Small die on one side 3.00 —

Morris Type

Inscribed "U.S. Domestic Rate"

1981

Precanceled with 3 printed lines

UY33 PC67 (13c +13c) **buff,** *Oct. 11,* unsevered 1.50 *2.00*
First day cancel, Memphis, TN 1.25

Inscribed "U.S. Postage 13¢"

UY34 PC67 13c +13c **buff,** *Nov. 10,* unsevered .85 .20
First day cancel, Philadelphia, PA 1.25
a. Message card normal, reply card blank 200.00

Charles Carroll Type

Inscribed: U.S. Domestic Rate

1985

Precanceled with 3 printed lines

UY35 PC79 (14c +14c) **pale green,** *Feb. 1,* unsevered 2.50 *2.00*
First day cancel, New Carrollton, MD 1.25

Inscribed: USA

UY36 PC79 14c +14c **pale green,** *Mar. 6,* unsevered 1.00 *2.00*
First day cancel, Annapolis, MD 1.25
a. One card blank *425.00*

George Wythe Type

1985, June 20
Precanceled with 3 printed lines

UY37 PC81 14c +14c **bright apple green,** unsevered .75 *2.00*
First day cancel, Williamsburg, VA 1.25
a. One card blank, preprinted 225.00

Flag Type

1987, Sept. 1

UY38 PC90 14c +14c **black, blue & red,** unsevered .75 *2.00*
First day cancel, Washington, DC *(22,314)* 1.25

America the Beautiful Type

1988, July 11

UY39 PC93 15c +15c **multicolored,** unsevered .75 *1.00*
First day cancel, Buffalo, WY *(24,338)* 1.25

Flag Type

1991, Mar. 27

UY40 PC122 19c +19c **rose, ultramarine & black,** unsevered .80 *1.00*
First day cancel, Washington, DC *(25,562)* 1.25
a. Printed on one side only *750.00*

Red Barn Type

1995, Feb. 1 **Litho.**

UY41 PC147 20c +20c **multi,** unsevered .80 *1.25*
First day cancel, Williamsburg, PA 1.50
a. One card blank —

Block Island Lighthouse Type

1999, Nov. 10 **Litho.**

UY42 PC165 20c +20c **multi,** unsevered .85 *1.25*
First day cancel, Block Island, RI 1.50

White Barn Type

2001, Sept. 20 **Litho.**

UY43 PC173 21c +21c **multi,** unsevered .90 *1.25*
First day cancel, Washington, DC 1.50

Carlsbad Caverns Type

2002, June 7 **Litho.**

UY44 PC174 23c+23c **multi,** unsevered 1.00 *1.25*
First day cancel, Carlsbad, NM 1.50
First day cancel, any other city 1.50

AIR POST POSTAL CARDS

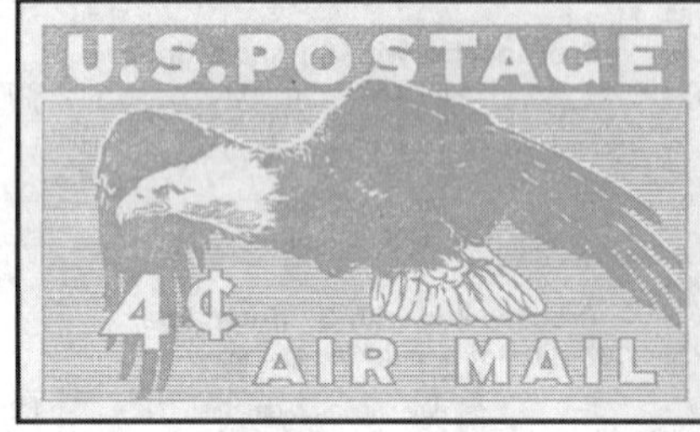

Eagle in Flight — APC1

1949, Jan.10 **Typo.**

UXC1 APC1 4c **red orange,** *buff* .50 *.75*
Preprinted .35
First day cancel, Washington, D.C. *(236,620)* 3.00
a. 4c **deep red,** *buff* *600.00* *400.00*

Expertization is recommended for No. UXC1a.

Type of Air Post Stamp, 1954

1958, July 31

UXC2 AP31 5c **red,** *buff* 1.75 .75
First day cancel, Wichita, Kans. *(156,474)* 1.00

Type of 1958 Redrawn

1960, June 18 **Lithographed (Offset)**

UXC3 AP31 5c **red,** *buff,* bicolored border 6.50 2.00
First day cancel, Minneapolis, Minn. *(228,500)* 1.50
a. Red omitted —

Size of stamp of No. UXC3: 18½x21mm; on No. UXC2: 19x22mm. White cloud around eagle enlarged and finer detail of design on No. UXC3. Inscription "AIR MAIL-POSTAL CARD" has been omitted and blue and red border added on No. UXC3.

Bald Eagle — APC2

1963, Feb. 15
Precanceled with 3 printed red lines

UXC4 APC2 6c **red,** bicolored border 1.10 *2.50*
First day cancel, Maitland, Fla. *(216,203)* 1.50

Emblem of Commerce Department's Travel Service — APC3

Issued at the Sixth International Philatelic Exhibition (SIPEX), Washington, D.C., May 21-30.

1966, May 27 **For International Use**

UXC5 APC3 11c **blue & red** .65 *20.00*
First day cancel, Washington, D.C. *(272,813)* 1.00

Four photographs at left on address side show: Mt. Rainier, New York skyline, Indian on horseback and Miami Beach. The card has blue and red border.
See Nos. UXC8, UXC11.

Virgin Islands and Territorial Flag — APC4

50th anniv. of the purchase of the Virgin Islands.

Designed by Burt Pringle

1967, Mar. 31 **Litho.**

UXC6 APC4 6c **multicolored** .75 *10.00*
First day cancel, Charlotte Amalie, V. I. *(346,906)* 1.00
a. Red & yellow omitted *1,700.*

No. UXC6 is known printed with an orange red ink instead of red. This is most easily seen in the two lines at the bottom of the card. Value is significantly greater thus.

Borah Peak, Lost River Range, Idaho, and Scout Emblem — APC5

12th Boy Scout World Jamboree, Farragut State Park, Idaho, Aug. 1-9.

Designed by Stevan Dohanos

1967, Aug. 4 **Litho.**

UXC7 APC5 6c **blue, yellow, black & red** .75 *10.00*
First day cancel, Farragut State Park, ID *(471,585)* 1.00
a. Blue omitted *11,000.*
b. Blue & black omitted *11,000.*
c. Red & yellow omitted —

Travel Service Type of 1966

Issued in connection with the American Air Mail Society Convention, Detroit, Mich.

1967, Sept. 8 **For International Use**

UXC8 APC3 13c **blue & red** 1.50 *25.00*
First day cancel, Detroit, Mich. *(178,189)* 1.00

Stylized Eagle — APC6

Designed by Muriel R. Chamberlain

1968, Mar. 1
Precanceled with 3 printed red lines

UXC9 APC6 8c **blue & red** .75 *2.50*
First day cancel, New York, N.Y. *(179,923)* 1.00
a. Tagged, *Mar. 19, 1969* 2.50 3.00
Tagged, first day cancel 15.00
b. **Blue & pale pink**, tagged *1,250.*

Tagged

Air Post Postal Cards from No. UXC10 onward are either tagged or printed with luminescent ink unless otherwise noted.

1971, May 15
Precanceled with 3 printed blue lines

UXC10 APC6 9c **red & blue** .50 *1.25*
First day cancel, Kitty Hawk, N.C. 1.00

Travel Service Type of 1966

1971, June 10
For International Use

UXC11 APC3 15c **blue & red** 1.75 *45.00*
First day cancel, New York, N.Y. 1.00

Grand Canyon APC7

Niagara Falls APC8

Tourism Year of the Americas 1972.

Designed by Melbourne Brindle

1972, June 29 **Litho.**

Size: 152½x108½mm

UXC12 APC7 9c **black,** *buff* (Statue of Liberty, Hawaii, Alaska, San Francisco on back) .75 —
First day cancel, any city 1.00
a. Red and blue lozenges omitted *2,250.*
b. Red lozenges omitted —
c. Tagging omitted —

For International Use

UXC13 APC8 15c **black,** *buff* (Mt. Vernon, Washington, D.C., Lincoln, Liberty Bell on back) .75 *75.00*
First day cancel, any city 1.00
a. Address side blank *400.00*
b. Double blue lozenges *6,000.*
c. Tagging omitted —
d. Red and blue lozenges omitted —

See note after No. UX63.

Stylized Eagle — APC9

Eagle Weather Vane — APC10

Designed by David G. Foote (11c) & Stevan Dohanos (18c)

1974, Jan. 4 **Litho.**

UXC14 APC9 11c **ultramarine & red** 1.10 *20.00*
First day cancel, State College, Pa. *(160,500)* 1.00

For International Use

UXC15 APC10 18c **multicolored** 1.10 *20.00*
First day cancel, Miami, Fla. *(132,114)* 1.00
a. Tagging omitted 350.00
b. **Black and yellow omitted** *7,000.*

All following issues are for international use.

Angel Gabriel Weather Vane — APC11

Designed by Stevan Dohanos

1975, Dec. 17 **Litho.**

UXC16 APC11 21c **multicolored** .85 *20.00*
First day cancel, Kitty Hawk, N.C. 1.00
a. Blue & red omitted *12,500.*
b. Tagging omitted 350.00

Curtiss (JN4H) Jenny — APC12

Designed by Keith Ferris

1978, Sept. 16 **Litho.**

UXC17 APC12 21c **multicolored** 1.00 *20.00*
First day cancel, San Diego, Cal. *(174,886)* 1.00

Gymnast APC13

22nd Olympic Games, Moscow, July 19-Aug. 3, 1980.

Designed by Robert M. Cunningham

1979, Dec. 1 **Litho.**

UXC18 APC13 21c **multicolored** 1.25 *20.00*
First day cancel, Fort Worth, Tex. 1.00

Pangborn, Herndon and Miss Veedol — APC14

First non-stop transpacific flight by Clyde Pangborn and Hugh Herndon, Jr., 50th anniv.

Designed by Ken Dallison

1981, Jan. 2 **Litho.**

UXC19 APC14 28c **multicolored** 1.00 *20.00*
First day cancel, Wenatchee, WA 1.25

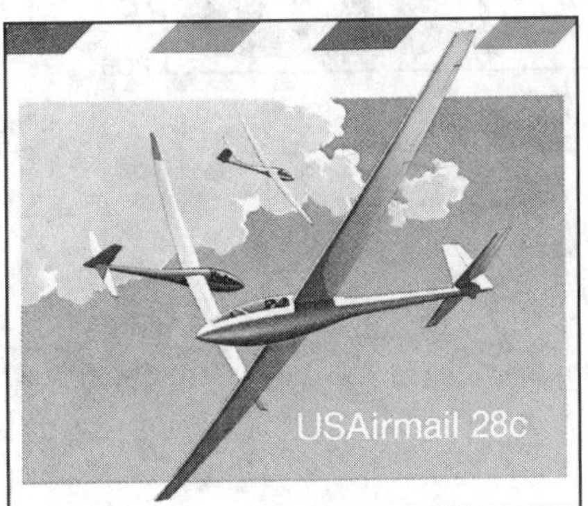

Gliders — APC15

Designed by Robert E. Cunningham

1982, Mar. 5 **Litho.**

UXC20 APC15 28c **magenta, yellow, blue & black** 1.00 *20.00*
First day cancel, Houston, TX *(106,932)* 1.25

Speedskater — APC16

Designed by Robert Peak

1983, Dec. 29 **Litho.**

UXC21 APC16 28c **multicolored** 1.00 *20.00*
First day cancel, Milwaukee, WI *(108,397)* 1.25

Martin M-130 China Clipper Seaplane — APC17

Designed by Chuck Hodgson

1985, Feb. 15 **Litho.**

UXC22 APC17 33c **multicolored** 1.00 *20.00*
First day cancel, San Francisco, CA 1.25

First day cancellation was applied to 269,229 of Nos. UXC22 and C115.

Chicago Skyline — APC18

AMERIPEX '86, Chicago, May 22-June 1.

Designed by Ray Ameijide

1986, Feb. 1 **Litho.**

UXC23 APC18 33c **multicolored** 1.00 *20.00*
First day cancel, Chicago, IL *(84,480)* 1.25

No. UXC23 was sold at Sudposta '87 by the U.S.P.S. with a show cachet.

DC-3 — APC19

Designed by Chuck Hodgson

1988, May 14 **Litho.**

UXC24 APC19 36c **multicolored** .85 *20.00*
First day cancel, San Diego, CA 1.25

No. UXC24 was sold at SYDPEX '88 by the USPS with a cachet for Australia's bicentennial and SYDPEX '88.

First day cancellations applied to 167,575 of Nos. UXC24 and C118.

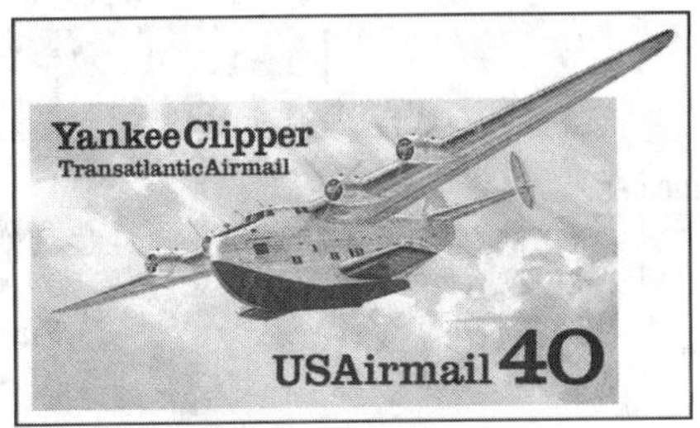

Yankee Clipper — APC20

Designed by Chuck Hodgson.

1991, June 28 **Litho.**

UXC25 APC20 40c **multicolored** .90 *20.00*
First day cancel, Flushing, NY *(24,865)* 1.25

Mt. Rainier — APC22

Designed by Ethel Kessler.

1999, May 15 **Litho.**

UXC27 APC22 55c **multicolored** 1.25 20.00
First day cancel, Denver, CO 1.50

First day cancellation was applied to 19,658 of Nos. UXC27 and UC65.

See note before No. C133.

Badlands Natl. Park, South Dakota — APC23

Designed by Ethel Kessler.

2001, Feb. 22 **Litho.**

UXC28 APC23 70c **multicolored** 1.40 10.00
First day cancel, Wall, SD 1.50

OFFICIAL POSTAL CARDS

PO1

1913, July

Size: 126x76mm

UZ1 PO1 1c **black** 550.00 350.00

All No. UZ1 cards have printed address and printed form on message side.

Used values are for contemporaneous usage without additional postage applied.

Great Seal — PO2

1983-85

UZ2 PO2 13c **blue,** *Jan. 12* .75 *80.00*
First day cancel, Washington, DC 1.00

UZ3 PO2 14c **blue,** *Feb. 26, 1985* .75 *70.00*
First day cancel, Washington, DC *(62,396)* 1.25

PO3

Designed by Bradbury Thompson

1988, June 10 **Litho.**

UZ4 PO3 15c **multicolored** .75 *80.00*
First day cancel, New York *(133,498)* 1.25

PO4

Designed by Bradbury Thompson

1991, May 24 **Litho.**

UZ5 PO4 19c **multicolored** .75 *80.00*
First day cancel, Seattle, WA *(23,097)* 1.25

PO5

1995, May 9 **Litho.**

UZ6 PO5 20c **multicolored** .75 *80.00*
First day cancel, Washington, DC 1.25

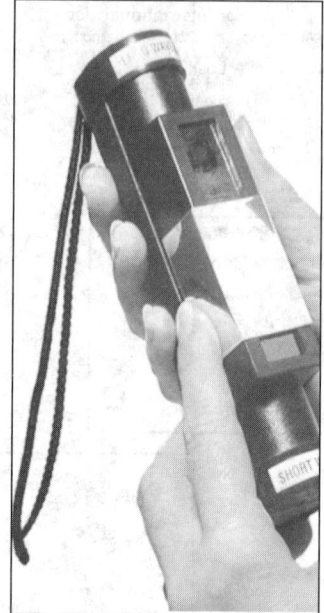

REVENUE STAMPS

The Commissioner of Internal Revenue advertised for bids for revenue stamps in August, 1862, and the contract was awarded to Butler & Carpenter of Philadelphia.

Nos. R1-R102 were used to pay taxes on documents and proprietary articles including playing cards. Until December 25, 1862, the law stated that a stamp could be used only for payment of the tax upon the particular instrument or article specified on its face. After that date, stamps, except the Proprietary, could be used indiscriminately.

Most stamps of the first issue appeared in the latter part of 1862 or early in 1863. The 5c and 10c Proprietary were issued in the fall of 1864, and the 6c Proprietary on April 13, 1871.

Plate numbers and imprints are usually found at the bottom of the plate on all denominations except 25c and $1 to $3.50. On these it is nearly always at the left of the plate. The imprint reads "Engraved by Butler & Carpenter, Philadelphia" or "Jos. R. Carpenter."

Plates were of various sizes: 1c and 2c, 210 subjects (14x15); 3c to 20c, 170 subjects (17x10); 25c to 30c, 102 subjects (17x6); 50c to 70c, 85 subjects (17x5); $1 to $1.90, 90 subjects (15x6); $2 to $10, 73 subjects (12x6); $15 to $50, 54 subjects (9x6); $200, 8 subjects (2x4). No. R132, one subject.

The paper varies, the first employed being thin, hard and brittle until September, 1869, from which time it acquired a softer texture and varied from medium to very thick. Early printings of some revenue stamps occur on paper which appears to have laid lines. Some are found on experimental silk paper, first employed about August, 1870.

Some of the stamps were in use eight years and were printed several times. Many color variations occurred, particularly if unstable pigments were used and the color was intended to be purple or violet, such as the 4c Proprietary, 30c and $2.50 stamps. Before 1868 dull colors predominate on these and the early red stamps. In later printings of the 4c Proprietary, 30c and $2.50 stamps, red predominates in the mixture and on the dollar values of red is brighter. The early $1.90 stamp is dull purple, imperforate or perforated. In a later printing, perforated only, the purple is darker.

In the first issue, canceling usually was done with pen and ink and all values quoted are for stamps canceled in that way. Handstamped cancellations as a rule sell for more than pen. Printed cancellations are scarce and command much higher prices. Herringbone, punched or other types of cancellation which break the surface of the paper adversely affect prices.

Many, but not all, of the pre-1898 revenue stamps exist unused with original gum. These are not valued in the listings, but they sell for more than used examples in the marketplace.

1862-72 revenue stamps from the first three issues were often used on large folded documents. As a result, multiples (blocks and strips of four or more) are not often found in sound condition. In addition, part perforate pairs of all but the most common varieties generally are off center. Catalogue values of the noted multiples are for items in fine condition or for very fine appearing examples with small faults. Examples of such multiples in a true very fine grade without any faults are scarce to rare and will sell for well above catalogue value.

Where a stamp is known in a given form or variety but insufficient information is available on which to base a value, its existence is indicated by a dash.

Part perforate stamps are understood to be imperforate horizontally unless otherwise stated.

Part perforate stamps with an asterisk (*) exist imperforate horizontally or vertically.

Part perforate PAIRS should be imperforate between the stamps as well as imperforate at opposite ends. See illustration **Type A** under "Information For Collectors-Perforations."

All imperforate or part perforate stamps listed are known in pairs or larger multiples. Certain unlisted varieties of this nature exist as singles and specialists believe them genuine. Exceptions are Nos. R13a, R22a and R60b, which have not been reported in multiples but are regarded as legitimate by most students.

Documentary revenue stamps were no longer required after December 31, 1967.

First Issue

George Washington

R1 R2

1862-71 **Engr.** ***Perf. 12***

				a. Imperf.	b. Part Perf.	Perforated c. Old Paper	d. Silk Paper
R1	R1	1c	**Express, red**	60.00	40.00*	1.25	100.00
			Pair	150.00	120.00	3.25	
			Block of 4	500.00	400.00	12.50	
			Dble. transfer			—	
			Short transfer, No. 156	—	—	85.00	
		e.	Vert. pair, imperf. btwn.			*200.00*	
R2	R1	1c	**Playing Cards, red**	1,200.	1,250.	160.00	
			Pair	*2,800.*	*2,800.*	350.00	
			Block of 4			825.00	
			Cracked plate	—		225.00	
R3	R1	1c	**Proprietary, red**	775.00	175.00*	.50	30.00
			Pair	*2,100.*	500.00	1.25	75.00
			Block of 4		—	3.25	
R4	R1	1c	**Telegraph, red**	450.00		12.00	
			Pair	1,250.		30.00	
			Block of 4			110.00	

Double transfer (T5)

No.			Description	Perforated a. Imperf.	b. Part Perf.	c. Old Paper	d. Silk Paper
R5	R2	2c	**Bank Check, blue**	1.00	1.75*	.25	
			Pair	17.50	9.00	.50	
			Block of 4	150.00	80.00	2.00	
			Double transfer (T5)	80.00	85.00	50.00	
			Cracked plate		22.50	10.00	
			Double impression			800.00	
		e.	Vert. pair, imperf. btwn.			400.00	
R6	R2	2c	**Bank Check, orange**		55.00*	.25	250.00
			Pair		—	.50	
			Block of 4			1.40	
			Double transfer (T5)			250.00	
			Vert. half used as 1c on document			—	
		e.	2c **orange,** *green*			475.00	

Double transfer (T7)

No.			Description	a. Imperf.	b. Part Perf.	c. Old Paper	d. Silk Paper
R7	R2	2c	**Certificate, blue**	12.50		30.00	
			Pair	45.00		75.00	
			Block of 4	180.00		240.00	
			Double transfer (T7)	300.00		300.00	
			Cracked plate			37.50	
R8	R2	2c	**Certificate, orange**			27.50	
			Pair			180.00	
			Block of 4			*825.00*	
			Double transfer (T7)			400.00	
R9	R2	2c	**Express, blue**	12.50	20.00*	.40	
			Pair	40.00	120.00	1.25	
			Block of 4	140.00	300.00	4.25	
			Dble. transfer	60.00		17.50	
			Cracked plate			20.00	
R10	R2	2c	**Express, orange**		*750.00*	8.50	100.00
			Pair			20.00	
			Block of 4			45.00	
			Dble. transfer			22.50	
R11	R2	2c	**Playing Cards, blue**		240.00	4.00	
			Pair		600.00	13.00	
			Block of 4			50.00	
			Cracked plate			30.00	
R12	R2	2c	**Playing Cards, orange**			42.50	
			Pair			*350.00*	

Double transfer (T13)

Double transfer (T13a)

No.			Description	a. Imperf.	b. Part Perf.	c. Old Paper	d. Silk Paper
R13	R2	2c	**Proprietary, blue**	500.	175.	.40	80.00
			Pair		400.	.90	
			Block of 4		*850.*	5.00	
			Double transfer (T13)			120.00	
			Complete double transfer (T13a)			180.00	
			Cracked plate			25.00	
			Horiz. half used as 1c on document			—	
		e.	2c **ultra**			200.00	
			Pair			500.00	
			Block of 4			—	
			Dble. transfer (T13)			—	
			Complete dble. transfer (T13a)			*700.00*	
R14	R2	2c	**Proprietary, orange**			40.00	
			Pair			275.00	
			Block of 4			—	
			Double transfer (T13)			200.00	
			Complete double transfer (T13a)			400.00	

Double transfer (T15)

Double transfer (T15a)

No.			Description	a. Imperf.	b. Part Perf.	c. Old Paper	d. Silk Paper
R15	R2	2c	**U. S. Internal Revenue, orange** ('64)	—		.20	.25
			Pair	—	—	.20	1.00
			Block of 4			.40	
			Double transfer (T15)			60.00	
			Double transfer (T15a)			45.00	
			Dble. transfer			12.00	
			Triple transfer			40.00	
			Cracked plate			10.00	
			Half used as 1c on document			—	
		e.	2c **orange,** *green*			650.00	

R3

No.			Description	a. Imperf.	b. Part Perf.	c. Old Paper	d. Silk Paper
R16	R3	3c	**Foreign Exchange, green**		300.00	4.50	80.00
			Pair		*1,275.*	10.50	
			Block of 4			75.00	
			Dble. transfer			—	
R17	R3	3c	**Playing Cards, green** ('63)	*15,000.*		150.00	
			Pair	*40,000.*		350.00	
			Block of 4			*900.00*	
R18	R3	3c	**Proprietary, green**		350.00	4.25	55.00
			Pair		*1,000.*	10.50	125.00
			Block of 4		—	35.00	
			Dble. transfer			9.00	
			Double impression			*1,000.*	
			Cracked plate			—	
		e.	Printed on both sides			*3,500.*	
R19	R3	3c	**Telegraph, green**	75.00	27.50	2.75	
			Pair	350.00	82.50	8.75	
			Block of 4	900.00	300.00	80.00	
R20	R3	4c	**Inland Exchange, brown** ('63)			1.75	80.00
			Pair			5.25	
			Block of 4			22.50	
			Double transfer at top			7.50	
R21	R3	4c	**Playing Cards, slate** ('63)			600.00	
			Pair			*1,250.*	
			Block of 4			*2,600.*	
R22	R3	4c	**Proprietary, purple**	—	250.00	6.50	110.00
			Pair		600.00	16.00	
			Block of 4		1,900.	55.00	
			Double transfer at top			17.50	
			Double transfer at bottom			12.50	

There are shade and color variations of Nos. R21-R22. See foreword of Revenue Stamps section.

No.			Description	a. Imperf.	b. Part Perf.	c. Old Paper	d. Silk Paper
R23	R3	5c	**Agreement, red**			.30	1.50
			Pair			.50	3.75
			Block of 4			1.25	17.50
			Dble. transfer in numerals			25.00	
R24	R3	5c	**Certificate, red**	2.50	13.00	.30	.35
			Pair	35.00	95.00	.55	1.00
			Block of 4	200.00	300.00	1.10	6.00
			Double transfer in upper label			10.00	
			Dble. transfer throughout			70.00	
			Triple transfer (No. 121)			35.00	
			Impression of #R3 on back			*2,750.*	
R25	R3	5c	**Express, red**	5.00	7.00*	.30	
			Pair	20.00	80.00	.70	
			Block of 4	150.00	225.00	2.25	
			Double transfer			5.00	
R26	R3	5c	**Foreign Exchange, red**		—	.30	325.00
			Pair		—	.85	
			Block of 4			15.00	
			Double transfer at top			20.00	
			Double transfer at bottom			10.00	
R27	R3	5c	**Inland Exchange, red**	7.50	5.00	.25	17.50
			Pair	37.50	26.00	.50	40.00
			Block of 4	110.00	80.00	2.00	
			Double transfer at top	77.50	47.50	27.50	
			Cracked plate	95.00	90.00	32.50	
R28	R3	5c	**Playing Cards, red** ('63)			25.00	
			Pair			55.00	
			Block of 4			110.00	
			Double impression			*750.00*	
R29	R3	5c	**Proprietary, red** ('64)			25.00	160.00
			Pair			55.00	
			Block of 4			150.00	
R30	R3	6c	**Inland Exchange, orange** ('63)			1.75	100.00

No.	Type	Denom.	Description	a. Imperf.	b. Part Perf.	c. Old Paper	d. Silk Paper
			Pair			18.50	
			Block of 4			100.00	
R31	R3	6c	**Proprietary, orange** ('71)			*1,700.*	

Nearly all copies of No. R31 are faulty and poorly centered. The Catalogue value is for a fine centered copy with minor faults which do not detract from its appearance.

No.	Type	Denom.	Description	a. Imperf.	b. Part Perf.	c. Old Paper	d. Silk Paper
R32	R3	10c	**Bill of Lading, blue**	47.50	325.00	1.00	
			Pair	175.00	750.00	2.40	
			Block of 4	525.00		7.50	
			Dble. transfer (#33 & 143)			—	
			Half used as 5c on document			*200.00*	
R33	R3	10c	**Certificate, blue**	150.00	400.00*	.25	5.00
			Pair	400.00	900.00	.55	
			Block of 4	*950.00*	—	1.90	
			Dble. transfer			7.50	
			Cracked plate			15.00	
			Half used as 5c on document			*200.00*	
R34	R3	10c	**Contract, blue**		225.00	.50	2.25
			Pair		650.00	1.25	6.00
			Block of 4		—	4.75	60.00
			Complete double transfer			70.00	
			Vertical half used as 5c on document			*200.00*	
e.			10c **ultra**		425.00	1.00	
			Pair			2.50	
			Block of 4			17.50	
R35	R3	10c	**Foreign Exchange, blue**			10.00	—
			Pair			25.00	
			Block of 4			85.00	
e.			10c **ultra**			12.50	
			Pair			37.50	
			Block of 4			95.00	
R36	R3	10c	**Inland Exchange, blue**	300.00	4.00*	.20	45.00
			Pair	700.00	15.00	.35	100.00
			Block of 4	*2,000.*	80.00	1.50	—
			Half used as 5c on document			*200.00*	
R37	R3	10c	**Power of Attorney, blue**	600.00	25.00	.75	
			Pair	1,500.	100.00	1.75	
			Block of 4	*3,500.*	300.00	8.00	
			Half used as 5c on document			*200.00*	
R38	R3	10c	**Proprietary, blue** ('64)			17.50	
			Pair			40.00	
			Block of 4			110.00	
R39	R3	15c	**Foreign Exchange, brown** ('63)			15.00	
			Pair			50.00	
			Block of 4			250.00	
			Double impression			*500.00*	
R40	R3	15c	**Inland Exchange, brown**	37.50	12.50	1.25	
			Pair	190.00	50.00	2.85	
			Block of 4	750.00	300.00	10.25	
			Dble. transfer			6.25	
			Cracked plate	60.00	37.50	14.00	
			Double impression		*1,200.*	550.00	
R41	R3	20c	**Foreign Exchange, red**	60.00		40.00	
			Pair	200.00		125.00	
			Block of 4	700.00		325.00	
R42	R3	20c	**Inland Exchange, red**	15.00	17.50	.35	—
			Pair	50.00	60.00	.80	
			Block of 4	200.00	200.00	14.00	
			Half used as 10c on document			*200.00*	

R4

R5

No.	Type	Denom.	Description	a. Imperf.	b. Part Perf.	Perforated c. Old Paper	d. Silk Paper
R43	R4	25c	**Bond, red**	200.00	6.00	2.50	
			Pair	500.00	60.00	6.50	
			Block of 4		300.00	60.00	
R44	R4	25c	**Certificate, red**	10.00	6.00*	.25	2.75
			Pair	50.00	40.00	.55	8.25
			Block of 4	400.00	200.00	4.00	27.50
			Double transfer, top or bottom			2.00	
			Triple transfer			—	
e.			Printed on both sides			*4,500*	
f.			Impression of No. R48 on back			—	
R45	R4	25c	**Entry of Goods, red**	17.50	80.00*	.75	40.00
			Pair	65.00	*700.00*	40.00	
			Block of 4	450.00		92.50	
			Top frame line double	72.50	105.00	11.00	
R46	R4	25c	**Insurance, red**	10.00	10.00	.25	4.50
			Pair	42.50	25.00	.65	11.00
			Block of 4	*600.00*	210.00	5.50	
			Double impression			*500.00*	
			Cracked plate			17.50	
R47	R4	25c	**Life Insurance, red**	35.00	400.00	6.50	
			Pair	125.00	1,000.	50.00	
			Block of 4	500.00		240.00	
R48	R4	25c	**Power of Attorney, red**	7.50	27.50	.30	
			Pair	50.00	75.00	.70	
			Block of 4	450.00	*475.00*	6.50	
			Dble. transfer			1.10	
			Bottom frame line double			5.50	

No.	Type	Denom.	Description	a. Imperf.	b. Part Perf.	Perforated c. Old Paper	d. Silk Paper
R49	R4	25c	**Protest, red**	30.00	500.00	6.75	
			Pair	150.00	1,200.	29.00	
			Block of 4	650.00		115.00	
R50	R4	25c	**Warehouse Receipt, red**	47.50	400.00	30.00	
			Pair	200.00	825.00	95.00	
			Block of 4	*1,000.*		325.00	
R51	R4	30c	**Foreign Exchange, lilac**	90.00	1,250.	52.50	—
			Pair	500.00	*3,000.*	225.00	
			Block of 4	*3,500.*		—	
			Dble. transfer			100.00	
			Top frame line double			—	
R52	R4	30c	**Inland Exchange, lilac**	60.00	70.00	3.50	—
			Pair	300.00	210.00	35.00	
			Block of 4	1,000.	—	140.00	
			Dble. transfer			30.00	

There are shade and color variations of Nos. R51-R52. See foreword of "Revenues" section.

No.	Design	Denom.	Description	a. Imperf.	b. Part Perf.	c. Old Paper (Perforated)	d. Silk Paper (Perforated)
R53	R4	40c	**Inland Exchange, brown**	800.00	7.00	3.50	—
			Pair	*1,700.*	30.00	8.50	
			Block of 4		210.00	140.00	
			Dble. transfer		50.00	30.00	
		f.	Double impression			—	
R54	R5	50c	**Conveyance, blue**	17.00	1.60	.20	3.00
			Pair	90.00	40.00	.25	6.50
			Block of 4	475.00	150.00	2.50	
			Dble. transfer			6.00	
			Cracked plate			15.00	
		e.	50c **ultra**			.25	—
			Pair			1.00	
			Block of 4			10.00	
R55	R5	50c	**Entry of Goods, blue**		12.00	.40	60.00
			Pair		250.00	1.60	160.00
			Block of 4		550.00	25.00	
			Dble. transfer			5.00	
			Cracked plate			20.00	
R56	R5	50c	**Foreign Exchange, blue**	55.00	75.00	6.50	
			Pair	140.00	400.00	42.50	
			Block of 4			140.00	
			Double impression			*500.00*	
			Double transfer at left			11.00	
			Half used as 25c on document			*200.00*	
R57	R5	50c	**Lease, blue**	25.00	100.00	8.50	
			Pair	200.00	400.00	67.50	
			Block of 4	*900.00*	900.00	225.00	
R58	R5	50c	**Life Insurance, blue**	40.00	60.00	1.00	
			Pair	160.00		7.50	
			Block of 4	750.00		45.00	
			Dble. transfer	47.50		11.00	
			Double impression			*800.00*	

Cracked Plate (C59)

No.	Design	Denom.	Description	a. Imperf	b. Part Perf.	c. Old Paper (Perforated)	d. Silk Paper (Perforated)
R59	R5	50c	**Mortgage, blue**	17.00	2.50	.50	—
			Pair	60.00	150.00	1.25	
			Block of 4	350.00	350.00	7.50	
			Cracked plate (C59)		37.50	12.50	
			Scratched plate, diagonal	35.00	25.00	12.50	
			Dble. transfer			3.50	
			Double impression	—		—	

Scratch is across three stamps. Value is for a single.

No.	Design	Denom.	Description	a. Imperf	b. Part Perf.	c. Old Paper	d. Silk Paper
R60	R5	50c	**Original Process, blue**	3.75	*600.00*	.60	1.60
			Pair	75.00		1.50	8.00
			Block of 4	*800.00*		6.00	—
			Double transfer at top			5.00	
			Double transfer at bottom			8.00	
			Scratched plate			10.00	
			Half used as 25c on document			—	
R61	R5	50c	**Passage Ticket, blue**	75.00	225.00	1.25	
			Pair	240.00	700.00	12.50	
			Block of 4	*900.00*		225.00	
R62	R5	50c	**Probate of Will, blue**	50.00	100.00	19.00	
			Pair	150.00	400.00	50.00	
			Block of 4	600.00	900.00	350.00	
R63	R5	50c	**Surety Bond, blue**	210.00	2.50	.30	
			Pair	*900.00*	15.00	1.75	
			Block of 4		100.00	10.00	
		e.	50c **ultra**			.75	
			Pair			5.50	
			Block of 4			55.00	
R64	R5	60c	**Inland Exchange, orange**	100.00	55.00	6.00	40.00
			Pair	275.00	125.00	14.00	95.00
			Block of 4	*750.00*	425.00	100.00	
R65	R5	70c	**Foreign Exchange, green**	450.00	125.00	11.00	65.00
			Pair	1,800.	600.00	40.00	150.00
			Block of 4		*1,325.*	250.00	
			Cracked plate		—	30.00	

Pairs and blocks of No. R65b are valued in the grade of fine.

R6

R7

No.	Design	Denom.	Description	a. Imperf	b. Part Perf.	c. Old Paper	d. Silk Paper
R66	R6	$1	**Conveyance, red**	17.50	500.00	24.00	100.00
			Pair	72.50	*1,875.*	65.00	
			Block of 4	500.00		160.00	
			Dble. transfer	35.00		37.50	
			Right frame line double	90.00		77.50	
			Top frame line double	—		60.00	
R67	R6	$1	**Entry of Goods, red**	37.50		1.90	80.00
			Pair	125.00		5.75	
			Block of 4	425.00		55.00	
R68	R6	$1	**Foreign Exchange, red**	80.00		.60	75.00
			Pair	225.00		1.50	
			Block of 4	*1,475.*		11.00	
			Dble. transfer			5.50	
			Left frame line double	180.00		19.00	
			Diagonal half used as 50c on document				*200.00*
R69	R6	$1	**Inland Exchange, red**	15.00	375.00*	.45	3.00
			Pair	72.50	*3,500.*	1.80	9.00
			Block of 4	725.00	—	9.50	35.00
			Double transfer at bottom			4.25	
			Double transfer of top shields	100.00		21.00	
R70	R6	$1	**Lease, red**	35.00		3.00	
			Pair	110.00		10.00	
			Block of 4	450.00		80.00	
			Double transfer at bottom	50.00		11.00	
			Cracked plate			26.00	
			Half used as 50c on document			—	
R71	R6	$1	**Life Insurance, red**	175.00		6.50	—
			Pair	425.00		16.50	
			Block of 4	*1,000.*		60.00	

			Right frame line double	275.00		20.00	
R72	R6	$1	**Manifest, red**	42.50		35.00	
			Pair	120.00		85.00	
			Block of 4	350.00		210.00	
R73	R6	$1	**Mortgage, red**	25.00		175.00	
			Pair	85.00		385.00	
			Block of 4	550.00		825.00	
			Double transfer at left	—		230.00	
			Bottom frame line double	60.00		350.00	
R74	R6	$1	**Passage Ticket, red**	275.00		275.00	
			Pair	600.00		600.00	
			Block of 4	*1,325.*		1,550.	
R75	R6	$1	**Power of Attorney, red**	90.00		2.10	
			Pair	225.00		5.50	
			Block of 4	500.00		26.00	
			Dble. transfer			9.50	
			Recut			11.50	
R76	R6	$1	**Probate of Will, red**	90.00		45.00	
			Pair	225.00		125.00	
			Block of 4	*800.00*		325.00	
			Right frame line double	160.00		72.50	
R77	R7	$1.30	**Foreign Exchange, orange** ('63)	*5,000.*		70.00	
			Pair			180.00	
			Block of 4			—	

Double transfer (T78)

R78	R7	$1.50	**Inland Exchange, blue**	27.50		4.50	
			Pair	125.00		65.00	
			Block of 4	375.00		375.00	
			Double transfer (T78)			12.50	
R79	R7	$1.60	**Foreign Exchange, green** ('63)	1,000.		120.00	
			Pair	*4,000.*		375.00	
R80	R7	$1.90	**Foreign Exchange, purple** ('63)	*7,000.*		100.00	—
			Pair			300.00	
			Block of 4			700.00	

There are many shade and color variations of No. R80. See foreword of "Revenues" section.

R8

R81	R8	$2	**Conveyance, red**	160.00	1,500.	2.75	27.50
			Pair	350.00	*5,500.*	10.00	65.00
			Block of 4	850.00		65.00	190.00
			Cracked plate			32.50	
			Half used as $1 on document			—	
R82	R8	$2	**Mortgage, red**	120.00		4.50	55.00
			Pair	250.00		10.50	125.00
			Block of 4	600.00		60.00	
			Dble. transfer			12.50	
			Half used as $1 on document			—	
R83	R8	$2	**Probate of Will, red** ('63)	*5,000.*		60.00	
			Pair	*11,000.*		150.00	
			Block of 4			350.00	
			Dble. transfer			75.00	
			Horiz. half used as $1 on document			*250.00*	
R84	R8	$2.50	**Inland Exchange, purple** ('63)	5,500.		11.00	25.00
			Pair	*12,000.*		30.00	65.00
			Block of 4			325.00	425.00
			Double impression			*1,400.*	

There are many shade and color variations of Nos. R84c and R84d. See foreword of "Revenues" section.

R85	R8	$3	**Charter Party, green**	175.00		6.50	110.00
			Pair	400.00		65.00	275.00
			Block of 4	2,000.		250.00	
			Double transfer at top			—	
			Double transfer at bottom			12.00	
			Half used as $1.50 on document			—	
	e.		Printed on both sides			*2,300.*	
	g.		Impression of No. RS208 on back			*4,000.*	
R86	R8	$3	**Manifest, green**	140.00		40.00	
			Pair	300.00		100.00	
			Block of 4	*2,000.*		275.00	
			Dble. transfer			210.00	
R87	R8	$3.50	**Inland Exchange, blue** ('63)	*5,500.*		60.00	
			Pair	*12,000.*		180.00	
			Block of 4			450.00	
	e.		Printed on both sides			*4,000.*	

R9

R10

				a. Imperf	b. Part Perf.	Perforated c. Old Paper	d. Silk Paper
R88	R9	$5	**Charter Party, red**	250.00		6.00	75.00
			Pair	575.00		65.00	
			Block of 4	*1,250.*		200.00	
			Right frame line double	275.00		60.00	
			Top frame line double	275.00		60.00	
R89	R9	$5	**Conveyance, red**	40.00		8.50	100.00
			Pair	140.00		21.00	250.00
			Block of 4	*650.00*		110.00	
R90	R9	$5	**Manifest, red**	150.00		90.00	
			Pair	375.00		250.00	
			Block of 4	*1,100.*		550.00	
			Left frame line double	190.00		150.00	
R91	R9	$5	**Mortgage, red**	125.00		20.00	
			Pair	550.00		87.50	
			Block of 4	—		—	
R92	R9	$5	**Probate of Will, red**	575.00		20.00	
			Pair	1,250.		100.00	
			Block of 4	*3,000.*		375.00	
R93	R9	$10	**Charter Party, green**	650.00		32.50	
			Pair	*1,500.*		95.00	
			Block of 4	—		450.00	
			Dble. transfer			85.00	
R94	R9	$10	**Conveyance, green**	125.00		70.00	
			Pair	275.00		175.00	
			Block of 4	650.00		700.00	
			Double transfer at top	140.00		95.00	
			Right frame line double			150.00	
R95	R9	$10	**Mortgage, green**	450.00		30.00	
			Pair	1,000.		120.00	
			Block of 4	*2,500.*		—	
			Top frame line double	475.00		52.50	
R96	R9	$10	**Probate of Will, green**	1,400.		30.00	
			Pair	*3,500.*		87.50	
			Block of 4			400.00	
			Double transfer at top			57.50	
R97	R10	$15	**Mortgage, blue**	1,800.		175.00	
			Pair	*4,000.*		450.00	
			Block of 4	*8,500.*		*2,750.*	
		e.	$15 **ultra**			250.00	
			Pair			500.00	
			Block of 4			—	
			Milky blue			250.00	
R98	R10	$20	**Conveyance, orange**	140.00		90.00	160.00
			Pair	400.00		225.00	350.00
			Block of 4	950.00		625.00	
R99	R10	$20	**Probate of Will, orange**	1,600.		1,600.	
			Pair	*3,500.*		*3,500.*	
			Block of 4	*7,250.*		*7,500.*	
R100	R10	$25	**Mortgage, red** ('63)	1,000.		150.00	200.00
			Pair	*2,400.*		360.00	
			Block of 4	*6,500.*		*1,250.*	
		e.	Horiz. pair, imperf. between			*1,100.*	
R101	R10	$50	**U.S. Internal Revenue, green** ('63)	200.00		125.00	
			Pair	450.00		275.00	
			Block of 4	1,500.		650.00	
			Cracked plate			160.00	
R102	R11	$200	**U.S. Internal Revenue, grn & red** ('64)	2,000.		750.00	
			Pair	*4,200.*		1,600.	
			Block of 4	*9,500.*		*3,750.*	

R11

DOCUMENTARY STAMPS

Second Issue

After release of the First Issue revenue stamps, the Bureau of Internal Revenue received many reports of fraudulent cleaning and re-use. The Bureau ordered a Second Issue with new designs and colors, using a patented "chameleon" paper which is usually violet or pinkish, with silk fibers.

While designs are different from those of the first issue, stamp sizes and make up of the plates are the same as for corresponding denominations.

George Washington
R12 R12a

Engraved and printed by Jos. R. Carpenter, Philadelphia.

Various Frames and Numeral Arrangements

1871 ***Perf. 12***

R103	R12	1c	**blue & black**	55.00
			Cut cancel	20.00
			Pair	150.00
			Block of 4	375.00
a.			Inverted center	*1,500.*
			Pair	*3,100.*
			Block of 4	—
R104	R12	2c	**blue & black**	2.00
			Cut cancel	.20
			Pair	6.25
			Block of 4	40.00
a.			Inverted center	*6,000.*
R105	R12a	3c	**blue & black**	25.00
			Cut cancel	10.00
			Pair	60.00
			Block of 4	210.00
R106	R12a	4c	**blue & black**	75.00
			Cut cancel	30.00
			Pair	160.00
			Block of 4	375.00
			Horiz. or vert. half used as 2c on document	*250.00*
R107	R12a	5c	**blue & black**	1.50
			Cut cancel	.50
			Pair	6.00
			Block of 4	22.50
a.			Inverted center	*2,750.*
R108	R12a	6c	**blue & black**	125.00
			Cut cancel	55.00
			Pair	325.00
			Block of 4	850.00
R109	R12a	10c	**blue & black**	1.00
			Cut cancel	.20
			Pair	4.00
			Block of 4	12.00
			Double impression of center	—
			Half used as 5c on document	*250.00*
a.			Inverted center	*2,000.*
			Pair	*4,500.*

No. R109a is valued in the grade of fine.

R110	R12a	15c	**blue & black**	35.00
			Cut cancel	17.50
			Pair	90.00
			Block of 4	190.00
R111	R12a	20c	**blue & black**	6.00
			Cut cancel	2.75
			Pair	22.50
			Block of 4	87.50
a.			Inverted center	*8,000.*
			Pair	—

Nos. R109a and R111a are valued in the grade of fine.

R13

R13a

R112	R13 25c **blue & black**		.60
	Cut cancel		.20
	Pair		1.90
	Block of 4		9.50
	Double transfer, position 57		15.00
a.	Inverted center		*10,000.*
b.	Sewing machine perf.		110.00
	Pair		300.00
	Block of 4		1,150.
c.	Perf. 8		275.00
R113	R13 30c **blue & black**		90.00
	Cut cancel		42.50
	Pair		200.00
	Block of 4		525.00
R114	R13 40c **blue & black**		75.00
	Cut cancel		22.50
	Pair		175.00
R115	R13a 50c **blue & black**		.60
	Cut cancel		.20
	Pair		1.70
	Block of 4		8.75
	Double transfer		25.00
a.	Sewing machine perf.		75.00
	Pair		200.00
	Block of 4		*900.00*
b.	Inverted center		900.00
	Pair		*2,000.*
	Inverted center, punch cancellation		275.00
	Pair		650.00
R116	R13a 60c **blue & black**		125.00
	Cut cancel		50.00
	Pair		275.00
	Foreign entry, design of 70c		175.00
R117	R13a 70c **blue & black**		50.00
	Cut cancel		17.50
	Pair		100.00
a.	Inverted center		*3,500.*
	Cut cancel		*2,000.*

R13b

R13c

R118	R13b $1 **blue & black**		4.00
	Cut cancel		1.60
	Pair		17.50
	Block of 4		50.00
a.	Inverted center		*5,000.*
	Punch cancel		*900.00*
R119	R13b $1.30 **blue & black**		400.00
	Cut cancel		150.00
	Pair		850.00
R120	R13b $1.50 **blue & black**		16.00
	Cut cancel		8.00
	Pair		65.00
	Block of 4		—
	Foreign entry, design of $1		350.00
a.	Sewing machine perf.		450.00
	Pair		—
R121	R13b $1.60 **blue & black**		450.00
	Cut cancel		300.00
	Pair		1,000.
R122	R13b $1.90 **blue & black**		300.00
	Cut cancel		110.00
	Pair		700.00
	Block of 4		—
R123	R13c $2 **blue & black**		15.00
	Cut cancel		7.50
	Pair		55.00
	Block of 4		180.00
	Double transfer		20.00
R124	R13c $2.50 **blue & black**		30.00
	Cut cancel		16.00
	Pair		95.00
	Block of 4		750.00
R125	R13c $3 **blue & black**		35.00
	Cut cancel		17.50
	Pair		110.00
	Block of 4		550.00
	Double transfer		—
R126	R13c $3.50 **blue & black**		250.00
	Cut cancel		100.00
	Pair		600.00

R13d

R13e

R127	R13d $5 **blue & black**		22.50
	Cut cancel		9.00
	Pair		70.00
	Block of 4		275.00
a.	Inverted center		*3,250.*
	Punch cancel		*950.00*
R128	R13d $10 **blue & black**		175.00
	Cut cancel		70.00
	Pair		400.00
	Block of 4		*875.00*
R129	R13e $20 **blue & black**		400.00
	Cut cancel		260.00
	Pair		850.00
R130	R13e $25 **blue & black**		500.00
	Cut cancel		260.00
	Pair		1,100.
R131	R13e $50 **blue & black**		500.00
	Cut cancel		275.00
	Pair		1,100.

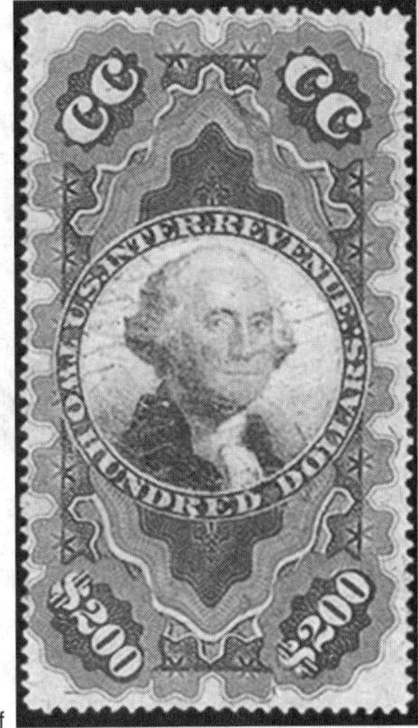
R13f

R132	R13f $200 **red, blue & black**		*5,000.*
	Cut cancel		*2,800.*

Printed in sheets of one.

R13g

R133	R13g	$500 **red orange, green & black**	*13,000.*

Printed in sheets of one.

Value for No. R133 is for a very fine appearing example with a light circular cut cancel or with minor flaws.

Inverted Centers: Fraudulently produced inverted centers exist, some excellently made.

Confusion resulting from the fact that all 1c through $50 denominations of the Second Issue were uniform in color, caused the ordering of a new printing with values in distinctive colors.

Plates used were those of the preceding issue.

Third Issue

Engraved and printed by Jos. R. Carpenter, Philadelphia.

Various Frames and Numeral Arrangements.

Violet "Chameleon" Paper with Silk Fibers.

1871-72 *Perf. 12*

R134	R12	1c **claret & black** ('72)	35.00
		Cut cancel	19.00
		Pair	90.00
		Block of 4	310.00
R135	R12	2c **orange & black**	.20
		Cut cancel	.20
		Pair	.40
		Block of 4	1.25
		Double transfer	—
		Double impression of frame	*1,500.*
		Frame printed on both sides	*1,600.*
		Double impression of center	*150.00*
a.		2c vermilion & black (error)	*650.00*
b.		Inverted center	375.00
		Pair	*1,100.*
		Block of 4	—
c.		Imperf., pair	—
R136	R12a	4c **brown & black** ('72)	50.00
		Cut cancel	21.00
		Pair	150.00
R137	R12a	5c **orange & black**	.25
		Cut cancel	.20
		Pair	.50
		Block of 4	1.10
a.		Inverted center	*3,500.*
		"Block" of 3	—

No. R137a is valued in the grade of fine.

R138	R12a	6c **orange & black** ('72)	60.00
		Cut cancel	25.00
		Pair	160.00
		Block of 4	450.00
R139	R12a	15c **brown & black** ('72)	12.50
		Cut cancel	5.00
		Pair	27.50
		Block of 4	130.00
a.		Inverted center	*15,000.*
		Pair	—
R140	R13	30c **orange & black** ('72)	17.50
		Cut cancel	7.50
		Pair	65.00
		Block of 4	250.00
		Double transfer	—
a.		Inverted center	*3,000.*
		Cut cancel	*1,750.*
R141	R13	40c **brown & black** ('72)	45.00
		Cut cancel	20.00
		Pair	120.00
		Block of 4	325.00
R142	R13a	60c **orange & black** ('72)	85.00
		Cut cancel	32.50
		Pair	250.00
		Block of 4	550.00
		Foreign entry, design of 70c	125.00
R143	R13a	70c **green & black** ('72)	60.00
		Cut cancel	22.50
		Pair	175.00
		Block of 4	450.00
R144	R13b	$1 **green & black** ('72)	1.35
		Cut cancel	.55
		Pair	8.50
		Block of 4	50.00
a.		Inverted center	*5,500.*
R145	R13c	$2 **vermilion & black** ('72)	22.50
		Cut cancel	14.00
		Pair	55.00
		Block of 4	155.00
		Double transfer	30.00
R146	R13c	$2.50 **claret & black** ('72)	40.00
		Cut cancel	22.00
		Pair	95.00
		Block of 4	210.00
a.		Inverted center	*25,000.*
R147	R13c	$3 **green & black** ('72)	40.00
		Cut cancel	21.00
		Pair	95.00
		Block of 4	250.00
		Double transfer	—
R148	R13d	$5 **vermilion & black** ('72)	27.50
		Cut cancel	12.50
		Pair	70.00
		Block of 4	150.00
R149	R13d	$10 **green & black** ('72)	125.00
		Cut cancel	45.00
		Pair	250.00
		Block of 4	850.00
R150	R13e	$20 **orange & black** ('72)	525.00
		Cut cancel	260.00
		Pair	1,250.
		Block of 4	*2,850.*
a.		$20 vermilion & black (error)	700.00

(See note on Inverted Centers after No. R133.)

1874 *Perf. 12*

R151	R12	2c **orange & black,** *green*	.20
		Cut cancel	.20
		Pair	.40
		Block of 4	.90
a.		Inverted center	400.00

Liberty — R14

1875-78

			Silk Paper a. Perf.	Wmkd. 191R b. Perf.	c. Roul. 6
R152	R14	2c **blue,** *blue*	.25	.25	32.50
		Pair	.50	.50	125.00
		"L" shaped strip of 3			600.00
		Block of 4	1.40	1.50	
		Double transfer	5.50	5.50	
d.		Vert. pair, imperf. horiz.	525.00		
e.		Imperf., pair		*275.00*	

The watermarked paper came into use in 1878.

Nos. 279, 267a, 267, 279Bg, 279B, 272-274 Overprinted in Red or Blue:

I.R. a - Rectangular Periods

I.R. a - Square Periods

I.R. b

I.R. b - Small Period

Overprint "a" exists in two (or possibly more) settings, with upright rectangular periods or with changed leg of "R" and square periods, both illustrated. Overprint "b" has 4 stamps with small period in each pane of 100 (pos. 41, 46, 91 & 96).

1898 **Wmk. 191** *Perf. 12*

R153	A87 (a)	1c **green,** red overprint	3.75	2.75
		Block of 4	22.50	12.00
		P# strip of 3, Impt.	27.50	
		P# block of 6, Impt.	75.00	
R154	A87 (b)	1c **green,** red overprint	.25	.25
		Block of 4	1.25	1.10
		P# strip of 3, Impt.	10.50	
		P# block of 6, Impt.	57.50	
a.		Overprint inverted	21.00	18.00
		Block of 4	110.00	—
		P# strip of 3, Impt.	115.00	
		P# block of 6, Impt.	275.00	
b.		Overprint on back instead of face, inverted	—	
c.		Pair, one without overprint	—	
R155	A88 (b)	2c **pink,** type III, blue overprint, *July 1, 1898*	.25	.25
		Block of 4	1.25	1.10
		P# strip of 3, Impt.	11.50	
		P# block of 6, Impt.	55.00	
		Dot in "S" of "CENTS"	1.10	
		P# strip of 3, Impt.	18.00	
b.		2c **carmine,** type III, blue overprint, *July 1, 1898*	.30	.25
		Block of 4	1.40	1.10
		P# strip of 3, Impt.	13.00	
		P# block of 6, Impt.	57.50	
		Dot in "S" of "CENTS"	1.40	
		P# strip of 3, Impt.	24.00	
c.		As No. R155, overprint inverted, *July 1898*	3.75	3.00
		Block of 4	16.00	13.00
		P# strip of 3, Impt.	42.50	
		P# block of 6, Impt.	110.00	
d.		Vertical pair, one without overprint	*750.00*	
e.		Horiz. pair, one without overprint	—	
f.		As No. R155, overprint on back instead of face, inverted	—	

NOTE: Old No. R155 is now Nos. R155b, R155Ag; old No. R155a is Nos. R155c, R155Ah; old No. R155b is Nos. R155d, R155e; old No. R155c is No. R155f.

R155A	A88 (b)	2c **pink,** type IV, blue overprint *July 1, 1898*	.25	.25
		Block of 4	1.25	1.10
		P# strip of 3, Impt.	10.50	
		P# block of 6, Impt.	52.50	
g.		2c **carmine,** type IV, blue overprint, *July 1, 1898*	.25	.25
		Block of 4	1.40	1.10
		P# strip of 3, Impt.	11.50	
		P# block of 6, Impt.	55.00	
h.		As No. R155A, overprint inverted, *July 1898*	2.75	2.00
		Block of 4	13.00	9.25
		P# strip of 3, Impt.	32.50	
		P# block of 6, Impt.	77.50	

Handstamped Type "b" in Magenta

R156	A93	8c *violet brown*		*4,500.*
R157	A94	10c *dark green*		*3,750.*
		Block of 6	—	
R158	A95	15c *dark blue*		*6,000.*

Nos. R156-R158 were emergency provisionals, privately prepared, not officially issued.

Privately Prepared Provisionals

No. 285 Overprinted in Red

I. R.

L. H. C.

1898 **Wmk. 191** *Perf. 12*

R158A	A100	1c **dark yellow green**	*12,500.*	*10,000.*

Same Overprinted "I.R./P.I.D. & Son" in Red

R158B	A100	1c **dark yellow green**	*25,000.*	*22,500.*

No. R158B is valued with small faults as each of the four recorded examples have faults.

Nos. R158A-R158B were overprinted with federal government permission by the Purvis Printing Co. upon order of Capt. L. H. Chapman of the Chapman Steamboat Line. Both the Chapman Line and P. I. Daprix & Son operated freight-carrying steamboats on the Erie Canal. The Chapman Line touched at Syracuse, Utica, Little Falls and Fort Plain; the Daprix boat ran between Utica and Rome. Overprintings of 250 of each stamp were made.

Dr. Kilmer & Co. provisional overprints are listed under "Private Die Medicine Stamps," Nos. RS307-RS315.

Newspaper Stamp No. PR121 Surcharged in Red

1898 *Perf. 12*

R159	N18	$5 **dark blue,** surcharge reading down	450.00	175.00
		Block of 4	1,950.	900.00
		P# strip of 3, Impt.	—	

R160 N18 $5 **dark blue,** surcharge reading up 110.00 97.50
Block of 4 450.00 *750.00*
P# strip of 3, Impt. 2,000.

Battleship — R15

There are two styles of rouletting for the proprietary and documentary stamps of the 1898 issue, an ordinary rouletting 5½ and one by which small rectangles of the paper are cut out, usually called hyphen-hole perforation 7. Several stamps are known with an apparent roulette 14 caused by slippage of a hyphen-hole 7 rouletting wheel.

1898 **Wmk. 191R**

Rouletted 5½, Hyphen Hole Perf 7

				Roul. 5½ Unused	Roul. 5½ Used	*p.* Hyphen Hole Perf. 7 Unused	*p.* Hyphen Hole Perf. 7 Used
R161	R15	½c	**orange**	2.75	*10.50*		
			Block of 4	12.50	*110.00*		
R162	R15	½c	**dark gray**	.30	.25		
			Block of 4	1.60	1.10		
			Double transfer		7.75		
a.			Vert. pair, imperf. horiz.	77.50			
R163	R15	1c	pale blue	.20	.20	.30	.25
			Block of 4	.40	.25	1.60	1.50
			Double transfer	10.00			
a.			Vert. pair, imperf. horiz.	8.00			
b.			Imperf., pair	*400.00*			
R164	R15	2c	**carmine rose**	.30	.30	.35	.25
			Block of 4	1.50	1.50	2.75	1.10
			Double transfer	1.10	.30		
a.			Vert. pair, imperf. horiz.	77.50			
b.			Imperf., pair	200.00			
c.			Horiz. pair, imperf. vert.	—			
R165	R15	3c	**dark blue**	2.10	.25	21.00	1.10
			Block of 4	9.75	1.25	95.00	5.00
			Double transfer	—			
R166	R15	4c	**pale rose**	1.40	.25	7.75	1.60
			Block of 4	6.25	1.25	40.00	7.75
a.			Vert. pair, imperf. horiz.	140.00			
R167	R15	5c	**lilac**	.55	.25	7.75	.25
			Block of 4	2.75	1.25	40.00	1.40
a.			Pair, imperf. horiz. or vert.	225.00	160.00		
b.			Horiz. pair, imperf. between		*475.00*		
R168	R15	10c	**dark brown**	1.60	.25	5.25	.25
			Block of 4	9.50	1.25	26.00	1.25
a.			Vert. pair, imperf. horiz.	35.00	30.00		
b.			Horiz. pair, imperf. vert.	—			
R169	R15	25c	**purple brown**	2.75	.25	8.25	.30
			Block of 4	16.00	1.25	42.50	1.40
			Double transfer	—			
R170	R15	40c	**blue lilac**	125.00	1.10	175.00	37.50
			Block of 4	600.00	52.50	875.00	275.00
			Cut cancel		.35		12.50
R171	R15	50c	**slate violet**	18.00	.25	37.50	.80
			Block of 4	87.50	2.25	190.00	6.25
a.			Imperf., pair	*300.00*			
b.			Horiz. pair, imperf. between			—	*250.00*
R172	R15	80c	**bister**	100.00	.30	210.00	50.00
			Block of 4	500.00	32.50	1,050.	240.00
			Cut cancel		.20		20.00

Numerous double transfers exist on this issue.

Commerce — R16

				Roul. 5½ Unused	Roul. 5½ Used	*p.* Hyphen Hole Perf. 7 Unused	*p.* Hyphen Hole Perf. 7 Used
R173	R16	$1	**dark green**	12.50	.20	20.00	.65
			Block of 4	60.00	.50		3.25
			Cut cancel		.20		.30
a.			Vert. pair, imperf. horiz.	—			
b.			Horiz. pair, imperf. vert.	—	325.00		
R174	R16	$3	**dark brown**	30.00	1.00	42.50	2.40
			Block of 4	—	5.25		12.00
			Cut cancel		.25		.30
a.			Horiz. pair, imperf. vert.		450.00		
R175	R16	$5	**orange red**	45.00	1.90		
			Block of 4	—	9.50		
			Cut cancel		.25		
R176	R16	$10	**black**	100.00	3.25		
			Block of 4		16.00		
			Cut cancel		.55		
a.			Horiz. pair, imperf. vert.		—		
R177	R16	$30	**red**	325.00	125.00		
			Block of 4		525.00		
			Cut cancel		47.50		
R178	R16	$50	**gray brown**	150.00	5.75		
			Block of 4		29.00		
			Cut cancel		2.10		

John Marshall — R17

Alexander Hamilton — R18

James Madison — R19

Various Portraits in Various Frames, Each Inscribed "Series of 1898"

1899 ***Imperf.***

Without Gum

R179	R17	$100	**yellow brown & black**	190.00	32.50
			Cut cancel		21.00
			Vertical strip of 4	—	150.
			Vertical strip of 4, cut cancel		90.
R180	R18	$500	**carmine lake & black**	1,200.	800.00
			Cut cancel		300.
			Vertical strip of 4	—	2,250.
			Vertical strip of 4, cut cancel		1,000.
R181	R19	$1000	**green & black**	925.	325.
			Cut cancel		140.
			Vertical strip of 4		1,400.
			Vertical strip of 4, cut cancel		500.

1900 ***Hyphen-hole perf. 7***

Allegorical Figure of Commerce

R182	R16	$1	**carmine**	25.00	.55
			Cut cancel		.30
			Block of 4	92.50	2.50
			Block of 4, cut cancel		1.25
R183	R16	$3	**lake** (fugitive ink)	175.00	47.50
			Cut cancel		7.25
			Block of 4	700.00	275.00
			Block of 4, cut cancel		32.50

Warning: The ink on No. R183 will run in water.

Surcharged in Black with Open Numerals of Value

No.	Type	Description	Unused	Used
R184	R16	$1 **gray**	17.50	.30
		Cut cancel		.25
		Block of 4	—	1.25
		Block of 4, cut cancel		1.10
a.		Horiz. pair, imperf. vert	—	
b.		Surcharge omitted	125.00	
		Surcharge omitted, cut cancel		82.50
R185	R16	$2 **gray**	17.50	.25
		Cut cancel		.25
		Block of 4	67.50	1.25
		Block of 4, cut cancel		1.10
R186	R16	$3 **gray**	85.00	11.50
		Cut cancel		4.25
		Block of 4	—	50.00
		Block of 4, cut cancel		18.00
R187	R16	$5 **gray**	55.00	7.75
		Cut cancel		1.40
		Block of 4	—	35.00
		Block of 4, cut cancel		7.00
R188	R16	$10 **gray**	110.00	20.00
		Cut cancel		3.25
		Block of 4	—	92.50
		Block of 4, cut cancel		15.00
R189	R16	$50 **gray**	925.00	450.00
		Cut cancel		92.50
		Block of 4		2,000.
		Block of 4, cut cancel		375.00

Surcharged in Black with Ornamental Numerals of Value

Warning: If Nos. R190-R194 are soaked, the center part of the surcharged numeral may wash off. Before the surcharging, a square of soluble varnish was applied to the middle of some stamps.

1902

No.	Type	Description	Unused	Used
R190	R16	$1 **green**	25.00	2.75
		Cut cancel		.25
		Block of 4	—	12.00
		Block of 4, cut cancel		1.10
a.		Inverted surcharge		*190.00*
R191	R16	$2 **green**	25.00	1.40
		Cut cancel		.30
		Block of 4	—	6.75
		Block of 4, cut cancel		1.40
a.		Surcharged as No. R185	110.00	75.00
b.		Surcharged as No. R185, in violet	*1,350.*	—
c.		As "a," double surcharge	*140.00*	
d.		As "a," triple surcharge	—	
R192	R16	$5 **green**	175.00	26.00
		Cut cancel		4.25
		Block of 4	—	115.00
		Block of 4, cut cancel		19.00
a.		Surcharge omitted	190.00	
b.		Pair, one without surcharge	*400.00*	
R193	R16	$10 **green**	375.00	125.00
		Cut cancel		47.50
		Block of 4		550.00
		Block of 4, cut cancel		210.00
R194	R16	$50 **green**	975.00	800.00
		Cut cancel		250.00
		Block of 4	—	—
		Block of 4, cut cancel		1,050.

R20

Wmk. 190

Inscribed "Series of 1914"

1914 Wmk. 190 Offset Printing *Perf. 10*

No.	Type	Description	Unused	Used
R195	R20	½c **rose**	9.00	3.75
		Block of 4	40.00	16.00
R196	R20	1c **rose**	1.90	.30
		Block of 4	8.25	1.25
		Creased transfer, left side		—
R197	R20	2c **rose**	2.40	.30
		Block of 4	10.00	1.25
		Double impression	—	
R198	R20	3c **rose**	57.50	30.00
		Block of 4	275.00	40.00
R199	R20	4c **rose**	17.00	2.10
		Block of 4	82.50	9.50
		Recut U. L. corner	*300.00*	
R200	R20	5c **rose**	5.25	.30
		Block of 4	22.50	1.25
R201	R20	10c **rose**	4.25	.25
		Block of 4	18.00	.45
R202	R20	25c **rose**	37.50	.55
		Block of 4	175.00	2.25
R203	R20	40c **rose**	21.00	1.40
		Block of 4	90.00	6.50
R204	R20	50c **rose**	7.25	.25
		Block of 4	35.00	.55
R205	R20	80c **rose**	125.00	10.50
		Block of 4	550.00	47.50

Wmk. 191R

No.	Type	Description	Unused	Used
R206	R20	½c **rose**	1.60	.50
		Block of 4	7.00	2.50
R207	R20	1c **rose**	.25	.20
		Block of 4	.70	.25
		Double impression	*300.00*	—
R208	R20	2c **rose**	.30	.25
		Block of 4	1.25	1.10
R209	R20	3c **rose**	1.50	.25
		Block of 4	6.50	1.10
R210	R20	4c **rose**	3.75	.50
		Block of 4	19.00	2.25
R211	R20	5c **rose**	1.75	.30
		Block of 4	8.00	1.25
R212	R20	10c **rose**	.80	.20
		Block of 4	3.75	.35
R213	R20	25c **rose**	5.25	1.50
		Block of 4	24.00	7.00
R214	R20	40c **rose**	92.50	13.00
		Cut cancel		.45
		Block of 4	500.00	57.50
R215	R20	50c **rose**	18.00	.25
		Cut cancel		.20
		Block of 4	82.50	1.10
R216	R20	80c **rose**	140.00	21.00
		Cut cancel		1.00
		Block of 4	625.00	210.00

Liberty — R21

Inscribed "Series 1914"

Engr.

No.	Type	Description	Unused	Used
R217	R21	$1 **green**	40.00	.45
		Cut cancel		.25
		Block of 4	—	2.75
		Block of 4, cut cancel		1.10
a.		$1 yellow green	40.00	.25
R218	R21	$2 **carmine**	60.00	.75
		Cut cancel		.20
		Block of 4	275.00	3.25
		Block of 4, cut cancel		.25
R219	R21	$3 **purple**	75.00	3.75
		Cut cancel		.50
		Block of 4	350.00	13.50
		Block of 4, cut cancel		2.10
R220	R21	$5 **blue**	65.00	3.00
		Cut cancel		.55
		Block of 4	300.00	13.50
		Block of 4, cut cancel		2.75
R221	R21	$10 **orange**	150.00	5.25
		Cut cancel		.80
		Block of 4	—	24.00
		Block of 4, cut cancel		3.75
R222	R21	$30 **vermilion**	325.00	17.50
		Cut cancel		2.10
		Block of 4	—	62.50
		Block of 4, cut cancel		10.50
R223	R21	$50 **violet**	1,350.	800.00
		Cut cancel		350.00
		Block of 4		*3,500.*

Portrait Types of 1899 Inscribed "Series of 1915" (#R224), or "Series of 1914"

1914-15 Without Gum *Perf. 12*

No.	Type	Description	Unused	Used
R224	R19	$60 **brown** *(Lincoln)*	190.00	140.00
		Vertical strip of 4		—
		Cut cancel		67.50
		Vertical strip of 4, cut cancel		300.00
R225	R17	$100 **green** *(Washington)*	62.50	42.50
		Vertical strip of 4		190.00
		Cut cancel		16.00
		Vertical strip of 4, cut cancel		70.00
R226	R18	$500 **blue** *(Hamilton)*	—	600.00
		Cut cancel		250.00
		Vertical strip of 4, cut cancel		1,000.
R227	R19	$1000 **orange** *(Madison)*	—	525.00
		Cut cancel		275.00
		Vert. strip of 4, cut cancel		1,150.

The stamps of types R17, R18 and R19 in this and subsequent issues are issued in vertical strips of 4 which are imperforate at the top, bottom and right side; therefore, single copies are always imperforate on one or two sides.

R22

Two types of design R22 are known.
Type I - With dot in centers of periods before and after "CENTS."
Type II - Without such dots.
First printings were done by commercial companies, later printings by the Bureau of Engraving and Printing.

1917 Offset Printing Wmk. 191R *Perf. 11*

No.	Type	Description	Unused	Used
R228	R22	1c **carmine rose**	.25	.20
		Block of 4	1.10	.50
		Double impression	20.00	4.00
R229	R22	2c **carmine rose**	.20	.20
		Block of 4	.50	.35
		Double impression	20.00	5.00
R230	R22	3c **carmine rose**	1.40	.40
		Block of 4	6.25	1.75
		Double impression	—	—
R231	R22	4c **carmine rose**	.70	.25
		Block of 4	3.50	1.10
		Double impression		
R232	R22	5c **carmine rose**	.30	.20
		Block of 4	1.25	.35
R233	R22	8c **carmine rose**	2.10	.35
		Block of 4	9.50	1.60
R234	R22	10c **carmine rose**	.40	.20
		Block of 4	1.90	.35
		Double impression		5.25
R235	R22	20c **carmine rose**	.65	.25
		Block of 4	3.00	1.10
		Double impression		—
R236	R22	25c **carmine rose**	1.25	.25
		Block of 4	5.75	1.10
		Double impression	—	—
R237	R22	40c **carmine rose**	2.10	.45
		Block of 4	10.50	2.00
		Double impression	8.00	5.00
R238	R22	50c **carmine rose**	2.10	.20
		Block of 4	9.50	.35
		Double impression	—	—
R239	R22	80c **carmine rose**	5.25	.25
		Block of 4	24.00	1.10
		Double impression	40.00	—

No. R234 is known used provisionally as a playing card revenue stamp in August 1932. Value for this use, authenticated, $300.

Liberty Type of 1914 without "Series 1914"

1917-33 Engr.

No.	Type	Description	Unused	Used
R240	R21	$1 **yellow green**	6.75	.25
		Block of 4	32.50	1.10
a.		$1 green	6.75	.20
R241	R21	$2 **rose**	11.50	.20
		Block of 4	52.50	.35
R242	R21	$3 **violet**	37.50	1.10
		Cut cancel		.25
		Block of 4	—	4.50
R243	R21	$4 **yellow brown**('33)	26.00	1.90
		Cut cancel		.25
		Block of 4	—	8.75
		Block of 4, cut cancel		1.00
R244	R21	$5 **dark blue**	18.00	.35
		Cut cancel		.25
		Block of 4	—	1.50
R245	R21	$10 **orange**	32.50	1.25
		Cut cancel		.25
		Block of 4	—	6.25
		Block of 4, cut cancel		1.10

Portrait Types of 1899 without "Series of" and Date

1917 Without Gum *Perf. 12*

No.	Type	Description	Unused	Used
R246	R17	$30 **deep orange, green numerals** *(Grant)*	47.50	13.00
		Cut cancel		2.10
		Vertical strip of 4		—

Cut cancel 3.50
a. Imperf., pair *750.00*
b. Numerals in blue 72.50 1.90
Cut cancel 1.40
R247 R19 $60 **brown** *(Lincoln)* 57.50 7.25
Cut cancel .85
Vertical strip of 4 —
Cut cancel 5.00
R248 R17 $100 **green** *(Washington)* 35.00 1.10
Cut cancel .40
Vertical strip of 4 —
Cut cancel 2.50
R249 R18 $500 **blue, red numerals** *(Hamilton)* 325.00 37.50
Cut cancel 12.50
Vertical strip of 4 *150.00*
Cut cancel 57.50
Double transfer — 52.50
a. Numerals in orange 375.00 52.50
Double transfer —
R250 R19 $1000 **orange** *(Madison)* 150.00 12.50
Cut cancel 4.25
Vertical strip of 4 75.00
Cut cancel 17.50
a. Imperf., pair *1,250.*

See note after No. R227.

1928-29 Offset Printing *Perf. 10*

R251 R22 1c **carmine rose** 2.10 1.60
Block of 4 9.50 7.50
R252 R22 2c **carmine rose** .60 .30
Block of 4 3.00 1.50
R253 R22 4c **carmine rose** 7.00 4.00
Block of 4 32.50 19.00
R254 R22 5c **carmine rose** 1.60 .55
Block of 4 7.75 2.50
R255 R22 10c **carmine rose** 2.40 1.25
Block of 4 11.00 5.50
R256 R22 20c **carmine rose** 5.50 4.50
Block of 4 25.00 20.00
Double impression —

Engr.

R257 R21 $1 **green** 125.00 32.50
Block of 4 — —
Cut cancel 5.00
R258 R21 $2 **rose** 55.00 2.75
Block of 4 — 13.50
R259 R21 $10 **orange** 175.00 42.50
Block of 4 — —
Cut cancel 26.00

1929 Offset Printing *Perf. 11x10*

R260 R22 2c **carmine rose**('30) 3.00 2.75
Block of 4 13.00 12.00
Double impression — —
R261 R22 5c **carmine rose**('30) 2.00 1.90
Block of 4 10.00 8.75
R262 R22 10c **carmine rose** 9.25 6.75
Block of 4 45.00 32.50
R263 R22 20c **carmine rose** 15.00 8.25
Block of 4 70.00 42.50

Types of 1917-33 Overprinted in Black

SERIES 1940

1940 Wmk. 191R Offset Printing *Perf. 11*

R264 R22 1c **rose pink** 3.50 2.40
Cut cancel .35
Perf. initial .25
R265 R22 2c **rose pink** 3.00 1.90
Cut cancel .40
Perf. initial .35
R266 R22 3c **rose pink** 9.25 4.25
Cut cancel .75
Perf. initial .50
R267 R22 4c **rose pink** 4.00 .60
Cut cancel .20
Perf. initial .25
R268 R22 5c **rose pink** 4.25 .95
Cut cancel .30
Perf. initial .20
R269 R22 8c **rose pink** 17.50 13.00
Cut cancel 3.00
Perf. initial 2.00
R270 R22 10c **rose pink** 1.90 .65
Cut cancel .25
Perf. initial .25
R271 R22 20c **rose pink** 2.50 .70
Cut cancel .20
Perf. initial .25
R272 R22 25c **rose pink** 6.00 1.10
Cut cancel .25
Perf. initial .25
R273 R22 40c **rose pink** 6.00 .70
Cut cancel .25
Perf. initial .25
R274 R22 50c **rose pink** 6.75 .55
Cut cancel .25
Perf. initial .25
R275 R22 80c **rose pink** 12.50 .95
Cut cancel .25
Perf. initial .25

Engr.

R276 R21 $1 **green** 50.00 .85
Cut cancel .25
Perf. initial .25
R277 R21 $2 **rose** 50.00 1.10
Cut cancel .25
Perf. initial .25
R278 R21 $3 **violet** 70.00 26.00
Cut cancel 3.50
Perf. initial 1.60
R279 R21 $4 **yellow brown** 125.00 32.50
Cut cancel 5.50
Perf. initial 2.10
R280 R21 $5 **dark blue** 62.50 11.50
Cut cancel 1.25
Perf. initial .55
R281 R21 $10 **orange** 160.00 35.00
Cut cancel 2.75
Perf. initial .55

Types of 1917 Handstamped "Series 1940" like R264-R281 in Green (Nos. R282-R284, R286) or Violet (No. R285)

1940 Wmk. 191R *Perf. 12*

Without Gum

R282 R17 $30 **vermilion** 700.
Cut cancel 375.
Perf. initial 325.
a. With black 2-line handstamp in larger type *9,000.*
R283 R19 $60 **brown** 1,000.
Cut cancel 700.
Perf. initial 500.
a. As #R282a, cut cancel —
R284 R17 $100 **green** 2,250.
Cut cancel 1,150.
Perf. initial 800.
R285 R18 $500 **blue** 1,750.
Cut cancel 1,250.
Perf. initial 1,000.
Double transfer 1,850.
a. As #R282a *3,250. 3,250.*
Cut cancel *2,500.*
Double transfer — *2,650.*
b. Blue handstamp; double transfer —
R286 R19 $1000 **orange** 675.
Cut cancel 400.
Perf. initial 275.
a. Double overprint, cut cancel —

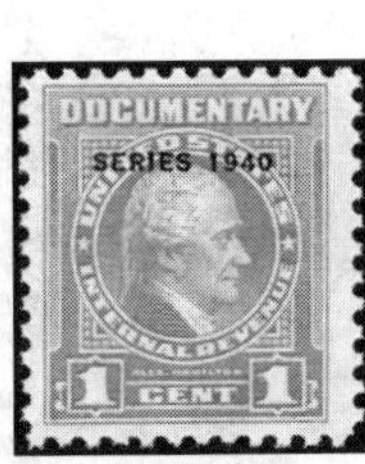

Alexander Hamilton — R23

Levi Woodbury — R24

Overprinted in Black SERIES 1940

Various Portraits: 2c, Oliver Wolcott, Jr. 3c, Samuel Dexter. 4c, Albert Gallatin. 5c. G. W. Campbell. 8c, Alexander Dallas. 10c, William H. Crawford. 20c, Richard Rush. 25c, S. D. Ingham. 40c. Louis McLane. 50c, William J. Duane. 80c, Roger B. Taney. $2, Thomas Ewing. $3, Walter Forward. $4, J. C. Spencer. $5, G. M. Bibb. $10, R. J. Walker. $20, William M. Meredith.

The "sensitive ink" varieties are in a bluish-purple overprint showing minute flecks of gold.

1940 Engr. Wmk. 191R *Perf. 11*

Plates of 400 subjects, issued in panes of 100

R288 R23 1c **carmine** 5.00 3.50
Cut cancel 1.40
Perf. initial .70
Sensitive ink 8.25 4.25
R289 R23 2c **carmine** 5.50 3.25
Cut cancel 1.40
Perf. initial .85
Sensitive ink 8.25 4.25
R290 R23 3c **carmine** 21.00 10.50
Cut cancel 3.50
Perf. initial 2.40
Sensitive ink 24.00 9.25
R291 R23 4c **carmine** 55.00 24.00
Cut cancel 4.75
Perf. initial 4.00
R292 R23 5c **carmine** 3.75 .70
Cut cancel .30
Perf. initial .25
R293 R23 8c **carmine** 80.00 52.50
Cut cancel 18.00
Perf. initial 13.00
R294 R23 10c **carmine** 3.00 .55
Cut cancel .25
Perf. initial .25
R295 R23 20c **carmine** 4.75 3.00
Cut cancel 1.10
Perf. initial .80
R296 R23 25c **carmine** 3.25 .60
Cut cancel .25
Perf. initial .25
R297 R23 40c **carmine** 55.00 24.00
Cut cancel 5.25
Perf. initial 2.40
R298 R23 50c **carmine** 5.50 .45
Cut cancel .25
Perf. initial .20
R299 R23 80c **carmine** 125.00 67.50
Cut cancel 26.00
Perf. initial 18.00

Plates of 200 subjects, issued in panes of 50

R300 R24 $1 **carmine** 37.50 .55
Cut cancel .20
Perf. initial .20
Sensitive ink 52.50 21.00
R301 R24 $2 **carmine** 52.50 .75
Cut cancel .20
Perf. initial .20
Sensitive ink 55.00 10.50
R302 R24 $3 **carmine** 150.00 87.50
Cut cancel 10.50
Perf. initial 7.25
Sensitive ink 150.00 87.50
R303 R24 $4 **carmine** 87.50 32.50
Cut cancel 6.25
Perf. initial 1.60
R304 R24 $5 **carmine** 52.50 2.00
Cut cancel .45
Perf. initial .25
R305 R24 $10 **carmine** 95.00 6.25
Cut cancel 1.00
Perf. initial .40
R305A R24 $20 **carmine** *2,000.* 900.00
Cut cancel 550.00
Perf. initial 425.00
b. Imperf., pair 600.00

Thomas Corwin — R25

Overprint: "SERIES 1940"

Various Frames and Portraits: $50, James Guthrie. $60, Howell Cobb. $100, P. F. Thomas. $500, J. A. Dix, $1,000, S. P. Chase.

Perf. 12

Plates of 16 subjects, issued in strips of 4

Without Gum

R306 R25 $30 **carmine** 140.00 42.50
Cut cancel 14.00
Perf. initial 10.50
R306A R25 $50 **carmine** — *3,250.*
Cut cancel 1,600.
Perf. initial 800.00
R307 R25 $60 **carmine** 275.00 62.50
Cut cancel 40.00
Perf. initial 21.00
a. Vert. pair, imperf. btwn. *2,500. 1,450.*
R308 R25 $100 **carmine** 200.00 67.50
Cut cancel 37.50
Perf. initial 13.00
R309 R25 $500 **carmine** — 3,250.
Cut cancel 1,600.
Perf. initial 800.00
R310 R25 $1000 **carmine** — 450.00
Cut cancel 210.00
Perf. initial 150.00

The $30 to $1,000 denominations in this and following similar issues, and the $2,500, $5,000 and $10,000 stamps of 1952-58 have straight edges on one or two sides. They were issued without gum through No. R723.

Nos. R288-R310 Overprinted: SERIES 1941

1941 Wmk. 191R *Perf. 11*

R311 R23 1c **carmine** 3.25 2.40
Cut cancel .75
Perf. initial .65
R312 R23 2c **carmine** 3.25 .95
Cut cancel .45
Perf. initial .40
R313 R23 3c **carmine** 8.25 3.75
Cut cancel 1.40
Perf. initial .90
R314 R23 4c **carmine** 5.50 1.40
Cut cancel .35
Perf. initial .25
R315 R23 5c **carmine** 1.10 .30
Cut cancel .25
Perf. initial .30
R316 R23 8c **carmine** 16.00 7.75
Cut cancel 3.25
Perf. initial 2.75
R317 R23 10c **carmine** 1.40 .25
Cut cancel .25
Perf. initial .25
R318 R23 20c **carmine** 3.25 .50
Cut cancel .25
Perf. initial .30

No.	Type	Description	Unused	Used
R319	R23	25c **carmine**	1.90	.55
		Cut cancel		.25
		Perf. initial		.25
R320	R23	40c **carmine**	12.00	2.75
		Cut cancel		1.10
		Perf. initial		.65
R321	R23	50c **carmine**	2.75	.25
		Cut cancel		.20
		Perf. initial		.20
R322	R23	80c **carmine**	60.00	10.50
		Cut cancel		3.00
		Perf. initial		2.40
R323	R24	$1 **carmine**	11.00	.25
		Cut cancel		.20
		Perf. initial		.20
R324	R24	$2 **carmine**	14.00	.45
		Cut cancel		.25
		Perf. initial		.25
R325	R24	$3 **carmine**	22.50	2.75
		Cut cancel		.35
		Perf. initial		.30
R326	R24	$4 **carmine**	37.50	17.50
		Cut cancel		.90
		Perf. initial		.70
R327	R24	$5 **carmine**	45.00	.95
		Cut cancel		.20
		Perf. initial		.20
R328	R24	$10 **carmine**	67.50	3.75
		Cut cancel		.30
		Perf. initial		.25
R329	R24	$20 **carmine**	800.00	275.00
		Cut cancel		67.50
		Perf. initial		42.50

Without Gum ***Perf. 12***

No.	Type	Description	Unused	Used
R330	R25	$30 **carmine**	140.00	42.50
		Cut cancel		16.00
		Perf. initial		10.50
R331	R25	$50 **carmine**	400.00	325.00
		Cut cancel		100.00
		Perf. initial		52.50
R332	R25	$60 **carmine**	190.00	62.50
		Cut cancel		26.00
		Perf. initial		13.00
R333	R25	$100 **carmine**	82.50	29.00
		Cut cancel		7.75
		Perf. initial		5.00
R334	R25	$500 **carmine**	—	240.00
		Cut cancel		140.00
		Perf. initial		55.00
R335	R25	$1000 **carmine**	—	125.00
		Cut cancel		40.00
		Perf. initial		29.00

Nos. R288-R310 Overprinted: SERIES 1942

1942 **Wmk. 191R** ***Perf. 11***

No.	Type	Description	Unused	Used
R336	R23	1c **carmine**	.55	.50
		Cut cancel		.25
		Perf. initial		.25
R337	R23	2c **carmine**	.50	.50
		Cut cancel		.25
		Perf. initial		.25
R338	R23	3c **carmine**	.75	.65
		Cut cancel		.30
		Perf. initial		.25
R339	R23	4c **carmine**	1.40	.95
		Cut cancel		.30
		Perf. initial		.25
R340	R23	5c **carmine**	.50	.25
		Cut cancel		.25
		Perf. initial		.20
R341	R23	8c **carmine**	6.00	4.50
		Cut cancel		1.25
		Perf. initial		1.10
R342	R23	10c **carmine**	1.40	.25
		Cut cancel		.25
		Perf. initial		.25
R343	R23	20c **carmine**	1.40	.50
		Cut cancel		.25
		Perf. initial		.25
R344	R23	25c **carmine**	2.25	.45
		Cut cancel		.25
		Perf. initial		.20
R345	R23	40c **carmine**	5.25	1.40
		Cut cancel		.55
		Perf. initial		.35
R346	R23	50c **carmine**	3.25	.25
		Cut cancel		.20
		Perf. initial		.20
R347	R23	80c **carmine**	19.00	10.50
		Cut cancel		3.00
		Perf. initial		2.00
R348	R24	$1 **carmine**	10.00	.25
		Cut cancel		.20
		Perf. initial		.20
R349	R24	$2 **carmine**	11.00	.25
		Cut cancel		.20
		Perf. initial		.20
R350	R24	$3 **carmine**	19.00	2.75
		Cut cancel		.35
		Perf. initial		.20
R351	R24	$4 **carmine**	27.50	5.25
		Cut cancel		.50
		Perf. initial		.30
R352	R24	$5 **carmine**	30.00	1.25
		Cut cancel		.25
		Perf. initial		.20
R353	R24	$10 **carmine**	72.50	2.75
		Cut cancel		.25
		Perf. initial		.20
R354	R24	$20 **carmine**	140.00	37.50
		Cut cancel		18.00
		Perf. initial		11.50

Without Gum ***Perf. 12***

No.	Type	Description	Unused	Used
R355	R25	$30 **carmine**	77.50	32.50
		Cut cancel		13.00
		Perf. initial		6.25
R356	R25	$50 **carmine**	1,400.	650.00
		Cut cancel		275.00
		Perf. initial		150.00
R357	R25	$60 **carmine**	1,600.	850.00
		Cut cancel		350.00
		Perf. initial		150.00
R358	R25	$100 **carmine**	175.00	120.00
		Cut cancel		52.50
		Perf. initial		40.00
R359	R25	$500 **carmine**	*1,600.*	225.00
		Cut cancel		140.00
		Perf. initial		77.50
R360	R25	$1000 **carmine**	—	110.00
		Cut cancel		52.50
		Perf. initial		42.50

Nos. R288-R310 Overprinted: SERIES 1943

1943 **Wmk. 191R** ***Perf. 11***

No.	Type	Description	Unused	Used
R361	R23	1c **carmine**	.65	.55
		Cut cancel		.25
		Perf. initial		.25
R362	R23	2c **carmine**	.50	.45
		Cut cancel		.25
		Perf. initial		.25
R363	R23	3c **carmine**	3.25	3.00
		Cut cancel		.55
		Perf. initial		.35
R364	R23	4c **carmine**	1.40	1.25
		Cut cancel		.35
		Perf. initial		.30
R365	R23	5c **carmine**	.55	.35
		Cut cancel		.25
		Perf. initial		.25
R366	R23	8c **carmine**	4.75	3.25
		Cut cancel		1.60
		Perf. initial		1.10
R367	R23	10c **carmine**	.75	.25
		Cut cancel		.25
		Perf. initial		.20
R368	R23	20c **carmine**	2.10	.70
		Cut cancel		.35
		Perf. initial		.30
R369	R23	25c **carmine**	2.25	.40
		Cut cancel		.25
		Perf. initial		.25
R370	R23	40c **carmine**	5.50	2.75
		Cut cancel		1.25
		Perf. initial		.65
R371	R23	50c **carmine**	1.60	.25
		Cut cancel		.20
		Perf. initial		.20
R372	R23	80c **carmine**	19.00	5.75
		Cut cancel		2.10
		Perf. initial		1.10
R373	R24	$1 **carmine**	6.75	.35
		Cut cancel		.25
		Perf. initial		.25
R374	R24	$2 **carmine**	12.50	.25
		Cut cancel		.25
		Perf. initial		.20
R375	R24	$3 **carmine**	22.50	2.40
		Cut cancel		.35
		Perf. initial		.20
R376	R24	$4 **carmine**	30.00	5.00
		Cut cancel		.45
		Perf. initial		.35
R377	R24	$5 **carmine**	40.00	.65
		Cut cancel		.35
		Perf. initial		.20
R378	R24	$10 **carmine**	60.00	4.25
		Cut cancel		1.60
		Perf. initial		.65
R379	R24	$20 **carmine**	125.00	29.00
		Cut cancel		5.25
		Perf. initial		3.25

Without Gum ***Perf. 12***

No.	Type	Description	Unused	Used
R380	R25	$30 **carmine**	60.00	19.00
		Cut cancel		5.00
		Perf. initial		4.50
R381	R25	$50 **carmine**	125.00	32.50
		Cut cancel		13.00
		Perf. initial		5.25
R382	R25	$60 **carmine**	275.00	87.50
		Cut cancel		35.00
		Perf. initial		11.50
R383	R25	$100 **carmine**	27.50	13.00
		Cut cancel		5.75
		Perf. initial		3.75
R384	R25	$500 **carmine**	—	210.00
		Cut cancel		110.00
		Perf. initial		87.50
R385	R25	$1000 **carmine**	—	175.00
		Cut cancel		52.50
		Perf. initial		40.00

Nos. R288-R310 Overprinted: **Series 1944**

1944 **Wmk. 191R** ***Perf. 11***

No.	Type	Description	Unused	Used
R386	R23	1c **carmine**	.45	.40
		Cut cancel		.25
		Perf. initial		.25
R387	R23	2c **carmine**	.50	.50
		Cut cancel		.25
		Perf. initial		.25
R388	R23	3c **carmine**	.55	.35
		Cut cancel		.25
		Perf. initial		.25
R389	R23	4c **carmine**	.60	.60
		Cut cancel		.25
		Perf. initial		.25
R390	R23	5c **carmine**	.35	.25
		Cut cancel		.25
		Perf. initial		.25
R391	R23	8c **carmine**	1.90	1.60
		Cut cancel		.45
		Perf. initial		.40
R392	R23	10c **carmine**	.45	.25
		Cut cancel		.20
		Perf. initial		.25
R393	R23	20c **carmine**	.80	.30
		Cut cancel		.20
		Perf. initial		.20
R394	R23	25c **carmine**	1.50	.25
		Cut cancel		.25
		Perf. initial		.25
R395	R23	40c **carmine**	3.00	.65
		Cut cancel		.35
		Perf. initial		.25
R396	R23	50c **carmine**	3.25	.25
		Cut cancel		.25
		Perf. initial		.25
R397	R23	80c **carmine**	17.00	4.25
		Cut cancel		1.40
		Perf. initial		.85
R398	R24	$1 **carmine**	8.25	.25
		Cut cancel		.25
		Perf. initial		.25
R399	R24	$2 **carmine**	11.00	.40
		Cut cancel		.30
		Perf. initial		.25
R400	R24	$3 **carmine**	17.50	2.10
		Cut cancel		.55
		Perf. initial		.25
R401	R24	$4 **carmine**	25.00	10.50
		Cut cancel		1.10
		Perf. initial		.95
R402	R24	$5 **carmine**	27.50	.40
		Cut cancel		.20
		Perf. initial		.30
R403	R24	$10 **carmine**	55.00	1.40
		Cut cancel		.30
		Perf. initial		.30
R404	R24	$20 **carmine**	110.00	16.00
		Cut cancel		3.25
		Perf. initial		2.10

Without Gum ***Perf. 12***

No.	Type	Description	Unused	Used
R405	R25	$30 **carmine**	82.50	29.00
		Cut cancel		7.75
		Perf. initial		6.00
R406	R25	$50 **carmine**	37.50	18.00
		Cut cancel		6.25
		Perf. initial		4.25
R407	R25	$60 **carmine**	225.00	62.50
		Cut cancel		26.00
		Perf. initial		9.25
R408	R25	$100 **carmine**	45.00	10.50
		Cut cancel		5.25
		Perf. initial		3.25
R409	R25	$500 **carmine**	—	*2,600.*
		Cut cancel		1,200.
		Perf. initial		775.00
R410	R25	$1000 **carmine**	—	275.00
		Cut cancel		110.00
		Perf. initial		57.50

Nos. R288-R310 Overprinted: **Series 1945**

1945 **Wmk. 191R** ***Perf. 11***

No.	Type	Description	Unused	Used
R411	R23	1c **carmine**	.30	.25
		Cut cancel		.25
		Perf. initial		.25
R412	R23	2c **carmine**	.30	.25
		Cut cancel		.25
		Perf. initial		.25
R413	R23	3c **carmine**	.55	.45
		Cut cancel		.25
		Perf. initial		.25
R414	R23	4c **carmine**	.35	.30
		Cut cancel		.30
		Perf. initial		.25
R415	R23	5c **carmine**	.40	.25
		Cut cancel		.20
		Perf. initial		.25
R416	R23	8c **carmine**	4.75	2.10
		Cut cancel		.65
		Perf. initial		.35
R417	R23	10c **carmine**	.90	.25
		Cut cancel		.25
		Perf. initial		.25
R418	R23	20c **carmine**	5.75	1.10
		Cut cancel		.45
		Perf. initial		.25
R419	R23	25c **carmine**	1.40	.30
		Cut cancel		.25
		Perf. initial		.20
R420	R23	40c **carmine**	6.00	1.10
		Cut cancel		.45
		Perf. initial		.40
R421	R23	50c **carmine**	3.00	.25
		Cut cancel		.20
		Perf. initial		.25
R422	R23	80c **carmine**	22.50	8.25
		Cut cancel		3.25
		Perf. initial		2.10
R423	R24	$1 **carmine**	9.50	.25
		Cut cancel		.20
		Perf. initial		.20
R424	R24	$2 **carmine**	10.00	.35
		Cut cancel		.20
		Perf. initial		.25
R425	R24	$3 **carmine**	19.00	2.40
		Cut cancel		.85
		Perf. initial		.65

No.	Type	Description	Unused	Used
R426	R24	$4 **carmine**	27.50	3.00
		Cut cancel		.55
		Perf. initial		.35
R427	R24	$5 **carmine**	27.50	.45
		Cut cancel		.25
		Perf. initial		.25
R428	R24	$10 **carmine**	55.00	1.50
		Cut cancel		.30
		Perf. initial		.25
R429	R24	$20 **carmine**	110.00	13.00
		Cut cancel		3.25
		Perf. initial		2.75

Without Gum *Perf. 12*

No.	Type	Description	Unused	Used
R430	R25	$30 **carmine**	140.00	35.00
		Cut cancel		8.75
		Perf. initial		5.75
R431	R25	$50 **carmine**	160.00	37.50
		Cut cancel		18.00
		Perf. initial		10.50
R432	R25	$60 **carmine**	275.00	57.50
		Cut cancel		29.00
		Perf. initial		13.00
R433	R25	$100 **carmine**	55.00	16.00
		Cut cancel		8.25
		Perf. initial		5.50
R434	R25	$500 **carmine**	325.00	190.00
		Cut cancel		72.50
		Perf. initial		52.50
R435	R25	$1000 **carmine**	225.00	92.50
		Cut cancel		29.00
		Perf. initial		17.50

Nos. R288-R310 Overprinted: **Series 1946**

1946 **Wmk. 191R** *Perf. 11*

No.	Type	Description	Unused	Used
R436	R23	1c **carmine**	.25	.30
		Cut cancel		.25
		Perf. initial		.25
R437	R23	2c **carmine**	.40	.35
		Cut cancel		.25
		Perf. initial		.25
R438	R23	3c **carmine**	.40	.35
		Cut cancel		.25
		Perf. initial		.25
R439	R23	4c **carmine**	.65	.55
		Cut cancel		.25
		Perf. initial		.25
R440	R23	5c **carmine**	.40	.25
		Cut cancel		.25
		Perf. initial		.25
R441	R23	8c **carmine**	1.40	1.25
		Cut cancel		.30
		Perf. initial		.25
R442	R23	10c **carmine**	.95	.25
		Cut cancel		.25
		Perf. initial		.25
R443	R23	20c **carmine**	1.40	.45
		Cut cancel		.25
		Perf. initial		.25
R444	R23	25c **carmine**	4.50	.30
		Cut cancel		.20
		Perf. initial		.20
R445	R23	40c **carmine**	2.75	.75
		Cut cancel		.35
		Perf. initial		.25
R446	R23	50c **carmine**	4.25	.25
		Cut cancel		.20
		Perf. initial		.20
R447	R23	80c **carmine**	14.00	4.50
		Cut cancel		.65
		Perf. initial		.50
R448	R24	$1 **carmine**	12.00	.25
		Cut cancel		.20
		Perf. initial		.20
R449	R24	$2 **carmine**	14.00	.25
		Cut cancel		.20
		Perf. initial		.20
R450	R24	$3 **carmine**	21.00	5.00
		Cut cancel		.90
		Perf. initial		.40
R451	R24	$4 **carmine**	27.50	10.50
		Cut cancel		2.10
		Perf. initial		1.00
R452	R24	$5 **carmine**	27.50	.45
		Cut cancel		.25
		Perf. initial		.25
R453	R24	$10 **carmine**	55.00	1.60
		Cut cancel		.35
		Perf. initial		.30
R454	R24	$20 **carmine**	110.00	13.00
		Cut cancel		2.75
		Perf. initial		1.60

Without Gum *Perf. 12*

No.	Type	Description	Unused	Used
R455	R25	$30 **carmine**	50.00	14.00
		Cut cancel		4.75
		Perf. initial		3.25
R456	R25	$50 **carmine**	37.50	10.50
		Cut cancel		4.25
		Perf. initial		2.75
R457	R25	$60 **carmine**	77.50	18.00
		Cut cancel		12.50
		Perf. initial		7.75
R458	R25	$100 **carmine**	55.00	10.00
		Cut cancel		3.75
		Perf. initial		3.00
R459	R25	$500 **carmine**	—	110.00
		Cut cancel		40.00
		Perf. initial		26.00
R460	R25	$1000 **carmine**	—	125.00
		Cut cancel		27.50
		Perf. initial		18.00

Nos. R288-R310 Overprinted: **Series 1947**

1947 **Wmk. 191R** *Perf. 11*

No.	Type	Description	Unused	Used
R461	R23	1c **carmine**	.75	.50
		Cut cancel		.25
		Perf. initial		.25
R462	R23	2c **carmine**	.60	.55
		Cut cancel		.25
		Perf. initial		.25
R463	R23	3c **carmine**	.75	.50
		Cut cancel		.25
		Perf. initial		.25
R464	R23	4c **carmine**	.75	.65
		Cut cancel		.25
		Perf. initial		.25
R465	R23	5c **carmine**	.40	.35
		Cut cancel		.25
		Perf. initial		.25
R466	R23	8c **carmine**	1.40	.75
		Cut cancel		.25
		Perf. initial		.25
R467	R23	10c **carmine**	1.25	.25
		Cut cancel		.25
		Perf. initial		.25
R468	R23	20c **carmine**	2.00	.50
		Cut cancel		.25
		Perf. initial		.25
R469	R23	25c **carmine**	2.60	.65
		Cut cancel		.25
		Perf. initial		.25
R470	R23	40c **carmine**	4.00	.95
		Cut cancel		.25
		Perf. initial		.25
R471	R23	50c **carmine**	3.25	.35
		Cut cancel		.25
		Perf. initial		.25
R472	R23	80c **carmine**	9.00	6.00
		Cut cancel		.65
		Perf. initial		.25
R473	R24	$1 **carmine**	6.75	.30
		Cut cancel		.25
		Perf. initial		.25
R474	R24	$2 **carmine**	10.50	.60
		Cut cancel		.25
		Perf. initial		.20
R475	R24	$3 **carmine**	13.50	5.00
		Cut cancel		1.10
		Perf. initial		.80
R476	R24	$4 **carmine**	15.00	4.50
		Cut cancel		.45
		Perf. initial		.35
R477	R24	$5 **carmine**	22.50	.55
		Cut cancel		.25
		Perf. initial		.25
R478	R24	$10 **carmine**	55.00	2.10
		Cut cancel		.65
		Perf. initial		.25
R479	R24	$20 **carmine**	82.50	10.50
		Cut cancel		1.10
		Perf. initial		.75

Without Gum *Perf. 12*

No.	Type	Description	Unused	Used
R480	R25	$30 **carmine**	110.00	21.00
		Cut cancel		5.25
		Perf. initial		2.75
R481	R25	$50 **carmine**	55.00	14.50
		Cut cancel		5.00
		Perf. initial		3.25
R482	R25	$60 **carmine**	140.00	42.50
		Cut cancel		21.00
		Perf. initial		9.25
R483	R25	$100 **carmine**	55.00	11.50
		Cut cancel		4.25
		Perf. initial		2.10
R484	R25	$500 **carmine**	—	150.00
		Cut cancel		62.50
		Perf. initial		37.50
R485	R25	$1000 **carmine**	—	82.50
		Cut cancel		35.00
		Perf. initial		24.00

Nos. R288-R310 Overprinted: **Series 1948**

1948 **Wmk. 191R** *Perf. 11*

No.	Type	Description	Unused	Used
R486	R23	1c **carmine**	.30	.30
		Cut cancel		.25
		Perf. initial		.25
R487	R23	2c **carmine**	.40	.40
		Cut cancel		.25
		Perf. initial		.25
R488	R23	3c **carmine**	.50	.35
		Cut cancel		.25
		Perf. initial		.25
R489	R23	4c **carmine**	.45	.35
		Cut cancel		.25
		Perf. initial		.25
R490	R23	5c **carmine**	.40	.25
		Cut cancel		.25
		Perf. initial		.20
R491	R23	8c **carmine**	.80	.35
		Cut cancel		.25
		Perf. initial		.25
R492	R23	10c **carmine**	.75	.25
		Cut cancel		.25
		Perf. initial		.20
R493	R23	20c **carmine**	1.90	.35
		Cut cancel		.25
		Perf. initial		.25
R494	R23	25c **carmine**	1.60	.25
		Cut cancel		.25
		Perf. initial		.25
R495	R23	40c **carmine**	4.75	1.75
		Cut cancel		.35
		Perf. initial		.25
R496	R23	50c **carmine**	2.25	.25
		Cut cancel		.20
		Perf. initial		.25
R497	R23	80c **carmine**	7.75	4.75
		Cut cancel		1.60
		Perf. initial		.55
R498	R24	$1 **carmine**	7.75	.25
		Cut cancel		.25
		Perf. initial		.25
R499	R24	$2 **carmine**	13.00	.30
		Cut cancel		.25
		Perf. initial		.25
R500	R24	$3 **carmine**	18.00	2.50
		Cut cancel		.40
		Perf. initial		.30
R501	R24	$4 **carmine**	26.00	2.75
		Cut cancel		.80
		Perf. initial		.55
R502	R24	$5 **carmine**	22.50	.50
		Cut cancel		.30
		Perf. initial		.25
R503	R24	$10 **carmine**	52.50	1.10
		Cut cancel		.30
		Perf. initial		.30
a.		Pair, one dated "1946"		—
R504	R24	$20 **carmine**	97.50	13.00
		Cut cancel		3.50
		Perf. initial		1.75

Without Gum *Perf. 12*

No.	Type	Description	Unused	Used
R505	R25	$30 **carmine**	72.50	24.00
		Cut cancel		6.25
		Perf. initial		3.75
R506	R25	$50 **carmine**	72.50	21.00
		Cut cancel		10.50
		Perf. initial		3.25
a.		Vert. pair, imperf. btwn.	—	
R507	R25	$60 **carmine**	140.00	37.50
		Cut cancel		18.00
		Perf. initial		7.25
a.		Vert. pair, imperf. btwn.	*1,150.*	
R508	R25	$100 **carmine**	55.00	10.00
		Cut cancel		5.00
		Perf. initial		3.25
a.		Vert. pair, imperf. btwn.	*875.00*	
R509	R25	$500 **carmine**	375.00	125.00
		Cut cancel		52.50
		Perf. initial		29.00
R510	R25	$1000 **carmine**	190.00	77.50
		Cut cancel		30.00
		Perf. initial		20.00

Nos. R288-R310 Overprinted: **Series 1949**

1949 **Wmk. 191R** *Perf. 11*

No.	Type	Description	Unused	Used
R511	R23	1c **carmine**	.30	.30
		Cut cancel		.25
		Perf. initial		.25
R512	R23	2c **carmine**	.60	.40
		Cut cancel		.25
		Perf. initial		.25
R513	R23	3c **carmine**	.45	.40
		Cut cancel		.25
		Perf. initial		.25
R514	R23	4c **carmine**	.65	.55
		Cut cancel		.25
		Perf. initial		.25
R515	R23	5c **carmine**	.40	.25
		Cut cancel		.25
		Perf. initial		.25
R516	R23	8c **carmine**	.75	.65
		Cut cancel		.25
		Perf. initial		.25
R517	R23	10c **carmine**	.45	.30
		Cut cancel		.25
		Perf. initial		.25
R518	R23	20c **carmine**	1.40	.65
		Cut cancel		.35
		Perf. initial		.30
R519	R23	25c **carmine**	2.00	.75
		Cut cancel		.30
		Perf. initial		.30
R520	R23	40c **carmine**	4.75	2.25
		Cut cancel		.45
		Perf. initial		.35
R521	R23	50c **carmine**	3.75	.35
		Cut cancel		.25
		Perf. initial		.25
R522	R23	80c **carmine**	11.00	5.00
		Cut cancel		1.60
		Perf. initial		.80
R523	R24	$1 **carmine**	9.25	.60
		Cut cancel		.25
		Perf. initial		.30
R524	R24	$2 **carmine**	12.00	2.10
		Cut cancel		.45
		Perf. initial		.30
R525	R24	$3 **carmine**	19.50	6.25
		Cut cancel		2.75
		Perf. initial		1.10
R526	R24	$4 **carmine**	22.50	6.25
		Cut cancel		3.00
		Perf. initial		1.60
R527	R24	$5 **carmine**	22.50	3.00
		Cut cancel		.65
		Perf. initial		.45
R528	R24	$10 **carmine**	55.00	3.75
		Cut cancel		1.10
		Perf. initial		.90
R529	R24	$20 **carmine**	110.00	11.50
		Cut cancel		2.10
		Perf. initial		1.40

Without Gum *Perf. 12*

No.	Type	Description	Unused	Used
R530	R25	$30 **carmine**	95.00	26.00
		Cut cancel		7.25
		Perf. initial		4.25

R531 R25 $50 **carmine**	110.00	42.50
Cut cancel		14.50
Perf. initial		7.50
R532 R25 $60 **carmine**	190.00	47.50
Cut cancel		24.00
Perf. initial		11.50
R533 R25 $100 **carmine**	55.00	16.00
Cut cancel		4.00
Perf. initial		2.75
R534 R25 $500 **carmine**	—	210.00
Cut cancel		110.00
Perf. initial		57.50
R535 R25 $1000 **carmine**	—	140.00
Cut cancel		42.50
Perf. initial		22.50

Nos. R288-R310 Overprinted: **Series 1950**

1950 **Wmk. 191R** ***Perf. 11***

R536 R23 1c **carmine**	.30	.25
Cut cancel		.25
Perf. initial		.25
R537 R23 2c **carmine**	.35	.30
Cut cancel		.25
Perf. initial		.25
R538 R23 3c **carmine**	.40	.35
Cut cancel		.25
Perf. initial		.25
R539 R23 4c **carmine**	.55	.45
Cut cancel		.25
Perf. initial		.25
R540 R23 5c **carmine**	.35	.25
Cut cancel		.25
Perf. initial		.25
R541 R23 8c **carmine**	1.40	.70
Cut cancel		.25
Perf. initial		.25
R542 R23 10c **carmine**	.65	.25
Cut cancel		.25
Perf. initial		.25
R543 R23 20c **carmine**	1.10	.40
Cut cancel		.30
Perf. initial		.30
R544 R23 25c **carmine**	1.60	.40
Cut cancel		.30
Perf. initial		.30
R545 R23 40c **carmine**	3.50	1.90
Cut cancel		.45
Perf. initial		.30
R546 R23 50c **carmine**	4.50	.25
Cut cancel		.25
Perf. initial		.25
R547 R23 80c **carmine**	10.00	5.00
Cut cancel		.90
Perf. initial		.55
R548 R24 $1 **carmine**	10.00	.35
Cut cancel		.30
Perf. initial		.25
R549 R24 $2 **carmine**	12.00	2.00
Cut cancel		.40
Perf. initial		.20
R550 R24 $3 **carmine**	14.00	5.00
Cut cancel		1.40
Perf. initial		.80
R551 R24 $4 **carmine**	19.00	6.25
Cut cancel		2.75
Perf. initial		1.40
R552 R24 $5 **carmine**	22.50	.85
Cut cancel		.30
Perf. initial		.25
R553 R24 $10 **carmine**	52.50	9.00
Cut cancel		.85
Perf. initial		.55
R554 R24 $20 **carmine**	110.00	10.00
Cut cancel		2.75
Perf. initial		1.90

Without Gum ***Perf. 12***

R555 R25 $30 **carmine**	77.50	50.00
Cut cancel		14.50
Perf. initial		10.50
R556 R25 $50 **carmine**	72.50	18.00
Cut cancel		8.50
Perf. initial		5.75
a. Vert. pair, imperf. horiz.		—
R557 R25 $60 **carmine**	160.00	57.50
Cut cancel		21.00
Perf. initial		9.75
R558 R25 $100 **carmine**	60.00	17.50
Cut cancel		5.25
Perf. initial		3.25
R559 R25 $500 **carmine**	—	100.00
Cut cancel		50.00
Perf. initial		32.50
R560 R25 $1000 **carmine**	—	77.50
Cut cancel		26.00
Perf. initial		19.00

Nos. R288-R310 Overprinted: **Series 1951**

1951 **Wmk. 191R** ***Perf. 11***

R561 R23 1c **carmine**	.30	.25
Cut cancel		.25
Perf. initial		.25
R562 R23 2c **carmine**	.35	.30
Cut cancel		.25
Perf. initial		.25
R563 R23 3c **carmine**	.30	.30
Cut cancel		.25
Perf. initial		.25
R564 R23 4c **carmine**	.35	.30
Cut cancel		.25
Perf. initial		.25
R565 R23 5c **carmine**	.35	.30
Cut cancel		.25
Perf. initial		.25
R566 R23 8c **carmine**	1.10	.40
Cut cancel		.25
Perf. initial		.25
R567 R23 10c **carmine**	.60	.30
Cut cancel		.25
Perf. initial		.25
R568 R23 20c **carmine**	1.40	.50
Cut cancel		.30
Perf. initial		.25
R569 R23 25c **carmine**	1.60	.45
Cut cancel		.30
Perf. initial		.25
R570 R23 40c **carmine**	4.00	1.40
Cut cancel		.45
Perf. initial		.30
R571 R23 50c **carmine**	3.00	.40
Cut cancel		.25
Perf. initial		.25
R572 R23 80c **carmine**	6.00	2.75
Cut cancel		1.60
Perf. initial		.80
R573 R24 $1 **carmine**	11.00	.25
Cut cancel		.25
Perf. initial		.25
R574 R24 $2 **carmine**	16.00	.50
Cut cancel		.25
Perf. initial		.30
R575 R24 $3 **carmine**	22.50	3.50
Cut cancel		1.90
Perf. initial		1.10
R576 R24 $4 **carmine**	27.50	6.25
Cut cancel		2.75
Perf. initial		1.40
R577 R24 $5 **carmine**	19.00	.70
Cut cancel		.35
Perf. initial		.25
R578 R24 $10 **carmine**	47.50	2.25
Cut cancel		1.10
Perf. initial		.80
R579 R24 $20 **carmine**	100.00	10.00
Cut cancel		4.25
Perf. initial		3.25

Without Gum ***Perf. 12***

R580 R25 $30 **carmine**	77.50	12.50
Cut cancel		5.25
Perf. initial		3.75
a. Imperf., pair	*1,750.*	*775.00*
R581 R25 $50 **carmine**	95.00	24.00
Cut cancel		7.75
Perf. initial		4.50
R582 R25 $60 **carmine**	150.00	47.50
Cut cancel		21.00
Perf. initial		16.00
R583 R25 $100 **carmine**	50.00	12.50
Cut cancel		7.00
Perf. initial		5.00
R584 R25 $500 **carmine**	275.00	110.00
Cut cancel		52.50
Perf. initial		26.00
R585 R25 $1000 **carmine**	—	100.00
Cut cancel		40.00
Perf. initial		29.00

No. R583 is known imperf horizontally. It exists as a reconstructed used vertical strip of 4 that was separated into single stamps.

Documentary Stamps and Types of 1940 Overprinted in Black

Series 1952

Designs: 55c, $1.10, $1.65, $2.20, $2.75, $3.30, L. J. Gage; $2500, William Windom; $5000, C. J. Folger; $10,000, W. Q. Gresham.

1952 **Wmk. 191R** ***Perf. 11***

R586 R23 1c **carmine**	.30	.30
Cut cancel		.25
Perf. initial		.25
R587 R23 2c **carmine**	.40	.30
Cut cancel		.25
Perf. initial		.25
R588 R23 3c **carmine**	.35	.30
Cut cancel		.25
Perf. initial		.25
R589 R23 4c **carmine**	.40	.30
Cut cancel		.25
Perf. initial		.25
R590 R23 5c **carmine**	.30	.30
Cut cancel		.25
Perf. initial		.25
R591 R23 8c **carmine**	.80	.50
Cut cancel		.25
Perf. initial		.25
R592 R23 10c **carmine**	.45	.25
Cut cancel		.25
Perf. initial		.20
R593 R23 20c **carmine**	1.10	.40
Cut cancel		.30
Perf. initial		.25
R594 R23 25c **carmine**	1.60	.45
Cut cancel		.30
Perf. initial		.30
R595 R23 40c **carmine**	3.25	1.40
Cut cancel		.55
Perf. initial		.45
R596 R23 50c **carmine**	3.00	.30
Cut cancel		.25
Perf. initial		.25
R597 R23 55c **carmine**	22.50	10.50
Cut cancel		1.40
Perf. initial		1.10
R598 R23 80c **carmine**	14.00	3.25
Cut cancel		.80
Perf. initial		.75
R599 R24 $1 **carmine**	5.50	1.50
Cut cancel		.75
Perf. initial		.40
R600 R24 $1.10 **carmine**	47.50	25.00
Cut cancel		10.50
Perf. initial		6.25
R601 R24 $1.65 **carmine**	160.00	47.50
Cut cancel		32.50
Perf. initial		21.00
R602 R24 $2 **carmine**	12.00	.70
Cut cancel		.25
Perf. initial		.25
R603 R24 $2.20 **carmine**	140.00	60.00
Cut cancel		32.50
Perf. initial		16.00
R604 R24 $2.75 **carmine**	160.00	62.50
Cut cancel		32.50
Perf. initial		16.00
R605 R24 $3 **carmine**	27.50	4.25
Cut cancel		1.60
Perf. initial		1.40
a. Horiz. pair, imperf. btwn.	*1,200.*	
R606 R24 $3.30 **carmine**	140.00	60.00
Cut cancel		32.50
Perf. initial		16.00
R607 R24 $4 **carmine**	25.00	4.25
Cut cancel		2.10
Perf. initial		1.60
R608 R24 $5 **carmine**	25.00	1.25
Cut cancel		.45
Perf. initial		.40
R609 R24 $10 **carmine**	50.00	1.25
Cut cancel		.45
Perf. initial		.35
R610 R24 $20 **carmine**	77.50	10.50
Cut cancel		3.75
Perf. initial		3.00

Without Gum ***Perf. 12***

R611 R25 $30 **carmine**	52.50	19.00
Cut cancel		5.25
Perf. initial		4.25
R612 R25 $50 **carmine**	47.50	16.00
Cut cancel		6.25
Perf. initial		5.25
R613 R25 $60 **carmine**	325.00	52.50
Cut cancel		16.00
Perf. initial		10.50
R614 R25 $100 **carmine**	42.50	8.00
Cut cancel		3.25
Perf. initial		2.10
R615 R25 $500 **carmine**	600.00	100.00
Cut cancel		60.00
Perf. initial		35.00
R616 R25 $1000 **carmine**	—	30.00
Cut cancel		16.00
Perf. initial		10.50
R617 R25 $2500 **carmine**	—	165.00
Cut cancel		140.00
Perf. initial		110.00
R618 R25 $5000 **carmine**	—	*3,250.*
Cut cancel		1,500.
Perf. initial		900.00
R619 R25 $10,000 **carmine**	—	*1,300.*
Cut cancel		825.00
Perf. initial		675.00

Documentary Stamps and Types of 1940 Overprinted in Black

Series 1953

1953 **Wmk. 191R** ***Perf. 11***

R620 R23 1c **carmine**	.30	.30
Cut cancel		.25
Perf. initial		.25
R621 R23 2c **carmine**	.30	.30
Cut cancel		.25
Perf. initial		.25
R622 R23 3c **carmine**	.35	.30
Cut cancel		.25
Perf. initial		.25
R623 R23 4c **carmine**	.55	.40
Cut cancel		.25
Perf. initial		.25
R624 R23 5c **carmine**	.40	.25
Cut cancel		.25
Perf. initial		.25
a. Vert. pair, imperf. horiz.		*650.00*
R625 R23 8c **carmine**	.95	.75
Cut cancel		.25
Perf. initial		.25
R626 R23 10c **carmine**	.55	.30
Cut cancel		.25
Perf. initial		.25
R627 R23 20c **carmine**	1.10	.45
Cut cancel		.25
Perf. initial		.25
R628 R23 25c **carmine**	1.25	.55
Cut cancel		.30
Perf. initial		.25
R629 R23 40c **carmine**	2.25	.80
Cut cancel		.45
Perf. initial		.35
R630 R23 50c **carmine**	2.75	.30
Cut cancel		.25
Perf. initial		.25

No.	Type	Description	Unused	Used
R631	R23	55c **carmine**	4.75	2.00
		Cut cancel		.80
		Perf. initial		.55
a.		Horiz. pair, imperf. vert.	*375.00*	
R632	R23	80c **carmine**	7.50	2.10
		Cut cancel		1.50
		Perf. initial		1.40
R633	R24	$1 **carmine**	4.50	.30
		Cut cancel		.25
		Perf. initial		.25
R634	R24	$1.10 **carmine**	8.75	2.50
		Cut cancel		2.10
		Perf. initial		1.60
a.		Horiz. pair, imperf. vert.	600.00	
b.		Imperf. pair	*600.00*	
R635	R24	$1.65 **carmine**	8.75	4.25
		Cut cancel		3.25
		Perf. initial		2.10
R636	R24	$2 **carmine**	6.75	.70
		Cut cancel		.30
		Perf. initial		.25
R637	R24	$2.20 **carmine**	16.00	6.00
		Cut cancel		2.75
		Perf. initial		2.10
R638	R24	$2.75 **carmine**	22.50	7.00
		Cut cancel		3.75
		Perf. initial		2.75
R639	R24	$3 **carmine**	13.50	3.25
		Cut cancel		1.60
		Perf. initial		1.40
R640	R24	$3.30 **carmine**	29.00	8.00
		Cut cancel		5.25
		Perf. initial		3.50
R641	R24	$4 **carmine**	27.50	8.75
		Cut cancel		2.40
		Perf. initial		2.10
R642	R24	$5 **carmine**	22.50	1.10
		Cut cancel		.55
		Perf. initial		.35
R643	R24	$10 **carmine**	50.00	1.90
		Cut cancel		1.10
		Perf. initial		.90
R644	R24	$20 **carmine**	95.00	18.00
		Cut cancel		3.25
		Perf. initial		2.40

Without Gum ***Perf. 12***

No.	Type	Description	Unused	Used
R645	R25	$30 **carmine**	72.50	16.00
		Cut cancel		6.75
		Perf. initial		4.25
R646	R25	$50 **carmine**	140.00	32.50
		Cut cancel		13.00
		Perf. initial		6.25
R647	R25	$60 **carmine**	500.00	210.00
		Cut cancel		125.00
		Perf. initial		67.50
R648	R25	$100 **carmine**	42.50	13.00
		Cut cancel		5.75
		Perf. initial		3.75
R649	R25	$500 **carmine**	550.00	140.00
		Cut cancel		62.50
		Perf. initial		29.00
R650	R25	$1000 **carmine**	275.00	67.50
		Cut cancel		24.00
		Perf. initial		16.00
R651	R25	$2500 **carmine**	1,900.	1,100.
		Cut cancel		475.00
		Perf. initial		325.00
R652	R25	$5000 **carmine**	—	*3,750.*
		Cut cancel		1,750.
		Perf. initial		1,100.
R653	R25	$10,000 **carmine**	—	*3,250.*
		Cut cancel		1,600.
		Perf. initial		650.00

Types of 1940
Without Overprint

1954 **Wmk. 191R** ***Perf. 11***

No.	Type	Description	Unused	Used
R654	R23	1c **carmine**	.30	.25
		Cut cancel		.25
		Perf. initial		.20
a.		Horiz. pair, imperf. vert.	—	
R655	R23	2c **carmine**	.30	.30
		Cut cancel		.25
		Perf. initial		.20
R656	R23	3c **carmine**	.30	.30
		Cut cancel		.25
		Perf. initial		.20
R657	R23	4c **carmine**	.30	.30
		Cut cancel		.25
		Perf. initial		.20
R658	R23	5c **carmine**	.30	.25
		Cut cancel		.20
		Perf. initial		.20
R659	R23	8c **carmine**	.30	.25
		Cut cancel		.25
		Perf. initial		.20
R660	R23	10c **carmine**	.30	.25
		Cut cancel		.25
		Perf. initial		.20
R661	R23	20c **carmine**	.55	.40
		Cut cancel		.30
		Perf. initial		.25
R662	R23	25c **carmine**	.65	.45
		Cut cancel		.30
		Perf. initial		.25
R663	R23	40c **carmine**	1.40	.60
		Cut cancel		.45
		Perf. initial		.35
R664	R23	50c **carmine**	1.90	.25
		Cut cancel		.20
		Perf. initial		.20
a.		Horiz. pair, imperf. vert.	250.00	
R665	R23	55c **carmine**	1.60	1.25
		Cut cancel		.55
		Perf. initial		.45
R666	R23	80c **carmine**	2.50	1.90
		Cut cancel		1.25
		Perf. initial		1.10
R667	R24	$1 **carmine**	1.60	.30
		Cut cancel		.30
		Perf. initial		.25
R668	R24	$1.10 **carmine**	3.50	2.50
		Cut cancel		1.60
		Perf. initial		1.10
R669	R24	$1.65 **carmine**	110.00	70.00
		Cut cancel		50.00
		Perf. initial		22.50
R670	R24	$2 **carmine**	1.90	.45
		Cut cancel		.25
		Perf. initial		.25
R671	R24	$2.20 **carmine**	5.00	3.75
		Cut cancel		2.75
		Perf. initial		1.60
R672	R24	$2.75 **carmine**	110.00	65.00
		Cut cancel		37.50
		Perf. initial		21.00
R673	R24	$3 **carmine**	3.25	2.00
		Cut cancel		1.10
		Perf. initial		.80
R674	R24	$3.30 **carmine**	7.25	5.00
		Cut cancel		3.25
		Perf. initial		2.10
R675	R24	$4 **carmine**	4.50	3.75
		Cut cancel		2.10
		Perf. initial		1.60
R676	R24	$5 **carmine**	6.00	.50
		Cut cancel		.35
		Perf. initial		.20
R677	R24	$10 **carmine**	11.00	1.50
		Cut cancel		.85
		Perf. initial		.70
R678	R24	$20 **carmine**	35.00	6.00
		Cut cancel		3.25
		Perf. initial		1.90

Documentary Stamps and Type of 1940 Overprinted in Black

Series 1954

1954 **Wmk. 191R** ***Perf. 12***
Without Gum

No.	Type	Description	Unused	Used
R679	R25	$30 **carmine**	55.00	14.00
		Cut cancel		4.75
		Perf. initial		3.25
R680	R25	$50 **carmine**	72.50	21.00
		Cut cancel		9.25
		Perf. initial		5.75
R681	R25	$60 **carmine**	110.00	24.00
		Cut cancel		13.00
		Perf. initial		9.25
R682	R25	$100 **carmine**	55.00	7.00
		Cut cancel		5.25
		Perf. initial		4.00
R683	R25	$500 **carmine**	—	75.00
		Cut cancel		24.00
		Perf. initial		19.00
R684	R25	$1000 **carmine**	325.00	62.50
		Cut cancel		19.00
		Perf. initial		16.00
R685	R25	$2500 **carmine**	—	210.00
		Cut cancel		92.50
		Perf. initial		62.50
R686	R25	$5000 **carmine**	—	875.00
		Cut cancel		550.00
		Perf. initial		475.00
R687	R25	$10,000 **carmine**	—	1,100.
		Cut cancel		350.00
		Perf. initial		210.00

Documentary Stamps and Type of 1940 Overprinted in Black

Series 1955

1955 **Wmk. 191R** ***Perf. 12***
Without Gum

No.	Type	Description	Unused	Used
R688	R25	$30 **carmine**	72.50	13.00
		Cut cancel		6.25
		Perf. initial		3.75
R689	R25	$50 **carmine**	72.50	17.00
		Cut cancel		9.25
		Perf. initial		6.50
R690	R25	$60 **carmine**	125.00	32.50
		Cut cancel		14.50
		Perf. initial		5.25
R691	R25	$100 **carmine**	60.00	7.50
		Cut cancel		5.00
		Perf. initial		3.75
R692	R25	$500 **carmine**	700.00	125.00
		Cut cancel		37.50
		Perf. initial		21.00
R693	R25	$1000 **carmine**	—	37.50
		Cut cancel		18.00
		Perf. initial		13.00
R694	R25	$2500 **carmine**	—	140.00
		Cut cancel		82.50
		Perf. initial		52.50
R695	R25	$5000 **carmine**	*1,900.*	1,300.
		Cut cancel		600.00
		Perf. initial		400.00
R696	R25	$10,000 **carmine**	—	1,100.
		Cut cancel		500.00
		Perf. initial		190.00

Documentary Stamps and Type of 1940 Overprinted in Black "Series 1956"

1956 **Wmk. 191R** **Without Gum** ***Perf. 12***

No.	Type	Description	Unused	Used
R697	R25	$30 **carmine**	95.00	16.00
		Cut cancel		9.25
		Perf. initial		4.75
R698	R25	$50 **carmine**	100.00	22.50
		Cut cancel		13.00
		Perf. initial		6.25
R699	R25	$60 **carmine**	125.00	42.50
		Cut cancel		16.00
		Perf. initial		7.25
R700	R25	$100 **carmine**	95.00	14.00
		Cut cancel		6.00
		Perf. initial		5.00
R701	R25	$500 **carmine**		87.50
		Cut cancel		26.00
		Perf. initial		16.00
R702	R25	$1000 **carmine**	600.00	67.50
		Cut cancel		21.00
		Perf. initial		13.00
R703	R25	$2500 **carmine**	—	475.00
		Cut cancel		210.00
		Perf. initial		110.00
R704	R25	$5000 **carmine**	—	1,700.
		Cut cancel		1,075.
		Perf. initial		700.00
R705	R25	$10,000 **carmine**	—	700.00
		Cut cancel		250.00
		Perf. initial		140.00

Documentary Stamps and Type of 1940 Overprinted in Black "Series 1957"

1957 **Wmk. 191R** ***Perf. 12***
Without Gum

No.	Type	Description	Unused	Used
R706	R25	$30 **carmine**	125.00	32.50
		Cut cancel		13.00
		Perf. initial		6.25
R707	R25	$50 **carmine**	95.00	35.00
		Cut cancel		13.00
		Perf. initial		5.75
R708	R25	$60 **carmine**	—	190.00
		Cut cancel		110.00
		Perf. initial		55.00
R709	R25	$100 **carmine**	82.50	15.00
		Cut cancel		8.00
		Perf. initial		4.25
R710	R25	$500 **carmine**	375.00	110.00
		Cut cancel		57.50
		Perf. initial		35.00
R711	R25	$1000 **carmine**	—	82.50
		Cut cancel		32.50
		Perf. initial		21.00
R712	R25	$2500 **carmine**	—	750.00
		Cut cancel		450.00
		Perf. initial		240.00
R713	R25	$5000 **carmine**	*2,250.*	1,100.
		Cut cancel		475.00
		Perf. initial		210.00
R714	R25	$10,000 **carmine**	—	475.00
		Cut cancel		175.00
		Perf. initial		110.00

Documentary Stamps and Type of 1940 Overprinted in Black "Series 1958"

1958 **Wmk. 191R** ***Perf. 12***
Without Gum

No.	Type	Description	Unused	Used
R715	R25	$30 **carmine**	87.50	21.00
		Cut cancel		16.00
		Perf. initial		8.25
R716	R25	$50 **carmine**	72.50	21.00
		Cut cancel		14.50
		Perf. initial		6.25
R717	R25	$60 **carmine**	125.00	32.50
		Cut cancel		16.00
		Perf. initial		10.50
R718	R25	$100 **carmine**	60.00	10.50
		Cut cancel		5.75
		Perf. initial		2.10
R719	R25	$500 **carmine**	275.00	77.50
		Cut cancel		37.50
		Perf. initial		21.00
R720	R25	$1000 **carmine**	—	70.00
		Cut cancel		32.50
		Perf. initial		21.00
R721	R25	$2500 **carmine**	—	900.00
		Cut cancel		525.00
		Perf. initial		350.00
R722	R25	$5000 **carmine**	—	*3,000.*
		Cut cancel		2,000.
		Perf. initial		1,750.
R723	R25	$10,000 **carmine**	—	1,500.
		Cut cancel		1,100.
		Perf. initial		650.00

Documentary Stamps and Type of 1940 Without Overprint

1958 **Wmk. 191R** ***Perf. 12***
With Gum

No.	Type	Description	Unused	Used
R724	R25	$30 **carmine**	40.00	7.00
		Cut cancel		6.00
		Perf. initial		4.25
a.		Vert. pair, imperf. horiz.	*2,250.*	
R725	R25	$50 **carmine**	42.50	7.00
		Cut cancel		4.00
		Perf. initial		3.25
a.		Vert. pair, imperf. horiz.		—
R726	R25	$60 **carmine**	80.00	21.00
		Cut cancel		10.50
		Perf. initial		5.25
R727	R25	$100 **carmine**	20.00	4.75
		Cut cancel		3.25
		Perf. initial		2.00

R728	R25 $500 **carmine**	87.50	26.00
	Cut cancel		10.50
	Perf. initial		7.75
R729	R25 $1000 **carmine**	57.50	21.00
	Cut cancel		10.50
	Perf. initial		7.75
a.	Vert. pair, imperf. horiz.		*1,550.*
R730	R25 $2500 **carmine**	—	160.00
	Cut cancel		90.00
	Perf. initial		55.00
R731	R25 $5000 **carmine**	—	150.00
	Cut cancel		87.50
	Perf. initial		62.50
R732	R25 $10,000 **carmine**	—	140.00
	Cut cancel		52.50
	Perf. initial		25.00

Internal Revenue Building, Washington, D.C. — R26

Centenary of the Internal Revenue Service.

Giori Press Printing

1962, July 2 **Unwmk.** ***Perf. 11***

R733	R26 10c **violet blue & bright green**	.80	.40
	Never hinged	1.10	
	Cut cancel		.20
	Perf. initial		.25
	P# block of 4	15.00	

1963

"Established 1862" Removed

R734	R26 10c **violet blue & bright green**	2.50	.60
	Never hinged	4.50	
	Cut cancel		.25
	Perf. initial		.25
	P# block of 4	30.00	

Documentary revenue stamps were no longer required after Dec. 31, 1967.

PROPRIETARY STAMPS

Stamps for use on proprietary articles were included in the first general issue of 1862-71. They are R3, R13, R14, R18, R22, R29, R31 and R38.

Several varieties of "violet" paper were used in printing Nos. RB1-RB10. One is grayish with a slight greenish tinge, called "intermediate" paper by specialists. It should not be confused with the "green" paper, which is truly green.

All values prior to 1898 are for used copies. Printed cancellations on proprietary stamps command sizable premiums.

George Washington
RB1 RB1a

Engraved and printed by Jos. R. Carpenter, Philadelphia.

1871-74 ***Perf. 12***

				a. Violet Paper (1871)	b. Green Paper (1874)
RB1	RB1	1c	**green & black**	5.00	10.00
			Pair	11.00	24.00
			Block of 4	25.00	60.00
		c.	Imperf.	80.00	
			Imperf. pair	175.00	
			Imperf. block of 4	475.00	
		d.	Inverted center	*3,000.*	
RB2	RB1	2c	**green & black**	6.00	22.50
			Pair	13.50	52.50
			Block of 4	30.00	110.00
			Double transfer	18.00	
			Vert. half used as 1c on document		—
		c.	Inverted center	*40,000.*	*8,500.*

No. RB2bc is valued with fine centering and small faults.

Only two examples recorded of the inverted center on violet paper, No. RB2ac.

				a. Violet Paper (1871)	b. Green Paper (1874)
RB3	RB1a	3c	**green & black**	22.50	55.00
			Pair	55.00	130.00
			Block of 4	110.00	275.00
			Double transfer	—	
		c.	Sewing machine perf.	275.00	
		d.	Inverted center	*16,000.*	

No. RB3d is valued with small faults as 6 of the 7 recorded examples have faults.

				a. Violet Paper (1871)	b. Green Paper (1874)
RB4	RB1a	4c	**green & black**	12.50	20.00
			Pair	30.00	50.00
			Block of 4	80.00	110.00
			Double transfer	—	
			Vert. half used as 2c on document		—
		c.	Inverted center	*19,000.*	

No. RB4c is valued with small faults as 6 of the 7 recorded examples have faults.

				a. Violet Paper (1871)	b. Green Paper (1874)
RB5	RB1a	5c	**green & black**	150.00	160.00
			Pair	325.00	375.00
			Block of 4	675.00	800.00
		c.	Inverted center	*130,000.*	

No. RB5c is unique. Value represents price realized in 2000 auction sale.

				a. Violet Paper (1871)	b. Green Paper (1874)
RB6	RB1a	6c	**green & black**	45.00	110.00
			Pair	100.00	260.00
			Block of 4	275.00	575.00
			Double transfer	—	
RB7	RB1a	10c	**green & black** ('73)	175.00	55.00
			Pair	425.00	125.00
			Block of 4	—	300.00
			Double transfer	—	

(See note on Inverted Centers after No. R133.)

RB1b

				a. Violet Paper	b. Green Paper (1874)
RB8	RB1b	50c	**green & black** ('73)	600.	1,000.
			Pair	*1,100.*	
RB9	RB1b	$1	**green & black** ('73)	*1,500.*	*8,000.*
			Pair	—	

RB1c

				a. Violet Paper	b. Green Paper (1874)
RB10	RB1c	$5	**green & black** ('73)	*7,000.*	*40,000.*
			Pair	*15,500.*	

No. RB10b is valued with small faults.

When the Carpenter contract expired Aug. 31, 1875, the proprietary stamps remaining unissued were delivered to the Bureau of Internal Revenue. Until the taxes expired, June 30, 1883, the B.I.R. issued 34,315 of the 50c, 6,585 of the $1 and 2,109 of the $5, Nos. RB8-RB10. No. RB19, the 10c blue, replaced No. RB7b, the 10c on green paper, after 336,000 copies were issued, exhausting the supply in 1881.

George Washington
RB2 RB2a

Plates prepared and printed by both the National Bank Note Co. and the Bureau of Engraving and Printing. No. RB11, and possibly others, also printed by the American Bank Note Co. All silk paper printings were by National, plus early printings of Nos. RB11b-RB14b, RB16b, RB17b. All rouletted stamps printed by the BEP plus Nos. RB15b, RB18b, RB19b. Otherwise, which company printed the stamps can be told only by guide lines (BEP) or full marginal inscriptions. ABN used National plates with A. B. Co. added on the second stamp to the left of the National inscription.

1875-81

				Silk Paper	Wmkd. 191R	
				a. Perf.	b. Perf.	c. Roul. 6
RB11	RB2	1c	**green**	1.90	.40	90.00
			Pair	4.50	1.10	225.00
			Block of 4	12.00	2.75	550.00
			Dble. transfer	—		
		d.	Vert. pair, imperf between		*250.00*	
RB12	RB2	2c	**brown**	2.50	1.40	110.00
			Pair	6.25	3.40	250.00
			Block of 4	62.50	8.00	575.00
RB13	RB2a	3c	**orange**	12.50	3.00	110.00
			Pair	27.50	6.75	250.00
			Block of 4	60.00	15.00	575.00
		d.	Horizontal pair, imperf. between			—
RB14	RB2a	4c	**red brown**	6.75	5.50	
			Pair	15.00	15.00	
			Block of 4	32.50	25.00	
RB15	RB2a	4c	**red**		4.50	175.00
			Pair		10.00	425.00
			Block of 4		25.00	
RB16	RB2a	5c	**black**	125.00	100.00	*1,500.*
			Pair	275.00	240.00	—
			Block of 4	—	—	—
RB17	RB2a	6c	**violet blue**	25.00	20.00	300.00
			Pair	62.50	50.00	*750.00*
			Block of 4	175.00	140.00	
RB18	RB2a	6c	**violet**		30.00	—
			Pair		80.00	
			Block of 4		225.00	
RB19	RB2a	10c	**blue** ('81)		300.00	
			Pair		700.00	
			Block of 4		—	

Many fraudulent roulettes exist.

Battleship — RB3

Inscribed "Series of 1898." and "Proprietary."

See note on rouletting preceding No. R161.

1898 **Wmk. 191R** **Engr.**

			Roul. 5½ Unused	Roul. 5½ Used	p. Hyphen Hole Perf. 7 Unused	p. Hyphen Hole Perf. 7 Used
RB20	⅛c	**yellow green**	.20	.20	.20	.20
		Block of 4	.50	.50	.75	.70
		Double transfer	—			

			Roul. 5½ Unused	Roul. 5½ Used	*p.* Hyphen Hole Perf. 7 Unused	*p.* Hyphen Hole Perf. 7 Used
a.		Vert. pair, imperf. horiz.	—			
RB21	¼c	**brown**	.20	.20	.20	.20
a.		¼c **red brown**	.20	.20		
b.		¼c **yellow brown**	.20	.20	.20	.20
c.		¼c **orange brown**	.20	.20	.20	.20
d.		¼c **bister**	.20	.20		
		Block of 4	.50	.25	.55	1.00
		Double transfer	—	—		
e.		Vert. pair, imperf. horiz.	—	—		
f.		Printed on both sides	—			
RB22	⅜c	**deep orange**	.25	.25	.30	.25
		Block of 4	1.10	1.00	1.40	—
a.		Horiz. pair, imperf. vert.	10.50			
b.		Vert. pair, imperf. horiz.	—			
RB23	⅝c	**deep ultra**	.25	.25	.30	.25
		Block of 4	1.25	1.10	1.50	1.25
		Double transfer	1.50			
a.		Vert. pair, imperf. horiz.	77.50	—		
b.		Horiz. pair, imperf. vert.	*325.00*			
RB24	1c	**dark green**	2.10	.25	26.00	13.00
		Block of 4	10.50	1.10	140.00	67.50
a.		Vert. pair, imperf. horiz.	*325.00*			
RB25	1¼c	**violet**	.25	.25	.30	.25
		Block of 4	1.10	1.00	1.40	1.25
a.		1¼c **brown violet**	.25	.20	.25	.25
b.		Vertical pair, imperf. between	—			
RB26	1⅞c	**dull blue**	12.00	1.60	32.50	7.75
		Block of 4	57.50	—	160.00	—
		Double transfer				
RB27	2c	**violet brown**	1.10	.25	6.25	.80
		Block of 4	5.00	—	27.50	—
		Double transfer		—		
a.		Horiz. pair, imperf. vert.	52.50			
RB28	2½c	**lake**	4.25	.25	5.25	.30
		Block of 4	21.00	1.10	29.00	—
a.		Vert. pair, imperf. horiz.	190.00			
RB29	3¾c	**olive gray**	42.50	10.50	72.50	21.00
		Block of 4	210.00	—	350.00	110.00
RB30	4c	**purple**	13.00	1.10	62.50	18.00
		Block of 4	62.50	5.50	325.00	90.00
		Double transfer	—			
RB31	5c	**brown orange**	13.00	1.10	67.50	21.00
		Block of 4	62.50	5.75	350.00	175.00

		Roul. 5½ Unused	Roul. 5½ Used	*p.* Hyphen Hole Perf. 7 Unused	*p.* Hyphen Hole Perf. 7 Used
a.	Vert. pair, imperf. horiz.	—	*325.00*		
b.	Horiz. pair, imperf. vert.	—	*425.00*		

See note after No. RS315 regarding St. Louis Provisional Labels of 1898.

RB4

Inscribed "Series of 1914"

1914 Wmk. 190 Offset Printing *Perf. 10*

				Unused	Used
RB32	RB4	⅛c	**black**	.25	.25
			Block of 4	1.25	1.10
RB33	RB4	¼c	**black**	2.10	1.10
			Block of 4	10.50	
RB34	RB4	⅜c	**black**	.25	.25
			Block of 4	1.25	1.10
RB35	RB4	⅝c	**black**	4.75	1.90
			Block of 4	21.00	
RB36	RB4	1¼c	**black**	3.25	1.10
			Block of 4	16.00	
RB37	RB4	1⅞c	**black**	42.50	16.00
			Block of 4	190.00	
RB38	RB4	2½c	**black**	9.25	2.75
			Block of 4	47.50	12.00
RB39	RB4	3⅛c	**black**	90.00	52.50
			Block of 4	400.00	
RB40	RB4	3¾c	**black**	42.50	21.00
			Block of 4	240.00	
RB41	RB4	4c	**black**	62.50	29.00
			Block of 4	325.00	
RB42	RB4	4⅜c	**black**	*1,500.*	—
			Block of 4	*10,000.*	
RB43	RB4	5c	**black**	120.00	72.50
			Block of 4	—	

Wmk. 191R

				Unused	Used
RB44	RB4	⅛c	**black**	.25	.25
			Block of 4	1.25	1.10
RB45	RB4	¼c	**black**	.25	.25
			Block of 4	1.25	1.10
			Double impression	25.00	
RB46	RB4	⅜c	**black**	.65	.35
			Block of 4	3.25	1.75
RB47	RB4	½c	**black**	3.50	3.00
			Block of 4	14.50	
RB48	RB4	⅝c	**black**	.25	.25
			Block of 4	1.25	1.10
RB49	RB4	1c	**black**	4.50	4.00
			Block of 4	19.00	17.50
RB50	RB4	1¼c	**black**	.40	.30
			Block of 4	1.75	1.25
RB51	RB4	1½c	**black**	3.25	2.50
			Block of 4	15.00	11.00
RB52	RB4	1⅞c	**black**	1.10	.65
			Block of 4	4.75	2.40
RB53	RB4	2c	**black**	5.25	4.25
			Block of 4	24.00	
RB54	RB4	2½c	**black**	1.40	1.10
			Block of 4	6.25	5.00
RB55	RB4	3c	**black**	4.25	3.00
			Block of 4	19.00	
RB56	RB4	3⅛c	**black**	5.25	3.25
			Block of 4	24.00	
RB57	RB4	3¾c	**black**	11.50	7.75
			Block of 4	50.00	
RB58	RB4	4c	**black**	.35	.25
			Block of 4	1.75	1.25
			Double impression	—	
RB59	RB4	4⅜c	**black**	16.00	8.25
			Block of 4	70.00	
RB60	RB4	5c	**black**	3.25	2.75
			Block of 4	15.00	
RB61	RB4	6c	**black**	57.50	42.50
			Block of 4	275.00	
RB62	RB4	8c	**black**	18.00	11.50
			Block of 4	77.50	
RB63	RB4	10c	**black**	11.50	7.25
			Block of 4	55.00	
RB64	RB4	20c	**black**	24.00	18.00
			Block of 4	100.00	

RB5

1919 Offset Printing *Perf. 11*

				Unused	Used
RB65	RB5	1c	**dark blue**	.25	.25
			Block of 4	1.25	1.10
			Double impression	30.00	20.00
RB66	RB5	2c	**dark blue**	.25	.25
			Block of 4	1.25	1.10
			Double impression	70.00	
RB67	RB5	3c	**dark blue**	1.10	.65
			Block of 4	5.00	3.00
			Double impression	70.00	
RB68	RB5	4c	**dark blue**	1.60	.55
			Block of 4	7.25	
RB69	RB5	5c	**dark blue**	1.40	.65
			Block of 4	6.25	3.00
RB70	RB5	8c	**dark blue**	14.50	9.25
			Block of 4	65.00	
RB71	RB5	10c	**dark blue**	5.25	2.10
			Block of 4	24.00	9.00
RB72	RB5	20c	**dark blue**	7.75	3.25
			Block of 4	37.50	
RB73	RB5	40c	**dark blue**	47.50	10.50
			Block of 4	210.00	

FUTURE DELIVERY STAMPS

Issued to facilitate the collection of a tax upon each sale, agreement of sale or agreement to sell any products or merchandise at any exchange or board of trade, or other similar place for future delivery.

Documentary Stamps of 1917 Overprinted in Black or Red

Type I

1918-34 Wmk. 191R Offset Printing *Perf. 11*

Overprint Horizontal (Lines 8mm apart)

				Unused	Used
RC1	R22	2c	**carmine rose**	6.00	.25
			Block of 4	26.00	1.10
RC2	R22	3c	**carmine rose** ('34)	32.50	24.00
			Cut cancel		13.00
RC3	R22	4c	**carmine rose**	10.00	.25
			Cut cancel		.20
			Block of 4	47.50	1.10
			Double impression of stamp		10.00
RC3A	R22	5c	**carmine rose** ('33)	77.50	6.00
			Block of 4	—	30.00
RC4	R22	10c	**carmine rose**	17.50	.25
			Block of 4	85.00	1.10
a.			Double overprint	—	5.25
b.			"FUTURE" omitted	—	*210.00*
c.			"DELIVERY FUTURE"		37.50
RC5	R22	20c	**carmine rose**	25.00	.25
			Cut cancel		.20
			Block of 4	125.00	1.10
a.			Double overprint		21.00
RC6	R22	25c	**carmine rose**	55.00	.45
			Cut cancel		.25
			Block of 4	250.00	2.25
			Block of 4, cut cancel		1.10
RC7	R22	40c	**carmine rose**	60.00	.80
			Cut cancel		.25
			Block of 4	275.00	4.00
			Block of 4, cut cancel		1.10
RC8	R22	50c	**carmine rose**	12.50	.25
			Cut cancel		.20
			Block of 4	60.00	1.10
a.			"DELIVERY" omitted	—	*110.00*
RC9	R22	80c	**carmine rose**	110.00	10.50
			Cut cancel		1.10
			Block of 4	525.00	52.50
			Block of 4, cut cancel		5.00
a.			Double overprint	—	37.50
			Double overprint, cut cancel		6.25

Engr.

Overprint Vertical, Reading Up (Lines 2mm apart)

				Unused	Used
RC10	R21	$1	**green** (R)	45.00	.30
			Cut cancel		.20
			Block of 4	210.00	1.40
a.			Overprint reading down	—	*300.00*
b.			Black overprint	—	—
			Cut cancel		125.00
RC11	R21	$2	**rose**	50.00	.30
			Cut cancel		.25
			Block of 4	225.00	1.40
RC12	R21	$3	**violet** (R)	110.00	2.75
			Cut cancel		.25
			Block of 4	—	12.50
			Block of 4, cut cancel		1.10
a.			Overprint reading down	—	52.50
RC13	R21	$5	**dark blue** (R)	90.00	.40
			Cut cancel		.25
			Block of 4	—	1.75
			Block of 4, cut cancel		1.10
RC14	R21	$10	**orange**	110.00	.80
			Cut cancel		.25
			Block of 4	500.00	3.25
			Block of 4, cut cancel		1.10
a.			"DELIVERY FUTURE"	—	*110.00*
RC15	R21	$20	**olive bister**	210.00	6.25
			Cut cancel		.55
			Perf initial		.30
			Block of 4		32.50
			Block of 4, cut cancel		2.50

Overprint Horizontal (Lines 11⅔mm apart)

Perf. 12

Without Gum

				Unused	Used
RC16	R17	$30	**vermilion,** green numerals	82.50	3.75
			Cut cancel		1.40
			Perf initial		1.00
			Vertical strip of 4		24.00
			Vertical strip of 4, cut cancel		6.50
a.			Numerals in blue	72.50	3.75
			Cut cancel		1.60
			Perf initial		1.25
b.			Imperf., blue numerals		*110.00*

RC17 R19 $50 **olive green** *(Cleveland)* 55.00 1.40
Cut cancel .65
Vertical strip of 4 13.00
Vertical strip of 4, cut cancel 2.75
a. $50 olive bister 55.00 2.10
Cut cancel .45
Perf initial .35
RC18 R19 $60 **brown** 82.50 2.40
Cut cancel .80
Perf initial .70
Vertical strip of 4 16.00
Vertical strip of 4, cut cancel 3.75
a. Vert. pair, imperf. horiz. — *425.00*
RC19 R17 $100 **yellow green** ('34) 140.00 32.50
Cut cancel 7.00
Perf initial 6.00
Vertical strip of 4 — *160.00*
Vertical strip of 4, cut cancel 30.00
RC20 R18 $500 **blue,** red numerals (R) 92.50 11.50
Cut cancel 4.75
Perf initial 4.00
Vertical strip of 4 *62.50*
Vertical strip of 4, cut cancel 21.00
Double transfer 15.00
a. Numerals in orange — 50.00
Cut cancel 11.50
Perf initial 10.00
Double transfer 75.00
RC21 R19 $1000 **orange** 125.00 5.75
Cut cancel 1.60
Perf initial 1.25
Vertical strip of 4 29.00
Vertical strip of 4, cut cancel 8.00
a. Vert. pair, imperf. horiz. — *1,100.*

See note after No. R227.

1923-24 Offset Printing *Perf. 11*
Overprint Horizontal (Lines 2mm apart)

RC22 R22 1c **carmine rose** 1.10 .25
Block of 4 5.50 1.25
RC23 R22 80c **carmine rose** 100.00 1.90
Cut cancel .40
Block of 4 — 8.50
Block of 4, cut cancel 1.75

Type II

1925-34 Engr.

RC25 R21 $1 **green** (R) 45.00 .80
Cut cancel .20
Block of 4 — 3.00
Block of 4, cut cancel .30
RC26 R21 $10 **orange** (Bk) ('34) 125.00 16.00
Cut cancel 10.50
Perf initial 9.00

Overprint Type I

1928-29 Offset Printing *Perf. 10*

RC27 R22 10c **carmine rose** *2,500.*
RC28 R22 20c **carmine rose** *2,500.*

STOCK TRANSFER STAMPS

Issued to facilitate the collection of a tax on all sales or agreements to sell, or memoranda of sales or delivery of, or transfers of legal title to shares or certificates of stock.

Documentary Stamps of 1917 Overprinted in Black or Red

1918-22 Offset Printing Wmk. 191R *Perf. 11*
Overprint Horizontal (Lines 8mm apart)

RD1 R22 1c **carmine rose** .90 .25
Block of 4 3.75 1.10
a. Double overprint — —
RD2 R22 2c **carmine rose** .20 .20
Block of 4 1.10 .20
a. Double overprint — 5.00
Double overprint, cut cancel 2.50
Double impression of stamp —
RD3 R22 4c **carmine rose** .25 .25
Block of 4 1.25 1.10
a. Double overprint — 4.25
Double overprint, cut cancel 2.10
b. "STOCK" omitted — 10.50
d. Ovpt. lines 10mm apart — —
Double impression of stamp 6.00
RD4 R22 5c **carmine rose** .30 .25
Block of 4 1.40 1.10
RD5 R22 10c **carmine rose** .30 .25
Block of 4 1.40 1.10
a. Double overprint — 5.25
Double overprint, cut cancel 2.75
b. "STOCK" omitted — —
Double impression of stamp —
RD6 R22 20c **carmine rose** .55 .25
Perf initial .20
Block of 4 2.25 1.10
a. Double overprint 6.25
b. "STOCK" double — —
Double impression of stamp 6.00
RD7 R22 25c **carmine rose** 1.60 .25
Cut cancel .20
Block of 4 7.50 1.10
RD8 R22 40c **carmine rose** ('22) 1.40 .25
Block of 4 6.75 1.10
RD9 R22 50c **carmine rose** .70 .25
Block of 4 3.25 1.10
a. Double overprint — —
Double impression of stamp —
RD10 R22 80c **carmine rose** 3.25 .35
Cut cancel .20
Block of 4 15.00 1.60

Engr.
Overprint Vertical, Reading Up (Lines 2mm apart)

RD11 R21 $1 **green** (R) 95.00 21.00
Cut cancel 3.00
Block of 4 — —
Block of 4, cut cancel 14.00
a. Overprint reading down 140.00 21.00
Overprint reading down, cut cancel 7.50
RD12 R21 $1 **green** (Bk) 2.75 .30
Block of 4 12.00 1.40
a. Pair, one without overprint — *160.00*
b. Overprinted on back instead of face, inverted — *110.00*
c. Overprint reading down — 6.00
d. $1 yellow green 3.00 .25
RD13 R21 $2 **rose** 2.75 .25
Perf initial .20
Block of 4 12.00 1.10
a. Overprint reading down — 10.50
Overprint reading down, cut cancel 1.50
b. Vert. pair, imperf. horiz. *500.00*
RD14 R21 $3 **violet** (R) 20.00 4.50
Cut cancel .20
Perf initial .20
Block of 4 90.00 —
Block of 4, cut cancel 1.00
RD15 R21 $4 **yellow brown** 11.00 .25
Cut cancel .20
Block of 4 47.50 1.10
RD16 R21 $5 **dark blue** (R) 7.00 .25
Cut cancel .20
Block of 4 35.00 1.10
Block of 4, cut cancel .20
a. Overprint reading down 21.00 1.10
Overprint reading down, cut cancel .20
RD17 R21 $10 **orange** 17.50 .35
Cut cancel .20
Block of 4 80.00 1.50
Block of 4, cut cancel .20
RD18 R21 $20 **olive bister** ('21) 95.00 18.00
Cut cancel 3.25
Perf initial 2.50
Block of 4 425.00 82.50
Block of 4, cut cancel 16.00

Shifted overprints on the $2, and $10 result in "TRANSFER STOCK," "TRANSFER" omitted, and possibly other varieties.

Overprint Horizontal (Lines 11½mm apart)

1918 Without Gum *Perf. 12*

RD19 R17 $30 **vermilion,** green numerals 18.00 4.75
Cut cancel 1.10
Perf initial 1.00
Vertical strip of 4 21.00
Vertical strip of 4, cut cancel 6.50
a. Numerals in blue — 57.50
RD20 R19 $50 **olive green** *(Cleveland)* 110.00 57.50
Cut cancel 21.00
Perf initial 22.50
Vertical strip of 4 260.00
Vertical strip of 4, cut cancel 85.00
RD21 R19 $60 **brown** 125.00 21.00
Cut cancel 9.25
Perf initial 6.00
Vertical strip of 4 90.00
Vertical strip of 4, cut cancel 42.50
RD22 R17 $100 **green** 24.00 5.75
Cut cancel 2.40
Perf initial 2.00
Vertical strip of 4 26.00
Vertical strip of 4, cut cancel 11.00
RD23 R18 $500 **blue** (R) 325.00 110.00
Cut cancel 65.00
Perf initial 50.00
Vertical strip of 4 —
Vertical strip of 4, cut cancel 275.00
Double transfer *500.00* 175.00
a. Numerals in orange 150.00
Numerals in orange, double transfer 190.00
RD24 R19 $1000 **orange** 175.00 75.00
Cut cancel 26.00
Perf initial 20.00
Vertical strip of 4 350.00
Vertical strip of 4, cut cancel 125.00

See note after No. R227.

1928 Offset Printing *Perf. 10*
Overprint Horizontal (Lines 8mm apart)

RD25 R22 2c **carmine rose** 2.75 .30
Block of 4 12.00 1.40
RD26 R22 4c **carmine rose** 2.75 .30
Block of 4 12.00 1.40
RD27 R22 10c **carmine rose** 2.10 .30
Block of 4 9.50 1.40
a. Inverted overprint *1,000.*
RD28 R22 20c **carmine rose** 3.25 .30
Perf initial .20
Block of 4 15.00 1.40
Double impression of stamp —
RD29 R22 50c **carmine rose** 3.75 .30
Block of 4 17.50 1.40

Engr.
Overprint Vertical, Reading Up (Lines 2mm apart)

RD30 R21 $1 **green** 35.00 .20
Cut cancel .20
Block of 4 — .90
a. $1 yellow green 35.00 .45
RD31 R21 $2 **carmine rose** 35.00 .25
Perf initial .20
Block of 4 — 1.10
a. Pair, one without overprint *225.00 190.00*
RD32 R21 $10 **orange** 37.50 .40
Cut cancel .20
Perf initial .20
Block of 4 — 1.90
Perf. 11 at top or bottom —

STOCK

Overprinted Horizontally in Black

TRANSFER

1920 Offset Printing *Perf. 11*

RD33 R22 2c **carmine rose** 7.75 .75
Block of 4 37.50 3.75

No.	Type	Description	Unused	Used
RD34	R22	10c **carmine rose**	2.75	.35
		Block of 4	13.00	1.50
b.		Inverted overprint	*1,550.*	—
RD35	R22	20c **carmine rose**	5.25	.25
		Block of 4	24.00	1.10
a.		Horiz. pair, one without overprint	175.00	
d.		Inverted overprint (perf. initials)		—
RD36	R22	50c **carmine rose**	3.25	.25
		Block of 4	15.00	1.10

Shifted overprints on the 10c, 20c and 50c result in "TRANSFER STOCK," "TRANFSER" omitted, "STOCK" omitted, pairs, and other varieties.

Engr.

No.	Type	Description	Unused	Used
RD37	R21	$1 **green**	55.00	9.75
		Cut cancel		.25
		Block of 4	250.00	45.00
		Block of 4, cut cancel		1.25
RD38	R21	$2 **rose**	50.00	8.25
		Cut cancel		.25
		Block of 4	225.00	42.50
		Block of 4, cut cancel		1.10

Offset Printing

Perf. 10

No.	Type	Description	Unused	Used
RD39	R22	2c **carmine rose**	6.75	.95
		Block of 4	35.00	4.25
		Double impression of stamp	—	
RD40	R22	10c **carmine rose**	1.60	.55
		Block of 4	7.50	2.50
RD41	R22	20c **carmine rose**	2.75	.25
		Cut cancel		.20
		Block of 4	13.50	1.10

Documentary Stamps of 1917-33 Overprinted in Black

1940 Offset Printing Wmk. 191R *Perf. 11*

No.	Type	Description	Unused	Used
RD42	R22	1c **rose pink**	3.25	.50
		Cut cancel		.20
		Perf. initial		.25
a.		"Series 1940" inverted	—	275.00
		Cut cancel		100.00

No. RD42a always comes with a natural straight edge at left.

No.	Type	Description	Unused	Used
RD43	R22	2c **rose pink**	3.25	.55
		Cut cancel		.20
		Perf. initial		.25
RD45	R22	4c **rose pink**	3.25	.35
		Cut cancel		.25
		Perf. initial		.25
RD46	R22	5c **rose pink**	3.75	.25
		Cut cancel		.25
		Perf. initial		.25
RD48	R22	10c **rose pink**	4.75	.25
		Cut cancel		.25
		Perf. initial		.25
RD49	R22	20c **rose pink**	7.75	.25
		Cut cancel		.25
		Perf. initial		.25
RD50	R22	25c **rose pink**	7.75	.65
		Cut cancel		.25
		Perf. initial		.25
RD51	R22	40c **rose pink**	5.25	.80
		Cut cancel		.25
		Perf. initial		.25
RD52	R22	50c **rose pink**	6.25	.30
		Cut cancel		.25
		Perf. initial		.25
RD53	R22	80c **rose pink**	97.50	60.00
		Cut cancel		35.00
		Perf. initial		24.00

Engr.

No.	Type	Description	Unused	Used
RD54	R21	$1 **green**	35.00	.40
		Cut cancel		.25
		Perf. initial		.25
RD55	R21	$2 **rose**	35.00	.65
		Cut cancel		.25
		Perf. initial		.25
RD56	R21	$3 **violet**	175.00	13.00
		Cut cancel		.35
		Perf. initial		.25
RD57	R21	$4 **yellow brown**	70.00	1.25
		Cut cancel		.30
		Perf. initial		.25
RD58	R21	$5 **dark blue**	60.00	1.40
		Cut cancel		.35
		Perf. initial		.25
RD59	R21	$10 **orange**	140.00	8.25
		Cut cancel		.80
		Perf. initial		.65
RD60	R21	$20 **olive bister**	300.00	100.00
		Cut cancel		16.00
		Perf. initial		10.50

Nos. RD19-RD24 Handstamped in Blue "Series 1940"

1940 Wmk. 191R *Perf. 12*

Without Gum

No.	Type	Description	Unused	Used
RD61	R17	$30 **vermilion**	*925.*	700.
		Cut cancel		325.
		Perf. initial		160.
RD62	R19	$50 **olive green**	*900.*	2,000.
		Cut cancel		900.
		Perf. initial		400.
a.		Double ovpt., perf. initial	—	*1,000.*
RD63	R19	$60 **brown**	*2,400.*	*2,200.*
		Cut cancel		675.
		Perf. initial		350.
RD64	R17	$100 **green**	*1,000.*	625.
		Cut cancel		225.
		Perf. initial		87.50
RD65	R18	$500 **blue**	—	2,250.
		Cut cancel		1,400.
		Perf. initial		775.
		Double transfer	*2,300.*	
RD66	R19	$1000 **orange**	—	*3,000.*
		Cut cancel		2,250.
		Perf. initial		1,750.

Alexander Hamilton — ST1

Levi Woodbury — ST2

Overprinted in Black SERIES 1940

Same Portraits as Nos. R288-R310.

1940 Engr. Wmk. 191R *Perf. 11*

No.	Type	Description	Unused	Used
RD67	ST1	1c **bright green**	12.00	3.25
		Cut cancel		.65
		Perf. initial		.40
RD68	ST1	2c **bright green**	7.75	1.75
		Cut cancel		.30
		Perf. initial		.30
RD70	ST1	4c **bright green**	14.00	4.50
		Cut cancel		.65
		Perf. initial		.35
RD71	ST1	5c **bright green**	8.75	1.75
		Cut cancel		.25
		Perf. initial		.25
a.		Without overprint, cut cancel	—	275.00
RD73	ST1	10c **bright green**	12.00	2.10
		Cut cancel		.25
		Perf. initial		.25
RD74	ST1	20c **bright green**	14.00	2.40
		Cut cancel		.25
		Perf. initial		.25
RD75	ST1	25c **bright green**	40.00	9.25
		Cut cancel		.75
		Perf. initial		.45
RD76	ST1	40c **bright green**	72.50	35.00
		Cut cancel		2.40
		Perf. initial		1.00
RD77	ST1	50c **bright green**	12.00	2.10
		Cut cancel		.45
		Perf. initial		.30
RD78	ST1	80c **bright green**	95.00	57.50
		Cut cancel		24.00
		Perf. initial		3.50
RD79	ST2	$1 **bright green**	42.50	4.25
		Cut cancel		.55
		Perf. initial		.30
a.		Without overprint, perf. initial	—	*240.00*
RD80	ST2	$2 **bright green**	47.50	10.50
		Cut cancel		.60
		Perf. initial		.30
RD81	ST2	$3 **bright green**	72.50	13.00
		Cut cancel		.70
		Perf. initial		.25
RD82	ST2	$4 **bright green**	300.00	210.00
		Cut cancel		92.50
		Perf. initial		50.00
RD83	ST2	$5 **bright green**	67.50	14.50
		Cut cancel		1.75
		Perf. initial		.30
RD84	ST2	$10 **bright green**	160.00	42.50
		Cut cancel		5.25
		Perf. initial		3.00
RD85	ST2	$20 **bright green**	900.00	82.50
		Cut cancel		13.00
		Perf. initial		5.75

Nos. RD67-RD85 exist imperforate, without overprint. Value, set of pairs, $1,100.

Thomas Corwin — ST3

Overprinted "SERIES 1940"

Various frames and portraits as Nos. R306-R310.

Without Gum *Perf. 12*

No.	Type	Description	Unused	Used
RD86	ST3	$30 **bright green**	650.00	160.00
		Cut cancel		72.50
		Perf. initial		37.50
RD87	ST3	$50 **bright green**	725.00	475.00
		Cut cancel		200.00
		Perf. initial		92.50
RD88	ST3	$60 **bright green**	*3,000.*	1,100.
		Cut cancel		450.00
		Perf. initial		120.00
RD89	ST3	$100 **bright green**	—	325.00
		Cut cancel		125.00
		Perf. initial		67.50
RD90	ST3	$500 **bright green**	—	*2,000.*
		Cut cancel		1,150.
		Perf. initial		700.
RD91	ST3	$1000 **bright green**	—	*2,000.*
		Cut cancel		1,050.
		Perf. initial		650.00

Nos. RD86-RD91 exist imperforate, without overprint.

Nos. RD67-RD91 Overprint Instead: SERIES 1941

1941 Wmk. 191R *Perf. 11*

No.	Type	Description	Unused	Used
RD92	ST1	1c **bright green**	.70	.55
		Cut cancel		.25
		Perf. initial		.25
RD93	ST1	2c **bright green**	.50	.30
		Cut cancel		.25
		Perf. initial		.25
RD95	ST1	4c **bright green**	.55	.25
		Cut cancel		.20
		Perf. initial		.20
RD96	ST1	5c **bright green**	.50	.25
		Cut cancel		.20
		Perf. initial		.20
RD98	ST1	10c **bright green**	.80	.25
		Cut cancel		.20
		Perf. initial		.20
RD99	ST1	20c **bright green**	1.90	.30
		Cut cancel		.25
		Perf. initial		.20
RD100	ST1	25c **bright green**	1.90	.45
		Cut cancel		.30
		Perf. initial		.30
RD101	ST1	40c **bright green**	2.75	.75
		Cut cancel		.30
		Perf. initial		.20
RD102	ST1	50c **bright green**	4.00	.35
		Cut cancel		.25
		Perf. initial		.25
RD103	ST1	80c **bright green**	25.00	7.75
		Cut cancel		.55
		Perf. initial		.50
RD104	ST2	$1 **bright green**	17.00	.20
		Cut cancel		.20
		Perf. initial		.20
RD105	ST2	$2 **bright green**	17.50	.30
		Cut cancel		.20
		Perf. initial		.25
RD106	ST2	$3 **bright green**	26.00	1.50
		Cut cancel		.35
		Perf. initial		.25
RD107	ST2	$4 **bright green**	47.50	7.75
		Cut cancel		.45
		Perf. initial		.30
RD108	ST2	$5 **bright green**	47.50	.65
		Cut cancel		.30
		Perf. initial		.25
RD109	ST2	$10 **bright green**	100.00	4.25
		Cut cancel		.75
		Perf. initial		.25
RD110	ST2	$20 **bright green**	275.00	67.50
		Cut cancel		18.00
		Perf. initial		4.25

Perf. 12

Without Gum

No.	Type	Description	Unused	Used
RD111	ST3	$30 **bright green**	250.00	240.00
		Cut cancel		77.50
		Perf. initial		29.00
RD112	ST3	$50 **bright green**	800.00	425.00
		Cut cancel		125.00
		Perf. initial		55.00
RD113	ST3	$60 **bright green**	*1,350.*	325.00
		Cut cancel		190.00
		Perf. initial		125.00

No.	Type	Description	Unused	Used
RD114	ST3	$100 **bright green**	—	175.00
		Cut cancel		57.50
		Perf. initial		24.00
RD115	ST3	$500 **bright green**	1,900.	*1,550.*
		Cut cancel		975.00
		Perf. initial		525.00
RD116	ST3	$1000 **bright green**	—	*1,400.*
		Cut cancel		850.00
		Perf. initial		575.00

Nos. RD67-RD91 Overprint Instead: **SERIES 1942**

1942 Wmk. 191R *Perf. 11*

No.	Type	Description	Unused	Used
RD117	ST1	1c **bright green**	.55	.30
		Cut cancel		.25
		Perf. initial		.25
RD118	ST1	2c **bright green**	.45	.35
		Cut cancel		.25
		Perf. initial		.25
RD119	ST1	4c **bright green**	3.25	1.10
		Cut cancel		.55
		Perf. initial		.45
RD120	ST1	5c **bright green**	.45	.20
		Cut cancel		.25
		Perf. initial		.20
a.		Overprint inverted, cut cancel	—	*240.00*
		Perf. initial		*200.00*
RD121	ST1	10c **bright green**	1.90	.20
		Cut cancel		.20
		Perf. initial		.20
RD122	ST1	20c **bright green**	2.25	.20
		Cut cancel		.20
		Perf. initial		.20
RD123	ST1	25c **bright green**	2.25	.20
		Cut cancel		.20
		Perf. initial		.20
RD124	ST1	40c **bright green**	4.75	.40
		Cut cancel		.25
		Perf. initial		.20
RD125	ST1	50c **bright green**	5.75	.20
		Cut cancel		.20
		Perf. initial		.20
RD126	ST1	80c **bright green**	25.00	6.00
		Cut cancel		1.50
		Perf. initial		.35
RD127	ST2	$1 **bright green**	17.00	.40
		Cut cancel		.25
		Perf. initial		.20
RD128	ST2	$2 **bright green**	27.50	.40
		Cut cancel		.25
		Perf. initial		.20
RD129	ST2	$3 **bright green**	32.50	1.10
		Cut cancel		.30
		Perf. initial		.20
RD130	ST2	$4 **bright green**	47.50	21.00
		Cut cancel		.40
		Perf. initial		.25
RD131	ST2	$5 **bright green**	42.50	.40
		Cut cancel		.25
		Perf. initial		.25
a.		Double overprint, perf. initial	—	—
RD132	ST2	$10 **bright green**	77.50	8.25
		Cut cancel		1.40
		Perf. initial		1.10
RD133	ST2	$20 **bright green**	175.00	37.50
		Cut cancel		7.75
		Perf. initial		3.50

Perf. 12

Without Gum

No.	Type	Description	Unused	Used
RD134	ST3	$30 **bright green**	225.00	62.50
		Cut cancel		24.00
		Perf. initial		16.00
RD135	ST3	$50 **bright green**	375.00	140.00
		Cut cancel		47.50
		Perf. initial		21.00
RD136	ST3	$60 **bright green**	450.00	200.00
		Cut cancel		80.00
		Perf. initial		52.50
RD137	ST3	$100 **bright green**	*550.00*	80.00
		Cut cancel		29.00
		Perf. initial		16.00
RD138	ST3	$500 **bright green**	—	*12,500.*
		Cut cancel		*9,500.*
		Perf. initial		*8,000.*
RD139	ST3	$1000 **bright green**	—	575.00
		Cut cancel		275.00
		Perf. initial		160.00

Nos. RD67-RD91 Overprint Instead: **SERIES 1943**

1943 Wmk. 191R *Perf. 11*

No.	Type	Description	Unused	Used
RD140	ST1	1c **bright green**	.45	.30
		Cut cancel		.25
		Perf. initial		.25
RD141	ST1	2c **bright green**	.55	.40
		Cut cancel		.20
		Perf. initial		.20
RD142	ST1	4c **bright green**	1.90	.20
		Cut cancel		.20
		Perf. initial		.20
RD143	ST1	5c **bright green**	.55	.20
		Cut cancel		.20
		Perf. initial		.20
RD144	ST1	10c **bright green**	1.10	.20
		Cut cancel		.20
		Perf. initial		.20
RD145	ST1	20c **bright green**	1.90	.20
		Cut cancel		.20
		Perf. initial		.20
RD146	ST1	25c **bright green**	5.00	.35
		Cut cancel		.25
		Perf. initial		.20
RD147	ST1	40c **bright green**	4.25	.25
		Cut cancel		.25
		Perf. initial		.20
RD148	ST1	50c **bright green**	4.25	.20
		Cut cancel		.20
		Perf. initial		.20
RD149	ST1	80c **bright green**	17.00	4.75
		Cut cancel		1.60
		Perf. initial		1.10
RD150	ST2	$1 **bright green**	17.00	.20
		Cut cancel		.20
		Perf. initial		.20
RD151	ST2	$2 **bright green**	19.00	.35
		Cut cancel		.20
		Perf. initial		.25
RD152	ST2	$3 **bright green**	22.50	1.40
		Cut cancel		.30
		Perf. initial		.25
RD153	ST2	$4 **bright green**	47.50	16.00
		Cut cancel		1.10
		Perf. initial		.30
RD154	ST2	$5 **bright green**	72.50	.40
		Cut cancel		.25
		Perf. initial		.25
RD155	ST2	$10 **bright green**	95.00	4.75
		Cut cancel		.80
		Perf. initial		.30
RD156	ST2	$20 **bright green**	160.00	40.00
		Cut cancel		14.50
		Perf. initial		3.75

Perf. 12

Without Gum

No.	Type	Description	Unused	Used
RD157	ST3	$30 **bright green**	350.00	150.00
		Cut cancel		52.50
		Perf. initial		24.00
RD158	ST3	$50 **bright green**	725.00	140.00
		Cut cancel		29.00
		Perf. initial		14.50
RD159	ST3	$60 **bright green**	—	1,000.
		Cut cancel		350.00
		Perf. initial		120.00
RD160	ST3	$100 **bright green**	125.00	62.50
		Cut cancel		18.00
		Perf. initial		13.00
RD161	ST3	$500 **bright green**	—	1,100.
		Cut cancel		400.00
		Perf. initial		210.00
RD162	ST3	$1000 **bright green**	—	260.00
		Cut cancel		175.00
		Perf. initial		140.00

Nos. RD67-RD91 Overprint Instead: **Series 1944**

1944 Wmk. 191R *Perf. 11*

No.	Type	Description	Unused	Used
RD163	ST1	1c **bright green**	.70	.65
		Cut cancel		.25
		Perf. initial		.25
RD164	ST1	2c **bright green**	.50	.25
		Cut cancel		.25
		Perf. initial		.25
RD165	ST1	4c **bright green**	.65	.25
		Cut cancel		.25
		Perf. initial		.25
RD166	ST1	5c **bright green**	.55	.20
		Cut cancel		.20
		Perf. initial		.25
RD167	ST1	10c **bright green**	.80	.20
		Cut cancel		.20
		Perf. initial		.20
RD168	ST1	20c **bright green**	1.40	.20
		Cut cancel		.25
		Perf. initial		.20
RD169	ST1	25c **bright green**	2.25	.30
		Cut cancel		.25
		Perf. initial		.25
RD170	ST1	40c **bright green**	8.75	5.25
		Cut cancel		2.40
		Perf. initial		1.60
RD171	ST1	50c **bright green**	5.00	.20
		Cut cancel		.20
		Perf. initial		.25
RD172	ST1	80c **bright green**	10.00	4.75
		Cut cancel		2.10
		Perf. initial		1.60
RD173	ST2	$1 **bright green**	11.00	.45
		Cut cancel		.25
		Perf. initial		.25
RD174	ST2	$2 **bright green**	42.50	.65
		Cut cancel		.25
		Perf. initial		.25
RD175	ST2	$3 **bright green**	37.50	1.40
		Cut cancel		.30
		Perf. initial		.25
RD176	ST2	$4 **bright green**	45.00	5.25
		Cut cancel		.25
		Perf. initial		.25
RD177	ST2	$5 **bright green**	42.50	1.10
		Cut cancel		.35
		Perf. initial		.25
RD178	ST2	$10 **bright green**	82.50	4.75
		Cut cancel		.50
		Perf. initial		.35
RD179	ST2	$20 **bright green**	140.00	9.25
		Cut cancel		4.25
		Perf. initial		3.50

Perf. 12

Without Gum

Designs: $2,500, William Windom. $5,000, C. J. Folger. $10,000, W. Q. Gresham.

No.	Type	Description	Unused	Used
RD180	ST3	$30 **bright green**	225.00	77.50
		Cut cancel		29.00
		Perf. initial		12.50
RD181	ST3	$50 **bright green**	150.00	62.50
		Cut cancel		16.00
		Perf. initial		11.50
RD182	ST3	$60 **bright green**	260.00	150.00
		Cut cancel		67.50
		Perf. initial		50.00
RD183	ST3	$100 **bright green**	225.00	62.50
		Cut cancel		24.00
		Perf. initial		11.50
RD184	ST3	$500 **bright green**	—	525.00
		Cut cancel		325.00
		Perf. initial		240.00
RD185	ST3	$1000 **bright green**	*2,500.*	825.00
		Cut cancel		325.00
		Perf. initial		190.00
RD185A	ST3	$2500 **bright green**		—
RD185B	ST3	$5000 **bright green**		—
RD185C	ST3	$10,000 **bright green**, cut cancel		—

Nos. RD67-RD91 Overprint Instead: **Series 1945**

1945 Wmk. 191R *Perf. 11*

No.	Type	Description	Unused	Used
RD186	ST1	1c **bright green**	.30	.25
		Cut cancel		.25
		Perf. initial		.25
RD187	ST1	2c **bright green**	.30	.30
		Cut cancel		.20
		Perf. initial		.20
RD188	ST1	4c **bright green**	.30	.20
		Cut cancel		.20
		Perf. initial		.20
RD189	ST1	5c **bright green**	.30	.20
		Cut cancel		.25
		Perf. initial		.20
RD190	ST1	10c **bright green**	.80	.35
		Cut cancel		.25
		Perf. initial		.25
RD191	ST1	20c **bright green**	1.40	.35
		Cut cancel		.25
		Perf. initial		.25
RD192	ST1	25c **bright green**	2.25	.35
		Cut cancel		.30
		Perf. initial		.25
RD193	ST1	40c **bright green**	3.25	.25
		Cut cancel		.20
		Perf. initial		.20
RD194	ST1	50c **bright green**	8.75	.30
		Cut cancel		.20
		Perf. initial		.25
RD195	ST1	80c **bright green**	8.25	3.25
		Cut cancel		.80
		Perf. initial		.70
RD196	ST2	$1 **bright green**	16.00	.30
		Cut cancel		.20
		Perf. initial		.25
RD197	ST2	$2 **bright green**	25.00	.50
		Cut cancel		.20
		Perf. initial		.25
RD198	ST2	$3 **bright green**	40.00	.95
		Cut cancel		.25
		Perf. initial		.25
RD199	ST2	$4 **bright green**	40.00	2.75
		Cut cancel		.80
		Perf. initial		.55
RD200	ST2	$5 **bright green**	26.00	.55
		Cut cancel		.20
		Perf. initial		.25
RD201	ST2	$10 **bright green**	60.00	6.75
		Cut cancel		.80
		Perf. initial		.75
RD202	ST2	$20 **bright green**	140.00	13.00
		Cut cancel		2.10
		Perf. initial		1.25

Perf. 12

Without Gum

No.	Type	Description	Unused	Used
RD203	ST3	$30 **bright green**	150.00	72.50
		Cut cancel		29.00
		Perf. initial		19.00
RD204	ST3	$50 **bright green**	72.50	26.00
		Cut cancel		6.50
		Perf. initial		5.25
RD205	ST3	$60 **bright green**	260.00	150.00
		Cut cancel		62.50
		Perf. initial		29.00
RD206	ST3	$100 **bright green**	95.00	42.50
		Cut cancel		17.00
		Perf. initial		8.75
RD207	ST3	$500 **bright green**	—	925.00
		Cut cancel		425.00
		Perf. initial		240.00
RD208	ST3	$1000 **bright green**	*1,650.*	1,000.
		Cut cancel		450.00
		Perf. initial		240.00
RD208A	ST3	$2500 **bright green**		
		Cut cancel		*30,000.*
		Perf. initial		*20,000.*
RD208B	ST3	$5000 **bright green**		*20,000.*
RD208C	ST3	$10,000 **bright green**		
		Cut cancel		*20,000.*

Stock Transfer Stamps and Type of 1940 Overprinted in Black

Series 1946

1946 Wmk. 191R *Perf. 11*

No.	Type	Description	Unused	Used
RD209	ST1	1c **bright green**	.25	.25
		Cut cancel		.25
		Perf. initial		.25
a.		Pair, one dated "1945"	*475.00*	
RD210	ST1	2c **bright green**	.40	.20
		Cut cancel		.25
		Perf. initial		.25
RD211	ST1	4c **bright green**	.35	.20
		Cut cancel		.20
		Perf. initial		.20

No.	Type	Description	Unused	Used
RD212	ST1	5c **bright green**	.40	.20
		Cut cancel		.20
		Perf. initial		.25
RD213	ST1	10c **bright green**	.80	.20
		Cut cancel		.20
		Perf. initial		.25
RD214	ST1	20c **bright green**	1.60	.20
		Cut cancel		.25
		Perf. initial		.20
RD215	ST1	25c **bright green**	1.90	.30
		Cut cancel		.25
		Perf. initial		.25
RD216	ST1	40c **bright green**	3.75	.65
		Cut cancel		.25
		Perf. initial		.25
RD217	ST1	50c **bright green**	5.00	.25
		Cut cancel		.20
		Perf. initial		.25
RD218	ST1	80c **bright green**	12.00	6.25
		Cut cancel		2.10
		Perf. initial		1.40
RD219	ST2	$1 **bright green**	11.00	.50
		Cut cancel		.20
		Perf. initial		.25
RD220	ST2	$2 **bright green**	12.00	.55
		Cut cancel		.25
		Perf. initial		.25
RD221	ST2	$3 **bright green**	22.50	1.40
		Cut cancel		.35
		Perf. initial		.25
RD222	ST2	$4 **bright green**	22.50	6.50
		Cut cancel		2.40
		Perf. initial		1.00
RD223	ST2	$5 **bright green**	35.00	1.40
		Cut cancel		.30
		Perf. initial		.25
RD224	ST2	$10 **bright green**	67.50	2.50
		Cut cancel		.80
		Perf. initial		.25
RD225	ST2	$20 **bright green**	160.00	47.50
		Cut cancel		13.00
		Perf. initial		7.25

Without Gum ***Perf. 12***

No.	Type	Description	Unused	Used
RD226	ST3	$30 **bright green**	140.00	45.00
		Cut cancel		18.00
		Perf. initial		16.00
RD227	ST3	$50 **bright green**	100.00	50.00
		Cut cancel		21.00
		Perf. initial		11.50
RD228	ST3	$60 **bright green**	225.00	100.00
		Cut cancel		37.50
		Perf. initial		13.00
RD229	ST3	$100 **bright green**	140.00	57.50
		Cut cancel		21.00
		Perf. initial		14.50
RD230	ST3	$500 **bright green**	—	175.00
		Cut cancel		110.00
		Perf. initial		85.00
RD231	ST3	$1000 **bright green**	—	200.00
		Cut cancel		125.00
		Perf. initial		85.00
RD232	ST3	$2500 **bright green**		*20,000.*
		Cut cancel		*13,500.*
RD233	ST3	$5000 **bright green**		
		Cut cancel		*12,500.*
RD234	ST3	$10 **bright green,**		
		Cut cancel		*10,000.*

Stock Transfer Stamps and Type of 1940 Overprinted in Black

Series 1947

1947 **Wmk. 191R** ***Perf. 11***

No.	Type	Description	Unused	Used
RD235	ST1	1c **bright green**	1.40	.60
		Cut cancel		.25
		Perf. initial		.25
RD236	ST1	2c **bright green**	1.40	.55
		Cut cancel		.25
		Perf. initial		.25
RD237	ST1	4c **bright green**	1.10	.45
		Cut cancel		.25
		Perf. initial		.25
RD238	ST1	5c **bright green**	1.10	.35
		Cut cancel		.25
		Perf. initial		.25
RD239	ST1	10c **bright green**	1.40	.55
		Cut cancel		.25
		Perf. initial		.25
RD240	ST1	20c **bright green**	2.25	.55
		Cut cancel		.25
		Perf. initial		.25
RD241	ST1	25c **bright green**	3.25	.65
		Cut cancel		.25
		Perf. initial		.25
RD242	ST1	40c **bright green**	3.75	.80
		Cut cancel		.30
		Perf. initial		.25
RD243	ST1	50c **bright green**	4.50	.30
		Cut cancel		.25
		Perf. initial		.20
RD244	ST1	80c **bright green**	22.50	10.50
		Cut cancel		4.25
		Perf. initial		3.75
RD245	ST2	$1 **bright green**	12.00	.55
		Cut cancel		.25
		Perf. initial		.25
RD246	ST2	$2 **bright green**	19.00	.80
		Cut cancel		.25
		Perf. initial		.25
RD247	ST2	$3 **bright green**	35.00	1.60
		Cut cancel		.40
		Perf. initial		.35
RD248	ST2	$4 **bright green**	45.00	6.25
		Cut cancel		1.25
		Perf. initial		.75
RD249	ST2	$5 **bright green**	37.50	1.60
		Cut cancel		.35
		Perf. initial		.25
RD250	ST2	$10 **bright green**	60.00	5.25
		Cut cancel		2.10
		Perf. initial		1.40
RD251	ST2	$20 **bright green**	110.00	32.50
		Cut cancel		7.50
		Perf. initial		6.25

Without Gum ***Perf. 12***

No.	Type	Description	Unused	Used
RD252	ST3	$30 **bright green**	110.00	52.50
		Cut cancel		16.00
		Perf. initial		10.50
RD253	ST3	$50 **bright green**	225.00	125.00
		Cut cancel		47.50
		Perf. initial		21.00
RD254	ST3	$60 **bright green**	325.00	150.00
		Cut cancel		52.50
		Perf. initial		37.50
RD255	ST3	$100 **bright green**	125.00	45.00
		Cut cancel		18.00
		Perf. initial		16.00
RD256	ST3	$500 **bright green**	—	400.00
		Cut cancel		160.00
		Perf. initial		100.00
RD257	ST3	$1000 **bright green**	—	110.00
		Cut cancel		52.50
		Perf. initial		32.50
RD258	ST3	$2500 **bright green**	—	—
		Cut cancel		450.00
		Perf. initial		—
RD259	ST3	$5000 **bright green**	—	—
		Cut cancel		325.00
		Perf. initial		—
RD260	ST3	$10,000 **bright green**	—	—
		Cut cancel		55.00
		Perf. initial		—
	a.	Horiz. pair, imperf. vert., cut cancel		—

Nos. RD67-RD91 Overprint Instead: **Series 1948**

1948 **Wmk. 191R** ***Perf. 11***

No.	Type	Description	Unused	Used
RD261	ST1	1c **bright green**	.30	.25
		Cut cancel		.25
		Perf. initial		.25
RD262	ST1	2c **bright green**	.30	.30
		Cut cancel		.25
		Perf. initial		.20
RD263	ST1	4c **bright green**	.50	.35
		Cut cancel		.25
		Perf. initial		.25
RD264	ST1	5c **bright green**	.35	.25
		Cut cancel		.20
		Perf. initial		.25
RD265	ST1	10c **bright green**	.35	.25
		Cut cancel		.20
		Perf. initial		.20
RD266	ST1	20c **bright green**	1.50	.35
		Cut cancel		.20
		Perf. initial		.20
RD267	ST1	25c **bright green**	1.50	.40
		Cut cancel		.25
		Perf. initial		.25
RD268	ST1	40c **bright green**	2.50	.80
		Cut cancel		.30
		Perf. initial		.25
RD269	ST1	50c **bright green**	4.75	.30
		Cut cancel		.20
		Perf. initial		.25
RD270	ST1	80c **bright green**	19.00	6.25
		Cut cancel		2.40
		Perf. initial		2.10
RD271	ST2	$1 **bright green**	13.00	.40
		Cut cancel		.20
		Perf. initial		.20
RD272	ST2	$2 **bright green**	22.50	.65
		Cut cancel		.25
		Perf. initial		.25
RD273	ST2	$3 **bright green**	27.50	4.00
		Cut cancel		1.75
		Perf. initial		1.40
RD274	ST2	$4 **bright green**	30.00	11.50
		Cut cancel		3.25
		Perf. initial		2.10
RD275	ST2	$5 **bright green**	35.00	2.75
		Cut cancel		.30
		Perf. initial		.25
RD276	ST2	$10 **bright green**	60.00	4.75
		Cut cancel		.80
		Perf. initial		.65
RD277	ST2	$20 **bright green**	110.00	19.00
		Cut cancel		6.25
		Perf. initial		4.25

Perf. 12

Without Gum

No.	Type	Description	Unused	Used
RD278	ST3	$30 **bright green**	160.00	62.50
		Cut cancel		26.00
		Perf. initial		16.00
RD279	ST3	$50 **bright green**	110.00	62.50
		Cut cancel		26.00
		Perf. initial		13.00
RD280	ST3	$60 **bright green**	275.00	140.00
		Cut cancel		55.00
		Perf. initial		21.00
RD281	ST3	$100 **bright green**	95.00	24.00
		Cut cancel		7.75
		Perf. initial		5.75
RD282	ST3	$500 **bright green**	—	240.00
		Cut cancel		140.00
		Perf. initial		47.50
RD283	ST3	$1000 **bright green**	—	140.00
		Cut cancel		47.50
		Perf. initial		29.00
RD284	ST3	$2500 **bright green**	725.00	375.00
		Cut cancel		190.00
		Perf. initial		140.00
RD285	ST3	$5000 **bright green**	—	300.00
		Cut cancel		175.00
		Perf. initial		140.00
RD286	ST3	$10,000 **bright green**	—	—
		Cut cancel		52.50
		Perf. initial		—

Nos. RD67-RD91 Overprint Instead: **Series 1949**

1949 **Wmk. 191R** ***Perf. 11***

No.	Type	Description	Unused	Used
RD287	ST1	1c **bright green**	1.60	.50
		Cut cancel		.25
		Perf. initial		.25
RD288	ST1	2c **bright green**	1.60	.50
		Cut cancel		.25
		Perf. initial		.25
RD289	ST1	4c **bright green**	1.90	.55
		Cut cancel		.25
		Perf. initial		.25
RD290	ST1	5c **bright green**	1.90	.55
		Cut cancel		.25
		Perf. initial		.25
RD291	ST1	10c **bright green**	3.25	.80
		Cut cancel		.25
		Perf. initial		.25
RD292	ST1	20c **bright green**	5.50	.65
		Cut cancel		.25
		Perf. initial		.25
RD293	ST1	25c **bright green**	6.50	.90
		Cut cancel		.25
		Perf. initial		.25
RD294	ST1	40c **bright green**	14.00	1.60
		Cut cancel		.25
		Perf. initial		.25
RD295	ST1	50c **bright green**	17.00	.30
		Cut cancel		.25
		Perf. initial		.25
RD296	ST1	80c **bright green**	22.50	6.75
		Cut cancel		3.00
		Perf. initial		2.75
RD297	ST2	$1 **bright green**	19.00	.80
		Cut cancel		.30
		Perf. initial		.25
RD298	ST2	$2 **bright green**	27.50	.95
		Cut cancel		.25
		Perf. initial		.25
RD299	ST2	$3 **bright green**	45.00	4.75
		Cut cancel		1.40
		Perf. initial		.95
RD300	ST2	$4 **bright green**	42.50	7.75
		Cut cancel		2.10
		Perf. initial		1.60
RD301	ST2	$5 **bright green**	52.50	2.10
		Cut cancel		.30
		Perf. initial		.25
RD302	ST2	$10 **bright green**	72.50	4.25
		Cut cancel		1.40
		Perf. initial		1.25
RD303	ST2	$20 **bright green**	150.00	16.00
		Cut cancel		6.25
		Perf. initial		5.25

Perf. 12

Without Gum

No.	Type	Description	Unused	Used
RD304	ST3	$30 **bright green**	190.00	87.50
		Cut cancel		35.00
		Perf. initial		16.00
RD305	ST3	$50 **bright green**	250.00	140.00
		Cut cancel		50.00
		Perf. initial		24.00
RD306	ST3	$60 **bright green**	425.00	250.00
		Cut cancel		110.00
		Perf. initial		47.50
RD307	ST3	$100 **bright green**	160.00	70.00
		Cut cancel		26.00
		Perf. initial		16.00
RD308	ST3	$500 **bright green**	—	250.00
		Cut cancel		92.50
		Perf. initial		57.50
RD309	ST3	$1000 **bright green**	—	100.00
		Cut cancel		45.00
		Perf. initial		29.00
RD310	ST3	$2500 **bright green**	—	
		Cut cancel		*475.00*
		Perf. initial		—
RD311	ST3	$5000 **bright green**	—	—
		Cut cancel		*475.00*
		Perf. initial		*350.00*
RD312	ST3	$10,000 **bright green**	—	425.00
		Cut cancel		45.00
		Perf. initial		—
	a.	Pair, one without ovpt., cut cancel		*8,000.*

No. RD312a is unique.

Nos. RD67-RD91 Overprint Instead: **Series 1950**

1950 **Wmk. 191R** ***Perf. 11***

No.	Type	Description	Unused	Used
RD313	ST1	1c **bright green**	.65	.35
		Cut cancel		.25
		Perf. initial		.25
RD314	ST1	2c **bright green**	.55	.30
		Cut cancel		.20
		Perf. initial		.20
RD315	ST1	4c **bright green**	.45	.35
		Cut cancel		.20
		Perf. initial		.20

No.	Type	Description	Unused	Used
RD316	ST1	5c **bright green**	.55	.20
		Cut cancel		.25
		Perf. initial		.25
RD317	ST1	10c **bright green**	2.75	.30
		Cut cancel		.25
		Perf. initial		.25
RD318	ST1	20c **bright green**	4.00	.55
		Cut cancel		.25
		Perf. initial		.20
RD319	ST1	25c **bright green**	5.50	.75
		Cut cancel		.25
		Perf. initial		.20
RD320	ST1	40c **bright green**	8.25	1.10
		Cut cancel		.25
		Perf. initial		.25
RD321	ST1	50c **bright green**	9.00	.40
		Cut cancel		.25
		Perf. initial		.25
RD322	ST1	80c **bright green**	17.00	5.25
		Cut cancel		2.10
		Perf. initial		1.40
RD323	ST2	$1 **bright green**	17.00	.50
		Cut cancel		.20
		Perf. initial		.20
RD324	ST2	$2 **bright green**	30.00	.80
		Cut cancel		.25
		Perf. initial		.25
RD325	ST2	$3 **bright green**	40.00	4.25
		Cut cancel		.65
		Perf. initial		.60
RD326	ST2	$4 **bright green**	47.50	9.00
		Cut cancel		3.50
		Perf. initial		2.10
RD327	ST2	$5 **bright green**	47.50	1.90
		Cut cancel		.25
		Perf. initial		.25
RD328	ST2	$10 **bright green**	150.00	5.25
		Cut cancel		1.60
		Perf. initial		.80
RD329	ST2	$20 **bright green**	150.00	26.00
		Cut cancel		17.00
		Perf. initial		4.75

Perf. 12

Without Gum

No.	Type	Description	Unused	Used
RD330	ST3	$30 **bright green**	150.00	72.50
		Cut cancel		32.50
		Perf. initial		16.00
RD331	ST3	$50 **bright green**	190.00	92.50
		Cut cancel		47.50
		Perf. initial		26.00
RD332	ST3	$60 **bright green**	275.00	150.00
		Cut cancel		67.50
		Perf. initial		42.50
RD333	ST3	$100 **bright green**	110.00	50.00
		Cut cancel		24.00
		Perf. initial		13.00
a.		Vert. pair, imperf. btwn.	2,250.	*1,750.*
RD334	ST3	$500 **bright green**	—	250.00
		Cut cancel		125.00
		Perf. initial		92.50
RD335	ST3	$1000 **bright green**	—	75.00
		Cut cancel		32.50
		Perf. initial		20.00
RD336	ST3	$2500 **bright green**	—	*1,250.*
		Cut cancel		900.00
		Perf. initial		—
RD337	ST3	$5000 **bright green**	—	750.00
		Cut cancel		425.00
		Perf. initial		—
RD338	ST3	$10,000 **bright green**	—	825.00
		Cut cancel		97.50
		Perf. initial		—

Nos. RD67-RD91 Overprint Instead: **Series 1951**

1951 Wmk. 191R *Perf. 11*

No.	Type	Description	Unused	Used
RD339	ST1	1c **bright green**	2.25	.40
		Cut cancel		.25
		Perf. initial		.25
RD340	ST1	2c **bright green**	1.90	.35
		Cut cancel		.25
		Perf. initial		.25
RD341	ST1	4c **bright green**	2.25	.55
		Cut cancel		.25
		Perf. initial		.25
RD342	ST1	5c **bright green**	1.60	.40
		Cut cancel		.25
		Perf. initial		.20
RD343	ST1	10c **bright green**	2.25	.35
		Cut cancel		.25
		Perf. initial		.20
RD344	ST1	20c **bright green**	5.50	.95
		Cut cancel		.25
		Perf. initial		.25
RD345	ST1	25c **bright green**	8.25	.95
		Cut cancel		.25
		Perf. initial		.25
RD346	ST1	40c **bright green**	32.50	9.25
		Cut cancel		3.00
		Perf. initial		1.60
RD347	ST1	50c **bright green**	14.00	.95
		Cut cancel		.25
		Perf. initial		.25
RD348	ST1	80c **bright green**	27.50	10.50
		Cut cancel		4.25
		Perf. initial		2.10
RD349	ST2	$1 **bright green**	29.00	.85
		Cut cancel		.25
		Perf. initial		.25
RD350	ST2	$2 **bright green**	35.00	1.40
		Cut cancel		.25
		Perf. initial		.25
RD351	ST2	$3 **bright green**	47.50	10.50
		Cut cancel		3.75
		Perf. initial		1.60
RD352	ST2	$4 **bright green**	55.00	12.50
		Cut cancel		5.00
		Perf. initial		2.10
RD353	ST2	$5 **bright green**	65.00	2.75
		Cut cancel		.30
		Perf. initial		.25
RD354	ST2	$10 **bright green**	110.00	8.75
		Cut cancel		2.10
		Perf. initial		1.60
RD355	ST2	$20 **bright green**	175.00	18.00
		Cut cancel		7.25
		Perf. initial		5.25

Perf. 12

Without Gum

No.	Type	Description	Unused	Used
RD356	ST3	$30 **bright green**	175.00	77.50
		Cut cancel		35.00
		Perf. initial		18.00
RD357	ST3	$50 **bright green**	160.00	67.50
		Cut cancel		26.00
		Perf. initial		18.00
RD358	ST3	$60 **bright green**	—	*1,400.*
		Cut cancel		525.00
		Perf. initial		240.00
RD359	ST3	$100 **bright green**	160.00	67.50
		Cut cancel		24.00
		Perf. initial		11.50
RD360	ST3	$500 **bright green**	—	375.00
		Cut cancel		160.00
		Perf. initial		110.00
RD361	ST3	$1000 **bright green**	—	100.00
		Cut cancel		67.50
		Perf. initial		52.50
RD362	ST3	$2500 **bright green**	—	*3,000.*
		Cut cancel		1,200.
		Perf. initial		500.00
RD363	ST3	$5000 **bright green**	—	*1,450.*
		Cut cancel		825.00
		Perf. initial		600.00
RD364	ST3	$10,000 **bright green**	*1,650.*	160.00
		Cut cancel		67.50
		Perf. initial		50.00

Nos. RD67-RD91 Overprint Instead: **Series 1952**

1952 Wmk. 191R *Perf. 11*

No.	Type	Description	Unused	Used
RD365	ST1	1c **bright green**	37.50	18.00
		Cut cancel		4.25
		Perf. initial		2.10
RD366	ST1	10c **bright green**	37.50	18.00
		Cut cancel		4.25
		Perf. initial		2.10
RD367	ST1	20c **bright green**	450.00	—
		Cut cancel		—
		Perf. initial		—
RD368	ST1	25c **bright green**	600.00	—
		Cut cancel		—
		Perf. initial		—
RD369	ST1	40c **bright green**	125.00	42.50
		Cut cancel		14.50
		Perf. initial		10.50
RD370	ST2	$4 **bright green**	*1,500.*	575.00
		Perf. initial		—
RD371	ST2	$10 **bright green**	*3,000.*	—
		Cut cancel		—
		Perf. initial		—
RD372	ST2	$20 **bright green**	*5,750.*	—
		Cut cancel		—
		Perf. initial		—

Stock Transfer Stamps were discontinued in 1952.

CORDIALS, WINES, ETC. STAMPS

RE1

Inscribed "Series of 1914"

1914 Wmk. 190 Offset Printing *Perf. 10*

No.	Type	Description	Unused	Used
RE1	RE1	¼c **green**	.95	.55
RE2	RE1	½c **green**	.50	.50
RE3	RE1	1c **green**	.50	.35
RE4	RE1	1½c **green**	2.40	1.60
RE5	RE1	2c **green**	4.00	3.75
RE6	RE1	3c **green**	3.25	1.40
RE7	RE1	4c **green**	2.75	1.60
RE8	RE1	5c **green**	1.10	.80
RE9	RE1	6c **green**	7.50	4.00
a.		Double impression		—
RE10	RE1	8c **green**	5.75	1.60
RE11	RE1	10c **green**	3.75	3.00
RE12	RE1	20c **green**	4.50	1.90
RE13	RE1	24c **green**	14.50	8.75
RE14	RE1	40c **green**	3.50	.90

RE1a

Without Gum *Imperf.*

No.	Type	Description	Unused	Used
RE15	RE1a	$2 **green**	7.75	.25
a.		Double impression		125.00

1914 Wmk. 191R *Perf. 10*

No.	Type	Description	Unused	Used
RE16	RE1	¼c **green**	6.25	5.25
RE17	RE1	½c **green**	4.75	3.25
RE18	RE1	1c **green**	.30	.20
RE19	RE1	1½c **green**	60.00	37.50
RE20	RE1	2c **green**	.25	.25
a.		Double impression		—
RE21	RE1	3c **green**	2.75	2.10
RE22	RE1	4c **green**	.90	1.10
RE23	RE1	5c **green**	15.00	11.50
a.		Double impression		—
RE24	RE1	6c **green**	.65	.30
RE25	RE1	8c **green**	2.10	.50
RE26	RE1	10c **green**	.70	.20
RE27	RE1	20c **green**	.80	.40
RE28	RE1	24c **green**	14.50	.80
RE29	RE1	40c **green**	32.50	11.50

Imperf

Without Gum

No.	Type	Description	Unused	Used
RE30	RE1a	$2 **green**	40.00	3.25

Perf. 11

No.	Type	Description	Unused	Used
RE31	RE1	2c **green**	82.50	92.50

WINE STAMPS

Issued Without Gum

RE2

Inscribed: "Series of 1916"

1916 Wmk. 191R Offset Printing ***Rouletted 3½***

Plates of 100 subjects

RE32	RE2	1c	**green**	.40	.35
a.	Double impression			200.00	
RE33	RE2	3c	**green**	5.50	4.25
RE34	RE2	4c	**green**	.30	.35
a.	Double impression				—
RE35	RE2	6c	**green**	2.10	.80
RE36	RE2	7½c	**green**	7.75	4.25
RE37	RE2	10c	**green**	1.25	.40
RE38	RE2	12c	**green**	3.00	4.25
RE39	RE2	15c	**green**	1.75	1.90
RE40	RE2	18c	**green**	24.00	24.00
RE41	RE2	20c	**green**	.30	.25
RE42	RE2	24c	**green**	5.25	3.75
a.	Double impression			150.00	
RE43	RE2	30c	**green**	3.25	3.00
a.	Double impression				—
RE44	RE2	36c	**green**	21.00	16.00
RE45	RE2	50c	**green**	.80	.40
RE46	RE2	60c	**green**	4.25	2.10
RE47	RE2	72c	**green**	35.00	29.00
RE48	RE2	80c	**green**	1.40	.60
RE49	RE2	$1.20	**green**	7.00	6.25
RE50	RE2	$1.44	**green**	9.25	3.25
RE51	RE2	$1.60	**green**	25.00	22.50
RE52	RE2	$2	**green**	1.75	1.60

For rouletted 7 see Nos. RE60-RE80, RE102-RE105.

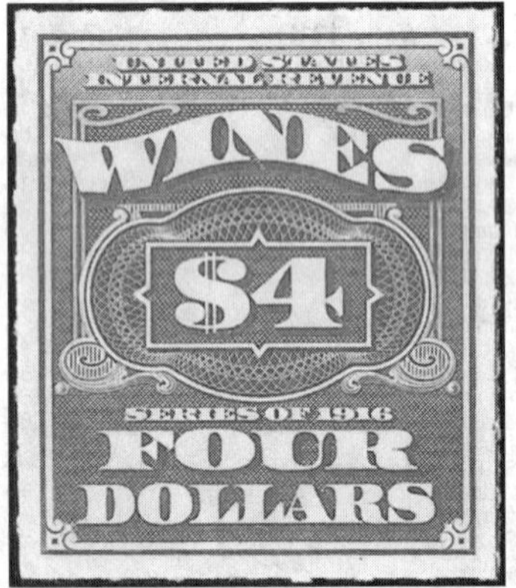

RE3

Engr.

Plates of 50 subjects

RE53	RE3	$4	**green**	1.00	.25
RE54	RE3	$4.80	**green**	3.50	3.25
RE55	RE3	$9.60	**green**	1.40	.35

Nos. RE32-RE55 exist in many shades. Size variations of 1c-$2 are believed due to offset printing. For rouletted 7 see Nos. RE81-RE83, RE106-RE107.

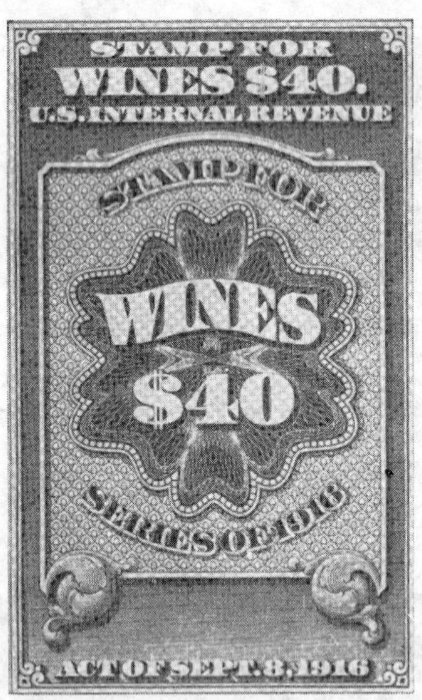

RE4

Plates of 6 subjects

Perf. 12 at left

RE56	RE4	$20	**green**	90.00	42.50
RE57	RE4	$40	**green**	175.00	52.50
RE58	RE4	$50	**green**	62.50	47.50
RE59	RE4	$100	**green**	250.00	140.00

Stamps of design RE4 have an adjoining tablet at right for affixing additional stamps. Values are for examples with the tablets attached. Examples with the tablets removed sell for much less. Used stamps with additional stamps tied on the tablet with cancels sell for about double the values given. See Nos. RE107A-RE107D.

Same designs as Issue of 1916

1933 Wmk. 191R Offset Printing ***Rouletted 7***

RE60	RE2	1c	**light green**	3.25	.45
a.	Double impression				—
RE61	RE2	3c	**light green**	7.50	2.50
RE62	RE2	4c	**light green**	2.00	.45
RE63	RE2	6c	**light green**	11.00	5.50
RE64	RE2	7½c	**light green**	5.25	1.10
RE65	RE2	10c	**light green**	2.10	.20
a.	Double impression				—
RE66	RE2	12c	**light green**	9.00	5.75
RE67	RE2	15c	**light green**	4.25	.30
RE69	RE2	20c	**light green**	5.25	.25
a.	Double impression			—	—
RE70	RE2	24c	**light green**	5.25	.20
a.	Double impression			—	*160.00*
RE71	RE2	30c	**light green**	5.25	.20
a.	Double impression				—
RE72	RE2	36c	**light green**	11.50	.65
RE73	RE2	50c	**light green**	4.50	.25
RE74	RE2	60c	**light green**	8.75	.20
RE75	RE2	72c	**light green**	13.00	.35
RE76	RE2	80c	**light green**	13.00	.35
RE77	RE2	$1.20	**light green**	10.50	1.50
RE78	RE2	$1.44	**light green**	13.00	4.25
RE79	RE2	$1.60	**light green**	350.00	190.00
RE80	RE2	$2	**light green**	35.00	4.00

Engr.

RE81	RE3	$4	**light green**	35.00	7.25
RE82	RE3	$4.80	**light green**	35.00	17.00
RE83	RE3	$9.60	**light green**	160.00	85.00

RE5

Offset Printing

1934-40 Wmk. 191R ***Rouletted 7***

Inscribed: "Series of 1934"

Plates of 200 and 224 subjects

Issued With and Without Gum

RE83A	RE5	⅕c	**green** ('40)	.75	.20
RE84	RE5	½c	**green**	.55	.20
RE85	RE5	1c	**green**	.70	.20
RE86	RE5	1¼c	**green**	1.00	.80
RE87	RE5	1½c	**green**	6.00	*6.75*
RE88	RE5	2c	**green**	1.75	.80
RE89	RE5	2½c	**green**	1.75	.60
RE90	RE5	3c	**green**	5.00	4.00
RE91	RE5	4c	**green**	2.75	.25
RE92	RE5	5c	**green**	.60	.20
RE93	RE5	6c	**green**	1.75	.50
RE94	RE5	7½c	**green**	2.40	.20
RE95	RE5	10c	**green**	.50	.20
RE96	RE5	12c	**green**	1.60	.25
RE96A	RE5	14⅖c	**green** ('40)	150.00	3.25
RE97	RE5	15c	**green**	.80	.20
RE98	RE5	18c	**green**	1.60	.20
RE99	RE5	20c	**green**	1.25	.20
RE100	RE5	24c	**green**	2.00	.20
RE101	RE5	30c	**green**	1.50	.20

Nos. RE83A-RE101 unused are valued without gum. Examples with gum sell for substantially more.

Nos. RE83A, RE86, RE96A were printed from plates of 200 only and all were issued without gum.

Plates of 100 subjects

Issued Without Gum

RE102	RE2	40c	**green**	3.50	.25
RE102A	RE2	43⅕c	**green** ('40)	14.50	2.75
RE103	RE2	48c	**green**	14.50	1.90
RE104	RE2	$1	**green**	21.00	11.00
RE105	RE2	$1.50	**green**	32.50	15.00
	Perforated initials				5.75

Engr.

Plates of 50 subjects.

RE106	RE3	$2.50	**green**	42.50	18.00
	Perforated initials				9.00
RE107	RE3	$5	**green**	32.50	7.50
	Perforated initials				2.50

Stamps of types RE5 and RE2 overprinted "Rectified Spirits / Puerto Rico" are listed under Puerto Rico.

Nos. RE102-RE204 issued without gum.

Inscribed: "Series of 1916"

Plates of 6 subjects

1934 ***Perf. 12 at left***

RE107A	RE4	$20	**yellow green**		1,800.
RE107B	RE4	$40	**yellow green**		*3,250.*

Perf. 12 or 12½ at left

RE107C	RE4	$50	**yellow green**	—	*2,000.*
RE107D	RE4	$100	**yellow green**	*1,050.*	375.00

The serial numbers of Nos. RE107A-RE107D are much thinner than on Nos. RE56-RE59. See valuing note after No. RE59.

RE6

Offset Printing

Inscribed "Series of 1941"

1942 Wmk. 191R ***Rouletted 7***

RE108	RE6	⅕c	**green & black**	.80	.55
RE109	RE6	¼c	**green & black**	2.50	1.90
RE110	RE6	½c	**green & black**	3.25	2.10
a.	Horiz. pair, imperf. vertically			200.00	
RE111	RE6	1c	**green & black**	1.25	1.25
RE112	RE6	2c	**green & black**	6.00	5.25
RE113	RE6	3c	**green & black**	6.00	4.50
RE114	RE6	3½c	**green & black**	—	*12,750.*
RE115	RE6	3¾c	**green & black**	11.50	7.25
RE116	RE6	4c	**green & black**	4.25	3.25
RE117	RE6	5c	**green & black**	3.00	2.40
RE118	RE6	6c	**green & black**	3.75	2.75
RE119	RE6	7c	**green & black**	7.50	5.50
RE120	RE6	7½c	**green & black**	11.00	6.00
RE121	RE6	8c	**green & black**	5.50	4.25
RE122	RE6	9c	**green & black**	15.00	9.50
RE123	RE6	10c	**green & black**	5.50	1.10
RE124	RE6	11¼c	**green & black**	6.00	6.00
RE125	RE6	12c	**green & black**	8.50	6.00
RE126	RE6	14c	**green & black**	37.50	26.00
RE127	RE6	15c	**green & black**	6.00	3.00
a.	Horiz. pair, imperf. vertically				*925.00*
RE128	RE6	16c	**green & black**	14.00	9.00
RE129	RE6	19⅕c	**green & black**	175.00	7.75
RE130	RE6	20c	**green & black**	7.50	2.10
RE131	RE6	24c	**green & black**	5.50	.25
RE132	RE6	28c	**green & black**	*2,100.*	*1,500.*
RE133	RE6	30c	**green & black**	1.50	.20
RE134	RE6	32c	**green & black**	175.00	7.50
RE135	RE6	36c	**green & black**	3.50	.25
RE136	RE6	40c	**green & black**	3.00	.20
RE137	RE6	45c	**green & black**	8.75	.25
RE138	RE6	48c	**green & black**	21.00	9.25
RE139	RE6	50c	**green & black**	12.00	7.50
RE140	RE6	60c	**green & black**	4.25	.20
RE141	RE6	72c	**green & black**	12.50	1.50
RE142	RE6	80c	**green & black**	*325.00*	10.50
RE143	RE6	84c	**green & black**	—	77.50
RE144	RE6	90c	**green & black**	25.00	.20
RE145	RE6	96c	**green & black**	15.00	.30

See Nos. RE182D-RE194.

Denomination Spelled Out in Two Lines — RE7

1942 **Engr.**

RE146	RE7	$1.20	**yel grn & blk**	7.50	.25
RE147	RE7	$1.44	**yel grn & blk**	1.75	.30
RE148	RE7	$1.50	**yel grn & blk**	130.00	67.50
RE149	RE7	$1.60	**yel grn & blk**	10.00	1.40
RE150	RE7	$1.68	**yel grn & blk**	120.00	50.00
	Perforated initials				35.00
RE151	RE7	$1.80	**yel grn & blk**	4.00	.20
a.	Vertical pair, one without denomination			—	—

	b.	Horiz. pair, one without denomination		—	
RE152	RE7	$1.92	**yel grn & blk**	72.50	42.50
RE153	RE7	$2.40	**yel grn & blk**	12.50	1.25
RE154	RE7	$3	**yel grn & blk**	87.50	42.50
RE155	RE7	$3.36	**yel grn & blk**	92.50	29.00
RE156	RE7	$3.60	**yel grn & blk**	*160.00*	6.25
RE157	RE7	$4	**yel grn & blk**	32.50	5.25
RE158	RE7	$4.80	**yel grn & blk**	*160.00*	3.75
RE159	RE7	$5	**yel grn & blk**	17.50	10.50
RE160	RE7	$7.20	**yel grn & blk**	20.00	.50
RE161	RE7	$10	**yel grn & blk**	240.00	200.00
RE162	RE7	$20	**yel grn & blk**	130.00	77.50
RE163	RE7	$50	**yel grn & blk**	130.00	77.50
		Perforated initials			21.00
RE164	RE7	$100	**yel grn & blk**	325.00	30.00
		Perforated initials			21.00
RE165	RE7	$200	**yel grn & blk**	190.00	24.00
		Perforated initials			8.75
RE165B	RE7	$400	**yel grn & blk**	—	*12,000.*
RE166	RE7	$500	**yel grn & blk**	—	150.00
		Perforated initials			35.00
RE167	RE7	$600	**yel grn & blk**	—	125.00
RE168	RE7	$900	**yel grn & blk**		*4,000.*
		Perforated initials			*1,500.*
RE169	RE7	$1000	**yel grn & blk**	—	200.00
RE170	RE7	$2000	**yel grn & blk**	—	*2,250.*
RE171	RE7	$3000	**yel grn & blk**	—	200.00
RE172	RE7	$4000	**yel grn & blk**		800.00

Denomination Repeated, Spelled Out in One Line

1949

RE173	RE7	$1	**yellow green & black**	4.25	1.60
RE174	RE7	$2	**yellow green & black**	7.25	2.10
RE175	RE7	$4	**yellow green & black**	925.00	425.00
		Perforated initials			175.00
RE176	RE7	$5	**yellow green & black**	—	82.50
RE177	RE7	$6	**yellow green & black**		500.00
RE178	RE7	$7	**yellow green & black**		47.50
RE179	RE7	$8	**yellow green & black**	875.00	450.00
		Perforated initials			85.00
RE180	RE7	$10	**yellow green & black**	10.00	5.25
		Perforated initials			2.10
RE181	RE7	$20	**yellow green & black**	25.00	5.25
		Perforated initials			1.90
RE182	RE7	$30	**yellow green & black**	1,550.	750.00

Other denominations of engraved stamps, type RE7, that were printed and delivered to the Internal Revenue Service were: $7.14, $9, $12, $40, $60, $70, $80, $300, $700 and $800. None are reported in collectors' hands.

Types of 1942-49

1951-54 **Offset Printing**

RE182D	RE6	1 7/10c	**green & black**		*25,000.*
RE183	RE6	3 2/5c	**green & black**	55.00	52.50
RE184	RE6	8 1/2c	**green & black**	30.00	20.00
RE185	RE6	13 2/5c	**green & black**	100.00	82.50
RE186	RE6	17c	**green & black**	16.00	15.00
RE187	RE6	20 2/5c	**green & black**	110.00	62.50
RE188	RE6	33 1/2c	**green & black**	90.00	92.50
RE189	RE6	38 1/4c	**green & black**	125.00	90.00
RE190	RE6	40 4/5c	**green & black**	3.75	.80
RE191	RE6	51c	**green & black**	4.00	1.40
RE192	RE6	67c	**green & black**	12.50	4.25
RE193	RE6	68c	**green & black**	3.75	.70
RE194	RE6	80 2/5c	**green & black**	140.00	110.00

Engr.

Denomination Spelled Out in Two Lines in Small Letters

Two types of $1.60 4/5:

I - The "4" slants sharply. Loop of "5" almost closes to form oval. Each numeral 2mm high.

II - The "4" is less slanted. Loop of "5" more open and nearly circular. Each numeral 2 1/2mm high.

RE195	RE7	$1.50 3/4	**yel grn & blk**	50.00	47.50
RE196	RE7	$1.60 4/5	**yel grn & blk** (I)	4.25	1.00
	a.	"DOLLLAR"		52.50	15.00
		Perforated initials			10.00
	b.	As "a," horiz. pair, one without denomination		*2,600.*	—
	c.	Type II		750.00	250.00
RE197	RE7	$1.88 3/10	**yel grn & blk**	300.00	85.00
		Perforated initials			35.00

Denomination Spelled Out in Two Lines in Slightly Larger Letters Same as Nos. RE146-RE172

RE198	RE7	$1.60 4/5	**yel grn & blk** (II)	32.50	6.25
	a.	First line larger letters, second line small letters		—	*3,000.*
	b.	Type I ('53)		75.00	25.00
RE199	RE7	$2.01	**yel grn & blk**	3.50	1.00
RE200	RE7	$2.68	**yel grn & blk**	3.50	1.40
RE201	RE7	$4.08	**yel grn & blk**	95.00	35.00
RE202	RE7	$5.76	**yel grn & blk**	275.00	115.00
RE203	RE7	$8.16	**yel grn & blk**	17.50	7.00
RE204	RE7	$9.60	**yel grn & blk**		*5,000.*

Other denominations that were printed but not delivered to the Internal Revenue Service were: 6 7/10c, 10 1/5c and $90. None are reported in collectors' hands.

Wine stamps were discontinued on Dec. 31, 1954.

BEER STAMPS

Basic stamps were printed by the Bureau of Engraving and Printing, unless otherwise noted.

All stamps are imperforate, unless otherwise noted.

Values for Nos. REA1-REA13 are for stamps with small faults, due to the fragile nature of the thin paper. Values for Nos. REA14-REA199 are for canceled stamps with small faults.

All copies of Nos. REA1-REA13 contain a circular pattern of 31 perforations in the design, 27 or 28½mm in diameter, often poorly punched.

Values for cut squares of Nos. REA1-REA13 are for margins clear of the design. Die cut and cut to shape stamps are valued for margins clear to slightly cutting into the design.

Eric Jackson, Michael Aldrich, Henry Tolman II and Thomas W. Priester helped the editors extensively in compiling the listings.

An excellent study of beer stamps by Frank Applegate appeared in *Weekly Philatelic Gossip* from Oct. 1-Nov. 26, 1927.

A List of the Beer Stamps of the United States of America by Ernest R. Vanderhoof appeared in the *American Philatelist* in June 1934. This was reprinted in pamphlet form.

United States Beer Stamps by Thomas W. Priester, published in 1979, comprised an illustrated and priced catalogue, illustrations of all known provisional surcharges, background notes on the stamps and tax laws, and a census of over 27,500 stamps. The catalogue and census portions were updated in the 1990 edition.

Printed by the Treasury Department. Tax rate $1 per barrel (bbl.).

12½c =	⅛ barrel	$1	= 1 barrel
16⅔c =	⅙ barrel	$2	= 1 hogshead
25c =	¼ barrel	$5	= 5 barrels
33⅓c =	⅓ barrel	$10	= 10 barrels
50c =	½ barrel	$25	= 25 barrels

1866 **Engr.**

No.	Description		
REA1	12½c **orange**	375.	500.
	Cut to shape		90.
a.	Die cut	300.	250.
b.	Silk paper		*1,500.*
REA2	16⅔c **dark green**	125.	200.
	Cut to shape		25.
a.	Die cut		75.
REA3	25c **blue**	75.	135.
	Cut to shape		25.
a.	Die cut		50.
b.	Silk paper		*2,000.*
	Double transfer		—
REA4	50c **orange brown**	30.	50.
	Printed cancellation, "A.S. 1869"		150.
	Cut to shape		10.
a.	Die cut		75.
REA5	$1 **black**	325.	250.
	Cut to shape		75.
a.	Die cut		225.
REA6	$2 **red**	900.	1,200.
	Cut to shape		150.
a.	Die cut		400.

Printed by the Treasury Department. See individual rates before No. REA1.

1867 **Engr.**

No.	Description		
REA7	12½c **orange**	*2,250.*	1,750.
	Cut to shape		750.
a.	Die cut		1,250.
REA8	16⅔c **dark green**	*2,500.*	*2,000.*
	Cut to shape		525.
a.	Die cut		1,500.
REA9	25c **blue**	250.	300.
	Cut to shape		50.
a.	Die cut		250.
REA10	33⅓c **violet brown**		*5,000.*
	Cut to shape		*2,500.*
b.	Silk paper		*3,500.*
c.	33⅓c **ocher red,** cut to shape		*3,500.*
d.	33⅓c **ocher red,** die cut		*4,000.*
REA11	50c **orange brown**	75.	125.
	Printed cancellation, "A.S. 1869"		350.
	Cut to shape		35.
a.	Die cut		150.
REA12	$1 **black**		1,250.
	Cut to shape		350.
a.	Die cut		750.
REA13	$2 **red**		*1,250.*
	Cut to shape		500.
a.	Die cut		1,100.

See individual rates before No. REA1.

1870 **Engr.** **Lilac Security Lines**

No.	Description	
REA14	12½c **brown**	200.
a.	Yellow security lines	1,000.
REA15	16⅔c **yellow orange**	250.
a.	Yellow security lines	*1,100.*
b.	Gray-green and yellow security lines	*1,750.*
c.	16⅔c **yellow ocher,** lilac security lines	750.
REA16	25c **green**	40.
a.	Yellow security lines	225.
REA17	50c **red**	100.
a.	Yellow security lines	500.
b.	Gray-green and yellow security lines	1,100.
c.	50c **brick red,** lilac security lines	600.
d.	50c **brick red,** yellow security lines	*2,500.*
REA18	$1 **blue**	750.
a.	Yellow security lines	225.
b.	Gray-green and yellow security lines	*1,500.*
REA19	$2 **black**	600.
a.	Yellow security lines	*2,500.*
b.	Gray-green and yellow security lines	*3,250.*

The security lines were printed across the center of the stamp where the cancel was to be placed.

Andrew Jackson

Designs: 16⅔c, Abraham Lincoln. 25c, Daniel Webster. 33⅓c, David G. Farragut. 50c, William T. Sherman. $1, Hugh McCulloch. $2, Alexander Hamilton.

Centers printed by the Bureau of Engraving and Printing. Frames printed by the National Bank Co.

See individual rates before No. REA1.

1871 **Engr.**

Centers, Plate Letters and Position Numbers in Black

No.	Description	
REA20	12½c **blue,** white silk paper	125.
a.	Pinkish gray silk paper	200.
b.	Gray silk paper	65.
c.	Green silk paper	150.
REA21	16⅔c **vermilion,** white silk paper	300.
a.	Pinkish gray silk paper	325.
b.	Gray silk paper	325.
c.	Green silk paper	325.
REA22	25c **green,** white silk paper	25.
a.	Pinkish gray silk paper	110.
b.	Gray silk paper	25.
c.	Green silk paper	25.
REA23	33⅓c **orange,** green silk paper	3,000.
b.	Gray silk paper	*4,000.*
REA24	33⅓c **violet brown,** white silk paper	2,000.
REA25	50c **brown,** gray silk paper	20.
a.	Pinkish gray silk paper	60.
c.	Green silk paper	75.
REA26	50c **red,** white silk paper	55.
REA27	$1 **yellow orange,** white silk paper	225.
a.	Pinkish gray silk paper	1,100.
b.	Gray silk paper	150.
REA28	$1 **scarlet,** gray silk paper	150.
a.	Pinkish gray silk paper	750.
c.	Green silk paper	300.
REA29	$2 **red brown,** white silk paper	175.
a.	Pinkish gray silk paper	*1,250.*
b.	Gray silk paper	250.
c.	Green silk paper	1,000.

Bacchus Serving the First Fermented Brew to Man

Printed by the National Bank Note Co. See individual rates before No. REA1.

1875 **Typo. & Engr.**

Center in Black

REA30 12½c **blue** 25.00
REA31 16⅔c **red brown** 150.00
REA32 25c **green** 20.00
a. Inverted center —
REA33 33⅓c **violet** 1,000.
REA34 50c **orange** 75.00
REA35 $1 **red** 175.00
REA36 $2 **brown** 300.00
a. Inverted center —

Designs: 12½c, Washington. 16⅔c, Corwin. 25c, Benton. 33⅓c, Thomas. 50c, Jefferson. $1, Johnson. $2, Wright.
Stamps on pale green paper have short greenish blue fibers. Plate designations for center consist of plate letter or number at left and position number at right.
See individual rates before No. REA1.

1878 **Typo. & Engr.** **Wmk. USIR**

Center, Plate Letters and Position Numbers in Black

REA37 12½c **blue**, *green* 7.50
b. Green silk paper, unwmkd. 1,250.
c. Pale green paper 200.00
With plate number and position number *1,250.*
d. Light blue paper, with plate number (and position number) 35.00
e. Blue paper, no plate letter or number or position number 30.00
f. Dark blue paper, no plate letter or number or position number 45.00
REA38 16⅔c **light brown**, *green* 7.50
One line under Cents 75.00
b. Green silk paper, unwmkd., one line under Cents 125.00
c. Pale green paper 75.00
With plate number 500.00
d. Light blue paper, with plate number (and position number) 40.00
e. Blue paper, no plate letter or number or position number 150.00
With plate number 1979 250.00
f. Dark blue paper, no plate letter or number or position number 75.00
REA39 25c **green**, *green* 5.00
a. Inverted center —
b. Green silk paper, unwmkd. 200.00
c. Pale green paper 90.00
With plate number 35.00
d. Light blue paper, with plate number (and position number) 7.50
e. Blue paper, no plate letter or number or position number 25.00
f. Dark blue paper, no plate letter or number or position number 27.50
REA40 33⅓c **violet**, *green* 75.00
b. Green silk paper, unwmkd. *2,000.*
c. Pale green paper 1,250.
d. Light blue paper, with plate number (and position number) 110.00
e. Blue paper, no plate letter or number or position number 120.00
f. Dark blue paper, no plate letter or number or position number 250.00
REA41 50c **orange**, *green* 11.00
One line under Cents 100.00
b. Green silk paper, unwmkd. 210.00
c. Pale green paper 90.00
With plate number 350.00
d. Light blue paper, with plate number (and position number) 30.00
e. Blue paper, no plate letter or number or position number 17.50
f. Dark blue paper, no plate letter or number or position number 20.00
REA42 $1 **red**, *green* 27.50
One line under Dollar 75.00
c. Pale green paper 200.00
One line under Dollar 400.00
d. Light blue paper, with plate number (and position number) 175.00
e. Blue paper, no plate letter or number or position number 125.00
One line under Dollar 200.00
f. Dark blue paper, no plate letter or number or position number 100.00
REA43 $2 **brown**, *green* 75.00
One line under Dollar 100.00
b. Green silk paper, unwmkd. 500.00
One line under dollar —
c. Pale green paper 650.00
One line under dollar *1,000.*
e. Blue paper, no plate letter or number or position number 175.00
f. Dark blue paper, no plate letter or number or position number 150.00

See Nos. REA58-REA64, REA65-REA71, REA75-REA81.

Stamps of 1878 Surcharged in Various Ways

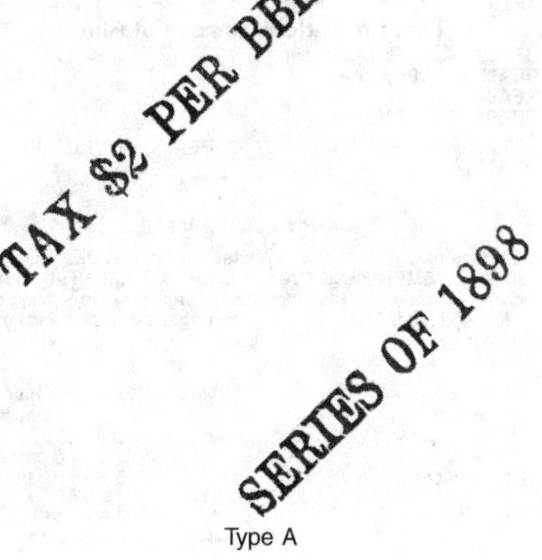

Type A

Four general surcharge types:
A - Bureau of Engraving and Printing surcharge "TAX $2 PER BBL./SERIES OF 1898" printed diagonally in red, letters 4¼mm high.
B - same, but letters 5½mm high.
C - handstamped provisional surcharge with similiar wording in 1-3 lines, more than 30 styles.
D - printed provisional 2-line surcharges, horizontal in various colors.
Tax rate $2 per bbl.

25c = ⅛ barrel
33⅓c = ⅙ barrel
50c = ¼ barrel
66⅔c = ⅓ barrel
$1 = ½ barrel
$2 = 1 barrel
$4 = 1 hogshead

1898 **Type A**

REA44 (25c) on 12½c #REA37f 350.00
a. Type C surcharge 250.00
b. Type D surcharge 750.00
REA45 (33⅓c) on 16⅔c #REA38e 75.00
a. on #REA38f 175.00
b. As "a," type C surcharge 250.00
c. As "a," type D surcharge 400.00
d. on #REA38d 750.00
REA46 (50c) on 25c #REA39f 90.00
a. Type C surcharge 150.00
b. Type D surcharge 750.00
c. on #REA39e 175.00
d. on #REA39, type C surcharge *2,000.*
REA47 (66⅔c) on 33⅓c #REA40 500.00
REA48 ($1) on 50c #REA41f 35.00
a. Type C surcharge 150.00
b. Type D surcharge 450.00
REA49 ($2) on $1 #REA42f 125.00
a. Type C surcharge 175.00
b. Type D surcharge 750.00
c. on #REA42e, type C surcharge 1,250.
REA50 ($4) on $2 #REA43f 500.00
a. Type C surcharge 500.00
b. Type D surcharge *2,000.*
c. on #REA43e, type C surcharge *2,500.*

Type B

REA51 (25c) on 12½c #REA37f 95.00
a. on #REA37e 100.00
b. As "a," type C surcharge *2,000.*
REA52 (33⅓c) on 16⅔c #REA38d 500.00
a. on #REA38f 500.00
b. on #REA38e 700.00
REA53 (50c) on 25c #REA39f 25.00
a. on #REA39e 25.00
REA54 (66⅔c) on 33⅓c #REA40f *2,500.*
a. Type D surcharge *2,500.*
b. On #REA40 *3,000.*
REA55 ($1) on 50c #REA41f 12.50
REA56 ($2) on $1 #REA42f 50.00
REA57 ($4) on $2 #REA43f 275.00

Counterfeit type C and D overprints exist.

Designs: 25c, Washington. 33⅓c, Corwin. 50c, Benton. 66⅔c, Thomas. $1, Jefferson. $2, Johnson. $4, Wright.
See individual rates before No. REA44.

1898 **Typo. & Engr.** **Wmk. USIR**

Center in Black, Dark Blue Paper

REA58 25c **blue** 95.
REA59 33⅓c **brown** 75.
REA60 50c **green** 25.
REA61 66⅔c **violet** *6,000.*
REA62 $1 **yellow** 20.
REA63 $2 **red** 25.
REA64 $4 **dark brown** 225.

Used values for 1901-51 issues are for stamps canceled by perforated company name (or abbreviation) and date.

Designs: 20c, Washington. 26⅔c, Corwin. 40c, Benton. 53⅓c, Thomas. 80c, Jefferson. $1.60, Johnson. $3.20, Wright.
Tax rate $1.60 per bbl.

20c = ⅛ barrel
26⅔c = ⅙ barrel
40c = ¼ barrel
53⅓c = ⅓ barrel
80c = ½ barrel
$1.60 = 1 barrel
$3.20 = 1 hogshead

Engr. (center) & Typo. (frame)

1901 **Wmk. USIR**

Dark Blue Paper

REA65 20c **blue** 75.
REA66 26⅔c **yellow orange** 75.
REA67 40c **green** 17.50
REA68 53⅓c **violet** 4,500.
REA69 80c **brown** 17.50
REA70 $1.60 **red** 75.
REA71 $3.20 **dark brown** 275.

Stamps of 1901 Provisionally Surcharged by Bureau of Engraving & Printing diagonally in red "TAX $1 PER BBL./SERIES OF 1902."

1902

REA72 (16⅔c) on 26⅔c #REA66 — 125.
REA73 (33⅓c) on 53⅓c #REA68 — *4,000.*
REA74 ($2) on $3.20 #REA71 — 600.

Designs: 12½c, Washington. 16⅔c, Corwin. 25c, Benton. 33⅓c, Thomas. 50c, Jefferson. $1, Johnson. $2, Wright.

Stamps on pale green paper have short greenish blue fibers.

See individual rates before No. REA1.

1902 **Typo. & Engr.** **Wmk. USIR**

Center in Black

REA75 12½c **blue**
a. Dark blue paper — 75.00
b. Pale green paper — 350.00
c. Light blue paper — 110.00
d. Bright blue paper — 50.00
REA76 16⅔c **yellow orange**
a. Dark blue paper — 225.00
b. Pale green paper — 350.00
c. Light blue paper — 200.00
d. Bright blue paper — 400.00
REA77 25c **green**
a. Dark blue paper — 25.00
b. Pale green paper — 80.00
c. Light blue paper — 25.00
d. Bright blue paper — 30.00
REA78 33⅓c **violet**
a. Dark blue paper — 200.00
c. Light blue paper — 450.00
d. Bright blue paper — 450.00
REA79 50c **brown**
a. Dark blue paper — 20.00
b. Pale green paper — 30.00
c. Light blue paper — 25.00
d. Bright blue paper — 20.00
REA80 $1 **red**
a. Dark blue paper — 110.00
b. Pale green paper — 300.00
c. Light blue paper — 75.00
d. Bright blue paper — 75.00
REA81 $2 **dark brown**
a. Dark blue paper — 750.00
b. Pale green paper — 900.00
c. Light blue paper — 500.00
d. Bright blue paper — 500.00

For surcharges see Nos. REA99a, REA100a, REA100b, REA141.

In the 1911-33 issues, the 5-25 barrel sizes were generally available only as center cutouts of the stamp. Values for these are for cutout portions that show enough of the denomination (or surcharge) to identify the item.

See individual rates before No. REA1.

1909-11 **Engr.** **Wmk. USIR**

Paper of Various Shades of Blue

REA82 12½c **black** — 500.00
REA83 16⅔c **black** — 150.00 90.00
REA84 25c **black** — 375.00
REA85 33⅓c **black** — *4,000.*
REA86 50c **black** — 6.00
REA87 $1 **black** — 750.00
REA88 $2 **black** — *4,500.*

Center Cutout Only

REA89 $5 **black,** *1911* — *150.00*
REA90 $10 **black,** *1911* — *125.00*
REA91 $25 **black,** *1911* — *100.00*

For surcharges see Nos. REA97, REA99-REA100, REA103-REA105, REA128.

1910 **Engr.** **Wmk. USIR**

Paper of Various Shades of Blue

REA92 12½c **red brown** — 75.00
REA93 25c **green** — 10.00
REA94 $1 **carmine** — 75.00
REA95 $2 **orange** — 125.00

For surcharges see Nos. REA96, REA98, REA101-REA102, REA126.

1914 Provisional Issue

Stamps of of 1902-11 with printed provisional BEP diagonal surcharge "EMERGENCY/TAX/UNDER ACT OF 1914" in red, black or yellow, or handstamped surcharge of value spelled out in full and separate "Roscoe Irwin" handstamped facsimile signature.

Tax rate $1.50 per bbl.

18¾c = ⅛ barrel	$1.50 = 1 barrel
25c = ⅙ barrel	$3 = 1 hogshead
37½c = ¼ barrel	$7.50 = 5 barrels
50c = ⅓ barrel	$15 = 10 barrels
75c = ½ barrel	$37.50 = 25 barrels

1914 **Entire Stamps**

REA96 (18¾c) on 12½ #REA92 — 65.00
REA97 (25c) on 16⅔c #REA83 — 60.00
REA98 (37½c) on 25c #REA93 — 7.50
a. 37½c handstamped; 50mm signature — 350.00
REA99 (50c) on 33⅓c #REA85 — 225.00
a. (50c) on 33⅓c #REA78d — 750.00
REA100 (75c) on 50c #REA86 — 7.50
a. (75c) On 50c #REA79c — 1,000.
b. (75c) On 50c #REA79b — *5,500.*
c. 75c handstamped on #REA86; 50mm signature — 175.00
d. As "c," 65mm signature — 325.00
REA101 ($1.50) on $1 #REA94 — 50.00
a. $1.50 handstamped; 50mm signature — 350.00
b. As "a," 65mm signature — *2,250.*
REA102 ($3.00) on $2 #REA95 — 75.00
a. $3 handstamped; 76mm signature — *2,750.*

Center Cutout Only

REA103 ($7.50) on $5 #REA89 — 17.50
REA104 ($15) on $10 #REA90 — 150.00
REA105 ($37.50) on $25 #REA91 — 225.00

For surcharges see Nos. REA119, REA123, REA133, REA140, REA140a.

See individual rates before No. REA96.

1914 **Engr.** **Wmk. USIR**

Paper of Various Shades of Blue

Entire Stamp

REA106 18¾c **red brown** — 85.00
REA107 25c **black** — 175.00
a. 25c **violet blue** — *2,000.*
REA108 37½c **green** — 17.50
a. 37½c **black** — *5,000.*
REA108B 50c **black** — —
REA109 75c **black** — 6.00
REA110 $1.50 **red orange** — 30.00
REA111 $3 **orange** — 200.00

Center Cutout Only

REA112 $7.50 **black** — 10.00
REA113 $15 **black** — 15.00
REA114 $37.50 **black** — 7.50

For surcharges see Nos. REA118, REA120, REA120a, REA121, REA124-REA125, REA127, REA129-REA131, REA134, REA134a, REA137, REA144, REA146-REA149.

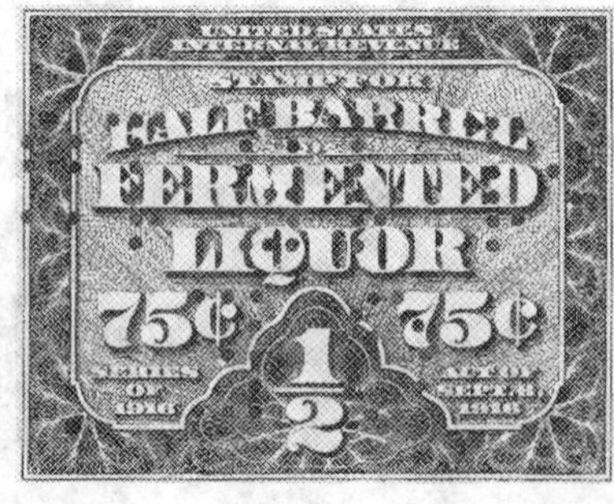

See individual rates before No. REA96.

1916 **Engr.** **Wmk. USIR**

Paper of Various Shades of Greenish Blue

Entire Stamp

REA115 37½c **green** — 110.00
REA116 75c **black** — 40.00

For surcharges see Nos. REA122, REA124, REA138.

Stamps of 1914-16 Provisionally Surcharged Types A, B & C

ACT OF 1917

Type C

Surcharge types:

A - "ACT OF 1917" handstamped in 1-3 lines in more than 30 styles.

B - "ACT OF 1917" locally printed horizontally in black or red.

C - "ACT OF 1917" printed in black or red by BEP, horizontally on ⅙ bbl-1 hhd and reading down on 5-25 bbl.

Surcharge also exists in manuscript on some values. Tax rate $3 per bbl.

37½c = ⅛ barrel	$3 = 1 barrel
50c = ⅙ barrel	$6 = 1 hogshead
75c = ¼ barrel	$15 = 5 barrels
$1 = ⅓ barrel	$30 = 10 barrels
$1.50 = ½ barrel	$75 = 25 barrels

1917 **Type A Surcharge**

Entire Stamp

REA117	(37½c) on #REA96	—
REA118	(37½c) on #REA106	200.00
b.	Type B surcharge	—
c.	Type C surcharge	500.00
REA119	(50c) on #REA97	150.00
REA120	(50c) on #REA107a	300.00
a.	On #107	500.00
REA121	(75c) on #REA108	110.00
REA122	(75c) on #REA115	50.00
b.	Type B surcharge	1,750.
c.	Type C surcharge	90.00
REA123	($1) on #REA99	175.00
REA124	($1.50) on #REA116	40.00
b.	Type B surcharge	1,750.
c.	Type C surcharge	7.50
d.	As "c," inverted surcharge	1,000.

$1.50 surcharge exists in manuscript on #REA109.

REA125	($3) on #REA110	100.
c.	Type C surcharge	40.
REA126	($6) on #REA102	2,000.
REA127	($6) on #REA111	500.

Center Cutout Only

REA128	($15) on #REA103	500.
REA129	($15) on #REA112, entire stamp, type C surcharge	*3,000.*
REA130	($30) on #REA113	100.
c.	Type C surcharge	45.
REA131	($75) on #REA114	225.
c.	Type C surcharge	12.50

For surcharges see Nos. REA132, REA132a, REA135-REA136, REA139-REA139b, REA142-REA143, REA145, REA150-REA151.

Stamps of 1914-17 provisionally surcharged "ACT OF 1918" or "Revenue Act of 1918" with rubber stamp in various colors in more than 20 styles.

A subtype has the incorrect date of 1919 due to the effective date of the act (at least five styles).

Tax rate $6 per bbl.

75c = ⅛ barrel	$6 = 1 barrel
$1 = ⅙ barrel	$12 = 1 hogshead
$1.50 = ¼ barrel	$30 = 5 barrels
$2 = ⅓ barrel	$60 = 10 barrels
$3 = ½ barrel	$150 = 25 barrels

1918 **Entire Stamp**

REA132	(75c) on #REA118	500.
a.	On #REA118c	750.
REA133	($1) on #REA97	900.
REA134	($1) on #REA107	*2,000.*
a.	On #REA107a	*2,750.*

Exists with additional overprint "Non-Intoxicating, containing not to/exceed 2¾% of Alcohol by weight." Value, *$1,750.*

REA135	($1) on #REA119	*2,500.*
REA136	($1) on #REA120	*2,500.*
REA137	($1.50) on #REA108	600.
a.	Surcharge dated "1919"	1,500.
REA138	($1.50) on #REA115	1,250.
REA139	($1.50) on #REA122c	75.
a.	Surcharge dated "1919"	60.
b.	On #REA122	350.
REA140	($2) on #REA99	800.
a.	On #REA99a	1,100.
REA141	($2) on #REA99a	2,500.

No. REA141 bears additional 1917 provisional surcharge, as well as the 1914 surcharge, but was not issued in that form without 1918 surcharge.

REA142	($2) on #REA123	*3,000.*
REA143	($3) on #REA124c	75.
a.	Surcharge dated "1919"	600.
REA144	($6) on #REA110	500.
REA145	($6) on #REA125c	50.
a.	Surcharge dated "1919"	500.
REA146	($12) on #REA111	500.
REA147	($12) on #REA111	75.

No. REA147 bears additional 1917 Type C provisional surcharge but was not issued in that form without 1918 surcharge.

Center Cutout Only

REA148	($30) on #REA112	75.
REA149	($60) on #REA113	75.
REA150	($60) on #REA130c	300.
a.	Entire stamp	*3,000.*
REA151	($150) on #REA131c	35.
a.	Entire stamp	*4,000.*

REA152-REA158

REA159-REA161

Tax rate $5 per barrel through Jan. 11, 1934. $6 rate also effective Dec. 5, 1933. Provisional handstamp "Surcharged $6.00 Rate" in 1-3 lines (seven styles).

1933 **Engr.** **Wmk. USIR**

Paper of Various Shades of Greenish Blue to Blue

Type A

Entire Stamp

REA152	⅛ bbl., **violet red**	17.50
a.	Provisional surcharge, $6 rate	1,500.
REA153	⅙ bbl., **purple**	450.00
REA154	¼ bbl., **green**	6.00
REA155	⅓ bbl., **brown orange**	1,000.
REA156	½ bbl., **orange**	4.00
a.	Provisional surcharge, $6 rate	750.00
REA157	1 bbl., **blue**	25.00
a.	Provisional surcharge, $6 rate	*3,000.*
REA158	1 hhd., **black**	5,000.
REA159	5 bbl., **black**, center cutout only	250.00
REA160	10 bbl., **black**, with cut-out center, rouletted 7 at left	*7,500.*
a.	Center cutout only	250.00
REA161	25 bbl., **black**, with cut-out center, rouletted 7 at left	7,500.
a.	Center cutout only	250.00

Center cutout portions of Nos. REA159-REA161 are on greenish blue paper. See Nos. REA177-REA178A for copies on bright blue paper.

Nos. REA152-REA159, REA161 Surcharged in Black

ACT OF MARCH 22, 1933 Type B

A - additional provisional handstamped surcharge.
B - additional manuscript and handstamped surcharges.
Tax rate same as Nos. REA152-REA161.

1933 **Engr.** **Wmk. USIR**

Entire Stamp

REA162	⅛ bbl., **violet red**	8.00
REA163	⅙ bbl., **purple**	175.00
REA164	¼ bbl., **green**	15.00
a.	With 1918 provisional handstamped surcharge, $6 rate	*2,250.*
b.	Type A surcharge, $6 rate	*2,750.*
REA165	⅓ bbl., **brown orange**	*6,000.*
REA166	½ bbl., **orange**	15.00
a.	Type A surcharge, $6 rate	*3,000.*
b.	Type B surcharge, $6 rate	*1,500.*
REA167	1 bbl., **blue**	25.00
REA168	1 hhd., **black**	*9,000.*
REA169	5 bbl., **black**, center cutout only	500.00
REA170	25 bbl., **black**, center cutout only	450.00

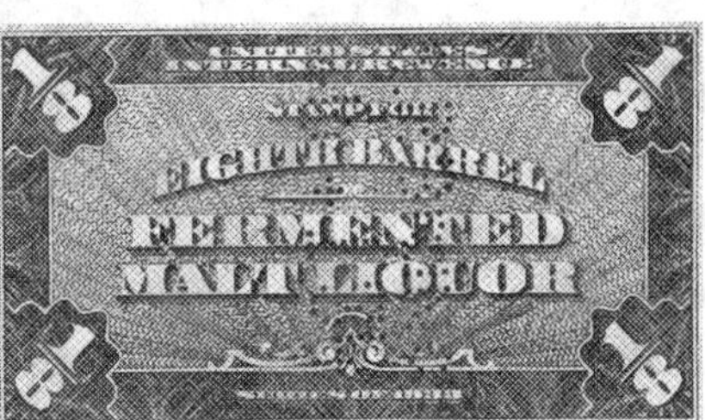

REA171-REA176

REA177-REA178A

Tax rate same as previous issue. Provisional handstamp reads "SOLD AT $5.00 RATE" or "$5.00 RATE."

1933 **Engr.** **Wmk. USIR**

Entire Stamp

REA171	⅛ bbl., **violet red**	35.00
REA172	⅙ bbl., **purple**	500.00
REA173	¼ bbl., **green**	6.00
a.	Provisional surcharge, $5 rate	*3,000.*
REA174	½ bbl., **brown orange**	5.00
a.	Provisional surcharge, $5 rate	800.00
REA175	1 bbl., **blue**	100.00
REA176	1 hhd., **black**	*5,000.*

Bright Blue Paper

REA177	5 bbl., **black**		1,000.
a.	Entire stamp with cut-out center		7.50
b.	Center cutout only		1.00
REA178	10 bbl., **black**	650.00	500.00
a.	Entire stamp with cut-out center		10.00
b.	Center cutout only		1.00
REA178A	25 bbl., **black**		500.00
b.	Entire stamp with cut-out center		4.50
c.	Center cutout only		1.00
d.	Rouletted 7 at left		—

For surcharge see No. REA199.

Nos. REA173-REA174 with BEP Printed Surcharge, "Act of March 22, 1933"

Additional provisional handstamped surcharge, $6 rate as previous issue.

1933

Entire Stamp

REA179	¼ bbl., **green**	27.50
a.	Handstamped "Surcharged $6 rate"	750.00
REA180	½ bbl., **brown orange**	12.50
a.	Handstamped "Surcharged $6 rate"	1,250.

REA181-REA187

REA188-REA189

Tax rates $5 per bbl; $6 from July 1, 1940; $7 from Nov. 1, 1942; $8 from Apr. 1, 1944.

1934-45 **Engr.** **Wmk. USIR**

With Black Control Numbers

REA181	⅛ bbl., **violet red**	7.50
a.	With cutout center	2.00
b.	Ovptd. "NOT LESS THAN 3⅞ GAL-LONS," uncut	—
REA182	⅙ bbl., **purple**	150.00
a.	With cutout center	100.00
b.	Ovptd. "NOT LESS THAN 4⅝ GAL-LONS," uncut	—
REA183	¼ bbl., **green**	4.00
a.	With cutout center	2.50
b.	Ovptd. "NOT LESS THAN 7¼ GAL-LONS," uncut	—
REA184	⅓ bbl., **brown orange**	*10,000.*
REA185	½ bbl., **orange**	3.00
a.	With cutout center	2.00
REA186	1 bbl., **blue**	7.50
a.	With cutout center	7.50
REA187	1 hhd., **black**	500.00
REA188	100 bbl., **carmine**, *1942*	200.00
a.	With cutout center	10.00
REA189	500 bbl., **dark brown**, with cutout center, *1945*	500.00

Most values also exist as center cutout portions only.

REA190-REA193

REA194-REA198

Tax rates $8 per bbl, $9 from Nov. 1, 1951.

1947 **Litho.**

Black Control Numbers

REA190	⅛ bbl., **carmine**	125.00	60.00
a.	With cutout center		15.00
REA191	¼ bbl., **green**	75.00	20.00
a.	With cutout center		22.50
REA192	½ bbl., **orange**	30.00	10.00
a.	With cutout center		12.50
REA193	1 bbl., **blue**	300.00	150.00
a.	With cutout center		15.00

Blue Paper

REA194	5 bbl., **black**	300.00	200.00
a.	With cutout center		12.50
REA195	10 bbl., **black**	450.00	300.00
a.	With cutout center		27.50
REA196	25 bbl., **black**	*3,200.*	*3,200.*
a.	With cutout center		*3,000.*

White Paper

REA197	100 bbl., **carmine**	350.00	250.00
a.	With cutout center		10.00
REA198	500 bbl., **dark brown**	1,000.	600.00
a.	With cutout center		60.00

All values also exist as center cutouts only.

No. REA158 Provisionally Handstamp Surcharged "Value increased under / Revenue Act of 1951" in black or purple.

Tax rate $9 per bbl.

1951

REA199 ($225) on 25 bbl., #REA178A, uncut *5,000.*

Also exists as center cutout only, showing portion of hand-stamped surcharge. Value, $150.

FERMENTED FRUIT JUICE STAMPS

Fermented fruit juice stamps were issued pending the ratification of the Repeal Amendment (Dec. 5, 1933) that made full-strength beer and wine legal again.

Congress, as a temporary measure, redefined intoxicating beverages by changing the legal definition from .5% to 3.2%, thus permitting the sale of 3.2 beer and wine beginning April 7, 1933.

Regular wine stamps were available to pay the Internal Revenue taxes. However, these Fermented Fruit Juice stamps were authorized for placement on individual bottles or containers of fermented fruit juice. Use was discontinued at the end of 1933.

Stamps are valued in the grade of very fine. Most stamps are found in average to fine condition. Unused stamps are valued with original gum.

REF1

Plates of 220 subjects in two panes of 110.

1933 **Wmk. USIR** **Engr.** ***Perf. 11***

REF1	REF1	4 oz	**gray**		75.00
REF3	REF1	8 oz	**light green**		60.00
REF4	REF1	12 oz	**light blue**	10.00	6.00
REF5	REF1	13 oz	**olive green**		50.00
REF6	REF1	16 oz	**lavender**		160.00
REF7	REF1	24 oz	**orange**		110.00
REF8	REF1	29 oz	**brown**		160.00
REF9	REF1	32 oz	**red**	85.00	65.00

A dark blue 7-ounce stamp was issued, but the only recorded examples currently are in the National Postal Museum collection.

Earliest known use: May 28, 1933.

Beer Stamp No. REA154 Overprinted "WINE OR FERMENTED FRUIT JUICE" in Red

1933 **Engr.** ***Imperf.***

REF10 ¼ bbl., **green**, *blue* —

The ½ barrel and 1 barrel stamps Beer Stamps, Nos. REA156-REA157, also were issued with this overprint, but no examples are currently recorded.

PLAYING CARDS

Stamps for use on packs of playing cards were included in the first general issue of 1862-71. They are Nos. R2, R11, R12, R17, R21 and R28. The tax on playing cards was repealed effective June 22, 1965.

"ON HAND . . ." — RF1

"ACT OF . . ." — RF2

1894 Engr. Unwmk. ***Rouletted 5½***

RF1 RF1 2c **lake** .75 .45
a. Horizontal pair, imperf. between *450.00* —
b. Horiz. pair, imperf. vert. —
RF2 RF2 2c **ultramarine** 21.00 2.75
a. 2c **blue** 30.00 3.75
b. Imperf., pair 500.00
c. Imperf. horizontally 160.00 160.00
d. Rouletted 12½ 100.00 100.00
e. Imperf. horizontally, rouletted 12½ vertically, pair 200.00 200.00

No vertical pairs of No. RF2e are known. Pairs will be horizontal. Singles are valued at 50% of the pair value.

1896-99 Wmk. 191R ***Rouletted 5½, 7***

RF3 RF2 2c **blue** 7.75 .65
a. 2c **ultramarine** ('99) 7.50 2.00
b. Imperf., pair 125.00

No. RF3 surcharged " VIRGIN / ISLANDS / 4 CTS" are listed under Danish West Indies.

1902 ***Perf. 12***

RF4 RF2 2c **deep blue** 52.50

No. RF4 is known with cancel date "1899" but that is due to the use of an old canceling plate. The stamp was first used in 1902.

ACT OF 1917
7
CENTS

Stamp of 1899 Surcharged in Rose

1917 Wmk. 191R ***Rouletted 7***

RF5 RF2 7c on 2c **ultramarine** *750.00* 600.00
a. Inverted surcharge —

The surcharge on No. RF5 was handstamped at the Internal Revenue Office in New York City. Different handstamps were used at other Internal Revenue Offices as well, values $250 to $300.

17

Surcharged in Black

1917

RF6 RF2 (7c) on 2c **blue** 52.50
a. Inverted surcharge 52.50

The "17" indicated that the 7 cent tax had been paid according to the Act of 1917.
Used by N. Y. Consolidated Card Co.
Cancellations are in red.

7

Surcharged in Black

RF7 RF2 7c on 2c **blue** 900.00
a. Inverted surcharge 550.00

Used by Standard Playing Card Co.

The surcharges on Nos. RF7-RF10, RF13, RF15, RF18 were applied by the manufacturers, together with their initials, dates, etc., thus forming a combination of surcharge and precancellation. The surcharge on No. RF16 was made by the Bureau of Engraving and Printing. After it appeared the use of some combinations was continued but only as cancellations.

7 CTS.

Surcharged Vertically Reading Up in Red or Violet

RF8 RF2 7c on 2c **blue** 1,250.
a. Double surcharge 1,800.
b. Reading down 2,000.

Used by Russell Playing Card Co.

Surcharged Vertically, Reading Up in Black, Violet or Red

RF9 RF2 7c on 2c **blue** 9.75
a. Double surcharge (violet) 100.00
b. Numeral omitted (black) 90.00
c. Surcharge reading down 11.50
d. As "c," numeral omitted (black) 77.50
e. As "c," double surcharge (violet) 275.00
f. Double surcharge, one down (red) 300.00
g. Surcharge and "A.D." in violet 375.00
h. Surcharge and "A.D." in red, "U.S.P.C. Co." in black *1,050.*
i. Surcharge and "A.D." in red reading up, "U.S.P.C. Co." in black reading down *775.00*
j. As "g," reading down —
k. Double surcharge (black) *1,000.*
l. Double surcharge (red) *400.00*
m. Double surcharge and "A.D.," both reading down (red) —

"A.D." (Andrew Dougherty Co.) printed in red, "S. P. C. Co." (Standard Playing Card Co.) printed in violet, "U.S.P.C. Co." printed in black. The first two became divisions of United States Playing Card Co.
See No. RF13.

Surcharged in Carmine

RF10 RF2 7c on 2c **blue** 77.50
a. Inverted surcharge 42.50
b. Double surcharge 550.00
c. Double surcharge, inverted 550.00
d. Triple surcharge —

Used by Russell Playing Card Co.

RF3

1918 Size: 21x40mm ***Imperf.***

RF11 RF3 **blue** 45.00 32.50
Block of 4 190.00 150.00

Private Roulette 14

RF12 RF3 **blue** 300.
a. Rouletted 13 in red *1,650.*
b. Rouletted 6½ 425.
c. Perf. 12 horiz., imperf. vert. 210.
d. Perf. 12 on 4 sides *1,600.*

Nos. RF11-RF12 served as 7c stamps when used before April 1, 1919, and as 8c stamps when used after that date.
No. RF11 is known handstamped "7" or "8," or both "7" and "8," as well as "Act of 1918" in black or magenta, either by the user to indicate the value when applied to the pack or by the IRS district offices at the time of sale.
No. RF12 was used by N. Y. Consolidated Card Co., Nos. RF12a, RF12b were used by Russell Playing Card Co., Nos. RF12, RF12d were used by Logan Printing House.

Surcharged like No. RF9 (but somewhat smaller) in Violet, Red or Black

Private Roulette 9½

RF13 RF3 7c **blue** 52.50
a. Inverted surcharge 52.50
b. Double surcharge 275.00
c. Double surcharge, inverted 325.00

REVENUE ACT
OF 1918
8
CENTS

Stamp of 1899 Surcharged in Magenta or Rose

1919 ***Rouletted 7***

RF14 RF2 8c on 2c **ultramarine** 110.00
a. Double surcharge 300.00
b. Inverted surcharge 325.00

The surcharge on No. RF14 was handstamped at the Internal Revenue Office in New York City. A handstamp in black is known.
Exists in pair, one double surcharge, also in pair, one with inverted surcharge.

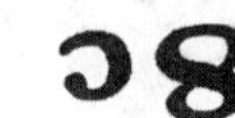

Inverted Surcharge in Carmine

RF15 RF2 8c on 2c **blue** 600.00
a. Double surcharge *1,000.*

No. RF15 is surcharged only with large "8c" inverted, and overprinted with date and initials (also inverted). No. RF16 is often found with additional impression of large "8c," as on No. RF15, but in this usage the large "8c" is a cancellation.
Used by Russell Playing Card Co.

Surcharged in Carmine or Vermilion 8 Cts.

RF16 RF2 8c on 2c **blue** 140.00 .90
a. Inverted surcharge —

See note after No. RF15.

RF4

1922 Size: 19x22mm ***Rouletted 7***

RF17 RF4 (8c) **blue** 20.00 1.50
Block of 4 100.00 —

No. RF17, rouletted 7 and perforated 11, surcharged " VIRGIN / ISLANDS / 4 cts." are listed under Danish West Indies.

Surcharged in Carmine, Blue or Black

RF18	RF4	8c on (8c) **blue**	62.50	
a.		Inverted surcharge	62.50	

Used by Pyramid Playing Card Co.

RF5

1924 ***Rouletted 7***

RF19	RF5	10c **blue**	13.00	.45
		Block of 4	72.50	

ROTARY PRESS COIL STAMP

1926 ***Perf. 10 Vertically***

RF20	RF5	10c **blue**		.30
		Pair		3.25
		Joint line pair		6.50

No. RF20 exists only precanceled. **Bureau precancels:** 11 different.

FLAT PLATE PRINTING

1927 ***Perf. 11***

RF21	RF5	10c **blue**	26.00	5.25
		Block of 4	125.00	

1929 ***Perf. 10***

RF22	RF5	10c **blue**	17.00	4.25
		Block of 4	80.00	—

RF6

ROTARY PRESS COIL STAMP

1929 ***Perf. 10 Horizontally***

RF23	RF6	10c **light blue**		.25
		Pair		2.50
		Joint line pair		5.00

No. RF23 exists only precanceled. **Bureau precancels:** 16 different.

FLAT PLATE PRINTING

1930 ***Perf. 10***

RF24	RF6	10c **blue**	17.00	1.40
		Block of 4	80.00	11.00
a.		Horiz. pair, imperf. vert.	175.00	

1931 ***Perf. 11***

RF25	RF6	10c **blue**	13.00	1.40
		Block of 4	62.50	—

No. R234 is known used provisionally as a playing card revenue stamp August 6 and 8, 1932. Value for this use, authenticated, $300.

RF7

ROTARY PRESS COIL STAMP

1940 ***Perf. 10 Vertically***

RF26	RF7	**blue,** wet printing	—	.45
		Pair		2.25
		Joint line pair		4.50
		Dry printing, unwatermarked	25.00	.40

See note after No. 1029.

Bureau precancels: 11 different.

RF8

ROTARY PRESS COIL STAMP

1940 **Wmk. 191R** ***Perf. 10 Horizontally***

RF27	RF8	**blue,** wet printing	3.00	.25
		Pair	7.50	
		Joint line pair	12.50	
		Dry printing, unwatermarked		3.25

Bureau precancels: 10 different.

FLAT PLATE PRINTING
Perf. 11

RF28	RF8	**blue,** wet printing	5.25	.80
		Block of 4	26.00	—
		Dry printing (rotary press)	5.25	4.25
		Dry printing (rotary press), unwatermarked		5.25
		Block of 4		—

ROTARY PRESS PRINTING
Perf. 10x11

RF29	RF8	**blue**	175.00	92.50
		Block of 4	750.00	—
a.		Imperforate (P.C. Co.)		900.00

SILVER TAX STAMPS

The Silver Purchase Act of 1934 imposed a 50 per cent tax on the net profit realized on a transfer of silver bullion occurring after May 15, 1934. The tax was paid by affixing stamps to the transfer memorandum. Congress authorized the Silver Tax stamps on June 19, 1934. They were discontinued on June 4, 1963.

Documentary Stamps of 1917 Overprinted

1934 **Offset Printing** **Wmk. 191R** ***Perf. 11***

RG1	R22	1c **carmine rose**	1.40	.95
RG2	R22	2c **carmine rose**	1.50	.65
		Double impression of stamp	—	
RG3	R22	3c **carmine rose**	1.75	.80
RG4	R22	4c **carmine rose**	1.90	1.60
RG5	R22	5c **carmine rose**	3.25	1.40
RG6	R22	8c **carmine rose**	4.25	3.25
RG7	R22	10c **carmine rose**	4.50	3.00
RG8	R22	20c **carmine rose**	6.25	3.75
RG9	R22	25c **carmine rose**	5.75	4.25
RG10	R22	40c **carmine rose**	6.75	6.00
RG11	R22	50c **carmine rose**	9.00	7.50
RG12	R22	80c **carmine rose**	16.00	10.50

Engr.

RG13	R21	$1 **green**	30.00	16.00
RG14	R21	$2 **rose**	37.50	25.00
RG15	R21	$3 **violet**	72.50	35.00
RG16	R21	$4 **yellow brown**	57.50	24.00
RG17	R21	$5 **dark blue**	72.50	27.50
RG18	R21	$10 **orange**	92.50	22.50

Perf. 12
Without Gum

RG19	R17	$30 **vermilion**	190.00	55.00
		Cut cancel		20.00
RG20	R19	$60 **brown**	210.00	82.50
		Cut cancel		27.50
		Vertical strip of 4		375.00
RG21	R17	$100 **green**	250.00	35.00
		Vertical strip of 4		150.00
RG22	R18	$500 **blue**	550.00	250.00
		Cut cancel		110.00
		Vertical strip of 4		—
RG23	R19	$1000 **orange**	—	110.00
		Cut cancel		60.00

See note after No. R227.

Same Overprint, spacing 11mm between words "SILVER TAX"
Without Gum

1936 ***Perf. 12***

RG26	R17	$100 **green**	475.00	82.50
		Vertical strip of 4		—
RG27	R19	$1000 **orange**		800.00

Documentary Stamps of 1917 Handstamped "SILVER TAX" in Violet, Large Block Letters, in Two Lines

1939 **Wmk. 191R** **Offset Printing** ***Perf. 10***

RG28	R22	1c **rose pink**		*12,500.*

Perf. 11

RG29	R22	3c **rose pink**		—
RG30	R22	5c **rose pink**		*750.*
RG31	R22	10c **rose pink**		*1,000.*
RG32	R22	80c **rose pink**		*6,000.*

Other handstamps exist on various values. One has letters 4mm high, 2mm wide with "SILVER" and "TAX" applied in separate operations. Another has "Silver Tax" in two lines in a box, but it is believed this handstamp was privately applied.

Overprint Typewritten in Black ($2, $3) or Red ($5)

1934-35 **Engr.** ***Perf. 11***

RG34	R21	$2 **carmine**		—
RG35	R21	$3 **violet**		*2,600.*
RG36	R21	$5 **dark blue**		—

Typewritten overprints also exist on 2c, 3c, 4c, 20c and 50c.

Type of Documentary Stamps 1917, Overprinted in Black

1940 **Offset Printing** ***Perf. 11***

RG37	R22	1c **rose pink**	25.00	—
RG38	R22	2c **rose pink**	25.00	—
RG39	R22	3c **rose pink**	25.00	—
RG40	R22	4c **rose pink**	27.50	—
RG41	R22	5c **rose pink**	17.50	—
RG42	R22	8c **rose pink**	27.50	—
RG43	R22	10c **rose pink**	25.00	—
RG44	R22	20c **rose pink**	27.50	—
RG45	R22	25c **rose pink**	25.00	—
RG46	R22	40c **rose pink**	42.50	—
RG47	R22	50c **rose pink**	42.50	—
RG48	R22	80c **rose pink**	42.50	—

Engr.

RG49	R21	$1 **green**	160.00	—
RG50	R21	$2 **rose**	250.00	—
RG51	R21	$3 **violet**	325.00	—
RG52	R21	$4 **yellow brown**	650.00	—
RG53	R21	$5 **dark blue**	775.00	—
RG54	R21	$10 **orange**	875.00	—

Nos. RG19-RG20, RG26 Handstamped in Blue "Series 1940"

1940 **Without Gum** ***Perf. 12***

RG55	R17	$30 **vermilion**	—	*6,250.*
RG56	R19	$60 **brown**	—	*15,000.*
RG57	R17	$100 **green**	—	*4,500.*

Alexander Hamilton — RG1

Levi Woodbury — RG2

Thomas Corwin — RG3

Overprinted in Black SERIES 1941

1941		Wmk. 191R	Engr.	*Perf. 11*	
RG58	RG1	1c	**gray**	6.00	2.40
RG59	RG1	2c	**gray** *(Oliver Wolcott, Jr.)*	6.00	3.00
RG60	RG1	3c	**gray** *(Samuel Dexter)*	6.00	3.00
RG61	RG1	4c	**gray** *(Albert Gallatin)*	8.50	5.25
RG62	RG1	5c	**gray** *(G.W. Campbell)*	11.00	9.25
RG63	RG1	8c	**gray** *(A.J. Dallas)*	12.00	—
RG64	RG1	10c	**gray** *(Wm. H. Crawford)*	15.00	8.50
RG65	RG1	20c	**gray** *(Richard Rush)*	25.00	7.75
RG66	RG1	25c	**gray** *(S.D. Ingham)*	29.00	—
RG67	RG1	40c	**gray** *(Louis McLane)*	50.00	37.50
RG68	RG1	50c	**gray** *(Wm. J. Duane)*	60.00	32.50
RG69	RG1	80c	**gray** *(Roger B. Taney)*	100.00	32.50
RG70	RG2	$1	**gray**	125.00	45.00
RG71	RG2	$2	**gray** *(Thomas Ewing)*	300.00	72.50
RG72	RG2	$3	**gray** *(Walter Forward)*	250.00	97.50
RG73	RG2	$4	**gray** *(J.C. Spencer)*	375.00	80.00
RG74	RG2	$5	**gray** *(G.M. Bibb)*	300.00	95.00
RG75	RG2	$10	**gray** *(R.J. Walker)*	575.00	97.50
RG76	RG2	$20	**gray** *(Wm. M. Meredith)*	825.00	300.00

Perf. 12

Without Gum

RG77	RG3	$30	**gray**	400.	250.
			Cut cancel		110.
RG78	RG3	$50	**gray** *(James Guthrie)*	*4,500.*	*4,000.*
RG79	RG3	$60	**gray** *(Howell Cobb)*	*1,800.*	275.
			Cut cancel		125.
RG80	RG3	$100	**gray** *(P.F. Thomas)*	*7,500.*	425.00
			Cut cancel		150.
			Vertical strip of 4		—
RG81	RG3	$500	**gray** *(J.A. Dix)*	—	*18,000.*
RG82	RG3	$1000	**gray** *(S.P. Chase)*	—	*2,500.*
			Cut cancel		*1,000.*

Nos. RG58-RG82 Overprinted Instead: SERIES 1942

1942		Wmk. 191R		*Perf. 11*	
RG83	RG1	1c	**gray**	2.50	—
RG84	RG1	2c	**gray**	2.50	—
RG85	RG1	3c	**gray**	2.50	—
RG86	RG1	4c	**gray**	2.50	—
RG87	RG1	5c	**gray**	2.10	—
RG88	RG1	8c	**gray**	5.00	—
RG89	RG1	10c	**gray**	6.00	—
RG90	RG1	20c	**gray**	12.00	—
RG91	RG1	25c	**gray**	21.00	—
RG92	RG1	40c	**gray**	30.00	—
RG93	RG1	50c	**gray**	35.00	—
RG94	RG1	80c	**gray**	90.00	—
RG95	RG2	$1	**gray**	125.00	72.50
a.			Overprint "SERIES 5942"	500.00	
RG96	RG2	$2	**gray**	125.00	72.50
a.			Overprint "SERIES 5942"	950.00	
RG97	RG2	$3	**gray**	240.00	140.00
a.			Overprint "SERIES 5942"	1,000.	
RG98	RG2	$4	**gray**	250.00	140.00
a.			Overprint "SERIES 5942"	1,000.	
RG99	RG2	$5	**gray**	250.00	175.00
a.			Overprint "SERIES 5942"	950.00	
RG100	RG2	$10	**gray**	650.00	425.00
RG101	RG2	$20	**gray**	825.00	—
a.			Overprint "SERIES 5942"	—	

Perf. 12

Without Gum

RG102	RG3	$30	**gray**	—	—
			Cut cancel		*2,250.*
RG103	RG3	$50	**gray**	*10,000.*	—
RG104	RG3	$60	**gray**	—	*1,750.*
			Cut cancel		750.
RG105	RG3	$100	**gray**	—	900.
			Cut cancel		525.
RG106	RG3	$500	**gray**	—	*6,000.*
			Cut cancel		*3,500.*
RG107	RG3	$1000	**gray**	—	*5,250.*
			Cut cancel		*4,000.*

Silver Purchase Stamps of 1941 without Overprint

1944		Wmk. 191R		*Perf. 11*	
RG108	RG1	1c	**gray**	.85	.30
RG109	RG1	2c	**gray**	.85	.65
RG110	RG1	3c	**gray**	1.10	1.00
RG111	RG1	4c	**gray**	1.40	1.25
RG112	RG1	5c	**gray**	2.75	2.75
RG113	RG1	8c	**gray**	4.50	2.75
RG114	RG1	10c	**gray**	5.00	3.25
RG115	RG1	20c	**gray**	8.25	5.50
RG116	RG1	25c	**gray**	14.00	6.00
RG117	RG1	40c	**gray**	20.00	11.50
RG118	RG1	50c	**gray**	22.50	14.00
RG119	RG1	80c	**gray**	30.00	20.00
RG120	RG2	$1	**gray**	60.00	21.00
RG121	RG2	$2	**gray**	87.50	47.50
RG122	RG2	$3	**gray**	100.00	37.50
RG123	RG2	$4	**gray**	140.00	85.00
RG124	RG2	$5	**gray**	150.00	47.50
RG125	RG2	$10	**gray**	225.00	35.00
			Cut cancel		19.00
RG126	RG2	$20	**gray**	700.00	500.00
			Cut cancel		250.00

Perf. 12

Without Gum

RG127	RG3	$30	**gray**	350.00	160.00
			Cut cancel		72.50
			Vertical strip of 4		—
RG128	RG3	$50	**gray**	775.00	625.00
			Cut cancel		325.00
			Vertical strip of 4		—
RG129	RG3	$60	**gray**	—	525.00
			Cut cancel		225.00
RG130	RG3	$100	**gray**	—	35.00
			Cut cancel		15.00
			Vertical strip of 4		—
RG131	RG3	$500	**gray**	—	500.00
			Cut cancel		250.00
RG132	RG3	$1000	**gray**	—	160.00
			Cut cancel		80.00
			Vertical strip of 4		—

CIGARETTE TUBES STAMPS

These stamps were for a tax on the hollow tubes of cigarette paper, with or without thin cardboard mouthpieces attached. They were sold in packages so buyers could add loose tobacco to make cigarettes.

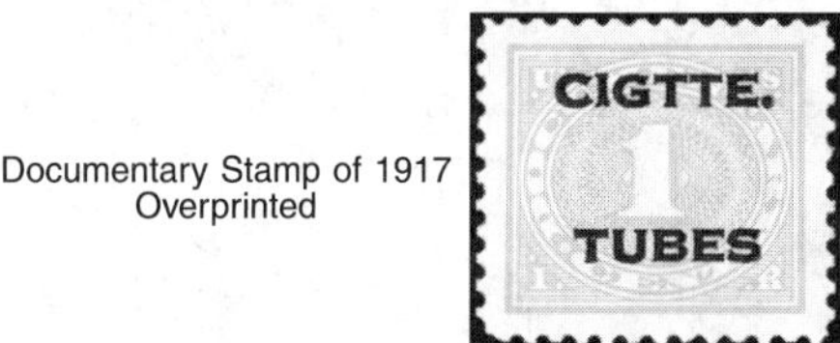

Documentary Stamp of 1917 Overprinted

1919	Offset Printing		Wmk. 191R	*Perf. 11*	
RH1	R22	1c	**carmine rose**	.65	.30
			Block of 4	3.25	1.50
			On package		20.00
			Pair on package		40.00
a.			Without period	13.00	8.25
			On package		—

1929				*Perf. 10*	
RH2	R22	1c	**carmine rose**	30.00	9.25
			On package		—

RH1

1933		Wmk. 191R		*Perf. 11*	
RH3	RH1	1c	**rose**	2.50	2.00
			Block of 4	15.00	
			On package		21.00
RH4	RH1	2c	**rose**	8.75	3.25
			On package		100.00

Cigarette tube on-package values are for fine undamaged stamps affixed to an empty package of Himyar Tobacco cigarette tubes manufactured by the Axton-Fisher Tobacco Co. Unopened packages containing cigarette tubes command a 50 to 100 percent premium. No. RH1 pairs are unseparated stamps.

POTATO TAX STAMPS

These stamps were required by the Potato Act of 1935, an amendment to the Agricultural Adjustment Act that became effective Dec. 1, 1935.

Potato growers were given allotments for which they were provided Tax Exempt Potato stamps. Growers exceeding their allotments would have paid for the excess with Tax Paid Potato stamps at the rate of ¾ cent per pound.

On Jan. 6, 1936, the U. S. Supreme Court declared the Agricultural Adjustment Act unconstitutional. Officially the Potato Act was in effect until Feb. 10, 1936, when it was repealed by Congress but, in essence, the law was ignored once the Supreme Court ruling was issued.

Because of the Act's short life, Tax Paid stamps were never used.

Young Woman from *The Bouquet* — RI1

RI2

Tax Paid Potatoes

1935		Engr.	Unwmk.	*Perf. 11*
RI1	RI1	¾c	**carmine rose**	.30
RI2	RI1	1½c	**black brown**	.45
RI3	RI1	2¼c	**yellow green**	.45
RI4	RI1	3c	**light violet**	.55
RI5	RI1	3¾c	**olive bister**	.60
RI6	RI1	7½c	**orange brown**	1.50
RI7	RI1	11¼c	**deep orange**	2.00
RI8	RI1	18¾c	**violet brown**	4.75
RI9	RI1	37½c	**red orange**	4.75
RI10	RI1	75c	**blue**	4.75
RI11	RI1	93¾c	**rose lake**	8.00
RI12	RI1	$1.12½	**green**	15.00
RI13	RI1	$1.50	**yellow brown**	14.50
			Nos. RI1-RI13 (13)	57.60

Tax Exempt Potatoes

1935		Engr.	Unwmk.	*Perf. 11x10½*	
RI14	RI2	2 lb	**black brown**	.65	*10.50*
a.		Booklet pane of 12		10.00	*250.00*
		Provisional booklet of 24, purple on pink cover		35.00	
		Provisional booklet of 96, purple on buff cover		100.00	
		Provisional booklet of 192, purple on white cover		300.00	
		Definitive booklet of 96, black on buff cover		100.00	
		Definitive booklet of 192, black on white cover		200.00	
RI15	RI2	5 lb	**black brown**	22.50	
a.		Booklet pane of 12		*375.00*	
		Provisional booklet of 192, purple on white cover		—	
RI16	RI2	10 lb	**black brown**	22.50	
a.		Booklet pane of 12		*375.00*	
		Provisional booklet of 192, purple on white cover		—	
RI17	RI2	25 lb	**black brown**	—	
a.		Booklet pane of 12		*1,500.*	
RI18	RI2	50 lb	**black brown**	1.10	*40.00*
a.		Booklet pane of 12		21.00	
		Provisional booklet of 24, purple on pink cover		50.00	
		Provisional booklet of 96, purple on buff cover		150.00	
		Provisional booklet of 192, purple on white cover		300.00	
		Definitive booklet of 96, black on buff cover		100.00	
		Definitive booklet of 192, black on white cover		200.00	
		Nos. RI14-RI16,RI18 (4)		*46.75*	

The booklet panes are arranged 4x3 with a tab at top. Edges are imperforate at left, right and bottom, yielding four stamps fully perforated, six stamps imperf. on one side and two stamps imperf. on two sides per pane.

These stamps were printed from 360-subject rotary booklet plates and cut into 30 panes of 12. The panes were stapled into booklets of 24 (2 panes, pink covers), 96 (8 panes, buff covers) and 196 (16 panes, white covers), with handstamped covers (provisionals) and later with covers printed with the Dept. of Agriculture seal in the center (definitives). Both types of cover were prepared by the Bureau of Engraving and Printing.

Values for booklets are for examples containing panes that have very good to fine centering, because the overwhelming majority of booklets are in this grade. It should be noted that Scott values for individual panes (listed above) are for very fine panes. For this reason, individual panes are valued higher than the per-pane value of panes in booklets. For example, a pane of No. RI14a is valued at $20, but the No. RI14 definitive booklet of 96 (8 panes) is valued at $100, or $12.50 per pane, which is a little more than what a collector would pay for an individual very good to fine pane. Booklets containing very fine panes will command a premium over the values given.

All recorded examples of No. RI17 are in three unbroken panes of 12. A 100 lb Tax Exempt stamp was printed, but all are believed to have been destroyed.

TOBACCO SALE TAX STAMPS

These stamps were required to pay the tax on the sale of tobacco in excess of quotas set by the Secretary of Agriculture. The tax was 25 per cent of the price for which the excess tobacco was sold. It was intended to affect tobacco harvested after June 28, 1934 and sold before May 1, 1936. The tax was stopped when the Agricultural Adjustment Act was declared unconstitutional by the Supreme Court on Dec. 1, 1935.

Values for unused stamps are for copies with original gum.

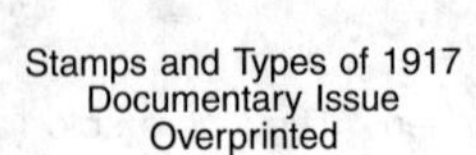

Stamps and Types of 1917 Documentary Issue Overprinted

1934		Offset Printing		Wmk. 191R	*Perf. 11*
RJ1	R22	1c	**carmine rose**	.30	.20
RJ2	R22	2c	**carmine rose**	.40	.20
RJ3	R22	5c	**carmine rose**	1.25	.45
RJ4	R22	10c	**carmine rose**	1.60	.40
a.		Inverted overprint		13.00	*15.00*
RJ5	R22	25c	**carmine rose**	4.25	1.60
RJ6	R22	50c	**carmine rose**	4.25	1.60
		Engr.			
RJ7	R21	$1	**green**	10.00	1.75
RJ8	R21	$2	**rose**	19.00	1.90
RJ9	R21	$5	**dark blue**	24.00	4.25
RJ10	R21	$10	**orange**	37.50	10.00
RJ11	R21	$20	**olive bister**	90.00	12.50
		Nos. RJ1-RJ11 (11)		192.55	34.85

On No. RJ11 the overprint is vertical, reading up.

No. RJ2 is known with a counterfeit inverted overprint.

NARCOTIC TAX STAMPS

The Revenue Act of 1918 imposed a tax of 1 cent per ounce or fraction thereof on opium, coca leaves and their derivatives. The tax was paid by affixing Narcotic stamps to the drug containers. The tax lasted from Feb. 25, 1919, through Apr. 30, 1971.
Members of the American Revenue Association compiled the listings in this section.

Documentary Stamps of 1914 Handstamped "NARCOTIC" in Magenta, Blue or Black

1919 Wmk. 191R Offset Printing *Perf. 10*

RJA1 R20 1c **rose** 85.00 75.00

The overprint was applied by District Collectors of Internal Revenue.

It is always in capital letters and exists in various type faces and sizes, including: 21½x2½mm, serif; 21x2¼mm, sans-serif boldface; 15½x 2½mm, sans-serif; 13x2mm, sans-serif.

The ½c, 2c, 3c, 4c, 5c, 10c, 25c and 50c with similar handstamp in serif capitals measuring about 20x2¼mm are bogus.

Documentary Stamps of 1917 Handstamped "NARCOTIC," "Narcotic," "NARCOTICS" or "ACT/NARCOTIC/1918" in Magenta, Black, Blue, Violet or Red

1919 Wmk. 191R Offset Printing *Perf. 11*

RJA9 R22 1c **carmine rose** 2.40 1.90
RJA10 R22 2c **carmine rose** 5.25 4.00
RJA11 R22 3c **carmine rose** 30.00 32.50
RJA12 R22 4c **carmine rose** 11.50 10.00
RJA13 R22 5c **carmine rose** 17.00 16.00
RJA14 R22 8c **carmine rose** 14.00 12.50
RJA15 R22 10c **carmine rose** 45.00 20.00
RJA16 R22 20c **carmine rose** *67.50 60.00*
RJA17 R22 25c **carmine rose** 40.00 32.50
RJA18 R22 40c **carmine rose** *125.00 100.00*
RJA19 R22 50c **carmine rose** 17.00 *19.00*
RJA20 R22 80c **carmine rose** *110.00 100.00*

Engr.

RJA21 R21 $1 **green** 100.00 52.50
RJA22 R21 $2 **rose** *1,000.*
RJA23 R21 $3 **violet** *1,200.*
RJA24 R21 $5 **dark blue** *1,000.*
RJA25 R21 $10 **orange** *1,200.*

The overprints were applied by District Collectors of Internal Revenue. They are known in at least 20 type faces and sizes of which the majority read "NARCOTIC" in capital letters. Two are in upper and lower case letters. Experts have identified 14 by city. The 3-line handstamp was used in Seattle; "NARCOTICS" in Philadelphia. Most handstamps are not found on all denominations.

Many fake overprints exist.

No. R228 Overprinted in Black: "NARCOTIC / E.L. CO. / 3-19-19"

1919 Wmk. 191R *Perf. 11*

"NARCOTIC" 14½mm wide

RJA26 R22 1c **carmine rose** *2,600.*

Overprinted by Eli Lilly Co., Indianapolis, for that firm's use.

No. R228 Overprinted in Black: "J W & B / NARCOTIC"

1919 Wmk. 191R *Perf. 11*

"NARCOTIC" 14½mm wide

RJA27 R22 1c **carmine rose** —
RJA27A R22 2c **carmine rose** *3,250.*

Overprinted by John Wyeth & Brother, Philadelphia, for that firm's use.

Nos. R228, R231-R232 Handstamped in Blue: "P-W-R-Co. / NARCOTIC"

1919 Wmk. 191R *Perf. 11*

RJA28 R22 1c **carmine rose** *625.00*
RJA28A R22 4c **carmine rose** *1,200.*
RJA29 R22 5c **carmine rose** —
RJA29A R22 25c **carmine rose** —
RJA29B R21 $1 **green** (violet handstamp) —

The handstamp was applied by the Powers-Weightmann-Rosengarten Co., Philadelphia, for that firm's use.

Proprietary Stamps of 1919 Handstamped "NARCOTIC" in Blue

1919 Wmk. 191R Offset Printing *Perf. 11*

RJA30 RB5 1c **dark blue** — —
RJA31 RB5 2c **dark blue** —
RJA32 RB5 4c **dark blue** —

No. RB65 is known with "Narcotic" applied in red ms.

Documentary Stamps of 1917 Overprinted in Black, "Narcotic" 17½mm wide

1919 Wmk. 191R Offset Printing *Perf. 11*

RJA33 R22 1c **carmine rose** *(6,900,000)* 1.00 .80
RJA34 R22 2c **carmine rose** *(3,650,000)* 2.00 1.10
RJA35 R22 3c **carmine rose** *(388,400)* 32.50 21.00
RJA36 R22 4c **carmine rose** *(2,400,000)* 5.25 4.75
RJA37 R22 5c **carmine rose** *(2,400,000)* 13.50 10.50
RJA38 R22 8c **carmine rose** *(1,200,000)* 21.00 18.00
RJA39 R22 10c **carmine rose** *(3,400,000)* 3.25 2.75
RJA40 R22 25c **carmine rose** *(700,000)* 21.00 16.00

Overprint Reading Up

Engr.

RJA41 R21 $1 **green** *(270,000)* 47.50 19.00

Fake overprints exist on Nos. RJA33-RJA41. In the genuine the C's are not slanted.

NT1

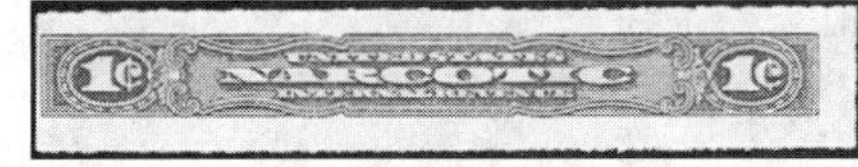
NT2

Imperf., Rouletted

1919-64 Offset Printing Wmk. 191R

Left Value- "a" Imperf.

Right Value- "b" Rouletted 7

RJA42 NT1 1c **violet** 5.25 .25
d. 1c purple 7.50 —
RJA43 NT2 1c **violet** .55 .30
d. 1c purple 5.00 5.25
RJA44 NT2 2c **violet** 1.40 .55
d. 2c purple 5.25
RJA45 NT2 3c **violet** ('64) 125.00

NT3

NT4

Left Value- "a" Imperf.

Right Value- "b" Rouletted 7

RJA46 NT3 1c **violet** 2.75 .65
d. 1c **purple** 9.00
RJA47 NT3 2c **violet** 1.60 .65
d. 2c **purple** 8.25
RJA48 NT3 3c **violet** 750.00
RJA49 NT3 4c **violet** ('42) — 10.00
d. 4c **purple** — 30.00
RJA50 NT3 5c **violet** 42.50 3.50
d. 5c **purple** 13.00
RJA51 NT3 6c **violet** .70
d. 6c **purple** 9.25
RJA52 NT3 8c **violet** 57.50 3.50
d. 8c **purple** 26.00
RJA53 NT3 9c **violet** ('53) 67.50 21.00
RJA54 NT3 10c **violet** 32.50 .50
d. 10c **purple** 7.00
RJA55 NT3 16c **violet** 52.50 4.00
d. 16c **purple** 14.50
RJA56 NT3 18c **violet** ('61) 110.00 10.50
RJA57 NT3 19c **violet** ('61) 125.00 26.00
RJA58 NT3 20c **violet** 375.00 200.00

Nos. RJA47-RJA58 have "CENTS" below the value.

Left Value- "a" Imperf.

Right Value- "b" Rouletted 7

RJA59 NT4 1c **violet** 47.50 10.50
c. Rouletted 3½ 4.25

RJA60	NT4	2c **violet**		50.00	20.00
RJA61	NT4	3c **violet**		52.50	62.50
RJA62	NT4	5c **violet**			26.00
RJA63	NT4	6c **violet**		62.50	21.00
RJA64	NT4	8c **violet**			47.50
RJA65	NT4	9c **violet** ('61)		26.00	21.00
RJA66	NT4	10c **violet**		15.00	15.00
RJA67	NT4	16c **violet**		16.00	10.00
RJA68	NT4	18c **violet** ('61)		400.00	425.00
RJA69	NT4	19c **violet**		16.00	190.00
RJA70	NT4	20c **violet**		325.00	240.00
RJA71	NT4	25c **violet**		—	21.00
c.		Rouletted 3½		—	4.25
RJA72	NT4	40c **violet**		400.00	*1,250.*
c.		Rouletted 3½			67.50
RJA73	NT4	$1 **green**			1.60
RJA74	NT4	$1.28 **green**		32.50	10.50

On Nos. RJA60-RJA74 the value tablet is solid.

Imperf., Rouletted

1963(?)-70 Offset Printing Unwatermarked

Left Value- "a" Imperf.

Right Value- "b" Rouletted 7

RJA75	NT1	1c **violet**	7.75	2.10+
RJA76	NT2	1c **violet**	1.10	1.10
RJA77	NT2	2c **violet**	5.25	2.10+
RJA78	NT2	3c **violet**		125.00
RJA79	NT3	1c **violet**	5.25	2.10
RJA80	NT3	2c **violet**		2.00
RJA81	NT3	4c **violet**		10.00
RJA82	NT3	5c **violet**	72.50	
RJA83	NT3	6c **violet**	—	10.50+
RJA84	NT3	8c **violet**		5.25
RJA85	NT3	9c **violet**	—	50.00
RJA86	NT3	10c **violet**	—	10.50+
RJA87	NT3	16c **violet**	150.00	4.25
RJA88	NT3	18c **violet**	—	52.50+
RJA89	NT3	20c **violet**		325.00+

Nos. RJA80-RJA89 have "CENTS" below the value.

+ Items so marked currently are only known unused with original gum and are valued thus.

Unwatermarked

Left Value- "a" Imperf.

Right Value- "b" Rouletted 7

RJA91	NT4	1c **violet**	67.50	15.00
RJA92	NT4	2c **violet**		52.50+
RJA93	NT4	3c **violet**	85.00	125.00+
RJA94	NT4	6c **violet**	100.00	52.50+
RJA95	NT4	9c **violet**		125.00+
RJA96	NT4	10c **violet**		60.00+
RJA97	NT4	16c **violet**	40.00	21.00
RJA98	NT4	19c **violet**	26.00	400.00
RJA99	NT4	20c **violet**	—	500.00+
RJA100	NT4	25c **violet**		250.00
RJA101	NT4	40c **violet**	*1,000.*	
RJA102	NT4	$1 **green**		32.50+
RJA103	NT4	$1.28 **green**		60.00+
RJA104	NT4	$4 **green** ('70)	*1,000.*	

On Nos. RJA92-RJA104 the value tablet is solid.

+ Items so marked currently are only known unused with original gum and are valued thus.

NT5

Denomination added in black by rubber plate in an operation similar to precanceling.

1963 Engr. Unwmk. *Imperf.*

Left Value- Unused

Right Value- Used

RJA105	NT5	1c **violet,** type 2	100.00	85.00
a.		Type 1	*140.00*	*140.00*

Type 1 was produced with four electric eye markings, one in each corner. Type 2 was produced later and has two electric eye markings, one in each corner on the left side of the stamp. Type 2 is the more common of the two varieties and, therefore, is listed as the major number.

Nos. RAJ105 and RAJ105a were issued in vertical coil strips.

Denomination on Stamp Plate

1964 Offset Printing *Imperf.*

RJA106	NT5	1c **violet**	90.00	5.25

RJA106 was issued in sheet of 80 stamps.

CONSULAR SERVICE FEE STAMPS

Act of Congress, April 5, 1906, effective June 1, 1906, provided that every consular officer should be provided with special adhesive stamps printed in denominations determined by the Department of State.

Every document for which a fee was prescribed had to have attached a stamp or stamps representing the amount collected, and such stamps were used to show payment of these prescribed fees.

These stamps were usually affixed close to the signature, or at the lower left corner of the document. If no document was issued, the stamp or stamps were attached to a receipt for the amount of the fee and canceled either with pen and ink or rubber stamp showing the date of cancellation and bearing the initials of the canceling officer or name of the Consular Office. These stamps were not sold to the public uncanceled. Their use was discontinued Sept. 30, 1955.

CSF1 CSF2

1906 Unwmk. Engr. *Perf. 12*

RK1	CSF1	25c **dark green**	70.00
RK2	CSF1	50c **carmine**	90.00
RK3	CSF1	$1 **dark violet**	7.50
a.		Diagonal half used as 50c with 2 #RK3, paying $2.50 fee, on document	*325.00*
RK4	CSF1	$2 **brown**	6.00
RK5	CSF1	$2.50 **dark blue**	1.90
RK6	CSF1	$5 **brown red**	26.00
a.		Horizontal or diagonal half used as $2.50, on document	*250.00*
RK7	CSF1	$10 **orange**	85.00

Perf. 10

RK8	CSF1	25c **dark green**	75.00
RK9	CSF1	50c **carmine**	90.00
RK10	CSF1	$1 **dark violet**	425.00
11	CSF1	$2 **brown**	100.00
a.		Diagonal half used as $1, on document	—
RK12	CSF1	$2.50 **dark blue**	24.00
RK13	CSF1	$5 **brown red**	175.00

Perf. 11

RK14	CSF1	25c **dark green**	80.00
RK15	CSF1	50c **carmine**	140.00
RK16	CSF1	$1 **dark violet**	2.00
a.		Diagonal half used as 50c, on document	*375.00*
RK17	CSF1	$2 **brown**	2.40
RK18	CSF1	$2.50 **dark blue**	.95
RK19	CSF1	$5 **brown red**	5.00
a.		Diagonal half used as $2.50, on document	50.00
RK20	CSF1	$9 **gray**	20.00
RK21	CSF1	$10 **orange**	40.00
a.		Diagonal half used as $5, on document	62.50

1924 *Perf. 11*

RK22	CSF2	$1 **violet**	100.00
RK23	CSF2	$2 **brown**	110.00
RK24	CSF2	$2.50 **blue**	15.00
RK25	CSF2	$5 **brown red**	85.00
RK26	CSF2	$9 **gray**	300.00
		Nos. RK22-RK26 (5)	610.00

CSF3

1925-52 *Perf. 10*

RK27	CSF3	$1 **violet**	30.00
RK28	CSF3	$2 **brown**	70.00
RK29	CSF3	$2.50 **ultramarine**	2.75
RK30	CSF3	$5 **carmine**	15.00
RK31	CSF3	$9 **gray**	50.00

Perf. 11

RK32	CSF3	25c **green** ('37)	85.00
RK33	CSF3	50c **orange** ('34)	85.00
RK34	CSF3	$1 **violet**	3.75
a.		Diagonal half used as 50c, on document	—
RK35	CSF3	$2 **brown**	4.25
RK36	CSF3	$2.50 **blue**	.45
a.		$2.50 ultramarine	.40
RK37	CSF3	$5 **carmine**	3.25
RK38	CSF3	$9 **gray**	20.00
RK39	CSF3	$10 **blue gray** ('37)	100.00
RK40	CSF3	$20 **violet** ('52)	110.00
		Nos. RK27-RK40 (14)	579.45

Consular Fee

The "Consular Fee stamp" on revenue stamped paper (previously listed as No. RN-Y1 but since deleted) was found to be nothing more than an illustration. Two identical copies are known.

CUSTOMS FEE STAMPS

New York Custom House

Issued to indicate the collection of miscellaneous customs fees. Use was discontinued on February 28, 1918. The stamps were not utilized in the collection of customs duties.

Silas Wright
CF1

Size: 48x34mm

1887 **Engr.** ***Rouletted 5½***

RL1	CF1 20c **dull rose**		110.00	1.00
a.	20c **red,** perf. 10			—
b.	Vert. half used as 10c, on document			*250.00*
c.	20c **red,** rouletted 7			*200.00*
RL2	CF1 30c **orange**		150.00	2.00
RL3	CF1 40c **green**		175.00	3.50
RL4	CF1 50c **dark blue**		175.00	5.50
RL5	CF1 60c **red violet**		140.00	2.00
RL6	CF1 70c **brown violet**		140.00	30.00
RL7	CF1 80c **brown**		200.00	77.50
RL8	CF1 90c **black**		250.00	90.00
	Nos. RL1-RL8 (8)		1,340.	211.50

Each of these stamps has its own distinctive background.

EMBOSSED REVENUE STAMPED PAPER

Some of the American colonies of Great Britain used embossed stamps in raising revenue, as Britain had done from 1694. The British government also imposed stamp taxes on the colonies, and in the early 19th century the U.S. government and some of the states enacted similar taxes.

Under one statue or another, these stamps were required on such documents as promissory notes, bills of exchange, insurance policies, bills of lading, bonds, protests, powers of attorney, stock certificates, letters patent, writs, conveyances, leases, mortgages, charter parties, commissions and liquor licenses.

A few of these stamps were printed, but most were colorless impressions resembling a notary public's seal.

The scant literature of these stamps includes E.B. Sterling's revenue catalogue of 1888, *The Stamps that Caused the American Revolution: The Stamps of the British Stamp Act for America,* by Adolph Koeppel, published in 1976 by the Town of North Hempstead (New York) American Revolution Bicentennial Commission, *New Discovery from British Archives on the 1765 Tax Stamps for America,* edited by Adolph Koeppel and published in 1962 by the American Revenue Association, *First Federal Issue 1798-1801 U.S. Embossed Revenue Stamped Paper,* by W.V. Combs, published in 1979 by the American Philatelic Society, *Second Federal Issue, 1801-1802,* by W.V. Combs, published in 1988 by the American Revenue Association, and *Third Federal Issue, 1814-1817,* by W.V. Combs, published in 1993 by the American Revenue Association.

Values are for stamps of clear impression on entire documents of the most common usage in good condition. The document may be folded. Unusual or rare usages may sell for much more. Parts of documents, cut squares or poor impressions sell for much less.

Colin MacR. Makepeace originally compiled the listings in this section.

INCLUDING COLONIAL EMBOSSED REVENUES

I. COLONIAL ISSUES

A. MASSACHUSETTS

Act of January 8, 1755
In effect May 1, 1755-April 30, 1757

ERP1 ERP2

ERP3 ERP4

Die 2 — ERP2

Typo.

RM1	ERP1	½p **red**	*2,300.*

Embossed

RM2	ERP2	2p	400.
RM3	ERP3	3p	200.
RM4	ERP4	4p	600.

A second die of ERP2 with no fin on the under side of the codfish has been seen. There were at least two dies of the ½p.

B. NEW YORK

Act of December 1, 1756
In effect January 1, 1757-December 31, 1760

ERP9

Typo.

RM9	ERP9	½p **red**	*2,500.*

Embossed

RM10	ERP9	1p	525.
RM11	ERP9	2p	300.
RM12	ERP9	3p	450.
RM13	ERP9	4p	375.

II. BRITISH REVENUES FOR USE IN AMERICA

Act of March 22, 1765
In effect November 1, 1765-May 1, 1766.

A. ALMANAC STAMPS

ERP15

Engr.

RM15	ERP15	2p **red**	
RM16	ERP15	4p **red**	—
RM17	ERP15	8p **red**	

Proofs of all of these stamps printed in the issued color are known. Full size facsimile reproductions in the color of the originals were made about 1876 of the proof sheets of the 8p stamp, Plates 1 and 2, Dies 1 to 50 inclusive.

B. PAMPHLETS AND NEWSPAPER STAMPS

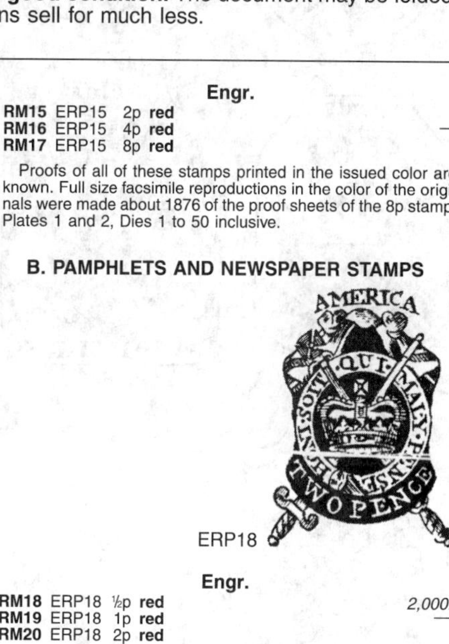

ERP18

Engr.

RM18	ERP18	½p **red**	*2,000.*
RM19	ERP18	1p **red**	—
RM20	ERP18	2p **red**	

Proofs of all of these stamps printed in the issued color are known. Full size facsimile reproductions in the color of the originals were made about 1876 of the proof sheets of the 1p stamp, Plates 3 and 4, Dies 51 to 100 inclusive.

C. GENERAL ISSUE

ERP24

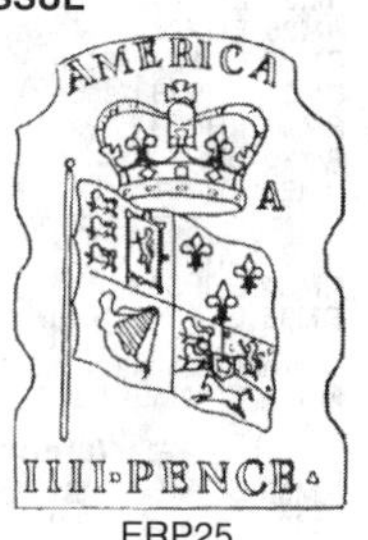

ERP25

ERP26 ERP27

ERP28 ERP29

ERP30 ERP31

ERP33 ERP34

ERP35

Embossed

RM24	ERP24	3p	*2,000.*
RM25	ERP25	4p	*3,000.*
RM26	ERP26	6p	*3,000.*
RM27	ERP27	1sh	*1,750.*
RM28	ERP28	1sh6p	*1,250.*
RM29	ERP29	2sh	*3,000.*
RM30	ERP30	2sh3p	*1,800.*
RM31	ERP31	2sh6p	*2,000.*
a.	Not on document		450.
RM33	ERP33	4sh	*1,750.*
RM34	ERP34	5sh	*2,500.*
RM35	ERP35	10sh	*3,250.*

Proofs exist of similar 1sh, 1sh6p and 2sh6p stamps inscribed "AMERICA CONT.& c."

Various Similar Designs

RM36	£1	
RM37	£2	—
RM38	£3	—
RM39	£4	
RM40	£6	—
RM41	£10	—

The £1 to £10 denominations probably exist only as proofs.

D. PLAYING CARDS STAMP

Type similar to EP29, with Arms of George III Encircled by Garter.

RM42 1sh —

All of these were embossed without color and most of them were embossed directly on the document except the 2sh 6p which was general embossed on a rectangular piece of bluish or brownish stiff paper or cardboard only slightly larger than the stamp which was attached to the document by a small piece of metal. Three dies exist of the 3p; two of the 4p, 6p, 1sh, 1sh 6p, 2sh and 2sh 3p.

All of these stamps have the word "America" somewhere in the design and this is the feature which distinguishes them from the other British revenues. The stamps of the general issue are occasionally found with a design of a British revenue stamp struck over the American design, as a number of them were afterwards re-struck and used elsewhere as British revenues.

These stamps are sometimes called the "Teaparty" or "Tax on Tea" stamps. This, however, is a misnomer, as the act under which these stamps were issued laid no tax on tea. The tax on tea was levied by an act passed two years later, and the duties imposed by that act were not collected by stamps.

It must be remembered that these stamps were issued under an act applicable to all of the British colonies in America which included many which are not now part of the United States. Copies have been seen which were used in Quebec, Nova Scotia and in the West Indies. So great was the popular clamor against taxation by a body in which the colonists had no representation that ships bringing the stamps from England were not allowed to land them in some of the colonies, the stamps were destroyed in others, and in practically all of those which are now a part of the United States the "Stamp Masters" who were to administer the act were forced to resign and to take oath that they would never carry out the duties of the offices. Notwithstanding the very general feeling about these stamps there is evidence that a very small number of them were actually used on ships' documents for one vessel clearing from New York and for a very small number of vessels clearing from the Savannah River. Florida was at this time under British authority and the only known copies of these stamps used in what is now the United States, a 4p (#RM25), a 1sh (#RM27), and two copies of the 5sh (#RM34) were used there.

III. ISSUES OF THE UNITED STATES

A. FIRST FEDERAL ISSUE

Act of July 6, 1797

In effect July 1, 1798-February 28, 1801

The distinguishing feature of the stamps of this issue is the name of a state in the design. These stamps were issued by the Federal Government, however, and not by the states. The design, with the exception of the name of the state, was the same for each denomination; but different denominations had the shield and the eagle in different positions. The design of only one denomination of these stamps is illustrated.

In addition to the eagle and shield design on the values from four cents to ten dollars there are two other stamps for each state, similar in design to one another, one of which is illustrated. All of these stamps are embossed without color.

Values are for clearly impressed examples.

RM45	4c	Connecticut	45.00
RM46	10c	Connecticut	125.00
RM47	20c	Connecticut	300.00
RM48	25c	Connecticut	45.00
RM49	30c	Connecticut	*2,750.*
RM50	50c	Connecticut	135.00
RM51	75c	Connecticut	—
RM52	$1	Connecticut	*1,750.*
RM54	$4	Connecticut	*1,250.*
RM58	4c	Delaware	300.00
RM59	10c	Delaware	350.00
RM60	20c	Delaware	500.00
RM61	25c	Delaware	450.00
RM62	30c	Delaware	—
RM63	50c	Delaware	550.00
RM64	75c	Delaware	700.00
RM65	$1	Delaware	—
RM71	4c	Georgia	275.00
RM72	10c	Georgia	200.00
RM73	20c	Georgia	—
RM74	25c	Georgia	250.00
RM75	30c	Georgia	*3,000.*
RM76	50c	Georgia	400.00
RM77	75c	Georgia	*1,750.*
RM78	$1	Georgia	—
RM84	4c	Kentucky	20.00
RM85	10c	Kentucky	25.00
RM86	20c	Kentucky	250.00
RM87	25c	Kentucky	40.00
RM88	30c	Kentucky	275.00
RM89	50c	Kentucky	50.00
RM90	75c	Kentucky	125.00
RM91	$1	Kentucky	—
RM97	4c	Maryland	75.00
RM98	10c	Maryland	50.00
RM99	20c	Maryland	500.00
RM100	25c	Maryland	75.00
RM101	30c	Maryland	600.00
RM102	50c	Maryland	125.00
RM103	75c	Maryland	15.00
RM104	$1	Maryland	—
RM106	$4	Maryland	—
RM110	4c	Massachusetts	20.00
RM111	10c	Massachusetts	50.00
RM112	20c	Massachusetts	80.00
RM113	25c	Massachusetts	35.00
RM114	30c	Massachusetts	950.00
RM115	50c	Massachusetts	125.00
RM116	75c	Massachusetts	400.00
RM117	$1	Massachusetts	200.00
RM123	4c	New Hampshire	25.00
RM124	10c	New Hampshire	25.00
RM125	20c	New Hampshire	350.00
RM126	25c	New Hampshire	70.00
RM127	30c	New Hampshire	425.00
RM128	50c	New Hampshire	80.00
RM129	75c	New Hampshire	50.00
RM130	$1	New Hampshire	550.00
RM136	4c	New Jersey	400.00
RM137	10c	New Jersey	175.00
RM138	20c	New Jersey	—
RM139	25c	New Jersey	110.00
RM140	30c	New Jersey	750.00
RM141	50c	New Jersey	125.00
RM142	75c	New Jersey	—
RM143	$1	New Jersey	—
RM147	$10	New Jersey	*4,750.*
RM149	4c	New York	35.00
RM150	10c	New York	20.00
RM151	20c	New York	25.00
RM152	25c	New York	20.00
RM153	30c	New York	25.00
RM154	50c	New York	30.00
RM155	75c	New York	35.00
RM156	$1	New York	350.00
RM157	$2	New York	—
RM159	$5	New York	—
RM160	$10	New York	—
RM162	4c	North Carolina	45.00
RM163	10c	North Carolina	50.00
RM164	20c	North Carolina	2,000.
RM165	25c	North Carolina	55.00
RM166	30c	North Carolina	2,500.
RM167	50c	North Carolina	175.00
RM168	75c	North Carolina	325.00
RM169	$1	North Carolina	*3,750.*
RM175	4c	Pennsylvania	30.00
RM176	10c	Pennsylvania	20.00
RM177	20c	Pennsylvania	27.50
RM178	25c	Pennsylvania	15.00
RM179	30c	Pennsylvania	30.00
RM180	50c	Pennsylvania	25.00
RM181	75c	Pennsylvania	75.00
RM182	$1	Pennsylvania	300.00
RM184	$4	Pennsylvania	13,000.
RM187		Pennsylvania, "Ten cents per centum"	—
RM188	4c	Rhode Island	35.00
RM189	10c	Rhode Island	50.00
RM190	20c	Rhode Island	200.00
RM191	25c	Rhode Island	65.00
RM192	30c	Rhode Island	900.00
RM193	50c	Rhode Island	150.00
RM194	75c	Rhode Island	*1,000.*
RM195	$1	Rhode Island	*1,750.*
RM201	4c	South Carolina	90.00
RM202	10c	South Carolina	200.00
RM203	20c	South Carolina	350.00
RM204	25c	South Carolina	125.00
RM205	30c	South Carolina	—
RM206	50c	South Carolina	175.00
RM207	75c	South Carolina	*2,500.*
RM208	$1	South Carolina	*6,000.*
RM211	$5	South Carolina	—
RM214	4c	Tennessee	350.00
RM215	10c	Tennessee	200.00
RM216	20c	Tennessee	—
RM217	25c	Tennessee	225.00
RM218	30c	Tennessee	—
RM219	50c	Tennessee	*900.00*
RM220	75c	Tennessee	—
RM221	$1	Tennessee	—
RM227	4c	Vermont	75.00
RM228	10c	Vermont	35.00
RM229	20c	Vermont	350.00
RM230	25c	Vermont	100.00
RM231	30c	Vermont	*1,350.*
RM232	50c	Vermont	130.00
RM233	75c	Vermont	*3,000.*
RM234	$1	Vermont	—
RM238	$10	Vermont	—
RM240	4c	Virginia	15.00
RM241	10c	Virginia	20.00
RM242	20c	Virginia	125.00
RM243	25c	Virginia	20.00
RM244	30c	Virginia	500.00
RM245	50c	Virginia	25.00
RM246	75c	Virginia	50.00
RM247	$1	Virginia	*1,000.*

The Act calls for a $2, $4, $5 and $10 stamp for each state, only the listed ones have been seen.

The Act also calls for a "Ten cents per centum" and a "Six mills per dollar" stamp for each state, none of which has been seen except No. RM187.

A press and a set of dies, one die for each denomination, were prepared and sent to each state where it was the duty of the Supervisors of the Revenue to stamp all documents presented to them upon payment of the proper tax. The Supervisors were also to have on hand for sale blank paper stamped with the different rates of duty to be sold to the public upon which the purchaser would later write or print the proper type of instrument corresponding with the value of the stamp impressed thereon. So far as is now known there was no distinctive watermark for the paper sold by the government. The Vermont set of dies is in the Vermont Historical Society at Montpelier.

B. SECOND FEDERAL ISSUE

Act of April 23, 1800
In effect March 1, 1801-June 30, 1802

RM260

RM261

		(a)Government watermark in italics; laid paper	(b)Government watermark in Roman; wove paper	(c)No Government watermark
RM260	4c	15.00	15.00	50.00
RM261	10c	20.00	20.00	50.00
RM262	20c	65.00	75.00	85.00
RM263	25c	15.00	15.00	17.50
RM264	30c	75.00	75.00	400.00
RM265	50c	65.00	45.00	85.00
RM266	75c	30.00	50.00	100.00
RM267	$1	200.00	150.00	175.00
RM269	$4			500.00
RM271	$10		*3,250.*	

The distinguishing feature of the stamps of this issue is the counter stamp, the left stamp shown in the illustration which usually appears on a document below the other stamp. In the right stamp the design of the eagle and the shield are similar to their design in the same denomination of the First Federal Issue but the name of the state is omitted and the denomination appears below instead of above the eagle and the shield. All of these stamps were embossed without color.

All the paper which was furnished by the government contained the watermark vertically along the edge of the sheet, "GEN STAMP OFFICE," either in Roman capitals on wove paper or in italic capitals on laid paper. The wove paper also had in the center of each half sheet either the watermark "W. Y. & Co." or "Delaware." William Young & Co. who owned the Delaware Mills made the government paper. The laid paper omitted the watermark "Delaware." The two stamps were separately impressed. The design of the eagle and shield differed in each value.

All the stamping was done in Washington, the right stamp being put on in the General Stamp Office and the left one or counter stamp in the office of the Commissioner of the Revenue as a check on the stamping done in the General Stamp Office. The "Com. Rev. C. S." in the design of the counter stamp stands for "Commissioner of the Revenue, Counter Stamp."

The Second Federal issue was intended to include $2 and $5 stamps, but these denominations have not been seen.

C. THIRD FEDERAL ISSUE

Act of August 2, 1813
In effect January 1, 1814-December 31, 1817

RM276

		a. Watermark	b. Unwmkd.
RM275	5c	10.00	15.00
RM276	10c	10.00	10.00
RM277	25c	15.00	15.00
RM278	50c	10.00	10.00
RM279	75c	13.00	17.50
RM280	$1	13.00	27.50
RM281	$1.50	13.00	65.00
RM282	$2	27.50	50.00
RM283	$2.50	27.50	110.00
RM284	$3.50	175.00	45.00
RM285	$4		200.00
RM286	$5	37.50	50.00

The distinguishing features of the stamps of this issue are the absence of the name of a state in the design and the absence of the counter stamp. Different values show different positions of the eagle.

All stamps of this issue were embossed without color at Washington. The paper with the watermark "Stamp U. S." was sold by the government. Unwatermarked paper may be either wove or laid.

IV. ISSUES BY VARIOUS STATES

DELAWARE

Act of June 19, 1793
In effect October 1, 1793-February 7, 1794

ERP50

ERP51

ERP53

RM291	EP50	5c	*1,700.*
RM292	EP51	20c	*1,350.*
RM294	EP53	50c	—

In some cases a reddish ink was used in impressing the stamp and in other cases the impressions are colorless.

Besides the denominations listed, 3c, 33c, and $1 stamps were called for by the taxing act. Stamps of these denominations have not been seen.

VIRGINIA

Act of February 20, 1813
In effect May 1, 1813-April 30, 1815
Act of December 21, 1814
In effect May 1, 1815-February 27, 1816

ERP60

ERP61

			a. Die cut	b. On Document
RM305	EP61	4c	17.50	90.00
RM306	EP60	6c	17.50	200.00
RM307	EP61	10c		200.00
RM308	EP60	12c	25.00	200.00
RM309	EP61	20c	40.00	500.00
RM310	EP61	25c	17.50	225.00
RM311	EP61	37c	17.50	300.00
RM312	EP61	45c	40.00	200.00
RM313	EP61	50c	17.50	225.00
RM314	EP61	70c	40.00	
RM315	EP61	75c	22.50	90.00
RM316	EP61	95c	40.00	300.00
RM317	EP61	100c	40.00	300.00
RM318	EP61	120c		225.00
RM319	EP61	125c	17.50	
RM323	EP60	175c	17.50	
RM325	EP61	200c	17.50	475.00

All of these stamps are colorless impressions and with some exceptions as noted below those issued under the 1813 Act cannot be distinguished from those issued under the 1814 Act. The 10c, 20c, 45c, 70c, 95c, 120c, 145c, 150c, 170c and 190c were issued only under the 1813 Act, the 6c, 12c, and 37c only under the 1814 Act.

No. RM311 has the large lettering of EP60 but the 37 is to the left and the XXXVII to the right as in EP61. The design of the dogwood branch and berries is similar but not identical in all values.

When the tax on the document exceeded "two hundred cents," two or more stamps were impressed or attached to the document. For instance a document has been seen with 45c and 200c to make up the $2.45 rate, and another with 75c and 200c.

Since both the Virginia and the Third Federal Acts to some extent taxed the same kind of document, and since during the period from Jan. 1, 1814 to Feb. 27, 1816, both Acts were in effect in Virginia, some instruments have both stamps on them.

The circular die cut Virginia stamps about 29mm in diameter were cut out of previously stamped paper which after the Act was repealed, was presented for redemption at the office of the Auditor of Public Accounts. They were threaded on fine twine and until about 1940 preserved in his office as required by law. Watermarked die cut Virginia stamps are all cut out of Third Federal watermarked paper.

Not seen yet, the 145c, 150c, and 170c stamps were called for by the 1813 Act, and 195c by both the 1813 and 1814 Acts.

MARYLAND

1. Act of February 11, 1818
In effect May 1, 1818-March 7, 1819

ERP70

RM362	EP70	30c **red** (printed), unused	400.
		Sheet of 4, unused	2,500.

The Act called for six other denominations, none of which has been seen. The Act imposing this tax was held unconstitutional by the United States Supreme Court in the case of McCulloch vs. Maryland.

2. Act of March 10, 1845
In effect May 10, 1845-March 10, 1856

ERP71

RM370	EP71	10c	12.50
RM371	EP71	15c	10.00
RM372	EP71	25c	10.00
RM373	EP71	50c	12.50
RM374	EP71	75c	10.00
RM375	EP71	$1	10.00
RM376	EP71	$1.50	12.50
RM377	EP71	$2	45.00
RM378	EP71	$2.50	17.50
RM379	EP71	$3.50	55.00
RM380	EP71	$4	90.00
RM381	EP71	$5.50	50.00
RM382	EP71	$6	100.00

Nos. RM370-RM382 are embossed without color with a similar design for each value. They vary in size from 20mm in diameter for the 10c to 33mm for the $6.

V. FEDERAL LICENSES TO SELL LIQUOR, ETC.

1. Act of June 5, 1794
In effect September 30, 1794-June 30, 1802

ERP80

RM400	EP80	$5	550.00

Provisionals are in existence using the second issue Connecticut Supervisors' stamp with the words "Five Dollars" written or printed over it or the second issue of the New Hampshire Supervisors' stamp without the words "Five Dollars."

2. Act of August 2, 1813
In effect January 1, 1814-December 31, 1817

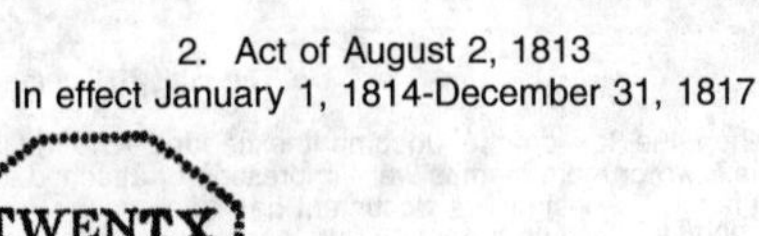

ERP81

RM451	EP81	$10	650.00
RM452	EP81	$12	625.00
RM453	EP81	$15	450.00
RM454	EP81	$18	800.00
RM455	EP81	$20	*1,200.*
RM456	EP81	$22.50	525.00
RM457	EP81	$25	425.00
RM458	EP81	$30	*1,400.*
RM459	EP81	$37.50	500.00

The Act of December 23, 1814, increased the basic rates of $10, $12, $15, $20 and $25 by 50 per cent, effective February 1, 1815. This increase applied to the unexpired portions of the year so far as licenses then in effect were concerned and these licenses were required to be brought in and to have the payment of the additional tax endorsed on them.

VI. FEDERAL LICENSES TO WORK A STILL

Act of July 24, 1813
In effect January 1, 1814-December 31, 1817

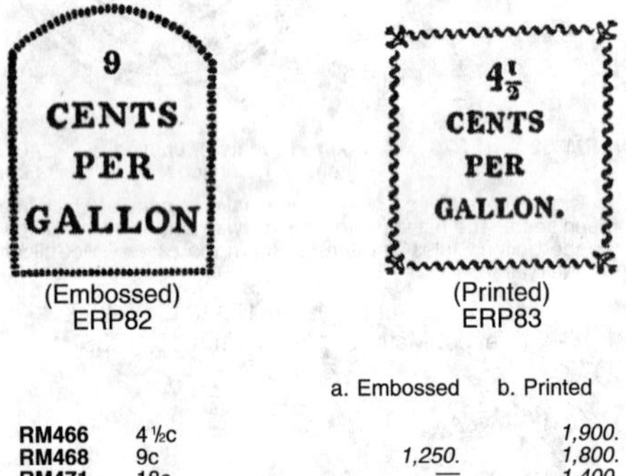

(Embossed) ERP82 (Printed) ERP83

		a. Embossed	b. Printed
RM466	4½c		*1,900.*
RM468	9c	*1,250.*	*1,800.*
RM471	18c	—	*1,400.*
RM477	36c		*2,100.*
RM480	52c	*2,000.*	
RM484	70c	*2,100.*	
RM488	$1.08	*2,000.*	

The statute under which these were issued provided for additional rates of 2½c, 5c, 10c, 16c, 21c, 25c, 26c, 32c, 35c, 42c, 50c, 54c, 60c, 64c, 84c, $1.04, $1.05, $1.20, $1.35, $1.40, $2.10, $2.16 and $2.70 per gallon of the capacity of the still. Stamps of these denominations have not been seen.

VII. SUPERVISORS' AND CUSTOM HOUSE SEALS

1. Supervisors' Seals Act of March 3, 1791.
In effect July 1, 1791-March 2, 1799.

ERP90

		Check Letter	State	
RM501	EP90	"B"	South Carolina	50.00
RM503	EP90	"D"	Virginia	*1,350.*
RM506	EP90	"G"	Pennsylvania	75.00
RM508	EP90	"I"	New York	22.50
RM509	EP90	"K"	Connecticut	30.00
RM510	EP90	"L"	Rhode Island	90.00
RM511	EP90	"M"	Massachusetts	22.50
RM512	EP90	"N"	New Hampshire	700.00
RM514	EP90	"P"	Kentucky	—

2. Supervisors' Seals Act of March 2, 1799
In effect from March 2, 1799

ERP91

RM552	EP91	North Carolina	500.00
RM553	EP91	Virginia	—
RM554	EP91	Maryland	200.00
RM556	EP91	Pennsylvania	250.00
RM558	EP91	New York	20.00
RM559	EP91	Connecticut	30.00
RM560	EP91	Rhode Island	35.00
RM561	EP91	Massachusetts	25.00
RM562	EP91	New Hampshire	90.00

3. Custom House Seals

ERP92

RM575	EP92	Custom House, Philadelphia	50.00

Although no value is expressed in the Supervisors' and Custom House seals, and they do not evidence the payment of a tax in the same way that the other stamps do, some collectors of stamped paper include them in their collections if they are on instruments evidencing the payment of a tax.

They were all embossed without color and, as to Supervisors' seals issued under the Act of 1791, the only difference in design is that at the left of the eagle there was a different check letter for each state. Custom House seals used in the other cities are in existence, but, in view of the doubtful status of Custom House seals as revenue stamps, it is not proposed to list them.

REVENUE STAMPED PAPER

These stamps were printed in various denominations and designs on a variety of financial documents, including checks, drafts, receipts, specie clerk statements, insurance policies, bonds and stock certificates.

They were authorized by Act of Congress of July 1, 1862, effective October 1, 1862, although regular delivery of stamped paper did not begin until July 1, 1865. The 2-cent tax on receipts ended Oct. 1, 1870. The 2-cent tax on checks and sight drafts ended July 1, 1883. All other taxes ended Oct. 1, 1872. The use of stamped paper was revived by the War Revenue Act of 1898, approved June 13, 1898. Type X was used July 1, 1898 through June 30, 1902.

Most of these stamps were typographed; some, types H, I and J, were engraved. They were printed by private firms under supervision of government representatives from dies loaned by the Bureau of Internal Revenue. Types A-F, P-W were printed by the American Phototype Co., New York (1865-75); type G, Graphic Co., New York (1875-83); types H-L, Joseph R. Carpenter, Philadelphia (1866-75); types M-N, A. Trochsler, Boston (1873-75); type O, Morey and Sherwood, Chicago (1874). Type X was printed by numerous regional printers under contract with the government.

Samples of these stamps are known for types B-G, P and Q with a section of the design removed and replaced by the word "Sample." Types G, P-Q, U-W exist with a redemption clause added by typography or rubber stamp. Redeemed type X's have a 5mm punched hole.

Multiples or single impressions on various plain papers are usually considered proofs or printers' waste.

For further information see "Handbook for United States Revenue Stamped Paper," published (1979) by the American Revenue Association.

Illustration size varies, with actual size quoted for each type.

Values for types A-O are for clear impressions on plain entire checks and receipts. Attractive documents with vignettes sell for more. The value of individual examples is also affected by the place of use. For example, territorial usage generally sells for more than a similar item from New York City.

Values for types P-W are for stamps on documents with attractive engravings, usually stock certificates, bonds and insurance policies. Examples on plain documents and cut squares sell for less.

Type A

Size: 22x25mm

RN-A1	2c **black**	90.	75.
	a. Printed on both sides		30.
RN-A2	2c **orange**		125.
RN-A3	2c **gray**		—
RN-A8	2c **purple** (shades)		*2,000.*
RN-A9	2c **green**		*1,250.*
	a. Inverted		—

The unique example of No. RN-A9a is on a partial document.

Same Type with 1 Entire and 53 or 56 Partial Impressions in Vertical Format ("Tapeworm") Left Col. - Full Document Right Col. - Strip with Bank Names

RN-A10	2c **orange**, 1 full plus 56 partial impressions	750.	100.
	Cut square (full strip without bank names)		45.
RN-A11	2c **orange**, 1 full plus 53 partial impressions	*1,250.*	250.

Nos. RN-A10 and RN-A11 were used by the Mechanics' National Bank of New York on a bank specie clerk's statement. It was designed so that the full stamp or one of the repeated bottom segments fell on each line opposite the name of a bank.

The three additional banks were added at the bottom of the form. No. RN-A11 must show white space below the "First National Bank" line.

Eagle Type B

Size: 31x48mm

RN-B1	2c **orange**	5.00	3.00
	yellow orange	5.00	3.00
	deep orange	5.00	3.00
a.	Printed on both sides	200.00	20.00
b.	Double impression	350.00	
c.	Printed on back		—
d.	With 10 centimes blue French handstamp, right	400.00	

All examples of the previously-listed "yellow" have some orange in them.

RN-B2	2c **black**	125.00	40.00
RN-B3	2c **blue**	125.00	40.00
	light blue	125.00	40.00
RN-B4	2c **brown**	125.00	40.00
RN-B5	2c **bronze**	125.00	40.00
RN-B6	2c **green** (shades)	110.00	15.00
RN-B10	2c **red** (shades)	200.00	22.50
RN-B11	2c **purple**	100.00	125.00
RN-B13	2c **violet** (shades)	125.00	40.00
a.	2c **violet brown**	110.00	45.00

"Good only for checks and drafts payable at sight." in Rectangular Tablet at Base

RN-B16	2c **orange**	45.00	12.50
a.	With 2c orange red Nevada	325.00	225.00

"Good only for checks and drafts payable at sight." in Octagonal Tablet at Base

RN-B17	2c **orange**	42.50	10.00
a.	Tablet inverted		1,250.
b.	With 2c orange red Nevada	85.00	35.00
c.	With 2c green Nevada	100.00	35.00
d.	With 2c dull violet Nevada		*1,500.*

"Good when issued for the payment of money." in Octagonal Tablet at Base

RN-B20	2c **orange**	70.00	12.50
a.	Printed on both sides	30.00	10.00
b.	As "a," one stamp inverted		*1,500.*
c.	Tablet inverted		*3,750.*

"Good when issued for the payment of money" in two lines at base in orange

RN-B23	2c **orange**		900.00

"Good when the amount does not exceed $100." in Octagonal Tablet at Base

RN-B24	2c **orange**	200.00	90.00

Washington-Type C

Size: 108x49mm

RN-C1	2c **orange**	7.00	4.00
	red orange	7.00	4.00
	yellow orange	7.00	4.00
	salmon	8.00	4.00
	brown orange	8.00	4.00
a.	"Good when used..." vert. at left black		*22.50*

All examples of the previously-listed "yellow" have some orange in them.

RN-C2	2c **brown**	30.00	12.00
a.	2c **buff**	30.00	12.00
RN-C5	2c **pale red** (shades)	50.00	25.00
RN-C8	2c **green**		—

"Good only for Sight Draft" in two lines in color of stamp

RN-C9	2c **orange,** legend at lower right	85.00	50.00
RN-C11	2c **brown,** legend at lower left	125.00	110.00
RN-C13	2c **orange,** legend at lower left	45.00	20.00

"Good only for Receipt for Money Paid" in two lines in color of stamp

RN-C15	2c **orange,** legend at lower right	*2,500.*	—
RN-C16	2c **orange,** legend at lower left		350.00

"Good when issued for the payment of money" in one line at base in color of stamp

RN-C17	2c **orange** (shades)		600.00

"Good when issued for the/Payment of Money" in two tablets at lower left and right

RN-C19	2c **orange**		550.00
a.	Printed on both sides		35.00

"Good/only for Bank/Check" in 3-part Band

RN-C21	2c **orange**	50.00	12.50
	salmon		12.50
	yellow orange		20.00
a.	Inverted		550.00
b.	With 2c red orange Nevada	140.00	65.00
c.	Printed on back		*2,900.*
RN-C22	2c **brown**	300.00	25.00
a.	Printed on back		500.00
RN-C23	2c **red**		—

"Good when the amount does not exceed $100" in tablet at lower right

RN-C26	2c **orange**		200.00

Franklin Type D

Size: 80x43mm

RN-D1	2c **orange** (shades)	5.00	2.00
a.	Double impression		—
b.	Printed on back	700.00	400.00
c.	Inverted		425.00

All examples of the previously-listed "yellow" have some orange in them and are included in the "shades."

RN-D3	2c **brown**	—	*500.00*
RN-D4	2c **buff** (shades)	9.00	5.00
RN-D5	2c **red**		*2,000.*

"Good only for/Bank Check" in panels within circles at left and right

RN-D7	2c **orange**	25.00	10.00
a.	Printed on back		2,100.

"Good only for/Bank Check" in two lines at lower right in color of stamp

RN-D8	2c **orange**		750.00

"Good only for Sight Draft" in two lines at lower left in color of stamp

RN-D9	2c **orange**	175.00	75.00

Franklin Type E

Size: 28x50mm

RN-E2	2c **brown**		*1,200.*
RN-E4	2c **orange**	12.50	5.00
	Broken die, lower right or left	40.00	20.00
a.	Double impression		*925.00*

"Good only for sight draft" in two lines at base in orange

RN-E5	2c **orange**	75.00	30.00

"Good only for Bank / Check" in two lines at base in orange

RN-E6	2c **orange**		—

"Good only for / Bank Check" in colorless letters in two lines above and below portrait

RN-E7	2c **orange**	75.00	17.50
a.	Double impression		—

Franklin Type F

Size: 56x34mm

RN-F1	2c **orange**	10.00	5.00
a.	Inverted		—

All examples of the previously-listed "yellow" have some orange in them

Liberty Type G

Size: 80x48mm

RN-G1	2c **orange**	2.00	1.00
a.	Printed on back	65.00	40.00
b.	Printed on back, inverted	125.00	50.00

All examples of the previously-listed "yellow" have some orange in them

Imprint: "Graphic Co., New York" at left and right in minute type

RN-G3	2c **orange**	110.00	100.00

Eagle Type H

Size: 32x50mm

No.	Description	Unused	Used
RN-H3	2c **orange**	15.00	5.00
	a. Inverted		—
	b. Double impression		600.00
	c. "Good when used. . ." added in 2 lines at base, black		400.00
	d. As "c," legend added in 1 line upward at left, black		*1,500.*
	e. As "c," legend added in 1 line horiz., black	800.00	600.00
	f. As "c," legend in yellow		*1,500.*
	g. As "c," legend in red		500.00
	h. "Good for bank check . . ." added in black		150.00
	i. As "e," inverted legend		—

"Good for check or sight draft only" at left and right in color of stamp

No.	Description	Unused	Used
RN-H5	2c **orange**		

Experts claim that No. RN-H5 exists only as a proof.

Type I

Design R2 of 1862-72 adhesive revenues

Size: 20x23mm

"BANK CHECK"

No.	Description	Unused	Used
RN-I1	2c **orange**		225.00

"U.S. INTER. REV."

No.	Description	Unused	Used
RN-I2	2c **orange**	650.00	350.00

Washington Type J

Size: 105x40mm

Background of medallion crosshatched, filling oval except for bust

No.	Description	Unused	Used
RN-J4	2c **orange**	20.00	10.00
	pale orange	20.00	10.00
	deep orange	50.00	12.50
	a. Double impression		—
	b. "Good only for . . ." added vertically at left in red orange		750.00
RN-J5	2c **red**	50.00	12.00
	a. Double impression		—

"Good for check or sight draft only" curved, below

No.	Description	Unused	Used
RN-J9	2c **red**	—	*2,000.*

Background shaded below bust and at left.

No.	Description	Unused	Used
RN-J11	2c **orange**	60.00	15.00

Washington Type K

Size: 84x33mm

No.	Description	Unused	Used
RN-K1	2c **blue**		—
RN-K4	2c **gray**	45.00	15.00
	pale gray	45.00	10.00
RN-K5	2c **brown**	175.00	125.00
RN-K6	2c **orange**	15.00	7.50
RN-K8	2c **red** (shades)	600.00	350.00
RN-K11	2c **olive**	200.00	175.00
	pale olive		110.00

Washington Type L

Size: 50x33mm

No.	Description	Unused	Used
RN-L1	2c **blue** (shades)	200.00	—
RN-L2	2c **turquoise**	250.00	200.00
RN-L3	2c **gray**	35.00	20.00
	pale gray	35.00	20.00
RN-L4	2c **green**	900.00	600.00
	light green	600.00	400.00
RN-L5	2c **orange**	15.00	10.00
RN-L6	2c **olive**		55.00
	gray olive		30.00
RN-L10	2c **red**	15.00	10.00
	a. 2c **violet red**	15.00	10.00
RN-L13	2c **brown**	—	300.00

Washington Type M

Size: 68x37mm

No.	Description	Unused	Used
RN-M2	2c **orange**	50.	10.
	a. Printed on back, inverted		*1,600.*

All examples of the previously-listed "yellow" have some orange in them

No.	Description	Unused	Used
RN-M3	2c **green**		475.
RN-M4	2c **gray**		1,250.

Eagle, Numeral and Monitor Type N

Size: 107x48mm

No.	Description	Unused	Used
RN-N3	2c **orange**	60.00	15.00
	a. Printed on back	300.00	225.00
	b. Inverted		900.00
RN-N4	2c **light brown**		150.00

Liberty Type O

Size: 75x35mm

No.	Description	Unused	Used
RN-O2	2c **orange**	1,750.	600.

Values for types P-W

are for stamps on documents with attractive engravings, usually stock certificates, bonds and insurance policies. Examples on plain documents sell for less.

Type P

Frame as Type B, Lincoln in center

Size: 32x49mm

No.	Description	Unused	Used
RN-P2	5c **brown**		350.00
	Cut square		90.00
RN-P5	5c **orange**	55.00	40.00
	Cut square		7.00

All examples of the previously-listed "yellow" have some orange in them.

No.	Description	Unused	Used
RN-P6	5c **red** (shades)	—	225.00
	Cut square		40.00

The 5c green, type P, only exists in combination with a 25c green or 50c green. The 5c pink, type P, only exists in combination with a $1 pink. See Nos. RN-T2, RN-V1 RN-W6.

Madison Type Q (See note before No. RN-P2)

Size: 28x56mm

No.	Description	Unused	Used
RN-Q1	5c **orange**	175.	150.
	Cut square		20.
	brownish orange	175.	150.
RN-Q2	5c **brown**		*2,750.*
	Cut square		500.

Type R

Frame as Type B, Lincoln in center

Size: 32x49mm

No.	Description	Unused	Used
RN-R1	10c **brown**		*2,500.*
RN-R2	10c **red**	—	675.
	Cut square		100.
RN-R3	10c **orange**		500.
	Cut square		50.

"Good when the premium does not exceed $10" in tablet at base

No.	Description	Unused	Used
RN-R6	10c **orange**	—	400.
	Cut square		50.

Motto Without Tablet

No.	Description	Unused	Used
RN-R7	10c **orange**		
	Cut square		500.

Washington Type S (See note before No. RN-P2)

Size: 33x54mm

No.	Description	Unused	Used
RN-S1	10c **orange**		*3,750.*

"Good when the premium does not exceed $10" in tablet at base

No.	Description	Unused	Used
RN-S2	10c **orange**		*4,750.*
	Cut square		400.

Eagle Type T (See note before No. RN-P2)

For type T design with Lincoln in center see type V, Nos. RN-V1 to RN-V10.

Size: 33x40mm

No.	Description	Unused	Used
RN-T1	25c **black**	—	
	Cut square		—
RN-T2	25c **green**		*7,500.*
RN-T3	25c **red**	175.00	*100.00*
	Cut square		9.00
RN-T4	25c **orange**	150.00	75.00
	Cut square		7.50
	light orange	150.00	75.00
	light orange, cut square		7.50
	brown orange		75.00
	brown orange, cut square		8.00

RN-T2 includes a 5c green, type P, and a 25c green, type T, obliterating an RN-V4.

"Good when the premium does not exceed $50" in tablet at base

No.	Description	Unused	Used
RN-T6	25c **orange**	450.	350.
	Cut square		50.
RN-T7	25c **orange,** motto without tablet		1,500.
	Cut square		400.

"Good when the amount insured shall not exceed $1000" in tablet at base

No.	Description	Unused	Used
RN-T8	25c **deep orange**	800.	700.
	Cut square		75.
RN-T9	25c **orange,** motto without tablet		
	Cut square		600.

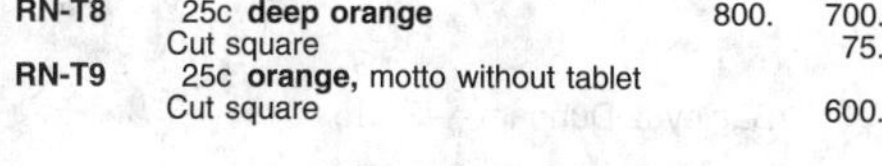

Franklin Type U (See note before No. RN-P2)

Size: 126x65mm

No.	Description	Unused	Used
RN-U1	25c **orange**	35.00	35.00
	Cut square		5.00
RN-U2	25c **brown**	45.00	35.00
	Cut square		5.00

"Good when the premium does not exceed $50" in tablet at lower right

No.	Description	Unused	Used
RN-U3	25c **orange**		*2,500.*
	Cut square		400.

Tablet at lower left

No.	Description	Unused	Used
RN-U5	25c **red**	800.	
	Cut square		250.
RN-U6	25c **orange**	500.	450.
	Cut square		65.

All examples of the previously-listed "yellow" have some orange in them

Tablet at base

No.	Description	Unused	Used
RN-U7	25c **brown**		*1,750.*
	Cut square		300.
RN-U9	25c **orange**		*1,000.*
	Cut square		400.

Type V

As Type T, Lincoln in center

Size: 32x41mm

No.	Description	Unused	Used
RN-V1	50c **green**		175.00
	Cut square		52.50
RN-V2	50c **brown**	—	400.00
	Cut square		125.00
RN-V4	50c **orange**	175.00	90.00
	Cut square		17.50
	deep orange	175.00	90.00
	deep orange, cut square		17.50
RN-V5	50c **red**	700.00	
	Cut square		250.00

RN-V1 includes a 50c green, type V, and a 5c green, type P, obliterating an RN-W2.

"Good when the amount insured shall not exceed $5000" in tablet at base

No.	Description	Unused	Used
RN-V6	50c **orange**	450.00	400.00
	Cut square		60.00
RN-V9	50c **red**		—
	Cut square		500.00

Motto Without Tablet

No.	Description	Unused	Used
RN-V10	50c **orange**		
	Cut square		500.00

Washington Type W (See note before No. RN-P2)

Size: 34x73mm

No.	Description	Unused	Used
RN-W2	$1 **orange**(shades)	150.00	90.00
	Cut square		15.00
RN-W5	$1 **brown**		*4,500.*
RN-W6	$1 **pink**		*3,750.*

The former light brown is now included with the orange shades.

SPANISH-AMERICAN WAR SERIES

Many of these stamps were used for parlor car tax and often were torn in two or more parts.

Liberty Type X

1898 **Size: 68x38mm**

No.	Description	Unused	Used
RN-X1	1c **rose**	800.00	—
	Partial		65.00
	dark red, partial		65.00
RN-X4	1c **orange**	165.00	
a.	On pullman ticket	600.00	—
	Partial		25.00
b.	As "a," printed on back		
	As "a," printed on back, partial		65.00
RN-X5	2c **green**	65.00	30.00
	Partial		25.00
a.	On parlor car ticket	65.00	15.00
b.	On pullman ticket	500.00	
	On pullman ticket, partial		15.00
RN-X6	2c **yellow**	2.00	1.00
	pale olive		*900.00*
RN-X7	2c **orange**	1.50	1.00
	pale orange	1.50	1.00
a.	Printed on back only	400.00	400.00
c.	Printed on front and back	—	—
d.	Vertical		85.00
e.	Double impression		—
f.	On pullman ticket	1,000.	200.00
g.	Inverted		550.00

The substantial reduction recently in catalogue value for No. RN-X7g is due to a new discovery of 25 additional examples.

No. RN-X1 exists only as a four-part unused pullman ticket, used as an unsevered auditor's and passenger's parts of the four-part ticket, or partial as a used half of a two-part ticket. Nos. RN-X4a and RN-X5b exist as unused two-part tickets and as used half portions. No. RN-X7f exists as an unused four-part ticket and as a used two-piece portion with nearly complete stamp design.

PRIVATE DIE PROPRIETARY STAMPS

The extraordinary demands of the Civil War upon the Federal Treasury resulted in Congress devising and passing the Revenue Act of 1862. The Government provided revenue stamps to be affixed to boxes or packages of matches, and to proprietary medicines, perfumery, playing cards -- as well as to documents, etc.

But manufacturers were permitted, at their expense, to have dies engraved and plates made for their exclusive use. Many were only too willing to do this because a discount or premium of from 5% to 10% was allowed on orders from the dies which often made it possible for them to undersell their competitors and too, the considerable advertising value of the stamps could not be overlooked. These are now known as Private Die Proprietary stamps.

The face value of the stamp used on matches was determined by the number, i.e., 1c for each 100 matches or fraction thereof. Medicines and perfumery were taxed at the rate of 1c for each 25 cents of the retail value or fraction thereof up to $1 and 2c for each 50 cents or fraction above that amount. Playing cards were first taxed at the same rate but subsequently the tax was 5c for a deck of 52 cards and 10c for a greater number of cards or double decks.

The stamp tax was repealed on March 3, 1883, effective July 1, 1883.

The various papers were:

a. Old paper, 1862-71. First Issue. Hard and brittle varying from thick to thin.

b. Silk paper, 1871-77. Second Issue. Soft and porous with threads of silk, mostly red, blue and black, up to ¼inch in length.

c. Pink paper, 1877-78. Third Issue. Soft paper colored pink ranging from pale to deep shades.

d. Watermarked paper, 1878-83. Fourth Issue. Soft porous paper showing part of "USIR." Roulettes on unwatermarked paper are rouletted 6.

e. Experimental silk paper. Medium smooth paper, containing minute fragments of silk threads either blue alone or blue and red (infrequent), widely scattered, sometimes but a single fiber on a stamp.

Early printings of some private die revenue stamps are on paper which appears to have laid lines.

These stamps were usually torn in opening the box or container. **Values quoted are for examples which are somewhat faulty but reasonably attractive, with the faults usually not readily apparent on the face.** Nos. RS278-RS306 are valued in the grade of very fine. Sound examples of these stamps (other than Nos. RS278-RS306) at a grade of fine-very fine can sell for 50% to 300% more than catalogue value. Outstanding examples of stamps in this section with a lower catalogue value can bring up to 10 times catalogue value.

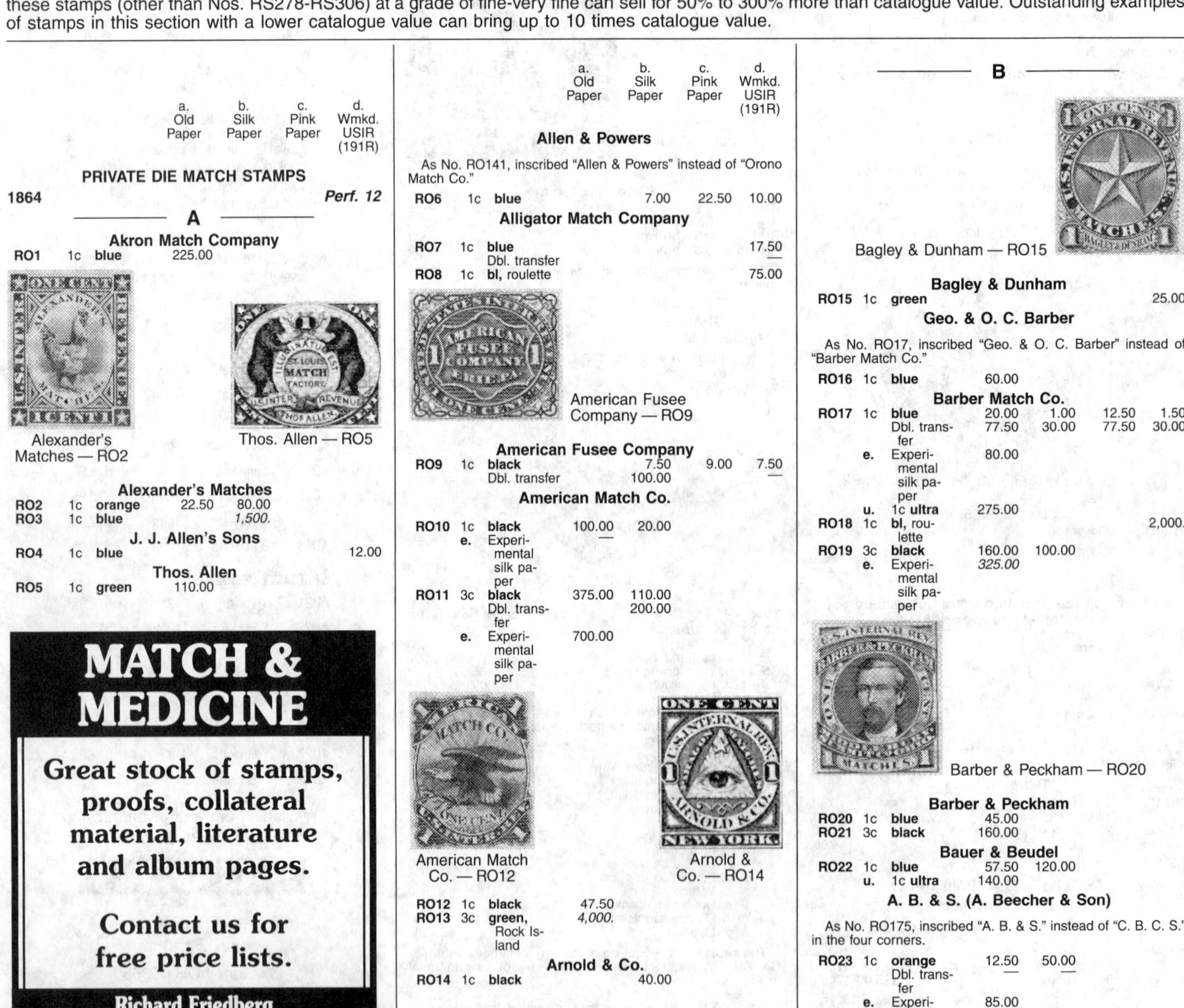

PRIVATE DIE MATCH STAMPS

1864 *Perf. 12*

A

			a. Old Paper	b. Silk Paper	c. Pink Paper	d. Wmkd. USIR (191R)
Akron Match Company						
RO1	1c	**blue**	225.00			

Alexander's Matches — RO2

Thos. Allen — RO5

			a. Old Paper	b. Silk Paper	c. Pink Paper	d. Wmkd. USIR (191R)
Alexander's Matches						
RO2	1c	**orange**	22.50	80.00		
RO3	1c	**blue**		*1,500.*		
J. J. Allen's Sons						
RO4	1c	**blue**				12.00
Thos. Allen						
RO5	1c	**green**	110.00			

Allen & Powers

As No. RO141, inscribed "Allen & Powers" instead of "Orono Match Co."

			a. Old Paper	b. Silk Paper	c. Pink Paper	d. Wmkd. USIR (191R)
RO6	1c	**blue**		7.00	22.50	10.00
Alligator Match Company						
RO7	1c	**blue**				17.50
		Dbl. transfer				—
RO8	1c	**bl,** roulette				75.00

American Fusee Company — RO9

			a. Old Paper	b. Silk Paper	c. Pink Paper	d. Wmkd. USIR (191R)
American Fusee Company						
RO9	1c	**black**		7.50	9.00	7.50
		Dbl. transfer		100.00		—
American Match Co.						
RO10	1c	**black**	100.00	20.00		
	e.	Experimental silk paper	—			
RO11	3c	**black**	375.00	110.00		
		Dbl. transfer		200.00		
	e.	Experimental silk paper	700.00			

American Match Co. — RO12

Arnold & Co. — RO14

			a. Old Paper	b. Silk Paper	c. Pink Paper	d. Wmkd. USIR (191R)
RO12	1c	**black**	47.50			
RO13	3c	**green,** Rock Island	*4,000.*			
Arnold & Co.						
RO14	1c	**black**		40.00		

B

Bagley & Dunham — RO15

			a. Old Paper	b. Silk Paper	c. Pink Paper	d. Wmkd. USIR (191R)
Bagley & Dunham						
RO15	1c	**green**				25.00

Geo. & O. C. Barber

As No. RO17, inscribed "Geo. & O. C. Barber" instead of "Barber Match Co."

			a. Old Paper	b. Silk Paper	c. Pink Paper	d. Wmkd. USIR (191R)
RO16	1c	**blue**	60.00			
Barber Match Co.						
RO17	1c	**blue**	20.00	1.00	12.50	1.50
		Dbl. transfer	77.50	30.00	77.50	30.00
	e.	Experimental silk paper	80.00			
	u.	1c **ultra**	275.00			
RO18	1c	**bl,** roulette				2,000.
RO19	3c	**black**	160.00	100.00		
	e.	Experimental silk paper	*325.00*			

Barber & Peckham — RO20

			a. Old Paper	b. Silk Paper	c. Pink Paper	d. Wmkd. USIR (191R)
Barber & Peckham						
RO20	1c	**blue**	45.00			
RO21	3c	**black**	160.00			
Bauer & Beudel						
RO22	1c	**blue**	57.50	120.00		
	u.	1c **ultra**	140.00			

A. B. & S. (A. Beecher & Son)

As No. RO175, inscribed "A. B. & S." instead of "C. B. C. S." in the four corners.

			a. Old Paper	b. Silk Paper	c. Pink Paper	d. Wmkd. USIR (191R)
RO23	1c	**orange**	12.50	50.00		
		Dbl. transfer	—	—		
	e.	Experimental silk paper	85.00			
		As "e," dbl. transfer	—			

B. Bendel & Co. — RO25

B. Bendel & Co.

RO24 1c brown 2.50 325.00
Dbl. transfer —
RO25 12c brown 210.00

H. Bendel

Nos. RO26-RO27 are RO24-RO25 altered to read "H. Bendel doing business as B. Bendel & Co."

RO26 1c brown 4.50 2.25 1.75
RO27 12c brown 375.00

H. & M. Bentz — RO28

Bent & Lea — RO29

H. & M. Bentz

RO28 1c blue 25.00

Bent & Lea

RO29 1c black 32.50
Double transfer at left 105.00
e. Experimental silk paper 25.00

B. J. & Co. — RO30

Bock, Schneider & Co. — RO31

B. J. & Co. (Barber, Jones & Co.)

As No. RO100 with "B. J. & Co." added above eagle.

RO30 1c green 85.00
Dbl. transfer 140.00

Bock, Schneider & Co.

RO31 1c black 16.00

Wm. Bond & Co. — RO32/RO33

Bousfield & Poole — RO34/RO35

Wm. Bond & Co.

RO32 4c black 250.00
RO33 4c green 140.00 150.00 14.00

Bousfield & Poole

RO34 1c lilac 125.00
Dbl. transfer 135.00
RO35 1c black 15.00 10.00
Dbl. transfer 62.50 82.50
e. Experimental silk paper 42.50
RO36 3c lilac 1,850.
RO37 3c black 160.00 125.00
Dbl. transfer 110.00
Experimental silk paper 275.00

Boutell & Maynard

RO38 1c black 140.00

Bowers & Dunham

As No. RO15, inscribed "Bowers & Dunham" instead of "Bagley & Dunham."

RO39 1c green 225.00
RO40 1c blue 75.00

B. & N. (Brocket & Newton)

RO41 1c lake, die I 35.00
RO42 1c lake, die II 6.50

The initials "B. & N." measure 5¼mm across the top in Die I, and 4¾mm in Die II.

Brown & Durling

RO43 1c black 1,400.
RO44 1c green 65.00

L. W. Buck & Co. — RO45

L. W. Buck & Co.

RO45 1c black 925.00
e. Experimental silk paper 800.00

D. Burhans & Co.

RO46 1c black 125.00 2,500.
Dbl. transfer 250.00
e. Experimental silk paper 650.00

Charles Busch — RO47

Byam, Carlton & Co. — RO49

Charles Busch

RO47 1c black 27.50

Byam, Carlton & Co.

RO48 1c black, imperf 2,000.

2 heads to left, 41x75mm.

RO49 1c black, 19x23mm 22.50 6.00 1.25
Dbl. transfer 125.00
e. Experimental silk paper 75.00
i. Vert. pair, imperf horiz. 125.00
RO50 1c black 1,350.

2 heads to left, buff wrapper, 131x99mm.

RO51 1c black 175.00

As #RO50, 131x89mm.

RO52 1c black 50.00

1 head to right, white wrapper, 94x54mm.

RO53 1c black 135.00

As #RO52, buff wrapper.

RO54 1c black 8.00
h. Up 45.00

2 heads to right, buff wrapper, 81x50mm. #RO54h has right block reading up.

RO55 1c black 25.00

1 head to left, white wrapper, 94x56mm.

RO56 1c black 6.00

As #RO50, 95x57mm.

C

Cannon Match Co.

As No. RO68, "Cannon Match Co." instead of "W. D. Curtis."

RO57 1c green 40.00

Cardinal Match Co. — RO58

Cardinal Match Co.

RO58 1c lake 25.00

F. E. C. (Frank E. Clark)

As No. RO41, "F.E.C." instead of "B. & N."

RO59 1c lake 65.00 65.00
e. Experimental silk paper 85.00

Chicago Match Co. — RO60

Henry A. Clark — RO61

Chicago Match Co.

RO60 3c black 275.00

Henry A. Clark

RO61 1c green 80.00

Jas. L. Clark — RO62/RO63

Clark Match Co. — RO64

Jas. L. Clark

RO62 1c green 2.50 20.00 1.50
Dbl. transfer 60.00
RO63 1c green, rouletted 325.00

The Clark Match Co.

RO64 1c lake 9.00

See No. RO64 for another "The Clark Match Co." design.

Cramer & Kemp — RO65/RO66

Crown Match Co. — RO67

Cramer & Kemp

RO65 1c black 40.00
RO66 1c blue, 100.00 6.00
e. Experimental silk paper 175.00
u. 1c ultra 300.00

Crown Match Co.

RO67 1c black 20.00

W. D. Curtis Matches — RO68

G. W. H. Davis — RO69/RO70

W. D. Curtis Matches

RO68 1c green 125.00 110.00

e. Experimental silk paper 140.00

D

G. W. H. Davis

RO69 1c **black** 37.50
RO70 1c **carmine** 70.00

W. E. Doolittle

RO71 1c **blue** 250.00

E. P. Dunham

RO72 1c **green** 70.00

E

Jas. Eaton

RO73 1c **black** 40.00 1.25 15.00 1.50
e. Experimental silk paper 120.00

RO74 1c **black,** rouletted 50.00

E. B. Eddy

RO75 1c **car,** die I 20.00
RO75A 1c **car,** die II 30.00

Die II shows eagle strongly recut; ribbon across bottom is narrower; color is deeper.

Aug. Eichele

RO76 1c **black** 75.00

P. Eichele & Co.

As No. RO78, "P. Eichele & Co." at top.

RO77 1c **blue** 50.00 6.50
e. Experimental silk paper 125.00
u. 1c **ultra** 275.00

Eichele & Co. — RO78/RO79

Eichele & Co.

RO78 1c **blue** 4.50 15.00 4.00
RO79 1c **blue,** rouletted 225.00

J. W. Eisenhart's Matches

RO80 1c **blue** 45.00 82.50 32.50

Excelsior Match Co. (Watertown) — RO81/RO82

Excelsior Match, Baltimore — RO83

Excelsior Match Co.

RO81 1c **black,** Watertown, N.Y. 85.00
RO82 1c **black,** Syracuse, N.Y. 9.00 14.00 9.00
Dbl. transfer 47.50

Excelsior Match, Baltimore, Md.

RO83 1c **blue** 75.00 100.00
u. 1c **ultra** 600.00

F

G. Farr & Co. — RO84

L. Frank — RO85

G. Farr & Co.

RO84 1c **black** 110.00

L. Frank

RO85 1c **brown** 90.00

G

Gardner, Beer & Co. — RO86

Gardner, Beer & Co.

RO86 1c **black** 175.00

Wm. Gates

RO87 1c **black,** die I 7.00 5.50
RO88 1c **black,** die II 40.00 4.00
Dbl. transfer 30.00
e. Experimental silk paper 140.00

The shirt collar is colorless in Die I and shaded in Die II. The colorless circle surrounding the portrait appears about twice as wide on Die I as it does on Die II.

RO89 3c **black** 50.00 37.50 —
Dbl. transfer 82.50 80.00
e. Experimental silk paper 150.00
RO90 6c **black** 150.00

RO91 3c **black,** 3 1c stamps 125.00

William Gates' Sons

The 1c is as No. RO87, 3c as No. RO91, "William Gates' Sons" replaces "Wm. Gates."

RO92 1c **black** 24.00 9.00 2.00
RO93 1c **black,** rouletted 1,100.
RO94 3c **black,** 3 1c stamps 90.00 135.00 75.00

A. Goldback & Co. — RO95

A. Goldback & Co.

RO95 1c **green** 40.00

A. Goldback

As No. RO95, "A. Goldback" instead of "A. Goldback & Co."

RO96 1c **green** 100.00 7,500.

T. Gorman & Bro.

As No. RO99, "T. Gorham & Bro." instead of "Thomas Gorham."

RO97 1c **black** 300.00
Dbl. transfer —
RO98 1c **green** 25.00 30.00
Dbl. transfer —

Thomas Gorman

RO99 1c **green** 3.75 30.00 60.00

Greenleaf & Co. — RO101/RO102

Griggs & Goodwill — RO103/RO104

Greenleaf & Co.

RO100 1c **green** 80.00 110.00
e. Experimental silk paper 475.00
RO101 3c **carmine** 75.00 140.00
e. Experimental silk paper 800.00
RO102 5c **orange** 140.00 1,400.
e. Experimental silk paper 325.00

Griggs & Goodwill

RO103 1c **black** 50.00
RO104 1c **green** 25.00
Dbl. transfer 150.00

Griggs & Scott

As No. RO69, inscribed "Griggs & Scott" instead of "G. W. H. Davis."

RO105 1c **black** 10.00 32.50
e. Experimental silk paper 40.00

H

Charles S. Hale — RO106

Charles S. Hale

RO106 1c **green** 175.00

Henning & Bonhack

RO107 1c **blue** 150.00

W. E. Henry & Co.

RO108 1c **red** 27.50
RO109 1c **black** 12.50

J. G. Hotchkiss RO110

L. G. Hunt RO113

The J. G. Hotchkiss Match Co.

RO110 1c **green** 12.50 40.00 9.00

B. & H. D. Howard

RO111 1c **lake** 85.00
RO112 1c **blue** 11.00
u. 1c **ultra** 190.00

L. G. Hunt

RO113 1c **black** 190.00 700.00
e. Experimental silk paper 175.00

D. F. Hutchinson Jr.

RO114 1c **lake** 12.50

I

Ives Matches

As No. RO116, "Ives Matches" instead of "P. T. Ives."

RO115 1c **blue** 5.00 5.00
Dbl. transfer —
u. 1c **ultra** 225.00

P. T. Ives — RO116/RO117

Ives & Judd — RO119

P. T. Ives

RO116 1c **blue** 3.00 35.00 3.00
RO117 1c **blue,** rouletted 300.00

RO118 8c **blue** 190.00
e. Experimental silk paper 700.00
u. 8c **ultra** 1,000.

Ives & Judd

RO119 1c **green** 20.00 50.00 125.00

Ives & Judd Match Co. — RO120

Leeds, Robinson & Co. — RO124

The Ives & Judd Match Co.

RO120 1c **green** 100.00
Dbl. transfer 250.00

K

Kirby & Sons

RO121 1c **green** 55.00

W. S. Kyle

RO122 1c **black** 17.50 12.50
Dbl. transfer 75.00

L

Lacour's Matches

RO123 1c **black** 15.00 45.00
Dbl. transfer 100.00
e. Experimental silk paper 55.00

Leeds, Robinson & Co.

RO124 1c **green** 65.00

H. Leigh

RO125 1c **blue** 8.00

Leigh & Palmer

As No. RO125, "Leigh & Palmer" replaces "H. Leigh."

RO126 1c **black** 20.00 60.00 37.50

John Loehr — RO127

John Loehr

RO127 1c **blue** 20.00

Joseph Loehr

As No. RO127, "Joseph" replaces "John."

RO128 1c **blue** 2.50 15.00 4.00

M

John J. Macklin & Co.

RO129 1c **blk,** roulette *6,000.*

F. Mansfield & Co. — RO130

Maryland Match Co. — RO131

F. Mansfield & Co.

RO130 1c **blue** 5.00 10.00 10.00

Maryland Match Co.

RO131 1c **blue** 100.00 8,000.

"Matches" — RO132

"Matches"

RO132 1c **blue** 5.00 4.00
Dbl. transfer 95.00
e. Experimental silk paper 110.00
u. 1c **ultra** *800.00*

See Nos. RO168-RO169.

A. Messinger

RO133 1c **black** 3.25 15.00 2.50

N

National Match Co. — RO134

F. P. Newton — RO135

National Match Co.

RO134 1c **blue** 65.00

Newbauer & Co. (N. & C.) follows No. RO140.

National Union Match Co. items are bogus.

F. P. Newton

RO135 1c **lake** 2.00 10.00 3.00

See No. RO64 for another "The Clark Match Co." design.

N.Y. Match Co.

No. RO136 is as No. RO22, "N.Y. Match Co." instead of "Bauer & Beudel."

RO136 1c **blue,** shield 240.00 7.50

No. RO137 is as No. RO111, "N.Y. Match Co." instead of "B. & H. D. Howard."

RO137 1c **ver,** eagle 75.00 5,000.
e. Experimental silk paper 110.00
As "e," dbl. transfer 240.00

New York Match Company

RO138 1c **green,** 22x60mm 50.00 8.50
e. Experimental silk paper 55.00

RO139 5c **blue,** 22x60mm 1,500.

N. & C. (Newbauer & Co.)

RO140 4c **green** 4.50 110.00 4.50

O

Orono Match Co.

RO141 1c **blue** 32.50 32.50
e. Experimental silk paper 220.00
u. 1c **ultra** 425.00

P

Park City Match Co. — RO143

Park City Match Co.

RO142 1c **green** 45.00 40.00
e. Experimental silk paper 225.00

RO143 3c **orange** 50.00

Penn Match Co. Limited

RO144 1c **blue** 40.00

Pierce Match Co.

RO145 1c **green** 1,750.

P. M. Co. (Portland M. Co.)

RO146 1c **black** 22.50

Portland Match Co.

RO147 1c **black,** wrapper 85.00

The value of No. RO147 applies to commonest date (Dec. 1866); all others are much rarer.

V.R. Powell
RO148 RO149-RO151

V. R. Powell

RO148 1c **blue** 7.50 10.00
Dbl. transfer 100.00
e. Experimental silk paper 110.00
u. 1c **ultra** 275.00

RO149 1c **black** *3,750.*
Buff wrapper, uncut.

RO150 1c **black** 900.00
Buff wrapper, cut to shape.

RO151 1c **black** 1,500.
White wrapper, cut to shape.

R

Reading Match Company

RO152 1c **black** 7.50

Reed & Thompson

RO153 1c **black** 18.00

D. M. Richardson

RO154 1c **red** 125.00
RO155 1c **black** 3.50 2.50
Dbl. transfer 40.00
e. Experimental silk paper 45.00

RO156 3c **ver** 150.00
RO157 3c **blue** 6.50 4.00
Dbl. transfer 27.50
e. Experimental silk paper 55.00

The Richardson Match Co.

The 1c is as No. RO154, 3c as No. RO156, inscribed "The Richardson Match Co." instead of "D. M. Richardson."

RO158 1c **black** 1.50 5.00 7.00
RO159 3c **blue** 75.00

H. & W. Roeber

RO160 1c **blue** 6.75 2.25
Dbl. transfer 175.00
e. Experimental silk paper *325.00*
u. 1c **ultra** 190.00

William Roeber

As No. RO160, "William Roeber" instead of "H. & W. Roeber."

RO161 1c **blue** 2.00 7.50 3.00
RO162 1c **bl,** roulette 95.00

E. T. Russell — RO163

E. T. Russell

RO163 1c **black** 7.50 15.00
e. Experimental silk paper 42.50

R. C. & W. (Ryder, Crouse & Welch)

RO164 1c **lake** 75.00

S

San Francisco Match Co. — RO165

San Francisco Match Company

RO165 12c **blue** 375.00

Schmitt & Schmittdiel — RO166/RO167

Schmitt & Schmittdiel

RO166 1c **ver** 4.00 75.00 4.00
RO167 3c **blue** 50.00

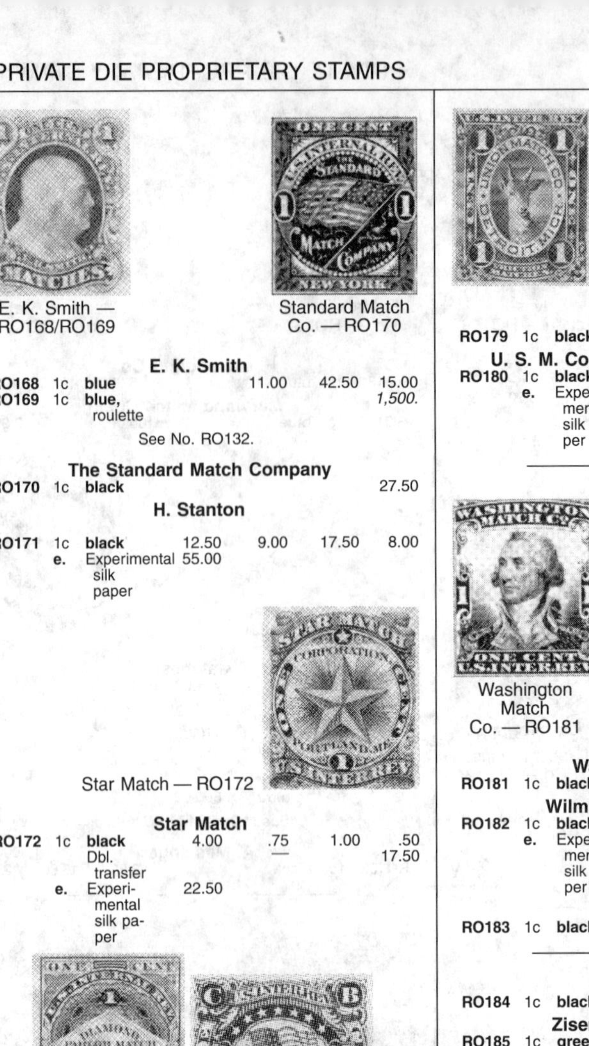

E. K. Smith — RO168/RO169

Standard Match Co. — RO170

E. K. Smith

RO168 1c **blue** 11.00 42.50 15.00
RO169 1c **blue,** roulette *1,500.*

See No. RO132.

The Standard Match Company

RO170 1c **black** 27.50

H. Stanton

RO171 1c **black** 12.50 9.00 17.50 8.00
e. Experimental silk paper 55.00

Star Match — RO172

Star Match

RO172 1c **black** 4.00 .75 1.00 .50
Dbl. transfer — 17.50
e. Experimental silk paper 22.50

Swift & Courtney & Beecher
RO174 RO175

Swift & Courtney

As No. RO174, "Swift & Courtney" in one line.

RO173 1c **blue** 2.50 2.50
Dbl. transfer — —
e. Experimental silk paper 22.50
u. 1c **ultra** 62.50

Swift & Courtney & Beecher Co.

RO174 1c **blue** 2.25 4.50 1.50
Dbl. transfer —
RO175 1c **black** 80.00

T

Trenton Match Co.

RO176 1c **blue** 9.00

E. R. T. (E. R. Tyler)

As No. RO120, inscribed "E. R. T." instead of "The Ives & Judd Match Co."

RO177 1c **green** 12.50 3.75
Dbl. transfer —
e. Experimental silk paper 67.50

U

Alex. Underwood & Co.

RO178 1c **green** 75.00 125.00
e. Experimental silk paper 275.00

Union Match Co. — RO179

Union Match Co.

RO179 1c **black** 50.00

U. S. M. Co. (Universal Safety Match Co.)

RO180 1c **black** 3.00 25.00
e. Experimental silk paper 57.50

W

Washington Match Co. — RO181

Wilmington Parlor Match Co. — RO182

Washington Match Co.

RO181 1c **black** 45.00

Wilmington Parlor Match Co.

RO182 1c **black** 110.00 *5,000.*
e. Experimental silk paper 190.00

Wise & Co.

RO183 1c **black** 1,100.

Z

F. Zaiss & Co.

RO184 1c **black** 1.75 7.00 1.75

Zisemann, Griesheim & Co.

RO185 1c **green** 800.00
RO186 1c **blue** 120.00 20.00
u. 1c **ultra** 675.00

PRIVATE DIE CANNED FRUIT STAMP

a. Old Paper	b. Silk Paper	c. Pink Paper	d. Wmkd. USIR (191R)

T. Kensett & Co. — RP1

1867 *Perf. 12*

T. Kensett & Co.

RP1 1c **green** 1,000.

a. Old Paper	b. Silk Paper	c. Pink Paper	d. Wmkd. USIR (191R)

PRIVATE DIE MEDICINE STAMPS

1862 *Perf. 12*

A

Anglo American Drug Co. — RS1

			a. Old Paper	b. Silk Paper	c. Pink Paper	d. Wmkd. USIR (191R)

Anglo American Drug Co.

			a	b	c	d
RS1	1c	**black**				60.00

J. C. Ayer & Co.

See illustration pages.

			a	b	c	d
RS2	1c	**brn car,** imperf	*5,250.*			
RS3	1c	**green,** imperf	*6,000.*			
RS4	1c	**black,** imperf, type 1	50.00	50.00		45.00
		Type 2	50.00	50.00	900.00	40.00
		Dbl. transfer		—		
	e.	Experimental silk paper	—			

Type 1: long, full-pointed "y" in "Ayers;" Type 2: short, truncated "y" in "Ayers."

			a	b	c	d
RS5	1c	**blue,** imperf	*8,000.*			
RS6	1c	**org,** imperf	*7,750.*			
RS6F	1c	**red,** imperf	—			
RS7	1c	**gray lilac,** imperf	*8,500.*			

J.C. Ayer & Co. — RS8/RS13

			a	b	c	d
RS8	4c	**red,** die cut	*5,750.*			
RS9	4c	**blue,** die cut	5.00	5.00		5.00
	e.	Experimental silk paper	—			
	u.	**4c ultra** (die cut)	525.00			
RS10	4c	**blue,** imperf	350.00	250.00		325.00
RS11	4c	**purple,** die cut	*7,000.*			
RS12	4c	**green,** die cut	*8,750.*			
RS13	4c	**ver,** die cut	*10,000.*			

The values of Nos. RS11-RS13 reflect the realizations at a 1991 auction sale. These three stamps are equally scarce.

The 4c in black was printed and sent to Ayer & Co. It may exist but has not been seen by collectors.

B

Barham Pile Cure Co.

			a	b	c	d
RS14	4c	**green,** wmkd. lozenges		75.00		

D. S. Barnes — RS15/RS20

D. S. Barnes

The 1c, 2c and 4c are about 184mm, 242mm and 304mm tall. The products mentioned differ. "D. S. Barnes" is in manscript.

			a
RS15	1c	**ver**	125.00
RS16	2c	**ver**	175.00
RS17	4c	**ver**	400.00
RS18	1c	**black**	22.50
RS19	2c	**black**	70.00
RS20	4c	**black**	60.00

Demas Barnes

Same as above but with "Demas Barnes" in serifed letters.

			a
RS21	1c	**black**	20.00
RS22	2c	**black**	55.00
RS23	4c	**black**	25.00

Demas Barnes & Co. — RS24/RS26

Demas Barnes & Co.

			a	b
RS24	1c	**black**	15.00	425.00
RS25	2c	**black**	15.00	325.00
	e.	Experimental silk paper	180.00	
RS26	4c	**black**	15.00	

T. H. Barr & Co. — RS27

T. H. Barr & Co.

			a
RS27	4c	**black**	25.00
		Dbl. transfer	200.00
	e.	Experimental silk paper	200.00

Barry's — RS28/RS29

D. M. Bennett — RS30

Barry's

			a	b	c	d
RS28	2c	**green,** Tricopherous	11.00	18.00		
RS29	2c	**grn,** Proprietary		6.50	160.00	5.50
		Dbl. transfer		250.00		

D. M. Bennett

			a	b	c	d
RS30	1c	**lake**	15.00			
	e.	Experimental silk paper	80.00			

W. T. Blow — RS31

W. T. Blow

			a	b	c	d
RS31	1c	**green**	240.00	60.00	275.00	75.00
	e.	Experimental silk paper	650.00			

B. Brandreth — RS32/RS35

B. Brandreth

			a	b	c	d
RS32	1c	**black,** perf	475.00	550.00		
RS33	1c	**black,** imperf	2.00	1.50		
	e.	Experimental silk paper	25.00			

Nos. RS32-RS33 inscribed "United States Certificate of Genuineness" around vignette.

			a	b	c	d
RS34	1c	**blk,** 41x50mm, imperf		125.00		
RS35	1c	**blk,** 24x30mm, imperf		1.50	7.50	1.50
	p.	Perf				425.00

Dr. C.F. Brown — RS36

Dr. C. F. Brown

			a	b	c	d
RS36	1c	**blue**	250.00	65.00		75.00

Fred Brown Co. — RS37/RS38

Fred Brown Co.

No.	Denom.	Description				
RS37	2c	**black,** imperf, die I	110.00	37.50	2,000.	30.00
	e.	Experimental silk paper	375.00			
RS38	2c	**black,** imperf, die II		65.00		

Die I has "E" of "Fred" incomplete. Die II shows recutting in the "E" of "Fred" and "Genuine."

John I. Brown & Son — RS39/RS41

John I. Brown & Son.

No.	Denom.	Description				
RS39	1c	**black**	9.00	35.00		8.00
RS40	2c	**green**	9.00	15.00	300.00	300.00
		Dbl. transfer	—			
	e.	Experimental silk paper	80.00			
RS41	4c	**brown**	225.00	85.00		1,100.

Dr. John Bull — RS42/RS43

Joseph Burnett & Co. — RS46

Dr. John Bull

No.	Denom.	Description				
RS42	1c	**black**	150.00	18.00	425.00	17.50
	e.	Experimental silk paper	325.00			
RS43	4c	**blue**	175.00	11.00	250.00	10.00
	e.	Experimental silk paper	325.00			
	u.	4c **ultra**	*1,000.*			

J. S. Burdsal & Co.

"J. S. Burdsal & Co." added to United States Proprietary Medicine Co. design.

No.	Denom.	Description				
RS44	1c	**blk,** wrapper, white paper		50.00		30.00
RS45	1c	**blk,** wrapper, orange paper		*1,000.*		425.00

Joseph Burnett & Co.

No.	Denom.	Description				
RS46	4c	**black**	85.00	12.50	225.00	6.00

C

J. W. Campion & Co.

See illustration pages.

No.	Denom.	Description				
RS47	4c	**black,** imperf		525.00		375.00
	p.	Pair, perf horiz.				2,500.
RS48	4c	**black,** die cut		125.00	250.00	100.00

Cannon & Co. — RS49

Cannon & Co.

No.	Denom.	Description				
RS49	4c	**green,** imperf		100.00	250.00	65.00

The Centaur Co. — RS50/RS52

The Centaur Co.

No.	Denom.	Description				
RS50	1c	**ver**			55.00	8.00
RS51	2c	**black**			12.50	3.50
RS52	4c	**black**				55.00

Dr. A. W. Chase, Son & Co. — RS53/RS55

Dr. A. W. Chase, Son & Co.

No.	Denom.	Description				
RS53	1c	**black**		90.00		3,000.
RS54	2c	**black**		125.00		
RS55	4c	**black**		125.00		

Wm. E. Clarke
RS56 RS57

Wm. E Clarke

No.	Denom.	Description				
RS56	3c	**blue**				140.00
RS57	6c	**black**				85.00

R. C. & C. S. Clark — RS58

R. C. & C. S. Clark

No.	Denom.	Description				
RS58	4c	**black**		17.50		22.50

Collins Bros.
RS59

W. H. Comstock
RS60

Collins Bros.

No.	Denom.	Description				
RS59	1c	**black**	22.50	275.00		

W. H. Comstock

No.	Denom.	Description				
RS60	1c	**black**				4.00

Cook & Bernheimer

No.	Denom.	Description				
RS61	4c	**blue**				100.00

Charles N. Crittenton — RS62/RS64

Charles N. Crittenton

No.	Denom.	Description				
RS62	1c	**black**		10.00		
RS63	1c	**blue**			12.50	6.50
RS64	2c	**black**		75.00	42.50	5.00

Oliver Crook & Co. (illustration reduced) — RS65

Oliver Crook & Co.

No.	Denom.	Description				
RS65	4c	**black**	100.00	22.50		
	e.	Experimental silk paper	50.00			

Jeremiah Curtis & Son — RS66/RS68

Jeremiah Curtis & Son

RS66	1c	**black**	80.00			
		Die I, small "1s."				
RS67	1c	**black**				100.00
		Die II, large "1s."				
RS68	2c	**black**	10.00	10.00	140.00	240.00
		Dbl. transfer		—		

Die II numerals nearly fill the circles.

Curtis & Brown

RS69	1c	**black**	5.75	4.00		
	e.	Experimental silk paper	—			
RS70	2c	**black**		125.00		

Curtis & Brown Mfg. Co.

These are identical to RS69-RS70 with "Mfg. Co. Limtd." instead of the right hand "TWO CENTS."

RS71	1c	**black**			225.00	8.00
RS72	2c	**black**		1,600.		800.00

D

Dalley's Galvanic Horse Salve

RS73	2c	**green**	110.00	200.00		150.00

Dalley's Magical Pain Extractor (Illustration reduced.) — RS74

Dalley's Magical Pain Extractor

RS74	1c	**black**	14.00	11.00		8.50
	h.	$100	225.00			17.50

#RS74h reads "$100" instead of "$1.00."

Perry Davis & Son — RS75/RS81

Perry Davis & Son

RS75	1c	**blue**	8.00	3.75	250.00	2.50
	e.	Experimental silk paper	110.00			
	u.	1c **ultra**	165.00			
RS76	2c	**brown red**	150.00			
RS77	2c	**black**	70.00			
RS78	2c	**dull pur**		10.00		
RS78A	2c	**slate**		12.50		6.50
RS79	2c	**dull red**		85.00		
RS80	2c	**brown**		*2,750.*		
RS81	4c	**brown**	13.00	4.00		3.00

P. H. Drake & Co.

RS82	2c	**black**	*2,750.*			
RS83	4c	**black**	50.00	60.00		
	e.	Experimental silk paper	140.00			

F

B. A. Fahnestock — RS84

B. A. Fahnestock

RS84	1c	**lake,** imperf	140.00	110.00		

Father Mathew Temperance & Manufacturing Co. — RS85

The Father Mathew Temperance & Manufacturing Company

RS85	4c	**black**				10.00

A. H. Flanders, M. D.

RS86	1c	**green,** perf		14.00		13.00
RS87	1c	**green,** part perf	25.00	2.00	35.00	3.00

Fleming Bros. — RS88/RS90

Fleming Bros.

Vermifuge

RS88	1c	**black,** imperf	14.00	22.50		50.00
	e.	Experimental silk paper	75.00			

L. Pills

RS89	1c	**black,** imperf	4,000.			
RS90	1c	**blue,** imperf	7.00	8.00		10.00
		Dbl. transfer		70.00		70.00
	e.	Experimental silk paper	—			
	u.	1c **ultra**	450.00			

Seth W. Fowle & Son — RS91

G. G. Green — RS92/RS93

Seth W. Fowle & Son, J. P. Dinsmore

RS91	4c	**black**	17.50	3.00		3.00

G

G. G. Green

RS92	3c	**black**				6.00
	h.	Tete beche pair				550.00
RS93	3c	**blk,** rouletted				140.00

H

Reuben P. Hall & Co.

RS94	4c	**black**	20.00	20.00		22.50
	e.	Experimental silk paper	*500.*			

Hall & Ruckel — RS95/RS96

Hall & Ruckel as agents for Xavier Bazin — RS95h/RS96h

Hall & Ruckel

RS95	1c	**green**	1.75	1.75	27.50	1.75
	e.	Experimental silk paper	25.00			
	h.	Handstamped "X.B." (Xavier Bazin) and obliteration				—
RS96	3c	**black**	3.25	3.00	50.00	3.00
	h.	Handstamped "X.B." (Xavier Bazin) and obliteration				—

Dr. Harter & Co.

RS97	1c	**black**	22.50	14.00		
	e.	Experimental silk paper	165.00			

Dr. Harter

As No. RS97, inscribed "Dr. Harter" instead of "Dr. Harter & Co."

RS98	1c	**black**		3.00	12.00	4.00
		Dbl. impression		*3,000.*		

(Dr.) S. B. Hartman & Co.

See illustration pages for illustration of No. RS99.

RS99	4c	**black**	325.00	65.00	275.00	1,250.
RS100	6c	**black**	325.00	225.00		

E. T. Hazeltine — RS101/RS103

E. T. Hazeltine

RS101	1c	**black**				18.00
RS102	2c	**blue**		32.50		
RS103	4c	**black**	475.00	24.00		17.50
	e.	Experimental silk paper	675.00			
	i.	Imperf, pair	950.00			

E. H. (Edward Heaton)

RS104	3c	**black**				45.00
RS105	3c	**brown**				15.00

Helmbold's — RS106/RS109

John F. Henry — RS112/RS116

Helmbold's

RS106	2c	**blue**	1.50	225.00		
		Dbl. transfer	—			
RS107	3c	**green**	45.00	30.00		
RS108	4c	**black**	4.00	140.00		
		Dbl. transfer	160.00			
RS109	6c	**black**	2.00	3.50		
	e.	Experimental silk paper	37.50			

A. L. Helmbold's

Same as "Helmbold's" but inscribed "A. L. Helmbold's."

RS110	2c	**blue**		110.00	160.00	90.00
RS111	4c	**black**		27.50	140.00	9.00

John F. Henry

RS112	2c	**violet**	400.00			
RS113	4c	**bister**	625.00			
RS114	1c	**black**	55.00	1.00	10.00	1.50
	e.	Experimental silk paper	140.00			
RS115	2c	**blue**	32.50	6.50	125.00	6.00
	u.	**ultra**	450.00			
RS116	4c	**red**	160.00	1.50	30.00	2.50
	e.	Experimental silk paper	85.00			

Herrick's Pills

RS117	1c	**black**	80.00	35.00	90.00	40.00
	e.	Experimental silk paper	160.00			
	i.	Imperf, pair	*3,500.*			

Horiz. pairs imperf between were issued of No. RS114d. All known pairs were originally separated, and some have been matched and rejoined. Three rejoined pairs are reported.

No. RS117i is valued in sound condition.

Most pairs are faulty and sell for much less.

Herrick's Pills & Plasters — RS118

Herrick's Pills & Plasters

RS118	1c	**red**	2.50	5.00	65.00	2.50
	e.	Experimental silk paper	—			

J. E. Hetherington

RS119	1c	**black**				15.00
RS120	2c	**black**				400.00
RS121	3c	**black**				20.00
	i.	Imperf, pair				550.00

Hiscox & Co.

RS122	2c	**black**				14.00
RS123	4c	**black**		100.00	225.00	1,200.

Holloway's Pills and Ointment — RS124/RS125

Holloway's Pills and Ointment

RS124	1c	**blue,** perf	9.00			
RS125	1c	**blue,** imperf	250.00			

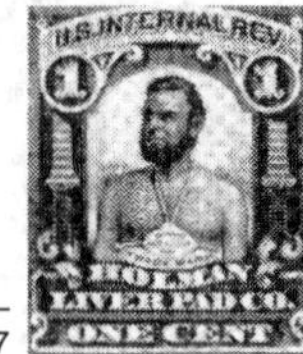

Holman Liver Pad Co. — RS126/RS127

Holman Liver Pad Co.

RS126	1c	**green**				20.00
RS127	4c	**green**				10.00

The Home Bitters Co.

RS128	2c	**blue**				200.00
		Dbl. transfer				—
RS129	3c	**green**		110.00	140.00	90.00
RS130	4c	**green**		225.00		225.00

Hop Bitters Co. RS131

Hop Bitters Co.

RS131	4c	**black**				7.00

Hostetter & Smith

RS132	4c	**blk,** imperf	65.00	37.50	90.00	27.50
		Dbl. transfer	—	50.00	87.50	37.50
	e.	Experimental silk paper	—			
RS133	6c	**blk,** imperf	80.00			
	e.	Experimental silk paper	240.00			

S. D. Howe — RS137

S. D. Howe

RS134	4c	**black,** Duponco's Pills	110.00	190.00		

No. RS134 in red or green exist but were not printed for use. Value, each $275.

RS137	4c	**blue,** Arabian Milk		8.00		140.00

C. E. Hull & Co.

RS138	1c	**black**	110.00	5.75	50.00	5.75

T. J. Husband — RS139/RS140

T. J. Husband

RS139	2c	**vio,** imperf	650.00			
RS140	2c	**ver,** imperf	15.00	10.00		9.00

Hutchings & Hillyer

RS141	4c	**grn,** imperf	20.00	27.50		
	e.	Experimental silk paper	160.00			

I

H. A. Ingham & Co.

RS142	1c	**black**				50.00

J

James A. Jackson & Co.

RS143	4c	**green**	900.00	225.00		
		Dbl. transfer		—		

Dr. D. Jayne & Son — RS144/RS149

Dr. D. Jayne & Son

RS144	1c	**blue,** imperf		850.00		550.00
	p.	Perf	800.00			*3,250.*
RS145	2c	**blk,** imperf	*3,250.*	1,500.		950.00
	p.	Perf	*3,500.*			—
RS146	4c	**grn,** imperf	*3,000.*	1,100.	1,200.	450.00
	p.	Perf	*4,000.*			—
RS146F	4c	**red,** imperf	—			
RS146G	4c	**org,** imperf	—			
RS147	1c	**bl,** die cut	6.00	5.00	200.00	5.00
	e.	Experimental silk paper	—			
	p.	Perf and die cut	150.00	250.00		—
		On horiz. laid paper	57.50			
RS148	2c	**blk,** die cut	10.00	8.00	90.00	5.00
		Dbl. transfer	55.00	55.00	110.00	75.00
	e.	Experimental silk paper	140.			
	p.	Perf & die cut	40.00	225.00	—	
RS149	4c	**grn,** die cut	7.00	5.00	90.00	8.50
		Dbl. transfer		—		
	e.	Experimental silk paper	110.			
	p.	Perf & die cut	45.00	210.00		—
		On vertically laid paper	30.00			

I. S. Johnson & Co. — RS150

Johnston Holloway & Co. — RS151/RS152

I. S. Johnson & Co.

RS150	1c	**ver**		1.25	14.00	.90
		Dbl. transfer		20.00	55.00	25.00

Johnston Holloway & Co.

RS151	1c	**black**		3.50		2.75

RS152 2c **green** 3.50 3.00

K

J. B. Kelly & Co. — RS153

J. B. Kelly & Co.

RS153 4c **blk,** imperf 1,750.
e. Experimental silk paper 1,900.

B. J. Kendall & Co.

RS154 4c **blue** 27.50

Dr. Kennedy

RS155 2c **green** 50.00 8.00 30.00 6.00
Dbl. transfer —
e. Experimental silk paper —
RS156 6c **black** 8.00 65.00 8.00

Kennedy & Co. RS157

Kennedy & Co.

RS157 2c **black** 7.00 100.00 8.50

K & Co. (Kennedy & Co.)

RS158 1c **green** 7.50

Dr. Jas. C. Kerr

RS159 4c **blue** *5,500.* 275.00 160.00
RS160 6c **black** 425.00

L

Lawrence & Martin

RS161 4c **black** 40.00

Lee & Osgood

RS162 1c **blue** 12.50 17.50 14.00

Jacob Lippman & Bro.

RS163 4c **blue** 1,500. 1,750.
e. Experimental silk paper 2,250.

Alvah Littlefield

RS164 1c **black** 1.50 1.00 20.00
Dbl. transfer 90.00 75.00
e. Experimental silk paper 110.00
On horiz. laid paper *500.00*

RS165 4c **green** 600.00 190.00

Prof. Low

RS166 1c **black** 3.00 16.00 3.00
Dbl. transfer — 55.00 40.00

Lyon Manufg. Co.

As No. RS24, inscribed "Lyon Manufg. Co." instead of "Demas Barnes & Co."

RS167 1c **black** 17.50 325.00 12.50
RS168 2c **black** 8.50 150.00 8.50
i. Vert. pair, imperf btwn. 650.00

M

J. McCullough

As No. RS137, inscribed "J. McCullough" instead of "S. D. Howe."

RS169 4c **black** 110.00 100.00

J. H. McLean — RS170

Manhattan Medicine Co. — RS171/RS172

Dr. J. H. McLean

RS170 1c **black** 2.50 1.50 15.00 1.50
Dbl. transfer 50.00 65.00 — 35.00
e. Experimental silk paper 80.00
i. Vert. pair, imperf horiz. —

Manhattan Medicine Co.

RS171 1c **violet** 37.50
u. 1c **purple** 60.00
RS172 2c **black** 27.50 37.50 14.00

Mansfield & Higbee

As No. RS174, inscribed "Mansfield & Higbee Memphis, Tenn."

RS173 1c **blue** 16.00
i. Pair, imperf btwn. 150.00
j. Block of 4, imperf btwn. 175.00

S. Mansfield & Co. — RS174

Merchant's Gargling Oil — RS178/RS179

S. Mansfield & Co.

RS174 1c **blue** 27.50 190.00 15.00
i. Pair, imperf btwn. 150.00 300.00 200.00
j. Block of 4, imperf btwn. 110.00 450.00 175.00

Nos. RS173-RS174 are perf on 4 sides. The i. and j. varieties served as 2c or 4c stamps. Straight edged copies from severed pairs or blocks are worth much less.

T. W. Marsden

RS175 2c **blue** *6,000.*
RS176 4c **black** 425.00

Mercado & Seully

See illustration pages.

RS177 2c **blk,** imperf *5,500.*

Merchant's Gargling Oil

RS178 1c **black** 225.00 35.00 425.00 27.50
e. Experimental silk paper *525.00*

RS179 2c **green** 225.00 25.00 325.00 22.50
Foreign entry *2,750.* *3,500.*
e. Experimental silk paper 400.00

Foreign entry is over design of #RO11.

Mette & Kanne

RS180 3c **black** 300.00

Mishler Herb Bitters Co.

See illustration pages.

RS181 4c **black** 125.00
p. Imperf at ends 150.00

Moody, Michel & Co.

See illustration pages.

RS182 4c **blk,** imperf 160.00

Dr. C. C. Moore — RS183

Dr. C. C. Moore

RS183 1c **ver,** Pilules 6.00
RS184 2c **black,** Sure Cure 65.00 *3,250.* 27.50

Morehead's — RS185/RS186

Morehead's

RS185 1c **black,** Magetic Plaster 22.50
RS186 4c **black,** Neurodyne 1,250.

N

New York Pharmacal Association — RS187

New York Pharmacal Association

RS187 4c **black** 15.00 32.50 9.00

P

Dr. M. Perl & Co.

RS188 6c **black,** cut to shape 1,100.

R. V. Pierce

RS189 1c **green** 20.00 125.00 22.50
RS190 2c **black** 25.00 7.50 30.00 7.00
Dbl. transfer —
e. Experimental silk paper 85.00

Bennett Pieters & Co.

RS191 4c **black** 350.00 1,450.
e. Experimental silk paper 550.00
RS192 6c **black** 1,250.
i. Imperf *1,400.*

R

Radway & Co.

RS193 2c **black** 4.50 3.00 11.00 5.00
Dbl. transfer 65.00 100.00 75.00
e. Experimental silk paper 45.00

D. Ransom & Co.

RS194 1c **blue** 4.50 2.75
Dbl. transfer —
e. Experimental silk paper 110.00
RS195 2c **black** 22.50 27.50
e. Experimental silk paper 110.00

D. Ransom, Son & Co.

As Nos. RS194-RS195 with "Son" added.

RS196 1c **blue** 4.00 15.00 6.00
Dbl. transfer —
RS197 2c **black** 16.00 65.00 10.00

Redding's Russia Salve — RS198

Ring's Vegetable Ambrosia — RS199/RS203

Redding's Russia Salve

RS198 1c **black** 8.00 8.00
Dbl. transfer 125.00

Ring's Vegetable Ambrosia

RS199 2c **blue,** imperf 2,750.
p. Perf *3,000.*
RS200 4c **blk,** imperf 1,600. 1,750.
RS201 2c **bl,** die cut 22.50
RS202 4c **black,** die cut 15.00 15.00 22.50
e. Experimental silk paper 95.00
RS203 4c **black,** perf 1,000. 1,400.
k. Perf & die cut 1,000.
p. Part perf 1,600. —

J. B. Rose & Co. — RS204/RS205

J. B. Rose & Co.

RS204 2c **black** 6.00 32.50
Dbl. transfer 140.00 200.00
RS205 4c **black** *8,000.* 140.00
Dbl. transfer —

Rumford Chemical Works

RS206 2c **green** 4.50
RS207 2c **grn,** imperf 25.00

S

A. B. & D. Sands

RS208 1c **green** 10.00 20.00
e. Experimental silk paper 70.00

M., P. J. & H. M. Sands

The #RS208 die was altered to make #RS209.

RS209 2c **green** 17.50 110.00 15.00

Scheetz's Celebrated Bitter Cordial

RS210 4c **black,** perf 450.00
RS211 4c **blk,** imperf *3,500.*

Schenck's Mandrake Pills

RS212 1c **grn,** imperf 5.00 10.00 125.00 5.00
Dbl. transfer 30.00 —
e. Experimental silk paper 280.
p. Perf —

Schenck's Pulmonic Syrup

RS213 6c **blk,** imperf 7.50 5.00 100.00 145.00
Dbl. transfer 57.50 —
e. Experimental silk paper 140.00
p. Perf 210.00

J. H. Schenck & Son — RS214

J. H. Schenck & Son

RS214 4c **black** 10.00

J. E. Schwartz & Co.

As No. RS84, inscribed "J. E. Schwartz & Co." instead of "B. A. Fahnestock."

RS215 1c **lake,** imperf 140.00 300.00 110.00

"A. L. Scovill" follows No. RS219.

Seabury & Johnson — RS216/RS218

Seabury & Johnson

RS216 1c **black** 75.00
RS217 1c **black,** printed obliteration over "porous" 5.00
h. "Porous" obliterated by pen 5.00
RS218 1c **lake** 1,750.

"Dr. D. H. Seelye & Co." follows No. RS221.

Dr. S. Brown Sigesmond

RS219 4c **blue** 87.50

A. L. Scovill & Co. — RS220/RS221

A. L. Scovill & Co.

RS220 1c **black** 1.75 2.50
Dbl. transfer — —
e. Experimental silk paper 67.50
r. Printed on both sides *2,250.*
RS221 4c **green** 2.00 5.00
e. Experimental silk paper 125.00

Dr. D. H. Seelye & Co. — RS222

Dr. D. H. Seelye & Co.

RS222 8c **blk,** imperf 25.00

Dr. M. A. Simmons

RS223 1c **black,** Iuka, Miss. 110.00 *6,000.*
RS224 1c **black,** St. Louis, Mo. 110.00

S. N. Smith & Co.

As No. RS65, inscribed "S. N. Smith & Co." instead of "Oliver Crook & Co."

RS225 4c **black** 50.00 50.00

Dr. E. L. Soule & Co.

N.Y. Wrapper

RS226 1c **blue** 75.00
For. entry —

Syracuse Wrapper

RS227 1c **blue** 75.00 35.00
For. entry — —
u. **ultra** 375.00
For. entry —

For Nos. RS226, RS227, the foreign entry is the design of No. RT1 (pos. 1).

H. R. Stevens — RS228/RS229

H. R. Stevens

RS228 1c **brown** 16.00
RS229 2c **choc** 6.00
RS230 6c **black** 110.00 6.00

Jas. Swaim

RS231 6c **org** *3,500.*

Die cut, ms signature.

RS232 8c **org,** imperf 1,750.
h. Ms. *2,000.* *5,500.*
RS233 8c **org,** die cut 350.00
e. Experimental silk paper 700.00
h. Ms. 1,200. —

No. RS232h, RS233h have manuscript signature.

Wm. Swaim

RS234 8c **org,** imperf *4,500.* *3,000.* 1,250.
k. None *3,250.* *1,750.*

No. RS234k is without signature. No. RS234d is found with signature "Suaim" or "Swaim." Also, No. RS234b is found with a period under the raised "m" of "Wm" and the right leg of "w" of "Swaim" retouched, both by pen.

RS235 8c **org,** die cut 650.00 190.00 200.00
h. Ms. 950.00
k. Invt. *2,750.*

Nos. RS235h has manuscript signature. No. RS235k has signature inverted.

Dr. G. W. Swett

RS236 4c **blk,** die cut 15.00
RS237 4c **green,** perf 225.00 1,050.
RS238 4c **green,** perf and die cut 275.00 1,200.

T

George Tallcot

RS239 2c **ver** 15.00
RS240 4c **black** 85.00 *2,750.* 20.00

Tarrant & Co. RS241

John L. Thompson RS242

Tarrant & Company

RS241 4c **red** 3.00 90.00 2.00

John L. Thompson

RS242 1c **black** 6.00 7.50 6.00
Dbl. transfer —
e. Experimental silk paper 110.00

U

United States Proprietary Medicine Co.

RS243 4c **black** 45.00 95.00
e. Experimental silk paper 175.00
RS244 6c **black** 825.00

U. S. Proprietary Medicine Co. Wrappers

See illustration pages.

No.	Denom.	Color				
RS245	1c	**black,** *white*	45.00	45.00		
	e.	Experimental silk paper	*450.00*			
RS246	1c	**black,** *yel*	120.00	220.00		
RS247	1c	**black,** *org*	220.00	2,000.		
RS248	1c	**black,** *org red*	*1,000.*	4,250.		

V

S. R. Van Duzer — RS249/RS250

S. R. Van Duzer

No.	Denom.	Color				
RS249	4c	**black**	40.00	35.00		190.00
RS250	6c	**black**				75.00

A. Vogeler & Co. — RS251

A. Vogeler & Co.

No.	Denom.	Color				
RS251	1c	**black**		1.50		2.00

Vogeler, Meyer & Co.

No.	Denom.	Color				
RS252	1c	**ver**			4.00	1.25

W

Dr. J. Walker

No.	Denom.	Color				
RS253	4c	**black**	40.00	20.00		20.00
		Dbl. transfer		50.00		40.00
	e.	Experimental silk paper	200.00			

H. H. Warner & Co. — RS254/RS255

H. H. W. & Co. (H. H. Warner & Co.)

No.	Denom.	Color				
RS254	1c	**brown**				6.00
RS255	6c	**brown,** 19x26mm				80.00
RS256	2c	**brown,** 88x11mm				30.00
RS257	4c	**brown,** 95x18mm				30.00
RS258	6c	**brown**				7.00
		Dbl. transfer				47.50

Weeks & Potter — RS259

Weeks & Potter

No.	Denom.	Color				
RS259	1c	**black**		7.00		5.00
RS260	2c	**black**		100.00		
RS261	4c	**black**		27.50	27.50	7.00
RS262	2c	**red**			35.00	7.00

Wells, Richardson & Co. — RS263

Edward Wilder — RS265/RS269

Wells, Richardson & Co.

No.	Denom.	Color				
RS263	4c	**black**				27.50

West India Manufacturing Co.

See illustration pages.

No.	Denom.	Color				
RS264	4c	**blk,** die I		225.00	275.00	400.00
RS264A	4c	**blk,** die II				350.00

Die II shows evidence of retouching, particularly in the central disk.

Edward Wilder

No.	Denom.	Color				
RS265	1c	**grn,** imperf	1,000.	220.00		275.00
	e.	Experimental silk paper	—			
RS266	1c	**grn,** die cut	50.00	45.00		22.50
	e.	Experimental silk paper	200.			
RS266A	4c	**ver,** imperf				
	e.	Experimental silk paper	*5,500.*			
RS267	4c	**ver,** die cut	175.00	500.00		
	e.	Experimental silk paper	100.			
RS268	4c	**lake,** imperf		190.00		1,100.
RS269	4c	**lake,** die cut	800.00	12.50		12.50

Rev. E. A. Wilson

No.	Denom.	Color				
RS270	12c	**blue**		75.00		375.00

Thos. E. Wilson, M. D.

No.	Denom.	Color				
RS271	4c	**black**	*25,000.*			

World's Dispensary Medical Assocn. — RS272/RS273

Wright's Indian Vegetable Pills — RS274

World's Dispensary Medical Assocn.

No.	Denom.	Color				
RS272	1c	**green**				25.00
RS273	2c	**black,** 56x256mm				8.00

Wright's Indian Vegetable Pills

No.	Denom.	Color				
RS274	1c	**green**	2.00	1.50	35.00	3.00
		Dbl. transfer				—
	e.	Experimental silk paper	100.			

Z

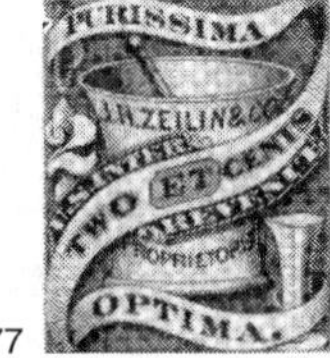

J.H. Zeilin & Co. — RS275/RS277

J.H. Zeilin & Co.

			Roul. 5½ Unused	Roul. 5½ Used	p. Hyphen Hole Perf. 7 Unused	p. Hyphen Hole Perf. 7 Used
RS275	2c	**red**		500.00		
RS276	2c	**green,** perf		40.00		—
RS277	2c	**grn,** imperf	175.00	7.50	125.00	5.00

1898-1900

See rouletting note preceding No. R161.

			Roul. 5½ Unused	Roul. 5½ Used	p. Hyphen Hole Perf. 7 Unused	p. Hyphen Hole Perf. 7 Used
The Antikamnia Chemical Co.						
RS278	2½c	**car**			3.00	3.00
Fernet Branca (Branca Bros.)						
RS279	4c	**black**	8.50	8.50	8.50	8.50
Emerson Drug Co.						
RS280	¼c	**car**			6.00	2.50
RS281	⅝c	**green**			6.00	3.00
RS282	1¼c	**vio brn**			8.00	6.50
RS283	2½c	**brn org**			7.50	4.50
Chas. H. Fletcher						
RS284	1¼c	**black**	.30	.30	.30	.30
Hostetter Co.						
RS285	2½c	**black,** imperf	.40	.40		
Johnson & Johnson						
RS286	⅝c	**car**	.30	.30	.30	.30
Lanman & Kemp						
RS287	⅝c	**green**	7.50	5.50	10.00	4.00
RS288	1¼c	**brown**	10.00	6.00	15.00	11.00
RS289	1⅞c	**blue**	10.00	7.50	20.00	10.00
J. Ellwood Lee Co.						
RS290	⅛c	**dk bl**			2.50	2.50
RS291	⅝c	**car**			2.00	1.50
RS292	1¼c	**dk grn**			1.50	1.50
RS293	2½c	**org**			2.00	2.00
RS294	5c	**chocolate**			2.25	2.25
Charles Marchand						
RS295	⅝c	**black**	7.50	7.50	8.00	8.00
RS296	1¼c	**black**	1.25	1.25	1.25	1.25
RS297	1⅞c	**black**	2.00	2.00	2.50	2.50
RS298	2½c	**black**	2.50	2.50	2.50	2.50
RS299	3⅛c	**black**	7.50	7.50	7.50	7.50
RS300	4⅜c	**black**	15.00	15.00	15.00	15.00
RS301	7½c	**black**	10.00	10.00	10.00	10.00
Od Chem. Co.						
RS302	2½c	**car**				1.00
The Piso Company (E. T. Hazletine)						
RS303	⅝c	**blue**	.30	.30	.30	.30
Radway & Co.						
RS304	⅝c	**blue**	1.00	1.00	1.00	1.00
Warner's Safe Cure Co.						
RS305	3⅛c	**brown**	1.00	1.00	1.00	1.00
Dr. Williams Medicine Co.						
RS306	1¼c	**pink**			2.00	2.00

Dr. Kilmer & Co., Provisionals

Postage Stamps of 1895, 1897-1903, Nos. 267a, 279, 279Bg and 268, Precancel Overprinted in Black:

Dr. K. & Co.

I. R.

7-5-'98.

a

b

c

1898 **Wmk. 191** ***Perf. 12***

Overprint "a," Large "I.R." Dated July 5, 1898.

No.	Design			Value
RS307	A87	1c	**deep green**	150.00
	a.		Red (trial) plus black ovpts.	—
RS308	A88	2c	**pink,** type III	145.00
RS308A	A88	2c	**pink,** type IV	150.00
	b.		Dark blue (trial) ovpt.	—
RS309	A89	3c	**purple**	140.00
	a.		Red (trial) ovpt.	—
	b.		Inverted ovpt.	—

A trial overprint in dark blue on the 2c stamp is known used on July 5.

Overprint "b," Small "I.R.," "Dr. K. & Co." with Serifs Dated July 6, 7, 9, 11 to 14, 1898

No.	Design			Value
RS310	A87	1c	**deep green**	125.00
RS311	A88	2c	**pink,** type III	135.00
RS311A	A88	2c	**pink,** type IV	70.00
RS312	A89	3c	**purple**	60.00
	a.		Inverted ovpt.	—

Overprint "c," Small "I.R.," "Dr. K. & Co." without Serifs Dated July 7, 9, 11 to 14, 1898

No.	Design			Value
RS313	A87	1c	**deep green**	130.00
RS314	A88	2c	**pink,** type III	135.00
RS314A	A88	2c	**pink,** type IV	90.00
RS315	A89	3c	**purple**	105.00
	a.		Inverted ovpt.	—

Nos. RS307a, RS308Ab and RS309a were all overprinted on July 5, the first day of overprinting. Though called "trials," there is every reason to believe they were used in the regular course of business, as they represented money spent by Dr. Kilmer & Co. and there was no reason not to use them. Three examples are recorded of No. RS307a, two of No. RS308Ab and one of No. RS309a.

For the inverted overprints, two examples are recorded of No. RS309b, 12 of No. RS312a and two of No. RS315a. Forgeries exist of No. RS312a, all dated July 6. The height of "I.R." is shorter on the forgeries, and the periods after these letters are circular rather than diamond shaped.

Many varieties of the Kilmer overprints exist. For the complete listing see "The Case of Dr. Kilmer's," by Morton Dean Joyce, 1954 (also serialized in "The Bureau Specialist," Mar.-Nov. 1957).

St. Louis Provisional Labels, 1898

INTERNAL REVENUE TAX.
II 1-4 CENTS.
Stamps not being obtainable at time of sale and shipment of this package, the tax will be paid on sworn returns thereof to Collector of Internal Revenue, 1st Dist. Mo.
Meyer Brothers Drug Co., St. Louis.

Ten proprietary drug companies of St. Louis (Antikamnia Chemical Co., W. R. Holmes, Lambert Pharmacal Co., Meyer Brothers Drug Co., Jno. T. Milliken & Co., Phenique Chemical Co., Prickly Ash Bitters Co., T. M. Sayman, Van Dyke Bitters Co. and Walker Pharmacal Co.) prepared and used labels to denote payment of July 1, 1898, Proprietary Revenue tax because the government issue of "Battleship" stamps (Nos. RB20-RB31) was not available on the effective date.

An illustrated descriptive list of these labels, compiled by Morton Dean Joyce, appeared in the December, 1970, issue of Scott's Monthly Journal.

a. Old Paper	b. Silk Paper	c. Pink Paper	d. Wmkd. USIR (191R)

PRIVATE DIE PERFUMERY STAMPS

1864 ***Perf. 12***

X. Bazin (Illustration reduced.) — RT1

X. Bazin

No.			a.	b.	c.	d.
RT1	2c	**blue,** die cut	700.00			

This stamp was never placed in use.

Corning & Tappan — RT2/RT4

E. W. Hoyt & Co. — RT6/RT11

Corning & Tappan

No.			a.	b.	c.	d.
RT2	1c	**black,** imperf				800.00
h.		Die cut, 19mm diameter				110.00
k.		Die cut, 21mm diameter				150.00
RT3	1c	**black,** perf				350.00
RT4	1c	**blue,** perf				4.00

Fetridge & Co.

No.			a.	b.	c.	d.
RT5	2c	**ver,** cut to shape	110.00			

E. W. Hoyt & Co.

No.			a.	b.	c.	d.
RT6	1c	**black,** imperf		*3,250.*	2,100.	140.00
RT7	1c	**black,** die cut		30.00	30.00	15.00
RT8	2c	**black,** imperf				450.00
RT9	2c	**black,** die cut				90.00
RT10	4c	**black,** imperf		2,500.	325.00	1,150.
RT11	4c	**black,** die cut		100.00	70.00	70.00

The 2c is larger than the 1c, 4c larger than 2c.

Kidder & Laird

No.			a.	b.	c.	d.
RT12	1c	**vermilion**				15.00
RT13	2c	**vermilion**				15.00

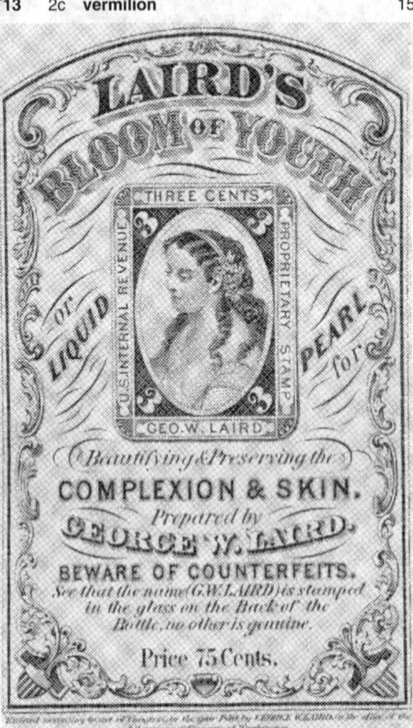

George W. Laird — RT14/RT15

George W. Laird

No.			a.	b.	c.	d.
RT14	3c	**blk,** imperf		700.00	1,000.	600.00
		Double transfer		1,000.	1,400.	1,000.
p.		Perf	1,500.	*3,750.*		
		As "p," double transfer	*1,600.*			
RT15	3c	**black,** die cut	1,500.	100.00	800.00	100.00
		Double transfer		250.00	900.00	300.00
p.		Perf and die cut	1,000.			

Lanman & Kemp — RT16/RT18

Tetlow's Perfumery — RT19

Lanman & Kemp

No.			a.	b.	c.	d.
RT16	1c	**black**		7.50	300.00	7.50
		Dbl. transfer		—		
RT17	2c	**brown**		30.00		10.00
RT18	3c	**green**		8.00		7.50
		Dbl. transfer		150.00		70.00

Tetlow's Perfumery

No.			a.	b.	c.	d.
RT19	1c	**vermilion**				3.50

C. B. Woodworth & Son — RT20/RT21

R. & G. A. Wright — RT22/RT25

C. B. Woodworth & Son

No.			a.	b.	c.	d.
RT20	1c	**green**		5.50	17.50	7.00
		Dbl. transfer		60.00	75.00	60.00
RT21	2c	**blue**		140.00	1,200.	9.00

R. & G. A. Wright

No.			a.	b.	c.	d.
RT22	1c	**blue**	6.00	8.00		60.00
e.		Experimental silk paper	85.00			
RT23	2c	**black**	11.00	20.00		200.00
RT24	3c	**lake**	30.00	110.00		290.00
RT25	4c	**green**	90.00	125.00		275.00

Young, Ladd & Coffin — RT26/RT33

Young, Ladd & Coffin

No.			a.	b.	c.	d.
RT26	1c	**green,** imperf		90.00	85.00	90.00
RT27	1c	**green,** perf		22.50	15.00	15.00
RT28	2c	**blue,** imperf		125.00	110.00	75.00
RT29	2c	**blue,** perf		55.00	85.00	15.00
RT30	3c	**ver,** imperf		110.00	130.00	80.00
RT31	3c	**ver,** perf		35.00	7.50	7.00
RT32	4c	**brown,** imperf		6,000.	145.00	50.00
RT33	4c	**brown,** perf		40.00	12.50	5.00

a. Old Paper	b. Silk Paper	c. Pink Paper	d. Wmkd. USIR (191R)

PRIVATE DIE PLAYING CARD STAMPS

1864

Caterson Brotz & Co.

No.			a.	b.	c.	d.
RU1	5c	**brown**				*9,000.*

This stamp was never placed in use.

A. Dougherty — RU2/RU6

Eagle Card Co. — RU7

A. Dougherty

RU2	2c	**orange**	70.00		
RU3	4c	**black**	45.00		
RU4	5c	**blue,** 20x26mm	1.50	1.50	12.50
		Double transfer		—	
	e.	Experimental silk paper	—		
		As "e," inverted dbl. transfer	—		
	u.	5c **ultra**	125.00		
RU5	5c	**blue,** 18x23mm			1.50
RU6	10c	**blue**	40.00		

The 2c, 4c and 5c have numerals in all four corners.

Eagle Card Co.

RU7	5c	**black**			85.00

Goodall (London, New York)

As No. RU13, "London Goodall New York" replaces both "American Playing Cards" and Victor E. Mauger and Petrie New York."

RU8	5c	**black**	150.00	4.00	
	e.	Experimental silk paper	425.00		

Samuel Hart & Co.

RU9	5c	**black**	6.00	6.00	
	e.	Experimental silk paper	240.00		

Lawrence & Cohen — RU10/RU11

Lawrence & Cohen

RU10	2c	**blue**	80.00		
RU11	5c	**green**	5.00	7.00	
	e.	Experimental silk paper	85.00		

Jn. J. Levy

RU12	5c	**black**	25.00	27.50	
	e.	Experimental silk paper	95.00		

Victor E. Mauger & Petrie — RU13

Victor E. Mauger and Petrie

RU13	5c	**blue**	1.75	1.75	.75

New York Consolidated Card Co.

RU14	5c	**black**	5.00	15.00	4.50

Paper Fabrique — RU15

Russell, Morgan & Co. — RU16

Paper Fabrique Company

RU15	5c	**black**	9.00	20.00	9.00

Russell, Morgan & Co.

RU16	5c	**black**			15.00

MOTOR VEHICLE USE REVENUE STAMPS

When affixed to a motor vehicle, permitted use of that vehicle for a stated period.

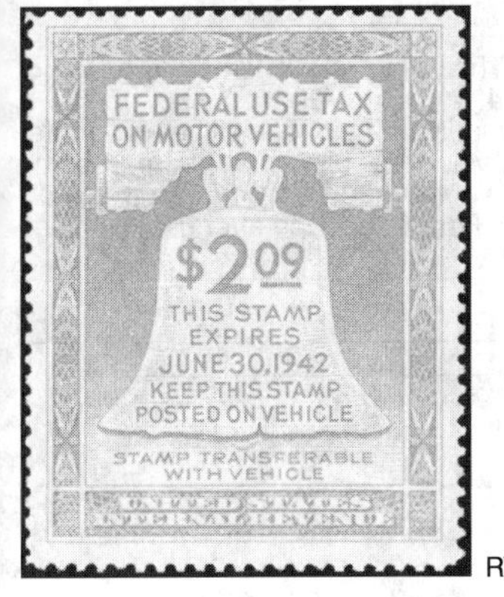

RV1

1942 Wmk. 191R OFFSET PRINTING *Perf. 11*

With Gum on Back

RV1	RV1	$2.09	**light green** *(February)*	1.60	.40

With Gum on Face

Inscriptions on Back

RV2	RV1	$1.67	**light green** *(March)*	24.00	8.00
RV3	RV1	$1.25	**light green** *(April)*	17.00	7.25
RV4	RV1	84c	**light green** *(May)*	19.00	7.00
RV5	RV1	42c	**light green** *(June)*	19.00	7.00

With Gum and Control Number on Face

Inscriptions on Back

RV6	RV1	$5	**rose red** *(July)*	3.25	1.10
RV7	RV1	$4.59	**rose red** *(August)*	40.00	12.50
RV8	RV1	$4.17	**rose red** *(September)*	45.00	15.00
RV9	RV1	$3.75	**rose red** *(October)*	40.00	12.00
RV10	RV1	$3.34	**rose red** *(November)*	40.00	12.00
RV11	RV1	$2.92	**rose red** *(December)*	40.00	12.00
			Nos. RV1-RV11 (11)	288.85	94.25

1943

RV12	RV1	$2.50	**rose red** *(January)*	47.50	15.00
RV13	RV1	$2.09	**rose red** *(February)*	32.50	10.50
RV14	RV1	$1.67	**rose red** *(March)*	27.50	12.00
RV15	RV1	$1.25	**rose red** *(April)*	27.50	8.75
RV16	RV1	84c	**rose red** *(May)*	27.50	8.75
RV17	RV1	42c	**rose red** *(June)*	22.50	9.50
RV18	RV1	$5	**yellow** *(July)*	3.75	.80
RV19	RV1	$4.59	**yellow** *(August)*	50.00	16.00
RV20	RV1	$4.17	**yellow** *(September)*	62.50	20.00
RV21	RV1	$3.75	**yellow** *(October)*	62.50	20.00
RV22	RV1	$3.34	**yellow** *(November)*	70.00	21.00
RV23	RV1	$2.92	**yellow** *(December)*	82.50	24.00
			Nos. RV12-RV23 (12)	516.25	166.30

1944

RV24	RV1	$2.50	**yellow** *(January)*	87.50	24.00
RV25	RV1	$2.09	**yellow** *(February)*	55.00	17.50
RV26	RV1	$1.67	**yellow** *(March)*	47.50	15.00
RV27	RV1	$1.25	**yellow** *(April)*	47.50	16.00
RV28	RV1	84c	**yellow** *(May)*	40.00	15.00
RV29	RV1	42c	**yellow** *(June)*	40.00	15.00

Gum on Face

Control Number and Inscriptions on Back

RV30	RV1	$5	**violet** *(July)*	2.40	.55
RV31	RV1	$4.59	**violet** *(August)*	72.50	20.00
RV32	RV1	$4.17	**violet** *(September)*	52.50	17.50
RV33	RV1	$3.75	**violet** *(October)*	52.50	17.50
RV34	RV1	$3.34	**violet** *(November)*	47.50	12.00
RV35	RV1	$2.92	**violet** *(December)*	47.50	12.00
			Nos. RV24-RV35 (12)	592.40	182.05

1945

RV36	RV1	$2.50	**violet** *(January)*	40.00	11.50
RV37	RV1	$2.09	**violet** *(February)*	35.00	11.50
RV38	RV1	$1.67	**violet** *(March)*	35.00	10.00
RV39	RV1	$1.25	**violet** *(April)*	35.00	10.00
RV40	RV1	84c	**violet** *(May)*	27.50	8.75
RV41	RV1	42c	**violet** *(June)*	24.00	7.00

Daniel Manning — RV2

Gum on Face

Control Number and Inscriptions on Back

1945 Wmk. 191R Offset Printing *Perf. 11*

Bright Blue Green & Yellow Green

RV42	RV2	$5	*(July)*	3.25	.55
RV43	RV2	$4.59	*(August)*	52.50	17.50
RV44	RV2	$4.17	*(Sept.)*	52.50	18.00
RV45	RV2	$3.75	*(October)*	47.50	12.00
RV46	RV2	$3.34	*(November)*	37.50	11.50
RV47	RV2	$2.92	*(December)*	32.50	8.75
			Nos. RV36-RV47 (12)	422.25	127.05

1946

Bright Blue Green & Yellow Green

RV48	RV2	$2.50	*(January)*	35.00	12.00
RV49	RV2	$2.09	*(February)*	35.00	11.50
RV50	RV2	$1.67	*(March)*	27.50	8.75
RV51	RV2	$1.25	*(April)*	22.50	8.75
RV52	RV2	84c	*(May)*	22.50	8.75
RV53	RV2	42c	*(June)*	17.00	1.10
			Nos. RV48-RV53 (6)	159.50	50.85

BOATING STAMPS

Required on applications for the certificate of number for motorboats of more than 10 horsepower, starting April 1, 1960. The pictorial upper part of the $3 stamp was attached to the temporary certificate and kept by the boat owner. The lower part (stub), showing number only, was affixed to the application and sent by the post office to the U.S. Coast Guard, which issues permanent certificates. The $3 fee was for three years. The $1 stamp covered charges for reissue of a lost or destroyed certificate of number. These stamps were used in the 12 states and the District of Columbia that had not passed laws in conformity with the Boating Act of 1958.

Catalogue value for unused stamps in this section are for Never Hinged items.

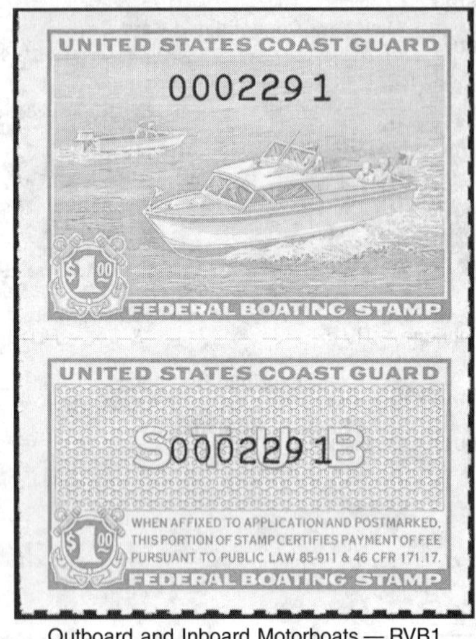

Outboard and Inboard Motorboats — RVB1

Offset Printing, Number Typographed

1960, Apr. 1			**Unwmk.**		***Rouletted***
RVB1	RVB1	$1	**rose red, black number**	37.50	*200.00*
			P# block of 4	160.00	
			On license		—
RVB2	RVB1	$3	**blue, red number**	42.50	30.00
			P# block of 4	180.00	
			On license		40.00
			First day license		*1,000.*

Nos. RVB1 and RVB2 unused stamp values are for MNH complete two-part stamps. Used values are for stamps, without the stubs, bearing a complete cancel dated between April 1, 1960, and January 31, 1964. On-license values are for clean licenses with undamaged stamps and a complete cancel. A license fold can be expected. Mute oval cancels are usually favor cancels.

CAMP STAMPS

The Camp Stamp program of the Department of Agriculture's National Forest Service was introduced in 1985. The public was offered the option of prepaying their recreation fees through the purchase of camp stamps. The fees varied but were typically $3 to $4.

The stamps were supplied in rolls with the backing roulетted 9 horizontally. The letter preceding the serial number indicated the face value and printer (A-D, Denver; E-J, Washington). The stamps were designed so that any attempt to remove them from the fee envelope would cause them to come apart.

The program ended in the summer of 1988. The envelopes containing the stamps were destroyed by the National Forerst Service after use. No used examples have been reported.

Catalogue value for unused stamps in this section are for Never Hinged items.

National Forest Service Logo — RVC1

Printed in Denver, CO.

Self-Adhesive, Coated Paper

1985		**Typo.**	***Die Cut***
RVC1	RVC1	50c **black,** *pink,* "A"	*27.50*
RVC2	RVC1	$1 **black,** *red,* "B"	*27.50*
RVC3	RVC1	$2 **black,** *yellow,* "C"	*27.50*
RVC4	RVC1	$3 **black,** *green,* "D"	*27.50*

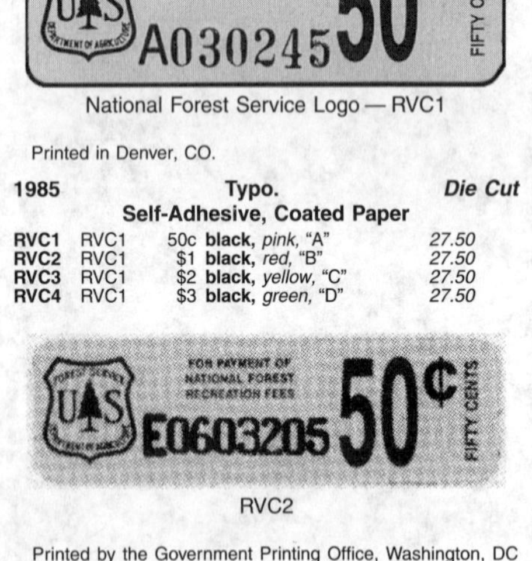

RVC2

Printed by the Government Printing Office, Washington, DC (?).

Self-Adhesive, Coated Paper

1986		**Typo.**	***Die Cut***
RVC5	RVC2	50c **black,** *pink,* "E"	75.00
RVC6	RVC2	$1 **black,** *red,* "F"	75.00
RVC7	RVC2	$2 **black,** *yellow,* "G"	75.00
RVC8	RVC2	$3 **black,** *green,* "H"	75.00
RVC9	RVC2	$5 **black,** *silver,* "I"	275.00
RVC10	RVC2	$10 **black,** *bronze,* "J"	—

TRAILER PERMIT STAMPS

Issued by the National Park Service of the Department of the Interior. Required to be affixed to "License to Operate Motor Vehicle" starting July 1, 1939, when a house trailer was attached to a motor vehicle entering a national park or national monument.

Issued to rangers in booklets of 50 (five 2x5 panes).

Use was continued at least until 1952.

Unused stamps may have a ranger's handwritten control number.

Trailer and Automobile RVT1

1939 Unwmk. Offset Printing *Perf. 11*

RVT1	RVT1	50c	**bright blue**	*1,100.*	*600.00*
			On license		*1,250.*
RVT2	RVT1	$1	**carmine**	*500.00*	175.00
			On license		*300.00*

Earliest known use: July 1939.

DISTILLED SPIRITS EXCISE TAX STAMPS

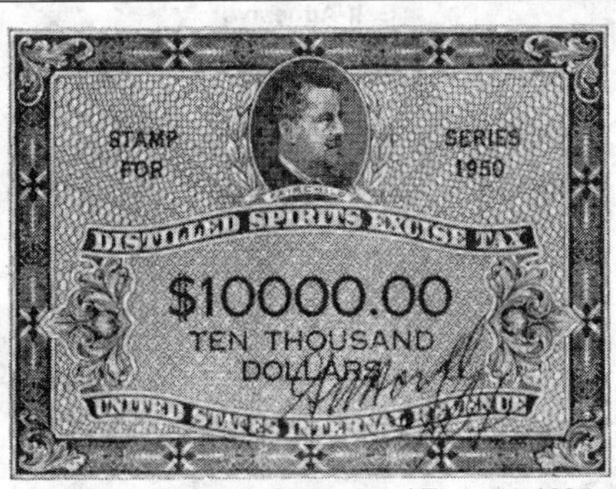

Charles S. Fairchild, Secretary of Treasury 1887-89 — DS1

Actual size: 89½x63½mm

Inscribed "STAMP FOR SERIES 1950"

1950 Wmk. 191R Offset Printing *Rouletted 7*

Left Value- Used

Right Value- Punched Cancel

RX1	DS1	1c	**yellow green & black**	25.00	21.00
RX2	DS1	3c	**yellow green & black**	100.00	92.50
RX3	DS1	5c	**yellow green & black**	20.00	17.50
RX4	DS1	10c	**yellow green & black**	17.50	15.00
RX5	DS1	25c	**yellow green & black**	9.00	7.25
RX6	DS1	50c	**yellow green & black**	9.00	7.25
RX7	DS1	$1	**yellow green & black**	2.00	1.25
RX8	DS1	$3	**yellow green & black**	20.00	15.00
RX9	DS1	$5	**yellow green & black**	5.00	3.75
RX10	DS1	$10	**yellow green & black**	3.00	1.50
RX11	DS1	$25	**yellow green & black**	12.50	9.25
RX12	DS1	$50	**yellow green & black**	6.00	5.00
RX13	DS1	$100	**yellow green & black**	4.00	2.75
RX14	DS1	$300	**yellow green & black**	25.00	21.00
RX15	DS1	$500	**yellow green & black**	15.00	10.00
RX16	DS1	$1,000	**yellow green & black**	9.00	7.50
RX17	DS1	$1,500	**yellow green & black**	50.00	40.00
RX18	DS1	$2,000	**yellow green & black**	4.50	3.50
RX19	DS1	$3,000	**yellow green & black**	21.00	15.00
RX20	DS1	$5,000	**yellow green & black**	21.00	16.00
RX21	DS1	$10,000	**yellow green & black**	27.50	22.50
RX22	DS1	$20,000	**yellow green & black**	32.50	30.00
RX23	DS1	$30,000	**yellow green & black**	70.00	50.00
RX24	DS1	$40,000	**yellow green & black**	1,000.	650.00
RX25	DS1	$50,000	**yellow green & black**	87.50	75.00

Inscription "STAMP FOR SERIES 1950" omitted

1952

Left Value- Used

Right Value- Punched Cancel

RX28	DS1	5c	**yellow green & black**		40.00
RX29	DS1	10c	**yellow green & black**	30.00	4.00
RX30	DS1	25c	**yellow green & black**	25.00	15.00
RX31	DS1	50c	**yellow green & black**	30.00	12.00
RX32	DS1	$1	**yellow green & black**	20.00	2.50
RX33	DS1	$3	**yellow green & black**	35.00	22.50
RX34	DS1	$5	**yellow green & black**	37.50	25.00
RX35	DS1	$10	**yellow green & black**	20.00	2.50
RX36	DS1	$25	**yellow green & black**	25.00	10.00
RX37	DS1	$50	**yellow green & black**	65.00	25.00
RX38	DS1	$100	**yellow green & black**	20.00	2.50
RX39	DS1	$300	**yellow green & black**	25.00	7.00
RX40	DS1	$500	**yellow green & black**		30.00
RX41	DS1	$1,000	**yellow green & black**	75.00	6.00
RX43	DS1	$2,000	**yellow green & black**		70.00
RX44	DS1	$3,000	**yellow green & black**	—	1,000.
RX45	DS1	$5,000	**yellow green & black**		50.00
RX46	DS1	$10,000	**yellow green & black**		80.00

Seven other denominations with "Stamp for Series 1950" omitted were prepared but are not known to have been put into use: 1c, 3c, $1,500, $20,000, $30,000, $40,000 and $50,000.

Copies listed as used have staple holes.

Distilled Spirits Excise Tax stamps were discontinued in 1959.

FIREARMS TRANSFER TAX STAMPS

Documentary Stamp of 1917 Overprinted Vertically in Black. Reading Up

1934 Engr. Wmk. 191R *Perf. 11*
Without Gum

RY1	R21	$1 **green**	350.00	—
		On license		—

RY1

RY2

Eagle, Shield and Stars from U.S. Seal

Two types of $200:

I - Serial number with serifs, not preceded by zeros. Tips of 6 lines project into left margin.

II - Gothic serial number preceded by zeros. Five line tips in left margin.

1934 Wmk. 191R Size: 28x42mm
Without Gum

RY2 RY1	$200 **dark blue & red,** type I, #1-1500	1,350.	750.00
	On license		*900.00*

Issued in vertical strips of 4 which are imperforate at top, bottom and right side.

See Nos. RY4, RY6-RY8.

1938 Size: 28x33½mm *Perf. 11*

RY3 RY2	$1 **green**	85.00	—
	On license		—

See No. RY5.

1950 (?) Wmk. 191R Size: 29x43mm

RY4 RY1	$200 **dull blue & red,** type II, #1501-3000	600.00	450.00
	On license		500.00

No. RY4 has a clear impression and is printed on white paper. No. RY2 has a "muddy" impression in much darker blue ink and is printed on off-white paper.

1960, July 1 Size: 29x34mm *Perf. 11*

RY5 RY2	$5 **red**	25.00	*40.00*
	On license		200.00

No. RY5 was issued in sheets of 50 (10x5) with straight edge on four sides of sheet.

The watermark is hard to see on many copies of #RY2-RY5.

1974 Unwmk. Size: 29x43mm

RY6 RY1	$200 **dull blue & red,** type II, #3001-up	225.00	110.00
	On license		140.00

Panes of 32

1990(?) Litho. Without Gum *Imperf.*

RY7 RY1	$200 **dull blue**	*500.00*
	On license	*650.00*

1990 *Perf. 12½*

RY8 RY1	$200 **dull blue**	75.00
	On license	100.00
RY9 RY2	$5 **red,** *1994*	125.00
	On license	200.00

Nos. RY7 and RY8 do not have a printed serial number or the tabs at left. Because the stamps do not have a serial number mint copies are not being sold to the public.

WARNING: Nos. RY7-RY9 are taped or glued to the transfer of title documents. The glue used is NOT water soluble. Attempts to soak the stamps may result in damage.

2001(?) *Serpentine Die Cut 11.5*
Self-Adhesive

RY10 RY2	$5 **dull red**	—
	On license	—

RECTIFICATION TAX STAMPS

Used to indicate payment of the tax on distilled spirits that were condensed and purified for additional blending through repeated distillations.

RZ1

Actual size: 89½x64mm

1946 Offset Printing Wmk. 191R *Rouletted 7*

RZ1	RZ1	1c **blue & black**	7.50	4.00
		Punched cancel		2.00
RZ2	RZ1	3c **blue & black**	25.00	8.00
		Punched cancel		7.50
RZ3	RZ1	5c **blue & black**	15.00	2.50
		Punched cancel		1.25
RZ4	RZ1	10c **blue & black**	15.00	2.75
		Punched cancel		1.25
RZ5	RZ1	25c **blue & black**	15.00	3.00
		Punched cancel		2.00
RZ6	RZ1	50c **blue & black**	20.00	5.00
		Punched cancel		3.50
RZ7	RZ1	$1 **blue & black**	20.00	4.00
		Punched cancel		2.50
RZ8	RZ1	$3 **blue & black**	100.00	18.00
		Punched cancel		9.00
RZ9	RZ1	$5 **blue & black**	30.00	10.00
		Punched cancel		6.00
RZ10	RZ1	$10 **blue & black**	25.00	3.00
		Punched cancel		1.25
RZ11	RZ1	$25 **blue & black**	100.00	10.00
		Punched cancel		3.00
RZ12	RZ1	$50 **blue & black**	100.00	7.50
		Punched cancel		3.00
RZ13	RZ1	$100 **blue & black**	—	9.50
		Punched cancel		3.50
RZ14	RZ1	$300 **blue & black**	*250.00*	10.00
		Punched cancel		7.50
RZ15	RZ1	$500 **blue & black**	—	10.00
		Punched cancel		7.00
RZ16	RZ1	$1000 **blue & black**	—	18.00
		Punched cancel		15.00
RZ17	RZ1	$1500 **blue & black**	—	52.50
		Punched cancel		37.50
RZ18	RZ1	$2000 **blue & black**	—	80.00
		Punched cancel		60.00

Copies listed as used have staple holes.

HUNTING PERMIT STAMPS

Authorized by an Act of Congress, approved March 16, 1934, to license hunters. Receipts go to maintain waterfowl life in the United States. Sales to collectors were made legal June 15, 1935.

No. RW1 used is valued with handstamp or manuscript cancel, though technically it was against postal regulations to deface the stamp. Beginning with No. RW2 the used value is for stamp with signature.

Plate number blocks of six have selvage on two sides.

Hunting permit stamps are valid from July 1 - June 30. Stamps have been made available prior to the date of validity, and stamps are sold through the philatelic agency after the period of validity has passed.

Catalogue values for all unused stamps in this section are for stamps with never-hinged original gum. Minor natural gum skips and bends are normal on Nos. RW1-RW20. No-gum stamps are without signature or other cancel.

Department of Agriculture

Mallards Alighting — HP1

Engraved: Flat Plate Printing
Issued in panes of 28 subjects.

1934 **Unwmk.** ***Perf. 11***

Inscribed "Void after June 30, 1935"

				Unused	Used
RW1	HP1	$1	**blue**	800.	130.
			Hinged	375.	
			No gum	160.	
			P# block of 6	16,500.	
a.			Imperf., pair	—	
b.			Vert. pair, imperf. horiz.	—	

Used value is for stamp with handstamp or manuscript cancel.

It is possible that No. RW1a is No. RW1b with vertical perfs. removed. Both varieties probably are printer's waste since copies exist with gum on front or without gum.

Canvasbacks Taking to Flight — HP2

1935 **Inscribed "Void after June 30, 1936"**

				Unused	Used
RW2	HP2	$1	**rose lake**	700.	150.
			Hinged	350.	
			No gum	200.	
			P# block of 6	11,500.	

Canada Geese in Flight — HP3

1936 **Inscribed "Void after June 30, 1937"**

				Unused	Used
RW3	HP3	$1	**brown black**	350.	75.00
			Hinged	175.	
			No gum	110.	
			P# block of 6	3,500.	

Scaup Ducks Taking to Flight — HP4

1937 **Inscribed "Void after June 30, 1938"**

				Unused	Used
RW4	HP4	$1	**light green**	300.	60.00
			Hinged	150.	
			No gum	75.	
			P# block of 6	2,750.	

Pintail Drake and Hen Alighting — HP5

1938 **Inscribed "Void after June 30, 1939"**

				Unused	Used
RW5	HP5	$1	**light violet**	425.	57.50
			Hinged	200.	
			No gum	75.	
			P# block of 6	3,500.	

Department of the Interior

Green-winged Teal — HP6

1939 **Inscribed "Void after June 30, 1940"**

				Unused	Used
RW6	HP6	$1	**chocolate**	250.00	45.00
			Hinged	110.	
			No gum	50.	
			P# block of 6	2,000.	

Black Mallards — HP7

1940 **Inscribed "Void after June 30, 1941"**

				Unused	Used
RW7	HP7	$1	**sepia**	225.	45.00
			Hinged	110.	
			No gum	50.	
			P# block of 6	2,000.	

Family of Ruddy Ducks — HP8

1941 **Inscribed "Void after June 30, 1942"**

				Unused	Used
RW8	HP8	$1	**brown carmine**	225.	45.00
			Hinged	110.	
			No gum	50.	
			P# block of 6	2,000.	

Baldpates — HP9

1942 **Inscribed "Void after June 30, 1943"**

				Unused	Used
RW9	HP9	$1	**violet brown**	225.	45.00
			Hinged	110.	
			No gum	50.	
			P# block of 6	2,000.	

Wood Ducks — HP10

1943 **Inscribed "Void After June 30, 1944"**

RW10	HP10	$1	**deep rose**	90.00	32.50
			Hinged	50.00	
			No gum	35.00	
			P# block of 6	625.00	

White-fronted Geese — HP11

1944 **Inscribed "Void after June 30, 1945"**

RW11	HP11	$1	**red orange**	95.00	25.00
			Hinged	55.00	
			No gum	37.50	
			P# block of 6	650.00	

Shoveller Ducks in Flight — HP12

1945 **Inscribed "Void after June 30, 1946"**

RW12	HP12	$1	**black**	60.00	25.00
			Hinged	35.00	
			No gum	27.50	
			P# block of 6	450.00	

Beginning with No. RW13, there is a message printed on the back of the sheet stamps telling hunters to sign their names on the face of the stamp. On Nos. RW13-RW17, offset plate no. 47510 for the printing on the backs of the stamps appears on the back of the selvage opposite the stamp in position 24 on the upper right panes. These are collected as plate blocks of six bearing the plate number on the back of the selvage opposite the center margin stamp. Value, mint never hinged $550 each for Nos. RW13-RW16, $1,500 for No. RW17.

Redhead Ducks — HP13

1946 **Inscribed "Void after June 30, 1947"**

RW13	HP13	$1	**red brown**	45.00	16.00
			No gum	18.00	
			P# block of 6	300.00	
a.		$1	**bright rose pink**	—	

Snow Geese — HP14

1947 **Inscribed "Void after June 30, 1948"**

RW14	HP14	$1	**black**	45.00	16.00
			No gum	18.00	
			P# block of 6	300.00	

Buffleheads in Flight — HP15

1948 **Inscribed "Void after June 30, 1949"**

RW15	HP15	$1	**bright blue**	50.00	15.00
			No gum	21.00	
			P# block of 6	350.00	

Goldeneye Ducks — HP16

1949 **Inscribed "Void after June 30, 1950"**

RW16 HP16 $2 **bright green** 65.00 14.00
No gum 22.50
P# block of 6 400.00

Trumpeter Swans in Flight — HP17

1950 **Inscribed "Void after June 30, 1951"**

RW17 HP17 $2 **violet** 80.00 12.00
No gum 22.50
P# block of 6 575.00

Gadwall Ducks — HP18

1951 **Inscribed "Void after June 30, 1952"**

RW18 HP18 $2 **gray black** 80.00 12.00
No gum 22.50
P# block of 6 575.00

Harlequin Ducks — HP19

1952 **Inscribed "Void after June 30, 1953"**

RW19 HP19 $2 **deep ultramarine** 80.00 12.00
No gum 22.50
P# block of 6 575.00

Blue-winged Teal — HP20

1953 **Inscribed "Void after June 30, 1954"**

RW20 HP20 $2 **deep brown rose** 80.00 12.00
No gum 22.50
P# block of 6 575.00

No. RW21 and following issues are printed on dry, pregummed paper and the back inscription is printed on top of the gum, except for the self-adhesive stamp issues starting in 1998.

Ring-necked Ducks — HP21

1954 **Inscribed "Void after June 30, 1955"**

RW21 HP21 $2 **black** 80.00 10.50
No gum 22.50
P# block of 6 575.00

Blue Geese — HP22

1955 **Inscribed "Void after June 30, 1956"**

RW22 HP22 $2 **dark blue** 80.00 10.50
No gum 22.50
P# block of 6 575.00
a. Back inscription inverted —

American Merganser — HP23

1956 **Inscribed "Void after June 30, 1957"**

RW23 HP23 $2 **black** 80.00 10.50
No gum 22.50
P# block of 6 575.00

American Eiders — HP24

1957 **Inscribed "Void after June 30, 1958"**

RW24 HP24 $2 **emerald** 80.00 10.50
No gum 22.50
P# block of 6 575.00
a. Back inscription inverted —

Canada Geese — HP25

1958 **Inscribed "Void after June 30, 1959"**

RW25 HP25 $2 **black** 80.00 10.50
No gum 22.50
P# block of 6 575.00

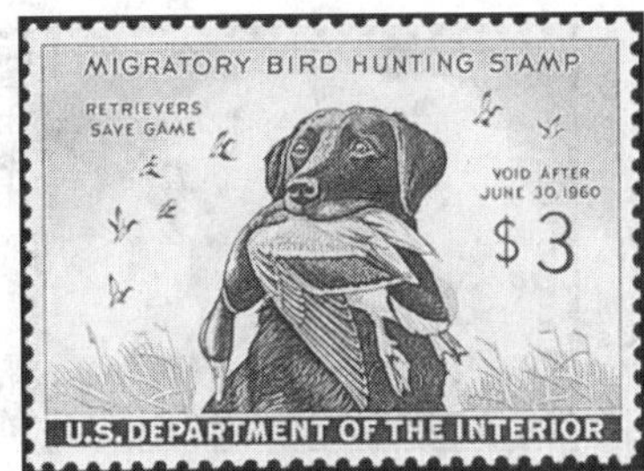

Labrador Retriever Carrying Mallard Drake — HP26

Giori Press Printing
Issued in panes of 30 subjects

1959 **Inscribed "Void after June 30, 1960"**

RW26 HP26 $3 **blue, ocher & black** 110.00 11.00
No gum 35.00
P# block of 4 550.00
a. Back inscription inverted —

Redhead Ducks — HP27

1960 **Inscribed "Void after June 30, 1961"**

RW27 HP27 $3 **red brown, dark blue & bister** 85.00 10.50
No gum 37.50
P# block of 4 425.00

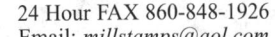

Mallard Hen and Ducklings — HP28

1961 **Inscribed "Void after June 30, 1962"**

RW28 HP28	$3 **multicolored**		85.00	10.50
	No gum		37.50	
	P# block of 4		425.00	

Pintail Drakes Coming in for Landing HP29

1962 **Inscribed "Void after June 30, 1963"**

RW29 HP29	$3 **dark blue, dark red brown & black**		110.00	10.50
	No gum		55.00	
	P# block of 4		575.00	
a.	Back inscription omitted		—	

Pair of Brant Landing — HP30

1963 **Inscribed "Void after June 30, 1964"**

RW30 HP30	$3 **multicolored**		105.00	10.50
	No gum		55.00	
	P# block of 4		500.00	

Hawaiian Nene Geese — HP31

1964 **Inscribed "Void after June 30, 1965"**

RW31 HP31	$3 **multicolored**		100.00	10.50
	No gum		55.00	
	P# block of 6		2,100.	

Three Canvasback Drakes — HP32

1965 **Inscribed "Void after June 30, 1966"**

RW32 HP32	$3 **multicolored**		100.00	10.50
	No gum		55.00	
	P# block of 4		500.00	

Whistling Swans — HP33

1966 **Inscribed "Void after June 30, 1967"**

RW33 HP33	$3 **multicolored**		100.00	10.50
	No gum		55.00	
	P# block of 4		500.00	

Old Squaw Ducks — HP34

1967 **Inscribed "Void after June 30, 1968"**

RW34 HP34	$3 **multicolored**		125.00	10.00
	No gum		55.00	
	P# block of 4		525.00	

Hooded Mergansers — HP35

1968 **Inscribed "Void after June 30, 1969"**

RW35 HP35	$3 **multicolored**		65.00	10.00
	No gum		25.00	
	P# block of 4		300.00	
a.	Back inscription omitted		—	

White-winged Scoters — HP36

1969 **Inscribed "Void after June 30, 1970"**

RW36 HP36	$3 **multicolored**		65.00	7.00
	No gum		25.00	
	P# block of 4		300.00	

Ross's Geese — HP37

1970 **Engraved & Lithographed**
Inscribed "Void after June 30, 1971"

RW37 HP37	$3 **multicolored**		65.00	7.00
	No gum		24.00	
	P# block of 4		300.00	

Three Cinnamon Teal — HP38

1971 **Inscribed "Void after June 30, 1972"**

RW38 HP38	$3 **multicolored**		42.50	7.75
	No gum		21.00	
	P# block of 4		200.00	

Emperor Geese — HP39

1972 **Inscribed "Void after June 30, 1973"**

RW39 HP39	$5 **multicolored**		25.00	7.00
	No gum		12.50	
	P# block of 4		110.00	

Steller's Eiders — HP40

1973 **Inscribed "Void after June 30, 1974"**

RW40 HP40	$5 **multicolored**		18.00	7.00
	No gum		11.50	
	P# block of 4		90.00	

Wood Ducks — HP41

1974 **Inscribed "Void after June 30, 1975"**

RW41	HP41	$5 **multicolored**	18.00	6.00
		No gum	9.50	
		P# block of 4	75.00	

Canvasback Decoy, 3 Flying Canvasbacks — HP42

1975 **Inscribed "Void after June 30, 1976"**

RW42	HP42	$5 **multicolored**	15.00	6.00
		No gum	7.50	
		P# block of 4	60.00	

Family of Canada Geese — HP43

1976 **Engr.**

Inscribed "Void after June 30, 1977"

RW43	HP43	$5 **green & black**	15.00	6.00
		No gum	7.50	
		P# block of 4	55.00	

Pair of Ross's Geese — HP44

1977 **Litho. & Engr.**

Inscribed "Void after June 30, 1978"

RW44	HP44	$5 **multicolored**	15.00	6.00
		No gum	7.50	
		P# block of 4	55.00	

Hooded Merganser Drake — HP45

1978 **Inscribed "Void after June 30, 1979"**

RW45	HP45	$5 **multicolored**	12.50	6.00
		No gum	7.00	
		P# block of 4	55.00	

Green-winged Teal — HP46

1979 **Inscribed "Void after June 30, 1980"**

RW46	HP46	$7.50 **multicolored**	14.00	7.00
		No gum	9.00	
		P# block of 4	55.00	

Mallards — HP47

1980 **Inscribed "Void after June 30, 1981"**

RW47	HP47	$7.50 **multicolored**	14.00	7.00
		No gum	8.50	
		P# block of 4	55.00	

Ruddy Ducks — HP48

1981 **Inscribed "Void after June 30, 1982"**

RW48	HP48	$7.50 **multicolored**	14.00	7.00
		No gum	8.50	
		P# block of 4	55.00	

Canvasbacks — HP49

1982 **Inscribed "Void after June 30, 1983"**

RW49	HP49	$7.50 **multicolored**	15.00	7.00
		No gum	8.50	
		P# block of 4	55.00	
a.		Orange and violet omitted	—	

Pintails — HP50

1983 **Inscribed "Void after June 30, 1984"**

RW50	HP50	$7.50 **multicolored**	15.00	7.00
		No gum	8.50	
		P# block of 4	60.00	

Widgeons — HP51

1984 **Inscribed "Void after June 30, 1985"**

RW51	HP51	$7.50 **multicolored**	15.00	7.00
		No gum	8.50	
		P# block of 4	62.50	

See Special Printings section that follows.

Cinnamon Teal — HP52

1985 **Inscribed "Void after June 30, 1986"**

RW52	HP52	$7.50 **multicolored**	15.00	7.00
		No gum	8.50	
		P# block of 4	60.00	

Fulvous Whistling Duck — HP53

1986 **Inscribed "Void after June 30, 1987"**

RW53	HP53	$7.50 **multicolored**	15.00	7.00
		No gum	8.50	
		P# block of 4	60.00	
a.		Black omitted	*3,750.*	

Redheads — HP54

1987 ***Perf. 11½x11***

Inscribed "Void after June 30, 1988"

RW54	HP54	$10 **multicolored**	17.50	9.50
		No gum	10.00	
		P# block of 4	65.00	

Snow Goose — HP55

1988 **Inscribed "Void after June 30, 1989"**

RW55 HP55 $10 **multicolored** 17.00 10.00
No gum 11.00
P# block of 4 75.00

Lesser Scaup — HP56

1989 **Inscribed "Void after June 30, 1990"**

RW56 HP56 $12.50 **multicolored** 19.00 10.00
No gum 12.00
P# block of 4 82.50

Black Bellied Whistling Duck — HP57

1990 **Inscribed "Void after June 30, 1991"**

RW57 HP57 $12.50 **multicolored**> 19.00 10.00
No gum 12.00
P# block of 4 82.50
a. Back inscription omitted *400.00*

The back inscription is on top of the gum so beware of copies with gum removed. Used examples of No. RW57a cannot exist.

King Eiders HP58

1991 **Inscribed "Void after June 30, 1992"**

RW58 HP58 $15 **multicolored** 24.00 11.00
No gum 15.00
P# block of 4 110.00
a. Black (engr.) omitted *8,500.*

Spectacled Eider — HP59

1992 **Inscribed "Void after June 30, 1993"**

RW59 HP59 $15 **multicolored** 24.00 12.50
No gum 15.00
P# block of 4 110.00

Canvasbacks — HP60

1993 **Inscribed "Void after June 30, 1994"**

RW60 HP60 $15 **multicolored** 24.00 11.00
No gum 15.00
P# block of 4 110.00
a. Black (engr.) omitted *3,250.*

Red-breasted Mergansers — HP61

1994 ***Perf. 11¼x11***

Inscribed "Void after June 30, 1995"

RW61 HP61 $15 **multicolored** 24.00 11.00
No gum 15.00
P# block of 4 110.00

Mallards — HP62

1995 **Inscribed "Void after June 30, 1996"**

RW62 HP62 $15 **multicolored** 24.00 11.00
No gum 15.00
P# block of 4 110.00

Surf Scoters — HP63

1996 **Inscribed "Void after June 30, 1997"**

RW63 HP63 $15 **multicolored** 24.00 11.00
No gum 15.00
P# block of 4 110.00

Canada Goose — HP64

1997 **Inscribed "Void after June 30, 1998"**

RW64 HP64 $15 **multicolored** 22.50 11.00
No gum 15.00
P# block of 4 110.00

Barrow's Goldeneye — HP65

1998 ***Perf. 11¼***

Inscribed "Void after June 30, 1999"

RW65 HP65 $15 **multicolored** 24.00 11.00
No gum 15.00
P# block of 4 110.00

Self-Adhesive

Die Cut Perf. 10

RW65A HP65 $15 *Barrow's Goldeneye* 20.00 12.50
No gum 18.00

Nos. RW65 and later issues were sold in panes of 30 (RW65 and RW66) or 20 (RW67 and later issues), with four plate numbers per pane. The self-adhesives starting with No. RW65A were sold in panes of 1. The self-adhesives are valued unused as complete panes and used as single stamps.

Greater Scaup — HP66

1999 ***Perf. 11¼***

Inscribed "Void after June 30, 2000"

RW66 HP66 $15 **multicolored** 22.50 11.00
No gum 15.00
P# block of 4 100.00

Self-Adhesive

Die Cut Perf. 10

RW66A HP66 $15 **multicolored** 22.50 12.50
No gum 20.00

Mottled Duck — HP67

2000 ***Perf. 11¼***

Inscribed "Void after June 30, 2001"

RW67 HP67 $15 **multicolored** 22.50 11.00
No gum 15.00
P# block of 4 100.00

Self-Adhesive

Die Cut 10

RW67A HP67 $15 **multicolored** 22.50 12.50
No gum 20.00

Northern Pintail — HP68

2001 ***Perf. 11¼***

Inscribed "Void after June 30, 2002"

RW68 HP68 $15 **multicolored** 22.50 11.00
No gum 15.00
P# block of 4 100.00

Self-Adhesive

Die Cut Perf. 10

RW68A HP68 $15 **multicolored** 22.50 12.50
No gum 20.00

Black Scoters
HP69

2002 ***Perf. 11¼***

Inscribed "Void after June 30, 2003"

RW69 HP69 $15 **multicolored** 22.50 11.00
No gum 15.00
P# block of 4 100.00

Self-Adhesive

Serpentine Die Cut 11x10¾

RW69A HP69 $15 **multicolored** 22.50 11.00
No gum 20.00

Snow Geese — HP70

Designed by Ron Louque.

2003 ***Perf. 11***

Inscribed "Void after June 30, 2004"

RW70 HP70 $15 **multicolored** 22.50 11.00
No gum 15.00
P# block of 4 100.00

Self-Adhesive

Serpentine Die Cut 11x10¾

RW70A HP70 $15 **multicolored** 22.50 11.00
No gum 20.00

SPECIAL PRINTING

After No. RW51 became void, fifteen uncut sheets of 120 (4 panes of 30 separated by gutters) were overprinted "1934-84" and "50th ANNIVERSARY" in the margins and auctioned by the U.S. Fish and Wildlife Service.

Bids were accepted from September 1 through November 1, 1985. Minimum bid for each sheet was $2,000. The face value of each sheet, had they still been valid, was $900. Each sheet also had the sheet number and pane position printed in the corner of each pane ("01 of 15-1," "01 of 15-2," etc.). Fourteen of the sheets were sold at this and one subsequent auction and one was donated to the Smithsonian.

An individual sheet could be broken up to create these identifiable collectibles: 4 margin overprint blocks of 10; cross gutter block of 4; 6 horizontal pairs with gutter between; 8 vertical pairs with gutter between.

Single stamps from the sheet cannot be distinguished from No. RW51. No used examples can exist.

RW51x $7.50 *Widgeons*

DESIGNERS

1934 - *RW1*	*J.N. Darling*
1935 - *RW2*	*Frank W. Benson*
1936 - *RW3*	*Richard E. Bishop*
1937 - *RW4*	*J.D. Knap*
1938 - *RW5*	*Roland Clark*
1939 - *RW6*	*Lynn Bogue Hunt*
1940 - *RW7*	*Francis L. Jaques*
1941 - *RW8*	*E.R. Kalmbach*
1942 - *RW9*	*A. Lassell Ripley*
1943 - *RW10*	*Walter E. Bohl*
1944 - *RW11*	*Walter A. Weber*
1945 - *RW12*	*Owen J. Bromme*
1946 - *RW13*	*Robert W. Hines*
1947 - *RW14*	*Jack Murray*
1948 - *RW15*	*Maynard Reece*
1949 - *RW16*	*"Roge" E. Preuss*
1950 - *RW17*	*Walter A. Weber*
1951 - *RW18*	*Maynard Reece*
1952 - *RW19*	*John H. Dick*
1953 - *RW20*	*Clayton B. Seagears*
1954 - *RW21*	*Harvey D. Sandstrom*
1955 - *RW22*	*Stanley Searns*
1956 - *RW23*	*Edward J. Bierly*
1957 - *RW24*	*Jackson Miles Abbott,*
1958 - *RW25*	*Leslie C. Kouba*
1959 - *RW26*	*Maynard Reece*
1960 - *RW27*	*John A. Ruthven,*
1961 - *RW28*	*Edward A. Morris*
1962 - *RW29*	*Edward A. Morris*
1963 - *RW30*	*Edward J. Bierly*
1964 - *RW31*	*Stanley Searns*
1965 - *RW32*	*Ron Jenkins*
1966 - *RW33*	*Stanley Searns*
1967 - *RW34*	*Leslie C. Kouba*
1968 - *RW35*	*C.G. Pritchard*
1969 - *RW36*	*Maynard Reece*
1970 - *RW37*	*Edward J. Bierly*
1971 - *RW38*	*Maynard Reece*
1972 - *RW39*	*Arthur M. Cook*
1973 - *RW40*	*Lee LeBlanc*
1974 - *RW41*	*David A. Maass*
1975 - *RW42*	*James L. Fisher*
1976 - *RW43*	*Alderson Magee*
1977 - *RW44*	*Martin R. Murk*
1978 - *RW45*	*Albert Earl Gilbert*
1979 - *RW46*	*Kenneth L. Michaelsen*
1980 - *RW47*	*Richard W. Plasschaert*
1981 - *RW48*	*John S. Wilson*
1982 - *RW49*	*David A. Maass*
1983 - *RW50*	*Phil Scholer*
1984 - *RW51*	*William C. Morris*
1985 - *RW52*	*Gerald Mobley*
1986 - *RW53*	*Burton E. Moore, Jr.*
1987 - *RW54*	*Arthur G. Anderson*
1988 - *RW55*	*Daniel Smith*
1989 - *RW56*	*Neal R. Anderson*
1990 - *RW57*	*Jim Hautman*
1991 - *RW58*	*Nancy Howe*
1992 - *RW59*	*Joe Hautman*
1993 - *RW60*	*Bruce Miller*
1994 - *RW61*	*Neal R. Anderson*
1995 - *RW62*	*Jim Hautman*
1996 - *RW63*	*Wilhelm Goebel*
1997 - *RW64*	*Robert Hautman*
1998 - *RW65*	*Robert Steiner*
1999 - *RW66*	*Jim Hautman*
2000 - *RW67*	*Adam Grimm*
2001 - *RW68*	*Robert Hautman*
2002 - *RW69*	*Joe Hautman*
2003 - *RW70*	*Ron Louque*

QUANTITIES ISSUED

RW1	**635,001**	*RW33*	**1,805,341**
RW2	**448,204**	*RW34*	**1,934,697**
RW3	**603,623**	*RW35*	**1,837,139**
RW4	**783,039**	*RW36*	**2,072,108**
RW5	**1,002,715**	*RW37*	**2,420,244**
RW6	**1,111,561**	*RW38*	**2,445,977**
RW7	**1,260,810**	*RW39*	**2,184,343**
RW8	**1,439,967**	*RW40*	**2,094,414**
RW9	**1,383,629**	*RW41*	**2,214,056**
RW10	**1,169,352**	*RW42*	**2,237,126**
RW11	**1,487,029**	*RW43*	**2,170,194**
RW12	**1,725,505**	*RW44*	**2,196,774**
RW13	**2,016,841**	*RW45*	**2,216,621**
RW14	**1,722,677**	*RW46*	**2,090,155**
RW15	**2,127,603**	*RW47*	**2,045,114**
RW16	**1,954,734**	*RW48*	**1,907,120**
RW17	**1,903,644**	*RW49*	**1,926,253**
RW18	**2,167,767**	*RW50*	**1,867,998**
RW19	**2,296,628**	*RW51*	**1,913,861**
RW20	**2,268,446**	*RW52*	**1,780,636**
RW21	**2,184,550**	*RW53*	**1,794,484**
RW22	**2,369,940**	*RW54*	**1,663,270**
RW23	**2,332,014**	*RW55*	**1,402,096**
RW24	**2,355,190**	*RW56*	**1,415,882**
RW25	**2,176,425**	*RW57*	**1,408,373**
RW26	**1,626,115**	*RW58*	**1,423,374**
RW27	**1,725,634**	*RW59*	**1,347,393**
RW28	**1,344,236**	*RW60*	**1,402,569**
RW29	**1,147,212**	*RW61*	**1,471,751**
RW30	**1,448,191**	*RW62*	**1,539,622**
RW31	**1,573,155**	*RW63*	**1,560,123**
RW32	**1,558,197**	*RW64*	**1,697,590**
		RW65	**1,685,002**

STATE HUNTING PERMIT STAMPS

These stamps are used on licenses for hunting waterfowl (ducks, geese, swans) by states and Indian reservations. Stamps which include waterfowl along with a variety of other animals are listed here. Stamps for hunting birds that exclude waterfowl are not listed.

A number of states print stamps in sheets as well as in booklets. The booklets are sent to agents for issuing to hunters. Both varieties are listed. The major listing is given to the sheet stamp since it generally is available in larger quantities and has been the more popularly collected item. In some cases the stamp removed from a booklet, with no tabs or selvage, is identical to a single sheet stamp (see Rhode Island). In these cases the identifiable booklet stamp with tabs and selvage receives an unlettered listing. If the single booklet stamp can be identified by type of perforation or the existence of one or more straight edges, the item receives a lettered listing (see Oregon).

Governor's editions are sold at a premium over the license fee with proceeds intended to help waterfowl habitats. Only those which differ from the regular stamp are listed.

After the period of validity, a number of these stamps were sold at less than face value. This explains the low values on stamps such as Montana Nos. 30, 33, and Flathead Indian Reservation Nos. 2-10.

When used, most stamps are affixed to licenses and signed by the hunter. Values for used stamps are for copies off licenses and without tabs. Although used examples may be extremely scarce, they will always sell for somewhat less than unused examples (two-thirds of the unused value would be the upper limit).

ALABAMA

Printed in sheets of 10.
Stamps are numbered serially.

Catalogue values for all unused stamps in this section are for Never Hinged items.

Artists: Barbara Keel, #1; Wayne Spradley, #2; Jack Deloney, #3; Joe Michelet, #4; John Lee, #5; William Morris, #6, 14; Larry Martin, #7; Danny W. Dorning, #8; Robert C. Knutson, #9, 16, 20; John Warr, #10; Elaine Byrd, #11; Steven Garst, #12; Larry Chandler, #13, 24; James Brantley, #15; Neil Blackwell, #17; Judith Huey, #18; E. Hatcher, #19; Eddie LeRoy, #21; David Sellers, #22; H. Andrew McNeely, #23.

1979-2002

No.	Description	Unused	Used
1	$5 Wood ducks, rouletted	10.00	3.00
2	$5 Mallards, *1980*	10.00	3.00
3	$5 Canada geese, *1981*	10.00	3.00
4	$5 Green-winged teal, *1982*	10.00	3.00
5	$5 Widgeons, *1983*	10.00	3.00
6	$5 Buffleheads, *1984*	10.00	3.00
7	$5 Wood ducks, *1985*	13.00	3.00
8	$5 Canada geese, *1986*	13.00	3.00
9	$5 Pintails, *1987*	13.00	3.00
10	$5 Canvasbacks, *1988*	10.00	3.00
11	$5 Hooded mergansers, *1989*	12.00	3.00
12	$5 Wood ducks, *1990*	10.00	2.50
13	$5 Redheads, *1991*	10.00	2.50
14	$5 Cinnamon teal, *1992*	10.00	2.50
15	$5 Green-winged teal, *1993*	10.00	2.50
16	$5 Canvasbacks, *1994*	10.00	2.50
17	$5 Canada geese, *1995*	10.00	2.50
18	$5 Wood ducks, *1996*	10.00	2.50
19	$5 Snow goose, *1997*	10.00	2.50
20	$5 Barrow's goldeneye, *1998*	10.00	2.50
21	$5 Redheads, *1999*	9.00	2.50
22	$5 Buffleheads, *2000*	9.00	2.50
23	$5 Ruddy duck, *2001*	9.00	2.50
24	$5 Pintail, *2002*	8.00	2.50

ALASKA

Printed in sheets of 30.
Stamps are numbered serially on reverse. Booklet pane stamps printed in panes of 5.

Catalogue values for all unused stamps in this section are for Never Hinged items.

Artist: Daniel Smith, #1; James Meger, #2; Carl Branson, #3; Jim Beaudoin, #4; Richard Timm, #5; Louis Frisino, #6; Ronald Louque, #7; Fred Thomas, #8; Ed Tussey, #9; George Lockwood, #10, 13; Cynthia Fisher, #11; Wilhelm Goebel, #12; Robert Steiner, #14, 18; Sherrie Russell Meline, #15; Adam Grimm, #16; Greg Alexander, #17.

1985-2002

No.	Description	Unused	Used
1	$5 Emperor geese	10.00	3.00
2	$5 Steller's eiders, *1986*	10.00	3.00
3	$5 Spectacled eiders, perforated, *1987*	10.00	
a.	Bklt. single, rouletted, with tab	10.00	2.50
4	$5 Trumpeter swans, perforated, *1988*	10.00	
a.	Bklt. single, rouletted, with tab	10.00	2.50
5	$5 Barrow's goldeneyes, perforated, *1989*	8.50	
a.	Bklt. single, rouletted, with tab	10.00	2.50
b.	Governor's edition	*125.00*	

No. 5b was sold in full panes through a sealed bid auction.

No.	Description	Unused	Used
6	$5 Old squaws, perforated, *1990*	8.50	
a.	Bklt. single, rouletted, with tab	9.50	2.50
7	$5 Snow geese, perforated, *1991*	8.25	
a.	Bklt. single, rouletted, with tab	9.50	2.50
8	$5 Canvasbacks, perforated, *1992*	8.25	
a.	Bklt. single, rouletted, with tab	9.00	2.50
9	$5 Tule white front geese, perforated, *1993*	8.25	
a.	Bklt. single, rouletted, with tab	9.00	2.50
10	$5 Harlequin ducks, perforated, *1994*	10.00	
a.	Bklt. single, rouletted, with tab	9.00	2.50
b.	Governor's edition	*90.00*	
11	$5 Pacific brant, perforated, *1995*	10.00	
a.	Bklt. single, rouletted, with tab	8.50	2.50
12	$5 Canada geese, *1996*	10.00	
a.	Bklt. single, rouletted, with tab	9.00	2.50
13	$5 King eiders, *1997*	10.00	
a.	Bklt. single, rouletted, with tab	8.50	2.50
14	$5 Barrow's goldeneye, *1998*	8.25	
a.	Bklt. single, with tab	8.50	2.50
15	$5 Pintail, *1999*	8.00	
a.	Bklt. single, with tab	8.50	2.50
16	$5 Common eider, *2000*	8.00	
a.	Bklt. single, with tab	8.50	2.50
17	$5 American wigeon, *2001*	8.00	
a.	Bklt. single, with tab	8.50	2.50
18	$5 Black scoters, *2002*	7.50	
a.	Bklt. single, with tab	8.50	2.50

ARIZONA

Printed in booklet panes of 5 with tab and in sheets of 30.
Stamps are numbered serially.

Catalogue values for all unused stamps in this section are for Never Hinged items.

Artists: Daniel Smith, #1; Sherrie Russell Meline, #2, 6-7, 9, 11-16; Robert Steiner, #3; Ted Blaylock, #4; Brian Jarvi, #5; Harry Adamson, #8, Larry Hayden, #10.

1987-2002

No.	Description	Unused	Used
1	$5.50 Pintails, perf. 4 sides	11.00	
a.	Bklt. single, perf. 3 sides, with tab	11.00	3.00
2	$5.50 Green-winged teal, perf. 4 sides, *1988*	11.00	
a.	Bklt. single, perf. 3 sides, with tab	11.00	3.00
3	$5.50 Cinnamon teal, perf. 4 sides, *1989*	11.00	
a.	Bklt. single, perf. 3 sides, with tab	11.00	2.50
b.	$5.50 +$50 Governor's edition	65.00	
4	$5.50 Canada geese, perf. 4 sides, *1990*	11.00	
a.	Bklt. single, perf. 3 sides, with tab	11.00	2.50
b.	$5.50 +$50 Governor's edition	72.50	
5	$5.50 Blue-winged teal, perf. 4 sides, *1991*	8.00	
a.	Bklt. single, perf. 3 sides, with tab	11.00	2.50
b.	$55.50 Governor's edition	72.50	
6	$5.50 Buffleheads, perf. 4 sides, *1992*	8.00	
a.	Bklt. single, perf. 3 sides, with tab	11.00	2.50
b.	$55.50 Governor's edition	72.50	
7	$5.50 Mexican ducks, perf. 4 sides, *1993*	8.00	
a.	Bklt. single, perf. 3 sides, with tab	9.00	2.50
b.	$55.50 Governor's edition	72.50	
8	$5.50 Mallards, perf. 4 sides, *1994*	8.00	
a.	Bklt. single, perf. 3 sides, with tab	9.00	2.50
b.	$55.50 Governor's edition	72.50	
9	$5.50 Widgeon, perf. 4 sides, *1995*	8.00	
a.	Bklt. single, perf. 3 sides, with tab	9.00	2.50
b.	$55.50 Governor's edition	72.50	
10	$5.50 Canvasbacks, perf. 4 sides, *1996*	8.00	
a.	Bklt. single, perf 3 sides, with tab	9.00	2.50
b.	$55.50 Governor's edition	75.00	
11	$5.50 Gadwalls, *1997*	8.00	
a.	Bklt. single, perf 3 sides, with tab	9.00	2.50
b.	$55.50 Governor's edition	75.00	
12	$5.50 Wood duck, *1998*	8.00	
a.	Bklt. single, perf 3 sides, with tab	9.00	2.50
b.	$55.50 Governor's edition	75.00	
13	$5.50 Snow goose, *1999*	7.50	
a.	Blkt. single, perf. 3 sides, with tab	8.50	2.50
b.	$55.50 Governor's edition	75.00	
14	$7.50 Ruddy duck, *2000*	10.50	
a.	Bklt. single, perf. 3 sides, with tab	10.50	2.50
b.	$55.50 Governor's edition	75.00	
15	$7.50 Redheads, *2001*	10.50	
a.	Bklt. single, perf. 3 sides, with tab	10.50	2.50
16	$7.50 Ring-necked ducks, *2002*	9.50	
a.	Bklt. single, perf. 2 sides, with tabs	10.50	2.50

ARKANSAS

Imperforate varieties of these stamps exist in large quantities. Imperforate copies of Nos. 1 and 2 were sold by the state for $1 each.

No. 1 printed in sheets and booklet panes of 30, others in sheets and booklet panes of 10.

Stamps are numbered serially on reverse.

Catalogue values for all unused stamps in this section are for Never Hinged items.

Artists: Lee LeBlanc, #1; Maynard Reece, #2, 8; David Maass, #3, 10, 21; Larry Hayden, #4, 15; Ken Carlson, #5, 13; John P. Cowan, #6; Robert Bateman. #7; Phillip Crowe, #9, 16, 22; Daniel Smith, #11, 14; Jim Hautman, #12, 19; L. Chandler, #17, 20; John Dearman, #18.

1981-2002

1	$5.50 Mallards	45.00	12.00
	Booklet single with top tab, Nos. 110,001-200,000 on back	50.00	
2	$5.50 Wood ducks, *1982*	37.50	9.00
3	$5.50 Green-winged teal, *1983*	55.00	12.00
4	$5.50 Pintails, *1984*	22.50	5.00
5	$5.50 Mallards, *1985*	13.00	2.50
6	$5.50 Black swamp mallards, *1986*	11.00	2.50
7	$7 Wood ducks, *1987*	11.00	2.50

Stamps like Nos. 7 and 8 with $5.50 face values were sold following an order of the state Supreme Court restoring the fee level of 1986. The stamps were sold after the 1988 season had ended. Value, $11 each.

8	$7 Pintails, *1988*	10.00	2.50

See footnote following No. 7.

9	$7 Mallards, *1989*	10.00	2.50
10	$7 Black ducks & mallards, *1990*	10.00	2.50
11	$7 Sulphur river widgeons, *1991*	10.00	2.50
12	$7 Shirey Bay shovelers, *1992*	10.00	2.50
13	$7 Grand prairie mallards, *1993*	10.00	2.50
14	$7 Canada goose, *1994*	10.00	2.50
15	$7 White River mallards, *1995*	10.00	2.50
16	$7 Mallards, black labrador, *1996*	10.00	2.00
17	$7 Labrador retriever, mallards, *1997*	10.00	2.00
18	$7 Labrador retriever, mallards, *1998*	10.00	2.00
19	$7 Wood duck, *1999*	10.00	2.00
20	$7 Mallards and golden retriever, *2000*	10.00	2.00
21	$7 Canvasbacks, *2001*	10.00	2.00
22	$7 Mallards, *2002*	9.00	2.00

CALIFORNIA

Honey Lake Waterfowl Stamps

Required to hunt waterfowl at Honey Lake. Valid for a full season. Stamps are rouletted. Used values are for signed copies. Unsigned stamps without gum probably were used. Values for these stamps are higher than used values, but lower than values shown for gummed unused stamps.

1956-86

A1	$5 black, *1956-1957*		—
A2	$5 black, *blue green, 1957-1958*		—
A3	$5 black, *dark yellow, 1958-1959*		—
A4	$5 black, *dark yellow, 1959-1960*	*1,250.*	*500.00*
A5	$5 black, *1960-1961*		*1,100.*
A6	$5 black, *bluish green, 1961-1962*	—	*1,000.*
A7	$5 black, *dark yellow, 1962-1963*		*550.00*
A8	$5 black, *1963-1964*		*375.00*
A9	$6.50 black, *pink, 1964-1965*	*1,500.*	*350.00*
A10	$6.50 black, *1965-1966*		*300.00*
A11	$6.50 black, *yellow,* Nos. 1-700, printer's information at bottom right, *1966-1967*		*325.00*
a.	Serial Nos. 701-1050, no printer's information		*5,500.*
A12	$10 black, *pink, 1967-1968*	—	*300.00*
A13	$10 black, *blue, 1968-1969*		*375.00*
A14	$10 black, *green, 1969-1970*	—	*400.00*
A15	$15 black, *dark yellow, 1970-1971*	—	*475.00*
A16	$15 black, *pink, 1971-1972*		*1,500.*
A17	$15 black, *blue, 1972-1973*		*1,950.*
A18	$15 black, *blue, 1973-1974*	—	—
A19	$15 black, *pink, 1974-1975*	50.00	*25.00*
A20	$15 black, *green, 1975-1976*	*150.00*	*35.00*
A21	$15 black, *light yellow, 1976-1977*	*150.00*	*35.00*
A22	$20 black, *blue, 1977-1978*	*150.00*	*35.00*
A23	$20 blk, *light yel brown, 1978-1979*	*150.00*	*35.00*
A24	$20 black, *light yellow, 1979-1980*	*150.00*	*35.00*
A25	$15 black, *light blue, 1980-1981*	*110.00*	*30.00*
A26	$20 black, *light yellow, 1981-1982*		—
A27	$20 black, *pink, 1982-1983*	*95.00*	*30.00*
A28	$20 black, *light green, 1983-1984*	45.00	*25.00*
A29	$20 black, *dark yellow, 1984-1985*	42.50	*25.00*
A30	$20 black, *light blue, 1985-1986*	37.50	*20.00*

Eighteen $5 black on dark yellow permit stamps were sold for hunting at the state-owned and operated Madeline Plains waterfowl management area for the 1956-57 season. No examples have been recorded.

Statewide Hunting License Validation Stamps

Fees are for resident, junior and non-resident hunters. "No fee" stamps were for disabled veterans. Stamps with special serial numbers for state officials are known for some years. Nos. 2A1-2A3 imperf on 3 sides, rouletted at top. Others die cut.

Stamps are numbered serially.

Used values are for written-upon copies. Starting with No. 2A4, unused values are for stamps on backing paper.

1962-1963

2A1	$4 black	*450.00*	7.00
a.	Ovptd. "NO FEE"	*475.00*	*300.00*
2A2	$1 black, *yellow*	*1,350.*	*75.00*
2A3	$25 black, *green*	*2,500.*	*150.00*

No. 2A25

1963-1964

2A4	$4 black, *green*		3.00
a.	Ovptd. "NO FEE"	—	—
2A5	$1 black, *gray*	—	20.00
2A6	$25 black, *yellow orange*		*300.00*

1964-1965

2A7	$4 black, *pink*	30.00	1.00
a.	Ovptd. "NO FEE"	*550.00*	*275.00*
2A8	$1 black, *yellow brown*	*225.00*	25.00
2A9	$25 black, *dark gray*		*70.00*

1965-1966

2A10	$4 black, *gray*	25.00	1.00
a.	Ovptd. "NO FEE"		—
2A11	$1 black, *yellow gray*		25.00
2A12	$25 black, *ivory*		*75.00*

1966-1967

2A13	$4 black, *salmon*	25.00	1.00
a.	Ovptd. "NO FEE"		*650.00*
2A14	$1 black, *lt blue*	75.00	10.00
2A15	$25 black, *burgundy*		*65.00*

1967-1968

2A16	$4 black, *yellow*	20.00	1.00
a.	Ovptd. "NO FEE"		*600.00*
2A17	$1 black, *green*	45.00	5.00
a.	black, *yellow gray*		—
2A18	$25 black, *brown*	75.00	25.00

1968-1969

2A19	$4 black, *pink*	55.00	1.00
a.	Ovptd. "NO FEE"		*650.00*
2A20	$1 black, *blue gray*	*175.00*	20.00
2A21	$25 black, *light orange*		*85.00*

1969-1970

2A22	$4 black	55.00	1.00
a.	Ovptd. "NO FEE"		*575.00*
2A23	$1 black, *dark pink*	*175.00*	20.00
2A24	$25 black, *light yellow*	70.00	25.00

1970-1971

2A25	$4 black, *manila*	70.00	2.00
a.	Ovptd. "NO FEE"	*1,350.*	*1,000.*
2A26	$1 black, *blue gray*	75.00	10.00
2A27	$25 black, *gray brown*	100.00	25.00

1971-1972

2A28	$4 black, *green*	45.00	1.00
a.	Ovptd. "NO FEE"		*600.00*
b.	Ovptd. "DISABLED VETERANS/NO FEE"		*750.00*
2A29	$1 black, *lavender*		20.00
2A30	$25 black, *peach*	*275.00*	*35.00*

1972-1973

2A31	$6 black, *pink*		1.00
a.	Ovptd. "DISABLED VETERANS/NO FEE"		*750.00*
2A32	$2 black, *light yellow*		30.00
2A33	$35 black, *lavender*	*225.00*	

1973-1974

2A34	$6 black, *blue*		1.00
a.	Ovptd. "DISABLED VETERANS/NO FEE"		*750.00*
2A35	$2 black, *lavender*	*175.00*	20.00
2A36	$35 black, *gray*	*275.00*	*35.00*

1974-1975

2A37	$6 black, *green*	35.00	1.00
a.	Ovptd. "DISABLED VETERANS/NO FEE"		*800.00*
2A38	$2 black, *orange*		20.00
2A39	$35 black, *reddish purple*	175.00	*25.00*

1975-1976

2A40	$10 red brown, *brown*	40.00	1.00
a.	Ovptd. "DISABLED VETERANS/NO FEE"	—	*800.00*
2A41	$2 black, *dark red*	80.00	20.00
2A42	$35 black, *yellow*	85.00	25.00

1976-1977

2A43	$10 black, *blue*	30.00	1.00
a.	Ovptd. "DISABLED VETERANS/NO FEE"		*900.00*
2A44	$2 black, *gray violet*	*100.00*	20.00
a.	Inscibed "Deer Tag No." instead of "Bear Tag No."		—
2A45	$35 black, *lavender*	85.00	25.00

1977-1978

2A46	$10 black, *red orange*	30.00	1.00
a.	Ovptd. "DISABLED VETERANS/NO FEE"		*850.00*
2A47	$2 black, *yellow green*	95.00	25.00
2A48	$35 black, *pink*	*95.00*	

1978-1979

2A49	$10 black, *yellow*	40.00	1.50
a.	Ovptd. "DISABLED VETERANS/NO FEE"		*800.00*
2A50	$2 black, *red*	80.00	20.00
2A51	$35 black, *light brown*	85.00	

1979-1980

2A52	$10 black, *red*	30.00	1.00
a.	Ovptd. "DISABLED VETERANS/NO FEE"		*900.00*
2A53	$2 black, *yellow green*	80.00	20.00
2A54	$35 black, *dark blue*	85.00	

1980-1981

2A55	$10.25 black, *blue*	30.00	1.00
a.	Ovptd. "DISABLED VETERANS/NO FEE"		*1,200.*
2A56	$2 black, *light brown*	75.00	15.00
2A57	$36.25 black, *tan*	75.00	25.00

1981-1982

2A58	$11.50 black, *dark green*	30.00	1.00
2A59	$2.25 black, *blue*	75.00	20.00
2A60	$40 black, *gray*	*200.00*	

1982-1983

2A61	$12.50 black, *pink*	30.00	1.00
2A62	$2.50 black, *brown*	75.00	20.00
2A63	$43.50 black, *orange*	*140.00*	

1983-1984

2A64	$13.25 black, *blue*	50.00	1.00
2A65	$2.75 black, *purple*	*150.00*	20.00
2A66	$46.50 black, *green*	*175.00*	

1984-1985

2A67	$13.25 black, *yellow*	*50.00*	1.00
2A68	$2.75 black, *green*	*150.00*	20.00
2A69	$49.25 black, *brown*	*175.00*	

1985-1986

2A70	$14 black, *blue*	*50.00*	1.00
2A71	$3.50 black, *yellow*	*150.00*	20.00
2A72	$51.75 black, *purple*	*175.00*	

1986-1987

2A73	$18.50 black, *green*		1.00
2A74	$4.50 black, *dark blue*		*15.00*

1987-1988

2A76	$17.50 black, *dark blue*		1.00
2A77	$4.50 black, *purple*		*15.00*

1988-1989

2A79	$19.25 black, *tan*		1.00
2A80	$5 black, *yellow*		*15.00*

1989-1990

2A82	$19.75 black, *blue gray*		1.00
2A83	$5 black, *dark green*		*15.00*

1990-1991

2A85	$21.50 black, *reddish gray*		1.00
2A86	$5.50 black, *yellow*		*15.00*
2A87	$73 black, *pink*		*25.00*

1991-1992

2A88	$23.10 black, *lime green*		*1.00*
2A89	$5.50 black, *bluish purple*		*15.00*
2A90	$79.80 black, *brown*		*25.00*

1992-1993

2A91	$24.15 black, *yellow*	—	1.00
2A92	$5.80 black, *greenish gold*		*15.00*
2A93	$83.75 black, *mauve*	—	*25.00*

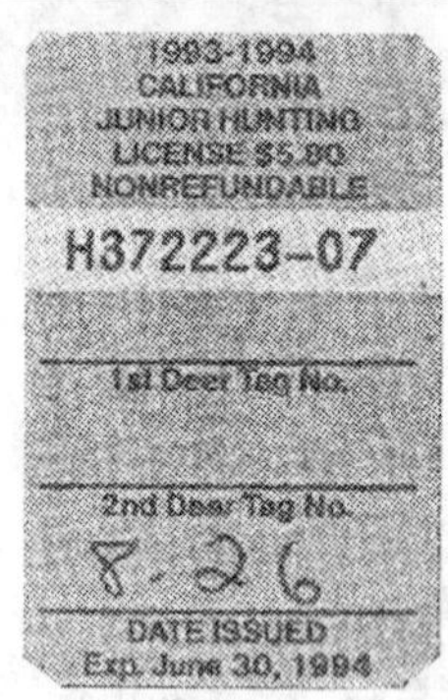

1993-1994

2A94	$24.40 black & white, *green*		1.00
2A95	$5.80 black & white, *light blue*		*15.00*

1994-1995

2A97	$24.95 black & white, *pale yellow*		1.00
2A98	$6.05 black & white, *lavender*		*15.00*
2A99	$86.90 black & white, *gray*		*25.00*

1996-1997

2A100	$25.45 black, *gray brown*		1.00
2A101	$6.30 black, *pink*		*15.00*
2A102	$88.70 black, *pale blue*		*25.00*

Statewide Waterfowl Issues

Nos. 1-24 printed in booklet panes of five, No. 25 in pane of 4.

Issues through 1978 are die cut and self-adhesive. Starting with the 1979 issue, stamps are rouletted. Stamps are numbered serially.

Catalogue values for all unused stamps in this section are for Never Hinged items.

Artists: Paul Johnson, #1-8; Ken Michaelson, #9; Walter Wolfe, #10-11; Robert Steiner, #12, 18-20, 26-33; Robert Richert, #13; Charles Allen, #14; Robert Montanucci, #15; Richard Wilson, #16; Sherrie Russell Meline, #17, 23; Ronald Louque, #21; Larry Hayden, #22; Richard Clifton, #24-25.

1971-2002

1	$1 Pintails	600.00	65.00
2	$1 Canvasbacks, *1972*	2,000.	150.00
3	$1 Mallards, *1973*	13.50	2.50
4	$1 White-fronted geese, *1974*	3.00	2.50
5	$1 Green-winged teal, backing paper with red wavy lines, *1975*	35.00	8.00
	Waxy backing paper without lines	140.00	

The gum bleeds through the stamp with red wavy lines resulting in a spotted or blotchy effect. Little or no gum bleeds through on stamps with waxy backing paper.

6	$1 Widgeons, *1976*	20.00	2.50
7	$1 Cinnamon teal, *1977*	45.00	9.00
8	$5 Cinnamon teal, *1978*	9.00	2.50
9	$5 Hooded mergansers, *1978*	100.00	15.00
10	$5 Wood ducks, *1979*	8.00	2.50
11	$5 Pintails, *1980*	8.00	2.50
12	$5 Canvasabacks, *1981*	9.00	2.50
13	$5 Widgeons, *1982*	9.00	2.50
14	$5 Green-winged teal, *1983*	9.00	2.50
15	$7.50 Mallard decoy, *1984*	11.00	2.50
16	$7.50 Ring-necked ducks, *1985*	11.00	2.50
17	$7.50 Canada goose, *1986*	11.00	3.00
18	$7.50 Redheads, *1987*	11.00	3.00
19	$7.50 Mallards, *1988*	11.00	3.00
20	$7.50 Cinnamon teal, *1989*	11.00	3.00
21	$7.50 Canada goose, *1990*	11.00	3.00
22	$7.50 Gadwalls, *1991*	11.00	3.00
23	$7.90 White-fronted goose, *1992*	11.00	3.00
24	$10.50 Pintails, *1993*	13.00	4.00

Rouletted Horiz.

25	$10.50 Wood duck, *1994*	13.00	4.00

Perf. Vertically

Birds in flight, denomination at: b, UL. c, UR. d, LL. e, LR.

26	$10.50 Snow geese, booklet pane of 4, #b.-e., *1995*	60.00	
a.	Souvenir sheet of 4, #b.-e. (decorative border)	*125.00*	
b.-e.	Booklet single, each	14.00	4.00

Stamps in No. 26a are perfed on all four sides.

Perf. Horizontally

27	$10.50 Mallards, *1996*	13.00	2.50

Issued in panes of 4.

28	$10.50 Pintails, *1997*	13.00	2.50
29	$10.50 Green-winged teal, pair, *1998*	28.00	
a.-b.	a, Female, b, Male, each	14.00	2.50

No. 29 issued in strips of 4 stamps.

30	$10.50 Wood duck, pair, *1999*	26.00	
a.-b.	a, Male, b, Male and female, each	13.00	2.50

No. 30 issued in strips of 2 pairs.

31	$10.50 Canada geese, mallard, widgeon *2000*	26.00	2.50
32	$10.50 Canvasbacks, *2001*	26.00	2.50
33	$10.50 Pintails, *2002*	26.00	2.50

COLORADO

North Central Goose Stamp

Used in an area extending from Ft. Collins to approximately 50 miles east of the city.

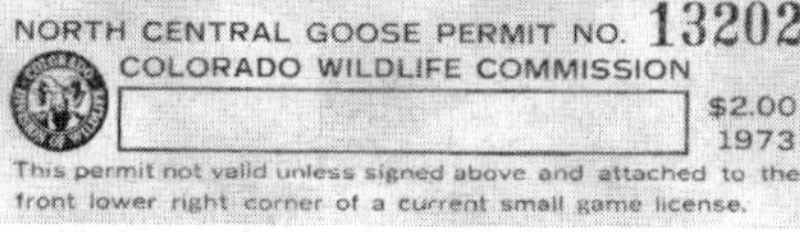

Illustration reduced.

1973

A1	$2 black	—	—

No. A1 is die cut and self-adhesive. Unused copies have glassine backing.

Statewide Issues

Printed in booklet panes of 5 and panes of 30. Stamps are numbered serially.

Imperforate varieties of these stamps are printer's proofs.

Catalogue values for all unused stamps in this section are for Never Hinged items.

Artists: Robert Steiner, #1-2; Charles Allen, #3; Dan Andrews, #4; Sarah Woods, #5; Cynthie Fisher, #6, 9-13; Bill Border, #7; Gerald G. Putt, #8.

1990-2002

1	$5 Canada geese	12.00	
	Bklt. single, with tab, Nos. 80,001-150,000	12.50	3.00
a.	$5 +$50 Governor's edition	60.00	
2	$5 Mallards, *1991*	16.00	
	Bklt. single, with tab, Nos. 80,001-150,000	16.00	3.00
a.	$5 +$50 Governor's edition	60.00	
3	$5 Pintails, *1992*	8.50	
	Bklt. single, with tab, Nos. 80,001-150,000	9.00	3.00
a.	$5 +$50 Governor's edition	60.00	
4	$5 Green-winged teal, *1993*	8.50	
	Bklt. single, with tab, Nos. 80,001-150,000	9.50	3.00
a.	$5 +$50 Governor's edition	60.00	
5	$5 Wood ducks, *1994*	8.50	
	Bklt. single, with tab	9.00	2.50
6	$5 Buffleheads, *1995*	8.00	
	Bklt. single, with tab	9.00	2.50
7	$5 Cinnamon teal, *1996*	8.00	
	Bklt. single, with tab and top selvage	9.00	2.50
8	$5 Widgeons, gold text, *1997*	8.00	
a.	Bklt. single, with tab and top selvage, text in black & white	8.50	2.50
9	$5 Redheads, *1998*	8.00	
	Bklt. single, with tab and top selvage	8.50	2.50

10	$5 Blue-winged teal, *1999*	7.50	
a.	Blkt. single, with tab and top selvage	8.00	2.50
11	$5 Gadwalls, *2000*	7.50	
a.	Bklt. single, with tab and top selvage	8.00	2.50
12	$5 Ruddy ducks, *2001*	7.50	
13	$5 Common goldeneyes, *2002*	7.50	

CONNECTICUT

Printed in booklet panes of 10 and sheets of 30.
Stamps are numbered serially.
Imperforate varieties are proofs.

Catalogue values for all unused stamps in this section are for Never Hinged items.

Artists: Thomas Hirata, #1; Robert Leslie, #2, 9; Phillip Crowe, #3; Keith Mueller, #4, 7; Robert Steiner, #5; Joe Hautman, #6; George Lockwood, #8; Robert Richert, #13.

1993-2002

1	$5 Black ducks	10.00	3.00
	Booklet pane pair with L & R selvage, Nos. 51,001-81,000	17.00	
a.	Sheet of 4	70.00	
b.	$5 +$50 Governor's edition	75.00	
2	$5 Canvasbacks, *1994*	10.00	3.00
	Booklet pair with L & R selvage, Nos. 53,000-up	17.00	
a.	Sheet of 4	42.50	
3	$5 Mallards, *1995*	10.00	3.00
	Booklet pair with L & R selvage	17.00	
4	$5 Old squaw ducks, *1996*	10.00	3.00
	Booklet pair with L & R selvage	17.00	
5	$5 Green-winged teal, *1997*	10.00	3.00
a.	$5 +$50 Governor's edition	*150.00*	
6	$5 Mallards, *1998*	10.00	3.00
7	$5 Canada geese, *1999*	10.00	3.00
a.	$5 +$50 Governor's edition	*400.00*	
8	$5 Wood duck, *2000*	9.00	3.00
a.	$5 +$50 Governor's edition	*425.00*	
9	$5 Buffleheads, *2001*	9.00	3.00
10	$5 Greater scaups, *2002*	8.00	3.00
a.	$5 +$50 Governor's edition	60.00	

DELAWARE

Printed in sheets of 10.
Starting in 1991, a portion of the printing is numbered serially on the reverse.

Catalogue values for all unused stamps in this section are for Never Hinged items.

Artists: Ned Mayne, #1; Charles Rowe, #2; Lois Butler, #3; John Green, #4; Nolan Haan, #5; Don Breyfogle, #6; Robert Leslie, #7, 10; Bruce Langton, #8; Jim Hautman, #9; Francis Sweet, #11; Ronald Louque, #12; Richard Clifton, #13, 17, 19; Robert Metropulos, #14; Louis Frisino, #15; Michael Ashman, #16, 21; Jeffrey Klinefelter, #18; Russ Duerksen, #20; Brian Blight, #22; George Lockwood, #23.

1980-2002

1	$5 Black ducks	85.00	20.00
2	$5 Snow geese, *1981*	70.00	20.00
3	$5 Canada geese, *1982*	70.00	20.00
4	$5 Canvasbacks, *1983*	30.00	10.00
5	$5 Mallards, *1984*	15.00	5.00
6	$5 Pintail, *1985*	12.00	3.00
7	$5 Widgeons, *1986*	11.00	3.00
8	$5 Redheads, *1987*	11.00	3.00
9	$5 Wood ducks, *1988*	9.00	3.00
10	$5 Buffleheads, *1989*	9.00	3.00
11	$5 Green-winged teal, *1990*	9.00	3.00
a.	$5 +$50 Governor's edition	85.00	
12	$5 Hooded merganser, no serial number on reverse, *1991*	9.00	
	With serial number on reverse	11.00	3.00
13	$5 Blue-winged teal, no serial number on reverse, *1992*	8.00	
	With serial number on reverse	9.00	2.50
14	$5 Goldeneye, no serial number on reverse, *1993*	8.00	
	With serial number on reverse	9.00	2.50
15	$5 Blue goose, no serial number on reverse, *1994*	8.00	
	With serial number on reverse	9.00	2.50
16	($6) Scaup, no serial number on reverse, *1995*	8.00	
	With serial number on reverse	9.00	2.50
17	$6 Gadwall, no serial number on reverse, *1996*	8.00	
	With serial number on reverse	9.00	2.50
18	$6 White-winged scoter, no serial number on reverse, *1997*	8.00	
	With serial number on reverse	9.00	2.50
19	$6 Blue-winged teal, *1998*	8.00	2.50
20	$6 Tundra swan, *1999*	8.00	
21	$6 American brant, *2000*	8.00	2.50
22	$6 Oldsquaw, *2001*	8.00	2.50
23	$6 Ruddy ducks, *2002*	8.00	2.50

FLORIDA

#1-7 issued in booklet panes of 5. Nos. 8-19 in sheets of 10. No. 20 in sheet of 12.
Stamps are numbered serially and rouletted. Serial numbers for stamps with survey tabs attached end in -04.

Catalogue values for all unused stamps in this section are for Never Hinged items.

Illustration reduced.

Artists: Bob Binks, #1, 7; Ernest Simmons, #2; Clark Sullivan, #3; Lee Cable, #4; Heiner Hertling, #5; John Taylor, #6; Robert Steiner, #8; Ronald Louque, #9-10; J. Byron Test, #11; Ben Test, #12; Richard Hansen, #13; Richard Clifton, #14; John Mogus, #15; Antonie Rossini, #16; Kenneth Nanney, #17; Wally Makuchal, #18; M. Frase, #19; Brian Blight, #20; John Harris, #21, 23; Jeffrey Klinefelter, #22; John Nelson Harris, #24.

1979-2002

1	$3.25 Green-winged teal	150.00	20.00
	With tab	175.00	
2	$3.25 Pintails, *1980*	15.00	5.00
	With tab	20.00	

3	$3.25 Widgeon, *1981*	15.00	5.00
	With tab	24.00	
4	$3.25 Ring-necked ducks, *1982*	20.00	5.00
	With tab	25.00	
5	$3.25 Buffleheads, *1983*	40.00	5.00
	With tab	45.00	
6	$3.25 Hooded merganser, *1984*	11.00	3.50
	With tab	17.50	
7	$3.25 Wood ducks, *1985*	11.00	3.50
	With tab	12.00	
8	$3 Canvasbacks, *1986*	10.00	3.50
	With small tab at top	10.00	
	With larger survey tab at side and small tab at top	17.50	
9	$3.50 Mallards, *1987*	9.00	3.50
	With small tab at top	9.00	
	With larger survey tab at side and small tab at top	15.00	
10	$3.50 Redheads, *1988*	9.00	2.50
	With small tab at top	9.00	
	With larger survey tab at side and small tab at top	15.00	
11	$3.50 Blue-winged teal, *1989*	7.50	2.50
	With small tab at top	7.50	
	With larger survey tab at side and small tab at top	15.00	
12	$3.50 Wood ducks, *1990*	7.50	2.50
	With small tab at top	7.50	
	With larger survey tab at side and small tab at top	15.00	
13	$3.50 Northern Pintails, *1991*	7.00	2.50
	With small tab at top	7.00	
	With larger survey tab at side and small tab at top	15.00	
14	$3.50 Ruddy duck, *1992*	7.00	2.50
	With small tab at top	7.00	
	With larger survey tab at side and small tab at top	12.00	
15	$3.50 American widgeon, *1993*	6.00	2.50
	With small tab at top	6.00	
	With larger survey tab at side and small tab at top	12.00	
16	$3.50 Mottled duck, *1994*	6.00	2.50
	With small tab at top	6.00	
	With larger survey tab at side and small tab at top	12.00	
17	$3.50 Fulvous whistling duck, *1995*	6.00	2.50
	With small tab at top	6.00	
	With larger survey tab at side and small tab at top	12.00	
18	$3.50 Goldeneyes, *1996*	6.00	2.50
	With small tab at top	6.00	
	With larger survey tab at side and small tab at top	12.00	
19	($3.00) Hooded merganser, *1997*	6.00	2.50
	With small tab at top	6.00	
	With larger survey tab at side and small tab at top	12.00	

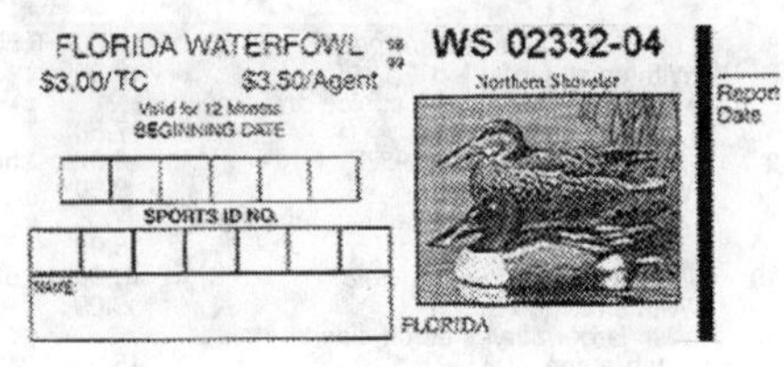

Self-Adhesive

20	$3 Shoveler, *1998*	12.00	2.50

Sold for $3.50 through agents.

21	$3 Pintail, *1999*	6.00	2.50

Sold for $3.50 through agents.

22	$3 Ring-necked duck, *2000*	6.00	2.50

Sold for $3.50 through agents.

23	$3 Canvasback, *2001*	6.00	2.50

Sold for $3.50 through agents.

24	$3 Mottled duck, *2002*	6.00	2.50

Sold for $3.50 through agents. No. 24 with rouletting and with duck facing right come from a special limited reprinting demanded by the artist to correct the appearance of his work.

GEORGIA

Not required to hunt waterfowl until 1989.
Nos. 1-4 printed in sheets of 30, others in sheets of 20.
Starting with No 5, stamps are numbered serially.

Catalogue values for all unused stamps in this section are for Never Hinged items.

Artists: Daniel Smith, #1; Jim Killen, #2, 14; James Partee, Jr., #3; Paul Bridgeford, #4; Ralph J. McDonald, #5; Guy Coheleach, #6; Phillip Crowe, #7-8, 11; Jerry Raedeke, #9, 13, 15; Herb Booth, #10; David Lanier, #12.

1985-99

1	$5.50 Wood ducks	15.00	
2	$5.50 Mallards, *1986*	8.50	
3	$5.50 Canada geese, *1987*	7.50	
4	$5.50 Ring-necked ducks, *1988*	8.00	
5	$5.50 Duckling & golden retriever puppy, *1989*	13.00	2.50
6	$5.50 Wood ducks, *1990*	8.00	2.50
7	$5.50 Green-winged teal, *1991*	8.00	2.50
8	$5.50 Buffleheads, *1992*	8.00	2.50
9	$5.50 Mallards, *1993*	8.00	2.50
10	$5.50 Ring-necked ducks, *1994*	11.00	2.50
11	$5.50 Widgeons, Labrador retreiver, *1995*	11.00	2.50
12	$5.50 Black ducks, *1996*	11.00	2.50
13	$5.50 Lesser scaup, Cockspur Island lighthouse, *1997*	11.00	2.50
14	$5.50 Labrador retreiver, ring-necked ducks, *1998*	10.00	2.50
15	$5.50 Pintails, *1999*	8.00	2.50

HAWAII

Required for the hunting of small game. Hunting birds is illegal in Hawaii.

Artists: Patrick Ching, #1, D. Van Zyle, #2; Michael Furuya, #3; Norman Nagai, #4, 7; Marion Berger, #5; Daniel Wang, #6.

1996-2002

1	$50Nene goose	10.00	
a.	$5 +$50 Governor's edition	75.00	
b.	As No. 1, sheet of 4	45.00	

No. 1b exists imperf.

2	$5 Hawaiian duck, *1997*	10.00	
	With tab	10.00	
a.	As No. 2, sheet of 4	45.00	

No. 2a exists imperf.

3	$5 Wild turkey, *1998*	10.00	
	With tab	10.00	
4	$5 Ring-necked pheasant, *1999*	9.00	
	With tab	9.00	
5	$5 Erckel's francolin, *2000*	8.00	
	With tab	8.00	
6	$5 Green pheasant, *2001*	7.50	
	With tab	7.50	2.50
7	$10Chukar partridge, *2002*	15.00	
	With tab	15.00	2.50

IDAHO

Printed in booklet panes of 5 and sheets of 30, except No. 5, which was issued in booklets of 10. Numbered serially except for No. 11.

Catalogue values for all unused stamps in this section are for Never Hinged items.

Artists: Robert Leslie, #1; Jim Killen, #2; Daniel Smith, #3; Francis E. Sweet, #4, Richard Clifton, #6, 11; Richard Plasschaert, #7; Sherrie Russell Meline, #8; Bill Moore, #9; David Gressard, #10; T. Smith, #12; Maynard Reece, #13.

1987-98

1	$5.50 Cinnamon teal, perforated	14.00	
a.	Bklt. single, rouletted, with 2-part tab	11.00	3.00
2	$5.50 Green-winged teal, perforated, *1988*	13.00	
a.	Bklt. single, rouletted, with 2-part tab	11.00	3.00
3	$6 Blue-winged teal, perforated, *1989*	10.00	
a.	Bklt. single, rouletted, with 2-part tab	10.00	3.00
4	$6 Trumpeter swans, perforated, *1990*	15.00	
a.	Bklt. single, rouletted, with 2-part tab	12.00	3.00

Die cut self-adhesive

5	$6 green, *1991*	140.00	*35.00*

No. 5 was used provisionally in 1991 when the regular stamps were delayed. Unused value is for stamp, remittance tab and selvage pieces on backing paper.

Designs like No. 1

6	$6 Widgeons, perforated, *1991*	8.50	
a.	Bklt. single, rouletted, with 2-part tab	9.50	2.50
7	$6 Canada geese, perforated, *1992*	10.00	
a.	Bklt. single, rouletted, with 2-part tab	9.50	2.50
8	A00 $6.00 Common goldeneye, perforated, *1993*	10.00	
a.	Bklt. single, rouletted, with 2-part tab	9.50	2.50
9	$6 Harlequin ducks, perforated, *1994*	10.00	
a.	Bklt. single, rouletted, with 2-part tab	9.50	2.50
10	$6 Wood ducks, perforated, *1995*	10.00	
a.	Bklt. single, rouletted, with 2-part tab	8.50	2.50
11	$6.50 Mallard, *1996*	10.00	2.50
12	$6.50 Shovelers, *1997*	10.00	2.50
13	$6.50 Canada geese, *1998*	9.00	2.50

ILLINOIS

Daily Usage Stamps for State-operated Waterfowl Areas.

Date and fee overprinted in black. $2 and $3 stamps were for hunting ducks, $5 stamps for hunting geese and pheasants. 1953-58 had separate pheasant stamps. No duck stamp was printed in 1971.
Some unused stamps have dry gum.
Used stamps have no gum or have staple holes.
Black printing.
Stamps are numbered serially.

1953-1972

A1	$2 orange, *blue*	—	—
A4	$2 green, *manila, 1956*	*9,500.*	*6,500.*
A5	$2 orange, *light blue green, 1957*	*950.*	*500.*
A6	$2 green, *manila, 1958*	*850.*	*400.*
A7	$3 green, *manila, 1959*	*775.*	*375.*
A8	$5 red brown, *light blue green, 1959*	*775.*	*375.*
A9	$3 red brown, *light blue green, 1960*	*775.*	*375.*
A10	$5 green, *manila, 1960*	*775.*	*375.*
A11	$3 green, *manila, 1961*	*775.*	*375.*
A12	$5 red brown, *light blue green, 1961*	*775.*	*375.*
A15	$3 green, *manila, 1962*	*775.*	*375.*
A14	$5 red brown, *light blue green, 1962*	*775.*	*375.*
A15	$3 orange, *light blue green, 1963*	*775.*	*375.*
A16	$5 green, *manila, 1963*	*775.*	*375.*
A17	$3 green, *manila, 1964*	*775.*	*375.*
A18	$5 red, *light blue green, 1964*	*775.*	*375.*
A19	$3 orange, *light blue green, 1965*	*775.*	*375.*
A20	$5 green, *manila, 1965*	*775.*	*375.*
A21	$3 green, *manila, 1966*	*775.*	*375.*
A22	$5 orange, *light blue green, 1966*	*775.*	*375.*
A23	$3 orange, *light blue green, 1967*	*775.*	*375.*
A24	$5 green, *yellow, 1967*	*775.*	*375.*
A25	$3 green, *yellow, 1968*	*775.*	*375.*
A26	$5 orange, *light blue, 1968*	*775.*	*375.*
A27	$3 orange, *light blue, 1969*	*775.*	*375.*
A28	$5 green, *manila, 1969*	*775.*	*375.*
A29	$3 green, *manila, 1970*	*1,250.*	*800.*
A30	$5 orange, *light blue, 1970*	*1,350.*	*800.*
A31	$5 green, *manila, 1971*	*1,650.*	*900.*
A32	$3 orange, *light blue green, 1972*	*3,750.*	
A33	$5 orange, *light blue green, 1972*	*3,750.*	

Catalogue values for unused stamps in this section, from this point to the end, are for Never Hinged items.

No. A34

No. A35

1977-91(?)

No.	Description	Unused	Used
A34	black, *light blue*, duck, *1991*	—	—
A35	black, *manila*, goose	—	—

Nos. A34-A35 do not show year or denomination and were used until 1994. No. A34 used before 1991 should exist but has not been reported yet. Separate pheasant and controlled quail and pheasant stamps of a similar design have also been used.

No. A36

No. A37

1996

No.	Description	Unused	Used
A36	black, *light blue*, duck	—	—
A37	black, *manila*, goose	—	—

Nos. A36-A37 do not show year or denomination.

Statewide Issues

Nos. 1-10 in sheets of 10. Starting with No. 11, in booklet panes of 5; starting with No. 22, in panes of 10.

Stamps are numbered serially and rouletted.

Catalogue values for all unused stamps in this section are for Never Hinged items.

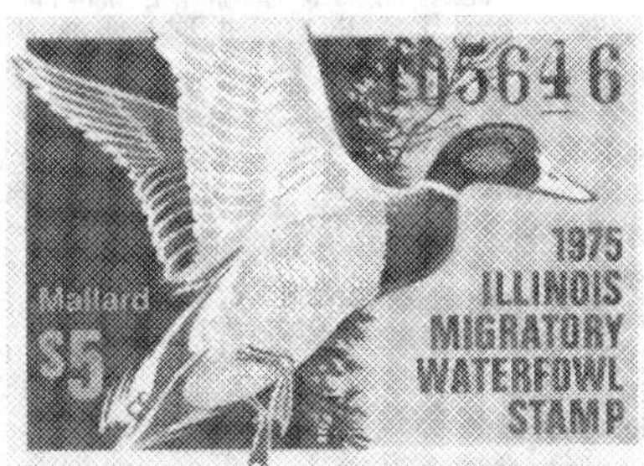

Artists: Robert Eschenfeldt, #1; Robert G. Larson, #2; Richard Lynch, #3; Everett Staffeldt, #4; John Eggert, #5; Bart Kassabaum, #6, 9, 11, 13; Jim Trindel, #7; Arthur Sinden, #8, 12, 14; George Kieffer, #10; Charles McKay Freeman, #15; John Henson, #16; Phillip Crowe, #17-21; Thomas Hirata, #22-24; Jim Killen, #25-28.

1975-2002

No.	Description	Unused	Used
1	$5 Mallard	*475.00*	85.00
2	$5 Wood ducks, *1976*	*225.00*	50.00
3	$5 Canada goose, *1977*	150.00	35.00
4	$5 Canvasbacks, *1978*	110.00	22.50
5	$5 Pintail, *1979*	100.00	16.00
6	$5 Green-winged teal, *1980*	100.00	16.00
7	$5 Widgeons, *1981*	100.00	16.00
a.	"Green-winged teal"	*375.00*	
8	$5 Black ducks, *1982*	60.00	12.50
9	$5 Lesser scaup, *1983*	45.00	10.00
10	$5 Blue-winged teal, *1984*	45.00	10.00
11	$5 Redheads, *1985*	15.00	3.00
	With 2-part tab	22.50	
12	$5 Gadwalls, *1986*	12.00	3.00
	With 2-part tab	14.00	
13	$5 Buffleheads, *1987*	11.00	3.00
	With 2-part tab	13.00	
14	$5 Common goldeneyes, *1988*	7.50	2.50
	With 2-part tab	10.00	
15	$5 Ring-necked ducks, *1989*	7.50	2.50
	With 2-part tab	8.50	
16	$10 Lesser snow geese, *1990*	15.00	3.00
	With 2-part tab	17.00	
17	$10 Labrador retriever & Canada goose, *1991*	14.00	3.00
	With 2-part tab	16.00	
a.	Governor's edition with tab	*85.00*	
18	$10 Retriever & mallards, *1992*	20.00	3.00
	With 2-part tab	21.00	
19	$10 Pintail decoys and puppy, *1993*	20.00	3.00
	With 2-part tab	21.00	
20	$10 Canvasbacks & retrievers, *1994*	20.00	3.00
	With 2-part tab	21.00	
21	$10 Retriever, green-winged teal, decoys, *1995*	20.00	3.00
	With 2-part tab	21.00	
22	$10 Wood ducks, *1996*	14.00	2.50
23	$10 Canvasbacks, *1997*	14.00	2.50
24	$10 Canada geese, *1998*	14.00	2.50
25	$10 Canada geese, black Labrador retriever, *1999*	14.00	2.50
a.	Anniversary edition, perforated	*92.50*	
b.	Governor's edition, perforated	*92.50*	
c.	Silver edition, perforated	*92.50*	

Nos. 25a-25c were sold as a set of three.

No.	Description	Unused	Used
26	$10 Mallards, golden retriever, *2000*	14.00	2.50
27	$10 Pintails, yellow Labrador retriever, *2001*	14.00	2.50
28	$10 Canvasbacks, Chesapeake retriever, *2002*	14.00	2.50

INDIANA

Issued in booklet panes of 4 (Nos. 1-10) and booklet panes of 2, starting with No. 11.

Stamps are numbered serially and rouletted.

Catalogue values for all unused stamps in this section are for Never Hinged items.

Artists: Justin H. (Sonny) Bashore, #1-2; Carl (Spike) Knuth, #3; Daniel Renn Pierce, #4; Dean Barrick, #5; Rodney Crossman, #6; George Metz, #7; Kieth Freeman, #8; Lyn Briggs, #9; Rick Pas, #10; Ronald Louque, #11; Susan Hastings Bates, #12.

Bruce Langton, #13, 17; Ann Dahoney, #14; Ken Bucklew, #15, 20, 22, 24; Richard Hansen, #16; Jeffrey Klinefelter, #18, 26; Jeffrey Mobley. #19; Charles Riggles, #21, 23; George Lockwood, #25; Biran Blight, 27.

1976-2002

No.	Description	Unused	Used
1	$5 Green-winged teal	8.00	2.50
2	$5 Pintail, *1977*	8.00	2.50
3	$5 Canada geese, *1978*	8.00	2.50
4	$5 Canvasbacks, *1979*	8.00	2.50
5	$5 Mallard ducklings, *1980*	8.00	2.50
6	$5 Hooded mergansers, *1981*	8.00	2.50
7	$5 Blue-winged teal, *1982*	8.00	2.50
8	$5 Snow geese, *1983*	8.00	2.50
9	$5 Redheads, *1984*	8.00	2.50
10	$5 Pintail, *1985*	8.00	2.50
	With tab	10.00	
11	$5 Wood duck, *1986*	8.00	2.50
	With tab	10.00	
12	$5 Canvasbacks, *1987*	8.00	2.50
	With tab	10.00	
13	$6.75 Redheads, *1988*	10.00	2.50
	With tab	10.50	
14	$6.75 Canada goose, *1989*	10.00	2.50
	With tab	10.50	
15	$6.75 Blue-winged teal, *1990*	10.00	2.50
	With tab	10.50	
16	$6.75 Mallards, *1991*	10.00	2.50
	With tab	10.50	
17	$6.75 Green-winged teal, *1992*	10.00	2.50
	With tab	10.50	
18	$6.75 Wood ducks, *1993*	10.00	2.50
	With tab	10.50	
19	$6.75 Pintail, *1994*	10.00	2.50
	With tab	10.50	
20	$6.75 Goldeneyes, *1995*	10.00	2.50
	With tab	10.50	
21	$6.75 Black ducks, *1996*	10.00	2.50
	With tab	10.50	
22	$6.75 Canada geese, *1997*	10.00	2.50
	With tab	10.50	
23	$6.75 Widgeon, *1998*	10.00	2.50
	With tab	10.50	
24	$6.75 Bluebills, *1999*	9.00	2.50
	With tab	10.00	
25	$6.75 Ring-necked duck, *2000*	9.00	2.50
	With tab	10.00	
26	$6.75 Hooded mergansers, *2001*	9.00	2.50
	With tab	10.00	
27	$6.75 Green-winged teal, *2002*	9.00	2.50
	With tab	10.00	

IOWA

Catalogue values for all unused stamps in this section are for Never Hinged items.

Issued in booklet pane of 5 (No. 1), 10 (others) and sheets of 10 (No. 19).

Artists: Maynard Reece, #1, 6, 22; Thomas Murphy, #2; James Landenberger, #3; Mark Reece, #4; Nick Klepinger, #5, 7; Andrew Peters, #8; Paul Brigford, #9, 12, 15; Brad Reece, #10; Tom Walker, #11; Larry Zach, #13.

Jack C. Hahn, #14, 18; John Heidersbach, #16; Mark Cary, #17; Patrick Murillo, #19; Jerry Raedeke, #20; Charlotte Edwards, #21, 26; Dietmar Krumrey, #23, 25; Cynthia Fisher, #24; Sherrie Russell Meline, #27, 29; Mark Anderson, #28; Darren Maurer, #30, 31.

1972-98

No.	Description	Unused	Used
1	$1 Mallards	125.00	25.00
2	$1 Pintails, *1973*	35.00	7.50
3	$1 Gadwalls, rouletted, *1974*	85.00	7.00
4	$1 Canada geese, *1975*	95.00	9.00
5	$1 Canvasbacks, *1976*	25.00	2.50
6	$1 Lesser scaup, rouletted, *1977*	21.00	2.50
7	$1 Wood ducks, rouletted, *1978*	50.00	5.00
8	$5 Buffleheads, *1979*	275.00	25.00
9	$5 Redheads, *1980*	27.50	6.00
10	$5 Green-winged teal, rouletted, *1981*	27.50	4.00
11	$5 Snow geese, rouletted, *1982*	16.00	2.50
12	$5 Widgeons, *1983*	15.00	2.75
13	$5 Wood ducks, *1984*	35.00	3.00
14	$5 Mallard & mallard decoy, *1985*	20.00	2.50
15	$5 Blue-winged teal, *1986*	15.00	2.50
16	$5 Canada goose, *1987*	13.00	2.50
17	$5 Pintails, *1988*	12.00	2.50
18	$5 Blue-winged teal, *1989*	12.00	2.50
19	$5 Canvasbacks, *1990*	8.00	2.50
20	$5 Mallards, *1991*	8.00	2.50
21	$5 Labrador retriever & ducks, *1992*	9.00	2.50
22	$5 Mallards, *1993*	9.00	2.50
23	$5 Green-winged teal, *1994*	9.00	2.50
24	$5 Canada geese, *1995*	8.50	2.50
25	$5 Canvasbacks, *1996*	8.50	2.50
26	$5 Canada geese, *1997*	8.00	2.50
27	$5 Pintails, *1998*	8.00	2.50

1999

No.	Description	Unused	Used
28	Trumpeter swan, *1999*	8.00	2.50

No. 28 not required for hunting. The Department of Natural Resources sent customers No. 28 upon receipt of a postcard given to the customer after paying license fee of $5.

2000

29	Hooded merganser, *2000*	8.50 2.50

No. 29 not required for hunting. The Department of Natural Resources sent customers No. 29 upon receipt of a postcard given to the customer after paying license fee of $5.

2001

Artist: Darren Maurer

30	Snow goose, *2001*	10.00 2.50

No. 30 not required for hunting. The Department of Natural Resources sent customers No. 30 upon receipt of a postcard given to the customer after paying license fee of $5.

2002

Artist: Darren Maurer

31	Shovelers, *2002*	13.00 4.00

No. 31 not required for hunting. The Department of Natural Resources sent customers No. 31 upon receipt of a postcard given to the customer after paying license fee of $8.50.

KANSAS

Marion County Resident Duck Stamps

Wording, type face, border and perforation/roulette differs.

Used values are for stamps without gum.

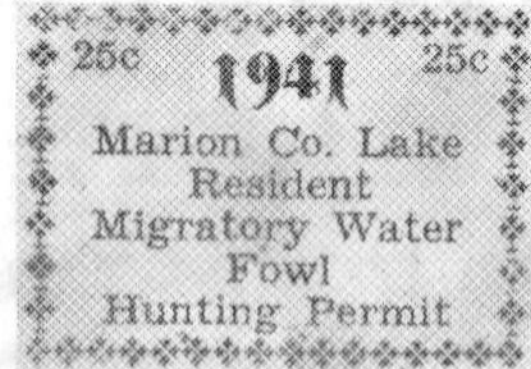

1941-42

A1	25c black	—
A2	25c black, *1942*	—

Remainders from 1941 were rubber stamped "1942" in purple and initialed "J.E.M." by the Park and Lake Supervisor.

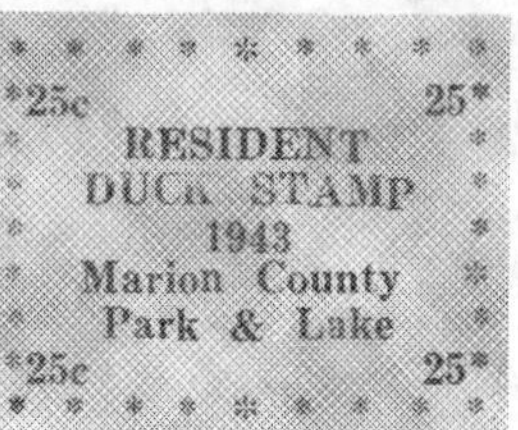

1943-73

A3	25c black, *pink*		—
A4	25c black, *green, 1944*		—
A5	25c green, *1945*		—
A6	25c black, *yellow, 1946*		*12,500.*
A7	25c black, *pink, 1947*		*8,500.*
A8	50c black, *blue, 1948*		*15,000.*
A9	50c black, *1949*		—
A10	50c black, *blue, 1950*		—
A11	50c black, *1951*		—
A13	50c black, *blue, 1953*		—
A14	50c black, *pink, 1954*	140.00	*65.00*
A15	50c black, *green, 1955*	125.00	*65.00*
A16	50c black, *1956*	150.00	*100.00*
A17	50c black, *blue, 1957*	125.00	*65.00*
a.	"1" instead of "I" in "RESIDENT," pos. 3	*1,750.*	*1,250.*
b.	1st 2 lines reversed, pos. 6	*2,250.*	*1,650.*
A18	50c black, *light yellow, 1958*	450.00	*225.00*
A19	50c black, *1959*	85.00	*65.00*
A20	50c black, *pink, 1960*	160.00	*110.00*
a.	Missing ornamental ball, pos. 9	*2,650.*	
A21	50c black, *1961*	175.00	*150.00*
A22	50c black, *1962*	250.00	*150.00*
A23	50c black, *pink, 1963*	750.00	*450.00*
A24	50c black, *pink, 1964*	750.00	*450.00*
a.	2nd & 3rd lines reversed, pos. 10	*7,500.*	
A25	50c black, *green, 1965*	475.00	*350.00*
A26	50c black, *yellow, 1966*	—	*5,500.*
A27	50c black, *green, 1967*	*2,750.*	*1,750.*
A28	50c black, *pink, 1968*	300.00	*250.00*
A29	50c black, *yellow, 1969*	325.00	*225.00*
a.	"Dusk" instead of "Duck," pos. 8	*10,500.*	
A30	50c black, *1970*	475.00	*375.00*
A31	50c black, *pink, 1971*	*2,200.*	*1,650.*
A32	50c black, *blue, 1972*	*2,200.*	*1,650.*
A33	50c black, *pink, 1972*	*4,750.*	*4,000.*

Statewide Issues

Issued in booklet panes of 10 (Nos. 1-5) and sheets of 30 (starting with No. 2). Starting with No. 11, issued in sheets of 10. No. 1 issued in booklets with one pane of 10 (serial number has prefix "DD") and booklets with two panes of 10 (serial number has prefix "SS").

Nos. 1-4 numbered serially.

Catalogue values for all unused stamps in this section are for Never Hinged items.

Artists: Guy Coheleach, #1; Ann Dahoney, #2, 8; Leon Parson, #3; Wes Dewey, #4; J. Byron Test, #5; Jerry Thomas, #6, 10; Jerry Roedeke, #7; Neal Anderson, #9; Dustin Teasley, #14-16.

1987-96

1	$3 Green-winged teal	8.00	2.50
	Pair from booklet pane with L & R selvage	17.00	
2	$3 Canada geese, *1988*	6.00	2.50
	Pair from booklet pane with L & R selvage	14.00	
3	$3 Mallards, *1989*	5.50	2.50
	Pair from booklet pane with L & R selvage	12.00	
4	$3 Wood ducks, *1990*	5.50	2.50
	Pair from booklet pane with L & R selvage	12.00	
5	$3 Pintail, rouletted, *1991*	5.25	2.50
	Pair from booklet pane with selvage at L & straight edge at R	12.00	
6	$3 Canvasbacks, *1992*	5.25	2.50
7	$3 Mallards, *1993*	5.25	2.50
8	$3 Blue-winged teal, *1994*	5.25	2.50
9	$3 Barrow's goldeneye, *1995*	5.25	2.50
10	$3 American widgeon, *1996*	5.25	2.50

Artist: Dustin Teasleys.

1997-2002	**Self-Adhesive**	***Die Cut***	
11	$3 blue	5.25	2.50
12	$3 green, *1998*	5.25	2.50
13	$3 red, *1999*	5.25	2.50
14	$3 red lilac, *2000*	5.25	2.50
15	$3 orange, *2001*	5.25	2.50

16	$5 blue, *2002*	8.75	2.50

KENTUCKY

Printed in booklet panes of 5, starting with No. 12 in panes of 30.

Stamps are numbered serially.

Catalogue values for all unused stamps in this section are for Never Hinged items.

Artists: Ray Harm, #1, 7; David Chapple, #2; Ralph J. McDonald, #3, 10; Lynn Kaatz, #4, 15; Phillip Crowe, #5, 9; Jim Oliver, #6; Phillip Powell, #8, 13; Jim Killen, #11; Laurie Parsons Yarnes, #12; Harold Roe, #14, 17; Tim Donovan, #16; Larry Chandler, #18.

1985-2002

1	$5.25 Mallards, rouletted	13.00	3.00
	With tab	14.00	
2	$5.25 Wood ducks, rouletted, *1986*	9.00	2.50
	With tab	10.00	
3	$5.25 Black ducks, *1987*	9.00	2.50
	With tab	10.00	
4	$5.25 Canada geese, *1988*	9.00	2.50
	With tab	10.00	
5	$5.25 Retriever & canvasbacks, *1989*	9.00	2.50
	With tab	10.00	
6	$5.25 Widgeons, *1990*	9.00	2.50
	With tab	10.00	
7	$5.25 Pintails, *1991*	9.00	2.50
	With tab	10.00	
8	$5.25 Green-winged teal, *1992*	9.00	2.50
	With tab	10.00	
9	$5.25 Canvasback & decoy, *1993*	9.00	2.50
	With tab	10.00	
10	$5.25 Canada goose, *1994*	9.00	2.50
	With tab	10.00	
11	$7.50 Retriever, decoy, ringnecks, *1995*	12.00	3.00
	With tab	10.00	
12	$7.50 Blue-winged teal, *1996*	10.00	3.00
13	$7.50 Shovelers, *1997*	10.00	3.00
14	$7.50 Gadwalls, *1998*	10.00	3.00
15	$7.50 Common goldeneyes, *1999*	9.50	3.00
16	$7.50 Hooded mergansers, *2000*	9.50	3.00
17	$7.50 Mallards, *2001*	9.50	3.00
18	$7.50 Pintails, *2002*	9.50	3.00

LOUISIANA

Printed in sheets of 30.
Stamps are numbered serially. Stamps without numbers are artist presentation copies.
Two fees: resident and non-resident.

Catalogue values for all unused stamps in this section are for Never Hinged items.

Artists: David Noll, #1-2; Elton Louviere, #3-4; Brett J. Smith, #5-6; Bruce Heard, #7-8; Ronald Louque, #9-10, 15-16, 21-22; Don Edwards, #11-12; John Bertrand, #13-14; R. Hall, #17-18; R. C. Davis, #19-20; Jude Brunet, #23-24; Edward Butler, #25-26; Reggie McLeroy, #27-28.

1989-2002

1	$5	Blue-winged teal	12.00	2.50
a.		Governor's edition	*100.00*	
2	$7.50	Blue-winged teal	8.50	2.50
a.		Governor's edition	*150.00*	

Nos. 1a and 2a were available only through a sealed bid auction where sheets of 30 of each denomination with matching serial numbers were sold as a unit.

3	$5	Green-winged teal, *1990*	8.50	2.50
4	$7.50	Green-winged teal, *1990*	12.00	2.50
5	$5	Wood ducks, *1991*	9.00	2.50
6	$7.50	Wood ducks, *1991*	10.50	2.50
7	$5	Pintails, *1992*	8.00	2.50
8	$7.50	Pintails, *1992*	10.50	2.50
9	$5	American widgeon, *1993*	12.00	2.50
10	$7.50	American widgeon, *1993*	10.50	2.50
11	$5	Mottled duck, *1994*	12.00	2.50
12	$7.50	Mottled duck, *1994*	10.50	2.50
13	$5	Speckle bellied goose, *1995*	12.00	2.50
14	$7.50	Speckle bellied goose, *1995*	10.50	2.50
15	$5	Gadwall, *1996*	12.00	2.50
16	$7.50	Gadwall, *1996*	10.50	2.50
17	$5	Ring-necked ducks, *1997*	8.00	2.50
18	$13.50	Ring-necked ducks, *1997*	17.00	2.50
19	$5.50	Mallards, *1998*	8.00	2.50
a.		Governor's edition	*150.00*	
20	$13.50	Mallards, *1998*	17.00	2.50
a.		Governor's edition	*200.00*	
21	$5.50	Snow geese, *1999*	8.00	2.50
22	$13.50	Snow geese, *1999*	15.00	2.50
23	$5.50	Lesser scaup, *2000*	8.00	2.50
24	$13.50	Lesser scaup, *2000*	30.00	2.50

No. 24 sold for $25 as stamps were printed before fee increase was finalized.

25	$5.50	Shovelers, *2001*	8.00	2.50
26	$25	Shovelers, *2001*	30.00	2.50
27	$5.50	Canvasbacks, *2002*	8.00	2.50
28	$25	Canvasbacks, *2002*		

MAINE

Printed in sheets of 10. Nos. 1-10 are numbered serially.

Catalogue values for all unused stamps in this section are for Never Hinged items.

Artists: David Maass, #1-3; Ron Van Gilder, #4; Rick Allen, #5; Jeannine Staples, #6, 10, 15, 18; Thea Flanagan, #7; Patricia D. Carter, #8; Persis Weirs, #9; Susan Jordan, #11; Richard Alley, #12, 19, 16; Paul Fillion, #13; T. Kemp, #14; Darby Mumford, #17.

1984-2002

1	$2.50	Black ducks	22.50	5.00
2	$2.50	Common eiders, *1985*	40.00	5.00
3	$2.50	Wood ducks, *1986*	8.50	2.50
4	$2.50	Buffleheads, *1987*	8.00	2.50
5	$2.50	Green-winged teal, *1988*	8.00	2.50
6	$2.50	Common goldeneyes, *1989*	5.00	2.50
7	$2.50	Canada geese, *1990*	5.00	2.50
8	$2.50	Ring-necked duck, *1991*	5.00	2.50
9	$2.50	Old squaw, *1992*	5.00	2.50
10	$2.50	Hooded merganser, *1993*	5.00	2.50
11	$2.50	Mallards, *1994*	5.00	2.50
12	$2.50	White-winged scoters, *1995*	5.00	2.50
13	$2.50	Blue-winged teal, *1996*	5.00	2.50
14	$2.50	Greater scaup, *1997*	5.00	2.50
15	$2.50	Surf scoters, *1998*	5.00	2.50
16	$2.50	Black duck, *1999*	5.00	2.50
17	$2.50	Common eider, *2000*	5.00	2.50
18	$2.50	Wood duck, *2001*	5.00	2.50
19	$2.50	Buffleheads, *2002*	5.00	2.50

MARYLAND

Nos. 1-19 printed in sheets of 10. Starting with No. 20, printed in sheets of 5 with numbered tab at bottom and selvage at top.
Each stamp has tab. Unused value is for stamp with tab. Many used copies have tab attached.

Catalogue values for all unused stamps in this section are for Never Hinged items.

Artists: John Taylor, #1, 6, 24; Stanley Stearns, #2, 5; Louis Frisino, #3, 13, 20; Jack Schroeder, #4, 7; Arthur Eakin, #8; Roger Bucklin, #9; Roger Lent, #10, 16; Carla Huber, #11, 17; David Turnbaugh, #12, 18, 23, 27; Francis Sweet, #14; Christopher White, #15; Will Wilson, #19; Robert Bealle, #21; Charles Schauck, #22; Paul Makuchal, #25; Wally Makuchal, #26; Wilhelm Goebel, #28; James Kinnett, #29.

1974-2002

1	$1.10	Mallards	11.00	2.50
2	$1.10	Canada geese, rouletted, *1975*	10.00	2.50
3	$1.10	Canvasbacks, rouletted, *1976*	10.00	2.50
4	$1.10	Greater scaup, *1977*	10.00	2.50
5	$1.10	Redheads, *1978*	10.00	2.50
6	$1.10	Wood ducks, rouletted, *1979*	10.00	2.50
7	$1.10	Pintail decoy, rouletted, *1980*	10.00	2.50
8	$3	Widgeon, rouletted, *1981*	6.00	2.50
9	$3	Canvasback, *1982*	6.00	2.50
10	$3	Wood duck, *1983*	10.00	2.50
11	$6	Black ducks, *1984*	10.00	2.50
12	$6	Canada geese, *1985*	9.50	2.50
13	$6	Hooded mergansers, *1986*	9.50	2.50
14	$6	Redheads, *1987*	9.50	2.50
15	$6	Ruddy ducks, *1988*	9.50	2.50
16	$6	Blue-winged teal, *1989*	9.00	2.50
17	$6	Lesser scaup, *1990*		
18	$6	Shovelers, *1991*	8.50	2.50
19	$6	Bufflehead, *1992*	8.50	2.50
20	$6	Canvasbacks, *1993*	8.50	2.50
21	$6	Redheads, *1994*	8.50	2.50
22	$6	Mallards, *1995*	8.50	2.50
23	$6	Canada geese, *1996*	8.50	2.50
24	$6	Canvasbacks, *1997*	8.50	2.50
25	$6	Pintails, *1998*	8.50	2.50
26	$6	Wood ducks, *1999*	8.00	2.50
27	$6	Oldsquaws, *2000*	8.00	2.50
28	$6	Wigeons, *2001*	8.00	2.50
29	$9	Black scoters, *2002*	12.00	2.50

Public Lands Hunting Stamps

Required to hunt waterfowl in state-managed wildlife areas.
Issued in booklet panes of 10.

1975-79

A1	$2	purple	*950.00*	75.00
A2	$2	black, *pink, 1976*	*850.00*	45.00
A3	$2	black, *yellow, 1977*	*750.00*	45.00
A4	$2	black, *1978*	*1,500.*	110.00
A5	$2	black, *yellow, 1979*	*650.00*	35.00

MASSACHUSETTS

Printed in sheets of 12.

Catalogue values for all unused stamps in this section are for Never Hinged items.

Artists: Milton Weiler, #1; Tom Hennessey, #2; William Tyner, #3-5; Randy Julius, #6, 8, 10, 12, 19, 27; John Eggert, #7, 9, 24; Joseph Cibula, #11; Robert Piscatori, #13, 15, 25; Peter Baedita, #14, 29; Lou Barnicle, #16; Warren Racket Shreve, #17; Benjamin Smith, #18; Donald Little, #20; Sergio Roffo, #21; David Brega, #22; Christine Wilkinson, #23; Stephen Badlam; Barry Julius, #28.

1974-2002

1	$1.25	Wood duck decoy, rouletted	15.00	3.00
2	$1.25	Pintail decoy, *1975*	13.00	3.00
3	$1.25	Canada goose decoy, *1976*	13.00	3.00
4	$1.25	Goldeneye decoy, *1977*	13.00	3.00
5	$1.25	Black duck decoy, *1978*	13.00	3.00
6	$1.25	Ruddy turnstone duck decoy, *1979*	13.00	3.00
a.		Imperf, pair	160.00	
7	$1.25	Old squaw decoy, *1980*	13.00	3.00
8	$1.25	Red-breasted merganser decoy, *1981*	12.00	3.00
9	$1.25	Greater yellowlegs decoy, *1982*	12.00	3.00
10	$1.25	Redhead decoy, *1983*	12.00	3.00
11	$1.25	White-winged scoter decoy, *1984*	12.00	3.00
12	$1.25	Ruddy duck decoy, *1985*	12.00	3.00
13	$1.25	Preening bluebill decoy, *1986*	12.00	2.50
14	$1.25	American widgeon decoy, *1987*	12.00	2.50
15	$1.25	Mallard decoy, *1988*	12.00	2.50
16	$1.25	Brant decoy, *1989*	9.50	2.50
17	$1.25	Whistler hen decoy, *1990*	9.50	2.50
18	$5	Canvasback decoy, *1991*	9.50	2.50
19	$5	Black-bellied plover decoy, *1992*	9.50	2.50
20	$5	Red-breasted merganser decoy, *1993*	9.50	2.50
21	$5	White-winged scoter decoy, *1994*	9.50	2.50
22	$5	Female hooded merganser decoy, *1995*	9.50	2.50
23	$5	Eider decoy, *1996*	9.50	2.50
24	$5	Curlew decoy, *1997*	9.50	2.50
25	$5	Canada goose decoy, *1998*	9.50	2.50
26	$5	Oldsquaw decoy, *1999*	9.50	2.50
27	$5	Merganser hen decoy, *2000*	8.00	2.50
28	$5	Black duck decoy, *2001*	9.50	2.50
29	$5	Bufflehead decoy, *2002*	8.00	2.50

MICHIGAN

Nos. 1-5 printed in sheets of 10 with center gutter, rouletted. Printed in sheets of 10 die cut self-adhesives on backing paper (Nos. 6-19), or sheets of 15 (starting with No. 20).
Nos. 1, 3-19 are serially numbered.

Catalogue values for all unused stamps in this section are for Never Hinged items.

Artist: Oscar Warbach.

1976

1 $2.10 Wood duck 5.00 2.50

Artists: Larry Hayden, #2, 5, 12; Richard Timm, #3; Andrew Kurzmann, #4; Dietmar Krumrey, #6, 14, 23-24; Gjisbert van Frankenhuyzen, #7; Rod Lawrence, #8, 15, 20, 25, 27; Larry Cory, #9, 16; Robert Steiner, #10; Russell Cobane, #11; John Martens, #13; Heiner Hertling, #17; Clark Sullivan, #18; David Bollman, #19; Rusty Fretner, #21; M. Monroe, #22; Kim Diment, #26.

1977-2002

2 $2.10 Canvasbacks 275.00 35.00
With numbered tab 325.00
3 $2.10 Mallards, *1978* 20.00 5.00
With tab 47.50
4 $2.10 Canada geese, *1979* 35.00 5.00
With tab 40.00
5 $3.75 Lesser scaup, *1980* 15.00 4.00
With tab 20.00
6 $3.75 Buffleheads, *1981* 20.00 4.00
7 $3.75 Redheads, *1982* 22.50 4.00

Unused value is for stamp with sufficient margin to show printed spaces for date and time the stamp was sold.

8 $3.75 Wood ducks, *1983* 25.00 4.00
9 $3.75 on $3.25 Pintails, *1984* 25.00 3.00

No. 9 not issued without surcharge.

10 $3.75 Ring-necked ducks, *1985* 25.00 3.00
11 $3.75 Common goldeneyes, *1986* 18.00 2.50
12 $3.85 Green-winged teal, *1987* 10.00 2.50
13 $3.85 Canada geese, *1988* 9.50 2.50
14 $3.85 Widgeons, *1989* 8.00 2.50
15 $3.85 Wood ducks, *1990* 7.00 2.50
16 $3.85 Blue-winged teal, *1991* 7.00 2.50
17 $3.85 Red-breasted merganser, *1992* 6.50 2.50
18 $3.85 Hooded merganser, *1993* 6.50 2.50
19 $3.85 Black duck, *1994* 6.50 2.50
20 $4.35 Blue winged teal, *1995* 7.00 3.00
21 $4.35 Canada geese, *1996* 7.00 3.00
22 $5 Canvasbacks, *1997* 7.50 3.00
23 $5 Pintail, *1998* 8.00 3.00
24 $5 Shoveler, *1999* 8.00 3.00
25 $5 Mallards, *2000* 8.00 3.00

Self-Adhesive Die Cut

26 $5 Ruddy ducks, *2001* 8.00 3.00
27 $5 Wigeons, *2002* 8.00 3.00

Nos. 24-27 not required for hunting.

MINNESOTA

License Surcharge Stamps

No. A1 printed in sheets of 10. These stamps served as a $1 surcharge to cover the cost of a license increase.

Nos. A1-A2 issued to raise funds for acquisition and development of wildlife lands.

1957 ***Perf. 12½***

A1 $1 Mallards & Pheasant 125.00 8.00

1971 MINNESOTA $1.00
Department of Natural Resources
Additional one dollar surcharge to be paid by sportsmen, pursuant to Laws 1971 Chapter 867, for the acquisition and development of wildlife lands.

1971 ***Rouletted 9½***

A2 $1 black, *dark yellow* *1,950.* 30.00

Regular Issues

Printed in sheets of 10.

Catalogue values for all unused stamps in this section are for Never Hinged items.

Artists: David Maass, #1, 3; Leslie Kouba, #2; James Meger, #4; Terry Redlin, #5, 9, Phil Scholer, #6, 17; Gary Moss, #7; Thomas Gross, #8; Brian Jarvi, #10; Ron Van Gilder, #11; Robert Hautman, #12, 16, 25; Jim Hautman, #13, 20; Kevin Daniel, #14, 21; Daniel Smith, #15; Edward DuRose, #18; Bruce Miller, #19; Thomas Moen, #22; John House, #23; Kim Norlien, #24; John Freiberg, #26.

1977-2002

1 $3 Mallards 15.00 2.50
2 $3 Lesser scaup, *1978* 10.00 2.50
3 $3 Pintails, *1979* 9.50 2.50
4 $3 Canvasbacks, *1980* 9.50 2.50
5 $3 Canada geese, *1981* 9.50 2.50
6 $3 Redheads, *1982* 10.00 2.50
7 $3 Blue geese & snow goose, *1983* 10.00 2.50
8 $3 Wood ducks, *1984* 10.00 2.50
9 $3 White-fronted geese, *1985* 8.50 2.50
10 $5 Lesser scaup, *1986* 9.50 2.50

Beginning with this issue, left side of sheet has an agent's tab, detachable from the numbered tab.

11 $5 Common goldeneyes, *1987* 11.00 2.50
With numbered tab 11.00
With agent's and numbered tabs 12.00
12 $5 Buffleheads, *1988* 11.00 2.50
With numbered tab 11.00
With agent's and numbered tabs 12.00
13 $5 Widgeons, *1989* 11.00 2.50
With numbered tab 11.00
With agent's and numbered tabs 12.00
14 $5 Hooded mergansers, *1990* 15.00 2.50
With numbered tab 15.00
With agent's and numbered tabs 20.00
15 $5 Ross's geese, *1991* 8.00 2.50
With numbered tab 8.00
With agent's and numbered tabs 9.00
16 $5 Barrow's goldeneyes, *1992* 8.00 2.50
With numbered tab 8.00
With agent's and numbered tabs 9.00
17 $5 Blue-winged teal, *1993* 8.00 2.50
With numbered tab 8.00
With agent's and numbered tabs 9.00
18 $5 Ringneck duck, *1994* 8.00 2.50
With numbered tab 8.00
With agent's and numbered tabs 9.00
19 $5 Gadwall, *1995* 8.00 2.50
With numbered tab 8.00
With agent's and numbered tabs 9.00
20 $5 Greater scaup, *1996* 8.00 2.50
With numbered tab 8.00
With agent's and numbered tabs 9.00
21 $5 Shovelers, *1997* 8.00 2.50
With numbered tab 8.00
With agent's and numbered tabs 9.00
22 $5 Harlequins, *1998* 8.00 2.50
With numbered tab 8.00
With agent's and numbered tabs 9.00
23 $5 Green-winged teal, *1999* 7.50 2.50
With numbered tab 7.50
With agent's and numbered tabs 9.00

Self- Adhesive Die Cut

24 $5 Red-breasted merganser, *2000* 7.50 2.50

No. 24 is on backing paper affixed to back of license form.

25 $5 Black duck, *2001* 7.50 2.50

No. 25 is on backing paper affixed to back of license form.

26 $5 Ruddy duck, *2002* 7.50 2.50

No. 26 is on backing paper affixed to mailing envelope.

MISSISSIPPI

Starting with No. 2, stamps are printed in sheets of 10. Nos. 2-14 are rouletted. All stamps are numbered serially.

Catalogue values for all unused stamps in this section are for Never Hinged items.

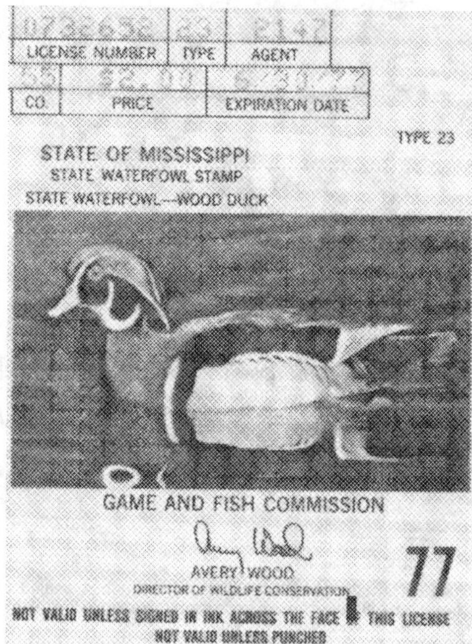

Illustration reduced.

Artists: Carroll & Gwen Perkins, #1; Allen Hughes, #2; John C. A. Reimers, #3, 6; Carole Pigott Hardy, #4; Bob Tompkins, #5, 13; Jerry Johnson, #7; Jerrie Glasper, #8; Tommy Goodman, #9; Lottie Fulton, #10; Joe Lattl, #11, 17, 22-23; Robert Garner, #12; Debra Aven Swartzendruber, #14; Kathy Dickson, #15; Phillip Crowe, #16; Eddie Suthoff, #18; Emitt Thames, #19-20; James Josey, #21; John MacHudspeth, #24, 25; Joe MacHudspeth, #26, 27.

1976 ***Without Gum***

1 $2 Wood duck 16.00 5.00
a. Complete 2-part data processing card 25.00

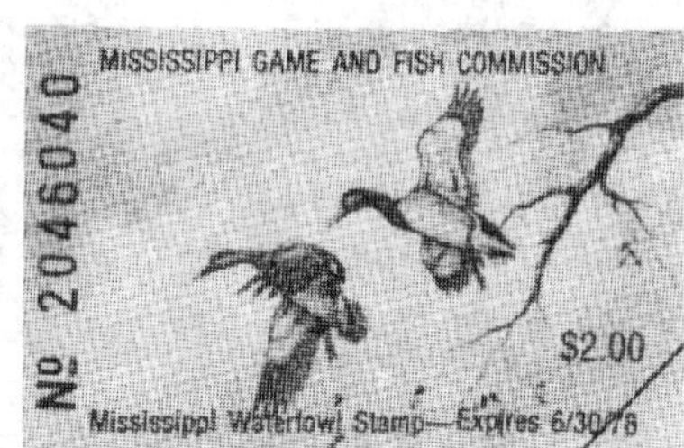

1977-2002

2 $2 Mallards 8.00 2.50
3 $2 Green-winged teal, *1978* 8.00 2.50
4 $2 Canvasbacks, *1979* 8.00 2.50
5 $2 Pintails, *1980* 8.00 2.50
6 $2 Redheads, *1981* 8.00 2.50
7 $2 Canada geese, *1982* 8.00 2.50
8 $2 Lesser scaup, *1983* 8.00 2.50
9 $2 Black ducks, *1984* 8.00 2.50
10 $2 Mallards, *1985* 8.00 2.50
a. Vert. serial No., imperf btwn. serial No. and stamp 125.00
b. Horiz. serial No., no vert. silver bar 425.00
11 $2 Widgeons, *1986* 8.00 2.50
12 $2 Ring-necked ducks, *1987* 8.00 2.50
13 $2 Snow geese, *1988* 8.00 2.50
14 $2 Wood ducks, *1989* 7.00 2.50
15 $2 Snow geese, *1990* 12.50 2.50
16 $2 Labrador retriever & canvasbacks, *1991* 5.00 2.50
17 $2 Green-winged teal, *1992* 5.00 2.50
18 $5 Mallards, *1993* 8.00 2.50
19 $5 Canvasbacks, *1994* 8.00 2.50
20 $5 Blue-winged teal, *1995* 8.00 2.50
21 $5 Hooded merganser, *1996* 8.00 2.50
22 $5 Pintail, *1997* 8.00 2.50
23 $5 Pintails, *1998* 8.00 2.50
24 $5 Ring-necked duck, *1999* 8.00 2.50
25 $5 Mallards, *2000* 8.00 2.50
26 $5 Gadwall, *2001* 8.00 2.50
27 $10 Wood duck, *2002* 14.00 2.50

MISSOURI

Issued in booklet panes of five with tab. Nos. 1-8 are rouletted. No. 18 issued in pane of 30.

Catalogue values for all unused stamps in this section are for Never Hinged items.

Artists: Charles Schwartz, #1; David Plank, #2; Tom Crain, #3, 8; Gary Lucy, #4; Doug Ross, #5; Glenn Chambers, #6; Ron Clayton, #7; Ron Ferkol, #9, 13, 18; Bruce Bollman, #10; Kathy Dickson, #11; Eileen Melton, #12; Kevin Guinn, #14; Thomas Bates, #15; Keith Alexander, #16; Ryan Peterson, #17.

1979-96

No.	Description	Unused	Used
1	$3.40 Canada geese	*450.00*	75.00
	With tab	*550.00*	
2	$3.40 Wood ducks, *1980*	*65.00*	18.00
	With tab	*150.00*	
3	$3 Lesser scaup, *1981*	57.50	9.00
	With tab	75.00	
4	$3 Buffleheads, *1982*	42.50	8.00
	With tab	52.50	
5	$3 Blue-winged teal, *1983*	37.50	8.00
	With tab	52.50	
6	$3 Mallards, *1984*	37.50	7.00
	With tab	47.50	
7	$3 American widgeons, *1985*	22.50	3.00
	With tab	25.00	
8	$3 Hooded mergansers, *1986*	12.00	3.00
	With tab	15.00	
9	$3 Pintails, *1987*	9.00	3.00
	With tab	13.00	
10	$3 Canvasback, *1988*	8.00	2.50
	With tab	11.00	
11	$3 Ring-necked ducks, *1989*	8.00	2.50
	With tab	9.25	

All copies of Nos. 12b, 13b, 14b, 15b, 16b, 17b are signed by the governor.

No.	Description	Unused	Used
12	$5 Redheads, *1990*	7.00	2.50
	With two part tab	9.00	
a.	$50 Governor's edition with tab	75.00	
b.	$100 Governor's edition with tab	—	
13	$5 Snow geese, *1991*	7.00	2.50
	With two part tab	9.00	
a.	$50 Governor's edition with tab	72.50	
b.	$100 Governor's edition with tab	—	
14	$5 Gadwalls, *1992*	7.00	2.50
	With tab	9.00	
a.	$50 Governor's edition with tab	75.00	
b.	$100 Governor's edition with tab	—	
15	$5 Green-winged teal, *1993*	7.00	2.50
	With tab	9.00	
a.	$50 Governor's edition with tab	75.00	
b.	$100 Governor's edition with tab	—	
16	$5 White-fronted goose, *1994*	7.00	2.50
	With 2-part tab	9.00	
a.	$50 Governor's edition with tab	75.00	
b.	$100 Governor's edition with tab	—	
17	$5 Goldeneyes, *1995*	7.00	2.50
	With 2-part tab	9.00	
a.	$50 Governor's edition with tab	75.00	
b.	$100 Governor's edition with tab	—	
18	$5 Black ducks, *1996*	7.00	2.50

MONTANA

Bird License Stamps

Required to hunt waterfowl.

Resident ($2, $4, $6), youth ($1, $2), and non-resident ($25, $30, $53) bird licenses. Licenses were no longer produced for youth, beginning in 1985, and non-resident, beginning in 1989.

Nos. 1-33 rouletted.

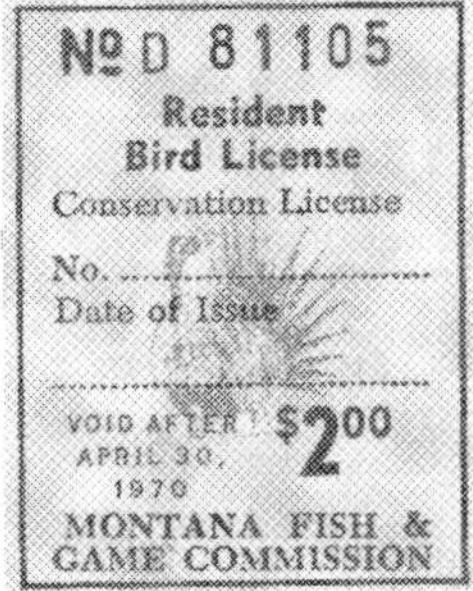

1969

No.	Description	Unused	Used
A1	$2 Sage grouse	475.00	15.00
A2	$1 Sage grouse	475.00	50.00
A3	$25 Sage grouse	475.00	75.00

1970

No.	Description	Unused	Used
A4	$2 Sage grouse	450.00	10.00
a.	Missing "1" in "1971," pos. 10		*450.00*
A5	$1 Sage grouse	*1,150.*	150.00
A6	$25 Sage grouse	—	275.00

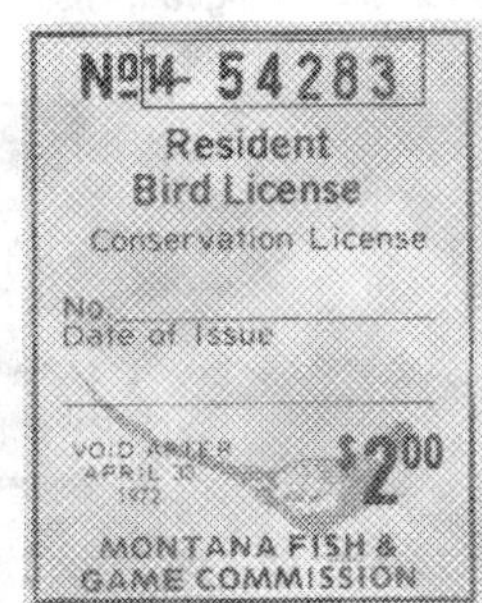

1971

No.	Description	Unused	Used
A7	$2 Pheasant	475.00	10.00
A8	$1 Pheasant	475.00	35.00
A9	$25 Pheasant	475.00	50.00

1972

No.	Description	Unused	Used
A10	$2 Pheasant	475.00	10.00
A11	$1 Pheasant	475.00	35.00
A12	$25 Pheasant	475.00	50.00

1973

No.	Description	Unused	Used
A13	$2 Pheasant	475.00	10.00
A14	$1 Pheasant	475.00	35.00
A15	$25 Pheasant	475.00	50.00

1974

No.	Description	Unused	Used
A16	$2 Pheasant	475.00	10.00
A17	$1 Pheasant	475.00	35.00
A18	$25 Pheasant	475.00	50.00

1975

No.	Description	Unused	Used
A19	$2 Pheasant	475.00	10.00
A20	$1 Pheasant	475.00	35.00
A21	$25 Pheasant	475.00	50.00

1976

No.	Description	Unused	Used
A22	$4 Pheasant	475.00	10.00
A23	$2 Pheasant	475.00	35.00
A24	$30 Pheasant	475.00	50.00

1977

No.	Description	Unused	Used
A25	$4 Pheasant	475.00	10.00
A26	$2 Pheasant	475.00	35.00
A27	$30 Pheasant	475.00	50.00

1978

No.	Description	Unused	Used
A28	$4 Sage grouse	8.00	2.00
A29	$2 Sage grouse	8.00	5.00
A30	$30 Sage grouse	8.00	5.50

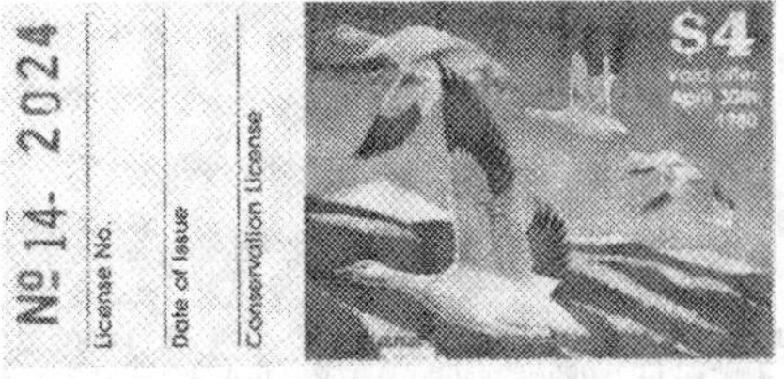

1979

No.	Description	Unused	Used
A31	$4 Snow geese	8.00	2.00
A32	$2 Snow geese	8.00	5.00
A33	$30 Snow geese	8.00	5.50

1980

No.	Description	Unused	Used
A36	$30 black, *gray green*		*35.00*

1982

No.	Description	Unused	Used
A40	$4 black, *yellow*		5.00

1983

No.	Description	Unused	Used
A43	$4 black, *yellow gray*	*200.00*	5.00
A44	$2 black, *gray*	*200.00*	
A45	$30 black, *light blue*	*200.00*	

1984

No.	Description	Unused	Used
A46	$4 black, *light blue green*	*175.00*	5.00
A47	$2 black, *light violet*	*250.00*	
A48	$30 black, *gray*	*175.00*	

1985

No.	Description	Unused	Used
A49	$4 black, *light blue*	*250.00*	5.00
A50	$30 black, *lavender*	*175.00*	

1986

No.	Description	Unused	Used
A51	$4 black, *orange*	*250.00*	5.00
A52	$30 black, *light blue*	*250.00*	

1987

No.	Description	Unused	Used
A53	$4 black, *orange brown*	*150.00*	3.00
A54	$30 black, *tan*	*200.00*	

1988

No.	Description	Unused	Used
A55	$6 black, *light blue*	*125.00*	3.00
A56	$53 black, *purple*	*200.00*	

1989-99

No.	Description	Unused	Used
A57	$6 black, *rose*	95.00	2.00
A58	$6 black, *lavender, 1990*	85.00	2.00
A59	$6 black, *pale blue, 1991*	75.00	2.00
A60	$6 black, *brown, 1992*	65.00	2.00
A61	$6 black, *blue, 1993*	50.00	1.50
A62	$6 black, *red orange, 1994*	45.00	1.50
A63	$6 black, *blue, 1995*	35.00	1.50
A64	$6 black, *purple, 1996*	25.00	1.00
A65	$6 black, *mauve, 1997*	15.00	1.00
A66	$6 black, *gray, 1998*	13.00	1.00
A67	$6 black, *green, 1999*	13.00	1.00

Waterfowl Stamps

Issued in booklet panes of 10 and sheets of 30.

Stamps are numbered serially.

Stamps with serial numbers above 31,000 (1986) and above 21,000 (other years) are from booklet panes.

Catalogue values for all unused stamps in this section are for Never Hinged items.

Artist: Joe Thornbrugh, #34, 38, 39, 45, 46, 48; Roger Cruwys, #35, 37, 42; Dave Samuelson, #36; Craig Philips, #40; Darrell Davis, #41; Wayne Dowdy, #43; Jim Borgreen, #44, 50; Cliff Rossberg, #47, 49.

1986-2002

34	$5 Canada geese	12.00	3.00
	Pair from booklet pane with L & R selvage	*1,850.*	
	Top pair from booklet pane with agent tabs and L & R selvage	—	
35	$5 Redheads, *1987*	12.50	3.00
	Pair from booklet pane with L & R selvage	25.00	
	Top pair from booklet pane with agent tabs and L & R selvage	55.00	
36	$5 Mallards, *1988*	11.00	3.00
	Pair from booklet pane with L & R selvage	25.00	
	Top pair from booklet pane with agent tabs and L & R selvage	40.00	
37	$5 Black Labrador retriever & pintail, *1989*	8.00	3.00
	Pair from booklet pane with L & R selvage	19.00	
	Top pair from booklet pane with agent tabs and L & R selvage	40.00	
a.	Governor's edition	*140.00*	

No. 37a was available only in full sheets only through a sealed bid auction.

38	$5 Blue-winged & cinnamon teal, *1990*	8.50	2.50
	Pair from booklet pane with L & R selvage	18.00	
	Top pair from booklet pane with agent tabs and L & R selvage	25.00	
39	$5 Snow geese, *1991*	8.00	2.50
	Pair from booklet pane with L & R selvage	17.50	
	Top pair from booklet pane with agent tabs and L & R selvage	25.00	
40	$5 Wood ducks, *1992*	8.00	2.50
	Pair from booklet pane with L & R selvage	17.50	
	Top pair from booklet pane with agent tabs and L & R selvage	25.00	
41	$5 Harlequin ducks, *1993*	8.00	2.50
	Pair from booklet pane with L & R selvage	17.50	
	Top pair from booklet pane with agent tabs and L & R selvage	25.00	
42	$5 Widgeons, *1994*	8.00	2.50
	Pair from booklet pane with L & R selvage	17.50	
	Top pair from booklet pane with agent tabs and L & R selvage	25.00	
43	$5 Tundra swans, *1995*	8.00	2.50
	Pair from booklet pane with L & R selvage	17.50	
	Top pair from booklet pane with agent tabs and L & R selvage	25.00	
44	$5 Canvasbacks, *1996*	7.50	2.50
	Pair from booklet pane with L & R selvage	17.50	
	Top pair from booklet pane with agent tabs and L & R selvage	30.00	
45	$5 Golden retriever, mallard, *1997*	7.50	2.50
	Pair from booklet pane with L & R selvage	17.50	
	Top pair from booklet pane with agent tabs and L & R selvage	30.00	
46	$5 Gadwalls, *1998*	7.50	2.50
	Pair from booklet pane with L & R selvage	17.50	
	Top pair from booklet pane with agent tabs and L & R selvage	30.00	
47	$5 Barrow's goldeneye, *1999*	7.50	2.50
	Pair from booklet pane with L & R selvage	17.50	
	Top pair from booklet pane with agent tabs and L & R selvage	30.00	
48	$5 Mallard decoy, Chesapeake retriever, *2000*	7.50	2.50
	Pair from booklet pane with L & R selvage	17.50	
	Top pair from booklet pane with agent tabs and L & R selvage	30.00	
49	$5 Canada geese, *2001*	7.50	2.50
	Pair from booklet pane with L & R selvage	17.50	
	Top pair from booklet pane with agent tabs and L & R selvage	30.00	
50	($5) Sandhill crane, *2002*	7.50	2.50

NEBRASKA

Habitat Stamps

Required to hunt waterfowl.
Printed in sheets of 20.

Catalogue values for all unused stamps in this section are for Never Hinged items.

1977-98

A1	$7.50 Ring-necked pheasant	12.00	1.50
A2	$7.50 White-tailed deer, *1978*	12.00	1.50
A3	$7.50 Bobwhite quail, *1979*	12.00	1.50
A4	$7.50 Pheasant, *1980*	12.00	1.50
A5	$7.50 Cottontail rabbit, *1981*	12.00	1.50
A6	$7.50 Coyote, *1982*	12.00	1.50
A7	$7.50 Wild turkey, *1983*	12.00	1.50
A8	$7.50 Canada goose, *1984*	12.00	1.50
A9	$7.50 Cardinal, *1985*	12.00	1.50
A10	$7.50 Sharp-tailed grouse, *1986*	12.00	1.50
A11	$7.50 Sandhill crane, *1987*	12.00	1.50
A12	$7.50 Snow geese, *1988*	12.00	1.50
A13	$7.50 Mallards, *1989*	12.00	1.50
A14	$7.50 Pheasants, *1990*	12.00	1.50
A15	$7.50 Canada geese, *1991*	12.00	1.50
A16	$10.00 Raccoon, *1992*	14.00	1.50
A17	$10.00 Fox squirrel, *1993*	14.00	1.50
A18	$10.00 Hungarian partridge, *1994*	14.00	1.50
A19	$10.00 Prairie pronghorns, *1995*	14.00	1.50
A20	$10.00 Ring-necked pheasant, *1996*	14.00	1.50
A21	$10.00 White-tailed deer, *1997*	14.00	1.50
A22	$10.00 Mourning doves, *1998*	14.00	1.50

Pictorial Labels

These stamps are not valid for any hunting fees.
Printed in sheets of 10.
Stamps are numbered serially.

Catalogue values for all unused stamps in this section are for Never Hinged items.

Artist: Neal Anderson.

1991-95

Artist: Neal Anderson

1	$6 Canada geese	10.00
2	$6 Pintails, *1992*	8.50
3	$6 Canvasbacks, *1993*	8.50
4	$6 Mallards, *1994*	8.50
5	$6 Wood ducks, *1995*	8.50

NEVADA

Printed in booklet panes of 4.
Stamps are rouletted and selvage is found above and below stamps on the pane. The tab portion of the panes in imperforate.
Starting with No. 4 stamps are numbered serially.

Catalogue values for all unused stamps in this section are for Never Hinged items.

Artists: Larry Hayden, #1; Dick Mcrill, #2; Phil Scholer, #3; Richard Timm, #4; Charles Allen, #5; Robert Steiner, #6; Richard Wilson, #7; Nolan Haan. #8, 12; Sherrie Russell Meline, #9, 21; Jim Hautman, #10; Robert Hautman, #11; Tak Nakamura, #13, 17; Richard Clifton, #14, 22; Steve Hopkins, #15; Mark Mueller, #16; Jeffrey Klinefelter, #18, 23; B. Blight, #19; Janie Kreutzjans, #20; Jeff Hoff, #24.

1979-2002

1	$2 Canvasbacks and decoy	40.00	12.00
	With numbered tab	50.00	

Copies with tabs without numbers are printer's waste.

2	$2 Cinnamon teal, *1980*	6.50	3.00
	With tab	10.00	
3	$2 Whistling swans, *1981*	7.00	3.00
	With tab	9.00	
4	$2 Shovelers, *1982*	7.00	3.00
	With tab	9.00	
5	$2 Gadwalls, *1983*	10.50	3.00
	With tab	11.00	
6	$2 Pintails, *1984*	10.50	3.00
	With tab	11.00	
7	$2 Canada geese, *1985*	13.00	3.00
	With tab	13.50	
8	$2 Redheads, *1986*	13.00	2.50
	With tab	13.50	
9	$2 Buffleheads, *1987*	11.00	2.50
	With tab	12.00	
10	$2 Canvasbacks, *1988*	11.00	2.50
	With tab	12.00	
11	$2 Ross's geese, *1989*	7.50	2.50
	With tab	8.00	
12	$5 Green-winged teal, *1990*	8.00	2.50
	With tab	10.00	
13	$5 White-faced ibis, *1991*	8.00	2.50
	With tab	10.00	
14	$5 American widgeon, *1992*	8.00	2.50
	With tab	8.50	
15	$5 Common goldeneye, *1993*	8.50	2.50
	With tab	9.00	
16	$5 Mallards, *1994*	8.00	2.50
	With tab	8.50	
17	$5 Wood duck, *1995*	8.00	2.50
	With tab	8.50	
18	$5 Ring-necked ducks, *1996*	8.00	2.50
	With tab	8.50	
19	$5 Ruddy ducks, *1997*	8.00	2.50
	With tab	8.50	
20	$5 Hooded merganser, *1998*	8.00	2.50
	With tab	8.50	
21	$5 Canvasback decoy, *1999*	7.50	2.50
22	$5 Canvasbacks, *2000*	7.50	2.50
23	$5 Lesser Scaups, *2001*	7.50	2.50
	With tab	8.00	
24	$5 Cinnamon teal, *2002*	7.50	2.50

NEW HAMPSHIRE

Printed in booklet panes of 1 with 2-part tab and in sheets of 30. Sheet stamps are perf on four sides.
Stamps are numbered serially.

Catalogue values for all unused stamps in this section are for Never Hinged items.

Artists: Richard Plasschaert, #1; Phillip Crowe, #2; Thomas Hirata, #3; Durrant Bell, #4; Robert Steiner, #5-9; Richard Clifton, #10-11, 15; Louis Frisino, #12; Matthew Scharle, #13; Jeffrey Klinefelter, #14; Jim Collins, #16, 20; Bruce Holloway, #17; Susan Knowles Jordan, #18; Charles Freeman, #19.

1983-2002

1	$4 Wood ducks	100.00	
a.	Booklet single with 2-part tab	95.00	25.00
2	$4 Mallards, *1984*	75.00	
a.	Booklet single with 2-part tab	125.00	20.00
3	$4 Blue-winged teal, *1985*	60.00	
a.	Booklet single with 2-part tab	85.00	20.00
4	$4 Hooded mergansers, *1986*	20.00	
a.	Booklet single with 2-part tab	25.00	6.00
5	$4 Canada geese, *1987*	12.00	
a.	Booklet single with 2-part tab	14.00	4.00
b.	$50 Governor's edition	*375.00*	
6	$4 Buffleheads, *1988*	8.00	
a.	Booklet single with 2-part tab	10.00	3.00
b.	$4 +$46 Governor's edition	60.00	
7	$4 Black ducks, *1989*	8.00	
a.	Booklet single with 2-part tab	9.50	3.00
b.	$4 +$50 Governor's edition	67.50	
8	$4 Green-winged teal, *1990*	7.25	
a.	Booklet single with 2-part tab	8.25	3.00
b.	$4 +$50 Governor's edition	62.50	

9 $4 Golden retriever & mallards, *1991* 7.25
a. Booklet single with 2-part tab 8.25 3.00
b. $4 +$50 Governor's edition 75.00

Governor's Editions that follow are so inscribed.

10 $4 Ring-necked ducks, *1992* 7.25
a. Booklet single with 2-part tab 8.25 3.00
b. Governor's edition *625.00*
11 $4 Hooded mergansers, *1993* 7.25
a. Booklet single with 2-part tab 8.00 3.00
b. Governor's edition *600.00*
12 $4 Common goldeneyes, *1994* 7.25
a. Bklt. single with 2-part tab 8.00 2.50
b. Governor's edition *175.00*
13 $4 Northern pintails, *1995* 7.25
a. Bklt. single with 2-part tab 8.00 2.50
b. Governor's edition *150.00*
14 $4 Surf scooters, *1996* 7.25
a. Bklt. single with 2-part tab 8.00 2.50
b. Governor's edition 150.00
15 $4 Wood ducks, *1997* 7.25
a. Bklt. single with 2-part tab 8.00 2.50
b. Governor's edition *125.00*
16 $4 Canada geese, *1998* 7.25
a. Bklt. single with 2-part tab 8.00 2.50
b. Governor's edition *110.00*
17 $4 Mallards, *1999* 6.00
a. Bklt. single with 2-part tab 8.00 2.50
b. Governor's edition *110.00*
18 $4 Black ducks, *2000* 6.00
a. Bklt. single with 2-part tab 8.00 2.50
19 $4 Blue-winged teal, *2001* 6.00
a. Bklt. single with 2-part tab 8.00 2.50
20 $4 Pintails, *2002* 6.00
a. Bklt. single with 2-part tab 8.00 2.50

NEW JERSEY

Resident and non-resident fees.
Printed in sheets of 30 (starting with No. 1) and booklet panes of 10 (all but Nos. 2, 4, 6, 17b, 18b).
Sheet stamps are perf on 4 sides.
Stamps are numbered serially.

Catalogue values for all unused stamps in this section are for Never Hinged items.

Artists: Thomas Hirata, #1-2, 17-18; David Maass, #3-4; Ronald Louque, #5-6; Louis Frisino, #7-8; Robert Leslie, #9-10, 19-20, 29-30; Daniel Smith, #11-12; Richard Plasschaert, #13-14; Bruce Miller, #21-22; Wilhelm Goebel, #23-24, 27-28; Joe Hautman, #25-26, 35-36; Phillip Crowe, #31-32; Richard Clifton, #33-34; Bob Hautman, #37-40.

1984-2002

1 $2.50 Canvasbacks 45.00
a. Booklet single, #51,000-102,000 60.00 10.00
2 $5 Canvasbacks 60.00 10.00
3 $2.50 Mallards, *1985* 15.00
a. Booklet single, #51,000-102,000 25.00 6.00
4 $5 Mallards, *1985* 18.00 5.00
5 $2.50 Pintails, *1986* 10.00
a. Booklet single, #51,000-102,000 10.00 3.00
6 $5 Pintails, *1986* 13.00 3.00
7 $2.50 Canada geese, *1987* 11.00
a. Booklet single, #51,000-102,000 11.00 3.00
8 $5 Canada geese, *1987* 11.00
a. Booklet single, #45,001-60,000 11.00 3.00
9 $2.50 Green-winged teal, *1988* 7.50
a. Booklet single, #51,000-102,000 7.50 3.00
10 $5 Green-winged teal, *1988* 10.00
a. Booklet single, #45,001-60,000 10.00 3.00
11 $2.50 Snow geese, *1989* 5.00
a. Booklet single, #45,001-60,000 6.00 3.00
b. Governor's edition *72.50*
12 $5 Snow geese, *1989* 10.00
a. Booklet single, #45,001-60,000 10.00 3.00
b. Governor's edition *140.00*

Nos. 11b and 12b were available only in sets of sheets of 30 stamps with matching serial numbers through a sealed bid auction.

13 $2.50 Wood ducks, *1990* 5.00
a. Booklet single, #45,001-60,000 5.00 3.00
14 $5 Wood ducks, *1990* 8.00
a. Booklet single, #45,001-60,000 8.50 3.00
17 $2.50 Atlantic brant, *1991* 5.00
a. Booklet single, #45,001-60,000 5.00 3.00
b. Atlantic "brandt" 14.00
18 $5 Atlantic brant, *1991* 9.00
a. Booklet single, #45,001-60,000 9.50 3.00
b. Atlantic "brandt" 27.50

Matching serial number sets of Nos. 17b and 18b were available for sale only with the purchase of matching serial number sets of Nos. 17 and 18.

19 $2.50 Bluebills, *1992* 5.00
a. Booklet single, #27,691-78,690 5.00 2.50
20 $5 Bluebills, *1992* 8.50
a. Booklet single, #27,691-57,690 9.00 2.50
21 $2.50 Buffleheads, *1993* 5.00
a. Booklet single, #27,691-78,690 5.00 2.50
b. Sheet of 4 *20.00*
c. Governor's edition, signed by Florio or Whitman 42.50
22 $5 Buffleheads, *1993* 7.50
a. Booklet single, #27,691-57,690 8.00 2.50
b. Sheet of 4 *40.00*
c. Governor's edition, signed by Florio or Whitman 82.50

Nos. 21b and 22b were available only in sets of sheets with matching serial numbers. The set of sheets sold for $35.
Nos. 21c and 22c were available only in sets with matching serial numbers.

23 $2.50 Black ducks, *1994* 5.00
a. Bklt. single, perf. 2 or 3 sides 5.00 2.50
24 $5 Black ducks, *1994* 7.50
a. Bklt. single, perf. 2 or 3 sides 8.00 2.50
25 $2.50 Widgeon, lighthouse, *1995* 5.00
a. Bklt. single, perf. 3 sides 5.00 2.50
26 $5 Widgeon, lighthouse, *1995* 7.50
a. Bklt. single, perf. 3 sides 8.00 2.50
27 $5 Goldeneyes, lighthouse, *1996* 7.50
a. Bklt. single, perf. 2 or 3 sides 7.50 2.50
28 $10 Goldeneyes, lighthouse, *1996* 12.50
a. Bklt. single, perf. 2 or 3 sides 13.00 2.50

The $2.50 was printed but not used as the rate no longer existed. Later they were sold to collectors. Value, unused $5.

29 $5 Old squaws, schooner, *1997* 7.50
a. Bklt. single, perf. 2 or 3 sides 7.50 2.50
30 $10 Old squaws, schooner, *1997* 12.50
a. Bklt. single, perf. 2 or 3 sides 13.00 2.50
31 $5 Mallards, *1998* 7.50
a. Bklt. single, perf. 2 or 3 sides 7.50 2.50
32 $10 Mallards, *1998* 12.50
a. Bklt. single, perf. 2 or 3 sides 13.00 2.50
33 $5 Redheads, perf. 4 sides, *1999* 7.50
a. Bklt. single, perf. 2 or 3 sides 7.50 2.50
34 $10 Redheads, perf. 4 sides, *1999* 12.50
a. Bklt. single, perf. 2 or 3 sides 13.00 2.50
35 $5 Canvasbacks, perf. 4 sides, *2000* 7.50
a. Bklt. single, perf. 2 or 3 sides 7.50 2.50
36 $10 Canvasbacks, perf. 4 sides, *2000* 12.50
a. Bklt. single, perf. 2 or 3 sides 13.00 2.50
37 $5 Tundra swans, perf. 4 sides, *2001* 7.50
a. Bklt. single, perf. 2 or 3 sides 7.50 2.50
38 $10 Tundra swans, perf. 4 sides, *2001* 12.50
a. Bklt. single, perf. 2 or 3 sides 13.00 2.50
39 $5 Wood ducks, perf. 4 sides, *2002* 7.50
a. Bklt. single, perf. 2 or 3 sides 7.50 2.50
40 $10 Wood ducks, perf. 4 sides, *2002* 12.50
a. Bklt. single, perf. 2 or 3 sides 13.00 2.50

NEW MEXICO

Printed in booklet panes of 5 and sheets of 30.
Stamps are numbered serially.

Catalogue values for all unused stamps in this section are for Never Hinged items.

Artist: Robert Steiner.

1991-94

1 $7.50 Pintails 10.00
Booklet single, with large tab and selvage 11.00 5.00
a. $7.50 +$50 Governor's edition 72.50
2 $7.50 American widgeon, *1992* 9.50
Booklet single, with large tab and selvage 10.00 4.00
a. $7.50 +$50 Governor's edition 65.00
3 $7.50 Mallard, *1993* 9.50
Booklet single, with large tab and selvage 10.00 4.00
a. Sheet of 4 50.00
b. $7.50 +$50 Governor's edition 65.00

No. 3a exists imperf.

No. 4: b, Three birds in flight. c, Two birds in flight. d, Two birds flying over land. e, Bird's head close-up.

4 $7.50 Green-winged teal, sheet of 4, #b.-e., *1994* 40.00
a. Souvenir sheet of 4, #b.-e. (decorative border) 40.00
b.-e. Bklt. single with large tab and selvage, each 10.00 4.00
f. Bklt. pane of 4, #b.-e. 40.00

Stamps in Nos. 4-4a are printed with continuous design and have serial numbers reading down. Stamps in No. 4f have framelines around each design, inscriptions at the top and serial numbers reading up.

NEW YORK

Not required to hunt. Printed in sheets of 30.

Catalogue values for all unused stamps in this section are for Never Hinged items.

Artists: Larry Barton, #1; David Maass, #2; Lee LeBlanc, #3; Richard Plasschaert, #4; Robert Bateman, #5; John Seerey-Lester, #6; Terry Isaac, #7; Anton Ashak, #8; Ron Kleiber, #9; Jerome Hageman, #10; Frederick Szatkowski, #11; Len Rusin, #12; R. Easton, #13; Barbara Woods, #14; Richard Clifton, #15; Rob Leslie, #16; Bruce Miller, #17; Adam Grimm, #18.

1985-2002

1 $5.50 Canada geese 13.00
2 $5.50 Mallards, *1986* 9.00
3 $5.50 Wood ducks, *1987* 8.00
4 $5.50 Pintails, *1988* 8.00
5 $5.50 Greater scaup, *1989* 8.00
6 $5.50 Canvasbacks, *1990* 8.00
7 $5.50 Redheads, *1991* 8.00
8 $5.50 Wood ducks, *1992* 8.00
9 $5.50 Blue-winged teal, *1993* 8.00
10 $5.50 Canada geese, *1994* 11.00
11 $5.50 Common goldeneye, *1995* 8.00
12 $5.50 Common loon, *1996* 8.00
13 $5.50 Hooded merganser, *1997* 8.00
14 $5.50 Osprey, *1998* 8.00
15 $5.50 Buffleheads, *1999* 7.50
16 $5.50 Wood ducks, *2000* 7.50
17 $5.50 Pintails, *2001* 7.50
18 $5.50 Canvasbacks, *2002* 7.50 3.00

NORTH CAROLINA

Not required to hunt until 1988. Printed in sheets of 30. Starting with No. 6, stamps are numbered serially.

Catalogue values for all unused stamps in this section are for Never Hinged items.

Artists: Richard Plasschaert, #1, 10; Jim Killen, #2, 13;Thomas Hirata, #3-4, 17-18; Larry Barton, #5; Ronald Louque, #6, 21-22, 23-26; Louis Frisino, #7; Robert Leslie, #8, 14; Phillip Crowe, #9, 12; Bruce Miller, #11; Wilhelm Goebel, #15-16; Robert Flowers, #19-20.

1983-2002

1 $5.50 Mallards 55.00
2 $5.50 Wood ducks, *1984* 35.00
3 $5.50 Canvasbacks, *1985* 20.00
4 $5.50 Canada geese, *1986* 16.00
5 $5.50 Pintails, *1987* 13.00
6 $5 Green-winged teal, *1988* 9.50 3.00
7 $5 Snow geese, *1989* 9.50 3.00
8 $5 Redheads, *1990* 9.50 3.00

No.	Description	Unused	Used
9	$5 Blue-winged teal, *1991*	9.50	3.00
10	$5 American widgeon, *1992*	9.50	3.00
11	$5 Tundra swans, *1993*	9.50	3.00
12	$5 Buffleheads, *1994*	9.50	3.00
13	$5 Brant, lighthouse, *1995*	9.50	3.00
14	$5 Pintails, *1996*	8.00	3.00
15	$5 Wood ducks, perf., *1997*	8.00	3.00
16	$5 As #15,, self-adhesive, die cut, *1997*	8.00	
17	$5 Canada geese, perf., *1998*	8.00	3.00
18	$5 As #17, self-adhesive, die cut, *1998*	8.00	
19	$5 Green-winged teal, perf., *1999*	8.00	3.00
20	$5 As #19, self-adhesive, die cut, *1999*	8.00	
21	$10 Green-winged teal, perf., *2000*	14.00	3.00
22	$10 Green-winged teal, self-adhesive, die cut, *2000*	14.00	
23	$10 Black duck, perf., *2001*	14.00	3.00
24	$10 Black duck, self-adhesive, die cut, *2001*	14.00	
25	$10 Pintails, hunters, dog, perf., *2002*	14.00	3.00
26	$10 Pintails, hunters, dog, self-adhesive, die cut, *2002*	14.00	

NORTH DAKOTA

Small Game Stamps

Required to hunt small game and waterfowl statewide. Resident and non-resident fees.

Values for 1967-70 non-resident stamps are for copies with staple holes.

Used values are for signed copies. Unused values for Nos. 12, 16, 18, 20, 22, 24, 26 and 28 are for stamps on backing.

1967-80

No.	Description	Unused	Used
1	$2 black, *green*	*850.00*	60.00
2	$25 black, *green*	*2,950.*	*350.00*
3	$2 black, *pink, 1968*	200.00	20.00
4	$25 black, *yellow, 1968*	*450.00*	
5	$2 black, *green, 1969*	190.00	20.00
6	$35 black, *1969*	*400.00*	
7	$2 blue, *1970*	160.00	15.00
8	$35 black, *pink, 1970*	*250.00*	*50.00*
9	$2 black, *yellow, 1971*	125.00	10.00
10	$35 black, *1971*		*150.00*
11	$3 black, *pink, 1972*	65.00	5.00
12	$35 red, *1972*	*450.00*	*75.00*
13	$3 black, *yellow, 1973*	65.00	5.00
14	$35 green, *1973*	*1,750.*	*125.00*
15	$3 black, *blue, 1974*	125.00	15.00
16	$35 red, *1974*	*400.00*	*50.00*
17	$3 black, *1975*	95.00	10.00
18	$35 green, *1975*	*300.00*	*40.00*
19	$3 black, *dark yellow, 1976*	55.00	5.00
20	$35 red, *1976*	*140.00*	25.00
21	$3 black, *1977*	90.00	10.00
22	$35 red, *1977*	*125.00*	25.00
23	$5 black, *1978*	45.00	5.00
24	$40 red, *1978*	85.00	20.00
25	$5 black, *1979*	35.00	5.00
26	$40 red, *1979*	45.00	15.00
27	$5 black, *1980*	35.00	5.00
28	$40 green, *1980*	45.00	15.00

Small Game and Habitat Stamps

Required to hunt small game and waterfowl statewide.

Resident ($9), youth ($6) and non-resident ($53) fees.

Resident stamps issued in booklet panes of 5 numbered 20,001-150,000 (1982-86 issues) or 20,001-140,000 (starting with 1987 issue) or sheets of 30 numbered 150,001 and up (1982-86 issues) or 140,001 and up (starting with 1987 issue).

Starting with 1984, resident booklet stamps have straight edges at sides.

Nos. 31, 34, 37, 40 are die cut self adhesives.

Unused values are for stamps on backing.

All youth stamps were issued in booklet panes of 5. Non-resident stamps for 1981, 1982, 1996 and following years were issued in booklet panes of 5.

The 1984-95 non-resident stamps were issued se-tenant with non-resident waterfowl and non-resident general game stamps (rouletted on three sides). The 1994 and 1995 non-resident stamps also were issued se-tenant with only the non-resident general game stamp (rouletted at sides), as well as in booklet panes of 5 (rouletted top and bottom).

Catalogue values for all unused stamps in this section, from this point to the end, are for Never Hinged items.

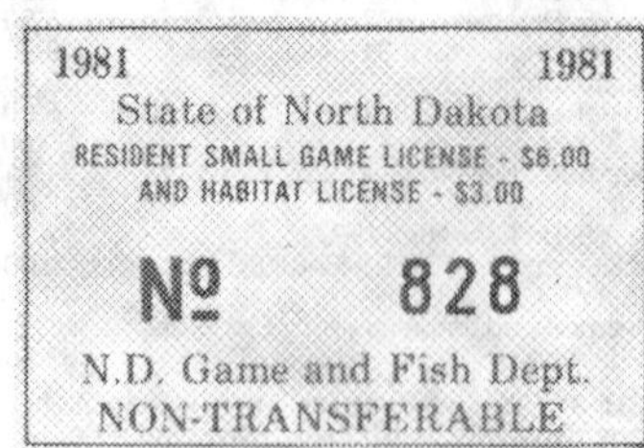

A1

1981

No.	Type	Description	Unused	Used
29	A1	$9 black	35.00	3.00
30	A1	$6 black, *blue green*	*175.00*	25.00
31	A1	$53 blue	110.00	20.00

A2

Artists: Richard Plaschaert, #32, 73; Terry Radlin, #35; David Maass, #38; Leslie Kouba, #41; Mario Fernandez, #44; Ronald Louque, #47, 75; Louis Frisino, #50; Robert Leslie, #53; Roger Cruwys, #56; Thomas Hirata, #59; Phillip Crowe, #62, 77, 81; Bruce Miller, #65; Darrell Davis, #67; Richard Clifton, #69; Wilhelm Goebel, #71; Jeffrey Klinefelter, #79.

1982

No.	Type	Description	Unused	Used
32	A2	$9 Canada geese	95.00	
		Booklet single with L & R selvage	*950.00*	25.00

Serial numbers 1-20,000 are from sheets of 10. Stamps without selvage from booklets sell for considerably less.

No.	Type	Description	Unused	Used
33	A1	$6 black, *blue*	*175.00*	25.00
34	A1	$53 black	35.00	15.00

1983

No.	Type	Description	Unused	Used
35	A2	$9 Mallards	55.00	
		Booklet single with L & R selvage	*2,000.*	25.00

Serial numbers 1-20,000 are from sheets. Stamps without selvage from booklets sell for considerably less.

No.	Type	Description	Unused	Used
36	A1	$6 black, *orange*		25.00
37	A1	$53 black		*40.00*

1984

No.	Type	Description	Unused	Used
38	A2	$9 Canvasbacks	30.00	
a.		Booklet single, perforated horiz. on 1 or 2 sides	*2,250.*	25.00
39	A1	$6 black, *light blue*		25.00
40	A1	$53 black		*40.00*

1985

No.	Type	Description	Unused	Used
41	A2	$9 Bluebills	20.00	
a.		Booklet single, perforated horiz. on 1 or 2 sides	*3,750.*	25.00
42	A1	$6 black, *light blue*		25.00
43	A1	$53 black		*40.00*

1986

No.	Type	Description	Unused	Used
44	A2	$9 Pintails	19.00	
a.		Booklet single, perforated horiz. on 1 or 2 sides	*400.00*	20.00
45	A1	$6 black, *light blue*		20.00
46	A1	$53 black		*35.00*

1987

No.	Type	Description	Unused	Used
47	A2	$9 Snow geese	16.00	
a.		Booklet single, perforated horiz. on 1 or 2 sides	*45.00*	18.00
48	A1	$6 black, *light blue*	—	25.00
49	A1	$53 black		*30.00*

1988

No.	Type	Description	Unused	Used
50	A2	$9 White-winged scoters	14.00	
a.		Booklet single, perforated horiz. on 1 or 2 sides	20.00	12.00
51	A1	$6 black, *light blue*	—	25.00
52	A1	$53 black		*30.00*

Stamps Inscribed "Small Game"

Resident ($6), youth ($3) and non-resident ($50, $75) fees.

1989

No.	Type	Description	Unused	Used
53	A2	$6 Redheads	10.00	
a.		Booklet single, perforated horiz. on 1 or 2 sides	15.00	8.00
54	A1	$3 black, *light blue*	—	25.00
55	A1	$50 black		30.00

1990

No.	Type	Description	Unused	Used
56	A2	$6 Labrador retriever & mallard	10.00	
a.		Booklet single, perforated horiz. on 1 or 2 sides	12.50	8.00
57	A1	$3 black, *light blue*	200.00	25.00
58	A1	$50 black		25.00

1991

No.	Type	Description	Unused	Used
59	A2	$6 Green-winged teal	9.00	
a.		Booklet single, perforated horiz. on 1 or 2 sides	10.00	6.00
60	A1	$3 black, *light blue*	200.00	25.00
61	A1	$50 black	*350.00*	25.00

1992

No.	Type	Description	Unused	Used
62	A2	$6 Blue-winged teal	8.00	
a.		Booklet single, perforated horiz. on 1 or 2 sides	10.00	6.00
63	A1	$3 black, *light blue*	325.00	
64	A1	$50 black		25.00

When supplies of No. 64 ran out, copies of No. 58 were used with the date changed by hand. Unused copies exist. Value, $300.

1993

No.	Type	Description	Unused	Used
65	A2	$6 Wood ducks	8.00	
a.		Booklet single, perforated horiz. on 1 or 2 sides	10.00	6.00
66	A1	$50 black	*550.00*	25.00

1994

No.	Type	Description	Unused	Used
67	A2	$6 Canada geese	8.00	
a.		Booklet single, perforated horiz. on 1 or 2 sides	10.00	6.00
68	A1	$75 black, rouletted on 2 adjacent sides	*400.00*	20.00
a.		Booklet single, rouletted top and bottom		—

1995

No.	Type	Description	Unused	Used
69	A2	$6 Widgeon	8.00	
a.		Booklet single, perforated horiz. on 1 or 2 sides	10.00	5.00
70	A1	$75 black, rouletted on 2 adjacent sides	*350.00*	20.00
a.		Booklet single, rouletted top and bottom		—

1996

No.	Type	Description	Unused	Used
71	A2	$6 Mallards	8.00	
a.		Booklet single, perforated horiz. on 1 or 2 sides	10.00	2.50
72	A1	$75 black, rouletted at top and bottom	—	

1997

No.	Type	Description	Unused	Used
73	A2	$6 White-fronted geese	8.00	
a.		Booklet single, perforated horiz. on 1 or 2 sides	10.00	2.50
74	A1	$75 black, rouletted at top and bottom	—	

1998

No.	Type	Description	Unused	Used
75	A2	$6 Blue-winged teal	8.00	
a.		Bklt. single, perforated horiz. on 1 or 2 sides	10.00	2.50
76	A1	$75 black, rouletted at top and bottom	—	

1999

No.	Type	Description	Unused	Used
77	A2	$6 Gadwalls	8.00	
a.		Bklt. single, perforated horiz. on 1 or 2 sides	10.00	2.50
78	A1	$75 black, rouletted at top and bottom	—	

2000

No.	Type	Description	Unused	Used
79		$6 Pintails, *2000*	8.00	
a.		Bklt. single, perforated horiz. on 1 or 2 sides	10.00	2.50
81	A2	$6 Canada geese, *2001*	8.00	
a.		Bklt. single, perforated horiz. on 1 or 2 sides	10.00	2.50

Expires June 30, 2003
State of North Dakota
Resident Small Game
$6.00
Nº 105573
N.D. Game and Fish Dept.
NON-TRANSFERABLE

A3

No.	Type	Description	Unused	Used
83	A3	$6 black, *green*	8.00	

Non-Resident Waterfowl Stamps

Required by non-residents to hunt waterfowl only. Unused copies of Nos. A1a, A13a-A19a have no serial number. Used copies have number written in. Nos. A1-A10 are self-adhesive, die cut. Others are rouletted.

Catalogue values for all unused stamps in this section are for Never Hinged items.

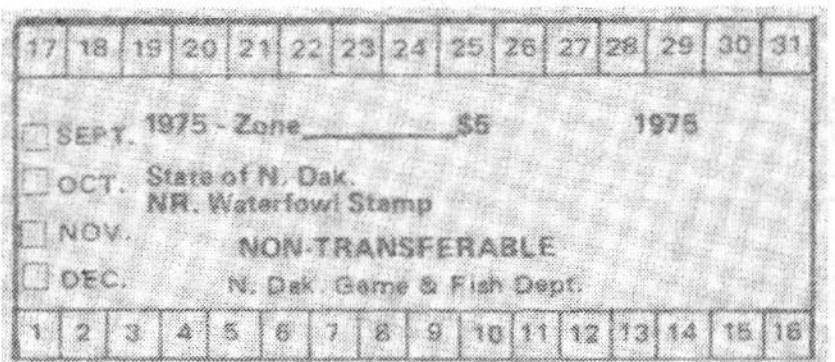

Illustration reduced.

1975-99

No.	Description	Unused	Used
A1	$5 green		*150.00*
a.	No serial number	175.00	—
A2	$5 red, *1976*	*500.00*	*100.00*
A3	$5 red, *1977*	325.00	*75.00*
A4	$5 red, *1978*	110.00	25.00
A5	$5 red, *1979*	85.00	20.00
A6	$5 green, *1980*	90.00	20.00
A7	$8 blue, *1981*	175.00	25.00
A8	$8 black, *1982*	27.50	15.00
A9	$8 black, *1983*		*55.00*
A10	$8 black, *1984*		*50.00*
A11	$8 black, *1985*		*45.00*
A12	$8 black, *1986*		*45.00*
A13	$8 black, *1987*		*40.00*
a.	No serial number	*400.00*	*50.00*
A14	$8 black, *1988*		35.00
a.	No serial number	*350.00*	*50.00*
A15	$8 black, *1989*		25.00
a.	No serial number, light green paper	*350.00*	*50.00*
A16	$8 black, *1990*		25.00
a.	No serial number	*300.00*	*50.00*
A17	$8 black, *1991*	*400.00*	25.00
a.	No serial number	250.00	*35.00*
A18	$8 black, *1992*		20.00
a.	No serial number	*200.00*	35.00

When supplies of No. A18 ran out copies of No. A16 were used with the date changed by hand. Values, unused $200, used $50.

No.	Description	Unused	Used
A19	$10 black, *1993*	*275.00*	20.00
a.	No serial number	*175.00*	30.00
A20	$10 black, rouletted on 2 adjacent sides, *1994*	*250.00*	20.00
a.	No serial number, rouletted top and bottom	175.00	30.00
A21	$10 black, rouletted on 2 adjacent sides, *1995*	*225.00*	20.00
a.	No serial number, rouletted top and bottom	100.00	25.00
A22	$10 black, rouletted top and bottom, *1996*	*95.00*	20.00
A23	$10 black, rouletted top and bottom, *1997*	*85.00*	14.00
A24	$10 black, rouletted top and bottom, *1998*	*75.00*	12.00
A25	$10 black, rouletted top and bottom, *1999*	*65.00*	12.00

Resident Sportsmen's Stamps

Required to hunt a variety of game, including waterfowl.

Catalogue values for all unused stamps in this section are for Never Hinged items.

1992-93 Resident
ND Sportsmens License
$25.00
Fishing - Small Game
General Game & Habitat
Furbearer
Nº 12969
NON-TRANSFERABLE

1992-98

No.	Description	Unused	Used
2A1	$25 black & purple, *1992-1993*	*3,500.*	75.00
2A2	$25 black & purple, *1993-1994*	*1,500.*	35.00
2A3	$25 black & purple, *1994-1995*	*325.00*	25.00
2A4	$25 black & purple, *1995-1996*	*200.00*	*20.00*
2A5	$25 black & purple, *1996-1997*	*150.00*	15.00
2A6	$27 black & purple, *1997-1998*	*100.00*	12.00

OHIO

Pymatuning Lake Waterfowl Hunting Stamps

Pymatuning Hunting License

Valid when attached to Resident Hunters and Trappers License. Authority H. B. 668.
YEAR 1938 $1.00 NO FEE

1938-45

No.	Description	Unused	Used
A1	$1 black, *light yellow*		—
A2	$1 black, *gray, 1939*		—
A3	$1 black, *blue, 1940*		—
A4	$1 black, *pink, 1941*		—
A5	$1 black, *green, 1942*		—
A6	$1 black, *1943*		—
A7	$1 black, *manila, 1944*		—
A8	$1 black, *manila, 1945*		—

Statewide Issues

Nos. 1-18 printed in sheets of 16. Starting with No. 19, stamps are printed in souvenir sheets of 1.

Catalogue values for all unused stamps in this section are for Never Hinged items.

Artists: John Ruthven, #1; Harry Antis, #2; Harold Roe, #3, 6, 15, 17; Ronald Louque, #4; Lynn Kaatz, #5, 8; Cynthia Fisher, #7; Jon Henson, #9; Gregory Clair, #10; Samuel Timm, #11; Kenneth Nanney, #12; Richard Clifton, #13; Ron Kleiber, #14; D. J. Cleland-Hura, #16: Timothy Donovan, #18; Mark Anderson, #19; Brian Bright, #20; Jeffrey Klinefelter, #21.

1982-2002

No.	Description	Unused	Used
1	$5.75 Wood ducks	65.00	10.00
2	$5.75 Mallards, *1983*	60.00	10.00
3	$5.75 Green-winged teal, *1984*	60.00	8.00
4	$5.75 Redheads, *1985*	30.00	6.00
5	$5.75 Canvasback, *1986*	27.50	5.00
6	$6 Blue-winged teal, *1987*	12.00	4.00
7	$6 Common goldeneyes, *1988*	11.00	4.00
8	$6 Canada geese, *1989*	11.00	3.00
9	$9 Black ducks, *1990*	13.00	3.00
10	$9 Lesser scaup, *1991*	13.00	3.00
11	$9 Wood duck, *1992*	12.00	3.00
12	$9 Buffleheads, *1993*	12.00	3.00
13	$11 Mallards, *1994*	15.00	2.50
14	$11 Pintails, *1995*	15.00	2.50
15	$11 Hooded mergansers, *1996*	15.00	2.50
16	$11 Widgeons, *1997*	15.00	2.50
17	$11 Gadwall, *1998*	14.00	2.50
18	$11 Mallard, *1999*	13.50	2.50
19	$11 Buffleheads, *2000*	13.50	2.50
20	$11 Canvasback, *2001*	13.50	2.50

Souvenir Sheet ***Rouletted***

No.	Description	Unused	Used
21	$11 Ring-necked ducks, *2002*	13.50	2.50

Nos. 19-21 not required for hunting.

OKLAHOMA

Printed in booklet panes of 10 (Nos. 1-3) and booklet panes of 5 (Starting with No. 4). No. 10 was the first to be printed in a sheet of 30, No. 17 in a sheet of 24.

Catalogue values for all unused stamps in this section are for Never Hinged items.

Artists: Patrick Sawyer, #1; Hoyt Smith, #2, 5, 7, 20; Jeffrey Frey, #3; Gerald Mobley, #4, 6; Rayburn Foster, #8, 12; Jim Gaar, #9; Wanda Mumm, #10; Ronald Louque, #11; Jeffrey Mobley, #13; Jerome Hageman, #14; Richard Kirkman, #15; Richard Clifton, #16; Greg Everhart, #17; M. Anderson, #18; Jeffrey Klinefelter, #19; Paul Makuchal, #21; Daniel Brevick, #22; Brian Blight, #23.

1980-2002

No.	Description	Unused	Used
1	$4 Pintails	45.00	10.00
2	$4 Canada goose, *1981*	20.00	8.00
3	$4 Green-winged teal, *1982*	10.00	4.00
4	$4 Wood ducks, *1983*	10.00	10.00
5	$4 Ring-necked ducks, *1984*	10.00	3.00
	With tab	9.00	
6	$4 Mallards, *1985*	7.00	3.00
	With tab	10.00	
7	$4 Snow geese, *1986*	7.00	3.00
	With tab	8.00	
8	$4 Canvasbacks, *1987*	7.00	3.00
	With tab	8.00	
9	$4 Widgeons, *1988*	7.00	3.00
	With tab	8.00	
10	$4 Redheads, *1989*	7.00	3.00
	Booklet single, with tab & selvage at L, selvage at R	7.50	
a.	Governor's edition	*125.00*	

No. 10a was available only in sheets of 30 through a sealed bid auction.

No.	Description	Unused	Used
11	$4 Hooded merganser, *1990*	7.00	3.00
	Booklet single, with tab & selvage at L, selvage at R	7.50	
12	$4 Gadwalls, *1991*	7.00	3.00
	Booklet single, with tab & selvage at L, selvage at R	7.50	
13	$4 Lesser scaup, *1992*	7.00	3.00
	Booklet single, with tab & selvage at L, selvage at R	7.50	
14	$4 White-fronted geese, *1993*	7.00	3.00
	Booklet single, with tab & selvage at L, selvage at R	7.50	
15	$4 Blue-winged teal, *1994*	7.00	3.00
	Booklet single, with tab & selvage at L, selvage at R	7.50	
16	$4 Ruddy ducks, *1995*	7.00	3.00
	Booklet single, with tab & selvage at L, selvage at R	7.50	
17	$4 Bufflehead, *1996*	6.50	3.00
	Booklet single, with selvage at L & R	7.00	
18	$4 Goldeneyes, *1997*	6.50	3.00
	Bklt. single, with selvage at L & R	7.00	
19	$4 Shovelers, *1998*	6.50	3.00
	Bklt. single, with selvage at L & R	7.00	
20	$4 Canvasbacks, *1999*	6.00	3.00
21	$4 Pintails, *2000*	6.00	3.00
22	$4 Canada goose, *2001*	6.00	3.00
23	$4 Green-winged teal, *2002*	6.00	3.00

OREGON

Non-resident fees begin in 1994.

Issued in sheets of 30, except for No. 6. Nos. 2-4 also exist from booklet panes of 5.

Stamps are numbered serially. Nos. 11b, 11c have serial numbers on sheet selvage.

Nos. 10 and 11 were issued on computer form. Unused values are for stamps on form.

Catalogue values for all unused stamps in this section are for Never Hinged items.

Artists: Michael Sieve, #1-3; Dorothy M. Smith, #4; Darrell Davis, #5; Phillip Crowe, #7; Roger Cruwys, #8; Louis Frisino,

#9; Kip Richmond, #10; R. Bruce Horsfall, #11; Richard Plasschaert, #12-13; Robert Steiner, #14-26.

1984-88

1 $5 Canada geese 20.00 7.00
2 $5 Lesser snow goose, *1985* 30.00 10.00
Booklet single, with 3 tabs (2 at left) *450.00*
3 $5 Pacific brant, perf. 4 sides, *1986* 14.00
a. Booklet single, with 2-part tab 15.00 4.00
4 $5 White-fronted geese, perf. 4 sides, *1987* 10.00
a. Booklet single, with 2-part tab 13.00 3.00
5 $5 Great Basin Canada geese, *1988* 9.00 3.00
a. Booklet pane of 1 10.00

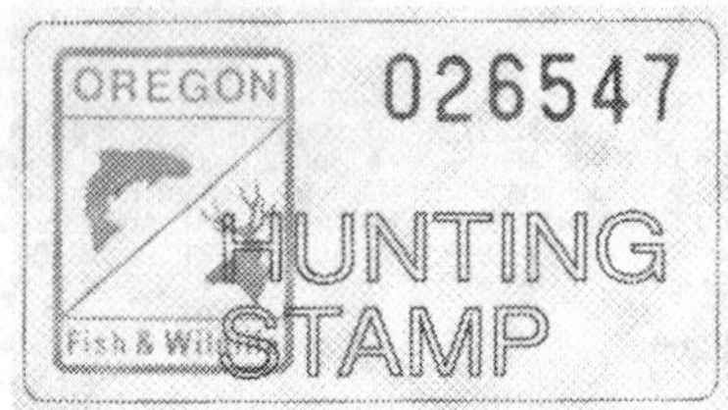

OR6

1989-2002 **Die cut self-adhesive**

6 ($5) Red Nos., 16,001 and up 12.50 *6.00*
a. Black Nos., 001-16,000 30.00 *12.50*

This provisional stamp was used in early 1989, when the regular stamps were delayed. Unused value is for stamp and adjacent label with serial number on backing paper.

Designs like No. 1

7 $5 Black Labrador retriever & pintails, *1989* 9.00 2.50
a. Booklet pane of 1 10.00
8 $5 Mallards & golden retriever, *1990* 10.00 2.50
a. Booklet pane of 1 11.00
9 $5 Buffleheads & Chesapeake Bay retriever, perf, *1991* 8.50
a. Rouletted at L 10.00 2.50

No. 9a is straight edged on 3 sides and stamp is attached to paper by selvage. Unused value is for stamp attached to paper.

10 $5 Green-winged teal, *1992* 8.50
a. Die cut, self-adhesive 10.00 2.50
11 $5 Mallards, vert., *1993* 8.00
a. Die cut self-adhesive 10.00 2.50
b. Sheet of 2 20.00
c. $50 Governor's edition sheet of 1 75.00

No. 11b contains No. 11 and the Oregon upland bird stamp. Nos. 11b, 11c exist imperf.

12 $5 Pintails, perf. 4 sides, *1994* 8.50
a. Die cut self-adhesive 10.00 2.50
13 $25 Pintails, diff., die cut self-adhesive, *1994* 32.50 —
14 $5 Wood ducks, *1995* 8.50
a. Booklet pane of 1 10.00 2.50
15 $25 Columbian sharp-tailed grouse, bklt. pane of 1, *1995* 50.00 —
16 $5 Mallards, *1996* 8.50
a. Booklet pane of 1 10.00 2.50
17 $25 Common snipe, booklet pane of 1, *1996* 45.00 —
18 $5 Canvasbacks, *1997* 8.50
a. Booklet pane of 1 10.00 2.50
19 $25 Canvasbacks, booklet pane of 1, *1997* 40.00
20 $5 Pintails, *1998* 8.50
a. Booklet pane of 1 10.00 2.50
21 $25 Pintails, booklet pane of 1, *1998* 37.50
22 $5 Canada geese, *1999* 6.00
a. Booklet pane of 1 10.00 2.50
23 $25 Canada geese, booklet pane of 1, *1999* 30.00
24 $7.50 Canada geese, mallard, widgeon, *2000* 12.00 2.50
25 $7.50 Redheads, *2001* 12.00 2.50
26 $7.50 American wigeon, *2002* 12.00 2.50

PENNSYLVANIA

Not required to hunt.
Printed in sheets of 10.

Catalogue values for all unused stamps in this section are for Never Hinged items.

Artists: Ned Smith, #1, 3; Jim Killen, #2; Robert Knutson, #4; Robert Leslie, #5; John Heldersbach, #6; Ronald Louque, #7; Thomas Hirata, #8, 12; Gerald W. Putt, #9, 14, 16, 18, 20; Robert Sopchick, #10; Glen Reichard, #11; Mark Bray, #13; Clark Weaver, #15, 17, 19.

1983-2002

1 $5.50 Wood ducks 12.00
2 $5.50 Canada geese, *1984* 10.00
3 $5.50 Mallards, *1985* 9.00
4 $5.50 Blue-winged teal, *1986* 9.00
5 $5.50 Pintails, *1987* 9.00
6 $5.50 Wood ducks, *1988* 9.00
7 $5.50 Hooded mergansers, *1989* 9.00
8 $5.50 Canvasbacks, *1990* 9.00
9 $5.50 Widgeons, *1991* 8.00
10 $5.50 Canada geese, *1992* 8.00
11 $5.50 Northern shovelers, *1993* 8.00
12 $5.50 Pintails, *1994* 8.00
13 $5.50 Buffleheads, *1995* 8.00
14 $5.50 Black ducks, *1996* 8.00
15 $5.50 Hooded merganser, *1997* 8.00
16 $5.50 Wood ducks, *1998* 8.00
17 $5.50 Ring-necked ducks, *1999* 8.00
18 $5.50 Green-winged teal, *2000* 7.50
19 ($5.50) Pintails, *2001* 7.50
20 $5.50 Snow geese, *2002* 7.50 2.50

RHODE ISLAND

Issued in booklet panes of 5 and sheets of 30. Starting with No. 8, the spacing of the reverse text of the booklet stamp differs from the sheet stamp. Stamps are numbered serially.

Catalogue values for all unused stamps in this section are for Never Hinged items.

Artists: Robert Steiner, #1-7, 9-10; Charles Allen, #8; Keith Mueller, #11-14.

1989-2002

1 $7.50 Canvasbacks 12.00 3.00
Booklet single, with tab 15.00
a. $7.50 +$50 Governor's edition 92.50

No. 1a exists without serial number.

2 $7.50 Canada geese, *1990* 12.00 3.00
Booklet single, with tab 15.00
a. $7.50 +$50 Governor's edition 72.50

No. 2a exists without serial number.

3 $7.50 Wood ducks & Labrador retriever, *1991* 15.00 3.00
Booklet single, with tab 15.00
a. $7.50 +$50 Governor's edition 60.00

No. 3a exists without serial number.

4 $7.50 Blue-winged teal, *1992* 12.00 3.00
Booklet single, with tab 12.50
a. $7.50 +$50 Governor's edition 60.00

No. 4a exists without serial number.

5 $7.50 Pintails, *1993* 10.00 3.00
Booklet single, with tab 12.00
a. Sheet of 4 55.00

No. 5a imperf. is printer's waste.

6 $7.50 Wood ducks, *1994* 10.00 2.50
Booklet single, with tab and selvage 12.00
7 $7.50 Hooded mergansers, *1995* 10.00 2.50
Booklet single, with tab and selvage 12.00
a. Governor's edition *110.00*

No. 7a inscribed "Governor's edition."

8 $7.50 Harlequin, *1996* 15.00 2.50
Booklet single, with tab and selvage 12.00
a. Governor's edition *125.00*

No. 8a inscribed "Governor's edition" and has serial number with "G" prefix.

9 $7.50 Greater scaup, *1997* 10.00 2.50
Booklet single, with tab and selvage 10.50
a. Governor's edition *110.00*

No. 9a inscribed "Governor's edition" and has serial number with "G" prefix.

10 $7.50 Black ducks, *1998* 10.00 2.50
Booklet single, with tab and selvage 10.50
a. Governor's edition *125.00*

No. 11-14 do not have a serial number.

Rouletted

11 $7.50 Common eiders, *1999* 9.50 2.50
Horiz. pair from booklet pane 21.00

Booklet pane contains 10 stamps.

12 $7.50 Canvasbacks, *2000* 9.50 2.50
a. Inscribed "Hunter" 9.50
a. Governor's edition —
13 $7.50 Mallard, black duck, *2001* 9.50 2.50
a. Inscribed "Hunter" 9.50
a. Governor's edition *125.00*
14 $7.50 White-winged scoter, lighthouse, *2002* 9.50 2.50
a. Inscribed "Hunter" 9.50

SOUTH CAROLINA

Issued in sheets of 30. Stamps with serial numbers were to be issued to hunters.

Catalogue values for all unused stamps in this section are for Never Hinged items.

Artists: Lee LeBlanc, #1; Bob Binks, #2; Jim Killen, #3, 8, 11; Al Dornish, #4; Rosemary Millette, #5; Daniel Smith, #6; Steve Dillard, #7; Lee Cable, #9; John Wilson, #10; Russell Cobane, #12; Bob Bolin, #13; Joe Hautman, #14; Rodney Huckaby, #15, 17, 22; D. J. Cleland-Hura, #16, 18; Denise Nelson, #19; Mark Constantine, #20; Jeffrey Klinefelter, #21.

1981-2002

1 $5.50 Wood ducks 60.00 15.00

No. 2-22 do not have a serial number.

2 $5.50 Mallards, *1982* 95.00
a. Serial number on reverse *450.00* 25.00
3 $5.50 Pintails, *1983* 95.00
a. Serial number on reverse *375.00* 25.00
4 $5.50 Canada geese, *1984* 62.50
a. Serial number on reverse *190.00* 15.00
5 $5.50 Green-winged teal, *1985* 52.50
a. Serial number on reverse 100.00 15.00
6 $5.50 Canvasbacks, *1986* 25.00
a. Serial number on reverse 42.50 10.00
7 $5.50 Black ducks, *1987* 19.00
a. Serial number on reverse 22.50 5.00
8 $5.50 Widgeon & spaniel, *1988* 20.00
a. Serial number on reverse 30.00 5.00
9 $5.50 Blue-winged teal, *1989* 11.00
a. Serial number on reverse 14.00 4.00
10 $5.50 Wood ducks, *1990* 8.50
a. Serial number on reverse 10.00 4.00
b. $5.50 +$44.50 Governor's edition 82.50
c. $5.50 +$94.50 Governor's edition 225.00

All copies of No. 10c are signed by the governor.

11 $5.50 Labrador retriever, pintails & decoy, *1991* 8.00
a. Serial number on reverse 9.00 4.00
12 $5.50 Buffleheads, *1992* 8.00
a. Serial number on front 9.00 3.00
13 $5.50 Lesser scaup, *1993* 8.00
a. Serial number on front 9.00 3.00
14 $5.50 Canvasbacks, *1994* 8.00
a. Serial number on front 9.00 2.50
15 $5.50 Shovelers, lighthouse, *1995* 8.00
a. Serial number on front 9.00 2.50
16 $5.50 Redheads, lighthouse, *1996* 8.00
a. Serial number on front 8.50 2.50
17 $5.50 Old squaws, *1997* 8.00
a. Serial number on front 8.50 2.50
18 $5.50 Green-winged teal, *1998* 8.00
a. Serial number on front 8.50 2.50

19	$5.50 Barrow's goldeneye, *1999*	8.00	
20	$5.50 Wood ducks, boykin spaniel, *2000*	8.00	2.50
21	$5.50 Mallard, decoy, yellow Labrador retriever, *2001*	8.00	2.50
22	$5.50 Wigeons, chocolate Labrador retriever, *2002*	8.00	2.50

SOUTH DAKOTA

Resident Waterfowl Stamps

Vertical safety paper (words read up)

1949-50

1	$1 blk, *grn*, vert. safety paper	*750.00*	85.00
a.	Horizontal safety paper	—	*150.00*
2	$1 blk, *lt brn*, vert. safety paper	*550.00*	65.00
a.	Horizontal safety paper	—	*175.00*

Safety paper design of Nos. 1 and 2 washes out if stamp is soaked. Washed out copies sell for considerably less. Used values are for copies showing safety paper design.

Printed in booklet panes of 5.
Stamps are numbered serially.

Catalogue values for all unused stamps in this section, from this point to the end of the Resident Waterfowl stamps, are for Never Hinged items.

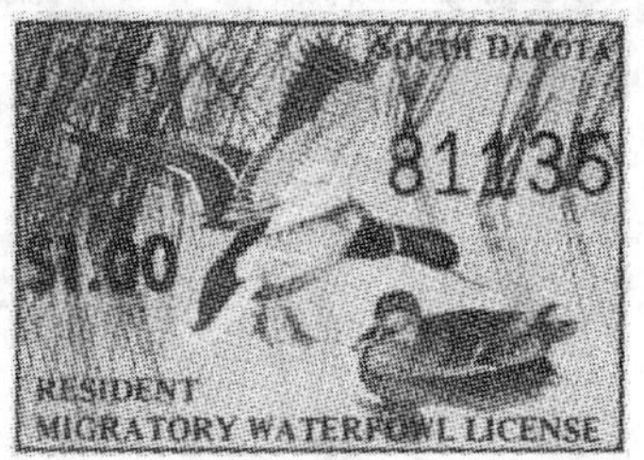

Artists: Robert Kusserow, #3; Don Steinbeck, #4; John Moisan, #5; John Wilson, #6, 12; Rosemary Millett, #7, 9; Marion Toillion, #8; John Green, #10, 17; Russell Duerksen, #11, 15-16, 19-20; Mark Anderson, #13, 18, 21, 22; Jeff Reuter, #14.

1976-2002

3	$1 Mallards	30.00	3.00
a.	Serial number 4mm high	65.00	10.00
4	$1 Pintails, *1977*	21.00	2.50
5	$1 Canvasbacks, *1978*	13.00	2.50
6	$2 Canada geese, *1988*	8.50	2.50
7	$2 Blue geese, *1987*	7.00	2.50
8	$2 White-fronted geese, *1988*	6.00	2.50
9	$2 Mallards, *1989*	5.00	2.50
10	$2 Blue-winged teal, *1990*	4.50	2.50
11	$2 Pintails, *1991*	4.50	2.50
12	$2 Canvasbacks, *1992*	4.50	2.50
13	$2 Lesser scaup, *1993*	4.50	2.50
14	$2 Redheads, *1994*	4.50	2.50
15	$2 Wood ducks, *1995*	4.50	2.50
16	$2 Canada geese, *1996*	4.00	2.50
17	$2 Widgeons, *1997*	4.00	2.50
18	$2 Green-winged teal, *1998*	4.00	2.50

Migratory Bird Certification Stamps

19	$3 Tundra swan, *1999*	4.00	2.50
20	$3 Buffleheads, *2000*	5.50	2.50
21	$3 Mallards, *2001*	5.50	2.50
22	$3 Canvasbacks, *2002*	5.50	2.50

Non-resident Waterfowl Stamps

Nos. A1-A7, A9 have serial No. in red. Nos. A1-A18 issued in booklet panes of 5. Type faces and designs of Nos. A1-A18 vary.

Unused values are for unpunched copies. Used values are for signed and punched copies.

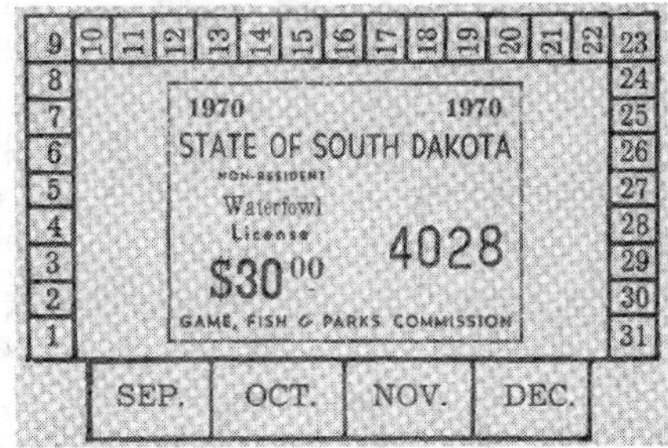

Illustration reduced.

1970-86

A1	$30 black, *pink*	20.00	
a.	Missing serial number	*3,750.*	
A2	$30 black, *pink, 1971*	9.00	
a.	Overprinted "3"		*275.00*
A3	$30 black, *1972*	3.75	
A4	$30 black, *blue, 1973*	8.00	
a.	Overprinted "2"	*325.00*	
A5	$30 black, *green, 1974*	5.50	
a.	Overprinted "1"	*25.00*	
b.	Overprinted "2"	*30.00*	
c.	Overprinted "4"	*30.00*	
A6	$30 black, *yellow, 1975*	6.50	
a.	Overprinted "UNIT 1"	*45.00*	
b.	Overprinted "UNIT 4"	*35.00*	
c.	Overprinted "UNIT 3"		—
A7	$30 black, *yellow, 1976*	5.00	
a.	Overprinted "1"	18.00	
b.	Overprinted "2"	30.00	*20.00*
c.	Serial No. 4mm high	*18.00*	
d.	As "c," overprinted "1"	*35.00*	
e.	As "c," overprinted "2"	*85.00*	
A8	$30 black, *red, 1977*	7.00	
a.	Overprinted "1"	*20.00*	
b.	Overprinted "2"	*30.00*	
c.	Overprinted "3"	*35.00*	
d.	Overprinted "4"	*30.00*	
e.	Overprinted "5"	*150.00*	
A9	$30 black, *yellow, 1978*	7.00	
a.	Overprinted "1" and 3 strikes of "UNIT 2"	*125.00*	
b.	Overprinted "1"	*150.00*	
A10	$30 black, *red, 1979*	2.50	
A11	$30 black, *light manila, 1980*	4.50	
a.	Overprinted "1"	6.00	
b.	Overprinted "2"	10.00	
A12	$30 black, *light yellow, 1981*	4.50	
a.	Overprinted "UNIT 1"	6.00	
b.	Overprinted "UNIT 2"	10.00	5.00
A13	$30 black, *blue, 1982*	6.50	
A14	$50 black, *dark yellow, 1982*	7.00	
a.	Overprinted "UNIT 2"		—
A15	$50 black, *red, 1983*	8.00	
a.	Overprinted "AREA 1"	*50.00*	
b.	Overprinted "AREA 2"	*65.00*	
c.	Serial No. with serifs	*675.00*	
A16	$50 black, *light manila, 1984*	16.00	
a.	Overprinted "A"	*225.00*	
b.	Overprinted "B"	*110.00*	
A17	$50 black, *red, 1985*	*2,950.*	*550.00*
A18	$50 black, *1986*	*9.00*	5.00

Bennett County Canada Goose Stamps

Type faces and designs vary. Nos. 2A1-2A2 imperf. Nos. 2A3-2A12 printed in booklet panes of 5, perforated horizontally. Some show vertical perforations.

Nos. 2A1-2A4 were free. No. 2A5 cost $5. Stamps were issued to hunters by means of a drawing.

Used values are for signed stamps.

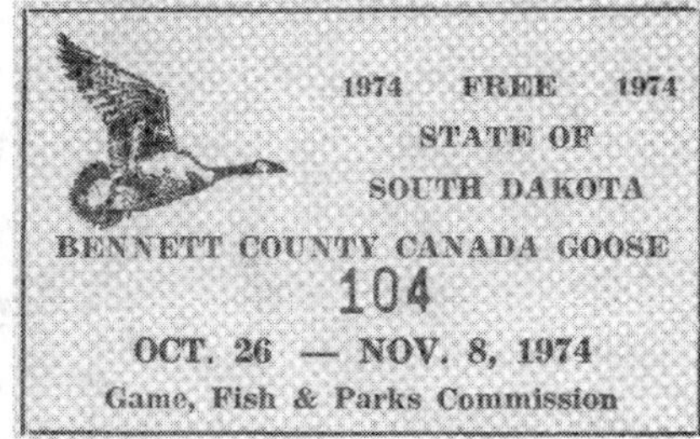

Illustration reduced.

1974-78

2A1	black	50.00	30.00
2A2	black, *pink, 1975*	*225.00*	

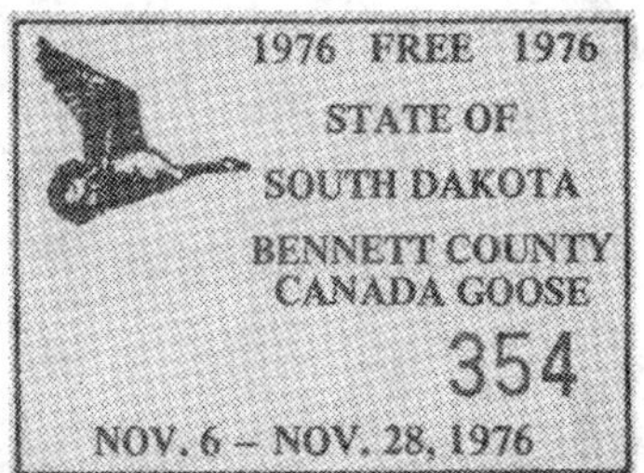

2A3	black, *blue, 1976*	47.50	25.00
2A4	black, *yellow, 1977*	42.50	25.00
2A5	black, *greenish blue, 1978*	*600.00*	

West River Unit Canada Goose

Counties handstamped.

Used values are for signed stamps.

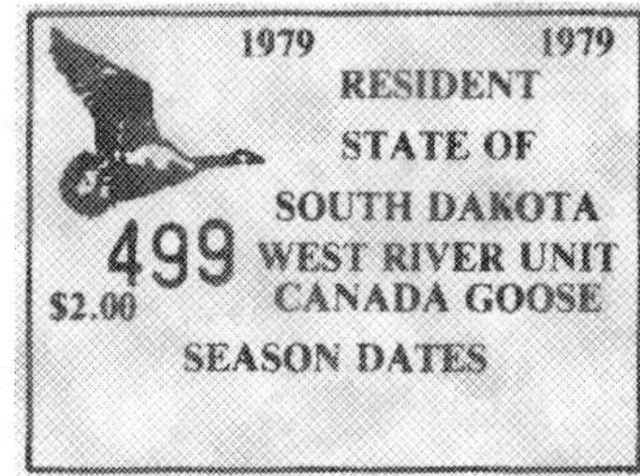

1979

2A6	$2 black, *yellow*	*350.00*	
a.	Bennettt County	400.00	*225.00*
b.	Haakon County	200.00	
c.	Jackson County	210.00	
d.	Pennington County	175.00	*85.00*

Stamps overprinted for Perkins County exist but may not have been regularly issued.

1980

2A7	$2 black, *blue*	75.00	
a.	Bennett County	200.00	*75.00*
b.	Haakon County	100.00	
c.	Jackson County	110.00	
d.	As "c," missing serial number	*3,750.*	
e.	Pennington County	90.00	*45.00*
f.	Perkins County	110.00	

Prairie Canada Geese

Counties or Units handstamped.

Used values are for signed stamps.

1981

Perf. 12

2A8	$2 black, *red*	8.00	
a.	Bennett County	80.00	*35.00*
b.	Haakon County	60.00	*20.00*
c.	Jackson County	60.00	*20.00*
d.	Pennington County	60.00	
e.	Perkins County	60.00	

1982

2A9	$2 black, *blue*	110.00	
a.	Bennett County	*450.00*	*175.00*
b.	Haakon County	*350.00*	
c.	Jackson County	*350.00*	
d.	Pennington County	*350.00*	
e.	Perkins County	*350.00*	

1983

Perf. 12

2A10	$2 black, *yellow*	60.00	
a.	UNIT 2A	70.00	
b.	UNIT 31	70.00	*35.00*
c.	UNIT 39	70.00	*35.00*
d.	UNIT 49	70.00	*35.00*
e.	UNIT 53	70.00	*35.00*
f.	UNIT 11, 3mm type	100.00	*50.00*
g.	UNIT 23	100.00	

Rouletted top and bottom

2A11	$2 black, *yellow*	11.00	
a.	UNIT 2A	65.00	
b.	UNIT 6	45.00	
c.	UNIT 11, 3mm type	60.00	
d.	UNIT 11, 4½mm type	45.00	
e.	UNIT 23	45.00	
f.	UNIT 31	65.00	
g.	UNIT 32	45.00	
h.	UNIT 39	65.00	
i.	UNIT 42	45.00	
j.	UNIT 49	65.00	
k.	UNIT 53, 3mm type	45.00	
l.	UNIT 53, 4½mm type	50.00	

1984

Perf. 12

2A12	$2 black, *green*	45.00	
a.	UNIT 6	75.00	
b.	UNIT 11, 3mm type	85.00	
c.	UNIT 11, 4½mm type	75.00	
d.	UNIT 23, 3mm type	85.00	
e.	UNIT 23, 4½mm type	75.00	*30.00*
f.	UNIT 32	85.00	
g.	UNIT 42	75.00	
h.	UNIT 47, 3mm type	85.00	
i.	UNIT 53, 3mm type	75.00	
j.	UNIT 47, 4½mm type		*65.00*
k.	UNIT 53, 4½mm type		*65.00*

1985

Rouletted two adjacent sides

2A13	$2 black, *red*		
a.	UNIT 47		*90.00*
b.	UNIT 53		*90.00*
c.	UNIT 23		*100.00*
d.	UNIT 32		*140.00*
e.	UNIT 42		*100.00*
f.	UNIT 11		*140.00*

1986 South Dakota

Prairie Canada Goose

№ 01300

1986

No fee printed on stamp

Imperf. on 3 sides, rouletted at top

2A14	black		
a.	UNIT 11		*95.00*
b.	UNIT 47		*95.00*
c.	UNIT 53		*95.00*
d.	UNIT 23		*125.00*

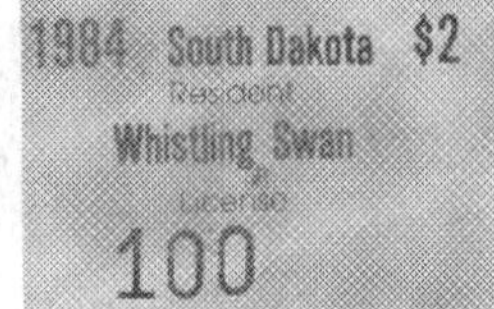

105 stamps for hunting whistling swans during the 1984 season exist. The season was canceled. Value, unused $300.

Pheasant Restoration Stamps

Required to hunt all small game, including waterfowl. Printed in booklet panes of 5. No. 3A4 rouletted, others perforated. Stamps are numbered serially.

Catalogue values for all unused stamps in this section, from this point to the end of the Wildlife Habitat stamps, are for Never Hinged items.

1977-88

3A1	$5 Pheasants	12.00	2.50
a.	Rubber-stamped serial number		—
3A2	$5 Pheasants, *1978*	12.00	1.50
3A3	$5 Pheasants, *1979*	12.00	1.50
3A4	$5 Pheasants, *1980*	10.00	2.00
a.	Serial number omitted	—	
3A5	$5 Pheasants, *1981*	10.00	1.50
3A6	$5 Pheasants, *1982*	10.00	1.50
a.	Pair, imperf. between	—	
3A7	$5 Pheasant, *1983*	10.00	1.00
3A8	$5 Pheasant, *1984*	10.00	2.00
3A9	$5 Pheasant, *1985*	10.00	2.00
3A10	$5 Pheasants, *1986*	10.00	2.50
3A11	$5 Pheasants, *1987*	10.00	2.00
3A12	$5 Pheasants, *1988*	10.00	2.00

Wildlife Habitat Stamps

Required to hunt all small game, including waterfowl. Printed in booklet panes of 5. Starting with No. 3A18 stamps are rouletted, others are perforated. Stamps are numbered serially.

1989-99

3A13	$8 Pheasants	12.00	2.00
3A14	$8 White-tailed deer, *1990*	12.00	2.00
3A15	$8 Greater prairie chicken, *1991*	12.00	2.00
3A16	$8 Mule Deer, *1992*	12.00	2.50
3A17	$8 Sharp-tailed grouse, *1993*	12.00	2.00
a.	Pair, imperf. between	—	
3A18	$8 Turkey, *1994*	12.00	2.00
3A19	$8 Elk, *1995*	12.00	2.00
3A20	$8 Pheasants, *1996*	10.00	2.00
3A21	$8 Antelope, *1997*	10.00	2.00
3A22	$8 Buffalo, *1998*	10.00	2.00
3A23	$8 Buffalo, *1999*	10.00	2.00

Resident Small Game Stamps

Required by residents wishing to hunt small game, including waterfowl. Nos. 4A1, 4A2 issued panes of 10. Others issued in booklet panes of 5. Stamps are numbered serially in red from 1960 to 1967 and 1978.

Catalogue values for all unused stamps in this section are for Never Hinged items.

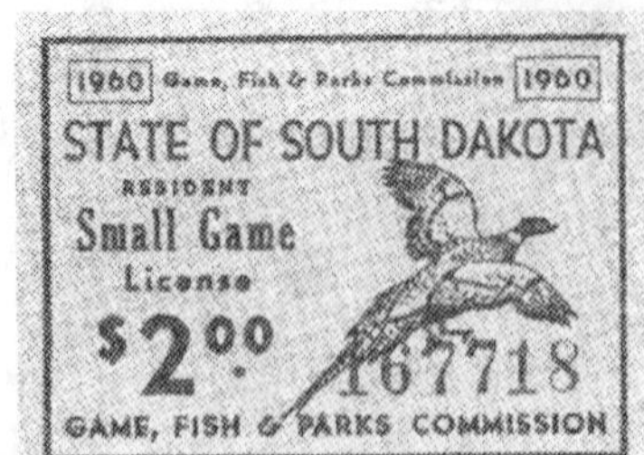

1960-79

4A1	$2 black, *pink*	12.00	2.00
4A2	$2 black, *blue, 1961*	25.00	3.00
4A3	$2 black, *dark yellow, 1962*	35.00	3.00
4A4	$2 black, *light yellow, 1963*	25.00	3.00
4A5	$2 black, *green, 1964*	25.00	3.00
4A6	$2 black, *1965*	25.00	3.00
4A7	$2 black, *yellow, 1966*	10.00	2.00
4A8	$2 black, *light green, 1967*	25.00	2.00
4A9	$2 black, *light yellow, 1968*	10.00	2.00
4A10	$3 black, *blue, 1969*	25.00	2.00
4A11	$3 black, *light yellow, 1970*	10.00	2.00
4A12	$3 black, *green, 1971*		3.00
4A13	$3 black, *light yellow, 1972*	10.00	2.00
4A14	$3 black, *light yellow, 1973*	9.00	2.00
4A15	$3 black, *1974*	10.00	2.00
4A16	$3 black, *pink, 1975*	8.00	2.00
4A17	$3 black, *gray, 1976*	6.00	1.00
4A18	$3 black, *red, 1977*	5.00	1.00
4A19	$3 black, *1978*	6.00	1.00
4A20	$3 black, *red, 1979*	7.00	1.00

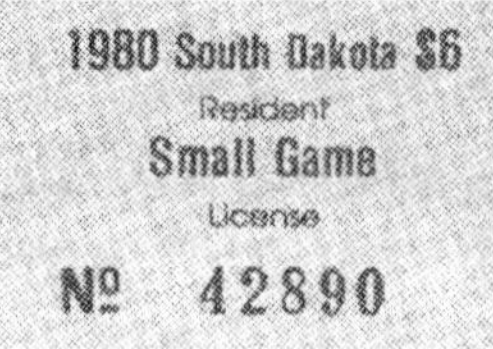

1980-98

4A21	$6 black	8.00	1.00
4A22	$6 black, *light yellow, 1981*	9.00	1.00
4A23	$6 black, *blue, 1982*	5.00	.50
4A24	$6 black, *green, 1983*	10.00	1.00
4A25	$6 black, *light blue, 1984*	*20.00*	1.00
4A26	$6 black, *light blue, 1985*	12.00	1.00
4A27	$6 black, *light blue green, 1986*		2.00
4A28	$6 black, *1987*		2.00
4A29	$6 black, *light green, 1988*	5.00	.50
4A30	$6 black, *1989*		1.00
4A31	$6 black, *light green, 1990*	8.00	.50
4A32	$6 black, *light blue green, 1991*	5.00	.50
4A33	$6 black, *light green, 1992*		1.00
4A34	$6 black, *light pink, 1993*	5.00	.50
4A35	$6 black, *light blue, 1994*	5.00	.50
4A36	$6 black, *yellow, 1995*		1.00
4A37	$6 black, *pink, 1996*	5.00	.50
4A38	$6 black, *light blue, 1997*		.50
4A39	$6 black, *pink, 1998*	8.00	.50

TENNESSEE

Stamps are die cut self-adhesives and are numbered serially.

Cards include both license cost and a fee of 30c (Nos. 1-5), 50c (Nos. 6-13) or $1 (starting with No. 14).

Nos. 3, 5, 7-15 come as 3-part card.

Starting with No. 12, cards come in four parts as well.

1979 and 1980 issues are for resident and non-resident fees.

Unused values are for stamps on original computer card stub.

Catalogue values for all unused stamps in this section are for Never Hinged items.

Artists: Dick Elliott, #1-2; Phillip Crowe, #3-4, 7, 17; Bob Gillespie, #5; Ken Schulz, #6; Allen Hughes, #8; Jimmy Stewart, #9; Ralph J. McDonald, #10, 18; Thomas Hirata, #11, 16; Jim Lamb, #12; Roger Cruwys, #13; Tom Freeman, #14; Richard Clifton, #15, 19; Bob Leslie, #20; Bethany Carter, #21; Beth Ann McMurray, #22; Nick Williamson, #23, 24.

1979-2002

1	$2 Mallards	75.00	25.00
2	$5 Mallards	*550.00*	*150.00*
3	$2 Canvasbacks, *1980*	50.00	15.00
	3-part card	325.00	

4	$5 Canvasbacks, *1980*	*325.00*	75.00
5	$2 Wood ducks, *1981*	30.00	10.00
	3-part card	—	
6	$6 Canada geese, *1982*	40.00	15.00
7	$6 Pintails, *1983*	40.00	15.00
	3-part card	45.00	
8	$6 Black ducks, *1984*	40.00	12.00
	3-part card	50.00	
9	$6 Blue-winged teal, *1985*	20.00	7.00
	3-part card	35.00	
10	$6 Mallard, *1986*	15.00	5.00
	3-part card	35.00	
11	$6 Canada geese, *1987*	12.00	5.00
	3-part card	18.00	

Card exists with 2/28/88 expiration date rather than correct 2/29 date.

12	$6 Canvasbacks, *1988*	12.00	4.00
	3-part card	20.00	
	4-part card	20.00	
13	$6 Green-winged teal, *1989*	11.00	4.00
	3-part card	14.00	
	4-part card	14.00	
14	$12 Redheads, *1990*	17.00	4.00
	3-part card	20.00	
	4-part card	20.00	
15	$12 Mergansers, *1991*	17.00	4.00
	3-part card	20.00	
	4-part card	20.00	
16	$13 Wood ducks, *1992*	17.00	4.00
	4-part card	20.00	
17	$13 Pintails & decoy, *1993*	18.00	4.00
	4-part card	20.00	
18	$15 Mallard, *1994*	20.00	5.00
	4-part card	22.50	
19	$16 Ring-necked duck, *1995*	20.00	5.00
	4-part card	22.50	
20	$17 Black ducks, *1996*	21.00	5.00
	4-part card	25.00	

Starting with No. 21 stamps are perforated. Not required for hunting.

21	$10 Mallard, *1999*	13.00	2.50
22	$10 Bufflehead, *2000*	13.00	2.50
23	$10 Wood ducks, *2001*	13.00	2.50
24	$10 Green-winged teal, *2002*	12.00	2.50

TEXAS

Printed in sheets of 10.
Nos. 1-4 are rouletted.
Stamps are numbered serially.

Catalogue values for all unused stamps in this section are for Never Hinged items.

Artists: Larry Hayden, #1, 12; Ken Carlson, #2, 14; Maynard Reece, #3; David Maass, #4, 9, 15; John Cowan, #5, 8; Herb Booth, #6; Gary Moss, #7; Robert Bateman, #10; Daniel Smith, #11, 16; Jim Hautman, #13, 17, 22; Phillip Crowe, #18; Robert Hautman, #19; Sherrie Russell Meline, #20; John Dearman, #21.

1981-2002

1	$5 Mallards	35.00	8.00
2	$5 Pintails, *1982*	25.00	5.00
3	$5 Widgeons, *1983*	125.00	18.00
4	$5 Wood ducks, *1984*	20.00	5.00
5	$5 Snow geese, *1985*	10.00	3.00
6	$5 Green-winged teal, *1986*	9.50	2.50
7	$5 White-fronted geese, *1987*	9.50	2.50
8	$5 Pintails, *1988*	9.50	2.50
9	$5 Mallards, *1989*	9.50	2.50
10	$5 American widgeons, *1990*	9.00	2.50
11	$7 Wood duck, *1991*	9.50	2.50
12	$7 Canada geese, *1992*	9.50	2.50
13	$7 Blue-winged teal, *1993*	9.50	2.50
14	$7 Shovelers, *1994*	9.50	2.50
15	$7 Buffleheads, *1995*	9.50	2.50

Beginning with No. 16, these stamps were sold only in booklets with seven other wildlife stamps and were not valid for hunting.

16	$3 Gadwalls, *1996*	12.50	
17	$3 Cinnamon teal, *1997*	12.50	
18	$3 Pintail, labrador retreiver, *1998*	12.50	
19	$3 Canvasbacks, *1999*	12.00	
20	$3 Hooded merganser, *2000*	12.00	
21	$3 Snow geese, *2000*	12.00	
22	$3 Redheads, *2002*	12.00	

UTAH

Game Bird Stamps

For hunting game birds, including waterfowl. In 1951 No. A1 or No. 2A1 were required, in 1952 No. A3 or 2A2. No. A1 printed in booklet panes of 25, others in booklet panes of 10. Perforated.

A1

A2

1951

A1	A1	$3 brown, resident	*65.00*	*7.00*
A2	A1	$15 red, non-resident	*350.00*	50.00

1952

A3	A2	$3 red, resident	*95.00*	
A4	A2	$15 blue, non-resident	*250.00*	*35.00*

Resident Fishing and Hunting Stamps

For hunting game birds, including waterfowl. Printed in sheets of 40. No. 2A1 printed on linen.
Unused values are for stamps with deer tags attached at left.

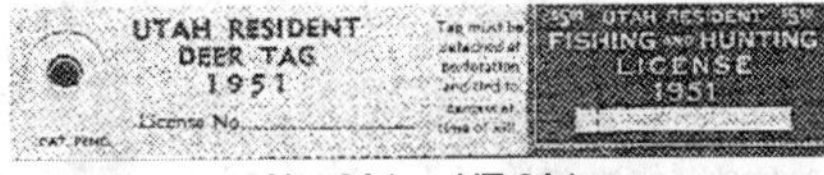

No. 2A1 — UT-2A1

No. 2A2 — UT-2A2

1951-52

2A1	$5 blue	3.00	.50
2A2	$5 green, *1952*	3.00	.50

Waterfowl Issues

Printed in sheets of 30 or in booklet panes of 5 (starting in 1990). No. 11 issued in sheets of 9.
Stamps are numbered serially.

Catalogue values for all unused stamps in this section are for Never Hinged items.

Artists: Leon Parsons, #1; Arthur Anderson, #2; David Chapple, #3; Jim Morgan, #4; Daniel Smith, #5; Robert Steiner, #6-12.

1986-97

1	$3.30 Whistling swans	9.50	3.00
2	$3.30 Pintails, *1987*	7.50	3.00
3	$3.30 Mallards, *1988*	7.50	2.50
4	$3.30 Canada geese, *1989*	6.50	2.50
5	$3.30 Canvasbacks, perf. 4 sides, *1990*	6.50	
a.	Booklet single, with 2-part tab	8.00	2.50
6	$3.30 Tundra swans, perf. 4 sides, *1991*	6.00	
a.	Booklet single, with 2-part tab	7.00	2.50
7	$3.30 Pintails, perf. 4 sides, *1992*	6.00	
a.	Booklet single, with 2-part tab	7.00	2.50
8	$3.30 Canvasbacks, perf. 4 sides, *1993*	6.00	
a.	Booklet single, with 2-part tab	7.00	2.50
9	$3.30 Chesapeake Retriever and ducks, perf. 4 sides, *1994*	*75.00*	
a.	Booklet single, with 2-part tab	*65.00*	2.50
10	$3.30 Green-winged teal, *1995*	6.00	
a.	Booklet single, with 2-part tab	7.00	2.50
11	$7.50 White-fronted goose, *1996*	12.00	2.50
a.	$97.50 Governor's edition	125.00	

Redheads: a, Male, serial # at UL. b, Female, serial # at LL.

12	Pair, *1997*	45.00	
a.-b.	$7.50 Any single	11.00	2.50
c.	$97.50 Governor's Edition	110.00	

No. 12c is No. 12 without the central perforations. The denomination appears only in the upper right corner. The bottom inscription has Governor's Edition plus a serial number.

VERMONT

Printed in sheets of 30.

Catalogue values for all unused stamps in this section are for Never Hinged items.

Artists: Jim Killen, #1-4; Richard Plasschaert, #5-8; Reed Prescott, #9, 11; Robert Mullen, #10; J. Collins, #12; George Lockwood, #13-17.

1986-2002

1	$5 Wood ducks	11.00	4.00
2	$5 Common goldeneyes, *1987*	8.00	3.00
3	$5 Black ducks, *1988*	8.00	2.50
4	$5 Canada geese, *1989*	8.00	2.50
5	$5 Green-winged teal, *1990*	8.00	2.50
6	$5 Hooded mergansers, *1991*	7.50	2.50
7	$5 Snow geese, *1992*	7.50	2.50
8	$5 Mallards, *1993*	10.00	2.50
9	$5 Ring-necked duck, *1994*	10.00	2.50
10	$5 Bufflehead, *1995*	10.00	2.50
11	$5 Lesser scaup, *1996*	10.00	2.50
12	$5 Pintails, *1997*	7.50	2.50
13	$5 Blue-winged teal, *1998*	7.00	2.50
14	$5 Canvasbacks, *1999*	7.00	2.50
15	$5 Widgeons, *2000*	7.00	2.50
16	$5 Oldsquaws, *2001*	7.00	2.50
17	$5 Greater scaups, *2002*	7.00	2.50

VIRGINIA

Printed in booklet panes of 10 and/or sheets of 30.
Stamps are numbered serially.

Catalogue values for all unused stamps in this section are for Never Hinged items.

Artists: Ronald Louque, #1; Arthur LeMay, #2; Louis Frisino, #3; Robert Leslie, #4, 11; Carl Knuth, #5, 12; Bruce Miller, #6; Francis Sweet, #7; Richard Clifton, #8; Wilhelm Goebel, #9; Roger Cruwys, #10; Tim Donovan, #13, 14; Jim Wilson, #15.

1988-2002

1	$5 Mallards, serial Nos. 1-40,000	12.00	2.50
	Booklet pair with L & R selvage, serial Nos. above 40,000	24.00	
2	$5 Canada geese, serial Nos. 1-40,000, *1989*	12.00	2.50
	Booklet pair with L & R selvage, serial Nos. above 40,000	24.00	
3	$5 Wood ducks, serial Nos. 1-20,000, *1990*	9.00	2.50
	Booklet pair with L & R selvage, serial Nos. above 20,000	18.00	
4	$5 Canvasbacks, serial Nos. 1-20,000, *1991*	8.50	2.50
	Booklet pair with L & R selvage, serial Nos. above 20,000	17.00	
5	$5 Buffleheads, serial Nos. 1-20,000, *1992*	8.00	2.50
	Booklet pair with L & R selvage, serial Nos. above 20,000	16.00	
6	$5 Black ducks, serial Nos. 1-20,000, *1993*	8.00	2.50
	Booklet pair with L & R selvage, serial Nos. above 20,000	16.00	
7	$5 Lesser scaup, *1994*	7.50	2.50
	Booklet pair with L & R selvage	15.00	
8	$5 Snow geese, *1995*	7.50	2.50
	Booklet pair with L & R selvage	15.00	
9	$5 Hooded mergansers, *1996*	7.50	2.50
10	($5) Pintail, Labrador retriever, *1997*	7.50	2.50
11	$5 Mallards, *1998*	7.50	2.50
12	$5 Green-winged teal, *1999*	7.50	2.50
13	$5 Mallards, *2000*	7.50	2.50
14	$5 Blue-winged teal, *2001*	7.50	2.50
15	$5 Canvasbacks, *2002*	7.50	2.50

WASHINGTON

Printed in booklet panes of 1 and sheets of 30. Stamps are numbered serially. Booklet panes starting with No. 7 without staple holes were sold to collectors.

Catalogue values for all unused stamps in this section are for Never Hinged items.

Artists: Keith Warrick, #1; Ray Nichol, #2; Robert Bateman, #3; Maynard Reece, #4; Thomas Quinn, #5; Ronald Louque, #6-7; Phillip Crowe, #8; Fred Thomas, #9; David Hagenbaumer, #10; Cynthie Fisher, #11; Greg Beecham, #12; A. Young, #13; Robert Steiner, #14-16; Adam Grimm, #17; Don Nicholson Miller, #18.

1986-2002

1	$5 Mallards, Nos. 1-60,000	9.00	
	Booklet pane of 1, Nos. 60,001-160,000	12.50	4.00
2	$5 Canvasbacks, Nos. 1-24,000, *1987*	9.50	
	Booklet pane of 1, Nos. 24,001-124,000	10.00	3.00
3	$5 Harlequin, Nos. 1-60,000, *1988*	9.00	
	Booklet pane of 1, Nos. 60,001-160,000	10.00	3.00
4	$5 American widgeons, Nos. 1-60,000, *1989*	9.00	
	Booklet pane of 1, Nos. 60,001-160,000	10.00	2.50
5	$5 Pintails & sour duck, Nos. 1-60,000, *1990*	9.00	
	Booklet pane of 1, Nos. 60,001-160,000	10.00	2.50
6	$5 Wood duck, Nos. 1-30,000, *1991*	9.00	
	Booklet pane of 1, Nos. above 30,000	10.00	4.00
7	$6 Wood duck, Nos. 100,000-130,000, *1991*	10.00	
	Booklet pane of 1, Nos. above 130,000	10.00	2.50
8	$6 Labrador puppy & Canada geese, Nos. 1-30,000, *1992*	9.00	
	Booklet pane of 1, Nos. above 30,000	10.00	2.50
9	$6 Snow geese, Nos. 1-30,000, *1993*	8.00	
	Booklet pane of 1, Nos. above 30,000	9.00	2.50
10	$6 Black brant, Nos. 1-30,000, *1994*	8.00	
	Booklet pane of 1, Nos. above 30,000	9.00	2.50
11	$6 Mallards, Nos. 1-30,000, *1995*	8.00	
	Booklet pane of 1, Nos. above 30,000	9.00	2.50
12	$6 Redheads, Nos. 1-25,050, *1996*	8.00	
	Booklet pane of 1, Nos. above 25,050	9.00	2.50
13	$6 Canada geese, Nos. 9600001-9625050, *1997*	8.00	
	Bklt. pane of 1, Nos. above 9625050	9.00	2.50
14	$6 Barrow's goldeneye Nos. 1-25,050 , *1998*	8.00	
	Bklt. pane of 1, Nos. 25,051-27,050	9.00	2.50
15	$6 Bufflehead, *1999*	8.00	
a.	Bklt. pane of 1	9.00	2.50
16	$6 Canada geese, mallard, widgeon, *2000*	8.00	
a.	Bklt. pane of 1	9.00	2.50
17	$6 Mallards, *2001*	8.00	
a.	Bklt. pane of 1	9.00	2.50
18	$10 Green-winged teal, *2002*	13.50	
a.	Souvenir sheet of 1	15.00	2.50

WEST VIRGINIA

Printed in sheets of 30 and booklet panes of 5. All booklet stamps have straight edges at sides. Starting in 1990, booklet stamps are numbered serially. Some, but not all, of the 1988 booklet stamps are numbered serially. Stamps from sheets are not numbered serially.

Catalogue values for all unused stamps in this section are for Never Hinged items.

Artists: Daniel Smith, #1-2; Steven Dillard, #3-4; Ronald Louque, #5-6; Louis Frisino, #7-8; Robert Leslie, #9-10; Thomas Hirata, #11-12; Phillip Crowe, #13-14; Richard Clifton, #15-16; Fran Sweet, #17-18; Karl Badgley, #19-20.

1987-96

1	$5 Canada geese, resident	13.00	8.00
	Booklet single with tab at top	75.00	
2	$5 Canada geese, non-resident	13.00	8.00
	Booklet single with tab at top	75.00	
3	$5 Wood ducks, resident, *1988*	10.00	4.00
	Booklet single with tab at top, no serial number	40.00	
a.	Booklet single with serial number on reverse	85.00	4.00
4	$5 Wood ducks, non-resident, *1988*	10.00	4.00
	Booklet single with tab at top, no serial number	40.00	
a.	Booklet single with serial number on reverse	85.00	4.00
5	$5 Decoys, resident, *1989*	9.50	3.00
	Booklet single with tab at top	35.00	
a.	Governor's edition	*70.00*	
6	$5 Decoys, non-resident, *1989*	9.50	3.00
	Booklet single with tab at top	35.00	
a.	Governor's edition	*70.00*	

Nos. 5a and 6a were available only in sheets of 30 through a sealed bid auction.

7	$5 Labrador retriever & decoy, resident, *1990*	9.00	
a.	Booklet single	9.00	3.00
8	$5 Labrador retriever & decoy, non-resident, *1990*	9.00	
a.	Booklet single	9.00	3.00
9	$5 Mallards, resident, *1991*	8.50	
a.	Booklet single	8.50	2.50
10	$5 Mallards, non-resident, *1991*	8.50	
a.	Booklet single	8.50	2.50
b.	Sheet, 3 each #9-10	50.00	

No. 10b is numbered serially; exists imperf. without serial numbers.

11	$5 Canada geese, resident, *1992*	8.50	
a.	Booklet single	8.50	2.50
12	$5 Canada geese, non-resident, *1992*	8.50	
a.	Booklet single	8.50	2.50
13	$5 Pintails, resident, *1993*	8.00	
a.	Booklet single	8.00	2.50
14	$5 Pintails, non-resident, *1993*	8.00	
a.	Booklet single	8.00	2.50
15	$5 Green-winged teal, resident, *1994*	8.00	
a.	Booklet single	8.00	2.50
16	$5 Green-winged teal, non-resident, *1994*	8.00	
a.	Booklet single	8.00	2.50
17	$5 Mallards, resident, *1995*	8.00	
a.	Booklet single	8.00	2.50
18	$5 Mallards, non-resident, *1995*	8.00	
a.	Booklet single	8.00	2.50
19	$5 Widgeons, resident, *1996*	8.00	
a.	Booklet single	8.00	2.50
20	$5 Widgeons, non-resident, *1996*	8.00	
a.	Booklet single	8.00	2.50

WISCONSIN

Printed in sheets of 10. Starting in 1980 the left side of the sheet has an agent tab and a numbered tab, the right side a numbered tab.

Catalogue values for all unused stamps in this section are for Never Hinged items.

Artists: Owen Gromme, #1; Rockne (Rocky) Knuth, #2, 6; Martin Murk, #3; Timothy Schultz, #4; William Koelpin, #5; Michael James Riddet, #7, 15; Greg Alexander, #8, 20; Don Moore, #9, 17, 23; Al Kraayvanger, #10; Richard Timm, #11; Rick Kelley, #12; Daniel Renn Pierce, #13; Terry Doughty, #14, 25; Frank Middlestadt, #16, 22; Les Didler, #18, 21, 24; Sam Timm, #19.

1978-2002

1	$3.25 Wood ducks	50.00	9.00
2	$3.25 Buffleheads, rouletted, *1979*	20.00	6.00
3	$3.25 Widgeons, *1980*	12.00	2.50
	With tab	15.00	
4	$3.25 Lesser Scaup, *1981*	9.50	2.50
	With tab	13.00	
5	$3.25 Pintails, *1982*	8.00	2.50
	With numbered tab	8.00	
	With agent's and numbered tab	10.00	
6	$3.25 Blue-winged teal, *1983*	8.00	2.50
	With numbered tab	8.00	
	With agent's and numbered tab	10.00	
7	$3.25 Hooded merganser, *1984*	8.00	2.50
	With numbered tab	8.00	
	With agent's and numbered tab	10.00	
8	$3.25 Lesser scaup, *1985*	8.50	2.50
	With numbered tab	8.50	
	With agent's and numbered tab	10.00	
9	$3.25 Canvasbacks, *1986*	8.50	2.50
	With numbered tab	8.50	
	With agent's and numbered tab	10.00	
10	$3.25 Canada geese, *1987*	6.00	2.50
	With numbered tab	6.00	
	With agent's and numbered tab	7.00	
11	$3.25 Hooded merganser, *1988*	6.00	2.50
	With numbered tab	6.00	
	With agent's and numbered tab	7.00	
12	$3.25 Common goldeneye, *1989*	6.00	2.50
	With numbered tab	6.00	
	With agent's and numbered tab	7.00	
13	$3.25 Redheads, *1990*	6.00	2.50
	With numbered tab	6.00	
	With agent's and numbered tab	7.00	
14	$5.25 Green-winged teal, *1991*	8.00	2.50
	With numbered tab	8.00	
	With agent's and numbered tab	9.00	
15	$5.25 Tundra swans, *1992*	8.00	2.50
	With numbered tab	8.00	
	With agent's and numbered tab	9.00	
16	$5.25 Wood ducks, *1993*	8.00	2.50
	With numbered tab	8.00	
	With agent's and numbered tab	9.00	
17	$5.25 Pintails, *1994*	8.00	2.50
	With numbered tab	8.00	
	With agent's and numbered tabs	9.00	
18	$5.25 Mallards, *1995*	8.00	2.50
	With numbered tab	8.00	
	With agent's and numbered tabs	9.00	
19	($5.25) Green-winged teal, *1996*	8.00	2.50
	With numbered tab	8.00	
	With agent's and numbered tabs	9.00	
20	($7) Canada geese, *1997*	9.50	2.50
	With numbered tab	9.50	
	With agent's and numbered tabs	10.00	
21	$7 Snow goose, *1998*	9.50	2.50
	With numbered tab	9.50	
	With agent's and numbered tabs	10.00	
22	$7 Greater scaups, *1999*	9.00	2.50
23	$7 Canvasbacks, *2000*	9.00	2.50
24	$7 Common goldeneyes, *2001*	9.00	2.50
25	$7 Shovelers, *2002*	9.00	2.50

WYOMING

00.00'>

Issued in panes of 5. Required to fish as well as to hunt all small and big game, including waterfowl. Stamps are numbered serially.

Catalogue values for all unused stamps in this section are for Never Hinged items.

Artists: From photo by Luroy Parker, #1; Robert Kusserow, #2; Dan Andrews, #3; Ted Feeley, #4; Clark Ostergaard, #5; Dave Wade, #6, 8, 10, 13, 17; Connie J. Robinson, #7; Sarah Rogers, #9; James Brooks, #11; Peter Eades, #12; D. Enright, #14; Garth Hegeson, #15; Nick Reitzel, #16; Brent Todd, #18; Paul Kay, #19.

No. 1 is in vertical format. All others are horizontal.

1984-2002

1	$5 Meadowlark	50.00	5.00
2	$5 Canada geese, *1985*	40.00	5.00
3	$5 Antelope, *1986*	50.00	4.00
4	$5 Grouse, *1987*	55.00	4.00
5	$5 Fish, *1988*	55.00	4.00
6	$5 Deer, *1989*	110.00	4.00
7	$5 Bear, *1990*	40.00	4.00
8	$5 Rams, *1991*	40.00	3.50
9	$5 Bald eagle, *1992*	40.00	3.50
10	$5 Elk, *1993*	25.00	3.50
11	$5 Bobcat, *1994*	15.00	3.50
12	$5 Moose, *1995*	15.00	3.50
13	$5 Turkey, *1996*	10.00	3.00
14	$5 Mountain goats, *1997*	10.00	3.00
15	$5 Trumpeter swan, *1998*	10.00	3.00
16	$5 Brown trout, *1999*	10.00	3.00
17	$5 Buffalo, *2000*	10.00	3.00
18	$10 White-tailed deer, *2001*	19.00	5.00
19	$10 River otters, *2002*	19.00	5.00

INDIAN RESERVATIONS

Stamps for other reservations exist and will be listed after more information is received about them.

CHEYENNE RIVER INDIAN RESERVATION

South Dakota
Birds and Small Game Stamps

Nos. A1-A2 issued in booklet panes of 6, rouletted. Nos. A3-A4 issued in booklet panes of 5, perforated, self-adhesive. Nos. A5-A6 issued in booklet panes of 5, perforated.

A1

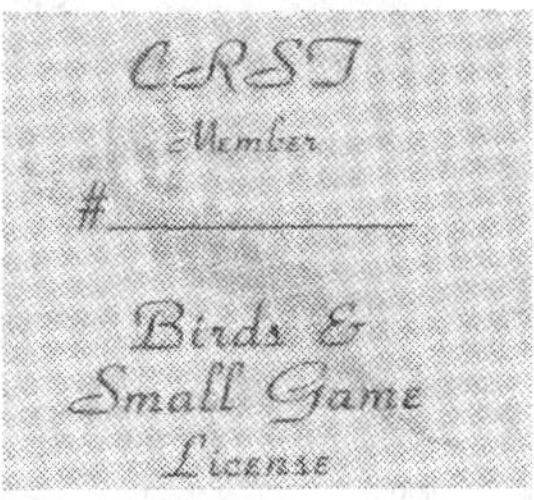

A2

A1	A1	black, *light yellow*, member	*1,350.*	*200.00*
A2	A1	black, *yellow*, non-member	*450.00*	*110.00*

Nos. A1-A2 probably issued starting in 1984.

Catalogue values for all unused stamps in this section, from this point to the end, are for Never Hinged items.

A3	A2	black, *yellow*, member	25.00	10.00
A4	A2	black, *yellow*, non-member	45.00	15.00
A5	A2	black, *light yellow*, member	13.00	5.00
A6	A2	black, *light yellow*, non-member	27.50	10.00

Nos. A3-A4 issued starting in 1989. Nos. A5-A6 issued starting in 1992.

Waterfowl Stamps

Issued starting in 1993 in panes of 5. Perforated.

Catalogue values for all unused stamps in this section are for Never Hinged items.

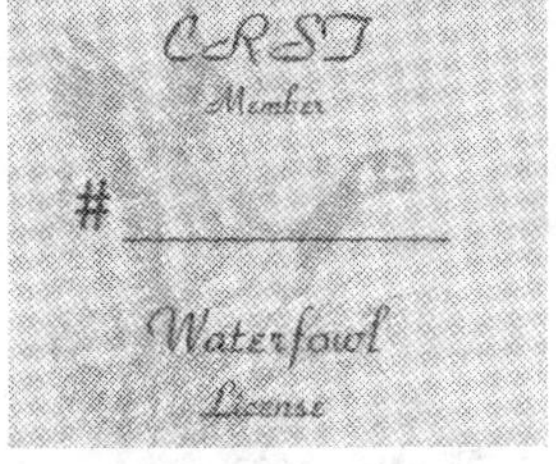

1	black, *light yellow*, member	15.00	5.00
2	black *light yellow*, non-member	27.50	10.00

COLVILLE INDIAN RESERVATION

Washington
Bird Stamps

Required by non-tribal members to hunt birds, including waterfowl. Stamps are die cut, self-adhesive. No. 2 is numbered serially in red.

Catalogue values for all unused stamps in this section are for Never Hinged items.

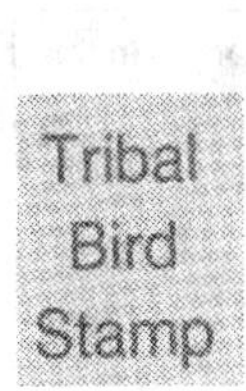

A1

1991 Tribal Bird Stamp Nº 0056 $20.00

A2

1990-91

1	A1		black, *yellow*	—
2	A2	$20	black, *yellow, 1992*	—

CROW INDIAN RESERVATION

Montana
Waterfowl Stamps

Issued in panes of 5 stamps (4 each No. 1, 1 No. 1a). Die cut, self-adhesive. Numbered serially in red.

Catalogue values for all unused stamps in this section are for Never Hinged items.

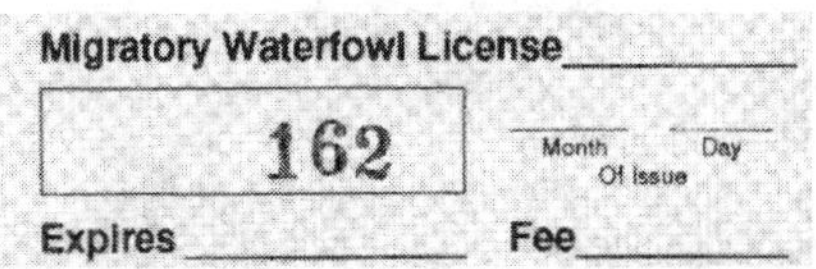

Migratory Waterfowl License
162
Month Day
Of Issue
Expires
Fee

1992

1	blue	*95.00*	*25.00*
a.	Inscribed "Apr. 30, 199_"	*300.00*	*75.00*

Stamps without serial numbers exist. Some may have been issue to hunters during an abbreviated 1993 season.

CROW CREEK SIOUX INDIAN RESERVATION

South Dakota
Non-Indian Small Game Hunting Stamps

Issued 1961-64. The 1961 fee was $2.50. No example is recorded. The 1962 stamps were changed by hand for use in 1963 and 1964. No example of the 1964 stamp is recorded.

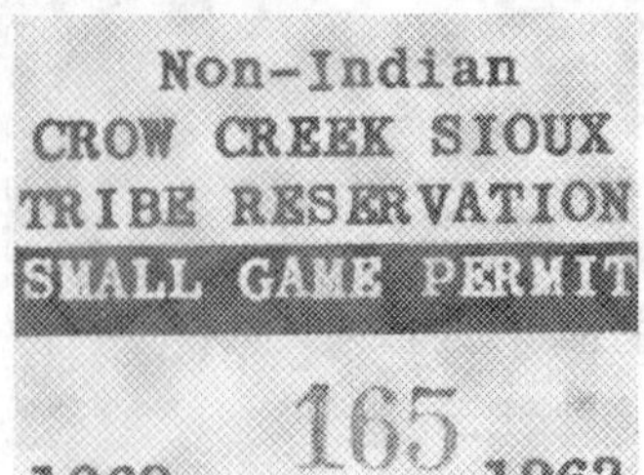

1962-63

2	$5 black	*13,500.*	—
3	$5 black, *1963*	—	—

Waterfowl Stamps

Fees: $10, reservation resident, non-tribal member; $30, South Dakota resident; $65, non-South Dakota resident.

Catalogue values for all unused stamps in this section, from this point to the end, are for Never Hinged items.

1989

5	$10 black	500.	*150.*
6	$30 black	*10,500.*	*1,000.*
7	$65 black	*1,350.*	*350.*

1990

8	$10 black	300.	*100.*
9	$30 black	250.	
10	$65 black	1,200.	*300.*

Fees: $5, tribal member; $15, affiliate, reservation resident; $30 ($35), South Dakota resident/non-resident daily use; $75 ($100), South Dakota resident/non-resident season.

1994

11	$5 green	75.00	15.00
12	$15 blue	100.00	
13	$30 red	125.00	
a.	$25 red (error)	—	
14	$75 red	200.00	65.00

1995

15	$5 green	35.00	10.00
16	$15 blue	55.00	
17	$30 red	95.00	
18	$75 red	150.00	40.00

1996

19	$5 green	27.50	10.00
20	$15 blue	45.00	
21	$35 red	75.00	
22	$100 red	125.00	35.00

1997

23	$5 green	12.00	
24	$15 blue	35.00	
25	$35 red	85.00	
26	$75 red	190.00	

No. 25 is inscribed $75, but sold for $35.

1998

27	$5 green	12.00	
28	$15 blue	35.00	
29	$35 red	85.00	
30	$75 red	190.00	

1999

31	$5 green	12.00	
32	$15 blue	35.00	
33	$35 red	85.00	
34	$75 red	190.00	

Sportsmen's Stamps

For hunting game including waterfowl.

Fees: $10, tribal member; $25, reservation resident, non-tribal member; $100, South Dakota resident; $250, non-South Dakota resident.

Used values are for signed stamps.

Catalogue values for all unused stamps in this section are for Never Hinged items.

1989

A1	$10 black	450.00	*100.00*
A2	$25 black	1,150.	*300.00*
A3	$100 black	450.00	*75.00*
A4	$250 black	450.00	*150.00*

1990

A5	$10 black	500.00	*100.00*
A6	$25 black	650.00	*150.00*
A7	$100 black	275.00	*125.00*
A8	$250 black	400.00	*150.00*

FLATHEAD INDIAN RESERVATION

Montana
Bird or Fish Stamps

The 1988 stamp was printed in booklet panes of 10. Starting in 1989, printed in booklet panes of 5 stamps se-tenant with 5 stamps marked "Duplicate." Numbered serially in red. Rouletted.

Catalogue values for all unused stamps in this section are for Never Hinged items.

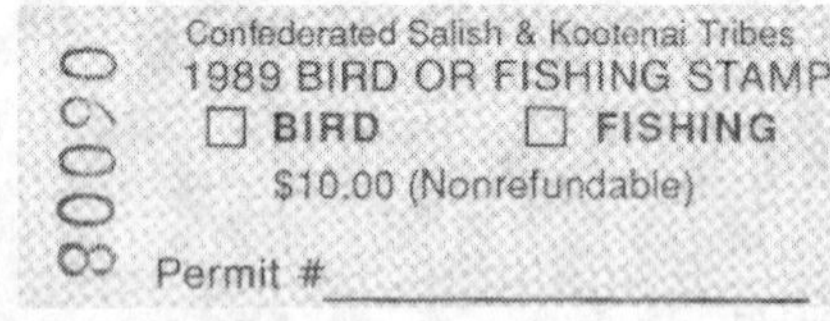

1987-90

1	$10 black	*1,450.*	*350.00*
1A	$10 black, *1988*	*1,650.*	*275.00*
2	$10 blue, *1989*	16.00	5.00
3	$10 blue, *1990*	16.00	5.00

Joint Bird License Stamps

Printed in booklet panes of 10. Die cut, self-adhesive. Numbered serially.

1991

4	$10 black, *green*	10.50	5.00

Bird License Stamps

Printed in booklet panes of 10. Die cut, self-adhesive. Numbered serially.

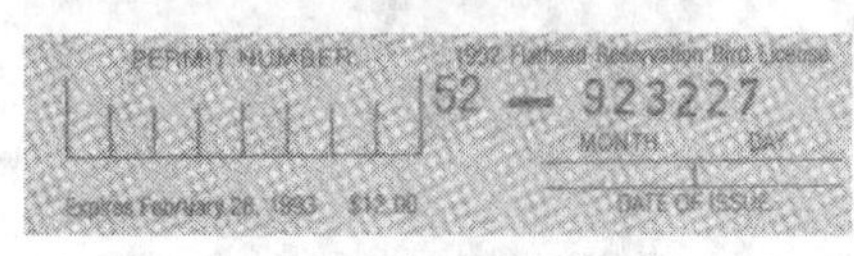

1992-2000

5	$12 black, *rose,* season	10.50	5.00
6	$12 black, *salmon,* 3-day	9.50	5.00
7	$12 black, *dark green,* season, *1993*	8.00	4.00
8	$12 black, *dark blue,* 3-day, *1993*	7.50	4.00
9	$12 black, *blue,* season, *1994*	8.00	4.00
10	$12 black, *orange,* 3-day, *1994*	7.00	3.00
11	$12 black, *yellow,* resident, *1995*	8.00	3.00
12	$55 black, *pale blue green,* non-resident, *1995*	*17.50*	*9.00*
13	$12 black, *turquoise,* resident, *1996*	11.00	3.00
14	$55 black, *pale orange,* non-resident, *1996*	*18.00*	*15.00*
15	$12 black, *pale yellow,* resident, *1997*	10.00	3.00
16	$55 black, *pale blue green,* non-resident, *1997*	*11.00*	
17	$13 black, *turquoise,* resident, *1998*	12.00	3.00
18	$56 black, *blue,* non-resident, *1998*	*12.00*	*3.00*
19	$13 black, *orange,* resident, *1999*	10.00	3.00
20	$56 black, *red,* non-resident, *1999*	*10.00*	*3.00*
21	$13 black, *yellow,* reservation, *2000*	12.00	3.00
22	$14 black, *green,* resident, *2000*	12.00	3.00
23	$110 black, *pink,* out-of-state, *2000*	*12.00*	*3.00*

FORT BERTHOLD INDIAN RESERVATION

North Dakota
Small Game Stamps

Stamps issued before 1990 may exist.

Issued in booklet panes of 6 stamps and 6 tabs. Required for hunting small game including waterfowl.

Values are for stamps with tabs. Fees varied, usually $6 for tribe members and $20-$30 for non-members.

Stamps are numbered serially.

Catalogue values for all unused stamps in this section are for Never Hinged items.

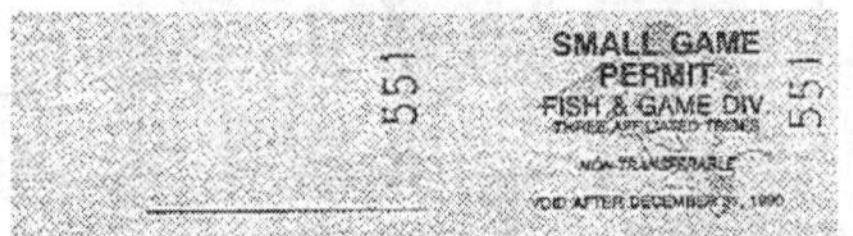

1990-98

Rouletted

A6	black, *pink*	*85.00*	*25.00*
A7	black, *green, 1991*	*80.00*	
A8	black, *pink, 1992*	*80.00*	
A9	black, *blue, 1993*	*175.00*	
A10	black, *pink, 1994*	70.00	
A11	black, *pink, 1995*	*100.00*	*25.00*
A12	black, *green, 1996*	*57.50*	
A13	black, *light green, 1997*	50.00	*12.00*
A14	black, *green,* 1998	30.00	

Waterfowl Stamps

Stamps issued before 1990 may exist.

Issued in booklet panes of 6 stamps and 6 tabs.

Required for non-member waterfowl hunters only.

Values are for stamps with tabs.

Fees varied, usually $20-$30.

Stamps are numbered serially.

Catalogue values for all unused stamps in this section are for Never Hinged items.

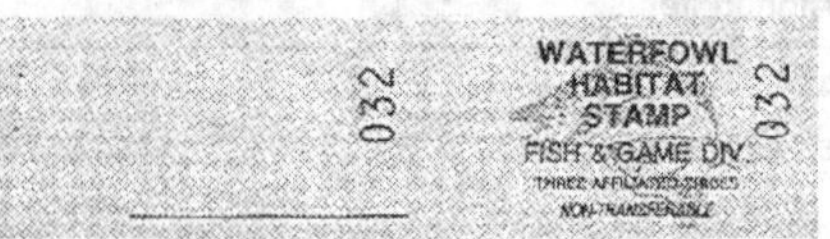

1990-2000

Rouletted

2A6	black	*2,750.*	
2A7	black, *blue, 1991*	*950.00*	
2A8	black, *yellow,* #1-60, *1992*	*4,000.*	
2A9	black, *yellow,* #61-120, *1993*	*650.00*	
2A10	black, *green,* #1-60, *1994*	*625.00*	
2A11	black, *green,* #61-120, *1995*	*275.00*	*50.00*
2A12	black, *green,* #121-198, *1996*	*225.00*	
2A13	black, *light green,* #199-276, *1997*	*250.00*	
2A14	black, *light green,* #277-, *1998*	*300.00*	
2A15	black, *light green,* #355-432, *1999*	*300.00*	
2A16	black, *light green,* #433-588, *2000*	*250.00*	

FORT PECK INDIAN RESERVATION

Montana
Stamps issued before 1975 may exist.

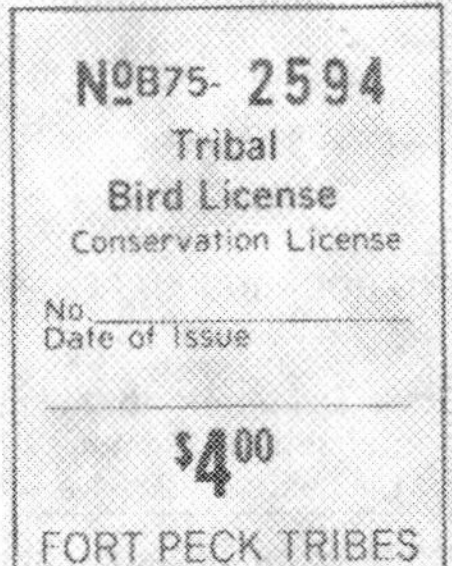

1975-78

Rouletted

2	$4 black	*1,650.*
3	$4 black, *1976*	100.
a.	Double impression	*4,250.*
4	$4 black, *1977*	—
5	$5 black, *orange, 1978*	325.

JICARILLA APACHE INDIAN RESERVATION

New Mexico
Wildlife Stamp

Believed to have been issued starting in 1988. Issued in booklet panes of 4. Numbered serially. Rouletted.

Catalogue values for all unused stamps in this section are for Never Hinged items.

1	$5 black & gold, *blue*	12.00

LAKE TRAVERSE (SISSETON-WAHPETON) INDIAN RESERVATION

South Dakota-North Dakota
Waterfowl Stamps

No examples are recorded of stamps from 1987-1990. No. 1 is die cut. Nos. 6, 8-9 are die cut, self-adhesive. No. 7 issued in booklet panes of 5, rouletted, numbered serially in red.

A1

1991 S.W.S.T.
WATERFOWL
License

A2

A3

A4

1986-2000

1	A1	green	200.00	75.00

Catalogue values for all unused stamps in this section, from this point to the end, are for Never Hinged items.

6	A2	black, *bright green, 1991*	*110.00*	
7	A3	Wood duck, *1992*	15.00	
8	A2	black, *bright red, 1993*	25.00	
9	A4	black, *yellow orange, 1994*	7.50	4.00

Inscribed SWST

10	A4	black, *red orange, 1995*	12.00	4.00
11	A4	black, *blue, 1996*	10.00	4.00
12	A4	black, *bright green, 1997*	11.00	3.00
13	A4	black, *red, 1998*	40.00	
14	A4	black, *orange, 1999*	10.00	
15	A4	black, *orange, 2000*	35.00	

LOWER BRULE INDIAN RESERVATION

South Dakota
Waterfowl Stamps

Serial Nos. are in red. Year and fee are written by hand or typewritten on each stamp. The $5 fee was for for non-members and non-Indians. There was a $2.50 fee for tribal members but no examples of these stamps are recorded.

Numbers have been reserved for the $2.50 stamps.

Since no year is on an unused copy, they are listed under the first year only.

1962-70

2	$5 black	—
4	$5 black, *1963*	—
6	$5 black, *1964*	*2,500.*
8	$5 black, *1965*	*2,500.*
10	$5 black, *1966*	*2,200.*
12	$5 black, *1967*	*1,950.*
14	$5 black, *1968*	*1,900.*
18	$5 black, *1969*	*3,250.*

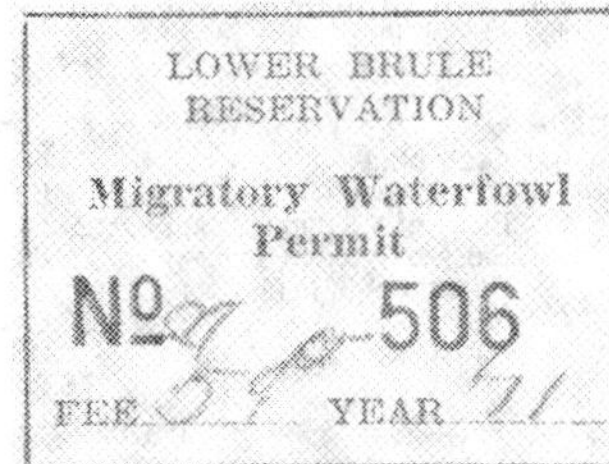

1969-71

20	$5 black	*3,750.*
24	$5 black, *1971*	—
26	$5 black, *1972*	—

Migratory Bird Hunting and Conservation Stamps

Issued in panes of 20.
All stamps have serial number on reverse.

Catalogue values for all unused stamps in this section, from this point to the end, are for Never Hinged items.

1995

27	$5 green, tribal member	7.00
28	$5 orange brown, resident deeded land owner / operator	7.00
29	$5 blue, resident government employee	7.00
30	$10 red, non-tribal S.D. resident	12.00
31	$10 purple, non-resident, out of state	12.00

1996

32	$5 multi, tribal / resident	7.00
33	$10 multi, non-tribal S.D. resident	12.00
34	$10 multi, non-resident, out of state	12.00

1997

35	$5 multi, tribal / resident	7.00
36	$10 multi, non-tribal S.D. resident	12.00
37	$10 multi, non-resident, out of state	12.00

Nos. 38-40 have been reserved for 1998 stamps which were printed, but use of which has not yet been verified.

1999

41	$5 multi, tribal / resident	7.00
42	$10 multi, non-tribal S. D. resident	14.00
43	$10 multi, non-resident, out of state	14.00

PINE RIDGE (OGLALA SIOUX) INDIAN RESERVATION

South Dakota
Waterfowl Stamps

Nos. 1-5 issued in booklet panes of 5, numbered serially in red.

No. 2 perforated, others rouletted. Nos. 4-5 have simulated perforations.

A1

A2

A3

1	A1	$4 black	*350.00*

Earliest known use of No. 1 is 1988.

Catalogue values for all unused stamps in this section, from this point to the end, are for Never Hinged items.

2	A1	$4 black, perforated	15.00
3	A2	$4 Canada geese, *1992*	11.00

$6 stamps picturing Canada geese were produced and sold for the 1993 season. The same stamp was rubber hand-stamped for the 1994 season. However, there was no hunting season those years. Value, each $15.

ROSEBUD INDIAN RESERVATION

South Dakota
Tribal Game Bird Stamps

Nos. 1, 3-4 have red serial number. Stamps for 1960, 1963-69 may exist.

Since no year is on an unused copy, they are listed under the first year only.

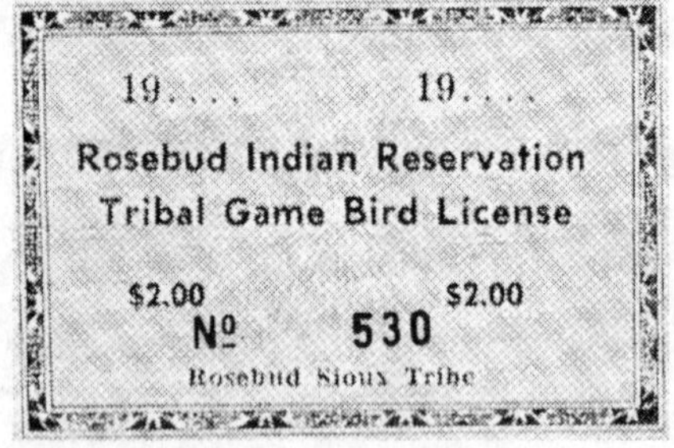

1959-62

1	$2 green	—	
3	$2 green, *1961*	*4,950.*	
4	$2 green, *1962*	*5,500.*	

Small Game Stamps

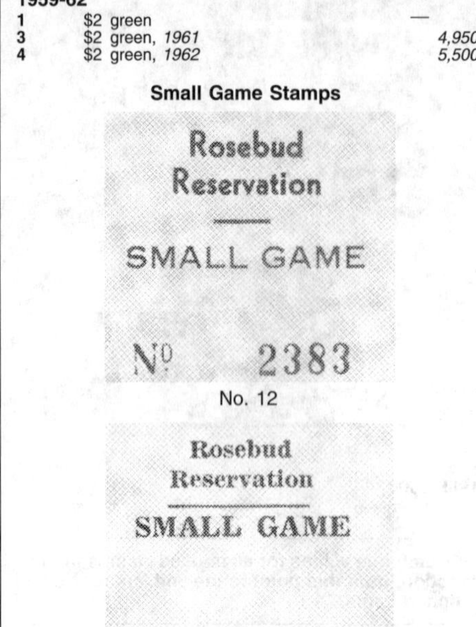

No. 12

No. 13

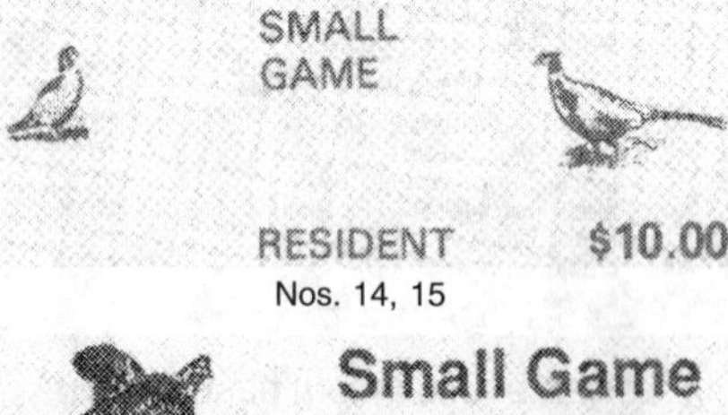

Nos. 14, 15

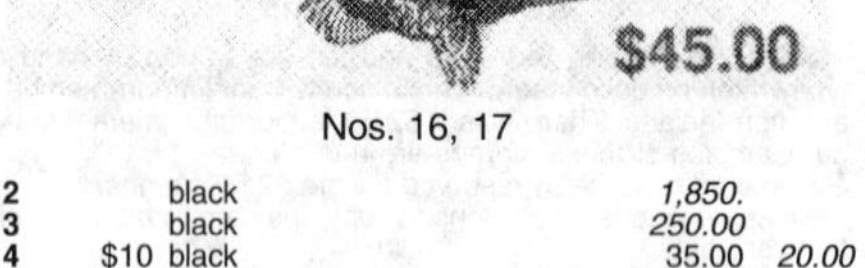

Nos. 16, 17

12		black	*1,850.*	
13		black	*250.00*	
14	$10	black	35.00	*20.00*

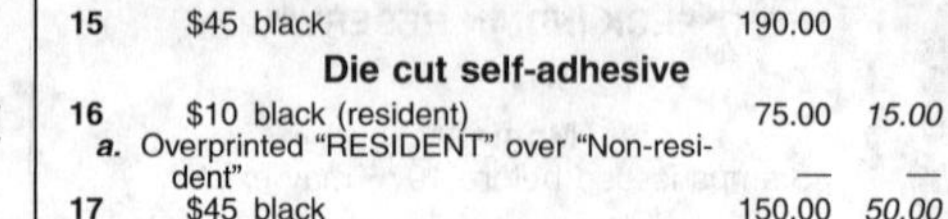

15	$45 black	190.00	

Die cut self-adhesive

16	$10 black (resident)	75.00	*15.00*
a.	Overprinted "RESIDENT" over "Non-resident"	—	—
17	$45 black	150.00	*50.00*

No. 12 was used in the 1970s, No. 13 in the early 1980s, Nos. 14 (resident) and 15 (non-resident) in the late 1980s, and Nos. 16 (resident) and 17 (non-resident) starting in 1990. Unused values for Nos. 16-17 are for never hinged copies.

STANDING ROCK INDIAN RESERVATION

South Dakota-North Dakota
Waterfowl Stamps
Die cut, self-adhesive.

Catalogue values for all unused stamps in this section are for Never Hinged items.

1992-98

1	black	16.00	5.00
2	black, *1993*	10.00	4.00
3	black, inscribed "SRST," *1994*	8.50	3.00
4	black, *1995*	15.00	5.00
5	black, *1996*	13.00	4.00
6	black, *1997*	9.00	4.00
7	black, *1998*	15.00	4.00

SAVINGS STAMPS

POSTAL SAVINGS STAMPS

Issued by the Post Office Department.

Redeemable in the form of credits to Postal Savings accounts. The Postal Savings system was discontinued Mar. 28, 1966.

PS1

Plates of 400 subjects in four panes of 100 each
FLAT PLATE PRINTING

1911, Jan. 3 Wmk. 191 Engr. *Perf. 12*
Size of design: 18x21½mm

PS1	PS1	10c	**orange**	8.50	1.40
			Never hinged	15.00	
			Block of 4, 2mm spacing	37.50	
			Block of 4, 3mm spacing	40.00	
			P# strip of 3, Impt. open star	57.50	
			P# block of 6, Impt. open star	525.00	

Plate Nos. 5504-5507, 5698, 5700, 5703-5704.

1911, Jan. 3 Unwmk.
Imprinted on Deposit Card
Size of design: 137x79mm

PS2	PS1	10c	**orange**	175.00	40.00

A 10c deep blue with head of Washington in circle imprinted on deposit card (design 136x79mm) exists, but there is no evidence that it was ever placed in use.

1911, Aug. 14 Wmk. 190 *Perf. 12*

PS4	PS1	10c	**deep blue**	5.00	1.00
			Never hinged	8.50	
			Block of 4, 2mm spacing	22.50	
			Block of 4, 3mm spacing	25.00	
			P# strip of 3, Impt. open star	30.00	
			P# block of 6, Impt. open star	175.00	

Plate Nos. 5504-5507, 5698, 5700, 5703-5704.

1911 Unwmk.
Imprinted on Deposit Card
Size of design: 133x78mm

PS5	PS1	10c	**deep blue**	150.00	22.50

Catalogue values for unused stamps in this section, from this point to the end, are for Never Hinged items.

1936 Unwmk. *Perf. 11*

PS6	PS1	10c	**deep blue**	5.50	1.25
			violet blue	5.50	1.25
			Block of 4	25.00	
			P# block of 6, Impt. solid star	135.00	

Plate Nos. 21485, 21486.

PS2

Plates of 400 subjects in four panes of 100 each
FLAT PLATE PRINTING

1940 **Unwmk.** **Engr.** ***Perf. 11***

Size of design: 19x22mm

No.	Design	Description	Unused	Used
PS7	PS2	10c **deep ultramarine,** *Apr. 3*	20.00	6.00
		Block of 4	85.00	
		P# block of 6	275.00	

Plate Nos. 22540, 22541.

No.	Design	Description	Unused	Used
PS8	PS2	25c **dark car rose,** *Apr. 1*	22.50	9.00
		Block of 4	95.00	
		P# block of 6	300.00	

Plate Nos. 22542, 22543.

No.	Design	Description	Unused	Used
PS9	PS2	50c **dark blue green,** *Apr. 1*	60.00	17.50
		Block of 4	250.00	
		P# block of 6	1,050.	

Plate No. 22544.

No.	Design	Description	Unused	Used
PS10	PS2	$1 **gray black,** *Apr. 1*	175.00	17.50
		Block of 4	725.00	
		P# block of 6	2,200.	

Plate No. 22545.

Nos. PS11-PS15 redeemable in the form of United States Treasury Defense, War or Savings Bonds.

Minute Man — PS3

E.E. Plates of 400 subjects in four panes of 100 each
ROTARY PRESS PRINTING

1941, May 1 **Unwmk.** ***Perf. 11x10½***

Size of design: 19x22½mm

No.	Design	Description	Unused
PS11	PS3	10c **rose red**	.60
a.		10c **carmine rose**	.60
		Block of 4	2.40
		P# block of 4	7.25
b.		Bklt. pane of 10, *July 30,* trimmed horizontal edges	50.00
		As "b," with Electric Eye marks at left	55.00
c.		Booklet pane of 10, perf. horizontal edges	100.00
		As "c," with Electric Eye marks at left	115.00

Plate Nos., sheet stamps, 22714-22715, 22722-22723, 148245-148246.
Plate Nos., booklet panes, 147084, 147086, 148241-148242.

No.	Design	Description	Unused
PS12	PS3	25c **blue green**	2.00
		Block of 4	8.25
		P# block of 4	22.50
b.		Bklt. pane of 10, *July 30*	60.00
		Booklet pane with Electric Eye marks at left	65.00

Plate Nos., sheet stamps, 22716-22717, 22724-22725, 148247-148248.
Plate Nos., booklet panes, 147087-147088, 148243-148244.

No.	Design	Description	Unused
PS13	PS3	50c **ultramarine**	7.50
		Block of 4	32.50
		P# block of 4	50.00

Plate Nos. 22718-22719, 22726-22727.

No.	Design	Description	Unused
PS14	PS3	$1 **gray black**	12.50
		Block of 4	52.50
		P# block of 4	75.00

Plate Nos. 22720, 22728.

FLAT PLATE PRINTING
Plates of 100 subjects in four panes of 25 each

Size: 36x46mm ***Perf. 11***

No.	Design	Description	Unused
PS15	PS3	$5 **sepia**	42.50
		Block of 4	175.00
		P# block of 6 at top or bottom	475.00

Plate Nos. 22730-22737, 22740.

SAVINGS STAMPS

Issued by the Post Office Department.

Redeemable in the form of United States Savings Bonds. Sale of Savings Stamps was discontinued June 30, 1970.

Catalogue values for unused stamps in this section are for Never Hinged items.

Minute Man — S1

E.E. Plates of 400 subjects in four panes of 100 each
ROTARY PRESS PRINTING

1954-57 **Unwmk.** ***Perf. 11x10½***

Size of design: 19x22½mm

No.	Design	Description	Unused
S1	S1	10c **rose red,** wet printing, *Nov. 30, 1954*	.50
		Block of 4	2.00
		P# block of 4	3.50
a.		Booklet pane of 10, *Apr. 22, 1955*	150.00
		Booklet pane with Electric Eye marks at left	165.00
b.		Dry printing	.50
		Block of 4	2.00
		P# block of 4	3.50
c.		As "b," booklet pane of 10	150.00
		Booklet pane with Electric Eye marks at left	165.00

Plate Nos., sheet stamps, 164991-164992 (wet), 165917-165918, 166643-166644, 167089-167090, 168765-168766 (dry).
Plate Nos., booklet panes, 165218-165219 (wet), 165954-165955, 167001-167002 (dry).

No.	Design	Description	Unused
S2	S1	25c **blue green,** wet printing, *Dec. 30, 1954*	7.50
		Block of 4	30.00
		P# block of 4	35.00
a.		Booklet pane of 10, *Apr. 15, 1955*	800.00
		Booklet pane with Electric Eye marks at left	825.00
b.		Dry printing	7.50
		Block of 4	30.00
		P# block of 4	35.00
c.		As "b," booklet pane of 10	800.00
		Booklet pane with Electric Eye marks at left	825.00

Plate Nos., sheet stamps, 165007-165008 (wet), 165919-165920 (dry), booklet panes, 165220-165221 (wet), 165956-165957 (dry).

No.	Design	Description	Unused
S3	S1	50c **ultramarine,** wet printing, *Dec. 31, 1956*	9.00
		Block of 4	37.50
		P# block of 4	50.00
a.		Dry printing	9.00
		Block of 4	37.50
		P# block of 4	50.00

Plate Nos. 165050-165051 (wet), 166741-166742, 166941-166942 (dry).

No.	Design	Description	Unused
S4	S1	$1 **gray black,** *Mar. 13, 1957*	25.00
		Block of 4	100.00
		P# block of 4	125.00

Plate Nos. 166097-166098, 166683-166684.

FLAT PLATE PRINTING
Plates of 100 subjects in four panes of 25 each

Size: 36x46mm ***Perf. 11***

No.	Design	Description	Unused
S5	S1	$5 **sepia,** *Nov. 30, 1956*	95.00
		Block of 4	400.00
		P# block of 6 at top or bottom	725.00

Plate No. 166068.

Minute Man and 48-Star Flag — S2

GIORI PRESS PRINTING
Plates of 400 subjects in four panes of 100 each

1958, Nov. 18 **Unwmk.** ***Perf. 11***

No.	Design	Description	Unused
S6	S2	25c **dark blue & carmine**	2.00
		Block of 4	8.00
		P# block of 4	10.00
a.		Booklet pane of 10	75.00

Plate Nos.: sheet stamps, 166921, 166925, 166946; booklet panes, 166913, 166916.

Minute Man and 50-Star Flag — S3

Plates of 400 subjects in four panes of 100 each.

1961 **Unwmk.** ***Perf. 11***

No.	Design	Description	Unused
S7	S3	25c **dark blue & carmine**	1.50
		Block of 4	6.00
		P# block of 4	11.00
a.		Booklet pane of 10	300.00

Plate Nos.: sheet stamps, 167473, 167476, 167486, 167489, 169089; booklet panes, 167495, 167502, 167508, 167516.

WAR SAVINGS STAMPS

Issued by the Treasury Department.

Redeemable in the form of United States Treasury War Certificates, Defense Bonds or War Bonds.

Unused values of War Savings stamps are for copies with full original gum. Used values are for stamps without gum that generally have been removed from savings certificates or booklets. **Caution:** beware of used stamps that have been regummed to appear unused.

WS1

Plates of 300 subjects in six panes of 50 each
FLAT PLATE PRINTING

1917, Dec. 1 **Unwmk.** **Engr.** ***Perf. 11***

Size of design: 28x18½mm

No.	Design	Description	Unused	Used
WS1	WS1	25c **deep green**	16.00	2.25
		Never hinged	25.00	
		Block of 4	70.00	
		Margin strip of 3, P#	80.00	
		P# block of 6	900.00	

Plate Nos. 56800, 56810-56811, 56817, 57074-57077, 57149-57152, 57336, 57382, 57395-57396, 57399, 57443, 58801-58804, 59044-59045, 59156, 61207-61210.

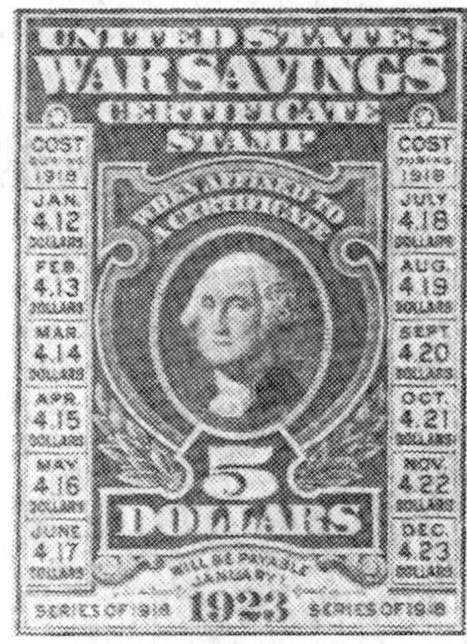

George Washington — WS2

Plates of 80 subjects in four panes of 20 each
FLAT PLATE PRINTING

1917 **Unwmk.** **Engr.** ***Perf. 11***

Size of design: 39x55mm

No.	Design	Description	Unused	Used
WS2	WS2	$5 **deep green,** *Nov. 17*	80.00	25.00
		Never hinged	125.00	
		Block of 4	325.00	
		Margin copy with P#	90.00	
		P# block of 6	*1,600.*	
b.		Vert. pair, imperf. horiz.	—	

Plate Nos. 56914-56917, 57066-57073, 57145-57148, 57169-57176, 57333-57334, 57343-57348, 58431, 58433-58438, 58726-58729, 59071, 60257-60260, 60659-60662, 60665-60668, 60846-60852, 60899, 61203-61206, 61265-61268, 61360-61367, 61388, 61435, 61502.

Rouletted 7

WS3 WS2 $5 **deep green** 1,200. 650.
Never hinged *2,250.*
Block of 4 5,000.
Margin copy with P# 1,500.

Benjamin Franklin — WS3

Plates of 150 subjects in six panes of 25 each
FLAT PLATE PRINTING

1919, July 3 Unwmk. Engr. *Perf. 11*
Size of design: 27x36mm

WS4 WS3 $5 **deep blue** 325. 160.
Never hinged 500.
Block of 4 1,350.
Margin copy with P# 350.
Margin copy with inverted P# 375.

Plate Nos. 61882-61885, 61910-61913, 61970-61972, 61997-61998, 62007-62013.

George Washington WS4

Plates of 100 subjects in four panes of 25 each
FLAT PLATE PRINTING

1919, Dec. 11 Unwmk. Engr. *Perf. 11*
Size of design: 36x41½mm

WS5 WS4 $5 **carmine** 800. 250.
Never hinged 1,300.
Block of 4 *3,500.*
Margin copy with P# 850.

Plate Nos. 67545-67552, 69349-69352, 69673-69675, 69677-69680, 69829.

Abraham Lincoln — WS5

Plates of 100 subjects in four panes of 25 each
FLAT PLATE PRINTING

1920, Dec. 21 Unwmk. Engr. *Perf. 11*
Size of design: 39½x42mm

WS6 WS5 $5 **orange,** *green* 3,500. 1,250.
Never hinged *6,500.*
Block of 4 *15,000.*
Margin copy with P# 3,750.

Plate Nos. 73129-73136.

Catalogue values for unused stamps in this section, from this point to the end, are for Never Hinged items.

Minute Man — WS6

Plates of 400 subjects in four panes of 100 each
ROTARY PRESS PRINTING

1942 Unwmk. *Perf. 11x10½*
Size of design: 19x22½mm

WS7 WS6 10c **rose red,** *Oct. 29* .50 .20
a. 10c carmine rose .50
Block of 4 2.00
P# block of 4 5.00
b. Booklet pane of 10, *Oct. 27* 50.00
Booklet pane with Electric Eye marks at left 55.00

Plate Nos., sheet stamps, 149492-149495, 150206-150207, 150706-150707, 155311-155312.
Plate Nos., booklet panes, 149655-149657, 150664.

WS8 WS6 25c **dark blue green,** *Oct. 15* 1.10 .25
Block of 4 5.00
P# block of 4 8.25
b. Booklet pane of 10, *Nov. 6* 50.00
Booklet pane with Electric Eye marks at left 55.00

Plate Nos., sheet stamps, 149587-149590, 150320-150321, 150708-150709, 155313-155314, 155812-155813, 156517-156518, booklet panes, 149658-149660, 150666.

WS9 WS6 50c **deep ultra,** *Nov. 12* 4.00 1.25
Block of 4 16.00
P# block of 4 22.50

Plate Nos. 149591-149594.

WS10 WS6 $1 **gray black,** *Nov. 17* 12.50 3.50
Block of 4 52.50
P# block of 4 70.00

Plate Nos. 149595-149598.

Type of 1942
FLAT PLATE PRINTING
Plates of 100 subjects in four panes of 25 each

1945 Unwmk. Size: 36x46mm *Perf. 11*

WS11 WS6 $5 **violet brown** 55.00 17.50
Block of 4 240.00
P# block of 6 at top or bottom 500.00

Plate Nos. 150131-150134, 150291.

Type of 1942
Coil Stamps

1943, Aug. 5 Unwmk. *Perf. 10 Vertically*

WS12 WS6 10c **rose red** 2.75 .90
Pair 6.00
Line pair 10.50

Plate Nos. 153286-153287.

WS13 WS6 25c **dark blue green** 5.00 1.75
Pair 10.50
Line pair 22.50

Plate Nos. 153289-153290.

TREASURY SAVINGS STAMP

Issued by the Treasury Department.

Redeemable in the form of War Savings Stamps or Treasury Savings Certificates.

Alexander Hamilton — TS1

FLAT PLATE PRINTING

1920, Dec. 21 Unwmk. Engr. *Perf. 11*
Size of design: 33½x33½mm

TS1 TS1 $1 **red,** *green* 3,500. 1,250.
Never hinged *6,500.*
Block of 4 *15,000.*
Margin copy with P# 3,750.

Plate Nos. 73196-73203.

TELEGRAPH STAMPS

These stamps were issued by the individual companies for use on their own telegrams, and can usually be divided into three classes: Free franking privileges issued to various railroad, newspaper and express company officials, etc., whose companies were large users of the lines; those issued at part cost to the lesser officials of the same type companies; and those bearing values which were usually sold to the general public. Occasionally, some of the companies granted the franking privilege to stockholders and minor State (not Federal) officials. Most Telegraph Stamps were issued in booklet form and will be found with one or more straight edges.

Serial numbers may show evidence of doubling, often of a different number. Such doubling is not scarce.

American Rapid Telegraph Company

Organized Feb. 21, 1879, in New York State. Its wires extended as far north as Boston, Mass., and west to Cleveland, Ohio. It was amalgamated with the Bankers and Merchants Telegraph Co., but when that company was unable to pay the fixed charges, the properties of the American Rapid Telegraph Company were sold on Mar. 11, 1891, to a purchasing committee comprised of James W. Converse and others. This purchasing committee deeded the property and franchise of the American Rapid Telegraph Company to the Western Union Telegraph Company on June 25, 1894. Issued three types of stamps: Telegram, Collect and Duplicate. Telegram stamps were issued in sheets of 100 and were used to prepay messages which could be dropped in convenient boxes for collection. Collect and duplicate stamps were issued in alternate rows on the same sheet of 100 subjects. Collect stamps were attached to telegrams sent collect, the receiver of which paid the amount shown by the stamps, while the Duplicate stamps were retained by the Company as vouchers. **Remainders with punched cancellations were bought up by a New York dealer.**

T1

T2

"Prepaid Telegram" Stamps

Engraved and Printed by the American Bank Note Co.

1881 *Perf. 12*

No.	Type	Description	Unused	Used
1T1	T1	1c **black**	9.00	3.00
		Punched		.20
		Block of 4	40.00	
		Punched		1.00
1T2	T1	3c **orange**	35.00	32.50
		Punched		1.50
		Block of 4, punched		10.00
1T3	T1	5c **bister brown**	2.10	.80
		Punched		.25
		Block of 4	9.50	
		Punched		1.10
a.		5c **brown**	2.10	.90
		Punched		.20
		Block of 4	9.50	
		Punched		1.00
1T4	T1	10c **purple**	12.00	5.00
		Punched		.20
		Block of 4	55.00	
		Punched		1.00
1T5	T1	15c **green**	3.50	1.60
		Punched		.20
		Block of 4	16.00	
		Punched		1.00
1T6	T1	20c **red**	3.50	1.60
		Punched		.20
		Block of 4, punched		.80
1T7	T1	25c **rose**	4.50	1.10
		Punched		.20
		Block of 4	21.00	
		Punched		1.00
1T8	T1	50c **blue**	24.00	12.50
		Punched		1.50
		Block of 4, punched		8.00

"Collect" Stamps

No.	Type	Description	Unused	Used
1T9	T2	1c **brown**	4.00	3.50
		Punched		.20
1T10	T2	5c **blue**	3.25	2.50
		Punched		.20
1T11	T2	15c **red brown**	3.50	2.00
		Punched		.25
1T12	T2	20c **olive green**	3.50	2.50
		Punched		.20

T3

"Office Coupon" Stamps

No.	Type	Description	Unused	Used
1T13	T3	1c **brown**	7.50	2.75
		Punched		.20
a.		Pair, #1T9, 1T13, punched		2.00
		As "a," block of 4, punched		4.50
1T14	T3	5c **blue**	6.50	3.25
		Punched		.20
a.		Pair, #1T10, 1T14	32.50	
		Punched		3.00
		As "a," block of 4	70.00	
		Punched		7.00
1T15	T3	15c **red brown**	11.00	3.00
		Punched		.25
a.		Pair, #1T11, 1T15	27.50	
		Punched		2.50
		As "a," block of 4	65.00	
		Punched		5.50
1T16	T3	20c **olive green**	11.00	3.00
		Punched		.20
a.		Pair, #1T12, 1T16, punched		2.75
		As "a," block of 4, punched		6.00

Atlantic Telegraph Company

Organized 1884 at Portland, Maine. Its lines extended from Portland, Me., to Boston, Mass., and terminated in the office of the Baltimore and Ohio Telegraph Company at Boston. Later bought out by the Baltimore and Ohio Telegraph Co. Stamps issued by the Atlantic Telegraph Company could also be used for messages destined to any point on the Baltimore and Ohio system. Stamps were printed in panes of six and a full book sold for $10. **Remainders of these stamps, without control numbers, were purchased by a Boston dealer and put on the market about 1932.**

T4

1888 *Perf. 13*

No.	Type	Description	Unused	Used
2T1	T4	1c **green**	4.75	—
		Remainders		2.25
		Pane of 6		—
		Remainders		14.00
2T2	T4	5c **blue**	6.50	—
		Remainders		2.25
		Pane of 6		—
		Remainders		14.00
a.		Horiz. pair, imperf. vert.		—
b.		Vert. pair, imperf. horiz.	25.00	—
2T3	T4	10c **purple brown**	8.00	—
		Remainders		2.25
		Pane of 6		—
		Remainders		14.00
a.		Horiz. pair, imperf. between	40.00	
2T4	T4	25c **carmine**	5.00	—
		Remainders		2.25
		Pane of 6, remainders		16.00

Baltimore & Ohio Telegraph Companies

"The Baltimore & Ohio Telegraph Co. of the State of New York" was incorporated May 17, 1882. Organization took place under similar charter in 26 other states. It absorbed the National Telegraph Co. and several others. Extended generally along the lines of the Baltimore & Ohio Railroad, but acquired interests in other states. Company absorbed in 1887 by the Western Union Telegraph Co. Stamps were issued in booklet form and sold for $5 and $10, containing all denominations.

T5

T6

Engraved by the American Bank Note Co.

1885 *Perf. 12*

No.	Type	Description	Unused	Used
3T1	T5	1c **vermilion**	60.00	25.00
		Pane of 6	350.00	
3T2	T5	5c **blue**	60.00	35.00
3T3	T5	10c **red brown**	30.00	12.50
		Pane of 6	190.00	
3T4	T5	25c **orange**	50.00	25.00
3T5	T6	**brown**	1.75	
		Pane of 4	12.50	

1886

No.	Type	Description	Unused	Used
3T6	T6	**black**	2.00	*25.00*
		Pane of 4	22.50	

Imprint of Kendall Bank Note Co.
Thin Paper

1886 *Perf. 14*

No.	Type	Description	Unused	Used
3T7	T5	1c **green**	6.00	3.00
a.		Thick paper	10.00	.85
b.		Imperf., pair	90.00	
3T8	T5	5c **blue**	4.00	1.25
a.		Thick paper	9.00	4.00
b.		Imperf., pair		55.00
3T9	T5	10c **brown**	6.00	.75
a.		Thick paper	10.00	1.50
3T10	T5	25c **deep orange**	35.00	.75
a.		Thick paper	40.00	1.50

Used copies of Nos. 3T7-3T20 normally have heavy grid cancellations. Lightly canceled copies command a premium.

Litho. by A. Hoen & Co.

1886 **Imprint of firm** *Perf. 12*

No.	Type	Description	Unused	Used
3T11	T5	1c **green**	3.00	.65
		Pane of 6	22.50	—
3T12	T5	5c **blue**	7.50	.65
		Pane of 6	50.00	—
a.		Imperf., pair	90.00	
3T13	T5	10c **dark brown**	7.50	.75
		Pane of 6	45.00	—
a.		Vert. pair, imperf. between	60.00	

Wmk. "A HOEN AND CO. BALTIMORE" in double lined capitals in sheet

Perf. 12

No.	Type	Description	Unused	Used
3T14	T5	1c **green**	12.50	1.25
		Pane of 6	70.00	—
3T15	T5	5c **blue**	20.00	1.50
		Pane of 6	125.00	—
a.		Imperf., pair	52.50	—
3T16	T5	10c **dark brown**	15.00	1.25
		Pane of 6	90.00	—

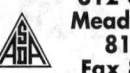

Lithographed by Forbes Co., Boston

1887			Imprint of firm	*Perf. 12½*	
3T17	T5	1c	**green**	25.00	2.75
3T18	T5	5c	**blue**	45.00	6.00
3T19	T5	10c	**brown**	45.00	5.50
3T20	T5	25c	**yellow**	45.00	8.25
a.		25c	**orange**	45.00	5.50

Baltimore & Ohio-Connecticut River Telegraph Companies

The Connecticut River Telegraph Co. ran from New Haven to Hartford. An agreement was entered wherein the Baltimore & Ohio System had mutual use of their lines. This agreement terminated when the Baltimore & Ohio System was absorbed by the Western Union. The Connecticut River Telegraph Company then joined the United Lines. In 1885 stamps (black on yellow) were issued and sold in booklets for $10. In 1887 the Connecticut River Telegraph Co. had extended its lines to New Boston, Mass., and new books of stamps (black on blue) were issued for use on this extension. **Remainders were canceled with bars and sold to a New York dealer.**

T7

1885				*Perf. 11*	
4T1	T7	1c	**black,** *yellow*	5.00	6.00
			Remainders		1.25
			Pane of 10	55.00	
			Remainders		6.00
a.			Imperf., pair	40.00	
b.			Vert. pair, imperf. horiz., remainders		—
4T2	T7	5c	**black,** *yellow*	3.00	10.00
			Remainders		1.00
			Pane of 10	35.00	
			Remainders		6.00
a.			Horizontal pair, imperf. between, remainders		—
b.			Vert. pair, imperf. between, remainders		35.00
c.			Imperf., pair, remainders		35.00
4T3	T7	1c	**black,** *blue*	7.50	—
			Remainders		4.00
			Pane of 10	80.00	
			Remainders		35.00
4T4	T7	5c	**black,** *blue*	11.00	9.00
			Remainders		4.00
			Pane of 10	110.00	
			Remainders		52.50

California State Telegraph Company

Incorporated June 17, 1854 as the California Telegraph Company and constructed a line from Nevada through Grass Valley to Auburn. Extended to run from San Francisco to Marysville via San Jose and Stockton. Later absorbed Northern Telegraph Co. and thus extended to Eureka. It was incorporated as the California State Telegraph Company on April 6, 1861. At the time of its lease to the Western Union on May 16, 1867 the California State consisted of the following companies which had been previously absorbed: Alta California Telegraph Co., Atlantic and Pacific States Telegraph Co., National Telegraph Co., Northern California Telegraph Co., Overland Telegraph Co., Placerville and Humboldt Telegraph Co., Tuolumne Telegraph Co. Stamps were issued in booklets, six to a pane. **Remainders of Nos. 5T1 and 5T4 are without frank numbers.**

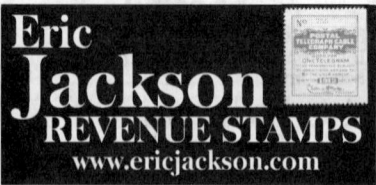

T8

1870			*Perf. 13½*	
5T1	T8	**black & blue**	450.	—
		Pane of 6	2,900.	
		Without number	150.	

T9

T10

1870			*Perf. 12, 13*	
5T2	T9	**black & red,** without number	225.00	160.00

1871			**Dated "1871"**	
5T3	T9	**black & red,** without number	500.00	
a.		Imperf., pair	—	—
5T4	T10	**black & salmon,** blue number	450.00	175.00
		Pane of 6	*2,900.*	
		Without number	175.00	

1872				
5T5	T10	**green & red,** red number (no year date)	210.00	—
		Pane of 6	—	

1873			**Dated "1873"**	
5T6	T10	**red & salmon,** blue number	300.00	225.00

1874			**Dated "1874"**	
5T7	T10	**blue & salmon,** black number	375.00	—
		Pane of 6	—	

1875			**Dated "1875"**	
5T8	T10	**brown & green,** black number	275.00	—
		Pane of 6	—	

City & Suburban Telegraph Company (New York City and Suburban Printing Telegraph Company)

Organized 1855. Extended only through New York City and Brooklyn. Sold out to the American Telegraph Co. Stamps were sold to the public for prepayment of messages, which could be dropped in convenient boxes for collection. Stamps were issued in sheets of 60 having a face value of $1. These were arranged in six vertical rows of ten, the horizontal rows having the following denominations: 2c, 1c, 1c, 1c, 2c, 3c.

Counterfeits are known both in black and blue, mostly on pelure or hard white paper. Originals are on soft wove paper, somewhat yellowish. Scalloped edge is more sharply etched on the counterfeits.

T11

			Typo.	*Imperf.*	
6T1	T11	1c	**black**	300.	200.
			Pair	—	
			Block of 4	—	
6T2	T11	2c	**black**	375.	250.
			Pair	—	
			Pair, 2c + 1c	600.	
6T3	T11	3c	**black**	600.	400.
			Pair	—	
			Strip of 3, 1c, 2c & 3c	*3,750.*	

Colusa, Lake & Mendocino Telegraph Company

Was organized in California early in 1873. First known as the Princeton, Colusa and Grand Island Telegraph Co. In May, 1873 they completed their line from Princeton through Colusa, at which point it was connected with the Western Union office, to Grand Island. On Feb. 10, 1875 it was incorporated as the Colusa, Lake & Mendocino Telegraph Co. Its lines were extended into the counties of Colusa, Lake, Mendocino and Napa. Eventually reached a length of 260 miles. Went out of business in 1892. Stamps were issued for prepayment of messages and were sold in books. When sold they were stamped "P.L.W." (the superintendent's initials) in blue. The 5c value was printed 10 to a pane, being two horizontal rows of five. Of the 10c and 25c nothing definite is known about the settings.

T11a

1876				*Perf. 12*	
7T1	T11a	5c	**black**	*800.*	—
			Block of 4	*3,550.*	
			Pane of 10	*8,750.*	
			Without "P.L.W."	*900.*	
7T2	T11a	10c	**black**	*9,000.*	—
7T3	T11a	25c	**red**	*9,000.*	—

Commercial Union Telegraph Company

Incorporated in New York State on March 31, 1886. Its lines ran from Albany through Troy to Berlin, N.Y., thence to North Adams, Mass. The lines of this Company, which was controlled by the Postal Telegraph Company, were later extended throughout Northern New York and the States of Massachusetts, Vermont, New Hampshire and Maine. Stamps issued in panes of four.

T12

T13

T14

1891			Lithographed by A. C. Goodwin	*Perf. 12*	
8T1	T12	25c	**yellow**	22.50	—
			Pane of 4	85.00	
8T2	T13	25c	**green**	22.50	10.00
			Pane of 4	85.00	
a.			Horiz. pair, imperf. vert.	52.50	
8T3	T14		**lilac rose**	55.00	—

Mutual Union Telegraph Company

Incorporated October 4, 1880. Extended over 22 states. Absorbed about 1883 by the Western Union Telegraph Co. Franks issued for use of stockholders, in books, four to a pane.

T15

Engr. by Van Campen Engraving Co., New York

1882-83				*Perf. 14*	
9T1	T15		**blue**	40.00	20.00
			Pane of 4	180.00	
a.			Vert. pair, imperf. horizontal	100.00	—
b.			Imperf., pair	110.00	
9T2	T15		**carmine**	40.00	—
			Pane of 4	180.00	

North American Telegraph Company

Incorporated October 15, 1885 to run from Chicago to Minneapolis, later being extended into North and South Dakota. Absorbed in 1929 by the Postal System.

Apparently these stamps were not canceled when used.

Issued in panes of four.

T15a

1899-1907				*Perf. 12*	
10T1	T15a		**violet** (1899)	175.00	
			Pane of 4	750.00	
10T2	T15a		**green** (1901)	175.00	
10T3	T15a		**dark brown** (1902)	300.00	
10T4	T15a		**blue** (1903)	300.00	
10T5	T15a		**violet** (1904)	140.00	
			Pane of 4	625.00	
a.			Horiz. pair, imperf. vertically	350.00	
10T6	T15a		**red brown** (1905)	200.00	
10T7	T15a		**rose** (1906)	225.00	
10T8	T15a		**green** (1907)	1,100.	

Nos. 10T1 to 10T8 are known imperforate.

Northern Mutual Telegraph Company

Incorporated in New York State as the Northern Mutual Telegraph and Telephone Company on June 20, 1882. Its line, which consisted of a single wire, extended from Syracuse to Ogdensburg via Oswego, Watertown and Clayton, a distance of 170 miles. It was sold to the Bankers and Merchants Telegraph Company in 1883. Stamps were in use for a few days only in April, 1883. Issued in panes of 35 having a face value of $5. Seven horizontal rows of five covering all denominations as follows: 2 rows of 25c, 1 of 20c, 2 of 10c, 2 of 5c. **The remainders and plates were purchased by a New York dealer in 1887.**

T16

1883				*Perf. 14*	
11T1	T16	5c	**yellow brown**	5.50	—
			Block of 4	25.00	
11T2	T16	10c	**yellow brown**	7.50	—
			Block of 4	30.00	
11T3	T16	20c	**yellow brown**	17.50	—
			Horizontal pair	40.00	
11T4	T16	25c	**yellow brown**	5.00	—
			Block of 4	25.00	
			Pane of 35	350.00	

The first reprints are lighter in color than the originals, perf. 14 and the gum is yellowish instead of white. The pane makeup differs in the reprints. The second reprints are darker than the original, perf. 12. Value $1 each.

Northern New York Telegraph Company

Organized about 1892. Extended from Malone, N.Y. to Massena, N.Y. Re-incorporated as the New York Union Telegraph Co. on April 2, 1896.

T16a

Typo. by Charles H. Smith, Brushton, N.Y.

1894-95				*Rouletted*
12T1	T16a		**green** (overprinted in red "Frank 1894")	45.
			Pane of 6	275.
a.			Imperf., pair	50.
12T2	T16a		**red** (overprinted in black "Frank 1895")	160.
			Pane of 6	1,500.
a.			Imperf., pair	50.
12T3	T16a	1c	**yellow** (overprinted in black "One")	80.
			Pane of 6	525.
a.			Imperf., pair	50.
12T4	T16a	10c	**blue** (overprinted in red "10")	150.
			Pane of 6	900.
a.			Imperf., pair	50.

Some specialists believe that Nos. 12T1-12T4 were not issued and probably are essays. However, one Northern New York stamp is recorded tied to a piece of a telegraph form by a punch cancel.

Pacific Mutual Telegraph Company

Incorporated in Missouri on June 21, 1883. Operated between St. Louis and Kansas City, Mo., during the years 1884 and 1885. It had 15 offices, 425 miles of poles and 850 miles of wire. The controlling interests were held by the Bankers and Merchants Telegraph Company. The name was changed on Sept. 10, 1910 to Postal Telegraph-Cable Company of Missouri. Stamps were issued in booklets having a face value of $10 and containing 131 stamps as follows: 50-1c, 20-5c, 45-10c, 16-25c. They are not known used.

T17

1883				*Perf. 12*
13T1	T17	1c	**black**	22.50
13T2	T17	1c	**slate**	.35
			Block of 4	1.50
a.			1c gray	.35
			Block of 4	1.50
13T3	T17	5c	**black,** *buff*	1.00
			Block of 4	4.50
13T4	T17	10c	**black,** *green*	.35
			Block of 4	1.75
a.			Horiz. pair, imperf. between	—
13T5	T17	25c	**black,** *salmon buff*	1.00
			Block of 4	4.50

Pacific Postal Telegraph-Cable Company

The Pacific Postal Telegraph-Cable Company was the Pacific Coast Department of the Postal Telegraph-Cable Company, and was organized in 1886. Its first wire ran from San Francisco to New Westminster, B.C., where it touched the lines of the Canadian Pacific Railway Company, then the only connection between the Eastern and Western Postal systems. Later the Postal's own wires spanned the continent and the two companies were united.

Stamps issued in booklet form in vertical panes of five.

T17a

			Perf. 12 Horiz.		
14T1	T17a	10c	**brown**	70.00	55.00
			Pane of 5	375.00	
14T2	T17a	15c	**black**	80.00	50.00
			Pane of 5	425.00	
14T3	T17a	25c	**rose red**	80.00	55.00
			Pane of 5	425.00	
14T4	T17a	40c	**green**	65.00	57.50
			Pane of 5	350.00	
14T5	T17a	50c	**blue**	65.00	55.00
			Pane of 5	350.00	

These stamps were issued with three sizes of frank numbers; large closely spaced, small closely spaced and small widely spaced figures. They also exist without frank numbers.

Postal Telegraph Company

Organized in New York in 1881. Reorganized in 1891 as the Postal Telegraph-Cable Co. The Postal Telegraph Co stamps of 1885 were issued in sheets of 100. **Some years after the reorganization a New York dealer purchased the remainders which were canceled with a purple star.** The Postal Telegraph-Cable Co. issued frank stamps in booklets, usually four stamps to a pane. This company was merged with the Western Union Telegraph Company in 1943.

T18

T19

T20

T21

Engraved by Hamilton Bank Note Co.

1885				*Perf. 14*	
15T1	T18	10c	**green**	3.50	—
			Remainders		.25
			Block of 4	15.00	
			Remainders		1.25
a.			Horiz. pair, imperf. btwn., remainders		20.00
b.			10c **deep green**	3.50	—
			Remainders		.25
			Block of 4	15.00	
			Remainders		1.25
15T2	T19	15c	**orange red**	3.50	—
			Remainders		.60
			Block of 4	15.00	—
			Remainders		3.00
a.			Horizontal pair, imperf. between	37.50	
15T3	T20	25c	**blue**	2.00	5.00
			Remainders		.20
			Block of 4	9.00	
			Remainders		.75
a.			Horizontal pair, imperf. between	37.50	
15T4	T21	50c	**brown**	1.75	—
			Remainders		.60
			Block of 4	8.00	
			Remainders		3.00

The 25c in ultramarine and the 50c in black were printed and perforated 16 but are not known to have been issued. Value about $7.50 each.

T22

T22a

Typographed by Moss Engraving Co.

1892-1920			*Perf. 14*	
		Signature of A.B. Chandler		
15T5	T22	**blue gray** (1892)	30.00	
a.		Imperf., pair	75.00	
		Perf. 13 to 14½ and Compound		
15T6	T22	**gray lilac** (1892)	35.00	
15T7	T22	**red** (1893)	17.50	10.00
		Pane of 4	75.00	
15T8	T22	**red brown** (1893)	6.00	4.00
		Perf. 12		
15T9	T22	**violet brown** (1894)	6.75	
15T10	T22	**gray green** (1894)	4.50	
a.		Imperf., pair	10.00	
15T11	T22	**blue** (1895)	30.00	
15T12	T22	**rose** (1895)	250.00	

Nos. 15T11 and 15T12 are from a new die resembling T22 but without shading under "Postal Telegraph Co."

15T13	T22a	**slate green** (1896)	5.50	
		Pane of 4	25.00	
15T14	T22a	**brown** (1896)	200.00	
		Signature of Albert B. Chandler		
15T15	T22a	**lilac brown** (1897)	1.50	*10.00*
		Pane of 4	6.50	
15T16	T22a	**orange** (1897)	160.00	

Typographed by Knapp & Co.

15T17	T22a	**pale blue** (1898)	2.25	
		Pane of 4	10.00	
15T18	T22a	**rose** (1898)	190.00	

Typographed by Moss Engraving Co.

Perf. 12

15T19	T22a	**orange brown** (1899)	1.75	
		Pane of 4	8.25	

Perf. 11

15T20	T22a	**blue** (1900)	3.00	3.00
a.		"I" of "Complimentary" omitted	.75	1.00
		Pane of 4	3.00	

The variety 15T20a represents a different die with many variations in the design.

Perf. 14

15T21	T22a	**sea green** (1901)	.60	.60
		Pane of 4	2.50	
a.		Horiz. pair, imperf. between	—	

Signature of John W. Mackay

15T22	T22a	**chocolate** (1902)	1.25	.65
		Pane of 4	5.50	
a.		Horiz. pair, imperf. vert.	—	

Signature of Clarence H. Mackay

15T23	T22a	**blue** (1903)	2.75	2.50
		Pane of 4		

Perf. 12

15T24	T22a	**blue,** *blue* (1904)	4.00	3.00
		Pane of 4	17.50	
15T25	T22a	**blue,** *yellow* (1905)	5.00	
		Pane of 4	22.50	
15T26	T22a	**blue,** *light blue* (1906)	5.00	5.00
		Pane of 4	22.50	
a.		Horiz. pair, imperf. vert.	—	

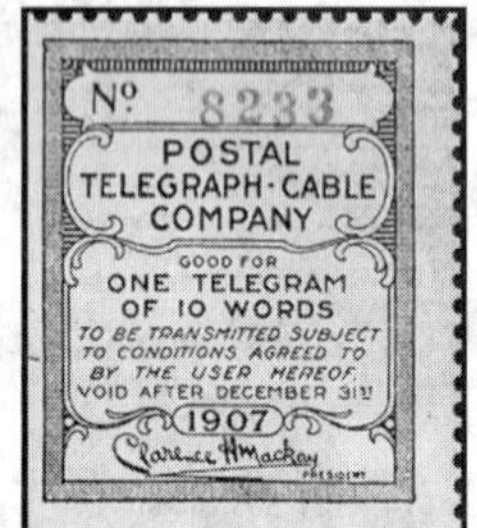

T22b

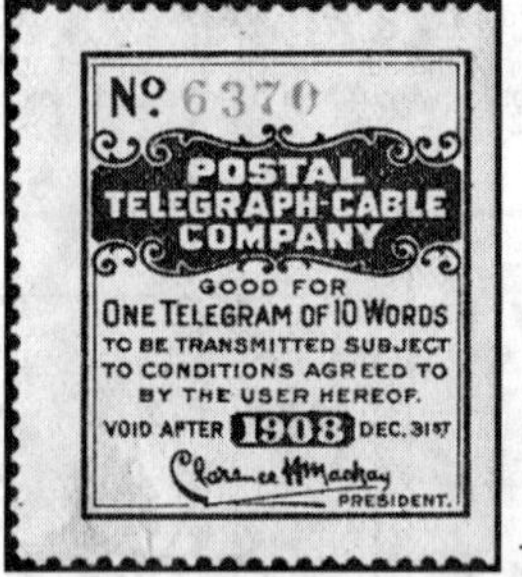

T22c

Perf. 12

15T27	T22b	**black,** *yellow* (laid paper) (1907)	50.00	
		Pane of 4	225.00	
15T28	T22b	**blue,** *pink* (laid paper) (1907)	30.00	
		Pane of 4	135.00	

"One Telegram of 10 Words"

15T29	T22c	**blue** (1908)	45.00	
		Pane of 4	200.00	
15T30	T22c	**yellow** (1908)	175.00	
		Pane of 4	750.00	
15T31	T22c	**black** (1908)	40.00	
		Pane of 4	175.00	
15T32	T22c	**brown** (1909)	30.00	
		Pane of 4	125.00	
a.		Date reads "1908"	*2,000.*	
15T33	T22c	**olive green** (1909)	15.00	
		Pane of 4	75.00	
15T34	T22c	**dark blue** (1910)	25.00	
15T35	T22c	**dark brown** (1910)	27.50	
		Pane of 4	125.00	
15T36	T22c	**violet** (1911)	225.00	
15T37	T22c	**blue** (1912)	450.00	
15T38	T22c	**violet** (1913)	500.00	

Perf. 14

15T39	T22c	**violet** (not dated) (1914)	160.00	
a.		Red violet	125.00	
		Pane of 4	625.00	

"One Telegram"

Perf. 12

15T40	T22c	**blue** (1908)	45.00	
		Pane of 4	200.00	
a.		Horiz. pair, imperf. between	350.00	
15T41	T22c	**lilac** (1909)	20.00	
		Pane of 4	87.50	
15T42	T22c	**black,** *yellow* (laid paper) (1910)	525.00	
a.		Date reads "1909"	—	
15T43	T22c	**violet** (1910)	15.00	
a.		**Red violet**	15.00	
		Pane of 4	—	
		Pane of 8	140.00	
15T44	T22c	**dark blue** (1911)	45.00	
		Pane of 4	200.00	
a.		Vert. pair, imperf between	*400.00*	
15T45	T22c	**light violet** (1912)	32.50	
		Pane of 4	150.00	

Perf. 14

15T46	T22c	**dark blue** (1913)	140.00	
		Pane of 8	1,100.	
a.		Imperf. vertically, pair	225.00	
b.		Perf. 12	75.00	
		Pane of 4	300.00	
15T47	T22c	**dark blue** (not dated) (1914)	.25	
		Pane of 4	2.50	
		Pane of 8	5.00	

In panes of four the stamps are 4½mm apart horizontally, panes of eight 5½mm. There are two types of design T22c, one with and one without spurs on colored curved lines above "O" of "Postal" and below "M" of "Company". No. 15T47 comes in both types.

Nos. 15T39 and 15T47 handstamped with date in double line numerals, all four numerals complete on each stamp.

15T47A	T22c	**violet** (1916)	*2,500.*	
15T48	T22c	**dark blue** (1917)	*1,250.*	
15T49	T22c	**dark blue** (1918)	*1,750.*	
15T49A	T22c	**dark blue** (1919)	90.00	
		Pane of 8	800.00	
15T49B	T22c	**dark blue** (1920)	70.00	
		Pane of 8	650.00	

No. 15T49B is handstamped "1920" in small single line numerals.

T22d

T22e

1907 ***Perf. 12***

15T50	T22d	1c	**dark brown**	30.00	20.00
			Pane of 4	125.00	
15T51	T22d	2c	**dull violet**	25.00	20.00
			Pane of 4	110.00	
15T52	T22d	5c	**green**	30.00	22.50
			Pane of 4	125.00	
15T53	T22d	25c	**light red**	32.50	20.00
			Pane of 4	140.00	

1931 ***Perf. 14***

15T54	T22e	25c	**gray blue** (1931)	.25	
			Pane of 6	2.00	

1932

No. 15T54 overprinted "1932" and control number in red

15T55	T22e	25c	**gray blue**	75.00	
			Pane of 6	500.00	

Many varieties between Nos. 15T5 and 15T55 are known without frank numbers.

OFFICIAL

1900-14 **Inscribed "Supts."** ***Perf. 11, 12***

15TO1	T22c	**black,** *magenta*	2.00	2.00

For Use of Railroad Superintendents

Perf. 12

"C. G. W." (Chicago, Great Western Railroad) at top

15TO2	T22c	**carmine** (1908)	40.00
		Pane of 4	175.00
15TO3	T22c	**carmine** (1909)	150.00
15TO4	T22c	**carmine** (1910)	125.00
15TO5	T22c	**carmine** (1911)	100.00
15TO6	T22c	**carmine** (1912)	110.00

Perf. 14

15TO7	T22c	**carmine** (1913)	160.00
a.		Perf. 12	—
15TO8	T22c	**dull red** (not dated) (1914)	.50
		Pane of 8	5.00

Perf. 12

"E. P." (El Paso and Northeastern Railroad) at top

15TO9	T22c	**orange** (1908)	175.00

"I. C." (Illinois Central Railroad) at top

15TO10	T22c	**green** (1908)	50.00
		Pane of 4	225.00
15TO11	T22c	**yellow green** (1909)	15.00
		Pane of 4	—
		Pane of 8	130.00
15TO12	T22c	**dark green** (1910)	125.00
15TO13	T22c	**dark green** (1911)	75.00
		Pane of 4	325.00
		Pane of 8	575.00
15TO14	T22c	**dark green** (1912)	700.00
15TO15	T22c	**dark green** (1913)	700.00

Perf. 14

15TO16	T22c	**dark green** (not dated) (1914)	2.50
		Pane of 4	11.00
		Pane of 8	22.50
a.		**Green** (spurs)	1.25
		Pane of 4	7.50
b.		Line under "PRESIDENT" (no spurs)	1.00
		Pane of 8	12.50

(See note after No. 15T47.)
Both types of design T22c are known of 15TO16.

Perf. 12

"O. D." (Old Dominion Steamship Co.) at top

15TO17	T22c	**violet** (1908)	1,250.

"P. R." (Pennsylvania Railroad) at top

15TO18	T22c	**orange brown** (1908)	25.00
		Pane of 4	110.00
		Pane of 8	225.00
15TO19	T22c	**orange brown** (1909)	30.00
		Pane of 4	125.00
		Pane of 8	275.00
15TO20	T22c	**orange brown** (1910)	30.00
		Pane of 4	125.00
		Pane of 8	275.00
15TO21	T22c	**orange brown** (1911)	110.00
15TO22	T22c	**orange brown** (1912)	65.00
		Pane of 4	*475.00*

Perf. 14

15TO23	T22c	**orange brown** (1913)	30.00
		Pane of 8	225.00
a.		Perf. 12	125.00

"P. R. R." (Pennsylvania Rail Road) at top

15TO24	T22c	**orange** (not dated) (1914)	22.50
		Pane of 4	110.00
		Pane of 8	200.00

Perf. 12

"S. W." (El Paso Southwestern Railroad) at top

15TO25	T22c	**yellow** (1909)	200.00
15TO26	T22c	**yellow** (1910)	900.00
15TO27	T22c	**yellow** (1911)	250.00
15TO28	T22c	**yellow** (1912)	250.00
		Pane of 4	1,050.

Nos. 15TO1-15TO17 and 15TO25-15TO28 are without frank numbers.

TO1

1942 **Litho.** **Unwmk.**

15TO29	TO1	5c	**pink**	6.50	3.00
			Pane of 8	55.00	
15TO30	TO1	25c	**pale blue**	7.75	4.00
			Pane of 8	65.00	

The stamps were issued in booklets to all Postal Telegraph employees in the Armed Forces for use in the United States. They were discontinued Oct. 8, 1943. Used copies normally bear manuscript cancellations.

Western Union Telegraph Company

Organized by consolidation in 1856. Now extends throughout the United States. Frank stamps have been issued regularly since 1871 in booklet form. The large size, early issues, were in panes of four, 1871-1913; the medium size, later issues, were in panes of six, 1914-32; and the recent small size issues are in panes of nine, 1933 to 1946.

T23

T24

Engraved by the National Bank Note Co.

1871-94 *Perf. 12*

Signature of William Orton

16T1 T23 **green** (not dated) (1871) 30.00 22.50
16T2 T23 **red** (not dated) (1872) 32.50 20.00
Pane of 4 150.00
16T3 T23 **blue** (not dated) (1873) 35.00 22.50
Pane of 4 160.00
16T4 T23 **brown** (not dated) (1874) 26.00 22.50
Pane of 4 120.00
16T5 T24 **deep green** (1875) 32.50 21.00
16T6 T24 **red** (1876) 32.50
Pane of 4 150.00
16T7 T24 **violet** (1877) 37.50 28.00
16T8 T24 **gray brown** (1878) 35.00

Signature of Norvin Green

16T9 T24 **blue** (1879) 35.00 28.00
Pane of 4 160.00

Engraved by the American Bank Note Co.

16T10 T24 **lilac rose** (1880) 22.50
Pane of 4 100.00
16T11 T24 **green** (1881) 20.00
Pane of 4 87.50
16T12 T24 **blue** (1882) 12.00
Pane of 4 55.00
16T13 T24 **yellow brown** (1883) 22.50
Pane of 4 100.00
16T14 T24 **gray violet** (1884) .40 .30
Pane of 4 2.00
16T15 T24 **green** (1885) 2.50 1.75
Pane of 4 12.00
16T16 T24 **brown violet** (1886) 2.50 2.00
Pane of 4 11.00
16T17 T24 **red brown** (1887) 4.50
Pane of 4 22.50
16T18 T24 **blue** (1888) 3.25
Pane of 4 15.00
16T19 T24 **olive green** (1889) 1.75 .80
Pane of 4 8.00
16T20 T24 **purple** (1890) .75 .40
Pane of 4 3.25
16T21 T24 **brown** (1891) 1.25
Pane of 4 5.50
16T22 T24 **vermilion** (1892) 1.75
Pane of 4 8.00
16T23 T24 **blue** (1893) 1.25 .40
Pane of 4 5.50

Signature of Thos. T. Eckert

16T24 T24 **green** (1894) .50 .40
Pane of 4 2.50

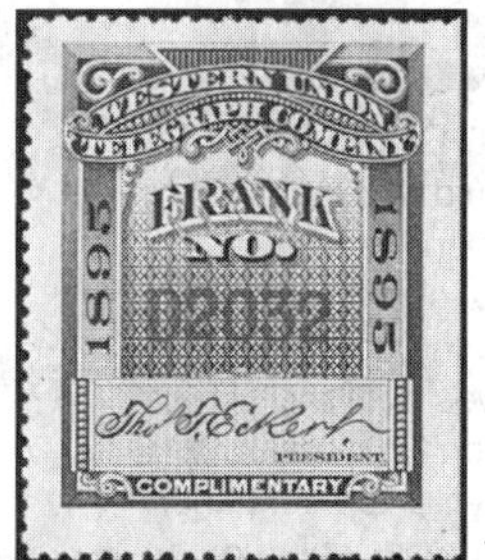

T25

Engraved by the International Bank Note Co.

1895-1913 *Perf. 14*

Signature of Thos. T. Eckert

16T25 T25 **dark brown** (1895) .50 .40
Pane of 4 2.50
16T26 T25 **violet** (1896) .50 .40
Pane of 4 2.50
16T27 T25 **rose red** (1897) .50 .40
Pane of 4 2.50
16T28 T25 **yellow green** (1898) .50 .40
Pane of 4 2.50
a. Vertical pair, imperf. between —
16T29 T25 **olive green** (1899) .50 .40
Pane of 4 2.25
16T30 T25 **red violet,** perf. 13 (1900) .50 .45
Pane of 4 3.00
16T31 T25 **brown,** perf. 13 (1901) .50 .40
Pane of 4 2.50
16T32 T25 **blue** (1902) 8.00
Pane of 4 40.00

Signature of R.C. Clowry

16T33 T25 **blue** (1902) 8.00
Pane of 4 40.00
16T34 T25 **green** (1903) .60 .40
Pane of 4 4.00
16T35 T25 **red violet** (1904) .60
Pane of 4 2.75
16T36 T25 **carmine rose** (1905) .60 .50
Pane of 4 2.75
16T37 T25 **blue** (1906) .80 .40
Pane of 4 4.00
a. Vertical pair, imperf. between *200.00*
16T38 T25 **orange brown** (1907) 1.75 .90
Pane of 4 10.00
16T39 T25 **violet** (1908) 2.00 1.00
Pane of 4 9.00
16T40 T25 **olive green** (1909) 2.00
Pane of 4 10.00

Perf. 12

16T41 T25 **buff** (1910) .75 .50
Pane of 4 3.25

Engraved by the American Bank Note Co.

Signature of Theo. N. Vail

16T42 T24 **green** (1911) 12.50
Pane of 4 60.00
16T43 T24 **violet** (1912) 8.50
Pane of 4 40.00

Imprint of Kihn Brothers Bank Note Company

Perf. 14

16T44 T24 **brown** (1913) 10.00
Pane of 4 50.00
a. Vert. pair, imperf. between 35.00
b. Horiz. pair, imperf. between 40.00

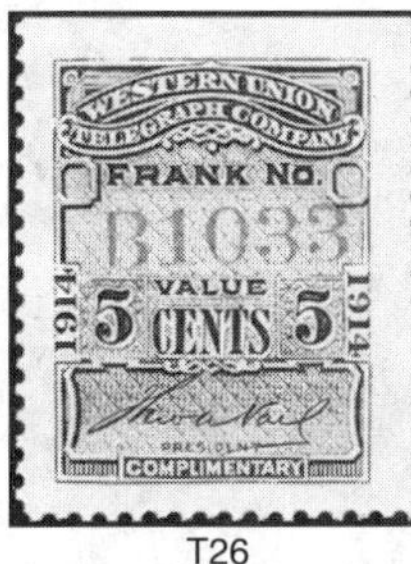

T26

T27

Engraved by the E.A. Wright Bank Note Co.

1914-15 Signature of Theo. N. Vail *Perf. 12*

16T45 T26 5c **brown** (1914) 1.10
Pane of 6 8.00
a. Vert. pair, imperf. between —
b. Horiz. pair, imperf. between —
16T46 T26 25c **slate** (1914) 7.00 5.00
Pane of 6 30.00

Signature of Newcomb Carlton

16T47 T26 5c **orange** (1915) 1.50
Pane of 6 10.00
orange yellow 5.00
16T48 T26 25c **olive green** (1915) 4.00
Pane of 6 30.00
a. Vert. pair, imperf. horizontally 45.00

Engraved by the American Bank Note Co.

1916-32

16T49 T27 5c **light blue** (1916) 1.50
Pane of 6 11.00
16T50 T27 25c **carmine lake** (1916) 1.75
Pane of 6 11.00

Engraved by the Security Bank Note Co.

Perf. 11

16T51 T27 5c **yellow brown** (1917) 1.00
Pane of 6 7.50
16T52 T27 25c **deep green** (1917) 3.00
Pane of 6 20.00
16T53 T27 5c **olive green** (1918) .60
Pane of 6 4.00
16T54 T27 25c **dark violet** (1918) 1.75
Pane of 6 12.50
16T55 T27 5c **brown** (1919) 1.25
Pane of 6 9.00
16T56 T27 25c **blue** (1919) 3.25
Pane of 6 22.50

Engraved by the E.A. Wright Bank Note Co.

Perf. 12

16T57 T27 5c **dark green** (1920) .65
Pane of 6 4.25
a. Vert. pair, imperf. between *300.00*
16T58 T27 25c **olive green** (1920) .65
Pane of 6 5.00

Engraved by the Security Bank Note Co.

16T59 T27 5c **carmine rose** (1921) .55
Pane of 6 4.25
16T60 T27 25c **deep blue** (1921) 1.30
Pane of 6 8.50
16T61 T27 5c **yellow brown** (1922) .55
Pane of 6 3.75
a. Horizontal pair, imperf. between 16.00
16T62 T27 25c **claret** (1922) 1.65
Pane of 6 11.50
16T63 T27 5c **olive green** (1923) .65
Pane of 6 4.25
16T64 T27 25c **dull violet** (1923) 1.35
Pane of 6 8.75
16T65 T27 5c **brown** (1924) 1.75
Pane of 6 12.00
16T66 T27 25c **ultramarine** (1924) 4.00
Pane of 6 30.00
16T67 T27 5c **olive green** (1925) .65
Pane of 6 4.25
16T68 T27 25c **carmine rose** (1925) 1.10
Pane of 6 7.00
16T69 T27 5c **blue** (1926) 1.00
Pane of 6 6.50
16T70 T27 25c **light brown** (1926) 2.00
Pane of 6 12.50
16T71 T27 5c **carmine** (1927) .85
Pane of 6 5.75
16T72 T27 25c **green** (1927) 7.25
Pane of 6 47.50

Engraved by the E. A. Wright Bank Note Co.

Without Imprint

16T73 T27 5c **yellow brown** (1928) .60
Pane of 6 4.00
16T74 T27 25c **dark blue** (1928) 1.00
Pane of 6 6.25

Engraved by the Security Bank Note Co.

Without Imprint

16T75 T27 5c **dark green** (1929) .30 .25
Pane of 6 2.00
16T76 T27 25c **red violet** (1929) .85 .50
Pane of 6 5.50
16T77 T27 5c **olive green** (1930) .25 .20
Pane of 6 1.75
16T78 T27 25c **carmine** (1930) .25 .25
Pane of 6 2.00
a. Horiz. pair, imperf. vertically 35.00
16T79 T27 5c **brown** (1931) .20 .20
Pane of 6 1.25
16T80 T27 25c **blue** (1931) .20 .20
Pane of 6 1.50
16T81 T27 5c **green** (1932) .20 .20
Pane of 6 1.50
16T82 T27 25c **rose carmine** (1932) .20 .20
Pane of 6 1.50

T28

1933-40

Lithographed by Oberly & Newell Co.

Without Imprint

Perf. 14x12½

16T83 T28 5c **pale brown** (1933) .25
Pane of 9 3.25
16T84 T28 25c **green** (1933) .25
Pane of 9 3.25

Lithographed by Security Bank Note Co.

Without Imprint

Perf. 12, 12½

Signature of R. B. White

16T85 T28 5c **lake** (1934) .20
Pane of 9 2.00
16T86 T28 25c **dark blue** (1934) .20
Pane of 9 2.50
16T87 T28 5c **yellow brown** (1935) .20
Pane of 9 1.75
16T88 T28 25c **lake** (1935) .20
Pane of 9 2.00
16T89 T28 5c **blue** (1936) .25 .20
Pane of 9 2.75
16T90 T28 25c **apple green** (1936) .20 .20
Pane of 9 2.50
16T91 T28 5c **bister brown** (1937) .20
Pane of 9 2.50
16T92 T28 25c **carmine rose** (1937) .20
Pane of 9 2.00
16T93 T28 5c **green** (1938) .25 .20
Pane of 9 3.00
16T94 T28 25c **blue** (1938) .30 .20
Pane of 9 3.50
16T95 T28 5c **dull vermilion** (1939) 1.00
Pane of 9 11.50
a. Horiz. pair, imperf. between —
16T96 T28 25c **bright violet** (1939) .50
Pane of 9 6.00
16T97 T28 5c **light blue** (1940) .55
Pane of 9 5.75
16T98 T28 25c **bright green** (1940) .50
Pane of 9 5.50

Samuel F. B. Morse
T29

Plates of 90 stamps.
Stamp designed by Nathaniel Yontiff.

Unlike the frank stamps, Nos. 16T99 to 16T103 were sold to the public in booklet form for use in prepayment of telegraph services.

Engraved by Security Bank Note Co. of Philadelphia

1940 **Unwmk.** ***Perf. 12, 12½x12, 12x12½***

No.	Type	Value	Description	Unused	Used
16T99	T29	1c	**yellow green**	1.25	
			Pane of 5	6.00	
a.			Imperf., pair	50.00	
16T100	T29	2c	**chestnut**	1.75	1.00
			Pane of 5	15.00	
a.			Imperf., pair	50.00	
16T101	T29	5c	**deep blue**	3.00	
			Pane of 5	18.00	
a.			Vert. pair, imperf. btwn.	65.00	
b.			Imperf., pair	50.00	
16T102	T29	10c	**orange**	5.00	
			Pane of 5	27.50	
a.			Imperf., pair	50.00	
16T103	T29	25c	**bright carmine**	4.00	
			Pane of 5	24.00	
a.			Imperf., pair	50.00	

Type of 1933-40

1941 **Litho.** ***Perf. 12½***

Without Imprint

Signature of R.B. White

No.	Type	Value	Description	Unused
16T104	T28	5c	**dull rose lilac**	.25
			Pane of 9	2.50
16T105	T28	25c	**vermilion**	.60
			Pane of 9	6.00

1942 **Signature of A.N. Williams**

No.	Type	Value	Description	Unused
16T106	T28	5c	**brown**	.30
			Pane of 9	3.50
16T107	T28	25c	**ultramarine**	.30
			Pane of 9	3.50

1943

No.	Type	Value	Description	Unused
16T108	T28	5c	**salmon**	.30
			Pane of 9	3.50
16T109	T28	25c	**red violet**	.30
			Pane of 9	3.50

1944

No.	Type	Value	Description	Unused
16T110	T28	5c	**light green**	.65
			Pane of 9	7.25
16T111	T28	25c	**buff**	.35
			Pane of 9	3.75

1945

No.	Type	Value	Description	Unused
16T112	T28	5c	**light blue**	.40
			Pane of 9	5.00
a.			Pair, imperf. between	—
16T113	T28	25c	**light green**	.35
			Pane of 9	3.75

1946

No.	Type	Value	Description	Unused
16T114	T28	5c	**light bister brown**	1.25
			Pane of 9	15.00
16T115	T28	25c	**rose pink**	1.00
			Pane of 9	12.00

Many of the stamps between 16T1 and 16T98 and 16T104 to 16T115 are known without frank numbers. Several of them are also known with more than one color used in the frank number and with handstamped and manuscript numbers. The numbers are also found in combination with various letters: O, A, B, C, D, etc.

Western Union discontinued the use of Telegraph stamps with the 1946 issue.

United States Telegraph-Cable-Radio Carriers

Booklets issued to accredited representatives to the World Telecommunications Conferences, Atlantic City, New Jersey, 1947. Valid for messages to points outside the United States. Issued by All America Cables & Radio, Inc., The Commercial Cable Company, Globe Wireless, Limited, Mackay Radio and Telegraph Company, Inc., R C A Communications, Inc., Tropical Radio Telegraph Company and The Western Union Telegraph Company.

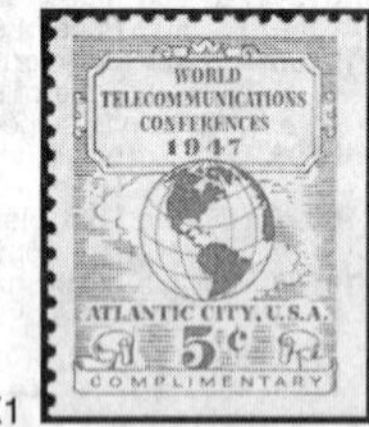

TX1

1947 **Litho.** **Unwmk.** ***Perf. 12½***

No.	Type	Value	Description	Unused
17T1	TX1	5c	**olive bister**	7.00
			Pane of 9	70.00
			Pane of 9, 8 5c + 1 10c	700.00
17T2	TX1	10c	**olive bister**	750.00
17T3	TX1	50c	**olive bister**	9.00
			Pane of 9	90.00

UNLISTED ISSUES

Several telegraph or wireless companies other than those listed above have issued stamps or franks, but as evidence of actual use is lacking, they are not listed. Among these are:

American District Telegraph Co.
American Telegraph Typewriter Co.
Continental Telegraph Co.
Los Angeles and San Gabriel Valley Railroad
Marconi Wireless Telegraph Co.
Mercantile Telegraph Co.
Telepost Co.
Tropical Radio Telegraph Co.
United Fruit Co. Wireless Service.
United Wireless Telegraph Co.

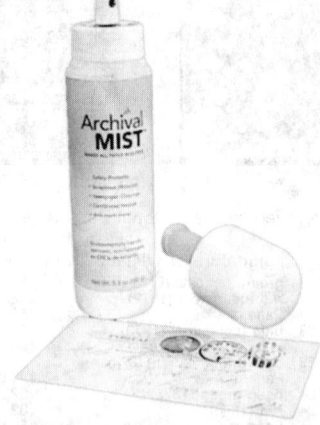

ESSAYS

An essay is a proposed design that differs in some way from the issued stamp.

During approximately 1845-1890, when private banknote engravers competed for contracts to print U.S. postage stamps, essays were produced primarily as examples of the quality of the firms' work and as suggestions as to what their finished product would look like. In most cases, dies were prepared, often with stock vignettes used in making banknotes. These dies were used to print essays for the Post Office Department. Rarely did the competitors go so far as to have essay plates made.

From 1894 onward, virtually all stamps were engraved and printed by the Bureau of Engraving and Printing (BEP). This usually required two types of essays. The first was a model design which was approved -- or disapproved -- by the Postmaster General. Sometimes preliminary drawings were made by the BEP designers, often in an enlarged size, subsequently photographically reduced to stamp size. An accepted stamp design usually became the engraver's model.

Occasionally during the course of engraving the die, a "progressive proof" was pulled to check the progress of the engraver's work. Because these were produced from an incompletely engraved die, they differ from the final design and are listed here as essays.

During approximately 1867-1870, various experiments were conducted to prevent the reuse of postage stamps. These included experimental grill types, safety papers, water-sensitive papers and inks, coupon essays, and others. These also differed in some way from issued stamps, even if the design was identical. A preliminary listing has been made here.

Because the essays in all their various colors have not been examined by the editors, traditional color names have been retained. Some color names have been taken from *Color Standards and Color Nomenclature,* by Robert Ridgway.

Only essays in private hands have been listed. Others exist but are not available to collectors. Some essays were produced after the respective stamps were issued. Year dates are given where information is available.

Essay papers and cards are white, unless described otherwise.

Values are for full-size essays, where they are known. Measurements are given where such information is available. Essays are valued in the grade of very fine, where such exist. Cut-down or faulty examples sell for less, often much less. A number of essays are unique or are reported in very limited quantities. Such items are valued in the conditions in which they exist.

The listings are by manufacturer. Basic stamps may appear in two or more places.

This listing is not complete. Other designs, papers and colors exist. The editors would appreciate reports of unlisted items, as well as photos of items listed herein without illustrations.

POSTMASTERS' PROVISIONALS

NON-CONTIGUOUS LISTINGS

Because many listings are grouped by manufacturer, some catalogue numbers are separated.

No. 5-E1 to 5-E2	**follow 11-E16**
No. 11-E17 to 72-E5	**follow 5-E2**
No. 65-E5 to 72-E8	**follow 72-E5**
No. 63-E13 to 113-E2	**follow 72-E8**
No. 112-E2 to 129-E2	**follow 113-E2**
No. 120-E1 to 122-E5	**follow 129-E2**
No. 115-E3a to 129-E6	**follow 122-E5**
No. 115-E11 to 116-E8	**follow 129-E6**
No. 115-E17 to 148-E1	**follow 116-E8**
No. 145-E2 to 179-E3	**follow 148-E1**
No. 156-E2 to 191-E2	**follow 179-E3**
No. 184-E8	**follows 191-E2**
No. 182-E4 to 190-E3	**follow 184-E8**
No. 184-E17 to 293-E11	**follow 190-E3**
No. 285-E10 to 856-E2	**follow 293-E11**

Albany, N.Y.
Gavit & Co.

1Xa-E1

Design size: 23½x25½mm
Die size: 58x48mm

Benjamin Franklin. With crosshatching about 2mm outside border (usually cut off).

1847

1Xa-E1 5c

a. Die on India die sunk on large card, printed through a mat to eliminate crosshatching

brownish black	*600.*
scarlet	*600.*
red brown	*600.*
blue	*600.*
green	*600.*

b. Die on India; some mounted on small card

bluish black	325.
scarlet	325.
brown	325.
yellow green	325.
gray blue	325.

c. Die on India cut close

black	250.
blue	250.
red brown	250.
scarlet	250.
green	250.
yellow green	250.
brown violet	250.
rose red	250.

d. Die on bond (1858)

bluish black	375.
scarlet	375.
brown	375.
blue	375.
blue green	375.
violet	375.

e. Die on white glazed paper (1905)

black	900.
dark brown	900.
scarlet	900.
blue	900.

New York, N.Y.
Rawdon, Wright & Hatch

9X1-E1

Design 22mm wide
Die size: 50x102mm

Vignette of Washington. Two transfers laid down vertically on the die 22mm apart; top one retouched, with frame around it (this is a proof). Values are for combined transfers. Vignette essay exists cut apart from proof, value $200 each.

1845

9X1-E1 5c

a. Die on India (1879)

black	450.
violet black	450.
gray black	450.
scarlet	450.
dull scarlet	450.
orange	450.
brown	450.
dull brown	450.
green	450.
dull green	450.
ultramarine	450.
dull blue	450.
red violet	450.

b. Die on white bond (1879)

gray black	550.
dull scarlet	550.
dull brown	550.
dull green	550.
dull blue	550.

c. Die on white glazed paper, die sunk (1879)

gray black	700.

POSTAGE

1847 ISSUE
Rawdon, Wright, Hatch & Edson

1-E1

Design size: 19x24mm

Original model. Engraved vignette of Franklin mounted on frame. Part of frame engraved, rest in pencil, ink and a gray wash.

1-E1 5c Die on card, black *21,000.*

No. 1-E1 is unique. Value represents 1997 auction sale.

Engraved vignette only, matted.

1-E2 5c Die on India (1895), brown *2,500.*

Engraved frame only, matted from complete die.

1-E3 5c Die on India (1895), brown 2,500.

The 1895 dates are in suppositional.

Design size: 19x23mm
Original model. Engraved vignette of Washington mounted (replaced) on frame. POST OFFICE and FIVE CENTS engraved as on No. 1-E1. U and S at top and X in bottom corners in black ink, rest in pencil, ink and a gray wash.

2-E1 10c Die on card, black *21,000.*

No. 2-E1 is unique. Value represents 1997 auction sale.

2-E2 2-E3

Engraved vignette only.

2-E2 10c Die on India (1895)
black *2,500.*
brownish black *2,500.*
brown *2,500.*

Engraved frame only.

2-E3 10c Die on India (1895)
black *2,500.*
brown orange *2,500.*

The 1895 dates are in suppositional.

1851 ISSUE
Attributed to
Rawdon, Wright, Hatch & Edson

11-E1 11-E2

Design size: 18½x23mm
Large 3 in vignette.

11-E1 3c Die on India
black *2,500.*
blue *2,500.*

Design size: 19x24mm
Vignette of Washington.

11-E2 3c
a. Die on India
black *4,500.*
b. Die on proof paper, die sunk on 40x51mm card
black *4,500.*

Attributed to
Gavit & Co.

11-E3 11-E4

Design size: 19x23mm
Vignette of Franklin. Three states of die. Second state has double line dash above P of POSTAGE, third state has single dash above P and dot in O of POSTAGE.

11-E3 3c
a. Die on India, die sunk on card
warm black *750.*
scarlet *750.*
red brown *750.*
blue green *750.*
b. Die on India, 41x43mm or smaller
black 300.
greenish black 300.
carmine 300.
scarlet 300.
yellow green 300.
brown 300.
blue green 300.
dull blue 300.
dark blue 300.
c. Die on India, cut to shape
warm black 225.
cool black 225.
black 225.
carmine 225.
orange 225.
brown 225.
dark green 225.
yellow green 225.
olive 225.
light blue 225.
dark blue 225.
violet 225.
scarlet 225.
d. Die on bond
cool black 225.
scarlet 225.
orange brown 225.
brown 225.
green 225.
blue 225.
e. Die on white glazed paper
black *750.*
dark brown *750.*
scarlet *750.*
blue *750.*
f. Die on thin card, dusky blue, cut to shape *200.*
g. Die on Francis Patent experimental paper with trial cancel
black *1,250.*
dark blue *1,250.*
brown *1,250.*

Design size: 19x22mm
Die size: 47x75mm
Vignette of Washington. Two states of die. Second state has small diagonal dash in top of left vertical border below arch.

11-E4 3c
a. Die on India, die sunk on card
black *750.*
scarlet *750.*
brown red *750.*
blue green *750.*
b. Die on India, about 30x40mm or smaller
orange 250.
orange brown 250.
brown 250.
dusky yellow brown 250.
yellow green 250.
blue green 250.
dull blue 250.
red violet 250.
deep red orange 250.
black 250.
c. Die on bond (1858)
black 250.
scarlet 250.
brown 250.
green 250.
blue 250.
d. Die on white glazed paper (1858)
black *750.*
dark brown *750.*
scarlet *750.*
blue *750.*
e. Die on proof paper (1858)
cool black *450.*
dull red *450.*
dull brown *450.*
dull blue green *450.*
dull blue *450.*

Bradbury, Wilkinson & Co., England

11-E5

Design size: 20½x23½mm
Vignette of Washington.

11-E5 3c
a. On stiff stamp paper about stamp size
black *1,250.*
violet red *1,250.*
deep carmine *1,250.*
dusky carmine *1,250.*
deep scarlet *1,250.*
orange brown *1,250.*
deep green *1,250.*
blue *1,250.*
ultramarine *1,250.*
brown *1,250.*
b. On card
violet black *1,250.*
dull scarlet *1,250.*
blue *1,250.*
green *1,250.*
brown *1,250.*
c. On stiff bond
brown *1,250.*
blue *1,250.*
violet black *1,250.*

Draper, Welsh & Co.

11-E6 11-E7

Design size: 18x23mm
Vignette of Washington.

11-E6 3c Surface printed on card, black *750.*

Design size: 17½x24mm
Die size: 44x106mm
Engraved vignette of Washington.

11-E7 3c
a. Die on India, about 44x105mm, die sunk on card, in vert. pair with No. 11-E8
black *1,250.*
scarlet *1,250.*
brown red *1,250.*
green *1,250.*
b. Die on India, about 40x45mm or smaller
warm black *250.*
cool black *250.*
dark carmine *250.*
scarlet *250.*
brown red *250.*
orange brown *250.*
brown *250.*
yellow green *250.*
blue green *250.*
blue *250.*
dull blue *250.*
brown violet *250.*
c. Die on India, stamp size
rose 150.
scarlet 150.
red brown 150.
brown 150.
green 150.
cool black 150.
warm black 150.
yellow green 150.
brown violet 150.
ultramarine blue 150.
d. Die on bond
black 200.
scarlet 200.
brown 200.
blue green 200.
blue 200.
e. Die on white glazed paper
black *750.*
dark brown *750.*
scarlet *750.*
blue *750.*

11-E8

Design size: 19½x24
Die size: 44x106mm
On same die 30mm below No. 11-E7
Vignette of Washington.

11-E8 3c
a. Die on India, 28x32mm or smaller
black *250.*
dark carmine *250.*
scarlet *250.*
brown red *250.*
red brown *250.*
orange brown *250.*
brown *250.*
yellow green *250.*
green *250.*
blue green *250.*
blue *250.*
b. Die on bond, about 32x40mm
black 225.
scarlet 225.
brown 225.
green 225.
blue 225.
c. Die on white glazed paper
black *750.*
dark brown *750.*
scarlet *750.*
blue *750.*

11-E8D

11-E9

Design size: 18x23mm
Vignette of Washington.
Washington vignette only. Same head as No. 11-E6 through 11-E8, but with more bust. No gridwork in background.

11-E8D 3c Die on proof paper, mounted on card, black —

Design size (No. 11-E9a): 18x33mm
Vignette design size (Nos. 11-E9b, 11-E9c): 18x22mm
As No. 11-E8D, gridwork added to background oval.

11-E9 3c
a. Die on India
black 350.
scarlet 350.
b. Die on India, single line frame
black 300.
blue 300.
dark carmine 300.
orange red 300.
lilac 300.
brown 300.
scarlet 300.
rose violet 300.
deep yellow green 300.
c. Die on India, imprint of Jocelyn, Draper, Welsh & Co., New York
black 300.
blue 300.
dark carmine 300.
orange red 300.
lilac 300.
brown 300.
scarlet 300.
rose violet 300.
deep yellow green 300.

Danforth, Bald & Co.

11-E10

11-E11

Vignette size: 18x22mm
Design size: 20x26mm
Die size: 57x74mm
Vignette of Washington. Double line frame.

11-E10 3c
a. Die on India, die sunk on card
black *750.*
scarlet *750.*
red brown *750.*
green *750.*
b. Die on India, off card, about 33x38mm
black *175.*
scarlet *175.*
brown *175.*
blue *175.*
green *175.*
dull violet *175.*
dull blue *175.*
red brown *175.*
rose *175.*
c. Die on bond, black *350.*
d. Die on white glazed paper
black *750.*
dark brown *750.*
scarlet *750.*
blue *750.*

Washington vignette only.

11-E11 3c Die on India
black 325.
dull rose 325.
scarlet 325.
orange 325.
brown orange 325.
brown 325.
green 325.
dark blue 325.
dull violet 325.
rose violet 325.

11-E12

Design size: 20x26mm
Die size: 62x66mm
Vignette of Washington. Single line frame. Two states of die. Second state shows scars in lathe lines in front of neck over T, and small dot below design. A third printing has more scars in front of neck.

11-E12 3c
a. Die on India, die sunk on card
black *750.*
scarlet *750.*
brown red *750.*
dusky brown yellow *750.*
brown *750.*
green *750.*
blue *750.*
dull blue *750.*
b. Die on India, about 43x45mm
black *300.*
scarlet *300.*
deep scarlet *300.*
brown *300.*
yellow brown *300.*
green *300.*
yellow green *300.*
blue *300.*
dull blue *300.*
dark blue *300.*
ultramarine blue *300.*
orange *300.*
red *300.*
c. Die on bond
dusky brown yellow *275.*
blue *275.*
d. Die on white glazed paper
black *750.*
dark brown *750.*
scarlet *750.*
blue *750.*
e. Plate on thick buff wove
rose 125.
violet brown 125.
orange 125.
dark orange 125.
pink orange 125.
f. Plate on India, dark red orange 150.
g. Plate on white wove (head more completely engraved, ruled lines between designs)
black 125.
dark carmine 125.
yellow 125.
blue 125.

Design size: 20x26mm
Die size: 62x66mm
Vignette of Washington. No. 11-E12 reengraved: more dark dots in forehead next to hair, thus line between forehead and hair more distinct.

11-E13 3c
a. Die on India, die sunk on card
black *750.*
scarlet *750.*
brown red *750.*
brown *750.*
green *750.*
b. Die on white glazed paper
black *750.*
dark brown *750.*
scarlet *750.*
blue *750.*

Bald, Cousland & Co.

11-E14

11-E15

Design size: 22x28mm
Die size: 95x43mm
Vignette of Washington. On same die with Nos. 11-E16 and incomplete 11-E14.

11-E14 3c
a. Die on India
black *450.*
scarlet *450.*
red brown *450.*
brown *450.*
yellow green *450.*
green *450.*
blue green *450.*
orange brown *450.*
rose pink *450.*
dull blue *450.*
violet *450.*
b. Die on bond
black 250.
scarlet 250.
brown 250.
blue green 250.
blue 250.

Design size: 28x22½mm
POSTAGE / 3 / CENTS in scalloped frame.

11-E15 3c
a. Die on India, die sunk on card
black *750.*
scarlet *750.*
red brown *750.*
green *750.*
slate *750.*
b. Die on bond, about 40x30mm
black 175.
scarlet 175.
brown 175.
green 175.
blue 175.
slate 275.
c. Die on white glazed paper
black *750.*
dark brown *750.*
scarlet *750.*
blue *750.*

11-E16

Design size: 28x22½mm
U.S. at sides of 3.

11-E16 3c
a. Die on India, cut small
black *275.*
light red *275.*
red brown *275.*
brown *275.*
yellow green *275.*
blue green *275.*
green *275.*
blue *275.*
red violet *275.*
b. Die on bond, about 40x30mm
black 175.
scarlet 175.
brown 175.
red brown 175.
green 175.
blue green 175.
blue 175.
violet 175.
slate 175.
c. Die on India, Nos. 11-E14 and 11-E16 with albino 11-E14
black *1,000.*
scarlet *1,000.*
brown *1,000.*
green *1,000.*
blue *1,000.*
red violet *1,000.*
d. Die on bond
black *225.*
scarlet *225.*
brown *225.*
green *225.*
blue green *225.*
gray blue *225.*
e. Die on white glazed paper, 64x78mm, black *650.*
f. Die on India, die sunk on card
black *900.*
scarlet *900.*

Toppan, Carpenter, Casilear & Co.

5-E1

5-E1E

5-E1f

Design size: 20½x26mm
Franklin vignette.

5-E1 1c
- ***a.*** Die on old proof paper, master die shortened to 18½x22½mm, black — *1,500.*
- ***b.*** Die on thick old proof paper, black — *1,500.*
- ***c.*** Pair, Nos. 5-E1b, 11-E23, black — *2,000.*

Design size: 20x24mm
Similar to No. 5-E1 but with no additional shaded oval border.

5-E1E 1c Die on thin card, black blue — —
- ***f.*** Block of 4 in combination with pair of No. 11-E23, on old proof paper, black — *3,500.*

5-E2

Complete design, but with SIX CENTS in value tablet.

5-E2 1c Die on India, black, cut to shape — 1,750.

11-E17

11-E18

Design size: 21½x25mm
Die size: 50½x60mm
Vignette of Washington.

11-E17 3c
- ***a.*** Die on India, 22x26mm, rose carmine — 1,500.
- ***b.*** Die on old ivory paper, rose carmine — 1,500.
- ***c.*** Die on proof paper, printed through a mat (1903)

black	125.
bright carmine	125.
dull carmine	125.
dark violet red	125.
dull scarlet	125.
dull violet	125.
dull red violet	125.
deep yellow	125.
deep orange	125.
orange brown	125.
dull brown olive	125.
deep green	125.
dark blue green	125.
ultramarine	125.
dark blue	125.
brown	125.

- ***d.*** Die on colored card (1903)

deep orange, *ivory*	200.
dark blue, *pale green*	200.
orange brown, *light blue*	200.

See note above No. 63-E1.

Design size: 20½x22½mm
Washington. Vignette has solid color background. Crack between N and T of CENTS.

11-E18 3c Die on India, card mounted, 24½x25mm

black	*2,000.*
carmine	*2,000.*

11-E19

11-E20

No. 11-E19
Design size: 20½x22½mm
Similar to No. 11-E18, but vignette background engraved horiz. and vert. lines. In pair with No. 11-E20.

No. 11-E20
Design size: 20x22½mm
Blank curved top and bottom labels. In pair with 11-E19. Also found in pair with 11-E21.

11-E19 3c Die on India, Nos. 11-E19, 11-E20 mounted on card, black — *6,000.*

11-E21

Straight labels. Similar to No. 11-E19 but labels erased and vignette cut out. In pair with No. 11-E20.

11-E21 3c Die on India, Nos. 11-E20, 11-E21 mounted on card, black — *4,500.*

11-E22

11-E23

Die size: 37½x46mm
Similar to issued stamp except lathework impinges on colorless oval.

11-E22 3c Die on India

dusky blue	*5,000.*
black	*5,000.*

Some students consider No. 11-E22 to be proof strikes of the die used to make the "Roosevelt" and Panama-Pacific small die proofs, as the lathework impinges on the colorless oval of Nos. 11P2 and 11P2a as well.

Design size: 18x22mm
Washington vignette only. From master die (21½mm high) with more robe and dark background.

11-E23 3c
- ***a.*** Master die impression, old proof paper, black — *900.*
- ***b.*** Block of 4, 2mm between ovals, thick old ivory paper, black — *3,000.*

13-E1

13-E2

Design as adopted but top label has pencil lettering only, also no lines in leaf ornaments around Xs in top corners.

13-E1 10c Die on India, black — *3,000.*

Similar to No. 13-E1 but vert. shading around Xs and lines added in leaf ornaments. No lettering in top label.

13-E2 10c Die on India, black — *3,000.*

17-E1

17-E2

Design size: 19x21½mm
Block sinkage size: 57x49mm
Engine engraved frame without labels or interior shadow lines from straight bands and left side rosettes. No small equilateral crosses in central row of diamonds. Original vignette cut out and replaced by engraved vignette of Washington as adopted.

17-E1 12c Die on India, cut close, mounted on block sunk card, 77x57mm, black — *6,000.*

Similar to adopted design but no small vertical equilateral crosses in center rows of diamond networks at top, sides and bottom.

17-E2 12c Die on India, brown violet, cut close — *750.*

37-E1

37-E2

Design size: 19½x25½mm
Die size: 46x49mm or larger
Probably not the die used to make the plates. No exterior layout lines. Oval outline recut at bottom of jabot and vignette background etched much darker. Light horizontal lines on stock below chin.

37-E1 24c Die on India, black — *2,500.*

Incomplete essay for frame only as adopted: no outer frameline and lathework not retouched. Also known with 37TC1 struck above it on same piece.

37-E2 24c Die on India, black — —

38-E1

Design size: 19x24mm
Incomplete engraving of entire design. Scrolls at each side of 30 have only one outer shading line.

38-E1 30c Die on India, black, cut to stamp size, black — *2,500.*

1861 ISSUE
Toppan, Carpenter & Co.

Examples on 1861 paper and in 1861 colors are rare. Most of the following listed on proof paper, colored card and bond paper are 1903 reprints. Ten sets of reprints on proof paper (and fewer on colored card, bond and pelure papers) supposedly were made for Ernest Schernikow, who bought the original dies about 1903. Similar reprints in similar colors on the same papers also were made of Nos. LO1-E2, 11-E18 and the Philadelphia sanitary fair stamps, plus several master dies of vignettes.

63-E1

63-E2

Vignette size: 18½x21½mm
Die size: 49x51mm
Franklin vignette only.

63-E1 1c
- ***a.*** Die on proof paper (1903)

black	75.
carmine	75.
dark carmine	75.

scarlet 75.
red brown 75.
orange 75.
yellow brown 75.
dark brown 75.
violet brown 75.
light green 75.
green 75.
dark blue 75.
ultramarine 75.
red violet 75.
dark violet 75.
dusky olive green 75.
b. Die on colored card (1903)
orange red, *pale yellow* *125.*
orange, *pale pink* *125.*
yellow brown, *buff* *125.*
dark blue, *pink* *125.*
dark violet, *pale olive* *125.*
dull violet, *blue* *125.*
deep green, *pale blue* *125.*
violet, *light green* *125.*
c. Die on green bond (1903)
black *125.*
dismal red *125.*
green *125.*

Franklin vignette with U S POSTAGE at top and ONE CENT at bottom.

63-E2 1c
a. Die on proof paper (1903)
black 100.
carmine 100.
dark carmine 100.
scarlet 100.
red brown 100.
orange 100.
yellow brown 100.
violet brown 100.
gray brown 100.
light green 100.
green 100.
blue 100.
red violet 100.
ultramarine 100.
dusky olive 100.
b. Die on old proof paper, outer line at sides of oval missing (1861), black *1,000.*
c. Die on green bond (1903)
orange *150.*
orange brown *150.*
violet *150.*
d. Die on colored card (1903)
deep green, *pale blue* *150.*
violet, *light green* *150.*
dark orange red, *pale dull green* *150.*
olive, *ivory* *150.*
brown, *pink* *150.*
scarlet, *yellow* *150.*

63-E3

Side ornaments added.

63-E3 1c
a. Die on old proof paper (1861)
black *1,250.*
blue *1,250.*
b. Die on stiff old ivory paper (1861), black *1,250.*
c. Die on colored card (1903)
black, *ivory* *150.*
brown, *pale pink* *150.*
blue, *blue* *150.*
orange brown, *pale pink* *150.*
gray olive, *ivory* *150.*
gray olive, *buff* *150.*
scarlet, *pale yellow* *150.*
d. Die on proof paper (1903)
black 85.
carmine 85.
dark carmine 85.
scarlet 85.
red brown 85.
orange 85.
yellow brown 85.
violet brown 85.
light green 85.
green 85.
blue 85.
violet 85.
red violet 85.
orange brown 85.
dusky olive 85.
ultramarine 85.
e. Die on green bond (1903)
carmine *150.*
orange *150.*
violet *150.*

63-E4

63-E4E

With upper and lower right corners incomplete. Serifs of 1s point to right.

63-E4 1c Die on old proof paper (1861), black *2,250.*

As No. 63-E4 but with pencil shading in upper right corner.

63-E4E 1c Die on old proof paper (1861), black *3,500.*

63-E5

63-E6

With four corners and numerals in pencil (ornaments differ in each corner).

63-E5 1c Die on old proof paper (1861), blue *2,750.*

As No. 63-E5 but ornaments different.

63-E6 1c Die on old proof paper (1861), blue *3,500.*

63-E7

As Nos. 63-E5 and 63-E6 but ornaments different.

63-E7 1c Die on old proof paper (1861), blue *3,250.*

Die proof of No. 5 with lower corners cut out of India paper and resketched in pencil on card beneath.

63-E8 1c Die on India, on card (1861), black *2,000.*

63-E9

Completely engraved design.

63-E9 1c
a. Die on India, cut to shape (1861)
black, on brown toned paper 1,000.
blue 600.
b. Die on India, about 58x57mm, die sunk on card (1861)
blue 2,000.
c. Die on old proof paper, about 48x55mm (1861)
black 2,000.
d. Die on large old white ivory paper (1861)
black 2,000.
blue 2,000.
e. Die on proof paper, printed through mat (1903)
black 100.
carmine 100.
dark carmine 100.
scarlet 100.
orange 100.
orange brown 100.
yellow brown 100.
light green 100.
green 100.
black blue 100.
violet 100.
red violet 100.
violet brown 100.
gray 100.
blue 100.
ultramarine 100.
f. Die on bond (1903)
orange *125.*
dismal blue green *125.*
g. Die on bond, Walls of Troy wmk. (1903)
carmine *200.*
orange red *200.*
orange *200.*
orange brown *200.*
dark green *200.*
light ultramarine *200.*
h. Die on bond, double line of scallops wmk. (1903)
orange red *200.*
dark green *200.*
i. Die on green bond (1903)
dismal carmine *125.*
dismal violet brown *125.*
dull dark green *125.*
j. Die on pinkish pelure (1903)
orange red *300.*
brown red *300.*
brown orange *300.*
dull blue green *300.*
violet *300.*
k. Die on colored card (1903)
black, *pale blue* *225.*
carmine, *pale yellow* *225.*
carmine, *pale pink* *225.*
brown red, *pale pink* *225.*
chestnut, *pale olive* *225.*
dismal olive, *buff* *225.*
ultramarine, *ivory* *225.*
l. Die on stiff card (1903), green *250.*

65-E1

65-E2

Vignette size: 16½x19mm
Die size: 49x50mm
1851 master die of Washington vignette only.

65-E1 3c
a. Die on proof paper (1903)
black 75.
carmine 75.
dark carmine 75.
scarlet 75.
red brown 75.
orange 75.
brown orange 75.
violet brown 75.
dusky olive 75.
light green 75.
green 75.
dark blue 75.
ultramarine 75.
lilac 75.
red violet 75.
b. Die on green bond (1903)
red *125.*
brown *125.*
blue *125.*
olive *125.*
c. Die on colored card (1903)
carmine, *pale green* *125.*
scarlet, *yellow* *125.*
orange, *ivory* *125.*
olive brown, *blue* *125.*
dark blue, *pink* *125.*
violet, *buff* *125.*
dark green, *pink* *125.*

With tessellated frame, bottom label and diamond blocks. Without rosettes, top label and diamond blocks.

65-E2 3c
a. Die on old proof paper (1861)
black *1,000.*
red *1,000.*
b. Die on proof paper, printed through a mat (1903)
black *85.*
carmine *85.*
dark carmine *85.*
scarlet *85.*
orange *85.*
yellow *85.*
yellow brown *85.*
dusky gray *85.*
light green *85.*
green *85.*
black blue *85.*
ultramarine *85.*
lilac *85.*
dark lilac *85.*
red violet *85.*
c. Die on green bond (1903)
black *150.*
dull orange red *150.*
orange *150.*
orange brown *150.*
blue violet *150.*
black blue *150.*
dusky green *150.*

d. Die on dull pale gray blue thin wove (1903)
dull red *300.*
orange *300.*
yellow brown *300.*
dusky green *300.*
black blue *300.*
e. Die on colored card (1903)
black, *light blue* *150.*
orange red, *yellow* *150.*
red brown, *ivory* *150.*
light green, *pink* *150.*
green, *light green* *150.*
blue, *buff* *150.*
f. Die on India
black —
rose —

65-E3

65-E4

With top label and diamond blocks.

65-E3 3c
a. Die on old proof paper (1861)
brown red *1,500.*
black *1,500.*
b. Same as No. 65-E3 with numerals in pencil, Die on old proof paper (1861), black *3,500.*
c. Die on proof paper, no numerals, printed through a mat (1903)
black 90.
carmine 90.
dark carmine 90.
scarlet 90.
orange 90.
yellow 90.
yellow brown 90.
dusky olive 90.
light green 90.
green 90.
black blue 90.
violet blue 90.
violet brown 90.
lilac 90.
red violet 90.
d. Die on green bond (1903)
dull scarlet *150.*
dim red *150.*
orange *150.*
yellow brown *150.*
green *150.*
dusky blue *150.*
violet *150.*
black *150.*
e. Die on colored card (1903)
black, *buff* *150.*
scarlet, *ivory* *150.*
orange, *light yellow* *150.*
brown, *light blue* *150.*
violet blue, *light pink* *150.*
violet, *light green* *150.*
f. Die on pink thin wove (1903)
dull yellow *300.*
dismal red *300.*
yellow brown *300.*
dusky blue green *300.*
dusky blue *300.*

Complete die, with numerals in rosette circles.

65-E4 3c
a. Die on India, 75x76mm die sinkage (1861)
black *1,500.*
carmine *1,500.*
b. Die on old proof paper (1861)
black *1,500.*
dark red *1,500.*
c. Die on India, cut to shape (1861)
black *1,000.*
carmine *1,000.*

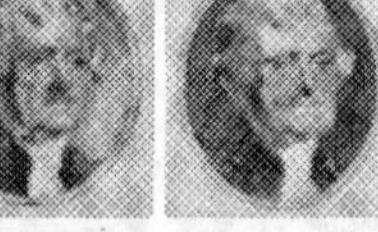

67-E1 — Die I 67-E1 — Die II

Vignette size: 13½x16mm
Jefferson vignette only. Two dies: die I incomplete, light background in vignette; die II background essentially complete.

67-E1 5c
a. Die I on proof paper, black *650.*
b. Die II on proof paper (1903)
black 75.
carmine 75.
dark carmine 75.
scarlet 75.
red brown 75.
orange brown 75.
brown 75.
dusky olive 75.
green 75.
dark green 75.
black blue 75.
ultramarine 75.
violet brown 75.
red violet 75.
lilac 75.
c. Die II on colored card (1903)
olive, *buff* *150.*
carmine, *pale yellow* *150.*
scarlet, *green* *150.*
brown, *pink* *150.*
black, *ivory* *150.*
ultramarine, *pale blue* *150.*
d. Die II on green bond (1903)
orange brown *150.*
dismal red brown *150.*
dark green *150.*
violet *150.*
black blue *150.*
e. Die II on old thin ivory paper (1903)
green 175.
dark carmine 175.
f. Die I on old thin ivory paper (1861), dark blue *1,000.*
g. Die I on old proof paper (1861)
black *750.*
dusky ultramarine *1,500.*
h. Die II on old ivory paper (1861), navy blue *750.*

67-E2

Vignette die II framed, with spaces for numerals.

67-E2 5c
a. Die II on proof paper (1903)
black 95.
carmine 95.
dark carmine 95.
scarlet 95.
red brown 95.
orange 95.
yellow brown 95.
dusky olive 95.
violet brown 95.
light green 95.
green 95.
blue 95.
ultramarine 95.
red violet 95.
lilac 95.
b. Die II on colored card (1903)
orange brown, *light yellow* *175.*
deep blue, *light pink* *175.*
dusky olive, *light buff* *175.*
dark green, *pale blue* *175.*
red violet, *ivory* *175.*
c. Die II on green bond (1903)
orange brown *160.*
olive green *160.*
violet *160.*
blue *160.*
ultramarine *160.*

67-E3 67-E4

With numerals.

67-E3 5c
a. Die I on proof paper, printed through a mat (1903)
black 125.
carmine 125.
dark carmine 125.
scarlet 125.
red brown 125.
yellow brown 125.
dark brown 125.
violet brown 125.
light green 125.
green 125.
dark blue 125.
lilac 125.
ultramarine 125.
red violet 125.
dusky olive 125.
b. Die I on soft laid paper (1861)
black *750.*
dark brown *750.*
orange brown *750.*
c. Die I on old proof paper, pencil designs drawn in corners (1861), black *1,500.*
d. Die I on old proof paper, outer lines on corner curves missing (1861), black *500.*
e. Die I on colored card (1903)
orange red, *buff* *175.*
orange red, *light yellow* *175.*
olive green, *pale green* *175.*
deep green, *ivory* *175.*
dark blue, *light pink* *175.*
violet brown, *light blue* *175.*
f. Die I on green bond (1903)
black *160.*
scarlet *160.*
brown *160.*
green *160.*
g. Die I on yellow pelure (1903)
scarlet *350.*
brown red *350.*
brown *350.*
dark green *350.*
violet *350.*
blue *350.*
h. Die I on bond, Walls of Troy wmk. (1903)
dark orange *250.*
blue *250.*
carmine *250.*
i. Die I on bond, two line scalloped border wmk. (1903)
dark blue green *250.*
scarlet *250.*

Complete die II design with corner ornaments.

67-E4 5c
a. Die II on India, cut to shape (1861), black *500.*
b. Die II on brown toned paper (1861)
black *1,000.*
brown *1,000.*
c. Die II on old proof paper (1861)
orange brown *1,000.*
black *1,000.*
d. Die II on old ivory paper (1861), black *1,000.*
e. Die II on old proof paper, additional frameline drawn on curved corners and small circle drawn in each corner (1861), black *1,500.*
f. Die II on proof paper, printed through a mat (1903)
black 125.
carmine 125.
dark carmine 125.
scarlet 125.
orange 125.
brown 125.
yellow brown 125.
dusky olive 125.
light green 125.
green 125.
blue 125.
black blue 125.
violet brown 125.
red violet 125.
lilac 125.
ultramarine 125.
g. Die II on colored card (1903)
red, *light yellow* *150.*
brown, *buff* *150.*
olive green, *light pink* *150.*
dark violet *150.*
violet brown, *pale green* *150.*
dusky yellow green, *dull pale* *150.*
blue green *150.*
brown, *ivory* *150.*
h. Die II on green bond (1903)
black *125.*
dull dark orange *125.*
violet *125.*
i. Die II on bond, Walls of Troy wmk. (1903)
scarlet *250.*
deep red *250.*
dark green *250.*
j. Die II on bond, two-line scalloped border wmk. (1903)
deep orange *250.*
blue *250.*
k. Die II on greenish pelure (1903)
orange *350.*
olive brown *350.*
dark green *350.*
l. Die II on bluish pelure (1903), red brown *450.*

69-E1

69-E2

Vignette size: 15x17mm
Washington vignette only. Two dies: die I incomplete, horiz. background lines irregularly spaced, space occurring about every 2mm; die II more engraving on face, horiz. background lines regularly spaced, outer oval border smudged. Die II known only as 1851 master die.

69-E1 12c
a. Die II on old proof paper (1851), black 650.
b. Die I on proof paper (1903)
black 60.
carmine 60.
dark carmine 60.

scarlet 60.
red brown 60.
orange 60.
yellow brown 60.
violet brown 60.
gray brown 60.
light green 60.
green 60.
blue 60.
black blue 60.
red violet 60.
lilac 60.
ultramarine 60.

c. Die I on green bond (1903)
black *150.*
red brown *150.*
brown *150.*

d. Die I on colored card (1903)
dark carmine, *ivory* *150.*
dark carmine, *light blue* *150.*
dark olive, *buff* *150.*
dark green, *light yellow* *150.*
dark blue, *pale green* *150.*
violet brown, *light pink* *150.*

Die II with curved labels at top and bottom.

69-E2 12c

a. Die II on proof paper, some printed through a mat (1903)
black 75.
carmine 75.
dark carmine 75.
scarlet 75.
orange 75.
yellow 75.
yellow brown 75.
violet brown 75.
gray brown 75.
light green 75.
green 75.
light blue 75.
black blue 75.
red violet 75.
lilac 75.
ultramarine 75.

b. Die I on old proof paper (1861)
dim red violet *500.*
red violet *500.*

c. Die I on dull light green bond (1903)
black *150.*
dull red *150.*
dim orange *150.*
yellow brown *150.*
dusky green *150.*
dusky blue *150.*
red violet *150.*

d. Die I on pale yellow thin wove (1903)
dim red *200.*
deep orange red *200.*
yellow brown *200.*
dusky blue *200.*
red violet *200.*

e. Die I on colored card (1903)
dull red, *light pink* *150.*
orange red, *buff* *150.*
brown, *light blue* *150.*
dark olive, *light yellow* *150.*
dull dark blue, *ivory* *150.*
violet, *pale green* *150.*

69-E3

Frame incomplete: all four rosettes blank.

69-E3 12c

a. Die on proof paper (1903)
black 125.
carmine 125.
dark carmine 125.
scarlet 125.
red brown 125.
orange 125.
orange brown 125.
violet brown 125.
light green 125.
green 125.
light blue 125.
black blue 125.
red violet 125.
lilac 125.
ultramarine 125.

b. Die on old proof paper (1861)
black *750.*
olive gray *750.*

c. Die on old ivory, top border and half of rosettes missing (1861), black *750.*

d. Die on stiff old ivory, top border missing (1861), bluish black *750.*

e. Die on colored card, top border missing (1903)
orange brown, *light blue* *175.*
deep green, *light yellow* *175.*
deep blue, *light pink* *175.*
violet, *ivory* *175.*
deep yellow orange, *pale yellow green* *175.*
brown, *buff* *175.*

f. Die on green bond, top border missing (1903)
orange *175.*
green *175.*
violet *175.*

g. Die on old proof paper, 1851 die with border lines complete, upper right rosette blank (1861)
orange *750.*
dark green *750.*
ultramarine *750.*
violet *750.*

h. Die I on old proof paper, vignette background incomplete or worn, stock on neck unfinished (1861)

i. Die I on old proof paper, as 69-E3h but both upper rosettes blank (1861), ultramarine *1,000.*

69-E3j

69-E3k

j. Die I on old proof paper, as No. 69-E3h but both upper plus lower left rosettes blank (1861), ultramarine *1,000.*

k. Die I on old proof paper, as No. 69-E3h but both lower plus upper left rosettes blank, corner borders removed around blank rosettes (1861), ultramarine *1,000.*

l. Die I on old proof paper, as No. 69-E3h but all rosettes blank, border lines complete (1861)
dim scarlet *750.*
orange *750.*
green *750.*
ultramarine *750.*
violet *750.*

m. Die I on white wove, as No. 69-E3l (1861), scarlet *750.*

n. Die I on old proof paper, complete design (1861)
orange *750.*
dark red *750.*
orange red *750.*
ultramarine *750.*

o. Die I on pale yellow thin wove (1903), dark red *750.*

p. Die I on pink thin wove (1903), blue *750.*

q. Die I on pale pink (1903), blue *750.*

69-E4

Original complete design with numerals in corners.

69-E4 12c

a. Die on India, card mounted (1861)
black *750.*
gray black *750.*

b. Die on India, cut to shape (1861), black *500.*

c. Die on old proof paper (1861), black *500.*

d. Die on old proof paper, corners drawn in pencil (1861), black *1,500.*

e. Die on old proof paper, as No. 69-E3a but numerals sketched in diagonally and vert. (1861), black *3,000.*

f. Die on stiff old ivory paper, as No. 69-E4e but without top border (1861), bluish black *1,500.*

g. Die on thin card, black —

70-E1

70-E2

Vignette size: 7x16mm
Washington die II vignette only.

70-E1 24c

a. Die II on proof paper (1903)
black 60.
carmine 60.
dark carmine 60.
scarlet 60.
orange 60.
yellow 60.
yellow brown 60.
violet brown 60.
gray olive 60.
light green 60.
green 60.
light blue 60.
black blue 60.
red violet 60.
lilac 60.

b. Die II on green bond (1903)
black *150.*
red brown *150.*
violet *150.*
orange *150.*

c. Die II on colored card (1903)
dull red, *ivory* *150.*
brown red, *buff* *150.*
brown orange, *light pink* *150.*
dark green, *light yellow* *150.*
blue, *pale green* *150.*
violet, *blue* *150.*

Washington vignette with oval label. Background complete, eyes retouched.

70-E2 24c

a. Die II on proof paper (1903)
black 60.
carmine 60.
dark carmine 60.
scarlet 60.
orange 60.
yellow 60.
yellow brown 60.
violet brown 60.
light green 60.
green 60.
light blue 60.
black blue 60.
red violet 60.
lilac 60.
gray olive 60.
ultramarine 60.

b. Die I on old proof paper, background lines incomplete (1861)
black *750.*
dim red violet *750.*

c. Die I on colored card (1903)
black, *light pink* *150.*
orange, *buff* *150.*
orange, *light blue* *150.*
dark green, *pale green* *150.*
violet blue, *light yellow* *150.*
violet, *ivory* *150.*

d. Die I on green bond (1903), brown *150.*

e. Die I on dull light blue green bond (1903)
black *150.*
orange red *150.*
orange *150.*
yellow brown *150.*
dusky green *150.*
dull blue *150.*
red violet *150.*

f. Die I on dull pale green blue thin wove (1903)
orange red *300.*
orange *300.*
yellow brown *300.*
dusky green *300.*
dull blue *300.*

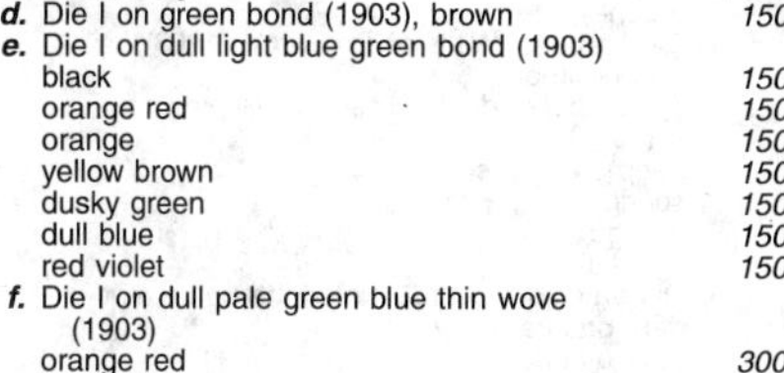
70-E3

70-E4

With frame. Blank areas in corners for numerals.

70-E3 24c

a. Die on proof paper (1903)
black 100.
carmine 100.
dark carmine 100.
scarlet 100.
orange 100.
yellow brown 100.
orange brown 100.
violet brown 100.
gray olive 100.
light green 100.
green 100.
light blue 100.
black blue 100.
red violet 100.
lilac 100.
ultramarine 100.

b. Die on old proof paper (1861), dusky red violet *1,000.*

c. Die on colored card (1903)
carmine, *light blue* *175.*
blue, *pale green* *175.*
scarlet, *buff* *175.*
yellow brown, *cream* *175.*
dull violet, *pink* *175.*
dusky green, *light yellow* *175.*
gray olive, *ivory* *175.*

d. Die on green bond (1903)

black 175.
orange brown 175.
green 175.

Complete design with numerals in corners.

70-E4 24c
a. Die on old proof paper, cut to shape (1861)
lilac 400.
black 400.
red violet 400.
b. Die on India, cut close (1861)
black 400.
lilac 400.
brown lilac 400.
c. Die on India (1861), dark blue 750.
d. Die on India, mounted on 80x115mm card (1861), lilac 750.
e. On stiff old ivory paper (1861)
black 1,000.
lilac 1,000.
f. Die on proof paper, printed through a mat (1903)
black 125.
carmine 125.
dark carmine 125.
scarlet 125.
red borwn 125.
yellow brown 125.
brown 125.
violet brown 125.
gray olive 125.
light green 125.
green 125.
light blue 125.
black blue 125.
red violet 125.
lilac 125.
ultramarine 125.
g. Die on blue pelure (1903)
dark carmine 300.
scarlet 300.
orange 300.
brown 300.
dusky green 300.
h. Die on bond (1903)
black 175.
scarlet 175.
orange 175.
dark green 175.
blue 175.
i. Die on green bond (1903)
black 250.
dark red 250.
green 250.
j. Die on bond, Walls of Troy wmk. (1903), dark green 300.
k. Die on bond, double line of scallops wmk. (1903)
deep orange red 300.
scarlet 300.
orange 300.
light blue 300.
l. Die on colored card, printed through a mat
dark orange, *ivory* 150.
dark orange, *light pink* 150.
brown, *light blue* 150.
dull dark blue, *pale green* 150.
violet, *light yellow* 150.
violet brown, *buff* 150.

72-E1

72-E2

Vignette size: 16x17½mm
Washington vignette only.

72-E1 90c
a. Die on proof paper (1903)
black 100.
carmine 100.
dark carmine 100.
scarlet 100.
red brown 100.
orange 100.
orange brown 100.
violet brown 100.
gray olive 100.
light green 100.
green 100.
dark blue 100.
lilac 100.
red violet 100.
yellow brown 100.
ultramarine 100.
b. Die on colored card (1903)
black, *light yellow* 165.
red brown, *light pink* 165.
carmine, *buff* 165.
brown, *pale green* 165.
dark brown, *light blue* 165.
ultramarine, *ivory* 165.
c. Die on dull light blue green bond (1903)
violet brown 165.
dusky green 165.
dusky blue 165.
red violet 165.

Vignette with blank top and bottom labels.

72-E2 90c
a. Die on proof paper (1903)
black 100.
carmine 100.
dark carmine 100.
scarlet 100.
orange 100.
yellow brown 100.
brown 100.
violet brown 100.
gray olive 100.
light green 100.
green 100.
dark blue 100.
red violet 100.
lilac 100.
ultramarine 100.
b. Die on green bond (1903)
dull orange 150.
dull orange brown 150.
red violet 150.
c. Die on colored card (1903)
black, *buff* 185.
orange red, *light yellow* 185.
brown, *ivory* 185.
olive green, *light pink* 185.
green, *light blue* 185.
violet brown, *pale green* 185.

72-E3

72-E5

U.S. POSTAGE in top label.

72-E3 90c
a. Die on proof paper (1903)
black 125.
carmine 125.
dark carmine 125.
scarlet 125.
yellow 125.
yellow brown 125.
brown 125.
violet brown 125.
gray olive 125.
light green 125.
green 125.
dark blue 125.
lilac 125.
red violet 125.
ultramarine 125.
b. Die on colored card (1903)
orange, *light blue* 185.
orange red, *light yellow* 185.
dark blue, *buff* 185.
violet, *pale green* 185.
violet brown, *ivory* 185.
orange brown, *pale pink* 185.
c. Die on green bond (1903)
black 175.
brown 175.
green 175.

Lower corners of vignette cut out, "NINETY 90 CENTS" in pencil in bottom label.

72-E4 90c Die on India (1861), black 2,000.

Complete design.

72-E5 90c
a. Die on India, cut to shape (1861)
black 300.
dark blue 300.
b. Die on India, die sunk on card (1861), blue 2,000.
c. Die on India, cut close (1861)
black 300.
blue 300.
d. Die on proof paper, printed through a mat (1903)
black 175.
carmine 175.
dark carmine 175.
scarlet 175.
orange 175.
yellow brown 175.
brown 175.
violet brown 175.
gray olive 175.
light green 175.
green 175.
dark blue 175.
lilac 175.
red violet 175.
ultramarine 175.
e. Die on colored card (1903)
carmine, *light blue* 250.
dismal brown, *light pink* 250.
orange brown, *buff* 250.
blue, *ivory* 250.
violet, *pale green* 250.
green, *pale yellow* 250.
f. Die on green bond (1903)
dark carmine 225.
red brown 225.
green 225.
g. Die on bond (1903), orange brown 250.
h. Die on bond, "Bond No. 1" wmk. (1903), orange brown 350.
i. Die on bond, "Bond No 2" wmk. (1903), orange brown 350.
j. Die on bond, Walls of Troy wmk. (1903)
carmine 300.
scarlet 300.
orange 300.
dark green 300.
ultramarine 300.
k. Die on pink pelure (1903)
brown red 350.
dull yellow 350.
very dark green 350.
dark blue 350.
dull violet 350.

American Bank Note Co.

65-E5

65-E6

Design size: 19x23½mm
Engraved frame with pencil border, center cut out, mounted over 22x27mm engraved vignette of Washington.

65-E5 3c Die on India, black 2,500.

Design size: 19x24½mm
Engraved frame with pencil border, center cut out, mounted over engraved ruled background with engraved Washington vignette mounted on it.

65-E6 Three Cents Die on India, on card about 23x27½mm, black 2,500.

65-E7

65-E8

Master die No. 80 of frame only.

65-E7 3c Die on India, card mounted
deep orange 1,250.
dark brown 1,250.
green 1,250.
dark blue 1,250.
black 1,250.

Design size: 19½x24½mm
Engraved lathework frame with Bald, Cousland & Co. engraved Washington vignette and engraved lettered labels and numerals mounted on it.

65-E8 3c Die on India, on 22x27mm card, black 2,500.

65-E9

65-E10

Master die No. 81 of frame only.

65-E9 3c Die on India
black 1,250.
brown yellow 1,250.
dark green 1,250.
orange red 1,250.

Engraved lathework frame with Bald, Cousland & Co. engraved Washington vignette and engraved lettered labels and numerals mounted on it.

65-E10 3c Die on India, on 28x35mm card, black 2,500.

67-E5

Design size: 21x25mm
Engraved frame used for the 1860 Nova Scotia 5c stamp cut to shape, with engraved lettered labels and Washington vignette No. 209-E7 mounted on it.

67-E5 Five Cents Die on India, on 23x27mm card, black *2,500.*

67-E6

67-E7

Design size: 19x24
Engraved lathework background with Bald, Cousland & Co. engraved Washington vignette and engraved lettered labels and numerals mounted on it.

67-E6 5c Die on India, mounted on 22x26mm card, black *2,500.*

Design size: 19x24mm
Engraved lathework background with Bald, Cousland & Co. engraved Washington vignette and engraved lettered labels and numerals mounted on it.

67-E7 5c Die on India, mounted on 21x26½mm card, black *2,500.*

National Bank Note Co.

The following essays include those formerly listed as Nos. 55-57, 59 and 62 in the Postage section, and the corresponding die and plate essays formerly listed in the Proof section. Former No. 58 is now No. 62B. Former Nos. 60 and 61 are now Nos. 70eTC and 71bTC in the Trial Color Proofs section.

Frame essay with blank areas for Franklin vignette, labels, numerals, U and S.

63-E10 1c Die on India, black 2,000.

63-E11

63-E12

Die size: 58x56mm
"Premiere Gravure" die No. 440.

63-E11 1c
- ***a.*** "Premiere Gravure" die essay on India (formerly Nos. 55P1, 55TC1)
  - black *3,250.*
  - indigo *1,350.*
  - ultramarine *2,250.*
- ***b.*** "Premiere Gravure" small die essay on white wove, 28x31mm (**formerly No. 55P2**), indigo *325.*
- ***c.*** "Premiere Gravure" plate essay on India (**formerly Nos. 55P3, 55TC3**)
  - indigo *250.*
  - blue —
  - ultramarine *300.*
  - violet ultramarine —
- ***d.*** "Premiere Gravure" plate essay on semi-transparent stamp paper (**formerly No. 55TC4**), ultramarine *400.*
- ***e.*** Finished "Premiere Gravure" plate essay on semitransparent stamp paper, perf. 12, gummed (**formerly No. 55**), indigo *29,000.*

No. 63-E11e is valued with perfs cutting slightly into design at top.

Die size: 47x55mm
Apparently complete die except value numerals have been cut out.

63-E12 1c Die on India, die sunk on card, black *1,500.*

65-E11

65-E12

Die size: 64x76½mm
Incomplete engraving of Washington head only.

65-E11 3c
- ***a.*** Die on India, on card, carmine *750.*
- ***b.*** Die on white glazed paper
  - black *750.*
  - scarlet *750.*
  - brown violet *750.*

Die size: 78x55mm
Incomplete engraved design, no scrolls outside framelines, no silhouette under chin, no ornaments on 3s, U and S.

65-E12 3c Die on India, die sunk on card
- black *1,000.*
- blue *1,000.*

65-E13

65-E14

As No. 65-E12 but ornaments on 3s, U and S. Shows traces of first border design erased. With imprint and No. 441 below design.

65-E13 3c Die on India, card mounted
- scarlet *1,000.*
- brown red *1,000.*
- ultramarine *1,000.*

Die size: 59x55mm
As No. 65-E13 but with ornaments outside frame.

65-E14 3c Die on India, die sunk on card
- black *750.*
- scarlet *750.*
- pink *1,250.*
- brown orange *750.*
- deep orange red *750.*
- deep red *750.*

As No. 65-E14 but top of head silhouetted, lines added or strengthened in hair at top of head, around eye, on chin, in hair behind ear. The three lines on bottom edge of bust extended to back. No imprint or die number.

65-E15 3c
- ***a.*** Die on India, card mounted, deep orange red *1,000.*
- ***b.*** "Premiere Gravure" die essay on semi-transparent stamp paper, 20x25mm-30x37mm
  - deep orange red *750.*
  - deep red orange *750.*
  - dim red *750.*
  - dim deep red *750.*
  - dim orange red *750.*
  - dull pink *750.*
  - dull violet red *750.*
- ***c.*** "Premiere Gravure" die essay on India (**formerly Nos. 56P1, 56TC1**)
  - red *1,350.*
  - black *2,000.*
  - scarlet *2,000.*
  - pink *2,850.*
  - orange red *2,000.*
  - dark orange red *2,000.*
- ***d.*** Small die essay on white wove, 28x31mm altered laydown die of complete design but with outer scrolls removed and replaced by ones similar to "Premiere Gravure" design (1903) (**formerly No. 56P2**), dim deep red *325.*
- ***e.*** As "c," small die essay on pale cream soft wove, 24x29mm (1915) (**formerly No. 56P2a**), deep red *1,250.*
- ***f.*** "Premiere Gravure" plate No. 2 essay on India (**formerly Nos. 56P3, 56TC3**)
  - red *250.*
  - scarlet *350.*
- ***g.*** "Premiere Gravure" plate essay on semi-transparent stamp paper (**formerly Nos. 56aP4, 56TC4**)
  - red, pair with gum *1,750.*
  - black *400.*
- ***h.*** Finished "Premiere Gravure" plate essay on semitransparent stamp paper, perf. 12, gummed (**formerly No. 56**)
  - brown rose *550.*
  - P# block of 8, Impt. *20,000.*
  - orange red *475.*
  - bright orange red *475.*
  - dark orange red *475.*
  - dim deep red *475.*
  - pink *475.*
  - deep pink *475.*

67-E8

67-E9

Incomplete impression from die No. 442, border lines and corner scrolls missing.

67-E8 5c Die on India, mounted on 34x50mm card, black *1,750.*

Size of die: 58x59mm
"Premiere Gravure" design, with corner scrolls but without leaflets.

67-E9 5c
- ***a.*** "Premiere Gravure" die essay on India, card mounted (formerly No. 57TC1)
  - black *1,750.*
  - scarlet *1,750.*
- ***b.*** Small die essay on white wove, 28x31mm, altered laydown die of complete design but with scrolls removed from corners to resemble "Premiere Gravure" (1903) (**formerly No. 57P2), brown** 325.
- ***c.*** As "b," die essay on pale cream soft wove, 24x29mm (1915) (**formerly No. 57P2a**), brown *1,350.*
- ***d.*** "Premiere Gravure" plate No. 3 essay on India (**formerly Nos. 57P3, 57TC3)**
  - brown *250.*
  - light brown *300.*
  - dark brown *300.*
  - red brown *300.*
- ***e.*** Finished "Premiere Gravure" plate essay on semitransparent stamp paper, perf. 12, gummed (**formerly No. 57**), brown *15,000.*

68-E1

68-E2

Design size: 14x17½mm
Die size: 26x31mm
Washington vignette only.

68-E1 10c Die on ivory paper, black *500.*

Incomplete die No. 443.

68-E2 10c Die on India, 22x26mm, dark green *2,500.*

Incomplete die of No. 68P1, thin lines missing on top of frame

68-E3 10c Die on India
- yellowish green *1,000.*
- dark green *1,000.*

69-E5

69-E6

Design size: 12½x16mm
Die size: about 62x65mm
Washington vignette only.

69-E5 12c
- ***a.*** Die on India, die sunk on card
  - black *400.*
  - dark red *400.*
  - orange red *400.*
- ***b.*** Die on ivory paper, about 24x28mm
  - black *500.*
  - scarlet *500.*
  - black brown *500.*
  - blue *500.*

Incomplete die No. 444, without corner ornaments.

69-E6 12c
a. "Premiere Gravure" die essay on India, mounted on card (**formerly Nos. 59P1, 59TC1**)
black *1,350.*
scarlet *1,750.*
dark green *1,500.*
b. "Premiere Gravure" small die essay on white wove, 28x31mm (1903) (**formerly No. 59P2**), black *450.*
c. "Premiere Gravure" small die essay on pale cream soft wove, 24x29mm (1915) (**formerly No. 59P2a**), black *1,750.*
d. "Premiere Gravure" plate No. 5 essay on India (**formerly No. 59P3**), black *350.*
e. Finished "Premiere Gravure" plate essay on semitransparent stamp paper, perf. 12, gummed (**formerly No. 59**), black *47,500.*

70-E5

70-E6

Washington vignette in incomplete frame.

70-E5 24c Die on India, black *3,250.*

Die size: 56½x56mm
Incomplete die (No. 445): silhouette unfinished, especially scrolls around numerals; shadows over numerals not acid etched.

70-E6 24c Die on India, die sunk on card
black *900.*
violet *900.*
gray violet *900.*
dark violet *900.*
scarlet *900.*
green *900.*
orange *900.*
red brown *900.*
orange brown *900.*
orange yellow *900.*
rose red *900.*
gray *900.*
steel blue *900.*
blue *900.*

For finished "Premiere Gravure" trial color plate proof on semitransparent stamp paper, perf 12, gummed (formerly No. 60), see 70eTC in the Trial Color Proof section.

71-E1

71-E2

Die size: 46x60mm
Incomplete die (No. 446): additional ornaments at top and bottom in pencil, as later engraved.

71-E1 30c Die on India, black *1,750.*

"Premiere Gravure" die: left side of frame and silhouette at lower right unfinished.

71-E2 30c
a. "Premiere Gravure" die essay on India, die sunk on card (**formerly No. 61TC1**)
black *1,750.*
green *1,750.*
dull gray blue *1,750.*
violet brown *1,750.*
scarlet *1,750.*
dull rose *1,750.*
b. "Premiere Gravure" plate essay on India (**formerly No. 61P3**), deep red orange *500.*
c. "Premiere Gravure" plate essay on card
black (split thin) *500.*
blue *750.*
d. "Premiere Gravure" plate essay on card, black 12x2mm SPECIMEN overprint,
blue *750.*
e. "Premiere Gravure" plate essay on semi-transparent stamp paper
deep red orange *1,250.*
yellow orange *1,250.*
lemon yellow *1,250.*
dark orange yellow *1,250.*
dull orange yellow *1,250.*

For finished "Premiere Gravure" trial color proof on semi-transparent stamp paper, perf 12, gummed (formerly No. 61), see No. 71bTC in the Trial Color Proof section.

72-E6

72-E7

Die size: 54x63mm
Incomplete die: without thin lines at bottom of frame and in upper left triangle between label and frame, and without leaves at left of U and right of S.

72-E6 90c Die on India, blue (shades) *1,000.*

Similar to 72-E6 but lines added in upper left triangle, leaves added at left of U and at right of S. Exists with and without imprint and Die No. 447 added below design.

72-E7 90c
a. Die on India, die sunk on card, black *1,750.*
b. "Premiere Gravure" die essay on India, thin line under bottom center frame (**formerly Nos. 62P1, 62TC1**)
blue *1,350.*
black *1,750.*
c. "Premiere Gravure" small die essay on white wove, 28x31mm (1903) (**formerly No. 62P2**), blue *500.*
d. "Premiere Gravure" small die essay on pale cream soft wove, 24x29mm (1915) (**formerly No. 62P2a**), blue *1,750.*
e. "Premiere Gravure" plate essay on India, blue *350.*
f. "Premiere Gravure" plate essay on card, black (split thin) *500.*
g. "Premiere Gravure" plate essay on semi-transparent stamp paper (**formerly Nos. 62aP4, 62TC4**)
blue, pair, gummed *5,500.*
blue green *275.*
h. Finished "Premiere Gravure" plate essay on semitransparent stamp paper, perf. 12, gummed (**formerly No. 62**), blue *32,500.*

Die size: 54x63mm
Similar to Nos. 72-E6 and 72-E7 but leaf at left of "U" only, no shading around "U" and "S," leaf and some shading missing at bottom right above "S," shading missing in top label, etc., faint ms. "8" at bottom of backing card.

72-E8 90c Die on India, die sunk on 3¼x3½-inch card, dark blue —

63-E13

Design size: 20x47mm
Die size: 57x95mm
Bowlsby patent coupon at top of 1c stamp design.

63-E13 1c
a. Die on India, die sunk on card
black *1,050.*
red *1,050.*
scarlet *1,050.*
orange *1,050.*
orange brown *1,050.*
brown *1,050.*
yellow brown *1,050.*
blue green *1,050.*
blue *1,050.*
violet *1,050.*
red violet *1,050.*
gray *1,050.*
gray brown *1,050.*
dull orange yellow *1,050.*
b. Die on white glazed paper
black *1,050.*
dark brown *1,050.*
scarlet *1,050.*
blue *1,050.*
c. Plate on pelure paper, gummed, red *225.*
d. Plate on white paper, red *175.*
e. Plate on white paper, with 13x16mm points-up grill, red *225.*
Split grill *500.*
f. Plate on white paper, perf. all around and between stamp and coupon
red *150.*
blue *150.*
g. Plate on white paper, perf. all around, imperf. between stamp and coupon
red *150.*
blue *150.*
h. Plate on white paper, perf. all around, rouletted between stamp and coupon
red *300.*
blue *300.*

1861-66 Essays
Authors Unknown

73-E2

73-E3

Design size: 21x26mm

73-E2 2c Pencil and watercolor on thick card, bright green *3,750.*

Design size: 21x26mm
Indian vignette. Typographed printings from woodcuts. Plates of three rows of three, one row each of Nos. 73-E3, 73-E4, 73-E5. Listings are of singles.

73-E3 2c
a. Plate on white wove
red *30.*
scarlet *30.*
violet *30.*
black *30.*
blue *30.*
green *30.*
b. Plate on mauve wove
red *50.*
violet *50.*
black *50.*
blue *50.*
green *50.*
c. Plate on yellow wove
red *50.*
violet *50.*
black *50.*
blue *50.*
green *50.*
d. Plate on yellow laid
red *50.*
violet *50.*
black *50.*
blue *50.*
green *50.*
e. Plate on pink laid
red *50.*
violet *50.*
black *50.*
blue *50.*
green *50.*
f. Plate on green laid
red *50.*
violet *50.*
black *50.*
blue *50.*
green *50.*
g. Plate on cream laid
red *50.*
violet *50.*
black *50.*
blue *50.*
green *50.*
h. Plate on pale yellow wove
red *50.*
green *50.*
blue *50.*
i. Plate on yellow-surfaced card, violet *50.*

73-E4

73-E5

Design size: 23x26½mm
Small head of Liberty in shield. Typographed printings from woodcuts. On plate with Nos. 73-E3 and 73-E5. Listings are of singles.

73-E4 3c
a. Plate on white wove
red *30.*
scarlet *30.*
violet *30.*
black *30.*
blue *30.*
green *30.*
b. Plate on mauve wove, violet *50.*

c. Plate on yellow wove
red 50.
violet 50.
black 50.
blue 50.
green 50.
d. Plate on yellow laid
red 50.
violet 50.
black 50.
blue 50.
green 50.
e. Plate on pink laid
carmine 50.
violet 50.
black 50.
blue 50.
green 50.
f. Plate on green laid
carmine 50.
green 50.
dull violet 50.
blue 50.
g. Plate on cream laid
red 50.
violet 50.
black 50.
blue 50.
green 50.
h. Plate on pale yellow wove
red 50.
green 50.
blue 50.
i. Plate on yellow-surfaced card, violet 50.
j. Plate on fawn wove, green 50.

Design size: 22½x25½mm
Large head of Liberty. Typographed impressions from woodcut. On plate with Nos. 73-E3 and 73-E4. Listings are of singles.

73-E5 5c
a. Plate on white wove
red 30.
scarlet 30.
violet 30.
black 30.
blue 30.
green 30.
b. Plate on mauve wove, violet 50.
c. Plate on yellow wove
red 50.
violet 50.
black 50.
blue 50.
green 50.
d. Plate on yellow laid
red 50.
violet 50.
black 50.
blue 50.
green 50.
e. Plate on pink laid
red 50.
black 50.
blue 50.
green 50.
f. Plate on green laid
red 50.
violet 50.
black 50.
blue 50.
green 50.
g. Plate on cream laid
red 50.
black 50.
blue 50.
green 50.
h. Plate on pale yellow wove
red 50.
blue 50.
green 50.
i. Plate on yellow-surfaced card, violet 50.

73-E6

Size of design: 21x27mm
Indian vignette. Typographed impressions from woodcut.

73-E6 10c
a. Die on proof paper
black 200.
gray black 200.
carmine 200.
dusky red 200.
brown 200.
green 200.
blue 200.
violet 200.
b. Plate on white paper (pane of 4)
red 600.
violet 600.
brown 600.
black 600.
blue 600.
green 600.
c. Plate on soft cream card (pane of 4)
black 600.
red 600.
blue 600.
green 600.
red violet 600.

1867 Essays
Re-use Prevention
Authors Unknown

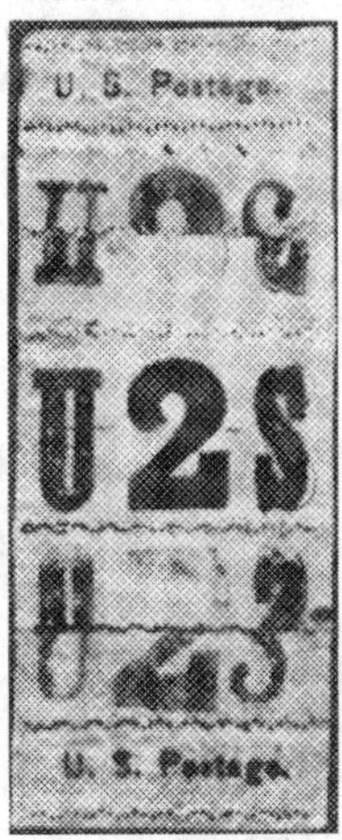

79-E1

Design size (folded): 18x23mm
Design size (unfolded): 18x58mm
Folded and scored four times, horiz. crease at center. Bronze overprint U 2 S, (2 punched out). Lower ⅔ gummed below second fold so top ⅓ could be torn off for canceling.

79-E1 2c On white paper, dull red violet 5,000.

79-E2

Similar to No. 79-E1 but larger and not folded. Pierced with S-shaped cuts as well as punched out 2.

79-E2 2c
a. On white paper, US 7½mm high, bronze, US in dull black 5,000.
b. On white paper, US 10mm high, bronze, US in violet 5,000.

79-E3

Cuts as on back

U.S. No. 73 as issued but pierced with S-shaped cuts, ovptd. in metallic color.

79-E3 2c Essay on 2c stamp, gold overprint 7,500.

79-E4

79-E6

Similar to No. 79-E1 but with punched out 3.

79-E4 3c
a. On white paper, U 3 S black above, bronze below and on face beneath folds 5,000.
b. On green paper, 3 not punched out, 3 black, POSTAGE blue 5,000.

Similar to No. 79-E4, with "3 U.S. 3 / Three Cents / Void if detached."

79-E5 3c On green paper, black 3,000.

Similar to No. 79-E2 but with punched out 3, gummed.

79-E6 3c
a. On white paper, bronze over viole 3,000.
b. On white paper, U S black, rest bronze 3,000.

79-E7

Vignette map of U.S.

79-E7 3c On thick white paper, rouletted, green, gold 3 on map 2,500.

1867 Essays
Henry Lowenberg

79-E8

79-E9

Washington vignette. Printed in reverse on back of transparent paper, reads correctly from front. Plate essays from sheets of 25.

79-E8 3c
a. Plate on onionskin paper, imperf., gummed
brown 10.
orange brown 10.
deep orange brown 10.
orange 10.
green 10.
light green 10.
blue green 10.
pale green 10.
red 10.
light red 10.
dark red 10.
violet red 10.
violet 10.
light violet 10.
dull pale violet 10.
blue 10.
dark blue 10.
deep blue 10.
pale blue 10.
dull blue 10.
gold 50.
gray 7.
black 7.
carmine 7.
b. Plate on onionskin paper, perf. 12, gummed
gray black 25.
gray 25.
gray violet 25.
dull violet 25.
brown red 25.
c. Plate on more opaque onionskin paper, imperf.
black 25.
red violet 25.
dull violet 25.
d. Plate on thick transparent paper
gray 25.
black 25.

Washington vignette. Printed with design reversed on front of various opaque papers, Plate essays are from sheets of 25.

79-E9 3c
a. Plate on white wove, imperf., gummed
blue 10.
red 10.
gray 10.
brown 10.
orange 10.
green 10.
yellow green 10.
b. Plate on clear white paper, imperf.
orange 10.

blue *10.*
gray *10.*
dark gray *10.*

c. Plate on thick wove, fugitive ink, perf., gummed
carmine *10.*
violet carmine *10.*
pale dull red *10.*
gray *10.*
pale gray *10.*
pale dull tan *10.*
green *10.*

d. As "c," strip of 3, signed Henry Lowenberg, pale tan *400.*

e. Plate on white chemically treated paper (turns blue if wet), imperf.
carmine *10.*
Prussian blue *10.*
orange *10.*
green *10.*
black *10.*

f. As "e," perf.
carmine *10.*
scarlet *10.*
orange *10.*
blue *10.*
green *10.*
brown *10.*

g. Plate on India
violet brown *10.*
green *10.*
blue *10.*
dark blue *10.*

h. Plate on India, signed D.H. Craig, red *350.*

i. On white card, 62x72mm, design deeply indented, green *15.*

j. On blue wove, red *15.*

k. On orange laid
black *15.*
gray *15.*

l. On blue laid, scarlet *15.*

m. On white laid, blue *15.*

n. On pink laid, blue *15.*

o. On linen cloth
green *50.*
red *50.*
blue *50.*

p. On glazed white paper, blue *20.*

1867 Essays
John M. Sturgeon

79-E10

Liberty vignette. Curved labels top and bottom. Self-canceling: CANCELLED in colorless sensitive ink, becomes colored when wet. Patented 1867, 1868.

79-E10 10c

a. Die on stiff card, cut close, clearly engraved, not canceled, both labels completely blank, dark carmine *350.*

b. Die on wove, rough impression, CANCELLED diagonally each way, dark carmine *350.*

c. Die on thick white or tinted paper, gummed, rough impression, about 21x26mm, two lines in upper label, one line in lower label
carmine *200.*
dark carmine *200.*
very dark carmine *200.*
green *200.*
dark green *200.*
dull red violet *200.*

d. As "c," on thick pinkish paper, dark green *250.*

g. Single centered in 6-inch wide strip of thick white paper, almost always cut in at top and bottom, dark carmine *400.*

h. Horiz. row of five designs on thick white paper, 10mm apart
dark carmine *1,200.*
dark purple *1,200.*
black *1,200.*

i. Single on blue card, ovptd. seal BRITISH CONSULATE, V.R. in center, black *1,250.*

American Bank Note Co.

79-E11

Design size: 18x21mm
Vignette of Columbia. Probably submitted by Charles F. Steel.

79-E11 2c and 3c

a. Engraved plate on thick yellowish wove, imperf. (usually found in upper left margin blocks)
rose scarlet *300.*
Block of 4 *1,250.*
blue green *300.*
Block of 4 *1,250.*

b. Engraved plate on stamp paper, perf. 12, gummed
black *175.*
rose scarlet *175.*
blue green *175.*
blue *175.*

Author Unknown

79-E12

Design size: 20x26mm
Vignette of Liberty in circle of stars. Vertical color lines outside design to 24x28mm. Curved labels blank. Lithographed.

79-E12 No denomination

a. Die on white paper, dull violet *1,000.*

b. Die on bluish paper, blue *1,000.*

1867 Grill Essays
National Bank Note Co.

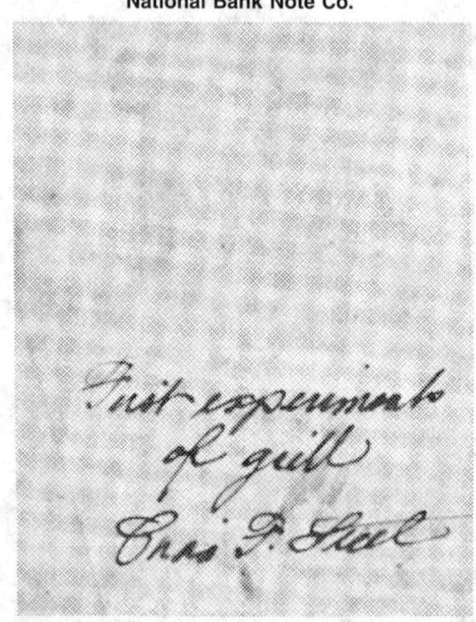

79-E13

Grill essays patented by Charles F. Steel.

79-E13

a. Wove paper, 80x140mm, impressed with four diff. seals, crossed lines and square dots down, circles 11 or 12mm *9,000.*

79-E13b

b. Grills in odd shapes on white wove, each about 20x25mm
cross *1,500.*
star in square *1,500.*
horizontal lined oval in square *1,500.*
diagonal lined oval in square *1,500.*

c. White wove, gummed, 15mm circle with points down grill, surrounded by 24 perforated holes *1,000.*

d. White wove, quadrille batonne watermark, 12mm colored circle with points down grill around 3, roughly grilled colorless 3 below, carmine *1,250.*

79-E13e

e. Colorless 12mm grilled circle as on "d," on tan wove, perf. 12 *200.*

f. As "e," yellow wove *200.*

g. As "e," white wove, block of 6 with ms. "Subject to a half hour pressure after embossing" *3,500.*

h. Colorless 15mm points down grilled circle on white wove, perf. 12 *200.*

79-E14

Allover grill.

79-E14

a. White wove, about 55x30mm, points down grill, stamped with red 6-digit number 450.

b. Wove paper in various colors, about 85x40mm, points up grill as adopted
white *200.*
pale pink *200.*
salmon *200.*
light yellow *200.*
light gray green *200.*
light blue *200.*
pale lilac *200.*
light gray *200.*

79-E15

Experimental grills on perf. or imperf. stamps or stamp-size pieces of paper.

79-E15

a. Allover grill of small squares, points down (points do not break paper as on issued stamp, No. 79)
on 3c rose, gummed (No. 65) *250.*
on 3c lake, imperf. pair, gummed (No. 66aP4) *250.*

b. As "a" but points up, on 3c stamp, perf. 12, gummed
black *200.*
rose *200.*

c. As "a" but points up, imperf pair, gummed
3c rose (**formerly No. 79P4**) *250.*
3c lake (**formerly No. 66aP4**) *250.*

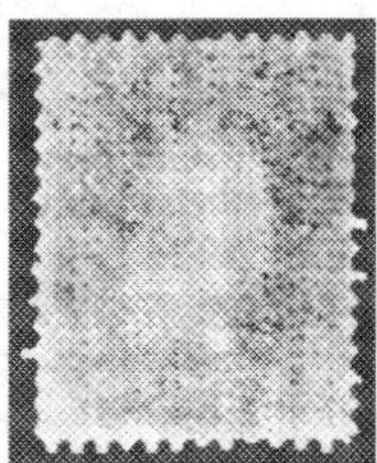
79-E15d

d. Allover pinpoint grill (so-called "Music Box" grill), points up, on No. 65 (plates 11, 34, 52) *75.*
e. As "d" but points down, on 3c rose (plate 11) *125.*
f. 15x16mm grill on stamp size white wove paper, perf. 12, gummed *125.*
g. C grill, 13x16mm, points down on stamp size wove paper, perf. 12, gummed
yellowish *100.*
pinkish *100.*
h. As "g" but points up, on white wove *100.*
i. C grill on 1c stamp (No. 63), points down *4,000.*
j. C grill on 3c stamp (No. 65)
points up *4,000.*
points down *4,000.*

The 3c C grill essay is almost identical to the issued stamp. There are slight differences in the essay grill which match those on No. 79-E15i and Nos. 79-E15k through 79-E15n.

k. C grill on 5c stamp (No. 76)
points up *4,000.*
points down *4,000.*
l. C grill on 10c stamp (No. 68)
points up *4,000.*
points down *4,000.*
m. C grill on 12c stamp (No. 69)
points up *4,000.*
points down *4,000.*
n. C grill on 30c stamp (No. 71)
points up *4,000.*
points down *4,000.*
o. E grill, 11x13mm, points up, on stamp size white wove paper, perf. 12, gummed *100.*
p. As "o," points down *100.*

79-E15q

q. Z grill, 11x14mm, points down on stamp size wove paper, perf. 12, partly gummed
white *100.*
salmon *100.*
yellow *100.*
greenish *100.*
dull violet *100.*
pale lilac *100.*

Some experts believe this is sheet selvage from other essays.

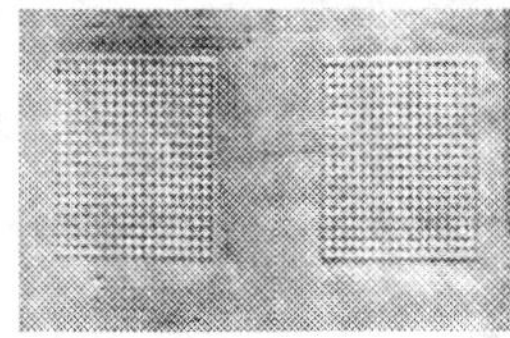
79-E15r

r. As "q," in sheet of white wove stamp paper, imperf., gummed 175.

Continental Bank Note Co.

White wove paper about 6x9 inches with 7x9½mm grills spaced as they would fall on centers of stamps in a sheet.

79-E16
a. End roller grill at left, ms. "Chas. F. Steel-Sample of Grill used by Continental Bank Note Co. in 1874. Alexander Reid. J.K. Myers." *1,250.*
b. Without end roller grill, ms. "Grill of Continental Bank Note Co. Chas. F. Steel." *1,750.*
c. End roller grill at right, same inscription as "b" *250.*
d. On soft card, six grills *450.*

Wilbur I. Trafton

79-E17

Coarse grill in 15mm circle with 7 points up in 11mm, found on 1873 1c, some with 18mm circular cancel, stuck down on printed ad circular along with black, red and albino grill impressions (two each) on paper labeled "The Security Impression from the plates."

79-E17 Entire ad circular with grill examples *750.*

Natonal Bank Note Co.

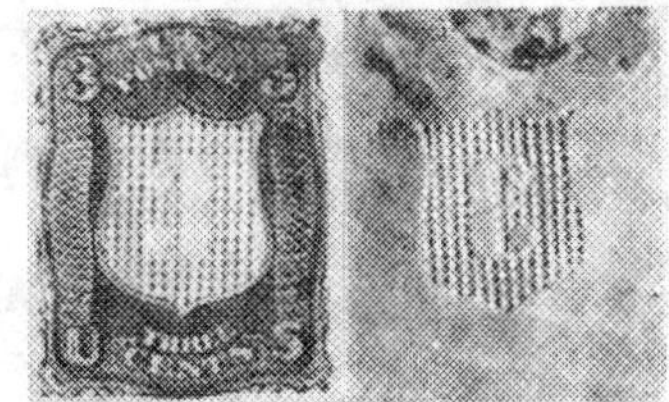
79-E18

Albino 3 in points down shield-shaped grill in lithographed frame of 3c 1861 stamp.

79-E18 3c
a. Die on thick white paper, gummed
black *1,000.*
deep pink *1,000.*
b. As "a," with Washington, D.C. Feb. 21 pmk.
black *1,250.*
deep pink *1,250.*

79-E18c

c. As "a" but grill with points up, black *1,000.*
d. As "a," perf. 12, gummed, black *1,000.*
e. Die on yellow wove, gummed
black *1,000.*
red *1,000.*
f. Die on orange wove
black *1,000.*
carmine *1,000.*
g. Die on yellow laid, black *1,000.*
h. Numeral handcolored, dull carmine *1,250.*
i. Frame only, no grill, on grayish wove with pencil "McDonald P.O. Dept. Steel Nature(?)", pale orange brown *1,500.*

79-E18j

79-E18k

Albino 3 in 13x14mm shield made up of embossed narrow spaced horiz. lines.

j. White wove stamp paper, 22x27mm, perf. 12, gummed 450.

Albino 3 in 13x14mm shield slightly different from No. 79-E18j.

k. As "j," different shield 250.

79-E19

Typographed impression of frame, lettering and numerals of 3c 1861 stamp with 3 in double lined shield in center. In strip of three about 20mm apart, impression of 3 and shield progressively lighter on impressions two and three.

79-E19 3c
a. Engraved (die No. 1570), green *3,000.*
b. Typographed in color on white paper
blue green *3,000.*
dark red brown *3,000.*
c. As "b," colored and colorless parts interchanged, on thick paper
blue green *3,000.*
dark red brown *3,000.*

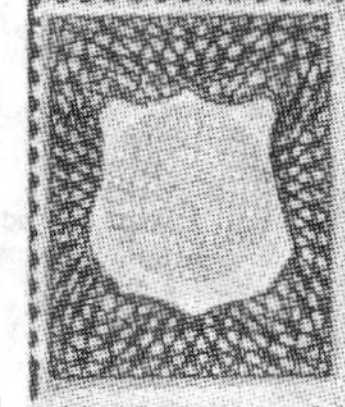
79-E21

Lathework frame with shield shaped vignette cut out, albino 3 in circular grill in center.

79-E21 3c
a. Thick paper, perf. 12
blue *500.*
carmine *500.*
b. At left in strip of 3 with 2 No. 79-E13f, latter black cancels, blue *3,500.*
c. Lathework frame on thin wove, allover diagonal grill, imperf., gummed, blue *500.*

Lathework frame similar to No. 79-E21 but vignette of 6 horiz. bars with 3 in center printed in glossy ink.

79-E22 3c On pink lilac paper, blue 2,250.

79-E23

Design of 3c 1861 stamp typographed in relief for surface printing. Single impression lightly block sunk 63x62mm in color. Design has 21x26½mm border inside 23x28½mm colorless rectangle.

79-E23 3c
a. Die on 64x75mm ivory paper, black *325.*
b. Die on India, dull violet-red red *325.*
c. Die on 59x54mm stiff white card, color about 40mm wide (not extending to edges)
light red violet *325.*
carmine *325.*
blue *325.*
d. Washington head only, lines on face around eye, on soft card
dim blue-green blue *250.*
dim orange-orange red *250.*

On 17x21mm plain colored rectangle printed through a mat, surrounded by 55x62mm colorless rectangle, vert. 4½mm wide color bands at sides inside 64x62mm die sinkage.

e. Washington head with dots around eye, on 17x42mm solid color, on 77x45mm stiff white paper, dull violet-red *250.*
f. India paper on soft white card block sunk 63x62mm, dull violet-red-red with solid color margins *250.*

Colored India generally cut away outside colorless rectangle 23x28½mm, design heavily embossed through to card beneath.

g. As "f," trimmed to shape
dark carmine *350.*
orange *350.*
blue green *350.*
red violet *350.*
h. Complete design on India, sunk on card, trimmed to shape
blue *100.*
dull green blue *100.*
i. Plate typographed on white wove, imperf., gummed
dim red *50.*
dim light orange red *50.*
dim blue green *50.*

dim pale blue 50.
dim dark blue 50.
dusky violet red 50.

Color outside design generally fills rectangle, design impression shows on back.

j. Complete design on glossy sticky paper, deep violet red 150.
k. As "j," on pelure, perf. 12, gummed, rose 175.
l. As "k," allover grill, dim red 150.
m. As "k," 13x16mm grill, gray black 150.

79-E24 79-E24c

Block sinkage: 65x76mm
Washington head only.

79-E24 3c
a. Lithographed, face dotted, on 65x76mm solid color background
black 750.
red violet 750.
olive black 750.
b. Typographed, background irregular edge, on card, gray black 750.
c. Face lined, on 64x72mm solid color background
black 750.
scarlet 750.

79-E25

Plate essays of complete 1861 3c design.

79-E25 3c
a. Plate on hard white transparent wove, dark red 50.
b. Plate on more opaque white wove, dim red 50.
c. Plate on Gibson patent starch coated opaque white paper, generally crinkled, lathework design usually poorly printed
orange red 25.
deep orange red 25.
pink 25.
dull yellow 25.
yellow orange 25.
dull yellow orange 25.
brown yellow 25.
brown 25.
green 25.
blue green 25.
blue 25.
light blue 25.
d. Plate on semitransparent white wove
dull pale blue 20.
green 20.
dull yellow orange 20.
e. Plate on pale green paper, clearly printed, dark g-b green 40.
f. Plate on white wove, 13x16mm points down grill, gummed, dark blue 40.
g. Plate on lilac gray paper, 13x16mm grill, gummed
dark blue 40.
dull red 40.
black 40.
h. Plate on white paper (ungrilled), perf. 12, gummed
red 25.
light red 25.
pale red 25.
light orange red 25.
deep yellow orange 25.
brown 25.
dark green 25.
deep blue 25.
dull g-b blue 25.
gray black 25.
i. As "h," ms. A or B in UL corner, red 50.
j. Plate on white paper, 13x16mm points down grill, perf. 12, gummed
black 25.
gray black 25.
pale red 25.
light red 25.
orange red 25.
deep orange yellow 25.
brown 25.
dark brown 25.
green 25.
blue 25.
dark blue 25.
k. As "j," ms. "s No. 6" on back
red 50.
gray black 50.
dark blue 50.
l. As "j," but grill points up
red 40.
pink 40.
pale rose 40.
brown 40.
orange yellow 40.
deep red orange 40.
green 40.
dull blue 40.
dull light blue 40.
m. As "l," pair with blue oval "American Bank Note Co. April 17, '79", pink 150.
n. Plate on greenish gray chemical paper, 13x16mm grill, perf. 12
black 50.
green 50.
dark blue 50.
orange red 50.
light yellow gray 50.
light red gray 50.
o. As "n," without grill
red 50.
rose 50.
p. Plate on pelure, without grill, imperf., gummed, dim red 50.
q. As "p," perf. 12, dim red 50.

79-E26

Plate imresssions of 1861 3c stamp overprinted with various safety network designs. Inks probably fugitive.

79-E26 3c
a. Vert. pair on 58x80mm India, overprint die 54x71mm or more, small ONE repeated in 41 vert. lines per 40mm, rose pink, overprint deep orange yellow 2,000.
b. As "a," block of 6 inscribed "J. Sangster Pat. 190376, Jan. 6, 1877" 3,500.
c. 65TC3, "VEINTE" overprint, in miniature sheet of 12, perf. 12, black, overprint orange 7,500.

3c 1861 printed in various colors in miniature sheets of 12 with safety ovpts. (Apparently only one sheet printed of each color combination, except two Type D combinations known both perf. and imperf.)

d. Type A
perf. 12, dull violet, overprint gray 425.
perf. 12, rose red, overprint gray blue 425.
perf. 12, violet, overprint gray tan 425.
imperf., pale olive, overprint pale tan 425.
imperf., green, overprint gray tan 425.

e. Type B
perf. 12, green, overprint pale tan 425.
perf. 12, violet, overprint gray tan 425.
perf. 12, dull red brown, ovpt. pale brown 425.
perf. 12, dark dull red brown, overprint pale brown 425.

Type C Type D

f. Type C
perf. 12, dull violet, overprint gray tan 550.
perf. 12, dull red, overprint gray blue 550.
perf. 12, rose red, overprint gray blue 550.
perf. 12, green, overprint gray tan 550.
imperf., rose red, overprint pale tan 550.
imperf., pale rose red, overprint pale tan 550.
imperf., yellow brown, overprint tan 550.

g. Type D
perf. 12, dull violet, overprint gray blue 550.
perf. 12, rose red, overprint gray blue 550.
perf. 12, light red brown, overprint pale brown 550.
perf. 12, dark green, overprint dull blue 550.
imperf., pale olive, overprint tan 550.
imperf., ultramarine, overprint tan 550.
imperf., dull violet, overprint gray blue 550.
imperf., dull violet, overprint pale green 550.
imperf., dark green, overprint dull blue 550.

79-E27

Design size: 20½x26½mm
Engraved in relief for surface printing, large 2 vignette, on same die with No. 79-E28, 20mm apart. Also essayed for envelopes on thick papers.

79-E27 2c
a. Untrimmed die, 30x42mm, on paper with "US" monogram, pale rose 850.
b. Die on stiff glazed paper, 63x50mm, black 600.
c. Trimmed die on India, on thick soft card, colorless parts in relief
black 450.
red 450.
orange 450.
violet red 450.
d. Die on 35x40mm white wove, imperf., gummed
blue 450.
albino 450.
e. Die on white wove, perf. 12, gummed, smoky violet red 450.
f. Untrimmed die on white wove, 61x42mm, black 550.

79-E28 79-E28g

Design size: 21x25½mm
Engraved in relief for surface printing, large 3 in shield vignette, on same die with No. 79-E27, 20mm apart. Also essayed for envelopes on thick papers.

79-E28 3c
a. Untrimmed die on stiff ivory paper, showing color 30x42mm
black 700.
rose 700.
orange 700.
blue 700.
b. Untrimmed die on India with No. 79-E27, both embossed, yellow orange 1,000.
c. Trimmed die heavily struck on India, card mounted, colorless parts in relief
black 250.
red 250.
orange 250.
d. Die on wide laid paper, "US" monogram, perf. 12, gummed
pale rose 250.
dull brown yellow 250.
e. Die on greenish wove, 10x12mm points down grill, imperf., gummed, dull brown 250.
f. Die on white paper, perf. 12, gummed
smoky violet red 250.
green 250.
g. Underprinted design only on thin white wove
light blue 350.
albino 350.

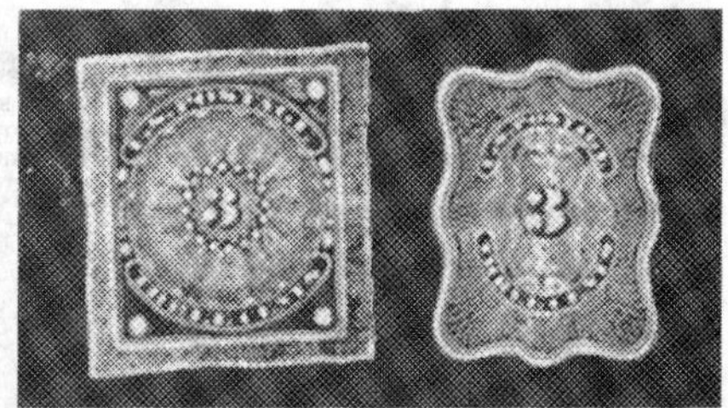

79-E28H

Design size: 68x38mm
Two compound surface-printed designs, "3" within ornate frame. Possibly included a third design at right.

79-E28H 3c Untrimmed die on wove paper, green *1,250.*

79-E29

1861 1c frame only.

79-E29 1c
- ***a.*** Die on thin crisp paper, safely design underprint, black on dull olive green *3,000.*
- ***b.*** Die on pink paper, 18x13mm points down grill, imperf., gummed, red brown *1,250.*
- ***c.*** Die on pink "laid" paper, red *1,250.*
- ***d.*** Die on pale pink paper, red brown *1,250.*
- ***e.*** Die on transparent white paper, red brown *1,250.*
- ***f.*** Die on thick yellow paper, red brown *1,250.*
- ***g.*** Die on thin transparent white paper, 11x13mm points down grill, perf. 12, gummed, red brown *1,250.*
- ***h.*** As "g," imperf. *2,000.*

79-E29i

As No. 79-E29 but with monogram in vignette.
- ***i.*** Die on transparent white stamp paper, perf. 12, gummed, red brown *3,500.*

79-E30

Design size: 20x26mm
Block size: 64x76½mm
Vignette of Liberty. Typographed.

79-E30 3c
- ***a.*** Head only on solid color (die size: 67x76mm), on 32x37mm stiff yellowish wove
  - black *600.*
  - blue green *600.*
- ***b.*** Vignette only, on 66x100mm card
  - black *600.*
  - blue green *600.*
  - blue *600.*
- ***c.*** Vignette only, on proof paper
  - bright blue *600.*
  - black *600.*
- ***d.*** Complete design, untrimmed block, colorless 22x27 rectangle around design, broad outer edge in color, on stiff yellowish wove
  - black *350.*
  - blue green *350.*
  - violet brown *350.*
  - bright violet red *350.*
  - red violet *350.*
  - buff *350.*
- ***e.*** As "d," on proof paper
  - buff *350.*
  - deep blue green *350.*
  - red brown *350.*
  - carmine *350.*
  - black *350.*
- ***f.*** Die on proof paper, perf. 12, vignette oval perf. 16, carmine *200.*
- ***g.*** Die on stiff ivory paper about 28x32mm
  - black *150.*
  - carmine *150.*
  - yellow *150.*
  - dark blue green *150.*
  - rose violet *150.*
- ***h.*** Die on stiff ivory paper, no color outside design, block of 4, carmine *500.*
  - Block of 8 with vert. pairs in orange, dull yellow green, dark green and dark violet *900.*
- ***i.*** Die on deep orange-surfaced white paper, carmine *150.*
- ***j.*** As "i," perf. 12, gummed, carmine *150.*
- ***k.*** Die on yellow-surfaced wove, carmine *150.*

79-E30l

- ***l.*** Die with outer color removed, on 64x90mm white wove stamp paper with imprint below, imperf., gummed
  - carmine *150.*
  - scarlet *150.*
  - dim orange red *150.*
  - orange *150.*
  - dull yellow orange *150.*
  - pale dull yellow *150.*
  - brown *150.*
  - lemon *150.*
  - yellow green *150.*
  - dull olive green *150.*
  - dull greenish gray *150.*
  - dim blue green *150.*
  - dull blue *150.*
  - dull red violet *150.*
  - pale red violet *150.*
- ***m.*** As "l," tete-beche pairs, each with imprint
  - carmine, orange *350.*
  - buff, pale lilac *350.*
  - dark orange brown, yellow *350.*
  - dull green gray *350.*
- ***n.*** As "l," perf. 12, vignette oval perf. 16 (also found without paper outside perfs.
  - carmine *150.*
  - pale rose *150.*
  - dim scarlet *150.*
  - dull scarlet *150.*
  - dim orange red *150.*
  - light red brown *150.*
  - dark brown *150.*
  - orange *150.*
  - dull orange *150.*
  - dismal orange *150.*
  - dull brown orange *150.*
  - pale dull yellow *150.*
  - dull brown *150.*
  - yellow brown *150.*
  - dull olive green *150.*
  - dim dark yellow orange *150.*
  - light yellow green *150.*
  - green *150.*
  - dim blue green *150.*
  - dark blue green *150.*
  - dull greenish gray *150.*
  - dull yellowish gray *150.*
  - dull blue *150.*
  - dim red violet *150.*
  - dull red violet *150.*
  - pale red violet *150.*
  - red violet *150.*
- ***o.*** Plate essay on wove, designs 7mm apart, in two colors shading into each other, imperf.
  - red brown to dark orange *150.*
  - dark orange to brown red *150.*
  - brown olive to red brown *150.*
  - red brown to yellow green *150.*
  - yellow green to dull carmine *150.*
  - dull carmine to yellow green *150.*
  - blue green to dull carmine *150.*
  - brown olive to dull carmine *150.*
  - dull carmine to orange *150.*
  - orange to deep blue *150.*
  - deep blue to orange brown *150.*
  - orange brown to dull orange *150.*
  - dull carmine to deep blue *150.*
- ***p.*** As "o," on transparent wove, imperf.
  - red violet to deep violet *150.*
  - deep violet to carmine *150.*
  - dull scarlet to gold *150.*
  - gold to carmine *150.*
  - dark violet to blue green *150.*
  - blue green to dark violet red *150.*
  - violet to yellow green *150.*
  - yellow green to red violet *150.*
- ***q.*** Plate on stiff yellowish wove, imperf.
  - dull carmine to orange *150.*
  - orange to deep blue *150.*
  - brown olive to brown red *150.*
  - brown red to yellow green *150.*
  - blue green to dull carmine *150.*
  - dull carmine to deep blue *150.*
  - deep blue to dark brown *150.*
  - dark brown to orange *150.*
- ***r.*** As "q," outside edge perf. 12
  - blue green to dull carmine *150.*
  - dull carmine to deep blue *150.*
  - deep blue to dark brown *150.*
  - dark brown to dull orange *150.*
  - dull carmine to dull orange *150.*
  - dull orange to deep blue *150.*
  - yellow green to dull carmine *150.*
  - dull carmine to yellow green *150.*
  - brown olive to brown red *150.*
  - brown red to yellow green *150.*
- ***s.*** Plate in single color, outside edge perf. 12, gummed
  - carmine *150.*
  - dull orange *150.*
  - orange brown *150.*
  - dark brown *150.*
  - brown olive *150.*
  - dark blue green *150.*
  - violet *150.*
- ***t.*** As "s," imperf., gummed
  - brown *125.*
  - brown orange *125.*
  - dull blue green *125.*
  - deep blue *125.*
  - carmine *125.*
- ***u.*** As "t," one color directly over another (gives effect of one color), black on scarlet *275.*
- ***v.*** As "b," heavily stamped on white card, only faint traces of vignette, albino *125.*
- ***w.*** As "v," printed design at right, very dark blue green *250.*

79-E31a

79-E31b

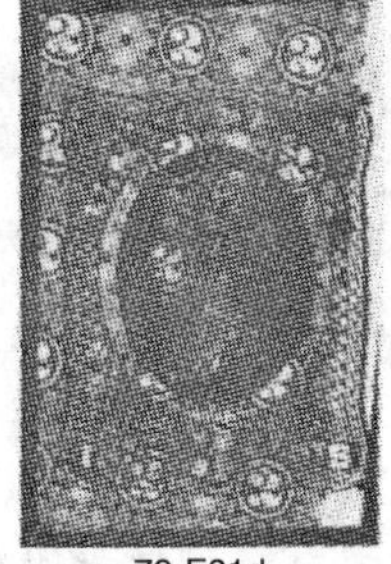

79-E31d

79-E31e

79-E31f

79-E31g

Same design as No. 79-E30, black green on white wove safety paper, underprinted with different designs in various colors, imperf.

79-E31 3c
- ***a.*** Red horiz. diamonds *1,400.*
- ***b.*** Dull yellow green with ONE repeated *1,400.*
- ***c.*** Red with 2 in circles *1,400.*
- ***d.*** Red with 2 in circular stars *1,400.*
- ***e.*** Red with 2 in ovals *1,400.*

f. Red with 3 in diamonds *1,400.*
g. Black with 5 in hexagons *1,400.*
h. Red with X repeated *1,400.*

79-E32

Similar to No. 79-E30f, but perf. vignette removed and frame mounted over 18x23mm Washington vignette.

79-E32 3c Die on 34x40mm white wove, black vignette, blueframe *1,000.*

1868 Essays
Experiments for bicolor printing

1c 1861 design, color reversed as adopted. Typographed frame with 43x60mm solid color border.

79-E33 1c Die on thin white paper, frame pink, vignette dark blue over pink *750.*

79-E35a

79-E35c

Frame lithographed, colored and colorless parts interchanged, vignette engraved and printed in another color.
Die I: colorless vignette oval (Nos. 79-E35a, 79-E35b)
Die II: vignette with horiz. lines (Nos. 79-E35d through 79-E35f)

79-E35 5c
a. Untrimmed die on thin white paper, 40x60mm (values for cut to stamp size)
frame buff, vignette black *2,000.*
frame buff, vignette blue *2,000.*
frame buff, vignette red brown *2,000.*
frame buff, vignette dark brown *2,000.*
frame buff, vignette orange *2,000.*
frame buff, vignette carmine *2,000.*
frame blue green, vignette dark brown *2,000.*
frame blue green, vignette red brown *2,000.*
frame blue green, vignette orange *2,000.*
frame carmine, vignette blue *2,000.*
frame carmine, vignette red brown *2,000.*
frame violet, vignette orange *2,000.*
frame light red, vignette deep orange red *2,000.*
frame light red, vignette yellow orange *2,000.*
b. Die on stiff wove, frame brown, vignette scarlet *2,000.*
c. 45x65mm die impression of lithographed frame only, on ivory paper
black *2,000.*
blue green *2,000.*
d. Die on thin white paper
frame violet, vignette carmine *2,000.*
frame violet, vignette brown *2,000.*
frame violet, vignette red brown *2,000.*
frame carmine, vignette black *2,000.*
e. Vignette only on white glazed paper
black *2,000.*
blue *2,000.*
scarlet *2,000.*
dark brown *2,000.*
f. As "e," without thin outer frameline, on India
lake *2,000.*
red *2,000.*
deep red orange *2,000.*
scarlet *2,000.*
deep green *2,000.*
ultramarine *2,000.*

79-E36

Die II vignette as No. 79-E35e, with gothic "United States" above.

79-E36 5c
a. Die on white glazed paper
black *450.*
scarlet *450.*
dark brown *450.*
green *450.*
blue *450.*

Die size: 51x63½
5c 1861 design, color reversed as adopted, vignette mounted on typographed frame.

79-E37 5c
a. Die on white card, frame light blue, vignette black *1,000.*
b. Vignette only, die on India, black *350.*
c. Vignette only, die on white glazed paper
blue *350.*
black *350.*
green *350.*

100-E1

Design size: 20½x24½mm
Engraved circular Franklin vignette mounted on 43x75mm white card, engraved Washington head mounted thereon; background, silhouette, etc., retouched in black ink. With engraved frame of No. 71-E1 (vignette cut out) mounted over the double vignette.

100-E1 30c Die on India, 30x34mm, black *6,000.*

1869 ISSUE
George T. Jones

112-E1

113-E1

Design size: 24x30mm
U.S. Grant vignette in frame with blank labels, ovals, etc. Paper overprinted with network of fine colored wavy lines in fugitive inks as on beer stamps.

112-E1 No Denomination
a. Die on India cut to stamp size, 1 color
black *2,250.*
blue *2,250.*
b. Die on India cut to stamp size, 2 colors (head in black)
blue, light gray overprint *2,750.*
red, light gray overprint *2,750.*
black, light violet overprint *2,750.*
black brown, pale red violet ovpt. *2,750.*
carmine, gray overprint *2,750.*
blue, yellow overprint *2,750.*

Design size: 24x30mm
U.S. Treasury Dept. seal in vignette oval.

113-E1 2c
a. Die on India cut to stamp size, 1 color
carmine *2,500.*
blue *2,500.*
b. Die on India cut to stamp size, 3 colors, black on pale red violet wavy lines and blue green lined vignette *3,750.*

Frame as 112-E1 but with Washington vignette and 2c denomination. Another Washington vignette below but in horiz. lined oval frame.

113-E2 2c Die on 1⅝x3½inch India, black *5,000.*

National Bank Note Co.

All values originally essayed with numerals smaller than adopted. All designs are same size as issued stamps. Sheets of 150 of 1c-12c, sheets of 50 of 24c-90c. Many colors of plate essays exist from one sheet only, some colors from two sheets and a few from three. Some plate essays exist privately perforated.

112-E2

112-E3

Die size: 40x65mm
Vignette size: 17mm diameter
Vignette of Franklin.

112-E2 1c Die of vignette only on India
orange *900.*
violet brown *900.*
black *900.*

Circle of pearls added to vignette, suggestion for frame and 1 in circle at bottom penciled in.

112-E3 1c Die on India, black *1,500.*

112-E4

112-E5

Complete design as issued but with small value numeral.

112-E4 1c
a. Die on India, die sunk on card
black *1,250.*
violet brown *1,250.*
dark brown *1,250.*
yellow brown *1,250.*
scarlet *1,250.*
carmine *1,250.*
deep violet *1,250.*
blue *1,250.*
green *1,250.*
yellow *1,250.*
b. Plate on stamp paper, imperf., gummed
buff *100.*
deep orange brown *100.*
orange brown *100.*
c. Plate on stamp paper, perf. 12, gummed
buff *100.*
orange brown *100.*
orange *125.*
d. As "c," with 9x9mm grill
buff *110.*
orange brown *85.*
red brown *85.*
chocolate *85.*
black brown *85.*
dull red *85.*
violet *110.*
dark violet *110.*
blue *110.*
deep blue *110.*
green *110.*
yellow *110.*
orange *110.*
rose red *110.*

Design size: 23x31mm
Die size: 51x55mm
Design as issued but surrounded by fancy frame with flags and shield. Also essayed for envelopes and wrappers on thick paper.

112-E5 1c
a. Die on stamp paper, perf. 12, gummed, gray *2,250.*
b. Die on white ivory paper
black *1,750.*
black brown *1,750.*
scarlet *1,750.*
blue *1,750.*
c. Die on India
blue *1,750.*
blue green *1,750.*
d. Die on India, cut to shape
carmine *600.*
yellow *600.*

113-E3

Die size: 41x50mm
Design as issued but with small value numeral. Nos. 113-E3a and 113-Eb have incomplete shading around "UNITED STATES."

113-E3 2c
a. Die on India, die sunk on card
black *1,500.*
yellow *1,500.*
red orange *1,500.*
deep scarlet *1,500.*
brown *1,500.*
green *1,500.*
dusky blue *1,500.*
deep blue *1,500.*
b. Die on India, cut to stamp size
deep orange red *400.*
deep orange yellow *400.*
blue green *400.*
gray black *400.*
light blue *400.*
rose *400.*
c. Complete die on India, die sunk on card
brown *1,500.*
rose *1,500.*
mauve *1,500.*
green *1,500.*
dark chocolate *1,500.*
red brown *1,500.*
d. Plate on stamp paper, perf. 12, gummed
brown *425.*
dark brown *425.*
yellow *425.*
e. As "d," with 9x9mm grill
brown *80.*
dark brown *80.*
orange brown *80.*
dark orange brown *80.*
rose *80.*
brown rose *80.*
copper red *80.*
deep copper red *80.*
green *80.*
deep green *80.*
blue green *80.*
yellow *80.*
orange *80.*
dull yellow orange *80.*
blue *80.*
light violet *80.*
violet *80.*
dark violet *80.*
f. As "e," double grill, orange *300.*

113-E4

Original sketch of postrider, printed "NATIONAL BANK NOTE COMPANY. BUSINESS DEPARTMENT. 1868" at top, pencil instructions at bottom, "Reduce to this length" and "2 copies on one plate. Daguerrotype."

113-E4 2c Drawing on paper, black —

114-E3

114-E4

Die size: 53x47mm
Design nearly as issued: larger motive above and below "POSTAGE" erased, no shading on numeral shield, top leaves and corner leaves do not touch, no dots in lower corners or scrolls beside bottom of shield, no vert. shading lines in "POSTAGE" label. Small value numeral.

114-E3 3c Die on 30x30mm ivory paper, black *1,500.*

Similar to 114-E3, but smaller motive around "POSTAGE," shield shaded.

114-E4 3c
a. Die on India, die sunk on card
black *1,500.*
carmine *1,500.*
scarlet *1,500.*
orange red *1,500.*
yellow orange *1,500.*
dull yellow *1,500.*
red sepia *1,500.*
blue green *1,500.*
blue *1,500.*
dull red *1,500.*
orange brown *1,500.*
b. Die on India, cut to stamp size
black *500.*
rose *500.*
scarlet *500.*
chocolate *500.*
dull dusky orange *500.*
red violet *500.*
blackish slate *500.*

Similar to No. 114-E4 but vert. shading lines added to "POSTAGE" frame.

114-E5 3c Die on India, dusky yellow orange *1,750.*

114-E6

114-E7

Completed small numeral die essay: leaves at top and sides touch, dots in lower corners added, vert. shading lines in frame around "POSTAGE," shield shaded darker at bottom, scrolls added to bottom of shield.

114-E6 3c
a. Die on India, card mounted
black *1,750.*
blue *1,750.*
deep orange red *1,750.*
b. Plate on stamp paper, imperf., gummed
ultramarine *125.*
dark ultramarine *125.*
light brown *85.*
red brown *85.*
dark red brown *85.*
pale rose *85.*
rose *85.*
brown rose *85.*
c. Plate on stamp paper, perf. 12, gummed
ultramarine *500.*
dark ultramarine *500.*
d. As "c," with 9x9mm grill
blue *80.*
deep blue *80.*
orange brown *80.*
black brown *80.*
deep black brown *80.*
rose red *80.*
green *80.*
yellow *80.*
orange *80.*
deep orange *80.*
dull violet *80.*
deep violet *80.*
red violet *80.*

Same design and color as issued stamp, but with allover essay grill of squares up.

114-E7 3c
a. Imperf., gummed, ultramarine *700.*
b. As "a," 23mm "NATIONAL BANK NOTE CO. N.Y. SEP 27, 1869" circular pmk., ultramarine *1,100.*
c. On thick paper, imperf., gummed, horiz. line defacement, ultramarine *700.*
d. Perf. 12, horiz. line defacement, ultramarine *700.*

115-E1

115-E2

Die size: 40x60mm
Vignette of Washington. Design as issued 6c stamp but with 5c denomination. Large lettering, large U and S in corners. Also essayed for envelopes on thick paper.

115-E1 6c
a. Die on India, no frameline, solid vignette background, corner spandrels short at centers
black *700.*
carmine *700.*
dismal red brown *700.*
smoky dusky brown *700.*
gray violet *700.*
b. Completed die on India, die sunk on card
black *600.*
carmine *600.*
deep rose *600.*
red violet *600.*
red brown *600.*
deep yellow brown *600.*
black brown *600.*
dull yellow *600.*
orange *600.*
dusky blue *600.*
dusky slate blue *600.*
green *600.*
blue green *600.*
scarlet *600.*
c. Die on proof paper, about 40x65mm
black *600.*
carmine *600.*
scarlet *600.*
red orange *600.*
orange *600.*
dull yellow *600.*
orange brown *600.*
olive brown *600.*
dusky green *600.*
dusky yellow green *600.*
light blue *600.*
deep blue *600.*
red violet *600.*
d. Die on pink bond
orange *600.*
brown *600.*
blue *600.*
e. Die on light yellow green bond, black *600.*
f. Die on pale olive buff bond
black *600.*
carmine *600.*
orange *600.*
red orange *600.*
brown *600.*
g. Die on cream wove
black *600.*
orange *600.*
brown *600.*
blue *600.*
h. Die on clear white bond
black *600.*
blue *600.*
orange *600.*
red orange brown *600.*
i. Die on thick cloudy bond
black *600.*
red *600.*
orange *600.*
orange brown *600.*
blue *600.*
reddish brown *600.*
j. Die on pale lilac bond
dark red orange *700.*
orange *700.*
blue *700.*
k. Die on glazed paper
black *550.*
scarlet *550.*
yellow *550.*
dark brown *550.*
blue *550.*
l. Die on marbled white card
green on red violet veined *1,750.*
black on green veined *1,750.*
red violet on green veined *1,750.*
m. Die on ivory card, black *1,500.*
n. Die on white card, cut to stamp size, red orange *250.*

Die size: 43x63mm
Similar to No. 115-E1 but lettering, U and S smaller.

115-E2 6c
a. Incomplete die on India (incomplete spandrel points, hair on top of head, etc.)
black *750.*
dull red brown *750.*
b. Complete die on India, die sunk on card
black *750.*
blue *750.*
dull dusky violet *750.*
scarlet *750.*
dark orange red *750.*
dim dusky red orange *750.*
dusky green *750.*
dusky green blue green *750.*
dusky blue green *750.*
c. Plate essay on wove, imperf., gummed
deep ultramarine *150.*
orange *150.*
dull red violet *80.*
deep red violet *80.*
red brown *80.*
dull red brown *80.*
buff *80.*
green *80.*
d. Plate essay on wove, perf. 12, gummed
orange *200.*
blue *200.*

115-E3

Vignette of Washington as used on stamp but with longer shirt front.

115-E3 6c Die on india, affixed to card, 35x37mm, black —

116-E1

Die size: 14x18mm

Vignette of Lincoln as on No. 77.

116-E1 10c Die on India, on card, black —

116-E1a

Design size:14x14½mm
Vignette of Lincoln as on No. 77, reduced.

116-E1a Die on India, on card, black *1,500.*

116-E1b

Design size: about 19½x19½mm
Die size: 64x68½mm
Head as on No. 77 but less bust, large unshaded collar, no cross shading in triangles between labels and fasces, no shading on diamonds at end of value label. Also essayed for envelopes on yellow laid paper.

116-E1b Incomplete die on India, on card, black *800.00*

116-E1c

Small collar, shading on diamonds at end of value label.

116-E1c Complete die on India, die sunk on card
black *1,000.*
brown black *1,000.*
gray black *1,000.*
carmine *1,000.*
scarlet *1,000.*
brown red *1,000.*
orange *1,000.*
deep orange *1,000.*
deep red *1,000.*
yellow brown *1,000.*
yellow *1,000.*
green *1,000.*
blue green *1,000.*
deep blue *1,000.*
red violet *1,000.*
brown *1,000.*

d. Die on proof paper
black *1,000.*
carmine *1,000.*
bright red *1,000.*
orange red *1,000.*
orange *1,000.*
dark chocolate *1,000.*
dusky yellow brown *1,000.*
green *1,000.*
blue *1,000.*
red violet *1,000.*

e. Die on ivory paper
black *1,000.*
scarlet *1,000.*
black brown *1,000.*
blue *1,000.*

f. Die on clear white thin bond, about 30x35mm
black *1,000.*
red orange *1,000.*

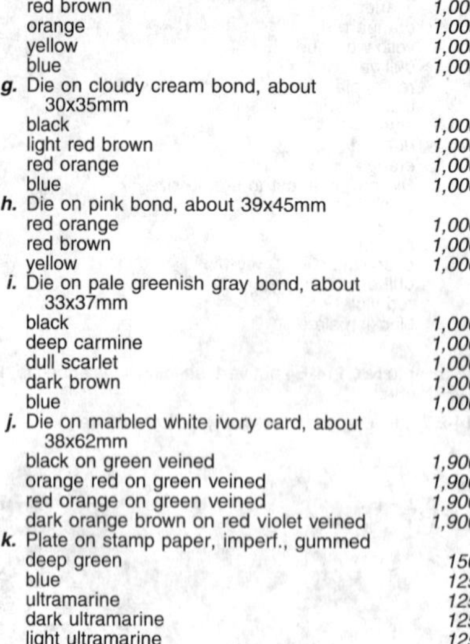

red brown *1,000.*
orange *1,000.*
yellow *1,000.*
blue *1,000.*

g. Die on cloudy cream bond, about 30x35mm
black *1,000.*
light red brown *1,000.*
red orange *1,000.*
blue *1,000.*

h. Die on pink bond, about 39x45mm
red orange *1,000.*
red brown *1,000.*
yellow *1,000.*

i. Die on pale greenish gray bond, about 33x37mm
black *1,000.*
deep carmine *1,000.*
dull scarlet *1,000.*
dark brown *1,000.*
blue *1,000.*

j. Die on marbled white ivory card, about 38x62mm
black on green veined *1,900.*
orange red on green veined *1,900.*
red orange on green veined *1,900.*
dark orange brown on red violet veined *1,900.*

k. Plate on stamp paper, imperf., gummed
deep green *150.*
blue *125.*
ultramarine *125.*
dark ultramarine *125.*
light ultramarine *125.*

l. Plate on stamp paper, perf. 12, gummed, orange *200.*

116-E2

Die size: 101x62mm
Vignette of signing the Declaration of Independence as adopted for 24c.

116-E2 10c

a. Die on India, die sunk on card
black *2,500.*
carmine *2,500.*
dim rose *2,500.*
dull scarlet *2,500.*
red orange *2,500.*
orange yellow *2,500.*
red brown *2,500.*
orange brown *2,500.*
green *2,500.*
blue *2,500.*
gray *2,500.*

b. Die on India, cut to stamp size
black *800.*
red orange *800.*
blue green *800.*
dim rose *800.*
brown *800.*
buff *800.*
dull scarlet *800.*

Other colors reported to exist.

116-E3

116-E4

Die size: 63x75mm
Design as adopted for issued stamp, but incomplete shading on bottom ribbon, thin shading lines behind "States," and center of "0" of "10" not filled in.

116-E3 10c Die on India on 61x53mm card, black *2,500.*

Similar to No. 116-E3 except shading lines added behind "Ten Cents" and center of "0" of "10" filled in.

116-E4 10c Die on India, die sunk on card
black *2,500.*
orange *2,500.*
blue *2,500.*

117-E1

117-E2

Die size: 47x51mm
Design as issued but with smaller value numerals.

117-E1 12c

a. Die on card, black *1,600.*

b. Vignette die on India, pencil "Adriatic", black *1,600.*

c. Complete die on India, die sunk on card
black *1,350.*
rose *1,350.*
yellow *1,350.*
scarlet *1,350.*
dark red brown *1,350.*
blue green *1,350.*
blue *1,350.*
dull violet *1,350.*
gray black *1,350.*
orange brown *1,350.*
yellow brown *1,350.*
dull orange red *1,350.*

d. Die on India, cut to stamp size
black *600.*
dusky red orange *600.*
deep orange red *600.*
dim blue *600.*

e. Plate on stamp paper, 9x9mm grill, perf. 12, gummed
green *125.*
rose red *125.*
pale rose red *125.*
yellow brown *125.*
red brown *125.*
orange *125.*
blue *125.*
dull violet *125.*
dull red violet *125.*
yellow orange *125.*

Similar to No. 117-E1, but small numeral not printed, large 12 drawn in pencil.

117-E2 12c Die on India, black *2,750.*

117-E3

117-E4

Typographed small numeral design similar to No. 117-E1, relief engraved for surface printing. Heavier lines, upper label with solid background, letters of "UNITED STATES POSTAGE" colorless. Nos. 117-E3a through 117-E3c from untrimmed die, heavily struck with uncolored areas in relief, color covering borders beyond white line exterior of frame. Untrimmed die size: 58x45mm.

117-E3 12c

a. Untrimmed die on card
brown red *750.*
green *750.*
black *750.*
red brown *750.*

b. Untrimmed die on thin pinkish wove
gray black *450.*
dull deep red orange *450.*
dark red orange *450.*

c. Untrimmed die on thick white wove
carmine *600.*
green *600.*

d. Die on white paper, stamp size
carmine *400.*
orange *400.*
brown *400.*
lilac *400.*
green *400.*

e. Die on thin white wove
carmine *400.*
gray black *400.*
dull deep red orange *400.*
deep orange red *400.*

g. Die on pinkish wove, perf. 12, gummed, red brown *400.*

h. Die on yellow wove, imperf.
gray black *400.*
carmine *400.*
red brown *400.*
dark red violet *400.*

i. Die on yellow wove, 11x13mm grill, imperf., red brown *400.*

j. Die on white laid
gray *400.*

gray black 400.
brown 400.
red brown 400.
k. Die on yellow laid
red brown 400.
brown 400.
dull red violet 400.
carmine 400.
l. Die on salmon laid, red brown 400.
m. Die on pinkish laid
red brown 400.
gray 400.
n. Die on pinkish laid, 11x13mm grill, gummed, red brown 400.
o. Die on dull red violet laid, gray 400.

Vignette size: 15x11mm
Untrimmed die size: 63x32mm
Vignette only, similar to No. 117-E3 but lithographed instead of typographed.

117-E4 12c
a. Die on white ivory paper, black 1,000.
b. Complete impression from untrimmed stone in solid color about 63x63mm, on white ivory paper, black 750.
c. Die on glossy-surfaced thin white wove, trimmed to stamp size
carmine 750.
rose pink 750.
yellow 750.
blue green 750.
dim red violet 750.
pale red violet 750.
deep red orange 750.
dull dark red orange 750.
dull dark yellow orange 750.
dark violet red 750.
pale gray 750.
d. Die on thick white wove
yellow 750.
violet red 750.
deep red violet 750.

118-E1

119-E1

Die size: 62x49mm
Type I design as issued but with smaller value numerals.

118-E1 15c
a. Die of vignette only on India, mounted on 62x62mm India, die sunk on card, dark blue 3,500.
b. Incomplete die (no outer frameline or shading outside frame scrolls) on India, black 4,500.
c. Complete die on India, die sunk on card
black 5,000.
scarlet 5,000.
orange brown 5,000.
green 5,000.
dull violet 5,000.
red brown 5,000.

Type II design with large value numerals as issued.

119-E1 15c
a. Type II frame only, die on India
black 3,000.
red brown 3,000.
b. Vignette only, die on India, blue —
c. Type II frame with vignette mounted in place, die on India, red brown frame, blue vignette 3,000.
d. Type II frame with vignette mounted at right, die on India, red brown frame, blue vignette —

129-E1

129-E2

Die size: 65x49
Type III design as adopted, except in various single colors, large "15" overprint in diff. color.

129-E1 15c
a. Die on India, die sunk on card
orange brown, red overprint 3,250.
blue green, red overprint 3,250.
ultramarine, red overprint 3,250.
violet, red overprint 3,250.
red brown, red overprint 3,250.
b. Die on India, die sunk on card
rose red, ultramarine overprint 3,250.
dull scarlet, ultramarine overprint 3,250.
dark red brown, ultramarine ovpt. 3,250.
c. Die on India, die sunk on card
scarlet, blue green overprint 3,250.
orange brown, blue green overprint 3,250.
dark red brown, blue green overprint 3,250.

Type III frame only.

129-E2 15c
a. Die on India, red brown 2,750.
b. Die on India, with vignette mounted in place, blue frame, yellow vignette 3,500.

120-E1

120-E2

Die size: 102x63mm
Design nearly as issued, but shading under leaves at top of frame and ribbon over "TWENTY" are unfinished. Small value numerals. Single color.

120-E1 24c Die on India, black 3,500.

Completed small numeral design in single color. No. 120-E2a has 8mm-high bands of shaded colored lines 31mm long overprinted above and below vignette, printed in various single colors with bands in contrasting color.

120-E2 24c
a. Die on India
black with carmine bands 4,000.
black with violet brown bands 4,000.
black with brown orange bands 4,000.
orange brown with deep dull violet bands 4,000.
orange brown with blue green bands 4,000.
b. Die on India
black 2,250.
scarlet 2,250.
dark red brown 2,250.
blue 2,250.
violet 2,250.
c. Plate on red salmon tinted paper, black 200.
d. Plate on orange buff tinted paper, black 250.
e. Plate on dull yellowish tinted paper, black 250.
f. Plate on blue tinted paper, black 250.
g. Plate on gray tinted paper, black 500.
h. Plate on India, black 300.
j. Plate on card, imperf., black 250.

120-E3

No. 120-E3a bicolor design as issued, except vignette printed separately and mounted in place; No. 120-E3b frame only with 3 border lines around vignette space; No. 120-E3c frame only with 2 border lines around vignette space as issued.

120-E3 24c
a. Die on India, card mounted
dull violet frame, green vignette 2,500.
violet frame, red vignette 2,500.
green frame, violet vignette 2,500.
rose frame, green vignette 2,500.
b. Frame die on India, card mounted
light green 2,500.
dark green 2,500.
c. Frame die on India, block sunk on India, green 2,500.

121-E1

Design size: 21½x22mm
Die Size: 71x51mm
Vignette of Surrender of Gen. Burgoyne in ornate frame.

121-E1 30c
a. Die on India, die sunk on card
black 800.
carmine 800.
rose red 800.
light brown red 800.
red brown 800.
brown orange 800.
orange 800.
red orange 800.
yellow green 800.

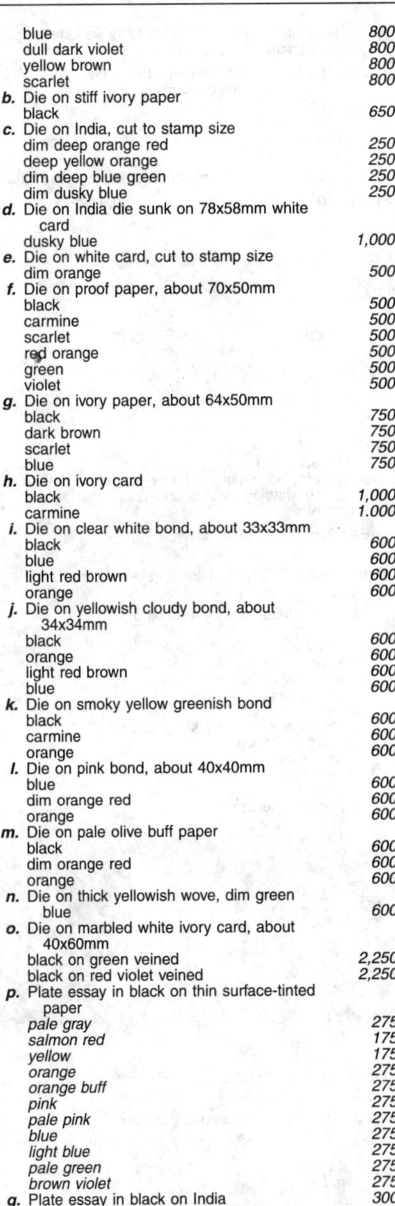

blue 800.
dull dark violet 800.
yellow brown 800.
scarlet 800.
b. Die on stiff ivory paper
black 650.
c. Die on India, cut to stamp size
dim deep orange red 250.
deep yellow orange 250.
dim deep blue green 250.
dim dusky blue 250.
d. Die on India die sunk on 78x58mm white card
dusky blue 1,000.
e. Die on white card, cut to stamp size
dim orange 500.
f. Die on proof paper, about 70x50mm
black 500.
carmine 500.
scarlet 500.
red orange 500.
green 500.
violet 500.
g. Die on ivory paper, about 64x50mm
black 750.
dark brown 750.
scarlet 750.
blue 750.
h. Die on ivory card
black 1,000.
carmine 1,000.
i. Die on clear white bond, about 33x33mm
black 600.
blue 600.
light red brown 600.
orange 600.
j. Die on yellowish cloudy bond, about 34x34mm
black 600.
orange 600.
light red brown 600.
blue 600.
k. Die on smoky yellow greenish bond
black 600.
carmine 600.
orange 600.
l. Die on pink bond, about 40x40mm
blue 600.
dim orange red 600.
orange 600.
m. Die on pale olive buff paper
black 600.
dim orange red 600.
orange 600.
n. Die on thick yellowish wove, dim green blue 600.
o. Die on marbled white ivory card, about 40x60mm
black on green veined 2,250.
black on red violet veined 2,250.
p. Plate essay in black on thin surface-tinted paper
pale gray 275.
salmon red 175.
yellow 175.
orange 275.
orange buff 275.
pink 275.
pale pink 275.
blue 275.
light blue 275.
pale green 275.
brown violet 275.
q. Plate essay in black on India 300.
r. Plate on thick rough pitted card, black 300.

121-E1s

s. Plate on bond, red bands overprinted top and bottom as on No. 120-E2a, dull red violet 350.

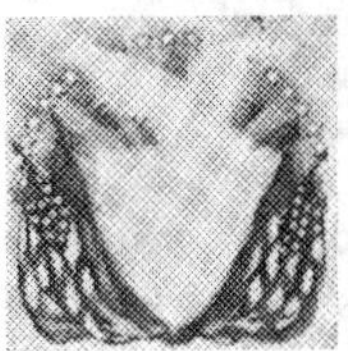
121-E2

121-E3

Flags, stars and rays only as adopted for issued stamp. Black essay shows traces of vignette also.

121-E2 30c Die on India, mounted on India, block sunk on card
black 7,500.
light ultramarine 6,000.
dark blue 6,000.

Eagle, shield and value only as adopted for issued stamp.

121-E3 30c Die on India, card mounted, black 8,500.

122-E1

Die size: 62x69mm
Vignette of Washington in frame similar to that of issued stamp but no shading over U and S in lower corners, small value numerals.

122-E1 90c Die on India, black 3,250.

Similar to No. 122-E1 but shading over U and S.

122-E2 90c
a. Die on India, die sunk on card
black 2,500.
carmine 2,500.
scarlet 2,500.
red brown 2,500.
blue green 2,500.
violet 2,500.
b. Plate essay with black vignette on stamp paper, imperf.
dull violet 275.
red brown 275.
orange red 275.
pale orange red 275.
blue 275.

122-E3

122-E4

Frame as No. 122-E2, vignette oval with narrow-spaced horiz. lines in same color as frame, but no head.

122-E3 90c Plate on stamp paper, imperf.
red brown 225.
blue 225.
dark blue 225.
red violet 225.
dull violet 225.
dark violet 225.
rose red 225.
deep rose red 225.
yellow 225.
orange brown 225.
dark navy blue 225.
blue green 225.
deep blue green 225.
dark blue green 225.
orange 225.

Small numeral frame but with Lincoln vignette from No. 77 mounted in place.

122-E4 90c
a. Die on India
yellow 2,000.
deep blue green 2,000.
dark navy blue 2,000.
b. Plate of Lincoln vignette only, on rough pitted thick gray paper, black 600.
c. Die on India, Lincoln vignette as used on No. 77, black 2,500.

122-E5

Similar to No. 122-E1, with Washington vignette but with large numerals as on issued stamp.

122-E5 90c
a. Die on India, die sunk on card
black 5,000.
carmine 2,500.
b. Plate of frame only, 2 lines at top, 3 lines at bottom, on India, mounted on block sunk card, rose red 1,250.
c. As "b," 3 lines at top, 2 lines at bottom
rose red 4,500.
red brown 1,250.

Safety essays: die essays on thin wove, underprinted with various engraved safety paper designs in another color, probably with fugitive ink.

Found on 5c (No. 115-E1), 10c (No. 116-E1), 15c (No. 129-E1 without overprint) and 30c (No. 121-E1). Stamp color given first.

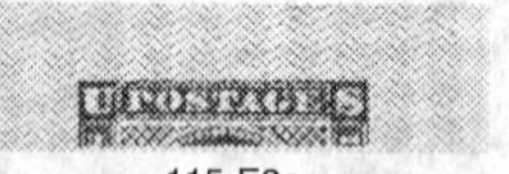

115-E3a

Design 1: wavy lines

115-E3
a. 5c
carmine on scarlet 3,250.
orange on scarlet 3,250.
b. 10c blue on scarlet 5,000.
c. 30c carmine on scarlet 3,500.

115-E4

Design 2: banknote type

115-E4
a. 5c
carmine on violet 3,250.
orange on violet 3,250.
b. 10c carmine on violet 5,000.
c. 30c
carmine on violet 3,500.
orange on violet 3,500.
orange on gray 3,500.

115-E5

Design 3: banknote type

115-E5
a. 5c
carmine on orange and red 3,250.
carmine on brown 3,250.
orange on brown 3,250.
b. 10c
carmine on orange and red 5,000.
blue on orange and red 5,000.
c. 30c
carmine on orange and red 3,500.
orange on brown 3,500.

115-E6

Design 4: continuous wavy lines

115-E6
a. 5c orange on scarlet 3,250.
b. 10c
blue on scarlet 5,000.
carmine on scarlet 5,000.
c. 30c black on scarlet 3,500.

115-E7

Design 5: wavy lines

115-E7
a. 5c
orange on scarlet 3,250.
orange on black 3,250.
b. 10c
dark brown on black 5,000.
orange red on black 5,000.
carmine on scarlet 5,000.
c. 30c
carmine on black 3,500.
carmine on scarlet 3,500.

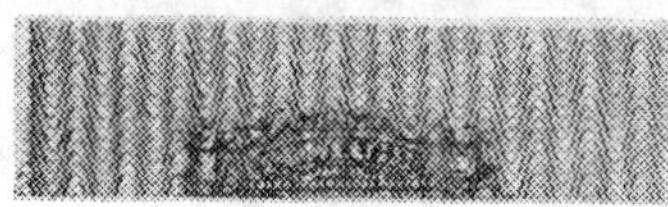

115-E8

Design 6: wavy lines

115-E8
a. 5c orange on black 3,250.
b. 10c blue on black 5,000.
c. 30c
carmine on black 3,500.
orange on black 3,500.

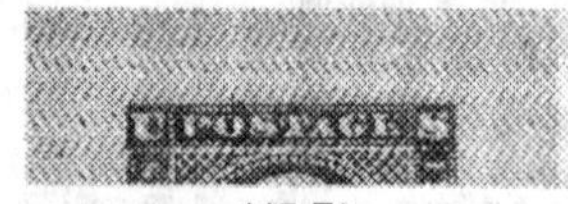

115-E9

Design 7: crossed wavy lines

115-E9
a. 5c
carmine on black 3,250.
orange on black 3,250.
b. 10c blue on black 5,000.
c. 30c orange on black 3,500.

115-E10

Design 8: wavy lines

115-E10
a. 5c carmine on scarlet 3,250.
b. 10c
blue on scarlet 5,000.
carmine on scarlet 5,000.
orange red on scarlet 5,000.

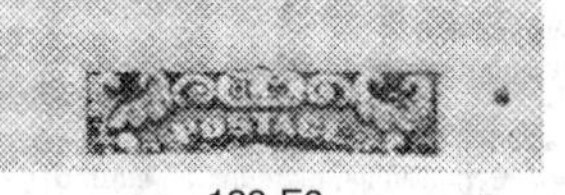

129-E3

Design 9: wavy lines

129-E3 15c
orange brown on orange, vert. 3,500.
blue green on orange, horiz. 3,500.
dark blue on orange, horiz. 3,500.

129-E4

Design 10: banknote type

129-E4 15c
orange brown on scarlet 3,500.
blue green on scarlet 3,500.
dark blue on scarlet 3,500.

129-E5

Design 11: banknote type

129-E5 15c
orange brown on light scarlet 3,500.
blue green on light scarlet, vert. 3,500.
dark blue on light scarlet 3,500.

129-E6

Design 12: banknote type

129-E6 15c
orange brown on deep scarlet 3,500.
blue green on deep scarlet 3,500.
dark blue on deep scarlet 3,500.

115-E11

Design 13: banknote type

115-E11
a. 5c orange on brown 3,250.
b. 10c
carmine on brown 5,000.
orange red on brown 5,000.
blue on brown (horiz. underprinting) 5,000.
blue on brown (vert. underprinting) 5,000.
c. 30c carmine on brown 3,500.

115-E12

Design 14: banknote type

115-E12
a. 5c
carmine on scarlet (horiz.) 3,250.
black on scarlet (vert.) 3,250.
b. 10c
carmine on scarlet 5,000.
orange on scarlet 5,000.
sepia on scarlet 5,000.
blue on scarlet 5,000.
c. 30c black on scarlet 3,500.

115-E13

Design 15: banknote type

115-E13
a. 5c carmine on orange brown 3,250.
b. 30c carmine on deep orange 3,500.

115-E14

Design 16: multiple rosettes

115-E14
a. 5c orange on scarlet 3,250.
b. 10c
carmine on scarlet 5,000.
orange red on scarlet 5,000.
sepia on scarlet 5,000.
blue on scarlet 5,000.

115-E15

Design 17: multiple oval rosettes

115-E15
a. 5c carmine on scarlet 3,250.
b. 30c
carmine on scarlet 3,500.
orange on scarlet 3,500.

115-E16

Design 18: negative stars in diagonal lines

115-E16
a. 5c
black on scarlet 3,250.
carmine on scarlet 3,250.
b. 10c
carmine on scarlet 5,000.
sepia on scarlet 5,000.
c. 30c carmine on scarlet 3,500.

116-E6

Design 19: multiple 6-point stars in lathework

116-E6
a. 10c blue on blue green 5,000.
b. 30c carmine on blue green 3,500.

116-E7

Design 20: banknote type

116-E7
a. 10c
brown on orange 5,000.
blue on orange 5,000.
b. 30c carmine on orange 3,500.

116-E8

Design 21: multiple "ONE"

116-E8 10c blue on scarlet 5,000.

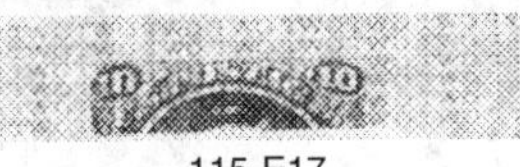
115-E17

Design 22: multiple "TWO"

115-E17
a. 5c orange on scarlet 3,250.
b. 10c carmine on scarlet 5,000.

115-E18

Design 23: multiple "5"s in oval rosettes

115-E18 5c black on carmine 3,250.

115-E19

Design 24: multiple "TEN 10"

115-E19
a. 5c
orange on scarlet 3,250.
carmine on scarlet 3,250.
b. 10c
carmine on scarlet 5,000.
orange red on scarlet 5,000.
blue on scarlet 5,000.
c. 30c
carmine on scarlet 3,500.
orange red on scarlet 3,500.
brown on scarlet 3,500.
blue on scarlet 3,500.

115-E20

Design 25: multiple "50"

115-E20 5c
black on black 3,250.
orange on black 3,250.

1870 ISSUE
Continental Banknote Co.

145-E1

Vignette of Washington in large ornate "1."

145-E1 One Cent
a. Die on India, die sunk on card
black 1,500.
scarlet 1,500.
green 1,500.
ultramarine 1,500.
blue 1,500.
b. On proof paper, about 25x30mm
black 1,000.
green 1,000.

146-E1

147-E1

Blank vignette in large ornate "2."

146-E1 2c Engraved die on India, die sunk on card
black 1,500.
scarlet 1,500.
ultramarine 1,500.
blue 1,500.
green 1,500.

Design size: 20x25mm

Die size: 43x48mm

Vignette of Lincoln in large ornate "3" with rounded top.

147-E1 3c Engraved die on proof paper
black 2,250.
scarlet 1,750.
ultramarine 1,750.
green 1,750.

147-E1A

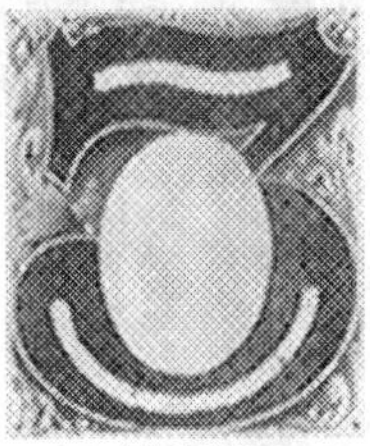

147-E1B

Design size: 11½x15½mm

Die size: 25x32mm

Vignette only of Columbia. Imprint and die number below design.

147-E1A 3c Engraved die on India, black —

Design size: 21x25mm

Blank vignette in frame of large ornate "3" with upper and lower labels not yet engraved.

147-E1B 3c Engraved die on India, die sunk on card
black 2,250.
green 2,000.

147-E1C

Design size: 21x25mm

No. 147-E1A cut to shape and mounted in frame of large ornate "3" with upper and lower labels not yet engraved.

147-E1C 3c Engraved die on India, die sunk on card
black 2,250.
green 2,000.

Design size: 21x25mm

Blank vignette in frame only as No. 147-E1B but with upper and lower labels engraved.

147-E2 3c Engraved die on India, die sunk on card
black 2,250.
green 2,000.

Vignette of Columbia mounted in place on No. 147-E2.

147-E3 3c Engraved die on India, die sunk on card
- black *2,250.*
- green *2,000.*

147-E4

Complete design with Columbia vignette in large ornate "3" surrounded by foliate ornamentation.

147-E4 3c Engraved die on India, die sunk on card
- black *2,250.*
- green *2,000.*

147-E5A

147-E5B

Design size: 22x27mm
Blank vignette in large ornate "3" without ornamentation.

147-E5A 3c Engraved die on India, die sunk on card backing, black *1,250.*

Design size: 22x27mm
Blank vignette in large ornate "3" surrounded by scrolled ornamentation.

147-E5B 3c Engraved die on India, die sunk on card
- black *2,250.*
- green *2,000.*

147-E6

Vignette of Columbia mounted in place on No. 147-E5B.

147-E6 3c Engraved die on India, die sunk on card
- black *2,250.*
- green *2,000.*

148-E1

Blank vignette in large ornate "6."

148-E1 6c
- ***a.*** Engraved die on India, die sunk on card
  - black *2,000.*
  - scarlet *2,000.*
  - green *2,000.*
  - dark green *2,000.*
  - ultramarine *2,000.*
- ***b.*** Engraved die on India, cut close
  - black *1,750.*
  - scarlet *1,750.*
  - blue *1,750.*
  - green *1,750.*

National Banknote Co.

145-E2

145-E3

Die size: 64x74mm
Engraved vignette of Franklin facing right.

145-E2 1c Die on India, die sunk on card
- black (with pencil lines on bust0 *700.*
- dull dark orange *700.*

Engraved incomplete Franklin vignette facing right mounted over pencil sketch of frame.

145-E3 1c Die on thin white card, 55x66mm, black *2,850.*

145-E4

145-E5

Incomplete Franklin vignette mounted on more complete pencil sketch of frame.

145-E4 1c Die on thin white card, orange brown *2,000.*

Design size: 20x26mm
Engraved vignette mounted on pencil and watercolor frame design.

145-E5 1c Die on thin white card, 45x51mm, dull dark orange *2,000.*

145-E6

Incomplete engraving of entire design; lower edge of bust vert. shading only.

145-E6 1c
- ***a.*** Die on 64x71mm India, die sunk on card
  - ultramarine *475.*
  - red *475.*
  - orange brown *475.*
  - red brown *475.*
  - blue green *475.*
  - mauve *475.*
  - dull lilac *475.*
  - black *475.*
  - gray *475.*
  - carmine *475.*
  - carmine rose *475.*
  - dull rose *475.*
  - dull yellow brown *475.*
  - brown violet *475.*
  - light green *475.*
  - green *475.*
  - gray olive *475.*
  - yellow *475.*
- ***b.*** Die on bond, die sunk on card, dark yellow *750.*

Completed die: additional shading lines in background, four horiz. shading lines at top of lower edge of bust.

145-E8 1c
- ***a.*** Die on India, die sunk on card
  - black *475.*
  - blue green *475.*
  - carmine *475.*
  - yellow *475.*
  - orange brown *475.*
  - orange *475.*
  - gray green *475.*
  - dull red violet *475.*
  - dark blue *475.*
- ***b.*** Die on white glazed paper, 65x72mm
  - black *425.*
  - black brown *425.*
  - scarlet *425.*
  - blue *425*
- ***c.*** Completed die on thick wove, dismal dusky yellow *425*

145-E9

145-E10

Die size: 50½x64mm
Engraved vignette of Franklin facing left, no shading lines at top of bust, etc.

145-E9 1c
- ***a.*** Die on white glazed paper, black *475.*
- ***b.*** Die on India, mounted on card stamped "J.I. PEASE.", black *450.*

Engraved Franklin vignette with 1 and value label.

145-E10 1c Die on India, on card (1873), black *2,000.*

May be essay for Official stamps.

146-E2

146-E3

Vignette size: 19½x25½mm
Die size: 62x76mm
Vignette only of Jackson in high stiff collar.

146-E2 2c Die on India, die sunk on card
- black *500.*
- orange brown *500.*

Engraved Jackson vignette mounted on watercolor frame.

146-E3 2c Die on thin white card, 46x89mm, black vignette, dark gray frame *2,500.*

146-E4

146-E5

Engraved Jackson vignette, mounted on watercolor frame (diff. from No. 146-E3).

146-E4 2c Die on thin white card, 46x89mm, black vignette, gray frame *2,500.*

Similar to No. 146-E4 but with pencil border around frame.

146-E5 2c Die on thin white card, 45x50mm, dark orange *2,500.*

Incomplete die; without shading lines under value ribbon, vert. lines in colorless strips, and broken horiz. lines at top and bottom of frame.

146-E6 2c Die on thin white card, dark orange *1,250.*

146-E7

Die size: 64½x73mm
Completed die of unadopted design.

146-E7 2c
- ***a.*** Die on India
  - carmine *650.*
  - deep rose *650.*
  - scarlet *650.*
  - dim dusky orange orange red *650.*
  - deep yellow orange *650.*

bone brown 650.
orange brown 650.
brown 650.
canary yellow 650.
yellow brown 650.
dark olive green 650.
green 650.
dim dusky blue green 650.
dark blue 650.
deep ultramarine 650.
bright blue 650.
dull violet 650.
smoky deep red violet red 650.
gray 650.
black 650.

b. Die on ivory paper, about 64x77mm
black 550.
brown black 550.
scarlet 550.
blue 550.

c. Die on thin wove, dark yellow 550.

146-E8

Die size: 62x76mm
Incomplete vignette of Jackson as on issued stamp: incomplete shading in eye and hair in front of ear, right neck tendon on chest not shaded.

146-E8 2c
a. Die on India, on 55x66mm card
black 600.
orange 600.
orange brown 600.
dark blue green 600.
red violet 600.

Also known on 87x143mm card showing full die sinkage, pencil inscribed "2c" above and "Jackson" below sinkage area. Value, *$750.*

b. Die on glazed paper, die sinkage 50x63mm, black 1,000.

Completed Jackson vignette.

146-E9 2c Die on glazed paper, black 550.

146-E10

146-E11

Engraved Jackson vignette with 2 and value label.

146-E10 2c Die on glazed paper (1873), black 1,000.

May be essay for Official stamps.

Engraved vignette with pencil and watercolor frame design, labels blank.

146-E11 2c Die on thin white card, 50x60mm, dim dusky bright blue green vignette, dark green frame 3,000.

146-E12

Die size: 62x75mm
Incomplete engraving of entire design: no leaves on wide bands at sides below vignette, neck tendon and hair in front of ear changed, top of head incomplete, ear hole too dark. This design essayed for envelopes on thick papers.

146-E12 2c Die on India, die sunk on card
carmine 550.
orange 550.
brown orange 550.

147-E7

Incomplete engraved vignette of Lincoln (horiz. line background), mounted on pencil and watercolor frame design.

147-E7 3c Die on thin white card, black vignette, gray black frame 3,500.

147-E8

147-E9

Design size: 20x25mm
Die Size: 62x72½mm
Incomplete engraving of head only of Washington.

147-E8 3c Die on white glazed paper, black 550.

Engraved Washington vignette only as adopted.

147-E9 3c Die on white glazed paper, black 650.

Nos. 147-E8 and 147-E9 may have been made from completed dies of No. 147 to produce Nos. 184-E9 and 184-E10.

147-E10

147-E11

Washington vignette, 3 and value label.

147-E10 3c Die on India, card mounted (1873), black 1,600.

May be essay for Official stamps.

Design size: 20x25½mm
Incomplete engraved vignette (horiz. lined background), mounted on pencil and watercolor frame design.

147-E11 3c Die on thin white card, 45x54mm, carmine vignette, dim light red violet red frame 5,000.

Incomplete engraving of entire design: no horizontal lines on nose, parts of hair, chin, collar, forehead unfinished.

147-E12 3c Die on India, die sunk on card
black 575.
deep red 575.
carmine 575.
yellow orange 575.
brown 575.
red brown 575.
dark red brown 575.
ultramarine 575.
dark blue 575.
dark violet blue 575.
blue green 575.
dark red violet 575.

Issued stamp, No. 147, in trial colors, underprinted network in fugitive ink.

147-E13 3c
a. On thick paper, perf. 12, gummed
gray blue, underprinting gray brown 150.
green, underprinting olive gray 150.
dim red, underprinting olive gray 150.
dull orange, underprinting olive gray 150.
brown, underprinting olive gray 150.

b. As "a," faint 6mm-high horiz. bar trial cancel
dim red 450.
dull orange 450.

c. As "a," underprinting omitted
gray blue —
dim red —
dull orange —
brown —

d. As "a," imperf, green, underprinting olive gray 325.
Pair 700.

e. As "d," underprinting omitted 325.
Pair 700.
P# block of 10 —

Multiples of the No. 147-E13 varieties can be found with fully or partially underprinted stamps in conjunction with underprinting-omitted stamps.

148-E2

148-E3

Design size: 19½x25½mm
Die size: 63x76mm
Engraved Lincoln vignette only, hair brushed back, horiz. line background.

148-E2 6c Die on India, die sunk on card
black 700.
blue 700.

Incomplete engraved Lincoln vignette (horiz. lined background) mounted on pencil and watercolor frame with blank labels.

148-E3 6c Die on thin white card, 45x52mm, dim blue vignette, dim dark blue frame 3,000.

148-E4

Incomplete engraving of entire design: horiz. line background in vignette, lines on cheek and hair unfinished.

148-E4 6c Die on India, on card, about 50x52mm
carmine 600.
rose 600.
dull rose 600.
red violet 600.
dull violet 600.
deep ultramarine 600.
dark black blue 600.
yellow 600.
green 600.
dark green 600.
dark red brown 600.
deep yellow brown 600.
yellow brown 600.
orange brown 600.

Incomplete engraving of entire design: horiz. line background in vignette, no shading directly under value label, shadows on "SIX CENTS" and shading on ornaments in upper corners unfinished.

148-E5 6c Die on India, on card, ultramarine 900.

Similar to No. 148-E5 but with diagonal lines added to vignette background. (Essay in orange brown has pencil notations for changes.)

148-E6 6c Die on India, die sunk on card
black 1,000.
dull carmine 1,000.
dark rose 1,000.
yellowish black 1,000.
brown 1,000.
gray brown 1,000.
black brown 1,000.
yellow 1,000.
gray olive green 1,000.
dark green 1,000.
ultramarine 1,000.
deep ultramarine 1,000.
dull ultramarine 1,000.
violet 1,000.
dark violet 1,000.
red violet 1,000.
orange brown 1,000.

Similar to No. 148-E6 but with dots added to top of hair.

148-E7 6c Die on India, on card
dark carmine 1,000.
dull rose 1,000.
orange 1,000.
yellow brown 1,000.
dark brown 1,000.
black brown 1,000.
yellow green 1,000.
blue green 1,000.
ultramarine 1,000.
dark red violet 1,000.

Completed die with lines on cheek softened to dots only.

148-E8 6c Die on India
- yellow green 250.
- brown 250.
- rose 250.

All known examples are much reduced.

Incomplete engraving of entire design, similar to No. 148-E10 but with hair brushed forward as on adopted design but shadow under hair in front of ear is round at bottom, not pointed as on approved design. Shading on cheek behind nostril is dotted instead of lined on completed design.

148-E9 6c Die on India, on card, red violet 750.

148-E10

Die size: 64x75mm
Frame as adopted, vignette similar to No. 148-E6 but with hair brushed back; lines on cheek.

148-E10 6c
- ***a.*** Die on India, die sunk on card, deep blue 850.
- ***b.*** Die on India, about 30x35mm, carmine 600.
- ***c.*** As "a," but no panels above top label, carmine 850.

Similar to No. 148-E10a but dots (not lines) on cheek and on lower lip. Shadow under hair in front of ear is rounded at bottom, not pointed as on approved design.

148-E11 6c Die on India, on card
- rose pink 700.
- deep rose 700.
- pale rose 700.
- brown rose 700.
- rose carmine 700.
- deep carmine 700.
- brown 700.
- yellow brown 700.
- blue 700.
- red violet 700.

Die of completed vignette only with hair brushed forward.

148-E12 6c Die on white glazed paper, black 1,500.

148-E13

Completed vignette with 6 and value label.

148-E13 6c Die on India, on card (1873), black 1,500.

May be essay for Official stamps.

149-E4

149-E4a

Die size: 62x75mm
Vignette of Stanton.

149-E4 7c Die on India, on card, black 1,000.

Engraved frame of adopted 30c design but with vignette cut out and mounted over Stanton vignette on India No. 149-E4.

149-E4a Stanton vignette with 30c frame on thin, stiff paper mounted on top, black 500.

The status of No. 149-E4a has been questioned.

149-E5

Die size: 62x76mm
Completed vignette with 7 and value label.

149-E5 7c
- ***a.*** Die on India, on card (1873), black 1,000.
- ***b.*** Die on white glazed paper, black 1,000.

May be essay for Official stamps.

149-E6

Design as issued but shading under ear incomplete.

149-E6 7c Die on India, die sunk on card
- black 500.
- dark red 500.
- light red 500.
- gray green 500.
- gray black 500.
- yellow brown 500.
- dark brown 500.
- dull yellow brown 500.
- dull red brown 500.
- blue green 500.
- ultramarine 500.
- dim blue 500.
- lilac 500.
- red orange 500.
- yellow orange 500.

Similar to No. 149-E6 but with dots added on forehead.

149-E7 7c Die on India, brown 1,000.

150-E1

150-E2

Design size: 20x25½mm
Incomplete engraved vignette of Jefferson (horiz. line background) mounted on pencil and watercolor frame design with blank labels.

150-E1 10c Die on thin white card, 45x51mm, black vignette, gray frame 3,000.

Design size: 19½x25½mm
Die size: 62x75mm
Jefferson vignette with incomplete engraving of frame: unfinished shading under "TEN" ribbon, under oval at ends of "U.S. POSTAGE," and under shield over ends of value label ribbons.

150-E2 10c Die on India, on card, deep blue green 2,500.

Similar to No. 150-E2 but showing horizontal shading lines only.

150-E2A 10c Die on India, die sunk on 152x225mm card
- blue green 750.
- red violet 750.

Completed engraving of unadopted design.

150-E3 10c
- ***a.*** Die on India, die sunk on card
  - carmine 650.
  - rose 650.
  - gray brown rose 650.
  - yellow 650.
  - yellow brown 650.
  - orange 650.
  - orange brown 650.
  - brown 650.
  - chocolate 650.
  - green 650.
  - blue green 650.
  - greenish gray 650.
  - blue 650.
  - dull violet 650.
  - dull red violet 650.
  - dark navy blue 650
  - ultramarine 650
  - deep ultramarine 650
  - dull dusky blue 650
  - navy blue 650
  - slate 650
- ***b.*** Die on bond
  - dull dusky brown 450
  - brown gray 450

All known examples of No. 153-E3b are reduced.

150-E4

150-E5

Three separate designs. Left one dark blue green, similar to No. 150-E3 but shows engraved attempt to remove coat collar to obtain nude neck (some coat still shows under chin). Middle one brown orange No. 150-E2 with coat collar and top of hair cut out, neck and bust drawn in. Right one black vignette of head finally adopted.

150-E4 10c Dies on India, on card 2,500.

Design size: 19½x25½mm
Same frame as No. 150-E2, but Jefferson vignette has hair arranged differently and bust has no clothing.

150-E5 10c
- ***a.*** Die on India, die sunk on card
  - black 600.
  - scarlet 600.
  - brown 600.
  - blue 600.
  - green 600.
- ***b.*** Die on glazed paper, 66x75mm
  - black 500.
  - black brown 500.
  - scarlet 500.
  - blue 500.
- ***c.*** Die on thin wove, dark yellow 500.

150-E6

150-E7

Frame of No. 150-E5 with vignette cut out and replaced by vignette as adopted.

150-E6 10c Die on India
- deep orange brown 850.
- black 850.

Die size: 62x76mm
Vignette of Jefferson as adopted.

150-E7 10c Die on India, die sunk on card
- dark ultramarine 700.
- yellow 700.
- brown 700.

151-E1

151-E2

Design size: 20x25½mm
Engraved vignette of Washington (No. 79-E37b) mounted on incomplete pencil drawing of frame design.

151-E1 12c Die on India, on 38x47½mm card, black vignette, pencil frame 2,500.

Design size: 20x25½mm
Engraved vignette of Washington (No. 79-E37b) mounted on pencil and watercolor frame design with blank labels.

151-E2 12c Die on card, 46x89mm, black vignette, gray frame 3,000.

151-E3

151-E4

Design size: 20x25½mm
Engraved vignette of Washington (No. 79-E37b) mounted on pencil and watercolor frame design with ribbons and blank labels.

151-E3 12c Die on card, 46x89mm, black vignette, gray frame *3,000.*

Design size: 20x25½mm
Engraved vignette of Washington (No. 79-E37b) mounted on pencil and watercolor frame design with "U, S, 12" and blank labels.

151-E4 12c Die on card, 46x89mm, black vignette, gray frame *3,000.*

151-E5

151-E6

Design size: 19½x25½mm
Die size: 62x74mm
Vignette of Henry Clay only.

151-E5 12c Die on India, die sunk on card
- black *600.*
- deep carmine *600.*
- yellow *600.*
- yellow brown *600.*
- brown orange *600.*
- dark orange brown *600.*
- black brown *600.*
- ultramarine *600.*
- dark blue green *600.*
- red violet *600.*

Incomplete Clay vignette mounted on watercolor shield-like frame design on gray background, pencil notation "background of stars to be gray."

151-E6 12c Die on card, 53x75mm, blue black vignette, blue frame *3,250.*

151-E7

Die sinkage size: 63x77mm
Completed die of unadopted design similar to No. 151-E6. This design essayed for envelopes on thick paper.

151-E7 12c
- ***a.*** Die on India, on card
  - deep orange brown *900.*
  - green *900.*
  - deep ultramarine *900.*
  - violet *900.*
  - deep red *900.*
  - deep orange red *900.*
  - dusky red *900.*
- ***b.*** Die on wove
  - carmine *700.*
  - orange *700.*
  - brown *700.*
  - orange brown *700.*
  - ultramarine *700.*
- ***c.*** Die on card colored yellow, black *700.*

Engraved vignette of Washington mounted on partly complete pencil drawing of frame, pencil notation "new border for clay 12c."

151-E8 12c Die on card, black, pencil frame *1,500.*

151-E9

151-E10

Die size: 55x63mm
Incomplete engraving of entire adopted design, without 3 vert. shading lines at left side of lower triangle.

151-E9 12c
- ***a.*** Die on India, die sunk on card
  - black *650.*
  - carmine *650.*
  - blue green *650.*
  - blue *650.*
  - light blue *650.*
  - orange *650.*
  - orange brown *650.*
  - dull red *650.*
  - brown red *650.*
- ***b.*** Die on proof paper, about 38x45mm
  - carmine *650.*
  - dull carmine *650.*
  - orange brown *650.*
  - dull red *650.*
  - ultramarine *650.*
- ***c.*** Die on India, on card, about 30x35mm, dark blue *650.*

Completed Clay vignette with 12 and value label.

151-E10 12c Die on white glazed paper (1873), black *1,250.*

May be essay for Official stamps.

152-E1

152-E2

Design size: 19½x25mm
Incomplete vignette of Webster with side whiskers bolder than as adopted, mounted on watercolor frame design with 15 and blank labels.

152-E1 15c Die on white card, 40x61mm, dim red vignette, light red violet frame *2,250.*

Design size: 19½x25mm
Die size: 63x76mm
Incomplete engraving of vignette only: missing shading under ear and at back of neck.

152-E2 15c Die on India, die sunk on card, black *750.*

152-E3

152-E4

Vignette similar to No. 152-E2 but with shading under ear, more shading at back of neck.

152-E3 15c Die on India, die sunk on card
- black *700.*
- dark orange *700.*
- orange *700.*
- yellow *700.*
- red violet *700.*
- ultramarine *700.*
- brown *700.*

Vignette of Webster with 15 below.

152-E4 15c Die on white glazed paper (1873), black *1,000.*

May be essay for Official stamps.

152-E5

Incomplete engraved design: shading on corner panel bevels incomplete, side whiskers bolder than as adopted. Also essayed for envelopes on thick paper.

152-E5 15c Die on India, die sunk on card, orange brown *750.*

Similar to No. 152-E5 but with pencil marks suggesting shading on corner panels.

152-E6 15c Die on India, orange brown *750.*

Similar to No. 152-E5 with engraved shading added to corner panels but white areas incomplete.

152-E7 15c Die on India
- orange *650.*
- orange yellow *650.*
- orange brown *650.*
- green *650.*
- red violet *650.*
- rose carmine *650.*

Similar to No. 152-E7 but shading on corner panels complete.

152-E8 15c Die on India, on card, black *1,000.*

153-E1

153-E2

Design size: 18x23mm
Incomplete engraved vignette of Scott mounted on pencil sketch of partial frame design.

153-E1 24c Die on white card, 33x39mm, dull red violet vignette, pencil frame *1,750.*

Design size: 19½x25mm
Complete engraved vignette mounted on pencil and watercolor frame design with "U.S. POSTAGE" in ink.

153-E2 24c Die on white card, 73x110mm, dim blue green *3,250.*

153-E3

153-E4

Die size: 62x76mm
Incomplete engraved vignette only.

153-E3 24c Die on India, die sunk on card
- black *600.*
- yellow *600.*
- yellow brown *600.*
- dark orange brown *600.*
- ultramarine *600.*
- dark ultramarine *600.*
- red violet *600.*

Die size: 62x77mm
Incomplete design as adopted: upper corners not squared outside scrolls, no periods after U and S in stars.

153-E4 24c Die on India, die sunk on card
- carmine *650.*
- orange *650.*
- brown orange *650.*
- yellow brown *650.*
- deep brown *650.*
- ultramarine *650.*
- dark red violet *650.*
- green *650.*

Value off card, cut down, $275.

Previous No. 154-E1 is now No. 149-E4a.

154-E2

Pencil drawing of entire design, labeled "Scott."

154-E2 30c Pencil drawing on white card, 53x92mm *2,000.*

Engraved vignette of Hamilton mounted on pencil drawing of frame.

154-E3 30c Die on card, yellow brown vignette, pencil frame *1,500.*

154-E4

Incomplete engraved vignette of Hamilton.

154-E4 30c Die on India, die sunk on card
yellow brown *700.*
dark ultramarine blue *700.*
orange *700.*

Vignette of Hamilton with more engraving on forehead, nose, neck, etc.

154-E5 30c Die on India, die sunk on card
dark red brown *700.*
dull carmine *700.*
ultramarine *700.*

154-E6

Completed vignette with 30 below.

154-E6 30c Die on white glazed paper (1873), black *1,250.*

May be essay for Official stamps.

155-E1

155-E2

Pencil drawing of entire design, labeled "Perry."

155-E1 90c Pencil drawing on white card, 53x92mm *2,000.*

Design size: 19½x25mm
Engraved vignette of Perry mounted on pencil and watercolor frame design.

155-E2 90c Die on white card, 73x110mm, dull dark violet vignette, dull red violet frame *3,250.*

155-E3

Die size: 58x79mm

Incomplete engraving of Perry vignette as adopted.

155-E3 90c
a. Die on India, die sunk on card
deep yellow orange *600.*
orange brown *600.*
dark brown *600.*
dull carmine *600.*
ultramarine blue *600.*
dark blue green *600.*
dark red violet *600.*
b. Die on white ivory paper, black *600.*

Similar to No. 155-E3 but more lines in hair above forehead.

155-E4 90c Die on India, on card, black *500.*

155-E5

Incomplete engraving of design as adopted: rope above vignette unfinished. Also essayed for envelopes on thick paper.

155-E5 90c Die on India, die sunk on card
black *750.*
carmine, off card *325.*
orange *750.*
dark orange *750.*
yellow brown *750.*
brown *750.*
deep orange brown *750.*
deep ultramarine *750.*
blue green *750.*
red violet *750.*

Value off card, cut down, $250.

1873 ISSUE
Continental Bank Note Co.

179-E1

179-E2

Die size: 20x25mm
Vignette of Taylor by Bureau of Engraving and Printing, in engraved frame.

179-E1 Five Cents, Die on India
black *3,000.*
blue *3,000.*

Design size: 24x29mm
Vignette of Taylor by Bureau of Engraving and Printing, in ornate wash drawing of frame ("FIVE CENTS" black, on shaded ribbon).

179-E2 5c Die on card, black *4,000.*

Incomplete vignette: hair, coat, background, etc., unfinished.

179-E3 5c Die on India, violet *2,000.*

George W. Bowlsby 1873 essay similar in concept to his No. 63-E13 but without coupon attached. It consisted of an unused 1c stamp (No. 156) with horiz. sewing machine perfs. through center, gummed on upper half only, as described in his Dec. 26, 1865 patent. Stamp was meant to be torn in half by postal clerk as cancellation, to prevent reuse.

156-E1 1c blue *250.*

1876 Experimental Ink and Paper Essays

Plate designs of 1873-75 issues in normal colors, printe on paper tinted with sensitive inks and on heavily lai (horiz.) colored papers (unless otherwise noted).

156-E2 1c Blue on:
carmine *150*
pale rose *150*
deep yellow *150*
pale violet *150*

158-E1 3c Green on:
pale rose *150.*
deep yellow *150.*
pale violet *150.*

158-E2 3c Green on paper covered with pink varnish which vanishes with the color *100.*

158-E3 3c Green on thick white blotting paper which absorbs canceling ink *100.*

161-E1 10c Brown on:
pale rose *150.*
deep yellow *150.*
pale violet *150.*

163-E1 15c Yellow orange on:
pale rose *200.*
deep yellow *200.*
pale violet *200.*

165-E1 30c Gray black on:
pale rose *200.*
deep yellow *200.*
pale violet *200.*

166-E1 90c Rose carmine on:
pale rose *200.*
deep yellow *200.*
pale violet *200.*

178-E1 2c Vermilion on:
pale rose *150.*
deep yellow *150.*
pale violet *150.*

179-E4 5c Blue on:
pale rose *300.*
deep yellow *300.*
pale violet *300.*

See No. 147-E13.

1877 Essays
Philadelphia Bank Note Co.

Die essays for this section were all engraved. The frame-only dies for all values of this series were engraved with two values appearing per die, except the 3c (No. 184-E1) which was engraved alone. In each case the listing is under the lower denomination. The Washington vignette associated with each value of the frames is from engraved master die No. 14. (No. 182-E1).

Except as noted, plate essays in this section are all lithographed from a composite stone plate of two panes. The left pane ("plate 1") consists of horiz. rows of four of the 1c, 3c, 7c, 24c and 90c. The right pane ("plate 2") consists of horiz. rows of four 2c, 6c, 12c and 30c. "Printed by Philadelphia Bank Note Co. Patented June 16, 1876" imprint below 2nd and 3rd designs on each row.

See note above No. 63-E1.

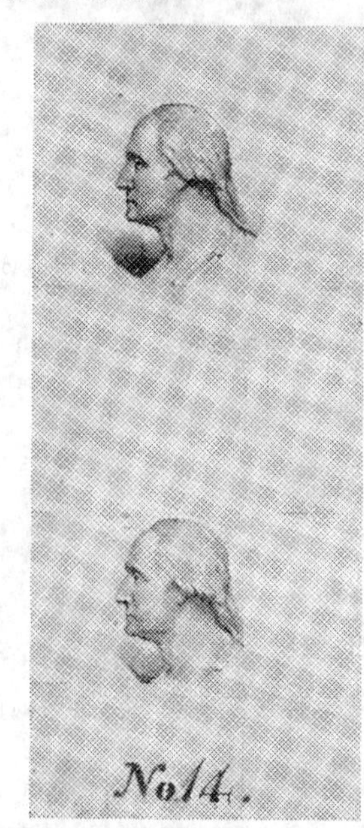

182-E1

Vignette master die "No. 14": two slightly diff. vignettes of Washington, one above the other, bottom one with truncated queue, bust and shading in front of neck.

182-E1

a. Die on old white glazed paper, black 500.

b. Die on proof paper (1903)
black 100.
carmine 100.
dull carmine 100.
dusky carmine 100.
yellow 100.
dull scarlet 100.
dull orange 100.
brown orange 100.
brown 100.
gray olive 100.
blue green 100.
dark green 100.
black blue 100.
ultramarine 100.
violet 100.
red violet 100.

182-E2

Design size: 20x25mm
Die size: 98x53mm
Frames of 1c and 2c side by side.

182-E2 1c + 2c

a. Die on white pelure
dark carmine 250.
orange 250.
brown 250.
blue green 250.
blue 250.

b. Die with vertical line between designs (die size 85x54mm), on India, die sunk on card
dusky red 400.
deep orange 400.
orange brown 400.
dark green 400.
dark blue 400.

c. Die on stiff glazed paper, black 400.

d. Die on proof paper, printed through a mat (1903)
black 100.
bright carmine 100.
dull carmine 100.
dim scarlet 100.
dark orange 100.
dull yellow 100.
dark orange brown 100.
black olive 100.
dark blue green 100.
dark blue 100.
ultramarine 100.
dark navy blue 100.
blue violet 100.
dull violet 100.
red violet 100.

e. Plate sheet of 1c, 2c, 3c, 12c, 24c, 30c, 90c frames only, on card, pale green blue 1,500.

182-E3

Complete 1c design, lithographed.

182-E3 1c

a. Plate on stamp paper, imperf., gummed
black 75.
blue green 75.
bright ultramarine 75.
yellow 75.

b. Plate on stamp paper, perf. 12, gummed
dark red orange 50.
orange brown 50.
red brown 50.
red violet 50.
violet blue 50.
ultramarine 50.

c. Plate 1 "sheet" of 20, complete designs, without imprint, on old glazed paper, imperf., deep brown orange 800.

d. As "c," with imprint, on old glazed paper, imperf., gummed
dull deep violet red 800.
ultramarine 800.
scarlet 800.
orange 800.
carmine 800.
dark carmine 800.
green 800.
bluish green 800.

e. As "d," perf. 12, gummed
dull deep violet red 700.
ultramarine 700.
red brown 700.
violet blue 700.

Concerning plate 1 sheets of 20, note that composite stone plates also contained the plate 2 sheets of 20 listed as Nos. 183-E2c to 183-E2e. Many such composite sheets remain intact. All separated plate 1 or plate 2 sheets originally were part of a composite sheet.

183-E2b

Complete 2c design, lithographed.

183-E2 2c

a. Plate on stamp paper, imperf.
blue green 60.
bright ultramarine 60.
brown 60.

b. Plate on stamp paper, perf. 12, gummed
bright red orange 35.
dull red orange 35.
dark red orange 35.
red brown 35.
dark red brown 35.
dark orange brown 35.
yellow brown 35.
dull yellow green 35.
green 35.
dull ultramarine 35.
bright ultramarine 35.
blue violet 35.
red violet 35.
light red violet 35.
violet red 35.

c. Plate 2 "sheet" of 16, complete designs, without imprint, on old glazed paper, imperf., deep brown orange 600.

d. As "c," with imprint, on old glazed paper, imperf., gummed, dull deep violet red 600.

e. As "d," perf. 12, gummed, dull deep violet red 500.

See note following No. 182-E3e.

Design size: 20x25mm
Die size: 54x55mm
Engraved frame of 3c alone on die.

184-E1 3c

a. Die on pelure paper
dark carmine 250.
dark orange 250.
orange brown 250.
bright blue 250.
bright blue 250.
green 250.
dark green 250.

b. Die on proof paper (1903)
black 100.
bright carmine 100.
dull carmine 100.
dim scarlet 100.
dark orange 100.
dull yellow 100.
dark orange brown 100.
black olive 100.
dark rose 100.
green 100.
yellow green 100.
dark blue green 100.
dark blue 100.
deep ultramarine 100.
dark navy blue 100.
blue violet 100.
dull violet 100.
red violet 100.

Built-up model of engraved frame cut to shape inside and out, mounted atop engraved vignette of the same color. Warning: fraudulent models combining engraved and lithographed materials exist.

184-E2 3c

a. Die on proof paper, cut close
dark scarlet 250.
blue green 250.
deep blue 250.

b. Four examples mounted 2½mm apart on stiff white card, 80x87mm
red 1,000.
orange brown 1,000.
green 1,000.
blue 1,000.
violet 1,000.
green frame, light blue vignette 1,000.

Built-up model as No. 184-E2, vignette as No. 184-E5 with dark background.

184-E3 3c Die on proof paper, scarlet 250.

184-E4

Complete 3c design, vignette with light background.

184-E4 3c

c. Plate lithographed on stamp paper, imperf.
black 75.
green 75.
dark green 75.
bright ultramarine 75.
orange 75.

No. 184-E4c exists in two plates of 9 tete-beche, in diff. colors, on same piece of paper. Value, $800 sheet of 18.

d. Plate lithographed on stamp paper, perf. 12, gummed
dark red orange 50.
red brown 50.
red voilet 50.
brown orange 50.
ultramarine 50.
violet blue 50.

e. Plate sheet of 9 (3x3), imprint below, on stiff white wove
carmine 300.
blue green 300.

f. Plate sheet of 9 (3x3), on glazed thin wove
carmine 300.
blue green 300.
blue 300.
orange 300.

g. Plate sheet of 9 (3x3), on yellowish wove
carmine 300.
blue green 300.
blue 300.

h. Die of complete design on old stiff glazed paper (die size: 55x66mm), black 350.

i. Complete die on glazed wove
deep carmine 200.
scarlet 200.
ultramarine 200.

j. Complete die on India, light orange red 200.

k. Complete die on proof paper (1903)
black 75.
bright carmine 75.
dull carmine 75.
dim scarlet 75.
dark orange 75.
dull yellow 75.
dark orange brown 75.
black olive 75.
green 75.
dark blue green 75.
deep ultramarine 75.
dark navy blue 75.
blue violet 75.
dull violet 75.
red violet 75.

l. Complete die on large colored card (1903)
black, *light green* 150.
deep scarlet, *ivory* 150.
red violet, *light blue* 150.
carmine, *pink* 150.

184-E5

Design size: 19x24½mm
Die No. 1 size: about 63x94mm Vignette of Washington slightly diff. from rest of series but with quite diff. frame design.

184-E5 3c

a. Die on glazed paper, about 50x75mm, black 350.

b. Die on proof paper (with and without printing through mats) (1903)
black 100.
dark carmine 100.
carmine 100.
bright carmine 100.
brown 100.
red brown 100.
yellow 100.
orange 100.
violet 100.
red violet 100.

violet brown 100.
blue 100.
steel blue 100.
light green 100.
dark green 100.
dull olive 100.

c. Die on colored card, 61x93mm (1903)
scarlet, *yellow* 150.
olive gray, *pale pink* 150.
dull violet, *buff* 150.

Plate proofs printed in sheets of 25 (plate size: 140x164mm). A horiz. crack extends through upper 3s from 2mm back of head on position 11 to vignette on position 12.

All plate essay items valued as singles except No. 184-E5d.

d. Engraved plate of 25 on India, mounted on large card, red brown 750.

e. Plate on proof paper (1903)
black 15.
blue black 15.
greenish black 15.
dull red violet 15.
dark red violet 15.
dull violet 15.
violet brown 15.
light red brown 15.
orange brown 15.
brown carmine 15.
brown 15.
dim orange 15.
yellow 15.
dull yellow 15.
carmine 15.
light carmine 15.
dark carmine 15.
dull carmine 15.
dull scarlet 15.
dark green 15.
light green 15.
dull olive green 15.
deep ultramarine 15.

f. Plate on proof paper, perf. 12, lithographed
carmine 100.
rose lilac 100.
red orange 100.

g. Plate on green bond, "Crane & Co. 1887" wmk. (1903)
black 25.
carmine 25.
dull carmine 25.
scarlet 25.
brown 25.
brown red 25.
orange brown 25.
red violet 25.
yellow 25.
orange 25.
dark green 25.
light green 25.
yellow green 25.
deep ultramarine 25.
dark navy blue 25.

h. Plate (printed before plate crack developed) on semiglazed yellowish wove, laid watermark
carmine 30.
dull red 30.
bright orange red 30.
deep orange red 30.
scarlet 30.
deep orange 30.
yellow orange 30.
orange brown 30.
orange yellow 30.
dark yellow green 30.
dusky blue green 30.
dull green blue 30.
violet blue 30.
red violet 30.
black 30.

i. Plate in sheets of 100 with imprint on yellowish glazed chemically prepared wove, lithographed
black 20.
brown 20.
scarlet 20.
light red 20.
rose pink 20.
carmine 20.
deep carmine 20.
violet rose 20.
deep violet rose 20.
violet red 20.
red violet 20.
violet 20.
blue 20.
pale blue 20.
pale dull blue 20.
yellow 20.
dull brown yellow 20.
orange 20.
red orange 20.

184-E6

Illustration with card margins reduced.

Similar to No. 184-E1 but engraved vignette of Lincoln on India facing ¾ to right. Each design has vignette attached to frame from behind.

184-E6 3c Four copies mounted on 80x89mm card to resemble block of 4
blue 3,500.
green 3,500.

Frame of No. 184-E5 with engraved vignette of Lincoln mounted in place.

184-E7 3c Die on card, brown —

There is some doubt whether No. 184-E7 exists as a genuine essay. The editors would like to see authenticated evidence of its existence.

Design size: 20x25mm
Die size: 92x50mm
Frames of 6c and 7c side by side (6c at right).

186-E1 6c + 7c

a. Die on white pelure, orange 375.

b. Die on proof paper, printed through a mat (1903)
black 100.
bright carmine 100.
dull carmine 100.
dim scarlet 100.
dark orange 100.
dull yellow 100.
dark orange brown 100.
black olive 100.
green 100.
dark blue green 100.
dark blue 100.
deep ultramarine 100.
dark navy blue 100.
blue violet 100.
dull violet 100.
red violet 100.

c. Die on white pelure, both 7s reversed on 7c frame, orange 750.

d. Die on old stiff glazed, black 400.

186-E2

Complete 6c design, lithographed.

186-E2 6c

a. Plate on stamp paper, perf. 12, gummed
bright red orange 35.
dull red orange 35.
dark red orange 35.
red brown 35.
dark red brown 35.
dark orange brown 35.
yellow brown 35.
dull yellow green 35.
green 35.
dull ultramarine 35.
bright ultramarine 35.
blue violet 35.
red violet 35.
light violet red 35.
violet red 35.

b. Plate on stamp paper, gummed
ultramarine 60.
lilac 60.
scarlet 60.
orange 60.
carmine 60.
dark carmine 60.
blue green 60.

186a-E2

Complete 7c design, lithographed.

186a-E2 7c

a. Plate on stamp paper, imperf.
black 75.
carmine 75.
red orange 75.
yellow orange 75.
green 75.
dark green 75.
dark blue 75.

b. Plate on stamp paper, perf. 12, gummed
red brown 50.
dark red orange 50.
brown orange 50.
red violet 50.
ultramarine 50.
violet blue 50.

Design size: 20x25mm
Die size: 78½x64mm
Frames of 12c and 24c side by side (12c on right).

188a-E1 12c + 24c

a. Die on white pelure
deep carmine 300.
brown orange 300.
orange brown 300.
blue green 300.
blue 300.

b. Die on proof paper, printed through a mat (1903)
black 100.
bright carmine 100.
dull carmine 100.
dim scarlet 100.
dark orange 100.
dull yellow 100.
dark orange brown 100.
black olive 100.
green 100.
dark blue green 100.
dark blue 100.
deep ultramarine 100.
dark navy blue 100.
blue violet 100.
dull violet 100.
red violet 100.

c. Die on old stiff glazed, black 400.

188a-E2

Complete 12c design, lithographed.

188a-E2 12c

a. Plate on stamp paper, perf. 12, gummed
bright red orange 35.
dull red orange 35.
dark red orange 35.
red brown 35.
dark red brown 35.
dark orange brown 35.
yellow brown 35.
dull yellow green 35.
green 35.
dull ultramarine 35.
bright ultramarine 35.
blue violet 35.
red violet 35.
light red violet 35.
violet red 35.

b. Plate on stamp paper, gummed
ultramarine 60.
lilac 60.
scarlet 60.
orange 60.
carmine 60.
dark carmine 60.
blue green 60.

189a-E2

Complete 24c design, lithographed.

189a-E2 24c
a. Plate on stamp paper, perf. 12, gummed
red brown 50.
dark red orange 50.
brown orange 50.
ultramarine 50.
violet blue 50.
red violet 50.
b. Plate on stamp paper, gummed
ultramarine 75.
lilac 75.
scarlet 75.
orange 75.
carmine 75.
dark carmine 75.
green 75.

Design size: 20x25mm
Die size: 79x64mm
Frames of 30c and 90c side by side.

190-E1 30c + 90c
a. Die on white pelure
dark carmine 300.
dark red orange 300.
dark orange brown 300.
brown 300.
blue green 300.
bright blue 300.
b. Die on stiff glazed paper, blue black 500.
c. Die on proof paper, printed through a mat (1903)
black 100.
bright carmine 100.
dull carmine 100.
dim scarlet 100.
dark orange 100.
dull yellow 100.
dark orange brown 100.
black olive 100.
green 100.
dark blue green 100.
dark blue 100.
deep ultramarine 100.
dark navy blue 100.
blue violet 100.
dull violet 100.
red violet 100.

190-E2

191-E2

Complete 30c design, lithographed.

190-E2 30c
a. Plate on stamp paper, perf. 12, gummed
bright red orange 35.
dull red orange 35.
dark red orange 35.
red brown 35.
dark red brown 35.
dark orange brown 35.
yellow brown 35.
dull yellow green 35.
green 35.
dull ultramarine 35.
bright ultramarine 35.
blue violet 35.
red violet 35.
light red violet 35.
violet red 35.
b. Plate on stamp paper, gummed
ultramarine 60.
lilac 60.
scarlet 60.
orange 60.
carmine 60.
dark carmine 60.
blue green 60.

Complete 90c design, lithographed.

191-E2 90c
a. Plate on stamp paper, perf. 12, gummed
black 50.
red brown 50.
dark red orange 50.
brown orange 50.
ultramarine 50.
violet blue 50.
red violet 50.
violet red 50.
dark blue green 50.
orange brown 50.
b. Plate on stamp paper, gummed
ultramarine 75.
lilac 75.
scarlet 75.
orange 75.
carmine 75.
dark carmine 75.
green 75.

1879 Coupon Essay
Azariah B. Harris

184-E8

Size of coupon design: 25x7½mm
A proposed $300 30-year Postal Revenue Bond with 3.65% interest. Daily coupons 3c each, "Receivable for Postage in all parts of the U.S>" after date thereon. Entire bond contained six pages of coupons with 16 rows of four (one for each day of two months); 20% bear month and day, others blank.

184-E8 3c
a. Coupon on bond (dated Jan. or Feb.), imperf., black 350.
b. Engraved die on old ivory paper (undated), black 900.
c. Single coupon on bond (dated), perf. 12, gummed, blue green 125.
d. Single coupon on bond (undated), perf. 12, gummed, blue green 50.

Continental Bank Note Co.

182-E4

Design size: 18x22mm
Die size: 59x67mm
Engraved vignette of Franklin on white background in unadopted frame.

182-E4 1c
a. Die on India, blue 575.
b. Die on proof paper
black 500.
dull scarlet 500.
dull brown 500.
dull green 500.
dull blue 500.
c. Die on white glazed paper
black 750.
black brown 750.
scarlet 750.
blue 750.

All known examples of "b" have reduced margins.

184-E9

184-E10

Die size: 61½x76½mm
Vignette of Washington on white background in incomplete frame as adopted: no veins in trifoliate ornaments in upper corners.

184-E9 3c Die on India, on card
black 750.
green 750.

Similar to No. 184-E9 but completed frame with veins in trifoliate ornaments.

184-E10 3c
a. Die on India, die sunk on card, green 750.
b. Die on proof paper, about 35x40mm
gray black 350.
dull red 350.
dull blue 350.
dull green 350.
dull brown 350.
c. Die on white glazed paper
black 600.
black brown 600.
scarlet 600.
blue 600.

Nos. 147-E8 and 147-E9 may have been made from completed dies of No. 147 to produce Nos. 184-E9 and 184-E10.

184-E11

184-E12

Design size: 17½x21½mm
Die size: 60x75mm
Complete unadopted design with vignette of Liberty on white background.

184-E11 Three Cents
a. Die on India
black 350.
brown red 350.
orange 350.
green 350.
blue 350.
scarlet 350.
b. Die on proof paper
brown 350.
green 350.
gray black 350.
dull red 350.
dull blue 350.
c. Die on white glazed paper
black 750.
black brown 750.
scarlet 750.
blue 750.

All known examples of Nos. 184-E11a, 184-E11b have reduced margins.

Design size: 19½x24½mm
Die size: 61x71mm
Complete unadopted design with vignette of Washington on white background in frame similar to No. 184-E11 but with numerals of value.

184-E12 3c
a. Die on India, die sunk on card
black 650.
dull scarlet 650.
brown 650.
green 650.
b. Die on white glazed paper
black 500.
black brown 500.
scarlet 500.
blue 500.
c. Plate on India (some adhering to original card backing), imperf.
black 100.
scarlet 100.
orange red 100.
green 100.
d. Plate on white paper, perf. 12, gummed
black 75.
green 75.
blue 75.
brown 75.
red brown 75.
orange 75.
dull scarlet 75.
orange brown 75.
e. Plate on Francis Patent bluish chemical paper, perf. 12, gummed
black 150.
scarlet 150.
red brown 150.
brown 150.
yellow 150.
green 150.
gray 150.
f. Plate on brown chemical paper, perf. 12, gummed
blue 150.
ultramarine 150.
g. Hybrid die on India, mounted on India, block sunk on card, green 400.

184-E13

184-E14

Design size: 18x22mm
Die size: about 61x62mm

Similar to No. 184-E12 but slightly different frame.

184-E13 3c
a. Die on India, die sunk on card
black *650.*
scarlet *650.*
green *650.*
blue *650.*
black brown *650.*
blue green *650.*
b. Die on white glazed paper
black *750.*
black brown *750.*
scarlet *750.*
blue *750.*
c. Plate on India, imperf.
black *100.*
deep scarlet *100.*
green *100.*
dark green *100.*
dark yellow brown *100.*
olive brown *100.*
violet brown *100.*
orange *100.*
d. Plate on stamp paper, perf. 12, gummed
black *75.*
dull scarlet *75.*
blue green *75.*
brown *75.*
red brown *75.*
dull blue *75.*
dark blue *75.*
orange *75.*
yellow *75.*
yellow brown *75.*
gray *75.*

Design size: 19x24½mm
Die size: about 67x71mm
Similar to No. 184-E13 but value label with "THREE" above "CENTS."

184-E14 3c
a. Hybrid die on India mounted on India, block sunk on card
brown red *400.*
green *400.*
b. Die on white glazed paper
black *500.*
black brown *500.*
scarlet *500.*
blue *500.*
c. Die on proof paper, about 35x35mm
black *300.*
dull scarlet *300.*
dull brown *300.*
dull green *300.*
dull blue *300.*
brown red *300.*
red brown *300.*

184-E15

184-E16

Design size: 20x25½mm
Die size: 60x73mm
Vignette of Indian maiden in headdress, "PORTAGE" error in top label.

184-E15 3c
a. Hybrid die on India, cut close, mounted on India, block sunk on card
black *900.*
dark green *900.*
b. Die on proof paper, about 28x35mm
black *600.*
dull scarlet *500.*
dull brown *500.*
dull blue *500.*
dull green *500.*
c. Die on white glazed paper
black *750.*
black brown *750.*
scarlet *750.*
blue *750.*
d. Die on India, scarlet —

Similar to No. 184-E15 but with spelling corrected to "POSTAGE."

184-E16 3c Die on India, cut close, mounted on India, block sunk on card
black *1,250.*
blue *1,250.*
steel blue *1,250.*
carmine *1,250.*
scarlet *1,250.*
brown *1,250.*
dark green *1,250.*

190-E3

Die size: 44½x71½mm
Vignette of Hamilton on white background in frame as adopted.

190-E3 30c
a. Die on proof paper, about 35x48mm
gray black *500.*
dull red *500.*
dull green *500.*
dull brown *500.*
dull blue *500.*
b. Die on white glazed paper
black *750.*
black brown *750.*
scarlet *750.*
blue *750.*

American Bank Note Co.

184-E17

Design size: 22x30mm
Silver photo print of engraved vignette of Washington mounted on pencil and ink frame design.

184-E17 3c
a. Die on white card, 38x49mm
light brown vignette, black frame *1,250.*
b. Die on white card, 38x50mm
light brown vignette, black frame *1,250.*

Frame ornaments extend beyond framelines, lettering less complete than on No. 184-E17a.

1881-82 ISSUE
American Bank Note Co.

Design size: 20x25mm
Die size: 59x74mm
Vignette of Garfield in lined oval.

205-E1 5c Die on India, die sunk on card, black *500.*

205-E2

205-E3

Die No. C-47 size: 70x83mm
Vignette of Garfield in beaded oval, in plain border of horiz. lines. Found with and without imprint and die number.

205-E2 5c Die on India, die sunk on card
gray brown *250.*
gray black *250.*

No. 205-E2 may not be a stamp essay.

Die size: 78x78mm
Vignette of Garfield in beaded oval with cutout at bottom for top of star.

205-E3 5c
a. Die on India, die sunk on card
black *750.*
deep red orange *750.*
red brown *750.*
blue *750.*
green *750.*
b. Die on white glazed paper
black *750.*
green *750.*
blue *750.*
scarlet *750.*
red brown *750.*
c. Negative impression, solid color outside design, die on India, bright red orange *1,000.*

Vignette of Garfield as No. 205-E1 in lined oval and finished frame as adopted.

205-E4 5c Die on India, 24x30mm, black *900.*

206-E1

206-E2

Design size: 21x26mm
Engraved frame of unadopted design.

206-E1 1c
a. Die on white glazed paper, 42x74mm, black *1,000.*
b. Die on surface-tinted glazed paper, cut close
green, *buff* *600.*
black, *orange* *600.*
brown orange, *blue* *600.*

Engraved frame almost identical to No. 206-E1 with small typographed vignette of Peace.

206-E2 1c Die on blue surface-tinted ivory paper, cut close, buff vignette, carmine frame *800.*

Vignette of Peace only.

206-E3 1c
a. Engraved vignette
black *350.*
dull red violet *350.*
b. Typographed vignette *350.*

206-E4

Engraved frame (No. 206-E1) with typographed vignette of Lincoln mounted on it. Four diff. colors (dull carmine, dull scarlet, dark brown, green) on cream white ivory paper, 22x27mm each, mounted together on 92x114mm thick white card, ms. "American Bank Note Co. N.Y." at lower right.

206-E4 1c Four designs on cream white ivory on card *2,500.*

Design size: 18x23½mm
Typographed vignette of Lincoln only.

206-E5 1c Die on white ivory paper
dull carmine *400.*
dark yellowish brown *400.*
dull purple *400.*
dull dark blue *400.*
orange *400.*

206-E6

Incomplete engraving of complete design as issued: no shading in upper arabesques.

206-E6 1c
a. Die on India
gray blue *750.*
green blue *750.*
b. Die on India, cut close, on India block sunk on card, deep gray blue *350.*

207-E1

207-E2

Design size: 20½x25½mm
Die size: 49x54½mm
Engraved unadopted frame design with 3's at sides and large 3 at top.

207-E1 3c
a. Die on India
yellow brown 750.
dull brown 750.
dull blue 750.
green 750.
b. Die on white glazed paper, 32x38mm
black 650.
dull dark yellow 650.
c. Die on surface-tinted ivory paper, cut close
black, *orange* 500.
green, *buff* 500.
violet blue, *orange* 500.

Engraved frame as No. 207-E1, with typographed vignette of Peace.

207-E2 3c Die on blue surface-tinted ivory paper, cut close, buff vignette, carmine frame 850.

Engraved frame (No. 207-E1) with typographed vignette of Peace mounted on it. Four diff. color combinations (orange red vignette, dull carmine frame; dull carmine vignette, dull red brown frame; yellow brown vignette and frame; blue green vignette and frame) on cream white ivory paper, 22x27mm each, mounted together on 92x114mm thick white card, ms. "American Bank Note Co. N.Y." at lower right.

207-E3 3c 4 designs on cream white ivory on card 2,500.

208-E1

Incomplete engraving of design as adopted: unfinished shading on top label and bottom ribbon, four lines between frame sinkage at right and left edges, horiz. line at bottom.

208-E1 6c Die on India, on card, black 1,500.

This is a new die engraved by the Bureau of Engraving & Printing for "Roosevelt" proof albums.

209-E1

Design size: 20x25mm
Die size: 58x76mm
Engraving of unadopted frame only, no horiz. lines in background.

209-E1 10c Die on thick white card, about 25x33mm
blue 800.
green 800.

Similar to No. 209-E1 but with horiz. lines added to background.

209-E2 10c
a. Die on thick white card
black 700.
red 700.
green 700.
blue 700.
b. Die on India, on 50x70mm card, black 800.
c. Die on white glazed paper, black 800.

209-E3

Engraved frame similar to No. 209-E2 with typographed vignette of Peace.

209-E3 10c
a. Die on blue surface-tinted glazed paper, cut close, buff vignette, carmine frame 650.
b. Die on orange surface-tinted glazed paper
dull carmine vignette, violet frame 650.
dull yellow vignette, violet frame 650.
yellow vignette, green frame 650.

209-E4

209-E5

Vignette diameter: 17mm
Engraved Franklin vignette.

209-E4 10c
a. Die on India
black 575.
dusky carmine 575.
dull scarlet 575.
dim orange 575.
orange brown 575.
yellow green 575.
dim blue green 575.
deep blue 575.
red brown on blue ground 575.
dark red violet 575.
b. Die sunk on glazed paper, approx. 51x69mm
dusky carmine 775.
dim scarlet 775.
dim orange 775.
deep blue 775.
dim blue green 775.

Design size: 21x26mm
Engraved frame with typographed vignette mounted on it. Four diff. color combinations (dull scarlet vignette, dull carmine frame; dull orange vignette, brown orange frame; yellow brown vignette, dark brown frame; blue green vignette and frame) on cream white ivory paper, 22x27mm each, mounted together on 92x114mm thick white card, ms. "American Bank Note Co. N.Y." at lower right.

209-E5 10c Four designs on cream white ivory on card 2,500.

209-E6

209-E7

Vignette diameter: 18mm
Engraved Washington vignette.

209-E6 10c
a. Die on India
black 600.
dim deep carmine 600.
dim deep scarlet 600.
dull orange 600.
dull brown 600.
dim blue green 600.
blue 600.
dusky red violet 600.
b. Die sunk on white ivory paper, 55x67mm
dusky carmine 800.
dull orange 800.
dull blue green 800.
scarlet 800.
dull brown 800.
red violet 800.

Design size: 21x26mm
Engraved frame with typographed vignette mounted on it. Four diff. color combinations (dull carmine vignette and frame; dull orange vignette, brown orange frame; yellow brown vignette, dark brown frame; blue green vignette and frame) on cream white ivory paper, 22x27mm each, mounted together on 92x114mm thick white card, ms. "American Bank Note Co. N.Y." at lower right.

209-E7 10c
a. Four designs on cream white ivory on card 2,500.
b. Single composite off card, dull carmine vignette, blue green frame 400.

Issued stamp, No. 209, in trial color, overprinted network in fugitive ink.

209-E8 10c On thick paper, perf. 12, gummed, sepia, overprint olive gray 150.

1883 ISSUE
American Bank Note Co.

210-E1

210-E2

Design size: 20x25½mm
Engraved vignette of Washington (from proof on India of No. 207) with watercolor frame design nearly as adopted but with "TWO" and "CENTS" at an angle, rubber stamp "Feb. 17, 1883" on back.

210-E1 2c Die on white card, 80x90mm, black vignette, gray and white frame 3,000.

Design size: 20x25mm
Engraved vignette of Washington (from proof on India of No. 207) mounted on unadopted watercolor and ink frame design. backstamped "American Bank Note Co. Feb. 27, 1883."

210-E2 2c Die on thick white card, 87x100mm, black and white 3,000.

210-E3

210-E4

Design size: 20x25½mm
Engraved vignette of Washington (from proof on India of No. 207) mounted on watercolor frame design as adopted, ms. "2 March 1883 No. 1."

210-E3 2c Die on white card, 80x90mm, black vignette, gray & white frame 3,000.

Design size: 20x25mm
Engraved vignette of Washington on white background mounted on a brush and pen watercolor drawing of unadopted fancy frame design, backstamped "American Bank Note Co. Mar. 2, 1883" and pencil "No. 2."

210-E4 2c Die on white card, 88x101mm, dusky blue green 3,000.

210-E5

Design size: 20x25mm
Engraved vignette of Washington (from revenue stamp No. RB17) mounted on wash drawing of unadopted ornate frame design, backstamped "American Bank Note Co. Mar. 2, 1883" and pencil "No. 3."

210-E5 2c Die on white card, 88x101mm, blue violet vignette, black frame 2,500.

211-E1

Design size: 20x25½mm
Engraved vignette of Jackson mounted on unadopted watercolor frame design.

211-E1 4c Die on white card, 70x70mm, blue green vignette and frame *3,500.*

Engraved head of Jackson only.

211-E2 4c Die on India, die sunk on card, black *1,000.*

211-E3

Incomplete engraved vignette of Jackson: lower edge of bust incomplete.

211-E3 4c Die on India, die sunk on card
black *2,500.*
green *2,500.*
red brown *2,500.*

Complete engraved vignette of Jackson.

211-E4 4c Die on India, die sunk on card, blue green *2,500.*

211-E5

Die size: 60x62mm
Complete design as adopted but with pencil sketch of pedestal top under bust.

211-E5 4c Die on India, die sunk on card, gray black *5,750.*

Similar to No. 211-E5 but with incomplete shading engraved on pedestal.

211-E6 4c Die on India, die sunk on card, blue green *2,500.*

1887 ISSUE
American Bank Note Co.

212-E1

Die size: 55x63mm
Incomplete engraved vignette of Franklin facing right: horiz. background lines only.

212-E1 1c Die on 32½x35mm card, India mounted, die sunk on card
black *600.*
ultramarine *600.*

Die size: 62x62mm
Franklin vignette similar to No. 212-E1 but diagonal lines (in one direction only) added to background.

212-E2 1c Die on India, die sunk on card
black *600.*
ultramarine *600.*

Die size: 55x64mm
Similar to No. 212-E2 but diagonal lines in both directions.

212-E3 1c Die on India, die sunk on card, black *500.*

212-E4

Complete design as issued except Franklin facing right.

212-E4 1c
a. Die on India, die sunk on card
black *600.*
ultramarine *600.*
b. Die on white glazed paper, about 64x76mm
black *750.*
black brown *750.*
scarlet *750.*
blue *750.*

Die size: 62x62mm
Incomplete vignette of Franklin facing left as adopted.

212-E5 1c Die on India, die sunk on card, ultramarine *450.*

212-E6

212-E7

Die size: 56x64½mm
Incomplete design as adopted except three lines below value label and taller numeral, shadow on edge of bust and in background below chin too dark.

212-E6 1c Die on India, die sunk on card
ultramarine *750.*
green *750.*

Similar to No. 212-E6 but with shadows lightened.

212-E7 1c Die on India, die sunk on card, ultramarine *750.*

1890 ISSUE
American Bank Note Co.

219-E1

Design size: 19x22½mm
Die size: 58x64mm
Engraved die of frame only with blank labels quite similar to adopted design.

219-E1 1c Die on ivory paper, 64x72mm, black *700.*

219-E2

219-E3

Design size: 19x22mm
Engraved Franklin vignette cut down from 1887 1c stamp (No. 212) mounted on watercolor frame design.

219-E2 1c Die on thick light buff card, ultramarine frame *3,500.*

Die size: 62x62mm
Engraved Franklin vignette with lettered label above.

219-E3 1c Die on India, die sunk on card, blue *800.*

220-E1

220-E2

Design size: 19x22mm
Engraved Washington vignette from 3c stamp (from proof on India of No. 184) mounted on watercolor frame design.

220-E1 2c Die on thick white card, 62x66mm, light carmine frame *3,750.*

Design size: 19x23mm
Engraved Washington vignette cut from 1887 2c stamp (No. 213) mounted on shield-like watercolor frame design.

220-E2 2c Die on thick light buff card, gray frame *3,000.*

220-E3

220-E4

Design size: 19x23mm
Engraved Washington vignette cut from 1887 2c stamp (No. 213) mounted on watercolor frame design.

220-E3 2c Die on white card, 105x135mm, gray black frame *3,000.*

Design size: 19x22mm
Die size: 56x63mm
Engraved unadopted frame only.

220-E4 2c Die on white ivory paper, black *1,250.*

220-E5

220-E6

Die size: 62x62mm
Engraved vignette of Washington in oval line frame.

220-E5 2c Die on India, die sunk on card, dark carmine *800.*

Engraved Washington vignette with lettered label above.

220-E6 2c Die on India, dusky carmine *1,250.*

220-E7

220-E8

Design size: 19x22½mm
Engraved Washington vignette and lettered top label mounted on pencil drawing of frame design adopted, ms. "J.J.M.--engraved background only without figures or words;" backstamped "Nov. 15, 1889 American Bank Note Co."

220-E7 2c Die on 50x55mm white card, mounted on thick white card, 119x122mm, black vignette, pencil frame *3,000.*

Design size: 19x22mm
Die size: 56x63mm
Engraved frame only as adopted with numerals, blank curved top label.

220-E8 2c
a. Die on ivory paper, 64x71mm, black *900.*
b. Die on India, 51x62mm
black *700.*
brown black *700.*
dark brown *700.*
dull scarlet *700.*
dark blue green *700.*
dark blue *700.*
red violet *700.*
red orange *700.*

220-E9

Incomplete engraving of entire design as adopted: no dots in rectangular spaces between shading lines on cheek under hair in front of ear and on back of neck.

220-E9 2c Die on India, die sunk on card, lake *1,250.*

(Probably by) The Times, Philadelphia

220-E11

Surface-printed essay for proposed business advertising on stamps.

220-E11 2c Die on India, on card, bright green blue —

American Bank Note Co.

221-E1

221-E2

Engraved 3c frame as adopted with vignette cut out, mounted over photo of James Madison.

221-E1 3c Die on India, cut close, dark green *2,500.*

Engraved vignette of Jackson with lettered label above.

221-E2 3c Die on India, die sunk on card, purple *750.*

Design size: 19x22mm
Incomplete engraved design as adopted except Lincoln facing ¾ left: unfinished shading under collar.

222-E1 4c Die on India, die sunk on card, black brown *1,250.*

222-E2

222-E3

Die No. C-226 size: 62½x62½mm
Completed design with die no. and impt., Lincoln facing ¾ left.

222-E2 4c Die on India, on 25x32mm card, black brown *1,000.*

Incomplete engraving as adopted: no wart on face, no lines on shirt.

222-E3 4c Die on India, die sunk on card, black brown *1,000.*

223-E1

Design size: 19x21½mm
Photo of Seward vignette mounted on watercolor frame design.

223-E1 5c Die on light buff paper in upper right corner of short envelope, gray & white *1,750.*

223-E2

223-E3

Design size: 19x26½mm
Die size: 63x62mm
Incomplete engraved design as adopted except Grant facing ¾ left: hair neatly combed.

223-E2 5c Die on India, die sunk on card
black *700.*
orange brown *700.*

Design size: 19x26½mm
Die size: 63x62mm
Incomplete engraving of complete bearded left-facing design: eye pupils not solid color, light shading on right side of face, only one diagonal shading line on left coat shoulder.

223-E3 5c Die on India, die sunk on card, chocolate *700.*

Similar to No. 223-E3 but more complete. Left beard has no diagonal lines and is light at top center.

223-E4 5c Die on India, die sunk on card, chocolate *700.*

Third state of die: no horiz. lines on left moustache or under lower lip.

223-E5 5c Die on India, die sunk on card, chocolate *700.*

223-E6

223-E7

Completed left-facing design: shows lines omitted from No. 223-E5, several diagonal shading lines on left shoulder of coat.

223-E6 5c Die on India, die sunk on card
black *700.*
chocolate *700.*

Design size: 19x26½mm
Die size: 62x62mm
Left-facing design with slightly diff. portrait, hair neatly combed. Horiz. shading lines on left coat shoulder, no wash-etched shadows on coat, beard and tie.

223-E7 5c
a. Die on India, die sunk on card
black *700.*
dark brown *700.*
b. Die on glazed paper, impt. and "ESSAY MARCH 1890"
black *750.*
black brown *750.*
scarlet *750.*
blue *750.*

Design size: 19x26½mm
Die similar to No. 223-E7 but diagonal shading lines on left coat shoulder, wash-etched shadows on coat, beard and tie.

223-E8 5c Die on India, on card, brown *700.*

223-E9

223-E10

Die size: 62x63mm
Engraving of right-facing Grant design diff. than adopted: light oval line around vignette, three diagonal lines on shirtfront under tie. Incomplete engraving: right collar unshaded.

223-E9 5c Die on India, dark orange brown *700.*

Similar to No. 223-E9 but engraving completed: right collar shaded.

223-E10 5c
a. Die on India, die sunk on card, dark orange brown *700.*
b. Die on ivory paper, impt. and "ESSAY MARCH 1890"
black *750.*
black brown *750.*
scarlet *750.*
blue *750.*

Ferrotype plate 39x51mm of Grant facing ¾ right, outlines engraved, filled with red.

223-E11 5c Metal plate *650.*

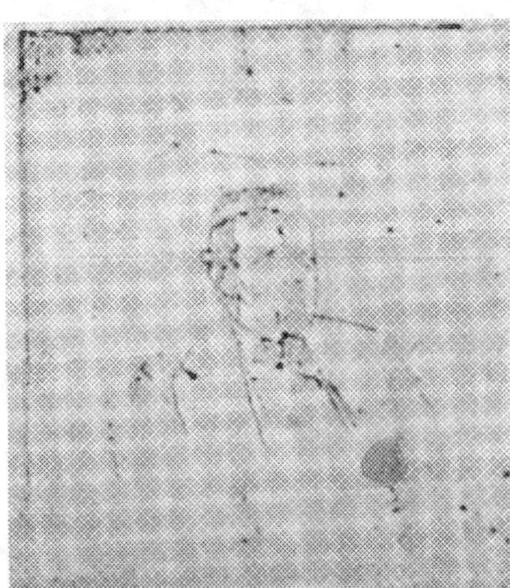
223-E12

Printing from ferrotype plate, No. 223-E11.

223-E12 5c Die on card, 43x56mm, red *650.*

226-E1

226-E2

Design size: 19x22½mm
Incomplete engraved vignette of Webster with curved label above, mounted on pencil drawing of frame design (includes additional pencil drawings of lower part of frame, value lettering), backstamped "D.S. Ronaldson," frame engraver.

226-E1 10c Die on white card, 51x55mm, black *6,000.*

Design size: 19x22½mm
Engraving of unadopted frame design.

226-E2 10c Die on white glazed paper, black *1,000.*

226-E3

226-E4

Design size: 19x22mm
Engraved 10c frame as adopted, vignette cut out and mounted over photo of John Adams.

226-E3 10c Die on India, cut close, dark green *2,500.*

Design size: 19x22mm
Engraved 10c frame as adopted, vignette cut out and mounted over photo of William T. Sherman.

226-E4 10c Die on India, cut close, dark green *2,500.*

227-E1

Design size: 19x22½mm
Engraved vignette of Henry Clay with curved label above, mounted on wash drawing of frame design (includes additional enlarged pencil and wash drawing of frame).

227-E1 15c Die on white card, mounted at left on light buff card, 110x123mm (frame drawing at right), black *1,750.*

228-E1

Design size: 19x22½mm
Die size: 62x61mm
Incomplete engraved vignette of Jefferson with curved lettered label at top: hair shading incomplete.

228-E1 30c Die on India, die sunk on card, black *750.*

Similar to No. 228-E1 but more shading on hair, vert. shading lines on chin.

228-E2 30c Die on India, die sunk on card, black *750.*

229-E1

Design size: 19x22½mm
Die size: 62x62mm
Engraved vignette of Perry with curved lettered label at top.

229-E1 90c Die on India, die sunk on card, red orange *750.*

COLUMBIAN ISSUE
Lyman H. Bagg

230-E1

237-E1

Design sizes: 22x22mm
Left: No. 230-E1 - pencil drawing of Columbus in armor, on paper. "I do not know whether these designs will be of any use to you or not -- they are so rough. L.H.B." written at top, "My idea illustrated" at bottom.
Right: No. 237-E1 - pencil drawing of North American continent, on paper.

230-E1 One Cent, Ten Cents, Drawings on 114x72mm white wove, Nos. 230-E1, 237-E1 *6,000.*

American Bank Note Co.

230-E2

230-E3

230-E4

Design size: 33x22mm

Silver print photo vignette of Columbus head mounted on watercolor drawing of unadopted frame design.

230-E2 1c Die on stiff white drawing paper, red violet *4,500.*
230-E3 1c Die on stiff white drawing paper, blue green *4,500.*
230-E4 1c Die on stiff white drawing paper, light red *4,500.*

230-E5

Ferrotype metal plate with outline of adopted vignette (reversed) and drawings of Indian man and woman at sides in single line frame 39mm long.

230-E5 1c Metal plate, 57x38mm 1,250.

230-E6

Vignette size: 16x15mm
Engraved vignette only as adopted.

230-E6 1c Die on 53x39mm India, on card
yellow brown *2,000.*
black *2,000.*

230-E7

Incomplete engraving of vignette, lettering, value numerals and tablet as issued: without palm tree, incomplete shading on and behind Indian and maiden, on Columbus' head, no shading on scrollwork, etc.

230-E7 1c Die on 39x28mm stiff wove, deep blue *2,000.*

230-E8

Incomplete engraving of entire design as issued: maiden's skirt only lightly engraved, chief's torso and shoulder incompletely engraved, incomplete shading in frame design at top, etc.

230-E8 1c Die on India, die sunk on 99x84mm card, deep blue *1,500.*

231-E1

Design size: 34x22mm
Silver print photo of vignette as adopted, mounted on watercolor drawing of unadopted frame design.

231-E1 2c Die on stiff white drawing paper, red violet *8,500.*

Die size: 74x61½mm
Incomplete engraving of adopted vignette only.

231-E2 2c Die on India, die sunk on card
black *1,500.*
sepia *1,500.*

231-E3

Design size: 35½x22mm
Engraved vignette of Columbus asking aid of Isabella as adopted for 5c, mounted on watercolor drawing of frame design similar to that adopted for 2c.

231-E3 2c Die on stiff white drawing paper, dark brown *4,000.*

231-E4

Vignette size: 29x15mm
Die size: 74x61½mm
Incomplete engraving of vignette as adopted (probably first state of die): cape on back of central figure incomplete, etc.

231-E4 2c Die on India, die sunk on card, black *2,500.*

231-E5

Incomplete engraving of vignette as adopted (probably second state of die): more shading on top right face, etc.; also pencil sketches for lengthening vignette.

231-E5 2c Die on India, die sunk on card, black *3,250.*

231-E6

Vignette size: 31½x15mm
Die size: 74x61½mm
Incomplete engraving of vignette, longer than Nos. 231-E4 and 231-E5, later shortened as adopted: Columbus' legs, central figure's cape, etc., are incomplete.

231-E6 2c Die on India, die sunk on card, black *2,500.*

231-E7

Design size: 33x22mm
Die size: 74x61½mm
Incomplete engraving of entire design almost as adopted: figures of value narrower, unfinished crosset shadows in lower corners.

Ridgway numbers used for colors of No. 231-E7.

231-E7 2c
a. ie on India, die sunk on card
13m/4 smoky dusky o-yellow-orange *1,250.*
b. Die on thin white wove card
69o/5 black *800.*
1m/0 dusky red *800.*
3k/2 dull dark orange-red *800.*
5i/0 deep o-orange-red *800.*
5j/1 deep v-deep o-orange-red *800.*
6i/0 deep m. red-orange *800.*
9i/0 deep o-yellow-orange *800.*
9m/0 dusky o-red-orange *800.*
9m/3 dismal dusky o-red-orange *800.*
9m/4 smoky dusky o-red-orange *800.*
9n/2 dull v. dusky o-red-orange *800.*
10k/0 m. dark orange *800.*
11i/0 deep orange *800.*
11k/1 dim dark orange *800.*
13m/1 dim dusky o-yellow-orange *800.*

13m/4 smoky dusky o-yellow-orange	*800.*
33m/2 dull dusky g-yellow-green	*800.*
37m/1 dim dusky g-blue-green	*800.*
43m/2 dull dusky green-blue	*800.*
49m/0 dusky blue	*800.*
49m/1 dim dusky blue	*800.*
55m/2 dull dusky blue-violet	*800.*
59m/2 dull dusky violet	*800.*
65m/2 dull dusky r-red-violet	*800.*
70i/0 deep violet-red-red	*800.*

231-E8

Design size: 33x22mm
Incomplete engraving of entire design as adopted: value numerals same as on issued stamp but without thick shading bars at ends of outer frame rectangles, etc.

231-E8 2c Die on India, card mounted, sepia *1,500.*

232-E1

Design size: 33½x22mm
Silver print photo of vignette unadopted for any value (Columbus embarking on voyage of discovery), mounted on watercolor drawing of unadopted frame design.

232-E1 3c Die on stiff white drawing paper, 41x29mm, orange brown *4,000.*

Ferrotype metal plate showing 19x15mm outline of *Santa Maria* (reversed) in 33x15mm vignette frame, outline engraved and filled with red ink.

232-E2 3c Metal plate, 51x30mm *1,250.*

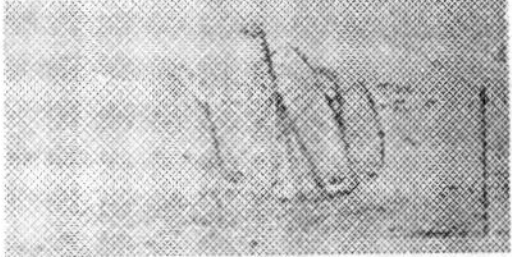
232-E3

Printing from ferrotype plate No. 232-E3.

232-E3 3c Die on stiff white card with rounded corners, 55x42mm, red *1,250.*

232-E4

Vignette size: 30x15mm
Die size: 74x61mm
Incomplete engraving of vignette as adopted: sky composed of horiz. ruled lines, no clouds.

232-E4 3c Die on India, die sunk on card

black	*1,250.*
dark yellow-orange	*1,250.*
sepia	*1,750.*

232-E5

Engraved vignette similar to No. 232-E4 but with "1492 UNITED STATES OF AMERICA 1892" and scrolls around numerals engraved in outline only, pencil outline of frame.

232-E5 3c Die on thick artist's card with beveled edges, 50x38mm, dark yellow orange *3,000.*

233-E1

Design size: 33½x22mm
Silver print photo of wash drawing of vignette as adopted, mounted on watercolor drawing of frame design as adopted but titled "COLUMBUS ON VOYAGE OF DISCOVERY. SHIPS AT SEA."

233-E1 4c Die on stiff white drawing paper, 41x29mm, brown red *4,750.*

233-E2

Design size: 33x22mm
Die size: 74x61½mm
Incomplete engraving of complete design as adopted: unfinished crosset shadows in lower corners.

Ridgway numbers used for some colors of No. 233-E2.

233-E2 4c

a. Die on India, die sunk on card

black	*1,250.*
dark yellow orange	*1,250.*

b. Die on thin white wove card, die sunk on card

1m/0 dusky red	*800.*
3i/1 dim deep orange-red	*800.*
3k/2 dull dark orange-red	*800.*
5i/0 deep o-orange-red	*800.*
9i/0 deep o-red-orange	*800.*
9m/1 dim dusky o-red-orange	*800.*
11i/0 deep orange	*800.*
11k/1 dim dark orange	*800.*
11m/2 dull dusky orange	*800.*
13k/1 dim dark o-yellow-orange	*800.*
13m/2 dull dusky o-yellow-orange	*800.*
13k/3 dismal dark o-yellow-orange	*800.*
13k/4 smoky dark o-yellow-orange	*800.*
13m/4 smoky dusky o-yellow-orange	*800.*
15m/2 dull dusky yellow-orange	*800.*
33m/2 dull dusky g-yellow-green	*800.*
35m/5 gloomy dusky green	*800.*
37m/1 dim dusky g-blue-green	*800.*
39m/1 dim dusky blue-green	*800.*
41m/1 dim dusky b-blue-green	*800.*
47m/0 dusky green-blue-blue	*800.*
55m/2 dull dusky blue-violet	*800.*
63m/2 dull dusky red-violet	*800.*
69m/1 dull dusky red-violet-red	*800.*
69k/3 dismal dark red-violet-red	*800.*
71i/0 deep violet-red-red	*800.*
71m/0 dusky violet-red-red	*800.*
71o/5 black	*800.*
ultramarine	*800.*
violet	*800.*
red violet	*800.*
brown violet	*800.*
orange brown	*800.*
dark brown	*800.*

234-E1

Design size: 38½x22mm
Engraved vignette as adopted, mounted on watercolor drawing of frame design similar to but longer than adopted. Vignette also used on No. 231-E3.

234-E1 5c Die on thick artist's card, block sunk as die essay, black brown *4,000.*

234-E2

Design size: 34x22½mm
Die size: 67x63mm
Engraved vignette as adopted, mounted on watercolor drawing of frame design as adopted, pencil "Oct. 5/92," approval monogram of J.D. Macdonough and ⅞x1 1/32 inches. Vignette also used on No. 231-E3.

234-E2 5c Die on thick artist's card, die sunk, black brown & white *4,000.*

234-E3

Vignette size: 29½x15mm
Die size: 74x61½mm
Engraved vignette only as adopted.

234-E3 5c Die on India, die sunk on card, sepia *1,250.*

234-E4

Incomplete engraving of entire design: bench at left has horiz. shading only, incomplete shading in Columbus' face, etc.

234-E4 5c Die on 74x60mm India, on card

sepia	*1,000.*
blue	*1,000.*

Ferrotype metal plate with engraved outline design (reversed) of vignette as used on 6c, engraved lines filled with red ink.

235-E1 6c Metal plate, 38x38mm *1,100.*

235-E2

Printing from ferrotype plate No. 235-E1.

235-E2 6c Die on stiff white card with rounded corners, 55x42mm, red *1,250.*

235-E3

Incomplete engraving of frame as adopted: unfinished crosset shadows in lower corners.

235-E3 6c Die on India, black *2,000.*

235-E4

Design size: 34x22mm
Die size: 73x60mm
Incomplete engraving of entire design as adopted: neck and shoulder of horse, side figures in niches, crosset shadows in lower corners all unfinished.

235-E4 6c Die on India, die sunk on card, blue violet *1,500.*

236-E1

Design size: 33½x22mm
Die size: 73x62mm
Design as adopted but frame incompletely engraved: unfinished crosset shadows in lower corners.

236-E1 8c Die on India, on card, black *2,500.*

236-E2

Design as adopted but frame incompletely engraved: unfinished crosset shadows in lower corners, incomplete gown at left and faces at right.

236-E2 8c Die on India, on card, black *1,000.*

237-E2

Ferrotype metal plate with engraved outline design (reversed) of vignette as used on 10c, engraved lines filled with red ink.

237-E2 10c Metal plate, 43x28mm *1,000.*

237-E3

Printing from ferrotype plate No. 237-E2.

237-E3 10c Die on stiff white card with rounded corners, 55x42mm, red *1,000.*

237-E4

Design size: 33x22mm
Die size: 74x62mm
Incomplete engraving of entire design as adopted: surroundings of Columbus, floor, etc., three figures behind King Ferdinand, crosset shadows in lower corners all unfinished.

237-E4 10c Die on India, card mounted
black brown *1,000.*
rose carmine *1,000.*

Similar to No. 237-E4 but more completely engraved: missing lines on ankle bracelet of Indian, many details in vignette and crosset shadows in lower corners.

237-E5 10c Die on India, die sunk on card
black brown *1,500.*
carmine *1,500.*

238-E1

Design size: 33½x22mm
Silver print photo of vignette unadopted for any value (Columbus relating incidents of voyage to Ferdinand and Isabella), mounted on watercolor drawing of frame design similar to that adopted.

238-E1 15c Die on stiff white drawing paper, 42x30mm, bright ultramarine *5,000.*

238-E2

Vignette size: 30x15mm
Die size: 71x59mm
Incomplete engraving of vignette only as adopted: shading on Columbus' tunic and arms, Isabella's sholder, Ferdinand's robe, seated Indian's robe, robe of kneeling figure in lower left corner, etc., all unfinished.

238-E2 15c Die on India, die sunk on card, black brown *1,500.*

Complete engraving of vignette adopted.

238-E3 15c Die on India, black brown *1,500.*

238-E4

Design size: 33½x22mm
Die size: 73½x62mm
Incomplete engraving of complete design as adopted: shading on Isabella's shoulder, Ferdinand's robe, seated Indian's blanket and crosset shadows in lower corners all unfinished.

238-E4 15c Die on India, on card
black brown *1,500.*
blue green *1,500.*

239-E1

Design size: 34½x22½mm
Silver print photo of vignette adopted for 15c, mounted on watercolor and ink drawing of unadopted frame design, titled "COLUMBUS PRESENTING NATIVES TO FERDINAND AND ISABELLA."

239-E1 30c Die on stiff white drawing paper, 42x30mm, bluish gray *5,000.*

239-E2

Ferrotype metal plate with engraved outline design (reversed) of vignette as used on 30c, engraved lines filled with red ink.

239-E2 30c Metal plate, 39x29mm *1,000.*

239-E3

Printing from ferrotype plate No. 239-E2.

239-E3 30c Die on stiff white card with rounded corners, 55x43mm, red *1,000.*

239-E4

Vignette size: 30x15mm
Die size: 74x62mm
Incomplete engraving of adopted vignette only: table cloth dark at top; horiz. lines on front edge of octagonal footstool, horiz. dots in shadow below windowsill at left, dots on top of head of man standing next to Columbus, etc., all missing.

239-E4 30c Die on India, die sunk on card, black *1,750.*

Similar to No. 239-E4 but further engraved: has horiz. lines on front of footstool, etc. Eight pencil instructions for finishing vignette engraving written on large card backing, e.g., "Too much color on table cloth near top."

239-E5 30c Die on India, die sunk on 177x117mm card
black *2,000.*
black brown *2,000.*

239-E6

Design size: 33½x22mm
Die size: 74x63mm
Incomplete engraving of entire design as adopted: table cloth dark at top, diagonal dashes in one direction only between horiz. lines at lower left of vignette, etc.

239-E6 30c Die on India, die sunk on card
black *2,000.*
black brown *2,000.*

Similar to No. 239-E6 but diagonal dashes in two directions, more dots on head and hand of man seated at near end of table.

239-E7 30c Die on India, die sunk on card
black brown *1,750.*
orange *1,750.*

Incomplete engraving of entire design: window frame, horiz. shading lines on shoulder of man at right, vert. lines on front of table cloth below Columbus all missing. Lighter shading at top of table cloth as on issued stamp.

239-E8 30c Die on India, on card, orange *2,500.*

240-E1

Design size: 34x22mm
Die size: Incomplete engraving of entire design as adopted: unfinished shadows between right arm and body of man on donkey, distant object in front of bowing man's head darker than on issued stamp.

240-E1 50c Die on India, on card, slate blue *1,500.*

240-E2

Incomplete engraving of entire design: missing dots on donkey's flank and long lines on wrist of bowing man, no etching on two riders or their mounts.

240-E2 50c Die on India, on card, slate blue *1,500.*

240-E3

Incomplete engraving of entire design: additional engraving on donkey's hindquarters and face of figure to left of Columbus.

240-E3 50c Die on India, on card, slate blue *1,500.*

241-E1

Ferrotype metal plate with engraved outline design (reversed) of vignette as used on $1, engraved lines filled with red ink.

241-E1 $1 Metal plate, 45x29mm *1,000.*

241-E2

Printing from ferrotype plate No. 241-E1.

241-E2 $1 Die on stiff white card with rounded corners, 55½x43mm, red *1,000.*

241-E3

Vignette size: 31x15mm
Die size: 72x59mm
Incomplete engraving of vignette only as adopted (very early state of die): very little shading on Isabella, floor, walls, etc.

241-E3 $1 Die on India, die sunk on card, black brown *2,000.*

241-E4

Incomplete engraving of entire design as adopted: shadow on table cloth, woman in front of table, crosslet shadows at lower corners all unfinished.

241-E4 $1 Die on India, on card, black brown *2,000.*

241-E5

Later state of complete design: horiz. lines in rectangle above Isabella missing.

241-E5 $1 Die on India, die sunk on 86x69mm card, black brown *2,000.*

242-E1

Design size: 33½x22mm
Die size: 75x62mm
Incomplete engraving of entire design as adopted: about 12 horiz. lines missing on back of cape of tall man at right, some vert. dashes missing on corselet of soldier at right, incomplete foliage over "C" of "COLUMBUS," etc.

242-E1 $2 Die on India, die sunk on card
dull yellow orange *2,000.*
olive brown *2,000.*

243-E1

Ferrotype metal plate with engraved outline design (reversed) of vignette as used on $3, engraved lines filled with red wax.

243-E1 $3 Metal plate, 45x29mm *1,250.*

243-E2

Printing from ferrotype plate No. 243-E1.

243-E2 $3 Die on stiff white card with rounded corners, 55x43mm, red *1,250.*

243-E3

Design size: 33½x22mm
Incomplete engraving of entire design as adopted: unshaded crossets in lower corners, shading lines on crossets and frame above title label too light. Pencil marks correct these.

243-E3 $3 Die on India, die sunk on card, dark yellow green *1,500.*

243-E4

Incomplete engraving of entire design as adopted, before etching of shadows on Columbus, Ferdinand, backs of chairs, etc.

243-E4 $3 Die on India, on card, dark red *2,000.*

Ferrotype metal plate with engraved outline design (reversed) of Queen Isabella vignette as used on $4, engraved lines filled with red wax.

244-E1 $4 Metal plate, 33x44mm *1,500.*

244-E2

Printing from ferrotype plate No. 244-E1.

244-E2 $4 Die on stiff white card with rounded corners, 43x55mm, red *1,500.*

244-E3

Vignette diameter: 14mm
Incomplete engraving of Isabella head with background of uniform ruled horiz. lines only, blank circle for Columbus vignette at right adjoining.

244-E3 $4 Die on India, on card, black *3,000.*

Similar to No. 244-E3 but background has diagonal shading also.

244-E4 $4 Die on India, on card, black *3,000.*

244-E5

Design size: about 34x21½mm
Die size: 74½x61½mm
Incomplete engraving of vignettes and lettering only: no diagonal shading lines in background of Columbus vignette.

244-E5 $4 Die on India, die sunk on card
black *3,500.*
dark red *4,000.*

244-E6

Design size: 34x22mm
Same engraving as No. 244-E5 but with wash drawing of frame design as adopted.

244-E6 $4 Die on thick artist's card with beveled edges, 50x39mm, gray black *3,000.*

244-E7

Incomplete engraving of entire design as adopted: shadow at top of vert. bar and lines on leaves at bottom between vignettes unfinished; no circular line bordering vignette at Isabella's right shoulder.

244-E7 $4 Die on India, on card, black brown *2,000.*

244-E8

More complete engraving than No. 244-E7 but still missing circular line at Isabella's shoulder; only light shading on Columbus' collar.

244-E8 $4 Die on India, on card
black brown *2,000.*
dark red —

245-E1

Design size: 34½x22½mm
Incomplete engraved vignette as adopted for 1c: missing sky, etc., with pencil drawing of part of frame design.

245-E1 $5 Die on 50x38mm artist's cardboard, on thicker card, 55x43mm, black *4,000.*

Design size: 34x22½mm
Die size: 74½x61½mm
Incomplete engraving of vignette, lettering and frame as adopted (side panels blank): shading unfinished on Columbus' neck, hair and background, and with white and black wash touches.

245-E2 $5 Die on India, die sunk on card, black *3,000.*

245-E3

Similar to No. 245-E2 but further engraved: shading lines on neck, diagonal lines in background, etc.

245-E3 $5 Die on India, on card, 49x38mm, black *3,000.*

Model with photos of female figures mounted each side of vignette, pencil "Design approved subject to inspection of engraved proof, color to be black. A.D.H. Dec. 6 '92" (A.D. Hazen, 3rd asst. PMG).

245-E4 $5 Die on thick white card, on 117x116mm card, black *3,000.*

245-E5

Engraving of No. 245-E3 with retouched photos of side subjects mounted in place.

245-E5 $5 Die on white artist's cardboard, 56½x46mm, die sunk on card, black *2,000.*

Design size: 33½x22mm
Incomplete engraving of entire design: one line under "POSTAGE FIVE DOLLARS", no lines outside and no diagonal lines in sky to upper right and upper left of vignette, etc.

245-E6 $5 Die on India, on card, black *2,000.*

245-E7

Similar to No. 245-E2 but with pencil marks to show engraver where to place diagonal shading lines behind head and in front of bust.

245-E7 $5 Die on 65x55mm India, card mounted, black *3,000.*

245-E8

Similar to No. 245-E6 but with pencil marks and white ink suggestions for further engraving.

245-E8 $5 Die on India, die sunk on 83x68mm card, black *2,000.*

245-E9

Similar to No. 245-E6 but further engraved: with diagonal shading above side figures, below numerals and around vignette circle, but still incomplete in arched band above vignette.

245-E9 $5 Die on India, die sunk on 110x83mm card, black *2,000.*

245-E10

Similar to No. 245-E9 but further engraved: with shading lines in arched band above vignette but no shading on pole of liberty cap, object below shield has dotted shading only, spear tip shading incomplete.

245-E10 $5 Die on India, die sunk on 85x70mm card, black *2,000.*

1894 ISSUE
Bureau of Engraving and Printing

The 1c-15c designs of the 1890 issue engraved by the American Bank Note Co. were worked over by the BEP, including the addition of triangles in the upper corners. The 1890 30c was changed to a 50c and the 90c to a $1. Some 1894 essays have American Bank Note Co. imprints below the design.

247-E1

Design size: 18½x22mm
Die size: 61x62mm
Large die engraving of 1890 1c with pencil drawing of UL triangle 3½mm high with straight side next to curved upper label, freehand horiz. ink line at UR.

247-E1 1c Die on India, die sunk on card, black *1,850.*

247-E2

Experimental laydown die with 1890 1c proof 4mm to left of similar design with 15-line high type I triangle in UR corner. Same laydown die also contains two 2c designs 18mm below, 5½mm apart, either uninked or lightly inked in color of 1c (sometimes found separated from 1c designs). No. 247-E2b nearly always found cracked horiz. through designs.

247-E2 1c
a. Die on semiglazed white wove with pencil notations
blue *1,750.*
ultramarine *1,750.*
b. Die on white card with pencil notations re color
"1-1 Antwerp, 4 Ultra." *1,500.*
"2--little lighter--" *1,500.*
"1 Antwerp blue, 1 Ultra." (not cracked) *1,750.*
"4 Cobalt and Indigo" *1,500.*
"No 5" *1,500.*
"No. 6--Antwerp blue" *1,500.*
"No. 6--with little Antwerp blue" *1,500.*

Die impression of 1890 1c with 15-line high type I triangle in UR corner.

247-E3 1c Die on India, 50x52mm, dusky green *2,000.*

Experimental die impression of single 1890 1c with 2c 18mm below, triangles added in ink to upper corners of both designs, ms. "Approved" notations.

247-E4 1c +2c, Die on India, mounted on 57x102mm card, mounted on another card, 144x195mm
green *2,500.*
dull violet (without added triangles) *2,400.*

247-E5

247-E6

Large die engraving of 1890 1c with 18-line high triangle in UL corner (inner lines very thick).

247-E5 1c Die on India, die sunk on card, dusky blue green *1,250.*

Similar to No. 247-E5 but inner line of triangle almost as thin as outer line.

247-E6 1c Die on India, die sunk on card, dusky blue green *1,250.*

247-E7

Similar to No. 247-E6 but inner line of triangle same thickness as adopted.

247-E7 1c Die on India, die sunk on card, dusky blue green *1,250.*

Incomplete engraving of entire design as adopted including triangles: coat collar, scroll under "U," horiz. lines on frame, oval line of vignette, etc., all unfinished; vignette background not re-etched.

247-E8 1c Die on India, die sunk on card
ultramarine *1,000.*
blue ("Cobalt 2--Indigo 4") *1,250.*

Design size: 18½x22mm
Die size: 61x62½mm
Large die engraving of 1890 2c with pencil drawing of UL triangle 2½mm high.

250-E1 2c Die on India, die sunk on card, black *1,850.*

Die width: 92mm
Experimental laydown die with 1890 2c proof 5½mm to left of similar design with 14-line high type I triangles in upper corners (found cut apart from No. 247-E2 and used for trial colors as noted thereon in pencil).

250-E2 2c Die on white card
"1 R&D Lake, 1½P. white" *1,750.*
"M3 1 white, 7 Gem Lake, ¼ Car. Lake" *1,750.*
"2 White, 4 Ger. Lake No. 1, ½ R&D Lake" *1,750.*
"Opal Red" *1,750.*
"Opal Orange" *1,750.*
"Opal Maroon" *1,750.*

250-E3

Die size: 61½x62½mm
American Banknote Co. die No. C-224 annealed, with 18-line high type I triangles engraved in upper corners, ms "No. 1" at lower left of card backing.

250-E3 2c Die on India, die sunk on card
medium deep red *1,000.*
deep red *1,000.*
dusky red *1,000.*
dim red *1,000.*
medium deep orange-red *1,000.*
deep o-orange-red *1,000.*
dusky g-blue-green *1,000.*
dark medium violet-red-red *1,000.*

Incomplete engraving of entire design: shadows on frame not etched; lines on foliage, front collar and oval line at vignette bottom not recut; dots instead of lines over corner of eye; only one line on truncated scroll at left of right 2 and no line on similar scroll at right of left 2; shadows of TWO CENTS not etched.

250-E4 2c Die on India, die sunk on card
bright red *1,000.*
light red *1,000.*
dark red *1,000.*
deep orange red *1,000.*

Similar to No. 250-E4 but line added to scroll at right of left 2, ms. "A.B.N.Co. Die worked over and ornaments put in" at top, ms. "No. 1" at lower left.

250-E5 2c medium deep red *1,250.*

Incomplete engraving of entire design: two lines on truncated scroll at left of right 2 (one later removed), scroll at left of right 2 unfinished, profile of nose and forehead darker than on issued stamp, shadows of "TWO CENTS" not etched, short dashes on inside of outer edge of white oval at lower right, veins on scrolls around 2s not recut. Pencil notations incl. "Old A.B.N.Co. annealed & triangles engraved and rehardened to take up roll for plate."

250-E6 2c Die on India, die sunk on card, medium deep red *1,250.*

Incomplete engraving of entire design: bottom of ear still angular and not yet rounded, dots on lobe not yet gathered into two lines, dot shading under corner of eye not yet gathered into four lines, shadows of "TWO CENTS" have been etched.

250-E7 2c Die on India, die sunk on card, medium deep red *1,000.*

Die size: 57x76mm
Incomplete engraving of entire design with type II triangles: top of head not silhouetted. Pencil notation "2/ Transfer from roll taken from No. 1 so as to change portrait and make cameo effect. Unfinished."

251-E1 2c Die on India, die sunk on card, dark violet red *1,250.*

Similar to No. 251-E1 but hair in front of ear unfinished, forehead and hair lightened.

251-E2 2c Die on India, die sunk on card, dusky gray *1,500.*

Die size: 57x81mm
Incomplete engraving of entire design with type III triangles: top of head not silhouetted, unfinished shadow over eye, etc.

252-E1 2c Die on India, die sunk on card, medium deep red *1,000.*

Incomplete engraving of entire design with type III triangles: unfinished shadow over eye, etc.

252-E2 2c Die on India, die sunk on card
dusky blue green *1,500.*
dark violet red *1,000.*

252-E3

Design size: 19x22mm
Die size: 56x80½mm
Discarded die, vignette overengraved: too much shading on front hair, cheek, nose, below eye; background too dark; hair in front of ear very prominent.

252-E3 2c Die on India, die sunk on card
light carmine *1,500.*
green *2,000.*

253-E1

Die size: 60x63mm
Complete engraved design as adopted but with type II triangles.

253-E1 3c
a. Die on India, die sunk on card
dusky blue green *1,500.*
dark red violet *1,000.*
dusky red violet *1,000.*
b. Die printed directly on card, die sunk on card, violet *1,250.*

254-E1

Design size: about 19x22mm
Die size: 61x63mm
Incomplete engraving of entire design: line under collar wings missing, oval line around vignette not recut; hair, beard, forehead, neck, collar, shirt, etc., all incomplete.

254-E1 4c Die on India, die sunk on card, dark yellow brown *1,500.*

Entire design engraved further than No. 254-E1 but still incomplete: shadows in lettering, etc., not etched, faint lines under collar incomplete, oval around vignette not recut.

254-E2 4c Die on India, die sunk on card, dark yellow brown *1,500.*

Entire design engraved further than No. 254-E2 but still incomplete: beard, collar and necktie, etc., unfinished. Some veins recut on foliage under oval label.

254-E3 4c Die on India, die sunk on card, dark brown *1,250.*

255-E1

Design size: 19x22mm
Engraved frame of American Bank Note Co. die No. C-227 with triangles, vignette cut out, mounted over engraved vignette of Washington.

255-E1 5c Die on 41x53mm India, on white wove, 48x75mm, black *3,000.*

Washington vignette only as on No. 255-E1.

255-E2 5c Die on India, green *2,000.*

255-E3

255-E4

Design size: 19x22mm
Engraved frame as adopted with William H. Seward photo mounted on it.

255-E3 5c Die on India, cut close, mounted on 74x84mm white card, black *3,000.*

Design size: about 19x22mm
Die size: 62½x75mm
Incomplete engraving of entire design as adopted: no oval border line around vignette.

255-E4 5c Die on India, die sunk on card, orange brown *1,250.*

256-E1

Design size: about 19x22mm
Die size: 62x61½mm
Incomplete engraving of entire design as adopted: white spot on eye and shadows not darkened, diagonal lines missing on beard under mouth, lines on coat unfinished.

256-E1 6c Die on India, die sunk on card, dark red *1,250.*

Entire design engraved further than No. 256-E1 but still incomplete: diagonal lines on beard under mouth incomplete, lines on coat not as dark as on issued stamp.

256-E2 6c Die on India, die sunk on card, dim dusky red *1,000.*

257-E1

Design size: about 19x22mm
Die size: 58½x60mm
Incomplete engraving of entire design as adopted: lines on coat not recut darker, vignette background not etched darker.

257-E1 8c Die on India, die sunk on card, dusky red violet *1,000.*

258-E1

Design size: about 19x22mm
Die size: 61½x61½mm
Incomplete engraving of entire design as adopted: shading unfinished on cheek, in ear, etc.

258-E1 10c Die on India, die sunk on card, dark brown *1,500.*

Entire design engraved further than No. 258-E1 but still incomplete: unfinished shading on cheek under eye.

258-E2 10c Die on India, die sunk on card, red brown *1,500.*

261-E1

Design size: 19x22mm
Die size: 50x101mm
Large die engraving of 1890 90c with value label and figure circles blank, no triangles.

261-E1 $1 Die on India, die sunk on card, black *2,750.*

Similar to No. 261-E1 but head further re-engraved and background shadows etched deeper.

261-E2 $1 Die on India, die sunk on card, blue green *3,000.*

261-E3

261-E4

Design size: 19x22mm
Model of engraved Perry vignette mounted on 1890 engraved frame with penciled in triangles, values painted in white and black. Ms. "O.K. July 14/94 TFM" below.

261-E3 $1 Die on India, cut close, mounted on 63x101mm white card, green vignette, black frame *3,250*

Similar to No. 261-E3 but with value lettering and circles added, background of circles unfinished, no triangles.

261-E4 $1 Die on India, die sunk on card, dark indigo blue *2,750.*

Incomplete engraving of entire design: hair on top and back of head, whiskers and back of neck, and shading in value circles all unfinished. Triangles are engraved.

261-E5 $1 Die on India, die sunk on card, black *1,600.*

Similar to No. 261-E5 but hair at back of head and whiskers darker, face in front of whiskers darker as on issued stamp. Circular lines extend into colorless vignette oval.

261-E6 $1 Die on India, die sunk on card
black *1,500.*
blue green *2,000.*

261-E7

Design size: 19x21½mm
Die size: 49x100mm
Incomplete engraving of unadopted dollar value design with portrait of Sen. James B. Beck: value label and numerals blank.

261-E7 $1 Die on India, die sunk on card, black *3,250.*

262-E1

262-E2

Design size: 19x22mm
Die size: 50x101mm
Incomplete engraving of frame only nearly as adopted: smaller $2's.

262-E1 $2 Die on India, die sunk on card, blue green *3,500.*

Design size: 19x22mm
Die size: 51x112mm
Incomplete engraving of entire design: left value circle blank, right circle engraved $2 outline only.

262-E2 $2 Die on India, die sunk on card, black *3,250.*

Die size: 51x112mm
Incomplete engraving of entire design: vignette shading unfinished, no veins in leaves around value circles.

262-E3 $2 Die on India, die sunk on card, black *2,850.*

262-E4

Incomplete engraving of entire design: inside of right border line above $2 unfinished.

262-E4 $2 Die on India, die sunk on card, black *2,600.*

Similar to No. 262-E4 but border line complete.

262-E5 $2 Die on India, die sunk on card, black *2,500.*

263-E1

Die size: 50x112½mm
Incomplete engraving of entire design: only one line in each scroll at right and left of $5, inner line of right border above $5 unfinished, etc., veins on leaves around right value circle unfinished.

263-E1 $5 Die on India, die sunk on card, black *2,750.*

Similar to No. 263-E1 but horiz. lines cut into oval line at top and inner oval line above L and R of DOLLARS required retouching as indicated by pencil instructions. Two lines in scrolls around value circles as adopted.

263-E2 $5 Die on India, die sunk on card, black *3,250.*

The bicolored essays commonly offered as No. 285-293 bicolored proofs can be found under the following listings: Nos. 285-E8, 286-E8, 287-E9, 288-E5, 289-E4, 290-E4, 291-E8, 292-E6, 293-E7. Values are for full-size cards (approximately 8x6 inches).

TRANS-MISSISSIPPI ISSUE

Die size: 79x68mm
Incomplete engraving of vignette only: initial state of die, no lines in sky or water.

285-E1 1c Die on India, die sunk on card, black *2,500.*

Vignette further engraved: lines in sky and water.

285-E2 1c Die on India, die sunk on card, black *2,500.*

Vignette further engraved: more background lines added.

285-E3 1c Die on India, die sunk on card, black *2,500.*

285-E4

Vignette further engraved: Indian at right darker, robe shadow etched.

285-E4 1c Die on India, die sunk on card, black *2,500.*

Vignette further engraved: rock in water more complete.

285-E5 1c Die on India, die sunk on card, black *2,500.*

Design size: 34x22mm
Die size: 73x62mm
Incomplete bicolor engraving of entire design: no second inner line in numerals.

285-E6 1c Die on India, die sunk on card, orange red & black *2,500.*

Die size: 83x68mm
Incomplete engraving of entire design: vignette unfinished and unetched, frame has second inner line in numerals.

285-E7 1c Die on India, die sunk on card, black *3,500.*

285-E8

Die size: 63x51mm
Complete bicolor engraving of entire design.

285-E8 1c Die with black vignette on India, die sunk on card
dark yellow green ("normal" bicolor) *300.*
dusky green *2,000.*
dusky blue green *2,000.*
brown *2,000.*

Incomplete engraving of entire design: corn husks and panels in ends of cartouche unfinished, lines under MARQUETTE and MISSISSIPPI not as thick as on completed die.

285-E9 1c Die on India, die sunk on card, dusky green *2,500.*

285-E10

Unfinished frame in red brown missing second inner line in numerals, with black unfinished "Cattle in the Storm" vignette as used on the $1 value, foreground snow at left incomplete.

285-E10 1c Die on India, red brown & black 3,500.

Die size: 78x68mm
Incomplete engraving of Mississippi River Bridge vignette (originally intended for 2c but eventually used on $2): initial state of die, very lightly engraved.

286-E1 2c Die on India, die sunk on card, black *3,750.*

Vignette further engraved but no lines on bridge beside two trolley cars.

286-E2 2c Die on India, die sunk on card, black *5,000.*

286-E3

Vignette further engraved but foreground between bridge and boat and foretopdeck incomplete, horse truck visible (later removed).

286-E3 2c Die on India, die sunk on card, black *3,000.*

Complete engraving of vignette only.

286-E4 2c Die on India, die sunk on card, black *3,000.*

286-E5

Design size: 137x88½mm
Pencil sketch by R. Ostrander Smith of 2c frame design as adopted except titled "ST. LOUIS BRIDGE."

286-E5 2c Sketch on tracing paper, 120x178mm *1,500.*

286-E6

Complete pencil drawing by R.O. Smith of frame design ("P" of "POSTAGE" in ink), titled "ST. LOUIS BRIDGE."

286-E6 2c Drawing on Whatman drawing board, 1889 wmk., 237x184mm *1,500.*

286-E7

Pencil drawing by R.O. Smith, no title.

286-E7 2c Drawing on 72x61mm tracing paper *1,500.*

286-E7A

Ink and wash drawing of frame, stamp size, similar to adopted design.

286-E7A 2c Drawing on hard, thick paper, black —

286-E8

Die size: 63x51mm
Complete bicolor engraving of 2c design but with Mississippi River Bridge vignette as used on $2.

Ridgway numbers used for colors of No. 286-E8.

286-E8 2c Die with black vignette on India, die sunk on card

dark red ("normal" bicolor)	*300.*
3k/0 dark orange red	*2,000.*
5k/0 dark o-orange-red	*2,000.*
5m/1 dim dusky o-orange-red	*2,000.*
7i/0 deep red orange	*2,000.*
7m/0 dusky red orange	*2,000.*
9m/0 dusky o-red-orange	*2,000.*
9k/2 dull dark o-red-orange	*2,000.*
13m/3 dismal dusky o-yellow-orange	*2,000.*
35m/1 dim dusky green	*2,000.*
49m/1 dim v. dusky blue	*2,000.*
63m/1 dim dusky red violet	*2,000.*
71-/0 deep violet-red-red	*2,000.*

286-E10

Die size: 82x68mm
Complete engraving with "FARMING IN THE WEST" vignette as adopted but from a die not used for the stamp: horses at left vignette border engraved dark up to border line which is solid complete line at both left and right.

286-E10 2c Die on India, die sunk on card (marked "Proof from 1st die.")

black	*2,500.*
dark orange red	*2,500.*

Design size: 34x22mm
Die No. 259 size: 63x51mm
Initial state of die, very lightly engraved.

287-E1 4c Die on India, die sunk on card, black *3,000.*

Vignette further engraved: sky lines ruled in.

287-E2 4c Die on India, die sunk on card, black *3,000.*

287-E3

Vignette further engraved: more lines added, no right forefoot on bison.

287-E3 4c Die on India, die sunk on card, black *3,750.*

Shadow under bison incomplete.

287-E4 4c Die on India, die sunk on card, black *3,750.*

Shadow under bison and foreground penciled in.

287-E5 4c Die on India, die sunk on card, black *3,750.*

Vignette further engraved: right forefoot added, shadow under bison engraved but not etched.

287-E6 4c Die on India, die sunk on card, black *3,750.*

287-E7

Die size: 83x67mm
Incomplete engraving of entire design: no lines in sky, frame shadow etching unfinished.

287-E7 4c Die on India, die sunk on card

black	*3,500.*
deep orange	*3,500.*

287-E8

Die size: 63x51mm
Incomplete engraving of entire design: corn husks at lower sides of frame unfinished.

Ridgway numbers used for colors of No. 287-E8.

287-E8 4c Die with black vignette on India, die sunk on card

5k/0 dark o-orange-red	*2,000.*
5m/0 dusky o-orange-red	*2,000.*
7m/0 dusky red orange	*2,000.*
11o/2 dull v. dusky orange	*2,000.*
13m/3 dismal dusky o-yellow-orange	*2,000.*
35m/1 dim dusky green	*2,000.*
39m/1 dim dusky blue green	*2,000.*
49o/1 dim v. dusky blue	*2,000.*
61k/1 dim dark violet-red violet	*2,000.*
63m/1 dim dusky red violet	*2,000.*
71m/0 dusky violet-red-red	*2,000.*

Complete bicolor engraving.

287-E9 4c Die with black vignette on India, die sunk on card

red orange ("normal" bicolor)	*300.*
deep red orange ("normal" bicolor)	*300.*

Die size: 77x69mm
Initial state of die, very lightly engraved.

288-E1 5c Die on India, die sunk on card, black *3,500.*

Vignette further engraved: lower clouds at right darkened.

288-E2 5c Die on India, die sunk on card, black *3,750.*

Vignette further engraved: shading penciled in on figures at right, etc.

288-E3 5c Die on India, die sunk on card, black *3,750.*

288-E4

Vignette further engraved but dots in sky at left of flag unfinished.

288-E4 5c Die on India, die sunk on card, black *3,750.*

288-E5

Design size: 34x22mm
Die size: 63x51mm
Incomplete bicolor engraving of entire design: unfinished crosshatching at left of "FREMONT," lines against bottom label and frame unfinished, no etching on flag.

Ridgway numbers used for colors of No. 288-E5.

288-E5 5c Die with black vignette on India, die sunk on card

49m/1 dim dusky blue ("normal" bicolor)	*300.*
49k/1 dim dark blue ("normal" bicolor)	*300.*
3k/0 dark orange red	*2,000.*
3m/0 dusky orange red	*2,000.*
7m/0 dusky red orange	*2,000.*
7m/1 dim dusky red orange	*2,000.*
9m/0 dusky o-red-orange	*2,000.*
11o/2 dull v. dusky orange	*2,000.*
37m/1 dim dusky g-blue-green	*2,000.*
39m/1 dim dusky blue green	*2,000.*
49o/1 dim v. dusky blue	*2,000.*
63m/1 dim dusky red violet	*2,000.*
71n/0 medium deep violet-red-red	*2,000.*
35m/1 dim dusky green	*2,000.*

Die size: 82x68½mm

Incomplete engraving of entire design: cornhusks, panels at ends of cartouche, mountains, foreground at sides of title label, sky, etc., all unfinished, figures and mountains not etched dark.

288-E7 5c Die on India, die sunk on card, black *3,250.*

Incomplete engraving of vignette: no dots on mountain tops next to right border, unfinished crosshatching at left end of title label.

288-E8 5c Die on India, die sunk on card, black *3,750.*

289-E1

Engraved vignette only of mounted Indian, not used for any value.

289-E1 8c Die on India, on card, black *5,000.*

Incomplete engraving of vignette only as adopted: blank area for label wider than completed bicolor vignette, knee of kneeling soldier unfinished, etc.

289-E2 8c Die on India, die sunk on card, black *3,000.*

289-E3

Design size: about 33½x21½mm
Incomplete engraving of frame only: shading of sunken center of cartouche at right of vignette unfinished.

289-E3 8c Die on India, 26x37mm, black *3,000.*

289-E4

Incomplete engraving of entire design: top row of distant shrubbery under "ERICA" missing, crosshatching on distant mountains at left, blades of grass at left end of label, some dots against top label all unfinished.

Ridgway numbers used for colors of No. 289-E4.

289-E4 8c Die with black vignette on India, die sunk on card

dark red ("normal" bicolor)	*375.*
dusky red ("normal" bicolor)	*375.*
3m/0 dusky orange red	*2,750.*
5m/0 dusky o-orange-red	*2,750.*
7i/0 deep red orange	*2,750.*
7m/0 dusky red orange	*2,750.*
9m/0 dusky o-red-orange	*2,750.*
11o/2 dull v. dusky orange	*2,750.*
35m/1 dim dusky green	*2,750.*
39m/1 dim dusky blue-green	*2,750.*
49o/1 dim v. dusky blue	*2,750.*
63m/1 dim dusky red violet	*2,750.*
71-/0 deep violet-red-red	*2,750.*

Die size: 77x64mm
Incomplete engraving of vignette only: two rows of dots in sky over wagon.

290-E1 10c Die on India, die sunk on card, black *3,750.*

290-E2

Vignette further engraved: three rows of dots in sky over wagon.

290-E2 10c Die on India, die sunk on card, black *3,750.*

Vignette further engraved: front of wagon canvas crosshatched.

290-E3 10c Die on India, die sunk on card, black *3,750.*

290-E4

Incomplete bicolor engraving of entire design: cornhusks unfinished, blades of grass to right of girl's feet and some to right of dark horse's feet are missing. Five lines of dots in sky over wagon.

Ridgway numbers used for colors of No. 290-E4.

290-E4 10c Die with black vignette on India, die sunk on card

dull dusky violet blue ("normal" bicolor)	*350.*
dusky blue violet ("normal" bicolor)	*350.*
1i/0 deep red	*2,500.*
3k/0 dark orange red	*2,500.*
5k/0 dark o-orange-red	*2,500.*
5m/0 dusky o-orange-red	*2,500.*
7i/0 deep red orange	*2,500.*
9m/0 dusky o-red-orange	*2,500.*
11o/2 dull v. dusky orange	*2,500.*
35m/1 dim dusky green	*2,500.*
39m/1 dim dusky blue green	*2,500.*
49o/1 dim v. dusky blue	*2,500.*
55m/2 smoky dark v.-blue violet	*2,500.*
63m/1 dim dusky red violet	*2,500.*
71-/0 deep violet-red-red	*2,500.*

Incomplete engraving of entire design: cornhusks unfinished, vignette from No. 290-E4 trimmed by engraving to fit frame.

290-E6 10c Die on India, die sunk on card, dark red orange *3,000.*

Incomplete engraving of entire design: cornhusks and panels at ends of cartouche and both sides and botton of vignette next to border unfinished.

290-E7 10c Die on India, die sunk on card, dull red violet *3,000.*

Incomplete engraving of entire design: cornhusks and both sides and bottom of vignette next to border are unfinished, vert. lines on cartouche frame at right of vignette missing.

290-E8 10c Die on India, dull red violet *3,000.*

Die size: 62x52mm
Incomplete engraving of vignette only: without sky or mountains.

291-E1 50c Die on India, die sunk on card, black *3,750.*

Vignette further engraved: sky ruled in.

291-E2 50c Die on India, die sunk on card, black *3,750.*

Vignette further engraved but no shading on distant mountains.

291-E3 50c Die on India, die sunk on card, black *3,750.*

Vignette further engraved: light shading on distant mountains.

291-E4 50c Die on India, die sunk on card, black *3,750.*

Vignette further engraved: more shading on distant mountains.

291-E5 50c Die on India, die sunk on card, black *3,750.*

291-E6

Vignette further engraved: shadows on miner's hat darker (etched).

291-E6 50c Die on India, die sunk on card, black *3,750.*

Vignette further engraved: girth under donkey darkened.

291-E7 50c Die on India, die sunk on card, black *3,750.*

291-E8

Design size: 34x22mm
Die size: 89x71mm
Incomplete bicolor engraving of entire design: shading lines on scroll in LR corner of frame and shrubbery in UL corner of vignette unfinished, sky incomplete.

Ridgway numbers used for colors of No. 291-E8.

291-E8 50c Die with black vignette on India, die sunk on card

dull dusky b-blue-green ("normal" bicolor; die size: 63x51mm)	*300.*
dull dusky g-blue-green ("normal" bicolor; die size: 63x51mm)	*300.*
1i/0 deep red	*2,500.*
3k/0 dark orange red	*2,500.*
5m/0 dusky o-orange-red	*2,500.*
7m/0 dusky red orange	*2,500.*
9i/0 deep o-yellow-orange	*2,500.*
9m/0 dusky o-red-orange	*2,500.*
11m/2 dull dusky orange	*2,500.*
13m/3 dismal dusky o-yellow-orange	*2,500.*
35m/1 dim dusky green	*2,500.*
39m/1 dim dusky blue green	*2,500.*
47n/2 dull v. dusky green-blue blue	*2,500.*
49o/1 dim v. dusky blue	*2,500.*
61k/1 dim dark violet-red-violet	*2,500.*
71m/0 dusky violet-red-red	*2,500.*

Incomplete engraving of entire design: vignette against top frame unfinished.

291-E9 50c Die on India, die sunk on card

black	*3,000.*
deep red orange	*3,000.*

Incomplete engraving of entire design: engraving on bottom of miner's pan dots only, not lines as on issued stamp.

291-E10 50c Die on wove, sage green *3,000.*

Incomplete engraving of vignette only: initial state of die, lightly engraved.

292-E1 $1 Die on India, die sunk on card, black *3,750.*

292-E2

Vignette further engraved: light shield-shaped vignette outline (later removed.)

292-E2 $1 Die on India, die sunk on card, black *3,750.*

Vignette further engraved: left front hoof of lead bull darker.

292-E3 $1 Die on India, die sunk on card, black *3,750.*

Vignette similar to No. 292-E3 but with penciled modeling in snow and among cattle.

292-E4 $1 Die on India, die sunk on card, black *3,750.*

Vignette further engraved: foreground snow at left darkened, shield outline removed.

292-E5 $1 Die on India, die sunk on card, black *3,750.*

292-E6

Incomplete engraving of entire bicolored design: right cornhusk and sky against top of frame unfinished, bull's right forefoot does not touch frame, foreground at right end of label unfinished.

Ridgway numbers used for colors of No. 292-E6, where available.

292-E6 $1 Die with black vignette on India, die sunk on card
dull violet blue ("normal" bicolor) *450.*
dull blue ("normal" bicolor) *450.*
dull violet ("normal" bicolor) *3,000.*
3k/0 dark orange red *3,000.*
5m/0 dusky-o-orange-red *3,000.*
7m/0 dusky red orange *3,000.*
9m/0 dusky o-red-orange *3,000.*
9n/3 dismal v. dusky o-red-orange *3,000.*
13n/3 dismal v. dusky o-yellow-orange *3,000.*
35m/1 dim dusky green *3,000.*
43m/1 dim dusky green blue *3,000.*
49m/1 dim dusky blue *3,000.*
57k/4 smoky dark violet-blue violet *3,000.*
63m/1 dim dusky red violet *3,000.*
71-/0 violet-red-red *3,000.*
47n/2 dull dusky green blue *3,000.*
dark brown *3,000.*

Incomplete engraving of entire design: left frameline, cornhusks and shading in frame over cornhusks all unfinished.

292-E7 $1 Die on India, die sunk on card, dusky red orange *3,000.*

293-E1

Design size: 34x22mm
Die size: 73x63mm
Vignette of Western mining prospector as used on 50c, but labeled HARVESTING IN THE WEST, frame shows $ same size as numeral 2.

293-E1 $2 Die on India, on card, dusky violet & black *3,500.*

Die size: 77x66mm
Incomplete engraving of Farming in the West vignette (originally intended for $2 but eventually used on 2c): initial state of die, very lightly engraved.

293-E2 $2 Die on India, die sunk on card, black *3,000.*

Vignette further engraved: four horses shaded.

293-E3 $2 Die on India, die sunk on card, black *3,000.*

Vignette further engraved: shading added to background figures and horses, pencil shading above and below half horse at left.

293-E4 $2 Die on India, die sunk on card, black *3,000.*

Vignette further engraved: foreground and shadows under horse teams darkened, no shading dots above half horse at left, etc.

293-E5 $2 Die on India, die sunk on card, black *3,000.*

293-E6

Vignette further engraved but foreground in front of plow wheel still unfinished.

293-E6 $2 Die on India, die sunk on card, black *3,000.*

293-E7

Die size: 62x51mm
Incomlpete engraving of entire bicolor design: only one plowshare shown, label longer, less foreground than on issued stamp.

Ridgway numbers used for colors of No. 293-E7.

293-E7 $2 Die with black vignette on India, die sunk on card
dusky orange red ("normal" bicolor; die size: 63x61mm) *450.*
dark red orange ("normal" bicolor; die size: 63x61mm) *450.*
1-/0 red *3,000.*
3k/0 dark orange red *3,000.*
7m/0 dusky red orange *3,000.*
35m/1 dim dusky green *3,000.*
39m/1 dim dusky blue green *3,000.*
45o/1 dim v. dusky blue-green blue *3,000.*
45m/2 dull dusky blue-green blue *3,000.*
63m/1 dim dusky red violet *3,000.*
71i/0 deep violet-red-red *3,000.*
47n/2 dull dusky green blue *3,000.*

Incomplete engraving of entire design as adopted: black wash over engraving on side of bridge and foreground (engraving under wash unfinished).

293-E9 $2 Die on India, die sunk on card, black *3,500.*

Complete design, vignette further engraved: engraving completed between title label and steamboat and city next to right frame, near side of bridge and smoke shadow on water lighter than on issued stamp.

293-E10 $2 Die on India, die sunk on card, black *3,500.*

Incomplete engraving of entire design: circles in upper corners of vignette next to value ovals, water next to right end of value label, panels at ends of cartouche all unfinished.

293-E11 $2 Die on India, die sunk on card, black *3,500.*

Edward Rosewater

Rosewater, of St. Louis, was asked by the Post Office Dept. in 1897 to submit proposed designs for the Trans-Mississippi Exposition issue. For that reason, they are listed here.
All are drawings on tracing paper, on 91x142mm buff card.

285-E11

Design size: 62x97mm
Wash drawing of cattle.

285-E11 1c dull orange —

286-E11

Design size: 57x98mm
Wash drawing of mounted Indian saluting wagon train.

286-E11 2c deep orange red —

288-E9

Design size: 61x100mm
Wash drawing of man plowing field.

288-E9 5c dark yellow —

290-E9

Design size: 62x99mm
Wash drawing of train coming around mountain.

290-E9 Ten Cents, dusky blue —

292-E9

Design size: 60x98mm
Wash drawing of woman holding light, standing on globe.

292-E9 $1 deep orange yellow —

PAN-AMERICAN ISSUE
Bureau of Engraving and Printing

294-E1

Design size: 108x82mm
Preliminary pencil drawing for frame design as adopted.

294-E1 1c Drawing on tracing paper, black *750.*

294-E2

Design size: 114x82½mm
Final ink drawing for frame design as adopted.

294-E2 1c Drawing on white card, about 6½x5 inches, black *750.*

294-E3

Die size: 87x68½mm
Incomplete engraving of vignette only.

294-E3 1c Die on India, die sunk on card, black *1,500.*

295-E1

Design size: 108x82mm
Preliminary pencil drawing of frame similar to that adopted (side ornaments, etc., different); UR corner, etc., unfinished.

295-E1 2c Drawing on tracing paper, black *750.*

295-E2

Design size: 114x83mm
Preliminary pencil drawing of frame similar to No. 295-E1 (minor differences) but with UR corner complete.

295-E2 2c Drawing on tracing paper, black *750.*

295-E3

Design size: 108x82mm
Preliminary pencil drawing of frame design similar to No. 295-E2 but with minor differences at top, in lettering, etc.

295-E3 2c Drawing on tracing paper, black *750.*

295-E4

Design size: 95x70mm
Ink and wash drawing model of frame design as adopted, side torchbearers engraved on India as on U.S. Series of 1901 $10 note.

295-E4 2c Die on white card, about 108x82mm, black *750.*

295-E4A

Design size: 88x69mm
Incomplete engraving of vignette only.

295-E4A 2c Die on India, die sunk on card, black *3,500.*

295-E5

295-E6

Design size: 27x19½mm
Die size: 88x68mm

Complete engraving of frame only as adopted.

295-E5 2c Die on India, die sunk on card, carmine *3,750.*

Die size: 88½x69mm
Engraving of entire design with vignette incomplete near frame and on cars.

295-E6 2c Die on India, die sunk on card, carmine & black *2,750.*

296-E1

Preliminary pencil drawing of unadopted frame design.

296-E1 4c Drawing on tracing paper, black *750.*

296-E2

Design size: 114x82½mm
Final ink drawing for frame design as adopted.

296-E2 4c Drawing on white card, about 6½x5 inches, black *750.*

296-E3

Design size: 27x19mm
Die size: 88x67mm
Incomplete engraving of entire design as adopted: lines missing at base of capitol dome, above driver's head.

296-E3 4c Die on India, die sunk on card, deep red brown & black *1,750.*

297-E1

Photo reproduction of pencil sketch of unadopted frame design on photosensitive tan paper, reduced to stamp size. Incomplete preliminary pencil drawing of frame design as adopted.

297-E1 5c Photo reproduction on tan paper *750.*

297-E2

Design size: 114x83mm
Incomplete preliminary pencil drawing of frame design as adopted.

297-E2 5c Drawing on tracing paper, black *750.*

297-E3

Design size: 114x82½mm
Final ink drawing for frame design as adopted.

297-E3 5c Drawing on white card, about 6½x5 inches, black *750.*

297-E4

Photo reproduction of sketch of adopted frame design on photosensitive paper, reduced to stamp size.

297-E4 5c Photo reproduction on tan paper *750.*

297-E5 297-E6

Die size: 87x68mm
Incomplete engraving of vignette only.

297-E5 5c Die on India, die sunk on card, black *1,500.*

Die size: 87x68mm
As No. 297-E5, but more completely engraved.

297-E6 5c Die on India, die sunk on card, black *1,500.*

297-E7

Design size: 27x19½mm
Die size: 87x68mm

Incomplete engraving of entire design as adopted: shading at bottom of battleaxes and scrolls at ends of title frame unfinished.

297-E7 5c Die on India, die sunk on card, blue & black *1,750.*

298-E1

Design size:108x82mm
Preliminary pencil drawing of unadopted frame design.

298-E1 8c Drawing on tracing paper, black *750.*

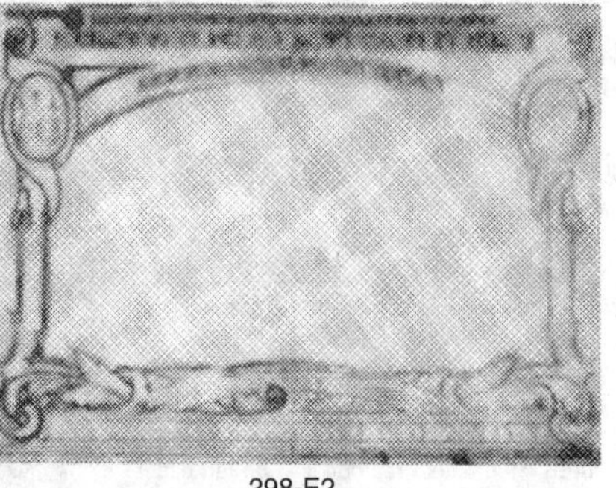

298-E2

Design size: 114x83mm
Incomplete preliminary pencil drawing of unadopted frame design.

298-E2 8c Drawing on tracing paper, black *750.*

298-E3

Design size: 114x83mm
Preliminary pencil drawing of unadopted frame design.

298-E3 8c Drawing on tracing paper, black *750.*

298-E4

Design size: 114x83mm
Preliminary pencil drawing of frame design as adopted.

298-E4 8c Drawing on tracing paper, black *750.*

298-E5

Design size: 114x82½mm
Final ink drawing for frame design as adopted.

298-E5 8c Drawing on white card, about 6½x5 inches, black *750.*

298-E6

Photo reproduction of sketch of adopted frame design on photosensitive paper, reduced to stamp size.

298-E6 8c Photo reproduction on tan paper *750.*

298-E7

Design size: 27x20mm
Die size: 87x69mm
Incomplete engraving of entire design: shading lines of ornaments, scrolls and ribbons at top unfinished, vignette incomplete at right, no etching on building in left foreground.

298-E7 8c Die on India, die sunk on card, bi-colored *1,750.*

299-E1

Design size: 114x83mm
Preliminary pencil drawing of unadopted frame design (small blank oval at center).

299-E1 10c Drawing on tracing paper, black *750.*

299-E2

Design size: 114x82½mm
Similar to No. 299-E1 but with outline of eagle and shield in center oval.

299-E2 10c Drawing on tracing paper, black *750.*

299-E3

Design size: 114x83mm
Preliminary pencil drawing for frame design as adopted.

299-E3 10c Drawing on tracing paper, black *750.*

299-E4

Design size: 114x82½mm
Final ink drawing for frame design as adopted.

299-E4 10c Drawing on white card, about 6½x9 inches, black *750.*

299-E5

Photo reproduction of sketch of adopted frame design on photosensitive paper, reduced to stamp size.

299-E5 10c Photo reproduction on tan paper *750.*

299-E6

Die size: 87x68mm
Incomplete engraving of entire design: frame complete but lines later engraved in the mast, smokestack and sky.

299-E6 10c Die on India, die sunk on card, bi-colored *1,750.*

1902 ISSUE

300-E1

300-E2

Incomplete engraving of vignette and lower part of frame.

300-E1 1c Die on India, die sunk on card, black *2,000.*

Design size: 19x22mm
Die size: 74½x88½mm
Incomplete engraving of entire design: vignette background has horiz. lines only, neckpiece, men at sides, etc., all unfinished.

300-E2 1c Die on India, die sunk on card, black *1,250.*

300-E3

Design size: 136x190mm
Preliminary ink drawing for 5c frame design but later adopted for 1c.

300-E3 1c Drawing on manila paper, black & blue green *1,000.*

300-E4

Design size: 116x135mm
Preliminary pencil and ink drawing for frame design as adopted.

300-E4 1c Drawing on white card, black *1,000.*

301-E1

Design size: 164x181mm
Paper size: 169x214mm
Preliminary pencil drawing of frame design (Raymond Ostrander Smith). Not adopted.

301-E1 2c Drawing on yellowed transparent tracing paper, black *1,000.*

301-E1A

Design size: 145x168mm
Preliminary pencil drawing of frame design as adopted.

301-E1A 2c Drawing on tracing paper, black *900.*

301-E2

301-E3

Model with vignette of Houdon bust of Washington, on wash drawing over photo reduced to stamp size for approval by PMG.

301-E2 2c Model mounted on card, black *750.*

Design size: 19x22mm
Die size: 75x87½mm
Incomplete engraving of entire design: head unfinished, horiz. background lines only, frame unfinished, lettering either blank or unfinished.

301-E3 2c Die on India, die sunk on card, black *1,250.*

301-E4

Design size: 60x88mm
Preliminary pencil drawing of right numeral 2 design as adopted.

301-E4 2c Drawing on tracing paper, black *900.*

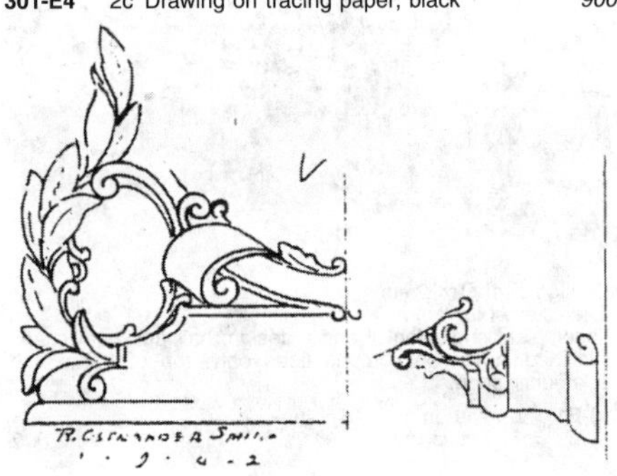

301-E5

Design size: 176x120mm
Preliminary pencil drawing of lower left and upper right design.

301-E5 2c Drawing on tracing paper, black *900.*

Design size: 19x22mm
Die size: 74x89mm
Incomplete engraving of entire design: head unfinished, horiz. background lines only, frame almost finished, lettering complete. No. 62057 on back.

301-E6 2c Die on India, die sunk on 153x202mm card, black —

302-E1

303-E1

Design size: 19x22mm
Die size: 74½x88mm
Incomplete engraving of entire design: vignette unfinished, horiz. background lines only, atlantes at sides unfinished. No. 66218 on back.

302-E1 3c Die on India, die sunk on card, black *1,750.*

Design size: 19x22mm
Die size: 75x88mm
Incomplete engraving of entire design: vignette unfinished on eyes, hair, beard, etc. No. 58920 on back.

303-E1 4c Die on India, die sunk on card, black *1,750.*

304-E1

Design size: 19x22mm
Die size: 74x87½mm
Rejected die: figure at right poorly draped, blank triangles below "UNITED STATES," no shading in frame around "POSTAGE/FIVE CENTS" except at extreme ends.

304-E1 5c Die on India, die sunk on card, blue *2,300.*

Incomplete engraving of entire design: shading on side figures unfinished.

304-E2 5c Die on India, die sunk on card, blue *1,250.*

Incomplete engraving of entire design as adopted.

305-E1 6c Die on India, lake *1,250.*

305-E2

Design size: 123x210mm
Preliminary ink drawing for unadopted frame design.

305-E2 6c Drawing on kraft paper, black & blue green *800.*

306-E1

Design size: 7x3½ inches
Preliminary pencil drawing of left side of frame design as adopted.

306-E1 8c Drawing on tracing paper, black *500.*

306-E2

Die size: 76x89mm
Incomplete engraving of vignette and numerals only: head drapery unfinished, horiz. background lines only.

306-E2 8c Die on India, die sunk on card, black *2,000.*

306-E3

Design size: 165x175mm
Preliminary ink drawing for unadopted frame design.

306-E3 8c Drawing on kraft paper, black, blue & green *800.*

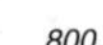

307-E1

Design size: 135x174mm
Preliminary ink drawing for unadopted frame design.

307-E1 10c Drawing on kraft paper, black, blue & green *800.*

308-E1

Design size: 19x22mm
Die size: 69x85½mm
Incomplete engraving of entire design: hair, beard, right cheek, eyes and right shoulder all unfinished, horiz. background lines only, name panel blank, ribbon shading unfinished, etc. No. 57796 on back.

308-E1 13c Die on India, die sunk on card, black *1,250.*

308-E2

Design size: 177x220mm
Preliminary ink drawing of 3c frame design but later adopted for 13c.

308-E2 13c Drawing on kraft paper, black & blue green *900.*

310-E1

Design size: 19x22mm
Die size: 74x87½mm
Incomplete engraving of entire design: hair and right cheek unfinished, horiz. background lines only, top of frame and eagles unfinished.

310-E1 50c Die on India, die sunk on card, black *2,000.*

Incomplete engraving of entire design, further engraved than No. 310-E1: oval line outside top label thinner at bottom ends than on issued stamp.

310-E2 50c Die on India, die sunk on card, black *2,000.*

312-E1

313-E1

Design size: 19x22mm
Die size: 76x88mm
Incomplete engraving of entire design: hair, neckpiece, etc., unfinished, horiz. background lines only; top of frame, leaves and numeral surrounds all unfinished.

312-E1 $2 Die on India, die sunk on card, black *2,000.*

Design size: 19x22mm
Die size: 75½x87½mm
Incomplete engraving of entire design: eyes, cheeks, hair, neckpiece all unfinished, horiz. background lines only, frame engraved in outlines only.

313-E1 $5 Die on India, die sunk on card, dark green *1,750.*

319-E1

Design size: 19½x22mm
Die size: 75x87½mm
Incomplete engraving of entire design from rejected die (central star between UNITED and STATES, four lines above small lettering, bottom of shield curved): name and date ribbon blank.

319-E1 2c Die on India, die sunk on card, carmine *2,000.*

319-E2

319-E3

Incomplete engraving of entire design from rejected die: shading on leaves and vignette completed, lettering added to bottom ribbon and started on label above vignette. Blue pencil note on card backing, "May 1903. This die was abandoned at this stage because of crowded condition of lettering above portrait. G.F.C.S." No. 83909 on back.

319-E2 2c Die on India, die sunk on card, carmine *1,500.*

Design size: 19½x22mm
Die I size: 75½x88mm
Incomplete engraving of entire design as adopted (no star between UNITED and STATES, bottom of shield straight): small label above vignette is blank.

319-E3 2c Die on India, die sunk on card, black *2,000.*

LOUISIANA PURCHASE ISSUE

324-E1

Incomplete engraving of entire design: head, hair, eyes, chin, coat all unfinished, horiz. background lines only, bottom label and upper corner labels blank, frame shading unfinished.

324-E1 2c Die on India, die sunk on card, black *2,500.*

325-E1

Incomplete engraving of entire design: head only lightly engraved, horiz. background lines only, laurel leaves unshaded, leaves' background and numeral shields blank.

325-E1 3c Die on India, die sunk on card, black *2,500.*

326-E1

Incomplete engraving of entire design: vignette unfinished, horiz. background lines only, much of frame blank or incomplete.

326-E1 5c Die on India, die sunk on card, black blue *2,500.*

JAMESTOWN ISSUE

328-E1

Incomplete engraving of entire design: vignette, shading on heads in upper corners, numerals and numeral shields all unfinished.

328-E1 1c Die on pale cream soft wove, 30x24mm, dusky green *1,250.*

330-E1

330-E2

Incomplete engraving of vignette only: collar, hat, corselet, etc., unfinished. No. 245910 on back.

330-E1 5c Die on India, die sunk on card, black *1,750.*

Incomplete engraving of entire design: no shading in frame background.

330-E2 5c Die on India, die sunk on card, blue *5,000.*

330-E3

Incomplete engraving of entire design: shading on corselet and arm of Pocahontas unfinished, horiz. background lines only, shading around date and name ribbon unfinished. No. 247606 on back.

330-E3 5c Die on card, die sunk, blue *4,250.*

Incomplete engraving of entire design: shading on ribbons unfinished.

330-E4 5c Die on India, die sunk on card, black *4,250.*

1908 ISSUE

331-E1

Photograph of wash drawing of entire design, head and vignette background retouched with black wash. Ms. "GVLM-Sept. 26th-1908" (PMG) in LR corner of backing card.

331-E1 1c Retouched photo on thick gray cardboard, 83x100mm, black *2,000.*

332-E1

332-E2

Design size: 6⅛x7¼ inches
Wash drawing of frame design with vignette cut out, mounted over retouched glossy black photo of Houdon bust of Washington.

332-E1 Two Cents, Design on drawing paper, black *1,250.*

Design size: 19x22mm
Photograph of wash drawing of entire design, almost completely retouched with black ink and wash. Pencil "GVLM" (PMG) at top of backing card.

332-E2 Two Cents, Retouched photo on thick gray cardboard, 81x100mm, black *2,000.*

332-E3

Design size: 19x22mm
Incomplete engraving of entire design: shading on leaves at right unfinished. Pencil "Oct 15 - 1908" at LR of backing card.

332-E3 Two Cents, Die on India, die sunk on card, carmine *1,250.*

333-E1

333-E2

Design size: 18½x22mm
Engraving of design as adopted except "THREE CENTS" at bottom.

333-E1 Three Cents, Die printed directly on card, deep violet *1,000.*

Design size: 19x22mm
Photograph of wash drawing of entire design with "3 CENTS 3" drawn in black and white wash. Ms. "Nov. 24/08. J.E.R." (BEP director) in LR corner of backing card.

333-E2 3c Retouched photo on thick gray cardboard, 80x100mm, black *2,000.*

334-E1

334-E2

Design size: 18½x22mm
Engraving of design as adopted except "FOUR CENTS" at bottom.

334-E1 Four Cents, Die printed directly on card, orange brown *1,000.*

Design size: 19x22mm
Photograph of wash drawing of entire design with "4 CENTS 4" drawn in black and white wash. Ms. "Nov. 24/08. J.E.R." (BEP director) in LR corner of backing card.

334-E2 4c Retouched photo on thick gray cardboard, 80x100mm, black *2,000.*

335-E1

335-E2

Design size: 18½x22mm
Engraving of design as adopted except "FIVE CENTS" at bottom.

335-E1 Five Cents, Die printed directly on card, blue *2,000.*

Design size: 19x22mm
Photograph of wash drawing of entire design with "5 CENTS 5" drawn in black and white wash. Ms. "Nov. 24/08. J.E.R." (BEP director) in LR corner of backing card.

335-E2 5c Retouched photo on thick gray cardboard, 80x100mm, black *2,000.*

Design size: 18½x22mm
Incomplete engraving of design with "SIX CENTS" at bottom.

336-E1 Six Cents, Die on India, on card, red orange *1,250.*

336-E2

Design size: 19x22mm
Photograph of wash drawing of entire design with "6 CENTS 6" drawn in black and white wash. Ms. "Nov. 24/08. J.E.R." (BEP director) in LR corner of backing card.

336-E2 6c Retouched photo on thick gray cardboard, 80x100mm, black *2,000.*

337-E1

338-E1

Design size: 19x22mm
Photograph of wash drawing of entire design with "8 CENTS 8" drawn in black and white wash. Ms. "Nov. 24/08. J.E.R." (BEP director) in LR corner of backing card.

337-E1 8c Retouched photo on thick gray cardboard, 80x100mm, black *2,000.*

Design size: 19x22mm
Photograph of wash drawing of entire design with "10 CENTS 10" drawn in black and white wash. Ms. "Nov. 24/08. J.E.R." (BEP director) in LR corner of backing card.

338-E1 10c Retouched photo on thick gray cardboard, 80x100mm, black *2,000.*

338a-E1

Design size: 18½x22mm
Complete engraving of entire adopted design but a value not issued: "12 CENTS 12" at bottom. Virtually all are stamp size, imperf.

Ridgway numbers used for colors of No. 338a-E1.

338a-E1 12c
- ***a.*** Die on bluish white wove
  - 41n/1 dim v. dusky b-blue-green *900.*
- ***b.*** Die on 1f/1 dim pale red wove
- ***c.*** Die on 7d/1 dim light red orange wove
  - 47m/1 dim dusky g-b. blue *900.*
- ***d.*** Die on 17b/1 dim bright o-y. yellow wove
  - 1i/0 deep red *900.*
  - 5i/0 deep o-orange-red *900.*
  - 27m/0 dusky green yellow *900.*
  - 37m/0 dusky g-blue-green *900.*
  - 41m/0 dusky b-blue-green *900.*
  - 55m/1 dim dusky blue violet *900.*
  - 59m/1 dim dusky violet *900.*
  - 69m/3 dismal dusky r-violet-red *900.*
- ***e.*** Die on 19f/0 pale y-orange yellow wove
  - 1i/0 deep red *900.*
  - 15i/1 dim deep yellow orange *900.*
  - 35m/0 dusky green *900.*
  - 43d/1 dim light green blue *900.*
  - 61m/3 dismal dusky v-red-violet *900.*
  - 69o/5 black *900.*
- ***f.*** Die on 31f/2 dull pale yellow green wove
  - 69o/5 black *900.*
- ***g.*** Die on 42d/1 dim bright green blue wove
  - 41m/1 dim dusky b-blue-green *900.*
- ***h.*** Die on 44-/1 dim medium green blue wove
  - 9k/2 dull dark o-r-orange *900.*
- ***i.*** Die on 45l/1 dim v. dark b-green-blue wove
  - 5i/0 deep o-orange-red *900.*
  - 27m/2 dull dusky green yellow *900.*
- ***j.*** Die on 69g/0 pale r-v. red wove *900.*
- ***k.*** Die on dark blue bond, 69o/5 black *900.*

339-E1

340-E1

Design size: 19x22mm

Photograph of wash drawing of entire design with "13 CENTS 13" drawn in black and white wash. Ms. "Oct. 7-08. J.E.R.-GVLM" (BEP director, PMG) in LL corner of backing card.

339-E1 13c Retouched photo on thick gray cardboard, 80x100mm, black *2,000.*

Design size: 19x22mm
Photograph of wash drawing of entire design with "15 CENTS 15" drawn in black and white wash. Ms. "Oct. 7-08. J.E.R.-GVLM" (BEP director, PMG) at bottom of backing card.

340-E1 15c Retouched photo on thick gray cardboard, 80x100mm, black *2,000.*

341-E1

342-E1

Design size: 19x22mm
Photograph of wash drawing of entire design with "50 CENTS 50" drawn in black and white wash. Ms. "Oct. 7-08. J.E.R.-GVLM" (BEP director, PMG) at bottom of backing card.

341-E1 50c Retouched photo on thick gray cardboard, 80x100mm, black *2,000.*

Design size: 19x22mm
Photograph of wash drawing of entire design with "1 DOLLAR 1" drawn in black and white wash. Ms. "Oct. 7-08. J.E.R.-GVLM" (BEP director, PMG) at bottom of backing card.

342-E1 $1 Retouched photo on thick gray cardboard, 80x100mm, black *2,000.*

LINCOLN MEMORIAL ISSUE

Design size: 7x8 inches
Photostat of 1980 2c frame design with wash drawing of ribbons and vignette photo of Lincoln's head.

367-E1 Two Cents, Model of Lincoln design, black *1,500.*

Photo of No. 367-E1 reduced to stamp size, retouched to highlight hair and beard.

367-E2 Two Cents, Retouched photo, black *1,500.*

367-E3

Design size: 19x22mm
Incomplete engraving of entire design: head, background, name/date ribbon all unfinished.

367-E3 Two Cents, Die on India, die sunk on card, carmine *2,500.*

ALASKA-YUKON-PACIFIC EXPOSITION ISSUE

Design size: 18½x22mm
Wash drawing of frame similar to 1908 2c design with photo of wash drawing of seal on ice cake as vignette. Ms. "#1" at UL corner of backing card.

370-E1 2c Model on card, about 3x4 inches, black *1,500.*

370-E2

Design size: 18½x22mm
Engraved frame similar to 1908 2c but with wash drawing of "1870 1909" in ribbons and "2 CENTS 2" at bottom, vignette cut out, mounted over engraved vignette of Wm. H. Seward from snuff stamp. Ms. "#2" at UL corner of backing card.

370-E2 2c Model on card, about 3x4 inches, black *1,500.*

370-E3

Design size: 27½x20½mm
Photo of seal on ice cake vignette as originally approved, mounted on ink and wash drawing of frame design as approved. Ms. "#3" at UL corner of backing card, engraved Seward vignette pasted on at bottom, "Approved April 3, 1909 FH Hitchcock Postmaster-General" at right.

370-E3 2c Model on glazed card, 93x70mm, black, white and gray *2,250.*

370-E4

Design size: 27½x20mm
Photo of wash drawing of frame and arched ribbon as adopted, vignette cut out, mounted over photo of engraved Seward vignette, background retouched with black wash. Ms. "Approved subject to addition of the name Seward, as indicated in letter of Director, Bureau of Engraving and Printing, dated April 24, 1909. F.H. Hitchcock Postmaster General."

370-E4 2c Model on 93x75mm thick gray card, black *2,250.*

370-E5

Design size: 27x20mm
Retouched photo of wash drawing of adopted frame with seal on ice cake vignette but pencil "WILLIAM H. SEWARD" on white wash ribbon below. Ms. "April 26/09 Approved J.E.R." (BEP director) at LR corner of backing card.

370-E5 2c Retouched photo and pencil on 94x66mm thick gray card, black *2,000.*

Incomplete engraving of entire design: no shading on head or vignette background, no shading lines on ribbons.

370-E6 2c Die on India, die sunk on 8x6 inch card, carmine *2,000.*

370-E7

Design size: 26½x19½mm
Similar to No. 370-E6 but further engraved: face and collar lightly engraved, horiz. background lines only, no shading lines on ribbons.

370-E7 2c Die on wove, 32x26½mm, carmine *2,000.*

372-E1

Wash drawing of adopted vignette design.

372-E1 2c Drawing on artist's cardboard, 11¼x6¾ inches, black *1,500.*

372-E2

Wash drawing of frame design as adopted except "HUDSON-FULTON CENTENARY" at top.

372-E2 2c Drawing on artist's cardboard, 7¾x6¾ inches, black *1,500.*

Design size: 33x21½mm
Wash drawing of frame design as adopted with dates "1609-1807" and photo of No. 372-E1 reduced to fit and worked over with wash.

372-E3 2c Model on card, 4x3 inches, black *2,000.*

Design size: 33x21½mm
Wash drawing of frame with vignette cut out, mounted over photo of No. 372-E1. Typed/ms. "Approved August 17, 1909 F.H. Hitchcock Postmaster General" and "August 19, 1909 Amend by substituting word 'Celebration' for 'Centenary.' F.H. Hitchcock Postmaster General." Pencil "P.O. 488" in LR corner.

372-E4 2c Model on white card, 129x103mm, black *2,000.*

372-E5

Incomplete engraving of entire design: lettering on flag at masthead of *Clermont* has "N" reversed and no "T."

372-E5 2c Die on wove, 38x27mm, carmine *2,000.*

PANAMA-PACIFIC ISSUE

397-E1

Design size: 27x20mm
Incomplete engraving of frame with engraved circular vignette as adopted, with wash drawing of palm trees on each side and "1 CENT 1" in wash. Ms. "Approved July 16, 1912 Frank H. Hitchcock Postmaster General" on backing card.

397-E1 1c Model on card, about 89x77mm, black *1,500.*

398-E1

Design size: about 29½x20mm
Ink and wash drawing of frame design longer than adopted with photo of wash drawing of Golden Gate as eventually used (reduced) on 5c. Backstamp "STAMP DIVISION FEB. 12, 1912 P.O. DEPT" on backing card.

398-E1 2c Model on card, about 4x3 inches, black *1,500.*

398-E2

Design size: 27x20mm

Incomplete engraving of frame with photo of wash drawing of vignette as adopted with engraved title "GATUN LOCKS," wash drawing of value numerals. Ms. "Approved Aug. 27, 1912 Frank H. Hitchcock Postmaster General" on backing card.

398-E2 2c Model on gray card, about 3¾x2⅞ inches, black *1,500.*

Completely engraved design as adopted except titled "GATUN LOCKS" in error (design pictures Pedro Miguel locks).

398-E3 2c
a. Large die on India, die sunk on card, 6x8 inches (formerly #398AP1), carmine *6,500.*
b. Small die on India (formerly #398AP2), carmine *6,000.*

398-E4

Design size: 27x20mm
Photo of incomplete engraving (no sky in vignette). Ms. "Approved Dec. 17, 1912 Frank Hitchcock Postmaster General" on backing card.

398-E4 2c Model on thick gray card, black *1,500.*

399-E1

Design size: 27x20mm
Photo of wash drawing of frame design as adopted with photo of wash drawing of adopted vignette mounted in place. Ms. "Approved July 16, 1912 Frank H., Hitchcock Postmaster General" on backing card.

399-E1 5c Model on 30x22mm white paper, mounted on card, about 3⅞x2⅞ inches, black *1,500.*

400-E1

Design size: 27x20mm
Photo of wash drawing of frame design as adopted with photo of painting adopted for vignette mounted in place. Ms. "Approved Aug. 22, 1912, Frank H. Hitchcock Postmaster General" on backing card.

400-E1 10c Model on 31x34mm white paper, on thick gray card, black *1,500.*

Design size: 27x20mm
Photo of wash drawing of frame design as adopted with photo of wash drawing of two galleons at anchor in bay, titled "CABRILLO 1542" mounted in place. Backing card marked "II."

400-E2 10c Model on white paper, on 91x85mm thick gray card, black *1,500.*

Design size: 27x20mm
Photo of wash drawing of frame design as adopted with photo of Liberty standing among palm fronds, two battleships in bay. Backing card marked "III."

400-E3 10c Model on white paper, on thick gray card, black *1,500.*

400-E4

Design size: 27x20mm
Similar to No. 400-E3 but steamships replace battleships. Backing card marked "IV."

400-E4 10c Model on white paper, on thick gray card, black *1,500.*

400-E5

Design size: 27x20mm
Similar to No. 400-E2 but two galleons under full sail at right in front of snowclad mountains. Backing card marked "V," paper with typed "Stamp Division Feb. 21, 1912. P.O. Dept." pasted on back.

400-E5 10c Model on white paper, on thick gray card, black *1,500.*

1912 ISSUE

Incomplete engraving of entire design: wash drawing of "1 CENT 1" at bottom. Ms. "Approved. July 17, 1911 Frank H. Hitchcock. P.M. Gen." on backing card.

405-E1 1c Model on 3½x3¾-inch card, black —

Wash drawing of design as adopted, worked over partial photo with "2 CENTS 2" at bottom drawn in wash. Ms. "Approved. July 17, 1911 Frank H. Hitchcock P. M. Gen." on backing card.

406-E1 2c Model on 3½x3¾-inch card, black —

Wash drawing of design as adopted, worked over partial photo with 8 in lower corners drawn in wash. Ms. "Approved. July 17, 1911 Frank H. Hitchcock Postmaster General" on backing card.

414-E1 8c Model on 3½x3¾-inch card, black —

Vignette of head only without background gridwork.

414-E2 8c Die on India, die sunk on 157x208mm, olive green —

416-E1

418-E1

Design size: 19x22mm
Photo of wash drawing of generic design with 10 in lower corners drawn in black ink. Ms. "July 17, 1911. (May, 1911 erased) Approved: Frank H. Hitchcock PM Gen" on backing card, backstamped "STAMP DIVISION P.O. DEPT. MAY 15, 1911."

416-E1 10c Model on 87x113mm thick gray card, black *1,000.*

Design size: 19x22mm
Photo of wash drawing of generic design with background of frame between oval and outer colorless line in dark gray wash and some colorless retouching, 15 in lower corners drawn in black ink. Ms. "July 17, 1911. (May, 1911 erased) Approved: Frank H. Hitchcock PM Gen" on backing card, backstamped "STAMP DIVISION P.O. DEPT. MAY 15, 1911."

418-E1 15c Model on 87x113mm thick gray card, black *1,000.*

421-E1

423-E1

Design size: 19x22mm
Photo of wash drawing of generic design with 50 in lower corners drawn in black ink. Ms. "July 17, 1911. (May, 1911 erased) Approved: Frank H. Hitchcock PM Gen" on backing card, backstamped "STAMP DIVISION P.O. DEPT. MAY 15, 1911."

421-E1 50c Model on 77x112mm thick gray card, black *1,000.*

Design size: 19x22mm
Photo of wash drawing of generic design with entire value label drawn in black ink. Ms. "July 17, 1911. (May, 1911 erased) Approved: Frank H. Hitchcock PM Gen" on backing card, backstamped "STAMP DIVISION P.O. DEPT. MAY 15, 1911."

423-E1 $1 Model on 87x113mm thick gray card, black *1,000.*

1922 PRECANCEL ESSAY

499-E1

Design size: 19x22mm
Die size: 90x88mm
"NEW YORK/N.Y." precancel engraved directly onto type I die, printed in one color. Ms. "8/16/22 J.S." in LR corner of backing card.

499-E1 2c Die on India, die sunk on card, lake —
Dark carmine (on bond) —

1918 ISSUE

Complete engraving of Franklin head only as on $2 and $5 values, no shading around head.

523-E2 $2 Die on India, die sunk on 151x103mm card, black —

523-E3

Design size: 16x18¾mm
Complete engraving of vignette only including shading. Pencil "837660 May 1917" on back of India paper, pencil "Schofield" at bottom of backing card.

523-E3 $2 Die on 32x33mm India, card mounted, black *1,000.*

PEACE ISSUE

537-E1

537-E2

Design size: 21½x18½mm
Stamp never issued due to World War I.

537-E1 2c Die on India, die sunk on card, deep red *1,500.*

Die size: 22x19mm
Stamp never issued due to World War I.

537-E2 5c Die on India, die sunk on card, dim dusky g-b-blue *1,500.*

SAMUEL F.B. MORSE ISSUE

537-E3

Design size: 21½x18½mm
Incomplete engraving of entire design: vignette and lettering finished but blank spaces beside vignette. Backstamped "932944" and "Jan. 1, 1919" or "932945" and "Jan. 7, 1919". Frame design subsequently used for 3c Victory issue, No. 537, though lettering and value numerals made slightly smaller.

537-E3 3c Die on India, die sunk on card, black *2,000.*

VICTORY ISSUE

537-E4

Design size: 21½x18½mm
Die size: 85½x75½mm
Incomplete engraving of entire design: no shading in border and some flags unfinished. Backstamped "936356 Jan. 25, 1919."

537-E4 3c Die on India, die sunk on card, black *1,500.*

PILGRIM ISSUE

548-E1

Design size: 26x19mm
Incomplete engraving of entire design: sky blank, sails unshaded.

548-E1 1c Die on India, die sunk on card, green *1,500.*

Incomplete engraving of frame only: "CENTS" engraved but numeral circles blank (probably an essay for both 2c and 5c).

549-E1 2c Die on India, die sunk on card
black *1,500.*
green *1,500.*

1922 ISSUE

551-E1

Design size: 19x22mm
Incomplete engraving of entire design as adopted: name label blank, vignette unfinished. Ms. "Approved--Harry S. New" on backing card.

551-E1 ½c Die on India, die sunk on 151x202mm card, olive brown *1,900.*

Incomplete engraving of entire design but further engraved than No. 551-E1: no lines in white oval over ends of title ribbon and ribbon foldunders not etched as darkly as on issued stamp.

551-E2 ½c Die on India, die sunk on 149x201mm card, olive brown *1,350.*

555-E2

Complete engraving with horizontal lines surrounding bust of Lincoln.

555-E2 3c Die on India, affixed to card, 26x30mm, violet *2,750.*

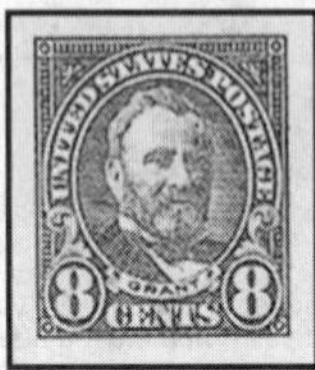

560-E1

Complete engraving with horizontal lines surrounding slightly larger bust of Grant.

560-E1 8c Die on India, die sunk on 97x111mm card, dark olive green *2,000.*

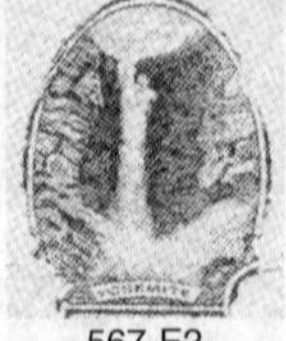

567-E2

568-E2

Design size: 19x22mm
Engraving of unadopted vignette with unadopted engraved frame cut away.

567-E2 20c Die on India, die sunk on 151x201mm card, cobalt blue *2,500.*

Design size: 19x15mm
Die size: 88x75mm
Engraving of adopted vignette with engraved frame cut away.

568-E2 25c Die on India, die sunk on 202x151mm card, green *2,500.*

Pencil drawings for unadopted frame design.

555-E1 3c black *1,150.*
557-E1 5c black *1,150.*
557-E2 5c black *1,150.*
566-E1 15c black *1,150.*
571-E1 $1 black *1,150.*

573-E1

Engraving of accepted vignette.

573-E1 $5 Die on India, affixed to card, 73x87mm, blue *3,750.*

HUGUENOT-WALLOON TERCENTENARY ISSUE

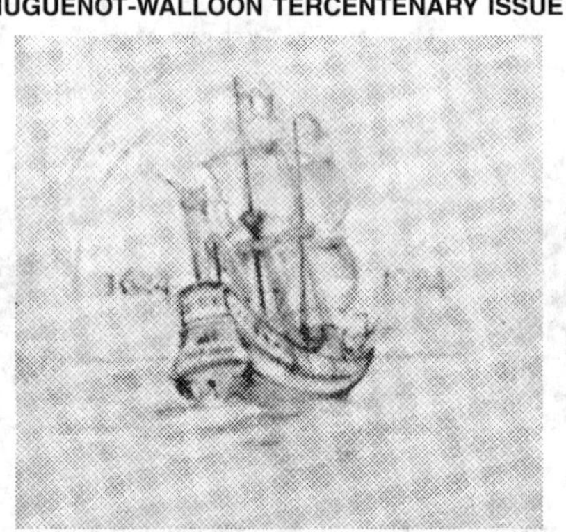

614-E1

Design size: 8½x7¼ inches
Preliminary pencil drawing of *Nieu Nederland* in circular frame. Pencil note: "Reverse--Sailing to America, not away from America--J. B. Stoudt."

614-E1 1c black *500.*

616-E1

Design size: 5½x3⅛ inches
Wash drawing of design adopted for vignette.

616-E1 5c black *1,500.*

618-E1

Design size: 36x21mm
Incomplete engraving of entire design as adopted: spaces between letters of "BIRTH OF LIBERTY" not solid color.

618-E1 2c Die on India, die sunk on card, carmine *1,250.*

Design size: 36x21mm
Incomplete engraving of entire design as adopted: numeral circles blank, many shading lines missing in vignette, no shading around "TWO CENTS," etc.

618-E2 2c Die on India, die sunk on 91x71mm card, black *1,500.*

ERICSSON MEMORIAL ISSUE

Wash drawing of design as adopted, stamp size.

628-E1 5c black *750.*

BATTLE OF WHITE PLAINS ISSUE

629-E1

Design size: 8⅜x9 inches
Preliminary ink and watercolor drawing of entire design quite similar to that adopted.

629-E1 2c black & red *750.*

BURGOYNE CAMPAIGN ISSUE

644-E1

Design size: 22x19mm
Essay size: 25x22mm
Card size: 78x98mm
Preliminary wash drawing of unadopted design, on white paper mounted on thick gray card with "Approved" in ink and "May 7, 1927" in pencil subsequently crossed out with "X's."

644-E1 2c black *2,000.*

683-E1

Design size: 13x17 inches
Preliminary ink drawing of design nearly as adopted.

683-E1 2c Drawing on artist's cardboard, black *500.*

704-E1

Design size: 119x150mm
Preliminary pencil sketch of unadopted ½c design.

704-E1 ½c Drawing on tracing paper, mounted on 195x192mm manila paper, black *750.*

718-E1

Design size: 6x7 inches
Watercolor drawing of unadopted design with 2c denomination.

718-E1 2c Drawing on thick artist's card, red *1,250.*

719-E1

Design size: 6x7 inches
Watercolor drawing of entire design similar to that eventually adopted for 5c but with 2c denomination.

719-E1 2c Drawing on thick artist's card, 150x175mm, blue *1,250.*

PANAMA CANAL ISSUE

856-E1

Design size: 37x21½mm
Essay size: 99x81mm
Card size: 141x117mm
Engraving of unadopted design: "3 CENTS 3" and "25th ANNIVERSARY PANAMA CANAL" changed for final design. "W. O. Marks" at lower right corner, "Engraver's Stock Proof 594256 / Authorized by 'OML'" on reverse.

856-E1 3c Die on India, die sunk on card, deep violet —

AIR POST

1918 ISSUE

Complete engraving of frame only as adopted. Backstamped "626646A ENGRAVER'S STOCK PROOF AUTHORIZED BY" (signature), plus pencil "663" and "Weeks" (?).

C3-E1 24c Die on India, die sunk on card, deep carmine *5,000.*

Incomplete engraving of entire design as adopted: unfinished plumes above value numerals and no serial number on biplane.

C3-E2 24c Die on wove, 40x37mm, black vignette, blue frame —

SPECIAL DELIVERY

1885 ISSUE
American Bank Note Co.

E1-E1

Incomplete engraving of entire design as adopted: ornaments missing at each side of "SPECIAL," line under messenger is in pencil, shading on left side of messenger tablet missing, leaves and vert. background lines unfinished (latter shaded over with pencil).

E1-E1 10c Die on India, dim dusky g-b. green *2,500.*

1888 ISSUE

No. E1P1 with "AT ANY OFFICE" drawn in wash on small piece of thin paper and mounted over "AT A SPECIAL / DELIVERY / OFFICE." Pencil "any post office" and ms. "At once O.K. / J.C.M. 14 Aug. 86" (?) on backing card.

E2-E1 10c Die on India, on card, black *2,500.*

1908 ISSUE
Bureau of Engraving and Printing

E7-E1

Design size: about 8½x7⅛ inches
Preliminary ink and pencil drawing of entire design somewhat similar to that adopted: ("V.S." for U.S. and other minor changes).

E7-E1 10c Drawing on vellum, black *750.*

E7-E2

Design size: about 8½x7⅛ inches
Preliminary ink and pencil drawing of entire design nearly as adopted: ("V.S." for U.S.)

E7-E2 10c Drawing on white drawing paper, black *750.*

E7-E3

Design size: 213½x179mm
Similar to No. E7-E2 but with "U.S."

E7-E3 10c Drawing on white drawing paper, black *750.*

E7-E4

E7-E5

Design size: 26x21½mm
Woodblock size: 45x42mm
Woodblock of entire design as adopted with about 5mm colorless border outside design, solid color beyond, engraved on wood by Giraldon of Paris. (One exists with ms. "Wood cut made in Paris by Mr. Whitney Warren -- The cuts and the impression therefrom were turned over to the Director of the Bureau of Engraving & Printing, and by him turned over to the Custodian of Dies, Rolls and Plates and given No. 446. They are now held by the Custodian." Another has typewritten "Prints made in Paris, France, from a wood-cut engraving by an unknown engraver from a design made by Mr. Whitney Warren, architect, of New York City." with ms. "Compliments J.E. Ralph" director of B.E.P. and pencil date "9/7/1917.")

Ridgeway numbers used for colors of Nos. E7-E4 and E7-E5.

E7-E4 10c
- ***a.*** Woodcut on 19g/2 yellowish wove
  - 43k/1 dim dark green blue *450.*
  - 44m/2 dull dusky m. g-blue *450.*
  - 45j/1 dim v. dark b-g-blue *450.*
  - 45m/1 dim dusky b-g-blue *450.*
- ***b.*** Woodcut on 19f/2 dull faint y-o-yellow wove
  - 43k/1 dim dark g-blue *450.*
  - 43m/1 dim dusky g-blue *450.*
  - 44k/1 dim dark m. g-blue *450.*
  - 44k/2 dull dark m. g-blue *450.*
  - 45m/1 dim dusky b-g-blue *450.*
  - 45m/2 dull dusky b-g-blue *450.*
- ***c.*** Woodcut on 19g/2 dull v. faint y-o-yellow wove
  - 43k/1 dim dark g-blue *450.*
  - 43m/1 dim dusky g-blue *450.*

Design size: 26x21½mm
Complete engraving of entire design fairly similar to that adopted but with minor differences.

E7-E5 10c
- ***a.*** Die on India, die sunk on card, 37m/0 dusky g-b. green blue *750.*
- ***b.*** Die on soft white wove, 30x35mm, 37m/0 dusky g-blue-green *750.*

REGISTRATION STAMP

F1-E1

Design size: 19x22½mm
Retouched circular photo of vignette mounted on wash drawing of frame design as adopted. Ms. "Approved July 8/11--Frank H. Hitchcock--Postmaster General" on backing card.

F1-E1 10c Model on white paper, mounted on thick gray cardboard, 81x92mm, black *1,250.*

POSTAGE DUE

1879 ISSUE
American Bank Note Co.

J1-E1

Design size: 19½x25½mm
Die size: 54x66½mm
Complete engraving of entire design as adopted except "UNPAID POSTAGE" instead of "POSTAGE DUE" above vignette oval.

J1-E1 1c

a. Die on India, die sunk on card
orange brown *850.*
slate gray *850.*
dark red violet *850.*
dull yellow *850.*
light orange *850.*
red brown *850.*
b. Die on India, cut small (1-4mm)
gray black *400.*
dull red *400.*
dull brown *400.*
dull green *400.*
dull blue *400.*
c. Die on India, cut close (0-1mm)
orange brown *400.*
slate gray *400.*
dark red violet *400.*
dull yellow *400.*
d. Die on white ivory paper, die sunk
black *700.*
black brown *700.*
scarlet *700.*
blue *700.*

Design size: 19½x25½mm
Die size: 53½x53½mm
Complete engraving of entire design as adopted except "UNPAID POSTAGE" instead of "POSTAGE DUE" above vignette oval.

J2-E1 2c

a. Die on India, die sunk on card
dark red violet *850.*
black *850.*
b. Die on India, cut small
gray black *400.*
dull red *400.*
dull brown *400.*
dull green *400.*
dull blue *400.*
c. Die on India, cut close
orange brown *400.*
dark red violet *400.*
slate gray *400.*
d. Die on white ivory paper, die sunk
black *700.*
black brown *700.*
scarlet *700.*
blue *700.*

Design size: 19½x25½mm
Die size: 53x53mm
Complete engraving of entire design as adopted except "UNPAID POSTAGE" instead of "POSTAGE DUE" above vignette oval.

J3-E1 3c

a. Die on India, die sunk on card, dull yellow *850.*
b. Die on India, cut small
gray black *400.*
dull red *400.*
dull brown *400.*
dull green *400.*
dull blue *400.*
c. Die on India, cut close, dull yellow *400.*
d. Die on white ivory paper, die sunk
black *700.*
black brown *700.*
scarlet *700.*
blue *700.*

Design size: 19½x25½mm
Complete engraving of entire design as adopted except "UNPAID POSTAGE" instead of "POSTAGE DUE" above vignette oval.

J4-E1 5c

a. Die on India, die sunk on card, slate gray *850.*
b. Die on India, cut small
gray black *400.*
dull red *400.*
dull brown *400.*
dull green *400.*
dull blue *400.*
c. Die on India, cut close
orange brown *400.*
slate gray *400.*
dark red violet *400.*
dull yellow *400.*
d. Die on white ivory paper, die sunk
black *700.*
black brown *700.*
scarlet *700.*
blue *700.*

1894 ISSUE
Bureau of Engraving and Printing

J31-E1

J31-E2

Design size: 18½x22½mm
Die size: 50x99mm
Incomplete engraving of entire design: no engraved lines on numeral, lathework unfinished on two inclined spots at each side of numeral.

J31-E1 1c Die on India, die sunk on card, deep claret *750.*

Design size: 18½x22½mm
Die size: 50x99mm
Incomplete engraving of entire design: engraved lines on numeral but lathework still unfinished on two inclined spots at each side of numeral.

J31-E2 1c Die on India, die sunk on card, claret *750.*

J33-E1

J33-E2

Incomplete engraving of entire design: blank space for numeral with "3" drawn in pencil.

J33-E1 3c Die on India, die sunk on card, black *1,000.*

Incomplete engraving of entire design: no engraved lines on numeral, bottom lettering in pencil only, no hand retouching of lathework around numeral.

J33-E2 3c Die on India, die sunk on card, black *1,000.*

J33-E3

Incomplete engraving of entire design: no engraved lines on numeral.

J33-E3 3c Die on India, die sunk on card, claret *750.*

J35-E1

J36-E1

Incomplete engraving of entire design: no engraved lines on numerals.

J35-E1 10c Die on India, die sunk on card, black *750.*

Incomplete engraving of entire design: no engraved lines on numerals.

J36-E1 30c Die on India, die sunk on card, claret *750.*

J37-E1

J37-E2

Incomplete engraving of entire design: 9x9mm blank space for numerals.

J37-E1 50c Die on India, die sunk on card
black *1,000.*
claret *850.*

Incomplete engraving of entire design: numerals engraved but hand engraving to retouch lathework around numerals missing.

J37-E2 50c Die on India, die sunk on card, black *1,000.*

OFFICIAL

Continental Bank Note Co.
AGRICULTURE

O2-E1

Design size: 20x25mm
Engraved vignette, numeral and value label from 1873 2c (No. 146-E10) mounted on pencil and wash drawing for frame design as adopted for Agriculture set. Pencil signature "J. Claxton" on backing card. Frame differs for each dept.

O2-E1 2c Model on yellowish card, 23x30mm, on 90x118mm white card, black vignette, gray black frame *1,500.*

EXECUTIVE

O12-E1

O12-E2

Design size: 20x25mm
See design note for No. O2-E1.

O12-E1 3c Model on yellowish card, 23x30mm, on 90x118mm white card, black *1,500.*

Design size: 19½x25mm
Die size: 64x76mm

Engraving of complete design of No. O12-E1 with "DEP'T" in top label.

O12-E2 3c
a. Die on India, die sunk on card, green *2,000.*
b. Die on India, cut close
black *1,250.*
green *1,250.*

INTERIOR

O17-E1

Design size: 20x25mm
See design note for No. O2-E1.

O17-E1 3c Model on yellowish card, 23x30mm, on 90x118mm white card, black *1,500.*

JUSTICE

O27-E1

Design size: 20x25mm
See design note for No. O2-E1.

O27-E1 3c Model on yellowish card, 23x30mm, on 90x118mm white card, black *1,500.*

NAVY

O37-E1

Design size: 20x25mm
See design note for No. O2-E1.

O37-E1 3c Model on yellowish card, 23x30mm, on 90x118mm white card, black *1,500.*

POST OFFICE

O47-E1

Design size: 19½x25mm
Complete engraving of entire design as adopted except with Franklin vignette instead of large numeral.

O47-E1 1c
a. Die on India, mounted on white ivory card
blue *1,500.*
b. Die on proof paper
gray black *1,250.*
dull scarlet *1,250.*
dull brown *1,250.*
dull green *1,250.*
dull blue *1,250.*
c. Die on white ivory paper
brown black *1,500.*
orange red *1,500.*
blue *1,500.*

Design size: 19½x25mm
Complete engraving of entire design as adopted except with Jackson vignette instead of large numeral.

O48-E1 2c
a. Die on India, mounted on white ivory card
orange brown *1,500.*
b. Die on proof paper
gray black *1,250.*
dull scarlet *1,250.*
dull brown *1,250.*
dull green *1,250.*
dull blue *1,250.*
c. Die on white ivory paper
brown black *1,500.*
orange red *1,500.*
blue *1,500.*

O49-E1

O49-E2

Design size: 20x25mm
Engraved vignette, numeral and value label from 1873 3c (No. 147-E10) mounted on pencil and wash drawing for frame design not adopted for Post Office set.

O49-E1 3c Model on yellowish card, 23x30mm, on 90x118mm white card, black *1,500.*
O49-E2 3c Model on yellowish card, 23x30mm, on 90x118mm white card, black *1,500.*

O49-E3

Design size: 20x25mm
See design note for No. O2-E1.

O49-E3 3c Model on yellowish card, 23x30mm, on 90x118mm white card, black *1,500.*

Design size: 19½x25mm
Complete engraving of entire design as adopted except with Washington vignette instead of large numeral.

O49-E4 3c
a. Die on India, mounted on white ivory card
green *1,500.*
b. Die on proof paper
gray black *1,250.*
dull scarlet *1,250.*
dull brown *1,250.*
dull green *1,250.*
dull blue *1,250.*
c. Die on white ivory paper
brown black *1,500.*
orange red *1,500.*
blue *1,500.*

O49-E5

1870 1c stamp (No. 145) with vignette cut out, "OFFICIAL 3 STAMP" drawn in pencil on envelope on which stamp is mounted. Blue pencil notation on backing envelope, "Design by Mr. J. Barber for P.O.D. Official."

O49-E5 1c Stamp frame mounted on envelope, ultramarine frame, black vignette *2,500.*

O49-E6

O49-E8

Model of engraved frame from No. O49-E4 with hollow oval engraved lathework band with "OFFICIAL / STAMP" drawn in wash mounted in place, numeral drawn in pencil and wash. Ms. "No. 1" on backing card.

O49-E6 3c Model on stiff white card, 50x75mm, black 1,750.

As No. O49-E6, Ms. "No. 3" on backing card.

O49-E8 3c Model on stiff white card, 50x75mm, black *1,750.*

O50-E1

Incomplete engraving of design with Lincoln vignette, without rectangular frame design.

O50-E1 6c Die on white ivory paper, black *2,250.*

Design size: 19½x25mm
Complete engraving of entire design as adopted except with Perry vignette instead of large numeral.

O56-E1 90c
a. Die on India, mounted on white ivory card, brown *1,500.*
b. Die on proof paper
gray black *1,500.*
dull scarlet *1,500.*
dull brown *1,500.*
dull green *1,500.*
dull blue *1,500.*
c. Die on white ivory paper, black *1,250.*

STATE

O59-E1

O68-E1

Design size: 20x25mm
Engraved vignette, numeral and value label from 1873 3c (No. 147-E10) mounted on pencil and wash drawing for frame design as adopted for State set. Pencil signature "J. Claxton" on backing card.

O59-E1 3c Model on yellowish card, 23x30mm, on 90x118mm white card, black *1,250.*

Design size: 25½x40mm
Engraved vignette of Seward mounted in watercolor drawing of adopted frame design. Ms. signatures of J. Claxton and Chas. Skinner on backing card.

O68-E1 Two Dollars, Model on 29x43mm grayish white card, mounted on 96x120mm white card, black *3,000.*

O68-E2

Complete engraving of adopted frame only with "TWO DOLLARS." in value label at bottom. With "FIVE DOLLARS." and "TEN DOLLARS." value labels outside design at left and "TWENTY DOLLs." value tablet at right.

O68-E2 Two Dollars, Die on India, black *3,000.*

O68-E3

Plate engraved frame only (occurs paired with complete bicolor plate proof of $2).

O68-E3 Two Dollars, Plate essay on India, green *3,000.*

WAR

O85-E1

Design size: 20x25mm

Engraved vignette, numeral and value label from 1873 3c (No. 147-E10) mounted on pencil and wash drawing for frame design as adopted for War set. Pencil signature "J. Claxton" on backing card.

O85-E1 3c Model on yellowish card, 23x30mm, on 90x118mm white card, black *2,500.*

NEWSPAPER AND PERIODICALS

1865 ISSUE
National Bank Note Co.

PR1-E1

Design size: 51x89mm

Typographed design somewhat similar to that adopted but with large Franklin vignette facing left, "PACKAGE" at bottom, other minor differences.

PR1-E1 5c Die on stiff white ivory paper

deep orange red	*1,000.*
dusky g-b. blue	*1,000.*
bright blue	*1,000.*
a. Die on paper with blue ruled lines	
deep orange red	*1,000.*
carmine	*1.000.*

1875 ISSUE
National Bank Note Co.

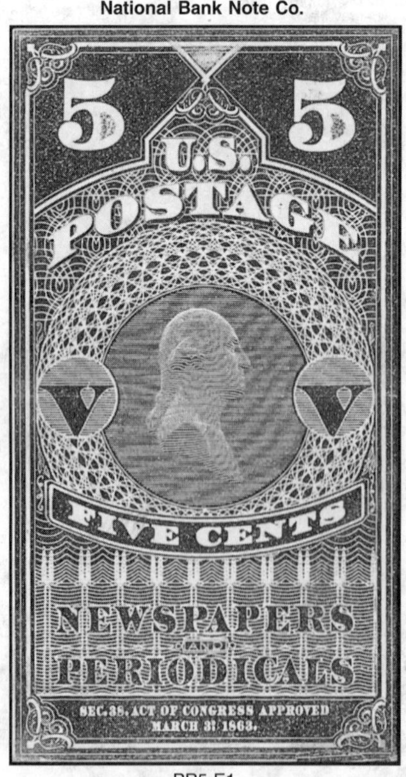

PR5-E1

Design size: 52x96½mm

Typographed design as issued but lacking "National Bank Note Company, New York" imprint at bottom.

PR5-E1 5c Die on wove paper, blue —

1875 ISSUE
Continental Bank Note Co.

PR9-E1

PR9-E2

Design size: 19½x25mm

Engraved vignette and numerals (25's) with pencil sketch of unadopted frame design.

PR9-E1 25c Die on India, on card, black *2,750.*

Design size: 19½x25mm

Complete engraving of unadopted design with "U S" at top and "25 CENTS 25" at bottom.

PR9-E2 25c

a. Die on India, on card	
black	*1,250.*
scarlet	*1,250.*
blue	*1,250.*
b. Die on white ivory paper	
black	*1,250.*
black brown	*1,250.*
scarlet	*1,250.*
blue	*1,250.*

PR14-E1

PR23-E1

Design size: 25x35mm

Wash drawing of complete design as adopted. Backing card signed by both designers, Chas. Skinner and Jos. Claxton.

PR14-E1 9c Drawing on 26x36mm card, on 56x74mm card, black *900.*

Design size: 24x35½mm

Wash drawing similar to that adopted, backing card signed by designers Skinner and Claxton, also has pencil "$12" and ms. "Continental Bank Note Co."

PR23-E1 96c Drawing on 88x121mm card, black *900.*

PR27-E1

PR28-E1

Design size: 24½x35mm

Incomplete engraving of entire design: unshaded (shading pencilled in) inside left, right and bottom framelines, value label, top of "9." Upper corners unfinished.

PR27-E1 $9 Die on India, die sunk on 76x82mm card, black *1,250.*

Design size: 24½x35mm

Incomplete engraving of entire design: no shading on dollar signs and numerals. No shading on frame around numerals and around value tablet.

PR28-E1 $12 Die on India, die sunk on 66x80mm card, black *1,250.*

PR29-E1

Design size: 24x35½mm
Wash drawing similar to that adopted but with "U S" in six-pointed stars instead of at top. Backing card signed by designers Skinner and Claxton, also pencil "31/32" and "8 13/32," pencil "Alter" with lines to stars.

PR29-E1 $24 Drawing on 88x121mm card, black *750.*

PR31-E1

PR31-E2

Vignette size: 13½x26mm
Engraved vignette only as adopted.

PR31-E1 $48 Die on India, die sunk on card, black *750.*

Design size: 24x36mm
Wash drawing similar to that adopted, backing card signed by designers Skinner and Claxton, also has pencil "$48" above each value numeral.

PR31-E2 $48 Drawing on 88x121mm card, black *1,350.*

PR32-E1

Design size: 24½x35½mm
Wash drawing similar to that adopted, backing card signed by designers Skinner and Claxton.

PR32-E1 $60 Drawing on 88x121mm card, black *750.*

1885 ISSUE
American Bank Note Co.

PR81-E1

Design size: 23x25mm
Complete engraving of entire design as adopted for 12c-96c.

PR81-E1 1c
- ***a.*** Die on India, die sunk on card
  black *1,350.*
- ***b.*** Die on white ivory paper
  black *600.*

black brown *600.*
scarlet *600.*
blue *600.*

1895 ISSUE
Bureau of Engraving and Printing

Incomplete engraving of entire design: background at upper ends of value label, shading on side lettering and numerals missing.

PR102-E2 1c Die on India, die sunk on card
black *600.*
green *600.*

Incomplete engraving of entire design but further engraved than No. PR102-E2: shading on PA is light, no shading on PE of NEWSPAPERS or IO of PERIODICALS and shading on OD is light.

PR102-E3 1c Die on India, die sunk on card, black *600.*

Incomplete engraving of entire design but further engraved than No. PR102-E3: shading on PERIODICALS is finished but not on PAPE.

PR102-E4 1c Die on India, die sunk on card, black *500.*

PR103-E1 PR103-E2

Design size: 21½x34½mm
Die size: 56x75½mm
Incomplete engraving of entire design: spaces for numerals and value label blank but with pencil outline of lettering.

PR103-E1 2c Die on India, die sunk on card, black *1,500.*

Incomplete engraving of entire design but further engraved than No. PR103-E1: shading on leaves at ends of value label unfinished, numerals unshaded, unfinished shading on APE of NEWSPAPERS and RIO of PERIODICALS.

PR103-E2 2c Die on India, black *1,250.*

Incomplete engraving of entire design but further engraved than No. PR103-E2: no shading on PE of NEWSPAPERS, unfinished shading on PA of NEWSPAPERS and RIO of PERIODICALS.

PR103-E3 2c Die on India, die sunk on card, black *1,250.*

PR104-E1

Design size: 21½x34½mm
Die size: 57x73mm
Incomplete engraving of entire design: spaces for numerals and value label blank but with pencil outline of lettering.

PR104-E1 5c Die on India, die sunk on card, black *1,250.*

PR105-E1 PR105-E2

Design size: 21½x34½mm
Die size: 56x75mm
Incomplete engraving of entire design: spaces for numerals and value label blank but with pencil outline of lettering.

PR105-E1 10c Die on India, die sunk on card, black *1,250.*

Incomplete engraving of entire design but further engraved than No. PR105-E1: numerals unfinished, lower corners blank.

PR105-E2 10c Die on India, die sunk on card, black *1,500.*

Incomplete engraving of entire design but further engraved than No. PR105-E2: lower right corner blank.

PR105-E3 10c Die on India, die sunk on card, black *1,250.*

Incomplete engraving of entire design but further engraved than No. PR105-E3: numerals blank, no inner lines.

PR105-E4 10c Die on India, die sunk on card, black *1,250.*

PR105-E5

Design size: 21½x34½mm
Die size: 56x75mm
Incomplete engraving of entire design (early state of die similar to No. PR105-E1) with "10" pencilled in upper right corner and "TEN CENTS" pencilled in at bottom. Pencil notes on India include "Make top of 1 a little larger and put on spur," "Work up Vignette" and "Use same scrolls as marked on 5c-."

PR105-E5 10c Die on India, die sunk on card, black *1,500.*

PR106-E1

PR106-E2

Vignette size: 13x25½mm
Die size: 56x72mm
Incomplete engraving of vignette only (transfer of Continental Banknote Co. die for 72c with left side cut off): eagle crest faces front and its right wing is not pointed, shading on left thigh near sword hilt incomplete, bottom of vignette straight instead of curved.

PR106-E1 25c Die on India, die sunk on card
black *1,750.*
deep red *1,750.*

Design size: about 21x34½mm
Die size: 57½x75mm
Entire design with frame incompletely engraved: vert. lines around CENTS label missing, no shading on TWENTY FIVE, colorless beads under E and FI of same.

PR106-E2 25c Die on India, die sunk on card
black *1,750.*
deep red *1,750.*

An impression from No. PR106-E2 with pencil shading on TWENTY FIVE and vert. ink lines in spaces around CENTS label, colorless beads also blacked out in ink. Below engraving are three diff. pencil sketches for shape and shading to be engraved.

PR106-E3 25c Die on India, die sunk on card, black *1,750.*

An impression from No. PR106-E2 but with shading suggestions from No. PR106-E3 partly engraved except colorless beads have pencil shading only. Below engraving is pencil sketch for corner of CENTS label.

PR106-E4 25c Die on India, die sunk on card
black *1,750.*
deep red *1,500.*

PR106-E5

Design size: 21½x34½mm
Die size: 55x72mm
Large die proof of PR107 with bottom value label cut out and "TWENTY-FIVE CENTS" pencilled in on backing card.

PR106-E5 25c Die on India, die sunk on card, black *1,250.*

PR107-E1

PR107-E3

Incomplete engraving of entire design: eagle's head and much of bottom of stamp's design unfinished, top of frame unfinished, value lettering sketched in pencil.

PR107-E1 50c Die on India, die sunk on card, black *1,750.*

Incomplete engraving of entire design: top of frame and scrolls below FIFTY CENTS unfinished.

PR107-E3 50c Die on India, die sunk on card, black *1,300.*

PR108-E1

PR108-E2

Design size: 24½x37mm
Die size: 75x76mm
Incomplete engraving of entire design: vignette and spaces around numerals incomplete, pencil sketch instructions for engraver at top and side for these spaces.

PR108-E1 $2 Die on India, die sunk on card, black *1,650.*

Design size: 24½x37mm
Die size: 75x76mm
Incomplete engraving of entire design but further engraved than No. PR108-E1: space for ornaments under POSTAGE blank, numerals unshaded.

PR108-E2 $2 Die on India, die sunk on card, scarlet *1,500.*

Further engraved than No. PR108-E2: scrolls under POSTAGE engraved but unfinished.

PR108-E3 $2 Die on India, die sunk on card, black *1,500.*

PR111-E1

PR112-E1

Design size (incomplete): 24½x30mm
Die size: 75x84mm
Incomplete engraving of partial design: spaces for stars and 0s of numerals blank, design missing below bottom of vignette.

PR111-E1 $20 Die on India, die sunk on card, black *1,250.*

Design size: 24½x35½mm
Die size: 72½x76mm
Incomplete engraving of entire design: upper corners around value numerals unfinished, etc.

PR112-E1 $50 Die on India, on card, black *1,850.*

PR113-E1

Design size: 24½x35½mm
Die size: 75x74mm
Incomplete engraving of entire design: spaces at lower inner corners of value shields blank, shading on numerals and letters at top unfinished.

PR113-E1 $100 Die on India, on card, black *1,350.*

Further engraved than No. PR113-E1: vignette completed but numerals not shaded, shadows on frame not etched dark.

PR113-E2 $100 Die on India
black *1,350.*
red-violet *1,350.*

Further engraved than No. PR113-E2: numerals shaded, shadows on frame not finally etched, especially above POSTAGE.

PR113-E3 $100 Die on India, black *1,350.*

PARCEL POST

Q1-E1

Design size: 35½x23mm
Photo of wash drawing of frame design with numerals, CENT and POST OFFICE CLERK in black ink, vignette in black wash. Ms. "Changed from 15c" and "Approved Nov. 15, 1912--Frank H. Hitchcock--Postmaster General" on backing card.

Q1-E1 1c Model on thick gray cardboard, 106x91mm, black *2,500.*

Q2-E1

Design size: 35x23½mm
Photo of wash drawing of frame only as adopted. Ms. "Approved Oct. 10, 1912, for border and size of stamps. Engraving to be ⅞ by 1⅜ inches. Frank H. Hitchcock. Postmaster General" on backing card.

Q2-E1 2c Model on thick gray cardboard, 122x110mm, black *1,500.*

Q2-E2

Design size: 35x23mm
Photo of wash drawing of frame design and retouched photo of ship vignette as eventually used for 10c, numerals and STEAMSHIP AND MAIL TENDER in black ink. Ms. "Changed to 10c" and "Approved Oct. 11, 1912. Frank H. Hitchcock. Postmaster General" on backing card.

Q2-E2 2c Model on thick gray cardboard, 110x83mm, black *2,500.*

Q2-E3

Design size: 34x22mm
Photo of wash drawing of entire design with adopted vignette, numerals in white wash and CITY CARRIER in black ink. Ms. "Changed from 5c" and "Approved Nov. 14, 1912. Frank H. Hitchcock. Postmaster General" on backing card.

Q2-E3 2c Model on thick gray cardboard, 111x92mm, black *2,500.*

Q3-E1

Design size: 35x23mm
Complete engraving of unadopted design: vignette shows mail truck backing up to railroad mail train with clerk about to handle pouches.

Q3-E1 3c Die on white wove, about 43x31mm, carmine *1,500.*

Q3-E2

Design size: 35x22mm
Photo of wash drawing of entire design with adopted vignette (retouched around door to mail car). Ms. "Approved Feb. 22, 1913. Frank H. Hitchcock. Postmaster General" on backing card.

Q3-E2 3c Model on thick gray cardboard, black *2,500.*

Q4-E1

Design size: 33½x22mm
Photo of wash drawing of entire design with adopted vignette, numerals drawn in white and RURAL CARRIER in black ink. Ms. "Changed from 10c" and "Approved Nov. 14, 1912. Frank H. Hitchcock. Postmaster General" on backing card.

Q4-E1 4c Model on thick gray cardboard, 116x92mm, black *2,500.*

Q5-E1

Design size: 35x23mm
Photo of wash drawing of entire design with vignette (retouched) eventually used for 2c, numerals and CITY LETTER CARRIER in black ink and white wash. Ms. "Changed to 2c.--City Carrier" and "Approved Oct. 10, 1912. Frank H. Hitchcock. Postmaster General" on backing card.

Q5-E1 5c Model on thick gray cardboard, 110x84mm, black *2,500.*

Q5-E2

Design size: 33½x21½mm
Photo of wash drawing of entire design with numerals in gray, unadopted vignette with MAIL TRAIN in black ink, first car retouched with wash. Ms. "Approved . . . 1912 / . . . Postmaster General" on backing card.

Q5-E2 5c Model on thick gray cardboard, 104½x92mm, black *1,500.*

Q5-E3

Design size: 33½x22mm
Photo of wash drawing of entire design with numerals in gray, MAIL TRAIN in black ink, first car retouched with wash. Ms. "Approved . . . 1912 / . . . Postmaster General" on backing card.

Q5-E3 5c Model on thick gray cardboard, 104½x92mm, black *1,500.*

Q5-E4

Design size: 33½x22mm
Photo of wash drawing of entire design with numerals in white with black background, MAIL TRAIN and pouch catcher in black ink. Ms. "Approved Nov. 19, 1912 Frank H. Hitchcock Postmaster General" on backing card.

Q5-E4 5c Model on thick gray cardboard, 94x90mm, black *2,500.*

Q6-E1

Design size: 35½x23mm
Photo of wash drawing of entire design with vignette (retouched) eventually used for 4c, numerals and RURAL DELIVERY in black ink and white wash. Ms. "Changed to 4c." and "Approved Oct. 10, 1912. Frank H. Hitchcock. Postmaster General" on backing card.

Q6-E1 10c Model on thick gray cardboard, 111x83mm, black *2,500.*

Q6-E2

Design size: 35x23mm
Photo of wash drawing of entire design with adopted vignette, numerals and STEAMSHIP AND MAIL TENDER in black ink and white wash. Ms. "Changed from 2c." and "Approved Nov. 8, 1912. Frank H. Hitchcock. Postmaster General" on backing card.

Q6-E2 10c Model on thick gray cardboard, 116x92mm, black *2,500.*

Q7-E1

Design size: 33½x22mm
Photo of wash drawing of entire design (redrawn in front of autocar and U S MAIL and STATION A) with AUTOMOBILE SERVICE in black ink. Ms. "Approved . . . 1912 / . . . Postmaster General" on backing card.

Q7-E1 15c Model on thick gray cardboard, 115x93mm, black *1,500.*

Design size:
Complete engraving of entire design with unadopted title label "COLLECTION SERVICE" instead of the adopted "AUTOMOBILE SERVICE."

Q7-E2 15c Die on white wove, card mounted, carmine *1,500.*

Q8-E1

Design size: 35x22mm
Incomplete engraved design nearly as adopted: aviator wears football helmet, head tilted far forward and one leg dangling over edge of plane, mail bag "No. 1" at his right while another sack hangs loosely out of plane.

Q8-E1 20c Die on white wove, about 37x24mm, carmine *1,500.*

Q8-E2

Design size: 35x22mm
Photo of incomplete engraved design as adopted. Ms. "Approved Nov. 19, 1912. Frank H. Hitchcock. Postmaster General" on backing card.

Q8-E2 20c Model on thick gray cardboard, 98x95mm, black *2,500.*

Q9-E1

Design size: 34½x22½mm
Photo of wash drawing of entire design with numerals and smoke at right painted in. Ms. "Changed from $1.00." and "Approved Nov. 14, 1912. Frank H. Hitchcock. Postmaster General" on backing card.

Q9-E1 25c Model on thick gray cardboard, 112x92mm, black *2,500.*

Q10-E1

Design size: 35x23mm
Photo of drawing of entire design with vignette eventually used for 25c with roof, smokestacks and smoke drawn in. Typed label "Stamp Division / Feb / 21 / 1912 / P.O. Dept" on back of backing paper.

Q10-E1 50c Model on thick white paper, black *1,500.*

Q10-E2

Design size: 33x21½mm
Photo of wash drawing of frame design with vignette cut out, mounted over photo of wash drawing of unadopted vignette design, retouched with wash on cows, etc., with DAIRYING in black ink. Pencil "Original" and ms. "Approved . . . 1912 / . . . Postmaster General" on backing card.

Q10-E2 50c Model on thick gray cardboard, 98x93mm, black *1,500.*

Q10-E3

Design size: 35x23mm
Complete engraving of entire design with unadopted vignette: silo and barns placed closer to front of design.

Q10-E3 50c Die on white wove, about 43x31mm, carmine *1,500.*

Q10-E4

Design size: 35x22mm
Photo of incomplete engraved design: no vert. lines on frame around corner foliate spandrels or in numeral circles. Ms. "Approved Jan. 8, 1913. Frank H. Hitchcock. Postmaster General" on backing card.

Q10-E4 50c Model on thick gray cardboard, 99x94mm, black *2,500.*

Q11-E1

Design size: 33½x21½mm
Photo of wash drawing of entire design with central horses and thresher retouched. Ms. "Approved Dec. 12, 1912. Frank H. Hitchcock. Postmaster General" on backing card.

Q11-E1 75c Model on thick gray cardboard, 108x89mm, black *2,500.*

Q12-E1

Photo of wash drawing of entire design with vignette much retouched in black ink, numerals, MANUFACTURING and DOLLAR drawn in black ink and white wash. Ms. "Changed to 25c" and "Approved Oct. 22, 1912. Frank H. Hitchcock. Postmaster General" on backing card.

Q12-E1 $1 Model on thick gray cardboard, 114x86mm, black *2,500.*

Q12-E2

Design size: 35x22mm
Photo of wash drawing of complete design with DOLLAR painted in white and black and FRUIT GROWING in black ink, vignette retouched with wash on fruit pickers. Ms. "Approved . . . 1912 . . . Postmaster General" on backing card.

Q12-E2 $1 Model on thick gray cardboard, 105x94mm, black *1,500.*

Q12-E3

Design size: 36x23½mm
Incomplete engraving of entire design: no shading lines in sky. This may be from a rejected die.

Q12-E3 $1 Die on white wove, about 43x31mm, carmine *1,500.*

Q12a-E1

Engraving of entire design as adopted for 1917 offset Documentary Revenues, etc., but with "U.S. PARCEL POST" around value oval.

Q12a-E1	1c Die on card, green	*700.*
Q12b-E1	2c Die on card, carmine	*700.*
Q12c-E1	3c Die on card, deep violet	*700.*
Q12d-E1	4c Die on card, brown	*700.*
Q12e-E1	5c Die on card, blue	*700.*
Q12f-E1	10c Die on card, orange yellow	*700.*
Q12g-E1	15c Die on card, gray	*700.*
Q12h-E1	20c Die on wove, carmine rose, affixed to card	*1,500.*

PARCEL POST POSTAGE DUE

Retouched photo of design as adopted, officially dated and approved.

QJQ5-E1a 25c Model, black *1,500.*

CARRIER'S STAMP

Essays by Toppan, Carpenter, Casilear & Co. in 1851

Die size: 50x57mm
Design as adopted, but distinguished by having top and bottom frame lines as well as horizontal and vertical guide lines and rosettes in lower right corner.

1851

LO1-E1 (1c)

a. Die on white ivory paper, black *1,000.*
b. Die on pale green India, red —

Essays by Schernikow in 1903 from a new soft steel die made from the original 1851 transfer roll.
See note above No. 63-E1.

LO1-E2

LO1-E3

Die size: 50x50mm
Engraving of Franklin vignette only.

1903

LO1-E2 (1c)

a. Die on proof paper
- black *75.*
- carmine *75.*
- red *75.*
- light red *75.*
- orange *75.*
- orange brown *75.*
- yellow *75.*
- olive *75.*
- green *75.*
- dark green *75.*
- dark blue *75.*
- violet *75.*
- violet brown *75.*

b. Die on colored card, about 75x75mm
- deep red, *pinkish white* *175.*
- yellow brown, *pale blue* *175.*
- violet brown, *pale green* *175.*
- dark green, *pale pink* *175.*
- dark blue, *pale pink* *175.*
- violet, *pale yellow* *175.*

c. Die on green bond (die size: 49x50mm)
- dull scarlet *175.*
- dull olive *175.*
- dark ultramarine *175.*

Design size: 19½x25mm
Die size: 50x50mm
Design as No. LO1-E1, but distinguished by addition of left and right inner frame lines.

1903

LO1-E3 (1c)

a. Die on proof paper
- black *100.*
- carmine *100.*
- dark carmine *100.*
- scarlet *100.*
- orange *100.*
- yellow *100.*
- yellow brown *100.*
- olive *100.*
- light green *100.*
- green *100.*
- steel blue *100.*
- violet *100.*
- red violet *100.*
- violet brown *100.*
- ultramarine *100.*

b. Die on colored card
- dull carmine, *pale olive* *175.*
- brown orange, *pink* *175.*
- brown, *pale buff* *175.*
- brown, *pale blue* *175.*
- gray green, *buff* *175.*
- gray green, *yellow* *175.*
- violet, *ivory* *175.*
- dull carmine, *pale blue* *175.*

c. Die on blue pelure
- carmine *200.*
- scarlet *200.*
- orange *200.*
- brown *200.*
- dark green *200.*

d. Die on green bond
- scarlet *250.*
- orange *250.*
- green *250.*
- dull violet *250.*

Essays by Clarence Brazer in 1952 using the Schernikow complete die with addition of two diagonal lines in upper right corner.

Die size: 50x50mm

1952

LO1-E4 (1c) Die on glazed card
- scarlet *500.*
- brown *500.*
- green *500.*
- red *500.*

POST OFFICE SEALS

Registry Seals
1872 ISSUE
National Bank Note Co.

Design size: 72x40mm
Block size: 100x56½mm
Typographed design similar to that adopted but inscription STAMP HERE DATE AND PLACE OF MAILING around central circular disk is in colorless capitals, remainder of lettering in solid colors without shading lines. The word REGISTERED obliterates other words where it touches them.

OXF1-E1

a. Block impression on white card, brown *2,000.*
b. Die on India, dark brown —

Similar to No. OXF1-E1 except REGISTERED appears to be under other words it touches and does not obliterate them, as in design adopted.

OXF1-E2

a. Block impression on white paper, card mounted, brown *2,000.*
b. Block impression on large card
- brown *2,000.*
- red *2,000.*
- yellow *2,000.*

Similar to adopted type but circular disk in center has a ground of concentric circles, REGISTERED without colorless shading and obliterates other words where it touches them.

OXF1-E3 Block impression on white card, red violet —

OXF1-E4

Similar to adopted design except REGISTERED obliterates other words where it touches them; colored shading as adopted.

OXF1-E4

a. Block on India, on card
- carmine *1,000.*
- yellow *1,000.*
- blue *1,000.*
- green *1,000.*
- red brown *1,000.*
- rose *1,000.*
- brown orange *1,000.*

b. Block on India, printed in two colors
- top dark green, bottom light green *1,000.*
- left half blue, right half green *1,000.*

c. Block sunk on white card, colored border around stamp (full size 57x100mm)
- deep carmine *1,000.*
- brown orange *1,000.*
- brown *1,000.*
- light green *1,000.*
- blue *1,000.*

d. Block sunk on white wove, colorless border, stamp size, imperf., dim dusky blue *1,000.*
e. As "d," perf. 12, gummed, dim dusky blue *1,000.*

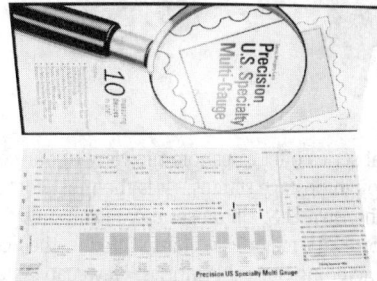

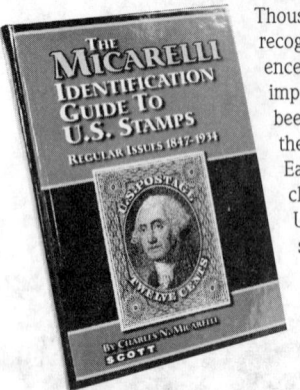

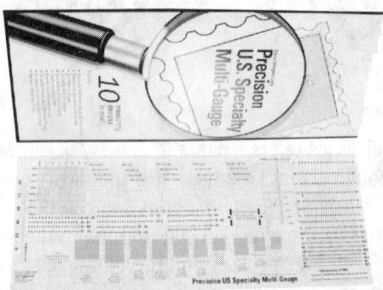

DIE AND PLATE PROOFS

PROOFS are known in many styles other than those noted in this section. For the present, however, listings are restricted to die proofs, large and small, and plate proofs on India paper and card, and occasionally on stamp paper. The listing of normal color proofs includes several that differ somewhat from the colors of the issued stamps.

Large Die Proofs are so termed because of the relatively large piece of paper on which they are printed which is about the size of the die block, 40mm by 50mm or larger. The margins of this group of proofs usually are from 15mm to 20mm in width though abnormal examples prevent the acceptance of these measurements as a complete means of identification.

These proofs were prepared in most cases by the original contracting companies and 19th century issues often show the imprint thereof and letters and numbers of identification. They are listed under "DIE-Large (1)." The India paper on which these proofs are printed is of an uneven texture and in some respects resembles hand-made paper. These large die proofs were usually mounted on cards though many are found removed from the card. Large Die Proofs autographed by the engraver or officially approved are worth much more, except for those of the 1922-29 period, which are generally approved and signed proofs.

Values for Large Die Proofs are for the full die proofs mounted on cards unless noted otherwise. Full large die proofs measure 5-6" x 7-8". Cut-down Large Die Proofs sell for less. Values for die proofs of the bicolored 1869 issue are for examples which are completely printed. Occasionally the vignette has been cut out and affixed to an impression of the border.

Die Proofs of all United States stamps of later issues exist. Only those known outside of government ownership are listed.

Small Die Proofs are so called because of the small piece of paper on which they are printed. Proofs of stamps issued prior to 1904, are reprints, and not in all cases from the same dies as the large die proofs.

Small Die Proofs (Roosevelt Album, "DIE-Small (2)") - These 302 small die proofs are from sets prepared for 85 ("Roosevelt presentation") albums in 1903 by the Bureau of Engraving and Printing but bear no imprint to this effect. The white wove paper on which they are printed is of a fibrous nature. The margins are small, seldom being more than from 3-5mm in width. Values are for proofs affixed to the original gray card backing from the Roosevelt album. Proofs without the card backing sell for less.

Small Die Proofs (Panama-Pacific Issue, "DIE-Small (2a)") - A special printing of 413 different small die proofs was made in 1915 for the Panama-Pacific Exposition. These have small margins (2½-3mm) and are on soft yellowish wove paper. They are extremely scarce as only 3-5 of each are known and a few exist only in this special printing. 6-10 exist of No. E6 in two slightly different colors.

Plate Proofs are, quite obviously, impressions taken from finished plates and differ from the stamps themselves chiefly in their excellence of impression and the paper on which they are printed. Some of the colors vary.

Hybrids are plate proofs of all issues before 1894 which have been cut to shape, mounted and pressed on large cards to resemble large die proofs. These sell for somewhat less than the corresponding large die proofs.

India Paper is a thin, soft, opaque paper which wrinkles when wet. It varies in thickness and shows particles of bamboo.

Card is a plain, clear white card of good quality, which is found in varying thicknesses for different printings. Plate proofs on card were made in five printings in 1879-94. Quantities range from 500 to 3,200 of the card proofs listed between Scott 3P and 245P.

Margin blocks with full imprint and plate number are indicated by the abbreviation "P# blk. of -."

Numbers have been assigned to all proofs consisting of the number of the regular stamp with the suffix letter "P" to denote Proof.

Proofs in other than accepted or approved colors exist in a large variety of shades, colors and papers produced at various times by various people for many different reasons. The field is large. The task of listing has been begun under "Trial Colors" following the regular proofs.

Some proofs are not identical to the issued stamps. Some of these are now listed in the Essay section. Others have been left in the proof section to keep sets together at this time.

Values are for items in very fine condition. Most "Panama-Pacific" small die proofs are toned. Values are for moderately toned examples. **Plate proof pairs on stamp paper are valued with original gum unless otherwise noted.**

NORMAL COLORS

1845 **New York**

			DIE (1) Large	DIE (2) Small	(2a)	PLATE (3) India	PLATE (4) Card
9X1P	5c	black on India paper	750.	350.		—	
	a.	With scar on neck		300.			
	b.	Dot in "P" of "POST" and scar on neck	525.	300.			
	c.	As "b," on Bond	525.	300.			—
	d.	As "b," on glazed paper	525.				
	e.	As "a," on Bond	525.				

The above listed Large Die varieties have an additional impression of the portrait medallion. Some experts question the existance of plate proofs from the sheets of 40. Plate proofs from the sheet of 9 exist on white and bluish bond paper. Value $125.

Providence, R.I.

			(1)	(2)	(2a)	(3)	(4)
10X1P	5c	black					300.
10X2P	10c	black					500.
		Sheet of 12					3,250.

General Issues

1847

			(1)	(2)	(2a)	(3)	(4)
1P	5c	red brown on India paper	800.			600.	
	a.	White bond paper	800.				
	b.	Colored bond paper	1,000.				
	c.	White laid paper	800.				
	d.	Bluish laid paper	800.				
	e.	Yellowish wove paper	800.				
	f.	Bluish wove paper	800.				
	g.	White wove paper	800.				
	h.	Card	1,000.				
	i.	Glazed paper	1,000.				
2P	10c	black on India paper	800.			900.	
		Double transfer (31R1)				—	
	a.	White bond paper	800.				
	b.	Colored bond paper	1,000.				
	c.	White laid paper	800.				
	d.	Bluish laid paper	800.				
	e.	Yellowish wove paper	800.				
	g.	White wove paper	800.				
	h.	Card	1,000.				
	i.	Glazed paper	1,000.				

Original die proofs are generally found cut to stamp size; full size die proofs sell at higher prices. Reprint proofs with cross-hatching are valued as full size; cut down examples sell for less. Plate proofs overprinted "Specimen" sell for about half the above figures.

Reproductions of 1847 Issue

Actually, official imitations made about 1875 from new dies and plates by order of the Post Office Department.

			(1)	(2)	(2a)	(3)	(4)
3P	5c	red brown	900.	425.	2,750.	225.	200.
		Block of 4				1,200.	750.
	a.	On bond paper		650.			
4P	10c	black	900.	425.	2,750.	225.	200.
		Block of 4				1,200.	750.
	a.	On bond paper		650.			

1851-60

			(1)	(2)	(2a)	(3)	(4)
5P	1c	blue, type I	*5,000.*				
11P	3c	red, type I	*5,000.*				
		brush obliteration				1,000.	
		Block of 4				5,000.	
		P# block of 8				—	
12P	5c	brn, type I	*7,500.*		2,000.		
13P	10c	grn, type I	*5,000.*				
17P	12c	black	*10,000.*				
24P	1c	blue, type V (pl. 9)				*1,250.*	
		Pair				*3,000.*	
26P	3c	red, type II (pl. 20)				*1,250.*	
		Pair				*3,000.*	
30P	5c	brn, type II				*1,250.*	
35P	10c	grn, type V				*1,250.*	
36bP	12c	black, plate III (broken frame lines)				*1,250.*	
		Block of 4				*5,500.*	
	d.	On stamp paper					—
		Pair					—
		Block of 4					—
37P	24c	lilac	—			*1,250.*	
		Pair				*3,000.*	
	c.	On stamp paper					*1,500.*
		Pair					*15,500.*
38P	30c	orange	—	—		*1,250.*	
		Pair				*3,000.*	
	a.	On stamp paper					*2,500.*
		Pair					*7,750.*
39P	90c	blue	—	—		*1,250.*	
		Pair				*3,000.*	
	a.	On stamp paper					*2,750.*
		Pair					*37,500.*

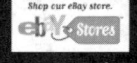

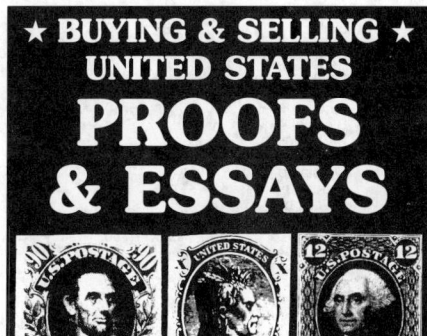

Plate proofs of 24P to 39P are from the original plates. They may be distinguished from the 40P to 47P by the type in the case of the 1c, 3c, 10c and 12c, and by the color in the case of the 5c, 24c, 30c and 90c.

The 3c plate proofs (No. 11) are on proof paper and all known copies have a vertical brush stroke obliteration.

Die proofs of the 30c show full spear point in corners of design.

Reprints of 1857-60 Issue

No.			DIE (1) Large	DIE (2) Small	(2a)	PLATE (3) India	PLATE (4) Card
40P	1c	bright blue, type I (new plate)	325.	350.	1,750.	80.	75.
		Block of 4				400.	300.
a.		On stamp paper					750.
41P	3c	scarlet, type I (new plate)	325.	350.	1,750.	80.	50.
		Block of 4				400.	250.
		Orange brown			*2,500.*		
42P	5c	orange brown type II (plate II)	325.	350.		80.	50.
		Block of 4				400.	250.
		P# blk. of 8				1,050.	—
43P	10c	blue green, type I (new plate)	325.	350.	1,750.	80.	50.
		Block of 4				400.	250.
44P	12c	greenish black (new plate, frame line complete)	325.	350.	2,500.	110.	50.
		Block of 4				550.	250.
45P	24c	blksh vio (pl. I)	325.	350.	1,750.	80.	50.
		Block of 4				400.	250.
		P# blk. of 8				1,050.	
46P	30c	yel org (pl. I)	325.	350.	1,750.	80.	50.
		Block of 4				400.	250.
		P# blk. of 8				1,050.	—
47P	90c	deep blue (pl. I)	325.	350.	1,750.	110.	75.
		Block of 4				550.	375.
		P# blk. of 8				1,150.	1,050.

Nos. 42P2-44P2 were printed from original dies, and the 5c shows type I projections at top and bottom.

Nos. 40P-47P, large die, exist only as hybrids.

SECOND DESIGNS (Regular Issue)

For "First Designs" see Essay section (former Nos. 55-57, 59, 62), Proofs and Trial Color Proofs (former No. 58) and Trial Color Proofs (former Nos. 60-61).

1861

No.			DIE (1) Large	DIE (2) Small	(2a)	PLATE (3) India	PLATE (4) Card
62BP	10c	dark green		*325.*		*325.*	
63P	1c	blue	700.	225.	2,000.	55.	40.
		Block of 4				225.	250.
		P# blk. of 8				1,100.	—
		Indigo			2,000.		
64P	3c	pink	3,500.	—			
65P	3c	rose	1,000.	—	1,750.	100.	130.
		Block of 4				550.	
		P# blk. of 8				1,400.	
a.		3c dull red				100.	
c.		On stamp paper, pair					*1,000.*
		P# blk. of 8					—
67P	5c	buff	*5,000.*		1,750.		
76P	5c	brown	700.	225.	1,750.	45.	30.
		Block of 4				225.	140.
		P# blk. of 8				875.	—
68P	10c	green	650.	225.	1,750.	65.	30.
		Block of 4				300.	140.
		P# blk. of 8				950.	—
69P	12c	black	700.	225.	2,000.	65.	30.
		Block of 4				300.	140.
		P# blk. of 8				950.	—
70P	24c	red lilac	—		2,750.		450.
78P	24c	lilac		225.	2,750.	80.	75.
		Block of 4				400.	375.
		P# blk. of 8				1,200.	—
71P	30c	orange	500.	225.	2,750.	50.	30.
		Block of 4				250.	140.
		P# blk. of 8				1,100.	—
72P	90c	blue	500.	225.	2,750.	50.	30.
		Block of 4				225.	140.
		P# blk. of 8				1,100.	—

1861-67

No.			DIE (1) Large	DIE (2) Small	(2a)	PLATE (3) India	PLATE (4) Card
73P	2c	black, die I	10,000.			150.	
		Block of 4				750.	
		P# blk. of 8				2,000.	—
a.		Die II	2,500.	1,350.	8,750.	110.	75.
		Block of 4				550.	400.
		P# blk. of 8				1,500.	—
77P	15c	black	1,250.	500.	2,750.	55.	45.
		Block of 4				250.	200.
		P# blk. of 8				950.	—
79P	3c	rose, A grill, on stamp paper, pair					*1,500.*
		Block of 4					*4,000.*
		P# blk. of 8					*10,000.*
83P	3c	rose, C grill, on stamp paper, pair					*1,850.*
94P	3c	red, F grill, on stamp paper, pair					*1,500.*

The listed plate proofs of the 1c (63P), 5c (76P), 10c (68P) and 12c (69P) are from the 100 subject re-issue plates of 1875. Single proofs of these denominations from the regular issue plates cannot be told apart from the reprints. As the reprint plates had wider spacing between the subjects, multiples can be differentiated. Values are for proofs from the reprint plates. The 2c Die II has a small dot on the left cheek.

1869

No.			DIE (1) Large	DIE (2) Small	(2a)	PLATE (3) India	PLATE (4) Card
112P	1c	buff	750.	350.	2,000.	55.	60.
		Block of 4				250.	275.
		P# blk. of 10				750.	
113P	2c	brown	750.	350.	2,000.	40.	45.
		Block of 4				175.	190.
		P# blk. of 10				600.	—
114P	3c	ultra.	900.	575.	2,000.	45.	75.
		Block of 4				190.	325.
		P# blk. of 10				800.	—
115P	6c	ultra.	900.	350.	2,000.	45.	75.
		Block of 4				190.	350.
		P# blk. of 10				800.	—
116P	10c	yellow	900.	350.	2,000.	45.	50.
		Block of 4				190.	235.
		P# blk. of 10				800.	—
117P	12c	green	900.	350.	2,000.	45.	50.
		Block of 4				190.	265.
		P# blk. of 10				875.	—
119P	15c	brown & blue (type II)	550.	450.	2,000.	120.	
		Block of 4				600.	
		P# blk. of 8				1,450.	
129P	15c	Reissue (type III)	550.	450.	2,000.	250.	125.
		Block of 4				1,200.	700.
		P# blk. of 8				3,000.	—
a.		Center inverted (100)					2,500.
		Block of 4					*11,000.*
		P# blk. of 8					*37,500.*
120P	24c	green & violet	550.	450.	2,000.	140.	125.
		Block of 4				625.	600.
		P# blk. of 8				1,450.	—
a.		Center inverted (100)					2,750.
		Block of 4					*12,000.*
		P# blk. of 8					*37,500.*
121P	30c	ultra & carmine	1,250.	450.	2,000.	140.	150.
		Block of 4				625.	825.
		P# blk. of 8				1,450.	—
a.		Flags inverted (100)					2,750.
		Block of 4					*12,000.*
		P# blk. of 8					*37,500.*
122P	90c	carmine & black	550.	450.	2,000.	180.	150.
		Block of 4				825.	825.
		P# blk. of 8				1,750.	—
a.		Center inverted (100)					2,750.
		Block of 4					*14,000.*
		P# blk. of 8					*37,500.*

Large die proofs of Nos. 119, 129, 120 and 122 exist only as hybrids.

1880

No.			DIE (1) Large	DIE (2) Small	(2a)	PLATE (3) India	PLATE (4) Card
133P	1c	dark buff	1,000.			100.	
		Block of 4				450.	
		P# blk. of 10				1,250.	

1870-71 National Bank Note Co.

No.			DIE (1) Large	DIE (2) Small	(2a)	PLATE (3) India	PLATE (4) Card
136P	3c	green, grill, on stamp paper, pair					*1,200.*
		P# blk. of 12					—
145P	1c	ultra	250.	175.	1,200.	20.	
		Block of 4				90.	
		P# blk. of 12				385.	
146P	2c	red brown	250.			20.	
		Block of 4				90.	
		P# blk. of 12				385.	
147P	3c	green	300.			20.	
		Block of 4				90.	
		P# blk. of 12				400.	

The former No. 147Pc4 is now listed in the Essay section as No. 147-E13e.

No.			DIE (1) Large	DIE (2) Small	(2a)	PLATE (3) India	PLATE (4) Card
148P	6c	carmine	450.			35.	
		Block of 4				150.	
		P# blk. of 12				650.	
149P	7c	vermilion	200.			15.	
		Block of 4				70.	
		P# blk. of 12				360.	
150P	10c	brown	300.			40.	
		Block of 4				165.	
		P# blk. of 12				750.	
151P	12c	violet	200.			16.	
		Block of 4				70.	
		P# blk. of 12				385.	
152P	15c	orange	250.			30.	
		Block of 4				135.	
		P# blk. of 12				550.	
153P	24c	purple	250.			30.	
		Block of 4				135.	
		P# blk. of 12				550.	
154P	30c	black	250.			40.	
		Block of 4				170.	
		P# blk. of 12				750.	
155P	90c	carmine	250.			45.	
		Block of 4				195.	
		P# blk. of 12				800.	

Secret Marks on 24, 30 and 90c Dies of the Bank Note Issues

National 24c - Rays of lower star normal.

Continental 24c - Rays of lower star strengthened.

National 30c - Lower line does not join point of shield.

Continental and American 30c - Lower line joins point of shield and bottom line of shield thicker.

National 90c - Rays of star in upper right normal.

Continental and American 90c - Rays of star in upper right strengthened.

1873 Continental Bank Note Co.

No.			DIE (1) Large	DIE (2) Small	(2a)	PLATE (3) India	PLATE (4) Card
156P	1c	ultra	450.			55.	150.
		Block of 4				250.	
		P# blk. of 14				1,150.	
157P	2c	brown	350.	175.	1,200.	35.	15.
		Block of 4				165.	80.
		P# blk. of 12				650.	—
a.		On stamp paper					—
158P	3c	green	350.	175.	1,200.	55.	150.
		Block of 4				250.	
		P# blk. of 14				1,150.	
f.		On stamp paper, pair					*750.*
g.		On stamp paper, grill, pair					*650.*
159P	6c	pink	750.	250.	1,400.	110.	200.
		Block of 4				525.	
		P# blk. of 12				2,000.	
160P	7c	orange vermilion	250.	175.	1,200.	35.	10.
		Block of 4				165.	50.
		P# blk. of 14				825.	—
161P	10c	brown	450.	200.	1,200.	60.	150.
		Block of 4				300.	
		P# blk. of 14				1,300.	
162P	12c	blackish violet	200.	175.	1,200.	38.	20.
		Block of 4				190.	100.
		P# blk. of 14				975.	—
a.		On stamp paper					—
163P	15c	yellow orange	400.	175.	1,200.	65.	20.
		Block of 4				250.	100.
		P# blk. of 12				1,000.	—
a.		On stamp paper					—
164P	24c	violet	400.	175.	1,200.	50.	30.
		Block of 4				225.	140.
		P# blk. of 12				975.	
165P	30c	gray black	400.	175.	1,200.	40.	20.
		Block of 4				200.	90.
		P# blk. of 12				825.	

No.			DIE (1) Large	(2) Small	(2a)	PLATE (3) India	(4) Card
166P	90c	rose carmine	400.	175.	1,200.	55.	40.
		Block of 4				250.	190.
		P# blk. of 12				1,000.	

Die proofs of the 24c, 30c and 90c show secret marks, as illustrated, but as plates of these denominations were not made from these dies, plate proofs can be identified only by color.

No.			Large	Small	(2a)	India	Card
178P	2c	vermilion	—				
a.		On stamp paper, pair					600.
		P# blk. of 12					—
179P	5c	blue	—				

1879 American Bank Note Co.

No.			Large	Small	(2a)	India	Card
182P	1c	gray blue	525.			60.	
		Block of 4				275.	
		P# blk. of 12				1,000.	
183P	2c	vermilion	300.	190.	1,200.	35.	20.
		Block of 4				160.	100.
		P# blk. of 12				600.	
184P	3c	green on stamp paper, pair					400.
		P# blk. of 12				—	
185P	5c	blue	450.	225.	1,200.	70.	25.
		Block of 4				325.	110.
		P# blk. of 12				1,300.	—
190P	30c	full black				—	150.
		Block of 4				—	600.
		P# blk. of 12					2,000.
191P	90c	carmine on stamp paper, pair					2,500.
		P# strip of 5					—

1881-82 American Bank Note Co.

No.			Large	Small	(2a)	India	Card
205P	5c	yellow brown	250.	190.	1,200.	40.	15.
		Block of 4				175.	75.
		P# blk. of 12				600.	—
206P	1c	blue	375.	190.	1,200.	40.	20.
		Block of 4				175.	90.
		P# blk. of 12				600.	—
207P	3c	blue green	375.	190.	1,200.	40.	20.
		Block of 4				175.	90.
		P# blk. of 12				600.	—
208P	6c	rose	800.	190.	1,200.	90.	60.
		Block of 4				425.	210.
		P# blk. of 12				—	—
a.		6c brown red			1,200.	100.	50.
209P	10c	brown	800.	190.	1,200.	40.	25.
		Block of 4				170.	110.
		P# blk. of 12				650.	—

1883

No.			Large	Small	(2a)	India	Card
210P	2c	red brown	400.	190.	1,200.	32.	20.
		Block of 4				145.	85.
		P# blk. of 12				600.	—
a.		On stamp paper, pair					—
211P	4c	green	500.	190.	1,200.	40.	25.
		Block of 4				165.	110.
		P# blk. of 12				750.	—
a.		On stamp paper, pair					—

1887-88

No.			Large	Small	(2a)	India	Card
212P	1c	ultra	650.	190.	1,200.	125.	2,000.
		Block of 4				600.	—
		P# blk. of 12				2,250.	
a.		On stamp paper, pair					1,000.

Copies of No. 212P3 mounted on card are frequently offered as No. 212P4.

No.			Large	Small	(2a)	India	Card
213P	2c	green	450.	190.	1,200.	40.	25.
		Block of 4				180.	110.
		P# blk. of 12				625.	—
a.		On stamp paper, pair					750.
214P	3c	vermilion	475.	190.	1,200.	40.	25.
		Block of 4				180.	110.
		P# blk. of 12				—	—

Nos. 207P1 & 214P1 inscribed: "Worked over by new company, June 29th, 1881."

No.			Large	Small	(2a)	India	Card
215P	4c	carmine	600.	190.	1,200.	95.	50.
		Block of 4				475.	225.
		P# blk. of 12					—
216P	5c	indigo	600.	190.	1,200.	60.	30.
		Block of 4				300.	130.
		P# blk. of 12					—
b.		On stamp paper, pair					1,400.
217P	30c	organge brown	625.	190.	1,200.	60.	30.
		Block of 4				300.	130.
		P# blk. of 10					—
a.		On stamp paper, pair					1,750.
218P	90c	purple	625.	190.	1,200.	90.	50.
		Block of 4				400.	225.
		P# blk. of 10					—
a.		On stamp paper, pair					—

1890-93

No.			Large	Small	(2a)	India	Card
219P	1c	ultra	225.	190.	1,100.	25.	40.
		Block of 4				110.	180.
		P# blk. of 12				500.	650.
c.		On stamp paper, pair					190.
219DP	2c	lake	550.	190.	1,100.	80.	165.
		Block of 4				385.	700.
		P# blk. of 12				1,650.	3,250.
e.		On stamp paper, pair					80.
220P	2c	carmine	450.	190.		300.	200.
		Block of 4				1,250.	825.
		P# blk. of 12				3,850.	2,500.
d.		On stamp paper, pair					80.
		As "d," without gum					40.
		P# blk. of 12					—
221P	3c	purple	225.	190.	1,100.	35.	25.
		Block of 4				160.	110.
		P# blk. of 12				650.	600.
a.		On stamp paper, pair					225.
222P	4c	dark brown	225.	190.	1,100.	35.	25.
		Block of 4				160.	110.
		P# blk. of 12				650.	600.
a.		On stamp paper, pair					210.
223P	5c	chocolate	225.	190.	1,100.	32.	25.
		Block of 4				135.	110.
		P# blk. of 12				600.	625.
b.		Yellow brown, on stamp paper, pair					225.
224P	6c	brown red	225.	190.	1,100.	32.	20.
		Block of 4				135.	85.
		P# blk. of 12				600.	775.
a.		On stamp paper, pair					225.
225P	8c	lilac	600.	190.	1,100.	55.	110.
		Block of 4				250.	500.
		P# blk. of 12				1,100.	2,000.
a.		On stamp paper, pair					1,000.
226P	10c	green	225.	190.	1,100.	45.	40.
		Block of 4				200.	180.
		P# blk. of 12				700.	750.
a.		On stamp paper, pair					325.
227P	15c	indigo	300.	190.	1,100.	45.	40.
		Block of 4				190.	180.
		P# blk. of 12				825.	875.
a.		On stamp paper, pair					625.
228P	30c	black	300.	190.	1,100.	45.	45.
		Block of 4				190.	190.
		P# blk. of 12				825.	875.
a.		On stamp paper, pair					1,000.
229P	90c	orange	300.	190.	1,100.	60.	50.
		Block of 4				275.	225.
		P# blk. of 12				1,100.	1,150.
a.		On stamp paper, pair					1,450.

COLUMBIAN ISSUE

1893

No.			Large	Small	(2a)	India	Card
230P	1c	blue	700.	325.	1,400.	40.	25.
		Block of 4				175.	125.
		P# blk. of 8				400.	350.
231P	2c	violet	800.	350.	1,750.	225.	65.
		Block of 4				1,000.	280.
		P# blk. of 8				2,250.	825.
b.		On stamp paper, pair					1,250.
c.		"Broken hat" variety					130.

Almost all examples of No. 231Pb are faulty. Value is for pair with minimal faults.

No.			Large	Small	(2a)	India	Card
232P	3c	green	700.	325.	2,000.	60.	50.
		Block of 4				260.	225.
		P# blk. of 8				675.	600.
233P	4c	ultra.	700.	325.	2,000.	60.	50.
		Block of 4				260.	225.
		P# blk. of 8				675.	600.
233aP	4c	blue (error) on thin card	2,750.				
234P	5c	chocolate	700.	325.	2,000.	60.	45.
		Block of 4				260.	200.
		P# blk. of 8				675.	550.
235P	6c	purple	700.	325.	2,000.	60.	50.
		Block of 4				260.	225.
		P# blk. of 8				675.	600.
236P	8c	magenta	700.	325.	2,000.	60.	100.
		Block of 4				260.	450.
		P# blk. of 8				675.	1,250.
237P	10c	black brown	700.	325.	2,000.	60.	50.
		Block of 4				260.	225.
		P# blk. of 8				675.	600.
238P	15c	dark green	700.	325.	2,000.	60.	55.
		Block of 4				260.	250.
		P# blk. of 8				675.	1,400.
239P	30c	orange brown	700.	325.	2,000.	90.	65.
		Block of 4				400.	300.
		P# blk. of 8				1,250.	1,100.
240P	50c	slate blue	700.	325.	2,000.	135.	75.
		Block of 4				575.	350.
		P# blk. of 8				1,500.	1,100.
241P	$1	salmon	900.	450.	2,000.	160.	130.
		Block of 4				775.	575.
		P# blk. of 8				1,900.	
242P	$2	brown red	900.	450.	2,000.	180.	125.
		Block of 4				750.	550.
		P# blk. of 8				2,050.	1,500.
243P	$3	yellow green	900.	450.	2,000.	225.	150.
		Block of 4				1,000.	675.
		P# blk. of 8				2,700.	1,900.
244P	$4	crimson lake	900.	450.	2,000.	275.	175.
		Block of 4				1,200.	775.
		P# blk. of 8				3,000.	2,500.
245P	$5	black	900.	450.	2,000.	325.	225.
		Block of 4				1,425.	1,000.
		P# blk. of 8				3,500.	3,000.

This set also exists as Large Die proofs, not die sunk, but printed directly on thin card. Set value $4,725. 1c through 50c, $225 each; $1 through $5, $450 each.

Nos. 234P1, 234P2 differ from issued stamp.

Bureau of Engraving and Printing

1894

No.			Large	Small	(2a)	India	Card
246P	1c	ultra	450.				
247P	1c	blue	250.	250.	1,100.		100.
		Block of 4					450.
		P# blk. of 6					950.
248P	2c	pink, type I					100.
		Block of 4					475.
		P# blk. of 6					950.
250P	2c	car, type I	250.	250.			
251P	2c	car, type II	250.	—			

The existence of No. 251P2 has been questioned by specialists. The editors would like to see evidence that the item exists.

No.			Large	Small	(2a)	India	Card
252P	2c	car, type III				350.	
		Block of 4				1,200.	
253P	3c	purple (triangle I)	750.				
a.		On stamp paper, pair					300.
		Block of 4					625.
		P# blk. of 6					—
253AP	3c	purple (triangle II)	325.	250.	1,100.		
254P	4c	dark brown	250.	250.	1,100.		
a.		On stamp paper, pair					300.
		Block of 4					625.
		P# blk. of 6					—
255P	5c	chocolate	250.	250.	1,100.		
b.		On stamp paper, pair					300.
		Block of 4					625.
		P# blk. of 6					—
256P	6c	brown	250.	250.	1,100.		450.
		Block of 4					1,900.
		P# blk. of 6					3,750.
257P	8c	violet brown	275.	250.	1,100.		
258P	10c	green	275.	250.	1,100.		
a.		On stamp paper, pair					500.
		Block of 4					1,100.
		P# blk. of 6					—
259P	15c	dark blue	300.	250.	1,100.		
260P	50c	orange	450.	210.	1,100.		
261AP	$1	black	475.	350.	1,100.		
262P	$2	dark blue	475.	350.	1,100.		450.
		Block of 4					2,250.
		Margin block of 4, arrow					2,750.
		P# blk. of 6					6,250.
263P	$5	dark green	650.	375.	1,100.		450.
		Block of 4					2,250.
		Margin block of 4, arrow					2,750.
		P# blk. of 6					6,250.

1895

Imperf, with gum

No.			
264P	1c	blue, on stamp paper, pair	275.
		Block of 4	600.
		P# blk. of 6	
b.		Horiz. P# strip of 3, perf horiz., imperf. vert.	7,500.
267P	2c	carmine, type III, on stamp paper, pair	225.
		Block of 4	475.
		P# blk. of 6	—
268P	3c	purple, on stamp paper, pair	275.
		Block of 4	600.
		P# blk. of 6	—
269P	4c	dark brown, on stamp paper, pair	275.
		Block of 4	600.
		P# blk. of 6	—
270P	5c	chocolate, on stamp paper, pair	275.
		Block of 4	600.
271P	6c	dull brown, on stamp paper, pair	300.
		Block of 4	650.
272P	8c	violet brown, on stamp paper, pair	450.
		Block of 4	1,000.
		P# blk. of 6	—
273P	10c	dark green, on stamp paper, pair	350.
		Block of 4	750.
274P	15c	dark blue, on stamp paper, pair	1,100.
		Block of 4	2,500.
275P	50c	orange, on stamp paper, pair	1,250.
		Block of 4	2,750.
276P	$1	black, type I, on stamp paper, pair	1,600.
		Block of 4	3,500.
277P	$2	bright blue, on stamp paper, pair	3,500.
		Block of 4	7,500.
278P	$5	dark green, on stamp paper, pair	3,500.
		Block of 4	7,500.

No. 264Pb exists only as a bottom margin P#24 and imprint strip of 3.

1897-1903

No.			Large	Small	(2a)
279P	1c	green	700.	375.	1,100.
279BdP	2c	orange red, type IV			1,100.
279BfP	2c	car, type IV	400.		1,100.
280P	4c	rose brown	700.		1,100.
281P	5c	blue	700.	375.	1,100.
282P	6c	lake	700.		1,100.
283P	10c	orange brown, type II	800.	375.	1,100.
283aP	10c	brown, type II	800.		
284P	15c	olive green, type II	800.	375.	1,100.

TRANS-MISSISSIPPI ISSUE

1898

285P	1c	green	650.	650.	1,250.	
286P	2c	copper red	650.	650.	1,250.	4,000.
287P	4c	orange	650.	650.	1,250.	
288P	5c	dull blue	650.	650.	1,250.	
289P	8c	violet brown	650.	650.	1,250.	
290P	10c	gray violet	650.	650.	1,250.	
291P	50c	sage green	650.	650.	1,250.	
292P	$1	black	750.	650.	1,250.	
293P	$2	orange brown	750.	650.	1,250.	6,000.
		Block of 4				30,000.

The bicolored items commonly offered as No. 285-293 bicolored proofs can be found under the following essay listings: No. 285-E8a, 286-E8a, 287-E9a, 288-E5a, 289-E4a, 290-E4a, 291-E8a, 292-E6a, 293-E7a.

PAN-AMERICAN ISSUE

1901

294P	1c	green & black	575.	575.	2,000.
295P	2c	carmine & black	575.	575.	2,000.
296P	4c	chocolate & black	575.	575.	2,000.
297P	5c	ultra & black	575.	575.	2,000.
298P	8c	brown violet & black	575.	575.	2,000.
299P	10c	yel brn & blk	575.	575.	2,000.

1902-03

300P	1c	green	750.	300.	1,750.
301P	2c	carmine	750.	300.	1,750.
302P	3c	purple	750.	300.	1,750.
303P	4c	orange brown	750.	300.	1,750.
304P	5c	blue	750.	300.	1,750.
305P	6c	lake	750.	300.	1,750.
306P	8c	violet black	750.	300.	1,750.
307P	10c	orange brown	750.	300.	1,750.
308P	13c	deep vio brn	750.	300.	1,750.
309P	15c	olive green	750.	300.	1,750.
310P	50c	orange	750.	300.	1,750.
311P	$1	black	750.	300.	1,750.
312P	$2	blue	925.	300.	1,750.
313P	$5	green	1,050.	375.	1,750.

1903

319P	2c	carmine, Type I	1,500.		
319aP	2c	lake, Type I	—		
319iP	2c	carmine, Type II	2,000.	1,000.	3,500.

LOUISIANA PURCHASE ISSUE

1904

323P	1c	green	1,400.	750.	1,250.
324P	2c	carmine	1,400.	750.	1,250.
325P	3c	violet	1,400.	750.	1,250.
326P	5c	dark blue	1,400.	750.	1,250.
327P	10c	brown	1,400.	750.	1,250.

JAMESTOWN EXPOSITION ISSUE

1907

328P	1c	green	1,000.	900.	1,250.
329P	2c	carmine	1,000.	900.	1,250.
330P	5c	blue	1,000.	900.	1,250.

1908-09

331P	1c	green	1,250.	725.	1,200.
332P	2c	carmine	1,250.	725.	1,200.
		carmine, *amber*	—		
		carmine, *lt blue*	—		
333P	3c	deep violet	1,250.	725.	1,200.
334P	4c	brown	1,250.	725.	1,200.
335P	5c	blue	1,250.	725.	1,200.
		blue, *salmon*	—		
336P	6c	red orange	1,250.	725.	1,200.
337P	8c	olive green	1,250.	725.	1,200.
		olive green, *yellow*	—		
338P	10c	yellow	1,250.	725.	1,200.
339P	13c	blue green	1,250.	725.	1,200.
340P	15c	pale ultramarine	1,250.	725.	1,200.
341P	50c	violet	1,250.	725.	1,200.
		violet, *pale lilac*	—		
		violet, *yellow*	—		
		violet, *greenish*	—		
342P	$1	violet black	1,500.	725.	1,200.

LINCOLN MEMORIAL ISSUE

1909

367P	2c	carmine	1,100.	1,000.	1,750.

ALASKA-YUKON ISSUE

1909

370P	2c	carmine	1,100.	1,000.	1,750.

HUDSON-FULTON ISSUE

1909

372P	2c	carmine	1,250.	1,000.	1,750.

PANAMA-PACIFIC ISSUE

1912-13

397P	1c	green	1,750.	1,500.	1,250.
398P	2c	carmine	1,750.	1,500.	1,250.
399P	5c	blue	1,750.	1,500.	1,250.
400P	10c	org. yellow	1,750.	1,500.	1,250.
400AP	10c	orange	1,750.	1,500.	1,250.

No. 398P inscribed "Gatun Locks" is listed in the Essay section as No. 398-E3.

1912-19

			DIE (1) Large	DIE (2) Small	(2a)
405P	1c	green	1,400.	650.	1,200.
406P	2c	carmine	1,400.	650.	1,200.
407P	7c	black	1,400.	650.	1,200.
414P	8c	olive green	1,400.	650.	1,200.
415P	9c	salmon red	1,400.	650.	1,200.
416P	10c	orange yellow	1,400.	650.	1,200.
434P	11c	dark green	1,500.		
417P	12c	claret brown	1,400.	650.	1,200.
513P	13c	apple green	1,500.		
418P	15c	gray	1,400.	650.	1,200.
419P	20c	ultramarine	1,400.	650.	1,200.
420P	30c	orange red	1,400.	650.	1,200.
421P	50c	violet	1,400.	650.	1,200.
423P	$1	violet black	1,400.	650.	1,200.

1918-20

524P	$5	deep green & black	1,500.	
547P	$2	carmine & black	1,500.	

VICTORY ISSUE

1919

537P	3c	violet	1,100.	850.

PILGRIM ISSUE

1920

548P	1c	green	1,250.	1,200.
549P	2c	carmine rose	1,250.	1,200.
550P	5c	deep blue	1,250.	1,200.

1922-26

			LARGE DIE (1) India	LARGE DIE (1a) White Wove	PLATE (3) White Wove	PLATE (4) Card
551P	½c	olive brown	1,500.		—	—
552P	1c	deep green	1,000.	700.	—	
553P	1 ½c	yel brn	1,500.		—	
554P	2c	carmine	1,000.	700.	—	
555P	3c	violet	1,250.	1,000.	—	
556P	4c	yel brn	1,200.	700.	—	
557P	5c	dark blue	1,000.	700.	—	
558P	6c	red orange	1,000.	700.	—	
559P	7c	black	1,000.	700.	—	
560P	8c	olive green	1,000.	700.	—	
561P	9c	rose	1,000.	700.	—	
562P	10c	orange	1,000.	700.	—	
563P	11c	light blue	1,500.	700.	—	
564P	12c	brn vio	1,000.	700.	—	
622P	13c	green	1,000.	700.	—	
565P	14c	dark blue	1,250.	700.	—	
566P	15c	gray	1,250.	700.	—	
623P	17c	black	1,000.		—	
567P	20c	car rose	1,000.	700.	—	
568P	25c	deep green	1,000.	700.	—	
569P	30c	olive brown	1,000.	700.	—	
570P	50c	lilac	1,250.	700.	—	
571P	$1	vio brn	1,500.	700.	—	
572P	$2	deep blue	2,500.	700.	—	
572P2		deep blue, small die on India	—			
573P	$5	carmine & dark blue	5,000.			

No. 573P1 exists only as a hybrid.

1923-26

		LARGE DIE (1) India	LARGE DIE (1a) White Wove	SMALL DIE (2) White or Yellowish Wove
610P	Harding, 2c black	1,400.	1,400.	1,000.
614P	Huguenot Walloon, 1c	750.	700.	700.
615P	Huguenot Walloon, 2c	750.	700.	700.
616P	Huguenot Walloon, 5c	750.	700.	700.
617P	Lexington Concord, 1c	750.	700.	700.
618P	Lexington Concord, 2c	750.	700.	700.
619P	Lexington Concord, 5c	750.	700.	700.
620P	Norse American, 2c	850.	850.	850.
621P	Norse American, 5c	850.	850.	850.
627P	Sesquicentennial, 2c	800.	750.	850.
628P	Ericsson, 5c	800.	750.	850.
629P	White Plains, 2c	800.	750.	850.

1927-29

643P	Vermont, 2c	800.	750.	850.
644P	Burgoyne, 2c	800.	750.	850.
645P	Valley Forge, 2c	800.	750.	850.
649P	Aeronautics, 2c	1,250.	900.	900.
650P	Aeronautics, 5c	1,250.	900.	900.
651P	Clark, 2c	900.	800.	750.
654P	Edison, 2c	900.	800.	750.
657P	Sullivan, 2c	850.	800.	750.
680P	Fallen Timbers, 2c	850.	800.	750.
681P	Ohio River Canalization, 2c	850.	800.	750.

1930-31

682P	Massachusetts Bay, 2c	850.	800.	750.
683P	Carolina Charleston, 2c	850.	800.	750.
684P	1 ½c brown	650.		
685P	4c brown	650.		
688P	Braddock's Field, 2c	850.	800.	750.
689P	von Steuben, 2c	850.	800.	750.
690P	Pulaski, 2c	850.	800.	750.
702P	Red Cross, 2c black & red		900.	900.
703P	Yorktown, 2c	1,250.	800.	750.

1932

Washington Bicentennial

704P	½c olive brown	1,000.	800.	750.
705P	1c green	1,000.	800.	750.
706P	1 ½c brown	1,000.	800.	750.
707P	2c carmine rose	1,000.	800.	750.
708P	3c deep violet	1,000.	800.	750.
709P	4c light brown	1,000.	800.	750.
710P	5c blue	1,000.	800.	750.
711P	6c red orange	1,000.	800.	750.
712P	7c black	1,000.	800.	750.
713P	8c olive bister	1,000.	800.	750.
714P	9c pale red	1,000.	800.	750.
715P	10c orange yellow	1,000.	800.	750.
716P	Winter Games, 2c	1,100.	950.	900.
717P	Arbor Day, 2c	900.	900.	800.
718P	Olympic Games, 3c violet	*10,000.*	950.	900.
719P	Olympic Games, 5c blue	*15,000.*	950.	900.
720P	3c deep violet	800.		
724P	Penn, 3c violet	800.	850.	750.
725P	Webster, 3c violet	800.	850.	750.

1933-34

726P	Georgia, 3c violet	700.	800.	650.
727P	Peace, 3c violet	700.	800.	650.
728P	Century of Progress, 1c	700.	800.	650.
729P	Century of Progress, 3c	700.	800.	650.
732P	N.R.A., 3c violet		900.	650.
733P	Byrd Antarctic, 3c	*1,150.*	900.	650.
734P	Kosciuszko, 5c blue	*1,150.*	800.	650.
736P	Maryland, 3c carmine rose	*1,150.*	800.	650.
737P	Mothers Day, 3c	800.	800.	650.
739P	Wisconsin, 3c deep violet		800.	650.
740P	Parks, 1c green		800.	650.
741P	Parks, 2c red			650.
742P	Parks, 3c violet		800.	650.
743P	Parks, 4c brown			650.
744P	Parks, 5c blue			650.
745P	Parks, 6c dark blue			650.
746P	Parks, 7c black		800.	650.
747P	Parks, 8c sage green			650.
748P	Parks, 9c red orange	800.		650.
749P	Parks, 10c gray black			650.

1935-37

772P	Conn., 3c violet	*1,150.*		650.
773P	San Diego, 3c purple			650.
774P	Boulder Dam, 3c purple			650.
775P	Michigan, 3c purple			650.
776P	Texas, 3c purple			650.
777P	Rhode Is., 3c purple			650.
782P	Arkansas, 3c pur.	800.	800.	650.
783P	Oregon, 3c purple	—	800.	650.
784P	Anthony, 3c violet			650.
785P	Army, 1c green		800.	800.
786P	Army, 2c carmine			800.
787P	Army, 3c purple	800.	800.	800.
788P	Army, 4c gray			800.
789P	Army, 5c ultramarine	*1,350.*	800.	800.
790P	Navy, 1c green			800.
791P	Navy, 2c car.	800.		800.
792P	Navy, 3c purple			800.
793P	Navy, 4c gray			800.
794P	Navy, 5c ultramarine			800.
795P	Ordinance, 3c red violet			650.
796P	Virginia Dare, 5c	800.		650.
797P	S.P.A. Sheet, 10c			650.
798P	Constitution, 3c red violet	800.		650.
799P	Hawaii, 3c violet	800.		650.
800P	Alaska, 3c violet			750.
801P	Puerto Rico, 3c	800.		650.
802P	Virgin Is., 3c light violet	—		650.

PRESIDENTIAL ISSUE

1938

803P	½c deep orange	*2,000.*		650.
804P	1c green			650.
805P	1 ½c bister brown			650.
806P	2c rose carmine		*1,800.*	650.
807P	3c deep violet			650.
a.	On glazed card	—		
808P	4c red violet			650.
809P	4 ½c dark gray	*1,500.*		650.
810P	5c bright blue	*1,500.*		650.
811P	6c red orange			650.
812P	7c sepia	*1,500.*		650.
813P	8c olive green		*1,800.*	650.
814P	9c olive green	*1,800.*	*1,800.*	650.
815P	10c brown red	*2,500.*		650.
816P	11c ultramarine			650.
817P	12c bright violet	*1,500.*		650.
818P	13c blue green			650.
819P	14c blue			650.
820P	15c blue gray	*1,800.*	*1,800.*	650.
821P	16c black	*1,500.*		650.
822P	17c rose red			650.
823P	18c brown carmine			650.
824P	19c bright violet	*1,800.*	*1,800.*	650.
825P	20c bright blue green	*1,800.*	*1,800.*	650.
826P	21c dull blue			650.
827P	22c vermilion			650.
828P	24c gray black	*1,800.*		650.
829P	25c deep red lilac			650.
830P	30c deep ultramarine			650.
831P	50c light red violet	*1,250.*		650.
832P	$1 purple & black			650.
833P	$2 yellow green & black			800.
834P	$5 carmine & black			800.

1938

835P	Constitution, 3c	—		600.
836P	Swedes & Finns, 3c	—		600.
837P	N.W. Territory, 3c			600.
838P	Iowa, 3c violet	*1,250.*		600.

1939

852P	Golden Gate, 3c	*1,800.*		600.
853P	World's Fair, 3c	*1,250.*		700.
854P	Inauguration, 3c	*1,250.*		650.
855P	Baseball, 3c violet	*1,500.*	*2,000.*	600.
856P	Panama Canal, 3c			600.
857P	Printing, 3c violet			600.
858P	Statehood, 3c rose violet			600.

FAMOUS AMERICANS ISSUE

1940

859P	Authors, 1c bright blue green			800.
860P	Authors, 2c rose carmine			800.
861P	Authors, 3c bright red violet			800.
862P	Authors, 5c ultramarine	*800.*		800.
863P	Authors, 10c dark brown	*2,500.*		800.
864P	Poets, 1c bright blue green	*1,300.*		800.
865P	Poets, 2c rose carmine			800.
866P	Poets, 3c bright red violet			800.
867P	Poets, 5c ultramarine	—		800.
868P	Poets, 10c dark brown	*1,450.*		800.
869P	Educators, 1c bright blue green	—		800.
870P	Educators, 2c rose carmine			800.
871P	Educators, 3c bright red violet			800.
872P	Educators, 5c ultramarine	*800.*		800.
873P	Educators, 10c dark brown	*900.*		800.
874P	Scientists, 1c bright blue green	*1,450.*		800.
875P	Scientists, 2c rose carmine	*800.*		800.
876P	Scientists, 3c bright red violet	*800.*		800.
877P	Scientists, 5c ultramarine			800.
878P	Scientists, 10c dark brown	*1,300.*		800.
879P	Composers, 1c bright blue green			800.
880P	Composers, 2c rose carmine	*900.*		800.
881P	Composers, 3c bright red violet			800.
882P	Composers, 5c ultramarine	*800.*		800.
883P	Composers, 10c dark brown			800.
884P	Artists, 1c bright blue green			800.
885P	Artists, 2c rose carmine			800.
886P	Artists, 3c bright red violet			800.
887P	Artists, 5c ultramarine	*800.*		800.
888P	Artists, 10c dark brown	*800.*		800.
889P	Inventors, 1c bright blue green			800.
890P	Inventors, 2c rose carmine	*1,275.*		800.
891P	Inventors, 3c bright red violet	*800.*		800.
892P	Inventors, 5c ultramarine			800.
893P	Inventors, 10c dark brown			800.

1940

894P	Pony Express, 3c henna brown	*1,100.*		600.
895P	Pan American, 3c light violet			600.
896P	Idaho, 3c bright violet	*800.*		600.
897P	Wyoming, 3c brown violet			600.
898P	Coronado, 3c violet	*1,100.*		600.
899P	Defense, 1c bright blue green	*800.*		600.
900P	Defense, 2c rose carmine	*800.*		600.
901P	Defense, 3c bright violet	*800.*		600.
902P	Emancipation, 3c deep violet	*800.*		750.

1941-44

903P	Vermont, 3c light violet			600.
904P	Kentucky, 3c violet	*750.*		600.
905P	Win the War, 3c violet			600.
906P	China, 5c bright blue			600.
907P	Allied Nations, 2c rose carmine			600.
908P	Four Freedoms, 1c br blue green	*800.*		600.
922P	Railroad, 3c violet	*800.*		600.
923P	Steamship, 3c violet	*1,500.*		600.
924P	Telegraph, 3c br red violet	*800.*		600.
925P	Corregidor, 3c deep violet	*1,275.*		600.
926P	Motion Picture, 3c deep violet	*800.*		600.

1945-46

927P	Florida, 3c br red violet	*1,100.*		600.
928P	United Nations, 5c ultramarine			600.
929P	Iwo Jima, 3c yellow green			600.
930P	Roosevelt, 1c blue green			600.
931P	Roosevelt, 2c carmine rose	*800.*		600.
932P	Roosevelt, 3c purple	*1,400.*		600.
933P	Roosevelt, 5c bright blue	—		
934P	Army, 3c olive	*1,250.*		600.
935P	Navy, 3c blue	*800.*		600.
939P	Merchant Marine, 3c blue green	—		
941P	Tennessee, 3c dark violet	*800.*		
942P	Iowa, 3c deep blue	*800.*		
944P	Kearny, 3c brown violet	*800.*		

1947-50

945P	Edison, 3c br red violet	*700.*	
946P	Pulitzer, 3c purple	*1,100.*	
947P	Stamp Centenary, 3c deep blue	—	
949P	Doctors, 3c brown violet	*1,325.*	
951P	Constitution, 3c blue green	*700.*	
955P	Mississippi, 3c brown violet	—	
956P	Four Chaplains, 3c gray black	—	
958P	Wisconsin, 5c deep blue	*700.*	
959P	Women, 3c dark violet	*700.*	
960P	White, 3c br red violet	*900.*	
962P	Key, 3c rose pink	*700.*	
965P	Stone, 3c bright violet	*700.*	
967P	Barton, 3c rose pink	*1,900.*	
972P	Indian Centennial, 3c dark brown	*900.*	
973P	Rough Riders, 3c violet brown	*700.*	
975P	Rogers, 3c br red violet	—	
976P	Fort Bliss, 3c henna brown	—	
977P	Michael, 3c rose pink	*1,150.*	
981P	Minnesota Terr., 3c blue green	*725.*	—
983P	Puerto Rico, 3c green	*1,000.*	
985P	G.A.R., 3c br rose carmine	*725.*	
988P	Gompers, 3c br red violet	*825.*	
989P	Statue of Freedom, 3c br blue	*1,325.*	
991P	Supreme Court, 3c light violet	*700.*	
992P	Capitol, 3c br red violet	*700.*	

1951-53

999P	Nevada, 3c lt olive green	*1,000.*	
1000P	Cadillac, 3c blue	*800.*	
1001P	Colorado, 3c blue violet	*700.*	
1002P	Chemical, 3c violet brown	*700.*	
1003P	Brooklyn, 3c violet	*1,325.*	
1004P	Betsy Ross, 3c carmine rose	*800.*	
1005P	4H Clubs, 3c blue green	*700.*	
1006P	B. & O. Railroad, 3c br blue	*1,750.*	
1007P	A.A.A., 3c deep blue	*700.*	—
1009P	Grand Coulee Dam, 3c blue green	*700.*	
1010P	Lafayette, 3c br blue	*800.*	
1011P	Mt. Rushmore, 3c blue green	*700.*	—
1012P	Engineering, 3c violet blue	—	
1013P	Service Women, 3c deep blue	*800.*	
1016P	Red Cross, 3c dp blue * carmine	—	
1017P	National Guard, 3c br blue	*700.*	
1018P	Ohio Statehood, 3c chocolate		—
1019P	Washington, 3c green	*700.*	
1020P	Louisiana, 3c violet brown	*800.*	
1021P	Japan, 5c green	*1,650.*	
1022P	American Bar, 3c rose violet	*700.*	
1025P	Trucking, 3c violet	*950.*	
1026P	Gen. Patton, 3c blue violet	*700.*	—

1954

1029P	Columbia, 3c blue	*700.*	

LIBERTY ISSUE

1030P	Franklin, ½c red orange	*1,500.*	
1031P	Washington, 1c dark green	*700.*	
1032P	Mount Vernon, 1½c brown carmine	*900.*	
1033P	Jefferson, 2c carmine rose	—	—
1036P	Lincoln, 4c red violet	*700.*	
1038P	Monroe, 5c dp blue	*700.*	
1039P	Roosevelt, 6c carmine	—	—
1044P	Independence Hall, 10c rose lake	—	
1047P	Monticello, 20c ultramarine	*1,100.*	
1049P	Lee, 30c black	*700.*	
1050P	Marshall, 40c brown red	*700.*	
1051P	Anthony, 50c br purple	*1,000.*	
1052P	Henry, $1 purple	*700.*	
1053P	Hamilton, $5 black	*1,200.*	

1954-61

1060P	Nebraska, 3c violet	*950.*	
1062P	Eastman, 3c brown orange	*900.*	
1063P	Lewis & Clark, 3c violet brown	*825.*	
1064P	Academy of Fine Arts, 3c rose brown	*800.*	
1067P	Armed Forces Reserve, 3c purple	*1,275.*	
1068P	New Hampshire, 3c green	*700.*	
1069P	Soo Locks, 3c blue	*825.*	
1071P	Fort Ticonderoga, 3c lt brown	*825.*	
1073P	Franklin, 3c br carmine	*700.*	
1074P	Washington, 3c dp blue	*700.*	
1076P	FIPEX, 3c & 8c S/S	*700.*	—
1077P	Turkey, 3c rose lake	*800.*	
1078P	Antelope, 3c brown	*700.*	
1079P	Salmon, 3c bl green	*700.*	
1080P	Pure Food & Drug Act, 3c dk bl green	*800.*	
1081P	Wheatland, 3c black brown	*700.*	
1082P	Labor Day, 3c dp blue	*700.*	
1083P	Nassau Hall, 3c black, *orange*	*700.*	
1085P	Children, 3c dk blue	*800.*	
1086P	Hamilton, 3c rose red	*700.*	—
1087P	Polio, 3c red lilac	*800.*	
1088P	Coast & Geodetic Survey, 3c dk blue	—	
1090P	Steel, 3c br ultramarine	*700.*	
1092P	Oklahoma, 3c dk blue	—	
1178P	Ft. Sumter, lt green	*1,250.*	

AIR POST

1918

			DIE	
			(1) Large	*(2)* Small
C1P	6c	orange	*8,500.*	
C2P	16c	green	*7,000.*	
C3P	24c	carmine rose & blue	*8,500.*	

1923

C4P	8c	dark green	*4,750.*	*6,500.*
C5P	16c	dark blue	*4,750.*	*6,500.*
C6P	24c	carmine	*4,750.*	*6,500.*

1926-27

C7P	10c	dark blue	*3,000.*	
C8P	15c	olive brown	*3,000.*	—
C9P	20c	yellow green	*3,000.*	

LINDBERGH ISSUE

1927

C10P	10c	dark blue	*6,000.*	*6,000.*

1928

C11P	5c	carmine & blue	*6,000.*	

1930

C12P	5c	violet	*3,000.*	

ZEPPELIN ISSUE

1930

C13P	65c	green	*15,000.*	*8,250.*
a.		on wove	*15,000.*	
C14P	$1.30	brown	*15,000.*	*8,500.*
a.		on wove	*15,000.*	
C15P	$2.60	blue	*15,000.*	*8,500.*
a.		on wove	*15,000.*	

1932

C17P	8c	olive bister	*4,000.*	

CENTURY OF PROGRESS ISSUE

1933

C18P	50c	green	*12,500.*	*8,250.*

1935-39

C20P	25c	blue on wove		*2,750.*
C21P	20c	green on wove		*2,750.*
C22P	50c	carmine on wove		*2,750.*
C23P	6c	dark blue & carm. on wove		*2,750.*
C24P	30c	dull blue	*3,500.*	*2,750.*

1941-53

C25P	6c	carmine on wove		*3,000.*
C26P	8c	olive green on wove		*3,000.*
C27P	10c	violet on wove	*5,000.*	*3,000.*
C28P	15c	brown carmine on wove		*3,000.*
C29P	20c	bright green on wove		*3,000.*
C30P	30c	blue on wove		*3,000.*
C31P	50c	orange on wove		*3,000.*
C33P	5c	carmine	—	
C40P	6c	carmine	*5,000.*	
C44P	25c	rose carmine	*5,000.*	*2,750.*
C45P	6c	magenta	*5,500.*	*5,000.*
C46P	80c	bright red violet	*5,000.*	—
C47P	6c	carmine	*5,000.*	
C48P	4c	bright blue	—	

AIR POST SPECIAL DELIVERY

1934

CE1P	16c	dark blue on wove		*3,000.*
CE2P	16c	red & blue on wove		*3,000.*

SPECIAL DELIVERY

1885

		DIE			PLATE	
		(1) Large	*(2)* Small	*(2a)*	*(3)* India	*(4)* Card
E1P	10c blue	600.	250.	2,250.	35.	30.
	Block of 4				175.	150.
	P# blk. of 8					—

1888

E2P	10c blue	750.	250.	2,250.	35.	30.
	Block of 4				200.	150.

		P# blk. of 8				525.	—

1893

E3P	10c	orange	1,100.	300.	2,250.	65.	70.
		Block of 4				280.	310.
		P# blk. of 8					875.

1894-95

E4P	10c	blue	500.	250.	2,250.		
	a.	On stamp paper, pair					*5,500.*
E5P	10c	blue, on stamp paper, pair					*4,500.*

1902

E6P	10c	ultra	900.	250.	1,250.		

1908

E7P	10c	green	2,250.	1,500.	2,250.		

1922

			LARGE DIE (1) India	(1a) White Wove	DIE (2) Small

1922

E12P	10c	deep ultra	1,850.	1,100.	

1925-54

E13P	15c	deep orange	1,750.		
E14P	20c	black	1,750.		
E17P	13c	blue			—
E20P	20c	deep blue	1,500.		

REGISTRATION

1911

			DIE (1) Large	(2) Small	(2a)	PLATE (3) India	(4) Card
F1P	10c	ultra	2,500.	1,000.	1,100.		

POSTAGE DUE

1879

J1P	1c	brown	250.	100.	500.	22.	10.
		Block of 4				105.	65.
		P# blk. of 12				450.	
J2P	2c	brown	250.	100.	500.	20.	10.
		Block of 4				90.	65.
		P# blk. of 12				425.	
		2c dark brown	—				
J3P	3c	brown	250.	100.	500.	20.	10.
		Block of 4				90.	65.
		P# blk. of 12				425.	
		3c dark brown	—	—			
J4P	5c	brown	250.	100.	500.	20.	10.
		Block of 4				90.	65.
		P# blk. of 12				425.	
		5c dark brown	—				
J5P	10c	brown	250.	100.	500.		10.
		10c dark brown	—			32.	
		Block of 4				145.	65.
		P# blk. of 12				675.	
J6P	30c	brown	250.	100.	500.		10.
		30c dark brown	—			32.	
		Block of 4				145.	65.
		P# blk. of 12				675.	
J7P	50c	brown	250.	100.	500.		10.
		50c dark brown	—			32.	
		Block of 4				145.	65.
		P# blk. of 12				675.	

1887

J15P	1c	red brown			500.		15.
		Block of 4					
		P# blk. of 12					
J16P	2c	red brown			500.		15.
		Block of 4					
		P# blk. of 12					
J17P	3c	red brown			500.		20.
		Block of 4					
		P# blk. of 12					
J18P	5c	red brown			500.		15.
		Block of 4					
		P# blk. of 12					
J19P	10c	red brown			500.	19.	25.
		Block of 4				90.	
		P# blk. of 12				360.	
J20P	30c	red brown			500.	19.	18.
		Block of 4				90.	
		P# blk. of 12				360.	
J21P	50c	red brown			500.	45.	25.
		Block of 4				210.	
		P# blk. of 12				900.	

1891-93

J22P	1c	bright claret	140.	125.	500.	12.	17.
		Block of 4				65.	80.
		P# blk. of 12					—
	a.	On stamp paper, pair					*425.*
J23P	2c	bright claret	140.	125.	500.	12.	17.
		Block of 4				65.	80.
		P# blk. of 12					—
	a.	On stamp paper, pair					*425.*
J24P	3c	bright claret	140.	125.	500.	12.	17.
		Block of 4				65.	80.
		P# blk. of 12					—
	a.	On stamp paper, pair					*425.*
J25P	5c	bright claret	140.	125.	500.	12.	17.
		Block of 4				65.	80.
		P# blk. of 12					—
	a.	On stamp paper, pair					*425.*
J26P	10c	bright claret	140.	125.	500.	12.	17.
		Block of 4				65.	80.
		P# blk. of 12					—
	a.	On stamp paper, pair					*425.*
J27P	30c	bright claret	140.	125.	500.	28.	17.
		Block of 4				140.	80.
		P# blk. of 12					—
	a.	On stamp paper, pair					*500.*
J28P	50c	bright claret	140.	125.	500.	19.	17.
		Block of 4				90.	80.
		P# blk. of 12					—
	a.	On stamp paper, pair					*500.*

Values for J22Pa-J28Pa are for pairs with original gum and minor faults.

1894

J31P	1c	claret	165.	120.	500.		
	a.	On stamp paper, pair					*225.*
		Block of 4					*500.*
J32P	2c	claret	165.	120.	500.		100.
		Block of 4					475.
		P# blk. of 6					3,000.
J33P	3c	claret	165.	120.	500.		
J34P	5c	claret	165.	120.	500.		
J35P	10c	claret	165.	120.	500.		
J36P	30c	claret	165.	120.	500.		
J37P	50c	claret	165.	120.	500.		

1925

J68P	½c	dull red	*5,750.*				

1930-31

J69P	½c	deep car	450.				
J70P	1c	deep car	450.				
J71P	2c	deep car	450.				
J72P	3c	deep car	450.				
J73P	5c	deep car	450.				
J74P	10c	deep car	450.				
J75P	30c	deep car	450.				
J76P	50c	deep car	450.				
J77P	$1	deep car	1,400.				
J78P	$5	deep car	1,400.				

PARCEL POST POSTAGE DUE

1912

			DIE (1) Large	(2) Small	(2a)	PLATE (3) India	(4) Card
JQ1P	1c	dark green	600.	500.	700.		
JQ2P	2c	dark green	600.	500.	700.		
JQ3P	5c	dark green	600.	500.	700.		
JQ4P	10c	dark green	600.	500.	700.		
JQ5P	25c	dark green	600.	500.	700.		

CARRIERS

1851

LO1P	1c	blue *(Franklin)*	800.	300.	1,500.	50.	25.
		Block of 4				165.	100.
		Cracked plate				—	—
LO2P	1c	blue *(Eagle)*	800.	300.	1,500.	50.	25.
		Block of 4				165.	100.
		P # blk. of 8				675.	

Nos. LO1P (1) and LO2P (1) exist only as hybrids.

OFFICIAL

AGRICULTURE

1873

O1P	1c	yellow	80.	100.	275.	10.	8.
		Block of 4				45.	50.
		P# blk. of 12					225.
O2P	2c	yellow	80.	100.	275.	10.	8.
		Block of 4				45.	50.
		P# blk. of 10					225.
O3P	3c	yellow	80.	100.	275.	10.	8.
		Block of 4				45.	50.
		P# blk. of 12					225.
O4P	6c	yellow	80.	100.	275.	10.	8.
		Block of 4				45.	50.
		P# blk. of 12					225.
O5P	10c	yellow	80.	100.	275.	10.	8.
		Block of 4				45.	50.
		P# blk. of 12					225.
O6P	12c	yellow	80.	100.	275.	10.	8.
		Block of 4				45.	50.
		P# blk. of 12					225.
O7P	15c	yellow	80.	100.	275.	10.	8.
		Block of 4				45.	50.
		P# blk. of 12					225.
O8P	24c	yellow	80.	100.	275.	10.	8.
		Block of 4				45.	50.
		P# blk. of 12					225.
O9P	30c	yellow	80.	100.	275.	10.	8.
		Block of 4				45.	50.
		P# blk. of 12					225.

EXECUTIVE

O10P	1c	carmine	100.	100.	275.	10.	10.
		Block of 4				45.	50.
		P# blk. of 14					225.
O11P	2c	carmine	100.	100.	275.	10.	10.
		Block of 4				45.	50.
		P# blk. of 12					225.
		Foreign entry of 6c Agriculture					—
O12P	3c	carmine	100.	100.	275.	10.	10.
		Block of 4				45.	50.
		P# blk. of 12					225.
O13P	6c	carmine	100.	100.	275.	20.	15.
		Block of 4				100.	85.
		P# blk. of 10					350.
O14P	10c	carmine	100.	100.	275.	10.	10.
		Block of 4				45.	50.
		P# blk. of 12					225.

INTERIOR

O15P	1c	vermilion	80.	100.	275.	10.	8.
		Block of 4				55.	50.
		P# blk. of 12					225.
O16P	2c	vermilion	80.	100.	275.	10.	8.
		Block of 4				55.	50.
		P# blk. of 10					200.
O17P	3c	vermilion	80.	100.	275.	10.	8.
		Block of 4				55.	50.
		P# blk. of 10					225.
O18P	6c	vermilion	80.	100.	275.	15.	10.
		Block of 4				55.	50.
		P# blk. of 12					250.
O19P	10c	vermilion	80.	100.	275.	10.	8.
		Block of 4				55.	45.
		P# blk. of 12					225.
O20P	12c	vermilion	80.	100.	275.	10.	8.
		Block of 4				55.	45.
		P# blk. of 10					225.
O21P	15c	vermilion	80.	100.	275.	10.	8.
		Block of 4				55.	45.
		P# blk. of 12					225.
O22P	24c	vermilion	80.	100.	275.	10.	8.
		Block of 4				55.	45.
		P# blk. of 12					225.
O23P	30c	vermilion	80.	100.	275.	10.	8.
		Block of 4				55.	45.
		P# blk. of 12					225.
O24P	90c	vermilion	80.	100.	275.	10.	8.
		Block of 4				55.	45.
		P# blk. of 12					225.

JUSTICE

O25P	1c	purple	80.	100.	275.	10.	8.
		Block of 4				50.	50.
		P# blk. of 12					225.
O26P	2c	purple	80.	100.	275.	10.	8.
		Block of 4				50.	50.
		P# blk. of 12					225.
O27P	3c	purple	80.	100.	275.	10.	8.
		Block of 4				50.	50.
		P# blk. of 12					225.
		Plate Scratches					—
O28P	6c	purple	80.	100.	275.	10.	8.
		Block of 4				50.	50.
		P# blk. of 12					225.
O29P	10c	purple	80.	100.	275.	10.	8.
		Block of 4				50.	50.
		P# blk. of 10					225.
O30P	12c	purple	80.	100.	275.	10.	8.
		Block of 4				50.	50.
		P# blk. of 12					225.
O31P	15c	purple	80.	100.	275.	10.	8.
		Block of 4				50.	50.
		P# blk. of 10					225.
O32P	24c	purple	80.	100.	275.	10.	8.
		Block of 4				50.	50.
		P# blk. of 12					225.
		Short transfer (pos. 98)					—
O33P	30c	purple	80.	100.	275.	10.	8.
		Block of 4				50.	50.
		P# blk. of 12					225.
O34P	90c	purple	80.	100.	275.	10.	8.
		Block of 4				50.	50.
		P# blk. of 10					225.

NAVY

O35P	1c	ultramarine	80.	100.	275.	10.	8.
		Block of 4				50.	50.
		P# blk. of 12					225.
O36P	2c	ultramarine	80.	100.	275.	10.	8.
		Block of 4				50.	50.
		P# blk. of 12					225.
O37P	3c	ultramarine	80.	100.	275.	10.	8.

		Block of 4				50.	50.
		P# blk. of 10					225.
O38P	6c	ultramarine	80.	100.	275.	15.	15.
		Block of 4				75.	75.
		P# blk. of 10					350.
O39P	7c	ultramarine	80.	100.	275.	10.	8.
		Block of 4				50.	50.
		P# blk. of 10					225.
O40P	10c	ultramarine	80.	100.	275.	10.	8.
		Block of 4				50.	50.
		P# blk. of 12				—	225.
O41P	12c	ultramarine	80.	100.	275.	10.	8.
		Block of 4				50.	50.
		P# blk. of 12					225.
O42P	15c	ultramarine	80.	100.	275.	10.	8.
		Block of 4				50.	50.
		P# blk. of 12					225.
O43P	24c	ultramarine	80.	100.	275.	10.	8.
		Block of 4				50.	50.
		P# blk. of 12					225.
O44P	30c	ultramarine	80.	100.	275.	10.	8.
		Block of 4				57.50	50.
		P# blk. of 12					225.
O45P	90c	ultramarine	80.	100.	275.	10.	8.
		Block of 4				50.	50.
		P# blk. of 12					225.
		Short transfer at upper left (106, pos. 1, 5)					—

POST OFFICE

O47P	1c	black	80.	100.	275.	10.	8.
		Block of 4				50.	50.
		P# blk. of 10					225.
O48P	2c	black	80.	100.	275.	10.	8.
		Block of 4				50.	50.
		P# blk. of 14					225.
O49P	3c	black	80.	100.	275.	10.	8.
		Block of 4				50.	50.
		P# blk. of 12					225.
O50P	6c	black	80.	100.	275.	10.	8.
		Block of 4				50.	50.
		P# blk. of 12					225.
O51P	10c	black	80.	100.	275.	10.	8.
		Block of 4				50.	50.
		P# blk. of 12					225.
O52P	12c	black	80.	100.	275.	10.	8.
		Block of 4				50.	50.
		P# blk. of 12					225.
O53P	15c	black	80.	100.	275.	10.	8.
		Block of 4				50.	50.
		P# blk. of 12					225.
O54P	24c	black	80.	100.	275.	10.	8.
		Block of 4				50.	50.
		P# blk. of 12					225.
O55P	30c	black	80.	100.	275.	10.	8.
		Block of 4				50.	50.
		P# blk. of 12					225.
O56P	90c	black	80.	100.	275.	10.	8.
		Block of 4				50.	50.
		P# blk. of 12					225.

STATE

O57P	1c	green	80.	100.	275.	10.	8.
		Block of 4				50.	50.
		P# blk. of 12					225.
O58P	2c	green	80.	100.	275.	10.	8.
		Block of 4				50.	50.
		P# blk. of 10					225.
O59P	3c	green	80.	100.	275.	10.	8.
		Block of 4				50.	50.
		P# blk. of 10					225.
O60P	6c	green	80.	100.	275.	20.	15.
		Block of 4				100.	85.
		P# blk. of 12					375.
O61P	7c	green	80.	100.	275.	10.	8.
		Block of 4				50.	50.
		P# blk. of 12					225.
O62P	10c	green	80.	100.	275.	10.	8.
		Block of 4				50.	50.
		P# blk. of 12					225.
O63P	12c	green	80.	100.	275.	10.	8.
		Block of 4				50.	50.
		P# blk. of 10					225.
O64P	15c	green	80.	100.	275.	10.	8.
		Block of 4				50.	50.
		P# blk. of 12					225.
O65P	24c	green	80.	100.	275.	10.	8.
		Block of 4				50.	50.
		P# blk. of 12					225.
O66P	30c	green	80.	100.	275.	10.	8.
		Block of 4				50.	50.
		P# blk. of 12					225.
O67P	90c	green	80.	100.	275.	10.	8.
		Block of 4				50.	50.
		P# blk. of 12					225.
O68P	$2	green & black	150.	125.	300.	70.	30.
		Block of 4				300.	150.
		Sheet of 10				1,000.	
a.		Invtd. center					2,500.
O69P	$5	green & black	150.	125.	300.	70.	30.
		Block of 4				300.	150.
		Sheet of 10				1,000.	
a.		Invtd. center					1,750.
		Sheet of 10					—
O70P	$10	green & black	150.	125.	350.	70.	30.
		Block of 4				300.	—
		Sheet of 10				1,000.	
O71P	$20	green & black	150.	125.	350.	70.	30.
		Block of 4				300.	150.
		Sheet of 10				1,000.	
a.		Invtd. center					1,750.
		Block of 4					*8,750.*

O68P to O71P Large Dies exist as hybrids only.

TREASURY

O72P	1c	brown	80.	100.	275.	10.	8.
		Block of 4				50.	50.
		P# blk. of 12					225.
O73P	2c	brown	80.	100.	275.	10.	8.
		Block of 4				50.	50.
		P# blk. of 12					225.
O74P	3c	brown	80.	100.	275.	10.	8.
		Block of 4				50.	50.
		P# blk. of 14					225.
O75P	6c	brown	80.	100.	275.	15.	15.
		Block of 4				75.	75.
		P# blk. of 12					375.
O76P	7c	brown	80.	100.	275.	10.	8.
		Block of 4				50.	50.
		P# blk. of 12					225.
O77P	10c	brown	80.	100.	275.	10.	8.
		Block of 4				50.	50.
		P# blk. of 12					225.
O78P	12c	brown	80.	100.	275.	10.	8.
		Block of 4				50.	50.
		P# blk. of 12					225.
O79P	15c	brown	80.	100.	275.	10.	8.
		Block of 4				50.	50.
		P# blk. of 12					275.
O80P	24c	brown	80.	100.	275.	10.	8.
		Block of 4				50.	45.
		P# blk. of 12					225.
O81P	30c	brown	80.	100.	275.	10.	8.
		Block of 4				50.	45.
		P# blk. of 12					225.
O82P	90c	brown	80.	100.	275.	10.	8.
		Block of 4				50.	50.
		P# blk. of 12					225.

WAR

O83P	1c	rose	80.	100.	275.	10.	8.
		Block of 4				50.	50.
		P# blk. of 12					225.
O84P	2c	rose	80.	100.	275.	10.	8.
		Block of 4				50.	50.
O85P	3c	rose	80.	100.	275.	10.	8.
		Block of 4				50.	50.
		Plate flaw at upper left (32R20)					—
O86P	6c	rose	80.	100.	275.	10.	8.
		Block of 4				50.	50.
		P# blk. of 12					225.
O87P	7c	rose	80.	100.	275.	10.	8.
		Block of 4				50.	50.
		P# blk. of 10					225.
O88P	10c	rose	80.	100.	275.	10.	8.
		Block of 4				50.	50.
		P# blk. of 10					225.
O89P	12c	rose	80.	100.	275.	10.	8.
		Block of 4				50.	50.
		P# blk. of 12					225.
O90P	15c	rose	80.	100.	275.	10.	8.
		Block of 4				50.	50.
		P# blk. of 12					225.
O91P	24c	rose	80.	100.	275.	10.	8.
		Block of 4				50.	50.
		P# blk. of 10					225.
O92P	30c	rose	80.	100.	275.	10.	8.
		Block of 4				50.	50.
		P# blk. of 10					225.
O93P	90c	rose	80.	100.	275.	10.	8.
		Block of 4				50.	50.
		P# blk. of 12					225.

O83-O93 exist in a plum shade.

POSTAL SAVINGS MAIL

1911

O124P	1c	dark violet	450.	275.	1,000.
O121P	2c	black	450.	275.	1,000.
O126P	10c	carmine	450.	275.	1,000.
O122P	50c	dark green	450.	275.	1,000.
O123P	$1	ultramarine	450.	275.	1,000.

NEWSPAPERS

1865

			DIE (1) Large	DIE (2) Small	(2a)	PLATE (3) Wove Paper	PLATE (4) Card
PR2P	10c	green	575.	225.		40.	60.
		Block of 4				200.	300.
		P# blk. of 6					—
PR3P	25c	orange red	575.	225.		45.	60.
		Block of 4				225.	300.
		P# blk. of 6					—
PR4P	5c	blue	575.	225.		40.	60.
		Block of 4				200.	300.
		P# blk. of 6					—

1875

PR5P	5c	dark blue			*1,750.*		60.
PR6P	10c	deep green			*1,750.*		60.
PR7P	25c	dark car red			*1,750.*		60.
PR9P	2c	black	80.	40.	250.	10.	8.
		Block of 4				45.	40.
		P# blk. of 8					—
PR10P	3c	black	80.	40.	250.	10.	8.
		Block of 4				45.	40.
		P# blk. of 8					—
PR11P	4c	black	80.	40.	250.	10.	8.
		Block of 4				45.	40.
		P# blk. of 8					—
PR12P	6c	black	80.	40.	250.	10.	8.
		Block of 4				45.	40.
		P# blk. of 8					—
PR13P	8c	black	80.	40.	250.	10.	8.
		Block of 4				45.	40.
		P# blk. of 8					—
PR14P	9c	black	80.	40.	250.	10.	8.
		Block of 4				45.	40.
		P# blk. of 8					—
PR15P	10c	black	80.	40.	250.	10.	8.
		Block of 4				45.	40.
		P# blk. of 8					—
PR16P	12c	rose	80.	40.	250.	10.	8.
		Block of 4				45.	40.
		P# blk. of 8					—
PR17P	24c	rose	80.	40.	250.	10.	8.
		Block of 4				45.	40.
		P# blk. of 8					—
PR18P	36c	rose	80.	40.	250.	10.	8.
		Block of 4				45.	40.
		P# blk. of 8					—
PR19P	48c	rose	80.	40.	250.	10.	8.
		Block of 4				45.	40.
		P# blk. of 8					—
PR20P	60c	rose	80.	40.	250.	10.	8.
		Block of 4				45.	40.
		P# blk. of 8					—
PR21P	72c	rose	80.	40.	250.	10.	8.
		Block of 4				45.	40.
		P# blk. of 8					—
PR22P	84c	rose	80.	40.	250.	10.	8.
		Block of 4				45.	40.
		P# blk. of 8					—
PR23P	96c	rose	80.	40.	250.	10.	8.
		Block of 4				45.	40.
		P# blk. of 8					—
PR24P	$1.92	dark brown	80.	40.	250.	12.	12.
		Block of 4				55.	60.
		P# blk. of 8					—
PR25P	$3	vermilion	80.	40.	250.	12.	12.
		Block of 4				55.	60.
		P# blk. of 8					—
PR26P	$6	ultra	80.	40.	250.	12.	12.
		Block of 4				55.	60.
		P# blk. of 8					—
PR27P	$9	yellow	80.	40.	250.	12.	12.
		Block of 4				55.	60.
		P# blk. of 8					—
PR28P	$12	blue green	80.	40.	250.	12.	12.
		Block of 4				55.	60.
		P# blk. of 8					—
PR29P	$24	dark gray violet	80.	40.	250.	12.	12.
		Block of 4				60.	60.
		P# blk. of 8					—
PR30P	$36	brown rose	80.	40.	250.	15.	12.
		Block of 4				75.	60.
		P# blk. of 8					—
PR31P	$48	red brown	80.	40.	250.	17.	12.
		Block of 4				80.	60.
		P# blk. of 8					—
PR32P	$60	violet	80.	40.	250.	20.	15.
		Block of 4				100.	75.
		P# blk. of 8					—

1879

PR57P	2c	deep black	80.			12.	4.
		Block of 4				60.	24.
a.		On stamp paper, pair					—
PR58P	3c	deep black	80.			12.	4.
		Block of 4				60.	24.
a.		On stamp paper, pair					—
PR59P	4c	deep black	90.			12.	4.
		Block of 4				60.	24.
a.		On stamp paper, pair					—
PR60P	6c	deep black	90.			12.	4.
		Block of 4				60.	24.
a.		On stamp paper, pair					—
PR61P	8c	deep black	90.			12.	4.
		Block of 4				60.	24.
a.		On stamp paper, pair					—
PR62P	10c	deep black	90.			12.	4.
		Block of 4				60.	24.
a.		On stamp paper, pair					—
PR63P	12c	red	90.			12.	6.
		Block of 4				60.	32.
PR64P	24c	red	90.			12.	6.
		Block of 4				60.	32.
PR65P	36c	red	90.			12.	6.
		Block of 4				60.	32.
PR66P	48c	red	90.			12.	6.
		Block of 4				60.	32.
PR67P	60c	red	90.			12.	6.
		Block of 4				60.	32.
PR68P	72c	red	90.			12.	6.
		Block of 4				60.	32.
PR69P	84c	red	90.			12.	6.
		Block of 4				60.	32.
PR70P	96c	red	90.			12.	6.
		Block of 4				60.	32.
PR71P	$1.92	pale brown	90.			15.	8.
		Block of 4				75.	45.
a.		On stamp paper, pair					—
PR72P	$3	red verm.	90.			15.	8.
		Block of 4				75.	45.
a.		On stamp paper, pair					—
PR73P	$6	blue	90.			15.	8.
		Block of 4				75.	45.
a.		On stamp paper, pair					—
PR74P	$9	orange	90.			15.	8.

			Die (1) Large	Die (2) Small	Die (2a)	Plate (3) India	Plate (4) Card
		Block of 4				75.	45.
a.		On stamp paper, pair					—
PR75P	$12	yel. green	90.			15.	8.
		Block of 4				75.	45.
a.		On stamp paper, pair					—
PR76P	$24	dark violet	90.			18.	8.
		Block of 4				90.	45.
a.		On stamp paper, pair					—
PR77P	$36	Indian red	90.			20.	8.
		Block of 4				100.	45.
a.		On stamp paper, pair					—
PR78P	$48	yellow brown	90.			24.	8.
		Block of 4				120.	45.
a.		On stamp paper, pair					—
PR79P	$60	purple	90.			24.	8.
		Block of 4				120.	45.
a.		On stamp paper, pair					—

1885

			Die (1) Large	Die (2) Small	Die (2a)	Plate (3) India	Plate (4) Card
PR81P	1c	black	100.	60.	250.	10.	8.
		Block of 4				50.	40.
		P# blk. of 8					200.
a.		On stamp paper, pair					—
PR82P	12c	carmine		80.	250.	17.	8.
		Block of 4				85.	
a.		On stamp paper, pair					—
PR83P	24c	carmine		80.	250.	17.	8.
		Block of 4				85.	
a.		On stamp paper, pair					—
PR84P	36c	carmine		80.	250.	17.	8.
		Block of 4				85.	
a.		On stamp paper, pair					—
PR85P	48c	carmine		80.	250.	17.	8.
		Block of 4				85.	
a.		On stamp paper, pair					—
PR86P	60c	carmine		80.	250.	17.	8.
		Block of 4				85.	
a.		On stamp paper, pair					—
PR87P	72c	carmine		80.	250.	17.	8.
		Block of 4				85.	
a.		On stamp paper, pair					—
PR88P	84c	carmine		80.	250.	17.	8.
		Block of 4				85.	
a.		On stamp paper, pair					—
PR89P	96c	carmine		80.	250.	17.	8.
		Block of 4				85.	
a.		On stamp paper, pair					—

1895

			Die (1) Large	Die (2) Small	Die (2a)
PR102P	1c	black	125.	100.	275.
PR103P	2c	black	125.	100.	275.
PR104P	5c	black	125.	100.	275.
PR105P	10c	black	125.	100.	275.
PR106P	25c	carmine	125.	100.	275.
PR107P	50c	carmine	125.	100.	275.
PR108P	$2	scarlet	125.	100.	275.
PR109P	$5	blue	125.	100.	275.
PR110P	$10	green	125.	100.	275.
PR111P	$20	slate	125.	100.	275.
PR112P	$50	carmine	125.	100.	275.
PR113P	$100	purple	125.	100.	275.

PARCEL POST

1912-13

			DIE ON INDIA (1) Large	(2) Small	(2a)	PLATE (3) India	(4) Card
Q1P	1c	car rose	1,400.	1,200.	1,200.		
Q2P	2c	car rose	1,400.	1,200.	1,200.		
Q3P	3c	car rose	1,400.	1,200.	1,200.		
Q4P	4c	car rose	1,400.	1,200.	1,200.		
Q5P	5c	car rose	1,400.	1,200.	1,200.		
Q6P	10c	car rose	1,400.	1,200.	1,200.		
Q7P	15c	car rose	1,400.	1,200.	1,200.		
Q8P	20c	car rose	1,400.	1,200.	1,200.		
Q9P	25c	car rose	1,400.	1,200.	1,200.		
Q10P	50c	car rose	1,400.	1,200.	1,200.		
Q11P	75c	car rose	1,400.	1,200.	1,200.		
Q12P	$1	car rose	1,400.	1,200.	1,200.		

SPECIAL HANDLING

1925-28

QE1P	10c	yel grn	900.
QE2P	15c	yel grn	900.
QE3P	20c	yel grn	900.
QE4P	25c	yel grn	*1,500.*
QE4aP	25c	deep grn	900.

LOCAL

1844

5L1P	5c	black	*2,250.*

TELEGRAPH

AMERICAN RAPID TELEGRAPH CO.

1881

			DIE (2) Small	PLATE (3) India
1T1P	1c	black	80.	32.
		Pair		68.
1T2P	3c	orange		32.
		Pair		68.
1T3P	5c	bister brown	80.	32.
		Pair		68.
1T4P	10c	purple		32.
		Pair		68.
1T5P	15c	green	80.	32.
		Pair		68.
1T6P	20c	red	80.	32.
		Pair		68.
1T7P	25c	rose	80.	32.
		Pair		68.
1T8P	50c	blue		32.
		Pair		68.

"Collect"

1T9P	1c	brown		32.
		Pair, Nos. 1T9P, 1T13P		68.
		Same, block of 4		145.
1T10P	5c	blue		32.
		Pair, Nos. 1T10P, 1T14P		68.
		Same, block of 4		145.
1T11P	15c	red brown		32.
		Pair, Nos. 1T11P, 1T15P		68.
		Same, block of 4		145.
1T12P	20c	olive green		32.
		Pair, Nos. 1T12P, 1T16P		68.
		Same, block of 4		145.

Office Coupon

1T13P	1c	brown		32.
1T14P	5c	blue		32.
1T15P	15c	red brown		32.
1T16P	20c	olive green		32.

BALTIMORE & OHIO TELEGRAPH CO.

1885

3T1P	1c	vermilion	32.
		Pair	68.
3T2P	5c	blue	32.
		Pair	68.
3T3P	10c	red brown	32.
		Pair	68.
3T4P	25c	orange	32.
		Pair	68.

1886

3T6P		black	32.
		Pair	68.
3T7P	1c	green	32.
3T8P	5c	blue	32.
3T9P	10c	brown	32.
3T10P	25c	orange	32.

POSTAL TELEGRAPH CO.

1885

			DIE (1) Large	DIE (2) Small	PLATE (3) India
15T1P	10c	green		55.	32.
15T2P	15c	orange red			32.
15T3P	25c	blue	65.		32.
15T4P	50c	brown		65.	32.

WESTERN UNION TELEGRAPH CO.

16T1P	(1871)	green			17.
		Pair			35.
16T2P	(1872)	red			17.
		Pair			35.
16T3P	(1873)	blue			17.
		Pair			35.
16T4P	(1874)	brown			17.
		Pair			35.
16T5P	(1875)	deep green			17.
16T6P	(1876)	red			17.
16T7P	(1877)	violet			—
16T8P	(1878)	gray brown			20.
16T9P	(1879)	blue			14.
16T10P	(1880)	lilac rose			16.
16T11P	(1881)	green			16.
16T12P	(1882)	blue			20.
16T13P	(1883)	yellow brown			16.
16T14P	(1884)	gray violet			20.
16T15P	(1885)	green			20.
16T16P	(1886)	brown violet			13.
		Pair			28.
16T17P	(1887)	red brown			13.
		Pair			28.
16T18P	(1888)	blue			13.
		Pair			28.
16T19P	(1889)	olive green			16.
16T22P	(1892)	vermilion			16.
16T30P	(1900)	red violet			28.
16T44P	(1913)	brown	—	—	—

REVENUE

NORMAL COLORS

1862-68 by Butler & Carpenter, Philadelphia.

1868-75 by Joseph R. Carpenter, Philadelphia.

In the following listing the so-called small die proofs on India paper may be, in fact probably are, plate proofs. The editors shall consider them die proofs, however, until they see them in pairs or blocks. Many revenue proofs on India are mounted on card.

FIRST ISSUE

1862-71

			DIE ON INDIA (1) Large	(2) Small	PLATE (3) India	(4) Card
R1P	1c	Express, red			70.	65.
		Block of 4				275.
R2P	1c	Playing Cards, red	600.		60.	65.
		Block of 4			250.	275.
R3P	1c	Proprietary, red			140.	45.
		Block of 4				200.
R4P	1c	Telegraph, red				28.
		Block of 4				125.
R5P	2c	Bank Check, blue		525.		33.
		Block of 4				140.
R6P	2c	Bank Check, orange			60.	
		Block of 4			250.	
R7P	2c	Certificate, blue				28.
		Block of 4				125.
R8P	2c	Certificate, orange			82.	
		Block of 4			350.	
R9P	2c	Express, blue				28.
		Block of 4				125.
R10P	2c	Express, orange	600.		60.	
		Pair			250.	
R11P	2c	Playing Cards, blue				38.
		Block of 4				160.
R13P	2c	Proprietary, blue		400.		28.
		Block of 4				125.
R15P	2c	U.S.I.R., orange			*1,250.*	
R16P	3c	Foreign Exchange, green	600.		225.	38.
		Block of 4				160.
		R16P1 + R19P1 composite	—			
R17P	3c	Playing Cards, green	*700.*	400.		100.
		Block of 4				425.
R18P	3c	Proprietary, green			60.	28.
		Block of 4			250.	125.
R19P	3c	Telegraph, green	600.		225.	28.
		Block of 4				125.
R20P	4c	Inland Exchange, brown			225.	28.
		Block of 4				125.
R21P	4c	Playing Cards, violet		400.		95.
		Block of 4				400.
R22P	4c	Proprietary, violet	600.		110.	60.
		Block of 4			475.	250.
R23P	5c	Agreement, red				33.
		Block of 4				140.
R24P	5c	Certificate, red			95.	110.
		Block of 4			400.	
		R24P1 + R25P1 composite	—			
R25P	5c	Express, red		250.		33.
		Block of 4				145.
R26P	5c	Foreign Exchange, red				300.
R27P	5c	Inland Exchange, red		250.		28.
		Block of 4				125.
R28P	5c	Playing Cards, red		—	105.	325.
		Block of 4			440.	
R29P	5c	Proprietary, red on blue wove, gummed				—
R30P	6c	Inland Exchange, orange			60.	33.
		Block of 4			250.	140.
R32P	10c	Bill of Lading, blue				33.
		Block of 4				140.

No.	Denom.	Description	Die on India (1) Large	Die on India (2) Small	Plate (3) India	Plate (4) Card
R33P	10c	Certificate, blue			140.	33.
		Block of 4				140.
R34P	10c	Contract, blue				33.
		Block of 4				140.
R35P	10c	Foreign Exchange, blue				33.
		Block of 4				140.
R36P	10c	Inland Exchange, blue				33.
		Block of 4				140.
R37P	10c	Power of Attorney, blue				33.
		Block of 4				140.
R38P	10c	Proprietary, blue	*700.*		70.	
		Block of 4			300.	
R39P	15c	Foreign Exchange, brown			90.	325.
		Block of 4			375.	1,600.
R40P	15c	Inland Exchange, brown			120.	33.
		Block of 4				140.
R41P	20c	Foreign Exchange, red	600.		90.	100.
		Block of 4			375.	425.
		R41P1 + R42P1 composite	—			
R42P	20c	Inland Exchange, red	600.	250.	260.	33.
		Block of 4				140.
R43P	25c	Bond, red				500.
		Block of 4				2,500.
R44P	25c	Certificate, red				33.
		Block of 4				140.
R45P	25c	Entry of Goods, red				550.
R46P	25c	Insurance, red			60.	33.
		Block of 4			250.	140.
R47P	25c	Life Insurance, red				33.
		Block of 4				140.
R48P	25c	Power of Attorney, red				33.
		Block of 4				140.
R49P	25c	Protest, red				33.
		Block of 4				140.
R50P	25c	Warehouse Receipt, red				33.
		Block of 4				140.
R51P	30c	Foreign Exchange, lilac			110.	100.
		Block of 4			475.	425.
R52P	30c	Inland Exchange, lilac			65.	55.
		Block of 4			275.	230.
R53P	40c	Inland Exchange, brown			150.	75.
		Block of 4				325.
R54P	50c	Conveyance, blue		250.		33.
		Block of 4				140.
R55P	50c	Entry of Goods, blue			65.	45.
		Block of 4			275.	190.
R56P	50c	Foreign Exchange, blue			65.	45.
		Block of 4			275.	190.
R57P	50c	Lease, blue			65.	38.
		Block of 4			275.	160.
R58P	50c	Life Insurance, blue			65.	38.
		Block of 4			275.	160.
R59P	50c	Mortgage, blue				110.
		Block of 4				475.
R60P	50c	Original Process, blue			65.	38.
		Block of 4			275.	160.
R61P	50c	Passage Ticket, blue				55.
		Block of 4				230.
R62P	50c	Probate of Will, blue			65.	55.
		Block of 4			275.	230.
R63P	50c	Surety Bond, blue				55.
		Block of 4				230.
R64P	60c	Inland Exchange, orange			55.	38.
		Block of 4				160.
R65P	70c	Foreign Exchange, green			120.	55.
		Block of 4				230.
R66P	$1	Conveyance, red				45.
		Block of 4				190.
R67P	$1	Entry of Goods, red	525.			45.
		Block of 4				190.
R68P	$1	Foreign Exchange red				33.
		Block of 4				140.
R69P	$1	Inland Exchange, red				55.
		Block of 4				230.
R70P	$1	Lease, red				*425.*
R71P	$1	Life Insurance, red				33.
		Block of 4				140.
R72P	$1	Manifest, red			55.	33.
		Block of 4			—	140.
R73P	$1	Mortgage, red				55.
		Block of 4				230.
R74P	$1	Passage Ticket, red				*425.*
		Block of 4				*1,850.*
R75P	$1	Power of Attorney, red				100.
		Block of 4				425.
R76P	$1	Probate of Will, red				33.
		Block of 4				140.
R77P	$1.30	Foreign Exchange, orange	*700.*		140.	100.
		Block of 4			575.	425.
R78P	$1.50	Inland Exchange, blue			110.	45.
		Block of 4			475.	190.
R79P	$1.60	Foreign Exchange green			140.	100.
		Block of 4				425.
R80P	$1.90	Foreign Exchange, violet			140.	100.
		Block of 4			575.	425.
R81P	$2	Conveyance, red			120.	33.
		Block of 4				140.
R82P	$2	Mortgage, red			120.	33.
		Block of 4			—	140.
R83P	$2	Probate of Will, red				110.
		Block of 4				—
R84P	$2.50	Inland Exchange, violet			250.	225.
		Block of 4				—
R85P	$3	Charter Party, green			120.	65.
		Block of 4			500.	275.
R86P	$3	Manifest, green	—	350.	180.	65.
		Block of 4				275.
R87P	$3.50	Inland Exchange, blue			180.	140.
		Block of 4				575.
R88P	$5	Charter Party, red			70.	55.
		Block of 4			300.	230.
R89P	$5	Conveyance, red			450.	55.
		Block of 4				230.
R90P	$5	Manifest, red		300.		55.
		Block of 4				230.
R91P	$5	Mortgage, red			650.	55.
		Block of 4				230.
R92P	$5	Probate of Will, red		300.		55.
		Block of 4				230.
R93P	$10	Charter Party, green			120.	55.
		Block of 4				230.
R94P	$10	Conveyance, green				55.
		Block of 4				230.
R95P	$10	Mortgage, green				55.
		Block of 4				230.
R96P	$10	Probate of Will, green	*700.*	300.		75.
		Block of 4				325.
R97P	$15	Mortgage, dark blue		—		180.
		Block of 4				800.
R97eP	$15	Mortgage, ultramarine		—		350.
		Block of 4				—
	$15	Mortgage, milky blue			290.	
R98P	$20	Conveyance, orange			220.	100.
		Block of 4			900.	425.
R99P	$20	Probate of Will, orange				220.
		Block of 4				—
R100P	$25	Mortgage, red			220.	160.
		Block of 4				675.
R101P	$50	U.S.I.R., green			220.	230.
		Block of 4				950.
R102P	$200	U.S.I.R., green & orange red			1,400.	

SECOND ISSUE

1871-72

No.	Denom.	Description	Die on India (1) Large	Die on India (2) Small	Plate (3) India	Plate (4) Card
R105P	3c	blue & black			20.	15.
		Block of 4			90.	65.
R109P	10c	blue & black			20.	15.
		Block of 4			90.	65.
R111P	20c	blue & black			20.	15.
		Block of 4			90.	65.
R112P	25c	blue & black			20.	15.
		Block of 4			90.	65.
R115P	50c	blue & black			50.	15.
		Block of 4			225.	65.
R119P	$1.30	blue & black			50.	38.
		Block of 4			225.	160.
R120P	$1.50	blue & black			28.	22.
		Block of 4			120.	100.
		Double transfer, design of $1				—
R121P	$1.60	blue & black			60.	60.
		Block of 4			260.	260.
R122P	$1.90	blue & black			50.	38.
		Block of 4			225.	170.
R126P	$3.50	blue & black			90.	100.
		Block of 4			400.	425.
R130P	$25	blue & black			150.	110.
		Block of 4			650.	500.
R131P	$50	blue & black			160.	140.
		Block of 4			700.	625.

The "small die proofs" formerly listed under Nos. R103P-R131P are plate proofs from the sheets listed under "Trial Color Proofs."

No.	Denom.	Description	Die on India (1) Large	Die on India (2) Small	Plate (3) India	Plate (4) Card
R132P	$200	red, blue & black	3,500.	2,750.	2,500.	
		Red (frame) inverted			—	
R133P	$500	red orange, green & black	3,750.			
R133AP	$5000	red orange, dark green & black	*7,500.*			

No. R133AP was approved in these colors but never issued. Shade differences of the red orange and dark green colors will be found. It comes both with and without manufacturer's imprints to the left and right of the design. One example exists on bond paper mounted on card with "853½" printed on the lower right card margin.

Due to the unusual manufacturing process of printing these tri-color stamps from single impression plates, proofs with imprints could also be considered to be plate proofs. All are extremely scarce or unique, and are valued in the grade, condition and scarcity in which they exist. For other colors see the trial color proofs listings under No. R133ATC.

THIRD ISSUE

1871-72

No.	Denom.	Description	Plate (3) India	Plate (4) Card
R134P	1c	claret & black		15.
		Block of 4		70.
R135P	2c	orange & black	16.	15.
		Block of 4	70.	70.
R136P	4c	brown & black	20.	15.
		Block of 4	85.	70.
R137P	5c	orange & black	20.	15.
		Block of 4	85.	70.
R138P	6c	orange & black	20.	15.
		Block of 4	85.	70.
R139P	15c	brown & black	20.	15.
		Block of 4	85.	70.
R140P	30c	orange & black	25.	18.
		Block of 4	105.	80.
R141P	40c	brown & black	25.	18.
		Block of 4	105.	80.
R142P	60c	orange & black	65.	50.
		Block of 4	270.	225.
		Foreign entry, design of 70c	200.	150.
a.		Center inverted		*1,250.*
		Block of 4		*5,500.*
		Foreign entry, design of 70c		—
R143P	70c	green & black	45.	38.
		Block of 4	190.	170.
R144P	$1	green & black	40.	38.
		Block of 4	170.	170.
R145P	$2	vermilion & black	80.	105.
		Block of 4	335.	450.
R146P	$2.50	claret & black	50.	40.
		Block of 4	210.	170.
R147P	$3	green & black	65.	70.
		Block of 4	270.	300.
R148P	$5	vermilion & black	65.	55.
		Block of 4	270.	240.
R149P	$10	green & black	80.	55.
		Block of 4	335.	240.
R150P	$20	orange & black	115.	150.
		Block of 4	500.	635.

The "small die proofs" formerly listed under Nos. R134P-R150P are plate proofs from the sheets listed under "Trial Color Proofs."

1875 National Bank Note Co., New York City

			DIE ON INDIA (1) Large	(2) Small	PLATE (3) India
R152P	2c	blue *(Liberty)*	450.		110.
		Block of 4			475.

DOCUMENTARY

1898

R173P	$1	dark green	*600.*
R174P	$3	dark brown	*600.*
R175P	$5	orange red	*600.*
R176P	$10	black	*600.*
R177P	$30	red	*600.*
R178P	$50	gray brown	*600.*

1899

R180P	$500	car lake & blk	*1,650.*

1914

			(1) Large	(2) Small
R197P	2c	rose		—

1914-15

R226P	$500	blue	*675.*

1917

R246P	$30	deep orange (without serial No.)	*650.*

1940

R298P	50c	car (without ovpt.)	*700.*
R305P	$10	carmine	*825.*
		Without overprint	—
R306AP	$50	carmine	*825.*
		Without overprint	—

1952

R597P	55c	carmine	*675.*

PROPRIETARY

1871-75 Joseph R. Carpenter, Philadelphia

			DIE ON INDIA (2) Small	(3) India	PLATE (4) Card	(5) Bond
RB1P	1c	grn & blk		—	12.	12.
		Block of 4			52.	52.
RB2P	2c	grn & blk		175.	12.	
		Block of 4			52.	
RB3P	3c	grn & blk		22.	12.	
		Block of 4		100.	52.	
RB4P	4c	grn & blk		22.	12.	
		Block of 4		100.	52.	
RB5P	5c	grn & blk		22.	12.	
		Block of 4		100.	52.	
RB6P	6c	grn & blk		22.	12.	
		Block of 4		100.	52.	
RB7P	10c	grn & blk		22.	12.	
		Block of 4		100.	52.	
RB8P	50c	grn & blk	1,000.		850.	
RB9P	$1	grn & blk	1,000.		1,250.	
RB10P	$5	grn & blk	2,000.	1,750.	2,000.	

The "small die proofs" formerly listed under Nos. RB1P-RB7P are from the composite plate proofs listed under "Trial Color Proofs."

National Bank Note Co., New York City

1875-83

			DIE ON INDIA (1) Large	(2) Small	PLATE (3) India	(4) Card
RB11P	1c	green	600.		65.	—
		Block of 4			325.	
RB12P	2c	brown	600.		65.	—
		Pair			160.	
RB13P	3c	orange	600.		65.	—
		Pair			160.	—
		Block of 4				—
RB14P	4c	red brown	600.		65.	—
		Pair			160.	—
		Block of 4				—
RB15P	4c	red	600.			
RB16P	5c	black	600.		65.	—
		Pair			160.	—
		Block of 4				—
RB17P	6c	violet blue	600.		65.	
		Pair			160.	
RB18P	6c	blue	600.		175.	
		Pair			400.	
RB19P	10c	blue	600.			

No. RB19P was produced by the Bureau of Engraving and Printing.

Wines

1916

RE56P	$20	green	*5,000.*

PLAYING CARDS

1896 Bureau of Engraving & Printing

RF2P	2c	ultramarine	*550.*
		a. 2c blue	*1,100.*

PRIVATE DIE PROPRIETARY

The editors are indebted to Eric Jackson and Philip T. Bansner for the compilation of the following listing of Private Die Proprietary die and plate proofs as well as the corrresponding trial color proofs. The large die proofs range in size and format from die impressions on India die sunk on cards generally up to 6x9 inches, through die impressions on India on or off card in medium to stamp size. Many individual listings are known in more than one size and format. Values reflect the size and format most commonly seen.

PRIVATE DIE MATCH STAMPS

1864

			DIE ON INDIA (1) Large	PLATE (3) India	(4) Card
RO1P	1c	blue	225.		
RO2P	1c	orange	500.	90.	
RO3P	1c	blue	225.		
RO4P	1c	blue	500.		
RO5P	1c	green	500.		
RO6P	1c	Blue	175.		
RO7P	1c	blue	175.		
RO9P	1c	black	175.		
RO10P	1c	black	175.		
RO11P	3c	Black	250.		
RO12P	1c	black	225.		
RO12/185P	1c	black	750.		
RO13P	3c	green	1000.		
RO14P	1c	black	175.		
RO15P	1c	green	300.		
RO16P	1c	blue	225.	60.	
RO17P	1c	blue	175.		
RO17/19P	1c/3c	blue	1000.		
RO17/19P	1c/3c	black	750.		
RO19P	3c	black	375.		
RO20P	1c	blue	175.		
RO21P	3c	black	250.		
RO23P	1c	orange	225.		
RO24P	1c	brown	225.		
RO28P	1c	blue	300.	90.	
RO29P	1c	black	175.		
RO30P	1c	green	175.		
RO31P	1c	black	175.		
RO32P	4c	black	300.		
RO33P	4c	green	225.		
RO35P	1c	black	175.		
RO37P	3c	black	225.		
RO38P	1c	black	350.		
RO39P	1c	blue	175.		
RO40P	1c	green	500.		
RO41P	1c	lake	225.		
RO42P	1c	lake	225.		
RO43P	1c	black	225.		
RO44P	1c	green	225.		
RO45P	1c	black	225.		
RO46P	1c	black	300.		
RO47P	1c	black	225.	90.	75.
RO48P	1c	black	500.		
RO49P	1c	black	175.		
RO50P	1c	black	375.		
RO55P	1c	black	250.		
RO56P	1c	black	250.		
RO57P	1c	green	300.		
RO58P	1c	lake	225.	75.	
RO60P	3c	black	300.		
RO61P	1c	green	300.		
RO62P	1c	green	175.		
RO64P	1c	lake	225.		
RO65P	1c	black	225.		
RO66P	1c	blue	175.		
RO67P	1c	black	175.		
RO68P	1c	green	225.		
RO69P	1c	black	175.		
RO72P	1c	green	500.		
RO73P	1c	black	175.		
RO75P	1c	carmine	450.		
RO76P	1c	black	175.		
RO77P	1c	blue	225.		
RO78P	1c	blue	225.		
RO80P	1c	blue	300.		
RO81P	1c	black	175.		
RO82P	1c	black	175.		
RO83P	1c	blue	175.		
RO84P	1c	black	175.		
RO85P	1c	brown	300.	100.	
RO86P	1c	black	250.	125.	
RO87P	1c	black	500.	50.	
RO88P	1c	black	175.		
RO89P	3c	black	175.		
RO90P	6c	black	175.	125.	
RO91P	3c	black	225.	125.	
RO92P	1c	black	175.		
RO94P	3c	black	175.	175.	
RO95P	1c	green	225.		
RO96P	1c	green	300.		
RO97P	1c	black	175.		
RO98P	1c	green	225.		
RO99P	1c	green	300.		
RO100P	1c	green	225.	65.	
RO101P	3c	carmine		75.	
RO102P	5c	orange		75.	
RO103P	1c	black	175.		
RO104P	1c	green	175.		
RO105P	1c	black	175.	100.	
RO106P	1c	green	300.		
RO107P	1c	blue	225.		
RO108P	1c	red	750.		
RO109P	1c	black	300.		
RO110P	1c	green	175.		
RO112P	1c	blue	225.	100.	
RO113P	1c	black	175.		
RO114P	1c	lake	750.		
RO115P	1c	blue	175.		
RO116P	1c	blue	175.		
RO118P	8c	blue	500.		
RO119P	1c	green	300.		
RO121P	1c	green	500.		
RO122P	1c	black	175.		
RO123P	1c	black	175.		
RO124P	1c	green	750.		
RO125P	1c	blue	300.		
RO126P	1c	black	175.		
RO127P	1c	blue	175.		
RO128P	1c	blue	225.		
RO130P	1c	blue	500.		
RO131P	1c	blue	300.		
RO132P	1c	blue	225.	125.	
RO133P	1c	black	225.		
RO134P	1c	blue	175.	75.	
RO135P	1c	lake	500.		
RO136P	1c	blue	175.		
RO138P	1c	green	175.		
RO139P	5c	blue	225.		
RO140P	4c	green	225.		
RO141P	1c	blue	175.		
RO142P	1c	green	225.		
RO143P	3c	orange	225.		
RO144P	1c	blue	400.		
RO146P	1c	black	175.		
RO148P	1c	blue	225.	100.	
RO152P	1c	black	175.	75.	
RO153P	1c	black	175.	75.	
RO155P	1c	black	175.	65.	
RO157P	3c	blue	225.	80.	
RO158P	1c	black	175.		
RO159P	3c	blue	175.		
RO160P	1c	blue	175.		
RO161P	1c	blue	500.		
RO163P	1c	black	175.		
RO164P	1c	lake	500.		
RO165P	12c	blue	750.		
RO166P	1c	vermilion	225.		
RO167P	3c	blue	175.		
RO168P	1c	blue	175.		
RO170P	1c	black	450.		
RO171P	1c	black	175.		
RO172P	1c	black	175.		
RO173P	1c	blue	225.	75.	
RO174P	1c	blue	175.		
RO175P	1c	black	225.		
RO176P	1c	blue	500.		
RO177P	1c	green	175.		
RO178P	1c	green	500.		
RO179P	1c	black	175.	75.	75.
RO180P	1c	black	175.	80.	
RO181P	1c	black	175.		
RO182P	1c	black	175.		
RO183P	1c	black	500.		
RO184P	1c	black	175.	75.	
RO186P	1c	blue	225.		

PRIVATE DIE CANNED FRUIT STAMP

RP1P	1c	green	375.

PRIVATE DIE MEDICINE STAMPS

			DIE ON INDIA (1) Large	PLATE (3) India	(4) Card
RS1P	1c	black	175.		
RS4P	1c	black	225.	125.	150.
RS5P	1c	blue	500.		
RS10P	4c	blue	225.	125.	150.
RS14P	4c	green	500.	10.	
RS16P	2c	vermilion	500.		
RS18P	1c	black	500.		125.
RS19P	2c	black			125.
RS20P	4c	black			125.
RS21P	1c	black	175.	125.	
RS22P	2c	black	225.	125.	
RS23P	4c	black	225.	125.	
RS24P	1c	black	175.		
RS25P	2c	black	175.		
RS26P	4c	black	175.		
RS27P	4c	black	175.		
RS28P	2c	green	175.		
RS29P	2c	green	225.		
RS29/RO120P	2c/1c	green	1250.		
RS30P	1c	lake	300.		
RS31P	1c	green	175.	100.	100.
RS33P	1c	black	175.	50.	50.
RS34P	1c	black	225.		
RS35P	1c	black	175.		
RS36P	1c	blue	175.		
RS37P	2c	black	450.		
RS38P	2c	black	300.		
RS39P	1c	black	175.	100.	100.
RS40P	2c	green	500.	100.	100.
RS41P	4c	brown		125.	125.
RS42P	1c	black	175.		
RS43P	4c	blue	225.		
RS44P	1c	black	600.		
RS46P	4c	black	175.		
RS47P	4c	black	175.	125.	
RS49P	4c	green	175.		

			DIE ON INDIA (1) Large	PLATE (3) India	PLATE (4) Card
RS50P	1c	vermilion	225.		
RS51P	2c	black	175.		
RS52P	4c	black	175.		
RS53P	1c	black	175.	125.	
RS54P	2c	black	175.	125.	
RS55P	4c	black	175.	125.	
RS56P	3c	blue	350.	125.	
RS57P	6c	black	175.	100.	
RS58P	4c	black	175.		
RS59P	1c	black	175.		
RS60P	1c	black	175.	65.	
RS61P	4c	blue	500.		
RS62P	1c	black	225.	125.	
RS63P	1c	blue	175.		
RS64P	2c	black	175.	125.	
RS65P	4c	black	175.		
RS66P	1c	black	500.		85.
RS67P	1c	black	175.		
RS68P	2c	black	175.	90.	
RS69P	1c	black	175.		
RS70P	2c	black	225.		
RS71P	1c	black	175.		
RS72P	2c	black	175.		
RS73P	2c	green	500.		
RS74P	1c	black	225.		
RS74hP	1c	black	175.		
RS75P	1c	blue	175.		
RS77P	2c	black	225.		
RS78P	2c	dull pur	750.		
RS81P	4c	brown	225.		
RS82P	2c	black	175.		
RS83P	4c	black	225.		
RS84P	1c	lake	500.	—	110.
RS85P	4c	black	250.	—	
RS86P	1c	green	175.		
RS88P	1c	black	225.	100.	100.
RS89P	1c	black	500.		
RS90P	1c	blue	225.	125.	125.
RS91P	4c	black	175.		
RS92P	3c	black	175.	—	
RS94P	4c	black	175.		
RS95P	1c	green	225.	90.	
RS96P	3c	black	175.	50.	
RS97P	1c	black	175.		
RS98P	1c	black	175.		
RS99P	4c	black	175.		
RS100P	6c	black	175.		
RS101P	1c	black	175.		
RS102P	2c	blue	175.		
RS103P	4c	black	175.		
RS104P	3c	black	750.		
RS105P	3c	brown	600.		
RS106P	2c	blue	225.	60.	
RS107P	3c	black	225.		
RS107/109P	3c/6c	black	1000.		
RS108P	4c	black	175.	45.	
RS109P	6c	black	225.		
RS110P	2c	blue	175.		
RS111P	4c	black	175.		
RS114P	1c	black	225.		
RS114/115P	1c/2c	black	1000.		
RS115P	2c	blue	225.		
RS116P	4c	red	225.		
RS117P	1c	black	250.		
RS118P	1c	red	300.	55.	50.
RS119P	1c	black	225.		
RS120P	2c	black	175.		
RS121P	3c	black	225.	75.	
RS122P	2c	black	175.	100.	
RS123P	4c	black	175.	125.	
RS124P	1c	blue	300.	90.	65.
RS126P	1c	green	175.		
RS127P	4c	green	175.	65.	
RS128P	2c	blue	275.	150.	
RS130P	4c	green	275.		
RS131P	4c	black	175.	75.	
RS132P	4c	black			75.
RS133P	6c	black	175.	125.	
RS134P	4c	blue	225.		
RS137P	4c	blue	500.		
RS138P	1c	black	175.		
RS141P	4c	green	300.	125.	
RS142P	1c	black	175.		
RS143P	4c	green	225.		
RS144P	1c	blue	175.	100.	100.
RS145P	2c	black	175.	100.	100.
RS146P	4c	green	225.	100.	100.
RS150P	1c	vermilion	225.	100.	
RS151P	1c	black	175.		
RS152P	2c	green	175.		
RS153P	4c	black	450.	175.	150.
RS154P	4c	blue	500.		
RS155P	2c	green	175.		
RS156P	6c	black	175.		
RS157P	2c	black	175.		
RS158P	1c	green	500.		
RS159P	4c	blue	225.		
RS160P	6c	black	225.		
RS161P	4c	black	300.	150.	
RS162P	1c	blue	300.		
RS163P	4c	blue	600.		
RS164P	1c	black	175.		
RS165P	4c	green	500.		
RS166P	1c	black	175.		
RS169P	4c	black	175.		
RS170P	1c	black	175.		
RS171P	1c	violet	175.		
RS171uP	1c	purple	500.		
RS172P	2c	black	175.	100.	
RS173P	1c	blue	175.		
RS174P	1c	blue	175.		
RS176P	4c	black	250.		
RS177P	2c	black	350.		
RS178P	1c	black	225.		
RS179P	2c	green	225.		
RS180P	3c	black	275.	125.	
RS181P	4c	black	225.		
RS182P	4c	black	175.		
RS183P	1c	vermilion	225.	85.	
RS184P	2c	black	175.	100.	
RS185P	1c	black	175.	100.	
RS186P	4c	black	175.		
RS187P	4c	black	175.	100.	
RS188P	6c	black	300.		
RS189P	1c	green	225.		
RS190P	2c	black	175.		
RS191P	4c	black	250.		
RS192P	6c	black	250.	125.	
RS193P	2	black	175.		
RS194P	1c	blue	175.		
RS195P	2c	black	175.		
RS196P	1c	blue	175.		
RS197P	2c	black	175.		
RS198P	1c	black	225.		
RS199P	2c	black	175.		
RS204P	2c	black	175.		
RS205P	4c	black	175.		
RS208P	1c	green	175.	100.	95.
RS209P	2c	green	225.		
RS210P	4c	black	225.		
RS212P	1c	green	225.	100.	
RS213P	6c	black	175.	100.	150.
RS214P	4c	black	175.	65.	
RS215P	1c	lake	300.		
RS216P	1c	black	175.	75.	
RS219P	4c	blue	300.		
RS220P	1c	black	175.	50.	
RS221P	4c	green	225.	50.	
RS222P	8c	black	175.		
RS223P	1c	black	175.	—	
RS224P	1c	black	175.	—	
RS225P	4c	black	175.		
RS226P	1c	blue		350.	
RS228P	1c	brown	225.	—	
RS229P	2c	chocolate	175.	75.	
RS230P	6c	black	175.	—	
RS231P	6c	orange	750.		750.
RS232P	8c	orange	750.		
RS236P	4c	black	175.		
RS239P	2c	vermilion	225.	100.	
RS240P	4c	black	175.	125.	50.

"USIR" & "4 cents" obliterated on #RS240P4.

			DIE ON INDIA (1) Large	PLATE (3) India	PLATE (4) Card
RS241P	4	red	225.		
RS242P	1c	black	175.	80.	75.
RS243P	4c	black	175.		
RS244P	6c	black	175.		
RS245P	1c	black	250.		
RS250P	6c	black	175.	100.	
RS251P	1c	black	175.		
RS252P	1c	ver	175.	100.	
RS253P	4c	black	175.		
RS258P	6c	brown	175.		
RS259P	1c	black	175.	90.	
RS260P	2c	black	225.	90.	
RS261P	4c	black	175.	100.	
RS262P	2c	black	175.		
RS263P	4c	black	225.	90.	
RS264P	4c	black	225.		
RS264AP	4c	black	300.		
RS265P	1c	green	225.		
RS267P	4c	lake	225.		
RS270P	12c	blue	175.		
RS271P	4c	black	2500.		
RS272P	1c	green	225.		
RS273P	2c	black	175.		
RS274P	1c	green	225.	65.	60.
RS276P	2c	green	175.		
RS300P	4 3/8c	black	*1,000.*		
RS306P	1 1/4c	pink	*1,000.*		

PRIVATE DIE PERFUMERY STAMPS

			DIE ON INDIA (1) Large	PLATE (3) India	PLATE (4) Card
RT1P	2c	blue		125.	125.
RT2P	1c	black	250.	95.	
RT4P	1c	blue	225.		
RT5P	2c	ver		100.	
RT6P	1c	black	250.	150.	
RT8P	2c	black	500.		
RT10P	4c	black	250.	150.	
RT12P	1c	ver	225.	—	
RT14P	3c	black	500.		
RT16P	1c	black	175.		
RT17P	2c	brown	175.		
RT18P	3c	green	175.		
RT19P	1c	ver	225.		
RT20P	1c	green	225.		
RT21P	2c	blue	175.		
RT22P	1c	blue	225.		
RT23P	2c	black	175.		
RT25P	4c	green	175.		
RT26P	1c	green	175.		
RT27P	1c	green		100.	
RT28P	2c	blue	175.		
RT30P	3c	ver	225.		
RT32P	4c	brown	175.		

PRIVATE DIE PLAYING CARD STAMPS

			DIE ON INDIA (1) Large	PLATE (3) India	PLATE (4) Card
RU1P	5c	black	2500.		
RU3P	4c	black	175.	100.	
RU4P	5c	blue	175.		
RU5P	5c	blue	175.		
RU6P	10c	blue	500.	100.	
RU7P	5c	black	250.	100.	
RU8P	5c	black	175.		
RU9P	5c	black	175.		
RU10P	2c	blue	175.		
RU11P	5c	green	225.		
RU12P	5c	black	175.		
RU13P	5c	blue	300.		
RU14P	5c	black	175.	—	
RU15P	5c	black	175.		
RU16P	5c	black	500.		

HUNTING PERMIT

				DIE (Wove) (1) Large	DIE (Wove) (2) Small
RW1P	1934	$1	blue	—	*2,750.*
RW2P	1935	$1	rose lake		*2,750.*
RW3P	1936	$1	brown black	*5,000.*	*2,750.*
RW4P	1937	$1	light green	—	*2,750.*
RW5P	1938	$1	light violet	—	*2,750.*
RW6P	1939	$1	chocolate		*2,750.*
RW7P	1940	$1	sepia		*2,750.*
RW8P	1941	$1	brown carmine	*5,500.*	*2,750.*
RW9P	1942	$1	violet brown		*2,750.*
RW10P	1943	$1	deep rose	*5,500.*	*2,750.*
RW11P	1944	$1	red orange		*2,750.*
RW12P	1945	$1	black	*3,850.*	*2,750.*
RW13P	1946	$1	red brown	*3,850.*	
RW14P	1947	$1	black	*3,850.*	
RW15P	1948	$1	bright blue	*3,850.*	
RW19P	1952	$2	deep ultra.	*3,850.*	
RW23P	1956	$2	black	—	

POSTAL SAVINGS

1911

			DIE (1) Large	DIE (2) Small	(2a)
PS1P	10c	orange	1,000.		750.
PS4P	10c	deep blue			750.

1940

			DIE (1) Large	DIE (2) Small	(2a)
PS7P	10c	deep ultra. on wove		1,200.	
PS8P	25c	dk. car. rose on wove		1,200.	
PS9P	50c	dk. bl. green on wove		1,200.	
PS10P	$1	gray black on wove		1,200.	

1941

			DIE (1) Large	DIE (2) Small	(2a)
PS11P	10c	rose red on wove		1,000.	
PS12P	25c	blue green on wove		1,000.	
PS13P	50c	ultramarine on wove		1,000.	
PS14P	$1	gray black on wove		1,000.	
PS15P	$5	sepia on wove		1,000.	

WAR SAVINGS STAMP

1942

			DIE (1) Large
WS7P	10c	rose red	1,400.

POST OFFICE SEALS

1872

OXF1P	green	275.	165.	60.	36.
	Block of 4			275.	
	a. Wove paper	*950.*			
	b. Glazed paper	190.			

1877

OX1P	brown	*1,750.*		18.	
	Block of 4			80.	

1879

OX2aP	brown	2,500.	110.	15.	
	Block of 4			65.	

1888-94

		DIE *Large*	DIE (2) Small
OX5P	chocolate		140.

1901-03

		DIE *Large*	DIE (2) Small
OX11P	red brown	650.	100.

	yellow brown	100.
OX11aP	gray brown	100.
OX11bP	dark brown	100.
OX11cP	orange brown	100.

1972

OX41P	Pane of 5, blue line proof	—

TRIAL COLOR PROOFS

Values are for items in very fine condition. The listings of trial color proofs include several that are similar to the colors of the issued stamps.

New York

All on India paper unless otherwise stated.

Original Die

1845

			DIE (1) Lg.	DIE (2) Sm.	PLATE (5) Bond
9x1TC	5c	dull dark violet		300.	
9x1TC	5c	brown violet		300.	
9x1TC	5c	deep rose violet		300.	
9x1TC	5c	deep blue		300.	200.
9x1TC	5c	dark green		300.	200.
9x1TC	5c	orange yellow		300.	
9x1TC	5c	brown		300.	200.
9x1TC	5c	scarlet			200.
		With "Scar" on Neck			
9x1TC	5c	dull blue		175.	
9x1TC	5c	vermilion		175.	
		With "Scar" and dot in "P" of "POST"			
9x1TC	5c	dull gray blue		300.	
9x1TC	5c	deep blue on Bond		250.	
9x1TC	5c	deep ultramarine on thin glazed card	450.		
9x1TC	5c	deep green		300.	
9x1TC	5c	deep green on Bond		250.	
9x1TC	5c	dull dark green		300.	
9x1TC	5c	orange vermilion on thin glazed card	450.		
9x1TC	5c	dull brown red on Bond		250.	
9x1TC	5c	dark brown red		300.	
9x1TC	5c	dull dark brown		300.	
9x1TC	5c	dull dark brown on Bond		250.	
9x1TC	5c	brown black on thin glazed card	450.		

Large die trial color proofs with additional impression of the portrait medallion are listed in the Essay section as Nos. 9X1-E1.

Plate proofs are from the small sheet of 9.

Providence, R. I.

1846

			Plate on Card
10x1TC	5c	gray blue	250.
10x1TC	5c	green	250.
10x1TC	5c	brown carmine	250.
10x1TC	5c	brown	250.

			Plate on Card
10x2TC	10c	gray blue	450.
10x2TC	10c	green	450.
10x2TC	10c	brown carmine	450.
10x2TC	10c	brown	450.
		Sheet of 12, any color	3,750.

General Issues

1847

			LARGE DIE India	LARGE DIE Bond	LARGE DIE Wove	Thin Glazed Card
1TC	5c	violet	1,000.			
1TC	5c	dull blue	1,000.			
1TC	5c	deep blue		800.	800.	
		Small, India				625.
1TC	5c	deep ultra				850.
1TC	5c	blue green	1,000.			
		Small, India				625.
1TC	5c	dull blue green		800.		
1TC	5c	dull green	1,000.			
		Small, bond				600.
1TC	5c	dark green	1,000.			
1TC	5c	yellow green, small India				625.
1TC	5c	orange yellow	1,000.	800.	800.	
		Small, India				625.
1TC	5c	deep yellow			800.	
1TC	5c	orange vermilion	1,000.	800.	800.	
1TC	5c	scarlet vermilion	1,000.	800.		850.
1TC	5c	rose lake	1,000.			
		Small, bond				625.
1TC	5c	black brown		800.		850.
1TC	5c	dull rose lake, small bond				625.
1TC	5c	brown red	1,000.			
1TC	5c	black	1,000.	800.		850.
		Small, India				675.
2TC	10c	violet	1,000.			
2TC	10c	dull blue				
2TC	10c	deep blue	1,000.	800.	800.	850.
		Small, India				675.
2TC	10c	dull gray blue, small bond				625.
2TC	10c	blue green		800.		
2TC	10c	dull blue green		800.		
2TC	10c	dull green		800.		
2TC	10c	dark green	1,000.			
2TC	10c	yel green, small India				675.
2TC	10c	dull yellow			800.	
2TC	10c	orange yellow	1,000.		800.	
2TC	10c	orange vermilion	1,000.	800.	800.	
		Small, India				625.
2TC	10c	scarlet vermilion				850.
2TC	10c	golden brown	1,000.	800.		850.
2TC	10c	light brown	1,000.			
2TC	10c	dark brown	1,000.	800.		
2TC	10c	red brown				675.
2TC	10c	dull red				675.
2TC	10c	rose lake	1,000.			
2TC	10c	dull rose lake, small bond				625.
2TC	10c	black brown				850.
2TC	10c	yellow green on blue pelure paper	1,000.			

Original die proofs are often cut down and reduced in size; full-size die proofs sell at higher prices. Reprint proofs with cross-haTChing are valued as full-size; cut down examples sell for less.

			DIE (1) Lg.	DIE (2) Sm.	PLATE (3) India	PLATE (4) Card
1TC	5c	orange				600.
1TC	5c	black				600.
		Double transfer (80R1)				—
		Double transfer (90R1)				—
2TC	10c	orange				600.
2TC	10c	deep brown				600.

Nos. 1TC3-2TC3 exist with and without "specimen" overprint. Values are for examples without the overprint. Examples with the overprint are equally as scarce but sell for slightly less.

1875

3TC	5c	dull rose lake		600.
3TC	5c	black	900.	
3TC	5c	green	900.	
4TC	10c	green	900.	750.

1851-60

			DIE (1) Lg.	DIE (2) Sm.	PLATE (3) India	PLATE (5) Wove Paper
5TC	1c	black	—			
7TC	1c	black on stamp paper				*3,750.*
11TC	3c	black on stamp paper				*3,000.*
12TC	5c	pale brown				300.
12TC	5c	rose brown				300.
12TC	5c	deep red brown				1,500.
12TC	5c	dark olive bister				300.
12TC	5c	olive brown				300.
12TC	5c	olive green				300.
12TC	5c	deep orange				300.
12TC	5c	black	*6,500.*			*5,000.*
13TC	10c	black	*5,000.*			1,500.
37TC	24c	claret brown				600.
37TC	24c	red brown				600.
37TC	24c	orange				600.
37TC	24c	deep yellow				600.
37TC	24c	yellow				600.
37TC	24c	deep blue				600.
37TC	24c	black	*7,000.*			—
37TC	24c	violet black				600.
37TC	24c	red lilac on stamp paper, perf. 15½, gummed (formerly No. 37b)				1,000.
		Block of 4				6,000.
38TC	30c	black	*5,000.*	1,250.	1,400.	600.
		Block of 4			9,000.	
39TC	90c	rose lake				625.
39TC	90c	henna brown				625.
39TC	90c	orange red				625.
39TC	90c	brown orange	*5,000.*			625.
39TC	90c	sepia				625.
39TC	90c	dark green				625.
39TC	90c	dark violet brown				625.
39TC	90c	black	*5,000.*	1,250.		675.

Former Nos. 55-57, 59, 62 are now in the Essay section. Former Nos. 60-61 will be found below as Nos. 70TCe and 71TCb, respectively.

1875

40TC	1c	orange vermilion	275.
40TC	1c	orange	275.
40TC	1c	yellow orange	275.
40TC	1c	orange brown	275.
40TC	1c	dark brown	275.
40TC	1c	dull violet	275.
40TC	1c	violet	275.
40TC	1c	red violet	275.
40TC	1c	gray	275.
41TC	3c	red	—

1861

			PLATE (5) Wove Paper, Imperf.	PLATE (6) Wove Paper, Perf.
63TC	1c	rose	30.	40.
63TC	1c	deep orange red	30.	40.
63TC	1c	deep red orange	30.	40.
63TC	1c	dark orange	30.	40.
63TC	1c	yellow orange	30.	40.
63TC	1c	orange brown	30.	40.
63TC	1c	dark brown	30.	40.
63TC	1c	yellow green	30.	40.
63TC	1c	green	30.	40.
63TC	1c	blue green	30.	40.
63TC	1c	gray lilac	30.	40.
63TC	1c	gray black	30.	40.
63TC	1c	slate black	30.	40.
63TC	1c	blue	30.	40.
63TC	1c	light blue	30.	40.
63TC	1c	deep blue	30.	40.

The perforated 1861 1c trial colors are valued with perfs cutting the design on two sides. Well centered examples are extremely scarce and sell for more.

There are many trial color impressions of the issues of 1861 to 1883 made for experimentation with various patent papers, grills, eTC. Some are fully perforated, gummed and with grill.

1861-62

			DIE (1) Lg.	(2) Sm.	(2a)	PLATE India (3)
62BTC	10c	black	*1,750.*			
62BTC	10c	green				300.
62BTC	10c	light green				300.
63TC	1c	black	*2,000.*	750.		
63TC	1c	red		750.		
63TC	1c	brown		750.		
63TC	1c	green		—		
63TC	1c	orange		—		
65TC	3c	black	1,400.			
65TC	3c	black on glazed	1,400.			
65TC	3c	blue green	1,400.			
65TC	3c	orange	1,400.			
65TC	3c	brown	1,400.			
65TC	3c	dark blue	1,400.			
65TC	3c	ocher	1,400.			
65TC	3c	green	1,400.			
65TC	3c	dull red	1,400.			
65TC	3c	slate	1,400.			
65TC	3c	red brown	1,400.			
65TC	3c	deep pink	1,400.			
65TC	3c	rose pink	1,400.			
65TC	3c	dark rose	1,400.			
67TC	5c	black	1,750.	—		
67TC	5c	dark orange	1,500.			
67TC	5c	green	1,500.			
67TC	5c	ultramarine	1,500.			
67TC	5c	gray	1,500.			
67TC	5c	rose brown	—			
68TC	10c	orange	1,400.			
68TC	10c	red brown	1,400.			
68TC	10c	dull pink	1,400.			
68TC	10c	scarlet	1,400.			
68TC	10c	black	1,750.	550.		
69TC	12c	scarlet verm.	1,400.			
69TC	12c	brown	1,400.			
69TC	12c	red brown	1,400.			
69TC	12c	green	1,400.			
69TC	12c	orange yellow	1,400.			
69TC	12c	black		550.		
70TC	24c	scarlet	2,250.			
70TC	24c	green	2,250.			
70TC	24c	orange	2,250.			
70TC	24c	red brown	2,250.			
70TC	24c	orange brown	2,250.			
70TC	24c	orange yellow	2,250.			
70TC	24c	rose red	2,250.			
70TC	24c	gray	2,250.			
70TC	24c	gray on bluish gray stamp paper				—
70TC	24c	steel blue	2,250.			
70TC	24c	blue	2,250.			
70TC	24c	black	2,250.	500.		
70TC	24c	violet	1,250.	375.	2,250.	250.
		Block of 4				1,125.
	e.	dark violet, semitransparent stamp paper, perf. 12, gummed **(formerly #60)**				*7,500.*
71TC	30c	rose	1,750.			
71TC	30c	black		600.		
71TC	30c	red orange	1,750.	375.	1,250.	
		Block of 4				
	b.	red orange, semitransparent stamp paper, perf. 12, gummed **(formerly #61)**				*25,000.*
72TC	90c	black	1,750.	600.		
72TC	90c	ultramarine	1,750.			
72TC	90c	bluish gray	1,750.			
72TC	90c	violet gray	1,750.			
72TC	90c	red brown	1,750.			
72TC	90c	orange	1,750.			
72TC	90c	yellow orange	1,750.			
72TC	90c	scarlet	1,750.			
72TC	90c	green	1,750.			

1861

			STAMP PAPER Unused	Used
66TC	3c	lake, perf. 12, gummed	*2,000.*	
		Pair	*4,500.*	
		Block of 4	*9,250.*	
		P# strip of 4	*10,000.*	
		Double transfer	*2,250.*	
	a.	Imperf, pair, gummed	*1,850.*	
		P# blk. of 8	—	

John N. Luff recorded the plate number as 34.

			STAMP PAPER Unused	Used
74TC	3c	scarlet, perf. 12, gummed	*7,000.*	
		Block of 4	*29,000.*	
		With 4 horiz. black pen strokes		*5,000.*
	a.	Imperf, pair, gummed	*4,000.*	

John N. Luff recorded the plate number as 19.

1861

			DIE (1) Large	(2) Small	(2a)	PLATE (3) India	(4) Card
66TC	3c	lake		250.	1,100.	125.	
		Block of 4				725.	
		P# blk. of 8				1,850.	
74TC	3c	scarlet	2,250.	375.	1,100.	100.	100.
		Block of 4				500.	450.
		P# blk. of 8					—

1863

			DIE (1) Lg.	(2) Sm.	PLATE (3) India	(4) Card
73TC	2c	light blue			250.	
73TC	2c	dull chalky blue	*8,000.*		500.	
73TC	2c	green	*8,000.*		250.	
73TC	2c	olive green			250.	
73TC	2c	blue green			*400.*	
73TC	2c	dull yellow	*8,000.*			
73TC	2c	dark orange	*8,000.*			
73TC	2c	vermilion			250.	
73TC	2c	scarlet	*8,000.*		250.	
73TC	2c	dull red			250.	
73TC	2c	dull rose	*8,000.*		250.	
73TC	2c	brown	*8,000.*			
73TC	2c	gray black			250.	
73TC	2c	ultramarine	*8,000.*			

1866

			DIE (1) Lg.	(2) Sm.	PLATE (3) India	(4) Card
77TC	15c	deep blue	2,500.		335.	
		Block of 4			1,650.	
77TC	15c	dark red	2,500.			
77TC	15c	orange red	2,500.			
77TC	15c	dark orange	2,500.			
77TC	15c	yellow orange	2,500.			
77TC	15c	yellow				
77TC	15c	sepia				
77TC	15c	orange brown	2,500.			
77TC	15c	red brown	2,500.			
77TC	15c	blue green	2,500.			
77TC	15c	dusky blue	2,500.			
77TC	15c	gray black	2,500.			

1869

			DIE (1) Lg.	(2) Sm.	PLATE (3) India	(4) Card
112TC	1c	black	2,500.			
113TC	2c	black	2,500.			
114TC	3c	black	2,500.			
115TC	6c	deep dull blue	2,500.			
115TC	6c	black	2,500.			
116TC	10c	black	2,500.			
116TC	10c	dull dark violet	2,500.			
116TC	10c	deep green	2,500.			
116TC	10c	dull dark orange	2,500.			
116TC	10c	dull rose	2,500.			
116TC	10c	copper red	2,500.			
116TC	10c	chocolate	2,500.			
116TC	10c	dk Prussian bl	2,500.			
117TC	12c	black	2,500.			
118TC	15c	dull dark violet	2,500.			
118TC	15c	deep blue	2,500.			
118TC	15c	dull red brown	2,500.			
118TC	15c	black	2,500.			
118TC	15c	dark blue gray	2,500.			
120TC	24c	black	3,500.			
121TC	30c	deep blue & deep green	3,500.			
121TC	30c	deep brown & blue	3,500.			
121TC	30c	golden brown & carmine lake	3,500.			
121TC	30c	carmine lake & dull violet	3,500.			
121TC	30c	car lake & green	3,500.			
121TC	30c	car lake & brown	3,500.			
121TC	30c	car lake & black	3,500.			
121TC	30c	dull orange red & deep green	3,500.			
121TC	30c	deep ocher & golden brown	3,500.			
121TC	30c	dull violet & golden brown	3,500.			
121TC	30c	black & deep green	3,500.			
122TC	90c	brown & deep green	3,500.			
122TC	90c	green & black				1,500.

1870-71

			DIE (1) Lg.	(2) Sm.	PLATE (3) India	(4) Card
145TC	1c	yellow orange	600.			
145TC	1c	red brown	600.			
145TC	1c	red violet	600.			
145TC	1c	black	—		—	
145TC	1c	green	600.			
146TC	2c	black	600.			
147TC	3c	brown	—		125.	
147TC	3c	dark brown			125.	
147TC	3c	red brown	—		125.	
147TC	3c	orange brown			125.	
147TC	3c	dark red	—		125.	
147TC	3c	deep red brown, wove paper			125.	
147TC	3c	light ultramarine	—		125.	
147TC	3c	yellow brown	—		125.	
147TC	3c	dull red violet	—		125.	
147TC	3c	dull grayish red	—			
147TC	3c	yellow orange	—		125.	
147TC	3c	red violet	—		125.	
147TC	3c	black	600.			

Former Nos. 147aTC and 147bTC are now listed in the Essay section as No. 147-E13c.

			DIE (1) Lg.	(2) Sm.	PLATE (3) India	(4) Card
148TC	6c	deep magenta	600.			
148TC	6c	ultramarine	600.			
148TC	6c	carmine	600.			
148TC	6c	maroon	600.			
149TC	7c	black	550.			
150TC	10c	blue	550.			
150TC	10c	dull pale blue	550.			
150TC	10c	ultramarine	550.			
150TC	10c	blue green	550.			
150TC	10c	carmine	550.			
150TC	10c	bister	550.			
150TC	10c	dull red	550.			
150TC	10c	red orange	550.			
150TC	10c	yellow brown	550.			
150TC	10c	brown orange	550.			
151TC	12c	orange	550.			
151TC	12c	orange brown	550.			
151TC	12c	brown red	550.			
151TC	12c	dull red	550.			
151TC	12c	carmine	550.			
151TC	12c	blue	550.			
151TC	12c	light blue	550.			
151TC	12c	ultramarine	550.			
151TC	12c	green	550.			
153TC	24c	dark brown	550.			
155TC	90c	carmine	550.			
155TC	90c	ultramarine	550.			
155TC	90c	black	550.			

1873

			DIE (1) Lg.	(2) Sm.	PLATE (3) India	(4) Card
156TC	1c	black			15.	30.
		Block of 4			65.	140.
156TC	1c	scarlet	—			
157TC	2c	black			15.	
		Block of 4			65.	
157TC	2c	dull blue	550.			
157TC	2c	rose	—			
158TC	3c	black	750.		12.	
		Block of 4			55.	
158TC	3c	orange red	—			
159TC	6c	black		300.	30.	
		Block of 4			150.	
159TC	6c	deep green		300.		
159TC	6c	deep brown		300.		
159TC	6c	dull red		300.		
159TC	6c	dull gray blue		300.		
160TC	7c	black		300.	75.	
		Block of 4			325.	
160TC	7c	deep green		300.		
160TC	7c	deep brown		300.		
160TC	7c	dull gray blue		300.		
160TC	7c	dull red		300.		
161TC	10c	black		300.		
161TC	10c	deep green		300.		
161TC	10c	deep brown		300.		
161TC	10c	dull gray blue		300.		
161TC	10c	dull red		300.		
162TC	12c	black		300.		
162TC	12c	deep green		300.		
162TC	12c	dull gray blue		300.		
162TC	12c	deep brown		300.		
162TC	12c	dull red		300.		
163TC	15c	black		300.		
163TC	15c	deep green		300.		
163TC	15c	dull gray blue		300.		
163TC	15c	deep brown		300.		
163TC	15c	dull red		300.		
164TC	24c	black		300.		
164TC	24c	deep green		300.		
164TC	24c	dull gray blue		300.		
164TC	24c	deep brown		300.		
164TC	24c	dull red		300.		
165TC	30c	black		300.		
165TC	30c	deep green		300.		
165TC	30c	dull gray blue		300.		
165TC	30c	deep brown		300.		
165TC	30c	dull red		300.		
166TC	90c	black		300.		
166TC	90c	deep green		300.		
166TC	90c	dull gray blue		300.		
166TC	90c	deep brown		300.		
166TC	90c	dull red		300.		

1875

			DIE (1) Lg.	(2) Sm.	PLATE (3) India	(4) Card
179TC	5c	black	650.	300.	25.	45.
		Block of 4			125.	200.
179TC	5c	deep green		300.		
179TC	5c	dull gray blue		300.		
179TC	5c	deep brown		300.		
179TC	5c	dull red		300.		
179TC	5c	scarlet	1,000.			

Small die proofs of 1873-75 issues are "Goodall" prints.

1879 On stamp paper, gummed *Perf. 12*

182TC	1c	ultramarine	300.
182TC	1c	green	300.
182TC	1c	deep green	300.
182TC	1c	vermilion	300.
182TC	1c	brown	300.
183TC	2c	ultramarine	300.
183TC	2c	blue	300.
183TC	2c	green	300.
184TC	3c	ultramarine	300.
184TC	3c	blue	300.
184TC	3c	vermilion	300.
		Block of 4	1,100.
184TC	3c	brown	300.
185TC	5c	ultramarine	300.
185TC	5c	green	300.
185TC	5c	vermilion	300.
186TC	6c	ultramarine	300.
186TC	6c	blue	300.
186TC	6c	vermilion	300.
187TC	10c	ultramarine	300.
187TC	10c	blue	300.
187TC	10c	vermilion	300.
189TC	15c	ultramarine	300.

189TC	15c	green				300.
189TC	15c	vermilion				300.
189TC	15c	brown				300.
189TC	15c	dull red				300.
190TC	30c	ultramarine				300.
190TC	30c	blue				300.
190TC	30c	green				300.

See Specimens for No. 189 in blue (No. 189S L), No. 209 in green (No. 209S L), No. 210 in rose lake (No. 210S L).

1881-82

206TC	1c	deep green	600.	125.		
206TC	1c	black	600.		125.	
206TC	1c	ultramarine	600.			
206TC	1c	dark yellow green	600.			

1882-87

			LARGE DIE		PLATE	
			(1) India	(2) Card	(3) India	(4) Card
212TC	1c	indigo	1,000.			
212TC	1c	carmine	1,000.			
212TC	1c	green	1,000.	450.		
212TC	1c	deep green	1,000.	450.		
212TC	1c	copper brown	1,000.	450.		
212TC	1c	chestnut brown	1,000.			
210TC	2c	brown red	1,000.	450.		
210TC	2c	deep dull orange	1,000.			
210TC	2c	chestnut brown	1,000.	450.		
210TC	2c	violet rose	1,000.	450.		
210TC	2c	indigo	1,000.	450.		
210TC	2c	black	1,000.			
210TC	2c	pale ultramarine	1,000.			
210TC	2c	olive green	1,000.	450.		
210TC	2c	olive brown		450.		
210TC	2c	lake				140.
210TC	2c	rose lake				140.
210TC	2c	dark carmine				140.
210TC	2c	deep red				140.
214TC	3c	green	1,000.	450.		
214TC	3c	dark green				—
214TC	3c	dark brown	1,000.	450.		
214TC	3c	chestnut brown	1,000.	450.		
214TC	3c	dull red brown	1,000.	450.		
214TC	3c	deep dull orange	—	—		

All of 214TC above bear inscription "Worked over by new company, June 29th, 1881."

211TC	4c	green	1,000.	450.		
211TC	4c	chestnut brown	1,000.	450.		
211TC	4c	orange brown	1,000.	450.		
211TC	4c	pale ultra.	1,000.	450.		
211TC	4c	dark brown	1,000.			
211TC	4c	black	1,000.	450.		
205TC	5c	chestnut brown	1,000.	—		
205TC	5c	deep dull orange	1,000.			
205TC	5c	pale ultra	1,000.	—		
205TC	5c	deep green	1,000.			
205TC	5c	green	1,000.		200.	
205TC	5c	carmine	1,000.	450.		
205TC	5c	carmine lake	1,000.		225.	
205TC	5c	blue black	1,000.			
205TC	5c	black on glazed	1,000.			
208TC	6c	deep dull orange	1,000.	450.		
208TC	6c	indigo	1,000.			
208TC	6c	orange vermilion	1,000.	450.		
208TC	6c	dark violet	1,000.	450.		
208TC	6c	chestnut brown	1,000.	450.		
208TC	6c	carmine	1,000.			
209TC	10c	carmine	1,000.	450.		
209TC	10c	orange brown	1,000.	450.		125.
209TC	10c	orange	1,000.			
209TC	10c	deep dull orange	1,000.	450.		
209TC	10c	chestnut brown	1,000.	450.		
209TC	10c	indigo	1,000.	450.		
209TC	10c	pale ultra	1,000.	450.		
209TC	10c	green				125.
209TC	10c	black (glazed)	1,000.			
189TC	15c	orange vermilion	1,000.	450.		
189TC	15c	orange brown	1,000.	450.		
189TC	15c	chestnut brown	1,000.	450.		
189TC	15c	dark brown	1,000.	450.		
189TC	15c	deep green	1,000.	450.		
189TC	15c	black	1,000.	450.		
190TC	30c	black	1,000.			
190TC	30c	orange vermilion	1,000.	450.		
190TC	30c	dark brown	1,000.	450.		
190TC	30c	deep green	1,000.	450.		
190TC	30c	dull red brown	1,000.	450.		
190TC	30c	green	1,000.	450.		
191TC	90c	carmine	1,000.	450.		
191TC	90c	dark brown	1,000.	450.		
191TC	90c	deep dull orange	1,000.	450.		
191TC	90c	indigo	1,000.	450.		
191TC	90c	dull red brown	1,000.	450.		
191TC	90c	black	1,000.	450.		

1890-93

			DIE		PLATE	
			(1) India	(2) Card	(3) India	(4) Card
219TC	1c	green	400.			
219TC	1c	dull violet	400.			
220TC	2c	dull violet	400.			
220TC	2c	blue green	400.			
220TC	2c	slate black	400.			
222TC	4c	orange brown on wove				—
222TC	4c	yellow brown on wove				—
222TC	4c	green	400.			
223TC	5c	blue on glossy wove	400.			
223TC	5c	dark brown on glossy wove	400.			
223TC	5c	bister on wove				—
223TC	5c	sepia on wove				—
223TC	5c	blk brown on wove				—
224TC	6c	deep orange red	400.			
224TC	6c	orange red on wove				120.
224TC	6c	vio. blk. on wove				120.
224TC	6c	yellow on wove				120.
224TC	6c	olive grn. on wove				120.
224TC	6c	purple on wove				120.
224TC	6c	red org. on wove				120.
224TC	6c	brown on wove				120.
224TC	6c	red brn. on wove				120.
224TC	6c	org. brn. on wove				120.
224TC	6c	blk. brn. on wove				120.
224TC	6c	slate grn. on wove				120.
224TC	6c	brn. olive on wove				120.
225TC	8c	dark violet red		400.		
225TC	8c	metallic green		400.		
225TC	8c	salmon		400.		
225TC	8c	yellow orange	—			
225TC	8c	orange brown		400.		
225TC	8c	green	—			
225TC	8c	light green		400.		
225TC	8c	blue		400.		
225TC	8c	steel blue		400.		

1893

231TC	2c	sepia	850.	850.		
231TC	2c	orange brown		850.		
231TC	2c	deep orange		850.		
231TC	2c	light brown		850.		
231TC	2c	blue green		850.		
231TC	2c	bright rose red		850.		
231TC	2c	rose violet		850.		
232TC	3c	sepia		850.		
232TC	3c	blackish green		850.	800.	
232TC	3c	black		850.		
233TC	4c	sepia		850.		
233TC	4c	deep orange		850.		
233TC	4c	light brown		850.		
233TC	4c	blue green		850.		
233TC	4c	rose red		850.		
233TC	4c	rose violet		850.		
234TC	5c	black	850.			
234TC	5c	dark violet	850.	850.		
234TC	5c	rose violet	850.	850.		
234TC	5c	red violet	850.			
234TC	5c	brown violet	850.			
234TC	5c	deep blue	850.			
234TC	5c	deep ultra	850.			
234TC	5c	green	850.			
234TC	5c	deep green	850.			
234TC	5c	blue green	—	850.		
234TC	5c	dark olive green	850.	—		
234TC	5c	deep orange	850.	—		
234TC	5c	orange red	850.			
234TC	5c	orange brown	850.	850.		
234TC	5c	bright rose red	850.			
234TC	5c	claret	850.	—		
234TC	5c	brown rose	850.			
234TC	5c	dull rose brown		850.		
234TC	5c	sepia	850.	850.		
234TC	5c	black brown		—		

The 5c trial color proofs differ from the issued stamp.

237TC	10c	bright rose red	1,250.			
237TC	10c	claret	1,250.			
239TC	30c	sepia		1,000.		
239TC	30c	black				350.
240TC	50c	sepia		1,000.		
242TC	$2	blackish brown			1,000.	
242TC	$2	sepia	—			
242TC	$2	red brown	—			

1894

			DIE		PLATE	
			(1) Lg.	(2) Sm.	(3) India	(4) Card
246TC	1c	dusky blue green	—			
246TC	1c	dark blue	—			
253TC	3c	light red violet	—			
253TC	3c	dark red violet	—			
255TC	5c	black	1,250.			
256TC	6c	dark brown	1,000.			
257TC	8c	black	1,250.			
258TC	10c	olive	1,250.			
259TC	15c	red violet	1,250.			
259TC	15c	dark red orange	1,250.			
261ATC	$1	lake	1,500.			
262TC	$2	black	1,500.			
262TC	$2	dull violet	1,500.			
262TC	$2	violet	1,500.			
262TC	$2	turquoise blue	1,500.			
262TC	$2	orange brown	1,500.			
262TC	$2	olive green	1,500.			
262TC	$2	sepia	1,500.			
262TC	$2	greenish black	1,500.			
263TC	$5	black	1,500.			
263TC	$5	dark yellow	1,500.			
263TC	$5	orange brown	1,500.			
263TC	$5	olive green	1,500.			
263TC	$5	dull violet	1,500.			
263TC	$5	sepia	1,500.			
263TC	$5	brown red	1,500.			

1898

283TC	10c	orange	1,250.			
283TC	10c	sepia	1,250.			
284TC	15c	yellowish olive	—			
284TC	15c	red violet	*2,000.*			

1898

285TC	1c	black	—			
286TC	2c	purple				1,750.
286TC	2c	black	—			1,750.
286TC	2c	blue				1,750.
286TC	2c	brown				1,750.
286TC	2c	deep carmine rose				1,750.
287TC	4c	black	—			
288TC	5c	black	—			
288TC	5c	orange brown	*2,500.*			
289TC	8c	black	—			
290TC	10c	black	1,500.	1,250.		
291TC	50c	black	1,500.	1,250.		
292TC	$1	black	—			
293TC	$2	black	5,000.			

1901

298TC	8c	violet & black on wove paper		*2,500.*		

1902-03

308TC	13c	gray violet, type I	1,000.			
319TC	2c	black, type I	3,250.			

1904

326TC	5c	black on glazed card	—			

1907

330TC	5c	ultramarine	1,600.			
330TC	5c	black	1,700.			

1908

332TC	2c	dull violet	750.			
332TC	2c	light ultra.	750.			
332TC	2c	bright ultra.	750.			
332TC	2c	light green	750.			
332TC	2c	dark olive green	750.			
332TC	2c	golden yellow	750.			
332TC	2c	dull orange	750.			
332TC	2c	rose carmine	750.			
332TC	2c	ultramarine	750.			
332TC	2c	black	—			
332TC	2c	dark blue	—			
332TC	2c	blue	850.			
332TC	2c	lilac brown	850.			
332TC	2c	lilac	850.			
332TC	2c	blue black	850.			
332TC	2c	sage green	850.			
332TC	2c	lilac black	850.			
332TC	2c	brown	850.			
332TC	2c	brown black	850.			
332TC	2c	purple	—			
332TC	2c	orange brown	850.			
332TC	2c	ultra. on orange brown	750.			
332TC	2c	ultra. on green	750.			
332TC	2c	green on pink	750.			
332TC	2c	green on rose	750.			
332TC	2c	dark green on grn	750.			
332TC	2c	green on orange brown	750.			
332TC	2c	purple on orange brown	750.			
332TC	2c	blue on yellow	750.			
332TC	2c	green on yellow	750.			
332TC	2c	brown on orange brown	750.			
332TC	2c	brown on yellow	750.			
332TC	2c	green on amber yel	—			
335TC	5c	green on pink	—			
336TC	6c	brown	—			
337TC	8c	green (shades) on yellow	—			
337TC	8c	orange (shades) on yellow	—			
337TC	8c	blue on buff	—			
337TC	8c	blue on yellow	—			
338TC	10c	carmine on pale yellow green	—			
338TC	10c	brown on yellow	—			
338TC	10c	green on pink	—			
338TC	10c	orange on greenish blue	—			
338TC	10c	brown on gray lavender	—			
338TC	10c	orange on orange	—			
338TC	10c	black on pink	—			
338TC	10c	orange on yellow	—			
338TC	10c	brown	—			
338TC	10c	carmine	—			
338TC	10c	blue on pink	—			
338TC	10c	brown on pink	—			
338TC	10c	black	—			
339TC	13c	blue on yellow	—			
339TC	13c	sea green on deep yellow	—			
339TC	13c	sea green on pale blue	—			
339TC	13c	deep violet on yellow	—			
340TC	15c	blue on pale lilac	—			
340TC	15c	blue on greenish blue	—			
340TC	15c	blue on pink	—			
340TC	15c	blue on yellow	—			
340TC	15c	dark blue on buff	—			
340TC	15c	orange brown on yellow	—			
340TC	15c	dark purple on yel	—			
340TC	15c	orange on yellow	—			
340TC	15c	violet on yellow	—			
340TC	15c	black on orange	—			
341TC	50c	lilac on light blue	—			
341TC	50c	dark violet on yellow	—			

341TC	50c	violet on yellow	—	
341TC	50c	orange on yellow	—	
341TC	50c	orange brown on yellow	—	
342TC	$1	brown on blue	—	

1909

342TC	$1	carmine lake	1,200.	1,100.
342TC	$1	pink	1,200.	1,100.
342TC	$1	brown on blue green	—	
342TC	$1	violet brown on pink	—	
342TC	$1	violet brown on gray	—	

1912-13

400TC	10c	brown red	1,750.	1,100.
414TC	8c	black	1,750.	

1918

524TC	$5	carmine & black	1,350.	

1919

513TC	13c	violet	650.	
513TC	13c	lilac	650.	
513TC	13c	violet brown	650.	
513TC	13c	light ultra	650.	
513TC	13c	ultramarine	650.	
513TC	13c	deep ultra	650.	
513TC	13c	green	650.	
513TC	13c	dark green	650.	
513TC	13c	olive green	650.	
513TC	13c	orange yellow	650.	
513TC	13c	orange	650.	
513TC	13c	red orange	650.	
513TC	13c	ocher	650.	
513TC	13c	salmon red	650.	
513TC	13c	brown carmine	650.	
513TC	13c	claret brown	650.	
513TC	13c	brown	650.	
513TC	13c	black brown	650.	
513TC	13c	gray	650.	
513TC	13c	black	650.	

1920

547TC	$2	green & black	1,500.	

1922-25

554TC	2c	black (bond paper)		1,250.
561TC	9c	red orange	2,250.	
563TC	11c	deep green	2,250.	
565TC	14c	dark brown	2,250.	
566TC	15c	black	2,250.	

1923

610TC	2c	Harding, green	*4,000.*	

1925

618TC	2c	Lexington Concord, black	*1,650.*	

1926

622TC	13c	black	2,250.	
628TC	5c	Ericsson, dull dusky blue	1,000.	
628TC		gray blue		1,000.

1932

718TC	3c	Olympic, carmine	*10,000.*	
720TC	3c	black (bond paper)		750.

1935

772TC	3c	Connecticut Tercentenary, black (thin glazed card)	*1,500.*	
773TC	3c	San Diego, org. red (yel. glazed card)	*1,500.*	

1936-43

785TC	1c	Army, black (bond paper)		750.
788TC	4c	Army, dark brown	1,000.	
789TC	5c	Army, blue	1,000.	
793TC	4c	Navy, dark brown	1,000.	
798TC	3c	Constitution, black (bond paper)		750.
799TC	3c	Hawaii, black (bond paper)		750.
800TC	3c	Alaska, black (bond paper)		750.
800TC		(India paper)		750.
801TC	3c	Puerto Rico, black (bond paper)	900.	750.
801TC		(India paper)	900.	
802TC	3c	Virgin Islands, black (bond paper)		750.
815TC	10c	sepia	900.	
829TC	25c	green	*2,000.*	
836TC	3c	Swedes & Finns, purple	900.	
837TC	3c	Northwest Terr., dark purple	900.	
854TC	3c	Inauguration, purple	900.	
855TC	3c	Baseball, red violet	*2,250.*	
862TC	5c	Authors, dull blue	900.	
866TC	3c	Poets, dark blue violet	900.	
897TC	3c	Wyoming, red violet	—	
929TC	3c	Iwo Jima, bright purple	*2,300.*	
959TC	3c	Progress of Women, brt. violet	*1,500.*	
963TC	3c	Youth, violet	900.	
964TC	3c	Oregon, dull violet	900.	
968TC	3c	Poultry, red brown	900.	

1923-47

AIR POST

			DIE (1) Lg.	(2) Sm.	PLATE (3) India	(4) Card
C5TC	16c	dark green	5,000.			
C8TC	15c	orange	4,500.			
C32TC	5c	blue	4,500.			
C35TC	15c	brown violet	4,500.			

1934

AIR POST SPECIAL DELIVERY

CE1TC	16c	black	3,500.			

1885-1902

SPECIAL DELIVERY

E1TC	10c	black	1,750.			
E1TC	10c	dark brown	1,750.			
E1TC	10c	org. yellow (wove paper)		*2,000.*		
E2TC	10c	black	1,750.			
E2TC	10c	green	1,750.			
E2TC	10c	olive yellow		800.		
E6TC	10c	orange	2,000.			
E6TC	10c	black	2,000.			
E6TC	10c	rose red	2,000.			

1922-25

E12TC	10c	black	1,500.			

1911

REGISTRATION

F1TC	10c	black (glazed card)	1,500.			

1851

CARRIERS

LO1TC	deep green			250.	
	Block of 4			1,250.	
	a. orange (wove paper)				350.
LO2TC	deep green			250.	
	Block of 4			1,250.	
	a. orange (wove paper)				350.

1879

POSTAGE DUE

			DIE (1) Lg.	(2) Sm.	PLATE (3) India	(4) Card
J1TC	1c	black	500.			50.
J1TC	1c	gray black	500.			
J1TC	1c	ultramarine	500.			
J1TC	1c	blue	500.			
J1TC	1c	blue green	500.			
J1TC	1c	orange	500.	100.		
J1TC	1c	red orange	500.			
J1TC	1c	olive bister	500.			
J2TC	2c	black	500.			
J2TC	2c	gray black	500.			
J2TC	2c	ultramarine	500.			
J2TC	2c	blue	500.			
J2TC	2c	blue green	500.			
J2TC	2c	orange	500.	100.		
J2TC	2c	red orange	500.			
J2TC	2c	sepia	500.			
J3TC	3c	black	500.			
J3TC	3c	gray black		100.		
J3TC	3c	ultramarine	500.			
J3TC	3c	blue	500.			
J3TC	3c	blue green	500.			
J3TC	3c	orange	500.	100.		
J3TC	3c	red orange	500.			
J3TC	3c	light brown	500.			
J4TC	5c	black	500.			
J4TC	5c	gray black	500.			
J4TC	5c	ultramarine	500.			
J4TC	5c	blue	500.			
J4TC	5c	blue green	500.			
J4TC	5c	orange	500.	100.		
J4TC	5c	red orange	500.			
J5TC	10c	black	500.			
J5TC	10c	gray black	500.			
J5TC	10c	blue	500.			
J5TC	10c	olive yellow	500.			
J5TC	10c	blue green	500.			
J5TC	10c	orange	500.	100.		
J5TC	10c	red orange	500.			
J5TC	10c	olive bister	500.			
J5TC	10c	sepia	500.			
J5TC	10c	gray	500.			
J6TC	30c	black	500.			
J6TC	30c	gray black	500.			
J6TC	30c	blue	500.			
J6TC	30c	olive yellow		100.		
J6TC	30c	blue green	500.			
J6TC	30c	orange	500.	100.		
J6TC	30c	red orange	500.			
J6TC	30c	olive bister	500.			
J6TC	30c	sepia		100.		
J7TC	50c	black	500.			
J7TC	50c	gray black	500.			
J7TC	50c	blue	500.	100.		
J7TC	50c	olive yellow		100.		
J7TC	50c	blue green	500.			
J7TC	50c	orange	500.	100.		
J7TC	50c	red orange	500.			
J7TC	50c	olive bister	500.			
J7TC	50c	sepia	500.			
J7TC	50c	gray	500.			

OFFICIAL

Agriculture

			DIE (1) Lg.	(2) Sm.	PLATE (3) India	(4) Card
O1TC	1c	black	350.		75.	
O2TC	2c	black	350.		75.	
O3TC	3c	black	350.			
O3TC	3c	deep green	350.			
O4TC	6c	black	350.		150.	
O5TC	10c	black	350.			
O6TC	12c	black	350.		75.	
O9TC	30c	black	350.			

Executive

O11TC	2c	black	350.		75.	
O11TC	2c	deep brown	350.			
O11TC	2c	brown carmine				75.
O12TC	3c	black	350.		75.	
O12TC	3c	deep green	350.			
O13TC	6c	black			90.	
O14TC	10c	black			90.	

Interior

O16TC	2c	black	350.			
O16TC	2c	deep brown	350.			
O17TC	3c	black	350.		90.	
O17TC	3c	deep green	350.			

Justice

O27TC	3c	black	350.		90.	
O27TC	3c	deep green	350.			
O27TC	3c	bister yellow			90.	
O27TC	3c	dull orange			90.	
O27TC	3c	black violet			90.	

Navy

O35TC	1c	black			90.	
O36TC	2c	black	350.			
O36TC	2c	deep brown	350.			
O36TC	2c	deep green on wove paper, perf.				250.
O36TC	2c	deep green on wove paper, imperf.				250.
O37TC	3c	black	350.		90.	
O37TC	3c	deep green	350.			

Post Office

O48TC	2c	deep brown	350.			
O49TC	3c	deep green	350.			
O50TC	6c	deep brown	350.			
O50TC	6c	brown carmine	350.			

State

O57TC	1c	black	350.			
O57TC	1c	light ultramarine	350.			
O58TC	2c	black	350.			
O58TC	2c	deep brown	350.			
O59TC	3c	black	350.			
O67TC	90c	black	350.			
O68TC	$2	violet & black	2,000.			
O68TC	$2	brown red & black	2,000.			
O68TC	$2	orange red & slate blue	2,000.			

Treasury

O72TC	1c	black	350.			
O72TC	1c	light ultramarine	350.			
O73TC	2c	black	350.			
O74TC	3c	black	350.			
O74TC	3c	deep green	350.			
O75TC	6c	black	350.			
O77TC	10c	black	350.			
O78TC	12c	black	350.			
O79TC	15c	black	350.			
O80TC	24c	black	350.			
O81TC	30c	black	350.			
O82TC	90c	black	350.			

War

O83TC	1c	black	350.		80.	
O83TC	1c	light ultramarine	350.			
O84TC	2c	black	350.		80.	75.
O84TC	2c	deep brown	350.			
O85TC	3c	black	350.			
O85TC	3c	deep green	350.			
O86TC	6c	black			80.	
O89TC	12c	black			80.	

1910

POSTAL SAVINGS MAIL

O121TC	2c	lake	500.			
O126TC	10c	black (on wove)	*1,250.*			

The so-called "Goodall" set of Small Die proofs on India Paper of Official Stamps in five colors

Agriculture

		(a) Black	(b) Deep green	(c) Dull gray blue	(d) Deep brown	(e) Dull red
O1TC	1c	150.	140.	140.	140.	140.
O2TC	2c	150.	140.	140.	140.	140.
O3TC	3c	150.	140.	140.	140.	140.
O4TC	6c	150.	140.	140.	140.	140.
O5TC	10c	150.	140.	140.	140.	140.
O6TC	12c	150.	140.	140.	140.	140.
O7TC	15c	150.	140.	140.	140.	140.
O8TC	24c	150.	140.	140.	140.	140.
O9TC	30c	150.	140.	140.	140.	140.

	(a) Black	(b) Deep green	(c) Dull gray blue	(d) Deep brown	(e) Dull red
Executive					
O10TC 1c	150.	140.	140.	140.	140.
O11TC 2c	150.	140.	140.	140.	140.
O12TC 3c	150.	140.	140.	140.	140.
O13TC 6c	150.	140.	140.	140.	140.
O14TC 10c	150.	140.	140.	140.	140.
Interior					
O15TC 1c	150.	140.	140.	140.	140.
O16TC 2c	150.	140.	140.	140.	140.
O17TC 3c	150.	140.	140.	140.	140.
O18TC 6c	150.	140.	140.	140.	140.
O19TC 10c	150.	140.	140.	140.	140.
O20TC 12c	150.	140.	140.	140.	140.
O21TC 15c	150.	140.	140.	140.	140.
O22TC 24c	150.	140.	140.	140.	140.
O23TC 30c	150.	140.	140.	140.	140.
O24TC 90c	150.	140.	140.	140.	140.
Justice					
O25TC 1c	150.	140.	140.	140.	140.
O26TC 2c	150.	140.	140.	140.	140.
O27TC 3c	150.	140.	140.	140.	140.
O28TC 6c	150.	140.	140.	140.	140.
O29TC 10c	150.	140.	140.	140.	140.
O30TC 12c	150.	140.	140.	140.	140.
O31TC 15c	150.	140.	140.	140.	140.
O32TC 24c	150.	140.	140.	140.	140.
O33TC 30c	150.	140.	140.	140.	140.
O34TC 90c	150.	140.	140.	140.	140.
Navy					
O35TC 1c	150.	140.	140.	140.	140.
O36TC 2c	150.	140.	140.	140.	140.
O37TC 3c	150.	140.	140.	140.	140.
O38TC 6c	150.	140.	140.	140.	140.
O39TC 7c	150.	140.	140.	140.	140.
O40TC 10c	150.	140.	140.	140.	140.
O41TC 12c	150.	140.	140.	140.	140.
O42TC 15c	150.	140.	140.	140.	140.
O43TC 24c	150.	140.	140.	140.	140.
O44TC 30c	150.	140.	140.	140.	140.
O45TC 90c	150.	140.	140.	140.	140.
Post Office					
O47TC 1c	150.	140.	140.	140.	140.
O48TC 2c	150.	140.	140.	140.	140.
O49TC 3c	150.	140.	140.	140.	140.
O50TC 6c	150.	140.	140.	140.	140.
O51TC 10c	150.	140.	140.	140.	140.
O52TC 12c	150.	140.	140.	140.	140.
O53TC 15c	150.	140.	140.	140.	140.
O54TC 24c	150.	140.	140.	140.	140.
O55TC 30c	150.	140.	140.	140.	140.
O56TC 90c	150.	140.	140.	140.	140.
State					
O57TC 1c	150.	140.	140.	140.	140.
O58TC 2c	150.	140.	140.	140.	140.
O59TC 3c	150.	140.	140.	140.	140.
O60TC 6c	150.	140.	140.	140.	140.
O61TC 7c	150.	140.	140.	140.	140.
O62TC 10c	150.	140.	140.	140.	140.
O63TC 12c	150.	140.	140.	140.	140.
O64TC 15c	150.	140.	140.	140.	140.
O65TC 24c	150.	140.	140.	140.	140.
O66TC 30c	150.	140.	140.	140.	140.
O67TC 90c	150.	140.	140.	140.	140.

O68TC $2 scarlet frame, green center	1,250.
O68TC $2 scarlet frame, black center	1,250.
O68TC $2 scarlet frame, blue center	1,250.
O68TC $2 green frame, brown center	1,250.
O68TC $2 brown frame, green center	1,250.
O68TC $2 brown frame, black center	1,250.

	(a) Black	(b) Deep green	(c) Dull gray blue	(d) Deep brown	(e) Dull red
Treasury					
O72TC 1c	150.	140.	140.	140.	140.
O73TC 2c	150.	140.	140.	140.	140.
O74TC 3c	150.	140.	140.	140.	140.
O75TC 6c	150.	140.	140.	140.	140.
O76TC 7c	150.	140.	140.	140.	140.
O77TC 10c	150.	140.	140.	140.	140.
O78TC 12c	150.	140.	140.	140.	140.
O79TC 15c	150.	140.	140.	140.	140.
O80TC 24c	150.	140.	140.	140.	140.
O81TC 30c	150.	140.	140.	140.	140.
O82TC 90c	150.	140.	140.	140.	140.
War					
O83TC 1c	150.	140.	140.	140.	140.
O84TC 2c	150.	140.	140.	140.	140.
O85TC 3c	150.	140.	140.	140.	140.
O86TC 6c	150.	140.	140.	140.	140.
O87TC 7c	150.	140.	140.	140.	140.
O88TC 10c	150.	140.	140.	140.	140.
O89TC 12c	150.	140.	140.	140.	140.
O90TC 15c	150.	140.	140.	140.	140.
O91TC 24c	150.	140.	140.	140.	140.
O92TC 30c	150.	140.	140.	140.	140.
O93TC 90c	150.	140.	140.	140.	140.

OFFICIAL SEALS

1872

OXF1TC ultra	Die on India	350.
OXF1TC blue	Die on card, colored border	350.
OXF1TC dp bl	Die on card, colored border	350.
OXF1TC green	Die on card, colored border	350.
OXF1TC choc	Die on glossy bond	350.
OXF1TC choc	Die on card, colored border	350.
OXF1TC car	Die on India	350.
OXF1TC brown	Die on India	350.
OXF1TC red vio	Die on India	—

1877

OX1TC blue	Die on India	200.
OX1TC green	Die on India	200.
OX1TC green	Plate on bond	200.
OX1TC green	Plate on bond, perforated and gummed	—
OX1TC orange	Die on India	200.
OX1TC red orange	Die on India	200.
OX1TC black	Die on India	200.

1879

OX2TC black	Die on India	—

POSTAL NOTE STAMPS

PN1TC 1c bister	imperf, on white wove	—

NEWSPAPERS

1865

			(1) Die on India	(5) Thick cream wove paper
PR1TC	5c	bright red	500.	
PR2TC	10c	brown	500.	
PR2TC	10c	dull red	500.	
PR2TC	10c	blue	500.	
PR2TC	10c	black		70.
PR2TC	10c	lake		70.
PR2TC	10c	blue green		70.
PR2TC	10c	blue		70.
PR3TC	25c	black		70.
PR3TC	25c	lake		70.
PR3TC	25c	blue green		70.
PR3TC	25c	blue		70.
PR3TC	25c	ocher	500.	
PR3TC	25c	brown	500.	
PR3TC	25c	brick red	500.	
PR4TC	5c	black		70.
PR4TC	5c	lake		70.
PR4TC	5c	blue green		70.
PR4TC	5c	blue		70.

1875

			(1) Die on India	(3) Plate on India
PR9TC	2c	dark carmine		35.
PR9TC	2c	brown rose		35.
PR9TC	2c	scarlet		35.
PR9TC	2c	orange brown	200.	35.
PR9TC	2c	black brown	200.	
PR9TC	2c	sepia		35.
PR9TC	2c	orange yellow		35.
PR9TC	2c	dull orange		35.
PR9TC	2c	green		35.
PR9TC	2c	blue green	200.	
PR9TC	2c	light ultramarine		35.
PR9TC	2c	light blue		35.
PR9TC	2c	dark violet		35.
PR9TC	2c	violet black		35.
PR10TC	3c	rose lake	200.	
PR16TC	12c	dark carmine		35.
PR16TC	12c	brown rose	200.	35.
PR16TC	12c	scarlet	200.	35.
PR16TC	12c	orange brown		35.
PR16TC	12c	sepia	200.	35.
PR16TC	12c	orange yellow		35.
PR16TC	12c	dull orange		35.
PR16TC	12c	green	200.	35.
PR16TC	12c	light ultramarine	200.	35.
PR16TC	12c	light blue		35.
PR16TC	12c	dark violet	200.	35.
PR16TC	12c	violet black	200.	35.
PR16TC	12c	black	200.	35.
PR17TC	24c	sepia		
PR17TC	24c	green	200.	
PR17TC	24c	black	200.	35.
PR18TC	36c	black	200.	35.
PR18TC	36c	sepia	200.	
PR18TC	36c	green	200.	
PR19TC	48c	black	200.	35.
PR19TC	48c	sepia	200.	
PR19TC	48c	green	200.	
PR20TC	60c	black	200.	35.
PR21TC	72c	black	200.	35.
PR22TC	84c	black	200.	35.
PR23TC	96c	black		35.
PR24TC	$1.92	dark carmine		35.
PR24TC	$1.92	brown rose		35.
PR24TC	$1.92	scarlet		35.
PR24TC	$1.92	orange brown	200.	35.
PR24TC	$1.92	sepia		35.
PR24TC	$1.92	orange yellow		35.
PR24TC	$1.92	dull orange		35.
PR24TC	$1.92	green	200.	35.
PR24TC	$1.92	light ultramarine		35.
PR24TC	$1.92	dark violet		35.
PR24TC	$1.92	violet black		35.
PR24TC	$1.92	black		35.
PR25TC	$3	dark carmine	200.	35.
PR25TC	$3	brown rose		35.
PR25TC	$3	scarlet		35.
PR25TC	$3	orange brown		35.
PR25TC	$3	sepia		35.
PR25TC	$3	orange yellow	200.	35.
PR25TC	$3	dull orange	200.	35.
PR25TC	$3	green	200.	35.
PR25TC	$3	light ultramarine	200.	35.
PR25TC	$3	light blue		35.
PR25TC	$3	dark violet	200.	35.
PR25TC	$3	violet black	200.	35.
PR25TC	$3	black	200.	35.
PR26TC	$6	dark carmine	200.	35.
PR26TC	$6	brown rose	200.	35.
PR26TC	$6	scarlet	200.	35.
PR26TC	$6	orange brown		35.
PR26TC	$6	dark brown		35.
PR26TC	$6	sepia	200.	35.
PR26TC	$6	orange yellow	200.	35.
PR26TC	$6	dull orange	200.	35.
PR26TC	$6	green	200.	35.
PR26TC	$6	light ultramarine		35.
PR26TC	$6	light blue	200.	35.
PR26TC	$6	dark violet	200.	35.
PR26TC	$6	violet black	200.	35.
PR26TC	$6	black	200.	35.
PR27TC	$9	dark carmine	200.	35.
PR27TC	$9	brown rose	200.	35.
PR27TC	$9	scarlet	200.	35.
PR27TC	$9	orange brown		35.
PR27TC	$9	sepia	200.	35.
PR27TC	$9	orange yellow	200.	35.
PR27TC	$9	dull orange	200.	35.
PR27TC	$9	green	200.	35.
PR27TC	$9	light ultramarine	200.	35.
PR27TC	$9	light blue		35.
PR27TC	$9	dark violet	200.	35.
PR27TC	$9	violet black	200.	35.
PR27TC	$9	black	200.	35.
PR28TC	$12	black	200.	
PR28TC	$12	sepia	200.	
PR28TC	$12	orange brown	200.	
PR29TC	$24	black	200.	35.
PR29TC	$24	black brown	200.	
PR29TC	$24	orange brown	200.	
PR29TC	$24	green	200.	
PR30TC	$36	dark carmine	200.	
PR30TC	$36	black	200.	35.
PR30TC	$36	black brown	200.	
PR30TC	$36	orange brown	200.	
PR30TC	$36	sepia	200.	
PR30TC	$36	violet	200.	
PR30TC	$36	green	200.	
PR31TC	$48	violet brown	200.	35.
PR31TC	$48	black	200.	35.
PR31TC	$48	sepia	200.	
PR31TC	$48	green	200.	
PR32TC	$60	dark carmine	200.	40.
PR32TC	$60	scarlet	200.	40.
PR32TC	$60	sepia	200.	40.
PR32TC	$60	green	200.	40.
PR32TC	$60	light ultramarine	200.	40.
PR32TC	$60	black	200.	40.
PR32TC	$60	violet black	200.	
PR32TC	$60	orange brown	200.	
PR32TC	$60	orange yellow	200.	
PR32TC	$60	dull orange	200.	
PR32TC	$60	brown rose	200.	

1885

			(1) Die on India	(3) Plate on India
PR81TC	1c	salmon	200.	
PR81TC	1c	scarlet		120.
PR81TC	1c	dark brown		120.
PR81TC	1c	violet brown		120.
PR81TC	1c	dull orange		120.
PR81TC	1c	green		120.
PR81TC	1c	light blue		120.

1894

			(1) Die on India	(3) Plate on India
PR106TC	25c	deep carmine	200.	
PR106TC	25c	dark carmine	200.	
PR107TC	50c	black	200.	
PR108TC	$2	deep scarlet	200.	
PR108TC	$2	dark scarlet	200.	
PR109TC	$5	light ultramarine	200.	
PR109TC	$5	dark ultramarine	200.	
PR110TC	$10	black	200.	
PR112TC	$50	black	200.	
PR112TC	$50	deep rose	200.	
PR112TC	$50	dark rose	200.	
PR113TC	$100	black	200.	

The so-called "Goodall" set of Small Die proofs on India Paper of Newspaper Stamps in five colors

		(a) Black	(b) Deep green	(c) Dull gray blue	(d) Deep brown	(e) Dull red
PR9TC	2c	150.	125.	125.	125.	125.
PR10TC	3c	150.	125.	125.	125.	125.
PR11TC	4c	150.	125.	125.	125.	125.
PR12TC	6c	150.	125.	125.	125.	125.
PR13TC	8c	150.	125.	125.	125.	125.
PR14TC	9c	150.	125.	125.	125.	125.
PR15TC	10c	150.	125.	125.	125.	125.
PR16TC	12c	150.	125.	125.	125.	125.
PR17TC	24c	150.	125.	125.	125.	125.
PR18TC	36c	150.	125.	125.	125.	125.
PR19TC	48c	150.	125.	125.	125.	125.
PR20TC	60c	150.	125.	125.	125.	125.
PR21TC	72c	150.	125.	125.	125.	125.
PR22TC	84c	150.	125.	125.	125.	125.
PR23TC	96c	150.	125.	125.	125.	125.
PR24TC	$1.92	150.	125.	125.	125.	125.
PR25TC	$3	150.	125.	125.	125.	125.
PR26TC	$6	150.	125.	125.	125.	125.
PR27TC	$9	150.	125.	125.	125.	125.
PR28TC	$12	150.	125.	125.	125.	125.
PR29TC	$24	150.	125.	125.	125.	125.
PR30TC	$36	150.	125.	125.	125.	125.
PR31TC	$48	150.	125.	125.	125.	125.

		(a) Black	(b) Deep green	(c) Dull gray blue	(d) Deep brown	(e) Dull red
PR32TC	$60	150.	125.	125.	125.	125.

1925

SPECIAL HANDLING

QE4TC	25c apple green	700.
QE4TC	25c olive green	700.
QE4TC	25c light blue green	700.
QE4TC	25c dark blue	700.
QE4TC	25c orange yellow	700.
QE4TC	25c orange	700.
QE4TC	25c dull rose	700.
QE4TC	25c carmine lake	700.
QE4TC	25c brown	700.
QE4TC	25c gray brown	700.
QE4TC	25c dark violet brown	700.
QE4TC	25c gray black	700.
QE4TC	25c black	700.

THE "ATLANTA" SET OF PLATE PROOFS

A set in five colors on thin card reprinted in 1881 for display at the International Cotton Exhibition in Atlanta, Ga.

1847 Designs (Reproductions)

		Black	Scarlet	Brown	Green	Blue
3TC	5c	300.	300.	300.	300.	300.
4TC	10c	300.	300.	300.	300.	300.
	1851-60 Designs					
40TC	1c	120.	100.	100.	100.	100.
41TC	3c	120.	100.	100.	100.	100.
42TC	5c	120.	100.	100.	100.	100.
43TC	10c	120.	100.	100.	100.	100.
44TC	12c	120.	100.	100.	100.	100.
45TC	24c	120.	100.	100.	100.	100.
46TC	30c	120.	100.	100.	100.	100.
47TC	90c	120.	100.	100.	100.	100.
	1861-66 Designs					
102TC	1c	100.	90.	90.	90.	90.
103TC	2c	175.	175.	175.	175.	175.
104TC	3c	100.	90.	90.	90.	90.
105TC	5c	100.	90.	90.	90.	90.
106TC	10c	100.	90.	90.	90.	90.
107TC	12c	100.	90.	90.	90.	90.
108TC	15c	100.	90.	90.	90.	90.
109TC	24c	100.	90.	90.	90.	90.
110TC	30c	100.	90.	90.	90.	90.
111TC	90c	100.	90.	90.	90.	90.
	1869 Designs					
123TC	1c	175.	150.	150.	150.	150.
124TC	2c	175.	150.	150.	150.	150.
125TC	3c	175.	150.	150.	150.	150.
126TC	6c	175.	150.	150.	150.	150.
127TC	10c	175.	150.	150.	150.	150.
128TC	12c	175.	150.	150.	150.	150.

129TC	15c black frame, scarlet center	375.
129TC	15c black frame, green center	375.
129TC	15c scarlet frame, black center	375.
129TC	15c scarlet frame, blue center	375.
129TC	15c brown frame, black center	375.
129TC	15c brown frame, green center	375.
129TC	15c brown frame, blue center	375.
129TC	15c green frame, black center	375.
129TC	15c green frame, blue center	375.
129TC	15c blue frame, black center	375.
129TC	15c blue frame, brown center	375.
129TC	15c blue frame, green center	375.
130TC	24c black frame, scarlet center	375.
130TC	24c black frame, green center	375.
130TC	24c black frame, blue center	375.
130TC	24c scarlet frame, black center	375.
130TC	24c scarlet frame, blue center	375.
130TC	24c brown frame, black center	375.
130TC	24c brown frame, blue center	375.
130TC	24c green frame, black center	375.
130TC	24c green frame, brown center	375.
130TC	24c green frame, blue center	375.
130TC	24c blue frame, brown center	375.
130TC	24c blue frame, green center	375.
131TC	30c black frame, scarlet center	375.
131TC	30c black frame, green center	375.
131TC	30c black frame, blue center	375.
131TC	30c scarlet frame, black center	375.
131TC	30c scarlet frame, green center	375.
131TC	30c scarlet frame, blue center	375.
131TC	30c brown frame, black center	375.
131TC	30c brown frame, scarlet center	375.
131TC	30c brown frame, blue center	375.
131TC	30c green frame, black center	375.
131TC	30c green frame, brown center	375.
131TC	30c blue frame, scarlet center	375.
131TC	30c blue frame, brown center	375.
131TC	30c blue frame, green center	375.
132TC	90c black frame, scarlet center	550.
132TC	90c black frame, brown center	550.
132TC	90c black frame, green center	550.
132TC	90c scarlet frame, blue center	550.
132TC	90c brown frame, black center	550.
132TC	90c brown frame, blue center	550.
132TC	90c green frame, brown center	550.
132TC	90c green frame, blue center	550.
132TC	90c blue frame, brown center	550.
132TC	90c blue frame, green center	550.

1873-75 Designs

		Black	Scarlet	Brown	Green	Blue
156TC	1c	55.	50.	50.	50.	50.
157TC	2c	55.	50.	50.	50.	50.
158TC	3c	60.	55.	55.	55.	55.
159TC	6c	65.	60.	60.	60.	60.
160TC	7c	55.	50.	50.	50.	50.
161TC	10c	55.	50.	50.	50.	50.
162TC	12c	55.	50.	50.	50.	50.
163TC	15c	55.	50.	50.	50.	50.
164TC	24c	55.	50.	50.	50.	50.
165TC	30c	60.	55.	55.	55.	55.
166TC	90c	55.	50.	50.	50.	50.
179TC	5c	80.	75.	75.	75.	75.
	POSTAGE DUE					
J1TC	1c	55.	50.	50.	50.	50.
J2TC	2c	55.	50.	50.	50.	50.
J3TC	3c	55.	50.	50.	50.	50.
J4TC	5c	55.	50.	50.	50.	50.
J5TC	10c	55.	50.	50.	50.	50.
J6TC	30c	55.	50.	50.	50.	50.
J7TC	50c	55.	50.	50.	50.	50.
	OFFICIALS					
	Agriculture					
O1TC	1c	43.	37.	37.	37.	37.
O2TC	2c	43.	37.	37.	37.	37.
O3TC	3c	43.	37.	37.	37.	37.
O4TC	6c	55.	50.	50.	50.	50.
O5TC	10c	43.	37.	37.	37.	37.
O6TC	12c	43.	37.	37.	37.	37.
O7TC	15c	43.	37.	37.	37.	37.
O8TC	24c	43.	37.	37.	37.	37.
O9TC	30c	43.	37.	37.	37.	37.
	Executive					
O10TC	1c	43.	37.	37.	37.	37.
O11TC	2c	43.	37.	37.	37.	37.
O12TC	3c	43.	37.	37.	37.	37.
O13TC	6c	55.	50.	50.	50.	50.
O14TC	10c	43.	37.	37.	37.	37.
	Interior					
O15TC	1c	43.	37.	37.	37.	37.
O16TC	2c	43.	37.	37.	37.	37.
O17TC	3c	43.	37.	37.	37.	37.
O18TC	6c	55.	50.	50.	50.	50.
O19TC	10c	43.	37.	37.	37.	37.
O20TC	12c	43.	37.	37.	37.	37.
O21TC	15c	43.	37.	37.	37.	37.
O22TC	24c	43.	37.	37.	37.	37.
O23TC	30c	60.	55.	55.	55.	55.
O24TC	90c	43.	37.	37.	37.	37.
	Justice					
O25TC	1c	43.	37.	37.	37.	37.
O26TC	2c	43.	37.	37.	37.	37.
O27TC	3c	43.	37.	37.	37.	37.
O28TC	6c	55.	50.	50.	50.	50.
O29TC	10c	43.	37.	37.	37.	37.
O30TC	12c	43.	37.	37.	37.	37.
O31TC	15c	43.	37.	37.	37.	37.
O32TC	24c	43.	37.	37.	37.	37.
O33TC	30c	60.	55.	55.	55.	55.
O34TC	90c	43.	37.	37.	37.	37.
	Navy					
O35TC	1c	43.	37.	37.	37.	37.
O36TC	2c	43.	37.	37.	37.	37.
O37TC	3c	43.	37.	37.	37.	37.
O38TC	6c	55.	50.	50.	50.	50.
O39TC	7c	43.	37.	37.	37.	37.
O40TC	10c	43.	37.	37.	37.	37.
O41TC	12c	43.	37.	37.	37.	37.
O42TC	15c	43.	37.	37.	37.	37.
O43TC	24c	43.	37.	37.	37.	37.
O44TC	30c	60.	55.	55.	55.	55.
O45TC	90c	43.	37.	37.	37.	37.
	Post Office					
O48TC	2c	43.	37.	37.	37.	37.
O49TC	3c	43.	37.	37.	37.	37.
O50TC	6c	43.	37.	37.	37.	37.
O51TC	10c	43.	37.	37.	37.	37.
O52TC	12c	43.	37.	37.	37.	37.
O53TC	15c	43.	37.	37.	37.	37.
O54TC	24c	43.	37.	37.	37.	37.
O55TC	30c	43.	37.	37.	37.	37.
O56TC	90c	43.	37.	37.	37.	37.
	State					
O57TC	1c	43.	37.	37.	37.	37.
O58TC	2c	43.	37.	37.	37.	37.
O59TC	3c	43.	37.	37.	37.	37.
O60TC	6c	55.	50.	50.	50.	50.
O61TC	7c	43.	37.	37.	37.	37.
O62TC	10c	43.	37.	37.	37.	37.
O63TC	12c	43.	37.	37.	37.	37.
O64TC	15c	43.	37.	37.	37.	37.
O65TC	24c	43.	37.	37.	37.	37.
O66TC	30c	60.	55.	55.	55.	55.
O67TC	90c	43.	37.	37.	37.	37.

O68TC	$2	scarlet frame, black center	1,000.
O68TC	$2	scarlet frame, blue center	1,000.
O68TC	$2	brown frame, black center	1,000.
O68TC	$2	brown frame, blue center	1,000.
O68TC	$2	green frame, brown center	1,000.
O68TC	$2	blue frame, brown center	1,000.
O68TC	$2	blue frame, green center	1,000.
O69TC	$5	scarlet frame, black center	1,000.
O69TC	$5	scarlet frame, blue center	1,000.
O69TC	$5	brown frame, black center	1,000.
O69TC	$5	brown frame, blue center	1,000.
O69TC	$5	green frame, brown center	1,000.
O69TC	$5	blue frame, brown center	1,000.
O69TC	$5	blue frame, green center	1,000.
O70TC	$10	scarlet frame, black center	1,000.
O70TC	$10	scarlet frame, blue center	1,000.
O70TC	$10	brown frame, black center	1,000.
O70TC	$10	brown frame, blue center	1,000.
O70TC	$10	green frame, brown center	1,000.
O70TC	$10	blue frame, brown center	1,000.
O70TC	$10	blue frame, green center	1,000.
O71TC	$20	scarlet frame, black center	1,000.
O71TC	$20	scarlet frame, blue center	1,000.
O71TC	$20	brown frame, black center	1,000.
O71TC	$20	brown frame, blue center	1,000.
O71TC	$20	green frame, brown center	1,000.
O71TC	$20	blue frame, brown center	1,000.
O71TC	$20	blue frame, green center	1,000.

Treasury

		Black	Scarlet	Brown	Green	Blue
O72TC	1c	43.	37.	37.	37.	37.
O73TC	2c	43.	37.	37.	37.	37.
O74TC	3c	43.	37.	37.	37.	37.
O75TC	6c	55.	50.	50.	50.	50.
O76TC	7c	43.	37.	37.	37.	37.
O77TC	10c	43.	37.	37.	37.	37.
O78TC	12c	43.	37.	37.	37.	37.
O79TC	15c	43.	37.	37.	37.	37.
O80TC	24c	43.	37.	37.	37.	37.
O81TC	30c	60.	55.	55.	55.	55.
O82TC	90c	43.	37.	37.	37.	37.
	War					
O83TC	1c	43.	37.	37.	37.	37.
O84TC	2c	43.	37.	37.	37.	37.
O85TC	3c	43.	37.	37.	37.	37.
	Plate flaw at upper left (32R20)			—		
O86TC	6c	55.	50.	50.	50.	50.
O87TC	7c	43.	37.	37.	37.	37.
O88TC	10c	43.	37.	37.	37.	37.
O89TC	12c	43.	37.	37.	37.	37.
O90TC	15c	43.	37.	37.	37.	37.
O91TC	24c	43.	37.	37.	37.	37.
O92TC	30c	60.	55.	55.	55.	55.
O93TC	90c	43.	37.	37.	37.	37.
	NEWSPAPERS					
PR9TC	2c	55.	37.	37.	37.	37.
PR10TC	3c	55.	37.	37.	37.	37.
PR11TC	4c	55.	37.	37.	37.	37.
PR12TC	6c	55.	37.	37.	37.	37.
PR13TC	8c	55.	37.	37.	37.	37.
PR14TC	9c	55.	37.	37.	37.	37.
PR15TC	10c	55.	37.	37.	37.	37.
PR16TC	12c	55.	37.	37.	37.	37.
PR17TC	24c	55.	37.	37.	37.	37.
PR18TC	36c	55.	37.	37.	37.	37.
PR19TC	48c	55.	37.	37.	37.	37.
PR20TC	60c	55.	37.	37.	37.	37.
PR21TC	72c	55.	37.	37.	37.	37.
PR22TC	84c	55.	37.	37.	37.	37.
PR23TC	96c	55.	37.	37.	37.	37.
PR24TC	$ 1.92	55.	37.	37.	37.	37.
PR25TC	$ 3	55.	37.	37.	37.	37.
PR26TC	$ 6	55.	37.	37.	37.	37.
PR27TC	$ 9	55.	37.	37.	37.	37.
PR28TC	$12	55.	37.	37.	37.	37.
PR29TC	$24	55.	37.	37.	37.	37.
PR30TC	$36	55.	37.	37.	37.	37.
PR31TC	$48	55.	37.	37.	37.	37.
PR32TC	$60	55.	37.	37.	37.	37.
	CARRIERS					
LO1TC	1c Franklin	120.	110.	110.	110.	110.
LO2TC	1c Eagle	120.	110.	110.	110.	110.

TELEGRAPH

American Rapid Telegraph Co.

			DIE (2) Small	PLATE (3) India	(4) Card
1T1TC	1c	green	55.		
1T1TC	1c	brown	55.		
1T1TC	1c	red	55.		
1T1TC	1c	blue	55.		
1T1TC	1c	bluish green	55.		
1T3TC	5c	green	55.		
1T3TC	5c	black	55.		
1T3TC	5c	red	55.		
1T3TC	5c	blue	55.		
1T3TC	5c	bluish green	55.		
1T5TC	15c	red	55.		
1T5TC	15c	black	55.		
1T5TC	15c	brown	55.		
1T5TC	15c	bluish green	55.		
1T6TC	20c	green	55.		
1T6TC	20c	black	55.		
1T6TC	20c	brown	55.		
1T6TC	20c	blue	55.		
1T6TC	20c	bluish green	55.		

Collect

			DIE (1) Large	(2) Small	PLATE (3) India	(4) Card
1T10TC	5c	red		55.		
1T10TC	5c	black		55.		
1T10TC	5c	brown		55.		
1T10TC	5c	green		55.		
1T10TC	5c	bluish green		55.		
1T11TC	15c	red		55.		
1T11TC	15c	black		55.		
1T11TC	15c	brown		55.		
1T11TC	15c	green		55.		
1T11TC	15c	blue		55.		
1T11TC	15c	bluish green		55.		
	Office Coupon					
1T14TC	5c	red		55.		

No.	Denom.	Color	DIE (1) Large	DIE (2) Small	PLATE (3) India	PLATE (4) Card
1T14TC	5c	black		55.		
1T14TC	5c	brown		55.		
1T14TC	5c	green		55.		
1T14TC	5c	bluish green		55.		
1T15TC	15c	red		55.		
1T15TC	15c	black		55.		
1T15TC	15c	brown		55.		
1T15TC	15c	green		55.		
1T15TC	15c	blue		55.		
1T15TC	15c	bluish green		55.		

Baltimore & Ohio Telegraph Co.

No.	Denom.	Color	Large	Small	India	Card
3T2TC	5c	dark olive		65.		
3T4TC	25c	dark olive		65.		

Postal Telegraph Co.

No.	Denom.	Color	Large	Small	India	Card
15T1TC	10c	brown red		65.		
15T1TC	10c	red	65.			
15T1TC	10c	blue	65.			
15T1TC	10c	black	65.			
15T1TC	10c	orange			65.	
15T2TC	15c	black	65.		55.	
15T2TC	15c	red	65.	55.		
15T2TC	15c	blue	65.	55.		
15T2TC	25c	brown red		65.		
15T3TC	25c	black	65.			
15T3TC	25c	red	65.			
15T3TC	25c	ultramarine			40.	
15T3TC	25c	brown		65.	40.	
15T4TC	50c	dull blue		65.		
15T4TC	50c	black	65.		40.	
15T4TC	50c	red	65.			
15T4TC	50c	blue	65.			
15T6TC		red brown			40.	

Western Union Telegraph Co.

No.	Color	Large	Small	India	Card
16T1TC	lilac (1871)			20.	20.
	Pair			45.	45.
16T1TC	orange			20.	20.
	Pair			45.	45.
16T1TC	black			20.	20.
	Pair			45.	45.
16T1TC	violet brown				20.
	Pair				45.
16T1TC	light olive				20.
	Pair				45.
16T1TC	brown				20.
	Pair				45.
16T1TC	orange brown				20.
	Pair				45.
16T1TC	blue green				20.
	Pair				45.
16T6TC	violet blue (1876)			20.	20.
16T7TC	orange yellow (1877)				20.
	Pair				45.
16T7TC	dark brown				20.
	Pair				45.
16T7TC	black				20.
	Pane of 4				—
16T8TC	dark brown (1878)				—
16T9TC	blue (1879)				—
16T10TC	violet brown (1880)				—
16T10TC	rose				—
16T22TC	black (1892)				—

Die Proof Printed Directly on Card

No.	Color	Price
16T44TC	dull red	—
16T44TC	orange	—
16T44TC	rose red	—
16T44TC	orange brown	—
16T44TC	ocher	—
16T44TC	dark blue	—
16T44TC	dark ultramarine	—
16T44TC	green	—
16T44TC	brown lake	—
16T44TC	reddish brown	—
16T44TC	sepia	—
16T44TC	sepia, unsurfaced card	—
16T44TC	dull violet	—
16T44TC	slate green	—
16T44TC	slate blue	—
16T44TC	black	—
16T44TC	black, unsurfaced card	—

On India

No.	Color	Price
16T44TC	deep rose	—
16T44TC	carmine lake	—
16T44TC	rose lake	—
16T44TC	deep ultramarine	—

Plate Proofs, Sheets of 16 on India or Bond

No.	Color	Price
16T44TC	deep rose, on India	—
16T44TC	deep rose, on Bond	—
16T44TC	orange, on India	—
16T44TC	orange, on Bond	—
16T44TC	dark blue, on India	—
16T44TC	dark blue, on Bond	—
16T44TC	slate green, on India	—
16T44TC	slate green, on Bond	—
16T44TC	rose lake, on India	—
16T44TC	rose lake, on Bond	—
16T44TC	sepia, on Bond	—

REVENUES

Several lists of revenue proofs in trial colors have been published, but the accuracy of some of them is questionable. The following listings are limited to items seen by the editors. The list is not complete.

1862-71 FIRST ISSUE

No.	Denom.	Design, Color	Proof	Price
R3TC	1c	**Proprietary,** black	Plate on India	80.
R3TC		carmine	Plate on Card	125.
R3TC		dull red	Plate on Bond	125.
R3TC		orange red	Plate on Bond	125.
R3TC		dull yel.	Plate on Bond	125.
R3TC		violet rose	Plate on Bond	125.
R3TC		deep blue	Plate on Bond	125.
R3TC		red on blue	Plate on Bond	125.
R3TC		blue, perf. & gum	Plate on Bond	125.
R3TC		green	Plate on buff wove	—
R3TC		black	Die on India	*950.*
R7TC	2c	**Certificate,** ultra.	Plate on Card	65.
R11TC	2c	**Playing Cards,** black	Die on India	500.
R13TC	2c	**Proprietary,** black	Plate on India	75.
R13TC		black	Die on India	650.
R13TC		carmine	Die on India	650.
R15TC	2c	**U.S.I.R.,** violet rose	Plate on Bond	110.
R15TC		light green	Plate on Bond	110.
R15TC		pale blue	Plate on Bond	110.
R15TC		pale rose	Plate on Bond	200.
R15TC		orange	Plate on blue Bond	—
R15TC		black	Plate on India	110.
R15TC		pale orange, perf. & gum	Plate on Bond	110.
R16TC	3c	**Foreign Exchange,** green on blue	Plate on Bond	140.
R16TC		blue	Plate on Goldbeater's Skin	110.
R18TC	3c	**Proprietary,** black	Die on India	300.
R21TC	4c	**Playing Cards,** black	Die (?) on India	300.
R22TC	4c	**Proprietary,** black	Plate on India	110.
R22TC		black	Die on India	350.
R22TC		deep red lilac	Die on India	400.
R22TC		red lilac	Plate on Card	110.
R24TC	5c	**Certificate,** carmine	Plate on India	110.
R25TC	5c	**Express,** pale olive	Plate on Wove	—
R26TC	5c	**Foreign Exchange,** orange	Plate on India	110.
R28TC	5c	**Playing Cards,** black	Die (?) on India	300.
R29TC	5c	**Proprietary,** red	Plate on blue Bond	—
R30TC	6c	**Inland Exchange,** black	Die on India	350.
R31TC	6c	**Proprietary,** black	Die on India	—
R32TC	10c	**Bill of Lading,** greenish blue	Die on India	350.
		R32TC+R37TC composite, dark green	Large Die on India	—
R35TC	10c	**Foreign Exchange,** black	Die (?) on India	350.
R37TC	10c	**Power of Attorney,** greenish blue	Die on India	350.
R38TC	10c	**Proprietary,** black	Die on India	350.
R43TC	25c	**Bond,** carmine	Plate on Card	90.
R44TC	25c	**Certificate,** blue	Plate on Bond	300.
R44TC		green	Plate on Bond	300.
R44TC		orange	Plate on Bond	300.
R45TC	25c	**Entry of Goods,** black	Hybrid Die on India	—
R46TC	25c	**Insurance,** dull red	Plate on Bond	150.
R46TC		dull red	Plate on Goldbeater's Skin	210.
R46TC		vermilion	Plate on Goldbeater's Skin	210.
R46TC		vermilion	Plate on Bond	170.
R46TC		blue	Plate on Bond	170.
R46TC		blue	Plate on Goldbeater's Skin	215.
R46TC		dark blue	Plate on Bond	155.
R46TC		dark blue	Plate on Goldbeater's Skin	215.
R46TC		green	Plate on Goldbeater's Skin	215.
R51TC	30c	**Foreign Exchange,** violet	Plate on India	130.
R51TC		violet gray	Plate on India	130.
R51TC		deep red lilac	Plate on India	155.
R51TC		slate blue	Plate on India	155.
R51TC		black	Plate on India	155.
R51TC		red	Plate on India	155.
R52TC		**Inland Exchange,** deep red lilac	Plate on India	155.
R53TC	40c	**Inland Exchange,** black	Hybrid Die on India	—
R55TC	50c	**Entry of Goods,** orange	Plate on Bond	275.
R55TC		green	Plate on Bond	275.
R55TC		red	Plate on Bond	340.
R55TC		deep blue	Plate on Bond	—
R58TC	50c	**Life Insurance,** ultramarine	Plate on India	85.
R60TC	50c	**Original Process,** black	Die (?) on India	280.
R64TC	60c	**Inland Exchange,** green	Die (?) on India	—
R65TC	70c	**Foreign Exchange,** orange	Die (?) on India	—
R65TC		black	Die (?) on India	285.
R66TC	$1	**Conveyance,** carmine	Plate on India	85.
R67TC	$1	**Entry of Goods,** carmine	Plate on India	60.
R68TC	$1	**Foreign Exchange,** carmine	Plate on India	60.
R69TC	$1	**Inland Exchange,** carmine	Plate on India	60.
R70TC	$1	**Lease,** carmine	Plate on India	130.
R71TC	$1	**Life Insurance,** carmine	Plate on India	75.
R72TC	$1	**Manifest,** carmine	Plate on India	80.
R73TC	$1	**Mortgage,** carmine	Plate on India	85.
R73TC		black	Hybrid Die on India	—
R74TC	$1	**Passage Ticket,** carmine	Plate on India	120.
R75TC	$1	**Power of Attorney,** carmine	Plate on India	120.
R76TC	$1	**Probate of Will,** carmine	Plate on India	60.
R78TC	$1.50	**Inland Exchange,** black	Die on India	475.
R80TC	$1.90	**Foreign Exchange,** black	Plate on India	155.
R81TC	$2	**Conveyance,** carmine	Plate on Card	85.
R82TC	$2	**Mortgage,** carmine	Plate on Card	85.
R83TC	$2	**Probate of Will,** black	Hybrid Die on India	—
R84TC	$2.50	**Inland Exchange,** black	Die (?) on India	120.
R85TC	$3	**Charter Party,** dark green	Plate on Thin Card	—
R87TC	$3.50	**Inland Exchange,** black	Die on India	400.
R88TC	$5	**Charter Party,** carmine	Plate on India	85.
R88TC		black	Hybrid Die on India	—
R89TC	$5	**Conveyance,** carmine	Plate on India	90.
R91TC	$5	**Mortgage,** carmine	Plate on India	90.
R95TC	$10	**Mortgage,** yellow green	Plate on Thin Card	—
R98TC	$20	**Conveyance,** red orange	Plate on Card	120.
R98TC		red orange	Plate on India	220.
R99TC	$20	**Probate of Will,** red orange	Plate on Card	275.
R99TC		black	Plate on Card	275.
R101TC	$50	**U.S.I.R.,** orange	Plate on Bond	275.
R101TC		deep blue	Plate on Bond	275.
		black	Hybrid Die on India	—
R102TC	$200	black & red	Plate on Card	1,600.
R102TC		gray brown & red	Plate on Bond	1,600.
R102TC		green & brown red	Plate on India	1,600.
R102TC		black	Plate on India	—

SECOND ISSUE

No.	Denom.	Color	Proof	Price
R104TC	2c	pale blue & black	Plate on Bond	60.
R132TC	$200	red, green & black	India	2,500.
R132TC		orange (master die)	India	2,500.
R132TC		blue (master die)	India	2,500.
R132TC		green (master die)	India	2,500.
R133TC	$500	black (master die)	India	7,000.
R133TC		yellow, green & black	India	5,000.

R133TC		bright green, orange brown & black	India	5,000.
R133TC		red, green & black	Bond	5,000.
R133TC		light green, light brown & black	Bond	5,000.
R133TC		blue, scarlet & black	Bond	5,000.
R133ATC	$5000	yel org, green & black	India	7,500.
R133ATC		olive brown, green & black	India	8,000.
R133ATC		org red, dark green & black	India	8,000.
R133ATC		org red, dark blue & black	India	8,000.

The master die is the completed stamp design prior to its division into separate color dies.

See note after No. R133AP in Die and Plate Proofs section.

THIRD ISSUE

R134TC	1c	brown & black	Plate on Card	60.

1875 National Bank Note Co., New York City

R152TC	2c	(Liberty), green	Die on India	600.
R152TC		(Liberty), brown	Die on India	600.
R152TC		(Liberty), black	Die on India	600.

1898

R161TC	½c	green	Lg. die on India	750.
R163TC	1c	green	Lg. die on India	750.
R163TC		black	Lg. die on India	750.
R165TC	3c	green	Sm. die on India	650.
R169TC	25c	green	Lg. die on India	650.
R170TC	40c	black	Lg. die on India	650.
R172TC	80c	green	Lg. die on India	650.

1898

R174TC	$3	black	Die on India	650.
R176TC	$10	green	Die on India	650.

1899

R179TC	$100	dark green & black	Die on India	1,250.
R181TC	$1000	dark blue & black	Die on India	1,250.

1914

R195TC	½c	black	Small die on Wove	—
R196TC	1c	blue green	Small die on Wove	—
R198TC	3c	ultramarine	Small die on Wove	—
R199TC	4c	brown	Small die on Wove	—
R200TC	5c	blue	Small die on Wove	—
R201TC	10c	yellow	Small die on Wove	—
R202TC	25c	dull violet	Small die on Wove	—
R203TC	40c	blue green	Small die on Wove	—
R204TC	50c	red brown	Small die on Wove	—
R205TC	80c	orange	Small die on Wove	—

PROPRIETARY

1871-75

RB1TC	1c	blue & black	Plate on Bond	70.
RB1TC		scarlet & black	Plate on Bond	70.
RB1TC		orange & black	Plate on Bond	70.
RB1TC		orange & ultramarine	Plate on Granite Bond	60.
RB3TC	3c	blue & black, with gum	Plate on Bond	60.
RB3TC		blue & black	Plate on Gray Bond	60.
RB3TC		blue & black	Plate on wove	—
RB8TC	50c	green & brown	Die on India	675.
RB8TC		green & purple	Die on India	675.
RB8TC		green & brown red	Die on India	675.
RB8TC		green & violet	Die on India	675.
RB8TC		green & dark carmine	Die on India	675.
RB8TC		ultramarine & red	Die on India	675.
RB9TC	$1	green & brown	Die on India	675.
RB9TC		green & purple	Die on India	675.
RB9TC		green & violet brown	Die on India	675.
RB9TC		green & brown red	Die on India	675.
RB9TC		green & violet	Die on India	675.
RB9TC		green & dark carmine	Die on India	675.

1875-83

RB11TC	1c	brown	Die on India	500.
RB11TC		red brown	Die on India	500.
RB11TC		blue	Die on India	500.
RB11TC		black	Die on India	500.
RB12TC	2c	green	Die on India	500.
RB12TC		black	Die on India	500.
RB12TC		brown	Die on India	500.
RB12TC		orange brown	Die on India	500.
RB12TC		blue	Die on India	500.
RB13TC	3c	brown	Die on India	500.
RB13TC		green	Die on India	500.
RB13TC		blue	Die on India	500.
RB13TC		black	Plate on India	150.
RB14TC	4c	dark brown	Die on India	450.
RB14TC		green	Die on India	450.
RB14TC		black	Die on India	450.
RB14TC		blue	Die on India	450.
RB14TC		black	Plate on India	150.
RB16TC	5c	green	Die on India	450.
RB16TC		dark slate	Die on India	450.
RB16TC		blue	Die on India	450.
RB17TC	6c	green	Plate on India	150.
RB17TC		black	Plate on India	150.
RB17TC		black	Die on India	500.
RB17TC		blue	Die on India	500.
RB17TC		purple	Die on India	500.
RB17TC		dull violet	Die on India	500.
RB17TC		violet	Die on India	500.
RB17TC		violet brown	Die on India	500.
RB17TC		dark brown	Die on India	500.
RB19TC	10c	black	Die on India	550.

SECOND, THIRD AND PROPRIETARY ISSUES

Stamps Nos. R103 to R131, R134 to R150 and RB1 to RB7.

A special composite plate was made and impressions taken in various colors and shades. Although all varieties in all colors must have been made, only those seen by the editors are listed.

PLATE PROOFS ON INDIA PAPER
CENTERS IN BLACK

1871-75

R103TC 1c

a.	dark purple	60.
b.	dull purple	60.
d.	brown	60.
e.	black brown	60.
g.	light blue	60.
h.	dark blue	70.
i.	ultramarine	70.
k.	yellow green	70.
n.	green	65.
o.	dark green	65.
p.	blue green	65.
q.	light orange	65.
r.	dark orange	65.
s.	deep orange	65.
t.	scarlet	65.
u.	carmine	65.
x.	dark brown red	65.
y.	dark brown orange, goldbeater's skin	90.

R104TC 2c

a.	dark purple	60.
b.	dull purple	60.
d.	brown	60.
e.	black brown	60.
g.	light blue	60.
h.	dark blue	70.
i.	ultramarine	70.
k.	yellow green	70.
l.	dark yellow green	70.
n.	green	65.
o.	dark green	65.
p.	blue green	65.
q.	light orange	65.
r.	dark orange	65.
s.	deep orange	65.
t.	scarlet	65.
u.	carmine	65.
x.	dark brown red	65.
y.	dark brown orange, goldbeater's skin	90.

R105TC 3c

a.	dark purple	60.
b.	dull purple	60.
d.	brown	60.
e.	black brown	60.
g.	light blue	60.
h.	dark blue	70.
i.	ultramarine	70.
k.	yellow green	70.
n.	green	65.
o.	dark green	65.
p.	blue green	65.
q.	light orange	65.
r.	dark orange	65.
s.	deep orange	65.
t.	scarlet	65.
u.	carmine	65.
x.	dark brown red	65.
y.	dark brown orange, goldbeater's skin	90.

R106TC 4c

a.	dark purple	60.
b.	dull purple	60.
d.	brown	60.
e.	black brown	60.
f.	orange brown	65.
g.	light blue	60.
h.	dark blue	70.
i.	ultramarine	70.
k.	yellow green	70.
n.	green	65.
o.	dark green	65.
p.	blue green	65.
q.	light orange	65.
r.	dark orange	65.
s.	deep orange	65.
t.	scarlet	65.
u.	carmine	65.
x.	dark brown red	65.
y.	dark brown orange, goldbeater's skin	90.

R107TC 5c

a.	dark purple	60.
b.	dull purple	60.
d.	brown	60.
e.	black brown	60.
f.	orange brown	65.
g.	light blue	60.
h.	dark blue	70.
i.	ultramarine	70.
k.	yellow green	70.
n.	green	65.
o.	dark green	65.
p.	blue green	65.
q.	light orange	65.
r.	dark orange	65.
s.	deep orange	65.
t.	scarlet	65.
u.	carmine	65.
v.	dark carmine	65.
w.	purplish carmine	65.
x.	dark brown red	65.
y.	dark brown orange, goldbeater's skin	90.

R108TC 6c

a.	dark purple	60.
b.	dull purple	60.
d.	brown	60.
e.	black brown	60.
f.	orange brown	65.
g.	light blue	60.
h.	dark blue	70.
i.	ultramarine	70.
k.	yellow green	70.
n.	green	65.
o.	dark green	65.
p.	blue green	65.
q.	light orange	65.
r.	dark orange	65.
s.	deep orange	65.
t.	scarlet	65.
u.	carmine	65.
v.	dark carmine	65.
w.	purplish carmine	65.
x.	dark brown red	65.
y.	dark brown orange, goldbeater's skin	90.

R109TC 10c

a.	dark purple	60.
b.	dull purple	60.
d.	brown	60.
e.	black brown	60.
g.	light blue	60.
h.	dark blue	70.
i.	ultramarine	70.
k.	yellow green	70.
n.	green	65.
o.	dark green	65.
p.	blue green	65.
q.	light orange	65.
r.	dark orange	65.
s.	deep orange	65.
t.	scarlet	65.
u.	carmine	65.
x.	dark brown red	65.

R110TC 15c

a.	dark purple	60.
b.	dull purple	60.
d.	brown	60.
e.	black brown	60.
f.	orange brown	65.
g.	light blue	60.
h.	dark blue	70.
i.	ultramarine	70.
k.	yellow green	70.
n.	green	65.
o.	dark green	65.
p.	blue green	65.
q.	light orange	65.
r.	dark orange	65.
s.	deep orange	65.
t.	scarlet	65.
u.	carmine	65.
w.	purplish carmine	65.
x.	dark brown red	65.

R111TC 20c

a.	dark purple	60.
b.	dull purple	60.
d.	brown	60.
e.	black brown	60.
g.	light blue	60.
h.	dark blue	70.
i.	ultramarine	70.
k.	yellow green	70.
n.	green	65.
o.	dark green	65.
p.	blue green	65.
q.	light orange	65.
r.	dark orange	65.
s.	deep orange	65.
t.	scarlet	65.
u.	carmine	65.
w.	purplish carmine	65.
x.	dark brown red	65.
y.	dark brown orange, goldbeater's skin	90.

R112TC 25c

a.	dark purple	60.
b.	dull purple	60.
d.	brown	60.
e.	black brown	60.

g. light blue 60.
h. dark blue 70.
i. ultramarine 70.
k. yellow green 70.
l. dark yellow green 70.
n. green 65.
o. dark green 65.
p. blue green 65.
q. light orange 65.
r. dark orange 65.
s. deep orange 65.
t. scarlet 65.
u. carmine 65.
x. dark brown red 65.
y. dark brown orange, goldbeater's skin 90.

R113TC 30c
a. dark purple 60.
b. dull purple 60.
d. brown 60.
e. black brown 60.
g. light blue 60.
h. dark blue 70.
i. ultramarine 70.
k. yellow green 70.
n. green 65.
o. dark green 65.
p. blue green 65.
q. light orange 65.
r. dark orange 65.
s. deep orange 65.
t. scarlet 65.
u. carmine 65.
v. dark carmine 65.
w. purplish carmine 65.
x. dark brown red 65.
y. dark brown orange, goldbeater's skin 90.

R114TC 40c
a. dark purple 60.
b. dull purple 60.
d. brown 60.
e. black brown 60.
f. orange brown 65.
g. light blue 60.
h. dark blue 70.
i. ultramarine 70.
k. yellow green 70.
n. green 65.
o. dark green 65.
p. blue green 65.
q. light orange 65.
r. dark orange 65.
s. deep orange 65.
t. scarlet 65.
u. carmine 65.
x. dark brown red 65.

R115TC 50c
a. dark purple 60.
b. dull purple 60.
d. brown 60.
e. black brown 60.
g. light blue 60.
h. dark blue 70.
i. ultramarine 70.
k. yellow green 70.
n. green 65.
o. dark green 65.
p. blue green 65.
q. light orange 65.
r. dark orange 65.
s. deep orange 65.
t. scarlet 65.
u. carmine 65.
x. dark brown red 65.

R116TC 60c
a. dark purple 60.
b. dull purple 60.
d. brown 60.
e. black brown 60.
g. light blue 60.
h. dark blue 70.
i. ultramarine 70.
k. yellow green 70.
n. green 65.
o. dark green 65.
p. blue green 65.
q. light orange 65.
r. dark orange 65.
s. deep orange 65.
t. scarlet 65.
u. carmine 65.
v. dark carmine 65.
x. dark brown red 65.
y. dark brown orange, goldbeater's skin 90.

R117TC 70c
a. dark purple 60.
b. dull purple 60.
d. brown 60.
e. black brown 60.
g. light blue 60.
h. dark blue 70.
i. ultramarine 70.
k. yellow green 70.
n. green 65.
o. dark green 65.
p. blue green 65.
q. light orange 65.
r. dark orange 65.
s. deep orange 65.
t. scarlet 65.
u. carmine 65.
x. dark brown red 65.

R118TC $1
a. dark purple 70.
b. dull purple 70.
d. brown 70.
e. black brown 70.
g. light blue 80.
h. dark blue 85.
i. ultramarine 85.
k. yellow green 80.
n. green 75.
o. dark green 75.
p. blue green 75.
q. light orange 75.
r. dark orange 75.
s. deep orange 75.
t. scarlet 80.
u. carmine 80.
w. purplish carmine 80.
x. dark brown red 80.
y. dark brown orange, goldbeater's skin 90.

R119TC $1.30
a. dark purple 70.
b. dull purple 70.
d. brown 70.
e. black brown 70.
g. light blue 80.
h. dark blue 85.
i. ultramarine 85.
k. yellow green 80.
n. green 75.
o. dark green 75.
p. blue green 75.
q. light orange 75.
r. dark orange 75.
s. deep orange 75.
t. scarlet 80.
u. carmine 80.
x. dark brown red 80.

R120TC $1.50
a. dark purple 70.
b. dull purple 70.
d. brown 70.
e. black brown 70.
g. light blue 80.
h. dark blue 85.
i. ultramarine 85.
j. bright yellow green, on card 75.
k. yellow green 80.
n. green 75.
o. dark green 75.
p. blue green 75.
q. light orange 75.
r. dark orange 75.
s. deep orange 75.
t. scarlet 80.
u. carmine 80.
x. dark brown red 80.

R121TC $1.60
a. dark purple 70.
b. dull purple 70.
d. brown 70.
e. black brown 70.
g. light blue 80.
h. dark blue 85.
i. ultramarine 85.
k. yellow green 80.
n. green 75.
o. dark green 75.
p. blue green 75.
q. light orange 75.
r. dark orange 75.
s. deep orange 75.
t. scarlet 80.
u. carmine 80.
x. dark brown red 80.

R122TC $1.90
a. dark purple 70.
b. dull purple 70.
d. brown 70.
e. black brown 70.
g. light blue 80.
h. dark blue 85.
i. ultramarine 85.
j. bright yellow green, on card 75.
k. yellow green 80.
n. green 75.
o. dark green 75.
p. blue green 75.
q. light orange 75.
r. dark orange 75.
s. deep orange 75.
t. scarlet 80.
u. carmine 80.
x. dark brown red 80.

R123TC $2
a. dark purple 70.
b. dull purple 70.
d. brown 70.
e. black brown 70.
g. light blue 80.
h. dark blue 85.
i. ultramarine 85.
j. bright yellow green, on card 75.
k. yellow green 80.
n. green 75.
o. dark green 75.
p. blue green 75.
q. light orange 75.
r. dark orange 75.
s. deep orange 75.
t. scarlet 80.
u. carmine 80.
w. purplish carmine 80.
x. dark brown red 80.
y. dark brown orange, goldbeater's skin 90.

R124TC $2.50
a. dark purple 70.
b. dull purple 70.
d. brown 70.
e. black brown 70.
g. light blue 80.
h. dark blue 85.
i. ultramarine 85.
k. yellow green 80.
n. green 75.
o. dark green 75.
p. blue green 75.
q. light orange 75.
r. dark orange 75.
s. deep orange 75.
t. scarlet 80.
u. carmine 80.
v. dark carmine 80.
x. dark brown red 80.

R125TC $3
a. dark purple 70.
b. dull purple 70.
d. brown 70.
e. black brown 70.
g. light blue 80.
h. dark blue 85.
i. ultramarine 85.
j. bright yellow green, on card 75.
k. yellow green 80.
n. green 75.
o. dark green 75.
p. blue green 75.
q. light orange 75.
r. dark orange 75.
s. deep orange 75.
t. scarlet 80.
u. carmine 80.
x. dark brown red 80.

R126TC $3.50
a. dark purple 70.
b. dull purple 70.
c. red purple 75.
d. brown 70.
e. black brown 70.
g. light blue 80.
h. dark blue 85.
i. ultramarine 85.
k. yellow green 80.
n. green 75.
o. dark green 75.
p. blue green 75.
q. light orange 75.
r. dark orange 75.
s. deep orange 75.
t. scarlet 90.
u. carmine 80.
x. dark brown red 80.

R127TC $5
a. dark purple 70.
b. dull purple 70.
d. brown 70.
e. black brown 70.
g. light blue 80.
h. dark blue 85.
i. ultramarine 85.
k. yellow green 80.
n. green 75.
o. dark green 75.
p. blue green 75.
q. light orange 75.
r. dark orange 75.
s. deep orange 75.
t. scarlet 75.
u. carmine 75.
w. purplish carmine 75.
x. dark brown red 80.
y. dark brown orange, goldbeater's skin 100.

R128TC $10
a. dark purple 70.
b. dull purple 70.
d. brown 70.
e. black brown 70.
g. light blue 80.
h. dark blue 85.
i. ultramarine 85.
j. bright yellow green, on card 75.
k. yellow green 75.
n. green 75.
o. dark green 75.
p. blue green 75.
q. light orange 75.
r. dark orange 75.
s. deep orange 75.
t. scarlet 75.
u. carmine 80.
x. dark brown red 80.

R129TC $20
a. dark purple 95.
b. dull purple 95.
d. brown 95.
e. black brown 95.
g. light blue 90.
h. dark blue 90.
i. ultramarine 90.
k. yellow green 85.
m. emerald green 85.
n. green 75.
o. dark green 75.
p. blue green 75.
q. light orange 75.
r. dark orange 85.
s. deep orange 85.
t. scarlet 90.
u. carmine 80.
v. dark carmine 90.
x. dark brown red 80.

R130TC $25
a. dark purple 100.
b. dull purple 100.

d.	brown	100.
e.	black brown	100.
g.	light blue	90.
h.	dark blue	90.
i.	ultramarine	90.
k.	yellow green	85.
m.	emerald green	85.
n.	green	75.
o.	dark green	75.
p.	blue green	75.
q.	light orange	75.
r.	dark orange	85.
s.	deep orange	85.
t.	scarlet	90.
u.	carmine	80.
w.	purplish carmine	90.
x.	dark brown red	300.
y.	dark brown orange, goldbeater's skin	100.

R131TC $50

a.	dark purple	95.
b.	dull purple	95.
d.	brown	95.
e.	black brown	95.
g.	light blue	90.
h.	dark blue	90.
i.	ultramarine	90.
j.	bright yellow green, on card	85.
k.	yellow green	85.
m.	emerald green	85.
n.	green	75.
o.	dark green	75.
p.	blue green	75.
q.	light orange	75.
r.	dark orange	85.
s.	deep orange	85.
t.	scarlet	90.
u.	carmine	80.
x.	dark brown red	80.

RB1TC 1c

a.	dark purple	70.
b.	dull purple	70.
d.	brown	65.
e.	black brown	65.
g.	light blue	75.
h.	dark blue	75.
i.	ultramarine	70.
k.	yellow green	70.
l.	dark yellow green	70.
n.	green	65.
o.	dark green	65.
p.	blue green	65.
q.	light orange	65.
r.	dark orange	65.
s.	deep orange	65.
t.	scarlet	65.
u.	carmine	65.
x.	dark brown red	65.

RB2TC 2c

a.	dark purple	70.
b.	dull purple	70.
d.	brown	65.
e.	black brown	65.
g.	light blue	70.
h.	dark blue	70.
i.	ultramarine	70.
j.	bright yellow green, on card	70.
k.	yellow green	70.
n.	green	65.
o.	dark green	65.
p.	blue green	65.
q.	light orange	65.
r.	dark orange	65.
s.	deep orange	65.
t.	scarlet	65.
u.	carmine	65.
x.	dark brown red	65.

RB3TC 3c

a.	dark purple	70.
b.	dull purple	70.
d.	brown	65.
e.	black brown	65.
g.	light blue	70.
h.	dark blue	70.
i.	ultramarine	70.
k.	yellow green	70.
l.	dark yellow green	70.
n.	green	65.
o.	dark green	65.
p.	blue green	65.
q.	light orange	65.
r.	dark orange	65.
s.	deep orange	65.
t.	scarlet	65.
u.	carmine	65.
x.	dark brown red	65.

RB4TC 4c

a.	dark purple	70.
b.	dull purple	70.
d.	brown	65.
e.	black brown	65.
g.	light blue	70.
h.	dark blue	70.
i.	ultramarine	70.
k.	yellow green	70.
n.	green	65.
o.	dark green	65.
p.	blue green	65.
q.	light orange	65.
r.	dark orange	65.
s.	deep orange	65.
t.	scarlet	65.
u.	carmine	65.
x.	dark brown red	65.

RB5TC 5c

a.	dark purple	70.
b.	dull purple	70.
d.	brown	65.
e.	black brown	65.
g.	light blue	70.
h.	dark blue	70.
i.	ultramarine	70.
j.	bright yellow green, on card	70.
k.	yellow green	70.
l.	dark yellow green	70.
n.	green	65.
o.	dark green	65.
p.	blue green	65.
q.	light orange	65.
r.	dark orange	65.
s.	deep orange	65.
t.	scarlet	65.
u.	carmine	65.
x.	dark brown red	65.

RB6TC 6c

a.	dark purple	70.
b.	dull purple	70.
d.	brown	65.
e.	black brown	65.
g.	light blue	70.
h.	dark blue	70.
i.	ultramarine	70.
k.	yellow green	70.
l.	dark yellow green	70.
n.	green	65.
o.	dark green	65.
p.	blue green	65.
q.	light orange	65.
r.	dark orange	65.
s.	deep orange	65.
t.	scarlet	65.
u.	carmine	65.
x.	dark brown red	65.

RB7TC 10c

a.	dark purple	70.
b.	dull purple	70.
d.	brown	65.
e.	black brown	65.
g.	light blue	70.
h.	dark blue	70.
i.	ultramarine	70.
k.	yellow green	70.
l.	dark yellow green	70.
n.	green	65.
o.	dark green	65.
p.	blue green	65.
q.	light orange	65.
r.	dark orange	65.
s.	deep orange	65.
t.	scarlet	65.
u.	carmine	65.
x.	dark brown red	65.

1898

RB21TC	¼c	green	Large die on India	1,300.
RB22TC	⅜c	green	Large die on India	750.
RB26TC	1 ⅞c	green	Large die on India	750.
RB26TC	1 ⅞c	black	Large die on India	750.
RB27TC	2c	green	Small die on India	500.
RB31TC	5c	green	Large die on India	500.

1918-29

Stock Transfer

RD20TC	$50	black	Die on India	*2,250.*
RD20TC	$50	blue	Die on India	*2,250.*

1894

Playing Cards

RF1TC	2c	black (On hand)	Die on India	*1,500.*
RF2TC	2c	lake (Act of)	Die on India	*1,000.*

PRIVATE DIE MATCH STAMPS

For important valuing information see the note before Private Die Proprietary die and plate proofs.

1864

			DIE ON INDIA (1) Large	PLATE (3) India	(4) Card
RO1TC	1c	black	175.		
RO1TC	1c	green	300.		
RO2TC	1c	black	225.		
RO2TC	1c	green	300.		
RO5TC	1c	black	275.		
RO5TC	1c	blue	500.		
RO6TC	1c	black	300.		
RO6TC	1c	green	500.		
RO7TC	1c	black	300.		
RO7TC	1c	dull green	300.		
RO7TC	1c	green	500.		
RO9TC	1c	blue	225.		
RO9TC	1c	brown	275.		
RO9TC	1c	dark green	500.		
RO9TC	1c	green	300.		
RO10TC	1c	blue	300.		
RO10TC	1c	green	500.		
RO11TC	3c	blue	500.		
RO11TC	3c	green	500.		
RO12TC	1c	blue	225.		
RO12TC	1c	green	500.		
RO13TC	3c	black	500.		
RO13TC	3c	blue	1000.		
RO14TC	1c	blue	225.		
RO14TC	1c	green	500.		
RO15TC	1c	black	225.		
RO15TC	1c	blue	225.		
RO16TC	1c	black	225.		
RO16TC	1c	green	300.		
RO17/19TC	1c/3c	green	1250.		
RO17TC	1c	black	225.		
RO17TC	1c	green	500.		
RO19TC	3c	blue	250.		
RO19TC	3c	green	600.		
RO20TC	1c	black	175.		
RO20TC	1c	green	500.		
RO21TC	3c	blue	375.		
RO21TC	3c	green	375.		
RO22TC	1c	black	300.		
RO23TC	1c	black	225.		
RO23TC	1c	blue	225.		
RO23TC	1c	green	500.		
RO24TC	1c	black	225.		
RO24TC	1c	blue	225.		
RO24TC	1c	green	500.		
RO25TC	12c	black	400.		
RO25TC	12c	blue	750.		
RO25TC	12c	green	750.		
RO26TC	1c	black	225.		
RO26TC	1c	blue	225.		
RO26TC	1c	dark brn	225.		
RO26TC	1c	green	300.		
RO26TC	1c	light brn	300.		
RO27TC	12c	black	400.		
RO27TC	12c	blue	500.		
RO27TC	12c	green	750.		
RO28TC	1c	black	175.		
RO28TC	1c	brown	300.		
RO28TC	1c	green	300.		
RO29TC	1c	blue	300.		
RO29TC	1c	green	300.		
RO30TC	1c	black	175.		
RO30TC	1c	blue	225.		
RO30TC	1c	green	300.		
RO30TC	1c	red	500.		
RO31TC	1c	blue	300.		
RO31TC	1c	green	225.		
RO31TC	1c	red	500.		
RO32TC	4c	blue	500.		
RO32TC	4c	brown	500.		
RO32TC	4c	orange	500.		
RO32TC	4c	vermilion	500.		
RO35TC	1c	blue	300.		
RO35TC	1c	green	500.		
RO37TC	3c	blue	400.		
RO37TC	3c	green	400.		
RO38TC	1c	blue	350.		
RO38TC	1c	dk bl	500.		
RO38TC	1c	green	375.		
RO38TC	1c	red	600.		
RO39TC	1c	black	300.		
RO41TC	1c	black	225.		
RO41TC	1c	green	300.		
RO42TC	1c	black	300.		
RO42TC	1c	blue	300.		
RO42TC	1c	green	500.		
RO43TC	1c	blue	500.		
RO45TC	1c	blue	350.		
RO45TC	1c	green	750.		
RO46TC	1c	blue	350.		
RO46TC	1c	dk bl	500.		
RO46TC	1c	green	500.		
RO46TC	1c	orange	300.		
RO47TC	1c	blue	300.		
RO47TC	1c	green	500.		
RO49TC	1c	blue	225.		
RO49TC	1c	brown	500.		
RO49TC	1c	brn red	300.		
RO49TC	1c	dk bl	500.		
RO49TC	1c	green	500.		
RO49TC	1c	red brn	500.		
RO55TC	1c	blue	375.		
RO56TC	1c	blue	750.		
RO56TC	1c	green	300.		
RO57TC	1c	black	175.		
RO57TC	1c	blue	225.		
RO58TC	1c	black	300.		
RO58TC	1c	blue	225.		
RO58TC	1c	dark rose	500.		
RO58TC	1c	green	500.		
RO58TC	1c	rose	300.		
RO59TC	1c	black	225.		
RO60TC	3c	blue	500.		
RO60TC	3c	green	500.		
RO61TC	1c	black	175.		
RO61TC	1c	blue	300.		
RO62TC	1c	black	175.		
RO62TC	1c	blue	175.		
RO64TC	1c	black	225.		
RO64TC	1c	blue	300.		
RO64TC	1c	green	300.		
RO65TC	1c	green	300.		
RO67TC	1c	blue	225.		
RO67TC	1c	green	300.		
RO67TC	1c	red	500.		
RO67TC	1c	rose	500.		
RO68TC	1c	black	225.		
RO68TC	1c	blue	225.		
RO69TC	1c	blue	300.		
RO69TC	1c	green	500.		
RO71TC	1c	black	250.		
RO71TC	1c	green	400.		
RO72TC	1c	black	500.		
RO73TC	1c	blue	225.		
RO73TC	1c	green	300.		

			DIE ON INDIA	PLATE	
			(1) Large	(3) India	(4) Card
RO73TC	1c	red	500.		
RO73TC	1c	red brn	225.		
RO76TC	1c	blue	500.		
RO76TC	1c	green	300.		
RO77TC	1c	black	225.		
RO77TC	1c	green	300.		
RO78TC	1c	black	225.		
RO78TC	1c	dk bl	500.		
RO78TC	1c	green	500.		
RO80TC	1c	black	225.		
RO80TC	1c	green	500.		
RO81TC	1c	blue	175.		
RO81TC	1c	dark green	500.		
RO81TC	1c	green	225.		
RO81TC	1c	lake	500.		
RO81TC	1c	red	300.		
RO82TC	1c	blue	175.		
RO82TC	1c	green	500.		
RO83TC	1c	black	175.		
RO83TC	1c	green	300.		
RO83TC	1c	red	500.		
RO84TC	1c	blue	300.		
RO84TC	1c	green	500.		
RO85TC	1c	black	250.		
RO85TC	1c	blue	300.		
RO85TC	1c	green	350.		
RO85TC	1c	orange	500.		
RO85TC	1c	vermilion	500.		
RO86TC	1c	blue	500.		
RO86TC	1c	brown	500.		
RO86TC	1c	green	400.		
RO86TC	1c	orange	500.		
RO86TC	1c	red	500.		
RO87TC	1c	dull rose	500.		
RO87TC	1c	orange	500.		
RO88TC	1c	blue	300.		
RO88TC	1c	green	500.		
RO89TC	3c	blue	300.		
RO89TC	3c	green	300.		
RO90TC	6c	blue	225.		
RO90TC	6c	brown	500.		
RO90TC	6c	green	500.		
RO90TC	6c	orange	500.		
RO91TC	3c	blue	225.		
RO91TC	3c	brown	500.		
RO91TC	3c	green	500.		
RO91TC	3c	orange	500.		
RO91TC	3c	red	500.		
RO92TC	1c	blue	300.		
RO92TC	1c	green	500.		
RO94TC	3c	blue	225.		
RO94TC	3c	brown	300.		
RO94TC	3c	green	225.		
RO94TC	3c	orange	300.		
RO94TC	3c	red	500.		
RO94TC	3c	vermilion	500.		
RO95TC	1c	black	175.		
RO95TC	1c	blue	175.		
RO95TC	1c	brown	225.		
RO95TC	1c	dk bl	500.		
RO96TC	1c	black	175.		
RO96TC	1c	blue	225.		
RO97TC	1c	blue	300.		
RO99TC	1c	black	175.		
RO99TC	1c	blue	500.		
RO100TC	1c	blue	500.		
RO101TC	3c	black	175.		
RO101TC	3c	green	300.		
RO101TC	3c	orange		75.	
RO102TC	5c	black	175.		
RO102TC	5c	blue	500.		
RO102TC	5c	green	500.		
RO103TC	1c	blue	225.		
RO103TC	1c	rose	300.		
RO105TC	1c	blue	300.		
RO105TC	1c	green	500.		
RO106TC	1c	black	175.		
RO106TC	1c	blue	225.		
RO107TC	1c	black	175.		
RO107TC	1c	green	300.		
RO110TC	1c	black	175.		
RO110TC	1c	blue	175.		
RO110TC	1c	orange	500.		
RO110TC	1c	red	225.		
RO112TC	1c	black	175.		
RO112TC	1c	green	500.		
RO113TC	1c	blue	300.		
RO113TC	1c	green	500.		
RO113TC	1c	orange	500.		
RO114TC	1c	black	750.		
RO115TC	1c	black	175.		
RO115TC	1c	green	500.		
RO116TC	1c	black	225.		
RO116TC	1c	green	300.		
RO118TC	8c	black	225.		
RO118TC	8c	dk bl	500.		
RO118TC	8c	green	500.		
RO119TC	1c	black	225.		
RO119TC	1c	blue	225.		
RO120TC	1c	black	500.		
RO121TC	1c	black	175.		
RO121TC	1c	blue	300.		
RO122TC	1c	blue	300.		
RO122TC	1c	green	500.		
RO123TC	1c	blue	500.		
RO125TC	1c	black	225.		
RO126TC	1c	blue	300.		
RO126TC	1c	green	500.		
RO127TC	1c	black	300.		
RO127TC	1c	green	225.		
RO128TC	1c	black	225.		
RO128TC	1c	green	500.		
RO130TC	1c	black	225.		
RO130TC	1c	green	300.		
RO131TC	1c	black	175.		
RO131TC	1c	green	225.		
RO131TC	1c	red	225.		
RO132TC	1c	black	225.		
RO132TC	1c	green	500.		
RO133TC	1c	blue	500.		
RO133TC	1c	green	300.		
RO134TC	1c	black	300.	150.	
RO134TC	1c	green	300.		
RO135TC	1c	black	500.		
RO135TC	1c	blue	300.		
RO135TC	1c	green	300.		
RO135TC	1c	rose	225.		
RO136TC	1c	black	225.		
RO136TC	1c	green	300.		
RO137TC	1c	black	175.		
RO137TC	1c	blue	175.		
RO137TC	1c	green	500.		
RO138TC	1c	black	175.		
RO138TC	1c	blue	500.		
RO139TC	5c	black	175.		
RO139TC	5c	green	500.		
RO140TC	4c	black	225.		
RO140TC	4c	blue	300.		
RO141TC	1c	black	175.		
RO141TC	1c	dk bl	300.		
RO141TC	1c	green	500.		
RO141TC	1c	yellow green	300.		
RO141TC	1c	green	500.		
RO142TC	1c	black	175.		
RO142TC	1c	blue	225.		
RO143TC	3c	black	175.		
RO143TC	3c	blue	225.		
RO143TC	3c	green	300.		
RO144TC	1c	black	500.		
RO145TC	1c	black	500.		
RO145TC	1c	blue	500.		
RO146TC	1c	blue	500.		
RO146TC	1c	green	300.		
RO148TC	1c	black	175.		
RO148TC	1c	green	300.		
RO148TC	1c	red	300.		
RO152TC	1c	blue	300.		
RO152TC	1c	green	300.		
RO153TC	1c	blue	225.		
RO153TC	1c	brown	300.		
RO153TC	1c	green	225.		
RO153TC	1c	orange	300.		
RO153TC	1c	red	300.		
RO155TC	1c	blue	225.		
RO155TC	1c	green	500.		
RO157TC	3c	black	175.		
RO157TC	3c	green	300.		
RO158TC	1c	blue	300.		
RO158TC	1c	green	500.		
RO159TC	3c	black	225.		
RO159TC	3c	green	500.		
RO160TC	1c	black	225.		
RO160TC	1c	brown	500.		
RO160TC	1c	green	300.		
RO161TC	1c	black	225.		
RO161TC	1c	green	300.		
RO163TC	1c	blue	300.		
RO163TC	1c	green	500.		
RO164TC	1c	black	500.		
RO165TC	12c	black	750.		
RO165TC	12c	green	1000.		
RO165TC	12c	red	1000.		
RO166TC	1c	black	300.		
RO166TC	1c	blue	225.		
RO166TC	1c	green	500.		
RO166TC	1c	red	175.		
RO167TC	3c	black	175.		
RO167TC	3c	green	300.		
RO167TC	3c	red	300.		
RO168TC	1c	black	500.		
RO168TC	1c	green	300.		
RO171TC	1c	blue	300.		
RO171TC	1c	green	300.		
RO172TC	1c	blue	225.		
RO172TC	1c	green	500.		
RO173TC	1c	black	225.		
RO173TC	1c	green	300.		
RO174TC	1c	black	300.		
RO174TC	1c	green	300.		
RO175TC	1c	blue	275.		
RO175TC	1c	green	350.		
RO175TC	1c	red	500.		
RO177TC	1c	black	175.		
RO177TC	1c	blue	225.		
RO177TC	1c	green	500.		
RO178TC	1c	black	175.		
RO178TC	1c	blue	300.		
RO179TC	1c	blue	500.		
RO179TC	1c	green	500.		
RO180TC	1c	blue	225.		
RO180TC	1c	green	500.		
RO181TC	1c	blue	500.		
RO181TC	1c	green	300.		
RO182TC	1c	blue	300.		
RO182TC	1c	green	300.		
RO183TC	1c	blue	650.		
RO183TC	1c	green	650.		
RO184TC	1c	blue	225.		
RO184TC	1c	brown	300.		
RO184TC	1c	green	225.		
RO184TC	1c	orange	300.		
RO184TC	1c	red	300.		
RO186TC	1c	black	175.		

PRIVATE DIE CANNED FRUIT STAMP

RP1TC	1c	black	375.		

PRIVATE DIE MEDICINE STAMPS

			DIE ON INDIA	PLATE	
			(1) Large	(3) India	(4) Card
RS1TC	1c	blue	300.		
RS1TC	1c	green	300.		
RS4TC	1c	green	500.		
RS10TC	4c	black	300.		
RS10TC	4c	green	500.		
RS14TC	4c	black	300.		
RS14TC	4c	blue	300.		
RS16TC	2c	green	500.		
RS21TC	1c	blue	500.		
RS21TC	1c	green	500.		
RS22TC	2c	blue	500.		
RS22TC	2c	green	500.		
RS23TC	4c	green	500.		
RS24TC	1c	blue	500.		
RS24TC	1c	green	500.		
RS25TC	2c	blue	500.		
RS25TC	2c	green	500.		
RS26TC	4c	blue	500.		
RS26TC	4c	green	500.		
RS27TC	4c	blue	225.		
RS27TC	4c	green	500.		
RS28TC	2c	black	225.		
RS28TC	2c	blue	225.		
RS29TC	1c	black	175.		
RS29/RO120TC	2c/1c	black	750.		
RS29TC	2c	blue	175.		
RS29TC	2c	dk bl	500.		
RS29TC	2c	green	500.		
RS29TC	2c	red	300.		
RS30TC	1c	black	175.		
RS30TC	1c	blue	500.		
RS30TC	1c	green	500.		
RS30TC	1c	red	500.		
RS31TC	1c	black	500.		
RS31TC	1c	blue	225.		
RS31TC	1c	red	500.		
RS33TC	1c	blue	175.		
RS33TC	1c	green	225.		
RS33TC	1c	red	500.		
RS34TC	1c	blue	500.		
RS34TC	1c	green	500.		
RS35TC	1c	blue	300.		
RS35TC	1c	green	500.		
RS36TC	1c	black	500.		
RS36TC	1c	dk bl	500.		
RS36TC	1c	green	500.		
RS36TC	1c	ultramarine	500.		
RS36TC	1c	yellow green	225.		
RS38TC	2c	blue	750.		
RS38TC	2c	green	750.		
RS39TC	1c	blue	300.		
RS39TC	1c	green	300.		
RS39TC	1c	orange	500.		
RS40TC	2c	black	225.		
RS40TC	2c	blue	300.		
RS41TC	4c	black	225.		
RS41TC	4c	blue	500.		
RS41TC	4c	green	500.		
RS42TC	1c	green	500.		
RS43TC	4c	black	225.		
RS43TC	4c	green	500.		
RS44TC	1c	green	750.		
RS46TC	4c	blue	225.		
RS46TC	4c	green	300.		
RS47TC	4c	blue	300.		
RS47TC	4c	brown	500.		
RS47TC	4c	green	300.		
RS47TC	4c	orange	500.		
RS47TC	4c	red	500.		
RS49TC	4c	black	225.		
RS49TC	4c	blue	300.		
RS50TC	1c	black	300.		
RS50TC	1c	blue	300.		
RS50TC	1c	green	500.		
RS51TC	2c	blue	500.		
RS51TC	2c	green	500.		
RS52TC	4c	blue	500.		
RS52TC	4c	green	500.		
RS53TC	1c	blue	225.		
RS53TC	1c	brown	300.		
RS53TC	1c	green	225.		
RS53TC	1c	orange	300.		
RS53TC	1c	red	300.		
RS54TC	2c	blue	225.		
RS54TC	2c	brown	300.		
RS54TC	2c	green	225.		
RS54TC	2c	orange	300.		
RS54TC	2c	red	500.		
RS55TC	4c	blue	225.		
RS55TC	4c	green	225.		
RS55TC	4c	orange	225.		
RS55TC	4c	red	500.		
RS56TC	3c	black	350.		
RS56TC	1c	green	500.		
RS57TC	6c	blue	225.		
RS57TC	6c	brown	300.		
RS57TC	6c	green	225.		
RS57TC	6c	orange	300.		
RS57TC	6c	red	300.		
RS58TC	4c	blue	225.		
RS58TC	4c	blue green	500.		
RS58TC	4c	dk bl	500.		
RS58TC	4c	green	225.		
RS58TC	4c	light blue	500.		
RS58TC	4c	red	225.		
RS59TC	1c	blue	300.		
RS59TC	1c	green	500.		
RS60TC	1c	blue	500.		
RS62TC	1c	brown	300.		
RS62TC	1c	green	225.		

			DIE ON INDIA (1) Large	PLATE (3) India	PLATE (4) Card
RS62TC	1c	orange	300.		
RS62TC	1c	red	500.		
RS62TC	1c	vermilion	500.		
RS64TC	2c	blue	225.		
RS64TC	2c	brown	300.		
RS64TC	2c	green	225.		
RS64TC	2c	orange	300.		
RS64TC	2c	red	500.		
RS64TC	1c	vermilion	500.		
RS65TC	4c	blue	500.		
RS65TC	4c	green	500.		
RS66TC	1c	blue	300.		
RS66TC	1c	green	500.		
RS66TC	1c	light green	500.		
RS66TC	1c	orange	500.		
RS66TC	1c	rose red	500.		
RS67TC	1c	green	500.		
RS69TC	1c	blue	500.		
RS69TC	1c	green	500.		
RS70TC	2c	blue	500.		
RS70TC	2c	green	500.		
RS71TC	1c	blue	500.		
RS71TC	1c	green	500.		
RS72TC	2c	blue	500.		
RS72TC	2c	green	500.		
RS73TC	2c	black	500.		
RS73TC	2c	blue	750.		
RS73TC	2c	red	1000.		
RS74TC	1c	blue	500.		
RS74TC	1c	green	500.		
RS74hTC	1c	blue	500.		
RS74hTC	1c	green	500.		
RS75TC	1c	black	300.		
RS75TC	1c	green	500.		
RS76TC	2c	blue	300.		
RS76TC	2c	green	300.		
RS81TC	4c	black	225.		
RS81TC	4c	blue	500.		
RS81TC	4c	green	500.		
RS83TC	4c	blue	500.		
RS83TC	4c	green	500.		
RS84TC	1c	black	250.		
RS84TC	1c	blue	350.		
RS84TC	1c	green	250.		
RS84TC	1c	orange	650.		
RS84TC	1c	red	650.		
RS84TC	1c	slate	650.		
RS85TC	4c	blue	275.		
RS85TC	4c	brown	275.		
RS85TC	4c	green	300.		
RS85TC	4c	orange	375.		
RS86TC	1c	black	225.		
RS86TC	1c	blue	225.		
RS88TC	1c	blue	500.		
RS88TC	1c	green	500.		
RS89TC	1c	green	300.		
RS91TC	4c	blue	225.		
RS91TC	4c	green	500.		
RS92TC	3c	blue	225.		
RS92TC	3c	brown	300.		
RS92TC	3c	green	225.		
RS92TC	3c	orange	300.		
RS92TC	3c	red	500.		
RS92TC	3c	vermilion	500.		
RS94TC	4c	blue	500.		
RS94TC	4c	green	500.		
RS95TC	1c	black	300.		
RS95TC	1c	blue	225.		
RS95TC	1c	dk bl	90.		
RS96TC	3c	blue	225.		
RS96TC	3c	green	500.		
RS97TC	1c	blue	300.		
RS97TC	1c	green	500.		
RS98TC	1c	blue	225.		
RS98TC	1c	green	175.		
RS98TC	1c	red	500.		
RS99TC	4c	blue	500.		
RS100TC	6c	green	500.		
RS101TC	1c	blue	500.		
RS101TC	1c	green	500.		
RS102TC	2c	black	175.		
RS102TC	2c	green	225.		
RS102TC	2c	rose	225.		
RS103TC	4c	blue	500.		
RS103TC	4c	green	500.		
RS106TC	2c	black	500.		
RS106TC	2c	green	300.		
RS107/109TC	3c/6c	green	1250.		
RS107TC	3c	blue	300.		
RS108TC	4c	blue	300.		
RS108TC	4c	green	500.		
RS109TC	6c	blue	300.		
RS110TC	2c	black	300.		
RS110TC	2c	green	300.		
RS111TC	4c	blue	300.		
RS111TC	4c	green	500.		
RS114TC	1c	green	300.		
RS116TC	4c	black	225.		
RS116TC	4c	blue	300.		
RS116TC	4c	brown	500.		
RS116TC	4c	green	500.		
RS116TC	4c	vermilion	500.		
RS117TC	1c	blue	350.		
RS117TC	1c	green	750.		
RS118TC	1c	black	175.		
RS118TC	1c	blue	225.		
RS118TC	1c	brn red	300.		
RS118TC	1c	green	300.		
RS120TC	2c	blue	225.		
RS120TC	2c	brown	300.		
RS120TC	2c	green	225.		
RS120TC	2c	orange	300.		

			DIE ON INDIA (1) Large	PLATE (3) India	PLATE (4) Card
RS120TC	2c	red	500.		
RS120TC	2c	vermilion	500.		
RS121TC	3c	blue	500.		
RS121TC	3c	green	500.		
RS122TC	2c	blue	500.		
RS122TC	2c	green	500.		
RS123TC	4c	blue	225.		
RS123TC	4c	brown	300.		
RS123TC	4c	green	225.		
RS123TC	4c	orange	300.		
RS123TC	4c	red	500.		
RS123TC	4c	vermilion	500.		
RS124TC	1c	black	175.		
RS124TC	1c	blue green	300.		
RS124TC	1c	green	500.		
RS124TC	1c	orange	500.		
RS124TC	1c	red	225.		
RS126TC	1c	black	225.		
RS126TC	1c	blue	225.		
RS126TC	1c	brown	300.		
RS126TC	1c	orange	300.		
RS126TC	1c	red	500.		
RS126TC	1c	vermilion	500.		
RS127TC	4c	black	225.		
RS127TC	4c	blue	225.		
RS127TC	4c	brown	225.		
RS127TC	4c	orange	300.		
RS127TC	4c	red	500.		
RS127TC	4c	vermilion	500.		
RS128TC	2c	black	600.		
RS128TC	2c	green	400.		
RS128TC	2c	pale blue	500.		
RS130TC	4c	black	275.		
RS130TC	4c	blue	350.		
RS131TC	4c	blue	225.		
RS131TC	4c	brown	500.		
RS131TC	4c	green	300.		
RS131TC	4c	orange	300.		
RS131TC	4c	red	500.		
RS131TC	4c	vermilion	500.		
RS132TC	4c	blue	500.		
RS132TC	4c	orange	500.		
RS133TC	6c	blue	500.		
RS133TC	6c	green	500.		
RS134TC	4c	black	300.		
RS134TC	4c	green	300.		
RS134TC	4c	red	500.		
RS138TC	1c	blue	300.		
RS138TC	1c	green	500.		
RS138TC	1c	red	500.		
RS138TC	1c	yel grn	500.		
RS139TC	2c	black	225.		
RS139TC	2c	blackish violet			90.
RS139TC	2c	blue	500.		
RS139TC	2c	green	500.		
RS139TC	2c	red	225.		
RS139TC	2c	rose	500.		
RS141TC	4c	black	225.		
RS141TC	4c	blue	300.		
RS142TC	1c	blue	225.		
RS142TC	1c	brown	300.		
RS142TC	1c	green	225.		
RS142TC	1c	orange	300.		
RS142TC	1c	red	500.		
RS142TC	1c	vermilion	500.		
RS143TC	4c	black	225.		
RS143TC	4c	blue	225.		
RS144TC	1c	black	500.		
RS144TC	1c	green	500.		
RS145TC	2c	blue	500.		
RS146TC	4c	black	300.		
RS146TC	4c	blue	300.		
RS150TC	1c	black	300.		
RS150TC	1c	blue	175.		
RS150TC	1c	carmine	500.		
RS150TC	1c	green	225.		
RS151TC	1c	blue	500.		
RS151TC	1c	green	500.		
RS152TC	2c	black	175.		
RS152TC	2c	blue	300.		
RS153TC	4c	blue	750.		
RS153TC	4c	green	750.		
RS154TC	4c	black	500.		
RS155TC	2c	black	300.		
RS155TC	2c	black	300.		
RS155TC	2c	blue	225.		
RS155TC	2c	red	500.		
RS156TC	6c	blue	225.		
RS156TC	6c	green	225.		
RS156TC	6c	red	225.		
RS157TC	2c	blue	225.		
RS157TC	2c	green	225.		
RS157TC	2c	red	500.		
RS157TC	2c	vermilion	300.		
RS158TC	1c	black	500.		
RS159TC	4c	black	375.		
RS160TC	6c	blue	300.		
RS160TC	6c	green	500.		
RS161TC	4c	blue	500.		
RS161TC	4c	green	750.		
RS162TC	1c	black	175.		
RS162TC	1c	green	300.		
RS162TC	1c	red	500.		
RS163TC	4c	black	300.		
RS163TC	4c	green	600.		
RS163TC	4c	yellow green	600.		
RS164TC	1c	blue	225.		
RS164TC	1c	green	500.		
RS165TC	4c	black	175.		
RS165TC	4c	blue	225.		
RS166TC	1c	blue	300.		

			DIE ON INDIA (1) Large	PLATE (3) India	PLATE (4) Card
RS166TC	1c	green	500.		
RS169TC	4c	blue	225.		
RS169TC	4c	green	500.		
RS169TC	4c	red	225.		
RS170TC	1c	blue	300.		
RS170TC	1c	green	500.		
RS171TC	1c	black	225.		
RS171TC	1c	blue	225.		
RS171TC	1c	brown	300.		
RS171TC	1c	dull blue	500.		
RS171TC	1c	green	225.		
RS171TC	1c	orange	300.		
RS171TC	1c	red	500.		
RS171TC	1c	vermilion	500.		
RS172TC	2c	blue	225.		
RS172TC	2c	brown	300.		
RS172TC	2c	green	225.		
RS172TC	2c	orange	225.		
RS172TC	2c	red	500.		
RS172TC	2c	vermilion	500.		
RS173TC	1c	black	225.		
RS173TC	1c	green	225.		
RS173TC	1c	red	300.		
RS174TC	1c	black	300.		
RS174TC	1c	dk bl	500.		
RS174TC	1c	green	300.		
RS175TC	2c	black	250.		
RS175TC	2c	blue	500.		
RS175TC	2c	green	500.		
RS176TC	4c	blue	375.		
RS176TC	4c	green	500.		
RS177TC	2c	blue	750.		
RS177TC	2c	green	1000.		
RS178TC	6c	blue	300.		
RS178TC	6c	green	500.		
RS179TC	2c	black	300.		
RS179TC	2c	blue	375.		
RS180TC	3c	blue	300.		
RS180TC	3c	green	300.		
RS181TC	4c	blue	225.		
RS181TC	4c	green	500.		
RS182TC	4c	blue	225.		
RS182TC	4c	green	225.		
RS182TC	4c	rose	300.		
RS183TC	1c	black	500.		
RS183TC	1c	blue	300.		
RS183TC	1c	green	500.		
RS183TC	1c	red	225.		
RS184TC	2c	blue	300.		
RS184TC	2c	brown	225.		
RS184TC	2c	green	225.		
RS184TC	2c	orange	300.		
RS184TC	2c	vermilion	300.		
RS185TC	1c	blue	300.		
RS186TC	4c	blue	225.		
RS186TC	4c	green	500.		
RS187TC	4c	blue	225.		
RS187TC	4c	brown	300.		
RS187TC	4c	green	300.		
RS187TC	4c	orange	500.		
RS187TC	4c	red	500.		
RS187TC	4c	vermilion	500.		
RS188TC	1c	blue	500.		
RS188TC	1c	green	500.		
RS189TC	1c	black	175.		
RS189TC	1c	blue	225.		
RS189TC	1c	red	225.		
RS190TC	2c	blue	500.		
RS190TC	2c	green	500.		
RS191TC	4c	blue	400.		
RS191TC	4c	green	400.		
RS192TC	6c	blue	400.		
RS192TC	6c	green	400.		
RS192TC	6c	rose	500.		
RS193TC	2c	blue	500.		
RS193TC	2c	green	500.		
RS194TC	1c	green	175.		
RS195TC	2c	blue	500.		
RS195TC	2c	green	500.		
RS196TC	1c	black	500.		
RS196TC	1c	green	225.		
RS197TC	2c	blue	300.		
RS198TC	1c	green	300.		
RS198TC	1c	red	500.		
RS199TC	2c	blue	225.		
RS199TC	2c	green	500.		
RS204TC	2c	blue	500.		
RS204TC	2c	green	500.		
RS205TC	4c	blue	225.		
RS205TC	4c	green	500.		
RS208TC	1c	black	225.		
RS208TC	1c	blue	225.		
RS208TC	1c	orange	300.		
RS209TC	2c	black	500.		
RS209TC	2c	blue	500.		
RS210TC	4c	blue	225.		
RS210TC	4c	green	225.		
RS210TC	4c	red	225.		
RS212TC	1c	black	225.		
RS212TC	1c	blue	300.		
RS212TC	1c	green	500.		
RS213TC	6c	blue	500.		
RS213TC	6c	green	500.		
RS214TC	4c	blue	300.		
RS214TC	4c	brown	300.		
RS214TC	4c	green	225.		
RS214TC	4c	orange	300.		
RS214TC	4c	red	500.		
RS214TC	4c	vermilion	500.		
RS215TC	1c	black	300.		
RS215TC	1c	blue	450.		
RS215TC	1c	dark red	500.		
RS215TC	1c	green	500.		

			DIE ON INDIA	PLATE	
			(1) Large	*(3)* India	*(4)* Card
RS216TC	1c	blue	500.		
RS216TC	1c	green	500.		
RS220TC	1c	blue	300.		
RS221TC	4c	black	175.		
RS221TC	4c	blue	225.		
RS222TC	8c	green	500.		
RS223TC	1c	blue	300.		
RS223TC	1c	brown	300.		
RS223TC	1c	green	225.		
RS223TC	1c	orange	300.		
RS223TC	1c	vermilion	300.		
RS224TC	1c	blue	500.		
RS224TC	1c	brown	300.		
RS224TC	1c	green	225.		
RS224TC	1c	orange	300.		
RS224TC	1c	red	500.		
RS225TC	4c	blue	500.		
RS225TC	4c	green	500.		
RS226TC	1c	black	350.		
RS228TC	1c	black	175.		
RS228TC	1c	blue	225.		
RS228TC	1c	brown	500.		
RS228TC	1c	green	225.		
RS228TC	1c	orange	500.		
RS228TC	1c	red	500.		
RS228TC	1c	vermilion	500.		
RS229TC	2c	black	225.		
RS229TC	2c	blue	225.		
RS229TC	2c	brown	300.		
RS229TC	2c	green	225.		
RS229TC	2c	orange	225.		
RS229TC	2c	red	300.		
RS229TC	2c	vermilion	500.		
RS230TC	6c	blue	225.		
RS230TC	6c	brown	300.		
RS230TC	6c	green	225.		
RS230TC	6c	orange	300.		
RS230TC	6c	vermilion	225.		
RS231TC	6c	black	1000.		
RS231TC	6c	blue	1000.		
RS231TC	6c	green	1000.		
RS231TC	6c	red	750.		
RS236TC	4c	blue	500.		
RS239TC	2c	black	225.		
RS239TC	2c	blue	300.		
RS239TC	2c	brown	500.		
RS239TC	2c	green	225.		
RS239TC	2c	orange	300.		
RS239TC	2c	vermilion	500.		
RS240TC	4c	red	500.		
RS240TC	4c	blue	175.		
RS240TC	4c	blue green	500.		
RS240TC	4c	brown	500.		
RS240TC	4c	green	225.		
RS240TC	4c	orange	225.		
RS240TC	4c	vermilion	225.		
RS241TC	4c	green	500.		
RS242TC	1c	blue	225.		
RS242TC	1c	green	500.		
RS243TC	4c	blue	500.		
RS243TC	4c	green	500.		
RS244TC	6c	blue	500.		
RS244TC	6c	green	500.		
RS245TC	1c	blue	500.		
RS250TC	6c	blue	500.		
RS250TC	6c	green	500.		
RS251TC	1c	blue	225.		
RS251TC	1c	brown	225.		
RS251TC	1c	green	225.		
RS252TC	1c	black	225.		
RS252TC	1c	blue	225.		
RS252TC	1c	brown	300.		
RS252TC	1c	green	225.		
RS252TC	1c	orange	500.		
RS252TC	1c	red	500.		
RS252TC	1c	rose	225.		
RS253TC	4c	blue	500.		
RS253TC	4c	green	500.		
RS258TC	6c	black	500.		
RS259TC	1c	blue	225.		
RS259TC	1c	brown	300.		
RS259TC	1c	green	225.		
RS259TC	1c	orange	300.		
RS259TC	1c	red	500.		
RS259TC	1c	vermilion	500.		
RS260TC	2c	blue	175.		
RS260TC	2c	brown	300.		
RS260TC	2c	green	225.		
RS260TC	2c	orange	300.		
RS260TC	2c	red	500.		
RS260TC	2c	rose	500.		
RS260TC	2c	vermilion	225.		
RS261TC	4c	blue	225.		
RS261TC	4c	brown	300.		
RS261TC	4c	green	225.		
RS261TC	4c	orange	300.		
RS261TC	4c	red	500.		
RS261TC	4c	vermilion	500.		
RS262TC	2c	blue	500.		
RS262TC	2c	green	500.		
RS264TC	4c	blue	300.		
RS264TC	4c	green	300.		
RS265TC	1c	black	225.		
RS265TC	1c	blue	500.		
RS267TC	4c	black	225.		
RS267TC	4c	blue	500.		
RS267TC	4c	green	300.		
RS270TC	12c	black	300.		
RS270TC	12c	blue green	500.		
RS270TC	12c	green	300.		
RS270TC	12c	red	225.		
RS271TC	4c	blue	2500.		
RS272TC	1c	black	300.		
RS272TC	1c	blue	300.		
RS273TC	2c	blue	500.		
RS274TC	1c	black	225.		
RS274TC	2c	blue	300.		
RS276TC	2c	black	225.		
RS276TC	2c	blue	300.		
RS278TC	2½c	black	*1,000.*		
RS280TC	¼c	black	*1,000.*		
RS302TC	2½c	black	*1,000.*		
RS303TC	⅝c	black	*1,000.*		

PRIVATE DIE PERFUMERY STAMPS

			DIE ON INDIA	PLATE	
			(1) Large	*(3)* India	*(4)* Card
RT2TC	1c	brown	500.		
RT2TC	1c	green	400.		
RT2TC	1c	orange	300.		
RT2TC	1c	red	500.		
RT5TC	2c	black	175.		
RT5TC	2c	blue	225.		
RT5TC	2c	green	500.		
RT5TC	2c	orange	500.	125.	
RT6TC	1c	blue	375.		
RT6TC	1c	brown	500.		
RT6TC	1c	green	375.		
RT6TC	1c	orange	500.		
RT6TC	1c	red	500.		
RT10TC	4c	blue	375.		
RT10TC	4c	brown	500.		
RT10TC	4c	green	400.		
RT10TC	4c	orange	500.		
RT10TC	4c	red	500.		
RT12TC	1c	black	225.		90.
RT12TC	1c	blue	225.		
RT12TC	1c	green	500.		
RT13TC	2c	black	225.	75.	
RT13TC	2c	blue	300.		
RT13TC	2c	green	300.		
RT13TC	2c	red	225.		
RT14TC	3c	blue	1000.		
RT16TC	1c	blue	175.		
RT16TC	1c	green	225.		
RT17TC	2c	black	300.		
RT17TC	2c	blue	300.		
RT17TC	2c	green	300.		
RT17TC	2c	orange	500.		
RT18TC	3c	black	175.		
RT18TC	3c	blue	175.		
RT18TC	3c	green	500.		
RT18TC	3c	orange	500.		
RT18TC	3c	red	300.		
RT19TC	1c	black	500.		
RT20TC	1c	black	225.		
RT20TC	1c	blue	300.		
RT20TC	1c	green	175.		
RT21TC	2c	black	500.		
RT21TC	2c	green	500.		
RT22TC	1c	black	175.		
RT22TC	1c	blue	300.		
RT22TC	1c	green	300.		
RT22TC	1c	red brn	300.		
RT22TC	1c	ultramarine	500.		
RT23TC	2c	blue	225.		
RT23TC	2c	green	500.		
RT24TC	3c	black	175.		
RT24TC	3c	blue	225.		
RT24TC	3c	green	300.		
RT24TC	3c	red	225.		
RT25TC	4c	black	175.		
RT25TC	4c	blue	225.		
RT26TC	1c	black	175.		
RT26TC	1c	blue	225.		
RT26TC	1c	brown	300.		
RT26TC	1c	green	500.		
RT26TC	1c	orange	300.		
RT26TC	1c	red	500.		
RT28TC	2c	black	225.		
RT28TC	2c	brown	300.		
RT28TC	2c	green	225.		
RT28TC	2c	orange	300.		
RT28TC	2c	red	300.		
RT30TC	3c	black	225.		
RT30TC	3c	blue	225.		
RT30TC	3c	brown	300.		
RT30TC	3c	green	225.		
RT30TC	3c	orange	300.		
RT30TC	3c	red	175.		
RT32TC	4c	black	225.		
RT32TC	4c	blue	225.		
RT32TC	4c	brown	500.		
RT32TC	4c	green	225.		
RT32TC	4c	orange	225.		
RT32TC	4c	red	300.		

PRIVATE DIE PLAYING CARD STAMPS

			DIE ON INDIA	PLATE	
			(1) Large	*(3)* India	*(4)* Card
RU2TC	2c	black	175.		
RU2TC	2c	blue	225.		
RU2TC	2c	green	300.		
RU3TC	4c	blue	225.		
RU3TC	4c	green	225.		
RU4TC	5c	black	225.		
RU4TC	5c	green	300.		
RU5TC	5c	black	225.		
RU5TC	5c	brown	300.		
RU5TC	5c	green	300.		
RU5TC	5c	light brn	500.		
RU5TC	5c	orange	500.		
RU5TC	5c	red	500.		
RU6TC	10c	black	175.		
RU6TC	10c	green	300.		
RU7TC	5c	blue	375.		
RU7TC	5c	green	375.		
RU8TC	5c	blue	225.		
RU8TC	5c	green	225.		
RU8TC	5c	orange	300.		
RU9TC	5c	blue	225.		
RU9TC	5c	green	500.		
RU10TC	2c	black	175.		
RU10TC	2c	brown	500.		
RU10TC	2c	green	500.		
RU11TC	5c	black	225.		
RU11TC	5c	blue	225.		
RU11TC	5c	brown	300.		
RU12TC	5c	blue	300.		
RU12TC	5c	green	300.		
RU13TC	5c	green	175.		
RU14TC	5c	blue	225.		
RU14TC	5c	brown	300.		
RU14TC	5c	green	300.		
RU14TC	5c	light brn	500.		
RU14TC	5c	orange	500.		
RU14TC	5c	red	300.		
RU15TC	5c	blue	300.		
RU15TC	5c	green	300.		

HUNTING PERMIT

			DIE ON INDIA
			(1) Large
RW4TC	$1	light violet	*5,500.*

SPECIMEN STAMPS

These are regular stamps overprinted "Specimen." Each number has a suffix letter "S" to denote "specimen." The Scott number is that of the stamp as shown in the regular listings and the second letter "A," etc., indicates the type of overprint. Values are for items of a grade of fine-very fine, with at least part original gum.

Specimen
Type A; 12mm long

Specimen.
Type B; 15mm long

Specimen.
Type C; 30mm long

SPECIMEN
Type D; Capital Letters

Specimen.
Type E; Initial Capital

Specimen.
Type F; 22mm long

SPECIMEN
Type G; 14mm long

SPECIMEN
Type H; 16mm long

Specimen
Type I; 20mm long

Specimen
Overprinted in Black

1851-56

7S	A	1c **blue,** type II	*2,500.*
11S	A	3c **dull red,** type I	*2,500.*

1857-60

21S	A	1c **blue,** type III	*1,500.*
24S	A	1c **blue,** type V	*1,000.*
26S	A	3c **dull red,** type II	*1,000.*
30S	A	5c **orange brown,** type II	*1,000.*
35S	A	10c **green,** type V	*1,250.*
36bS	A	12c **black**	*1,000.*
37S	A	24c **lilac**	*1,000.*
38S	A	30c **orange**	*1,000.*
26S	F	3c **dull red,** type II	*2,000.*
26S	I	3c **dull red,** type II	*4,000.*

1861

63S	A	1c **blue**	750.
65S	A	3c **rose**	750.
68S	A	10c **dark green**	750.
70S	A	24c **red lilac**	750.
72S	A	90c **blue**	750.
73S	A	2c **black**	*1,750.*
76S	A	5c **brown**	750.

Specimen.

Overprint Black, Except As Noted

1861-66

63S	B	1c **blue** *(1300)*	120.
		P# block of 8, Impt.	*1,750.*
		Without period	—
65S	B	3c **rose** *(1500)*	120.
68S	B	10c **dark green** *(1600)*	120.
		P# block of 8, Impt.	—
69S	B	12c **black** (orange) *(1300)*	120.
71S	B	30c **orange** *(1400)*	120.
		P# block of 8, Impt.	—
72S	B	90c **blue** *(1394)*	120.
		P# block of 8, Impt.	—
73S	B	2c **black** (vermilion) *(1306)*	250.
		Block of 4	*1,100.*
		Without period	*500.*
		Block of 4, one stamp without period	*1,500.*
76S	B	5c **brown** *(1306)*	120.
		P# block of 8, Impt.	—
77S	B	15c **black** (vermilion) *(1208)*	200.
		Block of 4	*900.*
78S	B	24c **lilac** *(1300)*	200.

1867-68

86S	A	1c **blue**	*1,000.*
85ES	A	12c **black**	*1,000.*
93S	A	2c **black**	*1,100.*
94S	A	3c **rose**	*1,000.*
95S	A	5c **brown**	*1,100.*
97S	A	12c **black**	—
98S	A	15c **black**	*1,000.*
99S	A	24c **gray lilac**	*1,250.*
		Split grill	—
100S	A	30c **orange**	*1,250.*

1869

112S	A	1c **buff**	*1,750.*
113S	A	2c **brown**	*1,250.*
115S	A	6c **ultramarine**	*1,250.*
116S	A	10c **yellow**	*1,250.*
117S	A	12c **green**	*1,250.*
119S	A	15c **brown & blue**	*1,500.*
120S	A	24c **green & violet**	*1,750.*
	a.	Without grill	—
121S	A	30c **blue & carmine**	*1,750.*
	a.	Without grill	—
122S	A	90c **carmine & black**	*2,000.*
	a.	Without grill	—
125S	B	3c **blue** (blue)	*3,500.*
126S	B	6c **blue** (blue)	*3,500.*
127S	B	10c **yellow** (blue)	—

1870-71

145S	A	1c **ultramarine**	*600.*
146S	A	2c **red brown**	*600.*
146S	B	2c **red brown**	*600.*
147S	A	3c **green**	*600.*
148S	A	6c **carmine**	*600.*
149S	A	7c **vermilion**	*600.*
150S	A	10c **brown**	*600.*
151S	A	12c **dull violet**	*600.*
152S	A	15c **bright orange**	*600.*
155S	A	90c **carmine**	*600.*
155S	B	90c **carmine** (blue)	*600.*

1873

158S	B	3c **green** (blue)	*750.*
159S	B	6c **dull pink**	*700.*
160S	B	7c **orange vermilion** (blue)	*700.*
162S	B	12c **blackish violet** (blue)	—
165S	B	30c **greenish black** (blue)	*700.*
166S	B	90c **carmine** (blue)	*750.*

SPECIMEN
Overprinted in Red

1879

Type D

189S	D	15c **red orange**	80.
190S	D	30c **full black**	80.
191S	D	90c **carmine**	80.
	a.	Overprint in black brown	80.

1881-82

205S	D	5c **yellow brown**	80.
206S	D	1c **gray blue**	80.
207S	D	3c **blue green**	80.
208S	D	6c **brown red**	80.
209S	D	10c **brown**	80.

1883

210S	D	2c **red brown**	100.
211S	D	4c **blue green**	100.

Specimen.
Handstamped in Dull Purple

1890-93

Type E

219S	E	1c **dull blue**	150.
220S	E	2c **carmine**	150.
221S	E	3c **purple**	150.
222S	E	4c **dark brown**	150.
223S	E	5c **chocolate**	150.
224S	E	6c **dull red**	150.
225S	E	8c **lilac**	150.
226S	E	10c **green**	150.
227S	E	15c **blue**	150.
228S	E	30c **black**	150.
229S	E	90c **orange**	175.

COLUMBIAN ISSUE

1893

230S	E	1c **deep blue**	400.
		Double overprint	—
231S	E	2c **violet**	400.
232S	E	3c **green**	400.
233S	E	4c **ultramarine**	400.
234S	E	5c **chocolate**	400.
235S	E	6c **purple**	400.
236S	E	8c **magenta**	400.
237S	E	10c **black brown**	400.
238S	E	15c **dark green**	400.
239S	E	30c **orange brown**	400.
240S	E	50c **slate blue**	400.
241S	E	$1 **salmon**	500.
242S	E	$2 **brown red**	500.
243S	E	$3 **yellow green**	550.
244S	E	$4 **crimson lake**	575.
245S	E	$5 **black**	675.

Specimen.
Overprinted in Magenta

Type F

230S	F	1c **deep blue**	550.
232S	F	3c **green**	550.
233S	F	4c **ultramarine**	550.
234S	F	5c **chocolate**	550.
235S	F	6c **purple**	550.
237S	F	10c **black brown**	550.
243S	F	$3 **yellow green**	700.

Overprinted Type H in Black or Red

231S	H	2c **violet** (Bk)	625.
233S	H	4c **ultramarine** (R)	625.
234S	H	5c **chocolate** (R)	625.

Overprinted Type I in Black or Red

231S	I	2c **violet** (R)	625.
232S	I	3c **green** (R)	625.
233S	I	4c **ultramarine** (R)	625.
234S	I	5c **chocolate** (Bk)	625.
235S	I	6c **purple** (R)	625.
236S	I	8c **magenta** (Bk)	625.
237S	I	10c **black brown** (R)	625.
238S	I	15c **dark green** (R)	625.
239S	I	30c **orange brown** (Bk)	625.
240S	I	50c **slate blue** (R)	625.

1895

Handstamped Type E in Purple

264S	E	1c **blue**	90.
267S	E	2c **carmine,** type III	90.
267aS	E	2c **pink,** type III	90.
268S	E	3c **purple**	90.
269S	E	4c **dark brown**	100.
270S	E	5c **chocolate**	90.
271S	E	6c **dull brown**	90.
272S	E	8c **violet brown**	90.
273S	E	10c **dark green**	90.
274S	E	15c **dark blue**	90.
275S	E	50c **orange**	90.
276S	E	$1 **black,** type I	325.
276AS	E	$1 **black,** type II	*2,000.*
277S	E	$2 **dark blue**	300.
278S	E	$5 **dark green**	400.

1897-1903

279S	E	1c **deep green**	90.
279BS	E	2c **light red,** type IV	90.
279BeS	E	2c Booklet pane of 6, **light red,** type IV (Bk)	525.
		Never hinged	750.
		With plate number	1,100.
		Never hinged	1,500.
	a.	As No. 279BeS, inverted overprint	—
	b.	As No. 279BeS, double impression of overprint on bottom two stamps	—
280S	E	4c **rose brown**	160.
281S	E	5c **dark blue**	80.
282S	E	6c **lake**	80.
282CS	E	10c **brown,** type I	80.
283S	E	10c **brown,** type II	—
284S	E	15c **olive green**	80.

Special Printing

In March 1900 one pane of 100 stamps of each of Nos. 279, 279B, 268, 280-282, 272, 282C, 284 and 275-278 were specially handstamped type E "Specimen" in black for displays at the Paris Exposition (1900) and Pan American Exposition (1901). The 2c pane was light red, type IV.

These examples were handstamped by H. G. Mandel and mounted by him in separate displays for the two Expositions. Examples from the panes in addition to those displayed were handstamped "Specimen," but most were destroyed after the Expositions. Examples of all issues that were handstamped are known.

Additional copies, not from the mounted display panes, do exist with a black "Specimen" handstamp, but it is believed Mandel applied such handstamps to regularly issued stamps from his personal collection. These include Nos. 267, 267a and 279B in pale red.

TRANS-MISSISSIPPI ISSUE

1898

Type F

285S	F	1c **dark yellow green**	250.

Type E

285S	E	1c **dark yellow green**	250.
286S	E	2c **copper red**	250.
287S	E	4c **orange**	250.
288S	E	5c **dull blue**	250.
289S	E	8c **violet brown**	250.
290S	E	10c **gray violet**	250.
291S	E	50c **sage green**	300.
292S	E	$1 **black**	600.
293S	E	$2 **orange brown**	750.

PAN-AMERICAN ISSUE

1901

294S	E	1c **green & black**	235.
295S	E	2c **carmine**	235.
296S	E	4c **chocolate & black**	235.
a.		Center inverted	*6,500.*
297S	E	5c **ultramarine & black**	235.
298S	E	8c **brown violet & black**	235.
299S	E	10c **yellow brown & black**	235.

1902

300S	E	1c **blue green**	90.
301S	E	2c **carmine**	90.
302S	E	3c **bright violet**	90.
303S	E	4c **brown**	90.
304S	E	5c **blue**	90.
305S	E	6c **claret**	90.
306S	E	8c **violet black**	90.
307S	E	10c **pale red brown**	90.
308S	E	13c **purple black**	90.
309S	E	15c **olive green**	90.
310S	E	50c **orange**	90.
311S	E	$1 **black**	200.
312S	E	$2 **dark blue**	300.
313S	E	$5 **dark green**	400.

1903

319S	E	2c **carmine**	110.

LOUISIANA PURCHASE ISSUE

1904

323S	E	1c **green**	350.
324S	E	2c **carmine**	350.
325S	E	3c **violet**	350.
326S	E	5c **dark blue**	350.
327S	E	10c **red brown**	350.

SPECIAL DELIVERY STAMPS

Overprinted in Red SPECIMEN

1885

Type D

E1S	D	10c **blue**	140.

Handstamped in Dull Purple Specimen.

1888

Type E

E2S	E	10c **blue**	150.

1893

E3S	E	10c **orange**	200.

1894

E4S	E	10c **blue**	300.

1895

E5S	E	10c **blue**	175.

1902

E6S	E	10c **ultramarine**	175.

POSTAGE DUE STAMPS

Overprinted in Red SPECIMEN

1879

Type D

J1S	D	1c **brown**	250.00
J2S	D	2c **brown**	250.00
J3S	D	3c **brown**	250.00
J4S	D	5c **brown**	250.00

1884

J15S	D	1c **red brown**	45.00
J16S	D	2c **red brown**	45.00
J17S	D	3c **red brown**	45.00
J18S	D	5c **red brown**	45.00
J19S	D	10c **red brown**	45.00
J20S	D	30c **red brown**	45.00
J21S	D	50c **red brown**	45.00

Handstamped in Dull Purple Specimen.

1895

Type E

J38S	E	1c **deep claret**	85.00
J39S	E	2c **deep claret**	85.00
J40S	E	3c **deep claret**	85.00
J41S	E	5c **deep claret**	85.00
J42S	E	10c **deep claret**	85.00
J43S	E	30c **deep claret**	85.00
J44S	E	50c **deep claret**	85.00

OFFICIAL STAMPS

Special printings of Official stamps were made in 1875 at the time the other Reprints, Re-issues and Special Printings were printed. The Official stamps reprints received specimen overprints, but philatelists believe they most properly should be considered to be part of the special printings. See Official section after No. O120.

NEWSPAPER STAMPS

Overprinted in Red Specimen.

1865-75

Type C - Overprint 30mm Long

PR5S	C	5c **dark blue**	300.00
a.		Triple overprint	900.00
PR2S	C	10c **blue green**	400.00
PR3S	C	25c **carmine red**	400.00

Handstamped in Black Specimen

1875

Type A

PR9S	A	2c **black**	300.00
PR11S	A	4c **black**	300.00
PR12S	A	6c **black**	300.00
PR16S	A	12c **rose**	300.00

Overprinted in Black, except as noted Specimen.

1875

Type B

Overprint 15mm Long

PR9S	B	2c **black**	45.00
PR10S	B	3c **black**	45.00
PR11S	B	4c **black**	45.00
PR12S	B	6c **black**	45.00
PR13S	B	8c **black**	45.00
PR14S	B	9c **black**	45.00
a.		Overprint in blue	—
PR15S	B	10c **black**	45.00
PR16S	B	12c **rose**	45.00
PR17S	B	24c **rose**	45.00
PR18S	B	36c **rose**	45.00
PR19S	B	48c **rose**	45.00
a.		Overprint in blue	62.50
PR20S	B	60c **rose**	45.00
PR21S	B	72c **rose**	45.00
a.		Overprint in blue	62.50
PR22S	B	84c **rose**	45.00
a.		Overprint in blue	—
PR23S	B	96c **rose**	45.00
a.		Overprint in blue	—
PR24S	B	$1.92 dark brown	45.00
PR25S	B	$3 **vermilion**	45.00
a.		Overprint in blue	62.50
PR26S	B	$6 **ultramarine**	45.00
a.		Overprint in blue	250.00
PR27S	B	$9 **yellow**	45.00
a.		Overprint in blue	250.00
PR28S	B	$12 **dark green**	45.00
a.		Overprint in blue	250.00
PR29S	B	$24 **dark gray violet**	45.00
a.		Overprint in blue	60.00
PR30S	B	$36 **brown rose**	62.00
PR31S	B	$48 **red brown**	62.00
PR32S	B	$60 **violet**	62.00

Overprinted in Red SPECIMEN

1875

Type D

PR14S	D	9c **black**	30.00

1879

PR57S	D	2c **black**	25.00
PR58S	D	3c **black**	25.00
PR59S	D	4c **black**	25.00
PR60S	D	6c **black**	25.00
PR61S	D	8c **black**	25.00
PR62S	D	10c **black**	25.00
a.		Double overprint	1,200.
PR63S	D	12c **red**	25.00
PR64S	D	24c **red**	25.00
PR65S	D	36c **red**	25.00
PR66S	D	48c **red**	25.00
PR67S	D	60c **red**	25.00
PR68S	D	72c **red**	25.00
PR69S	D	84c **red**	25.00
PR70S	D	96c **red**	25.00
PR71S	D	$1.92 **pale brown**	25.00
PR72S	D	$3 **red vermilion**	25.00
PR73S	D	$6 **blue**	25.00
PR74S	D	$9 **orange**	25.00
PR75S	D	$12 **yellow green**	25.00
PR76S	D	$24 **dark violet**	25.00
PR77S	D	$36 **Indian red**	25.00
PR78S	D	$48 **yellow brown**	25.00
PR79S	D	$60 **purple**	25.00

1885

PR81S	D	1c **black**	25.00

Handstamped in Dull Purple Specimen.

1879

Type E

PR57S	E	2c **black**	22.50
PR58S	E	3c **black**	22.50
PR59S	E	4c **black**	22.50
PR60S	E	6c **black**	22.50
PR61S	E	8c **black**	22.50
PR62S	E	10c **black**	22.50
PR63S	E	12c **red**	22.50
PR64S	E	24c **red**	22.50
PR65S	E	36c **red**	22.50
PR66S	E	48c **red**	22.50
PR67S	E	60c **red**	22.50
PR68S	E	72c **red**	22.50
PR69S	E	84c **red**	22.50
PR70S	E	96c **red**	22.50
PR71S	E	$1.92 **pale brown**	22.50
PR72S	E	$3 **red vermilion**	22.50
PR73S	E	$6 **blue**	22.50
PR74S	E	$9 **orange**	22.50
PR75S	E	$12 **yellow green**	22.50
PR76S	E	$24 **dark violet**	22.50
PR77S	E	$36 **Indian red**	22.50
PR78S	E	$48 **yellow brown**	22.50
PR79S	E	$60 **purple**	22.50

1885

PR81S	E	1c **black**	22.50

1895 **Wmk. 191**

PR114S	E	1c **black**	65.00
PR115S	E	2c **black**	65.00
PR116S	E	5c **black**	65.00
PR117S	E	10c **black**	65.00
PR118S	E	25c **carmine**	65.00
PR119S	E	50c **carmine**	65.00
PR120S	E	$2 **scarlet**	65.00
PR121S	E	$5 **dark blue**	65.00
PR122S	E	$10 **green**	75.00
PR123S	E	$20 **slate**	75.00
PR124S	E	$50 **dull rose**	75.00
PR125S	E	$100 **purple**	75.00

REVENUE STAMPS

SPECIMEN

1862

Overprint 14mm Long

R5S	G	2c Bank Check, **blue** (red)	375.00
R15S	A	2c U. S. I. R., **orange**	—

SPECIMEN

Overprint 16mm Long

R23S	H	5c Agreement, **red**	375.00
R34S	H	10c Contract, **blue** (red)	375.00
R35eS	H	10c Foreign Exchange, **ultra** (red)	375.00
R36S	H	10c Inland Exchange, **blue** (red)	375.00
R46S	H	25c Insurance, **red**	375.00
R52S	H	30c Inland Exchange, **lilac** (red)	375.00
R53S	H	40c Inland Exchange, **brown** (red)	375.00
R68S	H	$1 Foreign Exchange, **red**	375.00

Type I Specimen

1898 **Overprint 20mm Long**

R153S	I	1c **green** (red)	475.00

1875

RB11S	H	1c **green** (red)	300.00

PRIVATE DIE MATCH STAMP

Overprinted with Type G in Red SPECIMEN

RO133dS	G	1c **black,** A. Messinger	*500.00*

SAVINGS STAMPS

Overprinted Vertically Reading Down in Red — SPECIMEN

1911

PS4S	10c **deep blue**	—

1917-18 Handstamped "SPECIMEN" in Violet

WS1S	25c **deep green**	—
WS2S	$5 **deep green**	—

VARIOUS OVERPRINTS

Overprinted with control numbers in carmine — 7890

1861

Type J

63S	J A24	1c **pale blue** (overprint 9012)	200.00
65S	J A25	3c **brown red** (overprint 7890)	200.00
		Block of 4	*900.*
68S	J A27	10c **green** (overprint 5678)	200.00
69S	J A28	12c **gray black** (overprint 4567)	200.00
71S	J A30	30c **orange** (overprint 2345)	200.00
		Block of 4	*900.*
72S	J A31	90c **pale blue** (overprint 1234)	200.00
a.		Pair, one without overprint	—

1863-66

73S	J A32	2c **black** (overprint 8901)	300.00
		Block of 4	*1,400.*
76S	J A26	5c **brown** (overprint 6789)	200.00
77S	J A33	15c **black** (overprint 235)	250.00
		Block of 4	*1,150.*
78S	J A29	24c **gray lilac** (overprint 3456)	200.00

Special Printings Overprinted in Red or Blue — SAMPLE.

1889

Type K

212S	K A59	1c **ultramarine** (red)	75.00
210S	K A57	2c **red brown** (blue)	75.00
210S	K A57	2c **lake** (blue)	75.00
210S	K A57	2c **rose lake** (blue)	75.00
210S	K A57	2c **scarlet** (blue)	75.00
214S	K A46b	3c **vermilion** (blue)	75.00
211S	K A58	4c **blue green** (red)	75.00
205S	K A56	5c **gray brown** (red)	75.00
208S	K A47b	6c **brown red** (blue)	75.00
209S	K A49b	10c **brown** (red)	75.00
		Without overprint	80.00
189S	K A51a	15c **orange** (blue)	75.00
190S	K A53	30c **full black** (red)	75.00
191S	K A54	90c **carmine** (blue)	75.00

Special Printings Overprinted in Red or Blue — SAMPLE A.

Type L

212S	L A59	1c **ultramarine** (red)	75.00
210S	L A57	2c **rose lake** (blue)	75.00
		Without overprint	—
214S	L A46b	3c **purple** (red)	75.00
211S	L A58	4c **dark brown** (red)	75.00
205S	L A56	5c **yellow brown** (blue)	75.00
		Without overprint	—
208S	L A47b	6c **vermilion** (blue)	75.00
209S	L A49b	10c **green** (red)	75.00
		Without overprint	100.00
189S	L A51a	15c **blue** (red)	75.00
		Without overprint	100.00
190S	L A53	30c **full black** (red)	75.00
191S	L A54	90c **orange** (blue)	75.00

Overprinted with Type K Together with "A" in Black Manuscript

191S	M A54	90c **carmine** (blue)	140.00
209S	M A49b	10c **brown** (red)	140.00
211S	M A58	4c **blue green** (red)	140.00

"SAMPLE A" in Manuscript (red or black)

216S	N A56	5c **indigo**	160.00

Regular Issues Overprinted in Blue or Red — UNIVERSAL POSTAL CONGRESS

125 sets were distributed to delegates to the Universal Postal Congress held in Washington, D. C., May 5 to June 15, 1897.

1897 **Type O**

264S	O A87	1c **blue**	110.00
267S	O A88	2c **carmine,** type III	110.00
268S	O A89	3c **purple**	110.00
269S	O A90	4c **dark brown**	110.00
270S	O A91	5c **chestnut**	110.00
271S	O A92	6c **claret brown**	110.00
272S	O A93	8c **violet brown**	110.00
273S	O A94	10c **dark green**	110.00
274S	O A95	15c **dark blue**	110.00
275S	O A96	50c **red orange**	110.00
276S	O A97	$1 **black,** type I	350.00
276AS	O A97	$1 **black,** type II	300.00
277S	O A98	$2 **dark blue**	250.00
278S	O A99	$5 **dark green**	350.00

SPECIAL DELIVERY

E5S	O SD3	10c **blue** (R)	250.00

POSTAGE DUE

J38S	O D2	1c **deep claret**	125.00
J39S	O D2	2c **deep claret**	125.00
J40S	O D2	3c **deep claret**	125.00
J41S	O D2	5c **deep claret**	125.00
J42S	O D2	10c **deep claret**	125.00
J43S	O D2	30c **deep claret**	125.00
J44S	O D2	50c **deep claret**	125.00

NEWSPAPERS

PR114S	O N15	1c **black**	125.00
PR115S	O N15	2c **black**	125.00
PR116S	O N15	5c **black**	125.00
PR117S	O N15	10c **black**	125.00
PR118S	O N16	25c **carmine**	125.00
PR119S	O N16	50c **carmine**	125.00
PR120S	O N17	$2 **scarlet**	125.00
PR121S	O N18	$5 **dark blue**	125.00
PR122S	O N19	$10 **green**	125.00
PR123S	O N20	$20 **slate**	125.00
PR124S	O N21	$50 **dull rose**	125.00
PR125S	O N22	$100 **purple**	125.00

ENVELOPES

Overprinted — UNIVERSAL POSTAL CONGRESS

Type P

U294S	P	1c **blue**	100.00
U296S	P	1c **blue,** *amber*	100.00
U300S	P	1c **blue,** *manila*	100.00
W301S	P	1c **blue,** *manila*	100.00
U304S	P	1c **blue,** *amber manila*	100.00
U311S	P	2c **green,** Die 2	100.00
U312S	P	2c **green,** Die 2, *amber*	100.00
U313S	P	2c **green,** Die 2, *oriental buff*	100.00
U314S	P	2c **green,** Die 2, *blue*	100.00
U315S	P	2c **green,** Die 2, *manila*	100.00
W316S	P	2c **green,** Die 2, *manila*	100.00
U317S	P	2c **green,** Die 2, *amber manila*	100.00
U324S	P	4c **carmine**	100.00
U325S	P	4c **carmine,** *amber*	120.00
U330S	P	5c **blue,** Die 1	110.00
U331S	P	5c **blue,** Die 1, *amber*	110.00

Two settings of type P overprint are found. See the July\August 1949 issue of the Scott Monthly Stamp Journal for others.

POSTAL CARDS

Overprinted — UNIVERSAL POSTAL CONGRESS.

Type Q

UX12S	Q	1c **black,** *buff*	650.00
UX13S	Q	2c **blue,** *cream*	650.00

PAID REPLY POSTAL CARDS

Overprinted with Type Q

UY1S	Q	1c **black,** *buff*	650.00
UY2S	Q	2c **blue,** *grayish white*	650.00

As Nos. UY1S-UY2S were made by overprinting unsevered reply cards, values are for unsevered cards.

SOUVENIR CARDS

These cards were issued as souvenirs of the philatelic and numismatic gatherings at which they were distributed by the United States Postal Service (USPS), its predecessor the United States Post Office Department (POD), or the Bureau of Engraving and Printing (BEP). They were not valid for postage.

Most of the cards bear reproductions of United States stamps with the design enlarged, altered by removal of denomination, country name and "Postage" or "Air Mail" or defaced by diagonal bars. The cards are not perforated.

Numismatic cards are listed following the philatelic cards.

A forerunner of the souvenir cards is the 1939 Philatelic Truck souvenir sheet which the Post Office Department issued and distributed in various cities visited by the Philatelic Truck. It shows the White House, printed in blue on white paper. Issued with and without gum. Value, with gum, $50; without gum, $8.

Standard abbreviations:
APS- American Philatelic Society
ASDA- American Stamp Dealers Association

No. SC28

1954

SC1 Postage Stamp Design Exhibition, Natl. Philatelic Museum, Mar. 13, 1954, Philadelphia. Card of 4 monochrome views of Washington. Inscribed: "Souvenir sheet designed, engraved and printed by members, Bureau, Engraving and Printing. Reissued by popular request." *1,500.*

1960

SC2 Barcelona, 1st Intl. Philatelic Congress, Mar. 26-Apr. 5, 1960. Vignette, Landing of Columbus from #231. (POD) 350.00

1966

SC3 SIPEX, 6th Intl. Philatelic Exhibition, May 21-30, 1966, Washington. Card of 3 multicolored views of Washington. 160.00

1968

SC4 EFIMEX, Intl. Philatelic Exhibition, Nov. 1-9, 1968, Mexico City. #292. Spanish text. (POD) 1.50

1969

SC5 SANDIPEX, San Diego Philatelic Exhibition, July 16-20, 1969, San Diego, Cal. Card of 3 multicolored views of Washington. (BEP) 40.00

SC6 ASDA Natl. Postage Stamp Show, Nov. 21-23, 1969, New York. Card of 4 #E4. (BEP) 15.00

1970

SC7 INTERPEX, Mar. 13-15, 1970, New York. Card of 4, #1027, 1035, C35, C38. (BEP) 40.00

SC8 COMPEX, Combined Philatelic Exhibition of Chicagoland, May 29-31, 1970. Card of 4 #C18. (BEP) 10.00

SC9 PHILYMPIA, London Intl. Stamp Exhibition, Sept. 18-26 1970. Card of 3, #548-550. (POD) 1.25

SC10 HAPEX, APS Convention, Nov. 5-8, 1970, Honolulu. Card of 3, #799, C46, C55. (BEP) 10.00

1971

SC11 INTERPEX, Mar. 12-14, 1971, New York. Card of 4 #1193. Background includes #1331-1332, 1371, C76. (BEP) 1.40

SC12 WESTPEX, Western Philatelic Exhibition, Apr. 23-25, 1971, San Francisco. Card of 4, #740, 852, 966, 997. (BEP) 1.40

SC13 NAPEX 71, Natl. Philatelic Exhibition, May 21-23, 1971, Washington. Card of 3, #990, 991, 992. (BEP) 1.50

SC14 TEXANEX 71, Texas Philatelic Association and APS conventions, Aug. 26-29, 1971, San Antonio, Tex. Card of 3, #938, 1043, 1242. (BEP) 1.50

SC15 EXFILIMA 71, 3rd Inter-American Philatelic Exhibition, Nov. 6-14, 1971, Lima, Peru. Card of 3, #1111, 1126, Peru #360. Spanish text. (USPS) 1.00

SC16 ASDA Natl. Postage Stamp Show, Nov. 19-21, 1971, New York. Card of 3, #C13-C15. (BEP) 2.00

SC17 ANPHILEX '71, Anniv. Philatelic Exhibition, Nov. 26-Dec. 1, 1971, New York. Card of 2, #1-2. (BEP) 1.00

1972

SC18 INTERPEX, Mar. 17-19, 1972, New York. Card of 4 #1173. Background includes #976, 1434-1435, C69. (BEP) 1.00

SC19 NOPEX, Apr. 6-9, 1972, New Orleans. Card of 4 #1020. Background includes #323-327. (BEP) 1.00

SC20 BELGICA 72, Brussels Intl. Philatelic Exhibition, June 24-July 9, 1972, Brussels, Belgium. Card of 3, #914, 1026, 1104. Flemish and French text. (USPS) .75

SC21 Olympia Philatelie Munchen 72, Aug. 18-Sept. 10, 1972, Munich, Germany. Card of 4, #1460-1462, C85. German text. (USPS) .75

SC22 EXFILBRA 72, 4th Inter-American Philatelic Exhibition, Aug. 26-Sept. 2, 1972, Rio de Janeiro, Brazil. Card of 3 #C14, Brazil #C18-C19. Portuguese text. (USPS) .75

SC23 Natl. Postal Forum VI, Aug. 28-30, 1972, Washington. Card of 4 #1396. (USPS) .75

SC24 SEPAD '72, Oct. 20-22, 1972, Philadelphia. Card of 4 #1044. (BEP) 1.00

SC25 ASDA Natl. Postage Stamp Show, Nov. 17-19, 1972, New York. Card of 4, #883, 863, 868, 888. (BEP) 1.00

SC26 STAMP EXPO, Nov. 24-26, 1972, San Francisco. Card of 4 #C36. (BEP) 1.50

1973

SC27 INTERPEX, Mar. 9-11, 1973, New York. Card of 4 #976. (BEP) 1.00

SC28 IBRA 73 Intl. Philatelic Exhibition, Munich, May 11-20, 1973. #C13. (USPS) 1.10

SC29 COMPEX 73, May 25-27, 1973, Chicago. Card of 4 #245. (BEP) 2.00

SC30 APEX 73, Intl. Airmail Exhibition, Manchester, England, July 4-7, 1973. Card of 3, #C3a, Newfoundland #C4, Honduras #C12. (USPS) 1.10

SC31 POLSKA 73, World Philatelic Exhibition, Poznan, Poland, Aug. 19-Sept. 2, 1973. Card of 3, #1488, Poland #1944-1945. Polish text. (USPS) 1.10

SC32 NAPEX 73, Sept. 14-16, 1973, Washington. Card of 4 #C3. Background includes montage of #C4-C6. (BEP) 1.75

SC33 ASDA Natl. Postage Stamp Show, Nov. 16-18, 1973, New York. Card of 4 #908. Foreground includes #1139-1144. (BEP) .75

SC34 STAMP EXPO NORTH, Dec. 7-9, 1973, San Francisco. Card of 4 #C20. (BEP) 1.50

A card of 10, Nos. 1489-1498, was distributed to postal employees. Not available to public. Size: about 14x11 inches.

1974

SC35 Natl. Hobby Industry Trade Show, Feb. 3-6, 1974, Chicago. Card of 4, #1456-1459. Reproductions of silversmith (#1457) and glassmaker (#1456). (USPS) 1.40

SC36 MILCOPEX 1974, Mar. 8-10, 1974, Milwaukee. Card of 4 #C43. (BEP) 1.10

SC37 INTERNABA 1974, June 6, 1974, Basel, Switzerland. Card of 8, #1530-1537. German, French, and Italian text. (USPS) 2.25

SC38 STOCKHOLMIA 74, Intl. Philatelic Exhibition, Sept. 21-29, 1974, Stockholm. Card of 3, #836, Sweden #300, 767. Swedish text. (USPS) 2.25

SC39 EXFILMEX 74, Interamerican Philatelic Exposition, Oct. 26-Nov. 3, 1974, Mexico City. Card of 2, #1157, Mexico #910. Spanish text. (USPS) 2.25

1975

SC40 ESPANA 75, World Stamp Exhibition, Apr. 4-13, Madrid. Card of 3, #233, #1271, Spain #1312. Spanish text. (USPS) 1.10

SC41 NAPEX 75, May 9-11, 1975, Washington. Card of 4 #708. (BEP) 4.00

SC42 ARPHILA 75, June 6-16, 1975, Paris. Card of 3. Designs of #1187, #1207, France #1117. French text. (USPS) 1.75

SC43 Intl. Women's Year, 1975. Card of 3 #872, 878, 959. Reproduction of 1886 dollar bill. (BEP) 17.50

SC44 ASDA Natl. Postage Stamp Show, Nov. 21-23, 1975. Bicentennial series. Card of 4 #1003. (BEP) 15.00

1976

SC45 WERABA 76, 3rd Intl. Space Stamp Exhibition, Apr. 1-4, 1976, Zurich, Switzerland. Card of 2, #1434-1435. (USPS) 2.25

SC46 INTERPHIL 76, 7th Intl. Philatelic Exhibition, May 29-June 6, 1976. Philadelphia. Bicentennial series. Card of 4 #120. (BEP) 4.00

An Interphil '76 card issued by the American Revolution Bicentennial Administration was bound into the Interphil program. It shows an altered #1044 in black brown, the Bicentennial emblem and a view of Independence Hall. Printed by BEP

SC48 Bicentennial Exposition on Science and Technology, May 30-Sept. 6, 1976, Kennedy Space Center, Fla. #C76. (USPS) 2.50

SC49 STAMP EXPO 76, June 11-13, 1976, Los Angeles. Bicentennial series. Card of 4, #1351, 1352, 1345, 1348. (BEP) 4.50

SC50 Colorado Statehood Centennial, Aug. 1, 1976. Card of 3, #743, 288, 1670. (USPS) 2.25

SC51 HAFNIA 76, Intl. Stamp Exhibition, Copenhagen. Aug. 20-29, 1976. Card of 2, #5, Denmark #2. Danish and English text. (USPS) 2.25

SC52 ITALIA 76, Intl. Philatelic Exhibition, Oct. 14-24, Milan. Card of 3, #1168, Italy #578, 601. Italian text. (USPS) 2.25

SC53 NORDPOSTA 76, North German Stamp Exhibition, Oct. 30-31, Hamburg. Card of 3, #689, Germany #B366, B417. German text. (USPS) 2.00

1977

SC54 MILCOPEX, Milwaukee Philatelic Society, Mar. 4-6, Milwaukee. Card of 2, #733, 1128. (BEP) 1.75

SC55 ROMPEX 77, Rocky Mountain Philatelic Exhibition, May 20-22, Denver. Card of 4 #1001. (BEP) 1.50

SC56 AMPHILEX 77, Intl. Philatelic Exhibition, May 26-June 5, Amsterdam. Card of 3, #1027, Netherlands #41, 294. Dutch text. (USPS) 2.25

SC57 SAN MARINO 77, Intl. PhilatelicExhibition, San Marino, Aug. 28-Sept. 4. Card of 3, #1-2, San Marino #1. Italian text. (USPS) 2.25

SC58 PURIPEX 77, Silver Anniv. Philatelic Exhibit, Sept. 2-5, San Juan, P. R. Card of 4 #801. (BEP) 1.25

SC59 ASDA Natl. Postage Stamp Show, Nov. 15-20, New York. Card of 4 #C45. (BEP) 2.25

1978

SC60 ROCPEX 78, Intl. Philatelic Exhibition, Mar. 20-29, Taipei. Card of 6, #1706-1709, China #1812, 1816. Chinese text. (USPS) 2.50

SC61 NAPOSTA '78 Philatelic Exhibition, May 20-25, Frankfurt. Card of 3, #555, 563, Germany #1216. German text. (USPS) 2.25

SC62 CENJEX 78, Federated Stamp Clubs of New Jersey, 30th annual exhibition, June 23-25, Freehold, NJ. Card of 9, #646, 680, 689, 1086, 1716, 4 #785. (BEP) 2.00

1979

SC63 BRASILIANA 79, Intl. Philatelic Exhibition, Sept. 15-23, Rio de Janeiro. Card of 3, #C91-C92, Brazil #1295. Portuguese text. (USPS) 2.75

SC64 JAPEX 79, Intl. Philatelic Exhibition, Nov. 2-4, Tokyo. Card of 2, #1158, Japan #1024. Japanese text. (USPS) 3.00

1980

SC65 LONDON 1980, Intl. Philatelic Exhibition, May 6-14, London. #329. (USPS) 3.00

SC66 NORWEX 80, Intl. Stamp Exhibition, June 13-22, Oslo. Card of 3, #620-621, Norway #658. Norwegian text. (USPS) 3.00

SC67 NAPEX 80, July 4-6, Washington. Card of 4 #573. (BEP) 8.00

SC68 ASDA Stamp Festival, Sept. 25-28, 1980, New York. Card of 4 #962. (BEP) 9.50

SC69 ESSEN 80, 3rd Intl. Stamp Fair, Nov. 15-19, Essen. Card of 2, #1014, Germany #723. German text. (USPS) 3.00

1981

SC70 STAMP EXPO '81 SOUTH, Mar. 20-22, Anaheim, Calif. Card of 6, #1331-1332, 4 #1287. (BEP) 11.00

SC71 WIPA 1981, Intl. Stamp Exhibition, May 22-31, Vienna. Card of 2, #1252, Austria #789. German text. (USPS) 3.00

SC72 Natl. Stamp Collecting Month, Oct., 1981. Card of 2, #245, 1918. (USPS) 3.00

SC73 PHILATOKYO '81, Intl. Stamp Exhibition, Oct. 9-18. Tokyo. Card of 2, #1531, Japan #800. Japanese text. (USPS) 3.00

SC74 NORDPOSTA 81, North German Stamp Exhibition, Nov. 7-8. Hamburg. Card of 2, #923, Germany #B538. German text. (USPS) 3.00

1982

SC75 MILCOPEX '82, Milwaukee Philatelic Association Exhibition, Mar. 5-7. Card of 4 #1137. (BEP) 10.00

SC76 CANADA 82, Intl. Philatelic Youth Exhibition, May 20-24, Toronto. Card of 2, #116, Canada #15. French and English text. (USPS) 3.00

SC77 PHILEXFRANCE '82, Intl. Philatelic Exhibition, June 11-21, Paris. Card of 2, #1753, France #1480. French text. (USPS) 3.00

SC78 Natl. Stamp Collecting Month, Oct. #C3a. (USPS) 3.00

SC79 ESPAMER '82, Intl. Philatelic Exhibition, Oct. 12-17, San Juan, P.R. Card of 4 #244. English and Spanish text. (BEP) 20.00

SC80 ESPAMER '82, Intl. Philatelic Exhibition, Oct. 12-17, San Juan, P.R. Card of 3, #801, 1437, 2024. Spanish and English text. (USPS) 3.00

1983

SC81 Joint stamp issues, Sweden and US. Mar. 24. Card of 3, #958, 2036, Sweden #1453. Swedish and English text. (USPS) 3.00

SC82 Joint stamp issues, Germany and US. Apr. 29. Card of 2, #2040, Germany #1397. German and English text. (USPS) 3.00

SC83 TEMBAL 83, Intl. Philatelic Exhibition, Mar. 21-29, Basel. Card of 2, #C71, Basel #3L1. German text. (USPS) 3.00

SC84 TEXANEX-TOPEX '83 Exhibition, June 17-19, San Antonio. Card of 5, #1660, 4 #776. (BEP) 15.00

SC85 BRASILIANA 83, Intl. Philatelic Exhibition, July 29-Aug. 7, Rio de Janeiro. Card of 2, #2, Brazil #1. Portuguese text. (USPS) 3.00

SC86 BANGKOK 83, Intl. Philatelic Exhibition, Aug. 4-13, Bangkok. Card of 2, #210, Thailand #1. Thai text. (USPS) 3.00

SC87 Intl. Philatelic Memento, 1983-84. #1387. (USPS) 2.75

SC88 Natl. Stamp Collecting Month, Oct. #293 bicolored. (USPS) 3.75

SC89 Philatelic Show '83, Boston, Oct. 21-23. Card of 2, #718-719. (BEP) 9.00

SC90 ASDA 1983, Natl. Postage Stamp Show, New York, Nov. 17-20. Card of 4 #881. (BEP) 9.00

1984

SC91 ESPANA 84, World Exhibition of Philately. Madrid, Apr. 27-May 6. Card of 4 #241. Enlarged vignette, Landing of Columbus, from #231. English and Spanish text. (BEP) 15.00

SC92 ESPANA 84, Intl. Philatelic Exhibition, Madrid, Apr. 27-May 6. Card of 2, #233, Spain #428. Spanish text. (USPS) 3.00

SC93 Stamp Expo '84 South, Anaheim, CA, Apr. 27-29. Card of 4, #1791-1794. (BEP) 14.00

SC94 COMPEX '84, Rosemont, IL, May 25-27. Card of 4 #728. (BEP) 17.50

SC95 HAMBURG '84, Intl. Exhibition for 19th UPU Congress, Hamburg, June 19-26. Card of 2, #C66, Germany #669. English, French and German text. (USPS) 3.00

SC96 St. Lawrence Seaway, 25th anniv., June 26. Card of 2, #1131, Canada #387. English and French text. (USPS) 3.25

SC97 AUSIPEX '84, Australia's 1st intl. exhibition, Melbourne, Sept. 21-30. Card of 2, #290, Western Australia #1. (USPS) 3.00

SC98 Natl. Stamp Collecting Month, Oct. #2104, tricolored. (USPS) 2.75

SC99 PHILAKOREA '84, Seoul, Oct. 22-31. Card of 2, #741, Korea #994. Korean and English text. (USPS) 3.00

SC100 ASDA 1984, Natl. Postage Stamp Show, New York, Nov. 15-18. Card of 4 #1470. (BEP) 11.50

1985

SC101 Intl. Philatelic Memento, 1985. #2. (USPS) 3.00

SC102 OLYMPHILEX '85. Intl. Philatelic Exhibition, Lausanne. Mar. 18-24. Card of 2, #C106, Switzerland #746. French and English text. (USPS) 3.00

SC103 ISRAPHIL '85. Intl. Philatelic Exhibition, Tel Aviv, May 14-22. Card of 2, #566, Israel #33. Hebrew and English text. (USPS) 3.00

SC104 LONG BEACH '85, Numismatic and Philatelic Exposition, Long Beach, CA, Jan. 31-Feb. 3. Card of 4 #954, plus a Series 1865 $20 Gold Certificate. (BEP) 10.00

SC105 MILCOPEX '85, Milwaukee Philatelic Society annual stamp show, Mar. 1-3. Card of 4 #880. (BEP) 10.50

SC106 NAPEX '85, Natl. Philatelic Exhibition, Arlington, VA, June 7-9. Card of 4 #2014. (BEP) 9.00

SC107 ARGENTINA '85, Intl. Philatelic Exhibition, Buenos Aires, July 5-14. Card of 2, #1737, Argentina #B27. Spanish text. (USPS) 3.00

SC108 MOPHILA '85, Intl. Philatelic Exhibition, Hamburg, Sept. 11-15. Card of 2, #296, Germany #B595. German text. (USPS) 3.00

SC109 ITALIA '85, Intl. Philatelic Exhibition, Rome, Oct. 25-Nov. 3. Card of 2, #1107, Italy #830. Italian text. (USPS) 3.00

1986

SC110 Statue of Liberty Centennial, Natl. Philatelic Memento, 1986. #C87. (USPS) 4.50

SC111 Garfield Perry Stamp Club, Natl. Stamp Show, Cleveland, Mar. 21-23. Card of 4 #306. (BEP) 9.50

SC112 AMERIPEX '86, Intl. Philatelic Exhibition, Chicago, May 22-June 1. Card of 3, #134, 2052, 1474.(BEP) 9.50

SC113 STOCKHOLMIA '86, Intl. Philatelic Exhibition, Stockholm, Aug. 28-Sept. 7. Card of 2, #113, Sweden #253. Swedish text. (USPS) 4.50

SC114 HOUPEX '86, Natl. Stamp Show, Houston. Sept. 5-7. Card of 3, #1035, 1042, 1044A. (BEP) 10.00

SC115 LOBEX '86, Numismatic and Philatelic Exhibition, Long Beach, CA, Oct. 2-5. Long Beach Stamp Club 60th anniv. Card of 4, #291, plus a series 1907 $10 Gold Certificate. (BEP) 12.00

SC116 DCSE '86, Dallas Coin and Stamp Exhibition, Dallas, Dec. 11-14. Card of 4 #550, plus $10,000 Federal Reserve Note. (BEP) 12.50

1987

SC117 CAPEX '87, Intl. Philatelic Exhibition, Toronto, June 13-21. Card of 2, #569, Canada #883. English and French text. (USPS) 4.00

SC118 HAFNIA '87, Intl. Philatelic Exhibition, Copenhagen, Oct. 16-25. Card of 2, #299, Denmark #B52. English and Danish text. (USPS) 4.00

SC119 SESCAL '87, Stamp Exhibition of Southern California, Los Angeles, Oct. 16-18. #798. (BEP) 11.00

SC120 HSNA '87, Hawaii State Numismatic Association Exhibition, Honolulu, Nov. 12-15. #799 and a Series 1923 $5 Silver Certificate. (BEP) 17.50

SC121 MONTE CARLO, Intl. Philatelic Exhibition, Monte Carlo, Nov. 13-17. Card of 3, #2287, 2300, Monaco #1589. French and English text. (USPS) 4.00

1988

SC122 FINLANDIA '88, Intl. Philatelic Exhibition, Helsinki, June 1-12. Card of 2, #836, Finland #768. English and Finnish text. (USPS) 4.00

SC123 STAMPSHOW '88, APS natl. stamp show, Detroit, Aug. 25-28. #835. (BEP) 9.50

SC124 MIDAPHIL '88, Kansas City, Nov. 18-20. #627. (BEP) 9.00

1989

SC125 PHILEXFRANCE '89 intl. philatelic exhibition, Paris, July 7-17. Card of 2, #C120, France #2144. English and French text. (USPS) 7.75

SC126 STAMPSHOW '89, APS natl. stamp show, Anaheim, CA, Aug. 24-27. #565. Various reproductions of the portrait of Chief Hollow Horn Bear from which the stamp was designed. (BEP) 8.00

SC127 WORLD STAMP EXPO '89, Washington, Nov. 17-Dec. 3. Card of 4, #2433a-2433d. Embossed reproductions of Supreme Court, Washington Monument, Capitol and Jefferson Memorial. (USPS) 8.00

1990

SC128 ARIPEX 90, Arizona Philatelic Exhibition, Phoenix, Apr. 20-22. Card of 2, #285 and #285 with black vignette. (BEP) 9.00

SC129 STAMPSHOW '90, APS natl. stamp show, Cincinnati, Aug. 23-26. Card of 2, #286 and essay with frame of #286 in red with vignette of #293 in black. (BEP) 9.00

SC130 STAMP WORLD LONDON 90, London, England, May 3-13. Card of 2, #1, Great Britain #1. (USPS) 6.00

1991

SC131 STAMPSHOW '91, APS natl. stamp show, Philadelphia, Aug. 22-25. Card of 3, #537, Essays #537a-E1, 537b-E1. Embossed figure of "Freedom." (BEP) 10.00

1992

SC132 World Columbian Stamp Expo, Chicago, May 22-31. Card of 2, #118, 119b. (BEP) 10.00

SC133 Savings Bond, produced as gift to BEP employees, available to public. 1954 Savings stamp, Series E War Savings bond. (BEP) 12.00

SC134 STAMPSHOW '92. Oakland, CA (BEP) 8.50

1993

SC135 Combined Federal Campaign, produced as gift to BEP employees, available to public. #1016. Photos of 6 other stamps. (BEP) 10.00

SC136 ASDA stamp show, New York, May 1993. Card of 7 #859, 864, 869, 874, 879, 884, 889 (BEP) 10.00

SC137 Savings Bonds, produced as gift to BEP employees, available to the public Aug. 1993. $200 War Savings Bond, #WS8 (BEP) 10.00

SC138 Omaha Stamp Show, Sept. 1993. Card of 4, #E7, PR2, JQ5, QE4 (BEP) 11.00

SC139 ASDA New York Show, Oct. 1993. Card of 2, #499-E1a and similar with negative New York precancel (BEP) 9.00

1994

SC140 Sandical, San Diego, CA, Feb. 1994. Card of 4 #E4 (BEP) 8.50

SC140A Centennial of U.S. Stamp Production, July 1994, BEP Intaglio Print. Card of 13 Types A87-A99 in black 100.00

SC141 Savings Bonds, produced as a gift to BEP employees, available to the public Aug. 1, 1994. #WS7-WS11. 12.00

SC142 STAMPSHOW '94, APS National Stamp Show Pittsburgh, PA. Card of 3, 1c, 2c and 10c Type D2 9.00

SC143 American Stamp Dealers Association, Nov. 1994, New York, NY. Card of 4, 2c, 12c, $3, $6 Types N4-N5, N7-N8 9.00

1995

SC144 Natl. Exhibition of the Columbus Philatelic Club, Apr. 1995, Columbus, OH. Block of 4 of #261. 8.00

No. 144 was issued folded in half.

SC145 Centennial of U.S. Stamp Production, June 1995, BEP Intaglio Print. Card of 13 of Types A87-A99 in blue 70.00

SC146 Savings Bonds, produced as a gift to BEP employees, available to the public Aug. 1, 1995. Card of 3 #905, 907, 940 8.50

SC147 American Stamp Dealers Association, Nov. 1995, New York, NY. Block of 4, #292 8.50

No. SC147 issued folded in half.

1996

SC148 CAPEX '96, Toronto, Canada, June 1996. Block of 4, #291 9.50

SC149 Olymphilex '96, Atlanta, GA, July-August, 1996, Block of 4, #718 9.50

SC150 Billings Stamp Club, Billings, MT, Oct. 1996, Block of 4, #1130 9.50

1997

SC151 Long Beach Coin & Collectibles Expo, Feb. 1997, Lock Seal revenue stamp 10.00

SC152 PACIFIC 97, May 1997, Process or renovated butter revenue stamp 10.00

SC153 Milcopex, Milwaukee, WI, Sept. 1997, Newspaper Types N15, N16 and N19 10.00

1998

SC154	OKPEX 98, Oklahoma City, OK, May 1998, Block of 4, #922	10.00
SC155	Centennial of Trans-Mississippi Exposition Issue, Sept. 1998, BEP Engraved Print. Card of 9 die impressions in green of designs A100-A108	40.00

1999

SC156	Philadelphia National Stamp Exhibition, Oct. 1999, Card of 4, #RS281, RS284, RS290, RS306	10.50

NUMISMATIC SOUVENIR CARDS

Included in this section are cards issued by the Bureau of Engraving and Printing showing fractional currency, paper money or parts thereof, for numismatic shows. Not included are press samples sold or given away only at the shows and other special printings. Cards showing both money and stamps are listed in the preceeding section.

Standard abbreviations:

ANA- American Numismatic Association
IPMS- International Paper Money Show
FUN- Florida United Numismatists

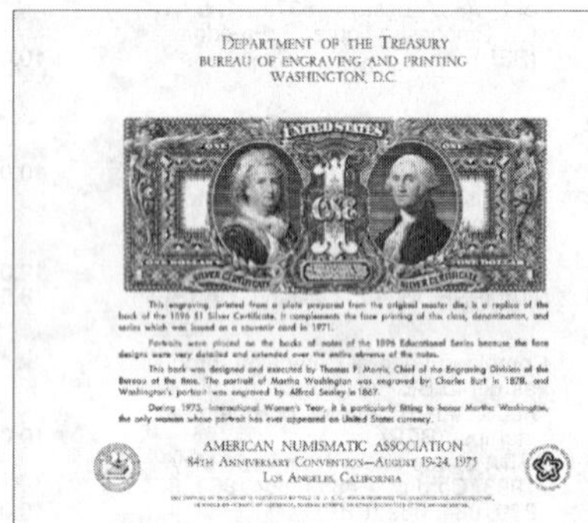

No. NSC8

1969-84

NSC1	ANA	52.50
NSC2	Fresno Numismatic Fair	*300.00*
NSC3	ANA ('70)	65.00
NSC4	ANA ('71)	4.50
NSC5	ANA ('72)	5.00
NSC6	ANA ('73)	7.00
NSC7	ANA ('74)	8.00
NSC8	ANA ('75)	8.50
NSC9	ANA ('76)	6.00
NSC10	ANA ('77)	7.50
NSC11	IPMS ('78)	3.50
NSC12	ANA ('80)	14.00
NSC13	IPMS ('80)	16.00
NSC14	IPMS ('81)	14.00
NSC15	ANA ('81)	10.00
NSC16	IPMS ('82)	10.00
NSC17	ANA ('82)	10.50
NSC18	FUN ('83)	18.00
NSC19	ANA ('83)	15.00
NSC20	FUN ('84)	18.00
NSC21	IPMS ('84)	17.50
NSC22	ANA ('84)	10.00

1985

NSC23	International Coin Club of El Paso	11.00
NSC24	Pacific Northwest Numismatic Assoc.	11.00
NSC25	IPMS	12.00
NSC26	ANA	12.00
NSC27	International Paper Money Convention (IPMC)	13.50

1986

NSC28	FUN	12.00
NSC29	ANA Midwinter	10.00
NSC30	IPMS	9.00
NSC31	ANA	10.00
NSC32	National World Paper Money Convention (NWPMC)	10.50

1987

NSC33	FUN	11.00
NSC34	ANA Midwinter	12.50
NSC35	BEP Fort Worth	15.00
NSC36	IPMS	10.00
NSC37	ANA	9.00
NSC38	Great Eastern Numismatic Association	12.50

1988

NSC39	FUN	10.00
NSC40	ANA Midwinter	14.00
NSC41	IPMS	10.00
NSC42	ANA	12.00
NSC43	Illinois Numismatic Association	10.00

1989

NSC44	FUN	9.50
NSC45	ANA Midwinter	10.00
NSC46	TNA	10.00
NSC47	IPMS	9.50
NSC48	ANA	13.00

1990

NSC49	FUN	9.00
NSC50	ANA Midwinter	9.00
NSC51	Central States Numismatic Society	9.00
NSC52	Dallas Coin and Stamp Exposition	10.00
NSC53	ANA, Seattle, WA	12.00
NSC54	Westex	11.00
NSC55	Honolulu State Numismatic Association	13.00

1991

NSC56	FUN	11.00
NSC57	ANA Midwinter, Dallas, Texas	10.00
NSC58	IPMS	10.00
NSC59	ANA Convention, Chicago, IL	14.00

1992

NSC60	FUN	8.50
NSC61	Central States Numismatics Society	11.00
NSC62	IPMS, Memphis, TN	10.00
NSC63	ANA Convention, Orlando, FL	11.00

1993

NSC64	FUN	11.00
NSC65	ANA Convention, Colorado Springs, CO	10.00
NSC66	Texas Numismatic Association Show	11.00
NSC67	Georgia Numismatic Association Show	11.00
NSC69	IPMS, Memphis, TN	10.00

1994

NSC70	FUN	9.00
NSC71	ANA Convention, New Orleans, LA	10.00
NSC72	European Paper Money Bourse, Netherlands	11.00
NSC73	IPMS, Memphis, TN	11.00
NSC74	ANA Convention, Detroit, MI	11.00

Nos. NSC75-NSC79 were issued folded in half.

1995

NSC75	FUN	11.00
NSC76	New York Intl. Numismatic Convention	10.00
NSC77	IPMS, Memphis, TN	10.00
NSC78	ANA Convention, Anaheim, CA	11.00
NSC79	Long Beach Numismatic/Philatelic Exposition, Long Beach, CA	10.00

1996

NSC80	FUN	10.00
NSC81	Suburban Washington/Baltimore Coin Show	10.00
NSC82	Central States Numismatic Association	10.00
NSC83	ANA Convention, Denver, CO	10.00

1997

NSC84	FUN	10.00
NSC85	Bay State Coin Show	10.00
NSC86	IPMS, Memphis, TN	10.00
NSC87	ANA Convention, New York, NY	10.00

1998

NSC88	FUN	10.00
NSC89	IPMS, Memphis, TN	10.00
NSC90	ANA Convention, Portland, OR	10.00
NSC91	Long Beach Coin & Collectibles Expo, Long Beach, CA	10.00

1999

NSC92	FUN	10.00
NSC93	Bay State Coin Club	10.00
NSC94	IPMS, Memphis, TN	10.00
NSC95	ANA Convention, Rosemont, IL	10.00

2001

NSC96	FUN	10.00
NSC97	Intl. Paper Money Show, Memphis, TN	10.00
NSC98	ANA Convention, Atlanta, GA	10.00
NSC99	Long Beach Coin & Collectibles Expo, Long Beach, CA	10.00

2002

NSC100	FUN	10.00
NSC101	Texas Numismatic Association, Fort Worth	10.00
NSC102	ANA Convention, New York, NY	10.00
NSC103	Long Beach Coin & Collectibles Expo, Long Beach, CA	10.00

2003

NSC104	FUN	45.00
NSC105	Georgia Numismatic Association, Dalton, GA (card of one #C45 in blue gray, without denomination and some inscriptions)	45.00

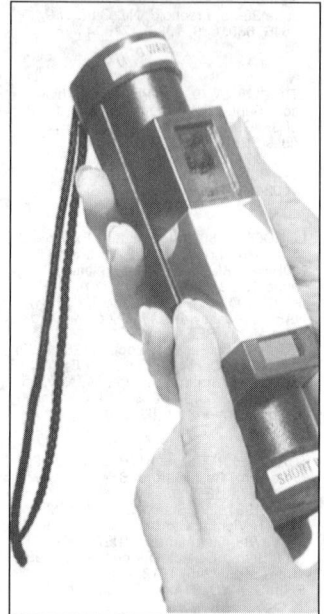

COMMEMORATIVE PANELS

The U.S. Postal Service began issuing commemorative panels September 20, 1972, with the Wildlife Conservation issue (Scott Nos. 1464-1467). Each panel is devoted to a separate issue. It includes unused examples of the stamp or stamps (usually a block of four), reproduction of steel engravings, and background information on the subject of the issue. Values are for panels without protective sleeves. Values for panels with protective sleeves are 10% to 25% higher.

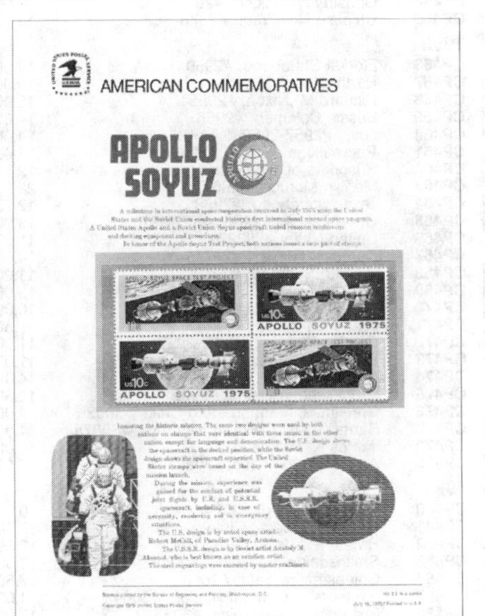

No. CP53

1972

CP1	Wildlife Conservation, #1467a	4.75
CP2	Mail Order, #1468	4.75
CP3	Osteopathic Medicine, #1469	6.50
CP4	Tom Sawyer, #1470	5.00
CP5	Pharmacy, #1473	6.00
CP6	Christmas (angel), #1471	8.00
CP7	Santa Claus, #1472	8.00
CP8	Stamp Collecting, #1474	5.50

1973

CP9	Love, #1475	6.75
CP10	Pamphleteers, #1476	5.50
CP11	George Gershwin, #1484	6.00
CP12	Posting a Broadside, #1477	5.50
CP13	Copernicus, #1488	5.50
CP14	Postal Service Employees, #1489-1498	5.25
CP15	Harry S Truman, #1499	6.50
CP16	Postrider, #1478	6.00
CP17	Boston Tea Party, #1483a	15.00
CP18	Electronics Progress, #1500-1502, C86	5.50
CP19	Robinson Jeffers, #1485	4.75
CP20	Lyndon B. Johnson, #1503	6.50
CP21	Henry O. Tanner, #1486	5.50
CP22	Willa Cather, #1487	5.00
CP23	Drummer, #1479	8.25
CP24	Angus and Longhorn Cattle, #1504	5.50
CP25	Christmas (Madonna), #1507	7.75
CP26	Christmas Tree, needlepoint, #1508	7.75

1974

CP27	Veterans of Foreign Wars, #1525	5.25
CP28	Robert Frost, #1526	5.25
CP29	EXPO }74, #1527	6.00
CP30	Horse Racing, #1528	8.00
CP31	Skylab, #1529	8.50
CP32	Universal Postal Union, #1537a	6.00
CP33	Mineral Heritage, #1541a	7.00
CP34	Kentucky Settlement (Ft. Harrod), #1542	5.25
CP35	First Continental Congress, #1546a	7.00
CP36	Chautauqua, #1505	5.75
CP37	Kansas Wheat, #1506	5.75
CP38	Energy Conservation, #1547	5.00
CP39	Sleepy Hollow Legend, #1548	5.75
CP40	Retarded Children, #1549	5.00
CP41	Christmas (Currier-Ives), #1551	7.50
CP42	Christmas (angel), #1550	7.50

1975

CP43	Benjamin West, #1553	5.50
CP44	Pioneer 10, #1556	8.50
CP45	Collective Bargaining, #1558	4.75
CP46	Contributors to the Cause, #1559-1562	6.25
CP47	Mariner 10, #1557	9.00
CP48	Lexington-Concord Battle, #1563	5.50
CP49	Paul Laurence Dunbar, #1554	6.00
CP50	D. W. Griffith, #1555	5.75
CP51	Battle of Bunker Hill, #1564	5.75
CP52	Military Services (uniforms), #1568a	5.00
CP53	Apollo Soyuz, #1569a	8.25
CP54	World Peace through Law, #1576	5.00
CP55	International Women's Year, #1571	5.75
CP56	Postal Service 200 Years, #1575a	5.50
CP57	Banking and Commerce, #1577a	6.25
CP58	Early Christmas Card, #1580	7.00
CP59	Christmas (Madonna), #1579	7.00

1976

CP60	Spirit of '76, #1631a	8.00
CP61	Interphil '76, #1632	7.00
CP62	State Flags, block of 4 from #1633-1682	15.00
CP63	Telephone Centenary, #1683	6.75
CP64	Commercial Aviation, #1684	9.25
CP65	Chemistry, #1685	7.00
CP66	Benjamin Franklin, #1690	7.00
CP67	Declaration of Independence, #1694a	7.00
CP68	12th Winter Olympics, #1698a	7.50
CP69	Clara Maass, #1699	8.00
CP70	Adolph S. Ochs, #1700	9.00
CP71	Christmas (Currier print), #1702	8.00
CP72	Christmas (Copley Nativity), #1701	8.75

1977

CP73	Washington at Princeton, #1704	9.00
CP74	Sound Recording, #1705	16.00
CP75	Pueblo Art, #1709a	45.00
CP76	Lindbergh Flight, #1710	45.00
CP77	Colorado Statehood, #1711	11.00
CP78	Butterflies, #1715a	12.00
CP79	Lafayette, #1716	10.50
CP80	Skilled Hands for Independence, #1720a	10.50
CP81	Peace Bridge, #1721	10.50
CP82	Battle of Oriskany, #1722	10.50
CP83	Energy Conservation-Development, #1723a	12.00
CP84	Alta California, #1725	11.00
CP85	Articles of Confederation, #1726	15.00
CP86	Talking Pictures, #1727	13.50
CP87	Surrender at Saratoga, #1728	15.00
CP88	Christmas (Washington at Valley Forge), #1729	18.00
CP89	Christmas (rural mailbox), #1730	24.00

1978

CP90	Carl Sandburg, #1731	6.50
CP91	Captain Cook, #1732a	12.00
CP92	Harriet Tubman, #1744	9.50
CP93	American Quilts, #1748a	14.00
CP94	American Dance, #1752a	10.00
CP95	French Alliance, #1753	10.00
CP96	Pap Test, #1754	8.25
CP97	Jimmie Rodgers, #1755	11.00
CP98	Photography, #1758	8.00
CP99	George M. Cohan, #1756	12.50
CP100	Viking Missions, #1759	27.50
CP101	American Owls, #1763a	27.50
CP102	American Trees, #1767a	26.00
CP103	Christmas (Madonna), #1768	10.50
CP104	Christmas (hobby-horse), #1769	10.50

1979

CP105	Robert F. Kennedy, #1770	7.25
CP106	Martin Luther King, Jr., #1771	7.50
CP107	Year of the Child, #1772	6.50
CP108	John Steinbeck, #1773	6.00
CP109	Albert Einstein, #1774	7.25
CP110	Pennsylvania Toleware, #1778a	6.75
CP111	American Architecture, #1782a	7.50
CP112	Endangered Flora, #1786a	7.00
CP113	Seeing Eye Dogs, #1787	6.25
CP114	Special Olympics, #1788	7.50
CP115	John Paul Jones, #1789	7.00
CP116	Olympic Games, #1794a	8.50
CP117	Christmas (Madonna), #1799	8.50
CP118	Christmas (Santa Claus), #1800	8.50
CP119	Will Rogers, #1801	7.00
CP120	Viet Nam Veterans, #1802	9.50
CP121	10c, 31c Olympics, #1790, C97	8.50

1980

CP122	Winter Olympics, #1798a	7.50
CP123	W.C Fields, #1803	7.50
CP124	Benjamin Banneker, #1804	7.25
CP125	Frances Perkins, #1821	5.50
CP126	Emily Bissell, #1823	6.00
CP127	Helen Keller, #1824	5.50
CP128	Veterans Administration, #1825	6.00
CP129	Galvez, #1826	5.25
CP130	Coral Reefs, #1830a	8.00
CP131	Organized Labor, #1831	5.50
CP132	Edith Wharton, #1832	5.25
CP133	Education, #1833	5.50
CP134	Indian Masks, #1837a	8.00
CP135	Architecture, #1841a	6.75
CP136	Christmas Window, #1842	8.00
CP137	Christmas Toys, #1843	8.00

1981

CP138	Dirksen, #1874	6.50
CP139	Young, #1875	7.00
CP140	Flowers, #1879a	7.00
CP141	Red Cross, #1910	7.00
CP142	Savings and Loan, #1911	6.75
CP143	Space Achievements, #1919a	11.00
CP144	Management, #1920	5.50
CP145	Wildlife, #1924a	8.00
CP146	Disabled, #1925	5.50
CP147	Millay, #1926	6.00
CP148	Architecture, #1931a	6.50
CP149	Zaharias, Jones, #1932, 1933	20.00
CP150	Remington, #1934	6.75
CP151	18c, 20c Hoban, #1935, 1936	5.50
CP152	Yorktown, Va. Capes, #1938a	5.25
CP153	Madonna and Child, #1939	7.00
CP154	Teddy Bear, #1940	8.00
CP155	John Hanson, #1941	5.50
CP156	Desert Plants, #1945a	8.00

1982

CP157	FDR, #1950	8.25
CP158	Love, #1951	10.00
CP159	Washington, #1952	9.50
CP160	Birds and Flowers, block of 4 from #1953-2002	27.50
CP161	US-Netherlands, #2003	10.00
CP162	Library of Congress, #2004	10.00
CP163	Knoxville World's Fair, #2009a	8.50
CP164	Horatio Alger, #2010	8.75
CP165	Aging, #2011	9.50
CP166	Barrymores, #2012	10.50
CP167	Dr. Mary Walker, #2013	9.00
CP168	Peace Garden, #2014	9.50
CP169	Libraries, #2015	8.00
CP170	Jackie Robinson, #2016	30.00
CP171	Touro Synagogue, #2017	9.50
CP172	Wolf Trap Farm, #2018	10.00
CP173	Architecture, #2022a	10.50
CP174	Francis of Assisi, #2023	10.50
CP175	Ponce de Leon, #2024	10.50
CP176	Puppy, Kitten, #2025	14.00
CP177	Madonna and Child, #2026	13.50
CP178	Children Playing, #2030a	13.50

1983

CP179	Science, #2031	5.25
CP180	Ballooning, #2035a	6.00
CP181	US-Sweden, #2036	5.25
CP182	CCC, #2037	5.25
CP183	Priestley, #2038	5.25
CP184	Voluntarism, #2039	5.25
CP185	German Immigration, #2040	5.25
CP186	Brooklyn Bridge, #2041	6.00
CP187	TVA, #2042	5.25
CP188	Fitness, #2043	5.25
CP189	Scott Joplin, #2044	7.25
CP190	Medal of Honor, #2045	8.00
CP191	Babe Ruth, #2046	22.50
CP192	Hawthorne, #2047	5.25
CP193	13c Olympics, #2051a	7.50
CP194	28c Olympics, #C104a	6.50
CP195	40c Olympics, #C108a	6.50
CP196	35c Olympics, #C112a	8.00
CP197	Treaty of Paris, #2052	5.50
CP198	Civil Service, #2053	5.50
CP199	Metropolitan Opera, #2054	6.50
CP200	Inventors, #2058a	6.75
CP201	Streetcars, #2062a	7.50
CP202	Madonna and Child, #2063	8.00
CP203	Santa Claus, #2064	8.00
CP204	Martin Luther, #2065	7.00

1984

CP205	Alaska, #2066	4.50
CP206	Winter Olympics, #2070a	5.00
CP207	FDIC, #2071	4.75
CP208	Love, #2072	4.00
CP209	Woodson, #2073	4.75
CP210	Conservation, #2074	4.75
CP211	Credit Union, #2075	4.75
CP212	Orchids, #2079a	5.50
CP213	Hawaii, #2080	6.25
CP214	National Archives, #2081	4.50
CP215	Olympics, #2085a	5.25
CP216	World Expo, #2086	5.00
CP217	Health Research, #2087	4.75
CP218	Fairbanks, #2088	4.75
CP219	Thorpe, #2089	8.25
CP220	McCormack, #2090	4.75
CP221	St. Lawrence Seaway, #2091	6.25
CP222	Waterfowl, #2092	9.00
CP223	Roanoke Voyages, #2093	4.75
CP224	Melville, #2094	4.75
CP225	Horace Moses, #2095	4.75
CP226	Smokey Bear, #2096	15.00
CP227	Roberto Clemente, #2097	25.00
CP228	Dogs, #2101a	6.25
CP229	Crime Prevention, #2102	5.25
CP230	Hispanic Americans, #2103	4.50
CP231	Family Unity, #2104	4.75
CP232	Eleanor Roosevelt, #2105	8.50
CP233	Readers, #2106	4.75
CP234	Madonna and Child, #2107	6.75
CP235	Child's Santa, #2108	6.75
CP236	Vietnam Memorial, #2109	8.25

1985

CP237	Jerome Kern, #2110	5.75
CP238	Bethune, #2137	5.75
CP239	Duck Decoys, #2141a	10.50
CP240	Winter Special Olympics, #2142	5.00
CP241	Love, #2143	5.00
CP242	REA, #2144	5.00
CP243	AMERIPEX '86, #2145	6.75
CP244	Abigail Adams, #2146	5.00
CP245	Bartholdi, #2147	6.50
CP246	Korean Veterans, #2152	6.00
CP247	Social Security, #2153	5.00
CP248	World War I Veterans, #2154	5.00
CP249	Horses, #2158a	9.00
CP250	Education, #2159	5.00
CP251	Youth Year, #2163a	8.25
CP252	Hunger, #2164	5.00
CP253	Madonna and Child, #2165	7.00

CP254	Poinsettias, #2166	7.00

1986

CP255	Arkansas, #2167	5.25
CP256	Stamp Collecting booklet pane, #2201a	6.75
CP257	Love, #2202	6.00
CP258	Sojourner Truth, #2203	7.50
CP259	Texas Republic, #2204	7.50
CP260	Fish booklet pane, #2209a	6.75
CP261	Hospitals, #2210	4.75
CP262	Duke Ellington, #2211	7.50
CP263	Presidents Souvenir Sheet No. 1, #2216	6.25
CP264	Presidents Souvenir Sheet No. 2, #2217	6.25
CP265	Presidents Souvenir Sheet No. 3, #2218	6.25
CP266	Presidents Souvenir Sheet No. 4, #2219	6.25
CP267	Arctic Explorers, #2223a	6.75
CP268	Statue of Liberty, #2224	7.50
CP269	Navajo Art, #2238a	8.00
CP270	T.S. Eliot, #2239	6.25
CP271	Woodcarved Figurines, #2243a	6.75
CP272	Madonna and Child, #2244	5.75
CP273	Village Scene, #2245	5.75

1987

CP274	Michigan, #2246	5.75
CP275	Pan American Games, #2247	3.50
CP276	Love, #2248	5.75
CP277	du Sable, #2249	5.75
CP278	Caruso, #2250	5.50
CP279	Girl Scouts, #2251	7.50
CP280	Special Occasions booklet pane, #2274a	5.50
CP281	United Way, #2275	4.75
CP282	Wildlife, #2286, 2287, 2296, 2297, 2306, 2307, 2316, 2317, 2326, 2327	6.50
CP283	Wildlife, #2288, 2289, 2298, 2299, 2308, 2309, 2318, 2319, 2328, 2329	6.50
CP284	Wildlife, #2290, 2291, 2300, 2301, 2310, 2311, 2320, 2321, 2330, 2331	6.50
CP285	Wildlife, #2292, 2293, 2302, 2303, 2312, 2313, 2322, 2323, 2332, 2333	6.50
CP286	Wildlife, #2294, 2295, 2304, 2305, 2314, 2315, 2324, 2325, 2334, 2335	6.50

1987-90

CP287	Delaware, #2336	5.75
CP288	Pennsylvania, #2337	5.25
CP289	New Jersey, #2338	5.25
CP290	Georgia, #2339	5.25
CP291	Connecticut, #2340	5.25
CP292	Massachusetts, #2341	5.25
CP293	Maryland, #2342	5.25
CP294	South Carolina, #2343	5.25
CP295	New Hampshire, #2344	5.25
CP296	Virginia, #2345	5.25
CP297	New York, #2346	5.25
CP298	North Carolina, #2347	5.25
CP299	Rhode Island, #2348	5.25

1987

CP300	U.S.-Morocco, #2349	4.75
CP301	William Faulkner, #2350	4.75
CP302	Lacemaking, #2354a	5.50
CP303	Drafting of the Constitution booklet pane, #2359a	5.00
CP304	Signing of the Constitution, #2360	5.00
CP305	Certified Public Accounting, #2361	20.00
CP306	Locomotives booklet pane, #2366a	7.50
CP307	Madonna and Child, #2367	6.25
CP308	Christmas Ornaments, #2368	5.50

1988

CP309	Winter Olympics, #2369	6.25
CP310	Australia Bicentennial, #2370	5.75
CP311	James Weldon Johnson, #2371	5.00
CP312	Cats, #2375a	6.50
CP313	Knute Rockne, #2376	9.00
CP314	New Sweden, #C117	5.75
CP315	Francis Ouimet, #2377	14.00
CP316	25c, 45c Love, #2378 and #2379	6.50
CP317	Summer Olympics, #2380	6.25
CP318	Classic Automobiles booklet pane, #2385a	7.00
CP319	Antarctic Explorers, #2389a	6.25
CP320	Carousel Animals, #2393a	7.00
CP321	Special Occasions booklet singles, #2395-2398	6.50
CP322	Madonna and Child, Sleigh, #2399, 2400	6.50

1989

CP323	Montana, #2401	6.25
CP324	A. Philip Randolph, #2402	8.00
CP325	North Dakota, #2403	6.25
CP326	Washington Statehood, #2404	6.25
CP327	Steamboats booklet pane, #2409a	7.50
CP328	World Stamp Expo, #2410	5.50
CP329	Arturo Toscanini, #2411	6.25

1989-90

CP330	House of Representatives, #2412	6.25
CP331	Senate, #2413	6.25
CP332	Executive Branch, #2414	6.25
CP333	Supreme Court, #2415	6.00

1989

CP334	South Dakota, #2416	6.25
CP335	Lou Gehrig, #2417	25.00
CP336	French Revolution, #C120	6.50
CP337	Ernest Hemingway, #2418	8.75
CP338	Letter Carriers, #2420	6.50
CP339	Bill of Rights, #2421	6.50
CP340	Dinosaurs, #2425a	13.50
CP341	Pre-Columbian Artifacts, #2426, C121	7.25
CP342	Madonna, Sleigh with Presents, #2427, 2428	8.50
CP343	Traditional Mail Delivery, #2437a	6.50
CP344	Futuristic Mail Delivery, #C125a	8.00

1990

CP345	Idaho, #2439	5.50
CP346	Love, #2440	7.25
CP347	Ida B. Wells, #2442	12.50
CP348	Wyoming, #2444	6.25
CP349	Classic Films, #2448a	13.00
CP350	Marianne Moore, #2449	5.50
CP351	Lighthouses booklet pane, #2474a	10.00
CP352	Olympians, #2500a	8.50
CP353	Indian Headdresses booklet pane, #2505c	10.00
CP354	Micronesia, Marshall Islands, #2507a	7.00
CP355	Sea Creatures, #2511a	11.50
CP356	Grand Canyon & Tropical Coastline, #2512, C127	7.50
CP357	Eisenhower, #2513	8.25
CP358	Madonna and Child, Christmas Tree, #2514-2515	8.00

1991

CP359	Switzerland, #2532	8.00
CP360	Vermont Statehood, #2533	6.00
CP361	Savings Bonds, #2534	6.25
CP362	Love, #2535-2536	8.00
CP363	William Saroyan, #2538	8.50
CP364	Fishing Flies, #2549a	10.00
CP365	Cole Porter, #2550	6.00
CP366	Antarctic Treaty, C130	5.50
CP367	Operations Desert Shield & Desert Storm, #2551	25.00
CP368	Summer Olympics, #2557a	7.50
CP369	Numismatics, #2558	6.50
CP370	World War II, #2559	12.00
CP371	Basketball, #2560	12.50
CP372	District of Columbia, #2561	7.00
CP373	Comedians, #2566c	9.50
CP374	Jan E. Matzeliger, #2567	7.50
CP375	Space Exploration, #2577a	11.50
CP376	Bering Land Bridge, #C131	6.50
CP377	Madonna and Child, Santa in Chimney, #2578-2579	9.50

1992

CP378	Winter Olympics, #2615a	8.50
CP379	World Columbian Stamp Expo '92, #2616	8.75
CP380	W.E.B. DuBois, #2617	10.00
CP381	Love, #2618	8.75
CP382	Olympic Baseball, #2619	30.00
CP383	Voyages of Columbus, #2623a	10.00
CP384	Columbus, #2624-2625	40.00
CP385	Columbus, #2626, 2629	40.00
CP386	Columbus, #2627-2628	40.00
CP387	New York Stock Exchange, #2630	11.00
CP388	Space Accomplishments, #2634a	10.00
CP389	Alaska Highway, #2635	7.50
CP390	Kentucky Statehood, #2636	6.50
CP391	Summer Olympics, #2641a	8.00
CP392	Hummingbirds, #2646a	10.00
CP393	World War II, #2697	10.00
CP394	Wildflowers, #2647, 2648, 2657, 2658, 2667, 2668, 2677, 2678, 2687, 2688	27.50
CP395	Wildflowers, #2649, 2650, 2659, 2660, 2669, 2670, 2679, 2680, 2689, 2690	27.50
CP396	Wildflowers, #2651, 2652, 2661, 2662, 2671, 2672, 2681, 2682, 2691, 2692	27.50
CP397	Wildflowers, #2653, 2654, 2663, 2664, 2673, 2674, 2683, 2684, 2693, 2694	27.50
CP398	Wildflowers, #2655, 2656, 2665, 2666, 2675, 2676, 2685, 2686, 2695, 2696	27.50
CP399	Dorothy Parker, #2698	6.50
CP400	Dr. Theodore von Karman, #2699	10.00
CP401	Minerals, #2703a	9.50
CP402	Juan Rodriguez Cabrillo, #2704	10.50
CP403	Wild Animals, #2709a	10.00
CP404	Madonna and Child, wheeled toys, #2710, 2714a	10.50
CP405	Chinese New Year, #2720	15.00

1993

CP406	Elvis Presley, #2721	20.00
CP407	Space Fantasy, #2745a	11.00
CP408	Percy Lavon Julian, #2746	10.00
CP409	Oregon Trail, #2747	9.00
CP410	World University Games, #2748	9.00
CP411	Grace Kelly, #2749	17.50
CP412	Oklahoma!, #2722	8.50
CP413	Circus, #2753a	9.00
CP414	Cherokee Strip, #2754	8.50
CP415	Dean Acheson, #2755	10.50
CP416	Sports horses, #2759a	10.00
CP417	Garden flowers, #2764a	8.50
CP418	World War II, #2765	12.00
CP419	Hank Williams, #2723	15.00
CP420	Rock & Roll/Rhythm & Blues, #2737b	20.00
CP421	Joe Louis, #2766	27.50
CP422	Broadway Musicals, #2770a	11.00
CP423	National Postal Museum, #2782a	9.00
CP424	American Sign Language, #2784a	9.00
CP425	Country & Western Music, #2778a	17.50
CP426	Christmas, #2789, 2794a	10.00
CP427	Youth Classics, #2788a	10.00
CP428	Mariana Islands, #2804	8.75
CP429	Columbus' Landing in Puerto Rico, #2805	10.50
CP430	AIDS Awareness, #2806	10.00

Starting with No. CP431, panels are shrink wrapped in plastic with cardboard backing. Values are for items with plastic intact.

1994

CP431	Winter Olympics, #2807-2811	15.00
CP432	Edward R. Murrow, #2812	9.00
CP434	Love, #2814	9.50
CP436	Dr. Allison Davis, #2816	10.00
CP437	Chinese New Year, #2817	14.00
CP438	Buffalo Soldiers, #2818	13.00
CP439	Silent Screen Stars, #2828a	14.00
CP440	Garden Flowers, #2829-2833	11.00
CP441	World Cup Soccer, #2837	12.00
CP442	World War II, #2838	15.00
CP443	Norman Rockwell, #2839	19.00
CP444	Moon Landing, #2841	16.00
CP445	Locomotives, #2843-2847	12.00
CP446	George Meany, #2848	8.00
CP447	Popular Singers, #2853a	12.50
CP448	Jazz/Blues Singers, block of 10, 2854-2861	15.00

Block of 10 on No. CP448 may contain different combination of stamps.

CP449	James Thurber, #2862	8.00
CP450	Wonders of the Sea, #2866a	11.00
CP451	Cranes, block of 2 #2868a	11.00
CP453	Christmas Madonna and Child, #2871	8.00
CP454	Christmas stocking, #2872	8.00
CP455	Chinese New Year, #2876	13.00

1995

CP456	Florida Statehood, #2950	10.00
CP457	Earth Day, #2954a	10.00
CP458	Richard M. Nixon, #2955	15.00
CP459	Bessie Coleman, #2956	14.00
CP460	Love, #2957-2958	14.00
CP461	Recreational Sports, #2965a	14.00
CP462	Prisoners of War/Missing in Action, #2966	12.50
CP463	Marilyn Monroe, #2967	22.50
CP464	Texas Statehood, #2968	12.50
CP465	Great Lakes Lighthouses, #2973a	14.00
CP466	United Nations, #2974	11.00
CP467	Carousel Horses, #2979a	14.00
CP468	Woman Suffrage, #2980	11.00
CP469	World War II, #2981	15.00
CP470	Louis Armstrong, #2982	16.00
CP471	Jazz Musicians, #2992a	17.50
CP472	Garden Flowers, #2993-2997	11.00
CP473	Republic of Palau, #2999	11.00
CP474	Naval Academy, #3001	14.00
CP475	Tennessee Williams, #3002	12.50
CP476	Christmas, Madonna and Child, #3003	14.00
CP477	Santa Claus, Children with toys, #3007a	14.00
CP478	James K. Polk, #2587	10.00
CP479	Antique Automobiles, 3023a	17.50

1996

CP480	Utah Statehood, #3024	10.00
CP481	Garden Flowers, #3029a	10.00
CP482	Ernest E. Just, #3058	12.50
CP483	Smithsonian Institution, #3059	10.00
CP484	Chinese New Year, #3060	17.50
CP485	Pioneers of Communication, #3064a	14.00
CP486	Fulbright Scholarships, #3065	10.00
CP487	Summer Olympic Games, #3068, 2 pages	30.00

Beginning with No. CP487, some items contain two pages. One has text and engraved illustrations, the second has the stamp(s).

CP488	Marathon, #3067	13.50
CP489	Georgia O'Keeffe, #3069	10.00
CP490	Tennessee Statehood, #3070	10.00
CP491	Indian Dances, #3076a	17.50
CP492	Prehistoric Animals, #3080a	17.50
CP493	Breast Cancer Awareness, #3081	11.00
CP494	James Dean, #3082	17.50
CP495	Folk Heroes, #3086a	17.50
CP496	Olympic Games, Cent., #3087	11.50
CP497	Iowa Statehood, #3088	10.00
CP498	Rural Free Delivery, #3090	10.00
CP499	Riverboats, #3095a	17.50
CP500	Big Band Leaders, #3099a	17.50
CP501	Songwriters, #3103a	17.50
CP502	F. Scott Fitzgerald, #3104	19.00
CP503	Endangered Species, #3105, 2 pages	27.50
CP504	Computer Technology, #3106	19.00
CP505	Madonna & Child, #3107	13.50
CP506	Family Scenes, #3111a	14.00
CP507	Hanukkah, #3118	15.00
CP507A	Cycling, #3119	15.00

1997

CP508	Chinese New Year, #3120	19.00
CP509	Benjamin O. Davis, Sr., #3121	14.00
CP510	Love Swans, #3123-3124	12.00
CP511	Helping Children Learn, #3125	10.50
CP512	PACIFIC 97 Stagecoach & Ship, #3131a	14.00
CP513	Thornton Wilder, #3134	12.00
CP514	Raoul Wallenberg, #3135	12.00
CP515	Dinosaurs, #3136	20.00
CP516	Bugs Bunny, #3137c	16.00
CP517	PACIFIC 97 Franklin, #3139	40.00
CP518	PACIFIC 97 Washington, #3140	40.00
CP519	Marshall Plan, #3141	10.00
CP520	Classic American Aircraft, #3142, 2 pages	27.50
CP521	Football Coaches, #3146a	17.50
CP522	American Dolls, #3151	25.00
CP523	Humphrey Bogart, #3152	14.00
CP524	"The Stars & Stripes Forever!," #3153	13.00
CP525	Opera Singers, #3157a	14.00
CP526	Composers & Conductors, #3165a	14.00
CP527	Padre Felix Varela, #3166	13.00
CP528	Department of the Air Force, #3167	13.50
CP529	Movie Monsters, #3172a	16.00
CP530	Supersonic Flight, #3173	16.00
CP531	Women in Military Service, #3174	13.00
CP532	Kwanzaa, #3175	14.00
CP533	Madonna & Child, #3176a	18.00
CP534	Holly, #3177a	18.00

1998

CP535	Chinese New Year, #3179	13.00
CP536	Alpine Skiing, #3180	13.00
CP537	Madam C.J. Walker, #3181	13.00

1998-2000

Celebrate the Century

CP537A	1900s, #3182, 2 pages	20.00
CP537B	1910s, #3183, 2 pages	20.00
CP537C	1920s, #3184, 2 pages	20.00
CP537D	1930s, #3185, 2 pages	20.00
CP537E	1940s, #3186, 2 pages	20.00

CP537F	1950s, #3187, 2 pages	20.00
CP537G	1960s, #3188, 2 pages	20.00
CP537H	1970s, #3189, 2 pages	20.00
CP537I	1980s, #3190, 2 pages	20.00
CP537J	1990s, #3191, 2 pages	20.00

1998

CP538	Remember the Maine,inscribed "Key West, Florida" #3192	13.00
a.	Inscribed "Scottsdale, Arizona."	20.00
CP539	Flowering Trees, #3197a	16.00
CP540	Alexander Calder, #3202a	16.00
CP541	Cinco de Mayo, #3203	13.00
CP542	Sylvester & Tweety, #3204c	17.00
CP543	Wisconsin Statehood, #3206	13.00
CP544	Trans-Mississippi, #3209-3210, 2 pages	20.00
CP545	Berlin Airlift, #3211	13.00
CP546	Folk Musicians, #3215a	14.00
CP547	Gospel Singers, #3219a	13.00
CP548	Spanish Settlement, #3220	14.00
CP549	Stephen Vincent Benét, #3221	13.00
CP550	Tropical Birds, #3225a	13.00
CP551	Alfred Hitchcock, #3226	13.00
CP552	Organ & Tissue Donation, #3227	13.00
CP553	Bright Eyes, #3234a	13.50
CP554	Klondike Gold Rush, #3235	13.00
CP555	American Art, #3236	20.00
CP556	American Ballet, #3237	13.00
CP557	Space Discovery, #3242a	13.50
CP558	Giving & Sharing, #3243	13.00
CP559	Madonna & Child, #3244a	18.00
CP560	Wreaths, #3252a	13.00
CP561	Breast Cancer Awareness, #B1	17.50

1999

CP562	Chinese New Year, #3272	15.00
CP563	Malcolm X, #3273	15.00
CP564	Love, #3274a	20.00
CP565	Love, #3275	15.00
CP566	Hospice Care, #3276	15.00
CP567	Irish Immigration, #3286	15.00
CP568	Lunt & Fontanne, #3287	15.00
CP569	Arctic Animals, #3292a	15.00
CP570	Sonoran Desert, #3293, 2 pages	22.50
CP571	Daffy Duck, #3306c	22.50
CP572	Ayn Rand, #3308	15.00
CP573	Cinco de Mayo, #3309	15.00
CP574	John & William Bartram, #3314	15.00
CP575	Prostate Cancer, #3315	15.00
CP576	California Gold Rush, #3316	15.00
CP577	Aquarium Fish, #3320a	15.00
CP578	Extreme Sports, #3324a	15.00
CP579	American Glass, #3328a	15.00
CP580	James Cagney, #3329	15.00
CP581	Honoring Those who Served, #3331	15.00
CP582	Famous Trains, #3337a	16.00
CP583	Frederick Law Olmsted, #3338	15.00
CP584	Hollywood Composers, #3344a	16.00
CP585	Broadway Songwriters, #3350a	16.00
CP586	Insects & Spiders, #3351, 2 pages	22.50
CP587	Hanukkah, #3352	15.00
CP588	NATO, #3354	15.00
CP589	Madonna & Child, #3355	15.00
CP590	Deer, #3359a	15.00
CP591	Kwanzaa, #3368	15.00
CP592	Year 2000, #3369	16.00

2000

CP593	Chinese New Year, #3370	15.00
CP594	Patricia Roberts Harris, #3371	15.00
CP595	Los Angeles Class Submarine, #3372	10.00
CP596	Pacific Coast Rain Forest, #3378, 2 pages	25.00
CP597	Louise Nevelson, #3383a	10.00
CP598	Hubble Space Telescope Images, #3388a	10.00
CP599	American Samoa, #3389	10.00
CP600	Library of Congress, #3390	10.00
CP601	Road Runner & Wile E. Coyote, #3391c	10.00
CP602	Distinguished Soldiers, #3396a	10.00
CP603	Summer Sports, #3397	10.00
CP604	Adoption, #3398	10.00
CP605	Youth Team Sports, #3402a	10.00
CP606	The Stars and Stripes, #3403, 2 pages	25.00
CP607	Legends of Baseball, #3408, 2 pages	25.00
CP608	Stampin' the Future, #3417a	10.00
CP609	California Statehood, #3438	10.00
CP610	Deep Sea Creatures, #3443a	10.00
CP611	Thomas Wolfe, #3444	10.00
CP612	White House, #3445	10.00
CP613	Edward G. Robinson, #3446	10.00
CP614	Non-denominated Love Letters, #3496	12.00
CP615	34c Love, #3497	12.00
CP615A	55c Love, #3499	12.00
CP616	Chinese New Year, #3500	12.00
CP617	Roy Wilkins, #3501	12.00
CP618	Nine-Mile Prairie, #C136	12.00
CP618A	American Illustrators, #3502, 2 pages	30.00
CP619	Diabetes Awareness, #3503	16.00
CP620	Nobel Prize, #3504	12.00
CP621	Pan-American Inverts, #3505, 2 pages	30.00
CP622	Mt. McKinley, #C137	12.00
CP623	Great Plains Prairie, #3506, 2 pages	30.00

2001

CP624	Peanuts Comic Strip, #3507	12.00
CP625	Honoring Veterans, #3508	12.00
CP626	Frida Kahlo, #3509	12.00
CP627	Legendary Playing Fields, #3510-3519	30.00

No. CP627 consists of 2 pages. One has text and engraved illustrations. The other consists of the pane of stamps.

CP628	Leonard Bernstein, #3521	12.00
CP629	Lucille Ball, #3523	12.00
CP630	Amish Quilts, #3527a	12.00
CP631	Carnivorous Plants, #3531a	12.00
CP632	Eid, #3532	12.00
CP633	Enrico Fermi, #3533	12.00
CP634	That's All Folks!, #3535c	12.00
CP635	Madonna & Child, #3536	12.00
CP636	Santas, #3540b	12.00
CP637	James Madison, #3545	12.00
CP638	Thanksgiving, #3546	12.00
CP639	Hanukkah, #3547	12.00
CP640	Kwanzaa, #3548	12.00
CP641	57c Love, #3551	12.00
CP648	Greetings from America, #3610a	40.00
CP649	Longleaf Pine Forest, #3611	30.00

Nos. CP648 and CP649 each consist of 2 pages. One has text and engraved illustrations. The other contains the pane of stamps.

2002

CP642	Winter Olympics, #3555a	12.00
CP643	Mentoring a Child, #3556	12.00
CP644	Langston Hughes, #3557	12.00
CP645	Happy Birthday, #3558	12.00
CP646	Chinese New Year, #3559	12.00
CP647	U.S. Military Academy Bicentennial, #3560	12.00
CP650	Heroes of 2001, #B2	12.00
CP651	Masters of American Photography, #3649	30.00

No. CP651 consists of 2 pages. One has text and engraved illustrations. The other consists of the pane of stamps.

CP652	John James Audubon, #3650	12.00
CP653	Harry Houdini, #3651	12.00
CP654	Andy Warhol, #3652	12.00
CP655	Teddy Bears, #3653-3656	12.00
CP656	37c Love, #3657	12.00
CP657	60c Love, #3658	12.00
CP658	Ogden Nash, #3659	12.00
CP659	Duke Kahanamoku, #3660	12.00
CP660	American Bats, #3664a	12.00
CP661	Women in Journalism, #3668a	12.00
CP662	Irving Berlin, #3669	12.00
CP663	Neuter or Spay, #3671a	12.00
CP664	Hanukkah, #3672	12.00
CP665	Kwanzaa, #3673	12.00
CP666	Eid, #3674	12.00
CP667	Madonna & Child, #3675	12.00
CP668	Christmas Snowmen, #3679a	12.00
CP669	Cary Grant, #3692	12.00
CP670	Hawaiian Missionary Stamps, #3694	30.00

No. CP670 consists of 2 pages. One has text and engraved illustrations. The other contains the pane of stamps.

CP671	Happy Birthday, #3695	12.00
CP672	Greetings from America, #3745a	42.50

No. CP672 consists of 2 pages. One has text and engraved illustrations. The other contains the pane of stamps.

2003

CP673	Thurgood Marshall, #3746	12.00
CP674	Chinese New Year, #3747	12.00
CP675	Zora Neale Hurston, #3748	12.00
CP676	Special Olympics, #3771	12.00
CP677	American Filmmaking: Behind the Scenes, #3772	30.00

No. CP677 consists of 2 pages. One has text and engraved illustrations. The other contains the pane of stamps.

CP678	Ohio Statehood, Bicent., #3773	12.00
CP679	Pelican Island National Wildlife Refuge, #3774	12.00

SOUVENIR PAGES

These are post office new-issue announcement bulletins, including an illustration of the stamp's design and informative text. They bear a copy of the stamp, tied by a first day of issue cancellation. Varieties of bulletin watermarks and text changes, etc., are beyond the scope of this catalogue.

Values for Scott Nos. SP1-SP295 are for folded copies. Values for Official Souvenir Pages (Nos. SP296 on) are for copies that never have been folded.

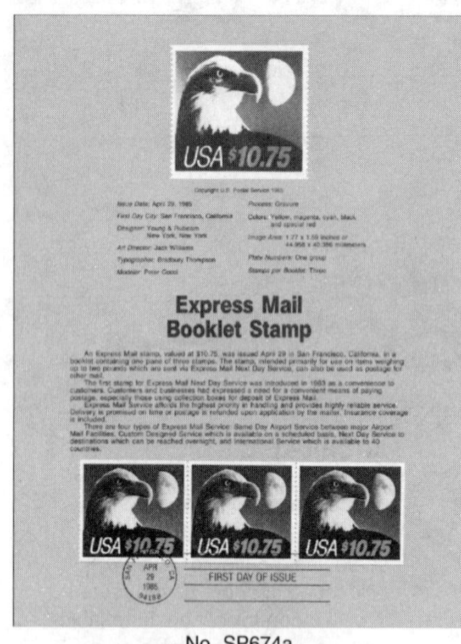

No. SP674a

UNOFFICIAL SOUVENIR PAGES

Liberty Issue

1960-65

SP1	1¼c Palace of Governors, sheet, coil, #1031A, 1054A	50.00
SP2	8c Pershing, #1042A	30.00
SP3	11c Statue of Liberty, #1044A	27.50
SP4	25c Revere coil, #1059A	6.00

1959

SP5	4c 49 Star Flag, #1132	—
SP6	7c Hawaii Statehood, #C55	—
SP7	4c Soil Conservation, #1133	—
SP8	10c Pan American Games, #C56	—
SP9	4c Petroleum, #1134	—
SP10	4c Dental Health, #1135	—
SP11	4c, 8c Reuter, #1136, 1137	—
SP12	4c McDowell, #1138	—

1960-61

SP13	4c Washington Credo, #1139	75.00
SP14	4c Franklin Credo, #1140	75.00
SP15	4c Jefferson Credo, #1141	75.00
SP16	4c F.S. Key Credo, #1142	75.00
SP17	4c Lincoln Credo, #1143	65.00
SP18	4c P. Henry Credo, #1144	35.00

1961

SP19	4c Boy Scout, #1145	75.00
SP20	4c Winter Olympics, #1146	75.00
SP21	4c, 8c Masaryk, #1147, 1148	75.00
SP22	4c Refugee Year, #1149	35.00
SP23	4c Water Consevation, #1150	20.00
SP24	4c SEATO, #1151	20.00
SP25	4c American Women, #1152	20.00
SP26	10c Liberty Bell, #C57	—
SP27	15c Statue of Liberty, #C58	—
SP28	25c Lincoln, #C59	—
SP29	4c 50 Star Flag, #1153	50.00
SP30	4c Pony Express, #1154	50.00
SP31	7c Jet, carmine, #C60	12.50
SP32	7c Booklet pane of 6, #C60a	30.00
SP33	7c Jet coil, #C61	17.50
SP34	4c Handicapped, #1155	50.00
SP35	4c Forestry Congress, #1156	50.00
SP36	4c Mexican Independence, #1157	35.00
SP37	4c U.S., Japan Treaty, #1158	20.00
SP38	4c, 8c Paderewski, #1159-1160	37.50
SP39	4c Sen. Taft, #1161	45.00
SP40	4c Wheels of Freedom, #1162	45.00
SP41	4c Boys' Clubs, #1163	45.00
SP42	4c Automated Post Office, #1164	45.00
SP43	4c, 8c Mannerheim, #1165-1166	45.00
SP44	4c Camp Fire Girls, #1167	45.00
SP45	4c, 8c Garibaldi, #1168-1169	45.00
SP46	4c Sen. George, #1170	45.00
SP47	4c Carnegie, #1171	45.00
SP48	4c Dulles, #1172	45.00
SP49	4c Echo I, #1173	20.00

1961

SP50	4c, 8c Gandhi, #1174-1175	20.00
SP51	4c Range Conservation, #1176	20.00
SP52	4c Greeley, #1177	20.00

1961-65

SP53	4c Ft. Sumter, #1178	20.00
SP54	4c Shiloh, #1179	27.50
SP55	5c Gettysburg, #1180	6.00
SP56	5c Wilderness, #1181	6.50
SP57	5c Appomattox, #1182	6.50

1961

SP58	4c Kansas, #1183	12.00
SP59	13c Liberty Bell, #C62	20.00
SP60	4c Sen. Norris, #1184	11.50
SP61	4c Naval Aviation, #1185	20.00
SP62	4c Workmen's Compensation, #1186	20.00
SP63	4c Remington, #1187	12.00
SP64	4c Sun Yat sen, #1188	20.00
SP65	4c Basketball, #1189	20.00
SP66	4c Nursing, #1190	15.00

1962

SP67	4c New Mexico, #1191	12.50
SP68	4c Arizona, #1192	12.50
SP69	4c Project Mercury, #1193	10.00
SP70	4c Malaria, #1194	12.50
SP71	4c Hughes, #1195	21.00
SP72	4c Seattle World's Fair, #1196	17.50
SP73	4c Louisiana, #1197	17.50
SP74	4c Homestead Act, #1198	17.50
SP75	4c Girl Scouts, #1199	20.00
SP76	4c McMahon, #1200	17.50
SP77	4c Apprenticeship, #1201	17.50
SP78	4c Rayburn, #1202	17.50
SP79	4c Hammarskjold, #1203	17.50
SP80	4c Hammarskjold, yellow inverted, #1204	40.00
SP81	4c Christmas, #1205	50.00
SP82	4c Higher Education, #1206	10.00
SP83	8c Capitol, #C64	9.00
SP83a	8c Capitol sheet, booklet, coil, #C64, C64b, C65	20.00
SP84	8c Capitol, tagged, #C64a	30.00
SP85	8c Capitol booklet single, #C64b	25.00
SP86	8c Capitol coil, #C65	15.00
SP87	4c Winslow Homer, #1207	15.00
SP88	5c Flag, #1208	12.50
SP89	1c Jackson, #1209	12.50
SP90	5c Washington, #1213	17.50
SP91	5c Washington booklet pane of 5 + label, #1213a	30.00
SP92	1c Jackson coil, #1225	17.50
SP93	5c Washington coil, #1229	17.50
SP94	15c Montgomery Blair, #C66	—

1963

SP96	5c Food for Peace, #1231	7.00
SP97	5c West Virginia, #1232	6.00
SP97A	6c Eagle, #C67	8.50
SP97B	8c Amelia Earhart, #C68	18.00
SP98	5c Emancipation Proclamation, #1233	12.50
SP99	5c Alliance for Progress, #1234	7.50
SP100	5c Cordell Hull, #1235	7.50
SP101	5c Eleanor Roosevelt, #1236	6.25
SP102	5c Science, #1237	6.00
SP103	5c City Mail Delivery, #1238	7.50
SP104	5c Red Cross, #1239	6.00
SP105	5c Christmas, #1240	7.50
SP106	5c Audubon, #1241	8.00

1964

SP107	5c Sam Houston, #1242	12.00
SP108	5c C.M. Russell, #1243	9.00
SP109	5c N.Y. World's Fair, #1244	7.50
SP110	5c John Muir, #1245	12.00
SP111	5c Kennedy (Boston, Mass.) (At least 4 other cities known), #1246	12.50
SP112	5c New Jersey, #1247	7.50
SP113	5c Nevada, #1248	7.50
SP114	5c Register and Vote, #1249	7.50
SP115	5c Shakespeare, #1250	7.50
SP116	5c Mayo Brothers, #1251	8.50
SP117	8c Goddard, #C69	5.00
SP118	5c Music, #1252	7.50
SP119	5c Homemakers, #1253	7.50
SP120	5c Christmas Plants, #1257b	17.50
SP121	5c Christmas, tagged, #1257c	90.00
SP122	5c Verrazano Narrows Bridge, #1258	7.50
SP123	5c Fine Arts, #1259	7.50
SP124	5c Amateur Radio, #1260	7.00

1965

SP125	5c New Orleans, #1261	6.00
SP126	5c Sokols, #1262	6.75
SP127	5c Cancer, #1263	6.00
SP128	5c Churchill, #1264	7.50
SP129	5c Magna Carta, #1265	6.00
SP130	5c I.C.Y., #1266	6.00
SP131	5c Salvation Army, #1267	6.50
SP132	5c Dante, #1268	6.00
SP133	5c Hoover, #1269	6.00
SP134	5c Fulton, #1270	6.00
SP135	5c Florida, #1271	7.50
SP136	5c Traffic Safety, #1272	6.00
SP137	5c Copley, #1273	7.50
SP138	11c I.T.U., #1274	7.50
SP139	5c Stevenson, #1275	6.00
SP140	5c Christmas, #1276	7.50

Prominent Americans

1965-73

SP141	1c Jefferson, #1278	7.50
SP141a	1c Jefferson sheet, booklet, coil, #1278, 1278a 1299	7.00
SP142	1c Jefferson booklet pane of 8, #1278a	8.25
SP143	1¼c Gallatin, #1279	7.50
SP144	2c Wright, #1280	5.25
SP145	2c Wright booklet pane of 5 + label, #1280a	9.50
SP146	3c Parkman, #1281	7.50
SP147	4c Lincoln, #1282	6.00
SP148	5c Washington, #1283	6.00
SP149	5c Washington, redrawn, #1283B	6.50
SP150	6c Roosevelt, #1284	6.00
SP151	6c Roosevelt booklet pane of 8, #1284b	13.00
SP151a	6c Roosevelt booklet, vert. coil, #1284b, 1298	5.00
SP151b	6c Roosevelt booklet, horiz. coil, #1284b, 1305	5.00
SP152	8c Einstein, #1285	10.00
SP153	10c Jackson, #1286	6.00
SP154	12c Ford, #1286A	9.00
SP155	13c Kennedy, #1287	20.00
SP156	15c Holmes, #1288	7.50
SP157	20c Marshall, #1289	9.00
SP158	25c Douglass, #1290	9.00
SP159	30c Dewey, #1291	30.00
SP160	40c Paine, #1292	40.00
SP161	50c Stone, #1293	35.00
SP162	$1 O'Neill, #1294	55.00
SP163	$5 Moore, #1295	125.00
SP164	6c Roosevelt, vert. coil, #1298	5.25
SP165	1c Jefferson, coil, #1299	5.75
SP166	4c Lincoln, coil, #1303	7.50
SP167	5c Washington, coil, #1304	7.00
SP168	6c Roosevelt, horiz. coil, #1305	6.50

Nos. 1297, 1305C and 1305E are known on unofficial pages. They are not listed here. For official pages of these issues, see Nos. SP296-SP298.

1966

SP169	5c Migratory Bird Treaty, #1306	7.00
SP170	5c ASPCA, #1307	7.00
SP171	5c Indiana, #1308	7.00
SP172	5c Circus, #1309	6.00
SP173	5c SIPEX, #1310	7.00
SP174	5c SIPEX Souvenir Sheet, #1311	7.25
SP175	5c Bill of Rights, #1312	7.50
SP176	5c Poland, #1313	7.50
SP177	5c National Park Service, #1314	7.50
SP178	5c Marine Corps Reserve, #1315	7.50
SP179	5c Women's Clubs, #1316	7.50
SP180	5c Johnny Appleseed, #1317	7.50
SP181	5c Beautifcation of America, #1318	7.50
SP182	5c Great River Road, #1319	7.50
SP183	5c Savings Bonds Servicemen, #1320	7.50
SP184	5c Christmas, #1321	6.00
SP185	5c Mary Cassatt, #1322	6.00

1967

SP186	8c Alaska, #C70	10.00
SP187	5c Grange, #1323	6.00
SP188	20c Audubon, #C71	4.00
SP189	5c Canada, #1324	5.25
SP190	5c Erie Canal, #1325	5.25
SP191	5c Search for Peace, #1326	6.50
SP192	5c Thoreau, #1327	5.50
SP193	5c Nebraska, #1328	5.25
SP194	5c VOA, #1329	5.25
SP195	5c Crockett, #1330	7.00
SP196	5c Space, #1332b	21.00
SP197	5c Urban Planning, #1333	5.25
SP198	5c Finland, #1334	6.00
SP199	5c Eakins, #1335	6.00
SP200	5c Christmas, #1336	7.00
SP201	5c Mississippi, #1337	5.50

1968-71

SP202	6c Flags, Giori Press, #1338	6.00
SP203	6c Flag, Huck Press, #1338D	5.00
SP204	8c Flag, #1338F	5.50
SP205	6c Flag coil, #1338A	5.75

1968

SP206	10c 50 star Runway, #C72	5.00
SP207	10c sheet, coil, booklet pane of 8, #C72, C72b, C73	25.00
SP207a	10c sheet, booklet single, coil, #C72, C72b, C73	7.00
SP208	10c 50 star Runway coil, #C73	9.00
SP209	6c Illinois, #1339	5.50
SP210	6c HemisFair, #1340	7.50
SP211	$1 Airlift, #1341	60.00
SP212	6c Youth, #1342	6.00
SP213	10c Air Mail Service, #C74	7.25
SP214	6c Law and Order, #1343	6.00
SP215	6c Register and Vote, #1344	6.00
SP216	6c Historic Flags, #1345-1354	70.00
SP217	6c Disney, #1355	10.00
SP218	6c Marquette, #1356	7.50
SP219	6c Daniel Boone, #1357	7.50

SP220	6c	Arkansas River Navigation, #1358	7.50
SP221	6c	Leif Erikson, #1359	15.00
SP222	6c	Cherokee Strip, #1360	7.50
SP223	6c	John Trumbull, #1361	6.00
SP224	6c	Waterfowl, #1362	7.50
SP225	6c	Christmas, #1363	7.50
SP226	6c	Chief Joseph, #1364	6.00
SP227	20c	USA, #C75	5.00

1969

SP228	6c	Beautification, #1368a	18.00
SP229	6c	American Legion, #1369	7.50
SP230	6c	Grandma Moses, #1370	6.00
SP231	6c	Apollo 8, #1371	15.00
SP232	6c	W.C. Handy, #1372	10.00
SP233	6c	California, #1373	6.00
SP234	6c	Powell, #1374	6.00
SP235	6c	Alabama, #1375	7.50
SP236	6c	Botanical Congress, #1379a	20.00
SP237	10c	Man on the Moon, #C76	14.00
SP238	6c	Dartmouth, #1380	7.50
SP239	6c	Baseball, #1381	40.00
SP240	6c	Football, #1382	10.00
SP241	6c	Eisenhower, #1383	6.00
SP242	6c	Christmas, #1384	7.50
SP243	6c	Hope, #1385	6.00
SP244	45c	Special Delivery, #E22	25.00
SP245	6c	Harnett, #1386	6.00

1970

SP246	6c	Natural History, #1390a	30.00
SP247	6c	Maine, #1391	7.50
SP248	6c	Wildlife Conservation, #1392	7.50

Regular Issue

1970-71

SP249	6c	Eisenhower, #1393	6.00
SP249a	6c	sheet, booklet, coil stamps, #1393, 1393a, 1401	7.00
SP249b	6c	sheet, coil stamps, #1393, 1401	6.00
SP250	6c	Eisenhower booklet pane of 8, #1393a	12.50
SP250a	6c	booklet, coil, #1393a, 1401	6.00
SP251	6c	Eisenhower booklet pane of 5 + label, #1393b	6.00
SP252	8c	Eisenhower, #1394	6.00
SP252a	8c	sheet, booklet, coil, #1394-1395, 1402	6.00
SP253	8c	Eisenhower booklet pane of 8, #1395a	15.00
SP254	8c	Eisenhower booklet pane of 8, #1395b	15.00
SP255	8c	U.S.P.S., #1396	10.00
SP256	16c	Pyle, #1398	6.00
SP257	6c	Eisenhower coil, #1401	6.00
SP258	8c	Eisenhower coil, #1402	5.00

1970

SP259	6c	Masters, #1405	7.50
SP260	6c	Suffrage, #1406	6.00
SP261	6c	So. Carolina, #1407	6.00
SP262	6c	Stone Mountain, #1408	6.00
SP263	6c	Ft. Snelling, #1409	6.00
SP264	6c	Anti pollution, #1413a	20.00
SP265	6c	Christmas Nativity, #1414	13.00
SP266	6c	Christmas Toys, #1418b	6.75
SP267	6c	Toys, precanceled, #1418c	35.00
SP268	6c	U.N., #1419	9.00
SP269	6c	Mayflower, #1420	7.50
SP270	6c	DAV, Servicemen, #1422a	27.50

1971

SP271	6c	Wool, #1423	7.50
SP272	6c	MacArthur, #1424	7.50
SP273	6c	Blood Donors, #1425	7.50
SP274	8c	Missouri, #1426	7.50
SP275	9c	Delta Wing, #C77	5.00
SP276	11c	Jet, #C78	3.50
SP276a	11c	sheet, booklet, coil, #C78, C78a, C82	5.00
SP277	11c	Jet booklet pane, #C78a	12.00
SP278	60c	Special Delivery, #E23	24.00
SP279	8c	Wildlife, #1430a	12.50
SP280	8c	Antarctic Treaty, #1431	10.00
SP281	8c	Bicentennial Emblem, #1432	12.50
SP282	17c	Statue of Liberty, #C80	15.00
SP283	21c	USA, #C81	20.00
SP284	11c	Jet coil, #C82	3.25
SP285	8c	Sloan, #1433	10.00
SP286	8c	Space, #1435b	15.00
SP287	8c	Dickenson, #1436	10.00
SP288	8c	San Juan, #1437	10.00
SP289	8c	Drug Abuse, #1438	10.00
SP290	8c	CARE, #1439	10.00
SP291	8c	Historic Preservation, #1443a	12.50
SP292	8c	Adoration, #1444	10.00
SP293	8c	Patridge, #1445	10.00

1972

SP294	8c	Lanier, #1446	10.00
SP295	8c	Peace Corps, #1447	10.00

OFFICIAL SOUVENIR PAGES

In 1972 the USPS began issuing "official" Souvenir pages by subscription. A few more "unofficials" were produced.

Prominent Americans

1970-78

SP296	3c	Parkman, coil, #1297	2.50
SP297	$1	O'Neill, coil, #1305C	10.00
SP298	15c	Holmes, coil, #1305E	3.50
SP299	7c	Franklin, #1393D	4.75
SP300	14c	LaGuardia, #1397	65.00
SP301	18c	Blackwell, #1399	2.00
SP302	21c	Giannini, #1400	3.50

1972

SP303	2c	Cape Hatteras, #1451a	65.00
SP304	6c	Wolf Trap Farm, #1452	22.50
SP305	8c	Yellowstone, #1453	80.00
SP306	11c	City of Refuge, #C84	70.00
SP307	15c	Mt. McKinley, #1454	17.50
SP308	8c	Family Planning, #1455	400.00
		Unofficials exist, value $150.	
SP309	8c	Colonial Craftsmen, #1459a	12.50
SP310		Olympics, #1460-1462, C85	9.00
SP311	8c	PTA, #1463	4.50
SP312	8c	Wildlife, #1467a	6.00
SP313	8c	Mail Order, #1468	4.50
SP314	8c	Osteopathic, #1469	4.50
SP315	8c	Tom Sawyer, #1470	6.00
SP316	8c	Christmas, #1471-1472	5.50
SP317	8c	Pharmacy, #1473	6.00
SP318	8c	Stamp Collecting, #1474	4.50

1973

SP319	8c	Love, #1475	5.50
SP320	8c	Printing, #1476	3.50
SP321	8c	Broadside, #1477	4.50
SP322	8c	Postrider, #1478	4.50
SP323	8c	Drummer, #1479	3.25
SP324	8c	Tea Party, #1483a	4.75
SP325	8c	Gershwin, #1484	4.50
SP326	8c	Jeffers, #1485	3.50
SP327	8c	Tanner, #1486	4.00
SP328	8c	Cather, #1487	3.25
SP329	8c	Copernicus, #1488	4.25
SP330	8c	Postal People, #1489-1498	4.75
SP331	8c	Truman, #1499	3.75
SP332		Electronics, #1500-1502, C86	5.75
SP333	8c	L.B. Johnson, #1503	2.75

1973-74

SP334	8c	Cattle, #1504	2.75
SP335	10c	Chautauqua, #1505	2.50
SP336	10c	Kansas Winter Wheat, #1506	1.90

1973

SP337	8c	Christmas, #1507	5.00

Regular Issues

1973-74

SP338	10c	Crossed Flags, #1509	2.25
SP339	10c	Jefferson Memorial, #1510	2.25
SP340	10c	ZIP, #1511	3.25
SP341	6.3c	Liberty Bell coil, #1518	2.25
SP341A	13c	Winged Envelope, #C79	2.00
SP341B	13c	Airmail, coil, #C83	2.50

1974

SP342	18c	Statue of Liberty, #C87	4.50
SP343	26c	Mt. Rushmore, #C88	4.00
SP344	10c	VFW, #1525	2.50
SP345	10c	Robert Frost, #1526	3.50
SP346	10c	EXPO '74, #1527	4.00
SP347	10c	Horse Racing, #1528	4.00
SP348	10c	Skylab, #1529	4.50
SP349	10c	UPU, #1537a	4.75
SP350	10c	Minerals, #1541a	4.75
SP351	10c	Ft. Harrod, #1542	2.25
SP352	10c	Continental Congress, #1546a	3.50
SP353	10c	Energy, #1547	2.00
SP354	10c	Sleepy Hollow, #1548	3.00
SP355	10c	Retarded Children, #1549	2.00
SP356	10c	Christmas, #1550-1552	4.25

1975

SP357	10c	Benjamin West, #1553	2.25
SP358	10c	Dunbar, #1554	3.00
SP359	10c	D.W. Griffith, #1555	2.50
SP360	10c	Pioneer, #1556	5.00
SP361	10c	Mariner, #1557	4.25
SP362	10c	Collective Bargaining, #1558	2.25
SP363	8c	Sybil Ludington, #1559	2.25
SP364	10c	Salem Poor, #1560	3.00
SP365	10c	Haym Salomon, #1561	2.25
SP366	15c	Peter Francisco, #1562	2.25
SP367	10c	Lexington & Concord, #1563	2.50
SP368	10c	Bunker Hill, #1564	2.50
SP369	10c	Military Uniforms, #1568a	5.00
SP370	10c	Apollo Soyuz, #1570a	5.00
SP371	10c	Women's Year, #1571	2.00
SP372	10c	Postal Service, #1575	3.00
SP373	10c	Peace through Law, #1576	2.00
SP374	10c	Banking and Commerce, #1578a	3.00
SP375	10c	Christmas, #1579-1580	3.00

Americana Issue

1975-81

SP376	1c, 2c, 3c, 4c	Americana, #1581-1585	2.00
SP377	9c	Capitol Dome, #1591	2.25
SP378	10c	Justice, #1592	2.25
SP379	11c	Printing Press, #1593	1.75
SP380	12c	Torch sheet, coil, #1594, 1816	2.25
SP381	13c	Eagle and Shield, #1596	2.50
SP382	15c	Flag sheet, coil, #1597, 1618C	2.00
SP383	16c	Statue of Liberty sheet, coil, #1599, 1619	1.90
SP384	24c	Old North Church, #1603	1.90
SP385	28c	Ft. Nisqually, #1604	2.00
SP386	29c	Lighthouse, #1605	1.90
SP387	30c	Schoolhouse, #1606	2.50
SP388	50c	"Betty" Lamp, #1608	3.00
SP389	$1	Candle Holder, #1610	3.50
SP390	$2	Kerosene Lamp, #1611	4.50
SP391	$5	R. R. Lantern, #1612	9.00
SP392	1c	Inkwell, coil, #1811	1.75
SP393	3.1c	Guitar, coil, #1613	3.50
SP394	3.5c	Violin, coil, #1813	2.50
SP395	7.7c	Saxhorns, coil, #1614	1.75
SP396	7.9c	Drum, coil, #1615	1.90
SP397	8.4c	Piano, coil, #1615C	2.00
SP398	9c	Capitol Dome, coil, #1616	1.75
SP398A	10c	Justice, coil, #1617	2.25
SP399	13c	Liberty Bell, coil, #1618	2.00
SP400	13c	13 star Flag sheet, coil, #1622, 1625	2.00
SP401	9c, 13c	Booklet pane, perf. 10, #1623Bc	14.00

1976

SP402	13c	Spririt of '76, #1631a	3.25
SP403	25c, 31c	Plane and Globes, #C89-C90	2.25
SP404	13c	Interphil 76, #1632	2.50
SP405	13c	State Flags, #1633-1642	5.50
SP406	13c	State Flags, #1643-1652	5.50
SP407	13c	State Flags, #1653-1662	5.50
SP408	13c	State Flags, #1663-1672	5.50
SP409	13c	State Flags, #1673-1682	5.50
SP410	13c	Telephone, #1683	1.75
SP411	13c	Aviation, #1684	1.75
SP412	13c	Chemistry, #1685	1.75
SP413	13c	Bicentennial Souvenir Sheet, #1686	7.00
SP414	18c	Bicentennial Souvenir Sheet, #1687	7.00
SP415	24c	Bicentennial Souvenir Sheet, #1688	7.00
SP416	31c	Bicentennial Souvenir Sheet, #1689	7.00
SP417	13c	Franklin, #1690	1.75
SP418	13c	Declaration of Independence, #1694a	3.50
SP419	13c	Olympics, #1698a	3.50
SP420	13c	Clara Maass, #1699	2.75
SP421	13c	Adolph Ochs, #1700	2.25
SP422	13c	Christmas, #1701-1703	2.25

1977

SP423	13c	Washington at Princeton, #1704	1.75
SP424	13c	Sound Recording, #1705	2.00
SP425	13c	Pueblo Pottery, #1709a	3.00
SP426	13c	Lindbergh Flight, #1710	2.25
SP427	13c	Colorado, #1711	1.90
SP428	13c	Butterflies, #1715a	2.25
SP429	13c	Lafayette, #1716	1.50
SP430	13c	Skilled Hands, #1720a	2.25
SP431	13c	Peace Bridge, #1721	1.60
SP432	13c	Oriskany, #1722	1.60
SP433	13c	Energy, #1724a	1.60
SP434	13c	Alta California, #1725	1.60
SP435	13c	Articles of Confederation, #1726	1.60
SP436	13c	Talking Pictures, #1727	2.00
SP437	13c	Saratoga, #1728	2.25
SP438	13c	Christmas, #1729-1730	1.60

1978

SP439	13c	Sandburg, #1731	2.00
SP440	13c	Capt. Cook, #1732, 1733	2.00
SP441	13c	Indian Head Penny, #1734	2.00
SP442	15c	A Sheet, coil, #1735, 1743	3.25
SP443	15c	Roses booklet single, #1737	2.00
SP444	15c	Windmills booklet pane of 10, #1742a	4.00
SP445	13c	Tubman, #1744	3.00
SP446	13c	Quilts, #1748a	2.50
SP447	13c	American Dance, #1752a	2.75
SP448	13c	French Alliance, #1753	1.90
SP449	13c	Cancer Detection, #1754	2.25
SP450	13c	Jimmie Rodgers, #1755	3.00
SP451	15c	George M. Cohan, #1756	1.60
SP452	13c	CAPEX '78 Souvenir Sheet, #1757	5.50
SP453	15c	Photography, #1758	1.90
SP454	15c	Viking Missions, #1759	3.75
SP455	15c	Owls, #1763a	2.50
SP456	31c	Wright Brothers, #C92a	2.50
SP457	15c	Trees, #1767a	2.75
SP458	15c	Madonna and Child, #1768	2.00
SP459	15c	Hobby Horse, #1769	2.00

1979

SP460	15c	Robert F. Kennedy, #1770	2.00
SP461	15c	Martin Luther King Jr., #1771	3.50
SP462	15c	Year of the Child, #1772	2.00
SP463	15c	John Steinbeck, #1773	2.50
SP464	15c	Einstein, #1774	3.00
SP465	21c	Chanute, #C94a	2.50
SP466	15c	Toleware, #1778a	2.50
SP467	15c	Architecture, #1782a	2.25
SP468	15c	Endangered Flora, #1786a	2.50
SP469	15c	Seeing Eye Dogs, #1787	1.90
SP470	15c	Special Olympics, #1788	1.90
SP471	15c	John Paul Jones, #1789	2.00
SP472	10c	Olympics, #1790	2.25
SP473	15c	Olympics, #1794a	3.75
SP474	31c	Olympics, #C97	3.00

1980

SP475	15c	Winter Olympics, #1798a	3.50

1979

SP476	15c	Madonna and Child, #1799	2.25
SP477	15c	Santa Claus, #1800	2.25
SP478	15c	Will Rogers, #1801	2.25
SP479	15c	Vietnam Veterans, #1802	2.75
SP480	25c	Wiley Post, #C96a	3.00

1980

SP481	15c	W.C. Fields, #1803	2.75
SP482	15c	Benjamin Banneker, #1804	2.75
SP483	15c	Letter Writing Week, #1805-1810	2.00
SP484	18c	B sheet, coil, #1818, 1820	2.00
SP485	18c	B booklet pane of 8, #1819a	2.00
SP486	15c	Frances Perkins, #1821	1.50
SP487	15c	Dolley Madison, #1822	2.25
SP488	15c	Emily Bissell, #1823	1.90
SP489	15c	Helen Keller, #1824	1.75
SP490	15c	Veterans Administration, #1825	1.50
SP491	15c	Galvez, #1826	1.75
SP492	15c	Coral Reefs, #1830a	2.75
SP493	15c	Organized Labor, #1831	2.25
SP494	15c	Edith Wharton, #1832	2.25

SP495	15c	Education, #1833	2.25
SP496	15c	Indian Masks, #1837a	2.50
SP497	15c	Architecture, #1841a	2.00
SP498	40c	Mazzei, #C98	2.00
SP499	15c	Christmas Window, #1842	2.00
SP500	15c	Christmas Toys, #1843	2.25
SP501	28c	Blanche Stuart Scott, #C99	1.60
SP502	35c	Curtiss, #C100	1.60

Great Americans

1980-85

SP503	1c	Dix, #1844	2.25
SP504	2c	Stravinsky, #1845	2.00
SP505	3c	Clay, #1846	1.50
SP506	4c	Schurz, #1847	1.50
SP507	5c	Buck, #1848	1.50
SP508	6c	Lippmann, #1849	1.50
SP509	7c	Baldwin, #1850	1.75
SP510	8c	Knox, #1851	1.50
SP511	9c	Thayer, #1852	1.75
SP512	10c	Russell, #1853	1.50
SP513	11c	Partridge, #1854	1.50
SP514	13c	Crazy Horse, #1855	1.75
SP515	14c	Lewis, #1856	1.50
SP516	17c	Carson, #1857	1.50
SP517	18c	Mason, #1858	1.50
SP518	19c	Sequoyah, #1859	1.50
SP519	20c	Bunche, #1860	4.00
SP520	20c	Gallaudet, #1861	1.75
SP521	20c	Truman, #1862	1.50
SP522	22c	Audubon, #1863	1.75
SP523	30c	Laubach, #1864	1.50
SP524	35c	Drew, #1865	1.75
SP525	37c	Millikan, #1866	1.50
SP526	39c	Clark, #1867	1.50
SP527	40c	Gilbreth, #1868	1.50
SP528	50c	Nimitz, #1869	1.75

1981

SP529	15c	Dirksen, #1874	1.50
SP530	15c	Young, #1875	2.75
SP531	18c	Flowers, #1879a	2.00
SP532	18c	Animals, #1889a	3.50
SP533	18c	Flag sheet, coil, #1890-1891	2.00
SP534	6c, 18c	Booklet pane, #1893a	2.00
SP535	20c	Flag sheet, coil, #1894-1895	3.00
SP536	20c	Flag booklet pane of 6, #1896a	2.50

1982

SP537	20c	Flag booklet pane of 10, #1896b	2.50

Transportation Coils

1981-84

SP538	1c	Omnibus, #1897	1.75
SP539	2c	Locomotive, #1897A	2.25
SP540	3c	Handcar, #1898	2.00
SP541	4c	Stagecoach, #1898A	2.50
SP542	5c	Motorcycle, #1899	3.75
SP543	5.2c	Sleigh, #1900	2.75
SP544	5.9c	Bicycle, #1901	4.75
SP545	7.4c	Baby Buggy, #1902	2.50
SP546	9.3c	Mail Wagon, #1903	2.50
SP547	10.9c	Hansom Cab, #1904	2.75
SP548	11c	Caboose, #1905	2.25
SP549	17c	Electric Auto, #1906	1.75
SP550	18c	Surrey, #1907	1.75
SP551	20c	Fire Pumper, #1908	3.25

1983

SP552	$9.35	Express Mail single, #1909	75.00
SP552a	$9.35	Express Mail booklet pane of 3, #1909a	125.00

1981

SP553	18c	Red Cross, #1910	1.50
SP554	18c	Savings and Loan, #1911	1.50
SP555	18c	Space Achievements, #1919a	6.75
SP556	18c	Management, #1920	1.50
SP557	18c	Wildlife, #1924a	2.00
SP558	18c	Disabled, #1925	1.50
SP559	18c	Millay, #1926	1.75
SP560	18c	Alcoholism, #1927	2.25
SP561	18c	Architecture, #1931a	2.50
SP562	18c	Zaharias, #1932	7.00
SP563	18c	Jones, #1933	8.00
SP564	18c	Remington, #1934	2.25
SP565	18c, 20c	Hoban, #1935-1936	1.50
SP566	18c	Yorktown, Va. Capes, #1938a	2.00
SP567	20c	Madonna and Child, #1939	2.00
SP568	20c	Teddy Bear, #1940	2.25
SP569	20c	John Hanson, #1941	1.50
SP570	20c	Desert Plants, #1945a	2.00
SP571	20c	C sheet, coil, #1946	2.50
SP572	20c	C Booklet pane of 10, #1948a	2.50

1982

SP573	20c	Bighorn Sheep, #1949a	3.00
SP574	20c	FDR, #1950	1.50
SP575	20c	Love, #1951	1.50
SP576	20c	Washington, #1952	2.25
SP577	20c	Birds and Flowers, #1953-1962	7.00
SP578	20c	Birds and Flowers, #1963-1972	7.00
SP579	20c	Birds and Flowers, #1973-1982	7.00
SP580	20c	Birds and Flowers, #1983-1992	7.00
SP581	20c	Birds and Flowers, #1993-2002	7.00
SP582	20c	US Netherlands, #2003	1.50
SP583	20c	Library of Congress, #2004	1.50
SP584	20c	Consumer Education, #2005	2.25
SP585	20c	Knoxville World's Fair, #2009a	1.50
SP586	20c	Horatio Alger, #2010	1.25
SP587	20c	Aging, #2011	1.25
SP588	20c	Barrymores, #2012	2.50
SP589	20c	Dr. Mary Walker, #2013	1.50
SP590	20c	Peace Garden, #2014	1.50
SP591	20c	Libraries, #2015	1.50
SP592	20c	Jackie Robinson, #2016	12.50
SP593	20c	Touro Synagogue, #2017	1.75
SP594	20c	Wolf Trap Farm, #2018	1.50
SP595	20c	Architecture, #2022a	1.75
SP596	20c	Francis of Assisi, #2023	1.40
SP597	20c	Ponce de Leon, #2024	1.40
SP598	13c	Puppy, Kitten, #2025	2.00
SP599	20c	Madonna and Child, #2026	2.25
SP600	20c	Children Playing, #2030a	2.25

1983

SP601	1c, 4c, 13c	Official Mail, #O127-O129	2.50
SP602	17c	Official Mail, #O130	2.25
SP603	$1	Official Mail, #O132	4.00
SP604	$5	Official Mail, #O133	9.50
SP605	20c	Official Mail coil, #O135	3.25
SP606	20c	Science, #2031	1.50
SP607	20c	Ballooning, #2035a	1.75
SP608	20c	US Sweden, #2036	1.50
SP609	20c	CCC, #2037	1.25
SP610	20c	Priestley, #2038	1.50
SP611	20c	Voluntarism, #2039	1.25
SP612	20c	German Immigration, #2040	1.50
SP613	20c	Brooklyn Bridge, #2041	2.00
SP614	20c	TVA, #2042	1.50
SP615	20c	Fitness, #2043	1.50
SP616	20c	Scott Joplin, #2044	2.50
SP617	20c	Medal of Honor, #2045	3.25
SP618	20c	Babe Ruth, #2046	10.00
SP619	20c	Hawthorne, #2047	1.50
SP620	13c	Olympics, #2051a	3.00
SP621	28c	Olympics, #C104a	3.00
SP622	40c	Olympics, #C108a	2.75
SP623	35c	Olympics, #C112a	2.75
SP624	20c	Treaty of Paris, #2052	1.25
SP625	20c	Civil Service, #2053	1.25
SP626	20c	Metropolitan Opera, #2054	1.75
SP627	20c	Inventors, #2058a	1.75
SP628	20c	Streetcars, #2062a	2.25
SP629	20c	Madonna and Child, #2063	1.50
SP630	20c	Santa Claus, #2064	1.50
SP631	20c	Martin Luther, #2065	2.25

1984-85

SP632	20c	Alaska, #2066	1.50
SP633	20c	Winter Olympics, #2070a	2.25
SP634	20c	FDIC, #2071	1.50
SP635	20c	Love, #2072	1.50
SP636	20c	Woodson, #2073	2.25
SP637	14c, 22c	D sheet, coil, #O138-O139	1.50
SP638	20c	Conservation, #2074	1.25
SP639	20c	Credit Union, #2075	1.50
SP640	20c	Orchids, #2079a	2.25
SP641	20c	Hawaii, #2080	2.00
SP642	20c	National Archives, #2081	1.25
SP643	20c	Olympics, #2085a	2.75
SP644	20c	World Expo, #2086	1.25
SP645	20c	Health Research, #2087	1.25
SP646	20c	Fairbanks, #2088	3.00
SP647	20c	Thorpe, #2089	7.00
SP648	20c	McCormack, #2090	3.00
SP649	20c	St. Lawrence Seaway, #2091	1.25
SP650	20c	Waterfowl, #2092	3.00
SP651	20c	Roanoke Voyages, #2093	1.25
SP652	20c	Melville, #2094	1.50
SP653	20c	Horace Moses, #2095	1.25
SP654	20c	Smokey Bear, #2096	7.00
SP655	20c	Clemente, #2097	11.00
SP656	20c	Dogs, #2101a	3.00
SP657	20c	Crime Prevention, #2102	1.50
SP658	20c	Hispanic Americans, #2103	1.25
SP659	20c	Family Unity, #2104	2.25
SP660	20c	Eleanor Roosevelt, #2105	2.50
SP661	20c	Readers, #2106	2.00
SP662	20c	Madonna and Child, #2107	2.00
SP663	20c	Child's Santa, #2108	2.00
SP664	20c	Vietnam Memorial, #2109	3.25

1985-87

SP665	20c	Jerome Kern, #2110	2.00
SP666	22c	D sheet, coil, #2111-2112	1.50
SP667	22c	D booklet pane of 10, #2113a	3.00
SP668	33c	Verville, #C113	1.25
SP669	39c	Sperry, #C114	1.75
SP670	44c	Transpacific, #C115	1.50
SP671	22c	Flags sheet, coil, #2114-2115	2.00
SP671a	22c	Flag "T" coil, #2115b	2.25
SP672	22c	Flag booklet pane of 5, #2116a	2.50
SP673	22c	Seashells, #2121a	3.50
SP674	$10.75	Express Mail single, #2122	30.00
SP674a	$10.75	Express Mail booklet pane of 3, #2122a	65.00

Transportation Coils

1985-89

SP675	3.4c	School Bus, #2123	3.00
SP676	4.9c	Buckboard, #2124	2.75
SP677	5.5c	Star Route Truck, #2125	3.00
SP678	6c	Tricycle, #2126	2.50
SP679	7.1c	Tractor, #2127	2.25
SP679a	7.1c	Tractor, Zip+4 precancel, #2127b	2.50
SP680	8.3c	Ambulance, #2128	2.75
SP681	8.5c	Tow Truck, #2129	1.50
SP682	10.1c	Oil Wagon, #2130	2.25
SP682a	10.1c	Red precancel, #2130a	2.00
SP683	11c	Stutz Bearcat, #2131	2.50
SP684	12c	Stanley Steamer, #2132	2.75
SP685	12.5c	Pushcart, #2133	2.50
SP686	14c	Iceboat, #2134	3.25
SP687	17c	Dog Sled, #2135	2.25
SP688	25c	Bread Wagon, #2136	3.00

1985

SP689	22c	Bethune, #2137	2.75
SP690	22c	Duck Decoys, #2141a	3.25
SP691	22c	Winter Special Olympics, #2142	1.25
SP692	22c	Love, #2143	2.25
SP693	22c	REA, #2144	1.25
SP694	14c, 22c	Official Mail, #O129A, O136	2.00
SP695	22c	AMERIPEX '86, #2145	1.25
SP696	22c	Abigail Adams, #2146	1.25
SP697	22c	Bartholdi, #2147	2.25
SP698	18c	Washington coil, #2149	2.25
SP699	21.1c	Letters coil, #2150	2.25
SP700	22c	Korean Veterans, #2152	2.00
SP701	22c	Social Security, #2153	1.50
SP702	44c	Serra, #C116	1.50
SP703	22c	World War I Veterans, #2154	1.75
SP704	22c	Horses, #2158a	3.25
SP705	22c	Education, #2159	1.50
SP706	22c	Youth Year, #2163a	2.50
SP707	22c	Hunger, #2164	1.60
SP708	22c	Madonna and Child, #2165	1.50
SP709	22c	Poinsettias, #2166	2.50

1986

SP710	22c	Arkansas, #2167	1.50

Great Americans

1986-94

SP711	1c	Mitchell, #2168	2.50
SP712	2c	Lyon, #2169	1.50
SP713	3c	White, #2170	1.50
SP714	4c	Flanagan, #2171	1.60
SP715	5c	Black, #2172	2.25
SP716	5c	Munoz Marin, #2173	2.00
SP717	10c	Red Cloud, #2175	1.75
SP718	14c	Howe, #2176	1.50
SP719	15c	Cody, #2177	1.75
SP720	17c	Lockwood, #2178	1.50
SP721	20c	Apgar, #2179	4.50
SP722	21c	Carlson, #2180	1.50
SP723	23c	Cassatt, #2181	1.50
SP724	25c	London, #2182	1.50
SP724a	25c	London, pane of 10, #2182a	4.25
SP725	28c	Sitting Bull, #2183	1.75
SP726	29c	Warren, #2184	3.00
SP727	29c	Jefferson, #2185	2.75
SP728	35c	Chavez, #2186	2.75
SP729	40c	Chennault, #2187	2.50
SP730	45c	Cushing, #2188	1.50
SP731	52c	Humphrey, #2189	2.00
SP732	56c	Harvard, #2190	2.00
SP733	65c	Arnold, #2191	2.25
SP734	75c	Willkie, #2192	2.25
SP735	$1	Revel, #2193	1.75
SP736	$1	Hopkins, #2194	2.25
SP737	$2	Bryan, #2195	3.25
SP739	$5	Harte, #2196	8.00
SP740	25c	London, #2197a	2.25

1986

SP741	22c	Stamp Collecting, #2201a	3.00
SP742	22c	Love, #2202	2.00
SP743	22c	Sojourner Truth, #2203	2.50
SP744	22c	Texas Republic, #2204	1.75
SP745	22c	Fish booklet pane of 5, #2209a	3.00
SP746	22c	Hospitals, #2210	1.50
SP747	22c	Duke Ellington, #2211	3.25
SP748	22c	Presidents Sheet #1, #2216	3.75
SP749	22c	Presidents Sheet #2, #2217	3.75
SP750	22c	Presidents Sheet #3, #2218	3.75
SP751	22c	Presidents Sheet #4, #2219	3.75
SP752	22c	Arctic Explorers, #2223a	2.75
SP753	22c	Statue of Liberty, #2224	2.25

1987

SP754	2c	Locomotive, reengraved, #2226	2.25

1986

SP755	22c	Navajo Art, #2238a	2.75
SP756	22c	T.S. Eliot, #2239	2.50
SP757	22c	Woodcarved Figurines, #2243a	2.75
SP758	22c	Madonna and Child, #2244	1.75
SP759	22c	Village Scene, #2245	1.75

1987

SP760	22c	Michigan, #2246	2.50
SP761	22c	Pan American Games, #2247	2.50
SP762	22c	Love, #2248	2.00
SP763	22c	du Sable, #2249	4.00
SP764	22c	Caruso, #2250	2.25
SP765	22c	Girl Scouts, #2251	3.50

Transportation Coils

1987-88

SP766	3c	Conestoga Wagon, #2252	2.50
SP767	5c, 17.5c	Milk Wagon, Racing Car, #2253, 2262	2.75
SP768	5.3c	Elevator, #2254	2.25
SP769	7.6c	Carreta, #2255	2.25
SP770	8.4c	Wheelchair, #2256	2.50
SP771	10c	Canal Boat, #2257	1.75
SP772	13c	Patrol Wagon, #2258	2.75
SP773	13.2c	Coal Car, #2259	2.75
SP774	15c	Tugboat, #2260	2.50
SP775	16.7c	Popcorn Wagon, #2261	2.50
SP776	20c	Cable Car, #2263	2.50
SP777	20.5c	Fire Engine, #2264	3.00
SP778	21c	Mail Car, #2265	3.00
SP779	24.1c	Tandem Bicycle, #2255	2.50

1987

SP780	22c	Special Occasions, #2274a	3.75
SP781	22c	United Way, #2275	1.50

1987-89

SP782	22c	Flag and Fireworks, #2276	1.50
SP783	22c	Flag, pair from booklet, #2276a	2.25
SP784	(25c)	"E" sheet, coil, #2277, 2279	2.75
SP785	(25c)	"E" booklet pane of 10, #2282a	3.25
SP786	25c	Flag with Clouds, #2278	1.50
SP787	25c	Flag with Clouds booklet pane of 6, #2285c	3.00
SP788	25c	Flag over Yosemite coil, block tagging, #2280	1.75
SP788a	25c	Flag over Yosemite, prephosphored uncoated paper (mottled tagging), #2280a	1.75
SP789	25c	Honeybee coil, #2281	3.00
SP790	25c	Pheasant, #2283a	3.25
SP791	25c	Owl and Grosbeak, #2285b	3.00
SP792	(25c)	"E" Official coil, #O140	2.25

SP793 20c Official coil, #O138B 1.75
SP794 15c, 25c Official coils, #O138A, O141 2.25

1987

SP795 22c Wildlife, #2286-2295 4.00
SP796 22c Wildlife, #2296-2305 4.00
SP797 22c Wildlife, #2306-2315 4.00
SP798 22c Wildlife, #2316-2325 4.00
SP799 22c Wildlife, #2326-2335 4.00

Ratification of the Constitution

1987-90

SP800 22c Delaware, #2336 2.00
SP801 22c Pennsylvania, #2337 1.50
SP802 22c New Jersey, #2338 1.75
SP803 22c Georgia, #2339 1.75
SP804 22c Connecticut, #2340 1.75
SP805 22c Massachusetts, #2341 2.25
SP806 22c Maryland, #2342 2.25
SP807 25c South Carolina, #2343 1.50
SP808 25c New Hampshire, #2344 1.75
SP809 25c Virginia, #2345 2.00
SP810 25c New York, #2346 2.00
SP811 25c North Carolina, #2347 2.00
SP812 25c Rhode Island, #2348 2.00

1987

SP813 22c U.S./Morocco, #2349 1.50
SP814 22c William Faulkner, #2350 1.50
SP815 22c Lacemaking, #2354a 3.50
SP816 22c Constitution, #2359a 2.50
SP817 22c Signing of Constitution, #2360 1.50
SP818 22c Certified Public Accounting, #2361 3.25
SP819 22c Locomotives, #2366a 6.75
SP820 22c Madonna and Child, #2367 1.50
SP821 22c Christmas Ornament, #2368 1.50

1988

SP822 22c Winter Olympics, #2369 1.50
SP823 22c Australia Bicentennial, #2370 1.75
SP824 22c James Weldon Johnson, #2371 2.75
SP825 22c Cats, #2375a 3.75
SP826 22c Knute Rockne, #2376 5.00
SP827 44c New Sweden, #C117 1.75
SP828 45c Samuel P. Langley, #C118 1.75
SP829 25c Francis Ouimet, #2377 4.00
SP830 36c Igor Sikorsky, #C119 2.00
SP831 25c Love, #2378 2.00
SP832 45c Love, #2379 1.75
SP833 25c Summer Olympics, #2380 1.75
SP834 25c Classic Automobiles, #2385a 3.75
SP835 25c Antarctic Explorers, #2389a 2.75
SP836 25c Carousel Animals, #2393a 3.00
SP837 $8.75 Express Mail, #2394 15.00
SP838 25c Special Occasions, #2396a 14.00
SP839 25c Special Occasions, #2398a 9.25
SP840 25c Madonna and Child, #2399 1.50
SP841 25c Village Scene, #2400 1.50

1989

SP842 25c Montana, #2401 1.75
SP843 25c A. Philip Randolph, #2402 3.00
SP844 25c North Dakota, #2403 1.50
SP845 25c Washington Statehood, #2404 1.50
SP846 25c Steamboats, #2409a 3.50
SP847 25c World Stamp Expo, #2410 1.50
SP848 25c Toscanini, #2411 2.00

Branches of Government

1989-90

SP849 25c House of Representatives, #2412 1.50
SP850 25c Senate, #2413 1.50
SP851 25c Executive, #2414 1.50
SP852 25c Supreme Court, #2415 1.50

1989

SP853 25c South Dakota, #2416 1.50
SP854 25c Lou Gehrig, #2417 10.00
SP855 1c Official, litho., #O143 2.25
SP856 45c French Revolution, #C120 2.25
SP857 25c Ernest Hemingway, #2418 2.50
SP858 $2.40 Moon Landing, #2419 11.00
SP859 25c Letter Carriers, #2420 1.50
SP860 25c Bill of Rights, #2421 1.50
SP861 25c Dinosaurs, #2425a 5.50
SP862 25c, 45c Pre-Columbian Artifacts, #2426, C121 2.00
SP863 25c Madonna sheet single, booklet pane of 10, #2427, 2427a 4.25
SP864 25c Sleigh single, booklet pane of 10, #2428, 2429a 4.25
SP865 25c Eagle & Shield, #2431 1.75
SP866 90c World Stamp Expo '89, #2433 7.00
SP867 25c Traditional Mail Delivery, #2437a 2.75
SP868 45c Futuristic Mail Delivery, #C126 3.25
SP869 45c Futuristic Mail Delivery, #C125a 3.25
SP870 25c Traditional Mail Delivery, #2438 3.50

1990

SP871 25c Idaho, #2439 1.50
SP872 25c Love single, booklet pane of 10, #2440, 2441a 3.00
SP873 25c Ida B. Wells, #2442 3.00
SP874 15c Beach Umbrella, #2443a 3.00
SP875 25c Wyoming, #2444 2.25
SP876 25c Classic Films, #2448a 4.25
SP877 25c Marianne Moore, #2449 1.50

Transportation Coils

1990-92

SP879 4c Steam Carriage, #2451 2.25
SP880 5c Circus Wagon, #2452 2.75
SP880A 5c Circus Wagon, #2452B 3.25
SP880B 5c Circus Wagon with cent sign, #2452D 5.00
SP881 5c, 10c Canoe, engr., Tractor Trailer, #2453, 2457 2.25
SP882 5c Canoe, photo., #2454 3.00
SP883 10c Tractor trailer, photo., #2458 5.00
SP891 20c Cog Railway, #2463 4.00
SP892 23c Lunch Wagon, #2464 2.25
SP893 32c Ferry Boat, #2466 4.00
SP895 $1 Seaplane, #2468 5.00

1990-94

SP897 25c Lighthouses, booklet pane of 5, #2474a 5.00
SP898 25c Flag, #2475 2.75

Flora and Fauna Series

SP899 1c, 3c, 30c Kestrel, Bluebird, Cardinal, #2476, 2478, 2480 2.25
SP900 1c Kestrel with cent sign, #2477 6.00
SP901 19c Fawn, #2479 2.25
SP902 45c Pumpkinseed Sunfish, #2481 2.75
SP903 $2 Bobcat, #2482 4.00
SP904 20c Blue jay, #2483 6.00
SP905 29c Wood Ducks booklet panes of 10, #2484a, 2485a 9.50
SP906 29c African Violets bklt. pane of 10, #2486a 4.25
SP907 32c Peach & Pear, #2488b, 2493-2494 4.50
SP908 29c Red Squirrel, #2489 2.75
SP909 29c Red Rose, #2490 2.50
SP910 29c Pine Cone, #2491 2.50
SP911 32c Pink rose, #2492 5.00
SP919 25c Olympians, #2496-2500 4.75
SP920 25c Indian Headdresses, #2505a 5.50
SP921 25c Micronesia, Marshall Islands, #2507a 2.25
SP922 25c Sea Creatures, #2511a 4.75
SP923 25c, 45c Grand Canyon, Tropical Coast-line, #2512, C127 2.25
SP924 25c Eisenhower, #2513 2.50
SP925 25c Madonna sheet single, booklet pane of 10, #2514, 2514a 5.00
SP926 25c Christmas Tree sheet single, booklet pane of 10, #2515, 2516a 5.00

1991-95

SP927 (29c) "F" Flower single, coil pair, #2517, 2518 2.50
SP928 (29c) "F" Flower booklet panes of 10, #2519a, 2520a 8.00
SP929 (4c) Make-up Rate, #2521 2.00
SP930 (29c) "F" Flag, #2522 2.25
SP931 (29c) "F" Official coil, #O144 2.50
SP932 29c Mt. Rushmore, #2523 2.50
SP933 29c Mt. Rushmore, photo., #2523A 2.25
SP934 29c Flower single, booklet pane of 10, #2524, 2527a 5.00
SP935 29c Flower coil, #2525 1.75
SP936 29c Flower coil, #2526 2.25
SP937 4c Official, #O146 2.00
SP938 29c Flag, Olympic Rings, #2528a 5.00
SP939 19c Fishing Boat coil, #2529 2.50
SP939A 19c Fishing Boat coil reissue, #2529C 3.75
SP940 19c Ballooning, #2530a 4.00
SP941 29c Flags on Parade, #2531 2.50
SP942 29c Liberty Torch, #2531A 2.50
SP943 50c Switzerland, #2532 2.25
SP944 20c Vermont Statehood, #2533 2.50
SP945 50c Harriet Quimby, #C128 2.25
SP946 29c Savings Bonds, #2534 2.00
SP947 29c, 52c Love, #2535, 2536a, 2537 6.00
SP948 40c William T. Piper, #C129 2.25
SP949 29c William Saroyan, #2538 2.75
SP950 Official 19c, 23c, 29c, #O145, O147-O148 2.50
SP951 $1.00 USPS/Olympic Rings, #2539 3.00
SP952 $2.90 Eagle, #2540 7.50
SP953 $9.95 Eagle, #2541 22.50
SP954 $14 Eagle, #2542 30.00
SP955 $2.90 Futuristic Space Shuttle, #2543 8.00
SP956 $3 Challenger Shuttle, #2544 10.00
SP956A $10.75 Endeavour Shuttle, #2544A 22.50
SP957 29c Fishing Flies, #2549a 5.25
SP958 29c Cole Porter, #2550 2.25
SP959 50c Antarctic Treaty, #C130 2.75
SP960 29c Desert Shield, Desert Storm, #2551 5.00
SP961 29c 1992 Summer Olympics, #2553-2557 4.00
SP962 29c Numismatics, #2558 2.50
SP963 29c World War II, #2559 6.50
SP964 29c Basketball, #2560 5.25
SP965 29c District of Columbia, #2561 2.25
SP966 29c Comedians, #2566a 5.00
SP967 29c Jan E. Matzeliger, #2567 4.00
SP968 29c Space Exploration, #2577a 6.75
SP969 50c Bering Land Bridge, #C131 2.25
SP970 29c Madonna and Child sheet single, booklet pane of 10, #2578, 2578a 7.50
SP971 29c Santa Claus sheet and booklet singles, #2579, 2580 or 2581, 2582-2585 11.00
SP973 32c James K. Polk, #2587 7.00
SP976 $1 Surrender of Gen. Burgoyne, #2590 4.75
SP978 $5 Washington and Jackson, #2592 10.00
SP980 29c Pledge of Allegiance, #2593a 7.00
SP982 29c Eagle & Shield self-adhesives, #2595-2597 4.00
SP983 29c Eagle self-adhesive, #2598 3.50
SP984 29c Statue of Liberty, #2599 3.50
SP990 (10c) Eagle and Shield coil, #2602 3.75
SP991 (10c) Eagle and Shield coils, #2603-2604 3.75
SP993 23c Stars and Stripes coil, #2605 2.50
SP994 23c USA coil, #2606 2.75
SP994A 23c USA coil, #2607 2.75
SP994B 23c USA coil, #2608 2.50
SP995 29c Flag over White House, #2609 2.50

1992

SP997 29c Winter Olympics, #2611-2615 3.75
SP998 29c World Columbian Stamp Expo '92, #2616 2.50
SP999 29c W.E.B. DuBois, #2617 3.75
SP1000 29c Love, #2618 2.50
SP1001 29c Olympic Baseball, #2619 10.00
SP1002 29c First Voyage of Columbus, #2623a 3.75
SP1003 1c, 4c, $1 First Sighting of Land souvenir sheet, #2624 7.50
SP1004 2c, 3c, $4 Claiming a New World souvenir sheet, #2625 7.50
SP1005 5c, 30c, 50c Seeking Royal Support souvenir sheet, #2626 7.50
SP1006 6c, 8c, $3 Royal Favor Restored souvenir sheet, #2627 7.50
SP1007 10c, 15c, $2 Reporting Discoveries souvenir sheet, #2628 7.50
SP1008 $5 Columbus souvenir sheet, #2629 7.50
SP1009 29c New York Stock Exchange, #2630 2.50
SP1010 29c Space Accomplishments, #2634a 4.00
SP1011 29c Alaska Highway, #2635 2.50
SP1012 29c Kentucky Statehood, #2636 2.50
SP1013 29c Summer Olympics, #2637-2641 3.75
SP1014 29c Hummingbirds, #2646a 5.00
SP1015 29c Wildflowers, #2647-2656 6.50
SP1016 29c Wildflowers, #2657-2666 6.50
SP1017 29c Wildflowers, #2667-2676 6.50
SP1018 29c Wildflowers, #2677-2686 6.50
SP1019 29c Wildflowers, #2687-2696 6.50
SP1020 29c World War II, #2697 6.00
SP1021 29c Dorothy Parker, #2698 2.75
SP1022 29c Dr. Theodore von Karman, #2699 3.50
SP1023 29c Minerals strip of 4, #2703a 4.00
SP1024 29c Juan Rodriguez Cabrillo, #2704 2.50
SP1025 29c Wild Animals, #2709a 5.00
SP1026 29c Madonna and Child sheet single, booklet pane of 10, #2710, 2710a 7.50
SP1027 29c Christmas Toys block of 4, booklet pane of 4 and booklet single, #2714a, 2718a, 2719 5.50
SP1028 29c Chinese New Year, #2720 7.75

1993

SP1029 29c Elvis Presley, #2721 10.00
SP1030 29c Oklahoma!, #2722 2.25
SP1030A 29c Hank Williams sheet stamp, #2723 5.00
SP1030B 29c Rock & Roll/Rhythm & Blues sheet single, booklet pane of 8, #2737b 10.00

No. SP1030B exists with any one of #2724-2730 affixed along with #2737b.

SP1034 29c Space Fantasy, #2745a 6.00
SP1035 29c Percy Lavon Julian, #2746 3.50
SP1036 29c Oregon Trail, #2747 2.75
SP1037 29c World University Games, #2748 2.75
SP1038 29c Grace Kelly, #2749 6.00
SP1039 29c Circus, #2753a 4.50
SP1040 29c Cherokee Strip, #2754 3.50
SP1041 29c Dean Acheson, #2755 3.00
SP1042 29c Sporting Horses, #2759a 5.50
SP1043 29c Garden Flowers, #2764a 3.50
SP1044 29c World War II, #2765 5.50
SP1045 29c Joe Louis, #2766 7.50
SP1046 29c Broadway Musicals, #2770a 4.50
SP1047 29c National Postal Museum strip of 4, #2782a 3.25
SP1048 29c American Sign Language, #2784a 2.75
SP1049 29c Country & Western Music sheet stamp and booklet pane of 4, #2778a 9.25

No. SP1049 exists with any one of #2771-2774 affixed along with #2778a.

SP1050 10c Official Mail, #O146A 2.75
SP1052 29c Classic Books strip of 4, #2788a 3.25
SP1053 29c Traditional Christmas sheet stamp, booklet pane of 4, #2789, 2790a 4.75
SP1054 29c Contemporary Christmas booklet pane of 10, sheet and self-adhesive single stamps, #2803 8.50

No. SP1054 exists with any one of #2791-2794, 2798a, 2798b, 2799-2802 affixed along with #2803.

SP1055 29c Mariana Islands, #2804 2.75
SP1056 29c Columbus' Landing in Puerto Rico, #2805 3.25
SP1057 29c AIDS Awareness, #2806, 2806b 4.75

1994

SP1058 29c Winter Olympics, #2811a 5.00
SP1059 29c Edward R. Murrow, #2812 3.25
SP1060 29c Love self-adhesive, #2813 3.25
SP1061 29c, 52c Love booklet pane of 10, single sheet stamp, #2814a, 2815 6.50
SP1062 29c Love sheet stamp, #2814C 3.25
SP1063 29c Dr. Allison Davis, #2816 4.50
SP1064 29c Chinese New Year, #2817 4.00
SP1065 29c Buffalo Soldiers, #2818 5.00
SP1066 29c Silent Screen Stars, #2819-2828 6.00
SP1067 29c Garden Flowers, #2833a 6.00
SP1068 29c, 40c, 50c World Cup Soccer, #2834-2836 6.00
SP1069 World Cup Soccer, #2837 6.00
SP1070 29c World War II, #2838 5.50
SP1071 29c, 50c Norman Rockwell stamp, souvenir sheet, #2839-2840 9.00

SP1072 29c, Moon Landing, #2841-2842 $9.95 15.00
SP1073 29c Locomotives, #2847a 6.50
SP1074 29c George Meany, #2848 3.25
SP1075 29c Popular Singers, #2853a 6.00
SP1076 29c Jazz and Blues Singers block of 10, #2854-2861 9.00

Block of 10 on No. SP1076 may contain different combinations of stamps.

SP1077 29c James Thurber, #2862 4.00
SP1078 29c Wonders of the Sea, #2866a 5.00
SP1079 29c Cranes, #2868a 3.25
SP1079A Legends of the West, #2869 12.00
SP1080 29c Traditional Christmas sheet stamp, booklet pane of 10, #2871, 2871b 8.50
SP1081 29c Contemporary Christmas sheet stamp, block of 4 from booklet pane, #2872 6.50
SP1082 29c Contemporary Christmas self-adhesive stamps, #2873--2874 7.00
SP1083 $2 Bureau of Engraving and Printing Souvenir Sheet, #2875 15.00

1995-96

SP1084 29c Chinese New Year, #2876 5.50
SP1085 G make-up rate, G stamps, #2877, 2884, 2890, 2893 4.00
SP1086 G make-up rate, G stamps, #2878, 2880, 2882, 2885, 2888, 2892 4.00
SP1087 G stamps, official G stamp, #2879, 2881, 2883, 2889, O152 4.00
SP1088 G self-adhesive stamps, #2886-2887 8.00
SP1091 32c Flag Over Porch, #2897, 2913, 2915-2916 5.50
SP1096 (5c) Butte coil, #2902 5.00
SP1097 (5c) Mountain coil, #2903, 2904 4.50
SP1099 Butte, Mountain, Juke Box, Auto Tail Fin, Auto, Flag over porch, #2902B, 2904A, 2906, 2910, 2912A, 2915B 5.50
SP1099A Mountain, Juke Box, Flag Over Porch coil and booklet stamps, #2904B, 2912B, 2915D, 2921b 9.00
SP1100 (10c) Auto coil, #2905 4.50
SP1102 Eagle & shield, Flag over porch, #2907, 2920D, 2921 4.50
SP1103 (15c) Auto Tail Fin, #2908-2909 4.50
SP1105 (25c) Juke Box, #2911-2912 3.00
SP1110 32c Flag over Field self-adhesive, # 2.75
SP1114 (32c) Non-denominated Love, #2948-2949 3.00
SP1115 32c Florida Statehood, #2950 2.75

Great Americans Series

1995-99

SP1126 32c Milton Hershey, #2933 2.75
SP1127 32c Cal Farley, #2934 3.25
SP1128 32c Henry R. Luce, #2935 5.50
SP1129 32c Lila & DeWitt Wallace, #2936 5.50
SP1131 46c Ruth Benedict, #2938 3.25
SP1133 55c Alice Hamilton, #2940 2.75
SP1134 55c Justin S. Morrill, #2941 5.50
SP1135 77c Mary Breckinridge, #2942 4.50
SP1136 78c Alice Paul, #2943 2.75

1995

SP1141 32c Kids Care, #2954a 3.50
SP1142 32c Richard Nixon, #2955 3.50
SP1143 32c Bessie Coleman, #2956 4.50
SP1144 1-32c Official, #O153-O156 3.00
SP1145 32c, 55c Love (with denominations), #2957-2960 3.50
SP1146 32c Recreational Sports, #2965a 9.00
SP1147 32c Prisoners of War/Missing in Action, #2966 4.50
SP1148 32c Marilyn Monroe, #2967 12.00
SP1149 32c Texas Statehood, #2968 4.00
SP1150 32c Great Lakes Lighthouses, #2973a 9.00
SP1151 32c United Nations, #2974 2.75
SP1152 32c Civil War, #2975 14.50
SP1153 32c Carousel Horses, #2979a 5.25
SP1154 32c Woman Suffrage, #2980 2.75
SP1155 32c World War II, #2981 6.00
SP1156 32c Louis Armstrong, #2982 4.50
SP1157 32c Jazz Musicians, #2992a 7.00
SP1158 32c Garden Flowers, #2997a 6.00
SP1159 60c Eddie Rickenbacker, #2998 4.50
SP1160 32c Republic of Palau, #2999 3.50
SP1161 32c Comic Strip Classics, #3000 15.00
SP1162 32c Naval Academy, #3001 4.50
SP1163 32c Tennessee Williams, #3002 4.50
SP1164 32c Traditional Christmas sheet stamp, booklet pane of 10, #3003, 3003b 5.50
SP1165 32c Contemporary Christmas block of 4, self-adhesive stamps, #3007a, 3010-3011 5.00

No. SP1165 may include different combinations of Nos. 3008-3011.

SP1166 32c Midnight Angel, #3012 4.75
SP1167 32c Children Sledding, #3013 4.75
SP1168 32c Antique Automobiles, #3023a 6.00

1996

SP1169 32c Utah Statehood, #3024 3.50
SP1170 32c Garden Flowers, #3029a 6.00
SP1171 1, 32c Flag Over Porch, Love self-adhesives, Kestrel coil, #2920e, 3030, 3044 16.00

1996-99

Flora and Fauna Series

SP1171A 1c Kestrel, self-adhesive, #3031 6.50
SP1172 2c Woodpecker, #3032 3.75
SP1173 3c Bluebird, #3033 3.75
SP1184 $1 Red Fox, #3036 7.00
SP1185 2c Woodpecker coil, #3045 6.00
SP1187 20c Bluejay self-adhesive coil, booklet stamps, #3048, 3053 5.00
SP1188 32c Yellow Rose, #3049 6.00
SP1189 20c Ring-necked Pheasant, #3050, 3055 7.00
SP1191A 33c Coral Pink Rose, serpentine die cut 10¾x10½, #3052E 7.00
SP1191 33c Coral Pink Rose, #3052 7.00
SP1192 32c Yellow Rose coil, #3054 7.00

1996

SP1197 32c Ernest E. Just, #3058 5.00
SP1198 32c Smithsonian Institution, #3059 3.75
SP1199 32c Chinese New Year, #3060 6.00
SP1200 32c Pioneers of Communication, #3064a 7.00
SP1201 32c Fulbright Scholarships, #3065 3.75
SP1202 50c Jacqueline Cochran, #3066 3.75
SP1203 32c Marathon, #3067 3.75
SP1204 32c Olympic Games, #3068 15.00
SP1205 32c Georgia O'Keeffe, #3069 4.75
SP1206 32c Tennessee Statehood, #3070 3.75
SP1207 32c American Indian Dances, #3076a 4.75
SP1208 32c Prehistoric Animals, #3080a 4.75
SP1209 32c Breast Cancer Awareness, #3081 4.75
SP1210 32c James Dean, #3082 6.00
SP1211 32c Folk Heroes, #3086a 5.00
SP1212 32c Centennial Olympic Games, #3087 5.00
SP1213 32c Iowa Statehood, #3088-3089 5.00
SP1214 32c Rural Free Delivery, #3090 4.00
SP1215 32c Riverboats, #3095a 5.50
SP1216 32c Big Band Leaders, #3099a 6.00
SP1217 32c Songwriters, #3103a 6.00
SP1218 23c F. Scott Fitzgerald, #3104 4.00
SP1219 32c Endangered Species, #3105 15.00
SP1220 32c Computer Technology, #3106 4.00
SP1221 32c Madonna & Child sheet & booklet stamps, #3107, 3112 6.00
SP1222 32c Contemporary Christmas block of 4, self-adhesive stamp, #3111a, 3113 6.00

#SP1222 may contain #3114-3116 instead of #3113.

SP1223 32c Skaters, #3117 6.00
SP1224 32c Hanukkah, #3118 5.00
SP1225 32c Cycling souvenir sheet, #3119 6.00

1997

SP1226 32c Chinese New Year, #3120 6.00
SP1227 32c Benjamin O. Davis, Sr., #3121 6.00
SP1228 32c Statue of Liberty, #3122 5.50
SP1229 32, 55c Love Swans, #3123-3124 5.50
SP1230 32c Helping Children Learn, #3125 5.00
SP1231 32c Merian Botanical Prints, #3126-3129 5.50
SP1232 32c PACIFIC 97 Triangles, #3131a 6.00
SP1233 (25c), 32c Flag Over Porch, Juke Box linerless coils, #3132-3133 5.50
SP1234 32c Thornton Wilder, #3134 5.00
SP1235 32c Raoul Wallenberg, #3135 5.00
SP1236 32c Dinosaurs, #3136 12.50
SP1237 32c Bugs Bunny, #3137 10.00
SP1238 50c PACIFIC 97 Franklin, #3139 10.00
SP1239 60c PACIFIC 97 Washington, #3140 10.00
SP1240 32c Marshall Plan, #3141 5.00
SP1241 32c Classic American Aircraft, #3142 12.50
SP1242 32c Football Coaches, #3146a 10.00
SP1242A 32c Vince Lombardi, #3147 8.00
SP1242B 32c Bear Bryant, #3148 8.00
SP1242C 32c Pop Warner, #3149 8.00
SP1242D 32c George Halas, #3150 8.00
SP1243 32c Classic American Dolls, #3151 10.00
SP1244 32c Humphrey Bogart, #3152 6.00
SP1245 32c The Stars and Stripes Forever!, #3153 6.00
SP1246 32c Opera Singers, #3157a 8.00
SP1247 32c Composers & Conductors, #3165a 9.00
SP1248 32c Padre Felix Varela, #3155 6.00
SP1249 32c Department of the Air Force, #3167 8.00
SP1250 32c Movie Monsters, #3172a 10.00
SP1251 32c Supersonic Flight, #3173 8.00
SP1252 32c Women in Military Service, #3174 6.00
SP1253 32c Kwanzaa, #3175 7.50
SP1254 32c Madonna and Child, #3176 7.50
SP1255 32c Holly, #3177 7.50
SP1256 32c Mars Pathfinder, #3178 12.00

1998

SP1257 32c Chinese New Year, #3179 6.00
SP1258 32c Alpine Skiing, #3180 6.00
SP1259 32c Madam C.J. Walker, #3181 6.00

1998-2000

Celebrate the Century

SP1259A 32c 1900s, #3182 10.00
SP1259B 32c 1910s, #3183 10.00
SP1259C 32c 1920s, #3184 10.00
SP1259D 32c 1930s, #3185 10.00
SP1259E 32c 1940s, #3186 10.00
SP1259F 33c 1950s, #3187 10.00
SP1259G 33c 1960s, #3188 10.00
SP1259H 33c 1970s, #3189 10.00
SP1259I 33c 1980s, #3190 10.00
SP1259J 33c 1990s, #3191 10.00

1998

SP1260 32c "Remember the Maine," #3192 6.00
SP1261 32c Flowering Trees, #3197a 8.00
SP1262 32c Alexander Calder, #3202a 8.00
SP1263 32c Cinco de Mayo, #3203 6.00
SP1264 32c Sylvester & Tweety, #3204a 6.00
SP1265 32c Wisconsin Statehood, #3206 6.00
SP1266 (5c), (25c) Wetlands, Diner Coils, #3207-3208 5.50
SP1266A (25c) Diner coil, #3208A 5.50
SP1267 1c-$2 Trans-Mississippi, #3209 10.00
SP1268 $1 Trans-Mississippi, #3209h 6.00
SP1269 32c Berlin Airlift, #3211 5.50
SP1270 32c Folk Musicians, #3215a 8.00
SP1271 32c Gospel Singers, #3219a 7.50
SP1272 32c Spanish Settlement, #3220 6.00
SP1273 32c Stephen Vincent Benét, #3221 6.00
SP1274 32c Tropical Birds, #3225a 8.00
SP1275 32c Alfred Hitchcock, #3226 6.00
SP1276 32c Organ & Tissue Donation, #3227 6.00
SP1277 (10c) Modern Bicycle, #3229 6.00
SP1278 32c Bright Eyes, #3234a 7.50
SP1279 32c Klondike Gold Rush, #3235 6.00
SP1280 32c American Art, #3236 10.00
SP1281 32c Ballet, #3237 6.00
SP1282 32c Space Discovery, #3242a 7.50
SP1283 32c Giving & Sharing, #3243 6.00
SP1284 32c Madonna & Child, #3244 6.00
SP1285 32c Wreaths, #3248a, 3252a 7.50
SP1286 (32+8c) Breast Cancer Awareness, #B1 6.00
SP1287 (1c), (33c) Weather Vane, Uncle Sam's Hat, #3257-3258, 3260 7.00
SP1288 22c Uncle Sam, #3259, 3263 6.00
SP1289 $3.20 Space Shuttle Landing, #3261 9.00
SP1290 $11.75 Piggyback Space Shuttle, #3262 17.50
SP1291 (33c) Uncle Sam's Hat, #3267-3269 7.50
SP1292 (33c) Uncle Sam's Hat, #3264, 3266 7.50
SP1293 (5c), (10c) Wetlands, Eagle & Shield, #3207A, 3270-3271 6.50

1999

SP1294 33c Chinese New Year, #3272 6.00
SP1295 33x Malcolm X, #3273 6.00
SP1296 33c Love, #3274 7.50
SP1297 55c Love, #3275 6.50
SP1298 33c Hospice Care, #3276 6.00
SP1299 33c Flag and City, #3279-3280, 3282 6.50
SP1300 33c Flag Over Chalkboard, #3283 6.00
SP1301 33c Irish Immigration, #3286 6.00
SP1302 33c Lunt & Fontanne, #3287 6.00
SP1303 33c Arctic Animals, #3292a 7.50
SP1304 33c Sonoran Desert, #3293 10.00
SP1305 33c Berries, #3294-3297 7.50
SP1306 33c Daffy Duck, #3306a 8.00
SP1307 33c Ayn Rand, #3308 6.50
SP1308 33c Cinco de Mayo, #3309 6.00
SP1309 33c Tropical Flowers, #3310-3313 7.50
SP1310 48c Niagara Falls, #C133 6.50
SP1311 33c John & William Bartram, #3314 6.00
SP1312 33c Prostate Cancer, #3315 6.00
SP1313 33c California Gold Rush, #3316 6.00
SP1314 33c Aquarium Fish, #3317-3320 7.50
SP1315 33c Extreme Sports, #3321-3324 7.50
SP1316 33c American Glass, #3328a 7.50
SP1317 33c James Cagney, #3329 7.50
SP1318 55c Billy Mitchell, #3330 7.50
SP1319 40c Rio Grande, #C134 6.00
SP1320 33c Honoring Those Who Served, #3331 6.00
SP1321 45c Universal Postal Union, #3332 6.00
SP1322 33c Famous Trains, #3337a 7.50
SP1323 33c Frederick Law Olmsted, #3338 6.00
SP1324 33c Hollywood Composers, #3344a 7.50
SP1325 33c Broadway Songwriters, #3350a 7.50
SP1326 33c Insects & Spiders, #3351 10.00
SP1327 33c Hanukkah, #3352 6.00
SP1328 22c Uncle Sam, #3353 6.00
SP1329 33c Official coil, #O157 6.00
SP1330 33c NATO, #3354 6.00
SP1331 33c Madonna & Child, #3355 6.00
SP1332 33c Christmas Deer, #3359a 7.50
SP1333 33c Kwanzaa, #3368 6.00
SP1334 33c Year 2000, #3369 6.00

2000

SP1335 33c Chinese New Year, #3370 6.00
SP1336 60c Grand Canyon, #C135 6.00
SP1337 33c Patricia Roberts Harris, #3371 6.00
SP1338 33c Berries, dated 2000, #3294a-3296a, 3297c 6.00
SP1339 33c Los Angeles Class Submarine (sheet stamp), #3372 6.00
SP1340 33c Pacific Coast Rain Forest, #3378 10.00
SP1341 33c Louise Nevelson, #3383a 7.50
SP1342 33c Hubble Space Telescope Images, #3388a 7.50
SP1343 33c American Samoa, #3389 6.00
SP1344 33c Library of Congress, #3390 6.00
SP1345 33c Road Runner & Wile E. Coyote, #3391a 7.50
SP1346 33c Distinguished Soldiers, 3396a 8.00
SP1347 33c Summer Sports, #3397 6.00
SP1348 33c Adoption, #3398 6.00
SP1349 33c Youth Team Sports, #3402a 6.50
SP1350 33c The Stars and Stripes, #3403 10.00
SP1351 33c Legends of Baseball, #3408 10.00
SP1352 33c Stampin' the Future, #3417a 6.50

Distinguished Americans Series

2000-02

SP1355 10c Gen. Joseph W. Stilwell, #3420 6.00
SP1361 33c Claude Pepper, #3426 6.00
SP1366 76c Hattie Caraway, #3431 6.00
SP1367 83c Edna Ferber, #3432 7.50

2000

SP1373	33c	California Statehood, #3438	6.00
SP1374	33c	Deep Sea Creatures, #3443a	7.50
SP1375	33c	Thomas Wolfe, #3444	6.00
SP1376	33c	White House, #3445	6.00
SP1377	33c	Edward G. Robinson, #3446	6.00
SP1378	(10c)	New York Public Library Lion, #3447	6.00
SP1379	(34c)	Flag Over Farm, #3448-3450	6.00
SP1380	(34c)	Statue of Liberty, #3451-3453	6.00
SP1381	(34c)	Flowers, #3454-3457	6.00

2001

SP1382	34c	Statue of Liberty self-adhesive coil, #3466	6.00
SP1382A	21c	American Buffalo, #3467, 3484	6.00
SP1383	21c	American Buffalo, #3468, 3475	6.00
SP1383A	23c	George Washington, #3468A, 3475A	6.00
SP1384	34c	Flag over Farm, #3469	6.00
SP1385	34c	Flag over Farm self-adhesive, #3470	6.00
SP1386	55c	Eagle, #3471	6.00
SP1386A	57c	Eagle, #3471A	7.50
SP1387	$3.50	US Capitol, #3472	10.00
SP1388	$12.25	Washington Monument, #3473	20.00
SP1389	34c	Statue of Liberty, #3476, 3477, 3485	7.50
SP1390	34c	Flowers, #3478-3481	7.50
SP1391	20c	George Washington, #3482	6.00
SP1392	34c	Apple and Orange, #3491, 3492	6.00
SP1393	34c	Flag over Farm self-adhesive booklet, #3495	6.00
SP1394	(34c)	Love, #3496	6.00
SP1395	34c, 55c	Love, #3497, 3499	7.50
SP1396	34c	Chinese New Year, #3500	6.00
SP1397	34c	Roy Wilkins, #3501	6.00
SP1398	34c	American Illustrators, #3502	10.00
SP1399	34c	Official, #O158	6.00
SP1400	70c	Nine-Mile Prairie, #C136	6.00
SP1401	34c	Diabetes Awareness, #3503	6.00
SP1402	34c	Nobel Prize, #3504	6.00
SP1403	1c-80c	Pan-American Inverts, #3505	10.00
SP1404	80c	Mt. McKinley, #C137	7.50
SP1405	34c	Great Plains Prairie, #3506	10.00
SP1406	34c	Peanuts Comic Strip, #3507	6.00
SP1407	34c	Honoring Veterans, #3508	6.00
SP1408	60c	Acadia National Park, #C138	7.50
SP1409	34c	Frida Kahlo, #3509	6.00
SP1410	34c	Legendary Playing Fields, #3510-3519	12.50
SP1411	(10c)	Atlas Statue, #3520	6.00
SP1412	34c	Leonard Bernstein, #3521	6.00
SP1413	(15c)	Woody Wagon, #3522	6.00
SP1414	34c	Lucille Ball, #3523	6.00
SP1415	34c	Amish Quilts, #3524-3527	7.50
SP1416	34c	Carnivorous Plants, #3528-3531	7.50
SP1417	34c	Eid, #3532	6.00
SP1418	34c	Enrico Fermi, #3533	6.00
SP1419	34c	That's All Folks!, #3534a	6.00
SP1420	34c	Christmas Madonna, #3536	6.00
SP1421	34c	Christmas Santas, #3537-3540	7.50
SP1422	34c	James Madison, #3545	6.00
SP1423	34c	Thanksgiving, #3546	6.00
SP1424	34c	Hanukkah, #3547	6.00
SP1425	34c	Kwanzaa, #3548	6.00
SP1426	34c	United We Stand booklet and coil, #3549, 3550	7.50
SP1427	57c	Love, #3551	6.00

2002

SP1428	34c	Winter Olympics, #3552-3555	7.50
SP1429	34c	Mentoring a Child, #3556	6.00
SP1430	34c	Langston Hughes, #3557	6.00
SP1431	34c	Happy Birthday, #3558	6.00
SP1432	34c	Chinese New Year, #3559	6.00
SP1433	34c	US Military Academy, Bicent., #3560	6.00
SP1434	34c	Greetings from America, #3561-3610	37.50
SP1435	34c	Longleaf Pine Forest, #3611	10.00
SP1436	5c	Toleware Coffeepot, #3612	6.00
SP1437	3c	Star, #3613-3615	6.00
SP1438	23c	George Washington, #3616-3618	7.50
SP1439	(37c)	Flag, #3620-3623	7.50
SP1440	(37c)	Toy coils, #3626-3629	7.50
SP1441	37c	Flag, #3630-3631, 3633, 3635	7.50

2003

SP1441A	37c	Flag, self-adhesive booklet stamp, #3637	6.00

2002

SP1442	37c	Toy coils, #3638-3641	7.50
SP1443	60c	Coverlet Eagle, #3646	6.00
SP1444	$3.85	Jefferson Memorial, #3647	10.00
SP1445	$13.65	Capitol Dome, #3648	21.00
SP1446	(34c+11c)	Heroes of 2001, #B2	6.00
SP1447	37c	Masters of American Photography, #3649	10.00
SP1448	37c	John James Audubon, #3650	6.00
SP1449	37c	Harry Houdini, #3651	6.00
SP1450	37c	Official coil, #O159	6.00
SP1451	37c	Andy Warhol, #3652	6.00
SP1452	37c	Teddy Bears, #3653-3656	7.50
SP1453	37c,60c	Love #3657-3658	7.50
SP1454	37c	Ogden Nash, #3659	6.00
SP1455	37c	Duke Kahanamoku, #3660	6.00
SP1456	37c	American Bats, #3661-3664	7.50
SP1457	37c	Women in Journalism, #3665-3668	7.50
SP1458	37c	Irving Berlin, #3669	6.00
SP1459	37c	Neuter and Spay, #3670-3671	7.50
SP1460	37c	Hanukkah, #3672	6.00
SP1461	37c	Kwanzaa, #3673	6.00
SP1462	37c	Eid #3674	6.00
SP1463	37c	Christmas Madonna, #3675	6.00
SP1464	37c	Christmas Snowmen, #3676-3679	7.50
SP1465	37c	Cary Grant, #3692	6.00
SP1466	(5c)	Sea Coast, #3693	6.00
SP1467	37c	Hawaiian Missionary Stamps, #3694	7.50
SP1468	37c	Happy Birthday, #3695	6.00
SP1469	37c	Greetings from America, #3696-3745	37.50

2003

SP1470	37c	Thurgood Marshall, #3746	6.00
SP1471	37c	Chinese New Year, #3747	6.00
SP1472	37c	Zora Neale Hurston, #3748	6.00
SP1475	10c	American Clock, #3751	6.00
SP1481	1c	Tiffany Lamp coil, #3757	6.00
SP1490	$1	Wisdom, #3766	7.50
SP1493	(10c)	New York Public Library Lion, perf. 10 vert, #3769	6.00
SP1495	80c	Special Olympics, #3771	7.50
SP1496	37c	American Filmmaking: Behind the Scenes, #3772	10.00
SP1497	37c	Ohio Statehood, Bicent., #3773	6.00
SP1498	37c	Pelican Island National Wildlife Refuge, #3774	6.00
SP1499	(5c)	Sea Coast perforated coil, #3775	6.00
SP1500	37c	Old Glory, #3776-3780	7.50
SP1501	37c	Cesar E. Chavez, #3781	6.00
SP1502	37c	Louisiana Purchase, #3782	6.00
SP1503	37c	First Flight of Wright Brothers, #3783	6.00
SP1504	37c	Purple Heart, #3784	6.00

COMPUTER VENDED POSTAGE

1992

SPCVP1	29c	Postage and Mailing Center (PMC) coil strip of 3, #31	3.50

1994

SPCVP2	29c	Postage and Mailing Center (PMC) horiz. coil strip of 3, #32	4.25

1996

SPCVP3	32c	Postage and Mailing Center (PMC) horiz. strip of 3, #33	4.75

INTERNATIONAL REPLY COUPONS

Coupons produced by the Universal Postal Union for member countries to provide for payment of postage on a return letter from a foreign country. Exchangeable for a stamp representing single-rate ordinary postage (and starting with the use of Type D3, airmail postage) to a foreign country under the terms of contract as printed on the face of the coupon in French and the language of the issuing country and on the reverse in four, five or six other languages.

Postmasters are instructed to apply a postmark indicating date of sale to the left circle on the coupon. When offered for exchange for stamps, the receiving postmaster is instructed to cancel the right circle.

Coupons with no postmark are not valid for exchange. Coupons with two postmarks have been redeemed and normally are kept by the post office making the exchange. **Coupons with one postmark are valued here.** Some coupons with a stamp added to pay an increased rate are listed in footnotes.

The following is a list of all varieties issued by the Universal Postal Union for any or all member countries.

Dates are those when the rate went into effect. The date that any item was put on sale in the United States can be very different.

Type A-Face

Wmk. "25c Union Postale Universelle 25c"

1907-20

A1 Face — Name of country in letters 1½mm high.
Reverse — Printed rules between paragraphs German text contains four lines.

1907-20

A2 Face — Same as A1.
Reverse — Same as A1 but without rules between paragraphs.

1910-20

A3 Face — Same as A1 and A2.
Reverse — Same as A2 except German text has but three lines.

1912-20

A4 Face — Name of country in bold face type; letters 2mm to 2½mm high.
Reverse — Same as A3.

1922-25

A5 Face — French words "le mois d'émission écoulé, deux mois encore."
Reverse — As A3 and A4 but overprinted with new contract in red; last line of red German text has five words.

Wmk. "50c Union Postale Universelle 50c"

1925-26

A6 Face — Same as A5.
Reverse — Four paragraphs of five lines each.

1926-29

A7 Face — French words "il est valable pendant un délai de six mois."
Reverse — As A6 but overprinted with new contract in red; last line of red German text has two words.

Wmk. "40c Union Postale Universelle 40c"

1926-29

A8 Face — Design redrawn. Without lines in hemispheres.
Reverse — Four paragraphs of four lines each.

Type B-Face

1931-35 — **Wmk. Double-lined "UPU"**

B1 Face — French words "d'une lettre simple."
Reverse — Four paragraphs of three lines each.

1935-36

B2 Face — French words "d'une lettre ordinaire de port simple."

Reverse Last line of German text contains two words.

1936-37

B3 Face Same as B2.
Reverse Last line of German text contains one word.

1937-40

B4 Face Same as B2 and B3. "Any Country of the Union."
Reverse German text is in German Gothic type.

1945

B5 Face "Any Country of the Universal Postal Union."
Reverse Each paragraph reads "Universal Postal Union."

Type B5 exists without central printing on face.

1950

B6 Face Same as B5.
Reverse Five paragraphs (English, Arabic, Chinese, Spanish, Russian).

1954

B7 Face Same as B5.
Reverse Six paragraphs (German, English, Arabic, Chinese, Spanish, Russian.)

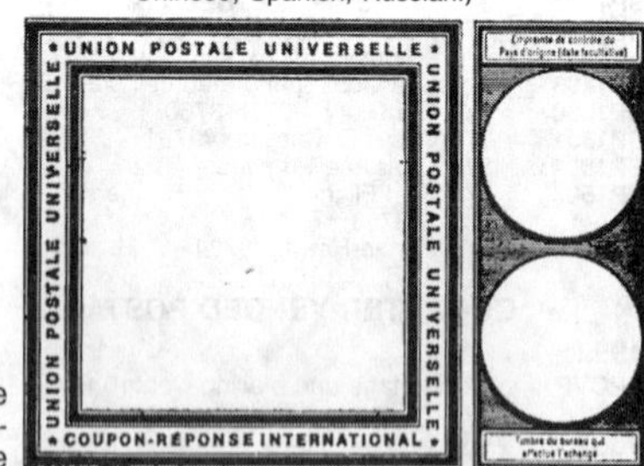

Type C-Face

1968 **Wmk. Single-lined "UPU" Multiple**

C1 Face French words "d'une lettre ordinaire de port simple."
Reverse Six paragraphs (German, English, Arabic, Chinese, Spanish, Russian).

Foreign coupons, but not U.S., of type C1 are known with large double-lined "UPU" watermark, as on type B coupons.

1971

C2 Face French words "d'une lettre ordinaire du premier échelon de poids."
Reverse Six paragraphs (German, English, Arabic, Chinese, Spanish, Russian).

Ce coupon est échangeable dans tous les pays de l'Union postale universelle contre un ou plusieurs timbres-poste représentant l'affranchissement minimal d'une lettre ordinaire, expédiée à l'étranger par voie de surface.

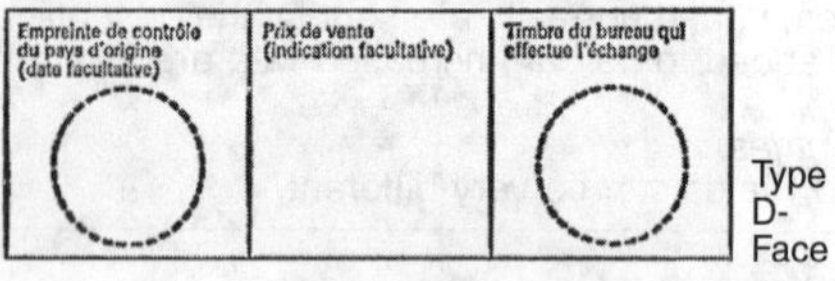

Type D-Face

1975 **Wmk. Single-lined "UPU" Multiple**

D1 Face French words "d'une lettre ordinaire, expédiée à l'étranger par voie de surface."
Reverse Six paragraphs (German, English, Arabic, Chinese, Spanish, Russian).
D2 Face Left box does not have third line of French and dotted circle.
Reverse Same as D1.

On D1 and D2 the watermark runs horizontally or vertically.

D3 Face ....aerienne. Left box as D2 with (faculative) added.
Reverse As D1, all references are to air service.
D4 Face As D3, "CN 01 / (ancien C22)" replaces "C22."

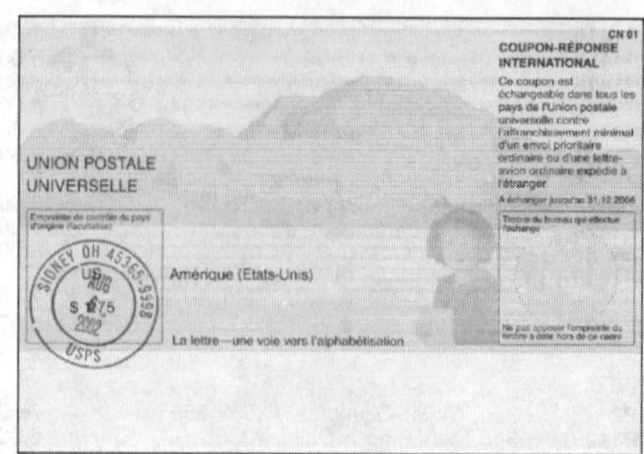

Type E—Face

Wmk. "UPU" in cross & 8-pointed star horiz. across sheet

2002

E1 Face Shown
Reverse Six paragraphs (German, English, Arabic, Chinese, Spanish, Russian), repeating expiration date paragraph in same languages, bar code.

Coupons exist without the validating origination markings. These have no validity and are beyond the scope of this catalogue.

REPLY COUPONS ISSUED FOR THE UNITED STATES

1907, Oct. 1

IRC2 A2 6c **slate green & gray green** 20.00

Rules omitted on reverse.
Earliest documented use: Oct. 10, 1907.

1912

IRC3 A4 6c **slate green & gray green** 28.00

Three line English paragraph on face.

1922, Jan. 1

IRC4 A5 11c **slate green & gray green,** name 81½mm long 20.00
a. Name 88½mm long 20.00

Five line English paragraph on face. Red overprint on reverse.

1925-26

IRC5 A6 11c **slate green & gray green** 17.50

Five line English paragraph on face. No overprint on reverse.

IRC6 A6 9c **slate green & gray green,** *Oct. 1, 1925* 17.50

1926

IRC7 A7 9c **slate green & gray green** 28.00

Four line English paragraph on face. Red overprint on reverse.

IRC8 A8 9c **slate green & gray green** 20.00

Without lines in hemispheres.

1935

IRC9 B2 9c **blue & yellow** 9.00

On reverse, last line of German text contains two words.

1936

IRC10 B3 9c blue and yellow 9.00

On reverse, last line of German text contains one word.

1937

IRC11 B4 9c **blue & yellow** 7.00

On reverse, German text in German Gothic type.

1945

IRC12 B5 9c **blue & yellow,** Italian text on reverse in 4 lines 5.00
a. Italian text on reverse in 3 lines 5.00

1948, Oct. 15

IRC13 B5 11c **blue & yellow** 5.00

On face, "Universal Postal Union" replaces "Union."

1950

IRC14 B6 11c **blue & yellow** 5.00

On reverse, text in English, Arabic, Chinese, Spanish, Russian.

1954, July 1

IRC15 B7 13c **blue & yellow** 5.00

On reverse, text in German, English, Arabic, Chinese, Spanish, Russian.

Varieties: period under "u" of "amount" in English text on reverse, and period under "n" of "amount." Also, country name either 47mm or 50mm long.

No. IRC15 Surcharged in Various Manners

1959, May 2

IRC16 B7 15c on 13c **blue & yellow** 5.50

Individual post offices were instructed to surcharge the 13c coupon, resulting in many types of surcharge in various inks. For example, "REVALUED 15 CENTS," reading vertically; "15," etc.

1959, May 2

IRC17 B7 15c **blue & yellow** 4.50

1964

IRC18 B7 15c **blue & yellow** 4.50
a. Reverse printing 60mm deep instead of 65mm (smaller Arabic characters) 4.50

On face, box at lower left: "Empreinte de contrôle / du Pays d'origine / (date facultative)" replaces "Timbre du / Bureau / d'Emission."

1969

IRC19 C1 15c **blue & yellow** 4.50

1971, July 1

IRC20 C2 22c **blue & yellow** 4.50

No. IRC20 Surcharged in Various Manners

1974, Jan. 5

IRC21 C2 26c on 22c **blue & yellow** 5.00

See note after No. IRC16.

1975, Jan. 2

IRC22 D1 26c **blue & yellow** 4.00

No. IRC22 Surcharged in Various Manners

1976, Jan. 3

IRC23 D1 42c on 26c **blue & yellow** 4.50

See note after No. IRC16. Several post offices are known to have surcharged No. IRC21 (42c on 26c on 22c).

Provisional surcharges on Nos. IRC24-IRC27 were not permitted.

1976, Jan. 3

IRC24 D1 42c **blue & yellow** 4.50

Some foreign countries use non-denominated IRCs. The U. S. has never ordered or used these "generic" items.

1981, July 1

IRC26 D1 65c **blue & yellow** 5.50

1986, Jan. 1

IRC27 D2 80c **blue & yellow** 5.50

1988, Apr. 3

IRC28 D2 95c **blue & yellow** 5.00
IRC29 D3 95c **blue & yellow** 5.00
a. "9.1992" in lower left corner 5.00

Post offices were authorized on July 11, 1995 to revalue remaining stock of 95c IRCs to $1.05 by applying 10c in stamps until new stock (No. 30) arrived. All 95c varieties are known revalued thus.

The date of issue of No. 29 is not known. Earliest documented use: Jan. 2, 1992.

No. 28 exists with inverted watermark (tops of letters facing right).

1995

IRC30	D4	$1.05 **blue & yellow**, "4.95" in lower left corner		3.75
a.		"10.98" in lower left corner		3.75
b.		As "a," with "United States of America" in left box		8.00

"1.05" comes 1½mm or 3mm high. 3mm height has numerals more widely spaced.

Earliest documented use: July 12, 1995.

Post offices were authorized on Jan. 7, 2001, to revalue remaining stock of $1.05 IRCs to $1.75 by applying 70c in stamps until new stock arrived. All $1.05 varieties are known revalued thus. Value $7.

2002, Jan. 1

IRC31	E1	$1.75 **multicolored**	3.50

POST OFFICE SEALS

Official Seals began to appear in 1872. They do not express any value, having no franking power.

The first seal issued was designed to prevent tampering with registered letters while in transit. It was intended to be affixed over the juncture of the flaps of the large official envelopes in which registered mail letters were enclosed or stamp requisitions were shipped to postmasters and was so used exclusively. Beginning in 1877 (No. OX1 and later), Post Office Seals were used to repair damaged letters, reseal those opened by mistake or by customs inspectors, and to seal letters received by the Post Office unsealed.

Values for unused Post Office Seals are for those without creases. Uncanceled seals without gum will sell for less.

Used Post Office Seals will usually have creases from being applied over the edges of damaged or accidentally opened covers but will have either cancels, precancels or a signature or notation indicating use on the seal. Creased, uncanceled seals without gum are considered used and will sell for less than either an unused or a canceled used seal.

Covers with Post Office Seals are almost always damaged except in cases when the seal was applied to a cover marked "Received Unsealed." The values shown are for covers where the damage is consistent with the application of the seal.

Post Office Seals must be tied or exhibit some auxiliary marking or docketing to qualify for "on cover" values. No. OXF1 must bear a circular date stamp cancel and the cover to which it is affixed must bear the identical cancel to qualify for the "on cover" value.

REGISTRY SEALS

RGS1

National Bank Note Co.

Typographed from a copper plate of 30 subjects (3x10) in two panes of 15 (3x5)

1872 Unwmk. White Wove Paper *Perf. 12*

OXF1	RGS1	**green**	30.00	7.50
		On cover, Barber signature		40.00
		On cover, Terrell signature		75.00
		Block of 4	*500.00*	
		Pane of 15	*2,500.*	
a.		**Yellow green,** pelure paper	75.00	40.00
b.		Imperf., pair	*1,500.*	
c.		Horizontally laid paper	*500.00*	
d.		Printed on both sides	*500.00*	
e.		Printed on both sides, back inverted	*800.00*	
f.		Double impression	*750.00*	—
g.		Double impression, one inverted	—	*750.00*

The second impression of Nos. OXF1d-OXF1g, is very faint.

Also issued as a pane of 9 (3x3) (attributed to Continental Bank Note Co.).

Cancellations

Black	7.50
Blue	+5.00
Red	+15.00
Green	+50.00
Magenta	+50.00
Carrier	+25.00
Panama	—
Shanghai	—

Special Printings

Continental Bank Note Co.

Plate of 30 subjects (5x6)

1875(?) Hard White Wove Paper Without Gum *Perf. 12*

OXF2	RGS1	**bluish green**	*1,000.*

American Bank Note Co.

Plate of 15 subjects (5x3)

1880 (?) Soft Porous Paper Without Gum *Perf. 12*

OXF3	RGS1	**bluish green**	*1,000.*

POSTAGE STAMP AGENCY SEALS

Used to seal registered pouches containing stamps for distribution to Post Offices.

PSA1

Background size: 102x52mm.

1875-93 Litho. Unwmk. *Die Cut*

Barber Signature

OXF4	PSA1	**brown & black**	20.00
		On cover	50.00

Hazen Signature, Text 87mm Wide

OXF5	PSA1	**brown & black,** *1877*	15.00
		On cover	50.00

Hazen Signature

OXF6	PSA1	**pink & red,** *1886*	50.00
		On cover	350.00
a.		**Salmon & red**	60.00
		On cover	*400.00*

Harris Signature

OXF7	PSA1	**pink & red,** *1887*	15.00
		On cover	50.00

Hazen Signature, Text 90½mm Wide

OXF8	PSA1	**pink & red,** *1889*	15.00
		On cover	50.00

Craige Signature

OXF9	PSA1	**pink & red,** *1893*	35.00
		On cover	90.00

PSA2

Background size: 120½x67mm.

1894 Litho. Unwmk. *Die Cut*

Craige Signature, "3rd Asst. P.M.G."

OXF10	PSA2	**pink & red**	20.00
		On cover	75.00

Craige Signature, "Third Assistant Postmaster General"

OXF11	PSA2	**pale pink & red**	15.00
		On cover	60.00
a.		**Deep pink & red**	15.00
		On cover	60.00

"John A. Merritt" in Sans-Serif Capitals at Left. Two Horizontal Lines Obliterating "Kerr Craige."

1897

OXF12	PSA2	**pale pink & red**	40.00
		On cover	150.00

Design of 1894

1897-1910(?)

Merritt Signature

OXF13	PSA2	**rose & black**	15.00
		On cover	60.00

Madden Signature

OXF14	PSA2	**rose & black**	35.00
		On cover	175.00

"Section 878"

OXF15	PSA2	**rose & black**	20.00
		On cover	85.00

"Section 970"

OXF16	PSA2	**rose & black,** *1910*	20.00
		On cover	110.00
a.		**Rose brown & black**	20.00
		On cover	110.00

DEAD LETTER OFFICE SEALS

No. OX1 supposedly was issued as a Dead Letter Office Seal. Most on-cover examples are normal Post Office usages from larger East Coast cities. New York and Philadelphia predominate. Very few examples with Dead Letter Office markings are recorded. For that reason, No. OX1 is listed with the other Post Office Seals.

"Hazen" — DLO1

1884 Litho. Unwmk. *Perf. 11, 12*

OXA1	DLO1	**black,** *tan*	27.50
		On cover	100.00

"Baird" DLO2

1889 *Perf. 10½, 12*

OXA2	DLO2	**black,** *tan*	27.50
		On cover	100.00

"Superintendent" — DLO3

1891 *Perf. 12*

OXA3	DLO3	**black,** *tan*	25.00
		On cover	90.00

"5-2807" — DLO4

1892 *Perf. 12*

OXA4	DLO4	**black,** *tan*	22.50
		On cover	85.00

"5-3282" — DLO5

1895 *Perf. 12*

OXA5	DLO5	**black,** *tan*	25.00
		On cover	90.00

1898(?) *Hyphen hole perf. 7*

OXA6	DLO5	**black,** *tan*	35.00
		On cover	110.00

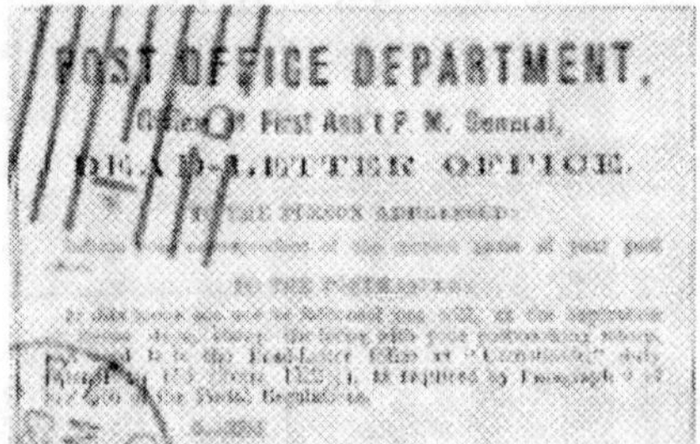

POST OFFICE DEPARTMENT,
Office of First Ass't P. M. General,
DEAD-LETTER OFFICE.

DLO6

Similar to DLO5 but smaller type used for instructions to the postmasters.

1900 *Perf. 12*

OXA7	DLO6	**black,** *tan*	20.00
		On cover	75.00

"5-3282" at Right — DLO7

1902(?) *Perf. 10½, 12*

OXA8	DLO7	**black,** *tan*	25.00
		On cover	85.00

"5-3282" at Center — DLO8

1902(?) *Perf. 12*

OXA9	DLO8	**black,** *tan*	25.00
		On cover	85.00

POST OFFICE SEALS

See introduction.

No. OX1 was prepared for use in the Dead Letter Office but was distributed to other offices and used in the same way as the later seals.

POS1

("Post Obitum" in background.)
National Bank Note Co.
Plate of 100 subjects (10x10)
Silk Paper

1877 **Engr.** *Perf. 12*

OX1	POS1	**brown**	45.00	25.00
		On cover		*1,200.*
		Block of 4	*500.00*	

POS2

American Bank Note Co.
Plate of 100 subjects (10x10) in two panes of 50 bearing imprint of American Bank Note Co.
(Also plates of 50 (10x5) subjects)

1879 **Engr.** *Perf. 12*

Thin, crisp, semi-translucent paper, yellowish gum

OX2	POS2	**red brown**	3.00	1.00
		On cover		85.00
		Block of 4	15.00	
		Margin block with imprint	25.00	
a.		**Brown**	10.00	5.00
		On cover		200.00
		Block of 4	60.00	
		Margin block with imprint	85.00	

Seal impression can be clearly seen when viewed from the back.

Plate of 50 subjects (5x10). Four imprints of the American Bank Note Co. centered on each side of the pane with a reversed "2" to the right of the top imprint.

1879(?)

Thick, opaque paper, clear transparent gum

OX3	POS2	**yellow brown**	20.00	20.00
		On cover		*1,000.*
		Block of 4	100.00	
		Margin block of 4 with imprint (side)	140.00	
		Margin block of 6 with imprint (bottom)	180.00	
		Margin block of 4 with imprint & reversed "2" (top)	225.00	

1881(?)

Thin, hard porous paper, clear transparent gum

OX4	POS2	**deep brown**	75.00
		Block of 4	350.00
		Margin block of 4 with imprint (side)	400.00
		Margin block of 6 with imprint (bottom)	550.00
		Margin block of 4 with imprint & reversed "2" (top)	575.00

No. OX4 is the so-called "Special Printing." It was produced from a new plate prepared from the original die. It received little usage, but at least three full panes are known to have existed.

Colors

Beginning with OX5, many Official Seals exhibit a wide variety of shades. Minimal care was exercised in their printing. It is not uncommon for seals within a single pane to vary in shade from dark to very light. No attempt is being made here to list all of the various shades separately.

POS3

Typographed
Without words in lower label.
Outer frame line at top and left is thick and heavy (compare with POS4).
Plate of 72 subjects (8x9)

1888 *Rough perf. 12*

Medium thick, crisp paper

OX5	POS3	**chocolate** (shades)	.75	.75
		On cover		50.00
		On cover with typeset seal No. LOX8		—
		Block of 4	5.00	
a.		Imperf, pair	50.00	
		Sheet of 72, imperf	—	

Imperforates

Imperforates of Nos. OX6, OX7, OX10 and OX13 are believed to be printer's waste. No seals were issued imperforate, though some may have been sent to post offices.

Plate of 42 subjects (7x6)

1889 *Rough perf. 12*

Thick to extremely thick paper

OX6	POS3	**chocolate** (shades)	.75	.50
		On cover		40.00
		Block of 4	5.00	

1889(?) *Perf. 12*

OX7	POS3	**bister brown** (shades)	.75	.50
		On cover		40.00
		Block of 4	5.00	
a.		**Rose brown**	4.00	2.50
		On cover		65.00
		Block of 4	22.50	
b.		**Yellow brown**	2.00	2.00
		On cover		50.00
		Block of 4	10.00	
c.		Imperf. vertically, pair	25.00	—
d.		Imperf. horizontally, pair	25.00	—
e.		Vertical pair, imperf. between	20.00	
f.		Horizontal pair, imperf. between	75.00	

g. Double impression —

Cancellation

Puerto Rico +75.00

Examples of No. OX7 with multiple impressions widely spaced or at angles to each other, are found on normal paper and various documents. These are printer's waste.

1892 ***Rouletted 5½***

OX8 POS3 **light brown** (shades) 20.00 15.00
On cover *1,250.*
Block of 4 300.00

1895 (?) ***Hyphen Hole Perf. 7***

OX9 POS3 **gray brown** 7.50 5.00
On cover 200.00
Block of 4 200.00

Earliest documented use: Feb. 3, 1897.

1898(?) ***Perf. 12***

Thin soft paper

OX10 POS3 **brown** (shades) 1.50 1.50
On cover 75.00
Block of 4 8.00

POS4

Plate of 143 (11x13)

Outer frame line at top and left is thin. Otherwise similar to POS3.

1900 **Litho.** ***Perf. 12***

OX11 POS4 **red brown** .50 .25
On cover 30.00
Block of 4 2.50
a. **Gray brown** 2.00 1.25
On cover 45.00
Block of 4 15.00
b. **Dark brown** 2.50 *4.50*
On cover 85.00
Block of 4 15.00
c. **Orange brown** .75 *2.00*
On cover 75.00
Block of 4 4.00

Most imperfs and part perfs are printers waste. Some genuine perforation errors may have been issued to post offices.

Watermarks

Watermarks cover only a portion of the panes. Many stamps in each pane did not receive any of the watermark. Values for watermarked panes are for examples with at least 50% of the watermark present.

Similar to POS4 but smaller.

Design: 38x23mm

Issued in panes of 20 (5x4)

1907 **Typo.** ***Perf. 12***

OX12 POS4 **bright royal blue** 2.00 2.00
On cover 45.00
Pane of 20 60.00

Earliest documented use: June 1, 1907.

OX13 POS4 **blue** (shades) .20 .20
On cover 25.00
Pane of 20 20.00
a. Wmkd. Seal of U.S. in sheet (2 types) 1.50 1.50
Pane of 20 50.00
b. Wmkd. "Rolleston Mills" in sheet 1.00 1.00
Pane of 20 40.00
c. Wmkd. "Birchwood Superfine" in sheet — —
Block of 4 —
d. Pelure paper *20.00* *20.00*
e. Toned paper *25.00* *25.00*
f. Printed on both sides —

Numerous varieties such as imperf., part perf., tete beche, and double impressions exist. These seem to be from printer's waste. Some genuine perforation errors may have been issued to post offices.

1912 ***Hyphen Hole 6½***

OX14 POS4 **blue** 1.75 1.50
On cover 50.00
Pane of 20 45.00
a. Wmkd. Seal of U.S. in sheet 10.00 10.00
Pane of 20 300.00
b. Wmkd. "Rolleston Mills" in sheet 2.50 2.50
Pane of 20 80.00

Panes of 10 were made from panes of 20 for use in smaller post offices. Complete booklets with covers exist.

1913 ***Perf. 12 x Hyphen Hole 6½***

OX15 POS4 **blue** 3.50 3.00
On cover 100.00
Pane of 20 110.00
a. Rouletted 6½ (right) x Perf. 12 (left, top, bottom) 15.00 —
Pane of 20 150.00
b. Wmkd. Seal of U.S. in sheet 4.50 4.00
Pane of 20 125.00
c. As "a" and "b" 20.00 —

No. OX15a comes from panes that are perfed between the left selvage and the stamps.

1913 ***Hyphen Hole 6½ x Perf. 12***

OX16 POS4 **blue** 5.25 5.25
On cover 150.00
Pane of 20 150.00
a. Wmkd. Seal of U.S. in sheet 6.50 6.50
Pane of 20 200.00
b. Wmkd. "Rolleston Mills" in sheet — —
Pane of 20 —

1916 ***Perf. 12***

OX17 POS4 **black,** *pink* 1.00 1.00
On cover 50.00
Pane of 20 40.00
a. Vert. pair, imperf. horizontally —

Three complete panes of No. OX17a have been reported.

1917 ***Perf. 12***

OX18 POS4 **gray black** .40 .40
On cover 27.50
Pane of 20 40.00
a. **Black** .50 .50
On cover 30.00
Pane of 20 45.00
b. Vert. pair, imperf horizontally 25.00
c. Horiz. pair, imperf vertically 20.00
d. Vertical pair, imperf between 60.00
e. Horizontal pair, imperf between 35.00
f. Imperf, pair 50.00

POS5

Quartermaster General's Office

Issued in panes of 10 (2x5) without selvage.

1919 ***Perf. 12***

OX19 POS5 **indigo** 300.
Block of 4 *1,500.*
Pane of 10 *3,600.*

Rouletted 7

OX20 POS5 **indigo** — *3,250.*

The pane format of No. OX20 is not known. One of the few reported examples is rouletted on four sides.

Nos. OX19-OX20 were used on mail to and from the Procurement Division of the Quartermaster General's Office. After five weeks of use the seals were withdrawn when the Mail and Records Section became a full branch of the Post Office.

POS6

Issued in panes of 20 (5x4) and 16 (4x4).

Panes of 10 were made from panes of 20 for use in smaller post offices.

1919 ***Perf. 12 (sometimes rough)***

Thin, white, crisp paper

OX21 POS6 **black** (shades) .20 .20
On cover 10.00
Pane of 20 10.00
a. Imperf, pair 15.00
On cover —
b. Vert. pair, imperf horiz. 10.00
c. Horiz. pair, imperf vert. 10.00
d. Vert. pair, imperf btwn. 25.00
e. Horiz. pair, imperf btwn. 25.00
f. Wmkd. eagle and star in sheet (1936?) 2.00 2.00
Pane of 20 70.00
g. As "f," imperf, pair 35.00
h. As "f," vert. pair, imperf horiz. 27.50
i. As "f," vert. pair, imperf btwn. 27.50
j. Wmkd. "Certificate Bond" in sheet (1936?) 10.00 10.00
Pane of 20 300.00

The paper used for Nos. OX21-OX27 is thin enough to allow reading text on the envelope.

Earliest documented use: 1920.

1936(?) ***Perf. 12x9***

OX22 POS6 **black** (shades) 7.50 7.50
On cover 85.00
Pane of 20 200.00
a. Vert. pair, imperf horiz. 50.00
b. Horiz. pair, imperf vert. 50.00
c. Wmkd. eagle and star in sheet 7.50 7.50
Pane of 20 200.00
d. As "c." vert. pair, imperf horiz. 50.00
e. As "c," horiz. pair, imperf vert. 50.00

Earliest documented use: Oct. 1936 (No. OX22 or OX23.)

1936(?) ***Perf. 12x8½***

OX23 POS6 **black** (shades) 2.50 2.50
On cover 40.00
Pane of 20 75.00
a. Wmkd. eagle and star in sheet 4.00 4.00
Pane of 20 110.00

1936(?) ***Perf. 12½***

OX24 POS6 **gray black,** pane of 20 —

1936(?) ***Perf. 8½***

OX25 POS6 **gray black** —
a. Wmkd. eagle and star in sheet —

1936(?) ***Perf. 12x9½***

OX26 POS6 **gray black,** pane of 20 —

1936(?) ***Perf. 11½***

OX27 POS6 **gray black** —
On cover —

Medium to thick, opaque, egg or cream colored paper

Perf. 12

1946(?)

OX28 POS6 **gray black** .40 .40
On cover 25.00
Pane of 20 22.50
a. Vert. pair, imperf btwn. 15.00

1946(?) ***Perf. 12½***

OX29 POS6 **gray black** .50 .50
On cover 25.00
Pane of 20 25.00

1947(?) ***Perf. 12½x8½***

OX30 POS6 **gray black** 1.50 1.50
On cover 45.00
Pane of 20 50.00

1947(?) ***Perf. 8½***

OX31 POS6 **gray black** 1.50 1.50
On cover 45.00
Pane of 20 50.00

1947(?) ***Perf. 8½x12***

OX32 POS6 **gray black** —

1947(?) ***Perf. 8x8½***

OX33 POS6 **gray black,** on cover —

Thick, gray, very soft paper

1948 ***Perf. 12½ (sometimes rough)***

OX34 POS6 **gray black** 1.00 1.00
On cover 35.00
Pane of 16 45.00

1948(?) ***Perf. 8½***

OX35 POS6 **gray black** 5.00 5.00
On cover 60.00
Pane of 16 —

1948(?) ***Perf. 12½x8½***

OX36 POS6 **gray black** — —
Pane of 10 —
Pane of 20 —

1948(?) ***Perf. 8½x12½***

OX37 POS6 **gray black** — —

1948 ***Hyphen Hole Perf. 9½***

OX38 POS6 **gray black** 15.00 15.00
On cover 100.00
Pane of 5, imperf at sides —
Pane of 16 350.00

Pane of 5, tab inscribed "16-56146-1 GPO."

1950(?) ***Hyphen Hole Perf. 9½ x Imperf***

Medium thick, cream paper

Design width: 37½mm

OX39 POS6 **gray black,** imperf at sides .25 .20
On cover 12.50
Pane of 5, imperf at sides 1.25
a. Vert. pair, imperf between 10.00
b. Pane of 5, imperf 15.00
c. Pane of 5, imperf at top & btwn. rows 2 & 3, 4 & 5 20.00

Pane of 5 tab inscribed, "16-56164-1 GPO."
Earliest documented use: Jan. 23, 1950.

1970(?) *Hyphen Hole Perf. 9½ x Imperf*

Medium thick, white paper

Design width: 38½mm

OX40	POS6	**gray black**	.25	.20
		On cover		*30.00*
		Pane of 5, imperf at sides	2.25	
a.		Vert. pair, imperf. btwn.	10.00	
b.		Pane of 5, Imperf	20.00	

Tab inscribed, "c43-16-56164-1 GPO"

POS7

On Nos. OX41-OX50, tab is inscribed, "LABEL 21, JULY 1971."

1972 **Litho.** *Rouletted 9½ x Imperf*

OX41	POS7	**black**	.20	.20
		On cover		12.50
		Pane of 5	2.00	
a.		Imperf, pair	10.00	

1972(?) *Rouletted 6½ x Imperf*

OX42	POS7	**black**	.20	.20
		On cover		5.00
		Pane of 5	2.75	

1973(?) **Litho.** *Hyphen Hole 7 x Imperf*

OX43	POS7	**black**	.30	.20
		On cover		7.50
		Pane of 5	9.00	

1976(?) **Litho.** *Rouletted 8½ x Imperf*

OX44	POS7	**black**	.20	.20
		On cover		7.50
		Pane of 5	2.00	

1979(?) **Litho.** *Perf. 12½ x Imperf*

OX45	POS7	**black**	.20	.20
		On cover		7.50
		Pane of 5	2.25	
		Small holes	.20	.20
		On cover		7.50
		Pane of 5	2.25	

1988(?) **Litho.** *Die Cut*

Self-Adhesive

OX46	POS7	**black,** 38x21mm, tagged, fluorescent paper	.25	.25
		On cover		*7.50*
		Pane of 5	3.50	
OX47	POS7	**bluish black,** 38x21mm, untagged, non-fluorescent paper	.25	.25
		On cover		*7.50*
		Pane of 5	3.50	
OX48	POS7	**gray** (shades), 37x21mm	.25	.25
		On cover		*7.50*
		Pane of 5	3.50	
OX49	POS7	**black,** 40x21mm	.50	.50
		On cover		*15.00*
		Pane of 5	10.00	
OX50	POS7	**purple,** 37x21mm	—	—
		On cover		—
		Pane of 5	—	

No. OX47 is on a creamier, thicker paper than No. OX46.

On No. OX49, BY is 2x1mm, P of POSTAL is left of P in POSTAL of Emblem. Tab inscribed as No. OX41, but 1's have no bottom serif.

Earliest documented use: No. OX50, Dec. 12, 1995.

POS8

Tab inscribed "LABEL 21, JAN. 1992."

1992 **Size: 44x22mm** *Die Cut*

Self-adhesive

OX51	POS8	**black**	1.00	1.00
		On cover		*25.00*
		Pane of 5	10.00	

Earliest documented use: Mar. 1992.

1992? *Die Cut*

Self-Adhesive

Size: 41x21mm

OX52	POS8	**black**	.25	.25
		On cover		*7.50*
		Pane of 5	3.50	

No. OX52 exists on both white and brown backing paper. Those on brown backing paper are worth more.

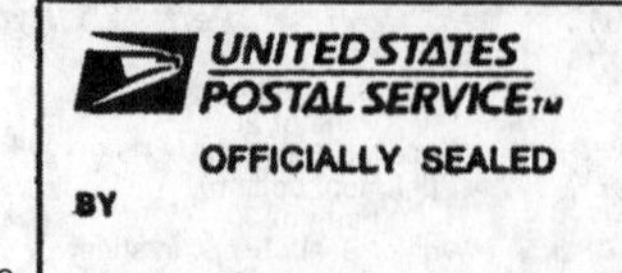

POS9

Tab inscribed "LABEL 21, April 1994."

1994 *Die Cut*

Self-Adhesive

OX53	POS9	**black**	.25	.25
		On cover		*7.50*
		Pane of 5	3.50	

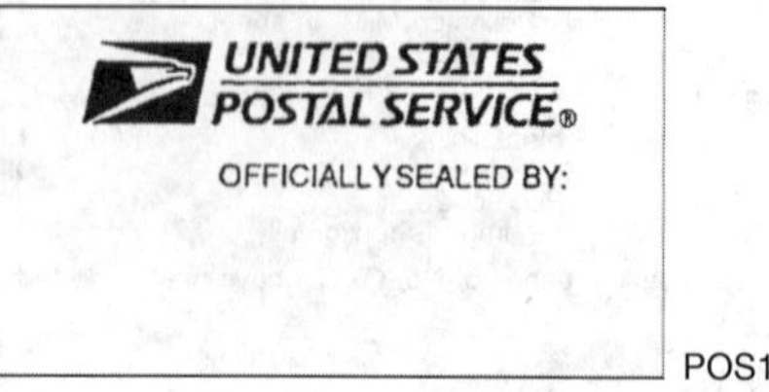

POS10

Tab inscribed "LABEL 21, August 1996."

1996 *Die Cut*

Self-Adhesive

OX54	POS10	**black**	.25	.25
		On cover		*7.50*
		Pane of 5	2.00	
a.		"OFFICALLY"	*1.00*	—
		On cover		—
		Pane of 5	*8.00*	

TYPESET SEALS

These seals were privately printed for sale to Fourth Class Post Offices. Many are extremely rare. Unquestioned varieties are listed. Many others exist.

All are imperf. except Nos. LOX7-LOX11.

TSS1

LOX1	TSS1	**black**	*500.00*	*500.00*

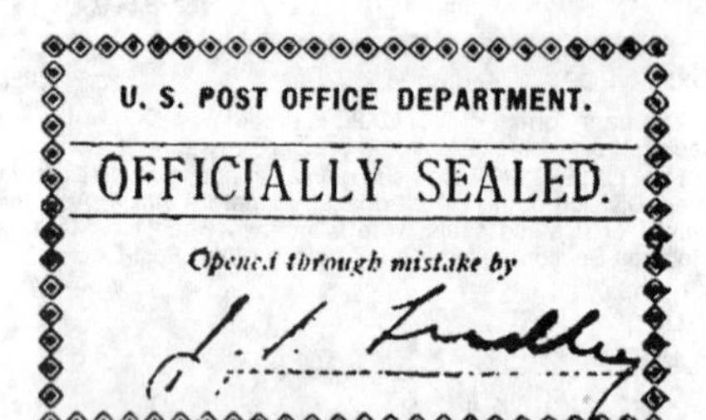

TSS2

LOX2	TSS2	**black**	*500.00*	*500.00*
a.		"OFFICALLY"	*750.00*	

TSS3

LOX3	TSS3	**black**		—
		On cover		—

TSS4

LOX4	TSS4	**black,** *pink*	*1,250.*

No. LOX4 used is valued with minor flaws.

TSS5

LOX5	TSS5	**black**	*500.00*	
LOX5A	TSS5	**black,** *pink*		—

TSS6

LOX6	TSS6	**black**	—

TSS7

Rouletted 9½ horizontally

LOX7	TSS7	**black**	*500.00*

TSS8

Printed and distributed by Morrill Bros., P.O. Supply Printers, Fulton, N.Y., in panes of 4, two tete beche pairs.

Rouletted 11½, 12½, 16½ in black at top & side

LOX8 TSS8 **black** 50.00 50.00
On cover *750.00*
a. Tete beche pair 100.00
Sheet of 4 600.00

TSS9

Solid lines above and below "OFFICIALLY SEALED" Printed in panes of 4, two tete beche pairs, and in pane of 2, rouletted 16½.

Rouletted 12½, 16½ in black between

LOX9 TSS9 **black** *500.00 500.00*
On cover *750.00*
a. Tete beche pair —
Pane of 4 —

TSS10

Dotted lines above and below "OFFICIALLY SEALED" Printed in pane of 4, two tete beche pairs, and pane of 2, tete beche.

Rouletted 11½, 12½ or 16½ in black

LOX10 TSS10 **black,** *pink* *500.00* —
LOX11 TSS10 **black** 1.50 —
On cover *1,000.*
a. Tete beche pair 3.00
Pane of 4 6.00
c. Dot after "OFFICIALLY" 2.50
d. Pair, Nos. LOX11, LOX11c 4.00
e. As "d," in tete beche pair 4.50
f. Pane of 4, one stamp with dot 37.50
g. As "c," blue, rouletted 12 *750.00*
h. Pane of 2, both stamps with dot —
i. Double impression, one inverted —

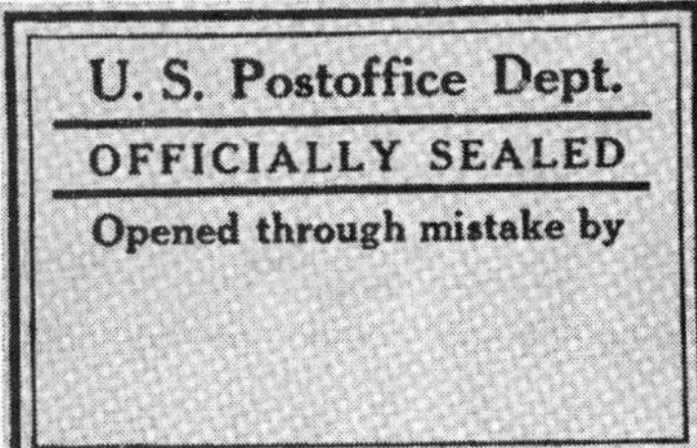

TSS11

Printed and distributed by The Lemoyne Supply Co., Lemoyne, Pa.
No. LOX13 has thin lines above and below 37¼mm long "OFFICIALLY SEALED"

LOX12 TSS11 **black** *250.00*
LOX13 TSS11 **blue** *250.00*

TSS12

LOX14 TSS12 **blue** *1,750.* —

TSS13

LOX15 TSS13 **black** *1,250.* —
blue —

No. LOX15 unused is valued with small faults and crease. The blue seal may be No. LOX29.

TSS14

LOX16 TSS14 **blue** *1,250.* 800.00

No. LOX16 used is valued with usual crease, thin spots and small tear.

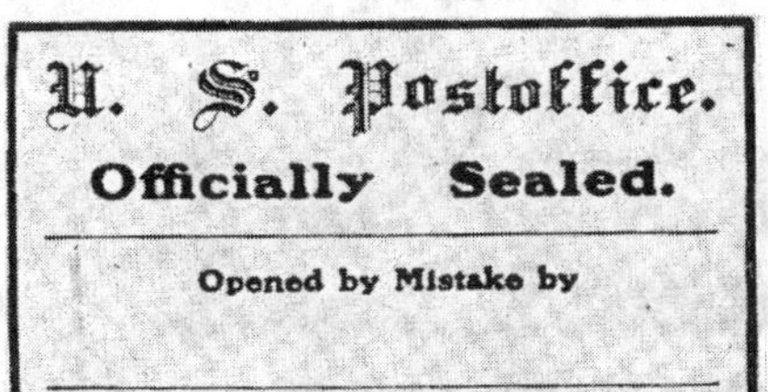

TSS15

LOX17 TSS15 **dark blue** 150.00 200.00
On cover *1,000.*
a. Printed on both sides 600.00
b. 2mm between "y" & "S," no period after "d" 200.00
LOX18 TSS15 **black** 400.00 —
On cover *1,000.*

TSS16

LOX19 TSS16 **black** *600.00*

TSS16a

LOX19A TSS16a **black** *2,750.*

No. LOX19A is unique. Valued based on 2000 auction sale.

Type I — TSS17

Type II - Bottom line in heavy type face. Period after "Office."

LOX20 TSS17 **black,** *light green* (Type I) — —

At least two different types or settings are known. The illustrated type has a dotted line above "BY" that does not show in the illustration.

LOX20A TSS17 **black,** *light green* (Type II) *2,000.* —

No. LOX20A is valued with major thin at top center.

TSS18

LOX21 TSS18 **black** *1,500.*

TSS18a

LOX21A TSS18a **black** *850.00* —
On cover *1,500.*

No. LOX21A unused is valued with crease and small faults.

TSS19

LOX22 TSS19 **black,** *blue* *2,000.*

No. LOX22 is unique. It is creased and is valued as such.

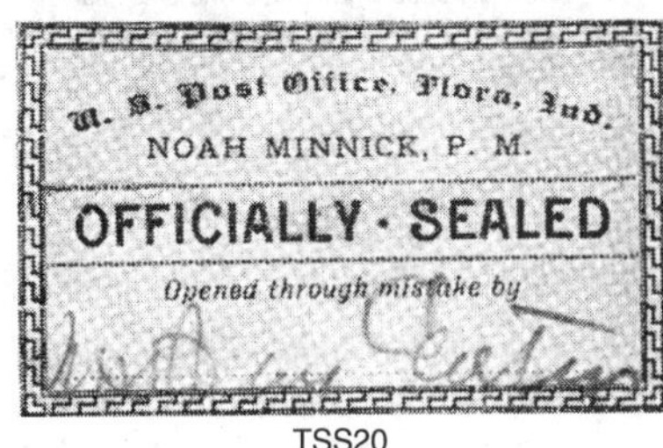

TSS20

LOX23 TSS20 **black** —

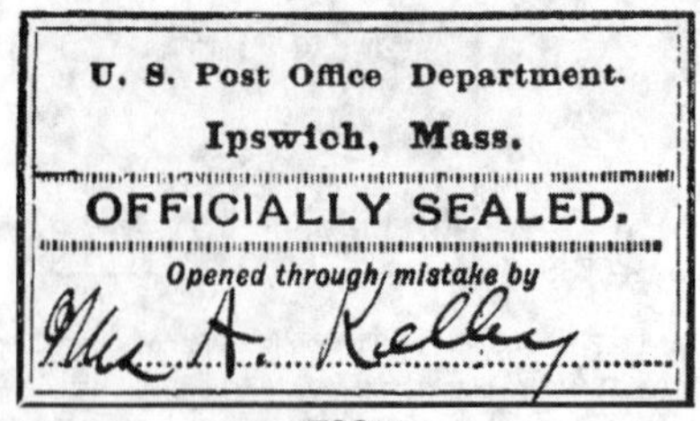

TSS21

LOX24 TSS21 **black,** on cover *3,000.*

TSS22

LOX25 TSS22 **black** *1,350.*

At least three examples of No. LOX25 exist. All have faults. Value is for the finest example.

TSS23

LOX26 TSS23 **black** *1,100.*

No. LOX26 used is valued with small fault.

TSS24

LOX27 TSS24 **black,** *dark brown red* *1,250.*

No. LOX27 is valued with crease and small flaws.

TSS25

LOX28 TSS25 **black,** on cover *4,000.*

No. LOX28 is unique. The seal was torn in half when the envelope was opened. Value is based on 2000 auction sale.

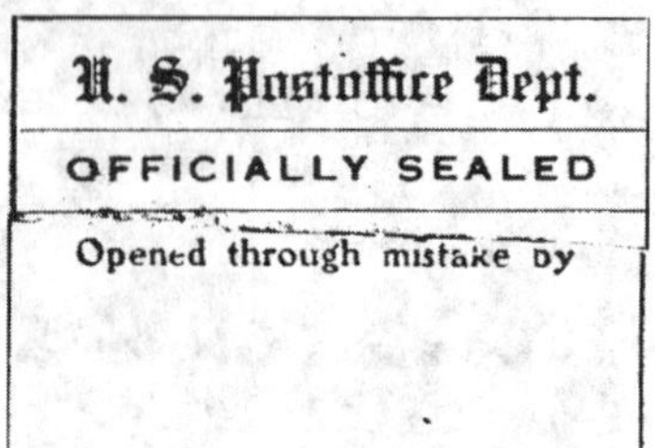

TSS26

LOX29 TSS26 **blue,** on cover *3,750.*

No. LOX29 is unique.
See note below No. LOX15.

TSS27

LOX30 TSS27 **black,** pair on cover *5,000.*

No. LOX30 is unique. The seals were torn in half when the envelope was opened. Value is based on 2000 auction sale.

TSS28

LOX31 TSS28 **red,** *cream* *1,000.*

No. LOX31 is unique. It has a thin spot and crease and is valued as such.

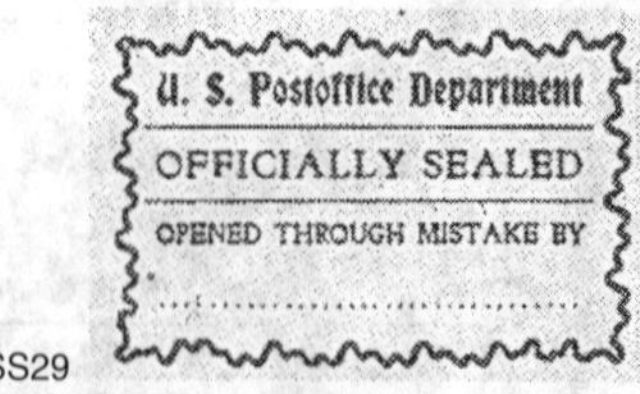

TSS29

LOX32 TSS29 **black** *700.00*

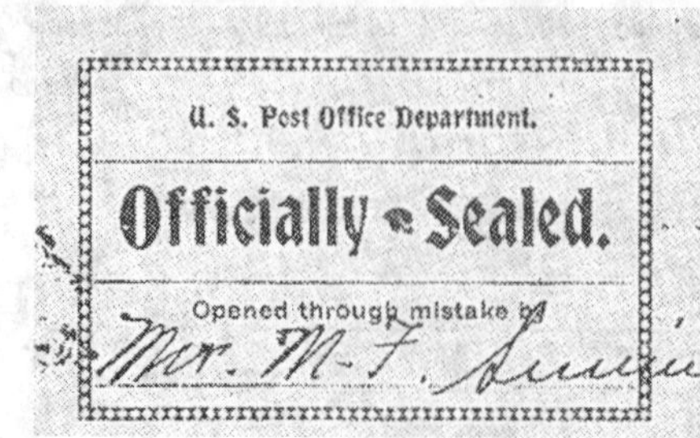

TSS30

LOX33 TSS30 **black** —

TSS31

LOX34 TSS31 **red,** *rose* — *3,250.*

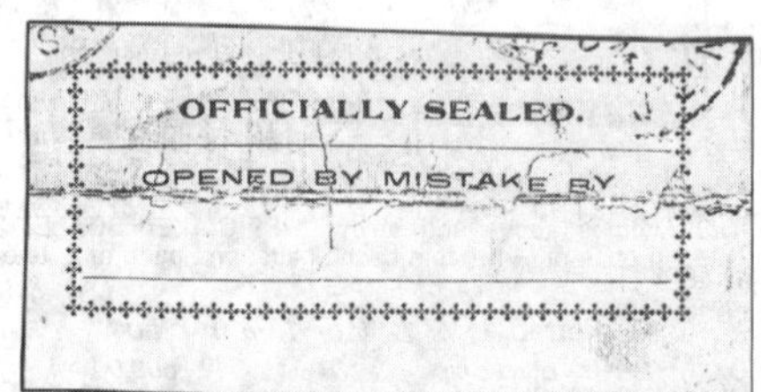

TSS32

LOX35 TSS32 **black,** on cover —

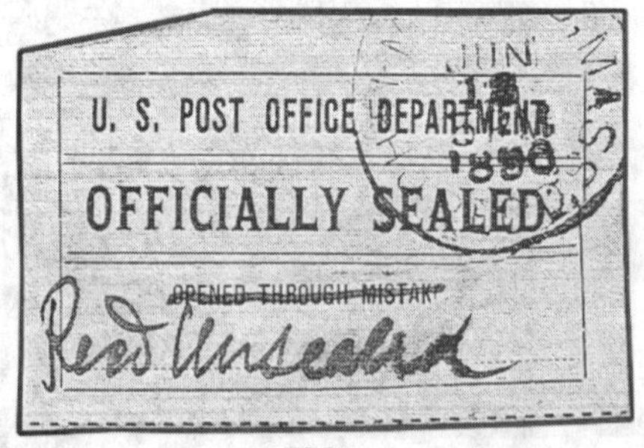

TSS33

LOX36 TSS33 **black** —

TSS34

LOX37 TSS34 **green** —

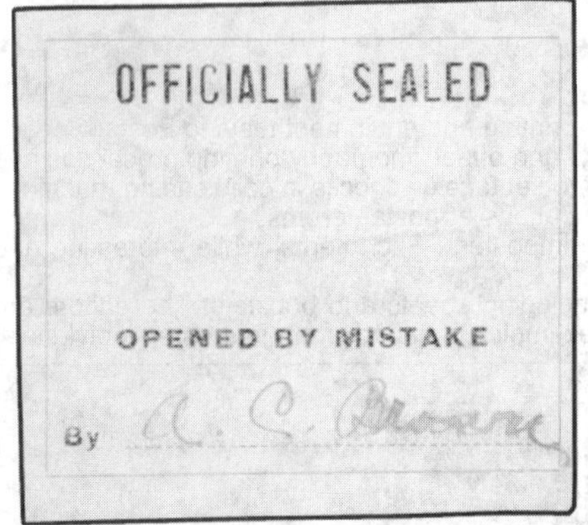

TSS35

LOX38 TSS35 **black,** *tan* *1,250.*

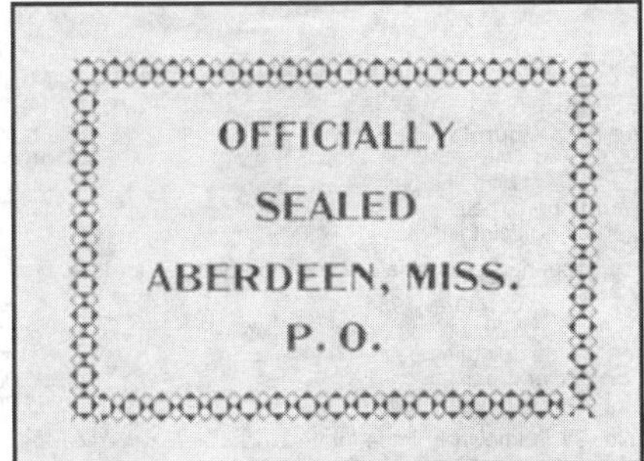

TSS36

LOX39 TSS36 **black,** *tan* *1,750.*

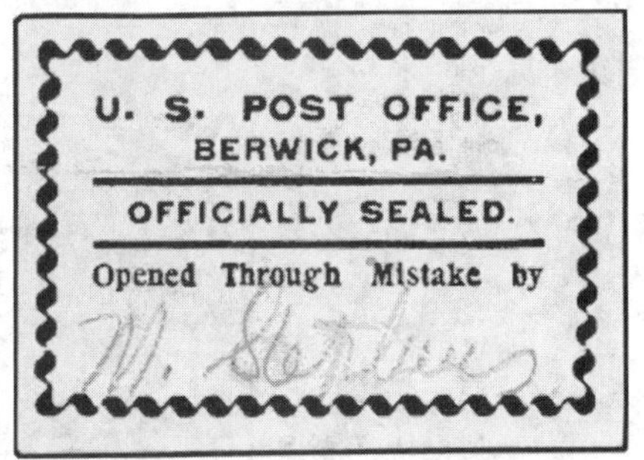

TSS37

LOX40 TSS37 **black,** *tan* *1,750.*

TSS38

LOX41 TSS38 **black** —

TEST STAMPS

The uses for Bureau of Engraving and Printing-produced test stamps have ranged from BEP internal printing and equipment tests to Postal Service and private mailer tests. The earliest test stamps were created to test engraving, letterpress (typography) and offset lithography printing processes and to test the coiling equipment being developed by the BEP. More recent coil test stamps are used mainly to set tension chocks in coil vending machines and stamp-affixing machines. Test stamps also are used for training purposes and for mailing demonstrations at postal forums.

In addition to BEP-produced test stamps, there are a number of private test stamps and lookalike imposters. Such items, while interesting and collectible, are beyond the scope of the Scott Catalogue.

There are other formats and designs of official U.S. test stamps than those currently listed here, including sheets and booklets. The editors are assembling data to correct, clarify and expand these listings, and they would welcome information and examples of stamps from interested individuals.

1909-10 BEP Test Stamps for Rotary Press Development

Hamilton

Design size: 19x22mm

Offset

1-E1a	Die on card, about 3x3½ inches, **black**	*2,000.*

Endorsed on back, "First die proof impression of experimental surface die from surface print. J.E.R. (BEP director) April 25/10" and stamped "420279."

b.	Die on thick glazed card, 73x83mm, deep red	*1,500.*

Endorsed on front, "Sample of surface printing from die: done by Bureau E&P 5/20/1910," with "420270" on back. Another example exists without notation and with "400894" on back.

c.	Essay cut to design size, on thick card with number on back, deep red	*1,000.*
d.	Plate, designs spaced 3½mm horiz., 2mm vert., imperf., deep red	—
e.	Coil plate, designs 2mm apart, perf. 10 horiz., gummed, deep red	—
	Pair	—
f.	As "e," perf. 12 vert., deep red	—
g.	Strip of 3, perf. 12, imperf. at top, deep red	—

Engr.

h.	Plate essay on soft wove, spaced 5mm apart, solid line vignettes, deep red *1909*	—

No. 1-E1h known in block of 12 with pencil on back: "first impression printed from an experimental press designed by J.E. Ralph & B.F. Stickney from intaglio roll. J.E.R." (BEP director).

1910 BEP Test Stamps for Offset Printing

No. 385a-E2 was made by BEP for the Harris company for demonstrating the Harris offset press at the BEP. The offset method of printing postage stamps was not adopted in 1910 but several Harris presses were used to print revenue stamps and the "offset" postage issues of 1918-20.

385a-E2b

Engraved vignette of Minerva in frame similar to No. 319 but with "HARRIS AUTOMATIC / PRESS COMPANY / SERIES 1010" above vignette and "NILES, / OHIO, U.S.A." below.

385a-E2a	3c white wove, imperf., red	*650.*
	Pair	*1,750.*
b.	As "a," design reversed, red	*500.*
	Pair	*1,500.*

TEST COILS
Blank Coils

11	Imperf.	
	Mail-O-Meter private perf., type I	*25.00*
	pair	*50.00*
	pasteup pair	*80.00*
	Schermack private perf., type III	*25.00*
	pair	*50.00*
	pasteup pair	*80.00*

Imperf. test coils are known only with private perforations. Private printing is known on both perforation types.

15	Perf. 10, horiz. ribbed gum	1.00
	Pair	1.50
a.	Smooth gum	1.25
	Pair	2.50

No. 15 is known with Multipost private printing.

17	Perf. 11	*4.00*
	Pair	*8.00*

Former No. 16 (perf 10½) was not produced by the BEP and therefore is beyond the scope of these listings.

Cottrell Press, 432-subject plates

1980(?)

18	Perf. 10, tagged, dull gum	*6.00*
	Pair	*12.00*
	Joint line pair	*50.00*

No. 18 was printed by an inked Cottrell Press. The ink was wiped, leaving some wiping marks and joint lines.

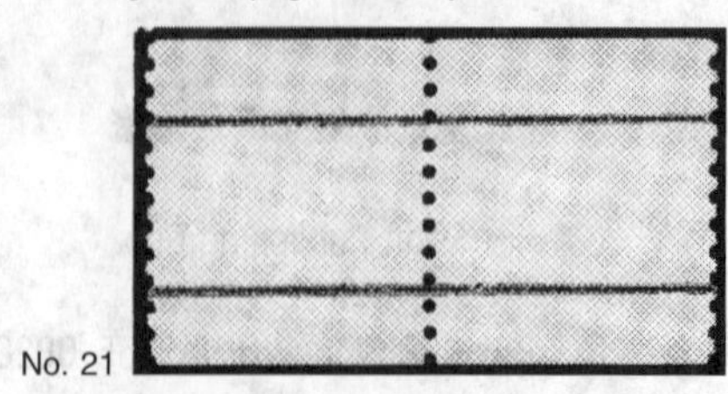

No. 21

Two Continuous Horiz. Red Lines

Stickney Rotary Press

21	Perf. 10	5.50
	Pair	11.00

Nos. 31-33

Vertical Framed Rectangle Design

1938-60 ***Perf. 10 Vert.***

31	**purple**	6.00
	Pair	18.00
	Joint line pair	30.00
a.	Imperf., pair	35.00
	Joint line pair	*85.00*

Misperfed examples are common and sell for less.

32	**carmine,** *1954*	—
	Pair	—
	Joint line pair	—
a.	Imperf., pair	*100.00*
	Joint line pair	*250.00*

No. 32 is known in imperforate blocks and in vertical pairs and blocks, imperforate horizontally.

Cottrell Press, 432-subject plates

33	**red violet,** small holes, *1960*	2.00
	Pair	4.00
	Joint line pair	*22.50*
	Large holes	7.00
	Pair	15.00
	Joint line pair	—
a.	Imperf., pair	*45.00*
	Joint line pair	*100.00*

Nos. 41-46, 49-50

Cottrell Press, 432-subject plates

1962-66 ***Perf. 10 Vert.***

Design size: approx. 19½mm wide

41	**black** (shades), untagged, shiny gum, *Nov. 8*	1.40
	Pair	3.00
	Joint line pair	11.00
a.	Tagged, shiny gum, *Sept. 8, 1966*	.60
	Pair	1.25
	Joint line pair	5.00
b.	Tagged, pebble-surface gum	*1.50*
	Pair	*3.00*
	Joint line pair	*22.50*
c.	As "b," imperf. pair	*50.00*
	Joint line pair	*150.00*
d.	Tagged, dull gum	2.25
	Pair	4.75
	Joint line pair	27.50
e.	Untagged, dull gum	.50
	Pair	1.00
	Joint line pair	10.00

No. 41 can be found with red, orange, blue, purple, gray graphite and black defacement lines; such copies sell for more. Also known on hi-brite fluorescent paper.

1970

42	**carmine,** tagged, *Feb. 17*	—
43	**green,** tagged, *pebble-surface gum*	75.00
	Pair	150.00
	Joint line pair	*450.00*
a.	Imperf., pair	*150.00*
	Joint line pair	*450.00*
b.	Vert. pair, imperf. between	*175.00*
c.	Untagged, dull gum	80.00
	Pair	160.00
	Joint line pair	*450.00*
d.	As "c," imperf., pair	*350.00*
	Joint line pair	*400.00*
e.	As "c," vert. pair, imperf. between	*300.00*

The tagging on No. 42 is orange red. All other tagged test stamps glow yellow green.

No. 43 was produced by BEP, distributed to Germany in large imperf. and part perf. sheets.

44	**brown,** untagged	3.00
	Pair	6.00
	Joint line pair	30.00
45	**orange,** tagged	*1,050.*
	Pair	—
	Joint line pair	—

B Press

1988

Design size: approx. 19mm wide

46	**black,** untagged	.50
	Pair	1.00

Also known on fluorescent paper.

1995

47	**blue,** untagged, shiny gum	*225.00*
	Pair	*450.00*

Design of No. 47 is a thick rectangular frame with mirror image row numbers on every 24th stamp.

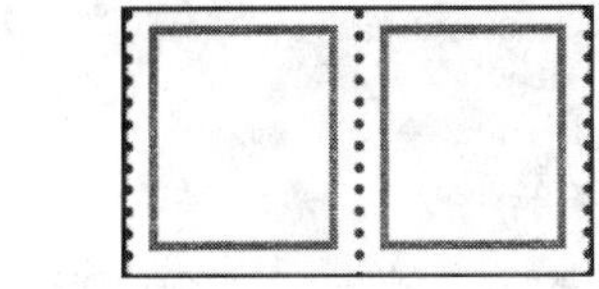

48	**gray black,** untagged, dull gum	*175.00*
	Pair	*375.00*

Design of No. 48 has a thick rectangular frame like No. 47, but does not have row numbers.

Self-Adhesive

1996 (?) ***Die Cut***

49	**black,** untagged	1.25
	P# strip of 5, #1111	9.00

Serpentine Die Cut 9.8 Vert.

50	**black,** untagged	1.00
	P# strip of 5, #1111	6.00

Nos. 49 and 50 appear to be printed on light blue paper. The blue color is caused by the buildup of white ink with a blue tint, which was applied to white paper containing brighteners.

A four-digit counting number appears behind every 20th stamp.

1999

51	**blue**	—
	Pair	—

The design of No. 51 is a thin rectangular frame measuring 18mm wide and 22.6mm tall. The row number of the printing plate appears on every 24th stamp.

Nos. 49-51 were produced on backing paper with a gap of 3.25mm between stamps.

CHRISTMAS SEALS

Issued by the American National Red Cross (1907-1919), the National Tuberculosis Association (1920-1967), the National Tuberculosis and Respiratory Disease Association (1968-1972) and the American Lung Association (1973-).

While the Christmas Seal is not a postage stamp, it has long been associated with the postal service because of its use on letters and packages.

Einar Holboell, an employee of the Danish Post Office, created the Christmas Seal. He believed that seal sales could raise money for charity. The post offices of Denmark, Iceland and Sweden began to sell such seals in the 1904 Christmas season. In the United States, Christmas Seals were first issued in 1907 under the guidance of Emily P. Bissell, following the suggestion of Jacob Riis, social service worker.

Until 1975, all seals (except those of 1907 and 1908 type I) were issued in sheets of 100. The grilled gum (1908) has small square depressions like a waffle. The broken gum (1922), devised to prevent paper curling, consists of depressed lines in the gum, ½mm. apart, forming squares. The vertical and horizontal broken gum (1922, 1923, 1925, 1927-1932) forms diamonds. The perf. 12.00 (1917-1919, 1923, 1925, 1931) has two larger and wider-spaced holes between every 11 smaller holes.

Values are for seals with original gum.

SEALS ISSUED BY THE DELAWARE CHAPTER OF THE AMERICAN NATIONAL RED CROSS

CS1 (Type II)

Designer - Emily P. Bissell.
Nearly $4,000 worth of seals were sold, $3,000 cleared.

Type I - "Merry Christmas" only.
Type II - "Merry Christmas" and "Happy New Year."

1907 ***Perf. 14***

WX1	CS1	Type I	16.00
WX2	CS1	Type II	15.00

Types I and II litho. by Theo. Leonhardt & Son, Philadelphia, Pa. The 1st seals were sold Dec. 7, 1907, in Wilmington, Del. Issued in sheets of 228 (19x12). Type II was issued to extend the sale of seals until New Year's Day, 1908.

Counterfeits of both types exist (perf. 12).

SEALS ISSUED BY THE AMERICAN NATIONAL RED CROSS

CS2 (Type II)

Designer - Howard Pyle. Sales $135,000.

Type I - frame lines with square corners, small "C" in "Christmas."

Type II - frame lines have rounded corners, large "C" in "Christmas," leaves veined.

1908 ***Perf. 12, 14***

WX3	CS2 Type I, perf. 14, smooth gum	35.00
a.	Perf. 12, smooth gum	45.00
c.	Perf. 14, grilled gum	75.00
d.	Perf. 12, grilled gum	50.00
e.	As #WX3, bklt. pane of 6	250.00
f.	As "c," bklt. pane of 6	250.00
g.	As #WX3, bklt. pane of 3	250.00
WX4	CS2 Type II, perf. 12	30.00
a.	Booklet pane of 6	175.00
b.	Booklet pane of 3	125.00

Type I litho. by Theo. Leonhardt & Son. Sheets of 250 (14x18), with the 1st space in the 9th and 18th rows left blank.

Type II litho. by American Bank Note Co., New York, N.Y. in sheets of 100 (10x10).

Booklet panes have straight edges on 3 sides and perforated on left side where there is a stub, except No. WX4b which is a vert. strip of 3 with stub at top. Panes of 6 were made up in books of 24 and 48 and sold for 25c and 50c, and panes of 3 in books of 9 sold for 10c. The grilled gum has small square depressions like on a waffle.

CS3

CS4

Designer - Carl Wingate. Sales $250,000.

1909 ***Perf. 12***

WX5	CS3	One type only	1.25

Litho. by The Strobridge, Cincinnati, Ohio. Seals with a round punched hole of 3½mm are printers' samples.

1910 ***Perf. 12***

Designer - Mrs. Guion Thompson. Sales $300,000.

WX6	CS4	One type only	20.00

Lithographed by The Strobridge Lithographing Co.

SEALS ISSUED BY THE AMERICAN NATIONAL RED CROSS (But sold by the National Association for the Study and Prevention of Tuberculosis)

"The Old Home Among the Cedars"—CS5 (Type II)

CS6

Designer - Anton Rudert under directions of F. D. Millet. Sales $320,000.

Type I - diameter of circle 22mm, solid end in house.
Type II - same circle but thinner, lined end to house.
Type III - diameter of circle 20mm, lined end to house.

1911 ***Perf. 12***

WX7	CS5	Type I	50.00
WX8	CS5	Type II	100.00

COIL STAMP

Perf. 8½ Vertically

WX9	CS5	Type III	75.00

Typo. by Eureka, Scranton, Pa. Type I has name and address of printer and union label in red in top margin. Type II has union label only in green on left margin.

1912 ***Perf. 12***

Designer - John H. Zeh. Sales $402,256.

WX10	CS6	One type only	10.00

Lithographed by The Strobridge Lithographing Co.

CS7 (Type I)

Designer - C. J. Budd. Sales $449,505.

Type I - with Poinsettia flowers and green circles around red crosses at either side.
Type II - the Poinsettia flowers have been removed.
Type III - the Poinsettia flowers and green circles have been removed.

1913 ***Perf. 12***

WX11	CS7	Type I	*1,250.*
WX12	CS7	Type II	7.50
WX13	CS7	Type III	8.50

Lithographed by American Bank Note Co.

CS8

CS9

Designer - Benjamin S. Nash. Sales $555,854.

1914 ***Perf. 12***

WX15	CS8	One type only	10.00

Lithographed by The Strobridge Lithographing Co.

1915

Designer - Benjamin S. Nash. Sales $760,000.

WX16	CS9	Perf. 12½	10.00
a.		Perf. 12	65.00

Lithographed by Andrew B. Graham Co., Washington, D.C.

CS10

CS11

Designer - T. M. Cleland. Sales $1,040,810.

1916

WX18	CS10	Perf. 12	5.00
a.		Perf. 12x12½	6.00
b.		Perf. 12½x12	15.00
c.		Perf. 12½	14.00

Lithographed by the Strobridge Lithographing Co.

Seals of 1917-21 are on coated paper.

1917

Designer - T. M. Cleland. Sales $1,815,110.

WX19	CS11	Perf. 12	2.00
a.		Perf. 12½	15.00
b.		Perf. 12x12.00	2.00
c.		Perf. 12x12½	*20.00*

Typographed by Eureka Specialty Printing Co.
Perf. 12.00 has two larger and wider-spaced holes between every eleven smaller holes.
Sheets come with straight edged margins on all four sides also with perforated margins at either right or left. Perforated margins have the union label imprint in green.

SEALS ISSUED BY THE AMERICAN NATIONAL RED CROSS (Distributed by the National Tuberculosis Association)

CS12

CS13 (Type II)

Designer - Charles A. Winter.
These seals were given to members and others in lots of 10, the Natl. Tuberculosis Assoc. being subsidized by a gift of $2,500,000 from the American National Red Cross.

Type I - "American Red Cross" 15mm long, heavy circles between date.
Type II - "American Red Cross" 15½mm long, periods between date.

1918

WX21	CS12	Type I, perf. 11½x12.00	7.50
a.		Perf. 12	8.50
b.		Perf. 12.00, booklet pane of 10	2.00
c.		Perf. 12x12.00, booklet pane of 10	2.00
d.		Perf. 12, booklet pane of 10	2.00
e.		Perf. 12.00x12, booklet pane of 10	65.00
WX22	CS12	Type II, booklet pane of 10, perf. 12½xRoulette 9½	.60
a.		Perf. 12½, booklet pane of 10	1.50
b.		Perf. 12½x12, bklt. pane of 10	—
d.		Roulette 9½xPerf. 12½, bklt. pane of 10	—
e.		Perf. 12½xRoulette 9½, bklt. pane of 10	20.00
f.		Perf. 12½, booklet pane of 10	20.00
h.		Roulette 9½xPerf. 12½, bklt. pane of 10	20.00
i.		Roulette 9½xPerf. 12½ and Roulette 12½, booklet pane of 10	—
j.		Perf. 12½, booklet pane of 10	50.00
k.		Perf. 12½x12½ and 12, bklt. pane of 10	—
l.		Roulette 9½xPerf. 12½, booklet pane of 10	—
m.		Perf. 12½, booklet pane of 10	—
n.		As "m," stub at bottom, bklt. pane of 10	50.00

For perf 12.00, see note following No. WX19.
Type I typographed by Eureka Specialty Printing Co.
Booklet panes of 10 (2x5) normally have straight edges on all four sides. They were cut from the sheets of 100 and can be plated by certain flaws which occur on both. Sheets have union label imprint on top margin in brown.
Type II lithographed by Strobridge Lithographing Co.
Booklet panes are the same but normally have a perforated margin at top and stub attached. These too can be plated by flaws. One or both vert. sides are rouletted on #WX22e; perforated on #WX22f and WX22h. #WX22i is rouletted 12½ on left, perf. 12½ on right. #WX22j, WX22k and WX22l are panes of 10 (5x2). #WX22m has a perforated margin at left.
Nos. WX21-WX21a are from sheet of 100, no straight edges.
The seal with "American Red Cross" 17¼mm long is believed to be an essay.

1919

Designer - Ernest Hamlin Baker. Sales $3,872,534.
Type I - plume at right side of Santa's cap.
Type II - no plume but a white dot in center of band.

WX24	CS13	Type I, perf. 12	.40
a.		Perf. 12x12.00	.60
b.		Perf. 12½x12	.50
c.		Perf. 12½x12.00	2.75
WX25	CS13	Type II, perf. 12½	.40

For perf 12.00, see note following No. WX19.
This is the first time the double barred cross, the emblem of the National Tuberculosis Association, appeared in the design of the seals. It is also the last time the red cross emblem of the American National Red Cross was used on seals.

Type I typo. by Eureka, and has union label on margin at left in dark blue. Type II litho. by Strobridge.

SEALS ISSUED BY THE NATIONAL TUBERCULOSIS ASSOCIATION

CS14

CS15

Designer - Ernest Hamlin Baker. Sales $3,667,834.

Type I - size of seal 18x22mm.
Type II - seal 18½x23½mm, letters larger & numerals heavier.

1920

WX26	CS14	Type I, perf. 12x12½	.50
a.		Perf. 12	.40
b.		Perf. 12½x12	13.50
c.		Perf. 12½	15.00
WX27	CS14	Type II, perf. 12½	.50

Type I typo. by Eureka, and has union label imprint and rings on margin at left in dark blue. Type II litho. & offset by Strobridge.

1921

Designer - George V. Curtis. Sales $3,520,303.
Type I - dots in the chimney shading and faces are in diagonal lines, dots on chimney are separate except between the 2 top rows of bricks where they are solid.
Type II - dots in the chimney shading and faces are in horiz. lines.
Type III - as Type I except red dots on chimney are mostly joined forming lines, dots between the 2 top rows of bricks are not a solid mass.

WX28	CS15	Type I, perf. 12½	.65
WX29	CS15	Type II, perf. 12½	.40
WX29A	CS15	Type III, perf. 12	.50

Type I typo. by Eureka. Type II offset by Strobridge. Type III typo. by Zeese-Wilkinson Co., Long Island City, N.Y.

CS16

CS17

Designer - T. M. Cleland. Sales $3,857,086.

1922

WX30	CS16	Perf. 12½, broken gum	.80
a.		Perf. 12, broken gum	3.00
b.		Perf. 12x12½, broken gum	7.50
c.		Perf. 12, smooth gum	3.00
d.		Perf. 12½, vertical broken gum	3.00

Typographed by Eureka Specialty Printing Co.
The broken gum, which was devised to prevent curling of paper, consists of depressed lines in the gum ½mm apart, forming squares, or vertical broken gum forming diamonds.

1923

Designer - Rudolph Ruzicka. Sales $4,259,660.

WX31	CS17	Perf. 12½, vertical broken gum	.30
a.		Perf. 12, horizontal broken gum	3.00
b.		Perf. 12x12.00, vertical broken gum	3.50
c.		Perf. 12½x12, vertical broken gum	6.50
d.		Perf. 12, vertical broken gum	.90
e.		Perf. 12.00x12, vertical broken gum	3.00

For perf 12.00, see note following No. WX19.
Typographed by Eureka Specialty Printing Co.
The broken gum on this and issues following printed by Eureka consists of very fine depressed lines forming diamonds.

CS18

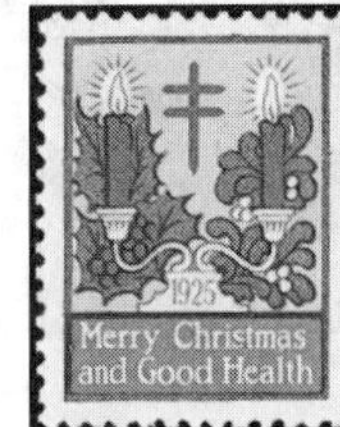

CS19 (Type II)

Designer - George V. Curtis. Sales $4,479,656.

1924

WX32 CS18 One type only .30

Offset by Strobridge, E.&D., and U.S.P.& L.

1925 ***Perf. 12½***

Designer - Robert G. Eberhard. Sales $4,937,786.

Type I - red lines at each side of "1925" do not join red tablet below.

Type II - red lines, as in type I, join red tablet below.

Type III - as type I but shorter rays around flames and "ea" of "Health" smaller.

WX35 CS19 Type I, vert. broken gum .30
a. Perf. 12, vertical broken gum 3.50
b. Perf. 12x12½ vertical broken gum .60
c. Perf. 12.00x12½ vert. broken gum —
WX36 CS19 Type II .30
WX37 CS19 Type III .75

For perf 12.00, see note following No. WX19.

Type I typo. by Eureka. Type II offset by E.&D. Type III litho. by Gugler Lithographing Co., Milwaukee.

CS20

CS21

Designer - George V. Curtis. Sales $5,121,872.

1926 ***Perf. 12½***

WX38 CS20 One type only .25

Offset by E.&D. and U.S.P.&L.

Printers' marks: E.&D. has a red dot at upper right on seal 91 on some sheets. U.S.P.&L. has a black dot at upper left on seal 56 on some sheets.

1927

Designer - John W. Evans. Sales $5,419,959.

WX39 CS21 Perf. 12, horizontal broken gum .20
a. Smooth gum (see footnote) 1.00
WX40 CS21 Perf. 12½, no dot .20
WX41 CS21 Perf. 12½, one larger red dot in background 1mm above right post of dashboard on sleigh .20

"Bonne Sante" added to design and #WX39a but with body of sleigh myrtle green instead of green were used in Canada.

Offset: #WX39, WX39a by Eureka. #WX40 by E.&D. #WX41 by U.S.P.&L.

Printer's marks: Eureka has no mark but can be identified by the perf. 12. E.&D. has red dot to left of knee of 1st reindeer on seal 92. U.S.P.&L. has 2 red dots in white gutter, one at lower left of seal 46 (and sometimes 41) and the other at upper right of seal 55. The perforations often strike out one of these dots.

The Gallant Ship "Argosy" — CS22

CS23

Designer - John W. Evans. Sales $5,465,738.

Type I - shading on sails broken, dots in flag regular.
Type II - shading on sails broken, dots in flag spotty.
Type III - shading on sails unbroken, dots in flag regular.

1928 ***Perf. 12½***

WX44 CS22 Type I, vertical broken gum .20
WX45 CS22 Type II .20
WX46 CS22 Type III .20

Seals inscribed "Bonne Annee 1929" or the same as type II but green in water, and black lines of ship heavier and deeper color were used in Canada.

Offset: Type I by Eureka, Type II by Strobridge, Type III by E.&D.

Printers' marks: Type I comes with and without a blue dash above seal 10, also with a blue and a black dash. Type II has 2 blue dashes below seal 100. Type III has red dot in crest of 1st wave on seal 92.

1929 ***Perf. 12½***

Designer - George V. Curtis. Sales $5,546,147.

WX49 CS23 Vertical broken gum .20
a. Perf. 12, vertical broken gum .50
b. Perf. 12½x12, vertical broken gum 1.25
WX50 CS23 Smooth gum .20

Seals inscribed "Bonne Sante 1929" or "Christmas Greetings 1929" were used in Canada.

Offset: #WX49-WX49b by Eureka, #WX50 by E.&D., U.S.P.&L., and R.R. Heywood Co., Inc., New York, N.Y.

Printers' marks: Eureka is without mark but identified by broken gum. E.&D. has a black dot in lower left corner of seal 92. U.S.P.&L. has blue dot above bell on seal 56. Heywood has a blue dot at lower right corner of seal 100.

CS24

CS25

Designer - Ernest Hamlin Baker, and redrawn by John W. Evans. Sales $5,309,352.

1930 ***Perf. 12½***

WX55 CS24 Vertical broken gum .20
a. Perf. 12, vert. broken gum .50
b. Perf. 12.00x12, vert. broken gum .25
c. Perf. 12½x12, vertical broken gum 2.50
d. Perf. 12, booklet pane of 10, horiz. broken gum .50
WX56 CS24 Smooth gum .20

Seals inscribed "Bonne Sante" or "Merry Christmas" on red border of seal were used in Canada.

Offset: #WX55-WX55d by Eureka, #WX56 by Strobridge, E.&D. and U.S.P.&L.

Printers' marks: Eureka has a dot between the left foot and middle of "M" of "Merry" on seal 1. Strobridge has 2 dashes below "ALL" on seal 100. E.&D. printed on Nashua paper has dot on coat just under elbow on seal 92, and on Gummed Products Co. paper has the dot on seals 91, 92. U.S.P.&L. has a dash which joins tree to top frame line just under "MA" of "Christmas" on seal 55.

The plate for booklet panes was made up from the left half of the regular plate and can be plated by certain flaws which occur on both.

1931 ***Perf. 12½***

Designer - John W. Evans. Sales $4,526,189.

WX61 CS25 Horiz. broken gum (see footnote) 2.00
WX62 CS25 Horizontal broken gum .20
a. Perf. 12x12½, horiz. broken gum .35
b. Perf. 12.00x12½, horizontal broken gum 2.50
c. Perf. 12, horizontal broken gum 1.00
g. Perf. 12, vertical broken gum, booklet pane of 10 .50
h. Perf. 12x12.00, vertical broken gum, booklet pane of 10 .60
WX63 CS25 Smooth gum .20

For perf 12.00, see note following No. WX19.

Offset: #WX61-WX62h by Eureka, #WX63 by Strobridge. #WX61 has a green dash across inner green frame line at bottom center on each seal in sheet except those in 1st and last vertical rows and the 2 rows at bottom.

Printers' marks: Eureka has none. Strobridge has the usual 2 dashes under seal 100.

The plate for booklet panes was made up from transfers of 60 seals (12x5). The panes can be plated by minor flaws.

CS26

CS27

Designer- Edward F. Volkmann. Sales $3,470,637.

1932

WX64 CS26 Perf. 12½x12¾ .20
a. Vertical broken gum .50
WX65 CS26 Perf. 12 .20
WX66 CS26 Perf. 12½ .20
WX67 CS26 Perf. 12½ .20

Offset: #WX64 by Eureka, #WX65 by E.&D., #WX66 by U.S.P.&L., #WX67 by Columbian Bank Note Co., Chicago. #WX64, WX67 have a little red spur on bottom inner frame line of each seal, at left corner.

Printers' marks: Eureka has a red dash, in each corner of the sheet, which joins the red border to the red inner frame line. E.&D. has a blue dot in snow at lower left on seal 91. U.S.P.&L. has a blue dot on top of post on seal 56. Columbian Bank Note has small "C" in lower part of girl's coat on seal 82.

1933

Designer - Hans Axel Walleen. Sales $3,429,311.

WX68 CS27 Perf. 12 .20
WX69 CS27 Perf. 12½ .20

Offset: #WX68 by Eureka, #WX69 by Strobridge, U.S.P.&L., and the Columbian Bank Note Co.

Printers' marks; Eureka has rope joining elbow of figure to left on seals 11, 20, 91, 100. Strobridge has the usual 2 dashes under seal 100. U.S.P.&L. has green dot on tail of "s" of "Greetings" on seal 55. Columbian has white "c" on margin, under cross, on seal 93.

CS28

CS29

Designer - Herman D. Giesen. Sales $3,701,344.

1934

WX72 CS28 Perf. 12½x12¼ .20
WX73 CS28 Perf. 12½ (see footnote) .20
WX74 CS28 Perf. 12½ (see footnote) .20
WX75 CS28 Perf. 12½ (see footnote) .20

Offset: #WX72 by Eureka, #WX73 by Strobridge, #WX74 by E.&D. and #WX75 by U.S.P.&L.

Cutting of blue plate for the under color: #WX72, WX73 (early printing) and WX74 have lettering and date cut slightly larger than ultramarine color. #WX73 (later printing) has square cutting around letters and date, like top part of letter "T". #WX75 has cutting around letters and date cut slightly larger.

Printers' marks: Eureka has 5 stars to right of cross on seal 10. Strobridge has 2 blue dashes in lower left corner of seal 91 or in lower right corner of seal 100. E.&D. has a red dot in lower left corner of seal 99. U.S.P.&L. has 5 stars to left of cross on seal 56.

Great Britain issued seals of this design which can be distinguished by the thinner and whiter paper. Sheets have perforated margins on all 4 sides but without any lettering on bottom margin, perf. 12½.

1935

Designer - Ernest Hamlin Baker. Sales $3,946,498.

WX76 CS29 Perf. 12½x12¼ .20
WX77 CS29 Perf. 12½ .20

Offset: #WX76 by Eureka, #WX77 by Strobridge, U.S.P.&L. and Columbian Bank Note Co.

Eureka recut their blue plate and eliminated the faint blue shading around cross, girl's head and at both sides of the upper part of post. U.S.P.& L. eliminated the 2 brown spurs which pointed to the base of cross, in all 4 corners of the sheet.

Printers' marks: Eureka has an extra vertical line of shading on girl's skirt on seal 60. Strobridge has 2 brown dashes in lower right corner of position 100 but sheets from an early printing are without this mark. U.S.P.&L. has a blue dot under post on seal 55. Columbian has a blue "c" under post on seal 99.

The corner seals carry slogans: "Help Fight Tuberculosis," "Protect Your Home from Tuberculosis," "Tuberculosis Is Preventable," "Tuberculosis Is Curable."

Printers' marks appear on seal 56 on sheets of 100 unless otherwise noted:

E Eureka Specialty Printing Co.
S Strobridge Lithographing Co. (1930-1958).
S Specialty Printers of America (1975-).
D Edwards & Deutsch Lithographing Co. (E.&D.)
U United States Printing & Lithographing Co. (U.S.P.&L.)
F Fleming-Potter Co., Inc.
W Western Lithograph Co.
B Berlin Lithographing Co. (1956-1969); I. S. Berlin Press (1970-1976); Barton-Cotton (1977-).
R Bradford-Robinson Printing Co.
N Sale-Niagara, Inc.

Seals from 1936 onward are printed by offset.

Seals with tropical gum (dull), starting in 1966, were used in Puerto Rico.

CS30

CS31

Designer - Walter I. Sasse. Sales $4,522,269.

1936 **Pair**

WX80 CS30 Perf. 12½x12 (E) .20
WX81 CS30 Perf. 12½ (S,D,U) .20

Seals with red background and green cap-band alternate with seals showing green background and red cap-band. The corner seals carry the same slogans as those of 1935.

Two of the three Strobridge printings show vertical green dashes in margin below seal 100, besides "S" on seal 56.

1937

Designer - A. Robert Nelson. Sales $4,985,697.

WX88 CS31 Perf. 12x12½ (E) .20
WX89 CS31 Perf. 12½ (S,D,U) .20

Positions 23, 28, 73 and 78, carry slogans: "Health for all," "Protect your home," "Preventable" and "Curable."

The "U" printer's mark of U.S.P.&L. appears on seal 55. It is omitted on some sheets.

CS32

CS33

Designer - Lloyd Coe. Sales $5,239,526.

1938

WX92 CS32 Perf. 12½x12 (E) .20
WX93 CS32 Perf. 12½ (S,D,U) .20
a. Miniature sheet, imperf. 2.50

The corner seals bear portraits of Rene T. H. Laennec, Robert Koch, Edward Livingston Trudeau and Einar Holboll.

No. WX93a contains the 4 corner seals, with the regular seal in the center. It sold for 25 cents.

1939

Designer - Rockwell Kent. Sales $5,593,399.

WX96 CS33 Perf. 12½x12 (E) .20
a. Booklet pane of 20, perf. 12 .50
WX97 CS33 Perf. 12½ (S,D,U) .20

The center seals, positions 45, 46, 55, 56, carry slogans: "Health to All," "Protect Your Home." "Tuberculosis Preventable Curable" and "Holiday Greetings."

Printers' marks appear on seal 57.

CS34

CS35

Designer- Felix L. Martini. Sales $6,305,979.

1940

WX100 CS34 Perf. 12½x12 (E) .20
WX101 CS34 Perf. 12½x13 (E) .20
WX103 CS34 Perf. 12½ (S,D,U) .20

Seals 23, 32 and 34 carry the slogan "Protect Us from Tuberculosis." Each slogan seal shows one of the 3 children.

1941

Designer - Stevan Dohanos. Sales $7,530,496.

WX104 CS35 Perf. 12½x12 (E) .20
WX105 CS35 Perf. 12½ (S,D,U) .20

"S" and "U" printers' marks exist on same sheet.

CS36

CS37

Designer - Dale Nichols. Sales $9,390,117.

1942

WX108 CS36 Perf. 12x12½ (E) .20
WX109 CS36 Perf. 12½ (S,D,U) .20

1943

Designer - Andre Dugo. Sales $12,521,494.

Pair

WX112 CS37 Perf. 12½x12 (E) .20
WX113 CS37 Perf. 12½ (S,D,U) .20

On alternate seals, the vert. frame colors (blue & red) are transposed as are the horiz. frame colors (buff & black).

Seals where "Joyeux Noel" replaces "Greetings 1943" and "1943" added on curtain or the same as #WX113 but darker colors were used in Canada.

CS38

CS39

Designer - Spence Wildey. Sales $14,966,227.

1944

WX118 CS38 Perf. 12½x12 (E) .20
WX119 CS38 Perf. 12½ (S,D,U) .20

Seals with "USA" omitted are for Canada.

1945 **"USA" at Lower Right Corner**

Designer - Park Phipps. Sales $15,638,755.

WX124 CS39 Perf. 12½x12 (E) .20
WX125 CS39 Perf. 12½ (S,D,U) .20

Seals with "USA" omitted are for Canada.

CS40

CS41

Designer - Mary Louise Estes and Lloyd Coe. Sales $17,075,608.

1946 **"USA" at Left of Red Cross**

WX130 CS40 Perf. 12½x12 (E) .20
WX131 CS40 Perf. 12½ (S,D,U) .20

Seals with "USA" omitted are for Canada and Bermuda.

Printers' marks are on seal 86.

The center seals (45, 46, 55, 56) bear portraits of Jacob Riis, Emily P. Bissell, E. A. Van Valkenburg and Leigh Mitchell Hodges.

1947

Designer - Raymond H. Lufkin. Sales $18,665,523.

WX135 CS41 Perf. 12x12½ (E) .20
WX136 CS41 Perf. 12½ (S,D,U) .20

Seals with "USA" omitted are for Canada and Great Britain.

The "U" printer's mark of U.S.P.&L. appears on seal 46.

CS42

CS43

Designer - Jean Barry Bart. Sales $20,153,834.

1948

WX140 CS42 Perf. 12x12½ (E) .20
WX141 CS42 Perf. 12½ (S,D,U) .20

Seals with "USA" omitted are for Canada and Great Britain.

1949

Designer - Herbert Meyers. Sales $20,226,794.

WX145 CS43 Perf. 12x12½ (E) .20
WX146 CS43 Perf. 12½ (S,D,U) .20

Seals with "USA" omitted are for Canada & Great Britain.

CS44

CS45

Designer - Andre Dugo. Sales $20,981,540.

1950

WX150 CS44 Perf. 12½x12 (E) .20
WX151 CS44 Perf. 12½ (S,D,U,F) .20

Seals with "USA" omitted are for Canada & Great Britain.

1951

Designer - Robert K. Stephens. Sales $21,717,953.

WX155 CS45 Perf. 12½x12 (E) .20
WX156 CS45 Perf. 12½ (S,D,U,F) .20

Seals with "USA" omitted are for Canada.

CS46

CS47

Designer - Tom Darling. Sales $23,238,148.

1952

WX159 CS46 Perf. 12½x12 (E) .20
WX160 CS46 Perf. 12½ (S,D,U,F) .20

Overprinted "Ryukyus" (in Japanese characters)

WX163 CS46 Perf. 12½x12, 12½ (U) 1.50

1953

Designers - Elmer Jacobs and E. Willis Jones. Sales $23,889,044.

WX164 CS47 Perf. 13 (E) .20
WX165 CS47 Perf. 12½ (S,D,U,F) .20

CS48

Designer - Jorgen Hansen. Sales $24,670,202.

1954			Block of 4
WX168	CS48	Perf. 13 (E)	.40
WX169	CS48	Perf. 12½ (S,U,F,W)	.40
WX170	CS48	Perf. 11 (D)	.50

CS49

Designer - Jean Simpson. Sales $25,780,365.

1955			Pair
WX173	CS49	Perf. 13 (E)	.25
WX174	CS49	Perf. 12½ (S,U,F,W)	.25
WX175	CS49	Perf. 11 (D)	.25

CS50

Designer - Heidi Brandt. Sales $26,310,491.

1956			Block of 4
WX178	CS50	Perf. 12½x12 (E)	.40
WX179	CS50	Perf. 12½ (E,S,U,F,W)	.50
WX180	CS50	Perf. 11 (D,B)	.40
WX183	CS50	"Puerto Rico," perf. 12½	3.00

CS51

Designer - Clinton Bradley. Sales $25,959,998.

1957			Block of 4
WX184	CS51	Perf. 13 (E)	.40
WX185	CS51	Perf. 12½ (S,U,F,W,R)	.40
WX186	CS51	Perf. 11 (D,B)	.50
WX187	CS51	Perf. 10½x11 (D)	.75
WX188	CS51	Perf. 10½ (D)	3.00
WX190	CS51	"Puerto Rico," perf. 13	3.00

CS52

Designer - Alfred Guerra. Sales $25,955,390.

1958			Pair
WX191	CS52	Perf. 13 (E)	.25
WX192	CS52	Perf. 12½ (S,U,F,W,R)	.25
WX193	CS52	Perf. 10½x11 (B,D)	.50
WX194	CS52	Perf. 11 (B,D)	.35
WX196	CS52	"Puerto Rico," perf. 13	1.50

CS53

Designer - Katherine Rowe. Sales $26,740,906.

1959			Pair
WX197	CS53	Perf. 13 (E)	.25
WX198	CS53	Perf. 12½ (F,R,W)	.25
a.		Horiz. pair, imperf. btwn. (D)	1.50
WX199	CS53	Perf. 10½x11 (B)	.40
WX200	CS53	Perf. 11 (B,D)	.25
WX201	CS53	Perf. 10½ (B)	2.00
WX203	CS53	"Puerto Rico," perf. 13	1.25

E.&D. omitted every other vertical row of perforation on a number of sheets which were widely distributed as an experiment. #WX198a (shown above in illustration) is from these sheets.

CS54

Designer - Philip Richard Costigan. Sales $26,259,030.

1960			Block of 4
WX204	CS54	Perf. 12½ (E,F,R,W)	.35
WX205	CS54	Perf. 12½x12 (E)	1.00
WX206	CS54	Perf. 11x10½ (B)	.35
WX207	CS54	Perf. 11 (D)	.35

Puerto Rico used No. WX204 (E).

CS55

Designer - Heidi Brandt. Sales $26,529,517.

1961			Block of 4
WX209	CS55	Perf. 12½ (E,F,R,W)	.35
WX209A	CS55	Perf. 12½x12 (E)	2.00
WX210	CS55	Perf. 11x10½ (B)	.35
WX211	CS55	Perf. 11 (D)	.35

Puerto Rico used No. WX209 (E).

CS56

Designer - Paul Dohanos. Sales $27,429,202.

1962			Block of 4
WX213	CS56	Perf. 12½ (F,R,W)	.35
WX214	CS56	Perf. 13 (E)	.35
WX215	CS56	Perf. 10½x11 (B)	.35
WX216	CS56	Perf. 11 (D,B)	.35

Puerto Rico used No. WX214.

CS57

Designer - Judith Campbell Piussi. Sales $27,411,806.

1963			Block of 4
WX218	CS57	Perf. 12½ (E,F,R,W)	.35
WX219	CS57	Perf. 11 (B,D)	.35

Puerto Rico used No. WX218 (E).

CS58

Designer - Gaetano di Palma. Sales $28,784,043.

1964			Block of 4
WX220	CS58	Perf. 12½ (E,F,R,W)	.35
WX221	CS58	Perf. 11 (B,D)	.35

Puerto Rico used No. WX221 (B).

CS59

Designer - Frede Salomonsen. Sales $29,721,878.

1965			Block of 4
WX222	CS59	Perf. 12½ (F,W)	.35
WX223	CS59	Perf. 11 (B,D)	.35
WX224	CS59	Perf. 13 (E)	.35

Puerto Rico used No. WX223 (B).

CS60

Designer - Heidi Brandt. Sales $30,776,586.

1966			Block of 8
WX225	CS60	Perf. 12½ (E,F,W)	.65
WX226	CS60	Perf. 10½x11 (B)	.65
WX227	CS60	Perf. 11 (D)	.65

Blocks of four seals with yellow green and white backgrounds alternate in sheet in checkerboard style.

Puerto Rico used No. WX226.

Holiday Train — CS61

Designer - L. Gerald Snyder. Sales $31,876,773.

The seals come in 10 designs showing a train filled with Christmas gifts and symbols. The direction of the train is reversed in alternating rows as are the inscriptions "Christmas 1967" and "Greetings 1967." The illustration shows first 2 seals of top row.

1967			Block of 20 (10x2)
WX228	CS61	Perf. 13 (E)	.65
WX229	CS61	Perf. 12½ (F,W)	.65
WX230	CS61	Perf. 10½ (B)	1.50
WX231	CS61	Perf. 11 (D)	.75
WX232	CS61	Perf. 11x10½ (B)	.75

Puerto Rico used No. WX229 (F).

SEALS ISSUED BY NATIONAL TUBERCULOSIS AND RESPIRATORY DISEASE ASSOCIATION

CS62

Designer - William Eisele. Sales $33,059,107.

1968			Block of 4
WX233	CS62	Perf. 13 (E)	.50
WX234	CS62	Perf. 10½x11 (B)	.50
WX234A	CS62	Perf. 10½ (B)	.50
WX235	CS62	Perf. 11 (D)	.50
WX236	CS62	Perf. 12½ (F,W)	.50

Pairs of seals with bluish green and yellow backgrounds alternate in sheet in checkerboard style.

Puerto Rico used No. WX236 (F).

CS63

Designer - Bernice Kochan. Sales $34,437,591.

1969			Block of 4
WX237	CS63	Perf. 13 (E)	.35
WX238	CS63	Perf. 12½ (F,W)	.35
WX239	CS63	Perf. 10½x11 (B)	.50
WX240	CS63	Perf. 11 (B)	.50

Puerto Rico used No. WX238 (F).

CS64

Designer - L. Gerald Snyder. Sales $36,237,977.

Sheets contain 100 different designs, Christmas symbols, toys, decorated windows; inscribed alternately "Christmas 1970" and "Greetings 1970." The illustration shows 6 seals from the center of the sheet.

1970			Sheet of 100 (10x10)
WX242	CS64	Perf. 12½ (E,F,W)	1.25
WX243	CS64	Perf. 11 (B)	1.25
WX244	CS64	Perf. 11x10½ (B)	1.25

Puerto Rico used No. WX242 (F).

CS65

Designer - James Clarke. Sales $36,120,000.

1971			Block of 8 (2x4)
WX245	CS65	Perf. 12½ (E,F)	.50
WX246	CS65	Perf. 11 (B)	.50

The 4 illustrated seals each come in a 2nd design arrangement: cross at left, inscriptions transposed, and reversed bugler, candle and tree ornaments. Each sheet of 100 has 6 horiz. rows as shown and 4 rows with 2nd designs.

Puerto Rico used No. WX245 (F).

Eureka printings are found with large "E," small "E" and without "E."

CS66

Designer - Linda Layman. Sales $38,000,557.

The seals come in 10 designs showing various holiday scenes with decorated country and city houses, carolers, Christmas trees and snowman. Inscribed alternately "1972 Christmas" and "Greetings 1972." Shown are seals from center of row.

1972			Strip of 10
WX247	CS66	Perf. 13 (E)	.50
WX248	CS66	Perf. 12½ (F)	.75
WX249	CS66	Perf. 11 (B)	.50

Seal 100 has designer's name. Puerto Rico used No. WX248.

SEALS ISSUED BY AMERICAN LUNG ASSOCIATION

CS67

Designer - Cheri Johnson. Sales $36,902,439.

The seals are in 12 designs representing "The 12 Days of Christmas." Inscribed alternately "Christmas 1973" and "Greetings 1973." Shown is block from center of top 2 rows.

1973			Block of 12
WX250	CS67	Perf. 12½ (F), 18x22mm	.50
a.		Size 16½x20½mm (E)	.50
WX251	CS67	Perf. 11 (B,W)	.50

Seal 100 has designer's name. Puerto Rico used #WX250 (F).

CS68

Designer - Rubidoux. Sales $37,761,745.

1974			Block of 4
WX252	CS68	Perf. 12½ (E,F)	.35
WX253	CS68	Perf. 11 (B)	.35

Seal 99 has designer's name. Puerto Rico used #WX252 (F).

value priced **stockbooks**

Stockbooks are a classic and convenient storage alternative for many collectors. These German-made stockbooks feature heavyweight archival quality paper with 9 pockets on each page. The 8½" x 11⅝" pages are bound inside a handsome leatherette grain cover and include glassine interleaving between the pages for added protection. The Value Priced Stockbooks are available in two page styles, the white page stockbooks feature glassine pockets while the black page variety includes clear acetate pockets

WHITE PAGE STOCKBOOKS GLASSINE POCKETS

ITEM	DESCRIPTION		RETAIL
SW16BL	Blue	16 pages	$6.95
SW16GR	Green	16 pages	$6.95
SW16RD	Red	16 pages	$6.95

BLACK PAGE STOCKBOOKS ACETATE POCKETS

ITEM	COLOR	PAGES	RETAIL
ST16RD	Red	16 pages	$10.95
ST16GR	Green	16 pages	$10.95
ST16BL	Blue	16 pages	$10.95
ST16BK	Black	16 pages	$10.95
ST32RD	Red	32 pages	$16.95
ST32GR	Green	32 pages	$16.95
ST32BL	Blue	32 pages	$16.95
ST32BK	Black	32 pages	$16.95
ST64RD	Red	64 pages	$29.95
ST64GR	Green	64 pages	$29.95
ST64BL	Blue	64 pages	$29.95
ST64BK	Black	64 pages	$29.95

The black page stockbook is available in three sizes:
16 pages
32 pages
64 pages.

Scott Value Priced Stockbooks are available from your favorite dealer or direct from:

SCOTT

P.O. Box 828
Sidney OH 45365-0828
www.amosadvantage.com
1-800-572-6885

SANITARY FAIR

The United States Sanitary Commission was authorized by the Secretary of War on June 9, 1861, and approved by President Lincoln on June 13, 1861. It was a committee of inquiry, advice and aid dealing with the health and general comfort of Union troops, supported by public contributions.

Many Sanitary Fairs were held to raise funds for the Commission, and eight issued stamps. The first took place in 1863 at Chicago, where no stamp was issued. Some Sanitary Fairs advertised on envelopes.

Sanitary Fair stamps occupy a position midway between United States semi-official carrier stamps and the private local posts. Although Sanitary Fair stamps were not valid for U.S. postal service, they were prepared for, sold and used at the fair post offices, usually with the approval and participation of the local postmaster.

The Commission undertook to forward soldiers' unpaid and postage due letters. These letters were handstamped "Forwarded by the U.S. Sanitary Commission."

Details about the Sanitary Fair stamps may be found in the following publications:
American Journal of Philately, Jan. 1889, by J. W. Scott
The Collector's Journal, Aug-Sept. 1909, by C. E. Severn
Scott's Monthly Journal, Jan. 1927 (reprint, Apr. 1973), by Elliott Perry
Stamps, April 24th, 1937, by Harry M. Konwiser
Pat Paragraphs, July, 1939, by Elliott Perry
Covers, Aug. 1952, by George B. Wray
Sanitary Fairs, 1992, by Alvin and Marjorie Kantor
The listings were compiled originally by H. M. Konwiser and Dorsey F. Wheless.

SF1

SF2

Albany, New York
Army Relief Bazaar

Setting A: narrow spacing, pane of 12.
Setting B: wider spacing, sheet of 25.

1864, Feb. 22-Mar. 30 Litho. *Imperf.*
Thin White Paper

WV1	SF1 10c **rose**	125.	
	Used on cover (tied "Albany")		9,500.
	Block of 4, setting A	1,200.	
	Pane of 12, setting A	4,800.	
	Block of 4, setting B	500.	
	Sheet of 25, setting B	2,500.	
WV2	SF1 10c **black**	700.	
	Block of 5	4,500.	

The No. WV1 tied by Albany cancel on cover is unique. One other cover exists in private hands with the stamp uncanceled and slightly damaged.

Imitations are typographed in red, blue, black or green on a thin white or ordinary white paper, also on colored papers and are:
(a) Eagle with topknot, printed in sheets of 30 (6x5).
(b) Eagle without shading around it.
(c) Eagle with shading around it, but with a period instead of a circle in "C" of "Cents," and "Ten Cents" is smaller.

Boston, Mass.
National Sailors' Fair

1864, Nov. 9-22 Litho.
Die Cut

WV3	SF2 10c **green**	350.

Brooklyn, N.Y.
Brooklyn Sanitary Fair

SF3

1864, Feb. 22-Mar. 8 Litho. *Imperf.*

WV4	SF3 (15c) **green**	1,250.	3,600.
	On cover, Fair postmark on envelope		3,000.
	Block of 4	6,500.	
	Block of 6	10,000.	
WV5	SF3 (25c) **black**	4,750.	
	On cover, with 1c local #28L2, Fair postmark on envelope		36,000.

No. WV4 used is valued canceled by the Fair postmark and is unique. One or more examples also exist with a manuscript cancel. No. WV5 unused is unique as is the usage on cover.

Imitations: *(a)* Typographed and shows "Sanitary" with a heavy cross bar to "T" and second "A" with a long left leg. *(b)* Is a rough typograph print without shading in letters of "Fair."

SF4

SF5

1863, Dec. Typeset *Imperf.*

WV6	SF4 5c **black,** *rosy buff*	750.	200.
WV7	SF5 10c **green**	1,150.	
	Tete beche pair	6,500.	

No. WV6 used is believed to be unique. It has a manuscript cancel and is faulty. It is valued thus.

SF6

SF7

New York, N. Y.
Metropolitan Fair

1864, Apr. 4-27 Engr. *Imperf.*
Thin White Paper

WV8	SF6 10c **blue**	250.
	Sheet of 4	1,500.
WV9	SF6 10c **red**	1,500.
	Pair	3,500.
WV10	SF6 10c **black**	14,000.

Engraved and printed by John E. Gavit of Albany, N.Y. from a steel plate composed of four stamps, 2x2. Can be plated by the positions of scrolls and dots around "Ten Cents."

No. WV10 is unique.

Philadelphia, Pa.
Great Central Fair

1864, June 7-28 Engr. *Perf. 12*
Printed by Butler & Carpenter, Philadelphia
Sheets of 126 (14x9)

WV11	SF7 10c **blue**	40.00	525.00
	On cover tied with Fair postmark		2,250.
	On cover with 3c #65, Fair and Philadelphia postmarks		36,000.
	On cover with 3c #65, New York postmark		42,500.
	Block of 4	250.00	
WV12	SF7 20c **green**	27.50	500.00
	On cover tied with Fair postmark		1,500.
	Block of 4	135.00	
	Block of 12	475.00	
WV13	SF7 30c **black**	35.00	400.00
	On cover tied with Fair postmark		1,500.
	Nos. WV11-WV13 on single cover, Fair postmark		7,500.
	Block of 4	160.00	
	Block of 6	240.00	

Imprint "Engraved by Butler & Carpenter, Philadelphia" on right margin adjoining three stamps.

Used examples of Nos. WV11-WV13 have Fair cancellation.

The No. WV11 covers used with 3c #65 are each unique. The New York usage is on a Metropolitan Fair illustrated envelope.

Imitation of No. WV13 comes typographed in blue or green on thick paper.

White and amber envelopes were sold by the fair inscribed "Great Central Fair for the Sanitary Commission," showing picture in several colors of wounded soldier, doctors and ambulance marked "U.S. Sanitary Commission." Same design and inscription are known on U.S. envelope No. U46.

SF8

SF9

Springfield, Mass.
Soldiers' Fair

1864, Dec. 19-24 Typo. *Imperf.*

WV14	SF8 10c **lilac**	210.00
	On unaddressed cover, Fair postmark on envelope	750.00
	Horizontal strip of 4	950.00

Design by Thomas Chubbuck, engraver of the postmaster provisional stamp of Brattleboro, Vt.

One cover exists pencil-addressed to Wm. Ingersoll, Springfield Armory; value slightly more than an unaddressed cover.

Imitations: (a) Without designer's name in lower right corner, in lilac on laid paper. *(b)* With designer's name, but roughly typographed, in lilac on white wove paper. Originals show 5 buttons on uniform.

Stamford, Conn.
Soldiers' Fair
Sheets of 8

1864, July 27-29

WV15	SF9 15c **pale brown**	2,000.	4,000.

Originals have tassels at ends of ribbon inscribed "SOLDIERS FAIR." Imitations have leaning "S" in "CENTS" and come in lilac, brown, green, also black on white paper, green on pinkish paper and other colors.

ESSAY
Great Central Fair, Philadelphia

1864

WV11-E1	Design as issued but value tablets blank, greenish black on glazed paper (unique)	—

PROOFS
Metropolitan Fair, New York

1864

WV10P	10c **black,** plate on India, mounted on card	900.

Great Central Fair, Philadelphia

1864

No.	Description	Value
WV11P	10c **blue,** card	32.50
	Block of 4	150.00
WV11TC/WV13TC	10c and 30c **grnsh blk,** se-tenant, glazed paper, large die	—
WV12P	20c **green,** card	35.00
	Block of 4	175.00
WV12TC	20c **carmine,** wove, perf.	35.00
	Block of 4	175.00
WV12TC	20c **vermilion,** India on card, large die	275.00
WV12TC	20c **vermilion,** wove, imperf.	22.50
	Block of 4	115.00
WV12TC	20c **vermilion,** wove, perf.	35.00
	Block of 4	175.00
WV12TC	20c **orange,** wove, imperf.	22.50
	Block of 4	115.00
WV12TC	20c **brown orange,** opaque paper	22.50
	Block of 4	115.00
WV12TC	20c **red brown,** wove, perf.	35.00
	Block of 4	175.00
WV12TC	20c **black brown,** wove, imperf.	25.00
	Block of 4	125.00
WV12TC	20c **olive,** wove, imperf.	22.50
	Block of 4	100.00
WV12TC	20c **yellow green,** wove, imperf.	22.50
	Block of 4	125.00
WV12TC	20c **light green,** wove, perf.	35.00
	Block of 4	175.00
WV12TC	20c **blue,** India on card, large die	275.00
WV12TC	20c **blue,** wove, perf.	175.00
WV12TC	20c **bright blue,** wove, imperf.	22.50
	Block of 4	125.00
WV12TC	20c **bright blue,** wove, perf.	35.00
	Block of 4	175.00
WV12TC	20c **lt. ultramarine,** wove, imperf.	22.50
	Block of 4	125.00
WV12TC	20c **purple,** wove, imperf.	22.50
	Block of 4	125.00
WV12TC	20c **claret,** wove, imperf.	35.00
	Block of 4	200.00
WV12TC	20c **brown black,** wove, perf.	35.00
	Block of 4	175.00
WV12TC	20c **greenish black,** glazed paper, large die	225.00
WV12TC	20c **gray black,** opaque paper, wove, imperf.	22.50
	Block of 4	125.00
WV12TC	20c **gray black,** wove, perf.	35.00
	Block of 4	175.00
WV12TC	20c **black,** experimental double paper, wove, imperf.	25.00
	Block of 4	140.00
WV13P	30c **black,** card	35.00
	Block of 4	175.00

Reprints (1903?) exist of WV11TC-WV13TC, se-tenant vertically, large die on glazed white, pink or yellow card and small die on India paper (mounted se-tenant) in carmine, red carmine, vermilion, orange, brown, yellow brown, olive, yellow green, blue green, gray blue, ultramarine, light violet, violet, claret and gray black.

There also exist large die essay reprints on India paper, green bond paper and glazed cardboard without denomination or with 20c. The 20c value has an added line below the center shield.

ENCASED POSTAGE STAMPS

In 1862 John Gault of Boston patented the idea of encasing postage stamps in metal frames behind a shield of transparent mica, and using them for advertising. The scarcity of small change during the Civil War made these encased stamps popular. Many firms impressed their names and products on the back of these stamp frames in embossed letters. Values are for very fine specimens with mica intact, although signs of circulation and handling are to be expected.

Grading encompasses three areas: 1. Case will show signs of wear or handling and signs of original toning. 2. Mica will be intact with no pieces missing. 3. Stamp will be fresh with no signs of toning or wrinkling.

Examples that came with silvered cases and still have some or all of the original silvering will sell for more than the values shown.

Aerated Bread Co., New York

EP1	1c	*2,500.*

Ayer's Cathartic Pills, Lowell, Mass.

Varieties with long and short arrows below legend occur on all denominations.

EP2	1c	210.
EP3	3c	225.
EP4	5c	310.
EP5	10c	475.
EP6	12c	850.
EP7	24c	*2,250.*

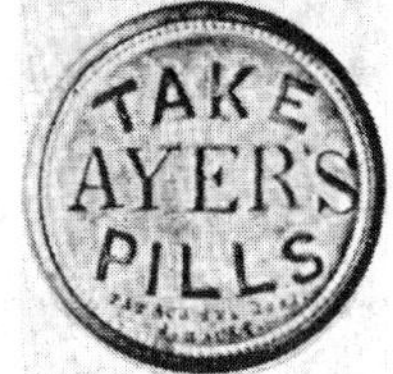

Take Ayer's Pills

EP8	1c	225.
EP9	3c	200.
EP10	5c	300.
a.	Ribbed frame	1,100.
EP11	10c	400.
EP12	12c	1,200.

Ayer's Sarsaparilla

Three varieties: "AYER'S" small, medium or large. Example illustrated is the medium variety.

EP13	1c medium "Ayer's"	240.
a.	Small	550.
EP14	2c	—
EP15	3c medium "Ayer's"	275.
a.	Small	475.
b.	Large	450.
c.	Ribbed frame, medium	850.
EP16	5c medium "Ayer's"	350.
a.	Large	675.
EP17	10c medium "Ayer's"	325.
a.	Ribbed frame, medium	950.
b.	Small	700.
c.	Large	575.
EP18	12c medium "Ayer's"	950.
a.	Small	1,300.
EP19	24c medium "Ayer's"	*1,750.*
EP20	30c medium "Ayer's"	*2,500.*

The authenticity of No. EP14 is questioned.

Bailey & Co., Philadelphia

EP21	1c	800.
EP22	3c	900.
EP23	5c	*2,000.*
EP24	10c	*2,000.*
EP25	12c	*2,750.*

"FANCYGOODS" as one word

"FANCY GOODS" as two words

Joseph L. Bates, Boston

EP26	1c one word	325.
a.	Two words	450.
EP27	3c one word	525.
a.	Two words	575.
EP28	5c two words	700.
a.	One word	800.
b.	Ribbed frame, one word	1,100.
EP29	10c two words	450.
a.	One word	525.
b.	Ribbed frame, one word	1,250.
EP30	12c two words	1,400.

Brown's Bronchial Troches

EP31	1c	800.
EP32	3c	400.
EP33	5c	400.
EP34	10c	750.
EP35	12c	1,400.
EP36	24c	*2,750.*
EP37	30c	*3,900.*

F. Buhl & Co., Detroit

EP38	1c	1,500.
EP39	3c	1,600.
EP40	5c	1,500.
EP41	10c	1,750.
EP42	12c	2,250.
EP43	24c	*5,000.*

Burnett's Cocoaine Kalliston

EP44	1c	325.
EP45	3c	325.
EP46	5c	525.
EP47	10c	575.
EP48	12c	1,100.
EP49	24c	*2,350.*
EP50	30c	*3,000.*
EP51	90c	*7,500.*

Burnett's Cooking Extracts

EP52	1c	275.
EP53	3c	300.
EP54	5c	500.
EP55	10c	575.
	a. Ribbed frame	1,250.
EP56	12c	1,400.
EP57	24c	*2,750.*
EP58	30c	*3,500.*

A. M. Claflin, Hopkinton, Mass.

EP59	1c	*12,500.*
EP60	3c	*4,750.*
EP61	5c	*6,000.*
EP62	10c	*5,000.*
EP63	12c	*6,000.*

H. A. Cook, Evansville, Ind.

EP64	5c	1,500.
EP65	10c	1,500.

Dougan, Hatter, New York

EP66	1c	*2,250.*
EP67	3c	*1,750.*
EP68	5c	*2,000.*
EP69	10c	*2,250.*

Drake's Plantation Bitters

EP70	1c	275.
EP71	3c	250.
EP72	5c	375.
	a. Ribbed frame	850.
EP73	10c	425.
	a. Ribbed frame	1,100.
EP74	12c	1,250.
EP75	24c	*2,250.*
EP76	30c	*3,000.*
EP77	90c	*8,500.*

Ellis, McAlpin & Co., Cincinnati

EP78	1c	1,750.
EP79	3c	1,750.
EP80	5c	1,200.
EP81	10c	1,200.
EP82	12c	*2,000.*
EP83	24c	*2,500.*

G. G. Evans, Philadelphia

EP84	1c	750.
EP85	3c	750.
EP86	5c	1,250.
EP87	10c	1,500.

Gage Bros. & Drake, Tremont House, Chicago

EP88	1c	375.
EP89	3c	500.
EP90	5c	575.
EP91	10c	500.
	a. Ribbed frame	1,250.
EP92	12c	1,750.

J. Gault

EP93	1c	475.
	a. Ribbed frame	—
EP94	2c	*9,000.*
EP95	3c	225.
	a. Ribbed frame	750.
EP96	5c	250.
	a. Ribbed frame	600.
EP97	10c	350.
	a. Ribbed frame	650.
EP98	12c	900.
	a. Ribbed frame	1,700.
EP99	24c	1,800.
	a. Ribbed frame	*2,750.*
EP100	30c	*2,400.*
	a. Ribbed frame	*3,750.*
EP101	90c	*6,500.*

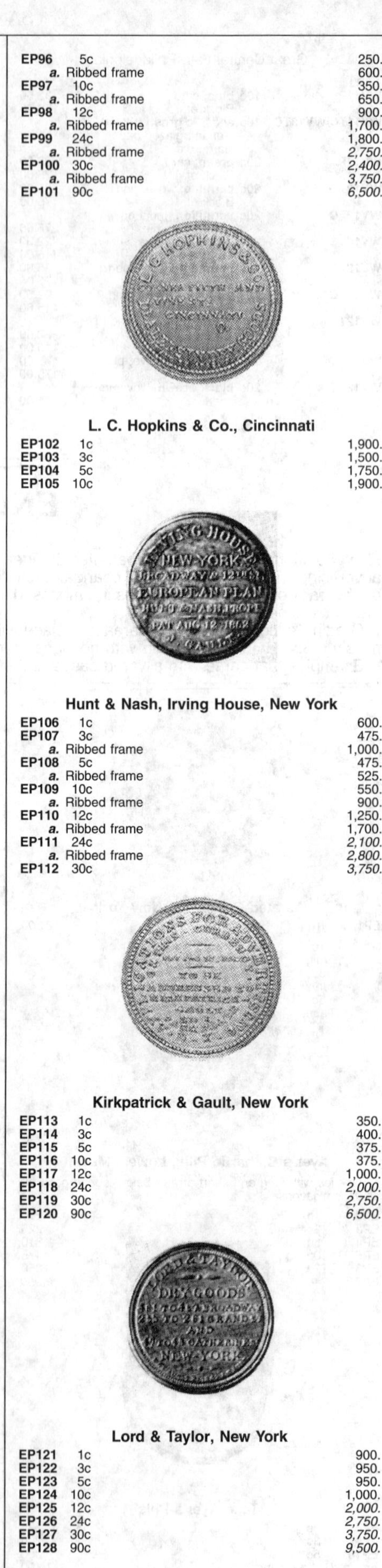

L. C. Hopkins & Co., Cincinnati

EP102	1c	1,900.
EP103	3c	1,500.
EP104	5c	1,750.
EP105	10c	1,900.

Hunt & Nash, Irving House, New York

EP106	1c	600.
EP107	3c	475.
	a. Ribbed frame	1,000.
EP108	5c	475.
	a. Ribbed frame	525.
EP109	10c	550.
	a. Ribbed frame	900.
EP110	12c	1,250.
	a. Ribbed frame	1,700.
EP111	24c	*2,100.*
	a. Ribbed frame	*2,800.*
EP112	30c	*3,750.*

Kirkpatrick & Gault, New York

EP113	1c	350.
EP114	3c	400.
EP115	5c	375.
EP116	10c	375.
EP117	12c	1,000.
EP118	24c	*2,000.*
EP119	30c	*2,750.*
EP120	90c	*6,500.*

Lord & Taylor, New York

EP121	1c	900.
EP122	3c	950.
EP123	5c	950.
EP124	10c	1,000.
EP125	12c	*2,000.*
EP126	24c	*2,750.*
EP127	30c	*3,750.*
EP128	90c	*9,500.*

Mendum's Family Wine Emporium, New York

EP129	1c	575.
EP130	3c	900.
EP131	5c	700.
EP132	10c	750.
a.	Ribbed frame	1,600.
EP133	12c	1,500.

B. F. Miles, Peoria

EP134	1c	*4,000.*
EP135	5c	*4,000.*

John W. Norris, Chicago

EP136	1c	*2,250.*
EP137	3c	*2,250.*
EP138	5c	*2,500.*
EP139	10c	*2,750.*

"INSURANCE" Curved "INSURANCE" Straight

North America Life Insurance Co., N. Y.

EP140	1c Curved	425.
a.	Straight	525.
EP141	3c Straight	600.
a.	Curved	700.
EP142	5c Straight	675.
a.	Ribbed frame	1,100.
EP143	10c Straight	625.
a.	Curved	800.
b.	Curved, ribbed frame	1,750.
EP144	12c Straight	1,750.

Pearce, Tolle & Holton, Cincinnati

EP145	1c	*2,250.*
EP146	3c	*2,250.*
EP147	5c	*1,800.*
EP148	10c	*2,700.*
EP149	12c	*3,250.*
EP150	24c	*3,750.*

Sands Ale

EP151	5c	*2,000.*
EP152	10c	*2,750.*
EP153	12c	*3,000.*
EP154	30c	—

No. EP154 may be unique. The case of the known example has been opened. It is possible that the 30c stamp has been substituted for the original stamp.

Schapker & Bussing, Evansville, Ind.

EP155	1c	600.
EP156	3c	675.
EP157	5c	600.
EP158	10c	575.
EP159	12c	1,600.

John Shillito & Co., Cincinnati

EP160	1c	725.
EP161	3c	1,000.
EP162	5c	600.
EP163	10c	675.
EP164	12c	1,950.

S. Steinfeld, New York

EP165	1c	*2,500.*
EP166	5c	*2,600.*
EP167	10c	*2,650.*
EP168	12c	*3,250.*

N. G. Taylor & Co., Philadelphia

EP169	1c	*2,250.*
EP170	3c	*2,000.*
EP171	5c	*2,350.*
EP172	10c	*2,500.*
EP173	12c	*3,100.*

Weir and Larminie, Montreal

EP174	1c	1,500.
EP175	3c	1,750.
EP176	5c	1,600.
EP177	10c	1,250.

White, the Hatter, New York

EP178	1c	*1,750.*
EP179	3c	*2,500.*
EP180	5c	*2,500.*
EP181	10c	*2,750.*

POSTAGE CURRENCY

Small coins disappeared from circulation in 1861-62 as cash was hoarded. To ease business transactions, merchants issued notes of credit, promises to pay, tokens, store cards, etc. U.S. Treasurer Francis E. Spinner made a substitute for small currency by affixing postage stamps, singly and in multiples, to Treasury paper. He arranged with the Post office to replace worn stamps with new when necessary.

The next step was to print the stamps on Treasury paper. On July 17, 1862, Congress authorized the issue of such "Postage Currency." It remained in use until May 27, 1863. It was not money, but a means of making stamps negotiable.

On Oct. 10, 1863 a second issue was released. These, and the later three issues, did not show stamps and are called Fractional Currency. In 1876 Congress authorized the minting of silver coins to redeem the outstanding fractional currency.

Values quoted are for notes in crisp, new condition, not creased or worn.

Creased or worn copies sell for 25 to 75 percent less.

Items valued with a dash are believed to be unique.

Front Engraved and Printed by the National Bank Note Co.
Back Engraved and Printed in Black by The American Bank Note Co.
"A B Co." on Back

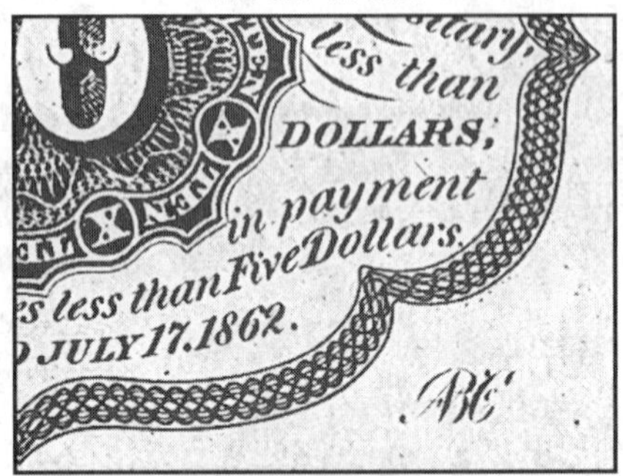

"ABCo." imprint, lower right corner of back (#1-8)

1862, Aug. 21

Perforated Edges-Perf. 12

PC1	5c Bust of Jefferson on 5c stamp, brown	62.50
a.	Inverted back	*500.00*
PC2	10c Bust of Washington on 10c stamp, green	45.00
PC3	25c Five 5c stamps, brown	57.50
PC4	50c Five 10c stamps, green	62.50
a.	Inverted back	*500.00*

Imperforate Edges

PC5	5c Bust of Jefferson on 5c stamp	22.50
a.	Inverted back	*200.00*
PC6	10c Bust of Washington on 10c stamp	20.00
a.	Inverted back	*350.00*
PC7	25c Five 5c stamps	40.00
a.	Inverted back	*300.00*
PC8	50c Five 10c stamps	62.50
a.	Inverted back	*400.00*

No. PC8 exists perforated 14, privately produced.

Front and Back Engraved and Printed by the the National Bank Note Co.

Without "A B Co." on Back

Perforated Edges-Perf. 12

PC9	5c Bust of Jefferson on 5c stamp	62.50
a.	Inverted back	—
PC10	10c Bust of Washington on 10c stamp	62.50
a.	Inverted back	—
PC11	25c Five 5c stamps	125.00
a.	Inverted back	*750.00*
PC12	50c Five 10c stamps	150.00
a.	Inverted back	—

Imperforate Edges

PC13	5c Bust of Jefferson on 5c stamp	62.50
a.	Inverted back	—
PC14	10c Bust of Washington on 10c stamp	110.00
a.	Inverted back	*750.00*
PC15	25c Five 5c stamps	150.00
PC16	50c Five 10c stamps	550.00
a.	Inverted back	—

CONFEDERATE STATES OF AMERICA

3¢ 1861 POSTMASTERS' PROVISIONALS

With the secession of South Carolina from the Union on Dec. 20, 1860, a new era began in U.S. history as well as its postal history. Other Southern states quickly followed South Carolina's lead, which in turn led to the formation of the provisional government of the Confederate States of America on Feb. 4, 1861.

President Jefferson Davis' cabinet was completed Mar. 6, 1861, with the acceptance of the position of Postmaster General by John H. Reagan of Texas. The provisional government had already passed regulations that required payment for postage in cash and that effectively carried over the U.S. 3c rate until the new Confederate Post Office Department took over control of the system.

Soon after entering on his duties, Reagan directed the postmasters in the Confederate States and in the newly seceded states to "continue the performance of their duties as such, and render all accounts and pay all moneys (sic) to the order of the Government of the U.S. as they have heretofore done, until the Government of the Confederate States shall be prepared to assume control of its postal affairs."

As coinage was becoming scarce, postal patrons began having problems buying individual stamps or paying for letters individually, especially as stamp stocks started to run short in certain areas. Even though the U.S. Post Office Department was technically in control of the postal system and southern postmasters were operating under Federal authority, the U.S.P.O. was hesitant in re-supplying seceded states with additional stamps and stamped envelopes.

The U.S. government had made the issuance of postmasters' provisionals illegal many years before, but the southern postmasters had to do what they felt was necessary to allow patrons to pay for postage and make the system work. Therefore, a few postmasters took it upon themselves to issue provisional stamps in the 3c rate then in effect. Interestingly, these were stamps and envelopes that the U.S. government did not recognize as legal, but they did do postal duty unchallenged in the Confederate States. Yet the proceeds were to be remitted to the U.S. government in Washington! Six authenticated postmasters' provisionals in the 3c rate have been recorded.

On May 13, 1861, Postmaster General Reagan issued his proclamation "assuming control and direction of postal service within the limits of the Confederate States of America on and after the first day of June," with new postage rates and regulations. The Federal government suspended operations in the Confederate States (except for western Virginia and the seceding state of Tennessee) by a proclamation issued by Postmaster General Montgomery Blair on May 27, 1861, effective from May 31, 1861, and June 10 for western and middle Tennessee. As Tennessee did not join the Confederacy until July 2, 1861, the unissued 3c Nashville provisional was produced in a state that was in the process of seceding, while the other provisionals were used in the Confederacy before the June 1 assumption of control of postal service by the Confederate States of America.

HILLSBORO, N.C.

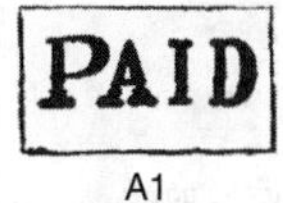

A1

Handstamped Adhesive

1AX1 A1 3c **bluish black,** on cover —

No. 1AX1 is unique. This is the same handstamp as used for No. 39X1. 3c usage is determined from the May 27, 1861 circular date stamp.

Cancellation: black town.

JACKSON, MISS.

E1

Handstamped Envelope

2AXU1 E1 3c **black** *1,000.*

See Nos. 43XU1-43XU4.

MADISON COURT HOUSE, FLA.

A1

"CNETS"

Typeset Adhesive

3AX1 A1 3c **gold** — *10,000.*
On cover *65,000.*
a. "CNETS" *14,000.*

No. 3AX1 on cover and No. 3AX1a are each unique.

Cancellations: black town, oblong paid, ms "Paid in Money."

See No. 137XU1.

NASHVILLE, TENN.

A1

Typeset Adhesive (5 varieties)

4AX1 A1 3c **carmine** 150.
Horizontal strip of 5 showing all varieties 900.

No. 4AX1 was prepared by Postmaster McNish with the U.S. rate, but the stamp was never issued.

See Nos. 61X2-61XU2.

SELMA, ALA.

E1

Handstamped Envelope

5AXU1 E1 3c **black** *1,750.*

See Nos. 77XU1-77XU3.

TUSCUMBIA, ALA.

E1

Handstamped Envelope, impression at upper right

6AXU1 E1 3c **dull red,** *buff* *16,500.*

No. 6AXU1 also exists with a 3c 1857 stamp affixed at upper right over the provisional handstamp, tied by black circular "TUSCUMBIA, ALA." town postmark. Value $15,000.

See Nos. 84XU1-84XU3.

CONFEDERATE POSTMASTERS' PROVISIONALS

These stamps and envelopes were issued by individual postmasters generally during the interim between June 1, 1861, when the use of United States stamps stopped in the Confederacy, and October 16, 1861, when the first Confederate Government stamps were issued. They were occasionally issued at later periods, especially in Texas, when regular issues of government stamps were unavailable.

Canceling stamps of the post offices were often used to produce envelopes, some of which were supplied in advance by private citizens. These envelopes and other stationery therefore may be found in a wide variety of papers, colors, sizes and shapes, including patriotic and semi-official types. It is often difficult to determine whether the impression made by the canceling stamp indicates provisional usage or merely postage paid at the time the letter was deposited in the post office. Occasionally the same mark was used for both purposes.

The *press-printed* **provisional envelopes are in a different category. They were produced in quantity, using envelopes procured in advance by the postmaster, such as those of Charleston, Lynchburg, Memphis, etc.** *The* **press-printed** *envelopes are listed and valued on all known papers.*

The **handstamped** *provisional envelopes are listed and valued according to type and variety of handstamp, but not according to paper. Many exist on such a variety of papers that they defy accurate, complete listing. The value of a handstamped provisional envelope is determined primarily by the clarity of the markings and its overall condition and attractiveness, rather than the type of paper.*

All handstamped provisional envelopes, when used, should also show the postmark of the town of issue.

Most handstamps are impressed at top right, although they exist from some towns in other positions.

Many illustrations in this section are reduced in size.

Values for envelopes are for entires. Values for stamps of provisional issues are for copies with little or no gum; original gum over a large portion of the stamp will increase the value substantially.

ABERDEEN, MISS.

E1

Handstamped Envelopes

1XU1	E1	5c **black**		6,000.
1XU2	E1	10c (ms.) on 5c **black**		*12,500.*

No. 1XU2 is unique.

ABINGDON, VA.

PAID 2 CENTS

E1

Handstamped Envelopes

2XU1	E1	2c **black**		*11,000.*
2XU2	E1	5c **black**		1,000.
		On patriotic cover		*2,750.*
2XU3	E1	10c **black**	2,200.	*3,500.*

The unused No. 2XU3 is a unique mint example, and the value represents the price realized in a 1997 auction sale. No. 2XU3 used also is unique.

ALBANY, GA.

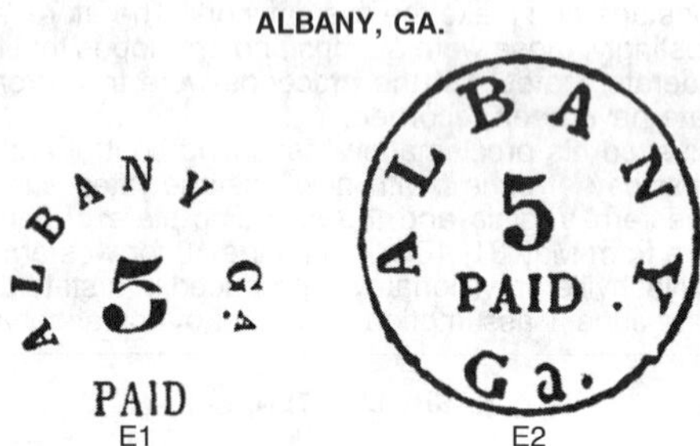

E1 E2

Handstamped Envelopes

3XU1	E1	5c **greenish blue**		700.
3XU2	E1	10c **greenish blue**		*2,000.*
3XU3	E1	10c on 5c **greenish blue**		*3,500.*
3XU5	E2	5c **greenish blue**		—
3XU6	E2	10c **greenish blue**		*2,500.*

Only one example each recorded of Nos. 3XU2, 3XU3 and 3XU6

ANDERSON COURT HOUSE, S.C.

E1

Handstamped Envelopes

4XU1	E1	5c **black**	500.	2,250.
4XU2	E1	10c (ms.) **black**		*3,000.*

ATHENS, GA

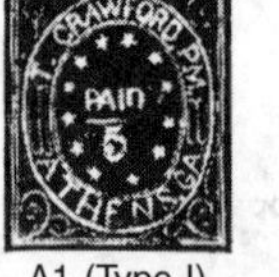

A1 (Type I)

A1 (Type II)

Typographed Adhesives
(from woodcuts of two types)

Pairs, both horizontal and vertical, always show one of each type.

5X1	A1	5c **purple** (shades)	900.	1,100.
		Pair	—	2,400.
		On cover		2,500.
		Pair on cover		4,750.
		Strip of 4 on cover (horiz.)		*10,000.*
a.		Tete beche pair (vertical)		*7,500.*
		Tete beche pair on cover		*27,500.*
5X2	A1	5c **red**	—	4,250.
		On cover		*15,000.*
		Pair on cover		—

Cancellations in black: grid, town, "Paid."

ATLANTA, GA.

E1

E2

Handstamped Envelopes

6XU1	E1	5c **red**		*3,500.*
6XU2	E1	5c **black**	175.	600.
		On patriotic cover		*3,500.*
6XU3	E1	10c on 5c **black**		1,500.
6XU4	E2	2c **black**		*3,000.*
6XU5	E2	5c **black**		1,500.
		On patriotic cover		3,500.
6XU6	E2	10c **black**		850.
6XU7	E2	10c on 5c **black**		2,500.

Only one example recorded of No. 6XU1.

E3

Handstamped Envelopes

6XU8	E3	5c **black**		3,500.
6XU9	E3	10c **black** ("10" upright)		2,750.

Only one example each recorded of Nos. 6XU1 and 6XU8.

AUGUSTA, GA.

E1

Handstamped Envelope

7XU1 E1 5c **black**

Provisional status questioned. Indistinguishable from a handstamp paid cover when used. The only known example purported to be a Postmaster Provisional has a general CSA issue used over the marking.

The editors intend to delist this item unless evidence of a certified unused envelope with the marking is furnished.

AUSTIN, MISS.

E1

Press-printed Envelope (typeset)

8XU1 E1 5c **red,** *amber* *75,000.*

One example recorded.

Cancellation: black "Paid."

AUSTIN, TEX.

E1

Handstamped Adhesive

9X1 E1 10c **black** —
On cover, uncanceled *1,500.*
On cover, tied —

Only one example of No. 9X1 tied on cover is recorded.

Handstamped Envelope

9XU1 E1 10c **black** 1,500.

Cancellation on Nos. 9X1 and 9XU1: black town.

AUTAUGAVILLE, ALA.

E1

E2

Handstamped Envelopes

10XU1 E1 5c **black** *10,000.*
10XU2 E2 5c **black** *12,500.*

No. 10XU2 is unique.

BALCONY FALLS, VA.

E1

Handstamped Envelope

122XU1 E1 10c **blue** *1,500.*

BARNWELL COURT HOUSE, S. C.

E1

Handstamped Envelope

123XU1 E1 5c **black** *1,500.*

These are two separate handstamps.

BATON ROUGE, LA.

A1

A2

Typeset Adhesives

Ten varieties of each

11X1 A1 2c **green** *5,250.* *5,000.*
On cover *20,000.*
a. "McCcrmick" *14,000.* *8,500.*
On cover —
11X2 A2 5c **green & carmine** (Maltese cross border) 1,500. 1,250.
On cover 2,750.
Strip of 3 *5,000.*
Strip of 5 *22,500.*
Canceled in New Orleans, on cover *20,000.*
a. "McCcrmick" — *2,000.*
On cover *6,500.*

Only one example each is recorded of No. 11X1a unused, used and on cover.

The "Canceled in New Orleans" examples entered the mails in New Orleans after having been placed (uncanceled) on riverboats in Baton Rouge. Two such covers are recorded.

A3

A4

Ten varieties of each

11X3 A3 5c **green & carmine** (crisscross border) *4,500.* *2,500.*
On cover *10,000.*
a. "McCcrmick" *3,250.*
11X4 A4 10c **blue** *6,000.*
On cover *75,000.*

No. 11X4 on cover is unique.

Cancellation on Nos. 11X1-11X4: black town.

BEAUMONT, TEX.

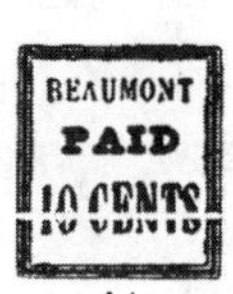

A1

A2

Typeset Adhesives

Several varieties of each

12X1 A1 10c **black,** *yellow* *12,500.*
On cover *55,000.*
12X2 A1 10c **black,** *pink* *12,500.*
On cover *27,500.*
12X3 A2 10c **black,** *yellow,* on cover *90,000.*

One example known of No. 12X3.

Cancellations: black pen; black town.

BLUFFTON, S. C.

E1

Handstamped Envelope

124XU1 E1 5c **black** *3,500.*

Only one example recorded of No. 124XU1.

BRIDGEVILLE, ALA.

A1

Handstamped Adhesive in black within red pen-ruled squares

13X1 A1 5c **black & red,** pair on cover *20,000.*

Cancellation is black pen.

CAMDEN, S. C.

E1

E2

Handstamped Envelopes

125XU1 E1 5c **black** *3,500.*
125XU2 E2 10c **black** *450.*

No. 125XU2 unused was privately carried and is addressed but has no postal markings. No. 125XU2 is indistinguishable from a handstamp paid cover when used.

CANTON, MISS.

E1

"P" in star is initial of Postmaster William Priestly.

Handstamped Envelopes

14XU1 E1 5c **black** 2,750.
14XU2 E1 10c (ms.) on 5c **black** 5,000.

CAROLINA CITY, N. C.

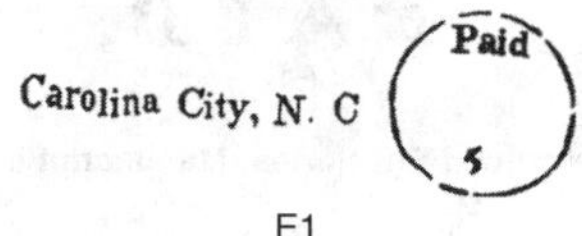

E1

Handstamped Envelope

118XU1 E1 5c **black** *3,500.*

CARTERSVILLE, GA.

E1

Handstamped Envelope

126XU1 E1 (5c) **red** *1,250.*

CHAPEL HILL, N. C.

E1

Handstamped Envelope

15XU1 E1 5c **black** 3,000.
On patriotic cover 5,000.

CHARLESTON, S. C.

A1

E1

E2

Lithographed Adhesive

16X1 A1 5c **blue** 900. 750.
Pair 1,750. 1,900.
On cover *2,250.*
On patriotic cover *5,000.*
Pair, on cover *5,000.*
On cover with No. 112XU1 —
Used on cover with C.S.A. 5c #6 to make 10c rate —

Values are for copies showing parts of the outer frame lines on at least 3 sides.

Cancellation: black town (two types).

Press-printed Envelopes (typographed from woodcut)

16XU1 E1 5c **blue** 1,100. 3,500.
16XU2 E1 5c **blue,** *amber* 1,100. 3,500.
16XU3 E1 5c **blue,** *orange* 1,100. 3,500.
16XU4 E1 5c **blue,** *buff* 1,100. 3,500.
16XU5 E1 5c **blue,** *blue* 1,100. 3,500.
16XU6 E2 10c **blue,** *orange* *77,500.*

The No. 16XU6 used entire is unique; value based on 1997 auction sale.

Handstamped Cut Square

16XU7 E2 10c **black** *3,000.*

There is only one copy of No. 16XU7. It is a cutout, not an entire. It may not have been mailed from Charleston, and it may not have paid postage.

CHARLOTTESVILLE, VA.

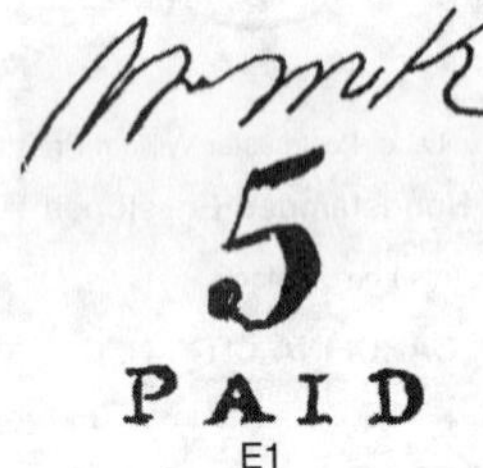

E1

Handstamped Envelopes, Manuscript Initials

127XU1 E1 5c **blue** —
127XU2 E1 10c **blue** —

CHATTANOOGA, TENN.

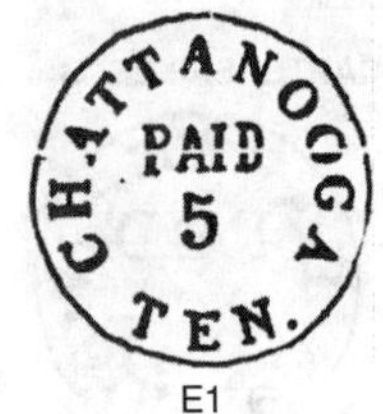

E1

Handstamped Envelopes

17XU2 E1 5c **black** 1,600.
17XU3 E1 5c on 2c **black** *3,250.*

CHRISTIANSBURG, VA.

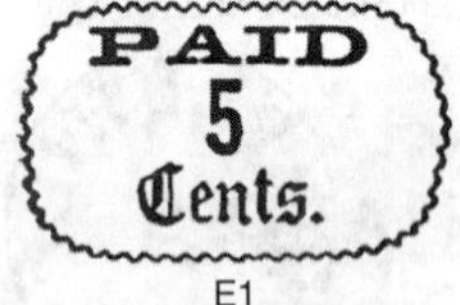

E1

Handstamped Envelopes

Impressed at top right

99XU1 E1 5c **black,** *blue* *2,000.*
99XU2 E1 5c **blue** *1,400.*
99XU3 E1 5c **black,** *orange* *2,000.*
99XU4 E1 5c **green** on U.S. envelope No. U27 *4,500.*
99XU5 E1 10c **blue** *3,500.*

COLAPARCHEE, GA.

E1

Control

Handstamped Envelope

119XU1 E1 5c **black** *3,500.*

There are only two recorded examples of No. 119XU1, and both are used with general issue stamp from Savannah.

COLUMBIA, S. C.

E1

E2

Handstamped Envelopes

18XU1 E1 5c **blue** 500. 900.
Used on cover with C.S.A. 5c #1 or #1c to make 10c rate *3,000.*
Used on cover with C.S.A. 5c #7 to make 10c rate *7,500.*
18XU2 E1 5c **black** 600. 900.
18XU3 E1 10c on 5c **blue** *3,500.*

Three types of "PAID," one in circle

18XU4 E2 5c **blue,** seal on front *2,500.*
a. Seal on back 1,000.
18XU5 E2 10c **blue,** seal on back *2,750.*

Three types of "PAID" for Nos. 18XU4-18XU5, one in circle.

Circular Seal similar to E2, 27mm diameter

18XU6 E2 5c **blue** (seal on back) *4,000.*

COLUMBIA, TENN.

E1

Handstamped Envelope

113XU1 E1 5c **red** *3,500.*

COLUMBUS, GA.

E1

Handstamped Envelopes

19XU1 E1 5c **blue** 700.
19XU2 E1 10c **red** *2,250.*

COURTLAND, ALA.

E1

Handstamped Envelopes (from woodcut)

103XU1 E1 5c **black** —
103XU2 E1 5c **red** *10,000.*

Provisional status of No. 103XU1 questioned.

DALTON, GA

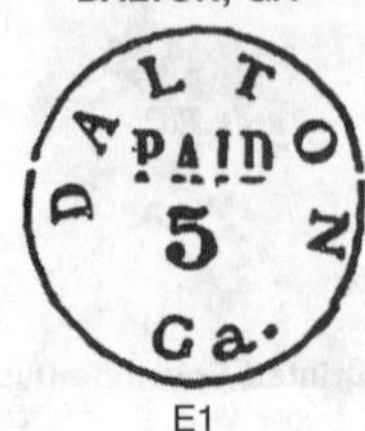

E1

Handstamped Envelopes

20XU1 E1 5c **black** 500.
a. Denomination omitted (5c rate) *650.*
20XU2 E1 10c **black** 700.
20XU3 E1 10c (ms.) on 5c **black** 1,500.

DANVILLE, VA.

A1

E1

E2

E3

PAID 10

E4

Typeset Adhesive
Wove Paper

21X1 A1 5c **red** *5,500.*
On cover —
Cut to shape *4,000.*
On cover, cut to shape *6,000.*

Two varieties known.

Only four rectangular-cut examples are recorded, one of which is reported to be on laid paper.

Cancellation: blue town.

Press-printed Envelopes (typographed)

Two types: "SOUTHERN" in straight or curved line
Impressed (usually) at top left

21XU1 E1 5c **black** *5,500.*
21XU2 E1 5c **black,** *amber* *5,500.*
21XU3 E1 5c **black,** *dark buff* *5,250.*

Unissued 10c envelopes (type E1, in red) are known. All recorded examples are envelopes on which added stamps paid the postage.

Handstamped Envelopes

21XU3A E4 5c **black** (ms "WBP" initials) *1,000.*
21XU4 E2 10c **black** *2,000.*
21XU5 E2 10c **blue**
21XU6 E3 10c **black** *2,750.*
21XU7 E4 10c **black** (ms "WBP" initials) —

Types E2 and E3 both exist on one cover. The existence of No. 21XU5 has been questioned.

DEMOPOLIS, ALA.

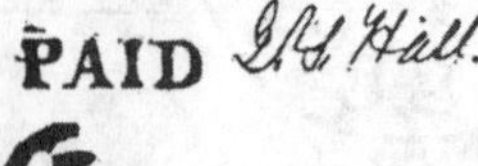

E1

Handstamped Envelopes, Signature in ms.

22XU1 E1 5c **black** ("Jno. Y. Hall") *3,500.*
22XU2 E1 5c **black** ("J. Y. Hall") *3,500.*
22XU3 E1 5c (ms.) **black** ("J. Y. Hall") *4,000.*

EATONTON, GA.

E1

Handstamped Envelopes

23XU1 E1 5c **black** *3,000.*
23XU2 E1 5c + 5c **black** *4,500.*

Only one example recorded of No. 23XU2.

EMORY, VA.

A1

Handstamped Adhesives ("PAID" and "5" in circle on selvage of U.S. 1c 1857 issue)

Perf. 15 on three sides

24X1 A1 5c **blue,** on cover, ms. tied *15,000.*

Also known with "5" above "PAID."

Cancellation: blue town.

E1

E2

Handstamped Envelopes

24XU1 E1 5c **blue** *2,000.*
24XU2 E2 10c **blue** *10,000.*

Only one example recorded of No. 24XU2.

FINCASTLE, VA.

E1

Press-printed Envelope (typeset)

Impressed at top right

104XU1 E1 10c **black** *20,000.*

One example known.

FORSYTH, GA.

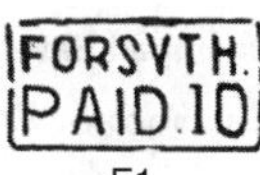

E1

Handstamped Envelope

120XU1 E1 10c **black** *1,350.*

Only one example recorded of No. 120XU1.

FRANKLIN, N. C.

E1

Press-printed Envelope (typeset)

Impressed at top right

25XU1 E1 5c **blue,** *buff* *30,000.*

The one known envelope shows black circular Franklin postmark with manuscript date.

FRAZIERSVILLE, S. C.

E1

Handstamped Envelope, "5" manuscript

128XU1 E1 5c **black** 2,250.

Only one example recorded of No. 128XU1.

FREDERICKSBURG, VA.

A1

Sheets of 20, two panes of 10 varieties each

Typeset Adhesives

Thin bluish paper

26X1 A1 5c **blue,** *bluish* 250. 750.
Block of 4 1,500.
Sheet of 20 10,000.
On cover *5,000.*
Pair on cover *12,000.*
26X2 A1 10c **red,** *bluish* 900.
Brown red, *bluish* 900.
Block of 4 —

Cancellation: black town.

GAINESVILLE, ALA.

E1

E2

Handstamped Envelopes

27XU1 E1 5c **black** *5,000.*
27XU2 E2 10c ("01") **black** *6,000.*

Postmark spells town name "Gainsville."

GALVESTON, TEX.

E1

Handstamped Envelopes

98XU1 E1 5c **black** 500. *1,500.*
98XU2 E1 10c **black** 2,000.

E2

Handstamped Envelopes

98XU3 E2 10c **black** 550. 2,400.
98XU4 E2 20c **black** *3,500.*

GASTON, N. C.

E1

Handstamped Envelope

129XU1 E1 5c **black** 4,500.

Only one example recorded of No. 129XU1.

GEORGETOWN, S. C.

E1

Control

Handstamped Envelope

28XU1 E1 5c **black** 800.

GOLIAD, TEX.

A1

A2

Typeset Adhesives

29X1 A1 5c **black** *7,000.*
29X2 A1 5c **black,** *gray* *6,500.*
29X3 A1 5c **black,** *rose* *7,000.*
On cover front *50,000.*
29X4 A1 10c **black** — *7,000.*
29X5 A1 10c **black,** *rose* *7,000.*

Type A1 stamps are signed "Clarke-P.M." vertically in black or red.

29X6 A2 5c **black,** *gray* *10,000.*
a. "GOILAD" *12,000.*
Pair, left stamp the error —
29X7 A2 10c **black,** *gray* *7,500.*
On cover *25,000.*
a. "GOILAD" *8,000.*
On cover *30,000.*
29X8 A2 5c **black,** *dark blue,* on cover *7,000.*
29X9 A2 10c **black,** *dark blue* —

Cancellations in black: pen, town, "Paid"

GONZALES, TEX.

Colman & Law were booksellers when John B. Law (of the firm) was appointed Postmaster. The firm used a small lithographed label on drugs and on the front or inside of books they sold.

A1

Lithographed Adhesives on colored glazed paper

30X1 A1 (5c) **gold,** *dark blue,* pair on cover, *1861* *15,000.*
30X2 A1 (10c) **gold,** *garnet,* on cover, *1864* *12,500.*
30X3 A1 (10c) **gold,** *black,* on cover, *1865* —

Cancellations: black town, black pen. No. 30X1 must bear double-circle town cancel as validating control. The control was applied to the labels in the sheet before their sale as stamps. When used, the stamps bear an additional Gonzales double-circle postmark.

GREENSBORO, ALA.

E1

E2

Handstamped Envelopes

31XU1	E1	5c **black**	*3,000.*
31XU2	E1	10c **black**	*2,750.*
31XU3	E2	10c **black**	*4,250.*

GREENSBORO, N. C.

E1

Handstamped Envelope

32XU1 E1 10c **red** 1,250.

GREENVILLE, ALA.

A1

A2

Typeset Adhesives
On pinkish surface-colored glazed paper.

33X1	A1	5c **blue & red**	*22,500.*	
		On cover		*40,000.*
33X2	A2	10c **red & blue**	—	
		On cover		*40,000.*

Two used examples each are known of Nos. 33X1-33X2, and all are on covers. Covers bear a postmark but it was not used to cancel the stamps.

The former No. 33X1a has been identified as a counterfeit.

GREENVILLE COURT HOUSE, S. C.

PAID 5
E1

Control

Handstamped Envelopes (Several types)

34XU1	E1	5c **black**	*2,000.*
34XU2	E1	10c **black**	*2,250.*
34XU3	E1	20c (ms.) on 10c **black**	*3,000.*

Envelopes must bear the black control on the back.

GREENWOOD DEPOT, VA.

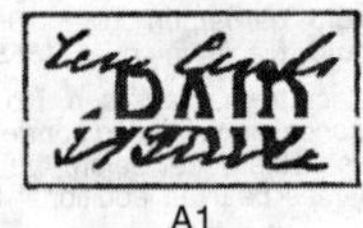

A1

"PAID" Handstamped Adhesive ("PAID" with value and signature in ms.)
Laid Paper

35X1	A1	10c **black,** *gray blue,* uncanceled, on cover	20,000.	
		On cover, tied		—

Six examples recorded of No. 35X1, all on covers. One of these is in the British Library collection. Of the remaining five, only one has the stamp tied to the cover.

Cancellation: black town.

GRIFFIN, GA.

E1

Handstamped Envelope

102XU1 E1 5c **black** 2,000.

GROVE HILL, ALA.

A1

Handstamped Adhesive (from woodcut)

36X1	A1	5c **black**		—
		On cover, tied		*75,000.*

Two examples are recorded. One is on cover tied by the postmark. The other is canceled by magenta pen on a cover front.

Cancellations: black town, magenta pen.

HALLETTSVILLE, TEX.

A1

Handstamped Adhesive
Ruled Letter Paper

37X1 A1 10c **black,** *gray blue,* on cover *15,000.*

One example known.

Cancellation: black ms.

HAMBURGH, S. C.

E1

Handstamped Envelope

112XU1	E1	5c **black**	*2,000.*	
		On cover with #16X1 (forwarded)		—

HARRISBURGH (Harrisburg), TEX.

E1

Handstamped Envelope

130XU1 E1 5c **black** —

No. 130XU1 is indistinguishable from a handstamp paid cover when used.

HELENA, TEX.

A1

Typeset Adhesives
Several varieties

38X1	A1	5c **black,** *buff*	*7,500.*	*6,000.*
38X2	A1	10c **black,** *gray*		*5,000.*

On 10c "Helena" is in upper and lower case italics.

Used examples are valued with small faults or repairs, as all recorded have faults.

Cancellation: black town.

HILLSBORO, N. C.

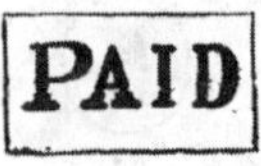

A1

Handstamped Adhesive

39X1 A1 5c **black,** on cover *15,000.*

No. 39X1 is unique.

See 3c 1861 Postmasters' Provisional No. 1AX1.

Cancellation: black town.

Ms./Handstamped Envelope

39XU1 10c "paid 10" in manuscript with undated blue town cancel as control on face —

HOLLANDALE, TEX.

E1

Handstamped Envelope

132XU1 E1 5c **black** —

HOUSTON, TEX.

E1

Handstamped Envelopes

40XU1	E1	5c **red**	—	700.
		On patriotic cover		—
40XU2	E1	10c **red**	—	*1,500.*
40XU3	E1	10c **black**		*2,250.*
40XU4	E1	5c +10c **red**		2,500.
40XU5	E1	10c +10c **red**		*2,500.*
40XU6	E1	10c (ms.) on 5c **red**		*3,000.*

Nos. 40XU2-40XU5 show "TEX" instead of "TXS."

HUNTSVILLE, TEX.

E1

Control

Handstamped Envelope

92XU1 E1 5c **black** *5,000.*

No. 92XU1 exists with "5" outside or within control circle.

INDEPENDENCE, TEX.

A1

Handstamped Adhesives

41X1 A1 10c **black,** *buff,* on cover, uncanceled, cut to shape — 20.000.
41X2 A1 10c **black,** *dull rose,* on cover

With small "10" and "Pd" in manuscript

41X3 A1 10c **black,** *buff,* on cover, uncanceled, cut to shape — 32,500.
On cover, uncanceled, cut square — —

No. 41X1 is unique.

All known examples of Nos. 41X1-41X3 are uncanceled on covers with black "INDEPENDANCE TEX." (sic) postmark.

The existence of No. 41X2 has been questioned by specialists. The editors would like to see authenticated evidence of the existence of this item.

ISABELLA, GA.

E1

Handstamped Envelope, "5" Manuscript

133XU1 E1 5c **black** — 2,000.

Only one example recorded of No. 133XU1.

IUKA, MISS.

I-U-KA
PAID 5CTS

E1

Handstamped Envelope

42XU1 E1 5c **black** — 1,600.
On patriotic cover — 4,000.

JACKSON, MISS.

E1

Handstamped Envelopes

Two types of numeral

43XU1 E1 5c **black** — 500.
On patriotic cover — 3,000.
43XU2 E1 10c **black** — 2,000.
43XU3 E1 10c on 5c **black** — *2,750.*
43XU4 E1 10c on 5c **blue** — *2,750.*

The 5c also exists on a lettersheet.
See 3c 1861 Postmasters' Provisional No. 2AXU1.

JACKSONVILLE, ALA.

E1

Handstamped Envelope

110XU1 E1 5c **black** — — 3,000.

JACKSONVILLE, FLA.

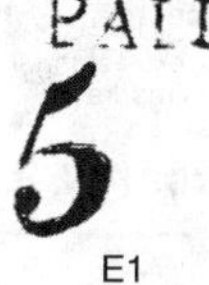

E1

Handstamped Envelope

134XU1 E1 5c **black** — —

Undated double circle postmark control on reverse.

JETERSVILLE, VA.

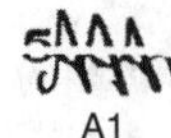

A1

Handstamped Adhesive ("5" with ms. "AHA." initials)

Laid Paper

44X1 A1 5c **black,** vertical pair on cover, uncanceled — 16,000.

Initials are those of Postmaster A. H. Atwood.

Cancellation: black town.

JONESBORO, TENN.

E1

Handstamped Envelopes

45XU1 E1 5c **black** — *3,750.*
45XU2 E1 5c **dark blue** — *7,000.*

KINGSTON, GA.

PAID
5
CENTS

E1

PAID
c 5 s
CENTS

E2

E3

E4

Typeset Envelopes (E1-E3 probably impressed by hand, possibly press printed); Handstamped Envelope (E4)

46XU1 E1 5c **black** — 2,000.
46XU2 E2 5c **black** — — 3,250.
a. No "C" or "S" at sides of numeral — —
46XU3 E2 5c **black,** *amber* — *2,750.*
46XU4 E3 5c **black** — —
46XU5 E4 5c **black** — *2,000.*

Only one example of No. 46XU3 is recorded.

KNOXVILLE, TENN.

A1 — Knxvle1

Typographed Adhesives (stereotype from woodcut)

Grayish Laid Paper

47X1 A1 5c **brick red** — *1,250.* 900.
Manuscript cancel — 325.
Horizontal pair — *3,750.* *1,850.*
Vertical pair — *3,100.*
Vertical strip of 3 — *6,000.*
On cover, tied by handstamp — *7,500.*
On cover, manuscript cancel — *2,100.*
Pair on cover — *7,500.*
47X2 A1 5c **carmine** — *1,750.* *1,500.*
Vertical strip of 3 — —
On cover, tied by handstamp — *7,500.*
On cover, manuscript cancel — *2,100.*
47X3 A1 10c **green,** on cover — *57,750.*

The #47X3 cover is unique. Value is based on 1997 auction sale.

The 5c has been reprinted in red, brown and chocolate on white and bluish wove and laid paper.

Cancellations in black: town, bars, pen or pencil.

E1

E2

Press-printed Envelopes (typographed)

47XU1 E1 5c **blue** — 750. *1,750.*
47XU2 E1 5c **blue,** *orange* — 750. *2,000.*
47XU3 E1 10c **red** (cut to shape) — *3,000.*
47XU4 E1 10c **red,** *orange* (cut to shape) — *3,000.*

Only one example each recorded of Nos. 47XU3 and 47XU4.

Handstamped Envelopes

47XU5 E2 5c **black** — 750. 1,500.
On patriotic cover — 3,000.
47XU6 E2 10c on 5c **black** — *3,500.*

Type E2 exists with "5" above or below "PAID."

LA GRANGE, TEX.

E1

Handstamped Envelopes

48XU1 E1 5c **black** — — 2,000.
48XU2 E1 10c **black** — 2,500.

LAKE CITY, FLA.

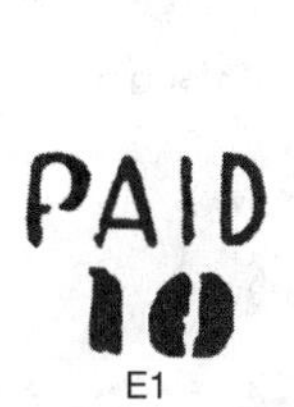

E1

Control

Handstamped Envelope

96XU1 E1 10c **black** — *2,000.*

Envelopes have black circle control mark, or printed name of E. R. Ives, postmaster, on face or back.

LAURENS COURT HOUSE, S. C.

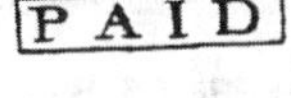

E1

Handstamped Envelope

116XU1 E1 5c **black** — *1,500.*

LENOIR, N. C.

LENOIR N 5 C PAID

A1

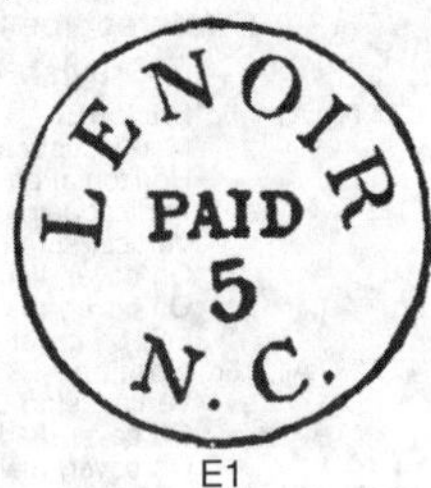

E1

Handstamped Adhesive (from woodcut)
White wove paper with cross-ruled orange lines

49X1 A1 5c **blue & orange** *3,250.* *2,750.*
On cover, pen canceled *7,000.*
On cover, tied by handstamp *20,000.*

Cancellations: blue town, blue "Paid" in circle, black pen.

Handstamped Envelopes

49XU1 A1 5c **blue** *3,500.*
49XU2 A1 10c (5c+5c) **blue** *25,000.*
49XU3 E1 5c **blue** *4,500.*
49XU4 E1 5c **black**

No. 49XU2 is unique. The existence of No. 49XU4 has been questioned.

LEXINGTON, MISS.

E1

Handstamped Envelopes

50XU1 E1 5c **black** *5,000.*
50XU2 E1 10c **black** *5,000.*

LEXINGTON, VA.

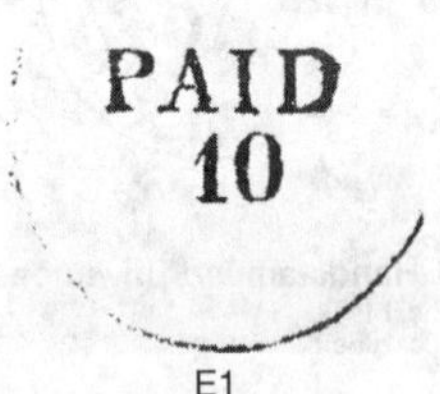

E1

Handstamped Envelopes

135XU1 E1 5c **blue** *500.*
Used with 5c #6 to make 10c rate *500.*
135XU2 E1 10c **blue** *750.*

Nos. 135XU1-135XU2 by themselves are indistinguishable from a handstamp paid cover when used.

LIBERTY, VA. (and Salem, Va.)

PAID
5cts.

A1

Typeset Adhesive (probably impressed by hand)
Laid Paper

74X1 A1 5c **black,** on cover, uncanceled, with Liberty postmark *35,000.*
On cover, uncanceled, with Salem postmark *40,000.*

Two known on covers with Liberty, Va. postmark; one cover known with the nearby Salem, Va. office postmark.

LIMESTONE SPRINGS, S. C.

A1

Handstamped Adhesive

121X1 A1 5c **black,** on cover *10,000.*
Two on cover *15,000.*

Stamps are cut round or rectangular, on white or colored paper. Covers are not postmarked.

LIVINGSTON, ALA.

A1

Lithographed Adhesive

51X1 A1 5c **blue** *8,000.*
On cover *60,000.*
Pair on cover *120,000.*

The pair on cover is unique.

Cancellation: black town.

LYNCHBURG, VA.

A1

E1

Typographed Adhesive
(stereotype from woodcut)

52X1 A1 5c **blue** (shades) *1,500.* 1,000.
Pair 2,250.
On cover *4,750.*
Pair on cover *20,000.*

Cancellations: black town, blue town.

Press-printed Envelopes (typographed)
Impressed at top right or left

52XU1 E1 5c **black** *2,500.*
52XU2 E1 5c **black,** *amber* 650. *2,500.*
52XU3 E1 5c **black,** *buff* *2,500.*
52XU4 E1 5c **black,** *brown* 900. *2,500.*
On patriotic cover —

MACON, GA.

A1

A2

A3

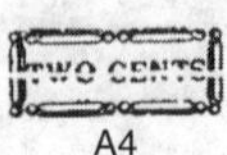

A4

Typeset Adhesives
Several varieties of type A1, 10 of A2, 5 of A3
Wove Paper

53X1 A1 5c **black,** *light blue green* (shades) 850. 600.
On cover *4,000.*
Pair on cover *9,000.*
Comma after "OFFICE" 900. 1,000.
Comma after "OFFICE," on cover *7,500.*

Warning: Dangerous forgeries exist of the normal variety and the Comma after "OFFICE" variety. Certificates of authenticity from recognized committees are strongly recommended.

53X3 A2 5c **black,** *yellow* 2,500. 800.
On cover *4,750.*
On patriotic cover *9,000.*
Pair on cover *8,000.*
53X4 A3 5c **black,** *yellow* (shades) 2,750. 1,250.
On cover *6,000.*
Pair on cover *10,000.*
a. Vertical tête bêche pair —
53X5 A4 2c **black,** *gray green* —
On cover *60,000.*

Laid Paper

53X6 A2 5c **black,** *yellow* *3,000.* *3,500.*
On cover *6,000.*
53X7 A3 5c **black,** *yellow* *6,000.*
On cover *9,000.*
53X8 A1 5c **black,** *light blue green* 1,750. *2,000.*
On cover *4,500.*

No. 53X4a is unique.

Cancellations: black town, black "PAID" (2 types).

E1

Handstamped Envelope
Two types: "PAID" over "5," "5" over "PAID"

53XU1 E1 5c **black** 250. 500.
On patriotic cover 1,900.

Values are for "PAID" over "5" variety. "5" over "PAID" is much scarcer.

MADISON, GA.

E1

Handstamped Envelope

136XU1 E1 5c **red** *500.*

No. 136XU1 is indistinguishable from a handstamp paid cover when used.

MADISON COURT HOUSE, FLA.

E1

Typeset Envelope

137XU1 E1 5c **black,** *yellow* *23,000.*

No. 137XU1 is unique.
See 3c 1861 Postmasters' Provisional No. 3AX1.

MARIETTA, GA.

E1

E2

Handstamped Envelopes
Two types of "PAID" and numerals

54XU1 E1 5c **black** 300.
54XU2 E1 10c on 5c **black** *1,750.*

With Double Circle Control

54XU3 E2 10c **black**
54XU4 E2 5c **black** *2,000.*

The existence of No. 54XU3 is questioned.

MARION, VA.

A1

Adhesives with Typeset frame and Handstamped numeral in center

55X1 A1 5c **black** *6,500.*
On cover *20,000.*
55X2 A1 10c **black** *16,500.* *10,000.*
On cover *60,000.*
55X3 A1 5c **black,** *bluish,* laid paper — —

The 2c, 3c, 15c and 20c are believed to be bogus items printed later using the original typeset frame.

Cancellations: black town, black "PAID."

MEMPHIS, TENN.

A1

A2

Typographed Adhesives (stereotyped from woodcut)

Plate of 50 (5x10) for the 2c. The stereotypes for the 5c stamps were set in 5 vertical rows of 8, with at least 2 rows set sideways to the right (see Thomas H. Pratt's monograph, "The Postmaster's Provisionals of Memphis").

56X1 A1 2c **blue** (shades) 90. *1,250.*
Block of 4 525.
On cover *10,000.*
Cracked plate (16, 17, 18) 150. *1,350.*

The "cracking off" (breaking off) of the plate at right edge caused incomplete printing of stamps in positions 5, 10, 15, 20, and 50. Poor make-ready also caused incomplete printing in position 50.

56X2 A2 5c **red** (shades) 140. 175.
Pair *325.* 450.
Block of 4 *1,000.*
On cover 1,750.
Pair on cover *3,500.*
Strip of 4 on cover *7,000.*
On patriotic cover *4,000.*
a. Tête bêche pair 1,500.
Pair on cover *10,000.*
b. Pair, one sideways 750.
c. Pelure paper — —

Cancellation on Nos. 56X1-56X2: black town.

Press-printed Envelopes (typographed)

56XU1 A2 5c **red** *2,500.*
Used with 5c #56X2 to make 10c rate *5,000.*
56XU2 A2 5c **red,** *amber* *4,000.*
Used with C.S.A. 5c #1 to make 10c rate *6,500.*
56XU3 A2 5c **red,** *orange* *2,500.*
On patriotic cover *4,000.*

MICANOPY, FLA.

E1

Handstamped Envelope

105XU1 E1 5c **black** *11,500.*

One example known.

MILLEDGEVILLE, GA.

E1

E2

E3

Handstamped Envelopes

57XU1 E1 5c **black** 250.
a. Wide spacing between "I" and "D" of "PAID" 400.
57XU2 E1 5c **blue** 800.
57XU3 E1 10c on 5c **black** 1,000.
57XU4 E2 10c **black** 225. 1,000.
a. Wide spacing between "I" and "D" of "PAID" 1,000.
57XU5 E3 10c **black** 700.

On No. 57XU4, the "PAID/10" virtually always falls outside the Milledgeville control marking (as in illustration E1).

Two types of No. 57XU5; with tall, thin "1" of "10" and with short, fat "1." The latter is about twice as scarce.

The existence of No. 57XU2 as a provisional has been questioned by specialists. The editors would like to see authenticated evidence of provisional use of this marking.

MILTON, N. C.

N. B. PATTON
PAID 5
E1

Handstamped Envelope, "5" Manuscript

138XU1 E1 5c **black** *2,000.*

MOBILE, ALA.

A1

Lithographed Adhesives

58X1 A1 2c **black** 2,000. 1,000.
Pair — *2,100.*
On cover *3,500.*
Pair on cover *16,500.*
Three singles on one cover *7,500.*
Five copies on one cover *20,000.*
58X2 A1 5c **blue** 275. 275.
Pair 675. 675.
On cover 1,800.
On cover, canceled in Claiborne, Ala. —
On cover, canceled in Montgomery, Ala. —
Pair on cover 2,400.
Strip of 3 on cover *14,000.*
Strip of 4 on cover —
Strip of 5 on cover —

Cancellations: black town, express company.

The existence of a strip of 5 of No. 58X2 has been questioned by specialists. The editors would like to see authenticated evidence of the existence of this strip either on or off cover.

MONTGOMERY, ALA.

E1

Handstamped Envelopes

59XU1 E1 5c **red** 1,000.
59XU2 E1 5c **blue** 400. 900.
59XU3 E1 10c **red** 800.
59XU4 E1 10c **blue** 1,500.
59XU5 E1 10c **black** 800.
59XU6 E1 10c on 5c **red** *2,750.*

The 10c design is larger than the 5c.

E2

E3

59XU7 E2 2c **red** *2,500.*
59XU7A E2 2c **blue** *3,500.*
59XU8 E2 5c **black** *2,250.*
59XU9 E3 10c **black** *2,750.*
59XU10 E3 10c **red** *1,500.*

MT. LEBANON, LA.

A1

Woodcut Adhesive (mirror image of design)

60X1 A1 5c **red brown,** on cover *385,000.*

One example known.

Cancellation: black pen.

NASHVILLE, TENN.

A2

Typographed Adhesives (stereotyped from woodcut)

Gray Blue Ribbed Paper

61X2 A2 5c **carmine** (shades) 850. 500.
Pair 1,250.
On cover 2,500.
On patriotic cover *4,500.*
Pair on cover *6,000.*
On cover with U.S. 3c 1857 (express) *25,000.*
a. Vertical tête bêche pair *3,000.*
On cover *30,000.*
61X3 A2 5c **brick red** 850. 450.
Pair 950.
On cover 3,500.
On patriotic cover *6,000.*
Pair on cover *7,500.*
On U.S. #U26 (express) *35,000.*
On U.S. #U27 with #26 (express) *25,000.*
61X4 A2 5c **gray** (shades) 950. 625.
On cover *5,500.*
Pair on cover *7,250.*
Strip of 5 on cover front *8,500.*
61X5 A2 5c **violet brown** 750. 475.
Block of 4 —
On cover 4,500.
On patriotic cover —
Pair on cover *6,000.*
a. Vertical tete beche pair *3,500.* *2,500.*
Pair on cover —
61X6 A2 10c **green** *3,000.* *3,000.*
On cover *15,000.*
On cover with U.S. 3c 1857 (express) *75,000.*
On U.S. #U26 (express) *100,000.*
On cover with No. 61X2 *17,500.*

Cancellations

Blue "Paid"
Blue "Postage Paid"
Blue town
Blue numeral "5"
Blue numeral "10"
Blue express company
Black express company

For the former 61X1, see No. 4AX1 in the 3c 1861 Postmasters' Provisional section.

E1

Handstamped Envelopes

61XU1 E1 5c **blue** 850.
On patriotic envelope 1,900.
61XU2 E1 5c +10c **blue** *2,750.*

NEW ORLEANS, LA.

A1

A2

Typographed Adhesives (stereotyped from woodcut)

Plate of 40

62X1 A1 2c **blue,** *July 14, 1861* 150. 500.
Pair 525. 1,150.
Block of 4 *6,500.*
On cover *4,250.*
On patriotic cover *8,000.*
Pair on cover *10,000.*
Three singles on one cover *20,000.*
Strip of 5 on cover *30,000.*
a. Printed on both sides —
On cover *7,500.*
62X2 A1 2c **red** (shades), *Jan. 6, 1862* 125. *1,000.*
Pair 300.
Block of 4 *1,500.*
On cover *25,000.*
62X3 A2 5c **brown,** *white, June 12, 1861* 250. 175.
Pair 525. 375.

No.		Description	Unused	Used
		Block of 4	1,750.	
		On cover		425.
		On cover from town other than N.O.		*5,000.*
		On patriotic cover		*5,500.*
		Pair on cover		850.
		Strip of 5 on cover		*5,000.*
		On cover with U.S. #26 (Southern Letter Unpaid)		*150,000.*
		On cover with U.S. No. 30A		—
a.		Printed on both sides		*2,250.*
		On cover		*7,500.*
b.		5c **ocher,** *June 18, 1861*	650.	600.
		Pair		1,450.
		On cover		2,250.
		On patriotic cover		*6,000.*
		Pair on cover		3,000.
62X4	A2	5c **red brn,** *bluish, Aug. 22, 1861*	280.	175.
		Pair	625.	425.
		Horizontal strip of 6		*3,500.*
		Block of 4		2,200.
		On cover		400.
		On patriotic cover		*5,500.*
		Pair on cover		675.
		Block of 4 on cover		*5,000.*
		Used on cover with C.S.A. 5c #1 to make 10c rate		*7,500.*
a.		Printed on both sides		*2,750.*
62X5	A2	5c **yel brn,** *off-white, Dec. 3, 1861*	125.	225.
		Pair	275.	500.
		Block of 4	650.	
		On cover		850.
		On patriotic cover		*3,000.*
		Pair on cover		1,000.
		Strip of 5 on cover		—
62X6	A2	5c **red**	—	*7,500.*
62X7	A2	5c **red,** *bluish*		*10,000.*

Cancellations

Black town (single or double circle New Orleans)
Red town (double circle New Orleans)
Town other than New Orleans
Postmaster's handstamp
Black "Paid"
Express Company
Packet boat, cover "STEAM"

J.L.RIDDELL.P.M
PD 5 CTS
N O.P.O

E1

These provisional handstamps were applied at the riverfront postal station.

Handstamped Envelopes

No.		Description	Unused	Used
62XU1	E1	5c **black**		4,500.
62XU2	E1	10c **black**		*12,500.*

"J. L. RIDDELL, P. M." omitted

No.		Description	Unused	Used
62XU3	E1	2c **black**		*9,500.*

NEW SMYRNA, FLA.

A1

Handstamped Adhesive

On white paper with blue ruled lines

No.		Description	Unused	Used
63X1	A1	10c ("O1") on 5c **black**		*45,000.*

One example known. It is uncanceled on a postmarked patriotic cover.

NORFOLK, VA.

E1

Handstamped Envelopes

Ms Initials on Front or Back

No.		Description	Unused	Used
139XU1	E1	5c **blue**	—	*1,250.*
139XU2	E1	10c **blue**		*1,750.*

OAKWAY, S. C.

A1

Handstamped Adhesive (from woodcut)

No.		Description	Unused	Used
115X1	A1	5c **black,** on cover		*66,000.*

Two used examples of No. 115X1 are recorded, both on cover. Value represents 1997 auction realization for the cover on which the stamp is tied by manuscript "Paid."

PENSACOLA, FLA.

E1

Handstamped Envelopes

No.		Description	Unused	Used
106XU1	E1	5c **black**		*3,750.*
106XU2	E1	10c (ms.) on 5c **black**		*4,250.*
		On patriotic cover		*13,500.*

PETERSBURG, VA.

A1

Typeset Adhesive

Ten varieties

Thick white paper

No.		Description	Unused	Used
65X1	A1	5c **red**	*1,750.*	500.
		Pair	*4,000.*	1,500.
		Block of 4	*9,000.*	
		On cover		2,000.
		On patriotic cover		—
		Pair on cover		*8,000.*
		Used on cover with C.S.A. 5c #1 to make 10c rate		*57,500.*

Cancellation: blue town.

PITTSYLVANIA COURT HOUSE, VA.

A1

Typeset Adhesives

No.		Description	Unused	Used
66X1	A1	5c **dull red,** wove paper	*6,000.*	*5,000.*
		Octagonally cut		*3,000.*
		On cover		*55,000.*
		On cover, octagonally cut		*20,000.*
66X2	A1	5c **dull red,** laid paper		*6,500.*
		Octagonally cut		*5,500.*
		On cover		*55,000.*
		On cover, octagonally cut		*40,000.*

Cancellation: black town.

PLAINS OF DURA, GA.

E1

Handstamped Envelopes, Ms. Initials

No.		Description	Unused	Used
140XU1	E1	5c **black**		—
140XU2	E1	10c **black**		—

PLEASANT SHADE, VA.

A1

Typeset Adhesive

Five varieties

No.		Description	Unused	Used
67X1	A1	5c **blue**	*2,750.*	*20,000.*
		On cover		*27,500.*
		Pair	*8,000.*	
		Pair on cover		*55,000.*
		Block of 6	*25,000.*	

Cancellation: blue town.

PLUM CREEK, TEX.

E1

Manuscript Adhesive

No.		Description	Unused	Used
141X1	E1	10c **black,** *blue,* on cover		—

The ruled lines and "10" are done by hand. Size and shape of the stamp varies.

PORT GIBSON, MISS.

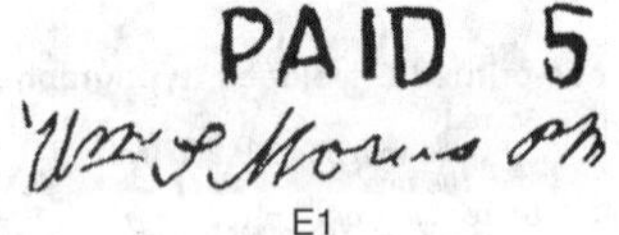

E1

Handstamped Envelope, Ms Signature

No.		Description	Unused	Used
142XU1	E1	5c **black**		—

PORT LAVACA, TEX.

A1

Typeset Adhesive

No.		Description	Unused	Used
107X1	A1	10c **black,** on cover		*25,000.*

One example known. It is uncanceled on a postmarked cover.

RALEIGH, N. C.

E1

Handstamped Envelopes

No.		Description	Unused	Used
68XU1	E1	5c **red**		500.
		On patriotic cover		2,750.
68XU2	E1	5c **blue**		*2,500.*

RHEATOWN, TENN.

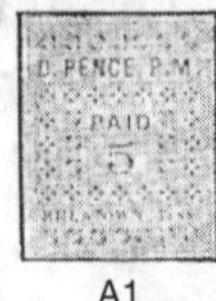

A1

Typeset Adhesive

Three varieties

No.		Description	Unused	Used
69X1	A1	5c **red**	*2,000.*	*2,750.*
		On cover, ms. cancel		*15,000.*
		On cover, tied by handstamp		*35,000.*
		Pair	*5,000.*	

Stamps normally were canceled in manuscript. One cover is known with stamp tied by red town postmark.

Cancellations: red town or black pen.

RICHMOND, TEX.

E1

Handstamped Envelopes or Letter Sheets

70XU1	E1	5c **red**	1,500.
70XU2	E1	10c **red**	1,000.
70XU3	E1	10c on 5c **red**	*5,000.*
70XU4	E1	15c (ms.) on 10c **red**	*5,000.*

RINGGOLD, GA.

E1

Handstamped Envelope

71XU1	E1	5c **blue black**	*3,000.*

RUTHERFORDTON, N. C.

A1

Handstamped Adhesive, Ms. "Paid 5cts"

72X1	A1	5c **black,** cut round, on cover (uncanceled)	*25,000.*

No. 72X1 is unique.

SALEM, N. C.

E1

E2

Handstamped Envelopes

73XU1	E1	5c **black**	1,150.
73XU2	E1	10c **black**	*1,500.*
73XU3	E2	5c **black**	*1,500.*
73XU4	E2	10c on 5c **black**	*2,800.*

Reprints exist on various papers. They either lack the "Paid" and value or have them counterfeited.

Salem, Va.
See No. 74X1 under Liberty, Va.

SALISBURY, N. C.

SALISBURY.
N. C.
POSTAGE

FIVE CENTS
P.M.

E1

Press-printed Envelope (typeset)

Impressed at top left

75XU1	E1	5c **black,** *greenish*	*5,000.*

One example known. Part of envelope is torn away, leaving part of design missing. Illustration E1 partly suppositional.

SAN ANTONIO, TEX.

E1 E2

Control

Handstamped Envelopes

76XU1	E1	10c **black**	275.	*2,000.*
76XU1A	E2	5c **black**		*1,500.*
76XU2	E2	10c **black**		*2,500.*

Black circle control mark is on front or back.

SAVANNAH, GA.

E1

Control

PAID 10

E2

Handstamped Envelopes

101XU1	E1	5c **black**	300.
101XU2	E2	5c **black**	600.
101XU3	E1	10c **black**	750.
101XU4	E2	10c **black**	750.
101XU5	E1	10c on 5c **black**	1,500.
101XU6	E2	20c on 5c **black**	*2,000.*

Envelopes must have octagonal control mark. One example is known of No.101XU6.

SELMA, ALA.

E1

Handstamped Envelopes; Signature in Ms.

77XU1	E1	5c **black**	*1,250.*
77XU2	E1	10c **black**	*2,500.*
77XU3	E1	10c on 5c **black**	*3,000.*

Signature is that of Postmaster William H. Eagar. See 3c 1861 Postmasters' Provisional No. 5AX1.

SPARTA, GA.

E1

Handstamped Envelopes

93XU1	E1	5c **red**	—	1,750.
93XU2	E1	10c **red**		*2,500.*

Only one example recorded of No. 93XU2.

SPARTANBURG, S. C.

A1

A2

Handstamped Adhesives

(on ruled or plain wove paper)

78X1	A1	5c **black**	*3,500.*
		On cover	*25,000.*
		Pair on cover	*30,000.*
		On patriotic cover	*30,000.*
a.		"5" omitted (on cover)	—
78X2	A2	5c **black,** *bluish*	*4,000.*
		On cover	*15,000.*
78X3	A2	5c **black,** *brown*	*4,000.*
		On cover	*18,000.*

Most examples of Nos. 78X1-78X3 are cut round. Cut square examples in sound condition are worth much more. The only recorded pair of No. 78X1 is on cover. The stamps are cut round, but are still connected.

Cancellations: black "PAID," black town.

STATESVILLE, N. C.

E1

Handstamped Envelopes

79XU1	E1	5c **black**	250.	*600.*
79XU2	E1	10c on 5c **black**		*2,250.*

Fakes exist of No. 79XU1 unused.

SUMTER, S. C.

E1

Handstamped Envelopes

80XU1	E1	5c **black**	400.	
80XU2	E1	10c **black**	500.	
80XU3	E1	10c on 5c **black**		*800.*
80XU4	E1	2c (ms.) on 10c **black**		*1,100.*

Used examples of Nos. 80XU1-80XU2 are indistinguishable from handstamped "Paid" covers.

TALBOTTON, GA.

E1

Handstamped Envelopes

94XU1	E1	5c **black**	1,000.
94XU2	E1	10c **black**	1,000.
94XU3	E1	10c on 5c **black**	*2,000.*

TALLADEGA, ALA.

IE
PAID10

E1

Handstamped Envelopes

143XU1	E1	5c **black**	—	—
143XU2	E1	10c **black**	—	—

TELLICO PLAINS, TENN.

A1

Typeset Adhesives
Settings of two 5c and one 10c
Laid Paper

81X1	A1	5c	**red**	1,250.	—
			On cover		*50,000.*
81X2	A1	10c	**red**	2,500.	
			Se-tenant with 5c	*4,000.*	
			Strip of 3 (5c+5c+10c)	*8,000.*	

Cancellation: black pen.

THOMASVILLE, GA.

PAID 

E1 Control

Handstamped Envelopes

82XU1	E1	5c	**black**	500.

On No. 82XU1, the control is on the reverse of the cover. The dated control is known with four different dates.

E2

82XU2	E2	5c	**black**	900.

TULLAHOMA, TENN.

E1

Control

Handstamped Envelope

111XU1	E1	10c	**black**	*3,000.*

TUSCALOOSA, ALA.

PAID
5
E1

Handstamped Envelopes

83XU1	E1	5c	**black**	250.
83XU2	E1	10c	**black**	250.

Used examples of Nos. 83XU1-83XU2 are indistinguishable from handstamped "Paid" covers. Some authorities question the use of E1 to produce provisional envelopes.

TUSCUMBIA, ALA.

E1

Handstamped Envelopes

84XU1	E1	5c	**black**	2,250.
			On patriotic cover	—
84XU2	E1	5c	**red**	*3,000.*
84XU3	E1	10c	**black**	*3,500.*

See 3c 1861 Postmasters' Provisional No. 6AXU1.

Union City, Tenn.

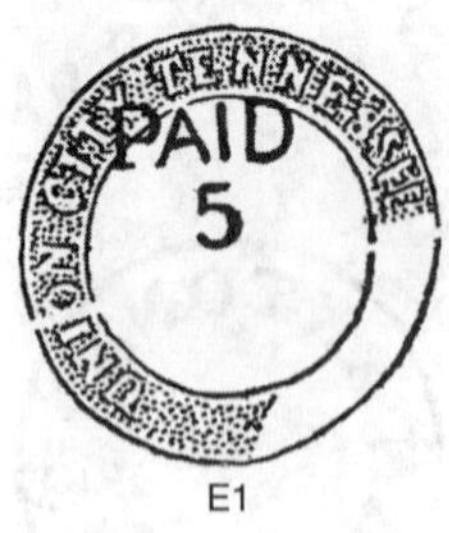

E1

The use of E1 to produce provisional envelopes is doubtful.

UNIONTOWN, ALA.

A1

Typeset Adhesives
(settings of 4 (2x2), 4 varieties of each value)
Laid Paper

86X1	A1	2c	**dark blue,** *gray blue,* on cover		—
86X2	A1	2c	**dark blue,** sheet of 4	*57,500.*	
86X3	A1	5c	**green,** *gray blue*	*3,000.*	*2,000.*
			Pair	—	
			On cover		*6,500.*
86X4	A1	5c	**green**	*3,000.*	*2,000.*
			On cover		*7,000.*
			Pair on cover		*18,500.*
86X5	A1	10c	**red,** *gray blue*		—
			On cover		*37,500.*

Two examples known of No. 86X1, both on cover (drop letters), one uncanceled and one pen canceled.
The only recorded examples of No. 86X2 are in a unique sheet of 4.
The item listed as No. 86X5 used is an uncanceled stamp on a large piece with part of addressee's name in manuscript.

Cancellation on Nos. 86X3-86X5: black town.

UNIONVILLE, S. C.

A1

Handstamped Adhesive
"PAID" and "5" applied separately
Paper with Blue Ruled Lines

87X1	A1	5c	**black,** *grayish*	—
			On cover, uncanceled	*17,500.*
			On cover, tied	—
			Pair on patriotic cover	*32,500.*

The pair on patriotic cover is the only pair recorded.

Cancellation: black town.

VALDOSTA, GA.

E1

Control

Handstamped Envelopes

100XU1	E1	10c	**black**	*2,000.*
100XU2	E1	5c +5c	**black**	—

The black circle control must appear on front or back of envelope.
There is one recorded cover each of Nos. 100XU1-100XU2.

VICTORIA, TEX.

A1

A2

Typeset Adhesives
Surface colored paper

88X1	A1	5c	**red brown,** *green*	*9,000.*	
88X2	A1	10c	**red brown,** *green*	*10,000.*	*5,500.*
			On cover		*115,000.*
88X3	A2	10c	**red brown,** *green,* pelure paper	*10,000.*	*10,000.*

WALTERBOROUGH, S. C.

E1

Handstamped Envelopes

108XU1	E1	10c	**black,** *buff*	*4,250.*
108XU2	E1	10c	**carmine**	*4,250.*

WARRENTON, GA.

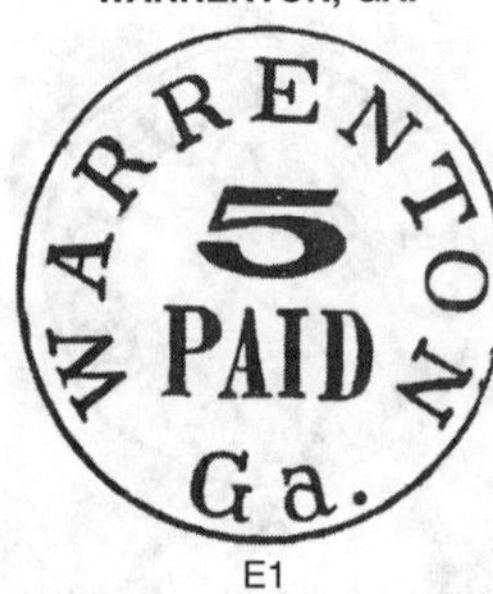

E1

Handstamped Envelopes

89XU1	E1	5c	**black**	1,250.
89XU2	E1	10c (ms.) on 5c	**black**	850.

Fakes of the Warrenton provisional marking based on the illustration shown are known on addressed but postally unused covers.

WASHINGTON, GA.

PAID 10
E1

Handstamped Envelope

117XU1	E1	10c	**black**	*2,000.*

Envelopes must have black circle postmark control on the back. Examples with the undated control on the front are not considered provisional unless a dated postmark is also present.

WEATHERFORD, TEX.

E1

Handstamped Envelopes
(woodcut with "PAID" inserted in type)

109XU1	E1	5c	**black**	*2,000.*
109XU2	E1	5c +5c	**black**	*11,000.*

One example is known of No. 109XU2.

WINNSBOROUGH, S. C.

PAID
5

E1 Control

Handstamped Envelopes

97XU1	E1	5c	**black**	*1,500.*
97XU2	E1	10c	**black**	*3,500.*

Envelopes must have black circle control on front or back.

WYTHEVILLE, VA.

5
PAID

E1 Control

Handstamped Envelope

114XU1	E1	5c	**black**	900.

For later additions, listed out of numerical sequence, see:

#74X1, **Liberty, Va.**
#92XU1, **Huntsville, Tex.**
#93XU1, **Sparta, Ga.**
#94XU1, **Talbotton, Ga.**
#96XU1, **Lake City, Fla.**
#97XU1, **Winnsborough, S. C.**
#98XU1, **Galveston, Tex.**
#99XU1, **Christiansburg, Va.**
#100XU1, **Valdosta, Ga.**
#101XU1, **Savannah, Ga.**
#102XU1, **Griffin, Ga.**
#103XU1, **Courtland, Ala.**
#104XU1, **Fincastle, Va.**
#105XU1, **Micanopy, Fla.**
#106XU1, **Pensacola, Fla.**
#107X1, **Port Lavaca, Tex.**
#108XU1, **Walterborough, S. C.**
#109XU1, **Weatherford, Tex.**
#110XU1, **Jacksonville, Ala.**
#111XU1, **Tullahoma, Tenn.**
#112XU1, **Hamburgh, S. C.**
#113XU1, **Columbia, Tenn.**
#114XU1, **Wytheville, Va.**
#115X1, **Oakway, S. C.**
#116XU1, **Laurens Court House, S. C.**
#117XU1, **Washington, Ga.**
#118XU1, **Carolina City, N.C.**
#119XU1, **Colaparchee, Ga.**
#120XU1, **Forsyth, Ga.**
#121XU1, **Limestone Springs, S.C.**
#122XU1, **Balcony Falls, Va.**
#123XU1, **Barnwell Court House, S.C.**
#124XU1, **Bluffton, S.C.**
#125XU1, **Camden, S.C.**
#126XU1, **Cartersville, Ga.**
#127XU1, **Charlottesville, Va.**
#128XU1, **Fraziersville, S.C.**
#129XU1, **Gaston, N.C.**
#130XU1, **Harrisburgh, Tex.**
#132XU1, **Hollandale, Tex.**
#133XU1, **Isabella, Ga.**
#134XU1, **Jacksonville, Fla.**
#135XU1, **Lexington, Va.**
#136XU1, **Madison, Ga.**
#137XU1, **Madison Court House, Fla.**
#138XU1, **Milton, N.C.**
#139XU1, **Norfolk, Va.**
#140XU1, **Plains of Dura, Ga.**
#141X1, **Plum Creek, Tex.**
#142XU1, **Port Gibson, Miss.**
#143XU1, **Talladega, Ala.**

CONFEDERATE STATES OF AMERICA, GENERAL ISSUES

The general issues are valued in the very fine grade, and unused stamps are valued both with and without original gum. As noted in the catalogue introduction, "original gum" for this era is defined as at least a majority part original gum, that is, at least 51% original gum. Stamps with substantially more than 51% original gum may be expected to sell for more than the values given, and stamps with less than a majority part original gum will sell for somewhat less.

For explanations of various terms used see the notes at the end of the postage listings.

Jefferson Davis — A1

1861 Litho. Soft Porous Paper *Imperf.*

All 5c Lithographs were printed by Hoyer & Ludwig, of Richmond, Va.

Stones A or B - First stones used. Earliest dated cancellation October 16, 1861. Plating not completed hence size of sheets unknown. These stones had imprints. Stamps from Stones A or B are nearly all in the olive green shade. Sharp, clear impressions. Distinctive marks are few and minute.

Stone 1 - Earliest dated cancellation October 18, 1861. Plating completed. Sheet consists of four groups of fifty varieties arranged in two panes of one hundred each without imprint. The first small printing was in olive green and later small printings appeared in light and dark green; the typical shade, however, is an intermediate shade of bright green. The impressions are clear though not as sharp as those from Stones A or B. Distinctive marks are discernible.

Stone 2 - Earliest dated cancellation December 2, 1861. Plating completed. Sheet consists of four groups of fifty varieties arranged in two panes of one hundred each without imprint. All shades other than olive green are known from this stone, the most common being a dull green. Poor impressions. Many noticeable distinctive marks.

Stone 2

1	A1	5c **green**	250.	150.
		No gum	175.	
		bright green	275.	150.
		dull green	250.	150.
a.		5c **light green**	250.	150.
		No gum	175.	
b.		5c **dark green**	300.	175.
		No gum	210.	
		On cover		250.
		Single on cover (overpaid drop letter)		350.
		On wallpaper cover		*1,500.*
		On prisoner's cover		—
		On prisoner's cover with U.S. #65		—
		On prisoner's cover with U.S. #U34		—
		On patriotic cover		1,250.
		Pair	600.	375.
		Pair on cover		400.
		Block of 4	1,450.	1,200.
		Pair with full horiz. gutter between		—

VARIETIES

Spur on upper left scroll (Pos. 21)	400.	260.
Side margin copy showing initials (Pos. 41 or 50)	1,100.	625.
Misplaced transfer (clear twin impressions of lower left scrolls - pos. 1 entered over pos. 10)	—	—
Roulетted unofficially	350.	700.
On cover		*1,600.*
Pair on cover		*2,500.*

Cancellations

Blue town	+10.
Red town	+125.
Green town	+175.
Orange town	+150.
Texas town	+35.
Arkansas town	+90.
Florida town	+110.
Kentucky town	+300.
Blue gridiron	+5.
Red gridiron	+50.
Blue concentric	+5.
Star or flowers	+100.
Numeral	+50.
"Paid"	+50.
"Steamboat"	+150.
Express Co.	+350.
Railroad	+300.
Pen	60.

Stone 1

1	A1	5c **green**	275.	150.
		No gum	200.	
		bright green	275.	150.
		dull green	250.	150.
a.		5c **light green**	250.	150.
		No gum	175.	
b.		5c **dark green**	275.	175.
		No gum	190.	
c.		5c **olive green**	350.	175.
		No gum	240.	
		On cover		250.
		On patriotic cover		1,250.
		Pair	700.	425.
		Pair on cover		525.
		Block of 4	1,500.	1,150.

VARIETIES

Acid flaw	325.	160.
Arrow between panes	575.	300.
Flaw on "at" of "States" (Pos. 38)	300.	200.

Cancellations

Blue town	+10.
Red town	+80.
Green town	+175.
Texas town	+35.
Arkansas town	+90.
Florida town	+110.
Kentucky town	+300.
October, 1861, year date	+40.
Blue gridiron	+5.
Red gridiron	+75.
Blue concentric	+5.
Numeral	+50.
"Paid"	+50.
"Steam"	+150.
"Steamboat"	+150.
Express Company	+350.
Railroad	+300.
Pen	60.

Stones A or B

1c	A1	5c **olive green**	375.	175.
		No gum	260.	
		On cover		300.
		On patriotic cover		1,400.
		Pair	800.	400.
		Pair on cover		650.
		Block of 4	2,150.	1,200.

VARIETIES

White curl back of head	400.	250.
Imprint	750.	450.

Cancellations

Blue town	+10.
Red town	+150.
October, 1861, year date	+50.
Blue gridiron	+5.
Blue concentric	+5.
Numeral	+60.
"Paid"	+50.
"Steam"	+150.
Express Co.	+400.
Pen	100.

Thomas Jefferson — A2

1861-62 Litho. Soft Porous Paper

Hoyer & Ludwig - First stone used. Earliest dated cancellation November 8, 1861. Sheet believed to consist of four groups of fifty varieties each arranged in two panes of one hundred each with imprint at bottom of each pane. Two different imprints are known. Hoyer & Ludwig printings are always in a uniform shade of dark blue. Impressions are clear and distinct, especially so in the early printings. Plating marks are distinct.

J. T. Paterson & Co. - Earliest dated cancellation July 25, 1862. Sheet consists of four groups of fifty varieties each arranged in two panes of one hundred each with imprint at bottom of each pane. Two different imprints are known and at least one pane is known without an imprint. Wide range of shades. Impressions are less clear than those from the Hoyer & Ludwig stone. Paterson stamps show small vertical colored dash below the lowest point of the upper left triangle.

Stone "Y" - Supposedly made by J. T. Paterson & Co., as it shows the distinctive mark of that firm. Plating not completed hence size of sheet unknown. No imprint found. Color is either a light milky blue or a greenish blue. Impressions are very poor and have a blurred appearance. Stone Y stamps invariably show a large flaw back of the head as well as small vertical colored dash beneath the upper left triangle.

Paterson

2	A2 10c **blue**	280.	190.
	No gum	200.	
a.	10c **light blue**	280.	190.
	No gum	200.	
b.	10c **dark blue**	550.	240.
	No gum	400.	
c.	10c **indigo**	*2,750.*	*2,250.*
	No gum	*2,000.*	
	On cover		250.
	On wallpaper cover		700.
	On patriotic cover		1,400.
	On prisoner's cover with U.S. #65		—
	Pair	725.	450.
	Pair on cover		950.
	Strip of 3 on cover		—
	Block of 4	1,750.	
	Horiz. pair, gutter btwn.	1,500.	
d.	Printed on both sides		—

VARIETIES

Malformed "O" of "POSTAGE" (Pos. 25)	400.	225.
J. T. Paterson & Co. imprint	1,000.	1,150.

Cancellations

Blue town	+10.
Red town	+100.
Green town	+200.
Violet town	—
Texas town	+125.
Arkansas town	+275.
Florida town	+325.
July, 1862, date	+300.
Straight line town	+500.
Blue gridiron	+10.
Red gridiron	+75.
Blue concentric	+10.
Numeral	+80.
"Paid"	+75.
Star or flower	+150.
Railroad	+350.
Express Co.	+300.
Pen	70.

Hoyer

2b	A2 10c **dark blue**	550.	240.
	No gum	400.	
	On cover		425.
	On wallpaper cover		725.
	On patriotic cover		2,100.
	On prisoner's cover with U.S. #65		—
	Pair	1,175.	800.
	Pair on cover		1,500.
	Strip of 3 on cover		3,500.
	Block of 4	2,750.	—
d.	Printed on both sides	—	

VARIETIES

Malformed "T" of "TEN" (Pos. 4)	575.	300.
"G" and "E" of "POSTAGE" joined (Pos. 10)	575.	300.
Circular flaw, upper left star (Pos. 11)	575.	300.
Third spiked ornament at right, white (Pos. 45)	575.	350.
Hoyer & Ludwig imprint	825.	825.
Rouletted unofficially, on cover		*3,000.*

Cancellations

Blue town	+30.
Red town	+100.
Texas town	+125.
Arkansas town	+275.
Florida town	+325.
Kentucky town	+400.
Nov., 1861, date	+300.
Straight line town	+500.
Blue gridiron	+10.
Red gridiron	+60.
Blue concentric	+10.
Numeral	+75.
"Paid"	+50.
Railroad	+350.
Express Company	+300.
Pen	75.

Stone Y

2e	A2 10c **greenish blue**	650.	300.
	No gum	450.	
	light milky blue	750.	300.
	No gum	575.	
	On cover		500.
	On patriotic cover		2,100.
	Pair	1,600.	—
	Block of 4	—	2,250.

Cancellations

Blue town	+10.
Red town	+125.
Violet town	+75.
Green town	+300.
Texas town	+125.
Arkansas town	+275.
Florida town	—
Straight line town	+500.
Blue gridiron	+10.
Red gridiron	+75.
Blue concentric	+10.
Numeral	+100.
"Paid"	+100.
Pen	90.

Andrew Jackson — A3

Sheet consists of four groups of fifty varieties arranged in two panes of 100 each.

One stone only was used. Printed by Hoyer & Ludwig, of Richmond, Va. Issued to prepay drop letter and circular rates. Strips of five used to prepay regular 10c rate, which was changed from 5c on July 1, 1862. Earliest known cancellation, March 21, 1862.

1862 (March?) Soft Porous Paper Litho.

3	A3 2c **green**	700.	650.
	light green	700.	650.
	dark green	700.	700.
	No gum	500.	
	dull yellow green	775.	800.
	No gum	575.	
	On cover		*2,750.*
	Pair on cover (double circular rate)		*3,250.*
	Strip of 5 on cover		*13,500.*
	On patriotic cover		*10,000.*
	Pair	1,500.	—
	Block of 4	3,250.	3,500.
	Block of 5	4,000.	*4,250.*
a.	2c **bright yellow green**	*1,750.*	—
	No gum	*1,400.*	
	On cover		—

VARIETIES

Diagonal half used as 1c with unsevered pair, on cover		—
Horiz. pair, vert. gutter between	—	—
Pair, mark between stamps (btwn. Pos. 4 and 5)	1,750.	1,900.
Mark above upper right corner (Pos. 30)	850.	850.
Mark above upper left corner (Pos. 31)	850.	850.
Acid flaw	800.	700.

Cancellations

Blue town	+500.
Red town	+800.
Arkansas town	—
Texas town	+1,250.
Blue gridiron	+250.
"Paid"	—
Express Company	—
Railroad	+3,000.
Pen	400.

1862 Soft Porous Paper Litho.

Stone 2 - First stone used for printing in blue. Plating is the same as Stone 2 in green. Earliest dated cancellation Feb. 26, 1862. Printings from Stone 2 are found in all shades of blue. Rough, coarse impressions are typical of printings from Stone 2.

Stone 3 - A new stone used for printings in blue only. Earliest dated cancellation April 10, 1862. Sheet consists of four groups of fifty varieties each arranged in two panes of one hundred each without imprint. Impressions are clear and sharp, often having a proof-like appearance, especially in the deep blue printing. Plating marks, while not so large as on Stone 2 are distinct and clearly defined.

Stone 2

4	A1 5c **blue**	180.	110.
	No gum	125.	
	light blue	210.	130.
	No gum	145.	
a.	5c **dark blue**	240.	160.
	No gum	170.	
b.	5c **light milky blue**	270.	200.
	No gum	190.	
	Pair	400.	400.
	Block of 4	1,000.	*1,900.*
	Horiz. pair, wide gutter between	1,250.	—
	Vert. pair, narrow gutter between	—	
	On cover		250.
	Single on cover (overpaid drop letter)		325.
	Pair on cover		450.
	On wallpaper cover		575.
	On patriotic cover		1,800.
	On prisoner's cover		*2,000.*
	On prisoner's cover with U.S. #65		—

VARIETIES

Spur on upper left scroll (Pos. 21)	225.	150.
Thin hard paper	—	140.
Misplaced transfer (faint twin impression of second lower left scroll at left - pos. 2 entered over pos. 10)		—

Cancellations

Blue town	+20.
Red town	+100.
Texas town	+300.
Arkansas town	+325.
Florida town	+200.
Straight line town	+300.
Blue gridiron	+10.
Red gridiron	+85.
Star or Flowers	+125.
Numeral	+85.
Railroad	—
"Paid"	+25.
"Steamboat"	+400.
Express Company	—
"Way"	+250.
Pen	65.

Stone 3

4	A1 5c **blue**	750.	250.
	No gum	550.	
a.	5c **dark blue**	750.	250.
	No gum	5500.	
b.	5c **light milky blue**	750.	250.
	No gum	550.	
	Pair	1750.	550.
	Block of 4	4,500.	*2,000.*
	On cover		500.
	Pair on cover		625.
	On patriotic cover		2,000.
	Horiz. pair, wide gutter btwn.	—	
	Vert. pair, narrow gutter between	—	

Stone 3 stamps can be positively identified by plating only. Color or shade is not a determinant.

VARIETIES

Tops of "C" and "E" of "cents" joined by flaw (Pos. 33)	850.	325.
"Flying bird" above lower left corner ornament (Pos. 19)	850.	325.

Cancellations

Blue town	+40.
Red town	+100.
Texas town	+300.
Arkansas town	+325.
Straight line town	+325.
Blue gridiron	+10.
Star or Flowers	+125.
"Paid"	+50.
Pen	80.

1862 (March?) Soft Porous Paper Litho.

Settings of fifty varieties repeated.

Printed by Hoyer & Ludwig, of Richmond, Va. One stone used, being the same as that used for the Hoyer & Ludwig 10c value in blue. Color change occured probably in March, 1862.

There are many shades of this stamp. The carmine is a very dark, bright color and should not be confused with the deeper shade of rose.

Earliest known cancellation, March 10, 1862. The earliest date of usage of the carmine shade is May 1, 1862.

5 A2 10c **rose**	1,400.	500.
No gum	1,000.	
dull rose	1,250.	500.
brown rose	1,750.	1,000.
deep rose	1,300.	650.
carmine rose	1,500.	875.
On cover		800.
On wallpaper cover		*2,000.*
On patriotic cover		*3,000.*
On prisoner's cover		*5,500.*
On prisoner's cover with U.S. #65		—
Pair	3,100.	2,250.
Strip of 3	—	*4,000.*
Block of 4	*11,000.*	*6,500.*
a. 10c **carmine**	*2,800.*	*1,750.*
No gum	*2,000.*	
On cover		*4,500.*

VARIETIES

Malformed "T" of "TEN" (Pos. 4)	1,250.	600.
"G" and "E" of "POSTAGE" joined (Pos. 10)	1,250.	600.
Circular flaw, upper left star (Pos. 11)	1,400.	675.
Third spiked ornament at right, white (Pos. 45)	1,400.	675.
Scratched stone (occurring on Pos. 40, 39, 49 and 48, one pane)	1,400.	925.
Imprint		1,750.
Horiz. pair, vert. gutter between		—
Side margin copy, initials (Pos. 41)		1,500.

Cancellations

Blue town	+50.
Red town	+125.
Green town	+350.
Texas town	+150.
Arkansas town	—
Straight line town	+500.
April, 1862, year date	—
Blue gridiron	+50.
Black concentric	+50.
Blue concentric	+50.
"Paid"	—
Railroad	—
Express Company	—
Pen	200.

Jefferson Davis — A4

Plate of 400 in four panes of 100 each. No imprint.

No. 6 represents London printings from De La Rue & Co., a number of sheets being sent over by blockade runners. Fine clear impressions. The gum is light and evenly distributed. Exact date of issue unknown. Earliest known cancellation, April 16, 1862.

Typographed by De La Rue & Co. in London, England

1862 (April) Hard Medium Paper

6 A4 5c **light blue**	10.00	27.50
No gum	6.50	
Single on cover used before July 1, 1862		125.00
Single on cover (overpaid drop letter)		240.00
Single on patriotic cover used before July 1, 1862		900.00
Single on prisoner's cover used before July 1, 1862		—
On wallpaper cover		350.00
On patriotic cover		1,100.
On prisoner's cover		1,250.
On prisoner's cover with U.S. #65		1,250.
Pair	21.00	75.00
Pair on cover		100.00
Pair on patriotic cover		*1,300.*
Block of 4	45.00	290.00
Block of 4 on cover		900.00

Cancellations

Blue town	+2.00
Red town	+55.00
Green town	+75.00
Texas town	+65.00
Arkansas town	+85.00
Straight line town	+150.00
Blue gridiron	+2.00
Red gridiron	+35.00
Blue concentric	+2.00
Express Company	+350.00
Railroad	+250.00
"Paid"	+50.00

1862 (August) Typo. Thin to Thick Paper

Plate of 400 in four panes of 100 each. No imprint.

Locally printed by Archer & Daly of Richmond, Va., from plates made in London, England, by De La Rue & Co. Printed on both imported English and local papers. Earliest known cancellation, August 15, 1862.

No. 7 shows coarser impressions than No. 6, and the color is duller and often blurred. Gum is light or dark and unevenly distributed.

7 A4 5c **blue**	13.00	20.00
No gum	8.50	
a. 5c **deep blue**	16.00	35.00
No gum	10.50	
Single on cover (overpaid drop letter)		200.00
On wallpaper cover		500.00
On patriotic cover		1,000.
On prisoner's cover		1,250.
On prisoner's cover with U.S. #65		—
Pair	30.00	47.50
Pair on cover		95.00
Block of 4	70.00	340.00
Block of 4 on cover		800.00
Eight on cover (Trans-Miss. rate)		—
b. Printed on both sides	*2,500.*	*950.00*
Pair		*2,100.*
Pair on cover		*3,250.*

VARIETIES

White tie (U.R. 30)	150.00	150.00
White tie on cover		350.00
De La Rue paper (thin)	27.50	45.00
No gum	20.00	
White tie, De La Rue paper	200.00	250.00
Thick paper	22.50	30.00
Horiz. pair, vert. gutter between	200.00	

Cancellations

Blue town	+2.00
Red town	+75.00
Brown town	+30.00
Violet town	+110.00
Green town	+150.00
Texas town	+90.00
Arkansas town	+110.00
Florida town	+140.00
Straight line town	+140.00
Blue gridiron	+2.00
Red gridiron	+60.00
Blue concentric	+2.00
Railroad	+250.00
Express Company	+400.00
Design (stars, etc.	+75.00
"Paid"	+50.00

The unissued 10c design A4 was privately printed in various colors for philatelic purposes. (See note below No. 14.)

Counterfeits of the 10c exist.

Andrew Jackson — A5

Sheet of 200 (two panes of 100 each).

One plate. Printed by Archer & Daly of Richmond, Va. Earliest known cancellation. Apr. 21, 1863. Issued to prepay drop letter and circular rates. Strips of five used to prepay regular 10c rate.

1863 (April) Soft Porous Paper Engraved

8 A5 2c **brown red**	70.	*350.*
No gum	52.50	
a. 2c **pale red**	90.	*450.*
No gum	65.	
Single on cover		*1,250.*
On prisoner's cover		*3,000.*
On prisoner's cover with U.S. #65		*4,000.*
Pair	150.	*1,000.*
Pair on cover		*3,250.*
On wallpaper cover		—
Block of 4	350.	—
Block of 5		—
Strip of 5 on cover		*5,000.*
Strip of 5 on wallpaper cover		—
Strip of 10 on cover		*13,000.*
Double transfer	125.	*450.*
Horiz. pair, vert. gutter between	325.	

Cancellations

Blue town	+35.
Red town	+225.
Army of Tenn.	—
Blue gridiron	+35.
Black numeral	—
Railroad	+325.

Jefferson Davis "TEN CENTS" — A6

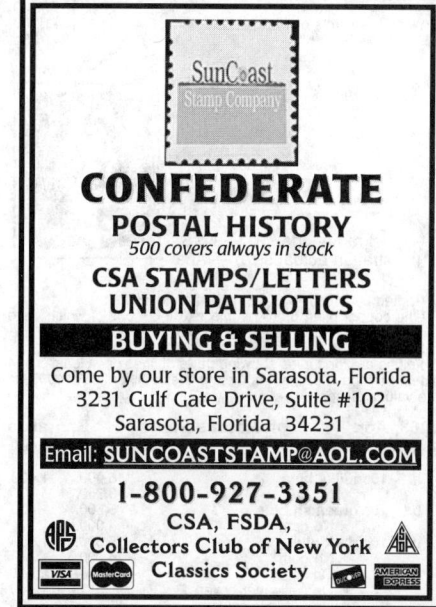

One plate of 200 subjects all of which were probably recut as every copy examined to date shows distinct recutting. Plating not completed.

Printed by Archer & Daly of Richmond, Va. First printings in milky blue. First issued in April, 1863. Earliest known cancellation, April 23, 1863.

1863, Apr. Soft Porous Paper Engraved

9 A6 10c **blue**	850.	525.
No gum	600.	
a. 10c **milky blue** (first printing)	850.	525.
No gum	600.	
b. 10c **gray blue**	900.	625.
No gum	650.	
On cover		1,600.
On wallpaper cover		*3,000.*
On patriotic cover		*3,500.*
On prisoner's cover		*4,250.*
On prisoner's cover with U.S. #65		—
Pair	1,850.	2,200.
Pair on cover		*3,000.*
Block of 4	*5,000.*	
Four stamps on one cover (Trans-Mississippi rate)		*13,500.*
Curved lines outside the labels at top and bottom are broken in the middle (Pos. 63R)	1,000.	750.
Double transfer	1,050.	1,000.
Damaged plate	1,150.	1,100.

Cancellations

Blue town	+25.
Red town	+150.
Green town	+600.
Violet town	—
Straight line town	+500.
April, 1863, year date	—
Black gridiron	+25.
Blue gridiron	+50.
Red gridiron	+200.

Railroad	+400.
Circle of wedges	+1,250.
Pen	350.

Frame Line "10 CENTS" (Illustration actual size) — A6a

Printed by Archer & Daly of Richmond, Va.

One copper plate of 100 subjects, all but one of which were recut. Earliest known use April 19, 1863.

Stamp design same as Die A (Pos. 11).

Values are for copies showing parts of lines on at least 3 of 4 sides. Stamps showing 4 complete lines sell for 300%-400% of the values given.

1863, Apr. Soft Porous Paper Engraved

10 A6a 10c **blue**	5,000.	1,400.
No gum	3,750.	
a. 10c **milky blue**	5,000.	1,400.
No gum	3,750.	
b. 10c **greenish blue**	5,500.	1,500.
No gum	4,000.	
c. 10c **dark blue**	5,500.	1,500.
No gum	4,000.	
On cover		*2,500.*
On wallpaper cover		*4,500.*
On patriotic cover		*6,000.*
On prisoner's cover		*7,000.*
On prisoner's cover with U.S. #65		—
Pair	*11,500.*	*5,500.*
Pair on cover		*6,500.*
Block of 4	*27,500.*	
Strip of 4	*26,000.*	
Strip of 6	—	*15,000.*
Strip of 7	*42,500.*	
Double transfer (Pos. 74)	5,500.	1,600.

Cancellations

Blue town	+100.
Red town	+500.
Straight line town	+750.
April, 1863, year date	—
Blue gridiron	+100.
Pen	750.

No Frame Line "10 CENTS" (Die A) — A7

There are many slight differences between A7 (Die A) and A8 (Die B), the most noticeable being the additional line outside the ornaments at the four corners of A8 (Die B).

Stamps were first printed by Archer & Daly, of Richmond, Va. In 1864 the plates were transferred to the firm of Keatinge & Ball in Columbia, S. C., who made further printings from them. Two plates, each with two panes of 100, numbered 1 and 2. First state shows numbers only, later states show various styles of Archer & Daly imprints, and latest show Keatinge & Ball imprints. Archer & Daly stamps show uniformly clear impressions and a good quality of gum evenly distributed (Earliest known cancellation, April 21, 1863); Keatinge & Ball stamps generally show filled in impressions in a deep blue, and the gum is brown and unevenly distributed. (Earliest known cancellation, Oct. 4, 1864). The so-called laid paper is probably due to thick streaky gum. (These notes also apply to No. 12.)

1863-64 Thick or Thin Paper Engraved

11 A7 10c **blue**	9.00	16.00
No gum	6.00	
a. 10c **milky blue**	22.50	37.50
No gum	15.00	
b. 10c **dark blue**	18.50	25.00
No gum	12.50	
c. 10c **greenish blue**	17.50	18.00
No gum	12.00	
d. 10c **green**	80.00	75.00
No gum	55.00	
deep blue, Keatinge & Ball ('64)	9.00	30.00
On cover		55.00
Single on cover (overpaid drop letter)		150.00
On wallpaper cover		400.00
On patriotic cover		650.00
On prisoner's cover		450.00
On prisoner's cover with U.S. #65		1,750.
On cover, dp. blue (K. & B.) ('64)		125.00
On wallpaper cover (K. & B.)		875.00
On prisoner's cover (K. & B.) with U.S. #65 ('64)		—
Pair	22.50	40.00
Pair on cover		175.00
Block of 4	47.50	290.00
Strip of 4 on cover (Trans-Mississippi rate)		—
Margin block of 12, Archer & Daly impt. & P#	375.00	
Margin block of 12, Keatinge & Ball impt. & P#	350.00	
Horiz. pair, vert. gutter between	110.00	
e. Officially perforated 12½	300.00	275.00
On cover		*500.00*
On wallpaper cover		—
Pair	650.00	600.00
Pair on cover		*2,750.*
Block of 4	1,350.	*2,250.*

VARIETIES

Double transfer	75.00	100.00
Rouletted unofficially		400.00
On cover		650.00

Cancellations

Blue town	+5.00
Red town	+35.00
Orange town	+110.00
Brown town	+60.00
Green town	+150.00
Violet town	+100.00
Texas town	+60.00
Arkansas town	+125.00
Florida town	+200.00
Straight line town	+300.00
Army of Tenn.	+300.00
April, 1863 year date	+75.00
"FREE"	+250.00
Blue gridiron	+5.00
Black concentric circles	+10.00
Star	+100.00
Crossroads	+150.00
"Paid"	+100.00
Numeral	+100.00
Railroad	+175.00
Steamboat	+1,500.

Jefferson Davis (Die B) — A8

Plates bore Nos. 3 and 4, otherwise notes on No. 11 apply. Earliest known use: Archer & Daly - May 1, 1863; Keatinge & Ball - Sept. 4, 1864.

1863-64 Thick or Thin Paper Engraved

12 A8 10c **blue**	11.00	18.00
No gum	7.50	
a. 10c **milky blue**	25.00	35.00
No gum	17.00	
b. 10c **light blue**	11.00	18.00
No gum	7.50	
c. 10c **greenish blue**	20.00	45.00
No gum	13.50	
d. 10c **dark blue**	11.00	20.00
No gum	7.50	
e. 10c **green**	175.00	150.00
No gum	130.00	
deep blue, Keatinge & Ball ('64)	11.00	40.00
On cover		75.00
Single on cover (overpaid drop letter)		150.00
On wallpaper cover		375.00
On patriotic cover		700.00
On prisoner's cover		450.00
On prisoner's cover with U.S. #65		1,750.
On cover, dp. blue (K. & B.) ('64)		130.00
Pair	27.50	52.50
Pair on cover		200.00
Block of 4	60.00	290.00
Strip of 4 on cover (Trans-Mississippi rate)		—
Margin block of 12, Archer & Daly impt. & P#	400.00	
Margin block of 12, Keatinge & Ball impt. & P#	350.00	
Horiz. pair, vert. gutter between	125.00	
f. Officially perforated 12½	325.00	300.00
On cover		*500.00*
Pair	700.00	600.00
Pair on cover		—
Block of 4	1,500.	

VARIETIES

Double transfer	95.00	110.00
Rouletted unofficially		375.00
On cover		850.00

Cancellations

Blue town	+5.00
Red town	+35.00
Brown town	+90.00
Green town	+120.00
Violet town	+85.00
Texas town	+125.00
Arkansas town	+150.00
Florida town	+200.00
Straight line town	+350.00

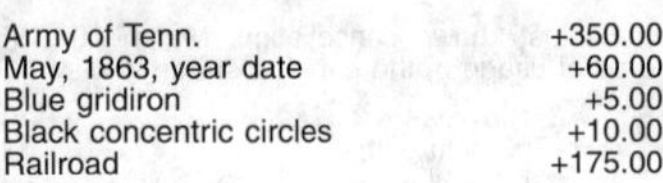

Army of Tenn.	+350.00
May, 1863, year date	+60.00
Blue gridiron	+5.00
Black concentric circles	+10.00
Railroad	+175.00

George Washington — A9

1863 (June?) Engraved by Archer & Daly

One plate which consisted of two panes of 100 each. First printings were from plates with imprint in Old English type under each pane, which was later removed. Printed on paper of varying thickness and in many shades of green. This stamp was also used as currency. Earliest known cancellation, June 1, 1863. Forged cancellations exist.

13 A9 20c **green**	37.50	*400.*
No gum	27.50	
a. 20c **yellow green**	70.00	*450.*
No gum	50.00	
b. 20c **dark green**	65.00	*500.*
No gum	45.00	
On cover		*1,250.*
On wallpaper cover		*1,750.*
On prisoner's cover		*4,000.*
On prisoner's cover with U.S. #65		*5,000.*
Pair	80.00	*900.*
Horizontal pair with gutter between	250.00	
Pair on cover (non-Trans-Mississippi rate)		*4,500.*
Pair on cover (Trans-Mississippi rate)		—
Block of 4	190.00	*3,500.*
Strip of 4 with imprint	400.00	
Block of 8 with imprint	1,000.	
c. Diagonal half used as 10c on cover		*2,000.*
Diagonal half on prisoner's cover		—
d. Horizontal half used as 10c on cover		*3,500.*

VARIETIES

Double transfer, 20 doubled (Pos. 24L and 35R)	250.	—
"20" on forehead	*3,000.*	—
Rouletted unofficially		*1,100.*
On cover		*3,750.*

Cancellations

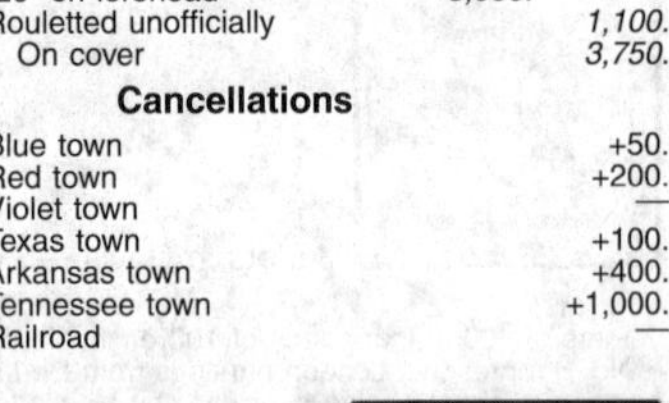

Blue town	+50.
Red town	+200.
Violet town	—
Texas town	+100.
Arkansas town	+400.
Tennessee town	+1,000.
Railroad	—

John C. Calhoun — A10

Typographed by De La Rue & Co., London, England

1862

14 A10 1c **orange**	100.00
No gum	70.00
Pair	200.00
Block of 4	375.00
a. 1c **deep orange**	125.00
No gum	90.00

This stamp was never put in use.

Upon orders from the Confederate Government, De La Rue & Co. of London, England, prepared Two Cents and Ten Cents typographed plates by altering the One Cent (No. 14) and the Five Cents (Nos. 6-7) designs previously made by them. Stamps were never officially printed from these plates although privately made prints exist in various colors.

Explanatory Notes

The following notes by Lawrence L. Shenfield explain the various routes, rates and usages of the general issue Confederate stamps.

"Across the Lines" Letters Carried by Private Express Companies

Adams Express Co. and American Letter Express Company Handstamps Used on "Across the Lines" Letters

PRIVATE LETTER MAIL.

Direct each letter to your correspondent as usual, envelope that with 15 cents in money and direct to

B. WHITESIDES,
Franklin, Ky.

Letters exceeding half an ounce or going over 500 miles must have additional amount enclosed. For single Newspapers enclose 10 cents.

B. Whitesides Label

About two months after the outbreak of the Civil War, in June, 1861, postal service between North and South and vice versa was carried on largely by Adams Express Company, and the American Letter Express Company. Northern terminus for the traffic was Louisville, Ky.; Southern terminus was Nashville, Tenn. Letters for transmission were delivered to any office of the express company, together with a fee, usually 20c or 25c per ½ ounce to cover carriage. The express company messengers carried letters across the lines and delivered them to their office on the other side, where they were deposited in the Government mail for transmission to addressees, postage paid out of the fee charged. Letters from North to South, always enclosed in 3c U. S. envelopes, usually bear the handstamp of the Louisville office of the express company, and in addition the postmark and "Paid 5" of Nashville, Tenn., indicating its acceptance for delivery at the Nashville Post Office. Letters from South to North sometimes bear the origin postmark of a Southern post office, but more often merely the handstamp of the Louisville express company office applied as the letters cleared through Louisville. The B. Whitesides South to North cover bears a "Private Letter Mail" label. In addition, these covers bear the 3c 1857 U.S. adhesive stamp, cancelled with the postmark and grid of Louisville, Ky., where they went into the Government mail for delivery. Some across-the-lines letters show the handstamp of various express company offices, according to the particular routing the letters followed. On August 26, 1861, the traffic ceased by order of the U. S. Post Office Dept. (Values are for full covers bearing the usual Louisville, Ky., or Nashville, Tenn., handstamps of the express company. Unusual express office markings are rarer and worth more.)

North to South 3c U.S. Envelope, Adams Exp. Co. Louisville, Ky., handstamp	1,500.
North to South 3c U.S. Envelope, American Letter Express Co., Ky., handstamp	2,100.
South to North 3c 1857, Adams Exp. Co., Louisville, Ky., handstamp	1,750.
South to North 3c 1857, American Letter Exp. 250, Nashville, Tenn., handstamp	2,500.
South to North 3c 1861, Adams Exp. Co., Louisville, Ky., handstamp	3,250.
South to North 3c 1857, B. Whitesides, Franklin, Ky., label	16,500.

Blockade-Run Letters from Europe to the Confederate States

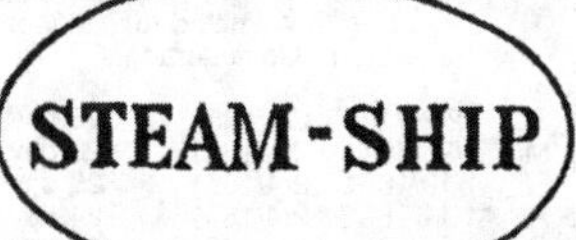

Charleston "STEAM-SHIP" in Oval Handstamp

As the Federal Fleet gradually extended its blockade of the Confederate States coastal regions, the South was forced to resort to blockade runners to carry letters to and from outside ports. These letters were all private-ship letters and never bore a foreign stamp if from Europe, nor a Confederate stamp if to Europe. The usual route from Europe was via a West Indies port, Nassau, Bahamas; Hamilton, Bermuda, or Havana, into the Southern ports of Wilmington, N.C. and Charleston, S.C. More rarely such letters came in to Savannah, Mobile and New Orleans. Letters from Europe are the only ones which are surely identified by their markings. They bore either the postmark of Wilmington, N.C., straightline "SHIP" and "12", "22", "32", etc., in manuscript; or the postmark of Charleston, S. C., "STEAMSHIP" in oval, and "12", "22", "32", etc., in manuscript. Very rarely Charleston used a straightline "SHIP" instead of "STEAMSHIP" in oval. All such letters were postage due; the single letter rate of 12c being made up of 2c for the private ship captain plus 10c for the regular single letter Confederate States rate. Over-weight letters were 22c (due), 32c, 42c, etc. A few examples are known on which Confederate General Issue stamps were used, usually as payment for forwarding postage. Covers with such stamps, or with the higher rate markings, 22c, 32, etc., are worth more.

Values are for full covers in fine condition.

Charleston, S.C. "6" handstamp	3,250.
Charleston, S.C., postmark, "STEAMSHIP," and "12" in ms.	2,750.
Charleston, S.C., postmark, "SHIP," and "12" in ms.	1,750.
Wilmington, N.C., postmark, "SHIP," and "12" in ms.	2,500.
Savannah, Ga., postmark "SHIP," and "7" in ms. (*)	4,000.
New Orleans, La. postmark, "SHIP" and "10" in ms.	5,000.

(* 7c rate: 5c postage before July 1, 1862, plus 2c for ship captain.)

Express Company Mail in the Confederacy

Southern Express Company Handstamps

Shortly after the outbreak of war in 1861, the Adams Express Company divisions operating in the South were forced to suspend operations and turned their Southern lines over to a new company organized under the title Southern Express Company. This express did the bulk of the express business in the Confederacy despite the continued opposition of the Post Office Dept. of the C.S.A. and the ravages of the contending armies upon railroads. Other companies operating in the Confederacy were: South Western Express Co. (New Orleans), Pioneer Express Company, White's Southern Express (only one example known) and some local expresses of limited operation. The first three used handstamps of various designs usually bearing the city name of the office. Postal regulation necessitated the payment of regular Confederate postal rates on letters carried by express companies, express charges being paid in addition. Important letters, particularly money letters, were entrusted to these express companies as well as goods and wares of all kinds. The express rates charged for letters are not known; probably they varied depending upon the difficulty and risk of transmittal. Covers bearing stamps and express company handstamps are very rare.

Prisoner-of-War and Flag-of-Truce Letters

Prison Censor Handstamps

By agreement between the United States and the Confederate States, military prisoners and imprisoned civilians of both sides were permitted to send censored letters to their respective countries. Such letters, if from North to South, usually bore a U.S. 3c 1861 adhesive, postmarked at a city near the prison, to pay the postage to the exchange ground near Old Point Comfort, Va.; and a 10c Confederate stamp, canceled at Richmond, Va. (or "due" handstamp) to pay the Confederate postage to destination. If from South to North, letters usually bore a 10c Confederate stamp canceled at a Southern city (or "paid" handstamp) and a U. S. 3c 1861 adhesive (or "due 3" marking) and the postmark of Old Point Comfort, Va. In addition, prison censor markings, handstamped or manuscript, the name and rank of the soldier, and "Flag of Truce, via Fortress Monroe" in manuscript usually appear on these covers. Federal prison censor handstamps of various designs are known from these prisons:

Camp Chase, Columbus, O.
David's Island, Pelham, N.Y.
Fort Delaware, Delaware City, Del.
Camp Douglas, Chicago, Ill.
Elmira Prison, Elmira, N.Y.
Johnson's Island, Sandusky, O.
Fort McHenry, Baltimore, Md.
Camp Morton, Indianapolis, Ind.
Fort Oglethorpe, Macon, Ga.
Old Capitol Prison, Washington, D.C.
Point Lookout Prison, Point Lookout, Md.
Fort Pulaski, Savannah, Ga.
Rock Island Prison, Rock Island, Ill.
Ship Island, New Orleans, La.
West's Hospital, Baltimore, Md.
U.S. General Hospital, Gettysburg, Pa.

Several other Federal prisons used manuscript censor markings.

Southern prison censor markings are always in manuscript, and do not identify the prison. The principal Southern prisons were at Richmond and Danville, Va.; Andersonville and Savannah, Ga.; Charleston, Columbia and Florence S.C.; Salisbury, N.C.; Hempstead and Tyler, Tex.

Civilians residing in both the North and the South were also, under exceptional circumstances, permitted to send Flag of Truce letters across the lines. Such covers bore no censor marking nor prison markings, but were always endorsed "via Flag of Truce".

Values will be found under various individual stamps for "on prisoner's cover" and are for the larger prisons. Prisoners' letters from the smaller prisons are much rarer. Only a very small percentage of prisoners' covers bore *both* a U.S. stamp and a Confederate stamp.

The "SOUTHERN LETTER UNPAID" Marking On Northbound Letters of Confederate Origin

DUE 3

SOUTHn LETTER
UNPAID.

By mid-May, 1861, correspondence between the North and South was difficult. In the South, postmasters were resigning and closing their accounts with Washington as the Confederacy prepared to organize its own postal system by June 1. From that date on, town marks and "paid" handstamps (and later postmasters' provisional stamps) were used in all post offices of the seceded states. The three most important Southern cities for clearing mail to the North were Memphis, Nashville and Richmond. The Richmond-Washington route was closed in April; Memphis was closed by June 1st, and mail attempting to cross the lines at these points generally ended up at the dead letter office. However, at Louisville, Kentucky, mail from the South via Nashville continued to arrive in June, July and August. On June 24, 1861, the Post Office Department advised the Louisville post office, "You will forward letters from the South for the Loyal States as unpaid, after removing postage stamps, but foreign letters in which prepayment is compulsory must come to the Dead Letter Office." However, Louisville avoided the task of "removing postage stamps," and instead prepared the "Southern Letter Unpaid" handstamp and special "due 3" markers for use. These markings were applied in the greenish-blue color of the Louisville office to letters of Southern origin that had accumulated, in addition to the usual town mark and grid of Louisville. The letters were delivered in the North as unpaid. Probably Louisville continued to forward such unpaid mail until about July 15. The marking is very rare. Other Southern mail was forwarded from Louisville as late as Aug. 27.

For listings see under U.S. 1857-61 issue, Nos. 26, 35-38. Values shown there are generally for this marking on off-cover stamps. Complete covers bearing stamps showing the full markings are valued from $7,500 upward depending upon the stamps, other postal markings and unusual usages, and condition. Fraudulent covers exist.

Trans-Mississippi Express Mail-the 40c Rate

From the fall of New Orleans on April 24, 1862, the entire reach of the Mississippi River was threatened by the Federal fleets. Late in 1862 the Confederacy experienced difficulty in maintaining regular mail routes trans-Mississippi to the Western states. Private express companies began to carry some mail, but by early 1863 when the Meridian-Jackson-Vicksburg-Shreveport route was seriously menaced, the Post Office Department of the Confederate States was forced to inaugurate an express mail service by contracting with a private company the name of which remains undisclosed. The eastern termini were at Meridian and Brandon, Miss.; the western at Shreveport and Alexandria, La. Letters, usually endorsed "via Meridian (or Brandon)" if going West; "via Shreveport (or Alexandria)" if going East were deposited in any Confederate post office. The rate was 40c per ½ ounce or less. Such Trans-Mississippi Express Mail upon arrival at a terminus was carried by couriers in a devious route across the Mississippi and returned to the regular mails at the nearest terminus on the other side of the river. The precise date of the beginning of the Trans-Mississippi service is not known. The earliest date of use so far seen is November 2, 1863 and the latest use February 9, 1865. These covers can be identified by the written endorsement of the route, but particularly by the rate since many bore no route endorsements.

Strips of four of 10c engraved stamps, pairs of the 20c stamp and various combinations of 10c stamps and the 5c London or Local prints are known; also handstamped Paid 40c marking. No identifying handstamps were used, merely the postmark of the office which received the letter originally. Values for Trans-Mississippi Express covers will be found under various stamps of the General Issues.

A 50c Preferred Mail Express rate, announced in April, 1863, preceded the Trans-Mississippi Express Mail 40c rate. One cover showing this rate is known.

Packet and Steamboat Covers and Markings

Letters carried on Confederate packets operating on coastal routes or up and down the inland waterways were usually handstamped with the name of the packet or marked STEAM or STEAMBOAT. Either United States stamps of the 1857 issue or stamped envelopes of the 1853 or 1860 issues have been found so used, as well as Confederate Postmasters' Provisional and General Issue stamps. Some specially designed pictorial or imprinted packet boat covers also exist. All are scarce and command values from $750 upward for handstamped United States envelopes and from $1,250 up for covers bearing Confederate stamps.

TABLE OF SECESSION

	Ordinance of Secession	Admitted to Confederacy	Period for Use of U.S. Stamps As Independent State	Total to 5/31/1861*
SC	12/20/1860	2/4/1861	46 days	163 days
MS	1/9/1861	2/4/1861	26 days	143 days
FL	1/10/1861	2/4/1861	25 days	142 days
AL	1/11/1861	2/4/1861	24 days	141 days
GA	1/19/1861	2/4/1861	16 days	133 days
LA	1/26/1861	2/4/1861	9 days	126 days
TX	2/1/1861	3/6/1861	33 days	120 days
VA	4/17/1861	5/7/1861	20 days	45 days
AR	5/6/1861	5/18/1861	12 days	26 days
TN	5/6/1861	7/2/1861	57 days	26 days
NC	5/20/1861	5/27/1861	7 days	12 days

* The use of United States stamps in the seceded States was prohibited after May 31, 1861.

TX- Ordinance of Secession adopted Feb. 1. Popular vote to secede Feb. 23, effective Mar. 2, 1861.

VA- Ordinance of Secession adopted. Admitted to Confederacy May 7. Scheduled election of May 23 ratified the Ordinance of Secession.

TN- Ordinance passed to "submit to vote of the people a Declaration of Independence, and for other purposes." Adopted May 6. Election took place June 8. General Assembly ratified election June 24.

The Confederate postal laws did not provide the franking privilege for any mail except official correspondence of the Post Office Department. Such letters could be sent free only when enclosed in officially imprinted envelopes individually signed by the official using them. These envelopes were prepared and issued for Post Office Department use.

The imprints were on United States envelopes of 1853-61 issue, and also on commercial envelopes of various sizes and colors. When officially signed and mailed, they were postmarked, usually at Richmond, Va., with printed or handstamped "FREE". Envelopes are occasionally found unused and unsigned, and more rarely, signed but unused. When such official envelopes were used on other than official Post Office Department business, Confederate stamps were used.

Semi-official envelopes also exist bearing imprints of other government departments, offices, armies, states, etc. Regular postage was required to carry such envelopes through the mails.

CONFEDERATE STATES OF AMERICA,
POST OFFICE DEPARTMENT,
OFFICIAL BUSINESS,
John H Reagan
POSTMASTER GENERAL.

Confederate States of America,
POST OFFICE DEPARTMENT,
OFFICIAL BUSINESS
John B. A. Dimitry
Act. CHIEF CLERK P. O. DEPARTMENT

Typical Imprints of Official Envelopes of the Post Office Department. (Many variations of type, style and wording exist.)

Office	Signature
Postmaster General	John H. Reagan
Chief of the Contract Bureau	H. St. Geo. Offutt
Chief of the Appointment Bureau	B. N. Clements
Chief of the Finance Bureau	Jno. L. Harrell
Chief of the Finance Bureau	J. L. Lancaster
Chief of the Finance Bureau	A. Dimitry
Dead Letter Office	A. Dimitry
Dead Letter Office	Jno. L. Harrell
Chief Clerk, P. O. Department	B. Fuller
Chief Clerk	W. D. Miller
Auditor's Office	W. W. Lester
Auditor's Office	B. Baker
Auditor's Office	J. W. Robertson
First Auditor's Office, Treasury Department	J. W. Robertson
First Auditor's Office, Treasury Department	B. Baker
Third Auditor's Office	A. Moise
Third Auditor's Office	I. W. M. Harris
Agency, Post Office Dept. Trans-Miss.	Jas. H. Starr

PROOFS

1861

(1)- Die on Glazed Card

(1a)- Die on Wove Paper

(5)- Plate on Wove Paper

(6)- Plate on Thin Card

(7)- Plate on Thick Ribbed Paper

1P	(5)	5c **green,** plate on wove paper	*1,500.*
2P	(5)	10c **blue,** plate on wove paper	*1,500.*
2TC	(5)	10c **black,** plate on wove paper (stone Y)	*3,000.*

1862

6P	(1)	5c **light blue,** die on glazed card	600.
6P, 14P	(1)	5c **blue** & 1c **orange**, composite die proof, 20x90mm card	*6,000.*
6P	(5)	5c **light blue,** plate on wove paper	150.
		Pair with gutter between	375.
6TC	(1a)	5c **dark blue,** die on woven paper	600.
6TC	(5)	5c **gray blue,** plate on wove paper	600.
6TC	(1)	5c **black,** die on glazed card	900.
6TC	(5)	5c **black,** plate on wove paper	1,000.
6TC	(1)	5c **pink,** die on glazed card	900.
7TC	(5)	5c **carmine,** plate on wove paper	850.
7TC	(6)	5c **carmine,** plate on thin card	750.

1863

8TC	(1a)	2c **black,** die on wove paper	1,750.
9TC	(1a)	10c **black,** die on wove paper	1,500.
11TC	(1a)	10c **black,** die on wove paper	1,100.
12P	(7)	10c **deep blue,** plate on thick ribbed paper	750.
13P	(1a)	20c **green,** die on wove paper	*4,000.*
13TC	(1a)	20c **red brown,** die on wove paper	*4,000.*

1862

14P	(1)	1c **orange,** die on glazed card	*2,000.*
14TC	(1)	1c **black,** die on glazed card	*2,500.*
14TC	(5)	1c **light yellow brown,** plate on wove paper	800.

Essay Die Proofs

In working up the final dies, proofs of incomplete designs in various stages were made. Usually dated in typeset lines, they are very rare. Others, of the 10c (No. 12) and the 20c (No. 13) were proofs made as essays from the dies. They are deeply engraved and printed in deep shades of the issued colors, but show only small differences from the stamps as finally issued. All are very rare.

Specimen Overprints

The De La Rue typographed 5c and 1c are known with "SPECIMEN" overprinted diagonally, also horizontally for 1c.

Counterfeits

In 1935 a set of 12 lithographed imitations, later known as the "Springfield facsimiles," appeared in plate form. They are in approximately normal colors on yellowish soft wove paper of modern manufacture.

CANAL ZONE

The Canal Zone, a strip of territory with an area of about 552 square miles following generally the line of the Canal, was under the jurisdiction of the United States, 1904-1979, and under the joint jurisdiction of the United States and Panama, 1979-1999, when the Canal, in its entirety, reverted to Panama.

The Canal organization underwent two distinct and fundamental changes. The construction of the Canal and the general administration of civil affairs were performed by the Isthmian Canal Commission under the provisions of the Spooner Act. This was supplanted in April, 1914, by the Panama Canal Act which established the organization known as The Panama Canal. This was an independent government agency which included both the operation and maintenance of the waterway and civil government in the Canal Zone. Most of the quasi-business enterprises relating to the Canal operation were conducted by the Panama Railroad, an adjunct of The Panama Canal.

A basic change in the mode of operations took effect July 1, 1951, under provisions of Public Law 841 of the 81st Congress. This in effect transferred the Canal operations to the Panama Railroad Co., which had been made a federal government corporation in 1948, and changed its name to the Panama Canal Co. Simultaneously the civil government functions of The Panama Canal, including the postal service, were renamed the Canal Zone Government. The organization therefore consisted of two units-the Panama Canal Co. and Canal Zone Government-headed by an individual who was president of the company and governor of the Canal Zone. His appointment as governor was made by the president of the United States, subject to confirmation by the Senate, and he was ex-officio president of the company.

The Canal Zone Government functioned as an independent government agency, and was under direct supervision of the president of the United States who delegated this authority to the Secretary of the Army.

The Panama Canal is 50 miles long from deep water in the Atlantic to deep water in the Pacific. It runs from northwest to southeast with the Atlantic entrance being 33.5 miles north and 27 miles west of the Pacific entrance. The airline distance between the two entrances is 43 miles. It requires about eight hours for an average ship to transit the Canal. Transportation between the Atlantic and Pacific sides of the Isthmus is available by railway or highway.

The Canal Zone Postal Service began operating June 24, 1904, when nine post offices were opened in connection with the construction of the Panama Canal. It ceased Sept. 30, 1979, and the Panama Postal Service took over.

Italicized numbers in parentheses indicate quantity issued.

100 CENTAVOS = 1 PESO
100 CENTESIMOS = 1 BALBOA
100 CENTS = 1 DOLLAR

Catalogue values for unused stamps are for Never Hinged items beginning with No. 118 in the regular postage section and No. C6 in the airpost section.

Map of Panama — A1

Violet to Violet Blue Handstamp on Panama Nos. 72, 72a-72c, 78, 79.

On the 2c "PANAMA" is normally 13mm long. On the 5c and 10c it measures about 15mm.

On the 2c, "PANAMA" reads up on the upper half of the sheet and down on the lower half. On the 5c and 10c, "PANAMA" reads up at left and down at right on each stamp.

On the 2c only, varieties exist with inverted "V" for "A," accent on "A," inverted "N," etc., in "PANAMA."

1904, June 24 Engr. Unwmk. *Perf. 12*

No.	Type	Description	Unused	Used
1	A1	2c **rose,** both "PANAMA" reading up or down *(2600)*	550.	425.
		Single on post card		*1,650.*
		Strip of 3 on cover		1,500.
		Block of 4	2,500.	2,100.
		"PANAMA" 15mm long *(260)*	600.	600.
		"P NAMA"	600.	600.
a.		"CANAL ZONE" inverted *(100)*	*950.*	850.
b.		"CANAL ZONE" double	*2,500.*	2,000.
c.		"CANAL ZONE" double, both inverted	*20,000.*	
d.		"PANAMA" reading down and up *(52)*	700.	650.
e.		As "d," "CANAL ZONE" invtd.	*9,000.*	*7,000.*
f.		Vert. pair, "PANAMA" reading up on top 2c, down on other	*2,100.*	*2,100.*
g.		As "f," "CANAL ZONE" inverted	*20,000.*	
2	A1	5c **blue** *(7800)*	250.	175.
		On cover		240.
		First day cover		*7,500.*
		Block of 4	1,200.	950.
		Left "PANAMA" 2¼mm below bar *(156)*	525.	500.
		Colon between right "PANAMA" and bar *(156)*	525.	500.
a.		"CANAL ZONE" inverted	725.	600.
		On cover		*800.*
b.		"CANAL ZONE" double	2,250.	1,500.
c.		Pair, one without "CANAL ZONE" overprint	*5,000.*	*5,000.*
d.		"CANAL ZONE" overprint diagonal, reading down to right	750.	700.
3	A1	10c **yellow** *(4946)*	350.	250.
		On cover		325.
		First day cover		*5,000.*
		Block of 4	1,500.	1,150.
		Left "PANAMA" 2¼mm below bar *(100)*	625.	575.
		Colon between right "PANAMA" and bar *(100)*	600.	550.
a.		"CANAL ZONE" inverted *(200)*	725.	600.
		On cover		*800.*
b.		"CANAL ZONE" double		*15,000.*
c.		Pair, one without "CANAL ZONE" overprint	6,000.	5,000.

Cancellations consist of town and/or bars in magenta or black, or a mixture of both colors.

Nos. 1-3 were withdrawn July 17, 1904.

Forgeries of the "Canal Zone" overprint and cancellations are numerous.

United States Nos. 300, 319, 304, 306 and 307 Overprinted in Black

CANAL ZONE
PANAMA

1904, July 18 Wmk. 191

No.	Type	Description	Unused	Used
4	A115	1c **blue green** *(43,738)*	32.50	22.50
		green	32.50	22.50
		On cover		75.00
		Block of 4	150.00	140.00
		P# strip of 3, Impt.	140.00	
		P# block of 6, Impt.	875.00	
5	A129	2c **carmine** *(68,414)*	30.00	25.00
		On cover		75.00
		Block of 4	125.00	125.00
		P# strip of 3, Impt.	125.00	
		P# block of 6, Impt.	950.00	
a.		2c **scarlet**	35.00	30.00
6	A119	5c **blue** *(20,858)*	110.00	65.00
		On cover		250.00
		Block of 4	525.00	325.00
		P# strip of 3, Impt.	475.00	
		P# block of 6, Impt.	1,450.	
7	A121	8c **violet black** *(7932)*	175.00	85.00
		On cover		—
		Block of 4	800.00	450.00
		P# strip of 3, Impt.	725.00	
		P# block of 6, Impt.	3,500.	
8	A122	10c **pale red brown** *(7856)*	150.00	90.00
		On cover		—
		Block of 4	675.00	475.00
		P# strip of 3, Impt.	650.00	
		P# block of 6, Impt.	2,750.	
		Nos. 4-8 (5)	497.50	287.50

Nos. 4-8 frequently show minor broken letters.

Cancellations consist of circular town and/or bars in black, blue or magenta.

Beware of fake overprints.

A2

A3

CANAL
ZONE
Regular Type

CANAL
ZONE
Antique Type

The Canal Zone overprint on stamps Nos. 9-15 and 18-20 was made with a plate which had six different stages, each with its peculiar faults and errors. Stage 1: Broken CA-L, broken L, A-L spaced, on Nos. 9, 10, 12-15. Stage 2: broken L, Z, N, E, on Nos. 9, 10, 12-14. Stage 3: same as 2 with additional antique ZONE, on Nos. 9, 11-14, 18. Stage 4: same as 3 with additional antique CANAL on Nos. 9, 12, 13. Stage 5: broken E and letters L, Z, N, and words CANAL and ZONE in antique type on Nos. 12-14, 19, 20. Stage 6: same as 5 except for additional antique Z on stamp which had antique L, on No. 12. The Panama overprints can be distinguished by the different shades of the red overprint, the width of the bar, and the word PANAMA. No.

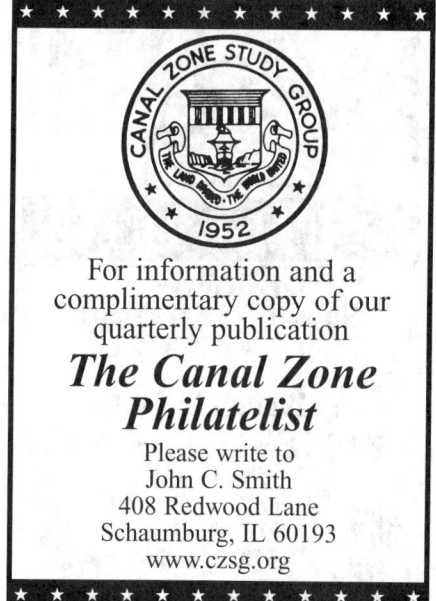

11 has two different Panama overprints; No. 12 has six; No. 13 five; No. 14 two; and Nos. 15, 18-20, one each. In the "8cts" surcharge of Nos. 14 and 15, there are three varieties of the figure "8." The bar is sometimes misplaced so that it appears on the bottom of the stamp instead of the top.

1904-06 **Unwmk.**

Black Overprint on Stamps of Panama

9	A2	1c **green** *(319,800) Dec. 12, 1904*	2.75	2.25
		On cover		12.50
		Block of 4	12.00	12.00
		Spaced "A L" in "CANAL" *(700)*	110.00	100.00
		"ON" of "ZONE" dropped	300.00	275.00
a.		"CANAL" in antique type *(500)*	100.00	100.00
b.		"ZONE" in antique type *(1500)*	70.00	70.00
c.		Inverted overprint	*5,000.*	*2,250.*
d.		Double overprint	*2,000.*	*1,500.*
10	A2	2c **rose** *(367,500) Dec. 12, 1904*	4.50	3.00
		On cover		17.50
		Block of 4	21.00	15.00
		Spaced "A L" of "CANAL" *(1700)*	85.00	85.00
		"ON" of "ZONE" dropped	400.00	400.00
a.		Inverted overprint	225.00	275.00
b.		"L" of "CANAL" sideways	2,500.	2,500.

"PANAMA" (15mm long) reading up at left, down at right

Overprint "CANAL ZONE" in Black, "PANAMA" and Bar in Red

11	A3	2c **rose** *(150,000) Dec. 9, 1905*	7.50	5.00
		On cover		50.00
		Block of 4	35.00	27.50
		Inverted "M" in "PANAMA" *(3,000)*	45.00	40.00
		"PANAMA" 16mm long *(3000)*	45.00	40.00
a.		"ZONE" in antique type *(1500)*	200.00	200.00
b.		"PANAMA" overprint inverted, bar at bottom *(200)*	375.00	375.00
12	A3	5c **blue** *(400,000) Dec. 12, 1904*	8.00	3.75
		On cover		100.00
		Block of 4	35.00	25.00
		Spaced "A L" in "CANAL" *(300)*	90.00	80.00
		"PAMANA" reading up *(2800)*	75.00	70.00
		"PAMANA" reading down *(400)*	200.00	180.00
		"PANAMA" 16mm long *(1300)*	40.00	37.50
		Inverted "M" in "PANAMA" *(1300)*	40.00	37.50
		Right "PANAMA" 5mm below bar *(600)*	75.00	70.00
		"PANAM"	70.00	65.00
		"PANAAM" at right	950.00	900.00
		"PAN MA"	75.00	70.00
		"ANAMA"	80.00	75.00
a.		"CANAL" in antique type *(2750)*	75.00	65.00
b.		"ZONE" in antique type *(2950)*	75.00	65.00
c.		"CANAL ZONE" double *(200)*	700.00	700.00
d.		"PANAMA" double *(120)*	1,050.	1,000.
e.		"PANAMA" inverted, bar at bottom		1,250.
13	A3	10c **yellow** *(64,900) Dec. 12, 1904*	22.50	12.50
		On cover		125.00
		Block of 4	110.00	62.50
		Spaced "A L" in "CANAL" *(200)*	200.00	180.00
		"PANAMA" 16mm long *(400)*	75.00	65.00
		"PAMANA" reading down *(200)*	200.00	180.00
		Invtd. "M" in "PANAMA" *(400)*	100.00	90.00
		Right "PANAMA" 5mm below bar *(398)*	150.00	140.00
		Left "PANAMA" touches bar *(400)*	200.00	160.00
a.		"CANAL" in antique type *(200)*	200.00	200.00
b.		"ZONE" in antique type *(400)*	175.00	160.00
c.		"PANAMA" ovpt. double *(80)*	650.00	650.00
d.		"PANAMA" overprint in red brown *(5000)*	27.50	27.50
		"PANAMA" ovpt. in orange red	32.50	32.50

With Added Surcharge in Red

a

There are three varieties of "8" in the surcharge on #14-15.

14	A3	8c on 50c **bister brown** *(27,900) Dec. 12, 1904*	32.50	22.50
		On cover		175.00
		Block of 4	190.00	140.00
		Spaced "A L" in "CANAL" *(194)*	175.00	160.00
		Right "PANAMA" 5mm below bar *(438)*	175.00	160.00
a.		"ZONE" in antique type *(25)*	1,100.	1,100.
b.		"CANAL ZONE" inverted *(200)*	425.00	400.00
c.		"PANAMA" overprint in rose brown *(6000)*	40.00	40.00
d.		As "c," "CANAL" in antique type *(10)*	2,000.	
e.		As "c," "ZONE" in antique type *(10)*	2,000.	
f.		As "c," "8 cts" double *(30)*	*850.00*	
g.		As "c," "8" omitted	*4,250.*	

Nos. 11-14 are overprinted or surcharged on Panama Nos. 77, 77e, 78, 78c, 78d, 78f, 78g, 78h, 79 79c, 79e, 79g and 81 respectively.

Panama No. 74a, 74b Overprinted "CANAL ZONE" in Regular Type in Black and Surcharged Type "a" in Red

Both "PANAMA" (13mm long) Reading Up

15	A3(a)	8c on 50c **bister brown** *(435) Dec. 12, 1904*	2,600.	*4,500.*
		On cover		*10,000.*
		Block of 4	*11,500.*	
		"PANAMA" 15mm long *(50)*	2,750.	*4,750.*
		"P NAMA"	5,000.	
		Spaced "A L" in "CANAL" *(5)*	5,000.	
a.		"PANAMA" reading down and up *(10)*	*7,500.*	—

On No. 15 with original gum the gum is almost always disturbed.

Map of Panama — A4

Panama Nos. 19 and 21 Surcharged in Black:

a b

c d e f

1906

There were three printings of each denomination, differing principally in the relative position of the various parts of the surcharges. Varieties occur with inverted "V" for the final "A" in "PANAMA," "CA" spaced, "ZO" spaced, "2c" spaced, accents in various positions, and with bars shifted so that two bars appear on top or bottom of the stamp (either with or without the corresponding bar on top or bottom) and sometimes with only one bar at top or bottom.

16	A4	1c on 20c **violet,** type a *(100,000) Mar.*	2.00	1.60
		On cover		10.00
		Block of 4	9.00	7.50
a.		Type b *(100,000) May*	2.00	1.60
		On cover		10.00
		Block of 4	9.00	7.50
b.		Type c *(300,000) Sept.*	2.00	1.60
		On cover		10.00
		Block of 4	10.50	7.50
		Spaced C A	13.00	12.00
c.		As No. 16, double surcharge		*2,000.*
17	A4	2c on 1p **lake,** type d *(200,000) Mar.*	2.75	2.75
		On cover		12.00
		Block of 4	14.00	12.50
a.		Type e *(200,000) May*	2.75	2.75
		On cover		12.00
		Block of 4	14.00	12.50
b.		Type f *(50,000) Sept.*	20.00	20.00
		On cover		75.00
		Block of 4	90.00	90.00

Panama Nos. 74, 74a and 74b Overprinted "CANAL ZONE" in Regular Type in Black and Surcharged in Red

8 cts. 8 cts
b c

1905-06

Both "PANAMA" Reading Up

18	A3(b)	8c on 50c **bister brown** *(17,500) Nov. 1905*	55.00	50.00
		On cover		225.00
		Block of 4	250.00	230.00
		"PANAMA" 15mm long *(1750)*	90.00	80.00
		"P NAMA"	125.00	110.00
a.		"ZONE" in antique type *(175)*	200.00	180.00
b.		"PANAMA" reading down and up *(350)*	175.00	160.00
19	A3(c)	8c on 50c **bister brown** *(19,000) Apr. 23, 1906*	55.00	45.00
		On cover		225.00
		Block of 4	250.00	200.00
		"PANAMA" 15mm long *(1900)*	85.00	70.00
		"P NAMA"	90.00	
a.		"CANAL" in antique type *(190)*	210.00	180.00
b.		"ZONE" in antique type *(190)*	210.00	180.00
c.		"8 cts" double	*1,100.*	*1,100.*
d.		"PANAMA" reading down and up *(380)*	110.00	90.00

On Nos. 18-19 with original gum, the gum is usually disturbed.

Panama No. 81 Overprinted "CANAL ZONE" in Regular Type in Black and Surcharged in Red Type "c" plus Period

"PANAMA" reading up and down

20	A3(c)	8c on 50c **bister brown** *(19,600) Sept. 1906*	45.00	40.00
		On cover		200.00
		Block of 4	190.00	175.00
		"PAMANA" reading up *(392)*	120.00	110.00
a.		"CANAL" antique type *(196)*	200.00	180.00
b.		"ZONE" in antique type *(196)*	200.00	180.00
c.		"8 cts" omitted *(50)*	750.00	750.00
d.		"8 cts" double	*1,500.*	
e.		"cts 8"		—

Nos. 14 and 18-20 exist without CANAL ZONE overprint but were not regularly issued. Forgeries of the overprint varieties of Nos. 9-15 and 18-20 are known.

Vasco Núñez de Balboa — A5

Fernández de Córdoba — A6

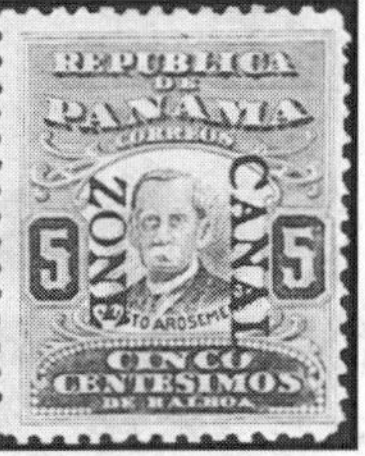
Justo Arosemena — A7

Manuel J. Hurtado — A8

José de Obaldía — A9

Engraved by Hamilton Bank Note Co.
Overprinted in Black by Isthmian Canal Commission Press.

1906-07 **Unwmk.** ***Perf. 12***

Overprint Reading Up

21 A6 2c **red & black** *(50,000) Oct. 29, 1906* 25.00 25.00
On cover 50.00
Block of 4 125.00 175.00
a. "CANAL" only *4,000.*

Overprint Reading Down

22 A5 1c **green & black** *(2,000,000) Jan. 14, 1907* 2.25 1.25
dull green & black 2.25 1.25
On cover 5.00
Block of 4 10.00 8.00
"ANA" for "CANAL" *(1000)* 70.00 70.00
"CAN L" for "CANAL" 80.00 80.00
"ONE" for "ZONE" *(3000)* 80.00 80.00
a. Horiz. pair, imperf. btwn. *(50)* 1,300. 1,300.
b. Vert. pair, imperf. btwn. *(20)* *1,750.* *1,750.*
c. Vert. pair, imperf. horiz. *(20)* *2,250.* *1,750.*
d. Inverted overprint reading up *(100)* 550.00 550.00
e. Double overprint *(300)* 275.00 275.00
f. Double overprint, one inverted 1,400. 1,350.
g. Invtd. center, ovpt. reading up *3,500.* *3,500.*
Pair on cover *10,000.*
h. Horiz. pair, imperf vert. —
23 A6 2c **red & black** *(2,370,000) Nov. 25, 1906* 3.25 1.40
scarlet & black, *1907* 3.25 1.40
On cover 6.00
Block of 4 14.00 9.00
"CAN L" for "CANAL" 45.00
a. Horizontal pair, imperf. between *(20)* 2,000. 1,750.
b. Vertical pair, one without overprint 1,750. 1,750.
c. Double overprint *(100)* 500.00 500.00
d. Double overprint, one diagonal 750.00 750.00
e. Double overprint, one diagonal, in pair with normal 1,750.
f. 2c carmine red & black, *Sept. 9, 1907* 5.00 2.75
g. As "f," inverted center and overprint reading up *6,000.*
On cover *12,000.*
h. As "d," one "ZONE CANAL" *4,000.*
i. "CANAL" double *4,000.*
24 A7 5c **ultramarine & black** *(1,390,000) Dec. 1906* 6.50 2.25
light ultramarine & black 6.50 2.25
blue & black, *Sept. 16, 1907* 6.50 2.25
dark blue & black 6.50 2.25
dull blue & black 6.50 2.25
light blue & black 6.50 2.25
On cover 40.00
Block of 4 27.50 20.00
"CAN L" for "CANAL" 60.00
c. Double overprint *(200)* 450.00 350.00
d. "CANAL" only *(10)* *4,000.*
e. "ZONE CANAL" *4,500.*
25 A8 8c **purple & black** *(170,000) Dec. 1906* 22.50 8.00
On cover 100.00
Block of 4 125.00 55.00
a. Horizontal pair, imperf. between and at left margin *(34)* *2,000.* —

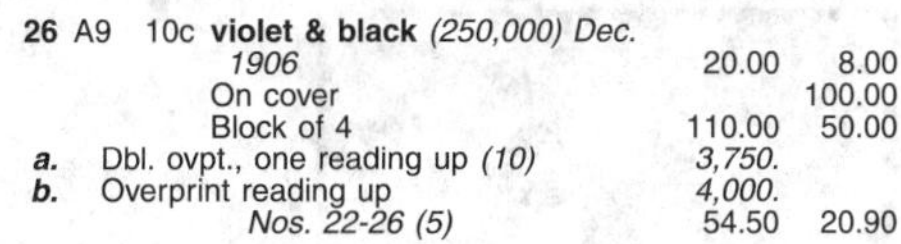

26 A9 10c **violet & black** *(250,000) Dec. 1906* 20.00 8.00
On cover 100.00
Block of 4 110.00 50.00
a. Dbl. ovpt., one reading up *(10)* *3,750.*
b. Overprint reading up *4,000.*
Nos. 22-26 (5) 54.50 20.90

The early printings of this series were issued on soft, thick, porous-textured paper, while later printings of all except No. 25 appear on hard, thin, smooth-textured paper.

Normal spacing of the early printings is 7¼mm between the words; later printings, 6¾mm. Nos. 22 and 26 exist imperf. between stamp and sheet margin. Nos. 22-25 occur with "CA" of "CANAL" spaced ½mm further apart on position No. 50 of the setting.

Córdoba — A11

Arosemena — A12

Hurtado — A13

José de Obaldía — A14

Engraved by American Bank Note Co.

1909

Overprint Reading Down

27 A11 2c **vermilion & black** *(500,000) May 11, 1909* 12.50 5.50
On cover 15.00
First day cover 750.00
Block of 4 57.50 30.00
a. Horizontal pair, one without overprint *2,600.*
b. Vert. pair, one without ovpt. *3,500.*
28 A12 5c **deep blue & black** *(200,000) May 28, 1909* 45.00 12.50
On cover 60.00
Block of 4 200.00 60.00
29 A13 8c **violet & black** *(50,000) May 25, 1909* 37.50 14.00
On cover 90.00
Block of 4 190.00 82.50
30 A14 10c **violet & black** *(100,000) Jan. 19, 1909* 40.00 15.00
On cover 85.00
Block of 4 200.00 85.00
a. Horizontal pair, one with "ZONE" omitted *2,400.*
b. Vertical pair, one without overprint *3,000.*

Nos. 27-30 occur with "CA" spaced (position 50).
Do not confuse No. 27 with Nos. 39d or 53a.
On No. 30a, the stamp with "ZONE" omitted is also missing most of "CANAL."

Vasco Núñez de Balboa — A15

Engraved, Printed and Overprinted by American Bank Note Co.
Black Overprint Reading Up

Type I

Type I Overprint: "C" with serifs both top and bottom. "L," "Z" and "E" with slanting serifs.

Compare Type I overprint with Types II to V illustrated before Nos. 38, 46, 52 and 55. Illustrations of Types I to V are considerably enlarged and do not show actual spacing between lines of overprint.

1909-10

31 A15 1c **dark green & black** *(4,000,000) Nov. 8, 1909* 4.00 1.60
On cover 5.00
Block of 4 17.50 8.50
a. Inverted center and overprint reading down *22,500.*
c. Bklt. pane of 6, handmade, perf. margins *575.00*
32 A11 2c **vermilion & black** *(4,000,000) Nov. 8, 1909* 4.50 1.60
On cover 5.00
Block of 4 20.00 8.50
a. Vert. pair, imperf. horiz. 1,000. 1,000.
c. Bklt. pane of 6, handmade, perf. margins *750.00*
d. Double overprint —
33 A12 5c **deep blue & black** *(2,000,000) Nov. 8, 1909* 15.00 4.00
On cover 40.00
Block of 4 70.00 20.00
a. Double overprint *(200)* 375.00 375.00
34 A13 8c **violet & black** *(200,000) Mar. 18, 1910* 11.00 5.25
On cover 75.00
Block of 4 50.00 27.50
a. Vertical pair, one without overprint *(10)* *1,500.*
35 A14 10c **violet & black** *(100,000) Nov. 8, 1909* 50.00 20.00

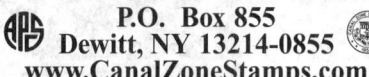

On cover 100.00
Block of 4 225.00 100.00
Nos. 31-35 (5) 84.50 32.45

Normal spacing between words of overprint on No. 31 is 10mm and on Nos. 32 to 35, 8½mm. Minor spacing variations are known.

A16

A17

1911, Jan. 14

36 A16 10c on 13c **gray** *(476,700)* 6.00 2.25
On cover 50.00
Block of 4 30.00 15.00
a. "10 cts" inverted 325.00 275.00
b. "10 cts" omitted 275.00

The "10 cts" surcharge was applied by the Isthmian Canal Commission Press after the overprinted stamps were received from the American Bank Note Co.

Many used stamps offered as No. 36b are merely No. 36 from which the surcharge has been removed with chemicals.

1914, Jan. 6

37 A17 10c **gray** *(200,000)* 55.00 12.50
On cover 85.00
Block of 4 230.00 65.00

Black Overprint Reading Up

Type II

Type II Overprint: "C" with serif at top only. "L" and "E" with vertical serifs. "O" tilts to left.

1912-16

38 A15 1c **green & black** *(3,000,000) July 1913* 11.00 3.00
On cover 5.50
Block of 4 50.00 20.00
a. Vertical pair, one without overprint 1,750. 1,750.
On cover *2,250.*
b. Booklet pane of 6, imperf. margins *(120,000)* 625.00
c. Booklet pane of 6, handmade, perf. margins *1,000.*

39 A11 2c **vermilion & black** *(7,500,000) Dec. 1912* 8.50 1.40
orange vermilion & black, *1916* 8.50 1.40
On cover 5.00
Block of 4 42.50 8.00
a. Horiz. pair, right stamp without overprint (20) *1,250.*
b. Horiz. pair, left stamp without overprint (10) *1,750.*
c. Booklet pane of 6, imperf. margins *(194,868)* 500.00
d. Overprint reading down 175.00
e. As "d," inverted center 575.00 *750.00*
f. As "e," booklet pane of 6, handmade, perf. margins *8,000.*
g. As "c," handmade, perf. margins *1,000.*
h. As No. 39, "CANAL" only 1,100.

40 A12 5c **deep blue & black** *(2,300,000) Dec. 1912* 22.50 3.25
On cover 35.00
Block of 4 105.00 15.00
a. With Cordoba portrait of 2c *8,750.*

41 A14 10c **violet & black** *(200,000) Feb. 1916* 47.50 8.50
On cover 80.00
Block of 4 240.00 40.00

Normal spacing between words of overprint on the first printing of Nos. 38-40 is 8½mm and on the second printing 9¼mm. The spacing of the single printing of No. 41 and the imperf. margin booklet pane printings of Nos. 38 and 39 is 7¾mm. Minor spacing variations are known.

Map of Panama Canal — A18

Balboa Taking Possession of the Pacific Ocean — A19

Gatun Locks — A20

Culebra Cut — A21

Engraved, Printed and Overprinted by American Bank Note Co.

1915, Mar. 1

Blue Overprint, Type II

42 A18 1c **dark green & black** *(100,000)* 8.50 6.50
On cover 17.50
Block of 4 37.50 30.00
First day cover 200.00

43 A19 2c **carmine & black** *(100,000)* 10.00 4.25
vermilion & black 10.00 4.25
On cover 25.00
First day cover 150.00
Block of 4 42.50 21.00

44 A20 5c **blue & black** *(100,000)* 11.00 5.75
On cover 55.00
Block of 4 50.00 29.00
First day cover 500.00

45 A21 10c **orange & black** *(50,000)* 22.50 11.00
On cover 60.00
Block of 4 95.00 55.00
First day cover 500.00

Normal spacing between words of overprint is 9¼mm on all four values except position No. 61 which is 10mm.

Black Overprint Reading Up

Type III

Type III Overprint: Similar to Type I but letters appear thinner, particularly the lower bar of "L," "Z" and "E." Impressions are often light, rough and irregular.

Engraved and Printed by American Bank Note Co.
Overprint applied by
Panama Canal Press, Mount Hope, C.Z.

1915-20

46 A15 1c **green & black**, *Dec. 1915* 160.00 95.00
light green & black, *1920* 225.00 160.00
On cover 160.00
Pair on cover *500.00*
Block of 4 725.00 500.00
a. Overprint reading down *(200)* 375.00
b. Double overprint *(180)* 275.00
c. "ZONE" double *(2)* *4,250.*
d. Double overprint, one reads "ZONE CANAL" *(18)* 1,750.

47 A11 2c **orange vermilion & black,** *Aug. 1920* 3,250. 100.00
On cover 375.00
Block of 4 *13,500.* 800.00

48 A12 5c **deep blue & black,** *Dec. 1915* 500.00 175.00
On cover 750.00
Block of 4 *2,400.* 850.00

Normal spacing between words of overprint on Nos. 46-48 is 9¼mm. This should not be confused with an abnormal 9¼mm spacing of the 2c and 5c values of type I, which are fairly common in singles, particularly used. Blocks of the abnormal spacing are rare.

A22

S. S. "Panama" in Culebra Cut — A23

S. S. "Cristobal" in Gatun Locks — A24

Engraved, Printed and Overprinted by American Bank Note Co.

1917, Jan. 23

Blue Overprint, Type II

49 A22 12c **purple & black** *(314,914)* 17.50 5.50
On cover 50.00
First day cover —
Block of 4 87.50 30.00

50 A23 15c **bright blue & black** 55.00 25.00
On cover 135.00
Block of 4 250.00 125.00

51 A24 24c **yellow brown & black** 45.00 15.00
On cover 325.00
Block of 4 200.00 90.00

Normal spacing between words of overprint is 11¼mm.

Black Overprint Reading Up

Type IV

Type IV Overprint: "C" thick at bottom, "E" with center bar same length as top and bottom bars.

Engraved, Printed and Overprinted by American Bank Note Co.

1918-20

52 A15 1c **green & black** *(2,000,000) Jan. 1918* 32.50 11.00
On cover 12.50
Block of 4 150.00 47.50
a. Overprint reading down 175.00 —
b. Booklet pane of 6 *(60,000)* 650.00
c. Booklet pane of 6, left vertical row of 3 without overprint *7,500.*
d. Booklet pane of 6, right vertical row of 3, with double overprint *7,500.*
e. Horiz. bklt. pair, left stamp without overprint *3,000.*
f. Horiz. bklt. pair, right stamp with double overprint *3,000.*

53 A11 2c **vermilion & black** *(2,000,000) Nov. 1918* 110.00 7.00
On cover 11.00
Block of 4 500.00 35.00
a. Overprint reading down 150.00 150.00
b. Horiz. pair, right stamp without ovpt. 2,000.
c. Booklet pane of 6 *(34,000)* 1,000.
d. Booklet pane of 6, left vertical row of 3 without overprint *15,000.*
e. Horiz. bklt. pair, left stamp without overprint *3,000.*
On cover (unique) *4,500.*

54 A12 5c **deep blue & black** *(500,000) Apr. 1920* 175.00 35.00
On cover 200.00
Block of 4 925.00 160.00

Normal spacing between words of overprint on Nos. 52 and 53 is 9¼mm. On No. 54 and the booklet printings of Nos. 52 and 53, the normal spacing is 9mm. Minor spacing varieties are known.

Black Overprint Reading Up

Type V

CANAL ZONE

Type V Overprint: Smaller block type 1¾mm high. "A" with flat top.

1920-21

55 A15	1c **light green & black,** *Apr. 1921*	22.50	3.50
	On cover		8.00
	Block of 4	100.00	17.50
a.	Overprint reading down	300.00	225.00
b.	Horiz. pair, right stamp without ovpt. (10)	*1,750.*	
c.	Horiz. pair, left stamp without ovpt. (21)	1,000.	
d.	"ZONE" only	*4,250.*	—
e.	Booklet pane of 6	*1,750.*	
f.	As No. 55, "CANAL" double (10)	*1,400.*	
56 A11	2c **orange vermilion & black,** *Sept. 1920*	8.50	2.25
	On cover		7.00
	Block of 4	37.50	10.50
a.	Double overprint *(100)*	600.00	
b.	Double overprint, one reading down *(100)*	650.00	
c.	Horiz. pair, right stamp without overprint (11)	1,500.	
d.	Horiz. pair, left stamp without overprint (20)	1,250.	
e.	Vertical pair, one without overprint	1,500.	
f.	"ZONE" double	1,250.	
g.	Booklet pane of 6	850.00	
h.	As No. 56, "CANAL" double	1,000.	
57 A12	5c **deep blue & black,** *Apr. 1921*	300.00	55.00
	On cover		225.00
	Block of 4	1,350.	250.00
a.	Horiz. pair, right stamp without overprint (10)	*2,500.*	
b.	Horiz. pair, left stamp without overprint (10)	*2,500.*	

Normal spacing between words of overprint on Nos. 55-57 is 9½mm. On booklet printings of Nos. 55 and 56 the normal spacing is 9¼mm.

Drydock at Balboa — A25

U.S.S. "Nereus" in Pedro Miguel Locks — A26

1920, Sept.

Black Overprint Type V

58 A25	50c **orange & black**	275.00	160.00
	On cover		*1,000.*
	Block of 4	1,375.	800.00
59 A26	1b **dark violet & black** *(23,014)*	160.00	65.00
	On cover		*1,000.*
	Block of 4	750.00	325.00

José Vallarino — A27

"Land Gate" — A28

Bolívar's Tribute — A29

Municipal Building in 1821 and 1921 — A30

Statue of Balboa — A31

Tomás Herrera — A32

José de Fábrega — A33

Engraved, Printed and Overprinted by American Bank Note Co.

Type V overprinted in black, reading up, on all values except the 5c which is overprinted with larger type in red

1921, Nov. 13

60 A27	1c **green**	3.75	1.40
	On cover		6.00
	Block of 4	17.50	6.75
a.	"CANAL" double	*2,500.*	
b.	Booklet pane of 6	*1,000.*	
61 A28	2c **carmine**	3.00	1.50
	On cover		15.00
	Block of 4	13.50	6.50
a.	Overprint reading down	200.00	*225.00*
b.	Double overprint	900.00	
c.	Vertical pair, one without overprint	*3,500.*	
d.	"CANAL" double	*1,900.*	
f.	Booklet pane of 6	*2,100.*	
62 A29	5c **blue** (R)	11.00	4.50
	On cover		30.00
	Block of 4	50.00	25.00
a.	Overprint reading down (R)	60.00	
63 A30	10c **violet**	18.00	7.50
	On cover		60.00
	Block of 4	100.00	35.00
a.	Overprint, reading down	90.00	
64 A31	15c **light blue**	47.50	17.50
	On cover		175.00
	Block of 4	225.00	95.00
65 A32	24c **black brown**	70.00	22.50
	On cover		*600.00*
	Block of 4	375.00	125.00
66 A33	50c **black**	150.00	100.00
	On cover		*600.00*
	Block of 4	725.00	475.00
	Nos. 60-66 (7)	303.25	154.90

Experts question the status of the 5c with a small type V overprint in red or black.

Type III overprint in black, reading up, applied by the Panama Canal Press, Mount Hope, C. Z.

Engraved and printed by the American Bank Note Co.

1924, Jan. 28

67 A27	1c **green**	500.	200.
	On cover		350.
	Block of 4	2,250.	900.
a.	"ZONE CANAL" reading down	850.	
b.	"ZONE" only, reading down	*1,900.*	

Arms of Panama — A34

1924, Feb.

68 A34	1c **dark green**	11.00	4.50
	On cover		12.00
	Block of 4	52.50	24.00
69 A34	2c **carmine**	8.25	2.75
	carmine rose	8.25	2.75
	On cover		15.00
	Block of 4	35.00	12.50

The following were prepared for use, but not issued.

A34 5c **dark blue** *(600)*	350.
Block of 4	1,750.
A34 10c **dark violet** *(600)*	350.
Block of 4	1,750.
A34 12c **olive green** *(600)*	350.
Block of 4	1,750.
A34 15c **ultramarine** *(600)*	350.
Block of 4	1,750.
A34 24c **yellow brown** *(600)*	350.
Block of 4	1,750.
A34 50c **orange** *(600)*	350.
Block of 4	1,750.
A34 1b **black** *(600)*	350.
Block of 4	1,750.

The 5c to 1b values were prepared for use but never issued due to abrogation of the Taft Agreement which required the Canal Zone to use overprinted Panama stamps. Six hundred of each denomination were not destroyed, as they were forwarded to the Director General of Posts of Panama for transmission to the UPU which then required about 400 sets. Only a small number of sets appear to have reached the public market.

All Panama stamps overprinted "CANAL ZONE" were withdrawn from sale June 30, 1924, and were no longer valid for postage after Aug. 31, 1924.

United States Nos. 551-554, 557, 562, 564-566, 569, 570 and 571 Overprinted in Red (No. 70) or Black (all others)

Printed and Overprinted by the U.S. Bureau of Engraving and Printing.

Type A

Letters "A" with Flat Tops

1924-25 **Unwmk.** ***Perf. 11***

70 A154	½c **olive brown** *(399,500) Apr. 15, 1925*	1.25	.75
	On cover		4.00
	First day cover		75.00
	Block of 4	5.50	3.50
	P# block of 6	18.00	
71 A155	1c **deep green** *(1,985,000) July 1, 1924*	1.40	.90
	On cover		4.00
	Block of 4	6.00	4.00
	P# block of 6	30.00	
a.	Inverted overprint	500.00	500.00
b.	"ZONE" inverted	350.00	325.00
c.	"CANAL" only *(20)*	1,750.	
d.	"ZONE CANAL" *(180)*	500.00	
e.	Booklet pane of 6 *(43,152)*	80.00	
72 A156	1½c **yellow brown** *(180,599) Apr. 15, 1925*	1.90	1.70
	brown	1.90	1.70
	First day cover, Nos. 70, 72		80.00
	Block of 4	8.25	9.50
	P# block of 6	35.00	
73 A157	2c **carmine** *(2,975,000) July 1, 1924*	7.50	1.70
	First day cover		80.00
	Block of 4	35.00	8.00
	P# block of 6	175.00	
a.	Booklet pane of 6 *(140,000)*	175.00	
74 A160	5c **dark blue** *(500,000) July 1, 1924*	19.00	8.50
	On cover		20.00
	Block of 4	80.00	37.50
	P# block of 6	325.00	
75 A165	10c **orange** *(60,000) July 1, 1924*	45.00	25.00
	On cover		45.00
	First day cover		500.00
	Block of 4	200.00	115.00
	P# block of 6	850.00	
76 A167	12c **brown violet** *(80,000) July 1, 1924*	35.00	32.50
	First day cover		600.00
	Block of 4	150.00	140.00
	P# block of 6	475.00	
a.	"ZONE" inverted	*3,750.*	*3,000.*
77 A168	14c **dark blue** *(100,000) June 27, 1925*	30.00	22.50
	On cover		50.00
	Block of 4	130.00	140.00
	P# block of 6	425.00	
78 A169	15c **gray** *(55,000) July 1, 1924*	50.00	37.50
	On cover		52.50
	Block of 4	225.00	190.00
	P# block of 6	850.00	
79 A172	30c **olive brown** *(40,000) July 1, 1924*	35.00	22.50
	On cover		50.00
	Block of 4	160.00	110.00
	P# block of 6	550.00	
80 A173	50c **lilac** *(25,000) July 1, 1924*	77.50	45.00
	On cover		*500.00*
	Block of 4	340.00	225.00
	P# block of 6	2,750.	
81 A174	$1 **violet brown** *(10,000) July 1, 1924*	225.00	95.00
	On cover		*1,000.*
	Block of 4	1,000.	500.00
	Margin block of 4, arrow, top or bottom	1,250.	
	P# block of 6	*4,250.*	
	Nos. 70-81 (12)	528.55	293.55

Normal spacing between words of the overprint is 9¼mm. Minor spacing variations are known. The overprint of the early printings used on all values of this series except No. 77 is a sharp, clear impression. The overprint of the late printings, used only on Nos. 70, 71, 73, 76, 77, 78 and 80 is heavy and smudged, with many of the letters, particularly the "A" practically filled.

Booklet panes Nos. 71e, 73a, 84d, 97b, 101a, 106a and 117a were made from 360 subject plates. The handmade booklet panes Nos. 102a, 115c and a provisional lot of 117b were made from Post Office panes from regular 400-subject plates.

United States Nos. 554, 555, 567, 562, 564-567, 569, 570, 571, 623 Overprinted in Red (No. 91) or Black (all others)

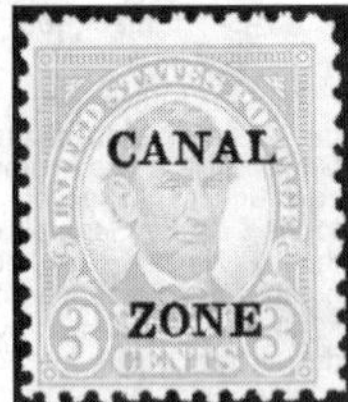

Type B
Letters "A" with Sharp Pointed Tops

1925-28 *Perf. 11*

84 A157 2c **carmine** *(1,110,000) May 1926* 30.00 8.00
On cover 11.00
Block of 4 125.00 37.50
P# block of 6 375.00
P# block of 6 & large 5 point star, side only *1,750.*
a. "CANAL" only *(20)* *1,600.*
b. "ZONE CANAL" *(180)* 325.00
c. Horizontal pair, one without overprint *3,500.*
d. Booklet pane of 6 *(82,000)* 175.00
e. Vertical pair, "a" and "b" se-tenant *2,750.*

85 A158 3c **violet** *(199,200) June 27, 1925* 4.00 3.25
On cover 6.00
Block of 4 17.50 13.50
P# block of 6 175.00
a. "ZONE ZONE" 600.00 550.00

86 A160 5c **dark blue** *(1,343,147) Jan. 7, 1926* 4.00 2.25
On cover 17.50
Block of 4 17.50 10.00
P# block of 6 165.00
Double transfer (15571 UL 86) — —
a. "ZONE ZONE" (LR18) 1,250.
b. "CANAL" inverted (LR7) 950.00
c. Inverted overprint *(80)* 500.00
d. Horizontal pair, one without overprint *3,250.*
e. Overprinted "ZONE CANAL" *(90)* 325.00
f. "ZONE" only *(10)* *2,000.*
g. Vertical pair, one without overprint, other overprint inverted *(10)* *2,250.*
h. "CANAL" only *2,250.*

87 A165 10c **orange** *(99,510) Aug. 1925* 35.00 12.00
On cover 40.00
Block of 4 160.00 70.00
P# block of 6 500.00
a. "ZONE ZONE" (LR18) *3,000.*

88 A167 12c **brown violet** *(58,062) Feb. 1926* 22.50 14.00
On cover 45.00
Block of 4 110.00 62.50
P# block of 6 375.00
a. "ZONE ZONE" (LR18) *5,250.*

89 A168 14c **dark blue** *(55,700) Dec. 1928* 20.00 16.00
On cover 50.00
Block of 4 90.00 75.00
P# block of 6 350.00

90 A169 15c **gray** *(204,138) Nov. 1925* 7.00 4.50
On cover 15.00
Block of 4 32.50 21.00
P# block of 6 200.00
P# block of 4, large 5 point star, side only —
a. "ZONE ZONE" (LR18) *5,500.*

Specialists believe a unique P# block of 4 with large 5-point star is the largest known P# multiple from the plate that shows the star. The editors would like to receive evidence to the contrary, if it exists.

91 A187 17c **black** *(199,500) Apr. 5, 1926* 4.00 3.00
On cover 12.50
Block of 4 17.50 14.00
P# block of 6 190.00
a. "ZONE" only *(20)* 900.00
b. "CANAL" only 1,700.
c. "ZONE CANAL" *(270)* 175.00

92 A170 20c **carmine rose** *(259,807) Apr. 5, 1926* 7.25 3.25
On cover 32.50
Block of 4 32.50 14.00
P# block of 6 175.00
a. "CANAL" inverted (UR48) *4,000.*
b. "ZONE" inverted (LL76) *4,250.*
c. "ZONE CANAL" (LL91) *3,600.*

93 A172 30c **olive brown** *(154,700) Dec. 1925* 5.00 4.00
On cover 60.00
Block of 4 22.50 20.00
P# block of 6 250.00

94 A173 50c **lilac** *(13,533) July 1928* 225.00 165.00
On cover *500.00*
Block of 4 1,100. 750.00
P# block of 6 2,500.

95 A174 $1 **violet brown** *(20,000) Apr. 1926* 125.00 60.00
On cover *1,000.*
Block of 4 550.00 265.00

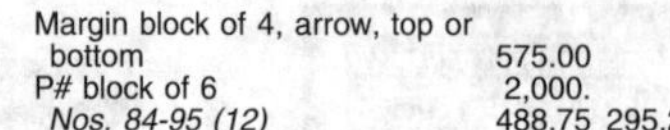

Margin block of 4, arrow, top or bottom 575.00
P# block of 6 2,000.
Nos. 84-95 (12) 488.75 295.25

Nos. 85-88, 90 and 93-95 exist with wrong-font "CANAL" and "ZONE." Positions are: Nos. 85-88 and 90, UL51 (CANAL) and UL82 (ZONE); Nos. 93-95, U51 (CANAL) and U82 (ZONE).

Normal spacing between words of the overprint is 11mm on No. 84; 9mm on Nos. 85-88, 90, first printing of No. 91 and the first, third and fourth printing of No. 92; 7mm on the second printings of Nos. 91-92. Minor spacing varieties exist on Nos. 84-88, 90-92.

Overprint Type B on U.S. Sesquicentennial Stamp No. 627

1926

96 A188 2c **carmine rose** *(300,000) July 6, 1926* 4.50 3.75
First day cover 60.00
Block of 4 20.00 18.00
P# block of 6 85.00

On this stamp there is a space of 5mm instead of 9mm between the two words of the overprint.

The authorized date, July 4, fell on a Sunday with the next day also a holiday, so No. 96 was not regularly issued until July 6. But the postmaster sold some copies and canceled some covers on July 4 for a few favored collectors.

Overprint Type B in Black on U.S. Nos. 583, 584, 591

1926-27 Rotary Press Printings *Perf. 10*

97 A157 2c **carmine** *(1,290,000) Dec. 1926* 62.50 11.00
On cover 14.00
Block of 4 290.00 50.00
P# block of 4 475.00
a. Pair, one without overprint *(10)* *3,250.*
b. Booklet pane of 6 *(58,000)* 525.00
c. "CANAL" only *(10)* *2,000.*
d. "ZONE" only *2,750.*

98 A158 3c **violet** *(239,600) May 9, 1927* 8.00 4.25
On cover 12.00
Block of 4 35.00 19.00
P# block of 4 120.00

99 A165 10c **orange** *(128,400) May 9, 1927* 17.50 7.50
On cover 35.00
Block of 4 80.00 40.00
P# block of 4 225.00

No. 97d is valued in the grade of fine. Very fine examples are not known.

Overprint Type B in Black on U.S. Nos. 632, 634 (Type I), 635, 637, 642

1927-31 Rotary Press Printings *Perf. 11x10½*

100 A155 1c **green** *(434,892) June 28, 1927* 2.25 1.40
On cover 3.00
Block of 4 10.00 6.75
P# block of 4 20.00
a. Vertical pair, one without overprint *(10)* *4,000.*

101 A157 2c **carmine** *(1,628,195) June 28, 1927* 2.50 1.00
On cover 3.00
Block of 4 11.00 4.75
P# block of 4 24.00
a. Booklet pane of 6 *(82,108)* 175.00

102 A158 3c **violet** *(1,250,000) Feb., 1931* 4.25 2.75
On cover 5.00
Block of 4 21.00 13.50
P# block of 4 90.00
a. Booklet pane of 6, handmade, perf. margins *6,500.*

103 A160 5c **dark blue** *(60,000) Dec. 13, 1927* 30.00 10.00
On cover 30.00
Block of 4 130.00 42.50
P# block of 4 200.00

104 A165 10c **orange** *(119,800) July, 1930* 17.50 10.00
On cover 35.00
Block of 4 77.50 45.00
P# block of 4 190.00
Nos. 100-104 (5) 56.50 25.15

Wet and Dry Printings

Canal Zone stamps printed by both the "wet" and "dry" process are Nos. 105, 108-109, 111-114, 117, 138-140, C21-C24, C26, J25, J27. Starting with Nos. 147 and C27, the Bureau of Engraving and Printing used the "dry" method exclusively, except for Nos. 152, 157 and 164.

See note on Wet and Dry Printings following U.S. No. 1029.

Maj. Gen. William Crawford Gorgas — A35

Maj. Gen. George Washington Goethals — A36

Gaillard Cut — A37

Maj. Gen. Harry Foote Hodges — A38

Lt. Col. David Du Bose Gaillard — A39

Maj. Gen. William Luther Sibert — A40

Jackson Smith — A41

Rear Adm. Harry Harwood Rousseau — A42

Col. Sydney Bacon Williamson — A43

Joseph Clay Styles Blackburn — A44

Printed by the U. S. Bureau of Engraving and Printing.

Plates of 400 subjects (except 5c), issued in panes of 100. The 5c was printed from plate of 200 subjects, issued in panes of 50. The 400-subject sheets were originally cut by knife into Post Office panes of 100, but beginning in 1948 they were separated by perforations to eliminate straight edges.

1928-40 Flat Plate Printing Unwmk. *Perf. 11*

105 A35 1c **green** *(22,392,147)* .20 .20
P# block of 6 2.25 —
a. Wet printing, yel grn, *Oct. 3, 1928* .20 .20
First day cover 17.50
P# block of 6 3.75 —

106 A36 2c **carmine** *(7,191,600) Oct. 1, 1928* .20 .20
First day cover 17.50
P# block of 6 2.50 —
a. Booklet pane of 6 *(284,640)* 15.00 *20.00*

107 A37 5c **blue** *(4,187,028) June 25, 1929* 1.00 .40
First day cover 5.00
P# block of 6 12.00 —

108 A38 10c **orange** *(4,559,788)* .20 .20
P# block of 6 4.00 —
a. Wet printing, *Jan. 11, 1932* .40 .25
First day cover 40.00
P# block of 6 5.50 —

109 A39 12c **brown violet** *(844,635)* .75 .60
P# block of 6 11.00 —
a. Wet printing, violet brown, *July 1, 1929* 1.50 1.00
First day cover 60.00
P# block of 6 19.00 —

110 A40 14c **blue** *(406,131) Sept. 27, 1937* .85 .85
First day cover 5.00
P# block of 6 14.00 —

111 A41 15c **gray black** *(3,356,500)* .40 .35
P# block of 6 8.00 —
a. Wet printing, gray, *Jan. 11, 1932* .80 .50
First day cover 45.00
P# block of 6 11.00 5.00

112 A42 20c **dark brown** *(3,619,080)* .60 .20

No.	Type	Denom.	Description	Unused	Used
			P# block of 6	8.00	—
a.			Wet printing, olive brown, *Jan. 11, 1932*	1.00	.30
			First day cover		45.00
			P# block of 6	14.00	—
113	A43	30c	**black** *(2,376,491)*	.80	.70
			P# block of 6	11.00	—
a.			Wet printing, brn blk, *Apr. 15, 1940*	1.25	1.00
			First day cover		10.00
			P# block of 6	19.00	—
114	A44	50c	**rose lilac**	1.50	.65
			P# block of 6	16.50	—
a.			Wet printing, lilac, *July 1, 1929*	2.50	.85
			First day cover		150.00
			P# block of 6	30.00	—
			Nos. 105-114 (10)	6.50	4.35

Nos. 105, 108, 112, 113 and 114 exist with both shiny gum and dull gum.

Coils are listed as Nos. 160-161.

United States Nos. 720 and 695 Overprinted type B

Rotary Press Printing

1933, Jan. 14 ***Perf. 11x10½***

No.	Type	Denom.	Description	Unused	Used
115	A226	3c	**deep violet** *(3,150,000)*	2.75	.25
			First day cover		12.00
			P# block of 4	35.00	—
b.			"CANAL" only	*2,600.*	
c.			Booklet pane of 6, handmade, perf. margins	210.00	—
116	A168	14c	**dark blue** *(104,800)*	4.50	3.50
			First day cover		20.00
			P# block of 4	60.00	—
a.			"ZONE CANAL" *(16)*	*1,500.*	

Maj. Gen. George Washington Goethals — A45

20th anniversary of the opening of the Panama Canal.

Flat Plate Printing

1934, Aug. 15 **Unwmk.** ***Perf. 11***

No.	Type	Denom.	Description	Unused	Used
117	A45	3c	**red violet**	.20	.20
			First day cover		3.00
			P# block of 6	1.00	—
a.			Booklet pane of 6	45.00	*32.50*
b.			As "a," handmade, perf. margins	175.00	—
c.			Wet printing, violet	.20	.20
			P# block of 6	1.00	—

Coil is listed as No. 153.

Catalogue values for unused stamps in this section, from this point to the end, are for Never Hinged items.

United States Nos. 803 and 805 Overprinted in Black

Rotary Press Printing

1939, Sept. 1 **Unwmk.** ***Perf. 11x10½***

No.	Type	Denom.	Description	Unused	Used
118	A275	½c	**red orange** *(1,030,000)*	.20	.20
			First day cover		1.00
			P# block of 4	2.75	—
119	A277	1½c	**bister brown** *(935,000)*	.20	.20
			brown	.20	.20
			First day cover		1.00
			P# block of 4	2.25	—

Balboa-Before A46

Balboa-After A47

Gaillard Cut-Before A48

Gaillard Cut-After A49

Bas Obispo-Before A50

Bas Obispo-After A51

Gatun Locks-Before A52

Gatun Locks-After A53

Canal Channel-Before A54

Canal Channel-After A55

Gamboa-Before A56

Gamboa-After A57

Pedro Miguel Locks-Before A58

Pedro Miguel Locks-After A59

Gatun Spillway-Before A60

Gatun Spillway-After A61

25th anniversary of the opening of the Panama Canal. Withdrawn Feb. 28, 1941; remainders burned Apr. 12, 1941.

Flat Plate Printing

1939, Aug. 15 **Unwmk.** ***Perf. 11***

No.	Type	Denom.	Description	Unused	Used
120	A46	1c	**yellow green** *(1,019,482)*	.65	.30
			First day cover		2.00
			P# block of 6	12.50	—
121	A47	2c	**rose carmine** *(227,065)*	.65	.35
			First day cover		2.00
			P# block of 6	12.50	—
122	A48	3c	**purple** *(2,523,735)*	.65	.20
			First day cover		2.00
			P# block of 6	12.50	—
123	A49	5c	**dark blue** *(460,213)*	1.60	1.25
			First day cover		2.50
			P# block of 6	20.00	—
124	A40	6c	**red orange** *(68,290)*	3.00	3.00
			First day cover		6.00
			P# block of 6	45.00	—
125	A51	7c	**black** *(71,235)*	3.25	3.00
			First day cover		6.00
			P# block of 6	45.00	—
126	A52	8c	**green** *(41,576)*	4.75	3.50
			First day cover		6.00
			P# block of 6	55.00	—
127	A53	10c	**ultramarine** *(83,571)*	3.50	3.00
			First day cover		6.00
			P# block of 6	55.00	—
128	A54	11c	**blue green** *(34,010)*	8.00	8.00
			First day cover		10.00
			P# block of 6	125.00	—
129	A55	12c	**brown carmine** *(66,735)*	7.50	7.50
			First day cover		10.00
			P# block of 6	100.00	—
130	A56	14c	**dark violet** *(37,365)*	7.50	7.50
			First day cover		10.00
			P# block of 6	125.00	—

131 A57 15c **olive green** *(105,058)* 10.00 6.00
First day cover 10.00
P# block of 6 160.00 —
132 A58 18c **rose pink** *(39,255)* 10.00 8.50
First day cover 10.00
P# block of 6 150.00 —
133 A59 20c **brown** *(100,244)* 12.50 7.50
First day cover 10.00
P# block of 6 190.00 —
134 A60 25c **orange** *(34,283)* 17.50 17.50
First day cover 20.00
P# block of 6 325.00 —
135 A61 50c **violet brown** *(91,576)* 22.50 6.00
First day cover 20.00
P# block of 6 350.00 —
Nos. 120-135 (16) 113.55 83.10

Maj. Gen. George W. Davis — A62

Gov. Charles E. Magoon — A63

Theodore Roosevelt — A64

John F. Stevens — A65

John F. Wallace — A66

1946-49 **Unwmk.** ***Perf. 11***
Size: 19x22mm

136 A62 ½c **bright red** *(1,020,000) Aug. 16, 1948* .40 .25
First day cover 1.25
P# block of 6 2.50 —
137 A63 1½c **chocolate** *(603,600) Aug. 16, 1948* .40 .25
First day cover 1.25
P# block of 6 2.25 —
138 A64 2c **light rose carmine** *(6,951,755)* .20 .20
P# block of 6 .65 —
a. Wet printing, rose carmine, *Oct. 27, 1949* .20 .20
First day cover 1.00
P# block of 6 1.00 —
139 A65 5c **dark blue** .35 .20
P# block of 6 2.25 —
a. Wet printing, deep blue, *Apr. 25, 1946* .60 .20
First day cover 1.00
P# block of 6 4.00 —
140 A66 25c **green** *(1,520,000)* .85 .55
P# block of 6 7.00 —
a. Wet printing, yel grn, *Aug. 16, 1948* 3.00 1.00
First day cover 3.50
P# block of 6 20.00 —
Nos. 136-140 (5) 2.20 1.45

See Nos. 155, 162, 164.

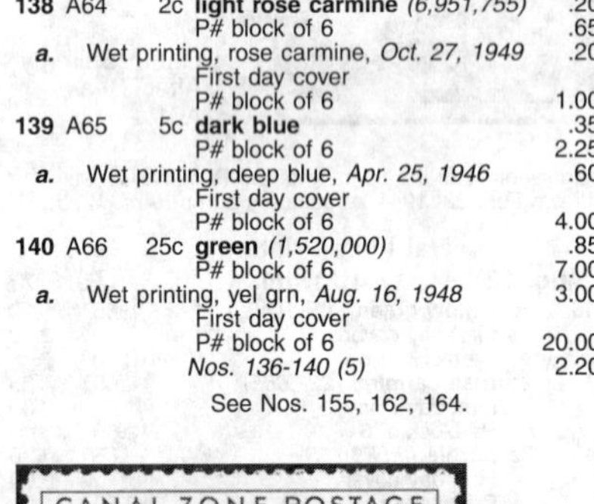

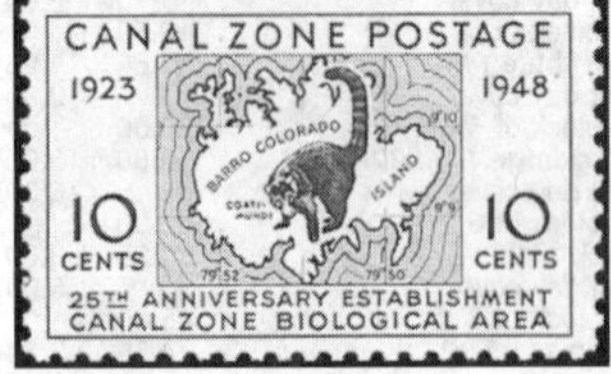

Map of Biological Area and Coati-mundi A67

25th anniversary of the establishment of the Canal Zone Biological Area on Barro Colorado Island.

Withdrawn Mar. 30, 1951, and remainders destroyed Apr. 10, 1951.

1948, Apr. 17 **Unwmk.** ***Perf. 11***
141 A67 10c **black** *(521,200)* 1.25 .80
First day cover 3.00
P# block of 6 8.50 —

"Forty-niners" Arriving at Chagres — A68

Journeying in "Bungo" to Las Cruces — A69

Las Cruces Trail to Panama — A70

Departure for San Francisco — A71

Centenary of the California Gold Rush.

Stocks on hand were processed for destruction on Aug. 11, 1952 and destroyed Aug. 13, 1952.

1949, June 1 **Unwmk.** ***Perf. 11***
142 A68 3c **blue** *(500,000)* .50 .25
First day cover 1.00
P# block of 6 6.00 —
143 A69 6c **violet** *(481,600)* .65 .30
First day cover 1.00
P# block of 6 6.50 —
144 A70 12c **bright blue green** *(230,200)* 1.10 .90
First day cover 2.00
P# block of 6 18.00 —
145 A71 18c **deep red lilac** *(240,200)* 2.00 1.50
First day cover 3.25
P# block of 6 20.00 —
Nos. 142-145 (4) 4.25 2.95

Workers in Culebra Cut — A72

Early Railroad Scene — A73

Contribution of West Indian laborers in the construction of the Panama Canal.

Entire issue sold, none withdrawn and destroyed.

1951, Aug. 15 **Unwmk.** ***Perf. 11***
146 A72 10c **carmine** *(480,000)* 2.25 1.50
First day cover 3.00
P# block of 6 22.50 —

1955, Jan. 28 **Unwmk.** ***Perf. 11***

Centenary of the completion of the Panama Railroad and the first transcontinental railroad trip in the Americas.

147 A73 3c **violet** *(994,000)* .60 .50
First day cover 1.50
P# block of 6 5.50 —

Gorgas Hospital and Ancon Hill — A74

75th anniversary of Gorgas Hospital.

1957, Nov. 17 **Unwmk.** ***Perf. 11***
148 A74 3c **black,** *dull blue green (1,010,000)* .45 .35
Light blue green paper .40 .35
First day cover 1.00
P# block of 4 4.25 —

S.S. Ancon — A75

1958, Aug. 30 **Unwmk.** ***Perf. 11***
149 A75 4c **greenish blue** *(1,749,700)* .40 .30
First day cover 1.00
P# block of 4 3.25 —

Roosevelt Medal and Canal Zone Map — A76

Centenary of the birth of Theodore Roosevelt (1858-1919).

1958, Nov. 15 **Unwmk.** ***Perf. 11***
150 A76 4c **brown** *(1,060,000)* .40 .30
First day cover 1.00
P# block of 4 3.00 —

Boy Scout Badge — A77

Administration Building, Balboa Heights — A78

50th anniversary of the Boy Scouts of America.

Giori Press Printing

1960, Feb. 8 **Unwmk.** ***Perf. 11***
151 A77 4c **dark blue, red & bister** *(654,933)* .50 .40
First day cover 1.50
P# block of 4 4.25 —

1960, Nov. 1 **Unwmk.** ***Perf. 11***
152 A78 4c **rose lilac** *(2,486,725)* .20 .20
First day cover 1.00
P# block of 4 .90 —

Types of 1934, 1960 and 1946
Coil Stamps

1960-62 **Unwmk.** ***Perf. 10 Vertically***
153 A45 3c **deep violet** *(3,743,959) Nov. 1, 1960* .20 .20
First day cover 1.00
Pair .40 .25
Joint line pair 1.10 —

Perf. 10 Horizontally
154 A78 4c **dull rose lilac** *(2,776,273) Nov. 1, 1960* .20 .20
First day cover 1.00
Pair .40 .25
Joint line pair 1.10 —

Perf. 10 Vertically
155 A65 5c **deep blue** *(3,288,264) Feb. 10, 1962* .25 .20
First day cover 1.00
Pair .50 .50
Joint line pair 1.25 —
Nos. 153-155 (3) .65 .60

Girl Scout Badge and Camp at Gatun Lake — A79

50th anniversary of the Girl Scouts.

Giori Press Printing

1962, Mar. 12 **Unwmk.** ***Perf. 11***

156 A79 4c	**blue, dark green & bister** *(640,000)*	.40	.30
	First day cover *(83,717)*		1.25
	P# block of 4	2.75	—

Thatcher Ferry Bridge and Map of Western Hemisphere A80

Opening of the Thatcher Ferry Bridge, spanning the Panama Canal.

Giori Press Printing

1962, Oct. 12 **Unwmk.** ***Perf. 11***

157 A80 4c	**black & silver** *(775,000)*	.35	.25
	First day cover *(65,833)*		1.00
	P# block of 4, 2P#	3.75	—
a.	Silver (bridge) omitted *(50)*	*7,500.*	
	P# block of 6, black P# only	*52,500.*	

Goethals Memorial, Balboa — A81

Fort San Lorenzo — A82

1968-71 **Giori Press Printing** ***Perf. 11***

158 A81 6c	**green & ultra.** *(1,890,000) Mar. 15, 1968*	.30	.30
	First day cover		1.00
	P# block of 4	2.00	—
159 A82 8c	**slate green, blue, dark brown & ocher** *(3,460,000) July 14, 1971*	.35	.20
	First day cover		1.00
	P# block of 4	2.75	—

Types of 1928, 1932 and 1948

Coil Stamps

1975, Feb. 14 **Unwmk.** ***Perf. 10 Vertically***

160 A35 1c	**green** *(1,090,958)*	.20	.20
	First day cover		1.00
	Pair	.40	.30
	Joint line pair	1.00	—
161 A38 10c	**orange** *(590,658)*	.70	.40
	First day cover		1.00
	Pair	1.40	.80
	Joint line pair	5.00	—
162 A66 25c	**yellow green** *(129,831)*	2.75	2.75
	First day cover		3.00
	Pair	5.50	5.50
	Joint line pair	20.00	—
	Nos. 160-162 (3)	3.65	3.35

Dredge Cascadas A83

1976, Feb. 23 **Giori Press Printing** ***Perf. 11***

163 A83 13c	**multicolored** *(3,653,950)*	.35	.20
	First day cover		1.00
	P# block of 4	2.00	—
a.	Booklet pane of 4 *(1,032,400) Apr. 19*	3.00	—

Stevens Type of 1946

1977 **Rotary Press Printing** ***Perf. 11x10½***

Size: 19x22½mm

164 A65 5c	**deep blue** *(1,009,612)*	.60	.85
	P# block of 4	3.50	—
a.	Tagged	12.00	15.00
	P# block of 4	125.00	—

No. 164 exists with both shiny gum and dull gum.

No. 164a exists even though there was no equipment in the Canal Zone to detect tagging.

Towing Locomotive, Ship in Lock, by Alwyn Sprague A84

1978, Oct. 25 ***Perf. 11***

165 A84 15c	**dp grn & bl grn** *(2,921,083)*	.35	.20
	First day cover *(81,405)*		1.00
	P# block of 4	2.00	—

AIR POST STAMPS

Regular Issue of 1928 Surcharged in Dark Blue

15 Type I- Flag of "5" pointing up

Type II- Flag of "5" curved **15**

1929-31 **Flat Plate Printing** **Unwmk.** ***Perf. 11***

C1 A35 15c	on 1c **green**, type I, *Apr. 1, 1929*	8.00	5.50
	First day cover		25.00
	Block of 4	35.00	25.00
	P# block of 6	120.00	—
C2 A35 15c	on 1c **yellow green**, type II, *Mar. 1931*	75.00	52.50
	On cover		175.00
	Block of 4	340.00	340.00
	P# block of 6	900.00	—
C3 A36 25c	on 2c **carmine** *(223,880) Jan. 11, 1929*	3.50	2.00
	First day cover		17.50
	Block of 4	15.00	9.00
	P# block of 6	115.00	—

Nos. 114 and 106 Surcharged in Black

1929, Dec. 31

C4 A44 10c	on 50c **lilac** *(116,666)*	7.50	6.50
	First day cover		25.00
	Block of 4	32.50	27.50
	P# block of 6	115.00	—
C5 A36 20c	on 2c **carmine** *(638,395)*	5.00	1.75
	First day cover		20.00
	Block of 4	20.00	8.00
	P# block of 6	110.00	—
a.	Dropped "2" in surcharge *(7,000)*	80.00	60.00

Catalogue values for unused stamps in this section, from this point to the end, are for Never Hinged items.

Gaillard Cut — AP1

Printed by the U. S. Bureau of Engraving and Printing.

Plates of 200 subjects, issued in panes of 50.

1931-49 **Unwmk.** ***Perf. 11***

C6 AP1 4c	**red violet** *(525,000) Jan. 3, 1949*	.75	.70
	First day cover		2.00
	P# block of 6	5.25	—
C7 AP1 5c	**yellow green** *(9,935,500) Nov. 18, 1931*	.60	.45
	green	.60	.45
	First day cover		10.00
	P# block of 6	4.50	—
C8 AP1 6c	**yellow brown** *(9,399,500) Feb. 15, 1946*	.75	.35
	First day cover		2.00
	P# block of 6	5.25	—
C9 AP1 10c	**orange** *(5,079,000) Nov. 18, 1931*	1.00	.35
	First day cover		10.00
	P# block of 6	10.00	—
C10 AP1 15c	**blue** *(11,072,700) Nov. 18, 1931*	1.25	.30
	pale blue	1.25	.30
	First day cover		15.00
	P# block of 6	11.00	—
C11 AP1 20c	**red violet** *(3,184,100) Nov. 18, 1931*	2.00	.30
	deep violet	2.00	.30
	First day cover		35.00
	P# block of 6	20.00	—
C12 AP1 30c	**rose lake** *(1,119,500) July 15, 1941*	3.50	1.00
	dull rose	3.50	1.00
	First day cover		22.50
	P# block of 6	32.50	—
C13 AP1 40c	**yellow** *(795,600) Nov. 18, 1931*	3.50	1.10
	lemon	3.50	1.10
	First day cover		75.00
	P# block of 6	32.50	—
C14 AP1 $1	**black** *(372,500) Nov. 18, 1931*	8.50	1.90
	First day cover		150.00
	P# block of 6	85.00	—
	Nos. C6-C14 (9)	21.85	6.45

Douglas Plane over Sosa Hill — AP2

Planes and Map of Central America AP3

Pan American Clipper and Scene near Fort Amador — AP4

Pan American Clipper at Cristobal Harbor — AP5

Pan American Clipper over Gaillard Cut — AP6

Pan American Clipper Landing — AP7

10th anniversary of Air Mail service and the 25th anniversary of the opening of the Panama Canal.

Withdrawn Feb. 28, 1941, remainders burned Apr. 12, 1941.

Flat Plate Printing

1939, July 15 Unwmk. *Perf. 11*

C15	AP2	5c	**greenish black** *(86,576)*	3.75	2.25
			First day cover		5.00
			P# block of 6	42.50	—
C16	AP3	10c	**dull violet** *(117,644)*	3.00	2.25
			First day cover		5.00
			P# block of 6	50.00	—
C17	AP4	15c	**light brown** *(883,742)*	4.25	1.25
			First day cover		3.00
			P# block of 6	55.00	—
C18	AP5	25c	**blue** *(82,126)*	13.00	8.00
			First day cover		17.50
			P# block of 6	250.00	—
C19	AP6	30c	**rose carmine** *(121,382)*	12.00	6.75
			First day cover		15.00
			P# block of 6	160.00	—
C20	AP7	$1	**green** *(40,051)*	35.00	22.50
			First day cover		60.00
			P# block of 6	525.00	—
			Nos. C15-C20 (6)	71.00	43.00

Globe and Wing — AP8

Flat Plate Printing

1951, July 16 Unwmk. *Perf. 11*

C21	AP8	4c	**lt red violet** *(1,315,000)*	.75	.35
			P# block of 6	7.00	—
a.			Wet printing, red violet	1.25	.40
			1st day card, Balboa Heights		1.50
			P# block of 6	10.00	—
C22	AP8	6c	**lt brown** *(22,657,625)*	.50	.25
			P# block of 6	5.00	—
a.			Wet printing, brown	.95	.35
			1st day cover, Balboa Heights		1.00
			P# block of 6	7.50	—
C23	AP8	10c	**lt red orange** *(1,049,130)*	.90	.35
			P# block of 6	8.00	—
a.			Wet printing, red orange	2.00	.50
			1st day cover, Balboa Heights		2.00
			P# block of 6	16.00	—
C24	AP8	21c	**lt blue** *(1,460,000)*	7.50	4.00
			P# block of 6	70.00	—
a.			Wet printing, blue	15.00	5.00
			1st day cover, Balboa Heights		7.50
			P# block of 6	125.00	—
C25	AP8	31c	**cerise** *(375,000)*	7.50	3.75
			1st day cover, Balboa Heights		7.50
			P# block of 6	70.00	—
a.			Horiz. pair, imperf. vert. *(98)*	1,000.	—
C26	AP8	80c	**lt gray black** *(827,696)*	4.50	1.50
			P# block of 6	35.00	—
a.			Wet printing, gray black	12.50	1.65
			1st day cover, Balboa Heights		12.50
			1st day cover, Balboa Heights, #C21-C26		20.00
			P# block of 6	100.00	—
			Nos. C21-C26 (6)	21.65	10.20

See note after No. 114. Total number of first day covers with one or more of Nos. C21-C26, about 12,000.

Flat Plate Printing

1958, Aug. 16 Unwmk. *Perf. 11*

C27	AP8	5c	**yellow green** *(899,923)*	1.00	.60
			First day cover *(2,176)*		4.50
			P# block of 4	6.00	—
C28	AP8	7c	**olive** *(9,381,797)*	1.00	.45
			First day cover *(2,815)*		4.50
			P# block of 4	6.00	—
C29	AP8	15c	**brown violet** *(359,923)*	3.75	2.75
			First day cover *(2,040)*		6.00
			P# block of 4	30.00	—
C30	AP8	25c	**orange yellow** *(600,000)*	10.00	2.75
			First day cover *(2,115)*		9.00
			P# block of 4	95.00	—
C31	AP8	35c	**dark blue** *(283,032)*	6.25	2.75
			First day cover *(1,868)*		11.00
			P# block of 4	40.00	—
			Nos. C27-C31 (5)	22.00	9.30
			Nos. C21-C31 (11)	43.65	19.50

Emblem of US Army Caribbean School — AP9

US Army Caribbean School for Latin America at Fort Gulick.

Giori Press Printing

1961, Nov. 21 Unwmk. *Perf. 11*

C32	AP9	15c	**red & blue** *(560,000)*	1.25	.75
			First day cover *(25,949)*		1.75
			P# block of 4	10.00	—

Malaria Eradication Emblem and Mosquito AP10

World Health Organization drive to eradicate malaria.

Giori Press Printing

1962, Sept. 24 Unwmk. *Perf. 11*

C33	AP10	7c	**yellow & black** *(862,349)*	.45	.40
			First day cover *(44,433)*		1.00
			P# block of 4	2.75	—

Globe-Wing Type of 1951

Rotary Press Printing

1963, Jan. 7 *Perf. 10½x11*

C34	AP8	8c	**carmine** *(5,054,727)*	.40	.30
			First day cover *(19,128)*		1.00
			P# block of 4	2.60	—

Alliance for Progress Emblem AP11

2nd anniv. of the Alliance for Progress, which aims to stimulate economic growth and raise living standards in Latin America.

Giori Press Printing

1963, Aug. 17 Unwmk. *Perf. 11*

C35	AP11	15c	**gray, grn & dk ultra** *(405,000)*	1.10	.85
			First day cover *(29,594)*		1.50
			P# block of 4	10.00	—

Jet over Cristobal AP12

50th anniversary of the opening of the Panama Canal. Designs: 8c, Gatun Locks. 15c, Madden Dam. 20c, Gaillard Cut. 30c, Miraflores Locks. 80c, Balboa.

Giori Press Printing

1964, Aug. 15 Unwmk. *Perf. 11*

C36	AP12	6c	**green & black** *(257,193)*	.45	.35
			1st day cover, Balboa		1.50
			P# block of 4	2.25	—
C37	AP12	8c	**rose red & black** *(3,924,283)*	.45	.35
			1st day cover, Balboa		1.00
			P# block of 4	2.25	—
C38	AP12	15c	**blue & black** *(472,666)*	1.00	.75
			1st day cover, Balboa		1.00
			P# block of 4	6.25	—
C39	AP12	20c	**rose lilac & black** *(399,784)*	1.50	1.00
			1st day cover, Balboa		2.00
			P# block of 4	8.00	—
C40	AP12	30c	**reddish brown & black** *(204,524)*	2.25	2.25
			1st day cover, Balboa		3.00
			P# block of 4	15.00	—
C41	AP12	80c	**olive bister & black** *(186,809)*	3.75	3.00
			1st day cover, Balboa		4.00
			1st day cover, Balboa, #C36-C41		10.00
			P# block of 4	20.00	—
			Nos. C36-C41 (6)	9.40	7.70

There were 57,822 first day covers with one or more of Nos. C36-C41.

Canal Zone Seal and Jet Plane — AP13

Giori Press Printing

1965, July 15 Unwmk. *Perf. 11*

C42	AP13	6c	**green & black** *(548,250)*	.35	.30
			First day cover, Balboa		2.00
			P# block of 4	1.90	—
C43	AP13	8c	**rose red & black** *(8,357,700)*	.30	.20
			First day cover, Balboa		1.00
			P# block of 4	1.75	—
C44	AP13	15c	**blue & black** *(2,385,000)*	.50	.20
			First day cover, Balboa		1.00
			P# block of 4	2.50	—
C45	AP13	20c	**lilac & black** *(2,290,699)*	.55	.30
			First day cover, Balboa		1.25
			P# block of 4	2.75	—
C46	AP13	30c	**redsh brn & blk** *(2,332,255)*	.80	.30
			First day cover, Balboa		1.25
			P# block of 4	4.00	—
C47	AP13	80c	**bister & black** *(1,456,596)*	2.00	.75
			First day cover, Balboa		2.50
			First day cover, Balboa, #C42-C47		7.00
			P# block of 4	12.50	—
			Nos. C42-C47 (6)	4.50	2.05

There were 35,389 first day covers with one or more of Nos. C42-C47.

1968-76

C48	AP13	10c	**dull orange & black** *(10,055,000) Mar. 15, 1968*	.25	.20
			First day cover, Balboa *(7,779)*		1.00
			P# block of 4	1.25	—
a.			Booklet pane of 4 *(713,390) Feb. 18, 1970*	4.25	—
			First day cover, Balboa *(5,054)*		5.00
C49	AP13	11c	**olive & black** *(3,335,000) Sept. 24, 1971*	.25	.20
			First day cover, Balboa *(10,916)*		1.00
			P# block of 4	1.25	—
a.			Booklet pane of 4 *(1,277,760) Sept. 24, 1971*	3.50	—
			First day cover, Balboa *(2,460)*		5.00
C50	AP13	13c	**emerald & black** *(1,865,000) Feb. 11, 1974*	.80	.25
			First day cover, Balboa *(7,646)*		1.00
			P# block of 4	4.75	—
a.			Booklet pane of 4 *(619,200) Feb. 11, 1974*	6.00	—
			First day cover, Balboa *(3,660)*		5.00
C51	AP13	22c	**vio & blk** *(363,720) May 10, 1976*	.75	*2.00*
			First day cover, Balboa		2.50
			P# block of 4	4.00	—
C52	AP13	25c	**pale yellow green & black** *(1,640,441) Mar. 15, 1968*	.60	.70
			First day cover, Balboa		1.00
			P# block of 4	2.75	—
C53	AP13	35c	**salmon & black** *(573,822) May 10, 1976*	.90	*2.00*
			First day cover, Balboa		2.50
			P# block of 4	4.75	—
			Nos. C48-C53 (6)	3.55	*5.35*

There were 5,047 first day covers with one or more of Nos. C51, C53.

AIR POST OFFICIAL STAMPS

Beginning in March, 1915, stamps for use on official mail were identified by a large "P" perforated through each stamp. These were replaced by overprinted issues in 1941. The use of official stamps was discontinued December 31, 1951. During their currency, they were not for sale in mint condition and were sold to the public only when canceled with a parcel post rotary canceler reading "Balboa Heights, Canal Zone" between two wavy lines.

After having been withdrawn from use, mint stamps (except Nos. CO8-CO12 and O3, O8) were made available to the public at face value for three months beginning Jan. 2, 1952. **Values for used examples of**

Nos. CO1-CO7, CO14, O1-O2, O4-O9, are for canceled-to-order specimens with original gum, postally used copies being worth more. Sheet margins were removed to facilitate overprinting and plate numbers are, therefore, unknown.

Air Post Stamps of 1931-41 Overprinted in Black

Two types of overprint.

Type I- "PANAMA CANAL" 19-20mm long

1941-42 Unwmk. *Perf. 11*

CO1 AP1 5c **yellow green** *(42,754) Mar. 31, 1941* 5.50 1.50
green 5.50 1.50
On cover 50.00
Block of 4 25.00 6.00
CO2 AP1 10c **orange** *(49,723) Mar. 31, 1941* 8.50 2.00
On cover 25.00
Block of 4 37.50 9.00
CO3 AP1 15c **blue** *(56,898) Mar. 31, 1941* 11.00 2.00
On cover 25.00
Block of 4 47.50 17.00
CO4 AP1 20c **red violet** *(22,107) Mar. 31, 1941* 12.50 4.00
deep violet 12.50 4.00
On cover 110.00
Block of 4 60.00 22.50
CO5 AP1 30c **rose lake** *(22,100) June, 4, 1942* 17.50 5.00
dull rose 17.50 4.50
On cover 40.00
Block of 4 80.00 22.50
CO6 AP1 40c **yellow** *(22,875) Mar. 31, 1941* 17.50 7.50
lemon yellow 17.50 7.50
On cover 75.00
Block of 4 80.00 37.50
CO7 AP1 $1 **black** *(29,525) Mar. 31, 1941* 20.00 10.00
On cover 150.00
Block of 4 90.00 45.00
Nos. CO1-CO7 (7) 92.50 32.00

Overprint varieties occur on Nos. CO1-CO7 and CO14: "O" of "OFFICIAL" over "N" of "PANAMA" (entire third row). "O" of "OFFICIAL" broken at top (position 31). "O" of "OFFICIAL" over second "A" of "PANAMA" (position 45). First "F" of "OFFICIAL" over second "A" of "PANAMA" (position 50).

1941, Sept. 22

Type II- "PANAMA CANAL" 17mm long

CO8 AP1 5c **yellow green** *(2,000)* — 160.00
On cover 500.00
Block of 4 675.00
CO9 AP1 10c **orange** *(2,000)* — 275.00
On cover 400.00
Block of 4 1,375.
CO10 AP1 20c **red violet** *(2,000)* — 175.00
On cover —
Block of 4 750.00
CO11 AP1 30c **rose lake** *(5,000)* — 65.00
On cover 125.00
Block of 4 — 275.00
CO12 AP1 40c **yellow** *(2,000)* — 180.00
On cover 500.00
Block of 4 750.00
Nos. CO8-CO12 (5) 855.00

1947, Nov.

Type I- "PANAMA CANAL" 19-20mm long

CO14 AP1 6c **yellow brown** *(33,450)* 12.50 5.00
On cover 50.00
Block of 4 57.50 22.50
a. Inverted overprint *(50)* *2,500.*

POSTAGE DUE STAMPS

Prior to 1914, many of the postal issues were handstamped "Postage Due" and used as postage due stamps.

Postage Due Stamps of the United States Nos. J45a, J46a, and J49a Overprinted in Black

CANAL ZONE

1914, Mar. Wmk. 190 *Perf. 12*

J1 D2 1c **rose carmine** *(23,533)* 85. 15.
On cover 275.
Block of 4 (2mm spacing) 350. 70.
Block of 4 (3mm spacing) 375. 80.
P# block of 6, impt. & star 700. —
J2 D2 2c **rose carmine** *(32,312)* 250. 45.
On cover 275.
Block of 4 1,100. 200.
P# block of 6 1,750. —
J3 D2 10c **rose carmine** *(92,493)* 850. 40.
On cover 725.
Block of 4 (2mm spacing) 3,700. 170.
Block of 4 (3mm spacing) 3,700. 170.
P# block of 6, Impt. & star *7,000.* —

Many examples of Nos. J1-J3 show one or more letters of the overprint out of alignment, principally the "E."

San Geronimo Castle Gate, Portobelo (See footnote) — D1

Statue of Columbus — D2

Pedro J. Sosa — D3

1915, Mar. Unwmk. *Perf. 12*

Blue Overprint, Type II, on Postage Due Stamps of Panama

J4 D1 1c **olive brown** *(50,000)* 12.50 5.00
On cover 150.00
Block of 4 55.00 22.50
J5 D2 2c **olive brown** *(50,000)* 225.00 17.50
On cover 175.00
Block of 4 975.00 90.00
J6 D3 10c **olive brown** *(200,000)* 50.00 10.00
On cover 175.00
Block of 4 225.00 45.00

Type D1 was intended to show a gate of San Lorenzo Castle, Chagres, and is so labeled. By error the stamp actually shows the main gate of San Geronimo Castle, Portobelo.

Surcharged in Red

CANAL 2 ZONE

1915, Nov. Unwmk. *Perf. 12*

J7 D1 1c on 1c **olive brown** *(60,614)* 110.00 15.00
On cover 160.00
Block of 4 500.00 70.00
J8 D2 2c on 2c **olive brown** 25.00 7.50
On cover 200.00
Block of 4 110.00 35.00
J9 D3 10c on 10c **olive brown** *(175,548)* 22.50 5.00
On cover 200.00
Block of 4 100.00 25.00

One of the printings of No. J9 shows wider spacing between "1" and "0." Both spacings occur on the same sheet.

D4

Capitol, Panama — D5

1919, Dec.

Surcharged in Carmine at Mount Hope

J10 D4 2c on 2c **olive brown** 30.00 12.50
On cover 110.00
Block of 4 130.00 55.00
J11 D5 4c on 4c **olive brown** *(35,695)* 35.00 15.00
On cover 190.00
Block of 4 160.00 75.00
a. "ZONE" omitted *8,250.*
b. "4" omitted *8,250.*

Blue Overprint, Type V, on Postage Due Stamp of Panama

1922

J11C D1 1c **dark olive brown** — 10.00
d. "CANAL ZONE" reading down 200.00

CANAL

United States Postage Due Stamps Nos. J61, J62b and J65b Overprinted

ZONE

Type A

Letters "A" with Flat Tops

1924, July 1 *Perf. 11*

J12 D2 1c **carmine rose** *(10,000)* 100.00 27.50
On cover 100.00
Block of 4 450.00 125.00
P# block of 6 1,150. —
J13 D2 2c **deep claret** *(25,000)* 55.00 10.00
On cover 95.00
Block of 4 275.00 45.00
P# block of 6 725.00 —
J14 D2 10c **deep claret** *(30,000)* 225.00 50.00
On cover 190.00
Block of 4 (2mm spacing) 1,150. 210.00
Block of 4 (3mm spacing) 1,150. 210.00
Margin block of 6, imprint, star and P# *3,250.* —

Values for Nos. J12-J29 on cover are for philatelically contrived items. Commercial usages on cover are much more valuable.

United States Nos. 552, 554 and 562 Overprinted Type A and Additionally Overprinted at Mount Hope in Red or Blue

POSTAGE DUE

1925, Feb. *Perf. 11*

J15 A155 1c **deep green** (R) *(15,000)* 90.00 13.00
On cover 95.00
Block of 4 400.00 55.00
P# block of 6 900.00 —
J16 A157 2c **carmine** (Bl) *(21,335)* 22.50 7.00
On cover 67.50
Block of 4 100.00 30.00
P# block of 6 225.00 —
J17 A165 10c **orange** (R) *(39,819)* 50.00 11.00
On cover 90.00
Block of 4 250.00 47.50
P# block of 6 500.00 —
a. "POSTAGE DUE" double 500.00
b. "E" of "POSTAGE" omitted 450.00
c. As "b," "POSTAGE DUE" double *3,250.*

Overprinted Type B

Letters "A" with Sharp Pointed Tops

On U.S. Postage Due Stamps Nos. J61, J62, J65, J65a

1925, June 24

J18 D2 1c **carmine rose** *(80,000)* 8.00 3.00
On cover 50.00
Block of 4 35.00 15.00
P# block of 6 90.00 —
a. "ZONE ZONE" (LR18) 1,250.
J19 D2 2c **carmine rose** *(146,430)* 15.00 4.00
On cover 47.50
Block of 4 65.00 17.50
P# block of 6 160.00 —
a. "ZONE ZONE" (LR18) 1,500.
J20 D2 10c **carmine rose** *(153,980)* 150.00 20.00
On cover 120.00
Block of 4, 2mm spacing 650.00 85.00
Block of 4, 3mm spacing 675.00 90.00
P# block of 6, Impt. & Star 1,250. —
a. Vert. pair, one without ovpt. *(10)* *3,000.*
P# block of 6, Impt. & Star *18,000.*
b. 10c **rose red** *250.00* 150.00
On cover —
c. As "b," double overprint *450.00* —

Nos. J18-J20 exist with wrong font "CANAL" (UL51) and "ZONE" (UL82).

Regular Issue of 1928-29 Surcharged

1929-30

J21 A37 1c on 5c **blue** *(35,990) Mar. 20, 1930* 4.50 1.75
On cover 37.50
P# block of 6 45.00 —
a. "POSTAGE DUE" omitted *(5)* *5,500.*
J22 A37 2c on 5c **blue** *(40,207) Oct. 18, 1930* 7.50 2.50
On cover 32.50
P# block of 6 75.00 —
J23 A37 5c on 5c **blue** *(35,464) Dec. 1, 1930* 7.50 2.75
On cover 32.50
P# block of 6 75.00 —

J24 A37 10c on 5c **blue** *(90,504) Dec. 16, 1929* 7.50 2.75
On cover 32.50
P# block of 6 75.00 —

On No. J23 the three short horizontal bars in the lower corners of the surcharge are omitted.

Canal Zone Seal — D6

Printed by the U.S. Bureau of Engraving and Printing.

Plates of 400 subjects, issued in panes of 100.

1932-41 **Flat Plate Printing**

J25 D6 1c **claret** *(378,300) Jan. 2, 1932* .20 .20
On cover 30.00
P# block of 6 2.00 —
a. Dry printing, red violet .25 .20
On cover 32.50
P# block of 6 3.00 —
J26 D6 2c **claret** *(413,800) Jan. 2, 1932* .20 .20
On cover 22.50
P# block of 6 3.00 —
J27 D6 5c **claret** *Jan. 2, 1932* .35 .20
On cover 25.00
P# block of 6 3.50 —
a. Dry printing, red violet 1.00 .30
On cover 22.50
P# block of 6 7.50 —
J28 D6 10c **claret** *(400,600) Jan. 2, 1932* 1.40 1.50
On cover 32.50
P# block of 6 15.00 —
J29 D6 15c **claret** *Apr. 21, 1941* 1.10 1.00
On cover 37.50
P# block of 6 12.00 —
Nos. J25-J29 (5) 3.25 3.10

See note after No. 114.

OFFICIAL STAMPS

See note at beginning of Air Post Official Stamps

Regular Issues of 1928-34 Overprinted in Black by the Panama Canal Press, Mount Hope, C.Z.

OFFICIAL
PANAMA
CANAL
Type 1

OFFICIAL
PANAMA CANAL
Type 2

Type 1- "PANAMA" 10mm long
Type 1a- "PANAMA" 9mm long

1941, Mar. 31 **Unwmk.** ***Perf. 11***

O1 A35 1c **yellow green,** type 1 *(87,198)* 2.25 .40
On cover 70.00
O2 A45 3c **deep violet,** type 1 *(34,958)* 4.00 .75
On cover 90.00
O3 A37 5c **blue,** type 2 *(19,105)* *1,000.* 32.50
On cover *110.00*
O4 A38 10c **orange,** type 1 *(18,776)* 7.00 1.90
On cover 200.00
O5 A41 15c **gray black,** type 1 *(16,888)* 12.50 2.25
gray 2.25
On cover 140.00
O6 A42 20c **olive brown,** type 1 *(20,264)* 15.00 2.75
On cover 100.00
O7 A44 50c **lilac,** type 1 *(19,175)* 37.50 5.50
rose lilac 5.50
On cover —
O8 A44 50c **rose lilac,** type 1a *(1000)* 550.00

No. O3 exists with "O" directly over "N" of "PANAMA."

No. 139 Overprinted in Black

1947, Feb.

O9 A65 5c **deep blue,** type 1 *(21,639)* 9.00 3.50
On cover 75.00

POST OFFICE SEALS

POS1

Issued in sheets of 8 without gum, imperforate margins.

1907 **Typo.** **Unwmk.** ***Perf. 11½***

OX1 POS1 **blue** 40.00 —
Block of 4 175.00
a. Wmkd. seal of U.S. in sheet 55.00 —

No. OX1 clichés are spaced 3½mm apart.

1910

OX2 POS1 **ultramarine** 70.00 —
Block of 4, cliches ½mm apart 325.00
Block of 4, cliches 1½mm apart horiz., 4mm vert. 800.00
a. Wmkd. "Rolleston Mills" in sheet 90.00 —
b. Wmkd. U.S. Seal in sheet 225.00 —

POS2

Printed by the Panama Canal Press, Mount Hope, C.Z.

Issued in sheets of 25, without gum, imperforate margins.

Rouletted 6 horizontally in color of seal, vertically without color

1917, Sept. 22

OX3 POS2 **dark blue** 4.00 —
Block of 4 17.50
a. Wmkd. double lined letters in sheet ("Sylvania") 35.00

1946 ***Rouletted 6, without color***

Issued in sheets of 20, without gum, imperforate margins.

OX4 POS2 **slate blue** 9.00 —
Block of 4 40.00

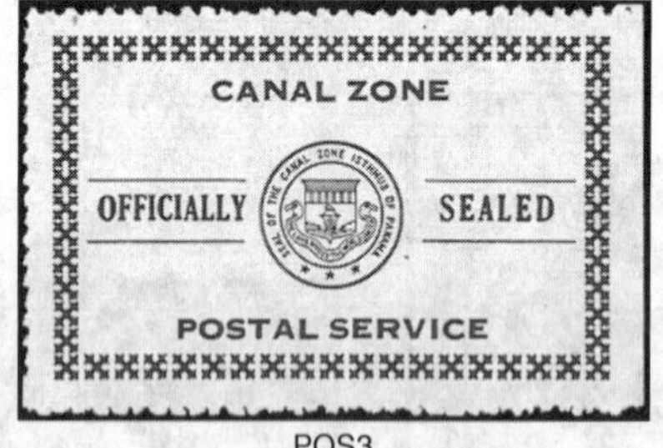

POS3

Typographed by the Panama Canal Press

Issued in sheets of 32, without gum, imperforate margins

except at top of sheet.

Size: 46x27mm

Seal Diameter: 13mm

1954, Mar. 8 **Unwmk.** ***Perf. 12½***

OX5 POS3 **black** *(16,000)* 5.00 —
a. Wmkd. Seal of U. S. in sheet 20.00 —

Seal Diameter: 11½mm

1961, May 16 ***Perf. 12½***

OX6 POS3 **black** (48,000) 3.00 —
b. Wmkd. Seal of U.S. in sheet, perf. 12½ 6.00
c. Double impression 80.00
d. As "b," double impression 100.00

1974, July 1 ***Rouletted 5***

OX7 POS3 **black** 3.00 —

ENVELOPES

Values for cut squares are for copies with fine margins on all sides. Values for unused entires are for those without printed or manuscript address. A "full corner" includes back and side flaps and commands a premium.

Vasco Núñez de Balboa — U1

Fernandez de Córdoba — U2

Envelopes of Panama Lithographed and Overprinted by American Bank Note Co.

1916, Apr. 24

On White Paper

U1 U1 1c **green & black** 15.00 10.00
Entire 95.00 35.00
a. Head and overprint only — —
Entire *2,000.* *2,000.*
b. Frame only — —
Entire *1,500.* *2,500.*
U2 U2 2c **carmine & black** 12.50 5.00
Entire 90.00 25.00
a. 2c **red & black** 12.50 5.00
Entire 85.00 45.00
b. Head and overprint only — —
Entire *1,500.* *2,000.*
c. Frame only (red) — —
Entire *1,000.* *2,000.*
d. Frame double (carmine) — —
Entire *2,500.* *2,250.*

José Vallarino — U3

"The Land Gate" — U4

1921, Nov. 13

On White Paper

U3 U3 1c **green** 140.00 100.00
Entire 700.00 375.00
U4 U4 2c **red** 35.00 20.00
Entire 275.00 125.00

Arms of Panama — U5

Typographed and embossed by American Bank Note Co. with "CANAL ZONE" in color of stamp.

1923, Dec. 15

On White Paper

U5 U5 2c **carmine** 55.00 32.50
Entire 200.00 125.00

U.S. Nos. U420 and U429 Overprinted in Black by Bureau of Engraving and Printing, Washington, D.C.

CANAL
ZONE

1924, July 1

U6 U92 1c **green** *(50,000)* 5.00 3.00
Entire 30.00 19.00
U7 U93 2c **carmine** *(100,000)* 5.00 3.00
Entire 30.00 19.00

Seal of Canal Zone — U6

Printed by the Panama Canal Press, Mount Hope, C.Z.

1924, Oct.

On White Paper

U8 U6 1c **green** *(205,000)* 2.00 1.00
Entire 24.00 15.00
U9 U6 2c **carmine** *(1,997,658)* .75 .40
Entire 27.50 15.00

Gorgas — U7

Goethals — U8

Typographed and Embossed by International Envelope Corp., Dayton, O.

1932, Apr. 8

U10 U7 1c **green** *(1,300,000)* .20 .20
Entire 3.00 1.10
Entire, 1st day cancel 35.00
U11 U8 2c **carmine** *(400,250)* .25 .20
Entire 3.50 1.75
Entire, 1st day cancel 35.00

No. U9 Surcharged in Violet by Panama Canal Press, Mount Hope, C.Z. Numerals 3mm high **3 3**

1932, July 20

U12 U6 3c on 2c **carmine** *(20,000)* 17.50 7.50
Entire 225.00 125.00

No. U11 Surcharged in Violet, Numerals 5mm high **3 3**

1932, July 20

U13 U8 3c on 2c **carmine** *(320,000)* 2.00 1.00
Entire 25.00 15.00
Entire, 1st day cancel 75.00

1934, Jan. 17

Numerals with Serifs

U14 U6 3c on 2c **carmine** (Numerals 4mm high) *(8,000)* 115.00 60.00
Entire 450.00 525.00
U15 U8 3c on 2c **carmine** (Numerals 5mm high) *(23,000)* 25.00 15.00
Entire 250.00 150.00

Typographed and Embossed by International Envelope Corp., Dayton, O.

1934, June 18

U16 U8 3c **purple** *(2,450,000)* .20 .20
Entire 1.20 1.40

1958, Nov. 1

U17 U8 4c **blue** *(596,725)* .20 .25
Entire 1.25 1.25
Entire, 1st day cancel, Cristobal 2.00

Surcharged at Left of Stamp in Ultra. as No. UX13

1969, Apr. 28

U18 U8 4c +1c **blue** *(93,850)* .20 *.25*
Entire 1.25 *1.60*
Entire, 1st day cancel 1.50
U19 U8 4c +2c **blue** *(23,125)* .50 *.65*
Entire 2.50 *4.00*
Entire, 1st day cancel 1.50

Ship Passing through Gaillard Cut — U9

Typographed and Embossed by United States Envelope Co., Williamsburg, Pa.

1971, Nov. 17

U20 U9 8c **emerald** *(121,500)* .25 *.30*
Entire .75 .65
Entire, 1st day cancel, Balboa *(9,650)* 1.50

Surcharged at Left of Stamp in Emerald as #UX13

1974, Mar. 2

U21 U9 8c +2c **emerald** .30 *.35*
Entire 1.00 *2.00*
Entire, 1st day cancel 1.25

1976, Feb. 23

U22 U9 13c **violet** *(638,350)* .35 *.40*
Entire .85 .85
Entire, 1st day cancel, Balboa *(9,181)* 1.25

Surcharged at Left of Stamp in Violet as No. UX13

1978, July 5

U23 U9 13c +2c **violet** *(245,041)* .35 *.40*
Entire .85 *2.00*
Entire, 1st day cancel 1.25

AIR POST ENVELOPES

No. U9 Overprinted with Horizontal Blue and Red Bars Across Entire Face. Overprinted by Panama Canal Press, Mount Hope. Boxed inscription in lower left with nine lines of instructions. Additional adhesives required for air post rate.

1928, May 21

UC1 U6 2c **red,** entire *(15,000)* 135.00 65.00
First day cancel 175.00

No. U9 with Similar Overprint of Blue and Red Bars, and "VIA AIR MAIL" in Blue, At Left, no box.

1929

UC2 U6 2c **red,** entire *(60,200)* 65.00 27.50
a. Inscription centered *(10,000) Jan. 11* 325.00 190.00

Earliest known use of No. UC2 is Feb. 6.

DC-4 Skymaster — UC1

Typographed and Embossed by International Envelope Corp., Dayton, O.

1949, Jan. 3

UC3 UC1 6c **blue** *(4,400,000)* .25 .25
Entire 4.00 3.00
Entire, 1st day cancel 2.00

1958, Nov. 1

UC4 UC1 7c **carmine** *(1,000,000)* .25 .20
Entire 4.00 3.50
Entire, 1st day cancel 1.50

No. U16 Surcharged at Left of Stamp and Imprinted "VIA AIR MAIL" in Dark Blue

Surcharged by Panama Canal Press, Mount Hope, C.Z.

1963, June 22

UC5 U8 3c + 5c **purple** *(105,000)* 1.00 1.00
Entire 6.00 *8.00*
Entire, 1st day cancel 5.00
a. Double surcharge *1,250.*

Jet Liner and Tail Assembly UC2

Typographed and Embossed by International Envelope Corp., Dayton, O.

1964, Jan. 6

UC6 UC2 8c **deep carmine** *(600,000)* .35 .35
Entire 2.25 2.50
Entire, 1st day cancel, Balboa *(3,855)* 2.25

No. U17 Surcharged at Left of Stamp as No. UC5 and Imprinted "VIA AIR MAIL" in Vermilion
Surcharged by Canal Zone Press, La Boca, C.Z.

1965, Oct. 15

UC7 U8 4c + 4c **blue** *(100,000)* .50 .40
Entire 4.50 *7.50*
Entire, 1st day cancel 5.00

Jet Liner and Tail Assembly — UC3

Typographed and Embossed by United States Envelope Co., Williamsburg, Pa.

1966, Feb.

UC8 UC3 8c **carmine** *(224,000)* .50 .45
Entire 5.00 5.00

Earliest known use: Feb. 23.

No. UC8 Surcharged at Left of Stamp as No. UX13 in Vermilion
Surcharged by Canal Zone Press, La Boca, C.Z.

1968, Jan. 18

UC9 UC3 8c + 2c **carmine** *(376,000)* .40 .35
Entire 2.75 *5.00*
Entire, 1st day cancel 4.50

No. UC7 with Additional Surcharge at Left of Stamp as No. UX13 and Imprinted "VIA AIR MAIL" in Vermilion
Surcharged by Canal Zone Press, La Boca, C.Z.

1968, Feb. 12

UC10 U8 4c + 4c + 2c **blue** *(224,150)* .60 .50
Entire 2.25 *6.00*
Entire, 1st day cancel 5.00

Type of 1966
Typographed and Engraved by United States Envelope Co., Williamsburg, Pa.

1969, Apr. 1

Luminescent Ink

UC11 UC3 10c **ultramarine** *(448,000)* .60 .40
Entire 4.00 *5.00*
Entire, 1st day cancel, Balboa *(9,583)* 2.00

No. U17 Surcharged at Left of Stamp as Nos. UC5 and UX13, and Imprinted "VIA AIR MAIL" in Vermilion

1971, May 17

UC12 U8 4c + 5c + 2c **blue** *(55,775)* .75 .50
Entire 4.00 *6.00*
Entire, 1st day cancel 5.00

No. UC11 Surcharged in Ultra. at Left of Stamp as No. UX13

1971, May 17

Luminescent Ink

UC13 UC3 10c + 1c **ultramarine** *(152,000)* .45 .40
Entire 4.00 *7.00*
Entire, 1st day cancel 3.50

Type of 1966
Typographed and Engraved by United States Envelope Co., Williamsburg, Pa.

1971, Nov. 17

UC14 UC3 11c **rose red** *(258,000)* .30 .20
Entire 1.10 1.25
Entire, 1st day cancel, Balboa *(3,451)* 1.50
a. 11c **carmine,** stamp tagged, *(395,000)* .30 .20
Entire 1.10 1.25
Entire, 1st day cancel, Balboa *(5,971)* 1.50

The red diamonds around the envelope edges are luminescent on both Nos. UC14 and UC14a. No. UC14 is size 10, No. UC14a size 6¾.

Surcharged at Left of Stamp in Rose Red as No. UX13

1974, Mar. 2

UC15 UC3 11c + 2c **carmine,** tagged *(305,000)*	.35	.30
Entire	1.50	*3.00*
Entire, 1st day cancel		1.25
a. 11c + 2c **rose red,** untagged, *(87,000)*	.35	.25
Entire	1.75	2.00

No. U21 with Additional Surcharge in Vermilion at Left of Stamp as No. UX13 and Imprinted "VIA AIR MAIL" in Vermilion

1975, May 3

UC16 U9 8c + 2c + 3c **emerald** *(75,000)*	.50	.30
Entire	1.25	*2.50*
Entire, 1st day cancel		1.50

REGISTRATION ENVELOPES

RE1

Panama Registration Envelope surcharged by Panama Canal Press, Mount Hope, C.Z.

1918, Oct. 8mm between CANAL & ZONE

UF1 RE1 10c on 5c **black & red,** *cream (10,000),* entire	*1,750.*	*2,000.*
a. 9¼mm between CANAL & ZONE *(25,000),* entire ('19)	*1,250.*	*2,000.*

Stamped envelopes inscribed "Diez Centesimos," surcharged with numerals "5" and with solid blocks printed over "Canal Zone," were issued by the Republic of Panama after being rejected by the Canal Zone. Parts of "Canal Zone" are often legible under the surcharge blocks. These envelopes exist without surcharge.

POSTAL CARDS

Values are for Entires

Map of Panama — PC1

Panama Card Lithographed by American Bank Note Co., revalued and surcharged in black by the Isthmian Canal Commission.

1907, Feb. 9

UX1 PC1 1c on 2c **carmine,** "CANAL" 15mm *(50,000)*	40.	25.
a. Double surcharge	*1,500.*	*1,500.*
b. Double surcharge, one reading down	*2,750.*	
c. Triple surcharge, one reading down	*3,300.*	
d. "CANAL" 13mm *(10,000)*	250.	200.
e. As "d," double surcharge	*2,400.*	

Balboa — PC2

Panama card lithographed by Hamilton Bank Note Co. Overprinted in black by Isthmian Canal Commission.

At least six types of overprint, reading down.

1908, Mar. 3

UX2 PC2 1c **green & black,** "CANAL" 13mm *(295,000)*	190.	80.
a. Double overprint	*2,000.*	*2,000.*
b. Triple overprint	*1,750.*	—
c. Period after "ZONE" *(40,000)*	200.	125.
d. "CANAL" 15mm *(30,000)*	200.	125.
e. "ZONE CANAL", reading up	*4,000.*	

Balboa

PC3 PC4

Lithographed by Hamilton Bank Note Co. Overprinted in Black by Panama Canal Press, Mount Hope, C.Z.

1910, Nov. 10

UX3 PC3 1c **green & black** *(40,000)*	190.	70.
a. Double overprint		*4,250.*

This card, with overprint reading up, is actually the fourth of seven settings of UX2.

Lithographed and Overprinted by American Bank Note Co.

1913, Mar. 27

UX4 PC4 1c **green & black** *(634,000)*	160.	60.

Design of Canal Zone Envelopes Overprinted in black by the American Bank Note Co.

1921, Oct.

UX5 U3 1c **green**	1,100.	450.

Typographed and embossed by American Bank Note Co. with "CANAL ZONE" in color of stamp.

1924, Jan.

UX6 U5 1c **green**	725.	*1,100.*

CANAL

U.S. No. UX27 Overprinted by U.S. Gov't. Printing Office at Washington, D.C.

ZONE

1924, July 1

UX7 PC17 1c **green,** *buff (Jefferson) (50,000)*	85.	35.

Design of Canal Zone Envelope Printed by Panama Canal Press.

1925, Jan.

UX8 U6 1c **green,** *buff (25,000)*	80.	35.
a. Background only	*1,800.*	

CANAL

U.S. No. UX27 Overprinted

ZONE

1925, May

UX9 PC17 1c **green,** *buff (Jefferson) (850,000)*	8.50	5.00

CANAL

U.S. No. UX27 Overprinted

ZONE

1935, Oct.

UX10 PC17 1c **green,** *buff (Jefferson) (2,900,000)*	1.80	1.80
a. Double overprint	*1,900.*	

Used values are for contemporaneous usage without additional postage applied.

Same on U.S. No. UX38

1952, May 1

UX11 PC22 2c **carmine rose,** *buff (Franklin) (800,000)*	2.00	2.00
1st day cancel, Balboa Heights		3.50

Ship in Lock — PC5

Printed by Bureau of Engraving & Printing, Washington, D.C.

1958, Nov. 1

UX12 PC5 3c **dark blue,** *buff (335,116)*	1.90	*3.00*
First day cancel, Cristobal		1.25

No. UX12 Surcharged at Left of Stamp in Green by Panama Canal Press, Mount Hope, C.Z.

1963, July 27

UX13 PC5 3c + 1c **dark blue,** *buff (78,000)*	4.00	*6.00*
First day cancel		3.50

CANAL ZONE POSTAGE

4c

Ship Passing through Panama Canal — PC6

Printed by Panama Canal Press, Mount Hope, C.Z.

1964, Dec. 1

UX14 PC6 4c **violet blue,** *buff (74,200)*	3.75	*7.50*
1st day cancel, Cristobal *(19,260)*		3.50

Ship in Lock (Towing locomotive at right redrawn) — PC7

Printed by Bureau of Engraving & Printing, Washington, D.C.

1965, Aug. 12

UX15 PC7 4c **emerald** *(95,500)*	1.10	*2.00*
1st day cancel, Cristobal *(20,366)*		1.00

No. UX15 Surcharged at Left of Stamp in Green as No. UX13 by Canal Zone Press, La Boca, C.Z.

1968, Feb. 12

UX16 PC7 4c + 1c **emerald** *(94,775)*	1.10	*4.00*
First day cancel		1.00

Ship-in-Lock Type of 1965

1969, Apr. 1

UX17 PC7 5c **light ultramarine** *(63,000)*	1.00	*2.50*
1st day cancel, Balboa *(11,835)*		1.00

No. UX17 Surcharged at Left of Stamp in Light Ultramarine as No. UX13

1971, May 24

UX18 PC7 5c + 1c **light ultramarine** *(100,500)*	.90	*3.50*
First day cancel		1.00

Ship-in-Lock Type of 1965

Printed by Bureau of Engraving & Printing, Washington, D.C.

1974, Feb. 11

UX19 PC7 8c **brown** *(90,895)*	.90	*2.00*
1st day cancel, Balboa *(10,375)*		1.00

No. UX19 Surcharged at Left of Stamp in Brown as No. UX13

1976, June 1

UX20 PC7 8c + 1c **brown** *(60,249)*	.65	*4.00*
First day cancel		1.00

No. UX19 Surcharged at Left of Stamp in Brown as No. UX13

1978, July 5

UX21 PC7 8c + 2c **brown** *(74,847)*	.85	*4.00*
First day cancel		1.00

AIR POST POSTAL CARDS

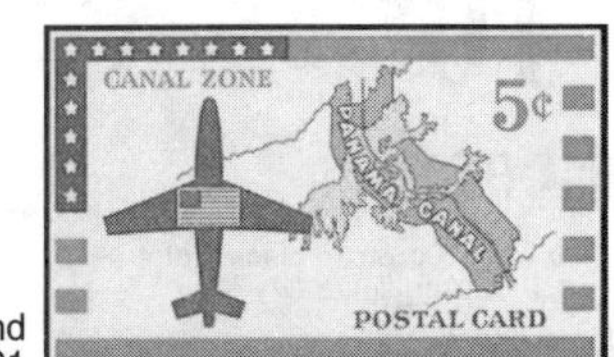

Plane, Flag and Map — APC1

Printed by Bureau of Engraving & Printing, Washington, D.C.

1958, Nov. 1

UXC1 APC1	5c **blue & carmine rose** *(104,957)*	3.75	*7.50*
	1st day cancel, Balboa		3.75

No. UXC1 Surcharged at Left of Stamp in Green as No. UX13 by Panama Canal Press, Mount Hope, C.Z.

1963, July 27

UXC2 APC1	5c + 1c **blue & carmine rose** *(48,000)*	9.50	*18.00*
a.	Inverted surcharge	*1,500.*	
	First day cancel		5.00

No. UX15 Surcharged at Left of Stamp as No. UX13 and Imprinted "AIR MAIL" in Vermilion

1965, Aug. 18

UXC3 PC7	4c + 2c **emerald** *(41,700)*	4.00	*20.00*
	First day cancel		6.00

No. UX15 Surcharged at Left of Stamp as No. UC5 and Imprinted "AIR MAIL" in Vermilion by Canal Zone Press, La Boca, C.Z.

1968, Feb. 12

UXC4 PC7	4c + 4c **emerald** *(60,100)*	2.75	*16.00*
	First day cancel		6.00

No. UX17 Surcharged at Left of Stamp as No. UC5 and Imprinted "AIR MAIL" in Vermilion

1971, May 24

UXC5 PC7	5c + 4c **light ultramarine** *(68,000)*	1.00	*15.00*
	First day cancel		6.00

PROOFS

1928-40

Column (1)- Large Die
Column (2)- Small Die

		(1)	(2)
106TC	2c **black**	*1,300.*	
113P	30c **brown black**		975.

1934

		(1)	(2)
117P	3c **deep violet** *(8)*		475.

1939

		(1)	(2)
120P	1c **yellow green**	*1,300.*	875.
121P	2c **rose carmine**		875.
122P	3c **purple**	*1,300.*	875.
123P	5c **dark blue**	*1,300.*	875.
124P	6c **red orange**		875.
125P	7c **black**		875.
126P	8c **green**	*1,300.*	875.
127P	10c **ultramarine**	*1,300.*	875.
128P	11c **blue green**	*1,300.*	875.
129P	12c **brown carmine**	*1,300.*	875.
130P	14c **dark violet**		875.
131P	15c **olive green**		875.
132P	18c **rose pink**		875.
133P	20c **brown**	*1,300.*	875.
134P	25c **orange**	*1,300.*	875.
135P	50c **violet brown**	*1,300.*	875.

1946-48

		(1)	(2)
136P	½c **bright red**	*1,300.*	
137P	1½c **chocolate**	*1,300.*	
139P	5c **deep blue**	*1,300.*	
140P	25c **yellow green**	*1,300.*	
141P	10c **black**	*825.*	

1949

		(1)	(2)
142P	3c **blue**	*1,150.*	
143P	6c **violet**	*1,150.*	
144P	12c **bright blue green**	*1,150.*	
145P	18c **deep red lilac**	*1,150.*	

1951

		(1)	(2)
146P	10c **carmine**	*1,500.*	

1955

		(1)	(2)
147P	3c **violet**	*1,500.*	

Air Post

1931-49

		(1)	(2)
C6P	4c **red violet**	*1,600.*	
C7P	5c **light green**	*1,600.*	
C8P	6c **yellow brown**	*1,600.*	
C13TC	40c **orange**	*1,600.*	

1939

		(1)	(2)
C15P	5c **greenish black**		925.
C15TC	5c **scarlet**	*1,300.*	
C16P	10c **dull violet**	*1,300.*	925.
C17P	15c **light brown**	*1,300.*	925.
C18P	25c **blue**		925.
C19P	30c **rose carmine**	*1,300.*	925.
C20P	$1 **green**	*1,300.*	925.

1951

		(1)	(2)
C21P	4c **red violet**	*1,300.*	

The Small Die proofs listed are on soft yellowish wove paper.
Only No. 117P has more than two copies reported in private collections.

CUBA

After the U.S. battleship "Maine" was destroyed in Havana harbor with a loss of 266 lives in February, 1898, the United States demanded the withdrawal of Spanish troops from Cuba. The Spanish-American War followed. With the peace treaty of Dec. 10, 1898, Spain relinquished Cuba to the United States in trust for its inhabitants. On Jan. 1, 1899, Spanish authority was succeeded by U.S. military rule which lasted until May 20, 1902, when Cuba, as a republic, assumed self-government.

The listings in this catalogue cover the U.S. Administration issue of 1899, the Republic's 1899-1902 issues under U.S. military rule and the Puerto Principe issue of provincial provisionals.

Values for Nos. 176-220 are for stamps in the grade of fine and in sound condition where such exist. Values for Nos. 221-UX2b are for very fine examples.

100 CENTS = 1 DOLLAR

Puerto Principe Issue

In December, 1898, Puerto Principe, a provincial capital now called Camagüey, ran short of 1c, 2c, 3c, 5c and 10c stamps. The Postmaster ordered Cuban stamps to be surcharged on Dec. 19, 1898.

The surcharging was done to horizontal strips of five stamps, so vertical pairs and blocks do not exist. Five types are found in each setting, and five printings were made. Counterfeits are plentiful.

First Printing

Black Surcharge, 17½mm high

Surcharge measures 17½mm high and is roughly printed in dull black ink.

HABILITADO HABILITADO HABILITADO
2 2 2
cents. cents. cents.
Position 1 Position 2 Position 3

HABILITADO HABILITADO
2 2
cents. cents.
Position 4 Position 5

Position 1	-No serif at right of "t"
Position 2	-Thin numeral except on 1c on 1m No. 176
Position 3	-Broken right foot of "n"
Position 4	-Up-stroke of "t" broken
Position 5	-Broken "DO"

This printing consisted of the following stamps:

176	1c on 1m orange brown, Pos. 1, 2, 3, 4 and 5
178	2c on 2m orange brown, Pos. 1, 3, 4 and 5
179	2c on 2m orange brown, Pos. 2
180	3c on 3m orange brown, Pos. 1, 3, 4 and 5
181	3c on 3m orange brown, Pos. 2
188	5c on 5m orange brown, Pos. 1, 3, 4 and 5
189	5c on 5m orange brown, Pos. 2

Second Printing

Black Surcharge, 17½mm high

This printing was from the same setting as used for the first printing, but the impression is much clearer and the ink quite shiny.

The printing consisted of the following stamps:

179F	3c on 2m orange brown, Pos. 1, 3, 4 and 5
179G	3c on 2m orange brown, Pos. 2
182	5c on 1m orange brown, Pos. 1, 3, 4 and 5
183	5c on 1m orange brown, Pos. 2
184	5c on 2m orange brown, Pos. 1, 3, 4 and 5
185	5c on 2m orange brown, Pos. 2
186	5c on 3m orange brown, Pos. 1, 3, 4 and 5
187	5c on 3m orange brown, Pos. 2
188	5c on 5m orange brown, Pos. 1, 3, 4 and 5
189	5c on 5m orange brown, Pos. 2
190	5c on ½m blue green, Pos. 1, 3, 4 and 5
191	5c on ½m blue green, Pos. 2

Third Printing

Red Surcharge, 20mm high

The same setting as for the first and second was used for the third printing. The 10c denomination first appeared in this printing and position 2 of that value has numerals same as on positions 1, 3, 4 and 5, while position 4 has broken "1" in "10."

The printing consisted of the following stamps:

196	3c on 1c black violet, Pos. 1, 3, 4 and 5
197	3c on 1c black violet, Pos. 2
198	5c on 1c black violet, Pos. 1, 3, 4 and 5
199	5c on 1c black violet, Pos. 2
200	10c on 1c black violet, Pos. 1, 2, 3 and 5
200a	10c on 1c black violet, Pos. 4

Fourth Printing

Black Surcharge, 19½mm high

The same type as before but spaced between so that the surcharge is 2mm taller. Clear impression, shiny ink.

HABILITADO HABILITADO HABILITADO
1 1 1
cents. cents. cents.
Position 1 Position 2 Position 3

HABILITADO HABILITADO
1 1
cents. cents.
Position 4 Position 5

Position 1	-No serif at right of "t"
Position 2	-Broken "1" on No. 177
Position 2	-Thin numerals on 5c stamps
Position 3	-Broken right foot of "n"
Position 4	-Up-stroke of "t" broken
Position 4	-Thin numeral on 3c stamps
Position 5	-Broken "DO"

This printing consisted of the following stamps:

177	1c on 1m orange brn, Pos. 1, 3, 4 and 5
177a	1c on 1m orange brn, Pos. 2
179B	3c on 1m orange brn, Pos. 1, 2, 3 and 5
179D	3c on 1m orange brn, Pos. 4
183B	5c on 1m orange brn, Pos. 1, 3, 4 and 5
189C	5c on 5m orange brn, Pos. 1, 3, 4 and 5
192	5c on ½m blue green, Pos. 1, 3, 4 and 5
193	5c on ½m blue green, Pos. 2

Fifth Printing

Black Surcharge, 19½mm high

HABILITADO 3 cents. Position 1
HABILITADO 3 cents. Position 2
HABILITADO 3 eents. Position 3
HABILITADO 3 cents. Position 4
HABILITADO 3 cents. Position 5

Position 1	-Nick in bottom of "e"and lower serif of "s"
Position 2	-Normal surcharge
Position 3	-"eents"
Position 4	-Thin numeral
Position 5	-Nick in upper part of right stroke of "n"

This printing consisted of the following stamps:

201	3c on 1m blue green, Pos. 1, 2 and 5
201b	3c on 1m blue green, Pos. 3
202	3c on 1m blue green, Pos. 4
203	3c on 2m blue green, Pos. 4
203a	3c on 2m blue green, Pos. 3
204	3c on 2m blue green, Pos. 4
205	3c on 3m blue green, Pos. 1, 2 and 5
205b	3c on 3m blue green, Pos. 3
206	3c on 3m blue green, Pos. 4
211	5c on 1m blue green, Pos. 1, 2 and 5
211a	5c on 1m blue green, Pos. 3
212	5c on 1m blue green, Pos. 4
213	5c on 2m blue green, Pos. 1, 2 and 5
213a	5c on 2m blue green, Pos. 3
214	5c on 2m blue green, Pos. 4
215	5c on 3m blue green, Pos. 1, 2 and 5
215a	5c on 3m blue green, Pos. 3
216	5c on 3m blue green, Pos. 4
217	5c on 4m blue green, Pos. 1, 2 and 5
217a	5c on 4m blue green, Pos. 3
218	5c on 4m blue green, Pos. 4
219	5c on 8m blue green, Pos. 1, 2 and 5
219b	5c on 8m blue green, Pos. 3
220	5c on 8m blue green, Pos. 4

Counterfeits exist of all Puerto Principe surcharges. Illustrations have been altered to discourage further counterfeiting.

Regular Issues of Cuba of 1896 and 1898 Surcharged:

HABILITADO 1 cent. a
HABILITADO 1 cents. b

Numeral in ( ) after color indicates printing.

1898-99

Black Surcharge on Nos. 156-158, 160

176	(a)	1 cent on 1m **orange brn** (1)	50.00	30.00
177	(b)	1 cents on 1m **org brn** (4)	45.00	35.00
a.		Broken figure "1"	75.00	65.00
b.		Inverted surcharge		200.00
d.		Same as "a" inverted		*250.00*

HABILITADO 2 cents. c
HABILITADO 2 cents. d

178	(c)	2c on 2m **orange brown** (1)	22.50	18.00
a.		Inverted surcharge	250.00	50.00
179	(d)	2c on 2m **orange brown** (1)	40.00	35.00
a.		Inverted surcharge	350.00	100.00

HABILITADO 3 cents. k
HABILITADO 3 cents. l

179B	(k)	3c on 1m **orange brown** (4)	300.	175.
c.		Double surcharge	1,500.	750.

An unused copy is known with "cents" omitted.

179D	(l)	3c on 1m **orange brown** (4)	*1,500.*	*750.*
e.		Double surcharge	—	—

HABILITADO 3 cents. e
HABILITADO 3 cents. f

179F	(e)	3c on 2m **orange brown** (2)		*1,500.*

Value is for copy with minor faults.

179G	(f)	3c on 2m **orange brown** (2)	—	*2,000.*

Value is for copy with minor faults.

180	(e)	3c on 3m **orange brown** (1)	27.50	30.
a.		Inverted surcharge		110.
181	(f)	3c on 3m **orange brown** (1)	75.	75.
a.		Inverted surcharge		*200.*

HABILITADO 5 cents. g
HABILITADO 5 cents. h
HABILITADO 5 cents. i
HABILITADO 5 cents. j

182	(g)	5c on 1m **orange brown** (2)	700.	200.
a.		Inverted surcharge		*500.*
183	(h)	5c on 1m **orange brown** (2)	*1,300.*	*500.*
a.		Inverted surcharge		*700.*
184	(g)	5c on 2m **orange brown** (2)	750.	250.
185	(h)	5c on 2m **orange brown** (2)	1,500.	500.
186	(g)	5c on 3m **orange brown** (2)	650.	175.
a.		Inverted surcharge	1,200.	700.
187	(h)	5c an 3m **orange brown** (2)		400.
a.		Inverted surcharge		1,000.
188	(g)	5c on 5m **orange brown** (1) (2)	80.	60.
a.		Inverted surcharge	400.	200.
b.		Double surcharge	—	—
189	(h)	5c on 5m **orange brown** (1) (2)	350.	250.
a.		Inverted surcharge		400.
b.		Double surcharge	—	—
189C	(i)	5c on 5m **orange brown** (4)		*7,500.*

Values for Nos. 188, 189 are for the first printing.

Black Surcharge on No. P25

190	(g)	5c on ½m **blue green** (2)	250.	75.
a.		Inverted surcharge	500.	150.
b.		Pair, one without surcharge		500.
191	(h)	5c on ½m **blue green** (2)	300.	90.
a.		Inverted surcharge		200.
192	(i)	5c on ½m **blue green** (4)	550.	200.
a.		Double surcharge, one diagonal		*11,500.*

Value for No. 190b is for pair with unsurcharged copy at right. One pair with unsurcharged copy at left is known.
No. 192a is unique.

193	(j)	5c on ½m **blue green** (4)	800.	300.

Red Surcharge on No. 161

196	(k)	3c on 1c **black violet** (3)	65.	35.
a.		Inverted surcharge		300.
197	(l)	3c on 1c **black violet** (3)	125.	55.
a.		Inverted surcharge		300.
198	(i)	5c on 1c **black violet** (3)	25.	30.
a.		Inverted surcharge		125.
b.		Vertical surcharge		*3,500.*
c.		Double surcharge	*400.*	*600.*
d.		Double inverted surcharge		—
199	(j)	5c on 1c **black violet** (3)	55.	55.
a.		Inverted surcharge		250.
b.		Vertical surcharge		*2,000.*
c.		Double surcharge	1,000.	600.

Value for No. 198b is for surcharge reading up. One copy is known with surcharge reading down.

HABILITADO 10 cents. m

200	(m)	10c on 1c **black violet** (3)	20.	*50.*
a.		Broken figure "1"	40.	*100.*

Black Surcharge on Nos. P26-P30

201	(k)	3c on 1m **blue green** (5)	350.	350.
a.		Inverted surcharge		450.
b.		"EENTS"	550.	450.
c.		As "b", inverted		850.
202	(l)	3c on 1m **blue green** (5)	550.	400.
a.		Inverted surcharge		850.
203	(k)	3c on 2m **blue green** (5)	850.	350.
a.		"EENTS"	1,250.	500.
b.		Inverted surcharge		850.
c.		As "a," inverted		950.
204	(l)	3c on 2m **blue green** (5)	1,250.	600.
a.		Inverted surcharge		750.
205	(k)	3c on 3m **blue green** (5)	900.	350.
a.		Inverted surcharge		500.
b.		"EENTS"	1,250.	450.
c.		As "b," inverted		700.
206	(l)	3c on 3m **blue green** (5)	1,200.	550.
a.		Inverted surcharge		700.
211	(i)	5c on 1m **blue green** (5)		1,800.
a.		"EENTS"	—	2,500.
212	(j)	5c on 1m **blue green** (5)		2,250.
213	(i)	5c on 2m **blue green** (5)		1,800.
a.		"EENTS"	—	1,900.
214	(j)	5c on 2m **blue green** (5)		1,750.
215	(i)	5c on 3m **blue green** (5)		550.
a.		"EENTS"		1,000.
216	(j)	5c on 3m **blue green** (5)	—	1,000.
217	(i)	5c on 4m **blue green** (5)	*2,500.*	900.
a.		"EENTS"	*3,000.*	1,500.
b.		Inverted surcharge		*2,000.*
c.		As "a," inverted		2,000.
218	(j)	5c on 4m **blue green** (5)		*1,250.*
a.		Inverted surcharge		*2,000.*
219	(i)	5c on 8m **blue green** (5)	*2,500.*	1,250.
a.		Inverted surcharge		1,500.
b.		"EENTS"	—	1,800.
c.		As "b," inverted		2,500.
220	(j)	5c on 8m **blue green** (5)		2,000.
a.		Inverted surcharge		2,500.

Puerto Principe pairs, strips and stamps properly canceled on cover are scarce and command high premiums.

Most copies of all but the most common varieties are faulty or have tropical toning. Values are for sound copies where they exist.

United States Stamps Nos. 279, 267, 267b, 279Bf, 279Bh, 268, 281, 282C and 283 Surcharged in Black

1899 Wmk. 191 *Perf. 12*

221	A87	1c on 1c **yellow green**	5.25	.35
		On cover		15.00
		Block of 4	27.50	4.50
		P# strip of 3, Impt.	57.50	
		P# block of 6, Impt.	300.00	
222	A88	2c on 2c **reddish carmine,** type III, *Feb.*	10.00	.75
		On cover		22.50
		Block of 4	55.00	8.00
		P# strip of 3, Impt.	115.00	
		P# block of 6, Impt.	650.00	
b.		2c on 2c **vermilion,** type III, *Feb.*	10.00	.75
222A	A88	2c on 2c **reddish carmine,** type IV, *Feb.*	5.75	.40
		On cover		12.50
		Block of 4	30.00	4.50
		P# strip of 3, Impt.	65.00	
		P# block of 6, Impt.	425.00	
		"CUBA" at bottom	*600.00*	
		"CUPA" (broken letter. pos. 99)	175.00	
c.		2c on 2c **vermilion,** type IV, *Feb.*	5.75	.40
d.		As No. 222A, inverted surcharge	*3,500.*	*5,000.*
223	A88	2½c on 2c **reddish carmine,** type III, *Jan. 2*	5.00	.80
		On cover		20.00
		Block of 4	27.50	8.00
		P# strip of 3, Impt.	90.00	
		P# block of 6, Impt.	350.00	
b.		2½c on 2c **vermilion,** type III, *Jan. 2*	5.00	.80
223A	A88	2½c on 2c **reddish carmine,** type IV, *Jan. 2*	3.50	.50
		On cover		12.50
		Block of 4	20.00	4.50
		P# strip of 3, Impt.	62.50	
		P# block of 6, Impt.	250.00	
c.		2½c on 2c **vermilion,** type IV, *Jan. 2*	3.50	.50

All 2½c stamps were sold and used as 2 centavo stamps.

224 A89 3c on 3c **purple** 12.50 1.75
On cover 25.00
Block of 4 62.50 14.00
P# strip of 3, Impt. 110.00
P# block of 6, Impt. 675.00
a. Period between "B" and "A" 37.50 35.00

Two types of surcharge
I - "3" directly over "P"
II - "3" to left over "P"

225 A91 5c on 5c **blue** 12.50 2.00
On cover 30.00
Block of 4 62.50 15.00
P# strip of 3, Impt. 190.00
P# block of 6, Impt. 800.00
"CUBA" at bottom — —
"CUPA" (broken letter) 80.00 40.00
226 A94 10c on 10c **brown,** type I 25.00 6.50
On cover 110.00
Block of 4 100.00 45.00
P# strip of 3, Impt. 260.00
P# block of 6, Impt. 1,000.
"CUBA" at bottom 325.00 500.00
b. "CUBA" omitted *5,500. 4,000.*
226A A94 10c on 10c **brown,** type II *6,000.*
Block of 4 —
Nos. 221-226 (8) 79.50 13.05

No. 226A exists only in the special printing.
The No. 225 "CUPA" variety always has a straight edge at the right.

Special Printing

In March 1900, one pane of 100 each of Nos. 221-225, 226A, J1-J4 and two panes of 50 of No. E1, were specially overprinted for displays at the Paris Exposition (1900) and Pan American Exposition (1901). The 2c pane was light red, type IV. Copies were handstamped type E "Specimen" in black ink by H. G. Mandel and mounted by him in separate displays for the two Expositions. Additional copies from each pane were also handstamped "specimen," but most were destroyed after the Expositions. Nearly all copies remaining bear impression of a dealer's handstamp reading "Special Surcharge" in red ink on the back. Value: Nos. 221-225, J1-J4, each $600; No. E1, $1,000.

Issues of the Republic under US Military Rule

Statue of Columbus — A20

Royal Palms — A21

Allegory, "Cuba" — A22

Ocean Liner — A23

Cane Field — A24

Re-engraved

The re-engraved stamps issued by the Republic of Cuba in 1905-07 may be distinguished from the Issue of 1899 as follows:
Nos. 227-231 are watermarked U S-C
The re-engraved stamps are unwatermarked.

1c: The ends of the label inscribed "Centavo" are rounded instead of square.
2c: The foliate ornaments, inside the oval disks bearing the numerals of value, have been removed.
5c: Two lines forming a right angle have been added in the upper corners of the label bearing the word "Cuba."
10c: A small ball has been added to each of the square ends of the label bearing the word "Cuba."

No. 227 Re-engraved

No. 228 Re-engraved

No. 230 Re-engraved

No. 231 Re-engraved

Printed by the US Bureau of Engraving and Printing

1899 **Wmk. US-C (191C)** ***Perf. 12***

227 A20 1c **yellow green** 3.50 .20
On cover 2.00
Block of 4 15.00 1.00
P# block of 10, Impt., type VII 225.00 —
228 A21 2c **carmine** 3.50 .20
On cover 2.00
Block of 4 15.00 1.00
P# block of 10, Impt., type VII 180.00 —
a. 2c **scarlet** 3.50 .20
b. Booklet pane of 6 *2,000.*
229 A22 3c **purple** 3.50 .20
On cover 4.00
Block of 4 15.00 2.50
P# block of 10, Impt., type VII 275.00 —
230 A23 5c **blue** 4.50 .20
On cover 4.00
Block of 4 21.00 2.50
P# block of 10, Impt., type VII 450.00 —
231 A24 10c **brown** 11.00 .50
On cover 6.50
Block of 4 52.50 5.50
P# block of 10, Impt., type VII 1,200. —
Nos. 227-231 (5) 26.00 1.30

SPECIAL DELIVERY

Issued under Administration of the United States

Special Delivery Stamp of the United States No. E5 Surcharged in Red

1899 **Wmk. 191** ***Perf. 12***

E1 SD3 10c on 10c **blue** 130. 100.
On cover 450.
Block of 4 575.
Margin block of 4, arrow 650.
P# strip of 3, Impt. 1,000.
P# block of 6, Impt. *6,000.*
Five dots in curved frame above messenger's head (Pl. 882) —
a. No period after "CUBA" 400. 400.

Issue of the Republic under US Military Rule

Special Delivery Messenger SD2

Printed by the US Bureau of Engraving and Printing

1899 **Wmk. US-C (191C)**

Inscribed: "Immediata"

E2 SD2 10c **orange** 50.00 15.00
On cover 150.00
Block of 4 250.00 —
P# strip of 3, Impt., type VII 300.00
P# block of 6, Impt., type VII 1,000.

Re-engraved

In 1902 the Republic of Cuba issued a stamp of design SD2 re-engraved with word correctly spelled "Inmediata." The corrected die was made in 1899 (See No. E3P). It was printed by the U.S. Bureau of Engraving and Printing.

POSTAGE DUE

Issued under Administration of the United States Postage Due Stamps of the United States Nos. J38, J39, J41 and J42 Surcharged in Black Like Regular Issue of Same Date

1899 **Wmk. 191** ***Perf. 12***

J1 D2 1c on 1c **deep claret** 45.00 5.25
Block of 4 210.00 45.00
P# block of 6, Impt. *900.00*
J2 D2 2c on 2c **deep claret** 45.00 5.25
Block of 4 200.00 30.00
P# block of 6, Impt. *900.00*
a. Inverted surcharge *4,000.*
J3 D2 5c on 5c **deep claret** 45.00 5.25
Block of 4 220.00 45.00
P# block of 6, Impt. *900.00*
"CUPA" (broken letter) 150.00 140.00
J4 D2 10c on 10c **deep claret** 27.50 2.50
Block of 4 125.00 27.50
P# block of 6, Impt. *800.00*

The No. J3 "CUPA" variety always has a straight edge at right.

ENVELOPES

Values are for Cut Squares

US Envelopes of 1887-99 Surcharged

a

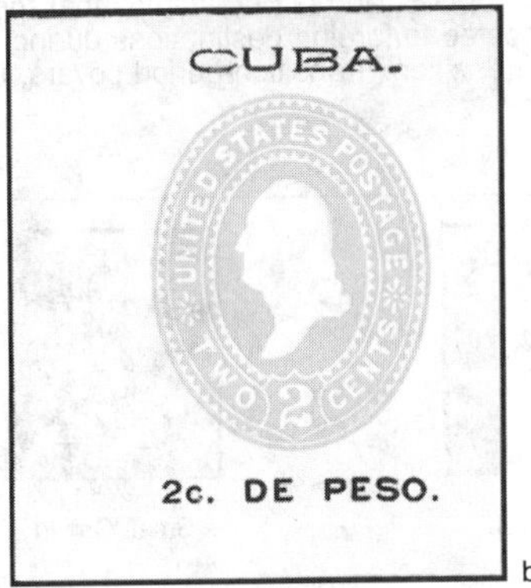

b

1899

U1 U77 (a) 1c on 1c **green,** *oriental buff* (No. U354) 5.00 3.50
Entire 12.00 15.00
U2 U77 (a) 1c on 1c **green,** *blue* (No. U355) 3.25 2.50
Entire 5.00 6.50
a. Double surcharge, entire *5,250.*
U3 U71 (b) 2c on 2c **green** (No. U311) 1.50 1.10
Entire 3.00 3.50
a. Double surcharge, entire *4,500. 6,500.*
U4 U71 (b) 2c on 2c **green,** *amber* (No. U312) 2.75 1.65
Entire 5.25 6.00
a. Double surcharge, entire *5,250.*
U5 U71 (a) 2c on 2c **green,** *oriental buff* (No. U313) 17.50 8.00

	Entire	47.50	47.50
U6	U79 (a) 2c on 2c **carmine,** *amber* (No. U363)	17.50	17.50
	Entire	47.50	47.50
U7	U79 (a) 2c on 2c **carmine,** *oriental buff* (No. U364)	25.00	25.00
	Entire	100.00	80.00
U8	U79 (a) 2c on 2c **carmine,** *blue* (No. U365)	3.00	2.00
	Entire	7.00	8.00
a.	Double surcharge, entire		*6,750.*
	Nos. U1-U8 (8)	75.50	61.25

In addition to the envelopes listed above, several others are known but were not regularly issued. They are:
1c on 1c green
1c on 1c green, *manila*
2c on 2c carmine
4c on 4c brown
5c on 5c blue

Issue of the Republic under US Military Rule

Columbus — E1

Similar envelopes without watermark on white and amber papers, were issued by the Republic after Military Rule ended in 1902.

1899 **Wmk. "US POD '99" in Monogram**

U9 E1	1c **green**	.75	.65
	Entire	4.00	4.00
U10 E1	1c **green,** *amber*	1.00	.65
	Entire	4.00	4.00
U11 E1	1c **green,** *buff*	17.50	13.00
	Entire	85.00	42.50
U12 E1	1c **green,** *blue*	25.00	15.00
	Entire	85.00	42.50
U13 E1	2c **carmine**	1.00	.70
	Entire	3.75	3.00
U14 E1	2c **carmine,** *amber*	1.00	.70
	Entire	3.75	3.00
U15 E1	2c **carmine,** *buff*	9.00	7.75
	Entire	35.00	21.00
U16 E1	2c **carmine,** *blue*	25.00	18.00
	Entire	60.00	52.50
U17 E1	5c **blue**	3.25	2.25
	Entire	5.00	2.75
U18 E1	5c **blue,** *amber*	6.00	4.00
	Entire	9.00	5.75
	Nos. U9-U18 (10)	89.50	62.70

WRAPPERS

Issue of the Republic under US Military Rule

1899

W1 E1	1c **green,** *manila*	4.00	10.00
	Entire	11.00	50.00
W2 E1	2c **carmine,** *manila*	12.00	10.00
	Entire	25.00	50.00

POSTAL CARDS

Values are for Entires

U.S. Postal Cards Nos. UX14, UX16 Surcharged

CUBA. 1c. de Peso.

UX1	PC8 1c on 1c **black,** *buff, Jefferson (1,000,000)*	15.00	16.50
a.	No period after "1c"	40.00	75.00
b.	No period after "Peso"	35.00	
c.	Surcharge "2c" (error)	*6,500.*	
UX2	PC3 2c on 2c **black,** *buff, Liberty (583,000)*	15.00	16.50
a.	No period after "Peso"	40.00	75.00
b.	Double surcharge		—

In 1904 the Republic of Cuba revalued remaining stocks of No. UX2 by means of a perforated numeral "1."

PROOFS

1899

Column (1)- Large Die
Column (2)- Small Die

		(1)	(2)
227P	1c **yellow green**	160.	160.
227TC	1c **blue green**	375.	
227TC	1c **black**	625.	
228P	2c **carmine**	160.	160.
228TC	2c **black**	625.	
229P	3c **purple**	160.	160.
229TC	3c **black**	375.	
230P	5c **blue**	160.	160.
230TC	5c **black**	625.	
231P	10c **nrown**	160.	160.
231TC	10c **gray**	625.	
231TC	10c **black**	625.	

Special Delivery

E2TC	10c **blue**	1,500.	
E3P	10c **orange**	375.	325.

SPECIMEN STAMPS

Overprinted Type E in Purple — Specimen.

1899

221S	E 1c on 1c **yellow green**	175.
222AS	E 2c on 2c **reddish carmine,** type IV	175.
223AS	E 2½c on 2c **reddish carmine,** type IV	175.
224S	E 3c on 3c **purple**	175.
225S	E 5c on 5c **blue**	175.
226S	E 10c on 10c **brown,** type I	175.
226AS	E 10c on 10c **brown,** type II	*3,500.*

See note after No. 226A for Special Printings with black "Specimen" overprints.

1899

227S	E 1c **yellow green**	200.
228S	E 2c **carmine**	200.
229S	E 3c **purple**	200.
230S	E 5c **blue**	200.
231S	E 10c **brown**	200.

Special Delivery

1899

E1S	E 10c on 10c **blue**	550.
a.	Five dots in curved frame above messenger's head	1,750.
E2S	E 10c **orange**	1,000.

Postage Due

1899

J1S	E 1c on 1c **deep claret**	250.
J2S	E 2c on 2c **deep claret**	250.
J3S	E 5c on 5c **deep claret**	250.
J4S	E 10c on 10c **deep claret**	250.

Black "Specimen" overprint known on all stamps of the Special Printing.

DANISH WEST INDIES

Formerly a Danish colony, these islands were purchased by the United States on March 31, 1917 and have since been known as the U.S. Virgin Islands. They lie east of Puerto Rico, have an area of 132 square miles and had a population of 27,086 in 1911. The capital is Charlotte Amalie (also called St. Thomas). Stamps of Danish West Indies were replaced by those of the United States in 1917. However, for the first six months of U.S. ownership, until September 30, 1917, a postal transition period existed. During this period, either U.S., D.W.I. or mixed frankings could be used. The domestic printed matter or postcard rate was 5 bits or 1 cent, and the foreign printed matter or postcard rate was 10 bits, 2 cents, or 5 bits + 1 cent. The domestic minimum weight letter rate was 10 bits, 2 cents, or 5 bits + 1 cent, while the foreign minimum letter rate was 25 bits, 5 cents, or any combination of U.S. and D.W.I. stamps that together totalled 25 bits or 5 cents.

Letters posted to foreign destinations during the transition period are rare because of World War I. Values for covers listed here are for the period before the transition. Transition-period covers, including those with mixed franking, sell for much more.

100 CENTS = 1 DOLLAR
100 BIT = 1 FRANC (1905)

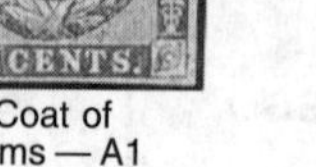

Coat of Arms — A1

Wmk. 111- Small Crown

1856 **Typo.** **Wmk. 111** ***Imperf.***

Yellowish Paper

Yellow Wavy-line Burelage, UL to LR

1 A1	3c **dark carmine,** brown gum	175.	190.
	On cover		3,000.
	Block of 4	1,250.	
a.	3c **dark carmine,** yellow gum	200.	210.
	On cover		3,000.
	Block of 4	2,750.	
b.	3c **carmine,** white gum	*4,000.*	—
	On cover		—

The brown and yellow gums were applied locally.

Reprint: 1981, carmine, back-printed across two stamps ("Reprint by Dansk Post og Telegrafmuseum 1978"), value, pair, $10.

1866

White Paper

Yellow Wavy-line Burelage UR to LL

2 A1	3c **rose**	40.	*60.*
	On cover		3,000.
	Block of 4	200.	*300.*
	Rouletted 4½ privately	350.	150.
	On cover, rouletted 4½		—
	Rouletted 9	450.	175.

The value for used blocks is for favor cancel (CTO).

No. 2 reprints, unwatermarked: 1930, carmine, value $75. 1942, rose carmine, back-printed across each row ("Nytryk 1942 G. A. Hagemann Danmark og Dansk Vestindiens Frimaerker Bind 2"), value $40.

1872 ***Perf. 12½***

3 A1	3c **rose**	75.	*175.*
	On cover		*7,500.*
	Block of 4	500.	

1873

Without Burelage

4 A1	4c **dull blue**	175.	*350.*
	On cover		—
	Block of 4	1,100.	
a.	Imperf., pair	750.	
b.	Horiz. pair, imperf. vert.	550.	

The 1930 reprint of No. 4 is ultramarine, unwatermarked and imperf., value $85.

The 1942 4c reprint is blue, unwatermarked, imperf. and has printing on back (see note below No. 2), value $50.

Numeral of Value — A2

NORMAL FRAME

INVERTED FRAME

The arabesques in the corners have a main stem and a branch. When the frame is in normal position, in the upper left corner the branch leaves the main stem half way between two little leaflets. In the lower right corner the branch starts at the foot of the second leaflet. When the frame is inverted the corner designs are, of course, transposed.

The central element in the fan-shaped scrollwork at the outside of the lower left corner of Nos. 5a and 7b looks like an elongated diamond.

Wmk. 112- Crown

1874-79 **Wmk. 112** ***Perf. 14x13½***

White Wove Paper, Printings 1-3 Thin, 4-7 Medium, 8-9 Thick
1c Nine printings
3c Eight printings
4c Two printings
5c Six printings
7c Two printings
10c Seven printings
12c Two printings
14c One printing
50c Two printings

Values for inverted frames, covers and blocks are for the cheapest variety.

5 A2 1c **green & brown red** 15.00 *22.50*
On cover 225.00
Block of 4 75.00 *225.00*
a. 1c **green & rose lilac,** thin paper 75.00 *125.00*
b. 1c **green & red violet,** medium paper 40.00 *65.00*
c. 1c **green & claret,** thick paper 15.00 *22.50*
e. As "c," inverted frame 15.00 *22.50*
f. As "a," inverted frame *425.00*

No. 5 exists with "b" surcharge, "10 CENTS 1895." See note below No. 15.

6 A2 3c **blue & carmine** 19.00 15.00
On cover 225.00
Block of 4 85.00 —
White "wedge" flaw 50.00 50.00
a. 3c **light blue & rose carmine,** thin paper 65.00 50.00
b. 3c **deep blue & dark carmine,** medium paper 35.00 16.00
c. 3c **greenish blue & lake,** thick paper 19.00 14.00
d. Imperf., pair 325.00 —
e. Inverted frame, thick paper 19.00 14.00
f. As "a," inverted frame *350.00*
7 A2 4c **brown & dull blue** 13.00 *14.00*
On cover 225.00
Block of 4 65.00 —
b. 4c **brown & ultramarine,** thin paper 150.00 200.00
c. Diagonal half used as 2c on cover 110.00
d. As "b," inverted frame *750.00* *1,250.*
8 A2 5c **green & gray** 17.50 16.00
On cover 250.00
Block of 4 90.00 —
a. 5c **yellow green & dark gray,** thin paper 45.00 30.00
b. Inverted frame, thick paper 17.50 15.00
9 A2 7c **lilac & orange** 22.50 *85.00*
On cover 1,100.
Block of 4 140.00 —
a. 7c **lilac & yellow** 77.50 77.50
b. Inverted frame 52.50 *125.00*
10 A2 10c **blue & brown** 21.00 *22.50*
On cover 300.00
Block of 4 100.00 —
a. 10c **dark blue & black brown,** thin paper 70.00 45.00
b. Period between "t" & "s" of "cents" 30.00 30.00
c. Inverted frame 21.00 *25.00*
11 A2 12c **red lilac & yellow green** 37.50 *125.00*
On cover 1,750.
Block of 4 225.00 —
a. 12c **lilac & deep green** 125.00 *140.00*
12 A2 14c **lilac & green** 500.00 *850.00*
On cover —
Block of 4 *3,250.*
a. Inverted frame *2,000.* *2,750.*
13 A2 50c **violet,** thin paper 160.00 *260.00*
On cover 2,500.
Block of 4 1,250.
a. 50c **gray violet,** thick paper 210.00 *350.00*

Issue dates: 1c, 3c, 4c, 14c, Jan. 15, 1874. 7c, July 22, 1874. 5c, 10c, 1876; 12c, 1877; 50c, 1879. Colors of major numbers are generally those of the least expensive of two or more shades, and do not indicate the shade of the first printing.

Nos. 9 and 13 Surcharged in Black:

a

b

1887
14 A2 (a) 1c on 7c **lilac & orange** 72.50 *175.00*
On cover 3,000.
Block of 4 350.00 —
a. 1c on 7c **lilac & yellow** 72.50 *175.00*
b. Double surcharge 175.00 *350.00*
c. Inverted frame 90.00 *300.00*

1895
15 A2 (b) 10c on 50c **violet,** thin paper 37.50 *60.00*
On cover 275.00
Block of 4 250.00 —

The "b" surcharge also exists on No. 5, with "10" found in two sizes. These are essays.

1896-1901 ***Perf. 13***
16 A2 1c **green & red violet,** inverted frame ('98) 12.00 *18.00*
On cover 150.00
Block of 4 60.00 —
a. Normal frame 225.00 *325.00*
17 A2 3c **blue & lake,** inverted frame ('98) 10.00 *13.00*
On cover 150.00
Block of 4 50.00 —
a. Normal frame 200.00 *325.00*
White "wedge" flaw 35.00 *45.00*
18 A2 4c **bister & dull blue** ('01) 12.50 12.50
On cover 150.00
Block of 4 60.00 —
a. Diagonal half used as 2c on cover 90.00
b. Inverted frame 45.00 *75.00*
On cover 250.00
c. As "b," diagonal half used as 2c on cover 300.00
19 A2 5c **green & gray,** inverted frame 30.00 30.00
On cover 325.00
Block of 4 140.00 —
a. Normal frame 600.00 *850.00*
20 A2 10c **blue & brown** ('01) 65.00 *110.00*
On cover 1,150.
Block of 4 400.00 —
a. Inverted frame 750.00 *1,300.*
b. Period between "t" and "s" of "cents" 160.00 150.00
Nos. 16-20 (5) 129.50 *183.50*

Two printings each of Nos. 18-19.

Arms — A5

1900
21 A5 1c **light green** 2.75 2.75
On cover, pair 80.00
On cover, single franking 300.00
Block of 4 11.50 11.50
22 A5 5c **light blue** 15.00 *20.00*
On cover 300.00
Block of 4 75.00 —

Nos. 6, 17 and 20 Surcharged in Black — c

1902 ***Perf. 14x13½***
23 A2 2c on 3c **blue & carmine,** inverted frame 300.00 350.00
On cover 4,000.
Block of 4 *1,800.*
a. "2" in date with straight tail 325.00 *375.00*
b. Normal frame 3,500.

Perf. 13
24 A2 2c on 3c **blue & lake,** inverted frame 9.00 *20.00*
On cover 160.00
Block of 4 40.00 —
White "wedge" flaw 55.00 55.00
a. "2" in date with straight tail 11.50 *22.50*
b. Dated "1901" 375.00 *400.00*
c. Normal frame 150.00 *225.00*
d. Dark green surcharge 1,750.
e. As "d" & "a" — —
f. As "d" & "c" —

One example recorded of No. 24f.

25 A2 8c on 10c **blue & brown** 20.00 *32.50*
On cover 225.00
Block of 4 82.50 —
a. "2" with straight tail 22.50 *35.00*
b. On No. 20b 20.00 *37.50*
c. Inverted frame 200.00 *325.00*

Nos. 17 and 20 Surcharged in Black — d

1902 ***Perf. 13***
27 A2 2c on 3c **blue & lake,** inverted frame 11.00 *30.00*
On cover 500.00
Block of 4 47.50 —
White "wedge" flaw 40.00 50.00
a. Normal frame 225.00 *375.00*
28 A2 8c on 10c **blue & brown** 11.00 11.00
On cover 175.00
Block of 4 47.50 —
a. On No. 20b 17.50 *20.00*
b. Inverted frame 175.00 *350.00*

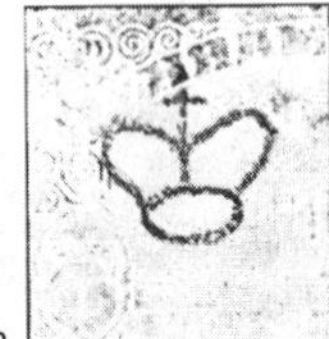
Wmk. 113- Crown

1903 **Wmk. 113**

29 A5	2c **carmine**		6.00	*17.50*
	On cover			125.00
	Block of 4		25.00	—
30 A5	8c **brown**		22.50	*42.50*
	On cover			250.00
	Block of 4		95.00	—

King Christian IX — A8

St. Thomas Harbor — A9

1905 **Typo.** ***Perf. 12½***

31 A8	5b **green**		3.50	3.00
	On cover			32.50
	Block of 4		16.00	—
32 A8	10b **red**		3.50	3.00
	On cover			32.50
	Block of 4		15.00	—
33 A8	20b **green & blue**		8.00	7.50
	On cover			140.00
	Block of 4		37.50	—
34 A8	25b **ultramarine**		8.00	8.50
	On cover			80.00
	Block of 4		37.50	—
35 A8	40b **red & gray**		8.00	7.50
	On cover			200.00
	Block of 4		35.00	—
36 A8	50b **yellow & gray**		9.00	10.00
	On cover			225.00
	Block of 4		37.50	—

Perf. 12

Wmk. Two Crowns (113)

Frame Typographed, Center Engraved

37 A9	1fr **green & blue**		17.50	*40.00*
	On cover			600.00
	Block of 4		75.00	—
38 A9	2fr **orange red & brown**		30.00	*55.00*
	On cover			1,000.
	Block of 4		150.00	—
39 A9	5fr **yellow & brown**		75.00	*225.00*
	On cover			1,600.
	Block of 4		350.00	—
	Nos. 31-39 (9)		162.50	*359.50*

On cover values are for commercial usages, usually parcel address cards. Philatelic covers are valued at approximately 25% of these figures.

Nos. 18, 22 and 30 Surcharged in Black

1905 **Wmk. 112** ***Perf. 13***

40 A2	5b on 4c **bister & dull blue**		13.50	*40.00*
	On cover			250.00
	Block of 4		67.50	—
a.	Inverted frame		40.00	*75.00*
41 A5	5b on 5c **light blue**		12.50	*32.50*
	On cover			250.00
	Block of 4		55.00	—

Wmk. 113

42 A5	5b on 8c **brown**		12.50	*32.50*
	On cover			250.00
	Block of 4		50.00	—

Favor cancels exist on Nos. 40-42. Value 25% less.

King Frederik VIII — A10

Frame Typographed, Center Engraved

1908 **Wmk. 113** ***Perf. 13***

43 A10	5b **green**		1.75	1.60
	On cover			20.00
	Block of 4		8.75	—
	Number block of 6		17.50	
44 A10	10b **red**		1.75	1.60
	On cover			22.50
	Block of 4		8.75	—
	Number block of 6		17.50	
45 A10	15b **violet & brown**		3.50	3.50
	On cover			125.00
	Block of 4		17.50	—
	Number block of 6		50.00	
46 A10	20b **green & blue**		30.00	24.00
	On cover			110.00
	Block of 4		130.00	—
	Number block of 6		375.00	
47 A10	25b **blue & dark blue**		1.50	*2.00*
	On cover			30.00
	Block of 4		7.25	—
	Number block of 6		17.50	
48 A10	30b **claret & slate**		42.50	42.50
	On cover			300.00
	Block of 4		190.00	190.00
	Number block of 6		500.00	
49 A10	40b **vermilion & gray**		4.50	*7.00*
	On cover			200.00
	Block of 4		22.50	—
	Number block of 6		50.00	
50 A10	50b **yellow & brown**		4.50	*11.00*
	On cover			200.00
	Block of 4		22.50	—
	Number block of 6		67.50	
	Nos. 43-50 (8)		90.00	93.20

Printing numbers appear in the selvage, once per pane, in Roman or Arabic numerals.

King Christian X — A11

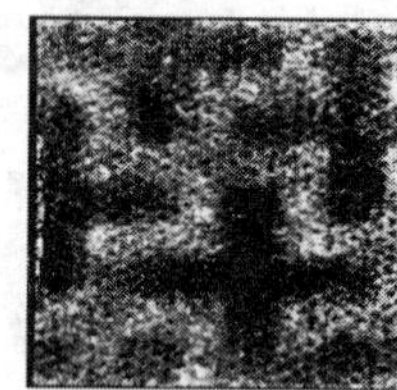

Wmk. 114 — Multiple Crosses

Frame Typographed, Center Engraved

1915 **Wmk. 114** ***Perf. 14x14½***

51 A11	5b **yellow green**		3.50	3.00
	On cover			45.00
	Block of 4		15.00	—
	Number block of 4		35.00	
52 A11	10b **red**		3.50	*35.00*
	On cover			100.00
	Block of 4		15.00	—
	Number block of 4		35.00	
53 A11	15b **lilac & red brown**		3.50	*40.00*
	On cover			300.00
	Block of 4		15.00	—
	Number block of 4		35.00	
54 A11	20b **green & blue**		3.50	*40.00*
	On cover			350.00
	Block of 4		15.00	—
	Number block of 4		35.00	
55 A11	25b **blue & dark blue**		3.50	*10.00*
	On cover			100.00
	Block of 4		15.00	
	Number block of 4		35.00	
56 A11	30b **claret & black**		3.50	*50.00*
	On cover			900.00
	Block of 4		15.00	—
	Number block of 4		35.00	
57 A11	40b **orange & black**		3.50	*50.00*
	On cover			550.00
	Block of 4		16.50	—
	Number block of 4		35.00	
58 A11	50b **yellow & brown**		3.50	*50.00*
	On cover			650.00
	Block of 4		16.50	—
	Number block of 4		35.00	
	Nos. 51-58 (8)		28.00	*278.00*

Forged and favor cancellations exist.

Plate identifications 11-D, 50-D or 50-O are located in the selvage in all four corners of the pane. The 50-D is on all denominations. 11-D, all but the 50b, 50-O, all but 15b, 20b, 25b.

POSTAGE DUE

Royal Cipher "Christian Rex" — D1

Numeral of Value — D2

1902 **Litho.** **Unwmk.** ***Perf. 11½***

J1 D1	1c **dark blue**		4.00	*11.00*
	On cover			400.00
	Block of 4		20.00	
J2 D1	4c **dark blue**		9.00	*17.50*
	On cover			350.00
	Block of 4		40.00	
J3 D1	6c **dark blue**		17.50	*45.0*
	On cover			450.0
	Block of 4		85.00	
J4 D1	10c **dark blue**		15.00	*45.0*
	On cover			400.0
	Block of 4		75.00	

There are five types of each value. On the 4c they may be distinguished by differences in the figure "4"; on the other values differences are minute.

Used values of Nos. J1-J8 are for canceled copies. Uncanceled examples without gum have probably been used. Value 60% of unused. On cover values are for copies tied by cancellation.

Excellent counterfeits of Nos. J1-J4 exist.

1905-13 ***Perf. 13***

J5 D2	5b **red & gray**		4.00	*6.25*
	On cover			*450.00*
	Block of 4		18.00	—
J6 D2	20b **red & gray**		7.00	*12.50*
	On cover			*450.00*
	Block of 4		30.00	—
J7 D2	30b **red & gray**		6.00	*12.50*
	On cover			*450.00*
	Block of 4		27.50	—
J8 D2	50b **red & gray**		5.50	*32.50*
	On cover			*900.00*
	Block of 4		25.00	—
a.	Perf. 14x14½ ('13)		35.00	*125.00*
	Block of 4		160.00	—
b.	Perf. 11½		300.00	

Nos. J5-J8 are known imperforate but were not regularly issued. Excellent counterfeits exist.

See notes following No. J4 for canceled copies.

ENVELOPES

E1

1877-78 **On White Paper**

U1	E1	2c **light blue** ('78)	5.50	*14.00*
		Entire	22.50	*65.00*
a.		2c **ultramarine**	20.00	*200.00*
		Entire	100.00	*800.00*
U2	E1	3c **orange**	5.50	*12.50*
		Entire	22.50	*65.00*
a.		3c **red orange**	5.50	*12.50*
		Entire	22.50	*65.00*

Three different Crown watermarks are found on entires of No. U1, four on entires of No. U2. Envelope watermarks do not show on cut squares.

POSTAL CARDS

Values are for entire cards.

Italicized numbers in parentheses indicate quantities issued.

Designs of Adhesive Stamps

"BREV-KORT" at top

1877

Inscription in Three Lines

UX1	A2	6c **violet**	40.00	*1,400.*

Used value is for card to foreign destination postmarked before April 1, 1879.

1878-85

Inscription in Four Lines

UX2	A2	2c **light blue** *(8,800)*	22.50	*50.00*
UX3	A2	3c **carmine rose** *(17,700)*	17.50	*35.00*

1888

Inscription in Five Lines

UX4	A2	2c **light blue** *(30,500)*	20.00	*32.50*
UX5	A2	3c **red** *(26,500)*	12.50	*22.50*

Card No. UX5 Locally Surcharged with type "c" but with date "1901"

1901

UX6	A2	1c on 3c **red** *(2,000)*	50.00	*200.00*

1902

Card No. UX4 Locally Surcharged with type "c"

UX7	A2	1c on 2c **light blue** *(3,000)*	37.50	*160.00*

Card No. UX5 Surcharged similar to type "c" but heavy letters

1902

UX8	A2	1c on 3c **red** *(7,175)*	12.50	*150.00*

1903

UX9 A5 1c **light green** *(10,000)* 12.50 *30.00*
UX10 A5 2c **carmine** *(10,000)* 19.00 *70.00*

1905

UX11 A8 5b **green** *(16,000)* 12.50 *22.50*
UX12 A8 10b **red** *(14,000)* 12.50 *35.00*

1907-08 **Unwmk.**

UX13 A10 5b **green** ('08) *(30,750)* 9.50 *30.00*
UX14 A10 10b **red** *(19,750)* 12.50 *40.00*

1913 **Wmk. Wood-grain**

UX15 A10 5b **green** *(10,000)* 90.00 *210.00*
UX16 A10 10b **red** *(10,000)* 100.00 *325.00*

1915-16 **Wmk. Wood-grain**

UX17 A11 5b **yellow green** *(8,200)* 80.00 *250.00*
UX18 A11 10b **red** ('16) *(2,000)* 100.00 —

PAID REPLY POSTAL CARDS

Designs similar to Nos. UX2 and UX3 with added inscriptions in Danish and French:
Message Card-Four lines at lower left.
Reply Card-Fifth line centered, "Svar. Réponse."
Italicized numbers in parentheses indicate quantities issued.

1883

UY1 A2 2c +2c **light blue,** unsevered *(2,600)* 25.00 *250.00*
m. Message card, detached 12.50 *35.00*
r. Reply card, detached 12.50 *35.00*
UY2 A2 3c +3c **carmine rose,** unsevered 21.00 *150.00*
m. Message card, detached 12.50 *20.00*
r. Reply card, detached 12.50 *25.00*

Designs similar to Nos. UX4 and UX5 with added inscription in fifth line, centered in French:
Message Card-"Carte postale avec réponse payée."
Reply Card-"Carte postale-réponse."

1888

UY3 A2 2c +2c **light blue,** unsevered *(26,000)* 25.00 *125.00*
m. Message card, detached 10.00 *20.00*
r. Reply card, detached 10.00 *100.00*
UY4 A2 3c +3c **carmine rose,** unsevered *(5,000)* 22.50 *175.00*
m. Message card, detached 11.00 *35.00*
r. Reply card, detached 11.00 *125.00*

No. UY4 Locally Surcharged with type "c" but with date "1901"

1902

UY5 A2 1c on 3c+1c on 3c **carmine rose,** unsevered *(1,000)* 35.00 *300.00*
m. Message card, detached 12.50 *50.00*
r. Reply card, detached 14.00 *75.00*

No. UY4 Surcharged in Copenhagen with type similar to "c" but heavy letters

UY6 A2 1c on 3c+1c on 3c **carmine rose,** unsevered *(975)* 50.00 *350.00*
m. Message card, detached 20.00 *60.00*
r. Reply card, detached 20.00 *75.00*

Designs similar to Nos. UX9 and UX10 with added inscriptions in Danish and English

1903

UY7 A5 1c +1c **light green,** unsevered *(5,000)* 35.00 *75.00*
m. Message card, detached 11.00 *20.00*
r. Reply card, detached 11.00 *25.00*
UY8 A5 2c +2c **carmine,** unsevered *(5,000)* 40.00 *400.00*
m. Message card, detached 15.00 *50.00*
r. Reply card, detached 15.00 *75.00*

Designs similar to Nos. UX11 and UX12 with added inscriptions

1905

UY9 A8 5b +5b **green,** unsevered *(5,000)* 21.00 *75.00*
m. Message card, detached 10.00 *20.00*
r. Reply card, detached 10.00 *30.00*
UY10 A8 10b +10b **red,** unsevered *(4,000)* 30.00 *90.00*
m. Message card 12.50 *25.00*
r. Reply card, detached 15.00 *35.00*

Designs similar to Nos. UX13, UX14 and UX15 with added inscriptions

1908 **Unwmk.**

UY11 A10 5b +5b **green,** unsevered *(7,150)* 25.00 *100.00*
m. Message card, detached 11.00 *30.00*
r. Reply card, detached 11.00 *35.00*
UY12 A10 10b +10b **red,** unsevered *(6,750)* 25.00 *100.00*
m. Message card, detached 12.50 *30.00*
r. Reply card, detached 11.00 *40.00*

1913 **Wmk. Wood-grain**

UY13 A10 5b +5b **green,** unsevered *(5,000)* —
m. Message card, detached —
r. Reply card, detached —

The 10b + 10b red type A10 with wood-grain watermark was authorized and possibly printed, but no example is known.

REVENUES

PLAYING CARDS

These stamps were overprinted by the Bureau of Engraving and Printing. Shipments of 10,000 each of Nos. RFV1-RFV3 were sent to the Virgin Islands on June 17, 1920, Jan. 16, 1926, and Mar. 5, 1934, respectively.

U. S. Playing Card Stamp No. RF3 Overprinted in Carmine

1920 **Engr.** **Wmk. 191R** ***Rouletted 7***

RFV1 RF2 4c on 2c **blue** 200.00

U. S. Playing Card Stamp No. RF17 Overprinted in Carmine

1926 ***Rouletted 7***

RFV2 RF4 4c on (8c) **blue** 45.00

RFV2 was surcharged with new value in "Bits" for use in collecting a tobacco tax.

Same Overprint on U.S. Type RF4

1934 ***Perf. 11***

RFV3 RF4 4c on (8c) **light blue** 200.00 110.00

The above stamp with perforation 11 was not issued in the United States without the overprint.

GUAM

A former Spanish island possession in the Pacific Ocean, one of the Mariana group, about 1,450 miles east of the Philippines. Captured June 20, 1898, and ceded to the United States by treaty after the Spanish-American War. Stamps overprinted "Guam" were used while the post office was under the jurisdiction of the Navy Department from July 7, 1899, until March 29, 1901, when a Postal Agent was appointed by the Post Office Department and the postal service passed under that Department's control. From this date on Guam was supplied with regular United States postage stamps, although the overprints remained in use for several more years.

Italicized numbers in parentheses indicate quantities issued.

Population 9,000 (est. 1899).

100 CENTS = 1 DOLLAR

United States Nos. 279, 279B, 279Bc, 268, 280a, 281, 282, 272, 282C, 283, 284, 275, 275a, 276 and 276A Overprinted

1899 **Wmk. 191** ***Perf. 12***

Black Overprint

1 A87 1c **deep green** *(25,000)* 20.00 *25.00*
On cover *200.00*
Block of 4 90.00 *140.00*
P# strip of 3, Impt. 90.00
P# block of 6, Impt. 350.00

A bogus inverted overprint exists.

2 A88 2c **red,** type IV, *Dec. (105,000)* 17.50 *25.00*
light red, type IV 17.50 *25.00*
On cover *200.00*
Block of 4 85.00 *140.00*
P# strip of 3, Impt. 75.00
P# block of 6, Impt. 300.00
a. 2c **rose carmine,** type IV, *Aug. 15* 30.00 *30.00*
On cover *225.00*
Block of 4 125.00 *175.00*
P# strip of 3, Impt. 100.00
P# block of 6, Impt. 375.00
3 A89 3c **purple** *(5000)* 140.00 *175.00*
On cover *400.00*
Block of 4 600.00 *850.00*
P# strip of 3, Impt. 575.00
P# block of 6, Impt. 1,600.
4 A90 4c **lilac brown** *(5000)* 135.00 *175.00*
On cover *450.00*
Block of 4 600.00 *825.00*
P# strip of 3, Impt. 550.00
P# block of 6, Impt. *2,000.*
Extra frame line at top (Plate 793 R62) —
5 A91 5c **blue** *(20,000)* 32.50 *45.00*
On cover *200.00*
Block of 4 140.00 *250.00*
P# strip of 3, Impt. 140.00
P# block of 6, Impt. 775.00
6 A92 6c **lake** *(5000)* 125.00 *200.00*
On cover *450.00*
Block of 4 550.00 *1,000.*
P# strip of 3, Impt. 500.00
P# block of 6, Impt. 1,600.
7 A93 8c **violet brown** *(5000)* 140.00 *200.00*
On cover *450.00*
Block of 4 600.00 *1,000.*
P# strip of 3, Impt. 600.00
P# block of 6, Impt. 1,700.
8 A94 10c **brown,** type I *(10,000)* 47.50 *55.00*
On cover *275.00*
Block of 4 210.00 *300.00*
P# strip of 3, Impt. 225.00
P# block of 6, Impt. 1,000.
9 A94 10c **brown,** type II *4,000.* —
Pair —
10 A95 15c **olive green** *(5000)* 150.00 *175.00*

On cover 900.00
Block of 4 650.00 875.00
P# strip of 3, Impt. 600.00
P# block of 6, Impt. 2,200.

11 A96 50c **orange** *(4000)* 350.00 *425.00*
On cover *1,500.*
Block of 4 1,600. *2,000.*
P# strip of 3, Impt. 1,600.
P# block of 6, Impt. 4,500.

a. 50c **red orange** 550.00 —

Red Overprint

12 A97 $1 **black,** type I *(3000)* 350.00 *400.00*
On cover *3,000.*
Block of 4 1,750. *1,750.*
P# strip of 3, Impt. 1,650.
P# block of 6, Impt. *12,500.*

13 A97 $1 **black,** type II *4,500.*
Block of 4 —
Nos. 1-8,10-12 (11) 1,507. *1,900.*

Counterfeits of overprint exist.
No. 13 exists only in the special printing.

Special Printing

In March 1900, one pane of 100 stamps of each of Nos. 1-8, 10-12 and two panes of 50 stamps of No. E1 were specially overprinted for displays at the Paris Exposition (1900) and Pan American Exposition (1901). The 2c pane was light red, type IV.

Copies were handstamped type E "Specimen" in black ink by H. G. Mandel and mounted by him in separate displays for the two Expositions. Additional copies from each pane were also handstamped "Specimen" but most were destroyed after the Expositions.

J. M. Bartels, a stamp dealer, signed some copies from these panes "Special Surcharge" in pencil on the gum to authenticate them as coming from the "Mandel" Special Printing panes. In 1904 or later, he handstamped additional surviving copies "Special Surcharge" in red ink on the back as his guarantee. Some of these guaranteed stamps had Mandel's "Specimen" handstamp on the face while others did not. Value (with or without "Specimen" handstamp): Nos. 1-8, 10, each $1,000; Nos. 11, E1, each $1,250; No. 12, $2,000.

SPECIAL DELIVERY STAMP

Special Delivery Stamp of the United States, No. E5 Overprinted diagonally in Red

1899 **Wmk. 191** ***Perf. 12***

E1 SD3 10c **blue** *(5000)* 150. *200.*
On cover *1,250.*
Block of 4 650.
Margin block of 4, arrow 750.
P# strip of 3, Impt. 900.
P# block of 6, Impt. *3,500.*
Dots in curved frame above messenger (Plate 882) 200.
P# block of 6, Impt. (Plate 882) *4,250.*

Counterfeits of overprint exist.

The special stamps for Guam were replaced by the regular issues of the United States.

GUAM GUARD MAIL

LOCAL POSTAL SERVICE

Inaugurated April 8, 1930, by Commander Willis W. Bradley, Jr., U.S.N., Governor of Guam, for the conveyance of mail between Agaña and the other smaller towns.

Philippines Nos. 290 and 291 Overprinted

GUAM
GUARD
MAIL

1930, Apr. 8 **Unwmk.** ***Perf. 11***

M1 A40 2c **green** *(2,000)* 400. 300.
On cover 600.
Block of 4 1,700.
P# block of 6 —

M2 A40 4c **carmine** *(3,000)* 225. 150.
On cover 400.
Block of 4 950.
P# block of 6 —

Counterfeits of overprint exist.

Seal of Guam — A1

1930, July **Unwmk.** ***Perf. 12***
Without Gum

M3 A1 1c **red & black** *(1,000)* 125.00 150.00
On cover 225.00
Block of 4 525.00

M4 A1 2c **black & red** *(4,000)* 75.00 95.00
On cover 250.00
Block of 4 325.00

a. Block of 4 with extra impression of vignette covering the intersection of the block *8,000.*

Copies are often found showing parts of watermark "CLEVELAND BOND."

Philippines Nos. 290 and 291 Overprinted in Black

1930, Aug. 10 **Unwmk.** ***Perf. 11***

M5 A40 2c **green** *(20,000)* 2.75 4.50
On cover 75.00
Block of 4 12.00
P# block of 6 *125.00*

a. 2c **yellow green** 2.50 4.50

M6 A40 4c **carmine** *(80,000)* .50 1.75
On cover 75.00
Block of 4 2.25
P# block of 6 *90.00*

Same Overprint in Red on Philippines Nos. 290, 291, 292, 293a, and 294

1930, Dec.

M7 A40 2c **green** *(50,000)* .80 2.00
On cover 50.00
Block of 4 3.50
P# block of 6 *125.00*

a. GRAUD (Pos. 63) *(500)* 425.00
b. MIAL (Pos. 84) *(500)* 425.00

M8 A40 4c **carmine** *(50,000)* .85 1.50
On cover 50.00
Block of 4 3.50
P# block of 6 *90.00*

M9 A40 6c **deep violet** *(25,000)* 2.50 4.50
On cover 60.00
Block of 4 11.00
P# block of 10, Impt. *250.00*

M10 A40 8c **orange brown** *(25,000)* 2.50 4.50
On cover 60.00
Block of 4 11.00
P# block of 10, Impt. *300.00*

M11 A40 10c **deep blue** *(25,000)* 2.50 4.50
On cover 60.00
Block of 4 11.00
P# block of 10, Impt. *350.00*

The local postal service was discontinued April 8th, 1931, and replaced by the service of the United States Post Office Department.

SPECIMEN STAMPS

Overprinted United States Type E in Purple — Specimen.

1899

1S	E	1c **deep green**	175.00
2aS	E	2c **rose carmine,** type IV	175.00
3S	E	3c **purple**	175.00
4S	E	4c **lilac brown**	175.00
5S	E	5c **blue**	175.00
6S	E	6c **lake**	175.00
7S	E	8c **violet brown**	175.00
8S	E	10c **brown,** type I	175.00
10S	E	15c **olive green**	175.00
11S	E	50c **orange**	350.00
12S	E	$1 **black,** type I	350.00
13S	E	$1 **black,** type II	—

Special Delivery

1899

E1S E 10c **blue** 500.00

Values for specimen stamps are for fine-very fine appearing copies with minor faults.

See note after No. 13 for Special Printings with black "Specimen" overprints.

HAWAII

Until 1893, Hawaii was an independent kingdom. From 1893-1898 it was a republic. The United States annexed Hawaii in 1898, and it became a Territory on April 30, 1900. Hawaiian stamps remained in use through June 13, 1900, and were replaced by U.S. stamps on June 14. In 1959 Hawaii became the 50th State of the Union. Hawaii consists of about 20 islands in the mid-Pacific, about 2,300 miles southwest of San Francisco. The area is 6,434 square miles and the population was estimated at 150,000 in 1899. Honolulu is the capital.

100 CENTS = 1 DOLLAR

Values of Hawaii stamps vary considerably according to condition. Quotations for Nos. 5-82 are for very fine copies. Extremely fine to superb examples sell at much higher prices, and inferior or poor copies sell at reduced prices, depending on the condition of the individual specimen.

A1

A2

A3

1851-52 Unwmk. Typeset Pelure Paper *Imperf.*

1 A1 2c **blue** *660,000.* *200,000.*
On cover *2,100,000.*
2 A1 5c **blue** *45,000.* *25,000.*
On cover *75,000.*
3 A2 13c **blue** *22,500.* *18,000.*
On cover *70,000.*
4 A3 13c **blue** *40,000.* *27,500.*
On cover *75,000.*

Nos. 1-4 are known as the "Missionaries."

Two varieties of each. Nos. 1-4, off cover, are almost invariably damaged. Values are for examples with minor damage which has been skillfully repaired.

No. 1 unused and on cover are each unique; the on-cover value is based on a 1995 auction sale.

A4

King Kamehameha III — A5

Printed in Sheets of 20 (4x5)

1853 Thick White Wove Paper Engr.

5 A4 5c **blue** 1,500. 1,100.
On cover *3,750.*
On cover with U.S. #17 *12,000.*
Pair *3,250.* *3,500.*
a. Line through "Honolulu" (Pos. 2) *2,850.* *2,500.*
6 A5 13c **dark red** 600. *1,100.*
On cover *27,500.*
On cover with U.S. #11 (pair) *25,000.*
On cover with U.S. #17 *35,000.*
On cover with #5 and U.S. #17 *35,000.*
On cover with #5 and U.S. #36b *38,500.*
Pair *1,750.* *4,000.*
Block of 4 *3,500.*

Black Manuscript Surcharge on Scott 6

1857

7 A6 5c on 13c **dark red** *6,750.* *9,000.*
On cover with pair U.S. #7 and 15 *57,500.*
On cover with pair U.S. #11, 14 *55,000.*
On cover with U.S. #14 *50,000.*
On cover with U.S. #17 *37,500.*

1857

Thin White Wove Paper

8 A4 5c **blue** 650. 625.
On cover *1,500.*
On cover with U.S. #11 —
On cover with U.S. #7, 15 —
On cover with U.S. #17 *10,000.*
On cover with U.S. #26 —
On cover with U.S. #35 *11,000.*
On cover with U.S. #36 *10,000.*
On cover with U.S. #69 *12,500.*
On cover with U.S. #76 —
Pair 1,600.
Pair on cover *15,000.*
a. Line through "Honolulu" (Pos. 2) *1,250.* *1,250.*
On cover with U.S. #17 *6,500.*
b. Double impression *3,500.* *3,500.*

1861

Thin Bluish Wove Paper

9 A4 5c **blue** 350. 250.
On cover *3,750.*
On cover with U.S. #36b *3,250.*
On cover with U.S. #65 *3,000.*
On cover with U.S. #65, 73 *6,500.*
On cover with U.S. #68 *4,250.*
On cover with U.S. #76 *7,000.*
Block of 4 2,000. —
a. Line through "Honolulu" (Pos. 2) *750.* *900.*

1868

RE-ISSUE

Ordinary White Wove Paper

10 A4 5c **blue** 25.
Block of 4 125.
a. Line through "Honolulu" (Pos. 2) 55.
11 A5 13c **dull rose** 250.
Block of 4 1,150.

Remainders of Nos. 10 and 11 were overprinted "SPECIMEN." See Nos. 10S-11Sb.

Nos. 10 and 11 were never placed in use but copies (both with and without overprint) were sold at face value at the Honolulu post office.

REPRINTS (Official Imitations) 1889

5c Originals have two small dots near the left side of the square in the upper right corner. These dots are missing in the reprints.

13c The bottom of the 3 of 13 in the upper left corner is flattened in the originals and rounded in the reprints. The "t" of "Cts" on the left side is as tall as the "C" in the reprints, but shorter in the originals.

10R A4 5c **blue** 60.
Block of 4 275.
11R A5 13c **orange red** 250.
Block of 4 1,100.

On August 19, 1892, the remaining supply of reprints was overprinted in black "REPRINT." The reprints (both with and without overprint) were sold at face value.

Quantities sold (including overprints) were 5c-3634 and 13c-1696. See Nos. 10R-S and 11R-S.

Unused values for the Numeral Stamps, Nos. 12-26, are for examples without gum.

A7

A8

A9

1859-62 Typeset from settings of 10 varieties

12 A7 1c **light blue,** *bluish white* *9,000.* *7,500.*
Pair *18,000.*
a. "1 Ce" omitted *16,500.*
b. "nt" omitted — —
13 A7 2c **light blue,** *bluish white* *6,250.* *3,750.*
On cover *10,500.*
Block of 4 *27,500.*
a. 2c **dark blue,** *grayish white* *6,750.* *4,000.*
On cover *11,500.*
b. Comma after "Cents" — *6,250.*
On cover *11,500.*
c. No period after "LETA" — —
14 A7 2c **black,** *greenish blue* ('62) *7,500.* *4,500.*
On cover *7,750.*
a. "2-Cents." — —

1863

15 A7 1c **black,** *grayish* 500. *1,050.*
On cover —
Block of 4 2,250.
a. Tête bêche pair *3,750.*
b. "NTER" —
c. Period omitted after "Postage" 725.
16 A7 2c **black,** *grayish* 925. 700.
On cover *3,500.*
Pair — —
a. "2" at top of rectangle *3,750.* *3,750.*
b. Printed on both sides — *21,000.*
c. "NTER" *3,250.* *3,250.*
d. 2c **black,** *grayish white* 975. 725.
e. Period omitted after "Cents" —
f. Overlapping impressions — —
g. "TAGE" — —
17 A7 2c **dark blue,** *bluish* *10,000.* *6,750.*
Pair *21,250.*
a. "ISL" — —
18 A7 2c **black,** *blue gray* *3,250.* *4,750.*
On cover *18,000.*
Pair *11,000.*
Thick paper —

1864-65

19 A7 1c **black** 500. *1,000.*
Pair 1,050.
Block of 4 2,400.
20 A7 2c **black** 725. 1,200.
On cover *16,500.*
Pair 1,550.
Block of 4 *4,000.*
21 A8 5c **blue,** *blue* ('65) 775. 575.
On cover with U.S. #65 —
On cover with U.S. #68 —
On cover with U.S. #76 *8,250.*
Block of 4 *3,400.* —
a. Tête bêche pair *10,500.*
b. 5c **bluish black,** *grayish white* *12,500.*

No. 21b is unique. Value based on 1995 auction sale.

22 A9 5c **blue,** *blue* ('65) 550. *875.*
On cover *13,000.*
On cover with U.S. #76 *9,250.*
On cover with U.S. #63 and 76 —
Block of 4 2,500.
a. Tête bêche pair *8,750.*
b. 5c **blue,** *grayish white* —
c. Overlapping impressions —

1864

Laid Paper

23 A7 1c **black** 275. *2,100.*
On cover with U.S. #76 —
Block of 4 1,150.
a. "HA" instead of "HAWAIIAN" *3,750.*
b. Tête bêche pair *6,250.*
c. Tête bêche pair, Nos. 23, 23a *18,000.*
24 A7 2c **black** 300. *1,050.*
Block of 4 1,250.
a. "NTER" *3,750.*
b. "S" of "POSTAGE" omitted *1,500.*
c. Tête bêche pair *5,500.*

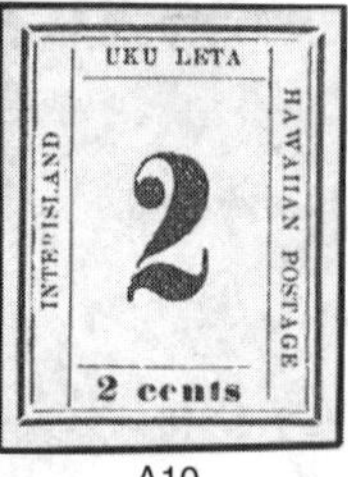

A10

King Kamehameha IV — A11

1865

Wove Paper

25 A10 1c **dark blue** 300.
Block of 4 1,350.
a. Double impression —
b. With inverted impression of No. 21 on face *11,000.*
26 A10 2c **dark blue** 300.
Block of 4 1,350.

Nos. 12 to 26 were typeset and were printed in sheets of 50 (5 settings of 10 varieties each). The sheets were cut into panes of 25 (5x5) before distribution to the post offices.

1861-63 Litho.

Horizontally Laid Paper

27 A11 2c **pale rose** 275. 250.
On cover *1,000.*
Pair —
a. 2c **carmine rose** ('63) 2,000. 2,000.

Vertically Laid Paper

28 A11 2c **pale rose** 275. 150.
On cover *1,500.*
Block of 4 1,500. 1,000.
a. 2c **carmine rose** ('63) 300. *350.*
On cover *2,000.*
Block of 4 1,750.

RE-ISSUE

1869 Engr. Thin Wove Paper

29 A11 2c **red** 45.00 —
Block of 4 225.00

No. 29 was not issued for postal purposes although canceled copies are known. It was sold only at the Honolulu post office, at first without overprint and later with overprint "CANCELLED." See No. 29S.

See note following No. 51.

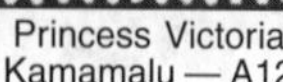
Princess Victoria Kamamalu — A12

King Kamehameha IV — A13

King Kamehameha V — A14

Kamehameha V — A15

Mataio Kekuanaoa — A16

1864-86 Engr. Wove Paper *Perf. 12*

No.	Type	Description	Unused	Used
30	A12	1c **purple** ('86)	9.00	7.50
		On cover		150.00
		Block of 4	50.00	
a.		1c **mauve** ('71)	40.00	20.00
b.		1c **violet** ('78)	17.50	10.00
31	A13	2c **rose vermilion**	15.00	9.00
		On cover		200.00
		On cover with U.S. #76		*1,000.*
		Block of 4	75.00	65.00
a.		2c **vermilion** ('86)	35.00	12.50
		On cover		150.00
b.		Half used as 1c on cover with H.I. #32		*8,500.*
32	A14	5c **blue** ('66)	175.00	30.00
		On cover		250.00
		On cover with any U.S. issues of 1861-67		*4,000.*
		On cover with U.S. #116		*17,500.*
		On cover with U.S. #116 and 69		*25,000.*
		Block of 4	800.00	175.00
33	A15	6c **yellow green** ('71)	25.00	9.00
		On cover		625.00
a.		6c **bluish green** ('78)	25.00	9.00
		On cover		650.00
		On cover with U.S. #179		*1,500.*
		On cover with U.S. #185		*800.00*
		Block of 4	140.00	—
34	A16	18c **dull rose** ('71)	85.00	35.00
		On cover		350.00
		Block of 4	375.00	
		Nos. 30-34 (5)	309.00	90.50

Half of No. 31 was used with a 5c stamp to make up the 6-cent rate to the United States.

No. 32 has traces of rectangular frame lines surrounding the design. Nos. 39 and 52C have no such frame lines.

King David Kalakaua — A17

Prince William Pitt Leleiohoku — A18

1875

No.	Type	Description	Unused	Used
35	A17	2c **brown**	7.50	3.00
		On cover		175.00
		Block of 4	37.50	40.00
36	A18	12c **black**	55.00	27.50
		On cover		400.00
		Block of 4	325.00	—

Princess Likelike (Mrs. Archibald Cleghorn) — A19

King David Kalakaua — A20

Queen Kapiolani — A21

Statue of King Kamehameha I — A22

King William Lunalilo — A23

Queen Emma Kaleleonalani — A24

1882

No.	Type	Description	Unused	Used
37	A19	1c **blue**	6.00	*10.00*
		On cover		60.00
		Block of 4	32.50	*52.50*
38	A17	2c **lilac rose**	125.00	45.00
		On cover		150.00
		Block of 4	625.00	
39	A14	5c **ultramarine**	15.00	3.25
		On cover		27.50
		Block of 4	75.00	60.00
a.		Vert. pair, imperf. horiz.	*4,250.*	*4,250.*
40	A20	10c **black**	35.00	20.00
		On cover		150.00
		Block of 4	160.00	130.00
41	A21	15c **red brown**	55.00	25.00
		On cover		200.00
		Block of 4	260.00	200.00
		Nos. 37-41 (5)	236.00	103.25

1883-86

No.	Type	Description	Unused	Used
42	A19	1c **green**	2.75	1.90
		On cover		25.00
		Block of 4	14.00	14.00
43	A17	2c **rose** ('86)	4.00	1.00
		On cover		25.00
		Block of 4	20.00	12.50
a.		2c **dull red**	62.50	21.00
		Block of 4	310.00	
44	A20	10c **red brown** ('84)	30.00	10.00
		On cover		125.00
		Block of 4	150.00	100.00
45	A20	10c **vermilion**	32.50	12.50
		On cover		125.00
		Block of 4	175.00	80.00
46	A18	12c **red lilac**	75.00	32.50
		On cover		425.00
		Block of 4	400.00	240.00
47	A22	25c **dark violet**	140.00	60.00
		On cover		375.00
		Block of 4	650.00	350.00
48	A23	50c **red**	160.00	85.00
		On cover		525.00
		Block of 4	850.00	
49	A24	$1 **rose red**	240.00	250.00
		On cover		650.00
		Block of 4	1,250.	
		Maltese cross cancellation		100.00
		Nos. 42-49 (8)	684.25	452.90

Other fiscal cancellations exist on No. 49.

Nos. 48-49 are valued used with postal cancels. Canceled-to-order cancels exist and are worth less.

REPRODUCTION and REPRINT

Yellowish Wove Paper

1886-89 Engr. *Imperf.*

No.	Type	Description	Unused	Used
50	A11	2c **orange vermilion**	160.00	
		Block of 4	800.00	
51	A11	2c **carmine** ('89)	25.00	
		Block of 4	125.00	

In 1885 the Postmaster General wished to have on sale complete sets of Hawaii's portrait stamps, but was unable to find either the stone from which Nos. 27 and 28, or the plate from which No. 29 was printed. He therefore sent a copy of No. 29 to the American Bank Note Company, with an order to engrave a new plate like it and print 10,000 stamps therefrom, of which 5000 were overprinted "SPECIMEN" in blue.

The original No. 29 was printed in sheets of fifteen (5x3), but the plate of these "Official Imitations" was made up of fifty stamps (10x5). Later, in 1887, the original die for No. 29 was discovered, and, after retouching, a new plate was made and 37,500 stamps were printed (No. 51). These, like the originals, were printed in sheets of fifteen. They were delivered during 1889 and 1890. In 1892 all remaining unsold in the Post Office were overprinted "Reprint".

No. 29 is red in color, and printed on very thin white wove paper. No. 50 is orange vermilion in color, on medium, white to buff paper. In No. 50 the vertical line on the left side of the portrait touches the horizontal line over the label "Elua Keneta", while in the other two varieties, Nos. 29 and 51, it does not touch the horizontal line by half a millimeter. In No. 51 there are three parallel lines on the left side of the King's nose, while in No. 29 and No. 50 there are no such lines. No. 51 is carmine in color and printed on thick, yellowish to buff, wove paper.

It is claimed that both Nos. 50 and 51 were available for postage, although not made to fill a postal requirement. They exist with favor cancellation. No. 51 also is known postally used. See Nos. 50S-51S.

Queen Liliuokalani — A25

1890-91 *Perf. 12*

No.	Type	Description	Unused	Used
52	A25	2c **dull violet** ('91)	4.50	1.50
		On cover		25.00
		Block of 4	21.00	12.00
a.		Vert. pair, imperf. horiz.	*4,000.*	
52C	A14	5c **deep indigo**	110.00	140.00
		On cover		500.00
		Block of 4	525.00	

Stamps of 1864-91 Overprinted in Red

Three categories of double overprints:
I. Both overprints heavy.
II. One overprint heavy, one of moderate strength.
III. One overprint heavy, one of light or weak strength.

1893

No.	Type	Description	Unused	Used
53	A12	1c **purple**	7.50	12.50
		On cover		35.00
		Block of 4	37.50	70.00
a.		"189" instead of "1893"	475.00	—
b.		No period after "GOVT"	*210.00*	*210.00*
f.		Double overprint (III)	*550.00*	
54	A19	1c **blue**	6.00	*12.50*
		On cover		40.00
		Block of 4	30.00	67.50
b.		No period after "GOVT"	*140.00*	*140.00*
e.		Double overprint (II)	*1,500.*	
f.		Double overprint (III)	*400.00*	
55	A19	1c **green**	1.50	*3.00*
		On cover		25.00
		Block of 4	7.50	15.00
d.		Double overprint (I)	*625.00*	*450.00*
f.		Double overprint (III)	*200.00*	
g.		Pair, one without ovpt.	*10,000.*	
56	A17	2c **brown**	10.00	*20.00*
		On cover		60.00
		Block of 4	50.00	120.00
b.		No period after "GOVT"	*300.00*	—
57	A25	2c **dull violet**	1.50	1.25
		On cover		25.00
		Block of 4	6.50	6.50
a.		"18 3" instead of "1893"	*650.00*	*500.00*
d.		Double overprint (I)	*1,300.*	*650.00*
f.		Double overprint (III)	*160.00*	
g.		Inverted overprint	*4,000.*	*4,500.*
58	A14	5c **deep indigo**	10.00	*25.00*
		On cover		100.00
		Block of 4	50.00	140.00
b.		No period after "GOVT"	*225.00*	*250.00*
f.		Double overprint (III)	*1,250.*	
59	A14	5c **ultramarine**	6.00	2.50
		On cover		40.00
		Block of 4	30.00	20.00
d.		Double overprint (I)	*6,500.*	
e.		Double overprint (II)	*4,000.*	*4,000.*
f.		Double overprint (III)		*600.00*
g.		Inverted overprint	*1,500.*	*1,500.*
60	A15	6c **green**	15.00	*25.00*
		On cover		140.00
		Block of 4	75.00	125.00
e.		Double overprint (II)	*1,000.*	
61	A20	10c **black**	9.00	*15.00*
		On cover		125.00
		Block of 4	45.00	82.50
e.		Double overprint (II)	*750.00*	
f.		Double overprint (III)	*200.00*	
61B	A20	10c **red brown**	*14,000.*	*29,000.*
		Block of 4	*60,000.*	
		Strip of 5, plate imprint	*75,000.*	
62	A18	12c **black**	9.00	*17.50*
		On cover		150.00
		Block of 4	50.00	110.00
d.		Double overprint (I)	*2,000.*	
e.		Double overprint (II)	*1,750.*	
63	A18	12c **red lilac**	150.00	*250.00*
		On cover		550.00
		Block of 4	900.00	—
64	A22	25c **dark violet**	26.00	*40.00*
		On cover		225.00
		Block of 4	125.00	200.00
b.		No period after "GOVT"	*325.00*	*325.00*
f.		Double overprint (III)	*1,000.*	
		Nos. 53-61,62-64 (12)	251.50	*424.25*

Virtually all known copies of No. 61B are cut in at the top.

Overprinted in Black

No.	Type	Description	Unused	Used
65	A13	2c **vermilion**	*67.50*	*75.00*
		On cover		*450.00*
		Block of 4	*325.00*	*400.00*
b.		No period after "GOVT"	*250.00*	*250.00*
66	A17	2c **rose**	1.25	*2.25*
		On cover		25.00
		Block of 4	6.50	*11.00*
b.		No period after "GOVT"	50.00	60.00
d.		Double overprint (I)	*4,000.*	
e.		Double overprint (II)	*2,750.*	
f.		Double overprint (III)	*300.00*	
66C	A15	6c **green**	*14,000.*	*29,000.*
		On cover		—
		Block of 4	*60,000.*	
67	A20	10c **vermilion**	15.00	*30.00*
		On cover		125.00
		Block of 4	80.00	180.00
f.		Double overprint (III)	*1,250.*	
68	A20	10c **red brown**	7.50	*12.50*
		On cover		100.00
		Block of 4	37.50	75.00
f.		Double overprint (III)	*1,750.*	
69	A18	12c **red lilac**	275.00	*500.00*
		On cover		950.00
		Block of 4	1,250.	*2,400.*
70	A21	15c **red brown**	20.00	*30.00*
		On cover		300.00
		Block of 4	110.00	*150.00*
e.		Double overprint (II)	*2,000.*	
71	A16	18c **dull rose**	25.00	*35.00*
		On cover		225.00
		Block of 4	125.00	*175.00*
a.		"18 3" instead of "1893"	*475.00*	*475.00*
b.		No period after "GOVT"	*300.00*	*300.00*
d.		Double overprint (I)	*600.00*	
f.		Double overprint (III)	*225.00*	
g.		Pair, one without ovpt.	*2,500.*	
72	A23	50c **red**	60.00	*90.00*
		On cover		600.00
		Block of 4	300.00	*500.00*
b.		No period after "GOVT"	*400.00*	*400.00*
f.		Double overprint (III)	*1,000.*	
73	A24	$1 **rose red**	110.00	*175.00*
		On cover		775.00
		Block of 4	500.00	*875.00*
b.		No period after "GOVT"	*450.00*	425.00
		Nos. 65-66,67-73 (9)	581.25	*949.75*

Coat of Arms — A26

View of Honolulu — A27

Statue of Kamehameha I — A28

Stars and Palms — A29

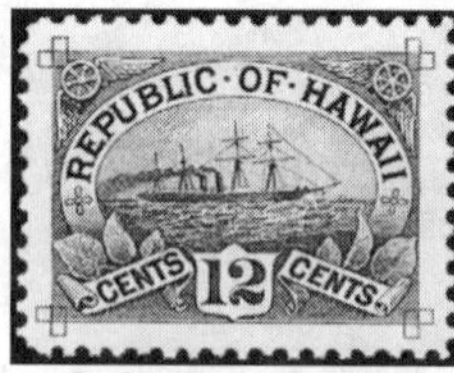

S. S. "Arawa" — A30

Pres. Sanford Ballard Dole — A31

"CENTS" Added — A32

1894

No.	Type	Description	Unused	Used
74	A26	1c **yellow**	2.00	1.25
		On cover		25.00
		Block of 4	8.50	8.00
75	A27	2c **brown**	2.25	.60
		On cover		25.00
		Block of 4	9.00	7.00
		"Flying goose" flaw (48 LR 2)	600.00	400.00
		Double transfer	5.00	5.00
76	A28	5c **rose lake**	4.00	1.50
		On cover		25.00
		Block of 4	20.00	15.00
77	A29	10c **yellow green**	6.00	4.50
		On cover		45.00
		Block of 4	30.00	25.00
78	A30	12c **blue**	12.50	*17.50*
		On cover		150.00
		Block of 4	55.00	*80.00*
		Double transfer	22.50	25.00
79	A31	25c **deep blue**	12.50	*17.50*
		On cover		100.00
		Block of 4	55.00	—
		Nos. 74-79 (6)	39.25	*42.85*

Numerous double transfers exist on Nos. 75 and 81.

1899

No.	Type	Description	Unused	Used
80	A26	1c **dark green**	1.50	1.25
		On cover		25.00
		Block of 4	7.00	7.00
81	A27	2c **rose**	1.40	1.00
		On cover		20.00
		Block of 4	6.00	6.00
		Double transfer	—	—
		"Flying goose" flaw (48 LR 2)	325.00	300.00
a.		2c **salmon**	1.50	1.25
b.		Vert. pair, imperf. horiz.	*4,500.*	
82	A32	5c **blue**	5.50	3.00
		On cover		25.00
		Block of 4	27.50	52.50

OFFICIAL STAMPS

Lorrin Andrews Thurston — O1

1896 Engr. Unwmk. *Perf. 12*

No.	Type	Description	Unused	Used
O1	O1	2c **green**	40.00	17.50
		On cover		400.00
		Block of 4	175.00	
O2	O1	5c **black brown**	40.00	17.50
		On cover		450.00
		Block of 4	175.00	
O3	O1	6c **deep ultramarine**	40.00	17.50
		On cover		—
		Block of 4	175.00	
O4	O1	10c **bright rose**	40.00	17.50
		On cover		500.00
		Block of 4	175.00	
O5	O1	12c **orange**	40.00	17.50
		On cover		—
		Block of 4	175.00	
O6	O1	25c **gray violet**	40.00	17.50
		On cover		—
		Block of 4	175.00	
		Nos. O1-O6 (6)	240.00	105.00

Used values for Nos. O1-O6 are for copies canceled-to-order "FOREIGN OFFICE/HONOLULU H.I." in double circle without date. Values of postally used copies: Nos. O1-O2, O4, $35, No. O3, $100, No. O5, $125, No. O6, $150.

ENVELOPES

Italicized numbers in parentheses indicate quantities issued.
All printed by American Bank Note Co., N.Y.

View of Honolulu Harbor — E1

Envelopes of White Paper, Outside and Inside

1884

No.	Type	Description	Unused	Used
U1	E1	1c **light green** *(109,000)*	2.50	3.00
		Entire	6.00	*15.00*
a.		1c **green** *(10,000)*	6.00	*15.00*
		Entire	15.00	*90.00*
b.		1c **dark green**	10.00	*10.00*
		Entire	25.00	*75.00*
U2	E1	2c **carmine** *(386,000 including U2a, U2b)*	2.50	4.00
		Entire	5.00	*17.50*
a.		2c **red**	2.50	4.00
		Entire	5.00	*17.50*
b.		2c **rose**	2.50	4.00
		Entire	5.00	*17.50*
c.		2c **pale pink** *(5,000)*	10.00	12.50

		Entire	35.00	*60.00*
U3	E1	4c **red** *(18,000)*	14.00	17.50
		Entire	30.00	*90.00*
U4	E1	5c **blue** *(90,775)*	6.50	7.50
		Entire	17.50	*30.00*
U5	E1	10c **black** *(3,500 plus)*	20.00	25.00
		Entire	50.00	*100.00*

Envelopes White Outside, Blue Inside

U6	E1	2c **rose**	150.00	200.00
		Entire	400.00	*1,500.*
U7	E1	4c **red**	150.00	200.00
		Entire	400.00	—
U8	E1	5c **blue**	150.00	200.00
		Entire	400.00	*1,250.*
U9	E1	10c **black**	250.00	400.00
		Entire	450.00	—
		Nos. U1-U9 (9)	745.50	1,057.

Nos. U1, U2, U4 & U5 Overprinted Locally "Provisional Government 1893" in Red or Black

1893

U10	E1	1c **light green** (R) *(16,000)*	3.50	7.00
		Entire	7.00	*20.00*
a.		Double overprint	*1,750.*	
		Entire	*6,000.*	
U11	E1	2c **carmine** (Bk) *(37,000)*	2.50	3.50
		Entire	4.50	*15.00*
a.		Double overprint	500.00	
		Entire	*1,100.*	*1,250.*
b.		Double overprint, one inverted, entire	*1,500.*	

No. U11 is known as an unused entire with a triple overprint, two of the overprints being at the bottom right portion of the envelope. Unique. Value, $9,500.

U12	E1	5c **blue** (R) *(34,891)*	4.25	5.00
		Entire	10.00	*15.00*
a.		Double overprint	375.00	*400.00*
		Entire	600.00	*3,000.*
b.		Triple overprint, entire		*7,500.*
U13	E1	10c **black** (R) *(17,707 incl. No. U14)*	12.50	16.00
		Entire	20.00	*90.00*
a.		Double overprint, entire	*1,800.*	*2,000.*

Envelope No. U9 with same overprint

U14	E1	10c **black** (R)	300.	*725.00*
		Entire	1,000.	—

SPECIAL DELIVERY ENVELOPE

Value is for Entire.

Envelope No. U5 with added inscription "Special Despatch Letter" etc. in red at top left corner

1885

UE1 E1 10c **black** *(2,000)* 175.

Envelope No. UE1 was prepared for use but never issued for postal purposes. Postally used examples exist, but no special delivery service was performed. Favor cancellations exist.

POSTAL CARDS

All printed by American Bank Note Co., N.Y. Values are for entires.

Queen Liliuokalani — PC1

View of Diamond Head — PC2

Royal Emblems — PC3

1882-92 **Engr.**

UX1	PC1	1c **red,** *buff (125,000)*	30.00	*75.00*
UX2	PC2	2c **black** *(45,000)*	50.00	*90.00*
a.		Lithographed ('92)	150.00	250.00
UX3	PC3	3c **blue green** *(21,426)*	60.00	*110.00*

1889 **Litho.**

UX4	PC1	1c **red,** *buff (171,240)*	25.00	*50.00*

Cards Nos. UX4, UX2a and UX3 overprinted locally "Provisional Government 1893" in red or black

1893

UX5	PC1	1c **red,** *buff* (Bk) *(28,760)*	30.00	*75.00*
a.		Double overprint	*4,000.*	*3,500.*
UX6	PC2	2c **black** (R) *(10,000)*	55.00	*95.00*

No. UX6 is known unused with double overprint, one inverted at lower left of card. Unique. Value, $16,000.

UX7	PC3	3c **blue green** (R) *(8,574)*	65.00	*250.00*
a.		Double overprint	*1,750.*	

Iolani Palace — PC4

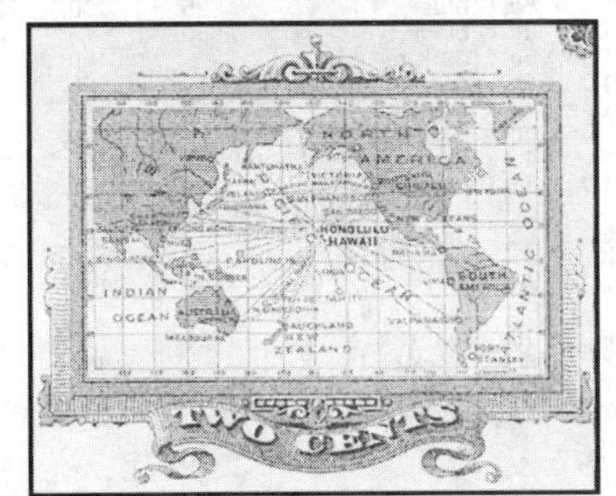

Map of Pacific Ocean, Mercator's Projection — PC5

1894-97 **Litho.**

Border Frame 131½x72½mm

UX8	PC4	1c **red,** *buff (100,000)*	20.00	*40.00*
a.		Border frame 132½x74mm ('97) *(200,000)*	20.00	*40.00*
UX9	PC5	2c **green** *(60,000)*	45.00	*80.00*
a.		Border frame 132½x74mm ('97) *(190,000)*	45.00	*80.00*

PAID REPLY POSTAL CARDS

Double cards, same designs as postal cards with added inscriptions on reply cards.

1883 **Litho.**

UY1	PC1	1c +1c **purple,** *buff,* unsevered *(5,000)*	400.00	*450.00*
m.		Message card, detached	35.00	*100.00*
r.		Reply card, detached	35.00	*100.00*
UY2	PC2	2c +2c **dark blue,** unsevered *(5,000)*	450.00	*500.00*
m.		Message card, detached	55.00	*140.00*
r.		Reply card, detached	55.00	*140.00*

1889

UY3	PC1	1c +1c **gray violet,** *buff,* unsevered *(5,000)*	400.00	*450.00*
m.		Message card, detached	35.00	*100.00*
r.		Reply card, detached	35.00	*100.00*
UY4	PC2	2c +2c **sapphire,** unsevered *(5,000)*	400.00	*450.00*
m.		Message card, detached	35.00	*80.00*
r.		Reply card, detached	35.00	*80.00*

Values for unused unsevered Paid Reply Postal Cards are for cards which have not been folded. Folded cards sell for about 33% of these values.

Detached card used values are for canceled cards with printed messages on the back.

REVENUE STAMPS

R1

R2

R3

R4

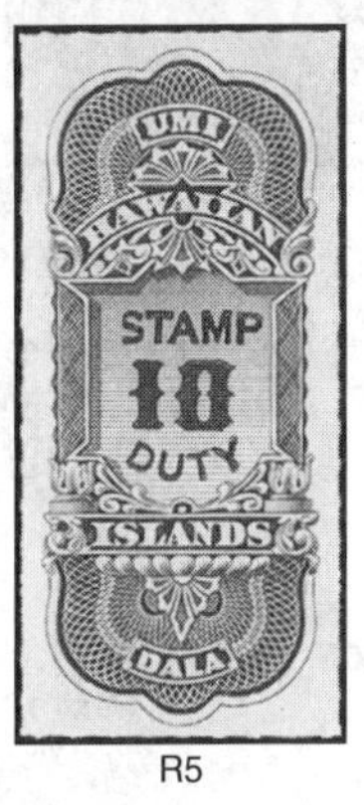

R5

R6

Printed by the American Bank Note Co.
Sheets of 70

1877		**Engr.**	**Unwmk.**	***Rouletted 8***	
R1	R1	25c **green** *(160,000)*		10.00	12.50
R2	R2	50c **yellow orange** *(190,000)*		25.00	10.00
R3	R3	$1 **black** *(580,000)*		25.00	5.00
a.		$1 gray		25.00	5.00

Denominations Typo.

R4	R4	$5 **vermilion & violet blue** *(21,000)*	100.00	25.00
R5	R5	$10 **reddish brown & green** *(14,000)*	100.00	25.00
R6	R6	$50 **slate blue & carmine** *(3,500)*	*400.00*	*250.00*

No. R6 unused is valued without gum, as all known examples come thus.

Unused values for all revenues except No. R6 are for stamps with original gum. Apparently unused copies without gum sell for less.

No. R1 Surcharged in Black or Gold

a

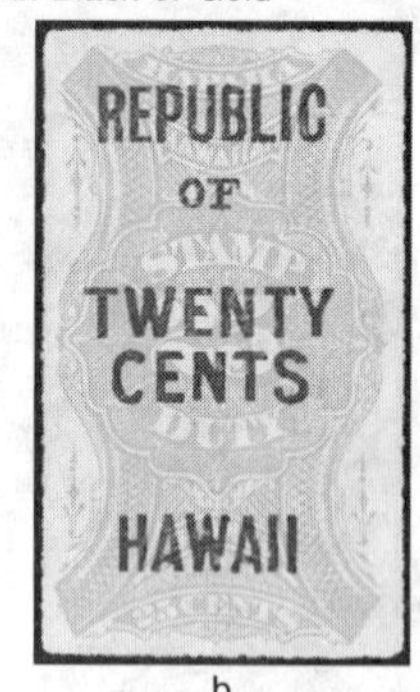
b

1893-94

R7	R1 (a) 20c on 25c **green**	20.00	12.50
a.	Inverted surcharge	*800.00*	*750.00*
R8	R1 (b) 20c on 25c **green** (G)	45.00	40.00
a.	Double surcharge	—	—
b.	Double surcharge, one black	—	*1,500.*
c.	Inverted surcharge		—

On No. R8b, the black surcharge is 20mm wide, while the normal gold surcharge is 15mm wide. Also known with second 20mm surcharge in red, with a "c" below "CENTS," and with a "c" below "CENTS" and another "c" above "TWENTY."

R7

Kamehameha I — R8

Sheets of 50

1894 **Litho.** ***Perf. 14***

R9	R7 20c **red** *(10,000)*	175.00	175.00
a.	Imperf. *(25,000)*	300.00	300.00
	Pair	800.00	
R10	R7 25c **violet brown**	750.00	675.00
a.	Imperf.	1,200.	—
	Pair	3,000.	
b.	As "a," tete beche pair	—	

Printed by the American Bank Note Co.
Sheets of 100

1897 **Engr.** ***Perf. 12***

R11	R8 $1 **dark blue** *(60,000)*	7.50	4.50

R9

1901 ***Rouletted 8***

R12	R9 $50 **slate blue & carmine** *(7,000)*	40.00	45.00

Types of 1877
Printed by the American Bank Note Co.
Sheets of 70

1910-13 **Engr.** ***Perf. 12***

R13	R2 50c **yellow orange** ('13) *(70,000)*	10.00	20.00
R14	R3 $1 **black** ('13) *(35,000)*	12.00	20.00
R15	R4 $5 **vermilion & violet blue** *(14,000)*	27.50	35.00
a.	Denomination inverted		—
R16	R5 $10 **reddish brown & green** *(14,000)*	27.50	35.00

PROOFS and TRIAL COLOR PROOFS

The large die proofs range in size and format from die impressions on India die sunk on cards generally up to 6x9 inches, through die impressions on India on or off card in medium to stamp size. Many individual listings are known in more than one size and format. Values reflect the size and format most commonly seen.

			DIE *(1)* Large	PLATE *(3)* India	PLATE *(4)* Card
1853					
5TC	5c	**black** on wove		*6,000.*	
6TC	13c	**black** on wove		*6,000.*	
1868-89					
10TC	5c	**orange red**	875.		
11TC	13c	**orange red**	875.	475.	
11RP	13c	**orange red**	*2,500.*	575.	
1861-63					
27TC	2c	**black**		875.	
1864-71					
30P	1c	**purple**	650.	190.	
		Block of 4		750.	
31P	2c	**rose vermilion**	650.	190.	225.
		Block of 4		—	
31TC	2c	**green**	*1,700.*		
32P	5c	**blue**	625.	190.	200.
32TC	5c	**black**	850.		
32TC	5c	**dark red**		190.	
32TC	5c	**orange red**		190.	
32TC	5c	**orange**		190.	
32TC	5c	**red brown**		190.	
		Block of 4		800.	
32TC	5c	**green**		190.	
		Block of 4		800.	
32TC	5c	**dark violet**		190.	
		Block of 4		800.	
33P	6c	**green**	650.	190.	
		Block of 4		800.	
34P	18c	**dull rose**	650.	190.	225.
		Block of 4		800.	
34TC	18c	**orange red**	875.	650.	
34TC	18c	**dark orange**	875.		
1875					
35P	2c	**brown**	650.	190.	225.
		Block of 4		800.	
35TC	2c	**black**	*2,600.*		
36P	12c	**black**	650.	190.	225.
36TC	12c	**violet blue**	875.		
1882					
37P	1c	**blue**		190.	
		Block of 4		800.	
37TC	1c	**black**	875.		
39P	5c	**ultramarine**	575.	190.	
40P	10c	**black**	575.	190.	
		Block of 4		800.	
41P	15c	**red brown**		190.	225.
		Block of 4		800.	
1883-86					
42P	1c	**green**		190.	225.
		Block of 4		800.	
43P	2c	**rose**		150.	225.
		Block of 4		700.	
47P	25c	**dark violet**	550.	190.	
		Block of 4		800.	
47TC	25c	**black**	*875.*		
48P	50c	**red**	550.	190.	
		Block of 4		800.	
48TC	50c	**lake**	*1,150.*	*375.*	
49P	$1	**rose red**	*1,750.*	190.	225.
		Block of 4		800.	
49TC	$1	**black**		190.	
49TC	$1	**orange red**	875.	*375.*	
49TC	$1	**carmine**		*375.*	
49TC	$1	**vermilion**		*375.*	
		Block of 4		*1,600.*	
1886-89					
50P	2c	**orange vermilion**	875.	250.	
51P	2c	**carmine**	875.		
1890-91					
52P	2c	**dull violet**	875.	250.	225.
52CP	5c	**deep indigo**		175.	
1894					
74P	1c	**yellow**	700.	150.	225.
75P	2c	**brown**	700.	150.	
75TC	2c	**dark green**	650.		
76P	5c	**rose lake**	700.	150.	225.
77P	10c	**yellow green**	700.	150.	225.
		Block of 4		625.	
77TC	10c	**deep blue green**	700.		
78P	12c	**blue**	700.	150.	225.
79P	25c	**deep blue**	700.	150.	225.
1899					
82P	5c	**blue**		190.	225.
		Block of 4		800.	

Official

1896					
O1P	2c		875.	300.	190.
O2P	5c	**black brown**	875.	300.	190.
O3P	6c	**deep ultramarine**	875.	300.	190.
O4P	10c	**bright rose**	875.	300.	190.
		Block of 4		—	
O4TC	10c	**black**	875.		
O5P	12c	**orange**	875.	300.	190.
O5TC	12c	**black**	875.		
O6P	25c	**gray violet**	875.	300.	190.
O6TC	25c	**black**	875.		

Envelopes

Uncleared indicia only

1884			
U1P	1c	**green**	*725.*
U1TC	1c	**black**	*725.*
U1TC	1c	**orange**	*725.*
U2P	2c	**carmine**	*725.*
U2TC	2c	**black**	*725.*
U2TC	2c	**blue**	*725.*
U3P	4c	**red**	*725.*
U3TC	4c	**black**	*725.*
U4P	5c	**blue**	*725.*
U4TC	5c	**black**	*725.*
U5P	10c	**black**	*725.*

Postal Cards

Large die proofs are of indicia only, India proofs are entire card.

1882-95				
UX1P	1c	**red**	*3,500.*	*1,700.*
UX1TC	1c	**green**		*1,950.*
UX2P	2c	**black**		*1,700.*
UX3P	3c	**blue green**		*3,000.*
UX8TC	1c	**orange**		*3,000.*
UX8TC	1c	**brown**		*3,000.*

Revenues

			DIE *(1)* Large	PLATE *(3)* India	PLATE *(4)* Card
1877-97					
R1P	25c	**green**		*300.*	*300.*
		Block of 4		*1,300.*	
R1TC	25c	**blue green**	*1,150.*		
R1TC	25c	**black**	*1,150.*		
R1TC	25c	**brown red**	*1,150.*		
R1TC	25c	**brown**	*1,150.*		
R1TC	25c	**grayish blue**	*1,150.*		
R2P	50c	**yellow orange**		*300.*	*350.*
		Block of 4		*1,300.*	
R2TC	50c	**blue green**	*1,150.*		
R2TC	50c	**black**	*1,150.*		
R2TC	50c	**brown red**	*1,150.*		
R2TC	50c	**brown**	*1,150.*		
R2TC	50c	**grayish blue**	*1,150.*		
R3P	$1	**black**	*1,150.*		*350.*
		Block of 4		*1,300.*	
R3TC	$1	**blue green**	*1,150.*		
R3TC	$1	**brown red**	*1,150.*		
R3TC	$1	**brown**	*1,150.*		
R3TC	$1	**grayish blue**	*1,150.*		
R4P	$5	**vermilion & violet blue**			*350.*
		Block of 4		*1,200.*	
R5P	$10	**reddish brown & green**		*300.*	*350.*
		Block of 4		*1,200.*	
R6P	$50	**slate blue & carmine**			*350.*
		Block of 4		*1,200.*	
R11P	$1	**dark blue**	*1,250.*	*300.*	*350.*

SPECIMEN

Overprinted in Black or Red — Type A

1868

10S	A 5c **blue** (R)	20.
	Block of 4	100.
a.	Line through "Honolulu" (Pos. 2)	75.
11S	A 13c **dull rose**	20.
	Block of 4	100.

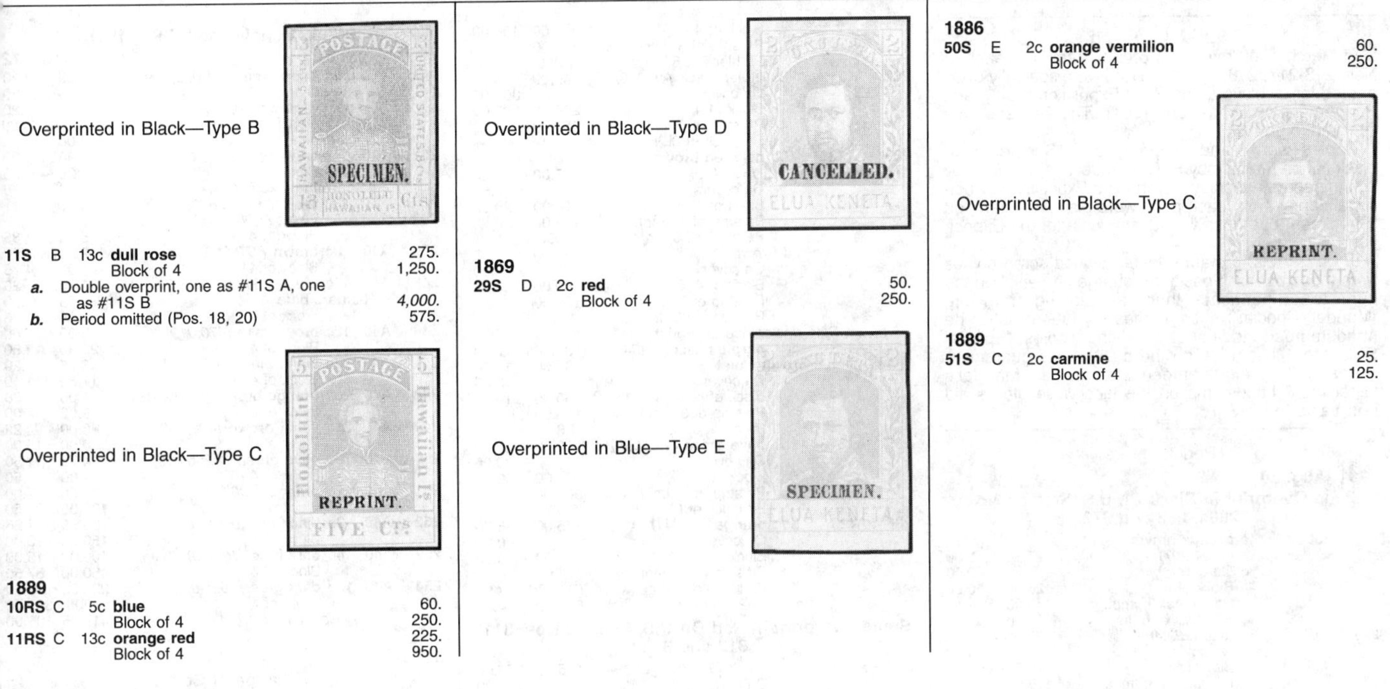

Overprinted in Black—Type B

11S	B	13c **dull rose**	275.
		Block of 4	1,250.
a.		Double overprint, one as #11S A, one as #11S B	*4,000.*
b.		Period omitted (Pos. 18, 20)	575.

Overprinted in Black—Type C

1889

10RS	C	5c **blue**	60.
		Block of 4	250.
11RS	C	13c **orange red**	225.
		Block of 4	950.

Overprinted in Black—Type D

1869

29S	D	2c **red**	50.
		Block of 4	250.

Overprinted in Blue—Type E

1886

50S	E	2c **orange vermilion**	60.
		Block of 4	250.

Overprinted in Black—Type C

1889

51S	C	2c **carmine**	25.
		Block of 4	125.

PHILIPPINES

Issued under U.S. Administration

Following the American occupation of the Philippines, May 1, 1898, after Admiral Dewey's fleet entered Manila Bay, an order was issued by the U. S. Postmaster General (No. 201, May 24, 1898) establishing postal facilities with rates similar to the domestic rates.

Military postal stations were established as branch post offices, each such station being placed within the jurisdiction of the nearest regular post office. Supplies were issued to these military stations through the regular post office of which they were branches.

Several post office clerks were sent to the Philippines and the San Francisco post office was made the nearest regular office for the early Philippine mail and the postmarks of the period point out this fact.

U.S. stamps overprinted "PHILIPPINES" were placed on sale in Manila June 30, 1899. Regular U.S. stamps had been in use from early March, and at the Manila post office Spanish stamps were also acceptable.

The first regular post office was established at Cavite on July 30, 1898, as a branch of the San Francisco post office. The first cancellation was a dated handstamp with "PHILIPPINE STATION" and "SAN FRANCISCO, CAL."

On May 1, 1899, the entire Philippine postal service was separated from San Francisco and numerous varieties of postmarks resulted. Many of the early used stamps show postmarks and cancellations of the Military Station, Camp or R.P.O. types, together with "Killers" of the types employed in the U.S. at the time.

The Philippines became a commonwealth of the United States on November 15, 1935, the High Commissioner of the United States taking office on the same day. The official name of the government was "Commonwealth of the Philippines" as provided by Article 17 of the Constitution. Upon the final and complete withdrawal of sovereignty of the United States and the proclamation of Philippine independence on July 4, 1946, the Commonwealth of the Philippines became the "Republic of the Philippines."

Italicized numbers in parenthesis indicate quantities issued.

Authority for dates of issue, stamps from 1899 to 1911, and some quantities issued-"The Postal Issues of the Philippines," by F. L. Palmer (New York, 1912). Authority for quantities issued - "NAPP's Numbers, Volume 2," by Joseph M. Napp (2001).

100 CENTS = 1 DOLLAR
100 CENTAVOS = 1 PESO (1906)

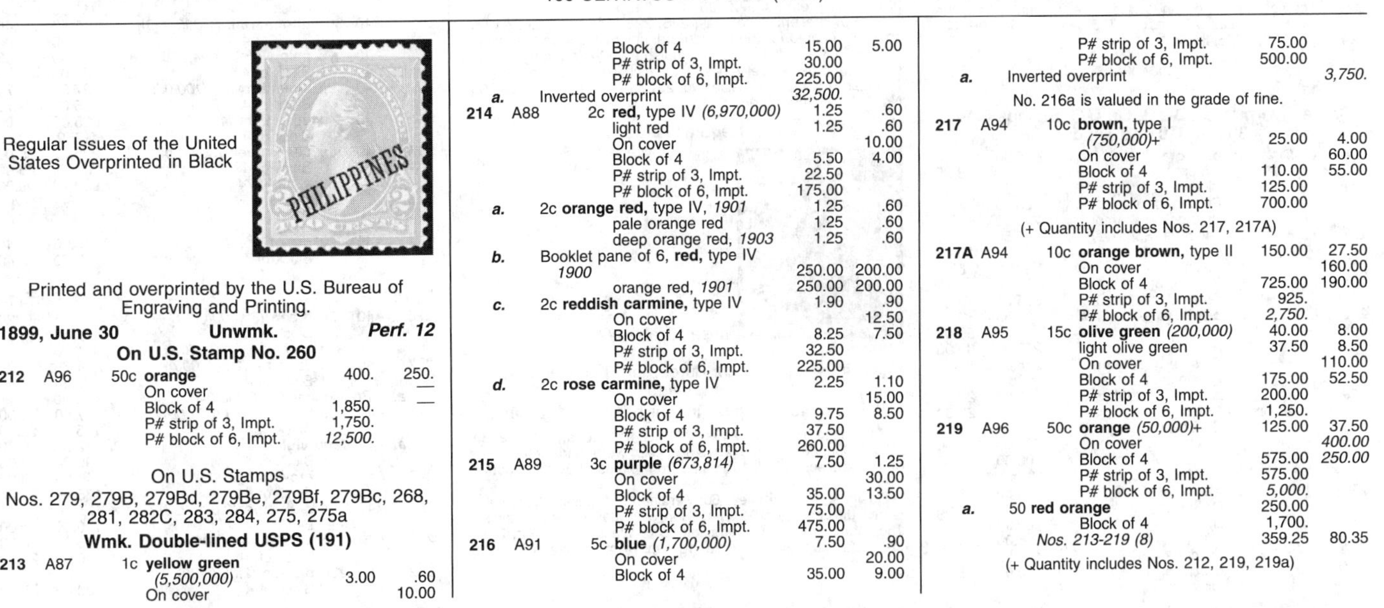

Regular Issues of the United States Overprinted in Black

Printed and overprinted by the U.S. Bureau of Engraving and Printing.

1899, June 30 **Unwmk.** ***Perf. 12***

On U.S. Stamp No. 260

212	A96	50c **orange**	400.	250.
		On cover		—
		Block of 4	1,850.	—
		P# strip of 3, Impt.	1,750.	
		P# block of 6, Impt.	*12,500.*	

On U.S. Stamps
Nos. 279, 279B, 279Bd, 279Be, 279Bf, 279Bc, 268, 281, 282C, 283, 284, 275, 275a

Wmk. Double-lined USPS (191)

213	A87	1c **yellow green** *(5,500,000)*	3.00	.60
		On cover		10.00
		Block of 4	15.00	5.00
		P# strip of 3, Impt.	30.00	
		P# block of 6, Impt.	225.00	
a.		Inverted overprint	*32,500.*	
214	A88	2c **red,** type IV *(6,970,000)*	1.25	.60
		light red	1.25	.60
		On cover		10.00
		Block of 4	5.50	4.00
		P# strip of 3, Impt.	22.50	
		P# block of 6, Impt.	175.00	
a.		2c **orange red,** type IV, *1901*	1.25	.60
		pale orange red	1.25	.60
		deep orange red, *1903*	1.25	.60
b.		Booklet pane of 6, **red,** type IV *1900*	250.00	200.00
		orange red, *1901*	250.00	200.00
c.		2c **reddish carmine,** type IV	1.90	.90
		On cover		12.50
		Block of 4	8.25	7.50
		P# strip of 3, Impt.	32.50	
		P# block of 6, Impt.	225.00	
d.		2c **rose carmine,** type IV	2.25	1.10
		On cover		15.00
		Block of 4	9.75	8.50
		P# strip of 3, Impt.	37.50	
		P# block of 6, Impt.	260.00	
215	A89	3c **purple** *(673,814)*	7.50	1.25
		On cover		30.00
		Block of 4	35.00	13.50
		P# strip of 3, Impt.	75.00	
		P# block of 6, Impt.	475.00	
216	A91	5c **blue** *(1,700,000)*	7.50	.90
		On cover		20.00
		Block of 4	35.00	9.00
		P# strip of 3, Impt.	75.00	
		P# block of 6, Impt.	500.00	
a.		Inverted overprint		*3,750.*

No. 216a is valued in the grade of fine.

217	A94	10c **brown,** type I *(750,000)+*	25.00	4.00
		On cover		60.00
		Block of 4	110.00	55.00
		P# strip of 3, Impt.	125.00	
		P# block of 6, Impt.	700.00	

(+ Quantity includes Nos. 217, 217A)

217A	A94	10c **orange brown,** type II	150.00	27.50
		On cover		160.00
		Block of 4	725.00	190.00
		P# strip of 3, Impt.	925.	
		P# block of 6, Impt.	*2,750.*	
218	A95	15c **olive green** *(200,000)*	40.00	8.00
		light olive green	37.50	8.50
		On cover		110.00
		Block of 4	175.00	52.50
		P# strip of 3, Impt.	200.00	
		P# block of 6, Impt.	1,250.	
219	A96	50c **orange** *(50,000)+*	125.00	37.50
		On cover		*400.00*
		Block of 4	575.00	*250.00*
		P# strip of 3, Impt.	575.00	
		P# block of 6, Impt.	*5,000.*	
a.		50 **red orange**	250.00	
		Block of 4	1,700.	
		Nos. 213-219 (8)	359.25	80.35

(+ Quantity includes Nos. 212, 219, 219a)

Special Printing

In March 1900 one pane of 100 stamps of each of Nos. 213-217, 218, 219 and J1-J5 were specially overprinted for displays at the Paris Exposition (1900) and Pan American Exposition (1901). The 2c pane was light red, type IV.

Copies were handstampd type E "Specimen" in black ink on the face by H. G. Mandel and mounted by him in separate displays for the two Expositions. Additional copies from each pane were also handstamped "Specimen" but most were destroyed after the Expositions.

J. M. Bartels, a stamp dealer, signed some copies from these panes "Special Surcharge" in pencil on the gum to authenticate them as coming from the "Mandel" Special Printing panes. In 1904 or later, he handstamped additional surviving copies "Special Surcharge" in red ink on the back as his guarantee. Some of these guaranteed stamps had Mandel's "Specimen" handstamp on the face while others did not. Value, each $775.

Regular Issue

1901, Aug. 30

Same Overprint in Black On U.S. Stamps Nos. 280b, 282 and 272

220 A90 4c **orange brown** *(404,907)* 27.50 5.00
On cover 50.00
Block of 4 125.00 50.00
P# strip of 3, Impt. 140.00
P# block of 6, Impt. 700.00
221 A92 6c **lake** *(223,465)* 35.00 7.00
On cover 65.00
Block of 4 175.00 50.00
P# strip of 3, Impt. 175.00
P# block of 6, Impt. 900.00
222 A93 8c **violet brown** *(248,000)* 35.00 7.50
On cover 50.00
Block of 4 175.00 55.00
P# strip of 3, Impt. 175.00
P# block of 6, Impt. 900.00

Same Overprint in Red On U.S. Stamps Nos. 276, 276A, 277a and 278

223 A97 $1 **black,** type I *(3,000)+* 475.00 275.00
On cover *800.00*
Block of 4 2,000.
P# strip of 3, Impt. *2,100.*
P# block of 6, Impt. —
Horiz. pair, types I & II *3,750.*
(+ Quantity includes Nos. 223, 223A)
223A A97 $1 **black,** type II 2,400. 750.00
On cover —
Block of 4 *10,500.* —
P# strip of 3, Impt., one stamp No. 223 8,500.
P# block of 6, Impt., two stamps No. 223 —
224 A98 $2 **dark blue** *(1800)* 475.00 350.00
On cover 3,250.
Block of 4 2,000. —
P# strip of 3, Impt. *2,600.*
P# block of 6, Impt. —
225 A99 $5 **dark green** *(782)* 825.00 *900.00*
On cover *12,500.*
Block of 4 *3,350.* —
P# strip of 3, Impt. *4,000.*
P# block of 6, Impt. —

Special Printing

Special printings exist of Nos. 227, 221, 223-225, made from defaced plates. These were made for display at the St. Louis Exposition. All but a few copies were destroyed. Most of the existing copies have the handstamp "Special Printing" on the back. Value: Nos. 227, 221, each $775; No. 223, $1,200; No. 224, $1,650; No. 225, $2,500.

Regular Issue

1903-04

Same Overprint in Black On U.S. Stamps Nos. 300 to 310 and shades

226 A115 1c **blue green** *(9,631,172)* 5.00 .30
On cover 8.25
Block of 4 17.50 4.00
P# strip of 3, Impt. 22.50
P# block of 6, Impt. 250.00
227 A116 2c **carmine** *(850,000)* 7.50 1.10
On cover 10.00
Block of 4 32.50 6.00
P# strip of 3, Impt. 32.50
P# block of 6, Impt. 325.00
228 A117 3c **bright violet** *(14,500)* 67.50 12.50
On cover 55.00
Block of 4 275.00 85.00
P# strip of 3, Impt. 275.00
P# block of 6, Impt. 1,650.
229 A118 4c **brown** *(13,000)* 75.00 22.50
a. 4c **orange brown** 75.00 20.00
On cover 40.00
Block of 4 325.00 150.00
P# strip of 3, Impt. 300.00
P# block of 6, Impt. 1,850.
230 A119 5c **blue** *(1,211,844)* 13.50 1.00
On cover 22.50
Block of 4 60.00 7.50
P# strip of 3, Impt. 65.00
P# block of 6, Impt. 450.00
231 A120 6c **brownish lake** *(11,500)* 80.00 22.50
On cover 65.00
Block of 4 325.00 150.00
P# strip of 3, Impt. 325.00
P# block of 6, Impt. 1,950.
232 A121 8c **violet black** *(49,033)* 45.00 15.00
On cover 300.00
Block of 4 225.00 100.00
P# strip of 3, Impt. 250.00
P# block of 6, Impt. 1,400.
233 A122 10c **pale red brown** *(300,179)* 25.00 2.25
On cover 27.50
Block of 4 110.00 20.00
P# strip of 3, Impt. 125.00
P# block of 6, Impt. 1,000.
a. 10c **red brown** 30.00 3.00
On cover 35.00
Block of 4 140.00 32.50
P# strip of 3, Impt. 150.00
P# block of 6, Impt. 1,200.
b. Pair, one without overprint *1,500.*
234 A123 13c **purple black** *(91,341)* 35.00 17.50
a. 13c **brown violet** 35.00 17.50
On cover 55.00
Block of 4 150.00 110.00
P# strip of 3, Impt. 175.00
P# block of 6, Impt. 1,350.
235 A124 15c **olive green** *(183,965)* 60.00 15.00
On cover 100.00
Block of 4 275.00 100.00
P# strip of 3, Impt. 300.00
P# block of 6, Impt. 2,000.
236 A125 50c **orange** *(57,641)* 125.00 35.00
On cover 300.00
Block of 4 575.00 275.00
P# strip of 3, Impt. 575.00
P# block of 6, Impt. *17,500.*
Nos. 226-236 (11) 538.50 144.65

Same Overprint in Red On U.S. Stamps Nos. 311, 312 and 313

237 A126 $1 **black** *(5617)* 475.00 275.00
On cover 750.00
Block of 4 2,100. 1,850.
P# strip of 3, Impt. 2,100.
P# block of 6, Impt. *7,500.*
238 A127 $2 **dark blue** *(695)* 800.00 *850.00*
Block of 4 *3,400.* —
P# strip of 3, Impt. *3,600.*
P# block of 6, Impt. *16,000.*
239 A128 $5 **dark green** *(746)* 975.00 *3,000.*
Block of 4 *4,000.* —
P# strip of 3, Impt. *4,750.*
P# block of 6, Impt. —

Same Overprint in Black On U.S. Stamp No. 319

240 A129 2c **carmine** *(862,245)* 5.50 2.25
On cover 3.50
Block of 4 25.00 15.00
P# strip of 3, Impt. 35.00
P# block of 6, Impt. 300.00
a. Booklet pane of 6 *1,100.*
b. 2c **scarlet** 6.25 2.75
On cover 4.00
Block of 4 27.50 17.50
P# strip of 3, Impt. 40.00
P# block of 6, Impt. 325.00
c. As "b," booklet pane of 6 —

Dates of issue:
Sept. 20, 1903, Nos. 226, 227, 236.
Jan. 4, 1904, Nos. 230, 234, 235, 237, 240a.
Nov. 1, 1904, Nos. 228, 229, 231, 232, 233, 238, 239, 240.
Nos. 212 to 240 became obsolete on Sept. 8, 1906, the remainders being destroyed.

Special Printing

Two sets of special printings exist of the 1903-04 issue. The first consists of Nos. 226, 230, 234, 235, 236, 237 and 240. These were made for display at the St. Louis Exposition. All but a few copies were destroyed. Most of the existing copies have the handstamp "Special Surcharge" on the back. Value: No. 237, $1,550; others $900; J6, J7, $1,150:

In 1907 the entire set Nos. 226, 228 to 240, J1 to J7 were specially printed for the Bureau of Insular Affairs on very white paper. They are difficult to distinguish from the ordinary stamps except the Special Delivery stamp which is on U.S. No. E6 (see Philippines No. E2A). Value: No. 237, $1,300; No. 238, $2,600; No. 239, $3,500; others, $775.

Regular Issue

José Rizal — A40

Printed by the U.S. Bureau of Engraving and Printing.

Plates of 400 subjects in four panes of 100 each.

Booklet panes Nos. 240a, 241b, 242b, 261a, 262b, 276a, 277a, 285a, 286a, 290e, 291b and 292c were made from plates of 180 subjects. No. 214b came from plates of 360 subjects.

Designs: 4c, McKinley. 6c, Ferdinand Magellan. 8c, Miguel Lopez de Legaspi. 10c, Gen. Henry W. Lawton. 12c, Lincoln. 16c, Adm. William T. Sampson. 20c, Washington. 26c, Francisco Carriedo. 30c, Franklin. 1p-10p, Arms of City of Manila.

Wmk. Double-lined PIPS (191)

1906, Sept. 8 *Perf. 12*

241 A40 2c **deep green** *(51,000,019)* .25 .20
Block of 4 1.10 .20
a. 2c **yellow green** ('10) .40 .20
Double transfer *40.00*
b. Booklet pane of 6 *(720,120)* 475.00
242 A40 4c **carmine** *(11,000,019)* .30 .20
Block of 4 1.25 .20
a. 4c **carmine lake** ('10) .60 .20
b. Booklet pane of 6*(300,600)* *650.00*
243 A40 6c **violet** *(1,980,019)* 1.25 .20
Block of 4 5.75 .85
244 A40 8c **brown** *(770,019)* 2.50 .70
Block of 4 11.00 4.75
245 A40 10c **blue** *(5,500,019)* 1.75 .20
a. 10c **dark blue** 1.75 .20
Block of 4 7.25 .85
246 A40 12c **brown lake** *(670,019)* 5.00 2.00
Block of 4 22.50 13.50
247 A40 16c **violet black** *(1,300,019)* 3.75 .20
Block of 4 17.50 1.40
248 A40 20c **orange brown** *(2,100,019)* 4.00 .30
Block of 4 19.00 2.00
249 A40 26c **violet brown** *(428,000)* 6.00 2.25
Block of 4 30.00 15.00
250 A40 30c **olive green** *(1,256,019)* 4.75 1.50
Block of 4 21.00 7.50
251 A40 1p **orange** *(200,019)* 27.50 7.00
Block of 4 125.00 37.50
252 A40 2p **black** *(100,000)* 35.00 1.25
Block of 4 150.00 10.00
253 A40 4p **dark blue** *(10,000)* 100.00 15.00
Block of 4 450.00 67.50
254 A40 10p **dark green** *(6,019)* 225.00 70.00
Block of 4 1,000. 350.00
Nos. 241-254 (14) 417.05 101.00

1909

Change of Colors

255 A40 12c **red orange** *(300,000)* 8.50 2.50
Block of 4 40.00 12.50
256 A40 16c **olive green** *(500,000)* 3.50 .75
Block of 4 15.00 3.50
257 A40 20c **yellow** *(800,000)* 7.50 1.25
Block of 4 35.00 7.50
258 A40 26c **blue green** *(250,000)* 1.75 .75
Block of 4 7.50 4.00
259 A40 30c **ultramarine** *(600,000)* 10.00 3.25
Block of 4 47.50 20.00
260 A40 1p **pale violet** *(100,000)* 30.00 5.00
Block of 4 150.00 32.50
260A A40 2p **violet brown** *(50,000)* 85.00 2.75
Block of 4 400.00 19.00
Nos. 255-260A (7) 146.25 16.25

1911 **Wmk. Single-lined PIPS (190)** *Perf. 12*

261 A40 2c **green** *(44,000,000)* .65 .20
Block of 4 4.25 .35
a. Booklet pane of 6 *(896,160)* *550.00*
262 A40 4c **carmine lake** *(6,000,000)* 2.50 .20
Block of 4 11.50 .35
a. 4c **carmine** — —
b. Booklet pane of 6 *(100,020)* *600.00*
263 A40 6c **deep violet** *(3,200,000)* 2.00 .20
Block of 4 9.00 .30
264 A40 8c **brown** *(1,400,000)* 8.50 .45
Block of 4 40.00 2.00
265 A40 10c **blue** *(3,700,000)* 3.25 .20
Block of 4 15.00 .30
266 A40 12c **orange** *(1,320,000)* 2.50 .45
Block of 4 11.50 2.10
267 A40 16c **olive green** *(1,000,000)* 2.50 .20
a. 16c **pale olive green** 2.50 .20
Block of 4 11.50 .65
268 A40 20c **yellow** *(3,000,000)* 2.00 .20
a. 20c **orange** 2.00 .20
Block of 4 8.00 .45
269 A40 26c **blue green** *(249,900)* 3.00 .20
Block of 4 12.50 1.00
270 A40 30c **ultramarine** *(1,000,000)* 3.50 .40
Block of 4 15.00 2.00
271 A40 1p **pale violet** *(694,000)* 22.50 .55
Block of 4 100.00 2.75
272 A40 2p **violet brown** *(100,000)* 27.50 .75
Block of 4 125.00 4.75
273 A40 4p **deep blue** *(10,000)* 625.00 80.00
Block of 4 2,750. 450.00
274 A40 10p **deep green** *(20,000)* 225.00 25.00
Block of 4 1,000. 125.00
Nos. 261-274 (14) 930.40 109.00

1914

275 A40 30c **gray** *(700,000)* 10.00 .40
Block of 4 47.50 2.40

1914 *Perf. 10*

276 A40 2c **green** *(60,000,000)* 1.75 .20
Block of 4 7.50 .30
a. Booklet pane of 6 *(400,080)* *450.00*
277 A40 4c **carmine** *(2,500,000)* 1.75 .20
Block of 4 7.50 .45
a. Booklet pane of 6 *(56,040)* *450.00*
278 A40 6c **light violet** *(700,000)* 37.50 9.00
Block of 4 175.00 52.50
a. 6c **deep violet** 42.50 6.00
Block of 4 190.00 35.00
279 A40 8c **brown** *(200,000)* 40.00 10.00
Block of 4 175.00 55.00
280 A40 10c **dark blue** *(2,000,000)* 25.00 .20
Block of 4 110.00 1.00
281 A40 16c **olive green** *(700,000)* 75.00 4.50
Block of 4 350.00 25.00
282 A40 20c **orange** *(2,000,000)* 22.50 .85
Block of 4 100.00 5.25

283 A40 30c **gray** *(1,300,000)* 55.00 2.75
Block of 4 250.00 16.50
284 A40 1p **pale violet** *(198,000)* 110.00 3.00
Block of 4 500.00 18.00
Nos. 276-284 (9) 368.50 30.70

1918 ***Perf. 11***

285 A40 2c **green** *(40,000,000)* 20.00 4.25
Block of 4 90.00 18.00
a. Booklet pane of 6 *(50,040)* *750.00*
286 A40 4c **carmine** *(3,000,000)* 25.00 2.50
Block of 4 110.00 12.50
a. Booklet pane of 6 *1,350.*
287 A40 6c **deep violet** *(1,000,000)* 35.00 1.75
Block of 4 140.00 8.50
287A A40 8c **light brown** *(200,000)* 200.00 25.00
Block of 4 825.00 160.00
288 A40 10c **dark blue** *(2,000,000)* 52.50 1.50
Block of 4 225.00 8.00
289 A40 16c **olive green** *(700,000)* 90.00 6.75
Block of 4 425.00 27.50
289A A40 20c **orange** *(1,000,000)* 60.00 7.50
Block of 4 275.00 40.00
289C A40 30c **gray** *(500,000)* 55.00 12.50
Block of 4 240.00 60.00
289D A40 1p **pale violet** *(200,000)* 70.00 14.00
Block of 4 300.00 77.50
Nos. 285-289D (9) 607.50 75.75

1917 Unwmk. ***Perf. 11***

290 A40 2c **yellow green** *(444,746,800)* .20 .20
Block of 4 .30 .20
a. 2c **dark green** .20 .20
green .20 .20
Double transfer — —
b. Vert. pair, imperf. horiz. *1,500.*
c. Horiz. pair, imperf. between *1,500.* —
d. Vertical pair, imperf. btwn. *1,750.*
e. Booklet pane of 6 *(3,251,080)* 27.50
291 A40 4c **carmine** *(50,579,100)* .20 .20
a. 4c **light rose** .20 .20
Block of 4 .30 .20
b. Booklet pane of 6 *(500,820)* 17.50 —
292 A40 6c **deep violet** *(8,803,600)* .30 .20
Block of 4 1.30 .30
a. 6c **lilac** .35 .20
b. 6c **red violet** .35 .20
c. Booklet pane of 6 *(75)* *550.00* —
293 A40 8c **yellow brown** *(6,036,700)* .35 .20
a. 8c **orange brown** .35 .20
Block of 4 1.75 .35
294 A40 10c **deep blue**(15,848,800) .20 .20
Block of 4 .85 .25
295 A40 12c **red orange** *(3,396,500)* .30 .20
Block of 4 1.25 .50
296 A40 16c **light olive green** *(3,249,600)* 55.00 .25
Block of 4 250.00 1.25
a. 16c **olive bister** 55.00 .40
297 A40 20c **orange yellow** *(10,814,600)* .30 .20
Block of 4 1.90 .30
298 A40 26c **green** *(1,595,400)* .45 .45
Block of 4 2.00 2.10
a. 26c **blue green** .55 .25
299 A40 30c **gray** *(6,031,300)* .55 .20
Block of 4 2.60 .35
Dark gray .55 .20
300 A40 1p **pale violet** *(1,173,200)* 27.50 1.00
Block of 4 115.00 4.50
a. 1p **red lilac** 27.50 1.00
b. 1p **pale rose lilac** 27.50 1.10
301 A40 2p **violet brown** *(475,300)* 25.00 .75
Block of 4 115.00 3.50
302 A40 4p **blue** *(541,800)* 22.50 .45
Block of 4 100.00 2.00
a. 4p **dark blue** 22.50 .45
Nos. 290-302 (13) 132.85 4.50

1923-26

303 A40 16c **olive bister** *(Adm. George Dewey) (13,524,300)* .90 .20
Block of 4 4.25 .45
a. 16c **olive green** 1.25 .20
304 A40 10p **deep green** *('26) (32,400)* 45.00 5.00
Block of 4 190.00 22.50

Legislative Palace Issue

Issued to commemorate the opening of the Legislative Palace.

Legislative Palace — A42

Printed by the Philippine Bureau of Printing.

1926, Dec. 20 Unwmk. ***Perf. 12***

319 A42 2c **green & black** *(502,300)* .40 .25
First day cover 3.50
Block of 4 1.75 1.10
a. Horiz. pair, imperf. between *300.00*
b. Vert. pair, imperf. between *575.00*
320 A42 4c **carmine & black** *(304,150)* .40 .35
First day cover 3.50
Block of 4 1.75 1.40
a. Horiz. pair, imperf. between *325.00*
b. Vert. pair, imperf. between *600.00*
321 A42 16c **olive green & black** *(203,500)* .75 .65
First day cover 10.00
Block of 4 3.75 3.00
a. Horiz. pair, imperf. between *350.00*
b. Vert. pair, imperf. between *625.00*
c. Double impression of center *675.00*
322 A42 18c **light brown & black** *(103,700)* .85 .50
First day cover 10.00
Block of 4 3.75 2.25
a. Double impression of center *(150)* *850.00*
b. Vertical pair, imperf. between *675.00*
323 A42 20c **orange & black** *(103,200)* 1.25 .80
Block of 4 5.50 4.00
a. 20c **orange & brown** *(100)* *600.00* —
b. As No. 323, imperf., pair *(50)* *575.00 575.00*
c. As "a," imperf., pair *(100)* *975.00*
d. Vert. pair, imperf. between *700.00*
324 A42 24c **gray & black** *(103,100)* .85 .55
Block of 4 3.75 2.50
a. Vert. pair, imperf. between *700.00*
325 A42 1p **rose lilac & black** *(10,800)* 45.00 30.00
Block of 4 190.00 140.00
a. Vert. pair, imperf. between *700.00*
First day cover, #319-325 85.00
Nos. 319-325 (7) 49.50 33.10

No. 322a is valued in the grade of fine.

Coil Stamp
Rizal Type of 1906
Printed by the U.S. Bureau of Engraving and Printing.

1928 Unwmk. ***Perf. 11 Vertically***

326 A40 2c **green** *(110,000)* 7.50 *15.00*
Pair 17.50 *37.50*
Line pair 55.00 *100.00*

Types of 1906-1923

1925-31 Unwmk. ***Imperf.***

340 A40 2c **yellow green** *('31) (99,986)* .20 .20
Block of 4 .25 .25
a. 2c **green** *('25) (51,000)* .30 .20
341 A40 4c **carmine rose** *('31) (49,855)* .20 .20
Block of 4 .40 .40
a. 4c **carmine** *('25) (25,500)* .50 .25
342 A40 6c **violet** *('31) (10,000)* 1.00 1.00
Block of 4 4.25 4.25
a. 6c **deep violet** *('25) (5,200)* 9.00 4.50
343 A40 8c **brown** *('31) (10,000)* .90 .90
Block of 4 3.75 3.75
a. 8c **yellow brown** *('25) (5,200)* 6.75 3.50
344 A40 10c **blue** *('31) (7,000)* 1.75 1.40
Block of 4 7.00 5.50
a. 10c **deep blue** *('25) (2,200)* 27.50 8.00
345 A40 12c **deep orange** *('31) (7,000)* 2.50 2.10
Block of 4 11.00 8.75
a. 12c **red orange** *('25) (2,200)* 27.50 8.00
346 A40 16c **olive green** *(Dewey) ('31) (7,000)* 2.00 1.50
Block of 4 8.25 6.75
a. 16c **bister green** *('25) (2,200)* 22.50 6.00
347 A40 20c **deep yellow orange** *('31) (7,000)* 2.00 1.50
Block of 4 8.25 6.75
a. 20c **yellow orange** *('25) (2,200)* 22.50 6.00
348 A40 26c **green** *('31) (7,000)* 2.00 1.50
Block of 4 8.25 6.75
a. 26c **blue green** *('25) (2,200)* 27.50 8.00
349 A40 30c **light gray** *('31) (7,000)* 2.25 1.75
Block of 4 9.25 7.25
a. 30c **gray** *('25) (2,200)* 27.50 8.00
350 A40 1p **light violet** *('31) (6,395)* 4.00 4.00
Block of 4 16.50 16.50
a. 1p **violet** *('25) (2,100)* 100.00 40.00
351 A40 2p **brown violet** *('31) (3,612)* 10.00 10.00
Block of 4 42.50 42.50
a. 2p **violet brown** *('25) (600)* 225.00 85.00
352 A40 4p **blue** *('31) (2,570)* 35.00 30.00
Block of 4 160.00 —
a. 4p **deep blue** *('25) (300)* 1,100. 425.00
353 A40 10p **green** *('31) (2,208)* 100.00 100.00
Block of 4 475.00
a. 10p **deep green** *('25) (200)* 2,250. 850.00
Nos. 340-353 (14) 163.80 156.05

Nos. 340a-353a were the original post office issue. These were reprinted twice in 1931 for sale to collectors (Nos. 340-353).

Mount Mayon, Luzon — A43

Post Office, Manila — A44

Pier No. 7, Manila Bay — A45

Vernal Falls, Yosemite Park, California (See Footnote) — A46

Rice Planting — A47

Rice Terraces — A48

Baguio Zigzag — A49

1932, May 3 Unwmk. ***Perf. 11***

354 A43 2c **yellow green**(5,432,000) .40 .20
First day cover 2.00
Block of 4 2.00 1.00
355 A44 4c **rose carmine** *(1,602,800)* .35 .25
First day cover 2.00
Block of 4 1.50 1.20
356 A45 12c **orange** *(483,000)* .50 .50
First day cover 6.50
Block of 4 2.25 2.00
357 A46 18c **red orange** *(983,400)* 25.00 9.00
First day cover 16.00
Block of 4 110.00 40.00
358 A47 20c **yellow** *(441,000)* .65 .55
First day cover 6.50
Block of 4 2.50 2.25
359 A48 24c **deep violet** *(425,000)* 1.00 .65
First day cover 6.50
Block of 4 4.00 3.75
360 A49 32c **olive brown** *(510,600)* 1.00 .70
First day cover 6.50
Block of 4 4.25 3.75
First day cover, #354-360 50.00
Nos. 354-360 (7) 28.90 11.85

The 18c vignette was intended to show Pagsanjan Falls in Laguna, central Luzon, and is so labeled. Through error the stamp pictures Vernal Falls in Yosemite National Park, California.

Nos. 302, 302a Surcharged in Orange or Red

1932

No.	Type	Description	Unused	Used
368	A40	1p on 4p **blue** (O) *(134,000)*	2.00	.45
		On cover		.60
		Block of 4	8.50	2.10
a.		1p on 4p **dark blue** (O)	2.75	1.25
369	A40	2p on 4p **dark blue** (R) *(80,000)*	3.50	.75
a.		2p on 4p **blue** (R)	3.50	.75
		On cover		.90
		Block of 4	15.00	3.50

Far Eastern Championship

Issued in commemoration of the Tenth Far Eastern Championship Games.

Baseball Players — A50

Tennis Player — A51

Basketball Players — A52

Printed by the Philippine Bureau of Printing.

1934, Apr. 14 **Unwmk.** ***Perf. 11½***

No.	Type	Description	Unused	Used
380	A50	2c **yellow brown** *(999,985)*	1.50	.80
		brown	1.50	.80
		First day cover		2.00
		"T" of "Eastern" malformed	2.00	1.25
381	A51	6c **ultramarine** *(800,000)*	.25	.20
		pale ultramarine	.25	.20
		First day cover		1.60
a.		Vertical pair, imperf. between	*1,250.*	
382	A52	16c **violet brown** *(500,000)*	.50	.50
		dark violet	.50	.50
		First day cover		2.25
a.		Imperf. horizontally, pair	*1,250.*	
		Nos. 380-382 (3)	2.25	1.50

José Rizal — A53

Woman and Carabao — A54

La Filipina — A55

Pearl Fishing — A56

Fort Santiago — A57

Salt Spring — A58

Magellan's Landing, 1521 — A59

"Juan de la Cruz" — A60

Rice Terraces — A61

Miguel Lopez de Legaspi and Chief Sikatuna Signing "Blood Compact," 1565 — A62

Barasoain Church, Malolos A63

Battle of Manila Bay, 1898 — A64

Montalban Gorge — A65

George Washington — A66

Printed by U.S. Bureau of Engraving and Printing.

1935, Feb. 15 **Unwmk.** ***Perf. 11***

No.	Type	Description	Unused	Used
383	A53	2c **rose** *(62,183,400)*	.20	.20
		First day cover		1.00
384	A54	4c **yellow green** *(14,238,193)*	.20	.20
		Light yellow green	.20	.20
		First day cover		1.00
385	A55	6c **dark brown** *(1,958,928)*	.20	.20
		First day cover		1.00
386	A56	8c **violet** *(792,000)*	.20	.20
		First day cover		1.60
387	A57	10c **rose carmine** *(341,400)*	.20	.20
		First day cover		1.60
388	A58	12c **black** *(319,500)*	.25	.20
		First day cover		1.60
389	A59	16c **dark blue** *(2,422,778)*	.25	.20
		First day cover		1.60
390	A60	20c **light olive green** *(1,061,400)*	.25	.20
		First day cover		2.25
391	A61	26c **indigo** *(212,000)*	.30	.25
		First day cover		3.00
392	A62	30c **orange red** *(171,200)*	.30	.25
		First day cover		3.00
393	A63	1p **red orange & black** *(80,000)*	1.75	1.25
		First day cover		8.25
394	A64	2p **bister brown & black** *(61,100)*	4.50	1.25
		First day cover		14.00
395	A65	4p **blue & black** *(59,000)*	5.00	3.00
		First day cover		20.00
396	A66	5p **green & black** *(54,000)*	10.00	3.00
		First day cover		27.50
		Nos. 383-396 (14)	23.60	10.60

USED VALUES

Used values in italics are for postally used examples with cancels of the proper function during the correct period of use.

Issues of the Commonwealth

Commonwealth Inauguration Issue

Issued to commemorate the inauguration of the Philippine Commonwealth, Nov. 15, 1935.

"The Temples of Human Progress" A67

1935, Nov. 15 **Unwmk.** ***Perf. 11***

397	A67	2c **carmine rose** *(1,531,000)*	.20	.20
		First day cover		1.00
398	A67	6c **deep violet** *(523,000)*	.20	.20
		First day cover		1.00
399	A67	16c **blue** *(313,500)*	.20	.20
		First day cover		1.00
400	A67	36c **yellow green** *(261,000)*	.35	.30
		First day cover		1.40
401	A67	50c **brown** *(218,500)*	.55	.55
		First day cover		2.00
		Nos. 397-401 (5)	1.50	1.45

Jose Rizal Issue

75th anniversary of the birth of Jose Rizal (1861-1896), national hero of the Filipinos.

Jose Rizal — A68

Printed by the Philippine Bureau of Printing.

1936, June 19 **Unwmk.** ***Perf. 12***

402	A68	2c **yellow brown** *(500,000)*	.20	.20
		light yellow brown	.20	.20
		First day cover		1.00
403	A68	6c **slate blue** *(300,000)*	.20	.20
		light slate green	.20	.20
		First day cover		1.00
a.		Imperf. vertically, pair	1,350.	
404	A68	36c **red brown** *(200,000)*	.50	.45
		light red brown	.50	.45
		First day cover		2.25
		Nos. 402-404 (3)	.90	.85

Commonwealth Anniversary Issue

Issued in commemoration of the first anniversary of the Commonwealth.

President Manuel L. Quezon — A69

Printed by U.S. Bureau of Engraving and Printing.

1936, Nov. 15 **Unwmk.** ***Perf. 11***

408	A69	2c **orange brown** *(4,946,816)*	.20	.20
		First day cover		1.00
409	A69	6c **yellow green** *(1,019,900)*	.20	.20
		First day cover		1.00
410	A69	12c **ultramarine** *(527,600)*	.20	.20
		First day cover		1.50
		Nos. 408-410 (3)	.60	.60

Stamps of 1935 Overprinted in Black

a

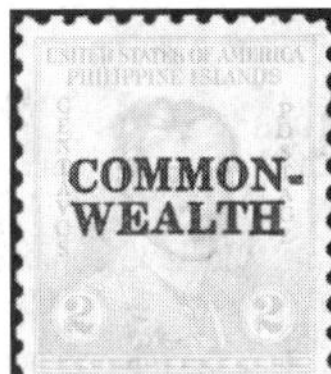

b

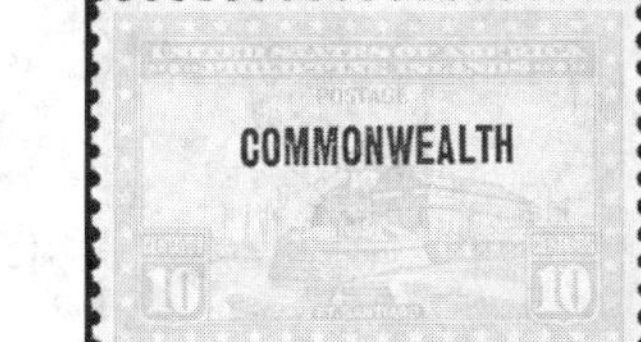

1936-37 **Unwmk.** ***Perf. 11***

411	A53(a)	2c **rose,** *Dec. 28, 1936 (84,092,400)*	.20	.20
		First day cover		35.00
a.		Bklt. pane of 6, *Jan. 15 1937 (239,492)*	2.50	2.00
		First day cover		40.00
412	A54(b)	4c **yellow green,** *Mar. 29, 1937 (100,000)*	.50	4.00
413	A55(a)	6c **dark brown,** *Oct. 7, 1936 (2,230,394)*	.20	.20
		On cover		.20
414	A56(b)	8c **violet,** *Mar. 29, 1937 (627,500)*	.25	.20
		On cover		.25
415	A57(b)	10c **rose carmine,** *Dec. 28, 1936 (1,687,550)*	.20	.20
		First day cover		35.00
a.		"COMMONWEALT"		—
416	A58(b)	12c **black,** *Mar. 29, 1937 (2,118,600)*	.20	.20
		On cover		.20
417	A59(b)	16c **dark blue,** *Oct. 7, 1936 (597,300)*	.20	.20
		On cover		.20
418	A60(a)	20c **lt olive green,** *Mar. 29, 1937 (100,000)*	.65	.40
		On cover		.45
419	A61(b)	26c **indigo,** *Mar. 29, 1937 (100,000)*	.45	.35
		On cover		.40
420	A62(b)	30c **orange red,** *Dec. 28, 1936 (836,252)*	.35	.20
		First day cover		35.00
421	A63(b)	1p **red org & blk,** *Oct. 7, 1936 (319,250)*	.65	.20
		On cover		.35
422	A64(b)	2p **bis brn & blk,** *Mar. 29, 1937 (50,000)*	5.00	2.75
		On cover		3.00
423	A65(b)	4p **blue & blk,** *Mar. 29, 1937 (30,000)*	22.50	5.00
		On cover		50.00
424	A66(b)	5p **green & blk,** *Mar. 29, 1937 (60,500)*	3.00	1.50
		On cover		35.00
		Nos. 411-424 (14)	34.35	15.60

Eucharistic Congress Issue

Issued to commemorate the 33rd International Eucharistic Congress held at Manila, Feb. 3-7, 1937.

Map, Symbolical of the Eucharistic Congress Spreading Light of Christianity — A70

FLAT PLATE PRINTING

Plates of 256 subjects in four panes of 64 each.

1937, Feb. 3 **Unwmk.** ***Perf. 11***

425	A70	2c **yellow green** *(4,102,848)*	.20	.20
		First day cover		1.00
426	A70	6c **light brown** *(2,626,240)*	.20	.20
		First day cover		1.00
427	A70	12c **sapphire** *(2,165,440)*	.20	.20
		First day cover		1.00
428	A70	20c **deep orange** *(1,640,640)*	.25	.20
		First day cover		1.00
429	A70	36c **deep violet** *(1,115,840)*	.50	.40
		First day cover		1.40
430	A70	50c **carmine** *(1,115,840)*	.65	.35
		First day cover		2.00
		Nos. 425-430 (6)	2.00	1.55

Arms of City of Manila — A71

1937, Aug. 27 **Unwmk.** ***Perf. 11***

431	A71	10p **gray** *(70,000)*	4.25	2.00
432	A71	20p **henna brown** *(90,600)*	2.25	1.40
		First day cover, #431-432		50.00

Stamps of 1935 Overprinted in Black:

a

b

1938-40 **Unwmk.** ***Perf. 11***

433	A53(a)	2c **rose,** *1939 (103,549,959)*	.20	.20
a.		Booklet pane of 6 *(157,176)*	3.50	2.50
b.		As "a," lower left-hand stamp overprinted "WEALTH COMMON-" *(24)*	4,000.	
c.		Hyphen omitted	—	—
434	A54(b)	4c **yellow green,** *1940 (72,500)*	1.25	30.00
435	A55(a)	6c **dark brown,** *May 12, 1939 (4,013,440)*	.20	.20
		First day cover		35.00
a.		6c golden brown	.20	.20
436	A56(b)	8c **violet,** *1939 (1,583,357)*	.20	.20
a.		"COMMONWEALT" (LR 31)	90.00	
437	A57(b)	10c **rose carmine,** *May 12, 1939 (2,695,242)*	.20	.20
a.		"COMMONWEALT" (LR 31)		—
438	A58(b)	12c **black,** *1940 (3,765,000)*	.20	.20
439	A59(b)	16c **dark blue** *(1,415,700)*	.20	.20
440	A60(a)	20c **light olive green,** *1939 (1,663,799)*	.20	.20
441	A61(b)	26c **indigo,** *1940 (597,500)*	.20	.20
442	A62(b)	30c **orange red,** *May 23, 1939 (643,100)*	1.40	.70
443	A63(b)	1p **red org & blk,** *Aug. 29, 1938 (1,065,629)>*	.40	.20
		First day cover		40.00
444	A64(b)	2p **bister brown & black,** *1939 (98,000)*	2.75	.75
445	A65(b)	4p **blue & black,** *1940 (6,500)*	275.00	275.00
		On cover		500.00
446	A66(b)	5p **green & black,** *1940 (31,500)*	6.00	3.25
		Nos. 433-446 (14)	288.40	311.50

Overprint *"b"* measures 18½x1¾mm.

No. 433b occurs in booklet pane, No. 433a, position 5; all copies are straight-edged, left and bottom.

First Foreign Trade Week Issue

Nos. 384, 298a and 432 Surcharged in Red, Violet or Black:

a

b

c

1939, July 5

449	A54(a)	2c on 4c **yellow green** (R) *(500,000)*	.20	.20
		First day cover		1.40
450	A40(b)	6c on 26c **blue green** (V) *(166,700)*	.20	.20
		First day cover		2.00
a.		6c on 26c **green**	.65	.30
451	A71(c)	50c on 20p **henna brown** (Bk) *(60,000)*	1.00	1.00
		First day cover		5.00

Commonwealth 4th Anniversary Issue (#452-460)

Triumphal Arch — A72

Printed by U.S. Bureau of Engraving and Printing.

1939, Nov. 15 **Unwmk.** ***Perf. 11***

452 A72 2c **yellow green** *(1,562,352)* .20 .20
First day cover 1.00
453 A72 6c **carmine** *(1,267,717)* .20 .20
First day cover 1.00
454 A72 12c **bright blue** *(971,724)* .20 .20
First day cover 1.40
Nos. 452-454 (3) .60 .60

Malacañan Palace — A73

1939, Nov. 15 **Unwmk.** ***Perf. 11***

455 A73 2c **green** *(1,578,600)* .20 .20
First day cover 1.00
456 A73 6c **orange** *(1,252,859)* .20 .20
First day cover 1.00
457 A73 12c **carmine** *(935,800)* .20 .20
First day cover 1.40
Nos. 455-457 (3) .60 .60

President Quezon Taking Oath of Office — A74

1940, Feb. 8 **Unwmk.** ***Perf. 11***

458 A74 2c **dark orange** *(1,572,400)* .20 .20
First day cover 1.00
459 A74 6c **dark green** *(1,257,900)* .20 .20
First day cover 1.00
460 A74 12c **purple** *(980,779)* .25 .20
First day cover 1.40
Nos. 458-460 (3) .65 .60

José Rizal — A75

ROTARY PRESS PRINTING

1941, Apr. 14 **Unwmk.** ***Perf. 11x10½***

Size: 19x22½mm

461 A75 2c **apple green** *(59,915,600)* .20 *.50*
First day cover 1.00
P# block of 4 1.00

FLAT PLATE PRINTING

1941-43 **Unwmk.** **Size: 18¾x22mm** ***Perf. 11***

462 A75 2c **apple green** .20 *.50*
a. 2c **pale apple green** ('41) .20 *.50*
b. As No. 462, booklet pane of 6 *(24,000)* 1.25 *5.00*
c. As "a," booklet pane of 6 ('41) *(114,960)* 2.50 *2.75*

This stamp was issued only in booklet panes and all copies have one or two straight edges.

Further printings were made in 1942 and 1943 in different shades from the first supply of stamps sent to the islands.

Stamps of 1935-41 Handstamped in Violet

1944 **Unwmk.** ***Perf. 11, 11x10½***

463 A53 2c **rose** (On 411), *Dec. 3 (168)* *325.00 160.00*
a. Booklet pane of 6 *(28)* *3,250.*
463B A53 2c **rose** (On 433), *Dec. 14 (41)* *1,400. 1,350.*
464 A75 2c **apple green** (On 461), *Nov. 8 (24,400)* 3.75 3.00
On cover 17.50
465 A54 4c **yellow green** (On 384), *Nov. 8 (807)* *42.50 42.50*
On cover —
466 A55 6c **dark brown** (On 385), *Dec. 14 (64)* *2,000. 2,000.*
On cover —
467 A69 6c **yellow green** (On 409), *Dec. 3* *150.00 110.00*
On cover —
468 A55 6c **dark brown** (On 413), *Dec. 28 (206)* *2,500. 825.00*
469 A72 6c **carmine** (On 453), *Nov. 8 (235)* *225.00 125.00*
On cover —
470 A73 6c **orange** (On 456), *Dec. 14 (141)* *1,250. 725.00*
On cover —
471 A74 6c **dark green** (On 459), *Nov. 8* *225.00 200.00*
On cover —
472 A56 8c **violet** (On 436), *Nov. 8 (1,643)* 17.50 *24.00*
On cover —
473 A57 10c **carmine rose** (On 415), *Nov. 8 (450)* *140.00 90.00*
On cover —
474 A57 10c **carmine rose** (On 437), *Nov. 8 (358)* *175.00 140.00*
On cover —
475 A69 12c **ultramarine** (On 410), *Dec. 3* *1,100. 400.00*
On cover —
476 A72 12c **bright blue** (On 454), *Nov. 8 (36)* *4,000. 2,250.*
On cover —
477 A74 12c **purple** (On 460), *Nov. 8* *275.00 190.00*
On cover —
478 A59 16c **dark blue** (On 389), *Dec. 3 (122)* *800.00*
479 A59 16c **dark blue** (On 417), *Nov. 8 (200)* *650.00 550.00*
On cover —
480 A59 16c **dark blue** (On 439), *Nov. 8 (500)* *300.00 200.00*
481 A60 20c **light olive green** (On 440), *Nov. 8 (1,401)* 110.00 35.00
On cover —
482 A62 30c **orange red** (On 420), *Dec. 3 (248)* *350.00 325.00*
On cover —
483 A62 30c **orange red** (On 442), *Dec. 3 (200)* *550.00 375.00*
On cover —
484 A63 1p **red orange & black** (On 443) *Dec. 3 (21)* *6,250. 4,500.*
On cover —

Nos. 463-484 are valued in the grade of fine to very fine.

No. 463 comes only from the booklet pane. All copies have one or two straight edges.

Types of 1935-37 Overprinted

a

b

c

1945 **Unwmk.** ***Perf. 11***

485 A53(a) 2c **rose,** *Jan. 19 (65,816,000)* .20 .20
First day cover 2.50
486 A54(b) 4c **yellow green,** *Jan. 19 (4,986,800)* .20 .20
First day cover 2.50
487 A55(a) 6c **golden brown,** *Jan. 19 (4,381,440)* .20 .20
First day cover 2.50
488 A56(b) 8c **violet,** *Jan. 19 (535,000)* .20 .20
First day cover 3.00
489 A57(b) 10c **rose carmine,** *Jan. 19 (1,060,000)* .20 .20
First day cover 3.00
490 A58(b) 12c **black,** *Jan. 19 (3,214,200)* .20 .20
First day cover 3.50
491 A59(b) 16c **dark blue,** *Jan. 19 (1,060,000)* .25 .20
First day cover 4.00
492 A60(a) 20c **light olive green,** *Jan. 19 (976,800)* .30 .20
First day cover 4.25
493 A62(b) 30c **orange red,** *May 1 (535,000)* .40 .35
First day cover 2.50
494 A63(b) 1p **red orange & black,** *Jan. 19 (1,434,400)* 1.10 .25
First day cover 6.50
495 A71(c) 10p **gray,** *May 1 (22,000)* 40.00 13.50
First day cover 20.00
496 A71(c) 20p **henna brown,** *May 1 (42,500)* 35.00 15.00
First day cover 25.00
Nos. 485-496 (12) 78.25 30.70

José Rizal — A76

ROTARY PRESS PRINTING

1946, May 28 **Unwmk.** ***Perf. 11x10½***

497 A76 2c **sepia** *(53,560,000)* .20 .20
P# block of 4 .50

Later issues, released by the Philippine Republic on July 4, 1946, and thereafter, are listed in Scott's Standard Postage Stamp Catalogue, Vol. 5.

AIR POST STAMPS

Madrid-Manila Flight Issue

Issued to commemorate the flight of Spanish aviators Gallarza and Loriga from Madrid to Manila.

Regular Issue of 1917-26 Overprinted in Red or Violet by the Philippine Bureau of Printing

1926, May 13 **Unwmk.** ***Perf. 11***

C1 A40 2c **green** (R) *(9,900)* 10.00 10.00
First day cover 26.00
Block of 4 47.50 47.50
C2 A40 4c **carmine** (V) *(8,900)* 13.50 13.50
First day cover 26.00
Block of 4 60.00 60.00
a. Inverted overprint *(100)* *2,500.* —
C3 A40 6c **lilac** (R) *(5,000)* 55.00 55.00
First day cover 40.00
Block of 4 240.00
C4 A40 8c **orange brown** (V) *(5,000)* 57.50 57.50
First day cover 40.00
Block of 4 250.00
C5 A40 10c **deep blue** (R) *(5,000)* 57.50 57.50
First day cover 40.00
Block of 4 250.00
C6 A40 12c **red orange** (V) *(4,000)* 57.50 57.50
First day cover 42.50
Block of 4 250.00
C7 A40 16c **light olive green** *(Sampson)* (V) *(300)* *2,100. 1,600.*

Block of 4 —
C8 A40 16c **olive bister** *(Sampson)* (R) *(100)* *4,250.* *3,000.*
Block of 4 —
C9 A40 16c **olive green** *(Dewey)* (V) *(3,600)* 70.00 70.00
First day cover 42.50
Block of 4 325.00
C10 A40 20c **orange yellow** (V) *(4,000)* 70.00 70.00
First day cover 42.50
Block of 4 325.00
C11 A40 26c **blue green** (V) *(3,900)* 70.00 70.00
First day cover 45.00
Block of 4 325.00
C12 A40 30c **gray** (V) *(4,000)* 70.00 70.00
First day cover 45.00
Block of 4 325.00
C13 A40 2p **violet brown** (R) *(900)* 550.00 300.00
On cover 300.00
Block of 4 —
C14 A40 4p **dark blue** (R) *(700)* 750.00 500.00
On cover *475.00*
Block of 4 —
C15 A40 10p **deep green** (V) *(500)* 1,350. 700.00
On cover *675.00*
Block of 4 —

Same Overprint on No. 269

Wmk. Single-lined PIPS (190)

Perf. 12

C16 A40 26c **blue green** (V) *(100)* *4,500.*
Block of 4 —

Same Overprint on No. 284

Perf. 10

C17 A40 1p **pale violet** (V) *(2,000)* 210.00 175.00
On cover 200.00
First day cover *225.00*
Block of 4 900.00

Overprintings of Nos. C1-C6, C9-C15 and C17 were made from two plates. Position No. 89 of the first printing shows broken left blade of propeller.

London-Orient Flight Issue

Issued Nov. 9, 1928, to celebrate the arrival of a British squadron of hydroplanes.

Regular Issue of 1917-25 Overprinted in Red

1928, Nov. 9 **Unwmk.** ***Perf. 11***

C18 A40 2c **green** *(101,200)* .50 .30
First day cover 7.75
C19 A40 4c **carmine** *(50,500)* .60 .50
First day cover 9.50
C20 A40 6c **violet** *(12,600)* 2.10 1.75
On cover 1.90
C21 A40 8c **orange brown** *(10,000)* 2.25 1.90
On cover 2.25
C22 A40 10c **deep blue** *(10,000)* 2.25 1.90
On cover 2.25
C23 A40 12c **red orange** *(8,000)* 3.25 2.75
On cover 3.25
C24 A40 16c **olive green** (No. 303a) *(12,600)* 2.40 1.90
On cover 2.40
C25 A40 20c **orange yellow** *(8,000)* 3.25 2.75
On cover 3.25
C26 A40 26c **blue green** *(7,000)* 9.50 6.50
On cover 8.50
C27 A40 30c **gray** *(7,000)* 9.50 6.50
On cover 8.50

Same Overprint on No. 271

Wmk. Single-lined PIPS (190)

Perf. 12

C28 A40 1p **pale violet** *(6,000)* 50.00 25.00
On cover 27.50
Nos. C18-C28 (11) 85.60 51.75

Von Gronau Issue

Issued commemoration of the visit of Capt. Wolfgang von Gronau's airplane on its round-the-world flight.

Nos. 354-360 Overprinted by the Philippine Bureau of Printing

1932, Sept. 27 **Unwmk.** ***Perf. 11***

C29 A43 2c **yellow green** *(100,000)* .50 .30
First day cover 2.00
C30 A44 4c **rose carmine** *(80,000)* .50 .30
First day cover 2.00
C31 A45 12c **orange** *(55,000)* .70 .50
On cover 1.00
C32 A46 18c **red orange** *(25,305)* 4.00 3.25
On cover 3.50
C33 A47 20c **yellow** *(30,000)* 2.00 1.50
On cover 1.60
C34 A48 24c **deep violet** *(30,000)* 2.00 1.50
On cover 1.60
C35 A49 32c **olive brown** *(30,000)* 2.00 1.50
On cover 1.60
First day cover, #C29-C35 35.00
Nos. C29-C35 (7) 11.70 8.85

Rein Issue

Commemorating the flight from Madrid to Manila of the Spanish aviator Fernando Rein y Loring.

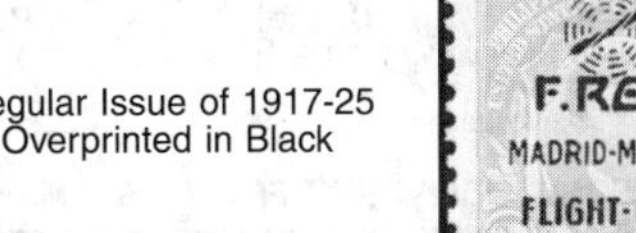

Regular Issue of 1917-25 Overprinted in Black

1933, Apr. 11

C36 A40 2c **green** *(95,000)* .40 .35
First day cover 1.60
C37 A40 4c **carmine** *(75,000)* .45 .35
First day cover —
C38 A40 6c **deep violet** *(65,000)* .80 .75
First day cover 3.00
C39 A40 8c **orange brown** *(35,000)* 2.50 1.50
C40 A40 10c **dark blue** *(35,000)* 2.25 1.00
C41 A40 12c **orange** *(35,000)* 2.00 1.00
C42 A40 16c **olive green** *(Dewey) (35,000)* 2.00 1.00
C43 A40 20c **yellow** *(35,000)* 2.00 1.00
C44 A40 26c **green** *(35,000)* 2.25 1.50
a. 26c **blue green** 3.00 1.75
C45 A40 30c **gray** *(30,000)* 3.00 1.75
First day cover, #C36-C45 40.00
Nos. C36-C45 (10) 17.65 10.20

Stamp of 1917 Overprinted by the Philippine Bureau of Printing

1933, May 26 **Unwmk.** ***Perf. 11***

C46 A40 2c **green** *(500,000)* .50 .40

Regular Issue of 1932 Overprinted

C47 A44 4c **rose carmine** *(799,878)* .20 .20
C48 A45 12c **orange** *(500,000)* .30 .20
C49 A47 20c **yellow** *(500,000)* .30 .20
C50 A48 24c **deep violet** *(500,000)* .40 .25
C51 A49 32c **olive brown** *(500,000)* .50 .35
First day cover, #C46-C51 35.00
Nos. C46-C51 (6) 2.20 1.60

Transpacific Issue

Issued to commemorate the China Clipper flight from Manila to San Francisco, Dec. 2-5, 1935.

Nos. 387, 392 Overprinted in Gold

1935, Dec. 2 **Unwmk.** ***Perf. 11***

C52 A57 10c **rose carmine** *(500,000)* .30 .20
First day cover 2.00
C53 A62 30c **orange red** *(300,000)* .50 .35
First day cover 3.00

Manila-Madrid Flight Issue

Issued to commemorate the Manila-Madrid flight by aviators Antonio Arnaiz and Juan Calvo.

Nos. 291, 295, 298a, 298 Surcharged in Various Colors by Philippine Bureau of Printing

1936, Sept. 6

C54 A40 2c on 4c **carmine** (Bl) *(2,000,000)* .20 .20
First day cover 1.00
C55 A40 6c on 12c **red orange** (V) *(500,000)* .20 .20
First day cover 3.00
C56 A40 16c on 26c **blue green** (Bk) *(300,000)* .25 .20
First day cover 5.00
a. 16c on 26c **green** 1.25 .70
Nos. C54-C56 (3) .65 .60

Air Mail Exhibition Issue

Issued to commemorate the first Air Mail Exhibition, held Feb. 17-19, 1939.

Nos. 298a, 298, 431 Surcharged in Black or Red by Philippine Bureau of Printing

1939, Feb. 17

C57 A40 8c on 26c **blue green** (Bk) *(200,000)* .75 .40
First day cover 3.50
a. 8c on 26c **green** (Bk) 3.00 .55
C58 A71 1p on 10p **gray** (R) *(30,000)* 3.00 2.25
First day cover 8.00

Moro Vinta and Clipper — AP1

Printed by the US Bureau of Engraving and Printing.

1941, June 30 **Unwmk.** ***Perf. 11***

C59 AP1 8c **carmine** *(210,000)* 1.00 .60
First day cover 2.00
C60 AP1 20c **ultramarine** *(25,000)* 1.25 .45
First day cover 2.50
C61 AP1 60c **blue green** *(50,000)* 1.75 1.00
First day cover 3.50
C62 AP1 1p **sepia** *(1,110,000)* .70 .50
First day cover 2.25
Nos. C59-C62 (4) 4.70 2.55

No. C47 Handstamped in Violet **VICTORY**

1944, Dec. 3 **Unwmk.** ***Perf. 11***

C63 A44 4c **rose carmine** *(122)* *2,750.* *2,750.*
On cover —

SPECIAL DELIVERY

U.S. No. E5 Overprinted in Red

a

Printed by U.S. Bureau of Engraving & Printing

Wmk. Double-lined USPS (191)

1901, Oct. 15 *Perf. 12*

E1 SD3 10c **dark blue** *(14,998)* 125. 100.
On cover 350.
Block of 4 550.
P# strip of 3, Impt. 550.
P# block of 6, Impt. *5,000.*
Dots in curved frame above messenger (Pl. 882) *175.* *160.*
P# block of 6, Impt. (Pl. 882) *5,250.*

Special Delivery Messenger SD2

Wmk. Double-lined PIPS (191)

1906, Sept. 8 *Perf. 12*

E2 SD2 20c **deep ultramarine** *(40,019)* 30.00 7.50
On cover 17.50
Block of 4 125.00
b. 20c **pale ultramarine** 30.00 7.50
On cover 17.50
Block of 4 125.00

SPECIAL PRINTING

U.S. No. E6 Overprinted Type "a" in Red

1907 Wmk. Double-lined USPS (191) *Perf. 12*

E2A SD4 10c **ultramarine** *2,750.*
Block of 4 *11,500.*
P# block of 6, Impt. *38,500.*

This stamp was part of the set specially printed for the Bureau of Insular Affairs in 1907. See note following No. 240.

There is only one intact plate block of No. E2A. It is fine and is valued thus.

1911, Apr. Wmk. Single-lined PIPS (190) *Perf. 12*

E3 SD2 20c **deep ultramarine** *(200,000)* 20.00 1.75
On cover 12.50
Block of 4 82.50

1916 *Perf. 10*

E4 SD2 20c **deep ultramarine** *(200,000)* 175.00 75.00
On cover 100.00
Block of 4 825.00
pale ultramarine —

Early in 1919 the supply of Special Delivery stamps in the Manila area was exhausted. A Government decree permitted the use of regular issue postage stamps for payment of the special delivery fee when so noted on the cover. This usage was permitted until the new supply of Special Delivery stamps arrived.

1919 Unwmk. *Perf. 11*

E5 SD2 20c **ultramarine** *(4,195,862)* .60 .20
On cover 5.00
Block of 4 2.50
a. 20c **pale blue** .75 .20
On cover 5.25
Block of 4 3.00
b. 20c **dull violet** .60 .20
On cover 5.00
Block of 4 2.50

Type of 1906 Issue

1925-31 Unwmk. *Imperf.*

E6 SD2 20c **dull violet** ('31) *(6,500)* 20.00 *50.00*
On cover 250.00
Block of 4 85.00
P# block of 6 350.00
a. 20c **violet blue** ('25) *(2,100)* 40.00 27.50
On cover —
Block of 4 200.00
P# block of 6 650.00

Type of 1919 Overprinted in Black

1939, Apr. 27 Unwmk. *Perf. 11*

E7 SD2 20c **blue violet** *(1,253,250)* .25 .20
First day cover 35.00

Nos. E5b and E7 Handstamped in Violet

1944 Unwmk. *Perf. 11*

E8 SD2 20c **dull violet** (On E5b) *(138)* *800.00 550.00*
E9 SD2 20c **blue violet** (On E7), *Nov. 8 (600)* *300.00 225.00*
On cover —

Type SD2 Overprinted "VICTORY" As No. 486

1945, May 1 Unwmk. *Perf. 11*

E10 SD2 20c **blue violet** *(578,600)* .70 .55
First day cover 10.00
a. "IC" close together 3.25 2.75

SPECIAL DELIVERY OFFICIAL STAMP

Type of 1906 Issue Overprinted

1931 Unwmk. *Perf. 11*

EO1 SD2 20c **dull violet** *(46,750)* .65 *75.00*
a. No period after "B" 20.00 15.00
b. Double overprint —

It is recommended that expert opinion be acquired for No. EO1 used.

POSTAGE DUE

U.S. Nos. J38-J44 Overprinted in Black

Printed by the US Bureau of Engraving and Printing.

Wmk. Double-lined USPS (191)

1899, Aug. 16 *Perf. 12*

J1 D2 1c **deep claret** *(340,892)* 6.50 1.50
On cover 30.00
On cover, used as regular postage 110.00
P# strip of 3, Impt. 125.00
P# block of 6, Impt. *650.00*
J2 D2 2c **deep claret** *(306,983)* 6.50 1.25
On cover 37.50
P# strip of 3, Impt. 125.00
P# block of 6, Impt. *650.00*
J3 D2 5c **deep claret** *(34,565)* 15.00 2.50
On cover *70.00*
P# strip of 3, Impt. 200.00
P# block of 6, Impt. *1,500.*
J4 D2 10c **deep claret** *(15,848)* 19.00 5.50
On cover 100.00
P# strip of 3, Impt. 175.00
P# block of 6, Impt. *1,100.*
J5 D2 50c **deep claret** *(6,168)* 200.00 100.00
On cover —
P# strip of 3, Impt. 1,100.
P# block of 6, Impt. *4,000.*

No. J1 was used to pay regular postage Sept. 5-19, 1902.

1901, Aug. 31

J6 D2 3c **deep claret** *(14,885)* 17.50 7.00
On cover 60.00
P# strip of 3, Impt. 175.00
P# block of 6, Impt. *875.00*
J7 D2 30c **deep claret** *(2,140)* 225.00 110.00
On cover —
P# strip of 3, Impt. 1,000.
P# block of 6, Impt. *4,000.*
Nos. J1-J7 (7) 489.50 227.75

Post Office Clerk — D3

1928, Aug. 21 Unwmk. *Perf. 11*

J8 D3 4c **brown red** *(948,054)* .20 .20
J9 D3 6c **brown red** *(255,490)* .20 .20
J10 D3 8c **brown red** *(508,621)* .20 .20
J11 D3 10c **brown red** *(254,195)* .20 .20
J12 D3 12c **brown red** *(407,457)* .20 .20
J13 D3 16c **brown red** *(253,215)* .20 .20
J14 D3 20c **brown red** *(259,665)* .20 .20
Nos. J8-J14 (7) 1.40 1.40

No. J8 Surcharged in Blue

1937, July 29 Unwmk. *Perf. 11*

J15 D3 3c on 4c **brown red** .20 .20
First day cover 35.00

See note after No. NJ1.

Nos. J8-J14 Handstamped in Violet **VICTORY**

1944, Dec. 3 Unwmk. *Perf. 11*

J16 D3 4c **brown red** *(306)* *140.00* —
J17 D3 6c **brown red** *(390)* *90.00* —
J18 D3 8c **brown red** *(379)* *95.00* —
J19 D3 10c **brown red** *(405)* *90.00* —
J20 D3 12c **brown red** *(423)* *90.00* —
J21 D3 16c **brown red** *(425)* *95.00* —
J22 D3 20c **brown red** *(375)* *95.00* —
Nos. J16-J22 (7) *695.00*

OFFICIAL

Official Handstamped Overprints

"Officers purchasing stamps for government business may, if they so desire, surcharge them with the letters O.B. either in writing with black ink or by rubber stamps but in such a manner as not to obliterate the stamp that postmasters will be unable to determine whether the stamps have been previously used." C.M. Cotterman, Director of Posts, December 26, 1905.

Beginning with January 1, 1906, all branches of the Insular Government, used postage stamps to prepay postage instead of franking them as before. Some officials used manuscript, some utilized the typewriting machines but by far the larger number provided themselves with rubber stamps. The majority of these read "O.B." but other forms were: "OFFICIAL BUSINESS" or "OFFICIAL MAIL" in two lines, with variations on many of these.

These "O.B." overprints are known on U. S. 1899-1901 stamps; on 1903-06 stamps in red and blue; on 1906 stamps in red, blue, black, yellow and green.

"O.B." overprints were also made on the centavo and peso stamps of the Philippines, per order of May 25, 1907.

Beginning in 1926 the Bureau of Posts issued press-printed official stamps, but many government offices continued to handstamp ordinary postage stamps "O.B."

During the Japanese occupation period 1942-45, the same system of handstamped official overprints prevailed, but the handstamp usually consisted of "K.P.", initials of the Tagalog words, "Kagamitang Pampamahalaan" (Official Business), and the two Japanese characters used in the printed overprint on Nos. NO1 to NO4.

Legislative Palace Issue of 1926 Overprinted in Red

Printed and overprinted by the Philippine Bureau of Printing.

1926, Dec. 20 Unwmk. *Perf. 12*

O1 A42 2c **green & black** *(90,500)* 2.25 1.00
On cover 2.00
Block of 4 9.50 5.50
O2 A42 4c **carmine & black** *(90,450)* 2.25 1.25

			On cover		2.00
			First day cover		10.00
			Block of 4	9.50	5.50
a.			Vertical pair, imperf. between	750.00	
O3	A42	18c	**light brown & black** *(70,000)*	7.00	4.00
			On cover		6.50
			Block of 4	35.00	20.00
O4	A42	20c	**orange & black** *(70,250)*	6.75	1.75
			On cover		2.25
			Block of 4	35.00	8.25
			First day cover, #O1-O4		50.00
			Nos. O1-O4 (4)	18.25	8.00

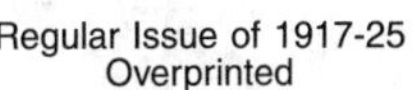

Regular Issue of 1917-25 Overprinted

Printed and overprinted by the U.S. Bureau of Engraving and Printing.

1931 Unwmk. *Perf. 11*

O5	A40	2c	**green** *(22,940,100)*	.20	.20
a.			No period after "B"	15.00	5.00
b.			No period after "O"		—
O6	A40	4c	**carmine** *(5,377,000)*	.20	.20
a.			No period after "B"	15.00	5.00
O7	A40	6c	**deep violet** *(616,500)*	.20	.20
O8	A40	8c	**yellow brown** *(706,700)*	.20	.20
O9	A40	10c	**deep blue** *(1,006,800)*	.30	.20
O10	A40	12c	**red orange** *(158,050)*	.25	.20
a.			No period after "B"	40.00	
O11	A40	16c	**light olive green** *(Dewey) (824,400)*	.25	.20
a.			16c olive bister	1.25	.20
O12	A40	20c	**orange yellow** *(509,050)*	.25	.20
a.			No period after "B"	35.00	15.00
O13	A40	26c	**green** *(68,600)*	.40	.30
a.			26c blue green	1.00	.65
O14	A40	30c	**gray** *(199,400)*	.30	.25
			Nos. O5-O14 (10)	2.55	2.15

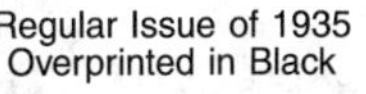

Regular Issue of 1935 Overprinted in Black

1935 Unwmk. *Perf. 11*

O15	A53	2c	**rose** *(7,927,800)*	.20	.20
a.			No period after "B"	15.00	5.00
O16	A54	4c	**yellow green** *(5,079,266)*	.20	.20
a.			No period after "B"	15.00	8.50
O17	A55	6c	**dark brown** *(786,896)*	.20	.20
a.			No period after "B"	25.00	17.50
O18	A56	8c	**violet** *(656,200)*	.20	.20
O19	A57	10c	**rose carmine** *(756,100)*	.20	.20
O20	A58	12c	**black** *(104,500)*	.20	.20
O21	A59	16c	**dark blue** *(254,800)*	.20	.20
O22	A60	20c	**light olive green** *(203,079)*	.20	.20
O23	A61	26c	**indigo** *(67,750)*	.25	.20
O24	A62	30c	**orange red** *(83,500)*	.30	.20
			Nos. O15-O24 (10)	2.15	2.00

Nos. 411 and 418 with Additional Overprint in Black

1937-38 Unwmk. *Perf. 11*

O25	A53	2c	**rose,** *Apr. 10, 1937 (11,580,800)*	.20	.20
			First day cover		50.00
a.			No period after "B"	10.00	2.25
b.			Period after "B" raised (UL 4)	175.00	
O26	A60	20c	**light olive green,** *Apr. 26, 1938 (174,929)*	.65	.50

Regular Issue of 1935 Overprinted In Black:

a

b

1938-40 Unwmk. *Perf. 11*

O27	A53(a)	2c	**rose** *(23,239,872)*	.20	.20
a.			Hyphen omitted	20.00	20.00
b.			No period after "B"	25.00	25.00
O28	A54(b)	4c	**yellow green** *(85,000)*	.20	.20
O29	A55(a)	6c	**dark brown** *(393,549)*	.20	.20
O30	A56(b)	8c	**violet** *(82,000)*	.20	.20
O31	A57(b)	10c	**rose carmine** *(1,188,735)*	.20	.20
a.			No period after "O"	30.00	30.00
O32	A58(b)	12c	**black** *(340,000)*	.20	.20
O33	A59(b)	16c	**dark blue** *(490,000)*	.20	.20
O34	A60(a)	20c	**light olive green** ('40) *(162,000)*	.25	.25
O35	A61(b)	26c	**indigo** *(77,000)*	.30	.30
O36	A62(b)	30c	**orange red** *(82,000)*	.25	.25
			Nos. O27-O36 (10)	2.20	2.20

No. 461 Overprinted in Black

c

ROTARY PRESS PRINTING

1941, Apr. 14 Unwmk. *Perf. 11x10½*

O37	A75	2c	**apple green** *(21,087,900)*	.20	.20
			First day cover		3.50
			Margin block of 4, P#	.25	

Nos. O27, O37, O16, O29, O31, O22 and O26 Handstamped in Violet

1944 Unwmk. *Perf. 11, 11x10½*

O38	A53	2c	**rose** (On O27) *(128)*	*250.00*	*150.00*
O39	A75	2c	**apple green** (On O37) *(13,100)*	6.50	3.00
			On cover		*10.00*
			Block of 4	32.50	—
O40	A54	4c	**yellow green** (On O16) *(2,634)*	*42.50*	*30.00*
			Block of 4	*190.00*	
O40A	A55	6c	**dark brown** (On O29)	*5,000.*	—
O41	A57	10c	**rose carmine** (On O31) *(665)*	*300.00*	
			Block of 4	*700.00*	
a.			No period after "O"	*4,000.*	
O42	A60	20c	**light olive green** (On O22)	*6,000.*	
O43	A60	20c	**light olive green** (On O26)	*1,550.*	

No. 497 Overprinted Type "c" in Black

1946, June 19 Unwmk. *Perf. 11x10½*

O44	A76	2c	**sepia** *(10,470,000)*	.20	.20
			Margin block of 4, P#	.40	

POST OFFICE SEALS

POS1

1906 Litho. Unwmk. *Perf. 12*

OX1	POS1	**light brown**	65.00	65.00

Wmk. "PIRS" in Double-lined Capitals

1907 *Perf. 12*

OX2	POS1	**light brown**	85.00	85.00

Hyphen-hole Perf. 7

OX3	POS1	**orange brown**	40.00	*45.00*

1911 *Hyphen-hole Perf. 7*

OX4	POS1	**yellow brown**	37.50	*40.00*
OX5	POS1	**olive bister**	75.00	75.00
a.		Unwatermarked		—
OX6	POS1	**yellow**	85.00	85.00

1913 Unwmk. *Hyphen-hole Perf. 7*

OX7	POS1	**lemon yellow**	2.00	*3.00*

Perf. 12

OX8	POS1	**yellow**	100.00	50.00

Wmk. "USPS" in Single-lined Capitals

Hyphen-hole Perf. 7

OX9	POS1	**yellow**	100.00	75.00

1934 Unwmk. *Rouletted*

OX10	POS1	**dark blue**	1.00	*1.50*

POS2

OX11	POS2	**dark blue**	1.00	*1.50*

POS3

1938 *Hyphen-hole Perf. 7*

OX12	POS3	**dark blue**	5.50	*5.50*

ENVELOPES

U.S. Envelopes of 1899 Issue Overprinted below stamp in color of the stamp, except where noted

PHILIPPINES.

1899-1900

Note: Many envelopes for which there was no obvious need were issued in small quantities. Anyone residing in the Islands could, by depositing with his postmaster the required amount, order any envelopes in quantities of 500, or multiples thereof, provided it was on the schedule of U.S. envelopes.

Such special orders are indicated by an plus sign after the quantity.

U1 U77 1c **green** (#U352) *(370,000)* 3.00 2.00
Entire 8.75 9.50
U2 U77 1c **green,** *amber* (#U353) *(1,000)*+ 18.00 14.00
Entire 40.00 40.00
U3 U77 1c **green,** *amber* (#U353) red overprint *(500)*+ 22.50 20.00
Entire 60.00 57.50
U4 U77 1c **green,** *oriental buff* (#U354) *(1,000)*+ 14.00 14.00
Entire 30.00 30.00
U5 U77 1c **green,** *oriental buff* (#U354) red overprint *(500)*+ 35.00 35.00
Entire 72.50 *72.50*
U6 U77 1c **green,** *blue* (#U355) *(1,000)*+ 9.00 9.00
Entire 30.00 30.00
U7 U77 1c **green,** *blue* (#U355) red overprint *(500)*+ 20.00 19.00
Entire 72.50 67.50
U8 U79 2c **carmine** (#U362) *(1,180,000)* 1.50 1.50
Entire 4.00 3.00
U9 U79 2c **carmine,** *amber* (#U363) *(21,000)* 5.25 5.00
Entire 15.00 12.50
U10 U79 2c **carmine,** *oriental buff* (#U364) *(10,000)* 5.25 4.75
Entire 17.00 13.50
U11 U79 2c **carmine,** *blue* (#U365) *(10,000)* 4.75 6.25
Entire 12.50 12.00
U12 U81 4c **brown,** *amber* (#U372) *(500)*+ 40.00 35.00
Entire 85.00 *92.50*
a. Double overprint —
Entire *4,000.*
U13 U83 4c **brown** (#U374) *(10,500)* 12.50 9.00
Entire 30.00 *40.00*
U14 U83 4c **brown,** *amber* (#U375) *(500)*+ 55.00 50.00
Entire 175.00 125.00
U15 U84 5c **blue** (#U377) *(20,000)* 6.25 6.00
Entire 13.00 13.00
U16 U84 5c **blue,** *amber* (#U378) *(500)*+ 35.00 35.00
Entire 87.50 *110.00*
Nos. U1-U16 (16) 287.00 265.50

1903 **Same Overprint on U.S. Issue of 1903**

U17 U85 1c **green** (#U379) *(300,000)* 1.50 1.25
Entire 4.25 4.25
U18 U85 1c **green,** *amber* (#U380) *(1,000)*+ 12.50 12.00
Entire 22.50 *25.00*
U19 U85 1c **green,** *oriental buff* (#U381) *(1,000)*+ 14.50 12.50
Entire 26.00 *24.00*
U20 U85 1c **green,** *blue* (#U382) *(1,500)*+ 12.00 11.00
Entire 26.00 *26.00*
U21 U85 1c **green,** *manila* (#U383) *(500)*+ 20.00 20.00
Entire 45.00 *47.50*
U22 U86 2c **carmine** (#U385) *(150,500)* 5.00 3.50
Entire 7.50 7.00
U23 U86 2c **carmine,** *amber* (#U386) *(500)*+ 17.50 14.00
Entire 35.00 42.50
U24 U86 2c **carmine,** *oriental buff* (#U387) *(500)*+ 17.50 *25.00*
Entire 45.00 —
U25 U86 2c **carmine,** *blue* (#U388) *(500)*+ 17.50 17.50
Entire 40.00
U26 U87 4c **chocolate,** *amber* (#U391) *(500)*+ 55.00 *75.00*
Entire 140.00 *190.00*
a. Double overprint, entire *7,000.*
U27 U88 5c **blue,** *amber* (#U394) *(500)*+ 55.00 —
Entire 125.00 125.00
Nos. U17-U27 (11) 228.00

1906

Same Overprint on Re-cut U.S. issue of 1904

U28 U89 2c **carmine** (#U395) 42.50 27.50
Entire 150.00 125.00
U29 U89 2c **carmine,** *Oriental buff* (#U397) 67.50 *110.00*
Entire 225.00 *275.00*

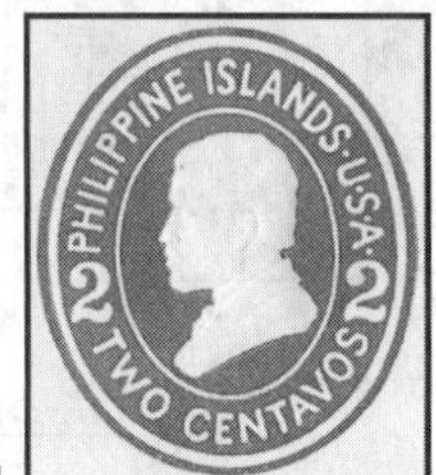

Rizal — E1

E2, McKinley.

1908

U30 E1 2c **green** .50 .25
Entire .85 1.50
U31 E1 2c **green,** *amber* 4.00 2.25
Entire 9.00 8.00
U32 E1 2c **green,** *oriental buff* 5.00 3.00
Entire 9.00 9.00
U33 E1 2c **green,** *blue* 5.00 3.00
Entire 9.00 9.00
U34 E1 2c **green,** *manila (500)* 7.25 —
Entire 15.00 20.00
U35 E2 4c **carmine** .50 .25
Entire 1.40 1.25
U36 E2 4c **carmine,** *amber* 4.00 2.50
Entire 9.00 7.00
U37 E2 4c **carmine,** *oriental buff* 4.25 3.50
Entire 9.00 17.00
U38 E2 4c **carmine,** *blue* 4.00 3.00
Entire 8.50 8.50
U39 E2 4c **carmine,** *manila (500)* 9.00 —
Entire 20.00 30.00
Nos. U30-U39 (10) 43.50

Rizal — E3

"Juan de la Cruz" — E4

1927, Apr. 5

U40 E3 2c **green** 11.50 9.50
Entire 30.00 25.00
Entire, 1st day cancel *37.50*

1935, June 19

U41 E4 2c **carmine** .35 .25
Entire 1.25 .75
U42 E4 4c **olive green** .50 .30
Entire 1.65 1.10

For surchages see Nos. NU1-NU2.

Nos. U30, U35, U41 and U42 Handstamped in Violet **VICTORY**

1944

U42A E1 2c **green** (On U30), Entire —
U43 E4 2c **carmine** (On U41) 17.50 14.00
Entire 47.50 *77.00*
U44 E2 4c **carmine,** *McKinley* (On U35) — —
Entire 950.00 *950.00*
U45 E4 4c **olive green** (On U42) 82.50 70.00
Entire 140.00 175.00

WRAPPERS

US Wrappers Overprinted in Color of Stamp PHILIPPINES.

1901

W1 U77 1c **green,** *manila* (No. W357) *(320,000)* 1.50 1.25
Entire 5.00 *10.00*

1905

W2 U85 1c **green,** *manila* (No. W384) 9.00 9.00
Entire 22.50 *25.00*
a. Double overprint, entire *4,500.*
W3 U86 2c **carmine,** *manila* (No. W389) 11.00 10.50
Entire 22.50 *27.50*

Design of Philippine Envelopes

1908

W4 E1 2c **green,** *manila* 2.00 2.00
Entire 11.00 *15.00*

POSTAL CARDS

Values are for Entires.
U.S. Cards Overprinted in Black below Stamp

a **PHILIPPINES.**

1900, Feb.

UX1 (a) 1c **black** (Jefferson) (UX14) *(100,000)* 17.50 15.00
a. Without period 47.50 75.00
UX2 (a) 2c **black** (Liberty) (UX16) *(20,000)* 40.00 30.00

b **PHILIPPINES**

1903, Sept. 15

UX3 (b) 1c **black** (McKinley) (UX18) *1,350.* *1,150.*
UX4 (b) 2c **black** (Liberty) (UX16) *800.* *700.*

c PHILIPPINES.

1903, Nov. 10

UX5 (c) 1c **black** (McKinley) (UX18) 47.50 40.00
UX6 (c) 2c **black** (Liberty) (UX16) 60.00 55.00

d **PHILIPPINES**

1906

UX7 (d) 1c **black** (McKinley) (UX18) *275.* *300.*
UX8 (d) 2c **black** (Liberty) (UX16) *2,000.* *1,500.*

Designs same as postage issue of 1906

1907

UX9 A40 2c **black,** *buff* (Rizal) 10.00 8.00
UX10 A40 4c **black,** *buff* (McKinley) 25.00 20.00

Color changes

1911

UX11 A40 2c **blue,** *light blue* (Rizal) 8.00 8.00
a. 2c blue on white 20.00 20.00
UX12 A40 4c **blue,** *light blue* (McKinley) 25.00 25.00

An impression of No. UX11 exists on the back of a U.S. No. UX21.

1915

UX13 A40 2c **green,** *buff* (Rizal) 3.00 2.00
UX14 A40 2c **yellow green,** *amber* 3.50 1.50
UX15 A40 4c **green,** *buff* (McKinley) 20.00 15.00

Design of postage issue of 1935

1935

UX16 A53 2c **red,** *pale buff* (Rizal) 2.50 1.60

No. UX16 Overprinted at left of Stamp **COMMONWEALTH**

1938

UX17 A53 2c **red,** *pale buff* 2.50 1.60

No. UX16 Overprinted **COMMONWEALTH**

UX18 A53 2c **red,** *pale buff* 45.00 45.00

No. UX16 Overprinted **COMMONWEALTH**

UX19 A53 2c **red,** *pale buff* 4.00 4.00

Nos. UX13, UX18 and UX19 Handstamped in Violet **VICTORY**

1944

UX20 A40 2c **green,** *buff, Rizal* (On UX13) *180.00* *225.00*
UX21 A53 2c **red,** *pale buff* (On UX18) *650.00* —
UX22 A53 2c **red,** *pale buff* (On UX19) *285.00* *550.00*

Overprinted in Black at left **VICTORY**

1945, Jan. 19

UX23 A76 2c **gray brown,** *pale buff* 1.25 .75
First day cancel 3.25
a. "IC" of "Victory" very close 5.00 3.00

This card was not issued without overprint.

PAID REPLY POSTAL CARDS

U.S. Paid Reply Cards of 1892-93 issues Overprinted with type "a" in blue

1900, Feb.

UY1 2c +2c **blue,** unsevered *(5,000)* *160.00* *500.00*
m. PM2 Message card, detached 27.50 50.00
r. PR2 Reply card, detached 27.50 50.00

Overprinted type "c" in black

1903

UY2 1c + 1c **black,** *buff,* unsevered *(20,000)* *150.00* *375.00*
m. PM1 Message card, detached 22.50 25.00
r. PR1 Reply card, detached 22.50 25.00
UY3 2c + 2c **blue,** unsevered *(20,000)* 300.00 *700.00*
m. PM2, Message card, detached 55.00 50.00
r. PR2, Reply card, detached 55.00 50.00

OFFICIAL CARDS

Overprinted at left of stamp **O. B.**

1925 **On postal card No. UX13**

UZ1 A40 2c **green,** *buff* (Rizal) 35.00 35.00

1935 **On postal card No. UX16**

UZ2 A53 2c **red,** *pale buff* 14.00 *17.50*

Overprinted at Left of Stamp **O. B.**

1938 **On postal card No. UX19**
UZ3 A53 2c **red,** *pale buff* 13.00 *17.50*

Overprinted Below Stamp **O. B.**

1941 **Design of postage issue of 1941**
UZ4 A75 2c **light green,** *pale buff* 160.00 *200.00*

This card was not issued without overprint.

Postal Card No. UX19 Overprinted at Left of Stamp **O. B.**

1941
UZ5 A53 2c **red,** *pale buff* 20.00 *25.00*

OCCUPATION

Issued Under Japanese Occupation

Nos. 461, 438 and 439 Overprinted with Bars in Black

1942-43 **Unwmk.** ***Perf. 11x10½, 11***
N1 A75 2c **apple green,** *Mar. 4, 1942 (3,000,000)* .20 .20
P# block of 4 .25
a. Pair, one without overprint —
N2 A58 12c **black,** *Apr. 30, 1943 (310,000)* .20 .20
N3 A59 16c **dark blue,** *Mar. 4, 1942 (160,000)* 5.00 3.75

Nos. 435a, 435, 442, 443, and 423 Surcharged in Black

1942-43 ***Perf. 11***
N4 A55(a) 5(c) on 6c **golden brown** *Sept. 1, 1942 (800,000)* .20 .20
First day cover, Manila 1.50
a. Top bar shorter and thinner *(200,000)* .20 .20
b. 5(c) on 6c **dark brown** .20 .20
c. As "b," top bar shorter and thinner .20 .20
N5 A62(b) 16(c) on 30c **orange red,** *Jan. 11, 1943 (210,000)* .25 .25
First day cover 1.75
N6 A63(c) 50c on 1p **red orange & black,** *Apr. 30, 1943 (20,000)* .60 .60
a. Double surcharge *300.00*
N7 A65(d) 1p on 4p **blue & black,** *Apr. 30, 1943 (19,975)* 125.00 *200.00*
Inverted "S" in "PESO;" position 4 150.00 *225.00*

On Nos. N4 and N4b, the top bar measures 1½x22½mm. On Nos. N4a and N4c, the top bar measures 1x21mm and the "5" is smaller and thinner.

The used value for No. N7 is for postal cancellation. Used stamps exist with first day cancellations. They are worth somewhat less.

1942, May 18
N8 A54 2(c) on 4c **yellow green** *(100,000)* 6.00 6.00
First day cover 4.00

Issued to commemorate Japan's capture of Bataan and Corregidor. The American-Filipino forces finally surrendered May 7, 1942. No. N8 exists with "R" for "B" in BATAAN.

No. 384 Surcharged in Black

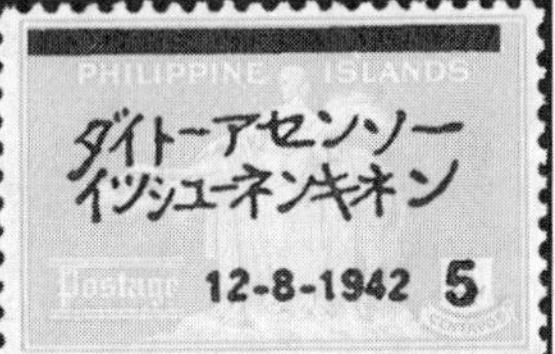

1942, Dec. 8
N9 A54 5(c) on 4c **yellow green** *(400,000)* .50 .50
First day cover 2.00

1st anniversary of the "Greater East Asia War."

Nos. C59 and C62 Surcharged in Black

1943, Jan. 23
N10 AP1 2(c) on 8c **carmine** *(400,000)* .25 .25
N11 AP1 5c on 1p **sepia** *(300,000)* .50 .50
First day cover, #N10-N11 2.00

1st anniv. of the Philippine Executive Commission.

Nipa Hut — OS1

Rice Planting — OS2

Mt. Mayon and Mt. Fuji — OS3

Moro Vinta — OS4

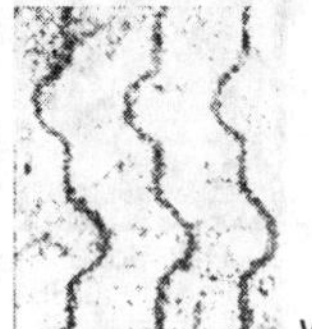

Wmk. 257

The "c" currency is indicated by four Japanese characters, "p" currency by two.

Engraved; Typographed (2c, 6c, 25c)

1943-44 **Wmk. 257** ***Perf. 13***
N12 OS1 1c **deep orange,** *June 7, 1943* .20 .20
N13 OS2 2c **bright green,** *Apr. 1, 1943* .20 .20
N14 OS1 4c **slate green,** *June 7, 1943* .20 .20
N15 OS3 5c **orange brown,** *Apr. 1, 1943* .20 .20
N16 OS2 6c **red,** *July 14, 1943* .20 .20
N17 OS3 10c **blue green,** *July 14, 1943* .20 .20
N18 OS4 12c **steel blue,** *July 14, 1943* 1.00 1.00
N19 OS4 16c **dark brown,** *July 14, 1943* .20 .20
N20 OS1 20c **rose violet,** *Aug. 16, 1943* 1.25 1.25
N21 OS3 21c **violet,** *Aug. 16, 1943* .20 .20
N22 OS2 25c **pale brown,** *Aug. 16, 1943* .20 .20
N23 OS3 1p **deep carmine,** *June 7, 1943* .75 .75
N24 OS4 2p **dull violet,** *Sept. 16, 1943* 5.50 5.50
First day cover *14.00*
N25 OS4 5p **dark olive,** *Apr. 10, 1944* 14.00 9.00
First day cover *14.00*
Nos. N12-N25 (14) 24.30 19.30

Map of Manila Bay Showing Bataan and Corregidor — OS5

1943, May 7 **Photo.** **Unwmk.**
N26 OS5 2c **carmine red** .20 .20
N27 OS5 5c **bright green** .25 .25
Colorless dot after left "5" 1.10 —
First day cover, #N26-N27, Manila 1.50

1st anniversary of the fall of Bataan and Corregidor.

No. 440 Surcharged in Black

1943, June 20 **Engr.** ***Perf. 11***
N28 A60 12(c) on 20c **light olive green** *(350,000)* .20 .20
First day cover 1.50
a. Double surcharge —

350th anniversary of the printing press in the Philippines. "Limbagan" is Tagalog for "printing press."

Rizal Monument, Filipina and Philippine Flag — OS6

1943, Oct. 14 **Photo.** **Unwmk.** ***Perf. 12***
N29 OS6 5c **light blue** .20 .20
a. Imperf. .20 .20
N30 OS6 12c **orange** .20 .20
a. Imperf. .20 .20

N31 OS6 17c **rose pink**	.20	.20
First day cover, #N29-N31, Manila		1.00
a. Imperf.	.20	.20
First day cover, #N29a-N31a, Manila		1.00
Nos. N29-N31 (3)	.60	.60

"Independence of the Philippines." Japan granted "independence" Oct. 14, 1943, when the puppet republic was founded. The imperforate stamps were issued without gum.

José Rizal — OS7

Rev. José Burgos — OS8

Apolinario Mabini — OS9

1944, Feb. 17 Litho. Unwmk. *Perf. 12*

N32 OS7 5c **blue**	.20	.20
a. Imperf.	.20	.20
N33 OS8 12c **carmine**	.20	.20
a. Imperf.	.20	.20
N34 OS9 17c **deep orange**	.20	.20
First day cover, #N32-N34, Manila		1.00
a. Imperf.	.20	.20
First day cover, #N32a-N34a, *Apr. 17,* Manila		1.50
Nos. N32-N34 (3)	.60	.60

Nos. C60 and C61 Surcharged in Black

1944, May 7 Unwmk. *Perf. 11*

N35 AP1 5(c) on 20c **ultramarine**	.50	.35
N36 AP1 12(c) on 60c **blue green** *(165,000)*	1.25	.85
First day cover, #N35-N36		2.50

2nd anniversary of the fall of Bataan and Corregidor.

José P. Laurel — OS10

1945, Jan. 12 Litho. Unwmk. *Imperf.*
Without Gum

N37 OS10 5c **dull violet brown**	.20	.20
N38 OS10 7c **blue green**	.20	.20
N39 OS10 20c **chalky blue**	.20	.20
First day cover, #N37-N39		1.00
Nos. N37-N39 (3)	.60	.60

Issued belatedly on Jan. 12, 1945, to commemorate the first anniversary of the puppet Philippine Republic, Oct. 14, 1944. "S" stands for "sentimos."

The special cancellation devices prepared for use on Oct. 14, 1944, were employed on "First Day" covers Jan. 12, 1945.

OCCUPATION SEMI-POSTAL

Woman, Farming and Cannery — OSP1

1942, Nov. 12 Litho. Unwmk. *Perf. 12*

NB1 OSP1 2c + 1c **pale violet**	.20	.20
NB2 OSP1 5c + 1c **bright green**	.25	.20
NB3 OSP1 16c + 2c **orange**	32.50	32.50
First day cover, #NB1-NB3		37.50
Nos. NB1-NB3 (3)	32.95	32.90

Issued to promote the campaign to produce and conserve food. The surtax aided the Red Cross.

Souvenir Sheet

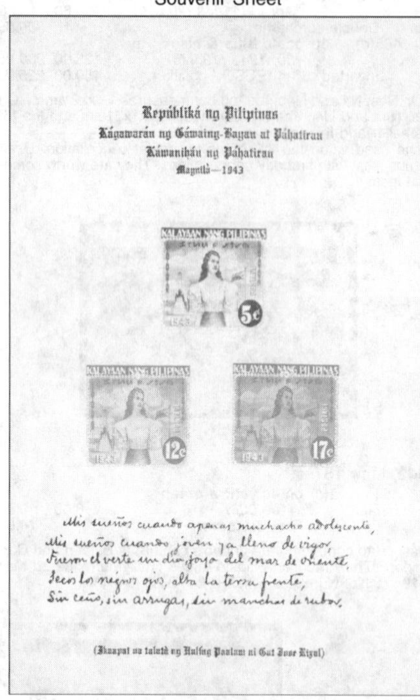

OSP2

Illustration reduced.

1943, Oct. 14 Without Gum *Imperf.*

NB4 OSP2 Sheet of 3	50.00	*10.00*
Sheet with first day cancel and cachet, Manila		2.50
First day cover, Manila		—

"Independence of the Philippines."

No. NB4 contains one each of Nos. N29a-N31a. Marginal inscription is from Rizal's "Last Farewell." Sold for 2.50p.

Nos. N18, N20 and N21 Surcharged in Black

1943, Dec. 8 Wmk. 257 *Perf. 13*

NB5 OS4 12c + 21c **steel blue**	.20	.20
NB6 OS1 20c + 36c **rose violet**	.20	.20
NB7 OS3 21c + 40c **violet**	.20	.20
First day cover, #NB5-NB7		1.25
Nos. NB5-NB7 (3)	.60	.60

The surtax was for the benefit of victims of a Luzon flood. "Baha" is Tagalog for "flood."

Souvenir Sheet

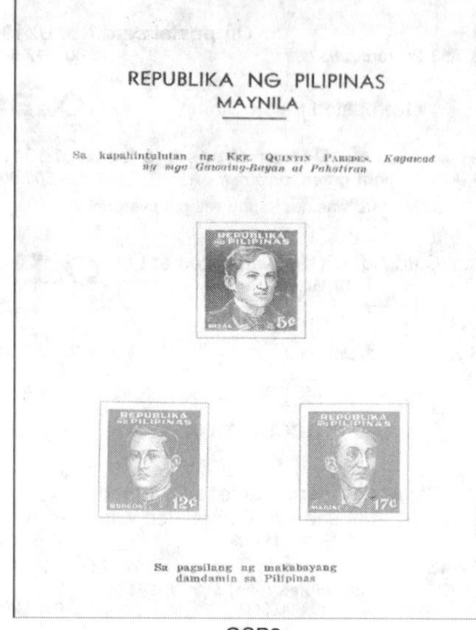

OSP3

Illustration reduced.

1944, Feb. 9 Litho. Unwmk. *Imperf.*
Without Gum

NB8 OSP3 Sheet of 3	5.00	*3.00*
First day cover		*4.00*

No. NB8 contains one each of Nos. N32a-N34a.

The sheet sold for 1p, the surtax going to a fund for the care of heroes' monuments. Size: 101x143mm. No. NB8 exists with 5c inverted.

OCCUPATION POSTAGE DUE

No. J15 Overprinted with Bar in Blue

1942, Oct. 14 Unwmk. *Perf. 11*

NJ1 D3 3c on 4c **brown red** *(40,000)*	35.00	*20.00*
First day cover		*27.50*
Double bar	—	—

On copies of No. J15, two lines were drawn in India ink with a ruling pen across "United States of America" by employees of the Short Paid Section of the Manila Post Office to make a provisional 3c postage due stamp which was used from Sept. 1, 1942 (when the letter rate was raised from 2c to 5c) until Oct. 14 when No. NJ1 went on sale. Value on cover, $125.

OCCUPATION OFFICIAL

Nos. 461, 413, 435, 435a and 442 Overprinted or Surcharged in Black with Bars and

1943-44 Unwmk. *Perf. 11x10½, 11*

NO1 A75 2c **apple green,** *Apr. 7, 1943 (200,000)*	.20	.20
P# block of 4	.25	
a. Double overprint	*500.00*	
On cover (double overprint)		*1,250.*
NO2 A55 5(c) on 6c **dark brown** (On No. 413), *June 26, 1944 (23,049)*	45.00	45.00
First day cover		*40.00*
NO3 A55 5(c) on 6c **golden brown** (On No. 435a), *Apr. 7, 1943 (250,000)*	.20	.20
a. Narrower spacing between bars *(249,951)*	.20	.20
b. 5(c) on 6c dark brown (On No. 435)	.20	.20
c. As "b," narrower spacing between bars	.20	.20
d. Double overprint	—	
NO4 A62 16(c) on 30c **orange red,** *Apr. 7, 1943 (100,000)*	.30	.30
a. Wider spacing between bars	.30	.30
First day cover, Nos. NO1, NO3-NO4		*35.00*

On Nos. NO3 and NO3b the bar deleting "United States of America" is 9¾ to 10mm above the bar deleting "Common." On Nos. NO3a and NO3c, the spacing is 8 to 8½mm.

On No. NO4, the center bar is 19mm long, 3½mm below the top bar and 6mm above the Japanese characters. On No. NO4a, the center bar is 20½mm long, 9mm below the top bar and 1mm above the Japanese characters.

"K.P." stands for Kagamitang Pampamahalaan, "Official Business" in Tagalog.

Nos. 435 and 435a Surcharged in Black

1944, Aug. 28 Unwmk. *Perf. 11*

NO5	A55	(5c) on 6c **golden brown** *(500,000)*	.20	.20
a.		5(c) on 6c **dark brown**	.20	.20

Nos. O34 and C62 Overprinted in Black

a

b

NO6	A60(a)	20c **light olive green** *(200,000)*	.25	.25
NO7	AP1(b)	1p **sepia** *(100,000)*	.65	.65
		First day cover, #NO5-NO7		2.00
		Nos. NO5-NO7 (3)	1.10	1.10

OCCUPATION ENVELOPES

5 5 No. U41 Surcharged in Black

1943, Apr. 1

NU1	E4	5c on 2c **carmine**	.50	.30
		Entire	1.90	1.25
		Entire, 1st day cancel		4.00

No. U41 Surcharged in Black

1944, Feb. 17

NU2	E4	5c on 2c **carmine**	.75	.50
		Entire	3.00	*5.00*
		Entire, 1st day cancel		7.50
a.		Inverted surcharged	—	
b.		Double surcharge	—	
c.		Both 5's missing	—	

OCCUPATION POSTAL CARDS

Values are for entire cards.

Nos. UX19 and UZ4 Overprinted with Bars in Black

1942

NUX1	A53	2c **red,** *pale buff, Mar. 4, 1942*	15.00	15.00
		First day cancel		*85.00*
a.		Vertical obliteration bars reversed	*140.00*	
NUX2	A75	2c **light green,** *pale buff, Dec. 12, 1942*	2.50	2.00
		First day cancel		6.00

Rice Planting—A77

1943, May 17

NUX3	A77	2c **green**	1.00	*1.00*
		First day cancel, Manila		2.00

OCCUPATION OFFICIAL CARDS

Nos. UX19, UX17 and UX18 Overprinted in Black with Bars and 公用 (K.P.)

1943, Apr. 7

NUZ1	A53	2c **red,** *pale buff*	4.00	3.00
		First day cancel		100.00
a.		On No. UX17	—	—
b.		On No. UX18	—	—

No. NUX3 Overprinted in Black REPUBLIKA NG PILIPINAS (K. P.)

1944, Aug. 28

NUZ2	A77	2c **green**	1.50	*1.00*
		First day cancel		2.00
a.		Double overprint	—	

FILIPINO REVOLUTIONARY GOVERNMENT

The Filipino Republic was instituted by Gen. Emilio Aguinaldo on June 23, 1899. At the same time he assumed the office of President. Aguinaldo dominated the greater part of the island of Luzon and some of the smaller islands until late in 1899. He was taken prisoner by United States troops on March 23, 1901.

The devices composing the National Arms, adopted by the Filipino Revolutionary Government, are emblems of the Katipunan political secret society or of Katipunan origin. The letters "K K K" on these stamps are the initials of this society whose complete name is "Kataas-taasang, Kagalang-galang Katipunan nang Mañga Anak nang Bayan," meaning "Sovereign Worshipful Association of the Sons of the Country."

The regular postage and telegraph stamps were in use on Luzon as early as Nov. 10, 1898. Owing to the fact that stamps for the different purposes were not always available together with a lack of proper instructions, any of the adhesives were permitted to be used in the place of the other. Hence telegraph and revenue stamps were accepted for postage and postage stamps for revenue or telegraph charges. In addition to the regular postal emission, there are a number of provisional stamps, issues of local governments of islands and towns.

POSTAGE ISSUES

A1

A2

Coat of Arms—A3

1898-99 Unwmk. *Perf. 11½*

Y1	A1	2c **red**	175.00	125.00
a.		Double impression	*225.00*	
Y2	A2	2c **red**	.20	.25
		On cover		450.00
b.		Double impression	—	
d.		Horiz. pair, imperf. between	—	
e.		Vert. pair, imperf. between	*200.00*	
Y3	A3	2c **red**	150.00	*200.00*
		On cover		*2,000.*

Imperf pairs and pairs, imperf horizontally, have been created from No. Y2e.

RS1

N1

REGISTRATION STAMP

YF1	RS1	8c **green**	1.00	*10.00*
		On cover with #Y2		*3,500.*
a.		Imperf., pair	400.00	
b.		Imperf. vertically, pair	—	

NEWSPAPER STAMP

YP1	N1	1m **black**	.20
a.		Imperf., pair	.20

PROOFS

			(1) Large	DIE (2) Small	(2a)
1906					
241P	2c	**yellow green**		500.	750.
242P	4c	**carmine lake**	*600.*	500.	750.
243P	6c	**violet**	*600.*	500.	750.
244P	8c	**brown**	*600.*	500.	750.
245P	10c	**dark blue**		500.	750.
246P	12c	**brown lake**		500.	750.
247P	16c	**violet black**	*600.*	500.	750.
248P	20c	**orange brown**		500.	750.
249P	26c	**violet brown**		500.	750.
250P	30c	**olive green**	*600.*	500.	750.
251P	1p	**orange**		500.	750.
252P	2p	**black**		500.	750.
253P	4p	**dark blue**		500.	750.
254P	10p	**dark green**		500.	750.
1909-13					
255P	12c	**red orange**		600.	625.
256P	16c	**olive green**		600.	625.
257P	20c	**yellow**		600.	625.
258P	26c	**blue green**		600.	625.
259P	30c	**ultramarine**		600.	625.
260P	1p	**pale violet**		600.	625.
260AP	2p	**violet brown**		600.	625.
275P	30c	**gray**		600.	625.
1923					
303P	16c	**olive bister**	450.		
303TC	16c	**olive green**	450.		
1926					
322P	18c	**light brown & black,** plate, glazed card			350.
1932					
357P	18c	**red orange**	450.		
357TC	18c	**orange red**	450.		
1935					
383P	2c	**rose**	600.		
384P	4c	**yellow green**	600.		
385P	6c	**dark brown**	600.		
386P	8c	**violet**	600.		
387P	10c	**rose carmine**	600.		
388P	12c	**black**	600.		
389P	16c	**dark blue**	600.		
390P	20c	**light olive green**	600.		
390TC	20c	**black**	—		
391P	26c	**indigo**	600.		
392P	30c	**orange red**	600.		
393P	1p	**red orange & black**	600.		
394P	2p	**bister brown & black**	600.		
395P	4p	**blue & black**	600.		
396P	5p	**green & black**	600.		

1936

408P	2c	**orange brown**	450.		
408TC	2c	**yellow green**	450.		

1937

425P	2c	**yellow green**		500.	

1939

452P	2c	**yellow green**		500.	
453P	6c	**carmine**		500.	
454P	12c	**bright blue**		500.	

1939

455P	2c	**green**	750.	500.	
456P	6c	**orange**		500.	
457P	12c	**carmine**		500.	

1940

458P	2c	**dark orange**	1,000.	600.	
459P	6c	**dark green**		600.	
460P	12c	**purple**		600.	

1941

461P	2c	**apple green**		600.	

1946

497P	2c	**sepia**	—		

AIR POST

1941

C59P	8c	**carmine**		500.	
C60P	20c	**ultramarine**		500.	
C61P	60c	**blue green**		500.	
C62P	1p	**sepia**		500.	

SPECIAL DELIVERY

1906

E2P	20c	**ultramarine**	800.	700.	550.
E2TC	20c	**green**		700.	

POSTAGE DUE

1899

J1P	1c	**deep claret**		1,100.	
J2P	2c	**deep claret**		1,100.	
J3P	5c	**deep claret**		1,100.	
J4P	10c	**deep claret**		1,100.	
J5P	50c	**deep claret**		1,100.	

1901

J6P	3c	**deep claret**		1,100.	
J7P	30c	**deep claret**		1,100.	

SPECIMEN STAMPS

Handstamped US Type E in Purple **Specimen.**

1899

213S E	1c	**yellow green**	175.00
214dS E	2c	**rose carmine**, type IV	175.00
215S E	3c	**purple**	175.00
216S E	5c	**blue**	175.00
217S E	10c	**brown**, type I	175.00
218S E	15c	**olive brown**	175.00
219S E	50c	**orange**	175.00

See note after No. 219 for Special Printings with black "Specimen" overprints.

Overprinted US Type R in Black *Specimen*

1917-25

290S R	2c	**green**	40.00
291S R	4c	**carmine**	40.00
292S R	6c	**deep violet**	40.00
293S R	8c	**yellow brown**	40.00
294S R	10c	**deep blue**	40.00
295S R	12c	**red orange**	40.00
297S R	20c	**orange yellow**	40.00
298S R	26c	**green**	40.00
299S R	30c	**gray**	40.00
300S R	1p	**pale violet**	40.00
301S R	2p	**violet brown**	40.00
302S R	4p	**blue**	40.00

1923-26

303S R	16c	**olive bister**	25.00
304S R	10p	**deep green**	25.00

1926 **Overprinted Type R in Red**

319S R	2c	**green & black**	65.00
320S R	4c	**carmine & black**	65.00
321S R	16c	**olive green & black**	65.00
322S R	18c	**light brown & black**	65.00
323S R	20c	**orange & black**	65.00
324S R	24c	**gray & black**	65.00
325S R	1p	**rose lilac & black**	65.00

Overprinted US Type S in Red *Cancelled*

1926

319S S	2c	**green & black**	65.00
320S S	4c	**carmine & black**	65.00
321S S	16c	**olive green & black**	65.00
322S S	18c	**light brown & black**	65.00
323S S	20c	**orange & black**	65.00
324S S	24c	**gray & black**	65.00
325S S	1p	**rose lilac & black**	65.00

Imperforate copies of this set, on glazed cards with centers in brown, are known with the "Cancelled" overprint.

Handstamped "SPECIMEN" in Red Capitals, 13x3mm

1925

340S S	2c	**green**	75.00
341S S	4c	**carmine**	75.00
342S S	6c	**deep violet**	75.00
343S S	8c	**yellow brown**	100.00
344S S	10c	**deep blue**	100.00
345S S	12c	**red orange**	100.00
346S S	16c	**olive bister**	100.00
347S S	20c	**yellow**	100.00
348S S	26c	**blue green**	100.00
349S S	30c	**gray**	100.00
350S S	1p	**violet**	100.00
351S S	2p	**violet brown**	100.00
352S S	4p	**deep blue**	150.00
353S S	10p	**deep green**	250.00

SPECIAL DELIVERY

1919 **Overprinted Type R in Black**

E5S R	20c	**ultramarine**	200.00
E5bS R	20c	**dull violet**	—

Handstamped "SPECIMEN" in Red Capitals, 13x3mm

1925

E6aS	20c	**violet blue**	300.00

POSTAGE DUE

1899 **Overprinted Type E in Black**

J1S E	1c	**deep claret**	225.00
J2S E	2c	**deep claret**	225.00
J3S E	5c	**deep claret**	225.00
J4S E	10c	**deep claret**	225.00
J5S E	50c	**deep claret**	225.00

OFFICIAL

1926 **Overprinted Type R in Red**

O1S R	2c	**green & black**	30.00
O2S R	4c	**carmine & black**	30.00
O3S R	18c	**light brown & black**	30.00
O4S R	20c	**orange & black**	30.00

1926 **Overprinted Type S in Red**

O1S S	2c	**green & black**	30.00
O2S S	4c	**carmine & black**	30.00
O3S S	18c	**light brown & black**	30.00
O4S S	20c	**orange & black**	30.00

PUERTO RICO

(Porto Rico)

United States troops landed at Guanica Bay, Puerto Rico, on July 25, 1898, and mail service between various points in Puerto Rico began soon after under the authority of General Wilson, acting governor of the conquered territory, who authorized a provisional service early in August, 1898. The first Military Postal Station was opened at La Playa de Ponce on August 3, 1898. Control of the island passed formally to the United States on October 18, 1898. Twenty-one military stations operating under the administration of the Military Postal Service, were authorized in Puerto Rico after the Spanish-American war. After the overprinted provisional issue of 1900, unoverprinted stamps of the United States replaced those of Puerto Rico.

Name changed to Puerto Rico by Act of Congress, approved May 17, 1932.

Italicized numbers in parentheses indicate quantities issued.

100 CENTS = 1 DOLLAR.

PROVISIONAL ISSUES

Ponce Issue

A11

1898 **Unwmk.** **Handstamped** ***Imperf.***

200 A11 5c **violet,** *yellowish* *7,500.* —

The only way No. 200 is known used is handstamped on envelopes. Both unused stamps and used envelopes have a violet control mark.

Uses on 2c U.S. stamps on cover were strictly as a cancellation, not as provisional postage.

Dangerous counterfeits exist.

Coamo Issue

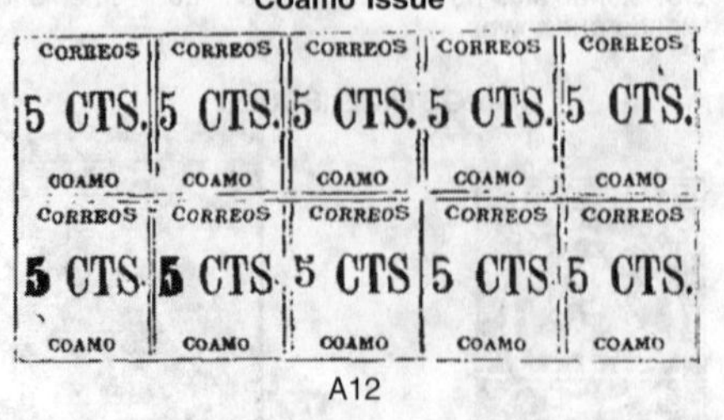

A12

Types of "5":
I - Curved flag. Pos. 2, 3, 4, 5.
II - Flag turns down at right. Pos. 1, 9, 10.
III - Fancy outlined "5." Pos. 6, 7.
IV - Flag curls into ball at right. Pos. 8.

Typeset, setting of 10

1898, Aug. **Unwmk.** ***Imperf.***

201 A12	5c	**black,** Type I	650.	*1,050.*
		Type II	700.	*1,100.*
		Type III	775.	*1,200.*
		Type IV	850.	*1,350.*
		Irregular "block" of 4 showing one of each type	3,750.	
		Sheet of 10	10,000.	
		On cover		*32,500.*
		Pair on cover		—

Blocks not showing all four types and pairs normally sell for 10-20% over the value of the individual stamps.

The stamps bear the control mark "F. Santiago" in violet. About 500 were issued.

Dangerous counterfeits exist.

Regular Issue

United States Nos. 279, 279Bf, 281, 272 and 282C Overprinted in Black at 36 degree Angle

1899		**Wmk. 191**		***Perf. 12***
210	A87	1c **yellow green,** *Mar. 15*	5.00	1.40
		On cover		22.00
		First day cover		—
		Block of 4	25.00	10.00
		P# strip of 3, Impt.	45.00	
		P# block of 6, Impt.	275.00	
a.		Overprint at 25 degree angle	7.50	2.25
		Pair, 36 degree and 25 degree angles	25.00	
		"PORTO RICU"	30.00	—
211	A88	2c **reddish carmine,** type IV, *Mar. 15*	4.25	1.25
		On cover		15.00
		Block of 4	22.50	10.00
		P# strip of 3, Impt.	37.50	
		P# block of 6, Impt.	350.00	
		"FORTO RICO" (pos. 77)	—	
a.		Overprint at 25 degree angle, *Mar. 15*	5.50	2.25
		On cover		20.00
		First day cover		—
		Block of 4	27.50	17.50
		P# strip of 3, Impt.	45.00	
		P# block of 6, Impt.	275.00	
		Pair, 36 degree and 25 degree angles	25.00	
		P# strip of 3, Impt.	95.00	
		P# block of 6, Impt.	700.00	
		"PORTU RICO" (pos. 46)	50.00	20.00
		"PORTO RICU" (pos. 3)	—	
		"PURTO RICO"	—	
		"FURTU RICO"	—	
212	A91	5c **blue**	12.50	2.50
		On cover		40.00
		Block of 4	55.00	27.50
		P# strip of 3, Impt.	70.00	
		P# block of 6, Impt.	350.00	
213	A93	8c **violet brown**	35.00	17.50
		On cover		125.00
		Block of 4	160.00	110.00
		P# strip of 3, Impt.	250.00	
		P# block of 6, Impt.	*1,750.*	
		"FORTO RICO"	90.00	60.00
a.		Overprint at 25 degree angle	40.00	19.00
		Pair, 36 degree and 25 degree angles	100.00	
c.		"PORTO RIC"	150.00	110.00
214	A94	10c **brown,** type I	25.00	6.00
		On cover		120.00
		Block of 4	110.00	45.00
		P# strip of 3, Impt.	160.00	
		P# block of 6, Impt.	1,250.	
		"FORTO RICO"	85.00	70.00
		Nos. 210-214 (5)	81.75	28.65

Misspellings of the overprint on Nos. 210-214 (PORTO RICU, PORTU RICO, FORTO RICO) are actually broken letters.

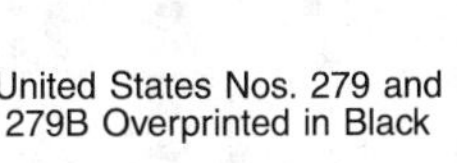

United States Nos. 279 and 279B Overprinted in Black

1900				
215	A87	1c **yellow green**	6.50	1.40
		On cover		17.50
		Block of 4	27.50	10.00
		P# strip of 3, Impt.	30.00	
		P# block of 6, Impt.	175.00	
216	A88	2c **red,** type IV, *Apr. 2*	4.75	2.00
		On cover		15.00
		Block of 4	22.50	15.00
		P# strip of 3, Impt.	32.50	
		P# block of 6, Impt.	175.00	
b.		Inverted overprint		*8,250.*

Special Printing

In March 1900 one pane of 100 stamps of each of the 1c (No. 215), 2c (No. 216) and 5c, 8c and 10c values, as well as 1c, 2c and 10c postage due stamps were specially overprinted for displays at the Paris Exposition (1900) and Pan American Exposition (1901). These last six items were never regularly issued with the PUERTO RICO overprint and therefore have no Scott catalogue number. The 2c pane was light red, type IV.

Copies were handstampd type E "Specimen" in black ink by H. G. Mandel and mounted by him in separate displays for the two Expositions. Additional copies from each pane were also handstamped "Specimen," but most were destroyed after the Expositions.

J. M. Bartels, a stamp dealer, signed some copies from these panes "Special Surcharge" in pencil on the gum to authenticate them as coming from the "Mandel" Special Printing panes. In 1904 or later, he handstamped additional surviving copies "Special Surcharge" in red ink on the back as his guarantee. Some of these guaranteed stamps had Mandel's "Specimen" handstamp on the face while others did not. Value, each $1,750.

No Special Printing panes overprinted "Porto Rico" were produced by the government. Copies do exist with a black type E "Specimen" handstamp, but it is believed that H. G. Mandel applied such handstamps to regularly issued overprinted "Porto Rico" stamps from his personal collection. Copies are known of the 2c type IV, in reddish carmine, 25 degree angle.

AIR POST

In 1938 a series of eight labels, two of which were surcharged, was offered to the public as "Semi-Official Air Post Stamps", the claim being that they had been authorized by the "Puerto Rican postal officials." These labels, printed by the Ever Ready Label Co. of New York, were a private issue of Aerovias Nacionales Puerto Rico, operating a passenger and air express service. Instead of having been authorized by the postal officials, they were at first forbidden but later tolerated by the Post Office Department at Washington.

In 1941 a further set of eight triangular labels was prepared and offered to collectors, and again the Post Office Department officials at Washington objected and forbade their use after September 16, 1941.

These labels represent only the charge for service rendered by a private enterprise for transporting matter outside the mails by plane. Their use did not and does not eliminate the payment of postage on letters carried by air express, which must in every instance be paid by United States postage stamps.

POSTAGE DUE STAMPS

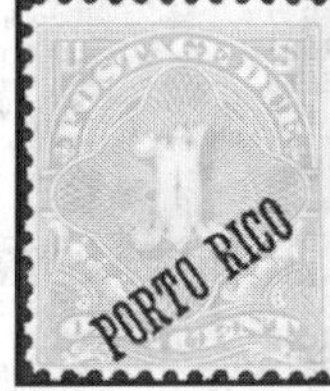

United States Nos. J38, J39 and J42 Overprinted in Black at 36 degree Angle

1899		**Wmk. 191**		***Perf. 12***
J1	D2	1c **deep claret**	22.50	5.50
		On cover		125.00
		Block of 4	100.00	35.00
		P# strip of 3, Impt.	120.00	
		P# block of 6, Impt.	*625.00*	
a.		Overprint at 25 degree angle	22.50	7.50
		Pair, 36 degree and 25 degree angles	65.00	
		P# strip of 3, Impt.	150.00	
		P# block of 6, Impt.	*750.00*	
J2	D2	2c **deep claret**	20.00	6.00
		On cover		250.00
		Block of 4	80.00	37.50
		P# strip of 3, Impt.	120.00	
		P# block of 6, Impt.	*800.00*	
a.		Overprint at 25 degree angle	20.00	7.00
		Pair, 36 degree and 25 degree angles	60.00	
		P# strip of 3, Impt.	140.00	
		P# block of 6, Impt.	*900.00*	
J3	D2	10c **deep claret**	190.00	60.00
		On cover		—
		Block of 4	800.00	—
		P# strip of 3, Impt.	*1,250.*	
		P# block of 6, Impt.	*3,750.*	
a.		Overprint at 25 degree angle	175.00	85.00
		Pair, 36 degree and 25 degree angles	650.00	

ENVELOPES

U.S. Envelopes of 1887 Issue Overprinted in Black

PORTO RICO.

20mm long

1899-1900

Note: Some envelopes for which there was no obvious need were issued in small quantities. Anyone residing in Puerto Rico could, by depositing with his postmaster the required amount, order any envelope in quantities of 500, or multiples thereof, provided it was on the schedule of U.S. envelopes. Such special orders are indicated by a plus sign, i. e., Nos. U15 and U18, and half the quantities of Nos. U16 and U17.

U1	U71	2c **green** (No. U311) *(3,000)*	16.00	*20.00*
		Entire	40.00	*350.00*
a.		Double overprint, entire	*3,500.*	
U2	U74	5c **blue** (No. U330) *(1,000)*	20.00	20.00
		Entire	55.00	*350.00*
a.		Double overprint, entire		—

U.S. Envelopes of 1899 Overprinted in color of the stamp

PORTO RICO.

21mm long

U3	U79	2c **carmine** (No. U362) *(100,000)*	3.00	3.00
		Entire	10.00	*12.00*
U4	U84	5c **blue** (No. U377) *(10,000)*	8.00	*9.00*
		Entire	17.50	*32.50*

Overprinted in Black **PORTO RICO.**

19mm long

U5	U77	1c **green,** *blue* (No. U355) *(1,000)*		750.
		Entire		1,900.
U6	U79	2c **carmine,** *amber* (No. U363), Die 2 *(500)*	450.	*500.*
		Entire	1,100.	1,250.
U7	U79	2c **carmine,** *oriental buff* (No. U364), Die 2 *(500)*		500.
		Entire		1,250.
U8	U80	2c **carmine,** *oriental buff* (No. U369), Die 3 *(500)*		600.
		Entire		1,300.
U9	U79	2c **carmine,** *blue* (No. U365), Die 2		
		Entire		*4,000.*
U10	U83	4c **brown** (No. U374), Die 3 *(500)*	200.	*500.*
		Entire	500.	*900.*

U.S. Envelopes of 1899 Issue Overprinted

PUERTO RICO.

23mm long

U11	U79	2c **carmine** (No. U362) red overprint *(100,000)*	4.00	3.00
		Entire	10.00	*11.00*
U12	U79	2c **carmine,** *oriental buff* (No. U364), Die 2, black overprint *(1,000)*	—	325.00
		Entire	*1,200.*	*1,300.*
U13	U80	2c **carmine,** *oriental buff* (No. U369), Die 3, black overprint *(1,000)*		375.00
		Entire		*1,750.*
U14	U84	5c **blue** (No. U377) blue overprint *(10,000)*	14.00	14.00
		Entire	42.50	*50.00*

Overprinted in Black **PUERTO RICO.**

U15	U77	1c **green,** *oriental buff* (No. U354) *(500)+*	20.00	*50.00*
		Entire	75.00	*80.00*
U16	U77	1c **green,** *blue* (No. U355) *(1,000)+*	25.00	*50.00*
		Entire	95.00	*125.00*
U17	U79	2c **carmine,** *oriental buff* (No. U364) *(1,000)+*	20.00	*50.00*
		Entire	95.00	*135.00*
U18	U79	2c **carmine,** *blue* (No. U365) *(500)+*	20.00	*50.00*
		Entire	75.00	*135.00*

There were two settings of the overprint, with minor differences, which are found on Nos. U16 and U17.

WRAPPER

U.S. Wrapper of 1899 Issue Overprinted in Green

PORTO RICO.

21mm long

W1	U77	1c **green,** *manila* (No. W357) *(15,000)*	8.00	*35.00*
		Entire	17.00	*110.00*

POSTAL CARDS

Values are for Entires.

Imprinted below stamp **PORTO RICO.**

1899-1900 U.S. Postal Card No. UX14

UX1	PC8 1c **black,** *buff,* imprint 21mm long	165.	*175.*
b.	Double imprint	*2,250.*	

Imprinted below stamp **PORTO RICO.**

UX1A	PC8 1c **black,** *buff,* imprint 20mm long	1,200.	*1,300.*

Imprinted below stamp **PORTO RICO.**

UX2	PC8 1c **black,** *buff,* imprint 26mm long	165.	*190.*

Imprinted below stamp **PUERTO RICO.**

UX3	PC8 1c **black,** *buff*	150.	*200.*

REVENUE

U.S. Revenue Stamps Nos. R163, R168-R169, R171 and Type of 1898 Surcharged in Black or Dark Blue

PORTO RICO 10 C. Excise Revenue
a

PORTO RICO $1 EXCISE REVENUE
b

1901 Wmk. 191R *Hyphen-hole Roulette 7*

R1	R15(a)	1c on 1c **pale blue** (Bk)	10.00	8.75
R2	R15(a)	10c on 10c **dark brown**	12.50	11.00
R3	R15(a)	25c on 25c **purple brown**	15.00	11.00
R4	R15(a)	50c on 50c **slate violet**	25.00	16.50
R5	R16(b)	$1 on $1 **pale greenish gray**	62.50	22.50
R6	R16(b)	$3 on $3 **pale greenish gray**	70.00	32.50
R7	R16(b)	$5 on $5 **pale greenish gray**	85.00	37.50
R8	R16(b)	$10 on $10 **pale greenish gray**	120.00	70.00
R9	R16(b)	$50 on $50 **pale greenish gray**	325.00	160.00
		Nos. R1-R9 (9)	725.00	369.75

Lines of 1c surcharge spaced farther apart; total depth of surcharge 15¾mm instead of 11mm.

RECTIFIED SPIRITS

U.S. Wine Stamps of 1933-34 Overprinted in Red or Carmine

RECTIFIED SPIRITS

1934 Offset Printing Wmk. 191R *Rouletted 7*

Overprint Lines 14mm Apart, Second Line 25mm Long

RE1	RE5	2c **green**	15.00
RE2	RE5	3c **green**	55.00
RE3	RE5	4c **green**	17.50
RE4	RE5	5c **green**	15.00
RE5	RE5	6c **green**	17.50

Overprint Lines 21½mm Apart, Second Line 23½mm Long

RE6	RE2	50c **green**	27.50
RE7	RE2	60c **green**	25.00

Handstamped overprints are also found on U.S. Wine stamps of 1933-34.

U.S. Wine Stamps of 1933-34 Overprinted in Black

RECTIFIED SPIRITS
a

RECTIFIED SPIRITS
b

1934 Offset Printing Wmk. 191R *Rouletted 7*

RE8	RE5(a)	1c **green**	22.50
RE9	RE5(a)	2c **green**	12.50
RE10	RE5(a)	3c **green**	60.00
RE11	RE5(a)	5c **green**	12.50
RE12	RE5(a)	6c **green**	15.00
RE13	RE2(b)	50c **green**	17.50
RE14	RE2(b)	60c **green**	15.00
RE15	RE2(b)	72c **green**	75.00
RE16	RE2(b)	80c **green**	40.00

RECTIFIED SPIRITS

U.S. Wine Stamps of 1933-34 Overprinted in Black

PUERTO RICO

1934 Offset Printing Wmk. 191R *Rouletted 7*

RE17	RE5	½c **green**		2.50
RE18	RE5	1c **green**	50.00	.60
RE19	RE5	2c **green**	50.00	.50
RE20	RE5	3c **green**	100.00	3.50
RE21	RE5	4c **green**		.75
RE22	RE5	5c **green**	50.00	1.00
RE23	RE5	6c **green**	50.00	1.25
RE24	RE5	10c **green**	100.00	3.50
RE25	RE5	30c **green**		30.00

Overprint Lines 12½mm Apart

RE26	RE2	36c **green**		6.00
RE27	RE2	40c **green**	150.00	5.00
RE28	RE2	50c **green**	150.00	2.50
RE29	RE2	60c **green**	125.00	.50
a.		Inverted overprint		—
RE30	RE2	72c **green**	150.00	3.00
RE31	RE2	80c **green**	150.00	4.00
RE32	RE2	$1 **green**	175.00	7.50

George Sewall Boutwell — R1

Engr. (8c & 58c); Litho.

1942-57 Wmk. 191 *Rouletted 7*

Without Gum

RE33	R1	½c **carmine**	3.50	1.25
RE34	R1	1c **sepia**	8.25	3.50
RE35	R1	2c **bright yellow green**	1.10	.20
RE36	R1	3c **lilac**	67.50	32.50
RE37	R1	4c **olive**	2.25	.50
RE38	R1	5c **orange**	5.50	1.00
RE39	R1	6c **red brown**	4.00	1.25
RE40	R1	8c **bright pink** ('57)	8.25	3.50
RE41	R1	10c **bright purple**	12.50	5.00
RE41A	R1	30c **vermilion**	190.00	
RE42	R1	36c **dull yellow**	250.00	65.00
RE43	R1	40c **deep claret**	20.00	7.00
RE44	R1	50c **green**	11.00	4.00
RE45	R1	58c **red orange**	82.50	6.00
RE46	R1	60c **brown**	1.40	.20
RE47	R1	62c **black**	3.50	.70
RE48	R1	72c **blue**	40.00	1.00
RE49	R1	77½c **olive gray**	11.00	3.50
RE50	R1	80c **brownish black**	14.00	6.00
RE51	R1	$1 **violet**	82.50	22.50
		Nos. RE33-RE51 (20)	818.75	

The 30c is believed not to have been placed in use.

SPECIMEN

Handstamped U.S. Type E in Purple **Specimen.**

1899

210S	E	1c **yellow green**	180.00
211S	E	2c **reddish carmine,** type IV	180.00
212S	E	5c **blue**	180.00
213S	E	8c **violet brown**	180.00
214S	E	10c **brown**	180.00

See note after No. 216 for Special Printings with **black** "Specimen" overprint.

Postage Due

1899

J1S	E	1c **deep claret**	225.00
J2S	E	2c **deep claret**	225.00
J3S	E	10c **deep claret**	225.00

Revenue

R1S	E	1c on 1c **pale blue**	40.00
R2S	E	10c on 10c **dark brown**	40.00
R3S	E	25c on 25c **purple brown**	40.00
R4S	E	50c on 50c **slate violet**	40.00
R5S	E	$1 on $1 **pale greenish gray**	40.00
R6S	E	$3 on $3 **pale greenish gray**	40.00
R7S	E	$5 on $5 **pale greenish gray**	40.00
R8S	E	$10 on $10 **pale greenish gray**	40.00
R9S	E	$50 on $50 **pale greenish gray**	40.00

RYUKYU ISLANDS

LOCATION — Chain of 63 islands between Japan and Formosa, separating the East China Sea from the Pacific Ocean.
GOVT. — Semi-autonomous under United States administration.
AREA — 848 sq. mi.
POP. — 945,465 (1970)
CAPITAL — Naha, Okinawa

The Ryukyus were part of Japan until American forces occupied them in 1945. The islands reverted to Japan May 15, 1972.

100 Sen = 1 Yen
100 Cents = 1 Dollar (1958).

In the Provisional Issues and Postal Stationery sections, italicized numbers in parentheses indicate quantity sold.

Values for First Day Covers are for unaddressed, cacheted covers. Values are for official cachets for Scott 1-26, C1-C3 and E1; and for commercial cachets for all others. Early cachets from the Japanese Philatelic Society command substantial premiums.

Catalogue values for unused stamps are for Never Hinged items beginning with Scott 1 in the regular postage section, Scott C1 in the air post section, Scott E1 in the special delivery section, Scott R1 in the revenue section, Scott 91S in the specimen section and Scott RQ1 in the unemployment insurance section.

Cycad — A1

Lily — A2

Sailing Ship — A3

Farmer — A4

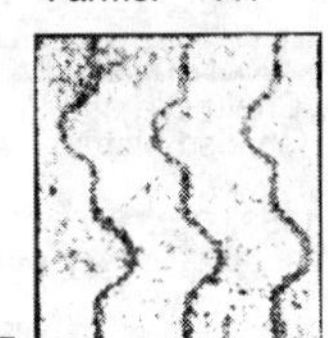

Wmk. 257

1948-49 Typo. Wmk. 257 *Perf. 13*

Second Printing, July 18, 1949

1	A1	5s	**magenta**	2.00	2.00
			Imprint block of 10	30.00	
2	A2	10s	**yellow green**	6.00	5.50
			Imprint block of 10	90.00	
3	A1	20s	**yellow green**	3.50	3.50
			Imprint block of 10	50.00	
4	A3	30s	**vermilion**	1.50	1.50
			Imprint block of 10	30.00	
5	A2	40s	**magenta**	1.50	1.50
			Imprint block of 10	25.00	
6	A3	50s	**ultramarine**	3.50	*3.00*
			Imprint block of 10	55.00	
7	A4	1y	**ultramarine**	6.00	5.50
			Imprint block of 10	90.00	
			Nos. 1-7 (7)	24.00	22.50

First Printing, July 1, 1948

1a	A1	5s	**magenta**	2.50	*3.50*
			First day cover		250.00
			Imprint block of 10	40.00	
2a	A2	10s	**yellow green**	1.50	*2.00*
			First day cover		250.00
			Imprint block of 10	25.00	
3a	A1	20s	**yellow green**	1.50	*2.00*
			First day cover		250.00
			Imprint block of 10	25.00	
4a	A3	30s	**vermilion**	2.50	*3.50*
			First day cover		250.00
			Imprint block of 10	40.00	
5a	A2	40s	**magenta**	55.00	55.00
			First day cover		250.00
			Imprint block of 10	750.00	
6a	A3	50s	**ultramarine**	3.00	3.00
			First day cover		250.00
			Imprint block of 10	45.00	
7a	A4	1y	**ultramarine**	450.00	350.00
			First day cover		250.00
			Imprint block of 10	*5,000.*	
			Nos. 1a-7a (7)	516.00	419.00

First printing: thick yellow gum, dull colors, rough perforations, grayish paper. Second printing: white gum, sharp colors, cleancut perforations, white paper.

A5

Ryukyu University — A6

Designs: 50s, Tile rooftop & Shishi. 1y, Ryukyu girl. 2y, Shuri Castle. 3y, Guardian dragon. 4y, Two women. 5y, Sea shells.

1950, Jan. 21 Photo. Unwmk. *Perf. 13x13½*

Off-white Paper

8	A5	50s	**dark carmine rose**	.20	.20
			First day cover		20.00
			Imprint block of 6	2.00	
a.			White paper, third printing, *Sept. 6, 1958*	.50	.50
			First day cover		27.50
			Imprint block of 10	6.50	
b.			"White Sky" variety (pos. 76)	2.50	2.50
9	A5	1y	**deep blue**	3.00	2.00
			First day cover		20.00
			Imprint block of 6	25.00	
10	A5	2y	**rose violet**	12.00	6.00
			First day cover		20.00
			Imprint block of 6	100.00	
11	A5	3y	**carmine rose**	30.00	11.00
			First day cover		20.00
			Imprint block of 6	275.00	
12	A5	4y	**greenish gray**	15.00	11.00
			First day cover		20.00
			Imprint block of 6	110.00	
13	A5	5y	**blue green**	7.50	5.00
			First day cover		20.00
			Imprint block of 6	60.00	
			First day cover, #8-13		200.00
			Nos. 8-13 (6)	67.70	35.20

No. 8a has colorless gum and an 8-character imprint in the sheet margin. The original 1950 first two printings on off-white paper have yellowish gum and a 5-character imprint.

For No. 8b, a defect in pos. 76 of the plates used for the first two printings resulted in the sky above the tile roof being predominantly white. A new master negative and plate was made for the third printing, so pos. 76 for this printing does not have the "white sky" variety.

For surcharges see Nos. 16-17.

1951, Feb. 12 *Perf. 13½x13*

14	A6	3y	**red brown**	60.00	25.00
			First day cover		60.00
			Imprint block of 6	450.00	

Opening of Ryukyu University, Feb. 12.

Pine Tree — A7

1951, Feb. 19 *Perf. 13*

15	A7	3y	**dark green**	55.00	25.00
			First day cover		60.00
			Imprint block of 6	450.00	

Reforestation Week, Feb. 18-24.

No. 8 surcharged in Black

16 Type II 16A Type I 16B Type III

There are three types of 10y surcharge:

Type I: narrow-spaced rules, "10" normal spacing, "Kai Tei" characters in 9-point type. First printing, Jan. 1, 1952.

Type II: wide-spaced rules, "10" normal spacing, "Kai Tei" characters in 9-point type. Second printing, June 5, 1952.

Type III: rules and "10" both wide-spaced, "Kai Tei" characters in 8-point type. Third printing, Dec. 8, 1952.

9 Point Kai Tei 8 Point Kai Tei

Both eight and nine point type were used in overprinting Nos. 16-17. In the varieties listed below, the first number indicates the size of the "Kai" character, and the second number is the size of the "Tei" character.

1952 ***Perf. 13½x13***

No.	Type	Description	Unused	Used
16	A5	10y on 50s **dark carmine rose** (II)	10.00	10.00
		Imprint block of 6	90.00	
		Top imprint block of 4, *Higa Seal* (pos. 8, 9, 18, 19)	75.00	
c.		8/8 point Kai Tei	10.00	10.00
d.		9/8 point Kai Tei	90.00	90.00
		9/9-9/8-8/8 se-tenant (horiz. strip of all 3 varieties)	75.00	75.00
e.		Surcharge transposed	600.00	—
f.		Legend of surcharge only (no obliteration bars)	600.00	
g.		Wrong font for "0" (pos. 59)	100.00	100.00
h.		Wrong font for "Yen" symbol (pos. 69)	150.00	150.00
i.		Surcharge on "white sky" variety (No. 8b)	100.00	100.00

On No. 16e, the entire obliteration-bars portion of the surcharge normally under the 10 Yen must be visible at the top of the stamp.

Forgeries to defraud the Postal Agency of revenue are known, used only, at the Gusikawa Post Office. Two types. Value, $350 each.

No.	Type	Description	Unused	Used
16A	A5	10y on 50s **dark carmine rose** (I)	40.00	40.00
		Imprint block of 6	275.00	
a.		8/8 point Kai Tei	40.00	40.00
		8/8-9/9 horiz. se-tenant pair (pos. 23-24)	250.00	250.00
		9/9-8/8 horiz. se-tenant pair	110.00	110.00
b.		Bottom two bars inverted (pos. 17)	100.00	100.00
c.		Wrong font for "0" (pos. 73)	250.00	250.00
d.		Surcharge on "white sky" variety (No. 8b)	250.00	250.00
16B	A5	10y on 50s **dark carmine rose** (III)	50.00	40.00
		Imprint block of 6	400.00	
a.		Wrong font for "Yen" symbol (pos. 25, 35, 85)	150.00	150.00
b.		Wrong font for "Tei" (pos. 26)	350.00	350.00
c.		Asterisk missing (pos. 54)	—	—
d.		"Kai Tei" 1.25mm above asterisk (pos. 54)	350.00	350.00
e.		"Kai" omitted (pos. 71)	—	
f.		Narrow spaced "10" (pos. 96)	350.00	350.00
		Strip of 3, narrow spaced "10" in center (pos. 95-97)	450.00	
g.		Surcharge on "white sky" variety (No. 8b)	350.00	350.00

The Kai Tei of the third printing measures the same as the 8-point type in the earlier printings but has differing characteristics. The Top curved line of the Kai is shorter and the lower curved line is also much shorter.

No. 10 surcharged 100y in black

No.	Type	Description	Unused	Used
17	A5	100y on 2y **rose violet,** Kai Tei characters in 9/9-point type, June 16, 1952	2,000.	1,600.
		Hinged	1,600.	
		Imprint block of 6	18,500.	
		Top imprint block of 4, *Higa Seal* (pos. 7, 8, 17, 18)	10,000.	
a.		8/8 point Kai Tei	2,000.	1,600.
b.		9/8 point Kai Tei	3,500.	3,500.
c.		Center "0" in wrong font, stamp with 9/9 Kai Tai (pos. 42)	5,000.	5,000.
d.		Center "0" in wrong font, stamp with 8/8 Kai Tai (pos. 67, 86)	3,500.	3,500.
e.		Center "0" in wrong font, stamp with 9/8 Kai Tai (pos. 53)	5,000.	5,000.
f.		Wrong font for last "0" (pos. 59)	5,000.	5,000.
g.		Wrong font for "yen" symbol (pos. 69)	5,000.	5,000.

Varieties of shifted and damaged surcharge characters exist, most notably a damaged ("clipped") Kai.

See note after 16B to differentiate between 8-point and 9-point charaters.

Surcharge forgeries are known. Authentication by competant experts is recommended.

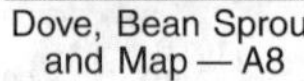

Dove, Bean Sprout and Map — A8

Madanbashi Bridge — A9

1952, Apr. 1 ***Perf. 13½x13***

No.	Type	Description	Unused	Used
18	A8	3y **deep plum**	120.00	40.00
		First day cover		80.00
		Imprint block of 10	1,800.	

Establishment of the Government of the Ryukyu Islands (GRI), April 1, 1952.

1952-53

Designs: 2y, Main Hall, Shuri Castle. 3y, Shurei Gate. 6y, Stone Gate, Soenji Temple, Naha. 10y, Benzaiten-do Temple. 30y, Sonohan Utaki (altar) at Shuri Castle. 50y, Tamaudun (royal mausoleum). Shuri. 100y, Stone Bridge, Hosho Pond, Enkaku Temple.

No.	Type	Description	Unused	Used
19	A9	1y **red,** *Nov. 20, 1952*	.20	.20
		Imprint block of 10	3.00	
20	A9	2y **green,** *Nov. 20, 1952*	.25	.25
		Imprint block of 10	3.50	
21	A9	3y **aquamarine,** *Nov. 20, 1952*	.30	.30
		First day cover, #19-21		35.00
		Imprint block of 10	5.00	
22	A9	6y **blue,** *Jan. 20, 1953*	2.50	2.50
		First day cover		27.50
		Imprint block of 10	40.00	
23	A9	10y **crimson rose,** *Jan. 20, 1953*	3.00	1.00
		First day cover		47.50
		Imprint block of 10	45.00	
24	A9	30y **olive green,** *Jan. 20, 1953*	12.00	6.50
		First day cover		75.00
		Imprint block of 10	150.00	
a.		30y **light olive green,** *1958*	50.00	
		Imprint block of 10	650.00	
25	A9	50y **rose violet,** *Jan. 20, 1953*	15.00	8.25
		First day cover		125.00
		Imprint block of 10	225.00	
26	A9	100y **claret,** *Jan. 20, 1953*	20.00	6.25
		First day cover		190.00
		Imprint block of 10	275.00	
		First day cover, #22-26		550.00
		Nos. 19-26 (8)	53.25	25.25

Issued: 1y, 2y and 3y, Nov. 20, 1952. Others, Jan. 20, 1953.

Reception at Shuri Castle — A10

Perry and American Fleet — A11

1953, May 26 ***Perf. 13½x13, 13x13½***

No.	Type	Description	Unused	Used
27	A10	3y **deep magenta**	14.00	6.50
		Imprint block of 6	120.00	
28	A11	6y **dull blue**	1.25	1.25
		First day cover, #27-28		11.00
		Imprint block of 6	9.50	

Centenary of the arrival of Commodore Matthew Calbraith Perry at Naha, Okinawa.

Chofu Ota and Pencil-shaped Matrix — A12

Shigo Toma and Pen — A13

1953, Oct. 1 ***Perf. 13½x13***

No.	Type	Description	Unused	Used
29	A12	4y **yellow brown**	11.00	5.00
		First day cover		17.50
		Imprint block of 10	150.00	

Third Newspaper Week.

1954, Oct. 1

No.	Type	Description	Unused	Used
30	A13	4y **blue**	13.00	7.50
		First day cover		22.50
		Imprint block of 10	175.00	

Fourth Newspaper Week.

Ryukyu Pottery — A14

Noguni Shrine and Sweet Potato Plant — A15

Designs: 15y, Lacquerware. 20y, Textile design.

1954-55 **Photo.** ***Perf. 13***

No.	Type	Description	Unused	Used
31	A14	4y **brown,** *June 25, 1954*	1.00	.60
		First day cover		9.00
		Imprint block of 10	11.00	
32	A14	15y **vermilion,** *June 20, 1955*	4.00	2.00
		First day cover		12.50
		Imprint block of 10	55.00	
33	A14	20y **yellow orange,** *June 20, 1955*	3.00	2.50
		First day cover		12.50
		Imprint block of 10	45.00	

First day cover, #32-33 35.00

Nos. 31-33 (3) 8.00 5.10

For surcharges see Nos. C19, C21, C23.

1955, Nov. 26

34	A15	4y **blue**	12.00	7.00
		First day cover		22.50
		Imprint block of 10	150.00	

350th anniv. of the introduction of the sweet potato to the Ryukyu Islands.

Stylized Trees — A16

Willow Dance — A17

1956, Feb. 18 **Unwmk.**

35	A16	4y **bluish green**	10.00	5.00
		First day cover		20.00
		Imprint block of 6	80.00	

Arbor Week, Feb. 18-24.

1956, May 1 ***Perf. 13***

8y, Straw hat dance. 14y, Dancer in warrior costume with fan.

36	A17	5y **rose lilac**	.90	.60
		First day cover		6.50
		Imprint block of 10	12.00	
37	A17	8y **violet blue**	2.00	1.65
		First day cover		6.50
		Imprint block of 10	27.50	
38	A17	14y **reddish brown**	3.50	2.00
		First day cover		6.50
		Imprint block of 10	45.00	
		First day cover, #36-38		35.00
		Nos. 36-38 (3)	6.40	4.25

For surcharges see Nos. C20, C22.

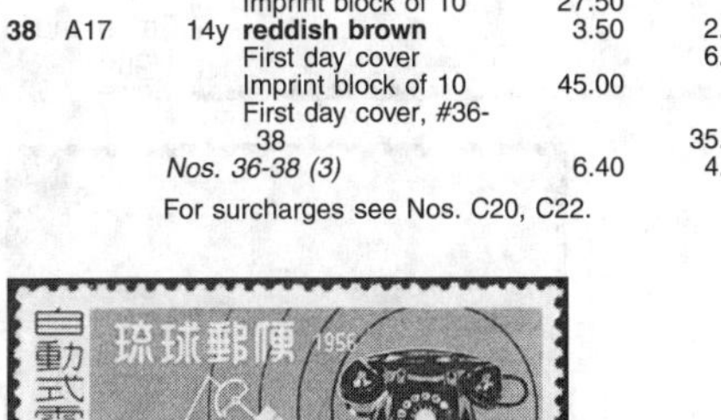

Telephone A18

1956, June 8

39	A18	4y **violet blue**	15.00	8.00
		First day cover		12.50
		Imprint block of 6	110.00	

Establishment of dial telephone system.

Garland of Pine, Bamboo and Plum — A19

Map of Okinawa and Pencil Rocket — A20

1956, Dec. 1 ***Perf. 13½x13***

40	A19	2y **multicolored**	2.00	2.00
		First day cover		3.00
		Imprint block of 10	27.50	

New Year, 1957.

1957, Oct. 1 **Photo.** ***Perf. 13½x13***

41	A20	4y **deep violet blue**	.75	.75
		First day cover		6.00
		Imprint block of 10	8.50	

7th annual Newspaper Week, Oct. 1-7.

Phoenix — A21

1957, Dec. 1 **Unwmk.** ***Perf. 13***

42	A21	2y **multicolored**	.25	.25
		First day cover		1.50
		Imprint block of 10	3.50	

New Year, 1958.

Ryukyu Stamps — A22

1958, July 1 ***Perf. 13½***

43	A22	4y **multicolored**	.80	.80
		First day cover		1.25
		Imprint block of 4	4.00	

10th anniv. of 1st Ryukyu stamps.

Yen Symbol and Dollar Sign — A23

Perf. 10.3, 10.8, 11.1 & Compound

1958, Sept. 16 **Typo.**

Without Gum

44	A23	½c **orange**	.90	.90
		Imprint block of 6	8.00	
a.		Imperf., pair	*1,000.*	
b.		Horiz. pair, imperf. between	100.00	
c.		Vert. pair, imperf. between	150.00	
d.		Vert. strip of 4, imperf. between	500.00	
45	A23	1c **yellow green**	1.40	1.40
		Imprint block of 6	11.00	
a.		Horiz. pair, imperf. between	150.00	
b.		Vert. pair, imperf. between	110.00	
c.		Vert. strip of 3, imperf. between	450.00	
d.		Vert. strip of 4, imperf. between	500.00	
e.		Block of 4, imperf. btwn. vert. & horiz.	—	
46	A23	2c **dark blue**	2.25	2.25
		Imprint block of 6	17.50	
a.		Horiz. pair, imperf. between	150.00	
b.		Vert. pair, imperf. between	*1,500.*	
c.		Horiz. strip of 3, imperf. between	300.00	
d.		Horiz. strip of 4, imperf. between	500.00	

Perforation and Paper Varieties of Ryukyu Islands Scott 44-53

Perforation	Perf. ID#	1/2¢ (No. 44) Paper Type 1	2	3	4	1¢ (No. 45) Paper Type 1	2	3	4	2¢ (No. 46) Paper Type 1	2	3	4	3¢ (No. 47) Paper Type 1	2	3	4	4¢ (No. 48) Paper Type 1	2	3	4	5¢ (No. 49) Paper Type 1	2	3	4	10¢ (No. 50) Paper Type 1	2	3	4	25¢ (No. 51) Paper Type 1	2	3	4	50¢ (No. 52) Paper Type 1	2	3	4	$1 (No. 53) Paper Type 1	2	3	4
11.1 x 11.1	M	*			*	*	*			*			*	*	*		*	*	*			*	*		*	*	*	*		*		*		*				*		*	
11.1 x 10.8	N	*			*	*	*			*			*	*	*		*	*	*		∞	*	?		*	*	*			*		*		*				*		*	
11.1 x 10.3	O	*			*	?	*			*			*	*	*			*				*	*			*				*		*		*				*			
10.8 x 11.1	P	*			*	*	*			*			*	*	*			*	*			*	*		*	*	*			*		*		*				*		*	
10.8 x 10.8	Q	*			*	*	*			*			*	*	*			*	*			*			*	*	*			*	*	*		*				*		*	
10.8 x 10.3	R	*			*	*	*			*			*	?	*			*	*			*				*	*			*				*							
10.3 x 11.1	S	*				*	*			*			*	*	*		*	?	*			*	*		*		*			*								*			
10.3 x 10.8	T	*			*	*	*			*			*	*	*		*		*			*	*			?	*	*										*		*	
10.3 x 10.3	U	*				?	*			*			*	?	*							*	*		*	?	*			\		*		\							

Paper Legend: 1= off-white; 2= white; 3= ivory; 4= thick

Specialists use a shorthand to refer to perf. and paper types: e.g., 50M3 =10¢ stamp, perf. 11.1 x 11.1, ivory paper.

Notes:

* = Verified variety

? = Reported in literature, but unverified variety.

∞ = 48N4 is unknown; however, a single example of 48N exists on a thick white paper unknown used for any other issue.

\ = These particular perf/paper combinations are known only in stamps of the Second (1961) Printing (51a and 52a)

The following are known unused only: 45R1, 45T2, 47O1, 48N4, 53O1.

The following are known used only: 47N4, 47T4, 50M3, 50Q2, 50R2, 50T2, 51P3, 51S1, 53T3.

Chart classifications and data supplied by courtesy of the Ryukyu Philatelic Specialist Society.

No.	Type	Value	Description	Unused	Used
47	A23	3c	**deep carmine**	1.75	1.50
			Imprint block of 6	14.00	
a.			Horiz. pair, imperf. between	150.00	
b.			Vert. pair, imperf. between	110.00	
c.			Vert. strip of 3, imperf. between	300.00	
d.			Vert. strip of 4, imperf. between	550.00	
e.			Block of 4, imperf. btwn. vert. & horiz.	—	
48	A23	4c	**bright green**	2.25	2.25
			Imprint block of 6	17.50	
a.			Horiz. pair, imperf. between	*500.00*	
b.			Vert. pair, imperf. between	150.00	
49	A23	5c	**orange**	4.25	3.75
			Imprint block of 6	35.00	
a.			Horiz. pair, imperf. between	150.00	
b.			Vert. pair, imperf. between	*750.00*	
50	A23	10c	**aquamarine**	5.75	4.75
			Imprint block of 6	42.50	
a.			Horiz. pair, imperf. between	200.00	
b.			Vert. pair, imperf. between	150.00	
c.			Vert. strip of 3, imperf. between	550.00	
51	A23	25c	**bright violet blue**	8.00	6.00
			Imprint block of 6	62.50	
a.			Gummed paper, perf. 10.3 ('61)	11.00	10.00
			Imprint block of 6	95.00	
b.			Horiz. pair, imperf. between	*1,500.*	
c.			Vert. pair, imperf. between	—	
d.			Vert. strip of 3, imperf. between	600.00	
52	A23	50c	**gray**	17.50	10.00
			Imprint block of 6	140.00	
a.			Gummed paper, perf. 10.3 ('61)	12.00	10.00
			Imprint block of 6	110.00	
			First day cover, #51a-52a		20.00
b.			Horiz. pair, imperf. between	*1,200.*	
53	A23	$1	**rose lilac**	12.50	5.50
			Imprint block of 6	100.00	
a.			Horiz. pair, imperf. between	400.00	
b.			Vert. pair, imperf. between	*1,750.*	
			Nos. 44-53 (10)	56.55	38.30

Printed locally. Perforation, paper and shade varieties exist. Nos. 51a and 52a are on off-white paper and perf 10.3.

First day covers come with various combinations of stamps: Nos. 44-48, 49-53, 44-53 etc. Values $10 for short set of low values (Nos. 44-48) to $50 for full set on one cover.

Gate of Courtesy — A24

1958, Oct. 15 **Photo.** ***Perf. 13½***

No.	Type	Value	Description	Unused	Used
54	A24	3c	**multicolored**	1.25	1.25
			First day cover		1.50
			Imprint block of 4	6.25	

Restoration of Shureimon, Gate of Courtesy, on road leading to Shuri City.

Imitations of this stamp were distributed in 1972 to discourage speculation in Ryukyuan stamps. The imitations were printed without gum and have a lengthy message in light blue printed on the back.

Lion Dance — A25

Trees and Mountains — A26

1958, Dec. 10 **Unwmk.** ***Perf. 13½***

No.	Type	Value	Description	Unused	Used
55	A25	1½c	**multicolored**	.30	.30
			First day cover		1.50
			Imprint block of 6	2.00	

New Year, 1959.

1959, Apr. 30 **Litho.** ***Perf. 13½x13***

No.	Type	Value	Description	Unused	Used
56	A26	3c	**blue, yellow green, green & red**	.70	.60
			First day cover		1.00
			Imprint block of 6	5.50	

"Make the Ryukyus Green" movement.

Yonaguni Moth — A27

1959, July 23 **Photo.** ***Perf. 13***

No.	Type	Value	Description	Unused	Used
57	A27	3c	**multicolored**	1.10	1.00
			First day cover		1.50
			Imprint block of 6	8.00	

Meeting of the Japanese Biological Education Society in Okinawa.

Hibiscus — A28

Toy (Yakaji) — A29

Designs: 3c, Fish (Moorish idol). 8c, Sea shell (Phalium bandatum). 13c, Butterfly (Kallinia Inachus Eucerca), denomination at left, butterfly going up. 17c, Jellyfish (Dactylometra pacifera Goette).

Inscribed:

琉球郵便

1959, Aug. 10 ***Perf. 13x13½***

No.	Type	Value	Description	Unused	Used
58	A28	½c	**multicolored**	.20	.20
			Imprint block of 10	3.25	
59	A28	3c	**multicolored**	.75	.40
			Imprint block of 10	9.00	
60	A28	8c	**light ultramarine, black & ocher**	11.00	5.50
			Imprint block of 10	150.00	
61	A28	13c	**light blue, gray & orange**	2.50	1.75
			Imprint block of 10	32.50	
62	A28	17c	**violet blue, red & yellow**	22.50	9.00
			Imprint block of 10	300.00	
			First day cover, #58-62		15.00
			Nos. 58-62 (5)	36.95	16.85

Four-character inscription measures 10x2mm on ½c; 12x3mm on 3c, 8c; 8½x2mm on 13c, 17c. See Nos. 76-80.

1959, Dec. 1 **Litho.**

No.	Type	Value	Description	Unused	Used
63	A29	1½c	**gold & multicolored**	.55	.45
			First day cover		1.50
			Imprint block of 10	8.00	

New Year, 1960.

University Badge A30

1960, May 22 **Photo.** ***Perf. 13***

No.	Type	Value	Description	Unused	Used
64	A30	3c	**multicolored**	.95	.75
			First day cover		1.25
			Imprint block of 6	7.25	

10th anniv. opening of Ryukyu University.

Dancer — A31

Designs: Various Ryukyu Dances.

1960, Nov. 1 **Photo.** ***Perf. 13***

Dark Gray Background

No.	Type	Value	Description	Unused	Used
65	A31	1c	**yellow, red & violet**	1.50	.80
			Imprint block of 10	18.00	
66	A31	2½c	**crimson, blue & yellow**	3.00	1.00
			Imprint block of 10	37.50	
67	A31	5c	**dark blue, yellow & red**	.65	.50
			Imprint block of 10	10.00	
68	A31	10c	**dark blue, yellow & red**	.80	.70
			Imprint block of 10	11.00	
			First day cover, #65-68		5.50
			Nos. 65-68 (4)	5.95	3.00

See Nos. 81-87, 220.

Torch and Nago Bay — A32

Runners at Starting Line — A33

1960, Nov. 8

No.	Type	Value	Description	Unused	Used
72	A32	3c	**light blue, green & red**	5.50	3.00
			First day cover		3.50
			Imprint block of 6	40.00	
73	A33	8c	**orange & slate green**	.75	.75
			First day cover		1.50
			Imprint block of 6	5.75	
			First day cover, #72-73		5.00

8th Kyushu Inter-Prefectural Athletic Meet, Nago, Northern Okinawa, Nov. 6-7.

Little Egret and Rising Sun — A34

1960, Dec. 1 **Unwmk.** ***Perf. 13***

No.	Type	Value	Description	Unused	Used
74	A34	3c	**reddish brown**	5.50	3.50
			First day cover		4.00
			Imprint block of 6	42.50	

National census.

Okinawa Bull Fight — A35

1960, Dec. 10 ***Perf. 13½***

No.	Type	Denom.	Description	Unused	Used
75	A35	1½c	**bister, dark blue & red brown**	1.75	1.50
			First day cover		2.00
			Imprint block of 6	12.50	

New Year, 1961.

Type of 1959 With Japanese Inscription Redrawn:

A28a

1960-61 **Photo.** ***Perf. 13x13½***

No.	Type	Denom.	Description	Unused	Used
76	A28a	½c	**multicolored,** *Oct. 1961*	.45	.45
			Imprint block of 10	5.50	
77	A28a	3c	**multicolored,** *Aug. 23, 1961*	.90	.35
			First day cover		1.50
			Imprint block of 10	12.50	
78	A28a	8c	**light ultramarine, black & ocher,** *July 1, 1960*	.90	.80
			Imprint block of 10	12.50	
79	A28a	13c	**blue, brown & red,** *July 1, 1960*	1.10	.90
			Imprint block of 10	15.00	
80	A28a	17c	**violet blue, red & yellow,** *July 1, 1960*	15.00	6.00
			Imprint block of 10	190.00	
			First day cover, #78-80		15.00
			Nos. 76-80 (5)	18.35	8.50

Size of Japanese inscription on Nos. 78-80 is 10½x1½mm. On No. 79 the denomination is at right, butterfly going down.

Dancer Type of 1960 with "RYUKYUS" Added in English

1961-64 ***Perf. 13***

No.	Type	Denom.	Description	Unused	Used
81	A31	1c	**multicolored,** *Dec. 5, 1961*	.20	.20
			First day cover		1.00
			Imprint block of 10	2.00	
82	A31	2½c	**multicolored,** *June 20, 1962*	.20	.20
			Imprint block of 10	2.25	
83	A31	5c	**multicolored,** *June 20, 1962*	.25	.25
			Imprint block of 10	3.00	
84	A31	10c	**multicolored,** *June 20, 1962*	.45	.40
			First day cover, #82-84		1.50
			Imprint block of 10	5.75	
84A	A31	20c	**multicolored,** *Jan. 20, 1964*	3.25	1.40
			First day cover		2.50
			Imprint block of 10	37.50	
85	A31	25c	**multicolored,** *Feb. 1, 1962*	1.00	.90
			First day cover		2.00
			Imprint block of 10	13.00	
86	A31	50c	**multicolored,** *Sept. 1, 1961*	2.50	1.40
			Imprint block of 10	32.50	
87	A31	$1	**multicolored,** *Sept. 1, 1961*	6.00	.25
			Imprint block of 10	70.00	
			First day cover, #86-87		35.00
			Nos. 81-87 (8)	13.85	5.00

Pine Tree — A36

1961, May 1 **Photo.** ***Perf. 13***

No.	Type	Denom.	Description	Unused	Used
88	A36	3c	**yellow green & red**	1.60	1.25
			First day cover		1.50
			Imprint block of 6	12.00	

"Make the Ryukyus Green" movement.

Naha, Steamer and Sailboat A37

1961, May 20

No.	Type	Denom.	Description	Unused	Used
89	A37	3c	**aquamarine**	2.10	1.50
			First day cover		1.75
			Imprint block of 6	16.00	

40th anniv. of Naha.

White Silver Temple — A38

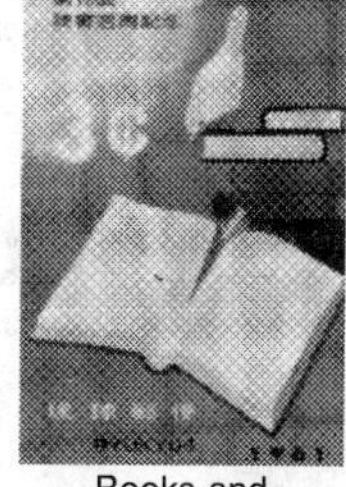

Books and Bird — A39

1961, Oct. 1 **Typo.** **Unwmk.** ***Perf. 11***

No.	Type	Denom.	Description	Unused	Used
90	A38	3c	**red brown**	2.25	1.50
			First day cover		1.75
			Imprint block of 6	15.00	
a.			Horiz. pair, imperf. between	*500.00*	
b.			Vert. pair, imperf. between	*600.00*	

Merger of townships Takamine, Kanegushiku and Miwa with Itoman.

A 3-cent stamp to commemorate the merger of two cities, Shimoji-cho and Hirara-shi of Miyako Island, was scheduled to be issued on Oct. 30, 1961. However, the merger was called off and the stamp never issued. It features a white chaplet on Kiyako linen on a blue background.

1961, Nov. 12 **Litho.** ***Perf. 13***

No.	Type	Denom.	Description	Unused	Used
91	A39	3c	**multicolored**	1.10	.90
			First day cover		1.25
			Imprint block of 6	10.00	

Book Week.

Rising Sun and Eagles — A40

Symbolic Steps, Trees and Government Building — A41

1961, Dec. 10 **Photo.** ***Perf. 13½***

No.	Type	Denom.	Description	Unused	Used
92	A40	1½c	**gold, vermilion & black**	2.00	2.00
			First day cover		2.50
			Imprint block of 6	16.00	

New Year, 1962.

1962, Apr. 1 **Unwmk.** ***Perf. 13½***

Design: 3c, Government Building.

No.	Type	Denom.	Description	Unused	Used
93	A41	1½c	**multicolored**	.60	.60
			Imprint block of 6	4.75	
94	A41	3c	**bright green, red & gray**	.80	.80
			Imprint block of 6	6.50	
			First day cover, #93-94		2.00

10th anniv. of the Government of the Ryukyu Islands (GRI).

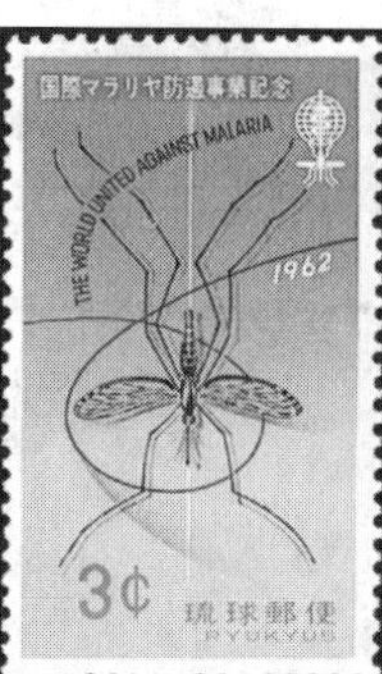

Anopheles Hyrcanus Sinensis — A42

Design: 8c, Malaria eradication emblem and Shurei gate.

1962, Apr. 7 ***Perf. 13½x13***

No.	Type	Denom.	Description	Unused	Used
95	A42	3c	**multicolored**	.60	.60
			Imprint block of 6	4.50	
96	A42	8c	**multicolored**	.90	.75
			Imprint block of 6	7.50	
			First day cover, #95-96		2.25

World Health Organization drive to eradicate malaria.

Dolls and Toys — A43

Linden or Sea Hibiscus — A44

1962, May 5 **Litho.** ***Perf. 13½***

No.	Type	Denom.	Description	Unused	Used
97	A43	3c	**red, black, blue & buff**	1.10	1.00
			First day cover		1.50
			Imprint block of 6	9.00	

Children's Day, 1962.

1962, June 1 **Photo.**

Flowers: 3c, Indian coral tree. 8c, Iju (Schima liukiuensis Nakal). 13c, Touch-me-not (garden balsam). 17c, Shell flower (Alpinia speciosa).

No.	Type	Denom.	Description	Unused	Used
98	A44	½c	**multicolored**	.20	.20
			Imprint block of 10	1.75	
99	A44	3c	**multicolored**	.35	.20
			Imprint block of 10	4.75	
100	A44	8c	**multicolored**	.50	.45
			Imprint block of 10	6.50	
101	A44	13c	**multicolored**	.70	.60
			Imprint block of 10	9.00	
102	A44	17c	**multicolored**	1.25	.80
			Imprint block of 10	15.00	
			First day cover, #98-102		3.75
			Nos. 98-102 (5)	3.00	2.25

See Nos. 107 and 114 for 1½c and 15c flower stamps. For surcharge see No. 190.

Earthenware A45

1962, July 5 ***Perf. 13½x13***

No.	Type	Denom.	Description	Unused	Used
103	A45	3c	**multicolored**	3.50	2.50
			First day cover		2.75
			Imprint block of 6	26.00	

Philatelic Week.

Japanese Fencing (Kendo) A46

1962, July 25 ***Perf. 13***

No.	Type	Denom.	Description	Unused	Used
104	A46	3c	**multicolored**	4.00	3.00
			First day cover		3.50
			Imprint block of 6	30.00	

All-Japan Kendo Meeting in Okinawa, July 25, 1962.

Rabbit Playing near Water, Bingata Cloth Design — A47

Young Man and Woman, Stone Relief — A48

1962, Dec. 10 *Perf. 13x13½*
105 A47 1½c **gold & multicolored** 1.00 .80
First day cover 1.50
Imprint block of 10 12.50

New Year, 1963.

1963, Jan. 15 **Photo.** *Perf. 13½*
106 A48 3c **gold, black & blue** .90 .80
First day cover 1.50
Imprint block of 6 6.75

Gooseneck Cactus — A49

Trees and Wooded Hills — A50

1963, Apr. 5 *Perf. 13x13½*
107 A49 1½c **dark blue green, yellow & pink** .20 .20
First day cover 1.25
Imprint block of 10 1.50

1963, Mar. 25 *Perf. 13½x13*
108 A50 3c **ultramarine, green & red brown** 1.00 .80
First day cover 1.25
Imprint block of 6 7.00

"Make the Ryukyus Green" movement.

Map of Okinawa — A51

Hawks over Islands — A52

1963, Apr. 30 **Unwmk.** *Perf. 13½*
109 A51 3c **multicolored** 1.25 1.00
First day cover 1.50
Imprint block of 6 9.00

Opening of the Round Road on Okinawa.

1963, May 10 **Photo.**
110 A52 3c **multicolored** 1.10 .95
First day cover 1.50
Imprint block of 6 9.00

Bird Day, May 10.

Shioya Bridge — A53

1963, June 5
111 A53 3c **multicolored** 1.10 .95
First day cover 1.40
Imprint block of 6 8.25

Opening of Shioya Bridge over Shioya Bay.

Tsuikin-wan Lacquerware Bowl — A54

1963, July 1 **Unwmk.** *Perf. 13½*
112 A54 3c **multicolored** 3.00 2.50
First day cover 2.75
Imprint block of 6 22.50

Map of Far East and JCI Emblem — A55

1963, Sept. 16 **Photo.** *Perf. 13½*
113 A55 3c **multicolored** .70 .70
First day cover 1.25
Imprint block of 6 6.00

Meeting of the International Junior Chamber of Commerce (JCI), Naha, Okinawa, Sept. 16-19.

Mamaomoto — A56

Site of Nakagusuku Castle — A57

1963, Oct. 15 *Perf. 13x13½*
114 A56 15c **multicolored** 2.00 .80
First day cover 1.25
Imprint block of 10 25.00

1963, Nov. 1 *Perf. 13½x13*
115 A57 3c **multicolored** .70 .60
First day cover 1.25
Imprint block of 6 5.25

Protection of national cultural treasures.

Flame — A58

Dragon (Bingata Pattern) — A59

1963, Dec. 10 *Perf. 13½*
116 A58 3c **red, dark blue & yellow** .70 .60
First day cover 1.25
Imprint block of 6 5.25

15th anniv. of the Universal Declaration of Human Rights.

1963, Dec. 10 **Photo.**
117 A59 1½c **multicolored** .60 .50
First day cover 1.50
Imprint block of 10 7.50

New Year, 1964.

Carnation — A60

Pineapples and Sugar Cane — A61

1964, May 10 *Perf. 13½*
118 A60 3c **blue, yellow, black & carmine** .40 .35
First day cover 1.25
Imprint block of 6 3.00

Mothers Day.

1964, June 1
119 A61 3c **multicolored** .40 .35
First day cover 1.25
Imprint block of 6 3.00

Agricultural census.

Minsah Obi (Sash Woven of Kapok) — A62

1964, July 1 **Unwmk.** *Perf. 13½*
120 A62 3c **deep blue, rose pink & ocher** .55 .50
First day cover 2.25
Imprint block of 6 4.50
a. 3c **deep blue, deep carmine & ocher** .70 .65
First day cover 2.75
Imprint block of 6 5.25

Philatelic Week.

Girl Scout and Emblem — A63

1964, Aug. 31 **Photo.**

121 A63 3c **multicolored** .40 .35
First day cover 1.25
Imprint block of 6 3.00

10th anniv. of Ryukyuan Girl Scouts.

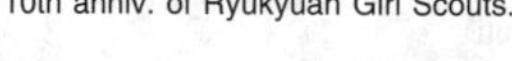

Shuri Relay Station — A64

Parabolic Antenna and Map — A65

1964, Sept. 1 **Unwmk.** ***Perf. 13½***

Black Overprint

122 A64 3c **deep green** .65 .65
Imprint block of 6 5.50
a. Figure "1" inverted 27.50 27.50
b. Overprint inverted *1,500.*
c. Overprint missing —
123 A65 8c **ultramarine** 1.25 1.25
Imprint block of 6 10.00
First day cover, #122-123 4.75
a. Overprint missing —

Opening of the Ryukyu Islands-Japan microwave system carrying telephone and telegraph messages. The overprints indicate the system was not actually opened until 1964.

Many of the stamps with overprint errors listed above are damaged. The values listed here are for stamps in very fine condition.

A number of different overprint shifts also exist with the shifts to greater and lesser degrees.

Gate of Courtesy, Olympic Torch and Emblem — A66

1964, Sept. 7 **Photo.** ***Perf. 13½x13***

124 A66 3c **ultramarine, yellow & red** .30 .20
First day cover (Sept. 7) 1.25
First day cover (Sept. 6 & 7) 25.00
Imprint block of 6 2.50

Relaying the Olympic torch on Okinawa en route to Tokyo.

Torch arrival was scheduled for Sept. 6. A typhoon delayed arrival until Sept. 7. A small number of covers received both Sept. 6 and 7 cancels.

"Naihanchi," Karate Stance — A67

"Makiwara," Strengthening Hands and Feet — A68

"Kumite," Simulated Combat — A69

1964-65 **Photo.** ***Perf. 13½***

125 A67 3c **dull claret, yel & blk,** *Oct. 5, 1964* .50 .45
First day cover 1.25
Imprint block of 6 3.25
126 A68 3c **yel & multi,** *Feb. 5, 1965* .40 .40
First day cover 1.25
Imprint block of 6 3.00
127 A69 3c **gray, red & blk,** *June 5, 1965* .40 .40
First day cover 1.25
Imprint block of 6 3.00
Nos. 125-127 (3) 1.30 1.25

Karate, Ryukyuan self-defense sport.

Miyara Dunchi — A70

Snake and Iris (Bingata) — A71

1964, Nov. 1 ***Perf. 13½***

128 A70 3c **multicolored** .30 .25
First day cover 1.25
Imprint block of 6 2.25

Protection of national cultural treasures. Miyara Dunchi was built as a residence by Miyara-pechin Toen in 1819.

1964, Dec. 10 **Photo.**

129 A71 1½c **multicolored** .30 .25
First day cover 2.00
Imprint block of 10 4.00

New Year, 1965.

Boy Scouts — A72

1965, Feb. 6 ***Perf. 13½***

130 A72 3c **light blue & multi** .45 .40
First day cover 1.50
Imprint block of 6 4.00

10th anniv. of Ryukyuan Boy Scouts.

Main Stadium, Onoyama A73

1965, July 1 ***Perf. 13x13½***

131 A73 3c **multicolored** .25 .25
First day cover 1.00
Imprint block of 6 2.00

Inauguration of the main stadium of the Onoyama athletic facilities.

Samisen of King Shoko — A74

1965, July 1 **Photo.** ***Perf. 13½***

132 A74 3c **buff & multicolored** .45 .40
First day cover 1.25
Imprint block of 6 3.25

Philatelic Week.

Kin Power Plant — A75

ICY Emblem, Ryukyu Map — A76

1965, July 1

133 A75 3c **green & multicolored** .25 .25
First day cover 1.00
Imprint block of 6 2.00

Completion of Kin power plant.

1965, Aug. 24 **Photo.** ***Perf. 13½***

134 A76 3c **multicolored** .20 .20
First day cover 1.00
Imprint block of 6 1.75

20th anniv. of the UN and International Cooperation Year, 1964-65.

Naha City Hall — A77

1965, Sept. 18 **Unwmk.** ***Perf. 13½***

135 A77 3c **blue & multicolored** .20 .20
First day cover 1.00
Imprint block of 6 1.75

Completion of Naha City Hall.

Chinese Box Turtle — A78

Horse (Bingata) — A79

Turtles: No. 137, Hawksbill turtle (denomination at top, country name at bottom). No. 138, Asian terrapin (denomination and country name on top).

1965-66 Photo. *Perf. 13½*

136 A78 3c **golden brown & multi,** *Oct. 20, 1965* .30 .30
First day cover 1.00
Imprint block of 6 2.50
137 A78 3c **black, yel & brown,** *Jan. 20, 1966* .30 .30
First day cover 1.00
Imprint block of 6 2.50
138 A78 3c **gray & multicolored,** *Apr. 20, 1966* .30 .30
First day cover 1.00
Imprint block of 6 2.50
Nos. 136-138 (3) .90 .90

1965, Dec. 10 Photo. *Perf. 13½*

139 A79 1½c **multicolored** .20 .20
First day cover 1.50
Imprint block of 10 2.25
a. Gold omitted *1,200.* —

New Year, 1966.

There are 92 unused and 2 used examples of No. 139a known.

NATURE CONSERVATION ISSUE

Noguchi's Okinawa Woodpecker — A80

Sika Deer — A81

Design: No. 142, Dugong.

1966 Photo. *Perf. 13½*

140 A80 3c **blue green & multi,** *Feb. 15* .20 .20
First day cover 1.00
Imprint block of 6 1.65
141 A81 3c **blue, red, black, brown & green,** *Mar. 15* .25 .25
First day cover 1.00
Imprint block of 6 1.75
142 A81 3c **blue, yellow green, black & red,** *Apr. 20* .25 .25
First day cover 1.00
Imprint block of 6 1.75
Nos. 140-142 (3) .70 .70

Ryukyu Bungalow Swallow — A82

1966, May 10 Photo. *Perf. 13½*

143 A82 3c **sky blue, black & brown** .20 .20
First day cover 1.00
Imprint block of 6 1.10

4th Bird Week, May 10-16.

Lilies and Ruins A83

1966, June 23 *Perf. 13x13½*

144 A83 3c **multicolored** .20 .20
First day cover 1.00
Imprint block of 6 1.00

Memorial Day, end of the Battle of Okinawa, June 23, 1945.

University of the Ryukyus A84

1966, July 1

145 A84 3c **multicolored** .20 .20
First day cover 1.00
Imprint block of 6 1.00

Transfer of the University of the Ryukyus from U.S. authority to the Ryukyu Government.

Lacquerware, 18th Century — A85

Tile-Roofed House and UNESCO Emblem — A86

1966, Aug. 1 *Perf. 13½*

146 A85 3c **gray & multicolored** .20 .20
First day cover 1.50
Imprint block of 6 1.30

Philatelic Week.

1966, Sept. 20 Photo. *Perf. 13½*

147 A86 3c **multicolored** .20 .20
First day cover 1.00
Imprint block of 6 1.10

20th anniv. of UNESCO.

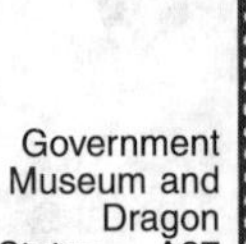

Government Museum and Dragon Statue — A87

1966, Oct. 6

148 A87 3c **multicolored** .20 .20
First day cover 1.00
Imprint block of 6 1.00

Completion of the GRI (Government of the Ryukyu Islands) Museum, Shuri.

Tomb of Nakasone-Tuimya Genga, Ruler of Miyako — A88

1966, Nov. 1 Photo. *Perf. 13½*

149 A88 3c **multicolored** .20 .20
First day cover 1.00
Imprint block of 6 1.00

Protection of national cultural treasures.

Ram in Iris Wreath — A89

Clown Fish — A90

1966, Dec. 10 Photo. *Perf. 13½*

150 A89 1½c **dark blue & multicolored** .20 .20
First day cover 1.50
Imprint block of 10 1.10

New Year, 1967.

1966-67

Fish: No. 152, Young boxfish (white numeral at lower left). No. 153, Forceps fish (pale buff numeral at lower right). No. 154, Spotted triggerfish (orange numeral). No. 155, Saddleback butterflyfish (carmine numeral, lower left).

151 A90 3c **orange red & multi,** *Dec. 20, 1966* .20 .20
First day cover 1.00
Imprint block of 6 1.75
152 A90 3c **orange yellow & multi,** *Jan. 10, 1967* .25 .20
First day cover 1.00
Imprint block of 6 1.75
153 A90 3c **multicolored,** *Apr. 10, 1967* .40 .25
First day cover 1.00
Imprint block of 6 2.75
154 A90 3c **multicolored,** *May 25, 1967* .35 .25
First day cover 1.00
Imprint block of 6 2.25
155 A90 3c **multicolored,** *June 10, 1967* .30 .25
First day cover 1.00
Imprint block of 6 1.90
Nos. 151-155 (5) 1.50 1.15

A 3-cent stamp to commemorate Japanese-American-Ryukyuan Joint Arbor Day was scheduled for release on March 16, 1967. However, it was not released. The stamp in light blue and white features American and Japanese flags joined by a shield containing a tree.

Tsuboya Urn — A91

Episcopal Miter — A92

1967, Apr. 20

156 A91 3c **yellow & multicolored** .20 .20
First day cover 1.25
Imprint block of 6 1.65

Philatelic Week.

1967-68 Photo. *Perf. 13½*

Seashells: No. 158, Venus comb murex. No. 159, Chiragra spider. No. 160, Green truban. No. 161, Euprotomus bulla.

157 A92 3c **light green & multi,** *July 20, 1967* .20 .20
First day cover 1.00
Imprint block of 6 1.25
158 A92 3c **greenish blue & multi,** *Aug. 30, 1968* .25 .20
First day cover 1.00
Imprint block of 6 1.75
159 A92 3c **emerald & multi,** *Jan. 18, 1968* .25 .20
First day cover 1.00
Imprint block of 6 1.65
160 A92 3c **light blue & multi,** *Feb. 20, 1968* .30 .25
First day cover 1.00
Imprint block of 6 1.65
161 A92 3c **bright blue & multi,** *June 5, 1968* .60 .50
First day cover 1.00
Imprint block of 6 4.00
Nos. 157-161 (5) 1.60 1.35

Red-tiled Roofs and ITY Emblem — A93

1967, Sept. 11 Photo. *Perf. 13½*

162 A93 3c **multicolored** .20 .20
First day cover 1.00
Imprint block of 6 1.25

International Tourist Year.

Mobile TB Clinic — A94

1967, Oct. 13 Photo. *Perf. 13½*

163 A94 3c **lilac & multicolored** .20 .20
First day cover 1.00
Imprint block of 6 1.25

15th anniv. of the Anti-Tuberculosis Society.

Hojo Bridge, Enkaku Temple, 1498 — A95

1967, Nov. 1

164 A95 3c **blue green & multicolored** .20 .20
First day cover 1.00
Imprint block of 6 1.50

Protection of national cultural treasures.

Monkey (Bingata) — A96

TV Tower and Map — A97

1967, Dec. 11 Photo. *Perf. 13½*

165 A96 1½c **silver & multicolored** .25 .20
First day cover 1.50
Imprint block of 10 3.00

New Year, 1968.

1967, Dec. 22

166 A97 3c **multicolored** .25 .25
First day cover 1.00
Imprint block of 6 1.50

Opening of Miyako and Yaeyama television stations.

Dr. Kijin Nakachi and Helper — A98

Pill Box (Inro) — A99

1968, Mar. 15 Photo. *Perf. 13½*

167 A98 3c **multicolored** .30 .25
First day cover 1.00
Imprint block of 6 1.75

120th anniv. of the first vaccination in the Ryukyu Islands, by Dr. Kijin Nakachi.

1968, Apr. 18

168 A99 3c **gray & multicolored** .45 .45
First day cover 1.25
Imprint block of 6 3.50

Philatelic Week.

Young Man, Library, Book and Map of Ryukyu Islands — A100

1968, May 13

169 A100 3c **multicolored** .30 .25
First day cover 1.00
Imprint block of 6 1.75

10th International Library Week.

Mailmen's Uniforms and Stamp of 1948 A101

1968, July 1 Photo. *Perf. 13x13½*

170 A101 3c **multicolored** .30 .25
First day cover 1.00
Imprint block of 6 1.75

First Ryukyuan postage stamps, 20th anniv.

Main Gate, Enkaku Temple — A102

1968, July 15 Photo. & Engr. *Perf. 13½*

171 A102 3c **multicolored** .30 .25
First day cover 1.00
Imprint block of 6 1.75

Restoration of the main gate Enkaku Temple, built 1492-1495, destroyed during World War II.

Old Man's Dance — A103

Mictyris Longicarpus — A104

1968, Sept. 15 Photo. *Perf. 13½*

172 A103 3c **gold & multicolored** .30 .25
First day cover 1.00
Imprint block of 6 2.00

Old People's Day.

1968-69 Photo. *Perf. 13½*

Crabs: No. 174, Uca dubia stimpson. No. 175, Baptozius vinosus. No. 176, Cardisoma carnifex. No. 177, Ocypode ceratophthalma pallas.

173 A104 3c **blue, ocher & black,** *Oct. 10, 1968* .30 .25
First day cover 1.25
Imprint block of 6 2.50
174 A104 3c **light blue green & multi,** *Feb. 5, 1969* .35 .30
First day cover 1.25
Imprint block of 6 2.75
175 A104 3c **light green & multi,** *Mar. 5, 1969* .35 .30
First day cover 1.25
Imprint block of 6 2.75
176 A104 3c **light ultra & multi,** *May 15, 1969* .45 .40
First day cover 1.25
Imprint block of 6 3.25
177 A104 3c **light ultra & multi,** *June 2, 1969* .45 .40
First day cover 1.25
Imprint block of 6 3.25
Nos. 173-177 (5) 1.90 1.65

Saraswati Pavilion — A105

1968, Nov. 1 **Photo.** ***Perf. 13½***

178 A105 3c **multicolored** .30 .25
First day cover 1.00
Imprint block of 6 2.00

Restoration of the Sarawati Pavilion (in front of Enkaku Temple), destroyed during World War II.

Tennis Player — A106

Cock and Iris (Bingata) — A107

1968, Nov. 3 **Photo.** ***Perf. 13½***

179 A106 3c **green & multicolored** .40 .35
First day cover 1.00
Imprint block of 6 3.25

35th All-Japan East-West Men's Soft-ball Tennis Tournament, Naha City, Nov. 23-24.

1968, Dec. 10

180 A107 1½c **orange & multicolored** .25 .20
First day cover 1.50
Imprint block of 10 3.50

New Year, 1969.

Boxer — A108

Ink Slab Screen — A109

1969, Jan. 3

181 A108 3c **gray & multicolored** .40 .30
First day cover 1.00
Imprint block of 6 2.75

20th All-Japan Amateur Boxing Championships held at the University of the Ryukyus, Jan. 3-5.

1969, Apr. 17 **Photo.** ***Perf. 13½***

182 A109 3c **salmon, indigo & red** .40 .35
First day cover 1.50
Imprint block of 6 2.75

Philatelic Week.

Box Antennas and Map of Radio Link — A110

Gate of Courtesy and Emblems — A111

1969, July 1 **Photo.** ***Perf. 13½***

183 A110 3c **multicolored** .25 .20
First day cover 1.00
Imprint block of 6 1.75

Opening of the UHF (radio) circuit system between Okinawa and the outlying Miyako-Yaeyama Islands.

1969, Aug. 1 **Photo.** ***Perf. 13½***

184 A111 3c **Prussian blue, gold & vermilion** .25 .20
First day cover 1.00
Imprint block of 6 1.75

22nd All-Japan Formative Education Study Conf., Naha, Aug. 1-3.

FOLKLORE ISSUE

Tug of War Festival A112

Hari Boat Race A113

Izaiho Ceremony, Kudaka Island A114

Mortardrum Dance A115

Sea God Dance A116

1969-70 **Photo.** ***Perf. 13***

185 A112 3c **multicolored,** *Aug. 1, 1969* .30 .25
First day cover 1.50
Imprint block of 6 2.00

186 A113 3c **multicolored,** *Sept. 5, 1969* .35 .30
First day cover 1.50
Imprint block of 6 2.25

187 A114 3c **multicolored,** *Oct. 3, 1969* .35 .30
First day cover 1.50
Imprint block of 6 2.25

188 A115 3c **multicolored,** *Jan. 20, 1970* .50 .45
First day cover 1.50
Imprint block of 6 3.50

189 A116 3c **multicolored,** *Feb. 27, 1970* .50 .45
First day cover 1.50
Imprint block of 6 3.50
Nos. 185-189 (5) 2.00 1.75

No. 99 Surcharged

1969, Oct. 15 **Photo.** ***Perf. 13½***

190 A44 ½c on 3c **multicolored** 1.00 1.00
First day cover 3.00
Imprint block of 10 13.50

Nakamura-ke Farm House, Built 1713-51 — A117

1969, Nov. 1 **Photo.** ***Perf. 13½***

191 A117 3c **multicolored** .20 .20
First day cover 1.00
Imprint block of 6 1.50

Protection of national cultural treasures.

Statue of Kyuzo Toyama, Maps of Hawaiian and Ryukyu Islands — A118

1969, Dec. 5 **Photo.** ***Perf. 13½***

192 A118 3c **light ultra & multi** .40 .40
First day cover 1.50
Imprint block of 6 2.75
a. Without overprint *2,500.*
b. Wide-spaced bars *725.00*

70th anniv. of Ryukyu-Hawaii emigration led by Kyuzo Toyama.

The overprint "1969" at lower left and bars across "1970" at upper right was applied before No. 192 was issued.

Dog and Flowers (Bingata) — A119

Sake Flask Made from Coconut — A120

1969, Dec. 10

193 A119 1½c **pink & multicolored** .20 .20
First day cover 1.50
Imprint block of 10 2.75

New Year, 1970.

1970, Apr. 15 **Photo.** ***Perf. 13½***

194 A120 3c **multicolored** .25 .25
First day cover 1.25
Imprint block of 6 1.75

Philatelic Week, 1970.

CLASSIC OPERA ISSUE

"The Bell" (Shushin Kaneiri) — A121

Child and Kidnapper (Chunusudu) A122

Robe of Feathers (Mekarushi) A123

Vengeance of Two Young Sons (Nidotichiuchi) A124

The Virgin and the Dragon (Kokonomaki) A125

1970 **Photo.** ***Perf. 13½***

195 A121 3c **dull blue & multi,** *Apr. 28* .40 .40
First day cover 1.75
Imprint block of 6 3.00
a. Souvenir sheet of 4 5.00 5.00
First day cover 5.00
196 A122 3c **light blue & multi,** *May 29* .40 .40
First day cover 1.75
Imprint block of 6 3.00
a. Souvenir sheet of 4 5.00 5.00
First day cover 5.00
197 A123 3c **bluish green & multi,** *June 30* .40 .40
First day cover 1.75
Imprint block of 6 3.00
a. Souvenir sheet of 4 5.00 5.00
First day cover 5.00
198 A124 3c **dull blue green & multi,** *July 30* .40 .40
First day cover 1.75
Imprint block of 6 3.00
a. Souvenir sheet of 4 5.00 5.00
First day cover 5.00
199 A125 3c **multicolored,** *Aug. 25* .40 .40
First day cover 1.75
Imprint block of 6 3.00
a. Souvenir sheet of 4 5.00 5.00
First day cover 5.00
Nos. 195-199 (5) 2.00 2.00
Nos. 195a-199a (5) 25.00 *25.00*

Underwater Observatory and Tropical Fish — A126

1970, May 22

200 A126 3c **blue green & multi** .30 .25
First day cover 1.25
Imprint block of 6 2.00

Completion of the underwater observatory of Busena-Misaki, Nago.

Noboru Jahana (1865-1908), Politician — A127

Great Cycad of Une — A129

Map of Okinawa and People — A128

Portraits: No. 202, Saion Gushichan Bunjaku (1682-1761), statesman. No. 203, Choho Giwan (1823-1876), regent and poet.

1970-71 **Engr.** ***Perf. 13½***

201 A127 3c **rose claret,** *Sept. 25, 1970* .50 .45
First day cover 2.50
Imprint block of 6 3.50
202 A127 3c **dull blue green,** *Dec. 22, 1970* .75 .65
First day cover 2.50
Imprint block of 6 6.00
203 A127 3c **black,** *Jan. 22, 1971* .50 .45
First day cover 2.50
Imprint block of 6 3.50

1970, Oct. 1 **Photo.**

204 A128 3c **red & multicolored** .25 .25
First day cover 1.00
Imprint block of 6 1.75

Oct. 1, 1970 census.

1970, Nov. 2 **Photo.** ***Perf. 13½***

205 A129 3c **gold & multicolored** .25 .25
First day cover 1.00
Imprint block of 6 1.75

Protection of national treasures.

Japanese Flag, Diet and Map of Ryukyus — A130

Wild Boar and Cherry Blossoms (Bingata) — A131

1970, Nov. 15 **Photo.** ***Perf. 13½***

206 A130 3c **ultramarine & multicolored** .80 .75
First day cover 2.00
Imprint block of 6 6.00

Citizen's participation in national administration to Japanese law of Apr. 24, 1970.

1970, Dec. 10

207 A131 1½c **multicolored** .20 .20
First day cover 1.50
Imprint block of 10 2.40

New Year, 1971.

Low Hand Loom (Jibata) — A132

Farmer Wearing Palm Bark Raincoat and Kuba Leaf Hat — A133

Fisherman's Wooden Box and Scoop — A134

Designs: No. 209, Woman running a filature (reel). No. 211, Woman hulling rice with cylindrical "Shiri-ushi."

1971 **Photo.** ***Perf. 13½***

208 A132 3c **light blue & multi,** *Feb. 16* .30 .25
First day cover 1.25
Imprint block of 6 2.00
209 A132 3c **pale green & multi,** *Mar. 16* .30 .25
First day cover 1.25
Imprint block of 6 2.00
210 A133 3c **light blue & multi,** *Apr. 30* .35 .30
First day cover 1.25
Imprint block of 6 2.25
211 A132 3c **yellow & multi,** *May 20* .40 .35
First day cover 1.25
Imprint block of 6 3.00
212 A134 3c **gray & multi,** *June 15* .35 .30
First day cover 1.25
Imprint block of 6 2.25
Nos. 208-212 (5) 1.70 1.45

Water Carrier (Taku) — A135

1971, Apr. 15 **Photo.** ***Perf. 13½***

213 A135 3c **blue green & multicolored** .35 .30
First day cover 1.50
Imprint block of 6 2.75

Philatelic Week, 1971.

Old and New Naha, and City Emblem A136

1971, May 20 ***Perf. 13***

214 A136 3c **ultramarine & multicolored** .25 .20
First day cover 1.00
Imprint block of 6 1.75

50th anniv. of Naha as a municipality.

Caesalpinia Pulcherrima — A137

Design: 2c, Madder (Sandanka).

1971 **Photo.** ***Perf. 13***

215	A137	2c **gray & multicolored,** *Sept. 30*	.20	.20
		First day cover		1.00
		Imprint block of 10	2.50	
216	A137	3c **gray & multicolored,** *May 10*	.20	.20
		First day cover		1.00
		Imprint block of 10	2.50	

GOVERNMENT PARK SERIES

View from Mabuni Hill — A138

Mt. Arashi from Haneji Sea — A139

Yabuchi Island from Yakena Port — A140

1971-72

217	A138	3c **green & multi,** *July 30, 1971*	.20	.20
		First day cover		1.25
		Imprint block of 6	1.50	
218	A139	3c **blue & multi,** *Aug. 30, 1971*	.20	.20
		First day cover		1.25
		Imprint block of 6	1.50	
219	A140	4c **multicolored,** *Jan. 20, 1972*	.25	.20
		First day cover		1.25
		Imprint block of 6	1.75	
		Nos. 217-219 (3)	.65	.60

For the 4-cent unissued "stamp" picturing Iriomote Park, originally planned for issue in 1971 but never released, see the note after No. R31.

Dancer — A141

Deva King, Torinji Temple — A142

1971, Nov. 1 **Photo.** ***Perf. 13***

220	A141	4c **Prussian blue & multicolored**	.20	.20
		First day cover		1.00
		Imprint block of 10	2.50	

1971, Dec. 1

221	A142	4c **deep blue & multicolored**	.20	.20
		First day cover		1.00
		Imprint block of 6	1.50	

Protection of national cultural treasures.

Rat and Chrysanthemums A143

Student Nurse A144

1971, Dec. 10

222	A143	2c **brown orange & multi**	.20	.20
		First day cover		1.50
		Imprint block of 10	2.50	

New Year, 1972.

1971, Dec. 24

223	A144	4c **lilac & multicolored**	.20	.20
		First day cover		1.00
		Imprint block of 6	1.50	

Nurses' training, 25th anniversary.

A145

A147

Coral Reef — A146

1972 **Photo.** ***Perf. 13***

224	A145	5c **bright blue & multi,** *Apr. 14*	.40	.35
		First day cover		1.25
		Imprint block of 6	2.75	
225	A146	5c **gray & multi,** *Mar. 30*	.40	.35
		First day cover		1.25
		Imprint block of 6	2.75	
226	A147	5c **ocher & multi,** *Mar. 21*	.40	.35
		First day cover		1.25
		Imprint block of 6	2.75	
		Nos. 224-226 (3)	1.20	1.05

Dove, U.S. and Japanese Flags — A148

1972, Apr. 17 **Photo.** ***Perf. 13***

227	A148	5c **bright blue & multi**	.80	.80
		First day cover		1.50
		Imprint block of 6	5.50	

Antique Sake Pot (Yushibin) — A149

1972, Apr. 20

228	A149	5c **ultramarine & multicolored**	.60	.60
		First day cover		1.25
		Imprint block of 6	4.50	

Ryukyu stamps were replaced by those of Japan after May 15, 1972.

AIR POST

Catalogue values for all unused stamps in this section are for Never Hinged items.

Dove and Map of Ryukyus — AP1

1950, Feb. 15 **Photo.** **Unwmk.** ***Perf. 13x13½***

C1	AP1	8y **bright blue**	150.00	60.00
		First day cover		35.00
		Imprint block of 6	1,250.	
C2	AP1	12y **green**	35.00	30.00
		First day cover		35.00
		Imprint block of 6	275.00	
C3	AP1	16y **rose carmine**	20.00	15.00
		First day cover		35.00
		Imprint block of 6	125.00	
		First day cover, #C1-C3		200.00
		Nos. C1-C3 (3)	205.00	105.00

Heavenly Maiden AP2

1951-54

C4	AP2	13y **blue,** *Oct. 1, 1951*	3.00	1.50
		First day cover		60.00
		Imprint block of 6, 5-character	225.00	
		Imprint block of 6, 8-character	37.50	
C5	AP2	18y **green,** *Oct. 1, 1951*	4.00	2.25
		First day cover		60.00
		Imprint block of 6, 5-character	55.00	
		Imprint block of 6, 8-character	45.00	
C6	AP2	30y **cerise,** *Oct. 1, 1951*	6.00	1.75
		First day cover		60.00
		First day cover, #C4-C6		250.00
		Imprint block of 6, 5-character	70.00	
		Imprint block of 6, 8-character	150.00	
C7	AP2	40y **red violet,** *Aug. 16, 1954*	8.00	5.50
		First day cover		35.00
		Imprint block of 6	90.00	
C8	AP2	50y **yellow orange,** *Aug. 16, 1954*	9.00	6.50
		First day cover		35.00
		Imprint block of 6	100.00	
		First day cover, #C7-C8		125.00
		Nos. C4-C8 (5)	30.00	17.50

Heavenly Maiden Playing Flute — AP3

1957, Aug. 1 **Engr.** ***Perf. 13½***

C9 AP3 15y **blue green** 9.00 3.50
Imprint block of 6 65.00
C10 AP3 20y **rose carmine** 15.00 5.50
Imprint block of 6 100.00
C11 AP3 35y **yellow green** 17.00 6.50
Imprint block of 6 130.00
a. 35y **light yellow green,** *1958* *150.00*
C12 AP3 45y **reddish brown** 20.00 8.00
Imprint block of 6 150.00
C13 AP3 60y **gray** 24.00 10.00
Imprint block of 6 210.00
First day cover, #C9-C13 45.00
Nos. C9-C13 (5) 85.00 33.50

On one printing of No. C10, position 49 shows an added spur on the right side of the second character from the left. Value unused, $150.

Same Surcharged in Brown Red or Light Ultramarine

1959, Dec. 20

C14 AP3 9c on 15y **blue green** (BrR) 3.00 1.50
Imprint block of 6 22.50
a. Inverted surcharge *950.00*
Imprint block of 6 *6,750.*
a. Pair, one without surcharge —
C15 AP3 14c on 20y **rose carmine** (L.U.) 4.00 3.00
Imprint block of 6 30.00
C16 AP3 19c on 35y **light yellow green** (BrR) 8.00 5.00
Imprint block of 6 57.50
C17 AP3 27c on 45y **reddish brown** (L.U.) 19.00 6.00
Imprint block of 6 150.00
C18 AP3 35c on 60y **gray** (BrR) 16.00 9.00
Imprint block of 6 125.00
First day cover, #C14-C18 35.00
Nos. C14-C18 (5) 50.00 24.50

No. C15 is found with the variety described below No. C13. Value unused, $100.

Nos. 31-33, 36 and 38 Surcharged in Black, Brown, Red, Blue or Green

1960, Aug. 3 **Photo.** ***Perf. 13***

C19 A14 9c on 4y **brown** 4.00 1.00
Imprint block of 10 50.00
a. Surcharge inverted and transposed *15,000.* *15,000.*
b. Inverted surcharge (legend only) *12,000.*
c. Surcharge transposed *1,500.*
d. Legend of surcharge only *4,000.*
e. Vert. pair, one without surcharge —

Nos. C19c and C19d are from a single sheet of 100 with surcharge shifted downward. Ten examples of No. C19c exist with "9c" also in bottom selvage. No. C19d is from the top row of the sheet.

No. C19e is unique, pos. 100, caused by paper foldover.

C20 A17 14c on 5y **rose lilac** (Br) 5.00 2.25
Imprint block of 10 65.00
C21 A14 19c on 15y **vermilion** (R) 3.50 2.00
Imprint block of 10 45.00
C22 A17 27c on 14y **reddish brown** (Bl) 10.50 2.75
Imprint block of 10 150.00
C23 A14 35c on 20y **yellow orange** (G) 7.50 4.50
Imprint block of 10 90.00
First day cover, #C19-C23 25.00
Nos. C19-C23 (5) 30.50 12.50

Wind God — AP4

Designs: 9c, Heavenly Maiden (as on AP2). 14c, Heavenly Maiden (as on AP3). 27c, Wind God at right. 35c, Heavenly Maiden over treetops.

1961, Sept. 21 **Unwmk.** ***Perf. 13½***

C24 AP4 9c **multicolored** .30 .20
Imprint block of 6 2.25
C25 AP4 14c **multicolored** .80 .60
Imprint block of 6 6.00
C26 AP4 19c **multicolored** .90 .70
Imprint block of 6 6.50
C27 AP4 27c **multicolored** 3.50 .60
Imprint block of 6 27.50
C28 AP4 35c **multicolored** 2.50 1.25
Imprint block of 6 20.00
First day cover, #C24-C28 35.00
Nos. C24-C28 (5) 8.00 3.35

AP5

AP6

1963, Aug. 28 ***Perf. 13x13½***

C29 AP5 5½c **multicolored** .25 .25
First day cover 1.00
Imprint block of 10 3.00
C30 AP6 7c **multicolored** .30 .30
First day cover 1.00
First day cover, #C29-C30 2.50
Imprint block of 10 3.50

SPECIAL DELIVERY

Catalogue value for the unused stamp in this section is for a Never Hinged item.

Sea Horse and Map of Ryukyus — SD1

1950, Feb. 15 **Unwmk.** **Photo.** ***Perf. 13x13½***

E1 SD1 5y **bright blue** 35.00 20.00
First day cover 100.00
Imprint block of 6 350.00

QUANTITIES ISSUED

Regular Postage and Commemorative Stamps

Cat. No.	*Quantity*	*Cat. No.*	*Quantity*
1	90,214	*87*	3,019,000
2	55,901	*88*	298,966
3	94,663	*89*	298,966
4	55,413	*90*	398,901
5	76,387	*91*	398,992
6	117,321	*92*	1,498,970
7	291,403	*93*	598,989
1a	61,000	*94*	398,998
2a-4a	181,000	*95*	398,993
5a	29,936	*96*	298,993
6a	99,300	*97*	398,997
7a	46,000	*98*	9,699,000
8	2,559,000	*99*	10,991,500
8a	300,000	*100*	1,549,000
9	1,198,989	*101*	799,000
10	589,000	*102*	1,299,000
11	479,000	*103*	398,995
12	598,999	*104*	298,892
13	397,855	*105*	1,598,949
14	499,000	*106*	348,989
15	498,960	*107*	10,099,000
16	199,197	*108*	348,865
16A	199,900	*109*	348,937
16B	39,900	*110*	348,962
17	9,800	*111*	348,974
18	299,500	*112*	398,974

Cat. No.	*Quantity*	*Cat. No.*	*Quantity*
19	3,014,427	*113*	398,911
20	3,141,777	*114*	1,199,000
21	2,970,827	*115*	398,948
22	191,917	*116*	398,943
23	1,118,617	*117*	1,698,912
24	276,218	*118*	550,000
24a	ca. 1,300	*119*	549,000
25	231,717	*120*	749,000
26	220,130	*121*	799,000
27	398,993	*122*	389,000
28	386,421	*123*	319,000
29	498,854	*124*	1,999,000
30	298,994	*125-127*	999,000
31	4,768,413	*128*	799,000
32	1,202,297	*129*	1,699,000
33	500,059	*130-131*	799,000
34	298,994	*132*	849,000
35	199,000	*133*	799,000
36	455,896	*134*	1,299,000
37	160,518	*135*	1,099,000
38	198,720	*136*	1,299,000
39	198,199	*137-138*	1,598,000
40	599,000	*139*	3,098,000
41	598,075	*140-142*	1,598,000
42	1,198,179	*143-148*	2,498,000
43	1,625,406	*149*	2,298,000
44	994,880	*150*	3,798,000
45	997,759	*151*	2,298,000
46	996,759	*152-156*	1,998,000
47	2,705,955	*157-158*	1,698,000
48	997,542	*159-160*	1,298,000
49	996,609	*161*	898,000
50	996,928	*162*	1,498,000
51	499,000	*163-164*	1,298,000
52	249,000	*165*	3,998,000
52a	78,415	*166-167*	1,298,000
53	248,700	*168*	998,000
54	1,498,991	*169-179*	898,000
55	2,498,897	*180*	3,198,000
56	1,098,972	*181-189*	898,000
57	998,918	*190*	1,773,050
58	2,699,000	*191*	898,000
59	2,499,000	*192*	864,960
60	199,000	*193*	3,198,000
61	499,000	*194*	898,000
62	199,000	*195-199*	598,000
63	1,498,931	*195a-199a*	124,500
64	798,953	*200-206*	898,000
65-68	999,000	*207*	3,198,000
72	598,912	*208-210*	1,098,000
73	398,990	*211-212*	1,298,000
74	598,936	*213*	1,098,000
75	1,998,992	*214*	1,298,000
76	1,000,000	*215-216*	4,998,000
77	2,000,000	*217*	1,498,000
78	500,000	*218-219*	1,798,000
79-80	400,000	*220*	2,998,000
81	12,599,000	*221*	1,798,000
82	11,979,000	*222*	4,998,000
83	6,850,000	*223*	1,798,000
84	5,099,000	*224-226*	2,498,000
84A	1,699,000	*227*	2,998,000
85	4,749,000	*228*	3,998,000
86	2,099,000		

AIR POST STAMPS

Cat. No.	*Quantity*	*Cat. No.*	*Quantity*
C1-C3	198,000	*C18*	96,650
C4	1,952,348	*C19*	1,033,900
C5	331,360	*C19a*	100
C6	762,530	*C20*	230,000
C7	76,166	*C21*	185,000
C8	122,816	*C22*	191,000
C9	708,319	*C23*	190,000
C10	108,824	*C24*	17,199,000
C11	164,147	*C25*	1,999,000
C12	50,335	*C26*	1,250,000
C13	69,092	*C27*	3,499,000
C14	597,103	*C28*	1,699,000
C15	77,951	*C29*	1,199,000
C16	97,635	*C30*	1,949,000
C17	98,353		

SPECIAL DELIVERY STAMP

Cat. No.	*Quantity*
E1	198,804

PROVISIONAL ISSUES

Stamps of Japan Overprinted by Postmasters in Four Island Districts

Trading Ship — A82

Rice Harvest — A83

Gen. Maresuke Nogi — A84

Admiral Heihachiro Togo — A86

War Worker & Planes — A147

Palms and Map of "Greater East Asia" — A148

Garambi Lighthouse, Taiwan — A88

Meiji Shrine, Tokyo — A90

Aviator Saluting & Japanese Flag — A150

Torii of Yasukuni Shrine — A151

Plane and Map of Japan — A92

Kasuga Shrine, Nara — A93

Mt. Fuji and Cherry Blossoms — A152

Torii of Miyajima — A153

Mount Fuji and Cherry Blossoms — A94

Horyu Temple, Nara — A95

Garambi Lighthouse, Taiwan — A154

Sun & Cherry Blossoms — A161

Miyajima Torii, Itsukushima Shrine — A96

Golden Pavilion, Kyoto — A97

Sunrise at Sea & Plane — A162

Coal Miners — A163

Great Budda, Kamakura — A98

Kamatari Fujiwara — A99

Yasukuni Shrine — A164

"Thunderstorm below Fuji," by Hokusai — A167

War Factory Girl — A144

Hyuga Monument & Mt. Fuji — A146

KUME ISLAND

Values are for unused stamps. Used copies sell for considerably more, should be expertized and are preferred on cover or document.

A1

Mimeographed
Seal Handstamped in Vermilion

1945, Oct. 1 Without Gum Unwmk. ***Imperf.***

1X1 A1 7s **black,** *cream (2,400)* 1,750. —
On cover —
a. "7" & "SEN" one letter space to left 2,500.

Printed on legal-size U.S. military mimeograph paper and validated by the official seal of the Kume Island postmaster, Norifume Kikuzato. Valid until May 4, 1946.

Cancellations "20.10.1" (Oct. 1, 1945) or "20.10.6" (Oct. 6, 1945) are by favor. See proofs section for copies on white watermarked U.S. official bond paper.

AMAMI DISTRICT

Inspection Seal ("Ken," abbreviation for *kensa zumi,* inspected or examined; five types)

Stamps of Japan 1937-46 Handstamped in Black, Blue, Purple, Vermilion or Red

Typographed, Lithographed, Engraved

1947-48 Wmk. 257 ***Perf. 13, Imperf***

2X1 A82 ½s **purple,** #257 800.
2X2 A83 1s **fawn,** #258 —
2X3 A144 1s **orange brown,** #325 *1,750.*
2X4 A84 2s **crimson,** #259 600.
a. 2s **vermilion,** #259c —
2X5 A84 2s **rose red,** imperf., #351 2,000.
2X6 A85 3s **green,** #260 *1,700.*
2X7 A84 3s **brown,** #329 —
2X8 A161 3s **rose carmine,** imperf., #352 *1,800.*
2X9 A146 4s **emerald,** #330 650.
2X10 A86 5s **brown lake,** #331 700.
2X11 A162 5s **green,** imperf., #353 *1,500.*
2X12 A147 6s **light ultramarine,** #332 —
2X13 A86 7s **orange vermilion,** #333 *1,250.*
2X14 A90 8s **dark purple & pale violet,** #265 *1,500.*
2X15 A148 10s **crimson & dull rose,** #344 550.
2X16 A152 10s **red orange,** imperf., #355 *(48)* *2,500.*
2X17 A93 14s **rose lake & pale rose,** #268 —
2X18 A150 15s **dull blue,** #336 550.
2X19 A151 17s **gray violet,** #337 *1,750.*
2X20 A94 20s **ultramarine,** #269 *1,750.*
2X21 A152 20s **blue,** #338 600.
2X22 A152 20s **ultramarine,** imperf., #356 *(48)* *1,750.*
2X23 A95 25s **dark brown & pale brown,** #270 900.
2X24 A151 27s **rose brown,** #339 —
2X25 A153 30s **bluish green,** #340 —
2X26 A153 30s **bright blue,** imperf., #357 *2,000.*
2X27 A88 40s **dull violet,** #341 *1,750.*
2X28 A154 40s **dark violet,** #342 *1,750.*
2X29 A97 50s **olive & pale olive,** #272 —
2X30 A163 50s **dark brown,** imperf., #358 *(48)* *2,000.*
2X31 A164 1y **deep olive green,** imperf., #359 *2,500.*
2X32 A167 1y **deep ultramarine,** imperf., #364 —
2X33 A99 5y **deep gray green,** #274 —
2X34 A99 5y **deep gray green,** imperf., #360 —

Nos. 2X5, 2X8, 2X11, 2X16, 2X22, 2X26, 2X30, 2X31, 2X32 and 2X34 were issued without gum.

MIYAKO DISTRICT

Personal Seal of Postmaster Jojin Tomiyama

Stamps of Japan 1937-46 Handstamped in Vermilion or Red

Typographed, Lithographed, Engraved

1946-47 Wmk. 257 ***Perf. 13***

3X1 A144 1s **orange brown,** #325 175.
3X2 A84 2s **crimson,** #259 125. —
a. 2s **vermilion** #259c ('47) 150.
b. 2s **pink** #259b ('47) 550.
3X3 A84 3s **brown,** #329 90. —
3X4 A86 4s **dark green,** #261 80.
3X5 A86 5s **brown lake,** #331 550. —
On cover with #3X17 —
3X6 A88 6s **orange,** #263 80. —
3X7 A90 8s **dark purple & pale violet,** #265 100. —
3X8 A148 10s **crimson & dull rose,** #334 90. —

On cover with #3X15 —
3X9 A152 10s **red orange,** imperf., #355 ('47) *(1,000)* 120.
3X10 A92 12s **indigo,** #267 80. —
3X11 A93 14s **rose lake & pale rose,** #268 80. —
3X12 A150 15s **dull blue,** #336 80. —
3X13 A151 17s **gray violet,** #337 90. —
3X14 A94 20s **ultramarine,** #269 —
3X15 A152 20s **blue,** #338 80. —
3X16 A152 20s **ultramarine,** imperf., #356 ('47) 175.
3X17 A95 25s **dark brown & pale brown,** #270 90. —
3X18 A153 30s **bluish green,** #340 90. —
3X19 A88 40s **dull violet,** #341 250.
3X20 A154 40s **dark violet,** #342 90. —
3X21 A97 50s **olive & pale olive,** #272 80. —
3X22 A163 50s **dark brown,** #358 ('47) *(750)* 200. —
3X23 A98 1y **brown & pale brown,** #273 *9,000.*
3X24 A167 1y **deep ultramarine,** #364 ('47) *(500)* 1,500. *600.*

Nos. 3X9, 3X16, 3X22 and 3X24 were issued without gum.

Nos. 3X22 and 3X24 have sewing machine perf.; No. 3X16 exists with that perf. also.

Nos. 3X1-3X2, 3X2a, 3X3-3X5, 3X8 Handstamp Surcharged with 2 Japanese Characters

1946-47

3X25 A144 1y on 1s **orange brown** 140. —
3X26 A84 1y on 2s **crimson** 3,000.
3X27 A84 1y on 3s **brown** ('47) 2,250.
3X28 A84 2y on 2s **crimson** 175. —
a. 2y on 2s **vermilion** ('47) 175. —
3X29 A86 4y on 4s **dark green** 140. —
3X30 A86 5y on 5s **brown lake** 140. —
3X31 A148 10y on 10s **crimson & dull rose** 140. —

The overwhelming majority of used examples of Miyako District stamps were used on Bulk Mailing Records documents and Letter Content Certification Records documents. Stamps affixed to such documents command a substantial premium above off-document used stamps.

Cancellation: black Miyako cds.

OKINAWA DISTRICT

Personal Seal of Postmaster Shiichi Hirata

R1

Japan Nos. 355-356, 358, 364 Overprinted in Black

1947, Nov. 1 Wmk. 257 Litho. *Imperf.*
Without Gum

4X1 A152 10s **red orange** *(13,997)* 1,200. *1,000.*
On cover, strip of 3 *9,500.*
On cover with #4X2 *7,500.*
4X2 A152 20s **ultramarine** *(13,611)* 600. *1,000.*
4X3 A163 50s **dark brown** *(6,276)* 900. *700.*
4X4 A167 1y **deep ultramarine** *(1,947)* 1,750. *1,000.*

On Revenue Stamp of Japan

4X5 R1 30s **brown** *(14,000)* *3,500. 3,500.*
On cover *7,500.*

No. 4X5 is on Japan's current 30s revenue stamp. The Hirata seal validated it for postal use.

Nos. 4X1-4X5 are known with rough sewing machine perforations, full or partial.

YAEYAMA DISTRICT

Personal Seal of Postmaster Kenpuku Miyara

Stamps of Japan 1937-46 Handstamped in Black

Typographed, Engraved, Lithographed

1948 Wmk. 257 *Perf. 13*

5X1 A86 4s **dark green,** #261 1,200.
5X2 A86 5s **brown lake,** #331 1,200.
5X3 A86 7s **orange vermilion,** #333 800.
5X4 A148 10s **crimson & dull rose,** #334 *5,000.*
5X5 A94 20s **ultramarine,** #269 150.
On cover with 2 #5X8 —
5X6 A96 30s **peacock blue,** #271 1,000.
5X7 A88 40s **dull violet,** #341 70.
5X8 A97 50s **olive & pale olive,** #272 100.
5X9 A163 50s **dark brown,** imperf., #358 *(250)* 1,350.
5X10 A99 5y **deep gray green,** #274 2,000.

No. 5X9 was issued without gum.

This handstamp exists double, triple, inverted and in pair, one stamp without overprint.

Provisional postal stationery of the four districts also exists.

LETTER SHEETS

Values are for entires.

Stylized Deigo Blossom — US1

Banyan Tree — US2

Typographed by Japan Printing Bureau.
Stamp is in upper left corner.

Designer: Shutaro Higa

1948-49

U1 US1 50s **vermilion,** *cream, July 18, 1949 (250,000)* 50.00 60.00
First day cancel —
a. 50s **orange red,** *gray, July 1, 1948 (1,000)* 1,200. —

Designer: Ken Yabu

1950, Jan. 21

U2 US2 1y **carmine red,** *cream (250,000)* 40.00 50.00
First day cancel —

AIR LETTER SHEETS

DC-4 Skymaster and Shurei Gate — UC1

UC2

Designer: Chosho Ashitomi
"PAR AVION" (Bilingual) below Stamp

Litho. & Typo. by Japan Printing Bureau

1952-53

UC1 UC1 12y **light rose,** *pale blue green, Mar. 9, 1953 (76,000)* 20.00 12.50
a. 12y **dull rose,** *pale blue green, Nov. 1, 1952 (50,000)* 30.00 15.00
First day cancel, No. UC1a 80.00

No. UC1a is on tinted paper with colorless overall inscription "RYUKYU FOREIGN AIRMAIL," repeated in parallel vertical lines, light and indistinct. Dull rose ink of imprinted design and legend "AIR LETTER" appears to bleed. No. UC1 has overall inscription darker and more distinct. Light rose ink of design and legend does not bleed. Model: U.S. No. UC16.

Litho. & Typo. by Nippon Toppan K.K.
"AEROGRAMME" below Stamp

1955, Sept. 10

UC2 UC2 15y **violet blue & bright red,** *pale yellow green (89,300)* 30.00 15.00
First day cancel 60.00
a. 15y **violet blue & dull red,** *pale blue green, Oct. 1957 (33,742)* 45.00 25.00

Printing on the envelope stamp is heavier on No. UC2a than on No. UC2.

No. UC2 surcharged in Red

"13" & "¢" aligned at bot.; 2 thick bars — a

"¢" raised; 2 thick bars — b

"13" & "¢" as in "a"; 4 thin bars — c

"¢" raised; 4 thin bars — d

Printers: Type "a," Nakamura Printing Co., "b" and "d," Okinawa Printing Co., "c," Sun Printing Co.

1958-60

UC3 UC2 13c on 15y type "a," *Sept. 16, 1958 (60,000)* 20.00 18.00
First day cancel 60.00
a. Type "b," on No. UC2, *June 1, 1959 (2,000)* 40.00 30.00
b. Type "b," on No. UC2a *(7,000)* 50.00 30.00
c. Type "c," on No. UC2, *Sept. 22, 1959 (1,000)* 80.00 80.00
d. As "c," small wrong font "¢" sign 1,000. —
e. Type "c," on No. UC2a *(1,000)* 80.00 80.00
f. As "e," double surcharge, one on reverse *2,000.*
g. Type "b" and No. 46 on No. UC2a, *Aug. 22, 1960 (1,000)* — —
h. Type "d" and Nos. 55, 58 on No. UC2, *Oct. 1, 1960 (1,000)* 450.00
i. Type "d" and Nos. 55, 58 on No. UC2a *(2,000)* 300.00 300.00

For Nos. UC3g, UC3h and UC3i, additional stamps have been affixed to make up the 15c rate.

UC3

Lithographed by Japan Printing Bureau

1959, Nov. 10

UC4 UC3 15c **dark blue,** *pale blue (560,000)* 4.00 2.50
First day cancel 10.00

POSTAL CARDS

Values are for entire cards.

Nos. UX1-UX9 are typo., others litho.

Printed by Japan Printing Bureau unless otherwise stated.

Quantities in parentheses; "E" means estimated.

Deigo Blossom Type

Designer: Shutaro Higa

1948, July 1

UX1 US1 10s **dull red,** *grayish tan (100,000)* 50.00 *60.00*

1949, July 1

UX2 US1 15s **orange red,** *gray (E 175,000)* 40.00 *70.00*
First day cancel —
a. 15s **vermilion,** *tan (E 50,000)* 110.00 *125.00*

Banyan Tree Type

Designer: Ken Yabu

1950, Jan. 21

UX3 US2 50s **carmine red,** *light tan (E 200,000)* 10.00 10.00
First day cancel 60.00
a. Grayish tan card (E 25,000) 25.00 *50.00*

Nos. UX2, UX2a Handstamp Surcharged in Vermilion

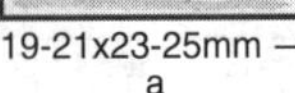

19-21x23-25mm — a

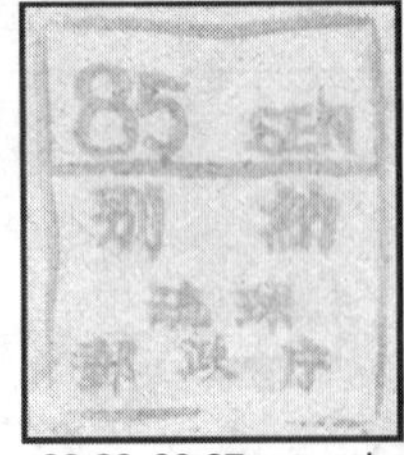

22-23x26-27mm — b

20-21x24-24½mm — c

22-23½x25-26mm — d

1951

UX4 US1 (c) 15s + 85s on #UX2 *(E 35,000)* 100. 100.
a. Type "c" on #UX2a *(E 5,000)* 150. 150.
b. Type "a" on #UX2 *(E 39,000)* 75. *100.*
c. Type "a" on #UX2a 1,000. —
d. Type "b" on #UX2 *1,000.* *1,000.*
e. Type "d" on #UX2 *(E 4,000)* 150. *200.*
f. Type "d" on #UX2a *(E 1,000)* 250. *300.*

Type "a" exists on the 15s cherry blossom postal card of Japan. Value $75.

Crown, Leaf Ornaments

Naha die 21x22mm PC3

Tokyo die 18½x19mm PC4

Designer: Masayoshi Adaniya Koshun Printing Co.

1952

UX5 PC3 1y **vermilion,** *tan, Feb. 8 (400,600)* 50.00 30.00
UX6 PC4 1y **vermilion,** *off-white, Oct. 6 (1,295,000)* 22.50 14.00
a. Tan card, coarse *(50,000)* 30.00 20.00
b. Tan card, smooth *(16,000)* 500.00 150.00

Naminoue Shrine

PC5

Naha die 23x25½mm

PC6

Tokyo die 22x24½mm

Designer: Gensei Agena

1953-57

UX7 PC5 2y **green,** *off-white, Dec. 2, 1953 (1,799,400)* 60.00 20.00
First day cancel 65.00
a. Printed both sides *500.00*
UX8 PC6 2y **green,** *off-white, 1955 (2,799,400)* 15.00 6.00
a. 2y **deep blue green,** *1956 (300,000)* 30.00 16.50
b. 2y **yellow green,** *1957 (2,400,000)* 12.50 3.50
c. As "a," printed on both sides *500.00*
d. As "b," printed on both sides *500.00*

Stylized Pine, Bamboo, Plum Blossoms — PC7

1956 New Year Card

Designer: Koya Oshiro Kotsura and Koshun Printing Companies

1955, Dec. 1

UX9 PC7 2y **red,** *cream* 100.00 45.00
First day cancel 125.00

No. UX9 was printed on rough card (43,400) and smooth-finish card (356,600)

Sun — PC8

Temple Lion — PC9

1957 New Year Card

Designer: Seikichi Tamanaha Kobundo Printing Co.

1956, Dec. 1

UX10 PC8 2y **brown carmine & yellow,** *off-white (600,000)* 5.00 3.75
First day cancel 10.00

1958 New Year Card

Designer: Shin Isagawa Fukuryu Printing Co.

1957, Dec. 1

UX11 PC9 2y **lilac rose,** *off-white (1,000,000)* 1.75 *2.25*
First day cancel 4.00
a. "1" omitted in right date 75.00 75.00
b. Printed on both sides 250.00 *300.00*

Nos. UX8, UX8a and UX8b "Revalued" in Red, Cherry or Pink by Three Naha Printeries

a

b

c

1958-59

UX12 PC6 1½c on 2y **green,** type "a," *Sept. 16 (600,000)* 4.50 4.50
First day cancel 10.00
a. Shrine stamp omitted *750.00* *1,000.*
b. Bar of ½ omitted, top of 2 broken 75.00 *100.00*
c. Type "b," *Nov. (1,000,000)* 8.00 *12.50*
d. Type "c," *1959 (200,000)* 15.00 *22.50*
e. Wrong font "¢," type "c" 30.00 *45.00*
f. "¢" omitted, type "c" *1,500.* 1,500.
g. Double surcharge, type "c" *1,000.* —

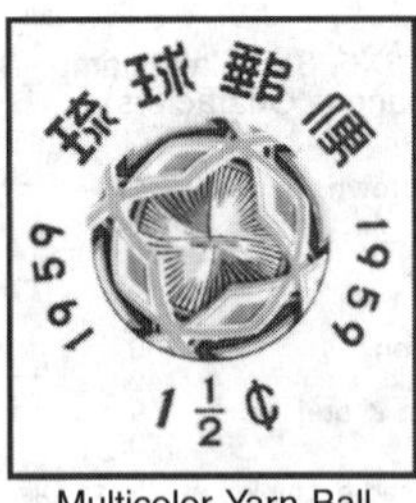

Multicolor Yarn Ball PC10

Toy Pony 19½x23mm PC11

1959 New Year Card

Designer: Masayoshi Adaniya Kobundo Printing Co.

1958, Dec. 10

UX13 PC10 1½c **black, red, yellow & gray blue,** *off-white (1,514,000)* 1.50 *1.90*
First day cancel 2.00
a. Black omitted —

1959, June 20

Designer: Seikichi Tamanaha Kobundo Printing Co.

UX14 PC11 1½c **dark blue & brown** *(1,140,000)* 1.50 1.25
First day cancel 1.50
a. Dark blue omitted 350.00

Toy Carp and Boy — PC12

Toy Pony 21x25mm — PC13

1960 New Year Card

Designer: Masayoshi Adaniya

1959, Dec. 1

UX15 PC12 1½c **violet blue, red & black,** *cream (2,000,000)* 1.25 *1.50*
First day cancel 1.75

1959, Dec. 30

UX16 PC13 1½c **gray violet & brown,** *cream (3,500,000)* 3.00 .75
First day cancel 2.75

Household Altar — PC14

Coral Head — PC15

1961 New Year Card

Designer: Shin Isagawa

1960, Nov. 20

UX17 PC14 1½c **gray, carmine, yellow & black,** *off-white (2,647,591)* 1.50 1.50
First day cancel 1.50

Summer Greeting Card

Designer: Shinzan Yamada Kidekuni Printing Co.

1961, July 5

UX18 PC15 1½c **ultramarine & cerise,** *off-white (264,900)* 2.25 *3.75*
First day cancel 4.00

Tiger — PC16

Inscribed "RYUKYUS" — PC17

1962 New Year Card

Designer: Shin Isagawa

1961, Nov. 15

UX19 PC16 1½c **ocher, black & red,** *off-white (2,891,626)* 1.50 *2.50*
First day cancel 1.65
a. Red omitted 750.00 —
b. Red inverted *500.00* —
c. Red omitted on face, inverted on back *500.00* —
d. Double impression of red, one inverted *500.00* —
e. Double impression of ocher & black, red inverted *500.00* —
f. Double impression of ocher & black, one inverted *500.00* —

1961-67

Designer: Seikichi Tamanaha

UX20 PC17 1½c **gray violet & brown,** *white ('67) (18,600,000)* 1.00 .50
a. Off-white card ('66) *(4,000,000)* 1.50 .75
b. Cream card, *Dec. 23 (12,500,000)* 1.00 .50
First day cancel 1.35

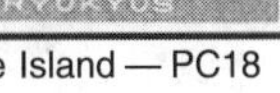
Ie Island — PC18

New Year Offerings — PC19

Summer Greeting Card

Designer: Shinzan Yamada Sakai Printing Co.

1962, July 10

UX21 PC18 1½c **bright blue, yellow & brown,** *off-white (221,500)* 1.50 *2.50*
First day cancel 3.00
Square notch at left 40.00 *45.00*

1963 New Year Card; Precanceled

Designer: Shin Isagawa Sakai Printing Co.

1962, Nov. 15

UX22 PC19 1½c **olive brown, carmine & black** *(3,000,000)* 1.50 *3.00*
First day cancel 2.25
a. Yellow brown background —
b. Brown ocher background —

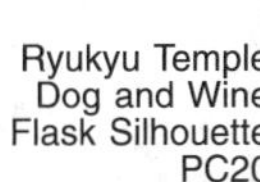
Ryukyu Temple Dog and Wine Flask Silhouette PC20

Water Strider — PC21

International Postal Card

Designer: Shin Isagawa

1963, Feb. 15

UX23 PC20 5c **vermilion, emerald & black,** *pale yellow (150,000)* 1.75 *2.75*
First day cancel 1.65
a. Black & emerald omitted 450.00

Summer Greeting Card

Designer: Seikichi Tamanaha

1963, June 20

UX24 PC21 1½c **Prussian green & black,** *off-white (250,000)* 4.00 *4.25*
First day cancel 3.50

Princess Doll — PC22

Bitter Melon Vine — PC23

1964 New Year Card; Precanceled

Designer: Koya Oshiro

1963, Nov. 15

UX25 PC22 1½c **orange red, yellow & ultra,** *off-white (3,200,000)* 2.00 2.00
First day cancel 2.00

Summer Greeting Card

Designer: Shinzan Yamada

1964, June 20

UX26 PC23 1½c **multicolored,** *off-white (285,410)* 1.40 *2.25*
First day cancel 1.75

Fighting Kite with Rider — PC24

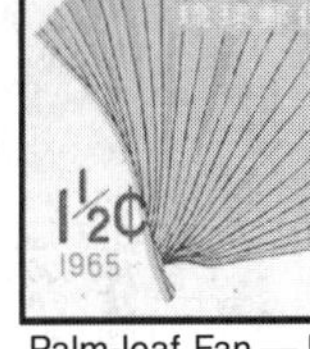

Palm-leaf Fan — PC25

1965 New Year Card; Precanceled

Designer: Koya Oshiro

1964, Nov. 15

UX27 PC24 1½c **multicolored,** *off-white (4,876,618)* 1.25 *1.75*
First day cancel 2.00

Summer Greeting Card

Designer: Koya Oshiro

1965, June 20

UX28 PC25 1½c **multicolored,** *off-white (340,604)* 1.40 *2.50*
First day cancel 1.65

Toy Pony Rider — PC26

Fan Palm Dipper — PC27

1966 New Year Card; Precanceled

Designer: Seikichi Tamanaha

1965, Nov. 15

UX29 PC26 1½c **multicolored,** *off-white (5,224,622)* 1.25 *1.75*
First day cancel 1.40
a. Silver (background) omitted 250.00

Summer Greeting Card

Designer: Seikichi Tamanaha

1966, June 20

UX30 PC27 1½c **multicolored,** *off-white (339,880)* 1.25 *2.00*
First day cancel 1.40

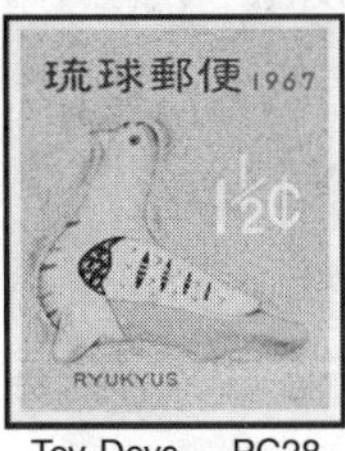

Toy Dove — PC28

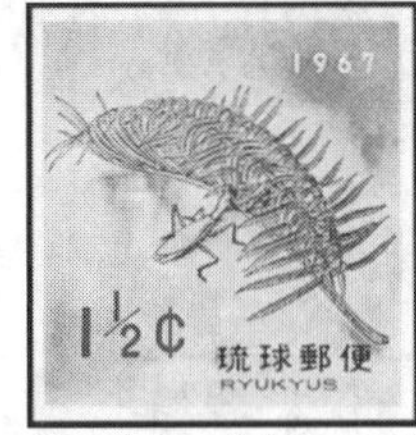

Cycad Insect Cage and Praying Mantis — PC29

1967 New Year Card; Precanceled

Designer: Seikichi Tamanaha

1966, Nov. 15

UX31 PC28 1½c **multicolored,** *off-white (5,500,000)* 1.25 *1.75*
First day cancel 1.65
a. Silver (background) omitted *500.00*
b. Gray blue & green omitted *750.00*

Summer Greeting Card

Designer: Shin Isagawa

1967, June 20

UX32 PC29 1½c **multicolored,** *off-white (350.000)* 1.50 *2.50*
First day cancel 1.75

Paper Doll Royalty — PC30

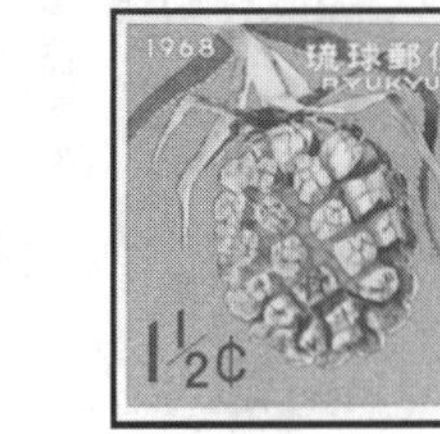

Pandanus Drupe — PC31

1968 New Year Card; Precanceled

Designer: Shin Isagawa

1967, Nov. 15

UX33 PC30 1½c **multicolored,** *off-white (6,200,000)* 1.10 *1.50*
First day cancel 1.75
a. Gold omitted 500.00

Summer Greeting Card

Designer: Seikan Omine

1968, June 20

UX34 PC31 1½c **multicolored,** *off-white (350,000)* 1.25 *2.25*
First day cancel 1.75

Toy Lion — PC32

Ryukyu Trading Ship — PC33

1969 New Year Card; Precanceled

Designer: Teruyoshi Kinjo

1968, Nov. 15
UX35 PC32 1½c **multicolored,** *off-white (7,000,000)* 1.10 *1.50*
First day cancel 1.50

Summer Greeting Card

Designer: Seikichi Tamanaha

1969, June 20
UX36 PC33 1½c **multicolored,** *(349,800)* 1.25 *2.25*
First day cancel 1.75

Toy Devil Mask — PC34

Ripe Litchis — PC35

1970 New Year Card; Precanceled

Designer: Teruyoshi Kinjo

1969, Nov. 15
UX37 PC34 1½c **multicolored** *97,200,000)* 1.10 *1.50*
First day cancel 1.25

Summer Greeting Card

Designer: Kensei Miyagi

1970, June 20
UX38 PC35 1½c **multicolored** *(400,000)* 1.40 *2.25*
First day cancel 1.50

Thread-winding Implements for Dance — PC36

Ripe Guavas — PC37

1971 New Year Card; Precanceled

Designer: Yoshinori Arakai

1970, Nov. 16
UX39 PC36 1½c **multicolored** *(7,500,000)* 1.10 *1.50*
First day cancel 1.25

Summer Greeting Card

Designer: Kensei Miyagi

1971, July 10
UX40 PC37 1½c **multicolored** *(400,000)* 1.25 *2.25*
First day cancel 1.25

Pony Type of 1961
Zip Code Boxes in Vermilion

1971, July 10
UX41 PC17 1½c **gray violet & brown** *(3,000,000)* 1.25 *3.50*
First day cancel 2.00

No. UX41 Surcharged below Stamp in Vermilion

"Revalued 2¢" applied by Nakamura Printing Co.

1971, Sept. 1
UX42 PC17 2c on 1½c **gray violet & brown** *(1,699,569)* 1.10 *2.25*
First day cancel 2.00
a. Inverted surcharge *500.00*
b. Double surcharge *500.00*
c. Surcharge on back *500.00*
e. Surcharge on back, inverted *500.00*

1972 New Year Card; Precanceled

Tasseled Castanets — PC38

Zip Code Boxes in Vermilion

Designer: Yoshinori Arakaki

1971, Nov. 15
UX43 PC38 2c **multicolored** *(8,000,000)* 1.00 *1.50*
First day cancel 1.25

Type of 1961
Zip Code Boxes in Vermilion

1971, Dec. 15
UX44 PC17 2c **gray violet & brown** *(3,500,000)* 1.25 *1.75*
First day cancel 1.65

PAID REPLY POSTAL CARDS

Sold as two attached cards, one for message, one for reply. The major listings are of unsevered cards except Nos. UY4-UY6.

Message

Reply

1948, July 1
UY1 US1 10s + 10s **dull red,** *grayish tan (1,000)* 1,800. —
m. Message card 500. 500.
r. Reply card 500. 500.

1949, July 18
UY2 US1 15s + 15s **vermilion,** *tan (E 150,000)* 30.00 *40.00*
a. Gray card *(E 75,000)* 75.00 —
First day cancel —
m. Message card 8.00 *16.50*
r. Reply card 8.00 *16.50*

1950, Jan. 21
UY3 US2 50s + 50s **carmine red,** *gray cream (E 130,000)* 25.00 *40.00*
a. Double impression of message card — —
b. Light tan card *(E 96,000)* 15.00 —
First day cancel —
m. Message card 3.50 *13.50*
r. Reply card 3.50 *13.50*

No. UY2a Handstamp Surcharged in Vermilion

1951
UY4 US1 1y (15s+85s) message, type "b" *(E 3,000)* 350. 350.
a. Reply, type "b" *(E 3,000)* 350. 350.
b. Message, type "a" *(E 300)* 600. —
c. Reply, type "a" *(E 300)* 600. —
d. Message, type "d" *(E 200)* 500. —
e. Reply, type "d" *(E 200)* 500. —
f. Message, UY2, type "a" *(E 3,000)* 150. *225.*
g. Reply, UY2, type "a" *(E 3,000)* 150. *225.*
h. Message, UY2, type "b" *(E 2,500)* 275. 275.
i. Reply, UY2, type "b" *(E 2,500)* 275. 275.
j. Message, UY2, type "d" *(E 2,800)* 150. *250.*
k. Reply, UY2, type "d" *(E 2,800)* 150. *250.*
l. 1y + 1y unsevered, type "b" *850.*
m. 1y + 1y unsevered, type "a" *1,450.*
n. 1y + 1y unsevered, type "d" *1,200.*
o. 1y + 1y unsevered, UY2, type "a" *360.*

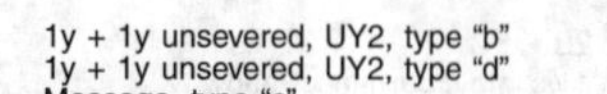
p. 1y + 1y unsevered, UY2, type "b" *650.*
q. 1y + 1y unsevered, UY2, type "d" *360.*
r. Message, type "c" —

e

f

g

h

Typographed Surcharge in Vermilion on No. UY2a

UY5 US1 1y (15s+85s) message, type "f" *(E 20,000)* 125. 125.
a. Reply, type "f" *(E 20,000)* 125. 125.
b. Message, type "e" *(E 12,500)* 225. 225.
c. Reply, type "e" *(E 12,500)* 225. 225.
d. Message, type "g" *(E 500)* *1,000.* *1,000.*
e. Reply, type "g" *(E 500)* *1,000.* *1,000.*
f. Message, UY2, type "e" *(E 15,000)* 125. 125.
g. Reply, UY2, type "e" *(E 15,000)* 125. 125.
h. Message, UY2, type "f" *(E 9,000)* 125. 125.
i. Reply, UY2, type "f" *(E 9,000)* 125. 125.
j. Message, UY2, type "g" *(E 500)* *1,000.* *1,000.*
k. Reply, UY2, type "g" *(E 500)* *1,000.* *1,000.*
l. 1y + 1y unsevered, type "e" *675.*
m. 1y + 1y unsevered, UY2, type "e" *375.*

Typographed Surcharge Type "h" in Vermilion on No. UY3

UY6 US2 1y (50s+50s) message *(E 35,000)* 125.00 *150.00*
a. Reply *(E 35,000)* 125.00 *150.00*
b. Message, UY3b *(E 10,000)* 125.00 *150.00*
c. Reply, UY3b *(E 10,000)* 125.00 *150.00*

Smooth or Coarse Card

1952, Feb. 8
UY7 PC3 1y + 1y **vermilion,** *gray tan (60,000)* 120.00 *140.00*
First day cancel 250.00
m. Message card 25.00 *50.00*
r. Reply card 25.00 *50.00*

1953
UY8 PC4 1y + 1y **vermilion,** *tan (22,900)* 30.00 *40.00*
First day cancel —
a. Off-white card *(13,800)* 40.00 *50.00*
m. Message card 7.50 *19.00*
r. Reply card 7.50 *26.50*

Off-white or Light Cream Card

1953, Dec. 2
UY9 PC5 2y + 2y **green** *(50,000)* 100.00 90.00
First day cancel 150.00
m. Message card 15.00 *25.00*
r. Reply card 15.00 *35.00*

1955, May
UY10 PC6 2y + 2y **green,** *off-white (280,000)* 10.00 —
a. Reply card blank 500.00
m. Message card 3.25 *11.00*
r. Reply card 3.25 *15.00*

No. UY10 Surcharged in Red

1958, Sept. 16
UY11 PC6 1½c on 2y, 1½c on 2y *(95,000)* 8.00 —
First day cancel 22.50
a. Surcharge on reply card only *500.00* —
b. Surcharge on message card only *500.00* —
c. Reply card double surcharge *750.00* —
d. Reply card stamp omitted (surcharge only) *1,000.* —
m. Message card 2.75 *10.00*
r. Reply card 2.75 *16.50*

Surcharge varieties include: "1" omitted; wrong font "2".

Pony Types

1959, June 20
UY12 PC11 1½c + 1½c **dark blue & brown** *(366,000)* 3.50 —
First day cancel 4.00
m. Message card .65 *3.50*
r. Reply card .65 *3.50*

1960, Mar. 10

UY13	PC13	1½c + 1½c **gray violet & brown,** *(150,000)*	7.00	—
		First day cancel		5.00
m.		Message card	1.50	*5.00*
r.		Reply card	1.50	*5.00*

International Type

1963, Feb. 15

UY14	PC20	5c + 5c **vermilion, emerald & black,** *pale yellow (70,000)*	2.50	—
		First day cancel		3.00
m.		Message card	.75	*3.75*
r.		Reply card	.75	*3.75*

Pony ("RYUKYUS") Type

1963-69

UY15	PC17	1½c + 1½c **gray violet & brown,** *cream, Mar. 15, (800,000)*	2.00	—
		First day cancel		2.50
a.		Off-white card, *Mar. 13, 1967 (100,000)*	2.25	—
b.		White card, *Nov. 22, 1969 (700,000)*	1.75	—
m.		Message card detached	.40	*4.00*
r.		Reply card detached	.40	*4.00*

No. UY14 Surcharged below Stamp in Vermilion

1971, Sept. 1

UY16	PC17	2c on 1½c + 2c on 1½c **gray violet & brown** *(80,000)*	1.50	—
		First day cancel		2.25
m.		Message card	.50	*2.50*
r.		Reply card	.50	*2.50*

Pony ("RYUKYUS") Type

Zip Code Boxes in Vermilion

1971, Nov. 1

UY17	PC17	2c + 2c **gray violet & brown** *(150,000)*	1.50	—
		First day cancel		2.50
m.		Message card	.50	*2.50*
r.		Reply card	.50	*2.50*

REVENUE

Upon its establishment Apr. 1, 1952, the government of the Ryukyu Islands assumed responsibility for the issuing and the profit from revenue stamps. The various series served indiscriminately as evidence of payment of the required fees for various legal, realty and general commercial transactions.

1 yen — R1

3

5

10

50

100

500

1000

Litho. by Japan Printing Bureau.
Designer: Eizo Yonamine

1952-54		**Wmk. 257**	***Perf. 13x13½***	
R1	R1	1y **brown**	15.00	10.00
R2	R1	3y **carmine**	20.00	12.00
R3	R1	5y **green**	25.00	15.00
R4	R1	10y **blue**	30.00	20.00
R5	R1	50y **purple**	35.00	25.00
R6	R1	100y **yellow brown**	50.00	30.00
R7	R1	500y **dark green**	250.00	100.00
R8	R1	1,000y **carmine**	200.00	150.00
		Nos. R1-R8 (8)	625.00	362.00

Issued: #R1-R6, July 15, 1952; #R7-R8, Apr. 16, 1954.

Denomination Vertical

"Cent"

"Dollar"

Litho. by Kobundo Printing Co., Naha

Perf. 10, 10½, 11 and combinations

1958, Sept. 16		**Without Gum**	**Unwmk.**	
R9	R1	1c **red brown**	25.00	25.00
a.		Horiz. pair, imperf. between	500.00	
R10	R1	3c **red**	35.00	35.00
a.		Horiz. pair, imperf. between	500.00	
R11	R1	5c **green**	45.00	45.00
R12	R1	10c **blue**	65.00	65.00
a.		Horiz. pair, imperf. between	500.00	
R13	R1	50c **purple**	120.00	120.00
R14	R1	$1 **sepia**	175.00	175.00
R15	R1	$5 **dark green**	300.00	300.00
R16	R1	$10 **carmine**	400.00	400.00
		Nos. R9-R16 (8)	1,165.	1,165.

R2

R3

R4

Litho. by Japan Printing Bureau.

1959-69		**Wmk. 257**	***Perf. 13x13½***	
R17	R2	1c **brown**	3.00	1.90
R18	R2	3c **red**	3.00	1.10
R19	R2	5c **purple**	5.50	3.25
R20	R2	10c **green**	10.00	6.00
R21	R2	20c **sepia** ('69)	70.00	55.00
R22	R2	30c **light olive** ('69)	80.00	65.00
R23	R2	50c **blue**	32.50	14.00
		Engr.		
R24	R3	$1 **olive**	45.00	12.50
R25	R3	$2 **vermilion** ('69)	200.00	50.00
R26	R3	$3 **purple** ('69)	350.00	70.00
R27	R3	$5 **orange**	100.00	50.00
R28	R3	$10 **dark green**	160.00	70.00
R29	R4	$20 **carmine** ('69)	1,000.	200.00
R30	R4	$30 **blue** ('69)	1,500.	—
R31	R4	$50 **black** ('69)	2,000.	—
		Nos. R17-R28 (12)	1,059.	398.75

A 4-cent "stamp" picturing Iriomote Park was originally planned for postage in 1971. Its use was changed, and it became a label that was used on the "Ryukyu Islands Emergency Conversion Confirmation Certificate." Value, $100 unused, $150 on document.

PROVISIONAL ISSUES MIYAKO

Stamps of Japan 1938-42 Handstamped in Black, Red or Orange

1948		**Typo., Litho., Engr.** **Wmk. 257**	***Perf. 13***	
3XR1	A84	3s **brown,** #329	75.00	—
3XR2	A86	5s **brown lake,** #331	75.00	—
3XR3	A152	20s **blue,** #338 (R)	60.00	—
3XR4	A95	25s **dark brown & pale brown,** #270 (R)	60.00	—
a.		Black overprint	600.00	—
3XR5	A96	30s **peacock blue,** #271 (R)	60.00	—
3XR6	A154	40s **dark violet,** #342 (R)	60.00	—
3XR7	A97	50s **olive & pale olive,** #272 (R)	135.00	
a.		Orange overprint	*500.00*	—

Doubled handstamps are known on all values and pairs with one stamp without handstamp exist on the 5s and 20s.

PROVISIONAL ISSUES YAEYAMA

In addition to the continued use of the then-current Japanese revenue stamps in stock from the wartime period, the varying authorities of the Yaeyama Gunto issued three district-specific revenue series, with a total of 28 values. Only those values at present verified by surviving copies are indicated. Numbers are reserved for other values believed to have been issued, but as yet not seen and verified.

No. 5XR2 — R5

壹 圓

No. 5XR3 — R6

No. 5XR5 — R7

No. 5XR27 — R8

1946 (?)		**Without Gum**	***Imperf.***
		Value printed, frame handstamped	
5XR1	R5	3s **vermilion & black**	—
5XR2	R5	10s **vermilion & black**	— —
		Validating handstamp below	
5XR3	R6	1y **vermilion & black**	— —

Civil Administration Issues

1947 (?)		**Without Gum**	***Imperf.***
		Value printed, frame handstamped	
		Cream Paper	
5XR5	R7	10s **vermilion & black**	—
5XR6	R7	50s **vermilion & black**	— —

Gunto Government Issues

1950 (?)		**Without Gum**	***Imperf.***
		Value printed, frame handstamped	
		Cream Paper	
5XR17	R8	10s **vermilion & black**	—
5XR18	R8	50s **vermilion & black**	—
a.		50s **vermilion & blue**	—
5XR20	R8	1.50y **vermilion & black**	—
5XR22	R8	5y **vermilion & black**	—
5XR24	R8	20y **vermilion & black**	—
5XR27	R8	100y **vermilion & black**	—

Nos. 5XR17-5XR27 are known with rough perforations, full or partial.

SPECIMEN

Regular stamps and postal cards of 1958-65 overprinted with three cursive syllabics *mi-ho-n* ("specimen").

Type A

1961-64

Overprinted in Black

91S	3c **multicolored** *(1,000)*	250.00
118S	3c **multicolored** *(1,100)*	450.00
119S	3c **multicolored** *(1,100)*	400.00

Type B

1964-65

Overprinted in Red or Black

120aS	3c **deep blue, deep carmine & ocher** (R) *(1,500)*	200.00
121S	3c **multicolored** (R) *(1,500)*	175.00
124S	3c **ultra, yel & red** (R) *(5,000)*	35.00
125S	3s **dull claret, yel & black** *(1,500)*	70.00
126S	3c **yellow & multi** *(2,000)*	60.00
127S	3c **gray, red & black** *(2,000)*	60.00
128S	3c **multicolored** *(1,500)*	70.00
129S	1½c **multicolored** (R) *(1,500)*	70.00
130S	3c **light blue & multi** (R) *(1,500)*	200.00
131S	3c **multicolored** (R) *(1,500)*	60.00
132S	3c **buff & multicolored** *(2,000)*	60.00
133S	3c **green & multi** (R) *(2,000)*	50.00
134S	3c **multicolored** *(2,000)*	50.00
135S	3c **blue & multicolored** *(2,000)*	50.00
136S	3c **golden brown & multi** *(2,000)*	50.00
139S	1½c **multicolored** (R) *(2,500)*	50.00

Postal Cards

1964-65

Overprinted Type A or B in Black or Red

UX26S A	1½c **multicolored** *(1,000)*	500.00
UX27S B	1½c **multicolored** *(1,000)*	350.00
UX28S A	1½c **multicolored** *(1,000)*	300.00
UX29S A	1½c **multicolored** *(1,100)*	250.00

UNEMPLOYMENT INSURANCE

These stamps, when affixed in an official booklet and canceled, certified a one-day contract for a day laborer. They were available to employers at certain post offices on various islands.

Dove — RQ1

Shield — RQ2

Lithographed in Naha

1961, Jan. 10 Without Gum Unwmk. *Rouletted*

RQ1	RQ1	2c **pale red**	700.00	—
RQ2	RQ2	4c **violet**	50.00	50.00

Redrawn

Lithographed by Japan Printing Bureau

1966, Feb. Unwmk. *Perf. 13x13½*

RQ3	RQ1	2c **pale red**	—	—
RQ4	RQ2	4c **violet**	30.00	30.00

Redrawn stamps have bolder numerals and inscriptions, and fewer, stronger lines of shading in background.

Cycad — RQ3

Lithographed by Japan Printing Bureau

1968, Apr. 19 Wmk. 257 *Perf. 13x13½*

RQ5	RQ3	8c **brown**	35.00	35.00

Nos. RQ3-RQ4 Surcharged with New Values and 2 Bars

1967-72

RQ6	RQ1	8c on 2c **pale red**	70.00	70.00
RQ7	RQ2	8c on 4c **violet** ('72)	35.00	35.00
RQ8	RQ2	12c on 4c **violet** ('71)	30.00	30.00

PROOFS AND TRIAL COLOR PROOFS

1948

Salmon Paper, Imperf.

1aP	5s **magenta**	—
2aP	10s **yellow green**	—
3aP	20s **yellow green**	—
5aP	40s **magenta**	—
6aP	50s **ultramarine**	—
7aP	1y **ultramarine**	—

Between the printing of Nos. 1a-7a and Nos. 1-7 essay sheets of the series were prepared in Tokyo and overprinted with a swirl-pattern of blue or red dots. These essays sell for about $800 each.

Except for No. 12TC 4y olive, the trial color proofs of Nos. 8-13, 18, C1-C3 and E1 are from blocks of 9.

1950

Soft White Paper, Imperf.

Proofs are Gummed, Trial Color Proofs are Without Gum

8P	50s **dark carmine rose**	1,500.
8TC	50s **rose**	1,750.
8TC	50s **green**	1,750.
9P	1y **deep blue**	1,500.
9TC	1y **rose**	1,750.
9TC	1y **green**	1,750.
10P	2y **rose violet**	1,500.
10TC	2y **rose**	1,750.
10TC	2y **green**	1,750.
11P	3y **carmine rose**	1,500.
11TC	3y **rose**	1,750.
11TC	3y **green**	1,750.
12P	4y **greenish gray**	1,500.
12TC	4y **rose**	1,750.
12TC	4y **olive**	1,750.
13P	5y **blue green**	1,500.
13TC	5y **rose**	1,750.
13TC	5y **green**	1,750.

1951

Soft White Paper, Imperf., Without Gum

14P	3y **red brown**	800.
15P	3y **dark green**	1,000.

1952

Whitish Paper, Imperf., With Gum

18TC	3y **pale salmon**	1,750.
18TC	3y **scarlet**	1,750.
18TC	3y **red orange**	1,900.

Perforated, gummed proof sheets of Nos. 18, 27 and 28 with oversized, untrimmed selvage were printed for display purposes.

1958

Off White Paper, Imperf., Without Gum

46TC	2c **black** (100)	650.
48TC	4c **black** (100)	650.

AIR POST

1950

Soft White Paper, Imperf.

Proofs are Gummed, Trial Color Proofs are Without Gum

C1P	8y **bright blue**	1,500.
C1TC	8y **rose**	1,750.
C1TC	8y **light green**	1,750.
C2P	12y **green**	1,500.
C2TC	12y **rose**	1,750.
C2TC	12y **light green**	1,750.
C3P	16y **rose carmine**	1,500.
C3TC	16y **rose**	1,750.

1951

Soft White Paper, Imperf., Without Gum

C4P	13y **blue**	1,000.
C5P	18y **green**	1,000.
C6P	30y **cerise**	800.

SPECIAL DELIVERY

1950

Soft White Paper, Imperf.

Proofs are Gummed, Trial Color Proofs are Without Gum

E1P	5y **bright blue**	1,500.
E1TC	5y **rose**	1,750.
E1TC	5y **green**	1,750.

Official proof folders contain one each of Nos. 8P-13P, 12TC in olive, C1P-C3P and E1P. The stamps are securely adhered to the folder. Value, $9,000.

Similar folders exist containing die proofs in black of the same issues and mockups of Nos. U2, UX3 and UY3.

KUME ISLAND

1945

U.S. Official Watermarked White Bond Paper

Seal Handstamped in Vermilion

Without Gum

1X1P	7s **black**	*2,500.*
	a. "7" and "SEN" one letter space to left, pos. 8	*4,000.*

SPECIMEN OVERPRINTS ON TRIAL COLOR PROOFS

1961

Overprinted in Vermillion

46TCS	2c **black** *(100)*	*750.*
48TCS	4c **black** *(100)*	*750.*

Cursive type used for these two trial color proofs is different from the mihon overprints.

UNITED NATIONS

United Nations stamps are used on UN official mail sent from UN Headquarters in New York City, the UN European Office in Geneva, Switzerland, or from the Donaupark Vienna International Center or Atomic Energy Agency in Vienna, Austria to points throughout the world. They may be used on private correspondence sent through the UN post offices.

UN mail is carried by the US, Swiss and Austrian postal systems.

See Switzerland official stamp listings in the Scott *Standard Postage Stamp Catalogue* for stamps issued by the Swiss Government for official use of the UN European Office and other UN affiliated organizations. See France official stamp listings for stamps issued by the French Government for official use of UNESCO.

+: When following the quantity, this indicates the total printed to date. Unless otherwise noted, these are the initial printing order. Final quantities frequently are not given for definitives and air post stamps. The total printed is shown here.

Blocks of four generally sell for four times the single stamp value.

Values for first day covers are for cacheted and unaddressed covers. Addressed covers sell for much less, and addressed and uncacheted first day covers sell for very little.

For imperforate stamps, see the Proofs section following U.N. Souvenir Cards.

Catalogue values for all unused stamps in this section are for Never Hinged items.

Peoples of the World — A1

UN Headquarters Building — A2

"Peace, Justice, Security" — A3

UN Flag — A4

UN International Children's Emergency Fund — A5

World Unity — A6

Printed by Thomas De La Rue & Co., Ltd., London (1c, 3c, 10c, 15c, 20c, 25c), and Joh. Enschedé and Sons, Haarlem, Netherlands (1½c, 2c, 5c, 50c, $1). The 3c, 15c and 25c have frame engraved, center photogravure; other denominations are engraved. Panes of 50. Designed by O. C. Meronti (A1), Leon Helguera (A2), J. F. Doeve (A3), Ole Hamann (A4), S. L. Hartz (5c) and Hubert Woyty-Wimmer (20c).

Perf. 13x12½, 12½x13

1951 Engr. and Photo. Unwmk.

No.	Type	Denomination / Description	Unused	Used
1	A1	1c **magenta,** *Oct. 24 (8,000,000)*	.20	.20
		First day cover		1.00
		Margin block of 4, UN seal	.20	—
2	A2	1½c **blue green,** *Oct. 24 (7,450,000)*	.20	.20
		First day cover		1.00
		Margin block of 4, UN seal	.20	—
		Precanceled *(361,700)*		*55.00*
3	A3	2c **purple,** *Nov. 16 (8,470,000)*	.20	.20
		First day cover		1.00
		Margin block of 4, UN seal	.25	—
4	A4	3c **magenta & blue,** *Oct. 24 (8,250,000)*	.20	.20
		First day cover		1.00
		Margin block of 4, UN seal	.25	—
5	A5	5c **blue,** *Oct. 24 (6,000,000)*	.20	.20
		First day cover		1.75
		Margin block of 4, UN seal	.40	—
6	A1	10c **chocolate,** *Nov. 16 (2,600,000)*	.25	.25
		First day cover		2.00
		Margin block of 4, UN seal	1.10	—
7	A4	15c **violet & blue,** *Nov. 16 (2,300,000)*	.25	.25
		First day cover		2.00
		Margin block of 4, UN seal	1.10	—
8	A6	20c **dark brown,** *Nov. 16 (2,100,000)*	.35	.35
		First day cover		2.00
		Margin block of 4, UN seal	1.90	—
9	A4	25c **olive gray & blue,** *Oct. 24 (2,100,000)*	.40	.40
		First day cover		2.00
		Margin block of 4, UN seal	1.90	—
10	A2	50c **indigo,** *Nov. 16 (1,785,000)*	2.25	2.25
		First day cover		8.00
		Margin block of 4, UN seal	13.00	—
11	A3	$1 **red,** *Oct. 24 (2,252,500)*	1.50	1.50
		First day cover		8.00
		Margin block of 4, UN seal	6.50	—
		Nos. 1-11 (11)	6.00	6.00

First day covers of Nos. 1-11 and C1-C4 total 1,113,216.

The various printings of Nos. 1-11 vary in sheet marginal perforation. Some were perforated through left or right margins, or both; some through all margins.

Sheets of this issue carry a marginal inscription consisting of the UN seal and "First UN/Issue 1951." This inscription appears four times on each sheet. The listing "Margin block of 4, UN seal" or "Inscription block of 4" in this and following issues refers to a corner block.

Sheets of the 1½c, 2c, 50c and $1 have a cut-out of different shape in one margin. The printer trimmed this off entirely on most of the 1½c third printing, and partially on the 1½c fourth printing and $1 fifth and sixth printings.

See UN Offices in Geneva Nos. 4, 14.

Forgeries of the 1½c precancel abound. Examination by a competent authority is necessary.

Veterans' War Memorial Building, San Francisco A7

Issued to mark the 7th anniversary of the signing of the United Nations Charter.

Engraved and printed by the American Bank Note Co., New York. Panes of 50. Designed by Jean Van Noten.

1952, Oct. 24 ***Perf. 12***

No.	Type	Denomination / Description	Unused	Used
12	A7	5c **blue** *(1,274,670)*	.20	.20
		First day cover *(160,117)*		1.00
		Inscription block of 4	.75	—

Globe and Encircled Flame — A8

4th anniversary of the adoption of the Universal Declaration of Human Rights.

Engraved and printed by Thomas De La Rue & Co., Ltd., London. Panes of 50. Designed by Hubert Woyty-Wimmer.

1952, Dec. 10 ***Perf. 13½x14***

No.	Type	Denomination / Description	Unused	Used
13	A8	3c **deep green** *(1,554,312)*	.20	.20
		First day cover		1.50
		Inscription block of 4	.75	—
14	A8	5c **blue** *(1,126,371)*	.20	.20
		First day cover		2.00
		First day cover, #13-14		5.75
		Inscription block of 4	1.10	—

First day covers of Nos. 13 and 14 total 299,309.

Refugee Family — A9

Issued to publicize "Protection for Refugees."

Engraved and printed by Thomas De La Rue & Co., Ltd., London. Panes of 50. Designed by Olav Mathiesen.

1953, Apr. 24 ***Perf. 12½x13***

No.	Type	Description	Unused	Used
15	A9	3c **dark red brown & rose brown** *(1,299,793)*	.20	.20
		First day cover		2.25
		Inscription block of 4	.75	—
16	A9	5c **indigo & blue** *(969,224)*	.25	.25
		First day cover		3.25
		First day cover, #15-16		7.50
		Inscription block of 4	2.00	—

First day covers of Nos. 15 and 16 total 234,082.

Envelope, UN Emblem and Map — A10

Issued to honor the Universal Postal Union.
Engraved and printed by Thomas De La Rue & Co., Ltd., London. Panes of 50. Designed by Hubert Woyty-Wimmer.

1953, June 12 ***Perf. 13***

No.	Type	Description	Unused	Used
17	A10	3c **black brown** *(1,259,689)*	.20	.20
		First day cover		5.00
		Inscription block of 4	1.25	—
18	A10	5c **dark blue** *(907,312)*	.50	.50
		First day cover		4.50
		First day cover, #17-18		9.00
		Inscription block of 4	3.00	—

First day covers of Nos. 17 and 18 total 231,627.
Plate number ("1A" or "1B") in color of stamp appears below 47th stamp of sheet.

Gearwheels and UN Emblem — A11

Hands Reaching Toward Flame — A12

Issued to publicize United Nations activities in the field of technical assistance.
Engraved and printed by Thomas De La Rue & Co. Ltd. London. Panes of 50. Designed by Olav Mathiesen.

1953, Oct. 24 ***Perf. 13x12½***

No.	Type	Description	Unused	Used
19	A11	3c **dark gray** *(1,184,348)*	.20	.20
		First day cover		2.00
		Inscription block of 4	.50	—
20	A11	5c **dark green** *(968,182)*	.30	.30
		First day cover		5.00
		First day cover, #19-20		9.00
		Inscription block of 4	1.75	—

First day covers of Nos. 19 and 20 total 229,211.

1953, Dec. 10 ***Perf. 12½x13***

Issued to publicize Human Rights Day.
Engraved and printed by Thomas De La Rue & Co., Ltd., London. Panes of 50. Designed by León Helguera.

No.	Type	Description	Unused	Used
21	A12	3c **bright blue** *(1,456,928)*	.20	.20
		First day cover		2.00
		Inscription block of 4	.70	—
22	A12	5c **rose red** *(983,831)*	.80	.40
		First day cover		4.00
		First day cover, #21-22		8.00
		Inscription block of 4	4.75	—

First day covers of Nos. 21 and 22 total 265,186.

Ear of Wheat — A13

UN Emblem and Anvil Inscribed "ILO" — A14

Issued to honor the Food and Agriculture Organization and printed by Thomas De La Rue & Co., Ltd., London. Panes of 50. Designed by Dirk Van Gelder.

1954, Feb. 11 ***Perf. 12½x13***

No.	Type	Description	Unused	Used
23	A13	3c **dark green & yellow** *(1,250,000)*	.30	.20
		First day cover		2.00
		Inscription block of 4	1.75	—
24	A13	8c **indigo & yellow** *(949,718)*	.75	.50
		First day cover		4.00
		First day cover, #23-24		5.00
		Inscription block of 4	3.75	—

First day covers of Nos. 23 and 24 total 272,312.

1954, May 10 ***Perf. 12½x13***

Design: 8c, inscribed "OIT."
Issued to honor the International Labor Organization.
Engraved and printed by Thomas De La Rue & Co., Ltd., London. Panes of 50. Designed by José Renau.

No.	Type	Description	Unused	Used
25	A14	3c **brown** *(1,085,651)*	.20	.20
		First day cover		2.00
		Inscription block of 4	.50	—
26	A14	8c **magenta** *(903,561)*	1.10	.65
		First day cover		4.00
		First day cover, #25-26		4.75
		Inscription block of 4	4.75	—

First day covers of Nos. 25 and 26 total 252,796.

UN European Office, Geneva — A15

Issued on the occasion of United Nations Day.
Engraved and printed by Thomas De La Rue & Co., Ltd., London. Panes of 50. Designed by Earl W. Purdy.

1954, Oct. 25 ***Perf. 14***

No.	Type	Description	Unused	Used
27	A15	3c **dark blue violet** *(1,000,000)*	1.50	1.10
		First day cover		1.75
		Inscription block of 4	8.50	—
28	A15	8c **red** *(1,000,000)*	.25	.25
		First day cover		2.25
		First day cover, #27-28		3.50
		Inscription block of 4	.75	—

First day covers of Nos. 27 and 28 total 233,544.

Mother and Child — A16

Issued to publicize Human Rights Day.
Engraved and printed by Thomas De La Rue & Co., Ltd. London. Panes of 50. Designed by Leonard C. Mitchell.

1954, Dec. 10 ***Perf. 14***

No.	Type	Description	Unused	Used
29	A16	3c **red orange** *(1,000,000)*	5.75	2.00
		First day cover		2.75
		Inscription block of 4	32.50	—
30	A16	8c **olive green** *(1,000,000)*	.25	.25
		First day cover		3.75
		First day cover, #29-30		8.00
		Inscription block of 4	1.10	—

First day covers of Nos. 29 and 30 total 276,333.

Symbol of Flight — A17

Design: 8c, inscribed "OACI."
Issued to honor the International Civil Aviation Organization.
Engraved and printed by Waterlow & Sons, Ltd., London. Panes of 50. Designed by Angel Medina Medina.

1955, Feb. 9 ***Perf. 13½x14***

No.	Type	Description	Unused	Used
31	A17	3c **blue** *(1,000,000)*	1.25	.65
		First day cover		2.00
		Inscription block of 4	7.00	—
32	A17	8c **rose carmine** *(1,000,000)*	.75	.75
		First day cover		3.00
		First day cover, #31-32		5.50
		Inscription block of 4	2.50	—

First day covers of Nos. 31 and 32 total 237,131.

UNESCO Emblem — A18

Issued to honor the UN Educational, Scientific and Cultural Organization.
Engraved and printed by Waterlow & Sons, Ltd., London. Panes of 50. Designed by George Hamori.

1955, May 11 ***Perf. 13½x14***

No.	Type	Description	Unused	Used
33	A18	3c **lilac rose** *(1,000,000)*	.20	.20
		First day cover		2.00
		Inscription block of 4	1.50	—
34	A18	8c **light blue** *(1,000,000)*	.20	.20
		First day cover		3.00
		First day cover, #33-34		5.00
		Inscription block of 4	.75	—

First day covers of Nos. 33 and 34 total 255,326.

United Nations Charter — A19

Design: 4c, Spanish inscription. 8c, French inscription.
10th anniversary of the United Nations.
Engraved and printed by Waterlow & Sons, Ltd., London. Panes of 50. Designed by Claude Bottiau.

1955, Oct. 24 ***Perf. 13½x14***

No.	Type	Description	Unused	Used
35	A19	3c **deep plum** *(1,000,000)*	.75	.50
		First day cover		3.00
		Inscription block of 4	4.00	—
36	A19	4c **dull green** *(1,000,000)*	.35	.20
		First day cover		3.00
		Inscription block of 4	1.75	—
37	A19	8c **bluish black** *(1,000,000)*	.20	.20
		First day cover		4.00
		First day cover, #35-37		11.00
		Inscription block of 4	.80	—
		Nos. 35-37 (3)	1.30	.90

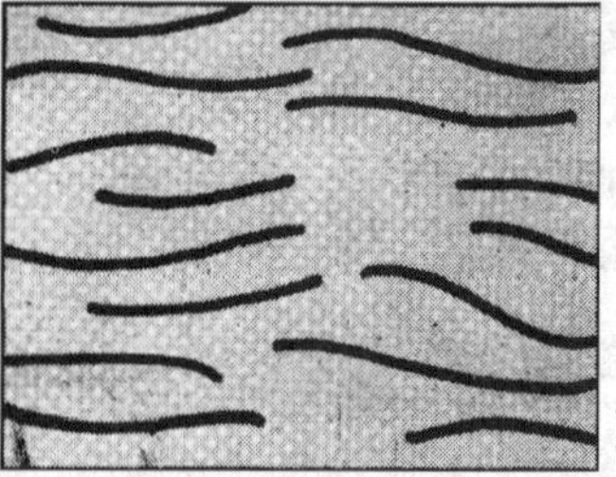

Wmk. 309-Wavy Lines

Souvenir Sheet

1955, Oct. 24		**Wmk. 309**		*Imperf.*
38	A19	Sheet of 3 *(250,000)*	95.00	20.00
		Hinged	60.00	
a.		3c **deep plum**	3.00	.50
b.		4c **dull green**	3.00	.50
c.		8c **bluish black**	3.00	.50
		First day cover		20.00
		Sheet with retouch on 8c	110.00	40.00

No. 38 measures 108x83mm and has marginal inscriptions in deep plum.

Two printings were made of No. 38. The first (200,000) may be distinguished by the broken line of background shading on the 8c. It leaves a small white spot below the left leg of the "n" of "Unies." For the second printing (50,000), the broken line was retouched, eliminating the white spot. The 4c was also retouched.

First day covers of Nos. 35-38 total 455,791.

Copies of No. 38 are known with the 4c and 8c stamps misaligned.

Hand Holding Torch — A20

Issued in honor of Human Rights Day.

Engraved and printed by Waterlow & Sons, Ltd., London. Panes of 50. Designed by Hubert Woyty-Wimmer.

1955, Dec. 9		**Unwmk.**		*Perf. 14x13½*
39	A20	3c **ultramarine** *(1,250,000)*	.20	.20
		First day cover		1.25
		Inscription block of 4	.55	—
40	A20	8c **green** *(1,000,000)*	.20	.25
		First day cover		1.25
		First day cover, #39-40		2.50
		Inscription block of 4	1.10	—

First day covers of Nos. 39 and 40 total 298,038.

Symbols of Telecommunication — A21

Design: 8c, inscribed "UIT."

Issued in honor of the International Telecommunication Union.

Engraved and printed by Thomas De La Rue & Co., Ltd., London. Panes of 50. Designed by Hubert Woyty-Wimmer.

1956, Feb. 17				*Perf. 14*
41	A21	3c **turquoise blue** *(1,000,000)*	.20	.20
		First day cover		1.50
		Inscription block of 4	.45	—
42	A21	8c **deep carmine** *(1,000,000)*	.20	.30
		First day cover		2.25
		First day cover, #41-42		3.50
		Inscription block of 4	1.40	—

Plate number ("1A" or "1B") in color of stamp appears below 47th stamp of sheet.

Globe and Caduceus — A22

Design: 8c, inscribed "OMS."

Issued in honor of the World Health Organization.

Engraved and printed by Thomas De La Rue & Co., Ltd., London. Panes of 50. Designed by Olav Mathiesen.

1956, Apr. 6				*Perf. 14*
43	A22	3c **bright greenish blue** *(1,250,000)*	.20	.20
		First day cover		1.00
		Inscription block of 4	.50	—
44	A22	8c **golden brown** *(1,000,000)*	.20	.25
		First day cover		1.50
		First day cover, #43-44		14.00
		Inscription block of 4	1.25	—

First day covers of Nos. 43 and 44 total 260,853.

General Assembly A23

Design: 8c, French inscription.

Issued to commemorate United Nations Day.

Engraved and printed by Thomas De La Rue & Co., Ltd., London. Panes of 50. Designed by Kurt Plowitz.

1956, Oct. 24				*Perf. 14*
45	A23	3c **dark blue** *(2,000,000)*	.20	.20
		First day cover		1.00
		Inscription block of 4	.30	—
46	A23	8c **gray olive** *(1,500,000)*	.20	.20
		First day cover		1.00
		First day cover, #45-46		7.50
		Inscription block of 4	.80	—

First day covers of Nos. 45 and 46 total 303,560.

Flame and Globe — A24

Issued to publicize Human Rights Day
Engraved and printed by Thomas De La Rue & Co., Ltd., London. Panes of 50. Designed by Rashid-ud Din.

1956, Dec. 10 ***Perf. 14***

47	A24	3c	**plum** *(5,000,000)*	.20	.20
			First day cover		1.00
			Inscription block of 4	.30	—
48	A24	8c	**dark blue** *(4,000,000)*	.20	.20
			First day cover		1.00
			First day cover, #47-48		2.00
			Inscription block of 4	.60	—

First day covers of Nos. 47 and 48 total 416,120.

Weather Balloon — A25

Badge of UN Emergency Force — A26

Design: 8c, Agency name in French.
Issued to honor the World Meterological Organization.
Engraved and printed by Thomas De La Rue & Co., Ltd., London. Panes of 50. Designed by A. L. Pollock.

1957, Jan. 28 ***Perf. 14***

49	A25	3c	**violet blue** *(5,000,000)*	.20	.20
			First day cover		1.00
			Inscription block of 4	.25	—
50	A25	8c	**dark carmine rose** *(3,448,985)*	.20	.20
			First day cover		1.00
			First day cover, #49-50		2.25
			Inscription block of 4	.65	—

First day covers of Nos. 49 and 50 total 376,110.

1957, Apr. 8 ***Perf. 14x12½***

Issued in honor of the UN Emergency Force.
Engraved and printed by Thomas De La Rue & Co., Ltd., London. Panes of 50. Designed by Ole Hamann.

51	A26	3c	**light blue** *(4,000,000)*	.20	.20
			First day cover		1.00
			Inscription block of 4	.30	—
52	A26	8c	**rose carmine** *(3,000,000)*	.20	.20
			First day cover		1.00
			First day cover, #51-52		1.75
			Inscription block of 4	.70	—

First day covers of Nos. 51 and 52 total 461,772.

Nos. 51-52 Re-engraved

1957, Apr.-May ***Perf. 14x12½***

53	A26	3c	**blue** *(2,736,206)*	.20	.20
			Inscription block of 4	.40	—
54	A26	8c	**rose carmine** *(1,000,000)*	.35	.20
			Inscription block of 4	1.40	—

On Nos. 53-54 the background within and around the circles is shaded lightly, giving a halo effect. The lettering is more distinct with a line around each letter.

UN Emblem and Globe — A27

Design: 8c, French inscription.
Issued to honor the Security Council.
Engraved and printed by Thomas De La Rue & Co., Ltd., London. Panes of 50. Designed by Rashid-ud Din.

1957, Oct. 24 ***Perf. 12½x13***

55	A27	3c	**orange brown** *(3,674,968)*	.20	.20
			First day cover		1.00
			Inscription block of 4	.25	—
56	A27	8c	**dark blue green** *(2,885,938)*	.20	.20
			First day cover		1.00
			First day cover, #55-56		2.25
			Inscription block of 4	.70	—

First day covers of Nos. 55 and 56 total 460,627.

Flaming Torch — A28

Issued in honor of Human Rights Day.
Engraved and printed by Thomas De La Rue & Co., Ltd., London. Panes of 50. Designed by Olav Mathiesen.

1957, Dec. 10 ***Perf. 14***

57	A28	3c	**red brown** *(3,368,405)*	.20	.20
			First day cover		1.00
			Inscription block of 4	.25	—
58	A28	8c	**black** *(2,717,310)*	.20	.20
			First day cover		1.00
			First day cover, #57-58		1.25
			Inscription block of 4	.65	—

First day covers of Nos. 57 and 58 total 553,669.

UN Emblem Shedding Light on Atom — A29

Design: 8c, French inscription.
Issued in honor of the International Atomic Energy Agency.
Engraved and printed by the American Bank Note Co., New York. Panes of 50. Designed by Robert Perrot.

1958, Feb. 10 ***Perf. 12***

59	A29	3c	**olive** *(3,663,305)*	.20	.20
			First day cover		1.00
			Inscription block of 4	.25	—
60	A29	8c	**blue** *(3,043,622)*	.20	.20
			First day cover		1.00
			First day cover, #59-60		1.00
			Inscription block of 4	.65	—

First day covers of Nos. 59 and 60 total 504,832.

Central Hall, Westminster — A30

UN Seal — A31

Design: 8c, French inscription.

Central Hall, Westminster, London, was the site of the first session of the United Nations General Assembly, 1946.
Engraved and printed by the American Bank Note Co., New York. Panes of 50. Designed by Olav Mathiesen.

1958, Apr. 14 ***Perf. 12***

61	A30	3c	**violet blue** *(3,353,716)*	.20	.20
			First day cover		1.00
			Inscription block of 4	.25	—
62	A30	8c	**rose claret** *(2,836,747)*	.20	.20
			First day cover		1.00
			First day cover, #61-62		2.00
			Inscription block of 4	.60	—

First day covers of Nos. 61 and 62 total 449,401.

1958, Oct. 24 ***Perf. 13½x14***

Engraved and printed by Bradbury, Wilkinson & Co., Ltd., England. Panes of 50. Designed by Herbert M. Sanborn.

63	A31	4c	**red orange** *(9,000,000)*	.20	.20
			First day cover		1.00
			First day cover of #63 also bearing #64		*75.00*
			Inscription block of 4	.20	—

1958, June 2 ***Perf. 13x14***

64	A31	8c	**bright blue** *(5,000,000)*	.20	.20
			First day cover *(219,422)*		1.00
			Inscription block of 4	.55	—
			Margin block of 4, Bradbury, Wilkinson imprint	3.00	—

Gearwheels — A32

Hands Upholding Globe — A33

Design: 8c, French inscription.
Issued to honor the Economic and Social Council.
Engraved and printed by the American Bank Note Co., New York. Panes of 50. Designed by Ole Hamann.

1958, Oct. 24 **Unwmk.** ***Perf. 12***

65	A32	4c	**dark blue green** *(2,556,784)*	.20	.20
			First day cover		1.00
			Inscription block of 4	.30	—
66	A32	8c	**vermilion** *(2,175,117)*	.20	.20
			First day cover		1.00
			First day cover, #65-66		1.00
			Inscription block of 4	.60	—

First day covers of Nos. 63, 65 and 66 total 626,236.

1958, Dec. 10 **Unwmk.** ***Perf. 12***

Issued for Human Rights Day and to commemorate the 10th anniversary of the signing of the Universal Declaration of Human Rights.
Engraved and printed by the American Bank Note Co., New York. Panes of 50. Designed by Leonard C. Mitchell.

67	A33	4c	**yellow green** *(2,644,340)*	.20	.20
			First day cover		1.00
			Inscription block of 4	.40	—
68	A33	8c	**red brown** *(2,216,838)*	.20	.20
			First day cover		1.00
			First day cover, #67-68		1.00
			Inscription block of 4	.75	—

First day covers of Nos. 67 and 68 total 618,124.

New York City Building, Flushing Meadows A34

Design: 8c, French inscription.

New York City Building at Flushing Meadows, New York, was the site of many General Assembly meetings, 1946-50.

Engraved and printed by Canadian Bank Note Company, Ltd., Ottawa. Panes of 50. Designed by Robert Perrot.

1959, Mar. 30 Unwmk. *Perf. 12*

69	A34	4c **light lilac rose** *(2,035,011)*	.20	.20
		First day cover		1.00
		Inscription block of 4	.30	—
70	A34	8c **aquamarine** *(1,627,281)*	.20	.20
		First day cover		1.00
		First day cover, #69-70		1.75
		Inscription block of 4	.70	—

First day covers of Nos. 69 and 70 total 440,955.

A35

A36

Design: UN emblem and symbols of agriculture, industry and trade.

Issued to honor the Economic Commission for Europe.

Engraved and printed by Canadian Bank Note Company, Ltd., Ottawa. Panes of 50. Designed by Ole Hamann.

1959, May 18 Unwmk. *Perf. 12*

71	A35	4c **blue** *(1,743,502)*	.20	.20
		First day cover		1.00
		Inscription block of 4	.60	—
72	A35	8c **red orange** *(1,482,898)*	.20	.20
		First day cover		1.00
		First day cover, #71-72		1.25
		Inscription block of 4	.75	—

First day covers of Nos. 71 and 72 total 433,549.

1959, Oct. 23 Unwmk. *Perf. 12*

Designs: 4c, Figure Adapted from Rodin's "Age of Bronze." 8c, same, French inscription.

Issued to honor the Trusteeship Council.

Engraved and printed by Canadian Bank Note Co., Ltd., Ottawa. Panes of 50. Designed by León Helguera; lettering by Ole Hamann.

73	A36	4c **bright red** *(1,929,677)*	.20	.20
		First day cover		1.00
		Inscription block of 4	.30	—
74	A36	8c **dark olive green** *(1,587,647)*	.20	.20
		First day cover		1.00
		First day cover, #73-74		1.50
		Inscription block of 4	1.00	—

First day covers of Nos. 73 and 74 total 466,053.

World Refugee Year Emblem — A37

Chaillot Palace, Paris — A38

Design: 8c, French inscription.

Issued to publicize World Refugee Year, July 1, 1959-June 30, 1960.

Engraved and printed by Canadian Bank Note Co., Ltd., Ottawa. Panes of 50. Designed by Olav Mathiesen.

1959, Dec. 10 Unwmk. *Perf. 12*

75	A37	4c **olive & red** *(2,168,963)*	.20	.20
		First day cover		1.00
		Inscription block of 4	.35	—
76	A37	8c **olive & bright greenish blue** *(1,843,886)*	.20	.20
		First day cover		1.00
		First day cover, #75-76		2.00
		Inscription block of 4	.75	—

First day covers of Nos. 75 and 76 total 502,262.

1960, Feb. 29 Unwmk. *Perf. 14*

Design: 8c, French inscription.

Chaillot Palace in Paris was the site of General Assembly meetings in 1948 and 1951.

Engraved and printed by Thomas De La Rue & Co., Ltd., London. Panes of 50. Designed by Hubert Woyty-Wimmer.

77	A38	4c **rose lilac & blue** *(2,276,678)*	.20	.20
		First day cover		1.00
		Inscription block of 4	.20	—
78	A38	8c **dull green & brown** *(1,930,869)*	.20	.20
		First day cover		1.00
		First day cover, #77-78		2.50
		Inscription block of 4	.70	—

First day covers of Nos. 77 and 78 total 446,815.

Map of Far East and Steel Beam — A39

Design: 8c, French inscription.

Issued to honor the Economic Commission for Asia and the Far East (ECAFE).

Printed by the Government Printing Bureau, Tokyo. Panes of 50. Designed by Hubert Woyty-Wimmer.

1960, Apr. 11 Photo. Unwmk. *Perf. 13x13½*

79	A39	4c **deep claret, blue green & dull yellow** *(2,195,945)*	.20	.20
		First day cover		1.00
		Inscription block of 4	.20	—
80	A39	8c **olive green, blue & rose** *(1,897,902)*	.20	.20
		First day cover		1.00
		First day cover, #79-80		2.00
		Inscription block of 4	.75	—

First day covers of Nos. 79 and 80 total 415,127.

Tree, FAO and UN Emblems — A40

UN Headquarters and Preamble to UN Charter — A41

Design: 8c, French inscription.

Issued to commemorate the Fifth World Forestry Congress, Seattle, Washington, Aug. 29-Sept. 10.

Printed by the Government Printing Bureau, Tokyo. Panes of 50. Designed by Ole Hamann.

1960, Aug. 29 Photo. Unwmk. *Perf. 13½*

81	A40	4c **dark blue, green & orange** *(2,188,293)*	.20	.20
		First day cover		1.00
		Inscription block of 4	.35	—
82	A40	8c **yellow green, black & orange** *(1,837,778)*	.20	.20
		First day cover		1.00
		First day cover, #81-82		2.00
		Inscription block of 4	.65	—

First day covers of Nos. 81 and 82 total 434,129.

1960, Oct. 24 Unwmk. *Perf. 11*

Design: 8c, French inscription.

Issued to commemorate the 15th anniversary of the United Nations.

Engraved and printed by the British American Bank Note Co., Ltd., Ottawa, Canada. Panes of 50. Designed by Robert Perrot.

83	A41	4c **blue** *(2,631,593)*	.20	.20
		First day cover		1.00
		Inscription block of 4	.35	—
84	A41	8c **gray** *(2,278,022)*	.20	.20
		First day cover		1.00
		First day cover, #83-84		1.50
		Inscription block of 4	.65	—

Souvenir Sheet

Imperf

85		Sheet of 2 *(1,000,000)*	.50	.50
a.	A41	4c **blue**	.25	.20
b.	A41	8c **gray**	.25	.20
		First day cover *(256,699)*		.50

No. 85 has dark gray marginal inscription. Size: 92x71mm. Broken "I" and "V" flaws occur in "ANNIVERSARY" in marginal inscription. Copies are known with the two stamps misaligned.

Block and Tackle — A42

Scales of Justice from Raphael's Stanze — A43

Design: 8c, French inscription.

Issued to honor the International Bank for Reconstruction and Development.

Printed by the Government Printing Bureau, Tokyo. Panes of 50. Designed by Angel Medina Medina.

1960, Dec. 9 Photo. Unwmk. *Perf. 13½x13*

86	A42	4c **multicolored** *(2,286,117)*	.20	.20
		First day cover		1.00
		Inscription block of 4	.35	—
87	A42	8c **multicolored** *(1,882,019)*	.20	.20
		First day cover		1.00
		First day cover, #86-87		1.25
		Inscription block of 4	.65	—

First day covers of Nos. 86 and 87 total 559,708.

1961, Feb. 13 Photo. Unwmk. *Perf. 13½x13*

Design: 8c, French inscription.

Issued to honor the International Court of Justice.

Printed by the Government Printing Bureau, Tokyo, Japan. Panes of 50. Designed by Kurt Plowitz.

88	A43	4c **yellow, orange brown & black** *(2,234,588)*	.20	.20
		First day cover		1.00
		Inscription block of 4	.35	—
89	A43	8c **yellow, green & black** *(2,023,968)*	.20	.20
		First day cover		1.00
		First day cover, #88-89		1.00
		Inscription block of 4	.65	—

First day covers of Nos. 88 and 89 total 447,467.

Seal of International Monetary Fund — A44

Design: 7c, French inscription.

Issued to honor the International Monetary Fund.

Printed by the Government Printing Bureau, Tokyo, Japan. Panes of 50. Designed by Roy E. Carlson and Hordur Karlsson, Iceland.

1961, Apr. 17 Photo. Unwmk. *Perf. 13x13½*

90	A44	4c **bright bluish green** *(2,305,010)*	.20	.20
		First day cover		1.00
		Inscription block of 4	.35	—
91	A44	7c **terra cotta & yellow** *(2,147,201)*	.20	.20
		First day cover		1.00
		First day cover, #90-91		1.00
		Inscription block of 4	.65	—

First day covers of Nos. 90 and 91total 448,729.

Abstract Group of Flags — A45

Printed by Courvoisier S.A., La Chaux-de-Fonds, Switzerland. Panes of 50. Designed by Herbert M. Sanborn.

1961, June 5 Photo. Unwmk. *Perf. 11½*

92 A45 30c **multicolored** *(3,370,000)* .40 .20
First day cover *(182,949)* 1.00
Inscription block of 4 1.75 —

See UN Offices in Geneva No. 10.

Cogwheel and Map of Latin America — A46

Design: 11c, Spanish inscription.
Issued to honor the Economic Commission for Latin America.
Printed by the Government Printing Bureau, Tokyo. Panes of 50. Designed by Robert Perrot.

1961, Sept. 18 Photo. Unwmk. *Perf. 13½*

93 A46 4c **blue, red & citron** *(2,037,912)* .20 .20
First day cover 1.00
Inscription block of 4 .45 —

94 A46 11c **green, lilac & orange vermilion** *(1,835,097)* .25 .20
First day cover 1.00
First day cover, #93-94 1.00
Inscription block of 4 1.25 —

First day covers of Nos. 93 and 94 total 435,820.

Africa House, Addis Ababa, and Map — A47

Design: 11c, English inscription.
Issued to honor the Economic Commission for Africa.
Printed by Courvoisier S.A., La Chaux-de-Fonds, Switzerland. Panes of 50. Designed by Robert Perrot.

1961, Oct. 24 Photo. Unwmk. *Perf. 11½*

95 A47 4c **ultramarine, orange, yellow & brown** *(2,044,842)* .20 .20
First day cover 1.00
Inscription block of 4 .30 —

96 A47 11c **emerald, orange, yellow & brown** *(1,790,894)* .25 .20
First day cover 1.00
First day cover, #95-96 1.00
Inscription block of 4 1.10 —

First day covers of Nos. 95 and 96 total 435,131.

Mother Bird Feeding Young and UNICEF Seal — A48

Designs: 3c, Spanish inscription. 13c, French inscription.
15th anniversary of the United Nations Children's Fund.
Printed by Courvoisier S.A., La Chaux-de-Fonds, Switzerland. Panes of 50. Designed by Minoru Hisano.

1961, Dec. 4 Photo. Unwmk. *Perf. 11½*

97 A48 3c **brown, gold, orange & yellow** *(2,867,456)* .20 .20
First day cover 1.00
Inscription block of 4 .25 —

98 A48 4c **brown, gold, blue & emerald** *(2,735,899)* .20 .20
First day cover 1.00
Inscription block of 4 .35 —

99 A48 13c **deep green, gold, purple & pink** *(1,951,715)* .20 .20
First day cover 1.00
First day cover, #97-99 1.40
Inscription block of 4 1.25 —
Nos. 97-99 (3) .60 .60

First day covers of Nos. 97-99 total 752,979.

Family and Symbolic Buildings A49

Design: 7c, inscribed "Services Collectifs".
Issued to publicize the UN program for housing and urban development, and in connection with the expert committee meeting at UN headquarters, Feb. 7-21.
Printed by Harrison and Sons, Ltd., London, England. Panes of 50. Designed by Olav Mathiesen.

1962, Feb. 28 Photo. Unwmk. *Perf. 14½x14*

Central design multicolored

100 A49 4c **bright blue** *(2,204,190)* .20 .20
First day cover 1.00
Inscription block of 4 .35 —
a. Black omitted 200.00
b. Yellow omitted —
c. Brown omitted —

101 A49 7c **orange brown** *(1,845,821)* .20 .20
First day cover 1.00
First day cover, #100-101 1.25
Inscription block of 4 .65 —
a. Red omitted —
b. Black omitted —
c. Gold omitted —

First day covers of Nos. 100-101 total 466,178.

"The World Against Malaria" — A50

Issued in honor of the World Health Organization and to call attention to the international campaign to eradicate malaria from the world.
Printed by Harrison and Sons, Ltd., London, England. Panes of 50. Designed by Rashid-ud Din.

1962, Mar. 30 Photo. Unwmk. *Perf. 14x14½*

Word frame in gray

102 A50 4c **orange, yellow, brown, green & black** *(2,047,000)* .20 .20
First day cover 1.00
Inscription block of 4 .35 —

103 A50 11c **green, yellow, brown & indigo** *(1,683,766)* .25 .20
First day cover 1.00
First day cover, #102-103 1.50
Inscription block of 4 1.10 —

First day covers of Nos. 102-103 total 522,450.

"Peace" — A51

UN Flag — A52

Hands Combining "UN" and Globe — A53

UN Emblem over Globe — A54

Printed by Harrison & Sons, Ltd. London, England (1c, 3c and 11c), and by Canadian Bank Note Co., Ltd., Ottawa (5c). Panes of 50. Designed by Kurt Plowitz (1c), Ole Hamann (3c), Renato Ferrini (5c) and Olav Mathiesen (11c).

Photo.; Engr. (5c)

1962, May 25 Unwmk. *Perf. 14x14½*

104 A51 1c **vermilion, blue, black & gray** *(5,000,000)* .20 .20
First day cover 1.00
Inscription block of 4 .25 —

105 A52 3c **light green, Prussian blue, yellow & gray** *(5,000,000)* .20 .20
First day cover 1.00
Inscription block of 4 .25 —

Perf. 12

106 A53 5c **dark carmine rose** *(4,000,000)* .20 .20
First day cover 1.00
Inscription block of 4 .65 —

Perf. 12½

107 A54 11c **dark & light blue & gold** *(4,400,000)* .25 .20
First day cover 1.00
First day cover, #104-107 6.00
Inscription block of 4 1.10 —
Nos. 104-107 (4) .85 .80

First day covers of Nos. 104-107 total 738,985.
Size of 5c, No. 106: 36½x23½mm.
See No. 167. See UN Offices in Geneva Nos. 2 and 6.

Flag at Half-mast and UN Headquarters — A55

World Map Showing Congo — A56

Issued on the 1st anniversary of the death of Dag Hammarskjold, Secretary General of the United Nations 1953-61, in memory of those who died in the service of the United Nations.

Printed by Courvoisier S. A., La Chaux-de-Fonds, Switzerland. Panes of 50. Designed by Ole Hamann.

1962, Sept. 17 Photo. Unwmk. *Perf. 11½*

108 A55 5c **black, light blue & blue** *(2,195,707)* .20 .20
First day cover 1.00
Inscription block of 4 .50 —
109 A55 15c **black, gray olive & blue** *(1,155,047)* .20 .20
First day cover 1.00
First day cover, #108-109 2.00
Inscription block of 4 .85 —

First day covers of Nos. 108-109 total 513,963.

1962, Oct. 24 Photo. Unwmk. *Perf. 11½*

Design: 11c inscribed "Operation des Nations Unies au Congo."
Issued to commemorate the United Nations Operation in the Congo.
Printed by Courvoisier S. A., La Chaux-de-Fonds, Switzerland. Panes of 50. Designed by George Hamori.

110 A56 4c **olive, orange, black & yellow** *(1,477,958)* .20 .20
First day cover 1.00
Inscription block of 4 .50 —
111 A56 11c **blue green, orange, black & yellow** *(1,171,255)* .20 .20
First day cover 1.00
First day cover, #110-111 1.75
Inscription block of 4 .95 —

First day covers of Nos. 110-111 total 460,675.

Globe in Universe and Palm Frond — A57

Development Decade Emblem — A58

Design: 4c, English inscription.
Issued to honor the Committee on Peaceful Uses of Outer Space.
Printed by Bradbury, Wilkinson and Co., Ltd., England. Panes of 50. Designed by Kurt Plowitz.

1962, Dec. 3 Engr. Unwmk. *Perf. 14x13½*

112 A57 4c **violet blue** *(2,263,876)* .20 .20
First day cover 1.00
Inscription block of 4 .35 —
113 A57 11c **rose claret** *(1,681,584)* .25 .20
First day cover 1.00
First day cover, #112-113 2.00
Inscription block of 4 1.25 —

First day covers of Nos. 112-113 total 529,780.

1963, Feb. 4 Photo. Unwmk. *Perf. 11½*

Design: 11c, French inscription.
UN Development Decade and UN Conference on the Application of Science and Technology for the Benefit of the Less Developed Areas, Geneva, Feb. 4-20.
Printed by Courvoisier S. A., La Chaux-de-Fonds, Switzerland. Panes of 50. Designed by Rashid-ud Din.

114 A58 5c **pale green, maroon, dark blue & Prussian blue** *(1,802,406)* .20 .20
First day cover 1.00
Inscription block of 4 .35 —
115 A58 11c **yellow, maroon, dark blue & Prussian blue** *(1,530,190)* .20 .20
First day cover 1.00
First day cover, #114-115 1.50
Inscription block of 4 .90 —

First day covers of Nos. 114-115 total 460,877.

Stalks of Wheat — A59

Design: 11c, French inscription.
Issued for the "Freedom from Hunger" campaign of the Food and Agriculture Organization.
Printed by Courvoisier S. A., La Chaux-de-Fonds, Switzerland. Panes of 50. Designed by Ole Hamann.

1963, Mar. 22 Photo. Unwmk. *Perf. 11½*

116 A59 5c **vermilion, green & yellow** *(1,666,178)* .20 .20
First day cover 1.00
Inscription block of 4 .35 —
117 A59 11c **vermilion, deep claret & yellow** *(1,563,023)* .25 .20
First day cover 1.00
First day cover, #116-117 1.50
Inscription block of 4 1.10 —

First day covers of Nos. 116-117 total 461,868.

Bridge over Map of New Guinea — A60

1st anniversary of the United Nations Temporary Executive Authority (UNTEA) in West New Guinea (West Irian).
Printed by Courvoisier S.A., La Chaux-de-Fonds, Switzerland. Panes of 50. Designed by Henry Bencsath.

1963, Oct. 1 Photo. Unwmk. *Perf. 11½*

118 A60 25c **blue, green & gray** *(1,427,747)* .45 .30
First day cover *(222,280)* 1.00
Inscription block of 4 2.00 —

General Assembly Building, New York — A61

Design: 11c, French inscription.
Since October 1955 all sessions of the General Assembly have been held in the General Assembly Hall, UN Headquarters, NY.
Printed by the Government Printing Bureau, Tokyo. Panes of 50. Designed by Kurt Plowitz.

1963, Nov. 4 Photo. Unwmk. *Perf. 13*

119 A61 5c **violet blue, blue, yellow green & red** *(1,892,539)* .20 .20
First day cover 1.00
Inscription block of 4 .35 —
120 A61 11c **green, yellow green, blue, yellow & red** *(1,435,079)* .20 .20
First day cover 1.00
First day cover, #119-120 1.25
Inscription block of 4 .85 —

First day covers of Nos. 119-120 total 410,306.

Flame — A62

Design: 11c inscribed "15e Anniversaire."
15th anniversary of the signing of the Universal Declaration of Human Rights.
Printed by the Government Printing Bureau, Tokyo. Panes of 50. Designed by Rashid-ud Din.

1963, Dec. 10 Photo. Unwmk. *Perf. 13*

121 A62 5c **green, gold, red & yellow** *(2,208,008)* .20 .20
First day cover 1.00
Inscription block of 4 .55 —
122 A62 11c **carmine, gold, blue & yellow** *(1,501,125)* .20 .20
First day cover 1.00
First day cover, #121-122 1.00
Inscription block of 4 .70 —

First day covers of Nos. 121-122 total 567,907.

Ships at Sea and IMCO Emblem — A63

Design: 11c, inscribed "OMCI."
Issued to honor the Intergovernmental Maritime Consultative Organization.
Printed by Courvoisier S.A., La Chaux-de-Fonds, Switzerland. Panes of 50. Designed by Henry Bencsath; emblem by Olav Mathiesen.

1964, Jan. 13 Photo. Unwmk. *Perf. 11½*

123 A63 5c **blue, olive, ocher & yellow** *(1,805,750)* .20 .20
First day cover 1.00
Inscription block of 4 .35 —
124 A63 11c **dark blue, dark green, emerald & yellow** *(1,583,848)* .20 .20
First day cover 1.00
First day cover, #123-124 1.00
Inscription block of 4 .85 —

First day covers of Nos. 123-124 total 442,696.

World Map, Sinusoidal Projection — A64

UN Emblem — A65

Three Men United Before Globe — A66

Stylized Globe and Weather Vane — A67

Printed by Thomas De La Rue & Co. Ltd., London (2c) and Courvoisier S.A., La Chaux-de-Fonds, Switzerland (7c, 10c and 50c). Panes of 50.
Designed by Ole Hamann (2c), George Hamori (7c, 10c) and Hatim El Mekki (50c).

1964-71 Photo. Unwmk. *Perf. 14*

125 A64 2c **light & dark blue, orange & yellow green** *(3,800,000)* .20 .20
First day cover 1.00
Inscription block of 4 .20 —
a. Perf. 13x13½, *Feb. 24, 1971 (1,500,000)* .20 .20

Perf. 11½

126 A65 7c **dark blue, orange brown & black** *(2,700,000)* .20 .20
First day cover 1.00
Inscription block of 4 .80 —
127 A66 10c **blue green, olive green & black** *(3,200,000)* .20 .25
First day cover 1.00
First day cover, #125-127 5.00
Inscription block of 4 .80 —
128 A67 50c **multicolored** *(2,520,000)* .75 .45
First day cover *(210,713)* 1.00
Inscription block of 4 3.75 —
Nos. 125-128 (4) 1.35 1.10

Issue dates: 50c, Mar. 6; 2c, 7c, 10c, May 29, 1964.
First day covers of 2c, 7c and 10c total 524,073.
See UN Offices in Geneva Nos. 3 and 12.

Arrows Showing Global Flow of Trade — A68

Design: 5c, English inscription.
Issued to commemorate the UN Conference on Trade and Development, Geneva, Mar. 23-June 15.
Printed by Thomas De La Rue & Co., Ltd., London. Panes of 50. Designed by Herbert M. Sanborn and Ole Hamann.

1964, June 15 Photo. Unwmk. *Perf. 13*

129 A68 5c **black, red & yellow** *(1,791,211)* .20 .20
First day cover 1.00
Inscription block of 4 .35 —
130 A68 11c **black, olive & yellow** *(1,529,526)* .20 .20
First day cover 1.00
First day cover, #129-130 1.50
Inscription block of 4 .85 —

First day covers of Nos. 129-130 total 422,358.

Poppy Capsule and Reaching Hands — A69

Design: 11c, Inscribed "Echec au Stupéfiants."
Issued to honor international efforts and achievements in the control of narcotics.
Printed by the Canadian Bank Note Co., Ottawa. Panes of 50. Designed by Kurt Plowitz.

1964, Sept. 21 Engr. Unwmk. *Perf. 12*

131 A69 5c **rose red & black** *(1,508,999)* .20 .20
First day cover 1.00
Inscription block of 4 .45 —
132 A69 11c **emerald & black** *(1,340,691)* .20 .20
First day cover 1.00
First day cover, #131-132 1.75
Inscription block of 4 1.10 —

First day covers of Nos. 131-132 total 445,274.

Padlocked Atomic Blast — A70

Education for Progress — A71

Signing of the nuclear test ban treaty pledging an end to nuclear explosions in the atmosphere, outer space and under water.
Printed by Artia, Prague, Czechoslovakia. Panes of 50. Designed by Ole Hamann.

Litho. and Engr.

1964, Oct. 23 Unwmk. *Perf. 11x11½*

133 A70 5c **dark red & dark brown** *(2,422,789)* .20 .20
First day cover *(298,652)* 1.00
Inscription block of 4 .45 —

1964, Dec. 7 Photo. Unwmk. *Perf. 12½*

Design: 11c, French inscription.
Issued to publicize the UNESCO world campaign for universal literacy and for free compulsory primary education.
Printed by Courvoisier, S. A., La Chaux-de-Fonds, Switzerland. Panes of 50. Designed by Kurt Plowitz.

134 A71 4c **orange, red, bister, green & blue** *(2,375,181)* .20 .20
First day cover 1.00
Inscription block of 4 .25 —
135 A71 5c **bister, red, dark & light blue** *(2,496,877)* .20 .20
First day cover 1.00
Inscription block of 4 .35 —
136 A71 11c **green, light blue, black & rose** *(1,773,645)* .20 .20
First day cover 1.00
First day cover, #134-136 1.25
Inscription block of 4 .75 —
Nos. 134-136 (3) .60 .60

First day covers of Nos. 134-136 total 727,875.

Progress Chart of Special Fund, Key and Globe — A72

UN Emblem, Stylized Leaves and View of Cyprus — A73

Design: 11c, French inscription.
Issued to publicize the Special Fund program to speed economic growth and social advancement in low-income countries.
Printed by the Government Printing Bureau, Tokyo. Panes of 50. Designed by Rashid-ud Din, Pakistan.

1965, Jan. 25 Photo. Unwmk. *Perf. 13½x13*

137 A72 5c **dull blue, dark blue, yellow & red** *(1,949,274)* .20 .20
First day cover 1.00
Inscription block of 4 .40 —
138 A72 11c **yellow green, dark blue, yellow & red** *(1,690,908)* .20 .20
First day cover 1.00
First day cover, #137-138 1.25
Inscription block of 4 .85 —
a. Black omitted (UN emblem on key) —

First day covers of Nos. 137-138 total 490,608.

1965, Mar. 4 Photo. Unwmk. *Perf. 11½*

Design: 11c, French inscription.
Issued to honor the United Nations Peace-keeping Force on Cyprus.
Printed by Courvoisier S.A., Switzerland. Panes of 50. Designed by George Hamori, Australia.

139 A73 5c **orange, olive & black** *(1,887,042)* .20 .20
First day cover 1.00
Inscription block of 4 .40 —
140 A73 11c **yellow green, blue green & black** *(1,691,767)* .20 .20
First day cover 1.00
First day cover, #139-140 1.25
Inscription block of 4 .80 —

First day covers of Nos. 139-140 total 438,059.

"From Semaphore to Satellite" — A74

Design: 11c, French inscription.
Centenary of the International Telecommunication Union.
Printed by Courvoisier S.A., Switzerland. Panes of 50. Designed by Kurt Plowitz, United States.

1965, May 17 Photo. Unwmk. *Perf. 11½*

141 A74 5c **aquamarine, orange, blue & purple** *(2,432,407)* .20 .20
First day cover 1.00
Inscription block of 4 .40 —
142 A74 11c **light violet, red orange, bister & bright green** *(1,731,070)* .20 .20
First day cover 1.00
First day cover, #141-142 1.25
Inscription block of 4 .80 —

First day covers of Nos. 141-142 total 434,393.

ICY Emblem — A75

Design: 15c, French inscription.
20th anniversary of the United Nations and International Cooperation Year.
Printed by Bradbury, Wilkinson and Co., Ltd., England. Panes of 50. Designed by Olav Mathiesen, Denmark.

1965, June 26 Engr. Unwmk. *Perf. 14x13½*

143 A75 5c **dark blue** *(2,282,452)* .20 .20
First day cover 1.00
Inscription block of 4 .40 —
144 A75 15c **lilac rose** *(1,993,562)* .20 .20
First day cover 1.00
First day cover, #143-144 1.00
Inscription block of 4 1.00 —

Souvenir Sheet

145 A75 Sheet of two *(1,928,366)* .35 .35
First day cover 1.00

No. 145 contains one each of Nos. 143-144 with dark blue and ocher marginal inscription, ocher edging. Size: 92x70mm.
First day covers of Nos. 143-145 total: New York, 748,876; San Francisco, 301,435.

"Peace" — A76

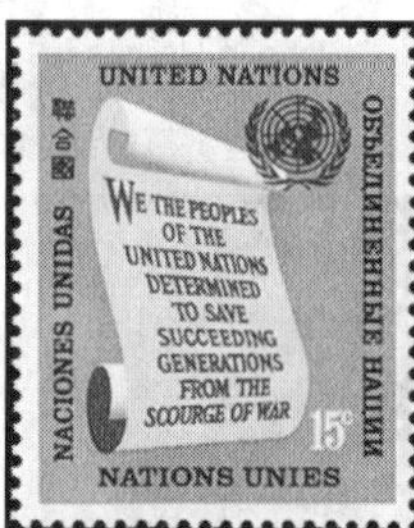

Opening Words, UN Charter — A77

UN Headquarters and Emblem — A78

UN Emblem — A79

UN Emblem Encircled — A80

Printed by Government Printing Bureau, Tokyo (1c); Government Printing Office, Austria (15c, 20c); Government Printing Office (Bundesdruckerei), Berlin (25c), and Courvoisier S.A., Switzerland ($1). Panes of 50.
Designed by Kurt Plowitz US (1c); Olav S. Mathiesen, Denmark (15c); Vergniaud Pierre-Noel, US (20c); Rashid-ud Din, Pakistan (25c), and Ole Hamann, Denmark ($1).

1965-66 Photo. Unwmk. *Perf. 13½x13*

146 A76 1c **vermilion, blue, black & gray** *(7,000,000)* .20 .20
First day cover 1.00
Inscription block of 4 .20 —

Perf. 14

147 A77 15c **olive bister, dull yellow, black & deep claret** *(2,500,000)* .25 .20
First day cover 1.00

Inscription block of 4 1.10 —

Perf. 12

148 A78 20c **dark blue, blue, red & yellow** *(3,000,000)* .30 .25
First day cover 1.00
First day cover, #147-148 1.25
Inscription block of 4 1.25 —
a. Yellow omitted —

Litho. and Embossed

Perf. 14

149 A79 25c **light & dark blue** *(3,200,000)* .35 .30
First day cover 1.25
First day cover, #146, 149 1.50
Inscription block of 4 1.50 —
Inscription block of 6, "Bundesdruckerei Berlin" imprint 20.00
First day cover, "Bundesdruckerei," margin block of 6 32.50

Photo.

Perf. 11½

150 A80 $1 **aquamarine & sapphire** *(2,570,000)* 1.75 1.60
First day cover *(181,510)* 2.00
Inscription block of 4 7.75 —
Nos. 146-150 (5) 2.85 2.55

Issued: 1c, 25c, Sept. 20, 1965; 15c, 20c, Oct. 25, 1965; $1, Mar. 25, 1966.

First day covers of Nos. 146 and 149 total 443,964. Those of Nos. 147-148 total 457,596.

The 25c has the marginal inscription (UN emblem and "1965") in two sizes: 1st printing (with Bundesdruckerei imprint), 6mm in diameter; 2nd printing, 8mm. In 1st printing, "halo" of UN emblem is larger, overlapping "25c."

See UN Offices in Geneva Nos. 5, 9 and 11.

Fields and People — A81

Globe and Flags of UN Members — A82

Design: 11c, French inscription.

Issued to emphasize the importance of the world's population growth and its problems and to call attention to population trends and development.

Printed by Government Printing Office, Austria. Panes of 50. Designed by Olav S. Mathiesen, Denmark.

1965, Nov. 29 Photo. Unwmk. *Perf. 12*

151 A81 4c **multicolored** *(1,966,033)* .20 .20
First day cover 1.00
Inscription block of 4 .25 —
152 A81 5c **multicolored** *(2,298,731)* .20 .20
First day cover 1.00
Inscription block of 4 .30 —
153 A81 11c **multicolored** *(1,557,589)* .20 .20
First day cover 1.00
First day cover, #151-153 1.75
Inscription block of 4 .90 —
Nos. 151-153 (3) .60 .60

First day covers of Nos. 151-153 total 710,507.

1966, Jan. 31 Photo. Unwmk. *Perf. 11½*

Design: 15c, French inscription.

Issued to honor the World Federation of United Nations Associations.

Printed by Courvoisier S.A., Switzerland. Panes of 50. Designed by Olav S. Mathiesen, Denmark.

154 A82 5c **multicolored** *(2,462,215)* .20 .20
First day cover 1.00
Inscription block of 4 .35 —
155 A82 15c **multicolored** *(1,643,661)* .20 .20
First day cover 1.00
First day cover, #154-155 1.25
Inscription block of 4 .90 —

First day covers of Nos. 154-155 total 474,154.

WHO Headquarters, Geneva — A83

Design: 11c, French inscription.

Issued to commemorate the opening of the World Health Organization Headquarters, Geneva.

Printed by Courvoisier, S.A., Switzerland. Panes of 50. Designed by Rashid-ud Din.

1966, May 26 Photo. *Perf. 12½x12*

Granite Paper

156 A83 5c **lt & dk blue, orange, green & bister** *(2,079,893)* .20 .20
First day cover 1.00
Inscription block of 4 .45 —
157 A83 11c **orange, lt & dark blue, green & bister** *(1,879,879)* .20 .20
First day cover 1.00
First day cover, #156-157 1.25
Inscription block of 4 .90 —

First day covers of Nos. 156-157 total 466,171.

Coffee — A84

UN Observer — A85

Design: 11c, Spanish inscription.

Issued to commemorate the International Coffee Agreement of 1962.

Printed by the Government Printing Bureau, Tokyo. Panes of 50. Designed by Rashid-ud Din, Pakistan.

1966, Sept. 19 Photo. *Perf. 13½x13*

158 A84 5c **orange, lt blue, green, red & dk brown** *(2,020,308)* .20 .20
First day cover 1.00
Inscription block of 4 .40 —
159 A84 11c **lt blue, yellow, green, red & dk brown** *(1,888,682)* .20 .20
First day cover 1.00
First day cover, #158-159 1.00
Inscription block of 4 .90 —

First day covers of Nos. 158-159 total 435,886.

1966, Oct. 24 Photo. *Perf. 11½*

Issued to honor the Peace Keeping United Nation Observers.

Printed by Courvoisier, S.A. Panes of 50. Designed by Ole S. Hamann.

Granite Paper

160 A85 15c **steel blue, orange, black & green** *(1,889,809)* .25 .20
First day cover *(255,326)* 1.00
Inscription block of 4 1.40 —

Children of Various Races — A86

Designs: 5c, Children riding in locomotive and tender. 11c, Children in open railroad car playing medical team (French inscription).

20th anniversary of the United Nations Children's Fund (UNICEF).

Printed by Thomas De La Rue & Co., Ltd. Panes of 50. Designed by Kurt Plowitz.

1966, Nov. 28 Litho. *Perf. 13x13½*

161 A86 4c **pink & multi** *(2,334,989)* .20 .20
First day cover 1.00
Inscription block of 4 .30 —
162 A86 5c **pale green & multi** *(2,746,941)* .20 .20
First day cover 1.00
Inscription block of 4 .35 —
a. Yellow omitted — —
163 A86 11c **light ultramarine & multi** *(2,123,841)* .20 .20
First day cover 1.00
First day cover, #161-163 1.00
Inscription block of 4 .85 —
b. Dark blue omitted —
Nos. 161-163 (3) .60 .60

First day covers of Nos. 161-163 total 987,271.

Hand Rolling up Sleeve and Chart Showing Progress — A87

Design: 11c, French inscription.

United Nations Development Program.

Printed by Courvoisier, S.A. Panes of 50. Designed by Olav S. Mathiesen.

1967, Jan. 23 Photo. *Perf. 12½*

164 A87 5c **green, yellow, purple & orange** *(2,204,679)* .20 .20
First day cover 1.00
Inscription block of 4 .35 —
165 A87 11c **blue, chocolate, light green & orange** *(1,946,159)* .20 .20
First day cover 1.00
First day cover, #164-165 1.00
Inscription block of 4 1.00 —

First day covers of Nos. 164-165 total 406,011.

Type of 1962 and

UN Headquarters, NY, and World Map — A88

Printed by Courvoisier, S.A. Panes of 50. Designed by Jozsef Vertel, Hungary (1½c); Renato Ferrini, Italy (5c).

1967 Photo. *Perf. 11½*

166 A88 1½c **ultramarine, black, orange & ocher** *(4,000,000)* .20 .20
First day cover *(199,751)* 1.00
Inscription block of 4 .20 —

Size: 33x23mm

167 A53 5c **red brown, brown & orange yellow** *(5,500,000)* .20 .20
First day cover *(212,544)* 1.00
Inscription block of 4 .40 —

Issue dates: 1½c, Mar. 17; 5c, Jan. 23.

For 5c of type A88, see UN Offices in Geneva No. 1.

Fireworks — A89

Design: 11c, French inscription.

Issued to honor all nations which gained independence since 1945.

Printed by Harrison & Sons, Ltd. Panes of 50. Designed by Rashid-ud Din.

1967, Mar. 17 Photo. *Perf. 14x14½*

No.	Type	Denom.	Description	Unused	Used
168	A89	5c	**dark blue & multi** *(2,445,955)*	.20	.20
			First day cover		1.00
			Inscription block of 4	.35	—
169	A89	11c	**brown lake & multi** *(2,011,004)*	.20	.20
			First day cover		1.00
			First day cover, #168-169		1.00
			Inscription block of 4	.85	—

First day covers of Nos. 168-169 total 390,499.

"Peace" — A90

UN Pavilion, EXPO '67 — A91

Designs: 5c, Justice. 10c, Fraternity. 15c, Truth.

EXPO '67, International Exhibition, Montreal, Apr. 28-Oct. 27, 1967.

Under special agreement with the Canadian Government Nos. 170-174 were valid for postage only on mail posted at the UN pavilion during the Fair. The denominations are expressed in Canadian currency.

Printed by British American Bank Note Co., Ltd., Ottawa. The 8c was designed by Olav S. Mathiesen after a photograph by Michael Drummond. The others were adapted by Ole S. Hamann from reliefs by Ernest Cormier on doors of General Assembly Hall, presented to UN by Canada.

1967, Apr. 28 Engr. & Litho. *Perf. 11*

No.	Type	Denom.	Description	Unused	Used
170	A90	4c	**red & red brown** *(2,464,813)*	.20	.20
			First day cover		1.00
			Inscription block of 4	.20	—
171	A90	5c	**blue & red brown** *(2,177,073)*	.20	.20
			First day cover		1.00
			Inscription block of 4	.20	—
			Litho.		
172	A91	8c	**multicolored** *(2,285,440)*	.20	.20
			First day cover		1.00
			Inscription block of 4	.35	—
			Engr. and Litho.		
173	A90	10c	**green & red brown** *(1,955,352)*	.20	.20
			First day cover		1.00
			Inscription block of 4	.50	—
174	A90	15c	**dark brown & red brown** *(1,899,185)*	.20	.20
			First day cover		1.00
			First day cover, #170-174		1.25
			Inscription block of 4	.60	
			Nos. 170-174 (5)	1.00	1.00

First day covers of Nos. 170-174 total 901,625.

Luggage Tags and UN Emblem A92

Issued to publicize International Tourist Year, 1967.

Printed by Government Printing Office, Berlin. Panes of 50. Designed by David Dewhurst.

1967, June 19 Litho. *Perf. 14*

No.	Type	Denom.	Description	Unused	Used
175	A92	5c	**reddish brown & multi** *(2,593,782)*	.20	.20
			First day cover		1.00
			Inscription block of 4	.35	—
176	A92	15c	**ultramarine & multi** *(1,940,457)*	.25	.20
			First day cover		1.00
			First day cover, #175-176		1.25
			Inscription block of 4	1.10	—

First day covers of Nos. 175-176 total 382,886.

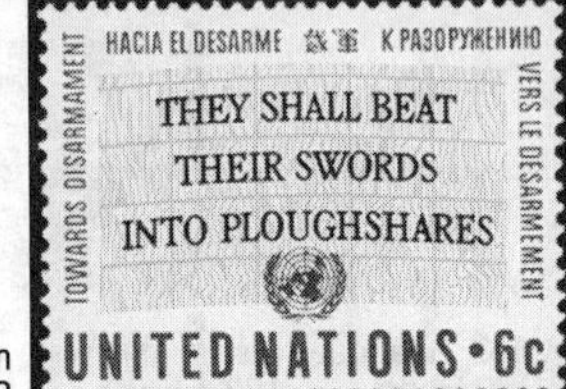

Quotation from Isaiah 2:4 — A93

Design: 13c, French inscription.

Issued to publicize the UN General Assembly's resolutions on general and complete disarmament and for suspension of nuclear and thermonuclear tests.

Printed by Heraclio Fournier S.A., Spain. Panes of 50. Designed by Ole Hamann.

1967, Oct. 24 Photo. *Perf. 14*

No.	Type	Denom.	Description	Unused	Used
177	A93	6c	**ultramarine, yellow, gray & brown** *(2,462,277)*	.20	.20
			First day cover		1.00
			Inscription block of 4	.45	—
178	A93	13c	**magenta, yellow, gray & brown** *(2,055,541)*	.20	.20
			First day cover		1.00
			First day cover, #177-178		1.00
			Inscription block of 4	.95	—

First day covers of Nos. 177-178 total 403,414.

Art at UN Issue

Miniature Sheet

Stained Glass Memorial Window by Marc Chagall, at UN Headquarters — A94

"The Kiss of Peace" by Marc Chagall — A95

Printed by Joh. Enschede and Sons, Netherlands. No. 180 issued in panes of 50. Design adapted by Ole Hamann from photograph by Hans Lippmann.

Sizes: a, 41x46mm. b, 24x46mm. c, 41x33½mm. d, 36x33½mm. e, 29x33½mm. f, 41½x47mm.

1967, Nov. 17 Litho. *Rouletted 9*

No.	Type	Denom.	Description	Unused	Used
179	A94	6c	Sheet of 6, #a.-f. *(3,178,656)*	.40	.40
			First day cover		1.00
			Perf. 13x13½		
180	A95	6c	**multicolored** *(3,438,497)*	.20	.20
			First day cover		1.00
			Inscription block of 4	.50	—

No. 179 contains six 6c stamps, each rouletted on 3 sides, imperf. on fourth side. Size: 124x80mm. On Nos. 179a-179c, "United Nations 6c" appears at top; on Nos. 179d-179f, at bottom. No. 179f includes name "Marc Chagall."

First day covers of Nos. 179-180 total 617,225.

Globe and Major UN Organs — A96

Statue by Henrik Starcke — A97

Design: 13c, French inscriptions.

Issued to honor the United Nations Secretariat.

Printed by Courvoisier, S. A., Switzerland. Panes of 50. Designed by Rashid-ud Din.

1968, Jan. 16 Photo. *Perf. 11½*

No.	Type	Denom.	Description	Unused	Used
181	A96	6c	**multicolored** *(2,772,965)*	.20	.20
			First day cover		1.00
			Inscription block of 4	.40	—
182	A96	13c	**multicolored** *(2,461,992)*	.20	.20
			First day cover		1.00
			First day cover, #181-182		1.00
			Inscription block of 4	.90	—

First day covers of Nos. 181-182 total 411,119.

Art at UN Issue

The 6c is part of the "Art at the UN" series. The 75c belongs to the regular definitive series. The teakwood Starcke statue, which stands in the Trusteeship Council Chamber, represents mankind's search for freedom and happiness.

Printed by Courvoisier, S.A., Switzerland. Panes of 50.

1968, Mar. 1 Photo. *Perf. 11½*

No.	Type	Denom.	Description	Unused	Used
183	A97	6c	**blue & multi** *(2,537,320)*	.20	.20
			First day cover		1.00
			Inscription block of 4	.50	—
184	A97	75c	**rose lake & multi** *(2,300,000)*	1.10	.90
			First day cover		1.25
			First day cover, #183-184		5.00
			Inscription block of 4	5.00	—

First day covers of Nos. 183-184 total 413,286.

See UN Offices in Geneva No. 13.

Factories and Chart — A98

UN Headquarters — A99

Design: 13c, French inscription ("ONUDI," etc.).

Issued to publicize the UN Industrial Development Organization.

Printed by Canadian Bank Note Co., Ltd., Ottawa. Panes of 50. Designed by Ole Hamann.

1968, Apr. 18 Litho. *Perf. 12*

No.	Type	Denom.	Description	Unused	Used
185	A98	6c	**greenish blue, lt greenish blue, black & dull claret** *(2,439,656)*	.20	.20
			First day cover		1.00
			Inscription block of 4	.35	—
186	A98	13c	**dull red brown, light red brown, black & ultra** *(2,192,453)*	.20	.20
			First day cover		1.00
			First day cover, #185-186		1.00
			Inscription block of 4	.80	—

First day covers of Nos. 185-186 total 396,447.

1968, May 31 Litho. *Perf. 12x13½*

Printed by Aspioti Elka-Chrome Mines, Ltd., Athens. Panes of 50. Designed by Olav S. Mathiesen.

No.	Type	Denom.	Description	Unused	Used
187	A99	6c	**green, blue, black & gray** *(4,000,000)*	.20	.20
			First day cover *(241,179)*		1.00
			Inscription block of 4	.50	—

Radarscope and Globe — A100

Design: 20c, French inscription.
Issued to publicize World Weather Watch, a new weather system directed by the World Meteorological Organization.
Printed by the Government Printing Bureau, Tokyo. Designed by George A. Gundersen and George Fanais, Canada.

1968, Sept. 19 Photo. *Perf. 13x13½*

188 A100 6c **green, black, ocher, red & blue** *(2,245,078)* .20 .20
First day cover 1.00
Inscription block of 4 .40 —
189 A100 20c **lilac, black, ocher, red & blue** *(2,069,966)* .30 .20
First day cover 1.00
First day cover, #188-189 1.25
Inscription block of 4 1.25 —

First day covers of Nos. 188-189 total 620,510.

Human Rights Flame — A101

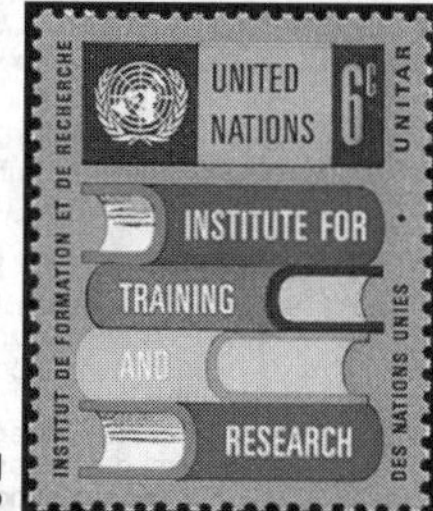

Books and UN Emblem — A102

Design: 13c, French inscription.
Issued for International Human Rights Year, 1968.
Printed by Harrison & Sons, Ltd., England. Designed by Robert Perrot, France.

1968, Nov. 22 Photo.; Foil Embossed *Perf. 12½*

190 A101 6c **bright blue, deep ultra & gold** *(2,394,235)* .20 .20
First day cover 1.00
Inscription block of 4 .40 —
191 A101 13c **rose red, dark red & gold** *(2,284,838)* .20 .20
First day cover 1.00
First day cover, #190-191 1.00
Inscription block of 4 .85 —

First day covers of Nos. 190-191 total 519,012.

1969, Feb. 10 Litho. *Perf. 13½*

Design: 13c, French inscription in center, denomination panel at bottom.
United Nations Institute for Training and Research (UNITAR).
Printed by the Government Printing Bureau, Tokyo. Panes of 50. Designed by Olav S. Mathiesen.

192 A102 6c **yellow green & multi** *(2,436,559)* .20 .20
First day cover 1.00
Inscription block of 4 .35 —
193 A102 13c **bluish lilac & multi** *(1,935,151)* .25 .20
First day cover 1.00
First day cover, #192-193 1.00
Inscription block of 4 1.00 —

First day covers of Nos. 192-193 total 439,606.

UN Building, Santiago, Chile A103

Design: 15c, Spanish inscription.
The UN Building in Santiago, Chile, is the seat of the UN Economic Commission for Latin America and of the Latin American Institute for Economic and Social Planning.
Printed by Government Printing Office, Berlin. Panes of 50. Design by Ole Hamann, adapted from a photograph.

1969, Mar. 14 Litho. *Perf. 14*

194 A103 6c **light blue, violet blue & light green** *(2,543,992)* .20 .20
First day cover 1.00
Inscription block of 4 .35 —
195 A103 15c **pink, cream & red brown** *(2,030,733)* .25 .20
First day cover 1.00
First day cover, #194-195 1.00
Inscription block of 4 1.10 —

First day covers of Nos. 194-195 total 398,227.

"UN" and UN Emblem — A104

UN Emblem and Scales of — A105

Printed by Government Printing Bureau, Tokyo. Panes of 50. Designed by Leszek Holdanowicz and Marek Freudenreich, Poland.

1969, Mar. 14 Photo. *Perf. 13½*

196 A104 13c **bright blue, black & gold** *(4,000,000)* .20 .20
First day cover *(177,793)* 1.00
Inscription block of 4 .90 —

See UN Offices in Geneva No. 7.

1969, Apr. 21 Photo. *Perf. 11½*

Design: 13c, French inscription.
20th anniversary session of the UN International Law Commission.
Printed by Courvoisier S.A., Switzerland. Panes of 50. Designed by Robert Perrot, France.

Granite Paper

197 A105 6c **bright green, ultra & gold** *(2,501,492)* .20 .20
First day cover 1.00
Inscription block of 4 .40 —
198 A105 13c **crimson, lilac & gold** *(1,966,994)* .20 .20
First day cover 1.00
First day cover, #197-198 1.00
Inscription block of 4 .90 —

First day covers of Nos. 197-198 total 439,324.

Allegory of Labor, Emblems of UN and ILO — A106

Design: 20c, French inscription.
Printed by Government Printing Bureau, Tokyo. Panes of 50. Designed by Nejat M. Gur, Turkey.
Issued to publicize "Labor and Development" and to commemorate the 50th anniversary of the International Labor Organization.

1969, June 5 Photo. *Perf. 13*

199 A106 6c **blue, deep blue, yellow & gold** *(2,078,381)* .20 .20
First day cover 1.00
Inscription block of 4 .40 —
200 A106 20c **orange vermilion, magenta, yellow & gold** *(1,751,100)* .25 .20
First day cover 1.00
First day cover, #199-200 1.25
Inscription block of 4 1.25 —

First day covers of Nos. 199-200 total 514,155.

Art at UN Issue

Ostrich, Tunisian Mosaic, 3rd Century — A107

Design: 13c, Pheasant; French inscription.
The mosaic "The Four Seasons and the Genius of the Year" was found at Haidra, Tunisia. It is now at the Delegates' North Lounge, UN Headquarters, New York.
Printed by Heraclio Fournier, S. A., Spain. Panes of 50. Designed by Olav S. Mathiesen.

1969, Nov. 21 Photo. *Perf. 14*

201 A107 6c **blue & multi** *(2,280,702)* .20 .20
First day cover 1.00
Inscription block of 4 .35 —
202 A107 13c **red & multi** *(1,918,554)* .20 .20
First day cover 1.00
First day cover, #201-202 1.00
Inscription block of 4 .90 —

First day covers of Nos. 201-202 total 612,981.

Art at UN Issue

Peace Bell, Gift of Japanese — A108

Design: 25c, French inscription.
The Peace Bell was a gift of the people of Japan in 1954, cast from donated coins and metals. It is housed in a Japanese cypress structure at UN Headquarters, New York.
Printed by Government Printing Bureau, Tokyo. Panes of 50. Designed by Ole Hamann.

1970, Mar. 13 Photo. *Perf. 13½x13*

203 A108 6c **violet blue & multi** *(2,604,253)* .20 .20
First day cover 1.00
Inscription block of 4 .35 —
204 A108 25c **claret & multi** *(2,090,185)* .35 .25
First day cover 1.25
First day cover, #203-204 1.25
Inscription block of 4 1.60 —

First day covers of Nos. 203-204 total 502,384.

Mekong River, Power Lines and Map of Mekong Delta — A109

Design: 13c, French inscription.
Issued to publicize the Lower Mekong Basin Development project under UN auspices.
Printed by Heraclio Fournier, S.A., Spain. Panes of 50. Designed by Ole Hamann.

1970, Mar. 13 *Perf. 14*

205 A109 6c **dark blue & multi** *(2,207,309)* .20 .20
First day cover 1.00
Inscription block of 4 .35 —
206 A109 13c **deep plum & multi** *(1,889,023)* .20 .20
First day cover 1.00
First day cover, #205-206 1.00
Inscription block of 4 .90 —

First day covers of Nos. 205-206 total 522,218.

"Fight Cancer" — A110

Design: 13c, French inscription.
Issued to publicize the fight against cancer in connection with the 10th International Cancer Congress of the International Union Against Cancer, Houston, Texas, May 22-29.
Printed by Government Printing Office, Berlin. Panes of 50. Designed by Leonard Mitchell.

1970, May 22 **Litho.** ***Perf. 14***

207 A110 6c **blue & black** *(2,157,742)* .20 .20
First day cover 1.00
Inscription block of 4 .35 —
208 A110 13c **olive & black** *(1,824,714)* .20 .20
First day cover 1.00
First day cover, #207-208 1.00
Inscription block of 4 .85 —

First day covers of Nos. 207-208 total 444,449.

UN Emblem and Olive Branch — A111

UN Emblem — A112

Design: 13c, French inscription.
25th anniv. of the UN. First day covers were postmarked at UN Headquarters, NY, and at San Francisco.
Printed by Courvoisier, S.A., Switzerland. Designed by Ole Hamann and Olav S. Mathiesen (souvenir sheet).

1970, June 26 **Photo.** ***Perf. 11½***

209 A111 6c **red, gold, dark & light blue** *(2,365,229)* .20 .20
First day cover 1.00
Inscription block of 4 .35 —
210 A111 13c **dark blue, gold, green & red** *(1,861,613)* .20 .20
First day cover 1.00
Inscription block of 4 .80 —

Perf. 12½

211 A112 25c **dark blue, gold & light blue** *(1,844,669)* .35 .25
First day cover 1.25
First day cover, #209-211 1.50
Inscription block of 4 1.50 —
Nos. 209-211 (3) .75 .65

Souvenir Sheet

Imperf

212 Sheet of 3 *(1,923,639)* .60 .60
a. A111 6c **red, gold & multicolored** .20 .20
b. A111 13c **violet blue, gold & multi** .20 .20
c. A112 25c **violet blue, gold & light blue** .30 .20
First day cover 1.25

No. 212 contains 3 imperf. stamps, gold border and violet blue marginal inscription. Size: 94½x78mm.
First day covers of Nos. 209-212 total: New York, 846,389; San Francisco, 471,100.

Scales, Olive Branch and Symbol of Progress — A113

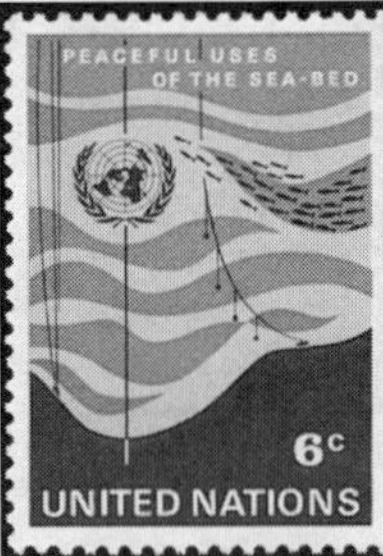

Sea Bed, School of Fish and Underwater Research — A114

Design: 13c, French inscription.
Issued to publicize "Peace, Justice and Progress" in connection with the 25th anniversary of the United Nations.
Printed by Government Printing Bureau, Tokyo. Panes of 50. Designed by Ole Hamann.

1970, Nov. 20 **Photo.** ***Perf. 13½***

213 A113 6c **gold & multi** *(1,921,441)* .20 .20
First day cover 1.00
Inscription block of 4 .40 —
214 A113 13c **silver & multi** *(1,663,669)* .20 .20
First day cover 1.00
First day cover, #213-214 1.00
Inscription block of 4 1.00 —

First day covers of Nos. 213-214 total 521,419.

1971, Jan. 25 **Photo. & Engr.** ***Perf. 13***

Issued to publicize peaceful uses of the sea bed.
Printed by Setelipaino, Finland. Panes of 50. Designed by Pentti Rahikainen, Finland.

215 A114 6c **blue & multi** *(2,354,179)* .20 .20
First day cover *(405,554)* 1.00
Inscription block of 4 .50 —

See UN Offices in Geneva No. 15.

Refugees, Sculpture by Kaare K. Nygaard — A115

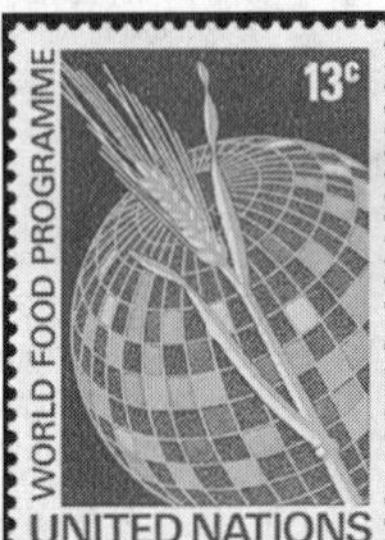

Wheat and Globe — A116

International support for refugees.
Printed by Joh. Enschede and Sons, Netherlands. Panes of 50. Designed by Dr. Kaare K. Nygaard and Martin J. Weber.

1971, Mar. 2 **Litho.** ***Perf. 13x12½***

216 A115 6c **brown, ocher & black** *(2,247,232)* .20 .20
First day cover 1.00
Inscription block of 4 .30 —
217 A115 13c **ultramarine, greenish blue & black** *(1,890,048)* .20 .20
First day cover 1.00
First day cover, #216-217 1.00
Inscription block of 4 .90 —

First day covers of Nos. 216-217 total 564,785.
See UN Offices in Geneva No. 16.

1971, Apr. 13 **Photo.** ***Perf. 14***

Publicizing the UN World Food Program.
Printed by Heraclio Fournier, S.A., Spain. Panes of 50. Designed by Olav S. Mathiesen.

218 A116 13c **red & multicolored** *(1,968,542)* .20 .20
First day cover *(409,404)* 1.00
Inscription block of 4 .90 —

See UN Offices in Geneva No. 17.

UPU Headquarters, Bern — A117

Opening of new Universal Postal Union Headquarters, Bern.
Printed by Courvoisier, S.A. Panes of 50. Designed by Olav S. Mathiesen.

1971, May 28 **Photo.** ***Perf. 11½***

219 A117 20c **brown orange & multi** *(1,857,841)* .35 .25
First day cover *(375,119)* 1.00
Inscription block of 4 1.40 —

See UN Offices in Geneva No. 18.

A118

"Eliminate Racial Discrimination" A119

International Year Against Racial Discrimination.
Printed by Government Printing Bureau, Tokyo. Panes of 50. Designers: Daniel Gonzague (8c); Ole Hamann (13c).

1971, Sept. 21 **Photo.** ***Perf. 13½***

220 A118 8c **yellow green & multi** *(2,324,349)* .20 .20
First day cover 1.00
Inscription block of 4 .60 —
221 A119 13c **blue & multi** *(1,852,093)* .20 .20
First day cover 1.00
First day cover, #220-221 1.00
Inscription block of 4 .90 —

First day covers of Nos. 220-221 total 461,103.
See UN Offices in Geneva Nos. 19-20.

UN Headquarters, New York — A120

UN Emblem and Symbolic Flags — A121

No. 222 printed by Heraclio Fournier, S.A., Spain. No. 223 printed by Government Printing Bureau, Tokyo. Panes of 50. Designers: O. S. Mathiesen (8c); Robert Perrot (60c).

1971, Oct. 22 **Photo.** ***Perf. 13½***

222 A120 8c **violet blue & multi** *(5,600,000)* .20 .20
First day cover 1.00
Inscription block of 4 .60 —

Perf. 13

223 A121 60c **ultra & multi** *(3,500,000)+* .75 .75
First day cover 1.25
First day cover, #222-223 3.00
Inscription block of 4 3.50 —

First day covers of Nos. 222-223 total 336,013.

Maia, by Pablo Picasso — A122

To publicize the UN International School.
Printed by Courvoisier, S.A. Panes of 50. Designed by Ole Hamann.

1971, Nov. 19 Photo. *Perf. 11½*

224 A122 8c **olive & multi** *(2,668,214)* .20 .20
First day cover 1.00
Inscription block of 4 .45 —
225 A122 21c **ultra & multi** *(2,040,754)* .30 .20
First day cover 1.00
First day cover, #224-225 1.75
Inscription block of 4 1.40 —

First day covers of Nos. 224-225 total 579,594.
See UN Offices in Geneva No. 21.

Letter Changing Hands A123

Printed by Bundesdruckerei, Berlin. Panes of 50. Designed by Olav S. Mathiesen.

1972, Jan. 5 Litho. *Perf. 14*

226 A123 95c **carmine & multi** *(2,000,000)* 1.25 1.10
First day cover *(188,193)* 1.25
Inscription block of 4 5.50 —

"No More Nuclear Weapons" A124

To promote non-proliferation of nuclear weapons.
Printed by Heraclio Fournier, S. A., Spain. Panes of 50. Designed by Arne Johnson, Norway.

1972, Feb. 14 Photo. *Perf. 13½x14*

227 A124 8c **dull rose, black, blue & gray** *(2,311,515)* .20 .20
First day cover *(268,789)* 1.00
Inscription block of 4 .55 —

See UN Offices in Geneva No. 23.

Proportions of Man, by Leonardo da Vinci — A125

"Human Environment" — A126

World Health Day, Apr. 7.
Printed by Setelipaino, Finland. Panes of 50. Designed by George Hamori.

1972, Apr. 7 Litho. & Engr. *Perf. 13x13½*

228 A125 15c **black & multi** *(1,788,962)* .25 .20
First day cover *(322,724)* 1.00
Inscription block of 4 1.00 —

See UN Offices in Geneva No. 24.

1972, June 5 Litho. & Embossed *Perf. 12½x14*

UN Conf. on Human Environment, Stockholm, June 5-16, 1972.
Printed by Joh. Enschede and Sons, Netherlands. Panes of 50. Designed by Robert Perrot.

229 A126 8c **red, buff, green & blue** *(2,124,604)* .20 .20
First day cover 1.00
Inscription block of 4 .50 —
230 A126 15c **blue green, buff, green & blue** *(1,589,943)* .25 .20
First day cover 1.00
First day cover, #229-230 1.00
Inscription block of 4 1.25 —

First day covers of Nos. 229-230 total 437,222.
See UN Offices in Geneva Nos. 25-26.

"Europe" and UN Emblem — A127

The Five Continents by José Maria Sert — A128

Economic Commission for Europe, 25th anniversary.
Printed by Government Printing Bureau, Tokyo. Panes of 50. Designed by Angel Medina Medina.

1972, Sept. 11 Litho. *Perf. 13x13½*

231 A127 21c **yellow brown & multi** *(1,748,675)* .35 .25
First day cover *(271,128)* 1.00
Inscription block of 4 1.60 —

See UN Offices in Geneva No. 27.

Art at UN Issue

Design shows part of ceiling mural of the Council Hall, Palais des Nations, Geneva. It depicts the five continents joining in space.
Printed by Courvoisier, S. A. Panes of 50. Designed by Ole Hamann.

1972, Nov. 17 Photo. *Perf. 12x12½*

232 A128 8c **gold, brown & golden brown** *(2,573,478)* .20 .20
First day cover 1.00
Inscription block of 4 .50 —
233 A128 15c **gold, blue green & brown** *(1,768,432)* .30 .20
First day cover 1.00
First day cover, #232-233 1.00
Inscription block of 4 1.25 —

First day covers of Nos. 232-233 total 589,817.
See UN Offices in Geneva Nos. 28-29.

Olive Branch and Broken Sword — A129

Poppy Capsule and Skull — A130

Disarmament Decade, 1970-79.
Printed by Ajans-Turk, Turkey. Panes of 50. Designed by Kurt Plowitz.

1973, Mar. 9 Litho. *Perf. 13½x13*

234 A129 8c **blue & multi** *(2,272,716)* .20 .20
First day cover 1.00
Inscription block of 4 .50 —
235 A129 15c **lilac rose & multi** *(1,643,712)* .35 .20
First day cover 1.00
First day cover, #234-235 1.00
Inscription block of 4 1.50 —

First day covers of Nos. 234-235 total 548,336.
See UN Offices in Geneva Nos. 30-31.

1973, Apr. 13 Photo. *Perf. 13½*

Fight against drug abuse.
Printed by Heraclio Fournier, S.A., Spain. Panes of 50. Designed by George Hamori.

236 A130 8c **deep orange & multi** *(1,846,780)* .20 .20
First day cover 1.00
Inscription block of 4 .60 —
237 A130 15c **pink & multi** *(1,466,806)* .35 .25
First day cover 1.00
First day cover, #236-237 1.00
Inscription block of 4 1.50 —

First day covers of Nos. 236-237 total 394,468.
See UN Offices in Geneva No. 32.

Honeycomb — A131

5th anniversary of the United Nations Volunteer Program.
Printed by Heraclio Fournier, S.A., Spain. Panes of 50. Designed by Courvoisier, S.A.

1973, May 25 Photo. *Perf. 14*

238 A131 8c **olive bister & multi** *(1,868,176)* .20 .20
First day cover 1.00
Inscription block of 4 .50 —
239 A131 21c **gray blue & multi** *(1,530,114)* .35 .25
First day cover 1.00
First day cover, #238-239 1.25
Inscription block of 4 1.50 —

First day covers of Nos. 238-239 total 396,517.
See UN Offices in Geneva No. 33.

Map of Africa with Namibia — A132

To publicize Namibia (South-West Africa) for which the UN General Assembly ended the mandate of South Africa and established the UN Council for Namibia to administer the territory until independence.

Printed by Heraclio Fournier, S.A., Spain. Panes of 50. Designed by George Hamori.

1973, Oct. 1 Photo. *Perf. 14*

No.	Type	Description	Unused	Used
240	A132	8c **emerald & multi** *(1,775,260)*	.20	.20
		First day cover		1.00
		Inscription block of 4	.50	—
241	A132	15c **bright rose & multi** *(1,687,782)*	.35	.25
		First day cover		1.00
		First day cover, #240-241		1.00
		Inscription block of 4	1.50	—

First day covers of Nos. 240-241 total 385,292.
See UN Offices in Geneva No. 34.

UN Emblem and Human Rights Flame — A133

25th anniversary of the adoption and proclamation of the Universal Declaration of Human Rights.
Printed by Government Printing Bureau, Tokyo. Panes of 50. Designed by Alfred Guerra.

1973, Nov. 16 Photo. *Perf. 13½*

No.	Type	Description	Unused	Used
242	A133	8c **deep carmine & multi** *(2,026,245)*	.20	.20
		First day cover		1.00
		Inscription block of 4	.50	—
243	A133	21c **blue green & multi** *(1,558,201)*	.35	.25
		First day cover		1.00
		First day cover, #242-243		1.25
		Inscription block of 4	1.50	—

First day covers of Nos. 242-243 total 398,511.
See UN Offices in Geneva Nos. 35-36.

ILO Headquarters, Geneva — A134

New Headquarters of International Labor Organization.
Printed by Heraclio Fournier, S.A., Spain. Panes of 50. Designed by Henry Bencsath.

1974, Jan. 11 Photo. *Perf. 14*

No.	Type	Description	Unused	Used
244	A134	10c **ultra & multi** *(1,734,423)*	.20	.20
		First day cover		1.00
		Inscription block of 4	.90	—
245	A134	21c **blue green & multi** *(1,264,447)*	.35	.25
		First day cover		1.00
		First day cover, #244-245		1.25
		Inscription block of 4	1.75	—

First day covers of Nos. 244-245 total 282,284.
See UN Offices in Geneva Nos. 37-38.

UPU Emblem and Post Horn Encircling Globe — A135

Centenary of Universal Postal Union.
Printed by Ashton-Potter Ltd., Canada. Panes of 50. Designed by Arne Johnson.

1974, Mar. 22 Litho. *Perf. 12½*

No.	Type	Description	Unused	Used
246	A135	10c **gold & multi** *(2,104,919)*	.25	.20
		First day cover *(342,774)*		1.00
		Inscription block of 4	1.10	—

See UN Offices in Geneva Nos. 39-40.

Art at UN Issue

Peace Mural, by Candido Portinari — A136

The mural, a gift of Brazil, is in the Delegates' Lobby, General Assembly Building.
Printed by Heraclio Fournier, S.A., Spain. Panes of 50. Design adapted by Ole Hamann.

1974, May 6 Photo. *Perf. 14*

No.	Type	Description	Unused	Used
247	A136	10c **gold & multi** *(1,769,342)*	.20	.20
		First day cover		1.00
		Inscription block of 4	.75	—
248	A136	18c **ultra & multi** *(1,477,500)*	.40	.30
		First day cover		1.00
		First day cover, #247-248		1.25
		Inscription block of 4	1.50	—

First day covers of Nos. 247-248 total 271,440.
See UN Offices in Geneva Nos. 41-42.

Dove and UN Emblem — A137

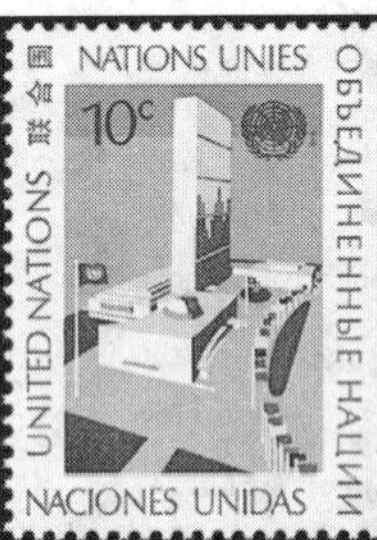

UN Headquarters — A138

Globe, UN Emblem, Flags — A139

Printed by Heraclio Fournier, S.A., Spain. Panes of 50.
Designed by Nejut M. Gur (2c); Olav S. Mathiesen (10c); Henry Bencsath (18c).

1974, June 10 Photo. *Perf. 14*

No.	Type	Description	Unused	Used
249	A137	2c **dark & light blue** *(6,900,000)*	.20	.20
		First day cover		1.00
		Inscription block of 4	.25	—
250	A138	10c **multicolored** *(4,000,000)*	.20	.20
		First day cover		1.00
		Inscription block of 4	.70	—
251	A139	18c **multicolored** *(2,300,000)*	.30	.20
		First day cover		1.00
		First day cover, #249-251		1.25
		Inscription block of 4	1.50	—
		Nos. 249-251 (3)	.70	.60

First day covers of Nos. 249-251 total 307,402.
+ Printing orders to Feb. 1990.

Children of the World — A140

Law of the Sea — A141

World Population Year
Printed by Heraclio Fournier, S.A., Spain. Panes of 50. Designed by Henry Bencsath.

1974, Oct. 18 Photo. *Perf. 14*

No.	Type	Description	Unused	Used
252	A140	10c **light blue & multi** *(1,762,595)*	.20	.20
		First day cover		1.00
		Inscription block of 4	1.00	—
253	A140	18c **lilac & multi** *(1,321,574)*	.40	.25
		First day cover		1.00
		First day cover, #252-253		1.25
		Inscription block of 4	1.75	—

First day covers of Nos. 253-254 total 354,306.
See UN Offices in Geneva Nos. 43-44.

1974, Nov. 22 Photo. *Perf. 14*

Declaration of UN General Assembly that the sea bed is common heritage of mankind, reserved for peaceful purposes.
Printed by Heraclio Fournier, S.A., Spain. Panes of 50. Designed by Asher Kalderon.

No.	Type	Description	Unused	Used
254	A141	10c **green & multi** *(1,621,328)*	.20	.20
		First day cover		1.00
		Inscription block of 4	.80	—
255	A141	26c **orange red & multi** *(1,293,084)*	.40	.30
		First day cover		1.25
		First day cover, #254-255		1.40
		Inscription block of 4	1.90	—

First day covers of Nos. 254-255 total 280,686.
See UN Offices in Geneva No. 45.

Satellite and Globe — A142

Peaceful uses (meteorology, industry, fishing, communications) of outer space.
Printed by Setelipaino, Finland. Panes of 50. Designed by Henry Bencsath.

1975, Mar. 14 Litho. *Perf. 13*

No.	Type	Description	Unused	Used
256	A142	10c **multicolored** *(1,681,115)*	.20	.20
		First day cover		1.00
		Inscription block of 4	.85	—
257	A142	26c **multicolored** *(1,463,130)*	.40	.30
		First day cover		1.25
		First day cover, #256-257		1.40
		Inscription block of 4	1.75	—

First day covers of Nos. 256-257 total 330,316.
See UN Offices in Geneva Nos. 46-47.

Equality Between Men and Women — A143

UN Flag and "XXX" — A144

International Women's Year
Printed by Questa Colour Security Printers, Ltd., England. Panes of 50. Designed by Asher Kalderon and Esther Kurti.

1975, May 9 Litho. *Perf. 15*

No.	Type	Description	Unused	Used
258	A143	10c **multicolored** *(1,402,542)*	.20	.20
		First day cover		1.00
		Inscription block of 4	.80	—
259	A143	18c **multicolored** *(1,182,321)*	.40	.30
		First day cover		1.00
		First day cover, #258-259		1.25
		Inscription block of 4	1.75	—

First day covers of Nos. 258-259 total 285,466.
See UN Offices in Geneva Nos. 48-49.

1975, June 26 Litho. *Perf. 13*

30th anniversary of the United Nations.
Printed by Ashton-Potter, Ltd., Canada. Nos. 260-261 panes of 50. Stamps designed by Asher Calderon, sheets by Olav S. Mathiesen.

No.	Type	Description	Unused	Used
260	A144	10c **olive bister & multi** *(1,904,545)*	.20	.20
		First day cover		1.00
		Inscription block of 4	.70	—
261	A144	26c **purple & multi** *(1,547,766)*	.50	.35
		First day cover		1.25
		First day cover, #260-261		1.40
		Inscription block of 4	2.25	—

Souvenir Sheet

Imperf

No.	Type	Description	Unused	Used
262		Sheet of 2 *(1,196,578)*	.65	.50
a.	A144	10c **olive bister & multicolored**	.20	.20
b.	A144	26c **purple & multicolored**	.40	.25
		First day cover		1.25

No. 262 has blue and bister margin with inscription and UN emblem.

First day covers of Nos. 260-262 total: New York 477,912; San Francisco, 237,159.
See Offices in Geneva Nos. 50-52.

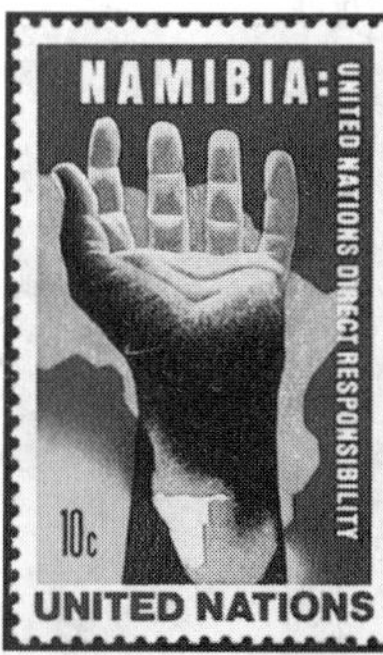

Hand Reaching up over Map of Africa and Namibia — A145

Wild Rose Growing from Barbed Wire — A146

"Namibia-United Nations direct responsibility." See note after No. 241.
Printed by Heraclio Fournier S.A., Spain. Panes of 50. Designed by Henry Bencsath.

1975, Sept. 22 Photo. *Perf. 13½*

263 A145 10c **multicolored** *(1,354,374)* .20 .20
First day cover 1.00
Inscription block of 4 .80 —
264 A145 18c **multicolored** *(1,243,157)* .35 .30
First day cover 1.00
First day cover, #263-264 1.25
Inscription block of 4 1.60 —

First day covers of Nos. 263-264 total 281,631.
See UN Offices in Geneva Nos. 53-54.

1975, Nov. 21 Engr. *Perf. 12½*

United Nations Peace-keeping Operations
Printed by Setelipaino, Finland. Panes of 50. Designed by Mrs. Eeva Oivo.

265 A146 13c **ultramarine** *(1,628,039)* .25 .20
First day cover 1.00
Inscription block of 4 1.00 —
266 A146 26c **rose carmine** *(1,195,580)* .50 .40
First day cover 1.25
First day cover, #265-266 1.40
Inscription block of 4 2.00 —

First day covers of Nos. 265-266 total 303,711.
See UN Offices in Geneva Nos. 55-56.

Symbolic Flags Forming Dove — A147

UN Emblem — A149

People of All Races A148

United Nations Flag — A150

Dove and Rainbow — A151

Printed by Ashton-Potter, Ltd., Canada (3c, 4c, 30c, 50c), and Questa Colour Security Printers, Ltd., England (9c). Panes of 50.
Designed by Waldemar Andrzesewski (3c); Arne Johnson (4c); George Hamori (9c, 30c); Arthur Congdon (50c).

1976 Litho. *Perf. 13x13½, 13½x13*

267 A147 3c **multicolored** *(4,000,000)* .20 .20
First day cover 1.00
Inscription block of 4 .25 —
268 A148 4c **multicolored** *(4,000,000)* .20 .20
First day cover 1.00
Inscription block of 4 .30 —

Photo.
Perf. 14

269 A149 9c **multicolored** *(3,270,000)+* .20 .20
First day cover 1.00
Inscription block of 4 .60 —

Litho.
Perf. 13x13½

270 A150 30c **blue, emerald & black** *(2,500,000)* .40 .35
First day cover 1.25
Inscription block of 4 1.75 —
271 A151 50c **yellow green & multi** *(2,000,000)* .70 .65
First day cover 1.25
First day cover, #267-268, 270-271 1.50
Inscription block of 4 3.25 —
Nos. 267-271 (5) 1.70 1.60

Issue dates: 3c, 4c, 30c, 50c, Jan. 6; 9c, Nov. 19.
First day covers of Nos. 267-268, 270-271 total 355,165; of Nos. 269 and 280 total 366,556.
See UN Offices in Vienna No. 8.

Interlocking Bands and UN Emblem — A152

World Federation of United Nations Associations.
Printed by Heraclio Fournier, S.A., Spain. Panes of 50. Designed by George Hamori.

1976, Mar. 12 Photo. *Perf. 14*

272 A152 13c **blue, green & black** *(1,331,556)* .20 .20
First day cover 1.00
Inscription block of 4 .80 —
273 A152 26c **green & multi** *(1,050,145)* .35 .30
First day cover 1.25
First day cover, #272-273 1.25
Inscription block of 4 1.60 —

First day covers of Nos. 272-273 total 300,775.
See UN Offices in Geneva No. 57.

Cargo, Globe and Graph — A153

Houses Around Globe — A154

UN Conference on Trade and Development (UNCTAD), Nairobi, Kenya, May 1976.
Printed by Courvoisier, S.A. Panes of 50. Designed by Henry Bencsath.

1976, Apr. 23 Photo. *Perf. 11½*

274 A153 13c **deep magenta & multi** *(1,317,900)* .20 .20
First day cover 1.00
Inscription block of 4 .80 —
275 A153 31c **dull blue & multi** *(1,216,959)* .40 .30
First day cover 1.25
First day cover, #274-275 1.40
Inscription block of 4 1.90 —

First day covers of Nos. 274-275 total 234,657.
See UN Offices in Geneva No. 58.

1976, May 28 Photo. *Perf. 14*

Habitat, UN Conference on Human Settlements, Vancouver, Canada, May 31-June 11.
Printed by Heraclio Fournier, S.A., Spain. Panes of 50. Designed by Eliezer Weishoff.

276 A154 13c **red brown & multi** *(1,346,589)* .20 .20
First day cover 1.00
Inscription block of 4 .75 —
277 A154 25c **green & multi** *(1,057,924)* .40 .30
First day cover 1.25
First day cover, #276-277 1.40
Inscription block of 4 1.75 —

First day covers of Nos. 276-277 total 232,754.
See UN Offices in Geneva Nos. 59-60.

Magnifying Glass, Sheet of Stamps, UN Emblem — A155

Grain — A156

United Nations Postal Administration, 25th anniversary.
Printed by Courvoisier, S.A. Designed by Henry Bencsath.

1976, Oct. 8 Photo. *Perf. 11½*

278 A155 13c **blue & multi** *(1,996,309)* .20 .20
First day cover 1.00
Inscription block of 4 .90 —
279 A155 31c **green & multi** *(1,767,465)* 1.40 1.40
First day cover 2.00
First day cover, #278-279 2.50
Inscription block of 4 6.25 —
Panes of 20, #278-279 32.50 —

First day covers of Nos. 278-279 total 366,784.
Upper margin blocks are inscribed "XXV ANNIVERSARY"; lower margin blocks "UNITED NATIONS POSTAL ADMINISTRATIONS."
See UN Offices in Geneva Nos. 61-62.

1976, Nov. 19 Litho. *Perf. 14½*

World Food Council.
Printed by Questa Colour Security Printers, Ltd., England. Panes of 50. Designed by Eliezer Weishoff.

280 A156 13c **multicolored** *(1,515,573)* .25 .20
First day cover 1.00
Inscription block of 4 1.10 —

See UN Offices in Geneva No. 63.

WIPO Headquarters, Geneva A157

World Intellectual Property Organization (WIPO).
Printed by Heraclio Fournier, S. A., Spain. Panes of 50. Designed by Eliezer Weishoff.

1977, Mar. 11 **Photo.** ***Perf. 14***

281 A157 13c **citron & multi** *(1,330,272)* .20 .20
First day cover 1.00
Inscription block of 4 .75 —
282 A157 31c **bright green & multi** *(1,115,406)* .45 .35
First day cover 1.25
First day cover, #281-282 1.25
Inscription block of 4 2.00 —

First day covers of Nos. 281-282 total 364,184.
See UN Offices in Geneva No. 64.

Drops of Water Falling into Funnel — A158

UN Water Conference, Mar del Plata, Argentina, Mar. 14-25.
Printed by Government Printing Bureau, Tokyo. Panes of 50. Designed by Elio Tomei.

1977, Apr. 22 **Photo.** ***Perf. 13½x13***

283 A158 13c **yellow & multi** *(1,317,536)* .20 .20
First day cover 1.00
Inscription block of 4 .75 —
284 A158 25c **salmon & multi** *(1,077,424)* .45 .35
First day cover 1.25
First day cover, #283-284 1.40
Inscription block of 4 2.00 —

First day covers of Nos. 283-284 total 321,585.
See UN Offices in Geneva Nos. 65-66.

Burning Fuse Severed — A159

UN Security Council.
Printed by Heraclio Fournier, S.A., Spain. Panes of 50. Designed by Witold Janowski and Marek Freudenreich.

1977, May 27 **Photo.** ***Perf. 14***

285 A159 13c **purple & multi** *(1,321,527)* .20 .20
First day cover 1.00
Inscription block of 4 .75 —
286 A159 31c **dark blue & multi** *(1,137,195)* .45 .30
First day cover 1.25
First day cover, #285-286 1.40
Inscription block of 4 2.00 —

First day covers of Nos. 285-286 total 309,610.
See UN Offices in Geneva Nos. 67-68.

"Combat Racism" — A160

Fight against racial discrimination.
Printed by Setelipaino, Finland. Panes of 50. Designed by Bruno K. Wiese.

1977, Sept. 19 **Litho.** ***Perf. 13½x13***

287 A160 13c **black & yellow** *(1,195,739)* .20 .20
First day cover 1.00
Inscription block of 4 .75 —
288 A160 25c **black & vermilion** *(1,074,639)* .40 .30
First day cover 1.25
First day cover, #287-288 1.40
Inscription block of 4 1.75 —

First day covers of Nos. 287-288 total 356,193.
See UN Offices in Geneva Nos. 60-70.

Atom, Grain, Fruit and Factory — A161

Peaceful uses of atomic energy.
Printed by Heraclio Fournier, S.A., Spain. Panes of 50. Designed by Henry Bencsath.

1977, Nov. 18 **Photo.** ***Perf. 14***

289 A161 13c **yellow bister & multi** *(1,316,473)* .20 .20
First day cover 1.00
Inscription block of 4 .90 —
290 A161 18c **dull green & multi** *(1,072,246)* .35 .25
First day cover 1.00
First day cover, #289-290 1.25
Inscription block of 4 1.50 —

First day covers of Nos. 289-290 total 325,348.
See UN Offices in Geneva Nos. 71-72.

Opening Words of UN Charter — A162

"Live Together in Peace" — A163

People of the World — A164

Printed by Questa Colour Security Printers, United Kingdom. Panes of 50. Designed by Salahattin Kanidinc (1c); Elio Tomei (25c); Paula Schmidt ($1).

1978, Jan. 27 **Litho.** ***Perf. 14½***

291 A162 1c **gold, brown & red** *(4,800,000)+* .20 .20
First day cover 1.00
Inscription block of 4 .25 —
292 A163 25c **multicolored** *(3,000,000)+* .35 .30
First day cover 1.25
Inscription block of 4 1.50 —
293 A164 $1 **multicolored** *(3,400,000)+* 1.10 1.10
First day cover 1.50
First day cover, #291-293 1.75
Inscription block of 4 5.25 —
Nos. 291-293 (3) 1.65 1.60

+ Printing orders to Sept. 1989.
First day covers of Nos. 291-293 total 264,782.
See UN Offices in Geneva No. 73.

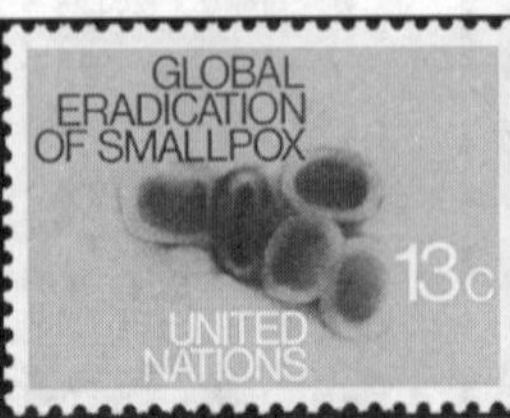

Smallpox Virus — A165

Global eradication of smallpox.
Printed by Courvoisier, S.A. Panes of 50. Designed by Herbert Auchli.

1978, Mar. 31 **Photo.** ***Perf. 12x11½***

294 A165 13c **rose & black** *(1,188,239)* .20 .20
First day cover 1.00
Inscription block of 4 .75 —
295 A165 31c **blue & black** *(1,058,688)* .45 .40
First day cover 1.25
First day cover, #294-295 1.40
Inscription block of 4 2.00 —

First day covers of Nos. 294-295 total 306,626.
See UN Offices in Geneva Nos. 74-75.

Open Handcuff — A166

Multicolored Bands and Clouds — A167

Liberation, justice and cooperation for Namibia.
Printed by Government Printing Office, Austria. Panes of 50. Designed by Cafiro Tomei.

1978, May 5 **Photo.** ***Perf. 12***

296 A166 13c **multicolored** *(1,203,079)* .20 .20
First day cover 1.00
Inscription block of 4 1.00 —
297 A166 18c **multicolored** *(1,066,738)* .30 .25
First day cover 1.00
First day cover, #296-297 1.25
Inscription block of 4 1.40 —

First day covers of Nos. 296-297 total 324,471.
See UN Offices in Geneva No. 76.

1978, June 12 **Photo.** ***Perf. 14***

International Civil Aviation Organization for "Safety in the Air."
Printed by Heraclio Fournier, S.A., Spain. Panes of 50. Designed by Cemalettin Mutver.

298 A167 13c **multicolored** *(1,295,617)* .20 .20
First day cover 1.00
Inscription block of 4 .85 —
299 A167 25c **multicolored** *(1,101,256)* .40 .30
First day cover 1.25
First day cover, #298-299 1.40
Inscription block of 4 1.75 —

First day covers of Nos. 298-299 total 329,995.
See UN Offices in Geneva Nos. 77-78.

General Assembly — A168

Printed by Government Printing Bureau, Tokyo. Panes of 50. Designed by Jozsef Vertel.

1978, Sept. 15 **Photo.** ***Perf. 13½***

300 A168 13c **multicolored** *(1,093,005)* .20 .20
First day cover 1.00
Inscription block of 4 1.00 —
301 A168 18c **multicolored** *(1,065,934)* .35 .30
First day cover 1.00
First day cover, #300-301 1.25
Inscription block of 4 1.50 —

First day covers of Nos. 300-301 total 283,220.
See UN Offices in Geneva Nos. 79-80.

Hemispheres as Cogwheels A169

Technical Cooperation Among Developing Countries Conference, Buenos Aires, Argentina, Sept. 1978.
Printed by Heraclio Fournier, S.A., Spain. Panes of 50. Designed by Simon Keter and David Pesach.

1978, Nov. 17 Photo. *Perf. 14*

302	A169 13c	**multicolored** *(1,251,272)*	.20	.20
		First day cover		1.00
		Inscription block of 4	1.00	—
303	A169 31c	**multicolored** *(1,185,213)*	.50	.40
		First day cover		1.25
		First day cover, #302-303		1.40
		Inscription block of 4	2.25	—

First day covers of Nos. 302-303 total 272,556.
See UN Offices in Geneva No. 81.

Hand Holding Olive Branch — A170

Various Races Tree — A171

Globe, Dove with Olive Branch — A172

Birds and Globe — A173

Printed by Heraclio Fournier, S.A., Spain. Panes of 50.
Designed by Raymon Müller (5c); Alrun Fricke (14c); Eliezer Weishoff (15c); Young Sun Hahn (20c).

1979, Jan. 19 Photo. *Perf. 14*

304	A170 5c	**multicolored** *(3,000,000)*	.20	.20
		First day cover		1.00
		Inscription block of 4	.35	—
305	A171 14c	**multicolored** *(3,000,000)+*	.20	.20
		First day cover		1.00
		Inscription block of 4	.90	—
306	A172 15c	**multicolored** *(3,000,000)+*	.30	.25
		First day cover		1.00
		Inscription block of 4	1.40	—
307	A173 20c	**multicolored** *(3,400,000)+*	.30	.25
		First day cover		1.00
		First day cover, #304-307		1.75
		Inscription block of 4	1.40	—
		Nos. 304-307 (4)	1.00	.90

First day covers of Nos. 304-307 total 295,927.
+ Printing orders to June 1990.

UNDRO Against Fire and Water — A174

Office of the UN Disaster Relief Coordinator (UNDRO).
Printed by Heraclio Fournier, S.A., Spain. Panes of 50. Designed by Gidon Sagi.

1979, Mar. 9 Photo. *Perf. 14*

308	A174 15c	**multicolored** *(1,448,600)*	.25	.20
		First day cover		1.00
		Inscription block of 4	1.00	—
309	A174 20c	**multicolored** *(1,126,295)*	.35	.30
		First day cover		1.00
		First day cover, #308-309		1.25
		Inscription block of 4	1.50	—

First day covers of Nos. 308-309 total 266,694.
See UN Offices in Geneva Nos. 82-83.

Child and IYC Emblem — A175

International Year of the Child.
Printed by Heraclio Fournier, S.A., Spain. Panes of 20 (5x4). Designed by Helena Matuszewska (15c) and Krystyna Tarkowska-Gruszecka (31c).

1979, May 4 Photo. *Perf. 14*

310	A175 15c	**multicolored** *(2,290,329)*	.20	.20
		First day cover		1.00
		Inscription block of 4	.90	—
311	A175 31c	**multicolored** *(2,192,136)*	.35	.35
		First day cover		1.25
		First day cover, #310-311		2.25
		Inscription block of 4	1.50	—
		Panes of 20, #310-311	11.50	

First day covers of Nos. 310-311 total 380,022.
See UN Offices in Geneva Nos. 84-85.

Map of Namibia, Olive Branch — A176

Scales and Sword of Justice — A177

For a free and independent Namibia.
Printed by Ashton-Potter Ltd., Canada. Panes of 50. Designed by Eliezer Weishoff.

1979, Oct. 5 Litho. *Perf. 13½*

312	A176 15c	**multicolored** *(1,470,231)*	.20	.20
		First day cover		1.00
		Inscription block of 4	.95	—
313	A176 31c	**multicolored** *(1,355,323)*	.40	.35
		First day cover		1.25
		First day cover, #312-313		1.50
		Inscription block of 4	1.75	—

First day covers of Nos. 312-313 total 250,371.
See UN Offices in Geneva No. 86.

1979, Nov. 9 Litho. *Perf. 13x13½*

International Court of Justice, The Hague, Netherlands.
Printed by Setelipaino, Finland. Panes of 50. Designed by Henning Simon.

314	A177 15c	**multicolored** *(1,244,972)*	.20	.20
		First day cover		1.00
		Inscription block of 4	.85	—
315	A177 20c	**multicolored** *(1,084,483)*	.40	.35
		First day cover		1.00
		First day cover, #314-315		1.25
		Inscription block of 4	1.75	—

First day covers of Nos. 314-315 total 322,901.
See UN Offices in Geneva Nos. 87-88.

Graph of Economic Trends — A178

Key — A179

New International Economic Order.
Printed by Questa Colour Security Printers, United Kingdom. Panes of 50. Designed by Cemalettin Mutver (15c), George Hamori (31c)

1980, Jan. 11 Litho. *Perf. 15x14½*

316	A178 15c	**multicolored** *(1,163,801)*	.20	.20
		First day cover		1.00
		Inscription block of 4	.85	—
317	A179 31c	**multicolored** *(1,103,560)*	.50	.35
		First day cover		1.25
		First day cover, #316-317		1.40
		Inscription block of 4	2.25	—

First day covers of Nos. 316-317 total 211,945.
See UN Offices in Geneva No. 89; Vienna No. 7.

Women's Year Emblem — A180

United Nations Decade for Women.
Printed by Questa Colour Security Printers, United Kingdom. Panes of 50. Designed by Susanne Rottenfusser.

1980, Mar. 7 Litho. *Perf. 14½x15*

318	A180 15c	**multicolored** *(1,409,350)*	.20	.20
		First day cover		1.00
		Inscription block of 4	1.00	—
319	A180 20c	**multicolored** *(1,182,016)*	.30	.25
		First day cover		1.00
		First day cover, #318-319		1.25
		Inscription block of 4	2.00	—

First day covers of Nos. 318-319 total 289,314.
See UN Offices in Geneva Nos. 90-91; Vienna Nos. 9-10.

UN Emblem and "UN" on Helmet — A181

Arrows and UN Emblem — A182

United Nations Peace-keeping Operations.
Printed by Joh. Enschede en Zonen, Netherlands. Panes of 50. Designed by Bruno K. Wiese (15c), James Gardiner (31c)

1980, May 16 Litho. *Perf. 14x13*

320	A181 15c	**blue & black** *(1,245,521)*	.25	.20
		First day cover		1.00
		Inscription block of 4	1.00	—
321	A182 31c	**multicolored** *(1,191,009)*	.40	.40
		First day cover		1.25
		First day cover, #320-321		1.40
		Inscription block of 4	2.25	—

First day covers of Nos. 320-321 total 208,442.
See UN Offices in Geneva No. 92; Vienna No. 11.

"35" and Flags — A183

Globe and Laurel — A184

35th Anniversary of the United Nations.
Printed by Ashton-Potter Ltd, Canada. Nos. 322-323, panes of 50. Designed by Cemalettin Matver (15c), Mian Mohammad Saeed (31c).

1980, June 26 Litho. *Perf. 13x13½*

322	A183 15c	**multicolored** *(1,554,514)*	.20	.20
		First day cover		1.00
		Inscription block of 4	1.00	—
323	A184 31c	**multicolored** *(1,389,606)*	.40	.35
		First day cover		1.25
		First day cover, #322-323		1.40

Inscription block of 4 2.00 —

Souvenir Sheet

Imperf

324 Sheet of 2 *(1,215,505)* .70 .60
a. A183 15c **multicolored** .20
b. A184 31c **multicolored** .40
First day cover 1.25

First day covers of Nos. 322-324 total: New York, 369,345; San Francisco, 203,701.

See UN Offices in Geneva Nos. 93-95; Vienna Nos. 12-14.

Flag of Turkey — A185

Printed by Courvoisier, S.A., Switzerland. Panes of 16. Designed by Ole Hamann.

Each pane contains 4 blocks of 4 (Nos. 325-328, 329-332, 333-336, 337-340). A se-tenant block of 4 designs centers each pane.

1980, Sept. 26 **Litho.** ***Perf. 12***

Granite Paper

325 A185 15c shown *(3,490,725)* .20 .20
326 A185 15c Luxembourg *(3,490,725)* .20 .20
327 A185 15c Fiji *(3,490,725)* .20 .20
328 A185 15c Viet Nam *(3,490,725)* .20 .20
a. Se-tenant block of 4, #325-328 .80 —
329 A185 15c Guinea *(3,442,633)* .20 .20
330 A185 15c Surinam *(3,442,633)* .20 .20
331 A185 15c Bangladesh *(3,442,633)* .20 .20
332 A185 15c Mali *(3,442,633)* .20 .20
a. Se-tenant block of 4, #329-332 .80 —
333 A185 15c Yugoslavia *(3,416,292)* .20 .20
334 A185 15c France *(3,416,292)* .20 .20
335 A185 15c Venezuela *(3,416,292)* .20 .20
336 A185 15c El Salvador *(3,416,292)* .20 .20
a. Se-tenant block of 4, #333-336 .80 —
337 A185 15c Madagascar *(3,442,497)* .20 .20
338 A185 15c Cameroon *(3,442,497)* .20 .20
339 A185 15c Rwanda *(3,442,497)* .20 .20
340 A185 15c Hungary *(3,442,497)* .20 .20
a. Se-tenant block of 4, #337-340 .80 —
First day covers of Nos. 325-340, each .75
Set of 4 diff. panes of 16 8.00
Nos. 325-340 (16) 3.20 3.20

First day covers of Nos. 325-340 total 6,145,595.

See Nos. 350-365, 374-389, 399-414, 425-440, 450-465, 477-492, 499-514, 528-543, 554-569, 690-697, 719-726, 744-751.

Symbolic Flowers — A186

Symbols of Progress — A187

Printed by Ashton-Potter Ltd., Canada. Panes of 50. Designed by Eliezer Weishoff (15c), Dietman Kowall (20c).

1980, Nov. 21 **Litho.** ***Perf. 13½x13***

341 A186 15c **multicolored** *(1,192,165)* .25 .25
First day cover 1.00
Inscription block of 4 1.25 —
342 A187 20c **multicolored** *(1,011,382)* .40 .35
First day cover 1.00
First day cover, #341-342 1.40
Inscription block of 4 1.75 —

First day covers of Nos. 341-342 total 232,149.

See UN Offices in Geneva, Nos. 96-97; Vienna Nos. 15-16.

Inalienable Rights of the Palestinian People — A188

Printed by Courvoisier S.A., Switzerland. Panes of 50. Designed by David Dewhurst.

1981, Jan. 30 **Photo.** ***Perf. 12x11½***

343 A188 15c **multicolored** *(993,489)* .25 .20
First day cover *(127,187)* 1.00
Inscription block of 4 1.25 —

See UN Offices in Geneva No. 98; Vienna No. 17.

Interlocking Puzzle Pieces — A189

Stylized Person — A190

International Year of the Disabled.

Printed by Heraclio Fournier S.A., Spain. Panes of 50. Designed by Sophia Van Heeswijk (20c) and G.P. Van der Hyde (35c).

1981, Mar. 6 **Photo.** ***Perf. 14***

344 A189 20c **multicolored** *(1,218,371)* .25 .20
First day cover 1.00
Inscription block of 4 1.25 —
345 A190 35c **black & orange** *(1,107,298)* .50 .45
First day cover 1.25
First day cover, #344-345 1.40
Inscription block of 4 2.25 —

First day covers of Nos. 344-345 total 204,891.

See UN Offices in Geneva Nos. 99-100; Vienna Nos. 18-19.

Desislava and Sebastocrator Kaloyan, Bulgarian Mural, 1259, Boyana Church, Sofia — A191

Art at UN Issue

Printed by Courvoisier. Panes of 50. Designed by Ole Hamann.

1981, Apr. 15 **Photo.** ***Perf. 11½***

Granite Paper

346 A191 20c **multicolored** *(1,252,648)* .25 .25
First day cover 1.00
Inscription block of 4 1.40 —
347 A191 31c **multicolored** *(1,061,056)* .45 .45
First day cover 1.25
First day cover, #346-347 1.40
Inscription block of 4 2.00 —

First day covers of Nos. 346-347 total 210,978.

See UN Offices in Geneva No. 101; Vienna No. 20.

Solar Energy — A192

Conference Emblem — A193

Conference on New and Renewable Sources of Energy, Nairobi, Aug. 10-21.

Printed by Setelipaino, Finland. Panes of 50. Designed by Ulrike Dreyer (20c); Robert Perrot (40c).

1981, May 29 **Litho.** ***Perf. 13***

348 A192 20c **multicolored** *(1,132,877)* .30 .25
First day cover 1.00
Inscription block of 4 1.40 —
349 A193 40c **multicolored** *(1,158,319)* .55 .50
First day cover 1.25
First day cover, #348-349 1.40
Inscription block of 4 2.50 —

First day covers of Nos. 348-349 total 240,205.

See UN Offices in Geneva No. 102; Vienna No. 21.

Flag Type of 1980

Printed by Courvoisier, S.A., Switzerland. Panes of 16. Designed by Ole Hamann.

Each pane contains 4 blocks of 4 (Nos. 350-353, 354-357, 358-361, 362-365). A se-tenant block of 4 designs centers each pane.

1981, Sept. 25 **Litho.**

Granite Paper

350 A185 20c Djibouti *(2,342,224)* .25 .20
351 A185 20c Sri Lanka *(2,342,224)* .25 .20
352 A185 20c Bolivia *(2,342,224)* .25 .20
353 A185 20c Equatorial Guinea *(2,342,224)* .25 .20
a. Se-tenant block of 4, #350-353 1.50 —
354 A185 20c Malta *(2,360,297)* .25 .20
355 A185 20c Czechoslovakia *(2,360,297)* .25 .20
356 A185 20c Thailand *(2,360,297)* .25 .20
357 A185 20c Trinidad & Tobago *(2,360,297)* .25 .20
a. Se-tenant block of 4, #354-357 1.50 —
358 A185 20c Ukrainian SSR *(2,344,755)* .25 .20
359 A185 20c Kuwait *(2,344,755)* .25 .20
360 A185 20c Sudan *(2,344,755)* .25 .20
361 A185 20c Egypt *(2,344,755)* .25 .20
a. Se-tenant block of 4, #358-361 1.50 —
362 A185 20c US *(2,450,537)* .25 .20
363 A185 20c Singapore *(2,450,537)* .25 .20
364 A185 20c Panama *(2,450,537)* .25 .20
365 A185 20c Costa Rica *(2,450,537)* .25 .20
a. Se-tenant block of 4, #362-365 1.50 —
First day covers, #350-365, each .60
Set of 4 diff. panes of 16 14.00
Nos. 350-365 (16) 4.00 3.20

First day covers of Nos. 350-365 total 3,961,237.

Seedling and Tree Cross-section A194

"10" and Symbols of Progress — A195

United Nations Volunteers Program, 10th anniv.

Printed by Walsall Security Printers, Ltd., United Kingdom. Pane of 50. Designed by Gabriele Nussgen (18c), Angel Medina Medina (28c).

1981, Nov. 13 **Litho.**

366 A194 18c **multicolored** *(1,246,833)* .30 .25
First day cover 1.00
Inscription block of 4 1.50 —
367 A195 28c **multicolored** *(1,282,868)* .60 .55
First day cover 1.25
First day cover, #366-367 1.40
Inscription block of 4 2.75 —

First day covers of Nos. 366-367 total 221,106.

See UN Offices in Geneva Nos. 103-104; Vienna Nos. 22-23.

A196

A197

A198

Respect for Human Rights (17c), Independence of Colonial Countries and People (28c), Second Disarmament Decade (40c).

Printed by Courvoisier, S.A., Switzerland. Panes of 50. Designed by Rolf Christianson (17c); George Hamori (28c); Marek Kwiatkowski (40c).

1982, Jan. 22 *Perf. 11½x12*

368 A196 17c **multicolored** *(3,000,000)+* .30 .25
First day cover 1.00
Inscription block of 4 1.25 —
369 A197 28c **multicolored** *(3,000,000)+* .50 .40
First day cover 1.25
Inscription block of 4 2.25 —
370 A198 40c **multicolored** *(3,000,000)* .80 .70
First day cover 1.25
First day cover, #368-370 1.25
Inscription block of 4 3.50 —
Nos. 368-370 (3) 1.60 1.35

First day covers of Nos. 368-370 total 243,073.

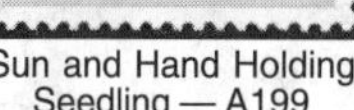
Sun and Hand Holding Seedling — A199

Sun, Plant Land and Water — A200

10th Anniversary of United Nations Environment Program.

Printed by Joh. Enschede En Zonen, Netherlands. Panes of 50. Designed by Philine Hartert (20c); Peer-Ulrich Bremer (40c).

1982, Mar. 19 **Litho.** *Perf. 13½x13*

371 A199 20c **multicolored** *(1,017,117)* .25 .25
First day cover 1.00
Inscription block of 4 1.25 —
372 A200 40c **multicolored** *(884,798)* .70 .65
First day cover 1.25
First day cover, #371-372 1.40
Inscription block of 4 3.25 —

First day covers of Nos. 371-372 total 288,721.

See UN Offices in Geneva Nos. 107-108; Vienna Nos. 25-26.

UN Emblem and Olive Branch in Outer Space — A201

Exploration and Peaceful Uses of Outer Space.

Printed By Enschede. Panes of 50. Designed by Wiktor C. Nerwinski.

1982, June 11 **Litho.** *Perf. 13x13½*

373 A201 20c **multicolored** *(1,083,426)* .55 .45
First day cover *(156,965)* 1.00
Inscription block of 4 2.40 —

See UN Offices in Geneva Nos. 109-110; Vienna No. 27.

Flag Type of 1980

Printed by Courvoisier. Panes of 16. Designed by Ole Hamann.

Issued in 4 panes of 16. Each pane contains 4 blocks of four (Nos. 374-377, 378-381, 383-385, 386-389). A se-tenant block of 4 designs centers each pane.

1982, Sept. 24 **Litho.** *Perf. 12*

Granite Paper

374 A185 20c Austria *(2,314,006)* .25 .20
375 A185 20c Malaysia *(2,314,006)* .25 .20
376 A185 20c Seychelles *(2,314,006)* .25 .20
377 A185 20c Ireland *(2,314,006)* .25 .20
a. Se-tenant block of 4, #374-377 1.50 —
378 A185 20c Mozambique *(2,300,958)* .25 .20
379 A185 20c Albania *(2,300,958)* .25 .20
380 A185 20c Dominica *(2,300,958)* .25 .20
381 A185 20c Solomon Islnads *(2,300,958)* .25 .20
a. Se-tenant block of 4, #378-381 1.50 —
382 A185 20c Philippines *(2,288,589)* .25 .20
383 A185 20c Swaziland *(2,288,589)* .25 .20
384 A185 20c Nicaragua *(2,288,589)* .25 .20
385 A185 20c Burma *(2,288,589)* .25 .20
a. Se-tenant block of 4, #382-385 1.50 —
386 A185 20c Cape Verde *(2,285,848)* .25 .20
387 A185 20c Guyana *(2,285,848)* .25 .20
388 A185 20c Belgium *(2,285,848)* .25 .20
389 A185 20c Nigeria *(2,285,848)* .25 .20
a. Se-tenant block of 4, #386-389 1.50 —
First day cover, #374-389, each .75
Set of 4 diff. panes of 16 16.00
Nos. 374-389 (16) 4.00 3.20

First day covers of Nos. 374-389 total 3,202,744.

Conservation and Protection of Nature — A202

Printed by Fournier. Panes of 50. Designed by Hamori.

1982, Nov. 19 **Photo.** *Perf. 14*

390 A202 20c Leaf *(1,110,027)* .35 .30
First day cover 1.00
margin block of 4, inscription 1.75 —
391 A202 28c Butterfly *(848,772)* .55 .50
First day cover 1.25
First day cover, #390-391 1.40
Inscription block of 4 2.40 —

First day covers of Nos. 390-391 total 214,148.

See UN Offices in Geneva Nos. 111-112; Vienna Nos. 28-29.

A203

A204

World Communications Year

Printed by Walsall. Panes of 50. Designed by Hanns Lohrer (A203) and Lorena Berengo (A204).

1983, Jan. 28 **Litho.** *Perf. 13*

392 A203 20c **multicolored** *(1,282,079)* .25 .25
First day cover 1.00
Inscription block of 4 1.25 —
393 A204 40c **multicolored** *(931,903)* .70 .65
First day cover 1.25
First day cover, #392-393 1.40
Inscription block of 4 3.50 —

First day covers of Nos. 392-393 total 183,499.

See UN Offices in Geneva No. 113; Vienna No. 30.

A205

A206

Safety at Sea.

Printed by Questa. Panes of 50. Designed by Jean-Marie Lenfant (A205), Ari Ron (A206).

1983, Mar. 18 **Litho.** *Perf. 14½*

394 A205 20c **multicolored** *(1,252,456)* .30 .25
First day cover 1.00
Inscription block of 4 1.50 —
395 A206 37c **multicolored** *(939,910)* .60 .55
First day cover 1.25
First day cover, #394-395 1.40
Inscription block of 4 2.75 —

First day covers of Nos. 394-395 total 199,962.

See UN Offices in Geneva Nos. 114-115; Vienna Nos. 31-32.

World Food Program — A207

Printed by Government Printers Bureau, Japan. Designed by Marek Kwiatkowski.

1983, Apr. 22 **Engr.** *Perf. 13½*

396 A207 20c **rose lake** *(1,238,997)* .35 .35
First day cover *(180,704)* 1.00
Inscription block of 4 1.60 —

See UN Offices in Geneva No. 116; Vienna Nos. 33-34.

A208

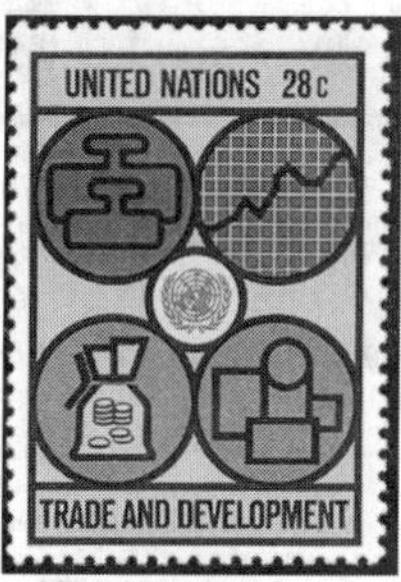

A209

UN Conference on Trade and Development.

Printed by Carl Uberreuter Druck and Verlag M. Salzer, Austria. Panes of 50. Designed by Dietmar Braklow (A208), Gabriel Genz (A209).

1983, June 6 **Litho.** *Perf. 14*

397 A208 20c **multicolored** *(1,060,053)* .35 .35
First day cover 1.10
Inscription block of 4 1.50 —
398 A209 28c **multicolored** *(948,981)* .70 .65
First day cover 1.40
First day cover, #397-398 1.50
Inscription block of 4 2.90 —

First day covers of Nos. 397-398 total 200,131.

See UN Offices in Geneva Nos. 117-118; Vienna Nos. 35-36.

Flag Type of 1980

Printed by Courvoisier. Panes of 16. Designed by Ole Hamann.

Issued in 4 panes of 16. Each pane contains 4 blocks of four (Nos. 399-402, 403-406, 407-410, 411-414). A se-tenant block of 4 designs centers each pane.

1983, Sept. 23 **Photo.** ***Perf. 12***

Granite Paper

399 A185 20c Great Britain *(2,490,599)* .25 .20
400 A185 20c Barbados *(2,490,599)* .25 .20
401 A185 20c Nepal *(2,490,599)* .25 .20
402 A185 20c Israel *(2,490,599)* .25 .20
a. Se-tenant block of 4, #399-402 1.60 —
403 A185 20c Malawi *(2,483,010)* .25 .20
404 A185 20c Byelorussian SSR *(2,483,010)* .25 .20
405 A185 20c Jamaica *(2,483,010)* .25 .20
406 A185 20c Kenya *(2,483,010)* .25 .20
a. Se-tenant block of 4, #403-406 1.60 —
407 A185 20c People's Republic of China *(2,474,140)* .25 .20
408 A185 20c Peru *(2,474,140)* .25 .20
409 A185 20c Bulgaria *(2,474,140)* .25 .20
410 A185 20c Canada *(2,474,140)* .25 .20
a. Se-tenant block of 4, #407-410 1.60 —
411 A185 20c Somalia *(2,482,070)* .25 .20
412 A185 20c Senegal *(2,482,070)* .25 .20
413 A185 20c Brazil *(2,482,070)* .25 .20
414 A185 20c Sweden *(2,482,070)* .25 .20
a. Se-tenant block of 4, #411-414 1.60 —
First day cover, #399-414, each .75
Set of 4 diff. panes of 16 17.00
Nos. 399-414 (16) 4.00 3.20

First day covers of Nos. 399-414 total 2,214,134.

Window Right — A210

Peace Treaty with Nature — A211

35th Anniversary of the Universal Declaration of Human Rights.
Printed by Government Printing Office, Austria. Panes of 16 (4x4). Designed by Friedensreich Hundertwasser, Austria.

1983, Dec. 9 **Photo. & Engr.** ***Perf. 13½***

415 A210 20c **multicolored** *(1,591,102)* .30 .25
First day cover 1.00
Inscription block of 4 1.25 —
416 A211 40c **multicolored** *(1,566,789)* .70 .65
First day cover 1.25
First day cover, #415-416 1.50
Inscription block of 4 3.00 —
Panes of 16, #415-416 16.00

First day covers of Nos. 415-416 total 176,269.
See UN Offices in Geneva Nos. 119-120; Vienna Nos. 37-38.

International Conference on Population — A212

Printed by Bundesdruckerei, Federal Republic of Germany. Panes of 50. Designed by Marina Langer-Rosa and Helmut Langer, Federal Republic of Germany.

1984, Feb. 3 **Litho.** ***Perf. 14***

417 A212 20c **multicolored** *(905,320)* .30 .25
First day cover 1.00
Inscription block of 4 1.40 —
418 A212 40c **multicolored** *(717,084)* .60 .55
First day cover 1.25
First day cover, #417-418 1.40
Inscription block of 4 2.50 —

First day covers of Nos. 417-418 total 118,068.
See UN Offices in Geneva No. 121; Vienna No. 39.

Tractor Plowing A213

Rice Paddy A214

World Food Day, Oct. 16
Printed by Walsall Security Printers, Ltd., United Kingdom. Panes of 50. Designed by Adth Vanooijen, Netherlands.

1984, Mar. 15 **Litho.** ***Perf. 14½***

419 A213 20c **multicolored** *(853,641)* .35 .30
First day cover 1.25
Inscription block of 4 1.60 —
420 A214 40c **multicolored** *(727,165)* .65 .65
First day cover 1.50
First day cover, #419-420 1.75
Inscription block of 4 2.75 —

First day covers of Nos. 419-420 total 116,009.

Grand Canyon — A215

Ancient City of Polonnaruwa, Sri Lanka — A216

World Heritage
Printed by Harrison and Sons, United Kingdom. Panes of 50. Designs adapted by Rocco J. Callari, U.S., and Thomas Lee, China.

1984, Apr. 18 **Litho.** ***Perf. 14***

421 A215 20c **multicolored** *(814,316)* .25 .20
First day cover 1.00
Inscription block of 4 1.10 —
422 A216 50c **multicolored** *(579,136)* .70 .70
First day cover 1.25
First day cover, #421-422 1.40
Inscription block of 4 3.25 —

First day covers of Nos. 421-422 total 112,036.

A217

A218

Future for Refugees
Printed by Courvoisier. Panes of 50. Designed by Hans Erni, Switzerland.

1984, May 29 **Photo.** ***Perf. 11½***

423 A217 20c **multicolored** *(956,743)* .40 .35
First day cover 1.00
Inscription block of 4 2.00 —
424 A218 50c **multicolored** *(729,036)* 1.00 .85
First day cover 1.25
First day cover, #423-424 1.40
Inscription block of 4 4.50 —

First day covers of Nos. 423-424 total 115,789.

Flag Type of 1980

Printed by Courvoisier. Panes of 16. Designed by Ole Hamann.
Issued in 4 panes of 16. Each pane contains 4 blocks of four (Nos. 425-428, 429-432, 433-436, 437-440). A se-tenant block of 4 designs centers each pane.

1984, Sept. 21 **Photo.** ***Perf. 12***

Granite Paper

425 A185 20c Burundi *(1,941,471)* .50 .45
426 A185 20c Pakistan *(1,941,471)* .50 .45
427 A185 20c Benin *(1,941,471)* .50 .45
428 A185 20c Italy *(1,941,471)* .50 .45
a. Se-tenant block of 4, #425-428 2.75 —
429 A185 20c Tanzania *(1,969,051)* .50 .45
430 A185 20c United Arab Emirates *(1,969,051)* .50 .45
431 A185 20c Ecuador *(1,969,051)* .50 .45
432 A185 20c Bahamas *(1,969,051)* .50 .45
a. Se-tenant block of 4, #429-432 2.75 —
433 A185 20c Poland *(2,001,091)* .50 .45
434 A185 20c Papua New Guinea *(2,001,091)* .50 .45
435 A185 20c Uruguay *(2,001,091)* .50 .45
436 A185 20c Chile *(2,001,091)* .50 .45
a. Se-tenant block of 4, #433-436 2.75 —
437 A185 20c Paraguay *(1,969,875)* .50 .45
438 A185 20c Bhutan *(1,969,875)* .50 .45
439 A185 20c Central African Republic *(1,969,875)* .50 .45
440 A185 20c Australia *(1,969,875)* .50 .45
a. Se-tenant block of 4, #437-440 2.75 —
First day cover, #425-440, each 1.00
Set of 4 diff. panes of 16 32.50
Nos. 425-440 (16) 8.00 7.20

First day covers of Nos. 425-440 total 1,914,972.

International Youth Year — A219

ILO Turin Center — A220

Printed by Waddingtons Ltd., United Kingdom. Panes of 50. Designed by Ramon Mueller, Federal Republic of Germany.

1984, Nov. 15 **Litho.** ***Perf. 13½***

441 A219 20c **multicolored** *(884,962)* .40 .35
First day cover 1.00
Inscription block of 4 2.00 —
442 A219 35c **multicolored** *(740,023)* 1.25 1.10
First day cover 1.25
First day cover, #441-442 1.40
Inscription block of 4 5.75 —

First day covers of Nos. 441-442 total 125,315.

1985, Feb. 1 **Engr.** ***Perf. 13½***

Printed by the Government Printing Bureau, Japan. Panes of 50. Engraved by Mamoru Iwakuni and Hiroshi Ozaki, Japan.

443 A220 23c **blue** *(612,942)* .55 .45
First day cover *(76,541)* 1.00
Inscription block of 4 2.50 —

See UN Offices in Geneva Nos. 129-130; Vienna No. 48.

UN University A221

Printed by Helio Courvoiser, Switzerland. Panes of 50. Designed by Moshe Pereg, Israel, and Hinedi Geluda, Brazil.

1985, Mar. 15 Photo. *Perf. 13½*

444 A221 50c Farmer plowing, discussion group *(625,043)* 1.10 1.00
First day cover *(77,271)* 1.25
Inscription block of 4 5.00 —

See UN Offices in Geneva Nos. 131-132; Vienna No. 49.

Peoples of the World United — A222

Painting UN Emblem — A223

Printed by Carl Ueberreuter Druck and Verlag M. Salzer, Austria. Panes of 50. Designed by Fritz Henry Oerter, Federal Republic of Germany (22c), and Rimondi Rino, Italy ($3).

1985, May 10 Litho. *Perf. 14*

445 A222 22c **multicolored** *(2,000,000)+* .35 .30
First day cover 1.00
Inscription block of 4 1.50 —
446 A223 $3 **multicolored** *(2,000,000)+* 4.00 1.00
First day cover 4.50
First day cover, #445-446 6.50
Inscription block of 4 17.00 —

First day covers of Nos. 445-446 total 88,613.

The Corner, 1947 — A224

Alvaro Raking Hay, 1953 — A225

UN 40th anniversary. Oil paintings (details) by American artist Andrew Wyeth (b. 1917). Printed by Helio Courvoisier, Switzerland. Nos. 447-448 panes of 50. Designed by Rocco J. Callari, U.S., and Thomas Lee, China (#449).

1985, June 26 Photo. *Perf. 12 x 11½*

447 A224 22c **multicolored** *(944,960)* .45 .35
First day cover 1.00
Inscription block of 4 2.25 —
448 A225 45c **multicolored** *(680,079)* 1.10 .85
First day cover 1.25
First day cover, #447-448 1.50
Inscription block of 4 5.50 —

Souvenir Sheet

Imperf

449 Sheet of 2 *(506,004)* 1.50 1.40
a. A224 22c **multicolored** .50 —
b. A225 45c **multicolored** .75 —
First day cover .75

First day covers of Nos. 447-449 total; New York, 210,189; San Francisco, 92,804.
See UN Offices in Geneva Nos. 135-137; Vienna Nos. 52-54.

Flag Type of 1980

Printed by Helio Courvoisier, Switzerland. Designed by Ole Hamann.
Issued in panes of 16; each contains 4 blocks of four (Nos. 450-453, 454-457, 458-461, 462-465). A se-tenant block of 4 designs is at the center of each pane.

1985, Sept. 20 Photo. *Perf. 12*
Granite Paper

450 A185 22c Grenada *(1,270,755)* .55 .50
451 A185 22c Federal Republic of Germany *(1,270,755)* .55 .50
452 A185 22c Saudi Arabia *(1,270,755)* .55 .50
453 A185 22c Mexico *(1,270,755)* .55 .50
a. Se-tenant block of 4, #450-453 3.25 —
454 A185 22c Uganda *(1,216,878)* .55 .50
455 A185 22c St. Thomas & Prince *(1,216,878)* .55 .50
456 A185 22c USSR *(1,216,878)* .55 .50
457 A185 22c India *(1,216,878)* .55 .50
a. Se-tenant block of 4, #454-457 3.25 —
458 A185 22c Liberia *(1,213,231)* .55 .50
459 A185 22c Mauritius *(1,213,231)* .55 .50
460 A185 22c Chad *(1,213,231)* .55 .50
461 A185 22c Dominican Republic *(1,213,231)* .55 .50
a. Se-tenant block of 4, #458-461 3.25 —
462 A185 22c Sultanate of Oman *(1,215,533)* .55 .50
463 A185 22c Ghana *(1,215,533)* .55 .50
464 A185 22c Sierra Leone *(1,215,533)* .55 .50
465 A185 22c Finland *(1,215,533)* .55 .50
a. Se-tenant block of 4, #462-465 3.25 —
First day covers, #460-465, each 1.00
Set of 4 diff. panes of 16 37.50
Nos. 450-465 (16) 8.80 8.00

First day covers of Nos. 450-465 total 1,774,193.

UNICEF Child Survival Campaign — A226

Africa in Crisis — A227

Printed by the Government Printing Bureau, Japan. Panes of 50. Designed by Mel Harris, United Kingdom (#466) and Dipok Deyi, India (#467).

1985, Nov. 22 Photo. & Engr. *Perf. 13½*

466 A226 22c Asian Toddler *(823,724)* .35 .30
First day cover 1.00
Inscription block of 4 1.50 —
467 A226 33c Breastfeeding *(632,753)* .65 .60
First day cover 1.25
First day cover, #466-467 1.75
Inscription block of 4 3.00 —

First day covers of Nos. 466-467 total 206,923.
See UN Offices in Geneva Nos. 138-139; Vienna Nos. 55-56.

1986, Jan. 31 Photo. *Perf. 11½x12*

Printed by Helio Courvoisier, Switzerland. Pane of 50. Designed by Wosene Kosrof, Ethiopia.

468 A227 22c **multicolored** *(708,169)* .50 .45
First day cover *(80,588)* 1.75
Inscription block of 4 2.50 —

Campaign against hunger. See UN Offices in Geneva No. 140; Vienna No. 57.

Water Resources A228

Printed by the Government Printing Bureau, Japan. Pane of 40, 2 blocks of 4 horizontal by 5 blocks of 4 vertical. Designed by Thomas Lee, China.

1986, Mar. 14 Photo. *Perf. 13½*

469 A228 22c Dam *(525,839)* 1.00 .90
470 A228 22c Irrigation *(525,839)* 1.00 .90
471 A228 22c Hygiene *(525,839)* 1.00 .90
472 A228 22c Well *(525,839)* 1.00 .90
a. Block of 4, #469-472 4.00 4.00
First day cover, #472a 7.00
First day cover, #469-472, each 2.00
Inscription block of 4, #469-472 7.50 —
Pane of 40, #469-472 55.00

UN Development Program. No. 472a has continuous design.
First day covers of Nos. 469-472 total 199,347.
See UN Offices in Geneva Nos. 141-144; Vienna Nos. 58-61.

Human Rights Stamp of 1954 — A229

Stamp collecting: 44c, Engraver. Printed by the Swedish Post Office, Sweden. Panes of 50. Designed by Czeslaw Slania and Ingalill Axelsson, Sweden.

1986, May 22 Engr. *Perf. 12½*

473 A229 22c **dark violet & bright blue** *(825,782)* .30 .25
First day cover 1.00
Inscription block of 4 1.50 —
474 A229 44c **brown & emerald green** *(738,552)* .80 .70
First day cover 1.25
First day cover, #473-474 1.50
Inscription block of 4 3.25 —

First day covers of Nos. 473-474 total: New York, 121,143; Chicago, 89,557.
See UN Offices in Geneva Nos. 146-147; Vienna Nos. 62-63.

Bird's Nest in Tree — A230

Peace in Seven Languages A231

Printed by the Government Printing Bureau, Japan. Panes of 50. Designed by Akira Iriguchi, Japan (#475), and Henryk Chylinski, Poland (#476).

1986, June 20 Photo. & Embossed *Perf. 13½*

475 A230 22c **multicolored** *(836,160)* .50 .40
First day cover 1.00
Inscription block of 4 2.50 —
476 A231 33c **multicolored** *(663,882)* 1.25 1.25
First day cover 2.00
First day cover, #475-476 4.50
Inscription block of 4 6.50 —

International Peace Year.
First day covers of Nos. 475-476 total 149,976.

Flag Type of 1980

Printed by Helio Courvoisier, Switzerland. Designed by Ole Hamann. Issued in panes of 16; each contains 4 blocks of four (Nos. 477-480, 481-484, 485-488, 489-492). A se-tenant block of 4 designs centers each pane.

1986, Sept. 19 Photo. *Perf. 12*
Granite Paper

477 A185 22c New Zealand *(1,150,584)* .55 .50
478 A185 22c Lao PDR *(1,150,584)* .55 .50
479 A185 22c Burkina Faso *(1,150,584)* .55 .50
480 A185 22c Gambia *(1,150,584)* .55 .50
a. Se-tenant block of 4, #477-480 3.25 —
481 A185 22c Maldives *(1,154,870)* .55 .50
482 A185 22c Ethiopia *(1,154,870)* .55 .50
483 A185 22c Jordan *(1,154,870)* .55 .50
484 A185 22c Zambia *(1,154,870)* .55 .50
a. Se-tenant block of 4, #481-484 3.25 —
485 A185 22c Iceland *(1,152,740)* .55 .50
486 A185 22c Antigua & Barbuda *(1,152,740)* .55 .50
487 A185 22c Angola *(1,152,740)* .55 .50
488 A185 22c Botswana *(1,152,740)* .55 .50
a. Se-tenant block of 4, #485-488 3.25 —
489 A185 22c Romania *(1,150,412)* .55 .50
490 A185 22c Togo *(1,150,412)* .55 .50
491 A185 22c Mauritania *(1,150,412)* .55 .50
492 A185 22c Colombia *(1,150,412)* .55 .50
a. Se-tenant block of 4, #489-492 3.25 —
First day covers, #477-492, each 1.00
Set of 4 diff. panes of 16 35.00
Nos. 477-492 (16) 8.80 8.00

First day covers of Nos. 477-492 total 1,442,284.

World Federation of UN Associations, 40th anniv. — A232

Printed by Johann Enschede and Sons, Netherlands. Designed by Rocco J. Callari, U.S.

Designs: 22c, Mother Earth, by Edna Hibel, U.S. 33c, Watercolor by Salvador Dali (b. 1904), Spain. 39c, New Dawn, by Dong Kingman, U.S. 44c, Watercolor by Chaim Gross, U.S.

1986, Nov. 14 Litho. *Perf. 13x13½*

Souvenir Sheet

No.	Description		
493	Sheet of 4 *(433,888)*	4.25	4.00
a.	A232 22c **multicolored**	.60	—
b.	A232 33c **multicolored**	.75	—
c.	A232 39c **multicolored**	1.10	—
d.	A232 44c **multicolored**	1.25	—
	First day cover *(106,194)*		2.00

No. 493 has inscribed margin picturing UN and WFUNA emblems.

See UN Offices in Geneva No. 150; Vienna No. 66.

Trygve Halvdan Lie (1896-1968), first Secretary-General — A233

1987, Jan. 30 Photo. & Engr. *Perf. 13½*

Printed by the Government Printing Office, Austria. Panes of 50. Designed by Rocco J. Callari, U.S., from a portrait by Harald Dal, Norway.

No.	Description		
494	A233 22c **multicolored** *(596,440)*	.90	.80
	First day cover *(84,819)*		1.75
	Inscription block of 4	4.00	—

See Offices in Geneva No. 151; Vienna No. 67.

International Year of Shelter for the Homeless A234

Printed by Johann Enschede and Sons, Netherlands. Panes of 50. Designed by Wladyslaw Brykczynski, Poland.

Designs: 22c, Surveying and blueprinting. 44c, Cutting lumber.

1987, Mar. 13 Litho. *Perf. 13½x12½*

No.	Description		
495	A234 22c **multicolored** *(620,627)*	.40	.35
	First day cover		1.60
	Inscription block of 4	1.75	—
496	A234 44c **multicolored** *(538,096)*	1.25	1.25
	First day cover		1.90
	First day cover, #495-496		2.75
	Inscription block of 4	5.50	—

First day covers of Nos. 495-496 total 94,090.

See Offices in Geneva Nos. 154-155; Vienna Nos. 68-69.

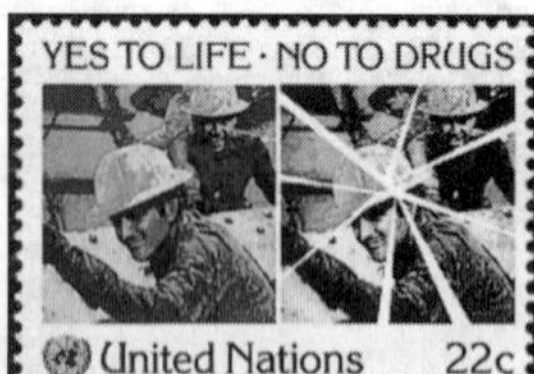

Fight Drug Abuse — A235

Printed by the House of Questa, United Kingdom. Panes of 50. Designed by Susan Borgen and Noel Werrett, U.S.

Designs: 22c, Construction. 33c, Education.

1987, June 12 Litho. *Perf. 14½x15*

No.	Description		
497	A235 22c **multicolored** *(674,563)*	.65	.50
	First day cover		1.75
	Inscription block of 4	2.75	—
498	A235 33c **multicolored** *(643,153)*	1.10	1.00
	First day cover		2.00
	First day cover, #497-498		2.25
	Inscription block of 4	5.25	—

First day covers of Nos. 497-498 total 106,941.

See Offices in Geneva Nos. 156-157; Vienna Nos. 70-71.

Flag Type of 1980

Printed by Courvoisier. Designed by Ole Hamann.

Issued in panes of 16; each contains 4 block of four (Nos. 499-502, 503-506, 507-510, 511-514). A se-tenant block of 4 designs centers each pane.

1987, Sept. 18 Photo. *Perf. 12*

Granite Paper

No.	Description		
499	A185 22c Comoros *(1,235,828)*	.55	.50
500	A185 22c Yemen PDR *(1,235,828)*	.55	.50
501	A185 22c Mongolia *(1,235,828)*	.55	.50
502	A185 22c Vanuatu *(1,235,828)*	.55	.50
a.	Se-tenant block of 4, #499-502	3.25	—
503	A185 22c Japan *(1,244,534)*	.55	.50
504	A185 22c Gabon *(1,244,534)*	.55	.50
505	A185 22c Zimbabwe *(1,244,534)*	.55	.50
506	A185 22c Iraq *(1,244,534)*	.55	.50
a.	Se-tenant block of 4, #503-506	3.25	—
507	A185 22c Argentina *(1,238,065)*	.55	.50
508	A185 22c Congo *(1,238,065)*	.55	.50
509	A185 22c Niger *(1,238,065)*	.55	.50
510	A185 22c St. Lucia *(1,238,065)*	.55	.50
a.	Se-tenant block of 4, #507-510	3.25	—
511	A185 22c Bahrain *(1,239,323)*	.55	.50
512	A185 22c Haiti *(1,239,323)*	.55	.50
513	A185 22c Afghanistan *(1,239,323)*	.55	.50
514	A185 22c Greece *(1,239,323)*	.55	.50
a.	Se-tenant block of 4, #511-514	3.25	—
	First day covers, #499-514, each		1.00
	Set of 4 diff. panes of 16	37.50	
	Nos. 499-514 (16)	8.80	8.00

United Nations Day — A236

Printed by The House of Questa, United Kingdom. Panes of 12. Designed by Elisabeth von Janota-Bzowski (#515) and Fritz Henry Oerter (#516), Federal Republic of Germany.

Designs: Multinational people in various occupations.

1987, Oct. 23 Litho. *Perf. 14½x15*

No.	Description		
515	A236 22c **multicolored** *(1,119,286)*	.40	.35
	First day cover		1.00
	Inscription block of 4	2.00	—
516	A236 39c **multicolored** *(1,065,468)*	.60	.65
	First day cover		2.00
	First day cover, #515-516		1.60
	Inscription block of 4	2.50	—
	Panes of 12, #515-516	12.00	

See Offices in Geneva Nos. 158-159; Vienna Nos. 74-75.

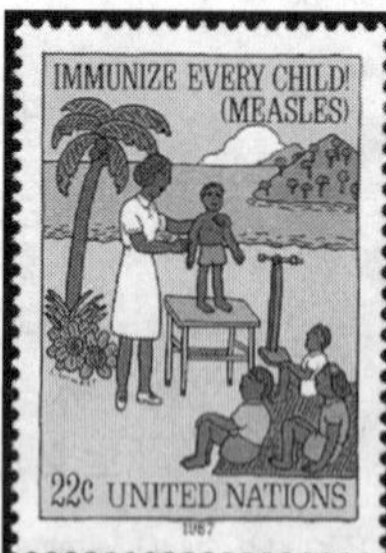

Immunize Every Child — A237

Printed by The House of Questa, United Kingdom. Panes of 50. Designed by Seymour Chwast, U.S.

Designs: 22c, Measles. 44c, Tetanus.

1987, Nov. 20 Litho. *Perf. 15x14½*

No.	Description		
517	A237 22c **multicolored** *(660,495)*	1.25	.60
	First day cover		2.00
	Inscription block of 4	5.00	—
518	A237 44c **multicolored** *(606,049)*	2.25	1.75
	First day cover		2.25
	First day cover, #517-518		3.50
	Inscription block of 4	11.00	—

See Offices in Geneva Nos. 160-161; Vienna Nos. 76-77.

Intl. Fund for Agricultural Development (IFAD) A238

Printed by CPE Australia Ltd., Australia. Panes of 50. Designed by Santiago Arolas, Switzerland.

Designs: 22c, Fishing. 33c, Farming.

1988, Jan. 29 Litho. *Perf. 13½*

No.	Description		
519	A238 22c **multicolored** *(392,649)*	.45	.40
	First day cover		1.00
	Inscription block of 4	2.25	—
520	A238 33c **multicolored** *(475,185)*	.90	.85
	First day cover		1.25
	First day cover, #519-520		3.00
	Inscription block of 4	4.75	—

See Offices in Geneva Nos. 162-163; Vienna Nos. 78-79.

A239

Printed by Heraclio Fournier, S.A., Spain. Panes of 50. Designed by David Ben-Hador, Israel.

1988, Jan. 29 Photo. *Perf. 13½x14*

No.	Description		
521	A239 3c **multicolored** *(3,000,000)+*	.20	.20
	First day cover		1.00
	Inscription block of 4	.75	—

Survival of the Forests — A240

Printed by The House of Questa, United Kingdom. Panes of six se-tenant pairs. Designed by Braldt Bralds, the Netherlands.

Tropical rain forest: 25c, Treetops. 44c, Ground vegetation and tree trunks. Printed se-tenant in a continuous design.

1988, Mar. 18 Litho. *Perf. 14x15*

No.	Description		
522	A240 25c **multicolored** *(647,360)*	1.25	1.25
	First day cover		5.00
523	A240 44c **multicolored** *(647,360)*	2.00	2.00
	First day cover		8.00
a.	Pair, #522-523	3.75	3.75
	First day cover, #523a		14.00
	Inscription block of 4	8.50	
	Pane of 12, #522-523	25.00	

See Offices in Geneva Nos. 165-166; Vienna Nos. 80-81.

Intl. Volunteer Day — A241

Printed by Johann Enschede and Sons, the Netherlands. Panes of 50. Designed by James E. Tennison, U.S.

Designs: 25c, Edurahon. 50c, Vocational training, horiz.

1988, May 6 Litho. *Perf. 13x14, 14x13*

524 A241 25c **multicolored** *(688,444)* .55 .50
First day cover 2.50
Inscription block of 4 2.50 —
525 A241 50c **multicolored** *(447,784)* 1.25 1.00
First day cover 3.00
First day cover, #524-525 3.25
Inscription block of 4 5.00 —

See Offices in Geneva Nos. 167-168; Vienna Nos. 82-83.

Health in Sports A242

Printed by the Government Printing Bureau, Japan. Panes of 50. Paintings by LeRoy Neiman, American sports artist.

Designs: 25c, Cycling, vert. 35c, Marathon.

1988, June 17 Litho. *Perf. 13½x13, 13x13½*

526 A242 25c **multicolored** *(658,991)* .50 .45
First day cover 2.25
Inscription block of 4 2.50 —
527 A242 38c **multicolored** *(420,421)* 1.10 1.10
First day cover 2.50
First day cover, #526-527 3.75
Inscription block of 4 6.50 —

See Offices in Geneva Nos. 169-170; Vienna Nos. 84-85.

Flag Type of 1980

Printed by Helio Courvoisier, Switzerland. Designed by Ole Hamann, Denmark. Issued in panes of 16; each contains 4 blocks of four (Nos. 528-531, 532-535, 536-539 and 540-543). A se-tenant block of 4 centers each pane.

1988, Sept. 15 Photo. *Perf. 12*

Granite Paper

528 A185 25c Spain *(1,029,443)* .60 .50
529 A185 25c St. Vincent & Grenadines *(1,029,443)* .60 .50
530 A185 25c Ivory Coast *(1,029,443)* .60 .50
531 A185 25c Lebanon *(1,029,443)* .60 .50
a. Se-tenant block of 4, #528-531 3.25 —
532 A185 25c Yemen (Arab Republic) *(1,010,774)* .60 .50
533 A185 25c Cuba *(1,010,774)* .60 .50
534 A185 25c Denmark *(1,010,774)* .60 .50
535 A185 25c Libya *(1,010,774)* .60 .50
a. Se-tenant block of 4, #532-535 3.25 —
536 A185 25c Qatar *(1,016,941)* .60 .50
537 A185 25c Zaire *(1,016,941)* .60 .50
538 A185 25c Norway *(1,016,941)* .60 .50
539 A185 25c German Democratic Republic *(1,016,941)* .60 .50
a. Se-tenant block of 4, #536-539 3.25 —
540 A185 25c Iran *(1,009,234)* .60 .50
541 A185 25c Tunisia *(1,009,234)* .60 .50
542 A185 25c Samoa *(1,009,234)* .60 .50
543 A185 25c Belize *(1,009,234)* .60 .50
a. Se-tenant block of 4, #540-543 3.25 —
First day covers, #528-543, each 1.25
Set of 4 diff. panes of 16 35.00
Nos. 528-543 (16) 9.60 8.00

Universal Declaration of Human Rights, 40th. Anniv. — A243

Printed by Helio Couvoisier, Switzerland. Panes of 50. Designed by Rocco J. Callari, U.S.

1988, Dec. 9 Photo. & Engr. *Perf. 11x11½*

544 A243 25c **multicolored** *(893,706)* .50 .45
First day cover 2.25
Inscription block of 4 2.40 —

Souvenir Sheet

545 A243 $1 **multicolored** *(411,863)* 1.50 1.50
First day cover 2.75

No. 545 has multicolored decorative margin inscribed with the preamble to the human rights declaration in English.

See Offices in Geneva Nos. 171-172; Vienna Nos. 86-87.

World Bank — A244

A245

Printed by Johann Enschede and Sons, the Netherlands. Panes of 50. Designed by Saturnino Lumboy, Philippines.

1989, Jan. 27 Litho. *Perf. 13x14*

546 A244 25c Energy and nature *(612,114)* .75 .45
First day cover 2.00
Inscription block of 4 3.00 —
547 A244 45c Agriculture *(528,184)* 1.50 1.00
First day cover 2.50
First day cover, #546-547 3.00
Inscription block of 4 7.00 —

First day covers of Nos. 546-547 total 103,087 (NYC), 56,501 (Washington).

See Offices in Geneva Nos. 173-174; Vienna Nos. 88-89.

1989, Mar. 17 Litho. *Perf. 14x13½*

UN Peace-Keeping Force, awarded 1988 Nobel Peace Prize. Printed by CPE Australia, Ltd., Australia. Panes of 50. Designed by Tom Bland, Australia.

548 A245 25c **multicolored** *(808,842)* .50 .40
First day cover *(52,115)* 2.25
Inscription block of 4 2.25 —

See Offices in Geneva No. 175; Vienna No. 90.

Aerial Photograph of New York Headquarters — A246

Printed by Johann Enschede and Sons, the Netherlands. Panes of 25. Designed by Rocco J. Callari, United States, from a photograph by Simon Nathan.

1989, Mar. 17 Litho. *Perf. 14½x14*

549 A246 45c **multicolored** *(2,000,000)+* .75 .65
First day cover *(41,610)* 2.00
Inscription block of 4 3.25 —

World Weather Watch, 25th Anniv. (in 1988) — A247

Printed by Johann Enschede and Sons, the Netherlands. Panes of 50.

Satellite photographs: 25c, Storm system off the U.S. east coast. 36c, Typhoon Abby in the north-west Pacific.

1989, Apr. 21 Litho. *Perf. 13x14*

550 A247 25c **multicolored** *(849,819)* .70 .60
First day cover 1.75
Inscription block of 4 3.00 —
551 A247 36c **multicolored** *(826,547)* 1.40 1.25
First day cover 2.50
First day cover, #550-551 3.00
Inscription block of 4 7.25 —

First day covers of Nos. 550-551 total 92,013.

See Offices in Geneva Nos. 176-177; Vienna Nos. 91-92.

Offices in Vienna, 10th Anniv.
A248 A249

Printed by the Government Printing Office, Austria. Panes of 25. Designed by Paul Flora (25c) and Rudolf Hausner (90c), Austria.

Photo. & Engr., Photo. (90c)

1989, Aug. 23 *Perf. 14*

552 A248 25c **multicolored** *(580,663)* 2.75 2.50
First day cover 2.50
Inscription block of 4 12.50 —
553 A249 90c **multicolored** *(505,776)* 2.25 2.00
First day cover 2.50
First day cover, #552-553 8.50
Inscription block of 4 9.00 —
Panes of 25, #552-553 150.00

First day covers of Nos. 552-553 total 89,068.

See Offices in Geneva Nos. 178-179; Vienna Nos. 93-94.

Flag Type of 1980

Printed by Helio Courvoisier, Switzerland. Designed by Ole Hamann, Denmark. Issued in panes of 16; each contains 4 blocks of 4 (Nos. 554-557, 558-561, 562-565, 566-569). A se-tenant block of 4 designs centers each pane.

1989, Sept. 22 Photo. *Perf. 12*

Granite Paper

554 A185 25c Indonesia *(959,076)* .65 .55
555 A185 25c Lesotho *(959,076)* .65 .55
556 A185 25c Guatemala *(959,076)* .65 .55
557 A185 25c Netherlands *(959,076)* .65 .55
a. Se-tenant block of 4, #554-557 3.75 —
558 A185 25c South Africa *(960,502)* .65 .55
559 A185 25c Portugal *(960,502)* .65 .55
560 A185 25c Morocco *(960,502)* .65 .55
561 A185 25c Syrian Arab Republic *(960,502)* .65 .55
a. Se-tenant block of 4, #558-561 3.75 —
562 A185 25c Honduras *(959,814)* .65 .55
563 A185 25c Kampuchea *(959,814)* .65 .55
564 A185 25c Guinea-Bissau *(959,814)* .65 .55
565 A185 25c Cyprus *(959,814)* .65 .55
a. Se-tenant block of 4, #562-565 3.75 —
566 A185 25c Algeria *(959,805)* .65 .55
567 A185 25c Brunei *(959,805)* .65 .55
568 A185 25c St. Kitts and Nevis *(959,805)* .65 .55
569 A185 25c United Nations *(959,805)* .65 .55
a. Se-tenant block of 4, #566-569 3.75 —
First day covers, #554-569, each 1.25
Set of 4 diff. panes of 16 42.50
Nos. 554-569 (16) 10.40 8.80

First day covers of Nos. 554-569 total 794,934.

Declaration of Human Rights, 40th Anniv. (in 1988) — A250

Printed by Johann Enschede and Sons, the Netherlands. Panes of 12+12 se-tenant labels containing Articles 1 (25c) or 2 (45c) inscribed in English, French or German. Designed by Rocco J. Callari and Robert Stein, US.

Paintings: 25c, The Table of Universal Brotherhood, by Jose Clemente Orozco. 45c, Study for Composition II, by Vassily Kandinsky.

1989, Nov. 17 Litho. *Perf. 13½*

570 A250 25c **multicolored** *(1,934,135)* .40 .30
First day cover 1.25
Inscription block of 3 + 3 labels 1.25 —
571 A250 45c **multicolored** *(1,922,171)* .90 .80
First day cover 1.25
First day cover, #570-571 2.00
Inscription block of 3 + 3 labels 2.75 —
Panes of 12, #570-571 17.00

First day covers of Nos. 570-571 total 146,489 (NYC), 46,774 (Washington).

See Nos. 582-583, 599-600, 616-617, 627-628; Offices in Geneva Nos. 180-181, 193-194, 209-210, 224-225, 234-235; Vienna Nos. 95-96, 108-109, 123-124, 139-140, 150-151.

Intl. Trade Center — A251

Printed by House of Questa, United Kingdom. Panes of 50. Designed by Richard Bernstein, US.

1990, Feb. 2 **Litho.** ***Perf. 14½x15***
572 A251 25c **multicolored** *(429,081)* 1.60 1.25
First day cover *(52,614)* 2.50
Inscription block of 4 6.50 —

See Offices in Geneva No. 182; Vienna No. 97.

Fight AIDS Worldwide A252

Printed by Johann Enschede and Sons, the Netherlands. Panes of 50. Designed by Jacek Tofil, Poland (25c) and Fritz Henry Oerter, Federal Republic of Germany (40c).
Design: 40c, Shadow over crowd.

1990, Mar. 16 **Litho.** ***Perf. 13½x12½***
573 A252 25c **multicolored** *(492,078)* .50 .40
First day cover 2.00
Inscription block of 4 2.25 —
574 A252 40c **multicolored** *(394,149)* 1.50 1.25
First day cover 3.50
First day cover, #573-574 6.50
Inscription block of 4 6.25 —

First day covers of Nos. 573-574 total 95,854.
See Offices in Geneva Nos. 184-185, Vienna Nos. 99-100.

Medicinal Plants — A253

Printed by Helio Courvoisier, Switzerland. Panes of 50. Designed by Rocco J. Callari & Robert Stein, US from illustrations from "Curtis's Botanical Magazine".

1990, May 4 **Photo.** **Granite Paper** ***Perf. 11½***
575 A253 25c Catharanthus roseus *(796,792)* .75 .65
First day cover 1.50
Inscription block of 4 2.75 —
576 A253 90c Panax quinquefolium *(605,617)* 1.75 1.50
First day cover 2.10
First day cover, #575-576 9.50
Inscription block of 4 8.00 —

First day covers of Nos. 575-576 total 100,548.
See Offices in Geneva Nos. 186-187, Vienna Nos. 101-102.

United Nations, 45th Anniv. A254

Printed by Johann Enschede and Sons, the Netherlands. Panes of 50. Designed by Kris Geysen, Belgium (25c), Nejat M. Gur, Turkey (45c), Robert Stein, US (No. 579).
Design: 45c, "45," emblem.

1990, June 26 **Litho.** ***Perf. 14½x13***
577 A254 25c **multicolored** *(581,718)* .75 .70
First day cover 1.25
Inscription block of 4 4.00 —
578 A254 45c **multicolored** *(582,769)* 2.50 2.50
First day cover 1.25
First day cover, #577-578 4.00
Inscription block of 4 12.00 —

Souvenir Sheet

579 Sheet of 2, #577-578 *(315,946)* 7.00 7.00
First day cover 4.00

First day covers of Nos. 577-579 total 129,011.
See Offices in Geneva Nos. 188-190; Vienna Nos. 103-105.

Crime Prevention — A255

Printed by Heraclio Fournier, S.A. Spain. Panes of 50. Designed by Josef Ryzec, Czechoslovakia.

1990, Sept. 13 **Photo.** ***Perf. 14***
580 A255 25c Crimes of youth *(533,089)* 1.10 1.00
First day cover 2.00
Inscription block of 4 4.75 —
581 A255 36c Organized crime *(427,215)* 2.50 2.25
First day cover 4.00
First day cover, #580-581 10.00
Inscription block of 4 10.00 —

First day covers of Nos. 580-581 total 68,660.
See Offices in Geneva Nos. 191-192; Vienna Nos. 106-107.

Human Rights Type of 1989

Printed by Johann Enschede and Sons, the Netherlands. Panes of 12+12 se-tenant labels containing Articles 7 (25c) or 8 (45c) inscribed in English, French or German. Designed by Rocco J. Callari and Robert Stein, US.
Artwork: 25c, Fragment from the sarcophagus of Plotinus, c. 270 A.D. 45c, Combined Chambers of the High Court of Appeal by Charles Paul Renouard.

1990, Nov. 16 **Litho.** ***Perf. 13½***
582 A250 25c **black, gray & tan** *(1,492,950)* .45 .35
First day cover 1.25
Inscription block of 3 + 3 labels 1.50 —
583 A250 45c **black & brown** *(1,490,934)* .90 .75
First day cover 1.25
First day cover, #582-583 3.75
Inscription block of 3 + 3 labels 4.00 —
Panes of 12, #582-583 17.50

First day covers of Nos. 582-583 total 108,560.
See Offices in Geneva Nos. 193-194; Vienna Nos. 108-109.

Economic Commission for Europe — A256

Printed by Heraclio Fournier, S.A., Spain. Panes of 40. Designed by Carlos Ochagavia, Argentina.

1991, Mar. 15 **Litho.** ***Perf. 14***
584 A256 30c Two storks *(590,102)* 1.10 .90
585 A256 30c Woodpecker, ibex *(590,102)* 1.10 .90
586 A256 30c Capercaille, plover *(590,102)* 1.10 .90
587 A256 30c Falcon, marmot *(590,102)* 1.10 .90
a. Block of 4, #584-587 4.50 3.75
First day cover, #587a 4.00
First day cover, #584-587, any single 3.00
Inscription block of 4, #587a 5.00 —
Pane of 40, #584-587 45.00

First day covers of Nos. 584-587 total 53,502.
See Offices in Geneva Nos. 195-198; Vienna Nos. 110-113.

Namibian Independence A257

Printed by Heraclio Fournier, S.A., Spain. Designed by Rocco J. Callari, US, from photographs by John Isaac, India.

1991, May 10 **Litho.** ***Perf. 14***
588 A257 30c Dunes, Namib Desert *(360,825)* .75 .65
First day cover 2.50
Inscription block of 4 3.50 —
589 A257 50c Savanna *(415,648)* 1.75 1.50
First day cover 3.50
First day cover, #588-589 6.50
Inscription block of 4 7.50 —

First day covers of Nos. 588-589 total 114,258.
See Offices in Geneva Nos. 199-200; Vienna Nos. 114-115.

A258

The Golden Rule by Norman Rockwell — A259

UN Headquarters, New York — A260

Printed by Johann Enschede and Sons, the Netherlands (30c), Helio Courvoisier, S.A., Switzerland (50c), and by Government Printing Bureau, Japan ($2). Panes of 50. Designed by Rocco J. Callari (30c), Norman Rockwell, US (50c), Rocco J. Callari and Robert Stein, US ($2).

1991 **Litho.** ***Perf. 13½***
590 A258 30c **multi,** *Sept. 11, (2,000,000)+* .90 .75
First day cover 1.25
Inscription block of 4 3.50 —

Photo.

Perf. 12x11½

591 A259 50c **multi,** *Sept. 11, (2,000,000)+* 1.50 1.25
First day cover 4.00
Inscription block of 4 6.50 —

Engr.

592 A260 $2 **dark blue,** *May 10, (2,000,000)+* 3.00 2.75
First day cover 5.50
Inscription block of 4 12.50 —

First day covers of Nos. 590-591 total 66,016, No. 592, 36,022.
See Offices in Geneva Nos. 199-200; Vienna Nos. 114-115.

Rights of the Child — A261

Printed by The House of Questa, United Kingdom. Panes of 50. Designed by Nicole Delia Legnani, US (30c) and Alissa Duffy, US (70c).

1991, June 14 **Litho.** ***Perf. 14½***
593 A261 30c Children, globe *(440,151)* 1.25 1.00
First day cover 2.00
Inscription block of 4 5.00 —
594 A261 70c House, rainbow *(447,803)* 3.25 2.25
First day cover 5.00
First day cover, #593-594 4.00
Inscription block of 4 12.00 —

First day covers of Nos. 593-594 total 96,324.
See Offices in Geneva Nos. 203-204; Vienna Nos. 117-118.

Banning of Chemical Weapons A262

Printed by Heraclio Fournier, S.A., Spain. Panes of 50. Designed by Oscar Asboth, Austria (30c), Michael Granger, France (90c).

Design: 90c, Hand holding back chemical drums.

1991, Sept. 11 **Litho.** ***Perf. 13½***

595	A262	30c	**multicolored** *(367,548)*	1.50	1.40
			First day cover		2.50
			Inscription block of 4	6.00	—
596	A262	90c	**multicolored** *(346,161)*	4.50	4.00
			First day cover		3.50
			First day cover, #595-596		3.00
			Inscription block of 4	19.00	—

First day covers of Nos. 595-596 total 91,552.

See Offices in Geneva Nos. 205-206; Vienna Nos. 119-120.

UN Postal Administration, 40th Anniv. — A263

Printed by The House of Questa, United Kingdom. Panes of 25. Designed by Rocco J. Callari, US.

1991, Oct. 24 **Litho.** ***Perf. 14x15***

597	A263	30c	No. 1 *(442,548)*	1.00	.90
			First day cover		1.25
			Inscription block of 4	4.50	—
598	A263	40c	No. 3 *(419,127)*	1.50	1.25
			First day cover		1.50
			First day cover, #597-598		2.00
			Inscription block of 4	7.50	—
			Panes of 25, #597-598	70.00	

First day covers of Nos. 597-598 total 81,177 (New York), 58,501 (State College, PA).

See Offices in Geneva Nos. 207-208; Vienna Nos. 121-122.

Human Rights Type of 1989

Printed by Johann Enschede and Sons, the Netherlands. Panes of 12+12 se-tenant labels containing Articles 13 (30c) or 14 (50c) inscribed in English, French or German. Designed by Robert Stein, US.

Artwork: 30c, The Last of England, by Ford Madox Brown. 40c, The Emigration to the East, by Tito Salas.

1991, Nov. 20 **Litho.** ***Perf. 13½***

599	A250	30c	**multicolored** *(1,261,198)*	.50	.45
			First day cover		1.25
			Inscription block of 3 + 3 labels	2.10	—
600	A250	50c	**multicolored** *(1,255,077)*	1.10	1.00
			First day cover		1.75
			First day cover, #599-600		2.25
			Inscription block of 3 + 3 labels	4.00	—
			Panes of 12, #599-600	17.50	

First day covers of Nos. 599-600 total 136,605.

See Offices in Geneva Nos. 209-210; Vienna Nos. 123-124.

World Heritage Type of 1984

Printed by Cartor S.A., France. Panes of 50. Designed by Robert Stein, U.S.

Designs: 30c, Uluru Natl. Park, Australia. 50c, The Great Wall of China.

1992, Jan. 24 **Litho.** ***Perf. 13***

Size: 35x28mm

601	A215	30c	**multicolored** *(337,717)*	.70	.60
			First day cover		2.50
			Inscription block of 4	3.00	—
602	A215	50c	**multicolored** *(358,000)*	1.10	1.00
			First day cover		3.75
			First day cover, #601-602		4.50
			Inscription block of 4	7.00	—

First day covers of Nos. 601-602 total 62,733.

See Offices in Geneva Nos. 211-212; Vienna Nos. 125-126.

Clean Oceans — A264

Printed by The House of Questa, United Kingdom. Panes of 12. Designed by Braldt Bralds, Netherlands.

1992, Mar. 13 **Litho.** ***Perf. 14***

603	A264	29c	Ocean surface *(983,126)*	.60	.55
604	A264	29c	Ocean bottom *(983,126)*	.60	.55
a.			Pair, #603-604	1.25	1.10
			First day cover, #604a		4.00
			First day cover, #603-604, any single		3.50
			Inscription block of 4, #603-604	4.00	—
			Pane of 12, #603-604	10.00	

First day covers of Nos. 603-604 total 75,511.

See Offices in Geneva Nos. 214-215, Vienna Nos. 127-128.

Earth Summit — A265

Printed by Helio Courvoisier S.A., Switzerland. Panes of 40. Designed by Peter Max, US.

Designs: No. 605, Globe at LR. No. 606, Globe at LL. No. 607, Globe at UR. No. 608, Globe at UL.

1992, May 22 **Photo.** ***Perf. 11½***

605	A265	29c	**multicolored** *(806,268)*	.60	.50
606	A265	29c	**multicolored** *(806,268)*	.60	.50
607	A265	29c	**multicolored** *(806,268)*	.60	.50
608	A265	29c	**multicolored** *(806,268)*	.60	.50
a.			Block of 4, #605-608	2.50	2.00
			First day cover, #608a		5.00
			First day cover, #605-608, each		2.50
			Inscription block of 4, #608a	3.50	—
			Pane of 40, #605-608	26.00	

First day covers of Nos. 605-608a total 110,577.

See Offices in Geneva Nos. 216-219, Vienna Nos. 129-132.

Mission to Planet Earth — A266

Printed by Helio Courvoisier, S.A., Switzerland. Designed by Attilla Hejja, US.

Designs: No. 609, Satellites over city, sailboats, fishing boat. No. 610, Satellite over coast, passenger liner, dolphins, whale, volcano.

1992, Sept. 4 **Photo.** ***Rouletted 8***

Granite Paper

609	A266	29c	**multicolored** *(643,647)*	2.75	2.50
610	A266	29c	**multicolored** *(643,647)*	2.75	2.50
a.			Pair, #609-610	5.75	5.50
			First day cover, #610a		4.00
			First day cover, #609-610, each		7.50
			Inscription block of 4	12.50	—
			Pane of 10, #609-610	32.50	

First day covers of Nos. 609-610a total 69,343.

See Offices in Geneva Nos. 220-221, Vienna Nos. 133-134.

Science and Technology for Development A267

Printed by Unicover Corp., US. Designed by Saul Mandel, US.

Design: 50c, Animal, man drinking.

1992, Oct. 2 **Litho.** ***Perf. 14***

611	A267	29c	**multicolored** *(453,365)*	.50	.45
			First day cover		2.00
			Inscription block of 4	2.75	—
612	A267	50c	**multicolored** *(377,377)*	.85	.70
			First day cover		3.00
			First day cover, #611-612		8.50
			Inscription block of 4	5.50	

First day covers of Nos. 611-612 total 69,195.

See Offices in Geneva Nos. 222-223, Vienna Nos. 135-136.

UN University Building, Tokyo A268

UN Headquarters, New York — A269

Printed by Cartor SA, France (4c, 40c), Walsall Security Printers, Ltd., UK (29c). Designed by Banks and Miles, UK (4c, 40c), Robert Stein, US (29c).

Design: 40c, UN University Building, Tokyo, diff.

1992, Oct. 2 **Litho.** ***Perf. 14, 13½x13 (29c)***

613	A268	4c	**multicolored** *(1,500,000)+*	.20	.20
			First day cover		2.00
			Inscription block of 4	1.00	—
614	A269	29c	**multicolored** *(1,750,000)+*	.70	.55
			First day cover		2.00
			Inscription block of 4	4.00	—
615	A268	40c	**multicolored** *(1,500,000)+*	.90	.75
			First day cover		2.00
			First day cover, #613-615		2.00
			Inscription block of 4	8.00	—
			Nos. 613-615 (3)	1.80	1.50

First day covers of Nos. 613-615 total 62,697.

Human Rights Type of 1989

Printed by Johann Enschede and Sons, the Netherlands. Panes of 12+12 se-tenant labels containing Articles 19 (29c) and 20 (50c) inscribed in English, French or German. Designed by Robert Stein, US.

Artwork: 29c, Lady Writing a Letter with her Maid, by Vermeer. 50c, The Meeting, by Ester Almqvist.

1992, Nov. 20 **Litho.** ***Perf. 13½***

616	A250	29c	**multicolored,** *(1,184,531)*	.80	.75
			First day cover		1.25
			Inscription block of 3 + 3 labels	2.75	—
617	A250	50c	**multicolored,** *(1,107,044)*	1.00	1.00
			First day cover		1.75
			First day cover, #616-617		7.00
			Inscription block of 3 + 3 labels	4.00	—
			Panes of 12, #616-617	12.00	

First day covers of Nos. 616-617 total 104,470.

See Offices in Geneva Nos. 224-225; Vienna Nos. 139-140.

Aging With Dignity — A270

Printed by Cartor SA, France. Designed by C.M. Dudash, US.
Designs: 29c, Elderly couple, family. 52c, Old man, physician, woman holding fruit basket.

1993, Feb. 5 Litho. *Perf. 13*

618	A270	29c	**multicolored** *(336,933)*	.90	.75
			First day cover		1.25
			Inscription block of 4	4.00	—
619	A270	52c	**multicolored** *(308,080)*	1.60	1.40
			First day cover		2.50
			First day cover, #618-619		4.00
			Inscription block of 4	8.00	—

First day covers of Nos. 618-619 total 52,932.
See Offices in Geneva Nos. 226-227; Vienna Nos. 141-142.

Endangered Species A271

Printed by Johann Enschede and Sons, the Netherlands. Designed by Rocco J. Callari and Norman Adams, US.
Designs: No. 620, Hairy-nosed wombat. No. 621, Whooping crane. No. 622, Giant clam. No. 623, Giant sable antelope.

1993, Mar. 2 Litho. *Perf. 13x12½*

620	A271	29c	**multicolored** *(1,200,000)+*	.55	.50
621	A271	29c	**multicolored** *(1,200,000)+*	.55	.50
622	A271	29c	**multicolored** *(1,200,000)+*	.55	.50
623	A271	29c	**multicolored** *(1,200,000)+*	.55	.50
a.			Block of 4, #620-623	2.25	2.25
			First day cover, #623a		4.50
			First day cover, #620-623, each		2.00
			Inscription block of 4, #623a	2.40	—
			Pane of 16, #620-623	11.00	

First day covers of Nos. 620-623a total 64,794.
See Nos. 639-642, 657-660, 674-677, 700-703, 730-733, 757-760, 773-776; Offices in Geneva Nos. 228-231, 246-249, 264-267, 280-283, 298-301, 318-321, 336-339, 352-355; Vienna Nos. 143-146, 162-165, 180-183, 196-199, 214-217, 235-238, 253-256, 269-272.

Healthy Environment A272

Printed by Leigh-Mardon Pty. Limited, Australia. Designed by Milton Glaser, US.
Designs: 29c, Personal. 50c, Family.

1993, May 7 Litho. *Perf. 15x14½*

624	A272	29c	Man *(430,463)*	.90	.70
			First day cover		1.50
			Inscription block of 4	4.00	—
625	A272	50c	Family *(326,692)*	1.25	1.10
			First day cover		2.00
			First day cover, #624-625		5.00
			Inscription block of 4	6.50	—

WHO, 45th anniv. First day covers of Nos. 624-625 total 55,139.
See Offices in Geneva Nos. 232-233; Vienna Nos. 147-148.

A273

Printed by House of Questa, Ltd., United Kingdom. Designed by Salahattin Kanidinc, US.

1993, May 7 Litho. *Perf. 15x14*

626	A273	5c	**multicolored** *(1,500,000)+*	.20	.20
			First day cover *(23,452)*		1.25
			Inscription block of 4	.85	—

Human Rights Type of 1989

Printed by Johann Enschede and Sons, the Netherlands. Panes of 12 + 12 se-tenant labels containing Articles 25 (29c) and 26 (35c) inscribed in English, French or German. Designed by Robert Stein, US.
Artwork: 29c, Shocking Corn, by Thomas Hart Benton. 35c, The Library, by Jacob Lawrence.

1993, June 11 Litho. *Perf. 13½*

627	A250	29c	**multicolored** *(1,049,134)*	.80	.65
			First day cover		1.25
			Inscription block of 3 + 3 labels	3.25	—
628	A250	35c	**multicolored** *(1,045,346)*	1.10	1.00
			First day cover		1.75
			First day cover, #627-628		6.00
			Inscription block of 3 + 3 labels	4.00	—
			Panes of 12, #627-628	22.50	

First day covers of Nos. 627-628 total 77,719.
See Offices in Geneva Nos. 234-235; Vienna Nos. 150-151.

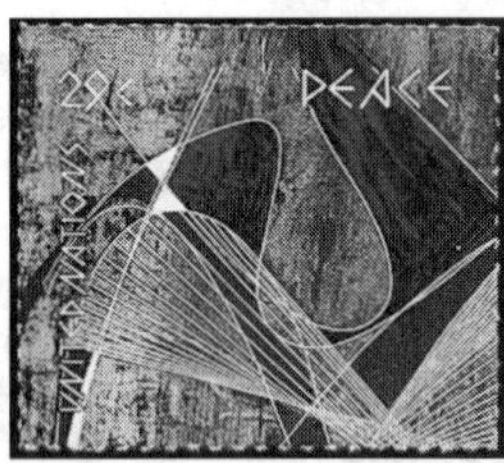

Intl. Peace Day — A274

Printed by the PTT, Switzerland. Designed by Hans Erni, Switzerland.
Denomination at: #629, UL. #630, UR. #631, LL. #632, LR.

1993, Sept. 21 Litho. & Engr. *Rouletted 12½*

629	A274	29c	**blue & multi** *(298,367)*	1.90	1.75
630	A274	29c	**blue & multi** *(298,367)*	1.90	1.75
631	A274	29c	**blue & multi** *(298,367)*	1.90	1.75
632	A274	29c	**blue & multi** *(298,367)*	1.90	1.75
a.			Block of 4, #629-632	8.00	7.00
			First day cover, #629-632, each		2.50
			First day cover, #632a		5.00
			Inscription block of 4, #632a	9.00	—
			Pane of 40, #629-632	*80.00*	

First day covers of Nos. 629-632a total 41,743.
See Offices in Geneva Nos. 236-239; Vienna Nos. 152-155.

Environment-Climate — A275

Printed by House of Questa, Ltd., United Kingdom. Designed by Braldt Bralds, Netherlands.
Designs: #633, Chameleon. #634, Palm trees, top of funnel cloud. #635, Bottom of funnel cloud, deer, antelope. #636, Bird of paradise.

1993, Oct. 29 Litho. *Perf. 14½*

633	A275	29c	**multicolored** *(383,434)*	1.00	.90
634	A275	29c	**multicolored** *(383,434)*	1.00	.90
635	A275	29c	**multicolored** *(383,434)*	1.00	.90
636	A275	29c	**multicolored** *(383,434)*	1.00	.90
a.			Strip of 4, #633-636	4.50	4.00
			First day cover, #636a		4.50
			First day cover, #633-636, each		3.00
			Inscription block, 2 #636a	9.00	—
			Pane of 24, #633-636	22.50	

First day covers of Nos. 633-636a total 38,182.
See Offices in Geneva Nos. 240-243; Vienna Nos. 156-159.

Intl. Year of the Family — A276

Printed by Cartor S.A., France. Designed by Rocco J. Callari, US.
Designs: 29c, Mother holding child, two children, woman. 45c, People tending crops.

1994, Feb. 4 Litho. *Perf. 13.1*

637	A276	29c	**green & multi** *(590,000)+*	1.40	1.25
			First day cover		1.25
			Inscription block of 4	5.75	—
638	A276	45c	**blue & multi** *(540,000)+*	2.25	2.00
			First day cover		1.75
			First day cover, #637-638		4.00
			Inscription block of 4	10.00	—

First day covers of Nos. 637-638 total 47,982. See Offices in Geneva Nos. 244-245; Vienna Nos. 160-161.

Endangered Species Type of 1993

Printed by Johann Enschede and Sons, the Netherlands. Designed by Rocco J. Callari, US (frame), and Kerrie Maddeford, Australia (stamps).
Designs: No. 639, Chimpanzee. No. 640, St. Lucia Amazon. No. 641, American crocodile. No. 642, Dama gazelle.

1994, Mar. 18 Litho. *Perf. 12.7*

639	A271	29c	**multicolored** *(1,200,000)+*	.55	.50
640	A271	29c	**multicolored** *(1,200,000)+*	.55	.50
641	A271	29c	**multicolored** *(1,200,000)+*	.55	.50
642	A271	29c	**multicolored** *(1,200,000)+*	.55	.50
a.			Block of 4, #639-642	2.25	2.25
			First day cover, #642a		4.50
			First day cover, #639-642, each		1.50
			Inscription block of 4, #642a	2.50	—
			Pane of 16, #639-642	11.00	

First day covers of Nos. 639-642 total 79,599. See Offices in Geneva Nos. 246-249; Vienna Nos. 162-165.

Protection for Refugees — A277

Printed by Leigh-Mardon Pty. Limited, Australia. Designed by Francoise Peyroux, France.

1994, Apr. 29 Litho. *Perf. 14.3x14.8*

643	A277	50c	**multicolored** *(600,000)+*	1.25	1.00
			First day cover *(33,558)*		3.00
			Inscription block of 4	5.75	—

See Offices in Geneva No. 250; Vienna No. 166.

Dove of Peace — A278

Sleeping Child, by Stanislaw Wyspianski — A279

Mourning Owl, by Vanessa Isitt — A280

Printed by Cartor S.A., France, and Norges Banks Seddeltrykkeri, Norway (#646).

1994, Apr. 29 Litho. *Perf. 12.9*

644 A278 10c **multicolored** *(1,000,000)+* .20 .20
First day cover 1.25
Inscription block of 4 1.00 —
645 A279 19c **multicolored** *(1,000,000)+* .80 .60
First day cover 2.00
Inscription block of 4 3.00 —

Engr.

Perf. 13.1

646 A280 $1 **red brown** *(1,000,000)+* 3.00 2.50
First day cover 4.00
Inscription block of 4 12.50 —
Nos. 644-646 (3) 4.00 3.30

First day covers of Nos. 644-646 total 48,946.

Intl. Decade for Natural Disaster Reduction — A281

Printed by The House of Questa, UK. Designed by Kenji Koga, Japan.

Earth seen from space, outline map of: #647, North America. #648, Eurasia. #649, South America, #650, Australia and South Asia.

1994, May 27 Litho. *Perf. 13.9x14.2*

647 A281 29c **multicolored** *(630,000)+* 1.75 1.50
648 A281 29c **multicolored** *(630,000)+* 1.75 1.50
649 A281 29c **multicolored** *(630,000)+* 1.75 1.50
650 A281 29c **multicolored** *(630,000)+* 1.75 1.50
a. Block of 4, #647-650 7.50 1.00
First day cover, #650a 5.00
First day cover, #647-650, each 2.00
Inscription block of 4, #650a 8.00 —
Pane of 40, #647-650 75.00

First day covers of Nos. 647-650 total 37,135. See Offices in Geneva Nos. 251-254; Vienna Nos. 170-173.

Population and Development A282

Printed by Johann Enschede and Sons, the Netherlands. Designed by Jerry Smath, US.

Designs: 29c, Children playing. 52c, Family with house, car, other possessions.

1994, Sept. 1 Litho. *Perf. 13.2x13.6*

651 A282 29c **multicolored** *(590,000)+* .75 .60
First day cover 1.25
Inscription block of 4 3.25 —
652 A282 52c **multicolored** *(540,000)+* 1.25 1.00
First day cover 1.75
First day cover, #651-652 2.25
Inscription block of 4 5.25 —

First day covers of Nos. 651-652 total 45,256.
See Offices in Geneva Nos. 258-259; Vienna Nos. 174-175.

UNCTAD, 30th Anniv. — A283

Printed by Johann Enschede and Sons, the Netherlands. Designed by Luis Sarda, Spain.

1994, Oct. 28

653 A283 29c **multicolored** *(590,000)+* .55 .50
First day cover 1.25
Inscription block of 4 2.75 —
654 A283 50c **multi, diff.** *(540,000)+* .95 .70
First day cover 1.75
First day cover, #653-654 2.25
Inscription block of 4 4.50

First day covers of Nos. 653-654 total 42,763. See Offices in Geneva Nos. 260-261; Vienna Nos. 176-177.

UN, 50th Anniv. — A284

Printed by Swiss Postal Service. Designed by Rocco J. Callari, US.

1995, Jan. 1 Litho. & Engr. *Perf. 13.4*

655 A284 32c **multicolored** *(938,644)* 1.50 1.25
First day cover *(39,817)* 7.00
Inscription block of 4 6.25 —

See Offices in Geneva No. 262; Vienna No. 178.

Social Summit, Copenhagen — A285

1995, Feb. 3 Photo. & Engr. *Perf. 13.6x13.9*

Printed by Austrian Government Printing Office.
Designed by Friedensreich Hundertwasser.

656 A285 50c **multicolored** *(495,388)* 1.10 1.00
First day cover *(31,797)* 3.00
Inscription block of 4 5.00 —

See Offices in Geneva No. 263; Vienna No. 179.

Endangered Species Type of 1993

Printed by Johann Enschede and Sons, the Netherlands. Designed by Chris Calle, US.

Designs: No. 657, Giant armadillo. No. 658, American bald eagle. No. 659, Fijian/Tongan banded iguana. No. 660, Giant panda.

1995, Mar. 24 Litho. *Perf. 13x12½*

657 A271 32c **multicolored** *(756,000)+* .55 .55
658 A271 32c **multicolored** *(756,000)+* .55 .55
659 A271 32c **multicolored** *(756,000)+* .55 .55
660 A271 32c **multicolored** *(756,000)+* .55 .55
a. Block of 4, 657-660 2.25 2.25
First day cover, #660a 3.25
First day cover, #657-660, each 1.75
Inscription block of 4, #660a 2.50 —
Pane of 16, #657-660 12.50

First day covers of Nos. 657-660 total 67,311. See Offices in Geneva Nos. 264-267; Vienna Nos. 180-183.

Intl. Youth Year, 10th Anniv. — A286

Printed by The House of Questa (UK). Designed by Gottfried Kumpf, Austria.

Designs: 32c, Seated child. 55c, Children cycling.

1995, May 26 Litho. *Perf. 14.4x14.7*

661 A286 32c **multicolored** *(358,695)* 1.00 .75
First day cover 1.25
Inscription block of 4 4.00 —
662 A286 55c **multicolored** *(288,424)* 1.60 1.50
First day cover 1.75
First day cover, #661-662 2.25
Inscription block of 4 7.00 —

First day covers of Nos. 661-662 total 42,846. See Offices in Geneva Nos. 268-269; Vienna Nos. 184-185.

UN, 50th Anniv. — A287

Printed by Johann Enschede Security Printing, the Netherlands. Designed by Paul and Chris Calle, US.

Designs: 32c, Hand with pen signing UN Charter, flags. 50c, Veterans' War Memorial, Opera House, San Francisco.

1995, June 26 Engr. *Perf. 13.3x13.6*

663 A287 32c **black** *(501,961)* 1.00 .85
First day cover 1.50
Inscription block of 4 5.00 —
664 A287 50c **maroon** *(419,932)* 2.00 2.00
First day cover 2.00
First day cover, #663-664 4.25
Inscription block of 4 6.50 —

Souvenir Sheet

Litho. & Engr.

Imperf

665 Sheet of 2, #663-664 *(347,963)+* 3.50 3.25
a. A287 32c **black** 1.25 .95
b. A287 50c **maroon** 1.60 1.40
First day cover 3.50

First day covers of Nos. 663-665 total: New York, 69,263; San Francisco, 53,354. See Offices in Geneva Nos. 270-272; Vienna Nos. 186-188.

4th World Conference on Women, Beijing — A288

Printed by Postage Stamp Printing House, MPT, People's Republic of China. Designed by Ting Shao Kuang, People's Republic of China.

Designs: 32c, Mother and child. 40c, Seated woman, cranes flying above.

1995, Sept. 5 Photo. *Perf. 12*

666 A288 32c **multicolored** *(561,847)* .80 .60
First day cover 1.25
Inscription block of 4 3.50 —

Size: 28x50mm

667 A288 40c **multicolored** *(499,850)* 1.25 1.00
First day cover 1.25
First day cover, #666-667 3.50
Inscription block of 4 5.25 —

First day covers of Nos. 666-667 total 103,963. See Offices in Geneva Nos. 273-274; Vienna Nos. 189-190.

UN Headquarters A289

Designed by John B. De Santis, Jr. US.

1995, Sept. 5 **Litho.** ***Perf. 15***

668 A289 20c **multicolored**		.40	.30
	First day cover *(18,326)*		2.00
	Inscription block of 4	2.00	—

Miniature Sheet

United Nations, 50th Anniv. — A290

Designed by Ben Verkaaik, Netherlands.
Printed by House of Questa, UK.
Designs: #669a-669 l, Various people in continuous design (2 blocks of six stamps with gutter between).

1995, Oct. 24 **Litho.** ***Perf. 14***

669	Sheet of 12 *(214,639 sheets)*	17.00	15.00
	First day cover		20.00
a.-l.	A290 32c any single	1.40	1.25
	First day cover, #669a-669l, each		7.00
670	Souvenir booklet *(85,256 booklets)*	17.50	
a.	A290 32c Booklet pane of 3, vert. strip of 3 from UL of sheet	4.25	3.50
b.	A290 32c Booklet pane of 3, vert. strip of 3 from UR of sheet	4.25	3.50
c.	A290 32c Booklet pane of 3, vert. strip of 3 from LL of sheet	4.25	3.50
d.	A290 32c Booklet pane of 3, vert. strip of 3 from LR of sheet	4.25	3.50

First day covers of Nos. 669-670 total 47,632. See Offices in Geneva Nos. 275-276; Vienna Nos. 191-192.

WFUNA, 50th Anniv. — A291

Designed by Rudolf Mirer, Switzerland.
Printed by Johann Enschede and Sons, the Netherlands.

1996, Feb. 2 **Litho.** ***Perf. 13x13½***

671 A291 32c **multicolored** *(580,000)+*		.55	.45
	First day cover		1.25
	Inscription block of 4	2.50	—

See Offices in Geneva No. 277; Vienna No. 193.

Mural, by Fernand Leger — A292

Designed by Fernand Leger, France.
Printed by House of Questa, UK.

1996, Feb. 2 **Litho.** ***Perf. 14½x15***

672 A292 32c **multicolored** *(780,000)+*		.50	.40
	First day cover		1.25
	Inscription block of 4	2.50	—
673 A292 60c **multi, diff.** *(680,000)+*		1.00	.80
	First day cover		1.75
	First day cover, #672-673		2.25
	Inscription block of 4	4.75	—

Endangered Species Type of 1993

Printed by Johann Enschede and Sons, the Netherlands. Designed by Diane Bruyninckx, Belgium.

Designs: No. 674, Masdevallia veitchiana. No. 675, Saguaro cactus. No. 676, West Australian pitcher plant. No. 677, Encephalartos horridus.

1996, Mar. 14 **Litho.** ***Perf. 12½***

674 A271 32c **multicolored** *(640,000)+*		.65	.65
675 A271 32c **multicolored** *(640,000)+*		.65	.65
676 A271 32c **multicolored** *(640,000)+*		.65	.65
677 A271 32c **multicolored** *(640,000)+*		.65	.65
a. Block of 4, #674-677		2.75	2.75
	First day cover, #677a		3.25
	First day cover, #674-677, each		1.25
	Inscription block of 4, #677a	3.00	—
	Pane of 16, #674-677	16.00	

See Offices in Geneva Nos. 280-283; Vienna Nos. 196-199.

City Summit (Habitat II) — A293

Printed by Johann Enschede and Sons, the Netherlands. Designed by Teresa Fasolino, US.

Designs: No. 678, Deer. No. 679, Man, child, dog sitting on hill, overlooking town. No. 680, People walking in park, city skyline. No. 681, Tropical park, Polynesian woman, boy. No. 682, Polynesian village, orchids, bird.

1996, June 3 **Litho.** ***Perf. 14x13½***

678 A293 32c **multicolored** *(475,000)+*		1.00	.90
679 A293 32c **multicolored** *(475,000)+*		1.00	.90
680 A293 32c **multicolored** *(475,000)+*		1.00	.90
681 A293 32c **multicolored** *(475,000)+*		1.00	.90
682 A293 32c **multicolored** *(475,000)+*		1.00	.90
a. Strip of 5, #678-682		5.00	4.50
	First day cover, #682a		10.00
	First day cover, #678-682, each		3.50
	Inscription block of 10, 2 #682a	11.00	
	Sheet of 25	26.00	

See Offices in Geneva Nos. 284-288; Vienna Nos. 200-204.

Sport and the Environment — A294

Printed by The House of Questa, UK. Designed by LeRoy Neiman, US.

Designs: 32c, Men's basketball. 50c, Women's volleyball, horiz.

1996, July 19 **Litho.** ***Perf. 14x14½, 14½x14***

683 A294 32c **multicolored** *(680,000)+*		1.00	.75
	First day cover		1.25
	Inscription block of 4	4.50	—
684 A294 50c **multicolored** *(680,000)+*		1.90	1.50
	First day cover		1.50
	First day cover, #683-684		2.25
	Inscription block of 4	9.00	—

Souvenir Sheet

685 A294	Sheet of 2, #683-684 *(370,000)+*	2.75	2.50
	First day cover		5.00

See Offices in Geneva Nos. 289-291; Vienna Nos. 205-207. 1996 Summer Olympic Games, Atlanta, GA.

Plea for Peace — A295

Printed by House of Questa, UK.
Designed by: 32c, Peng Yue, China. 60c, Cao Chenyu, China.

Designs: 32c, Doves. 60c, Stylized dove.

1996, Sept. 17 **Litho.** ***Perf. 14½x15***

686 A295 32c **multicolored** *(580,000)+*		.60	.45
	First day cover		1.25
	Inscription block of 4	3.00	—
687 A295 60c **multicolored** *(580,000)+*		1.10	.90
	First day cover		1.50
	First day cover, #686-687		2.25
	Inscription block of 4	5.50	—

See Offices in Geneva Nos. 292-293; Vienna Nos. 208-209.

UNICEF, 50th Anniv. — A296

Printed by The House of Questa, UK. Designed by The Walt Disney Co.

Fairy Tales: 32c, Yeh-Shen, China. 60c, The Ugly Duckling, by Hans Christian Andersen.

1996, Nov. 20 **Litho.** ***Perf. 14½x15***

688 A296 32c **multicolored** *(1,000,000)+*		.60	.50
	First day cover		1.25
	Pane of 8 + label	5.00	
689 A296 60c **multicolored** *(1,000,000)+*		1.40	1.25
	First day cover		1.50
	First day cover, #688-689		2.25
	Pane of 8 + label	15.00	

See Offices in Geneva Nos. 294-295; Vienna Nos. 210-211.

Flag Type of 1980

Printed by Helio Courvoisier, S.A., Switzerland. Designed by Oliver Corwin,US, and Robert Stein, UN. Each pane contains 4 blocks of 4 (Nos. 690-693, 694-697). A se-tenant block of 4 designs centers each pane.

1997, Feb. 12 **Photo.** ***Perf. 12***

Granite Paper

690 A185 32c Tadjikistan *(940,000)+*		1.00	.75
691 A185 32c Georgia *(940,000)+*		1.00	.75
692 A185 32c Armenia *(940,000)+*		1.00	.75
693 A185 32c Namibia *(940,000)+*		1.00	.75
a. Block of 4, #690-693		5.00	4.00
694 A185 32c Liechtenstein *(940,000)+*		1.00	.75
695 A185 32c Republic of Korea *(940,000)+*		1.00	.75
696 A185 32c Kazakhstan *(940,000)+*		1.00	.75
697 A185 32c Latvia *(940,000)+*		1.00	.75
a. Block of 4, #694-697		5.00	4.00
	First day cover, #690-697, each		3.00
	Set of 2 panes of 16	21.00	

First day covers of Nos. 690-697 total 136,114.

Cherry Blossoms, UN Headquarters — A297

Peace Rose — A298

Printed by The House of Questa, Ltd., UK.

1997, Feb. 12 Litho. *Perf. 14½*

698	A297 8c **multicolored** *(700,000)+*		.35	.35
	First day cover			2.50
	Inscription block of 4		1.50	—
699	A298 55c **multicolored** *(700,000)+*		1.50	1.40
	First day cover			1.50
	First day cover, #698-699			5.50
	Inscription block of 4		7.00	—

First day covers of Nos. 698-699 total 34,794.

Endangered Species Type of 1993

Printed by Johann Enschedé and Sons, the Netherlands. Designed by Rocco J. Callari, US.

Designs: No. 700, African elephant. No. 701, Major Mitchell's cockatoo. No. 702, Black-footed ferret. No. 703, Cougar.

1997, Mar. 13 Litho. *Perf. 12½*

700	A271 32c **multicolored** *(532,000)+*	.65	.50
701	A271 32c **multicolored** *(532,000)+*	.65	.50
702	A271 32c **multicolored** *(532,000)+*	.65	.50
703	A271 32c **multicolored** *(532,000)+*	.65	.50
a.	Block of 4, #700-703	2.75	2.00
	First day cover, #703a		3.50
	First day cover, #700-703, each		2.00
	Inscription block of 4, #703a	3.00	
	Pane of 16	11.00	

First day covers of Nos. 700-703 total 66,863.

See Offices in Geneva Nos. 298-301; Vienna Nos. 214-217.

Earth Summit, 5th Anniv. — A299

Printed by Helio Courvoisier SA, Switzerland. Designed by Peter Max, US.

Designs: No. 704, Sailboat. No. 705, Three sailboats. No. 706, Two people watching sailboat, sun. No. 707, Person, sailboat.

$1, Combined design similar to Nos. 704-707.

1997, May 30 Photo. *Perf. 11.5*

Granite Paper

704	A299 32c **multicolored** *(328,566)*	1.10	1.00
705	A299 32c **multicolored** *(328,566)*	1.10	1.00
706	A299 32c **multicolored** *(328,566)*	1.10	1.00
707	A299 32c **multicolored** *(328,566)*	1.10	1.00
a.	Block of 4, #704-707	4.50	4.25
	First day cover, #707a		3.50
	First day cover, #704-707, each		2.50
	Inscription block of 4, #707a	5.00	

Souvenir Sheet

708	A299 $1 **multicolored** *(181,667)*	4.00	4.00
	First day cover		6.00
a.	Ovptd. in sheet margin *(154,435)*	*20.00*	*20.00*
	First day cover, #708a		25.00

First day covers of Nos. 704-708 total: New York, 52,528; San Francisco, 49,197.

See Offices in Geneva Nos. 302-306; Vienna Nos. 218-222.

No. 708 contains one 60x43mm stamp. Overprint in sheet margin of No. 708a reads "PACIFIC 97 / World Philatelic Exhibition / San Francisco, California / 29 May - 8 June 1997".

Transportation — A300

Printed by The House of Questa, UK. Panes of 20. Designed by Michael Cockcroft, UK.

Ships: No. 709, Clipper ship. No. 710, Paddle steamer. No. 711, Ocean liner. No. 712, Hovercraft. No. 713, Hydrofoil.

1997, Aug. 29 Litho. *Perf. 14x14½*

709	A300 32c **multicolored** *(303,767)*	.65	.60
710	A300 32c **multicolored** *(303,767)*	.65	.60
711	A300 32c **multicolored** *(303,767)*	.65	.60
712	A300 32c **multicolored** *(303,767)*	.65	.60
713	A300 32c **multicolored** *(303,767)*	.65	.60
a.	Strip of 5, #709-713	3.25	2.75
	First day cover, #713a		5.00
	First day cover, #709-713, each		3.00
	Inscription block of 10, 2#713a	8.00	
	Sheet of 20	21.00	

First day covers of Nos. 709-713 total 29,287.

See Offices in Geneva Nos. 307-311; Vienna Nos. 223-227.

No. 713a has continuous design.

Philately — A301

Printed by Joh. Enschedé and Sons, the Netherlands. Panes of 20. Designed by Robert Stein, US.

Designs: 32c, No. 473. 50c, No. 474.

1997, Oct. 14 Litho. *Perf. 13½x14*

714	A301 32c **multicolored** *(363,237)*	2.25	2.25
	First day cover		1.25
	Inscription block of 4	10.00	—
715	A301 50c **multicolored** *(294,967)*	4.00	3.50
	First day cover		1.50
	First day cover, #714-715		2.50
	Inscription block of 4	16.00	—

First day covers of Nos. 714-715 total 43,684.

See Offices in Geneva Nos. 312-313; Vienna Nos. 228-229.

World Heritage Convention, 25th Anniv. — A302

Printed by Government Printing Office, Austria. Panes of 20. Designed by Robert Stein, US, based on photographs by Guo Youmin, People's Republic of China.

Terracotta warriors of Xian: 32c, Single warrior. 60c, Massed warriors. No. 718a, like #716. No. 718b, like #717. No. 718c, like Geneva #314. No. 718d, like Geneva #315. No. 718e, like Vienna #230. No. 718f, like Vienna #231.

1997, Nov. 19 Litho. *Perf. 13½*

716	A302 32c **multicolored** *(549,095)*	1.00	.75
	First day cover		1.25
	Inscription block of 4	4.50	—
717	A302 60c **multicolored** *(505,265)*	2.00	1.75
	First day cover		1.75
	First day cover, #716-717		2.75
	Inscription block of 4	8.50	—
718	Souvenir booklet *(304,406 booklets)*	8.50	
a.-f.	A302 8c any single	.30	.30
g.	Booklet pane of 4 #718a	.75	.50
h.	Booklet pane of 4 #718b	.75	.50
i.	Booklet pane of 4 #718c	.75	.50
j.	Booklet pane of 4 #718d	.75	.50
k.	Booklet pane of 4 #718e	.75	.50
l.	Booklet pane of 4 #718f	.75	.50

First day covers of Nos. 716-718 total 33,386.

See Offices in Geneva Nos. 314-316; Vienna Nos. 230-232.

Flag Type of 1980

Printed by Helio Courvoisier, S.A., Switzerland. Designed by Oliver Corwin, and Robert Stein, US. Each pane contains 4 blocks of 4 (Nos. 719-722, 723-726). A se-tenant block of 4 designs centers each pane.

1998, Feb. 13 Photo. *Perf. 12*

Granite Paper

719	A185 32c Micronesia *(718,000)+*	.75	.50
720	A185 32c Slovakia *(718,000)+*	.75	.50
721	A185 32c Democratic People's Republic of Korea *(718,000)+*	.75	.50
722	A185 32c Azerbaijan *(718,000)+*	.75	.50
a.	Block of 4, #719-722	5.00	—
723	A185 32c Uzbekistan *(718,000)+*	.75	.50
724	A185 32c Monaco *(718,000)+*	.75	.50
725	A185 32c Czech Republic *(718,000)+*	.75	.50
726	A185 32c Estonia *(718,000)+*	.75	.50
a.	Block of 4, #723-726	5.00	—
	First day cover, #719-726, each		3.00
	Set of 2 panes of 16	21.00	
	Nos. 719-726 (8)	6.00	4.00

A303

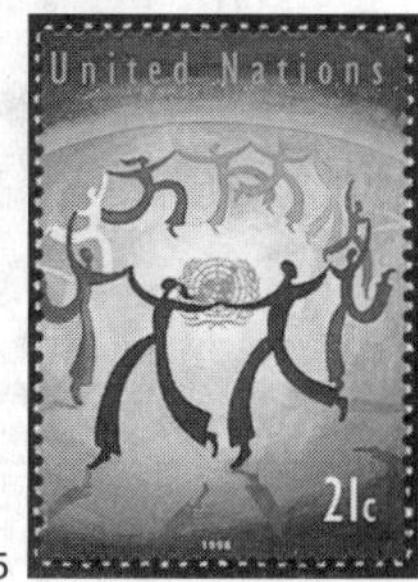

A304

A305

Printed by The House of Questa, UK. Designed by Zhang Le Lu, China (1c), Robert Stein, US (2c), Gregory Halili, Philippines (21c). Panes of 20.

1998, Feb. 13 Litho. *Perf. 14½x15, 15x14½*

727	A303 1c **multicolored** *(1,000,000)+*	.20	.20
	First day cover		1.00
	Inscription block of 4	.20	—
728	A304 2c **multicolored** *(1,000,000)+*	.20	.20
	First day cover		1.00
	Inscription block of 4	.20	—
729	A305 21c **multicolored** *(1,000,000)+*	.45	.35
	First day cover		1.00
	First day cover, #727-729		3.00
	Inscription block of 4	1.75	—
	Nos. 727-729 (3)	.85	.75

Endangered Species Type of 1993

Printed by Johann Enschedé and Sons, the Netherlands. Designed by Rocco J. Callari, US and Pat Medearis-Altman, New Zealand.

Designs: No. 730, Lesser galago. No. 731, Hawaiian goose. No. 732, Golden birdwing. No. 733, Sun bear.

1998, Mar. 13 Litho. *Perf. 12½*

730	A271 32c **multicolored** *(502,000)+*	.65	.50
731	A271 32c **multicolored** *(502,000)+*	.65	.50
732	A271 32c **multicolored** *(502,000)+*	.65	.50
733	A271 32c **multicolored** *(502,000)+*	.65	.50
a.	Block of 4, #730-733	2.75	2.25
	First day cover, #733a		3.50
	First day cover, #730-733, each		1.25
	Inscription block of 4, #733a	3.00	—
	Pane of 16	17.50	

See Offices in Geneva Nos. 318-321; Vienna Nos. 235-238.

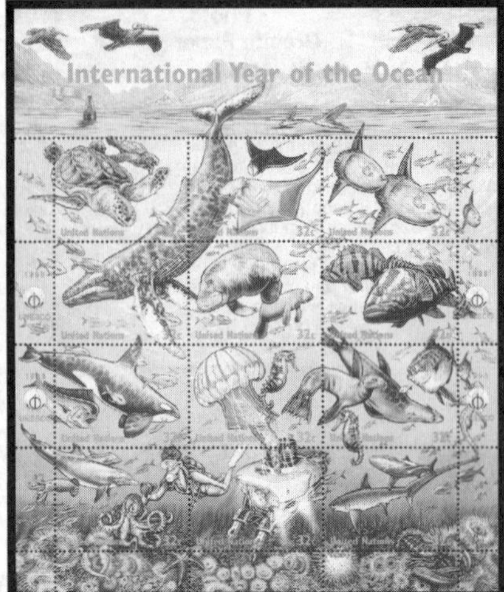

Intl. Year of the Ocean — A306

Printed by Johann Enschedé and Sons, the Netherlands. Designed by Larry Taugher, US.

1998, May 20 **Litho.** ***Perf. 13x13½***
734 A306 Sheet of 12 *(280,000)+* 9.00 7.50
First day cover 12.50
a.-l. 32c any single .75 .60
First day cover, #734a-734l, each 6.00

See Offices in Geneva No. 322; Vienna No. 239.

Rain Forests A307

Printed by Government Printing Bureau, Japan. Designed by Rick Garcia, US.

1998, June 19 **Litho.** ***Perf. 13x13½***
735 A307 32c Jaguar *(570,000)+* .75 .65
First day cover 2.50
Inscription block of 4 3.50 —

Souvenir Sheet

736 A307 $2 like #735 *(280,000)+* 4.00 1.00
First day cover 6.00

See Offices in Geneva Nos. 323-324; Vienna Nos. 240-241.

U.N. Peacekeeping Forces, 50th Anniv. — A308

Printed by Helio Courvoisier, S.A. (Switzerland). Designed by Andrew Davidson, UK.
Designs: 33c, Commander with binoculars. 40c, Two soldiers on vehicle.

1998, Sept. 15 **Photo.** ***Perf. 12***
737 A308 33c **multicolored** *(485,000)+* .75 .60
First day cover 1.25
Inscription block of 4 3.25 —
738 A308 40c **multicolored** *(445,000)+* 1.25 .90
First day cover 1.25
First day cover, #737-738 2.00
Inscription block of 4 5.00 —

See Offices in Geneva Nos. 325-326; Vienna Nos. 242-243.

Universal Declaration of Human Rights, 50th Anniv. — A309

Printed by Cartor Security Printing (France). Designed by Jean-Michel Folon, France.
Stylized people: 32c, Carrying flag. 55c, Carrying pens.

1998, Oct. 27 **Litho. & Photo.** ***Perf. 13***
739 A309 32c **multicolored** *(485,000)+* .75 .65
First day cover 1.25
Inscription block of 4 3.25 —
740 A309 55c **multicolored** *(445,000)+* 1.25 1.00
First day cover 1.50
First day cover, #739-740 2.50
Inscription block of 4 5.00 —

See Offices in Geneva Nos. 327-328; Vienna Nos. 244-245.

Schönbrunn Palace, Vienna — A310

Printed by the House of Questa, UK. Panes of 20. Designed by Robert Stein, US.
Designs: 33c, #743f, The Gloriette. 60c, #743b, Wall painting on fabric (detail), by Johann Wenzl Bergl, vert. No. 743a, Blue porcelain vase, vert. No. 743c, Porcelain stove, vert. No. 743d, Palace. No. 743e, Great Palm House (conservatory).

1998, Dec. 4 **Litho.** ***Perf. 14***
741 A310 33c **multicolored** *(485,000)+* .75 .65
First day cover 1.25
Inscription block of 4 3.00 —
742 A310 60c **multicolored** *(445,000)+* 1.50 1.25
First day cover 1.50
First day cover, #741-742 2.50
Inscription block of 4 6.00 —

Souvenir Booklet

743 Booklet *(110,000)+* 6.00
a.-c. A310 11c any single .40 .40
d.-f. A310 15c any single .50 .50
g. Booklet pane of 4 #743d 2.00
h. Booklet pane of 3 #743a 1.25
i. Booklet pane of 3 #743b 1.25
j. Booklet pane of 3 #743c 1.25
k. Booklet pane of 4 #743e 2.00
l. Booklet pane of 4 #743f 2.00

See Offices in Geneva Nos. 329-331; Vienna Nos. 246-248.

Flag Type of 1980

Printed by Helio Courvoisier S.A., Switzerland. Designed by Oliver Corwin, Robert Stein and Blake Tarpley, US. Each pane contains 4 blocks of 4 (Nos. 744-747, 748-751). A se-tenant block of 4 designs centers each pane.

1999, Feb. 5 **Photo.** ***Perf. 12***
744 A185 33c Lithuania *(524,000)+* .75 .60
745 A185 33c San Marino *(524,000)+* .75 .60
746 A185 33c Turkmenistan *(524,000)+* .75 .60
747 A185 33c Marshall Islands *(524,000)+* .75 .60
a. Block of 4, #744-747 5.00 —
748 A185 33c Moldova *(524,000)+* .75 .60
749 A185 33c Kyrgyzstan *(524,000)+* .75 .60
750 A185 33c Bosnia & Herzegovina *(524,000)+* .75 .60
751 A185 33c Eritrea *(524,000)+* .75 .60
a. Block of 4, #748-751 5.00 —
First day cover, #744-751, each 2.50
Set of 2 panes of 16 21.00
Nos. 744-751 (8) 6.00 4.80

First day covers of Nos. 744-751 total 102,040.

Flags and Globe — A311

Roses — A312

Designed by Blake Tarpley (#752), Rorie Katz, (#753), US.
Printed by Johann Enschedé and Sons, the Netherlands (#752), Helio Courvoisier SA, Switzerland (#753).

1999, Feb. 5 **Litho.** ***Perf. 14x13½***
752 A311 33c **multicolored** *(960,000)+* .65 .50
First day cover 1.25
Inscription block of 4 2.75 —

Photo.
Granite Paper
Perf. 11½x12

753 A312 $5 **multicolored** *(420,000)+* 8.00 1.00
First day cover 7.50
First day cover, #752-753 8.25
Inscription block of 4 30.00 —

First day covers of Nos. 752-753 total 32,142.

World Heritage Sites, Australia A313

Printed by House of Questa, UK. Panes of 20. Designed by Passmore Design, Australia.
Designs: 33c, #756f, Willandra Lakes region. 60c, #756b, Wet tropics of Queensland. No. 756a, Tasmanian wilderness. No. 756c, Great Barrier Reef. No. 756d, Uluru-Kata Tjuta Natl. Park. No. 756e, Kakadu Natl. Park.

1999, Mar. 19 **Litho.** ***Perf. 13***
754 A313 33c **multicolored** *(480,000)+* .85 .75
First day cover 1.25
Inscription block of 4 3.50 —
755 A313 60c **multicolored** *(440,000)+* 1.75 1.50
First day cover 1.50
First day cover, #754-755 2.50
Inscription block of 4 7.00 —

Souvenir Booklet

756 Booklet *(97,000)+* 5.25
a.-c. A313 5c any single .20 .20
d.-f. A313 15c any single .30 .30
g. Booklet pane of 4, #756a .40
h. Booklet pane of 4, #756d 1.25
i. Booklet pane of 4, #756b .40
j. Booklet pane of 4, #756e 1.25
k. Booklet pane of 4, #756c .40
l. Booklet pane of 4, #756f 1.25

First day covers of Nos. 754-756 total 42,385.
See Offices in Geneva Nos. 333-335; Vienna Nos. 250-252.

Endangered Species Type of 1993

Printed by Johann Enschedé and Sons, the Netherlands. Designed by Jimmy Wang, China.
Designs: No. 757, Tiger. No. 758, Secretary bird. No. 759, Green tree python. No. 760, Long-tailed chinchilla.

1999, Apr. 22 **Litho.** ***Perf. 12½***
757 A271 33c **multicolored** *(494,000)+* .65 .50
758 A271 33c **multicolored** *(494,000)+* .65 .50
759 A271 33c **multicolored** *(494,000)+* .65 .50

760 A271 33c **multicolored** *(494,000)+* .65 .50
a. Block of 4, #757-760 2.75
First day cover, #760a 3.50
First day cover, #757-760, each 1.25
Inscription block of 4, #760a 2.75 —
Pane of 16 15.00

First day covers of Nos. 757-760 total 49,656.
See Offices in Geneva Nos. 336-339; Vienna Nos. 253-256.

UNISPACE III, Vienna — A314

Printed by Helio Courvoisier SA, Switzerland. Designed by Attila Hejja, US.
Designs: No. 761, Probe on planet's surface. No. 762, Planetary rover. No. 763, Composite of #761-762.

1999, July 7 Photo. *Rouletted 8*

761 A314 33c **multicolored** *(1,000,000)+* .85 .60
762 A314 33c **multicolored** *(1,000,000)+* .85 .60
a. Pair, #761-762 1.75 1.50
First day cover, #762a 2.00
First day cover, #761-762, each 1.25
Inscription block of 4 4.00 —
Pane of 10, #761-762 9.00 —

Souvenir Sheet

Perf. 14½

763 A314 $2 **multicolored** *(530,000)+* 4.25 2.00
First day cover 5.00
a. Ovptd. in sheet margin 12.50 5.00
First day cover 13.00

No. 763a was issued 7/7/00 and is overprinted in violet blue "WORLD STAMP EXPO 2000 / ANAHEIM, CALIFORNIA / U.S.A./ 7-16 JULY 2000."
First day covers of Nos. 761-763 total 48,190.
See Offices in Geneva #340-342; Vienna #257-259.

UPU, 125th Anniv. — A315

Printed by Helio Courvoisier S.A., Switzerland. Panes of 24. Designed by Mark Hess, US.

Various people, 19th century methods of mail transportation, denomination at: No. 764, UL. No. 765, UR. No. 766, LL. No. 767, LR.

1999, Aug. 23 Photo. *Perf. 11¾*

764 A315 33c **multicolored** *(378,000)+* .85 .50
765 A315 33c **multicolored** *(378,000)+* .85 .50
766 A315 33c **multicolored** *(378,000)+* .85 .50
767 A315 33c **multicolored** *(378,000)+* .85 .50
a. Block of 4, #764-767 3.50 —
Inscription block of 4 3.75 —
First day cover, #767a 4.25
First day cover, #764-767, each 1.50
Sheet of 20 17.00

First day covers of Nos. 764-767 total 25,294.
See Offices in Geneva Nos. 343-346; Vienna Nos. 260-263.

In Memoriam — A316

Printed by Walsall Security Printers, Ltd., United Kingdom. Panes of 20. Designed by Robert Stein, US.

Designs: 33c, $1, UN Headquarters. Size of $1 stamp: 34x63mm.

1999, Sept. 21 Litho. *Perf. 14½x14*

768 A316 33c **multicolored** *(550,000)+* 2.00 1.75
Inscription block of 4 8.00 —
First day cover 1.25

Souvenir Sheet

Perf. 14

769 A316 $1 **multicolored** *(235,000)+* 2.00 1.00
First day cover 2.75

First day covers of Nos. 768-769 total 42,130.
See Offices in Geneva #347-348, Vienna #264-265.

Education, Keystone to the 21st Century — A317

Printed by Government Printing Office, Austria. Panes of 20. Designed by Romero Britto, Brazil.

1999, Nov. 18 Litho. *Perf. 13½x13¾*

770 A317 33c Two readers *(450,000)+* .65 .30
First day cover 1.25
Inscription block of 4 2.50 —
771 A317 60c Heart *(430,000)+* 1.25 .60
First day cover 1.50
First day cover, #770-771 2.50
Inscription block of 4 5.00 —

First day covers of Nos. 770-771 total 34,679.
See Offices in Geneva Nos. 349-350, Vienna Nos. 266-267.

International Year of Thanksgiving — A318

Printed by Cartor Security Printing, France. Panes of 20. Designed by Rorie Katz, US.

2000, Jan. 1 Litho. *Perf. 13¼x13½*

772 A318 33c **multicolored** *(550,000)+* .90 .75
First day cover 1.25
Inscription block of 4 3.75 —

On No. 772 portions of the design were applied by a thermographic process producing a shiny, raised effect. See Offices in Geneva No. 351, Vienna No. 268.

Endangered Species Type of 1993

Printed by Johann Enschedé and Sons, the Netherlands. Designed by Suzanne Duranceau, Canada.
Designs: No. 773, Brown bear. No. 774, Black-bellied bustard. No. 775, Chinese crocodile lizard. No. 776, Pygmy chimpanzee.

2000, Apr. 6 Litho. *Perf. 12¾x12½*

773 A271 33c **multicolored** *(490,000)+* .65 .30
774 A271 33c **multicolored** *(490,000)+* .65 .30
775 A271 33c **multicolored** *(490,000)+* .65 .30
776 A271 33c **multicolored** *(490,000)+* .65 .30
a. Block of 4, #773-776 2.50 2.00
First day cover, #776a 3.50
First day cover, #773-776, each 1.25
Inscription block of 4, #776a 2.75 —
Pane of 16 10.50

See Offices in Geneva Nos. 352-355; Vienna Nos. 269-272.

Our World 2000 — A319

Printed by Cartor Security Printing, France. Panes of 20. Designed by Robert Stein, US.
Winning artwork in Millennium painting competition: 33c, Crawling Toward the Millennium, by Sam Yeates, US. 60c, Crossing, by Masakazu Takahata, Japan, vert.

2000, May 30 Litho. *Perf. 13x13½, 13½x13*

777 A319 33c **multicolored** *(400,000)+* .65 .30
First day cover 1.25
Inscription block of 4 2.60 —
778 A319 60c **multicolored** *(360,000)+* 1.25 .60
First day cover 1.50
First day cover, #777-778 2.50
Inscription block of 4 7.00 —

See Offices in Geneva No. 356-357, Vienna No. 273-274.

UN, 55th Anniv. — A320

Printed by Cartor Security Printing, France. Panes of 20. Designed by Rorie Katz, US.
Designs: 33c, Workmen removing decorative discs in General Assembly Hall, 1956. 55c, UN Building in 1951.

2000, July 7 Litho. *Perf. 13¼x13*

779 A320 33c **multicolored** *(400,000)+* .65 .30
First day cover 1.25
Inscription block of 4 2.60 —
780 A320 55c **multicolored** *(360,000)+* 1.10 .55
First day cover 1.50
First day cover, #779-780 2.25
Inscription block of 4 4.50 —

Souvenir Sheet

781 A320 Sheet of 2, #779-780 *(277,000)+* 2.25 1.00
First day cover 3.00

See Offices in Geneva No. 358-360, Vienna No. 275-277.

International Flag of Peace — A321

Printed by House of Questa, UK. Panes of 20.
Designed by Mateja Prunk, Slovenia.

2000, Sept. 15 Litho. *Perf. 14½x14*

782 A321 33c **multicolored** *(400,000)+* .65 .30
First day cover 1.25
Inscription block of 4 2.60 —

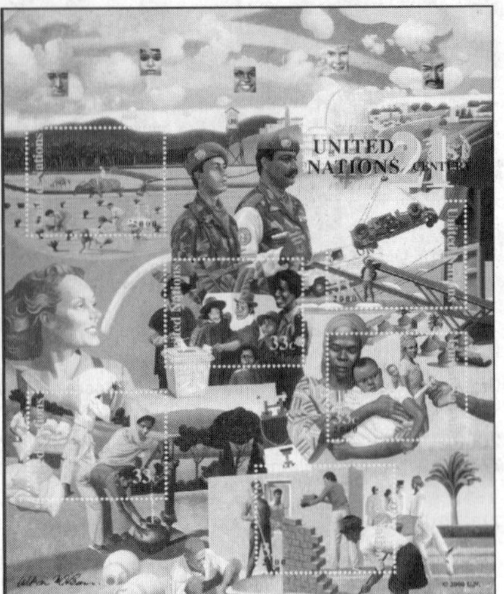

The UN in the 21st Century — A322

Printed by Government Printing Office, Austria. Designed by Wilson McLean, UK.

No. 783: a, Farmers, animals in rice paddy. b, Vehicle chassis being lifted. c, People voting. d, Baby reciving inoculation. e, Woman, man at pump. f, Mason, construction workers.

2000, Sept. 15 **Litho.** ***Perf. 14***

783	A322		Sheet of 6 *(274,000)+*	4.50	3.00
			First day cover		7.50
a.-f.		33c	any single	.75	.30

See Offices in Geneva No. 361; Vienna No. 278.

World Heritage Sites, Spain — A323

Printed by House of Questa, UK. Panes of 20. Designed by Robert Stein, US.

Designs: 33c, #786a, Alhambra, Generalife and Albayzin, Granada. 60c, #786d, Amphitheater of Mérida. #786b, Walled Town of Cuenca. #786c, Aqueduct of Segovia. #786e, Toledo. #786f, Güell Park, Barcelona.

2000, Oct. 6 **Litho.** ***Perf. 14¾x14½***

784	A323	33c	**multicolored** *(400,000)+*	.65	.30
			First day cover		1.25
			Inscription block of 4	2.60	—
785	A323	60c	**multicolored** *(360,000)+*	1.25	.60
			First day cover		1.50
			First day cover, #784-785		2.50
			Inscription block of 4	5.00	—

Souvenir Booklet

786			Booklet *(63,000)+*	5.00	
a.-c.	A323	5c	any single	.20	.20
d.-f.	A323	15c	any single	.30	.30
g.			Booklet pane of 4, #786a	.40	—
h.			Booklet pane of 4, #786d	1.25	—
i.			Booklet pane of 4, #786b	.40	—
j.			Booklet pane of 4, #786e	1.25	—
k.			Booklet pane of 4, #786c	.40	—
l.			Booklet pane of 4, #786f	1.25	—

See Offices in Geneva Nos. 362-364, Vienna Nos. 279-281.

Respect for Refugees — A324

Printed by Johann Enschedé and Sons, the Netherlands. Panes of 20. Designed by Yuri Gevorgian, Armenia.

2000, Nov. 9 **Litho.** ***Perf. 13¼x12¾***

787	A324	33c	**multicolored** *(540,000)+*	.65	.30
			First day cover		1.25
			Inscription block of 4	2.60	—

Souvenir Sheet

788	A324	$1	**multicolored** *(225,000)+*	2.00	1.00
			First day cover		2.50

See Offices in Geneva Nos. 365-366, Vienna Nos. 282-283.

Endangered Species Type of 1993

Printed by Johann Enschedé and Sons, the Netherlands. Designed by Grace DeVito, US.

Designs: No. 789, Common spotted cuscus. No. 790, Resplendent quetzal. No. 791, Gila monster. No. 792, Guereza.

2001, Feb. 1 **Litho.** ***Perf. 12¾x12½***

789	A271	34c	**multicolored** *(430,000)+*	.65	.30
790	A271	34c	**multicolored** *(430,000)+*	.65	.30
791	A271	34c	**multicolored** *(430,000)+*	.65	.30
792	A271	34c	**multicolored** *(430,000)+*	.65	.30
a.			Block of 4, #789-792	2.60	—
			First day cover, #792a		3.50
			First day cover, #789-792 each		1.25
			Inscription block of 4, #792a	2.75	—
			Pane of 16	10.50	

See Offices in Geneva Nos. 367-370; Vienna Nos. 284-287.

Intl. Volunteers Year — A325

Printed by Johann Enschedé and Sons, the Netherlands. Panes of 20. Designed by Rorie Katz and Robert Stein, US.

Paintings by: 34c, Jose Zaragoza, Brazil. 80c, John Terry, Australia.

2001, Mar. 29 **Litho.** ***Perf. 13¼***

793	A325	34c	**multicolored** *(390,000)+*	.65	.30
			First day cover		1.25
			Inscription block of 4	2.60	
794	A325	80c	**multicolored** *(360,000)+*	1.60	.80
			First day cover		2.40
			First day cover, #793-794		3.00
			Inscription block of 4	6.50	

See Offices in Geneva Nos. 371-372; Vienna Nos. 288-289.

Flag Type of 1980

Printed by Helio Courvoisier, Switzerland. Designed by Ole Hamann. Issued in panes of 16; each contains 4 blocks of 4 (Nos. 795-798, 799-802). A se-tenant block of 4 designs centers each pane.

2001, May 25 **Photo.** ***Perf. 12***

Granite Paper

795	A185	34c	Slovenia *(460,000)+*	.65	.30
796	A185	34c	Palau *(460,000)+*	.65	.30
797	A185	34c	Tonga *(460,000)+*	.65	.30
798	A185	34c	Croatia *(460,000)+*	.65	.30
a.			Block of 4, #795-798	2.60	—
799	A185	34c	Former Yugoslav Republic of Macedonia *(460,000)+*	.65	.30
800	A185	34c	Kiribati *(460,000)+*	.65	.30
801	A185	34c	Andorra *(460,000)+*	.65	.30
802	A185	34c	Nauru *(460,000)+*	.65	.30
a.			Block of 4, #799-802	2.60	—
			First day cover, #795-802, each		1.25
			Set of 2 panes of 16	21.00	
			Nos. 795-802 (8)	5.20	2.40

Sunflower — A326

Rose — A327

Printed by Johann Enschedé and Sons, the Netherlands. Panes of 20. Designed by Rorie Katz, US.

2001, May 25 **Litho.** ***Perf. 13¼x13¾***

803	A326	7c	**multicolored** *(550,000)+*	.20	.20
			First day cover		1.25
			Margin block of 4, inscription	.75	—
804	A327	34c	**multicolored** *(650,000)+*	.65	.30
			First day cover		1.25
			First day cover, #803-804		1.40
			Margin block of 4, inscription	3.00	—

World Heritage Sites, Japan — A328

Printed by Johann Enschedé and Sons, the Netherlands. Panes of 20. Designed by Rorie Katz, US.

Designs: 34c, #807a, Kyoto. 70c, #807d, Shirakawa-Go and Gokayama. #807b, Nara. #807c, Himeji-Jo. #807e, Itsukushima Shinto Shrine. #807f, Nikko.

2001, Aug. 1 **Litho.** ***Perf. 12¾x13¼***

805	A328	34c	**multicolored** *(380,000)+*	.65	.30
			First day cover		1.25
			Inscription block of 4	2.60	—
806	A328	70c	**multicolored** *(360,000)+*	1.40	.70
			First day cover		2.10
			First day cover, #805-806		2.75
			Inscription block of 4	5.75	—

Souvenir Booklet

807			Booklet *(51,000)+*	6.00	
a.-c.	A328	5c	any single	.20	.20
d.-f.	A328	20c	any single	.40	.40
g.			Booklet pane of 4, #807a	.40	—
h.			Booklet pane of 4, #807d	1.60	—
i.			Booklet pane of 4, #807b	.40	—
j.			Booklet pane of 4, #807e	1.60	—
k.			Booklet pane of 4, #807c	.40	—
l.			Booklet pane of 4, #807f	1.60	—

See Offices in Geneva Nos. 373-375, Vienna Nos. 290-292.

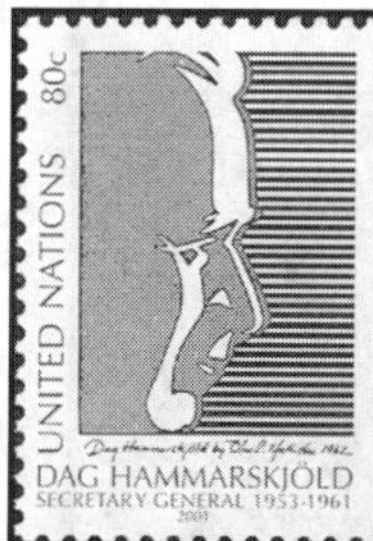

Dag Hammarskjöld (1905-61), UN Secretary General — A329

Printed by Banknote Corporation of America, US. Panes of 20. Designed by Robert Stein, US.

2001, Sept. 18 **Engr.** ***Perf. 11x11¼***

808 A329 80c **blue** *(530,000)+* 1.60 .80
First day cover 2.25
Inscription block of 4 6.50 —

See Offices in Geneva No. 376, Vienna No. 293.

A330

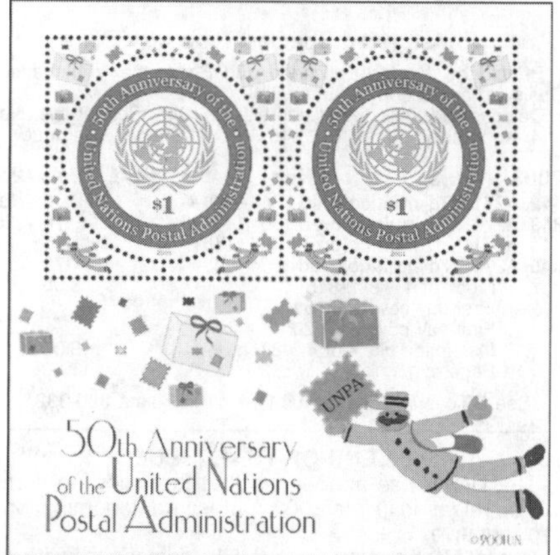

UN Postal Administration, 50th Anniv. — A331

Printed by Johann Enschedé and Sons, the Netherlands. Panes of 20. Designed by Rorie Katz, US.

2001, Oct. 18 **Litho.** ***Perf. 13½***

809 A330 34c Stamps, streamers *(350,000)+* .75 .40
First day cover 1.25
Inscription block of 4 3.00 —
810 A330 80c Stamps, gifts *(310,000)+* 1.75 1.00
First day cover 2.25
First day cover, #809-810 3.00
Inscription block of 4 7.00 —

Souvenir Sheet

811 A331 Sheet of 2 #811a *(180,000)+* 4.00 2.00
a. $1 **blue & light blue,** 38mm diameter 2.00 1.00
First day cover 16.00

See Offices in Geneva Nos. 377-379, Vienna Nos. 294-296.

Climate Change — A332

Printed by Walsall Security Printers Limited, UK. Panes of 24. Designed by Robert Giusti, US.

Designs: No. 812, Canada geese, greenhouses, butterfly, thistle. No. 813, Canada geese, iceberg, penguins, tomato plant. No. 814, Palm tree, solar collector. No. 815, Hand planting ginkgo cutting.

2001, Nov. 16 **Litho.** ***Perf. 13¼***

812 A332 34c **multicolored** *(70,500)+* .65 .30
813 A332 34c **multicolored** *(70,500)+* .65 .30
814 A332 34c **multicolored** *(70,500)+* .65 .30
815 A332 34c **multicolored** *(70,500)+* .65 .30
a. Horiz. strip, #812-815 2.75 2.50
Inscription block of 8 5.50 —
First day cover, #815a 3.50
Pane of 24 16.00 —

See Offices in Geneva Nos. 380-383, Vienna Nos. 297-300.

Awarding of Nobel Peace Prize to Secretary General Kofi Annan and UN — A333

Printed by Cartor S. A., France. Panes of 12. Designed by Robert Stein, US.

2001, Dec. 10 **Litho.** ***Perf. 13¼***

816 A333 34c **multicolored** *(840,000)+* .80 .60
Inscription block of 4 3.50 —
First day cover 1.25
Pane of 12 11.50 —

See Offices in Geneva Nos. 384, Vienna Nos. 301.

Children and Stamps — A334

Printed by Government Printing Office, Austria. Panes of 20. Designed by Jerry Smath, US.

2002, Mar. 1 **Litho.** ***Perf. 13¾***

817 A334 80c **multicolored** *(420,000)+* 1.60 .80
First day cover 2.25
Inscription block of 4 6.50 —

Endangered Species Type of 1993

Printed by Johann Enschedé and Sons, the Netherlands. Designed by Teresa Fasolino, US.

Designs: No. 818, Hoffmann's two-toed sloth. No. 819, Bighorn sheep. No. 820, Cheetah. No. 821, San Esteban Island chuckwalla.

2002, Apr. 4 **Litho.** ***Perf. 12¾x12½***

818 A271 34c **multicolored** *(414,000)+* .65 .30
819 A271 34c **multicolored** *(414,000)+* .65 .30
820 A271 34c **multicolored** *(414,000)+* .65 .30
821 A271 34c **multicolored** *(414,000)+* .65 .30
a. Block of 4, #818-821 2.60 —
First day cover, #821a 3.50
First day cover, #818-821 each 1.25
Inscription block of 4, #821a 2.75 —
Pane of 16 10.50 —

See Offices in Geneva Nos. 386-389; Vienna 308-311.

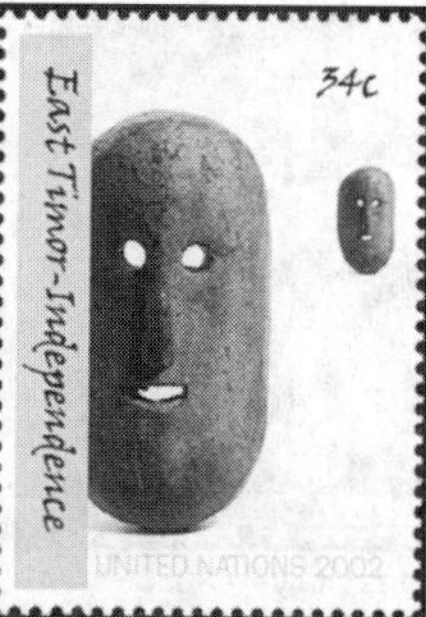

Independence of East Timor — A335

Printed by The House of Questa, UK. Designed by Karen Kelleher, US. Panes of 20

Designs: 34c, Wooden ritual mask. 57c, Decorative door panel.

2002, May 20 **Litho.** ***Perf. 14x14½***

822 A335 34c **multicolored** *(355,000)+* .65 .30
First day cover 1.25
Inscription block of 4 2.60 —
823 A335 57c **multicolored** *(325,000)+* 1.10 .55
First day cover 1.90
First day cover, #822-823 2.50
Inscription block of 4 4.50 —

See Offices in Geneva Nos. 390-391; Vienna Nos. 312-313.

Intl. Year of Mountains A336

Printed by Cartor Security Printing, France. Designed by Robert Stein and Rorie Katz, US.

Designs: No. 824, Khan Tengri, Kyrgyzstan. No. 825, Mt. Kilimanjaro, Tanzania. No. 826, Mt. Foraker, US. No. 827, Paine Grande, Chile.

2002, May 24 **Litho.** ***Perf. 13x13¼***

824 A336 34c **multicolored** *(1,362,000)+* .65 .30
First day cover 1.25
825 A336 34c **multicolored** *(1,362,000)+* .65 .30
First day cover 1.25
826 A336 80c **multicolored** *(1,362,000)+* 1.60 .80
First day cover 2.25
First day cover, #824, 826 3.2
827 A336 80c **multicolored** *(1,362,000)+* 1.60 .80
a. Vert. strip or block of four, #824-827 4.50 2.25
First day cover 2.25
First day cover, #825, 827 3.25
First day cover, #823-827 5.25
Pane of 12, 3 each #824-827 13.50 —

See Offices in Geneva Nos. 392-395; Vienna Nos. 314-317.

World Summit on Sustainable Development, Johannesburg A337

Printed by The House of Questa, UK. Designed by Peter Max, US.

Designs: No. 828, Sun, Earth, planets, stars. No. 829, Three women. No. 830, Sailboat. No. 831, Three faceless people.

2002, June 27 **Litho.** ***Perf. 14½x14***

828 A337 37c **multicolored** *(1,350,000)+* .75 .35
First day cover 1.25
829 A337 37c **multicolored** *(1,350,000)+* .75 .35
First day cover 1.25
830 A337 60c **multicolored** *(1,350,000)+* 1.25 .60
First day cover 2.00
First day cover, #828, 830 2.25
831 A337 60c **multicolored** *(1,350,000)+* 1.25 .60
a. Vert. strip or block of four, #828-831 4.00 1.90
First day cover 2.00
First day cover, #829, 831 2.25
First day cover, #828-831 4.50
Pane of 12, 3 each #828-831 12.00 —

See Offices in Geneva Nos. 396-399; Vienna Nos. 318-321.

World Heritage Sites, Italy — A338

Printed by Cartor Security Printing, France. Panes of 20. Designed by Rorie Katz, US.

Designs: 37c, #834d, Florence. 70c, #834a, Amalfi Coast. #834b, Aeolian Islands. #834c, Rome. #834e, Pisa. #834f, Pompeii.

2002, Aug. 30 Litho. *Perf. 13½x13¼*

No.	Description	Unused	Used
832	A338 37c **multicolored** *(365,000)+*	.70	.30
	First day cover		1.25
	Inscription block of 4	2.80	—
833	A338 70c **multicolored** *(345,000)+*	1.40	.70
	First day cover		2.40
	First day cover, #832-833		3.00
	Inscription block of 4	5.75	—

Souvenir Booklet

No.	Description	Unused	Used
834	Booklet *(52,000)+*	5.00	
a.-c.	A338 5c any single	.20	.20
d.-f.	A338 15c any single	.30	.30
g.	Booklet pane of 4, #834d	1.25	—
h.	Booklet pane of 4, #834a	.40	—
i.	Booklet pane of 4, #834e	1.25	—
j.	Booklet pane of 4, #834b	.40	—
k.	Booklet pane of 4, #834f	1.25	—
l.	Booklet pane of 4, #834c	.40	—

See Offices in Geneva Nos. 400-402, Vienna Nos. 322-324. See Italy Nos. 2506-2507.

AIDS Awareness — A339

Printed by Walsall Security Printers Limited, UK. Panes of 20. Designed by Rorie Katz, US.

2002, Oct. 24 Litho. *Perf. 13½*

No.	Description	Unused	Used
835	A339 70c **multicolored** *(365,000)+*	1.40	.70
	Inscription block of 4	5.75	
	First day cover, #835		2.10
	Pane of 20	30.00	

See No. B1, Offices in Geneva Nos. 403, B1, Vienna Nos. 325, B1.

Indigenous Art — A340

Printed by House of Questa, UK.
Designed by Rorie Katz and Robert Stein, US.

No. 836: a, Detail of Paracas textile, Peru. b, Sinu culture anthropo-zoomorphic pendant, Colombia. c, Hicholi Indian embroidery, Mexico. d, Rigpaktsa back ornament, Brazil. e, Wool crafts, Chile. f, Huari feathered woven hat, Bolivia.

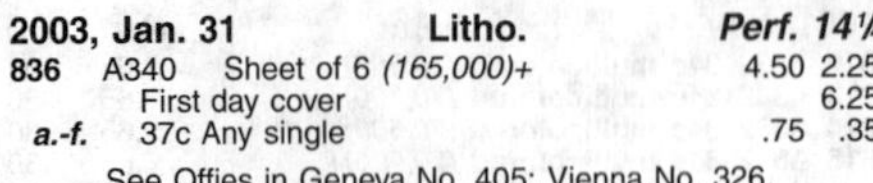

2003, Jan. 31 Litho. *Perf. 14¼*

No.	Description	Unused	Used
836	A340 Sheet of 6 *(165,000)+*	4.50	2.25
	First day cover		6.25
a.-f.	37c Any single	.75	.35

See Offies in Geneva No. 405; Vienna No. 326.

Clasped Hands — A341

UN Emblem — A342

UN Headquarters A343

Printed by House of Questa, UK (23c, 37c); Walsall Security Printers Ltd., UK (70c). Designed by Rorie Katz, US (23c, 37c), Robert Stein and Rorie Katz (70c). Panes of 20.

2003, Mar. 28 Litho. *Perf. 14¼*

No.	Description	Unused	Used
837	A341 23c **multicolored** *(870,000)+*	.45	.25
	First day cover		1.25
	Inscription block of 4	1.80	—

Litho. with Foil Application

No.	Description	Unused	Used
838	A342 37c **gold & multicolored** *(870,000)+*	.75	.35
	First day cover		1.25
	Inscription block of 4	3.00	—

Litho. with Hologram

No.	Description	Unused	Used
839	A343 70c **multicolored** *(910,000)+*	1.40	.70
	First day cover		2.50
	First day cover, #837-839		3.25
	Inscription block of 4	5.60	—

Powered Flight, Cent. — A344

Printed by Government Printing Office, Austria. Designed by Robert Stein, US. Panes of 16 (eight pairs).

2003, Mar. 28 Litho. *Perf. 13½x13¾*

No.	Description	Unused	Used
840	23c **multicolored** *(175,000)+*	.45	.25
841	70c **multicolored** *(175,000)+*	1.40	.70
a.	A344 Tete beche pair, #840-841	1.85	.95
	First day cover, #841a		2.60
	Inscription block of 4	3.75	

Endangered Species Type of 1993

Printed by Johann Enschedé and Sons, the Netherlands. Designed by Joseph Hautman, US.

Designs: No. 842, Great hornbill. No. 843, Scarlet ibis. No. 844, Knob-billed goose. No. 845, White-faced whistling duck.

2003, Apr. 3 Litho. *Perf. 12¾x12½*

No.	Description	Unused	Used
842	A271 37c **multicolored** *(364,000)+*	.75	.35
843	A271 37c **multicolored** *(364,000)+*	.75	.35
844	A271 37c **multicolored** *(364,000)+*	.75	.35
845	A271 37c **multicolored** *(364,000)+*	.75	.35
a.	Block of 4, #842-845	3.00	—
	First day cover, #845a		3.75
	First day cover, #842-845 each		1.25
	Inscription block of 4, #845a	3.00	—
	Pane of 16	12.00	—

See Offices in Geneva Nos. 407-410; Vienna 329-332.

2003 END-OF-YEAR ISSUES

The UNPA has announced that the following items will be released in late 2003. Dates and denominations are tentative.

Postal Stationery, *June 2,* 51c postal card with 4c surcharge; Geneva 51c envelope with 4c surcharge; Vienna €1.09 envelope with 16c surcharge

International Year of Fresh Water, *June 20,* setenant pair of 23c, 37c stamps; Geneva setenant pair of 70c, 1.30fr stamps; Vienna setenant pair of 55c, 75c stamps; souvenir card

Definitive, *Aug. 7,* Vienna 4c Schloss Eggenberg, Graz

Ralph Bunche, *Aug. 7,* 37c; Geneva 1.80fr; Vienna €2.10

World Heritage - United States, *Oct. 24,* 37c, 80c stamps, booklet containing 5c and 15c stamps; Geneva 90c and 1.30fr stamps, booklet containing 10c and 20c stamps; Vienna 51c and 75c stamps, booklet containing 10c and 15c stamps.

SEMI-POSTAL

Souvenir Sheet

AIDS Awareness — SP1

Printed by Walsall Security Printers Limited, UK. Designed by Rorie Katz, US.

2002, Oct. 24 **Litho.** ***Perf. 14½***

B1 SP1 37c + 6c **multicolored** *(175,000)+* .90 .90
First day cover, #B1 1.60

See Offices in Geneva No. B1, Vienna No. B1.

AIR POST

Plane and Gull — AP1

Swallows and UN Emblem AP2

Engraved and printed by Thomas De La Rue & Co., Ltd., London. Panes of 50. Designed by Ole Hamann (AP1) and Olav Mathiesen (AP2).

1951, Dec. 14 **Unwmk.** ***Perf. 14***

C1 AP1 6c **henna brown** *(2,500,000)* .20 .20
First day cover 2.00
Inscription block of 4 .25 —
C2 AP1 10c **bright blue green** *(2,750,000)* .20 .20
First day cover 2.00
Inscription block of 4 .60 —
C3 AP2 15c **deep ultramarine** *(3,250,000)* .20 .25
First day cover 3.00
Inscription block of 4 .75 —
a. 15c **Prussian blue** 75.00
C4 AP2 25c **gray black** *(2,250,000)* .60 .50
First day cover 7.50
First day cover, #C1-C4 30.00
Inscription block of 4 4.00 —
Nos. C1-C4 (4) 1.20 1.15

First day covers of Nos. 1-11 and C1-C4 total 1,113,216.
Early printings of Nos. C1-C4 have wide, imperforate sheet margins on three sides. Later printings were perforated through all margins.

Airplane Wing and Globe — AP3

Engraved and printed by Thomas De La Rue & Co., Ltd., London. Panes of 50. Designed by W. W. Wind.

1957, May 27 ***Perf. 12½x14***

C5 AP3 4c **maroon** *(5,000,000)* .20 .20
First day cover *(282,933)* 1.00
Inscription block of 4 .30 —

For 5c see No. C6.

Type of 1957 and

UN Flag and Plane — AP4

Engraved and printed by Waterlow & Sons, Ltd., London. Panes of 50. Designed by W. W. Wind (5c) and Olav Mathiesen (7c).

1959, Feb. 9 **Unwmk.** ***Perf. 12½x13½***

C6 AP3 5c **rose red** *(4,000,000)* .20 .20
First day cover 1.00
Inscription block of 4 .40 —

Perf. 13½x14

C7 AP4 7c **ultramarine** *(4,000,000)* .20 .20
First day cover 1.00
First day cover, #C6-C7 17.50
Inscription block of 4 .60 —

First day covers of Nos. C6 and C7 total 413,556.

Outer Space — AP5

UN Emblem — AP6

Bird of Laurel Leaves — AP7

Printed by Courvoisier S.A., La Chaux-de-Fonds, Switzerland. Panes of 50. Designed by Claude Bottiau (6c), George Hamori (8c) and Kurt Plowitz (13c).

1963, June 17 **Photo.** **Unwmk.** ***Perf. 11½***

C8 AP5 6c **black, blue & yellow green** *(4,000,000)* .20 .20
First day cover 1.00
Inscription block of 4 .45 —
C9 AP6 8c **yellow, olive green & red** *(4,000,000)* .20 .20
First day cover 1.00
Inscription block of 4 .60 —

Perf. 12½x12

C10 AP7 13c **ultra, aquamarine, gray & carmine** *(2,700,000)* .20 .20
First day cover 1.00
First day cover, #C8-C10 8.50
Inscription block of 4 .90 —

First day covers of Nos. C8-C10 total 535,824.

"Flight Across the Globe" — AP8

Jet Plane and Envelope — AP9

Printed by the Austrian Government Printing Office, Vienna, Austria. Panes of 50. Designed by Ole Hamann (15c) and George Hamori (25c).

Perf. 11½x12, 12x11½

1964, May 1 **Photo.** **Unwmk.**

C11 AP8 15c **violet, buff, gray & pale green** *(3,000,000)* .25 .20
First day cover 1.00
Inscription block of 4 1.25 —
a. Gray omitted —
C12 AP9 25c **yellow, orange, gray, blue & red** *(2,000,000)* .50 .30
First day cover 1.00
First day cover, #C11-C12 8.00
Inscription block of 4 2.50 —
Nos. C8-C12 (5) 1.35 1.10

First day covers of Nos. C11-C12 total 353,696.
For 75c in type AP8, see UN Offices in Geneva No. 8.

Jet Plane and UN Emblem — AP10

Printed by Setelipaino, Finland. Panes of 50. Designed by Ole Hamann.

1968, Apr. 18 **Litho.** ***Perf. 13***

C13 AP10 20c **multicolored** *(3,000,000)* .30 .25
First day cover *(225,378)* 1.00
Inscription block of 4 1.50 —

Wings, Envelopes and UN Emblem — AP11

Printed by Setelipaino, Finland. Panes of 50. Designed by Olav S. Mathiesen.

1969, Apr. 21 **Litho.** ***Perf. 13***

C14 AP11 10c **orange vermilion, orange, yellow & black** *(4,000,000)* .20 .20
First day cover *(132,686)* 1.00
Inscription block of 4 .75 —

UN Emblem and Stylized Wing — AP12

Birds in Flight — AP13

Clouds AP14

"UN" and Plane — AP15

Printed by Government Printing Bureau, Japan (9c); Heraclio Fournier, S. A., Spain (11c, 17c); Setelipaino, Finland (21c). Panes of 50. Designed by Lyell L. Dolan (9c), Arne Johnson (11c), British American Bank Note Co. (17c) and Asher Kalderon (21c).

1972, May 1 Litho. & Engr. *Perf. 13x13½*

C15 AP12 9c **light blue, dark red & violet blue** *(3,000,000)+* .20 .20
First day cover 1.00
Inscription block of 4 .50 —

Photo.

Perf. 14x13½

C16 AP13 11c **blue & multicolored** *(3,000,000)+* .20 .20
First day cover 1.00
Inscription block of 4 .75 —

Perf. 13½x14

C17 AP14 17c **yellow, red & orange** *(3,000,000)+* .25 .20
First day cover 1.00
Inscription block of 4 1.10 —

Perf. 13

C18 AP15 21c **silver & multi** *(3,500,000)* .25 .25
First day cover 1.00
First day cover, #C15-C18 3.50
Inscription block of 4 1.25 —
Nos. C15-C18 (4) .90 .85

First day covers of Nos. C15-C18 total 553,535.

Globe and Jet — AP16

Pathways Radiating from UN Emblem AP17

Bird in Flight, UN Headquarters AP18

Printed by Setelipaino, Finland. Panes of 50. Designed by George Hamori (13c), Shamir Bros. (18c) and Olav S. Mathiesen (26c).

1974, Sept. 16 Litho. *Perf. 13, 12½x13 (18c)*

C19 AP16 13c **multicolored** *(2,500,000)+* .20 .20
First day cover 1.00
Inscription block of 4 .80 —

C20 AP17 18c **gray olive & multicolored** *(2,000,000)* .25 .20
First day cover 1.00
Inscription block of 4 1.10 —

C21 AP18 26c **blue & multi** *(2,000,000)* .35 .30
First day cover 1.25
First day cover, #C19-C21 2.50
Inscription block of 4 1.60 —
Nos. C19-C21 (3) .80 .70

First day covers of Nos. C19-C21 total 309,610.

Winged Airmail Letter — AP19

Symbolic Globe and Plane — AP20

Printed by Heraclio Fournier, S.A. Panes of 50. Designed by Eliezer Weishoff (25c) and Alan L. Pollock (31c).

1977, June 27 Photo. *Perf. 14*

C22 AP19 25c **greenish blue & multi** *(2,000,000)+* .35 .25
First day cover 1.25
Inscription block of 4 1.60 —

C23 AP20 31c **magenta** *(2,000,000)* .40 .30
First day cover 1.25
First day cover, #C22-C23 1.50
Inscription block of 4 1.90 —

First day covers of Nos. C22-C23 total 209,060.

ENVELOPES

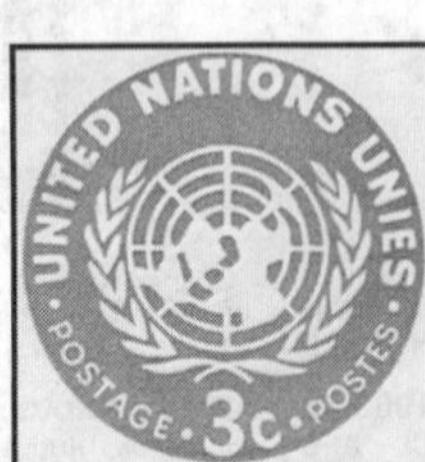

Emblem of United Nations — U1

Printed by the International Envelope Corp., Dayton, Ohio.

Die engraved by the American Bank Note Co., New York.

1953, Sept. 15 Embossed

U1 U1 3c **blue,** entire *(555,000)* .40 .40
Entire, first day cancel *(102,278)* 1.00

Printed by International Envelope Corp., Dayton, Ohio.

1958, Sept. 22 Embossed

U2 U1 4c **ultramarine,** entire *(1,000,000)* .40 .20
Entire, first day cancel *(213,621)* 1.00

Stylized Globe and Weather Vane — U2

Printed by United States Envelope Co., Springfield, Mass. Designed by Hatim El Mekki.

1963, Apr. 26 Litho.

U3 U2 5c **multicolored,** entire *(1,115,888)* .25 .20
Entire, first day cancel *(165,188)* 1.00

Printed by Setelipaino, Finland.

1969, Jan. 8 Litho.

U4 U2 6c **black, blue, magenta & dull yellow,** entire *(850,000)* .25 .20
Entire, first day cancel *(152,593)* 1.00

Headquarters Type of Regular Issue, 1968

Printed by Eureka Co., a division of Litton Industries.

1973, Jan. 12 Litho.

U5 A99 8c **sepia, blue & olive,** entire *(700,000)* .50 .20
Entire, first day cancel *(145,510)* 1.00

Headquarters Type of Regular Issue, 1974

Printed by United States Envelope Co., Springfield, Mass.

1975, Jan. 10 Litho.

U6 A138 10c **blue, olive bister & multi,** entire *(547,500)* .40 .20
Entire, first day cancel *(122,000)* 1.00

Bouquet of Ribbons — U3 UNITED NATIONS 22c

Printed by Carl Ueberreuter Druck and Verlag M. Salzer, Austria. Designed by George Hamori, Australia.

1985, May 10 Litho.

U7 U3 22c **multicolored,** entire *(250,000)* 8.50 .40
Entire, first day cancel *(28,600)* 5.00

New York Headquarters U4

Printed by Mercury Walch, Australia. Designed by Rocco J. Callari, United States.

1989, Mar. 17 Litho.

U8 U4 25c **multicolored,** entire *(350,000)* 2.75 .35
Entire, first day cancel *(28,567)* 6.00

For surcharge see No. U9A.

No. U8 Surcharged

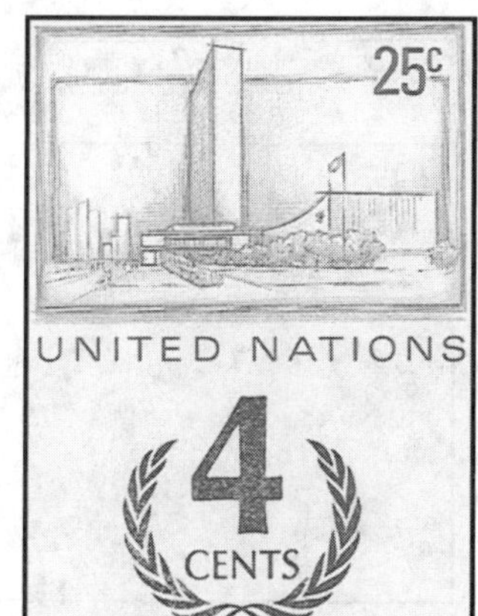

1991, Apr. 15 **Litho.**

U9 U4 25c +4c **multicolored,** entire *(50,000)+* 2.75 .40
Entire, first day cover 5.50

No. U8 Surcharged

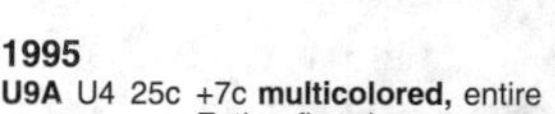

1995 **Litho.**

U9A U4 25c +7c **multicolored,** entire 3.00 .50
Entire, first day cover 6.00

Cripticandina, by Alfredo La Placa — U5

Illustration reduced.
Design sizes: No. U10, 79x38mm. No. U11, 89x44mm.

1997, Feb. 12 **Litho.**

U10 U5 32c **multicolored,** #6¾, entire *(65,000)+* 3.00 .45
Entire, first day cancel 5.50
U11 U5 32c **multicolored,** #10, entire *(80,000)+* 3.00 .45
Entire, first day cancel 5.50

Nos. U10-U11 Surcharged

1999, Jan. 10 **Litho.**

U12 U5 32c +1c **multicolored,** on #U10, entire 2.00 .45
First day cancel, entire 2.50
U13 U5 32c +1c **multicolored,** on #U11, entire 2.00 .45
First day cancel, entire 2.50

New York Headquarters — U6

Design sizes: No. U14, 34x34mm. No. U15, 36x36mm.

2001, May 25 **Litho.**

U14 U6 34c **multicolored,** #6¾, entire .90 .45
Entire, first day cancel 1.25
U15 U6 34c **multicolored,** #10, entire .90 .45
Entire, first day cancel 1.25

Nos. U14-U15 Surcharged

2002, June 30 **Litho.**

U16 U6 34c +3c **multicolored,** entire (#U14) 1.00 .50
Entire, first day cancel 1.25
U17 U6 34c +3c **multicolored,** entire (#U15) 1.00 .50
Entire, first day cancel 1.25

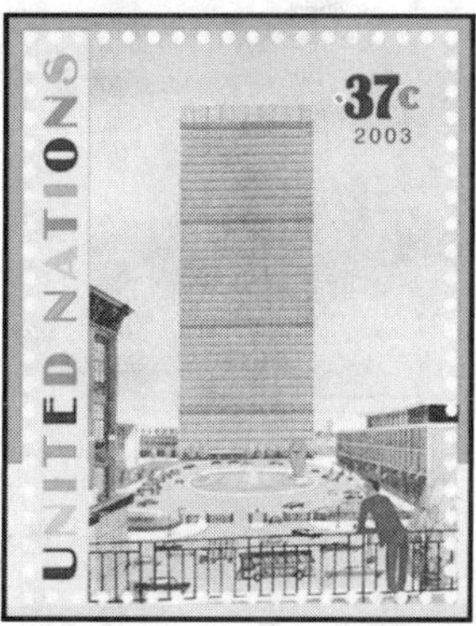

UN Headquarters U7

Printed by Australia Post Spintpak, Australia.
Design sizes: No. U18, 37x47mm. No. U19, 40x52mm.

2003, Mar. 28 **Litho.**

U18 U7 37c **multicolored,** #6¾, entire *(62,000)+* 1.00 .50
Entire, first day cancel 1.25
U19 U7 37c **multicolored,** #10, entire *(72,000)+* 1.00 .50
Entire, first day cancel 1.25

AIR POST ENVELOPES AND AIR LETTER SHEETS

Used values are for non-philatelic contemporaneous usages.

Letter Sheet
Type of Air Post Stamp of 1951
Inscribed "Air Letter" at Left
Printed by Dennison & Sons, Long Island City, NY.

1952, Aug. 29 **Litho.**

UC1 AP2 10c **blue,** *bluish,* entire *(187,000)* 22.50 *20.00*
Entire, 1st day cancel *(57,274)* 2.50

Designed by C. Mutver.

Letter Sheet
Inscribed "Air Letter" and "Aerogramme" at Left

1954, Sept. 14 **Litho.**

UC2 AP2 10c **royal blue,** *bluish,* entire, *(207,000)* 9.50 1.00
Entire, 1st day cancel *200.00*
a. No white border, *1958 (148,800)* 7.00 *6.00*

No. UC2 was printed with a narrow white border (½ to 1mm wide) surrounding the stamp. On No. UC2a, this border has been partly or entirely eliminated.

UN Flag and Plane — UC1

(UN Emblem Emblossed)

Printed by International Envelope Corp., Dayton, O.
Die engraved by American Bank Note Co., New York.

1959, Sept. 21 **Embossed**

UC3 UC1 7c **blue,** entire *(550,000)* 1.00 *1.25*
Entire, 1st day cancel *(172,107)* 1.00

Letter Sheet
Type of Air Post Stamp of 1959
Printed by Thomas De La Rue & Co., Ltd., London

1960, Jan. 18 **Litho.**

UC4 AP4 10c **ultramarine,** *bluish,* entire *(405,000)* .65 .65
Entire, 1st day cancel *(122,425)* .50

Printed on protective tinted paper containing colorless inscription "United Nations" in the five official languages of the UN.

Letter Sheet
Type of Air Post Stamp of 1951
Inscribed "Correo Aereo" instead of "Poste Aerienne"
Printed by Thomas De La Rue & Co., Ltd., London

1961, June 26 **Litho.**

UC5 AP1 11c **ultramarine,** *bluish,* entire *(550,000)* .50 .20
Entire, 1st day cancel *(128,557)* .50
a. 11c **dark blue,** *green* entire, *July 16, 1965 (419,000)* 1.25 1.25

Printed on protective tinted paper containing colorless inscription "United Nations" in the five official languages of the UN.

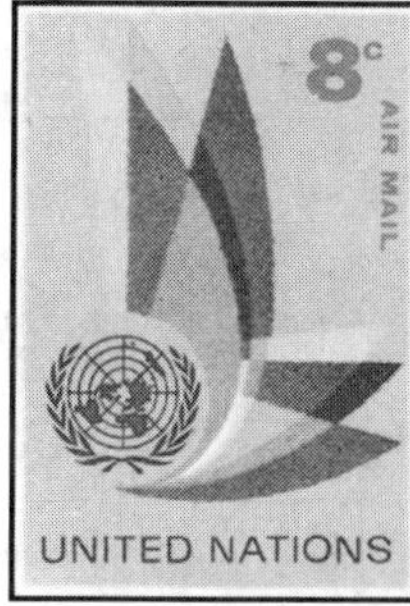

UN Emblem — UC2

Printed by United States Envelope Co., Springfield, Mass. Designed by George Hamori.

1963, Apr. 26 **Litho.**

UC6 UC2 8c **multicolored,** entire *(880,000)* .30 .20
Entire, 1st day cancel *(165,208)* 1.00

Letter Sheet

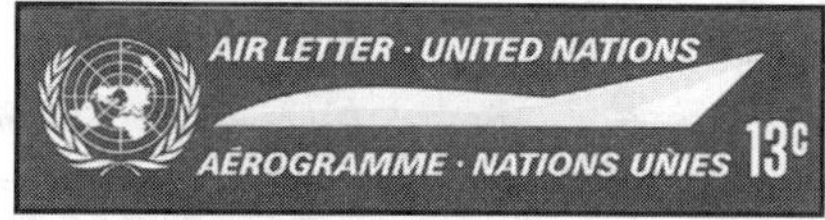

UN Emblem and Stylized Plane — UC3

Printed by Setelipaino, Finland. Designed by Robert Perrot.

1968, May 31 **Litho.**

UC7 UC3 13c **violet blue & light blue,** entire *(750,000)* .30 .25
Entire, 1st day cancel *(106,700)* .50

Type of 1963
Printed by Setelipaino, Finland.

1969, Jan. 8 **Litho.**
UC8 UC2 10c **pink, Prussian blue, orange & sepia,** entire *(750,000)* .35 .20
Entire, 1st day cancel *(153,472)* .50

Letter Sheet

UN Emblem, "UN," Globe and Plane — UC4

Printed by Joh. Enschede and Sons. Designed by Edmondo Calivis, Egypt. Sheet surface printed in greenish blue.

1972, Oct. 16 **Litho.**
UC9 UC4 15c **violet blue & greenish blue,** entire *(500,000)* .60 .20
Entire, 1st day cancel *(85,500)* 1.00

Bird Type of Air Post Stamp, 1972
Printed by Eureka Co., a division of Litton Industries

1973, Jan. 12 **Litho.**
UC10 AP13 11c **blue & multicolored,** entire *(700,000)* .40 .20
Entire, 1st day cancel *(134,500)* 1.00

Globe and Jet Air Post Type of 1974
Printod by United States Envelope Co., Springfield, Mass.

1975, Jan. 10 **Litho.**
UC11 AP16 13c **blue & multicolored,** entire *(555,539)* .60 .20
Entire, 1st day cancel *(122,000)* 1.00

Letter Sheet
Headquarters Type of Regular Issue, 1971
Printed by Joh. Enschede and Sons, Netherlands

1975, Jan. 10 **Photo.**
UC12 A120 18c **blue & multicolored,** entire *(400,000)* .60 .20
Entire, 1st day cancel *(70,500)* 1.00

Letter Sheet

"UN" Emblem and Birds UC5

Printed by Joh. Enschede and Sons. Designed by Angel Medina Medina.

1977, June 27 **Litho.**
UC13 UC5 22c **multicolored,** entire *(400,000)* .65 .20
Entire, 1st day cancel *(70,000)* 1.00

Letter Sheet

Paper Airplane UC6

Printed by Joh. Enschede and Sons.
Designed by Margaret-Ann Champion.

1982, Apr. 28 **Litho.**
UC14 UC6 30c **black,** *pale green,* entire *(400,000)* 1.50 .50
Entire, 1st day cancel *(61,400)* 1.25

Letter Sheet No. UC14 Surcharged

1987, July 7 **Litho.**
UC15 UC6 30c + 6c **black,** *green,* entire *(43,000)* *45.00* 4.25
Entire, 1st day cancel 18.00

New York Headquarters UC7

Printed by Mercury Walch, Australia. Designed by Thomas Lee, China.

1989, Mar. 17 **Litho.**
UC16 UC7 39c **multicolored,** entire *(350,000)* 3.50 1.50
Entire, 1st day cancel *(14,798)* 9.50

No. UC16 Surcharged

1991, Feb. 12 **Litho.**
UC17 UC7 39c + 6c **multicolored,** entire *(35,563)* 16.00 2.00
Entire, first day cancel 8.50

UC8

Designed by Robert Stein. Printed by Mercury-Walch, Australia.

1992, Sept. 4 **Litho.**
UC18 UC8 45c **multicolored,** entire, *(185,000)+* 3.00 .75
First day cancel 10.00

Letter Sheet No. UC18 Surcharged

1995, July 9 **Litho.**
UC19 UC8 45c +5c **multicolored,** entire 5.00 .60
First day cover 9.00

Cherry Blossoms — UC9

1997, Mar. 13 **Litho.**
UC20 UC9 50c **multicolored,** entire *(115,000)+* 2.50 .50
Entire, first day cancel 2.50

No. UC20 Surcharged

1999, Aug. 23 **Litho.**
UC21 UC9 50c +10c **multicolored,** entire 1.75 .65
Entire, first day cancel 2.00

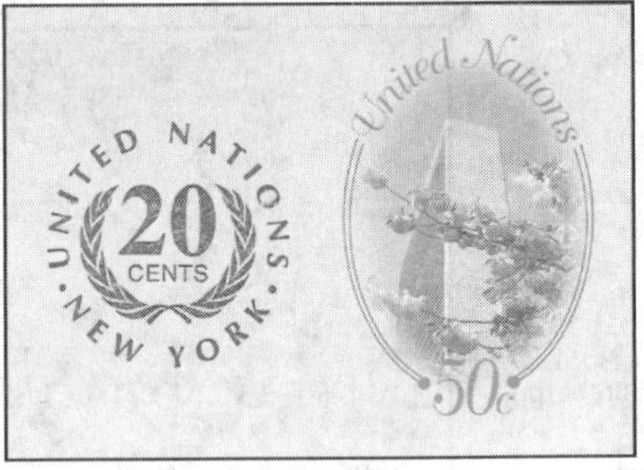

No. UC20 Surcharged

2001, Jan. 9 **Litho.**
UC22 UC9 50c +20c **multicolored,** entire 1.75 .70
Entire, first day cancel 2.00

Cherry Blossoms at New York Headquarters UC10

2001, May 25 **Litho.**
UC23 UC10 70c **multicolored,** entire 1.75 .70
Entire, first day cancel 1.75

POSTAL CARDS

Values are for entire cards.

Type of Postage Issue of 1951
Printed by Dennison & Sons, Long Island City, N.Y.

1952, July 18 **Litho.**
UX1 A2 2c **blue,** *buff (899,415)* .20 .20
First day cancel *(116,023)* 1.00

Printed by British American Bank Note Co., Ltd., Ottawa, Canada

1958, Sept. 22 **Litho.**
UX2 A2 3c **gray olive,** *buff (575,000)* .20 .20
First day cancel *(145,557)* .50

World Map, Sinusoidal Projection — PC1

Printed by Eureka Specialty Printing Co., Scranton, Pa.

1963, Apr. 26 **Litho.**

UX3 PC1 4c **light blue, violet blue, orange & bright citron** *(784,000)* .25 .20
First day cancel *(112,280)* .50
a. Bright citron omitted —

UN Emblem and Post Horn — PC2

"UN" — PC3

Printed by Canadian Bank Note Co., Ltd., Ottawa. Designed by John Mason.

1969, Jan. 8 **Litho.**

UX4 PC2 5c **blue & black** *(500,000)* .25 .20
First day cancel *(95,975)* .50

1973, Jan. 12 **Litho.**

Printed by Government Printing Bureau, Tokyo. Designed by Asher Kalderon.

UX5 PC3 6c **gray & multicolored** *(500,000)* .20 .20
First day cancel *(84,500)* .50

Type of 1973

Printed by Setelipaino, Finland.

1975, Jan. 10 **Litho.**

UX6 PC3 8c **light green & multi** *(450,000)* .60 .20
First day cancel *(72,500)* .50

UN Emblem — PC4

Printed by Setelipaino, Finland. Designed by George Hamori.

1977, June 27 **Litho.**

UX7 PC4 9c **multicolored** *(350,000)* .60 .20
First day cancel *(70,000)* .50

PC5

Printed by Courvoisier. Designed by Salahattin Kanidinc.

1982, Apr. 28 **Photo.**

UX8 PC5 13c **multicolored** *(350,000)* .50 .20
First day cancel *(59,200)* 1.00

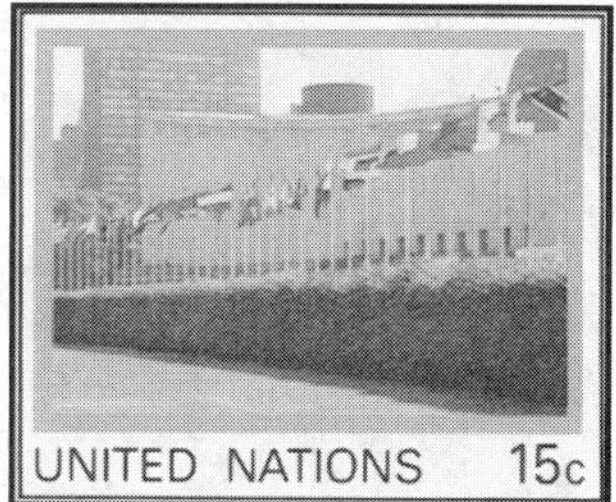

Views of New York Headquarters PC6

Designs: No. UX9, Spring at U.N. Headquarters, vert. No. UX10, Cherry Blossoms, U.N. Gardens, vert. No. UXC11, Row of Flags of member states. No. UX12, U.N. General Assembly. No. UX13, River view, U.N. Headquarters. No. UX14, U.N. Headquarters, vert. No. UX15, Row of flags of member states, vert. No. UX16, Night view, U.N. Headquarters, vert. No. UX17, U.N. Security Council. No. UX18, U.N. Gardens.

Printed by Johann Enschede and Sons, the Netherlands. Designed by Thomas Lee, China, from photographs.

1989, Mar. 17 **Litho.**

UX9 PC6 15c **multicolored** *(120,000)+* .80 .40
First day cancel 2.25
UX10 PC6 15c **multicolored** *(120,000)+* .80 .40
First day cancel 2.25
UX11 PC6 15c **multicolored** *(120,000)+* .80 .40
First day cancel 2.25
UX12 PC6 15c **multicolored** *(120,000)+* .80 .40
First day cancel 2.25
UX13 PC6 15c **multicolored** *(120,000)+* .80 .40
First day cancel 2.25
UX14 PC6 36c **multicolored** *(120,000)+* 1.20 .60
First day cancel 2.50
UX15 PC6 36c **multicolored** *(120,000)+* 1.20 .60
First day cancel 2.50
UX16 PC6 36c **multicolored** *(120,000)+* 1.20 .60
First day cancel 2.50
UX17 PC6 36c **multicolored** *(120,000)+* 1.20 .60
First day cancel 2.50
UX18 PC6 36c **multicolored** *(120,000)+* 1.20 .60
First day cancel 2.50
Nos. UX9-UX18 (10) 10.00 5.00

Nos. UX9-UX13 and UX14-UX18 sold only in sets. Nos. UX9-UX13 sold for $2 and Nos. UX14-UX18 sold for $3.

First day cancels of Nos. UX9-UX18 total 125,526.

New York Headquarters Type of 1991

Printed by Mercury-Walch, Australia.

1992, Sept. 4 **Litho.**

UX19 A260 40c **blue** *(150,000)+* 4.50 .40
First day cancel *(9,603)* 12.50

Secretariat Building, Roses — PC7

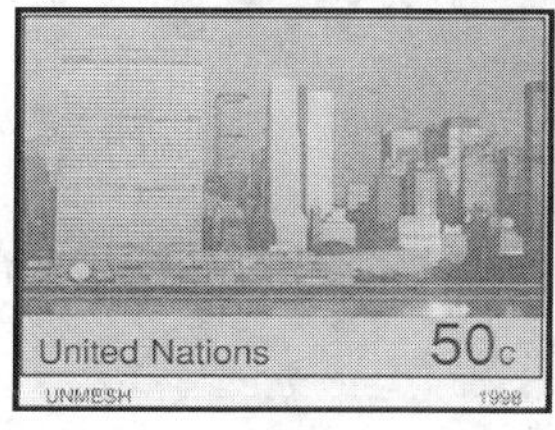

UN Complex — PC8

Printed by Mercury-Walsh, Australia.

1998, May 20 **Litho.**

UX20 PC7 21c **multicolored** *(150,000)+* 1.25 .25
First day cancel 1.75
UX21 PC8 50c **multicolored** *(150,000)+* 2.00 .50
First day cancel 2.25

Illustrations of the buildings and other scenes are shown on the back of each card.

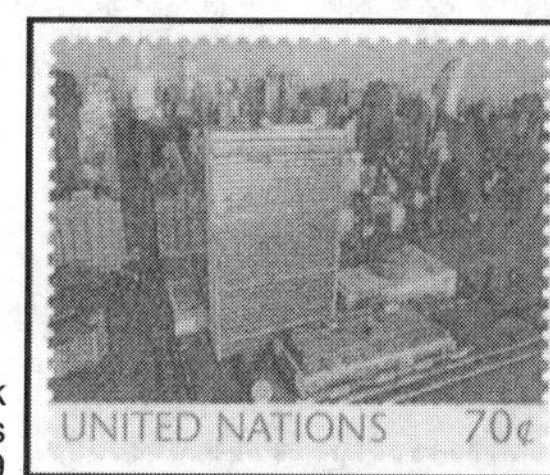

New York Headquarters PC9

2001, May 25 **Litho.**

UX22 PC9 70c **multicolored** 1.75 .70
Entire, first day cancel 1.75

No. UX20 Surcharged

2002, June 30 **Litho.**

UX23 PC7 21c +2c **multicolored** .50 .25
First day cancel 1.25

PC10

PC11

PC12

PC13

PC14

PC15

PC16

PC17

PC18

Illustrations from *This is the United Nations,* by M. Sasek — PC19

Printed by Banknote Corporation of America, US.

2003, Mar. 28 **Litho.**

UX24 PC10 23c **multicolored** *(61,500)+* .45 .25
Entire, first day cancel 1.00
UX25 PC11 23c **multicolored** *(61,500)+* .45 .25
Entire, first day cancel 1.00
UX26 PC12 23c **multicolored** *(61,500)+* .45 .25
Entire, first day cancel 1.00
UX27 PC13 23c **multicolored** *(61,500)+* .45 .25
Entire, first day cancel 1.00
UX28 PC14 23c **multicolored** *(61,500)+* .45 .25
Entire, first day cancel 1.00
UX29 PC15 70c **multicolored** *(86,500)+* 1.40 .70
Entire, first day cancel 1.40
UX30 PC16 70c **multicolored** *(86,500)+* 1.40 .70
Entire, first day cancel 1.40
UX31 PC17 70c **multicolored** *(86,500)+* 1.40 .70
Entire, first day cancel 1.40
UX32 PC18 70c **multicolored** *(86,500)+* 1.40 .70
Entire, first day cancel 1.40
UX33 PC19 70c **multicolored** *(86,500)+* 1.40 .70
Entire, first day cancel 1.40
Nos. UX24-UX33 (10) 9.25 4.75

Nos. UX24-UX28 and UX29-UX33 were sold only in shrink-wrapped sets.

AIR POST POSTAL CARDS

Values are for entire cards.

Type of Air Post Stamp of 1957

Printed by British American Bank Note Co., Ltd., Ottawa.

1957, May 27 **Litho.**

UXC1 AP3 4c **maroon,** *buff (631,000)* .25 .20
First day cancel *(260,005)* 1.00

No. UXC1 Surcharged in Maroon at Left of Stamp

1959, June 5 **Litho.**

UXC2 AP3 4c + 1c **maroon,** *buff (1,119,000)* .30 .20
Cancel first day of public use, June 8 *300.00*
a. Double surcharge —
b. Inverted surcharge —

Type of Air Post Stamp, 1957

Printed by Eureka Specialty Printing Co., Scranton, Pa.

1959, Sept. 21 **Litho.**

UXC3 AP3 5c **crimson,** *buff (500,000)* .65 .20
First day cancel *(119,479)* .50

Outer Space — APC1

Printed by Eureka Specialty Printing Co., Scranton, Pa.

1963, Apr. 26 **Litho.**

UXC4 APC1 6c **black & blue** *(350,000)* .60 .20
First day cancel *(109,236)* .00

APC2

Printed by Eureka-Carlisle Co., Scranton, Pa. Designed by Olav S. Mathiesen.

1966, June 9 **Litho.**

UXC5 APC2 11c **dark red, rose, yellow & brown** *(764,500)* .30 .20
First day cancel *(162,588)* .50

1968, May 31 **Litho.**

UXC6 APC2 13c **dark green, bright green & yellow** *(829,000)* .40 .20
First day cancel *(106,500)* 1.00

UN Emblem and Stylized Planes — APC3

Printed by Canadian Bank Note Co., Ltd., Ottawa. Designed by Lawrence Kurtz.

1969, Jan. 8 **Litho.**

UXC7 APC3 8c **gray, dull yellow, lt blue, indigo & red** *(500,000)* .65 .20
First day cancel *(94,037)* .50

Type of Air Post Stamp of 1972

Printed by Government Printing Bureau, Tokyo. Designed by L. L. Dolan.

1972, Oct. 16 **Litho.**

UXC8 AP12 9c **orange, red, gray & green** *(500,000)* .45 .20
First day cancel *(85,600)* .50

Type of 1969

Printed by Government Printing Bureau, Tokyo

1972, Oct. 16 **Litho.**

UXC9 APC3 15c **lilac, light blue, pink & carmine** *(500,000)* .50 .20
First day cancel *(84,800)* .50

Types of Air Post Stamps, 1972-74

Printed by Setelipaino, Finland.

1975, Jan. 10 **Litho.**

UXC10 AP14 11c **greenish blue, blue & dark blue** *(250,000)* .50 .20
First day cancel *(70,500)* .50
UXC11 AP17 18c **gray & multicolored** *(250,000)* .50 .20
First day cancel *(70,500)* .50

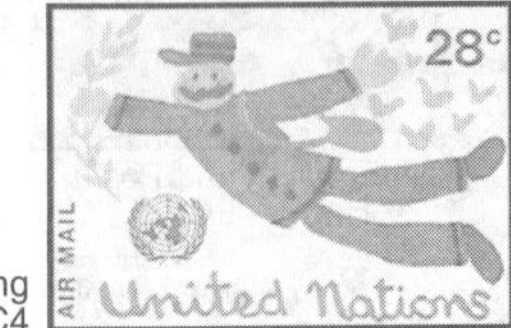

Flying Mailman — APC4

Printed by Courvoisier. Designed by Arieh Glaser.

1982, Apr. 28 **Photo.**

UXC12 APC4 28c **multicolored** *(350,000)* .45 .20
First day cancel *(58,700)* 1.40

OFFICES IN GENEVA, SWITZERLAND

For use only on mail posted at the Palais des Nations (UN European Office), Geneva. Inscribed in French unless otherwise stated.

100 Centimes = 1 Franc

Types of United Nations Issues 1961-69 and

United Nations European Office, Geneva — G1

Printed by Setelipaino, Finland (5c, 70c, 80c, 90c, 2fr, 10fr), Courvoisier, S.A., Switzerland (10c, 20c, 30c, 50c, 60c, 3fr). Government Printing Office, Austria (75c) and Government Printing Office, Federal Republic of Germany (1fr).

Panes of 50. 30c designed by Ole Hamann, others as before.

Designs: 5c, UN Headquarters, New York, and world map. 10c, UN flag. 20c, Three men united before globe. 50c, Opening words of UN Charter. 60c, UN emblem over globe. 70c, "un" and UN emblem. 75c, "Flight Across Globe." 80c, UN Headquarters and emblem. 90c, Abstract group of flags. 1fr, UN emblem. 2fr, Stylized globe and weather vane. 3fr, Statue by Henrik Starcke. 10fr, "Peace, Justice, Security."

The 20c, 80c and 90c are inscribed in French. The 75c and 10fr carry French inscription at top, English at bottom.

1969-70 Photo. Unwmk.

Perf. 13 (5c, 70c, 90c); 12½x12 (10c);

1 A88 5c **purple & multi,** *Oct. 4, 1969 (3,300,000)* .20 .20
First day cover 1.00
Inscription block of 4 .25 —
a. Green omitted —
2 A52 10c **salmon & multi,** *Oct. 4, 1969 (4,300,000)+* .20 .20
First day cover 1.00
Inscription block of 4 .25 —

Perf. 11½ (20c-60c, 3fr)

3 A66 20c **black & multi,** *Oct. 4, 1969 (4,500.000)* .20 .20
First day cover 1.00
Inscription block of 4 .45 —
4 G1 30c **dark blue & multi,** *Oct. 4, 1969 (3,000,000)* .20 .20
First day cover 1.00
Inscription block of 4 .60 —
5 A77 50c **ultra & multi,** *Oct. 4, 1969 (3,300,000)* .20 .20
First day cover 1.00
Inscription block of 4 .80 —
6 A54 60c **dark brown, salmon & gold,** *Apr. 17, 1970 (3,300,000)+* .20 .20
First day cover 1.00
Inscription block of 4 .90 —
7 A104 70c **red, black & gold,** *Sept. 22, 1970 (3,300,000)+* .20 .20
First day cover 1.00
Inscription block of 4 .90 —

Perf. 11½x12 (75c)

8 AP8 75c **carmine rose & multi,** *Oct. 4, 1969 (3,300,000)+* .25 .25
First day cover 1.00
Inscription block of 4 1.00 —

Perf. 13½x14 (80c)

9 A78 80c **blue green, red & yellow,** *Sept. 22, 1970 (3,300,000)* .25 .25
First day cover 1.00
Inscription block of 4 1.00 —
10 A45 90c **blue & multi,** *Sept. 22, 1970 (3,300,000)* .25 .25
First day cover 1.00
Inscription block of 4 1.10 —

Litho. & Embossed

Perf. 14 (1fr)

11 A79 1fr **light & dark green,** *Oct. 4, 1969 (3,000,000)* .30 .30
First day cover 1.00
Inscription block of 4 1.25 —

Photo.

Perf. 12x11½ (2fr)

12 A67 2fr **blue & multi,** *Sept. 22, 1970 (3,000,000)+* .60 .60
First day cover 2.00
Inscription block of 4 2.50 —
13 A97 3fr **olive & multi,** *Oct. 4, 1969 (3,000,000)+* .95 .95
First day cover 2.25
Inscription block of 4 4.00 —

Engr.

Perf. 12 (10fr)

14 A3 10fr **dark blue,** *Apr. 17, 1970 (2,250,000)+* 2.75 2.75
First day cover 8.50
Inscription block of 4 12.00 —
Nos. 1-14 (14) 6.75 6.75

+ Printing orders to June 1984.

First day covers of Nos. 1-5, 8, 11, 13 total 607,578; of Nos. 6 and 14, 148,055; of Nos. 7, 9-10 and 12, 226,000.

Sea Bed Type of UN

1971, Jan. 25 Photo. & Engr. *Perf. 13*

15 A114 30c **green & multi** *(1,935,871)* .20 .20
First day cover *(152,590)* 1.00
Inscription block of 4 .65 —

Refugee Type of UN

1971, Mar. 12 Litho. *Perf. 13x12½*

16 A115 50c **deep carmine, deep orange & black** *(1,820,114)* .20 .20
First day cover *(148,220)* 1.00
Inscription block of 4 .85 —

World Food Program Type of UN

1971, Apr. 13 Photo. *Perf. 14*

17 A116 50c **dark violet & multi** *(1,824,170)* .20 .20
First day cover *(151,580)* 1.00
Inscription block of 4 .85 —

UPU Headquarters Type of UN

1971, May 28 Photo. *Perf. 11½*

18 A117 75c **green & multi** *(1,821,878)* .30 .30
First day cover *(140,679)* 1.00
Inscription block of 4 1.40 —

Eliminate Racial Discrimination Types of UN

Designed by Daniel Gonzague (30c) and Ole Hamann (50c).

1971, Sept. 21 Photo. *Perf. 13½*

19 A118 30c **blue & multi** *(1,838,474)* .20 .20
First day cover 1.00
Inscription block of 4 .75 —
20 A119 50c **yellow green & multi** *(1,804,126)* .25 .25
First day cover 1.00
First day cover, #19-20 1.25
Inscription block of 4 1.10 —

First day covers of Nos. 19-20 total 308,420.

Picasso Type of UN

1971, Nov. 19 Photo. *Perf. 11½*

21 A122 1.10fr **multicolored** *(1,467,993)* .75 .75
First day cover *(195,215)* 1.25
Inscription block of 4 3.00 —

Palais des Nations, Geneva — G2

Printed by Courvoisier, S. A. Panes of 50. Designed by Ole Hamann.

1972, Jan. 5 Photo. *Perf. 11½*

22 G2 40c **olive, blue, salmon & dark green** *(3,500,000)+* .20 .20
First day cover *(152,300)* 1.00
Inscription block of 4 .70 —

+ Initial printing order.

Nuclear Weapons Type of UN

1972, Feb. 14 Photo. *Perf. 13½x14*

23 A124 40c **yellow, green, black, rose & gray** *(1,567,305)* .25 .25
First day cover *(151,350)* 1.00
Inscription block of 4 1.25 —

World Health Day Type of UN

1972, Apr. 7 Litho. & Engr. *Perf. 13x13½*

24 A125 80c **black & multi** *(1,543,368)* .40 .40
First day cover *(192,600)* 1.00
Inscription block of 4 1.75 —

Human Environment Type of UN

Lithographed & Embossed

1972, June 5 *Perf. 12½x14*

25 A126 40c **olive, lemon, green & blue** *(1,594,089)* .20 .20
First day cover 1.00
Inscription block of 4 .80 —
26 A126 80c **ultra, pink, green & blue** *(1,568,009)* .40 .40
First day cover 1.40
First day cover, #25-26 1.75
Inscription block of 4 1.60 —

First day covers of Nos. 25-26 total 296,700.

Economic Commission for Europe Type of UN

1972, Sept. 11 Litho. *Perf. 13x13½*

27 A127 1.10fr **red & multi** *(1,604,082)* 1.00 1.00
First day cover *(149,630)* 1.75
Inscription block of 4 4.25 —

Art at UN (Sert) Type of UN

1972, Nov. 17 Photo. *Perf. 12x12½*

28 A128 40c **gold, red & brown** *(1,932,428)* .30 .30
First day cover 1.00
Inscription block of 4 1.25 —
29 A128 80c **gold, brown & olive** *(1,759,600)* .60 .60
First day cover 1.25
First day cover, #28-29 1.75
Inscription block of 4 2.50 —

First day covers of Nos. 28-29 total 295,470.

Disarmament Decade Type of UN

1973, Mar. 9 Litho. *Perf. 13½x13*

30 A129 60c **violet & multi** *(1,586,845)* .40 .35
First day cover 1.00
Inscription block of 4 1.60 —
31 A129 1.10fr **olive & multi** *(1,408,169)* .85 .85
First day cover 1.40
First day cover, #30-31 1.75
Inscription block of 4 3.50 —

First day covers of Nos. 30-31 total 260,680.

Drug Abuse Type of UN

1973, Apr. 13 Photo. *Perf. 13½*

32 A130 60c **blue & multi** *(1,481,432)* .45 .40
First day cover *(144,760)* 1.00
Inscription block of 4 1.90 —

Volunteers Type of UN

1973, May 25 Photo. *Perf. 14*

33 A131 80c **gray green & multi** *(1,443,519)* .35 .35
First day cover *(143,430)* 1.10
Inscription block of 4 1.50 —

Namibia Type of UN

1973, Oct. 1 Photo. *Perf. 13½*

34 A132 60c **red & multi** *(1,673,898)* .35 .35
First day cover *(148,077)* 1.00
Inscription block of 4 1.50 —

Human Rights Type of UN

1973, Nov. 16 Photo. *Perf. 13½*

35 A133 40c **ultramarine & multi** *(1,480,791)* .30 .30
First day cover 1.00
Inscription block of 4 1.25 —
36 A133 80c **olive & multi** *(1,343,349)* .50 .50
First day cover 1.25
First day cover, #35-36 1.75
Inscription block of 4 2.10 —

First day covers of Nos. 35-36 total 438,260.

ILO Headquarters Type of UN

1974, Jan. 11 Photo. *Perf. 14*

37 A134 60c **violet & multi** *(1,212,703)* .45 .45
First day cover 1.00
Inscription block of 4 1.90 —
38 A134 80c **brown & multi** *(1,229,851)* .65 .60
First day cover 1.10
First day cover, #37-38 1.25
Inscription block of 4 2.75 —

First day covers of Nos. 37-38 total 240,660.

Centenary of UPU Type of UN

1974, Mar. 22 Litho. *Perf. 12½*

39 A135 30c **gold & multi** *(1,567,517)* .25 .20
First day cover 1.00
Inscription block of 4 1.25 —
40 A135 60c **gold & multi** *(1,430,839)* .60 .50
First day cover 1.25
First day cover, #39-40 1.50
Inscription block of 4 2.50 —

First day covers of Nos. 39-40 total 231,840.

Art at UN (Portinari) Type of UN

1974, May 6 Photo. *Perf. 14*

41 A136 60c **dark red & multi** *(1,202,357)* .40 .40
First day cover 1.00
Inscription block of 4 1.75 —
42 A136 1fr **green & multi** *(1,230,045)* .70 .70
First day cover 1.20
First day cover, #41-42 1.50
Inscription block of 4 3.00 —

First day covers of Nos. 41-42 total 249,130.

World Population Year Type of UN

1974, Oct. 18 Photo. *Perf. 14*
43 A140 60c **bright green & multi** *(1,292,954)* .50 .45
First day cover 1.00
Inscription block of 4 2.25 —
44 A140 80c **brown & multi** *(1,221,288)* .70 .70
First day cover 1.00
First day cover, #43-44 1.25
Inscription block of 4 3.25 —

First day covers of Nos. 43-44 total 189,597.

Law of the Sea Type of UN

1974, Nov. 22 Photo. *Perf. 14*
45 A141 1.30fr **blue & multicolored** *(1,266,270)* 1.00 .95
First day cover *(181,000)* 1.25
Inscription block of 4 4.00 —

Outer Space Type of UN

1975, Mar. 14 Litho. *Perf. 13*
46 A142 60c **multicolored** *(1,339,704)* .50 .50
First day cover 1.00
Inscription block of 4 2.00 —
47 A142 90c **multicolored** *(1,383,888)* .75 .75
First day cover 1.00
First day cover, #46-47 1.50
Inscription block of 4 3.25 —

First day covers of Nos. 46-47 total 250,400.

International Women's Year Type of UN

1975, May 9 Litho. *Perf. 15*
48 A143 60c **multicolored** *(1,176,080)* .40 .40
First day cover 1.00
Inscription block of 4 1.90 —
49 A143 90c **multicolored** *(1,167,863)* .70 .65
First day cover 1.00
First day cover, #48-49 1.50
Inscription block of 4 3.25 —

First day covers of Nos. 48-49 total 250,660.

30th Anniversary Type of UN

1975, June 26 Litho. *Perf. 13*
50 A144 60c **green & multi** *(1,442,075)* .40 .40
First day cover 1.00
Inscription block of 4 2.00 —
51 A144 90c **violet & multi** *(1,612,411)* .70 .70
First day cover 1.00
First day cover, #50-51 1.25
Inscription block of 4 3.25 —

Souvenir Sheet

Imperf

52 Sheet of 2 *(1,210,148)* .75 .75
a. A144 60c **green & multicolored** .25 .25
b. A144 90c **violet & multicolored** .50 .50
First day cover 1.25

No. 52 has blue and bister margin with inscription and UN emblem. Size: 92x70mm.
First day covers of Nos. 50-52 total 402,500.

Namibia Type of UN

1975, Sept. 22 Photo. *Perf. 13½*
53 A145 50c **multicolored** *(1,261,019)* .30 .30
First day cover 1.00
Inscription block of 4 1.25 —
54 A145 1.30fr **multicolored** *(1,241,990)* .85 .85
First day cover 1.10
First day cover, #53-54 1.25
Inscription block of 4 4.00 —

First day covers of Nos. 53-54 total 226,260.

Peace-keeping Operations Type of UN

1975, Nov. 21 Engr. *Perf. 12½*
55 A146 60c **greenish blue** *(1,249,305)* .35 .35
First day cover 1.00
Inscription block of 4 1.50 —
56 A146 70c **bright violet** *(1,249,935)* .65 .60
First day cover 1.00
First day cover, #55-56 1.25
Inscription block of 4 2.75 —

First day covers of Nos. 55-56 total 229,245.

WFUNA Type of UN

1976, Mar. 12 Photo. *Perf. 14*
57 A152 90c **multicolored** *(1,186,563)* .90 .85
First day cover 1.00
Inscription block of 4 4.00 —

First day covers of No. 57 total 121,645.

UNCTAD Type of UN

1976, Apr. 23 Photo. *Perf. 11½*
58 A153 1.10fr **sepia & multi** *(1,167,284)* .90 .90
First day cover *(107,030)* 1.25
Inscription block of 4 4.00 —

Habitat Type of UN

1976, May 28 Photo. *Perf. 14*
59 A154 40c **dull blue & multi** *(1,258,986)* .20 .20
First day cover 1.00
Inscription block of 4 1.00 —
60 A154 1.50fr **violet & multi** *(1,110,507)* .75 .75
First day cover 1.25
First day cover, #59-60 1.60
Inscription block of 4 3.50 —

First day covers of Nos. 59-60 total 242,530.

UN Emblem, Post Horn and Rainbow — G3

UN Postal Administration, 25th anniversary.
Printed by Courvoisier, S.A. Panes of 20 (5x4). Designed by Hector Viola.

1976, Oct. 8 Photo. *Perf. 11½*
61 G3 80c **tan & multicolored** *(1,794,009)* .50 .50
First day cover 2.00
Inscription block of 4 2.50 —
62 A3 1.10fr **light green & multi** *(1,751,178)* 1.60 1.60
First day cover 2.00
Inscription block of 4 8.00 —
First day cover, #61-62 3.00
Panes of 20, #61-62 37.50

Upper margin blocks are inscribed "XXVe ANNIVERSAIRE"; lower margin blocks "ADMINISTRATION POSTALE DES NATIONS UNIES."
First day covers of Nos. 61-62 total 152,450.

World Food Council Type of UN

1976, Nov. 19 Litho. *Perf. 14½*
63 A156 70c **multicolored** *(1,507,630)* .50 .45
First day cover *(170,540)* 1.00
Inscription block of 4 2.25 —

WIPO Type of UN

1977, Mar. 11 Photo. *Perf. 14*
64 A157 80c **red & multi** *(1,232,664)* .60 .60
First day cover *(212,470)* 1.00
Inscription block of 4 2.75 —

Drop of Water and Globe — G4

UN Water Conference, Mar del Plata, Argentina, Mar. 14-25.
Printed by Government Printing Bureau, Tokyo. Panes of 50. Designed by Eliezer Weishoff.

1977, Apr. 22 Photo. *Perf. 13½x13*
65 G4 80c **ultramarine & multi** *(1,146,650)* .50 .50
First day cover 1.00
Inscription block of 4 2.25 —
66 G4 1.10fr **dark carmine & multi** *(1,138,236)* .80 .75
First day cover 1.25
First day cover, #65-66 1.75
Inscription block of 4 3.50 —

First day covers of Nos. 65-66 total 289,836.

Hands Protecting UN Emblem — G5

UN Security Council.
Printed by Heraclio Fournier, S.A., Spain. Panes of 50. Designed by George Hamori.

1977, May 27 Photo. *Perf. 11*
67 G5 80c **blue & multi** *(1,096,030)* .50 .50
First day cover 1.00
Inscription block of 4 2.25 —
68 G5 1.10fr **emerald & multi** *(1,075,925)* .80 .75
First day cover 1.25
First day cover, #67-68 1.75
Inscription block of 4 3.50 —

First day covers of Nos. 67-68 total 305,349.

Colors of Five Races Spun into One Firm Rope — G6

Fight against racial discrimination.
Printed by Setelipaino, Finland. Panes of 50. Designed by M. A. Munnawar.

1977, Sept. 19 Litho. *Perf. 13½x13*
69 G6 40c **multicolored** *(1,218,834)* .25 .25
First day cover 1.00
Inscription block of 4 1.10 —
70 G6 1.10fr **multicolored** *(1,138,250)* .65 .65
First day cover 1.25
First day cover, #69-70 1.75
Inscription block of 4 2.75 —

First day covers of Nos. 69-70 total 308,722.

Atomic Energy Turning Partly into Olive Branch — G7

Peaceful uses of atomic energy.
Printed by Heraclio Fournier, S.A., Spain. Panes of 50. Designed by Witold Janowski and Marek Freudenreich.

1977, Nov. 18 Photo. *Perf. 14*
71 G7 80c **dark carmine & multi** *(1,147,787)* .55 .55
First day cover 1.00
Inscription block of 4 2.50 —
72 G7 1.10fr **Prussian blue & multi** *(1,121,209)* .75 .75
First day cover 1.20
First day cover, #71-72 1.50
Inscription block of 4 3.50 —

First day covers of Nos. 71-72 total 298,075.

"Tree" of Doves — G8

Printed by Questa Colour Security Printers, United Kingdom. Panes of 50. Designed by M. Hioki.

1978, Jan. 27 Litho. *Perf. 14½*
73 G8 35c **multicolored** *(3,000,000)*+ .20 .20
First day cover *(259,735)* 1.00
Inscription block of 4 .75 —

Globes with Smallpox Distribution — G9

Global eradication of smallpox.
Printed by Courvoisier, S.A. Panes of 50. Designed by Eliezer Weishoff.

1978, Mar. 31 Photo. *Perf. 12x11½*
74 G9 80c **yellow & multi** *(1,116,044)* .60 .60
First day cover 1.00
Inscription block of 4 2.50 —
75 G9 1.10fr **light green & multi** *(1,109,946)* .90 .85
First day cover 1.25
First day cover, #74-75 2.00
Inscription block of 4 3.75 —

First day covers of Nos. 74-75 total 254,700.

Namibia Type of UN

1978, May 5 Photo. *Perf. 12*
76 A166 80c **multicolored** *(1,183,208)* .85 .85
First day cover *(316,610)* 1.00
Inscription block of 4 3.50 —

Jets and Flight Patterns — G10

International Civil Aviation Organization for "Safety in the Air."
Printed by Heraclio Fournier, S.A., Spain. Panes of 50. Designed by Tomas Savrda.

1978, June 12 **Photo.** ***Perf. 14***

77 G10 70c **multicolored** *(1,275,106)* .40 .40
First day cover 1.00
Inscription block of 4 1.75 —
78 G10 80c **multicolored** *(1,144,339)* .70 .70
First day cover 1.00
First day cover, #77-78 1.60
Inscription block of 4 3.00 —

First day covers of Nos. 77-78 total 255,700.

General Assembly, Flags and Globe — G11

Printed by Government Printing Bureau, Tokyo. Panes of 50. Designed by Henry Bencsath.

1978, Sept. 15 **Photo.** ***Perf. 13½***

79 G11 70c **multicolored** *(1,204,441)* .45 .45
First day cover 1.00
Inscription block of 4 2.25 —
80 G11 1.10fr **multicolored** *(1,183,889)* .85 .85
First day cover 1.25
First day cover, #79-80 1.75
Inscription block of 4 3.75 —

First day covers of Nos. 79-80 total 245,600.

Technical Cooperation Type of UN

1978, Nov. 17 **Photo.** ***Perf. 14***

81 A169 80c **multicolored** *(1,173,220)* .70 .70
First day cover *(264,700)* 1.00
Inscription block of 4 3.25 —

Seismograph Recording Earthquake — G12

Office of the UN Disaster Relief Coordinator (UNDRO).
Printed by Heraclio Fournier, S.A., Spain. Panes of 50. Designed by Michael Klutmann.

1979, Mar. 9 **Photo.** ***Perf. 14***

82 G12 80c **multicolored** *(1,183,155)* .50 .50
First day cover 1.00
Inscription block of 4 2.00 —
83 G12 1.50fr **multicolored** *(1,168,121)* .80 .75
First day cover 1.40
First day cover, #82-83 1.90
Inscription block of 4 3.50 —

First day covers of Nos. 82-83 total 162,070.

Children and Rainbow — G13

International Year of the Child.
Printed by Heraclio Fournier, S.A., Spain. Panes of 20 (5x4). Designed by Arieh Glaser.

1979, May 4 **Photo.** ***Perf. 14***

84 G13 80c **multicolored** *(2,251,623)* .35 .35
First day cover 1.25
Inscription block of 4 1.60 —
85 G13 1.10fr **multicolored** *(2,220,463)* .65 .65
First day cover 1.75
Inscription block of 4 2.75 —
First day cover, #84-85 1.25
Panes of 20, #84-85 20.00

First day covers of Nos. 84-85 total 176,120.

Namibia Type of UN

1979, Oct. 5 **Litho.** ***Perf. 13½***

86 A176 1.10fr **multicolored** *(1,229,830)* .50 .50
First day cover *(134,160)* 1.25
Inscription block of 4 2.25 —

International Court of Justice, Scales — G14

International Court of Justice, The Hague, Netherlands.
Printed by Setelipaino, Finland. Panes of 50. Designed by Kyohei Maeno.

1979, Nov. 9 **Litho.** ***Perf. 13x13½***

87 G14 80c **multicolored** *(1,123,193)* .40 .40
First day cover 1.00
Inscription block of 4 1.75 —
88 G14 1.10fr **multicolored** *(1,063,067)* .60 .60
First day cover 1.25
First day cover, #87-88 1.75
Inscription block of 4 2.75 —

First day covers of Nos. 87-88 total 158,170.

New Economic Order Type of UN

1980, Jan. 11 **Litho.** ***Perf. 15x14½***

89 A179 80c **multicolored** *(1,315,918)* .85 .85
First day cover *(176,250)* 1.00
Inscription block of 4 3.50 —

Women's Year Emblem — G15

United Nations Decade for Women.
Printed by Questa Colour Security Printers, United Kingdom. Panes of 50. Designed by M.A. Munnawar.

1980, Mar. 7 **Litho.** ***Perf. 14½x15***

90 G15 40c **multicolored** *(1,265,221)* .30 .30
First day cover 1.00
Inscription block of 4 1.40 —
91 G15 70c **multicolored** *(1,240,375)* .70 .70
First day cover 1.10
First day cover, #90-91 1.25
Inscription block of 4 3.50 —

First day covers of Nos. 90-91 total 204,350.

Peace-keeping Operations Type of UN

1980, May 16 **Litho.** ***Perf. 14x13***

92 A181 1.10fr **blue & green** *(1,335,391)* .85 .75
First day cover *(184,700)* 1.00
Inscription block of 4 3.50 —

35th Anniversary Type of UN and Dove and "35" — G16

35th Anniversary of the United Nations.
Printed by Ashton-Potter Ltd., Canada. Panes of 50. Designed by Gidon Sagi (40c), Cemalattin Mutver (70c).

1980, June 26 **Litho.** ***Perf. 13x13½***

93 G16 40c **blue green & black** *(1,462,005)* .35 .30
First day cover 1.00
Inscription block of 4 1.40 —
94 A183 70c **multicolored** *(1,444,639)* .65 .60
First day cover 1.00
First day cover, #93-94 1.50
Inscription block of 4 3.00 —

Souvenir Sheet
Imperf

95 Sheet of 2 *(1,235,200)* .70 .70
a. G16 40c **blue green & black** .25 —
b. A183 70c **multicolored** .45 —
First day cover 1.00

First day covers of Nos. 93-95 total 379,800.

ECOSOC Type of UN and

Family Climbing Line Graph — G17

Printed by Ashton-Potter Ltd., Canada. Panes of 50. Designed by Eliezer Weishoff (40c), A. Medina Medina (70c).

1980, Nov. 21 **Litho.** ***Perf. 13½x13***

96 A186 40c **multicolored** *(986,435)* .30 .25
First day cover 1.00
Inscription block of 4 1.25 —
97 G17 70c **multicolored** *(1,016,462)* .60 .50
First day cover 1.00
First day cover #96-97 1.50
Inscription block of 4 2.50 —

Economic and Social Council.
First day covers of Nos. 96-97 total 210,460.

Palestinian Rights

Printed by Courvoisier S.A., Switzerland. Panes of 50. Designed by David Dewhurst.

1981, Jan. 30 **Photo.** ***Perf. 12x11½***

98 A188 80c **multicolored** *(1,031,737)* .55 .50
First day cover *(117,480)* 1.00
Inscription block of 4 2.75 —

International Year of the Disabled.

Printed by Heraclio Fournier S.A., Spain. Panes of 50. Designed by G.P. Van der Hyde (40c) and Sophia van Heeswijk (1.50fr).

1981, Mar. 6 **Photo.** ***Perf. 14***

99 A190 40c **black & blue** *(1,057,909)* .25 .25
First day cover 1.00
Inscription block of 4 1.00 —
100 V4 1.50fr **black & red** *(994,748)* 1.00 1.00
First day cover 1.25
First day cover, #99-100 1.75
Inscription block of 4 4.00 —

First day covers of Nos. 99-100 total 202,853.

Art Type of UN

1981, Apr. 15 **Photo.** ***Perf. 11½***
Granite Paper

101 A191 80c **multicolored** *(1,128,782)* .80 .80
First day cover *(121,383)* 1.00
Inscription block of 4 3.75 —

Energy Type of 1981

1981, May 29 **Litho.** ***Perf. 13***

102 A192 1.10fr **multicolored** *(1,096,806)* .75 .75
First day cover *(113,700)* 1.25
Inscription block of 4 3.50 —

Volunteers Program Type and

Symbols of Science, Agriculture and Industry — G18

Printed by Walsall Security Printers, Ltd., United Kingdom. Panes of 50.
Designed by Gabriele Nussgen (40c), Bernd Mirbach (70c).

1981, Nov. 13 **Litho.**

103 A194 40c **multicolored** *(1,032,700)* .45 .45
First day cover 1.00
Inscription block of 4 2.25 —
104 G18 70c **multicolored** *(1,123,672)* .90 .90
First day cover 1.00
First day cover, #103-104 1.50
Inscription block of 4 4.25 —

First day covers of Nos. 103-104 total 190,667.

Fight against Apartheid G19

Flower of Flags G20

Printed by Courvoisier, S.A., Switzerland. Panes of 50. Designed by Tomas Savrda (30c); Dietmar Kowall (1fr).

1982, Jan. 22			*Perf. 11½x12*	
105 G19	30c	**multicolored** *(3,000,000)+*	.25	.20
		First day cover		1.00
		Inscription block of 4	1.10	—
106 G20	1fr	**multicolored** *(3,000,000)+*	.80	.70
		First day cover		1.00
		First day cover, #105-106		1.25
		Inscription block of 4	3.25	—

First day covers of Nos. 105-106 total 199,347.

Human Environment Type of UN and:

Sun and Leaves — G21

10th Anniversary of United Nations Environment Program.
Printed by Joh. Enschede en Zonen, Netherlands. Panes of 50. Designed by Sybille Brunner (40c); Philine Hartert (1.20fr).

1982, Mar. 19		Litho.	*Perf. 13½x13*	
107 G21	40c	**multicolored** *(948,743)*	.30	.25
		First day cover		1.00
		Inscription block of 4	1.50	—
108 A199	1.20fr	**multicolored** *(901,096)*	1.10	1.10
		First day cover		1.10
		First day cover, #107-108		1.40
		Inscription block of 4	5.25	—

First day covers of Nos. 107-108 total 190,155.

Outer Space Type of UN and:

Satellite, Applications of Space Technology — G22

Exploration and Peaceful Uses of Outer Space.
Printed by Enschede. Panes of 50. Designed by Wiktor C. Nerwinski (80c) and George Hamori (1fr).

1982, June 11		Litho.	*Perf. 13x13½*	
109 A201	80c	**multicolored** *(964,593)*	.60	.60
		First day cover		1.00
		Inscription block of 4	3.00	—
110 G22	1fr	**multicolored** *(898,367)*	.80	.80
		First day cover		1.25
		First day cover, #109-110		1.50
		Inscription block of 4	3.75	—

First day covers of Nos. 109-110 total 205,815.

Conservation & Protection of Nature

1982, Nov. 19		Photo.	*Perf. 14*	
111 A202	40c	Bird *(928,143)*	.45	.40
		First day cover		1.00
		Inscription block of 4	2.10	—
112 A202	1.50fr	Reptile *(847,173)*	1.10	1.10
		First day cover		1.25
		First day cover, #111-112		1.75
		Inscription block of 4	5.25	—

First day covers of Nos. 111-112 total 198,504.

World Communications Year

1983, Jan. 28		Litho.	*Perf. 13*	
113 A204	1.20fr	**multicolored** *(894,025)*	1.25	1.10
		First day cover *(131,075)*		1.25
		Inscription block of 4	5.25	—

Safety at Sea Type of UN and

G23

Designed by Valentin Wurnitsch (A22).

1983, Mar. 18		Litho.	*Perf. 14½*	
114 A205	40c	**multicolored** *(892,365)*	.40	.40
		First day cover		1.00
		Inscription block of 4	1.75	—
115 G23	80c	**multicolored** *(882,720)*	.80	.80
		First day cover		1.00
		First day cover, #114-115		1.50
		Inscription block of 4	3.50	—

First day covers of Nos. 114-115 total 219,592.

World Food Program

1983, Apr. 22		Engr.	*Perf. 13½*	
116 A207	1.50fr	**blue** *(876,591)*	1.25	1.10
		First day cover		1.25
		Inscription block of 4	5.25	—

Trade Type of UN and

G24

Designed by Wladyslaw Brykczynski (A23).

1983, June 6		Litho.	*Perf. 14*	
117 A208	80c	**multicolored** *(902,495)*	.50	.50
		First day cover		1.00
		Inscription block of 4	2.50	—
118 G24	1.10fr	**multicolored** *(921,424)*	.90	.90
		First day cover		1.00
		First day cover, #117-118		1.40
		Inscription block of 4	4.00	—

First day covers of Nos. 117-118 total 146,507.

Homo Humus Humanitas — G25

Right to Create — G26

35th Anniversary of the Universal Declaration of Human Rights.
Printed by Government Printing Office, Austria. Designed by Friedensreich Hundertwasser, Austria. Panes of 16 (4x4).

1983, Dec. 9		Photo. & Engr.	*Perf. 13½*	
119 G25	40c	**multicolored** *(1,770,921)*	.45	.45
		First day cover		1.00
		Inscription block of 4	2.00	—
120 G26	1.20fr	**multicolored** *(1,746,735)*	.95	.90
		First day cover		1.10
		Inscription block of 4	4.25	—
		First day cover, #119-120		1.40
		Panes of 16, #119-120	22.50	

First day covers of Nos. 119-120 total 315,052.

International Conference on Population Type

1984, Feb. 3		Litho.	*Perf. 14*	
121 A212	1.20fr	**multicolored** *(776,879)*	.90	.90
		First day cover *(105,377)*		1.00
		Inscription block of 4	4.00	—

Fishing G27

Women Farm Workers, Africa — G28

World Food Day, Oct. 16
Printed by Walsall Security Printers, Ltd., United Kingdom. Panes of 50. Designed by Adth Vanooijen, Netherlands.

1984, Mar. 15		Litho.	*Perf. 14½*	
122 G27	50c	**multicolored** *(744,506)*	.30	.30
		First day cover		1.00
		Inscription block of 4	1.60	—
123 G28	80c	**multicolored** *(784,047)*	.60	.55
		First day cover		1.25
		First day cover, #122-123		1.75
		Inscription block of 4	2.75	—

First day covers of Nos. 122-123 total 155,234.

Valletta, Malta — G29

Los Glaciares National Park, Argentina — G30

World Heritage
Printed by Harrison and Sons, United Kingdom. Panes of 50. Designs adapted by Rocco J. Callari, US, and Thomas Lee, China.

1984, Apr. 18		Litho.	*Perf. 14*	
124 G29	50c	**multicolored** *(763,627)*	.60	.60
		First day cover		1.00
		Inscription block of 4	2.50	—
125 G30	70c	**multicolored** *(784,489)*	.85	.85
		First day cover		1.25
		First day cover, #124-125		1.75
		Inscription block of 4	4.50	—

First day covers of Nos. 124-125 total 164,498.

G31

G32

Future for Refugees
Printed by Courvoisier. Panes of 50. Designed by Hans Erni, Switzerland.

1984, May 29 **Photo.** ***Perf. 11½***
126 G31 35c **multicolored** *(880,762)* .30 .30
First day cover 1.00
Inscription block of 4 1.50 —
127 G32 1.50fr **multicolored** *(829,895)* 1.10 1.10
First day cover 1.25
First day cover, #126-127 1.75
Inscription block of 4 5.00 —

First day covers of Nos. 126-127 total 170,306.

International Youth Year — G33

Printed by Waddingtons Ltd., United Kingdom. Panes of 50. Designed by Eliezer Weishoff, Israel.

1984, Nov. 15 **Litho.** ***Perf. 13½***
128 G33 1.20fr **multicolored** *(755,622)* 1.25 1.25
First day cover *(96,680)* 1.00
Inscription block of 4 5.50 —

ILO Type of UN and

ILO Turin Center — G34

Printed by the Government Printing Bureau, Japan. Panes of 50. Engraved by Mamoru Iwakuni and Hiroshi Ozaki, Japan (#129) and adapted from photographs by Rocco J. Callari, US, and Thomas Lee, China (#130).

1985, Feb. 1 **Engr.** ***Perf. 13½***
129 A220 80c **blue** *(654,431)* .70 .70
First day cover 1.00
Inscription block of 4 3.00 —
130 G34 1.20fr U Thant Pavilion *(609,493)* 1.10 1.10
First day cover 1.50
First day cover, #129-130 2.25
Inscription block of 4 4.75 —

First day covers of Nos. 129-130 total 118,467.

UN University Type

1985, Mar. 15 **Photo.** ***Perf. 13½***
131 A221 50c Pastoral scene, advanced communications *(625,087)* .65 .60
First day cover 1.00
Inscription block of 4 2.75 —
132 A221 80c like No. 131 *(712,674)* 1.10 1.00
First day cover 1.25
First day cover, #131-132 1.75
Inscription block of 4 4.50 —

First day covers of Nos. 131-132 total 93,324.

Flying Postman — G35

Interlocked Peace Doves — G36

Printed by Carl Ueberreuter Druck and Verlag M. Salzer, Austria. Panes of 50. Designed by Arieh Glaser, Israel (#133), and Carol Sliwka, Poland (#134).

1985, May 10 **Litho.** ***Perf. 14***
133 G35 20c **multicolored** *(2,000,000)+* .25 .20
First day cover 1.00
Inscription block of 4 1.25 —
134 G36 1.20fr **multicolored** *(2,000,000)+* 1.50 1.50
First day cover 1.50
First day cover, #133-134 2.00
Inscription block of 4 6.50 —

First day covers of Nos. 133-134 total 103,165.

40th Anniversary Type

Designed by Rocco J. Callari, U.S., and Thomas Lee, China (No. 137).

1985, June 26 **Photo.** ***Perf. 12 x 11½***
135 A224 50c **multicolored** *(764,924)* .60 .60
First day cover 1.00
Inscription block of 4 2.50 —
136 A225 70c **multicolored** *(779,074)* .90 .90
First day cover 1.25
First day cover, #135-136 2.00
Inscription block of 4 4.00 —

Souvenir Sheet

Imperf

137 Sheet of 2 *(498,041)* 2.25 2.25
a. A224 50c **multicolored** .85 —
b. A225 70c **multicolored** 1.10 —
First day cover 1.25

First day covers of Nos. 135-137 total 252,418.

UNICEF Child Survival Campaign Type

Printed by the Government Printing Bureau, Japan. Panes of 50. Designed by Mel Harris, United Kingdom (#138) and Adth Vanooijen, Netherlands (#139).

1985, Nov. 22 **Photo. & Engr.** ***Perf. 13½***
138 A226 50c Three girls *(657,409)* .40 .40
First day cover 1.00
Inscription block of 4 2.00 —
139 A226 1.20fr Infant drinking *(593,568)* 1.10 1.10
First day cover 1.25
First day cover, #138-139 1.75
Inscription block of 4 4.50 —

First day covers of Nos. 138-139 total 217,696.

Africa in Crisis Type

Printed by Helio Courvoisier, Switzerland. Panes of 50. Designed by Alemayehou Gabremedhiu, Ethiopia.

1986, Jan. 31 **Photo.** ***Perf. 11½x12***
140 A227 1.40fr Mother, hungry children *(590,576)* 1.25 1.25
First day cover *(80,159)* 2.00
Inscription block of 4 5.25 —

UN Development Program Type

Forestry. Printed by the Government Printing Bureau, Japan. Pane of 40, 2 blocks of 4 horizontal and 5 blocks of 4 vertical. Designed by Thomas Lee, China.

1986, Mar. 14 **Photo.** ***Perf. 13½***
141 A228 35c Erosion control *(547,567)* 1.75 1.60
142 A228 35c Logging *(547,567)* 1.75 1.60
143 A228 35c Lumber transport *(547,567)* 1.75 1.60
144 A228 35c Nursery *(547,567)* 1.75 1.60
a. Block of 4, #141-144 7.50 7.00
First day cover, #144a 8.50
First day cover, #141-144, each 2.50
Inscription block of 4, #144a 8.50 —
Pane of 40, #141-144 80.00

No. 144a has a continuous design.

First day covers of Nos. 141-144 total 200,212.

Dove and Sun — G37

Printed by Questa Color Security Printers, Ltd., United Kingdom. Panes of 50. Designed by Ramon Alcantara Rodriguez, Mexico.

1986, Mar. 14 **Litho.** ***Perf. 15x14½***
145 G37 5c **multicolored** *(2,000,000)+* .20 .20
First day cover *(58,908)* 1.00
Inscription block of 4 .50 —

Stamp Collecting Type

Designs: 50c, UN Human Rights stamp. 80c, UN stamps. Printed by the Swedish Post Office, Sweden. Panes of 50. Designed by Czeslaw Slania and Ingalill Axelsson, Sweden.

1986, May 22 **Engr.** ***Perf. 12½***
146 A229 50c **dark green & henna brown** *(722,015)* 1.25 .90
First day cover 1.50
Inscription block of 4 5.50 —
147 A229 80c **dark green & yellow orange** *(750,945)* 1.75 1.40
First day cover 1.50
First day cover, #146-147 1.75
Inscription block of 4 7.50 —

First day covers of Nos. 146-147 total 137,653.

Flags and Globe as Dove — G38

Peace in French — G39

International Peace Year. Printed by the Government Printing Bureau, Japan. Panes of 50. Designed by Renato Ferrini, Italy (#148), and Salahattin Kanidinc, US (#149).

1986, June 20 **Photo. & Embossed** ***Perf. 13½***
148 G38 45c **multicolored** *(620,978)* .70 .70
First day cover 1.00
Inscription block of 4 3.00 —
149 G39 1.40fr **multicolored** *(559,658)* 1.50 1.50
First day cover 1.60
First day cover, #148-149 3.00
Inscription block of 4 6.50 —

First day covers of Nos. 148-149 total 123,542.

WFUNA Anniversary Type
Souvenir Sheet

Printed by Johann Enschede and Sons, Netherlands. Designed by Rocco J. Callari, US.

Designs: 35c, Abstract by Benigno Gomez, Honduras. 45c, Abstract by Alexander Calder (1898-1976), US. 50c, Abstract by Joan Miro (b. 1893), Spain. 70c, Sextet with Dove, by Ole Hamann, Denmark.

1986, Nov. 14 **Litho.** ***Perf. 13x13½***
150 Sheet of 4 *(478,833)* 4.00 3.75
a. A232 35c **multicolored** .55 —
b. A232 45c **multicolored** .75 —
c. A232 50c **multicolored** .95 —
d. A232 70c **multicolored** 1.25 —
First day cover *(58,452)* 2.00

No. 150 has inscribed margin picturing UN and WFUNA emblems.

Trygve Lie Type

1987, Jan. 30 Photo. & Engr. *Perf. 13½*

151 A233 1.40fr **multicolored** *(516,605)* 1.10 1.10
First day cover *(76,152)* 1.50
Inscription block of 4 5.50 —

Sheaf of Colored Bands, by Georges Mathieu — G40

Armillary Sphere, Palais des Nations — G41

Printed by Helio Courvoisier, Switzerland (#152), and the Government Printing Bureau, Japan (#153). Panes of 50. Designed by Georges Mathieu (#152) and Rocco J. Callari (#153), US.

Photo., Photo. & Engr. (#153)

1987, Jan. 30 *Perf. 11½x12, 13½*

152 G40 90c **multicolored** *(1,600,000)+* .65 .65
First day cover 1.00
Inscription block of 4 3.00 —
153 G41 1.40fr **multicolored** *(1,600,000)+* 1.25 1.25
First day cover 1.00
First day cover, #152-153 2.00
Inscription block of 4 5.00 —

First day covers of Nos. 152-153 total 85,737.

Shelter for the Homeless Type

Designs: 50c, Cement-making and brick-making. 90c, Interior construction and decorating.

1987, Mar. 13 Litho. *Perf. 13½x12½*

154 A234 50c **multicolored** *(564,445)* .50 .45
First day cover 1.00
Inscription block of 4 2.50 —
155 A234 90c **multicolored** *(526,646)* 1.00 .90
First day cover 1.10
First day cover, #154-155 2.00
Inscription block of 4 4.25 —

First day covers of Nos. 154-155 total 100,366.

Fight Drug Abuse Type

Designs: 80c, Mother and child. 1.20fr, Workers in rice paddy.

1987, June 12 Litho. *Perf. 14½x15*

156 A235 80c **multicolored** *(634,776)* .50 .50
First day cover 1.25
Inscription block of 4 3.00 —
157 A235 1.20fr **multicolored** *(609,475)* 1.00 1.00
First day cover 1.75
First day cover, #156-157 2.50
Inscription block of 4 4.75 —

First day covers of Nos. 156-157 total 95,247.

UN Day Type

Designed by Elisabeth von Janota-Bzowski (35c) and Fritz Oerter (50c).
Designs: Multinational people in various occupations.

1987, Oct. 23 Litho. *Perf. 14½x15*

158 A236 35c **multicolored** *(1,114,756)* .55 .55
First day cover 1.60
Inscription block of 4 2.50 —
159 A236 50c **multicolored** *(1,117,464)* .80 .80
First day cover 1.90
Inscription block of 4 3.50 —
First day cover, #158-159 2.50
Panes of 12, #158-159 15.00

Immunize Every Child Type

Designs: 90c, Whooping cough. 1.70fr, Tuberculosis.

1987, Nov. 20 Litho. *Perf. 15x14½*

160 A237 90c **multicolored** *(634,614)* 1.50 1.40
First day cover 1.00
Inscription block of 4 6.25 —
161 A237 1.70fr **multicolored** *(607,725)* 2.75 2.50
First day cover 1.25
First day cover, #160-161 2.50
Inscription block of 4 11.50 —

IFAD Type

Designs: 35c, Flocks, dairy products. 1.40fr, Fruit.

1988, Jan. 29 Litho. *Perf. 13½*

162 A238 35c **multicolored** *(524,817)* .40 .35
First day cover 1.00
Inscription block of 4 1.90 —
163 A238 1.40fr **multicolored** *(499,103)* 1.40 1.25
First day cover 1.50
First day cover, #162-163 2.00
Inscription block of 4 7.00 —

G42

Printed by Heraclio Fournier, S.A., Spain. Panes of 50. Designed by Bjorn Wiinblad, Denmark.

1988, Jan. 29 Photo. *Perf. 14*

164 G42 50c **multicolored** *(1,600,000)+* .80 .80
First day cover 2.00
Inscription block of 4 3.75 —

Survival of the Forests Type

Pine forest: 50c, Treetops, mountains. 1.10fr, Lake, tree trunks. Printed se-tenant in a continuous design.

1988, Mar. 18 Litho. *Perf. 14x15*

165 A240 50c **multicolored** *(728,569)* 1.50 1.40
First day cover 4.00
166 A240 1.10fr **multicolored** *(728,569)* 4.00 3.75
First day cover 6.00
a. Pair, #165-166 5.50 5.25
First day cover, #166a 10.00
Inscription block of 4, 2 #166a 12.50 —
Pane of 12, #165-166 30.00

Intl. Volunteer Day Type

Designed by Christopher Magadini, US.
Designs: 80c, Agriculture, vert. 90c, Veterinary medicine.

1988, May 6 Litho. *Perf. 13x14, 14x13*

167 A241 80c **multicolored** *(612,166)* .80 .80
First day cover 1.50
Inscription block of 4 4.00 —
168 A241 90c **multicolored** *(467,334)* 1.00 1.00
First day cover 1.75
First day cover, #167-168 3.50
Inscription block of 4 4.25 —

Health in Sports Type

Paintings by LeRoy Neiman, American sports artist: 50c, Soccer, vert. 1.40fr, Swimming.

1988, June 17 Litho. *Perf. 13½x13, 13x13½*

169 A242 50c **multicolored** *(541,421)* .40 .35
First day cover 1.25
Inscription block of 4 3.00 —
170 A242 1.40fr **multicolored** *(475,445)* 1.40 1.25
First day cover 2.40
First day cover, #169-170 3.00
Inscription block of 4 10.00 —

Universal Declaration of Human Rights 40th Anniv. Type

1988, Dec. 9 Photo. & Engr. *Perf. 12*

171 A243 90c **multicolored** *(745,508)* .75 .75
First day cover 2.50
Inscription block of 4 3.25 —

Souvenir Sheet

172 A243 2fr **multicolored** *(517,453)* 3.00 3.00
First day cover 4.00

World Bank Type

1989, Jan. 27 Litho. *Perf. 13x14*

173 A244 80c Telecommunications *(524,056)* 1.00 1.00
First day cover 1.50
Inscription block of 4 4.50 —
174 A244 1.40fr Industry *(488,058)* 2.25 2.25
First day cover 2.40
First day cover, #173-174 3.50
Inscription block of 4 9.50 —

First day covers of Nos. 173-174 total 111,004.

Peace-Keeping Force Type

1989, Mar. 17 *Perf. 14x13½*

175 A245 90c **multicolored** *(684,566)* 1.00 1.00
First day cover *(52,463)* 1.00
Inscription block of 4 5.00 —

World Weather Watch Type

Satellite photographs: 90c, Europe under the influence of Arctic air. 1.10fr, Surface temperatures of sea, ice and land surrounding the Kattegat between Denmark and Sweden.

1989, Apr. 21 Litho. *Perf. 13x14*

176 A247 90c **multicolored** *(864,409)* 1.25 1.10
First day cover 1.50
Inscription block of 4 5.50 —
177 A247 1.10fr **multicolored** *(853,556)* 2.00 1.90
First day cover 1.90
First day cover, #176-177 3.00
Inscription block of 4 9.00 —

First day covers of Nos. 176-177 total 83,343.

Offices in Geneva, 10th Anniv.
G43 G44

Printed by Government Printing Office, Austria. Panes of 25. Designed by Anton Lehmden (50c) and Arik Brauer (2fr), Austria.

Photo., Photo. & Engr. (2fr)

1989, Aug. 23 *Perf. 14*

178 G43 50c **multicolored** *(605,382)* 1.10 1.10
First day cover 1.25
Inscription block of 4 5.00 —
179 G44 2fr **multicolored** *(538,140)* 3.50 3.25
First day cover 2.75
Inscription block of 4 15.00 —
First day cover, #178-179 3.25
Panes of 25, #178-179 110.00

First day covers of Nos. 178-179 total 83,304.

Human Rights Type of 1989

Printed by Johann Enschede and Sons, the Netherlands. Panes of 12+12 se-tenant labels containing Articles 3 (35c) or 4 (80c) inscribed in English, French or German. Designed by Rocco J. Callari and Robert Stein, US.

Artwork: 35c, Young Mother Sewing, by Mary Cassatt. 80c, The Unknown Slave, sculpture by Albert Mangones.

1989, Nov. 17 Litho. *Perf. 13½*

180 A250 35c **multicolored** *(1,923,818)* .35 .30
First day cover 1.25
Inscription block of 3 + 3 labels 1.60 —
181 A250 80c **multicolored** *(1,917,953)* 1.00 .90
First day cover 3.00
Inscription block of 3 + 3 labels 4.50 —
First day cover, #180-181 4.50
Panes of 12, #180-181 17.50

First day covers of Nos. 180-181 total 134,469.
See Nos. 193-194, 209-210, 234-235.

Intl. Trade Center Type

1990, Feb. 2 Litho. *Perf. 14½x15*

182 A251 1.50fr **multicolored** *(409,561)* 2.50 2.40
First day cover *(61,098)* 3.50
Inscription block of 4 11.00 —

G45

Printed by Heraclio Fournier, S.A., Spain. Designed by Guy Breniaux, France and Elizabeth White, US.

1990, Feb. 2 Photo. *Perf. 14x13½*

183 G45 5fr **multicolored** *(1,600,000)+* 5.00 4.75
First day cover *(54,462)* 7.00
Inscription block of 4 21.00 —

G46

Fight AIDS Worldwide - G46a

Fight AIDS Type

Designed by Jacek Tofil, Poland (50c) and Lee Keun Moon, Korea (80c).

Designs: 50c, "SIDA." 80c, Proportional drawing of man like the illustration by Leonardo da Vinci.

1990, Mar. 16 Litho. *Perf. 13½x12½*

No.	Type	Denom.	Description	Unused	Used
184	G46	50c	**multicolored** *(480,625)*	1.10	1.10
			First day cover		1.25
			Inscription block of 4	5.00	—
185	G46a	80c	**multicolored** *(602,721)*	1.75	1.50
			First day cover		1.50
			First day cover, #184-185		2.00
			Inscription block of 4	7.75	—

First day covers of Nos. 184-185 total 108,364.

Medicinal Plants Type

1990, May 4 Photo. Granite Paper *Perf. 11½*

No.	Type	Denom.	Description	Unused	Used
186	A253	90c	Plumeria rubra *(625,522)*	1.10	1.10
			First day cover		1.40
			Inscription block of 4	5.00	—
187	A253	1.40fr	Cinchona officinalis *(648,619)*	2.25	2.00
			First day cover		2.25
			First day cover, #186-187		3.50
			Inscription block of 4	9.50	—

First day covers of Nos. 186-187 total 114,062.

UN 45th Anniv. Type

Designed by Fritz Henry Oerter and Ruth Schmidthammer, Federal Republic of Germany (90c), Michiel Mertens, Belgium (1.10fr), Robert Stein, US (No. 190).

"45," emblem and: 90c, Symbols of clean environment, transportation and industry. 1.10fr, Dove in silhouette.

1990, June 26 Litho. *Perf. 14½x13*

No.	Type	Denom.	Description	Unused	Used
188	A254	90c	**multicolored** *(557,253)*	1.25	1.25
			First day cover		1.40
			Inscription block of 4	5.25	—
189	A254	1.10fr	**multicolored** *(519,635)*	2.25	2.00
			First day cover		2.00
			First day cover, #188-189		3.00
			Inscription block of 4	9.50	—

Souvenir Sheet

No.	Type	Denom.	Description	Unused	Used
190			Sheet of 2, #188-189 *(401,027)*	6.50	5.00
			First day cover		4.50

First day covers of Nos. 188-190 total 148,975.

Crime Prevention Type

1990, Sept. 13 Photo. *Perf. 14*

No.	Type	Denom.	Description	Unused	Used
191	A255	50c	Official corruption *(494,876)*	1.50	1.40
			First day cover		1.40
			Inscription block of 4	5.50	—
192	A255	2fr	Environmental crime *(417,033)*	3.50	3.25
			First day cover		3.25
			First day cover, #191-192		4.50
			Inscription block of 4	15.00	—

First day covers of Nos. 191-192 total 76,605.

Human Rights Type of 1989

Panes of 12+12 se-tenant labels containing Articles 9 (35c) or 10 (90c) inscribed in French, German or English.

Artwork: 35c, The Prison Courtyard by Vincent Van Gogh. 90c, Katho's Son Redeems the Evil Doer From Execution by Albrecht Durer.

1990, Nov. 16 Litho. *Perf. 13½*

No.	Type	Denom.	Description	Unused	Used
193	A250	35c	**multicolored** *(1,578,828)*	.50	.50
			First day cover		1.25
			Inscription block of 3 + 3 labels	1.75	—
194	A250	90c	**black & brown** *(1,540,200)*	1.40	1.40
			First day cover		1.50
			Inscription block of 3 + 3 labels	4.50	—
			First day cover, #193-194		3.50
			Panes of 12, #193-194	22.50	

First day covers of Nos. 193-194 total 100,282.

Economic Commission for Europe Type

1991, Mar. 15 Litho. *Perf. 14*

No.	Type	Denom.	Description	Unused	Used
195	A256	90c	Owl, gull *(643,143)+*	1.40	1.25
			First day cover		2.00
196	A256	90c	Bittern, otter *(643,143)+*	1.40	1.25
			First day cover		2.00
197	A256	90c	Swan, lizard *(643,143)+*	1.40	1.25
			First day cover		2.00
198	A256	90c	Great crested grebe *(643,143)+*	1.40	1.25
			First day cover		2.00
a.			Block of 4, #195-198	6.00	5.50
			First day cover, #198a		5.50
			Inscription block of 4, #198a	6.50	—
			Pane of 40, #195-198	52.50	

First day covers of Nos. 195-198a total 75,759.

Namibian Independence Type

1991, May 10 Litho. *Perf. 14*

No.	Type	Denom.	Description	Unused	Used
199	A257	70c	Mountains *(328,014)*	1.50	1.40
			First day cover		1.60
			Inscription block of 4	6.25	—
200	A257	90c	Baobab tree *(395,362)*	2.50	2.25
			First day cover		2.25
			First day cover, #199-200		5.00
			Inscription block of 4	11.50	—

First day covers of Nos. 199-200 total 94,201.

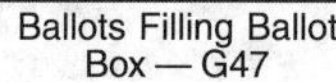

Ballots Filling Ballot Box — G47

UN Emblem — G48

Printed by House of Questa, United Kingdom. Designed by Ran Banda Mawilmada, Sri Lanka (80c), Maurice Gouju, France (1.50fr).

1991, May 10 Litho. *Perf. 15x14½*

No.	Type	Denom.	Description	Unused	Used
201	G46	80c	**multicolored** *(1,600,000)+*	1.60	1.50
			First day cover		1.75
			Inscription block of 4	6.50	—
202	G47	1.50fr	**multicolored** *(1,600,000)+*	3.00	2.75
			First day cover		3.25
			First day cover, #201-202		3.75
			Inscription block of 4	12.50	—

First day covers of Nos. 201-202 total 77,590.

G49

Rights of the Child — G50

Printed by The House of Questa. Panes of 50. Designed by Ryuta Nakajima, Japan (80c) and David Popper, Switzerland (1.10fr).

1991, June 14 Litho. *Perf. 14½*

No.	Type	Denom.	Description	Unused	Used
203	G48	80c	Hands holding infant *(469,962)*	1.50	1.40
			First day cover		1.75
			Inscription block of 4	6.25	—
204	G49	1.10fr	Children, flowers *(494,382)*	2.25	2.00
			First day cover		2.25
			First day cover, #203-204		3.25
			Inscription block of 4	9.50	—

First day covers of Nos. 203-204 total 97,732.

G51

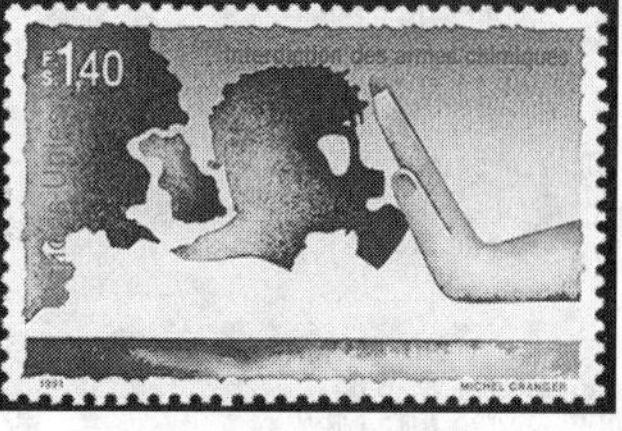

Banning of Chemical Weapons G52

Printed by Heraclio Fournier S.A. Panes of 50. Designed by Oscar Asboth, Austria (80c), Michel Granger, France (1.40fr).

1991, Sept. 11 Litho. *Perf. 13½*

No.	Type	Denom.	Description	Unused	Used
205	G50	80c	**multicolored** *(345,658)*	2.00	1.60
			First day cover		1.75
			Inscription block of 4	8.50	
206	G51	1.40fr	**multicolored** *(366,076)*	3.50	3.00
			First day cover		2.50
			First day cover, #205-206		3.50
			Inscription block of 4	14.50	—

First day covers of Nos. 205-206 total 91,887.

UN Postal Administration, 40th Anniv. Type

1991, Oct. 24 *Perf. 14x15*

No.	Type	Denom.	Description	Unused	Used
207	A263	50c	UN NY No. 7 *(506,839)*	1.25	1.10
			First day cover		1.25
			Inscription block of 4	5.00	—
208	A263	1.60fr	UN NY No. 10 *(580,493)*	2.75	2.50
			First day cover		3.00
			Inscription block of 4	12.00	—
			First day cover, #207-208		3.25
			Panes of 25, #207-208	75.00	

First day covers of Nos. 207-208 total 88,784.

Human Rights Type of 1989

Panes of 12+12 se-tenant labels containing Articles 15 (50c) or 16 (90c) inscribed in French, German or English.

Artwork: 50c, Early Morning in Ro...1925, by Paul Klee. 90c, Marriage of Giovanni (?) Arnolfini and Giovanna Cenami (?), by Jan Van Eyck.

1991, Nov. 20 Litho. *Perf. 13½*

No.	Type	Denom.	Description	Unused	Used
209	A250	50c	**multicolored** *(1,295,172)*	.90	.90
			First day cover		1.25
			Inscription block of 3 + 3 labels	2.75	—
210	A250	90c	**multicolored** *(1,324,091)*	1.50	1.40
			First day cover		2.00
			Inscription block of 3 + 3 labels	5.00	—
			First day cover, #209-210		2.75
			Panes of 12, #209-210	27.50	

First day covers of Nos. 209-210 total 139,904.

World Heritage Type of 1984

Designs: 50c, Sagarmatha Natl. Park, Nepal. 1.10fr, Stonehenge, United Kingdom.

1992, Jan. 24 Litho. *Perf. 13*

Size: 35x28mm

No.	Type	Denom.	Description	Unused	Used
211	G29	50c	**multicolored** *(468,647)*	1.25	1.10
			First day cover		1.25
			Inscription block of 4	5.25	—
212	G29	1.10fr	**multicolored** *(369,345)*	2.50	2.25
			First day cover		2.25
			First day cover, #211-212		3.00
			Inscription block of 4	11.00	—

First day covers of Nos. 211-212 total 77,034.

G53

Printed by The House of Questa. Panes of 50. Designed by Nestor Jose Martin, Argentina.

1992, Jan. 24 Litho. *Perf. 15x14½*
213 G53 3fr **multicolored** *(1,600,000)+* 3.75 3.50
First day cover *(36,135)* 4.00
Inscription block of 4 16.00 —

Clean Oceans Type

1992, Mar. 13 Litho. *Perf. 14*
214 A264 80c Ocean surface, diff. *(850,699)* .90 .90
215 A264 80c Ocean bottom, diff. *(850,699)* .90 .90
a. Pair, #214-215 1.80 *2.00*
First day cover, #215a 2.75
First day cover, #214-215, each 1.75
Inscription block of 4, 2 #215a 5.00 —
Pane of 12, #214-215 11.00

First day covers of Nos. 214-215a total 90,725.

Earth Summit Type

Designs: No. 216, Rainbow. No. 217, Two clouds shaped as faces. No. 218, Two sailboats. No. 219, Woman with parasol, boat, flowers.

1992, May 22 Photo. *Perf. 11½*
216 A265 75c **multicolored** *(826,543)* 1.10 1.00
217 A265 75c **multicolored** *(826,543)* 1.10 1.00
218 A265 75c **multicolored** *(826,543)* 1.10 1.00
219 A265 75c **multicolored** *(826,543)* 1.10 1.00
a. Block of 4, #216-219 5.25 5.00
First day cover, #219a 4.00
First day cover, #216-219, each 2.50
Inscription block of 4, #216-219 5.75 —
Pane of 40, #216-219 55.00

First day covers of Nos. 216-219a total 74,629.

Mission to Planet Earth Type

Designs: No. 220, Space station. No. 221, Probes near Jupiter.

1992, Sept. 4 Photo. *Rouletted 8*
Granite Paper
220 A266 1.10fr **multicolored** *(668,241)* 2.50 2.25
221 A266 1.10fr **multicolored** *(668,241)* 2.50 2.25
a. Pair, #220-221 5.00 4.50
First day cover, #221a 5.00
First day cover, #220-221, each 5.50
Inscription block of 4, 2 #220-221 12.00 —
Pane of 10, #220-221 27.50

First day covers of Nos. 220-221 total 76,060.

Science and Technology Type of 1992

Designs: 90c, Doctor, nurse. 1.60fr, Graduate seated before computer.

1992, Oct. 2 Litho. *Perf. 14*
222 A267 90c **multicolored** *(438,943)* 1.50 1.40
First day cover 1.60
Inscription block of 4 6.00 —
223 A267 1.60fr **multicolored** *(400,701)* 3.50 3.00
First day cover 2.50
First day cover, #222-223 3.25
Inscription block of 4 14.00 —

First day covers of Nos. 222-223 total 75,882.

Human Rights Type of 1989

Panes of 12+12 se-tenant labels containing Articles 21 (50c) and 22 (90c) inscribed in French, German or English.

Artwork: 50c, The Oath of the Tennis Court, by Jacques Louis David. 90c, Rocking Chair I, by Henry Moore.

1992, Nov. 20 Litho. *Perf. 13½*
224 A250 50c **multicolored,** *(1,201,788)* 1.00 1.00
First day cover 2.00
Inscription block of 3 + 3 labels 3.25 —
225 A250 90c **multicolored,** *(1,179,294)* 1.75 1.75
First day cover 4.00
Inscription block of 3 + 3 labels 5.50 —
First day cover, #224-225 2.75
Panes of 12, #224-225 30.00

First day covers of Nos. 224-225 total 104,491.

Aging With Dignity Type

Designs: 50c, Older man coaching soccer. 1.60fr, Older man working at computer terminal.

1993, Feb. 5 Litho. *Perf. 13*
226 A270 50c **multicolored** *(483,452)* .75 .75
First day cover 1.00
Inscription block of 4 3.50 —
227 A270 1.60fr **multicolored** *(331,008)* 2.40 2.40
First day cover 2.75
First day cover, #226-227 3.00
Inscription block of 4 10.50 —

First day covers of Nos. 226-227 total 61,361.

Endangered Species Type

Designed by Rocco J. Callari, US, and Betina Ogden, Australia.

Designs: No. 228, Pongidae (gorilla). No. 229, Falco peregrinus (peregrine falcon). No. 230, Trichechus inunguis (Amazonian manatee). No. 231, Panthera uncia (snow leopard).

1993, Mar. 2 Litho. *Perf. 13x12½*
228 A271 80c **multicolored** *(1,200,000)+* 1.10 1.00
229 A271 80c **multicolored** *(1,200,000)+* 1.10 1.00
230 A271 80c **multicolored** *(1,200,000)+* 1.10 1.00
231 A271 80c **multicolored** *(1,200,000)+* 1.10 1.00
a. Block of 4, #228-231 4.50 4.25
First day cover, #231a 5.00
First day cover, #228-231, each 2.00
Inscription block of 4, #228-231 4.50 —
Pane of 16, #228-231 19.00

First day covers of Nos. 228-231a total 75,363.

Healthy Environment Type

1993, May 7 Litho. *Perf. 15x14½*
232 A272 60c **Neighborhood** *(456,304)* 1.10 1.10
First day cover 1.25
Inscription block of 4 4.75 —
233 A272 1fr **Urban skyscrapers** *(392,015)* 2.25 2.00
First day cover 2.00
First day cover, #232-233 3.25
Inscription block of 4 10.00 —

First day covers of Nos. 232-233 total 59,790.

Human Rights Type of 1989

Printed in panes of 12 + 12 se-tenant labels containing Article 27 (50c) and 28 (90c) inscribed in French, German or English.

Artwork: 50c, Three Musicians, by Pablo Picasso. 90c, Voice of Space, by Rene Magritte.

1993, June 11 Litho. *Perf. 13½*
234 A250 50c **multicolored** *(1,166,286)* .90 .90
First day cover 1.25
Inscription block of 3 + 3 labels 2.75 —
235 A250 90c **multicolored** *(1,122,348)* 2.00 1.90
First day cover 2.00
Inscription block of 3 + 3 labels 6.25 —
First day cover, #234-235 3.50
Panes of 12, #234-235 30.00

First day covers of Nos. 234-235 total 83,432.

Intl. Peace Day Type

Denomination at: #236, UL. #237, UR. #238, LL. #239, LR.

1993, Sept. 21 Litho. & Engr. *Rouletted 12½*
236 A274 60c **purple & multi** *(357,760)* 2.25 2.00
237 A274 60c **purple & multi** *(357,760)* 2.25 2.00
238 A274 60c **purple & multi** *(357,760)* 2.25 2.00
239 A274 60c **purple & multi** *(357,760)* 2.25 2.00
a. Block of 4, #236-239 9.00 8.00
First day cover, #239a 5.50
First day cover, #236-239, each 2.50
Inscription block of 4, #239a 9.50 —
Pane of 40, #236-239 85.00

First day covers of Nos. 236-239a total 47,207.

Environment-Climate Type

1993, Oct. 29 Litho. *Perf. 14½*
240 A275 1.10fr Polar bears *(391,593)* 2.50 2.40
241 A275 1.10fr Whale sounding *(391,593)* 2.50 2.40
242 A275 1.10fr Elephant seal *(391,593)* 2.50 2.40
243 A275 1.10fr Penguins *(391,593)* 2.50 2.40
a. Strip of 4, #240-243 10.00 9.75
First day cover, #243a 7.25
First day cover, #240-243, each 6.00
Inscription blockof 8, 2 #243a 22.50 —
Pane of 24, #240-243 52.50

First day covers of Nos. 240-243a total 41,819.

Intl. Year of the Family Type of 1993

Designs: 80c, Parents teaching child to walk. 1fr, Two women and child picking plants.

1994, Feb. 4 Litho. *Perf. 13.1*
244 A276 80c **rose violet & multi** *(535,000)+* 1.25 1.25
First day cover 1.75
Inscription block of 4 5.75 —
245 A276 1fr **brown & multi** *(535,000)+* 1.75 1.75
First day cover 2.00
First day cover, #244-245 3.25
Inscription block of 4 7.25 —

First day covers of Nos. 244-245 total 50,080.

Endangered Species Type of 1993

Designed by Rocco J. Callari (frame) and Leon Parson, US (stamps).

Designs: No. 246, Mexican prairie dog. No. 247, Jabiru. No. 248, Blue whale. No. 249, Golden lion tamarin.

1994, Mar. 18 Litho. *Perf. 12.7*
246 A271 80c **multicolored** *(1,200,000)+* 1.10 1.10
247 A271 80c **multicolored** *(1,200,000)+* 1.10 1.10
248 A271 80c **multicolored** *(1,200,000)+* 1.10 1.10
249 A271 80c **multicolored** *(1,200,000)+* 1.10 1.10
a. Block of 4, #246-249 4.50 4.50
First day cover, #249a 5.50
First day cover, #246-249, each 1.75
Inscription block of 4, #246-249 4.50 —
Pane of 16, #246-249 20.00

First day covers of Nos. 246-249a total 82,043.

Protection for Refugees Type of 1994

Design: 1.20fr, Hand lifting figure over chasm.

1994, Apr. 29 Litho. *Perf. 14.3x14.8*
250 A277 1.20fr **multicolored** *(550,000)+* 2.75 2.50
First day cover *(33,805)* 2.50
Inscription block of 4 12.00 —

Intl. Decade for Natural Disaster Reduction Type of 1994

Earth seen from space, outline map of: No. 251, North America. No. 252, Eurasia. No. 253, South America. No. 254, Australia and South Pacific region.

1994, May 27 Litho. *Perf. 13.9x14.2*
251 A281 60c **multicolored** *(570,000)+* 2.00 1.75
252 A281 60c **multicolored** *(570,000)+* 2.00 1.75
253 A281 60c **multicolored** *(570,000)+* 2.00 1.75
254 A281 60c **multicolored** *(570,000)+* 2.00 1.75
a. Block of 4, #251-254 8.50 7.00
First day cover, #254a 7.00
First day cover, #251-254, each 2.50
Inscription block of 4, #254a 9.50 —
Pane of 40, #251-254 75.00

First day covers of Nos. 251-254a total 37,595.

Palais des Nations, Geneva — G54

Creation of the World, by Oili Maki — G55

Printed by House of Questa, United Kingdom. Designed by Rocco J. Callari, US.

1994, Sept. 1 Litho. *Perf. 14.3x14.6*
255 G54 60c **multicolored** *(1,075,000)+* .75 .75
First day cover 1.10
Inscription block of 4 3.50 —
256 G55 80c **multicolored** *(1,075,000)+* 1.00 1.00
First day cover 1.50
Inscription block of 4 4.50 —
257 G54 1.80fr **multi,** diff. *(1,075,000)+* 2.50 2.50
First day cover 2.75
Inscription block of 4 11.00 —
First day cover, #255-257 4.50

First day covers of Nos. 255-257 total 51,637.

Population and Development Type of 1994

Designs: 60c, People shopping at open-air market. 80c, People on vacation crossing bridge.

1994, Sept. 1 Litho. *Perf. 13.2x13.6*
258 A282 60c **multicolored** *(535,000)+* 1.25 1.10
First day cover 1.25
Inscription block of 4 5.00 —
259 A282 80c **multicolored** *(535,000)+* 1.75 1.60
First day cover 1.75
Inscription block of 4 7.50 —
First day cover, #258-259 3.00

First day covers of Nos. 258-259 total 50,443.

UNCTAD Type of 1994

1994, Oct. 28
260 A283 80c **multi,** diff. *(535,000)+* 1.25 1.25
First day cover 1.75
Inscription block of 4 5.50 —
261 A283 1fr **multi,** diff. *(535,000)+* 1.75 1.75
First day cover 2.00
Inscription block of 4 7.75 —
First day cover, #260-261 3.50
a. Grayish green omitted —
Inscription block of 4 —

First day covers of Nos. 260-261 total 48,122.

UN 50th Anniv. Type of 1995

1995, Jan. 1 Litho. & Engr. *Perf. 13.4*
262 A284 80c **multicolored** *(823,827)* 1.25 1.25
First day cover *(38,988)* 3.00
Inscription block of 4 5.75 —

Social Summit Type of 1995

1995, Feb. 3 Photo. & Engr. *Perf. 13.6x13.9*
263 A285 1fr **multi,** diff. *(452,116)* 1.50 1.40
First day cover *(35,246)* 2.00
Inscription block of 4 7.00 —

Endangered Species Type of 1993

Designed by Sibylle Erni, Switzerland.

Designs: No. 264, Crowned lemur, Lemur coronatus. No. 265, Giant Scops owl, Otus gurneyi. No. 266, Zetek's frog, Atelopus varius zeteki. No. 267, Wood bison, Bison bison athabascae.

1995, Mar. 24 Litho. *Perf. 13x12½*

264 A271 80c **multicolored** *(730,000)+* 1.40 1.25
265 A271 80c **multicolored** *(730,000)+* 1.40 1.25
266 A271 80c **multicolored** *(730,000)+* 1.40 1.25
267 A271 80c **multicolored** *(730,000)+* 1.40 1.25
a. Block of 4, 264-267 5.75 5.00
First day cover, #267a 4.50
First day cover, #264-267, each 1.60
Inscription block of 4, #267a 5.75 —
Pane of 16, #264-267 24.00

First day covers of Nos. 264-267a total 71,907.

Intl. Youth Year Type of 1995

Designs: 80c, Farmer on tractor, fields at harvest time. 1fr, Couple standing by fields at night.

1995, May 26 Litho. *Perf. 14.4x14.7*

268 A286 80c **multicolored** *(294,987)* 1.75 1.60
First day cover 1.75
Inscription block of 4 7.00 —
269 A286 1fr **multicolored** *(264,823)* 2.75 2.00
First day cover 2.00
First day cover, #268-269 4.00
Inscription block of 4 12.00 —

First day covers of Nos. 268-269 total 45,665.

UN, 50th Anniv. Type of 1995

Designs: 60c, Like No. 663. 1.80fr, Like No. 664.

1995, June 26 Engr. *Perf. 13.3x13.6*

270 A287 60c **maroon** *(352,336)* 1.00 .90
First day cover .90
Inscription block of 4 4.50 —
271 A287 1.80fr **green** *(377,391)* 3.25 3.00
First day cover 3.00
First day cover, #270-271 4.00
Inscription block of 4 14.00 —

Souvenir Sheet

Litho. & Engr.

Imperf

272 Sheet of 2, #270-271 *(251,272)* 4.25 4.25
a. A287 60c **maroon** 1.00 1.00
b. A287 1.80fr **green** 3.25 3.25
First day cover 8.00

First day covers of Nos. 270-272 total 72,666.

Conference on Women Type of 1995

Designs: 60c, Black woman, cranes flying above. 1fr, Women, dove.

1995, Sept. 5 Photo. *Perf. 12*

273 A288 60c **multicolored** *(342,336)* *1.50* 1.25
First day cover 1.25
Inscription block of 4 *6.50* —

Size: 28x50mm

274 A288 1fr **multicolored** *(345,489)* *2.50* .75
First day cover 2.25
First day cover, #273-274 3.25
Inscription block of 4 *11.00* —

First day covers of Nos. 273-274 total 57,542.

UN People, 50th Anniv. Type of 1995

1995, Oct. 24 Litho. *Perf. 14*

275 Sheet of 12 *(216,832 sheets)* 18.00 12.50
First day cover 20.00
a.-l. A290 30c each 1.40 1.25
First day cover, #275a-275l, each 5.00
276 Souvenir booklet, *(74,151 booklets)* 20.00
a. A290 30c Booklet pane of 3, vert. strip of 3 from UL of sheet 4.75 4.75
b. A290 30c Booklet pane of 3, vert. strip of 3 from UR of sheet 4.75 4.75
c. A290 30c Booklet pane of 3, vert. strip of 3 from LL of sheet 4.75 4.75
d. A290 30c Booklet pane of 3, vert. strip of 3 from LR of sheet 4.75 4.75

First day covers of Nos. 275-276d total 53,245.

WFUNA, 50th Anniv. Type

Design: 80c, Fishing boat, fish in net.

1996, Feb. 2 Litho. *Perf. 13x13½*

277 A291 80c **multicolored** *(550,000)+* 1.50 1.25
First day cover 2.00
Inscription block of 4 6.50 —

The Galloping Horse Treading on a Flying Swallow, Chinese Bronzework, Eastern Han Dynasty (25-220 A.D.) — G56

Palais des Nations, Geneva — G57

Printed by House of Questa, UK.

1996, Feb. 2 Litho. *Perf. 14½x15*

278 G56 40c **multicolored** *(1,125,000)+* .75 .60
First day cover 1.25
Inscription block of 4 3.50 —
279 G57 70c **multicolored** *(1,125,000+)* 1.25 1.10
First day cover 1.50
First day cover, #278-279 3.50
Inscription block of 4 6.00 —

Endangered Species Type of 1993

Designs: No. 280, Paphiopedilum delenatii. No. 281, Pachypodium baronii. No. 282, Sternbergia lutea. No. 283, Darlingtonia californica.

1996, Mar. 14 Litho. *Perf. 12½*

280 A271 80c **multicolored** *(680,000)+* 1.10 1.00
281 A271 80c **multicolored** *(680,000)+* 1.10 1.00
282 A271 80c **multicolored** *(680,000)+* 1.10 1.00
283 A271 80c **multicolored** *(680,000)+* 1.10 1.00
a. Block of 4, #280-283 4.50 4.25
First day cover, #280-283, each 2.00
First day cover, #283a 4.50
Inscription block of 4, #283a 4.50 —
Pane of 16, #280-283 18.00

City Summit Type of 1996

Designs: No. 284, Asian family. No. 285, Oriental garden. No. 286, Fruit, vegetable vendor, mosque. No. 287, Boys playing ball. No. 288, Couple reading newspaper.

1996, June 3 Litho. *Perf. 14x13½*

284 A293 70c **multicolored** *(420,000)+* 1.50 1.10
285 A293 70c **multicolored** *(420,000)+* 1.50 1.10
286 A293 70c **multicolored** *(420,000)+* 1.50 1.10
287 A293 70c **multicolored** *(420,000)+* 1.50 1.10
288 A293 70c **multicolored** *(420,000)+* 1.50 1.10
a. Strip of 5, #284-288 7.50 5.50
First day cover, #288a 11.00
First day cover, #284-288, each 5.00
Inscription block of 10, 2 #288a 20.00

Sport and the Environment Type

Designs: 70c, Cycling, vert. 1.10fr, Sprinters.

1996, July 19 Litho. *Perf. 14x14½, 14½x14*

289 A294 70c **multicolored** *(625,000)+* 1.40 1.40
First day cover 1.50
Inscription block of 4 5.75 —
290 A294 1.10fr **multicolored***(625,000)+* 2.00 1.75
First day cover 2.25
First day cover, #289-290 4.50
Inscription block of 4 8.75 —

Souvenir Sheet

291 A294 Sheet of 2, #289-290 *(345,000)+* 3.00 3.00
First day cover 12.00

Plea for Peace Type

Designed by: 90c, Chen Yu, China. 1.10fr, Zhou Jing, China.

Designs: 90c, Tree filled with birds, vert. 1.10fr, Bouquet of flowers in rocket tail vase, vert.

1996, Sept. 17 Litho. *Perf. 15x14½*

292 A295 90c **multicolored** *(550,000)+* 1.75 1.50
First day cover 1.50
Inscription block of 4 7.50 —
293 A295 1.10fr **multicolored** *(550,000)+* 2.50 2.00
First day cover 2.25
First day cover, #292-293 3.75
Inscription block of 4 11.00 —

UNICEF Type

Fairy Tales: 70c, The Sun and the Moon, South America. 1.80fr, Ananse, Africa.

1996, Nov. 20 Litho. *Perf. 14½x15*

294 A296 70c **multicolored** *(1,000,000)+* 1.00 .90
First day cover 1.50
Pane of 8 + label 8.50
295 A296 1.80fr **multicolored** *(1,000,000)+* 2.50 2.25
First day cover 3.00
First day cover, #294-295 4.00
Pane of 8 + label 21.00

UN Flag — G58

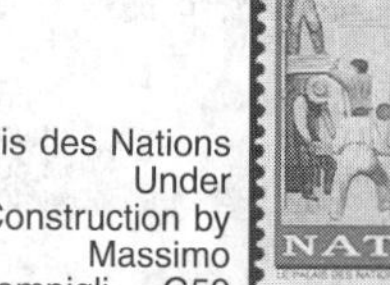

Palais des Nations Under Construction by Massimo Campigli — G59

Printed by The House of Questa, Ltd., UK.

1997, Feb. 12 Litho. *Perf. 14½*

296 G58 10c **multicolored** *(600,000)+* .20 .20
First day cover 1.25
Inscription block of 4 .55 —
297 G59 1.10fr **multicolored** *(700,000)+* 1.50 1.50
First day cover 2.25
First day cover, #296-297 3.50
Inscription block of 4 6.00 —

First day covers of Nos. 296-297 total 41,186.

Endangered Species Type of 1993

Designs: No. 298, Ursus maritimus (polar bear). No. 299, Goura cristata (blue-crowned pigeon). No. 300, Amblyrhynchus cristatus (marine iguana). No. 301, Lama guanicoe (guanaco).

1997, Mar. 13 Litho. *Perf. 12½*

298 A271 80c **multicolored** *(620,000)+* 1.10 1.00
299 A271 80c **multicolored** *(620,000)+* 1.10 1.00
300 A271 80c **multicolored** *(620,000)+* 1.10 1.00
301 A271 80c **multicolored** *(620,000)+* 1.10 1.00
a. Block of 4, #298-301 4.50 4.00
First day cover, #301a 5.00
First day cover, #298-301, each 2.50
Inscription block of 4, #301a 4.50
Pane of 16 20.00

First day covers of Nos. 298-301 total 71,905.

Earth Summit Anniv. Type

Designs: No. 302, Person flying over mountain. No. 303, Mountain, person's face. No. 304, Person standing on mountain, sailboats. No. 305, Person, mountain, trees.

1.10fr, Combined design similar to Nos. 302-305.

1997, May 30 Photo. *Perf. 11½*

Granite Paper

302 A299 45c **multicolored** *(227,187)* 1.50 1.25
303 A299 45c **multicolored** *(227,187)* 1.50 1.25
304 A299 45c **multicolored** *(227,187)* 1.50 1.25
305 A299 45c **multicolored** *(227,187)* 1.50 1.25
a. Block of 4, #302-305 7.00 5.50
First day cover, #305a 8.00
First day cover, #302-305, each 3.50
Inscription block of 4, #305a 7.25

Souvenir Sheet

306 A299 1.10fr **multicolored** *(176,386)* 3.50 3.50
First day cover 9.00

First day covers of Nos. 302-306 total 55,389.

Transportation Type of 1997

Air transportation: No. 307, Zeppelin, Fokker tri-motor. No. 308, Boeing 314 Clipper, Lockheed Constellation. No. 309, DeHavilland Comet. No. 310, Boeing 747, Illyushin jet. No. 311, Concorde.

1997, Aug. 29 Litho. *Perf. 14x14½*

307 A300 70c **multicolored** *(271,575)* 1.10 1.00
308 A300 70c **multicolored** *(271,575)* 1.10 1.00
309 A300 70c **multicolored** *(271,575)* 1.10 1.00
310 A300 70c **multicolored** *(271,575)* 1.10 1.00
311 A300 70c **multicolored** *(271,575)* 1.10 1.00
a. Strip of 5, #307-311 6.00 5.00
First day cover, #311a 7.00
First day cover, #307-311, each 3.00
Margin block of 10, 2#311a 12.50

No. 311a has continuous design.

First day covers of Nos. 307-311 total 33,303.

Philately Type

Designs: 70c, No. 146. 1.10fr, No. 147.

1997, Oct. 14 Litho. *Perf. 13½x14*

312 A301 70c **multicolored** *(254,406)* 2.00 1.75
First day cover 1.75
Inscription block of 4 8.50 —

313 A301 1.10fr **multicolored** *(303,125)* 2.75 2.75
First day cover 2.25
First day cover, #312-313 6.00
Inscription block of 4 11.50 —

First day covers of Nos. 312-313 total 47,528.

World Heritage Convention Type

Terracotta warriors of Xian: 45c, Single warrior. 70c, Massed warriors. No. 316a, like #716. No. 316b, like #717. No. 316c, like Geneva #314. No. 316d, like Geneva #315. No. 316e, like Vienna #230. No. 316f, like Vienna #231.

1997, Nov. 19 **Litho.** ***Perf. 13½***
314 A302 45c **multicolored** *(409,820)* 1.50 1.40
First day cover 1.40
Inscription block of 4 6.50 —
315 A302 70c **multicolored** *(414,059)* 2.50 2.50
First day cover 1.50
First day cover, #314-315 4.00
Inscription block of 4 11.00 —
316 Souvenir booklet *(275,114 booklets)* 8.50
a.-f. A302 10c any single .35 .35
g. Booklet pane of 4 #316a 1.40 1.40
h. Booklet pane of 4 #316b 1.40 1.40
i. Booklet pane of 4 #316c 1.40 1.40
j. Booklet pane of 4 #316d 1.40 1.40
k. Booklet pane of 4 #316e 1.40 1.40
l. Booklet pane of 4 #316f 1.40 1.40

First day covers of Nos. 314-316 total 40,366.

Palais des Nations, Geneva — G60

Printed by The House of Questa, UK. Designed by UN (2fr).

1998, Feb. 13 **Litho.** ***Perf. 14½x15***
317 G60 2fr **multicolored** *(550,000)+* 2.75 2.25
First day cover 6.00
Inscription block of 4 12.00 —

Endangered Species Type of 1993

Designed by Rocco J. Callari, US and Suzanne Duranceau, Canada.

Designs: No. 318, Macaca thibetana (short-tailed Tibetan macaque). No. 319, Phoenicopterus ruber (Caribbean flamingo). No. 320, Ornithoptera alexandrae (Queen Alexandra's birdwing). No. 321, Dama mesopotamica (Persian fallow deer).

1998, Mar. 13 **Litho.** ***Perf. 12½***
318 A271 80c **multicolored** *(560,000)+* 1.10 1.00
319 A271 80c **multicolored** *(560,000)+* 1.10 1.00
320 A271 80c **multicolored** *(560,000)+* 1.10 1.00
321 A271 80c **multicolored** *(560,000)+* 1.10 1.00
a. Block of 4, #318-321 4.50 4.00
First day cover, #321a 6.00
First day cover, #318-321, each 2.50
Inscription block of 4, #321a 4.50 —
Pane of 16 19.00

Intl. Year of the Ocean — G61

Designed by Jon Ellis, US.

1998, May 20 **Litho.** ***Perf. 13x13½***
322 G61 Sheet of 12 *(270,000)+* 12.00 11.00
First day cover 14.50
a.-l. 45c any single .80 .80
First day cover, #322a-322l, each 2.00

Rain Forests Type

1998, June 19 ***Perf. 13x13½***
323 A307 70c Orangutans *(430,000)+* 1.00 .75
First day cover 5.00
Inscription block of 4 4.00 —

Souvenir Sheet

324 A307 3fr like #323 *(250,000)+* 6.00 5.50
First day cover 10.00

Peacekeeping Type

Designs: 70c, Soldier with two children. 90c, Two soldiers, children.

1998, Sept. 15 **Photo.** ***Perf. 12***
325 A308 70c **multicolored** *(400,000)+* 1.50 1.10
First day cover 1.50
Inscription block of 4 6.00 —
326 A308 90c **multicolored** *(390,000)+* 2.00 1.75
First day cover 4.00
First day cover, #325-326 5.00
Inscription block of 4 8.50 —

Declaration of Human Rights Type of 1998

Designs: 90c, Stylized birds. 1.80fr, Stylized birds flying from hand.

1998, Oct. 27 **Litho. & Photo.** ***Perf. 13***
327 A309 90c **multicolored** *(400,000)+* 1.40 1.40
First day cover 2.00
Inscription block of 4 5.75 —
328 A309 1.80fr **multicolored** *(390,000)+* 2.75 2.75
First day cover 3.50
First day cover, #327-328 5.00
Inscription block of 4 12.00 —

Schönbrunn Palace Type

Designs: 70c, #331b, Great Palm House. 1.10fr, #331d, Blue porcelain vase, vert. No. 331a, Palace. No. 331c, The Gloriette (archway). No. 331e, Wall painting on fabric (detail), by Johann Wenzl Bergl, vert. No. 331f, Porcelain stove, vert.

1998, Dec. 4 **Litho.** ***Perf. 14***
329 A310 70c **multicolored** *(375,000)+* 1.00 1.00
First day cover 1.50
Inscription block of 4 4.00 —
330 A310 1.10fr **multicolored** *(375,000)+* 1.50 1.40
First day cover 2.25
First day cover, #329-330 5.00
Inscription block of 4 6.00 —

Souvenir Booklet

331 Booklet *(100,000)+* 7.00
a.-c. A310 10c any single .20 .20
d.-f. A310 30c any single .50 .40
g. Booklet pane of 4 #331a .75 .60
h. Booklet pane of 3 #331d 1.50 1.25
i. Booklet pane of 3 #331e 1.50 1.25
j. Booklet pane of 3 #331f 1.50 1.25
k. Booklet pane of 4 #331b .75 .60
l. Booklet pane of 4 #331c .75 .60

Palais Wilson, Geneva — G62

Designed and printed by Helio Courvoisier, SA, Switzerland.

1999, Feb. 5 **Photo.** ***Perf. 11½***
Granite Paper
332 G62 1.70fr **brown red** *(600,000)+* 3.00 2.75
First day cover *(25,568)* 3.50
Inscription block of 4 13.00 —

World Heritage, Australia Type

Designs: 90c, #335e, Kakadu Natl. Park. 1.10fr, #335c, Great Barrier Reef. No. 335a, Tasmanian Wilderness. No. 335b, Wet tropics of Queensland. No. 335d, Uluru-Kata Tjuta Natl. Park. No. 335f, Willandra Lakes region.

1999, Mar. 19 **Litho.** ***Perf. 13***
333 A313 90c **multicolored** *(420,000)+* 1.40 1.40
First day cover 2.00
Inscription block of 4 5.75 —
334 A313 1.10fr **multicolored** *(420,000)+* 1.50 1.40
First day cover 2.25
First day cover, #333-334 4.50
Inscription block of 4 8.00 —

Souvenir Booklet

335 Booklet *(90,000)+* 6.50
a.-c. A313 10c any single .20 .20
d.-f. A313 20c any single .40 .40
g. Booklet pane of 4, #335a .55 .40
h. Booklet pane of 4, #335d 1.60 1.40
i. Booklet pane of 4, #335b .55 .40
j. Booklet pane of 4, #335e 1.60 1.40
k. Booklet pane of 4, #335c .55 .40
l. Booklet pane of 4, #335f 1.60 1.40

First day covers of Nos. 333-335 total 44,622.

Endangered Species Type of 1993

Designed by Tim Barrall, US.

Designs: No. 336, Equus hemionus (Asiatic wild ass). No. 337, Anodorhynchus hyacinthinus (hyacinth macaw). No. 338, Epicrates subflavus (Jamaican boa). No. 339, Dendrolagus bennettianus (Bennetts' tree kangaroo).

1999, Apr. 22 **Litho.** ***Perf. 12½***
336 A271 90c **multicolored** *(488,000)+* 1.40 1.25
337 A271 90c **multicolored** *(488,000)+* 1.40 1.25
338 A271 90c **multicolored** *(488,000)+* 1.40 1.25
339 A271 90c **multicolored** *(488,000)+* 1.40 1.25
a. Block of 4, #336-339 5.75 5.50
First day cover, #339a 5.75
First day cover, #336-339, each 2.00
Inscription block of 4, #339a 6.00 —
Pane of 16 22.50

First day covers of Nos. 336-339 total 52,856.

UNISPACE III Type

Designs: No. 340, Farm, satellite dish. No. 341, City, satellite in orbit. No. 342, Composite of #340-341.

1999, July 7 **Photo.** ***Rouletted 8***
340 A314 45c **multicolored** *(925,000)+* .60 .60
341 A314 45c **multicolored** *(925,000)+* .60 .60
a. Pair, #340-341 2.00 2.00
First day cover, #341a 2.25
First day cover, #340-341, each 3.00
Inscription block of 4 5.00 —
Pane of 10, #340-341 9.50 —

Souvenir Sheet

Perf. 14½

342 A314 2fr **multicolored** *(275,000)+* 4.50 4.00
First day cover 6.00
a. Ovptd. in sheet margin 9.50 8.00
First day cover 19.00

No. 342a is ovptd. in violet blue "PHILEXFRANCE 99 / LE MONDIAL DU TIMBRE / PARIS / 2 AU 11 JUILLET 1999.

First day covers of Nos. 340-342 total 63,412.

UPU Type

Various people, early 20th century methods of mail transportation, denomination at: No. 343, UL. No. 344, UR. No. 345, LL. No. 346, LR.

1999, Aug. 23 **Photo.** ***Perf. 11¾***
343 A315 70c **multicolored** *(336,000)+* 1.00 .75
344 A315 70c **multicolored** *(336,000)+* 1.00 .75
345 A315 70c **multicolored** *(336,000)+* 1.00 .75
346 A315 70c **multicolored** *(336,000)+* 1.00 .75
a. Block of 4, #343-346 4.00 3.50
First day cover, #346a 3.50
First day cover, #343-346, each 1.50
Inscription block of 4, #346a 4.00 —

First day covers of Nos. 343-346 total 27,041.

In Memoriam Type

Designs: 1.10fr, 2fr, Armillary sphere, Palais de Nations. Size of 2fr stamp: 34x63mm.

1999, Sept. 21 **Litho.** ***Perf. 14½x14***
347 A316 1.10fr **multicolored** *(400,000)+* 1.60 1.40
First day cover 3.00
Inscription block of 4 6.50 —

Souvenir Sheet

Perf. 14

348 A316 2fr **multicolored** *(225,000)+* 3.00 3.00
First day cover 3.50

First day covers of Nos. 347-348 total 46,527.

Education Type

1999, Nov. 18 **Litho.** ***Perf. 13½x13¾***
349 A317 90c Rainbow over globe *(350,000)+* 1.40 1.25
First day cover 1.75
Inscription block of 4 5.75 —
350 A317 1.80fr Fish, tree, globe, book *(370,000)+* 2.50 2.50
First day cover 3.50
First day cover, #349-350 4.50
Inscription block of 4 10.50 —

First day covers of Nos. 349-350 total 37,925.

Intl. Year Of Thanksgiving Type

2000, Jan 1 **Litho.** ***Perf. 13¼x13½***
351 A318 90c **multicolored** *(450,000)+* 1.40 1.25
First day cover 3.00
Inscription block of 4 5.75 —

On No. 351 portions of the design were applied by a thermographic process producing a shiny, raised effect.

Endangered Species Type of 1993

Designed by Robert Hynes, US.

Designs: No. 352, Hippopotamus amphibius (hippopotamus). No. 353, Coscoroba coscoroba (Coscoroba swan). No. 354, Varanus prasinus (emerald monitor). No. 355, Enhydra lutris (sea otter).

2000, Apr. 6 **Litho.** ***Perf. 12¾x12½***
352 A271 90c **multicolored** *(488,000)+* 1.25 1.00
353 A271 90c **multicolored** *(488,000)+* 1.25 1.00
354 A271 90c **multicolored** *(488,000)+* 1.25 1.00

355 A271 90c **multicolored** *(488,000)+* 1.25 1.00
a. Block of 4, #352-355 5.00 4.50
First day cover, #355a 5.00
First day cover, #352-355, each 1.90
Inscription block of 4, #355a 5.25 —
Pane of 16 20.00

Our World 2000 Type

Winning artwork in Millennium painting competition: 90c, The Embrace, by Rita Adaimy, Lebanon. 1.10fr, Living Single, by Richard Kimanthi, Kenya, vert.

2000, May 30 Litho. *Perf. 13x13½, 13½x13*
356 A319 90c **multicolored** *(330,000)+* 1.25 1.00
First day cover 1.75
Inscription block of 4 5.00 —
357 A319 1.10fr **multicolored** *(330,000)+* 1.50 1.25
First day cover 2.25
First day cover, #356-357 3.50
Inscription block of 4 6.00 —

55th Anniversary Type

Designs: 90c, Trygve Lie, Harry S Truman, workers at cornerstone dedication ceremony, 1949. 1.40fr, Window cleaner on Secretariat Building, General Assembly Hall under construction, 1951.

2000, July 7 Litho. *Perf. 13¼x13*
358 A320 90c **multicolored** *(370,000)+* 1.25 .60
First day cover 1.75
Inscription block of 4 5.00 —
359 A320 1.40fr **multicolored** *(370,000)+* 2.00 1.00
First day cover 2.60
First day cover, #358-359 3.75
Inscription block of 4 8.00 —

Souvenir Sheet

360 A320 Sheet of 2, #358-359 *(235,000)+* 3.25 3.00
First day cover 5.00

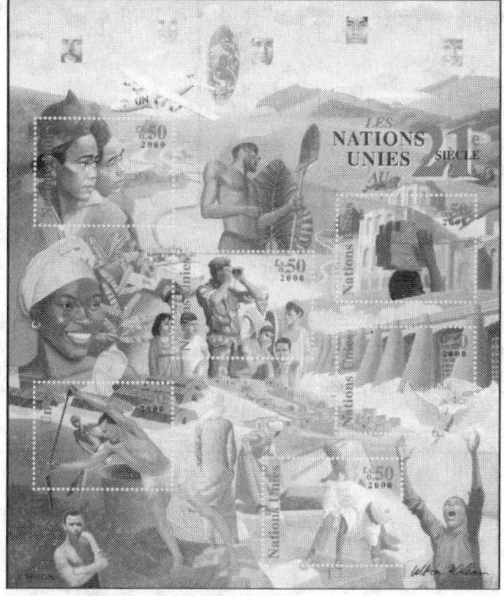

The UN in the 21st Century — G63

Printed by Government Printing Office, Austria. Designed by Wilson McLean, UK.

No. 361: a, Two people, terraced rice paddy. b, Man carrying bricks on head. c, UN Peacekeeper with binoculars. d, Dam, doves. e, Men with shovels. f, People working on irrigation system.

2000, Sept. 15 Litho. *Perf. 14*
361 G63 Sheet of 6 *(266,000)+* 5.50 5.25
First day cover 10.00
a.-f. 50c any single .65 .60

World Heritage, Spain Type

Designs: 1fr, #364b, Walled Town of Cuenca. 1.20fr, #364e, Toledo. #364a, Alhambra, Generalife and Albayzin, Granada. #364c, Aqueduct of Segovia. #364d, Amphitheater of Mérida. #364f, Güell Park, Barcelona.

2000, Oct. 6 Litho. *Perf. 14¾x14½*
362 A323 1fr **multicolored** *(340,000)+* 1.40 .70
First day cover 1.90
Inscription block of 4 5.75 —
363 A323 1.20fr **multicolored** *(340,000)+* 1.60 .80
First day cover 2.25
First day cover, #362-363 3.50
Inscription block of 4 6.50 —

Souvenir Booklet

364 Booklet *(64,000)+* 5.50
a.-c. A323 10c any single .20 .20
d.-f. A323 20c any single .30 .30
g. Booklet pane of 4, #364a .55 .50
h. Booklet pane of 4, #364d 1.25 1.10
i. Booklet pane of 4, #364b .55 .50
j. Booklet pane of 4, #364e 1.25 1.10
k. Booklet pane of 4, #364c .55 .50
l. Booklet pane of 4, #364f 1.25 1.10

Respect for Refugees Type

Designs: 80c, 1.80fr, Refugee with cane, four other refugees.

2000, Nov. 9 Litho. *Perf. 13¼x12¾*
365 A324 80c **multicolored** *(400,000)+* 1.10 .55
First day cover 1.75
Inscription block of 4 4.50 —

Souvenir Sheet

366 A324 1.80fr **multicolored** *(215,000)+* 2.40 1.25
First day cover 3.00

Endangered Species Type of 1993

Printed by Johann Enschedé and Sons, the Netherlands. Designed by Higgins Bond, US.

Designs: No. 367, Felis lynx canadensis (North American lynx). No. 368, Pavo muticus (green peafowl). No. 369, Geochelone elephantopus (Galapagos giant tortoise). No. 370, Lepilemur spp. (sportive lemur).

2001, Feb. 1 Litho. *Perf. 12¾x12½*
367 A271 90c **multicolored** *(448,000)+* 1.25 .60
368 A271 90c **multicolored** *(448,000)+* 1.25 .60
369 A271 90c **multicolored** *(448,000)+* 1.25 .60
370 A271 90c **multicolored** *(448,000)+* 1.25 .60
a. Block of 4, #367-370 5.00 —
First day cover, #370a 5.50
First day cover, #367-370 each 1.90
Inscription block of 4, #370a 5.25 —
Pane of 16 20.00

Intl. Volunteers Year — G64

Printed by Johann Enschedé and Sons, the Netherlands. Panes of 20. Designed by Rorie Katz and Robert Stein, US.

Paintings by: 90c, Ernest Pignon-Ernest, France. 1.30fr, Paul Siché, France.

2001, Mar. 29 Litho. *Perf. 13¼*
371 G64 90c **multicolored** *(350,000)+* 1.10 .55
First day cover 1.75
Inscription block of 4 4.50
372 G64 1.30fr **multicolored** *(340,000)+* 1.60 .80
First day cover 2.40
First day cover, #371-372 3.50
Inscription block of 4 6.50

World Heritage, Japan Type

Designs: 1.10fr, #375b, Nara. 1.30fr, #375e, Itsukushima Shinto Shrine. #375a, Kyoto. #375c, Himeji-Jo. #375d, Shirakawa-Go and Gokayama. #375f, Nikko.

2001, Aug. 1 Litho. *Perf. 12¾x13¼*
373 A328 1.10fr **multicolored** *(350,000)+* 1.40 .70
First day cover 2.00
Inscription block of 4 5.75 —
374 A328 1.30fr **multicolored** *(350,000)+* 1.60 .80
First day cover 2.40
First day cover, #373-374 3.75
Inscription block of 4 6.50 —

Souvenir Booklet

375 Booklet *(52,000)+* 6.00
a.-c. A328 10c any single .20 .20
d.-f. A328 30c any single .35 .35
g. Booklet pane of 4, #375a .50 —
h. Booklet pane of 4, #375d 1.50 —
i. Booklet pane of 4, #375b .50 —
j. Booklet pane of 4, #375e 1.50 —
k. Booklet pane of 4, #375c .50 —
l. Booklet pane of 4, #375f 1.50 —

Dag Hammarskjöld Type

2001, Sept. 18 Engr. *Perf. 11x11¼*
376 A329 2fr **carmine lake** *(380,000)+* 2.50 1.25
First day cover 3.25
Inscription block of 4 10.00 —

UN Postal Administration, 50th Anniv. Types

2001, Oct. 18 Litho. *Perf. 13½*
377 A330 90c Stamps, globe *(310,000)+* 1.10 .55
First day cover 1.60
Inscription block of 4 4.50 —
378 A330 1.30fr Stamps, horns *(310,000)+* 1.60 .80
First day cover 2.40
First day cover, #377-378 3.50
Inscription block of 4 6.50 —

Souvenir Sheet

379 A331 Sheet of 2 *(175,000)+* 4.00 2.00
a. 1.30fr **red & light blue,** 38mm diameter 1.75 .85
b. 1.80fr **red & light blue,** 38mm diameter 2.25 1.10
First day cover 4.50

Climate Change Type

Designs: No. 380, Lizard, flowers, shoreline. No. 381, Windmills, construction workers. No. 382, Non-polluting factory. No. 383, Solar oven, city, village, picnickers.

2001, Nov. 16 Litho. *Perf. 13¼*
380 A332 90c **multicolored** *(73,500)+* 1.10 .55
381 A332 90c **multicolored** *(73,500)+* 1.10 .55
382 A332 90c **multicolored** *(73,500)+* 1.10 .55
383 A332 90c **multicolored** *(73,500)+* 1.10 .55
a. Horiz. strip, #380-383 4.50 —
Inscription block of 8 9.00 —
First day cover, #383a 5.25
Pane of 24 27.00 —

Nobel Peace Prize Type

2001, Dec. 10 Litho. *Perf. 13¼*
384 A333 90c **multicolored** *(840,000)+* 1.10 .55
Inscription block of 4 4.50 —
First day cover 1.75
Pane of 12 13.50 —

Palais des Nations — G65

Printed by Government Printing Office, Austria. Panes of 20. Designed by Robert Stein, US.

2002, Mar. 1 Litho. *Perf. 13¾*
385 G65 1.30fr **multicolored** *(630,000)+* 1.75 .90
First day cover 2.25
Inscription block of 4 7.00 —

Endangered Species Type of 1993

Printed by Johann Enschedé and Sons, the Netherlands. Designed by Lori Anzalone, US.

Designs: No. 386, Cacajao calvus (white uakari). No. 387, Mellivora capensis (honey badger). No. 388, Otocolobus manul (manul). No. 389, Varanus exantematicus (Bosc's monitor).

2002, Apr. 4 Litho. *Perf. 12¾x12½*
386 A271 90c **multicolored** *(420,000)+* 1.25 .60
387 A271 90c **multicolored** *(420,000)+* 1.25 .60
388 A271 90c **multicolored** *(420,000)+* 1.25 .60
389 A271 90c **multicolored** *(420,000)+* 1.25 .60
a. Block of 4, #386-389 5.00 —
First day cover, #389a 5.50
First day cover, #386-389 each 1.90
Inscription block of 4, #389a 5.25 —
Pane of 16 20.00 —

Independence of East Timor Type

Designs: 90c, Wooden statue of male figure. 1.30fr, Carved wooden container.

2002, May 20 Litho. *Perf. 14x14½*
390 A335 90c **multicolored** *(305,000)+* 1.25 .60
First day cover 1.90
Inscription block of 4 5.00 —
391 A335 1.30fr **multicolored** *(295,000)+* 1.75 .85
First day cover 2.60
First day cover, #390-391 3.75
Inscription block of 4 7.00 —

Intl. Year of Mountains Type

Designs: No. 392, Weisshorn, Switzerland. No. 393, Mt. Fuji, Japan. No. 394, Vinson Massif, Antarctica. No. 395, Mt. Kamet, India.

2002, May 24 Litho. *Perf. 13x13¼*
392 A336 70c **multicolored** *(1,230,000)+* .90 .45
First day cover 1.40
393 A336 70c **multicolored** *(1,230,000)+* .90 .45
First day cover 1.40
394 A336 1.20fr **multicolored** *(1,230,000)+* 1.60 .80
First day cover 2.40
First day cover, #392, 394 3.25
395 A336 1.20fr **multicolored** *(1,230,000)+* 1.60 .80
a. Vert. strip or block of four, #392-395 5.00 2.50
First day cover 2.40
First day cover, #392, 395 3.25
First day cover, #392-395 6.00
Pane of 12, 3 each #392-395 15.00 —

World Summit on Sustainable Development (Peter Max) Type

Designs: No. 396, Sun, birds, flowers, heart. No. 397, Three faceless people, diff. No. 398, Three women, diff. No. 399, Sailboat, mountain.

2002, June 27 Litho. *Perf. 14½x14*
396 A337 90c **multicolored** *(1,215,000)+* 1.25 .60
First day cover 1.90
397 A337 90c **multicolored** *(1,215,000)+* 1.25 .60

First day cover 1.90
398 A337 1.80fr **multicolored** *(1,215,000)+* 2.40 1.25
First day cover 3.50
First day cover, #396, 398 4.00
399 A337 1.80fr **multicolored** *(1,215,000)+* 2.40 1.25
a. Vert. strip or block of four, #396-399 7.50 3.75
First day cover 3.50
First day cover, #397, 399 4.00
First day cover, #396-399 8.00
Pane of 12, 3 each #396-399 22.50 —

World Heritage, Italy Type

Designs: 90c, #402e, Pisa. 1.30fr, #402b, Aeolian Islands. #402a, Amalfi Coast. #402c, Rome. #402d, Florence. #402f, Pompeii.

2002, Aug. 30 Litho. *Perf. 13½x13¼*

400 A338 90c **multicolored** *(355,000)+* 1.25 .65
First day cover 1.90
Inscription block of 4 5.00 —
401 A338 1.30fr **multicolored** *(355,000)+* 1.90 .95
First day cover 2.75
First day cover, #400-401 4.00
Inscription block of 4 7.75 —

Souvenir Booklet

402 Booklet *(51,000)+* 5.00
a.-c. A338 10c any single .20 .20
d.-f. A338 20c any single .30 .30
g. Booklet pane of 4, #402d 1.25 —
h. Booklet pane of 4, #402a .40 —
i. Booklet pane of 4, #402e 1.25 —
j. Booklet pane of 4, #402b .40 —
k. Booklet pane of 4, #402f 1.25 —
l. Booklet pane of 4, #402c .40 —

AIDS Awareness Type

2002, Oct. 24 Litho. *Perf. 13½*

403 A339 1.30fr **multicolored** *(305,000)+* 1.90 .95
Inscription block of 4 7.75 —
First day cover, #403 2.60
Pane of 20 40.00 —

Entry of Switzerland into United Nations — G66

Printed by House of Questa, UK. Panes of 20. Designed by Thierry Clauson, Switzerland.

2002, Oct. 24 Litho. *Perf. 14½x14¾*

404 G66 3fr **multicolored** *(580,000)+* 4.25 2.10
Inscription block of 4 17.00 —
First day cover, #404 5.00
Pane of 20 85.00 —

Indigenous Art — G67

Printed by House of Questa, UK.
Designed by Rorie Katz and Robert Stein, US.

No. 405: a, Detail of Inca poncho, Peru. b, Bahia culture seated figure, Brazil. c, Blanket, Ecuador. d, Mayan stone sculpture, Belize. e, Embroidered fabric, Guatemala. f, Colima terra-cotta dog sculpture, Mexico.

2003, Jan. 31 Litho. *Perf. 14¼*

405 G67 Sheet of 6 *(168,000)+* 7.75 3.75
First day cover 9.75
a.-f. 90c Any single 1.25 .60

New Inter-Parliamentary Union Headquarters, Geneva — G68

Printed by House of Questa, UK. Panes of 20. Designed by Cyril Wursten, Switzerland.

2003, Feb. 20 Litho. *Perf. 14½x14*

406 G68 90c **multicolored** *(480,000)+* 1.25 .60
Inscription block of 4 5.00 —
First day cover 2.00
Pane of 20 25.00 —

Endangered Species Type of 1993

Printed by Johann Enschedé and Sons, the Netherlands. Designed by James Hautman, US.

Designs: No. 407, Branta ruficollis (red-breasted goose). No. 408, Geronticus calvus (bald ibis). No. 409, Dendrocygna bicolor (fulvous whistling duck). No. 410, Ramphastos vitellinus (channel-billed toucan).

2003, Apr. 3 Litho. *Perf. 12¾x12½*

407 A271 90c **multicolored** *(368,000)+* 1.40 .70
408 A271 90c **multicolored** *(368,000)+* 1.40 .70
409 A271 90c **multicolored** *(368,000)+* 1.40 .70
410 A271 90c **multicolored** *(368,000)+* 1.40 .70
a. Block of 4, #407-410 5.60 —
First day cover, #410a 6.25
First day cover, #407-410 each 2.10
Inscription block of 4, #410a 5.60 —
Pane of 16 22.50 —

2003 END-OF-YEAR ISSUES

See end of New York postage listings.

AIR LETTER SHEET

UN Type of 1968

Printed by Setelipaino, Finland. Designed by Robert Perrot.

1969, Oct. 4 Litho.

UC1 UC3 65c **ultra & light blue,** entire *(350,000)* .50 *1.50*
Entire, first day cancel *(52,000)* .75

SEMI-POSTAL STAMP

AIDS Awareness Semi-postal Type

Souvenir Sheet

2002, Oct. 24 Litho. *Perf. 14½*

B1 SP1 90c + 30c **multicolored** *(171,000)+* 1.75 1.75
First day cover, #B1 2.50

POSTAL CARDS

UN Type of 1969 and Type of Air Post Postal Card, 1966

Printed by Courvoisier, S.A., Switzerland. Designed by John Mason (20c) and Olav S. Mathiesen (30c).

Wmk. Post Horn, Swiss Cross, "S" or "Z"

1969, Oct. 4 Litho.

UX1 PC2 20c **olive green & black,** *buff (415,000)* .25 .20
First day cancel *(51,500)* .50
UX2 APC2 30c **violet blue, blue, light & dark green,** *buff (275,000)* .25 .20
First day cancel *(49,000)* .50

No. UX2, although of design APC2, is not inscribed "Poste Aerienne" or "Air Mail."

UN Emblem — GPC1

UN Emblem and Ribbons — GPC2

Printed by Setelipaino, Finland. Designed by Veronique Crombez (40c) and Lieve Baeten (70c).

1977, June 27 Litho.

UX3 GPC1 40c **multicolored** *(500,000)* .30 .20
First day cancel *(65,000)* 1.00
UX4 GPC2 70c **multicolored** *(300,000)* .40 .20
First day cancel *(65,000)* .50

A second printing of No. UX3 was made in 1984. It was released after the Swiss postal card rate had been increased to 50c so instructions were issued that all cards must have a 10c stamp affixed before being sold. A few were sold in NY without the added stamp. The card stock differs from the original printing.

Emblem of the United Nations — GPC3

Peace Dove — GPC4

Printed by Johann Enschede en Zonen, Netherlands.
Designed by George Hamori, Australia (50c) and Ryszard Dudzicki, Poland (70c).

1985, May 10 Litho.

UX5 GPC3 50c **multicolored** *(300,000)* 3.50 .75
First day cancel *(34,700)* 5.50
UX6 GPC4 70c **multicolored** *(300,000)* 3.25 .55
First day cancel *(34,700)* 4.50

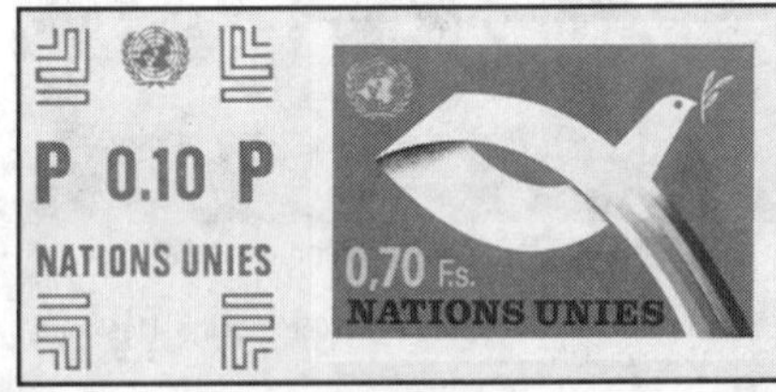

No. UX6 Surcharged in Lake

1986, Jan. 2 Litho.

UX7 GPC4 70c + 10c **multi** *(90,500)* 2.50 1.25
First day cancel *(8,000 est.)* 11.00

Type of 1990

Printed by Mercury-Walch, Australia.

1992, Sept. 4 Litho.

UX8 G45 90c **multicolored** *(150,000)+* 1.75 .60
First day cancel *(12,385)* 6.00

No. UX5 Surcharged in Lake like No. UX7

1993, May 7 Litho.

UX9 GPC3 50c +10c **multicolored** *(47,000)+* 1.50 .40
First day cancel 20.00

Palais des Nations — GPC5

Printed by Leigh Mardon Pty. Limited, Australia.

1993, May 7 **Litho.**
UX10 GPC5 80c **multicolored** *(200,000)+* 3.00 .50
First day cancel 7.50

#UX5, UX10 Surcharged in Carmine like #UX7

1996, Mar. 22 **Litho.**
UX11 GPC3 50c +20c **multi** 3.00 .55
First day cancel 4.00
UX12 GPC5 80c +30c **multi** 3.00 .85
First day cancel 4.00

Assembly Hall — GPC6

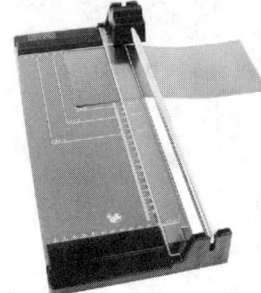

Palais des Nations — GPC7

Printed by Mercury-Walsh, Australia.

1998, May 20 **Litho.**
UX13 GPC6 70c **multicolored** *(80,000)+* 2.00 .50
First day cancel 3.00
UX14 GPC7 1.10fr **multicolored** *(80,000)+* 3.00 .75
First day cancel 3.25

Illustrations of the buildings are shown on the back of each card.

Type of 2002

Printed by Johann Enschedé and Sons, the Netherlands.

2002, Mar. 1 **Litho.**
UX15 G65 1.30fr **multicolored** *(68,000)+* 1.75 .50
First day cancel 2.00

SEMI-POSTAL

AIDS Awareness Semi-postal Type
Souvenir Sheet

2002, Oct. 24 **Litho.** ***Perf. 14½***
B1 SP1 90c + 30c multicolored 1.75 1.75

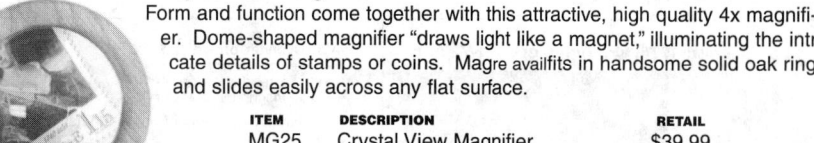

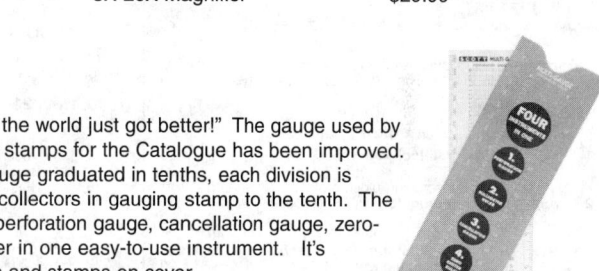

OFFICES IN VIENNA, AUSTRIA

For use only on mail posted at the Vienna International Center for the UN and the International Atomic Energy Agency.

100 Groschen = 1 Schilling
100 Cents = 1 Euro (2002)

Type of Geneva, 1978, UN Types of 1961-72 and

Donaupark, Vienna — V1

Aerial View — V2

Printed by Helio Courvoisier S.A., Switzerland. Panes of 50. Designed by Henryk Chylinski (4s); Jozsef Vertel (6s).

1979, Aug. 24 **Photo.** ***Perf. 11½***
Granite Paper

1 G8 50g **multicolored** *(3,500,000)+* .20 .20
First day cover 1.00
Inscription block of 4 .20 —
2 A52 1s **multicolored** *(3,800,000)+* .20 .20
First day cover 1.00
Inscription block of 4 .40 —
3 V1 4s **multicolored** *(3,500,000)+* .20 .20
First day cover 1.00
Inscription block of 4 .90 —
4 AP13 5s **multicolored** *(3,500,000)+* .25 .25
First day cover 1.00
Inscription block of 4 1.25 —
5 V2 6s **multicolored** *(4,500,000)+* .35 .35
First day cover 1.25
Inscription block of 4 1.50 —
6 A45 10s **multicolored** *(3,500,000)+* .50 .50
First day cover 2.00
Inscription block of 4 2.25 —
Nos. 1-6 (6) 1.70 1.70

+ Printing orders to Mar. 1993.
No. 4 is not inscribed "Air Mail," No. 6 has no frame.
First day covers of Nos. 1-6 total 1,026,575.

New Economic Order Type of UN

1980, Jan. 11 **Litho.** ***Perf. 15x14½***
7 A178 4s **multicolored** *(1,418,418)* .70 .70
First day cover 1.25
Inscription block of 4 *9.00* —

Value for margin inscription block is for one from bottom of sheet. One from top is about twice the value shown.

Dove Type of UN

1980, Jan. 11 **Litho.** ***Perf. 14x13½***
8 A147 2.50s **multicolored** *(3,500,000)+* .25 .25
First day cover 1.00
Inscription block of 4 1.25 —

First day covers of Nos. 7-8 total 336,229.

Women's Year Emblem on World Map — V3

United Nations Decade for Women.

Printed by Questa Colour Security Printers, United Kingdom. Panes of 50. Designed by Gunnar Janssen.

1980, Mar. 7 **Litho.** ***Perf. 14½x15***
9 V3 4s **light green & dark green** *(1,569,080)* .40 .40
First day cover 1.00
Inscription block of 4 1.75 —
10 V3 6s **bister brown** *(1,556,016)* .75 .75
First day cover 1.25
First day cover, #9-10 1.50
Inscription block of 4 3.25 —

First day covers of Nos. 9-10 total 443,893.

Peace-keeping Operations Type of UN

1980, May 16 **Litho.** ***Perf. 14x13***
11 A182 6s **multicolored** *(1,719,852)* .40 .40
First day cover *(323,923)* 1.00
Inscription block of 4 2.00 —

35th Anniversary Types of Geneva and UN

1980, June 26 **Litho.** ***Perf. 13x13½***
12 G16 4s **carmine rose & black** *(1,626,582)* .40 .40
First day cover 1.00
Inscription block of 4 1.60 —
13 A184 6s **multicolored** *(1,625,400)* .65 .65
First day cover 1.25
Inscription block of 4 2.75 —

Souvenir Sheet
Imperf

14 Sheet of 2 *(1,675,191)* .55 .55
a. G16 4s carmine rose & black .20
b. A184 6s multicolored .35
First day cover 1.00

First day covers of Nos. 12-14 total 657,402.

ECOSOC Types of UN and Geneva

Printed by Ashton-Potter Ltd., Canada. Panes of 50. Designed by Dietman Kowall (4s), Angel Medina Medina (6s).

1980, Nov. 21 **Litho.** ***Perf. 13½x13***
15 A187 4s **multicolored** *(1,811,218)* .30 .30
First day cover 1.00
Inscription block of 4 1.50 —
16 G17 6s **multicolored** *(1,258,420)* .60 .60
First day cover 1.00
First day cover #15-16 1.25
Inscription block of 4 2.50 —

Economic and Social Council (ECOSOC).
First day covers of Nos. 15-16 total 224,631.

Palestinian Rights Type of UN

Printed by Courvoisier S.A., Switzerland. Panes of 50. Designed by David Dewhurst.

1981, Jan. 30 **Photo.** ***Perf. 12x11½***
17 A188 4s **multicolored** *(1,673,310)* .45 .45
First day cover *(208,812)* 1.00
Inscription block of 4 2.00 —

Disabled Type of UN and

Interlocking Stitches — V4

International Year of the Disabled.
Printed by Heraclio Fournier S.A., Spain. Panes of 50. Designed by Sophia van Heeswijk.

1981, Mar. 6 **Photo.** ***Perf. 14***
18 A189 4s **multicolored** *(1,508,719)* .40 .40
First day cover 1.00
Inscription block of 4 1.75 —
19 V4 6s **black & orange** *(1,569,385)* .60 .60
First day cover 1.00
First day cover, #18-19 1.25
Inscription block of 4 2.75 —

First day covers of Nos. 18-19 total 290,603.

Art Type of UN

1981, Apr. 15 **Photo.** ***Perf. 11½***
Granite Paper

20 A191 6s **multicolored** *(1,643,527)* .75 .75
First day cover *(196,916)* 1.00
Inscription block of 4 3.25 —

Energy Type of UN

1981, May 29 **Litho.** ***Perf. 13***
21 A193 7.50s **multicolored** *(1,611,130)* .70 .70
First day cover *(216,197)* 1.00
Inscription block of 4 3.00 —

Volunteers Program Types

1981, Nov. 13 **Litho.**
22 A195 5s **multicolored** *(1,582,780)* .50 .45
First day cover 1.00
Inscription block of 4 2.25 —
23 G18 7s **multicolored** *(1,516,139)* 1.00 .90
First day cover 1.00
First day cover, #22-23 1.00
Inscription block of 4 4.25 —

First day covers of Nos. 22-23 total 282,414.

"For a Better World" — V5

Printed by Courvoisier, S.A., Switzerland. Sheets of 50. Designed by Eliezer Weishoff.

1982, Jan. 22 ***Perf. 11½x12***
24 V5 3s **multicolored** *(3,300,000)+* .35 .35
First day cover *(203,872)* 1.00
Inscription block of 4 1.75

Human Environment Types of UN

10th Anniversary of United Nations Environment Program.
Printed by Joh. Enschede en Zonen, Netherlands. Panes of 50. Designed by Peer-Ulrich Bremer (5s); Sybille Brunner (7s).

1982, Mar. 19 **Litho.** ***Perf. 13½x13***
25 A200 5s **multicolored** *(1,312,765)* .40 .40
First day cover 1.00
Inscription block of 4 1.90 —
26 G21 7s **multicolored** *(1,357,513)* .80 .80
First day cover 1.00
First day cover, #25-26 1.25
Inscription block of 4 3.75 —

First day covers of Nos. 25-26 total 248,576.

Outer Space Type of UN

Exploration and Peaceful Uses of Outer Space. Printed by Enschede. Panes of 50. Designed by George Hamori.

1982, June 11 **Litho.** ***Perf. 13x13½***
27 G22 5s **multicolored** *(1,339,038)* .60 .60
First day cover *(150,845)* 1.75
Inscription block of 4 3.00 —

Conservation & Protection of Nature Type

1982, Nov. 16 **Photo.** ***Perf. 14***
28 A202 5s Fish *(1,202,694)* .50 .50
First day cover 1.00
Inscription block of 4 2.50 —
29 A202 7s Animal *(1,194,403)* .70 .70
First day cover 1.00
First day cover, #28-29 1.40
Inscription block of 4 3.00 —

First day covers of Nos. 28-29 total 243,548.

World Communications Year Type

1983, Jan. 28 **Litho.** ***Perf. 13***
30 A203 4s **multicolored** *(1,517,443)* .40 .40
First day cover *(150,541)* 1.40
Inscription block of 4 2.10 —

Safety at Sea Type

1983, Mar. 18 **Litho.** ***Perf. 14½***
31 G23 4s **multicolored** *(1,506,052)* .40 .40
First day cover 1.00
Inscription block of 4 2.00 —
32 A206 6s **multicolored** *(1,527,990)* .65 .65
First day cover 1.00
First day cover, #31-32 2.25
Inscription block of 4 2.75 —

First day covers of Nos. 31-32 total 219,118.

World Food Program Type

1983, Apr. 22 **Engr.** ***Perf. 13½***

No.	Type	Value	Description	Unused	Used
33	A207	5s	**green** *(1,419,237)*	.50	.50
			First day cover		1.00
			Inscription block of 4	2.25	—
34	A207	7s	**brown** *(1,454,227)*	.70	.70
			First day cover		1.00
			First day cover, #33-34		1.25
			Inscription block of 4	2.75	—

First day covers of Nos. 33-34 total 212,267.

UN Conference on Trade and Development Type

1983, June 6 **Litho.** ***Perf. 14***

No.	Type	Value	Description	Unused	Used
35	G24	4s	**multicolored** *(1,544,973)*	.30	.30
			First day cover		1.00
			Inscription block of 4	1.90	—
36	A209	8.50s	**multicolored** *(1,423,172)*	.75	.75
			First day cover		1.00
			First day cover, #35-36		1.25
			Inscription block of 4	3.25	—

First day covers of Nos. 35-36 total 184,023.

The Second Skin — V6

Right to Think — V7

35th Anniversary of the Universal Declaration of Human Rights

Printed by Government Printing Office, Austria. Designed by Friedensreich Hundertwasser, Austria. Panes of 16 (4x4).

1983, Dec. 9 **Photo. & Engr.** ***Perf. 13½***

No.	Type	Value	Description	Unused	Used
37	V6	5s	**multicolored** *(2,163,419)*	.50	.50
			First day cover		1.25
			Inscription block of 4	2.25	
38	V7	7s	**multicolored** *(2,163,542)*	.75	.75
			First day cover		1.25
			First day cover, #37-38		2.25
			Inscription block of 4	3.25	
			Panes of 16, #37-38	20.00	

First day covers of Nos. 37-38 total 246,440.

International Conference on Population Type

Printed by Bundesdruckerei, Federal Republic of Germany. Panes of 50. Designed by Marina Langer-Rosa and Helmut Langer, Federal Republic of Germany.

1984, Feb. 3 **Litho.** ***Perf. 14***

No.	Type	Value	Description	Unused	Used
39	A212	7s	**multicolored** *(1,135,791)*	.65	.65
			First day cover *(80,570)*		1.50
			Inscription block of 4	2.75	—

Field Irrigation V8

Pest Control — V9

World Food Day, Oct. 16

Printed by Walsall Security Printers, Ltd., United Kingdom. Panes of 50. Designed by Adth Vanooijen, Netherlands.

1984, Mar. 15 **Litho.** ***Perf. 14½***

No.	Type	Value	Description	Unused	Used
40	V8	4.50s	**multicolored** *(994,106)*	.45	.45
			First day cover		1.00
			Inscription block of 4	2.00	—
41	V9	6s	**multicolored** *(1,027,115)*	.70	.70
			First day cover		1.00
			First day cover #40-41		2.25
			Inscription block of 4	2.50	—

First day covers of Nos. 40-41 total 194,546.

Serengeti Park, Tanzania — V10

Ancient City of Shiban, People's Democratic Rep. of Yemen — V11

World Heritage

Printed by Harrison and Sons, United Kingdom. Panes of 50. Designs adapted by Rocco J. Callari, US, and Thomas Lee, China.

1984, Mar. 15 **Litho.** ***Perf. 14***

No.	Type	Value	Description	Unused	Used
42	V10	3.50s	**multicolored** *(957,518)*	.25	.25
			First day cover		1.25
			Inscription block of 4	1.25	—
43	V11	15s	**multicolored** *(928,794)*	1.40	1.40
			First day cover		1.75
			First day cover, #42-43		2.50
			Inscription block of 4	5.75	—

First day covers of Nos. 42-43 total 193,845.

V12

V13

Future for Refugees

Designed by Hans Erni, Switzerland. Printed by Courvoisier. Panes of 50.

1984, Mar. 29 **Photo.** ***Perf. 11½***

No.	Type	Value	Description	Unused	Used
44	V12	4.50s	**multicolored** *(1,086,393)*	.55	.55
			First day cover		1.25
			Inscription block of 4	2.25	—
45	V13	8.50s	**multicolored** *(1,109,865)*	1.40	1.40
			First day cover		1.75
			First day cover, #44-45		2.25
			Inscription block of 4	5.75	—

First day covers of Nos. 44-45 total 185,349.

International Youth Year — V14

Printed by Waddingtons Ltd., United Kingdom. Panes of 50. Designed by Ruel A. Mayo, Phillipines.

1984, Nov. 15 **Litho.** ***Perf. 13½***

No.	Type	Value	Description	Unused	Used
46	V14	3.50s	**multicolored** *(1,178,833)*	.50	.50
			First day cover		1.25
			Inscription block of 4	2.10	—
47	V14	6.50s	**multicolored** *(1,109,337)*	.75	.75
			First day cover		1.50
			First day cover, #46-47		2.25
			Inscription block of 4	3.25	—

First day covers of Nos. 46-47 total 165,762.

ILO Type of Geneva

Printed by the Government Printing Bureau, Japan. Panes of 50. Adapted from photographs by Rocco J. Callari, US, and Thomas Lee, China.

1985, Feb. 1 **Engr.** ***Perf. 13½***

No.	Type	Value	Description	Unused	Used
48	G34	7.50s	U Thant Pavilion *(948,317)*	.85	.85
			First day cover *(115,916)*		1.75
			Inscription block of 4	3.50	—

UN University Type

Printed by Helio Courvoisier, Switzerland. Panes of 50. Designed by Moshe Pereg, Israel, and Hinedi Geluda, Brazil.

1985, Mar. 15 **Photo.** ***Perf. 13½***

No.	Type	Value	Description	Unused	Used
49	A221	8.50s	Rural scene, lab researcher *(863,673)*	.85	.85
			First day cover *(108,479)*		1.75
			Inscription block of 4	3.75	—

Ship of Peace — V15

Shelter under UN Umbrella — V16

Printed by Carl Ueberreuter Druck and Verlag M. Salzer, Austria. Panes of 50. Designed by Ran Banda Mawilmada, Sri Lanka (4.50s), and Sophia van Heeswijk, Federal Republic of Germany (15s).

1985, May 10 **Litho.** ***Perf. 14***

No.	Type	Value	Description	Unused	Used
50	V15	4.50s	**multicolored** *(2,000,000)+*	.35	.35
			First day cover		.75
			Inscription block of 4	1.50	—
51	V16	15s	**multicolored** *(2,000,000)+*	2.25	2.25
			First day cover		2.75
			First day cover, #50-51		3.50
			Inscription block of 4	9.50	—

First day covers of Nos. 50-51 total 142,687.

40th Anniversary Type

Designed by Rocco J. Callari, U.S., and Thomas Lee, China (No. 54).

1985, June 26 **Photo.** ***Perf. 12 x 11½***

No.	Type	Value	Description	Unused	Used
52	A224	6.50s	**multicolored** *(984,820)*	1.00	1.00
			First day cover		1.25
			Inscription block of 4	4.25	—
53	A225	8.50s	**multicolored** *(914,347)*	1.50	1.50
			First day cover		1.75
			First day cover, #52-53		2.50
			Inscription block of 4	6.25	—

Souvenir Sheet
Imperf

54 Sheet of 2 *(676,648)* 2.75 2.75
a. A224 6.50s **multi** .70 .70
b. A225 8.50s **multi** .90 .90
First day cover 2.50

First day covers of Nos. 52-54 total 317,652.

UNICEF Child Survival Campaign Type

Printed by the Government Printing Bureau, Japan. Panes of 50. Designed by Mel Harris, United Kingdom (No. 55) and Vreni Wyss-Fischer, Switzerland (No. 56).

1985, Nov. 22 Photo. & Engr. *Perf. 13½*
55 A226 4s Spoonfeeding children *(889,918)* .75 .75
First day cover 1.50
Inscription block of 4 3.50 —
56 A226 6s Mother hugging infant *(852,958)* 1.40 1.40
First day cover 1.50
First day cover, #55-56 2.50
Inscription block of 4 6.00 —

First day covers of Nos. 55-56 total 239,532.

Africa in Crisis Type

Printed by Helio Courvoisier, Switzerland. Panes of 50. Designed by Tesfaye Tessema, Ethiopia.

1986, Jan. 31 Photo. *Perf. 11½x12*
57 A227 8s **multicolored** *(809,854)* .80 .80
First day cover *(99,996)* 2.75
Inscription block of 4 3.50 —

UN Development Program Type

Agriculture. Printed by the Government Printing Bureau, Japan. Panes of 40, 2 blocks of 4 horizontal and 5 blocks of 4 vertical. Designed by Thomas Lee, China.

1986, Mar. 14 Photo. *Perf. 13½*
58 A228 4.50s Developing crop strains *(730,691)* 1.50 1.25
59 A228 4.50s Animal husbandry *(730,691)* 1.50 1.25
60 A228 4.50s Technical instruction *(730,691)* 1.50 1.25
61 A228 4.50s Nutrition education *(730,691)* 1.50 1.25
a. Block of 4, #58-61 6.25 5.50
First day cover, #61a 6.00
First day cover, #58-61, each 2.00
Inscription block of 4, #58-61 7.00 —
Pane of 40, #58-61 87.50

No. 61a has a continuous design.
First day covers of Nos. 58-61 total 227,664.

Stamp Collecting Type

Designs: 3.50s, UN stamps. 6.50s, Engraver. Printed by the Swedish Post Office, Sweden. Panes of 50. Designed by Czeslaw Slania and Ingalill Axelsson, Sweden.

1986, May 22 Engr. *Perf. 12½*
62 A229 3.50s **dk ultra & dk brown** *(874,119)* .50 .45
First day cover 1.50
Inscription block of 4 2.25 —
63 A229 6.50s **int blue & brt rose** *(877,284)* 1.10 1.10
First day cover 1.50
First day cover, #62-63 2.25
Inscription block of 4 4.50 —

First day covers of Nos. 62-63 total 150,836.

Olive Branch, Rainbow, Earth — V17

International Peace Year. Printed by the Government Printing Bureau, Japan. Panes of 50. Designed by Milo Schor, Israel (No. 64), and Mohammad Sardar, Pakistan (No. 65).

Photogravure & Embossed

1986, June 20 *Perf. 13½*
64 V17 5s shown *(914,699)* .90 .90
First day cover 1.50
Inscription block of 4 3.75 —
65 V17 6s Doves, UN emblem *(818,386)* 1.10 1.10
First day cover 1.50
First day cover, #64-65 2.50
Inscription block of 4 4.50 —

First day covers of Nos. 64-65 total 169,551.

WFUNA Anniversary Type
Souvenir Sheet

Printed by Johann Enschede and Sons, Netherlands. Designed by Rocco J. Callari, US.

Designs: 4s, White stallion by Elisabeth von Janota-Bzowski, Germany. 5s, Surrealistic landscape by Ernst Fuchs, Austria. 6s, Geometric abstract by Victor Vasarely (b. 1908), France. 7s, Mythological abstract by Wolfgang Hutter (b. 1928), Austria.

1986, Nov. 14 Litho. *Perf. 13x13½*
66 Sheet of 4 *(668,264)* 4.00 3.75
a. A232 4s **multicolored** .75 .60
b. A232 5s **multicolored** .85 .70
c. A232 6s **multicolored** 1.00 .80
d. A232 7s **multicolored** 1.25 1.00
First day cover *(121,852)* 4.00

No. 66 has inscribed margin picturing UN and WFUNA emblems.

Trygve Lie Type
Photogravure & Engraved

1987, Jan. 30 *Perf. 13½*
67 A233 8s **multicolored** *(778,010)* 1.00 .95
First day cover *(94,112)* 2.50
Inscription block of 4 4.50 —

Shelter for the Homeless Type

Designs: 4s, Family and homes. 9.50s, Family entering home.

1987, Mar. 13 Litho. *Perf. 13½x12½*
68 A234 4s **multicolored** *(704,922)* .65 .65
First day cover 1.25
Inscription block of 4 2.75 —
69 A234 9.50s **multicolored** *(671,200)* 1.25 1.25
First day cover 1.75
First day cover, #68-69 2.75
Inscription block of 4 5.25 —

First day covers of Nos. 68-69 total 117,941.

Fight Drug Abuse Type

Designs: 5s, Soccer players. 8s, Family.

1987, June 12 Litho. *Perf. 14½x15*
70 A235 5s **multicolored** *(869,875)* .60 .60
First day cover 1.40
Inscription block of 4 2.75 —
71 A235 8s **multicolored** *(797,889)* 1.00 1.00
First day cover 1.75
First day cover, #70-71 2.75
Inscription block of 4 4.25 —

First day covers of Nos. 70-71 total 117,964.

Donaupark, Vienna — V18

Peace Embracing the Earth — V19

Printed by The House of Questa, United Kingdom. Panes of 50. Designed by Henry Bencsath, US (2s), and Eliezer Weishoff, Israel (17s).

1987, June 12 Litho. *Perf. 14½x15*
72 V18 2s **multicolored** *(2,000,000)*+ .35 .35
First day cover 1.25
Inscription block of 4 1.50 —
73 V19 17s **multicolored** *(2,000,000)*+ 1.90 1.75
First day cover 2.50
First day cover, #72-73 3.50
Inscription block of 4 8.00 —

First day covers of Nos. 72-73 total 111,153.

UN Day Type

Designed by Elisabeth von Janota-Bzowski (5s) and Fritz Henry Oerter (6s), Federal Republic of Germany.
Designs: Multinational people in various occupations.

1987, Oct. 23 Litho. *Perf. 14½x15*
74 A236 5s **multicolored** *(1,575,731)* .85 .75
First day cover 1.40
Inscription block of 4 3.75 —
75 A236 6s **multicolored** *(1,540,523)* 1.00 1.00
First day cover 1.75
First day cover, #74-75 2.75
Inscription block of 4 4.25 —
Panes of 12, #74-75 24.00

Immunize Every Child Type

Designs: 4s, Poliomyelitis. 9.50s, Diphtheria.

1987, Nov. 20 Litho. *Perf. 15x14½*
76 A237 4s **multicolored** *(793,716)* .75 .75
First day cover 1.00
Inscription block of 4 4.00 —
77 A237 9.50s **multicolored** *(769,288)* 2.00 1.75
First day cover 1.90
First day cover, #76-77 2.75
Inscription block of 4 8.25 —

IFAD Type

Designs: 4s, Grains. 6s, Vegetables.

1988, Jan. 29 Litho. *Perf. 13½*
78 A238 4s **multicolored** *(697,307)* .50 .50
First day cover 1.25
Inscription block of 4 2.75 —
79 A238 6s **multicolored** *(701,521)* 1.00 1.00
First day cover 1.75
First day cover, #78-79 2.75
Inscription block of 4 4.25 —

Survival of the Forests Type

Deciduous forest in fall: 4s, Treetops, hills and dales. 5s, Tree trunks. Printed se-tenant in a continuous design.

1988, Mar. 18 Litho. *Perf. 14x15*
80 A240 4s **multicolored** *(990,607)* *2.25 2.25*
First day cover 4.50
81 A240 5s **multicolored** *(990,607)* *3.25 3.25*
First day cover 5.50
a. Pair, #80-81 *5.50 5.50*
First day cover, #81a 9.00
Inscription block of 4, #80-81 *12.00* —
Pane of 12, #80-81 *30.00*

Intl. Volunteer Day Type

Designed by George Fernandez, U.S.
Designs: 6s, Medical care, vert. 7.50s, Construction.

1988, May 6 Litho. *Perf. 13x14, 14x13*
82 A241 6s **multicolored** *(701,167)* .85 .80
First day cover 1.40
Inscription block of 4 4.00 —
83 A241 7.50s **multicolored** *(638,240)* 1.25 1.25
First day cover 1.60
First day cover, #82-83 3.00
Inscription block of 4 5.75 —

Health in Sports Type

Paintings by LeRoy Neiman, American Sports artist: 6s, Skiing, vert. 8s, Tennis.

1988, June 17 Litho. *Perf. 13½x13, 13x13½*
84 A242 6s **multicolored** *(668,902)* .85 .85
First day cover 1.40
Inscription block of 4 5.00 —
85 A242 8s **multicolored** *(647,915)* 1.25 1.25
First day cover 2.00
First day cover #84-85 4.00
Inscription block of 4 8.50 —

Universal Declaration of Human Rights 40th Anniv. Type

1988, Dec. 9 Photo. & Engr. *Perf. 11½*
86 A243 5s **multicolored** *(1,080,041)* .50 .50
First day cover 2.50
Inscription block of 4 3.00 —

Souvenir Sheet

87 A243 11s **multicolored** *(688,994)* 1.25 .50
First day cover 4.75

No. 87 has multicolored decorative margin inscribed with preamble to the human rights declaration in German.

World Bank Type

1989, Jan. 27 Litho. *Perf. 13x14*
88 A244 5.50s Transportation *(682,124)* 1.25 1.25
First day cover 1.40
Inscription block of 4 5.25 —
89 A244 8s Health care, education *(628,649)* 1.90 1.90
First day cover 2.00
First day cover, #88-89 3.00
Inscription block of 4 8.25 —

First day covers of Nos. 88-89 total 135,964.

Peace-Keeping Force Type

1989, Mar. 17 *Perf. 14x13½*
90 A245 6s **multicolored** *(912,731)* .90 .90
First day cover *(81,837)* 2.00
Inscription block of 4 4.00 —

World Weather Watch Type

Satellite photograph and radar image: 4s, Helical cloud formation over Italy, the eastern Alps, and parts of Yugoslavia. 9.50s, Rainfall in Tokyo, Japan.

1989, Apr. 21 Litho. *Perf. 13x14*
91 A247 4s **multicolored** *(948,680)* 1.00 1.00
First day cover 1.40
Inscription block of 4 4.50 —
92 A247 9.50s **multicolored** *(880,138)* 2.25 2.25
First day cover 2.00
First day cover, #91-92 4.00
Inscription block of 4 10.50 —

First day covers of Nos. 91-92 total 116,846.

Offices in Vienna, 10th Anniv.
V20 V21

Printed by the Government Printing Office, Austria. Panes of 25. Designed by Gottfried Kumpf (5s) and Andre Heller (7.50s), Austria.

Photo. & Engr., Photo. (7.50s)

1989, Aug. 23 *Perf. 14*

93 V20 5s **multicolored** *(958,339)* 4.50 4.00
First day cover 1.25
Inscription block of 4 18.00 —
94 V21 7.50s **multicolored** *(785,517)* 1.00 1.00
First day cover 3.00
First day cover, #93-94 4.00
Inscription block of 4 4.50 —
Panes of 25, #93-94 *140.00*

First day covers of Nos. 93-94 total 210,746.

Human Rights Type of 1989

Panes of 12+12 se-tenant labels containing Articles 5 (4s) or 6 (6s) inscribed in German, English or French.
Paintings: 4s, The Prisoners, by Kathe Kollwitz. 6s, Justice, by Raphael.

1989, Nov. 17 **Litho.** *Perf. 13½*

95 A250 4s **multicolored** *(2,267,450)* .65 .65
First day cover 2.00
Inscription block of 3 + 3 labels 2.00 —
96 A250 6s **multicolored** *(2,264,876)* .90 .90
First day cover 2.00
First day cover, #95-96 3.00
Inscription block of 3 + 3 labels 2.75 —
Panes of 12, #95-96 19.00

First day covers of Nos. 95-96 total 183,199.
See Nos. 108-109, 123-124, 150-151.

Intl. Trade Center Type

1990, Feb. 2 **Litho.** *Perf. 14½x15*

97 A251 12s **multicolored** *(559,556)* 2.00 1.90
First day cover *(77,928)* 4.00
Inscription block of 4 8.00 —

Painting by Kurt Regschek
V22

Printed by the National Postage Stamps and Fiduciary Printing Works, France. Designed by Robert J. Stein, US.

1990, Feb. 2 **Litho.** *Perf. 13x13½*

98 V22 1.50s **multicolored** *(1,000,000)+* .30 .30
First day cover *(64,622)* 2.50
Inscription block of 4 1.40 —

Fight AIDS Type

Designed by Jacek Tofil, Poland (5s), Orlando Pelaez, Colombia (11s).
Designs: 5s, "SIDA." 11s, Stylized figures, ink blot.

1990, Mar. 16 **Litho.** *Perf. 13½x12½*

99 A252 5s **multicolored** *(623,155)* 1.50 1.40
First day cover 1.50
Inscription block of 4 6.00 —
100 A252 11s **multicolored** *(588,742)* 2.75 2.50
First day cover 2.50
First day cover, #99-100 4.75
Inscription block of 4 11.50 —

First day covers of Nos. 99-100 total 123,657.

Medicinal Plants Type

1990, May 4 **Photo.** **Granite Paper** *Perf. 11½*

101 A253 4.50s Bixa orellana *(709,840)* 1.50 1.40
First day cover 1.50
Inscription block of 4 6.00 —
102 A253 9.50s Momordica charantia *(732,883)* 2.75 2.50
First day cover 2.50
First day cover, #101-102 4.75
Inscription block of 4 11.50 —

First day covers of Nos. 101-102 total 117,545.

UN 45th Anniv. Type

Designed by Talib Nauman, Pakistan (7s), Marleen Bosmans (9s), Robert Stein, US (No. 105).
Designs: 7s, 9s, "45" and emblem.

1990, June 26 **Litho.** *Perf. 14½x13*

103 A254 7s **multicolored** *(604,878)* 1.60 1.50
First day cover 1.75
Inscription block of 4 6.50 —
104 A254 9s **multicolored, diff.** *(550,902)* 2.50 2.40
First day cover 2.25
First day cover, #103-104 4.00
Inscription block of 4 12.00 —

Souvenir Sheet

105 Sheet of 2, #103-104 *(423,370)* 6.50 6.25
First day cover 5.00

First day covers of Nos. 103-105 total 181,174.

Crime Prevention Type

1990, Sept. 13 **Photo.** *Perf. 14*

106 A255 6s Domestic violence *(661,810)* 1.25 1.25
First day cover 1.50
Inscription block of 4 5.50 —
107 A255 8s Crimes against cultural heritage *(607,940)* 2.50 2.25
First day cover 2.25
First day cover, #106-107 3.00
Inscription block of 4 11.00 —

First day covers of Nos. 106-107 total 112,193.

Human Rights Type of 1989

Panes of 12+12 se-tenant labels containing Articles 11 (4.50s) or 12 (7s) inscribed in German, English or French.
Paintings: 4.50s, Before the Judge, by Sandor Bihari. 7s, Young Man Greeted by a Woman Writing a Poem, by Suzuki Harunobu.

1990, Nov. 16 **Litho.** *Perf. 13½*

108 A250 4.50s **multicolored** *(1,684,833)* .40 .40
First day cover 1.25
Inscription block of 3 + 3 labels 1.25 —
109 A250 7s **multicolored** *(1,541,022)* 1.25 1.25
First day cover 1.75
First day cover, #108-109 2.50
Inscription block of 3 + 3 labels 4.25 —
Panes of 12, #108-109 22.50

First day covers of Nos. 108-109 total 168,831.

Economic Commission for Europe Type

1991, Mar. 15 **Litho.** *Perf. 14*

110 A256 5s Weasel, hoopoe *(727,436)* 1.25 1.00
111 A256 5s Warbler, swans *(727,436)* 1.25 1.00
112 A256 5s Badgers, squirrel *(727,436)* 1.25 1.00
113 A256 5s Fish *(727,436)* 1.25 1.00
a. Block of 4, #110-113 5.50 4.75
First day cover, No. 113a 5.00
First day cover, Nos. 110-113, each 2.00
Inscription block of 4, #110-113 6.00 —
Pane of 40, #110-113 55.00

First day covers of Nos. 110-113 total 81,624.

Namibian Independence Type

1991, May 10 **Litho.** *Perf. 14*

114 A257 6s Mountains, clouds *(531,789)* 1.50 1.40
First day cover 2.50
Inscription block of 4 6.00 —
115 A257 9.50s Dune, Namib Desert *(503,735)* 3.50 3.50
First day cover 3.75
First day cover, #114-115 4.50
Inscription block of 4 14.50 —

First day covers of Nos. 114-115 total 111,184.

V24

Printed by House of Questa, United Kingdom. Designed by Marina Langer-Rosa, Germany.

1991, May 10 **Litho.** *Perf. 15x14½*

116 V24 20s **multicolored** *(1,750,000)+* 3.50 3.25
First day cover *(60,843)* 4.00
Inscription block of 4 15.00 —

V25

Rights of the Child — V26

Printed by The House of Questa. Panes of 50. Designed by Anna Harmer, Austria (7s) and Emiko Takegawa, Japan (9s).

1991, June 14 **Litho.** *Perf. 14½*

117 V25 7s Stick drawings *(645,145)* 1.50 1.50
First day cover 1.75
Inscription block of 4 6.75 —
118 V26 9s Child, clock, fruit *(568,214)* 2.00 2.00
First day cover 2.25
First day cover, #117-118 3.50
Inscription block of 4 10.00 —

First day covers of Nos. 117-118 total 120,619.

V27

Banning of Chemical Weapons
V28

Printed by Heraclio Fournier, S.A. Panes of 50. Designed by Oscar Asboth, Austria (5s), Michel Granger, France (10s).

1991, Sept. 11 **Litho.** *Perf. 13½*

119 V27 5s **multicolored** *(469,454)* 1.40 1.25
First day cover 1.40
Inscription block of 4 6.00 —
120 V28 10s **multicolored** *(525,704)* 2.75 2.40
First day cover 2.40
First day cover, #119-120 3.00
Inscription block of 4 11.50 —

First day covers of Nos. 119-120 total 116,862.

UN Postal Administration, 40th Anniv. Type

1991, Oct. 24 **Litho.** *Perf. 14x15*

121 A263 5s UN NY No. 8 *(564,450)* .85 .85
First day cover 1.40
Inscription block of 4 4.00 —
122 A263 8s UN NY No. 5 *(609,830)* 2.00 2.00
First day cover 2.10
First day cover, #121-122 3.25
Inscription block of 4 9.00 —
Panes of 25, #121-122 72.50

First day covers of Nos. 121-122 total 107,802.

Human Rights Type of 1989

Panes of 12+12 se-tenant labels containing Articles 17 (4.50s) or 18 (7s) inscribed in German, English or French.
Artwork: 4.50s, Pre-columbian Mexican pottery. 7s, Windows, by Robert Delaunay.

1991, Nov. 20 **Litho.** *Perf. 13½*

123 A250 4.50s **black & brown** *(1,717,097)* .75 .75
First day cover 2.25
Inscription block of 3 + 3 labels 3.00 —
124 A250 7s **multicolored** *(1,717,738)* 1.25 1.25
First day cover 3.50
First day cover, #123-124 3.50
Inscription block of 3 + 3 labels 5.00 —
Panes of 12+12 labels, #123-124 27.50

First day covers of Nos. 123-124 total 204,854.

World Heritage Type of 1984

Designs: 5s, Iguacu Natl. Park, Brazil. 9s, Abu Simbel, Egypt.

1992, Jan. 24 **Litho.** ***Perf. 13***
Size: 35x28mm

125 V10 5s **multicolored** *(586,738)* 1.25 1.25
First day cancel 1.50
Inscription block of 4 5.75 —
126 V10 9s **multicolored** *(476,965)* 2.25 2.25
First day cancel 2.75
First day cancel, #125-126 4.00
Inscription block of 4 9.00 —

First day covers of Nos. 125-126 total 93,016.

Clean Oceans Type

1992, Mar. 13 **Litho.** ***Perf. 14***

127 A264 7s Ocean surface, diff. *(1,121,870)* 1.10 1.10
128 A264 7s Ocean bottom, diff. *(1,121,870)* 1.10 1.10
a. Pair, #127-128 2.25 2.25
First day cover, #128a 3.25
First day cover, #127-128, any single 2.00
Inscription block of 4, 2 each #127-128 5.00 —
Pane of 12, #127-128 16.00

First day covers of Nos. 127-128 total 128,478.

Earth Summit Type

1992, May 22 **Photo.** ***Perf. 11½***

129 A265 5.50s Man in space *(784,197)* 1.25 1.00
130 A265 5.50s Sun *(784,197)* 1.25 1.00
131 A265 5.50s Man fishing *(784,197)* 1.25 1.00
132 A265 5.50s Sailboat *(784,197)* 1.25 1.00
a. Block of 4, #129-132 6.50 4.25
First day cover, #132a 6.00
First day cover, #129-132, any single 4.00
Inscription block of 4, #129-132 7.00 —
Pane of 40, #129-132 60.00

First day covers of Nos. 129-132a total 82,920.

Mission to Planet Earth Type

Designs: No. 133, Satellite, person's mouth. No. 134, Satellite, person's ear.

1992, Sept. 4 **Photo.** ***Rouletted 8***
Granite Paper

133 A266 10s **multicolored** *(881,716)* 2.90 2.75
134 A266 10s **multicolored** *(881,716)* 2.90 2.75
a. Pair, #133-134 6.00 5.50
First day cover, #134a 4.50
First day cover, #133-134, any single 7.50
Inscription block of 4, #133-134 12.50 —
Pane of 10, #133-134 30.00

First day covers of Nos. 133-134 total 99,459.

Science and Technology Type of 1992

Designs: 5.50s, Woman emerging from computer screen. 7s, Green thumb growing flowers.

1992, Oct. 2 **Litho.** ***Perf. 14***

135 A267 5.50s **multicolored** *(482,830)* .80 .80
First day cover 1.75
Inscription block of 4 3.75 —
136 A267 7s **multicolored** *(500,517)* 1.50 1.50
First day cover 2.00
First day cover, #135-136 4.00
Inscription block of 4 6.75 —

First day covers of Nos. 135-136 total 98,091.

V29

Intl. Center, Vienna — V30

Printed by Walsall Secruity Printers, Ltd., UK. Designed by Gundi Groh, Austria (5.50s), Rocco J. Callari, US (7s).

1992, Oct. 2 **Litho.** ***Perf. 13x13½***

137 V29 5.50s **multicolored** *(2,100,000)+* 1.00 1.00
First day cover 1.25
Inscription block of 4 5.00 —

Perf. 13½x13

138 V30 7s **multicolored** *(2,100,000)+* 1.50 1.50
First day cover 2.00
First day cover, #137-138 3.50
Inscription block of 4 7.50 —

First day covers of Nos. 137-138 total 151,788.

Human Rights Type of 1989

Panes of 12+12 se-tenant labels containing Articles 23 (6s) and 24 (10s) inscribed in German, English or French.

Artwork: 6s, Les Constructeurs, by Fernand Leger. 10s, Sunday Afternoon on the Island of Le Grande Jatte, by Georges Seurat.

1992, Nov. 20 **Litho.** ***Perf. 13½***

139 A250 6s **multicolored,** *(1,536,516)* 1.00 1.00
First day cover 3.50
Inscription block of 3 + 3 labels 4.00 —
140 A250 10s **multicolored,** *(1,527,861)* 1.75 1.75
First day cover 5.00
Inscription block of 3 + 3 labels 7.00 —
First day cover, #139-140 2.00
Panes of 12, #139-140 32.50

Aging With Dignity Type

Designs: 5.50s, Elderly couple, family working in garden. 7s, Older woman teaching.

1993, Feb. 5 **Litho.** ***Perf. 13***

141 A270 5.50s **multicolored** *(428,886)* 1.00 1.00
First day cover 1.60
Inscription block of 4 4.50 —
142 A270 7s **multicolored** *(459,471)* 1.60 1.60
First day cover 2.00
First day cover, #141-142 3.00
Inscription block of 4 7.50 —

First day covers of Nos. 141-142 total 87,052.

Endangered Species Type

Designed by Rocco J. Callari and Steve Brennan, US.

Designs: No. 143, Equus grevyi (Grevy's zebra). No. 144, Spheniscus humboldti (Humboldt's penguins). No. 145, Varanus griseus (desert monitor). No. 146, Canis lupus (gray wolf).

1993, Mar. 2 **Litho.** ***Perf. 13x12½***

143 A271 7s **multicolored** *(1,200,000)+* 1.25 1.10
144 A271 7s **multicolored** *(1,200,000)+* 1.25 1.10
145 A271 7s **multicolored** *(1,200,000)+* 1.25 1.10
146 A271 7s **multicolored** *(1,200,000)+* 1.25 1.10
a. Block of 4, #143-146 5.00 4.50
First day cover, #146a 5.25
First day cover, #143-146, any single 1.75
Inscription block of 4, #146a 5.00 —
Pane of 16, #143-146 20.00

First day covers of Nos. 143-146a total 106,211.

Healthy Environment Type

1993, May 7 **Litho.** ***Perf. 15x14½***

147 A272 6s **Wave in ocean** *(517,433)* 1.40 1.40
First day cover 1.50
Inscription block of 4 6.00
148 A272 10s **Globe** *(453,123)* 2.25 2.00
First day cover 2.25
First day cover, #147-148 3.50
Inscription block of 4 10.00 —

First day covers of Nos. 147-148 total 79,773.

V31

Designed by Marek Kwiatkowski, Poland. Printed by Helio Courvoisier S.A., Switzerland.

1993, May 7 **Photo.** ***Perf. 11½***
Granite Paper

149 V31 13s **multicolored** *(1,500,000)+* 3.00 2.50
First day cover *(41,489)* 2.50
Inscription block of 4 12.50 —

Human Rights Type of 1989

Printed in sheets of 12 + 12 se-tenant labels containing Article 29 (5s) and 30 (6s) inscribed in German, English or French.

Artwork: 5s, Lower Austrian Peasants' Wedding, by Ferdinand G. Waldmuller. 6s, Outback, by Sally Morgan.

1993, June 11 **Litho.** ***Perf. 13½***

150 A250 5s **multicolored** *(1,532,531)* 1.25 1.25
First day cover 2.50
Inscription block of 3 + 3 labels 4.00 —
151 A250 6s **multicolored** *(1,542,716)* 1.50 1.50
First day cover 3.50
First day cover, #150-151 1.50
Inscription block of 3 + 3 labels 5.00 —
Panes of 12, #150-151 32.50

First day covers of Nos. 150-151 total 128,687.

Intl. Peace Day Type

Denomination at: No. 152, UL. No. 153, UR. No. 154, LL. No. 155, LR.

1993, Sept. 21 **Litho. & Engr.** ***Rouletted 12½***

152 A274 5.50s **green & multi** *(445,699)* 2.00 1.75
153 A274 5.50s **green & multi** *(445,699)* 2.00 1.75
154 A274 5.50s **green & multi** *(445,699)* 2.00 1.75
155 A274 5.50s **green & multi** *(445,699)* 2.00 1.75
a. Block of 4, #152-155 8.50 7.00
First day cover, #155a 4.00
First day cover, #152-155, any single 2.25
Inscription block of 4, #155a 8.75 —
Pane of 40, #152-155 90.00

First day covers of Nos. 152-155a total 67,075.

Environment-Climate Type

Designs: No. 156, Monkeys. No. 157, Bluebird, industrial pollution, volcano. No. 158, Volcano, nuclear power plant, tree stumps. No. 159, Cactus, tree stumps, owl.

1993, Oct. 29 **Litho.** ***Perf. 14½***

156 A275 7s **multicolored** *(484,517)* 2.50 2.40
157 A275 7s **multicolored** *(484,517)* 2.50 2.40
158 A275 7s **multicolored** *(484,517)* 2.50 2.40
159 A275 7s **multicolored** *(484,517)* 2.50 2.40
a. Strip of 4, #156-159 10.00 9.50
First day cover, #159a 9.50
First day cover, #156-159, any single 4.00
Inscription block of 8, 2 #159a 21.00 —
Pane of 24, #156-159 60.00

First day covers of Nos. 156-159a total 61,946.

Intl. Year of the Family Type of 1993

Designs: 5.50s, Adults, children holding hands. 8s, Two adults, child planting crops.

1994, Feb. 4 **Litho.** ***Perf. 13.1***

160 A276 5.50s **blue green & multi** *(650,000)+* 1.25 1.25
First day cover 1.60
Inscription block of 4 5.75 —
161 A276 8s **red & multi** *(650,000)+* 2.00 2.00
First day cover 2.25
First day cover, #160-161 3.00
Inscription block of 4 8.75 —

First day covers of Nos. 160-161 total 78,532.

Endangered Species Type of 1993

Designed by Rocco J. Callari, US (frame), and Paul Margocsy, Australia (stamps).

Designs: No. 162, Ocelot. No. 163, White-breasted silver-eye. No. 164, Mediterranean monk seal. No. 165, Asian elephant.

1994, Mar. 18 **Litho.** ***Perf. 12.7***

162 A271 7s **multicolored** *(1,200,000)+* 1.40 1.40
163 A271 7s **multicolored** *(1,200,000)+* 1.40 1.40
164 A271 7s **multicolored** *(1,200,000)+* 1.40 1.40
165 A271 7s **multicolored** *(1,200,000)+* 1.40 1.40
a. Block of 4, #162-165 5.75 5.75
First day cover, #165a 6.00
First day cover, #162-165, each 2.25
Inscription block of 4, #165a 5.75 —
Pane of 16, #162-165 22.50

First day covers of Nos. 162-165a total 104,478.

Protection for Refugees Type

Design: 12s, Protective hands surround group of refugees.

1994, Apr. 29 **Litho.** ***Perf. 14.3x14.8***

166 A277 12s **multicolored** *(650,000)+* 1.50 1.50
First day cover *(49,519)* 3.00
Inscription block of 4 8.00 —

V32

V33

V34

Designed by Masatoshi Hioki, Japan (#167), Ramon Alcantara Rodriguez, Mexico (#168), Eliezer Weishoff, Israel (#169).
Printed by Cartor, S.A., France.

1994, Apr. 29 Litho. *Perf. 12.9*
167 V32 50g **multicolored** *(1,450,000)+* .20 .20
First day cover 1.25
Inscription block of 4 .40 —
168 V33 4s **multicolored** *(1,150,000)+* .70 .70
First day cover 1.25
Inscription block of 4 3.50 —
169 V34 30s **multicolored** *(560,000)+* 5.00 4.00
First day cover 5.00
Inscription block of 4 22.50 —

First day covers of Nos. 167-169 total 74,558.

Intl. Decade for Natural Disaster Reduction Type

Earth seen from space, outline map of: No. 170, North America. No. 171, Eurasia. No. 172, South America. No. 173, Australia and South Asia.

1994, May 27 Litho. *Perf. 13.9x14.2*
170 A281 6s **multicolored** *(690,000)+* 1.90 1.75
171 A281 6s **multicolored** *(690,000)+* 1.90 1.75
172 A281 6s **multicolored** *(690,000)+* 1.90 1.75
173 A281 6s **multicolored** *(690,000)+* 1.90 1.75
a. Block of 4, #170-173 8.00 7.00
First day cover, #173a 6.00
First day cover, #170-173, each 3.25
Inscription block of 4, #173a 8.50 —
Pane of 40, #170-173 82.50

First day covers of Nos. 170-173a total 52,502.

Population and Development Type

Designs: 5.50s, Women teaching, running machine tool, coming home to family. 7s, Family on tropical island.

1994, Sept. 1 Litho. *Perf. 13.2x13.6*
174 A282 5.50s **multicolored** *(650,000)+* 1.75 1.60
First day cover 2.00
Inscription block of 4 7.50 —
175 A282 7s **multicolored** *(650,000)+* 2.25 2.10
First day cover 2.00
First day cover, #174-175 5.00
Inscription block of 4 9.00 —

First day covers of Nos. 174-175 total 67,423.

UNCTAD Type

1994, Oct. 28
176 A283 6s **multi, diff.** *(650,000)+* 1.50 1.25
First day cover 1.25
Inscription block of 4 6.50 —
177 A283 7s **multi, diff.** *(650,000)+* 1.75 1.50
First day cover 1.75
First day cover, #176-177 3.00
Inscription block of 4 7.50 —

First day covers of Nos. 176-177 total 67,064.

UN 50th Anniv. Type

1995, Jan. 1 Litho. & Engr. *Perf. 13.4*
178 A284 7s **multicolored** *(742,052)* 1.60 1.50
First day cover *(118,537)* 2.00
Inscription block of 4 7.00 —

Social Summit Type

1995, Feb. 3 Photo. & Engr. *Perf. 13.6x13.9*
179 A285 14s **multi, diff.** *(595,554)* 2.50 2.50
First day cover *(51,244)* 3.50
Inscription block of 4 11.00 —

Endangered Species Type of 1993

Designed by Salvatore Catalano, US.
Designs: No. 180, Black rhinoceros, Diceros bicornis. No. 181, Golden conure, Aratinga guarouba. No. 182, Douc langur, Pygathrix nemaeus. No. 183, Arabian oryx, Oryx leucoryx.

1995, Mar. 24 Litho. *Perf. 13x12½*
180 A271 7s **multicolored** *(938,000)+* 1.25 1.25
181 A271 7s **multicolored** *(938,000)+* 1.25 1.25
182 A271 7s **multicolored** *(938,000)+* 1.25 1.25
183 A271 7s **multicolored** *(938,000)+* 1.25 1.25
a. Block of 4, 180-183 5.00 5.00
First day cover, #183a 4.50
First day cover, #180-183, each 2.00
Inscription block of 4, #183a 5.00 —
Pane of 16, #180-183 22.50

First day covers of Nos. 180-183a total 95,401.

Intl. Youth Year Type

Designs: 6s, Village in winter. 7s, Teepees.

1995, May 26 Litho. *Perf. 14.4x14.7*
184 A286 6s **multicolored** *(437,462)* 1.50 1.25
First day cover 1.50
Inscription block of 4 6.00 —
185 A286 7s **multicolored** *(409,449)* 1.75 1.75
First day cover 2.50
First day cover, #184-185 4.25
Inscription block of 4 7.50 —

First day covers of Nos. 184-185 total 60,979.

UN, 50th Anniv. Type

Designs: 7s, Like No. 663. 10s, Like No. 664.

1995, June 26 Engr. *Perf. 13.3x13.6*
186 A287 7s **green** *(433,922)* 1.40 1.40
First day cover 2.00
Inscription block of 4 6.50 —
187 A287 10s **black** *(471,198)* 2.00 1.75
First day cover 1.75
First day cover, #186-187 4.00
Inscription block of 4 11.00 —

Souvenir Sheet
Litho. & Engr.
Imperf

188 Sheet of 2, #186-187 *(367,773)* 4.50 4.50
a. A287 7s **green** 1.75 1.75
b. A287 10s **black** 2.50 2.50
First day cover 6.50

First day covers of Nos. 186-188b total 171,765.

Conference on Women Type

Designs: 5.50s, Women amid tropical plants. 6s, Woman reading, swans on lake.

1995, Sept. 5 Photo. *Perf. 12*
189 A288 5.50s **multicolored** *(549,951)* 1.25 1.25
First day cover 1.50
Inscription block of 4 5.50 —

Size: 28x50mm

190 A288 6s **multicolored** *(556,569)* 2.25 2.00
First day cover 1.50
First day cover, #189-190 3.50
Inscription block of 4 10.00 —

First day covers of Nos. 189-190 total 71,976.

UN People, 50th Anniv. Type

1995, Oct. 24 Litho. *Perf. 14*
191 Sheet of 12 *(280,528 sheets)* 19.00 19.00
First day cover 16.00
a.-l. A290 3s any single 1.50 1.25
First day cover, #191a-191 l, each 1.25
192 Souvenir booklet, *(95,449 booklets)* 21.00
a. A290 3s Booklet pane of 3, vert. strip of 3 from UL of sheet 5.00 5.00
b. A290 3s Booklet pane of 3, vert. strip of 3 from UR of sheet 5.00 5.00
c. A290 3s Booklet pane of 3, vert. strip of 3 from LL of sheet 5.00 5.00
d. A290 3s Booklet pane of 3, vert. strip of 3 from LR of sheet 5.00 5.00

First day covers of Nos. 191-192d total 107,436.

WFUNA, 50th Anniv. Type

Design: 7s, Harlequin holding dove.

1996, Feb. 2 Litho. *Perf. 13x13½*
193 A291 7s **multicolored** *(655,000)+* 1.40 1.00
First day cover 2.00
Inscription block of 4 6.75 —

UN Flag — V35

Abstract, by Karl Korab — V36

Printed by House of Questa, UK.

1996, Feb. 2 Litho. *Perf. 15x14½*
194 V35 1s **multicolored** *(1,180,000)+* .20 .20
First day cover 1.25
Inscription block of 4 1.00 —
195 V36 10s **multicolored** *(880,000)+* 2.00 2.00
First day cover 2.75
First day cover, #194-195 4.50
Inscription block of 4 10.00 —

Endangered Species Type of 1993

Designs: No. 196, Cypripedium calceolus. No. 197, Aztekium ritteri. No. 198, Euphorbia cremersii. No. 199, Dracula bella.

1996, Mar. 14 Litho. *Perf. 12½*
196 A271 7s **multicolored** *(846,000)+* 1.25 1.00
197 A271 7s **multicolored** *(846,000)+* 1.25 1.00
198 A271 7s **multicolored** *(846,000)+* 1.25 1.00
199 A271 7s **multicolored** *(846,000)+* 1.25 1.00
a. Block of 4, #196-199 5.25 4.25
First day cover, #199a 4.50
First day cover, #196-199, each 2.00
Inscription block of 4, #199a 5.50 —
Pane of 16, #196-199 21.00

City Summit Type

Designs: No. 200, Arab family selling fruits, vegetables. No. 201, Women beside stream, camels. No. 202, Woman carrying bundle on head, city skyline. No. 203, Woman threshing grain, yoke of oxen in field. No. 204, Native village, elephant.

1996, June 3 Litho. *Perf. 14x13½*
200 A293 6s **multicolored** *(500,000)+* 2.50 2.25
201 A293 6s **multicolored** *(500,000)+* 2.50 2.25
202 A293 6s **multicolored** *(500,000)+* 2.50 2.25
203 A293 6s **multicolored** *(500,000)+* 2.50 2.25
204 A293 6s **multicolored** *(500,000)+* 2.50 2.25
a. Strip of 5, #200-204 12.50 12.00
First day cover, #204a 11.50
First day cover, #200-204, each 3.00
Inscription block of 10, 2 #204a 25.00

Sport and the Environment Type

6s, Men's parallel bars (gymnastics), vert. 7s, Hurdles.

1996, July 19 Litho. *Perf. 14x14½, 14½x14*
205 A294 6s **multicolored** *(730,000)+* 1.25 1.25
First day cover 2.75
Inscription block of 4 5.50 —
206 A294 7s **multicolored** *(730,000)+* 1.75 1.75
First day cover 3.00
First day cover, #205-206 6.00
Inscription block of 4 7.75 —

Souvenir Sheet

207 A294 Sheet of 2, #205-206 *(500,000)+* 3.25 3.00
First day cover 10.00

Plea for Peace Type

Designed by: 7s, Du Keqing, China. 10s, Xu Kangdeng, China.

Designs: 7s, Dove and butterflies. 10s, Stylized dove, diff.

1996, Sept. 17 Litho. *Perf. 14½x15*
208 A295 7s **multicolored** *(655,000)+* 1.25 1.25
First day cover 1.50
Inscription block of 4 6.50 —
209 A295 10s **multicolored** *(655,000)+* 1.90 1.75
First day cover 2.50
First day cover, #208-209 5.00
Inscription block of 4 9.50 —

UNICEF Type

Fairy Tales: 5.50s, Hansel and Gretel, by the Brothers Grimm. 8s, How Maui Stole Fire from the Gods, South Pacific.

1996, Nov. 20 Litho. *Perf. 14½x15*
210 A296 5.50s **multicolored** *(1,160,000)+* 1.00 .90
First day cover 1.25
Pane of 8 + label 8.00
211 A296 8s **multicolored** *(1,160,000)+* 1.50 1.50
First day cover 2.00
First day cover, #210-211 4.00
Pane of 8 + label 12.00

V37

Phoenixes Flying Down (Detail), by Sagenji Yoshida — V38

Printed by The House of Questa, Ltd., UK.

1997, Feb. 12 Litho. *Perf. 14½*
212 V37 5s **multicolored** *(750,000)+* .85 .85
First day cover 1.25
Inscription block of 4 3.40 —
213 V38 6s **multicolored** *(1,050,000)+* 1.00 1.00
First day cover 1.50
First day cover, #212-213 4.00
Inscription block of 4 4.00 —

First day covers of Nos. 212-213 total 156,021.

Endangered Species Type of 1993

Designs: No. 214, Macaca sylvanus (Barbary macaque). No. 215, Anthropoides paradisea (blue crane). No. 216, Equus przewalskii (Przewalski horse). No. 217, Myrmecophaga tridactyla (giant anteater).

1997, Mar. 13 **Litho.** ***Perf. 12½***
214 A271 7s **multicolored** *(710,000)+* 1.50 1.25
215 A271 7s **multicolored** *(710,000)+* 1.50 1.25
216 A271 7s **multicolored** *(710,000)+* 1.50 1.25
217 A271 7s **multicolored** *(710,000)+* 1.50 1.25
a. Block of 4, #214-217 6.00 5.25
First day cover, #217a 6.00
First day cover, #214-217, each 2.50
Inscription block of 4, #217a 6.25
Pane of 16 25.00

First day covers of Nos. 214-217 total 86,406.

Earth Summit Anniv. Type

Designs: No. 218, Person running. No. 219, Hills, stream, trees. No. 220, Tree with orange leaves. No. 221, Tree with pink leaves.
11s, Combined design similar to Nos. 218-221.

1997, May 30 **Photo.** ***Perf. 11.5***

Granite Paper

218 A299 3.50s **multicolored** *(282,016)* 1.50 1.25
219 A299 3.50s **multicolored** *(282,016)* 1.50 1.25
220 A299 3.50s **multicolored** *(282,016)* 1.50 1.25
221 A299 3.50s **multicolored** *(282,016)* 1.50 1.25
a. Block of 4, #218-221 6.00 5.25
First day cover, #221a 10.00
First day cover, #218-221, each 3.50
Inscription block of 4, #221a 7.25

Souvenir Sheet

222 A299 11s **multicolored** *(221,434)* 2.75 2.75
First day cover 12.00

First day covers of Nos. 218-222 total 62,390.

Transportation Type

Ground transportation: No. 223, 1829 Rocket, 1901 Darraque. No. 224, Steam engine from Vladikawska Railway, trolley. No. 225, Double-decker bus. No. 226, 1950s diesel locomotive, semi-trailer. No. 227, High-speed train, electric car.

1997, Aug. 29 **Litho.** ***Perf. 14x14½***
223 A300 7s **multicolored** *(356,097)* 3.00 2.75
224 A300 7s **multicolored** *(356,097)* 3.00 2.75
225 A300 7s **multicolored** *(356,097)* 3.00 2.75
226 A300 7s **multicolored** *(356,097)* 3.00 2.75
227 A300 7s **multicolored** *(356,097)* 3.00 2.75
a. Strip of 5, #223-227 15.00 14.00
First day cover, #227a 16.00
First day cover, #223-227, each 3.75
Inscription block of 10, 2#227a 30.00

No. 227a has continuous design.
First day covers of Nos. 223-227 total 44,877.

Philately Type

Designs: 6.50s, No. 62. 7s, No. 63.

1997, Oct. 14 **Litho.** ***Perf. 13½x14***
228 A301 6.50s **multicolored** *(379,767)* 1.25 1.25
First day cover 2.50
Inscription block of 4 5.25 —
229 A301 7s **multicolored** *(378,107)* 1.75 1.75
First day cover 3.50
First day cover, #228-229 6.00
Inscription block of 4 7.00 —

First day covers of Nos. 228-229 total 57,651.

World Heritage Convention Type

Terracotta warriors of Xian: 3s, Single warrior. 6s, Massed warriors. No. 232a, like #716. No. 232b, like #717. No. 232c, like Geneva #314. No. 232d, like Geneva #315. No. 232e, like Vienna #230. No. 232f, like Vienna #231.

1997, Nov. 19 **Litho.** ***Perf. 13½***
230 A302 3s **multicolored** *(528,352)* 1.25 1.25
First day cover 1.50
Inscription block of 4 5.00 —
231 A302 6s **multicolored** *(530,947)* 2.50 2.25
First day cover 2.75
First day cover, #230-231 5.00
Inscription block of 4 10.00 —
232 Souvenir booklet *(298,055 booklets)* 8.00
a.-f. A302 1s any single .30 .30
g. Booklet pane of 4 #232a 1.25 1.25
h. Booklet pane of 4 #232b 1.25 1.25
i. Booklet pane of 4 #232c 1.25 1.25
j. Booklet pane of 4 #232d 1.25 1.25
k. Booklet pane of 4 #232e 1.25 1.25
l. Booklet pane of 4 #232f 1.25 1.25

First day covers of Nos. 230-232 total 71,708.

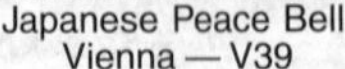

Japanese Peace Bell, Vienna — V39

Vienna Subway, Vienna Intl. Center — V40

Printed by The House of Questa, UK. Panes of 20.
Designed by Heinz Pfeifer, Austria (6.50s), Pigneter, Austria (9s).

1998, Feb. 13 **Litho.** ***Perf. 15x14½***
233 V39 6.50s **multicolored** *(670,000)+* 1.00 1.00
First day cover 3.25
Inscription block of 4 4.50 —
234 V40 9s **multicolored** *(770,000)+* 1.50 1.50
First day cover 4.50
First day cover, #233-234 3.00
Inscription block of 4 6.25 —

Endangered Species Type of 1993

Designed by Rocco J. Callari, US and Robert Hynes, US.
Designs: No. 235, Chelonia mydas (green turtle). No. 236, Speotyto cunicularia (burrowing owl). No. 237, Trogonoptera brookiana (Rajah Brooke's birdwing). No. 238, Ailurus fulgens (lesser panda).

1998, Mar. 13 **Litho.** ***Perf. 12½***
235 A271 7s **multicolored** *(620,000)+* 1.50 1.25
236 A271 7s **multicolored** *(620,000)+* 1.50 1.25
237 A271 7s **multicolored** *(620,000)+* 1.50 1.25
238 A271 7s **multicolored** *(620,000)+* 1.50 1.25
a. Block of 4, #235-238 6.00 5.00
First day cover, #238a 5.00
First day cover, #235-238, each 2.50
Inscription block of 4, #238a 6.25 —
Pane of 16 25.00

Intl. Year of the Ocean — V41

Designed by Yuan Lee, China.

1998, May 20 **Litho.** ***Perf. 13x13½***
239 V41 Sheet of 12 *(345,000)+* 12.00 11.00
a.-l. 3.50s any single 1.00 1.00
First day cover, 3239 17.00
First day cover, #239a-239l, each 2.00

Rain Forests Type

1998, June 19 ***Perf. 13x13½***
240 A307 6.50s Ocelot *(590,000)+* 1.00 1.00
First day cover 4.00
Inscription block of 4 5.00 —

Souvenir Sheet

241 A307 22s like #240 *(340,000)+* 3.50 3.25
First day cover 5.25

Peacekeeping Type of 1998

Designs: 4s, Soldier passing out relief supplies. 7.50s, UN supervised voting.

1998, Sept. 15 **Photo.** ***Perf. 12***
242 A308 4s multicolored *(555,000)+* .70 .70
First day cover 1.25
Inscription block of 4 2.80 —
243 A308 7.50s multicolored *(545,000)+* 1.25 1.25
First day cover 1.75
First day cover, #242-243 4.00
Inscription block of 4 5.25 —

Declaration of Human Rights Type

Designs: 4.50s, Stylized person. 7s, Gears.

1998, Oct. 27 **Litho. & Photo.** ***Perf. 13***
244 A309 4.50s multicolored *(555,000)+* .80 .80
First day cover 1.50
Inscription block of 4 3.25 —
245 A309 7s multicolored *(545,000)+* 1.25 1.25
First day cover 2.75
First day cover, #244-245 4.00
Inscription block of 4 5.00 —

Schönbrunn Palace Type

Designs: 3.50s, #248d, Palace. 7s, #248c, Porcelain stove, vert. No. 248a, Blue porcelain vase, vert. No. 248b, Wall painting on fabric (detail), by Johann Wenzl Bergl, vert. No. 248e, Great Palm House (conservatory). No. 248f, The Gloriette (archway).

1998, Dec. 4 **Litho.** ***Perf. 14***
246 A310 3.50s **multicolored** *(615,000)+* .60 .60
First day cover 2.00
Inscription block of 4 2.50 —
247 A310 7s **multicolored** *(615,000)+* 1.10 1.10
First day cover 2.75
First day cover, #246-247 4.00
Inscription block of 4 4.50 —

Souvenir Booklet

248 Booklet *(158,000)+* 6.50
a.-c. A310 1s any single .25 .25
d.-f. A310 2s any single .35 .35
g. Booklet pane of 4 #248d 1.40 1.25
h. Booklet pane of 3 #248a .75 .65
i. Booklet pane of 3 #248b .75 .65
j. Booklet pane of 3 #248c .75 .65
k. Booklet pane of 4 #248e 1.40 1.25
l. Booklet pane of 4 #248f 1.40 1.25

Volcanic Landscape — V42

Designed by Peter Pongratz, Austria. Printed by Johann Enschedé and Sons, the Netherlands.

1999, Feb. 5 **Litho.** ***Perf. 13x13½***
249 V42 8s **multicolored** *(660,000)+* 2.00 1.90
First day cover *(33,022)* 4.00
Inscription block of 4 9.00 —

World Heritage, Australia Type

Designs: 4.50s, #252d, Uluru-Kata Tjuta Natl. Park. 6.50s, #252a, Tasmanian Wilderness. No. 252b, Wet tropics of Queensland. No. 252c, Great Barrier Reef. No. 252e, Kakadu Natl. Park. No. 252f, Willandra Lakes region.

1999, Mar. 19 **Litho.** ***Perf. 13***
250 A313 4.50s **multicolored** *(540,000)+* .75 .75
First day cover 1.25
Inscription block of 4 3.00 —
251 A313 6.50s **multicolored** *(540,000)+* 1.10 1.10
First day cover 1.50
First day cover, #250-251 4.50
Inscription block of 4 4.50 —

Souvenir Booklet

252 Booklet *(116,000)+* 6.75
a.-c. A313 1s any single .20 .20
d.-f. A313 2s any single .35 .35
g. Booklet pane of 4, #252a .80
h. Booklet pane of 4, #252d 1.40
i. Booklet pane of 4, #252b .80
j. Booklet pane of 4, #252e 1.40
k. Booklet pane of 4, #252c .80
l. Booklet pane of 4, #252f 1.40

First day covers of Nos. 250-252 total 65,123.

Endangered Specied Type of 1993

Designed by Jeffrey Terreson, US.
Designs: No. 253, Pongo pygmaeus (oran-utan). No. 254, Pelecanus crispus (Dalmatian pelican). No. 255, Eunectes notaeus (yellow anaconda). No. 256, Caracal.

1999, Apr. 22 **Litho.** ***Perf. 12½***
253 A271 7s **multicolored** *(552,000)+* 1.10 1.10
254 A271 7s **multicolored** *(552,000)+* 1.10 1.10
255 A271 7s **multicolored** *(552,000)+* 1.10 1.10
256 A271 7s **multicolored** *(552,000)+* 1.10 1.10
a. Block of 4, #253-256 4.50 4.50

First day cover, #256a 6.00
First day cover, #253-256, each 2.25
Inscription block of 4, #256a 4.75 —
Pane of 16 20.00

First day covers of Nos. 253-256 total 66,733.

UNISPACE III Type

Designs: No. 257, Satellite over ships. No. 258, Satellite up close. No. 259, Composite of #257-258.

1999, July 7 Photo. *Rouletted 8*

257 A314 3.50s **multicolored** *(1,200,000)+* .75 .75
258 A314 3.50s **multicolored** *(1,200,000)+* .75 .75
a. Pair, #257-258 2.00 2.00
First day cover, #258a 3.00
First day cover, #257-258, each 2.50
Inscription block of 4 6.00 —
Pane of 10, #257-258 9.00 —

Souvenir Sheet

Perf. 14½

259 A314 13s **multicolored** *(350,000)+* 4.50 4.00
First day cover 5.00

First day covers of Nos. 257-259 total 72,143.

UPU Type

Various people, late 20th century methods of mail transportation, denomination at: No. 260, UL. No. 261, UR. No. 262, LL. No. 263, LR.

1999, Aug. 23 Photo. *Perf. 11¾*

260 A315 6.50s **multicolored** *(417,000)+* 1.10 1.10
261 A315 6.50s **multicolored** *(417,000)+* 1.10 1.10
262 A315 6.50s **multicolored** *(417,000)+* 1.10 1.10
263 A315 6.50s **multicolored** *(417,000)+* 1.10 1.10
a. Block of 4, #260-263 4.50 4.50
First day cover, #263a 4.50
First day cover, #260-263, each 2.00
Inscription block of 4 4.50 —

First day covers of Nos. 260-263 total 38,453.

In Memoriam Type

Designs: 6.50s, 14s, Donaupark. Size of 14s stamp: 34x63mm.

1999, Sept. 21 Litho. *Perf. 14½x14*

264 A316 6.50s **multicolored** *(530,000)+* 1.10 1.10
First day cover 3.00
Inscription block of 4 4.50 —

Souvenir Sheet

Perf. 14

265 A316 14s **multicolored** *(338,000)+* 2.40 2.25
First day cover 4.00

First day covers of Nos. 264-265 total 61,089.

Education Type

1999, Nov. 18 Litho. *Perf. 13½x13¾*

266 A317 7s Boy, girl, book *(490,000)+* 1.25 1.25
First day cover 1.60
Inscription block of 4 5.00 —
267 A317 13s Group reading *(490,000)+* 2.25 2.25
First day cover 3.00
First day cover, #266-267 4.00
Inscription block of 4 9.00 —

First day covers of Nos. 266-267 total 48,590.

Intl. Year of Thanksgiving Type

2000, Jan. 1 Litho. *Perf. 13¼x13½*

268 A318 7s **multicolored** *(510,000)+* 1.25 1.25
First day cover 3.00
Inscription block of 4 5.00 —

On No. 268 portions of the design were applied by a thermographic process producing a shiny, raised effect.

Endangered Species Type of 1993

Designed by Lori Anzalone, US.

Designs: No. 269, Panthera pardus (leopard). No. 270, Platalea leucorodia (white spoonbill). No. 271, Hippocamelus bisulcus (huemal). No. 272, Orcinus orca (killer whale).

2000, Apr. 6 Litho. *Perf. 12¾x12½*

269 A271 7s **multicolored** *(548,000)+* 1.10 1.10
270 A271 7s **multicolored** *(548,000)+* 1.10 1.10
271 A271 7s **multicolored** *(548,000)+* 1.10 1.10
272 A271 7s **multicolored** *(548,000)+* 1.10 1.10
a. Block of 4, #269-272 4.50 4.50
First day cover, #272a 6.00
First day cover, #269-272, each 2.00
Inscription block of 4, #272a 4.75 —
Pane of 16 18.00

Our World 2000 Type

Winning artwork in Millennium painting competition: 7s, Tomorrow's Dream, by Voltaire Perez, Philippines. 8s, Remembrance, by Dimitris Nalbandis, Greece, vert.

2000, May 30 Litho. *Perf. 13x13½, 13½x13*

273 A319 7s **multicolored** *(430,000)+* 1.10 1.10
First day cover 1.75
Inscription block of 4 4.50 —
274 A319 8s **multicolored** *(430,000)+* 1.25 1.25
First day cover 2.00
First day cover, #273-274 3.00
Inscription block of 4 5.00 —

55th Anniversary Type

Designs: 7s, Secretariat Building, unfinished dome of General Assembly Hall, 1951. 9s, Trygve Lie and Headquraters Advisory Committee at topping-out ceremony, 1949.

2000, July 7 Litho. *Perf. 13¼x13*

275 A320 7s **multicolored** *(440,000)+* 1.10 1.10
First day cover 1.75
Inscription block of 4 4.50 —
276 A320 9s **multicolored** *(440,000)+* 1.50 1.50
First day cover 2.25
First day cover, #275-276 3.00
Inscription block of 4 6.00 —

Souvenir Sheet

277 A320 Sheet of 2, #275-276 *(300,000)+* 2.60 2.25
First day cover 3.25

The UN in the 21st Century — V43

Printed by Government Printing Office, Austria. Designed by Wilson McLean, UK.

No. 278: a, Farm machinery. b, UN Peacekeepers and children. c, Oriental farm workers. d, Peacekeepers searching for mines. e, Medical research. f, Handicapped people.

2000, Sept. 15 Litho. *Perf. 14*

278 V43 Sheet of 6 *(330,000)+* 3.25 1.75
First day cover 3.75
a.-f. 3.50s any single .50 .25

World Heritage, Spain Type

Designs: 4.50s, #281c, Aqueduct of Segovia. 6.50s, #281f, Güell Park, Barcelona. #281a, Alhambra, Generalife and Albayzin, Granada. #281b, Walled Town of Cuenca. #281d, Amphitheater of Mérida. #281e, Toledo.

2000, Oct. 6 Litho. *Perf. 14¾x14½*

279 A323 4.50s **multicolored** *(430,000)+* .70 .35
First day cover 1.25
Inscription block of 4 3.00 —
280 A323 6.50s **multicolored** *(430,000)+* .95 .50
First day cover 1.75
First day cover, #279-280 2.40
Inscription block of 4 4.00 —

Souvenir Booklet

281 Booklet *(92,000)+* 5.50
a.-c. A323 1s any single .20 .20
d.-f. A323 2s any single .30 .30
g. Booklet pane of 4, #281a .55 .50
h. Booklet pane of 4, #281d 1.25 1.10
i. Booklet pane of 4, #281b .55 .50
j. Booklet pane of 4, #281e 1.25 1.10
k. Booklet pane of 4, #281c .55 .50
l. Booklet pane of 4, #281f 1.25 1.10

Respect for Refugees Type

Designs: 7s, 25s, Refugee with hat, three other refugees.

2000, Nov. 9 Litho. *Perf. 13¼x12¾*

282 A324 7s **multicolored** *(530,000)+* 1.10 .55
First day cover 1.75
Inscription block of 4 4.50 —

Souvenir Sheet

283 A324 25s **multicolored** *(273,000)+* 3.75 1.90
First day cover 4.50

Endangered Species Type of 1993

Printed by Johann Enschedé and Sons, the Netherlands. Designed by Betina Ogden, Australia.

Designs: No. 284, Tremarctos ornatus (spectacled bear). No. 285, Anas laysanensis (Laysan duck). No. 286, Proteles cristatus (aardwolf). No. 287, Trachypithecus cristatus (silvered leaf monkey).

2001, Feb. 1 Litho. *Perf. 12¾x12½*

284 A271 7s **multicolored** *(540,000)+* 1.00 .50
285 A271 7s **multicolored** *(540,000)+* 1.00 .50
286 A271 7s **multicolored** *(540,000)+* 1.00 .50
287 A271 7s **multicolored** *(540,000)+* 1.00 .50
a. Block of 4, #284-287 4.00 —
First day cover, #287a 5.00
First day cover, #284-287 each 1.75
Inscription block of 4, #287a 4.25 —
Pane of 16 16.00

Intl. Volunteers Year — V44

Printed by Johann Enschedé and Sons, the Netherlands. Panes of 20. Designed by Rorie Katz and Robert Stein, US.

Paintings by: 10s, Nguyen Thanh Chuong, Viet Nam. 12s, Ikko Tanaka, Japan.

2001, Mar. 29 Litho. *Perf. 13¼*

288 V44 10s **multicolored** *(440,000)+* 1.40 .70
First day cover 2.00
Inscription block of 4 5.75
289 V44 12s **multicolored** *(430,000)+* 1.75 .85
First day cover 2.40
First day cover, #288-289 3.75
Inscription block of 4 7.00

World Heritage, Japan Type

Designs: 7s, #290c, Himeji-Jo. 15s, #291f, Nikko. #292a, Kyoto. #292b, Nara. #292d, Shirakawa-Go and Gokayama. #292e, Itsukushima Shinto Shrine.

2001, Aug. 1 Litho. *Perf. 12¾x13¼*

290 A328 7s **multicolored** *(440,000)+* 1.00 .50
First day cover 1.40
Inscription block of 4 4.00 —
291 A328 15s **multicolored** *(440,000)+* 2.10 1.00
First day cover 3.00
First day cover, #290-291 3.75
Inscription block of 4 8.50 —

Souvenir Booklet

292 Booklet *(78,000)+* 5.00
a.-c. A328 1s any single .20 .20
d.-f. A328 2s any single .25 .25
g. Booklet pane of 4, #292a .55 —
h. Booklet pane of 4, #292d 1.10 —
i. Booklet pane of 4, #292b .55 —
j. Booklet pane of 4, #292e 1.10 —
k. Booklet pane of 4, #292c .55 —
l. Booklet pane of 4, #292f 1.10 —

Dag Hammarskjöld Type

2001, Sept. 18 Engr. *Perf. 11x11¼*

293 A329 7s **green** *(480,000)+* 1.00 .50
First day cover 1.60
Inscription block of 4 4.00 —

UN Postal Administration, 50th Anniv. Types

2001, Oct. 18 Litho. *Perf. 13½*

294 A330 7s Stamps, balloons *(380,000)+* 1.00 .50
First day cover 1.60
Inscription block of 4 4.00 —
295 A330 8s Stamps, cake *(380,000)+* 1.10 .55
First day cover 1.75
First day cover, #294-295 2.75
Inscription block of 4 4.50 —

Souvenir Sheet

296 A331 Sheet of 2 *(225,000)+* 4.00 2.00
a. 7s **green & light blue,** 38mm diameter 1.00 .50
b. 21s **green & light blue,** 38mm diameter 3.00 1.50
First day cover 4.50

Climate Change Type

Designs: No. 297, Solar panels, automobile at pump. No. 298, Blimp, bicyclists, horse and rider. No. 299, Balloon, sailboat, lighthouse, train. No. 300, Bird, train, traffic signs.

2001, Nov. 16 Litho. *Perf. 13¼*

297 A332 7s **multicolored** *(87,000)+* 1.00 .50
298 A332 7s **multicolored** *(87,000)+* 1.00 .50
299 A332 7s **multicolored** *(87,000)+* 1.00 .50
300 A332 7s **multicolored** *(87,000)+* 1.00 .50
a. Horiz. strip, #297-300 4.00 —
Inscription block of 8 8.00 —
First day cover, #300a 4.50
Pane of 24 24.00 —

Nobel Peace Prize Type

2001, Dec. 10 **Litho.** ***Perf. 13¼***
301 A333 7s **multicolored** *(1,260,000)+* 1.00 .50
Inscription block of 4 4.00 —
First day cover 1.60
Pane of 12 12.00 —

100 Cents = 1 Euro (€)

Austrian Tourist Attractions V45

Printed by House of Questa, UK. Panes of 20. Designed by Rorie Katz, US.

Designs: 7c, Semmering Railway. 51c, Pferdschwemme, Salzburg. 58c, Aggstein an der Donau Ruins. 73c, Hallstatt. 87c, Melk Abbey. €2.03, Kapitelschwemme, Salzburg.

2002, Mar. 1 **Litho.** ***Perf. 14½x14***
302 V45 7c **multicolored** *(860,000)+* .20 .20
First day cover 1.25
Inscription block of 4 .55 —
303 V45 51c **multicolored** *(960,000)+* 1.00 .50
First day cover 1.40
Inscription block of 4 4.00 —
304 V45 58c **multicolored** *(860,000)+* 1.10 .55
First day cover 1.60
Inscription block of 4 4.50 —
305 V45 73c **multicolored** *(760,000)+* 1.50 .75
First day cover 2.00
Inscription block of 4 6.00 —
306 V45 87c **multicolored** *(760,000)+* 1.75 .85
First day cover 2.40
Inscription block of 4 7.00 —
307 V45 €2.03 **multicolored** *(710,000)+* 4.00 2.00
First day cover 5.50
First day cover, #288-289 10.50
Inscription block of 4 16.00 —
Nos. 302-307 (6) 9.55 4.85

Endangered Species Type of 1993

Printed by Johann Enschedé and Sons, the Netherlands. Designed by Tim Barrall, US.

Designs: No. 308, Hylobates syndactylus (siamang). No. 309, Spheniscus demersus (jackass penguin). No. 310, Prionodon linsang (banded linsang). No. 311, Bufo retiformis (Sonoran green toad).

2002, Apr. 4 **Litho.** ***Perf. 12¾x12½***
308 A271 51c **multicolored** *(500,000)+* 1.00 .50
309 A271 51c **multicolored** *(500,000)+* 1.00 .50
310 A271 51c **multicolored** *(500,000)+* 1.00 .50
311 A271 51c **multicolored** *(500,000)+* 1.00 .50
a. Block of 4, #308-311 4.00 —
First day cover, #311a 4.75
First day cover, #308-311 each 1.75
Inscription block of 4, #311a 4.25 —
Pane of 16 16.00 —

Independence of East Timor Type

Designs: 51c, Deer horn container with carved wooden stopper. €1.09, Carved wooden tai weaving loom.

2002, May 20 **Litho.** ***Perf. 14x14½***
312 A335 51c **multicolored** *(384,000)+* 1.00 .50
First day cover 1.50
Inscription block of 4 4.00 —
313 A335 €1.09 **multicolored** *(374,000)+* 2.10 1.00
First day cover 3.25
First day cover, #312-313 4.00
Inscription block of 4 8.50 —

Intl. Year of Mountains Type

Designs: No. 314, Mt. Cook, New Zealand. No. 315, Mt. Robson, Canada. No. 316, Mt. Rakaposhi, Pakistan. No. 317, Mt. Everest (Sagarmatha), Nepal.

2002, May 24 **Litho.** ***Perf. 13x13¼***
314 A336 22c **multicolored** *(1,335,000)+* .45 .20
First day cover 1.25
315 A336 22c **multicolored** *(1,335,000)+* .45 .20
First day cover 1.25
316 A336 51c **multicolored** *(1,335,000)+* 1.00 .50
First day cover 1.50
First day cover, #314, 316 2.25
317 A336 51c **multicolored** *(1,335,000)+* 1.00 .50
a. Vert. strip or block of four, #314-317 3.00 1.50
First day cover 1.50
First day cover, #315, 317 2.25
First day cover, #314-317 3.75
Pane of 12, 3 each #314-317 9.00 —

World Summit on Sustainable Development (Peter Max) Type

Designs: No. 318, Rainbow. No. 319, Three women, diff. No. 320, Three faceless people. No. 321, Birds, wave.

2002, June 27 **Litho.** ***Perf. 14½x14***
318 A337 51c **multicolored** *(1,305,000)+* 1.00 .50
First day cover 1.50
319 A337 51c **multicolored** *(1,305,000)+* 1.00 .50
First day cover 1.50
320 A337 58c **multicolored** *(1,305,000)+* 1.10 .55
First day cover 1.60
First day cover, #318, 320 2.50
321 A337 58c **multicolored** *(1,305,000)+* 1.10 .55
a. Vert. strip or block of four, #318-321 4.25 2.10
First day cover 1.60
First day cover, #319, 321 2.50
First day cover, #318-321 3.75
Pane of 12, 3 each #318-321 13.00 —

World Heritage, Italy Type

Designs: 51c, #324f, Pompeii. 58c, #324c, Rome. #324a, Amalfi Coast. #324b, Aeolian Islands. #324d, Florence. #324e, Pisa.

2002, Aug. 30 **Litho.** ***Perf. 13½x13¼***
322 A338 51c **multicolored** *(400,000)+* 1.10 .55
First day cover 1.75
Inscription block of 4 4.50 —
323 A338 58c **multicolored** *(400,000)+* 1.25 .60
First day cover 2.00
First day cover, #322-323 3.00
Inscription block of 4 5.00 —

Souvenir Booklet

324 Booklet *(71,000)+* 5.50
a.-c. A338 7c any single .20 .20
d.-f. A338 15c any single .30 .30
g. Booklet pane of 4, #324d 1.25 —
h. Booklet pane of 4, #324a .55 —
i. Booklet pane of 4, #324e 1.25 —
j. Booklet pane of 4, #324b .55 —
k. Booklet pane of 4, #324f 1.25 —
l. Booklet pane of 4, #324c .55 —

AIDS Awareness Type

2002, Oct. 24 **Litho.** ***Perf. 13½***
325 A339 €1.53 **multicolored** *(370,000)+* 3.25 1.60
Inscription block of 4 13.00
First day cover, #325 4.00
Pane of 20 65.00

Indigenous Art — V46

Printed by House of Questa, UK.
Designed by Rorie Katz and Robert Stein, US.

No. 326: a, Mola, Panama. b, Mochican llama-shaped spouted vessel, Peru. c, Tarabuco woven cloth, Bolivia. d, Masks, Cuba. e, Aztec priest's feather headdress, Mexico. f, Bird-shaped staff head, Colombia.

2003, Jan. 31 **Litho.** ***Perf. 14¼***
326 V46 Sheet of 6 *(212,000)+* 6.50 3.25
First day cover 8.25
a.-f. 51c Any single 1.00 .50

Austrian Tourist Attractions Type of 2002

Printed by House of Quest, UK. Designed by Rorie Katz, US. Panes of 20.

Designs: 25c, Kunsthistorisches Museum, Vienna. €1, Belvedere Palace, Vienna.

2003, Mar. 28 **Litho.** ***Perf. 14½x14***
327 V45 25c **multicolored** *(650,000)+* .55 .30
First day cover 1.25
Inscription block of 4 2.25 —
328 V45 €1 **multicolored** *(650,000)+* 2.25 1.10
First day cover 3.25
First day cover, #327-328 3.50
Inscription block of 4 9.00 —

Endangered Species Type of 1993

Printed by Johann Enschedé and Sons, the Netherlands. Designed by Robert Hautman, US.

Designs: No. 329, Anas formosa (Baikal teal). No. 330, Bostrychia hagedash (Hadada ibis). No. 331, Ramphastos toco (toco toucan). No. 332, Alopochen aegyptiacus (Egyptian goose).

2003, Apr. 3 **Litho.** ***Perf. 12¾x12½***
329 A271 51c **multicolored** *(432,000)+* 1.10 .55
330 A271 51c **multicolored** *(432,000)+* 1.10 .55
331 A271 51c **multicolored** *(432,000)+* 1.10 .55
332 A271 51c **multicolored** *(432,000)+* 1.10 .55
a. Block of 4, #329-332 4.50 —
First day cover, #332a 5.25
First day cover, #329-332 each 1.90
Inscription block of 4, #332a 4.50 —
Pane of 16 18.00 —

2003 END-OF-YEAR ISSUES

See end of New York postage listings.

SEMI-POSTAL STAMP

AIDS Awareness Semi-postal Type

Souvenir Sheet

2002, Oct. 24 **Litho.** ***Perf. 14½***
B1 SP1 51c + 25c **multicolored** *(220,000)+* 1.60 1.60
First day cover, #B1 2.40

ENVELOPES

Donaupark, Vienna — VU1

Printed by Mercury-Walch Pty. Ltd. (Australia). Designed by Hannes Margreiter (Austria).

Design: 7s, Landscape. Design at lower left shows Vienna landmarks (6s), river scene (7s).

1995, Feb. 3 **Litho.**
U1 VU1 6s **multicolored,** entire *(128,000)+* 2.00 1.50
First day cancel *(14,132)* 2.75
U2 VU1 7s **multicolored,** entire *(128,000)+* 2.00 1.10
First day cancel *(9,684)* 3.50

VU2

Printed by Mercury-Walch Pty. Ltd. (Australia).

1998, Mar. 13 **Litho.**
U3 VU2 13s **multicolored,** entire *(87,000)+* 3.50 1.00
Entire, first day cancel 3.50

VU3

Vienna International Center — VU4

Printed by Australia Post Sprintpak (Australia). Designed by Robert Stein (US).

2002, June 27 **Litho.**
U4 VU3 51c **multicolored,** entire *(93,000)+* 1.50 1.00
Entire, first day cancel 2.00
U5 VU4 €1.09 **multicolored,** entire *(88,000)+* 2.60 1.75
Entire, first day cancel 3.25

AIR LETTER SHEETS

VLS1

Printed by Joh. Enschede and Sons. Designed by Ingrid Ousland.

1982, Apr. 28 **Litho.**
UC1 VLS1 9s **multi,** *light green,* entire *(650,000)* 2.50 1.75
First day cancel *(120,650)* 3.00

No. UC1 Surcharged in Lake

1986, Feb. 3 **Litho.**
UC2 VLS1 9s +2s **multi,** *light green,* entire *(131,190)* 52.50 5.00
First day cancel *(18,500)* 26.00

Birds in Flight, UN Emblem
VLS2

Printed by Mercury-Walch, Australia. Designed by Mieczyslaw Wasiliewski, Poland.

1987, Jan. 30 **Litho.**
UC3 VLS2 11s **bright blue,** entire *(414,000)* 3.00 1.25
First day cancel *(48,348)* 7.00

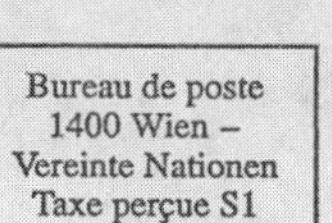

No. UC3 Surcharged

1992, Jan. 1 **Litho.**
UC4 VLS2 11s +1s **bright blue,** entire *(80,000)* 52.50 1.60
First day cancel 25.00

Donaupark, Vienna — VLS3

Designed by Rocco J. Callari. Printed by Mercury-Walch, Australia.

1992, Sept. 4 **Litho.**
UC5 VLS3 12s **multicolored,** entire *(200,000)+* 5.00 1.15
First day cancel *(16,261)* 27.50

POSTAL CARDS

Olive Branch — VPC1

Bird Carrying Olive Branch — VPC2

Printed by Courvoisier. Designed by Rolf Christianson (3s), M.A. Munnawar (5s).

1982, Apr. 28 **Photo.**
UX1 VPC1 3s **multicolored,** *cream (500,000)* 1.00 .65
First day cancel *(93,010)* 1.65
UX2 VPC2 5s **multicolored** *(500,000)* .75 .65
First day cancel *(89,502)* 1.65

Emblem of the United Nations — VPC3

Printed by Johann Enschede en Zonen, Netherlands. Designed by George Hamori, Australia.

1985, May 10 **Litho.**
UX3 VPC3 4s **multicolored** *(350,000)* 3.50 .30
First day cancel *(53,450)* 6.00

No. UX2 Surcharged Like No. UC4

1992, Jan. 1 **Photo.**
UX4 VPC2 5s +1s **multicolored** *(71,700)* 19.00 .55
First day cancel 14.50

Type of 1990

Printed by Mercury-Walch, Australia.

1992, Sept. 4 **Litho.**
UX5 V22 6s **multicolored** *(445,000)+* 3.00 .75
First day cancel *(16,359)* 13.00

See No. UX9.

Type of 1985

Printed by Leigh Mardon Pty. Limited, Australia.

1993, May 7 **Litho.**
UX6 A222 5s **multicolored** *(450,000)* 16.00 .45
First day cancel 10.00

Donaupark, Vienna — VPC4

Printed by Leigh Mardon Pty. Limited, Australia.

1993, May 7 **Litho.**
UX7 VPC4 6s **multicolored** *(450,000)+* 4.00 .50
First day cancel 7.50

See No. UX10.

No. UX6 with design of Vienna #1 Added

1994, Jan. 1 **Litho.**
UX8 A222+G8 5s +50g **multi** *(350,000)+* 4.00 .50
First day cancel 8.00

No. UX5 with design of Vienna #167 Added

1997, July 1 **Litho.**
UX9 V22+V32 6s +50g **multi** 2.50 .50
First day cancel 5.00

No. UX7 with design of Vienna #194 Added

UX10 VPC4+V35 6s +1s **multi** 3.00 .50
First day cancel 5.00

VPC5

Designed by Günter Leidenfrost.

1998, May 20 **Litho.**
UX11 VPC5 6.50s **multicolored** *(137,000)+* 1.50 .50
First day cancel 2.00

The Gloriette — VPC6

1999, Feb. 5 **Litho.**
UX12 VPC6 7s **multicolored** *(136,000)+* 2.00 .55
First day cancel 2.50

Type of 1983

2000, June 2 **Litho.**
UX13 V7 7s **multicolored** 2.25 .75
First day cancel 2.25

Clock Tower, Graz, Austria — VPC7

Printed by Johann Enschedé and Sons, the Netherlands. Designed by Robert Stein, US.

2002, Mar. 1 **Litho.**
UX14 VPC7 51c **multicolored** *(83,000)+* 1.00 .50
First day cancel 1.25

U.N. SOUVENIR CARDS

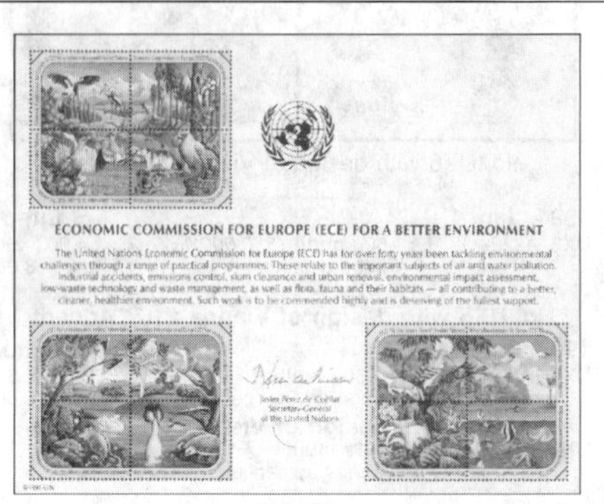

No. 39

These cards were issued by the United Nations Postal Administration and were not valid for postage.

Each card bears reproductions of UN stamps and a statement by the Secretary-General in English.

No.	Description	Value
SC1	World Health Day, Apr. 7, 1972. Card of 5: #43, 102, 156, 207, 228.	.65

A second printing shows several minor differences.

No.	Description	Value
SC2	Art on UN Stamps, Nov. 17, 1972. Card of 11: #170, 171, 173, 174, 180, 183, 201, 202, 203, 224, 232. #201, 202 form a simulated setenant pair	.45
SC3	Disarmament Decade, Mar. 9, 1973. Card of 5: #133, 147, 177, 227, 234	.50
SC4	Declaration of Human Rights, 25th Anniversary, Nov. 16, 1973. Card of 10: #13, 22, 29, 39, 47, 58, 68, 121, 190, 242	.75
SC5	UPU centenary, Mar. 22, 1974. Card of 7: #17, 18, 219, 246; Geneva 18, 39, 40.	.75
SC6	World Population Year, Oct. 18, 1974. Card of 7: #151, 152, 153, 252, 253; Geneva 43, 44.	4.00
SC7	Peaceful Uses of Outer Space, Mar. 14, 1975. Card of 6: #112, 113, 256, 257; Geneva 46, 47.	2.00
SC8	UN Peace Keeping Operations, Nov. 21, 1975. Card of 9: #52, 111, 118, 139, 160, 265, 266; Geneva 55, 56.	2.00
SC9	World Federation of United Nations Associations, Mar. 12, 1976. Card of 5: #154, 155, 272, 273; Geneva 57.	2.00
SC10	World Food Council, Nov. 19, 1976. Card of 6: #116, 117, 218, 280; Geneva 17, 63.	2.50
SC11	World Intellectual Property Organization (WIPO), Mar. 11, 1977. Card of 15: #17, 23, 25, 31, 33, 41, 43, 49, 59, 86, 90, 123, 281, 282; Geneva 64.	2.50
SC12	Combat Racism, Sept. 19, 1977. Card of 8: #220, 221, 287, 288; Geneva 19, 20, 69, 70.	2.50
SC13	Namibia, May 5, 1978. Card of 10: #240, 241, 263, 264, 296, 297; Geneva 34, 53, 54, 76.	1.00
SC14	Intl. Civil Aviation Organization, June 12, 1978. Card of 6: #31, 32, 298, 299; Geneva 77, 78.	2.50
SC15	Intl. Year of the Child, May 4, 1979. Card of 9: #5, 97, 161, 162, 163, 310, 311; Geneva 84, 85.	.75
SC16	Intl. Court of Justice, Nov. 9, 1979. Card of 6: #88, 89, 314, 315; Geneva 87, 88.	.75
SC17	UN Decade for Women, Mar. 7, 1980. Card of 4: #258, 318; Geneva 90; Vienna 9.	10.00
SC18	Economic and Social Council, Nov. 7, 1980. Card of 8; #65, 66, 341, 342; Geneva 96, 97; Vienna 15, 16.	.75
SC19	Intl. Year of Disabled Persons, Mar. 6, 1981. Card of 6; #344, 345; Geneva 99, 100; Vienna 18, 19.	.65
SC20	New and Renewable Sources of Energy, May 29, 1981. Card of 4; #348, 349; Geneva 102; Vienna 21.	1.00
SC21	Human Environment, Mar. 19, 1982. Card of 5: #230, 371; Geneva 26, 107; Vienna 25	.75
SC22	Exploration and Peaceful Uses of Outer Space, June 11, 1982. Card of 7: #112, 256, 373; Geneva 46, 109, 110; Vienna 27.	1.40
SC23	Safety at Sea, Mar. 18, 1983. Card of 8: #123, 124, 394, 395; Geneva 114, 115; Vienna 31, 32.	1.10
SC24	Trade and Development, June 6, 1983. Card of 11: #129, 130, 274, 275, 397, 398; Geneva 58, 117, 118; Vienna 31, 32.	2.00
SC25	Intl. Conference on Population, Feb. 3, 1984. Card of 10: #151, 153, 252, 253, 417, 418; Geneva 43, 44, 121; Vienna 39.	2.00
SC26	Intl. Youth Year, Nov. 15, 1984. Card of 5: #441, 442; Geneva 128; Vienna 46, 47.	3.00
SC27	ILO Turin Center, Feb. 1, 1985. Card of 8: #25, 200, 244, 443; Geneva 37, 129, 130; Vienna 48.	2.75
SC28	Child Survival Campaign, Nov. 22, 1985. Card of 6: #466, 467; Geneva 138, 139; Vienna 55, 56.	4.00
SC29	Stamp Collecting, May 22, 1986. Card of 5: #278, 473; Geneva 61, 147; Vienna 63.	*8.25*

No. 29 with stitch marks has been removed from the Ameripex program. Value is one-half that of unstitched copy.

No.	Description	Value
SC30	Intl. Peace Year, June 20, 1986. Card of 6: #475, 476; Geneva 148, 149; Vienna 64, 65.	4.00
SC31	Shelter for the Homeless, Mar. 13, 1987. Card of 6: #495, 496; Geneva 154, 155; Vienna 68, 69.	2.50
SC32	Immunize Every Child, Nov. 20, 1987. Card of 13: #44, 103, 157, 208, 294, 517, 518; Vienna 76, 77.	3.00
SC33	Intl. Volunteer Day, May 6, 1988. Card of 10; #239, 367, 524, 525; Geneva 103, 167, 168; Vienna 23, 82, 83.	4.00
SC34	Health in Sports, June 17, 1988. Card of 6; #526, 527; Geneva 169, 170; Vienna 84, 85.	5.00
SC35	World Bank, Jan. 27, 1989. Card of 8; #86-87, 546-547; Geneva 173-174; Vienna 88-89.	5.00
SC36	World Weather Watch, Apr. 21, 1989. Card of 10; #49-50, 188-189, 550-551; Geneva 176-177; Vienna 91-92.	5.00
SC37	Fight AIDS Worldwide, Mar. 16, 1990. Card of 6, #573-574; Geneva 184-185; Vienna 99-100	6.50
SC38	Crime Prevention, Sept. 13, 1990. Card of 6; #580-581; Geneva 191-192; Vienna 106-107.	6.00
SC39	Economic Commission for Europe, Mar. 15, 1991. Card of 12; #584-587; Geneva 195-198; Vienna 110-113.	6.00
SC40	Rights of the Child, June 14, 1991. Card of 6; #593-594; Geneva 203-204; Vienna 117-118.	7.00
SC41	Mission to Planet Earth, Sept. 4, 1992, Card of 6, #609-610; Geneva 220-221; Vienna 133-134	17.00
SC42	Science and Technology for Development, Oct. 2, 1992, Card of 6, #611-612; Geneva 222-223; Vienna 135-136	15.00
SC43	Healthy Environment, May 7, 1993, Card of 6, #624-625; Geneva #232-233; Vienna #147-148	17.50
SC44	Peace, Sept. 21, 1993, Card of 12, #629-632; Geneva #236-239; Vienna #152-155	16.00

No. 44 exists overprinted in gold with Hong Kong '94 emblem.

No.	Description	Value
SC45	Intl. Year of the Family, Feb. 4, 1994, Card of 6, #637-638; Geneva #244-245; Vienna #160-161	13.50
SC46	Population & Development, 1994, Card of 9, #151, 651-652; Geneva #43, 258-259; Vienna #39, 174-175	12.50
SC47	World Summit for Social Development, 1995, Card of 3, #656; Geneva #263; Vienna #179	10.50
SC48	Intl. Youth Year, 1995, Card of 9, #441, 661-662; Geneva #128, 268-269; Vienna #46, 184-185	16.00
SC49	WFUNA, 1996, Card of 3, #671; Geneva #277; Vienna #193	14.00
SC50	UNICEF, 1996, Card of 6, #688-689; Geneva #294-295; Vienna #210-211	7.50
SC51	Philately, 1997, Card of 6, #714-715; Geneva #312-313; Vienna #228-229	12.50
SC52	Peacekeeping, #737-738; Geneva #325-326; Vienna #242-243	9.00
SC53	Universal Declaration of Human Rights, #739-740; Geneva #327-328; Vienna #244-245	9.00
SC54	UPU, #767a; Geneva #346a; Vienna #263a	5.00
SC55	Respect for Refugees, #787; Geneva #365; Vienna #282	6.00
SC56	Intl. Volunteers Year, #793-794; Geneva #371-372; Vienna #288-289	3.00
SC57	Johannesburg Summit on Sustainable Development, #828-831; Geneva #396-399; Vienna #318-321	3.00

U.N. PROOFS

Proofs of United Nations stamps are known in four basic types: Die Proofs, Trial Color Proofs, Progressive Color Proofs, and Imperforate Plate Proofs on gummed stamp paper.

Die Proofs (PD suffix) for United Nations stamps show the design of the issued stamp. They are usually imperforate singles printed on stamp paper, that are either affixed to a backing paper that is a component of a printer's card, or affixed directly to a printer's card. These cards usually have a handstamp denoting the status of the proof (approved, approved with corrections, not approved, etc.). Many cards have signatures of UN Postal Administration officials. Cards with an "approved" handstamp and/or signature do not always contain proofs having the designs of the actual stamp produced for sale. As most proof cards have a handstamp, the listings mention specific handstamps only when it is critical to distinguishing items. Items not affixed to cards that are indistinguishable from imperforate singles of the issued stamps are not listed, even though they may have come from "stock sheet style" proof cards that have approval handstamps. Items affixed to art boards available to the general public are not considered to be proofs unless they are identified, usually by handstamps, that they are proofs. Die proofs of sheet layouts showing marginal inscriptions only exist, but are beyond the scope of these listings.

Trial Color Proofs (TC suffix) show the design of the stamp, but with one or more colors differing from that of the actual stamp. Items will be listed as trial color proofs when they differ significantly from the issued color. As evidenced by printer's identification numbers on some trial color proof cards, shades of individual items may differ slightly, but two similar yet discrete shades may fall under one color description. Trial colors can sometimes be found on cards with die proofs.

Progressive Color Proofs (PP suffix) are a set of color proofs containing the number of items stated in the listing. Values, therefore, are for the set of singles (unless otherwise mentioned in the description), not a single progressive color proof from that set. Numbers in parentheses represent the total number of complete sets that were created. Partial sets are not listed if complete sets are known.

Imperforate Plate Proofs (PI suffix) are usually found on gummed stamp paper. Any exceptions are noted in the listing description. Numbers in parentheses represent the total number of imperforate proof stamps created. Many items have inked fingerprints on the reverse as a security device. Values are for pairs unless otherwise stated. Many gutter pairs will have creases. Some gutter pairs will have marginal inscriptions. These are worth more.

Organization of listings Listings have all of the New York, Geneva and Vienna stamps and souvenir cards for any set all together. The first part of an item's catalogue number is the same catalogue number as shown in the listings for stamps and postal stationery. The prefix "G" is before the catalogue number for items from Geneva; prefix "V" for items from Vienna. Items with prefix "SC" are souvenir cards, and catalogue numbers without prefix are from New York. The suffix describing the type of proof follows the catalogue number. Die proofs (suffix PD) are the first proof category in the listings, and will be followed by the other categories in the same order as listed above. Each proof category will list New York items first, followed by Geneva items, Vienna items, and then souvenir cards.

Often cards of proofs will contain all of the items in an issued set. The catalogue numbers for cards that contain New York, Geneva and Vienna proofs are organized by the highest New York catalogue number of the various die proof items in the set. If there are no New York items in the card, then the numbering will be organized by the highest Geneva or Vienna catalogue number in the card of die proofs. Cards that contain both die proofs and trial color proofs are catalogued under the die proofs.

Numbers in parentheses represent the total number of items created. The number of items coming in part or in total from printer's archives are approximations. Listings for single proofs affixed to cards do not usually mention that they are affixed to a card. Cards containing more than one proof will have a minor letter following the PD suffix, and the listing will detail the component parts, as some cards may in the future be broken down by owners into individual proof items. Cutting up cards, however, may destroy their value, as listings are often based on the presence of the handstamp. Removing proofs from the card may also destroy their value, as it may then be impossible to distinguish them from imperforate singles.

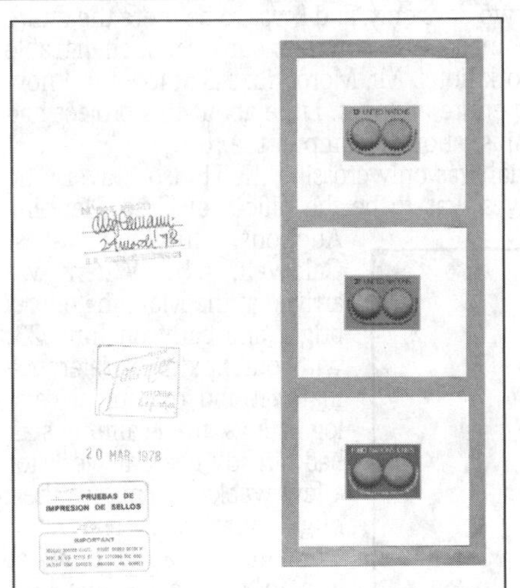

No. 303PDa - A Typical Die Proof Card

No. U1TC in Black - A Typical Trial Color Proof

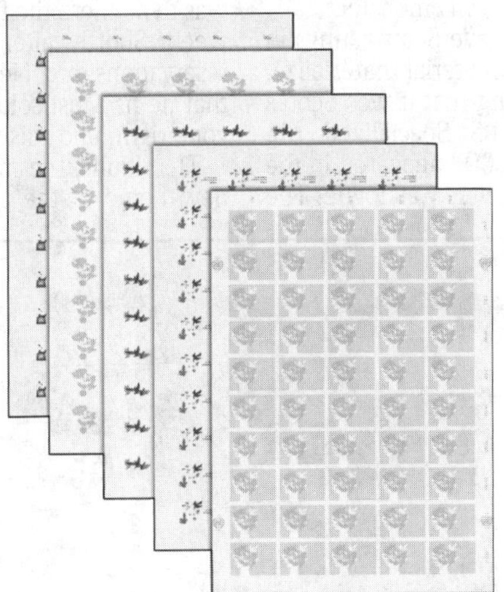
Sheets of 50 of No. V1PP - A Typical Progressive Proof Set

No. 1PI - A Typical Pair of Imperforate Plate Proofs

New York #1-11
Definitives

1951

1PD	(1)	—
2PD	(3)	—
3PD	(3)	—
3PDa	Card, #3PD, 3TC blue violet (1)	—
4PD	(1)	—
5PD	(1)	—
6PD	(1)	—
6PDa	Card, #1PD, 6PD (3)	—
7PD	(1)	—
8PD	(4)	—
9PD	(1)	—
9PDa	Card, #4PD, 7PD, 9PD, essays of #7, 9 (1)	—
10PD	(1)	—
11PD	(4)	—
2TC	indigo (1)	—
3TC	red violet (2)	—
3TC	dark red (2)	—
3TC	red orange (1)	—
3TC	carmine (3)	—
3TC	orange red (3)	—
3TCa	Card, #3TC carmine, #3TC orange red (1)	—
5TC	bright blue (1)	-
5TC	light blue (1)	

1952

12PD	(3)	—
12TC	dark blue (2)	—
12TC	black (2)	—
12TC	green (2)	—
12TC	light blue (1)	—

New York #13-14
Universal Declaration of Human Rights, 4th Anniv.

1952

13PDa	Card, #13PD and two #13TC in slightly different shades (1)	—
14PDa	Card, #14PD and two #14TC in slightly different shades (1)	—
14PDb	Card, #13PD, 14PD (1)	—

New York #15-16
Protection for Refugees

1953

15PD	(1)	—
16PD	(1)	—
16PDa	Card, #15PD, 16PD (3)	—
16PDb	Card, #15PD, 16PD, 16TC indigo (1)	—
16PDc	Card, #16PDb and card, #15PD, 15TC, 16PD (1)	—
15PI	(80 pairs)	—

2004 EDITION SPECIAL FEATURE

United Nations Proofs Added

By Martin J. Frankevicz
Scott Catalogue New Issues Editor

Sometime in early 2002, the David Feldman Galleries of Geneva, Switzerland acquired on consignment the archives from the United Nations Postal Administration, with plans to sell it in the spring of 2003.

On June 27, 2002, Mr. Feldman faxed Amos Press, Inc. President Bruce Boyd, relating his hope that the Scott catalog might be able to produce listings for the proof items that could be reproduced in his auction catalog. This request was passed down to Catalogue Editor James Kloetzel, who responded to Mr. Feldman on July 10. In his letter, Mr. Kloetzel agreed that this would be a beneficial project for all concerned, and he thought the job could be done in time for the Feldman sale the following year and that the listings would then appear in the 2004 U.S. Specialized Catalogue.

While Scott and the Feldman firm did their best to come up with catalog listings in time for them to appear in the Feldman auction catalog, it was not meant to be. All parties involved would now undoubtedly agree that the task was too large and complex to be done properly via e-mails and telephone calls. It seems evident to me that when the Feldman staff received the shipment of more than 70 large boxes from the United Nations Postal Administration, the shipment was beyond the terms "quite mixed up" that Mr. Feldman himself used in October 2002 to describe the order of the material in an e-mail to Scott Editor Kloetzel. We know that they tried to bring order to this massive mountain of philatelic material, but they no doubt underestimated the work that was needed to describe all of the component parts. Even we at Scott underestimated the amount of work that would be needed to tackle this monster.

While Mr. Feldman did not see his wish to have Scott listings in his May 12, 2003 auction catalog offering this material materialize, he did ask that Mr. Kloetzel write a letter stating that it was Scott's intention to list the UN proofs in the 2004 U.S. Specialized. Mr. Kloetzel's letter stating this, dated January 15, 2003 appeared in the Feldman United Nations Art and Archives Reference Catalogue. The information in this book served as a starting point for the Scott listings. The information the Feldman staff compiled was far better than a United Nations-generated inventory provided to us when we first embarked on the journey of listing this material. Still, study of the Feldman compilation left us with many questions. When we had received a rough draft of their compilation, the auction date was quickly approaching. When we received a printed copy of their work on April 25, a few short weeks before the sale, we saw pictures of items that made us realize immediately that Scott listings for UN proofs would come about only if the items could be viewed in person and described by Scott staff. That, however, might be a problem as Feldman's auction had seven lots (one of which was withdrawn) that could be going to different bidders around the globe. The only other option, and not a good one, was to not add the listings at all.

On the day of the sale, we were anxious to learn who had won the lots. Pre-sale interest among American stamp dealers was high, with one saying that Feldman's estimate was conservative. After the sale, we learned that dealer was an underbidder. We were quite relieved to learn that all of the material was returning to the U.S., and to one address. Arthur Morowitz of New York City purchased the entire archive, which was sold as one lot rather than six, for $3,068,000.

Upon hearing that news, Mr. Kloetzel asked Mr. Morowitz if we could look at his new purchase. Being a stamp dealer, Mr. Morowitz realized that accurate Scott catalog listings would benefit him and any future purchasers of his material, and he agreed.

With the deadlines for the U.S. Specialized Catalogue now rapidly approaching, we had to work quickly. Mr. Kloetzel and I made plans to view the material in New York the week of June 23-27. Mr. Kloetzel was to be there the first two days only, and I was to be there the entire week. Shortly after we made our non-refundable, non-changeable reservations for a New York hotel, Mr. Morowitz called to let us know that he had just sold the entire archives. Little about this project had gone right, and this was just another bump in the road.

Thankfully, the material was only crossing the Hudson River. The new home of the archives was to be the offices of Greg Manning Auctions, Inc., in West Caldwell, NJ. When we arrived at the Manning offices bright and early on June 23, with our boxful of reference material and our initial catalog listings, the Manning staff had already been at work for a few weeks sorting out their huge purchase. They too were making a list of what was in the boxes, and had been busy jotting down information in notebooks. Their plan was to break up the collection into individual lots for a sale in late 2003, and to place most progressive proof sheets and imperforate proof sheets privately.

The proofs were in long boxes scattered around a large room. Hard at work in that room that day amidst rolls of imperforate sheets was Robert Rothwell of the Manning staff. He knew where almost everything was in the jumble of cartons and large tubes, and if he didn't,

Illustration #1: No. V6PDa is a card with six proofs

he went on a safari in the box jungle to find it for us. He was there when we got there before 8 in the morning and was there when we left, usually around 7 or 8 in the evening. All of the Manning staffers were wonderful to work with, but Robert was almost always there assisting. Without him, I still might be there wading through boxes.

With our initial listings at hand, our goal was to try to verify every listing and every quantity in our notebook. As we slowly went through the boxes, we realized that Feldman's crew had missed items most probably because they lacked the time to analyze the material closely. We have to view the Feldman listings as the first real stab at organizing this massive collection. I have to shudder thinking about how they may have received the material from the U.N. While the Manning staff's notebooks were helpful, some of the information was still difficult to interpret, as a number of staffers had compiled it. Quantities of some se-tenants were given as singles, and at other times as blocks. It was important for us to see the material and be consistent in our descriptions. That is a difficult task when dealing with pressing time constraints and material produced by forty printers over a fifty-year span that saw printing technology advance from engraved dies to computer-manipulated images.

The first two days, Mr. Kloetzel looked at material, and I took notes as we tried to see something of each category. When we looked at the early die proofs, we saw trial color proofs in the first envelope. They looked much like the die proofs, and often they had subtle shade differences that were not all that obvious. For many issues it was necessary to splay all of these on the table, find approved cards, and compare them with items that were not approved. It didn't take long for us to encounter yet more surprises – essays. Like trial colors, many of them looked just like the die proofs, but they had subtle differences that distinguished them from the issued stamps. Essays are not listed, as the term can include the artwork that was in dozens of boxes that were not even looked at.

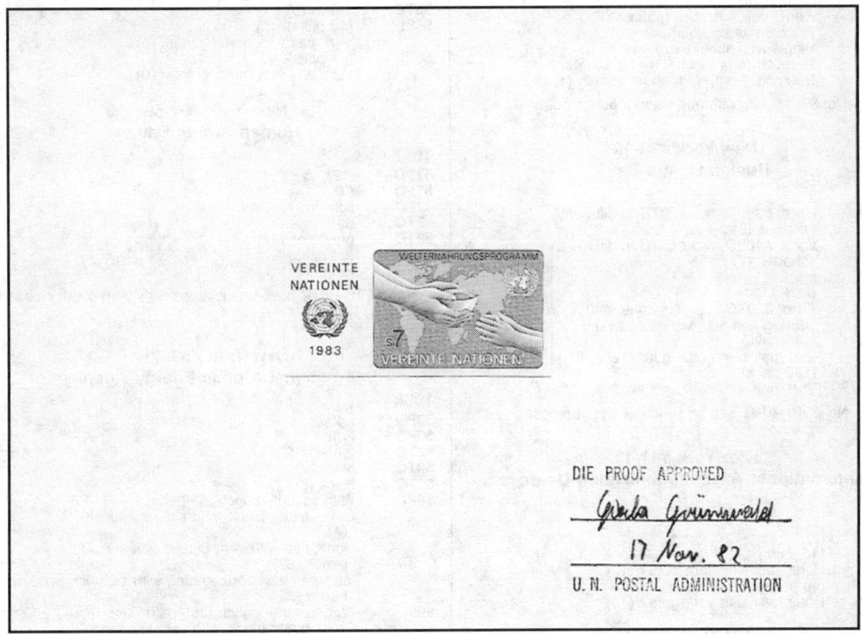

Illustration #2: No. V34PD is a card showing the stamp and the adjacent marginal imprint

All of this close analysis reduced the high counts of many items recorded on the Feldman list. What had been counted as 10 die proofs often ended up being three proofs, with the remainder trial color proofs and essays. Most die proof items have fewer than 10 items. There are more progressive proofs and imperforates, but even most of those are in quantities of 100 or less. Although much as the Flags series was printed in massive quantities that have depressed their catalog value for a number of years, there is only one set of progressive proof sheets for each of the yearly flag sets. Many cross gutter blocks from progressive proof sheets and imperforate sheets are one-only items.

Some of the items are indeed fascinating gems on a number of levels. No. 32PDb, a large card of die proofs, trial color proofs and essays of the UNESCO issue of 1955 shows how much attention was paid to getting the shading just right. No. 133TCc, a card of eleven trial color proofs for the Nuclear Test Ban Treaty of 1964, is a rainbow of colors to find the right effect for the stamp. The magic of the printer's art can be appreciated in the progressive proofs for the 1998 Rain Forest issue, wherein two different sets of progressive proofs were made with the blending of colors for each set producing an essentially identical final product. You can also see how "politically correct" the United Nations is when you realize the designers carefully removed anything that resembled a real national flag in the essays of Geneva No. 118 and Vienna No. 35, the 1983 U.N. Conference on Trade and Development issue.

One of the biggest surprises we had was in opening the package containing the 1973 New York 6c postal card die proof, No. UX5PD. Inside were seven pristine postal cards. They might have been tossed aside as yet another small group of issued items that occasionally made its way into the many envelopes. But a closer look at the cards showed that they were never-issued 7c cards, made up to match the 7c postal card rate that was briefly in effect in 1975, one of the few times that the U.S. Postal Service has decreased a postal rate.

One thing that Robert told us early on was that the condition of some items left a lot to be desired. Many early proofs were glued onto cards with what appeared to be mucilage, or some similar concoction that's even more hideous. Brown stains abounded. Many later items were taped down to cards, and at times staples would suffice. Many cards were cut up into pieces. Many imperforate and trial color proof sheets were folded and shoved into cramped envelopes. Often these had printer's smudgy fingerprints on the reverse - not the product of sloppy printers, but a deliberate security device. The faulty items certainly didn't look like stuff that would bring over $3 million in an auction, but most of the material is sound and very fine.

While it would have been ideal to see every proof item for a set at one time, this was not possible. As I was jotting down information, the Manning staff was shipping items out for placement. I tried to keep up with them, hoping that they would not end up sending out material that I had not yet seen. The imperforate items they sent out first were the simplest items in terms of the Scott listings. This left sheets that were more complex and difficult to figure out based on the data in the Manning notebooks. The imperforate sheets were the first items that were looked at in their entirety. The progressive proofs then followed, as many of these were to be sent out. The last items tackled would have to be the die proofs, as the Manning staff would not be touching them until it was time for them to write up their auction.

As it turned out, the week went quickly, but I was nowhere near done when Friday came, despite the long hours. In a call back to Sidney, Mr. Kloetzel asked me how long it might take for me to finish. I told him "Probably two weeks, but at least another week." It was not the news he wanted to hear, but it was my honest assessment.

Another week at a hotel was in the offing, but now the hotel was in New Jersey. And another week of long hours was to come. As the 4th of July was approaching, I wanted to work that entire weekend so I could again attend to matters in Ohio. Luckily, there were Manning staffers who were busy at the office that entire weekend. Still, at the end of that weekend, there were three big boxes to plod through. I would return again to New Jersey at the end of July for three days to finish up the final boxes.

Indeed, even my estimate of two additional weeks to finish was an underestimation. And my estimation of how long it would take to input the final data into the computer was off. Everything about this massive project was more massive than we and anyone involved with it thought. But the listing of this horde of fascinating proof material has been completed, and it is presented here as the first accurate and comprehensive listing to appear anywhere. We hope catalog users will find the listings to be interesting and useful.

	Vert. pair with horiz. gutter (20)	—
16PI	(80 pairs)	—
	Vert. pair with horiz. gutter (20)	—

New York #17-18
Universal Postal Union

1953

17PDa	Card, #17PD, 17TC violet brown (1)	—
18PDa	Card, #18PD, 18TC bright blue (1)	—
18PDb	Card, #17PDa, 18PDa (1)	—
17PI	(82 pairs)	—
	Horiz. pair with vert. gutter (8)	—
18PI	(84 pairs)	—
	Horiz. pair with vert. gutter (6)	—

Approximately half of PI items are stained and glued on cardboard. Imperforate printer's waste has No. 17 with No. 18 and impressions of other items on the reverse.

New York #19-20
Technical Assistance

1953

20PDa	Card, #19PD-20PD, #19TC-20TC in slightly different shades (2)	—

New York #21-22
Human Rights Day

1953

22PDa	Card, #23PD-24PD, two #23TC, two #24TC in slightly different shades (2)	—
21PI	(40 pairs)	—
	Vert. pair with horiz. gutter (10)	—
22PI	(40 pairs)	—
	Vert. pair with horiz. gutter (10)	—

New York #23-24
Food and Agricultural Organization

1954

24PDa	Card, #23PD-24PD, two #23TC-24TC in slightly different colors (2)	—
23PI	(40 pairs)	—
	Vert. pair with horiz. gutter (10)	—
24PI	(40 pairs)	—
	Vert. pair with horiz. gutter (120)	—

New York #25-26
International Labor Organization

1954

25PDa	Card, #25PD, two #25TC in slightly different shades, three #26TC in purple shades (2)	—
26PDa	Card, #25PD-26PD, #26TC in slightly different shade (2)	—
25PI	(40 pairs)	—
	Vert. pair with horiz. gutter (10)	—
26PI	(40 pairs)	—
	Vert. pair with horiz. gutter (10)	—

New York #27-28
United Nations Day

1954

27PI	(40 pairs)	—
	Horiz. pair with vert. gutter (10)	—
28PI	(40 pairs)	—
	Horiz. pair with vert. gutter (10)	—

New York #29-30
Human Rights Day

1954

29PD	(5)	—
30PD	(5)	—
29PI	(40 pairs)	—
	Vert. pair with horiz. gutter (10)	—
30PI	(40 pairs)	—
	Vert. pair with horiz. gutter (10)	—

New York #31-32
International Civil Aviation Organization

1955

31PDa	Card, #31PD, two #31TC in different blue shades (3)	—
32PDa	Card, #32PD, three #32TC in different red shades (3)	—
32PDb	Card, #31PD-32PD, #31TC-#32TC in different shades, three essays of #31-32 (1)	—
31TC	black (1)	—
32TC	black (1)	—
31PI	(171 pairs)	—
	Horiz. pair with vert. gutter (26)	—
32PI	(130 pairs)	—
	Horiz. pair with vert. gutter (20)	—

No. 31PI exists with and without punch holes.

New York #33-34
UN Educational, Scientific and Cultural Organization

1955

33PD	(1)	—
33PDa	Card, #33PD, two #33TC in different shades (3)	—
34PD	(1)	—
34PDa	Card, #34PD, two #34TC in different shades (3)	—
33TC	black (1)	—
34TC	black (1)	—
33PI	(128 pairs)	—
	Horiz. pair with vert. gutter (16)	—
34PI	(90 pairs)	—
	Horiz. pair with vert. gutter (10)	—

No. 33PI exists with and without punch holes.

New York #35-38
UN, 10th Anniv.

1955

35PDa	Card, #35PD, two #35TC in different shades (2)	—
35PDb	Card, #35PD, #35TC in lighter shade (1)	—
36PDa	Card, #36PD, two #36TC in different shades (3)	—
37PDa	Card, #37PD, two #37TC in different shades (3)	—
38PD	Sheet of #38 with security punches (2)	—
38bPD	Watermarked sheet of nine #38b and nine #38c with security punches (1)	—
38cPD	Watermarked sheet of nine #38c with security punches (1)	—
35TC	carmine (1)	—
35TC	black (1)	—
36TC	black (1)	—
37TC	black (1)	—
38PP	4 items (9 souvenir sheets)	—
38PP	Retouch, 2 items (9 souvenir sheets)	—
35PI	(130 pairs)	—
	Horiz. pair with vert. gutter (20)	—
36PI	(130 pairs)	—
	Horiz. pair with vert. gutter (20)	—
37PI	(180 pairs)	—
	Horiz. pair with vert. gutter (30)	—
38PI	(16 pairs of souvenir sheets)	—
	Single with sheet margin (4)	—
38PI	Retouch (4 pairs of souvenir sheets)	—
	Retouch, single with sheet margin (1)	—

No. 37PI exists with and without punch holes.

New York #39-40
Human Rights Day

1955

39PDa	Card, #39PD, two #39TC in different shades (2)	—
40PDa	Card, #40PD, two #40TC in different shades (2)	—
39TC	black (1)	—
40TC	black (1)	—
40TCa	Card, #39TC in aquamarine, #40TC in dark green and two essays (1)	—
39PI	(180 pairs)	—
	Vert. pair with horiz. gutter (20)	—
40PI	(130 pairs)	—
	Vert. pair with horiz. gutter (20)	—

No. 39PI exists with and without punch holes.

New York #41-42
International Telecommunication Union

1956

41PD	(2)	—
42PD	(2)	—
41PI	(40 pairs)	—
	Horiz. pair with vert. gutter (10)	—
42PI	(40 pairs)	—
	Horiz. pair with vert. gutter (10)	—

New York #43-44
World Health Organization

1956

43PD	(2)	—
44PD	(2)	—
43PI	(40 pairs)	—
	Vert. pair with horiz. gutter (10)	—
44PI	(40 pairs)	—
	Vert. pair with horiz. gutter (10)	—

Nos. 43PI-44PI have "Colour approved" handstamped in margin.

New York #45-46
General Assembly

1956

45PD	(7)	—
46PD	(7)	—
45PI	(40 pairs)	—
	Horiz. pair with vert. gutter (10)	—
46PI	(40 pairs)	—
	Horiz. pair with vert. gutter (10)	—

New York #47-48
Human Rights Day

1956

47PD	(2)	—
48PD	(2)	—
47TC	red (3)	—
47TC	carmine (3)	—
48TC	blue (6)	—
47PI	(40 pairs)	—
	Horiz. pair with vert. gutter (10)	—
48PI	(40 pairs)	—
	Horiz. pair with vert. gutter (10)	—

New York #49-50
World Meteorological Organization

1957

49PD	(2)	—
50PD	(2)	—
49TC	blue (3)	—
50TC	carmine rose (3)	—
49PI	(40 pairs)	—
	Vert. pair with horiz. gutter (10)	—
50PI	(40 pairs)	—
	Vert. pair with horiz. gutter (10)	—

Nos. 49PI-50PI have "Colour approved" handstamped in margin.

New York #51-52
UN Emergency Force

1957

51PD	(7)	—
52PD	(7)	—
51PI	(40 pairs)	—
	Horiz. pair with vert. gutter (10)	—
52PI	(40 pairs)	—
	Horiz. pair with vert. gutter (10)	—

New York #55-56
Security Council

1957

55PD	(6)	—
56PD	(11)	—
55TC	golden brown (6)	—
55TC	brown (5)	—
55PI	(40 pairs)	—
	Vert. pair with horiz. gutter (10)	—
56PI	(40 pairs)	—
	Vert. pair with horiz. gutter (10)	—

New York #57-58
Human Rights Day

1957

57PD	(12)	—
58PD	(9)	—
57TC	light red brown (1)	—
58TC	dark blue (3)	—
58TC	gray green (6)	—
57PI	(50 pairs)	—
58PI	(50 pairs)	—

Nos. 57TC-58TC have handstamps with "Approved" crossed out.

New York #59-60
International Atomic Energy Agency

1958

59PD	(12)	—
60PD	(13)	—
59TC	emerald (7)	—
59TC	black (7)	—
60TC	black (8)	—
59PI	With security punch (358 pairs)	—
	Cross gutter block, with security punch (4)	—
	Horiz. pair with vert. gutter, with security punch (52)	—
	Vert. pair with horiz. gutter, with security punch (32)	—
60PI	With security punch (358 pairs)	—
	Cross gutter block, with security punch (4)	—
	Horiz. pair with vert. gutter, with security punch (52)	—
	Vert. pair with horiz. gutter, with security punch (32)	—

New York #61-62
Central Hall, Site of First General Assembly Meeting

1958

61PD	(8)	—
62PD	(8)	—
61TC	black (3)	—
62TC	black (3)	—
61PI	With security punch (358 pairs)	—
	Cross gutter block, with security punch (4)	—
	Horiz. pair with vert. gutter, with security punch (32)	—
	Vert. pair with horiz. gutter, with security punch (52)	—
62PI	With security punch (358 pairs)	—
	Cross gutter block, with security punch (4)	—
	Horiz. pair with vert. gutter, with security punch (32)	—
	Vert. pair with horiz. gutter, with security punch (52)	—

New York #63-64
UN Emblem

1958

63PD	(21)	—
64PD	(7)	—
64PDa	Card, #64PD, #64TC Prussian blue, #64TC ultramarine (2)	—
63TC	brown orange (3)	—
64TC	light blue (1)	—
64TC	ultramarine (1)	—
63PI	(80 pairs)	—

	Vert. pair with horiz. gutter (20)	—
64PI	(80 pairs)	—
	Vert. pair with horiz. gutter (20)	—

No. 63TC is affixed to cards inscribed "D."

New York #65-66
Economic and Social Council

1958

65PD	(8)	—
66PD	(7)	—
65TC	black (2)	—
65TC	orange brown (1)	—
65TC	green (1)	—
65TC	red orange (1)	—
66TC	black (2)	—
65PI	With security punch (358 pairs)	—
	Cross gutter block, with security punch (4)	—
	Horiz. pair with vert. gutter, with security punch (32)	—
	Vert. pair with horiz. gutter, with security punch (52)	—
66PI	With security punch (358 pairs)	—
	Cross gutter block, with security punch (4)	—
	Horiz. pair with vert. gutter, with security punch (32)	—
	Vert. pair with horiz. gutter, with security punch (52)	—

New York #67-68
Human Rights Day

1958

67PD	(5)	—
68PD	(5)	—
67TC	black (2)	—
68TC	black (1)	—
67PI	(358 pairs)	—
	Cross gutter block, with security punch and "SPECIMEN" ovpt. (4)	—
	Horiz. pair with vert. gutter, with security punch and "SPECIMEN" ovpt. (52)	—
	Vert. pair with horiz. gutter, with security punch and "SPECIMEN" ovpt. (32)	—
68PI	(358 pairs)	—
	Cross gutter block, with security punch and "SPECIMEN" ovpt. (4)	—
	Horiz. pair with vert. gutter, with security punch and "SPECIMEN" ovpt. (52)	—
	Vert. pair with horiz. gutter, with security punch and "SPECIMEN" ovpt. (32)	—

Essays of Nos. 67 and 68 without denominations exist in issued colors and black.

New York #69-70
New York City Building, Flushing Meadows

1959

69PD	(7)	—
70PD	(7)	—
69PI	(216 pairs)	—
	Cross gutter block (3)	—
	Horiz. pair with vert. gutter (54)	—
	Vert. pair with horiz. gutter (24)	—
70PI	(216 pairs)	—
	Cross gutter block (3)	—
	Horiz. pair with vert. gutter (54)	—
	Vert. pair with horiz. gutter (24)	—

New York #71-72
Economic Commission for Europe

1959

71PD	(7)	—
72PD	(7)	—
71PI	(216 pairs)	—
	Cross gutter block (3)	—
	Horiz. pair with vert. gutter (24)	—
	Vert. pair with horiz. gutter (54)	—
72PI	(216 pairs)	—
	Cross gutter block (3)	—
	Horiz. pair with vert. gutter (24)	—
	Vert. pair with horiz. gutter (54)	—

New York #73-74
Trusteeship Council

1959

73PD	(5)	—
74PD	(5)	—
73TC	orange red (2)	—
73PI	(216 pairs)	—
	Cross gutter block (3)	—
	Horiz. pair with vert. gutter (24)	—
	Vert. pair with horiz. gutter (54)	—
74PI	(216 pairs)	—
	Cross gutter block (3)	—
	Horiz. pair with vert. gutter (24)	—
	Vert. pair with horiz. gutter (54)	—

No. 73TC has handstamps with words "Color and" crossed out.

New York #75-76
World Refugee Year

1959

75PD	(6)	—
76PD	(5)	—
75TC	purple & red (3)	—
76TC	olive & Prussian blue (2)	—
76TC	purple & green (3)	—
75PI	(216 pairs)	—
	Cross gutter block (3)	—
	Horiz. pair with vert. gutter (54)	—
	Vert. pair with horiz. gutter (24)	—
76PI	(216 pairs)	—
	Cross gutter block (3)	—
	Horiz. pair with vert. gutter (54)	—
	Vert. pair with horiz. gutter (24)	—

New York #77-78
Chaillot Palace

1960

77PD	(4)	—
78PD	(4)	—
78TC	brown & blue green(1)	—
78TC	blue & red (1)	—
78TCa	Card, #78TC brown & blue green, #78TC blue &red (1)	—
77PI	(25 pairs)	—
78PI	(25 pairs)	—

New York #79-80
Economic Commission for Asia and the Far East

1960

79PD	(1)	—
80PDa	Card, #79PD, #80PD (1)	—
80PDb	Card, two #79PD, two #80PD (1)	—
79PI	(50 pairs)	—
80PI	(50 pairs)	—

New York #81-82
World Forestry Congress

1960

81PD	(2)	—
82PDa	Card, #81PD-82PD (3)	—
81PI	(100 pairs)	—
82PI	(100 pairs)	—

New York #83-85
UN, 15th Anniv.

1960

83PD	(5)	—
84PD	(6)	—
85PD	(2)	—
83TC	black (1)	—
83TC	bright blue (2)	—
83PI	(144 pairs)	—
	Cross gutter block (2)	—
	Horiz. pair with vert. gutter (36)	—
	Vert. pair with horiz. gutter (16)	—
84PI	(119 pairs)	—
	Cross gutter block (2)	—
	Horiz. pair with vert. gutter (36)	—
	Vert. pair with horiz. gutter (16)	—
85PI	(16 pairs)	—
	Cross gutter block (2)	—
	Horiz. pair with vert. gutter (8)	—
	Vert. pair with horiz. gutter (8)	—

An essay in blue has diagonal lines in background rather than cross-hatching.

New York #86-87
International Bank for Reconstruction and Development

1960

87PDa	Card, 2 #86PD, 2 #87PD (2)	—
87PDb	Card, #86PD-87PD with simulated perforations (1)	—
86PI	(100 pairs)	—
87PI	(100 pairs)	—

New York #88-89
International Court of Justice

1961

89PDa	Card, #88PD-89PD affixed, dated 10/31/61 (2)	—
89PDb	Card, 2 #88PD, 2 #89PD, disapproved (2)	—
88PI	(100 pairs)	—
89PI	(100 pairs)	—

New York #90-91
International Monetary Fund

1961

91PDa	Card with 2 #90PD, 2 #91PD in slightly different shades (1)	—
90PI	(100 pairs)	—
91PI	(50 pairs)	—

New York #92
Abstract Flags

1961

92PI	(80 pairs)	—
	Horiz. pair with vert. gutter (20)	—

New York #93-94
Economic Commission for Latin America

1961

93PDa	Card, 2 #93PD, 2 essays of #94 (2)	—
94PDa	Card, 2 #94PD (1)	—

Essays of No. 94 lack serifs in "1's."

New York #95-96
Economic Commission for Africa

1961

96PDa	Card with #95PD-96PD affixed (8)	—
95PP	4 items (100)	—
96PP	8 items (100)	—
95PI	(100 pairs)	—
96PI	(100 pairs)	—

New York #97-99
UN Children's Fund (UNICEF)

1961

99PDa	Card, #97PD-99PD, with approval handstamp (3)	—
99PDb	Card, #97PD-99PD, no approval handstamp (5)	—
97PP	4 items (80)	—
	Vert. pair with horiz. gutter (10)	—
98PP	4 items (80)	—
	Vert. pair with horiz. gutter (10)	—
99PP	4 items (80)	—
	Vert. pair with horiz. gutter (10)	—
97PI	(80 pairs)	—
	Vert. pair with horiz. gutter (20)	—
98PI	(80 pairs)	—
	Vert. pair with horiz. gutter (20)	—
99PI	(80 pairs)	—
	Vert. pair with horiz. gutter (20)	—

New York #100-101
Housing and Urban Development Program

1962

100PD	With approval handstamp (3)	—
101PD	With approval handstamp (3)	—
100PI	With oval "Harrison's Photogravure Specimen" handstamp (25 pairs)	—
101PI	With oval "Harrison's Photogravure Specimen" handstamp (25 pairs)	—

Three essays each of Nos. 100 and 101 have larger numerals than issued stamps are are on cards marked "disapproved."

New York #102-103
Malaria Eradication Campaign

1962

102PD	(5)	—
103PD	(5)	—

New York #104-107
Definitives

1962

104PD	(5)	—
105PD	(7)	—
106PD	With approval handstamp & signature (2)	—
107PD	(3)	—
104PI	With oval "Harrison's Photogravure Specimen" handstamp (25 pairs)	—
105PI	With oval "Harrison's Photogravure Specimen" handstamp (25 pairs)	—
107PI	With oval "Harrison's Photogravure Specimen" handstamp (25 pairs)	—
	Same, without handstamp (25 pairs)	—

Three essays of No. 106 have indistinct line between "U" and "N," and are on cards marked "disapproved."

New York #108-109
Death of Dag Hammarskjold, 1st Anniv.

1962

108PDa	Card, #108PD, essay of #109 (1)	—
109PDa	Card, #109PD, essay of #108 (1)	—
109PDb	Card, #108PD-#109PD (2)	—
108PI	(80 pairs)	—
	Vert. pair with horiz. gutter (20)	—
109PI	(80 pairs)	—
	Vert. pair with horiz. gutter (20)	—

Essays of Nos 108-109 lack denomination.

New York #110-111
UN Operation in the Congo

1962

111PDa	Card, 3 #110PD, 3 #111PD (1)	—
111PDb	Card, #111PD, essay of #110 (2)	—
110PP	4 items (80)	—
	Horiz. pair with vert. gutter (10)	—
111PP	4 items (80)	—
	Horiz. pair with vert. gutter (10)	—
110PI	(80 pairs)	—
	Horiz. pair with vert. gutter (20)	—
111PI	(80 pairs)	—
	Horiz. pair with vert. gutter (20)	—

Essays of No. 110 have 5c denomination.

New York #112-113
Committee on Peaceful Uses of Outer Space

1962

112PD	(2)	—
113PD	(1)	—
113PDa	Card, #112PD-113PD (3)	—

Essays similar to Nos. 112PD-113PD have text in white panel below palm frond.

New York #114-115
UN Development Decade

1963

115PDa Card, #114PD, 2 #115PD (one in slightly different shade) with approval handstamp (3) —
115PDa Card, #114PD-115PD (3) —
114PP 4 items (80) —
Vert. pair with horiz. gutter (10) —
115PP 4 items (80) —
Vert. pair with horiz. gutter (10) —
114PI (80 pairs) —
Vert. pair with horiz. gutter (20) —
115PI (80 pairs) —
Vert. pair with horiz. gutter (20) —

New York #116-117
Freedom from Hunger Campaign

1963

116PD (1) —
117PD (1) —
117PDa Card, #116PD-117PD (5) —
116PP 3 items (80) —
Horiz. pair with vert. gutter (10) —
117PP 3 items (80) —
Horiz. pair with vert. gutter (10) —
116PI (80 pairs) —
Horiz. pair with vert. gutter (20) —
117PI (80 pairs) —
Horiz. pair with vert. gutter (20) —

Essays similar to Nos. 116PD-117PD have taller numerals and lettering.

New York #118
UN Temporary Executive Authority in West New Guinea

1963

118PD With approval handstamp (2) —
118PDa Card, #118PD (approved), #118TC (not approved) (3) —
118TCa Card, 2 #118TC (disapproved or with instructions to printer) (3) —
118PP 3 items (100) —
Horiz. pair with vert. gutter (10) —
118PI (100 pairs) —
Horiz. pair with vert. gutter (20) —

No. 118TC has right side of map in a lighter shade of green.

New York #119-120
General Assembly Building, New York

1963

120PDa Card, #119PD-120PD (2) —

New York #121-122
Universal Declaration of Human Rights, 15th Anniv.

1963

121PD (2) —
122PD (2) —
121PI (100 pairs) —
122PI (100 pairs) —

Essays similar to Nos. 121PD-122PD have top line of frame text flush left rather than centered, and are on a disapproved card.

New York #123-124
Intergovernmental Maritime Consultative Organization

1964

124PDa Card, #123PD-124PD (3) —
123PP 4 items (80) —
Horiz. pair with vert. gutter (10) —
124PP 4 items (80) —
Horiz. pair with vert. gutter (10) —
123PI (80 pairs) —
Horiz. pair with vert. gutter (20) —
124PI (80 pairs) —
Horiz. pair with vert. gutter (20) —

New York #125-128
Definitives

1964

125PD (3) —
125PDa Card, #125 perforated with approval handstamp (1) —
126PD (3) —
127PDa Card, #126PD-127PD with approval handstamp (3) —
127PDb Card, #127PD (approved), #127PD (not approved, in slightly different shade, #126PD (disapproved in slightly different shade (3) —
128PD (3) —
125PP 3 items (100) —
126PI 3 items (80) —
Vert. pair with horiz. gutter (10) —
127PP 4 items (80) —
Horiz. pair with vert. gutter (10) —
128PP 4 items (80) —
Horiz. pair with vert. gutter (10) —
125PI (65 pairs) —
Horiz. pair with vert. gutter (10) —
126PI (80 pairs) —
Vert. pair with horiz. gutter (20) —
127PI (80 pairs) —
Horiz. pair with vert. gutter (20) —
128PI (80 pairs) —
Horiz. pair with vert. gutter (20) —

Essays similar to No. 125PD have larger numerals and blue text.

New York #129-130
UN Conference on Trade and Development

1964

129PD (6) —
130PD (6) —
129PI (25 pairs) —
130PI (25 pairs) —

New York #131-132
Narcotics Control

1964

131PD (2) —
132PD (2) —
132PDa Card, #131PD-132PD (3) —

New York #133
Nuclear Test Ban Treaty

1964

133TC dark red & black, perforated, litho. & engr. (1) —
133TC lilac, perforated, engr. (20) —
133TCa Card, 2 #133TC dark red & dark brown, litho. & vignette essay, litho. (1) —
133TCb Card, #133TC dark red & black, engr. & 5 vignette essays, engr. (1) —
133TCc Card, 11 #133TC in red, claret, brown rose, brown, dark brown, dull blue, blue, blue violet, gray, dark gray, black, engr. (1) —

New York #134-136
Education for Progress Campaign

1964

135PD (1) —
136PDa Card, #134PD-136PD, with approval stamp (3) —
136PDb Card, #134PD-136PD, without approval stamp (2) —
136PDa Card, #134PD, #136PD, without approval stamp (1) —
134PP 4 items (80) —
Horiz. pair with vert. gutter (10) —
135PP 4 items (80) —
Horiz. pair with vert. gutter (10) —
136PP 4 items (80) —
Horiz. pair with vert. gutter (10) —
134PI (80 pairs) —
Horiz. pair with vert. gutter (20) —
135PI (80 pairs) —
Horiz. pair with vert. gutter (20) —
136PI (80 pairs) —
Horiz. pair with vert. gutter (20) —

New York #137-138
Special Fund Program

1965

137PD (2) —
138PD (2) —
138PDa Card, #137PD-138PD, with approval stamp (1) —
138PDb Card, #137PD-138PD, without approval stamp (1) —

New York #139-140
UN Peace-Keeping Force in Cyprus

1965

140PDa Card #139PD-140PD, with approval stamp (5) —
140PP 3 items (80) —
Vert. pair with horiz. gutter (10) —
139PI (40 pairs) —
Vert. pair with horiz. gutter (10) —
140PI (40 pairs) —
Vert. pair with horiz. gutter (10) —

Smaller-sized essays (30x38mm) of Nos. 139-140 are in three cards with approval stamps.

New York #141-142
International Telecommunication Union

1965

142PDa Card, #141PD-142PD, with approval stamp (3) —
142PDb Card, #141PD-142PD, no approval stamp (3) —
142PDcb Card, #141PD-142PD, #141TC dated "8.2.65" (3) —
141PP 4 items (80) —
Horiz. pair with vert. gutter (10) —
142PP 4 items (80) —
Horiz. pair with vert. gutter (10) —
141PI (80 pairs) —
Horiz. pair with vert. gutter (20) —
142PI (80 pairs) —
Horiz. pair with vert. gutter (20) —

No. 141TC has orange yellow lines instead of orange lines.

New York #143-145
UN, 20th Anniv. and International Cooperation Year

1965

143PD (3) —
143PDa Card, #143PD, 144TC orange red (3) —
144PD (3) —
144PDa Card, #143PD-144PD, with approval stamp (7) —
145PD Imperforate sheet with manuscript printer's instructions (4) —
Issued souvenir sheet, perforated (on printer's card) (1) —
145PDa #143PD, #144PD affixed to #145 souvenir sheet margin (5) —

New York #146-150
Definitives

1965-66

146PD (7) —
148PDa Block of 12 perforated stamps with approval handstamp in margin (2) —
148PDb Card, #147-148 perforated, with approval handstamp (3) —
149PD Perforated, with approval handstamp (2) —
149PDa Card, #149PD (2nd printing), #149PD, first printing, perforated, with approval handstamp (2) —
150PD (3) —
149TC Prussian blue & dark blue, perforated (1) —
150PP 3 items (80), affixed on cards —
Horiz. pair with vert. gutter (10) —
150PI (161 pairs) —
Horiz. pair with vert. gutter (19) —

Two cards without approval handstamp have perforated essays of both Nos. 147 and 148. The essay of No. 147 has larger numerals and the essay of No. 148 has bright yellow text at bottom. No. 150PI has had extra glue applied.

New York #151-153
Population Trends and Development

1965

152PDa Card, #151PD-152PD, 153TC, perforated, with approval handstamp (2) —

No. 153TC has "Nations Unies" in black instead of gray.

New York #154-155
World Federation of United Nations Associations

1966

155PDa Card, #154-155PD with approval handstamp (3) —
154PP 4 items (80) —
Vert. pair with horiz. gutter (10) —
155PP 4 items (80) —
Vert. pair with horiz. gutter (10) —
154PI (80 pairs) —
Vert. pair with horiz. gutter (20) —
155PI (80 pairs) —
Vert. pair with horiz. gutter (20) —

New York #156-157
World Health Organization

1966

157TCa Card, #156TC-157TC, with approval handstamp (3) —
156PP 4 items (50) —
157PP 4 items (80) —
Horiz. pair with vert. gutter (10) —
156PI (65 pairs) —
Horiz. pair with vert. gutter (10) —
157PI (80 pairs) —
Horiz. pair with vert. gutter (20) —

Nos. 156TC and 157TC have side and front of building the same shade of blue.

New York #158-159
International Coffee Agreement of 1962

1966

159PDa Card, #158PD-159PD (3) —

New York #160
UN Observers

1964

160PD (2) on cards dated "3.2.1966" —
160PP 4 items (50) —
160PI (65 pairs) —
Vert. pair with horiz. gutter (10) —

Two essays of No. 160 with white text lines larger and closer together are on cards dated "17.1.1966."

New York #161-163
UNICEF, 20th Anniv.

1966

161PD (3) —
162PD (3) —
163PD (3) —
161PI (72 pairs) —
Cross gutter block (1) —
Horiz. pair with vert. gutter (18) —
Vert. pair with horiz. gutter (8) —
162PI (72 pairs) —
Cross gutter block (1) —

	Horiz. pair with vert. gutter (18)	—
	Vert. pair with horiz. gutter (8)	—
163PI	(72 pairs)	—
	Cross gutter block (1)	—
	Horiz. pair with vert. gutter (18)	—
	Vert. pair with horiz. gutter (8)	—

New York #164-165
UN Development Program

1967

165PDa	Card, # 164PD-165PD, dated "6.9. 1966" (3)	—
165PDb	Card, #165PD, 2 #164PD, with approval handstamp, dated "4.10.66" (6)	—
164PI	(40 pairs)	—
	Horiz. pair with vert. gutter (10)	—
165PI	(40 pairs)	—
	Horiz. pair with vert. gutter (10)	—

New York #166-167
Definitives

1967

166PD	(6)	—
166PDa	Card, 2 #166PD (3)	—
167PD	(3)	—
166TC	With brown line separating "UN" in vignette, on card dated "27.4.1966" (3)	—
166PP	4 items (80)	—
	Vert. pair with horiz. gutter (10)	—
167PP	3 items (80)	—
	Horiz. pair with vert. gutter (10)	—
166PI	(80 pairs)	—
	Vert. pair with horiz. gutter (20)	—
167PI	(80 pairs)	—
	Horiz. pair with vert. gutter (20)	—

New York #168-169
Independence

1967

168PD	(2)	—
169PD	(3)	—

New York #170-174
EXPO '67

1967

170PD	(1)	—
171PD	(1)	—
172PD	(3)	—
173PD	(1)	—
174PD	(3)	—
170PP	2 items (144)	—
	Cross gutter block (1)	—
	Horiz. pair with vert. gutter (8)	—
	Vert. pair with horiz. gutter (18)	—
171PP	2 items (144)	—
	Cross gutter block (1)	—
	Horiz. pair with vert. gutter (8)	—
	Vert. pair with horiz. gutter (18)	—
172PP	3 items (144)	—
	Cross gutter block (1)	—
	Horiz. pair with vert. gutter (18)	—
	Vert. pair with horiz. gutter (8)	—
173PP	2 items (144)	—
	Cross gutter block (1)	—
	Horiz. pair with vert. gutter (8)	—
	Vert. pair with horiz. gutter (18)	—
174PP	2 items (144)	—
	Cross gutter block (1)	—
	Horiz. pair with vert. gutter (8)	—
	Vert. pair with horiz. gutter (18)	—
170PI	(72 pairs)	—
	Cross gutter block (1)	—
	Horiz. pair with vert. gutter (8)	—
	Vert. pair with horiz. gutter (18)	—
171PI	(72 pairs)	—
	Cross gutter block (1)	—
	Horiz. pair with vert. gutter (8)	—
	Vert. pair with horiz. gutter (18)	—
172PI	(72 pairs)	—
	Cross gutter block (1)	—
	Horiz. pair with vert. gutter (18)	—
	Vert. pair with horiz. gutter (8)	—
173PI	(72 pairs)	—
	Cross gutter block (1)	—
	Horiz. pair with vert. gutter (8)	—
	Vert. pair with horiz. gutter (18)	—
174PI	(72 pairs)	—
	Cross gutter block (1)	—
	Horiz. pair with vert. gutter (8)	—
	Vert. pair with horiz. gutter (18)	—

New York #175-176
International Tourist Year

1967

176PDa	#175-176, perforated, affixed to printer's card (2)	—

New York #177-178
Towards Disarmament

1967

177PD	(3)	—
178PD	(3)	—
178TC	Wall text in copper, gold lines in wall (1)	—
178TC	Wall text in copper, blue gray lines in wall (3)	—
178TC	Wall text in brown, silver lines in wall (1)	—
178TC	Wall text in brown, blue gray lines in wall (3)	—

New York #179-180
Chagall Stained Glass Windows

1967

179PP	8 items (29)	—
180PP	8 items (29)	—
179PI	On card stock (24 pairs)	—
180PI	On card stock (135 pairs)	—
	Horiz. pair with vert. gutter, on card stock (15)	—
180PI	On stamp paper (75 pairs)	—

Essays of Nos. 179-180 in 5c denomination exist.

New York #181-182
UN Secretariat

1968

181PD	(1)	—
182PD	(1)	—
182PDa	Card, #181PD-182PD (1)	—
181PP	5 items (160)	—
	Horiz. pair with vert. gutter (20)	—
182PP	5 items (160)	—
	Horiz. pair with vert. gutter (20)	—
181PI	(80 pairs)	—
	Horiz. pair with vert. gutter (20)	—
182PI	(80 pairs)	—
	Horiz. pair with vert. gutter (20)	—

New York #183-184
Art at the UN

1968

183PD	(1)	—
184PD	(1)	—
184PDa	Card, #183PD-184PD, dated "5.12.67" (2)	—
184TCa	Card, #183TC-184TC, dated "10.XI.67" (3)	—
183PP	5 items (80)	—
	Vert. pair with horiz. gutter (10)	—
184PP	5 items (80)	—
	Vert. pair with horiz. gutter (10)	—
183PI	(65 pairs)	—
	Vert. pair with horiz. gutter (10)	—
184PI	(80 pairs)	—
	Vert. pair with horiz. gutter (20)	—

No. 183TC has a bright blue frame; No. 184TC a birght red frame.

New York #185-186
UN Industrial Development Orgainzation

1968

185PD	(4)	—
186PD	(3)	—
186TC	brown frame, deep blue "ONUDI" (2)	—
185PP	4 items, affixed to cards (3)	—
186PP	4 items, affixed to cards (3)	—
185PI	with security punch (25 pairs)	—
186PI	with security punch (25 pairs)	—

New York #187
UN Headquarters

1964

187TC	light gray roof in foreground, numbered 34 or 38, dated July 7, 1967 (2)	—
187TC	With wide curved white line under window of General Assembly building, numbered 397 or 404, dated 11.8.1967 (2)	—
187TC	With halo around UN emblem, dated Feb. 12, 1968 (2)	—
187PP	11 items, on card with staple holes (3)	—
187PI	With "Specimen" overprint (80 pairs)	—
	Vert. pair with horiz. gutter, with "Specimen" overprint (20)	—
187PI	Without "Specimen" overprint (80 pairs)	—
	Vert. pair with horiz. gutter, without "Specimen" overprint (20)	—

New York #188-189
World Weather Watch

1968

189PDa	Card, #188PD-189PD (1)	—
188PP	5 items (100)	—
189PP	5 items (100)	—

New York #190-191
International Human Rights Year

1968

190PD	(6)	—
191PD	(6)	—
190PP	4 items (100)	—
191PP	4 items (100)	—
190PI	(50 pairs)	—
191PI	(50 pairs)	—

New York #192-193
UN Institute for Training and Research

1969

193PDa	Card, #192PD-193PD (2)	—
192PP	6 items (50)	—
193PP	6 items (100)	—
192PI	(15 pairs)	—
193PI	(15 pairs)	—

New York #194-195
Economic Commission for Latin America

1969

195PDa	#194-195, perforated, affixed to printer's card (4)	—

New York #196
"UN" and Emblem

1969

196PD	With approval handstamp (2)	—
196TC	Card, #196PD, 196TC dark blue background (2)	—
196PP	3 items (100)	—

New York #197-198
UN International Law Commission

1969

198PDa	Card, #197PD-198PD (9)	—
197PP	4 items (80)	—
	Horiz. pair with vert. gutter (10)	—
198PP	4 items (80)	—
	Horiz. pair with vert. gutter (10)	—
197PI	(40 pairs)	—
	Horiz. pair with vert. gutter (10)	—
198PI	(40 pairs)	—
	Horiz. pair with vert. gutter (10)	—

New York #199-200
Labor and Development

1969

199PD	With approval handstamp (1)	—
200PD	(1)	—
200PDa	Card, #199PD-200PD, with approval handstamp (1)	—
199TC	Men in dark blue, perforated (3)	—
200TC	Rose pink background, perforated (3)	—
200PP	4 items (91)	—

Geneva #1-14
Definitives

1969-70

G1PD	(2)	—
G3PD	(1)	—
G3PDa	Card, 2 #G3PD, with approval handstamp (2)	—
G4PD	(2)	—
G5PD	(3)	—
G7PD	(1)	—
G8PD	Perforated, on card with approval handstamp (2)	—
G8PDa	Perforated layout sheet proof with 4 #G8PD affixed (1)	—
G8PDb	Partial perforated layout sheet proof with 2 #G8PD affixed (1)	—
G9PD	(1)	—
G10PD	(1)	—
G11PD	(1)	—
G12PD	(1)	—
G13PD	(4)	—
G14PD	(3)	—
G1TC	Black panel behind "UN" (1)	—
G6TCa	Card, #G6PD, #G6TC pewter emblem, dated "7.10.69" (3)	—
G6TCb	Card, #G6TC silver emblem, 2 #G6PD dated "17.9.69" (3)	—
G6TCc	Card, #G6PD, #G6TC orange denomination, dated "27.8.69" (3)	—
G12TC	gray background, on card marked "Rejected" (2)	—
G1PP	3 items, perforated (100)	—
G2PP	5 items (160)	—
	Horiz. pair with vert. gutter (20)	—
G3PP	5 items (160)	—
	Horiz. pair with vert. gutter (20)	—
G4PP	5 items (151)	—
	Horiz. pair with vert. gutter (20)	—
G5PP	4 items (160)	—
	Vert. pair with horiz. gutter (20)	—
G6PP	3 items (160)	—
	Horiz. pair with vert. gutter (20)	—
G7PP	4 items (100)	—
G8PP	8 items (150)	—
G9PP	6 items (100)	—
G10PP	8 items (100)	—
G12PP	6 items (100)	—
G13PP	5 items (160)	—
	Vert. pair with horiz. gutter (20)	—
G2PI	(80 pairs)	—
	Horiz. pair with vert. gutter (20)	—
G3PI	(80 pairs)	—
	Horiz. pair with vert. gutter (20)	—
G4PI	(73 pairs)	—
	Horiz. pair with vert. gutter (20)	—
G5PI	(80 pairs)	—
	Vert. pair with horiz. gutter (20)	—
G6PI	(80 pairs)	—
	Horiz. pair with vert. gutter (20)	—
G7PI	(50 pairs)	—
G8PI	(75 pairs)	—
G9PI	(50 pairs)	—

G10PI	(50 pairs)	—
G13PI	(80 pairs)	—
	Vert. pair with horiz. gutter (20)	—

Four essays of No. G2 exist, having "0" below "F" jutting out to left. Two essays of No. G10 with small "F.S.re on rejected cards.

New York #201-202
Mosaic Art at the UN

1969

201PD	(3)	—
202PD	(3)	—
202PDa	Card, #201PD-202PD (2)	—
201PP	8 items (100)	—
202PP	8 items (100)	—
201PI	(50 pairs)	—
202PI	(50 pairs)	—

New York #203-204
Peace Bell

1970

204PDa	Card, 2 each #203PD-204PD (2)	—
203PP	5 items (100)	—
204PP	5 items (100)	—

About half of Nos. 203PP and 204PP have faults.

New York #205-206
Lower Mekong Basin Development Project

1970

205PD	(2)	—
206PD	(2)	—
205PP	10 items (100)	—
206PP	10 items (100)	—
205PI	(50 pairs)	—
206PI	(50 pairs)	—

New York #207-208
Fight Cancer

1970

207PD	Perforated, non-glossy paper, on piece of printer's card (1)	—
208PD	Perforated, non-glossy paper, on piece of printer's card (1)	—
208PDa	Card, #207PD-208PD, perforated, non-glossy paper (1)	—
208PDb	Card, 2 #207PD-208PD, perforated, non-glossy paper, with approval handstamp (1)	—
208PDc	#207-208, perforated, glossy paper, on printer's card (2)	—
207PP	2 items (50)	—
208PP	2 items (50)	—
207PI	(50 pairs)	—
208PI	(50 pairs)	—

New York #209-212
UN, 25th Anniv.

1970

209PD	(2)	—
210PD	(2)	—
211PD	On card (3)	—
211PDa	Card, #209PD-211PD (2)	—
212PD	(1)	—
212PDa	Card, #209PD-212PD (1)	—
209PP	4 items (180)	—
	Horiz. pair with vert. gutter (10)	—
210PP	5 items (180)	—
	Horiz. pair with vert. gutter (10)	—
211PP	3 items (180)	—
	Vert. pair with horiz. gutter (10)	—
212PP	5 items (22)	—
209PI	(80 pairs)	—
	Horiz. pair with vert. gutter (20)	—
210PI	(80 pairs)	—
	Horiz. pair with vert. gutter (20)	—
211PI	(80 pairs)	—
	Vert. pair with horiz. gutter (20)	—
212PI	(12 pairs)	—

New York #213-214
Peace, Justice and Progress

1970

214PDa	Card, #213PD-214PD (3)	—
214PDb	Card, 2 each #213PD-214PD (2)	—
213PP	4 items (50)	—
214PP	4 items (50)	—

New York #215, Geneva #15
Peaceful Uses of the Sea Bed

1971

215PD	(2)	—
G15PD	(1)	—
215PP	6 items (100)	—
G15PP	6 items (100)	—
215PI	(50 pairs)	—
G15PI	(50 pairs)	—

New York #216-217, Geneva #16
International Support for Refugees

1971

217PDa	Card, #216PD-217PD, #G16PD (2)	—
216PP	4 items (80)	—
	Horiz. pair with vert. gutter (10)	—
217PP	4 items (80)	—
	Horiz. pair with vert. gutter (10)	—
G16PP	4 items (160)	—
	Horiz. pair with vert. gutter (20)	—
216PI	(80 pairs)	—
	Horiz. pair with vert. gutter (20)	—
217PI	(80 pairs)	—
	Horiz. pair with vert. gutter (20)	—
G16PI	(80 pairs)	—
	Horiz. pair with vert. gutter (20)	—

New York #218, Geneva #17
World Food Program

1971

218PD	(4)	—
G17PD	(4)	—
218PP	6 items (100)	—
G17PP	6 items (100)	—
218PI	(50 pairs)	—
G17PI	(50 pairs)	—

New York #219, Geneva #18
Universal Postal Union

1971

219PDa	Card, #219PD, #G18PD (3)	—
219PP	5 items (130)	—
	Horiz. pair with vert. gutter (10)	—
G18PP	5 items (150)	—
219PI	(80 pairs)	—
	Horiz. pair with vert. gutter (20)	—
G18PI	(80 pairs)	—
	Horiz. pair with vert. gutter (20)	—

New York #220-221, Geneva #19-20
International Year Against Racial Discrimination

1971

221PDa	Card, #220PD-221PD, #G19PD-G20PD and 4 similar items with slightly different colors (1)	—
221PDb	Card with affixed plastic sheet with #220PD-221PD, #G19PD-G20PD affixed (1)	—
221PDc	Cut-up card, #220PD-221PD, G19PD-G20PD (1)	—
220PP	5 items (100)	—
221PP	5 items (75)	—
G19PP	5 items (100)	—
G20PP	5 items (100)	—

New York #222-223
UN Headquarters, New York

1971

222PD	(4)	—
223PD	(2)	—
222PP	8 items (91)	—
223PP	5 items (92)	—
222PI	(175 pairs)	—

Two sheets of 50 of No. 222PI are "approved."

New York #224-225, Geneva #21
UN International School

1971

225PDa	Card, #224PD-225PD, G21PD, with approval stamp (2)	—
225PDb	Card or sheet, #224PD-225PD, 1fr essay of #G21 (3)	—
224PP	5 items (180)	—
	Vert. pair with horiz. gutter (10)	—
225PP	5 items (100)	—
	Vert. pair with horiz. gutter (10)	—
G21PP	5 items (180)	—
	Vert. pair with horiz. gutter (10)	—
224PI	(80 pairs)	—
	Vert. pair with horiz. gutter (20)	—
225PI	(80 pairs)	—
	Vert. pair with horiz. gutter (20)	—
G21PI	(80 pairs)	—
	Vert. pair with horiz. gutter (20)	—

New York #226, Geneva #22
Definitives

1972

226PD	Perforated on printer's card (3)	—
G22PD	(5)	—
226PP	4 items (100)	—
G22PP	4 items (180)	—
	Horiz. pair with vert. gutter (10)	—
226PI	(50 pairs)	—
G22PI	(80 pairs)	—
	Horiz. pair with vert. gutter (20)	—

New York #227, Geneva #23
Non-proliferation of Nuclear Weapons

1972

227PD	(2)	—
G23PD	(2)	—
227PP	6 items (100)	—
G23PP	6 items (100)	—
227PI	(50 pairs)	—
G23PI	(50 pairs)	—

Two essays each of Nos. 227 and G23 lacking strong gray billowing in center of cloud exist on cards dated "22.Set.1971."

New York #228, Geneva #24, Souvenir Card #1
World Health Day

1972

228PD	Card, #228PD, #G24PD with approval handstamp (1)	—
G24PD	(1)	—
SC1PD	Card with stamps with simulated perforations and cancels (2)	—
228PP	8 items (80)	—
	Vert. pair with horiz. gutter (10)	—
G24PP	8 items (160)	—
	Vert. pair with horiz. gutter (20)	—
G24PI	(160 pairs)	—
	Vert. pair with horiz. gutter (20)	—

New York #229-230, Geneva #25-26
UN Conference on Human Environment

1972

229PD	(1)	—
230PDa	Card, #229PD-230PD, #G25PD-G26PD (3)	—
230PDb	Card, #230PD, #G25PD-G26PD (1)	—
229PP	6 items (288)	—
	Cross gutter block (2)	—
	Horiz. pair with vert. gutter (16)	—
	Vert. pair with horiz. gutter (36)	—
230PP	6 items (288)	—
	Cross gutter block (2)	—
	Horiz. pair with vert. gutter (16)	—
	Vert. pair with horiz. gutter (36)	—
G25PP	6 items (288)	—
	Cross gutter block (2)	—
	Horiz. pair with vert. gutter (16)	—
	Vert. pair with horiz. gutter (36)	—
G26PP	6 items (288)	—
	Cross gutter block (2)	—
	Horiz. pair with vert. gutter (16)	—
	Vert. pair with horiz. gutter (36)	—
229PI	(144 pairs)	—
	Cross gutter block (2)	—
	Horiz. pair with vert. gutter (16)	—
	Vert. pair with horiz. gutter (36)	—
230PI	(144 pairs)	—
	Cross gutter block (2)	—
	Horiz. pair with vert. gutter (16)	—
	Vert. pair with horiz. gutter (36)	—
G25PI	(144 pairs)	—
	Cross gutter block (2)	—
	Horiz. pair with vert. gutter (16)	—
	Vert. pair with horiz. gutter (36)	—
G26PI	(144 pairs)	—
	Cross gutter block (2)	—
	Horiz. pair with vert. gutter (16)	—
	Vert. pair with horiz. gutter (36)	—

New York #231, Geneva #27
Economic Commission for Europe

1972

231PDa	Card, #231PD, #G27PD (4)	—
231PP	8 items (100)	—
G27PP	8 items (50)	—

New York #232-233, Geneva #28-29, Souvenir Card #2
Art at the UN

1972

232PDa	Card, #232PD, #233TC text in dull blue green, #G28PD-G29PD (1)	—
G28PD	(1)	—
G29PDa	Card, #G28PD-G29PD, #233TC text in dull blue green (1)	—
G29PDb	Card, #G29PD, #233TC text in dull blue green (1)	—
SC2PD	(25)	—
SC2PDa	Defaced card, with corrections marked in blue (8)	—
SC2TC	Untrimmed card, signature in light blue(3)	—
G28PP	3 items (50)	—
G29PP	3 items (50)	—
232PI	(80 pairs)	—
	Vert. pair with horiz. gutter (20)	—
233PI	(80 pairs)	—
	Vert. pair with horiz. gutter (20)	—
G28PI	(80 pairs)	—
	Vert. pair with horiz. gutter (20)	—
G29PI	(80 pairs)	—
	Vert. pair with horiz. gutter (20)	—

New York #234-235, Geneva #30-31, Souvenir Card #3
Disarmament Decade

1973

235PDa	Card, #234PD-235PD, #G30PD-G31PD, with approval handstamp (1)	—
SC3PD	With printer's stamp or approval handstamp (9)	—
234PP	8 items (130)	—
	Horiz. pair with vert. gutter (20)	—
235PP	8 items (100)	—
G30PP	8 items (130)	—
	Horiz. pair with vert. gutter (20)	—
G31PP	8 items (100)	—
234PI	(230 pairs)	—
	Horiz. pair with vert. gutter (20)	—
235PI	(230 pairs)	—
	Horiz. pair with vert. gutter (20)	—
G30PI	(205 pairs)	—
	Horiz. pair with vert. gutter (20)	—
G31PI	(230 pairs)	—
	Horiz. pair with vert. gutter (20)	—

Two exapmles of #SC3PD are cut in half.

New York #236-237, Geneva #32
Fight Against Drug Abuse

1973

236PD	(1)	—
237PDa	Card, #236PD-237PD, #G32PD with approval handstamp (4)	—
237PDb	Card, #237PD, #G32PD with approval handstamp (1)	—
237PDc	Card, #237PD, #G32PD, 9c essay of #236 (6)	—
236PP	8 items (75)	—
237PP	8 items (100)	—
G32PP	8 items (50)	—
236PI	(50 pairs)	—
237PI	(50 pairs)	—
G32PI	(50 pairs)	—

New York #238-239, Geneva #33
UN Volunteer Program

1973

239PDa	Card, #238PD-239PD, #G33PD (9)	—
238PP	8 items (80)	—
239PP	8 items (100)	—
G33PP	8 items (50)	—
238PI	(50 pairs)	—
239PI	(50 pairs)	—
G33PI	(25 pairs)	—

New York #240-241, Geneva #34
Namibia

1973

241PDa	Card, #240PD-241PD, #G34PD (1)	—
241PDb	Card, #240PD-241PD, #G34PD, essays of #240-241, #G34 with Africa outlined in gold (3)	—
240PP	8 items (100)	—
241PP	8 items (100)	—
G34PP	8 items (50)	—
240PI	(50 pairs)	—
241PI	(50 pairs)	—
G34PI	(50 pairs)	—

Two cards containing the essays only exist.

New York #242-243, Geneva #35-36, Souvenir Card #4
Universal Declaration of Human Rights, 25th Anniv.

1973

242PD	(9)	—
243PDa	Card, #242PD-243PD, #G35PD-G36PD (6)	—
243PDb	Card, #242PD-243PD (9)	—
243PDc	Card, #243PD, #G35PD-G36PD (1)	—
SC4PD	With approval handstamp (3)	—
242PP	5 items (100)	—
243PP	5 items (100)	—
G35PP	5 items (100)	—
G36PP	5 items (50)	—
SC4PP	2 items (1)	—
SC4PI	untrimmed card (1)	—

No. SC4PP may not be a complete set of progressive proofs.

New York #244-245, Geneva #37-38
New International Labor Organization Headquarters

1974

245PDa	Card, #245PD, #G37PD-G38PD, 8c essay of #244 (4)	—
244PP	8 items (75)	—
245PP	8 items (75)	—
G37PP	8 items (50)	—
G38PP	8 items (50)	—
244PI	(50 pairs)	—
245PI	(50 pairs)	—
G37PI	(50 pairs)	—
G38PI	(50 pairs)	—

New York #246, Geneva #39-40, Souvenir Card #5
Universal Postal Union, Cent.

1974

246PD	(1)	—
246PDa	Card, #246PD, #G39PD-G40PD (7)	—
G40PDa	Card, #G39PD-G40PD (1)	—
SC5PD	Affixed to card (5)	—
SC5PDa	Card with printer instructions in ink (1)	—
SC5PDb	Progressive proof sheet with printer instructions in ink (1)	—
246PP	6 items (100)	—
G39PP	5 items (50)	—
G40PP	5 items (50)	—
246PI	(25 pairs)	—
G39PI	(25 pairs)	—
G40PI	(25 pairs)	—

New York #247-248, Geneva #41-42
Art at the UN

1974

247PDa	Card, #247PD, #G41PD-G42PD, 15c essay of #248 (5)	—
248PDa	Card, #247PD-248PD, #G41PD-G42PD (3)	—
247PP	8 items (100)	—
248PP	8 items (100)	—
G41PP	8 items (50)	—
G42PP	8 items (50)	—
247PI	(50 pairs)	—
248PI	(50 pairs)	—
G41PI	(50 pairs)	—
G42PI	(50 pairs)	—

New York #249-251
Definitives

1974

249PD	Affixed on perforated blank (1)	—
250PD	Affixed on perforated blank (1)	—
250PDa	Taped to card (1)	—
250PDb	Card, #250PD, 251TC with darker brown background, essay of #249 with flat top "S," with "21.DIC.1973" date and approval stamp (2)	—
251PD	Affixed on perforated blank (1)	—
251PDa	Card, #249PD, #251PD, with "17.ENE.1974" date and aproval stamp (3)	—
251TCa	Darker brown background, on cards dated "21.DIC.1973" (3)	—
250PP	10 items (50)	—
251PP	8 items (35)	—
249PI	(200 pairs)	—
250PI	(50 pairs)	—
251PI	(100 pairs)	—

New York #252-253, Geneva #43-44, Souvenir Card #6
World Population Year

1974

252PDa	Card, #252PD, #G44PD, 21c essay of #253, 40c essay of #G43 in se-tenant strip (3)	—
253PDa	Card, #252PD-253PD, G44PD, 40c essay of #G43 in se-tenant strip (4)	—
SC6PD	With approval handstamp (10)	—
252PP	10 items (50)	—
253PP	10 items (50)	—
G43PP	10 items (50)	—
G44PP	10 items (50)	—
252PI	(50 pairs)	—
253PI	(50 pairs)	—
G43PI	(50 pairs)	—
G44PI	(50 pairs)	—

All examples of No. SC6PD show the 40c essay.

New York #254-255, Geneva #45
Law of the Sea

1974

255PDa	Card, #254PD-255PD, #G45TC with blue green sky (3)	—
254PP	10 items (50)	—
255PP	10 items (50)	—
G45PP	10 items (50)	—
254PI	(50 pairs)	—
255PI	(50 pairs)	—
G45PI	(50 pairs)	—

New York #256-257, Geneva #46-47, Souvenir Card #7
Peaceful Uses of Outer Space

1975

256PDa	Card, #256PD, #G46PD-G47PD (1)	—
257PD	Cut from #256PDa (1)	—
257PDa	Card, #256PD-257PD, G46PD-G47PD (3)	—
SC7PD	with approval handstamp (4)	—
256PP	8 items (150)	—
257PP	8 items (150)	—
G46PP	8 items (50)	—
G47PP	8 items (50)	—
256PI	(100 pairs)	—
257PI	(100 pairs)	—
G46PI	(50 pairs)	—
G47PI	(50 pairs)	—

New York #258-259, Geneva #48-49
International Women's Year

1975

258PD	On card dated "16 Oct. 1974" (4)	—
259PD	(4)	—
G48PD	On card dated "16 Oct. 1974" (4)	—
G49PD	(4)	—
258TC	bright blue background (on cards dated "17 Sep. 1974") (4)	—
G48TC	red brown background (on cards dated "17 Sep. 1974") (4)	—
258PP	6 items (50)	—
259PP	6 items (50)	—
G48PP	6 items (50)	—
G49PP	6 items (50)	—
258PI	(50 pairs)	—
259PI	(50 pairs)	—
G48PI	(50 pairs)	—
G49PI	(50 pairs)	—

Six essays of the 18c stamp with "Nations Unies" inscription, and six essays of the 90c stamp with "United Nations" inscription exist.

New York #260-262, Geneva #50-52
UN, 30th Anniv.

1975

261PDa	Card, #260PD-261PD, #G51PD, #G50TC in olive green, se-tenant (4)	—
262PD	(5)	—
G52PD	(1)	—
G52TC	With #G52aTC olive green (5)	—
260PP	6 items (50)	—
261PP	6 items (50)	—
262PP	10 items (6)	—
G50PP	6 items (50)	—
G51PP	6 items (50)	—
G52PP	10 items (6)	—
260PI	(50 pairs)	—
261PI	(50 pairs)	—
262PI	(26 pairs of souvenir sheets)	—
G50PI	(50 pairs)	—
G51PI	(50 pairs)	—
G52PI	(26 pairs of souvenir sheets)	—

New York #263-264, Geneva #53-54
Namibia

1975

264PDa	Card, #263PD-264PD, #G53PD-G54PD (9)	—
263PP	8 items (50)	—
264PP	8 items (50)	—
G53PP	8 items (50)	—
G54PP	7 items (50)	—
263PI	(50 pairs)	—
264PI	(50 pairs)	—
G53PI	(50 pairs)	—
G54PI	(50 pairs)	—

New York #265-266, Geneva #55-56, Souvenir Card #8
UN Peace-keeping Operations

1975

266PDa	Card, #265PD-266PD, #G55PD-G56PD (3)	—
266PDb	Card, #266PD, #G55PD-G56PD, 10c essay of #265 (5)	—
SC8PD	With approval handstamp (5)	—
265PI	(25 pairs)	—
266PI	(25 pairs)	—
G55PI	(25 pairs)	—
G56PI	(25 pairs)	—

New York #267-271
Definitives

1976

267PD	(4)	—
268PD	(3)	—
269PD	(5)	—
270PD	(8)	—
271PD	(4)	—
271TC	Dark green background (not approved cards dated "30 June 1975" (5)	—
267PP	10 items (25)	—
268PP	8 items (50)	—
269PP	3 items (50)	—
270PP	6 items (50)	—
271PP	10 items (25)	—
267PI	(50 pairs)	—
268PI	(50 pairs)	—
269PI	(50 pairs)	—
270PI	(50 pairs)	—
271PI	(50 pairs)	—

New York #272-273, Geneva #57, Souvenir Card #9
World Federation of United Nations Associations

1976

273PDa	Card, #272PD-273PD, #G57PD (4)	—
SC9PD	With approval handstamp dated "18 Sep 1975" (4)	—
SC9TC	With light blue denominations on 1966 stamp (not approved) (5)	—
272PP	6 items (50)	—
273PP	6 items (50)	—
G57PP	6 items (50)	—
272PI	(50 pairs)	—
273PI	(50 pairs)	—
G57PI	(50 pairs)	—

New York #274-275, Geneva #58
UN Conference on Trade and Development

1976

G58PDa	Card, #G58PD, non-denominated essays of #274-275 (5)	—
274PP	5 items (130)	—
	Vert. pair with horiz. gutter (10)	—
275PP	5 items (130)	—
	Vert. pair with horiz. gutter (10)	—
G58PP	5 items (150)	—
274PI	(80 pairs)	—
	Vert. pair with horiz. gutter (20)	—
275PI	(80 pairs)	—
	Vert. pair with horiz. gutter (20)	—
G58PI	(80 pairs)	—
	Vert. pair with horiz. gutter (20)	—

New York #276-277, Geneva #59-60
UN Conference on Human Settlements

1976

277PDa	Card, #276PD-277PD, #G59PD-G60PD (4)	—
276PP	12 items (50)	—
277PP	12 items (50)	—
G59PP	12 items (50)	—
G60PP	12 items (50)	—
276PI	(50 pairs)	—
277PI	(50 pairs)	—
G59PI	(50 pairs)	—
G60PI	(50 pairs)	—

New York #278-279, Geneva #61-62
UN Postal Administration, 25th Anniv.

1976

279PDa	Card, #278PD-279PD, #G61PD-G62PD (5)	—
278PP	5 items (64)	—
	Horiz. pair with vert. gutter (4)	—
	Vert. pair with horiz. gutter (4)	—
279PP	5 items (64)	—
	Horiz. pair with vert. gutter (4)	—
	Vert. pair with horiz. gutter (4)	—
G61PP	5 items (72)	—
	Horiz. pair with vert. gutter (4)	—
G62PP	5 items (63)	—
	Horiz. pair with vert. gutter (4)	—
	Vert. pair with horiz. gutter (4)	—

New York #280, Geneva #63, Souvenir Card #10
World Food Council

1976

280PD	(5)	—
G63PD	(5)	—
SC10PD	With approval handstamp (12)	—
280PP	2 items (50)	—
G63PP	2 items (50)	—
280PI	(50 pairs)	—
G63PI	(50 pairs)	—

New York #281-282, Geneva #64, Souvenir Card #11
World Intellectual Property Organization

1977

282PDa	Card, #281PD-282PD, #G64PD (4)	—
SC11PD	With approval handstamp (4)	—
281PP	8 items (50)	—
282PP	8 items (50)	—
G64PP	8 items (50)	—
281PI	(50 pairs)	—
282PI	(50 pairs)	—
G64PI	(50 pairs)	—

New York #283-284, Geneva #65-66
UN Water Conference

1977

283PD	Cut out from #284PDb (1)	—
284PDa	Card, #283PD-284PD, #G65PD-G66PD (2)	—
284PDb	Card, #284PD, #G65PD-G66PD (1)	—
284PDc	Card, #284PD, #G66PD (1)	—
283PP	6 items (50)	—
284PP	6 items (50)	—
G65PP	5 items (50)	—
G66PP	5 items (50)	—
283PI	(50 pairs)	—
284PI	(50 pairs)	—
G65PI	(50 pairs)	—
G66PI	(50 pairs)	—

New York #285-286, Geneva #67-68
UN Security Council

1977

286PDa	Card, #285PD-286PD, essays of #G67-G68 with small top Chinese character (4)	—
G68PDa	Card, #G67PD-G68PD (large Chinese character) (4)	—
286PP	8 items (50)	—
G67PP	8 items (50)	—
G68PP	8 items (50)	—
285PI	(50 pairs)	—
286PI	(50 pairs)	—
G67PI	(50 pairs)	—
G68PI	(50 pairs)	—

A card with the two essays only (a cutout of No. 286PDa) with "not approved" handstamp exists.

New York #287-288, Geneva #69-70, Souvenir Card #12
Combat Racism

1977

288PDa	Card, #287PD-288PD (4)	—
G70PDa	Card, #G69PD-G70PD (4)	—
SC12PD	With approval handstamp and specimen perfin (5)	—
287PP	3 items (50)	—
288PP	3 items (50)	—
G69PP	6 items (150)	—
G70PP	6 items (150)	—
287PI	(175 pairs)	—
288PI	(175 pairs)	—
G69PI	(225 pairs)	—
G70PI	(225 pairs)	—

New York #289-290, Geneva #71-72
Peaceful Uses of Atomic Energy

1977

290PDa	Card, #289PD-290PD, #G71PD-G72PD (4)	—
290PDb	Card, #289PD-290PD, #G71PD, essay of #G72 with capital "F" in "Fins" (5)	—
289PP	8 items (50)	—
290PP	8 items (50)	—
G71PP	6 items (50)	—
G72PP	6 items (50)	—
289PI	(50 pairs)	—
290PI	(50 pairs)	—
G71PI	(50 pairs)	—
G72PI	(50 pairs)	—

New York #291-293, Geneva #73
Definitives

1978

291PD	(4)	—
292PD	(5)	—
293PD	(4)	—
G73PD	With approval handstamp (4)	—
G73TC	Tree in deep brown (with "not approved" handstamp (6)	—
G73PP	6 items (50)	—
291PI	(50 pairs)	—
292PI	(50 pairs)	—
293PI	(75 pairs)	—
G73PI	(50 pairs)	—

Six essays of No. 293 having "C" in Naciones not even with "A" exist on card with "not approved" handstamp.

New York #294-295, Geneva #74-75
Global Eradication of Smallpox

1978

295PDa	Card, #294PD-295PD, #G74PD-G75PD (5)	—
294PP	2 items (50)	—
295PP	2 items (50)	—
G74PP	4 items (50)	—
G75PP	4 items (50)	—
294PI	(50 pairs)	—
295PI	(50 pairs)	—
G74PI	(50 pairs)	—
G75PI	(50 pairs)	—

New York #296-297, Geneva #76, Souvenir Card #13
Liberation, Justice and Cooperation for Namibia

1978

296PD	On perforated sheet layout (2)	—
297PD	On perforated sheet layout (1)	—
297PDa	Card, #296-297, #G76, perforated (4)	—
297PDb	Card, #296-297 perforated, essay of #G76 ("F." and "S." same size, not approved) (5)	—
G76PD	On perforated sheet layout (9)	—
SC13PD	With approval handstamp (5)	—
296PP	6 items (50)	—
297PP	6 items (50)	—
G76PP	6 items (50)	—
296PI	(50 pairs)	—
297PI	(50 pairs)	—
G76PI	(50 pairs)	—

The essay of No. G76 exists on a not approved perforated sheet layout.

New York #298-299, Geneva #77-78, Souvenir Card #14
Safety in the Air

1978

298PDa	Card, #298PD, #G77PD-G78PD (1)	—
299PD	Cut out from #298PDa (1)	—
299PDa	Card, #298PD-299PD, #G77PD-G78PD (3)	—
SC14PD	With approval handstamp (4)	—
298PP	10 items (50)	—
299PP	10 items (50)	—
G77PP	6 items (50)	—
G78PP	6 items (50)	—
298PI	(50 pairs)	—
299PI	(50 pairs)	—
G77PI	(50 pairs)	—
G78PI	(50 pairs)	—

New York #300-301, Geneva #79-80
UN General Assembly

1978

301PDa	Card, #300PD-301PD, #G79PD-G80PD (4)	—
300PP	4 items (50)	—
301PP	5 items (50)	—
G79PP	6 items (50)	—
G80PP	6 items (50)	—
300PI	(25 pairs)	—
301PI	(25 pairs)	—
G79PI	(25 pairs)	—
G80PI	(25 pairs)	—

New York #302-303, Geneva #81
Technical Cooperation Conference

1978

303PDa	Card, #302PD-303PD, #G81PD (3)	—
302PP	10 items (50)	—
303PP	10 items (50)	—
G81PP	8 items (50)	—
302PI	(50 pairs)	—
303PI	(50 pairs)	—
G81PI	(50 pairs)	—

Five not approved cards have essays of the set showing black behind closer cogwheels and text close to bottom frame.

New York #304-307
Definitives

1979

304PD	(1)	—
304PDa	Card, #304PD-307PD (9)	—
304PDb	Card, #304PD, essays of #305, 306, 307 with inked-in corrections for printer (2)	—
307PDa	Card, #305PD-307PD (3)	—
304PP	8 items (50)	—
305PP	8 items (50)	—
306PP	6 items (50)	—
307PP	4 items (50)	—
304PI	(50 pairs)	—
305PI	(50 pairs)	—
306PI	(75 pairs)	—
307PI	(75 pairs)	—

Three cut-up not approved cards exist containing the three essays with inked-in corrections.

Nos. 306PI and 307PI include 25 pairs of reprints.

New York #308-309, Geneva #82-83
UN Disaster Relief Coordinator

1979

309PDa	Card, #308PD-309PD (4)	—
G83PDa	Card, #G82PD-G83PD (1)	—
G83PDb	Card, #G82PD-G83PD, essays of #308-309 with inked-in corrections for printer (3)	—
308PP	9 items (50)	—
309PP	9 items (50)	—
G82PP	4 items (50)	—
G83PP	4 items (50)	—
308PI	(50 pairs)	—
309PI	(50 pairs)	—
G82PI	(50 pairs)	—
G83PI	(50 pairs)	—

Two not approved cards contain the essays with inked-in corrections for printer.

New York #310-311, Geneva #84-85, Souvenir Card #15
International Year of the Child

1979

310PDa	Card, #310PD, essays of #G84-G85 (with IYC emblem above bottom of children's feet) (1)	—
311PD	Cut out from #310PDa (1)	—
311PDa	Card, #310PD-311PD, essays #G84-G85 (2)	—
G85PDa	Card, #G84PD-G85PD (4)	—
SC15PD	With manuscript approval (4)	—
310PP	9 items (20)	—
311PP	9 items (20)	—
G84PP	8 items (20)	—
G85PP	10 items (20)	—
310PI	(40 pairs)	—
311PI	(40 pairs)	—
G84PI	(40 pairs)	—
G85PI	(20 pairs)	—

One cut up not approved card contains the two essays. Five essays of No. SC15 marked "not approved" show the stamp essays.

Vienna #1-6
Definitives

1979

V6PDa	Card, #V1PD-V6PD (5)	—
V1PP	5 items (50)	—
V2PP	5 items (150)	—
V3PP	5 items (50)	—
V4PP	5 items (50)	—
V5PP	5 items (50)	—
V6PP	5 items (50)	—
V1PI	(50 pairs)	—
V2PI	(150 pairs)	—
V3PI	(50 pairs)	—
V4PI	(50 pairs)	—
V5PI	(50 pairs)	—
V6PI	(50 pairs)	—

New York #312-313, Geneva #86
Namibia

1979

313PDa	Card, #312PD-313PD, #G86PD (4)	—
312PP	8 items (50)	—
313PP	8 items (50)	—
G86PP	8 items (50)	—
312PI	(50 pairs)	—
313PI	(50 pairs)	—
G86PI	(50 pairs)	—

One card of No. 313PDa is badly damaged.

New York #314-315, Geneva #87-88, Souvenir Card #16
International Court of Justice

1979

315PDa	Card, #314PD-315PD, 2 each #G87PD-G88PD (4)	—
SC16PD	With "not approved" handstamp and "Specimen" perfin (5)	—
314PP	4 items (50)	—
315PP	4 items (50)	—
G87PP	6 items (50)	—
G88PP	7 items (50)	—
314PI	(50 pairs)	—

315PI	(50 pairs)	—
G87PI	(50 pairs)	—
G88PI	(50 pairs)	—

New York #316-317, Geneva #89, Vienna #7
New International Economic Order

1980

316PD	(11)	—
317PD	(5)	—
G89PD	With approval handstamp (5)	—
V7PD	(5)	—
316PP	4 items (50)	—
317PP	4 items (50)	—
G89PP	4 items (50)	—
V7PP	5 items (50)	—
316PI	(50 pairs)	—
317PI	(50 pairs)	—
G89PI	(50 pairs)	—
V7PI	(50 pairs)	—

Five cards of No. 316PD are marked "not approved" but there are no discernable differences between it and approved proofs. Six "not approved" cards have essays of No. G89 with text "Nouvel International Economique Ordre." Six "not approved" cards have essays of No. V7 with the same text.

Vienna #8
Definitive

1980

V8PD	(4)	—
V8PP	11 items, perforated (250)	—
V8PI	(25 pairs)	—

New York #318-319, Geneva #90-91, Vienna #9-10, Souvenir Card #17
Decade for Women

1980

318PD	(13)	—
319PD	(11)	—
G90PD	(13)	—
G91PD	(5)	—
V9PD	(5)	—
V10PD	(5)	—
SC17PD	With approval handstamp (5)	—
318PP	4 items (50)	—
319PP	4 items (50)	—
G90PP	4 items (50)	—
G91PP	4 items (50)	—
V9PP	3 items (50)	—
V10PP	2 items (50)	—
318PI	(50 pairs)	—
319PI	(50 pairs)	—
G90PI	(50 pairs)	—
G91PI	(50 pairs)	—
V9PI	(50 pairs)	—
V10PI	(50 pairs)	—

New York #320-321, Geneva #92, Vienna #11
UN Peace-keeping Operations

1980

321PDa	Card, #320PD-321PD, #V11PD, essay of #G92 with "de" on top line (3)	—
G92PD	(4)	—
320PP	2 items (50)	—
321PP	8 items (50)	—
G92PP	4 items (50)	—
V11PP	12 items (50)	—
320PI	(50 pairs)	—
321PI	(50 pairs)	—
G92PI	(50 pairs)	—
V11PI	(50 pairs)	—

New York #322-324, Geneva #93-95, Vienna #12-14
UN, 35th Anniv.

1980

324PDa	Card, #324PD, #G95D, #V14PD (4)	—
324PDb	Card, #322PD-324PD, #G93PD-G94PD, #V12PD-V14PD, essay of #G95 with incomplete marginal inscription (3)	—
322PP	8 items (50)	—
323PP	8 items (50)	—
G93PP	6 items (300)	—
G94PP	13 items (650)	—
V12PP	3 items (50)	—
V13PP	8 items (50)	—
322PI	(100 pairs)	—
323PI	(100 pairs)	—
G93PI	(100 pairs)	—
G94PI	(100 pairs)	—
V12PI	(175 pairs)	—
V13PI	(100 pairs)	—

New York #325-340
Flags

1980

325PD	Cut from #340PDa (1)	—
332PD	Cut from #340PDa (1)	—
340PDa	Card, #325PD-340PD (4)	—
340PDb	Card, #326PD-331PD, #333PD-340PD (1)	—
325-340PP	Set of 20 sheets (1)	—
325-340PI	Set of 4 sheets (2)	—

On Nos. 325-340PP, there are five progressive proof sheets per issued sheet.

New York #341-342, Geneva #96-97, Vienna #15-16, Souvenir Card #18
Economic and Social Council

1980

342PDa	Sheet, #341PD-342PD, #G96PD-G97PD, #V15PD-V16PD (4)	—
G96PD	(4)	—
G97PD	(4)	—
V15PD	(4)	—
V16PD	(4)	—
SC18PD	(4)	—
341PP	6 items (50)	—
342PP	6 items (50)	—
G96PP	6 items (50)	—
G97PP	6 items (50)	—
V15PP	6 items (50)	—
V16PP	6 items (50)	—
341PI	(50 pairs)	—
342PI	(50 pairs)	—
G96PI	(50 pairs)	—
G97PI	(50 pairs)	—
V15PI	(50 pairs)	—
V16PI	(50 pairs)	—

An essay of No. SC18 with curved cancel on 4s stamp has "not approved" handstamp.

New York #343, Geneva #98, Vienna #17
Inalienable Rights of the Palestinian People

1981

343PDa	Card, #343PD, #G98PD, #V17PD (1)	—
G98PD	(5)	—
V17PD	(5)	—
343PP	4 items (50)	—
G98PP	5 items (50)	—
V17PP	4 items (50)	—
343PI	(50 pairs)	—
G98PI	(50 pairs)	—
V17PI	(50 pairs)	—

New York #344-345, Geneva #99-100, Vienna #18-19, Souvenir Card #19
Intl. Year of the Disabled

1980

344PD	Cut out from #G100PDa (1)	—
344PDa	Card, #344PD, #G99PD-G100PD, #V18PD-V19PD, 31c essay of #345 (4)	—
344PDb	Card, #344PD, #G100PD, #V18PD-V19PD (4)	—
G100PDa	Card, #G100PD, #V18PD-V19PD (1)	—
SC19PD	With "not approved" handstamp (9)	—
344PP	6 items (50)	—
345PP	2 items (50)	—
G99PP	2 items (50)	—
G100PP	2 items (50)	—
V18PP	6 items (50)	—
V19PP	2 items (50)	—
344PI	(50 pairs)	—
345PI	(50 pairs)	—
G99PI	(50 pairs)	—
G100PI	(50 pairs)	—
V18PI	(50 pairs)	—
V19PI	(50 pairs)	—

All die proof cards are stamped "not approved." One example of No. SC19PD has "35c" covering "31c."

New York #346-347, Geneva #101, Vienna #20
Art at the UN

1981

347PDa	Card, #346PD-347PD, #G101PD, #V20PD (1)	—
347PDb	Card, #347PD, #G101PD, #V20PD, 15c essay of #346 (not approved) (6)	—
346PP	5 items (50)	—
347PP	5 items (50)	—
G101PP	5 items (50)	—
V20PP	5 items (50)	—
346PI	(50 pairs)	—
347PI	(50 pairs)	—
G101PI	(50 pairs)	—
V20PI	(50 pairs)	—

New York #348-349, Geneva #102, Vienna #21, Souvenir Card #20
Conference on New and Renewable Sources of Energy

1981

348PDa	Card, #348PD, #G102PD, #V21PD, 31c essay of #349 (3)	—
SC20PD	With approval and specimen handstamps (4)	—
348PP	6 items (50)	—
349PP	4 items (50)	—
G102PP	6 items (50)	—
V21PP	4 items (50)	—
348PI	(50 pairs)	—
349PI	(50 pairs)	—
G102PI	(50 pairs)	—
V21PI	(50 pairs)	—

All examples of No. SC20PD have the 31c essay.

New York #350-365
Flags

1981

357PDa	Card, #350PD-357PD (5)	—
365PDa	Card, #358PD-365PD (5)	—
350-365PP	Set of 19 sheets (1)	—
350-365PI	Set of 4 sheets (2)	—

On Nos. 350-365PP, there are four progressive sheets for the issued sheet containing Nos. 354-357, and five progressive proof sheets per issued sheet for the issued sheets containing Nos. 350-353, 358-361 and 362-365. Two sets of imperforate sheets of Nos. 350-353 and two sets of imperforate sheets of Nos. 354-357 exist with 15c denominations are essays.

New York #366-367, Geneva #103-104, Vienna #22-23
Volunteers Program, 10th Anniv.

1981

367PDa	Card, #367PD, #G103PD-G104PD, #V22PD-V23PD, 20c essay of #366 (3)	—
G103TC	white background (1)	—
V22TC	white background (1)	—
V23TC	white background (1)	—
366PI	(50 pairs)	—
367PI	(50 pairs)	—
G103PI	(50 pairs)	—
G104PI	(50 pairs)	—
V22PI	(50 pairs)	—
V23PI	(50 pairs)	—

New York #368-370, Geneva #105-106, Vienna #24
Definitives

1982

370PDa	Card, #368PD-370PD, #G106PD, #V24PD, essay of #G105 with no "l" before "apartheid" (5)	—
368PP	5 items (50)	—
369PP	5 items (50)	—
370PP	5 items (50)	—
G105PP	4 items (50)	—
G106PP	5 items (50)	—
V24PP	5 items (50)	—
368PI	(50 pairs)	—
369PI	(50 pairs)	—
370PI	(50 pairs)	—
G105PI	(50 pairs)	—
C106PI	(50 pairs)	—
V24PI	(50 pairs)	—

One example of No. 370PDa has all stamps canceled and #G105 altered.

New York #371-372, Geneva #107-108, Vienna #25-26, Souvenir Card #21
Environment Program, 10th Anniv.

1982

372PDa	Card, #371PD-372PD, #G107PD, #V25PD-V26PD, 1.30fr essay of #G108 (5)	—
372PDb	Card, #372PD, #G107PD-G108PD, #V25PD-V26PD, 18c essay of #371 (4)	—
SC21PD	(5)	—
371PP	8 items (50)	—
372PP	7 items (50)	—
G107PP	12 items (50)	—
G108PP	8 items (50)	—
V25PP	7 items (50)	—
V26PP	11 items (50)	—
371PI	(50 pairs)	—
372PI	(50 pairs)	—
G107PI	(50 pairs)	—
G108PI	(50 pairs)	—
V25PI	(50 pairs)	—
V26PI	(50 pairs)	—

One copy of No. 372PDb has had some stamps defaced. Five essays of No. SC21PD show the 18c essay, with one altered to change 18c to 20c.

New York #373, Geneva #109-110, Vienna #27, Souvenir Card #22
Exploration and Peaceful Uses of Outer Space

1982

373PDa	Card, #373PD, #G109PD-G110PD, #V27PD (4)	—
G109PD	(4)	—
G110PD	(4)	—
V27PD	(4)	—
SC22PD	(4)	—
373PP	6 items (50)	—
G109PP	6 items (50)	—
G110PP	14 items (50)	—
V27PP	14 items (50)	—
373PI	(50 pairs)	—
G109PI	(50 pairs)	—
G110PI	(50 pairs)	—
V27PI	(50 pairs)	—

New York #374-389
Flags

1982

381PDa	Card, #374PD-381PD (5)	—
389PDa	Card, #382PD-389PD (4)	—
374-389PP	Set of 20 sheets (1)	—
374-389PI	Set of 4 sheets (2)	—

On Nos. 374-389PP, there are five progressive proof sheets per issued sheet.

New York #390-391, Geneva #111-112, Vienna #28-29
Conservation and Protection of Nature

1982

390PDa	Card, #390PD, #G111PD, #V29PD, essays of #G112 and #V28 (1)	—
391PD	(1)	—
391PDa	Card, #390PD-391PD, #G111PD, #V29PD, essays of #G112 and #V28 (3)	—
G112PD	(3)	—
V29PD	(3)	—
390PP	10 items (50)	—
391PP	10 items (50)	—
G111PP	10 items (50)	—
G112PP	10 items (50)	—
V28PP	10 items (50)	—
V29PP	10 items (50)	—
390PI	(50 pairs)	—
391PI	(50 pairs)	—
G111PI	(50 pairs)	—
G112PI	(50 pairs)	—
V28PI	(50 pairs)	—
V29PI	(50 pairs)	—

Essays of No. G112 have snake with lighter stripes. Essays of No. V28 have umlaut missing one dot.

New York #392-393, Geneva #113, Vienna #30
World Communications Year

1983

392PD	(5)	—
393PD	(4)	—
G113PD	(4)	—
V30PD	(5)	—
392TC	Dark blue and green colors switched (4)	—
V30TC	Dark blue and green colors switched (3)	—
392PP	10 items (50)	—
393PP	15 items (50)	—
G113PP	15 items (50)	—
V30PP	10 items (50)	—
392PI	(50 pairs)	—
393PI	(50 pairs)	—
G113PI	(50 pairs)	—
V30PI	(50 pairs)	—

New York #394-395, Geneva #114-115, Vienna #31-32, Souvenir Card #23
Safety at Sea

1983

395PDa	Card, #394PD-395PD, #G114PD-G115PD, #V31PD-V32PD, #394TC-395TC, #G114TC (1)	—
395PDb	Card, #394PD-395PD, #G114PD (4)	—
G115PDa	Card, #G115PD, #V31PD-V32PD, #394TC-395TC,#G114TC(10)	—
SC23PD	(5)	—
SC23TC	(6)	—
394PP	10 items (50)	—
395PP	8 items (50)	—
G114PP	11 items (50)	—
G115PP	5 items (50)	—
V31PP	5 items (50)	—
V32PP	8 items (50)	—
394PI	(50 pairs)	—
395PI	(50 pairs)	—
G114PI	(50 pairs)	—
G115PI	(50 pairs)	—
V31PI	(50 pairs)	—
V32PI	(50 pairs)	—

Nos. 394TC and G114TC have orange buoy lights instead of red, and No. 395TC has red violet line in ship instead of orange. These appear on No. SC23TC.

New York #396, Geneva #116, Vienna #33-34 — World Food Program

1983

396PD	(3)	—
G116PD	(3)	—
V33PD	(3)	—
V34PD	(3)	—
396PI	(25 pairs)	—
G116PI	(25 pairs)	—
V33PI	(25 pairs)	—
V34PI	(25 pairs)	—

New York #397-398, Geneva #117-118, Vienna #35-36, Souvenir Card #24
UN Conference on Trade and Development

1983

398PDa	Card, #397PD-398PD, #G117PD-G118PD, #V35PD-V36PD, approval handstamp (4)	—
398PDb	Card, #397PD-398PD, #G117PD, #V36PD, essays of #G118 and #V35, (not approved, undated) (5)	—
398PDc	As #398PDb, with red dot essays (not approved, dated) (5)	—
SC24PD	With approval handstamp (4)	—
SC24TC	With "not approved" handstamp (5)	—
397PP	5 items (50)	—
398PP	7 items (50)	—
G117PP	5 items (50)	—
G118PP	6 items (50)	—
V35PP	6 items (50)	—
V36PP	7 items (50)	—
397PI	(50 pairs)	—
398PI	(50 pairs)	—
G117PI	(50 pairs)	—
G118PI	(50 pairs)	—
V35PI	(50 pairs)	—
V36PI	(50 pairs)	—

Essays of Nos. G118 and V35 have blue rectangle instead of blue and yellow triangles on bottom row of flags, along with other differences. No. 398PDb has essays showing flag with green dot in 3rd row; No. 398PDc has red dot on this flag. No. SC24TC has Nos. G118 and V35 with lighter box bottom.

New York #399-414
Flags

1983

403PD	With approval handstamp (1)	—
406PDa	Card, #399PD-402PD, 404PD-406PD, #403 essay (5)	—
414PDa	Card, #407PD, 409PD-414PD, #408 essay (5)	—
399-414PP	Set of 20 sheets (1)	—
399-414PI	Set of 4 sheets (2)	—

The essay of No. 403 has fewer sun rays than on the issued stamp. The essay of No. 408 has incomplete ring above crest and thinner garlands at left and right. Nos. 413PD-414PD are marked "not approved" on No. 414PDa, but there is no appreciable difference between these and the issued stamps. On Nos. 399-414PP, there are five progressive proof sheets per issued sheet.

New York #415-416, Geneva #119-120, Vienna #37-38
Universal Declaration of Human Rights, 35th Anniv.

1983

G120PDa	Card, #G119PD-G120PD (10)	—
415PP	7 items, with "Muster" overprint (32)	—
415PPa	6 items, without "Muster" overprint (24)	—
	Horiz. pair with vert. gutter, without "Muster" overprint (4)	—
416PP	7 items, with "Muster" overprint (24)	—
	Horiz. pair with vert. gutter, with "Muster" overprint (16)	—
416PPa	6 items, without "Muster" overprint (24)	—
	Horiz. pair with vert. gutter, without "Muster" overprint (4)	—
G119PP	7 items, with "Muster" overprint (24)	—
	Horiz. pair with vert. gutter, with "Muster" overprint (16)	—
G119PPa	6 items, without "Muster" overprint (24)	—
	Horiz. pair with vert. gutter, without "Muster" overprint (4)	—
G120PP	7 items, with "Muster" overprint (24)	—
	Horiz. pair with vert. gutter, with "Muster" overprint (16)	—
G120PPa	6 items, without "Muster" overprint (24)	—
	Horiz. pair with vert. gutter, without "Muster" overprint (4)	—
V37PP	7 items, with "Muster" overprint (24)	—
	Horiz. pair with vert. gutter, with "Muster" overprint (16)	—
V37PPa	6 items, without "Muster" overprint (24)	—
	Horiz. pair with vert. gutter, without "Muster" overprint (4)	—
V38PP	7 items, with "Muster" overprint (24)	—
	Horiz. pair with vert. gutter, with "Muster" overprint (16)	—
V38PPa	6 items, without "Muster" overprint (24)	—
	Horiz. pair with vert. gutter, without "Muster" overprint (4)	—
415PI	(64 pairs)	—
	Horiz. pair with vert. gutter (16)	—
416PI	(64 pairs)	—
	Horiz. pair with vert. gutter (16)	—
G119PI	(64 pairs)	—
	Horiz. pair with vert. gutter (16)	—
G120PI	(64 pairs)	—
	Horiz. pair with vert. gutter (16)	—
V37PI	(64 pairs)	—
	Horiz. pair with vert. gutter (16)	—
V38PI	(64 pairs)	—
	Horiz. pair with vert. gutter (16)	—

On Nos. 415PP-416PP, G119PP-G120PP, V37PP-V38PP, one of the items with "Muster" overprint is a finished imperforate.

New York #417-418, Geneva #121, Vienna #39, Souvenir Card #25
Intl. Conference on Population

1984

417PD	(4)	—
418PD	(4)	—
G121PD	(4)	—
V39PD	(4)	—
SC25PD	With "not approved" handstamp (9)	—
417PP	8 items (50)	—
418PP	7 items (50)	—
G121PP	8 items (50)	—
V39PP	8 items (50)	—
417PI	(50 pairs)	—
418PI	(50 pairs)	—
G121PI	(50 pairs)	—
V39PI	(50 pairs)	—

No. 418PP does not include the blue progressive proof found in No. 417PP.

New York #419-420, Geneva #122-123, Vienna #40-41
World Food Day

1984

419PD	(5)	—
420PDa	Card, #419PD-420PD, #G122PD-G123PD, #V40PD-V41PD with "not approved" handstamp (8)	—
419PP	6 items (50)	—
420PP	6 items (50)	—
G122PP	6 items (50)	—
G123PP	6 items (50)	—
V40PP	6 items (50)	—
V41PP	6 items (50)	—
419PI	(50 pairs)	—
420PI	(50 pairs)	—
G122PI	(50 pairs)	—
G123PI	(50 pairs)	—
V40PI	(50 pairs)	—
V41PI	(50 pairs)	—

There is no appreciable difference between approved and not approved examples of No. 419PD.

New York #421-422, Geneva #124-125, Vienna #42-43
World Heritage Sites

1984

422PDa	Card, #421PD-422PD, with approval handstamp (4)	—
G125PDa	Card, #G124PD-G125PD, with approval handstamp (4)	—
V43PDa	Card, #V42PD-V43PD, with approval handstamp (4)	—
V43TCa	Card, #V42PD (darker sky), V43PD prussian blue sky, "not approved" handstamp (8)	—
421PP	6 items (80)	—
	Horiz. pair with vert. gutter (10)	—
422PP	6 items (80)	—
	Horiz. pair with vert. gutter (10)	—
G124PP	6 items (80)	—
	Horiz. pair with vert. gutter (10)	—
G125PP	6 items (80)	—
	Horiz. pair with vert. gutter (10)	—
V42PP	6 items (80)	—
	Horiz. pair with vert. gutter (10)	—
V43PP	6 items (80)	—
	Horiz. pair with vert. gutter (10)	—
421PI	(80 pairs)	—
	Horiz. pair with vert. gutter (20)	—
422PI	(80 pairs)	—
	Horiz. pair with vert. gutter (20)	—
G124PI	(80 pairs)	—
	Horiz. pair with vert. gutter (20)	—
G125PI	(80 pairs)	—
	Horiz. pair with vert. gutter (20)	—
V42PI	(80 pairs)	—
	Horiz. pair with vert. gutter (20)	—
V43PI	(80 pairs)	—
	Horiz. pair with vert. gutter (20)	—

Four cards like No. 422PDa with "not approved" handstamp contain essays with slightly different vignettes having taller sky area that is brighter blue and with less distinct designs. Four cards like No. G125PDa contain essays lacking "F.S." before denominations.

New York #423-424, Geneva #126-127, Vienna #44-45
Future for Refugees

1984

424PDa	Card, #423PD-424PD, #G126PD-G127PD, #V44PD-V45PD (2)	—
424PDb	Card, #423PD, #G127PD, 2 each #424PD, #G126PD, #V44PD-V45PD (3)	—
424PDc	Card, #423PD-424PD, #G126PD-G127PD, #V44PD-V45PD, #423TC-424TC, #G126TC-G127TC, V44TC-V45TC (5)	—
424TCa	Card, #423TC-424TC, #G126TC-G127TC, #V44TC-V45TC (1)	—
423PP	2 items (50)	—
G126PP	2 items (50)	—
G127PP	2 items (50)	—
V44PP	2 items (50)	—
V45PP	2 items (50)	—
423PI	(50 pairs)	—
424PI	(25 pairs)	—
G126PI	(50 pairs)	—
G127PI	(50 pairs)	—
V44PI	(50 pairs)	—
V45PI	(50 pairs)	—

Trial color items have backgrounds in buff.

New York #425-440
Flags

1984

432PDa	Card, #429PD-432PD (1)	—
432PDb	Card, 2 each #429PD-432PD (2)	—
436PDa	Card, #425PD, 427PD, 433PD-436PD, essays of #426, 428 (5)	—
440PDa	Card, #437PD-440PD (1)	—
440PDb	Card, 2 each #437PD-440PD (2)	—
425-440PP	Set of 21 sheets (1)	—
425-440PI	Set of 4 sheets (2)	—

Essays of Nos. 426 and 428 have country name in smaller type. On Nos. 425-440PP, there are six progressive proof sheets for the issued sheet containing Nos. 429-432, and five progressive proof sheets for the issued sheets containing Nos. 425-428, 433-436 and 437-440.

New York #441-442, Geneva #128, Vienna #46-47, Souvenir Card #26
Intl. Youth Year

1984

441PD	With approval handstamp (4)	—
442PD	With approval handstamp (3)	—
G128PD	With approval handstamp (4)	—
V46PD	(4)	—
V47PD	(4)	—
SC26PD	With approval handstamp (4)	—
G128TC	Greenish black strand in center (not approved) (5)	—
SC26TC	With #G128TC "not approved" handstamp (5)	—
441PP	7 items (50)	—
442PP	9 items (50)	—
G128PP	9 items (50)	—
V46PP	7 items (50)	—
V47PP	7 items (50)	—
441PI	(50 pairs)	—
442PI	(50 pairs)	—
G128PI	(50 pairs)	—
V46PI	(50 pairs)	—
V47PI	(50 pairs)	—

Five "not approved" essays of No. 441 and four of No. 442 have "N" in "Nations" not touching white frame at bottom. A card with a cutout version of the approved No. 442, but with a "not approved" handstamp, and a card with a cutout essay of No. 442 with an "approved" handstamp exist, probably in error.

New York #443, Geneva #129-130, Vienna #48, Souvenir Card #27
Intl. Labor Organization

1985

443PD	Card, imperforate sheet of 50 stamps (1)	—
443PDa	Card, #443PD (single), #G129PD (single) (4)	—
G130PDa	Card, #G130PD (single), #V48PD (single) (4)	—
V48PD	Card, imperforate sheet of 50 stamps (4)	—
SC27PD	With approval handstamp (4)	—
443PI	(50 pairs)	—
G129PI	(50 pairs)	—
G130PI	(50 pairs)	—
V48PI	(50 pairs)	—

Essays of No. SC27 exist which have the 1954 stamp with a buff background.

New York #444, Geneva #131-132, Vienna #49
UN University

1985

444PDa	Card, #444PD, #G131PD-G132PD, #V49PD, with approval handstamp (5)	—
G132TC	Bright colors in background ("not approved" handstamp) (6)	—
444PP	6 items (50)	—
G131PP	6 items (50)	—
G132PP	6 items (50)	—
V49PP	6 items (50)	—
444PI	(50 pairs)	—
G131PI	(50 pairs)	—
G132PI	(50 pairs)	—
V49PI	(50 pairs)	—

New York #445-446, Geneva #133-134, Vienna #50-51
Definitives

1985

445PDa	Card, #445PD, #G133PD-G134PD, #V50PD-V51PD, #446TC ("not approved handstamp") (4)	—
446PDa	Card, #445PD-446PD, #G134PD (4)	—
445PP	4 items (50)	—
446PP	5 items (50)	—
G133PP	7 items (50)	—
G134PP	3 items (50)	—
V50PP	5 items (50)	—
V51PP	5 items (50)	—
V50PI	(50 pairs)	—
V51PI	(50 pairs)	—

No. 446TC has a lighter blue emblem. Other items in No. 445PDa were declared "not approved," but do not have any appreciable difference from approved items.

New York #447-449, Geneva #135-137, Vienna #52-54
UN, 40th Anniv.

1985

447PDa	Card, 4 each #447PD, #G135PD, #V52PD (1)	—
448PDa	Card, 4 each #448PD, #G136PD, #V53PD (1)	—
449PDa	Card, #447PD-449PD, #G135PD-G137PD, #V52PD-V54PD (1)	—
449PDb	Card, #449PD, #G137PD, #V54PD (4)	—
447PP	5 items (50)	—
448PP	5 items (50)	—
449PP	6 items (36)	—
G135PP	5 items (50)	—
G136PP	5 items (50)	—
G137PP	6 items (36)	—
V52PP	5 items (50)	—
V53PP	5 items (50)	—
V54PP	6 items (36)	—
447PI	(50 pairs)	—
448PI	(50 pairs)	—
449PI	(27 pairs of souvenir sheets)	—
G135PI	(50 pairs)	—
G136PI	(50 pairs)	—
G137PI	(27 pairs of souvenir sheets)	—
V52PI	(50 pairs)	—
V53PI	(50 pairs)	—
V54PI	(27 pairs of souvenir sheets)	—

New York #450-465
Flags

1985

465PDa	Card, #450PD-455PD, 457PD-465PD, essay of #456 (5)	—
450-465PP	Set of 24 sheets (1)	—
450-465PI	Set of 4 sheets (2)	—

Essay of Nos. 456 has thin-lined star. On Nos. 425-440PP, there are six progressive proof sheets per issued sheet.

New York #466-467, Geneva #138-139, Vienna #55-56, Souvenir Card #28
UNICEF Child Survival Campaign

1985

466PD	(4)	—
466PDa	Card, with cut-up pane of 50 (1)	—
467PD	(4)	—
467PDa	Card, with cut-up pane of 50 (1)	—
G138PD	(4)	—
G138PDa	Card, with cut-up pane of 50 (1)	—
G139PD	(4)	—
G139PDa	Card, with cut-up pane of 50 (1)	—
V55PD	(4)	—
V55PDa	Card, with cut-up pane of 50 (1)	—
V56PD	(4)	—
V56PDa	Card, with cut-up pane of 50 (1)	—
SC28PD	(4)	—
466PP	5 items (50)	—
467PP	5 items (50)	—
G138PP	5 items (50)	—
G139PP	5 items (50)	—
V55PP	5 items (50)	—
V56PP	5 items (50)	—
466PI	(50 pairs)	—
467PI	(50 pairs)	—
G138PI	(50 pairs)	—
G139PI	(50 pairs)	—
V55PI	(50 pairs)	—
V56PI	(50 pairs)	—

New York #468, Geneva #140, Vienna #57
Africa in Crisis

1986

468PDa	Card, #468PD, #G140PD, essay of #V57 (4)	—
468PP	5 items (50)	—
G140PP	4 items (50)	—
V57PP	4 items (50)	—
468PI	(50 pairs)	—
G140PI	(50 pairs)	—
V57PI	(50 pairs)	—

One example of No. 468PDa has essay of No. V57 corrected to show small loop of "8" at top as in the issued stamp.

New York #472a, Geneva #144a, Vienna #61a
UN Development Program

1986

472aPD	(4)	—
472aPDa	Card, pane of 10 blocks (2)	—
G144aPD	(4)	—
G144aPDa	Card, pane of 10 blocks (2)	—
V61aPD	(4)	—
V61aPDa	Card, pane of 10 blocks (2)	—
472aPP	6 items (10 blocks)	—
G144aPP	6 items (10 blocks)	—
V61aPP	6 items (10 blocks)	—
472aPI	(20 blocks)	—
G144aPI	(20 blocks)	—
V61aPI	(20 blocks)	—

Geneva #145
Definitive

1986

G145PD	(5)	—
G145PP	5 items (50)	—
G145PI	(50 pairs)	—

New York #473-474, Geneva #146-147, Vienna #62-63, Souvenir Card #29
Philately

1986

473PDa	Partial pane of 39 with approval handstamp on reverse (1)	—
473PDb	Full pane of 50 with approval handstamp on reverse (3)	—
474PDa	Imperforate pane of 50 with approval handstamp on reverse (4)	—
G146PDa	Imperforate pane of 50 with approval handstamp on reverse (4)	—
G147PDa	Partial pane of 41 with approval handstamp on reverse (1)	—
G147PDb	Full pane of 50 with approval handstamp on reverse (3)	—
V62PDa	Imperforate pane of 50 with approval handstamp on reverse (4)	—
V63PDa	Partial pane of 41 with approval handstamp on reverse (1)	—
V63PDb	Full pane of 50 with approval handstamp on reverse (4)	—
SC29PD	(3)	—
473TC	greenish black (5)	—
474TC	purple (1)	—
474TC	blue (1)	—
474TC	red brown (1)	—
474TC	olive brown (1)	—
474TC	dark green (1)	—
G146TC	purple (1)	—
G146TC	blue (1)	—
G146TC	reddish purple (1)	—
G146TC	greenish black (1)	—
G146TC	dark olive brown (1)	—
G147TC	dark blue (5)	—
V62TC	purple (1)	—
V62TC	blue (1)	—
V62TC	red brown (1)	—
V62TC	greenish black (1)	—
V62TC	dark olive brown (1)	—
V63TC	greenish black (5)	—

New York #475-476, Geneva #148-149, Vienna #64-65, Souvenir Card #30
International Peace Year

1986

475PD	(4)	—
475PDa	Card, imperforate pane of 50 (1)	—
476PD	(4)	—
476PDa	Card, imperforate pane of 50 (1)	—
G148PD	(4)	—
G148PDa	Card, imperforate pane of 50 (1)	—
G149PD	(4)	—
V64PD	(1)	—
V65PD	(4)	—
V65PDa	Card, imperforate pane of 50 (1)	—
SC30PD	(4)	—
475PP	4 items (50)	—
476PP	4 items (50)	—
G148PP	4 items (50)	—
G149PP	4 items (50)	—
V64PP	4 items (50)	—
V65PP	3 items (50)	—
475PI	(50 pairs)	—
476PI	(50 pairs)	—
G148PI	(50 pairs)	—
G149PI	(50 pairs)	—
V64PI	(50 pairs)	—
V65PI	(50 pairs)	—

Essays of No. V64 with 7s denominations exist in three cards with singles and one card with an imperforate pane of 50.

New York #477-492
Flags

1986

492PDa	Card, #477PD-492PD (5)	—
477-492PP	Set of 24 sheets (1)	—
477-492PI	Set of 4 sheets (2)	—

On Nos. 477-492PP, there are six progressive proof sheets per issued sheet.

New York #493, Geneva #150, Vienna #66
World Federation of UN Associations, 40th Anniv.

1986

493PD	(3)	—
493PDa	Imperforate souvenir sheet with cancel lines added (1)	—
G150PD	(3)	—
G150PDa	Imperforate souvenir sheet with cancel lines added (1)	—
V66PD	(3)	—
V66PDa	Imperforate souvenir sheet with cancel lines added (1)	—
493PP	8 items (16)	—
G150PP	11 items (16)	—
V66PP	6 items (16)	—
493PI	(32 souvenir sheets)	—
G150PI	(32 souvenir sheets)	—
V66PI	(32 souvenir sheets)	—

New York #494, Geneva #151, Vienna #67
Trygve Lie

1987

494PD	On imperforate sheet layout (1)	—
494PDa	Card, #494PD, #G151PD, V67PD (4)	—
G151PD	On imperforate sheet layout (1)	—
V67PD	On imperforate sheet layout (1)	—
494PP	10 items (50)	—
G151PP	10 items (50)	—
V67PP	10 items (50)	—
494PI	(50 pairs)	—
G151PI	(100 pairs)	—
V67PI	(50 pairs)	—

Geneva #152-153
Definitives

1987

G152PD	(1)	—
G153PD	(4)	—
G153TCa	Card, 2 #G153TC dark blue panel (5)	—
G153TCb	Card, imperforate pane of 50 #G153TC dark blue panel (2)	—
G152PP	6 items (50)	—
G153PP	5 items (50)	—
G152PI	(50 pairs)	—
G153PI	(50 pairs)	—

Six essays of No. G152 with design 33mm high exist on cards marked "approved text only."

New York #495-496, Geneva #154-155, Vienna #68-69, Souvenir Card #31
International Year of Shelter for the Homeless

1987

496PDa	Card, #495PD-496PD, #G154PD-G155PD, #V68PD-V69PD (4)	—
SC31PD	(3)	—
495PP	6 items (80)	—
	Horiz. pair with vert. gutter (10)	—
496PP	6 items (80)	—
	Horiz. pair with vert. gutter (10)	—
G154PP	6 items (80)	—
	Horiz. pair with vert. gutter (10)	—
G155PP	6 items (80)	—
	Horiz. pair with vert. gutter (10)	—
V68PP	6 items (80)	—
	Horiz. pair with vert. gutter (10)	—
V69PP	6 items (80)	—
	Horiz. pair with vert. gutter (10)	—
495PI	(80 pairs)	—
	Horiz. pair with vert. gutter (20)	—
496PI	(80 pairs)	—
	Horiz. pair with vert. gutter (20)	—
G154PI	(80 pairs)	—
	Horiz. pair with vert. gutter (20)	—
G155PI	(80 pairs)	—
	Horiz. pair with vert. gutter (20)	—
V68PI	(80 pairs)	—
	Horiz. pair with vert. gutter (20)	—
V69PI	(80 pairs)	—
	Horiz. pair with vert. gutter (20)	—

New York #497-498, Geneva #156-157, Vienna #70-71
Fight Drug Abuse

1987

498PDa	Card, #497PD-498PD, #G156PD-G157PD, #V70PD-V71PD with approval handstamp (5)	—
497PP	8 items (50)	—
498PP	8 items (50)	—
G156PP	8 items (50)	—
G157PP	8 items (50)	—
V70PP	8 items (50)	—
V71PP	8 items (50)	—
497PI	(100 pairs)	—
498PI	(100 pairs)	—
G156PI	(100 pairs)	—
G157PI	(100 pairs)	—
V70PI	(100 pairs)	—
V71PI	(100 pairs)	—

Six "not approved" cards contain essays of the six stamps, each lacking the white line separating the halves of the vignette.

Vienna #72-73
Definitives

1987

V73PDa	Card, #V72PD-V73PD (5)	—
V72PP	8 items (50)	—
V73PP	7 items (50)	—
V72PI	(100 pairs)	—
V73PI	(100 pairs)	—

New York #499-514
Flags

1987

511PDa	Card, #500PD, 501PD, 503PD, 507PD, 509PD, 511PD (1)	—
514PDa	Card, #499PD-514PD (5)	—
514PDb	Card, #499PD, 500PD, 502PD, 504PD-506PD, 508PD, 510PD, 512PD-514PD (1)	—
499-514PP	Set of 24 sheets (1)	—
499-502PI	Sheet (2)	—
503-506PI	Sheet (2)	—

On Nos. 499-514PP, there are six progressive proof sheets per issued sheet.

New York #515-516, Geneva #158-159, Vienna #74-75
United Nations Day

1987

515PDa	Card, #515PD, #V74PD, essay of #G158 (1)	—
516PDa	Card, #516PD, #G159PD, #V75PD (1)	—
516PDb	Card, #515PD-516PD, #G159PD, #V74PD-V75PD, essay of #G158 (4)	—
515PP	8 items (36)	—
	Cross gutter block (3)	—
	Horiz. pair with vert. gutter (6)	—
	Vert. pair with horiz. gutter (18)	—
516PP	8 items (36)	—
	Cross gutter block (3)	—
	Horiz. pair with vert. gutter (6)	—
	Vert. pair with horiz. gutter (18)	—
G158PP	8 items (36)	—
	Cross gutter block (3)	—
	Horiz. pair with vert. gutter (6)	—
	Vert. pair with horiz. gutter (18)	—
G159PP	8 items (36)	—
	Cross gutter block (3)	—
	Horiz. pair with vert. gutter (6)	—
	Vert. pair with horiz. gutter (18)	—
V74PP	8 items (36)	—
	Cross gutter block (3)	—
	Horiz. pair with vert. gutter (6)	—
	Vert. pair with horiz. gutter (18)	—
V75PP	8 items (36)	—
	Cross gutter block (3)	—
	Horiz. pair with vert. gutter (6)	—
	Vert. pair with horiz. gutter (18)	—
515PI	(12 pairs)	—
516PI	(12 pairs)	—
G158PI	(28 pairs)	—
	Cross gutter block (3)	—
	Horiz. pair with vert. gutter (6)	—
	Vert. pair with horiz. gutter (18)	—
G159PI	(28 pairs)	—
	Cross gutter block (3)	—
	Horiz. pair with vert. gutter (6)	—
	Vert. pair with horiz. gutter (18)	—
V74PI	(28 pairs)	—
	Cross gutter block (3)	—
	Horiz. pair with vert. gutter (6)	—
	Vert. pair with horiz. gutter (18)	—
V75PI	(28 pairs)	—
	Cross gutter block (3)	—
	Horiz. pair with vert. gutter (6)	—
	Vert. pair with horiz. gutter (18)	—

Essay of No. G158 lacks accent in "Journée."

New York #517-518, Geneva #160-161, Vienna #76-77, Souvenir Card #32
Immunize Every Child

1987

518PDa	Card, #517PD-518PD, #G161PD, #V76PD-V77PD, 35c essay of #G160 (11)	—
SC32PD	(11)	—
517PP	11 items (50)	—
518PP	11 items (50)	—
G160PP	11 items (50)	—
G161PP	12 items (50)	—
V76PP	12 items (50)	—
V77PP	9 items (50)	—
5178PI	(50 pairs)	—
518PI	(50 pairs)	—
G160PI	(75 pairs)	—
G161PI	(75 pairs)	—
V76PI	(75 pairs)	—
V77PI	(75 pairs)	—

All examples of No. SC32PD have the essay of No. G160. No appreciable difference could be found between approved and not approved examples of Nos. 518PDa or SC32PD.

New York #519-520, Geneva #162-163, Vienna #78-79
International Fund for Agricultural Development

1988

520PDa	Card, #519PD-520PD, #G162PD-G163PD, #V78PD-V79PD (4)	—
519PP	8 items (50)	—
520PP	8 items (50)	—
G162PP	9 items (50)	—
G163PP	9 items (50)	—
V78PP	9 items (50)	—
V79PP	9 items (50)	—
519PI	(50 pairs)	—
520PI	(50 pairs)	—
G162PI	(50 pairs)	—
G163PI	(50 pairs)	—
V78PI	(50 pairs)	—
V79PI	(50 pairs)	—

New York #521, Geneva #164
Definitives

1988

521PD	(4)	—
G164PD	(6)	—
521PP	6 items (50)	—
G164PP	11 items (50)	—
521PI	(50 pairs)	—
G164PI	(50 pairs)	—

New York #523a, Geneva #166a, Vienna #81a
Survival of the Forests

1988

523aPDa	Card, imperforate pane of 6 pairs with approval handstamp (6)	—
523aPDb	Card, perforated pane of 6 pairs with approval handstamp (1)	—
G166aPDa	Card, imperforate pane of 6 pairs with approval handstamp (7)	—
V81aPDa	Card, imperforate pane of 6 pairs with approval handstamp (7)	—
523aPP	8 items (6 pairs)	—
G166aPP	8 items (6 pairs)	—
V81aPP	8 items (6 pairs)	—
523aPI	(12 pairs)	—
G166aPI	(24 pairs)	—
V81aPI	(24 pairs)	—

Panes on Nos. 523aPDa, 523aPDb, G166aPDa, V81aPDa are not affixed to cards but are between stamp mounts.

New York #524-525, Geneva #167-168, Vienna #82-83, Souvenir Card #33
Intl. Volunteer Day

1988

524PDa	Card, #524PD, #G167PD-G168PD, #V82PD-V83PD with approval handstamp (4)	—
525PDa	Card, #525PD, #G168PD, #V83PD, essays of #524, #G167, #V82 with "not approved" handstamp (4)	—
SC33PD	(4)	—
SC33TC	light blue signature (4)	—
524PP	6 items (40)	—
525PP	6 items (40)	—
525PPa	Horiz. se-tenant pair with vert. gutter, #524PP-525PP (10)	—
G167PP	6 items (40)	—
G168PP	6 items (40)	—
G168PPa	Horiz. se-tenant pair with vert. gutter, #G167PP-G168PP (10)	—
V82PP	6 items (40)	—
V83PP	6 items (40)	—
V83PPa	Horiz. se-tenant pair with vert. gutter, #V82PP-V83PP (10)	—
524PI	(70 pairs)	—
525PI	(70 pairs)	—
G167PI	(70 pairs)	—
G168PI	(70 pairs)	—
V82PI	(70 pairs)	—
V83PI	(70 pairs)	—

Essays have incomplete dates at bottom.

New York #526-527, Geneva #169-170, Vienna #84-85, Souvenir Card #34
Health in Sports

1988

526PD	With approval handstamp(2)	—
526PDa	Card, #526PD, #527TC (1)	—
526PDb	Card, imperforate pane of 50 #526PD (1)	—
527PD	(6)	—
527PDa	Card, 2 #527PD (1)	—
527PDb	Card, imperforate pane of 50 #527PD (2)	—
G169PD	(6)	—
G169PDa	Card, 2 #G169PD (1)	—
G169PDb	Card, imperforate pane of 50 #G169PD (2)	—
G170PD	With approval handstamp (2)	—
G170PDa	Card, #G170PD, #G170TC (1)	—
G170PDb	Card, imperforate pane of 50 #G170PD (1)	—
V84PD	With approval handstamp (2)	—
V84PDa	Card, #V84PD, #V84TC (1)	—
V84PDb	Card, imperforate pane of 50 #V84PD (1)	—
V85PD	(6)	—
V85PDa	Card, 2 #V85PD (1)	—
V85PDb	Card, imperforate pane of 50 #V85PD (2)	—
SC34PD	With approval handstamp (5)	—
526TC	Card, darker brown in LL part of vignette (not approved) (4)	—
526TCa	Card, imperforate pane of 50 #526TC (1)	—
G170TC	Card, black "F.S." (not approved) (4)	—
G170TCa	Card, imperforate pane of 50 #G170TC (1)	—
V84TC	Card, red splotches in UL of vignette (not approved) (4)	—
V84TCa	Card, imperforate pane of 50 #V84TC (109)	—
SC34TC	With #526TC (not approved) (4)	—
526PP	4 items (50)	—
527PP	4 items (50)	—
G169PP	4 items (50)	—
G170PP	4 items (50)	—
V84PP	5 items (50)	—
V85PP	4 items (50)	—
526PI	(50 pairs)	—
527PI	(50 pairs)	—
G169PI	(50 pairs)	—
G170PI	(45 pairs)	—
V84PI	(50 pairs)	—
V85PI	(50 pairs)	—

No appreciable difference could be seen between approved and not approved examples of Nos. 527PD, G169PD and V85PD.

New York #528-543
Flags

1988

543PDa	Card, #540PD, 543PD (2)	—
543PDb	Card, #540PD, 543PD, 22c essays of #528-539, 541-542 (2)	—
528-543PP	Set of 24 sheets (1)	—
528-543PI	Set of 4 sheets (2)	—

Nine cards containing 22c essays of Nos. 528-543 exist. On Nos. 528-543PP, there are six progressive proof sheets per issued sheet.

New York #544-545, Geneva #171-172, Vienna #86-87
Universal Declaration of Human Rights, 40th Anniv.

1988

545PDa	Card, #544PD-545PD, #G171PD-G172PD, #V86PD-V87PD (5)	—
G172PDa	Card, #172PD, 90c essay of #G172 (6)	—
544PP	6 items (50)	—
545PP	6 items (1)	—
G171PP	6 items (50)	—
G172PP	6 items (1)	—
V86PP	6 items (50)	—
V87PP	6 items (1)	—
544PI	(50 pairs)	—
545PI	(2 souvenir sheets)	—
G171PI	(50 pairs)	—
G172PI	(2 souvenir sheets)	—
V86PI	(50 pairs)	—
V87PI	(2 souvenir sheets)	—

New York #546-547, Geneva #173-174, Vienna #88-89, Souvenir Card #35
World Bank

1989

547PDa	Card, #546PD-547PD, #G173PD-G174PD, #V88PD-V89PD with approval handstamp (4)	—
547PDb	Card, #547PD in slightly lighter colors, #V88PD, #G173TC, essays of #546, #G174, #V89 (5)	—
SC35PD	With "29 Aug. 1988" handstamp on back (4)	—
546PP	6 items (40)	—
547PP	6 items (40)	—
547PPa	Vert. se-tenant pair with horiz. gutter, #546PP-547PP (10)	—
G173PP	6 items (40)	—
G174PP	6 items (40)	—
G174PPa	Vert. se-tenant pair with horiz. gutter, #G173PP-G174PP (10)	—
V88PP	6 items (40)	—
V89PP	6 items (40)	—
V89PPa	Vert. se-tenant pair with horiz. gutter, #V88PP-V89PP (10)	—
546PI	(40 pairs)	—
547PI	(40 pairs)	—
G173PI	(70 pairs)	—
G174PI	(70 pairs)	—
G174PIa	Vert. se-tenant pair with horiz. gutter, #G173PI-G174PI (10)	—
V88PI	(50 pairs)	—
V89PI	(50 pairs)	—

No. G173TC has lighter orange background. Essays of Nos. 546, G174, and V89 have incomplete years at bottom.

New York #548, Geneva #175, Vienna #90
UN Peace-keeping Force

1989

548PD	Imperforate pane of 50 with "not approved" handstamp (1)	—
548PDa	Card, #548PD, #G175PD, #V90PD (5)	—
G175PD	Imperforate pane of 50 with "not approved" handstamp (1)	—
V90PD	Imperforate pane of 50 with "not approved" handstamp (1)	—
548PP	6 items (90)	—
	Horiz. pair with vert. gutter (5)	—
G175PP	6 items (90)	—
	Horiz. pair with vert. gutter (5)	—
V90PP	6 items (90)	—
	Horiz. pair with vert. gutter (5)	—
548PI	(50 pairs)	—
G175PI	(138 pairs)	—
	Horiz. pair with vert. gutter (10)	—
V90PI	(138 pairs)	—
	Horiz. pair with vert. gutter (10)	—

No appreciable difference could be seen between approved and not approved examples of No. 548PDa.

New York #549
Definitive

1989

549PD	(9)	—
549PP	6 items (64)	—
	Cross gutter block (1)	—
	Horiz. pair with vert. gutter (8)	—
	Vert. pair with horiz. gutter (8)	—
549PI	(24 pairs)	—

No appreciable difference could be seen between approved and not approved examples of No. 549PD.

New York #550-551, Geneva #176-177, Vienna #91-92, Souvenir Card #36
World Weather Watch

1989

551PDa	Card, #550PD-551PD, #G176PD-G177PD, #V91PD-V92PD (9)	—
SC36PD	(4)	—
550PP	6 items (40)	—
551PP	6 items (40)	—
551PPa	Vert. se-tenant pair with horiz. gutter, #550PP-551PP (10)	—
G176PP	6 items (40)	—
G177PP	6 items (40)	—
G177PPa	Vert. se-tenant pair with horiz. gutter, #G176PP-G177PP (10)	—
V91PP	6 items (40)	—
V92PP	6 items (40)	—
V92PPa	Vert. se-tenant pair with horiz. gutter, #V91PP-V92PP (10)	—
550PI	(50 pairs)	—
551PI	(50 pairs)	—
G176PI	(70 pairs)	—
G177PI	(70 pairs)	—
G177PIa	Vert. se-tenant pair with horiz. gutter, #G176PI-G177PI (10)	—
V91PI	(50 pairs)	—
V92PI	(50 pairs)	—

No appreciable difference could be seen between approved and not approved examples of No. 551PDa.

New York #552-553, Geneva #178-179, Vienna #93-94
Offices in Vienna, 10th Anniv.

1989

552PD	With approval handstamp (4)	—
553PD	(4)	—
G178PD	(4)	—
G179PDa	Card, #G179PD, #G179TC orange background, #G179TC dull green background (4)	—
V93PD	(4)	—
V94PD	(9)	—
552PP	10 items (25)	—
553PP	12 items (25)	—
G178PP	10 items (25)	—
G179PP	10 items (25)	—
V93PP	10 items (25)	—
V94PP	10 items (25)	—
552PI	(24 pairs)	—
553PI	(24 pairs)	—
G178PI	(24 pairs)	—
G179PI	(24 pairs)	—
V93PI	(24 pairs)	—
V94PI	(24 pairs)	—

Five not approved essays of #552 have clearly defined cross-hatching in background. There is no appreciable difference between approved and not approved examples of No. V94PD. One item from No. G179PP and V93PP is blank as it is from progressive proof sheet showing only black sheet margins.

New York #554-569
Flags

1989

568PDa	Card, #558PD-561PD, 563PD, 564PD, 566PD-568PD (6)	—
569PDa	Card, #554PD-569PD (5)	—
554-569PP	Set of 24 sheets (1)	—
554-569PI	Set of 4 sheets (2)	—

On Nos. 554-569PP, there are six progressive proof sheets per issued sheet.

New York #570-571, Geneva #180-181, Vienna #95-96
Human Rights

1989

570PD	Strip of 3 + 3 labels (4)	—
571PD	Strip of 3 + 3 labels (4)	—
571PDa	Card, #570PD-571PD, #G180PD-G181PD, #V95PD-V96PD (5)	—
G180PD	3 singles or strip of 3 + 3 labels (4)	—
G181PD	Strip of 3 + 3 labels (4)	—
V95PD	Strip of 3 + 3 labels (4)	—
V96PD	3 singles or strip of 3 + 3 labels (4)	—
570PP	6 items (20)	—
	Cross gutter block (1)	—
	Horiz. pair with vert. gutter (2)	—
	Vert. pair with horiz. gutter (10)	—
571PP	6 items (20)	—
	Cross gutter block (1)	—
	Horiz. pair with vert. gutter (2)	—
	Vert. pair with horiz. gutter (10)	—
G180PP	6 items (20)	—
	Cross gutter block (1)	—
	Horiz. pair with vert. gutter (2)	—
	Vert. pair with horiz. gutter (10)	—
G181PP	6 items (20)	—
	Cross gutter block (1)	—
	Horiz. pair with vert. gutter (2)	—
	Vert. pair with horiz. gutter (10)	—
V95PP	6 items (48)	—
	Cross gutter block (1)	—
	Horiz. pair with vert. gutter (2)	—
	Vert. pair with horiz. gutter (10)	—
V96PP	6 items (48)	—
	Cross gutter block (1)	—
	Horiz. pair with vert. gutter (2)	—
	Vert. pair with horiz. gutter (10)	—
570PI	(12 pairs)	—
	Cross gutter block (1)	—
	Horiz. pair with vert. gutter (2)	—
	Vert. pair with horiz. gutter (10)	—
571PI	(12 pairs)	—
	Cross gutter block (1)	—
	Horiz. pair with vert. gutter (2)	—
	Vert. pair with horiz. gutter (10)	—
G180PI	(20 pairs)	—
	Cross gutter block (1)	—
	Horiz. pair with vert. gutter (2)	—
	Vert. pair with horiz. gutter (10)	—
G181PI	(20 pairs)	—
	Cross gutter block (1)	—
	Horiz. pair with vert. gutter (2)	—
	Vert. pair with horiz. gutter (10)	—
V95PI	(20 pairs)	—
	Cross gutter block (1)	—
	Horiz. pair with vert. gutter (2)	—
	Vert. pair with horiz. gutter (10)	—
V96PI	(20 pairs)	—
	Cross gutter block (1)	—
	Horiz. pair with vert. gutter (2)	—
	Vert. pair with horiz. gutter (10)	—

New York #572, Geneva #182, Vienna #97
International Trade Center

1990

572PDa	Card, #572PD, #G182PD, #V97PD with approval handstamp (5)	—
572TCa	Card, #572TC blue green ship, #G182TC red orange ship, #V97TC light pink building, with "not approved" handstamp (6)	—
572PP	9 items (50)	—
G182PP	7 items (50)	—
V97PP	8 items (50)	—
572PI	(50 pairs)	—
G182PI	(75 pairs)	—
V97PI	(50 pairs)	—

Geneva #183, Vienna #98
Definitives

1990

G183PD	(6)	—
V98PD	Proof on large sheet with approval or "not approved" handstamp, and set of 7 progressive proofs on large sheets (9)	—
G183PP	9 items (1)	—
V98PP	7 items (50)	—
G183PI	(50 pairs)	—
V98PI	(50 pairs)	—

The not approved proofs of No. V98PD are slightly lighter than the approved proofs.

New York #573-574, Geneva #184-185, Vienna #99-100, Souvenir Card #37
Fight AIDS Worldwide

1990

573PDa	Card, #573PD, #G184PD, #V99PD (4)	—
574PDa	Card, #574PD, #G185PD, #573TC white background, #G184TC white background, #V99TC white background, 10s essay of #V100 (4)	—
SC37PD	(4)	—
573PP	7 items (50)	—
574PP	6 items (50)	—
G184PP	7 items (50)	—
G185PP	7 items (50)	—
V99PP	7 items (50)	—
V100PP	6 items (50)	—
573PI	(50 pairs)	—
574PI	(50 pairs)	—
G184PI	(75 pairs)	—
G185PI	(75 pairs)	—
V99PI	(75 pairs)	—
V100PI	(75 pairs)	—

New York #575-576, Geneva #186-187, Vienna #101-102
Medicinal Plants

1990

576PDa	Card, #575PD-576PD, #G186PD-G187PD, #V101PD-V102PD (4)	—
G187PD	(4)	—
G186PP	6 items (50)	—
G187PP	6 items (50)	—
V101PP	6 items (50)	—
V102PP	6 items (50)	—
575PI	(50 pairs)	—
576PI	(50 pairs)	—
G186PI	(50 pairs)	—
G187PI	(50 pairs)	—
V101PI	(50 pairs)	—
V102PI	(50 pairs)	—

New York #577-579, Geneva #188-190, Vienna #103-105
United Nations, 45th Anniv.

1990

578PDa	Card, #577PD-578PD, #G188PD-G189PD, 6s essay of #V103, 8s essay of #V104 (4)	—
579PDa	Card, #579PD, #G190PD, #V105PD (4)	—
577PP	8 items (320)	—
	Horiz. pair with vert. gutter (40)	—
578PP	8 items (320)	—
	Horiz. pair with vert. gutter (40)	—
579PP	8 items (100)	—
G188PP	10 items (160)	—
	Horiz. pair with vert. gutter (20)	—
G189PP	8 items (320)	—
	Horiz. pair with vert. gutter (40)	—
G190PP	9 items (100)	—
V103PP	8 items (320)	—
	Horiz. pair with vert. gutter (40)	—
V104PP	8 items (320)	—
	Horiz. pair with vert. gutter (40)	—
V105PP	8 items (100)	—
577PI	(80 pairs)	—
	Horiz. pair with vert. gutter (10)	—
578PI	(80 pairs)	—
	Horiz. pair with vert. gutter (10)	—
579PI	(100 souvenir sheets)	—
G188PI	(260 pairs)	—
	Horiz. pair with vert. gutter (40)	—
G189PI	(260 pairs)	—
	Horiz. pair with vert. gutter (40)	—
G190PI	(100 souvenir sheets)	—
V103PI	(260 pairs)	—
	Horiz. pair with vert. gutter (40)	—
V104PI	(260 pairs)	—
	Horiz. pair with vert. gutter (40)	—
V105PI	(100 souvenir sheets)	—

New York #580-581, Geneva #191-192, Vienna #106-107, Souvenir Card #38
Crime Prevention

1990

581PDa	Card, #580PD-581PD, #G191PD-G192PD, #V106PD-V107PD, #SC38PD (5)	—
580PP	8 items (50)	—
581PP	8 items (50)	—
G191PP	8 items (50)	—
G192PP	8 items (50)	—
V106PP	8 items (100)	—
V107PP	8 items (100)	—
580PI	(50 pairs)	—
581PI	(50 pairs)	—
G191PI	(75 pairs)	—
G192PI	(75 pairs)	—
V106PI	(75 pairs)	—
V107PI	(75 pairs)	—

New York #582-583, Geneva #193-194, Vienna #108-109,
Human Rights

1990

582PDa	Strip of 3 + 3 labels (9)	—
583PDa	Strip of 3 + 3 labels with approval handstamp (4)	—
G193PDa	Strip of 3 + 3 labels (9)	—
G194PDa	Strip of 3 + 3 labels (9)	—
V108PDa	Strip of 3 + 3 labels (9)	—
V109PDa	Strip of 3 + 3 labels (9)	—
583TCa	Strip of 3 + 3 labels (chocolate panels) with "not approved" handstamp (5)	—
582PP	6 items (20)	—
	Cross gutter block (1)	—
	Horiz. pair with vert. gutter (2)	—
	Vert. pair with horiz. gutter (10)	—
583PP	6 items (20)	—
	Cross gutter block (1)	—
	Horiz. pair with vert. gutter (2)	—
	Vert. pair with horiz. gutter (10)	—
G193PP	6 items (20)	—
	Cross gutter block (1)	—
	Horiz. pair with vert. gutter (2)	—
	Vert. pair with horiz. gutter (10)	—
G194PP	8 items (20)	—
	Cross gutter block (1)	—
	Horiz. pair with vert. gutter (2)	—
	Vert. pair with horiz. gutter (10)	—
V108PP	6 items (20)	—
	Cross gutter block (1)	—
	Horiz. pair with vert. gutter (2)	—
	Vert. pair with horiz. gutter (10)	—
V109PP	6 items (20)	—
	Cross gutter block (1)	—
	Horiz. pair with vert. gutter (2)	—
	Vert. pair with horiz. gutter (10)	—
582PI	(20 pairs)	—
	Cross gutter block (1)	—
	Horiz. pair with vert. gutter (2)	—
	Vert. pair with horiz. gutter (10)	—
583PI	(20 pairs)	—
	Cross gutter block (1)	—
	Horiz. pair with vert. gutter (2)	—
	Vert. pair with horiz. gutter (10)	—
G193PI	(20 pairs)	—
	Cross gutter block (1)	—
	Horiz. pair with vert. gutter (2)	—
	Vert. pair with horiz. gutter (10)	—
G194PI	(20 pairs)	—
	Cross gutter block (1)	—
	Horiz. pair with vert. gutter (2)	—
	Vert. pair with horiz. gutter (10)	—
V108PI	(20 pairs)	—
	Cross gutter block (1)	—
	Horiz. pair with vert. gutter (2)	—
	Vert. pair with horiz. gutter (10)	—
V109PI	(20 pairs)	—
	Cross gutter block (1)	—
	Horiz. pair with vert. gutter (2)	—
	Vert. pair with horiz. gutter (10)	—

There is no appreciable difference between approved and not approved examples of Nos. 582PD, G193PD, G194PD, V108PD and V109PD.

New York #587a, Geneva #198a, Vienna #113a, Souvenir Card #39
Economic Council for Europe

1991

587aPDa	Card, #587aPD, #G198aPD, #V113aPD with printed perforations (2)	—
587aPDb	Card, #587aPDa, SC39PD (1)	—
SC39PD	(1)	—
587aPP	13 items (20 blocks)	—
G198aPP	13 items (20 blocks)	—
V113aPP	13 items (20 blocks)	—
587aPI	(40 blocks)	—
G198aPI	(40 blocks)	—
V113aPI	(40 blocks)	—

Second sets of blocks of Nos. 587aPP and G198aPP with 10 items, and No. V113aPP with 11 items (some items differing from the 13 item set) exist.

New York #588-589, Geneva #199-200, Vienna #114-115
Namibian Independence

1991

588PDa	Card, #588PD, #G199PD-G200PD, #V114PD-V115PD, 36c essay of #589 (8)	—
589PDa	Card, #588PD-589PD, #G199PD-G200PD, #V114PD-V115PD (1)	—
588PP	7 items (50)	—
589PP	7 items (50)	—
G199PP	8 items (50)	—
G200PP	8 items (50)	—
V114PP	6 items (50)	—
V115PP	6 items (50)	—
588PI	(100 pairs)	—
589PI	(100 pairs)	—
G199PI	(75 pairs)	—
G200PI	(75 pairs)	—
V114PI	(75 pairs)	—
V115PI	(75 pairs)	—

New York #590-592, Geneva #201-202, Vienna #116
Definitives

1991

590PD	With approval handstamp (4)	—
592PD	(4)	—
592PDa	Card, imperforate pane of 50 (1)	—
G201PD	(5)	—
G202PDa	Card, #G201PD-G202PD, #G213PD, #V116PD (4)	—
590TC	deep blue background (not approved) (5)	—
592TC	black (1)	—
590PP	8 items (80)	—
	Horiz. pair with vert. gutter (10)	—
591PP	4 items (150)	—
G201PP	8 items (50)	—
G202PP	7 items (50)	—
V116PP	7 items (50)	—
590PI	(90 pairs)	—
	Horiz. pair with vert. gutter (10)	—
591PI	(175 pairs)	—
592PI	(50 pairs)	—
G201PI	(75 pairs)	—
G202PI	(100 pairs)	—
V116PI	(75 pairs)	—

An essay of No. 592 with emblem in solid color exists.

New York #593-594, Geneva #203-204, Vienna #117-118, Souvenir Card #40
Rights of the Child

1991

593PDa	Card, #593PD, #G203PD-G204PD, #V117PD-V118PD, 90c essay of #594 (6)	—
594PDa	Card, #593PD-594PD, #G203PD-G204PD, #V117PD-V118PD (4)	—
594PDb	Card, #593PD-594PD (4)	—
SC40PD	(4)	—
593PP	9 items (50)	—
594PP	9 items (50)	—
G203PP	8 items (50)	—
G204PP	7 items (50)	—
V117PP	7 items (50)	—
V118PP	7 items (50)	—
SC40PP	15 items (1)	—
593PI	(75 pairs)	—
594PI	(75 pairs)	—
G203PI	(75 pairs)	—
G204PI	(75 pairs)	—
V117PI	(75 pairs)	—
V118PI	(75 pairs)	—

No. SC40PP may not be a complete set of progressive proofs. Five essays of No. SC40PD with the 90c essay of No. 594 exist; one is attached to No. 593PDa.

New York #595-596, Geneva #205-206, Vienna #119-120,
Banning of Chemical Weapons

1991

596PDa	Card, #595PD-596PD, #G205PD-G206PD, #V119PD-V120PD with approval handstamp (5)	—
596PDb	Card, #596PD, #G206PD, #V120PD, essays of #595, #G205, #V119 (each with gray panels taller than numerals) with "not approved" handstamp (4)	—
595PP	9 items (50)	—
596PP	9 items (50)	—
G205PP	9 items (100)	—
G206PP	9 items (100)	—
V119PP	8 items (50)	—
V120PP	8 items (50)	—
595PI	(125 pairs)	—
596PI	(125 pairs)	—
G205PI	(125 pairs)	—
G206PI	(125 pairs)	—
V119PI	(125 pairs)	—
V120PI	(125 pairs)	—

Second sets of six items of Nos. 595PP-596PP, G205PP-G206PP, and V119PP-V120PP exist. Some items differ from those found in the listed sets.

New York #597-598, Geneva #207-208, Vienna #121-122
UN Postal Administration, 40th Anniv.

1991

598PDa	Card, #597PD-598PD, #G207PD-G208PD, #V121PD-V122PD (4)	—
597TCa	Card, #597TC, #G207TC-G208TCD, #V121TC-V122TC (each with white background), 36c essay of #598 (6)	—
597PP	2 items (64)	—
	Cross gutter block (1)	—
	Horiz. pair with vert. gutter (8)	—
	Vert. pair with horiz. gutter (8)	—
598PP	2 items (64)	—
	Cross gutter block (1)	—
	Horiz. pair with vert. gutter (8)	—
	Vert. pair with horiz. gutter (8)	—
G207PP	2 items (64)	—
	Cross gutter block (1)	—
	Horiz. pair with vert. gutter (8)	—
	Vert. pair with horiz. gutter (8)	—
G208PP	2 items (64)	—
	Cross gutter block (1)	—
	Horiz. pair with vert. gutter (8)	—
	Vert. pair with horiz. gutter (8)	—
V121PP	2 items (64)	—
	Cross gutter block (1)	—
	Horiz. pair with vert. gutter (8)	—
	Vert. pair with horiz. gutter (8)	—
V122PP	2 items (64)	—
	Cross gutter block (1)	—
	Horiz. pair with vert. gutter (8)	—
	Vert. pair with horiz. gutter (8)	—
597PI	(120 pairs)	—
	Cross gutter block (3)	—
	Horiz. pair with vert. gutter (24)	—
	Vert. pair with horiz. gutter (24)	—
598PI	(120 pairs)	—
	Cross gutter block (3)	—
	Horiz. pair with vert. gutter (24)	—
	Vert. pair with horiz. gutter (24)	—
G207PI	(120 pairs)	—
	Cross gutter block (3)	—
	Horiz. pair with vert. gutter (24)	—
	Vert. pair with horiz. gutter (24)	—
G208PI	(120 pairs)	—
	Cross gutter block (3)	—
	Horiz. pair with vert. gutter (24)	—
	Vert. pair with horiz. gutter (24)	—
V121PI	(120 pairs)	—
	Cross gutter block (3)	—
	Horiz. pair with vert. gutter (24)	—
	Vert. pair with horiz. gutter (24)	—
V122PI	(120 pairs)	—
	Cross gutter block (3)	—
	Horiz. pair with vert. gutter (24)	—
	Vert. pair with horiz. gutter (24)	—

Four cross gutter blocks, 32 horizontal pairs with vertical gutters and 32 vertical pairs with horizontal gutters can be cut from four perforated sheets of Nos. 597PI-598PI, G207PI-G208PI, V119PI-V120PI. No. 598PI is difficult to distinguish from one item from No. 598PP.

New York #599-600, Geneva #209-210, Vienna #123-124,
Human Rights

1991

599PDa	Strip of 3 + 3 labels with approval handstamp (4)	—
600PDa	Strip of 3 + 3 labels with approval handstamp (4)	—
G209PDa	Strip of 3 + 3 labels with approval handstamp (4)	—
G210PDa	Strip of 3 + 3 labels with approval handstamp (4)	—
V123PDa	Strip of 3 + 3 labels with approval handstamp (4)	—
V124PDa	Strip of 3 + 3 labels with approval handstamp (4)	—
599TC	Strip of 3 (dark gray background) + 3 labels with "not approved" handstamp (5)	—
600TC	Strip of 3 (dark green background) + 3 labels with "not approved" handstamp (5)	—
G209TC	Strip of 3 (light brown in painting) + 3 labels with "not approved" handstamp (5)	—
G210TC	Strip of 3 (dark green background) + 3 labels with "not approved" handstamp (5)	—
V124TC	Strip of 3 (black background) + 3 labels with "not approved" handstamp (5)	—
599PP	6 items (20)	—
	Cross gutter block (1)	—
	Horiz. pair with vert. gutter (2)	—
	Vert. pair with horiz. gutter (10)	—
600PP	6 items (20)	—
	Cross gutter block (1)	—
	Horiz. pair with vert. gutter (2)	—
	Vert. pair with horiz. gutter (10)	—
G209PP	6 items (20)	—
	Cross gutter block (1)	—
	Horiz. pair with vert. gutter (2)	—
	Vert. pair with horiz. gutter (10)	—
G210PP	6 items (20)	—
	Cross gutter block (1)	—
	Horiz. pair with vert. gutter (2)	—
	Vert. pair with horiz. gutter (10)	—
V123PP	6 items (20)	—
	Cross gutter block (1)	—
	Horiz. pair with vert. gutter (2)	—
	Vert. pair with horiz. gutter (10)	—

V124PP 6 items (20) —
Cross gutter block (1) —
Horiz. pair with vert. gutter (2) —
Vert. pair with horiz. gutter (10) —
599PI (56 pairs) —
Cross gutter block (1) —
Horiz. pair with vert. gutter (2) —
Vert. pair with horiz. gutter (10) —
600PI (56 pairs) —
Cross gutter block (1) —
Horiz. pair with vert. gutter (2) —
Vert. pair with horiz. gutter (10) —
G209PI (56 pairs) —
Cross gutter block (1) —
Horiz. pair with vert. gutter (2) —
Vert. pair with horiz. gutter (10) —
G210PI (56 pairs) —
Cross gutter block (1) —
Horiz. pair with vert. gutter (2) —
Vert. pair with horiz. gutter (10) —
V123PI (56 pairs) —
Cross gutter block (1) —
Horiz. pair with vert. gutter (2) —
Vert. pair with horiz. gutter (10) —
V124PI (56 pairs) —
Cross gutter block (1) —
Horiz. pair with vert. gutter (2) —
Vert. pair with horiz. gutter (10) —

New York #601-602, Geneva #211-212, Vienna #125-126
World Heritage

1992
602PDa Card, #601PD-602PD (5) —
G212PDa Card, #G211PD-G212PD (5) —
V126PDa Card, #V125PD-V126PD (5) —
601PP 6 items (50) —
602PP 6 items (50) —
G211PP 6 items (50) —
G212PP 6 items (50) —
V125PP 6 items (50) —
V126PP 6 items (50) —
601PI (50 pairs) —
602PI (50 pairs) —
G211PI (50 pairs) —
G212PI (50 pairs) —
V125PI (50 pairs) —
V126PI (50 pairs) —

Geneva #213
Definitive

1992
G213PP 6 items (50) —
G213PI (75 pairs) —

See No. G202PDa.

New York #604a, Geneva #215a, Vienna #128a
Clean Oceans

1992
604aPDa Card, imperforate pane of 6 #604aPD (2) —
604aPDb Card, as "a," with one pair removed (1) —
G215aPDa Card, imperforate pane of 6 #G215aPD (2) —
G215aPDb (Card, as "a," with one pair removed (1) —
V128aPDa Card, imperforate pane of 6 #V128aPD (2) —
V128aPDb Card, as "a," with one pair removed (1) —
604aPP 8 items, vert. pair of pairs with narrow horiz. gutter (20) —
Cross gutter block (1) —
Horiz. pair of pairs with vert. gutter (4) —
Vert. pair of pairs with wide horiz. gutter (10) —
G215aPP 8 items, vert. pair of pairs with narrow horiz. gutter (20) —
Cross gutter block (1) —
Horiz. pair of pairs with vert. gutter (4) —
Vert. pair of pairs with wide horiz. gutter (10) —
V128aPP 8 items, vert. pair of pairs with narrow horiz. gutter (20) —
Cross gutter block (1) —
Horiz. pair of pairs with vert. gutter (4) —
Vert. pair of pairs with wide horiz. gutter (10) —
604aPI Vert. pair of pairs with narrow horiz. gutter (20) —
Cross gutter block (1) —
Horiz. pair of pairs with vert. gutter (4) —
Vert. pair of pairs with wide horiz. gutter (10) —
G215aPI Vert. pair of pairs with narrow horiz. gutter (20) —
Cross gutter block (1) —
Horiz. pair of pairs with vert. gutter (4) —
Vert. pair of pairs with wide horiz. gutter (10) —
V128aPI Vert. pair of pairs with narrow horiz. gutter (20) —
Cross gutter block (1) —
Horiz. pair of pairs with vert. gutter (4) —
Vert. pair of pairs with wide horiz. gutter (10) —

New York #608a, Geneva #219a, Vienna #132a
Earth Summit

1992
608aPDa Card, #608aPD, #G219aPD, #V132aPD (5) —
608aPP 4 items (10) —
G219aPP 4 items (10) —
V132aPP 4 items (10) —
608aPI (20 blocks) —
G219aPI (20 blocks) —
V132aPI (20 blocks) —

New York #609-610, Geneva #220-221, Vienna #133-134
Mission to Planet Earth

1992
610PDa Card, #610aPD, G221aPD, #V134aPD (3) —
SC41PD (3) —
610aPP 6 items (5) —
G221aPP 6 items (5) —
V134aPP 6 items (5) —
610aPI (10 pairs) —
G221aPI (10 pairs) —
V134aPI (10 pairs) —

One item in No. G221aPP is a blank from a sheet showing marginal inscriptions only.

New York #611-612, Geneva #222-223, Vienna #135-136, Souvenir Card #42
Science and Technology for Development

1992
611PDa Card, 2 #611PD, 2 #V136PD (4) —
612PDa Card, #611PD-612PD, #G222PD-G223PD, #V135PD-V136PD (4) —
SC42PD (18) —
611PP 6 items (50) —
612PP 6 items (50) —
G222PP 6 items (50) —
G223PP 6 items (50) —
V135PP 6 items (50) —
V136PP 6 items (50) —
611PI (100 pairs) —
612PI (100 pairs) —
G222PI (100 pairs) —
G223PI (100 pairs) —
V135PI (100 pairs) —
V136PI (100 pairs) —

There is no appreciable difference between approved and not approved die proofs.

New York #613-615, Vienna #137-138
Definitives

1992
614PDa Card, #614PD, #V137PD-V138PD (4) —
615PDa Card, #613PD, #615PD (3) —
613PP 6 items (50) —
614PP 6 items (50) —
615PP 6 items (50) —
V137PP 6 items (50) —
V138PP 6 items (50) —
613PI (50 pairs) —
614PI (269 pairs) —
Cross gutter block (2) —
Horiz. pair with vert. gutter (36) —
Vert. pair with horiz. gutter (16) —
615PI (50 pairs) —
V137PI (269 pairs) —
Cross gutter block (2) —
Horiz. pair with vert. gutter (16) —
Vert. pair with horiz. gutter (36) —
V138PI (269 pairs) —
Cross gutter block (2) —
Horiz. pair with vert. gutter (36) —
Vert. pair with horiz. gutter (16) —

Three "not approved" cards containing essays of Nos. 613 and 615 lacking year date and designer inscriptions exist.

New York #616-617, Geneva #224-225, Vienna #139-140
Human Rights

1992
616PDa Strip of 3 + 3 labels (4) —
617PDa Strip of 3 + 3 labels (4) —
G224PDa Strip of 3 + 3 labels (4) —
G225PDa Strip of 3 + 3 labels (4) —
V139PDa Strip of 3 + 3 labels (4) —
V140PDa Strip of 3 + 3 labels (4) —
G225TCa Strip of 3 (dark brown background under chair) + 3 labels (not approved) (5) —
616PP 6 items (20) —
Cross gutter block (1) —
Horiz. pair with vert. gutter (2) —
Vert. pair with horiz. gutter (10) —
617PP 6 items (20) —
Cross gutter block (1) —
Horiz. pair with vert. gutter (2) —
Vert. pair with horiz. gutter (10) —
G224PP 6 items (20) —
Cross gutter block (1) —
Horiz. pair with vert. gutter (2) —
Vert. pair with horiz. gutter (10) —
G225PP 6 items (20) —
Cross gutter block (1) —
Horiz. pair with vert. gutter (2) —
Vert. pair with horiz. gutter (10) —
V139PP 6 items (20) —
Cross gutter block (1) —
Horiz. pair with vert. gutter (2) —
Vert. pair with horiz. gutter (10) —
V140PP 6 items (20) —
Cross gutter block (1) —
Horiz. pair with vert. gutter (2) —
Vert. pair with horiz. gutter (10) —
616PI (32 pairs) —
Cross gutter block (4) —
Horiz. pair with vert. gutter (8) —
Vert. pair with horiz. gutter (40) —
617PI (32 pairs) —
Cross gutter block (4) —
Horiz. pair with vert. gutter (8) —
Vert. pair with horiz. gutter (40) —
G224PI (32 pairs) —
Cross gutter block (4) —
Horiz. pair with vert. gutter (8) —
Vert. pair with horiz. gutter (40) —
G225PI (32 pairs) —
Cross gutter block (4) —
Horiz. pair with vert. gutter (8) —
Vert. pair with horiz. gutter (40) —
V139PI (32 pairs) —
Cross gutter block (4) —
Horiz. pair with vert. gutter (8) —
Vert. pair with horiz. gutter (40) —
V140PI (32 pairs) —
Cross gutter block (4) —
Horiz. pair with vert. gutter (8) —
Vert. pair with horiz. gutter (40) —

Five "not approved" cards contain 4.50s essays of No. V139, and five "not approved" cards contain 9.50s essays of No. V140.

New York #618-619, Geneva #226-227, Vienna #141-142
Aging With Dignity

1993
618PDa Card, #618PD, #G226PD-G227PD, #V141PD-V142PD, #619TC yellow flowers (not approved) (5) —
619PDa Card, #618PD-619PD, #V141PD-V142PD, #G226TC pink denomination, #G227TC yellow denomination, with approval handstamp (4) —
619TCb Card, #618TC-619TC, #G226TC-G227TC, #V141TC-V142TC, each with white denominations (5) —
618PP 7 items (50) —
619PP 7 items (50) —
G226PP 7 items (50) —
G227PP 7 items (50) —
V141PP 7 items (50) —
V142PP 7 items (50) —
618PI (50 pairs) —
619PI (50 pairs) —
G226PI (50 pairs) —
G227PI (50 pairs) —
V141PI (50 pairs) —
V142PI (50 pairs) —

New York #623a, Geneva #231a, Vienna #146a
Endangered Species

1993
623aPDa Card, imperforate pane of 4 blocks of #623aPD (3) —
G231aPDa Card, imperforate pane of 4 blocks of #G231aPD (4) —
V146aPDa Card, imperforate pane of 4 blocks of #V146aPD (3) —
G231aTCa Card, imperforate pane of 4 blocks of #G231aTC black (1) —
G231aPP 6 items (4 blocks) —
Cross gutter block (1) —
Horiz. pair with vert. gutter (2) —
Vert. pair with horiz. gutter (4) —
V146aPP 6 items (4 blocks) —
Cross gutter block (1) —
Horiz. pair with vert. gutter (2) —
Vert. pair with horiz. gutter (4) —
623aPI (20 blocks) —
Cross gutter block (8) —
Horiz. pair with vert. gutter (8) —
Vert. pair with horiz. gutter (16) —
G231aPI (44 blocks) —
Cross gutter block (10) —
Horiz. pair with vert. gutter (10) —
Vert. pair with horiz. gutter (20) —
V146aPI (20 blocks) —
Cross gutter block (8) —
Horiz. pair with vert. gutter (8) —
Vert. pair with horiz. gutter (16) —

New York #624-625, Geneva #232-233, Vienna #147-148, Souvenir Card #43
Healthy Environment

1993
625PDa Card, #624PD-625PD, #V147PD-V148PD, 90c essay of #G232, 1.10fr essay of #G233 (4) —
SC43PD (4) —
624PP 6 items (50) —
625PP 6 items (50) —
G232PP 6 items (50) —
G233PP 6 items (50) —
V147PP 6 items (50) —
V148PP 6 items (50) —
624PI (50 pairs) —
625PI (50 pairs) —
G232PI (50 pairs) —
G233PI (50 pairs) —
V147PI (50 pairs) —
V148PI (50 pairs) —

New York #626, Vienna #149
Definitives

1993

626PD	(5)	—
V149PD	(5)	—
626PP	8 items (144)	—
	Cross gutter block (1)	—
	Horiz. pair with vert. gutter (18)	—
	Vert. pair with horiz. gutter (8)	—
V149PP	5 items (50)	—
626PI	(194 pairs)	—
	Cross gutter block (2)	—
	Horiz. pair with vert. gutter (36)	—
	Vert. pair with horiz. gutter (16)	—
V149PI	(50 pairs)	—

New York #627-628, Geneva #234-235, Vienna #150-151
Human Rights

1993

627PDa	Strip of 3 + 3 labels (4)	—
628PDa	Strip of 3 + 3 labels (4)	—
G234PDa	Strip of 3 + 3 labels (4)	—
G235PDa	Strip of 3 + 3 labels (4)	—
V150PDa	Strip of 3 + 3 labels (3)	—
V151PDa	Strip of 3 + 3 labels (4)	—
627PP	6 items (20)	—
	Cross gutter block (1)	—
	Horiz. pair with vert. gutter (2)	—
	Vert. pair with horiz. gutter (10)	—
628PP	6 items (20)	—
	Cross gutter block (1)	—
	Horiz. pair with vert. gutter (2)	—
	Vert. pair with horiz. gutter (10)	—
G234PP	6 items (20)	—
	Cross gutter block (1)	—
	Horiz. pair with vert. gutter (2)	—
	Vert. pair with horiz. gutter (10)	—
G235PP	6 items (20)	—
	Cross gutter block (1)	—
	Horiz. pair with vert. gutter (2)	—
	Vert. pair with horiz. gutter (10)	—
627PI	(20 pairs)	—
	Cross gutter block (1)	—
	Horiz. pair with vert. gutter (2)	—
	Vert. pair with horiz. gutter (10)	—
628PI	(20 pairs)	—
	Cross gutter block (1)	—
	Horiz. pair with vert. gutter (2)	—
	Vert. pair with horiz. gutter (10)	—
G234PI	(20 pairs)	—
	Cross gutter block (1)	—
	Horiz. pair with vert. gutter (2)	—
	Vert. pair with horiz. gutter (10)	—
G235PI	(20 pairs)	—
	Cross gutter block (1)	—
	Horiz. pair with vert. gutter (2)	—
	Vert. pair with horiz. gutter (10)	—
V150PI	(6 pairs)	—
V151PI	(6 pairs)	—

New York #632a, Geneva #239a, Vienna #155a, Souvenir Card #44
International Peace Day

1993

632aPD	(4)	—
G239aPD	(4)	—
V155aPD	(4)	—
SC44PD	(4)	—
632aPP	7 items (10 blocks)	—
G239aPP	7 items (10 blocks)	—
V155aPP	7 items (10 blocks)	—
632aPI	(40 blocks)	—
G239aPI	(40 blocks)	—
V155aPI	(40 blocks)	—

New York #636a, Geneva #243a, Vienna #159a
Environment & Climate

1993

636aPDa	Card, #636aPD, #V159aPD (4)	—
G243aPD	(4)	—
636aPP	8 items (6 strips)	—
	Horiz. pair of strips with vert. gutter (6)	—
G243aPP	8 items (6 strips)	—
	Horiz. pair of strips with vert. gutter (6)	—
V155aPP	8 items (6 strips)	—
	Horiz. pair of strips with vert. gutter (6)	—
636aPI	(18 strips)	—
	Horiz. pair of strips with vert. gutter (18)	—
G243aPI	(18 strips)	—
	Horiz. pair of strips with vert. gutter (18)	—
V159aPI	(18 strips)	—
	Horiz. pair of strips with vert. gutter (18)	—

New York #637-638, Geneva #244-245, Vienna #160-161, Souvenir Card #45
International Year of the Family

1994

638PDa	Card, #637PD-638PD, #G244PD-G245PD, #V160PD-V161PD (4)	—
SC45PD	(4)	—
637PP	11 items (50)	—
638PP	11 items (50)	—
G244PP	10 items (50)	—
G245PP	10 items (50)	—
V160PP	11 items (50)	—
V161PP	11 items (50)	—
637PI	(100 pairs)	—
638PI	(100 pairs)	—
G244PI	(100 pairs)	—
G245PI	(100 pairs)	—
V160PI	(100 pairs)	—
V161PI	(100 pairs)	—

New York #642a, Geneva #249a, Vienna #165a
Endangered Species

1994

642aPDa	Card, imperforate pane of 4 #642aPD (9)	—
G249aPDa	Card, imperforate pane of 4 #G249aPD (4)	—
V165aPDa	Card, imperforate pane of 4 #V165aPD (4)	—
642aPP	6 items (4 blocks)	—
	Cross gutter block (2)	—
	Horiz. pair with vert. gutter (2)	—
	Vert. pair with horiz. gutter (4)	—
G249aPP	6 items (4 blocks)	—
	Cross gutter block (2)	—
	Horiz. pair with vert. gutter (2)	—
	Vert. pair with horiz. gutter (4)	—
V165aPP	6 items (4 blocks)	—
	Cross gutter block (2)	—
	Horiz. pair with vert. gutter (2)	—
	Vert. pair with horiz. gutter (4)	—
642aPI	(16 blocks)	—
	Cross gutter block (8)	—
	Horiz. pair with vert. gutter (8)	—
	Vert. pair with horiz. gutter (16)	—
G249aPI	(16 blocks)	—
	Cross gutter block (8)	—
	Horiz. pair with vert. gutter (8)	—
	Vert. pair with horiz. gutter (16)	—
V165aPI	(16 blocks)	—
	Cross gutter block (8)	—
	Horiz. pair with vert. gutter (8)	—
	Vert. pair with horiz. gutter (16)	—

There is no appreciative difference between appoved and not approved examples of No. 642aPD. Five cards with imperforate panes of 40c essays of No. G249a and five cards with imperforate panes of 5s essays of No. V165a exist.

New York #643, Geneva #250, Vienna #166
Protection for Refugees

1994

643PDa	Card, #643PD, #G250PD, #V166PD (4)	—
643PP	8 items (50)	—
G250PP	8 items (50)	—
V166PP	6 items (50)	—
643PI	(69 pairs)	—
	Horiz. pair with vert. gutter (8)	—
G250PI	(69 pairs)	—
	Horiz. pair with vert. gutter (8)	—
V166PI	(69 pairs)	—
	Horiz. pair with vert. gutter (8)	—

New York #644-646, Vienna #167-169
Definitives

1994

645PDa	Card, #644PD-645PD, #V167PD-V169PD (5)	—
646PD	(1)	—
644PP	6 items (50)	—
645PP	6 items (50)	—
V167PP	12 items (50)	—
V168PP	11 items (50)	—
V169PP	11 items (50)	—
644PI	(100 pairs)	—
645PI	(100 pairs)	—
646PI	(50 pairs)	—
V167PI	(100 pairs)	—
V168PI	(100 pairs)	—
V169PI	(100 pairs)	—

There is no appreciable difference between approved and not approved examples of No. 645PDa.

New York #650a, Geneva #254a, Vienna #173a
International Decade for Natural Disaster Reduction

1994

650aPDa	Card, #650aPD, #G254aPD, #V173aPD (5)	—
650aPP	6 items (16 blocks)	—
	Cross gutter block (1)	—
	Horiz. pair with vert. gutter (8)	—
	Vert. pair with horiz. gutter (2)	—
G254aPP	6 items (16 blocks)	—
	Cross gutter block (1)	—
	Horiz. pair with vert. gutter (8)	—
	Vert. pair with horiz. gutter (2)	—
V173aPP	6 items (16 blocks)	—
	Cross gutter block (1)	—
	Horiz. pair with vert. gutter (8)	—
	Vert. pair with horiz. gutter (2)	—
650aPI	(48 blocks)	—
	Cross gutter block (3)	—
	Horiz. pair with vert. gutter (24)	—
	Vert. pair with horiz. gutter (6)	—
G254aPI	(48 blocks)	—
	Cross gutter block (3)	—
	Horiz. pair with vert. gutter (24)	—
	Vert. pair with horiz. gutter (6)	—
V173aPI	(48 blocks)	—
	Cross gutter block (3)	—
	Horiz. pair with vert. gutter (24)	—
	Vert. pair with horiz. gutter (6)	—

Geneva #255-257
Definitives

1994

G257PDa	Card, #G255PD-G257PD (5)	—
G255PP	10 items (144)	—
	Cross gutter block (1)	—
	Horiz. pair with vert. gutter (18)	—
	Vert. pair with horiz. gutter (8)	—
G256PP	10 items (144)	—
	Cross gutter block (1)	—
	Horiz. pair with vert. gutter (18)	—
	Vert. pair with horiz. gutter (8)	—
G257PP	11 items (144)	—
	Cross gutter block (1)	—
	Horiz. pair with vert. gutter (18)	—
	Vert. pair with horiz. gutter (8)	—
G255PI	(288 pairs)	—
	Cross gutter block (4)	—
	Horiz. pair with vert. gutter (72)	—
	Vert. pair with horiz. gutter (32)	—
G256PI	(288 pairs)	—
	Cross gutter block (4)	—
	Horiz. pair with vert. gutter (72)	—
	Vert. pair with horiz. gutter (32)	—
G257PI	(288 pairs)	—
	Cross gutter block (4)	—
	Horiz. pair with vert. gutter (72)	—
	Vert. pair with horiz. gutter (32)	—

New York #651-652, Geneva #258-259, Vienna #174-175, Souvenir Card #46
Population and Development

1994

652PDa	Card, #651PD-652PD, #G258PD-G259PD, #V174PD-V175PD (4)	—
SC46PD	(4)	—
G258PP	6 items (40)	—
G259PP	6 items (40)	—
G259PPa	Horiz. se-tenant pair with vert. gutter, #G258PP-G259PP (10)	—
V174PP	6 items (40)	—
V175PP	6 items (40)	—
V175PPa	Horiz. se-tenant pair with vert. gutter, #V174PP-V175PP (10)	—
651PI	(50 pairs)	—
652PI	(50 pairs)	—
G258PI	(70 pairs)	—
G259PI	(70 pairs)	—
G259PIa	Horiz. se-tenant pair with vert. gutter, #G258PI-G259PI (10)	—
V174PI	(70 pairs)	—
V175PI	(70 pairs)	—
V175PIa	Horiz. se-tenant pair with vert. gutter, #V174PI-V175PI (10)	—

New York #653-654, Geneva #260-261, Vienna #176-177
UNCTAD, 30th Anniv.

1994

653PP	15 items (40)	—
654PP	15 items (40)	—
654PPa	Horiz. se-tenant pair with vert. gutter, #653PP-654PP (10)	—
G260PP	16 items (40)	—
G261PP	16 items (40)	—
G261PPa	Horiz. se-tenant pair with vert. gutter, #G260PP-G261PP (10)	—
V176PP	14 items (40)	—
V177PP	14 items (40)	—
V177PPa	Horiz. se-tenant pair with vert. gutter, #V176PP-V177PP (10)	—
653PI	(60 pairs)	—
654PI	(60 pairs)	—
654PIa	Horiz. se-tenant pair with vert. gutter, #653PI-654PI (30)	—
G260PI	(60 pairs)	—
G261PI	(60 pairs)	—
G261PIa	Horiz. se-tenant pair with vert. gutter, #G260PI-G261PI (30)	—
V176PI	(60 pairs)	—
V177PI	(60 pairs)	—
V177PIa	Horiz. se-tenant pair with vert. gutter, #V176PI-V177PI (30)	—

Two items from No. G260PP and one from No. V176PP are blank due to color arrangement on progressive proof sheet.

New York # 655, Geneva #262, Vienna #178
United Nations, 50th Anniv.

1995

655PD	(3)	—
G262PD	(3)	—
V178PD	(3)	—
655PP	8 items (50)	—
G262PP	8 items (50)	—
V178PP	8 items (50)	—
655PI	(100 pairs)	—
G262PI	(200 pairs)	—
V178PI	(200 pairs)	—

New York #656, Geneva #263, Vienna #179, Souvenir Card #47
World Summit for Social Development, Copenhagen

1995

656PDa	Card, #656PD, #G263PD, #V179PD (3)	—
SC47PD	Card, 4 #SC47PD (1)	—
656PP	12 items (25)	—
G263PP	8 items (25)	—
V179PP	8 items (25)	—

656PI	(24 pairs)	—
G263PI	(24 pairs)	—
V179PI	(24 pairs)	—

New York #660a, Geneva #267a, Vienna #183a Endangered Species

1995

660aPDa	Card, imperforate pane of 4 blocks, #660aPD (5)	—
660aPDb	Card, broken imperforate pane of 4 blocks, #660aPD (1)	—
660aPDc	Card, 2 imperforate panes of 4 blocks, #660aPD (1)	—
G267aPDa	Card, imperforate pane of 4 blocks, #G267aPD (6)	—
G267aPDb	Card, 2 imperforate panes of 4 blocks, #G267aPD (1)	—
V183aPDa	Card, imperforate pane of 4 blocks, #V183aPD with "14. Okt. 1994" handstamp (approved) (3)	—
V183aTCa	Card, imperforate pane of 4 blocks, #V183aTC (violet blue sky on #181TC), not approved (3)	—
V183aTCb	Card, 2 imperforate pane of 4 blocks, #V183aTC, not approved (1)	—
660aPP	6 items (9 blocks)	—
	Cross gutter block (3)	—
	Horiz. pair with vert. gutter (4)	—
	Vert. pair with horiz. gutter (7)	—
G267aPP	6 items (12 blocks)	—
	Cross gutter block (3)	—
	Horiz. pair with vert. gutter (4)	—
	Vert. pair with horiz. gutter (6)	—
V183aPP	6 items (12 blocks)	—
	Cross gutter block (3)	—
	Horiz. pair with vert. gutter (4)	—
	Vert. pair with horiz. gutter (7)	—
660aPI	(11 blocks)	—
	Cross gutter block (3)	—
	Horiz. pair with vert. gutter (4)	—
	Vert. pair with horiz. gutter (7)	—
G267aPI	(16 blocks)	—
	Cross gutter block (3)	—
	Horiz. pair with vert. gutter (4)	—
	Vert. pair with horiz. gutter (6)	—
V183aPI	(11 blocks)	—
	Cross gutter block (3)	—
	Horiz. pair with vert. gutter (4)	—
	Vert. pair with horiz. gutter (7)	—

Three cross gutter blocks, four horizontal pairs with vertical gutters, seven vertical pairs with horizontal gutters and nine blocks with untrimmed margins can be cut from perforated sheets of Nos. V180PI-V183PI.

New York #661-662, Geneva #268-269, Vienna #184-185, Souvenir Card #48 International Youth Year

1995

662PDa	Card, #661PD-662PD, #G268PD-G269PD, #V184PD-V185PD (6)	—
SC48PD	(6)	—
661PP	5 items (160)	—
	Cross gutter block (5)	—
	Horiz. pair with vert. gutter (25)	—
	Vert. pair with horiz. gutter (44)	—
662PP	8 items (160)	—
	Cross gutter block (5)	—
	Horiz. pair with vert. gutter (25)	—
	Vert. pair with horiz. gutter (44)	—
G268PP	6 items (208)	—
	Cross gutter block (5)	—
	Horiz. pair with vert. gutter (25)	—
	Vert. pair with horiz. gutter (44)	—
G269PP	5 items (208)	—
	Cross gutter block (5)	—
	Horiz. pair with vert. gutter (25)	—
	Vert. pair with horiz. gutter (44)	—
V184PP	7 items (101)	—
	Cross gutter block (2)	—
	Horiz. pair with vert. gutter (11)	—
	Vert. pair with horiz. gutter (12)	—
V185PP	6 items (197)	—
	Cross gutter block (5)	—
	Horiz. pair with vert. gutter (25)	—
	Vert. pair with horiz. gutter (44)	—
661PI	(128 pairs)	—
	Cross gutter block (5)	—
	Horiz. pair with vert. gutter (25)	—
	Vert. pair with horiz. gutter (44)	—
662PI	(128 pairs)	—
	Cross gutter block (5)	—
	Horiz. pair with vert. gutter (25)	—
	Vert. pair with horiz. gutter (44)	—
G268PI	(128 pairs)	—
	Cross gutter block (5)	—
	Horiz. pair with vert. gutter (25)	—
	Vert. pair with horiz. gutter (44)	—
G269PI	(128 pairs)	—
	Cross gutter block (5)	—
	Horiz. pair with vert. gutter (25)	—
	Vert. pair with horiz. gutter (44)	—
V184PI	(128 pairs)	—
	Cross gutter block (5)	—
	Horiz. pair with vert. gutter (25)	—
	Vert. pair with horiz. gutter (44)	—
V185PI	(128 pairs)	—
	Cross gutter block (5)	—
	Horiz. pair with vert. gutter (25)	—
	Vert. pair with horiz. gutter (44)	—

New York #663-665, Geneva #270-272, Vienna #186-188 United Nations, 50th Anniv.

1995

664PDa	Card, # 664PD, #663TC maroon, #663TC dark blue, #663TC green, #664TC dark blue, #664TC green (3)	—
663PI	(80 pairs)	—
664PI	(80 pairs)	—
664PIa	Horiz. se-tenant pair with vert. gutter, #663PI-664PI (40)	—
665PI	(8 pairs of souvenir sheets)	—
G270PI	(80 pairs)	—
G271PI	(80 pairs)	—
G271PIa	Horiz. se-tenant pair with vert. gutter, #G270PI-G271PI (40)	—
G272PI	(8 pairs of souvenir sheets)	—
V186PI	(80 pairs)	—
V187PI	(80 pairs)	—
V187PIa	Horiz. se-tenant pair with vert. gutter, #V186PI-V187PI (40)	—
V188PI	(8 pairs of souvenir sheets)	—

Three cards with non-engraved essays of No. 665 in red violet exist.

New York #666-667, Geneva #273-274, Vienna #189-190 Fourth World Conference on Women

1995

666PP	10 items, perforated (275)	—
667PP	10 items, perforated (250)	—
G273PP	10 items, perforated (100)	—
G274PP	10 items, perforated (250)	—
V189PP	9 items, perforated (275)	—
V190PP	9 items, perforated (275)	—
666PI	(144 pairs)	—
667PI	(144 pairs)	—
G273PI	(108 pairs)	—
G274PI	(144 pairs)	—
V189PI	(132 pairs)	—
V190PI	(144 pairs)	—

On No. V189PP and V190PP, 125 sets have a red and multicolored item while the remaining 150 sets have a blue and multicolored item.

New York #668 UN Headquarters

1995

668PD	(5)	—
668PP	6 items (162)	—
	Horiz. pair with vert. gutter (9)	—
	Vert. pair with horiz. gutter (5)	—
668PI	(85 pairs)	—
	Horiz. pair with vert. gutter (9)	—
	Vert. pair with horiz. gutter (5)	—

New York #669-670, Geneva #275-276, Vienna #191-192 United Nations, 50th Anniversary

1995

669PD	(4)	—
G275PD	(4)	—
V191PD	(4)	—
669PP	6 items (6)	—
G275PP	8 items (6)	—
V191PP	7 items (6)	—
669PI	(2 full panes)	—
669PIa	(3 pairs of full panes)	—
670PI	(3 booklets)	—
G275PI	(2 full panes)	—
G275PIa	(3 pairs of full panes)	—
G276PI	(3 booklets)	—
V191PI	(2 full panes)	—
V191PIa	(4 pairs of full panes)	—
V192PI	(3 booklets)	—

New York #671, Geneva #277, Vienna #193, Souvenir Card #49 World Federation of United Nations Associations, 50th Anniv.

1996

671PDa	Card, #671PD, #G277PD, #V193PD (3)	—
SC49PD	(4)	—
671PP	6 items (150)	—
	Horiz. pair with vert. gutter (25)	—
G277PP	6 items (150)	—
	Horiz. pair with vert. gutter (25)	—
V193PP	6 items (305)	—
	Cross gutter block (5)	—
	Horiz. pair with vert. gutter (40)	—
	Vert. pair with horiz. gutter (30)	—
671PI	(155 pairs)	—
	Horiz. pair with vert. gutter (55)	—
G277PI	(155 pairs)	—
	Horiz. pair with vert. gutter (55)	—
V193PI	(264 pairs)	—
	Cross gutter block (11)	—
	Horiz. pair with vert. gutter (88)	—
	Vert. pair with horiz. gutter (63)	—

New York #672-673, Geneva #278-279, Vienna #194-195 Definitives

1996

673PDa	Card, #672PD-673PD, #G278PD-G279PD, #V194PD-V195PD with approval handstamp (4)	—
673PDb	Card, #673PD, #672TC gray in vignette, #G278TC-G279TC tan background in panel, essays of #V194PD-V195PD (larger frames) (not approved) (4)	—
673PDc	#673PDa and 673PDb stapled together (1)	—
672PP	8 items (144)	—
	Cross gutter block (1)	—
	Horiz. pair with vert. gutter (18)	—
	Vert. pair with horiz. gutter (8)	—
673PP	8 items (144)	—
	Cross gutter block (1)	—
	Horiz. pair with vert. gutter (18)	—
	Vert. pair with horiz. gutter (8)	—
G278PP	8 items (144)	—
	Cross gutter block (1)	—
	Horiz. pair with vert. gutter (18)	—
	Vert. pair with horiz. gutter (8)	—
G279PP	8 items (144)	—
	Cross gutter block (1)	—
	Horiz. pair with vert. gutter (18)	—
	Vert. pair with horiz. gutter (8)	—
V194PP	8 items (144)	—
	Cross gutter block (1)	—
	Horiz. pair with vert. gutter (18)	—
	Vert. pair with horiz. gutter (8)	—
V195PP	8 items (144)	—
	Cross gutter block (1)	—
	Horiz. pair with vert. gutter (18)	—
	Vert. pair with horiz. gutter (8)	—
672PI	(216 pairs)	—
	Cross gutter block (3)	—
	Horiz. pair with vert. gutter (54)	—
	Vert. pair with horiz. gutter (16)	—
673PI	(144 pairs)	—
	Cross gutter block (3)	—
	Horiz. pair with vert. gutter (54)	—
	Vert. pair with horiz. gutter (16)	—
G278PI	(216 pairs)	—
	Cross gutter block (3)	—
	Horiz. pair with vert. gutter (54)	—
	Vert. pair with horiz. gutter (24)	—
G279PI	(216 pairs)	—
	Cross gutter block (3)	—
	Horiz. pair with vert. gutter (54)	—
	Vert. pair with horiz. gutter (24)	—
V194PI	(216 pairs)	—
	Cross gutter block (3)	—
	Horiz. pair with vert. gutter (24)	—
	Vert. pair with horiz. gutter (36)	—
V195PI	(216 pairs)	—
	Cross gutter block (3)	—
	Horiz. pair with vert. gutter (24)	—
	Vert. pair with horiz. gutter (36)	—

New York #677a, Geneva #283a, Vienna #199a Endangered Species

1996

677aPDa	Card, imperforate pane of 4 blocks, #677aPD (3)	—
677aPDb	Card, broken imperforate pane of 4 blocks, #677aPD (1)	—
G283aPDa	Card, imperforate pane of 4 blocks, #G283aPD (3)	—
G283aPDb	Card, broken imperforate pane of 4 blocks, #G283aPD (1)	—
V199aPDa	Card, imperforate pane of 4 blocks, #V199aPD (3)	—
V199aPDb	Card, broken imperforate pane of 4 blocks, #V199aPD (1)	—
677aPP	6 items (14 blocks)	—
	Cross gutter block (5)	—
	Horiz. pair with vert. gutter (6)	—
	Vert. pair with horiz. gutter (11)	—
G283aPP	6 items (14 blocks)	—
	Cross gutter block (5)	—
	Horiz. pair with vert. gutter (6)	—
	Vert. pair with horiz. gutter (11)	—
V199aPP	6 items (14 blocks)	—
	Cross gutter block (5)	—
	Horiz. pair with vert. gutter (6)	—
	Vert. pair with horiz. gutter (11)	—
677aPI	(25 blocks)	—
	Cross gutter block (11)	—
	Horiz. pair with vert. gutter (12)	—
	Vert. pair with horiz. gutter (23)	—
G283aPI	(25 blocks)	—
	Cross gutter block (11)	—
	Horiz. pair with vert. gutter (12)	—
	Vert. pair with horiz. gutter (23)	—
V199aPI	(25 blocks)	—
	Cross gutter block (11)	—
	Horiz. pair with vert. gutter (12)	—
	Vert. pair with horiz. gutter (23)	—

New York #682a, Geneva #288a, Vienna #204a City Summit

1996

682aPDa	Card, imperforate pane of 5 strips, #682aPD (4)	—
G288aPDa	Card, imperforate pane of 5 strips, #G288aPD (4)	—
V204aPDa	Card, imperforate pane of 5 strips, #V204aPD (4)	—
682aPP	10 items (15 horiz. pairs of strips with vert. gutter)	—

G288aPP 10 items (24 horiz. pairs of strips with vert. gutter) —
Cross gutter block of strips (3) —
V204aPP 10 items (15 horiz. pairs of strips with vert. gutter) —
682aPI (35 horiz. pairs of strips with vert. gutter) —
G288aPI (56 horiz. pairs of strips with vert. gutter) —
Cross gutter block of strips (7) —
V204aPI (35 horiz. pairs of strips with vert. gutter) —

New York #683-685, Geneva #289-291, Vienna #205-207
Sport and the Environment

1996

684PDa Card, #683PD-684PD (10) —
685PD (10) —
G290PDa Card, #G289PD-G290PD (10) —
G291PD (10) —
V206PDa Card, #V205PD-V206PD (10) —
V207PD (10) —
683PP 8 items (88) —
Cross gutter block (2) —
Horiz. pair with vert. gutter (16) —
Vert. pair with horiz. gutter (11) —
684PP 8 items (88) —
Cross gutter block (2) —
Horiz. pair with vert. gutter (11) —
Vert. pair with horiz. gutter (16) —
685PP 12 items (25 souvenir sheets) —
G289PP 8 items (88) —
Cross gutter block (2) —
Horiz. pair with vert. gutter (16) —
Vert. pair with horiz. gutter (11) —
G290PP 8 items (88) —
Cross gutter block (2) —
Horiz. pair with vert. gutter (11) —
Vert. pair with horiz. gutter (16) —
G291PP 10 items (25 souvenir sheets) —
V205PP 8 items (88) —
Cross gutter block (2) —
Horiz. pair with vert. gutter (16) —
Vert. pair with horiz. gutter (11) —
V206PP 8 items (88) —
Cross gutter block (2) —
Horiz. pair with vert. gutter (11) —
Vert. pair with horiz. gutter (16) —
V207PP 11 items (25 souvenir sheets) —
683PI (44 pairs) —
Cross gutter block (2) —
Horiz. pair with vert. gutter (16) —
Vert. pair with horiz. gutter (11) —
684PI (44 pairs) —
Cross gutter block (2) —
Horiz. pair with vert. gutter (11) —
Vert. pair with horiz. gutter (16) —
685PI (75 souvenir sheets) —
G289PI (88 pairs) —
Cross gutter block (4) —
Horiz. pair with vert. gutter (32) —
Vert. pair with horiz. gutter (22) —
G290PI (88 pairs) —
Cross gutter block (4) —
Horiz. pair with vert. gutter (22) —
Vert. pair with horiz. gutter (32) —
G291PI (75 souvenir sheets) —
V205PI (132 pairs) —
Cross gutter block (6) —
Horiz. pair with vert. gutter (48) —
Vert. pair with horiz. gutter (33) —
V206PI (132 pairs) —
Cross gutter block (6) —
Horiz. pair with vert. gutter (33) —
Vert. pair with horiz. gutter (48) —
V207PI (75 souvenir sheets) —

New York #686-687, Geneva #292-293, Vienna #208-209
Plea for Peace

1996

687PDa Card, #686PD-687PD, #G292PD-G293PD, #V208PD-V209PD (4) —
686PP 10 items (112) —
Cross gutter block (3) —
Horiz. pair with vert. gutter (14) —
Vert. pair with horiz. gutter (24) —
687PP 10 items (112) —
Cross gutter block (3) —
Horiz. pair with vert. gutter (14) —
Vert. pair with horiz. gutter (24) —
G292PP 10 items (112) —
Cross gutter block (3) —
Horiz. pair with vert. gutter (24) —
Vert. pair with horiz. gutter (14) —
G293PP 10 items (112) —
Cross gutter block (2) —
Horiz. pair with vert. gutter (24) —
Vert. pair with horiz. gutter (14) —
V208PP 10 items (112) —
Cross gutter block (3) —
Horiz. pair with vert. gutter (14) —
Vert. pair with horiz. gutter (24) —
V209PP 10 items (112) —
Cross gutter block (3) —
Horiz. pair with vert. gutter (14) —
Vert. pair with horiz. gutter (24) —
686PI (104 pairs) —
Cross gutter block (3) —
Horiz. pair with vert. gutter (14) —
Vert. pair with horiz. gutter (24) —
687PI (104 pairs) —
Cross gutter block (3) —
Horiz. pair with vert. gutter (14) —
Vert. pair with horiz. gutter (24) —
G292PI (80 pairs) —
Cross gutter block (3) —
Horiz. pair with vert. gutter (24) —
Vert. pair with horiz. gutter (14) —
G293PI (80 pairs) —
Cross gutter block (3) —
Horiz. pair with vert. gutter (24) —
Vert. pair with horiz. gutter (14) —
V208PI (80 pairs) —
Cross gutter block (3) —
Horiz. pair with vert. gutter (14) —
Vert. pair with horiz. gutter (24) —
V209PI (80 pairs) —
Cross gutter block (3) —
Horiz. pair with vert. gutter (14) —
Vert. pair with horiz. gutter (24) —

New York #688-689, Geneva #294-295, Vienna #210-211, Souvenir Card #50
UNICEF, 50th Anniv.

1996

689PDa Imperforate pane, #689PD (4) —
G294PDa Imperforate pane, #G294PD (4) —
G295PDa Imperforate pane, #G295PD (6) —
V210PDa Imperforate pane, #V210PD (on photographic paper) (2) —
V211PDa Imperforate pane, #V211PD (4) —
SC50PD (1) —
688PP 10 items (18) —
Cross gutter block (6) —
Horiz. pair with vert. gutter (12) —
Vert. pair with horiz. gutter (15) —
689PP 11 items (18) —
Cross gutter block (6) —
Horiz. pair with vert. gutter (12) —
Vert. pair with horiz. gutter (15) —
G294PP 9 items (18) —
Cross gutter block (6) —
Horiz. pair with vert. gutter (12) —
Vert. pair with horiz. gutter (15) —
G295PP 9 items (18) —
Cross gutter block (6) —
Horiz. pair with vert. gutter (12) —
Vert. pair with horiz. gutter (15) —
V210PP 9 items (18) —
Cross gutter block (6) —
Horiz. pair with vert. gutter (18) —
Vert. pair with horiz. gutter (14) —
V211PP 9 items (18) —
Cross gutter block (6) —
Horiz. pair with vert. gutter (18) —
Vert. pair with horiz. gutter (14) —
688PI (12 pairs) —
Cross gutter block (18) —
Horiz. pair with vert. gutter (36) —
Vert. pair with horiz. gutter (45) —
689PI (12 pairs) —
Cross gutter block (18) —
Horiz. pair with vert. gutter (36) —
Vert. pair with horiz. gutter (45) —
G294PI (12 pairs) —
Cross gutter block (18) —
Horiz. pair with vert. gutter (36) —
Vert. pair with horiz. gutter (45) —
G295PI (12 pairs) —
Cross gutter block (18) —
Horiz. pair with vert. gutter (36) —
Vert. pair with horiz. gutter (45) —
V210PI (12 pairs) —
Cross gutter block (18) —
Horiz. pair with vert. gutter (36) —
Vert. pair with horiz. gutter (45) —
V211PI (12 pairs) —
Cross gutter block (18) —
Horiz. pair with vert. gutter (36) —
Vert. pair with horiz. gutter (45) —

Two of the No. G295PDa items are on photographic paper. Four cards with imperforate panes of 32c Hansel & Gretel essays exist. Four cards with imperforate panes of 5.50s Yeh-Shen essays exist. Four essays of No. SC50 showing these two essay items exist.

New York #690-697
Flags

1997

690-697PP Set of 20 sheets (1) —
690-697PI Set of 2 sheets (3) —

On Nos. 690-697PP, there are ten progressive proof sheets per issued sheet.

New York #698-699, Geneva #296-297, Vienna #212-213
Definitives

1997

698PDa Card, #698PD, #G296PD-G297PD, #V212PD-V213PD (1) —
699PDa Card, #698PD-699PD, #G296PD-G297PD, #V212PD-V213PD (4) —
698PP 8 items (84) —
Cross gutter block (3) —
Horiz. pair with vert. gutter (18) —
Vert. pair with horiz. gutter (14) —
699PP 8 items (84) —
Cross gutter block (3) —
Horiz. pair with vert. gutter (14) —
Vert. pair with horiz. gutter (18) —
G296PP 8 items (84) —
Cross gutter block (3) —
Horiz. pair with vert. gutter (14) —
Vert. pair with horiz. gutter (18) —
G297PP 8 items (84) —
Cross gutter block (3) —
Horiz. pair with vert. gutter (14) —
Vert. pair with horiz. gutter (18) —
V212PP 10 items (84) —
Cross gutter block (3) —
Horiz. pair with vert. gutter (18) —
Vert. pair with horiz. gutter (14) —
V213PP 10 items (84) —
Cross gutter block (3) —
Horiz. pair with vert. gutter (18) —
Vert. pair with horiz. gutter (14) —
698PI (60 pairs) —
Cross gutter block (3) —
Horiz. pair with vert. gutter (18) —
Vert. pair with horiz. gutter (14) —
699PI (60 pairs) —
Cross gutter block (3) —
Horiz. pair with vert. gutter (14) —
Vert. pair with horiz. gutter (18) —
G296PI (60 pairs) —
Cross gutter block (3) —
Horiz. pair with vert. gutter (14) —
Vert. pair with horiz. gutter (18) —
G297PI (60 pairs) —
Cross gutter block (3) —
Horiz. pair with vert. gutter (14) —
Vert. pair with horiz. gutter (18) —
V212PI (60 pairs) —
Cross gutter block (3) —
Horiz. pair with vert. gutter (18) —
Vert. pair with horiz. gutter (14) —
V213PI (60 pairs) —
Cross gutter block (3) —
Horiz. pair with vert. gutter (18) —
Vert. pair with horiz. gutter (14) —

New York #703a, Geneva #301a, Vienna #217a
Endangered Species

1997

703aPDa Card, imperforate pane of 4 blocks #703aPD, imperforate pane of 4 blocks #G301aPD (4) —
V217aPDa Card, imperforate pane of 4 blocks #V217aPD (4) —
703aPP 6 items (4 blocks) —
Cross gutter block (2) —
Horiz. pair with vert. gutter (2) —
Vert. pair with horiz. gutter (4) —
G301aPP 6 items (4 blocks) —
Cross gutter block (2) —
Horiz. pair with vert. gutter (2) —
Vert. pair with horiz. gutter (4) —
V217aPP 6 items (4 blocks) —
Cross gutter block (2) —
Horiz. pair with vert. gutter (2) —
Vert. pair with horiz. gutter (4) —
703aPI (12 blocks) —
Cross gutter block (6) —
Horiz. pair with vert. gutter (6) —
Vert. pair with horiz. gutter (12) —
G301aPI (12 blocks) —
Cross gutter block (6) —
Horiz. pair with vert. gutter (6) —
Vert. pair with horiz. gutter (12) —
V217aPI (12 blocks) —
Cross gutter block (6) —
Horiz. pair with vert. gutter (6) —
Vert. pair with horiz. gutter (12) —

New York #707a, 708, Geneva #305a, 306, Vienna #221a, 222
Earth Summit

1997

707aPP 6 items (6 blocks) —
708PP 6 items (1 souvenir sheet) —
708aPP 6 items (1 souvenir sheet) —
G305aPP 6 items (6 blocks) —
V221aPP 6 items (6 blocks) —
707aPI (15 blocks) —
708PI (6 souvenir sheets) —
708aPI (6 souvenir sheets) —
G305aPI (15 blocks) —
G306PI (6 souvenir sheets) —
V221aPI (15 blocks) —
V222PI (6 souvenir sheets) —

New York #713a, Geneva #311a, Vienna #227a
Transportation

1997

713aPDa Imperforate pane, #713aPD (9) —
G311aPDa Imperforate pane, #G311aPD (9) —
V227aPDa Imperforate pane, #V227aPD (9) —
713aPP 9 items (6 strips) —
Cross gutter block of strips (1) —
Horiz. pair of strips with vert. gutter (6) —
Vert. pair of strips with horiz. gutter (1) —
G311aPP 10 items (6 strips) —
Cross gutter block of strips (1) —
Horiz. pair of strips with vert. gutter (6) —
Vert. pair of strips with horiz. gutter (1) —
V227aPP 9 items (6 strips) —
Cross gutter block of strips (1) —
Horiz. pair of strips with vert. gutter (6) —
Vert. pair of strips with horiz. gutter (1) —
713aPI (14 strips) —
Cross gutter block of strips (1) —
Horiz. pair of strips with vert. gutter (6) —
Vert. pair of strips with horiz. gutter (1) —

G311aPI	(14 strips)	—
	Cross gutter block of strips (1)	—
	Horiz. pair of strips with vert. gutter (6)	—
	Vert. pair of strips with horiz. gutter (1)	—
V227aPI	(14 strips)	—
	Cross gutter block of strips (1)	—
	Horiz. pair of strips with vert. gutter (6)	—
	Vert. pair of strips with horiz. gutter (1)	—

New York #714-715, Geneva #312-313, Vienna #228-229, Souvenir Card #51
Philately

1997

715TCa	Card, #714TC-715TC, #G312TC-G313TC, #V228TC-V229TC, all with white denominations (4)	—
715TCb	Card, #714TC-715TC, #G312TC-G313TC, #V228TC-V229TC, all with light blue green backgrounds (1)	—
SC51PD	(4)	—
714PP	11 items (33)	—
	Horiz. pair with vert. gutter (6)	—
715PP	11 items (33)	—
	Horiz. pair with vert. gutter (6)	—
715PPa	Cross gutter block, 2 each #714PP-715PP (2)	—
715PPb	Vert. pair with horiz. gutter, #714PP-715PP (11)	—
G312PP	11 items (33)	—
	Horiz. pair with vert. gutter (6)	—
G313PP	11 items (33)	—
	Horiz. pair with vert. gutter (6)	—
G313PPa	Cross gutter block, 2 each #G312PP-G313PP (2)	—
G313PPb	Vert. pair with horiz. gutter, #G312PP-G313PP (11)	—
V228PP	10 items (33)	—
	Horiz. pair with vert. gutter (6)	—
V229PP	10 items (33)	—
	Horiz. pair with vert. gutter (6)	—
V229PPa	Cross gutter block, 2 each #V228PP-V229PP (2)	—
V229PPb	Vert. pair with horiz. gutter, #V228PP-V229PP (11)	—
714PI	(48 pairs)	—
	Horiz. pair with vert. gutter (18)	—
715PI	(48 pairs)	—
	Horiz. pair with vert. gutter (18)	—
715PIa	Cross gutter block, 2 each #714PI-715PI (6)	—
715PIb	Vert. pair with horiz. gutter, #714PI-715PI (33)	—
G312PI	(48 pairs)	—
	Horiz. pair with vert. gutter (18)	—
G313PI	(48 pairs)	—
	Horiz. pair with vert. gutter (18)	—
G313PIa	Cross gutter block, 2 each #G312PI-G313PI (6)	—
G313PIb	Vert. pair with horiz. gutter, #G312PI-G313PI (33)	—
V228PI	(48 pairs)	—
	Horiz. pair with vert. gutter (18)	—
V229PI	(48 pairs)	—
	Horiz. pair with vert. gutter (18)	—
V229PIa	Cross gutter block, 2 each #V228PI-V229PI (6)	—
V229PIb	Vert. pair with horiz. gutter, #V228PI-V229PI (33)	—

On Nos. 714PP-715PP, G312PP-G313PP and V228PP-V229PP some progressive proof items are blank due to color arrangements on sheets.

New York #716-717, Geneva #314-315, Vienna #230-231
World Heritage

1997

717PDa	Stapled set of 6 layout sheets with #716PD-717PD, #G314PD-G315PD, #V230PD-V231PD affixed (3)	—
716PP	10 items (20)	—
717PP	10 items (20)	—
G314PP	10 items (20)	—
G315PP	10 items (20)	—
V230PP	10 items (20)	—
V231PP	10 items (20)	—
716PI	(30 pairs)	—
717PI	(30 pairs)	—
G314PI	(30 pairs)	—
G315PI	(30 pairs)	—
V230PI	(30 pairs)	—
V231PI	(30 pairs)	—

New York #719-726
Flags

1998

719-726PP	Set of 20 sheets (1)	—
719-726PI	Set of 2 sheets (3)	—

On Nos. 719-726PP, there are ten progressive proof sheets per issued sheet.

New York #727-729, Geneva #317, Vienna #233-234
Definitives

1998

727PDa	Card, #727PD, #G317TC black (1)	—
729PDa	Card, #727PD-729PD, #G317PD, #V233PD-V234PD (4)	—
727PP	10 items (84)	—
	Cross gutter block (3)	—
	Horiz. pair with vert. gutter (14)	—
	Vert. pair with horiz. gutter (18)	—
728PP	8 items (84)	—
	Cross gutter block (3)	—
	Horiz. pair with vert. gutter (14)	—
	Vert. pair with horiz. gutter (18)	—
729PP	9 items (84)	—
	Cross gutter block (3)	—
	Horiz. pair with vert. gutter (18)	—
	Vert. pair with horiz. gutter (14)	—
G317PP	10 items (84)	—
	Cross gutter block (3)	—
	Horiz. pair with vert. gutter (14)	—
	Vert. pair with horiz. gutter (18)	—
V233PP	8 items (84)	—
	Cross gutter block (3)	—
	Horiz. pair with vert. gutter (18)	—
	Vert. pair with horiz. gutter (14)	—
V234PP	10 items (84)	—
	Cross gutter block (3)	—
	Horiz. pair with vert. gutter (18)	—
	Vert. pair with horiz. gutter (14)	—
727PI	(60 pairs)	—
	Cross gutter block (3)	—
	Horiz. pair with vert. gutter (14)	—
	Vert. pair with horiz. gutter (18)	—
728PI	(60 pairs)	—
	Cross gutter block (3)	—
	Horiz. pair with vert. gutter (14)	—
	Vert. pair with horiz. gutter (18)	—
729PI	(60 pairs)	—
	Cross gutter block (3)	—
	Horiz. pair with vert. gutter (18)	—
	Vert. pair with horiz. gutter (14)	—
G317PI	(60 pairs)	—
	Cross gutter block (3)	—
	Horiz. pair with vert. gutter (14)	—
	Vert. pair with horiz. gutter (18)	—
V233PI	(60 pairs)	—
	Cross gutter block (3)	—
	Horiz. pair with vert. gutter (18)	—
	Vert. pair with horiz. gutter (14)	—
V234PI	(60 pairs)	—
	Cross gutter block (3)	—
	Horiz. pair with vert. gutter (18)	—
	Vert. pair with horiz. gutter (14)	—

New York #733a, Geneva #321a, Vienna #238a
Endangered Species

1998

733PDa	Card, imperforate pane of 4 blocks, #733aPD (1)	—
733PDb	Card, broken imperforate pane of 4 blocks, #733aPD (1)	—
G321PDa	Card, imperforate pane of 4 blocks, #G321aPD (1)	—
G321PDb	Card, broken imperforate pane of 4 blocks, #G321aPD (1)	—
V238PDa	Card, imperforate pane of 4 blocks, #V238aPD (1)	—
V238PDb	Card, broken imperforate pane of 4 blocks, #V238aPD (1)	—
733aPP	6 items (4 blocks)	—
	Cross gutter block (2)	—
	Horiz. pair with vert. gutter (2)	—
	Vert. pair with horiz. gutter (4)	—
G321aPP	4 items (4 blocks)	—
	Cross gutter block (2)	—
	Horiz. pair with vert. gutter (2)	—
	Vert. pair with horiz. gutter (4)	—
V238aPP	6 items (4 blocks)	—
	Cross gutter block (2)	—
	Horiz. pair with vert. gutter (2)	—
	Vert. pair with horiz. gutter (4)	—
733aPI	(12 blocks)	—
	Cross gutter block (2)	—
	Horiz. pair with vert. gutter (2)	—
	Vert. pair with horiz. gutter (4)	—
G321aPI	(12 blocks)	—
	Cross gutter block (2)	—
	Horiz. pair with vert. gutter (2)	—
	Vert. pair with horiz. gutter (4)	—
V238aPI	(12 blocks)	—
	Cross gutter block (2)	—
	Horiz. pair with vert. gutter (2)	—
	Vert. pair with horiz. gutter (4)	—

No. G321aPP is not a complete set, as there are no black only and cyan only items.

New York #734, Geneva #322, Vienna #239
International Year of the Ocean

1998

734PD	(not approved) (4)	—
G322PD	(4)	—
V239PD	(4)	—
734PP	6 items (6 panes)	—
G322PP	6 items (6 panes)	—
V239PP	6 items (6 panes)	—
734PI	(18 panes)	—
G322PI	(18 panes)	—
V239PI	(18 panes)	—

New York #735-736, Geneva #323-324, Vienna #240-241
Rain Forests

1998

735PDa	Card, imperforate pane of 20 #735PD (8)	—
736PDa	Card, #736PD, #G324PD, #V241PD (8)	—
G323PDa	Card, imperforate pane of 20 #G323PD (8)	—
V240PDa	Card, imperforate pane of 20 #V240PD (8)	—
735PP	6 items (see note)	—
G323PP	6 items (see note)	—
V240PP	6 items (see note)	—
735PI	(see note)	—
G323PI	(see note)	—
V240PI	(see note)	—

There are two types of Nos. 735PP and V240PP, one with cats lacking spots on the red item, the other with the cat with spots on the magenta item. There are 20 of each type.

There are two types of No. G323PP, one with orangutan with small dots in eyes on the cyan item, the other with large dots in eyes.

Similarly, there are two types of Nos. 735PI, G323PI and V240PI, one with a lighter background, the other with a bolder background. There are 20 pairs of each type.

New York #737-738, Geneva #325-326, Vienna #242-243, Souvenir Card #52
UN Peacekeeping Forces, 50th Anniv.

1998

737TC	Dark blue panel (on Cromalin paper) (5)	—
738TC	Dark blue panel (on Cromalin paper) (5)	—
G325TC	Dark blue panel (on Cromalin paper) (5)	—
G326TC	Dark blue panel (on Cromalin paper) (5)	—
V242TC	Dark blue panel (on Cromalin paper) (5)	—
V243TC	Dark blue panel (on Cromalin paper) (5)	—
SC52PD	(4)	—
737PP	10 items (20)	—
738PP	10 items (20)	—
G325PP	10 items (20)	—
G326PP	10 items (20)	—
V242PP	10 items (20)	—
V243PP	10 items (20)	—
737PI	(20 pairs)	—
738PI	(20 pairs)	—
G325PI	(20 pairs)	—
G326PI	(20 pairs)	—
V242PI	(20 pairs)	—
V243PI	(20 pairs)	—

New York #739-740, Geneva #327-328, Vienna #244-245, Souvenir Card #53
Universal Declaration of Human Rights, 50th Anniv.

1998

740PDa	Card, #739PD-740PD, #G327PD-G328PD, #V244PD-V245PD (4)	—
SC53PD	(4)	—
739PP	8 items (64)	—
	Cross gutter block (2)	—
	Horiz. pair with vert. gutter (8)	—
	Vert. pair with horiz. gutter (16)	—
740PP	8 items (64)	—
	Cross gutter block (2)	—
	Horiz. pair with vert. gutter (8)	—
	Vert. pair with horiz. gutter (16)	—
G327PP	8 items (64)	—
	Cross gutter block (2)	—
	Horiz. pair with vert. gutter (8)	—
	Vert. pair with horiz. gutter (16)	—
G328PP	8 items (64)	—
	Cross gutter block (2)	—
	Horiz. pair with vert. gutter (8)	—
	Vert. pair with horiz. gutter (16)	—
V244PP	8 items (64)	—
	Cross gutter block (2)	—
	Horiz. pair with vert. gutter (8)	—
	Vert. pair with horiz. gutter (16)	—
V245PP	8 items (64)	—
	Cross gutter block (2)	—
	Horiz. pair with vert. gutter (8)	—
	Vert. pair with horiz. gutter (16)	—
739PI	(52 pairs)	—
	Cross gutter block (2)	—
	Horiz. pair with vert. gutter (8)	—
	Vert. pair with horiz. gutter (16)	—
740PI	(52 pairs)	—
	Cross gutter block (2)	—
	Horiz. pair with vert. gutter (8)	—
	Vert. pair with horiz. gutter (16)	—
G327PI	(52 pairs)	—
	Cross gutter block (2)	—
	Horiz. pair with vert. gutter (8)	—
	Vert. pair with horiz. gutter (16)	—
G328PI	(52 pairs)	—
	Cross gutter block (2)	—
	Horiz. pair with vert. gutter (8)	—
	Vert. pair with horiz. gutter (16)	—
V244PI	(52 pairs)	—
	Cross gutter block (2)	—
	Horiz. pair with vert. gutter (8)	—
	Vert. pair with horiz. gutter (16)	—
V245PI	(52 pairs)	—

Cross gutter block (2) —
Horiz. pair with vert. gutter (8) —
Vert. pair with horiz. gutter (16) —

New York #741-743, Geneva #329-331, Vienna #246-248
Schönbrunn Palace

1998

742PDa Card, blocks of 4, #741PD-742PD (3) —
742PDb Card, cut apart blocks of 4, #741PD-742PD (1) —
G330PDa Card, blocks of 4, #G329PD-G330PD (3) —
G330PDb Card, cut apart blocks of 4, #G329PD-G330PD (1) —
V247PDa Card, blocks of 4, #V246PD-V247PD (3) —
V247PDb Card, cut apart blocks of 4, #V246PD-V247PD (1) —
742TCa Card, block of 4 #742TC dark blue denomination (on photographic paper) (1) —
743TCa Card, strips of 3, #743aTC-743cTC bright red violet denomination (on photographic paper) (1) —
743TCb Card, blocks of 4, #743dTC-743fTC bright red violet denomination (on photographic paper) (1) —
743TCc Entire booklet (black & white, on photographic paper) (1) —
G330TCa Card, blocks of 4, #G329TC-G330TC bright red violet denominations (on photographic paper) (1) —
G331TCa Card, blocks of 4, #G331aTC-G331cTC bright red violet denomination (on photographic paper) (1) —
G331TCb Card, strips of 3, #G331dTC-G331fTC bright red violet denomination (on photographic paper) (1) —
G331TCc Entire booklet (black & white, on photographic paper) (1) —
V247TCa Card, block of 4 #V247TC bright green denomination (on photographic paper) (1) —
V248TCa Card, strips of 3, #V248aTC-V248cTC bright red violet denomination (on photographic paper) (1) —
V248TCb Card, blocks of 4, #V248dTC-V248fTC bright red violet denomination (on photographic paper) (1) —
V248TCc Entire booklet (black & white, on photographic paper) (1) —
741PP 10 items (24) —
Vert. pair with horiz. gutter (3) —
742PP 10 items (24) —
Horiz. pair with vert. gutter (3) —
742PPa Cross gutter block, 2 #741PP-742PP (1) —
742PPb Vert. pair with horiz. gutter, #741PP-742PP (8) —
G329PP 10 items (24) —
Vert. pair with horiz. gutter (3) —
G330PP 10 items (24) —
Horiz. pair with vert. gutter (3) —
G330PPa Cross gutter block, 2 #G329PP-G330PP (1) —
G330PPb Vert. pair with horiz. gutter, #G329PP-G330PP (8) —
V246PP 10 items (24) —
Vert. pair with horiz. gutter (3) —
V247PP 10 items (24) —
Horiz. pair with vert. gutter (3) —
V247PPa Cross gutter block, 2 #V246PP-V247PP (1) —
V247PPb Vert. pair with horiz. gutter, #V246PP-V247PP (8) —
741PI (32 pairs) —
Vert. pair with horiz. gutter (3) —
742PI (32 pairs) —
Horiz. pair with vert. gutter (3) —
742PIa Cross gutter block, 2 #741PI-742PI (1) —
742PIb Vert. pair with horiz. gutter, #741PI-742PI (8) —
G329PI (32 pairs) —
Vert. pair with horiz. gutter (3) —
G330PI (32 pairs) —
Horiz. pair with vert. gutter (3) —
G330PIa Cross gutter block, 2 #G329PI-G330PI (1) —
G330PIb Vert. pair with horiz. gutter, #G329PI-G330PI (8) —
V246PI (32 pairs) —
Vert. pair with horiz. gutter (3) —
V247PI (32 pairs) —
Horiz. pair with vert. gutter (3) —
V247PIa Cross gutter block, 2 #V246PI-V247PI (1) —
V247PIb Vert. pair with horiz. gutter, #V246PI-V247PI (8) —

Five cards with blocks of four essays with gold frames over vignette exist for each of the New York, Geneva and Vienna pairings.

New York #744-751
Flags

1999

744-751PP Set of 20 sheets (1) —
744-751PI Set of 2 sheets (4) —

On Nos. 744-751PP, there are ten progressive proof sheets per issued sheet.

New York #752-753, Geneva #332, Vienna #249
Definitives

1999

752PDa Card, #752PD, #V249PD (3) —
752PDb Card, #752PD, #V249PD, #753TC lacking gray in pink frame boxes (1) —
753PDa Card, block of 4, #753PD (2) —
753TC Lacking gray in pink frame boxes (3) —
G332TC red (4) —
G332TC brown (4) —
752PP 9 items (48) —
Cross gutter block (1) —
Horiz. pair with vert. gutter (6) —
Vert. pair with horiz. gutter (8) —
753PP 10 items (20) —
V249PP 9 items (48) —
Cross gutter block (1) —
Horiz. pair with vert. gutter (6) —
Vert. pair with horiz. gutter (8) —
752PI (24 pairs) —
Cross gutter block (3) —
Horiz. pair with vert. gutter (18) —
Vert. pair with horiz. gutter (24) —
753PI (20 pairs) —
G332PI (20 pairs) —
V249PI (72 pairs) —
Cross gutter block (3) —
Horiz. pair with vert. gutter (18) —
Vert. pair with horiz. gutter (24) —

New York #754-756, Geneva #333-335, Vienna #250-252
World Heritage

1999

755PDa Card, pairs of #754PD-755PD, #G333PD-G334PD, #V250PD-V251PD (1) —
756PDa Card, pairs of #756aPD-756fPD (1) —
756PDb Sheet, pairs of #754PD-755PD, #756aPD-756fPD, #G333PD-G334PD, #G335aPD-G335fPD, #V250PD-V251PD, #V252aPD-V252fPD (2) —
756PDc Cut-up section of #756PDb with pairs of stamps issued in sheets (2) —
756PDd Cut-up section of #756PDb with pairs of stamps issued in booklets (2) —
754TC Black and white image on layout sheet of photographic paper (2) —
755TC Black and white image on layout sheet of photographic paper (2) —
G333TC Black and white image on layout sheet of photographic paper (2) —
G334TC Black and white image on layout sheet of photographic paper (2) —
V250TCa Black and white image on layout sheet of photographic paper (2) —
V250TCb 2 pairs of black and white images on layout sheet of photographic paper, affixed to card (1) —
V251TCa Black and white image on layout sheet of photographic paper (2) —
V251TCb 2 pairs of black and white images on layout sheet of photographic paper, affixed to card (1) —
754PP 6 items (32) —
Horiz. pair with vert. gutter (8) —
755PP 6 items (32) —
Horiz. pair with vert. gutter (8) —
755PPa Cross gutter block, 2 #754PP-755PP (2) —
755PPb Vert. pair with horiz. gutter, #754PP-755PP (8) —
G333PP 6 items (32) —
Horiz. pair with vert. gutter (8) —
G334PP 6 items (32) —
Horiz. pair with vert. gutter (8) —
G334PPa Cross gutter block, 2 #G333PP-G334PP (2) —
G334PPb Vert. pair with horiz. gutter, #G333PP-G334PP (8) —
V250PP 6 items (32) —
Horiz. pair with vert. gutter (8) —
V251PP 6 items (32) —
Horiz. pair with vert. gutter (8) —
V251PPa Cross gutter block, 2 #V250PP-V251PP (2) —
V251PPb Vert. pair with horiz. gutter, #V250PP-V251PP (8) —
754PI (52 pairs) —
Horiz. pair with vert. gutter (16) —
755PI (52 pairs) —
Horiz. pair with vert. gutter (16) —
755PIa Cross gutter block, 2 #754PI-755PI (4) —
755PIb Vert. pair with horiz. gutter, #754PI-755PI (16) —
G333PI (36 pairs) —
Horiz. pair with vert. gutter (8) —
G334PI (36 pairs) —
Horiz. pair with vert. gutter (8) —
G334PIa Cross gutter block, 2 #G333PI-G334PI (2) —
G334PIb Vert. pair with horiz. gutter, #G333PI-G334PI (8) —
V250PI (36 pairs) —
Horiz. pair with vert. gutter (8) —
V251PI (36 pairs) —
Horiz. pair with vert. gutter (8) —
V251PIa Cross gutter block, 2 #V250PI-V251PI (2) —
V251PIb Vert. pair with horiz. gutter, #V250PI-V251PI (8) —

New York #760a, Geneva #339a, Vienna #256a
Endangered Species

1999

760aPDa Card, imperf pane of 4 blocks, #760aPD (2) —
760aPDb Card, 2 each #757PD-760PD (1) —
G339aPDa Card, 2 each #G336PD-G339PD (on Cromalin paper), broken pane of 80c essays of #G336-G339 (1) —
V256aPDa Card, imperf pane of 4 blocks, #V256aPD (3) —
V256aPDb Card, 2 each #V253PD-V256PD (1) —
760aPP 6 items (4 blocks) —
Cross gutter block (2) —
Horiz. pair with vert. gutter (2) —
Vert. pair with horiz. gutter (4) —
G339aPP 6 items (4 blocks) —
Cross gutter block (2) —
Horiz. pair with vert. gutter (2) —
Vert. pair with horiz. gutter (4) —
V256aPP 6 items (4 blocks) —
Cross gutter block (2) —
Horiz. pair with vert. gutter (2) —
Vert. pair with horiz. gutter (4) —
760aPI (12 blocks) —
Cross gutter block (2) —
Horiz. pair with vert. gutter (2) —
Vert. pair with horiz. gutter (4) —
G339aPI (12 blocks) —
Cross gutter block (2) —
Horiz. pair with vert. gutter (2) —
Vert. pair with horiz. gutter (4) —
V256aPI (12 blocks) —
Cross gutter block (2) —
Horiz. pair with vert. gutter (2) —
Vert. pair with horiz. gutter (4) —

Three cards exist containing imperforate panes of four blocks of the 80c essays.

New York #762a, 763, Geneva #341a, 342, Vienna #258a, 259
UNISPACE III

1999

762aPDa Card, imperforate pane of 5 pairs, #762aPD (3) —
763PD With printed perforations on overlay (3) —
763aPD With printed perforations on overlay (2) —
G341aPDa Card, imperforate pane of 5 pairs, #G341aPD (4) —
G342PD With printed perforations on overlay (2) —
G342aPD With printed perforations on overlay (2) —
V258aPDa Card, imperforate pane of 5 pairs, #V258aPD (4) —
V259PD With printed perforations on overlay (2) —
762PP 8 items (5 pairs) —
762aPP 8 items (1 souvenir sheet) —
763PP 9 items (1 pair) —
763aPP 10 items (1 souvenir sheet) —
762aPI (10 pairs) —
763PI (3 souvenir sheets) —
763aPI (4 souvenir sheets) —
G341aPI (10 pairs) —
G342PI (3 souvenir sheets) —
V258aPI (10 pairs) —
V259PI (3 souvenir sheets) —

New York #767a, Geneva #346a, Vienna #263a, Souvenir Card #54
Universal Postal Union, 125th Anniv.

1999

767aPDa Card, #767aPD, #G346aPD, #V263aPD with approval handstamp (4) —
767aTCa Card, #767aTC, #G346aTCD, #V263aTC (dark blue denominations, not approved) (4) —
SC54PD (4) —
767aPP 8 items (6 blocks) —
G346aPP 8 items (6 blocks) —
V263aPP 8 items (6 blocks) —
767aPI (12 blocks) —
G346aPI (12 blocks) —
V263aPI (12 blocks) —

New York #768-769, Geneva #347-348, Vienna #264-265
In Memoriam

1999

769PDa Card, #768PD-769PD (4) —
G348PDa Card, #G347PD-G348PD (4) —
V265PDa Card, #V264PD-V265PD (4) —
768PP 10 items (66) —
Cross gutter block (2) —
Horiz. pair with vert. gutter (12) —
Vert. pair with horiz. gutter (11) —
769PP 10 items (24 souvenir sheets) —
G347PP 10 items (66) —
Cross gutter block (2) —
Horiz. pair with vert. gutter (12) —
Vert. pair with horiz. gutter (11) —
G348PP 10 items (24 souvenir sheets) —
V264PP 10 items (66) —
Cross gutter block (2) —
Horiz. pair with vert. gutter (12) —
Vert. pair with horiz. gutter (11) —
V265PP 10 items (24 souvenir sheets) —

768PI (52 pairs) —
Cross gutter block (2) —
Horiz. pair with vert. gutter (12) —
Vert. pair with horiz. gutter (11) —
769PI (24 souvenir sheets) —
G347PI (52 pairs) —
Cross gutter block (2) —
Horiz. pair with vert. gutter (12) —
Vert. pair with horiz. gutter (11) —
G348PI (24 souvenir sheets) —
V264PI (52 pairs) —
Cross gutter block (2) —
Horiz. pair with vert. gutter (12) —
Vert. pair with horiz. gutter (11) —
V265PI (24 souvenir sheets) —

New York #770-771, Geneva #349-350, Vienna #266-267
Education

1999

771PDa Card, #770PD-771PD, #G349PD-G350PD, #V266PD-V267PD with approval handstamp (4) —
771PDb Card, #770PD, #G350PD, #V266PD-V267PD, #771TC red denomination, #G349TC red violet denomination with "approved with corrections" handstamp (4) —
770PP 9 items (20) —
771PP 8 items (20) —
G349PP 7 items (20) —
G350PP 7 items (20) —
V266PP 7 items (20) —
V267PP 8 items (20) —
770PI (20 pairs) —
771PI (20 pairs) —
G349PI (30 pairs) —
G350PI (30 pairs) —
V266PI (30 pairs) —
V267PI (30 pairs) —

New York #772, Geneva #351, Vienna #268
International Year of Thanksgiving

2000

772PDa Card, #772PD, #G351PD, #V268PD (4) —
772TCa Card, #772TC, #G351TC, #V268TC, all with black background (4) —
772PP 12 items (32) —
Horiz. pair with vert. gutter (4) —
G351PP 12 items (32) —
Horiz. pair with vert. gutter (4) —
V268PP 12 items (32) —
Horiz. pair with vert. gutter (4) —
772PI (36 pairs) —
Horiz. pair with vert. gutter (4) —
G351PI (36 pairs) —
Horiz. pair with vert. gutter (4) —
V268PI (36 pairs) —
Horiz. pair with vert. gutter (4) —

New York #776a, Geneva #355a, Vienna #272a
Endangered Species

2000

776aPDa Card, imperforate pane of 4 blocks, #776aPD (3) —
776aPDb Card, 3 each #773PD-776PD (1) —
G355aPDa Card, imperforate pane of 4 blocks, #G355aPD, imperforate pane of 4 blocks, #V272aPD (3) —
G355aPDb Card, 3 each #G352PD-G355PD, #V269PD-V272PD (1) —
776aPP 6 items (4 blocks) —
Cross gutter block (2) —
Horiz. pair with vert. gutter (2) —
Vert. pair with horiz. gutter (4) —
G355aPP 6 items (4 blocks) —
Cross gutter block (2) —
Horiz. pair with vert. gutter (2) —
Vert. pair with horiz. gutter (4) —
V272aPP 6 items (4 blocks) —
Cross gutter block (2) —
Horiz. pair with vert. gutter (2) —
Vert. pair with horiz. gutter (4) —
776aPI (12 blocks) —
Cross gutter block (2) —
Horiz. pair with vert. gutter (2) —
Vert. pair with horiz. gutter (4) —
G355aPI (12 blocks) —
Cross gutter block (2) —
Horiz. pair with vert. gutter (2) —
Vert. pair with horiz. gutter (4) —
V272aPI (12 blocks) —
Cross gutter block (2) —
Horiz. pair with vert. gutter (2) —
Vert. pair with horiz. gutter (4) —

New York #777-778, Geneva #356-357, Vienna #273-274
Our World 2000

2000

778PDa Card, #777PD-778PD, #G356PD-G357PD, #V273PD-V274PD (4) —
778PDb Card, #777PD-778PD, #G356PD-G357PD, #V274PD, #V273TC black denomination, with "not approved" handstamp (2) —
777PP 8 items (64) —
Cross gutter block (2) —
Horiz. pair with vert. gutter (16) —
Vert. pair with horiz. gutter (8) —
778PP 8 items (64) —
Cross gutter block (2) —
Horiz. pair with vert. gutter (8) —
Vert. pair with horiz. gutter (16) —
G356PP 8 items (64) —
Cross gutter block (2) —
Horiz. pair with vert. gutter (8) —
Vert. pair with horiz. gutter (16) —
G357PP 8 items (64) —
Cross gutter block (2) —
Horiz. pair with vert. gutter (16) —
Vert. pair with horiz. gutter (8) —
V273PP 8 items (64) —
Cross gutter block (2) —
Horiz. pair with vert. gutter (16) —
Vert. pair with horiz. gutter (8) —
V274PP 8 items (64) —
Cross gutter block (2) —
Horiz. pair with vert. gutter (8) —
Vert. pair with horiz. gutter (16) —
777PI (52 pairs) —
Cross gutter block (2) —
Horiz. pair with vert. gutter (16) —
Vert. pair with horiz. gutter (8) —
778PI (52 pairs) —
Cross gutter block (2) —
Horiz. pair with vert. gutter (8) —
Vert. pair with horiz. gutter (16) —
G356PI (52 pairs) —
Cross gutter block (2) —
Horiz. pair with vert. gutter (16) —
Vert. pair with horiz. gutter (8) —
G357PI (52 pairs) —
Cross gutter block (2) —
Horiz. pair with vert. gutter (8) —
Vert. pair with horiz. gutter (16) —
V273PI (52 pairs) —
Cross gutter block (2) —
Horiz. pair with vert. gutter (16) —
Vert. pair with horiz. gutter (8) —
V274PI (52 pairs) —
Cross gutter block (2) —
Horiz. pair with vert. gutter (8) —
Vert. pair with horiz. gutter (16) —

New York #779-781, Geneva #358-360, Vienna #275-277
United Nations, 55th Anniv.

2000

780TCa Card, #779TC-780TC, #G358TC-G359TC, #V275TC-V276TC (all with white denominations with colored outlines (4) —
781TCa Card, #781TC, #G360TC, #V277TC (all with white denominations with colored outlines (4) —
781TCb Card, #779TC-781TC ultramarine & silver (2) —
781TCc Card, #779TC-781TC blue & silver (2) —
781TCd Card, #781TC, #G360TC silver backgrounds, white denominations with colored outlines (5) —
G359TCa Card, #G358TC-G359TC brown red & silver (2) —
G360TCa Card, #G358TC-G360TC carmine & silver (2) —
G360TCb Card, #G358TC-G360TC cerise & silver (2) —
V277TCa Card, #V275TC-V277TC green & silver (2) —
V277TCb Card, #V275TC-V277TC dark green & silver (2) —
V277TCc Silver background, white denominations with green outlines (5) —
779PP 7 items (128) —
Cross gutter block (4) —
Horiz. pair with vert. gutter (16) —
Vert. pair with horiz. gutter (32) —
780PP 7 items (128) —
Cross gutter block (4) —
Horiz. pair with vert. gutter (16) —
Vert. pair with horiz. gutter (32) —
781PP 6 items (60 souvenir sheets) —
G358PP 9 items (128) —
Cross gutter block (4) —
Horiz. pair with vert. gutter (16) —
Vert. pair with horiz. gutter (32) —
G359PP 9 items (128) —
Cross gutter block (4) —
Horiz. pair with vert. gutter (16) —
Vert. pair with horiz. gutter (32) —
G360PP 9 items (60 souvenir sheets) —
V275PP 10 items (128) —
Cross gutter block (4) —
Horiz. pair with vert. gutter (16) —
Vert. pair with horiz. gutter (32) —
V276PP 10 items (128) —
Cross gutter block (4) —
Horiz. pair with vert. gutter (16) —
Vert. pair with horiz. gutter (32) —
V277PP 10 items (60 souvenir sheets) —
779PI (84 pairs) —
Cross gutter block (4) —
Horiz. pair with vert. gutter (16) —
Vert. pair with horiz. gutter (32) —
780PI (84 pairs) —
Cross gutter block (4) —
Horiz. pair with vert. gutter (16) —
Vert. pair with horiz. gutter (32) —
781PI (60 souvenir sheets) —
G358PI (84 pairs) —
Cross gutter block (4) —
Horiz. pair with vert. gutter (16) —
Vert. pair with horiz. gutter (32) —
G359PI (84 pairs) —
Cross gutter block (4) —
Horiz. pair with vert. gutter (16) —
Vert. pair with horiz. gutter (32) —
V275PI (84 pairs) —
Cross gutter block (4) —
Horiz. pair with vert. gutter (16) —
Vert. pair with horiz. gutter (32) —
V276PI (84 pairs) —
Cross gutter block (4) —
Horiz. pair with vert. gutter (16) —
Vert. pair with horiz. gutter (32) —
781PI (60 souvenir sheets) —

One item in Nos. G358PP and G359PP is blank, coming from sheet with marginal inscriptions only.

New York #782
International Flag of Peace

2000

782PD With approval handstamp (4) —
782TC Black and white photocopy of layout of pane of 20, with approval handstamp and signature (1) —
782PP 9 items (96) —
Cross gutter block (2) —
Horiz. pair with vert. gutter (16) —
Vert. pair with horiz. gutter (8) —
782PI (96 pairs) —
Cross gutter block (6) —
Horiz. pair with vert. gutter (48) —
Vert. pair with horiz. gutter (24) —

An essay with "age 12" after artist's name exists in five cards and a black and white layout of the pane of 20 on photographic paper.

New York #783, Geneva #361, Vienna #278
UN in the 21st Century

2000

783PDa Card, #783PD, #G361PD, #V278PD with approval handstamp (4) —
783TCa Card, #783TC, #G361TC, #V278TC all with washed-out colors, with "not approved" handstamp (5) —
783PP 8 items (1) —
G361PP 8 items (1) —
V278PP 8 items (1) —
783PI (2 sheets) —
G361PI (2 sheets) —
V278PI (2 sheets) —

New York #784-786, Geneva #362-364, Vienna #279-281
World Heritage

2000

785PDa Card, #784PD-785PD, #G362PD-G364PD, #V279PD-V280PD (4) —
784TC Black and white image of pane of 20 on layout sheet on photographic paper (1) —
785TC Black and white image of pane of 20 on layout sheet on photographic paper (1) —
G362TC Black and white image of pane of 20 on layout sheet on photographic paper (1) —
G363TC Black and white image of pane of 20 on layout sheet on photographic paper (1) —
V279TC Black and white image of pane of 20 on layout sheet on photographic paper (1) —
V280TC Black and white image of pane of 20 on layout sheet on photographic paper (1) —
784PP 9 items (24) —
Vert. pair with horiz. gutter (3) —
785PP 9 items (24) —
Vert. pair with horiz. gutter (3) —
785PPa Cross gutter block, 2 #784PP-785PP (1) —
785PPb Horiz. pair with vert. gutter, #784PP-785PP (8) —
786iPPa 9 items, Strip of #786gPP-786iPP, with vert. gutters between (4) —
G362PP 9 items (24) —
Vert. pair with horiz. gutter (3) —
G363PP 9 items (24) —
Vert. pair with horiz. gutter (3) —
G363PPa Cross gutter block, 2 #G362PP-G363PP (1) —
G363PPb Horiz. pair with vert. gutter, #G362PP-G363PP (8) —
V279PP 7 items (24) —
Vert. pair with horiz. gutter (3) —
V280PP 7 items (24) —
Vert. pair with horiz. gutter (3) —
V280PPa Cross gutter block, 2 #V279PP-V280PP (1) —
V280PPb Horiz. pair with vert. gutter, #V279PP-V280PP (8) —
784PI (32 pairs) —
Vert. pair with horiz. gutter (3) —
785PI (32 pairs) —
Vert. pair with horiz. gutter (3) —
785PIa Cross gutter block, 2 #784PI-785PI (1) —
785PIb Horiz. pair with vert. gutter, #784PI-785PI (8) —
786gPI (5 booklet panes) —
786hPI (5 booklet panes) —
786iPI (5 booklet panes) —
786iPIa Strip of #786gPI-786iPI, with vert. gutters between (4) —
786jPI (5 booklet panes) —
786kPI (5 booklet panes) —
786lPI (5 booklet panes) —
G362PI (32 pairs) —

Vert. pair with horiz. gutter (3) —
G363PI (32 pairs) —
Vert. pair with horiz. gutter (3) —
G363PIa Cross gutter block, 2 #G362PI-G363PI (1) —
G363PIb Horiz. pair with vert. gutter, #G362PI-G363PI (8) —
G364gPI (5 booklet panes) —
G364hPI (5 booklet panes) —
G364iPI (5 booklet panes) —
G364jPI (5 booklet panes) —
G364kPI (5 booklet panes) —
G364lPI (5 booklet panes) —
V279PI (82 pairs) —
Vert. pair with horiz. gutter (3) —
V280PI (32 pairs) —
Vert. pair with horiz. gutter (3) —
V280PIa Cross gutter block, 2 #V279PI-V280PI (1) —
V280PIb Horiz. pair with vert. gutter, #V279PI-V280PI (8) —
V281gPI (5 booklet panes) —
V281hPI (5 booklet panes) —
V281iPI (5 booklet panes) —
V281jPI (5 booklet panes) —
V281kPI (5 booklet panes) —
V281lPI (5 booklet panes) —

Some pairs of No. V279PI are defaced with blue marker.

New York #787-788, Geneva #365-366, Vienna #282-283, Souvenir Card #55
Respect for Refugees

2000

787PDa Card, #787PD, #G365PD, #V282PD (4) —
788PDa Card, #788PD, #G366PD, #V283PD (4) —
SC55PD (4) —
787PP 6 items (32) —
Horiz. pair with vert. gutter (4) —
788PP 6 items (20 souvenir sheets) —
G365PP 6 items (32) —
Cross gutter block (1) —
Horiz. pair with vert. gutter (6) —
Vert. pair with horiz. gutter (8) —
G366PP 6 items (20 souvenir sheets) —
V282PP 6 items (32) —
Horiz. pair with vert. gutter (4) —
V283PP 6 items (20 souvenir sheets) —
787PI (36 pairs) —
Horiz. pair with vert. gutter (4) —
788PI (20 souvenir sheets) —
G365PI (44 pairs) —
Cross gutter block (1) —
Horiz. pair with vert. gutter (6) —
Vert. pair with horiz. gutter (8) —
G366PI (20 souvenir sheets) —
V282PI (36 pairs) —
Horiz. pair with vert. gutter (4) —
V283PI (20 souvenir sheets) —

AIR POST STAMPS

New York #C1-C4
Plane and Gull, Swallows and UN Emblem

1951

C1PD (1) —
C2PD (1) —
C3PD (1) —
C4PD (1) —
C1PI (25 pairs) —
C2PI (25 pairs) —
C3PI (25 pairs) —
C4PI (25 pairs) —

New York #C5
Airplane Wing and Globe

1957

C5PD (4) —
C5TC brown (not approved) (5) —
C5TC indigo (5) —
C5PI (40 pairs) —
Vert. pair with horiz. gutter (10) —

New York #C6-C7
Airplane Wing and Globe; UN Flag and Plane

1959

C6PD (1) —
C6PDa Card, #C6PD, 2 #C6TC in slightly different shades (2) —
C6PDb Card, 2 #C6PD, 2 #C7TC Prussian blue (1) —
C7PD (1) —
C7PDa Card, #C7PD, #C7TC Prussian blue, #C7TC dark blue (2) —
C6TC black (1) —
C7TC black (1) —
C6PI (115 pairs) —
Vert. pair with horiz. gutter (10) —
C7PI (90 pairs) —
Horiz. pair with vert. gutter (10) —

New York #C8-C10
Definitives

1963

C10PDa Card, #C8PD-C10PD (3) —
C10PDb Card, #C8PD, #C10PD, 3 #C9PD (3) —
C8PP 3 items (80) —
Horiz. pair with vert. gutter (10) —
C9PP 4 items (80) —
Vert. pair with horiz. gutter (10) —
C10PP 4 items (80) —
Horiz. pair with vert. gutter (10) —
C8PI (80 pairs) —
Horiz. pair with vert. gutter (20) —
C9PI (80 pairs) —
Vert. pair with horiz. gutter (20) —
C10PI (80 pairs) —
Horiz. pair with vert. gutter (20) —

New York #C11-C12
Definitives

1964

C11PDa Card, #C11PD, #C12TC peach and brown background (disapproved) (2) —
C12PD (2) —
C12PDa Card, #C11PD-C12PD (4) —
C11PI (25 pairs) —
C12PI (25 pairs) —

New York #C13
Jet and UN Emblem

1968

C13PD (3) —
C13PDa Card, #C13PD, 2 #C13TC with slightly different shades (2) —
C13PP 9 items, perforated, mounted on card (1) —

New York #C14
Wings, Envelopes and UN Emblem

1969

C14PD (4) —
C14PP 6 items, perforated (50) —

New York #C15-C18
Definitives

1972

C15PD (2) —
C16PD With approval handstamp (2) —
C17PD (2) —
C18PD (2) —
C16TC dark blue emblem (dated 16. Oct. 1971) (2) —
C15PP 4 items (100) —
C16PP 10 items (100) —
C17PP 4 items (100) —
C18PP 10 items (160) —
Horiz. pair with vert. gutter (20) —
C16PI (50 pairs) —
C17PI (50 pairs) —

New York #C19-C21
Definitives

1974

C19PD (3) —
C20PD (3) —
C21PD (3) —
C19PP 8 items (50) —
C21PP 5 items (50) —
C19PI (50 pairs) —
C20PI (50 pairs) —
C21PI (50 pairs) —

Five cards with essays of No. C21 with incorrect Russian inscription exist.

New York #C22-C23
Definitives

1977

C22PD With approval handstamp (4) —
C22TC Gray wings and envelope, with "not approved" handstamp (2) —
C23PD (1) —
C23PDa Card, #C23PD, #C22TC gray wings and envelope (3) —
C22PP 6 items (50) —
C22PI (50 pairs) —
C23PI (50 pairs) —

ENVELOPES

New York #U1
UN Emblem

1952

U1PD (1) —
U1TC black (1) —

New York #U2
UN Emblem

1958

U2PD with manuscript approval (2) —
U2TC black, on card, with manuscript approval (1) —

New York #U3
Stylized Globe and Weather Vane

1963

U3PD (2) —
U3PI Indicia only on small piece of paper (1) —

See No. UC6PI.

New York #U5
UN Headquarters

1973

U5PD (41) —
U5PP 6 items (5) —
U5PI Unfolded and uncut (2) —

New York #U6
UN Headquarters

1975

U6PD With approval handstamp (5) —
U6PDa Die cut and unfolded, without approval handstamp (4) —

New York #U7
Bouquet of Ribbons

1985

U7PD Indicia only, in folder (9) —

Vienna #U1-U2
Donaupark

1995

VU1PD On Cromalin paper (approved) (6) —
VU1PDa On AGFA paper (not approved) (5) —
VU2PD On Cromalin paper (approved) (6) —
VU2PDa On AGFA paper (not approved) (5) —

New York #U10-U11
Cripticandina

1997

U10PD On Cromalin paper (4) —
U11PD On Cromalin paper (4) —

Vienna #U3
Landscape

1998

VU3PD On Cromalin paper (4) —

AIR POST ENVELOPES & AIR LETTER SHEETS

New York #UC1 Swallows and UN Emblem

1952

UC1PI (32) —
UC1PIa On white paper (22) —

New York #UC3
UN Flag and Plane Envelope

1959

UC3PD (1) —

New York #UC4
UN Flag and Plane Letter Sheet

1960

UC4PD (1) —

Two "not approved" essays exist with diagonal lines rather than bars around envelope.

New York #UC5 Plane and Gull

1961

UC5PD With approval handstamp (1) —
UC5aPD With approval handstamp (3) —

New York #UC6
UN Emblem

1963

UC6PDa Sheet, #UC6PD, #U3PD, with approval handstamp (2) —
UC6PI (1) —
UC6PIa Sheet, #UC6PD (2 sizes), #U3PD (2 sizes) (6) —
UC6PIb As #UC6PIa with one #U3PI removed (1) —

New York #UC7
UN Emblem and Stylized Plane

1968

UC7PD With specimen perfin and approval handstamp (7) —

New York #UC8
UN Emblem

1969

UC8PD With specimen perfin at left (4) —

Geneva #UC1
UN Emblem and Stylized Plane

1969

GUC1PD With specimen perfin and approval handstamp (1) —
GUC1TC light blue (2) —
GUC1TC ultramarine (3) —

New York #UC9
UN Emblem, "UN," Globe and Plane

1972

UC9PD With approval handstamp (2) —

New York #UC10
Birds in Flight

1973

UC10PDa	Small envelope, die cut and folded, with approval handstamp (1)	—
UC10PDb	Large envelope, partially folded, with approval handstamp (2)	—
UC10PPa	Uncut and unfolded, large and small envelopes (6 items)	—

Three sets of essays exist with blue UN inscriptions close.

New York #UC11
Globe and Jet

1975

UC11PD	With approval handstamp (5)	—
UC11PDa	Die cut and unfolded, without approval handstamp (1)	—

New York #UC12
UN Headquarters

1975

UC12PD	With approval handstamp (1)	—

New York #UC13
UN Emblem and Birds

1977

UC13PD	With approval handstamp (2)	—

Five "not approved" essays have design flaw at end of orange line.

New York #UC14, Vienna #UC1
Paper Airplane, Dove

1982

UC14PD	With approval handstamp (3)	—
UC14PDa	On thin card stock (1)	—
VUC1PD	With approval handstamp (3)	—
VUC1PDa	On thin card stock (1)	—

Vienna #UC3
Birds in Flight and UN Emblem

1987

VUC3PD	On plastic, with approval handstamp (4)	—

New York #UC16
UN Headquarters

1989

UC16PD	With approval handstamp (approved) (3)	—
UC16PDa	With approval handstamp (not approved) (10)	—

Vienna #UC5
Donaupark

1992

VUC5PD	On Cromalin paper (3)	—

New York #UC19
Winged Hand With Envelopes Surcharge

1995

UC19PD	On Cromalin paper (1)	—

New York #UC20
Cherry Blossoms

1997

UC20PD	(5)	—

POSTAL CARDS

New York #UX1
UN Headquarters

1952

UX1TC	olive brown, on white paper (1)	—
UX1PI	(4 pairs)	—

New York #UX2
UN Headquarters

1958

UX2PD	With approval handstamp (2)	—

New York #UX3
World Map

1963

UX3PD	(2)	—

New York #UX4
UN Emblem and Post Horn

1969

UX4PD	With approval handstamp on reverse (1)	—

Geneva #UX1-UX2
UN Emblem and Post Horn, Stylized Space View

1969

GUX1PD	With approval handstamp (3)	—
GUX1PI	(53 pairs)	—
GUX2PI	(52 pairs)	—

New York #UX5
"UN"

1973

UX5PD	(1)	—

Five "not approved" essays similar to #UX5 exist. Ten 7c essays exist, three with approval handstamp, the others lacking any handstamp.

New York #UX6
"UN"

1975

UX6PD	With specimen perfin and approval handstamp (4)	—

Five "not approved" essays have incorrect Russian inscription.

New York #UX7, Geneva #UX3-UX4
UN Emblem, UN Emblem in Rectangles, UN Emblem and Ribbons

1977

UX7PD	With specimen perfin at left (4)	—
GUX3PD	With specimen perfin (5)	—
GUX4PD	With specimen perfin at left (4)	—

New York #UX8, Vienna #UX1-UX2
"United Nations," Olive Branch, Bird Carrying Olive Branch

1982

UX8PD	(2)	—
VUX1PD	With approval handstamp on reverse (4)	—
VUX2PD	With approval handstamp on reverse (16)	—

Geneva #UX5-UX6, Vienna #UX3
Peace Dove, UN Emblem

1985

GUX5PD	(3)	—
GUX6PD	With approval handstamp on reverse (3)	—
VUX3PD	(3)	—

One example of No. GUX5PD has inked lines at left of card. One example of No. GUX6PD has inked lines around address lines.

New York #UX9-UX18
Views of UN Headquarters

1989

UX9PD	Message side (4)	—
UX9PDa	Picture side (4)	—
UX10PD	Message side (4)	—
UX10PDa	Picture side (4)	—
UX11PD	Message side (4)	—
UX11PDa	Picture side (4)	—
UX12PD	Message side (4)	—
UX12PDa	Picture side (4)	—
UX13PD	Message side (4)	—
UX13PDa	Picture side (4)	—
UX14PD	Message side (4)	—
UX14PDa	Picture side (4)	—
UX15PD	Message side (4)	—
UX15PDa	Picture side (4)	—
UX16PD	Message side (4)	—
UX16PDa	Picture side (4)	—
UX17PD	Message side (4)	—
UX17PDa	Picture side (4)	—
UX18PD	Message side (4)	—
UX18PDa	Picture side (4)	—

New York #UX19, Geneva #UX8, Vienna #UX5
UN Headquarters, Palais des Nations, Regschek Painting

1992

UX19PD	On Cromalin paper (4)	—
GUX8PD	On Cromalin paper (4)	—
VUX5PD	On Cromalin paper (4)	—
VUX5PDa	Sheet, #GUX8PD, #VUX5PD on Cromalin paper (1)	—
UX19TC	ultramarine (1)	—

Geneva #UX10, Vienna #UX6-UX7
Palais des Nations, Peoples of the World United, Donaupark

1993

GUX10PD	On Cromalin paper (4)	—
VUX6PD	On Cromalin paper (4)	—
VUX7PD	On Cromalin paper (4)	—

Vienna #UX12
The Gloriette

1999

VUX12TCa	Light blue text (4)	—

AIR POST POSTAL CARDS

New York #UXC1
UN Flag and Plane

1957

UXC1PD	With printer and approval handstamps (6)	—
UXC1PI	(30 pairs)	—

New York #UXC3
Airplane Wing and Globe

1959

UXC3PD	With approval handstamp (3)	—

Six essays of No. UXC3 lacking outlined letters on "Airmail" and "Poste Aerienne" exist.

New York #UXC4
Outer Space

1963

UXC4PD	(2)	—

New York #UXC6
Outer Space

1968

UXC6PD	With "Canceled" perfin (2)	—
UXC6PDa	Strip of 3 cards with 2 "Canceled" perfins (2)	—

New York #UXC7
UN Emblem and Stylized Planes

1969

UXC7PD	(1)	—
UXC7TC	black (2)	—

New York #UXC8
UN Emblem and Stylized Wing

1972

UXC8PDa	Folder with mounted #UXC8PD with approval handstamp, and #UXC8 (2)	—

New York #UXC9
UN Emblem and Stylized Planes

1972

UXC9PD	Folder with mounted #UXC9, with approval handstamp (2)	—

New York #UXC10-UXC11
Clouds; Pathways

1975

UXC10PD	With specimen perfin and approval handstamp (4)	—
UXC11PD	With specimen perfin and approval handstamp (4)	—
UXC10TC	With manuscript "Lighter as on sample," and approval handstamp (not approved) (5)	—

New York #UXC12
Flying Mailman

1982

UXC12PD	With approval handstamp on reverse (5)	—

U.N. TEMPORARY EXECUTIVE AUTHORITY, WEST NEW GUINEA

Located in the western half of New Guinea, southwest Pacific Ocean, the former Netherlands New Guinea became a territory under the administration of the United Nations Temporary Executive Authority on Oct. 1, 1962. The size was 151,789 sq. mi. and the population was estimated at 730,000 in 1958. The capital was Hollandia.

The territory came under Indonesian administration on May 1, 1963. For stamps issued by Indonesia see West Irian in Vol. 6.

100 Cents = 1 Gulden

Catalogue values for all unused stamps in this country are for Never Hinged items.

First Printing (Hollandia)

Netherlands New Guinea Stamps of 1950-60 Overprinted

Overprint size: 17x3½mm. Top of "N" is slightly lower than the "U," and the base of the "T" is straight, or nearly so.

Photo.; Litho. (#4, 6, 8)

1962 **Unwmk.** ***Perf. 12½x12, 12½x13½***

1	A4	1c **vermilion & yellow,** *Oct. 1*	.20	.20
2	A1	2c **deep orange,** *Oct. 1*	.25	.25
3	A4	5c **chocolate & yellow,** *Oct. 1*	.25	.25
4	A5	7c **org red, bl & brn vio,** *Nov. 1*	.25	*.35*
5	A4	10c **aqua & red brown,** *Oct. 1*	.25	*.35*
6	A5	12c **green, bl & brn vio,** *Nov. 1*	.25	*.35*
7	A4	15c **deep yel & red brn,** *Nov. 1*	.50	.50
8	A5	17c **brown violet & blue,** *Oct. 1*	.60	*.75*
9	A4	20c **lt bl grn & red brn,** *Nov. 1*	.60	*.75*
10	A6	25c **red,** *Oct. 1*	.35	*.55*
11	A6	30c **deep blue,** *Oct. 1*	.80	.80
12	A6	40c **deep orange,** *Oct. 1*	.80	.80
13	A6	45c **dark olive,** *Nov. 1*	1.40	*1.60*
14	A6	55c **slate blue,** *Nov. 1*	15.00	1.10
15	A6	80c **dull gray violet,** *Nov. 1*	5.75	5.75
16	A6	85c **dark violet brown,** *Nov. 1*	3.00	3.00
17	A6	1g **plum,** *Oct. 1*	9.75	3.00
		Engr.		
18	A3	2g **reddish brown,** *Oct. 1*	9.75	22.50
19	A3	5g **green,** *Oct. 1*	7.75	5.50
		Nos. 1-19 (19)	57.50	48.35

Overprinted locally and sold in West New Guinea. Stamps of the second printing were used to complete sets sold to collectors.

Second Printing (Haarlen, Netherlands)

Overprint size: 17x3½mm. Top of the "N" is slightly higher than the "U," and the base of the "T" is concave.

Photo.; Litho. (#4a, 6a, 8a)

1962 **Unwmk.** ***Perf. 12½x12, 12½x13½***

1a	A4	1c **vermilion & yellow**	.20	.20
2a	A1	2c **deep orange**	.25	.20
3a	A4	5c **chocolate & yellow**	.25	.20
4a	A5	7c **org red, bl & brn vio**	.25	.20
5a	A4	10c **aqua & red brown**	.25	.20
6a	A5	12c **green, bl & brn vio**	.25	.20
7a	A4	15c **deep yel & red brn**	.50	.25
8a	A5	17c **brown violet & blue**	.60	.35
9a	A4	20c **lt blue grn & red brn**	.60	.35
10a	A6	25c **red**	.35	.30
11a	A6	30c **deep blue**	.80	.35
12a	A6	40c **deep orange**	.80	.35
13a	A6	45c **dark olive**	1.40	.75
14a	A6	55c **slate blue**	1.25	.55
15a	A6	80c **dull gray violet**	5.75	5.75
16a	A6	85c **dark violet brown**	3.00	3.00
17a	A6	1g **plum**	3.50	1.90
		Engr.		
18a	A3	2g **reddish brown**	9.75	13.00
19a	A3	5g **green**	6.00	3.50
		Nos. 1a-19a (19)	35.75	31.60

Overprinted in the Netherlands and sold by the UN in New York.

Third Printing

Overprint 14mm long.

Photo.; Litho. (#4b, 6b, 8b)

1963, Mar. **Photo.** **Unwmk.** ***Perf. 12½x12***

1b	A4	1c **vermilion & yellow**	*3.50*	*1.75*
3b	A4	5c **chocolate & yellow**	*4.00*	*2.50*
4b	A5	7c **org red, bl & brn vio**	*17.50*	*17.00*
5b	A4	10c **aqua & red brown**	*4.00*	*2.50*
6b	A5	12c **green, bl & brn vio**	*26.00*	*26.00*
7b	A4	15c **deep yel & red brn**	*80.00*	*87.50*
8b	A5	17c **brown violet & blue**	*9.50*	*9.50*
9b	A4	20c **lt blue grn & red brn**	*5.50*	*3.25*
		Nos. 1b-9b (8)	*150.00*	*150.00*

The third printing was applied in West New Guinea and it is doubtful whether it was regularly issued. Used values are for cto.

Fourth Printing

Overprint 19mm long.

Photogravure

1963, Mar. **Unwmk.** ***Perf. 12½x12***

1c	A4	1c **vermilion & yellow**	*40.00*	*40.00*
5c	A4	10c **aqua & red brown**	*110.00*	*110.00*

The fourth printing was applied in West New Guinea and it is doubtful whether it was regularly issued. Used values are for cto.

U.N. INTERIM ADMINISTRATION IN KOSOVO

These stamps were issued by the United Nations Interim Administration Mission in Kosovo and the Post & Telecommunications of Kosovo. Service was local for the first two months, with international use to start in mid-May.

100 pfennigs = 1 mark

Catalogue values for all unused stamps in this country are for Never Hinged items.

Peace in Kosovo — A1

Printed by La Poste, France. Panes of 40. Designed by Shyqri Nimani, Kosovo.

Designs: 20pf, Mosaic depicting Orpheus, c. 5th-6th cent., Podujeve. 30pf, Dardinian idol, Museum of Kosovo. 50pf, Silver coin of Damastion from 4th cent. B.C. 1m, Statue of Mother Teresa, Prizren. 2m, Map of Kosovo.

Perf. 13½x13, 13½x13¼ (30pf)

2000, Mar. 14 **Litho.** **Unwmk.**

1	A1	20pf	**multicolored**	.40	.40
			First day cover		1.25
2	A1	30pf	**multicolored**	.60	.60
			First day cover		1.25
3	A1	50pf	**multicolored**	1.00	1.00
			First day cover		1.50
4	A1	1m	**multicolored**	2.00	2.00
			First day cover		2.50
5	A1	2m	**multicolored**	4.00	4.00
			First day cover		5.00
			First day cover, #1-5		7.00
			Nos. 1-5 (5)	8.00	8.00

Peace in Kosovo — A2

Designs: 20pf, Bird. 30pf, Street musician. 50pf, Butterfly and pear. 1m, Children and stars. 2m, Globe and handprints.

2001, Nov. 12 **Litho.** ***Perf. 14***

6	A2	20pf	**multicolored**	1.25	1.25
7	A2	30pf	**multicolored**	1.75	1.75
8	A2	50pf	**multicolored**	3.00	3.00
9	A2	1m	**multicolored**	6.50	6.50
10	A2	2m	**multicolored**	12.50	12.50
			Nos. 6-10 (5)	25.00	25.00

Nos. 6-10 were not available to collectors through the United Nations Postal Administration.

100 Cents = 1 Euro (€)

Peace in Kosovo Type of 2001 With Denominations in Euros Only

2002, May 2 **Litho.** ***Perf. 14***

11	A2	10c	Like #6	.20	.20
12	A2	15c	Like #7	.30	.30
13	A2	26c	Like #8	.50	.50
14	A2	51c	Like #9	.95	.95
15	A2	€1.02	Like #10	1.90	1.90
			Nos. 11-15 (5)	3.85	3.85

Nos. 11-15 were not available to collectors through the United Nations Postal Administration.

Additions, Deletions & Number Changes

Number in 2003 Catalogue	Number in 2004 Catalogue
UNITED STATES	
Postage	
new	159a
new	248a
250c	deleted
319m	deleted
new	716a
new	1851a
new	2175f
new	2187b
2187b	2187c
new	2187d
new	2216m
new	2531a
new	2531Ad
new	2531Ae
new	2540b
2718c	deleted
new	2747b
new	2872e
2904Bc	deleted
new	2920j
new	3054f
new	3197b
new	3363c
new	3363d
new	3367d
new	3410g
new	3420a
3431a	3432
new	3472a
new	3485f
new	3492e
new	3540e
new	3540f
new	3540g
new	3611k
new	3613a
new	3619c
new	3619d
new	3619e
new	3619f
new	3619h
new	3622a
new	3632a
Offices in China	
new	K18a
new	K18b
Local Stamps	
new	131L1b
Envelopes	
new	U466D
new	U468m
new	U507A
new	U507B
new	U548Ab
new	U599b
new	U646a
new	U649a
new	U649b

Number in 2003 Catalogue	Number in 2004 Catalogue
UNITED STATES	
Postage	
new	UC61a
new	WO18A
Postal Cards	
new	UX125e
new	UY7s
new	UY20s
new	UXC9b
Revenue Stamps	
R285c	deleted
Beer Stamps	
new	REA182b
new	REA183b
Revenue Stamped Paper	
new	RN-E7a
new	RN-H3i
new	RN-K1
Private Die Proprietary Stamps	
new	RO10e
new	RS147e
new	RS205a
Duck Hunting Permit (Federal)	
new	RW35a
Duck Hunting Permit (State)	
new	Massachusetts 6a
Essays	
new	PR5-E1
Trial Color Proofs	
new	O80TC
new	O81TC
Telegraph Stamps	
new	15T44a
Souvenir Cards	
new	SC140A
International Reply Coupons	
new	IRC30a
new	IRC30b
Post Office Seals	
new	LOX41
Canal Zone	
new	1g
new	22h
new	84e
new	146P
new	147P

Number in 2003 Catalogue	Number in 2004 Catalogue
UNITED STATES	
Postage	
Danish West Indies	
new	5f
new	6f
Guam	
new	M4a
UNITED NATIONS	
81a	deleted
87a	deleted
new	101c
new	163a

value priced **stockbooks**

Stockbooks are a classic and convenient storage alternative for many collectors. These German-made stockbooks feature heavyweight archival quality paper with 9 pockets on each page. The 8½" x 11⅝" pages are bound inside a handsome leatherette grain cover and include glassine interleaving between the pages for added protection. The Value Priced Stockbooks are available in two page styles, the white page stockbooks feature glassine pockets while the black page variety includes clear acetate pockets

WHITE PAGE STOCKBOOKS GLASSINE POCKETS

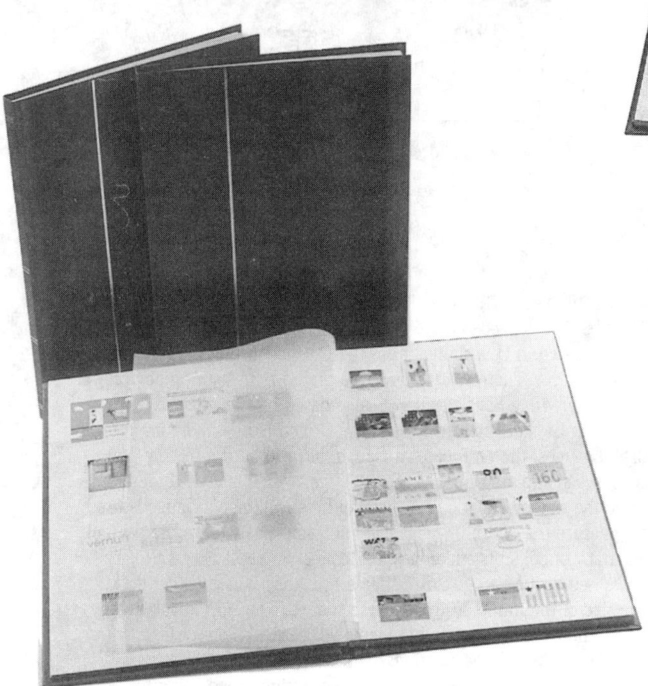

ITEM	DESCRIPTION		RETAIL
SW16BL	Blue	16 pages	$6.95
SW16GR	Green	16 pages	$6.95
SW16RD	Red	16 pages	$6.95

BLACK PAGE STOCKBOOKS ACETATE POCKETS

ITEM	COLOR	PAGES	RETAIL
ST16RD	Red	16 pages	$10.95
ST16GR	Green	16 pages	$10.95
ST16BL	Blue	16 pages	$10.95
ST16BK	Black	16 pages	$10.95
ST32RD	Red	32 pages	$16.95
ST32GR	Green	32 pages	$16.95
ST32BL	Blue	32 pages	$16.95
ST32BK	Black	32 pages	$16.95
ST64RD	Red	64 pages	$29.95
ST64GR	Green	64 pages	$29.95
ST64BL	Blue	64 pages	$29.95
ST64BK	Black	64 pages	$29.95

Scott Value Priced Stockbooks are available from your favorite dealer or direct from:

SCOTT

P.O. Box 828
Sidney OH 45365-0828
www.amosadvantage.com
1-800-572-6885

The black page stockbook is available in three sizes: 16 pages 32 pages 64 pages.

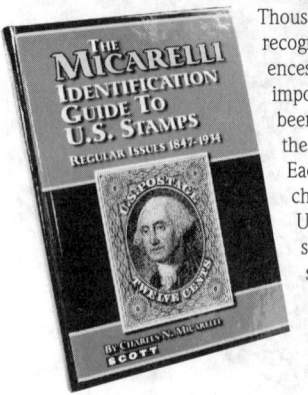

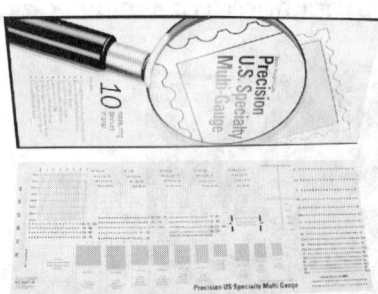

INDEX TO ADVERTISERS – 2004 U.S. SPECIALIZED

2004
UNITED STATES SPECIALIZED
DEALER DIRECTORY
YELLOW PAGE LISTINGS

This section of your Scott Catalogue contains advertisements to help you conveniently find what you need, when you need it...!

Accessories

BROOKLYN GALLERY COIN & STAMP
8725 4th Avenue
Brooklyn, NY 11209
718-745-5701
718-745-2775 Fax
Email:
info@brooklyngallery.com
Web: www.brooklyngallery.com

Albums

THE KEEPING ROOM
P.O. Box 257
Trumbull, CT 06611
203-372-8436

Appraisals

CONNEXUS
P.O. Box 819
Snow Camp, NC 27349
336-376-8207
Email:
Connexus1@world.att.net

Appraisals

RANDY SCHOLL STAMP CO.
Southhampton Square
7460 Jager Court
Cincinnati, OH 45230-4344
Email: randyscholl@fuse.net

Approvals-Personalized WW & US

THE KEEPING ROOM
P.O. Box 257
Trumbull, CT 06611
203-372-8436

Asia

MICHAEL ROGERS, INC.
199 E. Welbourne Ave.
Suite 3
Winter Park, FL 32789
407-644-2290 or 800-843-3751
407-645-4434 Fax
Email: mrogersinc@aol.com
Web:
www.michaelrogersinc.com

Auctions

SAM HOUSTON PHILATELICS
13310 Westheimer #150
Houston, TX 77077
281-493-6386 or 800-231-5926
281-496-1445 Fax
Email: shduck@aol.com
Web: www.shduck.com

DANIEL F. KELLEHER CO., INC.
24 Farnsworth Street
Suite 605
Boston, MA 02210
617-443-0033
617-443-0789 Fax

JACQUES C. SCHIFF, JR., INC.
195 Main Street
Ridgefield Park, NJ 07660
201-641-5566
From NYC: 212-662-2777
201-641-5705 Fax

R. MARESCH & SON LTD.
5th Floor - 6075 Yonge Street
Toronto, Ontario M2M 3W2
CANADA
416-363-7777
416-363-6511 Fax
Web: www.maresch.com

STAMP CENTER/DUTCH COUNTRY AUCTIONS
4115 Concord Pike
Wilmington, DE 19803
302-478-8740
302-478-8779 Fax
Email: scdca@dol.net
Web: www.thestampcenter.com

Auctions

SUBURBAN STAMP INC.
176 Worthington Street
Springfield, MA 01103
413-785-5348
413-746-3788 Fax
Email:
suburbanstamp@earthlink.net

Auctions-Internet

STEVE CRIPPE, INC.
PO Box 23413
Tampa, FL 33623
813-878-9845
813-877-8080 Fax
Email: stamp@stevecrippe.com
Web: www.stevecrippe.com

Auctions-Mail Bid

SUBURBAN STAMP INC.
176 Worthington Street
Springfield, MA 01103
413-785-5348
413-746-3788 Fax
Email:
suburbanstamp@earthlink.net

DALE ENTERPRISES INC.
P.O. Box 539-C
Emmaus, PA 18049
610-433-3303
610-965-6089 Fax
Email: daleent@ptd.net
Web: www.dalestamps.com

Auctions

Auctions - Public

ALAN BLAIR STAMPS/AUCTIONS
5407 Lakeside Ave.
Suite 4
Richmond, VA 23228
800-689-5602 Phone/Fax
Email: alanblair@prodigy.net

SUBURBAN STAMP INC.
176 Worthington Street
Springfield, MA 01103
413-785-5348
413-746-3788 Fax
Email:
suburbanstamp@earthlink.net

British Commonwealth

EMPIRE STAMP CO.
P.O. Box 8337
Calabasa, CA 91372-8337
800-616-7278 or 818-225-1181
818-225-1182 Fax
Email: info@empirestamps.com
Web: www.empirestamps.com

JAY'S STAMP CO.
Box 28484
Dept. S
Philadelphia, PA 19149-0184
215-743-0207 Phone/Fax
Email: jasc@comcast.net
Web: www.jaysco.com

METROPOLITAN STAMP CO., INC.
P.O. Box 1133
Chicago, IL 60690-1133
815-439-0142
815-439-0143 Fax
Email: metrostamp@aol.com

VICTORIA STAMP CO.
P.O. Box 745
Ridgewood, NJ 07451
201-652-7283
201-612-0024 Fax
Email:
VictoriaStampCo@aol.com
Web:
www.VictoriaStampCo.com

China

MICHAEL ROGERS, INC.
199 E. Welbourne Ave.
Suite 3
Winter Park, FL 32789
407-644-2290 or 800-843-3751
407-645-4434 Fax
Email: mrogersinc@aol.com
Web:
www.michaelrogersinc.com

Classics

GARY POSNER, INC.
1407 Avenue Z, PMB #535
Brooklyn, NY 11235
800-323-4279
718-241-2801 Fax
Email: garyposnerinc@aol.com
Web: www.garyposnerinc.com
www.gemstamps.com

HENRY GITNER PHILATELISTS, INC.
P.O. Box 3077-S
Middletown, NY 10940
845-343-5151 or 800-947-8267
845-343-0068 Fax
Email: hgitner@hgitner.com
Web: www.hgitner.com

Collections

HENRY GITNER PHILATELISTS, INC.
P.O. Box 3077-S
Middletown, NY 10940
845-343-5151 or 800-947-8267
845-343-0068 Fax
Email: hgitner@hgitner.com
Web: www.hgitner.com

BOB & MARTHA FRIEDMAN
624 Homestead Place
Joliet, IL 60435
815-725-6666
815-725-4134 Fax

DR. ROBERT FRIEDMAN & SONS
2029 West 75th Street
Woodridge, IL 60517
630-985-1515
630-985-1588 Fax

Confed. Stamps & Postal History

STANLEY M. PILLER & ASSOCIATES
3351 Grand Avenue
Oakland, CA 94610
510-465-8290
510-465-7121 Fax
Email: stmpdlr@aol.com
Web: www.smpiller.com

SUN COAST STAMP CO.
3231 Gulf Gate Drive
Suite 102
Sarasota, FL 34231
941-921-9761 or 800-927-3351
941-921-1762 Fax
Email:
email@suncoaststamp.com
Web: www.stampfinder.com

Auctions

Qualified Auctioneer

Conservation Stamps

SAM HOUSTON DUCK CO.
P.O. Box 820087
Houston, TX 77282
281-493-6386 or 800-231-5926
281-496-1445 Fax
Email: shduck@aol.com
Web: www.shduck.com

Covers-Zeppelins

HENRY GITNER PHILATELISTS, INC.
P.O. Box 3077-S
Middletown, NY 10940
845-343-5151 or 800-947-8267
845-343-0068 Fax
Email: hgitner@hgitner.com
Web: www.hgitner.com

Ducks

MICHAEL JAFFE
P.O. Box 61484
Vancouver, WA 98666
360-695-6161 or 800-782-6770
360-695-1616 Fax
Email:
mjaffe@brookmanstamps.com
Web:
www.brookmanstamps.com

SAM HOUSTON DUCK CO.
P.O. Box 820087
Houston, TX 77282
281-493-6386 or 800-231-5926
281-496-1445 Fax
Email: shduck@aol.com
Web: www.shduck.com

TRENTON STAMP & COIN CO./COASTAL BEND DUCK STAMP CO.
Thomas DeLuca
Mail: P.O. Box 8574
Trenton, NJ 08650
Store: Forest Glen Plaza
1804 Route 33
Hamilton Square, NJ 08690
800-446-8664
609-587-8664 Fax
Email: TOMD4TSC@aol.com

Ducks-Foreign

METROPOLITAN STAMP CO., INC.
P.O. Box 1133
Chicago, IL 60690-1133
815-439-0142
815-439-0143 Fax
Email: metrostamp@aol.com

Errors, Freaks & Oddities

STEVE CRIPPE, INC.
PO Box 23413
Tampa, FL 33623
813-878-9845
813-877-8080 Fax
Email: stamp@stevecrippe.com
Web: www.stevecrippe.com

SAM HOUSTON PHILATELICS
13310 Westheimer #150
Houston, TX 77077
281-493-6386 or 800-231-5926
281-496-1445 Fax
Email: shduck@aol.com
Web: www.shduck.com

Expertizing

STANLEY M. PILLER & ASSOCIATES
3351 Grand Avenue
Oakland, CA 94610
510-465-8290
510-465-7121 Fax
Email: stmpdlr@aol.com
Web: www.smpiller.com

First Day Covers

HENRY GITNER PHILATELISTS, INC.
P.O. Box 3077-S
Middletown, NY 10940
845-343-5151 or 800-947-8267
845-343-0068 Fax
Email: hgitner@hgitner.com
Web: www.hgitner.com

German Colonies

COLONIAL STAMP COMPANY
$1 million photo price list, $5.00
(refundable against purchase)
5757 Wilshire Blvd. PH #8
Los Angeles, CA 90036
323-933-9435
323-939-9930 Fax
Email: gwh225@aol.com
Web: www.colonialstamps.com

Insurance

COLLECTIBLES INSURANCE AGENCY
P.O. Box 1200 SSC
Westminster, MD 21158
888-837-9537
410-876-9233 Fax
Email:
info@insurecollectibles.com
Web: www.collectinsure.com

Italy

LO GIUDICE'S ITALY STAMPS & COVERS
2513 S. Gessner Road
Houston, TX 77063-2007
713-975-7401
713-975-7789 Fax

Japan

MICHAEL ROGERS, INC.
199 E. Welbourne Ave.
Suite 3
Winter Park, FL 32789
407-644-2290 or 800-843-3751
407-645-4434 Fax
Email: mrogersinc@aol.com
Web:
www.michaelrogersinc.com

Korea

MICHAEL ROGERS, INC.
199 E. Welbourne Ave.
Suite 3
Winter Park, FL 32789
407-644-2290 or 800-843-3751
407-645-4434 Fax
Email: mrogersinc@aol.com
Web:
www.michaelrogersinc.com

Lots & Collections

BOB & MARTHA FRIEDMAN
624 Homestead Place
Joliet, IL 60435
815-725-6666
815-725-4134 Fax

DR. ROBERT FRIEDMAN & SONS
2029 West 75th Street
Woodridge, IL 60517
630-985-1515
630-985-1588 Fax

Manchukuo

MICHAEL ROGERS, INC.
199 E. Welbourne Ave.
Suite 3
Winter Park, FL 32789
407-644-2290 or 800-843-3751
407-645-4434 Fax
Email: mrogersinc@aol.com
Web:
www.michaelrogersinc.com

New Issues

DALE ENTERPRISES INC.
P.O. Box 539-C
Emmaus, PA 18049
610-433-3303
610-965-6089 Fax
Email: daleent@ptd.net
Web: www.dalestamps.com

DAVIDSON'S STAMP SERVICE
P.O. Box 36355
Indianapolis, IN 46236-0355
317-826-2620
Email: davidson@in.net
Web: www.newstampissues.com

One of A Kind

DALE ENTERPRISES INC.
P.O. Box 539-C
Emmaus, PA 18049
610-433-3303
610-965-6089 Fax
Email: daleent@ptd.net
Web: www.dalestamps.com

Philatelic Literature

JAMES E. LEE
P.O. Drawer 250
Wheeling, IL 60090
800-696-8403
847-215-1231
847-215-7253 Fax
Email: philately2@earthlink.net
Web: www.jameslee.com

LEWIS KAUFMAN
P.O. Box 255
Kiamesha Lake, NY 12751
845-794-8013 Phone/Fax
800-491-5453 Phone/Fax
Email: mamet1@aol.com

Postal History

JAMES E. LEE
P.O. Drawer 250
Wheeling, IL 60090
800-696-8403
847-215-1231
847-215-7253 Fax
Email: philately2@earthlink.net
Web: www.jameslee.com

Postal History

LO GIUDICE'S ITALY STAMPS & COVERS
2513 S. Gessner Road
Houston, TX 77063-2007
713-975-7401
713-975-7789 Fax

STANLEY M. PILLER & ASSOCIATES
3351 Grand Avenue
Oakland, CA 94610
510-465-8290
510-465-7121 Fax
Email: stmpdlr@aol.com
Web: www.smpiller.com

Proofs & Essays

HENRY GITNER PHILATELISTS, INC.
P.O. Box 3077-S
Middletown, NY 10940
845-343-5151 or 800-947-8267
845-343-0068 Fax
Email: hgitner@hgitner.com
Web: www.hgitner.com

JAMES E. LEE
P.O. Drawer 250
Wheeling, IL 60090
800-696-8403
847-215-1231
847-215-7253 Fax
Email: philately2@earthlink.net
Web: www.jameslee.com

STANLEY M. PILLER & ASSOCIATES
3351 Grand Avenue
Oakland, CA 94610
510-465-8290
510-465-7121 Fax
Email: stmpdlr@aol.com
Web: www.smpiller.com

Publications-Collector

THE AMERICAN PHILATELIST
Dept. TZ
P.O. Box 8000
State College, PA 16803
814-237-3803
814-237-6128 Fax
Email: apsinfo@stamps.org
Web: www.stamps.org

Souvenir Cards

AALLSTAMPS
38 N. Main Street
P.O. Box 249
Milltown, NJ 08850
732-247-1093
732-247-1094 Fax
Email: mail@aallstamps.com
Web: www.aallstamps.com

Stamp Shows

CHRISTOPHER J. HRADIL, INC.
325 Main St.
Little Falls, NJ 07424
973-809-4606 or 973-890-0268
973-890-1596 Fax
Email: stamps@comcast.net
Web: www.dom17stamps.com

STAMP STORES

California

ASHTREE STAMP & COIN
2410 N. Blackstone
Fresno, CA 93703-1747
559-227-7167

BROSIUS STAMP & COIN
2105 Main Street
Santa Monica, CA 90405
310-396-7480
310-396-7455

FISCHER-WOLK PHILATELICS
24771 "G" Alicia Parkway
Laguna Hills, CA 92653
949-837-2932
Email:
fischerwolk@earthlink.net

STANLEY M. PILLER & ASSOCIATES
3351 Grand Avenue
Oakland, CA 94610
510-465-8290
510-465-7121 Fax
Email: stmpdlr@aol.com
Web: www.smpiller.com

Colorado

ACKLEY'S STAMPS
3230 N. Stone Ave.
Colorado Springs, CO 80907
719-633-1153
Email: ackl9@aol.com

SHOWCASE STAMPS
3865 Wadsworth
Wheat Ridge, CO 80033
303-425-9252
Email: kbeiner@colbi.net
Web:
www.showcasestamps.com

Connecticut

MILLER'S STAMP SHOP
41 New London Turnpike
Uncasville, CT 06382
860-848-0468 or 800-67-STAMP
860-848-1926 Fax
Email: millstamps@aol.com
Web: www.millerstamps.com

Connecticut

SILVER CITY COIN & STAMP
41 Colony Street
Meriden, CT 06451
203-235-7634
203-237-4915 Fax

Florida

CORBIN STAMP & COIN, INC.
108 West Robertson Street
Brandon, FL 33511
813-651-3266

R.D.C. STAMPS
7381 SW 24th Street
Miami, FL 33155-1402
305-264-4213
305-262-2919 Fax
Email: rdcstamps@aol.com

WINTER PARK STAMP SHOP
Ranch Mall (17-92)
325 S. Orlando Ave.
Suite 1-2
Winter Park, FL 32789-3608
407-628-1120 or 800-845-1819
407-628-0091 Fax
Email:
stamps@winterparkstampshop.c omWeb:
www.winterparkstampshop.com

Georgia

STAMPS UNLIMITED OF GEORGIA
133 Carnegie Way
Room 250
Atlanta, GA 30303
404-688-9161

Indiana

KNIGHT STAMP & COIN CO.
237 Main Street
Hobart, IN 46342
219-942-4341 or 800-634-2646
Email: knight@knightcoin.com
Web: www.knightcoin.com

Florida

STAMP STORES

Illinois

DR. ROBERT FRIEDMAN & SONS
2029 West 75th Street
Woodridge, IL 60517
630-985-1515
630-985-1588 Fax

DON CLARK'S STAMPS & COINS
937 1/2 W. Galena Blvd.
Aurora, IL 60506
630-896-4606

Kentucky

COLLECTORS STAMPS LTD.
4012 Dupont Circle #313
Louisville, KY 40207
502-897-9045
Email: csl@aye.net

Maryland

BALTIMORE COIN & STAMP EXCHANGE
10194 Baltimore National Pike
Unit 104
Ellicott City, MD 21042
410-418-8282
410-418-4813 Fax

BULLDOG STAMP COMPANY
4641 Montgomery Avenue
Bethesda, MD 20814
301-654-1138

Massachusetts

KAPPY'S COINS & STAMPS
534 Washington Street
Norwood, MA 02062
781-762-5552
781-762-3292 Fax
Email: kappyscoins@aol.com

SUBURBAN STAMP INC.
176 Worthington Street
Springfield, MA 01103
413-785-5348
413-746-3788 Fax
Email:
suburbanstamp@earthlink.net

Michigan

THE MOUSE AND SUCH
696 N. Mill Street
Plymouth, MI 48170
734-454-1515
734-454-9812 Fax
Email:
weluvstamps@hotmail.com

New Jersey

AALLSTAMPS
38 N. Main Street
P.O. Box 249
Milltown, NJ 08850
732-247-1093
732-247-1094 Fax
Email: mail@aallstamps.com
Web: www.aallstamps.com

BERGEN STAMPS & COLLECTIBLES
717 American Legion Drive
Teaneck, NJ 07666
201-836-8987

CHRISTOPHER J. HRADIL, INC.
325 Main St.
Little Falls, NJ 07424
973-809-4606 or 973-890-0268
973-890-1596 Fax
Email: stamps@comcast.net
Web: www.dom17stamps.com

New Jersey

RON RITZER STAMPS INC.
Millburn Mall
2933 Vauxhall Road
Vauxhall, NJ 07088
908-687-0007
908-687-0795 Fax
Email:
ritzerstamps@earthlink.net

TRENTON STAMP & COIN CO.
Thomas DeLuca
Store: Forest Glen Plaza
1804 Route 33
Hamilton Square, NJ 08690
Mail: P.O. Box 8574
Trenton, NJ 08650
800-446-8664
609-587-8664 Fax
Email: TOMD4TSC@aol.com

New York

CHAMPION STAMP CO., INC.
432 West 54th Street
New York, NY 10019
212-489-8130
212-581-8130 Fax
Email:
championstamp@aol.com
Web: www.championstamp.com

Ohio

FEDERAL COIN & STAMP EXCHANGE
P.O. Box 14579
401 Euclid Ave.
Suite 45
Cleveland, OH 44114
216-861-1160
216-861-5960 Fax

HILLTOP STAMP SERVICE
Richard A. Peterson
P.O. Box 626
Wooster, OH 44691
330-262-8907 or 330-262-5378
Email: hilltop@bright.net

THE LINK STAMP CO.
3461 E. Livingston Avenue
Columbus, OH 43227
614-237-4125 Phone/Fax
800-546-5726 Phone/Fax

Pennsylvania

PHILLY STAMP & COIN CO., INC.
1804 Chestnut Street
Philadelphia, PA 19103
215-563-7341
215-563-7382 Fax
Email: phillysc@netreach.net
Web:
www.phillystampandcoin.com

Tennessee

HERRON HILL, INC.
5007 Black Road
Suite 140
Memphis, TN 38117
901-683-9644

Texas

SAM HOUSTON PHILATELICS
13310 Westheimer #150
Houston, TX 77077
281-493-6386 or 800-231-5926
281-496-1445 Fax
Email: shduck@aol.com
Web: www.shduck.com

Virginia

KENNEDY'S STAMPS & COINS
7059 Brookfield Plaza
Springfield, VA 22150
703-569-7300
703-569-7644 Fax
Email: kennedy@patriot.net

LATHEROW & CO., INC.
5054 Lee Hwy.
Arlington, VA 22207
703-538-2727 or 800-647-4624
703-538-5210 Fax

Washington

TACOMA MALL BLVD. COIN & STAMP
5225 Tacoma Mall Blvd. E101
Tacoma, WA 98409
253-472-9632
253-472-8948 Fax
Email:
kfeldman01@sprynet.com

Wisconsin

JIM LUKES' STAMP & COIN
815 Jay Street
P.O. Box 1780
Manitowoc, WI 54221
920-682-2324 Phone/Fax

Supplies

CHRISTOPHER J. HRADIL, INC.
325 Main St.
Little Falls, NJ 07424
973-809-4606 or 973-890-0268
973-890-1596 Fax
Email: stamps@comcast.net
Web: www.dom17stamps.com

Topicals-Columbus

MR. COLUMBUS
Box 1492
Fennville, MI 49408
616-543-4755
Email: columbus@accn.org

United States

ARMSTRONG PHILATELICS
P.O. Box 4089
Chatsworth, CA 91313-4089
818-701-7380
818-701-5915 Fax
Email: armstrong@stamp1.com
Web: www.stamp1.com

B.J.'S STAMPS
Barbara J. Johnson
6342 W. Bell Road
Glendale, AZ 85308
623-878-2080
623-412-3456 Fax
Email: info@bjstamps.com
Web: www.bjstamps.com

United States

United States

BROOKMAN STAMP CO.
P.O. Box 90
Vancouver, WA 98666
360-695-1391 or 800-545-4871
360-695-1616 Fax
Email:
dave@brookmanstamps.com
Web:
www.brookmanstamps.com

STEVE CRIPPE, INC.
PO Box 23413
Tampa, FL 33623
813-878-9845
813-877-8080 Fax
Email: stamp@stevecrippe.com
Web: www.stevecrippe.com

DALE ENTERPRISES INC.
P.O. Box 539-C
Emmaus, PA 18049
610-433-3303
610-965-6089 Fax
Email: daleent@ptd.net
Web: www.dalestamps.com

DR. ROBERT FRIEDMAN & SONS
2029 West 75th Street
Woodridge, IL 60517
630-985-1515
630-985-1588 Fax

GARY POSNER, INC.
1407 Avenue Z, PMB #535
Brooklyn, NY 11235
800-323-4279
718-241-2801 Fax
Email: garyposnerinc@aol.com
Web: www. garyposnerinc.com
www.gemstamps.com

United States

HENRY GITNER PHILATELISTS, INC.
P.O. Box 3077-S
Middletown, NY 10940
845-343-5151 or 800-947-8267
845-343-0068 Fax
Email: hgitner@hgitner.com
Web: www.hgitner.com

U.S.-Back of Book

ARMSTRONG PHILATELICS
P.O. Box 4089
Chatsworth, CA 91313-4089
818-701-7380
818-701-5915 Fax
Email: armstrong@stamp1.com
Web: www.stamp1.com

U.S.-Booklets

LEWIS KAUFMAN
P.O. Box 255
Kiamesha Lake, NY 12751
845-794-8013 Phone/Fax
800-491-5453 Phone/Fax
Email: mamet1@aol.com

DALE ENTERPRISES INC.
P.O. Box 539-C
Emmaus, PA 18049
610-433-3303
610-965-6089 Fax
Email: daleent@ptd.net
Web: www.dalestamps.com

United States

U.S.-Classics

CHRISTOPHER J. HRADIL, INC.
325 Main St.
Little Falls, NJ 07424
973-809-4606 or 973-890-0268
973-890-1596 Fax
Email: stamps@comcast.net
Web: www.dom17stamps.com

DALE ENTERPRISES INC.
P.O. Box 539-C
Emmaus, PA 18049
610-433-3303
610-965-6089 Fax
Email: daleent@ptd.net
Web: www.dalestamps.com

STANLEY M. PILLER & ASSOCIATES
3351 Grand Avenue
Oakland, CA 94610
510-465-8290
510-465-7121 Fax
Email: stmpdlr@aol.com
Web: www.smpiller.com

SUBURBAN STAMP INC.
176 Worthington Street
Springfield, MA 01103
413-785-5348
413-746-3788 Fax
Email:
suburbanstamp@earthlink.net

U.S.-Classics/Moderns

LEWIS KAUFMAN
P.O. Box 255
Kiamesha Lake, NY 12751
845-794-8013 Phone/Fax
800-491-5453 Phone/Fax
Email: mamet1@aol.com

U.S.-Collections Wanted

CHRISTOPHER J. HRADIL, INC.
325 Main St.
Little Falls, NJ 07424
973-809-4606 or 973-890-0268
973-890-1596 Fax
Email: stamps@comcast.net
Web: www.dom17stamps.com

SUBURBAN STAMP INC.
176 Worthington Street
Springfield, MA 01103
413-785-5348
413-746-3788 Fax
Email:
suburbanstamp@earthlink.net

U.S.-Errors. Freaks & Oddities

STEVE CRIPPE, INC.
PO Box 23413
Tampa, FL 33623
813-878-9845
813-877-8080 Fax
Email: stamp@stevecrippe.com
Web: www.stevecrippe.com

GARY POSNER, INC.
1407 Avenue Z, PMB #535
Brooklyn, NY 11235
800-323-4279
718-241-2801 Fax
Email: garyposnerinc@aol.com
Web: www. garyposnerinc.com
www.gemstamps.com

SUBURBAN STAMP INC.
176 Worthington Street
Springfield, MA 01103
413-785-5348
413-746-3788 Fax
Email:
suburbanstamp@earthlink.net

U.S.-Fancy Cancels

JAMES E. LEE
P.O. Drawer 250
Wheeling, IL 60090
800-696-8403
847-215-1231
847-215-7253 Fax
Email: philately2@earthlink.net
Web: www.jameslee.com

U.S.-Federal Ducks Stamps

HENRY GITNER PHILATELISTS, INC.
P.O. Box 3077-S
Middletown, NY 10940
845-343-5151 or 800-947-8267
845-343-0068 Fax
Email: hgitner@hgitner.com
Web: www.hgitner.com

SAM HOUSTON DUCK CO.
P.O. Box 820087
Houston, TX 77282
281-493-6386 or 800-231-5926
281-496-1445 Fax
Email: shduck@aol.com
Web: www.shduck.com

U.S.-Mint

STEVE CRIPPE, INC.
PO Box 23413
Tampa, FL 33623
813-878-9845
813-877-8080 Fax
Email: stamp@stevecrippe.com
Web: www.stevecrippe.com

HENRY GITNER PHILATELISTS, INC.
P.O. Box 3077-S
Middletown, NY 10940
845-343-5151 or 800-947-8267
845-343-0068 Fax
Email: hgitner@hgitner.com
Web: www.hgitner.com

U.S.-Mint Sheets

HENRY GITNER PHILATELISTS, INC.
P.O. Box 3077-S
Middletown, NY 10940
845-343-5151 or 800-947-8267
845-343-0068 Fax
Email: hgitner@hgitner.com
Web: www.hgitner.com

METROPOLITAN STAMP CO., INC.
P.O. Box 1133
Chicago, IL 60690-1133
815-439-0142
815-439-0143 Fax
Email: metrostamp@aol.com

U.S.-Multiples Mint/Used

LEWIS KAUFMAN
P.O. Box 255
Kiamesha Lake, NY 12751
845-794-8013 Phone/Fax
800-491-5453 Phone/Fax
Email: mamet1@aol.com

U.S.-Plate Blocks

HENRY GITNER PHILATELISTS, INC.
P.O. Box 3077-S
Middletown, NY 10940
845-343-5151 or 800-947-8267
845-343-0068 Fax
Email: hgitner@hgitner.com
Web: www.hgitner.com

GARY POSNER, INC.
1407 Avenue Z, PMB #535
Brooklyn, NY 11235
800-323-4279
718-241-2801 Fax
Email: garyposnerinc@aol.com
Web: www. garyposnerinc.com
www.gemstamps.com

U.S.-Postal Stationery

ARMSTRONG PHILATELICS
P.O. Box 4089
Chatsworth, CA 91313-4089
818-701-7380
818-701-5915 Fax
Email: armstrong@stamp1.com
Web: www.stamp1.com

LEWIS KAUFMAN
P.O. Box 255
Kiamesha Lake, NY 12751
845-794-8013 Phone/Fax
800-491-5453 Phone/Fax
Email: mamet1@aol.com

U.S.-Price Lists

DALE ENTERPRISES INC.
P.O. Box 539-C
Emmaus, PA 18049
610-433-3303
610-965-6089 Fax
Email: daleent@ptd.net
Web: www.dalestamps.com

U.S.-Proofs & Essays

LEWIS KAUFMAN
P.O. Box 255
Kiamesha Lake, NY 12751
845-794-8013 Phone/Fax
800-491-5453 Phone/Fax
Email: mamet1@aol.com

CHRISTOPHER J. HRADIL, INC.
325 Main St.
Little Falls, NJ 07424
973-809-4606 or 973-890-0268
973-890-1596 Fax
Email: stamps@comcast.net
Web: www.dom17stamps.com

SUBURBAN STAMP INC.
176 Worthington Street
Springfield, MA 01103
413-785-5348
413-746-3788 Fax
Email:
suburbanstamp@earthlink.net

U.S.-Rare Stamps

GARY POSNER, INC.
1407 Avenue Z, PMB #535
Brooklyn, NY 11235
800-323-4279
718-241-2801 Fax
Email: garyposnerinc@aol.com
Web: www. garyposnerinc.com
www.gemstamps.com

SUBURBAN STAMP INC.
176 Worthington Street
Springfield, MA 01103
413-785-5348
413-746-3788 Fax
Email:
suburbanstamp@earthlink.net

U.S.-Revenues

ARMSTRONG PHILATELICS
P.O. Box 4089
Chatsworth, CA 91313-4089
818-701-7380
818-701-5915 Fax
Email: armstrong@stamp1.com
Web: www.stamp1.com

U.S.-Souvenir Pages/Panels

LEWIS KAUFMAN
P.O. Box 255
Kiamesha Lake, NY 12751
845-794-8013 Phone/Fax
800-491-5453 Phone/Fax
Email: mamet1@aol.com

U.S.-State Duck Stamps

SAM HOUSTON DUCK CO.
P.O. Box 820087
Houston, TX 77282
281-493-6386 or 800-231-5926
281-496-1445 Fax
Email: shduck@aol.com
Web: www.shduck.com

U.S.-Trust Territories

HENRY GITNER PHILATELISTS, INC.
P.O. Box 3077-S
Middletown, NY 10940
845-343-5151 or 800-947-8267
845-343-0068 Fax
Email: hgitner@hgitner.com
Web: www.hgitner.com

U.S.-Used

STEVE CRIPPE, INC.
PO Box 23413
Tampa, FL 33623
813-878-9845
813-877-8080 Fax
Email: stamp@stevecrippe.com
Web: www.stevecrippe.com

HENRY GITNER PHILATELISTS, INC.
P.O. Box 3077-S
Middletown, NY 10940
845-343-5151 or 800-947-8267
845-343-0068 Fax
Email: hgitner@hgitner.com
Web: www.hgitner.com

Want Lists

BROOKMAN INTERNATIONAL
P.O. Box 450
Vancouver, WA 98666
360-695-1391 or 800-545-4871
360-695-1616 Fax
Email:
dave@brookmanstamps.com

CHARLES P. SCHWARTZ
P.O. Box 165
Mora, MN 55051
320-679-4705
Email: charlesp@ecenet.com

Want Lists-U.S.

GARY POSNER, INC.
1407 Avenue Z, PMB #535
Brooklyn, NY 11235
800-323-4279
718-241-2801 Fax
Email: garyposnerinc@aol.com
Web: www. garyposnerinc.com
www.gemstamps.com

Wanted-Estates

CHRISTOPHER J. HRADIL, INC.
325 Main St.
Little Falls, NJ 07424
973-809-4606 or 973-890-0268
973-890-1596 Fax
Email: stamps@comcast.net
Web: www.dom17stamps.com

DALE ENTERPRISES INC.
P.O. Box 539-C
Emmaus, PA 18049
610-433-3303
610-965-6089 Fax
Email: daleent@ptd.net
Web: www.dalestamps.com

SUBURBAN STAMP INC.
176 Worthington Street
Springfield, MA 01103
413-785-5348
413-746-3788 Fax
Email:
suburbanstamp@earthlink.net

Wanted-Worldwide Collections

CHRISTOPHER J. HRADIL, INC.
325 Main St.
Little Falls, NJ 07424
973-809-4606 or 973-890-0268
973-890-1596 Fax
Email: stamps@comcast.net
Web: www.dom17stamps.com

SUBURBAN STAMP INC.
176 Worthington Street
Springfield, MA 01103
413-785-5348
413-746-3788 Fax
Email:
suburbanstamp@earthlink.net

Wanted to Buy

LEWIS KAUFMAN
P.O. Box 255
Kiamesha Lake, NY 12751
845-794-8013 Phone/Fax
800-491-5453 Phone/Fax
Email: mamet1@aol.com

DR. ROBERT FRIEDMAN & SONS
2029 West 75th Street
Woodridge, IL 60517
630-985-1515
630-985-1588 Fax

Wanted-U.S.

CHRISTOPHER J. HRADIL, INC.
325 Main St.
Little Falls, NJ 07424
973-809-4606 or 973-890-0268
973-890-1596 Fax
Email: stamps@comcast.net
Web: www.dom17stamps.com

STEVE CRIPPE, INC.
PO Box 23413
Tampa, FL 33623
813-878-9845
813-877-8080 Fax
Email: stamp@stevecrippe.com
Web: www.stevecrippe.com

GARY POSNER, INC.
1407 Avenue Z, PMB #535
Brooklyn, NY 11235
800-323-4279
718-241-2801 Fax
Email: garyposnerinc@aol.com
Web: www. garyposnerinc.com
www.gemstamps.com

SUBURBAN STAMP INC.
176 Worthington Street
Springfield, MA 01103
413-785-5348
413-746-3788 Fax
Email:
suburbanstamp@earthlink.net

Wanted-U.S. Collections

CHRISTOPHER J. HRADIL, INC.
325 Main St.
Little Falls, NJ 07424
973-809-4606 or 973-890-0268
973-890-1596 Fax
Email: stamps@comcast.net
Web: www.dom17stamps.com

SUBURBAN STAMP INC.
176 Worthington Street
Springfield, MA 01103
413-785-5348
413-746-3788 Fax
Email:
suburbanstamp@earthlink.net

Websites

ARMSTRONG PHILATELICS
P.O. Box 4089
Chatsworth, CA 91313-4089
818-701-7380
818-701-5915 Fax
Email: armstrong@stamp1.com
Web: www.stamp1.com

STEVE CRIPPE, INC.
PO Box 23413
Tampa, FL 33623
813-878-9845
813-877-8080 Fax
Email: stamp@stevecrippe.com
Web: www.stevecrippe.com

MILLER'S STAMP SHOP
41 New London Turnpike
Uncasville, CT 06382
860-848-0468 or 800-67-STAMP
860-848-1926 Fax
Email: millstamps@aol.com
Web: www.millerstamps.com

Wholesale

HENRY GITNER PHILATELISTS, INC.
P.O. Box 3077-S
Middletown, NY 10940
845-343-5151 or 800-947-8267
845-343-0068 Fax
Email: hgitner@hgitner.com
Web: www.hgitner.com

Wholesale-Dealers

GARY POSNER, INC.
1407 Avenue Z, PMB #535
Brooklyn, NY 11235
800-323-4279
718-241-2801 Fax
Email: garyposnerinc@aol.com
Web: www. garyposnerinc.com
www.gemstamps.com

Wholesale-U.S.

GARY POSNER, INC.
1407 Avenue Z, PMB #535
Brooklyn, NY 11235
800-323-4279
718-241-2801 Fax
Email: garyposnerinc@aol.com
Web: www. garyposnerinc.com
www.gemstamps.com

Worldwide-Collections

DR. ROBERT FRIEDMAN & SONS
2029 West 75th Street
Woodridge, IL 60517
630-985-1515
630-985-1588 Fax

Worldwide-Price Lists

ROBERT E. BARKER
P.O. Box 1100
Warren, ME 04864
207-273-6200 or 800-833-0217
207-273-4254 or 888-325-5158 Fax
Email: rebarker@rebarker.com
Web: www.rebarker.com